Football Outsiders Almanac 2014

THE ESSENTIAL GUIDE TO THE 2014 NFL AND COLLEGE FOOTBALL SEASONS

Edited by Aaron Schatz

With Bill Connelly, Doug Farrar, Nathan Forster, Brian Fremeau, Tom Gower, Matt Hinton, Scott Kacsmar, Jason Lisk, Rivers McCown, Christopher Price, Chase Stuart, Mike Tanier, Vince Verhei, and Robert Weintraub

ISBN-10: 1500628026

ISBN-13: 978-1500628024

Table of Contents

Player Comments

College Football

Further Data

Introduction

It was the best of times, it was the worst of times.

Last summer, Football Outsiders celebrated its tenth anniversary producing advanced analysis of the National Football League. As an anniversary present, the National Football League decided to have a season that was incredibly easy to analyze.

In 2013, we had none of this nonsense about 9-7 teams going on ridiculous playoff runs and taking home the Lombardi Trophy over teams that had dominated for the entire regular season. No, the best teams in 2013 were the best teams all year. In fact, they were the best teams for more than a year. Seattle and Denver finished in the top two spots of the Football Outsiders advanced DVOA ratings in 2012. They finished at the top of our season projections for 2013. They towered above the rest of the league from start to finish, the first time in the history of our DVOA ratings that the same two teams finished 1-2 for two straight seasons. They went into the playoffs as the No. 1 seeds in each conference. They met in the Super Bowl, and even that went as planned: the team that had led our ratings for two years beat the team that had finished second for two years.

It wasn't enough for one team to clearly dominate from wire to wire; we were also gifted with a championship team that represents so much of everything we've been saying about football for the last decade. The Seattle Seahawks combine excellent scouting with statistical analysis to unearth young talent. They represent the best of the "Moneyball" philosophy by identifying market inefficiencies ("Hey, if we have the best free safety in the game, we can sacrifice cornerback speed for size, physical strength, and intelligence") and building their team to maximize the value from every salary-cap dollar. Oh, and they also happen to be a team whose general manager has blurbed the back of this book for the last couple years.

So, it was a really, really good year to be Football Outsiders.

Unfortunately, it was a really, really bad year to be me.

If this is the first time you've ever read *Football Outsiders Almanac*, you may not know that the book came out really late this year. You can probably skip ahead a couple paragraphs. To the rest of you, to the dedicated readers who have stuck with us over the last 11 years, let me give one more round of apologies.

The somewhat vague summary is that I've dealt with serious illness and a lot of family issues over the past 12 months. It was very difficult to enjoy what should have been one of the most enjoyable NFL seasons in recent memory. (One of the two or three worst events in a cavalcade of awful events happened *the morning of the Super Bowl*. I didn't even see Manny Ramirez chuck the ball over Peyton Manning's head because I still wasn't done dealing with the crisis.) I tried not to allow my struggle to affect the quality of the writing at Football Outsiders, but it undoubtedly affected the quantity. I've got a lot of great guys writing for me, but the business dealings of Football Outsiders, and pretty much all the advanced stats—for the NFL, at least—still have to flow through me, and I didn't have enough time or mental energy to give.

The good news is that things have gotten better over the last couple of months. Although this year's *Football Outsiders Almanac* process got started much too late, we've worked as hard as possible to bring you all the good stuff you are used to every year: the best projections, the best scouting insights, the best writing, the best random statistical trivia, and the best completely obscure references to indie rock song lyrics. We're sorry it showed up a couple weeks late.

Thus endeth the navel-gazing. For the new people out there, let's get back to talking about what Football Outsiders is really about.

As we remind people each year, Football Outsiders is not founded on the idea that statistics are all-encompassing or can tell us everything about football. There's a lot more to our analysis than numbers, and you're going to find a lot of scouting knowledge in this book as well. There's a rumor that stat analysts don't watch game tape. In reality, stat analysts watch more tape than most beat writers or national Internet columnists, and *a lot* more tape than the average fan. We take everything we learn off the tape, synthesize it with the statistics, and deliver it to you. Occasionally, there are also jokes.

At its heart, the football analytics revolution is about learning more about the intricacies of the game instead of just accepting the boilerplate storylines produced by color commentators, lazy beat reporters, and crotchety old players from the past. It's about not accepting the idea that some guy "just wins." It's about understanding that the "skill players" aren't the only guys on the team with skills. It's about gaining insight into the complexity behind the modern offense, and that you don't just shove the ball into the line hoping to gain yardage. It's about understanding the dramatic way that strength of schedule affects the way we see a team's performance, especially at the college level. It's about figuring out which player skills translate from college to the pros, and which skills just produce meaningless scoutspeak. And it's about accepting that the pass dominates the run in the National Football League, and that it's been that way for 30 years.

Everybody who writes about football uses both statistics (whether they be basic yardage totals or more advanced stats like ours) and scouting (whether scouting reports by professionals or just their own eyes). The same goes for us, except that the statistics portion of our analysis is far more accurate than what you normally see from football coverage. Those numbers are based on two ideas:

1) **Conventional football statistics are heavily dependent on context.** If you want to see which teams are good and which are bad, which strategies work and which do not, you first need to filter out that context. Down and distance, field position, the current score, time left on the clock, the quality of the opponent—all of these elements influence the objective of the play and/or its outcome. Yet, the official NFL stats

add together all yardage gained by a specific team or player without considering the impact of that particular yardage on wins and losses.

A close football game can turn on a single bounce of the ball. In a season of only 16 games, those effects can have a huge impact on a team's win-loss record, thus obscuring the team's true talent level. If we can filter out these bits of luck and random chance, we can figure out which teams are really more likely to play better for the rest of the season, or even in the following season.

2) **On any one play, the majority of the important action is not tracked by the conventional NFL play-by-play.** That's why we started the Football Outsiders game charting project in 2005. A cadre of football-obsessed volunteers watches every single game and adds new detail to our record of each play. We know how many pass rushers teams send on each pass, how often teams go three-wide or use two tight ends, how often teams use a play-fake or a zone blitz, and which defensive backs are in coverage, even when they don't get a tackle in the standard play-by-play.

There's also a third important precept that governs the work we do at Football Outsiders, although it's more about how to interpret numbers and not the numbers themselves. **A player's production in one year does not necessarily equal his production the next year.** This also applies to teams, of course. Even when stats are accurate, they're often extremely variable from year to year and subject to heavy forces of regression to the mean. Field-goal percentage, red-zone performance, third-down performance on defense, interceptions and fumble recoveries—these are but a few examples. In addition, the age curves for football players are much steeper than in other sports. Old players break down faster, and young players often improve faster. A number of football analysts concentrate on looking at what players did last year. We'll talk about that as well, but we're more interested in what players are going to do *this* year. Which performances from a year ago are flukes, and which ones represent long-term improvement or decline? What will one more year of experience do to this player's production? And how will a player's role change this year, and what does it mean for the team?

As with past books, *Football Outsiders Almanac 2014* starts off with "Pregame Show" (reviewing the most important research we've done in past books) and "Statistical Toolbox" (explaining all our stats). Once again, we preserve the ridiculousness of the football season for posterity with another version of "The Year in Quotes" and we introduce you to some of the more promising (and lesser-known) young bench players with our seventh annual list of Top 25 Prospects chosen in the third round or later.

Each NFL team gets a full chapter covering what happened in 2013 and our projections for the upcoming season. Are there reasons to believe that the team was actually better or worse than its record last year? What did the team do in the offseason, and what does that mean for the team's chances to win in 2014? Each chapter also includes all kinds of advanced statistics covering 2013 performance and strategic tendencies, plus detailed commentary on each of the major units of the team: offensive line, defensive front seven, defensive secondary, and special teams.

"Skill players" (by which we mean "players who get counted in fantasy football") get their own section in the back of the book. We list the major players at each position alphabetically, along with commentary and a 2014 KUBIAK projection that will help you win your fantasy football league. We also have the most accurate projections anywhere for two fantasy football positions that people wrongly consider impossible to predict: kickers and team defense.

Next comes our preview of the college football season. We preview every team from the five major conferences as well as the top independents and mid-majors. Just like with our NFL coverage, the goal of our college previews is to focus as much as possible on "why" and how," not just "which team is better." We're not just here to rank the Football Bowl Subdivision teams from 1 to 128. We break things down to offense and defense, pass and run, and clutch situations compared to all plays.

We hope our book helps you raise your level of football expertise, win arguments with your friends, and win your fantasy football league—even if this year it is helping you do those things a couple weeks later than usual.

Aaron Schatz
Framingham, Mass.
July 23, 2014

P.S. Don't forget to visit FootballOutsiders.com every day for fresh coverage of the NFL and college football, plus the most intelligent football discussion threads on the Internet.

Pregame Show

It has now been 11 years since we launched Football Outsiders. In that time, we've done a lot of primary research on the National Football League, and we reference that research in many of the articles and comments in *Football Outsiders Almanac 2014*. New readers may come across an offhand comment in a team chapter about, for example, the idea that fumble recovery is not a skill, and wonder what in the heck we are talking about. We can't repeat all our research in every new edition of *Football Outsiders Almanac*, so we start each year with a basic look at some of the most important precepts that have emerged from Football Outsiders research. You will see these issues come up again and again throughout the book.

You can also find this introduction online at http://www.footballoutsiders.com/info/FO-basics, along with links to the original research in the cases in which that research appeared online instead of (or as well as) in print.

Our various methods for projecting NFL success for college prospects are not listed below, but are referenced at times during the book. Those methods are detailed in an essay on page xii.

You run when you win, not win when you run.

If we could only share one piece of anti-conventional wisdom with you before you read the rest of our book, this would be it. The first article ever written for Football Outsiders was devoted to debunking the myth of "establishing the run." There is no correlation whatsoever between giving your running backs a lot of carries early in the game and winning the game. Just running the ball is not going to help a team score; it has to run successfully.

There are two reasons why nearly every beat writer and television analyst still repeats the tired old school mantra that "establishing the run" is the secret to winning football games. The first problem is confusing cause and effect. There are exceptions, but for the most part, winning teams have a lot of carries because their running backs are running out the clock at the end of wins, not because they are running wild early in games.

The second problem is history. Most of the current crop of NFL analysts came of age or actually played the game during the 1970s. They believe that the run-heavy game of that decade is how football is meant to be, and today's pass-first game is an aberration. As we addressed in an essay in *Pro Football Prospectus 2006* on the history of NFL stats, it was actually the game of the 1970s that was the aberration. The seventies were far more slanted towards the run than any era since the arrival of Paul Brown, Otto Graham, and the Cleveland Browns in 1946. Optimal strategies from 1974 are not optimal strategies for 2014.

A sister statement to "you have to establish the run" is "team X is 5-1 when running back John Doe runs for at least 100 yards." Unless John Doe is possessed by otherworldly spirits the way Adrian Peterson was a couple years ago, the team isn't winning because of his 100-yard games. He's putting up 100-yard games because his team is winning.

A great defense against the run is nothing without a good pass defense.

This is a corollary to the absurdity of "establish the run." With rare exceptions, teams win or lose with the passing game more than the running game—and by stopping the passing game more than the running game. Ron Jaworski puts it best: "The pass gives you the lead, and the run solidifies it." The reason why teams need a strong run defense in the playoffs is not to shut the run down early; it's to keep the other team from icing the clock if they get a lead. You can't mount a comeback if you can't stop the run.

Note that "good pass defense" may mean "good pass rush" rather than "good defensive backs."

Running on third-and-short is more likely to convert than passing on third-and-short.

On average, passing will always gain more yardage than running, with one very important exception: when a team is just one or two yards away from a new set of downs or the goal line. On third-and-1, a run will convert for a new set of downs 36 percent more often than a pass. Expand that to all third or fourth downs with 1-2 yards to go, and the run is successful 40 percent more often. With these percentages, the possibility of a long gain with a pass is not worth the tradeoff of an incomplete that kills a drive.

This is one reason why teams have to be able to both run and pass. The offense also has to keep some semblance of balance so they can use their play-action fakes, and so the defense doesn't just run their nickel and dime packages all game. Balance also means that teams do need to pass occasionally in short-yardage situations; they just need to do it less than they do now. Teams pass roughly 60 percent of the time on third-and-2 even though runs in that situation convert 20 percent more often than passes. They pass 68 percent of the time on fourth-and-2 even though runs in that situation convert twice as often as passes.

Standard team rankings based on total yardage are inherently flawed.

Check out the schedule page on NFL.com, and you will find that each game is listed with league rankings based on total yardage. That is still how the NFL "officially" ranks teams, but these rankings rarely match up with common sense. That is because total team yardage may be the most context-dependent number in football.

It starts with the basic concept that rate stats are generally more valuable than cumulative stats. Yards per carry says more about a running back's quality than total yardage, completion percentage says more than just a quarterback's total number of completions. The same thing is true for teams; in fact, it is even more important because of the way football strategy influences the number of runs and passes in the game plan. Poor teams will give up fewer passing yards and more rushing yards because opponents will stop passing once they have a late-game lead and will run out the clock instead. For winning teams, the opposite is true. For example, which team had a better pass defense last year: Houston or San Francisco? The answer is obviously San Francisco, yet according to the official NFL rankings, Houston (3,123 net yards allowed on 516 pass attempts, 6.1 net yards per pass) was a better pass defense than San Francisco (3,819 net yards allowed on 623 passes, 5.7 net yards per pass).

Total yardage rankings are also skewed because some teams play at a faster pace than other teams. For example, last year Buffalo (5,410) had roughly the same number of yards as Pittsburgh (5,400). However, the Steelers were the superior offense and much more efficient; they gained those yards on only 183 drives while the Bills needed 207 drives.

A team will score more when playing a bad defense, and will give up more points when playing a good offense.

This sounds absurdly basic, but when people consider team and player stats without looking at strength of schedule, they are ignoring this. In 2004, Carson Palmer and Byron Leftwich had very similar numbers, but Palmer faced a much tougher schedule than Leftwich did. Palmer was better that year, and better in the long run. A similar comparison can be made between Russell Wilson and Robert Griffin III in their rookie years: Wilson had a higher DVOA rating because he faced a more difficult schedule, even though Griffin had slightly better standard stats.

If their overall yards per carry are equal, a running back who consistently gains yardage on every play is more valuable than a boom-and-bust running back who is frequently stuffed at the line but occasionally breaks a long highlight-worthy run.

Our brethren at Baseball Prospectus believe that the most precious commodity in baseball is outs. Teams only get 27 of them per game, and you can't afford to give one up for very little return. So imagine if there was a new rule in baseball that gave a team a way to earn another three outs in the middle of the inning. That would be pretty useful, right?

That's the way football works. You may start a drive 80 yards away from scoring, but as long as you can earn 10 yards in four chances, you get another four chances. Long gains have plenty of value, but if those long gains are mixed with a lot of short gains, you are going to put the quarterback in a lot of difficult third-and-long situations. That means more punts and more giving the ball back to the other team rather than moving the chains and giving the offense four more plays to work with.

The running back who gains consistent yardage is also going to do a lot more for you late in the game, when the goal of running the ball is not just to gain yardage but to eat clock time. If you are a Ravens fan watching your team with a late lead, you don't want to see three straight Ray Rice stuffs at the line followed by a punt. You want to see a game-icing first down.

A common historical misconception is that our preference for consistent running backs means that "Football Outsiders believes that Barry Sanders was overrated." Sanders wasn't just any boom-and-bust running back, though; he was the greatest boom-and-bust runner of all time, with bigger booms and fewer busts. Sanders ranked in the top five in DYAR five times (third in 1989, first in 1990, and second in 1994, 1996, and 1997).

Rushing is more dependent on the offensive line than people realize, but pass protection is more dependent on the quarterback himself than people realize.

Some readers complain that this idea contradicts the previous one. Aren't those consistent running backs just the product of good offensive lines? The truth is somewhere in between. There are certainly good running backs who suffer because their offensive lines cannot create consistent holes, but most boom-and-bust running backs contribute to their own problems by hesitating behind the line whenever the hole is unclear, looking for the home run instead of charging forward for the four-yard gain that keeps the offense moving.

As for pass protection, some quarterbacks have better instincts for the rush than others, and are thus better at getting out of trouble by moving around in the pocket or throwing the ball away. Others will hesitate, hold onto the ball too long, and lose yardage over and over.

Note that "moving around in the pocket" does not necessarily mean "scrambling." In fact, a scrambling quarterback will often take more sacks than a pocket quarterback, because while he's running around trying to make something happen, a defensive lineman will catch up with him.

Shotgun formations are generally more efficient than formations with the quarterback under center.

Over the past five seasons, offenses have averaged roughly 5.9 yards per play from Shotgun (or Pistol), but just 5.1 yards per play with the quarterback under center. This wide split exists even if you analyze the data to try to weed out biases like teams using Shotgun more often on third-and-long, or against prevent defenses in the fourth quarter. Shotgun offense is more efficient if you only look at the first half, on every down, and even if you only look at running back carries rather than passes and scrambles.

It's hard to think of a Football Outsiders axiom that has been better assimilated by the people running NFL teams since we started doing this a decade ago. In 2001, NFL teams only used Shotgun on 14 percent of plays. Five years later, in 2006, that had increased slightly, to 20 percent of plays. By 2012, Shotgun was used on a 47.5 percent of plays (including the Pistol, but not counting the Wildcat or other direct snaps to non-quarterbacks). Then last year, the league as a whole averaged a mind-blowing 59.1 percent of plays from Shotgun or Pistol. Remember, before 2007, no team had ever used Shotgun on more than half its offensive plays. Now, the league *averages* over 50 percent. At some point, defenses will adapt and the benefit of the formation will become less pronounced, but it doesn't look like it is happening yet. Success on Shotgun plays dropped slightly last year, but so did success on non-Shotgun plays.

A running back with 370 or more carries during the regular season will usually suffer either a major injury or a loss of effectiveness the following year, unless he is named Eric Dickerson.

Terrell Davis, Jamal Anderson, and Edgerrin James all blew out their knees. Larry Johnson broke his foot. Earl Campbell and Eddie George went from legendary powerhouses to plodding, replacement-level players. Shaun Alexander broke his foot *and* became a plodding, replacement-level player. This is what happens when a running back is overworked to the point of having at least 370 carries during the regular season.

The "Curse of 370" was expanded in our book *Pro Football Prospectus 2005*, and now includes seasons with 390 or more carries in the regular season and postseason combined. Research also shows that receptions don't cause a problem, only workload on the ground.

Plenty of running backs get injured without hitting 370 carries in a season, but there is a clear difference. On average, running backs with 300 to 369 carries and no postseason appearance will see their total rushing yardage decline by 15 percent the following year and their yards per carry decline by two percent. The average running back with 370 or more regular-season carries, or 390 including the postseason, will see their rushing yardage decline by 35 percent, and their yards per carry decline by eight percent. However, the Curse of 370 is not a hard and fast line where running backs suddenly become injury risks. It is more of a concept where 370 carries is roughly the point at which additional carries start to become more and more of a problem.

It's worth noting that the return to the committee backfields that dominated the '60s and '70s may mean an end to the Curse of 370. No running back has gone over 370 carries since Michael Turner in 2008.

Wide receivers must be judged on both complete and incomplete passes.

Last year, for example, Andre Holmes of the Raiders had 431 receiving yards, while Jarius Wright of the Vikings had 434 receiving yards. Both played for teams with poor quarterback situations, and both ran their average route at 14.4 yards downfield. But there was a big difference between them: Holmes caught 48 percent of intended passes, while Wright caught 60 percent.

Some work has been done on splitting responsibility for incomplete passes between quarterbacks and receivers, but not enough that we can incorporate this into our advanced stats at this time. We know that wide receiver catch rates are almost as consistent from year to year as quarterback completion percentages, but it is also important to look at catch rate in the context of the types of routes each receiver runs. Four years ago, we expanded on this idea with a new plus-minus metric, which is explained in the introduction to the chapter on wide receivers and tight ends.

The total quality of an NFL team is four parts offense, three parts defense, and one part special teams.

There are three units on a football team, but they are not of equal importance. For a long time, the saying from Football Outsiders was that the total quality of an NFL team is three parts offense, three parts defense, and one part special teams. Further recent research suggests that offense is even more important than we originally believed. Recent recent work by Chase Stuart, Neil Paine, and Brian Burke suggests a split between offense and defense of roughly 58-42, without considering special teams. Our research suggests that special teams contributes about 13 percent to total performance; if you measure the remaining 87 percent with a 58-42 ratio, you get roughly 4:3:1. When we compare the range of offense, defense, and special teams DVOA ratings, we get the same results, with the best and worst offenses roughly 130 percent stronger than the best and worst defenses, and roughly four times stronger than the best and worst special teams.

Offense is more consistent from year to year than defense, and offensive performance is easier to project than defensive performance. Special teams is less consistent than either.

Nobody in the NFL understood this concept better than former Indianapolis Colts general manager Bill Polian. Both the Super Bowl champion Colts and the four-time AFC champion Buffalo Bills of the early 1990s were built around the idea that if you put together an offense that can dominate the league year after year, eventually you will luck into a year where good health and a few smart decisions will give you a defense good enough to win a championship. (As the Colts learned in 2006, you don't even need a year, just four weeks.) Even the New England Patriots, who are led by a defense-first head coach in Bill Belichick, have been more consistent on offense than on defense since they began their run of success in 2001.

Field-goal percentage is almost entirely random from season to season, while kickoff distance is one of the most consistent statistics in football.

This theory, which originally appeared in the *New York Times* in October 2006, is one of our most controversial, but it is hard to argue against the evidence. Measuring every kicker from 1999 to 2006 who had at least ten field goal attempts in each of two consecutive years, the year-to-year correlation coefficient for field-goal percentage was an insignificant .05. Mike Vanderjagt didn't miss a single field goal in 2003, but his percentage was a below-average 74 percent the year before and 80 percent the year after. Adam Vinatieri has long been considered the best kicker in the game. But even he had never enjoyed two straight seasons with accuracy better than the NFL average of 85 percent until 2010 and 2011, and then in 2012 his field-goal percentage was back below 80 percent.

On the other hand, the year-to-year correlation coefficient for kickoff distance, over the same period as our measurement of field-goal percentage and with the same minimum of ten kicks per year, is .61. The same players consistently lead the league in kickoff distance. In recent years, that group includes Steven Hauschka, Billy Cundiff, Graham Gano, Stephen Gostkowski, and Michael Koenen.

Teams with more offensive penalties generally lose more games, but there is no correlation between defensive penalties and losses.

Specific defensive penalties of course lose games; we've all sworn at the television when the cornerback on our favorite team gets flagged for a 50-yard pass interference penalty. Yet overall, there is no correlation between losses and the total of defensive penalties or even the total yardage on defensive penalties. One reason is that defensive penalties often represent *good* play, not bad. Cornerbacks who play tight coverage may be just on the edge of a penalty on most plays, only occasionally earning a flag. Defensive ends who get a good jump on rushing the passer will gladly trade an encroachment penalty or two for ten snaps where they get off the blocks a split-second before the linemen trying to block them.

In addition, offensive penalties have a higher correlation from year to year than defensive penalties. The penalty that correlates highest with losses is the false start, and the penalty that teams will have called most consistently from year to year is also the false start.

Recovery of a fumble, despite being the product of hard work, is almost entirely random.

Stripping the ball is a skill. Holding onto the ball is a skill. Pouncing on the ball as it is bouncing all over the place is not a skill. There is no correlation whatsoever between the percentage of fumbles recovered by a team in one year and the percentage they recover in the next year. The odds of recovery are based solely on the type of play involved, not the teams or any of their players.

Fans like to insist that specific coaches can teach their teams to recover more fumbles by swarming to the ball. Chicago's Lovie Smith, in particular, is supposed to have this ability. However, in Smith's first three seasons as head coach of the Bears, their rate of fumble recovery on defense went from a league-best 76 percent in 2004 to a league-worst 33 percent in 2005, then back to 67 percent in 2006.

For an even better example, look at the New York Jets of the past two seasons. In 2012, the Jets defense forced 14 fumbles and recovered 11 of them. Last year, they forced 13 fumbles and recovered *only one.*

Fumble recovery is equally erratic on offense. In 2012, the Tennessee Titans fumbled 19 times on offense and only recovered seven. Last year, the same team fumbled 18 times on offense and recovered 13 of them.

Fumble recovery is a major reason why the general public overestimates or underestimates certain teams. Fumbles are huge, turning-point plays that dramatically impact wins and losses in the past, while fumble recovery percentage says absolutely nothing about a team's chances of winning games in the future. With this in mind, Football Outsiders stats treat all fumbles as equal, penalizing them based on the likelihood of each type of fumble (run, pass, sack, etc.) being recovered by the defense.

Other plays that qualify as "non-predictive events" include two-point conversions, blocked kicks, and touchdowns during turnover returns. These plays are not "lucky," per se, but they have no value whatsoever for predicting future performance.

Field position is fluid.

As discussed in the Statistical Toolbox, every yard line on the field has a value based on how likely a team is to score from that location on the field as opposed to from a yard further back. The change in value from one yard to the next is the same whether the team has the ball or not. The goal of a defense is not just to prevent scoring, but to hold the opposition so that the offense can get the ball back in the best possible field position. A bad offense will score as many points as a good offense if it starts each drive five yards closer to the goal line.

A corollary to this precept: The most underrated aspect of an NFL team's performance is the field position gained or lost on kickoffs and punts. This is part of why players like Devin Hester and Cordarrelle Patterson can have such an impact on the game, even when they aren't taking a kickoff or punt all the way back for a touchdown.

The red zone is the most important place on the field to play well, but performance in the red zone from year to year is much less consistent than overall performance.

Although play in the red zone has a disproportionately high importance to the outcome of games relative to plays on the rest of the field, NFL teams do not exhibit a level of performance in the red zone that is consistently better or worse than their performance elsewhere, year after year. The simplest explanation why is a small(er) sample size and the inherent variance of football, with contributing factors like injuries and changes in personnel.

Defenses which are strong on first and second down, but weak on third down, will tend to improve the following year. Defenses which are weak on first and second down, but strong on third down, will tend to decline the following year. This trend also applied to offenses through 2005, but may or may not still apply today.

We discovered this when creating our first team projection system in 2004. It said that the lowly San Diego Chargers would have of the best offenses in the league, which seemed a little ridiculous. But looking closer, our projection system treated the previous year's performance on different downs as different variables, and the 2003 Chargers were actually good on first and second down, but terrible on third.

Teams get fewer opportunities on third down, so third-down performance is more volatile—but it's also is a bigger part of a team's overall performance than first or second down, because the result is usually either very good (four more downs) or very bad (losing the ball to the other team with a punt). Over time, a team will play as well in those situations as it does in other situations, which will bring the overall offense or defense in line with the offense and defense on first and second down.

This trend is even stronger between seasons. Struggles on third down are a pretty obvious problem, and teams will generally target their off-season moves at improving their third-down performance ... which often leads to an improvement in third-down performance.

However, we have discovered something surprising over the past few years: The third-down rebound effect seems to have disappeared on offense, as we explained in the Philadelphia chapter of *Football Outsiders Almanac 2010*. We don't know yet if this change is temporary or permanent, and there is no such change on defense.

Injuries regress to the mean on the seasonal level, and teams that avoid injuries in a given season tend to win more games.

There are no doubt teams with streaks of good or bad health over multiple years. However, teams who were especially healthy or especially unhealthy, as measured by our Adjusted Games Lost (AGL) metric, almost always head towards league average in the subsequent season. Furthermore, injury—or the absence thereof—has a huge correlation with wins, and a significant impact on a team's success. There's no doubt that a few high-profile teams have resisted this trend in recent years. The Patriots seem to overcome injuries every year, and a number of recent Super Bowl champions such as the 2010 Packers and 2011 Giants have overcome a number of injuries to win the championship. Nonetheless, the overall rule still applies. Last year, the three teams that finished 1-2-3 in AGL were Philadelphia, Kansas City, and Cincinnati, all playoff teams.

In general, teams with a high number of injuries are a good bet to improve the following season. This year, that list would include Jacksonville, Pittsburgh, and the entire NFC East except for Philadelphia. However, while injury totals tend to regress towards the mean, there's also no doubt that certain teams have a record of staying healthier than others. We need to do more research on this issue, but teams with a consistent record of poor health include Indianapolis, New England, and Green Bay, while teams with a consistent record of good health include Tennessee, Minnesota, Chicago, and New Orleans (although last year was a major exception for the defenses of those last two teams, which ranked 30th and 32nd in Adjusted Games Lost).

By and large, a team built on depth is better than a team built on stars and scrubs.

Connected to the previous statement, because teams need to go into the season expecting that they will suffer an average number of injuries no matter how healthy they were the previous year. The Dallas Cowboys seem to go into every season with a number of big-name stars, only to come out at 8-8 because they have no depth. You cannot concentrate your salaries on a handful of star players because there is no such thing as avoiding injuries in the NFL. The game is too fast and the players too strong to build a team based around the idea that "if we can avoid all injuries this year, we'll win."

Running backs usually decline after age 28, tight ends after age 29, wide receivers after age 30, and quarterbacks after age 32.

This research was originally done by Doug Drinen (then editor of pro-football-reference.com) in 2000. In recent years, a few players have had huge seasons above these general age limits (most notably Tony Gonzalez), but the peak ages Drinen found a few years ago still apply to the majority of players.

As for "non-skill players," research we did in 2007 for *ESPN the Magazine* suggested that defensive ends and defensive backs generally begin to decline after age 29, linebackers and offensive linemen after age 30, and defensive tackles after age 31. However, because we still have so few statistics to use to study linemen and defensive players, this research should not be considered definitive.

The strongest indicator of how a college football team will perform in the upcoming season is their performance in recent seasons.

It may seem strange because graduation enforces constant player turnover, but college football teams are actually much more consistent from year to year than NFL teams. Thanks in large part to consistency in recruiting, teams can be expected to play within a reasonable range of their baseline program expectations each season. Our Program F/+ ratings, which represent a rolling five-year period of play-by-play and drive efficiency data, have an extremely strong (.76) correlation with the next year's F/+ rating.

Championship teams are generally defined by their ability to dominate inferior opponents, not their ability to win close games.

Football games are often decided by just one or two plays: a missed field goal, a bouncing fumble, the subjective spot of an official on fourth-and-1. One missed assignment by a cornerback or one slightly askew pass that bounces off a receiver's hands and into those of a defensive back five yards away and the game could be over. In a blowout, however, one lucky bounce isn't going to change things. Championship teams—in both professional and college football—typically beat their good opponents convincingly and destroy the cupcakes on the schedule.

Aaron Schatz

Statistical Toolbox

After 11 years of Football Outsiders, some of our readers are as comfortable with DVOA and ALY as they are with touchdowns and tackles. Yet to most fans, including our newer readers, it still looks like a lot of alphabet soup. That's what this chapter is for. The next few pages define and explain all of all the unique NFL statistics you'll find in this book: how we calculate them, what the numbers mean, and what they tell us about why teams win or lose football games. We'll go through the information in each of the tables that appear in each team chapter, pointing out whether those stats come from advanced mathematical manipulation of the standard play-by-play or simple counting of what see on television with the Football Outsiders game charting project. This chapter covers NFL statistics only. College metrics such as Adjusted POE and F/+ are explained in the introduction to the college football section on page 363.

We've done our best to present these numbers in a way that makes them easy to understand. This explanation is long, so feel free to read some of it, flip around the rest of the book, and then come back. It will still be here.

Defense-Adjusted Value Over Average (DVOA)

One running back runs for three yards. Another running back runs for three yards. Which is the better run?

This sounds like a stupid question, but it isn't. In fact, this question is at the heart of nearly all of the analysis in this book.

Several factors can differentiate one three-yard run from another. What is the down and distance? Is it third-and-2, or second-and-15? Where on the field is the ball? Does the player get only three yards because he hits the goal line and scores? Is the player's team up by two touchdowns in the fourth quarter and thus running out the clock, or down by two touchdowns and thus facing a defense that is playing purely against the pass? Is the running back playing against the porous defense of the Raiders, or the stalwart defense of the Bears?

Conventional NFL statistics value plays based solely on their net yardage. The NFL determines the best players by adding up all their yards no matter what situations they came in or how many plays it took to get them. Now, why would they do that? Football has one objective—to get to the end zone—and two ways to achieve that, by gaining yards and achieving first downs. These two goals need to be balanced to determine a player's value or a team's performance. All the yards in the world won't help a team win if they all come in six-yard chunks on third-and-10.

The popularity of fantasy football only exacerbates the problem. Fans have gotten used to judging players based on how much they help fantasy teams win and lose, not how much they help *real* teams win and lose. Typical fantasy scoring further skews things by counting the yard between the one and the goal line as 61 times more important than all the other yards on the field (each yard worth 0.1 points, a touchdown worth 6.0). Let's say Larry Fitzgerald catches a pass on third-and-15 and goes 50 yards but gets tackled two yards from the goal line, and then Rashard Mendenhall takes the ball on first-and-goal from the two-yard line and plunges in for the score. Has Mendenhall done something special? Not really. When an offense gets the ball on first-and-goal at the two-yard line, they are going to score a touchdown five out of six times. Mendenhall is getting credit for the work done by the passing game.

Doing a better job of distributing credit for scoring points and winning games is the goal of **DVOA**, or Defense-adjusted Value Over Average. DVOA breaks down every single play of the NFL season, assigning each play a value based on both total yards and yards towards a first down, based on work done by Pete Palmer, Bob Carroll, and John Thorn in their seminal book, *The Hidden Game of Football*. On first down, a play is considered a success if it gains 45 percent of needed yards; on second down, a play needs to gain 60 percent of needed yards; on third or fourth down, only gaining a new first down is considered success.

We then expand upon that basic idea with a more complicated system of "success points," improved over the past four years with a lot of mathematics and a bit of trial and error. A successful play is worth one point, an unsuccessful play zero points, with fractional points in between (for example, eight yards on third-and-10 is worth 0.54 "success points"). Extra points are awarded for big plays, gradually increasing to three points for 10 yards (assuming those yards result in a first down), four points for 20 yards, and five points for 40 yards or more. Losing three or more yards is -1 point. Interceptions average -6 points, with an adjustment for the length of the pass and the location of the interception (since an interception tipped at the line is more likely to produce a long return than an interception on a 40-yard pass). A fumble is worth anywhere from -1.7 to -4.0 points depending on how often a fumble in that situation is lost to the defense—no matter who actually recovers the fumble. Red zone plays get a bonus: 20 percent for team offense, five percent for team defense, and 10 percent for individual players. There is a bonus given for a touchdown that acknowledges that the goal line is significantly more difficult to cross than the previous 99 yards (although this bonus is nowhere near as large as the one used in fantasy football).

(Our system is a bit more complex than the one in *Hidden Game* thanks to our subsequent research, which added larger penalty for turnovers, the fractional points, and a slightly higher baseline for success on first down. The reason why all fumbles are counted, no matter whether they are recovered by the offense or defense, is explained in the essay "Pregame Show.")

Every single play run in the NFL gets a "success value" based on this system, and then that number gets compared to the average success values of plays in similar situations for all players, adjusted for a number of variables. These include down and distance, field location, time remaining in game, and the team's lead or deficit in the game score. Teams are always compared to the overall offensive average, as the team made its own choice whether to pass or rush. When it comes to individual players, however, rushing plays are compared to other rushing plays, passing plays to other passing plays, tight ends to tight ends, wideouts to wideouts, and so on.

Going back to our example of the three-yard rush, if Player A gains three yards under a set of circumstances in which the average NFL running back gains only one yard, then Player A has a certain amount of value above others at his position. Likewise, if Player B gains three yards on a play on which, under similar circumstances, an average NFL back gains four yards, that Player B has negative value relative to others at his position. Once we make all our adjustments, we can evaluate the difference between this player's rate of success and the expected success rate of an average running back in the same situation (or between the opposing defense and the average defense in the same situation, etc.). Add up every play by a certain team or player, divide by the total of the various baselines for success in all those situations, and you get VOA, or Value Over Average.

Of course, the biggest variable in football is the fact that each team plays a different schedule against teams of disparate quality. By adjusting each play based on the opposing defense's average success in stopping that type of play over the course of a season, we get DVOA, or Defense-adjusted Value Over Average. Rushing and passing plays are adjusted based on down and location on the field; passing plays are also adjusted based on how the defense performs against passes to running backs, tight ends, or wide receivers. Defenses are adjusted based on the average success of the *offenses* they are facing. (Yes, technically the defensive stats are actually "offense-adjusted." If it seems weird, think of the "D" in "DVOA" as standing for "opponent-Dependent" or something.)

The biggest advantage of DVOA is the ability to break teams and players down to find strengths and weaknesses in a variety of situations. In the aggregate, DVOA may not be quite as accurate as some of the other, similar "power ratings" formulas based on comparing drives rather than individual plays, but, unlike those other ratings, DVOA can be separated not only by player, but also by down, or by week, or by distance needed for a first down. This can give us a better idea of not just which team is better, but why, and what a team has to do in order to improve itself in the future. You will find DVOA used in this book in a lot of different ways—because it takes every single play into account, it can be used to measure a player or a team's performance in any situation. All Pittsburgh third downs can be compared to how an average team does on third down. Brian Hoyer and Johnny Manziel can each be compared to how an average quarterback performs in the red zone, or with a lead, or in the second half of the game.

Since it compares each play only to plays with similar circumstances, it gives a more accurate picture of how much better a team really is compared to the league as a whole. The list of top DVOA offenses on third down, for example, is more accurate than the conventional NFL conversion statistic because it takes into account that converting third-and-long is more difficult than converting third-and-short, and that a turnover is worse than an incomplete pass because it eliminates the opportunity to move the other team back with a punt on fourth down.

One of the hardest parts of understanding a new statistic is interpreting its scale, or what numbers represent good performance or bad performance. We've made that easy with DVOA. For each season, ratings are normalized so that 0% represents league average. A positive DVOA represents a situation that favors the offense, while a negative DVOA represents a situation that favors the defense. This is why the best offenses have positive DVOA ratings (last year, Denver led the league at 33.5%) and the best defenses have negative DVOA ratings (with Seattle on top at -25.9%).

In general, the scale of offensive ratings is slightly wider than the scale of defensive ratings, although the standard deviation of defenses has been particularly low for the last two seasons. In most years, the best and worst offenses tend to rate around +/- 30%, while the best and worst defenses tend to rate around +/- 25%. For starting players, the scale tends to reach roughly +/-40% for passing and receiving, and +/- 30% for rushing. As you might imagine, some players with fewer attempts will surpass both extremes.

Team DVOA totals combine offense and defense by subtracting the latter from the former because the better defenses will have negative DVOA ratings. (Special teams performance is also added, as described later in this essay.) Certain plays are counted in DVOA for offense and not for defense, leading to separate baselines on each side of the ball. In addition, although the league ratings for offense and defense are always 0%, the league averages for passing and rushing separately are *not* 0%. Because passing is more efficient than rushing, the average for team passing is almost always positive and the average for team rushing is almost always negative. However, ratings for individual players only compare passes to other passes and runs to other runs, so the league average for individual passing is 0%, as are the league averages for rushing and the three separate league averages for receiving by wide receivers, tight ends, and running backs.

Some other important notes about DVOA:

- Only four penalties are included in DVOA. Two penalties count as pass plays on both sides of the ball: intentional grounding and defensive pass interference. The other two penalties are included for offense only: false starts and delay of game. Because the inclusion of these penalties means a group of negative plays that don't count as either passes or runs, the league averages for pass offense and run offense are higher than the league averages for pass defense and run defense.
- Aborted snaps and incomplete backwards lateral passes are only penalized on offense, not rewarded on defense.
- Adjustments for playing from behind or with a lead in the fourth quarter are different for offense and defense, as are adjustments for the final two minutes of the first half when the offense is not near field-goal range.
- Offense gets a slight penalty and defense gets a slight bonus for games indoors.

Table 1. Correlation of Various Stats to Wins, 2000-2011

Stat	Offense	Defense	Total
Points Scored/Allowed	.744	-.678	.917
DVOA	.696	-.496	.856
Yards Gained/Allowed	.560	-.421	.694
Yards Gained/Allowed per Play	.540	-.363	.728

How well does DVOA work? Using correlation coefficients, we can show that only actual points scored are better than DVOA at indicating how many games a team has won (Table 1) and DVOA does a better job of predicting wins in the coming season than either wins or points scored in the previous season (Table 2).

(Correlation coefficient is a statistical tool that measures how two variables are related by using a number between 1 and -1. The closer to -1 or 1, the stronger the relationship, but the closer to 0, the weaker the relationship.)

Special Teams

The problem with a system based on measuring both yardage and yardage towards a first down is what to do with plays that don't have the possibility of a first down. Special teams are an important part of football and we needed a way to add that performance to the team DVOA rankings. Our special teams metric includes five separate measurements: field goals and extra points, net punting, punt returns, net kickoffs, and kick returns.

The foundation of most of these special teams ratings is the concept that each yard line has a different value based on the likelihood of scoring from that position on the field. In *Hidden Game*, the authors suggested that each additional yard for the offense had equal value, with a team's own goal line being worth -2 points, the 50-yard line 2 points, and the opposing goal line 6 points. (-2 points is not only the value of a safety, but also reflects the fact that when a team is backed up in its own territory, it is likely that its drive will stall, forcing a punt that will give the ball to the other team in good field position. Thus, the negative point value reflects the fact that the defense is more likely to score next.) Our studies have updated this concept to reflect the actual likelihood that the offense or defense will have the next score from a given position on the field based on actual results from the past few seasons. The line that represents the value of field position is not straight, but curved, with the value of each yard increasing as teams approach either goal line.

Our special teams ratings compare each kick or punt to league average based on the point value of the position of the kick, catch, and return. We've determined a league average for how far a kick goes based on the line of scrimmage for each kick (almost always the 35-yard line for kickoffs, variable for punts) and a league average for how far a return goes based on both the yard line where the ball is caught and the distance that it traveled in the air.

The kicking or punting team is rated based on net points

Table 2. Correlation of Various Stats to Wins Following Year, 2000-2011

Stat	Correlation	Stat	Correlation
DVOA	.374	Yards per Play Differential	.313
Point Differential	.329	Wins	.290
Pythagorean Wins	.324	Yardage Differential	.286

compared to average, taking into account both the kick and the return if there is one. Because the average return is always positive, punts that are not returnable (touchbacks, out of bounds, fair catches, and punts downed by the coverage unit) will rate higher than punts of the same distance which are returnable. (This is also true of touchbacks on kickoffs.) There are also separate individual ratings for kickers and punters that are based on distance and whether the kick is returnable, assuming an average return in order to judge the kicker separate from the coverage.

For the return team, the rating is based on how many points the return is worth compared to average, based on the location of the catch and the distance the ball traveled in the air. Return teams are not judged on the distance of kicks, nor are they judged on kicks that cannot be returned. As explained below, blocked kicks are so rare as to be statistically insignificant as predictors for future performance and are thus ignored. For the kicking team they simply count as missed field goals, for the defense they are gathered with their opponents' other missed field goals in Hidden value (also explained below).

Field goal kicking is measured differently. Measuring kickers by field goal percentage is a bit absurd, as it assumes that all field goals are of equal difficulty. In our metric, each field goal is compared to the average number of points scored on all field goal attempts from that distance over the past 16 years. The value of a field goal increases as distance from the goal line increases. Kickoffs, punts, and field goals are then adjusted based on weather and altitude. It will surprise no one to learn that it is easier to kick the ball in Denver or a dome than it is to kick the ball in Buffalo in December. Because we do not yet have enough data to tailor our adjustments specifically to each stadium, each one is assigned to one of four categories: Cold, Warm, Dome, and Denver. There is also an additional adjustment dropping the value of field goals in Florida (because the warm temperatures allow the ball to carry better) and raising the value of punts in San Francisco (because of those infamous winds).

The baselines for special teams are adjusted in each year for rule changes such as the introduction of the special-teams-use-only "k-ball" in 1999 as well as the move of the kickoff line from the 35 to the 30 in 1994 and then back to the 35 in 2011. Baselines have also been adjusted each year to make up for the gradual improvement of kickers over the last two decades.

Once we've totaled how many points above or below average can be attributed to special teams, we translate those points into DVOA so the ratings can be added to offense and defense to get total team DVOA.

There are three aspects of special teams that have an impact on wins and losses, but don't show up in the standard special teams rating because a team has little or no influence on them. The first is the length of kickoffs by the opposing team, with an asterisk. Obviously, there are no defenders standing on the 35-yard line, ready to block a kickoff after the whistle blows. However, over the past few years, some teams have deliberately kicked short in order to avoid certain top return men, such as Devin Hester and Cordarrelle Patterson. The special teams formula now includes adjustments to give teams extra credit for field position on kick returns if kickers are deliberately trying to avoid a return.

The other two items that special teams have little control over are field goals against your team, and punt distance against your team. Research shows no indication that teams can influence the accuracy or strength of field-goal kickers and punters, except for blocks. As mentioned above, although blocked field goals and punts are definitely skillful plays, they are so rare that they have no correlation to how well teams have played in the past or will play in the future, thus they are included here as if they were any other missed field goal or botched punt, giving the defense no additional credit for their efforts. The value of these three elements is listed separately as "Hidden" value.

Special teams ratings also do not include two-point conversions or onside kick attempts, both of which, like blocks, are so infrequent as to be statistically insignificant in judging future performance.

Defense-Adjusted Yards Above Replacement (DYAR)

DVOA is a good stat, but of course it is not a perfect one. One problem is that DVOA, by virtue of being a percentage or rate statistic, doesn't take into account the cumulative value of having a player producing at a league-average level over the course of an above-average number of plays. By definition, an average level of performance is better than that provided by half of the league and the ability to maintain that level of performance while carrying a heavy workload is very valuable indeed. In addition, a player who is involved in a high number of plays can draw the defense's attention away from other parts of the offense, and, if that player is a running back, he can take time off the clock with repeated runs.

Let's say you have a running back who carries the ball 300 times in a season. What would happen if you were to remove this player from his team's offense? What would happen to those 300 plays? Those plays don't disappear with the player, though some might be lost to the defense because of the associated loss of first downs. Rather those plays would have to be distributed among the remaining players in the offense, with the bulk of them being given to a replacement running back. This is where we arrive at the concept of replacement level, borrowed from our partners at Baseball Prospectus. When a player is removed from an offense, he is usually not replaced by a player of similar ability. Nearly every starting player in the NFL is a starter because he is better than the alternative. Those 300 plays will typically be given to a significantly worse player, someone who is the backup because he doesn't have as much experience and/or talent. A player's true value can then be measured by the level of performance he provides above that replacement level baseline, totaled over all of his run or pass attempts.

Of course, the *real* replacement player is different for each team in the NFL. Last year, the second-string running back in Arizona (Andre Ellington) had a higher DVOA than the original starter (Rashard Mendenhall). Sometimes a player like Ryan Grant or Danny Woodhead will be cut by one team and turn into a star for another. On other teams, the drop from the starter to the backup can be even greater than the general drop to replacement level. The 2011 Indianapolis Colts will now be the hallmark example of this until the end of time. The choice to start an inferior player or to employ a sub-replacement level backup, however, falls to the team, not the starter being evaluated. Thus we generalize replacement level for the league as a whole as the ultimate goal is to evaluate players independent of the quality of their teammates.

Our estimates of replacement level are computed differently for each position. For quarterbacks, we analyzed situations where two or more quarterbacks had played meaningful snaps for a team in the same season, then compared the overall DVOA of the original starters to the overall DVOA of the replacements. We did not include situations where the backup was actually a top prospect waiting his turn on the bench, since a first-round pick is by no means a "replacement-level" player.

At other positions, there is no easy way to separate players into "starters" and "replacements," since unlike at quarterback, being the starter doesn't make you the only guy who gets in the game. Instead, we used a simpler method, ranking players at each position in each season by attempts. The players who made up the final 10 percent of passes or runs were split out as "replacement players" and then compared to the players making up the other 90 percent of plays at that position. This took care of the fact that not every non-starter is a freely available talent. (Think of Shane Vereen or Ladarius Green, for example.)

As noted earlier, the challenge of any new stat is to present it on a scale that's meaningful to those attempting to use it. Saying that Tony Romo's passes were worth 91 success value points over replacement in 2012 has very little value without a context to tell us if 91 is good total or a bad one. Therefore, we translate these success values into a number called "Defense-adjusted Yards Above Replacement," or DYAR. Thus, Romo was seventh among quarterbacks with 1,156 passing DYAR. It is our estimate that a generic replacement-level quarterback, throwing in the same situations as Romo, would have been worth 1,156 fewer yards. Note that this doesn't mean the replacement level quarterback would have gained exactly 1,156 fewer yards. First downs, touchdowns, and turnovers all have an estimated yardage value in this system, so what we are saying is that a generic replacement-level quarterback would have fewer yards and touchdowns (and more turnovers) that would total up to be equivalent to the value of 1,156 yards.

Problems with DVOA and DYAR

Football is a game in which nearly every action requires the work of two or more teammates—in fact, usually 11 teammates all working in unison. Unfortunately, when it comes to individual player ratings, we are still far from the point at which we can determine the value of a player independent from the performance of his teammates. That means that when we say, "In 2013, Le'Veon Bell had a DVOA of -7.0%," what we really are saying is, "In 2013, Le'Veon Bell, playing in Todd Haley's offensive system with the Pittsburgh offensive line blocking for him and Ben Roethlisberger selling the fake when necessary, had a DVOA of -7.0%." (Or, in the case of the Steelers, perhaps this should read "not blocking for him.")

DVOA is limited by what's included in the official NFL play-by-play or tracked by the Football Outsiders game charting project (introduced below). Because we need to have the entire play-by-play of a season in order to compute DVOA and DYAR, these metrics are not yet ready to compare players of today to players throughout the league's history. As of this writing, we have processed 25 seasons, 1989 through 2013, and we add seasons at a rate of roughly two per year (the most recent season, plus one season back into history.)

Pythagorean Projection

The Pythagorean projection is an approximation of each team's wins based solely on their points scored and allowed. This basic concept was introduced by baseball analyst Bill James, who discovered that the record of a baseball team could be very closely approximated by taking the square of team runs scored and dividing it by the sum of the squares of team runs scored and allowed. Statistician Daryl Morey, now general manager of the Houston Rockets, later extended this theorem to professional football, refining the exponent to 2.37 rather than 2.

The problem with that exponent is the same problem we've had with DVOA in recent years: the changing offensive levels in the NFL. 2.37 worked great based on the league 20 years ago, but in the current NFL it ends up slightly underprojecting teams that play high-scoring games. The most accurate method is actually to adjust the exponent based on the scoring environment of each individual team. Saints games have a lot of points. Jaguars games feature fewer points.

This became known as Pythagenport when Clay Davenport of Baseball Prospectus started doing it with baseball teams. In the middle of the 2011 season, we switched our measurement of Pythagorean wins to a Pythagenport-style equation, modified for the NFL[1]. The improvement is slight, but noticeable due to the high-scoring teams that have dominated the last few years.

For a long time, Pythagorean projections did a remarkable job of predicting Super Bowl champions. From 1984 through 2004, 10 of 21 Super Bowls were won by the team that led the NFL in Pythagorean wins. Seven other Super Bowls during that time were won by the team that finished second. Super Bowl champions that led the league in Pythagorean wins but not actual wins include the 2004 Patriots, 2000 Ravens, 1999 Rams, and 1997 Broncos.

As noted in the Introduction, Super Bowl champions have been much less predictable over the last few seasons. As of 2004, the 1980 Oakland Raiders held the mark for the fewest Pythagorean wins by a Super Bowl champion, 9.7. In the past eight seasons, four different teams have won the Super Bowl with a lower Pythagorean win total: the 2006 Colts (9.6), the 2012 Ravens (9.4), the 2007 Giants (8.6), and the 2011 Giants (7.9), the first team in the 90-year history of the National Football League to ever be outscored during the regular season and still go on to win the championship.

Despite these recent trends, Pythagoras is still a useful metric, particularly as a predictor of year-to-year improvement. Teams that win a minimum of one full game more than their Pythagorean projection tend to regress the following year; teams that win a minimum of one full game less than their Pythagorean projection tend to improve the following year, particularly if they were at or above .500 despite their underachieving.

Adjusted Line Yards

One of the most difficult goals of statistical analysis in football is isolating the degree to which each of the 22 men on the field is responsible for the result of a given play. Nowhere is this as significant as the running game, in which one player runs while up to nine other players—including not just linemen but also wideouts and tight ends—block in different directions. None of the statistics we use for measuring rushing—yards, touchdowns, yards per carry—differentiate between the contribution of the running back and the contribution of the offensive line. Neither do our advanced metrics DVOA and DYAR.

We do, however, have enough play-by-play data amassed that we can try to separate the effect that the running back has on a particular play from the effects of the offensive line (and other offensive blockers) and the opposing defense. A team might have two running backs in its stable: RB A, who averages 3.0 yards per carry, and RB B, who averages 3.5 yards per carry. Who is the better back? Imagine that RB A doesn't just average 3.0 yards per carry, but gets exactly 3 yards on every single carry, while RB B has a highly variable yardage output: sometimes 5 yards, sometimes -2 yards, sometimes 20 yards. The difference in variability between the runners can be exploited not only to determine the difference between the runners, but the effect the offensive line has on every running play.

At some point in every long running play, the running back passes all of his offensive line blocks as well as additional blocking backs or receivers. From there on, the rest of the play is dependent on the runner's own speed and elusiveness

[1] The equation, for those curious, is 1.5 x log ((PF+PA)/G).

and the speed and tackling ability of the opposing defense. If Frank Gore breaks through the line for 50 yards, avoiding tacklers all the way to the goal line, his offensive line has done a great job—but they aren't responsible for the majority of the yards gained. The trick is figuring out exactly how much they *are* responsible for.

For each running back carry, we calculated the probability that the back involved would run for the specific yardage on that play based on that back's average yardage per carry and the variability of their yardage from play to play. We also calculated the probability that the offense would get the yardage based on the team's rushing average and variability using all backs *other* than the one involved in the given play, and the probability that the defense would give up the specific amount of yardage based on its average rushing yards allowed per carry and variability.

A regression analysis breaks the value for rushing yardage into the following categories: losses, 0-to-4 yards, 5-to-10 yards, and 11-plus yards. In general, the offensive line is 20 percent more responsible for lost yardage than it is for positive gains up to four yards, but 50 percent less responsible for additional yardage gained between five and ten yards, and not at all responsible for additional yardage past ten yards.

By applying those percentages to every running back carry, we were able to create **Adjusted Line Yards**, a statistic that measured offensive line performance. (We don't include carries by receivers, which are usually based on deception rather than straight blocking, or carries by quarterbacks, although we may need to reconsider that given the recent use of the read option in the NFL.) Those numbers are then adjusted based on down, distance, situation, opponent, and whether or not a team is in the shotgun. (Because defenses are generally playing pass when the quarterback is in shotgun, the average running back carry from shotgun last year gained 4.79 yards, compared to just 4.14 yards on other carries—and most years the difference is even greater than that.) The adjusted numbers are then normalized so that the league average for Adjusted Line Yards per carry is the same as the league average for RB yards per carry. (Historically, this is roughly 4.25 yards. Last year, it was only 4.10 yards; if lower numbers continue, we'll need to look at adjusting the way we normalize Adjusted Line Yards to account for this.)

The NFL distinguishes between runs made to seven different locations on the line: left/right end, left/right tackle, left/right guard, and middle. Further research showed no statistically significant difference between how well a team performed on runs listed as having gone up the middle or past a guard, so we separated runs into just five different directions (left/right end, left/right tackle, and middle). Note that there may not be a statistically significant difference between right tackle and middle/guard either, but pending further research (and for the sake of symmetry) we still list runs behind the right tackle separately. These splits allow us to evaluate subsections of a team's offensive line, but not necessarily individual linemen, as we can't account for blocking assignments or guards who pull towards the opposite side of the line after the snap.

Success Rate

Success rate is a statistic for running backs that measures how consistently they achieve the yardage necessary for a play to be deemed successful. Some running backs will mix a few long runs with a lot of failed runs of one or two yards, while others with similar yards-per-carry averages will consistently gain five yards on first down, or as many yards as necessary on third down. This statistic helps us differentiate between the two.

Since Success Rate compares rush attempts to other rush attempts, without consideration of passing, the standard for success on first down is slightly lower than those described above for DVOA. In addition, the standard for success changes slightly in the fourth quarter when running backs are used to run out the clock. A team with the lead is satisfied with a shorter run as long as it stays in bounds. Conversely, for a team down by a couple of touchdowns in the fourth quarter, four yards on first down isn't going to be a big help.

The formula for Success Rate is as follows:

- A successful play must gain 40 percent of needed yards on first down, 60 percent of needed yards on second down, and 100 percent of needed yards on third or fourth down.
- If the offense is behind by more than a touchdown in the fourth quarter, the benchmarks switch to 50 percent, 65 percent, and 100 percent.
- If the offense is ahead by any amount in the fourth quarter, the benchmarks switch to 30 percent, 50 percent, and 100 percent.

The league-average Success Rate in 2012 was 47.2 percent. Success Rate is not adjusted based on defenses faced, and is not calculated for quarterbacks and wide receivers who occasionally carry the ball.

Similarity Scores

Similarity scores were first introduced by Bill James to compare baseball players to other baseball players from the past. It was only natural that the idea would spread to other sports as statistical analysis spread to other sports. NBA analyst John Hollinger has created his own version to compare basketball players, and we have created our own version to compare football players.

Similarity scores have a lot of uses, and we aren't the only football analysts who use them. Doug Drinen of the website Footballguys.com has his own system that is specific to comparing fantasy football performances. The major goal of our similarity scores is to compare career progressions to try to determine when players have a higher chance of a breakout, a decline, or—due to age or usage—an injury (much like Baseball Prospectus's PECOTA player projection system). Therefore we not only compare numbers such as attempts, yards, and touchdowns, but also age and experience. We often are looking not for players who had similar seasons, but for players who had similar two- or three-year spans in their careers.

Similarity scores have some important weaknesses. The database for player comparison begins in 1978, the year the 16-game season began and passing rules were liberalized (a reasonable starting point to measure the "modern" NFL), thus the method only compares standard statistics such as yards and attempts, which are of course subject to all kinds of biases from strength of schedule to quality of receiver corps. For our comparisons, we project full-season statistics for the strike years of 1982 and 1987, although we cannot correct for players who crossed the 1987 picket line to play more than 12 games.

In addition to our similarity scores for skill players, we also have a similarity score system for defensive players based on FO's advanced statistics going back to 1997. It measures things like average distance on run tackles or pass tackles, as well as Stops and Defeats. It does not account for game-charting stats like hurries or Success Rate in coverage.

If you are interested in the specific computations behind our similarity scores system, we have listed the standards for each skill position online at http://www.footballoutsiders.com/stats/similarity. (The defensive system is not yet listed.) In addition, as part of our online premium package, all player pages for current players—both offensive and defensive—list the top ten similar players over one-, two-, and three-year spans.

KUBIAK Projection System

Most "skill position" players whom we expect to play a role this season receive a projection of their standard 2014 NFL statistics using the KUBIAK projection system. KUBIAK takes into account a number of different factors including expected role, performance over the past two seasons, age, height, weight, historical comparables, and projected team performance on offense and defense. When we named our system KUBIAK, it was a play on the PECOTA system used by our partners at Baseball Prospectus—if they were going to name their system after a long-time eighties backup, we would name our system after a long-time eighties backup. Little did we know that Gary Kubiak would finally get a head coaching job the very next season. After some debate, we decided to keep the name, although discussing projections for Houston players can be a bit awkward.

To clear up a common misconception among our readers, KUBIAK projects individual player performances only, not teams.

2014 Win Projection System

In this book, each of the 32 NFL teams receives a **2014 Mean Projection** at the beginning of its chapter. These projections stem from three equations that forecast 2014 DVOA for offense, defense, and special teams based on a number of different factors, including the previous two years of DVOA in various situations, improvement in the second half of 2013, recent draft history, coaching experience, injury history, specific coaching styles, and the combined tenure of the offensive line.

These three equations produce precise numbers representing the most likely outcome, but also produce a range of possibilities, used to determine the probability of each possible offensive, defensive, and special teams DVOA for each team. This is particularly important when projecting football teams, because with only 16 games in a season, a team's performance may vary wildly from its actual talent level due to a couple of random bounces of the ball or badly timed injuries. In addition, the economic structure of the NFL allows teams to make sudden jumps or drops in overall ability more often than in other sports.

To create our simulation, we used the range of DVOA possibilities to produce 1,000 different simulated seasons with 32 sets of DVOA ratings. We then plugged those season-long DVOA ratings into the same equation we use during the season to determine each team's likely remaining wins for our Playoff Odds Report. The simulation takes each season game-by-game, determining the home or road team's chance of winning each game based on the DVOA ratings of each team as well as home-field advantage, warm-weather or dome-stadium teams playing in the cold after November 1, and several other variables that can affect the outcome of each game. Then a random number between 0 and 100 determines whether the home or road team has won that game. Further tweaks adjust the simulation further to produce results closer to the historic distribution of wins in the NFL. While 8-8 is still more likely than any other record, historically more NFL teams end up with records between 2-14 and 4-12 or between 12-4 and 14-2 than you would otherwise expect from a normal distribution. We ran 1,000 simulations with each of the 1,000 sets of DVOA ratings, creating a million different simulations. The simulation was programmed by Mike Harris.

(Also, yes, we know that the first three teams in the book have the same numbers for this section. That's not a typo; it's partially a result of the simulation grouping teams so close together this season, and the numbers would not be the same if we showed decimal places.)

Football Outsiders Game Charting Project

Each of the formulas listed above relies primarily on the play-by-play data published by the NFL. When we began to analyze the NFL, this was all that we had to work with. Just as a television broadcast has a color commentator who gives more detail to the facts related by the play-by-play announcer, so too do we need some color commentary to provide contextual information that breathes life into these plain lines of numbers and text. The Football Outsiders Game Charting Project is our attempt to provide color for the simple play-by-play.

Providing color to 512 hours of football is a daunting task. To put it into perspective, there were more than 54,000 lines of play-by-play information in the 2013 NFL season and our goal is to add several layers of detail to nearly all of them. We recruited more than 50 volunteers to collectively chart each week's NFL games, and we've charted data on nearly every play since 2005. Through trial-and-error, we have gradually narrowed our focus to charting things both traceable and definitive. Charting a game, and rewinding to make sure mistakes are minimized, can take two to three hours. More than a couple of these per week can be hazardous to one's marriage. Our goal was to provide comprehensive information while understanding that our charters were doing this on a volunteer basis.

Over the last two seasons, there have been two huge changes to the Football Outsiders Game Charting Project. First, the NFL finally made coaches' film available publicly through their NFL Game Rewind project. That tape includes a sideline and end zone perspectives for each play, and shows all 22 players at all times, making it easier to see the cause-and-effect of certain actions taken on the field. The availability of coaches' film helped make our charting more accurate than ever before, although it is still imperfect. You often cannot tell which players did their jobs particularly well or made mistakes without knowing the play call and each player's assignment, particularly when it comes to zone coverage or pass rushers who reach the quarterback without being blocked. Therefore, the goal of Football Outsiders game charting is *not* to "grade" players, but rather to attempt to mark specific events: a pass pressure, a blown block, a dropped interception, and so on.

There are lots of things we would like to do with all-22 film that we simply haven't been able to do yet, such as charting coverage by cornerbacks when they aren't the target of a given pass, or even when pass pressure prevents the pass from getting into the air. Unfortunately, we are still limited by how much time our volunteers can give to the project, and the fact that our financial resources do not match those of our competitors.

The second major change for the game charting project in 2012 was an agreement to link our project up with the game charting done by the ESPN Stats & Information for internal ESPN use. ESPN charts games live on Sundays and our agreement allowed us to get access to their data immediately rather than waiting two to three weeks for our game charters to complete each game. In return, we provided suggestions to correct mistakes in the data—the more eyes we have on data like this, the more accurate it will be—and supplied ESPN with some of our older charting data, which allowed them to produce their new Total QBR metric for the 2006 and 2007 seasons. All data that comes from the ESPN Stats & Information is designated as such in the description of game charting that follows.

We emphasize that all data from the charting project is unofficial. Other sources for football statistics may keep their own measurements of yards after catch or how teams perform against the blitz. Our data will not necessarily match theirs. However, any other group that is publicly tracking this data is also working off the same footage, and thus will run into the same issues of difficulty.

The Football Outsiders game charting project tracks the following information:

Formation/Personnel

For each play, we have the number of running backs, wide receivers, and tight ends on the field courtesy of ESPN Stats & Information. Players were marked based on their designation on the roster, not based on where they lined up on the field. Obviously, this could be difficult with some hybrid players or players changing positions in 2013, but we did our best to keep things as consistent as possible.

Football Outsiders charters then added to ESPN's data by marking the names of players who were lined up in unexpected positions. This included marking tight ends or wide receivers in the backfield, and running backs or tight ends who were lined up either wide or in the slot (often referred to as "flexing" a tight end). Football Outsiders charters also marked when a fullback or tight end was actually a sixth (or sometimes even seventh) offensive lineman, and they marked the backfield formation as empty back, single back, I formation, offset I, split backs, full house, or "other." These notations of backfield formation were recorded directly before the snap and do not account for positions before pre-snap motion.

We also ask game charters to mark defensive formations by listing the number of linemen, linebackers, and defensive backs. There will be mistakes—a box safety may occasionally be confused for a linebacker, for example—but for the most part the data for defensive backs will be accurate. Figuring out how to mark whether a player is a defensive end or a linebacker can be a different story. The rise of hybrid defenses has led to a lot of confusion. Edge rushers in a 4-3 defense may play standing up because they used to play for a 3-4 defense and that's what they are used to. A player who is usually considered an outside linebacker for a 3-4 defense may put his hand on the ground on third down (thus looking like a 4-3 defensive end), but the tackle next to him is still two-gapping (which is generally a 3-4 principle). This year, instead of strictly separating defensive ends from outside linebackers based on whether the player lined up with his hand on the ground before the snap, we tried to ask our charters to mark 3-4 vs. 4-3 based on two-gap vs. one-gap principles. Honestly, this is really difficult for a bunch of volunteers who don't have hours and hours to analyze film, so we're going to need to figure out some sort of more coherent strategy to conquer this problem in the future.

Rushers and Blockers

ESPN Stats & Information provided us with two data points regarding the pass rush: the number of pass rushers on a given play, and the number defensive backs blitzing on a given play. Football Outsiders charters then added a count of blockers, although this has proved to be an art as much as a science. Offenses base their blocking schemes on how many rushers they expect. A running back or tight end's assignment may depend on how many pass-rushers cross the line at the snap. Therefore, an offensive player was deemed to be a blocker if he engaged in an actual block, or there was some hesitation before running a route. A running back who immediately heads out into the flat is not a blocker, but one who waits to verify that the blocking scheme is working and then goes out to the flat would, in fact, be considered a blocker.

Pass Play Details

ESPN Stats & Information recorded the following data for all pass plays:

• Did the play begin with a play-action fake, including read-option fakes that developed into pass plays instead of being handed to a running back. Football Outsiders charters also added notation of fake end-arounds and flea flickers.

- Was the quarterback in or out of the pocket.
- Was the quarterback hurried in making his pass.
- Was this a screen pass.

Football Outsiders charters then added to the ESPN data by identifying the defender who caused the pass pressure. Charters were allowed to list two names if necessary, and could also attribute a hurry to "overall pressure." No defender was given a hurry and a sack on the same play, but defenders were given hurries if they helped force a quarterback into a sack that was finished by another player. Football Outsiders charters also identified which defender(s) caused the pass pressure which forced a quarterback to scramble for yardage. If the quarterback wasn't under pressure but ran anyway, the play could be marked either as "coverage scramble" (if the quarterback ran because there were no open receivers) or "hole opens up" (if the quarterback ran because he knew he could gain significant yardage).

For the most part, Football Outsiders defaulted to ESPN's opinion on whether a play counted as pass pressure or not. The exception was for plays where the quarterback ran around solely because nobody was open; even if the quarterback eventually threw a pass, we changed these plays to "coverage scramble" and did not count them when counting up performance under pressure.

Some places in this book, we divide pass yardage into two numbers: distance in the air and yards after catch. This information is tracked by the NFL, but it can be hard to find and the official scorers often make errors, so we corrected the original data based on input from our charters as well as ESPN Stats & Information. Distance in the air is based on the distance from the line of scrimmage to the place where the receiver either caught or was supposed to catch the pass. We do not count how far the quarterback was behind the line or horizontal yardage if the quarterback threw across the field. All touchdowns are counted to the goal line, so that distance in the air added to yards after catch always equals the official yardage total kept by the league.

Incomplete Passes

Quarterbacks are evaluated based on their ability to complete passes. However, not all incompletes should have the same weight. Throwing a ball away to avoid a sack is actually a valuable incomplete, and a receiver dropping an otherwise quality pass is hardly a reflection on the quarterback.

This year, our evaluation of incomplete passes began with ESPN Stats & Information, which marked passes as Overthrown, Underthrown, Thrown Away, Batted Down at the Line, Defensed, or Dropped. Our charters then made changes to reflect a couple of additional categories we have kept in past years for Football Outsiders: Hit in Motion (indicating the quarterback was hit as his arm was coming forward to make a pass), Caught out of Bounds, and Hail Mary.

Our count of passes defensed will be different from the unofficial totals kept by the league, as well as the totals kept by ESPN Stats & Information, for reasons explained below in the section on Defensive Secondary tables.

ESPN Stats & Information also marked when a defender dropped an interception, and Football Outsiders then added the name of the defender responsible. When a play is close, we tend to err on the side of not marking a dropped interception, as we don't want to blame a defender who, for example, jumps high for a ball and has it tip off his fingers. This year for the first time, we also counted a few "defensed" interceptions, when a quarterback threw a pass that would have been picked off if not for the receiver playing defense on the ball. These passes counted as dropped interceptions for quarterbacks but not for the defensive players.

Defenders

The NFL play-by-play lists tackles and, occasionally, tipped balls, but it does not definitively list the defender on the play. Charters were asked to determine which defender was primarily responsible for covering either the receiver at the time of the throw or the location to which the pass was thrown, regardless of whether the pass was complete or not.

Every defense in the league plays zone coverage at times, some more than others, which leaves us with the question of how to handle plays without a clear man assigned to that receiver. We gave charters three alternatives:

- We asked charters to mark passes that found the holes in zone coverage as Hole in Zone, rather than straining to assign that pass to an individual defender. We asked the charter to also note the player who appeared to be responsible for that zone, and these defenders are assigned half credit for those passes. Some holes were so large that no defender could be listed along with the Hole in Zone designation.
- Charters were free to list two defenders instead of one. This could be used for actual double coverage, or for zone coverage in which the receiver was right between two close defenders rather than sitting in a gaping hole. When two defenders are listed, ratings assign each with half credit.
- Screen passes and dumpoffs are marked as Uncovered unless a defender (normally a linebacker) is obviously shadowing that specific receiver on the other side of the line of scrimmage.

Since we began the charting project in 2005, nothing has changed our analysis more than this information on pass coverage. However, even now with the ability to view all-22 film, it can be difficult to identify the responsible defender except when there is strict man-to-man coverage. We continue to hone our craft and do our best.

Additional Details from ESPN Stats & Information

All draw plays were marked, whether by halfbacks or quarterbacks. Option runs and zone reads were also marked.

ESPN tracked when the formation was pistol as opposed to shotgun; the official play-by-play simply marks these plays all as shotgun.

ESPN also marks the number of defenders in the box for each snap, and tags each play as either "loaded" or "not loaded." A loaded box is when the defense has more players in the box than the offense has available blockers for running plays. Finally, ESPN marks yards after contact for each play.

Additional Details from Football Outsiders Charters

Football Outsiders game charters marked each quarterback sack with one of the following terms: Blown Block, Coverage Sack, QB Fault, or Blitz/Overall Pressure. Blown Blocks were listed with the name of a specific offensive player who allowed the defender to come through. (Some blown block sacks are listed with two blockers, who each get a half-sack. There are also a handful of rare three-man blown blocks.) Coverage Sack denotes when the quarterback has plenty of time to throw but cannot find an open receiver. QB Fault represents "self sacks" listed without a defender, such as when the quarterback drops back, only to find the ball slip out of his hands with no pass-rusher touching him.

Our charters track "broken tackles" on all runs or pass plays. We define a "broken tackle" as one of two events: Either the ballcarrier escapes from the grasp of the defender, or the defender is in good position for a tackle but the ballcarrier jukes him out of his shoes. If the ballcarrier sped by a slow defender who dived and missed, that did not count as a broken tackle. If the defender couldn't bring the ballcarrier down but slowed him and still had his hand on him when another player made a tackle, this did not count as a broken tackle. It was possible to mark multiple broken tackles on the same play. Occasionally, the same defender would get a broken tackle, then recover, run upfield, and get a tackle on the same play, but we went through after the season to make sure no charter marked a broken tackle for contact that the league determined was an actual tackle. Broken tackles are not marked for special teams.

We track which defensive players draw offensive holding calls; the list of leaders for 2013 can be found in the appendix.

An additional column called Extra Comment allowed the charters to add any description they wanted to the play. These comments might be good blitz pickup by a running back, a missed tackle, a great hit, a description of a pass route, an angry tirade about the poor camera angles of network broadcasts, or a number of other possibilities.

Finally, we asked the game charters to mark when a mistake was made in the official play-by-play. These mistakes include missing quarterback hits, incorrect names on tackles or penalties, missing direction on runs or passes, or the absence of the "scramble" designation when a quarterback ran on a play that began as a pass. Thanks to the diligence of our volunteer game charters and a friendly contact at the league office, the NFL corrected more than 300 mistakes in the official play-by-play based on the data collected by our game charters.

Sack Timing Project

Separate from the regular game charting project is J.J. Cooper's sack timing project, which began as a series of columns for AOL Fanhouse in 2009-2010 and continued with Football Outsiders in 2011. Cooper has timed every sack in the NFL from the time of the snap to the time of initial contact on the sack. The median sack time is roughly 2.8 seconds. The project also assigns blame for blown blocks that lead to sacks or designates a sack as "QB/Play Call," roughly akin to when the regular game charting project designates a sack as "Rusher Untouched" or "QB Fault." We used this data to clean up some mistakes in our original game charting of sacks.

Acknowledgements

None of this would have been possible without the time spent by all the volunteer game charters. There are some specific acknowledgements at the end of the book, but we want to give a general thank you here to everyone who has helped collect data over the last few seasons. Without your unpaid time, the task of gathering all this information would have been too time-consuming to yield anything useful. If you are interested in participating in next year's charting project, please e-mail your contact information to gamecharting@gmail.com with the subject "New Game Charter." Please make sure to mention where you live, what team you follow, and whether or not you have the Sunday Ticket package.

Our thanks to lots of people at ESPN Stats & Information for helping us coordinate our sharing of data, particularly Edmundo Macedo, Allison Loucks, and Henry Gargiulo. Additional extra thanks to Peter Koski, who collects and compiles the data from all the other game charters.

How to Read the Team Summary Box

Here is a rundown of all the tables and stats that appear in the 32 team chapters. Each team chapter begins with a box in the upper-right hand corner that gives a summary of our statistics for that team, as follows:

2013 Record gives each team's actual win-loss record. **Pythagorean Wins** gives the approximate number of wins expected last year based on this team's raw totals of points scored and allowed, along with their NFL rank. **Snap-Weighted Age** gives the average age of the team in 2013, weighted based on how many snaps each player was on the field and ranked from oldest (Arizona, first at 27.8) to youngest (St. Louis, 32nd at 25.4). **Average Opponent** gives a ranking of last year's schedule strength based on the average DVOA of all 16 opponents faced during the regular season. Teams are ranked from the hardest schedule (Tampa Bay) to the easiest (Kansas City).

2014 Mean Projection gives the average number of wins for this team based on the 2013 Win Projection System described earlier in this chapter. Please note that we do not expect any teams to win the exact number of games in their mean projection. First of all, no team can win 0.8 of a game. Second, because these projections represent a whole range of possible values, the averages naturally tend to drift towards 8-8. (This was stronger than usual in 2013, and ended up *even stronger* for 2014, with the exception of Denver and Oakland as outlier teams, one on each end.) If every team were to hit its mean projection, the worst team in the league would finish 5-10-1 and the best team 10-5-1. Obviously, we're not expecting a season where no team goes 4-12 or 12-4. For a better way to look at the projections, we offer **Postseason Odds**, which give each team's chance of making the postseason based on our simulation, and **Super Bowl Appearance** odds, which give each team's chance of representing its conference in Super Bowl XLIX. The average team will make the playoffs in 37.5 percent of simulations, and the Super Bowl in 6.3

percent of simulations.

Projected Average Opponent gives the team's strength of schedule for 2014; like the listing for last year's schedule strength in the first column of the box, this number is based not on last year's record but on the mean projected DVOA for each opponent. A positive schedule is harder, a negative schedule easier. Teams are ranked from the hardest projected schedule (Oakland, first) to the easiest (Houston, 32nd). This strength of schedule projection does not take into account which games are home or away, or the timing of the bye week.

The final column of the box gives the team's chances of finishing in four different basic categories of success:

- On the Clock (0-4 wins; NFL average 11%)
- Mediocrity (5-7 wins; NFL average 33%)
- Playoff Contender (8-10 wins; NFL average 38%)
- Super Bowl Contender (11-plus wins; NFL average 19%)

The percentage given for each category is dependent not only on how good we project the team to be in 2013, but the level of variation possible in that projection, and the expected performance of the teams on the schedule.

You'll also find a table with the team's 2014 schedule placed within each chapter, along with a graph showing each team's 2013 week-to-week performance by single-game DVOA. The second, dotted line on the graph represents a five-week moving average of each team's performance, in order to show a longer-term view of when they were improving and declining. After the essays come statistical tables and comments related to that team and its specific units.

Weekly Performance

The first table gives a quick look at the team's week-to-week performance in 2013. (Table 1). This includes the playoffs for those teams that made the postseason, with the four weeks of playoffs numbered 18 (wild card) through 21 (Super Bowl). All other tables in the team chapters represent regular-season performance only unless otherwise noted.

Looking at the first week for the Atlanta Falcons in 2013, the first five columns are fairly obvious: the Falcons opened the season with a 23-17 loss in New Orleans. **YDF** and **YDA** are net yards on offense and net yards against the defense. These numbers do not include penalty yardage or special teams yardage. **TO** represents the turnover margin. Unlike other parts of the book in which we consider all fumbles as equal, this only represents actual turnovers: fumbles lost and interceptions. So, for example, the Falcons had two more turnovers than Carolina in Week 9, but then forced one more turnover than Carolina in the Week 17 rematch.

Finally, you'll see DVOA ratings for this game: Total **DVOA** first, then offense (**Off**), defense (**Def**), and special teams (**ST**). Note that these are DVOA ratings, adjusted for opponent, so a loss to a good team will often be listed with a higher rating than a close win over a bad team.

Table 1: 2013 Falcons Stats by Week

Wk	vs.	W-L	PF	PA	YDF	YDA	TO	Total	Off	Def	ST
1	at NO	L	17	23	367	419	-1	12%	7%	-4%	1%
2	STL	W	31	24	393	421	+1	25%	33%	17%	9%
3	at MIA	L	23	27	377	285	0	5%	20%	-1%	-16%
4	NE	L	23	30	457	448	-1	-8%	13%	29%	9%
5	NYJ	L	28	30	363	288	-1	-43%	4%	35%	-12%
6	BYE										
7	TB	W	31	23	291	337	0	28%	34%	-1%	-7%
8	at ARI	L	13	27	292	348	-3	-30%	-34%	3%	7%
9	at CAR	L	10	34	289	373	-2	-13%	-12%	2%	1%
10	SEA	L	10	33	226	490	-1	-38%	1%	39%	0%
11	at TB	L	28	41	420	410	-3	-58%	-11%	36%	-10%
12	NO	L	13	17	355	374	-1	2%	24%	19%	-3%
13	vs. BUF	W	34	31	423	405	+1	-10%	9%	27%	8%
14	at GB	L	21	22	285	334	0	-1%	-13%	-20%	-8%
15	WAS	W	27	26	243	476	+5	-35%	-24%	17%	6%
16	at SF	L	24	34	402	379	-2	-6%	20%	34%	8%
17	CAR	L	20	21	307	283	+1	10%	-9%	-14%	5%

Trends and Splits

Next to the week-to-week performance is a table giving DVOA for different portions of a team's performance, on both offense and defense. Each split is listed with the team's rank among the 32 NFL teams. These numbers represent regular season performance only.

Total DVOA gives total offensive, and defensive DVOA in all situations. **Unadjusted VOA** represents the breakdown of play-by-play considering situation but not opponent. A team whose offensive DVOA is higher than its offensive VOA played a harder-than-average schedule of opposing defenses; a team with a lower defensive DVOA than defensive VOA player a harder-than-average schedule of opposing offenses.

Weighted Trend lowers the importance of earlier games to give a better idea of how the team was playing at the end of the regular season. The final four weeks of the season are full strength; moving backwards through the season, each week is given less and less weight until the first three weeks of the season, which are not included at all. **Variance** is the same as noted above, with a higher percentage representing less consistency. This is true for both offense and defense: Oakland, for example, was very consistent on offense (3.7%, third) but one of the league's least consistent defenses (7.9%, 26th). **Average Opponent** is that the same thing that appears in the box to open each chapter, except split in half: the average DVOA of all opposing defenses (for offense) or the average DVOA of all opposing offenses (for defense).

Passing and **Rushing** are fairly self-explanatory. Note that rushing DVOA includes all rushes, not just those by running backs, including quarterback scrambles that may have began as pass plays.

The next three lines split out DVOA on **First Down, Second Down**, and **Third Down**. Third Down here includes fourth downs on which a team runs a regular offensive play instead of punting or attempting a field goal. **First Half** and **Second Half** represent the first two quarters and last two quarters (plus overtime), not the first eight and last eight games of the regular season. Next comes DVOA in the **Red Zone**, which is any offensive play starting from the defense's 20-yard line through the goal line. The final split is **Late and Close**, which includes any play in the second half or overtime when the teams are within eight points of each other in either direction. (Eight points, of course, is the biggest deficit that can be made up with a single score, a touchdown and two-point conversion.)

Five-Year Performance

This table gives each team's performance over the past five seasons (Table 2). It includes win-loss record, Pythagorean Wins, **Estimated Wins**, points scored and allowed, and turnover margin. Estimated wins are based on a formula that estimates how many games a team would have been expected to win based on 2013 performance in specific situations, normalized to eliminate luck (fumble recoveries, opponents' missed field goals, etc.) and assuming average schedule strength. The formula emphasizes consistency and overall DVOA as well as DVOA in a few specifically important situations. The next columns of this table give total DVOA along with DVOA for offense, defense, and special teams, and the rank for each among that season's 32 NFL teams.

The next four columns give the Adjusted Games Lost for starters on both offense and defense, along with rank. (Our total for starters here includes players who take over as starters due to another injury, such as Jordan Reed or Malcolm Smith last year, as well as important situational players who may not necessarily start, such as pass-rush specialists and slot receivers.) Adjusted Games Lost was introduced in *Pro Football Prospectus 2008*; it gives a weighted estimate of the probability that players would miss games based on how they are listed on the injury report. Unlike a count of "starter games missed," this accounts for the fact that a player listed as questionable who does in fact play is not playing at 100 percent capability. Teams are ranked from the fewest injuries (2013: Chicago on offense, Tampa Bay on defense) to the most (2013: New York Giants on offense, New Orleans on defense).

Individual Offensive Statistics

Each team chapter contains a table giving passing and receiving numbers for any player who either threw five passes or was thrown five passes, along with rushing numbers for any players who carried the ball at least five times. These numbers also appear in the player comments at the end of the book (except for wide-receiver rushing attempts). By putting them together in the team chapters we hope we make it easier to compare the performances of different players on the same team.

Players who are no longer on the team are marked with an asterisk. New players who were on a different team in 2013 are in italics. Changes should be accurate at least July 15. Rookies are not included.

All players are listed with DYAR and DVOA. Passing statistics (Table 3, next page) then list total pass plays (**Plays**), net yardage (**NtYds**), and net yards per pass (**Avg**). These numbers include not just passes (and the positive yardage from them) but aborted snaps and sacks (and the negative yardage from them). Then comes average yards after catch (**YAC**), as determined by the game charting project. This average is based on charted receptions, not total pass attempts. The final three numbers are completion percentage (**C%**), passing touchdowns (**TD**), and interceptions (**Int**).

It is important to note that the tables in the team chapters contain Football Outsiders stats, while the tables in the player comments later in the book contain official NFL totals, at least when it comes to standard numbers like receptions and yardage. This results in a number of differences between the two:

- Team chapter tables list aborted snaps as passes, not runs, although aborted handoffs are still listed as runs. Net yardage for quarterbacks in the team chapter tables includes the lost yardage from aborted snaps, sacks, and intentional grounding penalties. For official NFL stats, all aborted snaps are listed as runs.
- Football Outsiders stats omit kneeldowns from run totals and clock-stopping spikes from pass totals.
- In the Football Outsiders stats, we have changed a number of lateral passes to count as passes rather than runs, under the theory that a pass play is still a pass play, even if the receiver is standing five inches behind the quarterback. This results in some small differences in totals.
- Players who played for multiple teams in 2013 are only listed in team chapters with stats from that specific team; combined stats are listed in the player comments section.

Rushing statistics (Table 4) start with DYAR and DVOA, then list rushing plays and net yards along with average yards per carry and rushing touchdowns. The final two columns are fumbles (**Fum**)—both those lost to the defense and those recovered by the offense—and Success Rate (**Suc**), explained earlier in this chapter. Fumbles listed in the rushing table include all quarterback fumbles on sacks and aborted snaps, as well as running back fumbles on receptions, but not wide receiver fumbles.

Receiving statistics (Table 5) start with DYAR and DVOA and then list the number of passes thrown to this receiver (**Plays**), the number of passes caught (**Catch**) and the total receiving yards (**Yds**). Yards per catch (**Y/C**) includes total yardage per

Table 2: Minnesota Vikings' Five-Year Performance

Year	W-L	Pyth W	Est W	PF	PA	TO	Total	Rk	Off	Rk	Def	Rk	ST	Rk	Off AGL	Rk	Def AGL	Rk	Off Age	Rk	Def Age	Rk	ST Age	Rk
2009	12-4	11.8	10.4	470	312	+6	18.5%	7	12.9%	8	-1.0%	15	4.7%	3	9.4	7	13.1	4	28.3	3	27.5	8	26.9	8
2010	6-10	6.0	6.5	281	348	-11	-13.9%	25	-15.1%	27	-2.5%	12	-1.4%	19	35.7	25	19.7	14	28.5	5	28.3	4	27.4	2
2011	3-13	5.3	4.6	340	449	-3	-22.2%	29	-10.2%	24	8.0%	23	-4.1%	27	20.5	9	28.3	19	27.7	10	27.3	14	26.4	15
2012	10-6	8.8	8.8	379	348	-1	2.0%	14	0.3%	15	3.1%	21	4.7%	5	10.4	3	18.5	8	25.5	31	27.2	12	25.5	28
2013	5-10-1	6.1	6.5	391	480	-12	-11.4%	26	-4.7%	21	10.5%	27	3.8%	6	22.3	8	33.0	19	26.6	19	27.1	12	25.8	24

Table 3: Baltimore Ravens Passing

Player	DYAR	DVOA	Plays	NtYds	Avg	YAC	C%	TD	Int
J.Flacco	-296	-18.1%	661	3579	5.4	4.9	59.1%	19	22
T.Taylor	-75	-236.3%	5	2	0.4	1.0	20.0%	0	1

Table 4: Arizona Cardinals Rushing

Player	DYAR	DVOA	Plays	Yds	Avg	TD	Fum	Suc
R.Mendenhall*	-15	-10.2%	217	687	3.2	8	4	42%
A.Ellington	117	17.5%	118	657	5.6	3	1	46%
S.Taylor	-9	-14.7%	36	117	3.3	0	0	39%
A.Smith*	-16	-27.5%	18	54	3.0	1	2	50%
C.Palmer	-3	-30.4%	5	25	5.0	0	0	-
J.Dwyer	*-25*	*-18.7%*	*49*	*197*	*4.0*	*0*	*0*	*47%*

Table 5: Cincinnati Bengals Receiving

Player	DYAR	DVOA	Plays	Ctch	Yds	Y/C	YAC	TD	C%
A.J.Green	207	1.9%	178	98	1426	14.6	4.1	11	55%
M.Jones	279	32.4%	80	51	712	14.0	4.4	10	64%
M.Sanu	17	-10.0%	78	47	457	9.7	5.4	2	60%
A.Hawkins*	31	8.7%	18	12	199	16.6	11.3	0	67%
D.Sanzenbacher	13	9.2%	8	6	61	10.2	5.3	0	75%
J.Gresham	-47	-18.5%	67	46	458	10.0	5.8	4	69%
T.Eifert	-27	-14.0%	59	39	445	11.4	5.8	2	66%
A.Smith*	-36	-87.5%	6	3	12	4.0	2.0	1	50%
K.Brock	*-5*	*-23.0%*	*6*	*3*	*36*	*12.0*	*1.3*	*0*	*50%*
G.Bernard	167	29.4%	71	56	514	9.2	9.4	3	79%
B.Green-Ellis	-20	-61.0%	8	4	22	5.5	2.0	0	50%

reception, based on standard play-by-play, while yards after catch (**YAC**) is based on information from our game charting project. Finally we list total receiving touchdowns, and catch percentage (**C%**), which is the percentage of passes intended for this receiver which were caught. Wide receivers, tight ends, and running backs are separated on the table by horizontal lines.

Performance Based on Personnel

These tables provide a look at performance in 2013 based on personnel packages, as defined above in the section on marking formation/personnel as part of the Football Outsiders game charting project. There are four different tables, representing:

- Offense based on personnel
- Offense based on opponent's defensive personnel
- Defense based on personnel
- Defense based on opponent's offensive personnel

Most of these tables feature the top five personnel groupings for each team. Occasionally, we will list the personnel group which ranks sixth if the sixth group is either particularly interesting or nearly as common as the fifth group. Each personnel group is listed with its frequency among 2013 plays, yards per play, and DVOA. Offensive personnel are also listed with how often the team in question called a running play instead of a pass play from given personnel. (Quarterback scrambles are included as pass plays, not runs.)

Offensive personnel are given in the standard two-digit format where the first digit is running backs and the second digit is tight ends. You can figure out wide receivers by subtracting that total from five, with a couple of exceptions. Plays with six or seven offensive linemen will have a three-digit listing such as "611" or "622." Any play with a direct snap to a non-quarterback, or with a specific running quarterback taking the snap instead of the regular quarterback, was counted as "Wildcat." No team ends up with Wildcat listed among its top five offensive personnel groups.

When defensive players come in to play offense, defensive backs are counted as wide receivers and linebackers as tight ends. Defensive linemen who come in as offensive linemen are counted as offensive linemen; if they come in as blocking fullbacks, we count them as running backs.

When defensive personnel groups are listed in a number format such as "4-3-4," the first number is defensive linemen, the second number is linebackers, and the third number is defensive backs. Except for 4-4-3 and 3-5-3, all personnel groups with fewer than four defensive backs are combined and listed as "Goal Line." On the suggestion of some of our friends on coaching staffs and in front offices, we've grouped personnel groups with five defensive backs into two groups this year: "Nickel Odd" (1-5-5, 3-3-5, and the occasional 5-1-5) or "Nickel Even" (4-2-5 or 2-4-5). The 2-4-5 and 4-2-5 in particular are essentially the same, with the two outside linebackers in 2-4-5 usually rushing the passer. All personnel groups with at least six defensive backs are grouped together under the heading "Dime+."

11, or three-wide personnel, was by far the most common grouping in the NFL last year, used on 51 percent of plays, followed by the standard two-tight end set 12 personnel (21 percent of plays) and the more traditional (and slowly dying) 21 personnel (13 percent). The most common defensive setup was Nickel Even (40 percent), followed by 4-3-4 (20 percent) and 3-4-4 (19 percent), Dime (9.3 percent), and Nickel Odd (8.5 percent).

Strategic Tendencies

The Strategic Tendencies table (Table 6) presents a mix of information garnered from both the standard play by play and the Football Outsiders game charting project. It gives you an idea of what kind of plays teams run in what situations and with what personnel. Each category is given a league-wide **Rank** from most often (1) to least often (32) except as noted below. The sample table shown here lists the NFL average in each category for 2013.

The first column of strategic tendencies lists how often teams ran in different situations. These ratios are based on the type of play, not the actual result, so quarterback scrambles count as "passes" while quarterback sneaks, draws and option plays count as "runs."

Runs, first half and **Runs, first down** should be self evident. **Runs, second-and-long** is the percentage of runs on second down with seven or more yards to go, giving you an idea of how teams follow up a failed first down. **Runs, power situations** is the percentage of runs on third or fourth down with 1 or 2 yards to go, or at the goal line with 1 or 2 yards to go. **Runs, behind 2H** tells you how often teams ran when they were behind in the second half, generally a passing situation. **Pass, ahead 2H** tells you how often teams passed when they had the lead in the second half, generally a running situation.

In each case, you can determine the percentage of plays that were passes by subtracting the run percentage from 100 (the reverse being true for "Pass, ahead 2H," of course).

The second column gives information about offensive formations and personnel, as tracked by ESPN Stats & Information.

The first two entries detail formation, i.e. where players were lined up on the field. **Form: Single Back** lists how often the team lined up with only one player in the backfield, and **Form: Empty Back** lists how often the team lined up with no players in the backfield.

The next three entries are based on personnel, no matter where players were lined up in the formation. **Pers: 3+ WR** marks how often the team plays with three or more wide receivers. **Pers: 4+ WR** marks how often the team plays with four or more wide receivers. (Although announcers will often refer to a play as "five-wide," formations with five wide receivers are actually quite uncommon.) **Pers: 2+ TE/6+ OL** marks how often the team plays with either more than one tight end or more than five offensive linemen. Finally, we give the percentage of plays where a team used **Shotgun or Pistol** in 2013. This does not count "Wildcat" or direct snap plays involving a non-quarterback.

The third column shows how the defensive **Pass Rush** worked in 2013.

Rush 3/Rush 4/Rush 5/Rush 6+: The percentage of pass plays (including quarterback scrambles) on which our game charters recorded this team rushing the passer with three or fewer defenders, four defenders, five defenders, and six or more defenders. These percentages do not include goal-line plays on the one- or two-yard line.

Sacks by LB/Sacks by DB: The percentage of this team's sacks that came from linebackers and defensive backs. To figure out the percentage of sacks from defensive linemen, simply subtract the sum of these numbers from 100 percent.

The fourth column has more data on the use of defensive backs.

4 DB/5DB/6+ DB: The percentage of plays where this defense lined up with four, five, and six or more defensive backs.

CB by Sides: One of the most important lessons from game charting is that each team's best cornerback does not necessarily match up against the opponent's best receiver. Most cornerbacks play a particular side of the field and in fact cover a wider range of receivers than we assumed before we saw the charting data. This metric looks at which teams prefer to leave their starting cornerbacks on specific sides of the field. It replaces a metric from previous books called "CB1 on WR1," which looked at the same question but through the lens of how often the top cornerback covered the opponent's top receiver.

To figure CB by Sides, we took the top two cornerbacks from each team and looked at the percentage of passes where that cornerback was in coverage on the left or right side of the field, ignoring passes marked as "middle." For each of the two cornerbacks, we took the higher number, right or left, and then we averaged the two cornerbacks to get the final CB by Sides rating. Teams which prefer to leave their cornerbacks in the same place, such as Seattle, Atlanta, and Cincinnati, will have high ratings. Teams that do more to move their best cornerback around to cover the opponent's top targets, such as Arizona, Denver, and Houston, will have low ratings.

DB Blitz: We have data on how often the defense used at least one defensive back in the pass rush courtesy of ESPN Stats & Information.

Hole in Zone: The percentage of passes where this defense was listed with "Hole in Zone" in the column for pass coverage. Obviously, it can be hard to determine whether a defense is trying to play a man or zone coverage, so these numbers are imperfect, but we think they provide a general idea of whether a team's defense is more man- or zone-based.

Finally, in the final column, we have some elements of game strategy.

Play action: The percentage of pass plays (including quarterback scrambles) which began with a play-action fake to the running back. This percentage does not include fake end-arounds unless there was also a fake handoff. It does include flea flickers.

Average Box: Another item added to our charting courtesy of ESPN Stats & Information is the number of defenders in the box before the snap. We list the average box faced by each team's offense and the average box used by this team's defense.

Offensive Pace: Situation-neutral pace represents the seconds of game clock per offensive play, with the following restrictions: no drives are included if they start in the fourth quarter or final five minutes of the first half, and drives are only included if the score is within six points or less. Teams are ranked from quickest pace (Philadelphia, the quickest situation-neutral pace we've ever measured at 23.9 seconds) to

Table 6: League Average Strategic Tendencies

Run/Pass		Rk	Formation		Rk	Pass Rush		Rk	Secondary		Rk	Strategy		Rk
Runs, first half	38%	--	Form: Single Back	69%	--	Rush 3	5.8%	--	4 DB	40%	--	Play action	21%	--
Runs, first down	48%	--	Form: Empty Back	7%	--	Rush 4	62.0%	--	5 DB	49%	--	Avg Box (Off)	6.35	--
Runs, second-long	32%	--	Pers: 3+ WR	56%	--	Rush 5	23.9%	--	6+ DB	10%	--	Avg Box (Def)	6.35	--
Runs, power sit.	55%	--	Pers: 4+ WR	2%	--	Rush 6+	8.4%	--	CB by Sides	74%	--	Offensive Pace	29.79	--
Runs, behind 2H	27%	--	Pers: 2+ TE/6+ OL	32%	--	Sacks by LB	35.8%	--	DB Blitz	11%	--	Defensive Pace	29.79	--
Pass, ahead 2H	48%	--	Shotgun/Pistol	59%	--	Sacks by DB	8.2%	--	Hole in Zone	9%	--	Go for it on 4th	0.90	--

slowest pace (Pittsburgh, 32.3 seconds)

Defensive Pace: Situation-neutral pace based on seconds of game clock per defensive play. This is a representation of how a defense was approached by its opponents, not the strategy of the defense itself (an issue discussed in the Indianapolis chapter of *PFP 2006*). Teams are ranked from quickest pace (Cincinnati, 28.4 seconds) to slowest pace (Seattle, 31.9 seconds).

Go for it on fourth: This is the aggressiveness index (AI) introduced by Jim Armstrong in *Pro Football Prospectus 2006*, which measures how often a team goes for a first down in various fourth down situations compared to the league average. A coach over 1.00 is more aggressive, and one below 1.00 is less aggressive. Coaches are ranked from most aggressive to least aggressive. Contrary to popular wisdom, coaches on the whole have actually been less aggressive in recent seasons than they were five or six years ago. The AI for the league in 2013 was only 0.90. Aggressiveness Index has been slightly updated this season to include situations where a head coach chooses to take a Delay of Game penalty to move his punter five yards back on fourth-and-1 at midfield; previously, these plays were not counted for AI because they would be listed in the play-by-play as fourth-and-6.

Following each strategic tendencies table, you'll find a series of comments highlighting interesting data from that team's charting numbers. This includes DVOA ratings split for things like different formations, draw plays, or play-action passing. Please note that all DVOA ratings given in these comments are standard DVOA with no adjustments for the specific situation being analyzed, and the average DVOA for a specific situation will not necessarily be 0%. For example, the average offensive DVOA on play-action passes in 2013 was 20.9%. The average offensive DVOA when the quarterback was hurried was -75.2%; if we remove sacks, scrambles, and intentional grounding and only look at actual passes, the average offensive DVOA was -20.5%. On average last year, there was pressure marked on 24.7 percent of pass plays.

Previous books included an item in the Strategic Tendencies table called "max protect." Although we have not included it in the table this year, we do discuss it in some of the Strategic Tendencies comments. Max protect is defined as all passing plays where blockers outnumber pass rushers by at least two, with a minimum of seven blockers.

How to Read the Offensive Line Tables

This year's book includes the expanded offensive line tables we first introduced in 2013. For years, our game charters have marked blown blocks not just on sack but also on hurries, hits, and runs stuffed at the line. Unfortunately, in past years charters were so inconsistent about their frequency of marking blown blocks (except on sacks) that we couldn't really trust the numbers enough to present them to readers with any kind of confidence. For the past two seasons, however, we have gone back and dedicated time to checking plays with possible blown blocks in order to create more consistency between charters. The result is much more useful numbers for individual linemen.

However, while we have blown blocks to mark bad plays, we still don't have a metric that consistently marks good plays, so blown blocks should not be taken as the end all and be all of judging individual linemen. It's simply one measurement that goes into the conversation.

All offensive linemen who had at least 100 snaps in 2013 (not including special teams) are listed in the offensive line tables along with the position they played most often and their **Age** as of the 2014 season, listed simply as the difference between birth year and 2014. Players born in January and December of the same year will have the same listed age.

Then we list games, games started, snaps, and offensive penalties (**Pen**) for each lineman. Finally, there are three numbers for blown blocks in 2013.

- Blown blocks leading directly to sacks
- All blown blocks on pass plays, not only including those that lead to sacks but also those that lead to hurries, hits, or offensive holding penalties
- All blown blocks on run plays; generally this means plays where the running back is tackled for a loss or no gain, but it also includes a handful of plays where the running back would have been tackled for a loss if not for a broken tackle, as well as offensive holding penalties on running plays

Players are given half a blown block when two offensive players are listed with blown blocks on the same play; there are also a few plays where we assigned one-third of a blown

Table 7: Seattle Seahawks Offensive Line

Player	Pos	Age	GS	Snaps	Pen	Sk	Pass	Run	Player	Pos	Age	GS	Snaps	Pen	Sk	Pass	Run
J.R. Sweezy	RG	25	15/15	952	7	0.5	15.5	12.0	Breno Giacomini	RT	29	9/9	534	6	2.5	15.0	5.0
Paul McQuistan	G/T	29	16/10	773	4	6.8	21.3	8.0	Michael Bowie	RT	23	9/8	523	2	3.3	15.3	4.0
James Carpenter	LG	25	16/10	760	6	1.8	10.8	10.0	Russell Okung	LT	27	8/8	425	7	2.0	10.0	0.0
Max Unger	C	28	13/13	753	3	1.0	7.5	6.5	Lemuel Jeanpierre	C	27	16/3	274	0	0.0	1.5	0.0

Year	Yards	ALY	Rk	Power	Rk	Stuff	Rk	2nd Lev	Rk	Open Field	Rk	Sacks	ASR	Rk	Short	Long	F-Start	Cont.
2011	4.12	4.01	19	73%	2	18%	10	1.11	26	0.72	24	50	8.3%	24	19	18	35	27
2012	4.83	4.42	4	70%	4	15%	1	1.42	2	0.94	8	33	7.2%	20	9	19	23	23
2013	4.03	4.05	9	49%	32	19%	15	1.17	13	0.59	23	44	9.6%	32	10	21	21	29

2013 ALY by direction: Left End 3.80 (12) Left Tackle 4.52 (7) Mid/Guard 3.81 (19) Right Tackle 4.14 (11) Right End 4.13 (8)

block to three different players.

As with all player tables in the team chapters, players who are no longer on the team have an asterisk and those new to the team in 2014 are in italics. For offensive line and defensive player tables, players who spent time with multiple teams in 2012 are listed with the team where they ended the season.

The second offensive line table lists the last three years of our various line stats.

The first column gives standard yards per carry by each team's running backs (**Yards**). The next two columns give Adjusted Line Yards (**ALY**) followed by rank among the 32 teams.

Power gives the percentage of runs in "power situations" that achieved a first down or touchdown. Those situations include any third or fourth down with 1 or 2 yards to go, and any runs in goal-to-go situations from the two-yard line or closer. Unlike the other rushing numbers on the Offensive Line table, Power includes quarterbacks.

Stuff gives the percentage of runs that are stuffed for zero or negative gain. Since being stuffed is bad, teams are ranked from stuffed least often (1) to most often (32).

Second-Level (**2nd Lev**) Yards and **Open Field** Yards represent yardage where the running back has the most power over the amount of the gain. Second-Level Yards represent the number of yards per carry that come 5 to 10 yards past the line of scrimmage. Open-Field Yards represent the number of yards per carry that come 11 or more yards past the line of scrimmage. A team with a low ranking in Adjusted Line Yards but a high ranking in Open-Field Yards is heavily dependent on its running back breaking long runs to make the running game work, and therefore tends to have a less consistent running attack. Second Level Yards fall somewhere in between.

The next five columns give information about pass protection. That starts with total sacks, followed by Adjusted Sack Rate (**ASR**) and its rank among the 32 teams. Some teams allow a lot of sacks because they throw a lot of passes; Adjusted Sack Rate accounts for this by dividing sacks and intentional grounding by total pass plays. It is also adjusted for situation (sacks are much more common on third down, particularly third-and-long) and opponent, all of which makes it a better measurement than raw sack totals. Remember that quarterbacks share responsibility for sacks, and two different quarterbacks behind the same line can have very different Adjusted Sack Rates. We also give two specific totals that come from J.J. Cooper's sack-timing project. **Short Sacks** are the total of sacks that took shorter than 2.5 seconds; **Long Sacks** are the total of sacks that took longer than 3.0 seconds.

F-Start gives the number of false starts, which is the offensive penalty which best correlates to both wins and wins the following season. This total includes false starts by players other than offensive linemen, but it does not include false starts on special teams. Baltimore led the league with 25, the New York Giants were last with six, and the NFL average was 14.9. Finally, Continuity Score (**Cont.**) tells you how much continuity each offensive line had from game-to-game in that season. It was introduced in the Cleveland chapter of *Pro Football Prospectus 2007*. Continuity score starts with 48 and then subtracts:

- The number of players over five who started at least one game on the offensive line;
- The number of times the team started at least one different lineman compared to the game before; and
- The difference between 16 and that team's longest streak where the same line started consecutive games.

The perfect Continuity Score is 48, achieved last year by Chicago, Philadelphia, and Washington. The lowest Continuity Score belonged to Oakland at 22.

Finally, underneath the table in italics we give 2013 Adjusted Line Yards in each of the five directions with rank among the 32 teams. As noted earlier, these averages were down from past years. The league average was 3.63 on left end runs (**LE**), 3.97 on left tackle runs (**LT**), 3.93 on runs up the middle (**MID**), 3.83 on right tackle runs (**RT**), and 3.72 on right end runs (**RE**).

How to Read the Defensive Front Seven Tables

Defensive players make plays. Plays aren't just tackles—interceptions and pass deflections change the course of the game, and so does the act of forcing a fumble or beating the offensive players to a fumbled ball. While some plays stop a team on third down and force a punt, others merely stop a receiver after he's caught a 30-yard pass. We still cannot measure each player's opportunities to make a tackle. We can measure opportunities in pass coverage, however, thanks to the Football Outsiders game charting project.

Defensive players are listed in these tables if they made at least 20 plays during the 2013 season, or if they played at least eight games and played 25 percent of defensive snaps in those games.

Defensive Linemen/Edge Rushers

A major change in *Football Outsiders Almanac 2014* concerns how we are marking and ranking individual defensive players. As hybrid defenses become more popular, it becomes more and more difficult to tell the difference between a defensive end and an outside linebacker. What we do know is that there are certain players whose job is to rush the passer, even if they occasionally drop into coverage. We also know that the defensive ends in a two-gapping 3-4 system have a lot more in common with run-stuffing 4-3 tackles than with smaller 4-3 defensive ends.

Therefore, this year we have separated front seven players into three tables rather than two. All defensive tackles and defensive ends from 3-4 teams are listed as **Defensive Linemen**, and all ranked together. Defensive ends from 4-3 teams and outside linebackers from 3-4 teams are listed as **Edge Rushers**, and all ranked together. All 4-3 linebackers are ranked along with 3-4 inside linebackers, and listed simply as **Linebackers**. For the most part this categorization puts players with similar roles together, although you occasionally get a 4-3 outside linebacker who becomes a pass-rushing specialist on third downs (Von Miller being the best example).

The tables for defensive linemen and edge rushers are the same, although the players are ranked in two separate categories. Players are listed with the following numbers:

Age, position (**Pos**) and the number of defensive **Snaps** played in 2013.

Plays (**Plays**): The total defensive plays including tackles, pass deflections, interceptions, fumbles forced, and fumble recoveries. This number comes from the official NFL gamebooks and therefore does not include plays on which the player is listed by the Football Outsiders game charting project as in coverage, but does not appear in the standard play-by-play. Special-teams tackles are also not included.

Percentage of Team Plays (**TmPct**): The percentage of total team plays involving this defender. The sum of the percentages of team plays for all defenders on a given team will exceed 100 percent, primarily due to shared tackles. This number is adjusted based on games played, so an injured player may be fifth on his team in plays but third in **TmPct**.

Stops (**Stop**): The total number of plays which prevent a "success" by the offense (45 percent of needed yards on first down, 60 percent on second down, 100 percent on third or fourth down).

Defeats (**Dfts**): The total number of plays which stop the offense from gaining first down yardage on third or fourth down, stop the offense behind the line of scrimmage, or result in a fumble (regardless of which team recovers) or interception.

Broken Tackles (**BTkl**): The number of broken tackles recorded by our game charters.

The next five columns represent runs only, starting with the number of plays each player made on Runs. Stop Rate (**St%**) gives the percentage of these run Plays which were Stops. Average Yards (**AvYd**) gives the average number of yards gained by the runner when this player is credited with making the play.

Finally, we have pass rush numbers, starting with standard NFL **Sack** totals.

Hit: To qualify as a quarterback hit, the defender must knock the quarterback to the ground in the act of throwing or after the pass is thrown. We have listed hits on all plays, including those cancelled by penalties. (After all, many of the hardest hits come on plays cancelled because the hit itself draws a roughing the passer penalty.) Because official scorers are not entirely consistent, hits are adjusted slightly based on the home team of each game.

Hurries (**Hur**): The number of quarterback hurries recorded by the Football Outsiders game charting project. This includes both hurries on standard plays and hurries that force an offensive holding penalty that cancels the play and costs the offense yardage.

Tips: The number of plays where this player batted the ball down at the line of scrimmage or tipped it in the air, usually to force an incomplete pass. Occasionally tips lead to interceptions, and even more rarely they fall into the hands of offensive receivers. Some plays counted as tips by Football Outsiders were not counted as passes defensed by the NFL.

Defensive linemen and edge rushers are both ranked by percentage of team plays, Run Stop Rate, and average yards per run tackle. The lowest number of average yards earns the top rank (negative numbers indicate the average play ending behind the line of scrimmage). Defensive linemen and edge rushers are ranked if they played at least 40 percent of defensive snaps in the games they were active. There are 85 defensive linemen ranked, and 79 edge rushers.

Linebackers

Most of the stats for linebackers are the same as those for defensive linemen, except that the sections for pass rush and run tackles are reversed.[1] Linebackers are ranked in percentage of team plays, and also in Stop Rate and average yards for running plays specifically. Linebackers are ranked in these stats if they played at least 40 percent of defensive snaps in the games they were active; we also added two linebackers who just missed this threshold but did have at least 16 charted passes (Jamie Collins and Vincent Rey). There are 82 linebackers ranked.

The final six columns in the linebacker stats come from the Football Outsiders game charting project.

Targets (**Tgts**): The number of pass players on which our game charters listed this player in coverage.

Table 8: San Diego Chargers' Defensive Linemen, Edge Rushers

			Overall							vs. Run					Pass Rush				
Defensive Line	Age	Pos	G	Snaps	Plays	TmPct	Rk	Stop	Dfts	BTkl	Runs	St%	Rk	RuYd	Rk	Sack	Hit	Hur	Tips
Corey Liuget	24	DE	16	713	44	5.7%	32	26	11	0	28	57%	84	3.8	83	5.5	9	12.0	2
Kendall Reyes	25	DE	16	710	36	4.7%	53	23	8	2	23	65%	74	3.6	80	5.0	3	14.5	1
Cam Thomas*	28	DT	16	473	25	3.2%	77	18	5	5	22	68%	70	1.5	18	0.0	0	5.0	1
Sean Lissemore	27	DE	15	210	24	3.3%	--	16	5	0	20	65%	--	2.6	--	2.0	1	2.5	0
Lawrence Guy	24	DE	12	45	23	4.0%	--	18	3	1	19	74%	--	2.6	--	0.0	3	2.0	4

			Overall							vs. Run					Pass Rush				
Edge Rushers	Age	Pos	G	Snaps	Plays	TmPct	Rk	Stop	Dfts	BTkl	Runs	St%	Rk	RuYd	Rk	Sack	Hit	Hur	Tips
Jarret Johnson	33	OLB	11	434	37	7.0%	18	32	7	2	25	84%	18	2.4	40	3.0	2	6.5	2
Thomas Keiser	25	OLB	12	396	23	4.0%	69	14	7	0	12	50%	77	4.2	76	4.5	3	8.0	1
Larry English	28	OLB	9	370	18	4.1%	65	15	5	1	13	85%	16	1.5	12	2.5	2	9.5	1
Tourek Williams	23	OLB	13	215	10	1.6%	--	4	1	3	7	43%	--	4.3	--	1.0	0	2.0	0

1 To be honest, this is a vestigial remnant of how we built these tables in previous books. We were going to fix it this year and forgot.

Table 9: Tampa Bay Buccaneers' Linebackers

			Overall								Pass Rush			vs. Run					vs. Pass						
Linebackers	Age	Pos	G	Snaps	Plays	TmPct	Rk	Stop	Dfts	BTkl	Sack	Hit	Hur	Runs	St%	Rk	RuYd	Rk	Tgts	Suc%	Rk	AdjYd	Rk	PD	Int
Lavonte David	24	OLB	16	1022	154	18.7%	6	111	50	6	7.0	6	17.5	81	81%	5	2.1	6	52	58%	20	6.4	33	10	5
Mason Foster	25	MLB	15	770	98	12.7%	46	58	19	7	2.0	5	10.5	57	70%	21	3.1	27	27	39%	64	7.6	57	5	3
Dekoda Watson*	26	OLB	15	258	37	4.8%	--	21	8	1	2.0	3	4.5	22	68%	--	3.7	--	10	48%	--	6.3	--	1	1
Jonathan Casillas	27	OLB	12	197	27	4.4%	--	16	3	1	0.0	1	2	17	65%	--	3.2	--	6	51%	--	6.5	--	2	0

Success Rate (**Suc%**): The percentage plays of targeting this player on which the offense did not have a successful play. This means not only incomplete passes and interceptions, but also short completions which do not meet our baselines for success (45 percent of needed yards on first down, 60 percent on second down, 100 percent on third or fourth down). Success Rate is adjusted for the quality of the receiver covered.

Adjusted Yards per Pass (**AdjYd**): The average number of yards gained on plays on which this defender was the listed target, adjusted for the quality of the receiver covered.

Passes Defensed (**PD**): Football Outsiders' count of passes defensed. Unlike the official NFL count of passes defensed, this does not include passes batted down or tipped at the line.

These stats, including other differences between the NFL's count of passes defensed and our own, are explained in more detail in the section on secondary tables. Plays listed with two defenders or as "Hole in Zone" with this defender as the closest player count only for half credit in computing both Success Rate and Average Yards per Pass. Seventy-one linebackers are ranked in the charting stats, with a minimum of 16 charted passes. As a result of the different thresholds, some linebackers are ranked in standard stats but not charting stats, or vice versa.

Further Details

Just as in the offensive tables, players who are no longer on the team are marked with asterisks, and players who were on other teams last year are in italics. Other than the game charting statistics for linebackers, defensive front seven player statistics are not adjusted for opponent.

Numbers for defensive linemen and linebackers unfortunately do not reflect all of the opportunities a player had to make a play, but they do show us which players were most active on the field. A large number of plays could mean a strong defensive performance, or it could mean that the linebacker in question plays behind a poor part of the line. In general, defensive numbers should be taken as information that tells us what happened on the field in 2013, but not as a strict, unassailable judgment of which players are better than others—particularly when the difference between two players is small (for example, players ranked 20th and 30th) instead of large (players ranked 20th and 70th).

After the individual statistics for linemen and linebackers, the Defensive Front Seven section contains a table that looks exactly like the table in the Offensive Line section. The difference is that the numbers here are for all opposing running backs against this team's defensive front. As we're on the opposite side of the ball, teams are now ranked in the opposite order, so the number one defensive front seven is the one that allows the fewest Adjusted Line Yards, the lowest percentage in Power situations, and has the highest Adjusted Sack Rate. Directions for Adjusted Line Yards are given from the offense's perspective, so runs to left end and left tackle are aimed at the right defensive end and (assuming the tight end is on the other side) weakside linebacker.

How to Read the Secondary Tables

The first few columns in the secondary tables (Table 9) are based on standard play-by-play, not game charting, with the exception of Broken Tackles. Age, Total Plays, Percentage of Team Plays, Stops, and Defeats are computed the same way they are for other defensive players, so that the secondary can be compared to the defensive line and linebackers. That means that Total Plays here includes passes defensed, sacks, tackles after receptions, tipped passes, and interceptions, but not pass plays on which this player was in coverage but was not given a tackle or passed defense by the NFL's official scorer.

The middle five columns address each defensive back's role in stopping the run. Average Yardage and Stop Rate for run-

Table 10: Dallas Cowboys' Defensive Secondary

			Overall								vs. Run					vs. Pass									
Secondary	Age	Pos	G	Snaps	Plays	TmPct	Rk	Stop	Dfts	BTkl	Runs	St%	Rk	RuYd	Rk	Tgts	Tgt%	Rk	Dist	Suc%	Rk	AdjYd	Rk	PD	Int
Brandon Carr	28	CB	16	1116	83	9.6%	19	34	14	11	14	50%	25	5.9	25	107	21.3%	45	12.8	49%	62	8.9	73	12	3
Orlando Scandrick	27	CB	16	1088	76	8.8%	35	32	17	6	11	36%	49	10.5	68	91	18.6%	19	10.9	60%	11	6.6	16	10	2
Barry Church	26	SS	16	1015	139	16.1%	1	38	12	8	66	24%	70	7.2	47	34	7.4%	29	7.8	56%	36	6.4	26	6	1
Jeff Heath	23	FS	16	594	55	6.4%	70	14	4	6	26	19%	76	14.2	78	27	9.9%	61	11.5	55%	40	9.7	68	3	1
J.J. Wilcox	23	SS	13	515	34	4.9%	--	9	2	4	16	38%	--	7.6	--	18	7.8%	--	9.4	38%	--	9.1	--	1	0
Morris Claiborne	24	CB	10	506	31	5.8%	79	12	5	4	4	0%	84	11.0	72	51	22.4%	56	13.3	54%	37	9.2	75	5	1

Year	Pass D Rank	vs. #1 WR	Rk	vs. #2 WR	Rk	vs. Other WR	Rk	vs. TE	Rk	vs. RB	Rk
2011	22	14.0%	19	53.3%	31	-26.9%	6	19.1%	21	-3.6%	15
2012	25	-7.0%	12	11.5%	29	19.5%	28	28.9%	32	3.5%	18
2013	27	12.4%	25	17.6%	28	-11.4%	8	26.8%	32	9.6%	24

ning plays is computed in the same manner as for defensive linemen and linebackers.

The third section of statistics represents data from the game charting project. In all game charting coverage stats, passes where two defenders are listed and those listed as "Hole in Zone" with this player as the closest zone defender count for half credit. We do not count pass plays on which this player was in coverage, but the incomplete was listed as Thrown Away, Batted Down, or Hit in Motion. Hail Mary passes are also not included.

Targets (**Tgts**): The number of pass plays on which our game charters listed this player in coverage.

Target Percentage (**Tgt%**): The number of plays on which this player was targeted divided by the total number of charted passes against his defense, not including plays listed as Uncovered. Like Percentage of Team Plays, this metric is adjusted based on number of games played.

Distance (**Dist**): The average distance in the air beyond the line of scrimmage of all passes targeted at this defender. It does not include yards after catch, and is useful for seeing which defenders were covering receivers deeper or shorter.

Success Rate (**Suc%**): The percentage plays of targeting this player on which the offense did not have a successful play. This means not only incomplete passes and interceptions, but also short completions which do not meet our baselines for success (45 percent of needed yards on first down, 60 percent on second down, 100 percent on third or fourth down). Defensive pass interference is counted as a failure for the defensive player similar to a completion of equal yardage (and a new first down).

Adjusted Yards per Pass (**AdjYd**): The average number of yards gained on plays on which this defender was the listed target, adjusted for the quality of the receiver covered.

Passes Defensed (**PD**): This is our count of passes defensed, and will differ from the total found in NFL gamebooks. Our count includes:

- All passes listed by our charters as Defensed.
- All interceptions, or tipped passes leading to interceptions.
- Any pass on which the defender is given a pass defensed by the official scorer, and our game charter marked either Miscommunication or Caught Out of Bounds.

Our count of passes defensed does not include passes marked as defensed in the official gamebooks but listed by our charters as Overthrown, Underthrown, or Thrown Away. It also does not include passes tipped in the act of rushing the passer (which are listed in the defensive line and linebackers tables as **Tips**). In addition, we did a lot of work with both the NFL head office and the folks from ESPN Stats & Information to get the most accurate numbers possible for both drops and passes defensed. Official scorers and game charters will sometimes disagree on a drop vs. a pass defensed, or even an overthrown/underthrown ball vs. a pass defensed, and there are a number of passes where the league marked the official stats in one way and ESPN marked their stats the other way. We reviewed all these passes and on each one chose to either go with the NFL's decision or ESPN Stats & Information's decision, so we no longer have passes where we were unsure whether to give a pass defensed (as given by the NFL) or a drop (as given by charters). Each pass is marked as one or the other.

Interceptions (**Int**) represent the standard NFL interception total.

With more and more wide receivers playing, that means more and more cornerbacks are playing, so we've had to increase our minimums so we aren't ranking a zillion cornerbacks. Cornerbacks need 50 charted passes or eight games started to be ranked in the defensive stats, with 87 cornerbacks ranked in total. (Tarell Brock of San Francisco had no run tackles, so only 86 cornerbacks are ranked in run defense stats.) Safeties require 20 charted passes or eight games started, with 78 safeties ranked in total. Strong and free safeties are ranked together.

Just like the front seven, the secondary has a table of team statistics following the individual numbers. This table gives DVOA figured against different types of receivers. Each offense's wide receivers have had one receiver designated as No. 1, and another as No. 2. (Occasionally this is difficult, due to injury or an amorphous wide receiver corps like last year's Rams, but it's usually pretty obvious.) The other receivers form a third category, with tight ends and running backs as fourth and fifth categories. The defense is then judged on the performance of each receiver based on the standard DVOA method, with each rating adjusted based on strength of schedule. (Obviously, it's a lot harder to cover the No. 1 receiver of the Detroit Lions than to cover the No.1 receiver of the Jacksonville Jaguars—and in 2013, it was obviously much, much harder to cover the No. 1 receiver of the Cleveland Browns than to cover the No. 2 receiver of the Cleveland Browns.) **Pass D Rank** is the total ranking of the pass defense, as seen before in the Trends and Splits table, and combines all five categories plus sacks and passes with no intended target.

The "defense vs. types of receivers" table should be used to analyze the defense as a whole rather than individual players. The ratings against types of receivers are generally based on defensive schemes, not specific cornerbacks, except for certain defenses that really do move one cornerback around to cover the opponent's top weapon (i.e., Arizona). The ratings against tight ends and running backs are in large part due to the performance of linebackers.

How to Read the Special Teams Tables

The special teams tables list the last three years of kick, punt, and return numbers for each team.

The first two columns list total special teams DVOA and rank among the 32 teams (Table 10). The next two columns list the value in actual points of field goals and extra points (**FG/XP**) when compared to how a league average kicker would do from the same distances, adjusted for weather and altitude, and rank

Table 11: Philadelphia Eagles Special Teams

Year	DVOA	Rank	FG/XP	Rank	Net Kick	Rank	Kick Ret	Rank	Net Punt	Rank	Punt Ret	Rank	Hidden	Rank
2011	0.0%	17	3.9	9	7.5	5	-3.5	23	0.1	16	-7.9	27	1.7	14
2012	-2.2%	23	0.9	17	3.3	10	-0.5	18	-18.2	32	3.3	8	-9.1	29
2013	-2.8%	25	-2.8	24	-12.5	31	-0.9	15	5.4	10	-3.4	18	3.3	11

among the 32 teams. Next, we list the estimated value in actual points of field position over or under the league average based on net kickoffs (**Net Kick**), and rank that value among the 32 teams. That is followed by the estimated point values of field position for kick returns (**Kick Ret**), net punting (**Net Punt**), and punt returns (**Punt Ret**) and their respective ranks.

The final two columns represent the value of "**Hidden**" special teams, plays which throughout the past decade have usually been based on the performance of opponents without this team being able to control the outcome. We combine the opposing team's value on field goals, kickoff distance, and punt distance, adjusted for weather and altitude, and then switch the sign to represent that good special teams by the opponent will cost the listed team points, and bad special teams will effectively hand them points. We have to give the qualifier of "usually" because, as explained above, certain returners such as Devin Hester will affect opposing special teams strategy, and a handful of the missed field goals are blocked. Nonetheless, the "hidden" value is still "hidden" for most teams, and they are ranked from the most hidden value gained (Denver, 20.8 points) to the most value lost (New York Giants, -12.8 points).

We also have methods for measuring the gross value of kickoffs and punts. These measures assume that all kickoffs or punts will have average returns unless they are touchbacks or kicked out of bounds, then judge the kicker or punter on the value with those assumed returns. These metrics may be listed in special-teams comments as **KickPts+** and **PuntPts+**. We also count special-teams tackles; these include both tackles and assists, but do not include tackles on two-point conversions, tackles after onside kicks, or tackles of the player who recovers a fumble after the punt or kick returner loses the ball. The best and worst individual values for kickers, punters, returners, and kick gunners (i.e. tackle totals) are listed in the statistical appendix at the end of the book.

Administrative Minutia

Receiving statistics include all passes intended for the receiver in question, including those that are incomplete or intercepted. The word passes refers to both complete and incomplete pass attempts. When rating receivers, interceptions are treated as incomplete passes with no penalty.

For the computation of DVOA and DYAR, passing statistics include sacks as well as fumbles on aborted snaps. We do not include kneeldown plays or spikes for the purpose of stopping the clock. Some interceptions which we have determined to be "Hail Mary" plays that end the first half or game are counted as regular incomplete passes, not turnovers.

All statistics generated by ESPN Stats & Information or the Football Outsiders game charting project may be different from totals compiled by other sources.

Unless we say otherwise, when we refer to third-down performance in this book we are referring to a combination of third down and the handful of rushing and passing plays that take place on fourth down (primarily fourth-and-1).

Aaron Schatz

The Year In Quotes

THAT'S A TELEPOR ... EH, NEVERMIND

"A time machine. So if I wanted to be in Florida, it'd be like 'boom', I'm in Florida."

—New England Patriots tight end **Rob Gronkowski**, when asked what superpower he would want (Twitter)

I KNOW, I CAN'T BELIEVE THAT CHRIS JOHNSON GUY GETS ALL THOSE CARRIES EITHER

"No disrespect, I love Tennessee and would love to be in Tennessee. But I feel like I am wasting the prime years of my career if I am not used right. You feel me? It is crazy to look at backs around the league and see the opportunities they have."

—Tennessee Titans running back **Chris Johnson**, grumbling about the lack of opportunities he received this year (The Tennessean)

EVERYTHING'S SADDER IN TEXAS

"Sitting on the bench, I guess."

—Interim Houston Texans head coach **Wade Phillips**, on how third-string quarterback T.J. Yates got injured (Houston Chronicle)

THAT'S JUST LIKE, YOUR OPINION, MAN

"I've got a question for you: It was a 14-6 game. We played our ass off, and how anybody could pick the hammer and the nail, when in fact, that hammer, or that nail, or whatever the hell you got picked, we catch a ball down there, we're fixing to take the lead and we turn it over. I mean explain to me how Kevin Minter, who sets, damn near, the career tackle record in that game, how anybody could ever say 'hammer and nail.'"

"I can tell you right now, here's what happens: two very quality teams take the field and compete like a son-of-a-bitch for victory. And you know what? It's not a hammer and a nail relationship. It's an opportunity for an opponent to be equal, and to raise the level of play in such a fashion that they win."

"And that's how this thing works. That, in fact, you respect the opponent, and he's not the hammer and he's not the frickin' nail. OK, he's the opponent. Understand? I'm just letting you know I resent that. I resent the fact that suddenly we were nailed. You got it? I mean, honest to petes."

" [Expletive] we were a pretty good team last year. I thought we played like a son-of-a-bitch in the stadium. I'm just letting you know, I felt differently than the nail, so you know."

—LSU head coach **Les Miles**, taking exception to a reporter's reference that in last year's 14-6 loss to the Gators, LSU was a nail to Florida's hammer. (New Orleans Times-Picayune)

JUST IMAGINE WHAT DAVID TERRELL WOULD HAVE DONE TO PLAY WITH SID LUCKMAN ... NOT BUILD A TIME MACHINE I'M GUESSING

"I would have cut off both my balls. I'd give those up, no problem. You could have neutered me. I woulda been neutered with a smile."

—Former Bears receiver and No. 8 overall pick in the 2008 NFL Draft **David Terrell**, after being named one of the Chicago Bears' all-time draft busts by Chicago publication RedEye. This answer was in response to the question: "What would you have given to play with a quarterback like a Jay Cutler?" (Mile High Report)

THERE'S THE TRUTH (SHAKE HEAD) AND THE TRUTH (NOD SUGGESTIVELY)

"The key is, in those situations, is that the only way a team can beat you is to get the ball over your head; we let them do it one time in the game ... and one time is too many. So we don't use the term 'prevent defense.' We'll never use the term 'prevent defense.' But there is 'situational defense.'"

—Oakland Raiders head coach **Dennis Allen**, explaining why the Raiders don't use a 'prevent defense' (ESPN NFL Nation Blog)

THE DARK SIDE OF WINNING CHAMPIONSHIPS

"That damn game cost me a week of recruiting."

—Alabama head coach **Nick Saban**, after his golf buddy congratulated him on winning the 2012 national championship. (GQ)

DO NOT TAUNT HAPPY FUN STEVE SMITH

"I talk mess and I love talking mess and that's part of the game. But I would never walk up to a guy—first of all I don't really know outside of watching him on video—and Google his wife's name and her birthday and call her outside of her name and call that in the jest of sportsmanship or gamesmanship."

"That's not my deal. I take that as clear disrespect I feel like when you don't respect somebody well there's nothing much left. So if I don't respect you and you don't respect me there aren't any rules, there aren't any guidelines. I didn't like that. Second of all, I'm 34 years old. You're a couple of years older than my youngest son. We're not on the same level."

"It sounds like he needs to wear some condoms. That's what it sounds like he needs to wear."

—Carolina Panthers wide receiver **Steve Smith**, expressing his displeasure with the trash talk of St. Louis Rams cornerback Janoris Jenkins (Eye on Football)

THIS WAS WRITTEN ON A COCKTAIL NAPKIN. AND THIS STILL WASN'T HONEST. AND HONEST IS SPELLED WRONG.

"If [Robert Griffin] missed two offseasons in a row, that would be the hardest thing ... that would be devastating to him."

"Dan [Snyder] could care less about the other positions."

"What I'm trying to do is be as honest as I can [with the media], and I don't normally do that."

—Washington Redskins head coach **Mike Shanahan**, in a press conference explaining why quarterback Robert Griffin will be inactive for the rest of the season (Pro Football Talk)

I WOULD $*#% ON BARNEY

"She bought me diapers with Barney's face on them. She said, 'If you go to the bathroom in your diaper, you're going to the bathroom on Barney's face. And you don't want to do that.' So, I'm like, 'No, I don't want to do that, I wouldn't dare.' "

"Under Barney's diaper, I put another normal diaper on and went to the bathroom in that diaper. So, I guess, I decided I had to go to the bathroom, took my diaper off, went and found where the generic diapers were, put that one on, and then put Barney's diaper on."

—Penn State guard **John Urschel**, relaying a story of how his mother attempted to potty-train him (Dr. Saturday)

OR WE COULD DO WHAT THE NFL NORMALLY DOES: FINE EVERYBODY AND ACT LIKE THAT SOLVED IT

"[What's] going on in Miami goes on in every locker room. But it's time for us to start talking. Maybe have some group sessions where guys sit down and maybe talk about what's going on off the field or what's going on in the building and not mask everything. Because the [longer] it goes untreated, the worse it gets."

—Chicago Bears wide receiver **Brandon Marshall**, on the Richie Incognito/Jonathan Martin incident (Eye on Football)

(JOE WINS THE LOTTO, JUST LOOKS AT THE TICKET)

"It's a lot of money, man. Since I've been 18 years old, I've always played the lottery when it gets up to a couple $100 million. It's just for fun."

—Baltimore Ravens quarterback **Joe Flacco** on playing the Mega Millions lottery

"Not tell anybody."

—**Flacco**, on what he would do if he won the $600-plus million (Eye on Football)

SHARKNADO DEEPLY AFFECTED ALL OF US

"I really appreciate someone asking me what's my favorite food because I'm big, I gotta eat. There's so many topics about food you could be asking about."

"I'm definitely not a fish person, I don't like eating fish just for the fact, like, I used to catch fish and they probably eat disgusting things in the water. I would eat a shark, though, because a shark kills a lot of people. So, I mean, if I eat a shark, I feel like I'm avenging a lot of people's deaths or whatever. Sharks are so mean."

—University of Minnesota defensive lineman **Ra'Shede Hageman**, when asked what his favorite food was (Dr. Saturday)

IT'S GOOD TO HAVE DREAMS

"I want to play four more years."

—Cleveland Browns running back **Willis McGahee**, 32, saying that he wants to play another four years (Cleveland.com)

YEAH! AND HOW ABOUT SEASON TWO OF THE NEWSROOM! *DECOMMITS*

"I snapped on him. Told him I hadn't seen it yet and didn't want it ruined."

—Newly recruited Iowa State running back **Tommy Mister**, after ISU graduate assistant Derek Day asked him what he thought about the Red Wedding on Game of Thrones. (Ames Tribune)

URINATION MIGHT HAVE BEEN MORE EFFECTIVE

"I don't want to sit here and make excuses about anything. We've played well at times and we haven't played well and today is as bad as we've played this whole season. It's really embarrassing to be a part of it. We were like the Bad News Bears out there today. In saying that, I do want to give credit to our offense. They just kept fighting today and really gave us a chance to still be in the game. Defensively we went out there and basically peed down our legs."

—Oakland Raiders safety **Charles Woodson**, on why the Raiders defense struggled against the Jets (Inside Bay Area)

NEW DEFENSIVE COORDINATOR BRIAN MCCANN IS GOING TO GET TO THE BOTTOM OF THIS

"That's total [B.S.] that he threw the ball at the end of the game like he did. And you can print that and you can send it to him, and he can comment, too. I think it's low class and it's [B.S.] to throw the ball when the game is completely over against our kids that are basically our scout team."

—Oregon defensive coordinator **Nick Aliotti**, criticizing Washington State head coach Mike Leach for playing his starters the entire game, and continuing to throw the ball down to the final seconds. Oregon won the game 62-38 (The Oregonian)

THE YEAR IN THE BLACK UNICORN

"I think me and Coach Trestman are probably the only two people who understand each other. I always say Coach Trestman reminds me of the first Willy Wonka. Not the Johnny Depp one; the Johnny Depp one was really cool. But the first one. Before that. The 1943 version."

"If you really look at Coach, he's a genius. And a lot of times when you're around really, really smart people, you don't really understand them. I thought Willy Wonka was brilliant. I mean he had all kinds of candy. Who doesn't like chocolate and candies? Everybody wanted a Gobstopper. Ya know? I just think he's brilliant."

—Chicago Bears tight end **Martellus Bennett**, explaining his relationship with head coach Marc Trestman and the brilliance of Willy Wonka (Shutdown Corner)

"It's called 'Do Not Draft Me. Which is for fantasy football people who always come to me and are like 'Oh, I drafted you and... blah, blah, blah.'"

"[If] your team name is the 'Black Unicorns' or 'The Black Marty B's', [it's okay]."

—Chicago Bears tight end **Martellus Bennett**, addressing fantasy football players on the Jim Rome Show (Eye on Football)

THAT'S ONE OKRA PATCH YOU DON'T WANT TO RUN THROUGH

"I didn't say he shopped for bad groceries. He shopped for good players ... Like we said, he just cannot cook. You know, sometimes grandma gets too old. She know what to go in the grocery store and get, but she just cannot whip it up like she used to."

—Former Washington Redskin **Fred Smoot**, describing Mike Shanahan's coaching skills (Shutdown Corner)

WELL THE IMPORTANT THING IS THAT IT DIDN'T STOP YOU FROM SPECULATING WILDLY

"There's no doubt that Stanford did not play well. But I know coming from an academic institution, this is a time for midterm exams. Players are not focused, they don't get to practice on time, they're worn out, they're tired, they don't get much sleep, and you do not play very well. And that is exactly what it looked like to me with Stanford. I don't know that for a fact, but that looked like a football team that was in midterms."

—ESPN analyst **Lou Holtz**, claiming that Stanford's midterms were the reason for their upset loss to Utah. Stanford was not currently in midterms (Dr. Saturday)

IT COULD BE WORSE ... SHE COULD HAVE ASKED YOU ABOUT THE LOVE BOAT

"So my daughter is laying here under me and just out the blue she says... I can't believe you lost to the Browns Daddy! Smh"

—Minnesota Vikings running back **Adrian Peterson**, after Peterson's Vikings dropped to 0-3 against the Browns (For The Win)

LORD RYAN SHALL HEAR OF THIS, AND WE SHALL SEE IF HE FAVORS YOUR DAUGHTERS AND LIVESTOCK, AWAY!

"Whatever u do is not work you disrespectful little peasant"

—Atlanta Falcons wide receiver **Roddy White**, replying to someone on Twitter who in response to White's Labor Day tweet said, "Getting paid to play a kids game is not work." White later apologized (Kissing Suzy Kolber)

LANE KIFFIN HAS NEVER SEEN E.T. SO NO BIG DEAL

"The Washington State game."

—Film director **Steven Spielberg**, on a visit to USC, when asked what his favorite disaster movie was (Twitter)

YOU CAN'T QUITE SUM UP CLEVELAND ANY BETTER

"he said the interview went well and he's going back for a second! Its the Browns.. but hey, still pretty cool!"

—**Megan Pettine**, daughter of new Browns coach Mike Pettine, on the possibility of her dad getting a head coaching gig (Twitter)

I'M BETTER THAN THE NEW YORK TIMES' HEADLINE WRITER

"I'm better [than Jadeveon Clowney]. Let's put it like this. People like to talk about size all the time. Size is pretty much overrated in my eyes. You can look at guys like Robert Mathis, Elvis Dumervil, Von Miller. These are 6-2 guys and under. People are just looking at the fact that he's a physical specimen. Honestly if you watch the film, he plays like a blind dog in a meat market basically."

—Former Auburn defensive lineman **Dee Ford**, saying that he is better than Jadeveon Clowney (Eye on Football)

YES, BUT HIS SCREAMS ARE GRITTY AND HIS CUSSING IS QUICKER THAN FAST

"I've seen Tom Brady cuss and scream and do all kind of things but nobody looks at him like that. I just think it's unfair the way we see it and the way the media portrays certain things because of personal feelings about a person."

—Pittsburgh Steelers safety **Ryan Clark**, calling the criticism of Dallas Cowboys wide receiver Dez Bryant's sideline theatrics a double standard (ESPN)

HOW MANY AUTOGRAPHS DO WE GET OUT OF IT?

"If I ever get Manziel disease, I want all of you to smack me in the head with your microphones."

—Florida State quarterback **Jameis Winston**, at an FSU media availability

"I would not, BUT I'm gonna get some cheeseballs anyway."

—**Winston**, when asked if he would give up a national championship for a lifetime supply of cheeseballs (Deadspin)

NOT LIKE LONGTIME NFL STANDOUT TRAVIS JOHNSON HAS, ANYWAY

"Tony Romo has not earned a dollar he's been given in this league... but [Matt Schaub] can take his team to a Super Bowl. Tony Romo is not that guy. He's a thief; he needs to be brought up on federal charges."

—Former Houston Texans defensive lineman **Travis Johnson**, during a roundtable segment on CSN Houston (Shutdown Corner)

(FUMBLES PHONE INTO TOILET, TOILET RETURNS PHONE FOR A TOUCHDOWN)

"Ayy to fantasy participants and pissed Giants fans ur irrelevant to me!!! Nobody wants me to succeed more than ME!!! WATCH US WORK!"

—New York Giants running back **David Wilson**, ripping his critics in a tweet after he lost two fumbles and was benched on Sunday night (Twitter)

JUST WAIT 'TIL HE ENCOUNTERS THE KUBIAK PEOPLE

"You can print this: You can print that I don't really give a fuck what the 'Paterno people' think about what I do with this program. I've done everything I can to show respect to Coach Paterno. Everything in my power. So I could really care less about what the Paterno faction of people, or whatever you call them, think about what I do with the program. I'm tired of it. For any 'Paterno person' to have any objection to what I'm doing, it makes me wanna put my fist through this windshield right now."

—New Houston Texans head coach **Bill O'Brien**, in a conversation last month about his tenure at Penn State (The Patriot News)

REALLY WISH HE WAS PRESSED ON THE DIFFERENCES BETWEEN DIRTBAGS AND SCUMBAGS

"Absolutely. I don't think there's any question about that. They go after quarterbacks. Their entire defense takes cheap shots all the time, that's what they do, that's who they are. They're a bunch of dirtbags, or scumbags. I mean, that's how they play."

"It starts with their frickin' coach. Starts with the head coach. Schwartz, he's a [expletive], too, I wouldn't want to play for him. ... Starts with him, their D-coordinator and their D-line coach. They're all just scumbags, and so are the D-line."

—Green Bay Packers left guard **Josh Sitton**, calling the Lions dirtbags (Sporting News)

SO HE WAS A PAID VOLUNTEER

"I don't know if this will throw us into an NCAA investigation—my senior year, I was getting money on the side. I really didn't have any money. I had to either pay the rent or buy some food. I remember the feeling of like, 'Man, be careful.' But there's nothing wrong with it. And you're not going to convince me that there is something wrong with it."

..."Then I walk back, and reality sets in. I go to my dorm room, open my fridge, and there's nothing in my fridge. Hold up, man. What just happened? Why don't I have anything to show for what I just did? There was a point where we had no food, no money, so I called my coach and I said, 'Coach, we don't have no food. We don't have no money. We're hungry. Either you give us some food, or I'm gonna go do something stupid.' He came down and he brought like 50 tacos for like four or five of us. Which is an NCAA violation. [laughs] But then, the next day I walk up to the facility and I see my coach pull up in a brand new Lexus. Beautiful."

—Houston Texans running back **Arian Foster**, admitting he accepted money his senior year at the University of Tennessee (Sports Illustrated)

YES IT'S BEEN NOTHING BUT NON-STOP PRAISE FOR THE DOLPHINS OFFENSIVE LINE THIS YEAR

"I just don't feel that team was as good as everybody was saying they were. We just abused the offensive line all game."

—New Orleans Saints outside linebacker **Junior Galette**, who had one sack in the Saints' 38-17 win over the Miami Dolphins (Nanaimo Daily News)

MUST HAVE BEEN A CLOWN CAR! *SHOWS SELF OUT*

"I didn't know Jadeveon's car that could go that fast. He doesn't have a pretty car like those FSU guys used to drive."

—South Carolina head coach **Steve Spurrier**, commenting on Jadeveon Clowney's speeding ticket. Clowney was clocked at 110 MPH (Dr. Saturday)

RYAN CLARK WATCHED THIS PRESS CONFERENCE

"We make some good plays and we make plenty of shitty plays. Thank you."

—New England Patriots quarterback **Tom Brady**, in a 72-second postgame press conference after losing to the Dolphins (Eye on Football)

(TODD GRAHAM LOOKING ON IN AWE AT USE OF PHRASE "DESTINATION JOB")

"I've made mistakes professionally and personally. Something I'm not going to do again. My first mistake was leaving Louisville [in 2007]. I want everyone here to know this is my destination job."

—New Louisville head coach **Bobby Petrino**, in his introductory press conference (Eye on Football)

I MET MY GIRLFRIEND ON INSTANTFACE

"With all due respect, I hate to admit this but I don't think I've been online in a couple days or weeks or whatever, so that's not really an important thing to me. I don't even know what's online and what isn't online. But I would say we probably have, I can't even imagine, 10,000 pages of information. It's a lot of information. There's no way I can sit up here and tell you that I've read it all. I've read a fraction of it. But we have a ton of information on all the players that are in the draft. What's online, you should go talk to the geniuses that are online. I don't know. MyFace, YourFace, InstantFace. Go talk to whoever you want that does that stuff. I don't know."

—New England Patriots head coach **Bill Belichick**, on a leaked Patriots scouting report on Johnny Manziel (CSN New England)

WELL, BY DEFAULT, AREN'T THEY ALL?

Pam Oliver: "After you've gone through offseason training and all of that and to come up a little short, devastating?"

Jim Harbaugh: [Laughs] "A man can be destroyed but he cannot be defeated."

Pam Oliver: "Is that a quote?"

—Part of an interview between FOX's **Pam Oliver** and San Francisco 49ers head coach **Jim Harbaugh**, where Oliver was confused after Harbaugh quoted Hemingway's The Old Man and the Sea (For The Win)

JUST REPEAT AFTER ME: STANFORD COMMUNICATION DEGREE

"Well, I'm the best corner in the game! When you try me with a sorry receiver like Crabtree that's the result you're gonna get! Don't you ever talk about me!"

—Seattle Seahawks cornerback **Richard Sherman**, describing what happened on the final play of the NFC Championship game when he tipped a pass leading to an interception

"Crabtree! Don't you open your mouth about the best! Or I'm gonna shut it for you real quick!"

—**Sherman**, when asked who was talking about him (Pro Football Talk)

I REALLY LIKE APPETIZERS THOUGH

"OK, y'all listen to me loud and clear. Y'all listening? Y'all hear me? For all y'all who called us, the receiving corps, average, pedestrian, appetizers—I'm not going to say any names, but he knows who he is—I respect what you did on the field, but stick to playing football, because your analytical skills ain't up to par yet. You need to slow down and go back and not do it half-assed and put some effort into it, because you're saying some stuff that didn't really make sense."

"That dude who said that we were appetizers, he told me to Google him, and I did Google him, but I didn't see any Super Bowl appearances, and I also saw two losses in conference championships. I have a Super Bowl ring, and I would gladly show that to him. And if he doesn't have time to come see it, tell him he can Google it."

—Seattle Seahawks wide receiver **Doug Baldwin**, having some choice words directed at ESPN analyst Cris Carter (HeraldNet)

LIKE THAT RULE ABOUT DREADLOCKS, EXCEPT, NOT

"It should be a league rule saying that a defender can not tackle a player by his penis. #NFL the most painful thing ever! #NFL"

—San Francisco 49ers tight end **Vernon Davis**, in a tweet after Rams safety T.J. McDonald made a tackle, so to speak (Deadspin)

NOT A FOOTBALL OUTSIDERS READER QUOTE OF THE YEAR

"I'm never chasing points early in games... Riverboat Ron or not, check the analytics... take the points."

—FOX NFL analyst **Tim Ryan**, on the CAR-TB broadcast with :30 left in the second quarter, right before the Panthers sent Cam Newton over the top to score a touchdown on fourth-and-goal from the 1 (FOX broadcast)

Compiled by Rivers McCown

Arizona Cardinals

2013 Record: 10-6	**Total DVOA:** 10.0% (10th)	**2014 Mean Projection:** 7.3 wins	**On the Clock (0-4):** 13%
Pythagorean Wins: 9.5 (9th)	**Offense:** -2.4% (20th)	**Postseason Odds:** 23.8%	**Mediocrity (5-7):** 40%
Snap-Weighted Age: 27.8 (1st)	**Defense:** -16.4% (2nd)	**Super Bowl Odds:** 2.2%	**Playoff Contender (8-10):** 36%
Average Opponent: 5.9% (4th)	**Special Teams:** -4.1% (27th)	**Proj. Avg. Opponent:** 2.5% (6th)	**Super Bowl Contender (11+):** 11%

2013: The title of "best Arizona Cardinals team ever" is cold comfort when you're golfing in January.

2014: This may once again be among the five best Arizona Cardinals teams ever, and they might go 6-10 anyway.

The Arizona Cardinals picked a bad year to have a really good season.

Okay, so when the alternative is slogging through 4-12 and 5-11 campaigns, and watching the law firm of Lindley, Hall & Skelton at quarterback, ending up just one result short of a postseason berth is still a lot of fun. But still, the timing of when to have the franchise's best *regular* season in at least 25 years turned out less than ideal. Now, obviously, the two most important words in that sentence are *regular season.* We know the Cardinals came within a few plays of winning a Super Bowl just six seasons ago, but that came as a result of a postseason hot streak after backing into the playoffs as a 9-7 division champion back when the NFC West was slightly less strong than it is today. The following year, in Kurt Warner's final season in the desert, Arizona went 10-6. That 2009 season was the only time that the franchise had a positive overall DVOA since 1989 . . . until last year (Table 1). And when we find the time to complete more seasons from the 1980s, this will probably remain true going back to the 1984 season when the team was still playing in St. Louis.

Table 1. Best Single-Season DVOA, Phoenix/Arizona Cardinals (1989-2013)

Year	DVOA	Rk	W-L
2009	11.2%	12	10-6
2013	**10.0%**	**10**	**10-6**
1993	-0.1%	16	7-9
1992	-4.0%	15	4-12
2008	-5.0%	21	9-7
1990	-7.3%	16	5-11
1994	-9.1%	20	8-8
2005	-12.2%	22	5-11
2007	-12.8%	23	8-8
2001	-13.6%	24	7-9

These two seasons, 2009 and 2013, rank far ahead of every other year as the best regular seasons since the Cardinals franchise came to the Valley of the Sun. In fact, they are the only two seasons where the Cardinals franchise has managed double-digit wins since 1976, when the team was still coached by Don Coryell and playing at Busch Stadium. Your outlook on which of these two teams was better likely depends on your vantage point. Last year's Cardinals were one of the best defensive teams in the league, with an offense that mediocre, and played an extremely tough schedule (3-5 against teams that would reach the postseason). The 2009 team was the opposite: an offensive force with Kurt Warner, Larry Fitzgerald, and Anquan Boldin, coupled with a pedestrian defense and an easy schedule (only 1-2 against playoff teams).

The NFL's current postseason format can be cruel, and the eight-division setup combined with a short season can lead to plenty of inequities. The 2013 version of the Cardinals was light years better than the 1998 team that got into the postseason at 9-7 despite being outscored by 53 points. It was better than the 2008 team that rode roughshod over a division where the other three teams only won 13 games. Instead, the 2013 Cardinals became the first team since the 1985 Jets to win 10 or more games in a division where two other teams reached the conference championship game. For a team to play as well as Arizona did last year and still get stuck in traffic behind two other high-caliber teams is something that just doesn't happen very often.

How did Arizona turn things around after going 5-11 the previous season? The quarterback position was the most glaring change. Carson Palmer may not be a Hall of Famer or even a Pro Bowl-level quarterback. But the upgrade from the previous year's quarterback play, which made running the triple option look like a viable alternative, was massive. Palmer made some excellent throws, and some poor ones. He finished the year with 22 interceptions, but also stabilized the offense and allowed it to expand the variety of its playcalling as the year went on. His effect on the pass-protection schemes and his ability to cover for an offensive line that was very much in flux cannot be understated.

The team was always going to be improved so long as Palmer stayed healthy, but that improvement was expected to be more toward respectability rather than among the league's top teams. Instead, Bruce Arians managed the team so well that he became a Coach of the Year candidate for the second straight season. In 2012, he won the award serving as interim coach for the Indianapolis Colts during Chuck Pagano's cancer treatment. Last year, he may have done an even better job.

Even after Arians and general manager Steve Keim brought in Palmer, plenty of genuine questions remained. For example, how on earth would Arians fix the team's horrible offensive line? And how would the change in coaches affect the defense? Ray Horton had overseen the best defense in Arizona

2014 Cardinals Schedule

Week	Opp.	Week	Opp.	Week	Opp.
1	SD (Mon.)	7	at OAK	13	at ATL
2	at NYG	8	PHI	14	KC
3	SF	9	at DAL	15	at STL (Thu.)
4	BYE	10	STL	16	SEA
5	at DEN	11	DET	17	at SF
6	WAS	12	at SEA		

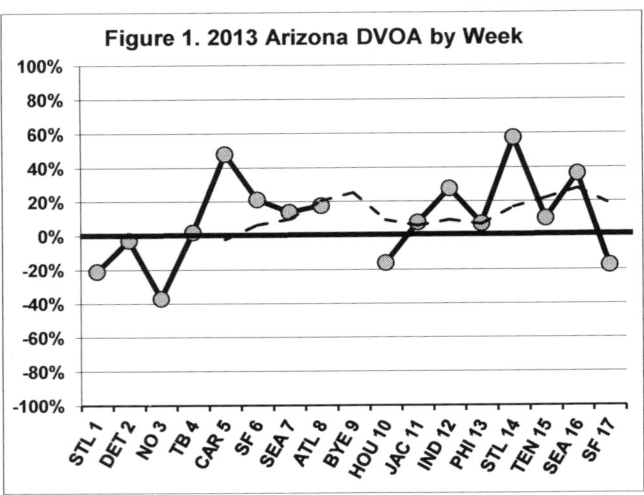

since Buddy Ryan's last year, and his departure turned the one team strength into a wild card. His replacement, Todd Bowles, was maligned after his previous stint in Philadelphia, and continued success was far from assured.

Arizona had managed a rare double the previous season—finishing 32nd in Adjusted Line Yards for both offense and defense. The offensive line could have been a disaster last year, and finishing even 32nd may have been ambitious. By year's end, four of the five starting spots were manned by players who were not projected as starters during OTAs. Two of them weren't even on the roster. Top pick Jonathan Cooper broke his leg near the end of the preseason, forcing veteran Daryn Colledge back into the lineup at left guard. Left tackle Levi Brown was such a disaster that the team traded him to Pittsburgh four games into the season, and instead went with Bradley Sowell, an undrafted free agent who had been cut by the Colts at the end of the preseason and claimed off waivers. The team signed veteran right tackle Eric Winston at the start of preseason to supplant 2012 fourth round pick Bobby Massie. Without Cooper, it was a unit very much lacking a top-end talent, relying on grizzled veterans and unproven castoffs from other teams.

So finishing 17th in Adjusted Line Yards and 13th in Adjusted Sack Rate was basically performing miracles. It was done with a combination of Palmer's ability to get rid of the ball with a less than ideal pocket, coaching and scheme to minimize the individual weaknesses on the line, and, as the season went on, the impact of Andre Ellington.

While the offensive line improvement was unexpected, the defensive front seven is where the biggest tangible leap for Arizona occurred. The Cardinals' defense went from dead last to first in Adjusted Line Yards, the first time that has happened during the period where Adjusted Line Yards data is available (1995 to present). It is also the second largest single-season improvement in Adjusted Line Yards allowed (Table 2), and Arizona fans can take heart that most of the teams that made similar progress carried that upgrade over to the following season.

Table 2. Biggest Year-to-Year Improvement in Defensive Adjusted Line Yards, 1995-2013

Team	Years	ALY Year 1	Rank	ALY Year 2	Rank	Change	ALY Year 3	Rank
TB	2011-12	4.37	26	2.96	1	1.41	3.62	7
ARI	**2012-13**	**4.49**	**32**	**3.09**	**1**	**1.40**	**--**	**--**
MIN	2005-06	3.98	17	2.75	1	1.23	3.27	1
SD	1997-98	3.95	15	2.78	1	1.17	3.25	2
WAS	2003-04	4.49	29	3.40	2	1.09	3.76	10
NYJ	2003-04	4.75	32	3.72	4	1.03	4.34	26
MIN	2001-02	4.38	29	3.35	1	1.03	3.88	11
MIA	1997-98	4.28	23	3.30	4	0.98	3.51	9
DAL	2000-01	4.93	31	3.99	19	0.94	3.96	12
GB	2008-09	4.51	28	3.65	4	0.86	4.22	20

What makes the improvement in Arizona more remarkable is that it came without making substantial changes to the defensive front personnel. Calais Campbell, Dan Williams, and Darnell Dockett had been the starters the previous year at the three line positions. The team did add veteran edge rusher John Abraham, and Karlos Dansby returned to play inside linebacker. The improvement, though, was due to Todd Bowles' aggressive style, allowing Campbell and Dockett to play one-gap technique and play to their strengths to penetrate and disrupt opponents in the backfield. Arizona led the league in stuffing run plays behind the line of scrimmage, at 28 percent.

Arizona was the first team since the 2002 Vikings to lead the league in Adjusted Line Yards but not send a player on the defensive line or at inside linebacker to the Pro Bowl (although John Abraham was selected at outside linebacker). That Vikings team is notable in that none of the players in its front seven ever made a Pro Bowl. The Cardinals should have had at least one, though. Calais Campbell was squeezed out of the popular voting because 3-4 defensive ends are grouped with 4-3 edge rushers. He had a fantastic season, disruptive against the run while also adding nine sacks. In the Week 16 upset of eventual Super Bowl champion Seattle, the Seahawks' line could not block Campbell, period. That was true even when they tried to tackle him, as one of his sacks came after a clear takedown brought him to his knees, and he bounced up and still got to Russell Wilson.

Arizona might have had the best defense in the league in 2013, except for one major Achilles' heel. They struggled covering the top tight ends, and it cost them (Table 3).

Table 3. Arizona Defense vs. Tight Ends, 2013

	DVOA	Passes	C %	Yards	TD	INT
Losses	36.0%	72	68%	721	12	1
Wins	-20.5%	84	59%	524	5	4

Arizona allowed 17 touchdowns to opposing tight ends, exactly half of all the offensive touchdowns they allowed all year. The splits in losses were even more extreme. In Arizona's six losses, 12 of the 18 touchdowns allowed were scored by tight ends. Jimmy Graham had 134 yards and scored twice. Vernon Davis had 180 yards in the first meeting with San Francisco, also scoring twice. The Philadelphia duo of Brent Celek and Zach Ertz scored all three of the Eagles' touchdowns in the narrow road loss.

The first-round selection of Deone Bucannon, safety out of Washington State, was a clear move to address this weakness. Bucannon has good size at 6-foot-1, and he also clocked a 4.49 forty-yard dash at the combine. He fits the personality of this defense under Bowles as an aggressive "in-the-box" strong safety who the team anticipates can match up with tight ends. Another factor will be the midseason return of Tyrann Mathieu, who suffered a serious knee injury in Week 14 but had been a revelation as a free safety and nickel defender (and blitzer).

While the secondary should be improved around all-everything cornerback Patrick Peterson (the team also added veteran Antonio Cromartie to replace Jerraud Powers, a move that will only increase the aggressiveness of the defense), major questions have arisen at inside linebacker. Karlos Dansby left for Cleveland in free agency to get paid "what I'm worth" after having a tremendous season in Arizona. That loss was compounded in late May when Daryl Washington cemented his place on the all-knucklehead team with a full-year suspension for yet another violation of the league's substance abuse policy. Kevin Minter had only played a single defensive snap as a second-round rookie out of LSU, but he was expected to replace Dansby in the lineup. And before the suspension was even handed down by the league office, the Cardinals had signed up some Washington insurance with 34-year-old veteran Larry Foote, who was released by Pittsburgh after missing almost all of last season with a torn biceps.

Foote's arrival means that the team will have three starters in the defensive front seven who are age 33 or older (Abraham, Dockett). Teams with three or more older starters in the front seven can be successful, as long as those veterans stay healthy (Table 4). We've seen teams like the 1996 Panthers build around experienced stars. The issue is what happens the next year, and the drop-off can be harsh.

Over half the teams that relied on older starters in the defensive front finished in the top seven in defensive DVOA. Those seven teams averaged a nearly 15% decline in defensive DVOA the next year, and their rank dropped on average from fifth to 19th.

So the future for this defense is right now, if the team can withstand the losses of Washington and Dansby at inside linebacker. Carson Palmer also turns 35 this December, so the window of opportunity for the offense is likely only open for a season or two before a replacement needs to be found for him as well.

While the defense is just trying to hold steady, the offense has potential to improve in 2014. The offensive line should be adding two superior talents, if they can stay healthy. Massive left tackle Jared Veldheer, signed as a free agent from Oakland, missed 11 games last year with a torn triceps. Jonathan Cooper should be ready to go from his broken leg. However, the biggest reason for optimism on offense is second-year running back Andre Ellington, the No. 1 player on this year's FOA Top 25 Prospects list. Ellington averaged 5.5 yards per carry and was fourth in rushing DVOA as a rookie. Teammate Rashard Mendenhall had 99 more carries, but the two produced almost identical yardage totals. The offense was more dynamic in 2013 with Ellington playing a larger role, and with Mendenhall gone, he should be a big factor this year.

Table 4: Teams With At Least Three Players Age 33 Or Older With 8 Or More Starts In The Defensive Front Seven, 1989-2013

Team	Year	Old Starters	DVOA	Rk	DVOA Y+1	Rk
CLE1	1989	3	-16.9%	3	12.2%	23
NO	1992	3	-18.3%	1	-5.2%	10
ATL	1995	4	5.8%	20	21.6%	30
CAR	1996	4	-12.2%	6	4.7%	23
OAK	2002	3	-6.2%	7	9.5%	26
OAK	2005	3	1.9%	20	-8.0%	8
CLE	2006	3	3.0%	19	6.3%	23
MIA	2006	3	-9.7%	5	12.6%	31
TB	2007	3	-11.7%	4	-10.7%	6
WAS	2009	3	-2.1%	12	5.8%	26
ARI	2010	4	5.6%	25	2.4%	20
PIT	2011	4	-9.4%	7	-2.9%	13
PIT	2012	3	-2.9%	13	4.0%	19
AVERAGE			-5.6%	11	4.0%	20

Ellington shares a lot of traits with Jamaal Charles, and both his performance last year and the time share with Mendenhall were similar to when Charles used to split time with an aging Thomas Jones. Both Ellington and Charles show great speed when they get to the edge, and an ability to make the first defender miss in the backfield to turn a sure loss into a three-yard gain. Ellington is also a tremendous receiver, and could very well line up exclusively as a slot receiver and have great success in the league. Not only did he catch passes out of the backfield as a rookie, but he also he lined up in the slot and caught downfield routes, and got the ball on bubble screens. Expect those to only increase with an offseason of preparation. If the offense is going to explode, it will be because the Cardinals figure out how to give Ellington the ball as many times as he can handle. He's a potential star waiting to emerge this year.

And yet, even a huge Jamaal Charles-sized Ellington breakout might not get this team into the postseason. Our statistical projections, as well as the current betting lines, see a regression for the Cardinals. A big part of this is the schedule. They still have to overcome San Francisco and Seattle while holding off the Rams, and none of those teams will get to beat up on the AFC South this year. The other factor is the aging core, with several key players in their mid-thirties. And let's be honest that in the court of public opinion, the lack of sustained success for this franchise also colors perception. Arizona has not earned the benefit of the doubt that other franchises have earned. To cash in on its current talent, this team needs to be even better than last year. It needs to be an even better best team in Arizona Cardinals history.

Jason Lisk

2013 Cardinals Stats by Week

Wk	vs.	W-L	PF	PA	YDF	YDA	TO	Total	Off	Def	ST
1	at STL	L	24	27	390	366	0	-21%	1%	4%	-18%
2	DET	W	25	21	348	322	0	-3%	-4%	7%	8%
3	AT NO	L	7	31	247	423	-1	-37%	-17%	10%	-10%
4	at TB	W	13	10	296	253	0	2%	-45%	-37%	10%
5	CAR	W	22	6	250	353	+1	48%	-8%	-48%	8%
6	at SF	L	20	32	403	387	-2	21%	6%	-17%	-2%
7	SEA	L	22	34	234	344	0	14%	2%	-5%	6%
8	ATL	W	27	13	348	292	+3	18%	-24%	-48%	-6%
9	BYE										
10	HOU	W	27	24	332	235	-2	-16%	-13%	0%	-4%
11	at JAC	W	27	14	416	274	+2	8%	5%	-18%	-15%
12	IND	W	40	11	410	239	+1	28%	11%	-22%	-6%
13	at PHI	L	21	24	350	307	-3	7%	-1%	-12%	-4%
14	STL	W	30	10	369	257	+1	57%	31%	-46%	-20%
15	at TEN	W	37	34	360	460	+3	10%	23%	21%	9%
16	at SEA	W	17	10	307	192	-2	36%	-30%	-60%	6%
17	SF	L	20	23	482	375	-2	-17%	3%	-5%	-26%

Trends and Splits

	Offense	Rank	Defense	Rank
Total DVOA	-2.4%	20	-16.4%	2
Unadjusted VOA	-7.2%	21	-14.6%	4
Weighted Trend	1.8%	15	-18.5%	2
Variance	3.7%	2	5.9%	19
Average Opponent	-4.0%	6	0.8%	10
Passing	10.8%	15	-11.2%	5
Rushing	-9.2%	25	-24.9%	1
First Down	-0.1%	15	-7.4%	11
Second Down	2.0%	14	-22.4%	2
Third Down	-14.3%	24	-24.2%	3
First Half	-0.2%	16	0.0%	16
Second Half	-4.4%	19	-33.7%	1
Red Zone	-9.4%	25	-13.9%	8
Late and Close	6.8%	11	-40.9%	1

Five-Year Performance

Year	W-L	Pyth W	Est W	PF	PA	TO	Total	Rk	Off	Rk	Def	Rk	ST	Rk	Off AGL	Rk	Def AGL	Rk	Off Age	Rk	Def Age	Rk	ST Age	Rk
2009	10-6	9.4	10.4	381	325	-7	11.2%	12	6.8%	13	-2.8%	11	1.7%	10	13.6	10	10.5	3	27.6	11	28.0	5	27.2	3
2010	5-11	4.3	3.1	289	434	-5	-37.1%	32	-35.6%	31	5.6%	25	4.2%	9	26.8	17	11.4	8	26.7	23	28.0	8	26.8	11
2011	8-8	6.9	4.9	312	348	-13	-19.7%	28	-18.4%	28	2.4%	20	1.2%	11	46.3	28	40.5	25	27.0	17	27.5	11	27.0	2
2012	5-11	4.8	4.8	250	357	-1	-16.3%	26	-30.9%	32	-13.5%	6	1.1%	11	50.3	28	22.0	12	26.7	18	27.6	8	27.1	4
2013	10-6	9.5	10.4	379	324	-1	10.0%	10	-2.4%	20	-16.4%	2	-4.1%	27	28.3	11	36.6	23	27.9	4	28.0	2	27.0	3

2013 Performance Based on Most Common Personnel Groups

ARI Offense					ARI Offense vs. Opponents				ARI Defense				ARI Defense vs. Opponents			
Pers	Freq	Yds	DVOA	Run%	Pers	Freq	Yds	DVOA	Pers	Freq	Yds	DVOA	Pers	Freq	Yds	DVOA
11	44%	6.7	9.5%	34%	Nickel Even	39%	6.4	7.3%	Nickel Even	37%	4.7	-26.7%	11	52%	4.9	-23.3%
12	29%	4.8	-2.6%	40%	4-3-4	24%	4.4	-15.2%	3-4-4	36%	5.0	-12.6%	12	23%	5.2	-13.7%
10	11%	5.4	16.6%	5%	3-4-4	21%	5.4	4.0%	Dime+	12%	5.0	-26.7%	21	13%	4.7	-17.5%
13	5%	3.2	-35.5%	77%	Dime+	11%	6.3	17.7%	Nickel Odd	8%	6.2	16.4%	22	3%	4.3	17.5%
21	3%	6.2	-7.5%	62%	Nickel Odd	4%	4.9	15.0%	4-4-3	4%	6.5	-0.2%	13	2%	4.4	-11.4%

Strategic Tendencies

Run/Pass		Rk	Formation		Rk	Pass Rush		Rk	Secondary		Rk	Strategy		Rk
Runs, first half	38%	19	Form: Single Back	71%	14	Rush 3	1.8%	30	4 DB	37%	17	Play action	14%	26
Runs, first down	48%	15	Form: Empty Back	16%	1	Rush 4	48.7%	31	5 DB	45%	24	Avg Box (Off)	6.26	23
Runs, second-long	34%	15	Pers: 3+ WR	58%	12	Rush 5	32.4%	1	6+ DB	12%	9	Avg Box (Def)	6.43	11
Runs, power sit.	56%	14	Pers: 4+ WR	12%	1	Rush 6+	17.1%	2	CB by Sides	55%	29	Offensive Pace	30.16	15
Runs, behind 2H	29%	10	Pers: 2+ TE/6+ OL	40%	7	Sacks by LB	58.5%	8	DB Blitz	14%	8	Defensive Pace	30.27	24
Pass, ahead 2H	50%	12	Shotgun/Pistol	38%	32	Sacks by DB	6.4%	19	Hole in Zone	6%	28	Go for it on 4th	0.75	23

Arizona used a tight end on 88.2 percent of plays, which was the highest figure we've ever recorded for the Cardinals, but still the lowest figure in the NFL for 2013. The Cardinals offense was better without a tight end on the field—in fact, the Cardinals got gradually worse in DVOA as they put more tight ends (or extra linemen) on the field (Table 5). The Cardinals led the league in using empty-backfield formations even though they actually had a below-average -9.3% DVOA from these formations. One of the surprising changes brought by Bruce Arians: the Cardinals went from ranking dead last in runs when behind on the second half (17 percent in 2012) to being above average (29 percent in 2013). Not only did Arians have the Cardinals using shotgun less than any other

Table 5: Arizona offense by number of tight ends/extra linemen

TE	Plays	DVOA	Avg Yds	Avg to go
0	122	16.0%	5.3	8.5
1	**495**	**5.4%**	**6.6**	**9.1**
2	327	-2.5%	4.8	8.8
3	82	-15.5%	3.5	7.0

team, but the Cardinals also had virtually the same DVOA from shotgun that they had the rest of the time. Arizona's use of shotgun on 38 percent of plays would have actually ranked first in the NFL, not last, just ten years ago (Indianapolis led at 32 percent in 2003). Once again, the Cardinals were terrible in "max protect" blocking schemes, with just 4.2 yards per play (29th) and -28.9% DVOA (27th). They were dead last in both categories in 2012. The Cardinals improved significantly on wide receiver screens, and used them a lot: 44 plays by our count, with just 5.5 yards per play but 31.9% DVOA. Arizona's defense was at its best when opponents ran from formations with three or more wide receivers, ranking second at -24.2% DVOA and first with just 3.35 yards allowed per carry. We don't know if it was random variation or a change made by Todd Bowles, but the Cardinals finally figured out how to defend against draw plays, allowing just 2.4 yards per carry after allowing an average of 7.1 yards per carry on draws between 2010 and 2012. Arizona's defense ranked 26th in DVOA in the first quarter of games, then was the best in the league from the second quarter on.

Passing

Player	DYAR	DVOA	Plays	NtYds	Avg	YAC	C%	TD	Int
C.Palmer	547	2.7%	614	3966	6.5	4.9	63.7%	24	22

Rushing

Player	DYAR	DVOA	Plays	Yds	Avg	TD	Fum	Suc
R.Mendenhall*	-15	-10.2%	217	687	3.2	8	4	42%
A.Ellington	117	17.5%	118	657	5.6	3	1	46%
S.Taylor	-9	-14.7%	36	117	3.3	0	0	39%
A.Smith*	-16	-27.5%	18	54	3.0	1	2	50%
C.Palmer	-3	-30.4%	5	25	5.0	0	0	-
J.Dwyer	*-25*	*-18.7%*	*49*	*197*	*4.0*	*0*	*0*	*47%*

Receiving

Player	DYAR	DVOA	Plays	Ctch	Yds	Y/C	YAC	TD	C%
L.Fitzgerald	132	-0.6%	136	84	962	11.5	4.2	10	62%
M.Floyd	220	12.9%	112	65	1041	16.0	4.3	5	58%
A.Roberts*	-15	-15.3%	76	43	471	11.0	2.6	2	57%
J.Brown	20	2.5%	18	11	140	12.7	2.9	1	61%
B.Golden	16	9.4%	10	4	136	34.0	18.8	0	40%
P.Peterson	-11	-29.8%	8	6	54	9.0	6.3	0	75%
T.Ginn	*65*	*0.3%*	*68*	*36*	*556*	*15.4*	*5.9*	*5*	*53%*
R.Housler	32	0.8%	57	39	456	11.7	5.1	1	68%
J.Dray*	21	2.3%	32	26	215	8.3	4.0	2	81%
J.Ballard	31	38.3%	9	7	75	10.7	5.4	2	78%
J.Carlson	*-24*	*-14.6%*	*47*	*32*	*344*	*10.8*	*4.8*	*1*	*68%*
A.Ellington	117	22.3%	57	39	371	9.5	6.7	1	68%
R.Mendenhall*	38	21.3%	21	18	134	7.4	8.7	0	86%
A.Smith*	24	18.8%	13	10	68	6.8	7.6	0	77%
S.Taylor	2	-10.7%	9	8	71	8.9	7.5	0	89%
J.Dwyer	*12*	*8.5%*	*11*	*8*	*64*	*8.0*	*6.4*	*0*	*73%*

Offensive Line

Player	Pos	Age	GS	Snaps	Pen	Sk	Pass	Run	Player	Pos	Age	GS	Snaps	Pen	Sk	Pass	Run
Paul Fanaika	RG	28	16/16	1084	1	5.5	20.5	10.0	Bradley Sowell	LT	25	16/12	825	3	9.0	29.0	5.0
Lyle Sendlein	C	30	16/16	1084	5	4.3	13.3	6.0	Levi Brown*	LT	30	5/4	262	2	4.5	14.0	0.0
Eric Winston*	RT	31	16/16	1063	9	5.8	20.8	4.0	*Ted Larsen*	*C/G*	*27*	*16/4*	*361*	*5*	*0.0*	*8.0*	*1.0*
Daryn Colledge*	LG	33	16/16	1027	5	1.5	9.5	4.0	*Jared Veldheer*	*LT*	*27*	*5/5*	*323*	*6*	*0.0*	*7.5*	*0.0*

Year	Yards	ALY	Rk	Power	Rk	Stuff	Rk	2nd Lev	Rk	Open Field	Rk	Sacks	ASR	Rk	Short	Long	F-Start	Cont.
2011	4.12	4.07	15	63%	16	20%	18	1.07	27	0.74	21	54	9.0%	27	21	22	16	31
2012	3.26	2.93	32	48%	31	27%	32	0.85	32	0.66	20	58	8.1%	26	25	16	17	31
2013	3.89	3.84	17	73%	6	19%	16	1.00	24	0.71	15	41	6.8%	13	18	7	19	42

2013 ALY by direction: Left End 4.96 (2) Left Tackle 3.34 (28) Mid/Guard 3.61 (28) Right Tackle 4.29 (8) Right End 3.69 (16)

Arizona only had four games (out of a possible 80) started by an offensive lineman who was drafted by the organization. Those were all by Levi Brown, who was jettisoned by the new coaching staff one month into the season. That easily qualifies as the lowest amount of drafted players starting on the line for any NFL team. St. Louis (nine starts by Roger Saffold), Washington (16 starts by Trent Williams), Oakland (22 starts by three different drafted players), and Indianapolis (28 starts by three different drafted players) were the only other teams with less than 32 starts by drafted linemen.

It wasn't supposed to be that way. The team invested a top-10 pick in guard Jonathan Cooper. Cooper flashed the athleticism and ability to get to the second level in the preseason, but suffered a broken leg before the season began. Bobby Massie, drafted in 2013, had started 16 games as a rookie at right tackle, but he struggled so much in the preseason that the new coaching staff signed up veteran Eric Winston to replace him.

Winston, along with veteran Daryn Colledge, served as the stopgaps for one season, but were not resigned. The other two starters last year were right guard Paul Fanaika, an Arizona State product who had played with four other teams since coming into the league in 2009, and Bradley Sowell, an undrafted waiver pickup who was pressed into action at left tackle when Brown was sent packing. Fanaika will be starting again at right guard, while Sowell will compete with Massie to start at right tackle. (The two played together as the two starting tackles at Mississippi.)

Free-agent addition Jared Veldheer was one of the more underappreciated and underrated left tackles in the league, toiling in Oakland, where he did block for Carson Palmer. He missed most of last season with a triceps injury. If Cooper and Veldheer play at a high level, they can team up with veteran center Lyle Sendlein, the one constant on the offensive line going back to the Super Bowl year in 2008, and form perhaps the best trio of linemen that Arizona has had in a long time. It's not a high standard. Arizona has also only finished higher than 15th in the Adjusted Line Yards metric once since 1995 (10th in 2007). The last Arizona lineman to get selected to a Pro Bowl was Lomas Brown in 1996.

Defensive Front Seven

			Overall								vs. Run					Pass Rush			
Defensive Line	**Age**	**Pos**	**G**	**Snaps**	**Plays**	**TmPct**	**Rk**	**Stop**	**Dfts**	**BTkl**	**Runs**	**St%**	**Rk**	**RuYd**	**Rk**	**Sack**	**Hit**	**Hur**	**Tips**
Calais Campbell	28	DE	16	963	64	7.8%	10	57	22	5	47	87%	12	1.4	14	9.0	14	24.0	6
Darnell Dockett	33	DE	16	865	45	5.5%	34	35	20	3	31	74%	52	1.6	22	4.5	9	17.0	0
Frostee Rucker	31	DE	16	357	11	1.3%	--	10	5	0	9	89%	--	1.8	--	2.0	6	10.0	0
Dan Williams	27	DT	14	285	25	3.5%	--	20	3	0	21	81%	--	1.9	--	1.0	5	2.0	1

			Overall								vs. Run					Pass Rush			
Edge Rushers	**Age**	**Pos**	**G**	**Snaps**	**Plays**	**TmPct**	**Rk**	**Stop**	**Dfts**	**BTkl**	**Runs**	**St%**	**Rk**	**RuYd**	**Rk**	**Sack**	**Hit**	**Hur**	**Tips**
John Abraham	36	OLB	16	863	38	4.7%	55	35	21	4	22	91%	6	0.4	1	10.5	5	32.0	1
Matt Shaughnessy	28	OLB	16	718	36	4.4%	61	24	11	0	21	86%	11	1.1	4	3.0	3	9.0	2

			Overall								Pass Rush			vs. Run					vs. Pass						
Linebackers	**Age**	**Pos**	**G**	**Snaps**	**Plays**	**TmPct**	**Rk**	**Stop**	**Dfts**	**BTkl**	**Sack**	**Hit**	**Hur**	**Runs**	**St%**	**Rk**	**RuYd**	**Rk**	**Tgts**	**Suc%**	**Rk**	**AdjYd**	**Rk**	**PD**	**Int**
Karlos Dansby*	33	ILB	16	1078	141	17.3%	12	87	31	9	6.5	5	9.5	69	67%	35	4.2	70	60	58%	21	6.2	25	16	4
Daryl Washington	26	ILB	12	799	84	13.7%	38	54	24	6	3.0	9	11.5	37	62%	52	3.1	28	44	58%	22	4.8	8	9	2
Jasper Brinkley*	29	ILB	15	202	24	3.1%	--	16	6	5	0.0	2	2	18	83%	--	2.8	--	7	15%	--	11.3	--	0	0
Ernie Sims	*30*	*OLB*	*12*	*380*	*41*	*6.3%*	*76*	*14*	*2*	*3*	*0.0*	*0*	*0*	*31*	*39%*	*80*	*6.5*	*82*	*12*	*48%*	*--*	*8.7*	*--*	*0*	*0*

Year	Yards	ALY	Rk	Power	Rk	Stuff	Rk	2nd Level	Rk	Open Field	Rk	Sacks	ASR	Rk	Short	Long
2011	4.23	4.11	19	71%	27	20%	13	1.27	23	0.69	10	42	6.4%	22	12	15
2012	4.58	4.49	32	55%	7	17%	25	1.31	28	0.80	17	38	7.2%	7	11	15
2013	3.19	3.09	1	48%	2	28%	1	1.01	8	0.46	7	47	7.2%	12	23	15
2013 ALY by direction:			*Left End 1.54 (1)*			*Left Tackle 2.56 (1)*			*Mid/Guard 3.39 (3)*			*Right Tackle 3.17 (7)*			*Right End 3.76 (17)*	

Daryl Washington's year-long suspension robs the middle of this 3-4 of its best interior rusher and run defender. But the hand-wringing ignores the fact that Arizona does have a player with pedigree to take his place in 2013 second-rounder Kevin Minter. The former LSU star didn't see much action last year, but not many linebackers would when playing behind Washington and the departed Karlos Dansby. Minter is a thumper first, and that could limit some of Arizona's more creative rushing schemes. Veteran Larry Foote is the favorite to start next to him. Flotsam Ernie Sims and special-teamer Lorenzo Alexander are also candidates to get playing time. They'll probably struggle to recreate Dansby's havoc in the passing game—he had four tipped passes, the only middle/inside linebacker with more than two—but the Cardinals are in a better position than most teams would be after losing their top linebacker.

As modern medicine and training techniques continue to improve, we're seeing more and more that pass rushers don't necessarily go gently into retirement at 30. Robert Mathis had a career year in 2013, Shaun Phillips was a big threat for a Broncos team that needed pass rush, and John Abraham had another vintage John Abraham year at age 35. There are currently four players on NFL rosters that were drafted in 2000: Abraham, Shane Lechler, Sebastian Janikowski, and Tom Brady. It's been a remarkable ride, and the Cardinals will need every last drop of his sweat to make this pass rush work again in 2014. Matt Shaughnessy is a technically sound gap defender, but isn't a sexy pass rusher. University of Texas fourth-round alums Sam Acho (2011) and Alex Okafor (2013) have their share of draftnik supporters, but Acho hasn't produced much and Okafor hasn't gotten much of a chance yet.

The defensive line is the real strength of this team. Calais Campbell is without flaw as a football player. He tips passes at the line, he can pressure the passer, and he ends pulling guards to ruin the running game. Darnell Dockett is past his prime on the field, but he's still a well above-average gap-shooter who anchors as well as anyone in the league. (Off the field, of course, his Twitter account is a national treasure.) Third-rounder Kareem Martin was a SackSEER favorite who will get some room to grow and eventually replace Dockett. While you probably wouldn't spend a first-round pick on a nose tackle in an ideal world, Dan Williams has returned on the investment. Williams can two-gap and hold his own, though it'd be nice if he could stay on the field more.

Defensive Secondary

			Overall								vs. Run					vs. Pass									
Secondary	Age	Pos	G	Snaps	Plays	TmPct	Rk	Stop	Dfts	BTkl	Runs	St%	Rk	RuYd	Rk	Tgts	Tgt%	Rk	Dist	Suc%	Rk	AdjYd	Rk	PD	Int
Patrick Peterson	24	CB	16	1074	55	6.7%	66	20	8	5	5	20%	73	9.8	65	84	17.5%	12	12.4	57%	23	6.4	13	12	3
Yeremiah Bell*	36	SS	16	1070	81	9.9%	39	35	14	6	38	50%	21	4.8	10	47	9.9%	59	9.3	57%	34	5.8	18	9	2
Jerraud Powers	27	CB	16	1030	82	10.0%	17	28	8	4	14	14%	82	13.1	80	102	22.1%	53	12.2	54%	40	8.0	55	16	1
Tyrann Mathieu	22	CB/FS	13	780	75	11.3%	6	27	13	3	22	32%	61	6.1	28	60	17.3%	10	11.0	47%	71	7.3	40	8	2
Rashad Johnson	28	FS	13	620	57	8.6%	57	18	7	6	16	44%	30	7.1	41	24	8.7%	49	11.9	62%	25	4.8	10	5	3
Antonio Cromartie	*30*	*CB*	*16*	*1064*	*46*	*5.7%*	*80*	*18*	*4*	*2*	*11*	*36%*	*49*	*11.4*	*77*	*84*	*17.8%*	*15*	*16.6*	*52%*	*44*	*11.8*	*87*	*11*	*3*

Year	Pass D Rank	vs. #1 WR	Rk	vs. #2 WR	Rk	vs. Other WR	Rk	vs. TE	Rk	vs. RB	Rk
2011	14	10.7%	17	4.4%	16	6.0%	24	9.6%	17	-26.8%	2
2012	2	-7.4%	11	-18.2%	4	-46.0%	1	-2.5%	15	-52.4%	1
2013	5	-27.3%	1	-10.5%	9	-9.3%	10	6.4%	20	-11.3%	8

The "Patrick Peterson vs. Richard Sherman vs. Darrelle Revis battle royale for the best cornerback in the NFL" argument really breaks down to what your definition of "best" is. Peterson and Revis both have the ability to cover one receiver all over the field. (Revis was not allowed to do so last year because Greg Schiano's moral code only tries to find weaknesses when quarterbacks are kneeling.) Sherman mostly stayed on one side, but was undoubtedly the best corner in the NFL last year from an empirical results standpoint. The winner of this ranking argument is not an important thing for the Cardinals. The important thing is that Peterson is in that company and will soon have to be paid like it.

2013 third-rounder Tyrann Mathieu gave the Cardinals a lot of flexibility last season with his ability to cover the slot in base packages. He reminded us of a quicker Glover Quin, and Todd Bowles was able to utilize that to create some unique conundrums for offensive coordinators. A torn ACL and LCL suffered late in the season will have the Honey Badger sidelined early, with head coach Bruce Arians saying he's aiming for a return after Arizona's Week 4 bye. This, of course, assumes that the Honey Badger doesn't just take what he wants and return to the field when he feels like it. Which is not always the correct assumption, if we are to believe YouTube.

In the meantime, the Cardinals will likely play a little more traditionally in the early going. Antonio Cromartie (ex-Jets) spent the year trying to play like Peterson and actually playing like DeAngelo Hall. Because of Cromartie's sterling track record in our advanced stats (top 20 in Success Rate in both 2012 and 2011), he does offer some bounce-back potential, but at age 30 he also carries some risk. Jerraud Powers is a perfectly serviceable, though injury-prone, No. 2 corner who now gets to play No. 3. First-round rookie Deone Bucannon (Washington State) will take over at strong safety for the flammable Yeremiah Bell. Arians said of Bucannon: "We've got some good guys here to help him and teach and give him opportunities to knock the crap out of people in our division," and with six interceptions for the Cougars last year, he also has some play-making ability. Rashad Johnson is a fine deep safety and is most well-known for defensing five passes with only nine fingers.

Special Teams

Year	DVOA	Rank	FG/XP	Rank	Net Kick	Rank	Kick Ret	Rank	Net Punt	Rank	Punt Ret	Rank	Hidden	Rank
2011	1.2%	11	-5.2	24	-0.7	20	-3.5	24	-4.7	22	20.0	1	14.7	2
2012	1.1%	11	4.4	10	-6.7	27	-2.5	20	19.7	1	-9.3	31	14.4	2
2013	-4.1%	27	-4.9	25	-1.0	18	-6.5	30	3.9	14	-11.8	31	3.4	10

Patrick Peterson was amazing on punt returns as a rookie. He was worth 21 estimated points worth of field position above average in 2011, *double* any other returner in the NFL. Yet over the last two years, he's been the worst punt returner in the league. This is one of the league's hidden mysteries, but we can safely ignore it because Ted Ginn will likely take over the role. Rookie wide receiver John Brown should be an improvement over Javier Arenas on kick returns.

It may be time for the Cardinals to consider replacing kicker Jay Feely. He's now 38, and while his decline in field-goal value last year was just typical oscillation, he's declined in gross kickoff value for two straight years. There will be two young kickers in camp to challenge him, Danny Hrapmann (Southern Miss) and Chandler Catanzaro (Clemson). Punter Dave Zastudil is almost as old (35) but still above average, though he wasn't as good in 2013 as he was in 2012. Justin Bethel earned the NFC's "all-purpose special-teamer" spot, and deservedly so, as our count has him with 21 special-teams tackles. Nobody else in the NFC had more than 15.

Atlanta Falcons

2013 Record: 4-12	**Total DVOA:** -10.4% (25th)	**2014 Mean Projection:** 7.3 wins	**On the Clock (0-4):** 13%
Pythagorean Wins: 5.9 (24th)	**Offense:** 3.2% (14th)	**Postseason Odds:** 23.3%	**Mediocrity (5-7):** 40%
Snap-Weighted Age: 26.9 (12th)	**Defense:** 13.5% (29th)	**Super Bowl Odds:** 2.2%	**Playoff Contender (8-10):** 36%
Average Opponent: 7.3% (2nd)	**Special Teams:** -0.1% (17th)	**Proj. Avg. Opponent:** 0.8% (14th)	**Super Bowl Contender (11+):** 11%

2013: Me and Julio down at the doctor's office.

2014: Me and Sean Weatherspoon down at the doctor's office.

For all intents and purposes, the Atlanta Falcons' 2013 campaign ended after just five games when Julio Jones underwent season-ending foot surgery. At that point the Falcons were 1-4; few teams have ever rebounded from that mark to make the postseason, and fewer still have done so with their best player on the sidelines. It was a brutally sudden end to a string of successful seasons that few teams in the league could match. Was it a sign that the Falcons' window of opportunity has closed, or a one-year fluke that will be forgotten about by December? Most likely the answer lies somewhere in the middle. The Falcons should win more games in 2014 than they did a year ago, but getting back into playoff contention may be too much to ask.

It has been six years now since the trio of general manager Thomas Dimitroff, head coach Mike Smith, and quarterback Matt Ryan arrived in Atlanta and rewrote the team's history. The Falcons had never before put together back-to-back winning seasons, but under the new regime they laid down five in a row. In those five seasons they had a combined record of 56-24, better than anyone in the NFL except New England. The perennial doormats became playoff regulars, and came up four points shy of a Super Bowl berth in 2012.

And then the wheels fell off. At the time of Jones' injury, the Falcons' passing offense DVOA was a robust 30.3%. In their next game, Matt Ryan went 20-of-26 for 273 yards and three touchdowns against Tampa Bay, and it looked like the team would survive. That Bucs game proved to be a fluke, however, and for the season's final ten games Atlanta's passing DVOA was just 2.2%.

There were other injuries—lots of them. At the fantasy positions, Roddy White missed three games, Steven Jackson four, Harry Douglas five. Offensive tackle Sam Baker started only four games. Six linebackers started at least one game for the Falcons (on a 4-3 team, at that), but only two of them started more than seven: undrafted rookies Joplo Bartu and Paul Worrilow. When all was said and done, Atlanta finished 27th in Adjusted Games Lost, and made the bottom five at wide receiver, offensive line, and linebacker.

If the Falcons' luck was bad in the trainers' room, it was even worse on the calendar. The Falcons played the second-most difficult schedule in the league last year, and the most difficult on offense. In fact, since 1989, only six other offenses have played a tougher slate of defenses than last year's Falcons. That's what happens when you play five games against the top four defenses in football, nine games against the top ten, and 12 games against the top 13 (Table 1).

The biggest takeaway from this table? Pittsburgh and Baltimore have made life rough on coordinators and quarterbacks in Ohio for many years. As it pertains to Atlanta, there's no consistent pattern on what happens to offensive DVOA the season after a tough schedule. This makes sense, since DVOA is schedule-adjusted. Basic stats, though, are not, and these offenses have usually won more games and scored more points in the following season.

Table 1: Most Difficult Offensive Schedules, 1989-2013

YEAR	TEAM	Year N				Year N+1		
		OFF SCHED	W-L	OFF DVOA	PF	W-L	OFF DVOA	PF
2004	CLE	-9.2%	4-12	-14.2%	276	6-10	-11.7%	232
2008	CIN	-8.2%	4-11-1	-18.3%	204	10-6	-0.9%	305
2008	CLE	-7.9%	4-12	-21.3%	232	5-11	-16.4%	245
2004	CIN	-7.7%	8-8	3.7%	374	11-5	22.9%	421
1991	DAL	-7.3%	11-5	17.6%	342	13-3	23.6%	409
2004	NYJ	-6.6%	10-6	20.8%	333	4-12	-19.8%	240
2013	ATL	-6.5%	4-12	3.2%	353	--	--	--
2008	NYG	-6.2%	12-4	18.9%	427	8-8	8.7%	402
1998	IND	-6.2%	3-13	-0.5%	310	13-3	14.2%	423
2000	PIT	-6.1%	9-7	7.9%	321	13-3	14.7%	352
AVERAGE		-7.2%	7.0-9.0	1.8%	317.2	9.2-6.8	3.9%	336.6

2014 Falcons Schedule

Week	Opp.	Week	Opp.	Week	Opp.
1	NO	7	at BAL	13	ARI
2	at CIN	8	DET (U.K.)	14	at GB (Mon.)
3	TB (Thu)	9	BYE	15	PIT
4	at MIN	10	at TB	16	at NO
5	at NYG	11	at CAR	17	CAR
6	CHI	12	CLE		

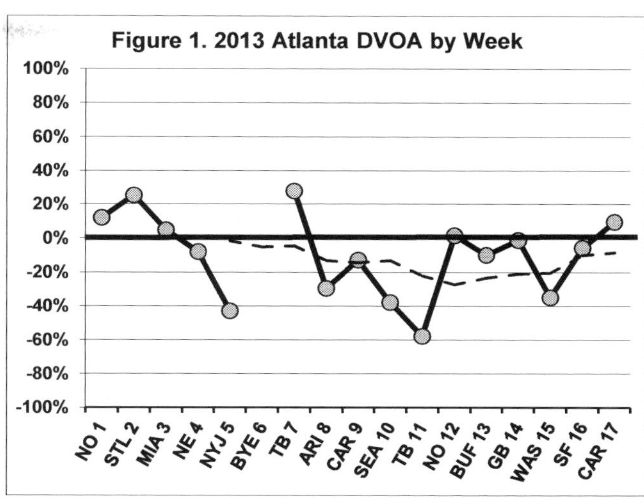

The Falcons should be healthier in 2014, and a schedule that doesn't include teams like the Seahawks, Cardinals, or Bills should make life easier on Matt Ryan and company. So why is our enthusiasm for a bounce-back season so restrained? For starters, this team was almost never as good during their five-year run as their sterling win-loss record would indicate. Though they ranked second in total wins between 2008 and 2012, they were just eighth in average DVOA and Estimated Wins, and sixth in Pythagorean Wins. In fact, if we subtract either Estimated Wins or Pythagorean Wins from actual wins, we find only one team (the Colts) in that timespan which over-achieved more than Atlanta did. The Falcons have failed to patch their holes, while the strengths of the roster have diminished with time.

The offense, for example, has never ranked higher than ninth in DVOA under this regime. Now, there is something to be said for consistency, and they've never ranked lower than 14th, either, even during last year's disaster. But even with the return of Julio Jones to the lineup and the addition of Jake Matthews at tackle, we still find question marks all over the field. Can Levine Toilolo fill the shoes of the departed Tony Gonzalez? Can a 31-year-old Steven Jackson play like he did with the Rams? Can Roddy White, at 33, pull out one more big year, or will he take another step towards retirement? Was Harry Douglas' first 1,000-yard season a fluke, or can he take White's role as No. 2 receiver? And God forbid any of the top wideouts get hurt again, because nobody wants to see more extended action from the likes of Drew Davis or Darius Johnson.

Wait, we haven't even gotten to the offensive line yet. Sam Baker was dreadful last year even before he went on injured reserve. Baker has been frequently injured throughout his career, and rarely better than adequate when he has played. Can the former first-round pick finally live up to his draft status? Joe Hawley started last season on Atlanta's bench, while Jon Asamoah finished the year on Kanasas City's. Can the Falcons count on either to be a full-time starter? And even if the talent is there, can a line that could have up to four new starters (counting Baker and Hawley) play with any kind of cohesion?

These questions, keep in mind, are on Atlanta's *better* side of the ball. Things have really fallen apart on defense. Atlanta's defensive DVOA last season was its worst since 1996. The injuries at linebacker didn't help, but there was plenty of blame to go around. The defensive line, for example, spent far too little time in the opponents' backfields. Our defensive line stats go back to 1996, and the 2013 Falcons set franchise-worst marks in both Stuff Rate and Adjusted Sack Rate. When they did get there, they failed to put the ballcarrier down; the Falcons' defensive linemen missed 20 tackles, the worst mark in the league. In fact, missed tackles were a problem that plagued this defense. The linebackers missed 24 and the defensive backs missed 39, with both figures ranking among the ten worst teams at each position. Atlanta missed 33 tackles on run plays (tied for eighth-most), 40 on completed passes (sixth-most), and 10 on attempted quarterback sacks (tied for second.)

So let's not blame everything on the front seven; there were plenty of problems in the secondary as well. The Falcons' corners were a mix of the very old (Asante Samuel) and the very young (Desmond Trufant, Robert Alford, Robert McClain), and the resulting mix was very bad. Though Trufant's game-charting metrics were shockingly good for a rookie, overall the team struggled to stop, well, anyone, ranking exactly 30th against No. 1 wide receivers, No. 2s, and No. 3/others. It's hard to separate the performance of a team's coverage from its pass rush, but what we can do is look at each defense's numbers when they failed to pressure the quarterback. And on those plays, the Falcons gave up a league-worst 8.7 yards per play and 58.2% DVOA. It's unfortunate, then, that they pressured the quarterback on just 21.5 percent of all pass plays, fourth-lowest rate in the league. So, to recap: they couldn't pressure the quarterback, they couldn't bring him down when they did get there, they couldn't cover receivers, and they couldn't tackle receivers after the catch. Other than that, they weren't too bad.

Clearly, an overhaul was in order. Defensive coordinator Mike Nolan wanted to move to something resembling a 3-4 scheme, a system he has used throughout his coaching career in stints with the Jets, Ravens, 49ers, Broncos, and Dolphins. That meant he needed more beef. So in free agency, the Falcons added big-body linemen Paul Soliai from Miami and Tyson Jackson from Kansas City, then drafted 6-foot-6, 310-pound Ra'Shede Hageman in the second round. It wasn't a terrible plan, but when a torn Achilles at OTAs knocked linebacker Sean Weatherspoon out for the entire 2014 season, it rendered the positive benefits of the scheme change largely moot. Meanwhile, for all the mass they added up front, the Falcons forgot to acquire a pass rusher. Who on this team is going to strike fear in quarterbacks' hearts? Osi Umenyiora, now 33 and limited to a third-down role? Jonathan Massaquoi, whose five sack plays last year (counting two half-sacks as one play each) included two plays listed as "overall pressure," and another listed as "coverage sack?" Kroy Biermann, the Real Househusband who missed 14 games last year with a torn Achilles, and has just 16.5 career sacks in 82 games? 2013 fourth- and fifth-rounders Malliciah Goodman and Stansly Maponga, who played just 429 total defensive snaps as rookies? The Falcons were probably thinking that fourth-round rookie Prince Shembo out of Notre Dame would fight for a spot, but they formally moved him inside after OTAs (and, perhaps not coincidentally, after Weatherspoon's injury). There is no good answer to this question. Nolan will have to rely on some very creative blitz schemes, or else the Falcons are likely to finish last in Adjusted Sack Rate again.

The plan in the secondary is that the young group will play better with another year of seasoning. And honestly, it's not a bad plan, certainly wiser than adding more youth in the draft or throwing more money at washed-up vets. The Falcons doubled up on corners in the 2013 draft with Trufant and Alford. McClain, meanwhile, is entering his fifth NFL season, but he's still only 26 years old. He had stellar numbers in 2012 (first among corners in Adjusted Yards per Pass, third in Adjusted Success Rate) although his terrible numbers in 2013 (85th and 84th, respectively) show how wildly charting stats can fluctuate for nickelbacks. Given the typical aging pattern of NFL cornerbacks, plus the likelihood of a rebound from McClain, improvement from this unit is quite likely.

At safety, William Moore enters his fifth season as a starter. His 2013 statline looks remarkably similar to his 2012 Pro Bowl campaign (13.9 percent of his team's plays, 33 Stops, 15 Defeats), though it took him four more games to get there. So he was healthier and on the field more often, but he apparently spent most of that extra time away from the ball and not making plays. Given the sorry state of the rest of the secondary, it's very hard to evaluate him. The Falcons are hoping that ex-Jaguar Dwight Lowery can make fewer mistakes than former free safety Thomas DeCoud, whose play last year slipped noticeably from his 2012 Pro Bowl season. Lowery played very well in 2011, but missed the lion's share of the last two years with an assortment of injuries.

All told, the Falcons have too many question marks to believe they'll make a serious charge for the playoffs. It's possible that the top three receivers will stay healthy, that Mathews' presence will solidify the line and give Jackson running lanes, and that Jackson has another 1,000-yard season left in his legs. The young players at linebacker and corner might take a collective step forward, and maybe somebody here turns out to be a quality pass rusher. That's a lot of "possibles" and "maybes." Most likely, some of it works out, some of it fails, and the team loses eight or nine games. Dimitroff and company have turned this team around before, but this looks like more than a one-year project.

Vince Verhei

2013 Falcons Stats by Week

Wk	vs.	W-L	PF	PA	YDF	YDA	TO	Total	Off	Def	ST
1	at NO	L	17	23	367	419	-1	12%	7%	-4%	1%
2	STL	W	31	24	393	421	+1	25%	33%	17%	9%
3	at MIA	L	23	27	377	285	0	5%	20%	-1%	-16%
4	NE	L	23	30	457	448	-1	-8%	13%	29%	9%
5	NYJ	L	28	30	363	288	-1	-43%	4%	35%	-12%
6	BYE										
7	TB	W	31	23	291	337	0	28%	34%	-1%	-7%
8	at ARI	L	13	27	292	348	-3	-30%	-34%	3%	7%
9	at CAR	L	10	34	289	373	-2	-13%	-12%	2%	1%
10	SEA	L	10	33	226	490	-1	-38%	1%	39%	0%
11	at TB	L	28	41	420	410	-3	-58%	-11%	36%	-10%
12	NO	L	13	17	355	374	-1	2%	24%	19%	-3%
13	vs. BUF	W	34	31	423	405	+1	-10%	9%	27%	8%
14	at GB	L	21	22	285	334	0	-1%	-13%	-20%	-8%
15	WAS	W	27	26	243	476	+5	-35%	-24%	17%	6%
16	at SF	L	24	34	402	379	-2	-6%	20%	34%	8%
17	CAR	L	20	21	307	283	+1	10%	-9%	-14%	5%

Trends and Splits

	Offense	Rank	Defense	Rank
Total DVOA	3.2%	14	13.5%	29
Unadjusted VOA	-2.5%	18	14.0%	29
Weighted Trend	-1.5%	18	14.3%	30
Variance	4.0%	6	3.6%	4
Average Opponent	-6.5%	1	1.3%	8
Passing	14.7%	11	24.7%	32
Rushing	-7.0%	21	1.2%	26
First Down	-7.5%	23	3.5%	19
Second Down	0.8%	16	15.5%	32
Third Down	27.5%	6	28.2%	30
First Half	8.5%	9	17.3%	32
Second Half	-2.2%	18	9.7%	23
Red Zone	-8.8%	24	12.0%	22
Late and Close	-4.9%	19	7.2%	22

Five-Year Performance

Year	W-L	Pyth W	Est W	PF	PA	TO	Total	Rk	Off	Rk	Def	Rk	ST	Rk	Off AGL	Rk	Def AGL	Rk	Off Age	Rk	Def Age	Rk	ST Age	Rk
2009	9-7	9.1	7.9	363	325	+3	0.5%	18	5.9%	14	4.1%	22	-1.3%	22	15.9	12	21.8	14	28.0	8	26.4	26	26.9	10
2010	13-3	11.4	11.3	414	288	+14	16.3%	7	8.0%	9	-2.1%	14	6.3%	3	5.2	1	10.9	6	28.6	4	26.6	19	27.1	6
2011	10 6	9.4	10.2	402	350	+8	13.9%	8	6.1%	11	-9.1%	8	-1.3%	22	22.2	13	26.4	16	28.0	4	26.7	20	26.4	12
2012	13-3	11.2	9.1	419	299	+13	9.1%	10	6.1%	12	-2.9%	12	0.1%	16	17.3	7	35.6	21	28.6	1	28.0	3	26.5	9
2013	4-12	5.9	6.5	353	443	-7	-10.4%	25	3.2%	14	13.5%	29	-0.1%	17	54.0	28	36.8	24	27.6	7	26.7	15	25.9	21

2013 Performance Based on Most Common Personnel Groups

ATL Offense					ATL Offense vs. Opponents				ATL Defense				ATL Defense vs. Opponents			
Pers	Freq	Yds	DVOA	Run%	Pers	Freq	Yds	DVOA	Pers	Freq	Yds	DVOA	Pers	Freq	Yds	DVOA
11	59%	6.0	18.0%	21%	Nickel Even	43%	5.5	14.2%	Nickel Even	47%	6.4	12.3%	11	49%	6.4	15.2%
21	16%	5.1	-11.3%	52%	Dime+	15%	6.8	35.8%	4-3-4	37%	6.4	13.4%	12	18%	5.6	-2.4%
12	14%	4.4	-8.6%	30%	3-4-4	15%	4.1	-1.6%	Nickel Odd	7%	6.4	20.4%	21	16%	6.5	19.5%
20	2%	4.3	-56.9%	9%	4-3-4	15%	5.4	-0.4%	3-4-4	3%	4.0	-14.4%	22	5%	7.5	15.5%
611	2%	6.6	46.6%	52%	Nickel Odd	11%	6.3	-18.0%	Goal Line	3%	2.3	20.2%	20	2%	7.6	25.0%
22	2%	3.9	13.2%	72%												

Strategic Tendencies

Run/Pass		Rk	Formation		Rk	Pass Rush		Rk	Secondary		Rk	Strategy		Rk
Runs, first half	34%	26	Form: Single Back	74%	12	Rush 3	7.4%	11	4 DB	40%	16	Play action	13%	31
Runs, first down	41%	31	Form: Empty Back	8%	10	Rush 4	54.7%	28	5 DB	54%	10	Avg Box (Off)	6.06	32
Runs, second-long	19%	32	Pers: 3+ WR	63%	7	Rush 5	28.6%	7	6+ DB	2%	23	Avg Box (Def)	6.44	8
Runs, power sit.	41%	32	Pers: 4+ WR	1%	18	Rush 6+	9.3%	10	CB by Sides	90%	5	Offensive Pace	31.69	27
Runs, behind 2H	20%	30	Pers: 2+ TE/6+ OL	21%	27	Sacks by LB	25.0%	19	DB Blitz	14%	7	Defensive Pace	30.18	23
Pass, ahead 2H	65%	1	Shotgun/Pistol	60%	16	Sacks by DB	9.4%	15	Hole in Zone	11%	14	Go for it on 4th	0.64	26

The Falcons threw only 11 percent of passes deep, i.e. over 15 yards past the line of scrimmage. That was the lowest figure in the league. Lest you think this was just a product of Julio Jones' injury, the Falcons threw only 17 percent of passes deep the year before, which was tied for the third lowest figure. Atlanta was much better running from single-back formations (4.1 yards per carry, -2.1% DVOA) than from two-back formations (3.4 yards per carry, -24.1% DVOA). A league-leading 20 percent of runs by Atlanta running backs were marked as draw plays, but the Falcons only averaged 4.3 yards per carry with -9.5% DVOA. (NFL average: 5.0 yards, -1.7% DVOA) Over the last three seasons, Atlanta's rate of blitzing (five or more pass rushers) has gone from 22 percent to 28 percent to 38 percent. The Falcons are blitzing more because they've become so desperate to bring pressure. Last year they gave up a league-worst 8.7 yards per pass and 58.2% DVOA without pressure, but ranked fourth in yards (2.2) and sixth in DVOA (-93.3%) on the rare occasions when they got pressure. Our charting suggested Atlanta used zone coverage much more than in other recent seasons; in 2012 they were just 29th in passes marked as Hole in Zone. Mike Smith, long one of the league's most aggressive coaches on fourth down, has been one of the least aggressive over the last couple seasons.

Passing

Player	DYAR	DVOA	Plays	NtYds	Avg	YAC	C%	TD	Int
M.Ryan	1124	13.3%	695	4195	6.0	4.8	67.7%	26	16
D.Davis	8	4.4%	7	34	4.9	3.0	71.4%	0	0
T.J. Yates	*-109*	*-78.0%*	*24*	*106*	*4.4*	*3.0*	*68.2%*	*0*	*2*

Rushing

Player	DYAR	DVOA	Plays	Yds	Avg	TD	Fum	Suc
S.Jackson	-2	-8.8%	157	543	3.5	6	0	40%
J.Rodgers	2	-8.1%	96	332	3.5	2	0	45%
J.Snelling*	19	1.2%	44	164	3.7	1	0	50%
M.Ryan	23	54.5%	8	71	8.9	0	0	-
A.Smith	78	392.3%	5	145	29.0	2	0	100%

Receiving

Player	DYAR	DVOA	Plays	Ctch	Yds	Y/C	YAC	TD	C%
H.Douglas	171	3.6%	132	85	1067	12.6	6.0	2	64%
R.White	118	2.7%	97	63	711	11.3	1.8	3	65%
J.Jones	60	0.4%	60	41	580	14.1	6.0	2	68%
D.Johnson	-40	-24.6%	43	22	210	9.5	3.8	1	51%
D.Davis	88	51.7%	17	12	216	18.0	9.2	2	71%
T.Gonzalez*	135	8.7%	121	83	859	10.3	2.7	8	69%
L.Toilolo	-19	-22.4%	14	11	55	5.0	2.5	2	79%
B.Pascoe	*-54*	*-52.0%*	*20*	*12*	*81*	*6.8*	*4.0*	*0*	*60%*
J.Rodgers	72	7.8%	62	52	340	6.5	7.0	2	84%
S.Jackson	-36	-26.0%	49	33	191	5.8	6.1	1	67%
J.Snelling*	109	46.2%	33	28	224	8.0	6.5	3	85%
P.DiMarco	5	-5.2%	10	8	49	6.1	4.5	0	80%

Offensive Line

Player	Pos	Age	GS	Snaps	Pen	Sk	Pass	Run	Player	Pos	Age	GS	Snaps	Pen	Sk	Pass	Run
Justin Blalock	LG	31	16/16	1077	2	3.0	14.0	4.0	Joe Hawley	C	26	16/7	539	1	0.5	3.5	1.0
Lamar Holmes	LT	25	16/15	1052	12	9.0	35.5	6.0	Ryan Schraeder	OT	26	13/4	306	2	4.0	11.0	1.0
Peter Konz	C/G	25	16/15	889	1	6.5	16.5	7.0	Sam Baker	LT	29	4/4	189	3	1.0	8.0	1.0
Garrett Reynolds	RG	27	15/10	682	3	3.5	11.0	2.0	*Jon Asamoah*	*RG*	*26*	*13/9*	*652*	*3*	*1.5*	*5.0*	*3.0*
Jeremy Trueblood	RT	31	14/10	628	3	1.5	10.0	2.0	*Gabe Carimi*	*G/T*	*26*	*14/2*	*209*	*1*	*1.0*	*5.0*	*1.0*

Year	Yards	ALY	Rk	Power	Rk	Stuff	Rk	2nd Lev	Rk	Open Field	Rk	Sacks	ASR	Rk	Short	Long	F-Start	Cont.
2011	4.21	3.83	27	59%	22	25%	31	1.16	17	1.05	6	26	5.1%	7	13	9	13	34
2012	3.69	3.87	24	39%	32	23%	27	1.03	26	0.66	21	28	5.1%	8	9	9	9	40
2013	3.91	3.74	24	63%	18	21%	25	0.98	25	0.76	14	44	5.9%	7	14	5	18	23
2013 ALY by direction:			*Left End 2.60 (28)*			*Left Tackle 4.16 (10)*			*Mid/Guard 3.64 (27)*				*Right Tackle 4.40 (4)*			*Right End 3.05 (26)*		

The Falcons' line this season will be bookended by a pair of first-round tackles: one a 22-year-old rookie full of potential, the other a seventh-year pro still trying to live up to his draft status. Jake Matthews, the latest member of football's first family to hit the NFL, arrives in Atlanta after an All-American career at Texas A&M. He has experience at all five line positions, and the Falcons plan to start him immediately at right tackle. The left tackle will once again be Sam Baker, whose career has been marked by too much time on the sidelines and too many mistakes when he has been healthy. Baker played in just four games last year, his season ending in November after an injury to his left patellar tendon. Following platelet rich plasma treatment and surgery, the team said he would be ready for the start of the 2014 season and dismissed the idea that he would be moved to right tackle. It seems inevitable, though, that Matthews will wind up on the left side at some point.

Left guard Justin Blalock will return for his eighth season in Atlanta. He hasn't missed a start since 2007. Peter Konz began last year at center, then moved to guard after Garrett Reynolds was benched. Joe Hawley, a fourth-round pick in 2010, took over at center. Hawley has bounced in and out of the lineup throughout his career, but he opened OTAs getting (delivering?) first-string snaps ahead of Konz. At right guard, Jon Asamoah joins the Falcons from Kansas City. He started for three years for the Chiefs, but by the last six games of 2013 he had been benched for Geoff Schwartz.

Atlanta's raw sack numbers, like so many of their offensive statistics in 2013, were skewed by schedule and other factors. The Falcons ran 60 more pass plays than they did in 2012, and many of those plays came against the league's most brutal pass rushers. When you account for those influences, Atlanta's ASR rank remained virtually unchanged from what they had done in prior seasons. The Falcons have surrendered only 23 long sacks the last three seasons, tied with New Orleans for the lowest total in the league. However, while he rarely gets sacked, there is evidence that Ryan needs to get rid of the ball more quickly. Last year, he was second in the league with 103 knockdowns, trailing only Andrew Luck. The year before, he was third behind Luck and Aaron Rodgers with 92 knockdowns. It's a bit remarkable he has never had a major injury.

Defensive Front Seven

			Overall								vs. Run					Pass Rush			
Defensive Line	**Age**	**Pos**	**G**	**Snaps**	**Plays**	**TmPct**	**Rk**	**Stop**	**Dfts**	**BTkl**	**Runs**	**St%**	**Rk**	**RuYd**	**Rk**	**Sack**	**Hit**	**Hur**	**Tips**
Jonathan Babineaux	33	DT	16	902	41	5.0%	42	32	8	9	37	81%	31	2.1	38	1.0	3	16.0	0
Peria Jerry	30	DT	16	663	33	4.0%	62	24	12	3	24	71%	63	2.1	39	3.5	2	8.5	1
Corey Peters	26	DT	15	654	47	6.1%	28	40	7	0	36	81%	33	2.3	48	5.0	2	5.5	1
Paul Soliai	*31*	*DT*	*15*	*523*	*39*	*4.7%*	*50*	*32*	*6*	*0*	*31*	*84%*	*21*	*1.7*	*31*	*1.0*	*3*	*5.5*	*5*
Tyson Jackson	*28*	*DE*	*15*	*500*	*37*	*4.7%*	*52*	*28*	*4*	*2*	*30*	*70%*	*65*	*2.1*	*42*	*4.0*	*0*	*5.0*	*3*

			Overall								vs. Run					Pass Rush			
Edge Rushers	**Age**	**Pos**	**G**	**Snaps**	**Plays**	**TmPct**	**Rk**	**Stop**	**Dfts**	**BTkl**	**Runs**	**St%**	**Rk**	**RuYd**	**Rk**	**Sack**	**Hit**	**Hur**	**Tips**
Osi Umenyiora	34	DE	16	726	50	6.1%	29	32	13	2	36	53%	76	5.1	79	7.5	5	17.5	1
Jonathan Massaquoi	26	DE	16	528	43	5.3%	44	26	14	2	26	58%	71	4.3	77	4.0	3	19.0	2
Malliciah Goodman	24	DE	14	302	8	1.1%	--	5	1	2	7	71%	--	2.3	--	0.0	3	3.5	0

			Overall								Pass Rush			vs. Run					vs. Pass						
Linebackers	**Age**	**Pos**	**G**	**Snaps**	**Plays**	**TmPct**	**Rk**	**Stop**	**Dfts**	**BTkl**	**Sack**	**Hit**	**Hur**	**Runs**	**St%**	**Rk**	**RuYd**	**Rk**	**Tgts**	**Suc%**	**Rk**	**AdjYd**	**Rk**	**PD**	**Int**
Paul Worrilow	24	OLB	16	772	128	15.7%	21	66	15	5	2.0	2	5.5	90	59%	63	3.8	60	24	37%	67	6.6	36	1	0
Joplo Bartu	24	OLB	16	771	86	10.5%	59	45	20	7	3.5	4	4	52	65%	43	2.7	20	27	56%	26	6.0	24	1	0
Sean Weatherspoon	27	OLB	7	391	40	11.2%	57	24	9	6	0.0	2	1	24	58%	65	4.0	64	24	59%	18	7.8	59	2	1
Akeem Dent*	27	MLB	15	364	47	6.1%	--	27	9	3	1.5	0	1	33	61%	--	3.3	--	12	30%	--	10.0	--	0	0
Stephen Nicholas*	31	OLB	14	130	30	4.2%	--	14	5	2	1.0	0	0	22	50%	--	3.1	--	6	21%	--	4.8	--	1	0

Year	Yards	ALY	Rk	Power	Rk	Stuff	Rk	2nd Level	Rk	Open Field	Rk	Sacks	ASR	Rk	Short	Long
2011	4.10	3.72	3	63%	17	23%	2	1.19	17	0.81	20	33	6.0%	24	11	15
2012	4.47	3.81	8	65%	21	20%	11	1.18	14	1.11	29	29	5.8%	26	10	15
2013	4.85	4.30	27	68%	20	16%	25	1.17	23	1.26	31	32	5.3%	32	7	14
2013 ALY by direction:			*Left End 3.95 (21)*			*Left Tackle 5.00 (32)*			*Mid/Guard 4.17 (23)*			*Right Tackle 4.73 (28)*			*Right End 4.17 (25)*	

Mike Smith confirmed at OTAs that the Falcons were moving to a 3-4 scheme, although he also told the team's website that they will operate from a nickel defense "65 percent of the snaps." (He still referred to that package as their "sub defense." This phrase… I do not think it means what you think it means.) Smith added that in the nickel, the outside linebackers will put a hand on the ground and play strictly as perimeter rushers. With that in mind, it appears the Falcons will be starting Tyson Jackson and Jonathan Babineaux as defensive ends, with Paul Soliai manning the nose and leaving the field on passing downs. Second-round rookie Ra'Shede Hageman (Minnesota) figures to see a heavy share of the load as well.

After that, who knows? Sean Weatherspoon ruptured his Achilles tendon in minicamps and is done for the season, leaving Paul Worrilow and Joplo Bartu the most likely starters inside. The two started 25 total games last year as undrafted rookies. Mind you, these were not especially *good* starts, but there's always a chance for improvement as sophomores. Smith has said that fourth-round rookie Prince Shembo (Notre Dame) could beat out Bartu for the starting spot next to Worrilow. Shembo was originally drafted to play on the perimeter, and whether he wins a starting spot or not, he figures to see a lot of time as an A-gap blitzer on third downs. Shembo won't be the only rookie fighting for playing time here; fifth-rounder Marquis Spruill (Syracuse) and seventh-rounder Yawin Smallwood (Connecticut) will get a chance to show what they can do. Nolan Nawrocki described Spruill as "duck-footed, tight-ankled, stiff-hipped and straight-linish." That sounds bad. He's also undersized at 6-foot-1 and 231 pounds. Smallwood has potential as a two-down run defender, but that's about it. Finally, the Falcons added veteran journeyman Tim Dobbins (110 career games for the Chargers, Dolphins, and Texans, but only 22 starts).

Our best guess is that the starters at outside linebacker will be Jonathan Massaquoi and Kroy Biermann. Both were undersized 4-3 ends, which theoretically makes them a decent fit as 3-4 linebackers. (The Falcons were already experimenting with Biermann at linebacker before a torn Achilles cost him most of last season) At 280 pounds, the larger Osi Umenyiora doesn't have a natural fit in the new scheme and could be limited to a situational third-down rushing role. Seventh-rounder Tyler Starr played defensive end and linebacker at South Dakota, amassing 27 career sacks and winning the 2013 Missouri Valley Conference Defensive Player of the Year award. He was one of the standout performers at the East-West Shrine Game.

Defensive Secondary

			Overall								vs. Run					vs. Pass									
Secondary	Age	Pos	G	Snaps	Plays	TmPct	Rk	Stop	Dfts	BTkl	Runs	St%	Rk	RuYd	Rk	Tgts	Tgt%	Rk	Dist	Suc%	Rk	AdjYd	Rk	PD	Int
William Moore	29	SS	16	1042	93	11.4%	26	33	13	11	43	37%	45	6.4	27	27	6.4%	18	14.0	55%	39	9.4	64	6	3
Desmond Trufant	24	CB	16	1000	86	10.5%	15	35	16	5	23	39%	47	11.1	74	81	20.4%	37	13.1	56%	24	6.2	8	17	2
Thomas DeCoud*	29	FS	15	890	65	8.5%	62	20	6	10	37	46%	27	9.3	68	28	7.8%	36	11.0	31%	76	11.2	72	1	0
Robert McClain	26	CB	16	575	68	8.3%	46	27	12	4	11	64%	5	6.5	33	53	23.2%	61	9.6	37%	84	11.3	85	3	0
Robert Alford	26	CB	16	569	46	5.6%	82	16	8	4	11	45%	33	8.2	57	55	24.1%	66	14.5	45%	78	8.2	59	8	2
Asante Samuel*	33	CB	11	499	33	5.9%	77	13	5	1	3	67%	3	2.3	1	33	16.4%	6	14.5	31%	87	11.5	86	4	1
Josh Wilson	*29*	*CB*	*16*	*965*	*96*	*12.2%*	*1*	*41*	*19*	*13*	*34*	*56%*	*17*	*4.4*	*7*	*64*	*16.2%*	*4*	*11.0*	*49%*	*63*	*8.9*	*72*	*6*	*1*

Year	Pass D Rank	vs. #1 WR	Rk	vs. #2 WR	Rk	vs. Other WR	Rk	vs. TE	Rk	vs. RB	Rk
2011	10	30.9%	30	-5.6%	12	-32.1%	2	-16.9%	1	-13.2%	7
2012	11	-15.2%	7	-28.5%	1	-3.0%	13	3.0%	21	-3.0%	14
2013	32	24.1%	30	18.6%	30	22.5%	30	9.1%	23	-8.8%	12

Desmond Trufant was one of the few bright spots for Atlanta in 2013. Rookie cornerbacks almost always struggle, especially those drafted highly and thrown into a starting role. Trufant, though, delivered in a big way, and he got better as the year went along, with a 52 percent Adjusted Success Rate in the first eight games but 62 percent in the last eight games. Robert Alford played more like a typical rookie, though his recovery speed and quickness have drawn praise from Mike Smith in this year's OTAs. This could still be one of the league's better corner duos in, say, 2015, but 2014 will likely see them struggle through some growing pains and rough patches. Incumbent Robert McClain will battle veteran signees Javier Arenas (ex-Arizona) and Josh Wilson (ex-Washington) for the nickelback spot. Arenas barely saw the field for the Cardinals last year, getting just 102 snaps on defense despite playing every game, but he had some success as a nickelback in Kansas City. Even in his best years, Wilson has been a boom-and-bust corner susceptible to missing tackles—which makes him kind of an odd candidate for a spot in the slot, where he would be called on for run support fairly often.

Thomas DeCoud has taken his tackle-missing abilities to Carolina, and the Falcons signed Dwight Lowery from the Jaguars to replace him. Lowery has versatility (he started his career with the Jets as a cornerback), speed, and ball skills, with three seasons with Adjusted Success Rates greater than 60 percent. What he does not have is health; he has played only 12 games the last two years due to head, shoulder, and ankle injuries, and he has never started 16 games in a season. Dezmen Southward, a third-round rookie out of Wisconsin, could also challenge for the free safety spot. William Moore returns at strong safety. His leadership could be the most critical aspect of his game, especially now as the senior member of such a young team.

Special Teams

Year	DVOA	Rank	FG/XP	Rank	Net Kick	Rank	Kick Ret	Rank	Net Punt	Rank	Punt Ret	Rank	Hidden	Rank
2011	-1.3%	22	4.0	8	-8.0	29	-1.9	21	-1.4	17	0.9	14	-10.7	29
2012	0.1%	16	-2.3	20	4.7	7	0.8	13	1.1	14	-3.7	21	-0.6	19
2013	-0.1%	17	0.0	18	-0.4	16	1.2	10	4.8	12	-6.2	25	-6.2	25

Matt Bosher handles kickoffs and punts for Atlanta, and his progression in both departments has been remarkably similar over the past three years: awful in 2011, a little below average in 2012, and above average in 2013. Matt Bryant also returns for field goals, where he went 21-for-22 inside 50 yards last year. Antone Smith was third in the league in punt return tackles and stops, but there's not much else to say about Atlanta's coverage units one way or another.

The Falcons franchise doesn't have a lot to boast about, historically, but they have featured a star-studded cast of great kick returners, from Billy "White Shoes" Johnson to Deion Sanders to Eric Metcalf to Allen Rossum. Devin Hester's resume, however, trumps them all. Hester is still dangerous as a punt returner, with one touchdown last year and two in 2011, finishing in the top ten in value both seasons according to our numbers. As a kickoff returner, however, he has been quite mediocre, finishing within two points of league-average value each of the last three years. Hester will be 32 this season, which is old for a returner, but continued success at this age not unprecedented. There have been 14 kickoff return touchdowns by players 32 or older in NFL history (most recently by Rossum, then with the 49ers in 2008) and 13 scores on punt returns (last by Joey Galloway for Tampa Bay in 2004).

Baltimore Ravens

2013 Record: 8-8	**Total DVOA:** -6.7% (23rd)	**2014 Mean Projection:** 7.4 wins	**On the Clock (0-4):** 13%
Pythagorean Wins: 7.1 (21st)	**Offense:** -21.7% (30th)	**Postseason Odds:** 25.8%	**Mediocrity (5-7):** 40%
Snap-Weighted Age: 26.8 (13th)	**Defense:** -8.7% (7th)	**Super Bowl Odds:** 2.1%	**Playoff Contender (8-10):** 36%
Average Opponent: -1.1% (20th)	**Special Teams:** 6.3% (3rd)	**Proj. Avg. Opponent:** -2.3% (26th)	**Super Bowl Contender (11+):** 11%

2013: Baltimore Ravens: The Phantom Menace.

2014: We have more faith in Ozzie Newsome than our statistical projections do.

Forget about NFL Films and *America's Game*. The story of the Baltimore Ravens begs to be told by Peter Jackson, director of the film adaptations of J.R.R. Tolkien's *The Hobbit* and *The Lord of the Rings*. All the elements of a great story are present. Ray Lewis was the perfect antihero you either loved or hated. Joe Flacco started out as the clumsy protagonist, accepting the challenge to become Baltimore's first true franchise quarterback. He carried out the clumsy role longer than you'd like until his heroic transformation finally came in the 2012 postseason with 11 touchdowns and zero interceptions. He was joined at the hip in 2008 by mentor John Harbaugh, who guided the Ravens on this long, five-year journey through the AFC's elite to that precious Super Bowl ring in 2012, creating a happy ending to one story and new beginnings for many key characters.

Just like how you thought *The Return of the King* would never end, Ray Lewis finally stopped dancing and allowed the credits to roll on his era in Baltimore, giving way to Flacco, king of all quarterback contracts for a brief moment in time. For a sequel, the Ravens were expected to become an offense-driven team. When Peyton Manning ravaged the defense on opening night with seven touchdown passes and Flacco attempted a career-high 62 passes in defeat, the makeover looked real. However, that quickly proved to be an outlier. The actual result looked more like a prequel based on what the Ravens looked like following their first Super Bowl win in 2000. Flacco threw a career-high 22 interceptions and the offense plummeted to 30th in DVOA, the lowest ranking ever for a Ravens offense. Yes, not even the likes of Stoney Case, Travis Taylor, Kyle Boller or Anthony Wright participated in a Baltimore offense that was statistically worse than this one. The 2013 Ravens also ranked No. 1 in offensive variance, meaning they were consistently terrible. Meanwhile the reworked defense finished a respectable seventh in DVOA and also first in variance. Once the Ravens got over the sting of not having Lewis to remind them it was game time, this was the same old Baltimore team of past years: a good defense trying to cover up for a putrid offense.

The Ravens finishing 8-8 and out of the playoffs did not come as a huge surprise. The last eight defending Super Bowl champions have failed to win a playoff game, partly because this era has been dominated by "they got hot at the right moment" teams, the 2012 Ravens included. Also, Baltimore was trying to become just the second team to win at least one playoff game in six consecutive seasons, after the 1991-96 Cowboys. Sustaining success is very difficult in the NFL, but it's even harder without top-notch quarterback play. Some will say that Flacco's postseason run allowed him to swindle the Ravens out of a fortune. He treated that postseason like a gambler good enough to count cards and have one incredible weekend in Vegas. One smarter play by a Denver safety and Flacco would have lost millions of dollars, and we would be writing in the Arizona chapter about how Flacco would fare in year two under Bruce Arians.

Nevertheless, a year after helping him win a Super Bowl and a huge contract, Flacco's teammates held him back from improving as a sixth-year starter in 2013. The defense may have gone through more noticeable changes, but the offense suffered the biggest declines in performance and that wasn't just because of the quarterback. There's plenty of blame to go around.

We can start with the running game that ranked as the fourth worst in our DVOA database going back to 1989. It's not like the Ravens traded for Trent Richardson, so how did they drop 25 spots in rushing DVOA with Ray Rice, Bernard Pierce and Vonta Leach combining to miss one game? Only three other teams have had such a precipitous fall in the rankings (including last year's Giants as well, who had an epic number of injured running backs). In raw numbers, Baltimore's decline was only outdone by the 1991 Eagles (Table 1), and of course that fall was easy to explain because team rushing DVOA includes quarterback runs as well. Randall Cunningham rushed for 942 yards and averaged 8.0 yards per carry in 1990, then tore his ACL in the opening game of 1991. The 2007 Falcons had a similar story, as Michael Vick took the only 1,000-yard rushing quarterback season in NFL history and went directly to jail without passing GO or collecting $200. That dynamic is not present with the 2012-2013 Ravens.

Rice and Pierce were young backs coming off a fine 2012 season in which both averaged at least 4.4 yards per carry. Last year, both averaged less than 3.1 yards per carry on more than 150 carries each. The only other teammates in NFL history with a similar rushing decline were Craig James (2.77) and Tony Collins (2.64) for the 1986 Patriots, coincidentally another defending AFC champion. James may be better known as a college football sportscaster or a politician, but his decline in New England was very sudden thanks to numerous shoulder injuries. He had just eight more carries after 1986. Collins also had a short career, rushing for 474 yards in 1987 and never getting

Table 1: Largest Declines in Rushing DVOA Since 1989

Team	Years	Rush DVOA Y1	Rush DVOA Y2	Decline
PHI	1990-91	14.0%	-23.0%	-37.0%
BAL	2012-13	7.5%	-27.2%	-34.7%
SF	2003-04	9.9%	-22.1%	-32.0%
SF	1993-94	30.5%	-0.8%	-31.3%
LARM	1993-94	17.7%	-13.4%	-31.1%
NYG	2012-13	9.2%	-21.2%	-30.4%
DEN	2005-06	26.8%	-2.0%	-28.8%
SEA	2005-06	20.1%	-7.2%	-27.3%
ATL	2006-07	14.9%	-12.2%	-27.1%
NYG	1995-96	7.2%	-19.6%	-26.8%

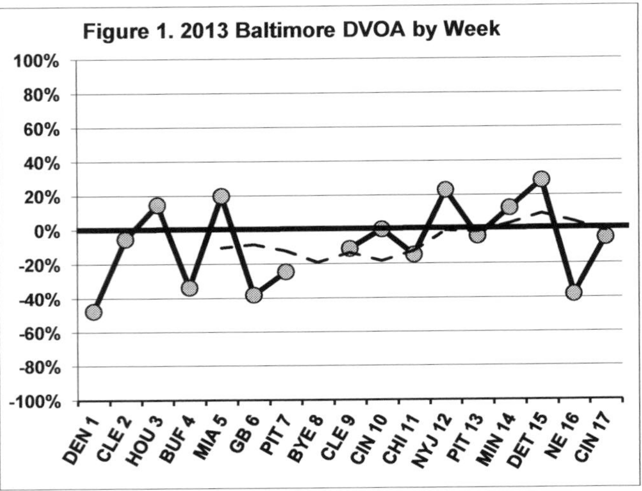

another carry because of his struggles with drug use.

When two backs have such a poor rushing average, the first thought is to blame the offensive line. That's what makes the 1986 Patriots an interesting comparison, because that team made only one significant change: guard John Hannah, believed by many to be the greatest guard in NFL history, retired after the Super Bowl XX loss. Hannah was replaced by the forgettable Paul Fairchild. For the next nine seasons (1986-94), the Patriots never averaged better than 3.7 yards per carry and never ranked higher than 21st in that category. They didn't hit 4.0 yards per carry again until the 2004 season. During Hannah's career (1973-85), the Patriots averaged 4.18 yards per carry, which ranked fifth in the league in that span. Now it would be crazy to give Hannah all the credit and pretend his absence alone caused years of misery, but the numbers suggest he meant a lot to his offense. For the Ravens, the closest thing was center Matt Birk retiring after the Super Bowl win. He had a very good career, but he was not Hannah. Leach's offensive snaps were cut in half (456 to 224) compared to the year before, as the Ravens used "11" personnel a league-high 75 percent of the time, but the running game might have been even worse had the Ravens used Leach more. They had a dreadful -40.0% DVOA when running with multiple backs.

Pierce was just a second-year back last season. The real concern may be with Rice, who has accumulated a lot of touches with Baltimore's annual deep playoff runs. Rice had four consecutive seasons with at least 250 carries and 60 receptions from 2009 to 2012. Marshall Faulk is the only other player with four such seasons, doing so in 1998-01. It's not likely Rice "got tired" at age 26, but we have seen running backs unexpectedly drop off before. Warrick Dunn made the Pro Bowl with Tampa Bay in 2000. A year later he averaged just 2.8 yards per carry and 34.4 rushing yards per game. His numbers shot right back up in Atlanta. Yards per carry can be a very volatile stat, but Rice is not a back who relies on huge gains to inflate his average like a Chris Johnson. He has consistently posted a rushing success rate in the mid-40s and does well in DVOA. In 2013, Rice's success rate was 35 percent and he ranked dead last in DYAR and next to last (only ahead of Pierce) in DVOA. Even his receiving was down, averaging 5.5 yards per catch (8.7 in his first five seasons). Flacco did have a league-worst 30.7 percent of his completions fail to gain enough yards to be considered a successful play, but that can happen when the running game leads the league in getting stuffed.

2014 Ravens Schedule

Week	Opp.	Week	Opp.	Week	Opp.
1	CIN	7	ATL	13	SD
2	PIT (Thu.)	8	at CIN	14	at MIA
3	at CLE	9	at PIT	15	JAC
4	CAR	10	TEN	16	at HOU
5	at IND	11	BYE	17	CLE
6	at TB	12	at NO (Mon.)		

Rice has been the heart of the offense the last few years, but let's get the elephant out of the room if we're going to talk about the chances for a rebound in 2014. Rice could face a personal-conduct suspension thanks to video footage that shows him dragging his unconscious wife (then fiancée) out of a casino elevator after allegedly assaulting her in February. One day after being indicted for third-degree aggravated assault, Rice married his fiancée. In May he did a bizarre press conference about the incident, featuring cringe-worthy statements like "Sometimes in life, you will get knocked down." This is not something that will just go away easily.

For Baltimore's sake, hopefully the running back position won't go through as much flux as the receivers did last year. Tight end Dennis Pitta missed most of the regular season due to offseason hip surgery. Pitta has caught 65.3 percent of his career targets from Flacco. It's not like anyone will confuse Pitta for Rob Gronkowski or Jimmy Graham, but he's a red-zone favorite for Flacco and the two were building chemistry. More importantly, Pitta's not Ed "Stone Hands" Dickson or a geriatric Dallas Clark, who the Ravens used in his absence. Owen Daniels (Texans) was a good insurance signing as well.

Torrey Smith was one constant, but he has only caught 48 percent of his career targets. That puts him in the bottom 10 for wide receivers since 1999 (minimum 200 targets), but it doesn't mean he's a bad player. Part of that number is Flacco's general inefficiency, and part of it is just the nature of being a vertical threat. He was the target of only three screens last year. He's at his best down the field and that's usually where Flacco tries to find him. The offense needs a player like that, but it's great to have someone to complement the deep threat by making all the short catches over the middle and keeping the offense on schedule.

Anquan Boldin was that kind of player, but he was traded to San Francisco for almost nothing after the Super Bowl. He helped Flacco play big in the postseason with his effort to win 50/50 balls. Baltimore will now look to another scrappy veteran in Steve Smith, who can be the vocal leader this offense lacks. He's like the offensive version of Old Ray Lewis: past his prime, but still a contributor who will draw the other team's attention. However, there is no way to overlook that Smith is a 35-year-old wide receiver joining his second team. There have only been 16 1,000-yard receiving seasons by a receiver age 35 or older, and the incredible Jerry Rice had three of them. The 500-yard barrier has been reached 57 times, but most of those seasons were by players in familiar situations at the end of their careers. It's very rare for an older receiver to have a big year with a new team (Table 2).

Table 2: Most Receiving Yards in Team Debut Season, Age 35-plus

Rk	Receiver	Age	Season	Team	Yards
1	Jerry Rice	39	2001	OAK	1,139
2	Terrell Owens	37	2010	CIN	983
3	Muhsin Muhammad*	35	2008	CAR	923
4	Isaac Bruce	36	2008	SF	835
5	Terrell Owens	36	2009	BUF	829
6	Drew Hill	36	1992	ATL	623
7	Art Monk	37	1994	NYJ	581
8	Tony Martin*	36	2001	ATL	548
9	Brandon Stokley*	36	2012	DEN	544
10	Randy Moss	35	2012	SF	434

**Second stint with team*

Ten receivers have debuted with at least 400 yards, which is a fine minimum benchmark for Smith. Naturally, Rice is the only 1,000-yard receiver and he did it at age 39. Smith to Baltimore is nothing like Rice to Oakland. It may actually be closer to the 2007 Falcons signing a 35-year-old Joe Horn. Expectations for Smith have to be low, even if he does end up starting over an improving Marlon Brown and deep threat Jacoby Jones. Despite standing just 5-foot-9, Smith has always been fascinating to watch down the field on deep balls. He only caught two passes thrown beyond 20 yards last season and averaged 11.6 yards per reception (second lowest of his career), but Flacco has the tendency to give his receivers shots. The days of vintage Steve Smith are likely over, but it's not like they'll turn him into a dink-and-dunk receiver in this offense. He'll still go deep and intermediate and at best could replicate the role Derrick Mason played in Flacco's first couple seasons.

Regardless of the skill players around him, one of Flacco's strong points has always been limiting interceptions. It often seemed strange since he's not a high-percentage passer and he takes a lot of deep shots. Still, he is the only quarterback in NFL history to have five straight seasons with no more than 12 interceptions (minimum 400 attempts each year). Could he really just be that lucky with dropped interceptions every year? In 2010, he only had four charted dropped interceptions, but that climbed to nine in 2011 and eight in 2012, numbers that would put him among the league leaders. So given he broke his career high by 10 interceptions in 2013, we expected not to find many dropped interceptions in last year's game charting. The number was nine, which even after adjusting for two tipped-ball interceptions still gives Flacco an adjusted total of 29 picks. He was both bad and lucky with his interceptions. Five picks were thrown in one game alone against Buffalo. The total will almost assuredly decrease to his normal range with more comfort around him on offense.

If the offense can just get back to mediocrity, then the Ravens can continue competing for the AFC North and taking another spin on the playoff roulette wheel. The defense still had them in position for that last year at 8-6, but the Patriots and Bengals destroyed Baltimore by a combined 75-24 score. Those blowouts were uncharacteristic for a team that played games so close the rest of the season. The defense certainly was not as dominant as some past Baltimore units. There were a few lapses, like that Week 1 pasting in Denver or two tough games with the Steelers that were high in points per drive. The Ravens even allowed 24 points in their first loss to Cleveland in 12 games under Harbaugh. The end of the Minnesota game—five touchdowns scored in 125 seconds—was easily one of the craziest moments in NFL history. Flacco did bail the defense out of that one with the final drive, but overall 2013 was another playoff-caliber defense led by a core group of Terrell Suggs, Haloti Ngata, Elvis Dumervil and Lardarius Webb. Jimmy Smith stepped up at cornerback and Daryl Smith was fantastic at replacing Ray Lewis. Not many teams have pieces like that in place on defense, especially after last year's Florida Marlins-esque turnover. Ozzie Newsome even made the 2014 draft defensive-focused with the first three picks being linebacker C.J. Mosley (Alabama), defensive tackle Timmy Jernigan (Florida State) and free safety Terrence Brooks (Florida State). That comes on the heels of four defenders to start the 2013 draft.

The Ravens haven't had consecutive non-winning seasons since their first four years in the league (1996-99). Projections for a quick rebound in 2014 aren't bright, but Newsome's track record suggests this team won't be down for long. Many franchises would allocate resources to the offense after last year, but the Ravens usually know what they are doing. They're going to keep a steady pipeline of defensive talent to fuel the team and ask the offense not to lose games. The only difference between this Baltimore team and those in the past is that this team is paying for premium quarterback play. The cap hit does not get grotesque until 2016 when it reaches $28.5 million, but the ramifications will soon start to limit the team in its ability to add talent. The whole point of paying a quarterback that much is to have someone who can cover up roster weaknesses, but Flacco's only been *that guy* in short bursts. If the Ravens are going to have a worthy sequel to the quest for a ring, Flacco first has to get back to his old level in the regular season. From there, it's just another case of catching fire at the right time. If Eli Manning and Jim Plunkett can do that twice, so can Flacco.

Scott Kacsmar

2013 Ravens Stats by Week

Wk	vs.	W-L	PF	PA	YDF	YDA	TO	Total	Off	Def	ST
1	at DEN	L	27	49	393	510	0	-48%	-17%	19%	-12%
2	CLE	W	14	6	296	259	-1	-5%	-7%	-8%	-6%
3	HOU	W	30	9	236	264	+1	15%	-14%	-5%	23%
4	at BUF	L	20	23	345	350	-2	-34%	-56%	-18%	4%
5	at MIA	W	26	23	384	294	-2	20%	2%	-15%	3%
6	GB	L	17	19	360	438	+1	-38%	-46%	-8%	0%
7	at PIT	L	16	19	287	286	+1	-25%	-3%	13%	-9%
8	BYE										
9	at CLE	L	18	24	278	315	-1	-11%	-16%	1%	6%
10	CIN	W	20	17	189	364	0	0%	-40%	-41%	-1%
11	at CHI	L	20	23	317	319	-2	-15%	-29%	-10%	4%
12	NYJ	W	19	3	312	220	+2	23%	-22%	-26%	19%
13	PIT	W	22	20	311	329	0	-4%	-17%	9%	22%
14	MIN	W	29	26	325	379	-2	12%	-25%	-10%	27%
15	at DET	W	18	16	305	349	+3	29%	-10%	-21%	18%
16	NE	L	7	41	358	300	-4	-38%	-33%	4%	-1%
17	at CIN	L	17	34	222	392	+1	-5%	-23%	-14%	4%

Trends and Splits

	Offense	Rank	Defense	Rank
Total DVOA	-21.7%	30	-8.7%	7
Unadjusted VOA	-19.0%	30	-5.9%	8
Weighted Trend	-24.2%	32	-11.1%	8
Variance	2.4%	1	2.3%	1
Average Opponent	1.4%	20	-0.1%	12
Passing	-9.0%	24	-4.8%	9
Rushing	-27.2%	32	-13.6%	10
First Down	-15.6%	27	0.0%	15
Second Down	-28.1%	30	-20.9%	3
Third Down	-22.9%	27	-6.1%	12
First Half	-30.0%	32	-11.8%	5
Second Half	-14.4%	25	-5.6%	12
Red Zone	-15.6%	28	-9.2%	10
Late and Close	-18.9%	27	-0.5%	18

Five-Year Performance

Year	W-L	Pyth W	Est W	PF	PA	TO	Total	Rk	Off	Rk	Def	Rk	ST	Rk	Off AGL	Rk	Def AGL	Rk	Off Age	Rk	Def Age	Rk	ST Age	Rk
2009	9-7	11.6	12.0	391	261	+10	29.1%	1	12.8%	9	-14.2%	4	2.2%	8	8.4	5	22.2	15	26.7	26	28.0	4	25.9	24
2010	12-4	10.6	12.1	357	270	+7	21.7%	5	5.4%	12	-10.3%	6	6.0%	4	23.8	15	27.1	19	27.9	9	28.2	6	25.8	23
2011	12-4	11.2	10.6	378	266	+2	14.5%	7	2.9%	13	-17.1%	1	-5.6%	30	8.0	1	10.9	4	27.8	9	28.2	3	26.6	6
2012	10-6	9.4	9.2	398	344	+9	9.8%	8	3.0%	13	2.2%	19	9.0%	1	8.1	2	46.4	25	27.3	10	27.7	7	26.9	7
2013	8-8	7.1	6.8	320	352	-5	-6.7%	23	-21.7%	30	-8.7%	7	6.3%	3	35.1	15	14.7	4	26.6	18	27.5	6	25.9	22

2013 Performance Based on Most Common Personnel Groups

BAL Offense					BAL Offense vs. Opponents				BAL Defense				BAL Defense vs. Opponents			
Pers	Freq	Yds	DVOA	Run%	Pers	Freq	Yds	DVOA	Pers	Freq	Yds	DVOA	Pers	Freq	Yds	DVOA
11	75%	5.1	-12.3%	26%	Nickel Even	49%	4.8	-18.5%	3-4-4	38%	4.9	-10.5%	11	51%	5.8	-0.4%
21	11%	2.6	-68.8%	68%	3-4-4	12%	3.5	-32.1%	Nickel Even	37%	5.8	-7.2%	12	26%	5.1	-19.1%
12	6%	7.1	18.9%	42%	Dime+	14%	5.9	0.3%	Nickel Odd	15%	5.3	-1.6%	21	11%	4.4	-13.3%
22	3%	3.9	-16.2%	97%	4-3-4	12%	5.0	-9.3%	4-3-4	5%	5.6	2.5%	611	4%	6.4	-11.1%
621	2%	3.7	23.4%	95%	Nickel Odd	9%	5.4	-23.2%	Dime+	3%	7.1	-13.9%	10	2%	5.1	-49.9%
													621	2%	4.9	12.4%

Strategic Tendencies

Run/Pass		Rk	Formation		Rk	Pass Rush		Rk	Secondary		Rk	Strategy		Rk
Runs, first half	35%	25	Form: Single Back	75%	11	Rush 3	2.9%	26	4 DB	43%	12	Play action	13%	29
Runs, first down	50%	13	Form: Empty Back	5%	22	Rush 4	66.4%	9	5 DB	52%	14	Avg Box (Off)	6.20	28
Runs, second-long	32%	18	Pers: 3+ WR	76%	2	Rush 5	21.9%	20	6+ DB	3%	20	Avg Box (Def)	6.40	12
Runs, power sit.	61%	10	Pers: 4+ WR	1%	21	Rush 6+	8.8%	14	CB by Sides	79%	13	Offensive Pace	28.28	5
Runs, behind 2H	28%	17	Pers: 2+ TE/6+ OL	14%	32	Sacks by LB	70.0%	3	DB Blitz	11%	20	Defensive Pace	30.15	21
Pass, ahead 2H	51%	11	Shotgun/Pistol	73%	4	Sacks by DB	2.5%	25	Hole in Zone	9%	23	Go for it on 4th	0.89	17

We could probably fill an entire page with nothing but stats showing the way the Baltimore running game collapsed in 2013, but we'll limit ourselves to a few examples. The Ravens went from using play action on 24 percent of 2012 pass plays (tenth) to just 13 percent of pass plays last year (29th). They went from facing an average box of 6.47 in 2012 (ninth) to 6.20 in 2013 (28th). And over the past three seasons, their use of three or more wide receivers has gone from 28 percent in 2011 (30th) to 45 percent in 2012 (26th) to 76 percent in 2013 (second). In another piece of evidence that success on play action doesn't seem to be at all associated with the quality of a team's running game, the Ravens actually passed better using play action in 2013 after years of having a good running game but struggling with play action. The Ravens had 8.2 yards per play and 30.5% DVOA with a play fake, but 5.4 yards per play and -11.9% DVOA otherwise. For the second straight year, the Ravens defense struggled against play action, allowing 8.3 yards per play and 26.4% DVOA with a play fake but just 5.8 yards per play with -11.9% otherwise. Only three teams had a bigger gap in yardage, and only two teams had a bigger gap in DVOA. The Ravens benefitted from a league-leading 143 penalties, roughly a flag per week more than any other team, and 1,196 penalty yards.

Passing

Player	DYAR	DVOA	Plays	NtYds	Avg	YAC	C%	TD	Int
J.Flacco	-296	-18.1%	661	3579	5.4	4.9	59.1%	19	22
T.Taylor	-75	-236.3%	5	2	0.4	1.0	20.0%	0	1

Rushing

Player	DYAR	DVOA	Plays	Yds	Avg	TD	Fum	Suc
R.Rice	-169	-27.9%	214	660	3.1	4	2	35%
B.Pierce	-131	-29.3%	152	436	2.9	2	0	38%
J.Flacco	53	37.4%	19	138	7.3	1	0	-
V.Leach*	-15	-33.6%	11	23	2.1	0	0	45%
T.Taylor	15	26.2%	7	64	9.1	0	0	-
J.Forsett	*7*	*20.8%*	*6*	*31*	*5.2*	*0*	*0*	*33%*

Receiving

Player	DYAR	DVOA	Plays	Ctch	Yds	Y/C	YAC	TD	C%
T.Smith	139	0.0%	137	65	1128	17.4	5.5	4	47%
M.Brown	117	4.9%	83	49	524	10.7	4.8	7	59%
J.Jones	30	-7.0%	67	37	449	12.1	2.8	2	55%
T.Doss*	17	-6.6%	36	19	305	16.1	4.5	0	53%
B.Stokley	-6	-16.5%	21	13	115	8.8	4.6	0	62%
D.Thompson	13	-4.3%	19	10	96	9.6	1.7	0	53%
S.Smith	*74*	*-3.7%*	*110*	*64*	*745*	*11.6*	*2.8*	*4*	*58%*
D.Clark*	-8	-9.7%	52	31	343	11.1	5.8	3	60%
E.Dickson*	-10	-10.8%	43	25	273	10.9	4.0	1	58%
D.Pitta	6	-4.6%	33	20	169	8.5	2.6	1	61%
O.Daniels	*14*	*-2.4%*	*41*	*24*	*252*	*10.5*	*3.5*	*3*	*59%*
R.Rice	-21	-19.1%	73	58	321	5.5	6.5	0	79%
B.Pierce	-27	-33.3%	25	20	104	5.2	5.7	0	80%
V.Leach*	-38	-43.0%	19	11	47	4.3	4.5	1	58%
J.Forsett	*-11*	*-28.0%*	*16*	*15*	*82*	*5.5*	*7.2*	*0*	*94%*

Offensive Line

Player	Pos	Age	GS	Snaps	Pen	Sk	Pass	Run
Gino Gradkowski	C	26	16/16	1137	4	1.8	11.8	6.5
Marshal Yanda	RG	30	16/16	1137	7	2.5	17.0	7.0
Michael Oher*	RT	28	16/16	1081	5	7.0	35.0	6.5
Eugene Monroe	LT	27	15/15	1031	6	4.5	16.5	3.0
A.Q. Shipley	LG	28	16/9	707	8	1.0	6.5	5.0
Kelechi Osemele	LG	25	7/7	423	5	0.5	5.5	2.0
Ricky Wagner	OT	25	16/2	131	1	2.3	2.3	0.0
Jeremy Zuttah	*C*	*28*	*16/16*	*1014*	*7*	*1.0*	*9.0*	*4.3*
Will Rackley	*LG*	*25*	*11/11*	*647*	*6*	*5.5*	*13.0*	*5.0*

Year	Yards	ALY	Rk	Power	Rk	Stuff	Rk	2nd Lev	Rk	Open Field	Rk	Sacks	ASR	Rk	Short	Long	F-Start	Cont.
2011	4.47	4.25	7	63%	15	18%	11	1.05	30	1.06	5	33	5.9%	12	4	19	23	36
2012	4.53	4.33	6	64%	14	16%	4	1.22	14	0.87	11	38	6.1%	13	9	13	23	30
2013	2.95	3.01	32	49%	31	26%	32	0.76	32	0.30	32	48	7.3%	16	14	20	25	37

2013 ALY by direction: Left End 2.06 (32) Left Tackle 3.48 (24) Mid/Guard 3.15 (32) Right Tackle 2.13 (32) Right End 3.87 (14)

Juan Castillo brought more zone blocking to Baltimore last year, but the results were very poor. Brighter days should be ahead for this unit, especially with new offensive coordinator Gary Kubiak implementing the proven zone-blocking schemes he learned so well in Denver from Mike Shanahan and Alex Gibbs. The running game needs the bigger boost. Not to say Flacco didn't suffer behind his protection at times, but only five of his 22 interceptions were thrown under pressure. Compared to other quarterbacks, the presence of pressure had an average impact on Flacco's statistics in terms of average gain and DVOA in 2013. The running game is where Baltimore led the league in stuffed run percentage and fell to 32nd in Adjusted Line Yards (32nd on runs off left end, middle and right tackle). In 2014, the Ravens will begin with better schemes, health and talent along the line.

If there was a Keyser Söze-esque mastermind behind 2013's poor line performance, it would have to be right tackle Michael Oher, who tied for the league lead with 41.5 blown blocks in 2013. His life story may have been adapted into an Oscar-nominated film called *The Blind Side*, but Oher spent much of his Baltimore career playing right tackle. Despite starting every one of his 80 games with the Ravens, he never quite lived up to the hype. After last year's performance, it's no surprise to see Oher now in Tennessee, where he can continue testing every referee's patience on false starts. Ricky Wagner, a 2013 fifth-round mauler out of Wisconsin, is the favorite to replace him, but left guard Kelechi Osemele made 16 starts at right tackle as a rookie in 2012 and could slide into Oher's spot should Wagner falter. Osemele missed nine games last season due to a herniated disk in his back.

Ever since it became clear that Mr. *Blind Side* couldn't actually play on the blind side, finding a left tackle has been Ozzie Newsome's greatest adventure. Bryant McKinnie was praised for his performance during the team's Super Bowl run, but the 34-year-old's struggles early last season led to an October trade with Jacksonville for Eugene Monroe, who then started the last 11 games. Monroe was solid, not spectacular last season, which is really the story of his whole career. His 52.9 snaps per blown block, nearly identical to his 54.9 average in 2012 with the Jaguars, ranked eighth among left tackles. In March, Monroe signed a five-year deal with Baltimore worth $37.5 million.

Right guard Marshal Yanda made the Pro Bowl for the third season in a row, but game charting makes it look like a selection based on reputation. His blown blocks increased from 8.5 to 24.0 (12th most among guards). Considering Yanda's past and that he was stuck between Oher and first-time starter Gino Gradkowski (seventh-most blown blocks among centers), we expect he'll be better in 2014. Gradkowski had big shoes to fill after the retirement of Matt Birk, who can now audition for *Hellboy* sequels at his leisure. Since he couldn't fill them, the Ravens traded a 2015 fifth-round pick to Tampa Bay for center Jeremy Zuttah, a versatile veteran with 76 career starts.

Defensive Front Seven

			Overall								vs. Run					Pass Rush			
Defensive Line	**Age**	**Pos**	**G**	**Snaps**	**Plays**	**TmPct**	**Rk**	**Stop**	**Dfts**	**BTkl**	**Runs**	**St%**	**Rk**	**RuYd**	**Rk**	**Sack**	**Hit**	**Hur**	**Tips**
Haloti Ngata	30	DT	15	700	54	7.0%	17	46	9	2	48	85%	15	2.1	44	1.5	6	4.0	4
Chris Canty	32	DE	15	564	33	4.3%	58	26	4	0	25	76%	49	2.5	57	2.0	5	6.0	3
Arthur Jones*	28	DE	14	521	53	7.3%	14	42	13	1	48	77%	45	2.4	52	4.5	3	9.5	0
Terrence Cody	26	DT	12	235	15	2.4%	--	13	1	0	14	86%	--	2.9	--	0.0	0	1.0	0

			Overall								vs. Run					Pass Rush			
Edge Rushers	**Age**	**Pos**	**G**	**Snaps**	**Plays**	**TmPct**	**Rk**	**Stop**	**Dfts**	**BTkl**	**Runs**	**St%**	**Rk**	**RuYd**	**Rk**	**Sack**	**Hit**	**Hur**	**Tips**
Terrell Suggs	32	OLB	16	903	79	9.5%	2	64	19	4	64	81%	24	2.3	32	10.0	10	24.0	0
Courtney Upshaw	25	OLB	16	640	31	3.7%	71	19	6	3	20	50%	77	3.9	74	1.5	3	8.5	1
Elvis Dumervil	30	OLB	15	557	32	4.1%	66	27	12	0	17	76%	36	2.6	47	9.5	6	19.5	2
Pernell McPhee	25	OLB	16	304	22	2.7%	--	18	8	0	17	82%	--	1.6	--	2.0	4	11.5	1

			Overall								Pass Rush			vs. Run					vs. Pass						
Linebackers	**Age**	**Pos**	**G**	**Snaps**	**Plays**	**TmPct**	**Rk**	**Stop**	**Dfts**	**BTkl**	**Sack**	**Hit**	**Hur**	**Runs**	**St%**	**Rk**	**RuYd**	**Rk**	**Tgts**	**Suc%**	**Rk**	**AdjYd**	**Rk**	**PD**	**Int**
Daryl Smith	32	ILB	16	1072	138	16.7%	16	83	32	8	4.5	1	7.5	71	58%	67	4.7	78	59	63%	9	5.6	13	14	3
Josh Bynes	25	ILB	15	454	44	5.7%	80	27	5	1	0.0	1	5	32	59%	61	4.5	76	16	42%	60	9.1	66	2	0
Jameel McClain*	29	ILB	10	369	50	9.7%	63	18	1	5	0.0	0	2	35	37%	81	4.6	77	12	53%	--	4.8	--	0	0

Year	Yards	ALY	Rk	Power	Rk	Stuff	Rk	2nd Level	Rk	Open Field	Rk	Sacks	ASR	Rk	Short	Long
2011	3.55	3.96	12	66%	22	17%	25	0.92	2	0.33	2	48	8.4%	2	14	18
2012	4.10	4.33	28	76%	29	14%	32	1.16	11	0.42	3	37	6.9%	10	11	14
2013	3.92	3.95	19	59%	8	18%	16	1.08	14	0.48	9	40	7.3%	10	16	11
2013 ALY by direction:			*Left End 4.47 (28)*			*Left Tackle 4.1 (19)*			*Mid/Guard 4.25 (28)*			*Right Tackle 2.88 (4)*			*Right End 2.75 (4)*	

We'll spare you a rendition of the "how can they replace such heart and leadership?" dirge for Ray Lewis' retirement, but he *was* the linchpin of this front seven for 17 seasons. It also did not help when Dannell Ellerbe left in free agency, or when the 23-year-old Rolando McClain decided to retire a month after signing with the Ravens. Newsome needed a backup plan, and Eugene Monroe was not his first attempt to take a talented player out of Jacksonville and put him in a better situation. Daryl Smith only played two games with the Jaguars in 2012 due to injury, and Newsome didn't sign him until early June. But he soon took over Lewis' spot, and by season's end, Smith's 32 Defeats at inside linebacker only trailed NaVorro Bowman (35) and Luke Kuechly (34) and were three more than the combined 2012 total for Lewis, Ellerbe and Jameel McClain. Smith also registered 18 official NFL passes defensed, easily breaking Lewis' franchise record for a linebacker.[1] That's about as good of a June addition as you can hope for in the NFL. The rich get even richer with the addition of pro-ready first-round pick C.J. Mosley from Alabama. He could start right away at weakside inside linebacker and position coach Don Martindale told *The Baltimore Sun* following the draft, "I put in my report how he uses his hands in getting off blocks better than anybody I've seen in the 10 years that I've been in this league."

Haloti Ngata and Terrell Suggs still provide the unit's star power. Ngata reportedly rejected a long-term deal in April, but something will have to be worked out given his 2014 cap hit of $16 million. Reserve Terrence Cody has only proven he can handle a full plate at the dinner table. Suggs already inked an extension to save the team money and is coming off another quality season where he tied Robert Quinn for the league lead with seven drawn holding penalties on his way to 10 sacks and the Pro Bowl. Pernell McPhee remains a solid backup going into his fourth season. Courtney Upshaw's Stops and Defeats decreased (from 43/13 to 19/6) but Elvis Dumervil, a prize won in the Great Denver Fax Fiasco, provided his usual pass-rushing production on a limited number of snaps.

Arthur Jones leaving for the Colts opened a hole on the line, but Brandon Williams might be able to fill it in his second season. A third-round pick in 2013, Williams has a good mixture of strength and quickness, but only played 91 defensive snaps as a rookie. Veteran Chris Canty will be the third starter on the line once again, making it five key contributors in the front seven age 30 or older, but this is still the strength of the defense and Newsome knows how to keep replenishing talent. Florida State's Timmy Jernigan had a first-round projection, but perhaps due to a diluted drug specimen at the combine and questions about consistency and conditioning, he fell to Baltimore in the second round.

1 For those wondering, the four passes defensed counted by the NFL but not by Football Outsiders include two passes that were clearly underthrown and had no chance to be caught as well as two dropped interceptions, one thrown way over the head over the intended receiver and one initially defended by Jimmy Smith before Daryl Smith dropped the carom

Defensive Secondary

			Overall								vs. Run					vs. Pass									
Secondary	Age	Pos	G	Snaps	Plays	TmPct	Rk	Stop	Dfts	BTkl	Runs	St%	Rk	RuYd	Rk	Tgts	Tgt%	Rk	Dist	Suc%	Rk	AdjYd	Rk	PD	Int
James Ihedigbo*	31	FS	16	1073	109	13.2%	11	53	19	12	57	53%	16	5.1	14	25	5.9%	11	16.6	60%	31	8.4	57	6	0
Jimmy Smith	26	CB	16	1040	73	8.8%	36	26	11	9	15	7%	83	10.5	67	90	21.8%	48	12.5	59%	12	6.3	10	15	2
Matt Elam	23	SS	16	1012	77	9.3%	49	21	12	11	41	32%	59	7.2	45	24	5.8%	10	16.8	49%	53	11.2	73	3	1
Lardarius Webb	29	CB	16	973	96	11.6%	3	49	19	8	24	54%	21	5.4	19	88	22.8%	59	11.9	56%	26	7.5	43	19	2
Corey Graham*	29	CB	16	688	78	9.4%	22	38	19	5	22	59%	9	7.2	45	60	22.0%	50	13.4	57%	18	6.6	15	12	4
Darian Stewart	*26*	*SS*	*13*	*567*	*39*	*5.6%*	*--*	*17*	*9*	*5*	*15*	*47%*	*--*	*5.3*	*--*	*13*	*6.0%*	*--*	*8.8*	*72%*	*--*	*3.3*	*--*	*5*	*0*

Year	Pass D Rank	vs. #1 WR	Rk	vs. #2 WR	Rk	vs. Other WR	Rk	vs. TE	Rk	vs. RB	Rk
2011	1	-4.5%	9	-4.2%	13	-28.8%	3	-0.4%	7	-18.0%	3
2012	13	6.4%	20	21.0%	30	-16.0%	6	-6.8%	9	-20.8%	7
2013	9	-27.2%	2	-1.8%	13	5.9%	22	2.1%	16	-10.6%	9

In their Super Bowl XLVII triumph, the Ravens' starting secondary included Corey Graham, Bernard Pollard, Ed Reed and Cary Williams. The latter three all played for a different team in 2013 and Graham lost his starting job to the athletic Jimmy Smith. The bright side in this extreme turnover was the return of Lardarius Webb, who was ascending to the ranks of elite corners before tearing his ACL after six games in 2012. While he did not reach the absurdly great level of play he displayed then, his 2013 Adjusted Yards per Pass and Adjusted Success Rate are on par with where they were in 2011. Webb also finished tied for second in the NFL with 19 passes defensed. But the tougher assignments actually tended to go to Smith, such as covering Calvin Johnson in Week 15. Smith allowed four catches for 43 yards on 10 targets, though those numbers do include one ugly drop by Johnson and two Matthew Stafford passes thrown so poorly they would have been caught out of bounds. Nonetheless, it was Smith and not a healthy Webb getting that assignment, and it is for this reason that we cannot ignore that Smith had the best pass coverage numbers (12th in Adjusted Success Rate) for Baltimore cornerbacks. The problem was that he defended the run about as well as retired Jacksonville receiver Jimmy Smith, who never played defense and is also 45 years old. Smith's 6.7 percent Stop Rate against the run ranked 83rd out of 84 ranked cornerbacks. Slot corner Graham had 12 more Stops and eight more Defeats on 352 fewer snaps than Smith, but the Ravens let Graham go to Buffalo and exercised the fifth-year option on Smith's rookie deal, expecting more great things to come from him. The Ravens are rather thin at cornerback behind Webb and Smith with only Asa Jackson (39 special teams snaps in 2013) and Chykie Brown (51 percent Success Rate on 23 targets in 2012) having previous experience with the team. Aaron Ross was signed in June, but he'll be 32 and missed 12 games last year with a back injury.

Free-agent addition Michael Huff did not work out at safety and rookie Matt Elam had to take over after just one regular-season game. The duo of Elam and James Ihedigbo combined for four interceptions, or what Ed Reed in his prime considered a good month. They also made enough mistakes that Chris and Snoop considered buying a new nail gun and lime. Ihedigbo had two interceptions of Andy Dalton in Week 10, but he infamously tipped a Hail Mary in the end zone right to A.J. Green to send the game into overtime. Elam and Ihedigbo were also one of just two safety duos to each rack up at least 11 broken tackles. (Oakland's Charles Woodson and Brandian Ross were the other.) Elam ranked 74th among safeties in YAC allowed and embarrassingly tripped over his own feet in the open field on a 79-yard bubble screen touchdown by Cordarrelle Patterson. With Ihedigbo now in Detroit, the Ravens could look at third-round rookie Terrence Brooks from Florida State as a potential starter, but he hasn't seen much action with the top two units at OTAs. Chances are veteran Darian Stewart will win the job. His best season in St. Louis was 2011 when he had 42 Stops, 10 passes defensed and ranked seventh among safeties in Adjusted Yards per Pass.

Special Teams

Year	DVOA	Rank	FG/XP	Rank	Net Kick	Rank	Kick Ret	Rank	Net Punt	Rank	Punt Ret	Rank	Hidden	Rank
2011	-5.6%	30	-5.3	25	-7.4	28	-5.9	29	-7.7	27	-1.6	19	-8.2	25
2012	9.0%	1	9.4	3	12.4	3	13.3	3	7.4	10	2.5	9	-21.7	32
2013	6.3%	3	11.4	2	-1.4	21	9.2	3	-2.9	24	15.5	2	-1.1	17

You may have heard a few dozen times how John Harbaugh earned his stripes by coaching special teams in Philadelphia. Nevertheless, his Ravens were all over the map in this area—as bad as 30th in 2011—before ranking No. 1 in 2012. They were great again in 2013 with a No. 3 ranking led by Justin Tucker, who after two years is already one of the best kickers in the NFL. Tucker tied Stephen Gostkowski for the league lead in field goals made (38) and attempted (41). He made a 61-yard game-winning field goal in Detroit: the third-longest winning kick in NFL history and the longest ever made in a dome. Tucker's 68 field goals are the most ever by a kicker in his first two seasons. With only six career misses, Tucker should officially replace Mike Vanderjagt (pour a drink) this season as the all-time leader in field goal percentage. If there's any criticism, it would be that Tucker's gross kickoff value dropped dramatically from 2012. The same can be said for punter Sam Koch, so kickoffs and punts were the weak links in Baltimore's special teams.

The return game and coverage units were again strengths. In 2012, Jacoby Jones led the league with 16.0 estimated points of field position on kickoffs. Injury made it impossible for him to match that mark in 2013, but he still finished third with 9.6 estimated points compared to an average returner. The Ravens were also second in yards per punt return (14.2). Jones (5.0 Pts+) shared these duties with Tandon Doss (10.4 Pts+) but will have to handle the full load now that Doss is in Jacksonville.

Buffalo Bills

2013 Record: 6-10	**Total DVOA:** -3.3% (18th)	**2014 Mean Projection:** 8.0 wins	**On the Clock (0-4):** 9%
Pythagorean Wins: 6.7 (22nd)	**Offense:** -11.5% (25th)	**Postseason Odds:** 35.7%	**Mediocrity (5-7):** 32%
Snap-Weighted Age: 26.2 (24th)	**Defense:** -13.8% (4th)	**Super Bowl Odds:** 4.8%	**Playoff Contender (8-10):** 43%
Average Opponent: 0.2% (15th)	**Special Teams:** -5.6% (30th)	**Proj. Avg. Opponent:** 0.6% (16th)	**Super Bowl Contender (11+):** 16%

2013: While nobody noticed, Buffalo turned into Philadelphia North—except without the winning.

2014: The offense won't improve enough to make up for defensive regression, but the Bills finally have hope and a long-term plan.

For years, the Bills were the vanilla-bland team of the AFC East: never good enough to mount a serious challenge to the Patriots while never being bad enough to really slide out of the picture. But in 2013, they truly offered up something new. First-year head coach Doug Marrone and quarterback EJ Manuel implemented a quicker offense—one of the fastest in the league—while defensive coordinator Mike Pettine helped push the Buffalo pass defense to become one of the best in the NFL. While it resulted in a 6-10 record, there was a feeling that after a handful of years, the Bills at least deserve some credit for trying something different.

The question now is: can the Bills build on that in 2014, and allow themselves to take a step forward when it comes to challenging the Patriots for the division title? Of course, it's not like Buffalo hasn't seen an uptempo approach previously. Jim Kelly and the Bills launched the K-Gun offense in the 1990s, which ultimately led to four straight Super Bowl appearances. But never has the turn been so dramatic from the middle-of-the-road pace employed by Chan Gailey in 2012 to the one favored by Marrone and offensive coordinator Nathaniel Hackett in 2013.

Chip Kelly made plenty of news installing his college-style, fast-tempo, run-first offense in Philadelphia a year ago. In fact, he made so much news that nobody noticed Marrone doing the exact same thing just 300 miles to the northwest. For example, the Bills went from 29th to second overall in our measurement of situation-neutral offensive pace, a formula that eliminates second-half plays when one team is far ahead or behind to get a truer idea of the offense's intentions when it comes to offensive pace. Using that formula, the Bills ran one play every 24.9 seconds, the third fastest of any team since 1997, trailing only the 2013 Eagles and the 2011 Patriots. The year before, Bills' situation-neutral pace ranked just 29th, with one play every 32.2 seconds. (Their total pace in 2013 was one play every 24.0 seconds, second fastest of any team since 1997 behind only the 2013 Eagles, and their pace in the second half of games was the highest of any team since 1997, one play every 23.4 seconds.)

Two years ago, the Bills used an empty backfield on 17 percent of plays, first in the NFL. Last year, they ranked dead last, going empty on just 1.4 percent of plays. To make up the difference, the Bills went from using a single-back set 66 percent of the time (17th in 2012) to 82 percent of the time (fourth in 2013). After all, you need a running back on the field if you want to run the ball. Buffalo led the league in use of running plays both in the first half (49 percent) and on first downs (60 percent), after being only slightly above average in 2012. As a result, they led the league in rush attempts by a wide margin (546, while the Seahawks were second at 509 attempts) even though they were almost never running out the clock, with ten losses and two wins in the final minute.

Ultimately, the offensive tweaks didn't result in wins: the Bills may have ranked second in rushing yardage, but they were 19th in total yardage, 22nd in points, and 29th in third-down conversions. Having two distinctly positive elements to your offense creates an interesting dynamic. In 2014, do the Bills want to lean on a steady running game—and presumably play more of a grind-it-out offense—or do they want to try and go more uptempo, as they did frequently last year? Of course, the two aren't necessarily mutually exclusive, but the two separate offensive philosophies often occupy different parts of the football universe. It'll be up to Manuel, Marrone and Hackett to find a middle ground for the 2014 Bills.

Manuel certainly showed enough in the 2013 preseason to win the starting job as a rookie. He was impressive in his first two starts of the season, taking the Patriots down to the last minute in the opener and knocking off the Panthers in the second game of the year. But the relatively rapid ascent of Manuel was a double-edged sword, as the young quarterback learned on the job and made the expected rookie mistakes. He also struggled with injury over the course of his rookie season, which forced Buffalo to turn to Jeff Tuel and Thad Lewis for five combined starts. And his season stats are significantly hit by one single really horrible game, the Week 14 loss to Tampa Bay, where Manuel threw four picks and took seven sacks. By DYAR, it was the second-worst performance by a quarterback all season.

As was the case with the offensive line—more on that shortly—the fact that the Bills were dealing with so much youth at quarterback over the course of the season made it hard to really get a handle on the overall offensive evolution of many of the younger skill position players. The Buffalo running game has been a fairly steady point of pride over the last few years with durable and dependable presences such as C.J. Spiller and Fred Jackson. Last year, things didn't go quite so smoothly—they ranked 14th in yards per carry at 4.2—but that could

2014 Bills Schedule

Week	Opp.	Week	Opp.	Week	Opp.
1	at CHI	7	MIN	13	CLE
2	MIA	8	at NYJ	14	at DEN
3	SD	9	BYE	15	GB
4	at HOU	10	KC	16	at OAK
5	at DET	11	at MIA (Thu.)	17	at NE
6	NE	12	NYJ		

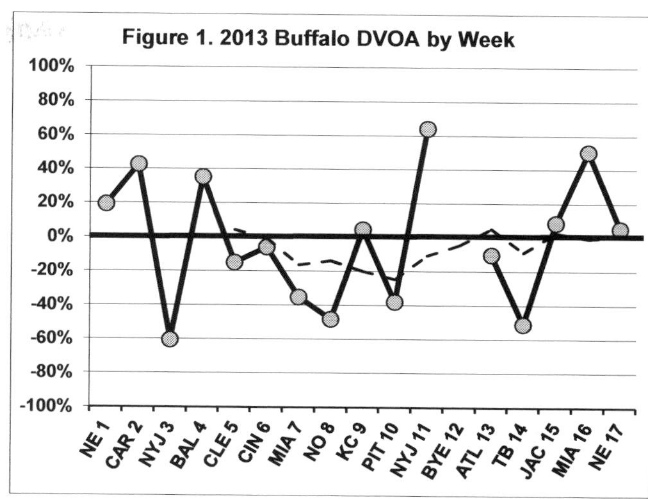

be a product of the fact that the Bills simply ran the ball a lot more than anyone else, and opponents knew it was coming. (The Bills went from facing an average of 6.00 men in the box in 2012—the lowest rate in the NFL—to an average of 6.46 in 2013, sixth in the league.) Despite a rapidly approaching expiration date, the 33-year-old Jackson proved he was able to carry the load in a year where Spiller had some issues. Because Jackson became a regular at the ripe old age of 28, the usual "running back window" rules might not necessarily apply to the Coe College product. Of course, that doesn't mean he's going to play dramatically longer than any other running back, but if he's utilized properly, there's no reason to think you couldn't squeeze another year or two of 800 to 900 rushing yards a season out of him.

If Buffalo can manage to run the ball consistently in 2014, that should take some of the pressure off Manuel in the passing game, and allow for the increased evolution of the quarterback. If they can't, it'll mean more on Manuel's plate. In particular, Manuel could benefit from a bounce-back year from Spiller, who suffered a sizable dropoff in a few statistical areas despite having almost as many carries in 2013 (202) as he had in 2012 (207). Those included rushing yards (1,244 to 933), yards per carry (6.0 to 4.6), DVOA (27.6% to -17.8%), yards per catch (10.7 to 5.6) and yards after the catch (11.8 to 6.9). It's questionable how much he was dogged by injury and how much might have been occasional misuse on the part of Marrone, but a resurgent season from Spiller would provide another boost for Manuel. While the Bills like Bryce Brown, acquired from Philadelphia in a trade this offseason, he may have more of an impact in 2015 and beyond, depending on health and personnel of the team over the next year.

Protecting Manuel was a challenge last year for a few reasons. Obviously, we start with the fact that the entire offense was working through a new system with a rookie quarterback. Like many young passers, Manuel was occasionally tentative, a big reason why the Bills' offensive line yielded a league-leading 17 coverage sacks. At the same time, it's important to note that the offensive line is a bit of a hodgepodge. First, the good: left tackle Cordy Glenn showed signs of becoming a foundational element up front, while center Eric Wood has played well over the course of the last five seasons, but still took seven holding penalties last year, tied for second-most in the league. (When it comes to Wood, it's worth mentioning that the Bills' coaching staff believes their best chance to move the ball on the ground came behind Wood, as a league-high 71 percent of their runs came either up the middle or over the guard.) Then, there's the questionable to not-so-good: the addition of rookie Cyrus Kouandijo at right tackle will likely be an upgrade over Erik Pears, while left guard Chris Williams has bounced around from team to team and position to position over the course of his inconsistent NFL career. Marrone first made his name as an offensive line coach, and so there's a cautious optimism that the O-line might get taken care of sooner rather than later. Still, the fact that Marrone told Spiller to chide the offensive line after it cleared the way for 68 yards on 38 carries in a November win over the Jets—and Spiller refused—might have some lingering aftereffects.

At receiver, Buffalo underwent a sizable change this offseason. Buffalo traded their 2015 first-round pick to Cleveland in order to move up to the fourth overall pick and take Clemson's Sammy Watkins. Then, to help make room for him, they jettisoned their veteran No. 1 receiver Stevie Johnson, shipping him to the Niners for a conditional fourth-round pick.

Watkins certainly has all the skills to be a game-breaking receiver in the NFL, but the decision to trade up for an elite-level talent like Watkins is usually the sort of move you see from a team that's one player away, which the Bills are emphatically *not*. This was also a really strange season to make that move. Both conventional wisdom among scouts and our Playmaker Score projection system considered this to be one of the deepest wide receiver draft classes in NFL history. Watkins didn't even have the highest Playmaker Projection in this class, ranking fourth behind Brandin Cooks, Odell Beckham, and Mike Evans. Sure, your scouts may be smarter than our projection system, but does it really make sense to give up a first-round pick next year to take that gamble, when both Cooks and Beckham were still on the board for Buffalo's original pick, ninth overall?

The departure of Johnson leaves Buffalo with a really young receiving corps that has a ton of potential and a ton of improvement required to reach it. Robert Woods, a 2013 second-round pick, is Manuel's top returning receiver from last season. He was inconsistent as a rookie, with 40 catches and only two drops but a catch rate under 50 percent and a game where he got tossed out for throwing a punch. He showed nice chemistry with Manuel in OTAs, and if the Bills are going to continue to run their up-tempo attack, look for Woods to have an even bigger role in 2014. Behind Watkins and Woods are two third-round picks. Marquise Goodwin is crazy fast; 36 percent of his pass targets as a rookie were "bombs" (i.e., more than 25 yards through the air), and he led the team in yards per catch at 16.6. If he can catch the ball consistently, he can develop into a serious deep threat who also makes room for Watkins and Woods to work underneath. The wild card here is third-year receiver T.J. Graham, who had very poor DVOA ratings in both his first two seasons, but with very different shapes. As a rookie, he had six drops and only 10.4 yards per catch because more than half his passes came within five yards of the line of scrimmage. In his second year, he was thrown a lot more mid-range stuff and suddenly was gaining more than 15 yards per catch, but his catch rate dropped to 40 percent because he had trouble getting open.

The old man of the receiving corps is the workmanlike tight end Scott Chandler, who is underrated and relatively dependable. While he's not exactly Rob Gronkowski, with roughly league-average DVOA in each of the last two seasons, he had career-bests in catches (53) and yards (655) for Buffalo in 2013, and became a nice fallback for Manuel when the young quarterback got into trouble. One area where Buffalo would like to see more from Chandler in 2014 is in the red zone—after catching nine touchdown passes inside the 20-yard line in 2011 and 2012, Chandler had just one red-zone catch in 2013.

With a young quarterback and so many young receivers, player development is hugely important for this team, and to that end, Marrone brought in two coaches this offseason to give Hackett further help. Hackett worked as both offensive coordinator and quarterbacks coach in 2013, but now, the new quarterbacks coach is former Lions assistant Todd Downing. Downing and Manuel built a relationship when the two worked together at the Senior Bowl, and will look to build on that in 2014. (Although we wonder if the guy who's been working with Matthew Stafford is the right one to help EJ Manuel improve his footwork.) Marrone also added former Ravens receivers coach Jim Hostler after he was turned down for the Baltimore offensive coordinator position. While it's unclear what exactly Hostler's duties will include—he has the vaguely-worded title of Senior Offensive Assistant—he's a well-regarded individual who has been credited with helping several members of the Baltimore receiving corps reach the next level over the last few seasons, including Anquan Boldin and Torrey Smith.

With so many reasons for optimism on the offensive side of the ball, it's a shame that the defense is likely to take a step backwards. Certainly, there's plenty to like about this defense, especially when it comes to defending against the pass. The front four is phenomenal, especially now that former Colts first-rounder Jerry Hughes has lived up to his potential. The Bills were second behind Carolina with 57 sacks, and three defenders (Mario Williams, Kyle Williams, and Hughes) each had at least ten. The Bills were also second in the league with 23 interceptions, as linebacker Kiko Alonso and safeties Jairus Byrd, Aaron Williams and Jim Leonhard all had four picks each.

Unfortunately, the Bills are a prime candidate for the Plexiglass Principle because their defensive improvement last year was so severe. For three straight years, Buffalo had ranked 24th or lower in defensive DVOA and 22nd or lower in pass defense. All of a sudden last year, they were fifth in defensive DVOA and second in pass defense behind only Seattle.

Making the regression even more likely are three huge losses suffered this offseason. First came the departure of Pettine, hired in late January as the new head coach of the Cleveland Browns. Then, Byrd left for the Saints in free agency. Finally, Alonso suffered a knee injury while working out early in the summer, which will likely cost him the entire 2014 season.

Even with the quality along the defensive line, Byrd and Alonso were arguably Buffalo's two best defensive players in 2013, and replacing them will be a major challenge. Projecting the best way to replace them becomes even more complicated because the hiring of Jim Schwartz will bring yet another defensive scheme change for a team that will now have its fourth defensive coordinator in four seasons. The front four personnel will stay the same, but most observers assume that the Pettine's multiple looks will be gone, replaced by the wide-9 front that Schwartz prefers. It should be said that Schwartz has told the media in the past that he would prefer to be more multiple if he had the right personnel for it, and the move of Manny Lawson from standard outside linebacker to edge rusher suggests there could be more wrinkles here than otherwise expected. But mostly, Schwartz brings the wide-9 because he wants to maximize the pass-rushing potential of his defensive ends and leave seven players in coverage as often as possible.

With Pettine as defensive coordinator, the 2013 Bills blitzed twice as often as they did the year before. That's likely going back down in 2014, as Jim Schwartz's Detroit defenses have been near the bottom of the league in blitz frequency every year. Although Buffalo brought pressure on 27.2 percent of pass plays, sixth in the NFL, the Bills didn't necessarily need it, as they were the only defense that actually had a negative DVOA when we *didn't* mark specific pass pressure, and only Cincinnati allowed fewer yards per pass without pressure than Buffalo's 6.6.

The loss of Byrd means the Bills could open the 2014 season with two starting safeties who aren't necessarily classic safeties, Aaron Williams and Da'Norris Searcy. Williams is a former cornerback who made a full-time switch to safety last season. Searcy was a big safety/small linebacker in Buffalo's system, and showed some nice playmaking ability, with two touchdowns, a fumble recovery, and 3.5 sacks. Provided they can stay healthy, the corner spot appears to be relatively deep for the Bills, as Leodis McKelvin and Stephon Gilmore enter camp as the two top options, while free-agent addition Corey Graham will take over the nickelback role from the much more properly-named Nickell Robey.

The improvement on pass defense last year didn't trickle over much into the run defense. The Bills tried to solve that problem by signing linebacker Brandon Spikes, who developed a rep as one of the best run-stoppers in the league in his four seasons in New England. With the Patriots, he struggled badly in coverage, but could be asked to work more on passing downs with the Bills in 2014 because of the absence of Alonso. Without Alonso, Keith Rivers and Nigel Bradham will round out the linebacking corps. Rivers has some positional versatility (he's played both strongside and weakside linebacker with the Bengals and Giants), while the speedy Bradham has played well in spurts over the last two seasons. While he might have been on the roster bubble if Alonso was available—he has trouble recognizing plays and being in proper position—Bradham now figures to be relatively secure going forward. Rookie Preston Brown saw some reps with the starters over the course of the spring and didn't look out of place while playing in the first-team nickel defense; could also end up taking many of the snaps that would have gone to Alonso.

Despite all the on-field change that's come to the Bills over the last 12 to 15 months, there's one other change that's completely under the radar: they'll fundamentally play one more home game in 2014. Though the Bills signed a new five-year contract for the "Bills Toronto Series" before the 2013 season, the 2014 game has been "postponed." In their quest to be the NFL's answer to Canadian Club, all the Bills got each year was essentially the chance to trade a home game for a road game with Rob Ford in attendance. The extra home game may not have a terrific impact on the Bills' playoff chances, but if it helps them take another positive step in the right direction in 2014—say, from 6-10 to 8-8—then it's a good thing.

But the best news for Bills fans is that it took us 3,000 words to get to the word "Toronto." For years, the most interesting thing about the Buffalo Bills was their attempt to become a regional franchise and resist a move when owner Ralph Wilson eventually passed away. Now, thanks to Marrone, Manuel, and Watkins, the situation on the field is finally more interesting than the situation off of it—even though the eventuality became reality on March 25 and the franchise is now officially for sale. They aren't going to make the playoffs this year, and certainly a lot can change over a couple of seasons. But as of right now, the Bills are the AFC East team best poised to finally challenge the Patriots when Tom Brady finally hits the wall and/or retires.

So when things seem even closer next April, they are *really* going to miss that first-round pick.

Christopher Price

2013 Bills Stats by Week

Wk	vs.	W-L	PF	PA	YDF	YDA	TO	Total	Off	Def	ST
1	NE	L	21	23	286	431	+1	19%	-4%	-22%	2%
2	CAR	W	24	23	436	308	-1	43%	26%	-17%	0%
3	at NYJ	L	20	27	328	513	+2	-61%	-29%	33%	1%
4	BAL	W	23	20	350	345	+2	35%	-12%	-51%	-5%
5	at CLE	L	24	37	343	290	-1	-15%	-10%	-18%	-23%
6	CIN	L	24	27	322	483	0	-6%	9%	14%	-1%
7	at MIA	W	23	21	268	293	+2	-35%	-53%	-22%	-4%
8	at NO	L	17	35	299	386	-3	-48%	-17%	22%	-9%
9	KC	L	13	23	470	210	-3	5%	-5%	-10%	0%
10	at PIT	L	10	23	227	300	0	-38%	-26%	-9%	-22%
11	NYJ	W	37	14	313	267	+4	64%	10%	-53%	1%
12	BYE										
13	vs. ATL	L	31	34	405	423	-1	-10%	-4%	-3%	-9%
14	at TB	L	6	27	214	246	-3	-51%	-80%	-35%	-7%
15	at JAC	W	27	20	366	354	+2	9%	5%	-7%	-4%
16	MIA	W	19	0	390	103	+1	50%	-13%	-72%	-9%
17	at NE	L	20	34	393	382	+1	5%	-2%	-8%	0%

Trends and Splits

	Offense	Rank	Defense	Rank
Total DVOA	-11.5%	25	-13.8%	4
Unadjusted VOA	-9.1%	23	-14.5%	5
Weighted Trend	-14.1%	26	-16.3%	5
Variance	6.4%	14	7.5%	25
Average Opponent	-1.1%	13	-2.7%	26
Passing	-14.0%	27	-22.8%	2
Rushing	-4.0%	17	-3.1%	19
First Down	-5.0%	21	-4.6%	12
Second Down	-13.1%	25	-19.0%	4
Third Down	-20.6%	25	-22.9%	4
First Half	-11.8%	27	-11.5%	6
Second Half	-11.2%	23	-16.3%	5
Red Zone	-13.7%	27	-26.0%	5
Late and Close	-12.0%	24	-9.7%	11

Five-Year Performance

Year	W-L	Pyth W	Est W	PF	PA	TO	Total	Rk	Off	Rk	Def	Rk	ST	Rk	Off AGL	Rk	Def AGL	Rk	Off Age	Rk	Def Age	Rk	ST Age	Rk
2009	6-10	5.9	6.6	258	326	+3	-10.4%	24	-20.7%	29	-9.2%	8	1.1%	13	60.7	32	62.1	32	26.9	21	27.5	9	26.9	11
2010	4-12	4.3	5.5	283	425	-17	-21.3%	29	-14.5%	26	6.8%	28	-0.1%	17	10.4	5	31.2	22	26.4	27	27.5	13	27.1	8
2011	6-10	6.4	7.1	372	434	+1	-9.7%	23	0.3%	16	8.3%	24	-1.7%	24	33.8	20	37.1	21	26.3	27	27.4	12	26.7	5
2012	6-10	5.7	6.5	344	435	-13	-12.1%	23	-4.2%	20	10.6%	27	2.7%	9	51.5	29	28.2	16	26.2	25	26.7	18	26.5	10
2013	6-10	6.7	7.1	339	388	+3	-3.3%	18	-11.5%	25	-13.8%	4	-5.6%	30	18.5	6	26.7	11	26.4	24	26.0	26	26.1	12

2013 Performance Based on Most Common Personnel Groups

BUF Offense					BUF Offense vs. Opponents				BUF Defense				BUF Defense vs. Opponents			
Pers	Freq	Yds	DVOA	Run%	Pers	Freq	Yds	DVOA	Pers	Freq	Yds	DVOA	Pers	Freq	Yds	DVOA
11	59%	5.3	-4.3%	30%	Nickel Even	40%	5.5	-5.8%	3-4-4	35%	4.8	-8.5%	11	46%	4.7	-27.4%
12	19%	4.4	-26.2%	61%	4-3-4	24%	4.9	-12.8%	Nickel Even	26%	5.7	-5.7%	12	23%	5.5	-6.6%
21	16%	5.7	9.8%	69%	3-4-4	20%	4.9	-5.5%	Dime+	22%	4.8	-40.6%	21	16%	6.0	5.5%
10	2%	4.3	-97.8%	45%	Dime+	9%	5.2	-4.0%	Nickel Odd	9%	5.1	-10.3%	22	3%	5.4	-3.7%
22	2%	1.8	-66.2%	100%	Nickel Odd	6%	4.2	-42.4%	4-3-4	6%	5.8	6.8%	611	3%	6.1	20.7%

Strategic Tendencies

Run/Pass		Rk	Formation		Rk	Pass Rush		Rk	Secondary		Rk	Strategy		Rk
Runs, first half	49%	1	Form: Single Back	82%	4	Rush 3	6.6%	14	4 DB	41%	13	Play action	16%	23
Runs, first down	60%	1	Form: Empty Back	1%	32	Rush 4	58.4%	23	5 DB	34%	29	Avg Box (Off)	6.46	6
Runs, second-long	32%	16	Pers: 3+ WR	62%	8	Rush 5	27.8%	11	6+ DB	22%	4	Avg Box (Def)	6.45	7
Runs, power sit.	52%	20	Pers: 4+ WR	2%	12	Rush 6+	7.2%	18	CB by Sides	80%	12	Offensive Pace	24.92	2
Runs, behind 2H	28%	16	Pers: 2+ TE/6+ OL	22%	26	Sacks by LB	12.3%	26	DB Blitz	14%	9	Defensive Pace	29.08	7
Pass, ahead 2H	40%	30	Shotgun/Pistol	66%	10	Sacks by DB	14.0%	4	Hole in Zone	5%	30	Go for it on 4th	0.54	29

The Bills are a very good draw team, averaging 7.0 yards per carry over the last two seasons. A dozen teams ran more than 25 running back screens last season, but only two of those teams had negative DVOA on screens: Jacksonville and Buffalo (-12.9% DVOA, 5.5 yards per play). Buffalo had the league's best Adjusted Sack Rate on third or fourth down. They had 30 sacks on third or fourth down; no other defense had more than 23. Buffalo had the league's best defense against short/medium passes (15 yards through the air or less) but were below average against deep passes (16-plus yards through the air). Though some defenses have been consistently good or bad against play action, the Bills offer some significant evidence that how well a defense does against play action could be entirely fluky (Table 1).

Table 1. Buffalo DVOA, Play Action vs. No Play Action, 2011-2013

Year	Freq.	Yds w/PA	Rank	DVOA w/PA	Rank	Yds, no PA	Rank	DVOA, no PA	Rank	DVOA Gap	Rank
2011	20%	8.5	27	31.4%	28	6.9	27	7.2%	22	24.3%	5
2012	20%	6.5	5	-11.2%	3	6.4	20	23.6%	29	-34.9%	32
2013	21%	7.1	13	19.2%	19	5.0	1	-32.9%	1	52.1%	1

Includes sacks, scrambles, and Defensive Pass Interference

Passing

Player	DYAR	DVOA	Plays	NtYds	Avg	YAC	C%	TD	Int
EJ Manuel	-190	-19.9%	335	1814	5.4	5.1	59.2%	11	9
T.Lewis	-84	-18.7%	176	990	5.6	5.1	59.2%	4	3
J.Tuel	-130	-43.4%	62	313	5.0	5.9	45.0%	1	3

Rushing

Player	DYAR	DVOA	Plays	Yds	Avg	TD	Fum	Suc
F.Jackson	163	9.1%	206	890	4.3	9	2	51%
C.J.Spiller	-70	-17.8%	202	933	4.6	2	4	36%
EJ Manuel	49	11.0%	39	217	5.6	2	1	-
T.Choice*	10	-1.8%	35	126	3.6	0	0	51%
T.Lewis	-47	-60.3%	17	57	3.4	1	2	-
F.Summers	14	19.4%	12	46	3.8	1	0	50%
B.Brown	*23*	*-1.2%*	*75*	*314*	*4.2*	*2*	*0*	*48%*
A.Dixon	*-13*	*-17.5%*	*28*	*56*	*2.0*	*2*	*0*	*39%*

Receiving

Player	DYAR	DVOA	Plays	Ctch	Yds	Y/C	YAC	TD	C%
S.Johnson*	-25	-15.6%	102	53	607	11.5	4.2	3	52%
R.Woods	6	-11.7%	85	40	587	14.7	2.8	3	47%
T.J.Graham	-55	-24.3%	57	23	366	15.9	3.6	2	40%
M.Goodwin	47	5.4%	32	17	286	16.8	2.8	3	53%
C.Hogan	-17	-25.3%	17	10	83	8.3	2.7	0	59%
M.Williams	*4*	*-11.4%*	*40*	*22*	*216*	*9.8*	*3.0*	*2*	*55%*
S.Chandler	32	-1.3%	81	53	655	12.4	5.2	2	65%
L.Smith	-4	-13.7%	9	5	78	15.6	8.2	0	56%
C.Gragg	17	21.8%	7	5	53	10.6	2.0	1	71%
F.Jackson	52	0.8%	66	47	390	8.3	8.8	1	71%
C.J.Spiller	-8	-17.8%	40	33	185	5.6	6.9	0	83%
F.Summers	56	108.6%	8	7	79	11.3	8.0	1	88%
T.Choice*	-20	-72.9%	8	4	10	2.5	4.8	0	50%
B.Brown	*12*	*8.7%*	*13*	*8*	*84*	*10.5*	*11.8*	*0*	*62%*

Offensive Line

Player	Pos	Age	GS	Snaps	Pen	Sk	Pass	Run
Cordy Glenn	LT	25	16/16	1161	6	1.5	15.5	6.0
Erik Pears	RT	32	16/16	1161	6	4.5	14.0	9.0
Eric Wood	C	28	16/16	1161	10	0.0	4.5	2.0
Kraig Urbik	RG	29	16/16	1143	2	4.0	14.0	6.0
Doug Legursky	LG	28	11/11	765	2	0.0	8.5	5.0
Colin Brown*	OT	29	6/5	396	1	2.5	15.5	3.5
Chris Williams	*LG*	*29*	*16/16*	*901*	*4*	*2.8*	*16.8*	*4.0*

Year	Yards	ALY	Rk	Power	Rk	Stuff	Rk	2nd Lev	Rk	Open Field	Rk	Sacks	ASR	Rk	Short	Long	F-Start	Cont.
2011	5.04	4.18	12	67%	7	18%	14	1.25	9	1.29	2	23	3.8%	1	8	10	9	25
2012	5.15	4.25	7	57%	26	17%	8	1.42	3	1.14	4	30	5.5%	10	11	13	22	27
2013	4.38	3.85	16	65%	14	18%	11	1.14	14	0.96	6	48	8.5%	29	14	22	12	41

2013 ALY by direction: Left End 2.13 (30) Left Tackle 3.94 (15) Mid/Guard 4.08 (11) Right Tackle 3.59 (22) Right End 2.30 (32)

It was a weird year for the Buffalo offensive line, which spent 2013 protecting rookies EJ Manuel and Jeff Tuel, as well as youngster Thad Lewis, all of whom were in their first year of running an uptempo offense at the NFL level. So it was hardly a surprise that the Bills allowed 17 coverage sacks in 2013, the most in the NFL. That's not to suggest that the group as a whole would definitely have been better if they were protecting a more seasoned signal-caller—only to suggest that while the line isn't great, it might not be as bad as the initial numbers might appear. The run blocking was particularly reasonable, especially considering the problems C.J. Spiller was having. (The Bills had a 25 percent Stuff rate when Spiller carried the ball, compared to just 14 percent with Fred Jackson.)

Center Eric Wood was the best of the Buffalo starters with just 6.5 blown blocks, and his count of one blown block every 179 snaps put him sixth among all starting interior linemen across the league. However, Wood was also tied for second in the league with seven holding penalties—only Green Bay's David Bakhtiari was flagged for more holding calls (nine), and he had the excuses of being both a left tackle and a rookie. Left tackle Cordy Glenn had a steady second season, starting all 16 games, and showed signs he could be the sort of foundational element around which you could build a line. (For what it's worth, Glenn saw reps at guard in the spring at OTAs. That's not to suggest he'd move to guard on a full-time basis; it may have been more about preparing for an emergency situation.) And Kraig Urbik is a solid if unspectacular presence at right guard who can also slide over to center in a pinch.

The rest of the line has some question marks. Second-round pick Cyrus Kouandijo (Alabama) is the likely starter at right tackle, taking over for Erik Pears, but he tore his right ACL in 2011, and the report of a "failed surgery" after he went down (combined with a sluggish combine performance) caused some to wonder about his ability to perform at the next level. (Dr. James Andrews ultimately weighed in, saying reports of a failed surgery for Kouandijo were "not even close to the truth.") Left guard Chris Williams has struggled over the course of his career, going from the 14th overall pick in the draft as a tackle to a journeyman guard who has bounced from Chicago to St. Louis. He's replacing Doug Legursky, who now projects as the top backup for the interior of the line.

Defensive Front Seven

			Overall								vs. Run					Pass Rush			
Defensive Line	Age	Pos	G	Snaps	Plays	TmPct	Rk	Stop	Dfts	BTkl	Runs	St%	Rk	RuYd	Rk	Sack	Hit	Hur	Tips
Kyle Williams	31	DT	16	939	68	7.9%	9	59	25	1	53	83%	25	1.7	28	10.0	12	23.3	1
Marcell Dareus	25	DT	16	824	73	8.5%	4	59	12	5	59	76%	47	2.7	63	7.5	5	14.5	2
Corbin Bryant	26	DT	15	329	14	1.7%	--	12	3	1	13	85%	--	3.5	--	1.0	1	3.0	0

			Overall								vs. Run					Pass Rush			
Edge Rushers	Age	Pos	G	Snaps	Plays	TmPct	Rk	Stop	Dfts	BTkl	Runs	St%	Rk	RuYd	Rk	Sack	Hit	Hur	Tips
Mario Williams	29	DE	16	999	41	4.8%	52	36	21	1	23	78%	29	1.7	15	12.5	4	26.3	3
Jerry Hughes	26	DE	16	604	44	5.1%	46	27	13	3	23	57%	73	2.6	46	10.0	8	21.8	2
Alan Branch	30	DE	16	596	40	4.7%	56	29	5	0	37	76%	40	2.5	44	0.0	4	9.0	1
Jarius Wynn	28	DE	15	361	13	1.8%	--	12	5	0	7	86%	--	2.0	--	2.0	3	7.0	2

			Overall								Pass Rush			vs. Run					vs. Pass						
Linebackers	Age	Pos	G	Snaps	Plays	TmPct	Rk	Stop	Dfts	BTkl	Sack	Hit	Hur	Runs	St%	Rk	RuYd	Rk	Tgts	Suc%	Rk	AdjYd	Rk	PD	Int
Kiko Alonso	24	MLB	16	1145	161	18.7%	5	96	28	4	2.0	2	4.5	115	62%	53	3.2	31	25	54%	34	7.3	52	4	4
Manny Lawson	30	OLB	15	706	73	9.1%	64	51	17	1	4.5	2	5	51	67%	35	3.3	32	13	65%	--	4.0	--	1	1
Arthur Moats*	26	OLB	16	293	48	5.6%	--	27	7	1	0.0	1	1	36	69%	--	2.3	--	8	21%	--	11.3	--	0	0
Nigel Bradham	25	OLB	16	284	38	4.4%	--	25	1	2	0.0	0	1	33	67%	--	3.1	--	4	98%	--	3.9	--	0	0
Brandon Spikes	*27*	*MLB*	*16*	*687*	*88*	*10.3%*	*61*	*59*	*13*	*1*	*0.0*	*1*	*2.5*	*72*	*74%*	*13*	*2.6*	*18*	*22*	*45%*	*52*	*6.0*	*22*	*2*	*1*
Keith Rivers	*28*	*OLB*	*16*	*418*	*43*	*5.0%*	*--*	*22*	*4*	*4*	*1.0*	*0*	*4*	*31*	*52%*	*--*	*4.0*	*--*	*8*	*76%*	*--*	*7.1*	*--*	*0*	*0*

Year	Yards	ALY	Rk	Power	Rk	Stuff	Rk	2nd Level	Rk	Open Field	Rk	Sacks	ASR	Rk	Short	Long
2011	4.79	4.46	28	62%	14	15%	32	1.30	26	1.02	24	29	5.9%	26	7	16
2012	4.77	4.30	24	68%	25	18%	17	1.40	32	1.05	28	36	6.0%	23	8	17
2013	4.54	3.99	20	65%	15	17%	24	1.13	20	1.07	28	57	8.7%	3	19	18
2013 ALY by direction:			*Left End 2.35 (4)*			*Left Tackle 4.22 (23)*			*Mid/Guard 4.17 (24)*			*Right Tackle 3.29 (9)*			*Right End 4.51 (29)*	

Buffalo emerged as one of the best defenses in the league in 2013, and much of that success began up front, where Buffalo finished second in the league to the Panthers with 57 sacks. The Bills spread around the pass rush as the only team where three defenders (Mario Williams, Kyle Williams, and Jerry Hughes) had at least ten sacks. Those three players will continue to start up front along with Marcell "Speed Racer" Dareus. Veterans Alan Branch and Jarius Wynn provide depth along with Manny Lawson, who will be making the switch from starting outside linebacker to backup defensive end. The Bills hope this will simplify his role and make him more of a pass-rushing presence.

The front seven's struggles came against the run, where they were distinctly middle of the road; the Bills finished 19th in the league in run defense DVOA and yielded an average of 128.9 yards per game, which ranked 28th. The run defense should get a jolt with the acquisition of Brandon Spikes, who emerged as one of the best run-stoppers in the league in his four years in New England. His 74 percent Stop Rate last season was 13th best in the league, and we have only charted him with four broken tackles in the last three seasons combined. Unfortunately, the addition of Spikes might be cancelled out by the loss of Kiko Alonso to a torn ACL suffered during offseason workouts. Alonso made 115 run plays in his phenomenal rookie year, when no other player in the NFL was above 100. (That number was slightly inflated by how often Buffalo opponents ran the ball, but Alonso led the league in percentage of his team's run plays as well, at 26.4 percent. NaVorro Bowman was second at 25.1 percent.) To add insult to injury, the long and rangy Alonso was also the best pass defender among the Buffalo linebackers. Veteran Keith Rivers will also figure into the mix as well, but will likely come off the field on third down and other passing situations for someone like Nigel Bradham. Bradham has had limited experience in his first two seasons in the league, but has shown great speed and good coverage skills, and could be a solid sideline-to-sideline defensive presence as part of a pass defense that is relying on two relatively inexperienced safeties. As a collegian at Louisville, third-round rookie Preston Brown showed himself as a physical and relatively stout presence against the run, but struggled in coverage.

Defensive Secondary

			Overall								vs. Run					vs. Pass									
Secondary	Age	Pos	G	Snaps	Plays	TmPct	Rk	Stop	Dfts	BTkl	Runs	St%	Rk	RuYd	Rk	Tgts	Tgt%	Rk	Dist	Suc%	Rk	AdjYd	Rk	PD	Int
Leodis McKelvin	29	CB	15	927	88	10.9%	11	36	8	3	20	40%	44	7.3	48	101	26.9%	82	12.5	55%	32	6.4	12	19	1
Aaron Williams	25	SS/CB	14	926	93	12.4%	20	30	13	1	40	30%	61	10.3	72	62	16.5%	74	12.8	55%	42	7.3	44	10	4
Da'Norris Searcy	26	SS	16	729	76	8.8%	55	33	15	8	38	37%	48	8.0	60	33	11.2%	66	10.5	55%	38	6.4	25	6	1
Stephon Gilmore	24	CB	11	648	45	7.6%	53	18	9	3	7	57%	14	5.4	20	69	26.1%	80	12.4	51%	55	7.6	44	7	2
Jairus Byrd*	28	FS	11	635	54	9.1%	53	19	11	2	21	29%	66	12.2	77	17	6.4%	19	9.6	68%	5	3.4	2	5	4
Jim Leonhard*	32	SS	16	613	43	5.0%	73	17	8	8	17	47%	25	6.6	30	20	7.8%	39	11.1	66%	9	4.3	8	6	4
Nickell Robey	22	CB	16	609	49	5.7%	81	29	17	2	11	36%	49	5.1	15	52	20.9%	41	10.8	68%	2	6.9	24	10	1
Justin Rogers*	26	CB	6	303	28	8.7%	--	14	3	2	5	80%	--	4.4	--	40	32.2%	--	18.0	43%	--	12.5	--	5	1
Corey Graham	*29*	*CB*	*16*	*688*	*78*	*9.4%*	*22*	*38*	*19*	*5*	*22*	*59%*	*9*	*7.2*	*45*	*60*	*22.0%*	*50*	*13.4*	*57%*	*18*	*6.6*	*15*	*12*	*4*

Year	Pass D Rank	vs. #1 WR	Rk	vs. #2 WR	Rk	vs. Other WR	Rk	vs. TE	Rk	vs. RB	Rk
2011	25	16.5%	22	33.3%	29	-41.0%	1	20.6%	23	5.1%	21
2012	22	20.7%	26	-2.7%	15	24.2%	29	-24.5%	2	20.1%	26
2013	2	1.9%	20	-45.2%	1	5.2%	20	-27.4%	4	-29.7%	2

The pass rush wasn't the only thing to like about the Buffalo pass defense; the Bills were also second in the league with 23 picks. However, three-time Pro Bowl safety Jairus Byrd will be a tough presence to replace along the back line. In his place, Aaron Williams and Da'Norris Searcy figure to open the year at safety. (Historically, the safeties have been interchangeable in a Jim Schwartz defense.) Both come by the position in different ways: the 5-foot-11, 218-pound Searcy worked as something of a hybrid safety/nickel linebacker in 2013, while Williams is an ex-cornerback who made the switch to safety last season (though injuries forced him back to corner in Weeks 4 through 7).

As a first-round cornerback entering his third season, Stephon Gilmore is a prime candidate for a big leap forward, *if* he can stay healthy—Gilmore lost part of last season to a wrist injury and had hip surgery this offseason. The new coaching staff stopped yanking Leodis McKelvin in and out of the lineup, and he responded with a strong season, tying for second in our count of passes defensed with 19. Meanwhile, it appears free-agent signing Corey Graham has bumped Nickell Robey from the primary role of nickel corner, at least based on OTAs. This despite the fact that Robey, an undrafted free agent out of USC and shortest player on the roster at 5-foot-8, surpassed expectations as a rookie with three sacks, one pick and an Adjusted Success Rate of 68 percent, tied with Byrd for best among Buffalo's defensive backs. Buffalo also added cornerback Ross Cockrell from Duke in the fourth round; he's a smart player with ball skills, but he'll need to build onto his slight frame if he wants to develop into an NFL starter.

Special Teams

Year	DVOA	Rank	FG/XP	Rank	Net Kick	Rank	Kick Ret	Rank	Net Punt	Rank	Punt Ret	Rank	Hidden	Rank
2011	-1.7%	24	-7.1	28	4.6	7	-0.1	17	-10.6	29	4.7	6	-11.5	30
2012	2.7%	9	1.1	15	-5.1	26	13.3	2	-12.3	26	16.2	2	4.0	6
2013	-5.6%	30	5.7	7	-1.5	23	-4.4	25	-15.7	29	-12.1	32	-9.8	29

Once upon a time, this was the one unit that Buffalo fans could rely on. When Bobby April was here, he guided Buffalo's special teams to the top ranking in DVOA three times in six years. Last year's bottom-three finish shows that those days are long past. For what it's worth, current special teams coordinator Danny Crossman has always been all over the map. His units in Carolina had DVOA rankings ranging from fifth to 30th during his five years in charge, and the Lions finished 29th and 30th in our special teams ratings during Crossman's two years in Detroit, 2011 and 2012. And so it should come as no surprise that the Bills' special teams were below average last year. With the exception of field goals, where Dan Carpenter was 10th overall with a 91.7 percent conversion rate despite the bad weather, the Bills were at or near the bottom of almost every major special teams category.

Buffalo went through two punters in 2013, cutting Shawn Powell after just five games and turning to old pal Brian Moorman.

Neither was very good, and it's debatable just how much the 38-year-old Moorman has left in his leg. Harvard's Jacob Dombrowski could get the call for 2014; the over-under on Pat McInally references is currently at 247. After rewatching Buffalo's return unit last year, it was difficult to try and find out exactly what sort of issues the Bills were having when it came to punt returns, but the dropoff was palpable: Leodis McKelvin returned three punts for touchdowns in 2011 and 2012 but averaged just 5.6 yards per return last year. Meanwhile, Marquise Goodwin has electric speed as a kick returner, but wasn't able to find any holes in 2013. Goodwin took 14 kickoffs out of the end zone and couldn't even make it past the 20 on half of them.

Marcus Easley was perhaps the best overall element to Buffalo's special teams unit in 2013, as he made a league-leading 23 plays on kickoffs or punts, 19 of them solo tackles. Easley is the sort of core special teamer around whom you can build coverage units, and maybe with that in mind, Buffalo added two veterans with significant special-teams experience, Corey Graham and Anthony Dixon.

Carolina Panthers

2013 Record: 12-4	**Total DVOA:** 24.6% (3rd)	**2014 Mean Projection:** 7.8 wins	**On the Clock (0-4):** 10%
Pythagorean Wins: 11.7 (3rd)	**Offense:** 7.9% (10th)	**Postseason Odds:** 32.1%	**Mediocrity (5-7):** 34%
Snap-Weighted Age: 27.3 (5th)	**Defense:** -15.7% (3rd)	**Super Bowl Odds:** 4.4%	**Playoff Contender (8-10):** 41%
Average Opponent: 3.2% (6th)	**Special Teams:** 1.0% (13th)	**Proj. Avg. Opponent:** 2.0% (8th)	**Super Bowl Contender (11+):** 15%

2013: Last season's biggest surprise, unless you read *Football Outsiders Almanac 2013.*

2014: Hey, can that kid from the Cam Newton *Play 60* commercial play wide receiver?

On the surface, this seems an odd time for the Carolina Panthers to rebuild. By any measure, their 2013 season was a rousing success. A franchise-best 12 regular-season wins. Club records in overall and defensive DVOA. Wins over playoff teams such as the 49ers, Patriots, and Saints, all leading to a division championship. Their playoff dreams were largely undone by a pair of failed goal-line opportunities, in the kind of loss that leaves the brass ring clearly in sight. This seemed like a team on the rise, not one to be torn down.

A closer look, though, shows that there were plenty of flaws on this team, weaknesses that were masked by their gaudy final numbers and substandard talent that was covered up by superstars elsewhere.

Perception says that the Panthers were a young team, largely because they had a young quarterback; that their passing attack, though nothing special, could at least stretch defenses and create opportunities in the running game; that any team with a defense this strong must have a talented secondary. In reality, only the Saints had an older offense last season; no team had more trouble getting receivers open downfield; and the defense was built on a conservative scheme that asked very little of its subpar defensive backs, relying instead on a dominant pass rush to stop opposing drives.

These were not minor holes that could be patched in one offseason. No, these repairs were going to take time, and attempts to get better in 2014 would likely leave Carolina treading water at best, and certainly not getting closer to a championship. So general manager David Gettleman made a difficult decision, opting to yank the Band-Aid off all at once. Wholesale sections of the roster were lopped off and replaced on the cheap. It was a painful measure, but one that might have been good for the long-term health of the team. By taking one step back now, Gettleman has positioned his team to take two steps forward in the future.

The problems with last year's team begin at receiver. It's no secret that the Panthers have been trying to find a complement to Steve Smith since Muhsin Muhammad left town, a goal they never really accomplished. Last year, the Panthers' depth chart at receiver was basically three names long: Smith, showing serious signs of aging in his 13th NFL season; Brandon LaFell, a fourth-year man known more for his blocking than for his receiving; and Ted Ginn, Jr., a decent returner and subpar wideout who was coming off a season with just two catches in 16 games for the 49ers. Expectations were low, but it proved to be a passable trio. Each player gained at least 500 yards and scored at least four touchdowns, and they were all close to average in DVOA. None of them, though, produced much of anything downfield.

The Panthers achieved all that they did last year despite the league's most impotent deep passing attack. They threw 89 deep passes (more than 15 yards beyond the line of scrimmage) last year; only two teams threw fewer, and no team had worse results. Not only was Carolina the league's worst deep passing team in every category, most of the time it wasn't even close (Table 1).

Table 1: NFL's Worst Deep Passing Game

Stat	CAR	Next Worst Team	Number
Receptions + DPI	21	JAC	29
Success Rate	23.6%	TEN	30.6%
Yards	621	JAC	804
Avg. Gain	7.0	WAS	9.4
DVOA	-13.9%	WAS	-1.3%

True, the Panthers didn't pass very often. Only Seattle and San Francisco had fewer pass plays last year. But the Seahawks gained 1,500 yards on deep passes last year, seventh-best in the league. The 49ers were 22nd with 1,112 yards, still nearly double Carolina's total. So we can't use play-calling as an excuse here. Then remember that the Panthers were usually ahead. They threw 214 passes (among the top ten teams in the league) with a lead, facing defenses that theoretically would have been crowding the line to stop the run. Finally, the most damning context of all, their quarterback is Cam Newton, an excellent deep-ball passer. The Panthers were in the top five in deep-pass frequency and DVOA in 2012.

No, we can't blame the passer here, so we must blame the receivers, and there is plenty of blame to go around. Smith, LaFell, and Ginn each had at least 18 deep targets last year, and none even averaged 9.0 yards per target. Tight end Greg Olsen was no help either, averaging 6.3 yards on 18 deep targets of his own. (The league average on deep targets is 11.7 yards.) And none of those players was particularly young, either. Smith was 34 last season, Ginn 28, and LaFell 27. Smith is clearly declining, and we've probably seen the best of what

2014 Panthers Schedule

Week	Opp.	Week	Opp.	Week	Opp.
1	at TB	7	at GB	13	at MIN
2	DET	8	SEA	14	at NO
3	PIT	9	NO (Thu.)	15	TB
4	at BAL	10	at PHI (Mon.)	16	CLE
5	CHI	11	ATL	17	at ATL
6	at CIN	12	BYE		

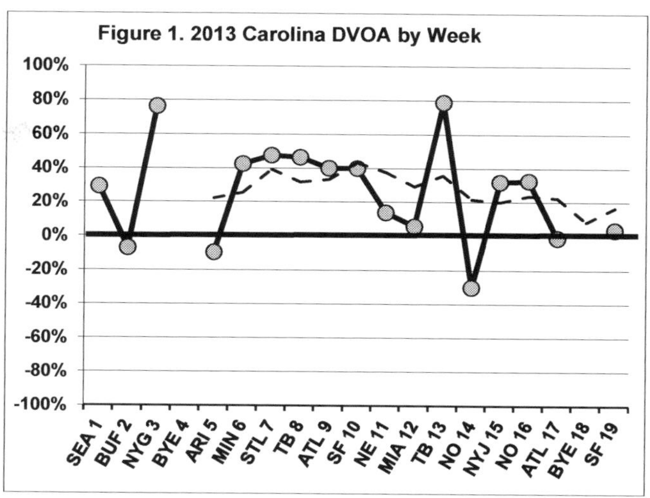

Ginn and LaFell had to offer too. And so Smith was released, a move that saved Carolina $7 million this season. He eventually joined the Ravens. LaFell was allowed to sign with the Patriots in free agency, while Ginn joined the Cardinals. Only one other wide receiver caught a pass for Carolina last year (Domenik Hixon, who had seven), and he was not re-signed after the season either. It's unusual to see a team this successful wipe out an entire position group like this, but each of the moves, in a vacuum, makes sense.

The Panthers replaced that group with some veteran free-agent signings of their own. Jerricho Cotchery, the leading receiver for the Jets many years ago, was just a slot receiver for the past few seasons in Pittsburgh, though he fared well in that role. By DVOA and DYAR, he actually had his best season in 2013, thanks largely to a career-high (and fairly fluky) ten touchdowns. Jason Avant had several productive seasons in Philadelphia, but he lacks the speed to survive in Chip Kelly's offense, finishing among the bottom 10 qualifying wideouts in DVOA and DYAR. Tiquan Underwood set a personal best in yards and DYAR with Tampa Bay last year, thanks in no small part to an 85-yard touchdown against Detroit that made up nearly 20 percent of his yardage.

It's not a sterling group, and with a combined age of 90, they're no younger than the Smith-Ginn-LaFell trio they're replacing. Can they solve the downfield passing problems? Cotchery had six receptions out of 15 deep targets last year; Avant, nine in 24. Those are better numbers than last year's Panthers, but hardly ideal. Underwood finished with nine receptions and one DPI in 14 targets, which is outstanding in a small sample size. Still, he has more drops (eight) than touchdowns (six) over the past three years, and if he was the answer to anyone's problems, he probably wouldn't be on his fourth team in the past five seasons.

Fortunately, there is a fourth option at receiver: Kelvin Benjamin, the 28th overall pick in this year's draft. Benjamin played only two seasons at Florida State, but twice finished in the top ten in the ACC in yards per catch, and led the conference in receiving touchdowns as a sophomore. A physical marvel at 6-foot-5 and 235 pounds, Benjamin should make a tantalizing target downfield and in the red zone. He doesn't have the best hands, and his limited agility won't help him in running routes or breaking tackles after the catch. Rob Rang of CBS Sports compared him to Plaxico Burress, certainly one of the better downfield threats of this century. Rookies, though, are never safe bets, especially not receivers. Between Benjamin's inexperience, Avant's plodding play, the unrepeatable nature of Cotchery's 2013 campaign, and Underwood, well, being Tiquan Underwood, the best-case scenario for this bunch is that they are just as good as last year's crew. And best-case scenarios rarely come to pass.

Speaking of coming to pass, that's what visiting teams in Carolina will do if the Panthers' changes in the secondary don't work out. Four of the top five defensive backs in snaps played—Captain Munnerlyn, Mike Mitchell, Quintin Mikell, and Drayton Florence—are no longer on the roster, though Mikell and Florence remain unsigned and could theoretically rejoin the team. (Of course, if the Panthers wanted them back, they probably would be signed by now.) Cornerback and safety are not fantasy positions like wide receiver, and so this turnover got much less attention than the departures on the other side of the ball. But these losses could hurt Carolina even more, because this is a team that is built on defense. A look at the individual charting numbers from last year would suggest that the Panthers were losing 80 percent of one of the better secondaries in the league.

Then again, maybe not. The Panthers play more deep zone and off-man coverage than almost any other team in football. By playing their defensive backs so far off the ball, they take away the big play, forcing opponents to march the length of the field to score, and giving the menacing front four more chances to put opposing quarterbacks on the ground. This is largely why they allowed the third-highest completion rate in the league, but the fourth-lowest average yards per completion. They also forced 126 "failed completions," 26 more than any other team.

It's a very forgiving scheme for defensive backs, one that rarely leaves them in one-on-one coverage against deeper pass patterns. It also leads to inflated individual pass-coverage numbers. The charting numbers for Carolina's cornerbacks say more about Charles Johnson and Greg Hardy than they do about Munnerlyn and Florence. When the pass rush got home before receivers could find seams in the zone, defenders were often able to break on the ball and make a play. When quarterbacks had time to throw, however, receivers had little trouble exploiting the cartoonishly large holes in Carolina's zones for big gains. All told, our game charters marked 91 passes by Carolina opponents as "Hole in Zone" (16 more than any other team), and 96 more were marked as "Uncovered" (28 more than any other team). Between those two numbers, nearly one-third of all passes (32.8 percent, to be precise) were listed with no defender in coverage. No other defense allowed even one-fourth of their passes to be thrown with no defender listed in coverage.

When one-third of opponents' passes end up going against air, there isn't much point in laying out big money to retain cornerbacks. It's better to go with cheap talent here and invest those resources elsewhere. So Carolina got frugal in the secondary too, letting Munnerlyn and Mitchell walk away and signing Antoine Cason and Thomas DeCoud to replace them.

The Panthers went into this offseason knowing they had to overhaul the receiving corps and the secondary, but the need to overhaul the offensive line was a bit of a surprise. Jordan Gross was still one of the better left tackles in football last season, and the Panthers were not expecting him to walk away from the game. Gross' retirement at the age of 34 started a domino effect that could result in new starters in up to four positions on the line. Gettleman did nothing to address the situation in free agency and very little in the draft, though he did add some college free agents when all was said and done. He did not, however, add a single player who cost more than the absolute bare minimum salary. (After OTAs, the Panthers did extend the contract of Nate Chandler, signing him to a three-year deal worth nearly $8 million, including $1.9 million in guarantees. Clearly they think he'll be the answer at left tackle.)

You can argue with Gettleman's moves from a talent perspective, but there's no doubt that he has saved the Panthers tons of cash. The five veteran departures (Smith, LaFell, Ginn, Munnerlyn, and Mitchell) received a total of $21.5 million in guarantees. Their five replacements (Cotchery, Avant, Underwood, Cason, and DeCoud) received just $3.3 million in guaranteed money. To put it another way, each of the departed players got more money *by himself* than the sum of the five guys who replaced them, except LaFell—who got "only" $3 million.

This is all very important, because a year from now the Panthers are going to need to do something with Cam Newton. The quarterback is currently on the books for 2015 with a cap number of $14.7 million. In all likelihood, Newton and the Panthers will sign a contract extension before that season starts, which will ensure Newton's long-term future with the club and also offer some short-term cap relief. On the downside, most onlookers project Newton to get somewhere around $18 million per season in the early years of his deal, with up to $50 million guaranteed. That's a lot of cash, and that's the biggest reason the Panthers had to play the tightwad this year.

Between the new holes on the roster and a difficult schedule, the Panthers seem like a longshot to make the playoffs. Most likely, the 2014 season will be about developing players for 2015. One year from now, Carolina will still have a dominant front seven and a developing franchise quarterback. They should have an emerging weapon at wide receiver, and they'll be in a better position to add talent at receiver, on the line, and in the secondary. And then they'll be ready for another run at a title.

Vince Verhei

2013 Panthers Stats by Week

Wk	vs.	W-L	PF	PA	YDF	YDA	TO	Total	Off	Def	ST
1	SEA	L	7	12	253	370	-1	29%	32%	-5%	-8%
2	at BUF	L	23	24	308	436	+1	-7%	7%	16%	2%
3	NYG	W	38	0	402	150	+1	76%	35%	-41%	1%
4	BYE										
5	at ARI	L	6	22	353	250	-1	-10%	-30%	-22%	-2%
6	at MIN	W	35	10	367	290	+2	42%	22%	-21%	0%
7	STL	W	30	15	282	317	+3	48%	16%	-29%	3%
8	at TB	W	31	13	324	297	+1	46%	43%	3%	6%
9	ATL	W	34	10	373	289	+2	40%	1%	-32%	7%
10	at SF	W	10	9	250	151	0	40%	-25%	-68%	-3%
11	NE	W	24	20	300	390	+2	14%	30%	15%	-1%
12	at MIA	W	20	16	295	332	0	6%	-4%	-12%	-2%
13	TB	W	27	6	426	206	0	79%	27%	-48%	3%
14	at NO	L	13	31	239	373	0	-30%	-21%	11%	1%
15	NYJ	W	30	20	392	297	+1	32%	40%	10%	2%
16	NO	W	17	13	222	365	+1	33%	-19%	-44%	8%
17	at ATL	W	21	20	283	307	-1	-1%	-21%	-20%	-1%
18	BYE										
19	SF	L	10	23	325	315	-2	4%	-2%	1%	7%

Trends and Splits

	Offense	Rank	Defense	Rank
Total DVOA	7.9%	10	-15.7%	3
Unadjusted VOA	5.5%	12	-14.6%	3
Weighted Trend	5.0%	11	-18.0%	3
Variance	6.5%	15	6.3%	20
Average Opponent	-4.0%	5	-0.9%	20
Passing	11.5%	14	-15.6%	3
Rushing	9.0%	4	-16.0%	6
First Down	8.8%	10	-18.5%	4
Second Down	-0.7%	17	-15.1%	6
Third Down	19.2%	7	-11.0%	8
First Half	6.7%	12	-23.1%	2
Second Half	9.3%	9	-8.4%	7
Red Zone	7.1%	14	-31.8%	2
Late and Close	8.0%	10	-4.0%	14

Five-Year Performance

Year	W-L	Pyth W	Est W	PF	PA	TO	Total	Rk	Off	Rk	Def	Rk	ST	Rk	Off AGL	Rk	Def AGL	Rk	Off Age	Rk	Def Age	Rk	ST Age	Rk
2009	8-8	8.2	8.3	315	308	+6	7.1%	15	-2.0%	20	-12.8%	6	-3.7%	29	28.9	20	39.8	25	27.4	14	26.1	28	25.9	25
2010	2-14	2.4	2.2	196	408	-8	-36.2%	31	-35.8%	32	-1.1%	16	-1.5%	22	39.8	27	35.2	24	25.7	30	25.4	32	25.0	32
2011	6-10	7.4	6.9	406	429	+1	-4.1%	20	18.2%	4	15.8%	32	-6.5%	32	47.6	29	61.5	32	27.2	15	25.3	32	26.0	25
2012	7-9	7.8	8.8	357	363	+1	5.5%	13	7.2%	10	-3.1%	11	-4.8%	29	23.1	10	53.0	27	27.1	15	25.7	28	26.0	19
2013	12-4	11.7	11.0	366	241	+11	24.6%	3	7.9%	10	-15.7%	3	1.0%	13	42.7	20	29.5	16	28.2	2	26.6	16	26.6	7

2013 Performance Based on Most Common Personnel Groups

CAR Offense					CAR Offense vs. Opponents				CAR Defense				CAR Defense vs. Opponents			
Pers	Freq	Yds	DVOA	Run%	Pers	Freq	Yds	DVOA	Pers	Freq	Yds	DVOA	Pers	Freq	Yds	DVOA
11	45%	6.0	20.7%	26%	4-3-4	29%	4.5	1.2%	Nickel Even	62%	5.1	-13.1%	11	56%	5.0	-10.3%
12	29%	4.9	7.0%	54%	Nickel Even	28%	6.8	42.7%	4-3-4	34%	5.0	-16.2%	21	17%	4.3	-42.7%
21	11%	5.0	-0.4%	41%	3-4-4	23%	4.8	3.5%	Nickel Odd	2%	4.6	-69.5%	12	14%	5.9	-7.6%
22	6%	3.9	-17.3%	85%	Nickel Odd	11%	5.6	-17.7%	3-4-4	1%	4.6	-9.9%	22	4%	5.0	-19.3%
13	4%	3.4	-4.3%	85%	Dime+	6%	3.3	-14.9%	Goal Line	1%	0.4	-36.7%	621	3%	5.6	-10.3%

Strategic Tendencies

Run/Pass		Rk	Formation		Rk	Pass Rush		Rk	Secondary		Rk	Strategy		Rk
Runs, first half	38%	17	Form: Single Back	61%	25	Rush 3	3.2%	25	4 DB	35%	20	Play action	29%	4
Runs, first down	52%	9	Form: Empty Back	3%	28	Rush 4	69.0%	6	5 DB	64%	5	Avg Box (Off)	6.54	4
Runs, second-long	32%	17	Pers: 3+ WR	47%	25	Rush 5	23.2%	17	6+ DB	0%	32	Avg Box (Def)	6.26	26
Runs, power sit.	66%	4	Pers: 4+ WR	1%	20	Rush 6+	4.5%	28	CB by Sides	68%	21	Offensive Pace	32.00	30
Runs, behind 2H	33%	4	Pers: 2+ TE/6+ OL	43%	6	Sacks by LB	13.6%	25	DB Blitz	14%	10	Defensive Pace	30.49	25
Pass, ahead 2H	41%	28	Shotgun/Pistol	61%	13	Sacks by DB	18.6%	2	Hole in Zone	21%	1	Go for it on 4th	1.20	7

Last year, Newton faced six or more pass rushers on 13.6 percent of passes—no other quarterback was above 12 percent—but Newton averaged 7.9 yards on these plays, seventh in the NFL. It was much better to send just five, as Newton averaged 4.1 yards per pass (31st) against a five-man pass rush. ⊜ The Panthers have led the league in yards per pass on running back screens for two straight seasons. They averaged 10.0 yards a year ago, with 65.8% DVOA (fifth in the NFL). ⊜ Along the same lines: Carolina averaged 11.8 yards after catch on passes thrown at or before the line of scrimmage (second to Philadelphia) and 3.7 yards after catch on passes thrown past the line of scrimmage (30th, ahead of only Tampa Bay and Chicago). ⊜ Spread out the Panthers, and you could run against them; try to power over their defensive line, and you were in trouble. Carolina allowed 4.7 yards per carry and -3.3% DVOA against running backs in one-back sets, but just 3.2 yards per carry and -36.8% DVOA against running backs in two-back sets. ⊜ Surprisingly, despite the huge year from Greg Hardy and the addition of the rookie defensive tackles, the Panthers actually blitzed more often (27.7 percent of passes) than the year before (19.7 percent of passes). One big change was that defensive-back blitzes nearly doubled, and the Panthers had a league-leading 11 sacks by defensive backs after zero in 2012. Oddly, Charles Godfrey is the only one of the defensive backs who had a sack for last year's Panthers who is still on the roster going into 2014. ⊜ Those defensive back blitzes were a big part of the Panthers becoming a much better team when big-blitzing six or more defenders. After getting killed on big blitzes in 2011 and 2012, the Panthers allowed just 4.4 yards per play when big-blitzing last year. They allowed a league-leading 3.8 yards per play when sending at least one defensive back. ⊜ For the second straight year, offenses threw to their running backs more often against Carolina than against any other defense. (Obviously, a small part of this is sharing a division with New Orleans, but neither Tampa Bay nor Atlanta is also in the top five.) ⊜ The Panthers somehow committed just one penalty on a kickoff all year, an unnecessary roughness call on Jordan Senn in the Week 5 game against Arizona.

Passing

Player	DYAR	DVOA	Plays	NtYds	Avg	YAC	C%	TD	Int
C.Newton	421	1.7%	513	3040	5.9	5.5	62.1%	24	13

Rushing

Player	DYAR	DVOA	Plays	Yds	Avg	TD	Fum	Suc
D.Williams	126	7.2%	201	843	4.2	3	1	43%
M.Tolbert	86	9.0%	101	361	3.6	6	0	50%
C.Newton	102	5.7%	100	597	6.0	6	2	-
J.Stewart	2	-7.4%	48	180	3.8	0	1	48%
K.Barner	-14	-67.2%	6	7	1.2	0	0	0%

Receiving

Player	DYAR	DVOA	Plays	Ctch	Yds	Y/C	YAC	TD	C%
S.Smith*	74	-3.7%	110	64	745	11.6	2.8	4	58%
B.LaFell*	44	-6.2%	85	49	620	12.7	5.2	5	58%
T.Ginn*	65	0.3%	68	36	556	15.4	5.9	5	53%
D.Hixon*	11	2.1%	9	7	55	7.9	1.3	1	78%
J.Cotchery	*235*	*26.2%*	*76*	*46*	*607*	*13.2*	*4.7*	*10*	*61%*
J.Avant	*-68*	*-24.5%*	*76*	*38*	*447*	*11.8*	*2.1*	*2*	*50%*
T.Underwood	*133*	*23.6%*	*45*	*24*	*440*	*18.3*	*4.3*	*4*	*53%*
J.Webb	*-25*	*-42.6%*	*11*	*5*	*33*	*6.6*	*0.6*	*0*	*45%*
G.Olsen	83	3.8%	111	73	816	11.2	4.5	6	66%
E.Dickson	*-10*	*-10.8%*	*43*	*25*	*273*	*10.9*	*4.0*	*1*	*58%*
De.Williams	57	16.0%	36	26	336	12.9	14.3	1	72%
M.Tolbert	77	29.0%	32	27	184	6.8	7.1	2	84%
J.Stewart	18	30.1%	7	7	44	6.3	6.0	0	100%

Offensive Line

Player	Pos	Age	GS	Snaps	Pen	Sk	Pass	Run	Player	Pos	Age	GS	Snaps	Pen	Sk	Pass	Run
Ryan Kalil	C	29	16/16	1016	3	2.5	6.5	2.0	Nate Chandler	RG	25	16/9	535	1	3.5	14.0	2.0
Byron Bell	RT	25	16/14	1014	4	7.5	23.0	3.0	Chris Scott	RG	27	10/8	499	1	0.0	4.0	2.5
Jordan Gross*	LT	34	16/16	1003	1	5.0	15.0	4.0	Amini Silatolu	LG	26	3/3	170	1	0.0	0.0	0.0
Travelle Wharton*	LG	33	16/12	841	3	0.0	7.5	5.5									

Year	Yards	ALY	Rk	Power	Rk	Stuff	Rk	2nd Lev	Rk	Open Field	Rk	Sacks	ASR	Rk	Short	Long	F-Start	Cont.
2011	5.30	4.32	5	71%	4	17%	6	1.38	5	1.40	1	35	7.2%	21	8	24	14	32
2012	3.88	3.49	30	75%	1	23%	26	1.08	22	0.72	19	36	7.6%	21	2	21	17	25
2013	3.87	3.91	14	72%	8	19%	14	1.04	22	0.54	25	43	8.2%	25	10	21	9	25
2013 ALY by direction:			*Left End 4.50 (7)*			*Left Tackle 3.69 (22)*			*Mid/Guard 3.79 (23)*			*Right Tackle 4.23 (9)*			*Right End 3.89 (13)*			

Jordan Gross, one of the top left tackles in football, surprised the Panthers by calling it a career in February, and the Panthers surprised everyone by not making a move in free agency or the draft to try to fill his spot. General manager David Gettleman explained why quite succinctly in an interview with Bryan Strickland of the team's website: he didn't like any of the available options any more than the options he already had on the roster. The early favorite to take over for Gross was Byron Bell, who joined Carolina in 2011 as an undrafted free agent out of New Mexico (where he played on the left side of the line), then started 41 games at right tackle over the next three seasons. Other options to compete with Bell (or take his old job at right tackle) are Nate Chandler, a former defensive lineman who started eight unimpressive games at guard last season, and 28-year-old Garry Williams, who started 11 games at right tackle in 2010, but has started only ten games since due to a myriad of ankle injuries. Chandler's contract extension makes it clear the Panthers expect him to start at one of the tackle spots.

Inside, All-Pro center Ryan Kalil remains the rock of the Panthers' line. Amini Silatolu, a 2012 second-rounder, should return at left guard after a knee injury limited him to three games last year. The right guard spot remains a mystery, especially if Chandler wins one of the tackle spots. Travelle Wharton spent his third straight offseason as an unrestricted free agent, and said that he might join Gross on the golf course. His retirement could open a spot for Trai Turner, a third-round rookie out of LSU, who looks better as a run blocker than he does as a pass protector.

Cam Newton escapes more sacks than any other quarterback in the NFL, but he also creates sacks with his tendency to hang on to the ball and look for the big play. The Panthers are the only team in the league to give up at least 20 long sacks in each of last three years.

Defensive Front Seven

			Overall								vs. Run					Pass Rush			
Defensive Line	Age	Pos	G	Snaps	Plays	TmPct	Rk	Stop	Dfts	BTkl	Runs	St%	Rk	RuYd	Rk	Sack	Hit	Hur	Tips
Star Lotulelei	25	DT	16	601	42	5.3%	37	39	14	2	35	91%	7	1.0	4	3.0	1	10.5	0
Kawann Short	25	DT	16	520	31	3.9%	68	25	11	2	24	75%	51	2.1	39	1.5	9	12.0	1
Dwan Edwards	33	DT	11	334	19	3.5%	75	14	5	0	13	69%	66	2.5	54	3.0	5	8.0	0
Colin Cole	34	DT	15	309	15	2.0%	--	13	2	0	12	92%	--	1.8	--	1.0	1	2.0	0
Drake Nevis	*25*	*DT*	*12*	*270*	*15*	*2.3%*	*--*	*12*	*2*	*1*	*12*	*92%*	*--*	*1.8*	*--*	*0.0*	*0*	*4.0*	*0*

			Overall								vs. Run					Pass Rush			
Edge Rushers	Age	Pos	G	Snaps	Plays	TmPct	Rk	Stop	Dfts	BTkl	Runs	St%	Rk	RuYd	Rk	Sack	Hit	Hur	Tips
Greg Hardy	26	DE	16	872	58	7.3%	14	48	26	4	36	78%	30	2.8	52	15.0	16	33.0	1
Charles Johnson	28	DE	14	718	31	4.4%	60	28	19	1	18	83%	21	1.6	13	11.0	6	26.5	0
Mario Addison	27	DE	16	259	13	1.6%	--	7	4	0	6	17%	--	6.5	--	2.5	5	11.0	0
Frank Alexander	25	DE	12	230	17	2.8%	--	16	3	0	13	92%	--	2.6	--	1.0	0	5.0	2
Wes Horton	24	DE	10	169	8	1.6%	--	4	3	0	5	40%	--	2.8	--	2.0	0	0.0	0

			Overall								Pass Rush			vs. Run					vs. Pass						
Linebackers	Age	Pos	G	Snaps	Plays	TmPct	Rk	Stop	Dfts	BTkl	Sack	Hit	Hur	Runs	St%	Rk	RuYd	Rk	Tgts	Suc%	Rk	AdjYd	Rk	PD	Int
Luke Kuechly	23	MLB	16	989	163	20.4%	3	88	34	13	2.0	0	4	82	60%	58	3.5	50	48	58%	19	5.8	17	8	4
Thomas Davis	31	OLB	16	988	129	16.2%	18	68	37	5	4.0	1	9	45	56%	69	6.4	81	52	61%	13	4.9	9	7	2
Chase Blackburn	31	OLB	13	199	23	3.5%	--	14	2	2	0.0	0	1	19	63%	--	2.4	--	5	41%	--	5.4	--	1	0

Year	Yards	ALY	Rk	Power	Rk	Stuff	Rk	2nd Level	Rk	Open Field	Rk	Sacks	ASR	Rk	Short	Long
2011	5.00	4.68	32	64%	18	17%	23	1.47	31	1.08	26	31	6.7%	16	4	13
2012	4.45	4.30	23	66%	23	16%	29	1.23	24	0.88	22	39	7.8%	5	9	20
2013	4.07	3.65	9	74%	27	22%	8	1.19	27	0.83	23	60	9.2%	2	20	11
2013 ALY by direction:			*Left End 3.69 (16)*			*Left Tackle 3.36 (5)*			*Mid/Guard 3.97 (18)*			*Right Tackle 2.42 (1)*			*Right End 2.12 (1)*	

If the Panthers are going to return to the playoffs this year, these are the men who will get them there. They were arguably the league's top front seven last season, they're all back for another year, they have a number of young players who are still developing, and they even added talent with second-round pick Kony Ealy out of Missouri. The only concerns are off the field. Greg Hardy was arrested on domestic violence charges just two months after signing his $13.1 million franchise player contract. The case is ongoing, and the threat of a league suspension still hangs over Hardy's head. Backup end Frank Alexander has been suspended for the first four games of the year due to a substance abuse violation.

At full strength, though, this unit is terrifying. It starts on the outside. Only eight players have at least 10 sacks in each of the last two seasons, and the Panthers have two of them in Hardy and Charles Johnson. Star Lotulelei, the 14th overall pick last year, collected 10 rushing Defeats, tied for third among defensive tackles. Fellow rookie Kawann Short, a second-rounder out of Purdue, technically didn't start a game, but still saw more playing time than veterans Colin Cole and Dwan Edwards. Cole, a prototypical space-eater, was out of the league for two years after multiple ankle injuries, and in fact he was the one who called the Panthers last year looking for work. They signed him to a one-year deal, and he entered the starting lineup after Edwards suffered a hamstring injury, playing well enough to earn another one-year deal for 2014. He was still getting first-team snaps in early OTAs. That would leave a second-string line of Alexander (a fourth-rounder who was our 2012 SackSEER sleeper and has shown flashes of pass-rush ability as a part-time player), Edwards (third among tackles in percentage of his team's plays in 2012), Short, and Ealy, who finished third in projected sacks in this year's SackSEER forecast. That quartet would be better than the starters on a handful of teams in the league, but they're all bench players in Carolina.

We've been praising the team's front seven for more than 300 words now, and we haven't even gotten to their best player. Luke Kuechly made 20.4 percent of Carolina's plays, exactly matching his figure from 2012, when he was the first rookie since Patrick Willis to lead the league in that category. Thomas Davis played in all 16 games for the first time since 2008 and had more Defeats than any defender in the league other than Lavonte David. Both Kuechly and Davis excel in pass coverage, especially coming up to tackle receivers on dumpoffs. Passes thrown to receivers behind the line of scrimmage averaged just 3.8 yards per play against Carolina, with only 7.0 yards after the catch per reception, both the lowest rates in the league.

Defensive Secondary

			Overall									vs. Run					vs. Pass									
Secondary	**Age**	**Pos**	**G**	**Snaps**	**Plays**	**TmPct**	**Rk**	**Stop**	**Dfts**	**BTkl**	**Runs**	**St%**	**Rk**	**RuYd**	**Rk**	**Tgts**	**Tgt%**	**Rk**	**Dist**	**Suc%**	**Rk**	**AdjYd**	**Rk**	**PD**	**Int**
Captain Munnerlyn*	26	CB	16	970	86	10.8%	13	47	18	4	22	50%	25	4.4	8	70	16.8%	8	12.6	60%	10	7.8	47	10	2
Mike Mitchell*	27	SS	15	899	73	9.8%	41	30	13	12	26	38%	40	9.1	66	28	7.1%	26	15.5	61%	28	5.8	17	7	4
Melvin White	24	CB	15	679	49	6.5%	68	22	10	7	6	50%	25	6.7	36	57	19.4%	25	9.4	55%	33	5.9	4	5	2
Quintin Mikell*	34	FS	14	672	64	9.2%	52	30	7	8	32	44%	30	6.3	26	25	8.5%	46	8.6	52%	46	7.4	46	5	0
Drayton Florence*	34	CB	14	584	35	5.0%	86	18	8	0	5	40%	44	9.6	63	50	19.8%	28	12.7	63%	3	6.1	6	8	2
Robert Lester	26	SS	12	294	22	3.7%	--	7	2	2	5	40%	--	9.0	--	8	6.4%	--	23.1	62%	--	4.5	--	4	3
Josh Thomas	25	CB	13	268	26	4.0%	--	11	3	1	9	56%	--	8.2	--	29	24.8%	--	14.9	55%	--	9.3	--	2	1
Thomas DeCoud	*29*	*FS*	*15*	*890*	*65*	*8.5%*	*62*	*20*	*6*	*10*	*37*	*46%*	*27*	*9.3*	*68*	*28*	*7.8%*	*36*	*11.0*	*31%*	*76*	*11.2*	*72*	*1*	*0*
Roman Harper	*32*	*SS*	*9*	*370*	*38*	*8.9%*	*--*	*19*	*7*	*0*	*19*	*58%*	*--*	*7.0*	*--*	*16*	*10.8%*	*--*	*10.9*	*54%*	*--*	*7.8*	*--*	*1*	*1*

Year	Pass D Rank	vs. #1 WR	Rk	vs. #2 WR	Rk	vs. Other WR	Rk	vs. TE	Rk	vs. RB	Rk
2011	29	26.5%	27	12.7%	22	-21.7%	8	40.2%	32	20.8%	27
2012	12	-4.9%	15	10.1%	26	-1.9%	15	-0.1%	19	-6.9%	13
2013	3	-2.3%	15	-20.0%	4	-28.1%	2	-4.0%	12	4.8%	18

There's not much point in talking about the guys who left, so let's talk about who's still here, and who's new in town. The only two incumbents in Carolina's starting lineup, cornerback Melvin White and strong safety Robert Lester, were both undrafted rookie free agents a year ago. White's charting numbers look good, but we've already discussed how they were influenced by scheme and circumstance. White's were influenced further because he saw time at nickelback and rarely had to cover receivers running deep routes. Antoine Cason enters camp as the likely starter at one corner. A former starter in San Diego, Cason's Adjusted Success Rate fell from 55 percent in 2010 to 49 percent the next year, and 40 percent in 2012. Last year, he could barely get on the field for Arizona, seeing only 17 targets despite playing in all 16 games. There is also Charles Godfrey, who played corner at Iowa, then moved to safety upon joining the Panthers in 2008. His 2013 season ended after just two games due to a torn Achilles tendon. Rivera has said that he likes Godfrey's potential as a nickelback. His background at safety should let him cover receivers while still offering effective run support.

Lester started four games last year, Weeks 3, 5, 12, and 13, intercepting a pass in two of those starts. Carolina's average defensive DVOA in those contests: -31.3%. Correlation does not equal causation, but it's safe to say his presence wasn't costing the team games or anything. New free safety Thomas DeCoud, late of Atlanta, has become a regular in some of Football Outsiders' leaderboards—unfortunately, they're the leaderboards for broken tackles. He's one of three players with at least 10 broken tackles in both of the last two seasons. (The others are Earl Thomas and Malcolm Jenkins. Thomas, obviously, makes enough big plays to atone for his missed tackles. DeCoud and Jenkins don't, which is why they both switched teams this offseason.) Broken tackles could hurt DeCoud badly in the Panthers' scheme, where safeties are usually asked to play as deep as possible, then come up and tackle receivers. The Panthers also signed Roman Harper away from the Saints. He was reduced to a part-time role for New Orleans last year, but that certainly doesn't mean he won't make key contributions to this defense—as long as nobody expects those contributions to come in man coverage.

Special Teams

Year	DVOA	Rank	FG/XP	Rank	Net Kick	Rank	Kick Ret	Rank	Net Punt	Rank	Punt Ret	Rank	Hidden	Rank
2011	-6.5%	32	-7.6	31	-0.8	21	2.2	10	-19.6	32	-6.7	24	6.7	8
2012	-4.8%	29	-6.3	30	4.6	8	-6.9	29	-13.4	28	-1.9	17	-15.5	31
2013	1.0%	13	2.4	14	5.0	8	-3.1	20	1.6	16	-1.0	17	-3.8	21

Graham Gano is the Panthers' secret weapon. A league-best 78 percent of his kickoffs resulted in touchbacks last season. Kicking in Carolina certainly helps, but our numbers account for weather, and Gano has still ranked among the top four kickoff men in each of the past three seasons. His field-goal kicking also bounced back after a dreadful 2012 season. (Olindo Mare was responsible for the even-more-dreadful 2011 season.) And speaking of bouncing back, Brad Nortman was the NFL's worst punter by our numbers in 2012, but made the top five last year. Carolina's coverage teams weren't very good, but Nortman and (especially) Gano were so good that they were rarely needed. Carolina opponents had a total of 54 returns on punts and kickoffs, lowest figure in the league.

Ted Ginn's departure leaves an opening at both punt and kickoff returner. First man up for the job: Kenjon Barner, a sixth-round pick a year ago, who scored one touchdown of each variety in his career with the Oregon Ducks. Kealoha Pilares returned kickoffs for the Panthers in 2011, with a 25.7-yard average and one touchdown.

Chicago Bears

2013 Record: 8-8	**Total DVOA:** 6.6% (11th)	**2014 Mean Projection:** 9.0 wins	**On the Clock (0-4):** 4%
Pythagorean Wins: 7.3 (20th)	**Offense:** 13.3% (6th)	**Postseason Odds:** 50.4%	**Mediocrity (5-7):** 19%
Snap-Weighted Age: 27.4 (3rd)	**Defense:** 8.7% (25th)	**Super Bowl Odds:** 9.7%	**Playoff Contender (8-10):** 49%
Average Opponent: -3.7% (27th)	**Special Teams:** 2.0% (11th)	**Proj. Avg. Opponent:** 1.3% (13th)	**Super Bowl Contender (11+):** 27%

2013: It was like the sack of Rome, but with fewer Visigoths and more Benny Cunningham.

2014: No more easy points in the paint.

The Bears had an outstanding defense from the founding of the NFL in 1920 until roughly 3 p.m. on October 20, 2013.

That's an oversimplification, of course. The Bears defense was not uniformly awesome for 90 years. Heck, it was pretty bad as recently as the late 1990s, during the Dave Wannstedt "Jim Flanagan is our star" era. And the cracks in the 2013 defense were evident before Lance Briggs got injured against the Redskins. But the thru-line of Bears history goes from George to Butkus to Singletary to Urlacher, from Halas to Ditka to Lovie, and when that line snapped in mid-October, it was a zeitgeist-shattering event for both Bears fans and NFL fans. Suddenly, the mighty Bears were vulnerable to runs up the gut. Seeing Rams no-names Zac Stacy and Benny Cunningham combine for nearly 200 yards against the Bears was like seeing a stampede of hippos down Broadway. "Now there's somethin' ya don't see every day," you mutter, then swear off booze forever.

The collapse of the Bears defense is easy to explain. Brian Urlacher retired, not quite voluntarily, and the team's replacement strategy involved oft-injured former Broncos middle linebacker D.J. Williams, rookie Jon Bostic, and a lot of finger crossing. While Urlacher was deemed too old to rock 'n' roll, Briggs (33 years old), Julius Peppers (33), and Charles Tillman (32) all retained their key defensive roles. With Lovie Smith ousted and on walkabout, new head coach Marc Trestman hired Mel Tucker to run the defense, and Tucker's Lovie Lite system proved easy for defenders to learn and easier for opponents to figure out. Early-season injuries to Henry Melton and Stephen Paea—a great young defensive tackle and a good one, respectively—were the foundational cracks that proved that the Bears defense was no longer up to code.

Melton and Paea's unexpected injuries were followed by more predictable injuries to Williams, Briggs, and Tillman. The depth-strapped Bears were suddenly playing multiple defenders out of position. Peppers, clearly on the decline, began sliding from defensive end to tackle on some snaps. Corey Wootton, a 270-pound end, saw even more action on the inside. Shea McClellin, a tweener best suited to a situational linebacker role, became a full-time, hand-in-the-dirt end. The rookie Bostic did not stand a chance with such a mixed-up, undersized defensive line in front of him, and with Tillman gone, Tucker could not load the box without worrying about his secondary. The cruel scheduling harpies showed no mercy, subjecting the Bears to Adrian Peterson and Shady McCoy when they were at their weakest. The Bears gave up over 150 rushing yards seven times in their final nine games. Their single-game run-defense DVOA wavered from 10.1% worse than league average to 80.2% (the Rams game) before a Week 17 reprieve against the Packers.

Obviously, something had to be done to restore balance to the cosmos. The Bears aggressively attacked their defensive problems in the offseason. Peppers was jettisoned, and Melton defected to Dallas when the Bears decided to spend their not-so-ample cap bucks elsewhere. In their place, the Bears acquired Lamarr Houston and Jared Allen, making them somewhat younger and more talented on the line while still minding the budget. The draft added vital puzzle piece Kyle Fuller in the secondary and even more insulation on the defensive line: tackles Ego Ferguson and Will Sutton, taken in the second and third rounds after Fuller.

Houston is the key acquisition among the free agents. He is a 300-pound matchup headache at defensive end with a run defender's mentality. He has great quickness for his size and gets inside his blocker well, allowing him to make more tackles on running plays than the typical defensive end. The Raiders used Houston at right end because they were terrible and had no better options, but at left end Houston can provide all the run support the Bears need, plus enough pass-rush capability to cause mismatches.

Houston may be the most vital piece, but Allen was the biggest name. The former Vikings All-Pro turned 32 in April, making him two years younger than Peppers, and is coming off an 11.5-sack season where he took over a handful of games (Eagles, Steelers). Allen became expendable in Minnesota because the Vikings are in the process of a much more invasive overhaul than the Bears, and Allen is unlikely to be around by the time the Vikings are good again. In Chicago, Allen joins another aging former star as part of the defensive line rebuild: Jay (now "Jeremiah") Ratliff joined the Bears during the Zac Stacy Crisis with something to prove after Jerry Jones tried to balance the Cowboys budget on his back. Ratliff is only a wave player at this point, but Paea is back, and newcomer Willie Young joins returnee Israel Idonije to give Tucker ample mix-and-match opportunities along the line. Factor in both Sutton and Ego the Living Planet, and the Bears have gone from having one of the thinnest lines in the league to one of the deepest.

2014 Bears Schedule

Week	Opp.	Week	Opp.	Week	Opp.
1	BUF	7	MIA	13	at DET (Thu.)
2	at SF	8	at NE	14	DAL (Thu.)
3	at NYJ (Mon.)	9	BYE	15	NO
4	GB	10	at GB	16	DET
5	at CAR	11	MIN	17	at MIN
6	at ATL	12	TB		

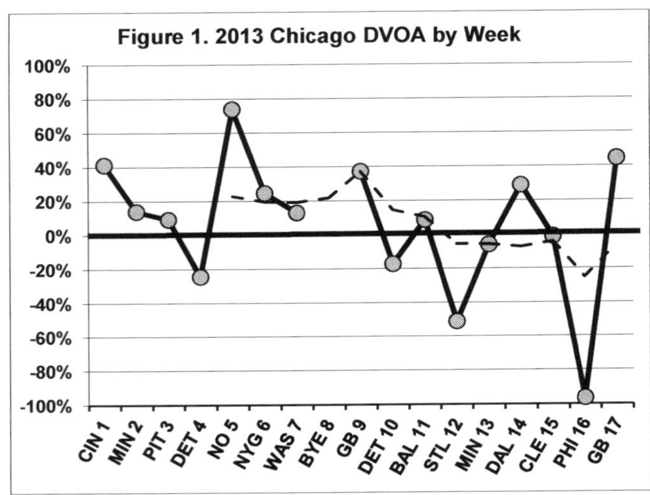

Figure 1. 2013 Chicago DVOA by Week

Behind the front four, the Bears are counting on familiar faces like Tillman, Briggs, and Williams to rebound and provide a year of moderate health and effectiveness until Fuller and young veterans like McClellin, Bostic, and Chris Conte can assume leadership roles. It's an imperfect solution, and the plans for succession are not perfect. Fuller is a natural replacement for Tillman, for example, but there is no obvious Briggs surrogate in the pipeline, and both McClellin and the safeties have some rebounding to do after regressing during the calamities of 2013. But the Bears did the best they could to reconstruct the defense with limited resources. The Bears' defense will not achieve 1985 or 2005 heights by a longshot, but it should be capable enough to support the team's other paradigm-obliterating unit: an efficient, creative, downright modern offense.

The professorial Marc Trestman did not try to install CFL strategies from his last job or outdated West Coast offense principles from his days with the 49ers. Trestman's devil was in the details. He spoke suspiciously like someone who read and understood analytical football research, explaining his clock management and down-and-distance strategies by citing probabilities and percentages. There was nothing superficially over-engineered about his scheme, except perhaps for his Alshon Jeffery end-around fetish, but the 2013 Bears appeared to be roughly 87.7 percent less hammer-headed about problem solving than they were during the Mike Tice administration.

Trestman did not try to solve the protection issues that plagued the Bears for half a decade by keeping everyone in to block so Jay Cutler had no one to throw to (the Tice solution). Instead, he fixed the line, with veteran free agents Jermon Bushrod and Matt Slauson taking over on Roberto Garza's left and rookies Kyle Long and Jordan Mills handling the right. Trestman and offensive coordinator Aaron Kromer (a Sean Payton disciple) mixed in some short passing and realistic blocking assignments for the youngsters, and suddenly the Bears were fifth in the NFL in Adjusted Sack Rate.

Jay Cutler also responded well to Trestman's soothing lectures, as well as fewer sacks and the sudden appearance of more than two receivers per passing play. Cutler's completion percentage, yards per attempt, and touchdown rate all improved. His interception rate also spiked, but there were fewer Smokin' Jay moments than usual, even though Cutler suddenly found himself going into shootout mode to beat the likes of the Browns. Josh McCown was even more efficient than Cutler, but those who are fooled by 34-year-old career backups with 13:1 touchdown-interception ratios should be forced to watch Damon Huard and Todd Collins play catch for all of eternity.

The entire Bears offense returns intact, with a full year of Trestman-Kromer science between its ears, so the formula for Bears 2014 success is obvious, though it is unfamiliar in a Bears context. The offense must lead the way. The defense must approach league average. The Packers are vulnerable, the Lions and Vikings pivoting, so a division crown is just a 25-touchdown Cutler season and a series of 27-20 victories away. It's plausible, even likely, but it is not 100 percent desirable: an NFC North title would be swell, but the Bears as they are currently fashioned would be Seahawks-Niners paste in the playoffs.

Last year's defensive collapse left general manager Phil Emery with two semi-conflicting offseason goals: improve a civic embarrassment of a run defense in the short term, and prepare for the real start of the post-Urlacher-Briggs-Peanut era in the not-so-short term. It required a delicate juggling act. Some of the moves were wise and timely: signing Houston, extending Cutler's contract to free cap space and set organizational priorities. Other moves are apparent stopgaps. Tillman is back for one more tour but was displeased about a potential move to safety until the team appeased him with a mentor role for Fuller. Williams and Ratliff are discount rentals at this point, and Allen will not be around forever. Tucker was allegedly on the chopping block, though his coaching performance was hard to evaluate when everyone was playing hurt or out of position. Retaining him was either evidence of patient wisdom, or like the Ratliff and Williams re-signing, a holding pattern decision.

By the time Brandon Marshall received his own restructured contract in mid-May, Emery's approach to the salary cap became more comprehensible. The Bears crammed bonus money and a substantial cap hit into 2014 for Cutler and Marshall, keeping the two most important players on the team happy without causing many long-term problems. Allen's deal is a strict two-year lease with obvious phony-baloney money afterward, while Houston's contract is more back-loaded. There is a long-term budgetary logic in place, and if everything falls into place, the 2016 Bears could have a strong-and-affordable Houston-Bostic-Fuller-etc. defense paired with a contentedly wealthy Cutler and Marshall, protected by the rebuilt line on the other side of the ball.

Everything rarely falls into place in the NFL, but Emery, like Trestman, has an apparent knack for long-range planning. The Bears addressed both short- and long-term needs aggressively and creatively. The team is poised to be competitive in 2014, and the blueprint for the immediate future is much more apparent than it was in December. The Bears bottomed out defensively in the second half of 2013, but they regrouped as efficiently as a modern NFL team can. They may not be ready to win with defense again, but they can do one more thing Bears fans will find highly unusual: they can win with balance.

Mike Tanier

2013 Bears Stats by Week

Wk	vs.	W-L	PF	PA	YDF	YDA	TO	Total	Off	Def	ST
1	CIN	W	24	21	323	340	+2	41%	39%	0%	3%
2	MIN	W	31	30	411	350	-1	14%	-1%	-11%	4%
3	at PIT	W	40	23	258	459	+5	9%	-14%	-19%	4%
4	at DET	L	32	40	417	387	-1	-24%	-19%	-12%	-17%
5	NO	L	18	26	434	347	-1	74%	57%	-11%	5%
6	NYG	W	27	21	372	355	+3	25%	49%	23%	-1%
7	at WAS	L	41	45	359	499	0	13%	26%	39%	25%
8	BYE										
9	at GB	W	27	20	442	312	+1	37%	14%	-29%	-6%
10	DET	L	19	21	338	364	0	-17%	-5%	20%	7%
11	BAL	W	23	20	319	317	+2	9%	1%	-5%	3%
12	at STL	L	21	42	424	406	-3	-51%	8%	49%	-10%
13	at MIN	L	20	23	480	496	0	-6%	6%	6%	-6%
14	DAL	W	45	28	490	328	0	29%	71%	38%	-4%
15	at CLE	W	38	31	440	366	-1	-1%	12%	29%	16%
16	at PHI	L	11	54	257	514	-1	-97%	-49%	52%	5%
17	GB	L	28	33	345	473	0	44%	29%	-9%	6%

Trends and Splits

	Offense	Rank	Defense	Rank
Total DVOA	13.3%	6	8.7%	25
Unadjusted VOA	14.0%	5	9.6%	25
Weighted Trend	13.8%	6	16.6%	31
Variance	9.4%	26	6.6%	23
Average Opponent	2.4%	23	-1.4%	21
Passing	28.0%	7	7.5%	17
Rushing	1.4%	15	9.8%	32
First Down	4.7%	13	12.1%	27
Second Down	13.5%	9	-0.2%	13
Third Down	31.6%	3	15.3%	26
First Half	7.3%	10	1.1%	18
Second Half	18.8%	6	16.4%	29
Red Zone	11.8%	11	-2.9%	14
Late and Close	28.4%	3	12.3%	28

Five-Year Performance

Year	W-L	Pyth W	Est W	PF	PA	TO	Total	Rk	Off	Rk	Def	Rk	ST	Rk	Off AGL	Rk	Def AGL	Rk	Off Age	Rk	Def Age	Rk	ST Age	Rk
2009	7-9	6.7	6.1	327	375	-6	-18.1%	25	-19.7%	28	3.0%	21	4.7%	4	8.2	4	42.7	26	26.9	20	27.0	20	26.8	12
2010	11-5	9.5	8.3	334	286	+4	2.4%	14	-15.8%	28	-10.9%	4	7.4%	1	6.8	3	5.5	2	27.1	21	28.3	5	27.6	1
2011	8-8	8.3	7.3	353	341	+2	1.3%	15	-21.4%	30	-14.2%	4	8.5%	1	42.2	24	12.4	6	26.9	18	28.0	4	26.5	9
2012	10-6	10.8	11.0	375	277	+20	20.5%	6	-10.9%	26	-26.7%	1	4.7%	6	17.6	8	13.6	4	27.2	12	27.9	4	26.9	6
2013	8-8	7.3	9.2	445	478	+5	6.6%	11	13.3%	6	8.7%	25	2.0%	11	6.9	1	55.7	30	27.5	8	27.3	10	27.5	1

2013 Performance Based on Most Common Personnel Groups

CHI Offense					CHI Offense vs. Opponents				CHI Defense				CHI Defense vs. Opponents			
Pers	Freq	Yds	DVOA	Run%	Pers	Freq	Yds	DVOA	Pers	Freq	Yds	DVOA	Pers	Freq	Yds	DVOA
11	49%	6.4	32.5%	26%	Nickel Even	48%	6.6	37.0%	4-3-4	50%	6.2	6.7%	11	43%	6.0	5.4%
12	16%	6.5	10.2%	23%	4-3-4	22%	5.7	10.5%	Nickel Even	48%	6.4	10.4%	12	24%	6.7	8.1%
21	15%	5.9	17.5%	61%	3-4-4	16%	5.5	-8.6%	Nickel Odd	1%	9.2	43.4%	21	18%	6.5	7.3%
611	7%	8.2	48.8%	37%	Nickel Odd	6%	5.8	-16.3%					22	5%	5.2	13.7%
610	5%	5.0	6.7%	59%	Dime+	6%	8.2	60.8%					20	3%	8.1	14.9%
													13	3%	7.3	13.9%

Strategic Tendencies

Run/Pass		Rk	Formation		Rk	Pass Rush		Rk	Secondary		Rk	Strategy		Rk
Runs, first half	34%	28	Form: Single Back	74%	13	Rush 3	1.0%	31	4 DB	51%	6	Play action	20%	17
Runs, first down	43%	26	Form: Empty Back	4%	25	Rush 4	66.5%	8	5 DB	49%	15	Avg Box (Off)	6.24	24
Runs, second-long	36%	11	Pers: 3+ WR	54%	21	Rush 5	21.3%	23	6+ DB	0%	30	Avg Box (Def)	6.62	1
Runs, power sit.	48%	25	Pers: 4+ WR	0%	31	Rush 6+	11.2%	8	CB by Sides	70%	19	Offensive Pace	31.21	25
Runs, behind 2H	32%	5	Pers: 2+ TE/6+ OL	35%	11	Sacks by LB	35.5%	15	DB Blitz	13%	13	Defensive Pace	29.73	15
Pass, ahead 2H	47%	16	Shotgun/Pistol	60%	15	Sacks by DB	0.0%	29	Hole in Zone	16%	3	Go for it on 4th	0.95	13

Chicago used six offensive linemen on 16 percent of plays last year—no other NFL team was above 10 percent—and they were excellent on these plays. In general, teams pass about one-fourth of the time when using an extra lineman, but the Bears passed on 47 percent of these plays. The Bears averaged 6.2 yards per play; of the ten teams to use an extra lineman most often, the closest in yards per play was Atlanta at 5.0. Chicago only had 2.8% DVOA with the extra lineman, but that number is depressed due to turnovers (two interceptions, two fumbles). Chicago was much better running from single-back formations (4.6 yards per carry, 3.3% DVOA) than from two-back formations (4.0 yards per carry, -17.5% DVOA). Despite a new coaching staff, Chicago's defensive tendencies stayed pretty much the same: they don't allow a lot of yards after the catch, they never play dime, they like to stack the box (boy, that didn't help, did it?), they tend to send the standard four pass rushers, and relative to other teams, more of their blitzes are big blitzes. When you can't stop the run, teams are going to run play-fakes on you, and the Bears faced play action on 31 percent of opponent passes. No other defense was above 25 percent. The Bears' defense was average on passes with no play fake, but got torched for 8.6 yards per play and 24.1% DVOA on passes with a play fake. For the second straight year, the Bears were dead last in penalties by opponents. Opponents drew just 4.7 flags per game, including declined or offsetting, the lowest average since the 2009 Jaguars. Opposing offenses drew just 23 penalties all year, while the Chicago offense has only drawn opponents offside five times in the last two years with no encroachments or neutral-zone infractions.

Passing

Player	DYAR	DVOA	Plays	NtYds	Avg	YAC	C%	TD	Int
J.Cutler	392	5.5%	371	2481	6.7	4.1	64.1%	19	11
J.McCown*	659	32.1%	236	1786	7.6	5.6	66.7%	13	1

Rushing

Player	DYAR	DVOA	Plays	Yds	Avg	TD	Fum	Suc
M.Forte	193	7.4%	288	1338	4.6	10	3	47%
M.Bush*	-56	-27.3%	63	197	3.1	3	0	35%
A.Jeffery	44	15.9%	16	105	6.6	0	0	-
J.Cutler	48	58.4%	14	124	8.9	0	0	-
J.McCown*	10	10.9%	9	70	7.8	1	1	-

Receiving

Player	DYAR	DVOA	Plays	Ctch	Yds	Y/C	YAC	TD	C%
B.Marshall	284	9.5%	163	100	1295	13.0	2.8	12	61%
A.Jeffery	248	8.3%	150	89	1421	16.0	4.7	7	59%
E.Bennett*	25	-5.5%	43	32	243	7.6	1.9	4	74%
J.Morgan	*-4*	*-14.1%*	*35*	*22*	*227*	*10.3*	*5.2*	*0*	*63%*
M.Bennett	65	3.4%	94	65	760	11.7	5.7	5	69%
J.Mastrud	*-16*	*-24.9%*	*13*	*6*	*88*	*14.7*	*9.2*	*0*	*46%*
M.Forte	113	8.5%	96	76	587	7.7	6.8	3	79%
M.Bush*	15	24.0%	8	4	48	12.0	11.8	1	50%

Offensive Line

Player	Pos	Age	GS	Snaps	Pen	Sk	Pass	Run
Jermon Bushrod	LT	30	16/16	1057	6	5.5	34.5	4.0
Roberto Garza	C	35	16/16	1057	4	0.0	5.5	8.0
Kyle Long	RG	26	16/16	1057	3	1.0	9.5	8.0
Matt Slauson	LG	28	16/16	1057	3	2.0	7.0	3.0
Jordan Mills	RT	24	16/16	1010	2	2.0	34.0	3.0
Eben Britton	OT	27	9/0	235	0	0.0	4.5	1.0
Brian De La Puente	*C*	*29*	*16/16*	*1126*	*4*	*2.0*	*9.0*	*3.5*

Year	Yards	ALY	Rk	Power	Rk	Stuff	Rk	2nd Lev	Rk	Open Field	Rk	Sacks	ASR	Rk	Short	Long	F-Start	Cont.
2011	4.39	3.92	24	61%	20	24%	30	1.24	11	1.03	8	49	9.8%	31	23	14	27	31
2012	4.08	4.05	16	57%	25	21%	25	1.12	19	0.73	18	44	8.0%	24	9	22	24	30
2013	4.37	3.80	20	50%	30	21%	26	1.23	11	1.03	3	30	5.5%	5	8	15	8	48

2013 ALY by direction: Left End 4.37 (9) · Left Tackle 4.02 (13) · Mid/Guard 3.65 (26) · Right Tackle 2.32 (31) · Right End 4.95 (1)

A people's history of the Bears offensive line, 2010-2013:

Mike Martz tried to repair the offensive line by pretending there was nothing wrong with the offensive line whatsoever. He sent five receivers into the pattern and asked J'Marcus Webb, Lance Louis, and Chris Williams to fake it until they could make it as NFL linemen. The result: 105 sacks in two seasons.

Mike Tice tried to repair the offensive line by treating it like it was the most terrible, dangerous thing on earth this side of Chernobyl. He adopted the Emperor's Bodyguards approach to pass protection, smothering Jay Cutler with seven or eight blockers per pass play. Cutler spent a season waiting for Brandon Marshall to get open against the entire opposing secondary. The result: 45 more sacks, one receiver with more than 400 receiving yards.

Marc Trestman and Aaron Kromer tried to repair the offensive line by *actually repairing the offensive line*, and by installing a scheme appropriate for an offensive line in transition. As a result, the offensive line was repaired, and a nation wondered what was so darned hard about that.

Jermon Bushrod looked like Jonathan Ogden after years of Webb, but he is simply a baseline-competent left tackle. Top edge rushers can tie him in knots—Robert Quinn in particular had a lively afternoon in November—but Kromer worked with Bushrod in New Orleans and knows how and when to provide extra support. Matt Slauson escaped the Jets on a low-priced one-year deal, provided his usual steady-Eddie performance, and earned a four-year, $12.8 million reward. Makes you wonder what the point of screwing around with Louis and Chilo Rachal for all those years was.

Kyle Long got baptized by Ndamukong Suh in Week 4, allowing a sack and essentially dropping Suh on Cutler on another play. He then settled down, holding opponents sackless for the rest of the year, though Cutler and Josh McCown both scrambled away from some Long mistakes. The original Bears plan to slide Long to tackle is on hold thanks to Jordan Mills, last year's fifth-round pick. Mills beat Webb for the right tackle job in camp; like Bushrod and Long, he had his troubles against better defenders, but the Trestman/Kromer schemes provided a logical balance of extra protection and quick throws to keep lineman in their comfort zones and quarterbacks upright. Mills had offseason foot surgery but will be ready for camp. Former Jaguars starter Eben Britton saw the field a lot in those six-lineman sets mentioned earlier.

Past Bears regimes were also in denial about the possibility that a center might get old and need to be replaced. Luckily, Roberto Garza moved from guard to center three years ago to provide a quality replacement for Olin Kreutz. Garza is now 35, but the Bears acquired another Kromer fave, Brian de la Puente, as Garza's eventual replacement. de la Puente has experience in the system and as a starter for a playoff team, yet he cost just $165,000 in guaranteed money to provide 2014 insurance and an extended tryout. Planning for the future: another concept the Mikes had trouble grasping

Defensive Front Seven

			Overall								vs. Run					Pass Rush			
Defensive Line	**Age**	**Pos**	**G**	**Snaps**	**Plays**	**TmPct**	**Rk**	**Stop**	**Dfts**	**BTkl**	**Runs**	**St%**	**Rk**	**RuYd**	**Rk**	**Sack**	**Hit**	**Hur**	**Tips**
Corey Wootton*	27	DT/DE	16	846	37	4.5%	55	31	14	2	29	79%	38	1.4	16	3.0	3	15.0	6
Stephen Paea	26	DT	13	474	26	3.9%	67	22	6	2	18	83%	23	1.6	21	1.5	0	5.5	2
Landon Cohen*	28	DT	15	381	15	2.0%	--	10	2	1	15	67%	--	1.2	--	0.0	0	3.5	0

			Overall								vs. Run					Pass Rush			
Edge Rushers	**Age**	**Pos**	**G**	**Snaps**	**Plays**	**TmPct**	**Rk**	**Stop**	**Dfts**	**BTkl**	**Runs**	**St%**	**Rk**	**RuYd**	**Rk**	**Sack**	**Hit**	**Hur**	**Tips**
Julius Peppers*	34	DE	16	851	46	5.6%	38	35	14	4	35	69%	56	2.9	53	7.0	2	14.5	3
Shea McClellin	25	DE	14	651	30	4.2%	64	18	8	3	22	55%	75	4.0	75	4.0	6	18.5	0
David Bass	24	DE	12	311	24	3.9%	--	16	8	1	22	64%	--	2.5	--	1.0	1	8.0	0
Jared Allen	*32*	*DE*	*16*	*1058*	*58*	*6.6%*	*23*	*43*	*22*	*5*	*38*	*63%*	*67*	*2.4*	*38*	*11.5*	*15*	*27.0*	*7*
Lamarr Houston	*27*	*DE*	*16*	*1020*	*69*	*8.4%*	*6*	*52*	*14*	*5*	*52*	*75%*	*44*	*2.3*	*34*	*6.0*	*11*	*21.0*	*0*
Willie Young	*29*	*DE*	*16*	*760*	*49*	*6.5%*	*24*	*45*	*12*	*2*	*37*	*89%*	*7*	*2.3*	*28*	*3.0*	*8*	*27.0*	*4*
Israel Idonije	*34*	*DE*	*15*	*330*	*11*	*1.5%*	*--*	*10*	*4*	*0*	*10*	*90%*	*--*	*0.6*	*--*	*0.5*	*2*	*10.5*	*0*

			Overall								Pass Rush			vs. Run					vs. Pass						
Linebackers	**Age**	**Pos**	**G**	**Snaps**	**Plays**	**TmPct**	**Rk**	**Stop**	**Dfts**	**BTkl**	**Sack**	**Hit**	**Hur**	**Runs**	**St%**	**Rk**	**RuYd**	**Rk**	**Tgts**	**Suc%**	**Rk**	**AdjYd**	**Rk**	**PD**	**Int**
James Anderson*	31	OLB	16	998	105	12.8%	43	53	20	4	4.0	1	7	59	59%	62	3.5	52	37	61%	15	5.0	10	3	0
Jon Bostic	23	MLB	16	605	56	6.8%	74	37	9	7	2.0	0	2	38	76%	10	3.3	35	11	40%	--	7.8	--	1	1
Lance Briggs	34	OLB	9	557	77	16.7%	15	49	22	9	3.0	1	4	41	78%	8	1.9	4	31	55%	29	6.4	32	3	0
Khaseem Greene	25	OLB	15	230	28	3.7%	--	13	2	4	0.0	0	2	19	58%	--	3.5	--	6	25%	--	12.9	--	1	1
D.J. Williams	32	MLB	6	212	27	8.8%	65	18	8	1	2.0	0	0	16	69%	27	2.9	24	7	58%	--	3.8	--	0	0

Year	Yards	ALY	Rk	Power	Rk	Stuff	Rk	2nd Level	Rk	Open Field	Rk	Sacks	ASR	Rk	Short	Long
2011	4.13	3.29	1	65%	20	26%	1	1.18	16	1.07	25	33	5.2%	29	7	12
2012	4.11	3.52	3	60%	14	24%	5	1.20	19	0.92	24	41	6.4%	15	6	13
2013	5.34	4.45	32	77%	31	20%	14	1.57	32	1.40	32	31	6.3%	23	10	13
2013 ALY by direction:			*Left End 3.60 (14)*			*Left Tackle 4.58 (28)*			*Mid/Guard 4.79 (32)*			*Right Tackle 4.73 (29)*			*Right End 3.92 (18)*	

As noted earlier in the chapter, the Bears' new front seven can be sorted into three bundles: the geezers, the young veterans, and the kids. Geezers Jared Allen, Lance Briggs, D.J. Williams and Jay Ratliff can all still play, Briggs and Allen at a very high level when healthy. Their combined age at the start of the season will be 130, so counting on them far beyond the 2014 season is crazy, which is why the Bears have been wisely pursuing replacements. Rookies Will Sutton and Ego "The Living Planet" Ferguson are the Bears starting defensive tackles of the future; for Sutton, that future may arrive in November. Sutton is similar in style to Henry Melton, whom the Bears lost to injuries in 2013 and the Cowboys in 2014. He's shorter than the prototype three-tech but is a quick-step penetrator who uses his leverage well. Ferguson is 315 pounds of hard labor as a nose tackle. Both are excellent system fits.

Jon Bostic will play behind Sutton and Ferguson in the Bears defense of the future. Bostic carried a lot of NEXT BUTKUS SINGLETARY URLACHER baggage out of camp last season, then started nine all-too-eventful games when Williams got hurt, finishing second-worst in the NFL in broken tackle rate for linebackers. Giving up on Bostic based on last season would not be fair: he practically had no line in front of him. He's a size-speed prospect with the potential to become a quality starter, and he is better off without the Hall of Fame expectations.

It will be up to the young veterans to glue this unit together. Stephen Paea's toe injury may have been the tipping-point event in the Bears' collapse last season. Paea has bulked up steadily and provides a fine mix of size and quickness at nose tackle. He returned to the lineup late in the season but was not much of a factor; toe injuries can do that to huge men, and Paea is expected back at full speed for camp. Shea McClellin lost 11 pounds and a few ticks off his 40 time in the offseason in an attempt to slide to Sam linebacker after a failed experiment at defensive end. McClellin displayed great range and coverage instincts in college, so the move is not as desperate as it sounds.

Lamarr Houston is expected to be a cornerstone of the next great Bears defense. With veteran scaffolding around him and quality prospects in the pipeline, he has a fighting chance.

Defensive Secondary

			Overall								vs. Run					vs. Pass									
Secondary	Age	Pos	G	Snaps	Plays	TmPct	Rk	Stop	Dfts	BTkl	Runs	St%	Rk	RuYd	Rk	Tgts	Tgt%	Rk	Dist	Suc%	Rk	AdjYd	Rk	PD	Int
Tim Jennings	31	CB	16	1032	71	8.7%	40	31	10	13	17	41%	43	10.7	70	83	20.3%	35	11.3	51%	51	8.3	62	13	4
Chris Conte	25	FS	16	1029	95	11.6%	25	18	9	15	51	18%	77	11.9	76	35	8.5%	45	15.5	46%	64	10.2	70	5	3
Major Wright*	26	SS	15	935	101	13.2%	10	27	8	8	58	38%	42	7.6	51	29	7.9%	40	14.1	29%	77	13.9	78	3	2
Zack Bowman	30	CB	16	593	53	6.5%	70	19	10	6	11	18%	79	7.9	53	55	23.5%	63	10.0	47%	70	6.7	19	6	3
Charles Tillman	33	CB	8	432	47	11.5%	5	21	10	5	21	57%	14	6.4	30	38	22.3%	55	13.0	50%	57	8.4	65	6	3
M.D. Jennings	*26*	*FS*	*16*	*789*	*69*	*8.5%*	*60*	*14*	*11*	*4*	*35*	*17%*	*78*	*10.3*	*73*	*13*	*3.7%*	*1*	*13.2*	*28%*	*78*	*12.2*	*75*	*1*	*0*
Ryan Mundy	*29*	*SS*	*16*	*653*	*72*	*8.4%*	*64*	*28*	*11*	*5*	*42*	*52%*	*17*	*4.4*	*7*	*22*	*7.6%*	*33*	*12.4*	*62%*	*24*	*6.3*	*24*	*2*	*1*

Year	Pass D Rank	vs. #1 WR	Rk	vs. #2 WR	Rk	vs. Other WR	Rk	vs. TE	Rk	vs. RB	Rk
2011	7	-9.1%	6	-18.9%	4	-26.7%	7	0.9%	8	-5.5%	13
2012	1	-31.0%	2	-5.2%	11	-30.2%	3	-24.7%	1	-27.2%	3
2013	17	-10.0%	10	6.6%	18	4.0%	19	18.8%	27	-14.3%	6

If the story of the 2013 Bears defense were rewritten as a zombie apocalypse movie, Tim Jennings would be the hero who barely survives to rebuild civilization. Jennings played through a dislocated shoulder in the final weeks of the season. He was often seen in the locker room wearing a sling, or needing help to get his shirt on, yet he was back in uniform the next week. Jennings somehow remained effective, and the Bears rewarded him with a four-year contract. The deal was loaded with up-front money, partially for cap reasons, partially because Jennings is a 5-foot-8 30-year-old whose body may be starting to betray him.

Charles Tillman resisted a team effort to move him to the assisted living community for cornerbacks known as "nickel safety;" after the draft, Phil Emery confirmed that Tillman will remain at cornerback this year. Tillman's most important task will be to mentor first-round pick Kyle Fuller (Virginia Tech). Fuller is a natural Cover-2 cornerback: smart, instinctive, and a sure tackler whose lack of pure deep speed is his greatest flaw. Fuller gets high marks for preparation, so the Tillman-Fuller Peanut-and-padawan relationship could yield huge dividends.

Safety was the one position the Bears could not address adequately in the offseason. Chris Conte is a polarizing figure in Chicago, judging by the fact that a stray May tweet of his name lit up my Twitter feed for hours. Conte was not quite gasoline on a fire; he was more like water on a grease fire, splattering a major problem everywhere instead of solving it. Conte had to clean up 29 runs of over 10 yards last season, and you don't blame the guy with the mop when the cooks keep spilling the soup. On the other hand, Conte had 15 broken tackles and failed to reach several ballcarriers enjoying a Sunday afternoon's sprint through empty pastures. The general Wild West mayhem of the Bears defense put Conte in untenable situations. Like Bostic, he deserves some benefit of the doubt for flailing with all his might in a no-win situation. M.D. Jennings took minicamp starter reps with Conte nicked up and could push for a role, though Jennings spent last season in Green Bay running around in circles.

Strong safety is an even bigger trouble spot, with journeyman Ryan Mundy replacing Major Wright. Mundy never got past nickel safety status in four seasons with the Steelers before cracking the Giants lineup last season and providing a few highlights. The inability to unseat Ryan Clark from a starting job is not something to put in your LinkedIn profile. Fourth-round pick Brock Vereen (Minnesota) is an undersized Combine champ who also has a good film-room rep. Vereen could challenge Mundy quickly, and Tillman may also prove willing to slide over for the sake of the children.

Special Teams

Year	DVOA	Rank	FG/XP	Rank	Net Kick	Rank	Kick Ret	Rank	Net Punt	Rank	Punt Ret	Rank	Hidden	Rank
2011	8.5%	1	7.5	3	0.4	18	4.4	5	19.7	1	10.5	2	-5.1	23
2012	4.7%	6	-4.4	24	13.0	2	0.5	14	18.8	2	-4.4	23	2.0	13
2013	2.0%	11	4.0	9	-4.1	26	-1.6	18	5.3	11	6.5	7	-5.6	23

For the first time in eight years, the Bears special teams comments will not focus on the awesomeness of Devin Hester. Hester is now with the Falcons, a victim of the caponomics necessary to retain Jay Cutler and Brandon Marshall while freeing enough cash for massive defensive renovations. Since 2010, only six opponent punts have been returned by Bears other than Hester, so there are some big, elusive shoes that must be filled.

Eric Weems was an effective all-purpose returner in Atlanta and has served as Hester's understudy for two seasons. Weems' primary jobs in Chicago have been as the "up" return man for short kickoffs and as a fair-catch machine when Hester was unavailable for punts, so it is not clear what he has left in terms of big-play ability. Reserve running back Michael Ford also saw some up-man duty and may get a crack at kickoff returns.

With Adam Podlesh in Pittsburgh, sixth-round pick Pat O'Donnell is the new Bears punter. O'Donnell is 6-foot-4, weighs 220 pounds, and benched 23 reps of 225 pounds at the Combine, far more than first-round cornerback Kyle Fuller. He also has a degree from Cincinnati in "organizational leadership," which sounds like "Management for Dummies" for dummies, but give the kid credit for getting his degree a year early, then transferring to the University of Miami to fulfill his childhood dream of punting for a slightly bigger program. O'Donnell is a well-regarded punting prospect, but his workout numbers and degree suggest that he may be suited for a role somewhere between strong safety and defensive coordinator.

Robbie Gould received a four-year, $15 million contract during Phil Emery's January cap-fu kata. He proved his worthiness during his ninja battle against Justin Tucker in the monsoon game against the Ravens in November. Tucker may have hit a 52-yarder by bending his kick around the edge of a Category 3 hurricane, but Gould blasted three field goals of his own during ever-changing conditions. Gould now ranks third on the all-time field goal accuracy list, and the two players above him played most of their games in a dome (Mike Vanderjagt) or America's best weather city (Nate Kaeding).

Cincinnati Bengals

2013 Record: 11-5	**Total DVOA:** 14.2% (9th)	**2014 Mean Projection:** 8.8 wins	**On the Clock (0-4):** 5%
Pythagorean Wins: 11.1 (5th)	**Offense:** 0.4% (17th)	**Postseason Odds:** 51.0%	**Mediocrity (5-7):** 22%
Snap-Weighted Age: 26.6 (19th)	**Defense:** -12.6% (5th)	**Super Bowl Odds:** 8.5%	**Playoff Contender (8-10):** 48%
Average Opponent: -3.5% (25th)	**Special Teams:** 1.2% (12th)	**Proj. Avg. Opponent:** -1.4% (23rd)	**Super Bowl Contender (11+):** 24%

2013: Another playoff pratfall leaves a bitter aftertaste.

2014: Sweet as ginger or bloody as the Red Wedding—it's up to Andy Dalton.

Any time a season has the phrase "or bust" appended to it, it's usually a recipe for disappointment. By that standard, the Bengals came up short in 2013.

Cincinnati entered the year with a simple mandate: to at long last win a playoff game (the franchise's first since 1990) after back-to-back losses in the wild-card round, and take the next step in what has been an otherwise exemplary display of team-building over the last few years. For the most part, everything leading up to the Bengals' playoff encounter at home against San Diego went according to plan. Cincinnati cruised to a division title, lapping perennial *bêtes noires* Baltimore and Pittsburgh by three games, and won the right to host the decidedly mediocre Chargers in the first round.

The game was played at Paul Brown Stadium, where the Bengals were undefeated and scored 37 points per game during the regular season. Even the timing of kickoff seemed to bode well. The Bengals had lost three consecutive playoff games played in the Saturday late-afternoon time slot, so Sunday at 1 p.m. was a positive omen. Indeed, Cincinnati led 10-7 at halftime after dominating the second quarter, and all signs pointed to an exorcism.

Then came one of the worst halves of football in franchise history, especially given the stakes. Quarterback Andy Dalton, who entered the game determined to shrug off his many doubters, instead imploded in a Delhommesque three-turnover meltdown, including two bad picks and an unforced fumble. San Diego won the second half 20-0, leaving the Striped Nation crushed and wondering about a future that had appeared so bright thirty minutes earlier. It was arguably the most traumatic event in Cincinnati since WKRP-FM rained turkeys on a shopping mall in a misguided Thanksgiving promotion back in the late 1970s.

In the aftermath, many observers felt that continued faith in Dalton as the franchise quarterback would be akin to believing turkeys can fly. Matters calmed as the offseason progressed, and it was clear that the Red Rifle (The "Ginger Ninja?" The "Scarlet Slinger?") would be the Bengals' signal caller for the immediate future. The Bengals passed on drafting a replacement in the first or second rounds, and the national media's dart-throwing suggestions of a trade for Kirk Cousins or Ryan Mallett were absurd on their face.

Now Dalton's contract is in its last season, and the pivotal decision of how to handle his re-signing is nigh. The franchise is caught between wanting to keep Dalton and not wanting to pay him anywhere close to the going rate for top quarterbacks. After all, the team's recent revival coincides directly with Carson Palmer voluntarily removing his enormous salary from the books after the 2010 season, allowing the Bengals to embark on the surest path to quality: having a good quarterback on a cheap contract. The signature feature of this team has been quality depth, as shown when the Bengals shrugged off the potentially devastating losses of Geno Atkins and Leon Hall last season. Giving Dalton big money, in addition to the coming paydays for A.J. Green and Vontaze Burfict, will eat into that core strength.

While head coach Marvin Lewis has been unwavering in his support for Dalton, owner Mike Brown has taken a more realpolitik approach, voicing a desire to re-sign Dalton, but only at the right price point. So the team may well walk the tightrope, à la the Ravens with Joe Flacco, a similarly "glass half-full or half-empty?" quarterback two years ago. That makes 2014 into a prove-it-or-lose-it campaign for Dalton. If he does re-sign before the season, the contract will most likely be loaded with incentives that protect the club in case the Chargers game has forever scarred the quarterback.

As is his frustrating wont, Dalton offered both sides of the "keep him or dump him" debate solid bullet points in 2013. The quarterback certainly had his moments. He was AFC Player of the Month after a scalding October, threw for franchise records in touchdowns and yards, and guided the team to an unprecedented third consecutive postseason appearance.

On the other hand, in three playoff games Dalton has thrown for six interceptions and just one touchdown, with a total DVOA of -30.4%. Add in six more nationally televised prime-time games, and he is 2-7, completing 56 percent of his passes, with six touchdowns and 11 picks, and a DVOA of -29.9%. It's a small sample, but part of a disturbing trend. When the lights are brightest and everyone is watching, Dalton tends to hyperventilate before curling up in a fetal position. If being a successful quarterback is in some respects playing a leadership role, regular failure in the big games gets you drummed out of Actor's Equity.

Dalton embodies the classic mid-pack quarterback conundrum: he's not good enough to embrace, but not bad enough to easily replace. For all his faults, real and imagined, not every backup or middling prospect throws for 33 touchdown

2014 Bengals Schedule

Week	Opp.	Week	Opp.	Week	Opp.
1	at BAL	7	at IND	13	at TB
2	ATL	8	BAL	14	PIT
3	TEN	9	JAC	15	at CLE
4	BYE	10	CLE (Thu.)	16	DEN (Mon.)
5	at NE	11	at NO	17	at PIT
6	CAR	12	at HOU		

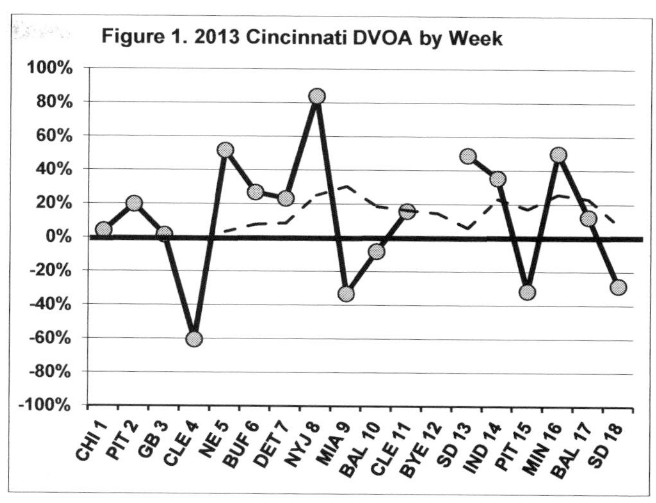

passes (only Peyton Manning and Drew Brees threw for more in 2013). In fact, hardly any of them do. Even elite prospects are unlikely to be so effective. Look back at Dalton's 2011 draft class for proof. Cam Newton was selected first overall, 34 spots before Dalton. After three seasons, his career passing DVOA is 4.5%, Dalton's 2.0%. Also drafted in the first round were Jake Locker, Blaine Gabbert, and Christian Ponder, who combined have thrown for two fewer touchdown passes than Dalton in their careers.

Quarterbacks picked in 2011's middle and lower rounds (Ricky Stanzi, Tyrod Taylor, T.J. Yates) have even less NFL pedigree, which dovetails with historical trends. The idea that Cincinnati could snag a Dalton facsimile in the lower rounds is unlikely, meaning those who cling to the belief that fifth-round pick A.J. McCarron will prove a magical anti-Dalton elixir have reality blowing in their faces at gale force.

For an essay supposedly about an entire franchise, this one has been disproportionately about a single player. But that's fitting in this case, for in large part the Bengals will rise or fall in 2014 in accordance with Dalton's play. Another year of improvement while eliminating the frustrating mistakes and the shrinkage in big moments, and Cincinnati is a Super Bowl contender. If he's maxed out, proven to be merely a creation of Jay Gruden's schematic protection, then the franchise will need to re-tool. The only question is how much it will cost for the Bengals to unshackle themselves from their quarterback.

Of course there *are* other areas of interest in Cincinnati, the most meaningful of which is the new flow chart under head coach Marvin Lewis. The 2014 Bengals will be an interesting test study in the power of coordinators. Both sides of the ball lost their gurus, with Gruden and Mike Zimmer accepting head coaching gigs elsewhere (the former's elevation seems premature, the latter's long overdue). It is a sign of the growth of the franchise that there were clear-cut replacements already on staff. Hue Jackson, the former Raiders head coach, will handle the offense, while linebackers coach Paul Guenther takes over for his mentor on defense. Both are highly respected within the league, proven in part when the Bengals had to fight off several suitors, including Zimmer, for Guenther's services.

It is rare for a team to see both coordinators hired away into head coaching jobs. If we include Charlie Weis leaving the Patriots for his dream job at Notre Dame, it has happened only four times since 1990 (Table 1). None of these teams suffered more than you would expect from normal regression towards the mean, and all four repeated as division champions. Meanwhile, the head-coaching records of these promoted coordinators are often not pretty, though there's one notable outlier.

The offensive side of the roster has already felt the effect of the change. Jackson has publicly declared his intention to embrace a faster tempo and, counterintuitively, a more physical running game designed to lighten Dalton's load on offense. The Bengals drafted Jeremy Hill, a punishing tailback out of LSU, to replace veteran BenJarvus Green-Ellis, whose effectiveness has diminished. Heady but injury-weakened center Kyle Cook was released, and North Carolina's Russell Bodine drafted in the fourth round to take his role. Implicit in all of this is that making Dalton's arm responsible for playoff victories, as the team did against San Diego when it threw 51 times (34 in the second half), is a losing proposition.

While this strategy seems to fly in the face of modern football (and the FO dictum "pass to set up the run"), certainly the argument can be made that the Bengals threw far too often in 2013. Dalton had 586 attempts, 170 more than Colin Kaepernick and 179 more than Russell Wilson, two quarterbacks who have been successful using the same formula the Bengals aim to use: winning on the back of a strong defense and running game. (Yes, both Wilson and Kaepernick are running quarterbacks, but Dalton ran it 61 times himself, ninth-most

Table 1. Teams with Both Coordinators Promoted Elsewhere, Year 1990-2012

Team	Year	W-L	W-L Y+1	OC	Team	Years	W-L	DC	Team	Years	W-L
SF	1994	13-3	11-5	Mike Shanahan	DEN	14	138-86	Ray Rhodes	PHI	4	29-34-1
JAC	1998	11-5	14-2	Chris Palmer	CLE	2	5-27	Dick Jauron	CHI	5	35-45
NE	2004	14-2	10-6	Charlie Weis	ND*	5	35-27	Romeo Crennel	CLE	4	24-40
SD	2006	14-2	11-5	Cam Cameron	MIA	1	1-15	Wade Phillips	DAL	3	29-19

*college, not NFL

in the league. Then again, few of those were designed runs, meaning he dropped back intending to heave it even more often.) All that throwing gave Dalton's efficiency numbers the expected beating. When it comes to the Rifle, less is almost certainly more.

Guenther is in the trickier spot. Philosophically and schematically, little is likely to change on defense, especially as head coach Marvin Lewis is the de facto decision maker on personnel and technique. Guenther has said he may blitz more, as befitting an old linebacker coach, but otherwise, the Bengals will still run a 4-3 defense, embrace press-man coverage, and employ frequent substitution at most positions.

What remains to be seen is whether Guenther can match Zimmer when it comes to player motivation. Zim was beloved in the locker room, an old-school, "don't tell me about the labor pains, just show me the baby" type who occasionally sprinkled in actual words among the expletives. Attributing inspirational powers to coaches often smacks of magical media nonsense, but there's plenty of evidence that Zimmer really was special. Zimmer's defenses weren't littered with highly-drafted studs. The only top-rotation guys the Bengals took in the first round are Rey Maualuga and Leon Hall. Zimmer unlocked the potential inside of Geno Atkins, figured out how to finally get through to Adam Jones, and turned around Terence Newman after he left Dallas as a smoldering piece of toast. Perhaps his best coaching effort was dedicated to developing undrafted defenders, highlighted by Vontaze Burfict.

As Burfict's position coach, Guenther got quite a bit of credit for Taze's metamorphosis from collegiate delinquent to NFL Pro Bowler, but can he match Zimmer, whom Chris Crocker called the Michael Jordan of coordinators? After all, the Bengals were fifth in defensive DVOA despite losing stalwarts Atkins and Hall by Halloween a year ago—in fact, the Bengals improved from -8.1% (sixth) in Weeks 1-9 to -18.7% (third) in Weeks 10-17.

"You can't replace him," Leon Hall said of Zimmer on Bengals.com this offseason. "Same system, same guys. On paper it sounds good. But it will definitely be different. We have to work harder, study harder, and we really have to play better."

Defensively, despite last season's heroics, any realistic chance the team has at a deep playoff run rests on the full recovery of Hall (who has now torn Achilles tendons twice in three years) and especially Atkins, who was among the best players in the entire league in 2012. His game is predicated upon dominant quickness and lower body drive. Whether or not he can return to full power after his knee ligament was rent asunder remains to be seen. If Geno is only good but not great, the Bengals will certainly feel the difference.

Meanwhile, the secondary is getting long in the tooth. It was this area that Zimmer's genius was best displayed, slapping together effective coverages using aging vets like Newman, Crocker, and Adam Jones. All are well past thirty, while safety Reggie Nelson will be 31 in September and Hall hits the big 3-0 this year as well. The Bengals addressed this concern in the draft, grabbing Darqueze Dennard from Michigan State, whose similarity to Hall is striking. Dennard's physical play and stickiness in press-man coverage will certainly help some, and if third-year man Dre Kirkpatrick can build upon the strides he showed late last year, the corners should be in good shape going forward. But that's a lot of ifs for such a critical position.

The defense that is supposedly the bedrock of the team was pushed around once again in the playoffs, giving up 196 yards and 4.9 yards per carry on the ground to San Diego. While it's far easier to spotlight Dalton's January ineptitude, it's also fair to call out Zimmer for the postseason failures of his unit. If Guenther can find a way for the defense to improve in those critical games, he will go a long way to carving out a niche for himself outside of "Michael Jordan's" shadow, even if he never pulls off the coordinator's equivalent of dunking from the free throw line.

That's assuming there is another postseason berth, of course. Cincinnati's ascension to the top of the AFC North has been the result of top-notch drafts, canny roster moves, and strong coaching. Also helping has been a rare mediocre stretch in Pittsburgh and Joe Flacco's deleterious effect on Baltimore's salary cap, surely a cautionary tale the Bengals are aware of when considering Dalton's future earnings. Neither franchise is unlikely to be down for long, while Cleveland shows ominous signs of stirring at last (Guenther's most important work may soon be devising anti-Manziel schemes). The Bengals face a first-place schedule in 2014 that is extremely backloaded; five of their final seven games are on the road, with the two home games coming against archrival Pittsburgh and the ultra-powerful Broncos.

The Bengals' record of three straight winless playoff appearances is actually quite rare throughout NFL history. Only three teams since 1978 had a similar run: the 1990-92 Saints, the 1992-94 Vikings, and the 1993-95 Lions. All three of those teams missed the postseason in the fourth year.

Of more recent vintage, the relevant analogue may be the 2008-2011 Falcons, who averaged 11 wins per year (barely missing the playoffs in 2009), but were creamed in their January games. Matt Ryan was clearly a good quarterback (better than Dalton, actually), but had legions of detractors criticizing his inability to raise his game when it mattered most. At last, the team managed to break through in 2012, albeit barely, and the heat was (temporarily) alleviated.

That same heat is now on the 2014 Bengals, and the flame setting is set to "sear." The dreaded "or bust" appendage has been attached to their season once again. Only this time, there is a whiff of "or else."

Robert Weintraub

2013 Bengals Stats by Week

Wk	vs.	W-L	PF	PA	YDF	YDA	TO	Total	Off	Def	ST
1	at CHI	L	21	24	340	323	-2	4%	-3%	2%	10%
2	PIT	W	20	10	407	278	+2	20%	9%	-18%	-7%
3	GB	W	34	30	297	399	0	1%	-10%	-17%	-5%
4	at CLE	L	6	17	266	336	-2	-61%	-44%	22%	5%
5	NE	W	13	6	341	248	0	52%	-21%	-69%	4%
6	at BUF	W	27	24	483	322	0	27%	27%	1%	0%
7	at DET	W	27	24	421	434	0	23%	35%	13%	1%
8	NY	W	49	9	402	240	+1	84%	42%	-33%	9%
9	at MIA	L	20	22	465	345	-3	-33%	-25%	15%	6%
10	at BAL	L	17	20	364	189	0	-8%	-32%	-30%	-6%
11	CLE	W	41	20	224	330	+2	16%	-44%	-44%	16%
12	BYE										
13	at SD	W	17	10	354	334	+1	49%	10%	-27%	11%
14	IND	W	42	28	430	389	0	35%	61%	43%	17%
15	at PIT	L	20	30	279	290	0	-32%	-5%	2%	-24%
16	MIN	W	42	14	426	209	+3	50%	16%	-50%	-16%
17	BAL	W	34	17	392	222	-1	12%	-9%	-20%	1%
18	SD	L	10	27	439	318	-4	-28%	-24%	9%	5%

Trends and Splits

	Offense	Rank	Defense	Rank
Total DVOA	0.4%	17	-12.6%	5
Unadjusted VOA	3.1%	15	-17.1%	2
Weighted Trend	3.7%	13	-13.1%	6
Variance	9.5%	27	8.6%	29
Average Opponent	2.9%	25	-2.1%	25
Passing	13.5%	12	-14.5%	4
Rushing	-5.7%	20	-9.8%	13
First Down	-9.1%	24	-19.7%	1
Second Down	14.5%	8	8.6%	25
Third Down	-4.5%	19	-33.6%	2
First Half	-6.5%	21	-12.4%	4
Second Half	6.9%	10	-12.9%	6
Red Zone	27.9%	3	1.4%	17
Late and Close	5.3%	13	-14.8%	7

Five-Year Performance

Year	W-L	Pyth W	Est W	PF	PA	TO	Total	Rk	Off	Rk	Def	Rk	ST	Rk	Off AGL	Rk	Def AGL	Rk	Off Age	Rk	Def Age	Rk	ST Age	Rk
2009	10-6	8.4	8.0	305	291	0	-0.1%	19	-0.9%	19	-2.0%	13	-1.3%	21	34.1	24	36.5	24	28.0	6	25.9	29	25.9	26
2010	4-12	6.0	6.6	322	395	-8	-3.4%	19	1.7%	17	1.5%	17	-3.5%	28	14.9	7	47.5	30	28.9	1	26.4	22	26.0	21
2011	9-7	8.6	8.5	344	323	0	0.10%	17	-1.4%	17	0.80%	17	2.3%	7	25.2	15	26.5	17	26.5	24	27.4	13	26.4	13
2012	10-6	9.9	8.7	391	320	+4	6.1%	12	-1.8%	17	-3.8%	10	4.1%	7	37.0	21	22.2	13	25.1	32	27.3	11	26.0	17
2013	11-5	11.1	10.1	430	305	+1	14.2%	9	0.4%	17	-12.6%	5	1.2%	12	12.1	2	31.3	17	26.0	29	27.4	8	26.3	9

2013 Performance Based on Most Common Personnel Groups

CIN Offense					CIN Offense vs. Opponents				CIN Defense				CIN Defense vs. Opponents			
Pers	Freq	Yds	DVOA	Run%	Pers	Freq	Yds	DVOA	Pers	Freq	Yds	DVOA	Pers	Freq	Yds	DVOA
12	43%	5.8	6.0%	44%	3-4-4	31%	5.1	5.5%	Nickel Even	66%	4.9	-13.9%	11	60%	4.9	-9.7%
11	40%	6.0	11.8%	26%	Nickel Even	31%	6.3	10.1%	4-3-4	25%	4.5	-12.3%	12	21%	5.6	-9.5%
13	9%	3.3	-15.4%	80%	4-3-4	19%	5.3	-3.0%	Dime+	5%	6.8	8.8%	21	6%	4.7	8.2%
611	3%	6.0	-12.9%	56%	Nickel Odd	9%	5.9	-14.6%	Nickel Odd	3%	5.3	-6.1%	22	4%	3.6	-18.9%
02	1%	6.3	24.5%	14%	Dime+	7%	6.6	34.2%	Goal Line	1%	1.1	-14.5%	10	2%	3.4	-109.7%

Strategic Tendencies

Run/Pass		Rk	Formation		Rk	Pass Rush		Rk	Secondary		Rk	Strategy		Rk
Runs, first half	38%	16	Form: Single Back	71%	15	Rush 3	2.0%	29	4 DB	25%	32	Play action	19%	21
Runs, first down	52%	10	Form: Empty Back	7%	13	Rush 4	72.5%	3	5 DB	69%	1	Avg Box (Off)	6.48	5
Runs, second-long	27%	23	Pers: 3+ WR	44%	28	Rush 5	18.5%	27	6+ DB	5%	18	Avg Box (Def)	6.16	29
Runs, power sit.	65%	5	Pers: 4+ WR	2%	11	Rush 6+	7.0%	20	CB by Sides	99%	1	Offensive Pace	30.00	13
Runs, behind 2H	24%	24	Pers: 2+ TE/6+ OL	58%	1	Sacks by LB	22.1%	20	DB Blitz	12%	17	Defensive Pace	28.42	1
Pass, ahead 2H	47%	17	Shotgun/Pistol	52%	24	Sacks by DB	9.3%	16	Hole in Zone	10%	17	Go for it on 4th	1.37	3

Here's one stat to best summarize Andy Dalton's weaknesses: the Bengals had exactly the same 43.2% DVOA on passes thrown behind the line of scrimmage that they had on passes thrown past the line of scrimmage. Leaguewide, teams average 7.7% DVOA on passes thrown behind the line of scrimmage, 51.3% DVOA on passes thrown past the line of scrimmage. (If you are wondering why both figures are positive, it is because many negative plays don't count in either category, such as sacks and passes batted down at the line.) With the arrival of Tyler Eifert and the move to use tight ends as fullbacks, the Bengals used two or more tight ends more than twice as often as they did in 2012. They were the only team to use 12 personnel more than any other personnel group. The Bengals also used six linemen much less often than in the previous two seasons. One reason the Bengals used five defensive backs more often than any other defense is that they tended to use a third safety rather than a linebacker to cover athletic tight ends like Antonio Gates or Coby Fleener. Bengals opponents threw 31 percent of their passes to their No. 1 receivers, the second highest rate in the league. The year before, the Bengals only faced 18 percent of passes to No. 1 receivers, the lowest rate in the league. The Bengals allowed a league-low 6.5 yards per pass when they weren't marked with pass pressure, and ranked third with 7.0% DVOA.

Passing

Player	DYAR	DVOA	Plays	NtYds	Avg	YAC	C%	TD	Int
A.Dalton	541	2.3%	615	4088	6.6	5.7	62.2%	33	20
J.Campbell	*-24*	*-12.2%*	*332*	*1912*	*5.8*	*5.8*	*57.1%*	*11*	*8*

Rushing

Player	DYAR	DVOA	Plays	Yds	Avg	TD	Fum	Suc
B.Green-Ellis	-27	-11.4%	220	756	3.4	7	2	49%
G.Bernard	28	-4.5%	170	700	4.1	5	1	48%
A.Dalton	52	13.0%	39	196	5.0	2	0	-
C.Peerman	-12	-55.5%	8	17	2.1	0	0	25%
M.Jones	32	25.8%	8	65	8.1	0	0	-
J.Johnson	-5	-28.2%	5	22	4.4	0	1	-
J.Campbell	*31*	*34.0%*	*13*	*108*	*8.3*	*0*	*0*	-

Receiving

Player	DYAR	DVOA	Plays	Ctch	Yds	Y/C	YAC	TD	C%
A.J.Green	207	1.9%	178	98	1426	14.6	4.1	11	55%
M.Jones	279	32.4%	80	51	712	14.0	4.4	10	64%
M.Sanu	17	-10.0%	78	47	457	9.7	5.4	2	60%
A.Hawkins*	31	8.7%	18	12	199	16.6	11.3	0	67%
D.Sanzenbacher	13	9.2%	8	6	61	10.2	5.3	0	75%
J.Gresham	-47	-18.5%	67	46	458	10.0	5.8	4	69%
T.Eifert	-27	-14.0%	59	39	445	11.4	5.8	2	66%
A.Smith*	-36	-87.5%	6	3	12	4.0	2.0	1	50%
K.Brock	*-5*	*-23.0%*	*6*	*3*	*36*	*12.0*	*1.3*	*0*	*50%*
G.Bernard	167	29.4%	71	56	514	9.2	9.4	3	79%
B.Green-Ellis	-20	-61.0%	8	4	22	5.5	2.0	0	50%

Offensive Line

Player	Pos	Age	GS	Snaps	Pen	Sk	Pass	Run
Andre Smith	RT	27	16/15	1098	4	4.5	17.5	5.5
Kyle Cook*	C	31	16/16	1050	4	3.0	11.0	2.5
Andrew Whitworth	LT	33	14/14	914	7	4.0	7.5	4.0
Kevin Zeitler	RG	24	12/11	809	3	2.5	8.0	4.0
Clint Boling	LG	25	12/12	776	1	1.0	5.5	2.0
Anthony Collins*	OT	29	15/7	578	1	0.5	3.0	1.5
Mike Pollak	RG	29	8/5	366	2	0.5	2.5	4.0
Marshall Newhouse	*LT*	*26*	*15/2*	*245*	*3*	*3.0*	*11.5*	*0.0*
Will Svitek	*OT*	*32*	*13/2*	*239*	*0*	*2.0*	*4.0*	*0.5*

Year	Yards	ALY	Rk	Power	Rk	Stuff	Rk	2nd Lev	Rk	Open Field	Rk	Sacks	ASR	Rk	Short	Long	F-Start	Cont.
2011	3.81	3.99	20	56%	25	22%	27	1.12	23	0.51	28	25	4.5%	4	10	11	25	32
2012	4.17	4.15	11	69%	5	17%	9	0.91	31	0.90	10	46	8.3%	28	9	26	16	35
2013	3.70	4.03	11	63%	19	18%	9	0.96	26	0.37	30	29	5.2%	3	11	8	17	32

2013 ALY by direction: Left End 3.08 (21) Left Tackle 3.73 (20) Mid/Guard 4.40 (4) Right Tackle 3.66 (21) Right End 3.33 (23)

Once Andrew Whitworth regained full health and mobility after offseason knee surgery, the line improved noticeably, going from 3.82 Adjusted Line Yards in the first half of the season to 4.22 afterwards. The line really found its stride, especially in pass blocking, after guard Clint Boling tore his ACL in Week 13 and Whitworth shifted inside from left tackle. Anthony Collins came off the bench and played well enough to earn himself a large free-agent payday from Tampa Bay. Whitworth shouldn't have a problem returning to his old position, but the depth takes a hit, as his backup is now Marshall Newhouse, the former Packers tackle whose main qualification appears to be being Andy Dalton's best pal from TCU. It remains to be seen whether losing Collins, who is technically excellent in pass blocking, causes the Adjusted Sack Rate to balloon back to 2012's high level, or if that year was an aberration.

For the second straight year the Bengals ranked fourth in ALY on runs up the middle, but that's where personnel is changing for 2014. Center Kyle Cook is smart and agile, but leg injuries have sapped his power. He was released in February. There are several options for his replacement. Trevor Robinson played well enough when Cook was hurt in 2012, and versatile Mike Pollak was re-signed specifically to play center if a better option didn't surface. But the preferred starter is fourth-rounder Russell Bodine, an immensely strong (he benched 42 reps at the combine, six more than anyone else there) and nasty character out of North Carolina. However, Bodine lacks second-level agility and the smarts to handle myriad protections, so he may be best suited for guard. The Bengals hadn't traded up in the draft since 2002, but moved up to grab Bodine, which speaks volumes.

Defensive Front Seven

			Overall								vs. Run					Pass Rush			
Defensive Line	Age	Pos	G	Snaps	Plays	TmPct	Rk	Stop	Dfts	BTkl	Runs	St%	Rk	RuYd	Rk	Sack	Hit	Hur	Tips
Domata Peko	30	DT	16	641	52	6.3%	25	40	9	1	42	81%	32	2.3	46	2.0	1	4.0	0
Geno Atkins	26	DT	9	454	20	4.3%	57	18	13	0	11	82%	30	1.0	4	6.5	6	8.3	0
Brandon Thompson	25	DT	16	386	24	2.9%	--	16	3	2	20	65%	--	2.7	--	1.5	1	2.5	1

			Overall								vs. Run					Pass Rush			
Edge Rushers	Age	Pos	G	Snaps	Plays	TmPct	Rk	Stop	Dfts	BTkl	Runs	St%	Rk	RuYd	Rk	Sack	Hit	Hur	Tips
Carlos Dunlap	25	DE	16	937	63	7.6%	12	52	21	3	41	85%	13	3.1	58	8.0	18	23.5	6
Michael Johnson*	27	DE	15	906	65	8.3%	7	50	18	4	45	73%	49	2.5	42	3.5	20	26.5	7
Wallace Gilberry	30	DE	16	508	27	3.2%	74	24	14	0	13	77%	34	3.1	59	7.5	6	9.3	3
Margus Hunt	27	DE	10	164	3	0.6%	--	1	1	0	2	0%	--	8.0	--	0.5	1	4.8	0

			Overall								Pass Rush			vs. Run					vs. Pass						
Linebackers	Age	Pos	G	Snaps	Plays	TmPct	Rk	Stop	Dfts	BTkl	Sack	Hit	Hur	Runs	St%	Rk	RuYd	Rk	Tgts	Suc%	Rk	AdjYd	Rk	PD	Int
Vontaze Burfict	24	OLB	16	1028	177	21.3%	1	93	26	6	3.0	2	6.5	90	63%	51	3.3	33	53	48%	43	6.3	30	7	1
Rey Maualuga	27	MLB	13	600	76	11.2%	56	38	2	6	1.0	0	1	47	62%	54	3.3	42	25	52%	38	4.7	7	1	1
James Harrison*	36	OLB	15	378	31	4.0%	--	20	8	2	1.5	4	7	20	65%	--	2.0	--	7	51%	--	7.8	--	1	1
Vincent Rey	27	OLB	16	342	51	6.1%	77	32	12	3	4.0	2	2	20	70%	22	2.3	8	23	61%	14	4.5	5	4	2

Year	Yards	ALY	Rk	Power	Rk	Stuff	Rk	2nd Level	Rk	Open Field	Rk	Sacks	ASR	Rk	Short	Long
2011	4.09	3.78	5	66%	23	20%	17	1.03	4	0.88	21	45	7.3%	10	15	20
2012	4.05	4.04	16	82%	32	18%	21	1.19	17	0.48	6	51	8.7%	2	13	22
2013	3.78	3.82	15	60%	10	15%	29	0.99	5	0.43	3	43	7.0%	14	18	16

2013 ALY by direction: Left End 3.44 (12) Left Tackle 4.82 (29) Mid/Guard 3.89 (12) Right Tackle 3.24 (8) Right End 3.41 (12)

Clearly the midseason loss of Geno Atkins was keenly felt, but the Bengals' superb depth kept the injury from being a death blow. Even without the departed Michael Johnson, this defensive line has no fewer than nine quality players. Whether the unit takes a step up into Seahawks or Rams territory depends on Atkins' full recovery, as well as the growth of young tackles Brandon Thompson (who impressed filling in for Atkins) and Devon Still (who did not), and especially end Margus Hunt. The Ivan Drago clone is immensely strong and creates pressure merely by leaning toward quarterbacks. But he is also incredibly raw, playing football as though he was still throwing the discus, which he did at a world-class level before taking up pigskin at SMU. If he can keep his pad level down and learn some technique, Johnson will be a distant memory. Just in case Hunt falters, the Bengals drafted MJ clone Will Clarke in the third round. Tall, long, and adept at batting down passes (seven his senior year at West Virginia, the same number Johnson swatted away in 2013), his skill set matches up with Johnson's to a scary degree.

Vontaze Burfict went from undrafted free agent to the cusp of a Defensive Player of the Year Award in two seasons. The Tazemanian Devil was everywhere, a sideline-to-sideline force even though he mostly played on the weak side. He will likely sign a (deserved) rich contract extension by the time you read this. UFAs are a key element of the linebacking corps even beyond Burfict. Vinny Rey filled in for Rey Maualuga when he was hurt, and showed tremendous instincts and burst (he had three sacks in his first start). Speedsters Jayson DiManche and Emannuel Lamur (who missed the season with a shoulder injury) are expected to be key contributors as well. Maualuga, no doubt paranoid over actually having been drafted, had a strong bounceback season after a 2012 dud. James Harrison, whom the Bengals chose over Karlos Dansby last summer, was often left out of the base nickel scheme the Bengals preferred to deploy. He has been released, his career presumably finished after ten seasons.

Defensive Secondary

			Overall								vs. Run					vs. Pass									
Secondary	Age	Pos	G	Snaps	Plays	TmPct	Rk	Stop	Dfts	BTkl	Runs	St%	Rk	RuYd	Rk	Tgts	Tgt%	Rk	Dist	Suc%	Rk	AdjYd	Rk	PD	Int
George Iloka	24	FS	16	1032	72	8.7%	56	27	9	7	35	51%	20	6.7	32	25	5.5%	9	16.9	48%	57	7.1	42	7	1
Adam Jones	31	CB	16	978	67	8.1%	50	31	16	7	12	58%	11	5.3	17	89	20.6%	39	12.9	58%	16	7.6	45	14	3
Reggie Nelson	31	FS	15	974	66	8.5%	63	25	14	3	29	34%	52	7.9	59	30	7.0%	23	18.9	61%	27	7.3	43	6	2
Terence Newman	36	CB	13	818	63	9.3%	27	27	12	6	10	60%	6	7.5	51	77	21.2%	44	13.1	49%	64	7.9	53	9	2
Isaiah Frey	24	CB	16	508	48	5.9%	--	23	8	3	18	56%	--	5.9	--	33	16.5%	--	8.4	58%	--	6.8	--	1	0
Chris Crocker*	34	SS	12	507	43	6.9%	68	22	13	4	15	53%	13	3.2	3	31	13.7%	72	8.7	62%	21	4.1	5	7	2
Dre Kirkpatrick	25	CB	14	302	32	4.4%	--	12	7	6	4	25%	--	6.8	--	27	19.9%	--	14.4	53%	--	9.1	--	4	3
Leon Hall	30	CB	5	274	25	9.6%	--	15	7	1	7	71%	--	9.4	--	24	19.9%	--	12.6	74%	--	3.6	--	5	1
Taylor Mays	26	FS	8	202	20	4.8%	--	10	5	0	6	33%	--	5.2	--	15	16.3%	--	10.0	63%	--	3.5	--	1	0
Danieal Manning	*32*	*FS*	*6*	*321*	*26*	*9.0%*	*--*	*12*	*4*	*4*	*15*	*47%*	*--*	*7.7*	*--*	*12*	*9.7%*	*--*	*16.1*	*78%*	*--*	*2.3*	*--*	*2*	*0*

Year	Pass D Rank	vs. #1 WR	Rk	vs. #2 WR	Rk	vs. Other WR	Rk	vs. TE	Rk	vs. RB	Rk
2011	18	14.9%	21	31.9%	28	-5.6%	15	11.4%	19	-11.8%	10
2012	9	-12.3%	9	7.3%	22	9.5%	24	-3.9%	12	-8.4%	10
2013	4	-21.9%	3	-27.6%	3	-19.6%	6	-11.7%	9	8.2%	23

Even without Leon Hall for much of the season, the defensive backfield was a strength. Only the Vikings and Jets had a higher percentage of sacks charted as "coverage sacks," which inverted the notion that the line made the back four look good. Terence Newman and Adam Jones are masters of the scheme, and Jones in particular plastered enemy receivers with sticky coverage. 2012 first-rounder Dre Kirkpatrick emerged from an injury black hole to shows flashes of his draft status at season's end. If he can develop as planned, and physical rookie Darqueze Dennard (Michigan State) is what everyone expects him to be, the balance of veteran smarts and young talent is ideal.

In a perfect world, Chris Crocker won't be required to come off his couch to provide crucial snaps at safety, as he has the last few seasons. Reggie Nelson is solid, but the other safety position takes a village. Just as Taylor Mays figured out how to play without knocking out his own teammates, he was lost for the year. He figures to be used on run downs as a hybrid box defender. George

Iloka played well but needs to improve his hands if he is to stick as a pass defense specialist. The player to watch is Danieal Manning, who came over from Houston with his position coach, Vance Joseph. Manning missed most of 2013 with a knee injury but he fits the profile of a veteran defender whose career is revived under Marvin Lewis—indeed, he'll likely play the hybrid safety/slot corner role Crocker inhabited. Shawn Williams, a strong special teamer, is on the bubble due to the depth.

Special Teams

Year	DVOA	Rank	FG/XP	Rank	Net Kick	Rank	Kick Ret	Rank	Net Punt	Rank	Punt Ret	Rank	Hidden	Rank
2011	2.3%	7	3.3	11	10.0	2	-7.5	31	0.7	15	4.8	5	4.8	10
2012	4.1%	7	5.9	8	-1.8	22	-6.3	26	18.0	3	4.9	7	4.2	5
2013	1.2%	12	-1.5	21	-1.2	19	4.0	6	3.4	15	1.5	12	-1.1	18

Kevin Huber was having an excellent season, ranking sixth in gross punt value, until his jaw was broken by a blindside shot against Pittsburgh. This was just the latest in a series of controversial hits the Steelers have foisted upon the Bengals over the years (we're looking right at you, Kimo von Oelhoffen and Hines Ward). The lefty is expected to be back to full health in 2014, presumably having spent the offseason working on keeping his head on a swivel during returns.

Otherwise, the status quo holds throughout the special teams. Few fans are excited by the prospects of another season of Brandon Tate handling return duties, but Tate was in the top ten for kickoff runbacks and is valued by the coaches for his sure hands and judgment on punts. Mid-pack kicker Mike Nugent is back for another season of watching from the sidelines while the Bengals eschew 50-plus-yard field goals, and the coverage units are strong, a reflection of the team's depth. Rookie linebacker DiManche led the team with 13 special-teams tackles.

Cleveland Browns

2013 Record: 4-12	**Total DVOA:** -21.8% (28th)	**2014 Mean Projection:** 6.8 wins	**On the Clock (0-4):** 18%
Pythagorean Wins: 5.5 (26th)	**Offense:** -14.4% (26th)	**Postseason Odds:** 18.7%	**Mediocrity (5-7):** 46%
Snap-Weighted Age: 25.8 (31st)	**Defense:** 8.2% (24th)	**Super Bowl Odds:** 1.1%	**Playoff Contender (8-10):** 28%
Average Opponent: -0.9% (19th)	**Special Teams:** 0.9% (14th)	**Proj. Avg. Opponent:** -2.9% (27th)	**Super Bowl Contender (11+):** 7%

2013: The latest reboot crashes yet again.

2014: The Johnny Cleveland Era begins.

Well, *that* was entertaining.

Cleveland's offseason was so full of incident, so speedily consuming of plot, and so packed with unexpected drama that it should have been available for binge-watching on Netflix. After stumbling through yet another underwhelming season in 2013, the Browns were the story of the NFL in the stretch between the year's final whistle and the opening thuds of training camp, thanks to a flurry of action; some of it genius, some of it mystifying, and some of it a great leap into the unknown.

A brief recap:

Owner Jimmy Haslem, who bought the team preaching stability, fired head coach Rob Chudzinski after a single 4-12 season. Haslem, along with general manager Mike Lombardi and CEO Joe Banner, were mocked by a local reporter as the "Three Stooges" following the move.

The coaching search to replace Chud went on for weeks, weaving unsuccessfully through pretty much every available candidate. At long last, the team settled on Mike Pettine, the Buffalo Bills' defensive coordinator best known for being a protege of Rex Ryan in Baltimore and New York. The Stooges seemed lost.

Moe then axed Larry and Curly. In a truly stunning move, given what had come before, Haslem showed both Banner and Lombardi the door a mere week before the scouting combine in February. The mocking was intense before this, but at this point the Browns became the NFL's version of Toronto Mayor Rob Ford—the franchise appeared to be operating while heavily under the influence.

Ray Farmer, a former Eagles linebacker turned respected personnel man, was elevated to run the team's football operations, just before Farmer was reportedly about to jump to Miami to take the GM job there.

Just when the dust began to settle, Pro Football Talk reported the Browns had nearly traded multiple draft picks to San Francisco in exchange for coach Jim Harbaugh, a move that would have been a stunning coup (and revealed cracks in the 49ers' fissure). But since the near-deal collapsed, and was revealed only after Pettine had been hired, the Browns were lampooned for their ineptitude once more.

Surprisingly enough, the Browns then had a superb draft, trading down and up with abandon in Farmer's first go-around. Building upon the fleecing of Indianapolis, who traded their first-rounder for Trent Richardson during the 2013 season, the Browns selected the best cornerback available as well as several other well-regarded prospects in spots that screamed "value," *and* added Buffalo's first-round pick in 2015.

But the Browns passed on taking any wide receivers, even though word leaked out during the draft that Josh Gordon, their fantastic but troubled wideout, would be suspended, perhaps as long as the entire season. Gordon is in Dutch with the NFL for flunking a third drug test while under double secret probation already.

Oh yeah—and they drafted Johnny Football.

Heck, events that would have defined the offseason in most other NFL cities, like the locking down of foundation players Alex Mack and Joe Haden to new long-term deals, or the free-agent signing of new lead back Ben Tate, were relegated to the agate type during Cleveland's Lollapalooza. And all of it, even the franchise-defining maneuverings in the front office, was utterly dwarfed when the Browns took Pigskin Elvis with the 22nd pick of the first round.

Ah, Johnny "Money" Manziel, aka Johnny Fat Stacks, aka Johnny Cleveland, aka Johnny (this space for rent or copyright)—what shall we do with you? Our projections forecast another bummer of a season by Lake Erie, but Manziel's impact is impossible to accurately predict. By now, you are surely all too familiar with the Manziel Mythology, and the wide range of opinion regarding his professional prospects. Manziel is at the epicenter of all those intangible memes that we generally frown upon here at your favorite metrics-based organization. "He's a winner with huge hands!" "He's too small and plays backyard football!" "He's great, but God hates Cleveland and the Browns always screw it up!" And so forth. We're all already tired of it, and he hasn't played a single down yet. Just wait until November, when Manziel is the topic of debate every single minute of every single ESPN program on every single platform, even during LPGA telecasts.

One thing is for sure: Manziel instantly makes the Browns compelling for the first time since they started up again in 1999. The Browns haven't merely been bad over the last fifteen years; they've also been deathly dull. Now they are about to be led by a player so cocksure he texted Browns quarterbacks coach Dowell Loggains, "Hurry up and draft me so we can wreck this league together." Usually, Red Zone Channel viewers could go an entire Sunday without seeing but a handful of Browns cut-ins. Now, virtually every snap will be spot-

2014 Browns Schedule

Week	Opp.	Week	Opp.	Week	Opp.
1	at PIT	7	at JAC	13	at BUF
2	NO	8	OAK	14	IND
3	BAL	9	TB	15	CIN
4	BYE	10	at CIN (Thu.)	16	at CAR
5	at TEN	11	HOU	17	at BAL
6	PIT	12	at ATL		

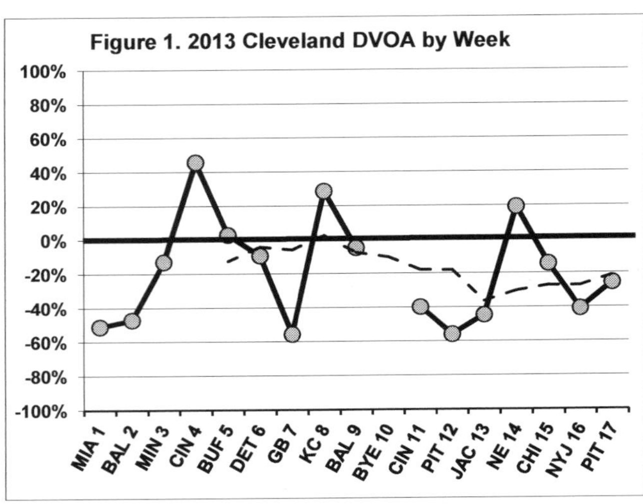

lighted. Such media saturation has already worn on the team, but they had best get used to it, as they ain't seen nuthin' yet.

Manziel's development is a project not only for Loggains but also for new offensive coordinator Kyle Shanahan and, to a lesser degree, Pettine, who as a defensive guru is more likely to spend time searching for holes in Manziel's game enemy teams might exploit. Shanahan is escaping from the toxic shadow he and his father Mike cast in Washington, where another celebrity quarterback with great running ability squabbled with the Shanaclan. Kyle has already compared Manziel to RG3, although he seemed to do it strictly because it was expected of him.

Otherwise, the team has kept to the official script that has Brian Hoyer returning from knee surgery to be the starter, with Manziel watching and learning from the bench. The first step is memorizing the playbook, starting with how to read one—according to Peter King, Manziel never had a playbook at Texas A&M, instead working off a mere handful of plays drawn up each week. That tidbit is just one of the multitude of reasons some analysts don't see Manziel's game translating to the "Lombardi Trophy is in the details" nature of the NFL. Nonetheless, it seems highly unlikely that the former Heisman Trophy winner will spend the whole season on the sidelines. Hoyer won both his 2013 starts before tearing up his knee, and by Browns standards that makes him Bernie Kosar. (Hoyer's Cleveland roots help, too.) But Manziel's ascendance seems preordained: he's the first-round pick, he's the explosive talent, and he's the man who sells tickets. If Johnny truly is Elvis, then Hoyer is Pat Boone, existing only to be displaced by the hot new thing.

Regardless of who plays quarterback, there won't be much of a passing game if Gordon is indeed out for a lengthy period. The fleet wideout established himself as the first true gamebreaker this franchise has trotted out since the days of Paul Warfield. Since the Browns were reborn in 1999, their leading receiver is the less-than-immortal Kevin Johnson. Gordon, in just 30 games, is already fifth on that list. His sophomore campaign was an out-of-nowhere sensation. Gordon improved in DYAR from 67 to 336, and in DVOA from -3.6% to 14.1%. His yardage and catches per game both doubled. Given the fact that Gordon's fellow wideouts were putrid (Greg Little and Davone Bess were the bottom two wide receivers in DYAR last season) and his quarterbacks were, well, Browns, his immense productivity was astonishing.

But Gordon's immaturity is rather astonishing in its own right, which is why he's in trouble with the league, and why he was pulled over for speeding shortly after word of his pending suspension broke, and why he was arrested for DWI a few weeks after *that*, and why the Browns were actively pursuing trades to rid themselves of their best player last season. The Browns passed on drafting help, despite the exceptional depth of this year's class at the wide receiver position, and instead brought in damaged goods like Miles Austin and Nate Burleson in free agency. Andrew Hawkins, a restricted free-agent signing who was the fourth wideout in Cincinnati, may now be the favorite to be Cleveland's leading receiver in 2014.

With the passing game questionable, running the ball could be the first, second, and third option in Cleveland, with the emphasis on "option" if Manziel is at the helm. Shanahan's zone blocking, one-cut run scheme that made Alfred Morris so effective in D.C. will be critical for Cleveland if it hopes to score at all. With the new scheme comes an all-new tandem of backs: the aforementioned Tate, who comes over from Houston after three solid seasons as Arian Foster's understudy, and rookie Terrance West, who put up eye-popping stats at FCS school Towson. The more important personnel are the three offensive linemen playing with Mack and All-Pro Joe Thomas. Second-round pick Joel Bitonio is presumably one of them, likely the left guard. Right tackle Mitchell Schwartz must improve after a horrid 2013, and all the linemen must pick up the new blocking scheme in a single summer.

While the offense tries to answer all these questions, the Browns will try to hang their hats on defense, which brings us to their new head coach. Pettine had a star turn in Nicholas Dawidoff's excellent behind-the-scenes book about the New York Jets, *Collision Low Crossers*, but he is otherwise mostly unknown, right down to the pronunciation of his surname (it's PETT-in, not Puh-TEE-knee).

Pettine took the fact that he was hardly Cleveland's first choice with equanimity, as any career assistant might, and expressed nothing but joy about landing the gig. His daughter Megan, conversely, succinctly summed up everyone else's feelings in 140 characters, tweeting, "It's the Browns...But hey, still pretty cool!"

Pettine may not be Bill Belichick to Rex Ryan's Bill Parcells, but his defenses have certainly been suffocating. Over the last five seasons, his units have finished fourth, ninth, second, fifth and first in DVOA, averaging -14.1% over that span. Last year,

Pettine proved he wasn't just riding Rex's coattails; he took over a Buffalo defense that ranked 27th in DVOA in 2012 and improved it to fourth in 2013, thanks in large part to 57 sacks.

Of course, if Pettine can't work wonders this season, he won't be the first well-regarded defensive mind to fail with these players. Ray Horton came to the AFC North with a sterling resume—his Arizona defense had ranked sixth in DVOA in 2012—but he was unable to generate consistent pass rush or further develop a proper partner for Joe Haden. Pettine will have longtime understudy Jim O'Neil as his coordinator. With those two calling the shots, the Browns will surely be bringing blitzers from all angles while hoping Haden and first-round draft pick Justin Gilbert (Oklahoma State) can hold up in press coverage. While neither corner figures to match Darrelle Revis, whose awesomeness propelled those Jets defenses to great heights, the hope is that they prove adept enough to allow the Browns' pass rush to affect the game more often. A breakthrough in linebacker Barkevious Mingo's second season would help; it would also be nice if pricey 2013 free-agent acquisition Paul Kruger would do a better job of playing up to his rich contract this year.

So yet again, we enter a season after a Cleveland overhaul—a more volatile and thorough one than usual, perhaps, but this is still well-trod terrain. Come September, the Browns will trot out their 12th different opening-day starting quarterback since their reboot in 1999, an incredible stat that neatly sums up the franchise's futility. The excitement the city felt over drafting Manziel was strongly tempered by cynicism that the Brownies would regardless find a way to botch things, just as they did with the previous passers they selected with the 22nd pick, Brandon Weeden and Brady Quinn. The job tasked to Farmer, Pettine, Shanahan, and Manziel is not merely to win games but to succeed against the run of play, at long last building something that isn't liable to be blown up two years hence. What is past is merely prologue, goes the saying. The Browns are desperately hoping this is the dawn of a new era. Their history suggests otherwise, but at least they've gone and drafted a potential change agent.

Robert Weintraub

2013 Browns Stats by Week

Wk	vs.	W-L	PF	PA	YDF	YDA	TO	Total	Off	Def	ST
1	MIA	L	10	23	291	275	-2	-51%	-51%	-3%	-3%
2	at BAL	L	6	14	259	296	+1	-47%	-19%	18%	-11%
3	at MIN	W	31	27	409	329	-1	-13%	-28%	-11%	4%
4	CIN	W	17	6	336	266	+2	46%	26%	-28%	-7%
5	BUF	W	37	24	290	343	+1	3%	-20%	8%	31%
6	DET	L	17	31	395	366	-1	-9%	12%	20%	-2%
7	at GB	L	13	31	216	357	-1	-56%	-44%	34%	23%
8	at KC	L	17	23	340	331	-1	29%	34%	7%	1%
9	BAL	W	24	18	315	278	+1	-5%	4%	7%	-1%
10	BYE										
11	at CIN	L	20	41	330	224	-2	-40%	-46%	-37%	-31%
12	PIT	L	11	27	367	302	-4	-56%	-41%	16%	2%
13	JAC	L	28	32	439	314	-2	-45%	-16%	22%	-7%
14	at NE	L	26	27	494	484	+2	19%	26%	13%	7%
15	CHI	L	31	38	366	440	+1	-14%	9%	18%	-5%
16	at NYJ	L	13	24	283	422	-2	-41%	-23%	34%	15%
17	at PIT	L	7	20	293	292	0	-26%	-31%	-6%	0%

Trends and Splits

	Offense	Rank	Defense	Rank
Total DVOA	-14.4%	26	8.2%	24
Unadjusted VOA	-13.9%	26	3.2%	21
Weighted Trend	-13.3%	25	12.0%	27
Variance	7.8%	20	3.9%	7
Average Opponent	-0.6%	14	-3.6%	30
Passing	-9.2%	25	14.1%	23
Rushing	-7.0%	22	0.7%	23
First Down	-15.4%	26	-2.0%	13
Second Down	-16.1%	27	3.3%	19
Third Down	-10.4%	21	33.9%	31
First Half	-12.7%	29	1.4%	19
Second Half	-16.2%	26	15.6%	28
Red Zone	-12.4%	26	55.0%	32
Late and Close	-15.0%	25	16.1%	31

Five-Year Performance

Year	W-L	Pyth W	Est W	PF	PA	TO	Total	Rk	Off	Rk	Def	Rk	ST	Rk	Off AGL	Rk	Def AGL	Rk	Off Age	Rk	Def Age	Rk	ST Age	Rk
2009	5-11	4.3	4.8	245	375	-12	-23.1%	16	-16.4%	24	16.4%	30	9.7%	1	37.4	25	43.3	27	27.3	15	27.5	10	26.6	17
2010	5-11	6.1	6.7	271	332	-1	-4.0%	20	-5.0%	22	1.7%	18	2.7%	10	42.7	31	52.0	32	27.7	13	27.7	9	27.4	3
2011	4-12	5.0	5.5	218	307	+1	-14.2%	25	-11.2%	25	4.2%	22	1.3%	10	45.5	27	26.3	15	26.1	29	26.6	24	26.1	23
2012	5-11	6.1	6.2	302	368	+3	-13.5%	24	-15.2%	27	4.5%	22	6.1%	2	26.4	13	57.0	29	25.7	30	26.1	26	25.2	30
2013	4-12	5.5	4.4	308	406	-8	-21.8%	28	-14.4%	26	8.2%	24	0.9%	14	25.9	9	18.4	7	26.6	21	25.4	30	24.9	31

2013 Performance Based on Most Common Personnel Groups

CLE Offense					CLE Offense vs. Opponents				CLE Defense				CLE Defense vs. Opponents			
Pers	Freq	Yds	DVOA	Run%	Pers	Freq	Yds	DVOA	Pers	Freq	Yds	DVOA	Pers	Freq	Yds	DVOA
11	51%	4.7	-22.6%	14%	Nickel Even	38%	4.8	-17.3%	3-4-4	46%	4.6	-6.8%	11	54%	5.1	10.0%
12	36%	5.7	-1.2%	42%	4-3-4	27%	5.6	-1.2%	Nickel Even	30%	4.9	5.6%	12	19%	5.4	6.5%
21	5%	5.1	12.8%	36%	3-4-4	15%	5.7	13.2%	Nickel Odd	17%	5.9	31.0%	21	11%	5.0	1.1%
22	3%	3.8	-3.2%	69%	Dime+	13%	5.3	-15.8%	Dime+	6%	7.0	45.0%	22	5%	3.7	-8.5%
13	3%	2.9	13.0%	75%	Nickel Odd	6%	3.2	-49.2%	4-3-4	1%	7.1	74.6%	13	4%	4.5	-8.5%

Strategic Tendencies

Run/Pass		Rk	Formation		Rk	Pass Rush		Rk	Secondary		Rk	Strategy		Rk
Runs, first half	35%	24	Form: Single Back	75%	10	Rush 3	4.7%	21	4 DB	47%	9	Play action	20%	18
Runs, first down	41%	30	Form: Empty Back	5%	20	Rush 4	58.6%	22	5 DB	47%	21	Avg Box (Off)	6.20	27
Runs, second-long	20%	31	Pers: 3+ WR	53%	23	Rush 5	27.1%	12	6+ DB	6%	16	Avg Box (Def)	6.37	17
Runs, power sit.	52%	19	Pers: 4+ WR	0%	26	Rush 6+	9.5%	9	CB by Sides	53%	31	Offensive Pace	28.90	9
Runs, behind 2H	17%	32	Pers: 2+ TE/6+ OL	43%	5	Sacks by LB	53.8%	9	DB Blitz	9%	24	Defensive Pace	28.45	2
Pass, ahead 2H	62%	2	Shotgun/Pistol	59%	17	Sacks by DB	15.0%	3	Hole in Zone	13%	10	Go for it on 4th	1.65	1

One big strategic change for Cleveland last year was the use of Joe Haden to shadow the opponent's best receiver, as the Browns dropped from 11th to 31st in our "CB by Sides" metric. For the second straight year, the Browns were excellent when they blitzed a defensive back. They allowed just 4.0 yards per play, third in the NFL, after leading the league with just 2.7 yards per play allowed on DB blitzes in 2012. The Browns were actually much better on defense when opponents used play action (-9.5% DVOA) compared to when they did not (24.6% DVOA), although they allowed 5.8 yards per pass either way. Cleveland showed a similar split on offense, with the league's third-biggest DVOA gap between play action (7.3 yards per pass, 25.6% DVOA) and passes without play action (5.2 yards per pass, -15.0% DVOA).

Passing

Player	DYAR	DVOA	Plays	NtYds	Avg	YAC	C%	TD	Int
J.Campbell*	-24	-12.2%	332	1912	5.8	5.8	57.1%	11	8
B.Weeden*	-443	-36.1%	293	1535	5.2	4.5	53.2%	9	9
B.Hoyer	5	-10.4%	103	553	5.4	5.5	60.4%	5	3

Rushing

Player	DYAR	DVOA	Plays	Yds	Avg	TD	Fum	Suc
W.McGahee*	-92	-22.6%	137	382	2.8	2	1	46%
C.Ogbonnaya	29	4.7%	49	240	4.9	0	1	53%
E.Baker	41	13.1%	43	171	4.0	2	0	51%
T.Richardson*	-14	-19.1%	31	105	3.4	0	0	48%
F.Whittaker*	-17	-25.2%	28	79	2.8	0	0	43%
J.Campbell*	31	34.0%	13	108	8.3	0	0	-
B.Rainey*	-14	-42.5%	13	34	2.6	0	0	23%
B.Weeden*	11	12.4%	9	46	5.1	0	0	-
M.Gray	13	56.8%	6	43	7.2	0	0	50%
J.Gordon	53	150.4%	5	88	17.6	0	0	-
B.Tate	*50*	*-2.0%*	*180*	*773*	*4.3*	*4*	*4*	*51%*

Receiving

Player	DYAR	DVOA	Plays	Ctch	Yds	Y/C	YAC	TD	C%
J.Gordon	336	14.4%	159	87	1646	18.9	7.3	9	55%
G.Little*	-171	-34.7%	99	41	465	11.3	4.6	2	41%
D.Bess*	-135	-32.3%	86	42	362	8.6	3.5	2	49%
J.Cooper	-17	-28.4%	14	9	60	6.7	2.2	0	64%
T.Benjamin	4	-8.3%	13	5	105	21.0	12.0	0	38%
N.Burleson	*56*	*0.4%*	*54*	*39*	*461*	*11.8*	*5.5*	*1*	*72%*
M.Austin	*-51*	*-25.9%*	*49*	*24*	*244*	*10.2*	*4.2*	*0*	*49%*
A.Hawkins	*31*	*8.7%*	*18*	*12*	*199*	*16.6*	*11.3*	*0*	*67%*
J.Cameron	99	5.6%	118	80	917	11.5	3.0	7	68%
G.Barnidge	-4	-10.7%	18	13	127	9.8	7.0	2	72%
J.Dray	*21*	*2.3%*	*32*	*26*	*215*	*8.3*	*4.0*	*2*	*81%*
C.Ogbonnaya	14	-10.2%	75	48	349	7.3	6.0	2	64%
F.Whittaker*	18	-5.5%	35	21	155	7.4	7.4	2	60%
W.McGahee*	-44	-74.5%	12	9	18	2.0	1.9	0	75%
T.Richardson*	-6	-24.0%	11	7	51	7.3	7.3	0	64%
E.Baker	23	30.3%	9	8	57	7.1	8.3	0	89%
M.Gray	-38	-84.2%	9	2	8	4.0	3.0	0	22%
B.Tate	*-125*	*-62.9%*	*50*	*35*	*138*	*3.9*	*4.7*	*0*	*70%*

Offensive Line

Player	Pos	Age	GS	Snaps	Pen	Sk	Pass	Run	Player	Pos	Age	GS	Snaps	Pen	Sk	Pass	Run
Alex Mack	C	29	16/16	1107	3	0.5	8.5	2.5	Shawn Lauvao*	RG	27	11/11	741	3	4.5	16.5	5.0
Mitchell Schwartz	RT	25	16/16	1107	3	10.0	37.5	4.0	Oniel Cousins*	G/T	30	16/4	311	4	0.0	9.5	3.0
Joe Thomas	LT	30	16/16	1106	11	3.0	12.5	3.5	Jason Pinkston	LG	27	3/2	152	0	0.0	2.0	1.0
John Greco	LG	29	14/14	921	2	4.0	15.0	1.5	*Paul McQuistan*	*G/T*	*29*	*16/10*	*773*	*4*	*6.8*	*21.3*	*8.0*

Year	Yards	ALY	Rk	Power	Rk	Stuff	Rk	2nd Lev	Rk	Open Field	Rk	Sacks	ASR	Rk	Short	Long	F-Start	Cont.
2011	3.60	3.94	23	66%	9	16%	2	0.85	32	0.41	31	39	6.4%	15	11	22	19	39
2012	3.79	4.03	20	53%	29	19%	16	1.08	23	0.40	31	36	6.0%	12	15	15	25	40
2013	3.53	3.83	18	70%	9	20%	18	0.95	28	0.36	31	49	7.5%	17	12	23	23	35

2013 ALY by direction: Left End 2.12 (31) Left Tackle 5.13 (1) Mid/Guard 3.80 (22) Right Tackle 3.40 (25) Right End 3.83 (15)

Offensive lines and basketball teams are both comprised of five players, but having two star linemen doesn't get a team nearly as far as having LeBron and D-Wade (or, to be more current, LeBron and Kyrie Irving). Lining up Joe Thomas at left tackle and Alex Mack at center hasn't translated into anything other than mediocrity in both Adjusted Line Yards and Adjusted Sack Rate the last three seasons. "No push at all by (Cleveland's) offensive line" came up in our game-charting comments far too often. Thomas is a bedrock player, and the fact we charted runs ostensibly his way as being so successful is some testimony to his sturdiness. But Thomas also was called for 11 penalties (seven of them false starts), giving him 27 in three seasons, a niggling bit of drive-stalling that dents his dauntless image a bit.

Still, he and the newly re-signed Mack are among the best in the league at their positions; it's the other three-fifths of the line that disappointed. Mitchell Schwartz struggled mightily at right tackle in his second season, with an astounding 41.5 blown blocks. (Only Michael Oher and Lamar Holmes caused equivalent damage.) The hope is that newly drafted Joel Bitonio (Nevada) can take over, though he projects better inside, most likely at left guard. A versatile player with quick feet and a nasty streak, Bitonio fits Shanahan's new outside zone scheme nicely, and at worst Bitonio will prod Schwartz to improve at tackle. If Schwartz merely gains some consistency, *dayenu*.

The question is really where Bitonio is needed most, for the guard play was atrocious last season. When Oniel Cousins was in there, a whiff was almost automatic. Clearly the incriminating photos he possessed were of Lombardi and Banner, not Farmer, for Cousins was released this offseason. Shaun Lauvao was also mediocre, and is also gone. Assuming Bitonio holds down one spot, there will be a four-way camp battle for the right guard slot. The contenders are John Greco, an effort guy who was the primary starter there a year ago; backup Jason Pinkston, talented but oft-injured; newcomer Paul McQuistan, who started 40 games for Seattle over the last three seasons; and feisty second-year man Garrett Gilkey, who may wind up the eventual starter.

Defensive Front Seven

			Overall								vs. Run					Pass Rush			
Defensive Line	**Age**	**Pos**	**G**	**Snaps**	**Plays**	**TmPct**	**Rk**	**Stop**	**Dfts**	**BTkl**	**Runs**	**St%**	**Rk**	**RuYd**	**Rk**	**Sack**	**Hit**	**Hur**	**Tips**
Ahtyba Rubin	28	DE	14	624	52	6.9%	19	34	7	1	48	63%	80	3.1	75	2.0	3	4.5	1
Desmond Bryant	29	DE	12	580	31	4.8%	47	24	10	1	26	73%	59	4.3	85	3.5	12	14.5	0
Phillip Taylor	26	DT	15	546	27	3.3%	76	23	7	0	22	91%	9	1.4	12	2.0	4	6.5	0
John Hughes	26	DE	15	400	36	4.5%	--	30	4	2	32	84%	--	2.1	--	1.0	0	6.0	1
Billy Winn	25	DE	11	311	21	3.5%	--	19	8	3	17	94%	--	0.8	--	2.0	2	5.0	0

			Overall								vs. Run					Pass Rush			
Edge Rushers	**Age**	**Pos**	**G**	**Snaps**	**Plays**	**TmPct**	**Rk**	**Stop**	**Dfts**	**BTkl**	**Runs**	**St%**	**Rk**	**RuYd**	**Rk**	**Sack**	**Hit**	**Hur**	**Tips**
Paul Kruger	28	OLB	16	877	51	5.9%	31	38	17	4	34	76%	36	2.5	43	4.5	6	26.5	3
Barkevious Mingo	24	OLB	15	663	43	5.3%	43	27	14	3	28	64%	64	3.0	56	5.0	7	12.5	4
Jabaal Sheard	25	OLB	13	651	40	5.7%	36	31	13	3	23	83%	22	1.9	19	5.5	5	15.0	3

			Overall								Pass Rush			vs. Run					vs. Pass						
Linebackers	**Age**	**Pos**	**G**	**Snaps**	**Plays**	**TmPct**	**Rk**	**Stop**	**Dfts**	**BTkl**	**Sack**	**Hit**	**Hur**	**Runs**	**St%**	**Rk**	**RuYd**	**Rk**	**Tgts**	**Suc%**	**Rk**	**AdjYd**	**Rk**	**PD**	**Int**
D'Qwell Jackson*	31	ILB	16	1147	148	17.2%	13	81	23	5	1.5	3	9.5	87	67%	35	3.2	29	36	54%	35	6.8	42	4	1
Craig Robertson	26	ILB	14	845	86	11.4%	53	47	13	4	3.0	2	5	42	69%	25	2.3	9	40	41%	62	8.8	65	3	1
Karlos Dansby	*33*	*ILB*	*16*	*1078*	*141*	*17.3%*	*12*	*87*	*31*	*9*	*6.5*	*5*	*9.5*	*69*	*67%*	*35*	*4.2*	*70*	*60*	*58%*	*21*	*6.2*	*25*	*16*	*4*

Year	Yards	ALY	Rk	Power	Rk	Stuff	Rk	2nd Level	Rk	Open Field	Rk	Sacks	ASR	Rk	Short	Long
2011	4.03	3.92	10	57%	10	22%	9	1.13	11	0.66	9	42	7.6%	6	14	18
2012	4.37	4.14	19	65%	20	16%	28	1.13	8	0.83	18	34	6.9%	9	10	16
2013	4.84	4.34	29	76%	29	18%	17	1.48	31	0.98	26	34	6.1%	26	12	10
2013 ALY by direction:			*Left End 3.74 (17)*			*Left Tackle 4.90 (31)*			*Mid/Guard 4.18 (25)*			*Right Tackle 4.63 (26)*			*Right End 4.42 (28)*	

Phil Taylor rebounded from missing the 2012 season (torn pectoral) to stuff the interior nicely as a 3-4 noseman, while Desmond Bryant came over from Oakland to provide a slashing pass rush. However, Bryant wasn't great against the run, a liability for a five-technique end. The weakest link up front was Ahtyba Rubin, a converted nose tackle who played more snaps than any other lineman but affected opposing offenses the least. The ends were the main culprit in Cleveland's league-worst showing in Power situations, a weakness that doesn't figure to improve greatly unless reserve ends Billy Winn and John Hughes get more playing time. Both backups were strong against the run and figure to push for more snaps in 2014.

The rap on sixth overall pick Barkevious Mingo coming out of LSU was that he needed to add size to his frame to withstand the NFL grind. Score one for the scouts, as Mingo wore down noticeably: after recording a sack in each of his first three games, "Kiki" had only two the rest of the season. The Browns hope an offseason spent packing on the pounds at Wing Stops across northeastern Louisiana allows Mingo to be more effective come winter. Paul Kruger's stellar 2012 was revealed to be partially a byproduct of playing in Baltimore. His numbers were decent but in the context of the large contract that lured him to Cleveland they were disappointing. Jabaal Sheard had more sacks in fewer snaps than either the highly-drafted Mingo or the highly-paid Kruger. However, better things should be ahead for Kruger: normally a player with 26.5 hurries and just 4.5 sacks is going to have more sacks the next season.

D'Qwell Jackson left for Indianapolis in free agency, but Karlos Dansby is as good a replacement as could be hoped for. Dansby went unsigned until late in the summer last season, then turned in a standout season in Arizona. Cleveland snapped him up to replace their leading tackler, and while Jackson's run defense will be missed, Dansby is more agile against the pass. (Dansby led all linebackers in FO's count of passes defensed, which doesn't include passes batted at the line—but he also batted down four passes at the line, the only inside/middle linebacker with more than two.) Third-rounder Christian Kirksey (Iowa) will compete with Craig Robertson at the other inside spot. Many in Cleveland are ready for an upgrade over the stiff and brittle Robertson, but his run numbers were actually pretty good. Kirksey is athletic but small for the position, and may make his more pivotal contributions on special teams for now.

Defensive Secondary

			Overall								vs. Run					vs. Pass									
Secondary	Age	Pos	G	Snaps	Plays	TmPct	Rk	Stop	Dfts	BTkl	Runs	St%	Rk	RuYd	Rk	Tgts	Tgt%	Rk	Dist	Suc%	Rk	AdjYd	Rk	PD	Int
T.J. Ward*	28	SS	16	1112	117	13.6%	8	61	24	8	66	59%	6	3.8	4	38	8.2%	42	9.7	66%	11	4.3	7	4	2
Tashaun Gipson	24	FS	16	1101	107	12.4%	19	40	13	10	55	36%	49	7.0	39	29	6.4%	17	18.1	62%	26	6.3	23	11	5
Buster Skrine	25	CB	16	1052	81	9.4%	24	33	14	13	21	33%	53	7.3	47	105	24.1%	67	11.9	54%	39	5.9	3	17	1
Joe Haden	25	CB	15	1051	74	9.2%	29	37	14	5	11	18%	79	8.3	58	88	20.3%	36	14.6	58%	15	6.1	7	19	4
Chris Owens	28	CB	13	539	53	7.6%	--	17	7	2	9	56%	--	7.0	--	44	19.6%	--	9.5	47%	--	5.7	--	3	0
Donte Whitner	*29*	*SS*	*16*	*1012*	*85*	*10.7%*	*32*	*30*	*12*	*7*	*28*	*32%*	*55*	*6.0*	*20*	*41*	*9.1%*	*54*	*13.7*	*62%*	*19*	*7.6*	*52*	*11*	*2*

Year	Pass D Rank	vs. #1 WR	Rk	vs. #2 WR	Rk	vs. Other WR	Rk	vs. TE	Rk	vs. RB	Rk
2011	17	1.1%	14	20.9%	26	-19.7%	9	22.1%	25	13.8%	25
2012	20	-2.9%	17	9.3%	24	10.3%	25	0.7%	20	-2.2%	15
2013	23	-17.8%	5	8.7%	20	2.9%	17	25.3%	31	20.7%	31

Take a deep breath before blindly assuming the Browns have a pair of lockdown corners in Joe Haden and top draft choice Justin Gilbert. The latter certainly is an outstanding prospect, one who matches blazing speed with terrific fluidity, and as we've noted in the past (primarily in the Dallas chapter of *FOA 2012*), even the most talented cornerbacks tend to struggle as rookies. One of the knocks on Gilbert at Oklahoma State was his tendency to cruise by on his natural talent and not mix it up on every play, especially against the run. That is a trait that needs to be beaten out of players at the pro level, and expecting brilliance out of the gate is unrealistic and unfair.

Still, Gilbert figures to be a future top-level player, at least on par with Joe Haden on the other side. Haden has the rep of an elite player, and just got paid like one, signing a new deal that pays him more than Richard Sherman in guarantees and signing bonus. Yet the numbers suggest Haden is more very good than great; in an article this offseason[1], our own Cian Fahey broke Haden down into little pieces, finding him good but hardly elite, especially in the areas of technique and footwork. Explosive, sharp-cutting receivers ate him up, and Haden is probably best suited to a Cover-2 zone scheme. But he's certainly better than anyone else the Browns trotted out last year. Buster Skrine will move down to the nickel after a year that combined a lot of good and bad moments. His charting stats came out pretty strong, but Skrine was horrific in short-area coverage, allowing a league-leading eight touchdowns in the red zone. Our charters noted a particular problem with falling for play-action fakes, though they also noted that Skrine shows extra hustle to try to get back into position after he realizes his mistake.

Fourth-round choice Pierre Desir is the wild card of the secondary. A big and explosive athlete, Desir looked great at Division II Lindenwood, and held his own at the Senior Bowl. From Port-au-Prince, Desir lost a pair of family members in the earthquakes that devastated Haiti in 2010, and it will truly be a feel-good story if he succeeds in the NFL. A Gilbert-Haden-Desir triumvirate could be making enemy passers weep come 2016 or so.

AFC North wideouts will surely be happy that strong safety T.J. Ward has left for Denver, taking his intimidating presence and powerful run support with him to the Rockies. Donte Whitner (*nee* "Hitner") replaces Ward, which is a slight downgrade. Rangy and athletic Tashaun Gipson holds down the free safety spot.

Special Teams

Year	DVOA	Rank	FG/XP	Rank	Net Kick	Rank	Kick Ret	Rank	Net Punt	Rank	Punt Ret	Rank	Hidden	Rank
2011	1.3%	10	5.0	6	-1.0	23	4.8	4	-2.3	19	-0.1	17	1.2	15
2012	6.1%	2	8.2	4	9.2	4	0.1	16	1.6	13	11.7	3	-4.8	24
2013	0.9%	14	-0.5	19	3.5	10	0.0	13	-2.4	23	4.1	10	-9.4	28

Billy Cundiff didn't kick off much, but when he did he boomed them. Travis Benjamin was a dangerous punt returner before blowing out his knee. The coverage units were solid enough. Those were the positives from 2013. On the flip side, kickoff returns were ugly, and Spencer Lanning was a disaster at punter. The aforementioned Gilbert, who averaged more than 26 yards and scored six touchdowns in four years returning kicks in college, figures to take over the kick return role. But for some reason, the Browns have not brought in any camp competition for Lanning.

1 http://www.footballoutsiders.com/extra-points/2014/joe-haden-numbers-tape-verdict-2014

Dallas Cowboys

2013 Record: 8-8	**Total DVOA:** -2.8% (17th)	**2014 Mean Projection:** 6.9 wins	**On the Clock (0-4):** 17%
Pythagorean Wins: 8.2 (15th)	**Offense:** 7.5% (11th)	**Postseason Odds:** 19.5%	**Mediocrity (5-7):** 44%
Snap-Weighted Age: 26.1 (26th)	**Defense:** 13.8% (30th)	**Super Bowl Odds:** 1.4%	**Playoff Contender (8-10):** 30%
Average Opponent: -1.3% (21st)	**Special Teams:** 3.4% (8th)	**Proj. Avg. Opponent:** 0.0% (20th)	**Super Bowl Contender (11+):** 8%

2013: Sustained mediocrity is a terrible place to be.

2014: So, does anyone want to drag Dat Nguyen out of retirement?

For three straight seasons, the Dallas Cowboys have gone into Week 17 and played an NFC East rival with the division on the line. And for three straight seasons, the Cowboys have lost that final game to finish 8-8. It's a trifecta unlikely to ever be duplicated. In the 94-year history of the NFL, only three other teams have finished .500 in three consecutive seasons: the 1932-34 Boston Braves/Redskins (before the team moved to Washington), the 1983-85 Green Bay Packers and the 1996-98 Oilers.

While the Oilers became the Tennessee Titans in 1999 and reached the Super Bowl, the bottom fell out on those other teams in year four. The Redskins went 2-8-1 and the Packers dropped to 4-12. With the Cowboys walking on fractured ground, it's easy to trace the fault lines in Dallas.

"I've been here when it was glory hole days and I've been here when it wasn't," Jerry Jones told reporters before the 2012 season. "Having said that, I want me some glory hole." Well, he sure ain't gettin' the glory hole he wants, and if he wants someone to blame, it's time to look in the mirror. (Hopefully, it is not a mirror anywhere near a glory hole.)

Football's usual scapegoats—a hand-picked coach, a polarizing quarterback and a scheme-miscast defense—are all present in Dallas right now, but the main driver of the Cowboys' struggles is still bad front-office decision-making. Every Dallas player wears a star on his helmet, but the team only has a few true stars and they are aging and/or disappearing at a rate that will make 8-8 a real achievement in 2014. Jason Garrett's decision-making in crucial situations continues to breed criticism. Tony Romo is 34 and coming off back surgery for a herniated disc. The defense has lost arguably its two best players. Dallas has gone four seasons without a winning record or a playoff appearance. The last time that happened, the Cowboys went through a transition period where Jones bought the team, fired Tom Landry and hired Jimmy Johnson. Another down year in 2014 and fans will expect wholesale changes again, but we know Jones will not fire himself. Nevertheless, it will take a lot of breaks for the Cowboys to exceed .500 given the hand Jones has dealt for his coach, quarterback and defense.

Since taking over for Wade Phillips during the 2010 season, Garrett has never lost more than two consecutive games. He's never won more than four in a row either. Garrett's record is 29-27 and the Cowboys have outscored their opponents by 34 points (0.6 points per game). Las Vegas odds-makers certainly cannot figure Garrett's Cowboys out.

- When favored, Garrett is 9-21-1 (.306) against the spread—the worst team record in the league since 2010.
- As an underdog, Garrett is 16-7 (.696) against the spread—the second-best team record in the league since 2010. (The Patriots are first at 7-1.)

The moral of the story: Dallas can make *any* game a nail-biter, even if it wasn't expected to be one. That makes the historic stream of 8-8 finishes less surprising. The high volume of close games tells us Dallas has not been good enough to pull away from many of its opponents, but Garrett still must be doing something right to keep his team competitive most weeks.

Forty of Garrett's 56 games (71.4 percent) have featured the Cowboys and/or their opponent having possession of the ball in the fourth quarter with a one-score deficit. The NFL average in this time is 58 percent. Garrett has coached Dallas to victory with a game-winning drive 16 times (28.6 percent of his games), but has also fallen victim to one in 15 losses (26.8 percent). Compared to the other ten head coaches with at least four seasons of tenure, those are the highest rates in each category (Table 1). So when the close wins are even with the close losses, why does Dallas have a stigma for not getting it done in crunch time? Well, try listing the 16 wins and 15 losses separately from memory and see which group is longer. We guarantee the losses have been more memorable, because frankly, they just have been.

Usually when an NFL team is losing a lot of close games, we recommend they stick with what they're doing, because the bounces may break their way soon. (Exhibit A: Ron Rivera's Carolina Panthers). However, the Cowboys are not losing close games in any normal fashion. Since 2011, 14 teams have rallied to win after trailing by at least 12 points in the fourth quarter. Dallas has allowed four of those comebacks, including three at home. Since 1999, home teams are 511-3 when leading by at least 23 points. Two of those three losses belong to Garrett and the Cowboys, in 2011 against the Lions and 2013 against the Packers. This stuff just doesn't happen to other coaches.

Teams usually find a way to close games with big leads, either with defense or with a ground game to drain the clock.

2014 Cowboys Schedule

Week	Opp.	Week	Opp.	Week	Opp.
1	SF	7	NYG	13	PHI (Thu.)
2	at TEN	8	WAS (Mon.)	14	at CHI
3	at STL	9	ARI	15	at PHI
4	NO	10	at JAC (U.K.)	16	IND
5	HOU	11	BYE	17	at WAS
6	at SEA	12	at NYG (Thu.)		

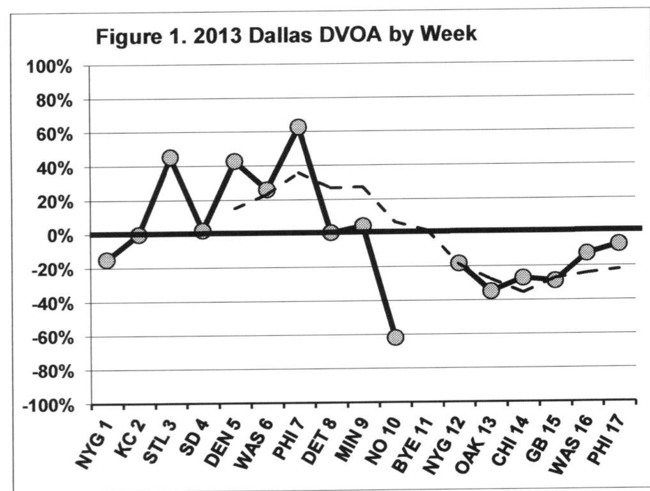

Figure 1. 2013 Dallas DVOA by Week

The Cowboys haven't cracked the top 15 in defensive DVOA since 2009, and the lack of commitment to the running game remains a story that goes back to Garrett's start as offensive coordinator in 2007. Last year he delegated playcalling duties to Bill Callahan, who has more experience with success on the ground. The Cowboys improved from 24th to fifth in rushing DVOA, one of the biggest yearly improvements in our database. However, the 336 runs were the fewest in any 16-game season in Dallas history. Part of that is because Dallas ran a league-low 957 offensive plays, which goes back to a bad defense that couldn't get off the field quickly enough. But part of that remains the unwillingness to stick with the run despite DeMarco Murray leading the league in rushing DVOA (24.0%).

In Garrett's three full seasons as coach, Dallas has ranked 30th, 32nd and 30th in play-action pass usage despite much success (Table 2). We have found no evidence that an effective running game is needed for an effective play-action game, but Garrett might subconsciously be limiting his offense's advantage because he thinks they don't have enough carries to keep defenses "honest." This kind of thinking would certainly match the rest of Garrett's risk-averse style. Dallas did not attempt a fourth-down play until Week 14—the latest any team has waited to do so in a season since at least 1999.

Even when he tries to be aggressive, Garrett usually draws criticism. After blowing a 26-3 lead against Green Bay (Week 15), Garrett came under fire for the offense calling 21 passes to seven runs in the second half after Murray's strong first-half performance (11 carries for 93 yards). Garrett cited Callahan as being responsible for play calls and noted that Romo probably should not have audibled late on a second-down run that became a huge interception for the Packers. In that one game the Cowboys showed everything they're about, from the potential to be great to the inescapable flaws that doom them on an annual basis. Garrett has yet to figure out how to maximize the little talent around him and to assert himself more so that the collapses cease.

Garrett might already be unemployed if he didn't have Romo at quarterback for this wild ride. For all the grief he gets, no quarterback since 2011 has led more fourth-quarter comebacks (11) or game-winning drives (13) than Romo. His 20 career fourth-quarter comeback wins are more than any quarterback in Dallas history, including Roger Staubach (15) and Troy Aikman (16). Garrett's overall record at game-winning drive opportunities is 16-19 (.457), sixth-best among active head coaches. Led by Romo, the Cowboys have consistently done well in tight games, but somehow he always finds a way to correlate his worst plays with the highest Nielsen ratings. The two late interceptions against Green Bay to seal the fall-from-ahead loss were the latest example.

At least no one can blame Romo for 2013's season-ending interception. Kyle Orton was the man who threw *that* back-breaking pick, when a field goal would have won the game. Romo had already injured his back the previous week after carrying the offense all season long. On his last play, fighting

Table 1. Coaches: Games Decided by a Game-Winning Drive (4Q/OT)

Coach	Team	Games	W-L	GWD Win	GWD Win%	Rk	GWD Loss	GWD Loss%	Rk
Jason Garrett	DAL	56	29-27	16	28.6%	1	15	26.8%	1
Mike Smith	ATL	101	61-40	25	24.8%	2	12	11.9%	9
Rex Ryan	NYJ	86	46-40	18	20.9%	3	7	8.1%	11
Mike Tomlin	PIT	120	76-44	24	20.0%	4	23	19.2%	3
Sean Payton	NO	122	79-43	23	18.9%	5	17	13.9%	7
Bill Belichick	NE	250	181-69	47	18.8%	6	22	8.8%	10
Marvin Lewis	CIN	181	90-90-1	34	18.8%	7	27	14.9%	6
Tom Coughlin	NYG	171	98-73	31	18.1%	8	21	12.3%	8
John Harbaugh	BAL	109	71-38	19	17.4%	9	20	18.3%	4
Pete Carroll	SEA	71	43-28	11	15.5%	10	11	15.5%	5
Mike McCarthy	GB	139	88-50-1	18	12.9%	11	28	20.1%	2

Includes head coaches who currently have more than four years of tenure with same team.

through pain against Washington, he found Murray on fourth-and-10 for a game-winning touchdown pass with 1:08 left. Isn't that what "clutch" is supposed to be about?

Last year's Week 5 shootout with Denver should go down as "The Quintessential Tony Romo Game." Romo led Dallas to a 14-0 lead before Peyton Manning started to terrorize the defense. Down 35-20, Romo put together his biggest passing day ever (506 yards and five touchdown passes on just 36 attempts) to lead Dallas to two more leads. The defense failed to hold both. Tied 48-48 with 2:39 left, Romo had a chance to lead the final drive and break the single-game record for passing yards (554). He took a sack and forced a bad throw that was intercepted, setting up Denver's easy game-winning field goal. Dallas lost 51-48. Since 1960, all other quarterbacks are 66-0 when they have a passer rating of at least 140.0 (minimum 30 attempts). Romo is 0-2. Only the Garrett/Romo-era Cowboys can have a game with a win probability chart that mirrors the life expectancy of the crew in *Das Boot*.

Year after year, Romo is the main reason fourth quarters and Week 17's still mean something in Dallas. With Romo and Jason Witten creeping up in age—maybe Jones will invest in a Lazarus Pit underneath Cowboys Stadium—their durability cannot be taken for granted. If we look only at the top level, Dallas has one of the best collections of skill players in the league, but there's not much depth behind players such as Dez Bryant and DeMarco Murray. Dallas' offense was the sixth healthiest in terms of Adjusted Games Lost in 2013. If any of these key players suffers a serious injury, then that's going to put even more pressure on the defense to keep the score down. Even with a perfectly healthy offense, there might be a couple of 51-48 games given this defensive lineup.

Before last season, the Cowboys were looking to simplify things after two tough seasons with Rob Ryan's 3-4 defense, and to install a scheme that could bring more turnovers. So they shifted to the Tampa-2 scheme, hiring defensive coordinator Monte Kiffin, who had not coached in the NFL since 2008. Six takeaways against the Giants in Week 1 was a promising start, but we quickly learned that game said more about the 2013 Giants than the 2013 Cowboys. It's also clear Barry Church and Bruce Carter are not quite the same as John Lynch and Derrick Brooks. The 2013 Cowboys were the first team in NFL history to allow four 400-yard passers in one season, and that happened in the first eight games. They also allowed an NFL-record 40 first downs against New Orleans and surrendered 51 points to Denver to break the franchise record for points allowed at home.

In January, Kiffin was demoted to an assistant as pupil/defensive line coach Rod Marinelli, from "0-16 Detroit" fame, took over his job. Despite the players having a season of scheme familiarity, Marinelli may face even more problems than Kiffin did a year ago. How does a team get to the point where a retired Brian Urlacher is explored as a backup plan in 2014? Maybe even worse, the Cowboys kicked off July by acquiring Rolando McClain in a trade from Baltimore. His biggest claims to fame are smiling during an arrest photo and retiring at the age of 23. The only way a team falls to these depths on defense is a slew of bad draft picks, poor contracts, injuries and bad luck. Soon the Cowboys will be looking under a bridge to see if Zach Thomas feels like making a comeback.

From 1992 to 2007, the Cowboys used 11 of 12 first-round picks on defense. Since 2008, defense has gotten just two of their seven first-round picks. The most recent of those defensive first-rounders was Morris Claiborne, chosen sixth overall in 2012. The Dallas brass compared him to Deion Sanders; so far, it's even a stretch to compare him to 37-year-old Ravens-era Deion Sanders. Claiborne has struggled with injuries and when he's on the field, there hasn't been a lot of playmaking. In fact, the best cornerback in Dallas the past two seasons hasn't been Claiborne or the big-money free-agent signing of that same offseason, Brandon Carr. It's been the forgotten Orlando Scandrick. The fact that it took six seasons for Scandrick to impress on a large number of snaps because the Cowboys devoted more time and resources to players that haven't been as good speaks to the core problems in the team-building department.

The secondary issues are magnified because of the disintegration of the Cowboys' defensive line. All-time Cowboys sack leader DeMarcus Ware is now gone; he was successfully able to transition to 4-3 end last season, but the Cowboys felt they had to release the 32-year-old Ware because injury issues and a high salary. Ware's old running mate, Anthony Spencer, is now a question because of microfracture surgery. Defensive tackle Jay Ratliff couldn't stay healthy, and is now in Chicago. Tyrone Crawford has barely been able to see the field due to injury. Josh Brent was supposed to be the future, but retired after his intoxication manslaughter claimed the life of teammate Jerry Brown in 2012. It took eight years for Jason Hatcher, playing the Warren Sapp role, to break out with 11.0 sacks in 2013. Given he'll be 32 this season, Dallas was probably wise to let him walk in free agency. The hopes of the defensive line rest on Henry Melton, who tore his ACL last year in Chicago and has a limited track record of success.

Many mock drafts had Dallas selecting a blue-chip defender with the 16th pick in the 2014 draft, but the Cowboys instead drafted Zack Martin—their third first-round offensive lineman since 2011 after not choosing any from 1982 to 2010. Despite Romo's quick release and ability to extend plays, Dallas has used consecutive first-round picks on interior linemen. That's bad positional value made even worse by a team that's shown little commitment to the running game. Travis Frederick had a nice rookie year, but this defense could really have

Table 2. Cowboys' Play-Action Passing Under Jason Garrett

Year	PA Pct.	Rk	PA* Yds	PA* DVOA	Rk	No PA Yds	No PA DVOA	Rk	Yds Dif	DVOA Dif	Rk
2011	14%	30	7.5	46.2%	7	6.9	28.0%	7	0.6	18.2%	15
2012	11%	32	8.8	53.0%	5	6.7	23.0%	9	2.1	30.0%	5
2013	13%	30	6.8	39.0%	8	6.4	14.5%	13	0.4	24.6%	9

Play-action plays include passes and scrambles

used Eric Reid (the player San Francisco chose with the pick the Cowboys sent them to trade down) or Matt Elam (chosen one pick after Frederick by the Baltimore Ravens).

As fate would have it, Martin was the player Sean Lee was trying to avoid when he tore his ACL during a May "non-contact" practice. Should Lee miss the entire 2014 season as is expected, he will have played in 46 of a potential 80 career games. With Ware gone, Lee was the defense's best player with ideal range to play middle linebacker in the Tampa-2 scheme. He had four interceptions in 11 games last season. Dallas' random cast of linebackers (Carter, McClain, Justin Durant, Anthony Hitchens, Kyle Wilber, DeVonte Holloman, etc.) has three career interceptions combined. Carter, playing the crucial Derrick Brooks role at weakside linebacker, has none and hasn't shown much playmaking ability in three seasons. Like many Dallas defenders, he's also missed time with injuries.

When the defense needs a splash play or one big stop to win an inevitably tight game, where on this roster could it possibly come from? Great Dallas defenses of the past took on the nickname "Doomsday Defense," with the third (and last) incarnation in the '90s. We might be looking at Doomsday Defense IV in 2014, but this time it's a reference to the impending doom awaiting Dallas. Our projection is barely any bleaker than it was last year, but as long as the comeback wins are canceled out by the monumental collapses, it's hard to see Dallas not fall in that six- to eight-win range again. The offense will have to deal with four games against NFC West defenses and the defense should see improved versions of Eli Manning and Robert Griffin III. Overall, the schedule is projected to be just a tad tougher than last season. Three road games and a Week 16 visit from the Colts that just screams "blown 20-point lead" should make for another difficult December for the Cowboys. But they should still be relevant by that time in a division no one runs away with.

Then again, records be damned, when is Dallas *not* relevant? Even in a downtrodden state, people still love to tune in for the drama and the schadenfreude. Once Jones hires an elite Glasses Cleaning Specialist, he'll see the same thing we have seen the last few years: the Cowboys are back to glory hole days, but they're stuck on the other side of the partition.

Scott Kacsmar

2013 Cowboys Stats by Week

Wk	vs.	W-L	PF	PA	YDF	YDA	TO	Total	Off	Def	ST
1	NYG	W	36	31	331	478	+5	-15%	-5%	16%	5%
2	at KC	L	16	17	318	313	-2	0%	0%	10%	9%
3	STL	W	31	7	396	232	0	45%	40%	-22%	-16%
4	at SD	L	21	30	319	506	0	2%	20%	15%	-3%
5	DEN	L	48	51	522	517	0	43%	65%	20%	-3%
6	WAS	W	31	16	213	433	+1	26%	-1%	11%	38%
7	at PHI	W	17	3	368	278	+1	63%	-15%	-71%	6%
8	at DET	L	30	31	268	623	+4	0%	8%	19%	12%
9	MIN	W	27	23	350	393	+1	4%	2%	2%	4%
10	at NO	L	17	49	193	625	+1	-62%	-13%	57%	9%
11	BYE										
12	at NYG	W	24	21	311	356	0	-18%	12%	28%	-3%
13	OAK	W	31	24	352	305	+1	-35%	13%	30%	-18%
14	at CHI	L	28	45	328	490	0	-27%	28%	61%	5%
15	GB	L	36	37	466	433	-1	-29%	-4%	28%	3%
16	at WAS	W	24	23	309	297	-1	-13%	-10%	11%	8%
17	PHI	L	22	24	414	366	-2	-7%	-11%	-5%	-1%

Trends and Splits

	Offense	Rank	Defense	Rank
Total DVOA	7.5%	11	13.8%	30
Unadjusted VOA	8.9%	8	14.6%	31
Weighted Trend	2.4%	14	19.3%	32
Variance	4.7%	8	9.2%	31
Average Opponent	2.3%	22	2.9%	5
Passing	15.9%	10	20.7%	27
Rushing	7.7%	5	4.3%	28
First Down	13.4%	8	12.7%	28
Second Down	15.5%	7	10.5%	26
Third Down	-21.7%	26	21.2%	28
First Half	9.3%	8	3.8%	21
Second Half	5.7%	14	22.9%	31
Red Zone	29.3%	2	12.8%	23
Late and Close	5.3%	12	-2.5%	17

Five-Year Performance

Year	W-L	Pyth W	Est W	PF	PA	TO	Total	Rk	Off	Rk	Def	Rk	ST	Rk	Off AGL	Rk	Def AGL	Rk	Off Age	Rk	Def Age	Rk	ST Age	Rk
2009	11-5	11.3	11.9	361	250	+2	25.5%	5	21.7%	3	-2.9%	10	1.0%	14	14.5	11	7.7	2	28.5	2	27.1	18	25.7	27
2010	6-10	7.0	6.8	394	436	0	-10.5%	23	-4.7%	21	6.3%	27	0.6%	15	20.7	12	11.1	7	28.7	2	27.4	15	25.6	27
2011	8-8	8.6	8.4	369	347	+4	3.5%	14	5.9%	12	0.4%	16	-2.1%	25	43.5	25	19.0	11	26.6	22	28.2	2	26.0	27
2012	8-8	7.4	7.9	376	400	-13	-0.4%	17	6.1%	11	6.7%	23	0.2%	15	29.0	17	57.5	30	27.2	11	26.7	19	25.6	26
2013	8-8	8.2	8.2	439	432	+8	-2.8%	17	7.5%	11	13.8%	30	3.4%	8	16.6	5	51.4	29	26.5	22	26.1	24	25.3	28

2013 Performance Based on Most Common Personnel Groups

DAL Offense					DAL Offense vs. Opponents				DAL Defense				DAL Defense vs. Opponents			
Pers	Freq	Yds	DVOA	Run%	Pers	Freq	Yds	DVOA	Pers	Freq	Yds	DVOA	Pers	Freq	Yds	DVOA
11	44%	5.4	-0.1%	29%	Nickel Even	42%	5.7	10.8%	Nickel Even	60%	6.5	12.1%	11	58%	6.5	15.9%
12	33%	5.7	18.4%	38%	3-4-4	22%	5.1	3.0%	4-3-4	32%	5.7	8.1%	21	15%	5.9	6.4%
01	8%	9.3	52.9%	1%	4-3-4	17%	6.1	31.8%	Dime+	3%	6.4	47.6%	12	13%	5.6	2.2%
02	4%	7.5	81.6%	0%	Dime+	10%	6.9	8.5%	Nickel Odd	3%	8.3	86.2%	22	5%	6.4	18.1%
13	4%	5.4	24.1%	64%	Nickel Odd	8%	7.3	26.1%	3-4-4	1%	6.5	44.4%	10	2%	4.6	-58.9%
21	3%	6.2	-16.1%	76%									20	2%	10.1	80.9%

Strategic Tendencies

Run/Pass		Rk	Formation		Rk	Pass Rush		Rk	Secondary		Rk	Strategy		Rk
Runs, first half	33%	29	Form: Single Back	76%	8	Rush 3	4.2%	22	4 DB	33%	24	Play action	13%	30
Runs, first down	43%	25	Form: Empty Back	14%	2	Rush 4	71.5%	4	5 DB	63%	6	Avg Box (Off)	6.24	25
Runs, second-long	23%	29	Pers: 3+ WR	56%	19	Rush 5	15.5%	30	6+ DB	3%	22	Avg Box (Def)	6.35	18
Runs, power sit.	45%	30	Pers: 4+ WR	8%	2	Rush 6+	8.8%	13	CB by Sides	67%	22	Offensive Pace	30.84	21
Runs, behind 2H	24%	26	Pers: 2+ TE/6+ OL	45%	4	Sacks by LB	12.1%	27	DB Blitz	6%	28	Defensive Pace	30.16	22
Pass, ahead 2H	60%	3	Shotgun/Pistol	61%	14	Sacks by DB	6.1%	20	Hole in Zone	11%	15	Go for it on 4th	0.18	32

The Cowboys used a lot of empty-backfield formations last year, which they had never really done before, and they were actually very good at it. Only Arizona used empty backfields more often, and the Cowboys averaged 8.3 yards per play and 59.8% DVOA, both second in the league behind Denver. The Dallas defense didn't just switch from a three-man front to a four-man front last season. They also switched to using nickel almost twice as often, going from 34 percent of defensive plays (30th in 2012) to 63 percent (sixth in 2013). The Cowboys used four defensive backs about two-thirds as often as the year before, and used dime about one-fourth as often. One thing that didn't change, however: the Cowboys' secondary is not good enough to hold when Dallas has to blitz. The Cowboys gave up 6.8 yards per pass with three or four pass rushers, but 9.1 yards per pass with five and 9.4 yards per pass with six or more. The Cowboys had the worst defensive DVOA in the NFL against passes thrown to the middle of the field. For the second straight year, the Cowboys' run defense was reasonable against running backs in one-back formations (4.2 yards per carry, -10.6% DVOA) but got completely trampled when opponents had multiple backs (5.8 yards per carry, 16.1% DVOA). Dallas recovered 11 of 14 fumbles on defense.

Passing

Player	DYAR	DVOA	Plays	NtYds	Avg	YAC	C%	TD	Int
T.Romo	839	11.5%	572	3556	6.2	5.2	64.2%	31	9
K.Orton	51	4.0%	51	398	7.8	6.7	64.7%	2	2
B.Weeden	*-443*	*-36.1%*	*293*	*1535*	*5.2*	*4.5*	*53.2%*	*9*	*9*

Rushing

Player	DYAR	DVOA	Plays	Yds	Avg	TD	Fum	Suc
D.Murray	295	24.0%	217	1119	5.2	9	2	53%
J.Randle	1	-8.1%	54	164	3.0	2	0	44%
L.Dunbar	31	16.8%	30	150	5.0	0	0	60%
P.Tanner*	-19	-53.1%	9	12	1.3	1	1	33%
T.Romo	17	44.3%	8	47	5.9	0	0	-
B.Weeden	*11*	*12.4%*	*9*	*46*	*5.1*	*0*	*0*	-

Receiving

Player	DYAR	DVOA	Plays	Ctch	Yds	Y/C	YAC	TD	C%
D.Bryant	215	3.7%	160	93	1251	13.5	5.7	13	58%
T.Williams	92	3.0%	75	45	733	16.3	4.6	5	60%
C.Beasley	59	1.5%	54	39	370	9.5	4.7	2	72%
M.Austin*	-51	-25.9%	49	24	244	10.2	4.2	0	49%
D.Harris	20	7.3%	14	9	80	8.9	4.0	2	64%
J.Witten	134	11.2%	111	73	851	11.7	4.3	8	66%
G.Escobar	30	24.8%	15	9	134	14.9	4.1	2	60%
J.Hanna	-19	-28.3%	15	12	73	6.1	5.1	0	80%
D.Murray	40	-3.5%	66	53	354	6.7	7.2	1	80%
J.Randle	2	-10.6%	10	8	61	7.6	7.6	0	80%
L.Dunbar	-1	-17.3%	7	7	59	8.4	8.7	0	100%

Offensive Line

Player	Pos	Age	GS	Snaps	Pen	Sk	Pass	Run	Player	Pos	Age	GS	Snaps	Pen	Sk	Pass	Run
Travis Frederick	C	23	16/16	997	3	3.0	10.5	4.0	Ronald Leary	LG	25	16/16	990	8	6.0	19.5	2.5
Doug Free	RT	30	16/16	997	8	2.5	15.0	3.0	Mackenzy Bernadeau	RG	28	16/11	675	1	3.5	9.5	2.0
Tyron Smith	LT	24	16/16	995	7	3.0	21.5	6.5	Brian Waters*	RG	37	7/5	329	1	1.0	4.0	0.5

Year	Yards	ALY	Rk	Power	Rk	Stuff	Rk	2nd Lev	Rk	Open Field	Rk	Sacks	ASR	Rk	Short	Long	F-Start	Cont.
2011	4.63	4.26	6	57%	23	19%	16	1.31	8	0.97	9	39	6.1%	13	10	19	23	36
2012	3.78	3.92	22	63%	15	19%	12	1.04	25	0.52	26	36	5.8%	11	11	14	26	28
2013	4.66	4.23	4	68%	11	15%	2	1.29	6	1.02	4	35	6.2%	10	14	12	16	37
2013 ALY by direction:			*Left End 3.30 (19)*			*Left Tackle 4.72 (5)*			*Mid/Guard 4.21 (8)*				*Right Tackle 5.09 (1)*			*Right End 4.32 (6)*		

There wasn't much difference in the total number of blown blocks accredited to the offensive line in 2012 (83.5 pass, 21.5 run) versus 2013 (81.0 pass, 18.5 run). At tackle, the numbers for Tyron Smith and Doug Free basically switched from 2012, an encouraging sign for Free but disappointment for the more talented Smith, who ranked 26th among left tackles in snaps per blown block. It's easy to forget that after three years as an NFL starter, Smith is still just 24. The Cowboys were the most left-focused rushing attack in the NFL (42 percent of runs went off left end or left tackle) and fared very well behind Smith at the point of attack.

Last year's first-round rookie center Travis Frederick was middle-of-the-pack statistically, but that beats the days of watching Phil Costa fail to get the snap to Romo. Frederick will line up next to Notre Dame rookie Zack Martin, who has the versatility to play tackle and guard. He only played tackle in college, but is expected to take over initially at right guard in Dallas. The biggest knock on Martin is his limited arm length (32 7/8 inches), but that won't be so noticeable if he's inside the trenches. Remember, the Cowboys once convinced us Leonard Davis was a Pro Bowl guard after he was a bust as a tackle in Arizona.

Left guard remained a problem in pass protection last season with Ronald Leary offering little improvement over Nate Livings. Mackenzy Bernadeau, last year's right guard, will compete with Leary for his spot. In June, Bernadeau told ESPN.com the difference between playing the left and right guard was "like learning to write with your left hand instead of your right hand." As is the case with most of the other Dallas linemen, Bernadeau has been ambidextrous. He was a left guard in Carolina in 2009-11 and he's also been taking practice snaps at center. Romo's ability to help his line by extending the play will come in very handy if one of these players gets injured.

Defensive Front Seven

				Overall							vs. Run					Pass Rush			
Defensive Line	Age	Pos	G	Snaps	Plays	TmPct	Rk	Stop	Dfts	BTkl	Runs	St%	Rk	RuYd	Rk	Sack	Hit	Hur	Tips
Nick Hayden	28	DT	16	821	43	5.0%	43	28	8	1	32	66%	73	2.5	55	0.0	3	8.5	0
Jason Hatcher*	32	DT	15	747	44	5.4%	35	38	24	2	28	86%	13	1.3	10	11.0	5	19.5	1
Drake Nevis*	25	DT	12	270	15	2.3%	--	12	2	1	12	92%	--	1.8	--	0.0	0	4.0	0

				Overall							vs. Run					Pass Rush			
Edge Rushers	Age	Pos	G	Snaps	Plays	TmPct	Rk	Stop	Dfts	BTkl	Runs	St%	Rk	RuYd	Rk	Sack	Hit	Hur	Tips
George Selvie	27	DE	16	744	46	5.3%	42	37	18	2	31	81%	26	1.9	20	7.0	8	21.0	1
DeMarcus Ware*	32	DE	13	628	41	5.9%	33	34	13	0	31	84%	20	1.8	18	6.0	6	24.0	1
Kyle Wilber	25	DE	16	501	42	4.9%	49	29	9	0	33	73%	50	3.8	71	2.0	2	5.5	0
Jarius Wynn*	28	DE	15	361	13	1.8%	--	12	5	0	7	86%	--	2.0	--	2.0	3	7.0	2
Jeremy Mincey	*31*	*DE*	*10*	*298*	*17*	*3.1%*	*77*	*16*	*6*	*1*	*13*	*92%*	*3*	*1.5*	*11*	*2.0*	*2*	*12.5*	*1*

			Overall								Pass Rush			vs. Run					vs. Pass						
Linebackers	Age	Pos	G	Snaps	Plays	TmPct	Rk	Stop	Dfts	BTkl	Sack	Hit	Hur	Runs	St%	Rk	RuYd	Rk	Tgts	Suc%	Rk	AdjYd	Rk	PD	Int
Bruce Carter	26	OLB	15	874	99	12.3%	48	49	21	5	2.0	3	5	54	54%	73	3.9	62	44	55%	28	6.2	28	2	0
Sean Lee	28	MLB	11	702	105	17.7%	9	51	16	2	0.0	1	2	55	73%	16	3.0	25	36	46%	50	7.2	51	6	4
DeVonte Holloman	23	OLB	9	207	24	4.9%	--	14	3	2	2.0	0	0	14	64%	--	1.9	--	13	34%	--	11.0	--	0	0
Justin Durant	29	OLB	10	197	25	4.6%	--	14	3	4	0.0	0	0	14	50%	--	4.5	--	6	38%	--	8.1	--	1	0

Year	Yards	ALY	Rk	Power	Rk	Stuff	Rk	2nd Level	Rk	Open Field	Rk	Sacks	ASR	Rk	Short	Long
2011	4.03	3.92	10	57%	10	22%	9	1.13	11	0.66	9	42	7.6%	6	14	18
2012	4.37	4.14	19	65%	20	16%	28	1.13	8	0.83	18	34	6.9%	9	10	16
2013	4.84	4.34	29	76%	29	18%	17	1.48	31	0.98	26	34	6.1%	26	12	10
2013 ALY by direction:			*Left End 3.74 (17)*			*Left Tackle 4.90 (31)*			*Mid/Guard 4.18 (25)*			*Right Tackle 4.63 (26)*			*Right End 4.42 (28)*	

If the Cowboys were that bad defensively in 2013 *with* DeMarcus Ware, Jason Hatcher and Sean Lee, then how much worse can things get *without* them in 2014? That's about the most optimistic way of looking at this barren wasteland of talent that will try to form a front seven. Let's attempt to lay out the absolute best-case scenario for where this 4-3 unit can go.

During free agency in March, Henry Melton received a holographic recording from Jerry Jones. "Help me, Henry Melton. You're my only hope." If Melton can once again be the interior force in Marinelli's defense in the same way that earned him a franchise tag in Chicago two years ago, then that's one big piece in place to help Nick Hayden inside. George Selvie was serviceable in his first year as a starter at defensive end. His 21 hurries were only three less than Ware. Veteran Anthony Spencer played only 36 snaps last season and had microfracture surgery on his knee. He re-signed on a one-year deal, but there is no timetable for his return or any way of knowing if he'll ever be the same player. Jeremy Mincey was a good veteran signing; he charted very well against the run and had as many hurries (12.5) as last year's depth (Kyle Wilber and Jarius Wynn) combined. The pass rush will also get some snaps out of Tyrone Crawford, a 2012 third-round pick who missed last season, and rookie Demarcus Lawrence, a second-round pick out of Boise State with a poor 36.0 percent SackSEER rating.

Due to Lee's ACL tear, linebacker requires a stronger spin doctor. Justin Durant has plenty of experience (74 starts) with bad 4-3 defenses in Jacksonville and Detroit, so he should unassumingly fade into obscurity just fine. He won't be as noticeably inept as Ernie Sims, but he'll never be Lee if he does in fact win that middle linebacker job. The Cowboys also have fourth-round rookie Anthony Hitchens, but he played on the outside at Iowa and has a big learning curve ahead of him. DeVonte Holloman notched two sacks in two starts in place of Lee last year, but don't get too excited about those. The first sack came when Philadelphia failed to pick him up and the second involved Nick Foles evading Holloman before intentionally taking a dive to keep the clock running.

Weakside linebacker Bruce Carter has come out very poorly in our run metrics the last two years, but he's better suited to pass coverage. He's physically gifted, the most talented linebacker on the team, but he's underachieved and hasn't stayed healthy. He'll have to step up in Lee's absence.

Defensive Secondary

			Overall								vs. Run					vs. Pass									
Secondary	Age	Pos	G	Snaps	Plays	TmPct	Rk	Stop	Dfts	BTkl	Runs	St%	Rk	RuYd	Rk	Tgts	Tgt%	Rk	Dist	Suc%	Rk	AdjYd	Rk	PD	Int
Brandon Carr	28	CB	16	1116	83	9.6%	19	34	14	11	14	50%	25	5.9	25	107	21.3%	45	12.8	49%	62	8.9	73	12	3
Orlando Scandrick	27	CB	16	1088	76	8.8%	35	32	17	6	11	36%	49	10.5	68	91	18.6%	19	10.9	60%	11	6.6	16	10	2
Barry Church	26	SS	16	1015	139	16.1%	1	38	12	8	66	24%	70	7.2	47	34	7.4%	29	7.8	56%	36	6.4	26	6	1
Jeff Heath	23	FS	16	594	55	6.4%	70	14	4	6	26	19%	76	14.2	78	27	9.9%	61	11.5	55%	40	9.7	68	3	1
J.J. Wilcox	23	SS	13	515	34	4.9%	--	9	2	4	16	38%	--	7.6	--	18	7.8%	--	9.4	38%	--	9.1	--	1	0
Morris Claiborne	24	CB	10	506	31	5.8%	79	12	5	4	4	0%	84	11.0	72	51	22.4%	56	13.3	54%	37	9.2	75	5	1

Year	Pass D Rank	vs. #1 WR	Rk	vs. #2 WR	Rk	vs. Other WR	Rk	vs. TE	Rk	vs. RB	Rk
2011	22	14.0%	19	53.3%	31	-26.9%	6	19.1%	21	-3.6%	15
2012	25	-7.0%	12	11.5%	29	19.5%	28	28.9%	32	3.5%	18
2013	27	12.4%	25	17.6%	28	-11.4%	8	26.8%	32	9.6%	24

Seven defensive backs played at least 178 defensive snaps for the Cowboys last season and all of them return this year with zero notable additions to the unit. One look at that lineup and calling it Doomsday Defense IV feels more legitimate. To be at least average, this unit is going to need breakout years from Morris Claiborne and at least one of the safeties—and that's going to be hard if the front seven is not generating a pass rush or containing the run. Claiborne, the sixth overall pick in the 2012 draft, tried to play through a left-shoulder dislocation, but quickly lost his starting job to Orlando Scandrick. It was a season filled with adversity for Claiborne; not only did he lose six games to injury, but he also dealt with a newborn child at home and the death of his father. When he played, Claiborne improved his Adjusted Success Rate from 41 percent as a rookie to 54 percent, but his Adjusted Yards per Pass soared from 7.9 to 9.2 and he again made just one interception. Jason Garrett has said that Claiborne has shown flashes of the player the Cowboys thought they were getting in 2012, but you don't take a player sixth overall so you can just see some flashes.

When Dallas drafted Claiborne and signed Brandon Carr to a five-year deal worth $50 million, expectations were not for these man-coverage covers to be in a zone-based Tampa-2 scheme. While there was certainly more zone played last year under Monte Kiffin, consider that the average depth of coverage target practically remained unchanged: Carr went from 12.9 to 12.8 and Claiborne went from 13.4 to 13.3. Neither played as well as Scandrick, who had great charting stats on limited snaps in 2012 and then had excellent stats in 2013 after being given his biggest role in six years. Dallas can't wait much longer for Claiborne to develop. His third season is crucial to the secondary's success.

The safeties are a bigger problem, and nobody there has a pedigree like "former sixth overall pick." Barry Church looks to have a grip on the strong safety job after starting all 16 games last year. No safety in the NFL was involved in more plays than his 139, but his performance left much to be desired, especially against the run. The Cowboys like 2012 fourth-round pick Matt Johnson, but he has yet to play a regular-season game due to injuries. J.J. Wilcox, a third-round pick in 2013, is the favorite to start at free safety. He would have started last year, but his mother tragically passed away in August and that slowed his development. Defensive coordinator Rod Marinelli told the *Dallas Morning News* this spring, "I just sense he's going to make a step. You feel good about it, but now he's got to go do it."

Jeff Heath started nine games last year, but he's a limited athlete who was outmatched in coverage. Heath allowed four touchdown passes and the receiver broke his tackle on three of them. He's the Dallas version of former Jets safety Eric Smith. Both players are listed at 6-foot-1 with Heath weighing 210 pounds and Smith at 209 pounds. In 2011 with the Jets, Smith's Adjusted Yards per Pass was 11.3. Heath's was 11.5 last season. Wilcox will win the job because he's the ultimate "upside" choice. He's young, he's raw (converted wide receiver from a small school), but he's a good athlete and that's what the Cowboys need right now on defense.

Special Teams

Year	DVOA	Rank	FG/XP	Rank	Net Kick	Rank	Kick Ret	Rank	Net Punt	Rank	Punt Ret	Rank	Hidden	Rank
2011	-2.1%	25	1.6	13	1.6	14	1.2	14	-5.0	23	-9.7	30	3.6	11
2012	0.2%	15	7.8	5	-3.1	24	-10.9	32	-1.4	17	8.4	4	2.5	10
2013	3.4%	8	7.0	5	1.2	14	3.2	7	-1.5	21	7.3	5	0.9	14

Last year, the Cowboys had top-ten rated special teams for the first time since 1998. Most would commend special teams coordinator Rich Bisaccia for his debut season, but in some dark corners of the Internet, this is merely seen as Romo blowing the best special teams performance since the Troy Aikman era. Two players drove the special teams success. Kicker Dan Bailey missed only twice all season for the second year in a row. He's made 89-of-98 field goals (90.8 percent) in his career. His kickoffs are still below average, but they have improved every season. The other player is Dwayne Harris, truly, the Cowboys' special-teams ace. He ranked in the top 10 in kickoff and punt return value, including a 90-yard kick return and a punt return touchdown. Harris' average of 30.6 yards per kick return in 2013 set a franchise record for highest average in a season (minimum 12 returns). In addition, all nine of Harris' special-teams tackles qualified as "Stops" by ending a return with below-average value. No other Dallas player had even half as many Stops on special teams. Other than Harris, the Dallas coverage teams were pretty average, while third-year player Chris Jones was a little below average in his debut season as the full-time punter.

Denver Broncos

2013 Record: 13-3	**Total DVOA:** 32.7% (2nd)	**2014 Mean Projection:** 10.7 wins	**On the Clock (0-4):** 1%
Pythagorean Wins: 11.7 (2nd)	**Offense:** 33.5% (1st)	**Postseason Odds:** 85.2%	**Mediocrity (5-7):** 4%
Snap-Weighted Age: 27.1 (9th)	**Defense:** -0.2% (15th)	**Super Bowl Odds:** 33.7%	**Playoff Contender (8-10):** 38%
Average Opponent: -6.6% (31st)	**Special Teams:** -1.0% (21st)	**Proj. Avg. Opponent:** 0.4% (18th)	**Super Bowl Contender (11+):** 56%

2013: One of the most amazing offensive seasons in NFL history, from September 5 through February 1.

2014: The clear AFC favorite, but they better hope they match up better with *this* year's NFC champion.

So, what the heck do you do after a season that ends like *that?*

The 2013 Denver Broncos scored 30 or more points in 13 of their 16 regular season games en route to setting an NFL record by scoring 606 points in a season. They went 13-3, tied for the best record in the league. They avenged two regular-season losses by defeating the San Diego Chargers and the New England Patriots en route to a Super Bowl appearance.

And then, *that.*

That was of course their 43-8 Super Bowl defeat at the hands of the Seattle Seahawks. *That* was a game that started inauspiciously, with a self-inflicted safety on the first play from scrimmage. *That* was a game where the Seahawks scored three times before the Broncos' oh-so-accomplished offense could even manage a first down. *That* was a game where Peyton Manning, he of the 55 regular-season passing touchdowns, threw as many passes that ended up as Seattle touchdowns as he did passes that ended up as Denver touchdowns (one of each). *That* was humiliating.

Most importantly for 2014, *that* created a number of questions. How good were the Broncos in 2013, *really?* Was the offense really as good as the gaudy numbers suggested they were? Just how good was the defense? Did the lack of some ineffable "it" factor, so beloved by some portions of the sports commentariat, prevent the Broncos from reaching the ultimate in postseason glory?

Fortunately, those questions were not all that hard to answer. The 2013 Denver Broncos were a very good team, the best in the AFC. They were not quite as good as the Seattle Seahawks, even just looking at the games played only from September through January, but they were good. The offense was really, really, really good, even if it may not have been quite as great as it looked early in the season. The defense was good against the run most of the time, but good against the pass some of the time and bad against the pass too much of the time, with an explanation both simple and complicated for the divide. And the absence of whatever "it" factor the Broncos might have been lacking did not seem to bother them too much in their first two playoff games.

Put simply, the best response to *that* is this: there was nothing fundamentally wrong with the 2013 Broncos, except they had a bad game against a great opponent at an awful time. Executive vice president of football operations John Elway saw this and understood that as long as Peyton Manning came back, there was no reason to dismantle the team. The ultra-competitive quarterback unsurprisingly did not retire, and Elway limited his offseason moves to tinkering at the edges rather than making major changes.

That means this great offense will be largely the same as it was last year. The nature of the modern NFL and free agency inevitably mean a certain degree of transition will occur, but the Broncos worked to minimize the changeover. Eight starters return, Emmanuel Sanders replaces Eric Decker as the second wide receiver, left guard Zane Beadles was not a major loss, and the departure of Knowshon Moreno just means a bigger role for last year's second-round pick Montee Ball, who was eased into the backfield as a rookie.

What are the question marks on offense? The first and most important is Peyton Manning, who turned 38 in March. NFL quarterbacks generally decline as they get older. Peyton obviously does not have the arm strength he did early in his career—it was particularly apparent late in the season—but he continues to throw the ball well enough that, combined with his work before the snap, he can be a great quarterback. The good news is that 38 does not appear to be any sort of cliff. Even beyond Brett Favre and Warren Moon, the two best "old" quarterbacks in NFL history, Joe Montana, Phil Simms, and Kurt Warner all played well at 38. His neck injury will always be a concern, but until it or another injury (unlikely, as Peyton rarely takes big hits and is sacked as little as any passer in the league) comes up, the outlook is bright.

Important for Peyton's continued health is the return of left tackle Ryan Clady, who suffered a season-ending knee injury in Week 2. His replacement, Chris Clark, shifts to the right side, where he will be better suited.

The only real issue is running back. Ball is a more explosive, better runner than Moreno and more experience should help him improve in the passing-game elements so important to the up-tempo Denver attack. The real question is his backup. Speedy Ronnie Hillman fell completely out of favor the second half of the season and may have been surpassed on the depth chart by former undrafted free agent C.J. Anderson. But if backup running back is an offense's biggest concern, that team is well-positioned indeed.

This does not mean that the Broncos will be as good as they were last year, or that they were as good as they looked last year. Those gaudy statistics came against the third-easiest slate of op-

2014 Broncos Schedule

Week	Opp.	Week	Opp.	Week	Opp.
1	IND	7	SF	13	at KC
2	KC	8	SD (Thu.)	14	BUF
3	at SEA	9	at NE	15	at SD
4	BYE	10	at OAK	16	at CIN (Mon.)
5	ARI	11	at STL	17	OAK
6	at NYJ	12	MIA		

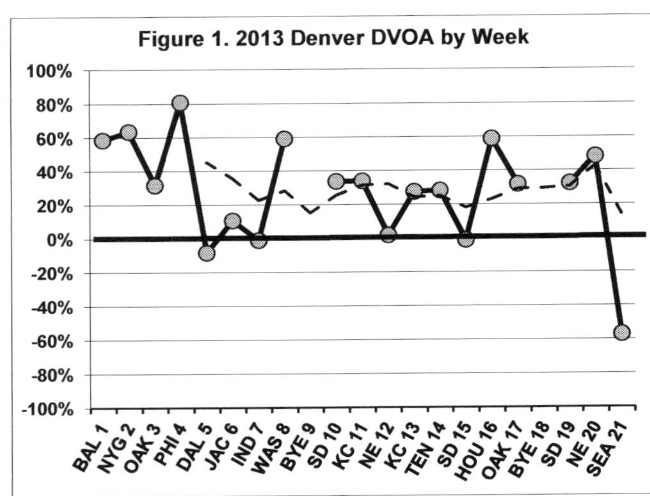

posing defenses in the league. With Seattle and the rest of the NFC West defenses on the schedule in 2014, a Broncos offense just as good as last year's will not match last year's numbers.

Furthermore, raw statistics like 55 touchdown passes and 5,447 passing yards are in part a function of volume, and the Broncos had a *lot* of volume. Manning threw 71 more passes than Tom Brady did when he had 50 touchdowns in 2007 and 162 more passes than he himself had when he threw for 49 touchdowns in 2004. By DVOA, last year was "only" Peyton's third-best season and the eighth-best passing season of the DVOA era (Table 1). Add in running plays, false starts, and the like, and the Broncos were "only" the sixth-best offense since 1989. Still great, but not quite as great as those NFL records might indicate (Table 2).

One look at Table 2 will provide evidence for one of the core theories at Football Outsiders, namely that offenses tend to be relatively consistent from year to year. Only three of the ten best offenses saw a drop of at least 20 percentage points of DVOA, and all three of those teams lost either their starting quarterback or their head coach. The 2008 Patriots lost Tom Brady to a torn ACL in Week 1. John Elway retired after the 1998 Broncos won the Super Bowl. New Orleans Saints head coach and offensive maestro Sean Payton missed the 2012 season with a suspension for Bountygate. The Broncos return Peyton Manning, offensive coordinator Adam Gase, and head coach John Fox (and the offense was still perfectly fine in the games Fox missed recovering from his heart attack). The Broncos will score plenty of points. The key variable is just how many they will give up.

On defense, what seemed to define the Broncos in 2013 was the presence or absence of star outside linebacker Von Miller. Coming off an 18.5-sack season, Miller only played in nine of the Broncos' 19 contests. He missed the first six games thanks to a suspension for violation of the NFL's substance-abuse policy, then the final four (including the postseason) after tearing his ACL in Week 16.

Miller is an excellent run defender, and the Broncos were an excellent run defense with him in the lineup, posting a DVOA of -11.4%. In the games he missed, though, they were even better, posting a DVOA of -17.9% when we combine both the regular season and the playoffs. Run defense was not the problem. Rather, the pass defense was a problem. Denver's -10.0% pass defense DVOA with Miller would have ranked sixth in the NFL. Without him, the Broncos had 29.4% DVOA on pass defense, which would have ranked worst in the league.

Miller is a talented player, so it makes sense that the Broncos played worse without him. Pinpointing just *why* the Broncos were worse without him is more difficult. It would make sense if the Broncos struggled to get pressure on opposing quarterbacks without Miller in the lineup, but that is not what our numbers tell us. The Broncos did have a slightly higher Adjusted Sack Rate in the games Miller played, but the difference—6.7 percent with him, 6.3 percent without him—was negligible. The picture is the same if you look at hurries instead of just sacks. The Broncos also did not force turnovers at a much higher rate. In the regular season, they actually intercepted passes at a higher rate in the games Miller did not play, though they did not manage to intercept Philip Rivers, Tom Brady, or Russell Wilson in the playoffs.

Table 1. Best Passing DVOA, 1989-2013 (min. 300 attempts)

Player	Team	Year	DVOA	Yd/At	Comp%	TD	INT
Peyton Manning	IND	2004	58.9%	9.2	67.6%	49	10
Tom Brady	NE	2007	54.1%	8.3	68.9%	50	8
Peyton Manning	IND	2006	51.3%	7.9	65.0%	31	9
Tom Brady	NE	2010	46.7%	7.9	65.9%	36	4
Aaron Rodgers	GB	2011	46.6%	9.2	68.3%	45	6
Steve Young	SF	1992	45.1%	8.6	66.7%	25	7
Randall Cunningham	MIN	1998	45.1%	8.7	60.9%	34	10
Peyton Manning	DEN	2013	43.2%	8.3	68.3%	55	10
Vinny Testaverde	NYJ	1998	42.2%	7.7	61.5%	29	7
Mark Rypien	WAS	1991	41.9%	8.5	59.1%	28	11

Table 2. Best Offensive DVOA, 1989-2013

Team	Year	DVOA	DVOA Y+1
NE	2007	43.5%	12.5%
NE	2010	42.2%	31.9%
KC	2002	35.4%	33.4%
DEN	1998	34.5%	3.4%
GB	2011	33.8%	19.5%
DEN	2013	33.7%	???
KC	2003	33.4%	31.6%
SF	1992	33.1%	31.4%
NO	2011	33.0%	11.9%
NE	2011	31.9%	30.8%

These statistics do not mean Miller is not a good player, or that his presence was not important. Rather, it points to a limitation of the statistics we have and the way we measure things. We can be pretty confident opposing offenses were impacted by Miller's presence. Statistics other than pass pressure and turnovers show this. With a DVOA difference of almost 40 percentage points, we can be pretty certain Miller's presence or absence meant a lot to how good Denver's pass defense was. And, of course, he jumps off the film.

Ancillary statistics, ones that can be influenced by pressure, suggest the real difference Miller's presence made. Opposing quarterbacks completed 63.0 percent of their passes in the games Miller missed, for 13.1 yards per completion. With Miller in the lineup, they completed just 58.4 percent of passes for 10.9 yards per completion. The average opponent completion was farther downfield in the games he missed. That could easily be a story about the pass rush with and without Miller. If you believe Miller's presence carries with it some sort of "it" factor, note that the Broncos were much more likely to have at least one broken tackle on a pass play in the games he missed, which created more yards after catch even though the completions came further downfield. The average completion produced 6.3 yards after catch in the games Miller missed, only 4.6 in the games he played in. (Typically, longer completions would result in fewer yards after contact, not more.)

As constant as the pressure statistics may have been, the Broncos noted the need for a second key pass rusher after losing Elvis Dumervil before last season. While Shaun Phillips contributed 9.5 sacks, none of them came from beating a left tackle. Enter one of three major free-agent acquisitions on defense, DeMarcus Ware. The Cowboys star had a somewhat quiet, injury-plagued season, recording only 6.0 sacks. But his 24 hurries suggest that his season was not quite as quiet as the raw sack total made it seem. Even if Miller does have a slow start to the 2014 season coming off that torn ACL (and we will probably not know until the season actually begins just how close he is to 100 percent), the Broncos should have an upgraded pass rush. As the numbers with and without Miller indicate, that may be true even if our raw pressure numbers do not indicate as much.

Of course, pass rush is only part of pass defense. The Broncos also upgraded their pass coverage personnel. The flashy acquisition was plucking cornerback Aqib Talib away from the arch-rival Patriots, but that signing was probably higher visibility than impact. The Broncos needed a starting-level corner after Dominique Rodgers-Cromartie, who had an outstanding season by our charting statistics, departed in free agency. The good news is that for the first time in his career, Talib will be a member of a secondary whose coverages will not revolve specifically around his presence. The bad news is that if he doesn't stay on the straight and narrow, his next NFL suspension will be for an entire season.

The more important signing, in terms of *really* upgrading the secondary from 2013 to 2014, is adding T.J. Ward from the Browns. Safety was a bit of a trouble spot for the Broncos in 2013, especially the strong safety role Ward is likely to play. Duke Ihenacho, an undrafted free-agent success story, started the season at the position. He was followed by Mike Adams, who also spent some time at free safety once Rahim Moore went down. Omar Bolden also got his shot at the job. Especially if Moore is not ready for Week 1, Ward's presence could have a major positive impact on the Broncos defense.

Just in case personnel upgrades don't make enough of an argument for an improved Broncos defense this season, there are also strong big-picture statistical indicators. As we note each year, defenses that are much stronger on first and second down compared to third down tend to improve the following season. Last year, the Broncos ranked seventh in DVOA on first down, 11th on second down, and 29th on third downs.

So, forget *that*. Instead, remember that the best team in the AFC replaced its key free-agent losses and made two major additions on defense that addressed its biggest trouble spot from the previous season. That makes the Broncos once again the favorite in a tough AFC West and a strong contender to head into the maelstrom of the postseason with home-field advantage.

Tom Gower

2013 Broncos Stats by Week

Wk	vs.	W-L	PF	PA	YDF	YDA	TO	Total	Off	Def	ST
1	BAL	W	49	27	510	393	0	59%	63%	-1%	-5%
2	at NYG	W	41	23	414	376	+3	64%	52%	14%	26%
3	OAK	W	37	21	536	342	-2	32%	51%	24%	4%
4	PHI	W	52	20	472	450	0	81%	71%	7%	17%
5	at DAL	W	51	48	517	522	0	-8%	40%	53%	5%
6	JAC	W	35	19	407	362	-1	11%	9%	-3%	-1%
7	at IND	L	33	39	429	334	-2	-1%	2%	0%	-3%
8	WAS	W	45	21	446	266	+1	59%	14%	-48%	-3%
9	BYE										
10	at SD	W	28	20	397	329	-1	34%	31%	-6%	-3%
11	KC	W	27	17	427	344	0	34%	32%	-10%	-8%
12	at NE	L	31	34	412	440	-1	2%	-3%	-14%	-9%
13	at KC	W	35	28	535	452	-1	28%	61%	11%	-23%
14	TEN	W	51	28	551	254	+2	28%	29%	-8%	-9%
15	SD	L	20	27	295	337	-1	-1%	5%	10%	3%
16	at HOU	W	37	13	511	240	+2	59%	39%	-29%	-9%
17	at OAK	W	34	14	458	255	+1	32%	49%	18%	1%
18	BYE										
19	SD	W	24	17	363	259	-2	32%	6%	-18%	9%
20	NE	W	26	16	507	320	0	48%	50%	7%	5%
21	vs. SEA	L	8	43	306	341	-4	-57%	-6%	27%	-23%

Trends and Splits

	Offense	Rank	Defense	Rank
Total DVOA	33.5%	1	-0.2%	15
Unadjusted VOA	37.0%	1	-2.7%	14
Weighted Trend	26.7%	1	-5.6%	10
Variance	5.4%	9	5.1%	16
Average Opponent	4.2%	30	-1.9%	23
Passing	60.3%	1	10.2%	21
Rushing	4.2%	10	-14.3%	9
First Down	23.8%	2	-11.4%	7
Second Down	37.0%	1	-1.6%	11
Third Down	51.1%	1	25.5%	29
First Half	35.3%	1	0.7%	17
Second Half	31.7%	1	-1.2%	17
Red Zone	50.4%	1	15.2%	25
Late and Close	37.0%	2	-24.6%	3

Five-Year Performance

Year	W-L	Pyth W	Est W	PF	PA	TO	Total	Rk	Off	Rk	Def	Rk	ST	Rk	Off AGL	Rk	Def AGL	Rk	Off Age	Rk	Def Age	Rk	ST Age	Rk
2009	8-8	8.1	9.2	326	324	+7	10.6%	13	1.3%	18	-9.8%	7	-0.4%	18	16.5	13	3.3	1	27.7	10	29.1	2	26.4	19
2010	4-12	4.9	5.3	344	471	-9	-17.1%	26	2.1%	15	16.6%	30	-2.6%	27	11.0	6	40.8	28	26.6	24	28.9	2	25.6	28
2011	8-8	5.8	7.0	309	390	+1	-11.8%	24	-9.9%	23	1.6%	18	-0.2%	18	15.0	5	40.4	24	25.6	32	27.5	10	25.9	28
2012	13-3	12.5	14.7	481	289	-1	36.5%	2	22.1%	2	-13.8%	5	0.6%	13	27.8	15	21.4	11	28.3	5	27.0	15	25.9	21
2013	13-3	11.7	14.1	606	399	0	32.7%	2	33.5%	1	-0.2%	15	-1.0%	21	37.9	19	47.5	27	27.9	3	26.3	18	26.8	5

2013 Performance Based on Most Common Personnel Groups

DEN Offense					DEN Offense vs. Opponents				DEN Defense				DEN Defense vs. Opponents			
Pers	Freq	Yds	DVOA	Run%	Pers	Freq	Yds	DVOA	Pers	Freq	Yds	DVOA	Pers	Freq	Yds	DVOA
11	71%	6.9	39.8%	34%	Nickel Even	54%	6.6	32.8%	Nickel Even	36%	5.7	7.9%	11	52%	5.3	-0.2%
12	24%	6.3	32.4%	47%	Nickel Odd	22%	7.4	58.1%	4-3-4	28%	4.9	-7.5%	12	18%	5.8	0.9%
13	3%	3.2	-6.9%	61%	3-4-4	9%	5.3	18.7%	Nickel Odd	22%	5.6	-3.5%	21	17%	4.7	-14.2%
02	1%	5.4	-21.8%	0%	Dime+	7%	7.1	42.3%	Dime+	10%	6.5	6.2%	20	5%	4.6	-32.5%
23	1%	0.9	58.4%	50%	4-3-4	7%	5.8	18.6%	3-4-4	2%	5.1	-9.8%	22	3%	6.4	30.9%

Strategic Tendencies

Run/Pass		Rk	Formation		Rk	Pass Rush		Rk	Secondary		Rk	Strategy		Rk
Runs, first half	34%	27	Form: Single Back	91%	2	Rush 3	6.9%	13	4 DB	30%	27	Play action	25%	9
Runs, first down	47%	17	Form: Empty Back	6%	18	Rush 4	59.1%	21	5 DB	59%	7	Avg Box (Off)	6.07	31
Runs, second-long	27%	24	Pers: 3+ WR	72%	5	Rush 5	26.8%	13	6+ DB	10%	12	Avg Box (Def)	6.17	28
Runs, power sit.	46%	27	Pers: 4+ WR	0%	25	Rush 6+	7.2%	17	CB by Sides	58%	26	Offensive Pace	25.86	3
Runs, behind 2H	25%	22	Pers: 2+ TE/6+ OL	29%	20	Sacks by LB	25.6%	18	DB Blitz	15%	5	Defensive Pace	30.06	19
Pass, ahead 2H	53%	6	Shotgun/Pistol	78%	2	Sacks by DB	0.0%	29	Hole in Zone	7%	27	Go for it on 4th	1.12	8

The book of conventional strategy still says not to blitz Peyton Manning, and he only faced more than four pass rushers on 25 percent of plays last year. However, for the second straight year, Manning wasn't quite as good against blitzes as he was the rest of the time, dropping from 8.4 yards per pass with three or four pass rushers to 7.5 yards per pass with five or more pass rushers. And Manning averaged only 5.1 yards per pass when opponents blitzed at least one defensive back. They're never going to be using the read-option, but the Broncos actually used pistol last year on 18.3 percent of plays, more than any other team except Washington. As good as the offense was all the time, the Broncos were just on another planet entirely when they used play-action, with an absurd 11.1 yards per play and 89.7% DVOA. Other than play-action, the biggest difference for Denver wasn't in the downfield passes but in the short ones. Last year, the Broncos had the best DVOA in the league on both passes behind the line of scrimmage and passes beyond the line of scrimmage. In 2012, however, the Broncos had been fourth in DVOA on passes beyond the line of scrimmage but just 26th in DVOA on passes thrown behind the line of scrimmage. Denver was the only offense that didn't use an extra offensive lineman on a single play all year.

Passing

Player	DYAR	DVOA	Plays	NtYds	Avg	YAC	C%	TD	Int
P.Manning	2475	43.2%	679	5347	7.9	5.7	68.5%	55	10
B.Osweiler	3	-8.5%	18	87	4.8	6.2	68.8%	0	0

Rushing

Player	DYAR	DVOA	Plays	Yds	Avg	TD	Fum	Suc
K.Moreno*	171	8.4%	241	1038	4.3	10	1	50%
M.Ball	86	7.5%	120	559	4.7	4	2	54%
R.Hillman	4	-6.9%	55	218	4.0	1	2	55%
C.Anderson	19	53.0%	7	38	5.4	0	0	86%

Receiving

Player	DYAR	DVOA	Plays	Ctch	Yds	Y/C	YAC	TD	C%
D.Thomas	430	26.5%	142	92	1431	15.6	7.6	14	65%
E.Decker*	381	21.3%	136	87	1288	14.8	4.3	11	64%
W.Welker	194	9.3%	111	73	778	10.7	4.4	10	66%
A.Caldwell	35	2.0%	29	16	200	12.5	2.6	3	55%
E.Sanders	*22*	*-10.2%*	*113*	*68*	*740*	*10.9*	*4.4*	*6*	*60%*
J.Thomas	214	27.0%	90	65	788	12.1	6.2	12	72%
J.Tamme	56	23.7%	25	20	184	9.2	3.3	1	80%
V.Green	-44	-61.0%	12	9	45	5.0	1.9	0	75%
J.Dreessen	-5	-14.2%	9	7	47	6.7	3.9	1	78%
K.Moreno*	192	31.0%	74	60	548	9.1	7.9	3	81%
M.Ball	-7	-18.3%	27	20	148	7.4	7.0	0	74%
R.Hillman	45	41.1%	14	12	119	9.9	6.3	0	86%

Offensive Line

Player	Pos	Age	GS	Snaps	Pen	Sk	Pass	Run	Player	Pos	Age	GS	Snaps	Pen	Sk	Pass	Run
Louis Vasquez	RG	27	16/16	1207	3	0.0	2.3	3.0	Chris Clark	LT	29	16/16	1057	7	6.5	22.8	1.0
Zane Beadles*	LG	28	16/16	1198	4	1.0	20.8	4.0	Ryan Clady	LT	28	2/2	141	1	1.0	3.0	1.0
Manny Ramirez	C	31	16/16	1198	5	1.5	10.0	10.0	Chris Kuper*	G	32	4/1	106	0	1.5	3.5	1.0
Orlando Franklin	RT	27	15/15	1092	11	4.5	16.5	4.0	*Will Montgomery*	*C*	*31*	*16/16*	*1144*	*9*	*3.0*	*10.5*	*4.0*

Year	Yards	ALY	Rk	Power	Rk	Stuff	Rk	2nd Lev	Rk	Open Field	Rk	Sacks	ASR	Rk	Short	Long	F-Start	Cont.
2011	4.67	4.19	11	56%	26	17%	9	1.31	7	0.94	10	42	9.5%	29	9	25	7	48
2012	4.07	4.13	12	67%	9	20%	20	1.19	16	0.53	25	21	4.2%	2	10	5	12	29
2013	4.38	4.07	8	64%	17	16%	3	1.30	4	0.63	20	20	3.6%	1	9	6	14	36

2013 ALY by direction: Left End 4.66 (6) Left Tackle 4.13 (12) Mid/Guard 4.03 (13) Right Tackle 3.67 (20) Right End 4.25 (7)

The most important part of the Broncos' offensive line is not listed in the table above, because it isn't an offensive lineman. Rather, it's Peyton Manning, who can compensate for almost any offensive line deficiency in pass protection and excels at getting the team into the right run or out of the wrong one. We have a lot of evidence that quarterbacks have more influence on their own Adjusted Sack Rate than the offensive line does; compare 2011's ASR to 2012's above, as the Broncos went from Tim Tebow to Manning.

That showed that even Peyton has his limitations, though. The good news for 2014 is the return of veteran Ryan Clady, who makes the line much better both at left tackle and overall. Chris Clark, game but a bit overmatched as Clady's replacement, shifts to right tackle. Orlando Franklin, badly exposed at times at right tackle, shifts inside to left guard. Manny Ramirez remains at center, where he played more consistently than he previously did at guard. Louis Vasquez had the fewest blown blocks per snap of any guard in the league by a considerable margin; next to No. 18, he may be the best veteran free-agent signing in Broncos history. The loss of Zane Beadles is almost addition by subtraction, as he ranked among the least effective left guards in the league.

Depth beyond the top five should be good enough. Third-round pick Michael Schofield (Michigan) may compete with Clark at right tackle but is better off as a backup, as is veteran Winston Justice. Will Montgomery was a starter for the Redskins and is a more natural center than Ramirez but may be better off as a versatile interior reserve.

Defensive Front Seven

			Overall								vs. Run					Pass Rush			
Defensive Line	Age	Pos	G	Snaps	Plays	TmPct	Rk	Stop	Dfts	BTkl	Runs	St%	Rk	RuYd	Rk	Sack	Hit	Hur	Tips
Terrance Knighton	28	DT	16	597	31	3.7%	71	27	7	1	27	85%	16	1.3	11	3.0	4	14.0	0
Kevin Vickerson	31	DT	11	390	24	4.2%	60	23	10	3	20	95%	2	0.9	1	1.0	2	9.5	3
Mitch Unrein	27	DT	16	354	20	2.4%	--	13	2	2	20	65%	--	2.6	--	0.0	3	5.0	0
Sylvester Williams	26	DT	13	297	18	2.6%	--	14	6	0	13	77%	--	2.2	--	2.0	1	3.0	0

			Overall								vs. Run					Pass Rush			
Edge Rushers	Age	Pos	G	Snaps	Plays	TmPct	Rk	Stop	Dfts	BTkl	Runs	St%	Rk	RuYd	Rk	Sack	Hit	Hur	Tips
Shaun Phillips*	33	DE	16	770	40	4.8%	53	32	19	4	19	68%	57	3.5	65	9.5	3	17.3	4
Malik Jackson	24	DE	16	591	45	5.4%	41	35	18	1	30	77%	35	2.4	36	6.0	8	12.8	5
Derek Wolfe	24	DE	11	553	15	2.6%	78	14	8	0	10	100%	1	0.7	2	3.5	4	15.5	0
Robert Ayers*	29	DE	15	506	28	3.6%	73	23	9	2	21	76%	38	2.2	26	5.5	5	17.5	0
Jeremy Mincey*	31	DE	10	298	17	3.1%	77	16	6	1	13	92%	3	1.5	11	2.0	2	12.5	1
DeMarcus Ware	*32*	*DE*	*13*	*628*	*41*	*5.9%*	*33*	*34*	*13*	*0*	*31*	*84%*	*20*	*1.8*	*18*	*6.0*	*6*	*24.0*	*1*

			Overall								Pass Rush			vs. Run					vs. Pass						
Linebackers	Age	Pos	G	Snaps	Plays	TmPct	Rk	Stop	Dfts	BTkl	Sack	Hit	Hur	Runs	St%	Rk	RuYd	Rk	Tgts	Suc%	Rk	AdjYd	Rk	PD	Int
Danny Trevathan	24	OLB	16	948	133	15.9%	20	83	23	4	2.0	4	4.5	85	68%	29	3.5	48	42	50%	41	6.8	41	9	3
Wesley Woodyard*	28	MLB	14	752	87	11.9%	50	52	18	2	2.0	6	9	44	66%	40	3.4	46	45	52%	39	6.2	27	4	1
Von Miller	25	OLB	9	541	34	7.2%	69	28	16	2	5.5	9	22	24	83%	1	1.3	1	3	62%	--	8.0	--	0	0
Nate Irving	26	OLB	15	275	34	4.3%	--	24	9	1	1.0	2	2	22	73%	--	2.2	--	11	44%	--	9.4	--	1	0
Paris Lenon*	37	MLB	14	237	22	3.0%	--	11	2	0	0.0	0	1	14	64%	--	2.9	--	8	32%	--	10.7	--	1	0

Year	Yards	ALY	Rk	Power	Rk	Stuff	Rk	2nd Level	Rk	Open Field	Rk	Sacks	ASR	Rk	Short	Long
2011	4.26	3.88	9	60%	12	22%	8	1.28	24	0.78	18	41	7.8%	5	18	14
2012	3.69	3.91	14	52%	6	18%	18	1.02	3	0.35	1	52	8.7%	1	19	18
2013	3.61	3.23	3	64%	13	22%	9	1.03	9	0.63	16	41	6.5%	22	11	16

2013 ALY by direction: Left End 3.93 (19) Left Tackle 3.80 (11) Mid/Guard 2.91 (1) Right Tackle 2.70 (3) Right End 4.22 (26)

Versatility is the watchword for the Broncos' defensive line. Defensive coordinator Jack Del Rio mixes up his fronts regularly. Terrance Knighton and Kevin Vickerson were excellent against the run in the interior, with Knighton also displaying pass-rush proficiency he had not showed in Jacksonville. First-round pick Sylvester Williams was eased into the lineup as a rookie, finally seeing a bigger role after Vickerson was lost for the season after Week 12. He has more potential as a pass rusher than the two veterans, but needs to improve leverage and technique.

Derek Wolfe will be looking for better health after a disappointing sophomore season that began with multiple bouts of food poisoning, continued with a neck injury, and was eventually ended by a seizure and general nervous system issues which combined to knock him down almost 40 pounds. Malik Jackson moved into a bigger role after Wolfe went down. Robert Ayers' departure likely means more playing time for both Jackson and Wolfe as ends with run-stuffing responsibilities who also provide pass rush threats, though the addition of DeMarcus Ware will limit their upside.

Danny Trevathan had an excellent season at weakside linebacker, regularly playing in all roles. While his charting numbers were unspectacular, he did a good job getting from place to place and was not a physical liability. The Broncos will have to replace middle linebacker Wesley Woodyard, who had a solid overall season as the other cover linebacker. The strongest candidate is Nate Irving, who saw his most regular work filling in for Von Miller on the strong side last year. Irving was capable against the run, though like Woodyard he will fare much better if the defensive line is able to protect him and not force him to take on blocks. Whether he can fill Woodyard's shoes playing the pass in nickel sets is an open question.

Defensive Secondary

			Overall									vs. Run					vs. Pass									
Secondary	Age	Pos	G	Snaps	Plays	TmPct	Rk	Stop	Dfts	BTkl	Runs	St%	Rk	RuYd	Rk	Tgts	Tgt%	Rk	Dist	Suc%	Rk	AdjYd	Rk	PD	Int
Chris Harris	25	CB	16	1042	79	9.4%	23	39	18	4	17	53%	24	4.4	9	81	17.4%	11	11.7	62%	6	7.3	38	13	3
D. Rodgers-Cromartie*	28	CB	15	776	44	5.6%	83	28	14	5	7	71%	1	6.9	40	66	18.9%	22	14.0	63%	4	7.8	51	14	3
Duke Ihenacho	25	SS	15	772	77	9.8%	40	28	9	6	35	37%	46	6.7	34	39	11.3%	67	11.2	62%	23	6.8	35	5	0
Mike Adams	33	FS	16	692	67	8.0%	65	25	14	3	34	38%	41	7.9	57	23	7.4%	28	12.7	60%	29	5.0	12	5	1
Rahim Moore	24	FS	10	660	50	9.5%	45	13	5	3	16	31%	60	7.6	53	23	7.8%	37	15.3	48%	56	6.6	30	4	2
Kayvon Webster	23	CB	14	478	47	6.4%	74	21	8	3	7	71%	1	6.1	29	57	26.4%	81	13.9	52%	48	8.6	68	7	1
Tony Carter	28	CB	12	266	17	2.7%	--	8	5	1	0	0%	--	0.0	--	33	27.7%	--	16.2	48%	--	10.2	--	4	1
Quentin Jammer*	35	CB	11	217	15	2.6%	--	8	3	0	3	100%	--	3.3	--	22	22.2%	--	12.7	50%	--	8.6	--	2	0
T.J. Ward	*28*	*SS*	*16*	*1112*	*117*	*13.6%*	*8*	*61*	*24*	*8*	*66*	*59%*	*6*	*3.8*	*4*	*38*	*8.2%*	*42*	*9.7*	*66%*	*11*	*4.3*	*7*	*4*	*2*
Aqib Talib	*28*	*CB*	*13*	*845*	*55*	*7.9%*	*52*	*23*	*14*	*5*	*9*	*44%*	*35*	*5.7*	*22*	*70*	*18.9%*	*23*	*13.0*	*52%*	*43*	*8.4*	*63*	*15*	*4*

Year	Pass D Rank	vs. #1 WR	Rk	vs. #2 WR	Rk	vs. Other WR	Rk	vs. TE	Rk	vs. RB	Rk
2011	24	21.7%	23	-1.2%	14	2.5%	22	6.1%	14	26.3%	30
2012	5	-12.5%	8	-20.3%	3	-18.1%	4	6.9%	24	-7.7%	11
2013	21	-1.1%	17	-4.5%	11	13.7%	27	3.8%	17	-8.7%	13

This is the tenth annual Football Outsiders has put out. One thing we have learned in all that time is that players with great charting numbers in a nickel role will often crash down to earth the next season. Sometimes, though, those great nickel charting numbers are a sign of a future quality starter, and Chris Harris is an example of that. He played very well in his transition to outside corner in base defense, while continuing to play inside when the Broncos went to nickel, at least until he tore his ACL in the playoff win against San Diego. Early expectations are for Harris to return and be ready to start Week 1. If Harris isn't ready to return, there will likely be two jobs available in nickel instead of just one. The leading candidate among returning players is Kayvon Webster, who had an inconsistent season in a limited role as a rookie, while the top newcomer is first-round pick Bradley Roby, a very talented player who is probably capable of playing inside if need be. Tony Carter, who was benched last season after the Cowboys' 48-point effort in Week 5, provides additional depth. Foot injuries limited to Champ Bailey to only 188 regular season snaps, so his offseason release was more noteworthy for the player he once was than for the player he was in 2013.

Even with the addition of T.J. Ward, Rahim Moore plays a pivotal role for the Broncos as by far the best fit for the single-high safety role. Though the pass defense was still strong in the first couple games he missed after the scary Week 11 leg injury that nearly required amputation, his absence for the rest of the season clearly affected how and how effectively the Broncos mixed up their coverages. Quinton Carter, who started 10 games as a rookie in 2011 before missing most of the past two seasons after a nasty knee injury, may figure in sub package situations if the Broncos cannot find a second cover linebacker.

Special Teams

Year	DVOA	Rank	FG/XP	Rank	Net Kick	Rank	Kick Ret	Rank	Net Punt	Rank	Punt Ret	Rank	Hidden	Rank
2011	-0.2%	18	-6.4	27	1.8	13	0.6	16	-5.3	24	8.2	4	4.8	9
2012	0.6%	13	-4.7	26	-1.6	20	0.9	12	13.2	5	-4.6	24	-0.1	18
2013	-1.0%	21	10.7	3	-11.7	29	5.4	5	-1.9	22	-7.6	28	20.8	1

Matt Prater has a strong leg, and he was truly excellent last year, but like all other kickers there is massive year-to-year inconsistency in his performance on field goals. Prater was phenomenal on long kicks last year, going 8-for-8 from 40-to-49 yards and 8-for-10 from 50 yards and beyond, including an NFL-record 64-yarder. However, that long accuracy was a big change from the recent past, as he hit only 8-of-16 field goals from 40-to-49 yards in 2011 and 2012. He did hit 3-of-4 field goals from 50 yards or more each year, but that's just a reminder that kickers don't usually get more than three or four opportunities per year to hit from that kind of distance. So we expect Prater to have both a lower field-goal percentage and fewer long field goals in 2014. We wouldn't mind also seeing fewer 19-yard field goals... say, zero instead of three. (John Fox, you have a good offense. Go for it on fourth-and-goal from the one!) Prater also had his best season on kickoffs, ranking sixth in the league with 3.1 points of gross kickoff value over average. As we saw in the Super Bowl, though, problems came when teams actually returned one of his kickoffs, as the Broncos had the fifth-worst kick coverage unit in the league. The Broncos lacked a standout gunner, with tight end Jacob Tamme leading the team in special teams tackles.

The Broncos gave punter Britton Colquitt a four-year, $13 million contract before the 2013 season, and he celebrated by going from slightly above average to a hair below average. Punt coverage was better than kickoff coverage, but not nearly as good as it was in 2012. When you have a great offense and play in an exceptionally favorable environment for kicking the ball, paying a punter that much money is probably not the best use of resources.

Trindon Holliday's explosiveness as a returner will be missed, while his occasional poor decisions and trouble handling the football will not be. Emmanuel Sanders has experience returning both punts and kicks, if he is not judged too valuable on offense to fill those roles. Wes Welker returned punts last year when Fox was looking for someone with more reliable hands than Holliday, though that did not work out so well against Welker's former team in the regular season. Among the lower profile options are rookie cornerback Roby, fourth receiver Andre Caldwell, and backup defensive back Omar Bolden.

Detroit Lions

2013 Record: 7-9	**Total DVOA:** -1.5% (16th)	**2014 Mean Projection:** 6.5 wins	**On the Clock (0-4):** 20%
Pythagorean Wins: 8.5 (13th)	**Offense:** -1.9% (19th)	**Postseason Odds:** 14.0%	**Mediocrity (5-7):** 48%
Snap-Weighted Age: 27.0 (10th)	**Defense:** -0.8% (14th)	**Super Bowl Odds:** 0.9%	**Playoff Contender (8-10):** 26%
Average Opponent: -3.7% (28th)	**Special Teams:** -0.4% (20th)	**Proj. Avg. Opponent:** 2.8% (3rd)	**Super Bowl Contender (11+):** 6%

2013: The Lions shot themselves in the foot by aiming at the scar left from the last time they shot themselves in the foot.

2014: "Culture change" may actually turn out to be a thing.

Some people have five years of experience at a job. Others experience the same year five times.

The Jim Schwartz Lions fell into the latter category. They were brimming with potential after Schwartz's first season in 2009: they just needed to mature, eliminate mistakes, and figure out how to convert talent into success. They were the same team in 2013, still making dumb mistakes, still approaching excellence like a dog with a shock collar creeping up on an electrified fence.

The Lions experienced a season just like 2013 before Schwartz even arrived. In 2007, the team started the season 6-2, lost a few close games, then lost a bunch of not-so-close ones as they descended into finger pointing and despair. Last year, the team started 5-3 and appeared to eradicate its demons with a last-second win against the Cowboys. You may recall Mathew Stafford gesturing to kill the clock then sneaking over the goal line in a move that surprised not only the Cowboys but even his own teammates. Two weeks later, the Lions held off a late Bears charge at Soldier Field to improve to 6-3. Like the 2007 Lions, they looked like a team that had grown smarter and more focused. With quarterbacks around the NFC North getting injured, the Lions were a playoff lock.

But just as Icarus flew too close to the sun, the Lions began to melt as soon as they approached the heat lamp of the postseason.

Leading the Steelers 27-23 early in the fourth quarter, Schwartz called a fake field goal that sent rookie punter Sam Martin on a doomed quest to gain five yards against the Steelers' field-goal block unit (a bunch of defensive regulars) in a steady drizzle. Martin fumbled. The Steelers drove for a touchdown, Stafford threw an interception, the Steelers drove for another touchdown, and the collapse was on.

Stafford followed with four interceptions against a Buccaneers team that would have let the Lions win if they promised to take Greg Schiano away from them forever. The Lions still led by three early in the fourth quarter, but Tiquan Underwood beat Chris Houston for an 85-yard touchdown, and the Lions turned the remainder of the quarter into a comedy routine featuring blocked punts and bobbled catches that turned into Buccaneers interceptions.

An unexpected snowstorm struck Philadelphia when the Lions arrived in early December. On a day when visibility was an arm's length and the field was a slip-n-slide, Schwartz's defensive strategy was to deploy the Wide-9 front as often as possible, granting Shady McCoy and his teammates plenty of interior gaps to blast through. Meanwhile, Stafford fumbled snaps like he was an Australian Bushman experiencing snow for the first time. The Lions fumbled seven times, the Eagles rushed for 299 yards, and suddenly the playoffs were in doubt.

Stafford then embarked on an interception jag, with the defense making matters worse by failing to get off the field in critical situations. A sidearm special into the belly of defender Daryl Smith, coupled with a third-and-15 conversion allowed during a Ravens desperation drive, led to two Justin Tucker field goals and a Ravens win in Week 15. A Stafford pick-six (off-target, though also off Joseph Fauria's fingertips) allowed the Giants to tie the Lions in the fourth quarter, and a third-and-13 Eli Manning conversion in overtime became a Giants win in Week 16. Forget the playoffs: the Lions were suddenly playing to preserve .500, but even that was too much, and they lost to the Adrian Peterson-less Vikings in the season finale.

There was some bad luck mixed in to all of the losses: Tucker and others converted more than their share of long field goals, the Giants' overtime third-down catch should have been reviewed (Rueben Randle appeared to trap the ball), the Philadelphia weather was a freak outlier, and so on. Still, the Lions proved that despite five years of Schwartz, Stafford, and Calvin Johnson, and four with their storied Ndamukong Suh-anchored defensive line, they firmly belonged in the same category as last year's Steelers, Ravens, and Cowboys: problem-plagued playoff outsiders. The only difference is that those teams have past glories to point to. The Lions just have five years of failing to correct the same mistakes. Stafford kept channeling Dan Quisenberry and acting like it was not a problem. The defensive line was never as good as its billing and never really got better. Late-game situational football remained an absolute train wreck. And the late-season losses to the Giants and Vikings spoke volumes about the team's lack of resilience once things went wrong.

With Schwartz gone, it is up to Jim Caldwell to solve the Lions problems. The good news is that the Lions problems have been problems for so long that they are easy to identify. Some of them should even be easy to solve.

Stafford may not be the biggest problem, but he is the most noticeable. He threw 13 interceptions in his final eight games, with another six dropped by defenders. His primary issues are mechanical: he is in love with his sidearm throws, which of-

2014 Lions Schedule

Week	Opp.	Week	Opp.	Week	Opp.
1	NYG (Mon.)	7	NO	13	CHI (Thu.)
2	at CAR	8	at ATL (U.K.)	14	TB
3	GB	9	BYE	15	MIN
4	at NYJ	10	MIA	16	at CHI
5	BUF	11	at ARI	17	at GB
6	at MIN	12	at NE		

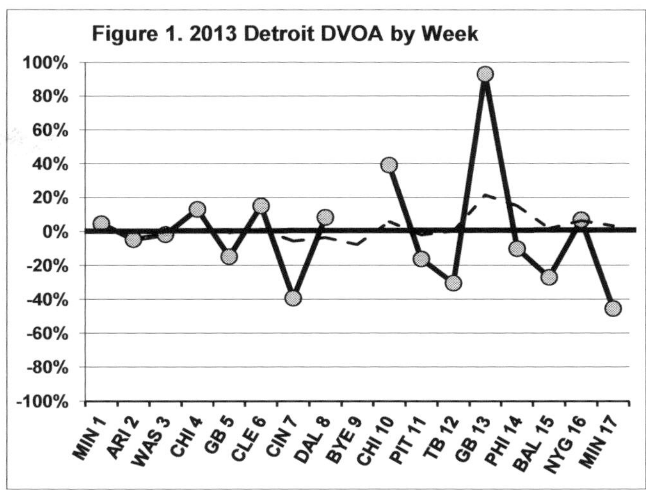

ten tail away from receivers, and he delivers too many high hard ones on short crossing routes. Stafford has one of the three strongest arms in the NFL, exceptional passing talent, and enough field smarts to eradicate interception sprees. Past coaches have simply been unwilling or unable to correct fundamental kinks that cause ill-timed disasters.

Caldwell arrives with Peyton Manning bona fides, and two years ago he worked short-term wonders with Joe Flacco, another pocket flamethrower. Caldwell's Super Bowl cred may be as important as the mechanical lessons he will impart. Stafford's delivery had become something between a low priority and a case of institutional denial for the Lions; the team too often joined Stafford in publically writing off his mechanics as a big deal about nuttin'. Caldwell's first step will be Stafford admitting there's a problem.

A rebuilt receiving corps will help Stafford achieve his potential. Too many game plans hinged on Kris Durham getting targeted six to 13 times last year after injuries to Ryan Broyles and Nate Burleson left Megatron without a Starscream. Golden Tate, signed away from Seattle, is an excellent complement to Johnson with the ability to both beat corners up the sideline and baffle opponents' second-best cornerbacks. Rookie Eric Ebron will play a role somewhere between second tight end and slot receiver. Brandon Pettigrew, miscast as a seam-stretcher for years, was re-signed to work the short middle, where he will be a matchup headache for most linebackers. This is one of the three or four best receiving corps in the NFL, if not the deepest, and Ebron's (and Reggie Bush's) versatility will limit Caldwell and Stafford's reliance on stopgap options like Durham. The potential for a 5,500-yard passing season is here, but pure passing yardage has never been the problem. Caldwell and the new weapons must make Stafford more efficient, and the defense must make sure record-breaking passing heroics are not necessary.

The on-scholarship Lions defensive line and the perpetually-underachieving secondary are the next recurring problems on the Caldwell agenda. Defensive coordinator Teryl Austin takes the point on these issues. Austin coached defensive backs in Baltimore, and the Lions signed James Ihedigbo as an Austin binky and on-field mentor for young defenders like Darius Slay and Bill Bentley. Austin's Super Bowl cred should also help him reach Suh and Nick Fairley, both of whom started the 2013 season playing smart football and ended it with their usual mix of penalties and inconsistency.

Austin's Ravens-flavored ideas will also improve a defense that grew incredibly predictable in recent years. Teams knew what they were getting from Schwartz' Lions: minimal blitzing and lots of Wide-9 fronts, even when conditions (a snowstorm) called for some flexibility. Austin comes from the Pagano family tree, meaning there will be more blitzing and front multiplicity in Detroit —though since he is practically working from baselines of "none" and "one," that's not saying much. Second-round pick Kyle Van Noy may be a sign of things to come. Van Noy is a pass rushing linebacker, not an edge-rushing end or a gaps-and-coverage linebacker. The old regime had no use for such a player, but Austin has a more dynamic imagination.

General manager Martin Mayhew could not make all of the upgrades that were necessary on offense and defense. In fact, it was remarkable what they accomplished under the circumstances. The Suh-Stafford-Megatron triplets eat up $50 million in cap space this season, meaning that the Lions entered the offseason with over 40 percent of the salary cap tied behind their backs. As outlined in last year's *Almanac*, the Lions were in the unique position of selecting players in the top five draft slots in 2008 through 2010, the exact years when top-five rookie contracts grew so out of control that the rookie salary cap became a lockout-worthy bargaining chip.

The Big Three remain far too good to part with but are almost too expensive to build around, which is why streamlining Stafford's approach and keeping Suh on the straight and narrow are such mandates for the coaching staff. Just acquiring this year's supporting class was something of a cap high-wire act. Tate's contract is insanely backloaded to accommodate his signing bonus: his base salary is just $1.5 million, with $13 million in silliness hidden on the 2017 and 2018 spreadsheets. Pettigrew also let the Lions be cap cute, with his salary going up by nearly a million dollars per year through 2017, when everything turns into bonus-proration Monopoly money. Ebron and Van Noy are a fine one-two draft punch, but there was little left to address the secondary beyond journeyman Ihedigbo and fourth-rounder Nevin Lawson. The Lions are paper-thin nearly everywhere, including backup quarterback (Kellen Moore and Dan Orlovsky) and kicker (seventh-round pick Nate Freese likely has the job).

Ignore the depth and the history, and the Lions look like a playoff team. That should not be surprising, because they looked like a playoff team as recently as early November. The 2012 and 2013 seasons are an impact crater where a success cycle should have stood, a testament to stubbornly stunted development. A team that gets to line up Stafford, Suh, and Megatron week after week, with a somewhat stable and reasonably reliable supporting cast, has no excuse to stumble around the way the Lions have.

Football Outsiders essays should never end with clichéd "learn how to win" hogwash. But the Lions need just such learning: the tiny details of the passing motion, focus and preparation, late-game and late-season tactical adjustments, and a swift jolt to the complacency centers of the brain. Those are also the lessons Caldwell and Austin promise to bring from their times with Peyton and Sugar Ray in Indy and Bawl'mer. If it really is impossible to "find a way" to win, the Lions must at least stop finding so many unique and depressing ways to lose. They don't have to grow up a lot, just a little, to return to a playoff picture they should always have been in.

Mike Tanier

2013 Lions Stats by Week

Wk	vs.	W-L	PF	PA	YDF	YDA	TO	Total	Off	Def	ST
1	MIN	W	34	24	469	330	2	5%	4%	-9%	-9%
2	at ARI	L	21	25	322	348	0	-5%	15%	2%	-18%
3	at WAS	W	27	20	441	420	1	-2%	18%	15%	-5%
4	CHI	W	40	32	387	417	1	13%	-22%	-20%	14%
5	at GB	L	9	22	286	449	0	-15%	-13%	6%	4%
6	at CLE	W	31	17	366	395	1	15%	18%	13%	10%
7	CIN	L	24	27	434	421	0	-39%	23%	52%	-10%
8	DAL	W	31	30	623	268	-4	8%	9%	-8%	-8%
9	BYE										
10	at CHI	W	21	19	364	338	0	39%	16%	-31%	-8%
11	at PIT	L	27	37	451	398	-3	-16%	-7%	13%	4%
12	TB	L	21	24	390	229	-5	-31%	-31%	-9%	-9%
13	GB	W	40	10	561	126	-1	93%	15%	-91%	-13%
14	at PHI	L	20	34	231	478	-2	-10%	-43%	13%	47%
15	BAL	L	16	18	349	305	-3	-27%	-12%	9%	-6%
16	NYG	L	20	23	355	279	-1	7%	-5%	-8%	4%
17	at MIN	L	13	14	245	345	2	-46%	-36%	6%	-3%

Trends and Splits

	Offense	Rank	Defense	Rank
Total DVOA	-1.9%	19	-0.8%	14
Unadjusted VOA	-0.9%	17	-2.8%	13
Weighted Trend	-5.5%	21	-2.5%	13
Variance	4.5%	7	9.1%	30
Average Opponent	2.9%	26	-0.7%	19
Passing	9.9%	16	9.6%	20
Rushing	-11.9%	27	-16.9%	5
First Down	-6.8%	22	7.2%	24
Second Down	-1.5%	18	-6.4%	8
Third Down	7.5%	11	-9.1%	10
First Half	-7.2%	23	-2.4%	13
Second Half	4.0%	15	0.7%	18
Red Zone	10.8%	12	-29.4%	3
Late and Close	-1.6%	15	-2.5%	15

Five-Year Performance

Year	W-L	Pyth W	Est W	PF	PA	TO	Total	Rk	Off	Rk	Def	Rk	ST	Rk	Off AGL	Rk	Def AGL	Rk	Off Age	Rk	Def Age	Rk	ST Age	Rk
2009	2-14	2.7	0.0	262	494	-18	-51.6%	32	-28.4%	31	17.9%	32	-5.3%	31	20.4	14	55.1	31	27.2	16	26.9	21	26.7	14
2010	6-10	7.8	7.5	362	369	+4	-1.1%	18	-0.8%	19	2.9%	22	2.6%	11	26.6	16	24.4	17	27.7	12	26.1	26	27.2	5
2011	10-6	10.1	9.4	474	387	+11	10.1%	11	7.1%	10	-8.1%	9	-5.1%	29	13.3	4	14.8	8	27.9	7	26.0	28	27.5	1
2012	4-12	6.4	7.6	372	437	-16	0.1%	16	12.3%	8	7.1%	24	-5.1%	30	23.2	11	58.3	31	28.3	4	26.7	17	27.8	1
2013	7-9	8.5	7.7	395	376	-12	-1.5%	16	-1.9%	19	-0.8%	14	-0.4%	20	32.5	14	32.0	18	27.0	14	27.0	13	26.8	6

2013 Performance Based on Most Common Personnel Groups

DET Offense					DET Offense vs. Opponents				DET Defense				DET Defense vs. Opponents			
Pers	Freq	Yds	DVOA	Run%	Pers	Freq	Yds	DVOA	Pers	Freq	Yds	DVOA	Pers	Freq	Yds	DVOA
11	68%	6.0	1.5%	38%	Nickel Even	62%	5.8	-2.7%	Nickel Even	64%	5.9	2.7%	11	60%	5.7	2.8%
12	21%	5.5	-4.3%	39%	3-4-4	13%	5.5	1.7%	4-3-4	31%	5.8	-9.3%	12	16%	5.4	-16.9%
21	4%	6.7	20.2%	29%	Dime+	12%	6.8	31.2%	Dime+	2%	5.5	53.6%	21	10%	7.1	7.4%
20	3%	4.4	-15.9%	48%	4-3-4	7%	5.0	-14.1%	Goal Line	1%	3.4	-31.8%	02	2%	10.5	75.7%
610	1%	6.2	37.8%	60%	Nickel Odd	6%	5.3	6.6%	Nickel Odd	1%	8.9	47.7%	10	2%	5.1	7.8%

Strategic Tendencies

Run/Pass		Rk	Formation		Rk	Pass Rush		Rk	Secondary		Rk	Strategy		Rk
Runs, first half	37%	21	Form: Single Back	83%	3	Rush 3	0.5%	32	4 DB	31%	26	Play action	23%	14
Runs, first down	54%	5	Form: Empty Back	13%	5	Rush 4	79.8%	1	5 DB	66%	4	Avg Box (Off)	6.13	30
Runs, second-long	26%	25	Pers: 3+ WR	73%	4	Rush 5	13.2%	32	6+ DB	2%	26	Avg Box (Def)	6.27	25
Runs, power sit.	49%	24	Pers: 4+ WR	1%	19	Rush 6+	6.5%	22	CB by Sides	79%	14	Offensive Pace	30.95	23
Runs, behind 2H	34%	2	Pers: 2+ TE/6+ OL	25%	24	Sacks by LB	10.6%	29	DB Blitz	8%	25	Defensive Pace	29.16	10
Pass, ahead 2H	51%	10	Shotgun/Pistol	68%	8	Sacks by DB	12.1%	8	Hole in Zone	7%	26	Go for it on 4th	1.06	9

The Lions dropped a league-high 46 passes, or 7.8 percent of all Matthew Stafford's passes. That's far beyond the next-highest offense, which was either New England (38) or St. Louis (6.4 percent). Golden Tate should help things; he had only four drops last year. The Lions ran 39 percent of the time when they had at least three wide receivers on the field, more than any team except the Jets, even though they had just 4.1 yards per carry (29th in the NFL) and -12.6% DVOA (27th) from those formations. Detroit was one of six teams to use empty backfields on at least 10 percent of plays, and they gained 7.8 yards per play with 23.2% DVOA. Matthew Stafford was blitzed less often than any other quarterback other than Peyton Manning even though his yards per pass dropped from 7.6 against a standard pass rush to 5.2 against five pass rushers and 4.5 against six or more pass rushers. The Lions ranked third in DVOA passing in the red zone but a dismal 29th when running in the red zone. Detroit's defense had -26.3% DVOA against passes thrown behind the line of scrimmage (fifth in the NFL) but 54.1% DVOA against passes thrown past the line of scrimmage (25th).

Passing

Player	DYAR	DVOA	Plays	NtYds	Avg	YAC	C%	TD	Int
M.Stafford	690	4.9%	658	4431	6.7	6.1	59.1%	29	19

Rushing

Player	DYAR	DVOA	Plays	Yds	Avg	TD	Fum	Suc
R.Bush	7	-7.8%	223	1006	4.5	4	5	47%
J.Bell	78	2.0%	166	653	3.9	8	4	51%
M.Stafford	-41	-40.3%	23	70	3.0	1	4	-
T.Riddick	9	16.2%	9	25	2.8	1	0	44%

Receiving

Player	DYAR	DVOA	Plays	Ctch	Yds	Y/C	YAC	TD	C%
C.Johnson	347	14.9%	156	84	1492	17.8	5.5	12	54%
K.Durham	-39	-18.5%	85	38	490	12.9	3.2	2	45%
N.Burleson*	56	0.4%	54	39	461	11.8	5.5	1	72%
K.Ogletree*	32	2.7%	25	13	199	15.3	5.3	1	52%
R.Broyles	-11	-23.0%	14	8	85	10.6	4.8	0	57%
P.Edwards	-21	-37.9%	11	5	46	9.2	5.0	0	45%
J.Ross	4	-8.2%	10	5	59	11.8	2.8	1	50%
G.Tate	*196*	*12.9%*	*100*	*66*	*920*	*13.9*	*7.6*	*5*	*66%*
B.Pettigrew	-37	-16.6%	63	41	416	10.1	4.6	2	65%
J.Fauria	64	24.2%	30	18	207	11.5	2.9	7	60%
T.Scheffler*	-16	-26.9%	12	7	82	11.7	4.0	0	58%
R.Bush	94	5.8%	80	54	506	9.4	8.7	3	68%
J.Bell	196	40.3%	69	53	547	10.3	10.3	0	77%
T.Riddick	-4	-22.0%	8	4	26	6.5	4.3	0	50%

Offensive Line

Player	Pos	Age	GS	Snaps	Pen	Sk	Pass	Run
Rob Sims	LG	31	16/16	1126	5	0.5	10.5	7.0
Larry Warford	RG	23	16/16	1126	3	0.0	10.0	5.0
Dominic Raiola	C	36	16/16	1124	1	0.0	3.0	1.0
Riley Reiff	LT	26	16/16	1097	4	6.5	22.5	1.0
LaAdrian Waddle	RT	23	12/8	536	2	0.0	10.0	2.0
Corey Hilliard	RT	29	9/7	452	0	0.0	4.5	1.0
Jason Fox*	OT	26	7/3	192	1	1.0	3.0	1.0

Year	Yards	ALY	Rk	Power	Rk	Stuff	Rk	2nd Lev	Rk	Open Field	Rk	Sacks	ASR	Rk	Short	Long	F-Start	Cont.
2011	4.22	3.70	31	52%	28	21%	24	1.13	21	0.89	14	36	5.8%	11	11	19	19	43
2012	4.01	4.05	15	56%	27	17%	5	1.10	20	0.49	27	29	3.7%	1	5	18	19	39
2013	4.23	3.94	13	76%	3	19%	12	1.26	9	0.68	17	23	4.5%	2	10	7	11	33

2013 ALY by direction: Left End 2.95 (24) Left Tackle 3.99 (14) Mid/Guard 4.00 (14) Right Tackle 4.50 (3) Right End 2.71 (30)

Larry Warford would have gotten Rookie of the Year notice if there was any mechanism for noticing guards as rookie of the year candidates. Warford did not allow a sack all season long despite playing beside a revolving cast of right tackles. Veteran Rob Sims, who has not missed a start in four years with the Lions, took an active role in helping Warford adjust to the NFL and returns for another tour at left guard.

LaAdrian Waddle, an undrafted rookie last year, took over the right tackle job after Jason Fox and Corey Hilliard suffered injuries. Waddle had a handful of exceptional games before an elbow injury limited his effectiveness during the Lions' December swoon. Hilliard, a veteran swing tackle, will push Waddle in camp but is likely to settle back into his reserve role.

With all of his backups injured or starting on the right side, Riley Reiff had to gut through a hamstring injury for the second half of the season. Reiff made great strides from his mistake-prone rookie year (which had the Lions considering a move to guard), and was playing more consistently in the second half of the year despite the aches and pains. Some defenders go right through Reiff, however, and in the fine Lions tradition, there are times when he does not even seem to know he has an assignment, let alone how to handle it. Add "clarification of assignments" to Jim Caldwell's to-do list.

When Dominic Raiola finally retires from the Lions, he may take 13 years of sins and frustration away with him, like a whitening strip removing decades of brown tar from a smoker's teeth. That will not happen this year. Raiola signed a one-year deal to remain the team's starting center, and he remains effective in a decidedly Lions sort of way. Raiola made headlines in October of last season by making fun of overweight members of the Wisconsin marching band, then issuing a boilerplate apology. His shining 2012 moment was a decision to snap the ball during an overtime attempt to draw an opponent offsides, causing a fumble. There are still times when Matthew Stafford reacts with genuine surprise when the ball hits him in the hands; in Detroit, they call this "distinguished veteran leadership." Travis Swanson arrived in the third round as Raiola's heir apparent. He survived playing under John L. Smith and Bret Bielema, so he is ready for the worst that Detroit can throw at him.

Defensive Front Seven

			Overall								vs. Run					Pass Rush			
Defensive Line	**Age**	**Pos**	**G**	**Snaps**	**Plays**	**TmPct**	**Rk**	**Stop**	**Dfts**	**BTkl**	**Runs**	**St%**	**Rk**	**RuYd**	**Rk**	**Sack**	**Hit**	**Hur**	**Tips**
Ndamukong Suh	27	DT	16	867	54	7.1%	16	45	18	1	40	80%	34	3.3	78	5.5	15	23.0	4
Nick Fairley	26	DT	15	659	34	4.8%	48	28	15	0	18	78%	41	3.7	81	6.0	13	17.0	1
C.J. Mosley	31	DT	16	321	16	2.1%	--	9	1	0	15	60%	--	3.7	--	0.0	5	4.0	0

			Overall								vs. Run					Pass Rush			
Edge Rushers	**Age**	**Pos**	**G**	**Snaps**	**Plays**	**TmPct**	**Rk**	**Stop**	**Dfts**	**BTkl**	**Runs**	**St%**	**Rk**	**RuYd**	**Rk**	**Sack**	**Hit**	**Hur**	**Tips**
Willie Young*	29	DE	16	760	49	6.5%	24	45	12	2	37	89%	7	2.3	28	3.0	8	27.0	4
Ezekiel Ansah	25	DE	14	547	32	4.8%	50	28	13	1	18	89%	8	1.4	9	8.0	3	15.5	1
Israel Idonije*	34	DE	15	330	11	1.5%	--	10	4	0	10	90%	--	0.6	--	0.5	2	10.5	0
Devin Taylor	25	DE	14	299	15	2.3%	--	11	7	1	11	64%	--	2.5	--	2.5	5	8.0	1

			Overall								Pass Rush			vs. Run					vs. Pass						
Linebackers	**Age**	**Pos**	**G**	**Snaps**	**Plays**	**TmPct**	**Rk**	**Stop**	**Dfts**	**BTkl**	**Sack**	**Hit**	**Hur**	**Runs**	**St%**	**Rk**	**RuYd**	**Rk**	**Tgts**	**Suc%**	**Rk**	**AdjYd**	**Rk**	**PD**	**Int**
Stephen Tulloch	29	MLB	16	1021	138	18.2%	7	79	30	5	3.5	3	5.5	79	61%	56	4.2	69	45	54%	30	6.9	45	4	1
DeAndre Levy	27	OLB	16	1011	131	17.3%	11	73	27	8	0.0	3	4	61	66%	42	3.9	61	52	60%	17	6.2	26	12	6
Ashlee Palmer	28	OLB	16	349	28	3.7%	--	20	7	1	0.0	1	1	17	94%	--	0.5	--	11	41%	--	8.1	--	1	0

Year	Yards	ALY	Rk	Power	Rk	Stuff	Rk	2nd Level	Rk	Open Field	Rk	Sacks	ASR	Rk	Short	Long
2011	4.60	3.99	14	52%	5	21%	11	1.23	19	1.16	28	41	6.4%	21	16	16
2012	4.30	3.69	5	72%	28	26%	2	1.33	29	1.03	27	34	5.2%	29	5	20
2013	4.08	3.13	2	50%	3	26%	4	1.13	19	1.07	29	33	5.8%	31	7	14
2013 ALY by direction:			*Left End 1.80 (2)*			*Left Tackle 3.50 (8)*			*Mid/Guard 3.20 (2)*			*Right Tackle 2.91 (5)*			*Right End 3.96 (19)*	

Ndamukong Suh and Nick Fairley combined for 17 penalties in 2013, up from 14 in 2012 but down from the 19 Suh and Avril combined to commit in the *Ryan Seacrest's Curb Stompin' Thanksgiving* halcyon days of 2011. Through Week 8, the pair combined for just eight flags, five of them harmless encroachment and neutral zone variations. Then the Lions went into their tailspin, and wouldn't you know it, Fairley reverted to form with three roughness fouls. Suh committed just one facemask grab during the grand collapse but took December off from recording sacks, and managed only four quarterback hits after Week 10. Suh remains one of the best defensive tackles in the game, and Fairley is not far behind him. The Lions need them to stop acting like the kids waiting for the substitute teacher to arrive so they can either set the boy's room on fire or take a nap.

Ziggy Ansah led the team in sacks, but like everyone else in Detroit hit the wall in December. Shoulder and ankle injuries slowed Ansah late in the year, and he remains a developmental speed rusher in need of a complete game. Ansah stands to benefit from a less-predictable defensive scheme: he is a natural Wide-9 edge rusher, but he could also do some damage standing up or shooting an inside gap. Former Seahawk Jason Jones, who tore a patellar tendon after three games last season, is expected to start opposite Ansah. He is a traditional 4-3 left end: stout against the run, nimble enough to get by as a pass rusher. Second-year end Devin Taylor racked up 1.5 sacks and a strip in the Matt Flynn feeding frenzy last year. He's a bull-rusher with a profile similar to Jones. Developmental pass rusher Larry Webster, a fourth-round pick out of Division II Bloomsburg, is also in the mix and could earn a third-and-long role. Fifth-round rookie Caraun Reid (Princeton) is a compact, tough multi-position backup who handled himself well at the Senior Bowl. With his Ivy League credentials, Reid can try to shush Suh and Fairley and tell them to pay attention.

DeAndre Levy bounced back from a miserable, hamstring-plagued 2012 season to enjoy a career year. The interceptions and passes defensed are not really a fluke: Levy is outstanding in zone coverage and can easily man up on the Martellus Bennett-Andrew Quarless class of tight ends. Stephen Tulloch attacks the line of scrimmage well and remains rock-steady in the middle. Ashlee Palmer, the first linebacker to leave the field in nickel situations last year, will likely lose his job to second-round pick Kyle Van Noy, Ansah's BYU teammate. Van Noy provides edge-blitz capability that rivals Ansah's, but he is much more versatile and polished, allowing him to provide value in coverage and as a run defender. Van Noy provides an exciting new dimension to a scheme that became straight-jacketed in recent years: opponents will not be able to set their watches by the Wide-9 formation and endless four-man rushes, with occasional jolts of Tulloch.

Defensive Secondary

			Overall								vs. Run					vs. Pass									
Secondary	Age	Pos	G	Snaps	Plays	TmPct	Rk	Stop	Dfts	BTkl	Runs	St%	Rk	RuYd	Rk	Tgts	Tgt%	Rk	Dist	Suc%	Rk	AdjYd	Rk	PD	Int
Louis Delmas*	27	FS	16	1011	72	9.5%	46	32	14	10	25	56%	9	4.6	9	28	6.1%	13	14.7	65%	14	6.9	36	8	3
Glover Quin	28	SS	16	986	65	8.6%	58	31	11	5	30	53%	13	5.4	15	28	6.3%	15	15.7	70%	3	2.9	1	10	3
Rashean Mathis	34	CB	15	762	62	8.7%	37	29	12	4	11	55%	18	4.3	6	76	22.2%	54	15.0	55%	34	7.5	42	15	0
Chris Houston*	30	CB	12	717	53	9.3%	25	21	10	8	8	50%	25	2.8	2	77	23.9%	64	15.2	51%	53	10.8	83	9	2
Bill Bentley	25	CB	13	471	33	5.4%	--	16	9	5	6	50%	--	4.3	--	38	17.8%	--	10.9	53%	--	6.6	--	5	0
Darius Slay	23	CB	13	339	36	5.9%	--	16	9	2	8	38%	--	8.8	--	45	29.8%	--	12.8	48%	--	10.2	--	5	0
Don Carey	27	FS	14	197	19	2.9%	78	12	7	4	9	89%	1	1.7	1	21	23.9%	78	10.0	42%	69	7.6	53	1	0
James Ihedigbo	*31*	*FS*	*16*	*1073*	*109*	*13.2%*	*11*	*53*	*19*	*12*	*57*	*53%*	*16*	*5.1*	*14*	*25*	*5.9%*	*11*	*16.6*	*60%*	*31*	*8.4*	*57*	*6*	*0*
Cassius Vaughn	*27*	*CB*	*16*	*404*	*34*	*4.1%*	*--*	*11*	*5*	*1*	*8*	*38%*	*--*	*5.8*	*--*	*38*	*22.6%*	*--*	*13.7*	*48%*	*--*	*9.8*	*--*	*6*	*3*

Year	Pass D Rank	vs. #1 WR	Rk	vs. #2 WR	Rk	vs. Other WR	Rk	vs. TE	Rk	vs. RB	Rk
2011	4	-18.3%	3	-18.5%	5	-4.8%	16	1.1%	9	-12.9%	8
2012	21	-5.1%	13	24.6%	31	2.0%	20	14.3%	26	-37.1%	2
2013	20	11.2%	24	-8.7%	10	12.5%	23	-20.6%	5	2.9%	16

A lot rests on the shoulders of second-year cornerback Darius Slay. Slay played mostly press-man coverage at Mississippi State, and when the Lions asked him to play off coverage and zone, the result was a mixed bag at best. Slay consistently turned to get upfield at exactly the wrong time, and he let too much happen in front of him in zone. Teryl Austin plans to meet Slay halfway by dialing up more tight man, and Slay worked with Rod Woodson in the offseason to develop everything from his "zone eyes" (Woodson's term) to a new approach at the top of the receiver's stem. It's usually a good sign when the improvement plan can be expressed so specifically, and May minicamp produced the usual huzzahs about how much more comfortable Slay looks and feels.

Chris Houston remains an adequate zone cornerback who keeps short passes in front of him and uses anticipation to break up some plays. Houston can get beaten deep and guesses wrong at times, which is probably why he was released in June. Rashean Mathis swapped the starting job opposite Houston with Slay most of the year and was terrible. Once a "safe veteran" for zone-heavy schemes, Mathis may now be the slowest cornerback in the NFL—Brandon Marshall throttled past him like he was standing still on one bomb—and has lost the agility needed to consistently clean up tackles in front of him. Lots of zone assignments, with safety help up top, kept his charting metrics from bottoming out. Bill Bentley earned some starts when other cornerbacks were injured and played reasonably well before suffering a season-ending concussion of his own. Bentley is an adequate match-up defender against shifty receivers. Fourth-round pick Nevin Lawson is a tiny technician who appears custom-built for a slot role. He played inside often at Utah State and gets high marks for read-and-recognition skills.

Safety is a trouble spot with Louis Delmas now in Miami. Glover Quin held his own as an undersized strong safety last year and will benefit from more of a centerfielder role this year. James Ihedigbo had a surprisingly effective season for Austin's Ravens last year. Ihedigbo gets by on brains and technique, not pure talent, and must be matched up carefully to prevent up-the-seam toastings. There is no real depth behind Quin and Ihedigbo, and the whole secondary is a Quin injury or Slay backslide away from a crisis.

Special Teams

Year	DVOA	Rank	FG/XP	Rank	Net Kick	Rank	Kick Ret	Rank	Net Punt	Rank	Punt Ret	Rank	Hidden	Rank
2011	-5.1%	29	-2.5	21	-8.8	30	-0.6	18	-6.8	26	-7.1	26	-8.6	27
2012	-5.1%	30	4.5	9	-9.4	30	-4.8	24	-9.1	25	-6.9	29	0.2	16
2013	-0.4%	20	-11.1	30	-1.6	24	5.7	4	-0.7	20	5.8	8	-11.2	31

David Akers' downhill slide, which began in 2011, finally rolled to a dead stop last year, leaving the Lions in the kicker market with their credit cards maxed. Seventh-round pick Nate Freese was 20-for-20 in his senior season at Boston College, including two 50-yarders, all the while handling kickoff and punting duties adequately. Freese is not a cannon leg but gets good grades for his mechanics and approach from those who understand kicker fundamentals. The alternative is Giorgio Tavecchio, who may have the greatest kicker name ever. Lions fans embraced "Kickalicious" Havard Rugland last year, and Tavecchio could be Kickalizioso. Tavecchio has had extended tryouts with the 49ers and Packers and has been working with former NFL kicker Michael Husted, so the competition is on!

Rookie Sam Martin was a reliable punter and holder who should not be asked to execute fake field goals in the rain against the Steelers again until he gets another year or two of experience under his belt. He replaced Akers as the kickoff specialist early in the year and led the NFL in yards per kickoff, helped a bit by the fact that he attempted no onside kicks and only squibbed it once. Martin produces consistent seven-yard deep kickoffs, though not as many touchbacks as the top specialists, and his line drives are often returnable. Packers castoff Jeremy Ross replaced Micheal Spurlock as the Lions' return man last year and was a revelation. Both of his return touchdowns came in the snow against the Eagles (making him the only Lions player who seemed to know what he was doing that afternoon), but Ross added long punt returns against the Giants and Bucs to his resume, proving that he was more than a tiny snowplow. The coverage units were solid in 2013, but with depth and cash flow as issues, new coordinator John Bonamego may have to be creative about cobbling units together.

Green Bay Packers

2013 Record: 8-7-1	**Total DVOA:** -6.0% (20th)	**2014 Mean Projection:** 9.7 wins	**On the Clock (0-4):** 3%
Pythagorean Wins: 7.8 (16th)	**Offense:** 8.6% (9th)	**Postseason Odds:** 65.2%	**Mediocrity (5-7):** 12%
Snap-Weighted Age: 26.0 (29th)	**Defense:** 14.4% (31st)	**Super Bowl Odds:** 17.3%	**Playoff Contender (8-10):** 47%
Average Opponent: -3.0% (24th)	**Special Teams:** -0.3% (19th)	**Proj. Avg. Opponent:** 1.8% (11th)	**Super Bowl Contender (11+):** 38%

2013: Wait, you mean we might need more than one quarterback?

2014: A clear choice to be one of this year's "new" playoff teams, except they somehow snuck into the playoffs last year.

Albert Einstein often forgot where his car was parked. Ned Brainard missed his own wedding because he was too busy inventing flubber. Ted Thompson forgot to sign a decent backup quarterback.

The absent-minded professor is a stock narrative character, and at his worst, the Packers general manager could hang and *Bang!* (the sound of an experiment gone wrong) with the wackiest and wiftiest of them. He's Professor Farnsworth causing a space-time rift with a cream meant to cure hemorrhoids, Dr. Doofenshmirtz wiring a giant "off" switch onto his Backup Quarterbackinator. Thompson's mad science has won a Super Bowl and kept the Packers at the top of the standings in fascinating and unique ways, but boy, there sure are some head-smacking moments. The Backup Quarterback Crisis of 2013 was an all-time flub.

The Packers entered training camp last season with Graham Harrell and B.J. Coleman as Aaron Rodgers' backups. Harrell was a college spread-offense hero with an al dente arm, Coleman a big developmental guy. Neither was Earl Morrall, but both had also been in camp in 2012, and there were crazier thoughts than Harrell scattering enough completions to keep the Packers competitive for a game or two. Thompson did sense trouble and decided to add an additional arm, but flaky geniuses have terrible taste in contingency plans, so that arm turned out to be attached to Vince Young.

All three quarterbacks were dreadful at the start of the preseason. Harrell flailed sadly in early-game reps, playing so poorly that young running backs Eddie Lacy and Jonathan Franklin could hardly get enough carries to be evaluated. Young, looking like the emotionally-stunted stepdad playing in a junior high sandlot game, had a few successful second halves. Mike McCarthy soured on B.J. and the Unbearable, giving Young a long final-week appearance to cement his position as Rodgers' backup. Young instead went 14-for-30 with some unproductive scrambles, cementing his position as Vince Young.

It was at this moment, days before the start of the season, that the Packers decided to cut all of their backups: Harrell was already gone, Coleman and Young were axed in the final round of cuts. Thompson scavenged the bottom of the 49ers depth chart for replacements and found two of them: Seneca Wallace, who was given just two preseason snaps as Jim Harbaugh considered him more of a den father than quarterback, and Scott Tolzien, a size-speed-arm prospect roughly equivalent to Coleman, but without the benefit of two training camps under McCarthy. In early October, Matt Flynn became available, but the Packers decided to ignore the Matt Flynn sized-and-shaped hole in their depth chart.

As you probably know, Rodgers suffered a fractured collarbone in October, just after Flynn signed with the Bills. The Packers were 5-2, but would go 0-3-1 in games started by or prominently featuring Wallace and Tolzien. Wallace looked like he was in his late forties and Tolzien appeared closer to 19. While the Packers were probably not going to beat the Eagles with anyone but Rodgers at quarterback, a capable backup could have beaten the Bears (a 27-20 final score) and Giants (as three Tolzien picks turned the game into a 27-13 groaner).

Flynn replaced Tolzien in the Vikings tie, looking initially like a wobbly backup who had just endured unproductive stints with the Raiders and Bills. But Flynn rediscovered his comfort with McCarthy's system in time to help beat bad Falcons and Cowboys defenses, holding the fort down for Rodgers' triumphant return and a backward stumble into the playoffs. The Packers narrowly lost to the 49ers in the first round. Who knows what an easier draw or a first-round bye might have sparked in the postseason? Both may have been possible if the Packers had a Flynn-level backup for the duration of Rodgers' injury.

The backup quarterback disaster was just the latest example of organizational absent-mindedness in Green Bay. In 2011, the team neglected to acquire anyone who could help Clay Matthews rush the passer. With Cullen Jenkins gone and opponents wise to the modest talents of Erik Walden and Frank Zombo, the Packers' sack total plummeted from 47 in the 2010 Super Bowl season to just 29.

In 2012, the Packers forgot all about running backs, reckoning that committee-guy James Starks could handle things all by himself until Thompson grabbed Cedric Benson in mid-August, the 2012 version of the Vince Young gambit. That was the season of Alex Green and a desperate Ryan Grant recall from the Redskins, of Randall Cobb running draw plays and Rodgers sometimes leading the team in rushing with 27 scramble yards. The Packers somehow finished 13th in run DVOA in 2012, but take out Rodgers and Cobb and they would have ranked 19th. Just as it is easy to wonder what

2014 Packers Schedule

Week	Opp.	Week	Opp.	Week	Opp.
1	at SEA (Thu.)	7	CAR	13	NE
2	NYJ	8	at NO	14	ATL (Mon.)
3	at DET	9	BYE	15	at BUF
4	at CHI	10	CHI	16	at TB
5	MIN (Thu.)	11	PHI	17	DET
6	at MIA	12	at MIN		

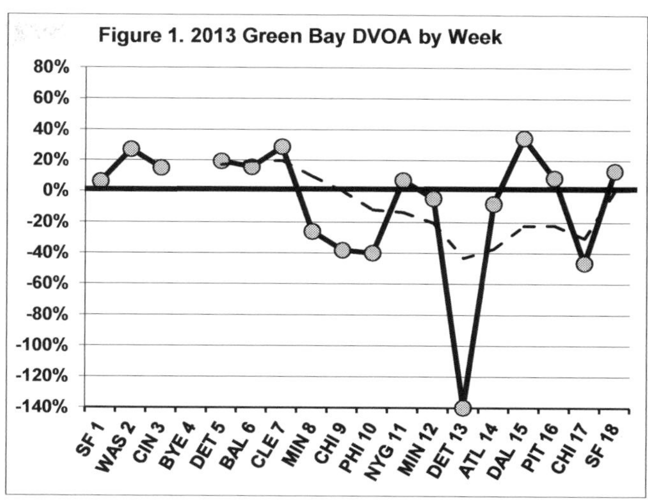

Figure 1. 2013 Green Bay DVOA by Week

2013 would have looked like without the Seneca Tolzien experience, 2012 might not have ended with a journey to San Francisco if the Packers had been able to run the football at the start of the season.

Rolling mental blackouts have been going on for so long that Thompson and his staff have started to develop compensation techniques. Rodgers and Matthews cover for a lot of lost car keys and mismatched socks, of course. Thompson's ability to dumpster dive for other team's practice-squad castoffs was a blessing in 2010, providing Starks, Walden, and many others, and it still drops a DuJuan Harris into McCarthy's lap in times of great need, but it also makes the Packers a little too confident in their ability to plug Tolzien types immediately into the lineup.

Thompson has now adopted saturation drafting as an additional coping mechanism. After leaving Matthews unsupported in 2011, the Packers drafted Nick Perry, Jerel Worthy, and Mike Daniels. The running back crisis of 2012 brought Eddie Lacy and Jonathan Franklin, plus Datone Jones for extra defensive reinforcement. Only Lacy has panned out as a true blue-chip prospect, but all of the defenders except the oft-injured Worthy have made contributions. The Packers learn from their mistakes, though they often seem bound and determined to make new ones.

So the summer of 2014 finds us looking at a strong Packers roster and wondering what glaring oversight will doom the team this year. It will not be backup quarterback: Flynn was re-signed, and Tolzien was retained to enjoy the benefits of an offseason in McCarthy's complex system. It will also not be running back. The team is suddenly waist-deep in quality runners and prospects, led by Lacy and supplemented by Starks, Harris and fullback John Kuhn: a Rookie of the Year backed up by a Who's Who of partial solutions of the past. (Johnathan Franklin retired in the offseason due to a neck injury.) The time of Seneca sadness forced the Packers to recommit to running game basics, and McCarthy can now use power tactics as successfully as wide-open aerial assaults, another feature of the 2010 champions that disappeared in 2011 and 2012.

The front seven also appears to have been amnesia-proofed, thanks to the arrival of Julius Peppers. Peppers is the bookend pass rusher Matthews has never had, and he is still capable of exploiting mismatches and punishing opponents that think the H-back can block him. Peppers should adapt to a position shift well—after getting shoved around as a tackle for the Bears last season, outside linebacker will feel like a vacation—and there are plenty of Perry and Andy Mulamba types on the depth chart to keep Peppers fresh. We can also toss out "oops, we did not notice that some teams use the read option" as a source of oversight: Dom Capers' fact-finding mission last offseason clearly stuck, and Packers defenders now understand the basics of defending the back side of a play.

No, Thompson is too brilliant to make the same mistake twice, which is why the Packers' Achilles heel keeps moving around the body. Its most likely 2014 location is smack in the middle of the offensive line. The team let Evan Dietrich-Smith sign with the Buccaneers, and in the fine Thompson tradition, initially embraced the loopiest possible solution. J.C. Tretter started his Cornell career at tight end, then moved to left tackle for his final two seasons. It's a short hop from Ivy League tackle to NFL center in Thompson's mind, so Tretter shifted positions after Green Bay took him in the fourth round of last year's. Tretter then broke his leg early in training camp, so it is not like he got hundreds of practice snaps under his belt. Nonetheless, as of the morning of May 10th, two days into this year's draft, Tretter was the Packers' incumbent center.

But then someone nudged Thompson, and the Packers selected Ohio State's Corey Linsley in the fifth round. The best thing about the Linsley scouting report is that it exists: only a select few humans on earth have seen Tretter snap a football. Linsley started in 2012 and 2013, handled all of the line calls in front of Braxton Miller, and has proven beyond all doubt that he can shotgun snap and identify a blitzing linebacker. Linsley is also a pretty quick-footed lateral and second-level blocker, skills that are essential now that Lacy gives the Packers a consistent rushing threat. Linsley gets bent backward by better defensive tackles and is a lunger at times, but the Packers won't have to resort to signing a Jeff Saturday in desperation: at worst, Linsley can be the Matt Flynn, James Starks, or Frank Zombo of centers.

Never has the fifth-round selection of an offensive lineman meant so much to a perennial playoff team. Maybe Thompson has decided to start filling holes before they open! The fissures that remain in the Packers' roster infrastructure are now small and manageable. Jermichael Finley will be replaced by a scheme, not a player: Andrew Quarless and Ryan Taylor block well enough to support Lacy, and a revamped receiving corps alleviates the need for a seam-stretching tight end. The return of Bryan Bulaga and emergence of David Bakhtiari transform tackle into a position of strength after years of thinness. Safety was a problem position last year, but the Packers drafted Ha Ha Clinton-Dix—again, before catastrophe truly struck—and are developing Micah Hyde as a Capers-style blitz safety. Mason Crosby is still a worry on both field goals and kickoffs, but when we are down to the kicker as a source of trouble, then there is not much trouble to be found.

After three post-Super Bowl years of outsmarting themselves, the Packers appear to have finally balanced their professorial general manager's strengths with his weaknesses. For Thompson, drafting a Clinton-Dix or Linsley is the equivalent of donning safety goggles before mixing dangerous chemicals. Maybe Tretter and Hyde are new examples of late-round alchemy, but it helps to have conventional solutions handy if things go wrong. The Packers are more equipped than any other NFC contender to challenge the Seahawks and 49ers for supremacy; with the NFC West powerhouses bludgeoning each other, they could even force the playoffs to roll through Lambeau if they can avoid the completely avoidable problems that held them back in the past. The Packers were a laboratory without a fire extinguisher from 2011 through 2013. This season, we get to discover just how successful they can be when not operating on the brink of disaster.

Mike Tanier

2013 xxx Stats by Week

Wk	vs.	W-L	PF	PA	YDF	YDA	TO	Total	Off	Def	ST
1	at SF	L	28	34	385	494	-2	6%	33%	24%	-2%
2	WAS	W	38	20	580	422	0	27%	76%	48%	-1%
3	at CIN	L	30	34	399	297	0	15%	4%	-6%	5%
4	BYE										
5	DET	W	22	9	449	286	0	19%	13%	-3%	4%
6	at BAL	W	19	17	438	360	-1	16%	9%	-2%	4%
7	CLE	W	31	13	357	216	+1	29%	41%	-17%	-29%
8	at MIN	W	44	31	464	243	0	-26%	31%	50%	-7%
9	CHI	L	20	27	312	442	-1	-38%	-28%	14%	4%
10	PHI	L	13	27	396	415	-1	-40%	-9%	19%	-12%
11	at NYG	L	13	27	394	334	-2	7%	16%	18%	8%
12	MIN	T	26	26	494	447	+1	-5%	13%	16%	-1%
13	at DET	L	10	40	126	561	+1	-140%	-101%	38%	-1%
14	ATL	W	22	21	334	285	0	-8%	-24%	-9%	8%
15	at DAL	W	37	36	433	466	+1	35%	26%	6%	15%
16	PIT	L	31	38	370	343	0	8%	6%	9%	12%
17	at CHI	W	33	28	473	345	0	-46%	-7%	31%	-9%
18	SF	L	20	23	281	381	+1	13%	10%	-7%	-4%

Trends and Splits

	Offense	Rank	Defense	Rank
Total DVOA	8.6%	9	14.4%	31
Unadjusted VOA	12.0%	7	11.5%	28
Weighted Trend	0.6%	16	14.1%	29
Variance	14.6%	31	4.0%	8
Average Opponent	3.0%	27	-0.5%	17
Passing	12.2%	13	21.4%	28
Rushing	11.0%	3	6.4%	30
First Down	-4.3%	19	14.2%	29
Second Down	24.0%	3	14.9%	30
Third Down	9.1%	10	14.0%	25
First Half	-4.5%	19	4.9%	22
Second Half	21.5%	4	24.1%	32
Red Zone	2.8%	15	34.2%	30
Late and Close	14.5%	7	12.6%	29

Five-Year Performance

Year	W-L	Pyth W	Est W	PF	PA	TO	Total	Rk	Off	Rk	Def	Rk	ST	Rk	Off AGL	Rk	Def AGL	Rk	Off Age	Rk	Def Age	Rk	ST Age	Rk
2009	11-5	12.0	11.0	461	297	+24	29.1%	2	18.8%	5	-17.7%	2	-7.5%	32	22.4	15	25.3	16	27.1	18	27.4	14	25.3	31
2010	10-6	12.1	10.9	388	240	+10	23.0%	4	11.5%	7	-13.9%	2	-2.4%	26	40.4	28	45.9	29	27.2	19	26.5	21	25.8	26
2011	15-1	12.2	13.3	560	359	+24	27.0%	1	33.8%	1	8.6%	25	1.8%	8	21.3	11	37.5	22	26.3	26	26.7	23	25.1	32
2012	11-5	10.5	11.8	433	336	+7	26.3%	5	19.5%	3	-7.0%	8	-0.2%	18	38.7	23	62.8	32	26.9	16	25.8	27	24.9	32
2013	8-7-1	7.8	7.3	417	428	-3	-6.0%	20	8.6%	9	14.4%	31	-0.3%	19	49.3	25	45.1	25	26.0	30	26.3	19	25.2	29

2013 Performance Based on Most Common Personnel Groups

GB Offense					GB Offense vs. Opponents				GB Defense				GB Defense vs. Opponents			
Pers	Freq	Yds	DVOA	Run%	Pers	Freq	Yds	DVOA	Pers	Freq	Yds	DVOA	Pers	Freq	Yds	DVOA
11	68%	6.2	15.5%	29%	Nickel Even	65%	6.2	14.9%	Nickel Even	56%	6.2	17.3%	11	52%	6.3	23.5%
12	12%	6.5	15.4%	62%	4-3-4	13%	5.7	-25.7%	3-4-4	26%	5.5	5.8%	12	22%	6.3	18.6%
21	8%	5.5	-33.4%	63%	3-4-4	12%	6.8	42.4%	Dime+	15%	6.4	22.8%	21	12%	6.7	18.6%
20	6%	6.5	21.5%	56%	Dime+	5%	6.7	12.0%	4-4-3	2%	1.5	-33.0%	22	5%	4.3	-27.6%
22	2%	3.6	-13.7%	76%	Nickel Odd	4%	4.9	-13.6%	Nickel Odd	1%	7.7	78.9%	621	1%	2.6	-21.0%

Strategic Tendencies

Run/Pass		Rk	Formation		Rk	Pass Rush		Rk	Secondary		Rk	Strategy		Rk
Runs, first half	37%	22	Form: Single Back	76%	9	Rush 3	7.6%	9	4 DB	26%	31	Play action	24%	13
Runs, first down	50%	12	Form: Empty Back	2%	31	Rush 4	55.6%	27	5 DB	57%	9	Avg Box (Off)	6.27	21
Runs, second-long	32%	19	Pers: 3+ WR	77%	1	Rush 5	31.2%	5	6+ DB	15%	7	Avg Box (Def)	6.16	30
Runs, power sit.	51%	21	Pers: 4+ WR	1%	17	Rush 6+	5.6%	23	CB by Sides	59%	23	Offensive Pace	28.92	10
Runs, behind 2H	37%	1	Pers: 2+ TE/6+ OL	17%	31	Sacks by LB	62.5%	7	DB Blitz	17%	2	Defensive Pace	30.91	28
Pass, ahead 2H	53%	7	Shotgun/Pistol	62%	11	Sacks by DB	12.5%	7	Hole in Zone	13%	11	Go for it on 4th	0.99	11

Although the Packers were fourth in the league with 36.0 yards per drive, they scored touchdowns on just 50.8 percent of red-zone opportunities, tied for 26th in the NFL. Green Bay had one of the league's largest gaps between running from single-back formations (4.4 yards per carry, 0.2% DVOA) and running from two-back formations (4.8 yards per carry, 20.5% DVOA). The Packers led the league with 22 passes we categorized as "smoke," either an audible or a package play where the quarterback throws to an outside receiver with no blockers. Green Bay's defense will need to figure out how to stop passes in the middle of the field. Opponents threw up the middle on 32 percent of passes—only Washington was higher, because the Washington official scorers mark more passes as "middle" than scorers in other cities—and the Packers ranked 30th in defense against passes up the middle, ahead of only Dallas and Minnesota. Although the Packers blitzed a defensive back more than almost any other team, it wasn't necessarily that effective. We only recorded quarterback pressure 22 percent of the time on a Green Bay DB blitz, the second lowest figure in the NFL. Although the Packers still used dime more than most defenses, they used it about half as much as they did in 2012, and used nickel much more often. The Green Bay defense benefitted from a league-high 42 dropped passes and recovered nine of 11 fumbles.

Passing

Player	DYAR	DVOA	Plays	NtYds	Avg	YAC	C%	TD	Int
A.Rodgers	740	25.4%	310	2413	7.8	6.5	66.8%	18	6
M.Flynn	-110	-20.3%	187	1115	6.0	5.8	61.4%	7	4
S.Tolzien	13	-9.1%	91	691	7.6	6.1	62.5%	1	5
S.Wallace*	-75	-54.2%	28	114	4.1	3.4	66.7%	0	1

Rushing

Player	DYAR	DVOA	Plays	Yds	Avg	TD	Fum	Suc
E.Lacy	160	5.3%	284	1178	4.1	11	1	46%
J.Starks	110	19.2%	89	493	5.5	3	1	54%
A.Rodgers	23	6.8%	21	124	5.9	0	1	-
J.Franklin	19	12.2%	19	109	5.7	1	2	58%
M.Flynn	-23	-55.4%	11	66	6.0	0	1	-
J.Kuhn	32	51.1%	10	38	3.8	1	0	70%
S.Tolzien	33	117.5%	5	55	11.0	1	0	-
M.Hill	*-8*	*-38.5%*	*9*	*23*	*2.6*	*0*	*0*	*44%*

Receiving

Player	DYAR	DVOA	Plays	Ctch	Yds	Y/C	YAC	TD	C%
J.Nelson	402	26.7%	127	85	1314	15.5	4.8	8	67%
J.Jones*	110	2.1%	93	59	817	13.8	6.2	3	63%
J.Boykin	146	9.3%	83	49	681	13.9	5.2	3	59%
R.Cobb	121	21.1%	47	31	433	14.0	5.6	4	66%
M.White	-21	-36.0%	12	9	66	7.3	6.1	0	75%
A.Quarless	-25	-14.4%	53	32	312	9.8	4.3	2	60%
J.Finley*	68	25.8%	34	25	300	12.0	9.0	3	74%
B.Bostick	-3	-11.0%	14	7	120	17.1	8.9	1	50%
R.Taylor	-33	-56.3%	9	6	30	5.0	2.5	0	67%
E.Lacy	26	-3.5%	44	35	257	7.3	8.9	0	80%
J.Kuhn	-6	-19.7%	19	13	81	6.2	6.4	0	68%
J.Starks	36	38.0%	13	10	89	8.9	10.9	1	77%

Offensive Line

Player	Pos	Age	GS	Snaps	Pen	Sk	Pass	Run	Player	Pos	Age	GS	Snaps	Pen	Sk	Pass	Run
Josh Sitton	LG	28	16/16	1122	6	0.5	6.5	1.3	Evan Dietrich-Smith	C	28	16/16	1055	3	4.0	6.0	4.5
David Bakhtiari	LT	23	16/16	1119	11	5.5	19.5	5.0	Don Barclay	RT	25	14/14	964	5	7.5	25.0	7.0
T.J. Lang	RG	27	16/16	1093	5	0.5	12.0	3.8	Marshall Newhouse*	RT	26	15/2	245	3	3.0	11.5	0.0

Year	Yards	ALY	Rk	Power	Rk	Stuff	Rk	2nd Lev	Rk	Open Field	Rk	Sacks	ASR	Rk	Short	Long	F-Start	Cont.
2011	4.06	4.05	17	61%	21	21%	25	1.15	18	0.63	26	41	7.4%	23	13	19	28	30
2012	3.58	3.86	25	68%	7	19%	13	0.97	29	0.28	32	51	8.6%	31	9	29	13	35
2013	4.52	4.11	5	83%	1	16%	5	1.24	10	0.95	8	45	8.3%	26	14	14	13	38
2013 ALY by direction:			*Left End 3.52 (16)*			*Left Tackle 4.37 (8)*				*Mid/Guard 4.58 (2)*			*Right Tackle 4.33 (7)*			*Right End 3.37 (22)*		

As soon as Mike McCarthy rediscovered the running game, the Packers offensive line rediscovered run blocking. Guards T.J. Lang and Josh Sitton excel at on-the-move blocks. Lang is particularly effective as a pull blocker and when sliding laterally for outside zone-type plays, and a few of his blown blocks on the tables above come from very difficult assignments. Both guards are also effective on the linebacker level and root gap-shooters out of holes well, contributing to the Packers' exceptional Power Success and low Stuff Rate.

Rookie left tackle David Bakhtari is also very effective as a quick lateral blocker. He is very good at beating edge defenders off the snap and sealing them inside or riding them to the sideline. Bakhtari's excellent initial quickness gives him the potential to be an outstanding pass protector, but there is a lot of work to be done. He committed nine holds, sometimes lost track of who to block during blitzes, and too often lunged or slipped when coping with a quality Wide-9 rusher. A year of experience should work wonders for a talented player who mixed stretches of excellence among his errors.

Don Barclay was a disaster at right tackle early in the season—Elvis Dumervil did things to him that are edited out of nature documentaries—but developed some coping mechanisms as the season wore on. Marshall Newhouse was worse in two mid-season starts, and McCarthy got intricate at times to make sure there was ample pass protection on the right side. Luckily for the Packers, Bryan Bulaga was back at minicamp after missing all of 2013 with an ACL tear. Bulaga's presence will prevent McCarthy from having to keep Andrew Quarless or John Kuhn in the protection package, or having to ask Lang or Sitton to execute a challenging "molly block."

As noted earlier in the chapter, the Packers have a ragtag collection of contenders to replace center Evan Dietrich-Smith, who had a fine 2013 season. As of minicamp, converted Ivy League tight end/tackle J.C. Tretter was making most of the first-team snaps, with fifth-round pick Corey Linsley expected to make a heavy push and Garth Gerhart (a 2012 UDFA out of Arizona State) staying in the conversation. Aaron Rodgers, who has gone from Scott Wells to a kindly old pudgy guy wearing a Jeff Saturday jersey to Dietrich-Smith to the newbies in four years, said in June that he hopes someone wins the job outright and keeps it. "Hopefully, we can get a guy who can stick for five or six years," he said on the team website. "As a quarterback, you appreciate when you can have some continuity there and some consistency."

Defensive Front Seven

			Overall								vs. Run					Pass Rush			
Defensive Line	**Age**	**Pos**	**G**	**Snaps**	**Plays**	**TmPct**	**Rk**	**Stop**	**Dfts**	**BTkl**	**Runs**	**St%**	**Rk**	**RuYd**	**Rk**	**Sack**	**Hit**	**Hur**	**Tips**
B.J. Raji	28	DE	16	606	17	2.1%	85	16	3	0	16	94%	3	1.3	8	0.0	1	6.5	0
Mike Daniels	25	DE	16	506	23	2.8%	79	22	14	0	16	94%	3	0.9	2	6.5	4	15.0	0
Ryan Pickett*	35	DT	16	488	21	2.6%	82	16	1	1	19	74%	55	2.4	53	0.0	0	1.0	2
Johnny Jolly*	31	DE	13	287	22	3.3%	--	17	6	0	16	81%	--	1.4	--	1.0	1	1.0	1
Letroy Guion	*27*	*DT*	*13*	*388*	*21*	*2.9%*	*--*	*16*	*6*	*2*	*19*	*74%*	*--*	*2.5*	*--*	*1.0*	*0*	*4.0*	*1*

			Overall								vs. Run					Pass Rush			
Edge Rushers	**Age**	**Pos**	**G**	**Snaps**	**Plays**	**TmPct**	**Rk**	**Stop**	**Dfts**	**BTkl**	**Runs**	**St%**	**Rk**	**RuYd**	**Rk**	**Sack**	**Hit**	**Hur**	**Tips**
Mike Neal	27	OLB	16	730	48	5.9%	32	36	14	8	37	70%	54	3.4	64	5.0	4	16.0	0
Clay Matthews	28	OLB	11	559	42	7.5%	13	36	18	3	31	87%	10	1.1	5	7.5	4	6.5	1
Nick Perry	24	OLB	11	368	28	5.0%	48	20	6	0	18	78%	30	2.9	54	4.0	0	11.0	1
Andy Mulumba	24	OLB	14	298	23	3.2%	--	14	3	1	18	67%	--	2.8	--	1.0	0	1.0	0
Nate Palmer	25	OLB	8	196	16	3.9%	--	9	1	0	16	56%	--	2.9	--	0.0	1	3.0	0
Julius Peppers	*34*	*DE*	*16*	*851*	*46*	*5.6%*	*38*	*35*	*14*	*4*	*35*	*69%*	*56*	*2.9*	*53*	*7.0*	*2*	*14.5*	*3*

			Overall								Pass Rush			vs. Run					vs. Pass						
Linebackers	**Age**	**Pos**	**G**	**Snaps**	**Plays**	**TmPct**	**Rk**	**Stop**	**Dfts**	**BTkl**	**Sack**	**Hit**	**Hur**	**Runs**	**St%**	**Rk**	**RuYd**	**Rk**	**Tgts**	**Suc%**	**Rk**	**AdjYd**	**Rk**	**PD**	**Int**
A.J. Hawk	30	ILB	16	994	122	15.0%	27	68	17	8	5.0	1	11	73	64%	48	3.7	55	44	52%	37	6.7	39	5	1
Brad Jones	28	ILB	12	584	84	13.8%	37	44	12	3	3.0	2	2.5	55	58%	66	3.8	58	28	46%	49	7.5	55	0	0
Jamari Lattimore	26	ILB	15	265	32	4.2%	--	22	6	0	2.0	0	1	20	75%	--	3.3	--	14	38%	--	5.1	--	1	0

Year	Yards	ALY	Rk	Power	Rk	Stuff	Rk	2nd Level	Rk	Open Field	Rk	Sacks	ASR	Rk	Short	Long
2011	4.49	4.50	29	67%	24	16%	30	1.30	27	0.70	12	29	4.8%	32	6	16
2012	4.40	4.25	22	51%	4	17%	24	1.17	12	0.80	16	47	8.0%	4	12	23
2013	4.67	4.26	26	77%	30	17%	22	1.38	29	0.88	24	44	8.1%	5	15	20
2013 ALY by direction:			*Left End 4.49 (29)*			*Left Tackle 4.47 (27)*			*Mid/Guard 4.10 (20)*			*Right Tackle 4.05 (19)*			*Right End 4.62 (30)*	

A.J. Hawk is really good. That's the first thing you have to adjust to if you only check in on the Packers defense once or twice per season. The Hawk we expected in 2006, the one we assumed we would never see as of about 2009 or so (even though the Packers kept shoveling money at him), finally blossomed into borderline awesomeness just before his 30th birthday. Hawk shot gaps with authority, making plays in the backfield and blowing up blockers to free other defenders. He has improved substantially in coverage, sometimes dropping into deep zones, and he is alert to the misdirection plays that are popular with teams such as the Eagles. Hawk still sometimes takes a bad open-field angle and lunges heroically instead of staying on his feet to pursue a ballcarrier, and he cannot handle above-average tight ends in man coverage, but he has become a heck of a defender. He still draws some criticism, but after eight years some of it is just habitual fault-finding.

The Packers needed a Hawk renaissance because Clay Matthews was injured or limited for much of last season. Matthews remains one of the best pure edge rushers in the NFL when playing with all of his appendages, but when he was out of the lineup, Dom Capers was forced to create pass rush off the whiteboard. That should change with Julius Peppers' arrival. Peppers was worn out and miscast last season with the Bears, who needed him to slide inside at times to quell a defensive line catastrophe. Capers will use Peppers as a situational pass rusher, a role the Packers have struggled to fill with Erik Walden types in recent years. Peppers can still power through tight ends and blocking backs or dip around slow right tackles; he could record double-digit sacks just by catching the quarterbacks Matthews flushes into him.

Peppers' arrival and Matthews' health will push Mike Neal and Nick Perry into situational roles. Both are useful system fits: hustle-and-effort edge defenders who can drop into coverage adequately and will disengage from blockers to record coverage sacks. Brad Jones and Jamari Lattimore are both capable stay-at-home inside linebackers who leave the field on passing downs.

B.J. Raji was effective as a spot-duty run defender last season, though he hardly had a "comeback" year. Raji got ambitious and tested the free agent market, but NFL teams appear convinced that Raji has to stay hungry to remain effective, so the Packers signed him to another one-year deal. Johnny Jolly was having something closer to a legit comeback before suffering a neck injury. He remains a free agent, but the market is light for 31-year-olds with neck ailments and criminal records. Ryan Pickett has retired, leaving the defensive line to Raji and youngsters. Datone Jones came on strong late last season, and Mike Daniels was a very effective situational player. Both are lighter and quicker than the Jolly-Pickett generation of Packers linemen. Letroy Guion arrives from Minnesota to provide 30 snaps per game of beef; Jerel Worthy, who combines size with excellent first-step quickness, will be a fine addition if he ever gets healthy.

Capers still uses more late-'90s style zone blitzes than any other coordinator, so players like Daniels, Jones, and even Raji or Guion will drop into coverage far more often than the typical 3-4 defensive lineman. Capers has closed some of the E-ZPass lanes that opened up when the Packers got flummoxed by read options in 2012—opponents averaged a manageable 4.6 yards per zone-read or quarterback option in 2013, with Shady McCoy doing most of the damage—but it is common to see running backs and receivers turning upfield after shallow drag receptions with only 290-pounders in immediate pursuit. It's a byproduct of having to creatively generate pass rush too often, something Capers can dial back on with Matthews and Peppers in the mix.

Defensive Secondary

			Overall								vs. Run					vs. Pass									
Secondary	Age	Pos	G	Snaps	Plays	TmPct	Rk	Stop	Dfts	BTkl	Runs	St%	Rk	RuYd	Rk	Tgts	Tgt%	Rk	Dist	Suc%	Rk	AdjYd	Rk	PD	Int
Tramon Williams	31	CB	16	1037	95	11.7%	2	45	21	7	28	54%	23	6.8	37	73	16.6%	7	12.7	57%	20	8.3	61	10	3
Sam Shields	27	CB	14	878	77	10.8%	12	25	7	6	21	19%	76	12.2	79	79	21.2%	43	17.2	55%	35	7.8	49	17	4
Morgan Burnett	25	SS	13	855	99	15.0%	2	36	13	6	56	38%	43	6.6	28	29	7.8%	38	15.1	50%	50	9.6	67	6	0
M.D. Jennings*	26	FS	16	789	69	8.5%	60	14	11	4	35	17%	78	10.3	73	13	3.7%	1	13.2	28%	78	12.2	75	1	0
Davon House	25	CB	16	465	41	5.0%	85	15	7	3	4	50%	25	9.0	59	50	25.0%	73	12.6	49%	61	6.6	14	10	1
Micah Hyde	24	CB	16	419	49	6.0%	--	19	12	2	16	31%	--	5.8	--	36	20.2%	--	7.9	55%	--	8.1	--	2	0

Year	Pass D Rank	vs. #1 WR	Rk	vs. #2 WR	Rk	vs. Other WR	Rk	vs. TE	Rk	vs. RB	Rk
2011	23	14.1%	20	-16.2%	7	-28.2%	4	23.2%	26	1.4%	18
2012	7	16.3%	24	-25.1%	2	-31.6%	2	-11.6%	6	22.8%	27
2013	28	20.0%	28	16.7%	27	-8.1%	11	15.4%	25	13.3%	27

News of the third *Star Wars* trilogy reached Tramon Williams quickly, as he donned his old Admiral Armbar costume and method-acted his way to 133 yards worth of interference and holding penalties. It was a discouraging sign for a cornerback who turned 31 this offseason. Williams is active in run support and blitzes well, so he may be eased into Charles Woodson's old "slot enforcer" role so he does not have to shove and claw receivers 40 yards downfield too often. The other starter, Sam Shields, signed a hefty four-year contract despite an up-and-down season. Ted Thompson feels that the 26-year-old converted college receiver is still improving, and after seeing A.J. Hawk, it is easy to believe in an extra-long gestation cycle in Green Bay. Casey Hayward missed most of 2013 with a chronic hamstring issue after earning lots of all-rookie status when he ranked first among cornerbacks in Adjusted Success Rate in 2012. Devon House was effective in nickel coverage last season but appears maxed out in that role.

Morgan Burnett missed the start of last season with a hamstring injury, then needed several weeks to round into form. At his best, he is an incredibly active safety who can handle man coverage assignments and clean up messes in the middle. Rookie Ha Ha Clinton-Dix replaces a cast of regrettable choices at free safety. Clinton-Dix passes the specimen test and earned his bachelor's degree in safety science from Saban University; worries about his stiff change-of-direction quickness aside, he is an immediate upgrade, and Burnett will look much better when not playing two positions at once.

Micah Hyde, who is about to feature in the special teams comments, took minicamp reps as the "starting" nickel safety in a package Capers frequently deploys. Hyde also played the role at times in 2013, and he has incredible burst and reaction quickness when blitzing or pursuing laterally. Hyde was also a roving hybrid player in college, and while he may not be a natural fit at cornerback or safety, he could not ask for a better coach to craft a specialized role for him.

Special Teams

Year	DVOA	Rank	FG/XP	Rank	Net Kick	Rank	Kick Ret	Rank	Net Punt	Rank	Punt Ret	Rank	Hidden	Rank
2011	1.8%	8	3.0	12	1.4	15	3.1	8	-2.2	18	3.8	9	-2.8	18
2012	-0.2%	18	-11.8	31	-1.5	18	0.0	17	9.7	7	2.5	10	3.4	8
2013	-0.3%	19	4.0	10	-12.3	30	-4.2	23	5.4	9	5.6	9	7.5	6

Hyde ran a 4.56 forty during last season's pre-draft run-up. Because nothing is more statistically significant than one-tenth of a second measured in isolation under conditions irrelevant to actual performance, he was branded as "slow," a label that sticks with him despite a 93-yard punt return touchdown last year, a 70-yard kickoff return, and other evidence that Hyde can, in fact, run with exceeding swiftness. Hyde is still tentative as a returner, prone to fair catches or misjudging the ball in flight in bad weather, but he has exceptional start-stop speed and acceleration through the hole. Yes, he can be chased down by an opponent's top coverage gunners, but only after he has run a long way.

Mason Crosby rebounded from an ugly 2012 season (two misses inside 40 yards, 2-of-9 from beyond 50 yards) to convert field goals consistently throughout 2013. Crosby took over kickoff duties from punter Tim Masthay at midseason after Masthay, in his first year on the job, dropped easy-to-return kicks into the hands of Travis Benjamin and Cordarelle Patterson. Masthay mixed line drives and easy-to-return 58-yard lobs among his touchbacks and had problems with drizzly weather. Crosby produced just 13 touchbacks (compared to 17 by Masthay in two-thirds as many attempts) but provided better hang time and the ability to angle Devin Hester types into a corner near the pylon. Masthay, a serviceable punter, may get another crack at kickoffs this season.

All of the returnable kickoffs put pressure on the coverage units, though they improved as the season progressed, and the returns yielded a bonanza in meaningless special teams tackle totals. Davon House recorded 13 total tackles, Chris Banjo seven, and both are fine gunners (Banjo has the look, style, and name of a special teams ace) who could use fewer opportunities. Micah Hyde recorded six tackles of his own, chasing down the blazing Benjamin to save a touchdown in the Browns game. Not bad for such a slow guy.

Houston Texans

2013 Record: 2-14	**Total DVOA:** -26.5% (30th)	**2014 Mean Projection:** 7.3 wins	**On the Clock (0-4):** 14%
Pythagorean Wins: 4.2 (31st)	**Offense:** -18.9% (29th)	**Postseason Odds:** 27.6%	**Mediocrity (5-7):** 41%
Snap-Weighted Age: 26.6 (18th)	**Defense:** 2.5% (18th)	**Super Bowl Odds:** 1.6%	**Playoff Contender (8-10):** 35%
Average Opponent: 1.4% (10th)	**Special Teams:** -5.1% (29th)	**Proj. Avg. Opponent:** -5.5% (32nd)	**Super Bowl Contender (11+):** 10%

2013: Pick-six sinks ships.

2014: Clowney, Watt, and some afterthoughts.

The end of the Gary Kubiak Texans was long in the making. But it sure didn't take long. Houston started the year 2-0, with tight wins against mid-tier AFC teams San Diego and Tennessee. The spin was that this was a playoff team just shaking off some early rust.

Then they lost 14 straight games.

After a humiliating loss at Jacksonville, Kubiak and special teams coordinator Joe Marciano both got the axe. Defensive coordinator Wade Phillips was let go at the end of the season, after serving as interim head coach. There has been some matter of speculation about just how much power general manager Rick Smith had, but it was rather peculiar that he avoided the fate of Kubiak despite presiding over the two personnel moves that anchored Houston to that 2-14 record.

The first came on September 9, 2012. The Texans won their season opener against Miami, then handed quarterback Matt Schaub, who was coming off a Lisfranc injury, a four-year extension with $30 million in guaranteed money. It's hard to argue against signing Schaub in the moment as a matter of course. We know as NFL scholars that non-special quarterbacks tend to fall off the cliff much earlier than special ones, as Jake Delhomme so artfully demonstrated. We also know that, despite the injury, Schaub was playing more or less how he'd played since his peak 2009 season. The Texans weren't going to change horses after they'd made the Divisional Round with T.J. Yates under center.

It wasn't necessarily that the extension was bad—it was that the extension was made with only the best-case scenario in mind. The Texans never had a serious plan for an orderly succession at quarterback despite employing the exact kind of quarterback that often needs one. Sure enough, Schaub began to fall apart near the end of the 2012 season. Schaub finished the year with a 7.4% DVOA, but from Week 13 on, he'd posted a -13.3% DVOA while showing a noticeable reduction in his ability to throw deep. The Texans went from 11-1 home-field favorites to 12-4, memorably getting shellacked by New England on Monday Night Football and again in the Divisional Round.

Rather than look at Schaub's trend, which was evident from both tape and statistics, the Texans decided to double-down on their quarterback. Kubiak repeatedly extolled the virtues of his signal-caller, saying on multiple occasions that he "believed" in Schaub. Houston did not select a quarterback in the 2013 draft, nor did they even bother to employ an experienced backup.

What followed was an exercise in dink and dunk. Schaub finished with a -16.2% DVOA—roughly equivalent to his post-Week 12 showing in 2012—but the real trick was just how little the Texans or Schaub himself believed in his arm. Schaub finished the season with an average pass distance of 7.95 yards, about half a yard lower than the league average. But if you look at the average pass distance on deep balls (i.e., more than 15 yards through the air), Schaub could muster only 22.0 yards against a league average of 25.1. He finished below every quarterback with more than 50 attempts, and beat most of them comfortably (Table 1).

Table 1. Playing it Safe: Bottom 10 Quarterbacks in Average Depth of Deep Pass, 2013

Name	Team	Deep Pass Depth	Deep Passes
Aaron Rodgers	GB	24.2	59
Matt Ryan	ATL	24.2	75
Matt Cassel	MIN	23.8	57
Peyton Manning	DEN	23.8	123
Colin Kaepernick	SF	23.6	90
Matt Stafford	DET	23.5	131
Philip Rivers	SD	23.1	101
Alex Smith	KC	23.0	83
Kellen Clemens	STL	22.5	51
Matt Schaub	HOU	22.0	62

Minimum 50 deep pass attempts.

How rare was Schaub's season? In the years that we have average depth of target data for, 2005-2013, only four quarterback seasons finished with 22 yards per deep pass or lower with a minimum of 50 attempts (Table 2). Even notably weak-armed players like Colt McCoy and Chad Pennington threw deeper than Schaub did last season. NFL teams, having scouting departments, began to figure this out and adjust to it. Other teams flooded the underneath areas against the Texans with zone defenders, often leading to what you most likely remember Schaub's season for: pick-sixes. If you weaned your child on football for the first time by making him watch this team, the child would grow up thinking that underneath zone defenders were the keys to NFL victory. Kubiak never made

Table 2. NFL Quarterbacks with Average Deep Pass of 22.0 Yards or Less, 2005-2013

Name	Team	Year	Deep Pass Depth	Deep Passes
Chad Henne	JAC	2012	22.0	60
Matt Schaub	HOU	2013	22.0	62
Shaun Hill	DET	2010	21.9	73
Derek Anderson	CLE	2007	21.6	110

Minimum 50 deep pass attempts.

a material adjustment with Schaub under center. The quarterbacks behind Schaub were overmatched—as you'd expect given their pedigree—and at the end of the season the Texans turned back to Schaub to play out the string.

The other personnel move of significance came in the 2013 offseason, when Houston flew private jets all over the country to court Ravens safety Ed Reed. The worst part about the Reed move wasn't that the Texans signed a perpetually hurt 35-year-old who tackled like a lawnmower. It was that they let one of their core players—safety Glover Quin—walk at a lesser per-year price for the privilege to pay Reed.

Quin has a fairly unique skill set for a safety, in that as a former cornerback, he could be counted on to provide man-cover skills at the line of scrimmage. This was especially important for the Texans because the Phillips defense calls for a ton of man coverage when it generates pressure. Having Quin opened up the ability to be more aggressive with those calls, because three receivers could be covered at the line of scrimmage with just base personnel.

When Reed was brought in, the Texans shifted Danieal Manning to Quin's old role. Manning has some skill as a box safety, and had also converted from cornerback back in his younger years. But Manning was, like Reed, an older player with durability questions. Manning fractured his fibula in Week 6, leaving the Texans to aggressively promote rookie second-rounder D.J. Swearinger to a passing-down role he wasn't ready to play.

Meanwhile, Reed signed his contract and had arthroscopic surgery on his hip before the Texans could even get him to training camp. Houston continually threw out overly optimistic timetables on the injury, and Pro Football Talk even speculated that while the Ravens knew of Reed's hip problems, the Texans didn't before they inked Reed to a three-year, $15 million deal. Reed hit the PUP list and didn't play his first game until Houston's return to Baltimore in Week 3. He made it to Week 10 before the Texans canned him. So not only was the contract a bust, but they lost a core player to make it happen.

2014 Texans Schedule

Week	Opp.	Week	Opp.	Week	Opp.
1	WAS	7	at PIT (Mon.)	13	TEN
2	at OAK	8	at TEN	14	at JAC
3	at NYG	9	PHI	15	at IND
4	BUF	10	BYE	16	BAL
5	at DAL	11	at CLE	17	JAC
6	IND (Thu.)	12	CIN		

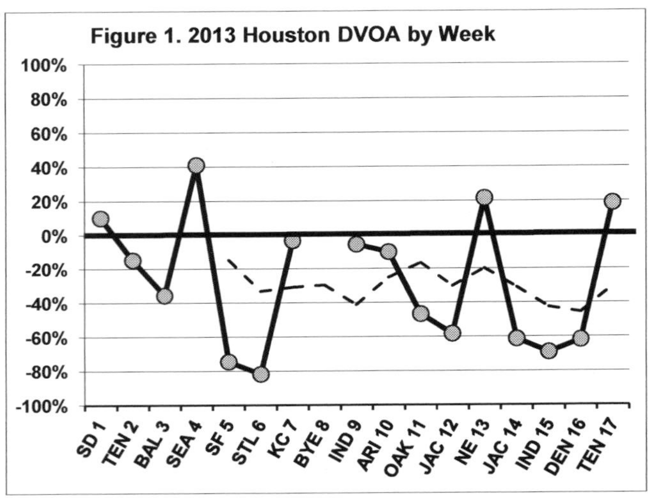

In that light, it's arguably the worst free-agent signing in Texans history. At the very least, it's up there with Ahman Green and Todd Wade.

Of course, these are only a couple of the reasons why the Texans went 2-14. The Texans were a bad football team, but they also had an inordinate share of bad luck. The Texans allowed 38 points directly off turnovers, went 2-9 in games decided by a touchdown or less, and had the league's largest gap between Pythagorean record and real record, at -2.2 wins. They also became the third team since 2006 to have a turnover margin of minus-20 or higher.

And that's where the optimistic signs for 2014 begin. Teams that managed that feat between 1991 and 2006 went from an average turnover differential of minus-22.9 to minus-2.4 the following season. The two teams that came into last season with minus-20 turnover differentials, the Chiefs and Eagles, rebounded to the opposite side of the spectrum. The Chiefs had a plus-19 turnover differential in 2013, and the Eagles settled in at plus-14.

Houston has also been gifted with a rather fortunate schedule—the easiest in the NFL based on DVOA projections. The AFC is by far the weaker conference at this point in time, and the AFC South is by far the weakest division. We have projected the division to play four of the five easiest schedules in the NFL in 2014, mostly due to playing each other. (Pittsburgh has the third-easiest.) Having a last-place schedule in 2014 gifts the Texans with games against the Raiders and Bills as well.

So we know that, based on statistical regression and schedule, Houston likely won't be as bad as they were last season. But what empirical evidence do we have that Houston has improved on the field?

Start with new head coach Bill O'Brien, who managed to make an above-.500 team out of a Penn State squad still working on a limited scholarship count thanks to the atrocities committed by Jerry Sandusky. Gary Kubiak had a long history of game-theory transgressions, as almost any NFL head coach not named Chip Kelly or Bill Belichick has accumulated over the years. O'Brien has brought a Belichick-style system to the Texans, hiring Romeo Crennel as defensive coordinator and immediately clamping down on outside media access. Hopefully, a Belichick-style grasp of game theory comes along with it.

When it comes to the roster, Houston's problem can be succinctly described in a *South Park* anecdote. Charged with creating a functioning dance troupe to help Stan serve the people who served his father into a hospital bed, Chef remarks: "You have the heart, but you don't have the soul. No, no wait… You have the soul, but you don't have the heart. No, no, scratch that… You have the heart and the soul. But you don't have the talent."

Certainly Houston has some top-notch individual talent. Johnathan Joseph was one of the 10 best cornerbacks in the NFL last season. Duane Brown had an off season, but is a top-of-the-line left tackle. Brian Cushing is one of the best linebackers in the NFL when he's actually healthy. Assuming Andre Johnson is actually going to play for the Texans this year—he didn't show up at OTAs and is frustrated with the direction of the team—he's one of the best receivers even at his advanced age. No. 1 overall pick Jadeveon Clowney is such a physical specimen that he'll likely be one of the top edge rushers in the NFL right away. J.J. Watt is probably the league's most valuable non-quarterback.

But outside of that core, most of this roster has stagnated. There are a troubling number of roster spots where Houston cannot point at a clear solution with a track record of success. The arrested development of Whitney Mercilus and Brooks Reed created a situation where picking Clowney addressed a need. But they're both still likely to start, with Reed moving inside to play next to Cushing. Nobody knows what to expect out of Kareem Jackson after a down season that left his sterling 2012 as an outlier among the rest of his work. Nickel corner Brandon Harris has barely played over the past three seasons and there's nothing behind him. The slot-receiver battle consists of a pair of players—Keshawn Martin and DeVier Posey—who have combined for minus-154 DYAR over their first two seasons in the league. All three of Houston's second-day picks are expected to be handed immediate starting roles.

Then there's the quarterback spot, where Houston ignored both the top-tier and middle-tier draft options on their way to creating a depth chart that Matt Schaub could still top, if he hadn't already been dealt to Oakland. Ryan Fitzpatrick is in town to play the role of "caretaker with a heart of gold," and fourth-round rookie Tom Savage will be "physically talented rookie with a one percent chance to develop into something worthwhile." Case Keenum returns as "local kid without a future." T.J. Yates will play the role of "backup linebacker Akeem Dent."

Because of those issues, Houston will likely spend the year getting served. The good news is that it may not show up on a surface level thanks to the schedule. It wouldn't even be a complete surprise to see the Texans winning a bad division if the Colts somehow falter. And either way, thanks to the impossibly low bar set by 2013, this year will be looked at as progress on a purely narrative level.

But in many ways, the 2014 Texans are a trial balloon. It's a situation where O'Brien can test the limits of his offense and where Crennel can figure out the best ways to use Watt and Clowney together: a situation without any expectations for immediate success.

Rivers McCown

2013 Texans Stats by Week

Wk	vs.	W-L	PF	PA	YDF	YDA	TO	Total	Off	Def	ST
1	at SD	W	31	28	449	263	0	10%	-4%	-20%	-6%
2	TEN	W	30	24	452	248	-2	-15%	-11%	-17%	-21%
3	at BAL	L	9	30	264	236	-1	-36%	-14%	6%	-16%
4	SEA	L	20	23	476	270	-1	41%	5%	-39%	-3%
5	at SF	L	3	34	313	284	-4	-75%	-54%	9%	-11%
6	STL	L	13	38	420	216	-4	-82%	-25%	40%	-17%
7	at KC	L	16	17	294	357	+1	-3%	-8%	-7%	-3%
8	BYE										
9	IND	L	24	27	483	314	0	-6%	46%	16%	-36%
10	at ARI	L	24	27	235	332	+2	-10%	-2%	1%	-7%
11	OAK	L	23	28	394	341	-2	-47%	-51%	18%	22%
12	JAC	L	6	13	218	333	-1	-58%	-50%	12%	3%
13	NE	L	31	34	385	453	0	21%	31%	15%	6%
14	at JAC	L	20	27	406	281	-2	-61%	-20%	40%	-1%
15	at IND	L	3	25	239	331	-1	-69%	-83%	-22%	-8%
16	DEN	L	13	37	240	511	-2	-62%	-48%	22%	8%
17	at TEN	L	10	16	288	311	-3	19%	-9%	-19%	8%

Trends and Splits

	Offense	Rank	Defense	Rank
Total DVOA	-18.9%	29	2.5%	18
Unadjusted VOA	-18.2%	29	4.2%	23
Weighted Trend	-23.5%	31	7.7%	23
Variance	10.9%	28	5.1%	17
Average Opponent	-0.2%	17	-0.3%	15
Passing	-19.7%	30	15.1%	24
Rushing	-8.9%	24	-11.4%	12
First Down	-21.0%	29	3.3%	17
Second Down	-11.4%	23	4.3%	21
Third Down	-26.2%	30	-1.7%	15
First Half	-4.7%	20	6.1%	25
Second Half	-32.1%	32	-1.3%	15
Red Zone	-23.3%	30	24.5%	26
Late and Close	-38.7%	30	-4.4%	13

Five-Year Performance

Year	W-L	Pyth W	Est W	PF	PA	TO	Total	Rk	Off	Rk	Def	Rk	ST	Rk	Off AGL	Rk	Def AGL	Rk	Off Age	Rk	Def Age	Rk	ST Age	Rk
2009	9-7	9.5	10.0	388	333	-1	9.7%	14	9.9%	10	2.5%	20	2.4%	7	39.9	28	17.5	7	26.4	28	25.3	32	26.9	7
2010	6-10	7.1	7.9	390	427	0	2.5%	13	21.7%	2	17.5%	31	-1.7%	23	31.0	20	24.2	16	27.4	15	25.5	30	26.2	15
2011	10-6	10.9	10.0	381	278	+7	18.6%	5	8.4%	9	-9.5%	6	0.7%	13	31.3	17	18.9	10	28.1	2	25.7	29	26.1	24
2012	12-4	10.2	8.3	416	331	+12	6.7%	11	0.1%	16	-14.2%	4	-7.7%	32	6.7	1	30.6	19	28.1	6	26.5	22	26.4	11
2013	2-14	4.2	3.9	276	428	-20	-26.5%	30	-18.9%	29	2.5%	18	-5.1%	29	37.2	18	33.1	20	27.5	9	26.2	22	25.7	26

2013 Performance Based on Most Common Personnel Groups

HOU Offense					HOU Offense vs. Opponents				HOU Defense				HOU Defense vs. Opponents			
Pers	Freq	Yds	DVOA	Run%	Pers	Freq	Yds	DVOA	Pers	Freq	Yds	DVOA	Pers	Freq	Yds	DVOA
1.1	35%	4.9	-14.4%	22%	Nickel Even	30%	5.1	-13.3%	3-4-4	54%	5.5	-3.2%	1.1	36%	6.2	20.2%
2.1	28%	5.5	-10.3%	61%	4-3-4	28%	5.2	-11.4%	Dime+	28%	6.2	16.8%	1.2	27%	5.6	-7.6%
1.2	24%	5.2	-12.9%	38%	3-4-4	22%	5.4	-15.1%	Nickel Odd	7%	7.1	28.3%	2.1	17%	5.0	-7.4%
0.2	6%	5.5	-38.6%	0%	Dime+	11%	3.5	-64.5%	Nickel Even	6%	4.8	-12.6%	2.2	8%	4.5	-3.5%
2.2	2%	2.2	-51.1%	56%	Nickel Odd	8%	7.2	10.0%	3-5-3	4%	1.9	-56.8%	1.3	4%	5.1	-23.1%

Strategic Tendencies

Run/Pass		Rk	Formation		Rk	Pass Rush		Rk	Secondary		Rk	Strategy		Rk
Runs, first half	42%	10	Form: Single Back	58%	26	Rush 3	2.3%	28	4 DB	54%	3	Play action	19%	20
Runs, first down	46%	20	Form: Empty Back	13%	4	Rush 4	49.0%	30	5 DB	13%	32	Avg Box (Off)	6.37	15
Runs, second-long	25%	26	Pers: 3+ WR	43%	29	Rush 5	28.2%	9	6+ DB	28%	3	Avg Box (Def)	6.55	2
Runs, power sit.	62%	8	Pers: 4+ WR	2%	10	Rush 6+	20.4%	1	CB by Sides	54%	30	Offensive Pace	30.82	20
Runs, behind 2H	29%	11	Pers: 2+ TE/6+ OL	35%	14	Sacks by LB	41.9%	14	DB Blitz	11%	19	Defensive Pace	30.08	20
Pass, ahead 2H	49%	15	Shotgun/Pistol	53%	22	Sacks by DB	3.2%	24	Hole in Zone	4%	32	Go for it on 4th	0.88	18

The Texans need to figure out how to stop the run when opponents spread them out. Last year, they allowed 6.42 yards per carry and 14.1% DVOA when opponents ran with three or more wide receivers in the game. The year before, it was 5.14 yards per carry and 8.9%, a little better but still much worse than average. Houston used a lot of empty backfields, and it wasn't really a good idea, as the Texans gained just 5.2 yards per play with -26.7% DVOA (compared to NFL averages of 6.3 and 17.0%). Despite ranking 29th in offensive DVOA, the Texans actually went three-and-out on just 20.5 percent of drives, sixth best in the NFL. Oddly enough, when they had an average overall offense in 2012, the Texans went three-and-out on 27.3 percent of drives, which ranked 27th.

Passing

Player	DYAR	DVOA	Plays	NtYds	Avg	YAC	C%	TD	Int
M.Schaub*	-123	-16.2%	380	2128	5.6	4.2	61.3%	10	14
C.Keenum	-191	-22.4%	270	1550	5.7	5.0	55.2%	9	6
T.J.Yates*	-109	-78.0%	24	106	4.4	3.0	68.2%	0	2
R.Fitzpatrick	*179*	*-3.6%*	*369*	*2359*	*6.4*	*5.1*	*62.5%*	*14*	*12*

Rushing

Player	DYAR	DVOA	Plays	Yds	Avg	TD	Fum	Suc
B.Tate*	50	-2.0%	180	773	4.3	4	4	51%
A.Foster	99	11.4%	121	542	4.5	1	0	50%
D.Johnson	-10	-12.8%	49	183	3.7	0	0	45%
J.Grimes	27	21.7%	21	73	3.5	1	0	48%
C.Keenum	27	23.8%	13	73	5.6	1	0	-
D.Karim*	10	15.9%	12	51	4.3	0	0	50%
A.Brown	*-44*	*-16.3%*	*139*	*494*	*3.6*	*3*	*3*	*50%*
R.Fitzpatrick	*85*	*34.8%*	*35*	*232*	*6.6*	*3*	*0*	*-*

Receiving

Player	DYAR	DVOA	Plays	Ctch	Yds	Y/C	YAC	TD	C%
A.Johnson	150	-2.3%	181	109	1407	12.9	3.7	5	60%
D.Hopkins	139	6.9%	91	52	802	15.4	3.5	2	57%
K.Martin	-1	-13.0%	40	22	253	11.5	4.0	2	55%
D.Posey	-38	-33.7%	25	15	155	10.3	4.9	0	60%
L.Jean*	-6	-23.0%	8	4	35	8.8	0.8	0	50%
G.Graham	-84	-21.3%	89	49	545	11.1	4.2	5	55%
O.Daniels*	14	-2.4%	41	24	252	10.5	3.5	3	59%
R.Griffin	38	13.9%	28	19	244	12.8	5.2	1	68%
B.Tate*	-125	-62.9%	50	35	138	3.9	4.7	0	70%
A.Foster	9	-9.2%	35	22	183	8.3	9.5	1	63%
D.Johnson	-18	-39.3%	12	8	46	5.8	6.8	0	67%
G.Jones*	-26	-55.6%	11	5	34	6.8	2.0	0	45%
J.Grimes	10	22.0%	6	6	76	12.7	9.7	0	100%
A.Brown	*-49*	*-46.7%*	*29*	*20*	*103*	*5.2*	*5.9*	*0*	*69%*

Offensive Line

Player	Pos	Age	GS	Snaps	Pen	Sk	Pass	Run	Player	Pos	Age	GS	Snaps	Pen	Sk	Pass	Run
Chris Myers	C	33	16/16	1121	2	1.0	14.2	4.5	Derek Newton	RT	27	16/16	830	13	6.3	28.7	1.5
Brandon Brooks	RG	25	15/15	1043	5	2.8	18.3	5.0	Ryan Harris*	OT	29	16/2	479	3	2.0	11.3	0.5
Wade Smith*	LG	33	16/16	972	0	4.0	25.3	7.0	Ben Jones	G	25	16/1	228	2	1.0	8.0	2.0
Duane Brown	LT	29	16/14	953	6	3.8	14.7	6.5									

Year	Yards	ALY	Rk	Power	Rk	Stuff	Rk	2nd Lev	Rk	Open Field	Rk	Sacks	ASR	Rk	Short	Long	F-Start	Cont.
2011	4.66	4.37	4	64%	14	18%	12	1.43	4	0.93	11	33	7.3%	22	15	15	15	43
2012	4.34	4.17	9	61%	18	20%	23	1.26	10	0.85	12	28	5.3%	9	14	7	18	33
2013	4.20	4.10	6	56%	26	20%	17	1.31	3	0.53	26	42	6.6%	11	13	14	19	38
2013 ALY by direction:			*Left End 3.56 (14)*			*Left Tackle 3.29 (29)*			*Mid/Guard 4.47 (3)*			*Right Tackle 3.68 (18)*			*Right End 4.82 (3)*			

The Texans had three Pro Bowlers on their offensive line in 2012. In 2013, their line was a clear weakness.

Duane Brown, one of the NFL's top left tackles, suffered through an injury-plagued season. He was noticeably slow over the first half. Brown put on 20 pounds in the offseason in the hopes of being a more impactful run blocker in 2014. Sometimes a weight shift can do wonders for a player, and sometimes you wind up with 2013 Ray Rice. Brown will be hoping for the former. Center Chris Myers has two years left on his deal, and at 32, what you see is what you get. Myers is a zone technician without the bulk to stand up to huge noses. Thankfully, he's playing in 2014 rather than 1994. Wade Smith's nod to Hawaii was laughable in 2012, and he was a complete liability in 2013. He fell so far off the map that he was still unsigned as we go to press.

Right guard Brandon Brooks had a solid, if not spectacular, first season as a full-time starter. He's more of a power blocker than a zone specialist, mostly because he has a lot of weight on his frame, but he moves well for his size. Ben Jones is the returning depth at guard, but he's struggled to deal with NFL pass-rush moves. Second-round pick Xavier Su'a-Filo (UCLA) will likely be an instant starter inside, assuming he isn't tried at right tackle. Su'a-Filo is a bruiser with an attitude, and he has the agility to get to the second level quickly. Derek Newton's counting stats don't make him out to be a Lamar Holmes-esque problem, but this is because the Texans rotated his snaps with journeyman Ryan Harris. Newton has survived as a starter because the Texans haven't been able to draft anyone healthy enough to push him. 2013 third-rounder Brennan Williams is coming off microfracture surgery, and 2013 sixth-rounder David Quessenberry was diagnosed with leukemia in OTAs. The Texans named Newton the starter before training camp. As Homer Simpson can attest, the two sweetest words in the English language are "default."

Defensive Front Seven

			Overall								vs. Run					Pass Rush			
Defensive Line	**Age**	**Pos**	**G**	**Snaps**	**Plays**	**TmPct**	**Rk**	**Stop**	**Dfts**	**BTkl**	**Runs**	**St%**	**Rk**	**RuYd**	**Rk**	**Sack**	**Hit**	**Hur**	**Tips**
J.J. Watt	25	DE	16	960	87	11.3%	1	79	35	4	63	92%	5	1.7	27	10.5	36	38.5	7
Antonio Smith*	33	DE	15	739	29	4.0%	65	25	14	3	20	85%	17	1.2	7	5.0	9	16.8	0
Earl Mitchell*	27	DT	16	534	48	6.2%	26	38	5	1	43	84%	22	2.5	56	1.5	2	5.8	0
Jared Crick	25	DE	16	266	23	3.0%	--	14	1	1	19	53%	--	4.1	--	0.0	2	3.5	3
*Ricardo Mathews**	*27*	*DT*	*16*	*428*	*19*	*2.3%*	*84*	*12*	*3*	*0*	*17*	*59%*	*82*	*3.0*	*69*	*0.5*	*2*	*6.5*	*0*

			Overall								vs. Run					Pass Rush			
Edge Rushers	**Age**	**Pos**	**G**	**Snaps**	**Plays**	**TmPct**	**Rk**	**Stop**	**Dfts**	**BTkl**	**Runs**	**St%**	**Rk**	**RuYd**	**Rk**	**Sack**	**Hit**	**Hur**	**Tips**
Brooks Reed	27	OLB	16	999	53	6.9%	19	37	13	2	41	76%	43	3.8	70	3.0	5	16.3	0
Whitney Mercilus	24	OLB	16	932	47	6.1%	30	31	11	3	33	64%	65	3.1	57	7.0	10	20.8	0

			Overall								Pass Rush			vs. Run					vs. Pass						
Linebackers	**Age**	**Pos**	**G**	**Snaps**	**Plays**	**TmPct**	**Rk**	**Stop**	**Dfts**	**BTkl**	**Sack**	**Hit**	**Hur**	**Runs**	**St%**	**Rk**	**RuYd**	**Rk**	**Tgts**	**Suc%**	**Rk**	**AdjYd**	**Rk**	**PD**	**Int**
Darryl Sharpton*	26	ILB	15	718	88	12.2%	49	48	13	9	0.0	5	6.5	56	68%	30	3.4	44	34	33%	70	10.3	70	1	0
Joe Mays*	29	ILB	14	545	69	10.2%	62	47	10	4	1.0	4	2	49	73%	14	2.5	16	18	73%	1	2.9	1	3	0
Brian Cushing	27	ILB	7	329	50	14.8%	29	37	12	5	1.5	2	5.5	36	83%	1	1.8	3	8	17%	--	8.0	--	1	1
Jeff Tarpinian	27	ILB	8	180	21	5.4%	--	13	6	0	0.5	1	1	15	60%	--	3.3	--	9	79%	--	3.7	--	1	0
Akeem Dent	*27*	*MLB*	*15*	*364*	*47*	*6.1%*	*--*	*27*	*9*	*3*	*1.5*	*0*	*1*	*33*	*61%*	*--*	*3.3*	*--*	*12*	*30%*	*--*	*10.0*	*--*	*0*	*0*

Year	Yards	ALY	Rk	Power	Rk	Stuff	Rk	2nd Level	Rk	Open Field	Rk	Sacks	ASR	Rk	Short	Long
2011	4.04	3.85	7	67%	25	20%	15	1.07	8	0.75	14	44	8.4%	3	14	18
2012	3.93	3.62	4	59%	11	25%	4	1.22	23	0.67	12	44	7.3%	6	11	15
2013	4.27	3.68	12	53%	6	22%	10	1.10	16	1.04	27	32	6.7%	18	12	8
2013 ALY by direction:			*Left End 4.66 (30)*			*Left Tackle 3.70 (9)*			*Mid/Guard 3.60 (8)*			*Right Tackle 3.71 (13)*			*Right End 3.23 (9)*	

By way of comparison, sometimes good things look even better when they are placed next to something undesirable. You'll never appreciate a cable company as much as you appreciate the second one in your area. You know, the one that's not Comcast. By this principle, J.J. Watt was the *Godfather* to the rest of the Houston front seven's *Godfather III*. As expected, Watt didn't replicate his amazing 2013 season, because nobody could have. But he was still among the league leaders in tipped passes (seven, tied for third in the league), Defeats (35, tied for third in the league), and hurries (38.5, fourth). He led the league with 36 quarterback hits when no other player had more than 21. He did this while mostly playing as a 5-technique lineman or an interior rusher on passing downs.

First overall pick Jadeveon Clowney will rejuvenate a pass rush that was almost entirely dependent on Watt. No non-quarterback was as scrutinized during the draft process as Clowney was, but reports that he was playing through a sports hernia help ease some of the concerns about effort and dwindling stats in his final season at South Carolina. Antonio Smith, a solid third banana on a good team, fled to Oakland for more money, and Jared Crick will be promoted to take his place. Former first-rounder Whitney Mercilus was, to use a John McClain-ism, "pathetic." On the opposite side, Brooks Reed was such a good pass rusher that the Texans are trying to move him to inside linebacker. Defensive tackle will essentially be handed to third-rounder Louis Nix III (Notre Dame) right away, because the only other player on the roster with the heft for the nose is castoff Jerrell Powe, who played just 40 snaps last season.

Houston will be hoping that Brian Cushing can rebound from another season lost to injury: both because they have essentially nobody else inside, and because they are on the hook for a six-year, $55 million extension that will be impossible to unload off their cap for a few years. Houston will be hoping to cobble together an acceptable second middle linebacker between Reed, challenge trade participant Akeem Dent, Jeff "Tarpy" Tarpinian, and undrafted free agent Max Bullough (Michigan State). Houston will be hoping to squeeze some form of depth out of a collection of late-round picks, UDFAs, and players recovering from injuries. Houston will be doing a lot of hoping.

Defensive Secondary

					Overall						vs. Run					vs. Pass									
Secondary	**Age**	**Pos**	**G**	**Snaps**	**Plays**	**TmPct**	**Rk**	**Stop**	**Dfts**	**BTkl**	**Runs**	**St%**	**Rk**	**RuYd**	**Rk**	**Tgts**	**Tgt%**	**Rk**	**Dist**	**Suc%**	**Rk**	**AdjYd**	**Rk**	**PD**	**Int**
Johnathan Joseph	30	CB	15	832	63	8.7%	39	27	11	3	12	25%	69	10.8	71	79	24.5%	70	13.3	63%	5	6.9	25	16	3
D.J. Swearinger	23	SS	16	797	71	9.2%	51	39	16	8	38	63%	3	4.9	11	37	11.9%	69	8.2	50%	52	9.0	62	4	1
Shiloh Keo	27	SS	16	769	66	8.5%	59	18	9	12	25	28%	68	10.8	75	21	7.1%	24	15.8	65%	12	8.7	61	6	1
Kareem Jackson	26	CB	14	760	65	9.6%	20	25	11	3	19	42%	39	6.6	34	76	26.0%	78	11.9	42%	81	8.5	66	8	0
Brice McCain*	28	CB	16	605	35	4.5%	87	15	9	6	7	29%	67	19.3	85	59	25.1%	74	10.8	51%	54	6.2	9	6	1
Danieal Manning*	32	FS	6	321	26	9.0%	--	12	4	4	15	47%	--	7.7	--	12	9.7%	--	16.1	78%	--	2.3	--	2	0
Brandon Harris	26	CB	16	205	21	2.7%	--	8	7	1	7	29%	--	7.1	--	17	21.5%	--	13.5	52%	--	9.8	--	3	0
Chris Clemons	29	FS	16	1136	98	11.1%	28	32	10	9	58	33%	54	6.8	35	18	3.8%	2	12.5	80%	1	5.2	13	6	1
Kendrick Lewis	26	FS	16	1042	60	7.1%	67	17	7	9	30	23%	72	10.1	70	24	5.2%	6	8.1	47%	58	7.9	55	3	1

Year	Pass D Rank	vs. #1 WR	Rk	vs. #2 WR	Rk	vs. Other WR	Rk	vs. TE	Rk	vs. RB	Rk
2011	9	24.0%	24	-15.9%	8	-14.7%	13	5.1%	12	-12.5%	9
2012	4	-26.7%	4	11.3%	28	1.8%	19	-12.2%	4	-23.1%	5
2013	24	-1.0%	18	5.4%	17	-10.5%	9	24.9%	30	17.6%	30

Johnathan Joseph received a lot of blame from the Houston press for the debacle that was the Texans defense in 2013, and that was really strange given how much heavy lifting Houston made him do last year. Joseph, playing with a toe injury that bothered him all year, shadowed receivers to the slot on a routine basis and finished with one of the best Adjusted Success Rates in the league. Perhaps it's easy to believe a cornerback is the problem when he's always the one tackling somebody—Texans corners were often thrown on an island in 2013 as Wade Phillips desperately tried to find pass rush.

The player who actually struggled last year was Kareem Jackson. Jackson fell from 12th in Success Rate in 2012 to 81st in 2013. Jackson is at a crossroads. This is his last year under contract in Houston, and outside of 2012 he has been downright abysmal. But 2012 was such a high peak that another boom year will have teams circling. Houston's coaching staff has floated the idea of Jackson covering the slot more in 2014, which would take advantage of what a physical player he is in run defense. Shining one-year fluke-turned-whipping boy Brice McCain is gone, so 2011 second-rounder Brandon Harris is the leader to take over as the nickel corner. Harris was more adequate last season than he had been in previous trials, but he committed so many penalties over the past two years that they may as well give him a yellow jersey.

At safety, the Texans clearly committed to upgrading on the debacle that was Ed Reed. D.J. Swearinger had an up-and-down rookie season highlighted by some overaggressive angles. The second starter will likely be former Dolphins safety Chris "not the defensive end" Clemons, who is well-suited to the deep safety role he'll likely play. Kansas City refugee Kendrick Lewis will play in dime packages and give Romeo Crennel the option of playing a Heavy Nickel, though Lewis has always been more filler than difference-maker. Shiloh Keo is around to do what Shiloh Keo always does: play 30 yards off the line of scrimmage and take poor tackling angles when one of the safeties ahead of him gets hurt.

Special Teams

Year	DVOA	Rank	FG/XP	Rank	Net Kick	Rank	Kick Ret	Rank	Net Punt	Rank	Punt Ret	Rank	Hidden	Rank
2011	0.7%	13	-3.6	22	3.7	10	-1.9	20	0.9	14	4.6	7	-3.2	20
2012	-7.7%	32	-5.8	29	-25.9	32	-6.9	28	-1.2	16	1.4	13	5.7	4
2013	-5.1%	29	-12.2	31	-1.4	20	-5.0	27	-7.8	27	0.6	13	1.3	13

The Texans finished dead last in special teams DVOA in 2012, but didn't fire long-time special teams coordinator Joe Marciano until the Kubiak purge following Week 14 of last year. Of course, the coordinator doesn't play the snaps, but Marciano's steadfast refusal to generate anything out of otherwise successful personnel like Jacoby Jones and Trindon Holliday was emblematic of the problems of the Kubiak era.

The Texans traded Shayne Graham's well-below average kickoff leg for Randy Bullock's adventures in field goals. Bullock did such a good job that he'll face a training camp challenge from undrafted free agent Chris Boswell (Rice). Shane Lechler's punts weren't a problem—he actually finished second in gross punt value, behind only Brandon Fields of Miami—but the team had zero gunners of note after Bryan Braman, and that's borderline inexcusable given how many of the backups were non-factors on defense or offense. Braman fled to the Eagles in free agency, so what new coordinator Bob Ligashesky can do with the bottom of the roster will be important. Keshawn Martin should return both punts (track record of success!) and kicks (track record of comical errors!).

Indianapolis Colts

2013 Record: 11-5	**Total DVOA:** 3.2% (13th)	**2014 Mean Projection:** 8.7 wins	**On the Clock (0-4):** 5%
Pythagorean Wins: 9.4 (10th)	**Offense:** 4.3% (13th)	**Postseason Odds:** 53.4%	**Mediocrity (5-7):** 23%
Snap-Weighted Age: 26.6 (20th)	**Defense:** 0.9% (16th)	**Super Bowl Odds:** 7.3%	**Playoff Contender (8-10):** 48%
Average Opponent: -2.6% (23rd)	**Special Teams:** -0.1% (18th)	**Proj. Avg. Opponent:** -3.4% (29th)	**Super Bowl Contender (11+):** 23%

2013: *The Andrew Luck Show* starring Andrew Luck and, um... some other people, apparently.

2014: Still very little time-slot competition, but they won't be playing into February sweeps.

The Andrew Luck Show (2012—current) is an American football drama that mixes the life of a burgeoning superstar quarterback with the basic plot of *The Truman Show*. The lead star, Luck, is forced into nigh-unwinnable circumstances. He is meant to replace one of the best quarterbacks of all time, Peyton Manning. He is selected with the first pick of the NFL Draft. He and the rest of his rookie class head to Indianapolis and find a roster that is roughly 10 percent Manning's war buddies and 90 percent filler.

Other factors begin to conspire against young Luck as well. His coach (Chuck Pagano, played by Tim Daly) contracts leukemia during the first season of the show, leading to the creation of the brand-phrase "ChuckStrong." The Colts run off a 9-2 record during Pagano's absence, but fall to Baltimore in the playoffs. The second season then took the dramatic narrative of the initial episodes and flipped it on its head. The Colts jumped out to a 6-2 start, with wins over power teams Seattle, San Francisco, and Denver. They came back to dispatch the reeling Texans, the former kings of the AFC South. But the team began to struggle down the stretch. Reggie Wayne (Larenz Tate) went down with a torn ACL, ending his season. With promising dual-threat tight end Dwayne Allen (Chiwetel Ejiofor) sidelined by a hip injury, Luck struggled to find targets from the rag-tag cast of extras surrounding fellow 2012 draftee T.Y. Hilton (D.B. Woodside). The running back for whom the team saw fit to trade a first-round pick, Trent Richardson (Jaden Smith), couldn't muster more than three yards a carry. Ultimately the team fell to the New England Patriots, as so many Colts teams have before, in a game that wasn't close.

A key conflict in *The Andrew Luck Show* is that Andrew Luck is rarely allowed to have any teammates of equivalent value. In this way, we experience the weekly struggle of a man trying to atone for mistakes that were never his own. All one needs to do to see how much Luck is accountable for is to research the history of roster construction in Indianapolis.

General managers Bill Polian (played by himself) and Ryan Grigson (Dave Annable) both have contributed to the roster malaise that surrounds Luck. After years of poor drafting, Polian left a bare-bones depth chart that was slaughtered by the league when the Colts took the field without Manning in 2011. Grigson took over that roster and added Luck, Hilton, and Allen. Every other move Grigson has made since that point has been a wash at best (Table 1).

Table 1: Colts in 2011, Colts in 2014

Name	Position	AV (2012-2013)
Reggie Wayne	WR	16
Robert Mathis	DE	19
Anthony Castonzo	OT	16
Joe Reitz	G	7
Fili Moala*	DL	7
Pat McAfee	P	5
Adam Vinatieri	K	6

**- will miss 2014 season due to ligament tear*

Table 1 lists the players that were on the team in 2011 and will still be on the team in 2014. It's a short list. We've used pro-football-reference's AV, or Approximate Value, as a tool to show how impactful those players were. AV is meant to be a smarter stat than games started or seasons played; a good season will score around 10, and Peyton Manning led the league last year with 19. The 2011 Colts that are still on the current roster combined for just 76 total AV over the past two years. More importantly, there are reasons to doubt that some of the players had as much value as their listed AV. For instance, Anthony Castonzo has struggled to be anything more than league-average since he began playing, but the AV system gives him credit for just being a starting left tackle for a winning team. Punters and kickers are a strange test of the AV system, and while McAfee has been more valuable than the average punter, Vinatieri has essentially been league-average the last few seasons. Joe Reitz wouldn't have played for most NFL teams at all. We could get into all the bad draft picks that left the Colts in this position, but this isn't a ten-page essay. And it wasn't like good players were running away from Indianapolis left and right. Antoine Bethea, Pierre Garcon, Donald Brown, and Phillip Wheeler have all since escaped the set. Those are nice complimentary players, but not the core of a successful team.

Luck's dilemma is simple: most of his teammates are extras, and Grigson has shown little capacity to find players who aren't. If we era-adjust for how running backs are valued today, the Trent Richardson trade is the modern equivalent of the Herschel Walker trade. But much like smaller tests of character show more about us than the crises in our lives, the trade that really demonstrated the flaws in Grigson's long-

2014 Colts Schedule

Week	Opp.	Week	Opp.	Week	Opp.
1	at DEN	7	CIN	13	WAS
2	PHI (Mon.)	8	at PIT	14	at CLE
3	at JAC	9	at NYG (Mon.)	15	HOU
4	TEN	10	BYE	16	at DAL
5	BAL	11	NE	17	at TEN
6	at HOU (Thu.)	12	JAC		

term thinking was not the Richardson deal but the Vontae Davis deal, which sent a second-round pick to the Dolphins for the former first-round cornerback.

Davis just had his best season by FO's cornerback charting stats. He compiled a 62 percent Adjusted Success Rate in 2013, seventh in the NFL. He was at 41 percent in 2012 and 57 percent in 2011. While he has historically been an underachiever, Davis put it all together in 2013 and became one of the only Colts defenders worth his salt. Then, after the season, he signed a four-year, $36 million deal, and immediately became a commodity rather than an asset.

Because Grigson traded for Davis two years into his career, he only received two seasons of pay on a cheap rookie deal. The asset he gave away, the second-round pick, would have given him four seasons of that—and at a bargain rate, as well. The player the Dolphins picked in that slot, Jamar Taylor, won't have a cap number higher than $1.15 million in any of those four seasons. In 2015, Davis' cap number will be $11.2 million. Grigson traded away that future asset because he felt he had to get a starting cornerback, despite the fact that there was zero internal pressure to compete for a playoff berth as the Colts broke in Luck during the 2012 season.

When a team is as bereft of assets as the Colts were after Grigson took over, they have two options to accumulate more of them. They can draft players that turn into serviceable stars, or they can sign undervalued free agents to bargain contracts. By trading two high picks away, Grigson forfeited two of his best shots to find a young star at a draft-level salary. Instead, he ended up with a talented-but-inconsistent cornerback who carries a big cap figure and the worst starting running back of 2013.

Grigson's work in free agency has been similarly uninspiring. He certainly has been trying to follow a blueprint that features undervalued free agents with bargain contracts. Beyond Davis, Mathis, Wayne, and Luck, no Colts have a cap figure above $6 million this season. But he has scouted poorly and inefficiently. Cory Redding, Ricky Jean-Francois, D'Qwell Jackson, Arthur Jones, and Erik Walden take up $24 million in cap space this season. They combined for 16 sacks in 2013, and only Jones has much on-field talent for rushing the passer.

Instead, the Indianapolis brain trust devotes its attention to snuffing out opposing running games. Between the myopic ramblings of Pagano about stopping the run and the payroll space allocated to it, you would forgive Colts fans for believing it was actually important. All that emphasis on the run game just for the Patriots to roll the Colts' defense for 234 rushing yards and six touchdowns in the playoffs? That only

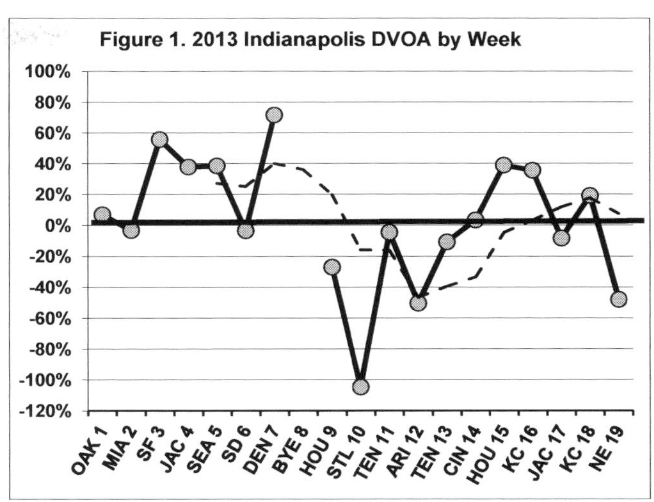

further emboldened Grigson and Pagano, which is why they signed Jones and Jackson rather than doing any work on the already-questionable pass defense.

Indianapolis finished 13th in pass defense DVOA last season, thanks primarily to standout seasons from Mathis and Davis (Table 2). Davis has always been a boom-or-bust corner, as the high Adjusted Yards per Pass figure shows. Even while he was having his best season in 2013, he allowed some humongous gains and big games. Tavon Austin and Andre Johnson both torched him in the middle of the season. Meanwhile, Mathis essentially stuffed his two previous seasons worth of sacks and hurries into one über-season. Given his advanced age (33), he was a good bet to regress even before a four-game substance abuse suspension was announced this offseason. With those four games gone, a worst-case scenario where Mathis plays as he did in 2012 could knock his sack total closer to six or seven.

Table 2: Here Comes the Pass Defense Regression!

	Robert Mathis			Vontae Davis		
	Sacks	Hits	Hurries	Target Rate (Rk)	Adj. Yards per Pass (Rk)	Success Rate (Rk)
2011	9.5	9	19	17.6% (40)	8.1 (54)	57% (21)
2012	8	6	8.5	19.4% (30)	9.9 (85)	41% (82)
2013	19.5	7	33.5	19.9% (30)	7.1 (33)	62% (7)

If the Colts had spent the last few years stockpiling intriguing pieces that played well in limited time around Mathis, that might have been acceptable. But they lost their only competent safety, Bethea, to free agency. Indianapolis signed no safeties of note and drafted none either, so they'll be starting either 33-year-old journeyman Mike Adams or a UDFA pizza party contest winner. 2013 first-round pick Bjoern Werner has a fine pedigree, but as a rookie he generated just five hurries and 2.5 sacks in 306 snaps. This is where we'd tell you about the other young contributors on Indy's defense, but if you skip ahead to the tables in the unit comments, you can see there aren't any. Josh Chapman is the only other player under 27 who played any real role for the Colts last season, and he's just a hulking nose tackle, not a burgeoning sackmaster. It speaks poorly for the few recent defensive draft picks that they weren't even able to beat out the collection of mediocrities the Colts trotted out in 2013. Was the issue here injuries? No: while Indianapolis finished 31st in Adjusted Games Lost in 2013, that was mostly contained to the offensive side of the ball. The only place Indianapolis had devastating injury problems on defense was in the secondary, and that's mostly because they made a conscious choice to target veterans Greg Toler and LaRon Landry in free agency. If Donte Whitner can threaten to change his name to Hitner, the least Landry and Toler could do is add "-Doubtful" to the end of their surnames. If Mathis is anything less than the Defensive Player of the Year candidate he was last season once he finally gets on the field, this defense could completely collapse.

The good news is that we are projecting the Colts offense to take a step forward in 2014. There are individual question marks about Wayne (age, injury comeback), Hakeem Nicks (diminished skill set from previous injury) and Allen (injury comeback), but surely the Colts can bank on at least one of them providing value. That's an improvement on the 2013 receiving corps colloquially known as "Hilton, Fleener, then drink drain cleaner." If the offensive line can have a year where they don't subject Luck to the most quarterback knockdowns in football—something that has been empirically beyond them so far—that would also help.

Despite Luck, the Colts actually ranked higher in run offense DVOA than pass offense DVOA in 2013. When you think of the 2013 Colts, you probably don't think of a dominant red-zone team. But they actually had the highest red-zone rushing DVOA in the NFL last year. While that is sure to regress in 2014, the good news is that most of the teams that led the league in this stat (Table 3) were still above-average the next season.

Let's list out the leading rushers by red zone DVOA, in reverse order: Richardson (-20.9% on 16 carries), Ahmad Bradshaw (17.7% on nine carries), and Brown (54.7% on 14 carries). Wait, that doesn't add up at all. Oh, right, it's because Luck rushed for a 61.5% DVOA in the red zone. Luck is not thought of as a running quarterback, perhaps because he lacks certain pigments, but he's every bit as talented at scrambling as Colin Kaepernick or Russell Wilson. (OK, we'll admit... he also isn't thought of as a running quarterback because the team doesn't want to expose him to injury on zone reads.)

In season three of *The Andrew Luck Show*, we're projecting the Colts to again return to the playoffs. However, because the team around him continues to be poor, there should be plenty of room for fourth-quarter suspense on a week-to-week basis. Only playing in the AFC South threatens to remove any of the dramatic tension.

Table 3: League Leaders in Red Zone Rushing DVOA, 2002-2013

Team	Year	Red Zone Rush DVOA	Red Zone Rush DVOA Y+1	Difference
2002	KC	63.0%	71.8%	8.8%
2003	KC	71.8%	22.5%	-49.3%
2004	ATL	33.0%	16.0%	-17.0%
2005	SEA	61.3%	10.0%	-51.3%
2006	SD	65.7%	37.3%	-28.4%
2007	MIN	59.6%	-8.6%	-68.2%
2008	CAR	56.2%	-17.9%	-74.1%
2009	ARI	40.4%	4.6%	-35.8%
2010	DET	38.6%	10.7%	-27.9%
2011	NYG	38.6%	25.2%	-13.4%
2012	WAS	38.3%	10.6%	-27.7%
2013	IND	56.0%	--	--
02-12 AVERAGE		*51.5%*	*16.6%*	*-34.9%*

But spectators do eventually tire of the same old, same old. There is only so much the Colts can wring from what is left of the Manning core. There is a cost for the producers of *The Andrew Luck Show* to stay married to the poor casting techniques they've used so far. Time is like a river, and repeating the same roster strategies Grigson has employed so far will lead Indianapolis directly back to 2011.

The emerging crisis point for this show, then, is how poor management will be corrected or punished. Grigson has been extraordinarily lucky thus far. His boss, Jim Irsay, has enough problems of his own to deal with, so oversight has been minimal. The star of the show has suspected nothing so far, mostly because he's so good that even a team of complete nobodies around him could win seven or eight games. But the Colts must construct a team worthy of changing the narrative around Luck before he comes to his senses and realizes that he can leave. That may be a ways off given Indianapolis' recent success and exclusive bargaining position, but if Grigson continues uncorrected, Luck may have no choice but to seek a show that's actually worthy of his talents.

The Colts simply have to create the correct roster around Luck to get a repeat of *The Peyton Manning Show*. Grigson's touch as general manager has instead given us a hi-def modernization of *The Archie Manning Show.*

Rivers McCown

2013 Colts Stats by Week

Wk	vs.	W-L	PF	PA	YDF	YDA	TO	Total	Off	Def	ST
1	OAK	W	21	17	274	372	+2	7%	18%	13%	2%
2	MIA	L	20	24	448	398	0	-3%	21%	19%	-6%
3	at SF	W	27	7	336	254	+2	56%	30%	-18%	8%
4	at JAC	W	37	3	437	205	+2	38%	-2%	-46%	-6%
5	SEA	W	34	28	317	423	0	39%	43%	-2%	-6%
6	at SD	L	9	19	267	374	-1	-4%	-15%	-1%	11%
7	DEN	W	39	33	334	429	+2	72%	16%	-34%	22%
8	BYE										
9	at HOU	W	27	24	314	483	0	-27%	16%	51%	7%
10	STL	L	8	38	406	372	-4	-105%	-56%	13%	-36%
11	at TEN	W	30	27	366	340	+1	-5%	31%	40%	4%
12	at ARI	L	11	40	239	410	-1	-51%	-26%	25%	1%
13	TEN	W	22	14	264	347	+3	-11%	-41%	-28%	2%
14	at CIN	L	28	42	389	430	0	3%	74%	51%	-20%
15	HOU	W	25	3	331	239	+1	39%	-25%	-54%	10%
16	at KC	W	23	7	367	287	+3	36%	15%	-20%	1%
17	JAC	W	30	10	379	350	+2	-8%	-13%	-1%	4%
18	KC	W	45	44	536	513	-3	19%	29%	13%	3%
19	at NE	L	22	43	386	419	-4	-48%	-32%	18%	1%

Trends and Splits

	Offense	Rank	Defense	Rank
Total DVOA	4.3%	13	0.9%	16
Unadjusted VOA	5.9%	11	-1.2%	16
Weighted Trend	-3.5%	20	1.9%	19
Variance	11.2%	29	10.5%	32
Average Opponent	-0.4%	15	-2.9%	27
Passing	8.3%	17	1.8%	13
Rushing	3.1%	11	-0.1%	22
First Down	5.4%	12	4.3%	20
Second Down	5.4%	13	3.3%	18
Third Down	0.5%	14	-8.9%	11
First Half	-2.0%	17	5.4%	24
Second Half	11.4%	7	-4.0%	14
Red Zone	12.8%	10	9.8%	20
Late and Close	21.0%	6	-18.0%	6

Five-Year Performance

Year	W-L	Pyth W	Est W	PF	PA	TO	Total	Rk	Off	Rk	Def	Rk	ST	Rk	Off AGL	Rk	Def AGL	Rk	Off Age	Rk	Def Age	Rk	ST Age	Rk
2009	14-2	10.9	11.1	416	307	+2	16.5%	8	16.8%	6	-0.8%	16	-1.1%	19	30.1	21	51.9	30	27.8	9	25.7	30	25.2	32
2010	10-6	9.2	8.2	435	388	-4	1.3%	16	13.1%	6	5.5%	24	-6.3%	31	42.5	30	48.1	31	28.0	8	26.4	23	25.4	31
2011	2-14	3.2	3.0	243	430	-12	-32.8%	31	-17.2%	27	9.3%	26	-6.2%	31	37.5	22	47.2	28	27.9	8	26.0	27	25.4	30
2012	11-5	7.2	6.2	357	387	-12	-16.0%	25	-2.9%	18	14.0%	31	0.9%	12	44.4	24	43.1	24	25.9	28	26.6	20	25.2	31
2013	11-5	9.4	9.5	391	336	+13	3.2%	13	4.3%	13	0.9%	16	-0.1%	18	76.4	30	33.9	21	25.8	31	27.7	4	26.0	20

2013 Performance Based on Most Common Personnel Groups

IND Offense					IND Offense vs. Opponents				IND Defense				IND Defense vs. Opponents			
Pers	Freq	Yds	DVOA	Run%	Pers	Freq	Yds	DVOA	Pers	Freq	Yds	DVOA	Pers	Freq	Yds	DVOA
11	50%	6.4	11.9%	18%	Nickel Even	36%	5.9	0.5%	3-4-4	45%	4.9	-2.6%	11	47%	6.4	1.0%
12	15%	4.2	-22.3%	41%	4-3-4	22%	5.7	13.2%	Nickel Even	30%	6.2	0.9%	12	23%	5.1	10.2%
21	11%	6.7	25.1%	44%	3-4-4	17%	4.9	-8.2%	Nickel Odd	14%	7.0	0.1%	21	16%	5.2	-7.8%
20	7%	5.4	5.3%	37%	Dime+	11%	6.3	20.8%	4-3-4	4%	6.8	35.9%	22	3%	5.1	2.9%
22	5%	5.6	12.7%	58%	Nickel Odd	10%	6.2	27.2%	Dime+	4%	5.4	-26.3%	13	3%	2.2	-34.7%
621	4%	4.0	6.4%	83%												

Strategic Tendencies

Run/Pass		Rk	Formation		Rk	Pass Rush		Rk	Secondary		Rk	Strategy		Rk
Runs, first half	29%	31	Form: Single Back	58%	27	Rush 3	5.4%	19	4 DB	49%	7	Play action	19%	22
Runs, first down	42%	27	Form: Empty Back	6%	17	Rush 4	62.2%	15	5 DB	44%	25	Avg Box (Off)	6.36	16
Runs, second-long	25%	28	Pers: 3+ WR	57%	15	Rush 5	23.6%	16	6+ DB	4%	19	Avg Box (Def)	6.39	16
Runs, power sit.	54%	15	Pers: 4+ WR	0%	28	Rush 6+	8.8%	12	CB by Sides	86%	7	Offensive Pace	28.50	7
Runs, behind 2H	19%	31	Pers: 2+ TE/6+ OL	33%	16	Sacks by LB	76.2%	1	DB Blitz	10%	21	Defensive Pace	29.78	16
Pass, ahead 2H	42%	26	Shotgun/Pistol	52%	23	Sacks by DB	2.4%	26	Hole in Zone	5%	31	Go for it on 4th	0.67	25

Despite the injury to Dwayne Allen, the Colts used two-tight end sets just as often as they did the year before. But Pep Hamilton brought in a big change in how many players were in the backfield, as the Colts went from using single-back formations on 76 percent of plays (fourth in 2012) to 58 percent (26th in 2013). And the Colts went from targeting running backs on a league-low 8.1 percent of passes in 2012 to targeting running backs on 19.0 percent of passes (12th in the league) in 2013. The Colts used at least six offensive linemen on 9.7 percent of plays, second only to Chicago. They were particularly successful when they used the extra lineman on a short-yardage run, converting 19 of 24 opportunities. Shades of the old Colts defense that was built to destroy quarterbacks once the Colts got the lead: the 2013 Colts had -10.8% defensive DVOA (sixth in NFL) when playing with a lead but 12.9% defensive DVOA (30th) when the game was tied or the Colts were behind. The Colts allowed just 3.4 yards per pass with a big blitz (six or more pass rushers).

Passing

Player	DYAR	DVOA	Plays	NtYds	Avg	YAC	C%	TD	Int
A.Luck	650	4.6%	606	3612	6.0	5.6	60.5%	23	9
M.Hasselbeck	-15	-28.6%	12	130	10.8	12.9	58.3%	0	1

Rushing

Player	DYAR	DVOA	Plays	Yds	Avg	TD	Fum	Suc
T.Richardson	-95	-22.8%	157	459	2.9	3	3	41%
D.Brown*	117	19.2%	101	533	5.3	6	0	54%
A.Luck	151	47.6%	48	392	8.2	4	1	-
A.Bradshaw	33	9.3%	41	186	4.5	2	0	54%
V.Ballard	22	34.3%	13	63	4.8	0	0	46%
T.Choice*	-2	-13.1%	11	44	4.0	0	0	27%
S.Havili	-21	-75.5%	7	7	1.0	0	0	29%
D.Herron	19	63.6%	5	33	6.6	0	0	60%

Receiving

Player	DYAR	DVOA	Plays	Ctch	Yds	Y/C	YAC	TD	C%
T.Y.Hilton	155	1.1%	140	84	1089	13.0	4.8	5	60%
D.Heyward-Bey*	-63	-24.5%	64	29	309	10.7	4.5	1	45%
R.Wayne	104	8.6%	59	39	508	13.0	4.6	2	66%
G.Whalen	32	-2.7%	40	24	259	10.8	5.0	2	60%
L.Brazill	-37	-30.2%	27	12	161	13.4	4.4	2	44%
D.Rogers	60	18.5%	23	14	192	13.7	8.4	2	61%
H.Nicks	*83*	*-2.4%*	*101*	*56*	*896*	*16.0*	*4.8*	*0*	*55%*
C.Fleener	-24	-11.3%	87	52	608	11.7	4.9	4	60%
W.Saunders	-17	-27.6%	11	4	46	11.5	3.3	0	36%
J.Doyle	-30	-67.9%	7	5	19	3.8	2.6	0	71%
T.Richardson	39	2.1%	41	28	265	9.5	9.1	1	68%
D.Brown*	44	6.2%	36	28	218	7.8	8.8	2	78%
S.Havili	32	11.4%	21	18	128	7.1	6.4	1	86%
A.Bradshaw	10	8.6%	8	7	42	6.0	5.6	0	88%

Offensive Line

Player	Pos	Age	GS	Snaps	Pen	Sk	Pass	Run
Gosder Cherilus	RT	30	16/16	1068	4	4.8	23.2	0.5
Anthony Castonzo	LT	26	16/16	1065	6	4.0	23.0	3.0
Mike McGlynn*	RG	29	15/14	887	2	3.0	29.7	3.5
Hugh Thornton	LG	23	14/12	868	2	5.3	21.2	8.0
Samson Satele*	C	30	13/13	820	2	0.0	9.3	3.0
Jeff Linkenbach*	G	27	11/4	385	1	1.5	5.5	1.5
Xavier Nixon	OT	24	4/1	152	0	1.0	3.3	3.0
Joe Reitz	G	29	13/3	146	0	0.0	2.0	0.0

Year	Yards	ALY	Rk	Power	Rk	Stuff	Rk	2nd Lev	Rk	Open Field	Rk	Sacks	ASR	Rk	Short	Long	F-Start	Cont.
2011	4.12	3.91	25	50%	30	20%	17	1.13	20	0.72	23	35	6.9%	18	17	8	19	22
2012	3.78	3.76	26	72%	2	25%	30	1.23	13	0.48	28	41	6.8%	17	8	17	10	22
2013	3.96	3.89	15	65%	15	18%	10	1.09	19	0.63	21	32	5.6%	6	12	9	8	29

2013 ALY by direction: Left End 3.33 (18) Left Tackle 4.94 (3) Mid/Guard 3.80 (21) Right Tackle 4.81 (2) Right End 2.98 (28)

Tackles Anthony Castonzo and Gosder Cherilus have similar resumes. They're both 6-foot-7. They were both selected in the bottom half of the first round out of Boston College. They've both proven capable of having good games at the NFL level. But the consistency isn't there. Another similarity: they both finished among the bottom 20 tackles in blown pass blocks last season. They'll both be here for a while. The Colts picked up Castonzo's fifth-year option over the offseason. Meanwhile, cutting Cherilus before 2016 would lead the Colts to take a salary cap hit. Both players have mildly improved since their futile early years, but complimenting either of them leads to reaching for synonyms of "they show up and play every day." Castonzo and Cherilus: they're as tangible as tackles can be.

There will be upheaval in the middle of the line. Indianapolis spent their second-round pick on Ohio State lineman Jack Mewhort. Mewhort played left tackle last year for the Buckeyes, but will likely move inside. Ryan Grigson compared Mewhort to Logan Mankins noting, "He's kind of a similar-type guy to me. You thought, he's probably not a left tackle but if you left him there, he would probably be a good, solid starter." Setting aside the idea that it's not smart to make fans expect Mewhort to turn into Mankins, it sounds like versatility was a calling card for Grigson. Hugh Thornton will be trying to build on a rough first season. Donald Thomas, who tore his quadriceps in Week 2 and missed the rest of the season, will also join the fray. Lance Louis is lurking at the bottom of the depth chart—so things could be worse. Assuming Thomas is healthy, he'll likely win one spot and the two youngsters will battle for the other. The guards can't help but be better than the Mike McGlynn-Thornton tandem was last season—they were first in the NFL in blown blocks per snap among right guards and left guards, respectively.

The Colts released Samson Satele after the season, so they did show some mercy for their fans. Center will fall into the hands of 2013 fourth-rounder Khaled Holmes. Holmes had 12 more snaps than you did last season. He is also the only real game in town after free-agent veteran Phil Costa signed with the Colts and then abruptly retired. Look for Indianapolis to send out feelers for an experienced center as training camp approaches.

Defensive Front Seven

			Overall								vs. Run					Pass Rush			
Defensive Line	Age	Pos	G	Snaps	Plays	TmPct	Rk	Stop	Dfts	BTkl	Runs	St%	Rk	RuYd	Rk	Sack	Hit	Hur	Tips
Cory Redding	34	DE	15	625	36	4.6%	54	28	15	3	27	74%	53	1.0	6	4.5	5	10.5	2
Fili Moala	29	DE	16	508	20	2.4%	83	16	5	2	15	73%	57	4.0	84	1.5	2	13.0	1
Ricardo Mathews*	27	DE	16	428	19	2.3%	84	12	3	0	17	59%	82	3.0	69	0.5	2	6.5	0
Ricky Jean-Francois	28	DE	10	393	20	3.9%	69	18	6	0	14	86%	13	1.9	33	2.5	2	6.8	2
Aubrayo Franklin*	34	DT	16	334	29	3.5%	--	20	1	0	27	67%	--	2.7	--	0.0	0	0.0	2
Josh Chapman	25	DT	13	237	15	2.2%	--	13	1	0	14	93%	--	1.6	--	0.0	0	2.0	0
Arthur Jones	*28*	*DE*	*14*	*521*	*53*	*7.3%*	*14*	*42*	*13*	*1*	*48*	*77%*	*45*	*2.4*	*52*	*4.5*	*3*	*9.5*	*0*

			Overall								vs. Run					Pass Rush			
Edge Rushers	Age	Pos	G	Snaps	Plays	TmPct	Rk	Stop	Dfts	BTkl	Runs	St%	Rk	RuYd	Rk	Sack	Hit	Hur	Tips
Erik Walden	29	OLB	15	843	48	6.2%	28	32	13	2	34	65%	62	3.6	66	3.0	6	23.8	1
Robert Mathis	33	OLB	16	841	59	7.1%	17	52	33	2	33	85%	15	1.7	16	19.5	7	33.3	2
Bjoern Werner	24	OLB	13	306	19	2.8%	--	17	9	3	10	90%	--	2.0	--	2.5	0	5.0	2

			Overall								Pass Rush			vs. Run					vs. Pass						
Linebackers	Age	Pos	G	Snaps	Plays	TmPct	Rk	Stop	Dfts	BTkl	Sack	Hit	Hur	Runs	St%	Rk	RuYd	Rk	Tgts	Suc%	Rk	AdjYd	Rk	PD	Int
Jerrell Freeman	28	ILB	16	958	132	15.9%	19	77	23	10	5.5	3	8	83	66%	38	4.0	66	45	45%	57	5.8	16	5	2
Pat Angerer*	27	ILB	11	493	65	11.4%	54	38	7	5	0.5	1	1	45	60%	57	3.4	47	29	66%	5	7.5	56	2	1
Kelvin Sheppard	26	ILB	15	333	43	5.5%	--	28	6	4	1.0	1	1	35	69%	--	2.5	--	9	42%	--	6.1	--	0	0
D'Qwell Jackson	*31*	*ILB*	*16*	*1147*	*148*	*17.2%*	*13*	*81*	*23*	*5*	*1.5*	*3*	*9.5*	*87*	*67%*	*35*	*3.2*	*29*	*36*	*54%*	*35*	*6.8*	*42*	*4*	*1*

Year	Yards	ALY	Rk	Power	Rk	Stuff	Rk	2nd Level	Rk	Open Field	Rk	Sacks	ASR	Rk	Short	Long
2011	4.36	4.41	27	65%	19	17%	24	1.27	22	0.70	11	29	6.8%	15	12	12
2012	5.10	4.32	27	64%	19	16%	30	1.15	10	1.49	32	32	5.8%	27	14	9
2013	4.25	4.30	28	53%	5	16%	26	1.18	24	0.58	14	42	7.6%	8	16	12
2013 ALY by direction:			*Left End 5.14 (32)*			*Left Tackle 3.79 (10)*			*Mid/Guard 4.14 (21)*			*Right Tackle 5.06 (31)*			*Right End 4.11 (23)*	

As noted earlier, Robert Mathis will regress in 2014, both because of aging and his four-game suspension for desire to procreate. But he won't be the problem with this unit. Opposite him is Erik Walden, a stopgap solution who has problems setting the edge. Walden managed a few more hurries than expected last year. We should note that 11 of those hurries were against Ryan Fitzpatrick, Case Keenum, and Russell Wilson without Russell Okung and Max Unger. The Colts were hoping that Bjoern Werner would push Walden for snaps, but that didn't happen in 2013. Werner is an odd fit at outside linebacker given that his work at defensive end in college was more on the strong side. There were questions about his burst coming out, and he did nothing to answer them in year one. He'll be the starter outside for those first four games, but likely reverts to the bench once Mathis returns.

The Colts reinforced the line with Arthur Jones, a multi-dimensional end who came over in free agency. Despite a virus that robbed him of 15 pounds before the season, Jones was still Baltimore's most effective lineman last year. If you follow the money, Indianapolis now has three 3-4 ends making more than $4 million: Jones, Ricky Jean-Francois, and Cory Redding. Expect Jones to see some time at nose tackle against lighter centers and in nickel sets. The regular nose tackle job will likely fall to Josh Chapman with Aubrayo Franklin walking in free agency. Chapman fell to the fifth round in the 2012 draft due to a torn ACL, but when healthy, he's a 350-pound boulder. Behind him is Montori Hughes, a third-rounder from the 2013 draft class who didn't play much last year. So, he was just like every other Colts draft pick from 2013, is what we're saying.

At inside linebacker, the Colts replaced Pat Angerer with D'Qwell Jackson. We hope that quelled whoever was angered. Handing Jackson $10 million in guarantees is an odd move for a team that had more glaring weaknesses, but at least the Colts can release him without repercussions after 2015. Jerrell Freeman, a decent inside linebacker, finished second on the team in sacks in 2013. That says more about Chuck Pagano's ability to create pressure—and the lack of edge rusher talent on the roster—than it does about Freeman.

Defensive Secondary

			Overall								vs. Run					vs. Pass									
Secondary	Age	Pos	G	Snaps	Plays	TmPct	Rk	Stop	Dfts	BTkl	Runs	St%	Rk	RuYd	Rk	Tgts	Tgt%	Rk	Dist	Suc%	Rk	AdjYd	Rk	PD	Int
Antoine Bethea*	30	FS	16	1028	116	14.0%	5	40	19	6	65	40%	37	7.5	50	30	7.1%	25	13.3	41%	72	13.2	76	5	2
Vontae Davis	26	CB	16	930	58	7.0%	62	29	7	2	13	38%	48	7.2	44	76	19.9%	30	13.6	62%	7	7.1	33	12	1
LaRon Landry	30	SS	12	787	88	14.1%	4	23	5	6	47	30%	63	6.9	38	27	8.2%	43	8.6	41%	71	6.9	40	2	0
Darius Butler	28	CB	16	693	67	8.1%	49	33	16	4	13	31%	63	7.5	50	70	24.6%	71	10.6	52%	49	8.0	56	13	4
Greg Toler	29	CB	9	437	30	6.4%	--	10	2	3	8	25%	--	8.0	--	39	21.4%	--	13.0	54%	--	6.0	--	6	1
Cassius Vaughn*	27	CB	16	404	34	4.1%	--	11	5	1	8	38%	--	5.8	--	38	22.6%	--	13.7	48%	--	9.8	--	6	3

Year	Pass D Rank	vs. #1 WR	Rk	vs. #2 WR	Rk	vs. Other WR	Rk	vs. TE	Rk	vs. RB	Rk
2011	28	26.2%	26	25.3%	27	33.7%	32	19.6%	22	-2.5%	17
2012	27	11.0%	22	3.0%	17	28.5%	31	22.2%	30	-22.3%	6
2013	13	-6.5%	14	7.6%	19	13.4%	26	17.7%	26	-0.9%	15

The Colts did what they had to do in re-signing Vontae Davis. He's proven himself capable of big things, both good and bad, in his two seasons in Indianapolis. Davis was undeniably good in 2013, justifying years of scouting hype despite playing through a groin injury. (This injury thing, you might hear about it again soon.)

Indianapolis' other projected starter at corner is Greg Toler. Toler led the NFL in circular finger-spins around the earhole of his helmet after incomplete passes at his assignment. Yes, the NFL competition committee does want to cast him down into the core of the Earth. How did you know? Toler is an adequate corner when on the field, but spent more than half of the season rehabbing his own groin injury that never healed. He had offseason sports hernia surgery, and still hasn't returned to practice as we go to press. Nickelback Darius Butler plays some terrific games (Sunday Night Football against the Broncos in Week 7, where his aggressive slot play helped slow Denver). He also plays some awful ones (Andy Dalton went 5-for-5 for 74 yards and a DPI targeting him).

Ryan Grigson brought on LaRon Landry last season to provide toughness and tackling. He did neither. He also (surprise!) missed time with a high-ankle sprain and concussion. Landry plays safety like your kid brother plays video games. Sometimes all that button-mashing works, and you're surprised. More often, he's just flailing around and getting little out of maximum effort. Antoine Bethea had started 16 games for the Colts in each of the past six years. They let him go since that didn't fit the theme of this secondary. Grigson failed to sign, draft, or trade for a replacement of any notable worth. He did do the absolute bare minimum by signing 33-year-old Mike Adams after the draft. Behind Adams is an untested field of Delano Howell, Corey Lynch, and Sergio Brown. Howell is the most likely candidate to challenge Adams for the starting job going into training camp. The winner of this battle would be the good quarterbacks playing for Indy's three AFC South rivals, except there aren't any.

Special Teams

Year	DVOA	Rank	FG/XP	Rank	Net Kick	Rank	Kick Ret	Rank	Net Punt	Rank	Punt Ret	Rank	Hidden	Rank
2011	-6.2%	31	-0.1	16	-2.8	25	-9.1	32	-10.9	30	-8.3	28	-5.8	24
2012	0.9%	12	-3.1	22	4.4	9	0.1	15	-2.4	19	5.3	6	1.4	14
2013	-0.1%	18	2.9	12	4.4	9	-3.3	21	-3.9	26	-0.6	16	6.2	7

Punters and kickers aren't worth the franchise tag. There are so many plausible replacements that it's silly to waste bargaining position on a specialist. That said, if one punter is worth the tag, it's Pat McAfee. McAfee handles kickoffs for the Colts, which means Indianapolis gets more out of his leg than most teams do of their punters. After playing out 2013 under the franchise tender, McAfee landed a five-year, $14 million contract. It's a fair deal as long as he continues to handle both roles. Adam Vinatieri, who you've heard plenty about at this point, handles field goals and extra points. Jeff Feagles was the last Tecmo Super Bowl player to hang 'em up. Vinatieri has a shot to be the last player mentioned in the first *Pro Football Prospectus* to do the same.

Kick returns were a bit of an adventure for Indianapolis last season. David Reed's insistence on returning every kickoff he could was his undoing. (Nine times, Reed took the ball at least five yards into the end zone and eschewed a touchback, but he never made it past the 22-yard line.) Replacement Chris Rainey got hurt after just a few games. Cassius Vaughn and LaVon Brazill had small cameos. Griff Whalen returned the last kickoff chance in the playoffs. Brazill's year-long substance abuse policy suspension got him released, as he does not own the Colts, so Whalen should be the top in-house candidate for the role in 2014. T.Y. Hilton returned punts, and did a decent job of it. But Hilton has become enough of a focal point for the offense that Indianapolis would likely prefer someone else do that job.

Jacksonville Jaguars

2013 Record: 4-12	**Total DVOA:** -38.2% (32nd)	**2014 Mean Projection:** 6.3 wins	**On the Clock (0-4):** 23%
Pythagorean Wins: 3.1 (32nd)	**Offense:** -29.8% (32nd)	**Postseason Odds:** 15.1%	**Mediocrity (5-7):** 50%
Snap-Weighted Age: 26.1 (27th)	**Defense:** 10.9% (28th)	**Super Bowl Odds:** 0.5%	**Playoff Contender (8-10):** 22%
Average Opponent: 0.5% (14th)	**Special Teams:** 2.5% (9th)	**Proj. Avg. Opponent:** -3.4% (28th)	**Super Bowl Contender (11+):** 5%

2013: I could be your flower, rise up in the dirt.

2014: Started from the bottom, now we're here... which is still very close to the bottom.

The gospel of tanking continues to spread throughout the world of sports. The Houston Astros have tanked their way into three straight No. 1 overall picks. The Philadelphia 76ers are tanking so hard that they're intentionally drafting players that are injured or can be stashed overseas, so as to spare the production they might get next year. Better draft picks and saving money; what's not to like?

The 2013 Jacksonville Jaguars weren't quite tanking to the extent of those clubs—an NFL roster isn't quite as top-heavy as it is in MLB or the NBA. But it wouldn't be disingenuous to call the first month of Jacksonville's 2013 season an extended tryout camp. The Jaguars broke camp with 12 street or undrafted free agents who had barely sniffed an NFL roster, 12 players who had been claimed off waivers in the last calendar year, one player who'd been signed off another team's practice squad, and four late-round picks of their own. Those players were supplemented not by a successful roster core, but by the failings of the Gene Smith administration: Blaine Gabbert, Tyson Alualu, Will Rackley, Chris Prosinski, and the enormous contracts of Marcedes Lewis, Jeremy Mincey, and Paul Posluszny. The only players Jacksonville had at the start of the year that had proven themselves deserving of a big contract were fading franchise back Maurice Jones-Drew and solid left tackle Eugene Monroe. Smith had so devastated the roster that it was akin to an expansion team. A completely new coaching staff led by Gus Bradley was left to pick up the pieces.

It showed quickly.

After four weeks, Jacksonville was the worst team DVOA had ever tracked to that point in a season (Table 1). It was mostly weighed down by a startlingly inept offense—another DVOA-era worst through four games—led by Gabbert, who DVOA believes is the worst quarterback of the past thirty years. (You'll find the grisly details on that in the quarterback player comments.)

At that point, it seemed like things would get worse before they got better. Jacksonville's rookies were struggling. A trade that sent Monroe to the Ravens for fourth- and fifth-round picks was finalized before Jacksonville played its fifth game. Second overall pick Luke Joeckel would break his leg in Week 5, leaving Jacksonville with nothing but UDFA protection for their quarterbacks. After Week 4, our playoff odds generator gave the Jaguars a better than two-thirds chance to wind up with the No. 1 pick. Jacksonville became the stand-in for every "Could Alabama beat the worst team in the NFL?" argument.

The Jaguars fell to 0-8 after a 42-10 trouncing at the hands of the 49ers in London, but a tough schedule masked some underlying improvement. Six of Jacksonville's first eight games were against playoff teams, and the only one of these opponents to finish the season lower than 14th in DVOA was Oakland. Faced with the largest point spread in NFL history, getting 28 points at Denver in Week 6, the Jaguars covered easily.

After their Week 9 bye, things started going right. Jacksonville reeled off wins in four of five games, and only two of their remaining four losses were by multiple touchdowns. Jacksonville's turnaround formula boiled down to two things: time and scouting.

The first step towards improvement came when Gus Bradley figured out who *not* to play. With Gabbert deposed after a Week 5 hamstring injury, journeyman backup quarterback Chad Henne took the helm. The Jaguars finished dead last in the NFL in passing DVOA, but the two games where Gabbert took the majority of the snaps are the abominations that weigh that rating down. The Jaguars averaged a pass DVOA of -106.9% in those two games, a 28-2 loss to Kansas City in Week 1 and a 37-3 loss to Indianapolis in Week 4. Jacksonville's offense improved to merely bad—their passing DVOA scoots up to 26th if you remove the games with Gabbert, despite one of the most abominable offensive lines in recent

Table 1. Worst DVOA through Four Games, 1989-2013

WORST TOTAL DVOA			WORST OFFENSIVE DVOA		
Year	Team	DVOA	Year	Team	DVOA
2013	**JAC**	**-83.8%**	**2013**	**JAC**	**-67.1%**
2001	WAS	-71.6%	2002	HOU	-61.5%
2008	DET	-69.8%	2004	MIA	-60.4%
2008	STL	-65.1%	2001	WAS	-56.5%
1989	DAL	-64.2%	2009	OAK	-45.1%
2002	CIN	-60.3%	2007	CHI	-44.8%
2000	CIN	-59.6%	1999	PHI	-41.8%
1999	CLE	-57.4%	2005	MIN	-40.2%
1999	CIN	-57.0%	2002	CIN	-40.2%
2005	HOU	-55.1%	1999	ARI	-39.7%
2006	TEN	-54.0%	1996	STL	-39.1%
2006	HOU	-54.0%	2006	OAK	-39.0%

2014 Jaguars Schedule

Week	Opp.	Week	Opp.	Week	Opp.
1	at PHI	7	CLE	13	NYG
2	at WAS	8	MIA	14	HOU
3	IND	9	at CIN	15	at BAL
4	at SD	10	DAL (U.K.)	16	TEN (Thu.)
5	PIT	11	BYE	17	at HOU
6	at TEN	12	at IND		

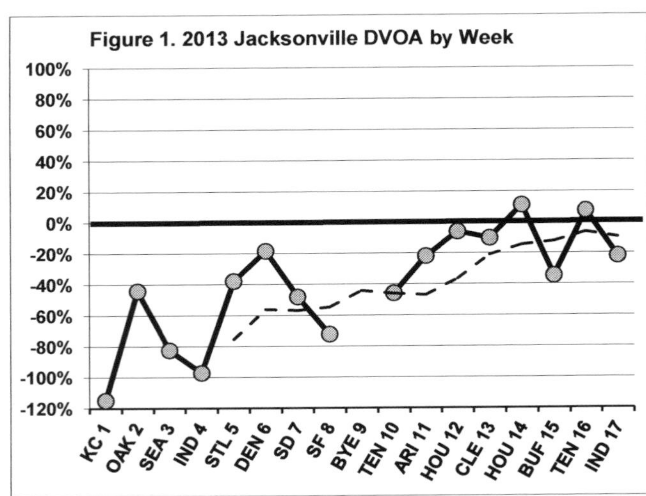

Figure 1. 2013 Jacksonville DVOA by Week

memory. The only thing that kept people from talking about the horrific Jaguars line is that the defending Super Bowl champion Ravens were getting line play that was equally horrific. Our Adjusted Line Yards stat, which measures the impact an offensive line has on its run game, had Jacksonville with the fourth-lowest average since 1996 (Table 2). Not that a physically limited Maurice Jones-Drew was any great shakes on the rare occasions he actually found the open field, but the impotent blocking ruined Bradley's plan to establish a power running game.

Table 2. Worst Adjusted Line Yards, 1996-2013

Team	Year	ALY
2012	ARI	2.93
2013	**BAL**	**3.01**
2002	HOU	3.04
2013	**JAC**	**3.13**
2001	CLE	3.17
1999	DET	3.18
1998	NO	3.25
2013	**NYG**	**3.27**
1997	OAK	3.27
2005	ARI	3.28

Bradley earned his chops as a defensive coordinator, and the changes he made on defense paid dividends faster than those he made on offense. Moves like scooping up Alan Ball and Sen'Derrick Marks were single-engine planes on the radar of the NFL, but these are the kinds of players that held the defense together until the rookies had enough experience under their belts to contribute on their own.

Cornerback Dwayne Gratz epitomizes Jacksonville's growth on defense. A third-round pick out of Connecticut, Gratz saw his snaps siphoned off to Mike Harris and Demetrius McCray after Week 1 until he was brought back for the Week 7 San Diego game. Gratz took his lumps from receivers like Josh Gordon and Andre Johnson once he was re-inserted into the lineup, but when you look at the big picture, you start to think Jacksonville might have something here. Gratz is the sort of tough, physical corner that fits the Seahawks' model. Now he's one of the building blocks for a defense that is trying to become them. With more time on the field, second-round safety Jonathan Cyprien began to grow after appearing totally overmatched early in the season, and second-year defensive end Andre Branch started to show more than mere hints of his ability as a pass rusher.

The Jaguars improved their defensive DVOA from 19.4% in Weeks 1-to-9 to 3.1% in Weeks 10-to-17. Our past studies on second-half improvements show the exact opposite of what you'd expect—that the narrative often means very little going forward. But in eight games of football, sometimes you'll find improvement governed almost exclusively by small sample sizes and fluke turnover rates. Jacksonville's defense has a youth movement that matches the narrative that such a leap is supposed to mean. That doesn't mean regression isn't possible, but it does seem less likely given the results can be traced to young players playing better rather than fluky strong performance from veterans.

To take another phrase you'll often hear from tanking teams, the Jaguars are currently in "asset accumulation" mode. To that end, they spent this spring finding more players like Marks and Ball—young veterans who may have some upside if properly utilized. Thus, former Pittsburgh 3-4 defensive end Ziggy Hood will get pushed inside and asked to penetrate. Second-string Minnesota runner Toby Gerhart, who has been kept remarkably fresh behind Adrian Peterson, will be given a shot as a three-down starting back. Dekoda Watson, a linebacker who has played fewer than 400 defensive snaps for Tampa Bay over the past two years, will be given a chance to win a starting job. If these moves don't pan out, they cost Jacksonville little. If the players prove to be good fits for their roles, Jacksonville takes one more step away from the Gene Smith era.

The most important assets that Jacksonville acquired this year, though, were their first- and second-round picks. The Jaguars were quick to understand that the lack of talent in their passing game needed to be addressed. They selected Central Florida quarterback Blake Bortles with the third overall pick, then added USC receiver Marqise Lee and Penn State wideout Allen Robinson in the second round.

Jacksonville's front office doesn't seem to always find the best value out there. For instance, it seems likely that Monroe could have fetched more than fourth- and fifth-round picks given the lucrative market he had in the offseason. But credit general manager Dave Caldwell for his convictions. He didn't even entertain a lucrative offer to trade down from the Buffalo

Bills, because he was certain that Bortles was the next Jaguars quarterback of the future. When the Jaguars believe they've got their man, they go get him.

Both our scouting and analytical wings are mixed on Bortles' potential. Our Long-Term Career Forecast quarterback projection system rated Bortles as a middle-of-the-pack quarterback—not a guy it was in love with, but someone who it expected to be productive (Table 3). The LCF score it comes up with is based on a three-year passing DYAR score in the player's prime. 353 DYAR per season would project him to be a little better than Alex Smith was last season, around the fringes of Flaccodom.

Table 3. LCF Forecast, 2014 Quarterbacks

Player	Team	Rnd	Pick	Projection
Jimmy Garoppolo	NE	2	62	1,530 DYAR
Teddy Bridgewater	MIN	1	32	1,411 DYAR
Derek Carr	OAK	2	36	1,223 DYAR
Blake Bortles	JAC	1	3	1,059 DYAR
Johnny Manziel	CLE	1	21	983 DYAR

Matt Waldman, who writes a weekly college scouting column for our site and also releases the *Rookie Scouting Portfolio* looking at skill position players every year before the draft, doesn't have Bortles on the same career trajectory as Teddy Bridgewater or Johnny Manziel. Waldman loved both of those players though, so that's no slight to Bortles, who he says is stylistically a mix of Ben Roethlisberger and Matt Hasselbeck. "Bortles has neither the freakish arm nor the mastery of reading defenses that the NFL seeks from a top-flight prospect. He's good enough in all three departments to become a starter, but unless one of these components of his game improves his upside is limited," quoth the 2014 *RSP*.

The Jaguars believe that a quarterback with Bortles' strong physical tools can be molded into something more than he was at Central Florida. To that end, they've adamantly insisted to reporters that Bortles will be learning on the bench in his rookie season. As hard as it can be to scout quarterbacks, it's even harder to do any sort of study that tries to figure out whether it's better for a quarterback to play immediately or to learn from the bench. We've tried to do this study numerous times, and the results are always inconclusive. Your mind may instinctively think of the success stories like Aaron Rodgers, Philip Rivers, and Carson Palmer. But did it remember Brady Quinn, Tim Tebow, or Jake Locker? And just how much of each success or failure is related to pure talent versus the player development staff?

It's very easy to become cynical about the Jaguars. There's the London angle, the tarp-covered sections at EverBank Field, and the fact that they haven't made the playoffs since 2007. Even Stephen Colbert bags on them. But there's something not to be overlooked while they're on the path back to relevance: while the players Jacksonville picks may or may not pan out, they've got the strongest vision of any franchise in the division. They're the ones spinning players like Marks into gold while the Colts, Texans, and Titans struggle to find low-cost contributors. As the dwindling remainder of Smith's roster is jettisoned, this will only become more pronounced.

This is the only team in the AFC South that acts like it understands the importance of depth. That doesn't do them much good today. But it will in the future.

Rivers McCown

2013 Jaguars Stats by Week

Wk	vs.	W-L	PF	PA	YDF	YDA	TO	Total	Off	Def	ST
1	KC	L	2	28	178	292	-2	-115%	-93%	16%	-6%
2	at OAK	L	9	19	248	340	1	-44%	-41%	1%	-3%
3	at SEA	L	17	45	265	479	-1	-83%	-41%	39%	-3%
4	IND	L	3	37	205	437	-2	-97%	-91%	10%	3%
5	at STL	L	20	34	363	351	-3	-38%	-22%	15%	-1%
6	at DEN	L	19	35	362	407	1	-18%	-21%	-7%	-5%
7	SD	L	6	24	353	434	-1	-48%	-20%	31%	2%
8	vs. SF	L	10	42	318	398	0	-72%	-22%	54%	5%
9	BYE										
10	at TEN	W	29	27	214	362	2	-46%	-58%	0%	11%
11	ARI	L	14	27	274	416	-2	-22%	-27%	12%	17%
12	at HOU	W	13	6	333	218	1	-6%	-21%	-24%	-9%
13	at CLE	W	32	28	314	439	2	-10%	-4%	14%	8%
14	HOU	W	27	20	281	406	2	11%	14%	6%	3%
15	BUF	L	20	27	354	366	-2	-35%	-15%	22%	2%
16	TEN	L	16	20	289	346	0	7%	-4%	-5%	6%
17	at IND	L	10	30	350	379	-2	-22%	-34%	-2%	11%

Trends and Splits

	Offense	Rank	Defense	Rank
Total DVOA	-29.8%	32	10.9%	28
Unadjusted VOA	-29.7%	32	11.5%	27
Weighted Trend	-19.9%	29	7.4%	22
Variance	8.4%	23	3.6%	5
Average Opponent	-1.4%	12	-0.2%	13
Passing	-24.2%	32	20.1%	26
Rushing	-27.1%	31	1.1%	24
First Down	-28.1%	32	15.9%	31
Second Down	-28.2%	31	12.2%	29
Third Down	-34.9%	32	-0.3%	18
First Half	-29.2%	31	7.7%	26
Second Half	-30.4%	31	14.9%	27
Red Zone	-44.4%	32	29.0%	29
Late and Close	-17.1%	26	10.7%	25

Five-Year Performance

Year	W-L	Pyth W	Est W	PF	PA	TO	Total	Rk	Off	Rk	Def	Rk	ST	Rk	Off AGL	Rk	Def AGL	Rk	Off Age	Rk	Def Age	Rk	ST Age	Rk
2009	7-9	5.5	7.0	290	380	+2	-9.3%	23	3.8%	17	11.3%	28	-1.8%	25	4.5	2	43.5	28	26.9	22	25.5	31	25.5	29
2010	8-8	6.3	6.5	353	419	-15	-9.0%	22	3.9%	14	17.7%	32	4.8%	7	19.7	9	17.8	11	27.2	20	25.8	29	26.0	22
2011	5-11	5.3	5.5	243	329	+5	-17.4%	27	-26.5%	31	-11.3%	5	-2.2%	26	20.5	10	52.8	29	26.2	28	26.9	18	26.5	8
2012	2-14	3.3	2.7	255	444	-3	-33.0%	31	-18.4%	28	11.7%	28	-3.0%	25	63.7	30	36.2	22	26.5	20	27.0	14	25.8	23
2013	4-12	3.1	3.2	247	449	-6	-38.2%	32	-29.8%	32	10.9%	28	2.5%	9	48.0	23	28.9	15	26.6	20	26.2	23	24.7	32

2013 Performance Based on Most Common Personnel Groups

JAC Offense					JAC Offense vs. Opponents				JAC Defense				JAC Defense vs. Opponents			
Pers	Freq	Yds	DVOA	Run%	Pers	Freq	Yds	DVOA	Pers	Freq	Yds	DVOA	Pers	Freq	Yds	DVOA
11	53%	5.0	-17.9%	21%	Nickel Even	36%	4.8	-17.4%	4-3-4	54%	5.6	8.8%	11	39%	6.1	14.3%
21	18%	4.0	-31.0%	62%	3-4-4	27%	4.3	-30.7%	Nickel Even	38%	6.4	16.5%	12	24%	5.6	3.4%
12	13%	5.4	-29.2%	44%	Dime+	16%	4.9	-44.6%	Nickel Odd	2%	2.7	-61.0%	21	14%	6.7	31.1%
22	5%	2.0	-58.5%	45%	4-3-4	13%	4.6	-27.1%	3-4-4	2%	6.5	20.2%	22	8%	4.7	0.3%
20	5%	4.6	-33.0%	44%	Nickel Odd	6%	4.8	-11.6%	Dime+	2%	3.9	-20.6%	13	3%	3.9	-6.2%
									Goal Line	2%	1.0	25.8%	02	3%	7.3	12.2%

Strategic Tendencies

Run/Pass		Rk	Formation		Rk	Pass Rush		Rk	Secondary		Rk	Strategy		Rk
Runs, first half	38%	18	Form: Single Back	63%	20	Rush 3	7.9%	7	4 DB	56%	2	Play action	25%	11
Runs, first down	40%	32	Form: Empty Back	7%	12	Rush 4	73.6%	2	5 DB	40%	26	Avg Box (Off)	6.33	19
Runs, second-long	37%	10	Pers: 3+ WR	61%	10	Rush 5	14.3%	31	6+ DB	2%	25	Avg Box (Def)	6.52	3
Runs, power sit.	58%	12	Pers: 4+ WR	2%	9	Rush 6+	4.2%	29	CB by Sides	91%	4	Offensive Pace	28.37	6
Runs, behind 2H	28%	13	Pers: 2+ TE/6+ OL	21%	28	Sacks by LB	16.1%	24	DB Blitz	6%	27	Defensive Pace	28.51	3
Pass, ahead 2H	53%	8	Shotgun/Pistol	62%	12	Sacks by DB	9.7%	14	Hole in Zone	13%	7	Go for it on 4th	1.31	6

The Jaguars were even more horrible than usual when they went without a tight end, which they did on 7.3 percent of plays. They gained just 4.5 yards per play and had -40.1% DVOA. They were also awful when they went empty backfield, with just 4.2 yards per play and -62.5% DVOA. (At least that was better than the year before, when they had 3.1 yards per play and -71.3% DVOA from an empty backfield.) Offensive coordinator Jedd Fisch loves screen passes. The Jaguars used wide receiver screens more than any team except Pittsburgh, and they were also in the top ten for running back screens. The wide receiver screens went well, with 5.6 yards per pass and 27.5% DVOA. The running back screens didn't go quite as well, with just 3.4 yards per pass and -23.1% DVOA. One bright spot: Jacksonville cut down dropped passes from a league-leading 7.9 percent of passes in 2012 to 5.0 percent (slightly more than average) in 2013. The Jaguars used play action on 37 percent of first-down pass plays, eighth in the NFL, even though they ran on first down less often than any other team. The Jaguars used just three pass rushers more than twice as often as they had the year before.

Passing

Player	DYAR	DVOA	Plays	NtYds	Avg	YAC	C%	TD	Int
C.Henne	-94	-13.9%	541	2972	5.5	5.9	61.0%	13	14
B.Gabbert*	-429	-84.1%	98	410	4.2	6.6	48.8%	1	7

Rushing

Player	DYAR	DVOA	Plays	Yds	Avg	TD	Fum	Suc
M.Jones-Drew*	-49	-13.6%	234	803	3.4	5	1	37%
J.Todman	13	-4.2%	76	256	3.4	2	0	37%
C.Henne	-37	-39.9%	22	80	3.6	0	0	-
D.Robinson	-61	-86.1%	20	64	3.2	0	3	35%
B.Gabbert*	-8	-29.2%	9	32	3.6	0	0	-
J.Forsett*	7	20.8%	6	31	5.2	0	0	33%
T.Gerhart	*105*	*73.6%*	*36*	*283*	*7.9*	*2*	*1*	*50%*

Receiving

Player	DYAR	DVOA	Plays	Ctch	Yds	Y/C	YAC	TD	C%
C.Shorts	-36	-16.3%	125	66	777	11.8	4.2	3	53%
A.Sanders	-99	-28.0%	86	51	484	9.5	5.8	1	59%
M.Brown	27	-6.6%	56	32	447	14.0	4.8	2	57%
J.Blackmon	33	-4.2%	48	29	415	14.3	7.6	1	60%
K.Taylor	17	-5.3%	30	19	189	9.9	4.3	1	63%
S.Burton	-1	-13.2%	13	8	76	9.5	4.4	0	62%
J.Ebert	-43	-90.4%	8	3	18	6.0	2.0	0	38%
T.Doss	*17*	*-6.6%*	*36*	*19*	*305*	*16.1*	*4.5*	*0*	*53%*
M.Lewis	-3	-8.1%	47	25	359	14.4	9.0	4	53%
C.Harbor*	18	0.4%	35	24	292	12.2	5.3	2	69%
A.Reisner	-22	-48.4%	9	5	40	8.0	2.0	0	56%
M.Jones-Drew*	32	-3.7%	60	43	314	7.3	7.7	0	72%
J.Todman	2	-12.6%	26	14	116	8.3	6.9	1	54%
J.Forsett*	-11	-28.0%	16	15	82	5.5	7.2	0	94%
W.Ta'ufo'ou	-33	-50.0%	15	10	40	4.0	3.7	0	67%
T.Gerhart	*22*	*10.7%*	*19*	*13*	*88*	*6.8*	*6.4*	*0*	*68%*

Offensive Line

Player	Pos	Age	GS	Snaps	Pen	Sk	Pass	Run	Player	Pos	Age	GS	Snaps	Pen	Sk	Pass	Run
Brad Meester*	C	37	16/16	1056	5	3.5	9.0	5.5	Luke Joeckel	RT	23	5/5	272	2	2.0	11.5	3.0
Uche Nwaneri*	RG	30	16/16	1056	4	2.5	11.5	6.0	Michael Brewster	C	25	14/3	225	0	1.0	3.0	2.0
Cameron Bradfield	LT	27	15/11	793	5	7.0	25.0	2.5	Jacques McClendon	G	27	5/2	186	2	0.0	0.0	1.0
Austin Pasztor	RT	24	15/12	790	3	5.5	11.5	2.0	*Zane Beadles*	*LG*	*28*	*16/16*	*1198*	*4*	*1.0*	*20.8*	*4.0*
Will Rackley*	LG	25	11/11	647	6	5.5	13.0	5.0									

Year	Yards	ALY	Rk	Power	Rk	Stuff	Rk	2nd Lev	Rk	Open Field	Rk	Sacks	ASR	Rk	Short	Long	F-Start	Cont.
2011	4.28	4.14	13	64%	13	17%	8	1.19	16	0.76	20	44	8.9%	26	12	19	10	31
2012	3.89	4.05	17	61%	20	19%	15	1.01	28	0.58	23	50	7.8%	22	17	13	16	25
2013	3.43	3.13	31	58%	24	25%	30	0.93	30	0.59	24	50	7.9%	24	23	9	16	30

2013 ALY by direction: Left End 2.24 (29) Left Tackle 2.04 (32) Mid/Guard 3.40 (31) Right Tackle 3.67 (19) Right End 3.22 (25)

Looking back at last year's offensive line is fairly irrelevant. Of the five players that took the most snaps in 2013, only Austin Pastzor is a projected starter in 2014. So let's trade our jokes about how old Brad Meester is for jokes about Brad Meester's camouflage jacket and move on.

At left tackle, the Jaguars are hoping Luke Joeckel's opening salvo was a small sample-size fluke caused by playing out of position on the right side, some good defenses, and Blaine Gabbert. Among linemen with 250 or more snaps, only Levi Brown blew more blocks per snap. Pastzor had a good rookie season for the Jaguars, and Cameron Bradfield is a credible candidate to be a swing tackle, though he's stretched as a starter. Former Ohio State UDFA Mike Brewster is first in line at center. The former Rimington Trophy award winner has played poorly at guard, mostly because of a lack of functional strength. Even if he's a liability, Meester's last season wasn't much to live up to.

Jacksonville extended a five-year, $30 million contract to former Peyton Manning protector Zane Beadles. Beadles led the Denver line in blown pass blocks, but was much more effective in 2012. Considering how far Uche Nwaneri fell last season, Beadles should be a huge upgrade. Waiver claim Jacques McClendon and rookie third-rounder Brandon Linder (Miami) are the combatants for the other guard spot. The Jaguars almost can't help but improve given how poorly they played last season, but you can raise legitimate questions about every lineman they plan to start. Regression will only take them up so far.

Defensive Front Seven

			Overall								vs. Run					Pass Rush			
Defensive Line	Age	Pos	G	Snaps	Plays	TmPct	Rk	Stop	Dfts	BTkl	Runs	St%	Rk	RuYd	Rk	Sack	Hit	Hur	Tips
Sen'Derrick Marks	27	DT	16	931	41	4.7%	49	35	17	2	25	84%	20	1.7	29	4.0	8	18.0	8
Roy Miller	27	DT	14	575	24	3.2%	78	19	5	0	23	78%	39	1.3	9	0.0	3	5.0	0
Brandon Deaderick*	27	DT	13	301	10	1.4%	--	6	1	0	8	50%	--	4.1	--	0.5	0	1.0	1
Ziggy Hood	*27*	*DE*	*16*	*633*	*39*	*4.9%*	*46*	*32*	*6*	*2*	*30*	*80%*	*34*	*2.6*	*59*	*3.0*	*1*	*4.5*	*0*

			Overall								vs. Run					Pass Rush			
Edge Rushers	Age	Pos	G	Snaps	Plays	TmPct	Rk	Stop	Dfts	BTkl	Runs	St%	Rk	RuYd	Rk	Sack	Hit	Hur	Tips
Jason Babin*	34	DE	16	764	40	4.6%	57	28	16	3	27	63%	68	2.7	50	7.5	17	21.0	0
Tyson Alualu	27	DE	16	744	44	5.1%	47	30	8	2	40	68%	58	2.4	37	1.5	8	8.5	1
Andre Branch	25	DE	16	592	40	4.6%	57	29	12	1	26	69%	55	3.8	73	6.0	3	10.5	2
Chris Clemons	*33*	*DE*	*14*	*570*	*25*	*3.6%*	*72*	*14*	*8*	*3*	*17*	*41%*	*79*	*3.8*	*72*	*4.5*	*6*	*23.0*	*3*
Red Bryant	*30*	*DE*	*15*	*481*	*30*	*4.0%*	*68*	*26*	*6*	*3*	*26*	*85%*	*16*	*2.0*	*23*	*1.5*	*2*	*11.5*	*1*

			Overall								Pass Rush			vs. Run					vs. Pass						
Linebackers	Age	Pos	G	Snaps	Plays	TmPct	Rk	Stop	Dfts	BTkl	Sack	Hit	Hur	Runs	St%	Rk	RuYd	Rk	Tgts	Suc%	Rk	AdjYd	Rk	PD	Int
Paul Posluszny	30	MLB	15	1037	170	21.0%	2	94	26	5	3.0	4	9	96	70%	23	3.3	38	52	43%	58	8.0	62	8	2
Geno Hayes	27	OLB	14	920	80	10.6%	58	39	13	8	1.0	1	5	41	59%	64	3.3	37	38	53%	36	5.7	15	5	2
Russell Allen*	28	OLB	14	596	63	8.3%	66	33	9	5	1.0	0	3	37	65%	46	3.3	41	16	32%	71	8.5	64	0	0
Dekoda Watson	*26*	*OLB*	*15*	*258*	*37*	*4.8%*	*--*	*21*	*8*	*1*	*2.0*	*3*	*4.5*	*22*	*68%*	*--*	*3.7*	*--*	*10*	*48%*	*--*	*6.3*	*--*	*1*	*1*

Year	Yards	ALY	Rk	Power	Rk	Stuff	Rk	2nd Level	Rk	Open Field	Rk	Sacks	ASR	Rk	Short	Long
2011	3.94	3.82	6	68%	26	21%	10	1.03	3	0.77	16	31	7.2%	13	13	12
2012	4.16	4.31	26	69%	26	18%	20	1.14	9	0.67	10	20	4.0%	32	6	10
2013	4.12	4.01	21	74%	28	18%	19	1.09	15	0.75	19	31	6.0%	30	9	11

2013 ALY by direction: Left End 3.94 (20) Left Tackle 4.11 (20) Mid/Guard 4.19 (26) Right Tackle 3.73 (14) Right End 3.16 (6)

Gus Bradley is building this unit in the image of the one he ran in Seattle, so it's not surprising that Jacksonville was first in line to pick up Seattle's cap casualties this offseason. Big Red Bryant will play five-technique end on run downs and be a load to move. Chris Clemons becomes the starter at the "Leo" edge-rusher position, though Andre Branch started to break out towards the end of last season—seven of his hurries and five of his sacks occurred after Week 11—and will mount a challenge to the job. Coming off a 2012 ACL tear, the Clemons of 2013 wasn't the same dominant player he was in the past, but he can't help but better a Jacksonville unit that was lacking pass rush the last two seasons.

One reclamation project that worked out quite well for the Jaguars was Sen'Derrick Marks. Rescued from a rotation in Tennessee, Marks bumped his hurries up from four to 18, and led the league in tipped passes. Jacksonville quietly rewarded him with a contract extension towards the end of the season, but managed to make Marks a very easy cut in 2015 should he turn back into a pumpkin. This year's reclamation project is Ziggy Hood, who got a four-year deal after being as anonymous as any Pittsburgh lineman can be. Jacksonville will see if he has any juice in his tank with a change to a one-gap scheme and a rotational role with Marks. Roy Miller's job remains eating up the blockers.

Linebacker is fairly wide open. Paul Posluszny is still around to thump and clog up the middle. Posluszny is a heady player who makes adjustments well, but doesn't have the speed to stay with most receivers in pass coverage. After Russell Allen's abrupt retirement due to an in-game stroke, free-agent signee Dekoda Watson will be counted on to play close to the line of scrimmage. (Bradley's staff has scrapped the "Sam" linebacker to create the "Otto" role for him. We think this means Watson is led to believe the line of scrimmage is really the line for Metallica tickets.) Geno Hayes will play the Will role, though fifth-rounder Telvin Smith (Florida State) could push for that job in a hurry. Smith has the speed and tenacity to be a three-down linebacker, and if he has problems tackling, well, so does Hayes.

Defensive Secondary

			Overall									vs. Run					vs. Pass									
Secondary	Age	Pos	G	Snaps	Plays	TmPct	Rk	Stop	Dfts	BTkl	Runs	St%	Rk	RuYd	Rk	Tgts	Tgt%	Rk	Dist	Suc%	Rk	AdjYd	Rk	PD	Int
Johnathan Cyprien	24	SS	15	1044	103	12.7%	16	33	8	10	49	41%	35	6.7	33	45	10.9%	65	11.6	46%	62	7.5	49	6	1
Alan Ball	29	CB	15	1005	61	7.5%	54	30	11	6	17	18%	81	13.5	82	69	17.6%	14	14.2	60%	9	6.9	23	14	2
Josh Evans	23	FS	15	675	55	6.8%	69	12	3	10	31	19%	75	8.5	63	16	5.9%	12	14.5	32%	75	13.5	77	2	0
Will Blackmon	30	CB	15	670	52	6.4%	73	23	7	4	11	55%	18	3.8	5	48	18.1%	17	15.5	47%	69	11.3	84	11	1
Dwayne Gratz	24	CB	10	485	35	6.5%	69	12	5	1	11	55%	18	5.7	23	43	22.7%	57	12.0	54%	38	8.3	60	4	2
Mike Harris	25	CB	16	403	36	4.2%	--	18	5	2	10	40%	--	11.1	--	28	17.8%	--	7.8	53%	--	7.6	--	3	0
Winston Guy	24	SS	14	353	25	3.3%	--	6	1	2	11	18%	--	7.7	--	12	8.7%	--	16.2	39%	--	16.1	--	1	0

Year	Pass D Rank	vs. #1 WR	Rk	vs. #2 WR	Rk	vs. Other WR	Rk	vs. TE	Rk	vs. RB	Rk
2011	6	-14.4%	4	14.2%	24	2.9%	23	18.5%	20	-38.8%	1
2012	29	16.8%	25	4.9%	18	36.6%	32	-1.5%	18	1.7%	17
2013	26	13.3%	26	8.9%	21	16.1%	28	19.9%	28	-9.0%	11

One of the reasons that Jacksonville experienced such a dramatic turnaround on defense over the last half of the season was rapid growth by a pair of rookies in the secondary. Third-rounder Dwayne Gratz, who almost always parked out at left cornerback, immediately justified his selection. He got better on a weekly basis despite often being matched up against the likes of Josh Gordon, Andre Johnson, and Michael Floyd. Johnathan Cyprien, Jacksonville's second rounder in 2013, looked like he didn't even belong on an NFL field for the first half of the season. Heading from Florida International to the NFL was quite the culture shock. By the end of the season, though, Cyprien was the most promising player in the secondary. His ballhawking prowess was evident.

The Jaguars got surprisingly good production out of journeymen Will Blackmon and Alan Ball at corner. Blackmon strip-sacked Ryan Fitzpatrick to seal Jacksonville's first win, stealing the ball out from Fitzpatrick's hands and running the distance of the field. Ball can be grabby, but was a top-10 corner in the eyes of Adjusted Success Rate. Both were extremely good system fits for Gus Bradley, and both came for a song: Blackmon came off waivers, and Ball as a free agent after a year spent mainly on special teams in Houston. Fourth-rounder Aaron Colvin (Oklahoma) might've gone two rounds higher had he not torn his ACL during the Senior Bowl, but Jacksonville will likely put him on PUP and reap the rewards later. There is adequate depth on hand in slot corner Mike Harris, and keep an eye out for UDFA Rashaad Reynolds (Oregon State), who got a mid-round grade from some draftniks.

The gaping wound in the comparison from Seattle to Jacksonville is that where Seattle has Earl Thomas, Jacksonville has a vacuum at free safety. 2013 sixth-rounder Josh Evans opened the season as the starter but quickly blew enough coverages to find himself watching from the sidelines. Winston Guy, a waiver claim from the Seahawks, was better, but hardly unimpeachable. Former Jags GM Gene Smith's answer to the question, 2011 fourth-rounder Chris Prosinski, wasn't given an opportunity because scouts watch game tape and have eyes. (He led Jacksonville with eight special-teams plays, so at least the guy isn't totally useless.) The only move of consequence Jacksonville made at the position was unearthing former Panthers safety Sherrod Martin from the free-agent scrap heap; he hasn't played since tearing his ACL and MCL during the 2012 season.

Special Teams

Year	DVOA	Rank	FG/XP	Rank	Net Kick	Rank	Kick Ret	Rank	Net Punt	Rank	Punt Ret	Rank	Hidden	Rank
2011	-2.2%	26	5.4	5	3.0	11	-5.3	28	-3.8	21	-10.5	31	15.6	1
2012	-3.0%	25	1.9	13	-3.6	25	-3.8	23	-3.2	21	-5.9	28	1.0	15
2013	2.5%	9	1.9	15	7.2	5	2.9	8	7.3	8	-6.6	26	9.2	5

At Football Outsiders, our belief is that teams are four parts offense, three parts defense, and one part special teams. So if you want to be optimistic, the Jaguars only need to improve the other seven-eighths of their roster!

Bryan Anger (drafted in the third round) has been a reasonably good punter since his rookie year (when he was drafted in the third round), but had his best season to date in 2013 (when Russell Wilson, drafted after him, won a Super Bowl). The narrative around him will probably never change. (The narrative was drafted in the third round.) But hey, at least he wasn't a total bust. Josh Scobee continues to be one of the best distance kickers in the NFL, even if the accuracy comes and goes at times. One of the perks of having a very young roster is that Jacksonville had good coverage teams—Anger and Scobee were basically average on gross yardage totals, but the Jaguars prevented most long returns. Jordan Todman was above-average on kickoff returns and the signing of Toby Gerhart will keep him fresh for the role in 2014. Ace Sanders was a bit of a disappointment as a punt returner, but will get a second chance for the role as the Jaguars didn't draft anyone of note to push him.

Kansas City Chiefs

2013 Record: 11-5	**Total DVOA:** 17.5% (6th)	**2014 Mean Projection:** 6.8 wins	**On the Clock (0-4):** 18%
Pythagorean Wins: 11.1 (6th)	**Offense:** 3.0% (15th)	**Postseason Odds:** 19.6%	**Mediocrity (5-7):** 45%
Snap-Weighted Age: 26.2 (25th)	**Defense:** -6.7% (9th)	**Super Bowl Odds:** 1.3%	**Playoff Contender (8-10):** 29%
Average Opponent: -7.0% (32nd)	**Special Teams:** 7.8% (1st)	**Proj. Avg. Opponent:** 3.4% (2nd)	**Super Bowl Contender (11+):** 8%

2013: Andy Reid and Bob Sutton combine to make the most out of a team with more than two-win talent.

2014: With tougher opponents and little help in the offseason, is regression an inevitability?

On January 4, 2013, the Kansas City Chiefs hired Andy Reid to be their new head coach and started a season of transformation that was like few others in recent NFL history.

On January 4, 2014, exactly one year later, Reid's team suffered the kind of playoff loss that seemingly negates an entire year of good feelings.

Up 38-10 in the third quarter of their wild-card game against the Indianapolis Colts, the Chiefs kept the historic tone of their season going in all the wrong ways by engineering the second-biggest postseason collapse in NFL annals. Instead of a huge win on the road, the season ended in a crushing 45-44 defeat. Yes, Andrew Luck played out of his mind in the second half (as he is wont to do), but this was obviously not the way to end a great year.

Kansas City's defense, so multiple and effective through most of the season, was stuck in a base dime defense that Luck was able to solve in the second half. Defensive coordinator Bob Sutton used safeties Husain Abdullah and Eric Berry as satellite blitzers and slot defenders, but those blitzes were easy to pick up, and after halftime Luck went 8-of-9 for 217 yards on passes of 10 yards or more. That Alex Smith had a transcendent game of his own, completing 30 of 46 passes for 346 yards, four touchdowns and no interceptions, simply didn't matter. The Chiefs watched player after player go down over the course of the afternoon, including running backs Jamaal Charles and Knile Davis, receiver Donnie Avery, cornerback Brandon Flowers, and linebacker Justin Houston. The cascade of injuries echoed the second half of the Chiefs' regular season, when a couple of key injuries on defense led the pass rush to collapse and set the franchise on a 2-6 path (including the postseason loss) after a 9-0 start.

"I sat there and talked to them this morning and there were a lot of long faces," Chiefs coach Andy Reid said the day after the Colts game. "They had their hearts ripped out. I can work with that. They should hurt. That'll make us better."

The question is, will the Chiefs get better, or will the wild swing from the bottom of the NFL's barrel to playoff contention settle in the middle for 2014? As Andy Benoit pointed out in *Football Outsiders Almanac 2013*, the pre-Reid Chiefs largely underperformed because they couldn't win the turnover battle. Kansas City's minus-24 turnover margin (ironically, tied for the league's worst with the Philadelphia Eagles in Reid's last year there) led to the team's final record in 2012 about as much as their plus-18 margin (second in the NFL to Seattle's plus-20) helped them to relevancy in 2013. In his first season in Kansas City, Sutton created defensive schemes conducive to turnovers, and that could continue—but regression could just as easily occur, especially with questions along the secondary.

In addition, the Chiefs had a remarkably easy schedule in the first half of last season. They played a bunch of teams in the throes of bad seasons (the Giants and Texans), and bad decades (the Jaguars, Raiders, Browns, and Bills). Things got a bit more complex when the Broncos and Chargers showed up twice each in the last seven games of the schedule, along with the same Colts team that would provide such heartbreak a few weeks later. Kansas City's only two post-bye wins came against the Redskins and Raiders; hardly a Murderer's Row unless we've taken the Wayback Machine to 1983. This year, things are going to be hard all year long, not just in the final few weeks. The Chiefs face the NFC West and the AFC East, as well as their own division; there are 11 games against opponents that finished at or above .500 in 2013.

Injury regression should also be a problem for the Chiefs in 2014. (Actually, it already has been; apparently, injury regression didn't even feel like waiting for the next regular season to bite the Chiefs right in the butt.) In 2013, Kansas City had the second-lowest Adjusted Games Lost in the league, behind only Philadelphia—and they weren't really equipped to deal with the injuries that *did* happen. Losing linebacker Justin Houston to a dislocated elbow from Week 13 until the end of the regular season really hurt, as an already banged-up Tamba Hali found himself double-teamed, and Sutton's formerly outstanding pass rush fell off mightily. The Chiefs had an 8.7 percent Adjusted Sack Rate and pressured quarterbacks on 28.7 percent of plays from Weeks 1-to-12, but that dropped to 6.2 percent and 19.6 percent in Weeks 13-to-17.

Thus, the Chiefs found out that the problem with a pass rush that consists of only two guys is that you sort of need both guys. In 2013, Hali and Houston combined for 54 percent of the sacks and 53 percent of the quarterback hurries among Kansas City's front-seven defenders. To prevent another drop-off, the Chiefs took Auburn end Dee Ford in the first round, hoping that his edge speed and confidence will bring absolutely necessary depth.

"This is the home of Derrick Thomas," Ford said at his

2014 Chiefs Schedule

Week	Opp.	Week	Opp.	Week	Opp.
1	TEN	7	at SD	13	DEN
2	at DEN	8	STL	14	at ARI
3	at MIA	9	NYJ	15	OAK
4	NE (Mon.)	10	at BUF	16	at PIT
5	at SF	11	SEA	17	SD
6	BYE	12	at OAK (Thu.)		

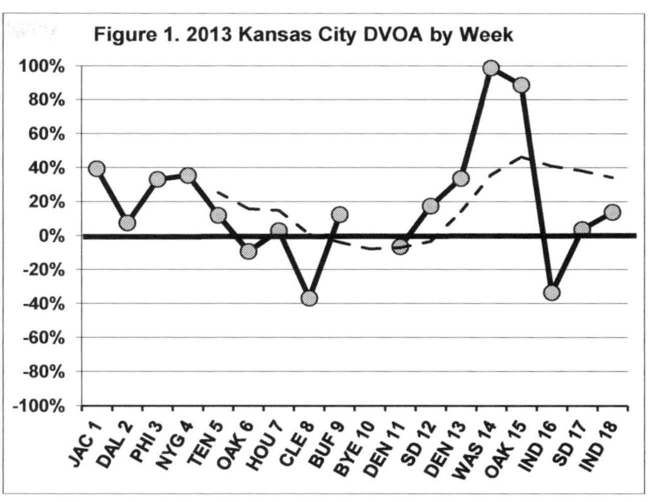

post-draft press conference, invoking the name of the franchise's all-time best pass-rusher. "I know you all remember that speed. That get-off is so vital and so deadly. I have a lot of counters, and there are definitely a lot of things I'm going to learn in the league, all of the vets here. I love speed rush. Love the speed and power. Love to spin. Pass rush is an art and it's all about what you put into it."

Unfortunately, that speed and power didn't result in much success until Ford's senior year, a big reason why our SackSEER projection system designated Ford as this year's biggest potential bust. We can't fault his athleticism—he does great in SackSEER's "explosion index"—but he had more sacks as a senior than he did in the rest of his collegiate career, and only three passes defensed. It's also a bit of a worry that the back problem that forced a medical redshirt in 2011 also kept Ford from working out at the combine.

If the pass rush falters in any way, it will create issues for a secondary that will now be without Flowers, who was released in mid-June. Flowers had been an above-average cornerback for a number of seasons, but something about Sutton's defense didn't hit him the right way—or, more likely, the other way around. Flowers spent a large part of the 2013 season playing in the slot for the first time in his career, and he wasn't very good at it. He toughed his way through a knee injury and did improve in his new role as the season progressed, but he appeared to be on the wrong side of Dorsey's preference for larger and more aggressive press cornerbacks. Flowers' 5-foot-9 stature won't work if a team is looking to adopt the new paradigm of "everyone try to be like the Seahawks." Only three of the 11 cornerbacks who spent time on Kansas City's roster last season stood less than six feet tall. The Chiefs will save $7.5 million in cap space this year with Flowers' release, and the move puts more pressure on third-round rookie Phillip Gaines, the 6-foot-0 Rice alum with blazing speed and some development needed when it comes to the advanced aspects of coverage at the NFL level. Gaines still bites on play action, runs on stilts too often, and can't always trail more angular routes. If he's thrown into the fire right away, Gaines might struggle even more than usual for a highly-drafted rookie cornerback.

On offense, the primary question for the Chiefs is what to put into the contract of one Alexander D. Smith, the veteran quarterback who set career highs in attempts, completions, and touchdowns in Reid's offense. Smith enters 2014 in the last year of the three-year, $24-million contract he signed in San Francisco before Kansas City acquired him in trade. There are legitimate questions regarding Smith's ceiling as a player, and what that ceiling deserves financially. Smith has reportedly said that he wants a contract that will pay him somewhere in the region of the $18.1 million given to Chicago's Jay Cutler in January. The problem is, of course, that Smith has never been the kind of quarterback who would inspire such generosity. He has never been a system-transcendent player, and he's far from the most important player in his own offense.

That honor goes most assuredly to running back Jamaal Charles, who had an outstanding season in 2013. Charles set career highs in yards from scrimmage (1,980) and combined rushing and receiving touchdowns (a league-leading 19). Charles was already a great player before Reid's arrival, but he's become perhaps the most effective version of the kind of back Reid prefers in his offense—versatile enough to do everything from running power (which Charles does better than his "scatback" image would suggest) to splitting out wide and catching passes in several different ways. Only the Saints had more running back screens than Kansas City's 48 last season, and Kansas City's 92.9% DVOA on such plays ranked second behind the Eagles. Charles was the epicenter of the offense; Smith was what he's always been at his best: a caretaker.

What Smith can do is distribute the ball to different targets consistently, and in that regard, he was an ideal Reid quarterback. Four different receivers had at least 13.0 percent of the team's receptions, with Charles leading the way. Smith's receivers were generally unspectacular—Donnie Avery finished 52nd in DVOA among qualifying wideouts, and Dwayne Bowe finished 61st. Meanwhile, Charles finished 17th in receiving DVOA among running backs—and eighth in receiving DYAR—so maybe, when the Chiefs are talking about the player deserving of a lucrative extension, they should be looking at the main man in their backfield. Charles is set to make $2.25 million in the penultimate year of the extension he signed in 2010. Smith, meanwhile, is due a base salary of $7.5 million. Charles' style of play makes him more valuable in the long term than you might think; not only will he not turn 28 until late December, but because he runs outside so much and is a prolific receiver (especially in Reid's offense), he's got a good chance to decline later and slower than most franchise-defining backs.

Field-position numbers provide further evidence that Smith was not the engine that powered the Chiefs' winning season. Sutton's defense combined with a tremendously productive special-teams unit (No. 1 in our ratings) to give the Chiefs a phenomenal field-position advantage all year. The Chiefs offense had the league's best starting field position (averaging a start just past their own 34-yard line) while their defense faced the worst average start since the kickoff was moved back to the 35 three years ago (with opponents averaging just past their own 23-yard line). That's more than four yards better on defense from the year before, and more than seven yards better on offense. Turnovers and special teams are two elements that tend to heavily regress towards the mean from year to year, and just a little bit of regression would put more pressure on an offense that isn't really built to sustain extended drives.

It's not that the 2013 Chiefs were a paper tiger. Some of the improvements were real, some were simply talent busting out around better coaching on both sides of the ball, and some were due to an easy schedule and the vagaries of single-season luck. Now the Chiefs will face a far more difficult slate of opponents, the possibility of regression in several crucial areas, and questions about maxing out the talent they had last season. The gravity of mediocrity won't just pull the Chiefs towards 8-8; like a space probe slingshotting around another planet, they're likely to get pulled a little bit past it.

Doug Farrar

2013 Chiefs Stats by Week

Wk	vs.	W-L	PF	PA	YDF	YDA	TO	Total	Off	Def	ST
1	at JAC	W	28	2	292	178	+2	39%	-1%	-43%	-3%
2	DAL	W	17	16	313	318	+2	7%	-3%	-11%	0%
3	at PHI	W	26	16	394	431	+5	33%	4%	-22%	7%
4	NYG	W	31	7	390	298	0	35%	24%	13%	24%
5	at TEN	W	26	17	353	339	+1	12%	-21%	-26%	7%
6	OAK	W	24	7	216	274	+2	-9%	-41%	-32%	-1%
7	HOU	W	17	16	357	294	-1	3%	-10%	-3%	10%
8	CLE	W	23	17	331	340	+1	-37%	-1%	34%	-1%
9	at BUF	W	23	13	210	470	+3	12%	7%	0%	5%
10	BYE										
11	at DEN	L	17	27	344	427	0	-7%	-6%	-2%	-3%
12	SD	L	38	41	395	491	-2	17%	35%	21%	4%
13	DEN	L	28	35	452	535	+1	34%	24%	19%	29%
14	at WAS	W	45	10	346	257	+1	99%	29%	-28%	41%
15	at OAK	W	56	31	384	461	+6	89%	71%	-7%	10%
16	IND	L	7	23	287	367	-3	-34%	-28%	-3%	-9%
17	at SD	L	24	27	332	405	+1	4%	-13%	-11%	5%
18	at IND	L	44	45	513	536	+3	14%	22%	10%	2%

Trends and Splits

	Offense	Rank	Defense	Rank
Total DVOA	3.0%	15	-6.7%	9
Unadjusted VOA	6.8%	10	-6.9%	6
Weighted Trend	6.3%	10	-2.2%	14
Variance	7.5%	19	4.5%	12
Average Opponent	5.0%	32	0.6%	11
Passing	6.7%	18	-7.0%	7
Rushing	11.1%	2	-6.4%	15
First Down	14.1%	7	-9.0%	10
Second Down	-9.0%	20	1.5%	15
Third Down	-1.8%	15	-14.8%	6
First Half	14.7%	6	-7.0%	7
Second Half	-11.1%	22	-6.5%	11
Red Zone	18.7%	6	-15.1%	7
Late and Close	-23.8%	28	-11.7%	10

Five-Year Performance

Year	W-L	Pyth W	Est W	PF	PA	TO	Total	Rk	Off	Rk	Def	Rk	ST	Rk	Off AGL	Rk	Def AGL	Rk	Off Age	Rk	Def Age	Rk	ST Age	Rk
2009	4-12	4.6	3.5	294	424	+1	-29.2%	28	-18.0%	25	9.2%	27	-2.1%	27	13.0	9	15.3	6	27.1	17	26.5	23	25.4	30
2010	10-6	9.1	8.3	366	326	+9	0.3%	17	4.4%	13	2.1%	20	-2.1%	24	5.8	2	4.2	1	27.9	10	25.9	28	25.8	24
2011	7-9	4.2	6.3	212	338	-2	-16.9%	26	-19.3%	29	-3.2%	13	-0.9%	19	43.8	26	21.7	13	28.0	5	26.3	25	26.1	22
2012	2-14	2.5	2.4	211	425	-24	-40.1%	32	-25.1%	31	13.0%	30	-2.0%	22	50.0	27	29.3	17	26.3	24	26.1	25	26.0	14
2013	11-5	11.1	10.0	430	305	+18	17.5%	6	3.0%	15	-6.7%	9	7.8%	1	30.6	13	11.2	2	26.1	27	26.4	17	25.8	23

2013 Performance Based on Most Common Personnel Groups

KC Offense					KC Offense vs. Opponents				KC Defense				KC Defense vs. Opponents			
Pers	Freq	Yds	DVOA	Run%	Pers	Freq	Yds	DVOA	Pers	Freq	Yds	DVOA	Pers	Freq	Yds	DVOA
11	45%	5.5	12.0%	19%	3-4-4	28%	5.5	11.9%	Dime+	43%	6.1	-1.1%	11	60%	6.0	-1.7%
21	17%	6.0	10.3%	59%	Nickel Even	26%	5.1	5.1%	3-4-4	31%	4.9	-12.0%	12	22%	5.4	-5.3%
12	16%	4.9	1.1%	39%	4-3-4	16%	5.1	4.6%	Nickel Even	13%	5.7	-2.2%	21	8%	5.5	-21.0%
22	8%	6.0	12.0%	74%	Nickel Odd	16%	5.5	27.5%	Nickel Odd	10%	6.5	-4.4%	22	2%	6.5	-1.9%
20	8%	5.1	0.1%	38%	Dime+	11%	6.1	-12.4%	4-4-3	1%	0.4	-44.7%	13	2%	3.1	-26.8%

Strategic Tendencies

Run/Pass		Rk	Formation		Rk	Pass Rush		Rk	Secondary		Rk	Strategy		Rk
Runs, first half	33%	30	Form: Single Back	62%	21	Rush 3	8.2%	6	4 DB	32%	25	Play action	25%	10
Runs, first down	48%	14	Form: Empty Back	5%	21	Rush 4	64.6%	12	5 DB	23%	30	Avg Box (Off)	6.45	8
Runs, second-long	30%	22	Pers: 3+ WR	57%	14	Rush 5	21.6%	22	6+ DB	43%	2	Avg Box (Def)	6.27	24
Runs, power sit.	63%	6	Pers: 4+ WR	4%	6	Rush 6+	5.5%	24	CB by Sides	72%	18	Offensive Pace	29.28	11
Runs, behind 2H	24%	25	Pers: 2+ TE/6+ OL	26%	22	Sacks by LB	62.8%	6	DB Blitz	12%	18	Defensive Pace	29.24	11
Pass, ahead 2H	52%	9	Shotgun/Pistol	54%	20	Sacks by DB	12.8%	6	Hole in Zone	9%	20	Go for it on 4th	0.68	24

Andy Reid Self-Parody Department: Kansas City ranked first in the league, running on 50 percent of first downs in 2012. That plummeted to 33 percent (30th) last season. And yet… Kansas City's use of play action actually went up, from 20 percent of pass plays in 2012 to 25 percent of pass plays in 2013. The Chiefs' offensive DVOA was basically the same whether they used play action or not. In 2012, the Chiefs had scored a touchdown on just 27 percent of red-zone opportunities. Last year, that improved to 60 percent, fifth best in the NFL. Kansas City was one of the few teams better running from two-back formations (4.9 yards per carry, 9.0% DVOA) than running from single-back formations (4.2 yards per carry, 1.1% DVOA). A heavy pass rush and a lot of dime packages left the Chiefs very susceptible to running back draws. They faced more of them than any other defense and allowed 7.3 yards per carry with 45.6% DVOA. Kansas City had the league's best DVOA against passes thrown to the middle of the field.

Passing

Player	DYAR	DVOA	Plays	NtYds	Avg	YAC	C%	TD	Int
A.Smith	262	-3.7%	545	3080	5.7	5.7	61.2%	23	7
C.Daniel	-6	-13.6%	40	237	5.9	5.9	65.8%	1	1

Rushing

Player	DYAR	DVOA	Plays	Yds	Avg	TD	Fum	Suc
J.Charles	247	13.7%	259	1288	5.0	12	4	51%
K.Davis	-29	-19.4%	70	242	3.5	4	1	34%
A.Smith	96	18.7%	61	434	7.1	1	1	-
C.Gray	-2	-14.6%	9	24	2.7	0	0	44%
D.McCluster*	-25	-89.6%	8	5	0.6	0	0	-
C.Daniel	18	47.0%	7	59	8.4	0	0	-

Receiving

Player	DYAR	DVOA	Plays	Ctch	Yds	Y/C	YAC	TD	C%
D.Bowe	71	-4.4%	103	57	673	11.8	3.4	5	55%
D.McCluster*	-22	-16.0%	83	53	511	9.6	4.9	2	64%
D.Avery	68	-0.8%	72	40	596	14.9	4.6	2	56%
J.Hemingway	-15	-22.9%	19	13	125	9.6	1.9	2	68%
A.J.Jenkins	-18	-27.4%	17	8	130	16.3	5.5	0	47%
C.Hall*	-23	-51.9%	7	2	20	10.0	8.5	0	29%
K.Williams	*-68*	*-46.8%*	*27*	*12*	*113*	*9.4*	*4.8*	*0*	*44%*
S.McGrath	21	1.0%	40	26	302	11.6	5.4	2	65%
A.Fasano	-12	-12.7%	33	23	200	8.7	3.2	3	70%
K.Brock*	-5	-23.0%	6	3	36	12.0	1.3	0	50%
J.Charles	135	8.5%	104	70	693	9.9	9.4	7	67%
A.Sherman	43	19.7%	24	18	155	8.6	9.0	1	75%
K.Davis	-11	-27.0%	15	11	76	6.9	8.3	0	73%
C.Gray	2	-10.0%	10	7	46	6.6	7.4	0	70%

Offensive Line

Player	Pos	Age	GS	Snaps	Pen	Sk	Pass	Run	Player	Pos	Age	GS	Snaps	Pen	Sk	Pass	Run
Rodney Hudson	C	25	15/15	1006	3	3.0	6.0	2.0	Geoff Schwartz*	RG	28	16/7	542	4	1.0	4.0	3.0
Jeff Allen	LG	24	15/14	880	4	5.0	15.0	1.0	Donald Stephenson	OT	26	16/7	534	7	0.5	13.0	2.0
Eric Fisher	RT	23	14/13	789	6	7.0	28.0	5.0	*Jeff Linkenbach*	*G*	*27*	*11/4*	*385*	*1*	*1.5*	*5.5*	*1.5*
Branden Albert*	LT	30	12/12	775	10	3.5	9.5	3.0	*J'Marcus Webb*	*OT*	*26*	*8/1*	*106*	*0*	*0.0*	*1.0*	*1.0*
Jon Asamoah*	RG	26	13/9	652	3	1.5	5.0	3.0									

Year	Yards	ALY	Rk	Power	Rk	Stuff	Rk	2nd Lev	Rk	Open Field	Rk	Sacks	ASR	Rk	Short	Long	F-Start	Cont.
2011	3.89	3.81	28	62%	18	20%	21	1.11	25	0.55	27	34	7.1%	19	6	20	26	39
2012	4.84	4.04	19	59%	23	20%	19	1.33	8	1.25	2	40	8.2%	27	10	20	20	30
2013	4.58	4.33	2	65%	16	16%	7	1.27	8	0.91	9	41	7.7%	20	14	15	19	28

2013 ALY by direction: Left End 4.48 (8) Left Tackle 3.81 (17) Mid/Guard 4.35 (5) Right Tackle 4.35 (6) Right End 4.35 (5)

Andy Reid's April assertion that all was well after Kansas City lost several key offensive linemen in free agency is yet another example of how he is the Optimist Prime. With left tackle Branden Albert and guards John Asamoah and Geoff Schwartz headed out the door, Reid had to scramble a few weeks before the draft when he told the media, "We kept a load of offensive linemen on the roster knowing something like this could happen. Some of them are young guys but they were able to get some experience and they'll have an opportunity to compete in there."

Sure, but *who* will be competing *where?* Reid intimated at the league meetings in March that 2013 first-overall pick Eric Fisher would move from right tackle back to his natural spot as Albert's replacement on the left. Hopefully, that move will bring some distinction to Fisher's game, because he struggled mightily at times in his rookie campaign. At Central Michigan, Fisher played with a nasty streak, a wide base, and excellent technique that allowed him to deal with defenders of every stripe. Against more consistently high-quality opponents, and working at a new position—the mechanical divide between left and right tackle is more complex that many fans realize—Fisher looked out of sorts too often. He struggled to plant blocks both when pulling and on the second level, his footwork was problematic in pass protection, and he didn't always use his power adroitly. We marked Fisher with 33 total blown blocks, and his figure of 23.9 snaps per blown block was the worst of any lineman with over 500 snaps. The Chiefs may soon realize that having Albert in 2013, after trying and failing to trade him and his onerous contract, was a blessing in disguise.

Jeff Allen manned the left guard position last season, and he proved to be a reasonably reliable blocker, especially in slide protection. The 2012 second-round pick out of Illinois now leads this line with 27 career NFL starts. Donald Stephenson, selected one round after Allen in that draft, performed surprisingly well on the left side late in the season in place of Albert, who was dealing with a back injury. Stephenson would be an ideal right tackle in Reid's offense, because he strikes forward with tremendous power in run-blocking. He's not especially agile in pass protection, but he could be a real asset against run-stopping ends and linebackers on the edge, and when pinching inside against defensive tackles. Both Fisher and Stevenson are recovering from off-season surgeries.

It's an open issue as to who will replace the tandem of Asamoah and Schwartz at right guard—veterans Jeff Linkenbach and Ricky Henry are available, as is sixth-round rookie Zach Fulton (Tennessee), though Rishaw Johnson may have the inside edge based on his Week 17 performance against the Chargers. Johnson is a powerful run-blocker who strikes well at the second level, though he needs work in pass protection; San Diego's Kendall Reyes absolutely clowned him with a spin move for a sack in that regular-season finale. Another interesting depth option is sixth-round rookie tackle Laurent Duvernay-Tardif out of Montreal's McGill University. The projected first overall pick in the CFL draft, Duvernay-Tardif impressed a lot of people at the East-West Shrine Game, but he'll be a developmental prospect unless the depth here falls completely apart.

Defensive Front Seven

			Overall									vs. Run					Pass Rush			
Defensive Line	**Age**	**Pos**	**G**	**Snaps**	**Plays**	**TmPct**	**Rk**	**Stop**	**Dfts**	**BTkl**	**Runs**	**St%**	**Rk**	**RuYd**	**Rk**	**Sack**	**Hit**	**Hur**	**Tips**
Dontari Poe	24	DT	15	975	55	6.9%	18	43	13	0	42	76%	48	2.4	51	4.5	3	12.0	5
Tyson Jackson*	28	DE	15	500	37	4.7%	52	28	4	2	30	70%	65	2.1	42	4.0	0	5.0	3
Allen Bailey	25	DE	15	438	32	4.0%	63	24	3	0	27	78%	41	3.3	77	1.0	1	6.0	2
Mike DeVito	30	DE	14	438	29	3.9%	66	19	4	1	28	64%	78	2.1	43	0.0	0	3.5	0
Vance Walker	*27*	*DT*	*15*	*766*	*40*	*5.2%*	*39*	*36*	*11*	*1*	*33*	*91%*	*9*	*1.7*	*30*	*3.0*	*2*	*13.0*	*0*

			Overall								vs. Run					Pass Rush			
Edge Rushers	**Age**	**Pos**	**G**	**Snaps**	**Plays**	**TmPct**	**Rk**	**Stop**	**Dfts**	**BTkl**	**Runs**	**St%**	**Rk**	**RuYd**	**Rk**	**Sack**	**Hit**	**Hur**	**Tips**
Tamba Hali	31	OLB	15	942	45	5.7%	37	35	20	1	25	80%	27	2.1	24	11.0	4	31.5	0
Justin Houston	25	OLB	11	696	48	8.3%	9	43	21	4	25	88%	9	2.3	30	11.0	6	24.5	3
Frank Zombo	27	OLB	16	421	25	3.0%	--	19	4	0	16	75%	--	2.8	--	2.0	4	5.5	0

			Overall								Pass Rush			vs. Run					vs. Pass						
Linebackers	**Age**	**Pos**	**G**	**Snaps**	**Plays**	**TmPct**	**Rk**	**Stop**	**Dfts**	**BTkl**	**Sack**	**Hit**	**Hur**	**Runs**	**St%**	**Rk**	**RuYd**	**Rk**	**Tgts**	**Suc%**	**Rk**	**AdjYd**	**Rk**	**PD**	**Int**
Derrick Johnson	32	ILB	15	1009	113	14.2%	33	69	27	7	4.5	6	10	66	65%	44	3.5	49	41	61%	12	5.9	20	7	2
Akeem Jordan*	29	ILB	16	469	63	7.4%	68	36	5	1	0.0	0	0	50	64%	49	3.3	40	6	34%	--	7.1	--	0	0
Joe Mays	*29*	*ILB*	*14*	*545*	*69*	*10.2%*	*62*	*47*	*10*	*4*	*1.0*	*4*	*2*	*49*	*73%*	*14*	*2.5*	*16*	*18*	*73%*	*1*	*2.9*	*1*	*3*	*0*

Year	Yards	ALY	Rk	Power	Rk	Stuff	Rk	2nd Level	Rk	Open Field	Rk	Sacks	ASR	Rk	Short	Long
2011	4.13	4.31	24	55%	9	16%	29	1.06	7	0.57	7	29	6.3%	23	12	11
2012	4.48	4.18	20	52%	5	18%	23	1.17	13	0.99	25	27	6.5%	14	4	17
2013	4.27	3.67	11	56%	7	18%	18	1.03	10	0.94	25	47	7.9%	6	14	20
2013 ALY by direction:			*Left End 3.38 (10)*			*Left Tackle 3.84 (13)*			*Mid/Guard 3.82 (10)*			*Right Tackle 3.04 (6)*			*Right End 3.00 (5)*	

Just as Kansas City's 2013 campaign morphed into a tale of two very different half-seasons, the Chiefs' ability to pressure opposing passers was the definition of feast-and-famine. When Tamba Hali and Justin Houston were on their game, Bob Sutton's defense worked very well, and the Chiefs finished the season with 47 sacks, tied with Arizona for the sixth-best mark in the league. But in the team's six regular-season losses, they had just six sacks. Hali had nine sacks through Week 7, but then only two sacks the rest of the way, both against Washington in Week 14. Meanwhile, Houston dislocated an elbow in Week 12 and missed the rest of the regular season. Thus, Kansas City's pass defense DVOA dropped from second in the first half of the season to 17th in Weeks 9-to-17, and the overall defense plummeted from fifth to 15th. Frank Zombo was game, but not exactly an optimal replacement for Houston in the talent department. First-round pick Dee Ford from Auburn improves the depth despite the SackSEER worries detailed earlier in the chapter. Ford played end in college but projects well as an outside linebacker in a hybrid defense like Sutton's because of his size and speed around the edge.

Sutton uses a lot of different personnel in odd fronts—as one would expect of a Rex Ryan disciple—so Kansas City's defensive linemen were tested in different ways. Dontari Poe, coming off a solid rookie season in 2012, picked up 3.5 sacks in the first two games of the 2013 season (against the offensive lines of the Jaguars and Cowboys, it must be said) and then settled into his preferred and indispensable role as a player who can both provide interior pressure and put up a wall against opposing running games.

Tyson Jackson left the Chiefs for Atlanta in free agency after an unsatisfying five seasons as one of Scott Pioli's most underwhelming draft picks. To replace him, the Chiefs signed former Raiders lineman Vance Walker to a three-year, $13 million deal. In Oakland, the 6-foot-2, 305-pound Walker played primarily as a defensive tackle. Allen Bailey and Mike DeVito were primarily a sub-package combo—Bailey worked well as a nickel and dime tackle, while DeVito made his bones as a run-stopper.

Only San Francisco's NaVorro Bowman had more Run Stops than Derrick Johnson among 3-4 inside linebackers last season, and Philly's DeMeco Ryans was the only 3-4 inside linebacker with more Run Defeats. Johnson also proved to be adept in coverage, a requirement in Sutton's defense, especially later in the season when more blitzes were the order of the day. At 31, Johnson still has the athleticism to cover slot receivers and tight ends on short routes, and enough awareness to peel off and stop the run. And when Sutton went heavy nickel and dime, Johnson was the primary 'backer on the field. To replace Akeem Jordan, who moved on from Kansas City after one season, the Chiefs will look at both journeyman Joe Mays and 2013 fourth-rounder Nico Johnson, a starter on two National Championship teams at Alabama.

Defensive Secondary

			Overall								vs. Run					vs. Pass									
Secondary	Age	Pos	G	Snaps	Plays	TmPct	Rk	Stop	Dfts	BTkl	Runs	St%	Rk	RuYd	Rk	Tgts	Tgt%	Rk	Dist	Suc%	Rk	AdjYd	Rk	PD	Int
Kendrick Lewis*	26	FS	16	1042	60	7.1%	67	17	7	9	30	23%	72	10.1	70	24	5.2%	6	8.1	47%	58	7.9	55	3	1
Eric Berry	26	SS	15	1010	84	10.6%	33	51	23	3	32	59%	5	4.3	6	46	10.3%	64	8.6	65%	13	4.9	11	11	3
Sean Smith	27	CB	13	866	60	7.1%	61	22	9	3	15	27%	68	20.0	86	87	19.7%	27	14.0	57%	19	7.1	30	11	2
Brandon Flowers*	28	CB	13	866	76	11.1%	9	23	11	3	9	44%	35	7.2	46	88	23.3%	62	11.9	47%	75	9.2	76	9	1
Marcus Cooper	24	CB	16	645	59	7.0%	63	23	11	0	5	20%	73	16.2	84	83	29.5%	87	13.4	53%	41	9.3	77	15	3
Quintin Demps*	29	FS	16	637	41	4.8%	75	21	11	5	9	56%	10	6.9	37	26	9.4%	56	10.6	74%	2	4.0	3	9	4
Husain Abdullah	29	FS	16	280	21	2.5%	--	13	7	0	6	67%	--	6.0	--	12	9.8%	--	7.7	46%	--	7.5	--	2	1
Dunta Robinson	32	CB	8	264	17	4.0%	--	12	6	3	2	50%	--	6.5	--	19	16.5%	--	10.4	52%	--	10.8	--	4	0

Year	Pass D Rank	vs. #1 WR	Rk	vs. #2 WR	Rk	vs. Other WR	Rk	vs. TE	Rk	vs. RB	Rk
2011	13	-22.9%	2	6.8%	19	-27.2%	5	6.5%	16	34.5%	31
2012	31	22.1%	28	7.0%	21	2.8%	22	-4.0%	11	33.4%	32
2013	7	-11.7%	8	-4.4%	12	2.8%	16	-36.9%	2	-7.1%	14

The June release of Brandon Flowers adds a question mark to this defense. In a system like the one Sutton prefers, cornerbacks must play aggressive press coverage consistently, and safeties have to take a number of different roles. Of the cornerbacks Sutton had in 2013, only Flowers is capable of playing on an island and delivering reasonable coverage from the seam to the boundary. Flowers' third-quarter concussion and the Chiefs' second-half defensive debacle against the Colts in the wild-card round? That was not a coincidence. Flowers isn't a complete cornerback—and he really suffered when Sutton tried to move him all over the field last season—but he was still the best defensive back the Chiefs had.

Sean Smith had a decent first year in Kansas City and fits Sutton's preference for more physical cornerbacks. Smith is good through the first few yards when press coverage is the order of the day, though he tends to lose traction as routes develop. Dunta Robinson was the team's third corner in 2013, and the Chiefs are moving on from that experiment. The addition of third-round pick Phillip Gaines from Rice, who ran a 4.31 40-yard dash at the scouting combine at 6-foot-0 and 193 pounds, will make things interesting. Gaines' technique, especially on boundary routes, allows him to match his track speed to the field most of the time, and he's the odds-on favorite to get a bulk of reps as Flowers' replacement. If that's the case, the Chiefs now need reinforcement at slot corner, a particularly important role with a defense that plays so much dime. The Chiefs played it on 43 percent of snaps; only the Steelers used dime more often, and none of the other 30 teams used it more than 30 percent of the time.

Eric Berry played everywhere from inside blitzer to linebacker depth to outside corner on a few snaps last season, and he's now working on improving his pass coverage. He actually provides more versatility than fellow 2010 first-rounder Earl Thomas, though not Thomas' nonpareil range in center field. "I see the praise and the accolades that other safeties around the league get, but at the same time, I can't be concerned with that because for a fact, I know I can do that—I've done that in the past," Berry told the *Kansas City Star* in April. "...There's not a lot of guys at my position that can do what I do. There's a lot of guys that can't blitz, there's a lot of guys that can't cover tight ends, there's a lot of guys that can't cover the deep middle. I just happen to be one of the guys that can do all that."

Berry may well be doing that at free safety in 2014 following the departure of Kendrick Lewis, who was regarded more highly for his ability to make calls on the field than his ability to perform at a high level in coverage. Lewis will likely be replaced by either veteran Husain Abdullah or Sanders Cummings, a fifth-round pick in 2013.

Special Teams

Year	DVOA	Rank	FG/XP	Rank	Net Kick	Rank	Kick Ret	Rank	Net Punt	Rank	Punt Ret	Rank	Hidden	Rank
2011	-0.9%	19	-2.3	20	-1.0	22	-6.6	30	3.2	12	2.1	12	-15.4	32
2012	-2.0%	22	-2.2	19	-1.5	19	-9.8	31	8.8	8	-5.4	26	2.4	12
2013	7.8%	1	-5.6	26	3.0	12	19.8	2	4.6	13	17.2	1	5.2	9

Kansas City's rousing ascension to prominence in special teams had its roots in three areas: Quintin Demps and Knile Davis combined to give Kansas City a league-leading 29.9 yards per kick return, Dexter McCluster logged two punt return touchdowns when no other team had more than one, and the Chiefs' average of 6.5 return yards allowed per punt ranked fourth in the league. That final stat was the primary factor in Kansas City's ninth-best ranking in net punting average, as Dustin Colquitt was just average in our gross punt value metric. Colquitt did tie Arizona's Dave Zastudil with a league-leading 35 punts inside the opponents' 20-yard line, and only New England's Ryan Allen had more touchbacks than Colquitt's 11. 2009 Mr. Irrelevant Ryan Succop is the weakness of this unit, as he's average on kickoffs and has never been among the league leaders in field-goal accuracy. He doesn't have a deep leg either; last year he hit just one of four attempts from 50 or more yards, and he has only nine 50-plus-yard field goals in five seasons.

Miami Dolphins

2013 Record: 8-8	**Total DVOA:** -6.5% (22nd)	**2014 Mean Projection:** 6.5 wins	**On the Clock (0-4):** 20%
Pythagorean Wins: 7.5 (19th)	**Offense:** -1.8% (18th)	**Postseason Odds:** 15.6%	**Mediocrity (5-7):** 48%
Snap-Weighted Age: 26.7 (14th)	**Defense:** 2.4% (17th)	**Super Bowl Odds:** 0.8%	**Playoff Contender (8-10):** 26%
Average Opponent: 2.5% (8th)	**Special Teams:** -2.4% (23rd)	**Proj. Avg. Opponent:** 1.6% (12th)	**Super Bowl Contender (11+):** 6%

2013: No sacks in the champagne room.

2014: Will Ryan Tannehill have time to throw to the NFL's highest-paid wide receiver corps?

OK, Miami Dolphins, take a seat while we roast you with the facts. From the 1970 merger through Dan Marino's swan song in 1999, you had the best winning percentage (.645) in the NFL. Since the turn of the century, you've become an afterthought. Your winning percentage (.478) ranks 19th since 2000. Once a proud offensive team either by ground or air, you rank 27th in points per game (19.6). You've hired more head coaches (five) than you've had playoff berths (three), and you've had more stadium names (five) than playoff wins (one). Don't even get us started on those 1972 geriatrics and their annual celebration of perfection.

Arnold Schwarzenegger predicted your collapse against the Jets on *Monday Night Football* in 2000. Ricky Williams would rather smoke weed than stick around in his prime with your team. You chose Daunte Culpepper over Drew Brees in 2006, so no wonder you've appeared on NBC's *Sunday Night Football* only one time in the last eight seasons. Cam Cameron and Ted Ginn? Enough said. You drafted Pat White in the second round, thinking the Wildcat was here to stay. The Wildcat was exciting... for about a month. Tony Sparano celebrated field goals like he won the Super Bowl and Powerball at the same time. Forget Jacksonville, let's ship *you* off to London.

What's that, Miami? Oh, you don't like being bullied? Well, now you know how Jonathan Martin felt...

The NFL has had its share of controversies over the years, whether it's been dog-fighting (Michael Vick), Spygate (Patriots) or Bountygate (Saints). The Jonathan Martin-Richie Incognito bullying scandal was a whole different beast. We won't recount the full story here due to space. There's lengthy documentation on the Internet; just search for the Ted Wells report. However, we will look at the significant impact the scandal had on the Dolphins' 2013 season and the team moving forward.

While we started in jest, the facts in the introduction are the unshakeable truth about the Miami Dolphins since Marino retired. This has not been a successful franchise for years now, and last year's embarrassment is another black eye for the organization. The Dolphins have long tried to develop Marino's successor while the defense has never been good enough to compensate for that difficult process—hence more than a decade of mediocrity. Embattled general manager Jeff Ireland parted ways with the team after six seasons and was replaced by Dennis Hickey, who must hope this year's moves will offer a better fix than last year's disastrous spending spree.

Other than Martin, obviously, no one was probably hurt more by the bullying scandal than second-year quarterback Ryan Tannehill. Still relatively new to the position after playing part of his college career at wide receiver, Tannehill suffered a league-high 58 sacks. By comparison, Marino was sacked 63 times total on 2,216 more passes in years two-through-six of his career. Not that anyone will mistake Tannehill for Marino, but clearly his line couldn't hold up in pass protection last season. Of the 58 sacks, only seven were charted as a coverage sack or a failed scramble. Tannehill could afford to get rid of the ball quicker at times, but generally, his sacks were the result of piss-poor blocking.

It's not like the offensive line wasn't expected to be a problem. Left tackle Jake Long left in free agency after five seasons of making fans wish Miami had taken Matt Ryan with the first overall pick in 2008. Martin, who had his share of struggles as a rookie, took on the responsibility of replacing Long at left tackle. Tyson Clabo, Ryan's right tackle in Atlanta, joined the Dolphins in the same capacity. The concerns were evident in the preseason. Martin struggled in pass protection and soon returned to right tackle. The Dolphins traded a conditional late-round pick to Baltimore for Bryant McKinnie, who moved into the left tackle spot. McKinnie had a good Super Bowl run, but in 2013 he looked like another old man who found his retirement home in Miami. The McKinnie-Martin experiment lasted one game before Martin left the team, citing "emotional" reasons. A few days later, the bullying story exploded and Martin never played another game for Miami. He was traded to San Francisco in the offseason. McKinnie and Clabo finished the season with a combined 19.5 sacks allowed, each player finishing second at his position in that statistic. When the season ended, they were told their services were no longer required.

Anyone that's followed his career knows we didn't need the vile text messages and threats sent to Martin to realize Richie Incognito is a big turd. For someone with a last name that's supposed to convey a sense of anonymity, Incognito sure is infamous. His big mouth and short fuse have given him a reputation as a dirty player who takes some of the dumbest penalties to hurt his teams. Charting stats suggest he was one of the worst left guards in the league. At midseason, once the extent of his abuse of Martin hit the media, the Dolphins had but no choice to suspend him indefinite-

2014 Dolphins Schedule

Week	Opp.	Week	Opp.	Week	Opp.
1	NE	7	at CHI	13	at NYJ (Mon.)
2	at BUF	8	at JAC	14	BAL
3	KC	9	SD	15	at NE
4	at OAK (U.K.)	10	at DET	16	MIN
5	BYE	11	BUF (Thu.)	17	NYJ
6	GB	12	at DEN		

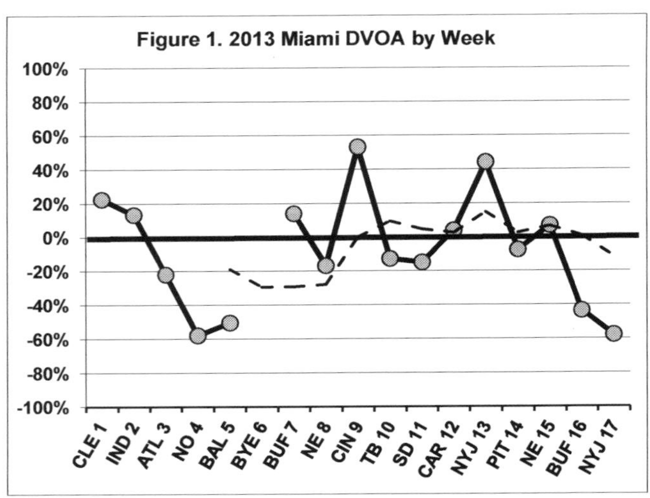

ly. Incognito never played for Miami again and remains a free agent. Think any team will want a player who called his teammate a "half-n***** piece of shit" in a threatening voicemail? And to think, Incognito was on Miami's six-man "leadership council" last year.

The whole story does make it appear like the inmates were running the prison while Warden Joe Philbin sat idle and oblivious. The investigative report revealed Incognito was not alone in the bullying, nor was Martin the only target. Linemen Mike Pouncey and John Jerry also bullied Martin in addition to repeated racial slurs and taunting of an assistant trainer from Japan.

Jerry, who had started all 32 games since Philbin took over, left for the Giants in free agency; Pouncey is still here. It's hard to get rid of one of the best centers in the league, but if the Dolphins and Philbin are trying to change the values of this organization, then it's a scary thought to have Pouncey as a franchise cornerstone. This is a guy that has shown public support of Aaron Hernandez, his former teammate at the University of Florida, *after* the tight end was charged with first-degree murder. Last July, the Pouncey brothers wore "Free Hernandez" hats in public. Maurkice apologized for that, but Mike, who still has a framed Hernandez jersey in his home according to May media reports, would not. He also doesn't think he needs to undergo any of the psychological testing that the league required him to do before taking the field again. He could face a suspension, which might be the only way he'll learn to grow up. After the Dolphins drafted offensive tackle Ja'Wuan James in April, Pouncey tweeted: "Great pick! I can't wait for our gifts he's getting us lol." We'll see what the future holds, but so far, Pouncey looks like a guy that "just doesn't get it." Some coaches are content with keeping players like that around as long as they play well. Other coaches are Chip Kelly.

Miami is in desperate need of leadership, which is a terrible segue into a discussion of Mike Wallace's $60 million contract. Wallace was the prized free-agent signing for Miami last year, but the only way to maximize his value is to take advantage of his speed down the field on the deep ball. Given the lack of protection time for Tannehill, Wallace was a terrible fit. Brian Hartline edged out Wallace in receptions and yards, and Wallace had the worst DVOA of Miami's four primary wide receivers, including Brandon Gibson and Rishard Matthews. The failure to connect deep was not for a lack of trying, but Wallace caught just six of his 35 targets (17.1 percent) that were thrown more than 20 yards beyond the line of scrimmage. In his heyday in Pittsburgh, he would have double that amount with a better catch rate. Overall, the Miami deep passing game actually worked better when someone other than Wallace was the target (Table 1).

Tannehill and Wallace did not make a good connection last season no matter how you slice it. With Wallace's cap hit ballooning to $17.25 million this year, the Dolphins are spending an insane $29.6 million on their 2014 wide receivers—by far the most in the league, according to a June study by CBS Sports.

Free-agent spending sprees can be deadly. Hickey's first offseason as general manager almost demanded another one to fix the offensive line, but he used free agency as a half measure. Kansas City tackle Branden Albert was on Miami's radar last season, but it took a year to get him on the team with a five-year deal worth $47 million. If he plays like he did last year, then this should work well. While the old Dolphins conducted meetings at strip clubs, new Dolphin Shelley Smith was getting married the weekend he signed with Miami to play right guard. He only has eight career starts at age 27, but his strength is in the running game. The starter between Albert and Pouncey at left guard is an open competition, but Miami would love for third-round rookie Billy Turner to win the job. He's aggressive, but not in the Incognito way. In an odd twist, Turner's demeanor was actually nurtured through the bullying he received as a kid. "The anger I had built up from getting mad and [peeved] at my older brother was what came out in my play. That's how I developed that strategy and that style of playing with a chip on my shoulder," Turner

Table 1. Miami's Downfield Passing Plays (20-plus Yards), 2013

Target	Att	Cmp	C%	Yds	Avg	TD	INT	DPI	Drop	Dist	Pressure Freq.	PA Pct.
Mike Wallace	35	6	17.1%	261	7.46	1	4	1	2	39.6	20.0%	31.4%
Other	30	9	30.0%	305	10.17	1	1	0	3	28.7	20.0%	6.7%

told the *Miami Herald.* If it's not Turner's job, the Dolphins have in-house options like last year's third-round pick Dallas Thomas or veteran Nate Garner. The selection of right tackle Ja'Wuan James with the 19th overall pick did receive a lot of "reach" criticism, but he's likely to be a Week 1 starter and has plenty of experience from Tennessee.

Just like that, the Dolphins have four new starters on the offensive line. While it's usually best to build continuity on the line and only replace one or two players at a time, mass replacement is often the best way to fix a really terrible line, and we don't have to go back far to find an example of it working. The 2013 Bears kept center Roberto Garza, but rebuilt the left side in free agency with Jermon Bushrod and Matt Slauson, then rebuilt the right side in the draft with Kyle Long and Jordan Mills. The result was one of the best Chicago offenses ever, though of course head coach Marc Trestman deserves much of the credit. The Miami line looks much improved on paper, but new offensive coordinator Bill Lazor and offensive line coach John Benton will be responsible for molding individual talent into a cohesive unit that works together.

Lazor comes from Philadelphia and looks to implement some elements of what made the Eagles so successful a year ago. Running an up-tempo offense is one goal, which shouldn't be a problem for Tannehill, who often operated from the no huddle even as a rookie. Nevertheless, there's a big adjustment for Tannehill to make, since for the first time since high school he won't have Mike Sherman around. Sherman coached Tannehill at Texas A&M and then came with him to Miami as offensive coordinator the last two years. Now Lazor looks to bring more diversity to the offense. Some of the zone-read designs that made the Eagles hard to defend can be employed in Miami, especially since Tannehill is a better athlete than Nick Foles. One of Miami's biggest plays last year had Tannehill gaining 48 yards on a simple zone-read keeper against New Orleans. Lost in all the sacks is the fact that there was no push in an equally unproductive running game. The Eagles didn't have the greatest pass protection last year, but the run blocking was very successful, and that's another way Lazor can help keep the pressure off Tannehill. The Dolphins also signed Knowshon Moreno to join Lamar Miller in the backfield.

In theory, Wallace should be better with an improved offensive line as Lazor will be able to use him in a manner similar to speedster DeSean Jackson, who had a career year in 2013. However, the ball still has to arrive with accuracy. Tannehill has the arm strength, but he can be erratic. Even on shorter throws, he's often too high with the ball and the receivers have to make odd adjustments. Eliminating any complacency that's set in with Sherman and getting a fresh set of eyes on Tannehill could be exactly what he needs to progress.

Improving the defense has been a secondary objective in Miami, but the unit's not good enough to grind out many low-scoring battles. Last year, Ireland opened up the checkbook in free agency in an attempt to sign three instant starters. Cornerback Brent Grimes received a one-year deal worth $5.5 million after missing most of 2012 with an Achilles injury. Linebacker Philip Wheeler spun a career year on a bad Oakland defense into $13 million fully guaranteed. Linebacker Dannell Ellerbe did what many have done before him: turned a Super Bowl win into a payday (five years, $35 million).

Initially, there was cause for excitement. In Week 2, the Dolphins thwarted an Andrew Luck comeback by doing things no one else had done to Luck in crunch time. Grimes picked him off in the end zone and Wheeler's rush on fourth-and-ball-game clinched the win with a sack. By season's end, Grimes made the Pro Bowl, though our game charting does not agree with the perception that he had a great year: he ranked only 73rd in Adjusted Success Rate. For context, of the 48 receptions Grimes allowed, 45 were a successful play for the offense based on down and distance. It's not like teams were shying away from him. Nonetheless, Grimes turned his 2013 season into a new contract including $16 million guaranteed.

On the other hand, no one will argue that Wheeler and Ellerbe lived up to their deals in 2013, nor did they adequately replace veterans Kevin Burnett and Karlos Dansby. Sure, Wheeler and Ellerbe brought youth and supposedly more pass-rushing ability, but our charting results show a disparity in impact plays (Table 2). Wheeler and Ellerbe were more productive per play on their old teams in 2012 than they were in their Miami debut. Burnett and Dansby thrived after leaving the Dolphins last season, and despite their age, their 2012 production in Miami was on par with what Ellerbe and Wheeler gave the Dolphins. Miami paid more to get less in return.

Table 2. Tag-Team Match: Burnett/Dansby vs. Ellerbe/Wheeler

Player	Year	Team	Snaps	Plays	Stop	Dfts	BTkl	Sack	Hur	INT	FF
Kevin Burnett	2012	MIA	1071	113	62	11	5	2.5	8	0	0
Karlos Dansby	2012	MIA	1099	143	81	24	7	1	3.5	0	1
2012 TOTAL			***2170***	***256***	***143***	***35***	***12***	***3.5***	***11.5***	***0***	***1***
Philip Wheeler	2012	OAK	1015	116	63	18	8	3.5	14	0	2
Dannell Ellerbe	2012	BAL	651	90	56	21	8	4.5	8.5	0	1
2012 TOTAL			***1666***	***206***	***119***	***39***	***16***	***8***	***23***	***0***	***3***
Kevin Burnett	2013	OAK	918	108	67	30	9	2.5	12.3	1	3
Karlos Dansby	2013	ARI	1078	141	87	31	9	6.5	9.5	4	1
2013 TOTAL			***1996***	***249***	***154***	***61***	***18***	***9***	***21.8***	***5***	***4***
Philip Wheeler	2013	MIA	1033	124	61	19	9	0.5	13.5	0	0
Dannell Ellerbe	2013	MIA	1009	106	42	14	8	1.0	5	2	0
2013 TOTAL			***2042***	***230***	***103***	***33***	***17***	***2***	***19***	***2***	***0***

Miami literally can't afford more offseason shopping sprees if the return is only going to be what Wallace, Ellerbe, and Wheeler did last year. If the offensive line rebuilding plan brings the same results, then Philbin's going to have more concerns than just reshaping the team's image and locker room culture. He's going to be viewed as a coach who hasn't developed talent or won in three years, and that's plenty of time in today's NFL to make a positive mark.

Reaction to our pessimistic projection for Miami depends on which narrative you want to believe. Are the Dolphins that team who beat Pittsburgh and New England in back-to-back weeks and fixed their biggest hole, or are they still mired in mediocrity with the clouds of last year's scandal and horrific offensive performances in Weeks 16 and 17 hanging overhead? Keep in mind, we projected Miami with 6.1 wins last year. Realistically, we can take any NFL team's record and add or subtract two wins and that's the range of team they likely were. Miami was 8-8, but Antonio Brown just had to stay in bounds down the sideline and Danny Amendola needed to hold onto the ball in front of the end zone. Then the Dolphins likely finish 6-10 and fire Philbin after a four-game losing streak to end the season (seven points scored in the last two games combined). We were a matter of inches away from that.

When a team's been stuck in prolonged mediocrity, something big has to push them into more probable playoff territory. Have the Dolphins found that addition, or does this still feel like a team in the range of six to nine wins? Reaching the upper end of that might still get Miami in the playoffs as a wild card. But as we have come accustomed to this century, even when the Dolphins say the right things and make moves that look good on paper, come September it's the same bland results. Regaining good PR is one thing, but ending this culture of being an irrelevant NFL franchise is what Philbin, or the next coach, has to change most in Miami.

Scott Kacsmar

2013 Dolphins Stats by Week

Wk	vs.	W-L	PF	PA	YDF	YDA	TO	Total	Off	Def	ST
1	at CLE	W	23	10	275	291	+2	22%	-14%	-29%	8%
2	at IND	W	24	20	398	448	0	13%	23%	13%	4%
3	ATL	W	27	23	285	377	0	-22%	-11%	19%	8%
4	at NO	L	17	38	331	465	-3	-58%	-14%	37%	-7%
5	BAL	L	23	26	294	384	+2	-51%	-19%	22%	-10%
6	BYE										
7	BUF	L	21	23	293	268	-2	14%	-7%	-25%	-4%
8	at NE	L	17	27	301	252	-2	-17%	-18%	-15%	-14%
9	CIN	W	22	20	345	465	+3	53%	33%	-25%	-5%
10	at TB	L	19	22	213	264	0	-13%	2%	6%	-9%
11	SD	W	20	16	343	435	0	-15%	-10%	3%	-2%
12	CAR	L	16	20	332	295	0	4%	-1%	-9%	-4%
13	at NYJ	W	23	3	453	177	+2	44%	24%	-23%	-2%
14	at PIT	W	34	28	367	412	0	-8%	12%	15%	-4%
15	NE	W	24	20	378	453	0	7%	32%	19%	-6%
16	at BUF	L	0	19	103	390	-1	-44%	-61%	-2%	16%
17	NYJ	L	7	20	296	374	-3	-58%	-26%	28%	-4%

Trends and Splits

	Offense	Rank	Defense	Rank
Total DVOA	-1.8%	18	2.4%	17
Unadjusted VOA	-2.7%	19	1.9%	18
Weighted Trend	-0.6%	17	0.7%	18
Variance	6.0%	12	4.4%	9
Average Opponent	-2.2%	10	-0.5%	18
Passing	4.0%	20	0.2%	12
Rushing	-4.3%	18	4.9%	29
First Down	-1.1%	17	1.4%	16
Second Down	10.8%	10	7.1%	24
Third Down	-24.5%	28	-3.1%	14
First Half	1.6%	15	-0.6%	14
Second Half	-5.6%	20	5.0%	21
Red Zone	25.5%	5	0.0%	16
Late and Close	2.8%	14	-0.5%	19

Five-Year Performance

Year	W-L	Pyth W	Est W	PF	PA	TO	Total	Rk	Off	Rk	Def	Rk	ST	Rk	Off AGL	Rk	Def AGL	Rk	Off Age	Rk	Def Age	Rk	ST Age	Rk
2009	7-9	7.2	8.4	360	390	-8	4.4%	16	4.1%	16	1.5%	18	1.8%	9	26.9	18	21.2	13	26.2	30	27.5	11	26.1	23
2010	7-9	6.2	8.5	273	333	-12	1.8%	15	0.7%	18	-4.8%	9	-3.7%	29	27.1	19	24.0	15	26.5	26	26.3	24	25.8	25
2011	6-10	8.5	7.7	329	313	-6	-1.3%	18	-7.5%	20	-3.7%	12	2.5%	6	22.1	12	9.6	3	26.6	21	27.7	6	26.3	16
2012	7-9	7.1	7.6	288	317	-10	-7.2%	21	-8.4%	22	-0.8%	14	0.4%	14	19.7	9	18.0	7	25.7	29	26.8	16	25.7	25
2013	8-8	7.5	6.8	317	335	-2	-6.5%	22	-1.8%	18	2.4%	17	-2.4%	23	42.8	21	19.4	8	26.5	23	27.3	11	26.0	18

2013 Performance Based on Most Common Personnel Groups

MIA Offense					MIA Offense vs. Opponents				MIA Defense				MIA Defense vs. Opponents			
Pers	Freq	Yds	DVOA	Run%	Pers	Freq	Yds	DVOA	Pers	Freq	Yds	DVOA	Pers	Freq	Yds	DVOA
11	67%	5.4	0.0%	22%	Nickel Even	42%	5.1	1.6%	Nickel Even	48%	5.3	-1.7%	11	48%	5.4	-5.8%
12	24%	5.0	5.6%	48%	3-4-4	20%	4.3	-6.6%	4-3-4	44%	5.2	2.4%	12	24%	5.7	5.0%
13	2%	2.5	-21.9%	95%	Dime+	16%	5.1	-10.3%	Nickel Odd	5%	8.3	-7.4%	21	17%	4.9	-3.3%
21	2%	3.5	-12.8%	68%	4-3-4	12%	5.6	4.1%	3-4-4	1%	7.3	39.0%	22	4%	4.3	1.6%
01	1%	4.3	27.3%	15%	Nickel Odd	10%	6.2	23.0%	Goal Line	1%	1.2	103.8%	621	2%	3.3	8.2%

Strategic Tendencies

Run/Pass		Rk	Formation		Rk	Pass Rush		Rk	Secondary		Rk	Strategy		Rk
Runs, first half	36%	23	Form: Single Back	69%	16	Rush 3	4.9%	20	4 DB	45%	10	Play action	14%	25
Runs, first down	45%	23	Form: Empty Back	9%	7	Rush 4	56.3%	26	5 DB	53%	11	Avg Box (Off)	6.18	29
Runs, second-long	25%	27	Pers: 3+ WR	69%	6	Rush 5	32.1%	3	6+ DB	0%	31	Avg Box (Def)	6.50	5
Runs, power sit.	45%	28	Pers: 4+ WR	1%	16	Rush 6+	6.8%	21	CB by Sides	74%	17	Offensive Pace	30.08	14
Runs, behind 2H	21%	29	Pers: 2+ TE/6+ OL	30%	17	Sacks by LB	8.3%	31	DB Blitz	16%	3	Defensive Pace	29.09	8
Pass, ahead 2H	60%	4	Shotgun/Pistol	68%	6	Sacks by DB	10.7%	11	Hole in Zone	8%	24	Go for it on 4th	0.55	28

For the second straight year, the Dolphins had a huge gap between performance with play action (7.3 yards per play, 50.0% DVOA) and pass plays without it (5.4 yards per play, -0.9% DVOA). That was the biggest gap in the league; they had the third-biggest gap in 2012. Miami was much better running from single-back formations (4.4 yards per carry, -4.2% DVOA) than from two-back formations (3.1 yards per carry, -18.1% DVOA). The Dolphins used three or more wide receivers 50 percent more often than they had in 2012. The Dolphins went "max protect" more than any other offense in the league, 15.2 percent of plays. They had been very successful in max protect in 2012, but they weren't in 2013, with just 5.3 yards per play and -7.6% DVOA (NFL average: 6.7 yards, 11.6% DVOA). Miami's offense benefitted from a league-low 26 opponent penalties. Even stranger, 12 of those were either defensive offside or neutral zone infraction, twice the usual NFL rate. The percentage of passes where the Dolphins defense was marked with "Hole in Zone" dropped from third in 2012 to 24th in 2013.

Passing

Player	DYAR	DVOA	Plays	NtYds	Avg	YAC	C%	TD	Int
R.Tannehill	54	-9.8%	643	3508	5.5	4.4	60.8%	24	17
M.Moore	-36	-120.6%	6	53	8.8	6.5	33.3%	0	2

Rushing

Player	DYAR	DVOA	Plays	Yds	Avg	TD	Fum	Suc
L.Miller	6	-7.7%	177	709	4.0	2	1	46%
D.Thomas	4	-7.7%	109	406	3.7	5	0	47%
R.Tannehill	46	19.0%	29	245	8.4	1	2	-
C.Clay	-6	-23.2%	7	15	2.1	1	0	29%
M.Gillislee	8	29.1%	6	21	3.5	0	0	50%
M.Thigpen	-2	-15.8%	6	18	3.0	0	0	33%
K.Moreno	*171*	*8.4%*	*241*	*1038*	*4.3*	*10*	*1*	*50%*

Receiving

Player	DYAR	DVOA	Plays	Ctch	Yds	Y/C	YAC	TD	C%
M.Wallace	-24	-14.8%	141	73	930	12.7	3.9	5	52%
B.Hartline	123	-0.7%	133	76	1016	13.4	3.7	4	57%
R.Matthews	27	-7.7%	67	41	448	10.9	3.9	2	61%
B.Gibson	103	16.3%	43	30	326	10.9	3.9	3	70%
M.Moore*	-9	-23.2%	11	6	56	9.3	2.0	0	55%
D.Williams	*46*	*12.8%*	*23*	*15*	*178*	*11.9*	*3.1*	*0*	*65%*
C.Clay	88	6.0%	102	69	759	11.0	5.2	6	68%
M.Egnew	-9	-21.2%	11	7	69	9.9	4.3	0	64%
D.Sims	-12	-22.0%	10	6	32	5.3	0.7	1	60%
L.Miller	11	-7.9%	35	26	170	6.5	6.8	0	74%
D.Thomas	27	12.3%	17	15	63	4.2	5.6	2	88%
M.Thigpen	48	66.2%	11	8	97	12.1	9.4	1	73%
K.Moreno	*192*	*31.0%*	*74*	*60*	*548*	*9.1*	*7.9*	*3*	*81%*

Offensive Line

Player	Pos	Age	GS	Snaps	Pen	Sk	Pass	Run	Player	Pos	Age	GS	Snaps	Pen	Sk	Pass	Run
Bryant McKinnie*	LT	35	14/14	1018	3	10.5	19.5	8.0	Nate Garner	LG	29	16/6	412	0	2.5	4.5	1.0
John Jerry*	RG	28	16/16	1013	5	4.5	11.0	5.0	Sam Brenner	C	24	7/4	283	2	1.0	5.5	0.5
Tyson Clabo*	RT	33	15/15	947	2	9.0	26.5	1.5	*Branden Albert*	*LT*	*30*	*12/12*	*775*	*10*	*3.5*	*9.5*	*3.0*
Mike Pouncey	C	25	14/14	899	3	0.5	2.0	2.0	*Shelley Smith*	*G*	*27*	*13/2*	*363*	*1*	*3.0*	*7.0*	*1.0*
Richie Incognito*	LG	31	8/8	467	1	4.0	7.0	2.0	*Jason Fox*	*OT*	*26*	*7/3*	*192*	*1*	*1.0*	*3.0*	*1.0*
Jonathan Martin	LT	25	7/7	453	3	5.5	9.0	0.0									

Year	Yards	ALY	Rk	Power	Rk	Stuff	Rk	2nd Lev	Rk	Open Field	Rk	Sacks	ASR	Rk	Short	Long	F-Start	Cont.
2011	4.28	4.05	16	46%	32	18%	13	1.14	19	0.82	17	52	9.6%	30	22	20	13	29
2012	4.15	3.93	21	63%	17	18%	11	1.14	17	0.76	17	37	6.8%	18	14	14	14	42
2013	3.83	3.62	28	56%	27	21%	27	1.00	23	0.64	19	58	8.6%	30	24	8	9	29

2013 ALY by direction: Left End 3.00 (23) Left Tackle 3.09 (31) Mid/Guard 3.81 (20) Right Tackle 3.46 (24) Right End 4.88 (2)

In this space last year, Danny Tuccitto wrote two things worth highlighting again. First, he prophetically claimed we should cut Jonathan Martin some slack for his rookie performance. Of course no one ever imagined bullying would be one of the biggest stories of the 2013 season, but we really should give Martin a break and think about how we treat other human beings and how we want to be treated in return. Second, we mentioned that Tyson Clabo was not who Dolphins fans really wanted; they wanted Branden Albert from Kansas City. Well, good things *can* come to those who wait. Albert's going to be 30, he's signed up for five years and he's coming off arguably the best season of his career.

Left guard is the competition to watch. Dallas Thomas played 11 offensive snaps last season after being drafted in the third round. He's taken some first-team reps at OTAs, but he's not a guarantee to start with Nate Garner and Billy Turner in the mix. Garner started in place of Richie Incognito last year and fared OK. Turner is a third-round pick from North Dakota State and he's transitioning from tackle to guard. He has been quoted as saying "I like to hit people." As long as he keeps his aggression on the field and between the whistles, he'll have a chance to contribute.

Adding four new starters to the offensive line makes training camp and the preseason extra vital to developing chemistry, but 2013's lone returning starter, center Mike Pouncey, will not be available this summer after having hip surgery in late June. The timetable for his return is about three months, which likely means the Dolphins will have five new starters on the line in Week 1. Sam Brenner is Pouncey's backup and he started four games as a rookie last year. Miami spent plenty of resources to fix this line, but between the rookies, the new arrivals, and Pouncey's recovery, the Dolphins may want to wait until the whole season has played out before judging how successful the rebuilding plan has been.

Defensive Front Seven

			Overall									vs. Run					Pass Rush			
Defensive Line	**Age**	**Pos**	**G**	**Snaps**	**Plays**	**TmPct**	**Rk**	**Stop**	**Dfts**	**BTkl**	**Runs**	**St%**	**Rk**	**RuYd**	**Rk**	**Sack**	**Hit**	**Hur**	**Tips**
Jared Odrick	27	DT	16	856	44	5.0%	45	36	14	5	35	77%	44	2.1	41	4.5	10	18.5	2
Randy Starks	31	DT	16	728	50	5.7%	33	41	15	1	42	83%	23	1.5	20	4.0	4	10.0	1
Paul Soliai*	31	DT	15	523	39	4.7%	50	32	6	0	31	84%	21	1.7	31	1.0	3	5.5	5
Earl Mitchell	*27*	*DT*	*16*	*534*	*48*	*6.2%*	*26*	*38*	*5*	*1*	*43*	*84%*	*22*	*2.5*	*56*	*1.5*	*2*	*5.8*	*0*

			Overall								vs. Run					Pass Rush			
Edge Rushers	**Age**	**Pos**	**G**	**Snaps**	**Plays**	**TmPct**	**Rk**	**Stop**	**Dfts**	**BTkl**	**Runs**	**St%**	**Rk**	**RuYd**	**Rk**	**Sack**	**Hit**	**Hur**	**Tips**
Olivier Vernon	24	DE	16	908	57	6.5%	25	39	16	2	40	63%	69	3.7	67	11.5	5	15.0	0
Cameron Wake	32	DE	15	681	36	4.3%	63	29	12	8	27	74%	46	3.1	61	8.5	16	26.5	0
Derrick Shelby	25	DE	16	438	32	3.6%	--	24	7	1	27	78%	--	2.3	--	2.5	2	3.5	0
Dion Jordan	24	DE	16	330	25	2.8%	--	18	9	0	15	67%	--	3.6	--	2.0	3	11.5	0

			Overall								Pass Rush			vs. Run					vs. Pass						
Linebackers	**Age**	**Pos**	**G**	**Snaps**	**Plays**	**TmPct**	**Rk**	**Stop**	**Dfts**	**BTkl**	**Sack**	**Hit**	**Hur**	**Runs**	**St%**	**Rk**	**RuYd**	**Rk**	**Tgts**	**Suc%**	**Rk**	**AdjYd**	**Rk**	**PD**	**Int**
Philip Wheeler	30	OLB	16	1033	124	14.0%	35	61	19	9	0.5	5	13.5	75	55%	70	4.1	68	43	42%	59	7.2	50	3	0
Dannell Ellerbe	29	MLB	15	1009	106	12.8%	44	42	14	8	1.0	4	5	63	37%	82	5.0	79	49	68%	4	4.2	4	4	2
Koa Misi	27	OLB	15	474	57	6.9%	73	36	13	3	2.0	2	4.5	38	66%	41	2.7	21	17	72%	2	3.9	3	2	0

Year	Yards	ALY	Rk	Power	Rk	Stuff	Rk	2nd Level	Rk	Open Field	Rk	Sacks	ASR	Rk	Short	Long
2011	3.79	3.96	13	73%	29	20%	14	1.15	14	0.38	3	41	7.6%	7	15	22
2012	3.88	3.85	11	64%	18	21%	10	1.04	5	0.63	9	42	6.3%	19	15	14
2013	4.25	4.24	25	64%	14	15%	28	1.20	28	0.58	13	42	6.8%	16	14	13
2013 ALY by direction:			*Left End 4.25 (26)*			*Left Tackle 3.89 (15)*			*Mid/Guard 4.16 (22)*			*Right Tackle 5.07 (32)*			*Right End 3.34 (10)*	

Miami has a bit of a logjam at defensive end involving a star, a top draft pick, and a breakout player. By now we can drop "former CFL star" and just go with "NFL star" to describe Cameron Wake, who notched at least 20 hurries and 20 quarterback knockdowns for the fourth year in a row. He's the best player on this defense, but if there is a concern, it would be the fact that he's already 32 and injuries limited him to just 681 snaps in 15 games last season. It's imperative for Wake to stay on the field, because Dion Jordan, the third overall pick in the 2013 draft, has been very unreliable. Beat writers took notice of how he bulked up this offseason, and coach Philbin said Jordan was playing faster because he's "doing less thinking." Well, he'll have plenty of time to think this September when he serves a four-game suspension for violating the league's performance enhancing drugs policy. So much for that planned duo of 4-3 ends with Wake and Jordan. It did not come to fruition last year either, as Jordan's playing time was limited. He sometimes found himself at linebacker, because second-year defensive end Olivier Vernon earned his snaps opposite of Wake with 11.5 sacks. Jordan's athletic enough to play linebacker and cover tight ends, but his draft value merits a more important role. Miami risks the development of two young players if it can't figure out the best way to split playing time between Vernon, Jordan, and Wake. If Jordan doesn't clean up his act, that will obviously simplify the issue.

Veteran Paul Soliai left for Atlanta in free agency, and the Dolphins have replaced him with the younger Earl Mitchell. Despite being 55 pounds lighter, Mitchell charted very similar numbers to Soliai last year, albeit as Houston's nose tackle in a 3-4 defense. Miami also still has Randy Starks and Jared Odrick, with the latter generating 32 hurries the last two seasons. If the Dolphins lose anything against the run without Soliai's size, they should make up for it in better pass-rush ability if Odrick continues to play the most snaps up front.

The defensive line has to live up to its potential, because Miami's trio of linebackers (Dannell Ellerbe, Philip Wheeler and Koa Misi) give the Sean Lee-less Cowboys a run for their money as the most insignificant corps in the league. The difference is that Miami's trio is grossly overpaid. Misi was about the same forgettable player he was in 2012, but he's set to make a third of what the Dolphins give Ellerbe and Wheeler. Ellerbe had flashed potential in Baltimore, especially when Ray Lewis was injured, so his mediocrity was a surprise. Wheeler was playing for his third team in three years, so his mediocrity was not. Veteran Jason Trusnik is the only other linebacker on the roster to ever start a NFL game, so there's even more pressure on this trio to stay healthy and produce. Count on Miami's 2015 draft to address the linebacker position and right the wrongs of Jeff Ireland's last ill-advised spending spree.

Defensive Secondary

			Overall									vs. Run					vs. Pass									
Secondary	Age	Pos	G	Snaps	Plays	TmPct	Rk	Stop	Dfts	BTkl	Runs	St%	Rk	RuYd	Rk	Tgts	Tgt%	Rk	Dist	Suc%	Rk	AdjYd	Rk	PD	Int
Reshad Jones	26	SS	16	1145	111	12.6%	17	37	12	9	49	39%	39	7.9	58	36	7.8%	34	11.3	43%	68	10.3	71	4	1
Chris Clemons*	29	FS	16	1136	98	11.1%	28	32	10	9	58	33%	54	6.8	35	18	3.8%	2	12.5	80%	1	5.2	13	6	1
Brent Grimes	31	CB	16	1105	77	8.7%	38	25	14	8	9	22%	71	8.1	56	92	20.4%	38	13.4	47%	73	8.1	58	19	4
Nolan Carroll*	27	CB	16	791	57	6.5%	72	24	16	2	9	67%	3	3.4	3	78	24.3%	69	15.2	52%	46	8.0	54	11	3
Jimmy Wilson	28	FS	16	614	42	4.8%	77	16	8	1	14	36%	50	7.1	43	52	20.9%	77	9.1	50%	49	6.7	34	5	2
Dimitri Patterson*	32	CB	6	237	25	7.6%	--	12	7	3	4	25%	--	7.0	--	27	27.6%	--	11.0	60%	--	6.7	--	6	4
Louis Delmas	*27*	*FS*	*16*	*1011*	*72*	*9.5%*	*46*	*32*	*14*	*10*	*25*	*56%*	*9*	*4.6*	*9*	*28*	*6.1%*	*13*	*14.7*	*65%*	*14*	*6.9*	*36*	*8*	*3*
Cortland Finnegan	*30*	*CB*	*7*	*361*	*28*	*7.5%*	*--*	*5*	*1*	*6*	*5*	*60%*	*--*	*7.2*	*--*	*29*	*20.8%*	*--*	*9.7*	*34%*	*--*	*9.2*	*--*	*1*	*1*

Year	Pass D Rank	vs. #1 WR	Rk	vs. #2 WR	Rk	vs. Other WR	Rk	vs. TE	Rk	vs. RB	Rk
2011	12	2.0%	15	0.5%	15	13.7%	29	1.7%	10	-13.9%	6
2012	17	5.2%	19	10.0%	25	-2.4%	14	-3.4%	13	22.9%	28
2013	12	-12.6%	7	11.9%	25	-39.3%	1	24.5%	29	4.6%	17

The Brent Grimes bandwagon has taken an odd path over the years. Grimes actually made the Pro Bowl in 2010 with Atlanta, but may have had a better year in 2011, ranking third in Adjusted Success Rate and second in Adjusted Yards per Pass. He tore his Achilles in 2012 and quietly signed with Miami on a one-year deal. By season's end, he was back in the Pro Bowl, but our charting figures suggest a pretty subpar year: 73rd in Adjusted Success Rate and 58th in Adjusted Yards per Pass. Grimes isn't an asset against the run and he didn't always shadow the opponent's best receiver. Generally, zone corners tend to get less recognition than man corners. Grimes, a smaller corner at 5-foot-10, did not allow a touchdown pass, but the Dolphins as a whole only allowed 17 of those and seven were marked with "Uncovered" or "Hole in Zone" for the primary defender. In terms of recovering from a serious injury at age 30 and performing on a new team, Grimes was very good last year, but the reality of his season does not match perception.

Miami is hoping lightning strikes twice with another 30-year-old cornerback coming off injury, but Cortland Finnegan just had a difficult tenure in St. Louis. He signed a five-year deal worth $27 million guaranteed, but only lasted two injury-plagued seasons while failing to excel despite his aggressive style. In his last two full seasons (2011-12), Finnegan's average target in coverage was the shortest depth (measured by yards past the line of scrimmage) among all qualified cornerbacks: 7.7 in 2011 and 8.0 in 2012. We'll see if he can keep receivers in front of him on short routes for a third team. Nolan Carroll left in free agency, leaving second-year players Jamar Taylor and Will Davis, who combined for 107 defensive snaps in 2013, as the depth.

At safety, both Reshad Jones and Chris Clemons ranked in the top 10 for Adjusted Success Rate in 2012. A year later, Clemons soared to No. 1 at 80 percent while Jones fell to 68th. Keep in mind, however, that we only marked Clemons with 18 targets. He's gone to Houston in free agency and will be replaced by veteran Louis Delmas, who comes in from Detroit on yet another one-year deal. The hard-hitting safety finally played a full 16-game season last year, but Detroit released him after five seasons. He's a marginal upgrade to Clemons if you can trust him to stay healthy. If not, nickel cornerback Jimmy Wilson can always play safety. That's the position he's still listed at, but last year he took over as the nickelback and held his own.

Special Teams

Year	DVOA	Rank	FG/XP	Rank	Net Kick	Rank	Kick Ret	Rank	Net Punt	Rank	Punt Ret	Rank	Hidden	Rank
2011	2.5%	6	-0.4	18	2.5	12	1.3	13	8.7	9	0.7	15	11.5	4
2012	0.4%	14	-4.9	27	0.5	16	7.4	6	-2.8	20	2.0	12	3.7	7
2013	-2.4%	23	-10.9	28	0.5	15	-6.1	28	9.4	5	-4.6	24	11.9	3

Punter Brandon Fields was involved in the funniest special teams play of 2013 when a snap hit him right in the face as he was holding for a field-goal attempt against the Patriots. Otherwise, pretty much everything went right, and Fields deservingly made his first Pro Bowl. His gross punt value of 10.1 estimated points above average led all punters and he has the third-highest career punt average (46.8) in NFL history. Rookie kicker Caleb Sturgis, a fifth-round pick from Florida, was not as consistent. He made his first 10 kicks, but missed a tough 57-yard, game-tying attempt against Baltimore. That sent him into a funk, and he missed five of his next six kicks before finishing 15-of-18 the rest of the way.

Marcus Thigpen handled all of Miami's return duties, but he ranked as the fourth-worst returner for both punts and kickoffs in terms of estimated points worth of field position. He was in the top seven for both categories in 2012. Last year, he only averaged 7.8 yards per punt return and 22.5 yards per kick return. That's a far cry from 2012 when he averaged 12.2 yards per punt return and 27.4 yards per kick return, with one touchdown of each type.

Minnesota Vikings

2013 Record: 5-10-1	**Total DVOA:** -11.4% (26th)	**2014 Mean Projection:** 7.4 wins	**On the Clock (0-4):** 13%
Pythagorean Wins: 6.1 (23rd)	**Offense:** -4.7% (21st)	**Postseason Odds:** 23.8%	**Mediocrity (5-7):** 39%
Snap-Weighted Age: 26.7 (16th)	**Defense:** 10.5% (27th)	**Super Bowl Odds:** 2.4%	**Playoff Contender (8-10):** 37%
Average Opponent: 1.3% (11th)	**Special Teams:** 3.8% (6th)	**Proj. Avg. Opponent:** 2.0% (7th)	**Super Bowl Contender (11+):** 11%

2013: If you have two quarterbacks, you really have no quarterbacks ... and if you have three quarterbacks, you may actually have negative quarterbacks.

2014: Strong signs of offensive rebound, but making this defense playoff-ready would take Mike Zimmer's best coaching performance ever.

You can make a bad situation far worse simply by overreacting to it. The 2013 Vikings quarterback controversy was a great proof of this axiom.

The Vikings had a bad quarterback situation last year. They did not, however, have a historic, league-worst, spoken-of-in-hushed-whispers quarterback situation. Christian Ponder had a droopy arm and a love of locking on to his first receiver, but rushing ability and an up-tempo, fearless style gave him a little usefulness. Matt Cassel also had a dead arm and looked like he was playing in a whirlpool full of mushroom soup at times, but he could read defenses and crank up a wisp of his former foot speed when absolutely necessary. Josh Freeman was one of the league's best prospects just a few seasons ago, though he was banged up and coping with Post-Schiano Stress Disorder when he arrived in Minnesota.

So the Vikings quarterbacks were more a problem than a crisis. The Bills and Browns dealt with worse quarterback situations all season long. The Packers were in more dire straits from the moment Aaron Rodgers got hurt until the moment he returned. The Vikings simply had to choose between a scatter-armed pepperpot and a game manager. With Adrian Peterson as your running back, there are worse fates.

Unfortunately, the Vikings could not choose, and Leslie Frazier made sure his waffling became the story of the Vikings' season.

Ponder began the year by spraying footballs around the way he always does, wedging a pretty solid effort against the Bears between ugly games against the Lions (three interceptions) and Browns (six sacks). Ponder broke a rib against the Browns, and when Cassel played fairly well against the Steelers (16-of-25, 248 yards, two touchdowns) in the Vikings' first win, Frazier appeared content to settle on (and for) Cassel, using the rib injury as an excuse to quietly sideline Ponder.

Frazier quickly soured on Cassel during a lopsided loss to the Panthers, though one ugly interception was Cassel's only major mistake in a game where the Panthers controlled the clock from the opening kickoff. No matter: Frazier had a secret weapon up his sleeve. The Vikings claimed Freeman off waivers from the Buccaneers after Greg Schiano threw all of Freeman's clothes and vintage vinyl onto the front lawn, and a week later, Freeman was named the starting quarterback for a Monday night game against the Giants. Freeman had just two weeks to learn Bill Musgrave's system and was probably in need of a breather from the limelight after his public flensing by Strategic Leak Schiano. Cassel was healthy, Ponder nearly so, but the Vikings were eager to try something new and ridiculous.

Sigmund Bloom of footballguys.com referred to watching Freeman that Monday night as "like watching your parents fight." Freeman was lost and helpless, but Frazier-Musgrave made him throw 53 passes (completing 20) before a concussion took him out of action. Frazier turned back to Ponder, then to Cassel, sometimes juggling them during a game and never ruling Freeman out of the picture until late in the year. Frazier and Musgrave reacted to every interception as if Ponder or Cassel had crashed an oil tanker into the Great Barrier Reef, calling long strings of Peterson handoffs until the vapors passed.

Peterson's carry totals blossomed into the low 30s per game, and the Vikings forgot about free-agent splurge Greg Jennings and first-round pick Cordarrelle Patterson at wide receiver. The Vikings rarely threw downfield—Cassel attempted just 18 passes of 20-plus yards in his first five starts, five of them while trailing late in fourth quarters—so defenses felt comfortable crowding safeties in the box and using creative blitzes.

The predictability of the Vikings offense caused lots of strange stat-sheet residue. The Vikings registered the worst second-and-short offensive DVOA in history (Table 1). Peterson and the other rushers managed just eight first downs on 15 second-and-short carries, but the passing situation was brutal: 19 attempts, 11 completions, nine first downs, two interceptions, two sacks—and here's the kicker—just 66 yards. Imagine a second-and-short pass for a moment. Did you see a fake handoff, followed by a bomb? The Vikings didn't. It looks even worse if we expand "short" past our usual definition of 1 or 2 yards to go. Thirty times, the Vikings put the ball in the air on second down with less than five yards to go. Only four of those passes were thrown over 10 yards through the air, and only one of those four was actually caught: a 57-yard bomb to Greg Jennings that didn't even start with a play fake. When you think of the personnel at their disposal, the inability to generate a single deep play-action pass on second-and-short is just ridiculous.

2014 Vikings Schedule

Week	Opp.	Week	Opp.	Week	Opp.
1	at STL	7	at BUF	13	CAR
2	NE	8	at TB	14	NYJ
3	at NO	9	WAS	15	at DET
4	ATL	10	BYE	16	at MIA
5	at GB (Thu.)	11	at CHI	17	CHI
6	DET	12	GB		

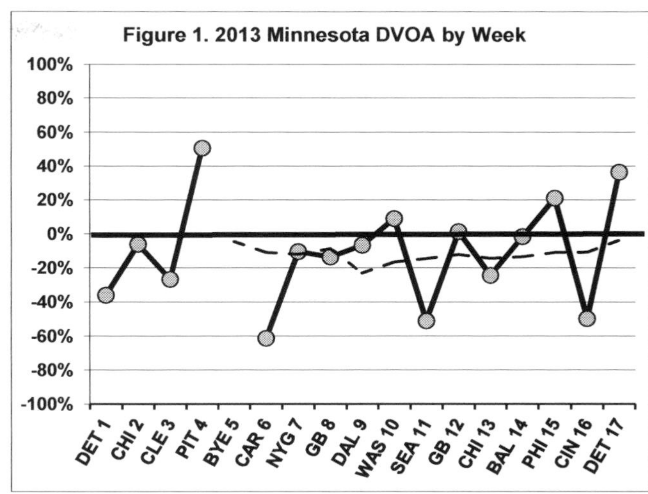

It was a vicious cycle that continued until Peterson got hurt and backup Toby Gerhart quickly followed him. With tight end Kyle Rudolph already on IR, all of the pieces of the Vikings' handoff-and-boot-pass offense were out of duty.

Then a Christmas season miracle happened. Left with no choice but to let Matt Cassel throw real downfield passes late in the season, Frazier and Musgrave did just that. The results weren't outstanding, but Cassel mixed a legitimately great game against the Eagles and serviceable ones against the Ravens and Lions in with a dud against the Bengals. The Vikings had problems in other areas, most notably the secondary and kickoff coverage, but the revelation that Cassel could ride to the corner without training wheels made you wonder what other games the Vikings might have won—the Giants game, perhaps, or the hockey-on-the-road tie against the Packers—if they didn't act so stubbornly like all of their quarterbacks had cooties.

Frazier and Musgrave are gone, of course, but their quarterback neurosis hid several secrets about the Vikings roster from the public eyes. The Vikings offensive line has fine young talent at several positions and no gaping holes. Their receiving corps can be very capable when not twiddling its thumbs. The Vikings defense got old late in the Frazier era and crumbled under the pressure of a weekly time-of-possession drubbing (the Vikings finished 30th in the NFL in net time of possession differential), but there was top talent sprinkled around the

Table 1. Worst Offensive DVOA on Second-and-Short, 1989-2013

Team	Year	2nd-Short	2nd-Short Y+1	All Offense	All Offense Y+1	Change
MIN	2013	-77.2%	--	-4.7%	--	
DET	2003	-64.0%	-25.0%	-21.7%	-10.1%	+11.6%
ARI	1996	-58.3%	11.6%	-4.2%	-13.8%	-9.6%
SD	2011	-55.7%	1.1%	13.0%	-10.0%	-23.1%
TB	2009	-52.6%	-22.9%	-19.3%	8.0%	+27.3%
ARI	2000	-52.1%	21.6%	-19.6%	5.2%	+24.8%
NYG	2001	-51.6%	6.5%	0.2%	3.8%	+3.6%
STL	1996	-49.7%	-29.2%	-26.8%	-14.6%	+12.2%
ARI	2005	-48.2%	-23.5%	-9.5%	-9.4%	+0.1%
PHI	2005	-47.2%	-13.4%	-7.5%	21.1%	+28.7%
STL	2004	-46.1%	-26.7%	-4.1%	-7.9%	-3.8%
NE	1992	-43.2%	-12.4%	-27.6%	-12.2%	+15.4%
OAK	2009	-42.4%	-9.0%	-25.8%	-8.3%	+17.6%
AVERAGE		**-50.9%**	**-10.1%**	**-12.7%**	**-4.0%**	**+8.7%**

Defined as 1-2 yards to go; 2013 Vikings not included in average.

line and secondary. By juggling quarterbacks and installing panicky game plans, the outgoing coaches concealed just how much infrastructure had been built over the last two seasons. This was not a desperate team. It just acted that way.

The Vikings ended 2013 as a disorganized collection of talent in need of direction. Direction will now come from Mike Zimmer, Norv Turner, and Teddy Bridgewater, as unlikely a trio as you could ask for. Zimmer is a long-time defensive X-and-O guru who waited a long time for his first head coaching chance. Turner is a long-time offensive nuts-and-bolts fundamentalist who will forever shine as the living embodiment of the Peter Principle. Bridgewater was the nose-diver of the draft board, a prospect who caused a panic among the draftnik community and prompted dozens of "media scout versus team scout" and "tape versus Pro Day" epistemological arguments on Twitter, all of which were uninteresting and horrible to be a part of.

To summarize the spring's lamest controversy: Bridgewater threw for 31 touchdowns and four interceptions in his senior season, lit up Miami like a display kitchen in the Russell Athletic Bowl, and became the consensus top quarterback among the roughly 80 percent of media draftniks of the sub-Mayock strata, from Doug Farrar to Eric Edholm to yours truly. He then had a weak Pro Day, with several wobbly passes and poor velocity on many throws. Mike Mayock savaged him for a news cycle, numerous reports suggested that he had fallen down draft boards, and in a draft season that lingered two weeks too long, the disconnect between Bridgewater's status among Internet drafniks and his reported status among teams (by late April, anonymous sources were playing the "may never become a starter" angle) became a thing.

Into the fray came Turner, according to a Sports on Earth article by Dan Pompei.[1] Turner, watching the Pro Day live with general manager Rick Spielman and others, spotted a slight mechanical flaw in Bridgewater's delivery, a mistake the young quarterback did not typically make in live action. Turner was also more impressed by the Pro Day than Mayock

1 http://bit.ly/VYSyry

or those of us watching streaming video: what looked to many of us like an off-target deep pass, for example, appeared to Turner to be a receiver's error.

Turner invited Bridgewater to a series of private workouts, coached him up on the tiny errors, and let the quarterback wear the glove he used throughout his college career but went without at the infamous Pro Day workout. Voila! Bridgewater was back. Turner and the other coaches gave him playbook snippets to study and other tasks, finally convincing themselves that Bridgewater was franchise quarterback material. The team selected Anthony Barr ahead of Bridgewater to help Zimmer with his defensive renovations, but Spielman traded back into the first round to secure Bridgewater and prove conclusively that when media scouts bicker with team scouts, only Norv Turner comes out a winner.

Turner has been taking lumps since the dawn of the Football Outsiders era because his reputation bears almost no similarity to the average-at-best performances of nearly all of his offenses. So it is important to point out that the two things the Vikings are asking Turner to do are the two things he has generally done very well. Turner excels at teaching quarterback and wide receiver "how to distribute your weight" basics, so fixing Bridgewater's little hitches and getting the most from Patterson are well within his wheelhouse. Turner also designs structurally-sound game plans; he may not outsmart the best opponents, but he never outsmarts himself, putting Turner a big step up from Musgrave and Frazier. Turner knows how to use second-and-short to his advantage, for example, and history shows that terrible second-and-short teams typically improve in offensive DVOA the next year. It's an easy fix, and Turner is good at easy fixes.

This is Zimmer's team, however, not Turner's. That's a good thing, as Turner's limitations as a motivator, late-game strategist, and long-term planner are well documented from previous stops. Zimmer, like Turner, has deep good ol' days Cowboys roots, though their tenures never overlapped (Zimmer was a Barry Switzer hire). Zimmer has switched from 4-3 to 3-4 base defenses and back again over the years; his current preference is for a 4-3 with a healthy dose of perimeter pass rushing, which is why Barr was such an important acquisition. Zimmer is more creative defensively and more outwardly dynamic than Frazier, a Dungy-Lovie disciple who started as an interim coach in 2010 and still seemed like an interim coach three seasons later.

While Turner adjusts Bridgewater, Zimmer orchestrates a more complex renovation on defense. The Vikings jettisoned Kevin Williams and Jared Allen, two still-capable defenders too old and expensive to keep through a construction project. Everson Griffen and Sharrif Floyd, a pair of tremendous prospects (Griffen a perma-prospect long trapped behind Allen), inherit jobs from the last of the Williams Wall holdouts. The incumbent cornerbacks were deplorable, with the exception of 2013 first-rounder Xavier Rhodes, so Zimmer and Spielman have imported Captain Munnerlyn from the Panthers. Barr adds youth and speed to an old-and-slow linebacker corps, and Zimmer has plans to vary fronts and roles, but the Vikings are not yet dealing with a full deck defensively, just as they are transitioning to a rookie quarterback and relearning the basics on offense.

The 2014 season, then, will be an old-fashioned rebuilding year. But signs of life should appear swiftly. Both Patterson and Rhodes showed that they were worth first-round investments last season, with Floyd also having his moments. Matt Kalil is settling in at left tackle, while Harrison Smith was brilliant in a dunce-cap secondary, so the 2012 draft is also reaping high-end rewards. Bridgewater should supplant Cassel as the Vikings starter early in the year, and when that happens, Vikings fans will get a taste of what they should have enjoyed in 2013: Adrian Peterson, fine receivers, and a strong line supporting a bad—but not spectacularly bad—young quarterback. The biggest difference is that Bridgewater, unlike Ponder, has the potential to get much better, and Zimmer and Turner, unlike the last administration, have both the imagination and the attention to detail to make it happen.

Mike Tanier

2013 Vikings Stats by Week

Wk	vs.	W-L	PF	PA	YDF	YDA	TO	Total	Off	Def	ST
1	at DET	L	24	34	330	469	-2	-36%	-14%	19%	-3%
2	at CHI	L	30	31	350	411	+1	-6%	-16%	-9%	1%
3	CLE	L	27	31	329	409	+1	-27%	-26%	-2%	-3%
4	vs. PIT	W	34	27	393	434	+2	51%	44%	10%	17%
5	BYE										
6	CAR	L	10	35	290	367	-2	-61%	-36%	25%	0%
7	at NYG	L	7	23	206	257	-2	-10%	-24%	1%	14%
8	GB	L	31	44	243	464	0	-14%	10%	29%	6%
9	at DAL	L	23	27	393	350	-1	-7%	-2%	1%	-3%
10	WAS	W	34	27	307	433	-1	9%	24%	26%	11%
11	at SEA	L	20	41	336	323	-4	-51%	-23%	26%	-3%
12	at GB	T	26	26	447	494	-1	1%	5%	19%	15%
13	CHI	W	23	20	496	480	0	-24%	-13%	7%	-4%
14	at BAL	L	26	29	379	325	+2	-2%	6%	-7%	-15%
15	PHI	W	48	30	455	475	0	21%	36%	20%	5%
16	at CIN	L	14	42	209	426	-3	-50%	-39%	23%	12%
17	DET	W	14	13	345	245	-2	36%	-1%	-28%	10%

Trends and Splits

	Offense	Rank	Defense	Rank
Total DVOA	-4.7%	21	10.5%	27
Unadjusted VOA	-5.0%	20	10.3%	26
Weighted Trend	-2.0%	19	11.9%	26
Variance	5.9%	11	2.6%	2
Average Opponent	0.3%	18	1.5%	7
Passing	-8.3%	23	22.1%	30
Rushing	5.8%	8	-6.2%	16
First Down	-4.3%	20	3.4%	18
Second Down	-11.0%	21	2.2%	16
Third Down	4.1%	13	36.1%	32
First Half	-7.8%	25	10.1%	29
Second Half	-1.6%	17	10.9%	24
Red Zone	-7.6%	22	7.9%	19
Late and Close	-7.8%	20	0.5%	20

Five-Year Performance

Year	W-L	Pyth W	Est W	PF	PA	TO	Total	Rk	Off	Rk	Def	Rk	ST	Rk	Off AGL	Rk	Def AGL	Rk	Off Age	Rk	Def Age	Rk	ST Age	Rk
2009	12-4	11.8	10.4	470	312	+6	18.5%	7	12.9%	8	-1.0%	15	4.7%	3	9.4	7	13.1	4	28.3	3	27.5	8	26.9	8
2010	6-10	6.0	6.5	281	348	-11	-13.9%	25	-15.1%	27	-2.5%	12	-1.4%	19	35.7	25	19.7	14	28.5	5	28.3	4	27.4	2
2011	3-13	5.3	4.6	340	449	-3	-22.2%	29	-10.2%	24	8.0%	23	-4.1%	27	20.5	9	28.3	19	27.7	10	27.3	14	26.4	15
2012	10-6	8.8	8.8	379	348	-1	2.0%	14	0.3%	15	3.1%	21	4.7%	5	10.4	3	18.5	8	25.5	31	27.2	12	25.5	28
2013	5-10-1	6.1	6.5	391	480	-12	-11.4%	26	-4.7%	21	10.5%	27	3.8%	6	22.3	8	33.0	19	26.6	19	27.1	12	25.8	24

2013 Performance Based on Most Common Personnel Groups

MIN Offense					MIN Offense vs. Opponents				MIN Defense				MIN Defense vs. Opponents			
Pers	Freq	Yds	DVOA	Run%	Pers	Freq	Yds	DVOA	Pers	Freq	Yds	DVOA	Pers	Freq	Yds	DVOA
11	40%	6.0	5.5%	14%	Nickel Even	38%	5.9	5.9%	Nickel Even	68%	6.5	20.9%	11	56%	6.6	21.7%
21	19%	5.2	-11.7%	54%	4-3-4	28%	5.4	-15.3%	4-3-4	29%	4.5	-9.3%	12	19%	5.2	-6.8%
12	19%	5.6	-14.7%	41%	3-4-4	25%	5.2	-5.8%	Goal Line	2%	0.5	-21.7%	21	9%	5.1	-5.9%
22	13%	5.2	-5.8%	76%	Dime+	4%	7.7	67.2%	Dime+	0%	6.4	49.9%	20	3%	6.8	40.0%
00	2%	5.7	30.0%	0%	Nickel Odd	2%	4.5	-31.9%					22	3%	2.1	-13.8%

Strategic Tendencies

Run/Pass		Rk	Formation		Rk	Pass Rush		Rk	Secondary		Rk	Strategy		Rk
Runs, first half	39%	15	Form: Single Back	48%	31	Rush 3	2.4%	27	4 DB	29%	29	Play action	29%	3
Runs, first down	47%	19	Form: Empty Back	4%	24	Rush 4	70.1%	5	5 DB	68%	2	Avg Box (Off)	6.59	2
Runs, second-long	44%	2	Pers: 3+ WR	45%	27	Rush 5	18.9%	25	6+ DB	0%	29	Avg Box (Def)	6.31	20
Runs, power sit.	50%	23	Pers: 4+ WR	4%	7	Rush 6+	8.6%	15	CB by Sides	82%	9	Offensive Pace	28.64	8
Runs, behind 2H	28%	14	Pers: 2+ TE/6+ OL	36%	10	Sacks by LB	19.5%	22	DB Blitz	6%	29	Defensive Pace	30.52	26
Pass, ahead 2H	46%	20	Shotgun/Pistol	44%	29	Sacks by DB	0.0%	29	Hole in Zone	15%	5	Go for it on 4th	0.92	15

Minnesota ranked ninth in DVOA throwing to the right side of the field, but 27th throwing to the middle and dead last throwing to the left. The left/right split was there for both Matt Cassel and Christian Ponder, although Cassel was much better throwing up the middle than Ponder was. Minnesota was one of only two teams to use 22 personnel on more than 10 percent of plays (San Francisco was the other). Minnesota was also the only team to run more than five plays that really were "five wide," as long as we count Joe Webb as a wideout. There were 18 five-wide plays, plus five plays with 00 personnel but Webb or Cordarrelle Patterson in the backfield. The Vikings blitzed a defensive back less often than almost any other team, and for good reason; they allowed a league-worst 9.2 yards per pass when sending a DB blitz.

Passing

Player	DYAR	DVOA	Plays	NtYds	Avg	YAC	C%	TD	Int
M.Cassel	92	-5.9%	271	1718	6.3	5.2	60.2%	11	9
C.Ponder	-42	-13.5%	267	1523	5.7	4.7	63.8%	7	9
J.Freeman*	-64	-30.0%	55	198	3.6	4.4	37.7%	0	1

Rushing

Player	DYAR	DVOA	Plays	Yds	Avg	TD	Fum	Suc
A.Peterson	60	-3.1%	278	1264	4.5	10	3	44%
M.Asiata	41	12.9%	44	166	3.8	3	1	55%
T.Gerhart*	105	73.6%	36	283	7.9	2	1	50%
C.Ponder	-31	-32.3%	31	145	4.7	4	3	-
C.Patterson	118	144.3%	12	158	13.2	3	0	-
M.Cassel	10	5.2%	12	62	5.2	1	0	-

Receiving

Player	DYAR	DVOA	Plays	Ctch	Yds	Y/C	YAC	TD	C%
G.Jennings	127	2.6%	105	68	804	11.8	5.0	4	65%
J.Simpson	20	-10.1%	100	48	726	15.1	3.5	1	48%
C.Patterson	4	-12.0%	77	45	469	10.4	6.1	4	58%
J.Wright	117	22.7%	43	26	434	16.7	4.5	3	60%
J.Webb*	-25	-42.6%	11	5	33	6.6	0.6	0	45%
L.Jean	*-6*	*-23.0%*	*8*	*4*	*35*	*8.8*	*0.8*	*0*	*50%*
J.Carlson*	-24	-14.6%	47	32	344	10.8	4.8	1	68%
K.Rudolph	-21	-13.9%	46	30	313	10.4	4.0	3	65%
C.Ford	6	-1.2%	16	11	133	12.1	5.5	0	69%
R.Ellison	3	-3.1%	10	5	61	12.2	8.0	1	50%
A.Peterson	-20	-22.8%	41	30	174	5.8	5.5	1	73%
T.Gerhart*	22	10.7%	19	13	88	6.8	6.4	0	68%
J.Felton	-2	-16.9%	8	6	37	6.2	3.8	0	75%
M.Asiata	-26	-67.7%	8	5	13	2.6	4.4	0	63%

Offensive Line

Player	Pos	Age	GS	Snaps	Pen	Sk	Pass	Run	Player	Pos	Age	GS	Snaps	Pen	Sk	Pass	Run
Matt Kalil	LT	25	16/16	1041	5	5.5	22.5	8.0	Brandon Fusco	RG	25	15/15	904	4	3.5	11.5	3.5
John Sullivan	C	29	16/16	1020	1	2.5	12.0	6.0	Joe Berger	OT	32	16/2	214	1	0.0	2.0	0.0
Charlie Johnson	LG	30	15/15	986	3	3.0	13.0	1.0	J'Marcus Webb*	OT	26	8/1	106	0	0.0	1.0	1.0
Phil Loadholt	RT	28	15/15	954	3	4.0	16.5	5.0	*Vladimir Ducasse*	*OT*	*27*	*16/4*	*317*	*5*	*3.0*	*10.0*	*2.0*

Year	Yards	ALY	Rk	Power	Rk	Stuff	Rk	2nd Lev	Rk	Open Field	Rk	Sacks	ASR	Rk	Short	Long	F-Start	Cont.
2011	4.72	4.05	18	73%	1	23%	28	1.43	3	1.15	3	49	9.8%	32	13	24	18	33
2012	5.67	4.17	10	53%	30	24%	29	1.41	4	2.08	1	32	6.5%	16	7	15	14	48
2013	4.78	4.04	10	79%	2	20%	20	1.29	7	1.26	1	44	7.8%	23	14	16	11	34

2013 ALY by direction: Left End 3.63 (13) Left Tackle 3.79 (18) Mid/Guard 4.18 (9) Right Tackle 3.98 (15) Right End 4.09 (10)

The Vikings committed just ten holding penalties last year, the lowest total in the NFL. That's pretty impressive for a line that had to block for three different quarterbacks who looked downfield with the confused apprehension of toddlers entering their first amusement park. The Vikings line was stable and reasonably effective under the circumstances, and it is the one unit most likely to look much better as soon as other minor problems are sorted out.

Matt Kalil faced some no-win situations last year when trying to keep Jason Pierre-Paul off Josh Freeman or coping with blitzers firing off the edge. Kalil can still get beaten by pure speed on an edge rush but takes care of business against any defender he can reach and has only one holding penalty in the last two seasons. Phil Loadholt has grown into one of the best run-blocking right tackles in the NFL and has cut down on his pass protection mistakes in recent seasons.

Brandon Fusco has grown from a sixth-rounder from Slippery Rock into one of the league's most reliable guards. Like Kalil, Fusco gave up a few "lost cause" sacks when Christian Ponder was trying to survive a blowout and the opposing defense was in a feeding frenzy. Center John Sullivan is no match for Brandon Mebane but can handle most defensive tackles. Both Fusco and Sullivan suffered a few blown blocks that were really I-formation handoffs up the middle that a drunk in the cheap seats could have predicted pre-snap.

Charlie Johnson was solid and consistent last season, but he turned 30 in May, and fifth-round rookie David Yankey is likely to push him soon. Yankey is the typical Stanford guard of the post-Harbaugh era: a pull-and-trap specialist with an ornery streak, but with undeveloped footwork and fundamentals. Guard depth is outstanding, with prospect Jeff Baca and longtime Jets reserve Vlad Ducasse joining Yankey on the bench. Tackle depth is a much bigger problem; in the event of an emergency, Johnson would likely slide to one of the tackle positions and let Yankey or Ducasse take over inside.

Defensive Front Seven

			Overall								vs. Run					Pass Rush			
Defensive Line	Age	Pos	G	Snaps	Plays	TmPct	Rk	Stop	Dfts	BTkl	Runs	St%	Rk	RuYd	Rk	Sack	Hit	Hur	Tips
Kevin Williams*	34	DT	15	718	33	4.0%	64	27	10	3	23	78%	39	2.3	50	3.5	4	12.0	3
Sharrif Floyd	23	DT	16	459	21	2.4%	--	18	9	0	14	79%	--	2.0	--	2.5	3	6.0	1
Letroy Guion*	27	DT	13	388	21	2.9%	--	16	6	2	19	74%	--	2.5	--	1.0	0	4.0	1
Fred Evans	31	DT	14	350	22	2.9%	--	18	5	2	18	83%	--	1.1	--	0.0	1	6.5	3
Corey Wootton	*27*	*DT/DE*	*16*	*846*	*37*	*4.5%*	*55*	*31*	*14*	*2*	*29*	*79%*	*38*	*1.4*	*16*	*3.0*	*3*	*15.0*	*6*
Linval Joseph	*26*	*DT*	*15*	*578*	*59*	*7.3%*	*13*	*38*	*12*	*1*	*53*	*64%*	*79*	*3.1*	*71*	*3.0*	*4*	*4.5*	*0*
Tom Johnson	*30*	*DE*	*12*	*223*	*12*	*2.1%*	*--*	*8*	*3*	*1*	*9*	*67%*	*--*	*3.7*	*--*	*2.0*	*2*	*7.0*	*0*

			Overall								vs. Run					Pass Rush			
Edge Rushers	Age	Pos	G	Snaps	Plays	TmPct	Rk	Stop	Dfts	BTkl	Runs	St%	Rk	RuYd	Rk	Sack	Hit	Hur	Tips
Jared Allen*	32	DE	16	1058	58	6.6%	23	43	22	5	38	63%	67	2.4	38	11.5	15	27.0	7
Brian Robison	31	DE	16	971	40	4.6%	59	34	16	3	26	81%	25	2.5	41	9.0	10	46.5	4
Everson Griffen	27	DE	16	697	28	3.2%	76	20	10	1	18	67%	59	2.3	29	5.5	5	25.0	0

			Overall								Pass Rush			vs. Run					vs. Pass						
Linebackers	Age	Pos	G	Snaps	Plays	TmPct	Rk	Stop	Dfts	BTkl	Sack	Hit	Hur	Runs	St%	Rk	RuYd	Rk	Tgts	Suc%	Rk	AdjYd	Rk	PD	Int
Chad Greenway	31	OLB	16	1152	136	15.5%	23	62	24	14	3.0	2	9.5	68	66%	39	2.8	23	53	45%	55	7.9	60	4	3
Erin Henderson	28	MLB	14	848	114	14.9%	28	63	24	5	4.0	2	4	71	68%	32	2.4	11	24	46%	51	9.2	67	4	2
Audie Cole	25	MLB	13	323	43	6.0%	--	25	8	5	1.0	4	6	22	68%	--	4.1	--	13	63%	--	7.3	--	1	0
Marvin Mitchell*	30	OLB	16	304	40	4.6%	--	26	5	2	0.0	0	2	31	68%	--	3.2	--	13	53%	--	6.1	--	1	0
Jasper Brinkley	*29*	*ILB*	*15*	*202*	*24*	*3.1%*	*--*	*16*	*6*	*5*	*0.0*	*2*	*2*	*18*	*83%*	*--*	*2.8*	*--*	*7*	*15%*	*--*	*11.3*	*--*	*0*	*0*

Year	Yards	ALY	Rk	Power	Rk	Stuff	Rk	2nd Level	Rk	Open Field	Rk	Sacks	ASR	Rk	Short	Long
2011	3.91	3.85	8	62%	16	22%	7	1.26	21	0.51	5	50	8.7%	1	20	21
2012	3.75	3.87	12	59%	12	24%	6	1.11	7	0.46	4	44	6.4%	16	9	21
2013	3.89	3.67	10	60%	9	23%	7	1.19	26	0.64	17	41	6.8%	17	12	17
2013 ALY by direction:			*Left End 3.53 (13)*			*Left Tackle 4.21 (21)*			*Mid/Guard 3.47 (5)*			*Right Tackle 4.71 (27)*			*Right End 2.74 (3)*	

The Vikings still asked too much of the old Williams Wall holdovers and had grown too slow at linebacker last year. Jared Allen and Kevin Williams could still play at a high level (Allen regularly, Williams in spurts), but it was obvious that the team would need to rebuild before they got good again. At linebacker, Erin Henderson looked sluggish all season before disappearing into a haze of DUI arrests, while Chad Greenway slammed hard into the wrong side of 30.

Allen, Williams, and Henderson are gone, and Mike Zimmer is revamping and rethinking everything. Sharrif Floyd and Linval Joseph are the new defensive tackles. Joseph has developed steadily over the last three years; by 2013, he was one of the Giants' bright spots in a season when everything else went dim. Joseph brings the same combination of pure hugeness (he hovers around 330 pounds), initial quickness, and willingness to attack double teams that made Pat Williams so effective. Floyd, one of the Vikings' first-round Three Amigos in 2013, takes over Kevin Williams' three-tech role after showing brief flashes last season. The Williams Wall metaphor should only be taken so far, however, as Zimmer likes to shuffle fronts and packages. Fred Evans is back for his eighth year as the Vikings' nose tackle off the bench.

Everson Griffen received a five-year deal with $20 million guaranteed once the Vikings decided to part ways with the old-timers. Griffen has been on "what a specimen" watch lists for years (including ours; he was No. 1 on last year's "Top 25 Prospects" list) but has never been able to slip past Allen or Brian Robison for an every-down role.

Robison's sack totals never fluctuate—they have crept up from eight to nine over the course of three seasons—but he led the NFL with 46.5 hurries. He had 15 "half-hurries" shared with Allen or other defenders, which creates a bit of a "chicken-and-egg" argument for the Vikings pass rush moving forward: what good is half a hurry, which is not quite a sack, which was shared with a now-absent teammate? Robison would have finished third in hurries even without those 15 plays, but of course some of his "full hurries" also were the product of opponents' keying on Allen. For the Vikings pass rush to evolve, Robison must elevate from second-fiddle status, or Griffen must finally make the most of his genetic advantages.

Neither end is an ideal every-down player, so the Vikings grabbed Corey Wootton from the Bears and drafted Scott Crichton. Wootton was the closest thing the Bears front seven had to a reliable run defender for much of last season but was lost in their reshuffle. Crichton draws comparison to Robison and was a versatile performer at Oregon State.

Versatility was what made Anthony Barr so appealing to Zimmer; the coach has a specialized role in mind for his top first-round pick, a natural outside linebacker with both pass-rush chops and range. Barr also has excellent speed, which will be welcome on a defense where linebackers were routinely a step behind the play on any run or throw to the sidelines. Look for Barr to take over Greenway's role as the Vikings' most likely blitzer, with Greenway serving as more of a signal caller and in-space reactor.

Jasper Brinkley, a longtime Vikings prospect who spent a season with the Cardinals last year, is the penciled-in starter at middle linebacker. Brinkley is a 275-pounder best suited for thumping between the tackles in a 4-3; Zimmer's ability to hybridize and mix-and-match should keep him out of bad situations. Audie Cole could compete for a nickel linebacker role. Cole replaced Henderson late in the year and did a credible job chasing down Ray Rice, Eddie Lacy, and Matt Forte after catches for minimal gains.

Defensive Secondary

			Overall								vs. Run					vs. Pass									
Secondary	Age	Pos	G	Snaps	Plays	TmPct	Rk	Stop	Dfts	BTkl	Runs	St%	Rk	RuYd	Rk	Tgts	Tgt%	Rk	Dist	Suc%	Rk	AdjYd	Rk	PD	Int
Jamarca Sanford	29	SS	13	790	71	10.0%	38	18	5	6	34	35%	51	8.1	61	18	5.2%	7	7.1	36%	73	5.9	19	1	0
Chris Cook*	27	CB	12	734	48	7.3%	58	15	5	7	11	36%	49	7.0	41	43	13.9%	2	12.0	35%	85	10.5	82	2	0
Andrew Sendejo	27	FS	16	725	81	9.2%	50	31	10	8	48	42%	34	7.2	46	21	6.7%	21	10.4	45%	67	8.1	56	2	1
Xavier Rhodes	24	CB	13	674	57	8.0%	51	23	7	5	9	33%	53	6.4	32	79	27.6%	83	12.1	53%	42	5.9	5	9	0
Josh Robinson	23	CB	10	653	58	10.6%	14	24	7	1	12	58%	11	5.5	21	45	16.3%	5	10.3	35%	86	10.2	81	3	0
Marcus Sherels	27	CB	16	527	48	5.5%	84	22	10	2	6	33%	53	11.0	72	56	25.2%	75	10.3	51%	56	7.5	41	5	1
Harrison Smith	25	FS	8	526	59	13.5%	9	24	9	5	26	54%	11	5.7	16	20	9.0%	52	10.8	50%	51	6.6	31	3	2
Robert Blanton	25	SS	16	391	50	5.7%	72	19	6	1	19	63%	3	5.8	19	30	17.9%	76	11.5	51%	47	7.4	47	0	0
Shaun Prater	25	CB	9	158	7	1.4%	--	4	4	4	0	0%	--	0.0	--	15	21.7%	--	20.4	67%	--	4.0	--	1	1
Captain Munnerlyn	*26*	*CB*	*16*	*970*	*86*	*10.8%*	*13*	*47*	*18*	*4*	*22*	*50%*	*25*	*4.4*	*8*	*70*	*16.8%*	*8*	*12.6*	*60%*	*10*	*7.8*	*47*	*10*	*2*
Derek Cox	*28*	*CB*	*16*	*554*	*45*	*5.8%*	*78*	*13*	*4*	*3*	*5*	*0%*	*84*	*15.6*	*83*	*59*	*24.0%*	*65*	*13.1*	*46%*	*76*	*9.4*	*78*	*7*	*1*

Year	Pass D Rank	vs. #1 WR	Rk	vs. #2 WR	Rk	vs. Other WR	Rk	vs. TE	Rk	vs. RB	Rk
2011	32	30.4%	28	41.1%	30	33.6%	31	21.5%	24	15.5%	26
2012	24	3.9%	18	38.6%	32	-8.7%	9	4.6%	22	18.4%	25
2013	30	5.1%	22	8.9%	22	44.8%	32	0.1%	15	15.2%	29

The Vikings cornerback situation was a mirror image of their quarterback situation. A group of mid-tier prospects kept trading the jobs and performing terribly. Injuries played a role, and the coaching staff avoided both clear decisions and obvious solutions (like admitting Xavier Rhodes was the best cover cornerback and just letting him take his rookie lumps). The Vikings even pulled a dude off the waiver wire and gave him a few starts: former Bengals and Eagles quasi-prospect Shaun Prater played mirrorverse Josh Freeman. It was ugly, and it would have looked far worse if fewer opponents were squatting safely on second-half leads.

Josh Robinson and Chris Cook were two of the worst starting cornerbacks in the NFL last year. They will be replaced by Rhodes and Captain Munnerlyn. Rhodes has talent to burn but looked like a rookie running around in confusion at times last year; in fairness, so did Cook and Robinson, but only Rhodes had the excuse. Charting analysis reveals that Rhodes' play deteriorated substantially as the quality of the receivers improved: he had a 68 percent Adjusted Success Rate and allowed 3.9 Adjusted Yards per Pass against slot receivers, but those numbers dropped to 58 percent and 6.2 against No. 2s and 40 percent and 7.6 versus No. 1s. Then again, as you can see by the table above, all of those numbers are better than Cook and Robinson's raw figures.

Munnerlyn has worked his way up from tough little special-teamer to solid starter to coveted free-agent acquisition. Munnerlyn is competent and always brings the effort, but the Panthers front seven protected him at times last year. Prater and Robinson are still around. Marcus Sherels also earned a few starts and looked like an ace return man playing cornerback. If the rest of the secondary settles down, Sherels can handle slot receivers in a pinch but probably will not have to.

Jamarca Sanford spent a lot of time cleaning up the messes of the cornerbacks last season. Sanford is effective in coverage but can get crossed up in the open field. In March, he took a pay cut to remain with the Vikings, and Antone "Don't Call Me Dante" Exum is expected to push him. Exum played safety and cornerback for Virginia Tech, as well as a specialized "Rover" role, before suffering an ACL tear in the 2013 offseason. The Hokies tried to Shanahan Exum back too early, resulting in another sprain that allowed Exum to slide down to the sixth round. Rick Spielman said after the draft that he prefers converted cornerbacks at safety, and Exum could provide more versatility and reliability than Sanford, at least in the long term.

Harrison Smith was the Vikings' best defensive back by far before getting sidelined by a concussion/turf-toe one-two punch for much of the season. Like Sanford, Smith was stuck doing a lot of cleanup duty, but he was a reliable fly-around blitzer and gap shooter in the rare instances when Leslie Frazier could trust his cornerbacks without two-deep protection. Defensive backs coach Jerry Gray compared Smith to Seahawks safeties Kam Chancellor and Earl Thomas in May, and while that is pushing things a bit, Smith falls into the Vikings' "vital building block" category.

Special Teams

Year	DVOA	Rank	FG/XP	Rank	Net Kick	Rank	Kick Ret	Rank	Net Punt	Rank	Punt Ret	Rank	Hidden	Rank
2011	-4.1%	27	-9.1	32	-13.2	31	11.7	1	-6.7	25	-3.0	20	-11.5	31
2012	4.7%	5	9.5	2	2.5	11	7.9	5	4.0	12	-0.1	16	-3.4	23
2013	3.8%	6	-0.6	20	-15.4	32	22.4	1	0.6	17	11.8	3	-4.6	22

Cordarelle Patterson's tackle-breaking ability makes him unique. Patterson has exceptional open-field speed and can make quick cuts to avoid defenders, but he is not Percy Harvin or Devin Hester when it comes to jukes. Instead, he rips though arm tackles like a man 30 pounds heavier. Opponents started giving Patterson the star treatment in the second half of the year, and you can tell who the blockers on the Vikings' kickoff units were by seeing who earned a nine-yard return of an avoid-Patterson shorty: Joe Webb, Jerome Felton, Rhett Ellison, Joe Banyard, and several of the other members of the Vikings' H-back legion.

Marcus Sherels returned a punt for a touchdown last season and brings a fine mix of elusiveness and runaway speed to the job. The Vikings lost many of their best return blockers, including Webb, John Carlson, and Toby Gerhart, but plenty remain, most notably special teams ace Robert Blanton. Blanton made 10 solo tackles on special teams, but he made an even more significant contribution as a blocker, often springing Sherels or creating a lane for Patterson. Patterson and Sherels kept several games close with their long returns; Blanton and the blocking units gave Patterson and Sherels what they needed to succeed.

Blair Walsh fell off from his 10-of-10 magic from 50-plus yards in 2012 to go 2-of-5 in 2013, because randomization and central tendency are two ladies you never want to have a threesome with. Walsh is middle-of-the-pack on kickoffs but can still slap 50s as well as any NFL kicker. Vikings kickoff coverage was terrible, with seven kickoffs allowed of over 40 yards. Devin Hester and ice may have combined to make the Vikings coverage units look worse than they appear, however. Hester cruised to 76 and 80 yarders in one game and a 57-yarder in the rematch, inspiring a few short keepaway kickoffs in between. Jacoby Jones sledded to a touchdown for the Ravens while a Walsh kickoff in the slush sailed out of bounds.

Jeff Locke replaced Chris Kluwe and provided reliable punting without uttering a single sociopolitical theory; it's debatable whether that final point was what the Vikings were really seeking, though those of us who tired of Kluwe's increasing Olbermannization enjoyed the respite. (We may agree with your opinions, but we defend to the death our right to ask you to STFU about them.) Blanton and others made the punt coverage team nasty; the kickoff coverage got the yips whenever they saw Hester.

New England Patriots

2013 Record: 12-4	Total DVOA: 18.9% (5th)	2014 Mean Projection: 9.7 wins	On the Clock (0-4): 3%
Pythagorean Wins: 10.5 (8th)	Offense: 16.4% (4th)	Postseason Odds: 67.9%	Mediocrity (5-7): 12%
Snap-Weighted Age: 26.5 (22nd)	Defense: 4.2% (20th)	Super Bowl Odds: 16.5%	Playoff Contender (8-10): 47%
Average Opponent: -0.9% (18th)	Special Teams: 6.7% (2nd)	Proj. Avg. Opponent: 0.6% (15th)	Super Bowl Contender (11+): 39%

2013: The clear No. 2 team in the AFC, and just as clearly not No. 1.

2014: Preparing for life beyond Brady, and trying to send him out a champion, all at the same time.

In the moments after the Patriots' divisional playoff win over the Colts last January, Charles Barkley suddenly materialized in the middle of the New England locker room. In a surreal moment, he woozily passed from locker to locker, stopping to congratulate players and talking with the media.

In the midst of his tour, Barkley stopped and spoke with the media. A longtime friend of Bill Belichick, he delivered a dire warning for New England fans.

"In New England, y'all have a chance to win every year," he said. "I'm impressed with the Patriots organization because they've lost so many people—and y'all take winning for granted. Y'all do.

"[But] let me tell you guys something," he added. "When Bill Belichick leaves and Tom Brady leaves, y'all team is going to fucking suck."

While it's widely presumed that Belichick isn't going anywhere, the quarterback does have a finite shelf life, a point that has been hammered home over the course of the last year-plus. And despite the fact that Brady's per-season numbers in his thirties are better than they were when he was in his twenties, it's undeniable that the quarterback is closer to the end of his career than the start. That means the Patriots need to start formulating a transition plan sooner rather than later.

So to Barkley's point, how do you avoid sucking when the franchise quarterback leaves? You start planning for the future *now*. In New England, it's been a gradual adding of parts, creating a mix of talent the franchise hopes will translate to a competitive roster whenever the post-Brady era begins. One of the biggest additions came this past spring, when the Patriots took Eastern Illinois quarterback Jimmy Garoppolo with their second-round pick, 62nd overall. No quarterback has ever been taken higher by Belichick. In a perfect world for the Patriots, Garoppolo would play the role of Aaron Rodgers to Brady's Brett Favre, minus the tiresome Hamlet act and creepy old-man scruff. He would sit and wait for three seasons, learning and absorbing knowledge from Brady, and then take over when Brady eases into retirement. Regardless of what you think of Garoppolo at this stage of his career, he certainly has the sort of pedigree that would appeal to New England for a few reasons, not the least of which is the fact that he was tutored by quarterback guru Jeff Christiansen, a former NFL quarterback who learned all of *his* teaching methods from Brady's late mentor, Tom Martinez.

"When Jimmy came to me, he was a sophomore linebacker in high school," Christensen said shortly after Garoppolo was drafted by the Patriots. "He was sent to me by his high school coach Doug Milsaps, and I started working with him and teaching him proper techniques and arm angles and footwork, and so on and so forth. Everything we did, we trained him off film of Tom. Every video, every drill, every routine was all based off Tom Brady, and what he did with Tom Martinez.

"This is so surreal to me, it's almost frightening," he added. "EVERYTHING we did was off Tom Brady. Brady set the standard for perfect technique, and so it just made sense for us to follow everything that Tom Martinez did with Brady."

But history tells us that identifying, drafting and developing The Next Guy is just one part of the process that needs to happen from a franchise to move into a new era. How did other teams prepare themselves for life after their franchise quarterback called it a career? And can the Patriots learn from these previous scenarios and apply those lessons to their own situation?

Here are four examples of how teams handled the final years of a once-in-a-generation quarterbacking talent, and how they prepared for a superstar's eventual departure. Who are the Patriots emulating—and who should they emulate?

Indianapolis (Peyton Manning): In 2011, the Colts weren't yet really concerned with the apocalyptic scenario of Life After Peyton. Following the 2010 season, Manning had just turned 34, and was coming off a year where he set personal marks for completions (450) and yardage (4,700) while leading Indy to its ninth straight postseason appearance. In addition, given the fact that he had been incredibly durable to that point in his career, there was little reason to think that the Colts would have to worry about a transition plan for at least the next few seasons. But at the same time, they had fundamentally ignored the backup quarterback position for the better part of a decade. Indy had only drafted two quarterbacks since taking Manning first overall in 1998: Jim Sorgi in the sixth round of the 2004 draft and Curtis Painter in the sixth round of the 2009 draft. That sort of planning is exactly what landed them in hot water when Manning went down for the year.

Of course, it all worked out for the Colts, but they can almost entirely thank random timing. If Manning's injury had come a year earlier, the Colts would have likely drafted Cam Newton with their top pick. Newton is a very talented quarter-

2014 Patriots Schedule

Week	Opp.	Week	Opp.	Week	Opp.
1	at MIA	7	NYJ (Thu.)	13	at GB
2	at MIN	8	CHI	14	at SD
3	OAK	9	DEN	15	MIA
4	at KC (Mon.)	10	BYE	16	at NYJ
5	CIN	11	at IND	17	BUF
6	at BUF	12	DET		

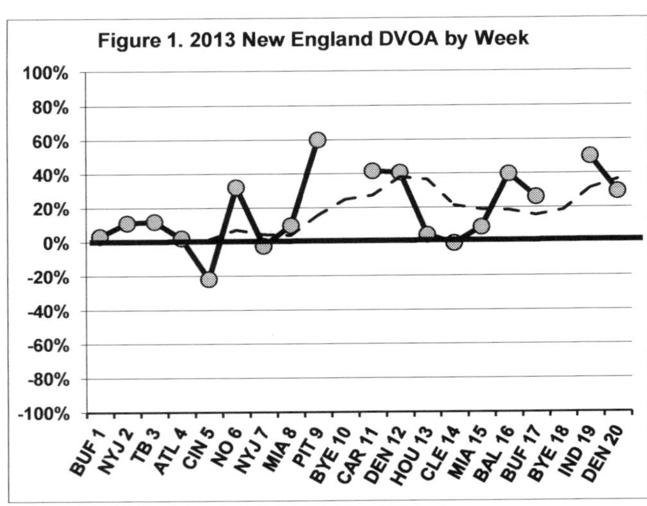

Figure 1. 2013 New England DVOA by Week

back, but nobody in the league would take him over Andrew Luck right now. If the injury comes a year later, the Colts are trying to trade around the board to use a pick somewhere in the first three rounds on EJ Manuel, Geno Smith, or Mike Glennon. Of course, the Colts' master plan wasn't to fall into Andrew Luck all along. And Belichick certainly isn't betting that the same thing will happen with the Patriots.

"I don't think we would put together a team the way Indianapolis did it when they lost [Peyton] Manning and they go (2-14)," Belichick told the media this spring, twisting a psychic knife into Bill Polian's back. "I don't think that's really what we're looking for. Fortunately, when we lost Tom [Brady] in 2008, we had a player that could step in, and we won 11 games... I don't think we'd be happy going 1-15 if we had an injury at one position. But other people have different philosophies."

Because Manning's career in Indy came to a screeching halt, there was no loading up for a late-career run. Instead, the real lesson learned here was the fact that you neglect the backup quarterback position at your own peril. For the Patriots, some backup quarterbacks have worked out (Matt Cassel), many others have not (Rohan Davey), and others have gone on to become pretty good college coaches (Kliff Kingsbury), but you should always be looking to draft a quarterback. You never know when you kick over a rock and discover a two-time MVP.

Green Bay (Brett Favre): When it came to cultivating backup quarterbacks, Green Bay was the exact opposite of Indy. Favre was every bit as durable as Manning, but the Packers were vigilant when it came to the backup quarterback spot. For many years, Green Bay was an assembly line for drafting quality signal-callers. Over the years, the Packers drafted and developed future starters Matt Hasselbeck, Mark Brunell, Aaron Brooks, and, of course, Rodgers, all of whom began their careers behind Favre. (For what it's worth, they also signed a young Kurt Warner.)

Like New England, Green Bay offered a relatively stable environment where there was no pressure on the successor to win, or even play immediately. Like Brady, Favre was years removed from the idea of moving on. (Remember, Favre got Green Bay to the NFC Championship game in 2007, and had them within overtime of a Super Bowl rematch with the Patriots. By that game, Rodgers had been in the league for three seasons.)

Since the Packers had an heir apparent on board at all times, it's not surprising that there was no attempt to load up with veterans for one last Brett Favre run. Despite knowing that Favre was on his way out the door (eventually), the Packers selected an astounding 33 players in the draft between 2005 and 2007. A number of these players would go on to have a significant impact once they turned the page, including Greg Jennings and James Jones. Two big pieces of the post-Favre offense, Jordy Nelson and Jermichael Finley, came in the 2008 draft, the first one where the Packers knew Aaron Rodgers would be their starting quarterback in the fall.

The best lesson here for the Patriots is that there is no such thing as too many offensive options for a young quarterback taking over from a legend. But when it comes to the quarterback transition itself, the Favre-to-Rodgers transition is likely an exception, rather than the rule. Much like Andrew Luck, the Rodgers pickup was a case of good timing. (One year later, the quarterbacks chosen in the first two rounds were Vince Young, Matt Leinart, Jay Cutler, Kellen Clemens and Tarvaris Jackson.) Green Bay was able to also take advantage of a collective brain fart by scouting departments around the league. A number of quarterback-hungry teams passed on Rodgers in 2005, including the Niners, Texans and Bears.

Dallas (Troy Aikman): Once the whole Steve Walsh-Troy Aikman nonsense was settled, Jimmy Johnson neglected the position. Dallas chose Bill Musgrave out of Oregon in the fourth round of the 1991 draft and then didn't draft another quarterback for Aikman's entire career.

As a result, following Aikman's retirement, the Cowboys were stuck reaching for Quincy Carter in the second round with no fallback plan if he failed. (Although to be fair, some of that was likely because they were caught unawares by the fact that Aikman retired at the relatively young age of 34 because of recurring concussion issues.) They went on to employ a series of terrible young quarterbacks and over-the-hill veterans until undrafted free agent Tony Romo matured into an NFL starter in 2006.

There was no loading up, and there was no change in organizational philosophy. (With Jerry Jones at the controls, is this a surprise?) Instead, the lesson here is fundamentally the same one that was learned roughly 15 years later in Indy: neglect the quarterback situation at your own peril. Johnson was a forward thinker who shares many of the same organizational philosophies as Belichick, but like Indy, the neglect of the backup quarterback position left the Cowboys wholly unprepared to deal with life after Aikman.

Denver (John Elway): Much more than the three teams we've discussed so far, the Broncos appeared to be loading up their roster with an eye toward landing a championship before Elway retired. Denver dealt away the majority of its draft picks in 1997, selecting only three players: Trevor Pryce, Dan Neil and Cory Gilliard. First-round pick Pryce would go on to become a major part of the Denver defense, as the defensive tackle had 35.5 sacks in his first four years with the Broncos. The rest of the draft was mostly built around protecting Elway. Their second-round pick went to Baltimore for veteran tackle Tony Jones, while their fifth- and sixth-round picks were part of a package to move up 21 spots in the third round to take Neil. Jones started all 16 games in both Super Bowl seasons, while Neil easily slid into the right guard spot for Elway's second title.

One year later, the Broncos drafted Brian Griese with the 91st overall pick in the 1998 draft. Much like Belichick's pick of Garoppolo, that third-round pick used on Griese was the highest pick Shanahan used on a quarterback during his time in Denver. The Broncos were fully aware that Griese was going to have to sit behind an aging Elway for at least a year. Griese tends to get lost in the fog of history simply because he wasn't Elway, but truthfully, he wasn't a bad quarterback. He had an average DVOA in 1999, his first year as the starter. In 2000 he was fifth in DYAR, second in DVOA (lower in DYAR because he missed some games). In 2001 he was slightly below average again, then above average in 2002. After Elway retired, the Broncos rebuilt their offense the next few seasons behind a stout offensive line and a steady and consistent ground game that featured a variety of backs. When Terrell Davis broke down, Shanahan and the Broncos plugged in a series of new faces, including Olandis Gary (1,159 rush yards in 1999), Mike Anderson (1,487 rush yards in 2000) and Clinton Portis (1,508 rush yards in 2002). They weren't a Super Bowl team, but they certainly remained competitive, and they got all the way to the AFC title game against the Steelers shortly after Jake Plummer assumed the starting role in 2003.

Ultimately, there are elements here that the Patriots can apply to their own team-building process, and based on how they have operated the last few seasons, it certainly looks like Belichick took note of Shanahan's approach. He's primarily known for defense, but Belichick has shown remarkable offensive flexibility over the last decade plus. He's taken remarkably pedestrian running backs like Antowain Smith, BenJarvus Green-Ellis and LeGarrette Blount, plugged them into the system and watched them become successful. Granted, a portion of that is due to Brady's successes, but there's also the fairly steady work of the offensive line over the last decade-plus, as well as the fact that those backs have been kept fresh by a rotation that includes third-down and short-yardage specialists ranging from Kevin Faulk and Sammy Morris to Danny Woodhead and Brandon Bolden.

Belichick's apparent distaste for Indy's situation—and how the Patriots approached the 2014 draft—pretty much rules out the Colts' template. The stunning lack of foresight offered by the Cowboys pretty much rules out that scenario as well. And while it would be nice to get lucky with a Rodgers-type of scenario with Garoppolo, the Denver example appears to be the most likely transition scenario in New England, particularly when you consider how the Patriots have loaded up on running backs in recent years. Garoppolo playing the role of Griese isn't a stretch—would that make Ryan Mallett the 21st century Bubby Brister?—and the Patriots also followed the late-'90s Broncos by drafting three offensive linemen this spring. Though the Patriots go for bigger blockers while the Broncos always liked undersized linemen, the overall similarities are striking.

Ultimately, for the Denver approach to work with the Patriots—and for the Patriots to prove Barkley wrong—they must build a steady and consistent backfield, develop solid and dependable run blockers, and craft a defense to carry the load if/when the offense stalls out. This past offseason, New England took significant steps in that direction by drafting three offensive linemen and signing two of the best cornerbacks on the market in Darrelle Revis and Brandon Browner.

No coach preaches complementary football more than Bill Belichick, but New England lost sight of that over the last few seasons. This year, however, there's legitimate reason to believe that the Patriots will put a balanced team on the field and perhaps even finish in the top ten of defensive DVOA for the first time since 2006. The young defensive talent drafted in 2012 and 2013 has had time to mature. Linebacker Jerod Mayo and defensive tackles Vince Wilfork and Tommy Kelly look like they've returned to full strength after ending the year on IR. Signing Revis actually gives the Patriots an upgrade on the departed Aqib Talib, while signing Browner provides depth to help avoid a repeat of last year's AFC Championship Game—when New England's ghastly lack of depth at corner was exposed after Talib went down with an injury.

The Patriots won't be at full strength until Browner returns from the four-game suspension he'll have to serve for a substance abuse violation last year, but considering the fact that the Patriots face the Dolphins, Vikings, Raiders and Chiefs right out of the gate, it shouldn't be an issue if they have to utilize Alfonzo Dennard at one outside corner spot until Browner steps into the starting lineup on a full-time basis. For the first time since 2007, New England goes into a year with a secondary that possesses pretty good ball skills, with the only question there being who will play the strong safety role. Steve Gregory was cut loose after two decent seasons, and while there was a steady parade of possibilities over the course of the spring, it now appears that the job will be Duron Harmon's to lose. Harmon has good instincts, is a steady and consistent tackler, and has shown toughness, all assets in the New England system. At the same time, he's not as rangy and doesn't have quite the ball skills of someone like McCourty.

The biggest question for the New England defense is depth at linebacker, with both Brandon Spikes and Dane Fletcher lost in free agency. Spikes was a massive liability in coverage, but one of the best interior run-stoppers in the AFC; Fletcher was a core special-teamer and backup coverage linebacker. In their place, the Patriots added veteran James Anderson, who does have some coverage skills and should help a group that was middle of the pack last year when it came to slowing tight ends and running backs in the passing game. But with little depth past Anderson, New England has to hope that the starting trio of Mayo, Dont'a Hightower and Jamie Collins stays healthy. Mayo is an interesting study in that there's no one area where he's considered an elite linebacker by either scouts or stats; instead, he's just very good at a lot of things, including working in coverage and occasionally stopping the run. His loss was felt across the board last season, but no more so than when it came to Hightower's overall evolution. By his own admission, Hightower tried to do too much when Mayo went out of the lineup last season. As a result, he got outside his comfort zone, and he spent much of midseason on the bench. (For example, he barely saw the field in the second half or overtime of New England's dramatic regular-season win over the Broncos.) Down the stretch, he entered into a nice groove, and if he can continue to build on that, it would go a ways toward ensuring he will stick as an every-down linebacker in the league. Collins progressed nicely over the course of his rookie year as a versatile defender who can run with many (though not all) tight ends while providing support as a potential pass rusher.

On the other side of the ball, it's easy to tie the success or failure of the New England offense to Rob Gronkowski. But while you can draw a line between the struggles of the Patriots early in 2013 and the fact that the big fella was still sidelined, there were plenty of other issues while the Patriots passing game adjusted to numerous new elements. Gronkowski certainly delivered a seismic jolt when he returned, but the numbers from last season suggest that there wasn't much slippage when he went down late in the year (Table 1).

Table 1. Patriots Offense with and without Rob Gronkowski, 2012-2013

Time Period	DVOA	PPG	Yds/Play
2012 with Gronk (1-11, 17)	34.7%	35.1	5.93
2012 w/o Gronk (12-16, 19-20)*	27.3%	32.1	5.86
2013 w/o Gronk Part I (1-6)	-2.4%	20.8	5.04
2013 with Gronk (7-14)	27.5%	32.0	5.94
2013 w/o Gronk Part II (15-20)*	30.9%	30.8	5.82

**Includes playoffs*

That's not to suggest the Patriots didn't miss Gronkowski in 2013—the red zone was an Achilles' heel for New England while he was on the sidelines, and his skill as a blocker remains underrated. But there's certainly a case to be made that the consistency from Week 7 through the end of the year is a product of an offense that had finally gotten used to playing without him. Others emerged as key parts of the offense, including LeGarrette Blount, Julian Edelman and Shane Vereen, all of whom played key roles down the stretch and into the playoffs. When it comes to the makeup of their current roster, trying to win a Super Bowl without a healthy Gronkowski for a full 16 games and into the playoffs probably isn't a sustainable philosophy. But what they have on offense without him is likely still good enough to separate them from most of the rest of the AFC.

And they still have Brady. Despite some struggles last season, it's shortsighted to say the 2013 season was the first sign the end is near. The fits of Marinoesque rage directed toward his younger receivers aside, it was a year of personal and professional growth for Brady, who was all over the map statistically but still a legitimate part of the MVP discussion in early December. He's not the same quarterback he was 10 years ago. The accuracy on his deep ball has clearly deteriorated, and two big throws missed early in the AFC Championship Game put the Patriots into a big hole. His pocket awareness, which had always been one of his most important assets, betrayed him at times last year, leading to some very bad sacks. But to use a half-season of woe as an indication that Brady will soon slip into the depths of mediocrity because he struggled with pressure and a group of new pass catchers—in a year when the Patriots essentially asked him to hit the reset button in the passing game—misses the big picture. Now he must build on the chemistry he forged last year with young receivers like Aaron Dobson, Josh Boyce, Kenbrell Thompkins and Danny Amendola. We already saw the progress through Brady's improvement in the second half of 2013. In the first eight games of the regular season, Brady struggled with a shockingly low passing DVOA of -12.4%. In the final eight, Brady was back at 32.9%, in line with his recent career numbers. From Week 9 on, only Peyton Manning and Nick Foles were more efficient according to our metrics.

It's debatable if the addition of Brandon LaFell and the continued maturation of young receivers like Dobson, Boyce, and Thompkins will be enough to lift the offense. On the other hand, Gronkowski isn't the only player who could lift the offense with a full season of health. Danny Amendola certainly needs a rebound year after struggling with a torn adductor longus tendon in 2013. (This is us trying to avoid the painful words "groin injury.") Another important piece is Shane Vereen, a dynamic offensive weapon who reached the 40-catch/40-carry plateau last season despite only playing eight games. If he can stay healthy for the 2014 season, he could be a Sprolesian matchup nightmare that could give opposing defensive coordinators ice-cream headaches. As for the rest of New England's running backs, the closest thing the Patriots will offer as a feature back will be Stevan Ridley, who had serious ball security issues in 2013—so much so, he was benched toward the end of the season.

On paper, the Patriots will head into the 2014 season more balanced than they have been since the halcyon days of 2007. As always, health will play a vital role in the overall success or failure of New England—this was a team that ended the 2013 season with $28 million in guaranteed contractual money on injured reserve—but there's no reason not to include them on the short list of Super Bowl contenders again in 2014. As for the long term, only time will tell if Belichick and the Patriots can avoid Barkley's apocalyptic scenario of a post-Brady landscape. While there's been a lot of talk about how New England's team-building approach became the gold standard across the league over the last decade-plus, how the Patriots execute the delicate procedure of the Life After Brady could provide Belichick with his greatest legacy as a crafter of champions.

Christopher Price

2013 Patriots Stats by Week

Wk	vs.	W-L	PF	PA	YDF	YDA	TO	Total	Off	Def	ST
1	at BUF	W	23	21	431	286	-1	3%	0%	7%	9%
2	NYJ	W	13	10	232	318	+4	11%	-21%	-34%	-3%
3	TB	W	23	3	358	323	0	12%	6%	2%	8%
4	at ATL	W	30	23	448	457	+1	2%	16%	16%	2%
5	at CIN	L	6	13	248	341	0	-22%	-41%	-11%	8%
6	NO	W	30	27	376	361	+1	32%	14%	-7%	11%
7	at NYJ	L	27	30	295	383	0	-2%	-18%	-7%	8%
8	MIA	W	27	17	252	301	+2	10%	-7%	-10%	7%
9	PIT	W	55	31	610	479	+2	60%	75%	13%	-2%
10	BYE										
11	at CAR	L	20	24	390	300	-2	42%	57%	25%	9%
12	DEN	W	34	31	440	412	+1	41%	13%	-21%	7%
13	at HOU	W	34	31	453	385	0	4%	39%	39%	4%
14	CLE	W	27	26	484	494	-2	-1%	31%	44%	11%
15	at MIA	L	20	24	453	378	0	8%	39%	29%	-1%
16	at BAL	W	41	7	300	358	+4	40%	30%	-6%	4%
17	BUF	W	34	20	382	393	-1	26%	13%	12%	24%
18	BYE										
19	IND	W	43	22	419	386	+4	50%	35%	-26%	-11%
20	at DEN	L	16	26	320	507	0	29%	35%	16%	10%

Trends and Splits

	Offense	Rank	Defense	Rank
Total DVOA	16.4%	4	4.2%	20
Unadjusted VOA	14.5%	4	2.1%	19
Weighted Trend	26.2%	2	9.3%	24
Variance	8.9%	24	4.6%	13
Average Opponent	-3.5%	8	-3.6%	29
Passing	28.2%	6	4.1%	14
Rushing	6.9%	6	4.3%	27
First Down	29.6%	1	5.8%	21
Second Down	16.4%	4	-1.2%	12
Third Down	-11.7%	23	10.0%	23
First Half	7.1%	11	-4.0%	10
Second Half	25.7%	2	11.7%	25
Red Zone	16.7%	7	-1.7%	15
Late and Close	21.4%	5	10.9%	27

Five-Year Performance

Year	W-L	Pyth W	Est W	PF	PA	TO	Total	Rk	Off	Rk	Def	Rk	ST	Rk	Off AGL	Rk	Def AGL	Rk	Off Age	Rk	Def Age	Rk	ST Age	Rk
2009	10-6	11.7	11.2	427	285	+6	28.8%	4	26.4%	1	-1.1%	14	1.3%	12	27.1	19	19.1	10	29.4	1	27.0	19	26.2	22
2010	14-2	12.6	14.6	518	313	+28	44.6%	1	42.2%	1	2.3%	21	4.7%	8	32.9	23	39.5	27	28.3	6	25.5	31	26.2	18
2011	13-3	11.9	12.2	513	342	+17	22.8%	3	31.9%	3	13.2%	30	4.1%	5	40.0	23	57.5	31	28.5	1	26.7	22	26.1	21
2012	12-4	12.7	13.4	557	331	+25	34.9%	3	30.8%	1	1.4%	15	5.5%	4	46.7	25	28.0	15	27.9	7	25.6	29	26.2	12
2013	12-4	10.5	11.0	444	338	+9	18.9%	5	16.4%	4	4.2%	20	6.7%	2	50.1	26	49.8	28	27.6	6	25.8	29	25.6	27

2013 Performance Based on Most Common Personnel Groups

NE Offense					NE Offense vs. Opponents				NE Defense				NE Defense vs. Opponents			
Pers	Freq	Yds	DVOA	Run%	Pers	Freq	Yds	DVOA	Pers	Freq	Yds	DVOA	Pers	Freq	Yds	DVOA
11	47%	5.6	12.4%	29%	Nickel Even	32%	5.5	10.4%	Nickel Even	49%	5.3	-2.9%	11	62%	5.6	6.2%
12	20%	5.4	9.3%	56%	3-4-4	21%	6.4	31.8%	4-3-4	20%	6.0	16.6%	12	18%	6.0	3.8%
21	19%	6.3	36.0%	47%	4-3-4	18%	5.9	29.2%	3-4-4	13%	4.7	-0.9%	21	10%	4.8	1.4%
10	6%	5.0	15.6%	3%	Nickel Odd	15%	5.2	9.7%	Nickel Odd	9%	4.9	-0.4%	20	3%	6.2	-42.0%
22	4%	4.5	29.5%	80%	Dime+	11%	5.7	19.4%	Dime+	7%	7.8	34.9%	22	2%	5.8	17.0%

Strategic Tendencies

Run/Pass		Rk	Formation		Rk	Pass Rush		Rk	Secondary		Rk	Strategy		Rk
Runs, first half	42%	8	Form: Single Back	76%	7	Rush 3	10.1%	2	4 DB	33%	23	Play action	25%	8
Runs, first down	47%	18	Form: Empty Back	7%	14	Rush 4	65.6%	10	5 DB	58%	8	Avg Box (Off)	6.41	13
Runs, second-long	38%	9	Pers: 3+ WR	55%	20	Rush 5	18.9%	26	6+ DB	7%	13	Avg Box (Def)	6.09	31
Runs, power sit.	57%	13	Pers: 4+ WR	6%	4	Rush 6+	5.4%	25	CB by Sides	58%	24	Offensive Pace	26.59	4
Runs, behind 2H	24%	23	Pers: 2+ TE/6+ OL	26%	21	Sacks by LB	10.9%	28	DB Blitz	5%	30	Defensive Pace	29.09	9
Pass, ahead 2H	47%	18	Shotgun/Pistol	45%	27	Sacks by DB	9.8%	12	Hole in Zone	6%	29	Go for it on 4th	1.06	10

One of the oddest trends of the past few years is that while almost every team in the NFL has shifted dramatically towards using more shotgun formations, the Patriots have actually been using *fewer* shotgun formations. In 2011, the Patriots went shotgun 51 percent of the time, which ranked sixth in the NFL. That dropped to 48 percent in 2012, then 45 percent in 2013. It doesn't seem like a big drop, until you realize that 26 different offenses used shotgun (or pistol) more often than the Patriots last year. And the drop may make sense, because last year the Pats were one of the rare teams to be better in standard formations, with 5.3 yards per play and 11.3% DVOA from shotgun but 5.9 yards per play and 19.8% DVOA otherwise. By the way, "shotgun or pistol" for the Patriots means "shotgun," as New England was one of just two teams to never trot out the pistol formation. Over the past three years, the Patriots' use of two-tight end sets has gone from 74 percent to 49 percent to 26 percent. Some explanation for why Bill Belichick keeps James Develin around: The Pats were one of the few teams to run better from two-back formations

(5.0 yards per carry, 16.6% DVOA) than from single-back formations (4.6 yards per carry, 4.7% DVOA). Patriots receivers dropped 38 passes, more than any team except Detroit. But the Patriots' defense benefitted from 40 opponent drops, more than any team except Green Bay. We only marked pressure on 18.1 percent of pass plays where Patriots opponents sent five or more pass rushers, the lowest rate in the league. Somewhat connected: the Patriots didn't send a lot of big blitzes of six or more pass rushers, but they were absolutely eviscerated when they did, giving up a league-worst 10.1 yards per pass.

Passing

Player	DYAR	DVOA	Plays	NtYds	Avg	YAC	C%	TD	Int
T.Brady	979	10.9%	665	4065	6.1	5.3	61.0%	25	10

Rushing

Player	DYAR	DVOA	Plays	Yds	Avg	TD	Fum	Suc
S.Ridley	135	10.2%	178	774	4.3	7	3	52%
L.Blount*	117	9.4%	153	776	5.1	7	3	54%
B.Bolden	54	13.1%	55	271	4.9	3	0	49%
S.Vereen	6	-5.0%	44	208	4.7	1	1	39%
T.Brady	-5	-19.4%	11	37	3.4	0	2	-

Receiving

Player	DYAR	DVOA	Plays	Ctch	Yds	Y/C	YAC	TD	C%
J.Edelman	204	4.3%	151	105	1056	10.1	4.7	6	70%
D.Amendola	163	12.3%	83	54	633	11.7	4.7	2	65%
A.Dobson	46	-5.4%	72	37	519	14.0	5.0	4	51%
K.Thompkins	4	-11.9%	70	32	466	14.6	4.3	4	46%
J.Boyce	9	-6.9%	19	9	121	13.4	8.7	0	47%
A.Collie*	6	-5.5%	11	6	63	10.5	0.7	0	55%
B.LaFell	*44*	*-6.2%*	*85*	*49*	*620*	*12.7*	*5.2*	*5*	*58%*
R.Gronkowski	91	12.9%	66	39	592	15.2	5.0	4	59%
M.Hoomanawanui	3	-4.4%	19	12	136	11.3	6.9	1	63%
S.Vereen	151	25.1%	69	47	427	9.1	5.9	3	68%
B.Bolden	-1	-14.6%	29	21	152	7.2	7.6	0	72%
S.Ridley	-9	-27.6%	12	10	62	6.2	5.7	0	83%

Offensive Line

Player	Pos	Age	GS	Snaps	Pen	Sk	Pass	Run	Player	Pos	Age	GS	Snaps	Pen	Sk	Pass	Run
Ryan Wendell	C	28	16/16	1197	5	5.0	22.8	5.5	Marcus Cannon	RT	26	14/6	571	5	0.0	5.0	7.0
Logan Mankins	LG	32	16/16	1184	7	6.0	15.8	0.0	Sebastian Vollmer	RT	30	8/8	500	0	1.5	9.5	1.0
Dan Connolly	RG	32	16/16	1117	3	3.0	17.5	2.0	Will Svitek*	OT	32	13/2	239	0	2.0	4.0	0.5
Nate Solder	LT	26	15/15	1085	4	8.5	22.3	6.0	Josh Kline	G	25	7/1	113	1	0.0	1.0	0.0

Year	Yards	ALY	Rk	Power	Rk	Stuff	Rk	2nd Lev	Rk	Open Field	Rk	Sacks	ASR	Rk	Short	Long	F-Start	Cont.
2011	4.17	4.53	2	61%	19	17%	7	1.22	14	0.45	30	32	5.4%	9	13	15	17	24
2012	4.32	4.45	3	66%	13	18%	10	1.33	9	0.63	22	27	4.5%	5	9	8	13	23
2013	4.69	4.63	1	59%	23	16%	4	1.39	2	0.80	12	40	6.1%	9	23	9	11	32

2013 ALY by direction: Left End 3.54 (15) Left Tackle 5.10 (2) Mid/Guard 4.88 (1) Right Tackle 3.99 (14) Right End 4.10 (9)

While there are several other notable units Patriots fans will be fixated on this season, perhaps the most interesting is the offensive line. They currently project to be able to run the same five guys out there that they had at the start of the 2013 season, yet it's clear that the Patriots are in flux up front. For the first time since shortly after the earth cooled, Dante Scarnecchia isn't New England's offensive line coach—instead, that job will fall to former Jets line coach Dave DeGuglielmo. While it remains to be seen how the veterans will react to a new position coach, it's also important to note that the Patriots selected three offensive linemen—tying a record for a Bill Belichick-led draft—and all of them have the sort of pedigree that suggests they could contribute sooner rather than later.

Health issues with the veteran linemen could make that depth very useful. Right tackle Sebastian Vollmer returns from a leg injury that prematurely ended his 2013 season, while left tackle Nate Solder missed a game because of a head injury and was working with a rehab group this spring for an undetermined reason. In addition, Logan Mankins is coming off a year where he suffered plenty of bumps and bruises but managed to hold up while playing left guard as well as left tackle when Solder went down. Mankins' pass blocking is no longer at an All-Pro level, but his leadership, toughness and overall attitude still set the tone for the group, and make him one of the most valuable players on the roster. (Belichick has said that in his nearly 40 years in the NFL, he hasn't coached anyone tougher than Mankins.)

One position that certainly bears watching in 2014 is center. Ryan Wendell is the incumbent, and has ably manned the spot since he took over on a full-time basis in 2012. However, he's slightly undersized for the position, and has played a tremendous amount of snaps the last two years for New England. (He was fourth among all offensive linemen last year with 1,197 snaps, and second in the league with 1,231 in 2012, trailing only Solder.) In addition, Wendell was second on the team with 42.3 snaps per blown block. Only Solder had a higher rate, at one blown block per 38.3 snaps, but left tackles almost always blow the most blocks because they face the best defenders. Wendell had the worst blown block rate of any center with at least 400 snaps last season: a stark contrast from 2012, when we marked Wendell with a blown block only once every 91.2 attempts. Has he worn down slightly from overuse? It's debatable—the Patriots faced some of the best defensive fronts in the league over the course of the 2013 season—but New England's decision to use a fourth-round pick on Rimington Award-winning center Bryan Stork out of Florida State, as well as the fact that Wendell drew almost zero attention on the market as a free agent this offseason, could be a sign his days as a starter are numbered. Among the two other rookies, expect fourth-round pick Cameron Fleming (a bona fide rocket scientist out of Stanford) to push for the job of backup swing tackle as a rookie. And sixth-rounder Jon Halapio (Florida) should provide some level of competition for starting right guard Dan Connolly, who is going into the last year of a three-year deal he signed in 2012.

Defensive Front Seven

			Overall								vs. Run					Pass Rush			
Defensive Line	**Age**	**Pos**	**G**	**Snaps**	**Plays**	**TmPct**	**Rk**	**Stop**	**Dfts**	**BTkl**	**Runs**	**St%**	**Rk**	**RuYd**	**Rk**	**Sack**	**Hit**	**Hur**	**Tips**
Chris Jones	24	DT	13	780	53	7.6%	11	37	12	1	44	66%	72	2.8	64	6.0	2	6.5	0
Joe Vellano	26	DT	16	664	53	6.2%	27	36	8	1	48	71%	63	2.9	66	2.0	3	10.0	0
Sealver Siliga	24	DT	5	218	23	8.6%	3	20	4	2	19	84%	18	2.9	67	3.0	0	3.0	0
Tommy Kelly	34	DT	5	218	22	8.2%	6	14	4	0	19	58%	83	3.1	70	2.0	3	8.0	0

			Overall								vs. Run					Pass Rush			
Edge Rushers	**Age**	**Pos**	**G**	**Snaps**	**Plays**	**TmPct**	**Rk**	**Stop**	**Dfts**	**BTkl**	**Runs**	**St%**	**Rk**	**RuYd**	**Rk**	**Sack**	**Hit**	**Hur**	**Tips**
Chandler Jones	24	DE	16	1125	79	9.2%	3	55	23	5	63	63%	66	2.7	49	11.5	12	32.5	1
Rob Ninkovich	30	DE	16	1097	92	10.8%	1	65	18	2	72	74%	47	3.1	60	8.0	10	31.5	1

			Overall								Pass Rush			vs. Run					vs. Pass						
Linebackers	**Age**	**Pos**	**G**	**Snaps**	**Plays**	**TmPct**	**Rk**	**Stop**	**Dfts**	**BTkl**	**Sack**	**Hit**	**Hur**	**Runs**	**St%**	**Rk**	**RuYd**	**Rk**	**Tgts**	**Suc%**	**Rk**	**AdjYd**	**Rk**	**PD**	**Int**
Dont'a Hightower	24	OLB	16	857	98	11.5%	52	46	9	2	1.0	4	11	60	52%	74	4.2	72	49	55%	27	6.5	34	3	0
Brandon Spikes*	27	MLB	16	687	88	10.3%	61	59	13	1	0.0	1	2.5	72	74%	13	2.6	18	22	45%	52	6.0	22	2	1
Jerod Mayo	28	OLB	6	399	56	17.5%	10	25	10	2	2.0	0	2	36	47%	79	4.2	71	24	61%	11	6.6	35	1	0
Jamie Collins	24	OLB	16	298	41	4.8%	81	24	7	1	0.0	3	3	21	71%	20	4.0	64	21	46%	48	8.3	63	4	0
James Anderson	*31*	*OLB*	*16*	*998*	*105*	*12.8%*	*43*	*53*	*20*	*4*	*4.0*	*1*	*7*	*59*	*59%*	*62*	*3.5*	*52*	*37*	*61%*	*15*	*5.0*	*10*	*3*	*0*

Year	Yards	ALY	Rk	Power	Rk	Stuff	Rk	2nd Level	Rk	Open Field	Rk	Sacks	ASR	Rk	Short	Long
2011	4.48	4.51	30	58%	11	16%	27	1.28	25	0.66	8	40	6.5%	19	9	23
2012	3.97	3.83	10	50%	2	19%	13	1.29	27	0.49	7	37	6.0%	24	4	20
2013	4.24	4.37	30	60%	11	13%	32	1.12	17	0.43	4	48	7.5%	9	8	20
2013 ALY by direction:			*Left End 3.98 (22)*			*Left Tackle 4.22 (22)*			*Mid/Guard 4.62 (31)*			*Right Tackle 3.93 (18)*			*Right End 3.48 (13)*	

Last August, this area was projected to be the strength of the team. With so many of Tom Brady's old offensive options stripped away, the defense was counted on to lead the way. But by the end of the 2013 season, the front seven was a shell of itself: three important starters (defensive tackles Vince Wilfork and Tommy Kelly and linebacker Jerod Mayo) all went down to season-ending injuries before the end of October. The Patriots were able to get some surprise performances out of some new faces, but more often it felt the whole thing was being held together with bubble gum and baling wire, especially in the AFC title game when the pass rush couldn't get anywhere near Peyton Manning. It's a small sample size, but for comparison's sake, the loss of Wilfork and Kelly was sizable when it came to run defense. Through the first four games—with Wilfork and Kelly—the Patriots yielded an average of 105 rushing yards per game, 13th in the league. By the end of the regular season, that number had jumped to 134 rushing yards per game allowed, 30th in the league. Their run defense DVOA went from -7.3% in the first four games to 7.6% the rest of the year. Chris Jones, Joe Vellano and Sealver Siliga did as well as could be expected up front and certainly did enough to warrant consideration as depth players in 2014, but they remain backups at best.

Provided the Wilfork/Kelly/Mayo combo returns in good health, this should be an area of strength for New England in 2014. Rob Ninkovich and Chandler Jones will continue to work on the edge as defensive ends, but look for Jones to also play some defensive tackle, as was the case in 2013. (His long frame frequently gave guards problems when he kicked inside on passing downs.) One youngster who will see an expanded role in 2014 is linebacker Jamie Collins, who started his rookie year slowly but was a regular down the stretch and into the postseason. In 2014, he will be expected to be a three-down presence, alongside Mayo and Hightower, the latter of whom started slowly and almost dropped off the radar screen completely (he sat for virtually the entire second half and into overtime in the November win over the Broncos) before rebounding to finish the year strong. With the loss of run stuffer Brandon Spikes and backup/special teamer Dane Fletcher in free agency, the Patriots are still a little thin at linebacker, but the spring additions of veterans James Anderson (ex-Bears) and Darius Fleming (ex-49ers) could ultimately rectify that issue. Ninkovich also provides flexibility; he has played a lot of strongside linebacker over the course of his career in New England and spent some of the spring OTA sessions working out at that spot.

First-round pick Dominique Easley, a versatile, aggressive defender, has massive boom/bust potential. When healthy, he was a disruptive force at Florida. However, he's coming off two torn ACLs over the course of his college career, which dampens some of the enthusiasm that's surrounded his arrival in New England. Speaking of ACL tears, this year's annual Patriots "See What He Has Left in the Tank" signing is defensive end Will Smith, who was discarded in the Great New Orleans Salary Purge of 2014. If Smith proves to be healthy enough, he will join a long line of veteran defensive linemen who made the trek to Foxboro at the tail end of their careers to try and win a ring. Over the last decade-plus, the group includes the likes of Ted Washington, Keith Traylor, Anthony Pleasant, Steve Martin, Albert Haynesworth, Shaun Ellis and Tommy Kelly. Needless to say, some vets have worked out better than others.

Defensive Secondary

			Overall									vs. Run					vs. Pass									
Secondary	Age	Pos	G	Snaps	Plays	TmPct	Rk	Stop	Dfts	BTkl	Runs	St%	Rk	RuYd	Rk	Tgts	Tgt%	Rk	Dist	Suc%	Rk	AdjYd	Rk	PD	Int
Devin McCourty	27	FS	15	1024	76	9.5%	47	22	9	5	25	24%	71	10.1	71	29	6.3%	16	18.3	62%	18	6.7	33	8	1
Aqib Talib*	28	CB	13	845	55	7.9%	52	23	14	5	9	44%	35	5.7	22	70	18.9%	23	13.0	52%	43	8.4	63	15	4
Steve Gregory*	31	SS	14	835	82	11.0%	29	33	5	4	44	50%	21	6.0	22	33	9.0%	53	10.6	52%	45	7.5	48	4	0
Kyle Arrington	28	CB	16	828	71	8.3%	47	28	15	5	15	33%	53	6.4	31	76	20.8%	40	12.7	47%	74	9.0	74	12	1
Alfonzo Dennard	25	CB	13	716	47	6.8%	65	17	7	5	13	31%	63	9.1	60	59	18.8%	21	15.5	51%	52	8.4	64	7	1
Logan Ryan	23	CB	16	600	45	5.3%	--	19	14	0	12	25%	--	7.9	--	46	17.3%	--	12.8	58%	--	7.0	--	10	5
Duron Harmon	23	FS	15	427	35	4.4%	--	9	5	2	13	15%	--	12.1	--	16	8.5%	--	13.8	54%	--	6.1	--	4	2
Darrelle Revis	*29*	*CB*	*16*	*948*	*61*	*7.4%*	*56*	*31*	*12*	*3*	*17*	*59%*	*10*	*5.1*	*14*	*50*	*13.4%*	*1*	*14.2*	*57%*	*22*	*6.4*	*11*	*11*	*2*
Patrick Chung	*27*	*SS*	*12*	*721*	*60*	*8.9%*	*54*	*13*	*3*	*7*	*25*	*28%*	*68*	*7.2*	*44*	*28*	*8.6%*	*48*	*14.4*	*58%*	*33*	*9.8*	*69*	*3*	*0*
Brandon Browner	*30*	*CB*	*8*	*453*	*29*	*7.3%*	*57*	*16*	*7*	*1*	*3*	*33%*	*53*	*7.3*	*49*	*41*	*22.1%*	*51*	*13.7*	*57%*	*17*	*7.1*	*32*	*8*	*1*

Year	Pass D Rank	vs. #1 WR	Rk	vs. #2 WR	Rk	vs. Other WR	Rk	vs. TE	Rk	vs. RB	Rk
2011	27	45.4%	32	7.0%	20	6.5%	25	25.8%	29	-14.7%	5
2012	23	-5.0%	14	-16.4%	6	27.3%	30	21.3%	29	14.8%	23
2013	14	-1.9%	16	17.9%	29	5.5%	21	-1.1%	13	5.1%	19

The secondary had a good season when the New England defensive backs were slotted into the appropriate spots. Alfonzo Dennard was more than competitive as the No. 2 corner, while Kyle Arrington held up well in the slot. Meanwhile, Logan Ryan did well to kind of cover all the bases as a rookie—while none of his five team-leading interceptions were especially worthy of a highlight reel, he made the plays when it counted. The problems arose when Aqib Talib went down, and the group as a whole was forced to step up (Dennard into the role of lead corner, Arrington moved out wide and Ryan wherever needed). That's when the house of cards collapsed—especially in the AFC Championship Game, when they appeared wholly unprepared for the offensive onslaught that Peyton Manning and the Broncos rained down upon them. Now, the arrivals of Darrelle Revis and Brandon Browner mean that it's unlikely the New England secondary will face this predicament again in 2014.

This offseason, the Patriots basically exchanged Talib for Revis, and while Revis might only be around Foxboro for one year because of his contract, it's a gamble the Patriots were willing to take. Despite the fact that he was coming off a serious knee injury and was being utilized mostly in zone coverage in Greg Schiano's Tampa schemes, Revis was still one of the best corners in the NFL. He ranked No. 1 in our "estimated target percentage" metric, which uses snap counts to estimate the number of passes when Revis was on the field that had him listed in coverage.

Revis enters the picture in New England as the acknowledged No. 1 cornerback, but the most intriguing new addition for the Patriots is Brandon Browner. The 6-foot-4, 221-pound Browner, who will sit out the first four games of the season because of a violation of league PED rules last year, is the biggest cornerback ever acquired by Bill Belichick. It's debatable how much of his success over the last two seasons has been because he plays opposite Richard Sherman and in front of Earl Thomas, but he has flashed enough impressive numbers while working in Seattle to indicate he could serve in a similar complementary role with Revis in New England. What isn't debatable is the fact that Browner is one of the best corners in the league when it comes to limiting yards after the catch. In his eight games in 2013, he yielded an average of just 1.8 yards after the catch, tied for the league lead with Jabari Greer. (For comparisons sake, Talib yielded an average of 5.4 YAC, 77th in the league, while Revis was at 3.3, 24th in the league.) In 2012, he was 15th in the league with an average of 2.5 yards allowed after the catch.

The addition of Revis and Browner generated a lot of buzz, but the steady anchor of the secondary remains Devin McCourty. He's not the most talented defensive back on the roster, but he's the acknowledged leader of the group. Like Jerod Mayo at linebacker, McCourty isn't particularly outstanding in one specific part of his game, but he remains very good in multiple areas, particularly diagnosing plays and working as a leader along the back line of the defense. The two second-year defensive backs, Ryan and Duron Harmon, both appear to be options to take over Steve Gregory's old role at strong safety, the biggest remaining question mark for the New England defense. Harmon is a second-year pro out of Rutgers who took most of the snaps at the spot throughout spring OTAs and minicamp. The sight of Harmon standing with Revis, Browner and McCourty working together as a group while the rest of the defense was working on other aspects of the game was one positive sign for the defensive backs. Meanwhile, one stat that suggests Ryan could move from cornerback to safety: in 600 snaps as a rookie, he was the only Patriots' defensive back to finish the year with zero broken tackles.

Special Teams

Year	DVOA	Rank	FG/XP	Rank	Net Kick	Rank	Kick Ret	Rank	Net Punt	Rank	Punt Ret	Rank	Hidden	Rank
2011	4.1%	5	1.2	14	8.3	3	-3.7	25	15.2	2	-0.3	18	0.0	16
2012	5.5%	4	-1.8	18	15.0	1	2.2	11	6.2	11	5.9	5	0.0	17
2013	6.7%	2	11.4	1	10.5	2	2.0	9	9.0	6	0.5	14	-9.9	30

This may be the only special teams unit in the league headlined by a gunner. Matthew Slater's combination of speed, experience, and football IQ makes him a tremendously active force on kickoffs and punts—and for good measure, he's also one of the team's locker-room leaders. Nate Ebner and Tavon Wilson also figure as core members of New England's special teams, which ranked in the top ten for four of the five major special-teams categories last season. The exception was punt returns because of a slightly down year for Julian Edelman, which figures to be a bit of an anomaly: Edelman was worth a combined 16 field-position points more than the average punt returner over the previous three seasons. Kick returner, meanwhile, will be one of the few positional battles of the New England preseason, now that the LeGarrette Blount Experience has moved on to Pittsburgh. Possibilities to take Blount's position include Devin McCourty, Shane Vereen, Josh Boyce, and Jeremy Gallon, a seventh-round pick out of Michigan who was an all-purpose yardage machine for the Wolverines.

For all his faults—and his critics are quick to remind you that *he's no Adam Vinatieri*—Stephen Gostkowski remains a very reliable kicker. He ended the year with several clutch field goals, including game-winners to beat the Bills and Broncos and big late kicks home against the Jets and on the road against the Texans. In addition, he had a field goal to force overtime against the Jets, as well as his career-best 54-yarder against the Saints, and he successfully executed an onside kick in the dramatic win over the Browns. Ryan Allen was middle-of-the-pack as a punter and holder for Gostkowski, finishing the regular-season with 29 punts landing inside the 20 (good for 10th in the league) and a 45.9 average, 14th in the NFL. (For what it's worth, Allen was one of the only stars for the Patriots in the AFC title game, dropping three first-half punts inside the 20 and doing his part to help tilt the field for New England in the early going.)

One other note about the 2013 Patriots' special teams: they finished 30th in "hidden" special teams because they faced the best gross punting in the league—opposing punters had just two touchbacks, and one of those was a 64-yard punt. Ultimately, this is one of those things that regresses to the mean from year to year.

New Orleans Saints

2013 Record: 11.5	**Total DVOA:** 19.3% (4th)	**2014 Mean Projection:** 9.4 wins	**On the Clock (0-4):** 4%
Pythagorean Wins: 10.8 (7th)	**Offense:** 16.0% (5th)	**Postseason Odds:** 60.3%	**Mediocrity (5-7):** 15%
Snap-Weighted Age: 27.1 (7th)	**Defense:** -5.8% (10th)	**Super Bowl Odds:** 12.6%	**Playoff Contender (8-10):** 48%
Average Opponent: 5.8% (5th)	**Special Teams:** -2.5% (24th)	**Proj. Avg. Opponent:** -0.4% (21st)	**Super Bowl Contender (11+):** 34%

2013: Sean Payton returns, and brings the wins back with him.

2014: Like Colin Kaepernick and Frances Farmer, Drew Brees seeks revenge on Seattle.

Welcome to the NFC South, where the Saints have passed their division rivals by standing still. As the Bucs have turned over their front office, the Falcons have turned over their front seven, and the Panthers have turned over every rock in the Carolinas trying to find a wide receiver, the Saints return most of the same players who reached the divisional round last season. It's a perfect window for New Orleans, but windows don't stay open forever. The Saints' offensive core is quickly aging, and there could be some dark financial times in the future. If New Orleans can't win a Super Bowl this year, will this team as we know it get another chance?

Since Sean Payton and Drew Brees arrived in 2006, the Saints have been an offensive mainstay, never finishing lower than 12th in DVOA and making the top five four times. It has been eight years of success, but it has also been eight years of aging, and the wrinkles on this team are starting to show. By snap-weighted age, the 2013 Saints were the eighth-oldest team in the league, and the oldest team on offense. And things aren't likely to change this season. The Saints only plan to have two or three new starters on offense this fall, and one of those moves may actually make them significantly older.

Can the Saints keep winning as their offense ages? Recent history says it will be a challenge. Let's take a look at the ten oldest offenses we've measured since 2006 (Table 1), the first season for which we have compiled snap-weighted age, along with their DVOA that season and over the next three years.

Table 1: Oldest Offenses by Snap-Weighted Age, 2006-2013

Team	Year	Age	DVOA	Year N+1	Year N+2	Year N+3
KC	2006	30.0	6.3%	-19.4%	-9.2%	-18.0%
CHI	2007	29.6	-22.1%	-9.0%	-19.7%	-15.8%
WAS	2008	29.6	8.2%	-8.3%	-11.3%	-7.0%
WAS	2007	29.4	-1.0%	8.2%	-8.3%	-11.3%
NE	2009	29.4	26.4%	42.2%	31.9%	30.8%
KC	2007	29.3	-19.4%	-9.2%	-18.0%	-9.2%
SEA	2006	29.2	-11.2%	6.6%	-14.2%	-19.6%
CHI	2006	29.1	-5.0%	-22.1%	-9.0%	-19.7%
NYJ	2008	29.1	0.0%	-12.5%	2.1%	-8.3%
SEA	2007	29.0	6.6%	-14.2%	-19.6%	-17.3%
AVERAGE		29.4	-1.1%	-3.8%	-7.5%	-9.5%
MEDIAN		29.4	-0.5%	-9.1%	-10.3%	-13.6%

We'll also examine both the average and median DVOA ratings of these offenses over each season. The medians are necessary to ensure that the results are not skewed by one radical outlier (which we shall get to shortly).

For one year, at least, these old offenses had mixed results. Some were good, some were bad, most were pretty mediocre. And then, usually, the bottom dropped out. Seven of the ten offenses had negative DVOAs one year later. Eight of them were negative two years later, and three years down the road, nine of the ten teams had offensive DVOAs of -7.0% of worse.

If we're going to compare the 2013 Saints to prior teams, though, we'll need to dig a little deeper. First of all, the Saints weren't *that* old. Though they were the oldest offense in the NFL last year, their snap-weighted age of 28.4 would not make a list of the top 20 oldest offenses of the past eight years. This is part of a general trend where teams are keeping more young offensive players on the roster; the average snap-weighted age has declined four of the past five years. Second, and more importantly, ten teams is a pretty small sample size.

We only have snap-weighted age going back to 2006, but we have starting lineups going back to 2000. By sacrificing a bit of accuracy in the age of each team, we can get a much larger sample size. Looking at the 25 oldest offenses from 2000 to 2010 (cutting off at that point so we can see what happened to each team over the ensuing three seasons) shows a clear pattern (Table 2). As a group, these offenses declined steadily, with fewer teams at the top of our rankings and more teams at the bottom.

Table 2: 25 Oldest Offenses by Average Age of Starters, 2000-2010

	Yr N	Yr N+1	Yr N+2	Yr N+3
Avg. DVOA	6.1%	1.3%	-4.8%	-5.5%
Teams >10% DVOA	9	6	3	2
Teams <-10% DVOA	4	5	10	9

There is a lot of variation and noise in the data, and the numbers are less extreme than those in Table 1, but we can still see a fairly clear pattern of decline. If we limit this table only to the 12 offenses since 2000 that have averaged at least 30 years of age (the 2000-04 Raiders; the Chiefs from 2000-03 and again in 2007; the 2004 Rams; the 2004-05 Seahawks;

2014 Saints Schedule

Week	Opp.	Week	Opp.	Week	Opp.
1	at ATL	7	at DET	13	at PIT
2	at CLE	8	GB	14	CAR
3	MIN	9	at CAR (Thu.)	15	at CHI (Mon.)
4	at DAL	10	SF	16	ATL
5	TB	11	CIN	17	at TB
6	BYE	12	BAL (Mon.)		

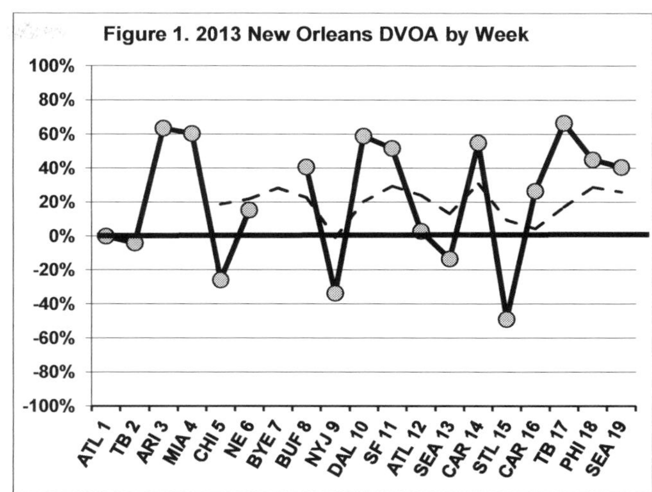

and the Redskins in 2008), we get an average DVOA of 11.3% that fell to 5.4%, then to -5.7%, and then to -9.3% over the next three seasons.

Only two of our oldest offenses had offenses greater than 10.0% DVOA three seasons later: the 2009 Patriots and the 2005 Broncos. The Broncos actually crashed and burned, going from a 26.9% DVOA in 2005 to a -4.8% DVOA in 2006. Then they put Jay Cutler in the starting lineup and put up DVOAs of 9.5% and 19.2%. This rapid improvement was so impressive that they traded Cutler away after that season.

The 2009 Patriots, meanwhile, bucked several trends here; as Table 1 shows, they were actually *better* in each of the three seasons following their old year. They somehow managed to improve even as they were overhauling their entire offense. Only two starters (Tom Brady and Logan Mankins) from the 2009 team were still on board in 2012. In theory, the Saints have their own Hall of Fame candidates at quarterback and guard around whom they could build, but whereas Brady and Mankins were 32 and 27 in 2009, Drew Brees will be 35 this year, and Jahri Evans will be 31.

It's that former number that is most concerning. The Saints are completely built around Brees. If he's not one of the top five quarterbacks in the league, they're not going to win a championship. So how many more excellent seasons does he have left?

Since 1989, quarterbacks have passed for at least 1,000 DYAR in a season 135 times, or about five or six times each year. (Remember that the baselines for DYAR are normalized for each season, so we can compare Brees and his contemporaries to those who played decades before with some degree of accuracy.) Five did it last year: Peyton Manning, Philip Rivers, Matt Ryan, Nick Foles, and Brees himself.

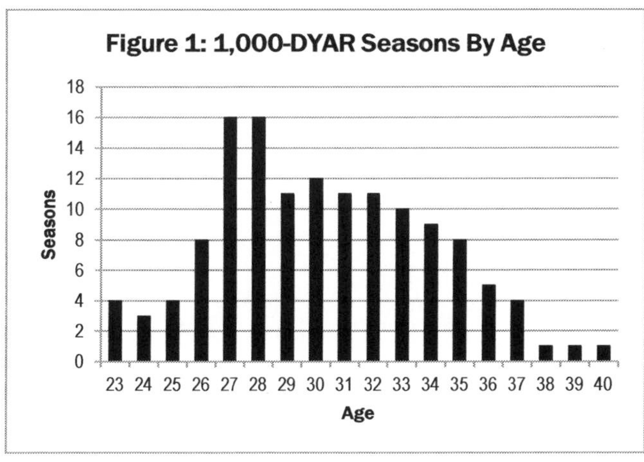

A graph showing the number of 1,000-DYAR seasons thrown by quarterbacks of each age shows that most big seasons come at age 27 or 28. There's a big drop-off after that, and then the numbers tend to get worse with each passing year (Figure 1).

There are reasons to think Brees can hold off Father Time, starting with the fact that he is *Drew Brees*. This is a man who has gone over 1,000 DYAR nine times; only Peyton Manning (13) has done it more often. If anything, Brees appears to be peaking. His 1,701 DYAR in 2013 represent his second-best season, and his 5,400-DYAR spree since 2011 represents the best three-year stretch of his Hall of Fame career. And he is not the only old quarterback playing so well right now. Peyton Manning just completed one of the great passing seasons of all time at age 37, and Tom Brady just missed the 1,000-DYAR threshold at age 36. Between the three of them, we're virtually certain to see some swelling at the right side of that bar graph.

If there is one crack showing in Brees' armor, it's in his ability to avoid sacks. Brees went down 37 times last year, ten more than he ever had in a season before. When we look at the Saints' blocking over the past three seasons, we see that long sacks have generally stayed stable while short and medium-length sacks have soared (Table 3).

Table 3: Saints' Soaring Sacks

Season	Sacks	Short	Medium	Long
2011	24	10	5	9
2012	26	12	7	7
2013	37	17	13	7

This suggests that opponents are getting early pressure on Brees a lot more often. It also suggests that Brees is hesitating to pull the trigger on quicker pass routes. Regardless, if the trend continues, it could be the downfall of the Saints' season. Brees can't throw touchdowns from his back—or from the sidelines.

Barring injury, Brees will obviously be the Saints' quarterback. Is there a chance to get younger elsewhere? Of the three returning starters on the line, left guard Ben Grubbs will be 30, while right guard Jahri Evans and right tackle Zach Strief will both be 31. The Saints will get four years younger at left tackle by swapping out Charles Brown for Terron Armstead. At center, it's not clear who will be starting, but one way or the other there will be a big change in age. Brian de la Puente (who will be 29 this year) is out. Taking his place will be either Tim Lelito (25), who started two games at guard last year as an undrafted free agent out of Grand Valley State, or Jonathan Goodwin (36), who returns to New Orleans after three years in San Francisco. If Goodwin winds up winning the job, then the average age of New Orleans' starting offense next year will climb over the dreaded 30-year threshold.

At least there will be some youth at the fantasy positions. Darren Sproles, the oldest of last year's running back group, is gone. Top runner Pierre Thomas will be 30, but Mark Ingram, Khiry Robinson, and Travaris Cadet, each of whom could see significant action, will all be 25. Top wideout Marques Colston will be 31, but thanks to first-round draft pick Brandin Cooks (21) and last year's rookie surprise Kenny Stills (22), the Saints will have at least two starters born after Reagan left the White House.

And of course, there is tight end—or, as they call it in New Orleans, tight end*. Despite his listing on the roster, Jimmy Graham wasn't often lined up with a hand on the ground. According to our charting numbers, Graham took a three-point stance on fewer than half his snaps, spending the bulk of his time in the slot or lined up wide, not as a traditional in-line tight end.

For Graham and the Saints, the distinction is neither trivial nor arbitrary. The Saints used the franchise tag to stop Graham from leaving in free agency, but they tagged him as a tight end, guaranteeing him a 2014 salary of $7.1 million. Graham argued that he was a wide receiver, which would have upped that guarantee by about $5 million. An arbitrator ruled in favor of New Orleans. Graham appealed the ruling, which might have dragged the conflict into the season, but he and the Saints beat a July 15 deadline to sign a new deal by just a few hours. The four-year, $40 million deal (including $21 million in guarantees) makes him the highest paid tight end in the league. (For the record, it would make him the seventh highest-paid wideout.)

The good news is that Graham is in the fold. The bad news is that his new deal is going to eat up a lot of cap space, of which there is precious little to be found in the Crescent City these days. Joel Corry of CBS Sports wrote that the Saints have already committed a league-high $142 million to their 2015 salary cap, and that doesn't include Graham's new deal.

All of that is going to make it hard for New Orleans to add any talent in free agency, and that means the Saints as we know them could be a radically different team in a few years. For while last year's offense was the oldest in the league, the defense was just 25th in snap-weighted age. If anything they're getting even younger, as every starter over thirty from last year's team is gone, replaced by twentysomethings like Jairus Byrd, Patrick Robinson, Victor Butler, and John Jenkins. Not since the Dome Patrol days of Rickey Jackson and Sam Mills have the Saints made the playoffs as a defense-first team, but that might be the route they need to travel in coming years. Even here, though, the menace of the salary cap looms over the team. Will they be able to afford players like Cameron Jordan and Kenny Vaccaro when deals for those stars come due? Between the age of the offense and the restraints of the salary cap, there is a day of reckoning coming for this team, and it is going to hit hard.

All of this makes it imperative that the Saints strike while the iron is hot. The NFC South is ripe for the picking, and a division title would mean a playoff game at home, where they played so well last year. That would give them their best shot at knocking off Seattle and the other powerhouses in the NFC. If everything falls into place, there's still time for one more parade down Canal Street before the good times end.

Vince Verhei

2013 Saints Stats by Week

Wk	vs.	W-L	PF	PA	YDF	YDA	TO	Total	Off	Def	ST
1	ATL	W	23	17	419	367	+1	0%	-4%	-7%	-3%
2	at TB	W	16	14	371	273	0	-4%	-14%	-12%	-2%
3	ARI	W	31	7	423	247	+1	63%	38%	-21%	4%
4	MIA	W	38	17	465	331	+3	60%	43%	-19%	-1%
5	at CHI	W	26	18	347	434	+1	-26%	5%	35%	4%
6	at NE	L	27	30	361	376	-1	15%	5%	-11%	0%
7	BYE										
8	BUF	W	35	17	386	299	+3	41%	41%	-12%	-12%
9	at NYJ	L	20	26	407	338	-2	-34%	-10%	21%	-3%
10	DAL	W	49	17	625	193	-1	59%	54%	-20%	-16%
11	SF	W	23	20	387	196	-2	52%	6%	-42%	4%
12	at ATL	W	17	13	374	355	+1	3%	13%	13%	3%
13	at SEA	L	7	34	188	429	-1	-14%	-7%	7%	1%
14	CAR	W	31	13	373	239	0	55%	42%	-19%	-6%
15	at STL	L	16	27	432	302	-3	-49%	-9%	26%	-15%
16	at CAR	L	13	17	365	222	-1	26%	-9%	-31%	4%
17	TB	W	42	17	468	290	+1	66%	61%	-8%	-3%
18	at PHI	W	26	24	434	256	-2	45%	30%	-11%	4%
19	at SEA	L	15	23	409	277	-1	41%	39%	-13%	-12%

Trends and Splits

	Offense	Rank	Defense	Rank
Total DVOA	16.0%	5	-5.8%	10
Unadjusted VOA	13.7%	6	-3.8%	12
Weighted Trend	17.5%	5	-5.8%	9
Variance	6.7%	17	4.4%	11
Average Opponent	-3.8%	7	1.0%	9
Passing	35.9%	3	-9.2%	6
Rushing	-5.3%	19	-1.5%	20
First Down	19.3%	4	-17.3%	5
Second Down	10.7%	11	10.6%	27
Third Down	17.7%	8	-9.2%	9
First Half	22.1%	4	3.5%	20
Second Half	9.7%	8	-17.6%	4
Red Zone	13.4%	9	-4.8%	11
Late and Close	-3.5%	18	-12.7%	9

Five-Year Performance

Year	W-L	Pyth W	Est W	PF	PA	TO	Total	Rk	Off	Rk	Def	Rk	ST	Rk	Off AGL	Rk	Def AGL	Rk	Off Age	Rk	Def Age	Rk	ST Age	Rk
2009	13-3	11.8	11.2	510	341	+11	21.3%	6	24.3%	2	-0.4%	17	-3.4%	28	45.6	30	32.9	21	27.5	12	27.7	6	27.4	2
2010	11-5	9.3	9.2	384	307	-6	9.2%	10	6.4%	11	-4.3%	10	-1.5%	21	19.8	10	25.2	18	28.2	7	27.6	12	27.0	10
2011	13-3	12.4	12.0	547	339	-3	23.8%	2	33.0%	2	10.2%	28	1.0%	12	17.4	7	7.2	1	27.7	11	26.9	19	26.2	18
2012	7-9	8.2	6.4	461	454	+2	-5.2%	19	11.9%	9	14.8%	32	-2.3%	24	11.5	4	23.6	14	28.3	3	26.6	21	25.9	22
2013	11-5	10.8	10.0	414	304	0	19.3%	4	16.0%	5	-5.8%	10	-2.5%	24	14.2	3	74.4	32	28.4	1	26.0	25	26.2	10

2013 Performance Based on Most Common Personnel Groups

NO Offense					NO Offense vs. Opponents				NO Defense				NO Defense vs. Opponents			
Pers	Freq	Yds	DVOA	Run%	Pers	Freq	Yds	DVOA	Pers	Freq	Yds	DVOA	Pers	Freq	Yds	DVOA
11	39%	6.8	43.0%	18%	Nickel Even	37%	6.9	30.8%	Nickel Even	27%	5.8	7.5%	11	54%	5.0	-6.3%
21	23%	5.9	15.0%	46%	4-3-4	30%	5.1	5.2%	Dime+	20%	5.2	-10.8%	12	12%	5.9	-3.3%
12	14%	6.4	4.5%	23%	3-4-4	11%	6.4	10.1%	Nickel Odd	20%	5.4	-19.0%	21	10%	6.2	0.6%
22	9%	5.3	4.4%	54%	Dime+	10%	6.8	42.2%	3-4-4	20%	4.7	-9.7%	22	7%	3.0	-41.1%
621	6%	5.5	9.2%	89%	Nickel Odd	8%	7.1	58.2%	4-3-4	9%	6.4	9.1%	13	4%	5.5	-4.1%

Strategic Tendencies

Run/Pass		Rk	Formation		Rk	Pass Rush		Rk	Secondary		Rk	Strategy		Rk
Runs, first half	28%	32	Form: Single Back	51%	30	Rush 3	7.6%	10	4 DB	28%	30	Play action	24%	12
Runs, first down	42%	29	Form: Empty Back	13%	3	Rush 4	60.8%	19	5 DB	47%	19	Avg Box (Off)	6.29	20
Runs, second-long	22%	30	Pers: 3+ WR	43%	30	Rush 5	20.3%	24	6+ DB	20%	5	Avg Box (Def)	6.29	23
Runs, power sit.	51%	22	Pers: 4+ WR	0%	29	Rush 6+	11.4%	5	CB by Sides	81%	10	Offensive Pace	30.26	16
Runs, behind 2H	30%	8	Pers: 2+ TE/6+ OL	35%	13	Sacks by LB	44.9%	13	DB Blitz	16%	4	Defensive Pace	29.42	12
Pass, ahead 2H	55%	5	Shotgun/Pistol	48%	26	Sacks by DB	7.1%	18	Hole in Zone	11%	16	Go for it on 4th	1.35	4

The Saints' home-field advantage is often overstated, but not last year. At home, the Saints had a league-best 35.1% offensive DVOA and -18.2% defensive DVOA (seventh in the NFL). On the road, the Saints had -3.7% offensive DVOA (16th) and 6.3% defensive DVOA (21st). Drew Brees faced a defensive back blitz on just 7.2 percent of passes, a significant decrease from 13.0 percent of passes the year before. It was a smart move by opposing defensive coordinators because he has crushed DB blitzes with 8.4 yards per pass over the last two seasons. New Orleans led the league with 65 screen passes to running backs; no other team used more than 50. But the Saints only threw six screen passes to tight ends or wide receivers. The New Orleans defense was much better against runs from two-back formations (3.7 yards per carry, -22.9% DVOA) than against runs from single-back formations (5.0 yards per carry, 9.9% DVOA). The Saints defense forced three-and-outs on a league-leading 29.4 percent of drives. Fumbles on special teams, particularly muffed punts, are usually recovered by the team that fumbled the ball. However, the Saints had three fumbles on special teams last year (one strip, two muffs) and didn't recover any of them.

Passing

Player	DYAR	DVOA	Plays	NtYds	Avg	YAC	C%	TD	Int
D.Brees	1701	26.9%	687	4906	7.1	5.5	68.9%	39	12

Rushing

Player	DYAR	DVOA	Plays	Yds	Avg	TD	Fum	Suc
P.Thomas	6	-7.6%	148	554	3.7	2	0	53%
M.Ingram	45	4.6%	78	386	4.9	1	0	49%
K.Robinson	-7	-11.9%	54	224	4.1	1	0	41%
D.Sproles*	21	1.4%	53	220	4.2	2	1	49%
J.Collins	18	9.3%	15	45	3.0	1	0	67%
D.Brees	36	33.6%	15	82	5.5	3	0	-

Receiving

Player	DYAR	DVOA	Plays	Ctch	Yds	Y/C	YAC	TD	C%
M.Colston	276	19.5%	110	75	943	12.6	3.4	5	68%
L.Moore*	150	22.1%	54	37	457	12.4	1.8	2	69%
K.Stills	206	40.1%	51	33	644	19.5	6.2	5	65%
R.Meachem	66	15.7%	30	16	324	20.3	5.4	2	53%
N.Toon	-23	-39.9%	12	4	68	17.0	2.3	0	33%
J.Graham	223	15.7%	143	86	1215	14.1	4.7	16	60%
B.Watson	22	2.5%	30	19	226	11.9	4.9	2	63%
J.Hill	-6	-14.7%	10	6	44	7.3	5.5	1	60%
D.Sproles*	174	23.9%	89	71	604	8.5	7.3	2	80%
P.Thomas	128	13.2%	84	77	513	6.7	8.3	3	92%
J.Collins*	-15	-25.6%	18	14	54	3.9	4.7	0	78%
M.Ingram	5	-5.4%	11	7	68	9.7	10.9	0	64%
E.Lorig	*-27*	*-43.6%*	*14*	*11*	*47*	*4.3*	*5.0*	*0*	*79%*

Offensive Line

Player	Pos	Age	GS	Snaps	Pen	Sk	Pass	Run	Player	Pos	Age	GS	Snaps	Pen	Sk	Pass	Run
Brian de la Puente*	C	29	16/16	1126	4	2.0	9.0	3.5	Bryce Harris	OT	25	16/1	239	2	0.0	6.5	2.0
Ben Grubbs	LG	30	16/16	1126	5	3.5	13.0	8.0	Tim Lelito	G	25	16/2	159	1	4.0	5.5	1.0
Zach Strief	RT	31	15/15	1035	4	3.0	12.5	1.0	Terron Armstead	OT	23	6/2	137	2	2.5	4.5	0.0
Jahri Evans	RG	31	14/14	974	6	1.5	17.0	6.5	*Jonathan Goodwin*	*C*	*36*	*16/16*	*970*	*3*	*3.0*	*15.5*	*3.5*
Charles Brown*	LT	27	16/14	951	12	5.0	24.0	4.5									

Year	Yards	ALY	Rk	Power	Rk	Stuff	Rk	2nd Lev	Rk	Open Field	Rk	Sacks	ASR	Rk	Short	Long	F-Start	Cont.
2011	5.02	4.95	1	65%	12	15%	1	1.50	1	0.91	13	24	4.5%	3	10	9	16	34
2012	4.40	4.04	18	71%	3	19%	14	1.25	12	0.90	9	26	4.9%	7	12	7	22	32
2013	4.11	4.08	7	67%	13	21%	23	1.22	12	0.65	18	37	5.3%	4	17	7	13	26

2013 ALY by direction: *Left End 4.18 (10)* *Left Tackle 4.54 (6)* *Mid/Guard 4.15 (10)* *Right Tackle 4.17 (10)* *Right End 3.04 (27)*

This unit was more stable last season than its low continuity score would suggest. Though there were lots of small tweaks in the lineup throughout the year, all five starters (even Charles Brown, who was benched by the end of the year) played at least 85 percent of the Saints' offensive snaps. Big change came in the offseason, though, as Brown joined the Giants in free agency, while center Brian de la Puente signed with the Bears.

Terron Armstead, a third-round rookie out of Arkansas-Pine Bluff, took Brown's spot at left tackle in the last two games of the regular season and both playoff contests. Forcing a rookie to start his first game against Carolina doesn't quite seem fair, and Greg Hardy drank his milkshake, beating the rookie for two sacks and two hurries. Armstead was much better in Week 17, giving up just half a sack to Tampa Bay's Adrian Clayborn, and he also looked good in the bright lights of the postseason, so this looks to be an upgrade for the Saints in 2014.

At center, a pessimist would say that the Saints must choose between a has-been and a never-was. The Saints reunited with Jonathan Goodwin very late in free agency, after the June 1 deadline once he no longer cost New Orleans a draft pick. Goodwin played for the Saints from 2006-10, so he's familiar with Sean Payton and the Saints offense. He's also durable, starting every game since 2008. That's all well and good, but he's still a 36-year-old lineman that the 49ers let walk away, and then he sat around for three months because nobody else wanted him either. Option B would be Tim Lelito, who joined the team last season as an undrafted rookie out of Grand Valley State and started two games at guard. The only other center on the roster is Matthew Armstrong, a college teammate of Lelito's who joined the Saints as an undrafted free agent this year.

Only five guards have started at least 100 games since 2007, and the Saints have two of them in Jahri Evans and Ben Grubbs. Both players, though, slipped noticeably last year. Grubb's blown block total climbed from 14.5 in 2012 to 21.0 in 2013; Evans' climbed from 12.0 to 23.5. Evans missed the All-Pro team for the first time since 2008, and he turns 31 in August. Right tackle Zach Strief, meanwhile, deserves more respect than he gets, especially for his run blocking. We credited him with just one blown block on a running play in each of the last two seasons, and his rate of blown blocks per snap was second best at his position in 2013.

Do not underestimate the value of Drew Brees and the effect he has on the Saints' pass blocking numbers. In the eight years since he arrived in New Orleans, the Saints have never ranked worse than seventh in ASR. In the eight years prior, they never ranked better than 15th.

Defensive Front Seven

			Overall								vs. Run					Pass Rush			
Defensive Line	Age	Pos	G	Snaps	Plays	TmPct	Rk	Stop	Dfts	BTkl	Runs	St%	Rk	RuYd	Rk	Sack	Hit	Hur	Tips
Cameron Jordan	25	DE	16	896	49	6.5%	24	36	19	1	31	61%	81	3.1	73	12.5	13	33.0	3
Akiem Hicks	25	DE	16	647	55	7.3%	15	46	11	3	50	82%	29	1.9	34	4.5	2	7.5	0
John Jenkins	25	DT	16	432	21	2.8%	80	13	5	0	17	53%	85	3.4	79	0.0	2	5.0	1
Brodrick Bunkley	31	DT	12	248	13	2.3%	--	12	3	0	12	92%	--	1.5	--	0.0	1	2.0	0
Tom Johnson*	30	DE	12	223	12	2.1%	--	8	3	1	9	67%	--	3.7	--	2.0	2	7.0	0
Glenn Foster	24	DE	12	207	8	1.4%	--	8	5	0	4	100%	--	1.0	--	3.0	3	4.0	1
Brandon Deaderick	*27*	*DT*	*13*	*301*	*10*	*1.4%*	*--*	*6*	*1*	*0*	*8*	*50%*	*--*	*4.1*	*--*	*0.5*	*0*	*1.0*	*1*

			Overall								vs. Run					Pass Rush			
Edge Rushers	Age	Pos	G	Snaps	Plays	TmPct	Rk	Stop	Dfts	BTkl	Runs	St%	Rk	RuYd	Rk	Sack	Hit	Hur	Tips
Junior Galette	26	OLB	16	835	42	5.6%	40	36	19	1	25	84%	18	2.1	24	12.0	12	25.5	0
Parys Haralson	30	OLB	16	360	31	4.1%	--	28	10	2	24	92%	--	1.0	--	3.5	4	3.5	1

			Overall								Pass Rush			vs. Run					vs. Pass						
Linebackers	Age	Pos	G	Snaps	Plays	TmPct	Rk	Stop	Dfts	BTkl	Sack	Hit	Hur	Runs	St%	Rk	RuYd	Rk	Tgts	Suc%	Rk	AdjYd	Rk	PD	Int
Curtis Lofton	28	ILB	16	933	129	17.1%	14	82	21	8	2.0	0	5	74	72%	19	2.5	17	51	56%	24	6.7	38	3	0
David Hawthorne	29	ILB	16	680	89	11.8%	51	52	14	7	3.0	1	4.5	59	69%	24	2.5	13	23	46%	47	6.6	37	0	0
Ramon Humber	27	ILB	16	155	23	3.0%	--	14	6	0	0.5	1	1	10	80%	--	3.6	--	9	49%	--	4.0	--	1	0

Year	Yards	ALY	Rk	Power	Rk	Stuff	Rk	2nd Level	Rk	Open Field	Rk	Sacks	ASR	Rk	Short	Long
2011	5.20	4.13	21	73%	30	18%	20	1.42	30	1.45	32	33	6.0%	25	13	16
2012	5.29	4.47	31	60%	15	18%	19	1.38	31	1.48	31	30	5.5%	28	6	18
2013	4.40	3.75	14	69%	23	21%	12	1.06	12	1.13	30	49	8.6%	4	13	16
2013 ALY by direction:			*Left End 3.61 (15)*			*Left Tackle 4.05 (17)*			*Mid/Guard 3.88 (11)*			*Right Tackle 3.41 (12)*			*Right End 3.67 (15)*	

The Saints' defensive front showed significant improvement last year without making any major acquisitions. The upgrade came not by adding outside names, but by promoting from within. Then they got through the offseason without losing any pieces of their puzzle. As a result, the Saints' front seven in 2014 will look a lot like their front seven in 2013, which looked a lot like the front seven in 2012. And all of these players are still under thirty, so it will probably still look familiar in 2015.

Rob Ryan's 3-4 defense moved Akiem Hicks from defensive tackle to defensive end, and Junior Galette from end to linebacker. Those transitions moved both from the bench to the front lines, and they performed much better than the veterans they replaced. Hicks, one of the league's most active interior linemen, played best in back-to-back close wins over San Francisco and Atlanta, racking up 15 tackles and 2.5 sacks, monster numbers for a 3-4 end. Galette, meanwhile, gave New Orleans a promising bookend rusher to Cam Jordan, collecting six sacks in the Saints' six games against NFC South foes. Jordan remains the star of the defense, finishing fifth in the NFL in sacks, sixth in hurries, and tying for eighth in quarterback knockdowns.

All of the Saints' linebackers posted excellent Run Stop Rates. That's a credit to Jordan, Hicks, Brodrick Bunkley, and third-round rookie John Jenkins, who did a fine job occupying blockers. (Jenkins and Parys Haralson, a free-agent signee from San Francisco, were the only prominent front seven players making their Saints debuts last year.) It's also a credit to Curtis Lofton, David Hawthorne, and the rest of the linebackers, who made plenty of plays near the line of scrimmage. It's the plays they didn't make, however, that caused so many problems. When Saints linebackers made a tackle on a running play last year, the average gain was just 2.6 yards, the lowest such rate in the league. However, when a defensive back made the tackle, the average gain was 8.6 yards, fourth-highest. Given the trouble they've had giving up long runs over the years, the Saints would surely give up some of those stuffs if it meant keeping opposing runners out of the open field more often.

Defensive Secondary

			Overall								vs. Run					vs. Pass									
Secondary	Age	Pos	G	Snaps	Plays	TmPct	Rk	Stop	Dfts	BTkl	Runs	St%	Rk	RuYd	Rk	Tgts	Tgt%	Rk	Dist	Suc%	Rk	AdjYd	Rk	PD	Int
Keenan Lewis	28	CB	16	891	56	7.4%	55	20	10	2	10	30%	65	9.4	61	61	17.1%	9	14.2	51%	50	6.9	26	9	4
Malcolm Jenkins*	27	FS	14	818	72	10.9%	30	27	19	12	27	37%	47	8.7	65	41	12.5%	70	10.2	47%	61	7.8	54	6	2
Kenny Vaccaro	23	SS	14	791	85	12.8%	14	35	17	3	34	53%	15	7.0	40	30	9.3%	55	11.7	60%	30	7.4	45	7	1
Corey White	24	CB	16	551	45	6.0%	--	24	7	2	14	57%	--	7.6	--	44	19.9%	--	11.8	57%	--	5.7	--	5	1
Jabari Greer*	32	CB	10	540	42	8.9%	34	19	7	1	9	33%	53	11.3	76	42	19.4%	26	13.9	57%	21	7.0	27	10	1
Rafael Bush	27	FS	13	513	42	6.8%	--	13	5	1	19	26%	--	11.5	--	15	7.1%	--	15.0	70%	--	5.1	--	5	0
Roman Harper*	32	SS	9	370	38	8.9%	--	19	7	0	19	58%	--	7.0	--	16	10.8%	--	10.9	54%	--	7.8	--	1	1
Jairus Byrd	*28*	*FS*	*11*	*635*	*54*	*9.1%*	*53*	*19*	*11*	*2*	*21*	*29%*	*66*	*12.2*	*77*	*17*	*6.4%*	*19*	*9.6*	*68%*	*5*	*3.4*	*2*	*5*	*4*

Year	Pass D Rank	vs. #1 WR	Rk	vs. #2 WR	Rk	vs. Other WR	Rk	vs. TE	Rk	vs. RB	Rk
2011	26	12.8%	18	-6.6%	11	9.3%	27	9.8%	18	21.5%	28
2012	28	38.3%	32	8.5%	23	-4.1%	12	-7.4%	8	17.5%	24
2013	6	-9.2%	12	10.7%	24	-5.0%	12	-15.6%	7	-10.4%	10

Keenan Lewis' play after arriving in New Orleans from Pittsburgh was one of the most pleasant surprises of the 2013 season. In 2012, his only season as a starter for the Steelers, Lewis' charting stats were quite good (54 percent Adjusted Success Rate, 6.3 Adjusted Yards per Pass), but opponents showed no fear of him; he was one of four corners in the league with more than 100 targets. In New Orleans, while his rate stats took a bit of a hit, his targets plummeted, even though he was the Saints cornerback most likely to be covering opponents' top receivers.

Jabari Greer's season ended with a knee injury in Week 11, and his Saints career ended when he was released in February. It's not clear who will take his place in the starting lineup. Patrick Robinson started 16 games in 2012, with a pretty good Success Rate but a horrible Adjusted Yards per Pass number that suggests an all-or-nothing, gambling style. His 2013 season ended in Week 2 when he tore his patellar tendon against Tampa Bay. Corey White improved greatly in his second season, but he has mostly played nickelback and hasn't spent much time covering the top receivers in the league. And then, on opposite ends of the age spectrum, we have Champ Bailey and Stanley Jean-Baptiste. A foot injury limited Bailey to just five regular-season games (and only two starts) in his last season in Denver. Bailey is a Hall of Famer, but he also has 15 NFL seasons under his belt. He broke into the league in 1999, in the middle of Bill Clinton's second presidential term, when John Elway was reigning Super Bowl champion and Jean-Baptiste was nine years old. Jean-Baptiste, the Saints' second-round pick out of Nebraska, has drawn comparisons to Richard Sherman as a converted wide receiver with a 6-foot-3, 215-pound frame. He also has freaky athletic ability, leading all corners at the combine this year with a 41.5-inch vertical jump.

Rookie safeties in our database most similar to Kenny Vaccaro: LaRon Landry, Greg Wesley, Eric Berry, Louis Delmas, Ed Reed. That's five long-term starters, two who went on to be All-Pros, and at least one Hall of Famer. Vaccaro figures to finish somewhere in the middle of that pack. The Saints have also added Jairus Byrd, the top safety in free agency. A three-time Pro Bowler, Byrd has 22 interceptions since entering the league in 2009; only Asante Samuel (25) has more over the past five seasons. Roman Harper was part of the Saints' veteran purge this offseason, but Rob Ryan's defense often puts three safeties on the field at the same time, which should mean another season of significant time for Rafael Bush, or perhaps fifth-round rookie Vinnie Sunseri out of Alabama.

Special Teams

Year	DVOA	Rank	FG/XP	Rank	Net Kick	Rank	Kick Ret	Rank	Net Punt	Rank	Punt Ret	Rank	Hidden	Rank
2011	1.0%	12	-4.1	23	-6.2	26	1.9	11	10.2	6	3.0	11	2.3	12
2012	-2.3%	24	-4.1	23	-7.3	28	-6.2	25	8.6	9	-2.5	18	14.2	3
2013	-2.5%	24	-13.8	32	-2.1	25	-0.5	14	11.1	2	-7.3	27	-8.0	27

Garrett Hartley handled most of the field-goal kicking duties in 2013, and he's most responsible for the Saints' last-place ranking in this category. Shayne Graham joined the club with two weeks left in the regular season and made each of his first six kicks, then went 0-for-2 in the playoff loss to Seattle. The Saints are bringing Graham back for what will be his 14th season in the league. It might seem like a dubious decision, but the random fluctuations in field-goal accuracy suggest that New Orleans should see a big improvement here regardless. Of the 24 teams that finished last in our values for FG/XP from 1989-2012, 15 finished with positive value the following season, and the average team improved by 16.1 points. Only one team has ever finished last in kicking for points two years in a row: Atlanta, during the "let's have our punter try field goals" era of 2006-07. (For completely unrelated reasons, the Falcons were last again in 2009.)

Thomas Morstead has finished second in punting value in each of the last two seasons, though he is just average on kickoffs. Kevin Reddick has been the top tackler on the Saints' nondescript coverage teams.

Darren Sproles had negative value on punt and kickoff returns last year. His departure likely leaves Travaris Cadet in charge of both duties. Cadet has only one punt return in his NFL career. He returned 50 punts at Appalachian State, but averaged only 5.9 yards per return. He has returned kickoffs in the NFL, averaging 26.5 yards on 35 returns, including a 75-yarder in 2012 and an 82-yarder last year. Oddly, he didn't score on either play.

New York Giants

2013 Record: 7-9	**Total DVOA:** -15.7% (27th)	**2014 Mean Projection:** 7.8 wins	**On the Clock (0-4):** 10%
Pythagorean Wins: 5.6 (25th)	**Offense:** -22.0% (31st)	**Postseason Odds:** 30.5%	**Mediocrity (5-7):** 34%
Snap-Weighted Age: 27.2 (6th)	**Defense:** -11.4% (6th)	**Super Bowl Odds:** 2.9%	**Playoff Contender (8-10):** 41%
Average Opponent: 3.0% (7th)	**Special Teams:** -5.1% (28th)	**Proj. Avg. Opponent:** -2.3% (25th)	**Super Bowl Contender (11+):** 14%

2013: The team in New York with the bad quarterback and the shutdown defense.

2014: Guaranteed to stay healthier, throw fewer interceptions. Not guaranteed to post a better record.

For years, each Giants regular season played out along more or less the same lines. New York would start the season strong before slumping in the second half of the season. Sometimes, the Giants would get hot again and go on a Super Bowl run, but just as often New York would wind up staying home for all of January.

Last year, Big Blue completely flipped the script, starting the season 0-6 but finishing with a 7-9 record.

Just as in other recent seasons, it was easy for the media to come up with a sequential narrative for the 2013 Giants. And just as in other recent seasons, the hidden driver for most of New York's apparently streaky play was really just strength of schedule. In fact, the Giants were one of the most consistent teams in the NFL if you measure the team's performance not chronologically, but by opponent.

- The Giants played four games against teams that ranked in the top seven in DVOA. New York went 0-4, with an average bludgeoning of 33-8.
- New York played four games against teams that ranked in the bottom seven in DVOA, and went 4-0. These games were a bit closer, with an average score of 23-13.
- The Giants beat the Eagles in a game where Matt Barkley took the majority of the snaps, and defeated Green Bay with Scott Tolzien at quarterback.
- New York played three other teams that had positive DVOA ratings, and lost all three games.
- Finally, the Giants played three games against slightly below average teams: Dallas twice, plus Detroit. New York went 1-2, with all three games decided by less than a touchdown.

The ice-cold start and hot finish may have dominated the headlines, but in between New York was a mediocre team that was about as predictable as an Eli Manning interception. Speaking of which, the 2013 season was undoubtedly the toughest of his career. Manning ranked 38th in passing DVOA and 42nd in passing DYAR, and was just as poor in traditional stats. But there are more extenuating circumstances than you might think, and roster turnover and some bad luck tell much of the story. The good news for Giants fans is that there's reason to believe the old Eli will be back in 2014. The bad news may be that the old Eli isn't quite as good as Giants fans tend to think.

For starters, let's put something in perspective: Manning averaged 6.9 yards per pass attempt in 2013, only a hair behind both the league average and his career average (7.1 in both cases). In other words, it's not as though Manning had a terrible year across the board. Rather, it was Manning's interception and sack rates that torpedoed his season. Manning has always been an interception-prone quarterback, of course: he has now led the league in that metric three times. But there's always a fair bit of luck involved with interceptions, and in 2012, Manning was the beneficiary of nine dropped interceptions. As a result, his adjusted interception rate went up only half as much as his actual interception rate. He's never going to be confused with his brother, but no Manning—heck, no starting quarterback—is going to throw 27 interceptions per year in today's NFL. No quarterback has even put up more than 20 interceptions in consecutive seasons since Jake Plummer in 1999 and 2000.

One area where you rightfully could confuse Peyton and Eli is sack rate. From 2010 to 2012, the Mannings and Drew Brees had the best sack rates in the NFL: all three were below 3.7 percent, while no other passer (minimum 800 attempts) was under 4.2 percent. In 2012, Eli led the NFL in sack rate, but last season, he was sacked on a career-high 6.6 percent of his passes. At age 32, Manning didn't suddenly forget how to avoid sacks: he was the victim of one of the league's worst (and most injury-wracked) offensive lines. Chris Snee and David Baas each missed 13 games, David Diehl missed five more, and William Beatty had a miserable year (which ended with him breaking his leg in a Week 17 game against Washington). Manning took 20 more sacks in 2013, but he doesn't deserve scorn for that figure.

The Giants look to be in much better shape on the line in 2014. New York signed Geoff Schwartz from Kansas City to play left guard, and hit the center position in free agency (J.D. Walton) and the draft (second-round pick Weston Richburg). Snee, who retired in July, will be replaced by either former Dolphin John Jerry or 2012 fourth-round pick Brandon Mosley. Jerry, who may be most famous for his ugly role in the Jonathan Martin scandal, is also recovering from knee surgery. While neither Jerry nor Mosley is the blocker Snee was in his prime, the Giants should still get better play out of the position compared to last year's disaster. The other two line spots have in-house solutions, with the team expecting improvement from 2013 first-round right tackle Justin Pugh and finger-crossing that Beatty plays more like he did in 2012 than in 2013.

2014 Giants Schedule

Week	Opp.	Week	Opp.	Week	Opp.
1	at DET	7	at DAL	13	at JAC
2	ARI	8	BYE	14	at TEN
3	HOU	9	IND (Mon.)	15	WAS
4	at WAS (Thu.)	10	at SEA	16	at STL
5	ATL	11	SF	17	PHI
6	at PHI	12	DAL		

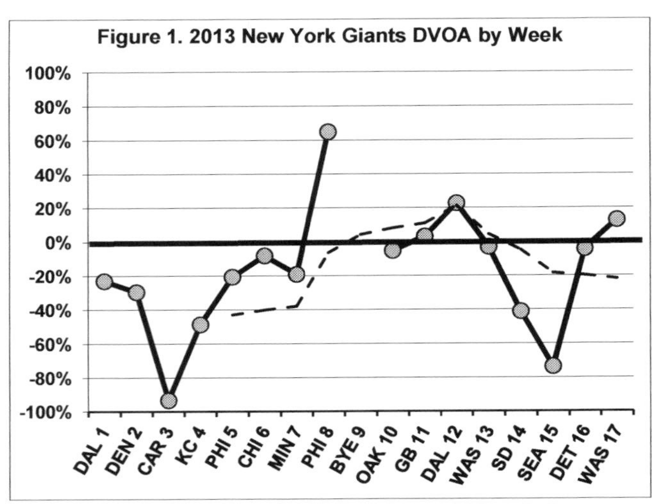

Another interesting part of Manning's decline was how clearly it was tied to the departure of two underrated players: wide receiver Domenik Hixon and running back Ahmad Bradshaw. Yes, Manning's completion percentage was an ugly 57.5 percent, but he's played in a vertical offense most of his career. He ranked in the top seven in both average length of pass and average length of completion in each of the past two years, so New York can live with a lower completion percentage in exchange for more big plays. But when it comes to Manning's specific decline in accuracy last year, it's Reuben Randle, not Manning, who bears the brunt of the blame. Consider that in 2012, the Giants' No. 3 receiver (Hixon) caught 39 of 59 passes (66 percent), while last season, Randle caught just 41 of 79 targets (52 percent). Catch rate can be a tricky stat to interpret, but most of those concerns are minimized when analyzing the same role in the same offense. Hixon's average pass in 2012 (11.1 air yards) even came a yard farther downfield than Randle's last year (10.1 air yards), which makes Randle's poor catch rate look even worse.

Both Victor Cruz and Hakeem Nicks posted similar catch rates in 2012 and 2013, as did the tight end (Martellus Bennett in 2012, Brandon Myers in 2013), which makes it plausible to blame much of Randle's struggle on the fact that he was a first-year starter who just wasn't nearly as experienced as Hixon was. Remove all passes to the No. 3 receivers, and Manning completed 59.1 percent of his throws in 2012 and 58.4 percent in 2013. Randle himself wasn't bad—his 14.9 yards per catch average justified his poor catch rate—but he does help explain why Manning's completion percentage dropped so significantly.

As for the departure of Ahmad Bradshaw, the issue was not Bradshaw as a runner but rather the Giants losing an unheralded asset in their passing game. Manning threw 75 passes in his direction in 2011 and 2012 combined, and Bradshaw gained 512 yards. Last season, New York's top four running backs saw 80 targets, and gained just 332 yards. Giants receivers and tight ends posted very similar efficiency numbers in 2012 and 2013, but the drop-off in effectiveness of the backs in the passing game was largely responsible for Manning's decline in yards per attempt. Don't think these are just numbers on a page in an advanced analytics book: general manager Jerry Reese saw the same thing, and that's why New York gave 29-year-old Rashad Jennings a very generous contract. In a market where all running backs had trouble getting paid, Jennings somehow got a four year deal with more guaranteed money that Knowshon Moreno and Maurice Jones-Drew *combined.* Jennings is a very good receiving back, and that production should be enough to put Manning north of seven yards per attempt in 2014.

Manning's interceptions tended to dominate the back pages in New York, but a wave of injuries was the truly important story of the 2013 season. The Giants didn't just suffer more injuries than the average team last year. And the Giants didn't just record more Adjusted Games Lost (AGL) in our database than any team in 2013. No, New York obliterated the record for AGL in a season with 144.6, moving the 2009 Bills (122.8 AGL) into second place in the Football Outsiders record books. With an incredible 82.1 AGL on offense, New York set the single-season record in that department, too. Here's one way to think of that number: since Manning started all 16 games last year, New York's other ten starters on average each missed more than half the season. That's incredible.

The defense wasn't much healthier: with 62.5 AGL, New York lost more games to injury than every defense other than New Orleans. The positive spin on this is that historically, New York has generally been pretty healthy on offense, ranking in the top half of the league in fewest AGL in four of the five years prior to 2013 (the defense sports a less successful track record). New York also ranked 28th in special teams DVOA, in part because injuries to starters often lead teams to turn special teamers into starters, and anybody left standing into special teamers. So there are reasons to be optimistic about the team going forward.

A more obvious reason to be excited about the team's offense this year is the addition of offensive coordinator Ben McAdoo, who replaces the polarizing Kevin Gilbride. McAdoo comes from Green Bay, so we should expect more short passes, an emphasis on yards after the catch, and a more conservative approach to the passing game. It remains to be seen whether this actually suits Manning—after all, he's a gunslinger who's never been a precision passer—but at a minimum, it should help cut down on his interceptions. On the other hand, despite what you might hear from those who count the #RINGZ, Manning has almost never been a superlative quarterback. The 2011 season looks even more like an anomaly with the benefit of hindsight. That year, Manning averaged 8.4 yards per attempt and threw for 4,933 yards, and both numbers are big outliers on his career averages. And, as you probably recall, Victor Cruz had a historic year with five touchdown catches of 65 yards or more. As a result, Cruz averaged a whopping 7.2 yards after the catch (he's been at 3.8 and 3.4 the past two years), a number he's unlikely to ever approach again.

It's time to acknowledge what Manning is: a streaky quarterback who can look like a top-five quarterback one week and a bottom-five quarterback the next. So even with three new starters on the line and a new running back, don't expect 2011 Manning to walk through that door. The Giants let Hakeem Nicks move on to Indianapolis, and drafted Odell Beckham, Jr., to replace him. Long-term, Cruz, Randle, and Beckham could be an excellent set of targets, but there will still be growing pains in 2014. Nicks didn't endear himself to Giants fans by the end of his stay in New York, but he still averaged an impressive 16.0 yards per catch last season while maintaining a respectable catch rate (56 percent) for a downfield receiver.

This doesn't mean we don't think the Giants can have a strong year: it's just that if the team returns to the playoffs, it will probably be because of the players on the other side of the ball. Football Outsiders projects the Giants' defense in the same tier as the Panthers and the Jets, with all three chasing the Seahawks for the right to be considered the best defense in the league. Does that sound surprising to you, that New York could wind up with the second best defense in the NFL? After all, Big Blue ranked just 18th in points allowed in 2013. But as is often the case, conventional statistics don't tell the true story.

The Giants allowed nine touchdowns last year when the offense wasn't on the field, the most in the NFL. So while the team ranked 18th in points allowed, New York ranked ninth in points allowed per drive, which better explains how the defense actually fared.

Because of the team's struggles on offense and in special teams coverage, Giants opponents began their average drive at the 30-yard line, the third worst average starting field position for any defense in the league. So even points allowed on a per-drive basis is a bit unfair to the defense. Another reason those 2013 numbers look better than you might remember is that New York faced the toughest schedule of opposing offenses in the league according to DVOA. Add it all up, and the Giants actually finished with the sixth best defensive DVOA last season.

Of course, with regression towards the mean, the Giants probably can't be that good again this year, right? Actually, they could be better, because the personnel will be better. It starts with regression towards the mean in a good way: we can't project the defense to rank second in AGL again. Then we also have to consider new players that were added. The additions of Dominique Rodgers-Cromartie, Quintin Demps, Walter Thurmond, and Stevie Brown (back after missing all of 2013 with a torn ACL) should give the Giants one of the league's top secondaries, especially if Trumaine McBride can once again put up strong play in spot duty. And New York had a top-ten defense on first and second downs while ranking just 17th on third downs. Historically that tends to lead to better overall play the following year, and this trend should be reinforced by the additions in the secondary. On top of all that, the defense's best player when healthy is still Jason Pierre-Paul. And JPP wasn't healthy last year, which makes it that much easier for him to make a bigger contribution in 2014 than he did in 2013.

The fact that the Giants were able to rank sixth in DVOA last season despite a lack of healthy talent is a testament to defensive coordinator Perry Fewell, who had a bounceback year after a rough 2012. The Giants had the best defense and the worst offense in New York last year, as odd as that might sound, and there's a good chance of that happening again in 2014. But given that the offense, when much healthier, ranked 11th in DVOA two years ago, it's also reasonable to picture a scenario where both the offense and special teams rebound to league average or better. We can count on the defense being very good this year, which means the Giants are one strong Eli Manning season away from another playoff run.

Chase Stuart

2013 Giants Stats by Week

Wk	vs.	W-L	PF	PA	YDF	YDA	TO	Total	Off	Def	ST
1	at DAL	L	31	36	478	331	-5	-23%	-23%	-11%	-11%
2	DEN	L	23	41	376	414	-3	-30%	-14%	-5%	-21%
3	at CAR	L	0	38	150	402	-1	-93%	-66%	18%	-9%
4	at KC	L	7	31	298	390	0	-49%	-8%	7%	-34%
5	PHI	L	21	36	383	439	-4	-21%	-15%	7%	1%
6	at CHI	L	21	27	355	372	-3	-8%	-2%	16%	10%
7	MIN	W	23	7	257	206	+2	-19%	-28%	-33%	-25%
8	at PHI	W	15	7	325	200	+2	65%	2%	-73%	-11%
9	BYE										
10	OAK	W	24	20	251	213	-1	-5%	-21%	-28%	-12%
11	GB	W	27	13	334	394	+2	3%	-14%	-13%	4%
12	DAL	L	21	24	356	311	0	23%	0%	-10%	12%
13	at WAS	W	24	17	286	323	0	-3%	5%	7%	0%
14	at SD	L	14	37	333	388	-2	-41%	-31%	14%	3%
15	SEA	L	0	23	181	327	-4	-74%	-84%	-14%	-3%
16	at DET	W	23	20	279	355	+1	-4%	-32%	-18%	10%
17	WAS	W	20	6	278	251	+1	13%	-53%	-61%	5%

Trends and Splits

	Offense	Rank	Defense	Rank
Total DVOA	-22.0%	31	-11.4%	6
Unadjusted VOA	-20.5%	31	-5.9%	7
Weighted Trend	-23.3%	30	-16.7%	4
Variance	6.3%	13	7.0%	24
Average Opponent	3.6%	29	7.3%	1
Passing	-17.9%	29	-7.0%	8
Rushing	-21.2%	30	-17.0%	4
First Down	-25.0%	30	-19.1%	3
Second Down	-24.1%	29	-8.8%	7
Third Down	-11.5%	22	-0.9%	17
First Half	-16.4%	30	-4.6%	9
Second Half	-27.7%	29	-18.2%	3
Red Zone	-38.9%	31	-3.1%	13
Late and Close	-45.5%	32	-40.1%	2

Five-Year Performance

Year	W-L	Pyth W	Est W	PF	PA	TO	Total	Rk	Off	Rk	Def	Rk	ST	Rk	Off AGL	Rk	Def AGL	Rk	Off Age	Rk	Def Age	Rk	ST Age	Rk
2009	8-8	7.4	8.4	402	427	-7	4.2%	17	8.7%	12	2.4%	19	-2.0%	26	8.5	6	47.2	29	26.9	23	26.7	22	26.4	20
2010	10-6	10.1	10.4	394	347	-3	13.0%	9	7.5%	10	-11.2%	3	-5.8%	30	39.7	26	18.4	13	27.3	18	27.2	16	26.0	20
2011	9-7	7.8	9.1	394	400	+7	8.5%	12	10.5%	7	2.4%	19	0.3%	15	25.2	14	53.1	30	27.4	13	27.6	8	26.1	20
2012	9-7	10.2	9.5	429	344	+14	13.4%	7	12.8%	7	1.5%	16	2.0%	10	26.1	12	56.6	28	27.8	8	27.2	13	26.2	13
2013	7-9	5.6	5.5	294	383	-15	-15.7%	27	-22.0%	31	-11.4%	6	-5.1%	28	82.1	32	62.5	31	27.4	12	27.4	7	26.1	15

2013 Performance Based on Most Common Personnel Groups

NYG Offense					NYG Offense vs. Opponents				NYG Defense				NYG Defense vs. Opponents			
Pers	Freq	Yds	DVOA	Run%	Pers	Freq	Yds	DVOA	Pers	Freq	Yds	DVOA	Pers	Freq	Yds	DVOA
11	53%	5.7	-16.4%	21%	Nickel Even	40%	6.1	-12.0%	Nickel Even	64%	5.2	-4.1%	11	55%	5.1	-15.6%
12	16%	4.8	-22.4%	45%	3-4-4	21%	4.6	-10.2%	4-3-4	29%	4.9	-17.6%	12	24%	5.4	-0.6%
21	16%	4.7	-15.9%	51%	4-3-4	21%	4.1	-34.6%	Nickel Odd	2%	5.3	-19.8%	21	8%	4.4	-30.5%
22	6%	2.5	-54.4%	89%	Dime+	11%	5.2	-22.4%	Dime+	2%	4.4	-139.5%	13	3%	4.1	-13.4%
02	3%	6.2	-25.3%	4%	Nickel Odd	5%	4.3	-63.3%	Goal Line	1%	0.6	-10.9%	22	3%	5.6	-9.0%

Strategic Tendencies

Run/Pass		Rk	Formation		Rk	Pass Rush		Rk	Secondary		Rk	Strategy		Rk
Runs, first half	38%	20	Form: Single Back	65%	18	Rush 3	4.2%	23	4 DB	30%	28	Play action	15%	24
Runs, first down	45%	24	Form: Empty Back	3%	27	Rush 4	61.9%	16	5 DB	66%	3	Avg Box (Off)	6.38	14
Runs, second-long	39%	6	Pers: 3+ WR	57%	13	Rush 5	24.8%	15	6+ DB	2%	27	Avg Box (Def)	6.32	19
Runs, power sit.	52%	18	Pers: 4+ WR	1%	14	Rush 6+	9.2%	11	CB by Sides	89%	6	Offensive Pace	31.08	24
Runs, behind 2H	29%	12	Pers: 2+ TE/6+ OL	29%	19	Sacks by LB	6.1%	32	DB Blitz	9%	22	Defensive Pace	29.50	13
Pass, ahead 2H	49%	14	Shotgun/Pistol	58%	18	Sacks by DB	12.1%	8	Hole in Zone	10%	18	Go for it on 4th	0.80	21

Big Blue had the best offense in the league on third/fourth-and-short, even though they ranked 25th in DVOA on all other third or fourth downs. The Giants ran 50 running back draws, more than any team other than San Diego or Atlanta, even though they were awful on these plays, with just 3.3 yards per carry and -52.2% DVOA. After two seasons where he completely destroyed big blitzes of six or more pass rushers, Eli Manning somewhat struggled against them in 2013, gaining just 5.1 yards per pass. The Giants had a league-leading -28.3% DVOA run defense against runs from formations with three or four wide receivers. The Giants had the worst offense in the league in "late and close" situations, but ranked second on defense behind only Arizona.

Passing

Player	DYAR	DVOA	Plays	NtYds	Avg	YAC	C%	TD	Int
E.Manning	-335	-20.2%	590	3471	5.9	4.6	58.1%	18	26
C.Painter	-103	-91.2%	19	45	2.4	3.4	50.0%	0	1

Rushing

Player	DYAR	DVOA	Plays	Yds	Avg	TD	Fum	Suc
A.Brown*	-44	-16.3%	139	494	3.6	3	3	50%
P.Hillis	-14	-13.3%	73	246	3.4	2	1	49%
B.Jacobs	21	-0.2%	58	239	4.1	4	1	47%
D.Wilson	-40	-30.4%	44	144	3.3	1	2	45%
M.Cox	-27	-41.3%	22	43	2.0	0	0	23%
D.Scott*	-7	-17.4%	20	73	3.7	0	0	30%
E.Manning	-27	-76.6%	9	42	4.7	0	3	-
R.Jennings	*164*	*15.8%*	*163*	*733*	*4.5*	*6*	*0*	*47%*

Receiving

Player	DYAR	DVOA	Plays	Ctch	Yds	Y/C	YAC	TD	C%
V.Cruz	133	1.0%	121	73	998	13.7	3.4	4	60%
H.Nicks*	83	-2.4%	101	56	896	16.0	4.8	0	55%
R.Randle	71	-1.5%	79	41	611	14.9	4.8	6	52%
J.Jernigan	40	0.0%	44	29	329	11.3	4.3	2	66%
L.Murphy*	-50	-61.2%	13	6	37	6.2	1.0	1	46%
M.Manningham	*-45*	*-38.8%*	*23*	*9*	*85*	*9.4*	*1.9*	*0*	*39%*
B.Myers*	7	-5.9%	75	47	522	11.1	3.6	4	63%
B.Pascoe*	-54	-52.0%	20	12	81	6.8	4.0	0	60%
L.Donnell	-5	-19.2%	6	3	31	10.3	3.3	0	50%
A.Brown*	-49	-46.7%	29	20	103	5.2	5.9	0	69%
P.Hillis	0	-13.5%	21	13	96	7.4	7.9	0	62%
D.Scott*	26	13.7%	19	11	102	9.3	10.2	1	58%
J.Conner	-25	-53.1%	11	6	31	5.2	4.8	0	55%
B.Jacobs	-9	-41.3%	7	2	13	6.5	7.5	0	29%
D.Wilson	-20	-89.5%	6	2	8	4.0	5.5	0	33%
R.Jennings	*66*	*10.8%*	*52*	*42*	*351*	*8.4*	*9.4*	*4*	*81%*

Offensive Line

Player	Pos	Age	GS	Snaps	Pen	Sk	Pass	Run	Player	Pos	Age	GS	Snaps	Pen	Sk	Pass	Run
Justin Pugh	RT	24	16/16	1026	3	3.5	17.0	4.0	Chris Snee	RG	32	3/3	186	1	3.0	9.0	1.0
Kevin Boothe*	LG	31	16/16	1021	2	1.3	11.3	6.5	David Baas*	C	33	3/3	142	1	0.0	2.0	5.0
William Beatty	LT	29	16/16	1003	9	11.3	31.8	3.0	Dallas Reynolds	C	30	3/0	101	0	0.0	4.0	1.0
David Diehl*	RG	34	11/11	707	0	2.0	17.0	9.0	*John Jerry*	*RG*	*28*	*16/16*	*1013*	*5*	*4.5*	*11.0*	*5.0*
Jim Cordle*	C	27	11/7	483	2	2.5	7.5	2.0	*Charles Brown*	*LT*	*27*	*16/14*	*951*	*12*	*5.0*	*24.0*	*4.5*
James Brewer	G/T	27	16/8	434	1	0.3	6.3	2.0	*Geoff Schwartz*	*RG*	*28*	*16/7*	*542*	*4*	*1.0*	*4.0*	*3.0*

Year	Yards	ALY	Rk	Power	Rk	Stuff	Rk	2nd Lev	Rk	Open Field	Rk	Sacks	ASR	Rk	Short	Long	F-Start	Cont.
2011	3.77	3.81	29	53%	27	19%	15	1.05	29	0.49	29	28	5.0%	6	11	10	16	26
2012	4.75	4.47	2	67%	8	19%	18	1.38	7	0.96	7	20	4.4%	3	1	11	13	33
2013	3.48	3.27	30	70%	10	25%	31	1.10	18	0.45	28	40	7.6%	18	10	11	6	23
2013 ALY by direction:			*Left End 2.72 (27)*			*Left Tackle 3.71 (21)*				*Mid/Guard 3.46 (30)*			*Right Tackle 2.91 (29)*			*Right End 2.93 (29)*		

This was the Giants' biggest weakness in 2013. The unit ranked 30th in Adjusted Line Yards and only 18th in Adjusted Sack Rate despite Eli Manning being excellent at avoiding sacks. Injuries devastated the team, and the offensive line was no exception with 36.3 Adjusted Games Lost, the second most in the league behind Oakland. And while Will Beatty remained healthy, he turned in one of the worst performances by a left tackle in 2013. We marked him with 35 blown blocks, roughly ten more than we would expect from an average left tackle with Beatty's snap count. He led all linemen with 11.3 blown blocks that led directly to sacks, and was one of just seven linemen flagged for holding six or more times. Beatty was a much better player in 2012, so the Giants are banking on a return to form. An upgrade next to Beatty should help. Geoff Schwartz was very good as a right guard for the Chiefs a year ago, and will move to the left side with the Giants to replace Kevin Boothe.

Center was a revolving door in 2012, and this year's starter will be decided in a camp battle between a pair of players who didn't play in the NFL last year: second-round draft pick Weston Richburg (Colorado State) and veteran J.D. Walton (ex-Broncos), who missed most of the past two seasons following leg injuries. Whoever plays at center will be asked to help revitalize the interior ground game. In 2012, the Giants led the league with 4.76 Adjusted Line Yards on runs in the middle of the line; that figured dropped to 3.46 last year, third worst in the league, although the Giants did remain strong converting short-yardage opportunities.

Right guard was a nightmare for the Giants last season, too, regardless of whether Chris Snee or David Diehl was lining up at the position. Both are now retired. We charted Snee with ten blown blocks on just 186 snaps last year, the worst percentage of any player with more than 30 snaps in 2013. Right tackle Justin Pugh had an uneventful rookie season, which is often the best you can hope for from a rookie tackle, but the team constantly struggled to run the ball on the right side.

Defensive Front Seven

			Overall								vs. Run					Pass Rush			
Defensive Line	Age	Pos	G	Snaps	Plays	TmPct	Rk	Stop	Dfts	BTkl	Runs	St%	Rk	RuYd	Rk	Sack	Hit	Hur	Tips
Cullen Jenkins	33	DT	16	696	30	3.5%	74	27	10	4	22	91%	9	1.5	17	5.0	6	13.0	0
Linval Joseph*	26	DT	15	578	59	7.3%	13	38	12	1	53	64%	79	3.1	71	3.0	4	4.5	0
Mike Patterson	31	DT	16	401	23	2.7%	--	17	3	3	22	77%	--	1.6	--	0.0	0	1.0	0
Johnathan Hankins	22	DT	11	191	16	2.7%	--	14	3	0	15	93%	--	1.2	--	0.0	2	1.5	0

			Overall								vs. Run					Pass Rush			
Edge Rushers	Age	Pos	G	Snaps	Plays	TmPct	Rk	Stop	Dfts	BTkl	Runs	St%	Rk	RuYd	Rk	Sack	Hit	Hur	Tips
Justin Tuck*	31	DE	16	873	66	7.7%	11	50	22	4	44	70%	53	2.3	31	11.0	12	32.0	3
Mathias Kiwanuka	31	DE	16	869	41	4.8%	54	35	13	3	28	86%	11	2.0	22	6.0	14	17.5	1
Jason Pierre-Paul	25	DE	11	567	31	5.2%	45	29	11	1	24	92%	5	1.4	10	2.0	5	18.0	3
*Robert Ayers**	*29*	*DE*	*15*	*506*	*28*	*3.6%*	*73*	*23*	*9*	*2*	*21*	*76%*	*38*	*2.2*	*26*	*5.5*	*5*	*17.5*	*0*

			Overall								Pass Rush			vs. Run					vs. Pass						
Linebackers	Age	Pos	G	Snaps	Plays	TmPct	Rk	Stop	Dfts	BTkl	Sack	Hit	Hur	Runs	St%	Rk	RuYd	Rk	Tgts	Suc%	Rk	AdjYd	Rk	PD	Int
Jon Beason	29	MLB	15	782	105	13.0%	42	45	13	5	0.0	1	1	57	60%	59	3.3	39	37	37%	68	9.5	69	1	1
Spencer Paysinger	26	OLB	16	691	66	7.7%	67	38	5	2	1.0	1	2.5	39	72%	18	3.3	34	29	62%	10	5.9	19	0	0
Jacquian Williams	26	OLB	16	604	60	7.0%	72	36	11	4	0.0	1	6	25	80%	6	2.4	12	34	56%	25	6.3	31	7	0
Keith Rivers*	28	OLB	16	418	43	5.0%	--	22	4	4	1.0	0	4	31	52%	--	4.0	--	8	76%	--	7.1	--	0	0
Mark Herzlich	27	MLB	16	191	31	3.6%	--	17	2	2	0.0	0	1	20	70%	--	3.4	--	4	27%	--	11.6	--	0	0
Jameel McClain	29	ILB	10	369	50	9.7%	63	18	1	5	0.0	0	2	35	37%	81	4.6	77	12	53%	--	4.8	--	0	0

Year	Yards	ALY	Rk	Power	Rk	Stuff	Rk	2nd Level	Rk	Open Field	Rk	Sacks	ASR	Rk	Short	Long
2011	4.60	3.99	14	52%	5	21%	11	1.23	19	1.16	28	41	6.4%	21	16	16
2012	4.30	3.69	5	72%	28	26%	2	1.33	29	1.03	27	34	5.2%	29	5	20
2013	4.08	3.13	2	50%	3	26%	4	1.13	19	1.07	29	33	5.8%	31	7	14
2013 ALY by direction:			*Left End 1.80 (2)*			*Left Tackle 3.50 (8)*			*Mid/Guard 3.20 (2)*			*Right Tackle 2.91 (5)*			*Right End 3.96 (19)*	

The Coughlin-era Giants will always be remembered for their relentless pass rush and dominant defensive lines. In 2007, New York led the league with 53 sacks and won the Super Bowl. Four years later, the Giants finished third with 48 sacks and won it again. But the team has recorded just 67 combined sacks in the past two seasons, and New York ranked tied for 25th in sacks in 2013. Most of the top pass rushers from the 2011 team are now gone, and the two that remain have seen their fortunes fall hard.

Some players age like fine wine, and then there's Jason Pierre-Paul. After recording 16.5 sacks and 32 Defeats at age 22 in 2011, those numbers dropped to 6.5 and 23 in 2012 before falling off the ledge in 2013. A combination of back, knee, and shoulder injuries torpedoed his season. Nobody doubts his talent, but neither we nor the Giants know what to expect out of JPP this year. In June, he told the media that he was "going to shut a whole bunch of people up," but even then acknowledged that he still feels some back pain. Mathias Kiwanuka has bounced between defensive end and outside linebacker for most of his career; he was never an elite pass rusher, but at 31, even his days as a "pretty good" pass rusher are behind him. Kiwanuka and Pierre-Paul will rotate with 2013 third-round pick Damontre Moore, who was relegated to special teams most of the season before recording three quarterback hits in Week 17, his only game with more than 25 defensive snaps. A new addition is former Denver first-round pick Robert Ayers, who totaled just 12 sacks in five seasons with the Broncos; however, 5.5 of those sacks were last season, so perhaps he'll be a useful player for the Giants.

A year ago, we praised Linval Joseph as a big reason for New York's first-place ranking stopping short-yardage (a.k.a. "Power") runs. Well, the Giants fell to 19th against Power runs in 2013, and the unit could be in more trouble in 2014 now that Joseph is in Minnesota. Last year, Joseph was one of the top interior defenders in the NFL: for the second straight year, he was in on 59 plays, which ranked fourth among defensive tackles behind fellow Empire Staters Marcell Dareus, Kyle Williams, and Damon Harrison. The task of replacing him will fall to a pair of unproven players, Johnathan Hankins (a 2013 second-round pick from Ohio State) or Jay Bromley (this year's third-rounder out of Syracuse). Hankins played well against the run in limited action last year, but replacing Joseph is a tall task. The other tackle spot is manned by Cullen Jenkins, who had a fine first season in New York after years in Green Bay and Philadelphia.

October's trade for Panthers veteran Jon Beason turned out very well, as Beason was able to stay healthy all season and was a big hit in New York. The Giants showed a commitment to the oft-injured run stuffer with a three-year deal in the offseason, despite his struggles as a pass defender. Beason's 37 percent Adjusted Success Rate in coverage put him among the bottom five linebackers with at least 16 charted passes last year. Still, while it may have worked out in 2013, the Beason acquisition is symptomatic of a bigger issue: the Giants like to treat the linebacker position the way most teams deal with kickers and punters. The Giants rarely spend significant draft capital or free-agent dollars on linebackers, preferring to fill out the starting lineup with spare parts. In that regard, handing out a nice contract to an aging, injury-prone linebacker who struggles in coverage was a move that was easy to criticize at the time, and looks even worse after Beason suffered a foot injury in June that will keep him out until at least September. Beason was acquired for a seventh-round pick, Spencer Paysinger and Mark Herzlich were undrafted free agents, Jacquian Williams was a sixth-round pick, and Jameel McClain was signed by New York in March after he was released by the Ravens. Investing so little in the linebacker position has combined with the departure of several veteran pass rushers to leave the front seven devoid of playmakers other than Pierre-Paul. New York largely ignored the position in the draft in 2014, too, taking only Devon Kennard (USC) in the fifth round. Jesse Armstead, drafted in 1993, is the last player drafted by New York to make a Pro Bowl at linebacker.

Defensive Secondary

			Overall								vs. Run					vs. Pass									
Secondary	Age	Pos	G	Snaps	Plays	TmPct	Rk	Stop	Dfts	BTkl	Runs	St%	Rk	RuYd	Rk	Tgts	Tgt%	Rk	Dist	Suc%	Rk	AdjYd	Rk	PD	Int
Antrel Rolle	32	FS	16	1124	106	12.3%	21	44	20	9	41	44%	29	6.6	29	56	11.6%	68	10.3	56%	35	6.1	20	10	6
Prince Amukamara	25	CB	16	1078	97	11.3%	7	36	14	6	28	39%	46	7.7	52	90	19.3%	24	11.0	48%	68	6.9	22	13	1
Will Hill*	24	FS	12	764	68	10.5%	34	25	13	2	30	43%	33	8.7	64	25	7.4%	31	11.8	63%	17	4.1	4	2	2
Ryan Mundy*	29	SS	16	653	72	8.4%	64	28	11	5	42	52%	17	4.4	7	22	7.6%	33	12.4	62%	24	6.3	24	2	1
Trumaine McBride	29	CB	15	606	50	6.2%	75	23	10	4	8	25%	69	7.0	41	72	27.6%	84	13.3	69%	1	4.2	1	13	2
Terrell Thomas*	29	CB	16	567	74	8.6%	43	31	12	6	15	60%	6	5.3	18	56	22.7%	58	9.6	56%	28	6.8	21	5	1
D.Rodgers-Cromartie	*28*	*CB*	*15*	*776*	*44*	*5.6%*	*83*	*28*	*14*	*5*	*7*	*71%*	*1*	*6.9*	*40*	*66*	*18.9%*	*22*	*14.0*	*63%*	*4*	*7.8*	*51*	*14*	*3*
Quintin Demps	*29*	*FS*	*16*	*637*	*41*	*4.8%*	*75*	*21*	*11*	*5*	*9*	*56%*	*10*	*6.9*	*37*	*26*	*9.4%*	*56*	*10.6*	*74%*	*2*	*4.0*	*3*	*9*	*4*
Walter Thurmond	*27*	*CB*	*12*	*468*	*39*	*6.6%*	*--*	*21*	*11*	*3*	*7*	*29%*	*--*	*12.7*	*--*	*41*	*21.1%*	*--*	*6.7*	*60%*	*--*	*5.8*	*--*	*5*	*1*

Year	Pass D Rank	vs. #1 WR	Rk	vs. #2 WR	Rk	vs. Other WR	Rk	vs. TE	Rk	vs. RB	Rk
2011	19	0.6%	13	5.7%	17	18.2%	30	5.1%	13	9.0%	23
2012	16	11.9%	23	-4.0%	13	18.2%	26	-20.2%	3	-7.6%	12
2013	8	-11.6%	9	-33.7%	2	-22.0%	5	-18.7%	6	14.9%	28

In this space last year, we opened with the line: "Injuries in the secondary have been responsible for some of the problems in coverage over the last two years." The 2013 Giants defensive backs laughed in the face of regression to the mean, recording an unthinkable 44.9 Adjusted Games Lost. Safety Stevie Brown was a breakout star in 2012, but missed all of last year after tearing his ACL in the preseason. Cornerbacks Corey Webster and Aaron Ross each missed 12 games. Safety Will Hill, meanwhile, was suspended for four games due to marijuana use.

The secondary will look much different in 2014, with only Antrel Rolle and Prince Amukamara returning in notable capacities. Rolle's high-risk, high-reward play has mostly worked out, but at age 32, those scales could tip at any moment. While Rolle's six interceptions in 2013 were a career high, he took a step back in our other pass defense metrics, and he's had nine or ten broken tackles in each of the past three seasons. Amukamara is in a critical year: the Giants chose to exercise his fifth-year option based more on potential than performance. He's not a top-tier cornerback, but he's too good to let hit the open market. The former Cornhusker plays a lot of soft coverage, allowing defenders to rack up short catches, but rarely gets beat deep. When surrounded by other talented players, that approach could be part of a top pass defense. And there's reason for optimism that the Giants secondary in 2014 will fully qualify as "surrounding Amukamara with other talented players."

Joining Amukamara at cornerback are Dominique Rodgers-Cromartie and Walter Thurmond, each of whom are coming off strong seasons for Super Bowl teams. DRC ranked fourth in Adjusted Success Rate among cornerbacks last season, and he's the type of long, athletic defender that the Giants need in the NFC East. Thurmond, mostly at nickel for Seattle last season, allowed just 5.1 yards per pass on his targets; he fell a few targets short of qualifying, but otherwise would have ranked second overall in that metric. Who ranked first in that category? The hidden star of the Giants' 2013 defense, Trumaine McBride. In fact, McBride ranked first in both Adjusted Yards per Attempt and Adjusted Success Rate, which is just plain weird… and incredible. Despite being on the field for 606 snaps, he was responsible for only three receptions of more than 16 yards. And this wasn't because McBride was a nickelback who got lucky: he started 10 games and spent much of his time guarding outside receivers. Was it a one-year fluke? Almost certainly, given McBride's non-existent pedigree entering the year. But he's a big reason why the Giants defense ranked eighth in pass DVOA last year, despite an inept pass rush and a decimated secondary.

The addition of safety Quintin Demps—who ranked in the top three in both Adjusted Yards per Attempt and Adjusted Success Rate in Kansas City—looks brilliant after Will Hill's career in New York flamed out. Add in a healthy Brown, and the Giants could have a trio of players at both cornerback and safety that rank in the top quarter of the league.

Special Teams

Year	DVOA	Rank	FG/XP	Rank	Net Kick	Rank	Kick Ret	Rank	Net Punt	Rank	Punt Ret	Rank	Hidden	Rank
2011	0.3%	15	-1.7	19	4.2	8	-3.4	22	10.9	5	-8.4	29	-3.8	21
2012	2.0%	10	-3.0	21	1.5	13	14.6	1	0.9	15	-4.0	22	-3.1	22
2013	-5.1%	28	0.7	17	3.3	11	-4.2	24	-20.5	31	-4.6	23	-12.8	32

The Giants had the second worst punting unit in the league last year, but don't blame Steve Weatherford. Big Blue's punter ranked in our top ten for gross punter value, only to be betrayed by the Giants' appalling coverage teams. The Giants became the first team since 1970 to allow three punt returns of 80 or more yards in the same season. (Washington was the only other team to allow more than one punt return touchdown last year, and somehow their punt coverage overall was actually *worse* than New York's.) The rest of the Giants' special teams were nondescript, with a mediocre performance by kicker Josh Brown and a rotating cast of kick returners.

The Giants then added poor luck to poor performance, as evidenced by their rank of 32nd in "Hidden" special teams value. New York was one of four teams that saw opposing field goal kickers miss just once all year, and that one miss was a 53-yard attempt by Minnesota's Blair Walsh. The Giants were even more unlucky when you consider that they play half their games in the windy Meadowlands; at least when Detroit and Atlanta only saw opponents miss a single field goal, they could partly blame their domed stadiums. In a year where everything seemed to go wrong for the Giants, just about everything went right for opposing kickers, too.

New York Jets

2013 Record: 8-8	**Total DVOA:** -7.7% (24th)	**2014 Mean Projection:** 7.6 wins	**On the Clock (0-4):** 12%
Pythagorean Wins: 5.4 (27th)	**Offense:** -15.3% (27th)	**Postseason Odds:** 29.5%	**Mediocrity (5-7):** 36%
Snap-Weighted Age: 26.4 (23rd)	**Defense:** -5.6% (12th)	**Super Bowl Odds:** 3.2%	**Playoff Contender (8-10):** 39%
Average Opponent: -0.4% (17th)	**Special Teams:** 2.1% (10th)	**Proj. Avg. Opponent:** 1.9% (10th)	**Super Bowl Contender (11+):** 13%

2013: A winding, serendipitous path to 8-8 takes Rex Ryan off the hot seat.

2014: A fourth straight season without the playoffs would put Rex Ryan back on the hot seat.

Leave it to Rex Ryan to field one of the weirdest 8-8 teams in NFL history. The Jets were ranked 32nd in ESPN's preseason power rankings, a fact that Ryan brought up repeatedly throughout the season. And in some ways, Ryan's "us against the world" mantra worked: after all, the Jets nearly made the playoffs, and Ryan was widely praised for getting a not-so-talented team to eight wins.

But in some ways, the 2013 Jets really *were* one of the worst teams in the NFL. Consider:

- In six games, the Jets never held a lead, tied for the most such games in 2013 with Houston, Jacksonville, and St. Louis.
- The Jets were outscored by 97 points, the most of any team in NFL history that didn't post a losing record. Based purely on points differential, we have the Jets as a team with 5.4 Pythagorean wins.
- New York ranked 28th in pass offense DVOA and just 18th in DVOA pass defense. As a result, the Jets ranked 27th in DVOA pass differential, and the five teams below them won an average of just 3.6 games.
- The team was embarrassed in roughly half of its games: New York's average loss came by 18.75 points, the most in the NFL.

So how exactly did the Jets *win* eight games? New York went 5-1 in games decided by seven or fewer points, and Geno Smith was tied for the league lead (with Tom Brady and Russell Wilson) with five game-winning drives. That helps to explain why the Jets recorded 2.6 more actual wins than Pythagorean wins, easily the most in the NFL last year.

But points differential doesn't tell the whole story, and DVOA wasn't nearly as harsh on the Jets. While points differential and DVOA are generally closely correlated, New York was also one of the biggest outliers when comparing the two metrics. So what explains the divergent ratings?

- New York forced 18 fumbles but recovered just two of them. Incredibly, the Jets became the first team in NFL history to recover fewer than three opponent fumbles in a season. Since our research suggests that recovering fumbles is almost purely a function of luck, that hurt New York's points differential, but not its DVOA.
- The Jets converted just one of eight fourth-down attempts, ranking 32nd in both conversions and conversion ratio. That's also more likely to harm the team's points differential than DVOA.
- Opposing defenses scored six touchdowns (five pick-sixes, one fumble return score), the second most in the NFL behind Chicago (seven). The NFL average was just 2.8, and since return touchdowns are among the flukiest types of scores in the game, the penalty is mitigated in DVOA.
- New York ranked 30th in DVOA variance, which helps us understand why a below-average team could still win eight games. As a general rule, above-average teams want to have low variances and below-average teams want to have a high variance. For the Jets, one might wonder if in some of the blowouts, the team simply stopped putting forth maximum effort. We're thinking of the Bengals game, the Titans game, the second Buffalo game, the first Miami... OK, you get the point. The Jets at least *looked* like a team that had quit in a handful of games last year.

So the Jets were a below-average team, but not as bad as the Pythagorean record would indicate. The Jets, as usual, were also a one-sided team. For the fifth time in Ryan's five years as head coach, the offense ranked at least 10 spots lower in DVOA than the defense did. And, for the fifth time in five years, the pass offense ranked worse in DVOA than the rushing offense. How bad was the passing attack? Last year's team joined the 2011 Jaguars as the only teams in the last nine years to fail to have a single player gain 550 receiving yards. So after doing little to retool the offense in the 2013 offseason, general manager John Idzik went out and signed the top wide receiver on the free-agent market in March.

It has been said that Eric Decker Is Not A Number One Receiver so frequently that you might think he has the longest name in the NFL. There's not much of a sample size for top receivers moving on from Peyton Manning, but history doesn't suggest that Decker is doomed to failure. Reggie Wayne gained 1,355 yards in 2010 with Manning, 960 yards playing for the Painter/Orlovsky Colts, and then 1,355 again with Andrew Luck in 2012. Pierre Garcon's two best years have come with Robert Griffin rather than Manning, and... well, that's pretty much the full list of top receivers who moved on from Manning.

2014 Jets Schedule

Week	Opp.	Week	Opp.	Week	Opp.
1	OAK	7	at NE (Thu.)	13	MIA (Mon.)
2	at GB	8	BUF	14	at MIN
3	CHI (Mon.)	9	at KC	15	at TEN
4	DET	10	PIT	16	NE
5	at SD	11	BYE	17	at MIA
6	DEN	12	at BUF		

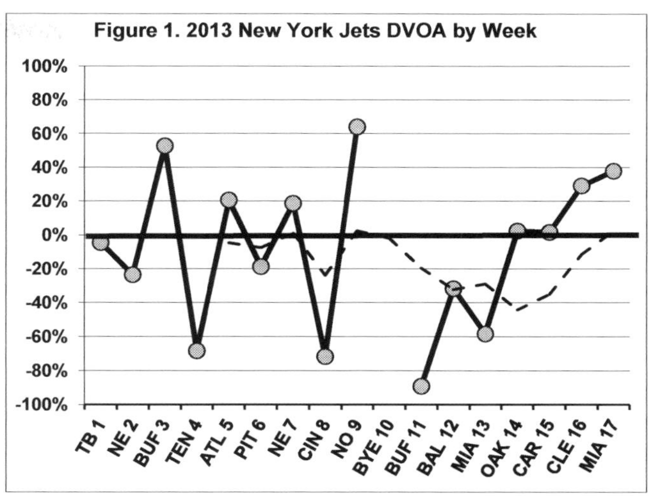

Taking a broader view, no top receiver has ever gone from a passing attack that ranked first in passing yards to one that ranked 31st. But one of the closest comparisons in recent history does involve the Jets. In 209, Santonio Holmes gained 1,248 yards as the nominal number two behind Hines Ward in Pittsburgh. Holmes was traded to the Jets in the offseason, after New York ranked 31st in passing yards during Mark Sanchez's rookie season. In 2010, Holmes gained 746 yards in 12 games, and that's the type of per-game production the Jets would gladly take from Decker. Decker doesn't need to be a "true" No. 1 receiver (whatever that means) for his signing to work out: he just needs to be better than David Nelson and Stephen Hill.

Decker obviously won't have the type of support he had in Denver, but is it possible that one of his new teammates is a hidden gem? Only three tight ends averaged at least ten yards per target last year (minimum 20 targets). One was Vernon Davis (10.1); another was everyone's favorite fantasy sleeper for 2013, Ladarius Green (12.5). And the third was... Jeff Cumberland?

What's going on here? How did Cumberland produce such strong numbers, and wind up second in DVOA among tight ends? Among the 52 tight ends with at least 20 targets, Cumberland ranked fifth in yards gained through the air (per reception) and seventh in yards gained after the catch (per reception). Incredibly, Green ranked first in both of those metrics, but there's generally an inverse relationship between those two statistics: you either catch passes downfield, or you gain a lot of yards after the catch, but rarely both. In fact, Green and Cumberland were the only two tight ends to rank in the top 15 in both categories, which underscores just how impressive Cumberland's efficiency numbers were in 2013.

So is Cumberland coming off a sneaky strong season and about to break out? There's no denying that his efficiency numbers were great, but sometimes, the best course of action is to take a step back and look at the bigger picture. In 2012, Cumberland finished second on the team with 53 targets. In the offseason, New York allowed Dustin Keller to head to Miami, but instead of handing the job to Cumberland, signed Kellen Winslow. As a result, Cumberland wound up seeing only 40 targets in 2013. If the Jets were as high on Cumberland as his numbers would suggest, he would have managed to pick up more than 2.5 targets per game in one of the league's most anemic passing attacks. Then, New York drafted Texas Tech tight end Jace Amaro in the second round of the 2014 draft. Efficiency numbers are fun to look at, but the revealed preference of the Jets organization would seem to trump those metrics. And it appears as though the organization views Cumberland as a role player and little more.

If there's a player Jets fans are hoping will break out, it's probably not Cumberland, but former second-round pick Stephen Hill. So far, Hill has been one of the biggest busts in recent Jets history—and if you've seen that video online of Jets fans reacting to their team's draft picks each year, you know there's a *lot* of competition in this category. Last year, Hill was one of the worst starting wide receivers in the NFL, and at least partially to blame for the team's ugly passing attack. Hill had a catch rate of 41 percent and averaged 5.8 yards per target; on all other passes to Jets wide receivers, the team completed 57 percent and averaged 7.6 yards per target.

Sure, some receivers take time to develop, but the frustrating part with Hill is that he's been given significant opportunities. Hill had more snaps than any other wide receiver on the team last year, but ranked fourth among Jets wideouts in receiving yards. It's the lack of success despite the opportunity that seems to have the organization ready to move on. Idzik wasn't in New York when the Jets drafted Hill, and Ryan was uncharacteristically negative when he talked about benching Hill last year, telling the media "By now I think we're all expecting... Jet fans are all expecting him to take the next step and for whatever reason it (hasn't) been there yet."

Rex Ryan will defend just about any of his players, so that sort of honesty is a sign of how confused the Jets really are with Hill's lack of development. But is there any hope? We looked at all wide receivers drafted in the first two rounds since 1990. Then, we limited the group to only players who had at least 15 starts in their first two seasons, since the most troubling issue with Hill is his lack of production despite significant playing time. Among that group, Hill has the second fewest receiving yards through two seasons (Table 1).

The optimist would note that several of those players had strong seasons in year three. A couple of them, Pickens and Conway, used that breakout season as a springboard to a pretty good career. (So did Ike Hilliard, though his breakout year was really his second.) Look at the rest of the list, however, and you'll see a pessimistic mix of one-year wonders and outright busts. In any event, it's clear that year three is the make-or-break campaign for the combine superstar. There are reasons the organization continues to hold out hope for Hill: he's suffered through serious knee injuries each of his first two years, and has had to deal with changing schemes and quarterbacks. Hill was raw coming out of college, but that excuse won't hold water for any longer.

When talking about the Jets, it's always a lot more fun to talk about the defense than the passing attack. And there are a few reasons for that. One is that the team's last six first-round picks have been either defensive backs or defensive linemen. Regardless of how Rex Ryan's tenure in New York ends, the coach certainly got a chance to build his team in his vision. The Jets are just the third team in NFL history to spend six straight first-round picks on defensive players, joining the 1998 to 2002 49ers (six straight) and the 1998 to 2007 Cowboys (eight).

Was this a prudent course of action? The offense has consistently been among the worst in the league, and despite the draft capital utilized, the pass defense still has a bunch of question marks. One school of thought is that the benefit of having a defensive guru like Ryan is the ability for a team to devote most of its resources to offense; instead, the Jets have gone in the other direction, and still haven't been able to build a dream-team defense.

Drafting Muhammad Wilkerson, Sheldon Richardson, and Quinton Coples has undoubtedly been a boon to the run defense, but in today's world, defending the pass is king. And that's still an open issue for the team heading into the fall.

The performance of the secondary has trailed behind what New York's seen from its defensive line. Kyle Wilson has alternated between promising slot corner and outright disappointment, and he's far enough in his career to assume he's never going to be a consistent corner; as a result, 2014 is likely his final year in New York. As we'll discuss later on when we specifically discuss the secondary, Dee Milliner had a disastrous rookie season, and he and Antonio Cromartie are the reasons the Jets struggled to stop opposing quarterbacks. In a vacuum, drafting Calvin Pryor makes a ton of sense, as New York had a glaring hole at strong safety. But for a team that's devoted so many resources to one side of the ball *and* has Ryan as head coach, the pass defense has more questions than most fans realize.

For starters, the Jets don't even know who their No. 2 cornerback will be. And Milliner as the No. 1 could be a stretch, even if he did end the 2013 season on a high note. If Darrin Walls wins the other starting corner job, New York's starting secondary will enter the year with a combined 25 career starts.

Table 1. The Year Three Wide Receiver Breakout is a Thing, Right?

Player	Team	Year	Yr 1 Yds	Yr 2 Yds	Total	Yr 1-2 GS	Yr 3 Yds
Darrius Heyward-Bey	OAK	2009	124	366	490	25	975
Stephen Hill	NYJ	2012	252	342	594	19	--
Rae Carruth	CAR	1997	545	59	604	15	200
Dennis Northcutt	CLE	2000	422	211	633	15	601
Jerome Pathon	IND	1998	511	163	674	17	646
Reggie Williams	JAC	2004	268	445	713	22	616
Ike Hilliard	NYG	1997	42	715	757	18	996
Todd Pinkston	PHI	2000	181	586	767	16	798
Curtis Conway	CHI	1993	231	546	777	19	1,037
Travis Taylor	BAL	2000	276	560	836	21	869
Arrelious Benn	TB	2010	395	441	836	23	26
Jabar Gaffney	HOU	2002	483	402	885	25	632
Alvin Harper	DAL	1991	326	562	888	18	777
Carl Pickens	CIN	1992	326	565	891	22	1,127
Kevin Dyson	TEN	1998	263	658	921	25	104
Bryant Johnson	ARI	2003	438	537	975	19	432
Average			**322**	**454**	**776**	**20**	**656**

Table shows first- and second-round wide receivers since 1990 with fewest yards in their first two seasons (minimum 15 games started).

Ryan has never been afraid to bet on himself, but the defense may need to revert to top-five form for the Jets to make the playoffs. For that to happen, Ryan, defensive coordinator Dennis Thurman and position coach Tim McDonald will have to quickly groom a talented but raw secondary.

Overall, the Jets should be a slightly better team in 2014, but that may not be reflected in the win column (though it almost certainly will be reflected in the team's points differential). The run defense should be very good, but the offense looks to again be one of the weakest in the league. The Jets have ranked in the bottom five in pass offense DVOA three times under Ryan, including in each of the last two years. Adding Decker will help, but the offensive talent remains decidedly below average. In the modern NFL, teams can be successful with a below-average passing attack only if everything else breaks right. It's a challenging task that only a few coaches—Rex Ryan, Jeff Fisher, and Lovie Smith—seem to embrace. New York may challenge for the playoffs in a weak AFC, but the Jets won't be consistent contenders for something greater until the offense gets significantly better.

Chase Stuart

2013 Jets Stats by Week

Wk	vs.	W-L	PF	PA	YDF	YDA	TO	Total	Off	Def	ST
1	TB	W	18	17	304	250	0	-5%	-30%	-18%	7%
2	at NE	L	10	13	318	232	-4	-24%	-56%	-34%	-2%
3	BUF	W	27	20	513	328	-2	53%	27%	-21%	4%
4	at TEN	L	13	38	330	322	-4	-68%	-63%	9%	3%
5	at ATL	W	30	28	288	363	+1	21%	14%	-2%	4%
6	PIT	L	6	19	267	328	-2	-19%	-31%	-7%	6%
7	NE	W	30	27	383	295	0	19%	-25%	-39%	4%
8	at CIN	L	9	49	240	402	-1	-72%	-38%	36%	2%
9	NO	W	26	20	338	407	+2	64%	20%	-28%	16%
10	BYE										
11	at BUF	L	14	37	267	313	-4	-89%	-73%	14%	-2%
12	at BAL	L	3	19	220	312	-2	-32%	-33%	-3%	-2%
13	MIA	L	3	23	177	453	-2	-58%	-45%	15%	1%
14	OAK	W	37	27	352	383	0	2%	2%	12%	13%
15	at CAR	L	20	30	297	392	-1	2%	21%	17%	-3%
16	CLE	W	24	13	422	283	+2	29%	26%	-13%	-10%
17	at MIA	W	20	7	374	296	+3	38%	19%	-27%	-9%

Trends and Splits

	Offense	Rank	Defense	Rank
Total DVOA	-15.3%	27	-5.6%	12
Unadjusted VOA	-13.6%	25	-4.3%	10
Weighted Trend	-10.9%	24	-0.9%	16
Variance	11.9%	30	4.6%	14
Average Opponent	-1.5%	11	-1.5%	22
Passing	-15.9%	28	7.5%	18
Rushing	-8.0%	23	-23.0%	2
First Down	-27.1%	31	-15.4%	6
Second Down	-14.2%	26	-5.8%	9
Third Down	6.4%	12	11.5%	24
First Half	-12.6%	28	-3.3%	11
Second Half	-17.7%	27	-8.2%	8
Red Zone	1.9%	17	-20.5%	6
Late and Close	-11.1%	23	-19.7%	5

Five-Year Performance

Year	W-L	Pyth W	Est W	PF	PA	TO	Total	Rk	Off	Rk	Def	Rk	ST	Rk	Off AGL	Rk	Def AGL	Rk	Off Age	Rk	Def Age	Rk	ST Age	Rk
2009	9-7	11.4	9.2	342	236	+1	25.8%	9	-12.5%	22	-25.5%	1	2.8%	6	4.1	1	21.0	12	28.1	4	27.6	7	27.0	5
2010	11-5	9.8	10.1	367	304	+9	18.7%	6	2.1%	16	-10.9%	5	5.8%	5	8.9	4	33.0	23	27.6	14	28.1	7	26.5	13
2011	8-8	8.4	8.4	377	363	-3	13.5%	10	-8.3%	21	-16.1%	2	5.6%	4	9.2	2	21.2	12	27.6	12	27.5	9	26.2	17
2012	6-10	5.3	5.6	281	375	-14	-18.0%	27	-20.7%	30	-4.2%	9	-1.5%	21	37.7	22	41.0	23	26.6	19	28.1	2	26.0	16
2013	8-8	5.4	7.5	290	387	-14	-7.7%	24	-15.3%	27	-5.6%	12	2.1%	10	35.9	16	20.7	9	26.2	26	26.7	14	26.1	13

2013 Performance Based on Most Common Personnel Groups

NYJ Offense					NYJ Offense vs. Opponents				NYJ Defense				NYJ Defense vs. Opponents			
Pers	Freq	Yds	DVOA	Run%	Pers	Freq	Yds	DVOA	Pers	Freq	Yds	DVOA	Pers	Freq	Yds	DVOA
11	47%	5.7	-1.4%	43%	Nickel Even	38%	5.0	-15.5%	Nickel Even	24%	5.2	-16.7%	11	47%	5.6	-2.3%
21	18%	4.3	-22.9%	52%	4-3-4	21%	4.6	-13.8%	4-3-4	19%	4.6	-13.8%	12	25%	5.2	-0.7%
12	11%	4.6	-32.6%	26%	3-4-4	18%	3.9	-27.7%	Nickel Odd	14%	5.8	-1.6%	21	13%	4.8	-16.4%
20	7%	6.4	-12.1%	28%	Dime+	11%	6.5	-11.2%	Dime+	7%	5.8	39.1%	13	4%	4.4	-27.7%
22	4%	4.0	-40.9%	82%	Nickel Odd	11%	7.8	23.7%	4-4-3	2%	2.7	-36.5%	22	4%	5.5	-22.6%
WC	4%	4.2	-17.1%	84%					Goal Line	2%	1.7	-41.3%				

Strategic Tendencies

Run/Pass		Rk	Formation		Rk	Pass Rush		Rk	Secondary		Rk	Strategy		Rk
Runs, first half	45%	3	Form: Single Back	62%	23	Rush 3	7.7%	8	4 DB	51%	4	Play action	21%	16
Runs, first down	57%	2	Form: Empty Back	6%	19	Rush 4	63.5%	13	5 DB	38%	28	Avg Box (Off)	6.43	10
Runs, second-long	38%	8	Pers: 3+ WR	61%	11	Rush 5	21.7%	21	6+ DB	7%	15	Avg Box (Def)	6.50	4
Runs, power sit.	78%	2	Pers: 4+ WR	4%	5	Rush 6+	7.1%	19	CB by Sides	58%	25	Offensive Pace	29.38	12
Runs, behind 2H	34%	3	Pers: 2+ TE/6+ OL	19%	30	Sacks by LB	52.5%	10	DB Blitz	13%	14	Defensive Pace	28.55	4
Pass, ahead 2H	43%	24	Shotgun/Pistol	68%	7	Sacks by DB	5.0%	21	Hole in Zone	9%	21	Go for it on 4th	0.44	30

Geno Smith averaged a league-low 3.1 yards per pass when opponents sent a big blitz of six or more pass rushers. For the second straight year, the Jets were actually worse when they used a play-action fake, gaining just 5.1 yards per pass with -20.9% DVOA when using play action but 6.1 yards per pass with -3.7% DVOA otherwise. Gang Green was much better running from single-back formations (4.9 yards per carry, -6.2% DVOA) than from two-back formations (3.6 yards per carry, -22.4% DVOA). The Jets pass rush got worse last year in definite passing situations: they ranked third in the league in Adjusted Sack Rate on first downs, but 21st on second downs and dead last on third or fourth downs. The Jets pressured the quarterback only 14 percent of the time when sending a four-man rush, the lowest rate in the league. Weirdly, we actually marked pressure more often when they sent only three (nine of 45 plays, or 20 percent).

Passing

Player	DYAR	DVOA	Plays	NtYds	Avg	YAC	C%	TD	Int
G.Smith	-371	-23.6%	485	2739	5.6	5.1	55.9%	12	21
M.Simms	-27	-24.6%	35	133	3.8	4.1	51.6%	1	1
M.Vick	*40*	*-6.9%*	*157*	*1098*	*7.0*	*7.4*	*55.0%*	*5*	*3*

Rushing

Player	DYAR	DVOA	Plays	Yds	Avg	TD	Fum	Suc
C.Ivory	2	-8.3%	182	833	4.6	3	2	44%
B.Powell	-1	-8.7%	176	700	4.0	1	1	43%
G.Smith	65	9.5%	60	388	6.5	6	4	-
T.Bohanon	5	-2.7%	17	62	3.6	0	0	47%
J.Cribbs*	12	16.6%	13	55	4.2	0	0	54%
A.Green	-5	-17.5%	11	35	3.2	0	0	45%
M.Goodson	16	60.0%	7	61	8.7	0	0	43%
M.Simms	-12	-73.4%	5	35	7.0	0	1	-
C.Johnson	*110*	*1.5%*	*279*	*1067*	*3.8*	*7*	*2*	*46%*
M.Vick	*128*	*70.0%*	*29*	*316*	*10.9*	*2*	*0*	*-*
J.Ford	*0*	*-37.9%*	*5*	*15*	*3.0*	*0*	*0*	*-*

Receiving

Player	DYAR	DVOA	Plays	Ctch	Yds	Y/C	YAC	TD	C%
J.Kerley	97	6.0%	72	43	523	12.2	4.1	3	60%
D.Nelson	67	2.4%	61	36	423	11.8	3.0	2	59%
S.Holmes*	27	-6.7%	59	23	456	19.8	5.4	1	39%
S.Hill	-74	-28.8%	59	24	342	14.3	3.8	1	41%
E.Gates	-43	-36.2%	24	12	122	10.2	2.2	0	50%
G.Salas	40	28.5%	13	8	143	17.9	9.8	0	62%
E.Decker	381	21.3%	136	87	1288	14.8	4.3	11	64%
J.Ford	*-78*	*-56.5%*	*24*	*13*	*99*	*7.6*	*5.6*	*0*	*54%*
K.Winslow*	52	9.9%	47	31	388	12.5	4.1	2	66%
J.Cumberland*	112	38.0%	39	26	398	15.3	5.9	4	67%
B.Powell	-20	-20.2%	57	36	272	7.6	8.7	0	63%
T.Bohanon	-6	-20.3%	16	11	69	6.3	5.5	0	69%
C.Ivory	-19	-58.2%	7	2	10	5.0	4.0	0	29%
C.Johnson	*66*	*10.8%*	*52*	*42*	*351*	*8.4*	*9.4*	*4*	*81%*

Offensive Line

Player	Pos	Age	GS	Snaps	Pen	Sk	Pass	Run
D'Brickashaw Ferguson	LT	31	16/16	1051	3	4.5	14.5	3.0
Austin Howard*	RT	27	16/16	1049	3	1.0	18.0	3.0
Nick Mangold	C	30	16/16	1049	0	0.0	3.0	2.0
Willie Colon	RG	31	16/16	1038	11	0.0	6.0	8.0
Brian Winters	LG	23	16/12	763	7	9.0	15.0	6.0
Vladimir Ducasse*	OT	27	16/4	317	5	3.0	10.0	2.0
Breno Giacomini	*RT*	*29*	*9/9*	*534*	*6*	*2.5*	*15.0*	*5.0*

Year	Yards	ALY	Rk	Power	Rk	Stuff	Rk	2nd Lev	Rk	Open Field	Rk	Sacks	ASR	Rk	Short	Long	F-Start	Cont.
2011	3.87	4.23	8	66%	10	16%	4	1.06	28	0.32	32	40	6.7%	17	16	19	26	41
2012	4.00	4.38	5	67%	10	16%	2	1.06	24	0.45	29	47	8.6%	30	16	19	16	48
2013	4.27	3.79	21	68%	12	17%	8	0.95	27	0.80	11	47	8.4%	27	13	21	14	42

2013 ALY by direction: Left End 4.81 (3) Left Tackle 3.61 (23) Mid/Guard 3.99 (15) Right Tackle 3.16 (28) Right End 3.26 (24)

D'Brickashaw Ferguson and Nick Mangold have been fixtures of the offensive line since 2006. At some point, both players will decline, but neither showed any age-related concerns in 2013. Each player ranked fourth at his position in snaps per blown block if we only look at players with a minimum of 800 snaps: Ferguson was behind Andrew Whitworth, Joe Thomas, and Branden Albert, while Mangold trailed Dominic Raiola, Nick Hardwick, and Mike Pouncey.

But the rest of the line has been less reliable in recent seasons, and questions continue for 2014. New York has concerns at both guard spots: Willie Colon racked up 11 penalties last year, and is tied with the Cowboys' Doug Free with a league-high 23 flags over the past two seasons. The former Steeler tore his biceps in week 17 and is also recovering from May knee surgery; the big concern is that the Jets have youth but little else behind him. Right guard Brian Winters struggled mightily in transition from the MAC to the NFL: he allowed nine sacks on his blown blocks last year, easily the most by any interior lineman in 2013. William Campbell (sixth round, 2013), Oday Aboushi (fifth round, 2013), and Dakota Dozier (fourth round, 2014) will fight for the third guard spot, and it's likely that at least one of those players will see significant action this year. At right tackle, the Jets chose to replace Austin Howard with Breno Giacomini. On the surface, it's a downgrade. Giacomini is older, has a spottier injury history (knee issues limited him to just 534 snaps for the 2013 Seahawks), and struggles with penalties (in 2012, he ranked second—in between Free and Colon—with 13 penalties). Depth on the line may be more important than ever for the Jets this year, as four of the team's starters will be 29 or older.

The offensive line is not necessarily the primary culprit for the Jets' rank of 27th in Adjusted Sack Rate. In fact, we have the Jets in the top eight for fewest sacks allowed due to blown blocks. The real issue was that New York had a league-high 15.5 sacks we registered as "Rusher Untouched" or "Overall Pressure." There are a few possible explanations here. Rookie quarterback Geno Smith may have been responsible for an unblocked man but failed to get the ball out quickly. It also could have been a coaching issue, but New York has brought back line coach Mike Devlin. The other explanation is that those sacks were mental mistakes of the individual linemen rather than blown blocks: with two new guards and a new offensive system, there were bound to be some mistakes. But the feeling here is that Smith was responsible for many of those sacks: that's acceptable for a rookie, but he'll have to improve on that area of the game to keep his job in 2014. Of course, if Michael Vick gets the job, all bets are off on the number of sacks the Jets will take this year.

Defensive Front Seven

			Overall								vs. Run					Pass Rush			
Defensive Line	Age	Pos	G	Snaps	Plays	TmPct	Rk	Stop	Dfts	BTkl	Runs	St%	Rk	RuYd	Rk	Sack	Hit	Hur	Tips
Muhammad Wilkerson	25	DE	16	1039	65	8.1%	8	51	25	3	44	80%	37	1.6	24	10.5	10	26.0	3
Sheldon Richardson	24	DE	16	880	77	9.6%	2	54	22	2	60	72%	62	2.0	37	4.0	5	14.5	1
Damon Harrison	26	DT	16	497	68	8.5%	5	56	11	0	63	84%	19	1.8	32	1.0	0	5.5	1
Leger Douzable	28	DE	16	236	20	2.5%	--	16	6	0	15	80%	--	1.1	--	1.5	2	5.0	0

			Overall								vs. Run					Pass Rush			
Edge Rushers	Age	Pos	G	Snaps	Plays	TmPct	Rk	Stop	Dfts	BTkl	Runs	St%	Rk	RuYd	Rk	Sack	Hit	Hur	Tips
Calvin Pace	34	OLB	16	869	54	6.7%	22	43	16	4	28	71%	52	2.9	55	10.0	4	6.0	1
Quinton Coples	24	OLB	14	814	39	5.6%	39	31	15	2	31	77%	32	1.3	8	4.5	15	14.5	2
Garrett McIntyre	30	OLB	13	266	17	2.6%	--	13	3	3	12	83%	--	2.6	--	2.0	0	3.5	0

			Overall								Pass Rush			vs. Run					vs. Pass						
Linebackers	Age	Pos	G	Snaps	Plays	TmPct	Rk	Stop	Dfts	BTkl	Sack	Hit	Hur	Runs	St%	Rk	RuYd	Rk	Tgts	Suc%	Rk	AdjYd	Rk	PD	Int
David Harris	30	ILB	16	1098	125	15.6%	22	76	23	9	2.0	2	6	73	73%	17	3.2	30	38	45%	54	7.7	58	1	0
Demario Davis	25	ILB	16	1046	102	12.7%	45	59	13	9	1.0	4	10	56	79%	7	2.4	10	44	45%	53	7.1	49	1	1

Year	Yards	ALY	Rk	Power	Rk	Stuff	Rk	2nd Level	Rk	Open Field	Rk	Sacks	ASR	Rk	Short	Long
2011	3.86	3.65	2	45%	2	22%	6	1.04	6	0.72	13	35	7.3%	12	6	23
2012	4.33	4.09	18	56%	8	16%	27	1.10	6	0.89	23	30	6.2%	20	9	19
2013	3.21	3.23	4	39%	1	26%	3	0.80	1	0.48	8	41	6.2%	24	14	21
2013 ALY by direction:			*Left End 2.66 (6)*			*Left Tackle 3.27 (3)*			*Mid/Guard 3.53 (7)*			*Right Tackle 2.49 (2)*			*Right End 3.51 (14)*	

The strength of the team is the defensive line, where two former first-round picks surround one of the game's unknown stars. Despite playing a 3-4, the Jets were the only team to have three defensive linemen record at least 10-plus Defeats in the run game in 2013. In this space last year, we noted that nose tackle Damon "Big Snacks" Harrison was a sleeper to watch. Well, in his first year as a starter, Harrison turned in a monster performance, helping to anchor one of the league's best run defenses. He was a big part of the team's success in power-running situations. His 50 tackles were the most of any lineman with zero broken tackles. On one side of Harrison, Muhammad Wilkerson reached double-digit sacks last year and is one of the best defensive linemen in the NFL. If you're looking to pick nits, Wilkerson had nine penalties last year, including five offside flags. That wasn't an issue with him earlier in his career, and it is unlikely to be a recurring problem. On the other side, Sheldon Richardson earned AP Defensive Rookie of the Year honors, and his impact was most clear in the running game. Scouts viewed Richardson as a pass-rushing star in a one-gap system because of his quick first step: that skill wasn't on display much in 2013, but Richardson should mature into a better pass rusher in time (after all, Wilkerson recorded just three sacks as a rookie). For most teams, Kenrick Ellis would have earned significant playing time by now. Instead, the Jets' third-round pick in 2011 has just five career starts despite playing very well in spot duty. The athletic nose tackle enters his contract year without much of a chance to see starting time, but he could be a bargain for some team in 2015.

Did Calvin Pace have the least exciting double-digit sack season ever? Among all other edge rushers with double-digit sacks, the average player recorded 12.1 sacks, 11.1 quarterback hits, and 29.0 hurries. Pace had just four hits and six hurries to go along with his ten sacks. Every other player with at least eight sacks last season also had at least 14 hurries. He'll turn 34 in October, so it wouldn't be a surprise if Pace's sack numbers drop dramatically this year. The Jets hope that will be offset by improvement from Quinton Coples, who converted from end to outside linebacker last year. Even after dropping 15 pounds, Coples remains one of the biggest outside linebackers in the league, and lacks the pure burst to be an elite 3-4 edge rusher. On the bright side, he recorded 3.5 sacks in December last year, and should at least be more comfortable with his role this season. Antwan Barnes, who played for Ryan in Baltimore, provides some insurance if he can stay healthy. Barnes had 11 sacks with San Diego in 2011, but injuries have limited him the last two years; he played just 145 defensive snaps for the Jets in 2013 before a knee injury ended his season.

Not only do the Jets lack explosive outside linebackers, but inside linebacker isn't a settled position, either. David Harris had a bounce-back year in 2013, but he hasn't lived up to the big contract the team gave him in 2011. Harris will either be with a new team in 2015 or back on a drastically reduced salary, which makes this a big year for the 30-year-old run-stuffer. Demario Davis had a magnificent Run Stop Rate, but his play didn't leap off the film. Perhaps it was growing pains as Davis was thrust into a full-time role after just spot duty as a rookie in 2012, but Davis' advanced numbers are more a reflection of the dominance of the Jets front three.

Defensive Secondary

			Overall									vs. Run					vs. Pass									
Secondary	**Age**	**Pos**	**G**	**Snaps**	**Plays**	**TmPct**	**Rk**	**Stop**	**Dfts**	**BTkl**	**Runs**	**St%**	**Rk**	**RuYd**	**Rk**	**Tgts**	**Tgt%**	**Rk**	**Dist**	**Suc%**	**Rk**	**AdjYd**	**Rk**	**PD**	**Int**
Dawan Landry	32	SS	16	1081	102	12.7%	15	36	11	6	46	52%	18	4.9	12	36	7.6%	32	10.5	49%	54	7.5	50	6	1
Antonio Cromartie*	30	CB	16	1064	46	5.7%	80	18	4	2	11	36%	49	11.4	77	84	17.8%	15	16.6	52%	44	11.8	87	11	3
Dee Milliner	23	CB	13	722	73	11.2%	8	32	12	9	19	42%	39	6.6	34	93	29.3%	86	14.4	56%	31	7.0	29	16	3
Ed Reed*	36	FS	14	629	42	6.0%	71	11	7	6	20	30%	61	9.1	67	11	4.2%	3	13.0	47%	59	12.1	74	4	3
Antonio Allen	26	FS	16	534	68	8.5%	61	24	11	4	23	39%	38	6.7	31	41	17.2%	75	13.0	51%	48	6.6	32	7	1
Kyle Wilson	27	CB	16	466	25	3.1%	--	9	3	1	5	60%	--	3.2	--	45	21.7%	--	11.4	64%	--	6.1	--	1	0
Darrin Walls	26	CB	16	288	22	2.7%	--	12	6	4	5	60%	--	4.6	--	30	23.7%	--	10.4	58%	--	5.0	--	4	0
Jaiquawn Jarrett	25	FS	16	276	17	2.1%	--	10	3	2	6	67%	--	6.7	--	15	12.4%	--	8.7	66%	--	8.0	--	0	0
Johnny Patrick	*26*	*CB*	*13*	*474*	*36*	*5.7%*	*--*	*13*	*8*	*4*	*11*	*36%*	*--*	*9.0*	*--*	*37*	*17.3%*	*--*	*9.5*	*39%*	*--*	*9.8*	*--*	*2*	*1*
Dimitri Patterson	*32*	*CB*	*6*	*237*	*25*	*7.6%*	*--*	*12*	*7*	*3*	*4*	*25%*	*--*	*7.0*	*--*	*27*	*27.6%*	*--*	*11.0*	*60%*	*--*	*6.7*	*--*	*6*	*4*

Year	Pass D Rank	vs. #1 WR	Rk	vs. #2 WR	Rk	vs. Other WR	Rk	vs. TE	Rk	vs. RB	Rk
2011	2	-32.5%	1	-25.1%	2	-3.1%	18	23.3%	27	-14.7%	4
2012	10	-19.4%	5	-4.9%	12	-0.9%	16	-3.1%	14	4.1%	19
2013	18	-0.6%	19	13.5%	26	-1.3%	13	5.5%	19	-22.3%	3

With the decline of the secondary in 2013, it's easy to forget that New York operated without Darrelle Revis for nearly all of 2012, too. The big culprit was Antonio Cromartie, who overnight turned from one of the league's top corners to one of its worst. Dee Milliner was handed the starting job after the Jets selected him with the ninth overall pick in 2013, but he had a rough year even by rookie cornerback standards. Kansas City's Marcus Cooper—a seventh-round pick in the same draft who was cut by the 49ers, who originally drafted him—was the only main corner to see a higher percentage of estimated targets than Milliner in 2013. Milliner was a better player in the final third of the season, and he ended things on a high note by snatching AFC Defensive Player of the Week honors in Week 17, but he still finished his rookie year with more benchings than awards.

The Jets didn't try very hard to retain Cromartie (now in Arizona), but they tried even less hard to find a proper replacement. Despite significant cap room and a free-agent market flooded with starting cornerbacks, the team's big splash was signing journeyman Dimitri Patterson, now on his seventh team. He will compete with Darrin Walls and Maryland's Dexter McDougle, whom the Jets selected in the third round in May's draft. Walls was very effective in spot duty last year—Ryan often called on him to replace a struggling Milliner—and is most likely to win the job.

Safety has been a revolving door for New York for years: Jim Leonhard and Eric Smith in 2011 were replaced by LaRon Landry and Yeremiah Bell in 2012, who were replaced by Dawan Landry and Antonio Allen last year. First-round pick Calvin Pryor is the new face this year, and his nickname—the Louisville Slugger—gives you some pretty good insight into his game. Allen will return as a starter, but for a team with issues at cornerback, going with a pair of young safeties is a risky move. Then again, after allowing Andy Dalton to throw for five touchdowns in three quarters, things can't get much worse in 2014.

Special Teams

Year	DVOA	Rank	FG/XP	Rank	Net Kick	Rank	Kick Ret	Rank	Net Punt	Rank	Punt Ret	Rank	Hidden	Rank
2011	5.6%	4	-0.1	15	11.2	1	10.8	2	13.2	3	-7.0	25	-8.3	26
2012	-1.5%	21	-5.0	28	-0.2	17	4.4	8	-7.9	24	1.3	14	-6.7	26
2013	2.1%	10	8.4	4	1.6	13	0.8	12	-0.4	19	-0.1	15	-3.7	20

Nick Folk started the year 23-for-23 before missing badly in the face of swirling winds in Buffalo (it's a shame the *FOA* doesn't support .gif files). In the first half of the season, Folk kicked a 48-yard game-winner against Tampa Bay and a 43-yard game-winner against Atlanta: both kicks not only came in the final seconds, but came with the Jets trailing. He also connected from 42 yards out to beat the Patriots in overtime, though he needed a little help from Patriots' defensive lineman Chris Jones not understanding the rule book. It was one of the best kicker seasons in Jets history, even though Folk was only average on kickoffs.

Trivia time: the Jets returned a kickoff for a touchdown in 11 straight seasons from 2002 to 2012. The streak ended last year, but that doesn't make it any less remarkable; it's the longest streak in NFL history by a good margin. (The second longest streak belongs to the Browns, who returned a kickoff for a score in six straight years from 2004 to 2009.) The 2013 season also marked the Jets' first year without legendary special teams coach Mike Westhoff, who not coincidentally joined the team in 2001. New York added Jacoby Ford (ex-Raiders) in the offseason, and he should help revitalize the return game. Even though Ford hasn't returned a kickoff for a score since 2011, his four return scores since 2010 are tied with Leon Washington for the most in the league over that span. Ryan Quigley, who isn't a former Aussie Rules football player but really sounds like he should be, had a very average first season as the Jets' punter.

Oakland Raiders

2013 Record: 4-12	**Total DVOA:** -34.1% (31st)	**2014 Mean Projection:** 5.2 wins	**On the Clock (0-4):** 39%
Pythagorean Wins: 4.9 (29th)	**Offense:** -16.7% (28th)	**Postseason Odds:** 5.4%	**Mediocrity (5-7):** 52%
Snap-Weighted Age: 27.0 (11th)	**Defense:** 10.3% (26th)	**Super Bowl Odds:** 0.2%	**Playoff Contender (8-10):** 8%
Average Opponent: 0.6% (13th)	**Special Teams:** -7.1% (31st)	**Proj. Avg. Opponent:** 3.9% (1st)	**Super Bowl Contender (11+):** 1%

2013: Lots of mediocre veterans get another year toward their pensions; unfortunately, none of them play quarterback.

2014: The worst DVOA projection with the hardest schedule. Have fun, kids!

When Reggie McKenzie became general manager of the Oakland Raiders in January 2012, he inherited a team that was coming off back-to-back 8-8 seasons. For most franchises, this would not have been much of an accomplishment. For the Raiders in the late days of Al Davis, those two .500 records were better than what the team had done in the previous seven seasons.

What quickly became apparent to McKenzie and most nonpartisan observers of the Raiders was the chimerical nature of those moderately successful seasons. Those teams may have gone .500, but they were not particularly good, finishing 21st and 22nd by DVOA. Further, that relative success was not sustainable. Instead, those teams were built primarily with aging non-star players signed to big-money deals, in some cases acquired for high draft choices.

Faced with this situation, McKenzie and new owner Mark Davis had a choice. On one hand, they could continue with the core of those 8-8 teams, retaining as many players as possible and kicking the proverbial salary cap can down the road. Given the age of the standout players of those teams, this likely would have resulted in several seasons that approached but failed to reach that coveted winning record. Alternatively, the Raiders could blow the roster up. That would mean a great deal of short-term pain and a return to those darker days of the mid-2000s, but at the end there would be a chance to develop what could be a real contender.

McKenzie and Davis chose option number two. The aftermath of that decision was as painful as expected. The big-money contracts were shed, but at an immense cost. Some 44 percent of the Raiders' 2013 salary cap was devoted to players who were no longer on the roster. That $56 million was more dead money than the next two highest teams had combined, and was nearly triple the dead money of each of the fourth and fifth place teams. Oh, and by the way, the Raiders had already given up their natural first-, second-, and third-round picks in 2012 and their second-round pick in 2013.

Of course, the NFL was not going to cancel games until the Raiders could once again field a quality team. McKenzie and his head coach Dennis Allen had to cobble together a roster despite the difficult circumstances. They found a series of stopgap veterans to wear the Silver and Black, typically on modest one-year deals. 2013's free-agent haul included eventual starting defensive linemen Jason Hunter, Pat Sims, and Vance Walker, plus starting cornerbacks Mike Jenkins and Tracy Porter. It is very difficult to have success when almost half the starters were not there the previous season and will likely not be there the next season. While the offense did not see the same number of departures and arrivals, the snap counts approached a similar level of turnover.

This year, that was all supposed to be over. McKenzie finally entered the offseason with his full complement of draft picks and as much cap room as any team in the league. So naturally, the Raiders began their offseason by losing their two most prominent free agents, both younger players McKenzie had stated publicly he was interested in retaining and both players the Raiders had discussed extensions with prior to the 2013 season. True, Jared Veldheer had missed much of the season with a triceps injury and may not have been better than an average starting left tackle after he returned late in the year. Yes, the Raiders would have needed to upgrade the pass rush even if they had retained Lamarr Houston. And yet, while the Raiders had the money and apparently the willingness to retain each player, and neither player had a natural replacement already on the roster, Veldheer will be playing in Arizona in 2014 while Houston is now in Chicago.

At least the departures of Veldheer and Houston would open up even more of the budget for new arrivals, but Oakland's first attempt to use that money was an embarrassing faceplant. The Raiders agreed to terms with free agent offensive lineman Rodger Saffold, a competent tackle who had started on both the left and right sides for the Rams, for what seemed like an exorbitant amount (five years, $42.5 million). They then flunked Saffold on his physical to void his contract, a move almost never seen with a big-dollar free agent.

McKenzie arrived in Oakland with much promise. He had learned his craft helping Ron Wolf and Ted Thompson build Super Bowl teams in Green Bay. It was hard to question him when he was dealing with such significant limitations in his first two seasons. But these three huge off-field defeats started to cast his previous decisions in a new light. Even after accounting for the salary limitations, it's clear that McKenzie's first two years featured several clear missteps that helped make the Raiders even worse. The 2013 quarterback situation was completely botched: the Raiders traded with Seattle to get Matt Flynn, reworked his contract to give him $6.5 million in guaranteed money, watched him blow the starting job in train-

2014 Raiders Schedule

Week	Opp.	Week	Opp.	Week	Opp.
1	at NYJ	7	ARI	13	at STL
2	HOU	8	at CLE	14	SF
3	at NE	9	at SEA	15	at KC
4	MIA (U.K.)	10	DEN	16	BUF
5	BYE	11	at SD	17	at DEN
6	SD	12	KC (Thu.)		

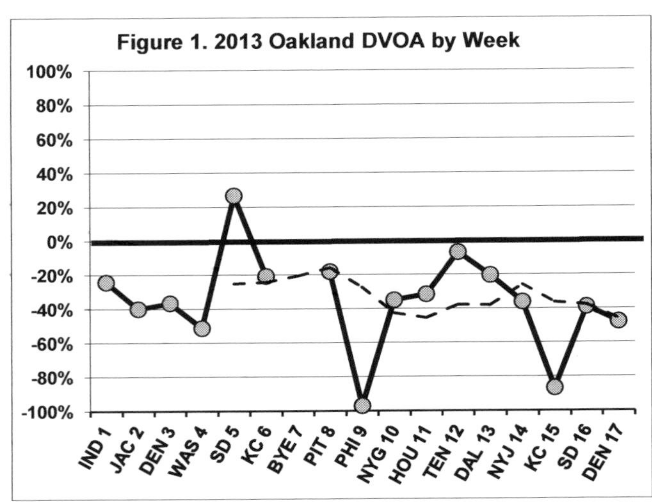

ing camp, and eventually cut him after his only regular-season start resulted in seven sacks and three turnovers. As an extra bonus mistake, the Raiders cut fourth-round quarterback pick Tyler Wilson before the season even began. He was just one of a number of unimpressive draft picks in 2012 and 2013. Tony Bergstrom, a compensatory third-round pick in 2012, was uninspiring as a rookie before spending his second season on injured reserve. Linebacker Miles Burris, chosen one round later, started as a rookie but also spent most of his second season injured. 2013 first-round pick D.J. Hayden had a cornerback's typically trouble-filled introduction to the NFL, while second-round selection Menelik Watson spent most of the season as the fourth offensive tackle while battling injuries.

McKenzie eventually recovered to spend some of that prodigious amount of cap room, and his vision for the team became clear. While there were more of those one-year stopgap-type deals, a great deal of the guaranteed money displayed evidence of a particular vision: upgrade from the lines out so that powerful players in the trenches could propel the other units on the team to success.

If there was a single adjective to describe how the Oakland Raiders played offense in 2013, it would be "unsubtle." New offensive coordinator Greg Olson called for Darren McFadden and Rashad Jennings to plunge into the line on power and dive over and over again, just one season after the Raiders tried to implement a zone blocking scheme that attacked primarily on the perimeter. In 2012, 36 percent of Raiders runs were marked as Mid/Guard, 30th in the NFL. Last year, that number was 67 percent, which ranked third.

The lack of subtlety extended to the passing game, particularly the quarterback position. Terrelle Pryor started and ended the season. When Pryor began his NFL career, he was simply a physical specimen. He's advanced as a passer, but subtler aspects of the game like reading defenses beyond a simple initial read and pocket movement remain elusive. Matt McGloin, an undrafted free agent whose surprisingly good training camp forced draftee Wilson off the team, brought more of a willingness to pull the trigger on throws, but wasn't any more refined than Pryor when it came to completing those throws to his teammates rather than the opponents. When you add on the league's most injury-riddled offensive line (by Adjusted Games Lost), it comes as no surprise that the Raiders had a below-average offensive DVOA in 13 of 16 games.

That beleaguered offensive line was bolstered by three prospective new starters in the offseason. The biggest contract (five years, $30 million) went to former Jets right tackle Austin Howard. More or less the Saffold backup plan, the Raiders apparently view Howard as a player capable of playing on the outside (unlike Saffold, the right side only) but prefer his potential value at right guard. That will depend on the development of the aforementioned Menelik Watson. Both Watson's improvement and the transition of Howard from tackle to guard will be major responsibilities for offensive line coach Tony Sparano, retained in the face of a determined effort to bring him to Tampa. Sparano previously coached Howard with the Jets and was presumably instrumental in the decision to bring him in and shift his position. Former Bucs tackle Donald Penn arrives to fill Veldheer's vacant spot on the left side. Like Howard, he brings great size and strength but perhaps not the best work when it comes to pass blocking. There will also be a new left guard, either third-round pick Gabe Jackson or stopgap veteran Kevin Boothe, formerly of the Giants.

Whether the quintet up front becomes Penn, Jackson, Stefen Wisniewski, Howard, and Watson—as the Raiders wish—or not, there isn't going to be much continuity in 2014. This is especially important on the offensive line, where teamwork and coordination is so important. Even if each offensive lineman is individually better than his counterpart among last year's Week 1 starters, it will probably take some time for that individual talent to translate into an effective and cohesive unit. That would likely be bad news for new quarterback Matt Schaub.

Schaub is the Raiders' latest Quarterback Matt of the Present, and McKenzie is hoping he will be a more durable solution than last year's Quarterback Matt of the Present. It is definitely a risky move after a season in which "Schaubing" became a neologism widely understood to mean "throwing a pick-six." (It had previously been an obscure neologism used to denote the accumulation of impressive cumulative statistics in a losing effort.) Schaub will also be learning a new offensive scheme after spending the past seven years in the sort of zone-blocking boot-heavy scheme the Raiders tried to run in 2012, and he will be operating without a superstar receiver like Andre Johnson to bail him out when things break down or pressure comes. (Free-agent addition James Jones is a quality player and should form a solid starting tandem with Rod Streater, but let's not kid ourselves.) At least he brings a quality play-fake and an acquaintance with some of the subtleties of the quarterback position so missing from Flynn, McGloin, and Pryor in 2013. Sooner or later, Schaub will give way to the latest Quarterback of the Future, second-round pick Derek Carr, but the Raiders are hoping that will not be until 2015 so that Carr has time to adjust to a drop-back passing game with multiple reads.

Just as they did on offense, the Raiders made a commitment to overhauling the defensive line. This was partly mandated by circumstances, with Houston departing and Hunter, Sims, and Walker on one-year deals, but the caliber of players they added indicated improvement was a priority. Enter a new trio of veterans: Texans defensive end Antonio Smith, Giants defensive end Justin Tuck, and Steelers outside linebacker LaMarr Woodley. For the Raiders' base 4-3 scheme, Smith, who lined up at 3-technique as the weakside end in the Texans' 3-4, will likely be a defensive tackle, while Tuck and Woodley will play on the edges. Houston was often a stand-up rusher or edge-setter in both base and sub packages last year, so it is not much of a surprise to see the Raiders add a career 3-4 outside linebacker like Woodley. The surprise was to hear Allen stress the Raiders would remain a base 4-3 scheme and to imply that the injury issues that hampered Woodley's production in 2013 may have been a result of keeping his weight down so he could stand up and be an outside linebacker.

Smith, Tuck, and Woodley combined for 21.0 sacks and 60.8 hurries in 2013, more than every single defensive lineman on last year's Raiders roster combined. The downside is that they are a combined 92 years old, with Woodley, who turns 30 in November, the youngest of the trio. So it's good news that the fifth overall pick in the draft brought the Raiders a much-needed younger pass rusher with great potential, University of Buffalo linebacker Khalil Mack. Mack isn't just an explosive edge rusher for defensive coordinator Jason Tarver's blitz packages; few collegians enter the NFL with such a complete defensive skill set. Too often Tarver had to manufacture whatever pressure the Raiders got in 2013. He was effective doing so, with returning linebackers Kevin Burnett, Sio Moore, and Nick Roach each hitting double-digit hurries, but sometimes that came at the cost of coverage. A more effective defensive line should have an impact on the defense as a whole.

Unfortunately, our projections suggest that impact won't matter much. The secondary is still mediocre and the offense is a mess. Plus, how much can incremental improvement help when the Raiders are stuck in the now-powerful AFC West? The NFC East drops off the schedule, replaced by the much more formidable NFC West. The last-place schedule isn't a bonus when it means the new offensive line has to figure out how to block both J.J. Watt and Jadeveon Clowney by Week 2, and the rest of the AFC South has been replaced on the schedule by the more difficult AFC East. Plus, the Raiders raised the degree of difficulty that extra little bit by shipping one of their home games off to London. Even an average team could easily go 6-10 against a schedule we project to be the most difficult in the league—and despite all of their additions this offseason, the Raiders are likely to be below average on both sides of the ball. There should be improvement on the field, but another 4-12 mark is a real possibility. Just as the Raiders required a multi-year teardown, so too will they require a multi-year rebuild.

Tom Gower

2013 Raiders Stats by Week

Wk	vs.	W-L	PF	PA	YDF	YDA	TO	Total	Off	Def	ST
1	at IND	L	17	21	372	274	-2	-24%	3%	15%	-13%
2	JAC	W	19	9	340	248	-1	-40%	-17%	15%	-8%
3	at DEN	L	21	37	342	536	+2	-37%	7%	39%	-5%
4	WAS	L	14	24	298	339	-2	-51%	-44%	6%	-2%
5	SD	W	27	17	299	427	+5	27%	-3%	-19%	11%
6	at KC	L	7	24	274	216	-2	-21%	-46%	-28%	-3%
7	BYE										
8	PIT	W	21	18	279	276	-1	-18%	-31%	-25%	-12%
9	PHI	L	20	49	560	542	-2	-97%	-20%	70%	-7%
10	at NYG	L	20	24	213	251	+1	-35%	-32%	-1%	-4%
11	at HOU	W	28	23	341	394	+2	-32%	-4%	-9%	-36%
12	TEN	L	19	23	353	426	-2	-7%	16%	21%	-2%
13	at DAL	L	24	31	305	352	-1	-20%	-17%	16%	13%
14	at NYJ	L	27	37	383	352	0	-36%	-1%	12%	-23%
15	KC	L	31	56	461	384	-6	-87%	-11%	65%	-12%
16	at SD	L	13	26	265	344	+1	-39%	-46%	-6%	1%
17	DEN	L	14	34	255	458	-1	-48%	-16%	21%	-12%

Trends and Splits

	Offense	Rank	Defense	Rank
Total DVOA	-16.7%	28	10.3%	26
Unadjusted VOA	-15.0%	27	14.4%	30
Weighted Trend	-18.1%	28	10.2%	25
Variance	3.1%	28	4.0%	4
Average Opponent	3.1%	28	4.0%	4
Passing	-20.3%	31	21.7%	29
Rushing	0.9%	16	-3.2%	18
First Down	-2.6%	18	9.5%	25
Second Down	-28.2%	32	6.0%	23
Third Down	-25.7%	29	19.7%	27
First Half	-7.8%	24	8.0%	27
Second Half	-26.3%	28	12.7%	26
Red Zone	0.4%	19	26.1%	28
Late and Close	-34.6%	29	13.3%	30

Five-Year Performance

Year	W-L	Pyth W	Est W	PF	PA	TO	Total	Rk	Off	Rk	Def	Rk	ST	Rk	Off AGL	Rk	Def AGL	Rk	Off Age	Rk	Def Age	Rk	ST Age	Rk
2009	5-11	2.9	3.9	197	379	-13	-34.0%	30	-25.8%	30	7.9%	24	-0.3%	17	32.4	23	18.9	8	26.4	29	27.3	16	27.0	6
2010	8-8	9.0	7.1	410	371	-2	-4.1%	21	-8.3%	23	-2.3%	13	1.8%	13	15.1	8	15.4	10	26.6	25	26.2	25	27.1	7
2011	8-8	6.1	7.3	359	433	-4	-8.0%	22	2.6%	14	9.6%	27	-1.0%	20	36.7	21	41.4	26	26.8	19	27.1	16	26.8	4
2012	4-12	4.1	3.7	290	443	-7	-27.8%	29	-9.5%	23	12.5%	29	-5.8%	31	31.8	19	35.0	20	27.1	13	27.5	9	26.6	8
2013	4-12	4.9	2.1	322	453	-9	-34.1%	31	-16.7%	28	10.3%	26	-7.1%	31	50.7	27	27.2	12	26.7	17	27.6	5	26.1	16

2013 Performance Based on Most Common Personnel Groups

OAK Offense					OAK Offense vs. Opponents				OAK Defense				OAK Defense vs. Opponents			
Pers	Freq	Yds	DVOA	Run%	Pers	Freq	Yds	DVOA	Pers	Freq	Yds	DVOA	Pers	Freq	Yds	DVOA
21	36%	6.2	0.4%	34%	3-4-4	34%	5.6	0.3%	Nickel Even	32%	7.1	20.3%	11	52%	6.7	20.0%
11	34%	4.9	-36.3%	20%	4-3-4	21%	5.6	-6.1%	4-3-4	22%	4.0	-11.5%	12	25%	5.0	0.8%
22	8%	4.4	-24.4%	64%	Nickel Even	19%	6.1	-5.9%	Nickel Odd	21%	6.1	22.2%	21	10%	4.4	-14.3%
12	7%	4.8	-20.8%	58%	Dime+	13%	4.1	-61.5%	3-4-4	14%	4.5	-7.9%	22	5%	4.8	-5.3%
20	4%	7.5	31.0%	42%	Nickel Odd	10%	5.1	-40.3%	Dime+	10%	6.4	20.9%	621	2%	5.6	42.5%
													20	2%	3.1	-29.3%

Strategic Tendencies

Run/Pass		Rk	Formation		Rk	Pass Rush		Rk	Secondary		Rk	Strategy		Rk
Runs, first half	43%	5	Form: Single Back	55%	29	Rush 3	10.1%	3	4 DB	35%	21	Play action	26%	7
Runs, first down	48%	16	Form: Empty Back	5%	23	Rush 4	43.8%	32	5 DB	53%	13	Avg Box (Off)	6.58	3
Runs, second-long	39%	7	Pers: 3+ WR	38%	31	Rush 5	31.9%	4	6+ DB	10%	11	Avg Box (Def)	6.30	21
Runs, power sit.	53%	16	Pers: 4+ WR	0%	30	Rush 6+	14.2%	4	CB by Sides	79%	15	Offensive Pace	31.94	28
Runs, behind 2H	25%	21	Pers: 2+ TE/6+ OL	25%	23	Sacks by LB	32.9%	16	DB Blitz	22%	1	Defensive Pace	29.54	14
Pass, ahead 2H	44%	21	Shotgun/Pistol	68%	9	Sacks by DB	23.7%	1	Hole in Zone	12%	12	Go for it on 4th	0.35	31

Department of Universal Truths Re-Establish Themselves: After ranking tenth in penalties in 2012, the Raiders returned to their rightful place near the top of the league, finishing second behind Seattle in 2013. The Raiders have finished first or second in the NFL in penalties (including declined and offsetting) in six of the past seven seasons. For some reason, Dennis Allen went from one of the league's most aggressive coaches in 2012 to one of the least aggressive in 2013, despite the fact that Oakland had a better running game than it did the year before. Oakland only "went for it" twice on fourth down when they weren't losing in the fourth quarter, and both of those plays were fake punts. Oakland used "conventional" 21 personnel more than any other team in the league. The Oakland offense would have been even worse if not for doing a good job in the red zone. The Raiders were just 25th with 27.3 yards per drive, but converted 59.5 percent of red-zone opportunities, sixth in the NFL. The Raiders faced more running back screens than any other defense and were terrible at stopping this tactic, allowing 8.5 yards per play with 84.5% DVOA.

Passing

Player	DYAR	DVOA	Plays	NtYds	Avg	YAC	C%	TD	Int
T.Pryor*	-388	-31.6%	304	1542	5.1	5.8	58.0%	8	11
M.McGloin	-11	-11.9%	219	1495	6.8	5.5	55.9%	8	8
M.Flynn*	-86	-42.8%	41	212	5.2	6.0	64.7%	1	1
M.Schaub	*-123*	*-16.2%*	*380*	*2128*	*5.6*	*4.2*	*61.3%*	*10*	*14*

Rushing

Player	DYAR	DVOA	Plays	Yds	Avg	TD	Fum	Suc
R.Jennings*	164	15.8%	163	733	4.5	6	0	47%
D.McFadden	-38	-17.0%	114	379	3.3	5	1	34%
T.Pryor*	105	16.1%	77	580	7.5	2	0	-
M.Reece	31	7.0%	46	218	4.7	2	0	39%
T.Jones	-2	-15.5%	5	23	4.6	0	0	20%
J.Ford*	0	-37.9%	5	15	3.0	0	0	-
M.Jones-Drew	*-49*	*-13.6%*	*234*	*803*	*3.4*	*5*	*1*	*37%*

Receiving

Player	DYAR	DVOA	Plays	Ctch	Yds	Y/C	YAC	TD	C%
R.Streater	204	13.6%	100	61	888	14.6	5.1	4	61%
D.Moore	107	3.1%	86	46	695	15.1	5.6	5	53%
A.Holmes	42	-2.1%	52	25	431	17.2	4.4	1	48%
J.Ford*	-78	-56.5%	24	13	99	7.6	5.6	0	54%
B.Butler	-19	-28.1%	17	9	103	11.4	3.4	0	53%
J.Criner	-19	-45.2%	8	3	32	10.7	3.0	0	38%
J.Jones	110	2.1%	93	59	817	13.8	6.2	3	63%
G.Little	*-171*	*-34.7%*	*99*	*41*	*465*	*11.3*	*4.6*	*2*	*41%*
M.Rivera	60	8.1%	60	38	407	10.7	2.4	4	63%
J.Mastrud*	-16	-24.9%	13	6	88	14.7	9.2	0	46%
M.Reece	38	-1.1%	54	32	331	10.3	7.1	2	59%
R.Jennings*	66	10.8%	52	42	351	8.4	9.4	4	81%
D.McFadden	34	-2.6%	52	35	316	9.0	8.8	1	67%
J.Olawale	0	-13.6%	11	7	63	9.0	7.1	0	64%
M.Jones-Drew	*32*	*-3.7%*	*60*	*43*	*314*	*7.3*	*7.7*	*0*	*72%*

Offensive Line

Player	Pos	Age	GS	Snaps	Pen	Sk	Pass	Run	Player	Pos	Age	GS	Snaps	Pen	Sk	Pass	Run
Khalif Barnes	G/T	32	16/16	1034	13	4.5	22.0	1.0	Andre Gurode	C/G	36	10/4	275	4	1.0	3.0	2.0
Stefen Wisniewski	C	25	14/14	904	3	0.0	4.0	2.0	Matt McCants	OT	25	13/3	256	1	0.0	3.0	0.0
Mike Brisiel	RG	31	15/15	871	7	0.0	6.5	2.0	Menelik Watson	OT	26	5/3	173	2	1.0	3.0	1.0
Tony Pashos	RT	34	12/12	713	3	5.0	11.5	0.0	*Austin Howard*	*RT*	*27*	*16/16*	*1049*	*3*	*1.0*	*18.0*	*3.0*
Lucas Nix	LG	25	14/10	642	3	3.5	18.0	2.0	*Donald Penn*	*LT*	*31*	*16/16*	*1032*	*5*	*8.5*	*21.5*	*6.0*
Jared Veldheer*	LT	27	5/5	323	6	0.0	7.5	0.0	*Kevin Boothe*	*LG*	*31*	*16/16*	*1021*	*2*	*1.3*	*11.3*	*6.5*

Year	Yards	ALY	Rk	Power	Rk	Stuff	Rk	2nd Lev	Rk	Open Field	Rk	Sacks	ASR	Rk	Short	Long	F-Start	Cont.
2011	4.52	4.13	14	67%	8	16%	3	1.12	24	1.05	7	25	5.0%	5	10	8	18	37
2012	3.90	3.52	29	55%	28	21%	24	1.10	21	0.78	15	27	4.4%	4	10	7	16	32
2013	4.09	3.71	26	61%	20	16%	6	0.88	31	0.83	10	44	8.5%	28	7	24	23	22

2013 ALY by direction: Left End 2.87 (25) Left Tackle 4.30 (9) Mid/Guard 3.73 (24) Right Tackle 2.90 (30) Right End 4.04 (11)

According to our blown block numbers, both Mike Brisiel and Tony Pashos were excellent last year, with Brisiel ranking second among right guards in fewest blown blocks per snap and Pashos third among right tackles. Why then were the Raiders so interested in moving on from both players? Because blown blocks tell only a very small part of the story. Any ineffectiveness in the run game was masked by Rashad Jennings' ability to power forward for a couple yards rather than getting stopped for a loss. The Raiders' excellent Stuff Rate last year is all Jennings (10 percent) and Marcel Reece (13 percent), because Darren McFadden got stuffed at the line constantly (25 percent). Meanwhile, struggles in the passing game were masked by their teammates and the quarterbacks. No team in the league had a lower percentage of their sacks allowed come from blown blocks. But just as with the running backs and Stuff Rate, the Oakland quarterbacks had very, very different sack rates from each other and the composite team Adjusted Sack Rate figure shown in the table. Terrelle Pryor's personal ASR was 11.2 percent while Matt McGloin's was 3.1 percent. When Pryor didn't throw the ball on his initial read, his instinct was often to escape the pocket in an attempt to buy time. That resulted in a lot of sacks we listed as coverage sacks and failed scrambles. His struggles on hot reads also resulted in an above-average rate of sacks from untouched rushers. McGloin, meanwhile, excelled at getting the ball out quickly, generally before anything other than a total protection breakdown could have gotten to him. The Raiders offensive line will look a lot different this season, and their Adjusted Sack Rate will probably end up looking more like Matt Schaub's usual ASR of 5.0 to 6.5 percent rather than Pryor's or McGloin's 2013 ASR.

Defensive Front Seven

			Overall								vs. Run					Pass Rush			
Defensive Line	Age	Pos	G	Snaps	Plays	TmPct	Rk	Stop	Dfts	BTkl	Runs	St%	Rk	RuYd	Rk	Sack	Hit	Hur	Tips
Vance Walker*	27	DT	15	766	40	5.2%	39	36	11	1	33	91%	9	1.7	30	3.0	2	13.0	0
Pat Sims	29	DT	16	676	53	6.5%	23	38	9	1	48	69%	68	2.2	45	1.5	5	7.5	0
Stacy McGee	24	DT	15	349	20	2.6%	--	14	4	0	15	87%	--	1.5	--	0.5	4	4.0	0
Daniel Muir*	31	DT	10	212	17	3.3%	--	13	3	0	15	73%	--	3.9	--	1.0	2	2.8	0
Antonio Smith	*33*	*DE*	*15*	*739*	*29*	*4.0%*	*65*	*25*	*14*	*3*	*20*	*85%*	*17*	*1.2*	*7*	*5.0*	*9*	*16.8*	*0*

			Overall								vs. Run					Pass Rush			
Edge Rushers	Age	Pos	G	Snaps	Plays	TmPct	Rk	Stop	Dfts	BTkl	Runs	St%	Rk	RuYd	Rk	Sack	Hit	Hur	Tips
Lamarr Houston*	27	DE	16	1020	69	8.4%	6	52	14	5	52	75%	44	2.3	34	6.0	11	21.0	0
Jason Hunter	31	DE	13	614	27	4.1%	67	18	5	0	17	65%	62	3.2	63	3.5	5	7.0	2
Justin Tuck	31	DE	16	873	66	7.7%	11	50	22	4	44	70%	53	2.3	31	11.0	12	32.0	3
LaMarr Woodley	*30*	*OLB*	*11*	*574*	*37*	*6.8%*	*20*	*24*	*8*	*2*	*26*	*58%*	*71*	*3.8*	*69*	*5.0*	*7*	*12.0*	*1*

			Overall								Pass Rush			vs. Run					vs. Pass						
Linebackers	Age	Pos	G	Snaps	Plays	TmPct	Rk	Stop	Dfts	BTkl	Sack	Hit	Hur	Runs	St%	Rk	RuYd	Rk	Tgts	Suc%	Rk	AdjYd	Rk	PD	Int
Nick Roach	29	MLB	16	1074	115	14.1%	34	53	17	6	5.5	0	11.3	67	49%	77	4.5	75	24	52%	40	7.3	53	2	1
Kevin Burnett	32	OLB	16	918	108	13.2%	39	67	30	9	2.5	4	12.3	60	73%	15	2.2	7	41	45%	56	6.8	43	5	1
Sio Moore	24	OLB	15	577	46	6.0%	79	32	10	1	4.5	5	11	31	65%	47	2.5	14	8	90%	--	6.4	--	0	0

Year	Yards	ALY	Rk	Power	Rk	Stuff	Rk	2nd Level	Rk	Open Field	Rk	Sacks	ASR	Rk	Short	Long
2011	4.87	4.04	18	72%	28	19%	18	1.33	28	1.28	30	39	6.4%	20	12	18
2012	4.27	3.80	6	58%	9	22%	9	1.01	2	1.18	30	25	4.9%	30	8	11
2013	3.96	3.95	18	73%	25	17%	21	1.16	21	0.45	6	38	7.3%	11	15	11

2013 ALY by direction: Left End 3.42 (11) Left Tackle 3.85 (14) Mid/Guard 3.89 (14) Right Tackle 4.78 (30) Right End 4.11 (22)

For the second consecutive season, the Raiders return only one of their starting defensive linemen from the previous season. There was no guarantee Pat Sims would return, despite some solid work as a run-stopper in the middle of the line, but a modest market in free agency made it possible. Joining him on the interior on run downs should be 2013 sixth-rounder Stacy McGee, who flashed at times. Antonio Smith in particular will be a much more effective player if the Raiders can play him primarily on passing downs, as he is not an impact player against the run. (Compare his 20 run plays to the 63 J.J. Watt had on the other side, even though teams were usually running away from Watt.) C.J. Wilson and Jack Crawford provide additional support on run downs.

Nick Roach was one of McKenzie's biggest offseason acquisitions last year, and he acquitted himself reasonably well in his first season as a full-time middle linebacker after spending most of his career on the strong side. He was probably no better than an average starter, but after years of Rolando McClain, things like "diagnosing and attacking a play" and " shedding second-level blockers" came as a breath of fresh air. While he lacks the range to be an ideal pass defender, he did some very good work going forward as a blitzer, especially using his power to overwhelm running backs. With fifth overall pick Khalil Mack likely a lock on one side of Roach, the weakside linebacker job is an open competition. Kevin Burnett is the incumbent, even if he is not the favorite. Like Roach, he brought a needed measure of professionalism in 2013. His 18 Defeats on runs tied him for fourth in the league, though he did not jump off the film as the high-impact run defender his stats seem to suggest. Burnett's competition includes 2013 third-round pick Sio Moore, who started on the strong side as a rookie and spent most of his nickel snaps as an edge rusher rather than as a pass defender, and 2012 fourth-round selection Miles Burris, who started 15 games as a rookie before suffering through an injury-riddled sophomore campaign.

Defensive Secondary

			Overall									vs. Run					vs. Pass									
Secondary	**Age**	**Pos**	**G**	**Snaps**	**Plays**	**TmPct**	**Rk**	**Stop**	**Dfts**	**BTkl**	**Runs**	**St%**	**Rk**	**RuYd**	**Rk**	**Tgts**	**Tgt%**	**Rk**	**Dist**	**Suc%**	**Rk**	**AdjYd**	**Rk**	**PD**	**Int**
Charles Woodson	38	FS	16	1067	100	12.2%	22	27	12	12	36	22%	73	8.2	62	20	4.8%	5	11.4	59%	32	8.7	60	3	1
Tracy Porter*	28	CB	16	985	79	9.7%	18	39	16	9	27	59%	8	3.8	4	78	20.9%	42	9.4	59%	13	7.1	31	12	2
Brandian Ross	25	SS	16	954	76	9.3%	48	18	5	14	28	32%	55	7.4	49	32	8.7%	50	10.0	47%	60	7.6	51	3	0
Mike Jenkins*	29	CB	15	903	70	9.1%	30	25	11	5	21	19%	76	8.0	54	68	19.9%	29	11.2	41%	82	8.7	69	6	2
Phillip Adams*	26	CB	16	340	28	3.4%	--	10	1	5	10	40%	--	9.6	--	28	21.7%	--	12.0	51%	--	8.8	--	1	0
D.J. Hayden	24	CB	8	337	26	6.4%	--	7	4	4	2	50%	--	6.5	--	41	31.7%	--	13.7	48%	--	9.9	--	2	1
Usama Young	29	FS	12	196	23	3.8%	--	10	8	1	7	29%	--	5.6	--	5	6.7%	--	16.7	53%	--	4.2	--	2	1
Carlos Rogers	*33*	*CB*	*16*	*1046*	*55*	*6.9%*	*64*	*23*	*8*	*6*	*9*	*44%*	*35*	*5.2*	*16*	*83*	*18.0%*	*16*	*11.4*	*50%*	*58*	*7.8*	*48*	*8*	*2*
Tarell Brown	*29*	*CB*	*13*	*755*	*42*	*6.5%*	*71*	*16*	*8*	*4*	*6*	*33%*	*53*	*9.8*	*66*	*73*	*21.9%*	*49*	*12.2*	*50%*	*59*	*6.7*	*18*	*10*	*0*

Year	Pass D Rank	vs. #1 WR	Rk	vs. #2 WR	Rk	vs. Other WR	Rk	vs. TE	Rk	vs. RB	Rk
2011	21	-1.1%	11	20.8%	25	-1.7%	19	-2.3%	5	-2.9%	16
2012	30	25.9%	30	5.0%	19	-13.4%	7	15.3%	28	11.0%	21
2013	29	10.8%	23	20.2%	31	28.4%	31	3.9%	18	10.8%	25

McKenzie making D.J. Hayden the 12th overall pick in last year's draft was an interesting selection, as he was coming off a major injury that would not let him participate fully until training camp. When the season began, Hayden was only used at right cornerback, and even then, only in nickel situations with Tracy Porter moving inside. (Although Oakland was overall average in our "CB by Sides" metric, most passes with Hayden in coverage are listed on the offensive left side, with only eight passes in the middle and none on the right.) Like most rookie cornerbacks, he struggled in his transition to the different rules of the NFL game, and our charters suggested that "Hayden's tackling style is best described as 'over-enthusiastic.'" The more concerning news is his continuing injuries, as a groin injury knocked him out for the year after Week 9 and an ankle injury in May had him in a walking boot for June minicamp. As that offseason after the rookie season is generally when good cornerbacks learn the technique needed to play well in the NFL, this missed time is a concern. The Raiders' plan is for Hayden to start at corner this year, with 49ers refugees Tarell Brown and Carlos Rogers traveling across the Bay to be the other starter and nickel corner.

At safety, the Raiders badly missed Tyvon Branch's presence after he broke his fibula in Week 2. He was replaced in the lineup by Brandian Ross. Branch was a solid man coverage defender and box safety before his injury. His return will provide a major upgrade to the Raiders defense, as Ross was a good example of the type of player a team with no cap space and a recent history of squandering draft picks must resort to. The second-year former undrafted free agent was at times an effective blitzer for Jason Tarver's exotic schemes, but beyond that was one of the NFL's least effective regular players in 2013.

The other starting safety was Charles Woodson. Physically, he is a far cry from the player he was a couple years ago. He provided a much-needed steadying presence for the Raiders, as he knew where he needed to be and when he needed to be there, and generally had a good idea of how to get there from where he was. Often deployed well off the line of scrimmage, he showed a veteran's instinct for coming up in run support. Like Ross, though, Woodson was in his own way a good example of what the 2013 Raiders were. He knew what he was doing. He was an effective player at times. As a veteran who has enjoyed success in the league and won a Super Bowl, he was probably a good player to have around in the locker room. He was not, though, a high-impact player on the field. While his deep safety role meant that game charters didn't assign him many specific pass targets, teams were able to throw to his side or target him effectively. While he came up in run support, his broken tackle count rightly suggests he was not always effective when he did so. On a better team, one with greater depth, he could be a useful chess piece for Jason Tarver in sub package situations. Instead, he seems poised to start at free safety after signing another one-year deal in the offseason.

Special Teams

Year	DVOA	Rank	FG/XP	Rank	Net Kick	Rank	Kick Ret	Rank	Net Punt	Rank	Punt Ret	Rank	Hidden	Rank
2011	-1.0%	20	16.6	1	-14.0	32	4.0	7	-8.3	28	-3.1	21	9.2	5
2012	-5.8%	31	11.8	1	-12.1	31	-2.8	21	-15.3	31	-10.4	32	-7.4	27
2013	-7.1%	31	-11.1	29	6.0	6	-10.4	32	-16.1	30	-4.1	22	13.5	2

Field goal kickers are inconsistent. Field goal kickers are inconsistent. Field goal kickers are inconsistent. We keep repeating this because it is true. A season after he was perfect inside of 50 yards and 6-of-9 beyond 50, Sebastian Janikowski was only 3-of-7 from 50-plus and 19-of-23 inside it. Some of the difficulty may have been attributable to having a new holder in Marquette King after spending his first 13 seasons with Shane Lechler, but this is not the first time Janikowski's performance has declined significantly from one season to the next. He still has a strong leg on field goals and should rebound in 2014. He hasn't shown a strong leg on kickoffs in some time, but the Raiders were above average in that area thanks to strong coverage work. Taiwan Jones earned a contract extension for his strong work on special teams, including a team-leading 13 return stops.

In his first year as Lechler's replacement, King's biggest issue was getting the ball off. He was a bit below average on punts actually kicked, and the Raiders were right around average when it came to covering punts. That 30th-place ranking was the result of a couple punt blocks.

The return jobs were both problematic for the Raiders in 2013 and each featured a revolving cast of characters. Jones, Jacoby Ford, Greg Jenkins, and Jeremy Stewart each tried their hand returning kicks, while Ford, Jenkins, and Philip Adams got a shot to return punts. Both jobs are open to competition in 2014, with seven players including Darren McFadden getting reps at kick returner in June while Maurice Jones-Drew and seventh-round rookie corner T.J. Carrie were among the potential punt returners.

Philadelphia Eagles

2013 Record: 10-6	**Total DVOA:** 15.2% (8th)	**2014 Mean Projection:** 9.3 wins	**On the Clock (0-4):** 4%
Pythagorean Wins: 9.4 (11th)	**Offense:** 22.9% (3rd)	**Postseason Odds:** 59.4%	**Mediocrity (5-7):** 16%
Snap-Weighted Age: 26.7 (17th)	**Defense:** 4.9% (23rd)	**Super Bowl Odds:** 11.1%	**Playoff Contender (8-10):** 48%
Average Opponent: -4.6% (29th)	**Special Teams:** -2.8% (25th)	**Proj. Avg. Opponent:** -1.9% (24th)	**Super Bowl Contender (11+):** 32%

2013: The NFL's most innovative offense goes forward by going back… to the days when the run came first.

2014: Will another year bring further refinement of the system, or statistical regression?

The Philadelphia Eagles are now Chip Kelly's team. Blame it on the lack of a defensive superstar or how Nick Foles looks like Napoleon Dynamite, but the Eagles are going to be defined by their head coach perhaps in the way Vince Lombardi once defined the Green Bay Packers.

Okay, maybe that's taking things way too far after one season, but there's a lot to be excited about. The buildup to 2013 mostly consisted of questions asking what Kelly would bring from Oregon and the college game to the Eagles. After Kelly stamped his brand on a division title, the focus shifts to what NFL teams can do this offseason to "figure him out" since the dreaded "year of tape" now exists. But what makes anyone think Kelly's done figuring the NFL out? Kelly has more to learn to take the Eagles to the upper echelon of the NFC that's recently been dominated by defensive-minded teams like Seattle and San Francisco. The Eagles played neither last year and will face both in 2014. That will serve as a good litmus test for where the Eagles are, but wherever they are going, they will get there behind Kelly.

His story is not like that of most coaches. Kelly is the first head coach since Steve Spurrier (2002) to be hired without spending any time on an NFL coaching staff—but at least Spurrier was a NFL quarterback many moons ago with the 49ers and Buccaneers. Kelly's a loner, Dottie. A rebel. He didn't even coach major college football until Oregon hired him as offensive coordinator in 2007. When Barry Switzer was hired by Dallas without any previous NFL experience, he had a 16-year run as Oklahoma's head coach. Kelly's only been a head coach since 2009, but in that short period of time he's developed an offensive system that maximizes speed, spacing, and tempo; has been adaptable to just about any quarterback not named Matt Barkley (small sample, but last year was brutal for the rookie); and is seemingly impervious to turnovers, all while built around the running game in an era that would rather pass.

Okay, we better put the lotion in the basket, but consider some of the feats this offense reached in one season.

Pace: The fast tempo was a hallmark of Kelly's Oregon offenses and he transferred it beautifully to the NFL. The Eagles averaged 23.38 seconds per play—the fastest pace of any offense in our database, which goes back to 1997. If we remove situations prone to the hurry-up and look at situation-neutral pace, the Eagles are still the fastest at 23.88 seconds per play. The top of these lists are dominated by teams from the last two years as the league picks up the pace, but Kelly set the gold standard on his first try. His first game (Monday night in Washington) saw the Eagles run 53 plays in the first half—the second highest total for any team in a first half since 1991.

Yards after catch (YAC): The Eagles fielded an offense with great speed, so getting the ball to these players in space is a must. Philadelphia averaged 7.04 yards after catch, the highest average since 1992 based on data from STATS LLC. There's no supporting evidence that a passing game built on YAC will be more successful than one that's built on air yards, but this further demonstrates that Kelly's style adapted to the pro game with great success last year.

Zone read: The zone read kept the Eagles balanced and their opponents off-balance. Though it was 2012's trendiest offensive wrinkle, the zone read was used on just 1.4 percent of all offensive plays that season, and no team used it more than Carolina (141 runs). In 2013, according to charting data from ESPN Stats & Information, the Eagles used the zone read on 304 runs. That's 135 more plays than the next team (Buffalo), and after excluding kneeldowns, that's 63.6 percent of the Eagles' rushes. In Week 1 at Washington, the Eagles had 41 zone-read runs for 245 yards—the most any team has had in five years. Obviously, those were season-best numbers. The Eagles led the league in rushing yards (2,566), yards per carry (5.13) and DVOA (23.6%), but the zone read produced a more dynamic attack.

- Zone-read runs: 304 carries for 1,713 yards (5.63 yards per carry)
- Other runs: 174 carries for 881 yards (5.06 yards per carry)

Kelly also disproved the myth that he needs a mobile quarterback to run his offense. Once Michael Vick inevitably went down with injury, Foles was far more efficient, and he even had 17 zone-read runs for 82 yards. (Vick had nine runs for 126 yards). He's not overly mobile, but he's not a statue either. An argument could be made that a mobile quarterback would make the offense better, but passing is still the first priority. Foles used the success of the zone read to his advantage with

2014 Eagles Schedule

Week	Opp.	Week	Opp.	Week	Opp.
1	JAC	7	BYE	13	at DAL (Thu.)
2	at IND (Mon.)	8	at ARI	14	SEA
3	WAS	9	at HOU	15	DAL
4	at SF	10	CAR (Mon.)	16	at WAS (Sat.)
5	STL	11	at GB	17	at NYG
6	NYG	12	TEN		

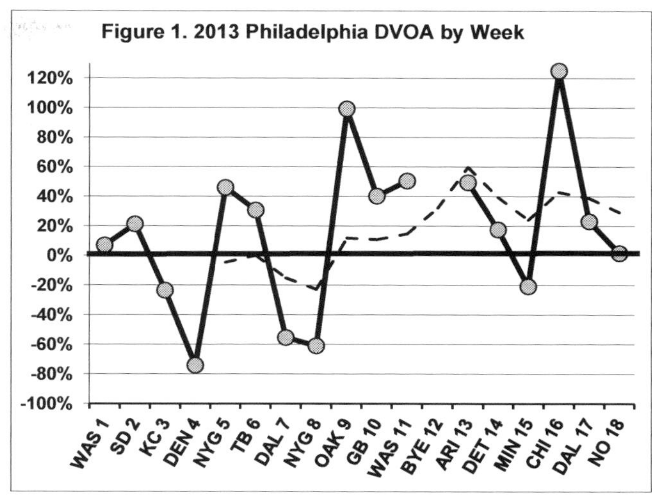

Figure 1. 2013 Philadelphia DVOA by Week

packaged plays involving the play-action passing game. That delayed reaction from the defense watching the mesh point led to numerous big plays for this offense, especially when Foles was healthy in the second half of the season. The Eagles went from using play action on 24 percent of their passes in their first eight games to 39 percent in the final eight games, a period in which Foles averaged 10.2 yards per attempt and threw 12 touchdowns on play-action passes. Only Peyton Manning finished the season with more touchdown passes off play action (17) than Foles' 15. Defenses may not respect Foles as a runner, but they can't just crash the mesh point for fear of the play being a pass.

Despite the innovative offense, Kelly's first year was far from flawless. The defense was roasted when facing top offenses like Denver and San Diego. The offensive line could not block Kansas City in a five-turnover mess. The Eagles were 2013's least consistent (highest variance) team in terms of their weekly DVOA performance. In back-to-back home losses against the Cowboys and Giants, Kelly's vaunted offense scored a combined three points on 25 drives. Granted, Vick and Foles were injured for parts of those games, but that type of scoring efficiency would disgust even the 1976 Tampa Bay Buccaneers. The only scoring drive came in a 17-3 loss to Dallas, an unusual 10-play, 17-yard field-goal drive right before Foles left the game with a concussion.

That ugly stretch put the Eagles at 3-5, making them the 15th team in NFL history to start no better than 3-5 and still make the playoffs. It certainly helped to play the year's fourth easiest schedule, which included a gimpy Robert Griffin III in Week 1, Scott Tolzien instead of Aaron Rodgers in Week 10, and Kyle Orton over Tony Romo in Week 17's division clincher. Right after those two abysmal home performances, Foles returned and threw seven touchdown passes against Oakland, starting a 7-1 run to finish the season. The lone loss again showed the team's inconsistency. No one would have ever expected Minnesota, with Matt Cassel and *without* Adrian Peterson, to pull off a 48-30 upset in Week 15.

In the Wild Card loss at home against New Orleans, problems in the trenches impacted both sides of the ball. Kelly was also not as aggressive as some would like. Trailing 20-14 in the fourth quarter with 11:24 to play, Kelly was content with sending out the field goal unit on fourth-and-1 at the New Orleans 7. In the regular season, Kelly's Aggressiveness Index, which quantifies fourth-down decisions based on game situation, was 1.46, ranked second in the league. However, even ranking second in the league still meant the Eagles had only 14 fourth-down attempts all year. Analytical fans hoping for Kelly to carry the torch for the "Fourth-Down Revolution" may have to wait for another hero to emerge.

That's not to say Kelly doesn't bring brass balls to the job. How many coaches would simply cite "football reasons" when releasing their best wide receiver in his prime after a career season? LeSean McCoy told NFL.com in June that DeSean Jackson's release sent a message to the team that "no matter how good you are, you gotta follow these guidelines. And if you don't, you could be gone. ...You gotta buy in."

But should we buy into the 2014 Eagles without Jackson, who was a bigger loss than anything they gained this offseason? As unexpectedly great as Foles' season was, he did only throw 317 passes and has 16 career regular-season starts. He might never come close to last season's level of play again, especially if the schedule's a bit tougher and he's lost a few receivers. Add in the fact the Eagles had a great bounce-back year in both injuries and turnovers, two things likely to regress, and there's cause for concern. The Eagles were just 4-12 in 2012, and a step back would not be unprecedented.

Since 2001, 21 teams have increased their win total by at least six games to make the playoffs, including last year's Eagles and Chiefs. The following season, only six of those teams returned to the playoffs, and teams on average declined by 3.6 wins (Table 1). Only the 2006 Bears increased their win total again. Many of these turnarounds were led by changes at head coach and/or quarterback, but that doesn't always mean instantly repeatable success. The best comparison for the Eagles might be the 2006 Saints, who looked great with Sean Payton and Drew Brees taking over the offense, but had a suspect defense. Brees had a lousy start in 2007 and the Saints never recovered, finishing 7-9. Even Bill Belichick and Tom Brady missed the playoffs for the only time together in 2002. If Eagles fans want some optimism, at least they can look at their own history. Andy Reid improved on his 5-11 rookie record in 1999 with an 11-5 record in 2000, which started a five-year run of 11-win seasons.

In *Football Outsiders Almanac 2013*, Chase Stuart wrote how the Eagles should improve in injuries and turnovers. That happened in a big way, which makes us wonder how far they'll fall back to the pack in 2014. Or does Kelly truly have methods that will keep the Eagles healthy and in control of the ball?

Turnovers were a huge problem at the end of Reid's tenure. Last year the Eagles had 19 giveaways, tied for the fourth fewest in the league. That's good, but consider that eight of the 19 came with Vick at quarterback, while Barkley had five turnovers on just 52 pass plays. That means the Eagles only had six turnovers when Foles played his 703 snaps. Including the playoff loss, the Eagles had five turnovers in their final nine games, a pace that would break the NFL record of 10 turnovers in a full season. Foles led the way with just two interceptions on 317 passes, setting the all-time record with a 27:2 touchdown-to-interception ratio. What makes that even more incredible is that he led all qualified passers in the highest rate of passes thrown at least 15 yards (27.4 percent). Sure, it helps the stats when Oakland's defensive backs are falling down or not even covering anyone, but Foles was the ultimate high-risk, high-reward passer in 2013—except without any of the risk.

It's not a bold prediction to say that Foles will throw more interceptions in 2014, but there may not be a lot more. Foles had a 1.9 interception percentage in 2012, although he also got away with eight passes that were dropped/defensed interceptions. Last year, Foles only had two passes that we charted as dropped interceptions. Both were defensed by his receiver, including a great break-up by Jackson on Arizona's Patrick Peterson. He may just be a quarterback who routinely posts low-interception seasons like Donovan McNabb once did for the Eagles. Kelly may help with that too. In his last four years at Oregon, Kelly's offense alternated between seven and nine interceptions with the rate never exceeding 2.4 percent.

On the injury front, the Eagles led the league with 33.6 Adjusted Games Lost (AGL). This comes a year after the offense alone ranked 32nd in AGL (65.2). The players have bought into Kelly's effort to reduce soft tissue injuries by focusing on rest, recovery and proper nutrition. Kelly remains tight-lipped over the details on what the Eagles are actually doing with sports science, but year one seemed to be a success. Of course, the more serious injuries like broken bones and torn ligaments can happen at any given moment, but reducing minor problems like hamstring strains should help any team's performance. For reference, teams finishing first in AGL have ranked 15.0 on average the following season since 2002. If Foles gets injured and Kelly gets a strong performance out of new backup Mark Sanchez, he'll *really* cement his legacy.

Jeremy Maclin (torn ACL) was the big injury last year, and his recovery is crucial to this season after the Eagles said goodbye to both Jackson and the reliable Jason Avant. Maclin's been good, but he's never been a No. 1 receiver and he lacks the speed as a deep threat and explosion to make big YAC plays. Kelly did get career years out of Jackson and Riley Cooper, so Maclin may top 1,000 yards for the first time in his career, but the decision to release Jackson could come back to haunt the Eagles.

It's an extremely rare decision. Jackson, who turns 28 in December, is the first receiver under 30 to be released after a 1,200-yard season. Receivers under the age of 30 have had 1,200 receiving yards in a season 211 times in NFL history. This will mark only the 10th time one of those receivers did not return to his team the following season (Table 2). Sometimes they wear out their welcome (Santonio Holmes), sometimes they argue over money (John Jefferson) and sometimes they're deemed replaceable No. 2's—Eric Decker, say hello to Peerless Price—but only in Jackson's case are they flat out cut in their prime. Only Muhsin Muhammad with the 2004 Panthers had more yards (1,405) than Jackson in a season before getting cut, but he was going on 32.

Kelly's putting a lot of faith in his system with this move. Different types of talent will have to replace Jackson's production. Darren Sproles can catch out of the backfield with the best of them. Zach Ertz should show more in his second season at tight end. But there is still a lot of pressure on rookie wide receivers Jordan Matthews (Vanderbilt) and Josh Huff (Oregon) to produce something this year. Huff played under Kelly at Oregon and had his best season as a senior in 2013. Draft analyst Mike Mayock said Huff "plays receiver like an old running back." Matthews has the better shot to play a big role right away. He has the best measurables of any Philadelphia receiver, but we know that doesn't always translate to the field. Matthews dropped 10 passes last season, or nearly half of Philadelphia's 2013 total (21).

Getting production out of this rookie class would help quiet perhaps the biggest criticism of Kelly's short career: talent procurement. The offensive scheme worked last year and the Eagles are an offense-first team, but playmakers are also needed to make the 3-4 defense work. Last year's success came mostly through the players acquired in the Reid era. Kelly's additions did not pan out well. We wrote last year how James Casey could be an intriguing piece in the offense, but he basically was an expensive No. 3 tight end. Kenny Phillips was waived in August. Felix Jones was traded to Pittsburgh. Isaac Sopoaga was traded to New England. Cary Williams and

Table 1. How Turnaround Playoff Teams Fared the Following Year, 2002-2014

Team	Year	W-L	Win Incr.	W-L Y+1	Win Diff.	Y+1 Result
PHI	2013	10-6	6	--	--	--
KC	2013	11-5	9	--	--	--
MIN	2012	10-6	7	5-10-1	-4.5	No Playoffs
IND	2012	11-5	9	11-5	0	Lost AFC-DIV
SF	2011	13-3	7	11-4-1	-1.5	Lost SB
KC	2010	10-6	6	7-9	-3	No Playoffs
CIN	2009	10-6	6	4-12	-6	No Playoffs
BAL	2008	11-5	6	9-7	-2	Lost AFC-DIV
ATL	2008	11-5	7	9-7	-2	No Playoffs
MIA	2008	11-5	10	7-9	-4	No Playoffs
NYJ	2006	10-6	6	4-12	-6	No Playoffs
BAL	2006	13-3	7	5-11	-8	No Playoffs
NO	2006	10-6	7	7-9	-3	No Playoffs
CHI	2005	11-5	6	13-3	2	Lost SB
TB	2005	11-5	6	4-12	-7	No Playoffs
ATL	2004	11-5	6	8-8	-3	No Playoffs
SD	2004	12-4	8	9-7	-3	No Playoffs
PIT	2004	15-1	9	11-5	-4	Won SB
SF	2001	12-4	6	10-6	-2	Lost NFC-DIV
NE	2001	11-5	6	9-7	-2	No Playoffs
CHI	2001	13-3	8	4-12	-9	No Playoffs
AVERAGE (2001-2012)		**11.4**	**7.0**	**7.8**	**-3.6**	

Table 2. Young Receivers Who Did Not Return After a 1,200 Yard-Season

Receiver	Team	Year	Age	Rec	Yds	TD	Tm PASS DVOA	Rk	Tm PASS DVOA Y+1	Rk	Reason
Yancey Thigpen	PIT	1997	28	79	1398	7	15.0%	12	-10.8%	25	FA
John Jefferson	SD	1980	24	82	1340	13	N/A	--	N/A	--	Trade
DeSean Jackson	PHI	2013	27	82	1332	9	30.0%	5	TBD	--	Cut
Jeff Graham	CHI	1995	26	82	1301	4	46.9%	2	15.7%	13	FA
Buddy Dial	PIT	1963	26	60	1295	9	N/A	--	N/A	--	Trade
Eric Decker	DEN	2013	26	87	1288	11	60.3%	1	TBD	--	FA
Laveranues Coles	NYJ	2002	25	89	1264	5	42.7%	2	21.5%	9	RFA/Trade*
Peerless Price	BUF	2002	26	94	1252	9	11.2%	15	-16.2%	27	Trade
Santonio Holmes	PIT	2009	25	79	1248	5	34.5%	7	40.6%	3	Trade
Brandon Marshall	MIA	2011	27	81	1214	6	3.0%	18	-1.8%	23	Trade

**Washington sent a first-round pick to the Jets for Coles in 2003.*

Bradley Fletcher were targeted frequently at corner while an improving Brandon Boykin continues to earn just a nickel assignment. Patrick Chung was a one-and-done signing. Connor Barwin had a passable debut, but there's an alarming lack of pieces firmly in place on defense. This year's "big" signing of safety Malcolm Jenkins feels like another case of applying a band-aid to a large gash.

Then there's Lane Johnson, the first draft pick (No. 4 overall) of the Kelly era. Every analyst had him pegged as a project at right tackle, and the early results lived up to that billing. Johnson struggled mightily with his pass protection in the first half of the season, but calmed down and played at a more respectable level during the 7-1 finish. He's still much better at run blocking, but perhaps his pass protection will come around in year two after getting used to the speed of this offense. Experience and continuity going into year two also has linebacker Mychal Kendricks hopeful on defense. "It's the second year with the same guys, the same coaches. It's a great thing," Kendricks said in June.

Any coach, from Lombardi to Kelly, will ultimately succeed or fail on the efforts of his players. Kelly's offensive system will not suddenly stop working in 2014 just because the league's had an offseason to analyze his success. It may not work as well due to factors not fully in his control, such as schedule, injuries and turnovers, but the players have fully bought into Kelly's methods and the Eagles should be glad to have a coach that's willing to be an innovator. Kelly's ability to grow the Eagles' talent core will be the deciding factor in just how long his scheme succeeds, but there's enough talent in place now to continue being the favorite in the NFC East, a division where nine or ten wins is really all that's necessary. His methods may be unique, but at the end of the day, Kelly's plan for success is as simple as what he told Cooper last season: "F---ing score points, what's your plan?"

Scott Kacsmar

2013 Eagles Stats by Week

Wk	vs.	W-L	PF	PA	YDF	YDA	TO	Total	Off	Def	ST
1	at WAS	W	33	27	443	382	+1	7%	25%	28%	10%
2	SD	L	30	33	522	539	+2	21%	32%	14%	3%
3	KC	L	16	26	431	394	-5	-24%	-6%	2%	-15%
4	at DEN	L	20	52	450	472	0	-74%	23%	41%	-57%
5	at NYG	W	36	21	439	383	+4	46%	41%	6%	11%
6	at TB	W	31	20	425	351	0	31%	50%	12%	-7%
7	DAL	L	3	17	278	368	-1	-55%	-64%	-9%	0%
8	NYG	L	7	15	200	325	-2	-61%	-45%	22%	5%
9	at OAK	W	49	20	542	560	+2	99%	96%	12%	15%
10	at GB	W	27	13	415	396	+1	40%	27%	-15%	-2%
11	WAS	W	24	16	402	427	+2	50%	42%	5%	13%
12	BYE										
13	ARI	W	24	21	307	350	+3	49%	24%	-8%	17%
14	DET	W	34	20	478	231	+2	17%	46%	-21%	-49%
15	at MIN	L	30	48	475	455	0	-21%	19%	38%	-2%
16	CHI	W	54	11	514	257	+1	125%	64%	-55%	6%
17	at DAL	W	24	22	366	414	+2	23%	5%	-11%	7%
18	NO	L	24	26	256	434	+2	2%	18%	13%	-3%

Trends and Splits

	Offense	Rank	Defense	Rank
Total DVOA	22.9%	3	4.9%	23
Unadjusted VOA	22.1%	3	2.9%	20
Weighted Trend	25.4%	3	-1.4%	15
Variance	14.9%	32	5.7%	18
Average Opponent	2.7%	24	-0.2%	14
Passing	30.0%	5	16.5%	25
Rushing	23.6%	1	-11.4%	11
First Down	23.5%	3	6.5%	22
Second Down	30.7%	2	3.7%	20
Third Down	9.1%	9	3.6%	21
First Half	23.5%	3	5.2%	23
Second Half	22.3%	3	4.6%	20
Red Zone	1.7%	18	-4.2%	12
Late and Close	44.1%	1	8.7%	24

Five-Year Performance

Year	W-L	Pyth W	Est W	PF	PA	TO	Total	Rk	Off	Rk	Def	Rk	ST	Rk	Off AGL	Rk	Def AGL	Rk	Off Age	Rk	Def Age	Rk	ST Age	Rk
2009	11-5	10.4	11.2	429	337	+15	28.8%	3	9.7%	11	-14.3%	3	4.8%	2	37.4	26	31.5	20	26.0	32	27.4	15	26.9	9
2010	10-6	9.5	11.9	439	377	+9	23.2%	5	17.3%	3	-3.6%	11	2.3%	12	41.4	29	28.7	21	25.6	32	26.6	18	26.2	16
2011	8-8	9.8	9.0	396	328	-14	13.5%	9	9.8%	8	-3.7%	11	0.0%	17	10.5	3	11.4	5	26.7	20	26.9	17	25.7	29
2012	4-12	3.9	4.5	280	444	-24	-22.4%	28	-10.8%	25	9.4%	26	-2.2%	23	65.2	32	8.1	2	26.8	17	26.5	23	25.6	27
2013	10-6	9.4	10.2	442	382	+12	15.2%	8	22.9%	3	4.9%	23	-2.8%	25	21.4	7	12.2	3	27.5	11	26.2	21	26.0	19

2013 Performance Based on Most Common Personnel Groups

PHI Offense					PHI Offense vs. Opponents				PHI Defense				PHI Defense vs. Opponents			
Pers	Freq	Yds	DVOA	Run%	Pers	Freq	Yds	DVOA	Pers	Freq	Yds	DVOA	Pers	Freq	Yds	DVOA
11	72%	6.4	21.1%	37%	Nickel Even	76%	6.5	25.5%	3-4-4	50%	5.1	4.3%	11	51%	6.4	14.1%
12	22%	6.3	41.1%	54%	4-3-4	11%	6.7	35.4%	Nickel Even	27%	5.9	10.8%	12	20%	4.8	-2.9%
21	4%	9.1	62.3%	77%	Nickel Odd	6%	8.3	28.5%	Nickel Odd	21%	6.0	0.2%	21	11%	5.5	14.8%
13	1%	4.3	6.9%	78%	3-4-4	4%	3.9	28.9%	Dime+	1%	12.2	92.5%	22	4%	3.1	-45.6%
22	1%	14.2	48.2%	50%	Dime+	2%	6.0	-11.2%	4-3-4	1%	0.9	-120.8%	13	3%	4.0	-4.1%

Strategic Tendencies

Run/Pass		Rk	Formation		Rk	Pass Rush		Rk	Secondary		Rk	Strategy		Rk
Runs, first half	39%	14	Form: Single Back	93%	1	Rush 3	9.4%	5	4 DB	51%	5	Play action	31%	2
Runs, first down	45%	22	Form: Empty Back	3%	30	Rush 4	54.2%	29	5 DB	48%	16	Avg Box (Off)	6.26	22
Runs, second-long	43%	3	Pers: 3+ WR	73%	3	Rush 5	27.8%	10	6+ DB	1%	28	Avg Box (Def)	6.40	13
Runs, power sit.	84%	1	Pers: 4+ WR	0%	23	Rush 6+	8.6%	16	CB by Sides	92%	3	Offensive Pace	23.88	1
Runs, behind 2H	27%	18	Pers: 2+ TE/6+ OL	23%	25	Sacks by LB	65.8%	5	DB Blitz	12%	16	Defensive Pace	30.58	27
Pass, ahead 2H	38%	32	Shotgun/Pistol	86%	1	Sacks by DB	3.9%	22	Hole in Zone	10%	19	Go for it on 4th	1.46	2

Where to begin with the dramatic changes that Chip Kelly brought to the Eagles' strategic tendencies? Philadelphia used shotgun/pistol formations more often than any team in modern NFL history. They ran more often in short-yardage situations than any team in the last decade. They went from passing on a league-high 63 percent of plays when ahead in the second half to passing on a league-low 38 percent of plays when ahead in the second half. They used max protect blocking one-third as often as they had the year before. On defense, they went from rushing four more often than any other team to rushing four less often than 28 other teams, and they sent a defensive back blitz more than twice as often as they did in 2012. The Eagles averaged 6.6 yards after catch, the highest figure since we started tracking YAC in 2005. Particularly impressive was their average 12.1 yards after catch on passes thrown at or behind the line of scrimmage (NFL average: 8.9 YAC). However, the Eagles weren't just about the short pass. They threw 28 percent of passes deep, i.e. over 15 yards past the line of scrimmage. No other offense was above 24 percent. The Eagles had a league-best 29.9% DVOA when running the ball on second-and-long (scrambles not included). Only Tampa Bay and Minnesota ran more often on second-and-long. The Eagles drew seven intentional grounding flags; no other defense drew more than three. Eagles opponents threw 24 percent of passes to "Other" receivers (i.e. not No. 1 or No. 2 receivers); no other defense was above 20 percent last year.

Passing

Player	DYAR	DVOA	Plays	NtYds	Avg	YAC	C%	TD	Int
N.Foles	1011	35.6%	347	2690	7.8	6.8	64.4%	27	2
M.Vick*	40	-6.9%	157	1098	7.0	7.4	55.0%	5	3
M.Barkley	-84	-34.9%	52	274	5.3	2.9	61.2%	0	4

Rushing

Player	DYAR	DVOA	Plays	Yds	Avg	TD	Fum	Suc
L.McCoy	341	18.1%	314	1607	5.1	9	1	52%
B.Brown*	23	-1.2%	75	314	4.2	2	0	48%
N.Foles	72	23.1%	39	242	6.2	3	0	-
M.Vick*	128	70.0%	29	316	10.9	2	0	-
C.Polk	64	120.4%	11	98	8.9	3	0	64%
D.Sproles	*21*	*1.4%*	*53*	*220*	*4.2*	*2*	*1*	*49%*

Receiving

Player	DYAR	DVOA	Plays	Ctch	Yds	Y/C	YAC	TD	C%
D.Jackson*	358	23.7%	125	82	1332	16.2	5.9	9	66%
R.Cooper	212	20.6%	84	47	835	17.8	4.9	8	56%
J.Avant*	-68	-24.5%	76	38	447	11.8	2.1	2	50%
J.Maehl	11	3.5%	9	4	67	16.8	8.5	1	44%
Z.Ertz	60	9.8%	56	36	469	13.0	4.4	4	64%
B.Celek	89	18.3%	51	32	502	15.7	8.8	6	63%
J.Casey	-9	-29.4%	6	3	31	10.3	8.0	0	50%
L.McCoy	137	23.8%	64	52	539	10.4	11.3	2	81%
B.Brown*	12	8.7%	13	8	84	10.5	11.8	0	62%
D.Sproles	*174*	*23.9%*	*89*	*71*	*604*	*8.5*	*7.3*	*2*	*80%*

Offensive Line

Player	Pos	Age	GS	Snaps	Pen	Sk	Pass	Run	Player	Pos	Age	GS	Snaps	Pen	Sk	Pass	Run
Todd Herremans	RG	32	16/16	1104	5	3.5	27.5	3.0	Jason Kelce	C	27	16/16	1096	5	1.0	8.0	8.0
Evan Mathis	LG	33	16/16	1104	7	1.0	13.0	7.0	Jason Peters	LT	32	16/16	1019	4	4.0	22.5	2.5
Lane Johnson	RT	24	16/16	1103	8	9.0	34.0	5.0									

Year	Yards	ALY	Rk	Power	Rk	Stuff	Rk	2nd Lev	Rk	Open Field	Rk	Sacks	ASR	Rk	Short	Long	F-Start	Cont.
2011	4.54	3.89	26	67%	6	25%	32	1.43	2	1.10	4	32	5.8%	10	7	20	21	31
2012	4.47	3.56	28	69%	6	26%	31	1.39	6	1.06	6	48	8.1%	25	17	19	15	31
2013	5.02	3.71	25	72%	7	20%	21	1.57	1	1.24	2	46	9.4%	31	10	24	14	48
2013 ALY by direction:			*Left End 3.16 (20)*			*Left Tackle 3.37 (25)*			*Mid/Guard 4.29 (6)*			*Right Tackle 3.39 (26)*			*Right End 3.57 (17)*			

The starting five remained intact through every game last season and all five return in 2014, though Lane Johnson could face a four-game suspension for violating the league's performance enhancing drug policy. Johnson did not live up to his draft status in year one, but neither did Eric Fisher and Luke Joeckel after a bizarre draft that was top-heavy on right tackles. Thought to be a perfect fit for Kelly's offense, pass protection was Johnson's biggest problem. His 34 blown pass blocks tied for the fifth most in the league. To Johnson's credit, he was a different player in the second half of the season. After allowing 26 blown blocks in the first eight games, he allowed 13 in the last eight and his run blocking was consistent all year.

That was a common theme for this unit: strong run blocking, suspect pass protection. Johnson's improvement coincided with the Eagles' 7-1 finish, but so did the return of a healthy Nick Foles at quarterback. Clearly the offense runs differently with Foles rather than a frenetic Michael Vick or inexperienced Matt Barkley behind center. The Eagles and Colts were the only teams to have three linemen in the top 30 for most blown pass blocks. Veteran Todd Herremans moved to right guard and ranked 28th out of 35 right guards in snaps per blown block. Like Johnson, he picked up the slack in the second half of the season. On the other hand, left tackle Jason Peters' so-so numbers were consistent throughout the year. Peters has had an interesting career where the individual accolades (six Pro Bowls and two First-Team All-Pro selections) haven't always matched his performance. In 2008 with Buffalo, Peters allowed 11.5 sacks, made the Pro Bowl, and then was traded to Philadelphia for a first-round pick (and then some) in 2009. He missed all of 2012 after twice rupturing his Achilles tendon in the offseason. He was again named an All-Pro for 2013, though our charting numbers have him ranked 22nd among left tackles in snaps per blown block.

Left guard Evan Mathis received individual honors (Pro Bowl and All-Pro) for the first time in his career last season. He's charted better in past seasons, but he is the line's most reliable starter. Center Jason Kelce was the third starter to return from a 2012 injury and impressed the Eagles enough to earn a six-year contract worth $37.5 million. Keeping the continuity up front will be very important, especially when Allen Barbre and Dennis Kelly are the only backups with any NFL starting experience.

Defensive Front Seven

			Overall								vs. Run					Pass Rush			
Defensive Line	Age	Pos	G	Snaps	Plays	TmPct	Rk	Stop	Dfts	BTkl	Runs	St%	Rk	RuYd	Rk	Sack	Hit	Hur	Tips
Fletcher Cox	24	DE	16	882	42	4.7%	51	31	8	3	36	72%	61	2.7	62	3.0	7	26.0	1
Cedric Thornton	26	DE	16	713	62	6.9%	20	46	15	2	59	73%	60	2.3	47	1.0	0	7.0	2
Bennie Logan	25	DT	16	477	26	2.9%	--	20	6	0	20	70%	--	2.9	--	2.5	3	9.5	0
Vinny Curry	26	DE	14	317	24	3.0%	--	16	8	0	16	63%	--	2.0	--	4.0	3	12.5	2

			Overall								vs. Run					Pass Rush			
Edge Rushers	Age	Pos	G	Snaps	Plays	TmPct	Rk	Stop	Dfts	BTkl	Runs	St%	Rk	RuYd	Rk	Sack	Hit	Hur	Tips
Connor Barwin	28	OLB	16	1128	65	7.2%	16	42	17	4	35	66%	60	2.5	45	5.0	4	21.5	8
Trent Cole	32	OLB	16	876	58	6.4%	26	47	19	4	44	77%	33	2.4	35	8.5	6	23.0	2
Brandon Graham	26	OLB	16	323	15	1.7%	--	12	6	1	9	78%	--	2.2	--	2.5	2	11.5	0

			Overall								Pass Rush			vs. Run					vs. Pass						
Linebackers	Age	Pos	G	Snaps	Plays	TmPct	Rk	Stop	Dfts	BTkl	Sack	Hit	Hur	Runs	St%	Rk	RuYd	Rk	Tgts	Suc%	Rk	AdjYd	Rk	PD	Int
DeMeco Ryans	30	ILB	16	1156	133	14.8%	30	59	21	5	4.0	1	2.5	69	51%	75	4.0	67	50	54%	32	6.0	23	7	2
Mychal Kendricks	24	ILB	15	991	110	13.0%	41	58	21	9	4.0	4	11	61	64%	50	3.4	45	45	40%	63	9.2	68	4	3

Year	Yards	ALY	Rk	Power	Rk	Stuff	Rk	2nd Level	Rk	Open Field	Rk	Sacks	ASR	Rk	Short	Long
2011	4.53	4.02	16	47%	3	23%	3	1.35	29	0.98	22	50	8.3%	4	22	18
2012	4.06	3.82	9	60%	16	22%	8	1.26	26	0.67	13	30	6.5%	12	7	11
2013	3.61	3.89	17	68%	21	18%	20	0.98	3	0.33	1	37	6.7%	19	16	10
2013 ALY by direction:			*Left End 4.35 (27)*			*Left Tackle 4.02 (16)*			*Mid/Guard 3.89 (13)*			*Right Tackle 4.47 (24)*			*Right End 2.67 (2)*	

Four years ago, the Eagles gave up two third-round picks and the No. 24 selection so they could move up to No. 13 and take pass-rusher Brandon Graham. Those picks only happened to become Dez Bryant, Ed Dickson, and Eric Decker. Does that make Graham's total of 11.5 sacks in four seasons feel disappointing? What if we tell you that Seattle took Earl Thomas one pick later at No. 14? By this point, Eagles fans reading this probably feel like they've been whacked in the face with a Lebanon bologna. Entering the final year of his rookie contract, Graham finds himself buried on a depth chart loaded with 3-4 outside linebackers to whom the team would rather give his snaps. Last year's starters, Connor Barwin and Trent Cole, both produced at higher levels than 2012, but didn't quite match their peak seasons. Cole's 19 Defeats more than doubled his 2012 output. Barwin tied for the league lead with eight passes batted down or tipped at the line of scrimmage and was also useful dropping into coverage; no edge rusher was charted with more pass targets (17). Add first-round pick Marcus Smith (Louisville) to the mix and the writing's on the wall for Graham, who has said his weight was an issue last year in making the switch to linebacker.

Smith arrives with less fanfare than Graham once did, but he's the only big addition to the front seven. However, perhaps even more than Lane Johnson last year, this pick comes with a "project" warning and a "reach" alert. CBS Sports wrote that Smith is "raw in terms of developing a repertoire of moves, but he has the initial burst you like to see, plays with intensity, and understands how to utilize his superb length (34-inch arms) to beat bigger blockers." Smith will battle Cole and Barwin for snaps, so it's hard to see him having a big impact in 2014. This is more of a pick for the future, but it's also one many feel could have been made in a later round. SackSEER projected Smith as a mid-second-round pick with 16.3 sacks in his first five years.

Outside linebackers are the stars in this scheme, but the defensive ends do the dirty work in setting the edge and eating up blockers. Both Fletcher Cox and Cedric Thornton impressively converted from 4-3 tackles to full-time 3-4 defensive ends. Cox, 2012's first-round pick, didn't get much glory with sacks (3.0), but he still produced 26 quarterback hurries. Thornton was strong against the run with the third-most Defeats (14) among defensive linemen on running plays. Nose tackle is another crucial position in the 3-4, but rookie Bennie Logan didn't dominate the middle after taking over as starter in the second half of the season. In the playoff loss to the Saints, Drew Brees put the game away with two quarterback sneaks up the gut on the game-winning drive. Logan should be better in year two after adding some weight, but there's virtually no competition to push him in training camp.

We haven't forgotten about inside linebacker DeMeco Ryans, but sometimes the opponent did. He was an untouched rusher on three of his four sacks and the other was a prison break no one alerted Carson Palmer about. Ryans and Mychal Kendricks are mostly there for pass coverage and run cleanup. Kendricks has had problems with finishing tackles (20 broken tackles since 2012), but he flashed some pass-rush skills with four sacks and 11 hurries.

Defensive Secondary

			Overall									vs. Run					vs. Pass									
Secondary	Age	Pos	G	Snaps	Plays	TmPct	Rk	Stop	Dfts	BTkl	Runs	St%	Rk	RuYd	Rk	Tgts	Tgt%	Rk	Dist	Suc%	Rk	AdjYd	Rk	PD	Int
Cary Williams	30	CB	16	1132	77	8.6%	44	26	8	4	11	45%	33	6.0	26	110	21.5%	47	13.4	48%	67	7.0	28	11	3
Nate Allen	27	FS	16	1096	87	9.7%	42	20	9	10	24	21%	74	7.8	54	34	6.9%	22	11.9	46%	65	5.6	15	3	1
Bradley Fletcher	28	CB	13	916	80	10.9%	10	22	9	4	7	0%	84	13.1	81	96	23.2%	60	13.1	47%	72	7.3	39	13	2
Patrick Chung*	27	SS	12	721	60	8.9%	54	13	3	7	25	28%	68	7.2	44	28	8.6%	48	14.4	58%	33	9.8	69	3	0
Brandon Boykin	24	CB	16	614	59	6.6%	67	29	17	1	5	20%	73	7.0	41	79	28.4%	85	11.4	56%	27	7.9	52	15	6
Earl Wolff	25	SS	11	524	48	7.8%	66	15	5	3	16	38%	43	7.8	55	23	9.8%	58	11.5	45%	66	9.3	63	2	1
Malcolm Jenkins	*27*	*FS*	*14*	*818*	*72*	*10.9%*	*30*	*27*	*19*	*12*	*27*	*37%*	*47*	*8.7*	*65*	*41*	*12.5%*	*70*	*10.2*	*47%*	*61*	*7.8*	*54*	*6*	*2*
Nolan Carroll	*27*	*CB*	*16*	*791*	*57*	*6.5%*	*72*	*24*	*16*	*2*	*9*	*67%*	*3*	*3.4*	*3*	*78*	*24.3%*	*69*	*15.2*	*52%*	*46*	*8.0*	*54*	*11*	*3*

Year	Pass D Rank	vs. #1 WR	Rk	vs. #2 WR	Rk	vs. Other WR	Rk	vs. TE	Rk	vs. RB	Rk
2011	11	-0.5%	12	7.9%	21	-15.2%	12	-8.2%	3	22.5%	29
2012	32	35.5%	31	11.1%	27	19.2%	27	-2.5%	16	11.0%	22
2013	25	2.6%	21	2.3%	16	12.8%	24	10.0%	24	5.8%	21

Cary Williams has a large tract of land in front of him, and he would like to invite you to visit. Williams leads all players with 303 charted targets since 2011, and he's the only cornerback to be targeted at least 90 times in each of the last three seasons. His first year in Philadelphia was no different as he led the league with 110 charted targets. He's never ranked higher than 47th in Adjusted Success Rate, but he always fares better in Adjusted Yards per Pass. But while Williams offers more cushions than Jerusalem Furniture, he does a solid job of limiting big plays and yards after the catch. Bradley Fletcher had a similar debut after four years in St. Louis. He was targeted 96 times in just 13 games. The best cornerback in Philadelphia may be 2012 fourth-round pick Brandon Boykin. Playing mostly in the slot, he led the team with six interceptions, including the division-clinching pick off Kyle Orton in Week 17. Despite playing hundreds of fewer snaps than Williams and Fletcher, Boykin had more Stops, Defeats and passes defensed. He has the ball skills and playmaking ability the rest of this secondary lacks, so it'll be hard to keep him relegated to a lesser role for much longer. Nolan Carroll comes over from Miami as a fine backup and dime option.

There are still issues at safety, which any Eagles fan clenching his Brian Dawkins jersey knows all too well. Nate Allen, returning on a one-year deal, had a poor Success Rate, but was good at Adjusted Yards per Pass. Patrick Chung was the opposite and had some tackling issues. He's been replaced by the outspoken Malcolm Jenkins from New Orleans. Jenkins quickly trashed each NFC East rival's offseason and told the media that Boykin needs to see the field more. He can be a leader in the secondary and was a defensive captain the last two years with the Saints, but Jenkins has never been a consistent playmaker. He's had 12 broken tackles in each of the last two years. He has six interceptions in 71 career games and has never played a full 16-game season. Kelly cited the former cornerback's versatility after the signing. "He can line up at either safety spot, can come in and make a tackle and can play man-to-man as well," said Kelly. In other words, Jenkins is a jack of all trades, master of none.

Special Teams

Year	DVOA	Rank	FG/XP	Rank	Net Kick	Rank	Kick Ret	Rank	Net Punt	Rank	Punt Ret	Rank	Hidden	Rank
2011	0.0%	17	3.9	9	7.5	5	-3.5	23	0.1	16	-7.9	27	1.7	14
2012	-2.2%	23	0.9	17	3.3	10	-0.5	18	-18.2	32	3.3	8	-9.1	29
2013	-2.8%	25	-2.8	24	-12.5	31	-0.9	15	5.4	10	-3.4	18	3.3	11

In a league where half the kickers convert at least 85 percent of their field goals, Alex Henery does little to stand out. He doesn't have a big leg (just 2-of-5 from 50-plus yards in his career) and he had 2013's lowest gross kickoff value (6.5 estimated points below average), though he was slightly above average in 2011 and 2012. Only seven kickoffs were returned for a touchdown last season and the Eagles were the only team to allow two. However, veteran punter Donnie Jones helped the punting unit climb from 32nd to 10th in field position value.

The return units were both average and Kelly will have options for improvement. The departed DeSean Jackson split punt-return duties with primary kick returner Damaris Johnson, but he's not a lock to resume duties. On kick returns, Brandon Boykin actually generated more return points above average (0.6) than Johnson (-1.4) on eight fewer returns. Darren Sproles could take some returns, though his return value dropped last season and he will be 31 years old. Rookie receiver Josh Huff had some kick-return experience at Oregon.

Speaking of Oregon, Kelly tried his swinging gate shenanigans with the extra-point team for a two-point conversion just once. The Chiefs easily snuffed out the direct snap in Week 3.

Pittsburgh Steelers

2013 Record: 8-8	**Total DVOA:** 0.9% (15th)	**2014 Mean Projection:** 9.0 wins	**On the Clock (0-4):** 5%
Pythagorean Wins: 8.2 (14th)	**Offense:** 4.4% (12th)	**Postseason Odds:** 53.7%	**Mediocrity (5-7):** 20%
Snap-Weighted Age: 27.1 (8th)	**Defense:** 4.0% (19th)	**Super Bowl Odds:** 7.2%	**Playoff Contender (8-10):** 48%
Average Opponent: -5.0% (30th)	**Special Teams:** 0.5% (16th)	**Proj. Avg. Opponent:** -4.0% (30th)	**Super Bowl Contender (11+):** 27%

2013: 0-4 September is just too much of a hole to climb out of.

2014: There has to be at least *one* new division champion in the AFC, right?

For 10 straight seasons, the Pittsburgh Steelers have outscored their opponents and avoided a losing record, just the eighth team in the Super Bowl era to do so. They extended this run to 10 seasons by the skin of their teeth, outscoring opponents last year by just nine points and winning their final three games to finish 8-8.

The foundation for this run of success started in 2004 with the drafting of Ben Roethlisberger and insertion of Troy Polamalu into the starting lineup. Since then each player has been the Steelers' MVP on his side of the ball. Their ad-lib style of play covers up many roster and scheme weaknesses, but their sometimes reckless nature has also led to an abundance of injuries. When they're not on the field with their unit, things look drastically different. But last year both Roethlisberger and Polamalu played 100 percent of the snaps for the first time in their careers. When the Steelers face the third-easiest schedule in the league with their two best players healthy as ever and *still* finish 8-8, someone has to be held accountable.

Pittsburgh almost never changes coaches because the Steelers are rarely down for long. This team has not had a three-year stretch without a winning record since Chuck Noll's first three years on the job (1969-71) when expectations were nonexistent. Mike Tomlin has expectations and enough talent to meet them. He can't be content with last year's 6-2 second-half finish where the losses tested the boundary lines of "a game of inches." Tomlin was fined $100,000 by the league for his shady sideline step that obstructed the path of Baltimore kick returner Jacoby Jones during a Thanksgiving game. The Steelers lost 22-20 after Emmanuel Sanders failed to haul in a two-point conversion pass. The following week against Miami, Antonio Brown took a lateral down the sideline and narrowly stepped out of bounds at the 12-yard line, denying one of the most improbable game-winning touchdowns in recent memory. In Week 17, the Chiefs could have sent Pittsburgh to the playoffs with a 41-yard field goal in San Diego, but Ryan Succop was just wide right and the officials missed a penalty on the play. A convicted murderer in Pennsylvania filed an injunction against the NFL to delay the playoffs and do a re-kick, but that's not the type of playoff expansion Roger Goodell has in mind.

The eternal optimist would cite these close calls as a sign of a team poised for improvement. After all, had the ball bounced their way just once or twice more, the Steelers would have made the playoffs. Of course, the same could be said about most 8-8 teams in the NFL, including the 2012 Steelers. In fact, Pittsburgh fans have probably been saying "if only" *a lot* over the past few years. The Steelers have had an opportunity for a game-winning drive in 14 of their last 16 losses. Over the past decade, no team has been as likely to lose close as the Steelers (Table 1). Nearly 80 percent of their losses since 2004 featured a fourth-quarter comeback and/or game-winning drive opportunity, defined as possession of the ball in a tied or one-score game in the fourth quarter/overtime. The league average is 57.7 percent. The Steelers are the only team to gain more yards than their opponents in losses and have the second-smallest margin of defeat. Only 12 times in the last decade have the Steelers been unable to fight back to a one-score margin, with the Ravens and Patriots responsible for eight of those losses (four each). While the Steelers have had seven failed fourth-quarter comebacks in each of the last two seasons, the offense had 23 drives in 2012 with an opportunity for a fourth-quarter comeback, versus just nine in 2013.When six of those nine drives required a touchdown drive of at least 78 yards, that leaves almost no margin for error.

Table 1: Most Close Losses Decided in Fourth Quarter (2004-13; Playoffs Included)

Team	Losses	Margin of Defeat (PPG)	Rk	Yds Margin	Rk	Failed 4QC/ GWD	Losses Pct.	Rk
PIT	59	-8.5	2	+5.0	1	47	79.7%	1
SD	66	-7.7	1	-30.9	6	50	75.8%	2
GB	69	-10.1	6	-21.8	3	50	72.5%	3
WAS	97	-9.9	4	-38.4	10	68	70.1%	4
DAL	76	-10.7	8	-33.8	7	49	64.5%	5
CIN	82	-11.0	10	-43.7	13	52	63.4%	6
MIN	86	-11.1	11	-37.4	9	54	62.8%	7
NE	44	-9.0	3	-30.8	5	27	61.4%	8
CHI	74	-11.8	14	-76.7	28	45	60.8%	9
PHI	76	-11.2	12	-22.1	4	46	60.5%	10
ATL	75	-12.0	16	-55.3	21	45	60.0%	11
IND	57	-12.4	22	-36.6	8	34	59.6%	12
AVG	83.3	-11.8	-	-49.0	-	47.4	57.7%	

2014 Steelers Schedule

Week	Opp.	Week	Opp.	Week	Opp.
1	CLE	7	HOU (Mon.)	13	NO
2	at BAL (Thu.)	8	IND	14	at CIN
3	at CAR	9	BAL	15	at ATL
4	TB	10	at NYJ	16	KC
5	at JAC	11	at TEN (Mon.)	17	CIN
6	at CLE	12	BYE		

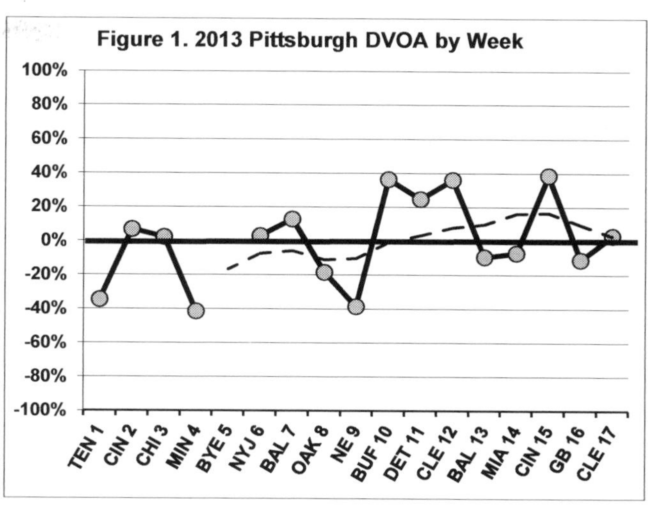

Figure 1. 2013 Pittsburgh DVOA by Week

We're used to seeing the Steelers fight admirably in defeat, but the qualities that made them a consistent winner are what they have to recapture in 2014. In the past, the roster was deep thanks to solid drafts. The team was built so that Roethlisberger didn't have to carry the offense without a running game and Polamalu didn't have to make every big play on defense. Retooling an aging machine combined with a limited return on recent drafts has created hardship on both sides of the ball. Naturally, Pittsburgh has plans to fix the problems, but it's not just a matter of developing better players. The coaching staff may have to make the biggest strides to get the Steelers back on a winning path.

Offensively, the problems still center around an offensive line that hasn't been right since the Steelers won Super Bowl XL. When the Steelers didn't have a franchise quarterback, they drafted All-Pro offensive linemen like Dermontti Dawson and Alan Faneca. Those are two examples of players who fit the mold of "draft him high and start him for a decade without any concerns" perfectly. Maurkice Pouncey and David DeCastro were supposed to be that caliber of player too, but so far neither has lived up to expectations. In June, Pouncey signed a five-year contract worth $44 million, making him the highest-paid center in the league. The Steelers obviously value him highly and he's made three Pro Bowls already, but do not be fooled here. Pouncey has never charted as an elite center and Fernando Velasco literally came off the street as a free agent to successfully replace him last season. Pouncey is a perfect case of the inability to accurately judge offensive line play due to a lack of traditional statistics, so things like draft status (first-round pick) and the fact that the Steelers have had great centers in the past play a large role in inflating his value.

A lineman can only have value if he's playing and the Steelers have had some bad luck with injuries in recent years. In addition to Pouncey and DeCastro, the Steelers spent second-round picks on Marcus Gilbert (2011) and Mike Adams (2012). The four have managed to get on the field together for a whopping eight snaps in two seasons. The Steelers spent the whole preseason hyping up their new outside zone-blocking scheme last year, then abandoned it after one run when DeCastro's cut-block ended Pouncey's season with a torn ACL. The Steelers have said they will not use cut-blocking this year with the outside zone-blocking scheme.

The Steelers essentially forced Bruce Arians out of his offensive coordinator position in 2012, much to the chagrin of Roethlisberger. Since leaving Pittsburgh, Arians was named Coach of the Year as interim boss of the 2012 Colts, then won 10 games in Arizona last season. Todd Haley was hired to revive the running game, but his two offenses have ranked 31st and 29th in rushing DVOA and the Steelers have not rushed for 1,600 yards or cracked 3.75 yards per carry in either season. During September's 0-4 start, the Steelers rushed for 232 yards, the fewest in team history through four games. It didn't help that Le'Veon Bell started the season with an injury, but the rookie rarely dazzled due in large part to the lack of continuity amongst his blockers.

If the offensive line has anything going for it, it's that no one knows if it can play well together or not because of all the injuries. Mike Munchak brings credibility as an offensive line coach and as a Hall of Fame guard himself. He returns home to Pennsylvania after spending every season since 1982 as a player or coach for the Oilers/Titans. He's one of four members on the coaching staff with experience as a NFL head coach (the others being Tomlin, Haley and Dick LeBeau). Munchak's used to coaching good lines, but he may never have had a better group of skill players to block for.

The onus still falls on Haley to utilize the pieces properly. Roethlisberger, as he has every year since 2006, wants to run more no-huddle offense this year, but that green light has to come from Haley. Their relationship has been rocky from the start, but in June Roethlisberger told 93.7 The Fan the growing period is over. "I enjoy working with him. I think we have a good relationship now. You see it on the field and you will continue to see that when we get out there because my play will be better and the play-calling will really be better." Interesting selective use of "really" aside, these two have to find common ground on the no-huddle, because it has been an effective change of pace for the offense over the years. According to the *Pittsburgh Tribune-Review*, the Steelers used the no-huddle on at least 15 plays in each of the final nine games last season—a stretch that ended with a 6-3 record. The fact that the Steelers waited until they were 2-5 and trailing the Patriots in Week 9 to indulge the no-huddle doesn't bode well for changing things up this September, but there's actual optimism this year for something different. Results usually talk.

Right before the Week 10 game against Buffalo in November, there were reports (mostly from NFL Network) that Roethlisberger wanted a trade out of Pittsburgh in the offseason. Later that week, Mike Silver used an always trustworthy "unnamed team source" for this observation of Roethlisberger:

"When he is away from the facility, he is no Peyton Manning. That is the biggest obstacle to him staying." A few days later against Detroit, Roethlisberger opened in a Manning-like no-huddle and had his most complete game under Haley. That started a stretch of more no-huddle and much improved pass protection (Table 2). The blocking in general was a joke in the first nine games when Roethlisberger was sacked 35 times, but that number dropped to seven over the last seven games. Blown blocks (rushes included), quarterback hits and pressures all decreased after the offense started utilizing more quick passes to get the ball out of Roethlisberger's hands. His average pass traveled 9.0 yards in Weeks 1-to-10, but dropped to 7.8 in the final seven weeks. This wasn't just schedule-biased either. The average defense the Steelers played ranked 16.4 in DVOA in Weeks 1-to-10 and 17.4 in Weeks 11-to-17.

Table 2. Pittsburgh's Improved Blocking in 2013

Weeks	W-L	Pass Plays	Sacks	ASR	Blown Blocks	QB Hits	Hurries
1-10	3-6	371	35*	9.8%*	77	23	95
11-17	5-2	254	7	3.4%	38	15	47

**Does not include a sack of Antonio Brown on a trick play.*

Now the big question is whether the offense that ended the season can carry over into 2014. One of the primary receivers (Martavis Bryant or Markus Wheaton) will be inexperienced, but Lance Moore is familiar with great offenses from his time in New Orleans. Heath Miller should be healthier than last year since he's not recovering from a major knee injury. Antonio Brown has proven he can be a No. 1 receiver. The offensive line will get back Pouncey, and Kelvin Beachum, who started most of the improved stretch last year, seems to have won the left tackle job from a demoted Adams. That's about as close as a team can get in keeping things constant from season to season, because as history shows, too many variables in the NFL change each year, which makes carrying over late-season improvement very difficult.

Since 1988, 26 teams cut down their sack total by at least 20 in the last seven games of the season. The 2013 Steelers (29) had the second-best improvement, trailing only the 2009 Packers (31). Like Roethlisberger, we know Aaron Rodgers takes his share of sacks. The Packers still allowed 38 sacks (6.6 percent sack rate) in 2010, but that was an improvement over the previous year and the team won the Super Bowl. Of the 26 teams in this sample, 22 of them had a sack rate under 6.5 percent in the final seven games. However, only four teams finished the following season with a sack rate under 6.5 percent. Three of those teams can attribute their improvement to a switch at quarterback late in the initial season: 1988 Chiefs (Bill Kenney to Steve DeBerg), 1993 Browns (Bernie Kosar to Vinny Testaverde) and 2004 Giants (Kurt Warner to Eli Manning). The lone team which kept the same head coach, same offensive coordinator and same starting quarterback and rode that wave of sack improvement through the next season: the 1994-95 Pittsburgh Steelers with Neil O'Donnell. Now we're not going to predict Roethlisberger grows another neckbeard and tosses two of the ugliest interceptions ever when the Steelers face the Cowboys in this year's Super Bowl,[1] but there's the precedent and it belongs to Pittsburgh.

The 1995 season was also Dick LeBeau's debut as the team's defensive coordinator and the height of the "Blitzburgh" front seven. That was when the zone-blitz scheme was still fresh and "exotic." For two decades, the Steelers were excellent at finding late-round gems and "tweeners" to replenish one of the league's best defenses: players such as Greg Lloyd (sixth round), Jason Gildon (third round), James Harrison (undrafted), Aaron Smith (fourth round), Joey Porter (third round) and Brett Keisel (seventh round). This was always a good run defense that also created pressure to help a secondary that rarely had elite talent—Rod Woodson was the only All-Pro cornerback in this era. Free agency for the Steelers often involved other teams snatching up their players, only for the backup to become the next success story.

That hasn't been happening lately, as the Steelers have been unable to find younger, capable replacements in the draft. With the advent of pass-happy spread offenses in the NFL, LeBeau's scheme looks a bit antiquated and everyone knows the defense has been "too old" for too long. The Steelers have had the oldest defense by Snap-Weighted Age for the last seven years, though that will change this season out of necessity.

In the Tomlin era, the Steelers have loaded up the front seven with first- and second-round picks. Thanks to Bill Cowher's linebacker factory, the Steelers never drafted a linebacker in the first round from 1992 through 2006. Ryan Shazier will be the third first-round linebacker in the starting lineup when he joins Jarvis Jones and Lawrence Timmons this season. The Steelers also picked up defensive end Stephon Tuitt in the second round. Ziggy Hood was once a first-round heir apparent to Aaron Smith and Brett Keisel, but he turned out to be general manager Kevin Colbert's least productive first-round pick in his first 10 drafts. If Hood was better, he would have a new deal and the Steelers could have used that 46th overall pick this year on a cornerback instead. Likewise, Jason Worilds was the replacement plan for an aging Harrison in 2010. Had he shown more flashes earlier, the Steelers probably wouldn't have drafted Jones 17th overall in 2013. They instead could have had safety Eric Reid, who went one pick later to San Francisco. In this passing era, the Steelers and Colts are the only teams not to use a first or second-round pick on a defensive back since 2007. The draft is not just about the players you take; it's the players you miss out on that hurt as well. Worilds unexpectedly made often-injured LaMarr Woodley expendable this past year, but that was not the intended plan.

Add in Mike Mitchell from Carolina to replace Ryan Clark at safety and this year's defensive plan is simple: younger and faster. Shazier's speed—yes, they have that at Ohio State—helped him climb the draft boards and he should be a Week 1 starter next to Timmons on the inside. He can cover receivers and blitz, which should allow Polamalu to return to his regular duties at strong safety. Mitchell's the only big change in the secondary, but the splash plays he had with Carolina last year are exactly what the Steelers have been missing.

Last year, the defense ranked 19th in DVOA—the lowest

---

1 And we're <u>really</u> not going to predict that the Cowboys are going to represent the NFC in the Super Bowl.

ranking for Pittsburgh going back to 1989. Even the run defense fell to 21st in DVOA, tied for the lowest ranking since 1989. Uncharacteristically, the Steelers allowed too many big runs. On the opening play of a Week 8 loss in Oakland, the Steelers allowed the longest quarterback run in NFL history when Terrelle Pryor went 93 yards on a simple zone-read keeper. But the lowest point came when Tom Brady led New England to the most points (55) and yards (610) ever allowed by the Steelers in a single game. Now, the Patriots have spent the last decade-plus exposing the holes in LeBeau's defense unlike any other offense. The use of the spread and quick, short passing game gets the Steelers out of their base defense, limits the amount of blitzes and puts more strain on a secondary that likes to give receivers a cushion. But this wasn't exactly the most explosive of recent Patriots teams.

The Patriots are one problem, but other teams with capable quarterbacks have also shredded the Pittsburgh defense. Since 2004, the standout group of Brady, Peyton Manning, Drew Brees and Aaron Rodgers has combined to throw 35 touchdowns and only six interceptions in 16 games against LeBeau's defense. When a great quarterback faces a top defense, the last thing you expect to happen is for the quarterback to produce statistics *better* than his average output. It's hard to avoid those teams if you have Super Bowl aspirations, though the Steelers did avoid New England in the playoffs for all three Super Bowl seasons. They couldn't avoid Rodgers, who shredded the defense in Super Bowl XLV without turning the ball over once.

Creating turnovers has become a huge problem for LeBeau's defense in recent seasons. The 2013 Steelers are the second team in NFL history to not register a takeaway through four games (the other: Houston in 2005). While turnover totals usually have a lot of variation from year to year, the Steelers have failed to get more than 20 takeaways in three consecutive years, joining the 2001-03 Bills and 2010-12 Dolphins as the only teams to do that since 1940. A declining pass rush is exacerbated by Polamalu being the only player in the secondary with any real ball skills. Last season, Polamalu looked more like a linebacker as the Steelers often used him in the box with a 2-3-6 dime look. The Steelers used dime on a league-high 45 percent of their snaps, making it sometimes hard to still recognize them as a 3-4 defense. The problem was their defensive DVOA in dime (5.2%) was no better than the NFL average (3.4%). If the Steelers can return to more base looks and get impact from their new additions, then LeBeau's defense should be back to being great against 75 percent of the league. On the bright side, the only top quarterback on the 2014 regular-season schedule is Brees, and that game is at home on the last day of November.

So why does our mean projection have the Steelers winning more games than last year? They still have some great players, including the best quarterback in the division. The AFC North is not loaded and we don't foresee a difficult schedule. Of course, the same elements were present last year for a potential 10-win season, but history suggests the Steelers will figure at least some of their problems out this year. Munchak should maximize the talent on the offensive line. Either Wheaton or Bryant will be the next mid-round breakout star at wide receiver. LeBeau will find ways to utilize Shazier and Mitchell. Rookie Dri Archer could be a special-teams dynamo. Roethlisberger will finally get his Red Ryder, err, no-huddle offense. This team is nowhere close to being the AFC favorite, but if they slip into the tournament, Roethlisberger is certainly the kind of quarterback who could go on a hot streak and lead a low-probability Super Bowl run to rival the 2011 Giants or 2012 Ravens. They're a flawed team and not a dominant one like they were in 2005, but in the top-heavy AFC, this is a second-level playoff-caliber squad.

However, what if things don't magically perk up this year? "The standard is the standard" as Tomlin likes to say, but standards *do change*. The Steelers have just enough to remain competitive in almost every game they play, but if the end result continues to be a team stuck in mediocrity, then it's about time for the Rooney family to make wholesale changes. That means firing Tomlin and Haley, retiring LeBeau, and replacing Colbert in the front office. The Steelers are the last organization anyone would expect that type of house cleaning from, but complacency breeds mediocrity. This is Pittsburgh. Mediocrity's only acceptable when it's the Pirates.

Scott Kacsmar

2013 Steelers Stats by Week

Wk	vs.	W-L	PF	PA	YDF	YDA	TO	Total	Off	Def	ST
1	TEN	L	9	16	194	229	-2	-35%	-40%	-11%	-5%
2	at CIN	L	10	20	278	407	-2	7%	8%	12%	11%
3	CHI	L	23	40	459	258	-5	2%	-18%	-18%	1%
4	vs. MIN	L	27	34	434	393	-2	-42%	13%	35%	-20%
5	BYE										
6	at NYJ	W	19	6	328	267	+2	3%	-6%	-11%	-2%
7	BAL	W	19	16	286	287	-1	13%	15%	18%	15%
8	at OAK	L	18	21	276	279	+1	-19%	-31%	-24%	-12%
9	at NE	L	31	55	479	610	-2	-39%	14%	57%	4%
10	BUF	W	23	10	300	227	0	36%	6%	-14%	17%
11	DET	W	37	27	398	451	+3	25%	24%	1%	2%
12	at CLE	W	27	11	302	367	+4	36%	15%	-15%	6%
13	at BAL	L	20	22	329	311	0	-9%	30%	22%	-18%
14	MIA	L	28	34	412	367	0	-7%	21%	21%	-7%
15	CIN	W	30	20	290	279	0	39%	12%	-5%	21%
16	at GB	W	38	31	343	370	0	-11%	-2%	4%	-5%
17	CLE	W	20	7	292	293	0	3%	-9%	-12%	0%

Trends and Splits

	Offense	Rank	Defense	Rank
Total DVOA	4.4%	12	4.0%	19
Unadjusted VOA	4.4%	13	-0.7%	17
Weighted Trend	9.1%	8	3.8%	20
Variance	3.8%	4	4.9%	15
Average Opponent	0.5%	19	-5.2%	32
Passing	23.5%	9	8.1%	19
Rushing	-14.9%	29	-1.0%	21
First Down	5.8%	11	6.8%	23
Second Down	7.5%	12	3.1%	17
Third Down	-3.5%	17	0.7%	19
First Half	2.4%	14	9.5%	28
Second Half	6.4%	11	-1.3%	16
Red Zone	2.0%	16	1.9%	18
Late and Close	14.0%	9	4.1%	21

Five-Year Performance

Year	W-L	Pyth W	Est W	PF	PA	TO	Total	Rk	Off	Rk	Def	Rk	ST	Rk	Off AGL	Rk	Def AGL	Rk	Off Age	Rk	Def Age	Rk	ST Age	Rk
2009	9-7	9.2	10.0	368	324	-3	14.2%	10	14.4%	7	-4.6%	9	-4.8%	30	23.9	16	29.2	17	27.0	19	29.4	1	26.6	16
2010	12-4	12.1	12.1	375	232	+17	35.4%	2	14.3%	5	-20.7%	1	0.4%	16	32.0	22	17.9	12	27.0	22	29.2	1	26.7	12
2011	12-4	11.1	11.3	325	227	-13	22.6%	4	11.4%	6	-9.4%	7	1.7%	9	33.2	19	27.3	18	26.4	25	29.1	1	26.2	19
2012	8-8	8.7	7.4	336	314	-10	-1.2%	18	-4.0%	19	-2.9%	13	-0.1%	17	64.3	31	19.1	9	26.5	21	29.2	1	25.9	20
2013	8-8	8.2	8.3	379	370	-4	0.9%	15	4.4%	12	4.0%	19	0.5%	16	55.8	29	27.7	14	26.4	25	28.4	1	25.7	25

2013 Performance Based on Most Common Personnel Groups

PIT Offense					PIT Offense vs. Opponents				PIT Defense				PIT Defense vs. Opponents			
Pers	Freq	Yds	DVOA	Run%	Pers	Freq	Yds	DVOA	Pers	Freq	Yds	DVOA	Pers	Freq	Yds	DVOA
11	59%	5.8	15.5%	23%	Nickel Even	50%	5.9	14.7%	3-4-4	40%	5.2	3.8%	11	55%	5.8	10.7%
12	17%	5.7	-7.6%	49%	3-4-4	19%	4.5	3.8%	Dime+	45%	5.7	5.2%	12	20%	5.0	-0.5%
21	5%	5.7	22.5%	40%	4-3-4	15%	4.6	-21.6%	Nickel Even	9%	5.7	14.3%	21	9%	6.1	15.2%
22	5%	4.0	2.2%	73%	Nickel Odd	9%	7.0	41.5%	Nickel Odd	3%	4.8	4.2%	22	5%	3.7	-3.1%
621	4%	3.8	0.8%	72%	Dime+	5%	4.8	9.7%	Goal Line	1%	0.7	3.3%	13	5%	4.4	-14.2%
611	3%	4.0	-3.7%	72%												

Strategic Tendencies

Run/Pass		Rk	Formation		Rk	Pass Rush		Rk	Secondary		Rk	Strategy		Rk
Runs, first half	40%	13	Form: Single Back	81%	6	Rush 3	10.0%	4	4 DB	40%	14	Play action	13%	27
Runs, first down	42%	28	Form: Empty Back	11%	6	Rush 4	57.8%	24	5 DB	13%	31	Avg Box (Off)	6.35	18
Runs, second-long	31%	21	Pers: 3+ WR	61%	9	Rush 5	28.3%	8	6+ DB	45%	1	Avg Box (Def)	6.39	15
Runs, power sit.	63%	7	Pers: 4+ WR	1%	15	Rush 6+	3.9%	31	CB by Sides	57%	27	Offensive Pace	32.31	32
Runs, behind 2H	22%	28	Pers: 2+ TE/6+ OL	33%	15	Sacks by LB	50.0%	11	DB Blitz	13%	12	Defensive Pace	28.81	5
Pass, ahead 2H	49%	13	Shotgun/Pistol	56%	19	Sacks by DB	8.8%	17	Hole in Zone	9%	22	Go for it on 4th	0.75	22

Injuries in the front seven had the Steelers using six defensive backs to a ridiculous extent; they used dime defense *20 times* more often than they had in 2012. For the second straight year, the Steelers' pass rush got much stronger on third and fourth down. The Steelers had 3.9 percent Adjusted Sack Rate on first down (31st) and 4.4 percent ASR on second down (32nd) but 10.6 percent ASR on third and fourth down (fourth in the NFL). For some reason, nobody wants to run a draw play against the Steelers. They've faced only 34 running back draws over the last three seasons combined, even though they've allowed at least 6.0 yards per carry on draws each season. The Steelers led the league in wide receiver screens, though they were only average on these plays. Pittsburgh was one of six teams to use empty backfields on at least 10 percent of plays, and they gained 6.8 yards per play with 39.2% DVOA.

Passing

Player	DYAR	DVOA	Plays	NtYds	Avg	YAC	C%	TD	Int
B.Roethlisberger	724	6.6%	621	3981	6.4	5.4	64.9%	28	14

Rushing

Player	DYAR	DVOA	Plays	Yds	Avg	TD	Fum	Suc
Player	DYAR	DVOA	Plays	Yds	Avg	TD	Fum	Suc
L.Bell	17	-7.0%	244	860	3.5	8	1	47%
J.Dwyer*	-25	-18.7%	49	197	4.0	0	0	47%
F.Jones*	-9	-13.4%	48	184	3.8	0	1	40%
B.Roethlisberger	-26	-41.5%	17	110	6.5	1	3	-
I.Redman*	-46	-132.3%	10	13	1.3	0	1	10%
L.Stephens-Howling*	-6	-40.5%	6	19	3.2	0	0	33%
A.Brown	1	-35.8%	6	3	0.5	0	0	-
L.Blount	*117*	*9.4%*	*153*	*776*	*5.1*	*7*	*3*	*54%*

Receiving

Player	DYAR	DVOA	Plays	Ctch	Yds	Y/C	YAC	TD	C%
A.Brown	361	15.0%	167	111	1444	13.0	5.2	8	66%
E.Sanders*	22	-10.2%	113	68	740	10.9	4.4	6	60%
J.Cotchery*	235	26.2%	76	46	607	13.2	4.7	10	61%
M.Wheaton	-18	-30.5%	13	6	64	10.7	6.0	0	46%
D.Moye	-1	-14.8%	6	2	20	10.0	0.5	1	33%
D.Heyward-Bey	-63	-24.5%	64	29	309	10.7	4.5	1	45%
L.Moore	*150*	*22.1%*	*54*	*37*	*457*	*12.4*	*1.8*	*2*	*69%*
H.Miller	23	-2.8%	78	58	593	10.2	3.9	1	74%
D.Paulson	-15	-28.9%	10	6	102	17.0	5.7	0	60%
D.Johnson	18	41.8%	6	4	70	17.5	7.8	0	67%
L.Bell	28	-5.9%	65	44	408	9.3	10.0	0	68%
F.Jones*	0	-14.3%	13	9	63	7.0	4.8	0	69%
W.Johnson	15	5.9%	11	8	41	5.1	4.6	1	73%
J.Dwyer*	12	8.5%	11	8	64	8.0	6.4	0	73%

Offensive Line

Player	Pos	Age	GS	Snaps	Pen	Sk	Pass	Run	Player	Pos	Age	GS	Snaps	Pen	Sk	Pass	Run
Marcus Gilbert	RT	26	16/16	950	8	5.0	18.5	6.0	Fernando Velasco*	C	29	11/11	748	1	1.5	11.0	1.0
David DeCastro	RG	24	15/15	948	2	2.0	16.5	2.0	Mike Adams	OT	24	10/5	480	2	3.5	20.5	3.0
Ramon Foster	LG	28	15/15	842	2	1.0	9.0	1.0	Cody Wallace	C	30	9/4	288	3	0.5	0.5	2.0
Kelvin Beachum	LT	25	14/11	828	4	7.3	20.8	6.0	Guy Whimper	OT	31	10/2	265	2	2.3	4.3	4.0

Year	Yards	ALY	Rk	Power	Rk	Stuff	Rk	2nd Lev	Rk	Open Field	Rk	Sacks	ASR	Rk	Short	Long	F-Start	Cont.
2011	4.49	4.44	3	57%	24	21%	23	1.32	6	0.82	16	42	7.2%	20	17	19	18	22
2012	3.71	3.72	27	61%	19	19%	17	0.95	30	0.54	24	37	6.3%	15	12	18	13	26
2013	3.57	3.79	22	60%	21	21%	24	0.94	29	0.39	29	43	7.3%	15	13	15	11	27

2013 ALY by direction: Left End 4.69 (5) Left Tackle 3.19 (30) Mid/Guard 3.82 (18) Right Tackle 3.96 (16) Right End 3.53 (19)

After going through years of stop-gaps (Sean Mahan) and signing players no other team wanted (Jonathan Scott), the Steelers finally began rebuilding the line with high draft picks. Now they continue to wait for better results than underachievement and injuries. The Steelers have not started the same offensive line combination in more than five consecutive games since 2010.

Maurkice Pouncey was the literal centerpiece, drafted in the first round in 2010, but he did not survive the first drive of the 2013 season before tearing his ACL. While most offenses would consider the loss of a three-time Pro Bowl center a huge blow, Pouncey's been very replaceable in his career, whether it was by Doug Legursky in the past or last year by Fernando Velasco, a street free agent who wasn't even signed until Pouncey went down. In 2012, Pouncey averaged a blown block every 54.6 snaps (worst among centers with at least 500 snaps). Velasco went 62.3 snaps per blown block last year before he too suffered a season-ending injury (Achilles tendon). Cody Wallace finished the season at center and he only had 2.5 blown blocks on 288 snaps. Whether the Steelers bring back Velasco, who averaged 124.6 snaps per blown block with Mike Munchak in Tennessee in 2012, or stick with Wallace as the main reserve, they'll be just fine should Pouncey suffer an injury for the fifth consecutive season.

Marcus Gilbert was just the second Pittsburgh offensive lineman over the past three seasons to start all 16 games at the same position. When he's not falling into his teammates' legs and causing serious injuries, he approaches the level of mediocre starter. David DeCastro was healthy in 2013 after an injury slowed his rookie development, but he hasn't quite lived up to the lofty expectations that came with his first-round pick status. With his talent he's likely to make the biggest leap forward after working with Munchak, who has been focusing his players on technique this offseason. "What he knows about the game, the little stuff (he shows his players) in technique, I can't speak enough to him," DeCastro told the *Pittsburgh Tribune-Review* of Munchak.

It would be almost impossible for Mike Adams to have a worse year than 2013 when he was stabbed in the offseason and benched after a poor start. He did get to see the field when the Steelers used a sixth lineman, but Kelvin Beachum looks to be the favorite at left tackle. Beachum would be the fourth different Week 1 starter at left tackle for the Steelers in the last four seasons. Veteran guard Ramon Foster is another cap-friendly starter with experience on both the left and right sides. Guy Whimper can play at any guard or tackle position, but he's a backup with easily the worst name in the league for an offensive lineman.

Defensive Front Seven

			Overall								vs. Run					Pass Rush			
Defensive Line	**Age**	**Pos**	**G**	**Snaps**	**Plays**	**TmPct**	**Rk**	**Stop**	**Dfts**	**BTkl**	**Runs**	**St%**	**Rk**	**RuYd**	**Rk**	**Sack**	**Hit**	**Hur**	**Tips**
Cameron Heyward	25	DE	16	828	65	8.2%	7	43	19	3	43	65%	75	3.7	82	5.0	5	17.0	6
Ziggy Hood*	27	DE	16	633	39	4.9%	46	32	6	2	30	80%	34	2.6	59	3.0	1	4.5	0
Brett Keisel*	36	DE	12	564	30	5.0%	41	22	9	1	22	68%	70	2.5	58	4.0	3	7.5	1
Steve McLendon	28	DT	14	350	33	4.8%	--	25	4	0	32	75%	--	3.0	--	0.0	1	5.5	0
Cam Thomas	*28*	*DT*	*16*	*473*	*25*	*3.2%*	*77*	*18*	*5*	*5*	*22*	*68%*	*70*	*1.5*	*18*	*0.0*	*0*	*5.0*	*1*

			Overall								vs. Run					Pass Rush			
Edge Rushers	**Age**	**Pos**	**G**	**Snaps**	**Plays**	**TmPct**	**Rk**	**Stop**	**Dfts**	**BTkl**	**Runs**	**St%**	**Rk**	**RuYd**	**Rk**	**Sack**	**Hit**	**Hur**	**Tips**
Jason Worilds	26	OLB	15	771	54	7.3%	15	43	11	3	42	76%	38	2.7	48	8.0	17	25.5	0
Jarvis Jones	25	OLB	14	631	40	5.8%	35	24	7	1	27	59%	70	3.7	68	1.0	2	8.0	3
LaMarr Woodley*	30	OLB	11	574	37	6.8%	20	24	8	2	26	58%	71	3.8	69	5.0	7	12.0	1

			Overall								Pass Rush			vs. Run					vs. Pass						
Linebackers	**Age**	**Pos**	**G**	**Snaps**	**Plays**	**TmPct**	**Rk**	**Stop**	**Dfts**	**BTkl**	**Sack**	**Hit**	**Hur**	**Runs**	**St%**	**Rk**	**RuYd**	**Rk**	**Tgts**	**Suc%**	**Rk**	**AdjYd**	**Rk**	**PD**	**Int**
Lawrence Timmons	28	ILB	16	1070	130	16.4%	17	86	20	7	3.0	3	6	75	77%	9	2.5	15	47	54%	31	5.9	21	5	2
Vince Williams	25	ILB	15	398	53	7.1%	--	29	7	3	0.0	0	0.5	39	62%	--	3.1	--	7	36%	--	5.7	--	0	0
Arthur Moats	*26*	*OLB*	*16*	*293*	*48*	*5.6%*	*--*	*27*	*7*	*1*	*0.0*	*1*	*1*	*36*	*69%*	*--*	*2.3*	*--*	*8*	*21%*	*--*	*11.3*	*--*	*0*	*0*

Year	Yards	ALY	Rk	Power	Rk	Stuff	Rk	2nd Level	Rk	Open Field	Rk	Sacks	ASR	Rk	Short	Long
2011	3.91	4.00	15	62%	15	18%	22	1.04	5	0.55	6	35	6.8%	14	16	14
2012	3.78	3.89	13	66%	22	19%	14	1.03	4	0.47	5	37	6.7%	11	11	15
2013	4.07	4.16	24	65%	16	15%	30	0.98	4	0.60	15	34	6.1%	27	6	16
2013 ALY by direction:			*Left End 3.98 (23)*			*Left Tackle 4.90 (30)*			*Mid/Guard 3.94 (17)*			*Right Tackle 4.27 (22)*			*Right End 4.68 (31)*	

Last year in this space we wrote how nose tackle Steve McClendon was an important player no one was talking about. The Steelers then gave us few reasons to talk about McClendon or *any* defensive tackle on the roster due to personnel usage that so often used just two defensive ends on the line. McClendon's in better shape than predecessor Casey Hampton ever was, but he played roughly 125 fewer snaps than what Hampton averaged in his final five seasons. With reserve Al Woods off to Tennessee, Cam Thomas was signed in March; he lost his starting job in San Diego late last season. There's no indication that Dick LeBeau's defense is seeking a stronger commitment to the nose tackle position. Defensive end is also going through a transition period with the departure of 2009 first-round pick Ziggy Hood. His 2013 was more productive than past seasons, but he never impressed enough to earn a second contract. Part of Hood's difficulty adapting to the NFL was his inability to unseat veteran Brett Keisel (110 career starts). At age 36, Keisel can still stop the run and grow the best beard in football, but this offseason has seen an emphasis on Pittsburgh getting younger and faster, so he remains a free agent.

Cameron Heyward was elevated to a starting position in his third season and he delivered. The only remaining question is which inexperienced player will man the other end. Nick Williams was a seventh-round pick in 2013, but missed his entire rookie season due to a knee injury. Thomas is a possibility, as the Steelers have discussed moving him over from the nose. But the favorite should be second-round rookie Stephon Tuitt. No rookie defensive lineman has started a season opener for Pittsburgh since defensive line coach John Mitchell took over in 1994, but Tuitt is versatile and a perfect body fit for the five-technique. He had 20.5 sacks in 28 career starts at Notre Dame, and we know those service academies rarely throw the football!

The Steelers have sure spent enough on the linebacker corps, so it needs to be the main attraction in 2014. Lawrence Timmons and rookie Ryan Shazier can both claim they were the 15th pick in the draft, expected to shine at inside linebacker in a 3-4 defense. Normally it's the outside guys who rush the passer that get the big bucks and fame, but these are athletic playmakers capable of playing the run and pass on every down. With LaMarr Woodley off to Oakland after another injury-plagued year, youngsters Jarvis Jones and Jason Worilds will hope to become the pass-rushing duo Woodley and James Harrison were for past Pittsburgh defenses. Flashes from Jones were infrequent as a rookie, but he can look no further than at Worilds for encouragement, because Worilds took four years to make a considerable impact in this defense. Worilds had 25.5 quarterback hurries last season, but 23.5 of them came in Weeks 10-17. If he sustained that pace for a whole season, he would have led the league in creating pressure. Worilds is scheduled to make $9.75 million on the transition tag this year before becoming a free agent in 2015, so the Steelers are in a pickle: do they work out a long-term deal based on half a season of outstanding production or risk losing him after a big 2014 season? Chris Carter will battle veteran Arthur Moats, best known for ending Brett Favre's consecutive starts streak, for a top reserve role.

Defensive Secondary

			Overall								vs. Run					vs. Pass									
Secondary	**Age**	**Pos**	**G**	**Snaps**	**Plays**	**TmPct**	**Rk**	**Stop**	**Dfts**	**BTkl**	**Runs**	**St%**	**Rk**	**RuYd**	**Rk**	**Tgts**	**Tgt%**	**Rk**	**Dist**	**Suc%**	**Rk**	**AdjYd**	**Rk**	**PD**	**Int**
Troy Polamalu	33	SS	16	1070	80	10.1%	36	42	21	4	38	50%	21	6.0	21	35	7.8%	35	10.9	69%	4	4.4	9	9	2
Ryan Clark*	35	FS	16	1061	108	13.6%	7	34	9	9	66	45%	28	5.7	17	21	4.6%	4	15.8	46%	63	8.6	59	3	2
Ike Taylor	34	CB	16	1045	74	9.3%	26	24	10	9	7	57%	14	11.1	75	109	24.6%	72	12.7	43%	80	8.9	71	8	0
William Gay	29	CB	16	910	72	9.1%	31	34	19	6	19	58%	13	5.8	24	82	21.4%	46	11.9	58%	14	5.8	2	11	1
Cortez Allen	26	CB	14	701	62	8.9%	33	22	8	7	10	30%	65	6.8	38	76	25.6%	77	12.5	52%	47	7.3	37	12	2
Will Allen	32	FS	17	532	44	4.8%	76	16	7	4	12	67%	2	3.2	2	29	12.7%	71	13.6	49%	55	9.6	66	4	2
Shamarko Thomas	23	SS	14	189	22	3.2%	--	9	3	2	7	57%	--	6.0	--	16	19.5%	--	8.8	38%	--	8.6	--	0	0
Mike Mitchell	*27*	*SS*	*15*	*899*	*73*	*9.8%*	*41*	*30*	*13*	*12*	*26*	*38%*	*40*	*9.1*	*66*	*28*	*7.1%*	*26*	*15.5*	*61%*	*28*	*5.8*	*17*	*7*	*4*
Brice McCain	*28*	*CB*	*16*	*605*	*35*	*4.5%*	*87*	*15*	*9*	*6*	*7*	*29%*	*67*	*19.3*	*85*	*59*	*25.1%*	*74*	*10.8*	*51%*	*54*	*6.2*	*9*	*6*	*1*

Year	Pass D Rank	vs. #1 WR	Rk	vs. #2 WR	Rk	vs. Other WR	Rk	vs. TE	Rk	vs. RB	Rk
2011	3	-5.5%	8	-9.9%	10	-0.8%	20	-6.9%	4	-5.1%	14
2012	15	-30.1%	3	-1.8%	16	0.5%	17	23.4%	31	4.5%	20
2013	19	23.9%	29	0.6%	15	-24.2%	4	-0.5%	14	-15.2%	5

With only ten interceptions, the 2013 Steelers tied the franchise record for fewest picks in a 16-game season. They tied the 2012 Steelers, who broke the record of 11 set by the 2011 and 2007 teams. See the trend? Interceptions usually have a good amount of variation from season to season, but the Steelers have struggled to get more than a dozen in five of the last seven seasons. The other two seasons, 2008 and 2010, were Super Bowl years, but Troy Polamalu had seven picks himself in both years. Big plays can't just be about one player.

For better or worse, most of this unit remains intact from last season. The biggest change is Carolina's Mike Mitchell replacing Ryan Clark after eight years of big hits and doing his best to cover up for a roaming Polamalu. This makes the Steelers eight years younger at the position and gives them a reliable starter should they play in Denver again. It also makes them faster, as Mitchell's first claim to fame was fulfilling Al Davis' speed fetish in the second round of the 2009 draft despite NFL Network's Mike Mayock having a seventh-round grade on him. In Carolina last year, Mitchell had four interceptions (Clark's best season was three) and made several other splash plays. He has no track record of sustaining 2013's level of play, but for a defense that's been dying for takeaways and big plays, Mitchell was a fine signing. Polamalu and Timmons were the only Steelers to play every defensive snap in 2013; given his age (33) and injury history, Polamalu is unlikely to do that again in 2014. Fortunately, the Steelers have veteran Will Allen and intriguing sophomore Shamarko Thomas, who could be a natural replacement as the secondary's "freelance guesser."

The three-man band at cornerback returns—we'd call them "The Dirty Three" if it wasn't already taken—with a 34-year-old Ike Taylor still holding onto his No. 1 spot. Of course, those hands are still not holding onto many interceptions. It's often difficult to judge if it's Taylor or LeBeau's scheme that's the problem, but there were too many lapses in 2013 where his receiver was wide open for big plays. Teams knew it too; we charted 109 targets for Taylor, second only to Philadelphia's Cary Williams (110). Taylor told Jim Rome this summer he was "pissed" about taking a $4.25 million pay cut to play this year, but we like to think of this as a rare example of performance-based pay.

Losing Keenan Lewis to New Orleans a year ago was supposed to be a curse and blessing for the Steelers. On one hand, they lost a potential long-term starter at corner, but his absence opened the door for Cortez Allen in his third season. Allen was supposed to be ascending to Taylor's job, but he couldn't even surpass William Gay, who is a fan of allowing a 10-yard cushion no matter if it's first-and-10 or third-and-3. At least Gay's improved from his early days and based on the charting he was easily Pittsburgh's best corner in 2013. Adding a nickel corner like Houston's Brice McCain (he allowed eight touchdowns in the red zone in 2013) or drafting Arizona's Shaquille Richardson (perfect name for an Orlando Magic player) in the fifth round is unlikely to make a dent on the cornerback depth chart.

Special Teams

Year	DVOA	Rank	FG/XP	Rank	Net Kick	Rank	Kick Ret	Rank	Net Punt	Rank	Punt Ret	Rank	Hidden	Rank
2011	1.7%	9	-7.3	29	8.0	4	-1.1	19	4.5	10	4.6	8	-9.0	28
2012	-0.1%	17	6.8	6	-1.8	21	5.6	7	-6.3	23	-4.8	25	-9.4	30
2013	0.5%	16	2.4	13	-1.5	22	1.0	11	-11.1	28	11.8	4	-6.0	24

For the Steelers to neglect a need at cornerback and use the 97th pick in the 2014 draft on tiny ball of speed Dri Archer, there must be a plan to use him on special teams. Archer only had two kick returns at Kent State last year, but he still returned one for a touchdown (one of four scores in his career). This could be the deluxe version of Stefan Logan from a few years ago. The Steelers primarily used Felix Jones and Emmanuel Sanders on kick returns last year, but both have departed. Antonio Brown will likely continue pulling double duty as primary receiver and punt returner. He does both very well, but the Steelers may want to look at Archer here to conserve some energy for Brown.

Shaun Suisham hopes to continue his career renaissance in Pittsburgh, converting on 87.2 percent of his field goals the last four years. He's only four-of-13 from 50-plus yards in his career, but it's not like many long field goals are even attempted at Heinz Field. His limited range does hurt on kickoffs, where he ranked next to last in gross kickoff value.

The biggest problem with last year's special teams was the punters. Punters Zoltan Mesko and Mat McBriar both ranked in the bottom seven in gross punting value and both are gone. This year's competition is between veteran Adam Podlesh, formerly of the Bears and Jaguars, and Brad Wing, an LSU standout with no NFL experience. Wing would cost half as much in salary, so that just about solves that battle.

San Diego Chargers

2013 Record: 9-7	**Total DVOA:** 6.4% (12th)	**2014 Mean Projection:** 9.4 wins	**On the Clock (0-4):** 4%
Pythagorean Wins: 9.2 (12th)	**Offense:** 23.1% (2nd)	**Postseason Odds:** 62.0%	**Mediocrity (5-7):** 15%
Snap-Weighted Age: 26.6 (21st)	**Defense:** 17.5% (32nd)	**Super Bowl Odds:** 11.4%	**Playoff Contender (8-10):** 48%
Average Opponent: -3.6% (26th)	**Special Teams:** 0.8% (15th)	**Proj. Avg. Opponent:** 0.3% (19th)	**Super Bowl Contender (11+):** 34%

2013: The resurrection of Philip Rivers.

2014: The offense will stay strong; the Broncos will stay stronger.

The primary question regarding the San Diego Chargers coming into the 2013 season seemed to be whether Philip Rivers was "fixable," or whether his window as an elite player had closed. In 2011 and 2012, Rivers had produced his two worst seasons in years from a statistical perspective, dropping from second to seventh in DYAR in 2011, and from seventh to 22nd in 2012. Rivers has always been an idiosyncratic quarterback with some mechanical limitations, and his odd three-quarters delivery is hardly the delight of those who study such things. Add in former head coach Norv Turner's justified reputation as a quarterback redeemer and maintenance man, and it was hard for some to place the blame for Rivers' decline on anyone but Rivers. But Turner's limitations as a designer of offensive schemes, combined with an attrition of personnel that can be laid at the feet of former general manager A.J. Smith, were the real reasons. And anyone who thought Rivers was on the wrong side of done got a quick education in the truth when, with new head coach Mike McCoy and general manager Tom Telesco at the helm, he finished second in DYAR to Peyton Manning and third in DVOA to Manning and Nick Foles.

McCoy's genius when it comes to quarterbacks is seemingly simple in concept, but rare in actual execution to the degree that he does it. Instead of molding his throwers to a book, McCoy takes the player he has, and molds the offense and playbook to that quarterback's strengths while moving plays away from his weaknesses. With Tim Tebow, McCoy relied not only on heavy option, but formations that kept Tebow's first read open as much as possible. Anything else was too much for Tebow's rudimentary understanding of NFL offenses, and would have taxed him beyond his limitations. With Rivers, McCoy relied far more on three- and five-step drops, understanding that he had a quarterback who is not at all mobile behind an offensive line that was very much under construction. The Chargers also saw a serious uptick in shotgun formations and shotgun effectiveness under McCoy—from 54.2 percent shotgun (ninth most in the NFL) and a 2.6% DVOA (19th) in 2012 to a 73.5 percent shotgun and a 29.2% DVOA in 2013, both good for third in the league.

Just as important to the best season Rivers enjoyed in years was the performance of offensive coordinator Ken Whisenhunt, the former Steelers offensive coordinator and Cardinals head coach whom both Rivers and McCoy endorsed without hesitation when the time came for Whisenhunt to leave and become a head coach again—this time, with the Tennessee Titans. On tape, it was clear that Whisenhunt's long-held preference for trips and bunch concepts created separation for Rivers' receivers in ways that Turner's three-vert paradigms simply did not. Rivers specifically cited Whisenhunt's steadiness and consistency, and McCoy said that it was no surprise that he would have to find a replacement sooner than later.

He didn't have to look far. Frank Reich, the third member of the Philip Rivers Rehabilitation Project as the team's quarterbacks coach in 2013, replaced Whisenhunt and immediately pointed to tempo as a primary component of his offensive philosophy. That led some to assume that Reich, who called plays as Jim Kelly's backup for years in Buffalo's "K-Gun" offense, would be going hurry-up all the time.

Not so, according to the source.

"In that offense, the quarterbacks called their own plays," Reich said of the no-huddle in his first press conference from his new position. "Things are a little bit more sophisticated now as far as what offenses do, but there's some strong experience that will help me."

Certainly, there are few quarterbacks who prepare more thoroughly than Rivers, which would seem to make this a fairly natural fit.

"When Philip Rivers steps out onto the field, he's the smartest person on the field," Reich said. "He's got great processing speed, and he's got a big capacity. It would be foolish not to use every ounce of that."

Ideally, as Reich has said, it will be about a mixture of tempo with crisp execution, which ties to the McCoy dogma, and further separates Rivers from the travails of the Norv downside.

In addition, Rivers had a new key target for the first time in years: rookie Keenan Allen, a steal out of Cal in the third round of the 2013 draft. Downgraded because of a knee injury and less than optimal field speed, Allen proved to be a highly valuable target who produced particularly well on third down (41 targets, 11.8 yards per pass, a 45.5% DVOA, and a 68 percent catch rate). He set the team's rookie receptions record with 71, and gained 1,046 yards and scored eight touchdowns in the regular season, adding eight catches for 163 yards and two touchdowns in San Diego's two postseason games.

In his first season with the Chargers, do-it-all back Danny Woodhead proved to be nearly as valuable as all those an-

2014 Chargers Schedule

Week	Opp.	Week	Opp.	Week	Opp.
1	at ARI (Mon.)	7	KC	13	at BAL
2	SEA	8	at DEN (Thu.)	14	NE
3	at BUF	9	at MIA	15	DEN
4	JAC	10	BYE	16	at SF (Sat.)
5	NYJ	11	OAK	17	at KC
6	at OAK	12	STL		

nouncers who perpetuate a man-crush on this "gritty little guy" always insist that he is. He posted high DVOA numbers in rushing and receiving on every down, with the exception of third-down rushing. For that particular specialty, there was Ryan Mathews, who put together his best NFL season after three years of relative disappointment since the Chargers took him in the first round of the 2010 draft. And Ladarius Green, the third-year tight end from Louisiana-Lafayette, is expected to take his impressive athleticism to another level in the new season. San Diego put two tight ends on the field 38 percent of the time, and having both Green and Antonio Gates on the field adds more security to Rivers' arsenal.

Put a smart, talented quarterback on the field with a coaching staff willing to tailor the game to his attributes and better talent around him, and a renaissance season is the result. No surprise there. Instead, the surprise of the 2013 Chargers' season was that their defense fell off so spectacularly from the previous year's league-average performance, and that the team made the postseason nonetheless. In John Pagano's second season as defensive coordinator, any improvements seen in 2012 were cast aside. From the defensive front to the secondary, just about everything regressed.

The secondary was the most obvious issue. As Andy Benoit observed in *Football Outsiders Almanac 2013*, former San Diego cornerbacks Quentin Jammer and Antoine Cason struggled to play tight coverage, limiting what Pagano could do with his blitzes. So, the Chargers jettisoned Jammer and Cason, promoting Shareece Wright and signing ex-Jaguar Derek Cox in their places. As a disappointment, Cox ran somewhere between *Godfather III* and sales of the Wii U. He started the first 11 games of the season, but was benched in three of the last four games, and had to be replaced by Richard Marshall and Crezdon Butler. *Crezdon Butler?* Yeah, that's kind of the point. The Chargers released Cox after just the one year, accepting a \$3.9 million dead-money hit to have him not play cornerback for them anymore. Marshall was a reasonably acceptable fill-in, though most of his trail speed is gone. So, the pressure was on Wright to deal with most opposing No. 1 receivers, which is a tall task for a guy who had never started a game before the 2013 season.

It was expected that Wright would be the No. 1 corner when the 2014 season started until a lovely bit of good fortune jumped in the Chargers' collective lap, by way of a division rival. The Chiefs released Brandon Flowers on June 13, and San Diego signed the veteran cornerback 11 days later to a one-year deal worth up to \$5 million. Flowers had his worst season in 2013 (despite making the Pro Bowl), but that was

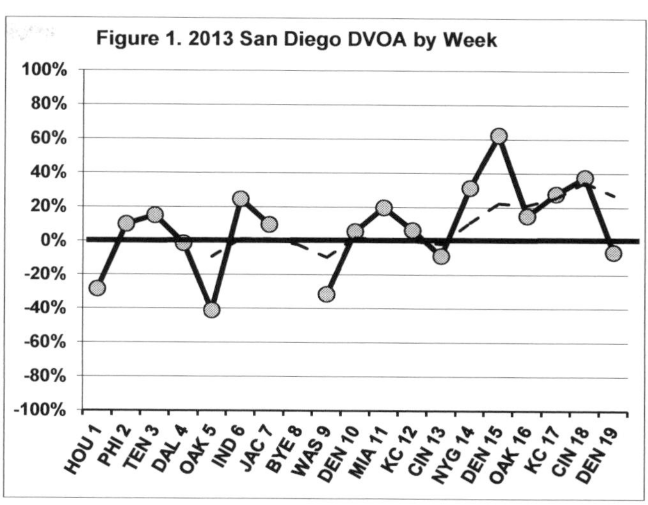

Figure 1. 2013 San Diego DVOA by Week

in part because new Chiefs defensive coordinator Bob Sutton gave Flowers a lot of time in the slot, preferring bigger cornerbacks outside. As an outside defender, Flowers still has something in the tank—and he immediately becomes the team's best player at that position.

Wright can become a good cornerback over time—he plays press pretty well, but he's not consistent with his footwork and will occasionally look fairly disastrous when dealing with more complex routes. The Chargers hope that TCU's Jason Verrett, the team's first-round pick, will be ready to start on the outside soon. But with Flowers and Wright in the equation, Verrett might start his NFL career in the slot. First, Verrett has to recover from surgery to repair a torn labrum, which puts him behind the curve in the process.

The trio of Flowers, Wright, and Verrett puts San Diego on the opposite end of the trend that has NFL teams looking for bigger cornerbacks. Flowers is 5-foot-9 and weighs 187 pounds, Wright stands 5-foot-11 and weighs 182 pounds, and Verrett measured 5-foot 10 and 189 at the scouting combine. That's not a liability in and of itself, but it does put more pressure on these players to stay sticky in coverage without a physical presence. Verrett did display that in his college tape—he's a mini-Richard Sherman in some ways—but facing 6-foot-5 receivers who run 4.4 40s and understand advanced route concepts is a different beast entirely.

The defensive problems continued in the front seven, where inside linebacker Donald Butler was the only consistent factor. Next to Butler, rookie Manti Te'o played through the season with a foot injury that cost him his first three regular-season games, and he proved to be pretty much the same player he was at Notre Dame—an instinctive asset in pass coverage, and an occasional liability against the run. He struggled specifically with motion plays that required advanced diagnosis, and he's never been particularly stout in power situations, but Te'o has vowed to be better in 2014.

"I'm really focused on fine-tuning my skills, getting all the little things right and making sure I am getting better," he told the team's official site in May. "But yeah, one year has made a whole lot of difference. I'm a lot calmer now and a lot more confident."

Realistically, confidence is tough to find when analyzing the front five. Ideally, the Chargers would have had Dwight Freeney and Melvin Ingram as their primary outside pass-rushing linebackers, but each player missed serious time with injuries. In their stead, Jarrett Johnson was better than serviceable, while Larry English was frequently invisible. Ends Corey Liuget and Kendall Reyes—who played inside frequently when the Chargers went to their sub packages—were pushed around too often. With nose tackle Cam Thomas off to Pittsburgh, San Diego hopes that Ryan Carrethers, the fifth-round pick from Arkansas State who showed up well against tougher competition, can become the true nose tackle this defense is built to require. Fellow rookie Jeremiah Attaochu will be tasked with adding to the pass rush, which could be a challenge for the talented but raw second-round pick out of Georgia Tech.

For those keeping score at home, what we have here is the defense that was the worst in the league by our metrics relying on three rookies to make major strides right away to fill significant personnel gaps. One could argue that even with the new kids, things couldn't be much worse. Pagano spoke late in the season about improved defensive effort, but that was a relative concept—just because they weren't allowing 452 total yards to the Titans or 346 passing yards to the Matt Schaub-led Texans anymore doesn't mean things were going well. Pagano will have to find more ways to be effectively creative, because with McCoy, the current Chargers have proven that they will overthrow tenure in favor of intelligent innovation.

Even with those questions on Pagano's side of things, we project the Chargers to be the AFC West's second-best team in 2014. That has something to do with the idea that regression to the mean should be at least slightly favorable to any defense this bad, but far more to do with our faith in McCoy, Rivers, and what the franchise is putting together on that side of the ball. San Diego is the only team with all projected starters returning on offense, including situational entities such as third receivers and second tight ends. And in this case, continuity is a good thing.

The Chargers find themselves in an interesting and unexpected place these days. It was thought a year ago that the passing offense was in need of an overhaul, and that Rivers might have seen his best days. In truth, it is a defense recovering from too many of A.J. Smith's capricious mistakes over the years that will have the Chargers reaching for the keys to the kingdom in vain. Unless everything comes together at an unusual level in 2014, the problems are not likely to be solved in a single season—but Chargers fans should enjoy more happy Sundays than sad ones this fall.

Doug Farrar

2013 Chargers Stats by Week

Wk	vs.	W-L	PF	PA	YDF	YDA	TO	Total	Off	Def	ST
1	HOU	L	28	31	263	449	0	-29%	0%	28%	-1%
2	at PHI	W	33	30	539	522	-2	10%	41%	31%	0%
3	at TEN	L	17	20	277	452	-1	15%	44%	24%	-5%
4	DAL	W	30	21	506	319	0	-1%	30%	28%	-4%
5	at OAK	L	17	27	427	299	-5	-41%	-11%	20%	-10%
6	IND	W	19	9	374	267	+1	25%	15%	-5%	5%
7	at JAC	W	24	6	434	353	+1	10%	35%	26%	0%
8	BYE										
9	at WAS	L	24	30	410	500	-1	-32%	7%	39%	0%
10	DEN	L	20	28	329	397	+1	6%	16%	10%	0%
11	at MIA	L	16	20	435	343	0	20%	27%	16%	9%
12	at KC	W	41	38	491	395	+2	6%	59%	51%	-2%
13	CIN	L	10	17	334	354	-1	-9%	4%	18%	5%
14	NYG	W	37	14	388	333	+2	31%	43%	14%	2%
15	at DEN	W	27	20	337	295	+1	62%	37%	-20%	5%
16	OAK	W	26	13	344	265	-1	15%	-2%	-8%	9%
17	KC	W	27	24	405	332	-1	28%	21%	-7%	-1%
18	at CIN	W	27	10	318	439	+4	38%	32%	-5%	1%
19	at DEN	L	17	24	259	363	+2	-6%	9%	-4%	-20%

Trends and Splits

	Offense	Rank	Defense	Rank
Total DVOA	23.1%	2	17.5%	32
Unadjusted VOA	22.7%	2	17.9%	32
Weighted Trend	23.7%	4	12.6%	28
Variance	4.0%	5	3.5%	3
Average Opponent	1.7%	21	-0.4%	16
Passing	52.5%	2	24.0%	31
Rushing	2.9%	12	8.6%	31
First Down	17.7%	5	29.1%	32
Second Down	16.0%	6	11.2%	28
Third Down	46.2%	2	3.3%	20
First Half	25.2%	2	15.3%	31
Second Half	21.0%	5	19.5%	30
Red Zone	10.1%	13	35.9%	31
Late and Close	22.7%	4	24.1%	32

Five-Year Performance

Year	W-L	Pyth W	Est W	PF	PA	TO	Total	Rk	Off	Rk	Def	Rk	ST	Rk	Off AGL	Rk	Def AGL	Rk	Off Age	Rk	Def Age	Rk	ST Age	Rk
2009	13-3	11.3	10.4	454	320	+8	13.5%	11	19.7%	4	6.5%	23	0.2%	16	26.6	17	29.5	18	26.8	25	26.5	24	26.5	18
2010	9-7	11.0	9.4	441	322	-6	15.4%	8	15.5%	4	-10.0%	7	-10.2%	32	26.8	18	12.7	9	27.4	16	27.5	14	27.1	9
2011	8-8	8.7	7.4	406	377	-7	0.70%	16	13.0%	5	10.8%	29	-1.6%	23	32.6	18	40.0	23	28.0	6	28.0	5	26.4	10
2012	7-9	8.0	6.6	350	350	+2	-9.0%	22	-10.0%	24	2.0%	18	3.0%	8	30.2	18	19.3	10	28.4	2	27.8	6	27.1	2
2013	9-7	9.2	8.8	396	348	-4	6.4%	12	23.1%	2	17.5%	32	0.8%	15	48.2	24	34.3	22	27.5	10	25.8	28	26.0	17

2013 Performance Based on Most Common Personnel Groups

SD Offense					SD Offense vs. Opponents				SD Defense				SD Defense vs. Opponents			
Pers	Freq	Yds	DVOA	Run%	Pers	Freq	Yds	DVOA	Pers	Freq	Yds	DVOA	Pers	Freq	Yds	DVOA
11	56%	6.9	39.1%	31%	Nickel Even	41%	6.6	36.1%	3-4-4	34%	5.9	11.1%	11	53%	7.0	27.3%
12	31%	5.8	22.7%	48%	Dime+	17%	7.7	59.8%	Nickel Even	28%	5.8	15.0%	12	21%	5.0	-3.3%
21	6%	3.0	-19.3%	80%	3-4-4	14%	4.9	-5.6%	Dime+	19%	6.3	22.6%	21	12%	6.9	21.5%
22	4%	3.4	8.8%	98%	4-3-4	14%	4.5	14.0%	Nickel Odd	18%	7.9	25.4%	13	4%	6.4	28.1%
13	2%	10.0	49.3%	57%	Nickel Odd	13%	6.4	26.4%	Goal Line	1%	2.3	33.9%	20	3%	6.0	8.0%
													22	3%	3.5	-18.2%

Strategic Tendencies

Run/Pass		Rk	Formation		Rk	Pass Rush		Rk	Secondary		Rk	Strategy		Rk
Runs, first half	44%	4	Form: Single Back	81%	5	Rush 3	6.1%	15	4 DB	34%	22	Play action	12%	32
Runs, first down	54%	7	Form: Empty Back	8%	11	Rush 4	61.2%	18	5 DB	45%	23	Avg Box (Off)	6.20	26
Runs, second-long	35%	12	Pers: 3+ WR	56%	16	Rush 5	28.7%	6	6+ DB	19%	6	Avg Box (Def)	6.29	22
Runs, power sit.	53%	17	Pers: 4+ WR	0%	31	Rush 6+	4.0%	30	CB by Sides	69%	20	Offensive Pace	31.96	29
Runs, behind 2H	27%	19	Pers: 2+ TE/6+ OL	38%	8	Sacks by LB	45.7%	12	DB Blitz	14%	11	Defensive Pace	31.00	30
Pass, ahead 2H	39%	31	Shotgun/Pistol	73%	3	Sacks by DB	12.9%	5	Hole in Zone	16%	4	Go for it on 4th	0.57	27

We often praise Philip Rivers for playing well despite the unknown names in his receiving corps, but those unknown receivers sure do know how to hold onto the ball. Last year, Chargers receivers dropped just 15 passes, ranking them third in drop rate behind Arizona and Houston. It was the fourth straight season where Chargers receivers ranked among the top four teams in lowest drop rate. Although the Chargers led the league with 40.1 yards per drive, they scored touchdowns on just 50.8 percent of red-zone opportunities, tied for 26th in the NFL. The Chargers recovered only three of their 10 fumbles on offense. San Diego led the league with 60 running back draws; they were slightly above average with 5.4 yards per carry and 22.9% DVOA. The terrible San Diego defense improved significantly with a big pass rush. They allowed only 5.5 yards per pass with six or more pass rushers, and only 4.7 yards per pass on any play where they blitzed at least one defensive back.

Passing

Player	DYAR	DVOA	Plays	NtYds	Avg	YAC	C%	TD	Int
P.Rivers	1799	34.8%	575	4363	7.6	5.7	69.6%	32	11
K.Clemens	*60*	*-7.5%*	*262*	*1526*	*5.8*	*5.2*	*58.9%*	*8*	*7*

Rushing

Player	DYAR	DVOA	Plays	Yds	Avg	TD	Fum	Suc
R.Mathews	141	3.6%	285	1255	4.4	6	2	49%
D.Woodhead	104	13.7%	106	432	4.1	2	1	60%
R.Brown*	-5	-11.3%	45	157	3.5	1	0	36%
P.Rivers	-5	-17.6%	17	81	4.8	0	0	-
L.McClain*	20	23.1%	11	32	2.9	0	0	73%
D.Brown	117	19.2%	101	533	5.3	6	0	54%
K.Clemens	*-35*	*-52.9%*	*16*	*69*	*4.3*	*0*	*2*	*-*

Receiving

Player	DYAR	DVOA	Plays	Ctch	Yds	Y/C	YAC	TD	C%
K.Allen	343	28.2%	104	71	1053	14.8	5.9	8	68%
V.Brown	49	-4.1%	69	41	472	11.5	2.3	1	59%
E.Royal	238	31.6%	67	47	625	13.3	7.1	8	70%
M.Floyd	47	40.9%	11	6	149	24.8	2.0	0	55%
A.Gates	63	0.7%	113	77	872	11.3	4.8	4	68%
L.Green	113	45.3%	30	17	376	22.1	9.8	3	57%
J.Phillips	-15	-42.9%	6	4	30	7.5	5.3	0	67%
D.Woodhead	282	41.2%	87	76	609	8.0	6.1	6	87%
R.Matthews	61	19.9%	33	26	189	7.3	7.3	1	79%
R.Brown*	23	37.6%	8	8	60	7.5	6.9	0	100%
D.Brown	*44*	*6.2%*	*36*	*28*	*218*	*7.8*	*8.8*	*2*	*78%*

Offensive Line

Player	Pos	Age	GS	Snaps	Pen	Sk	Pass	Run	Player	Pos	Age	GS	Snaps	Pen	Sk	Pass	Run
Nick Hardwick	C	33	16/16	1075	2	0.0	3.0	1.0	Chad Rinehart	LG	29	11/10	669	2	1.0	7.0	1.0
D.J. Fluker	RT	23	15/15	1047	6	5.5	30.0	4.5	Johnnie Troutman	LG	27	14/7	629	7	1.5	11.0	2.0
Jeromey Clary	RG	31	15/15	1039	7	4.0	12.5	7.0	Michael Harris	OT	26	5/3	189	2	1.0	5.0	0.0
King Dunlap	LT	29	11/11	672	4	4.5	9.5	0.0	Rich Ohrnberger	G	28	14/1	155	4	0.5	1.5	1.0

Year	Yards	ALY	Rk	Power	Rk	Stuff	Rk	2nd Lev	Rk	Open Field	Rk	Sacks	ASR	Rk	Short	Long	F-Start	Cont.
2011	4.42	4.21	9	69%	5	16%	5	1.23	13	0.85	15	30	5.4%	8	8	13	15	28
2012	3.71	3.91	23	60%	21	17%	6	1.01	27	0.41	30	49	8.9%	32	14	19	22	22
2013	4.20	4.26	3	74%	5	12%	1	1.10	17	0.50	27	30	5.9%	8	11	12	21	28

2013 ALY by direction: Left End 5.51 (1) Left Tackle 4.91 (4) Mid/Guard 4.04 (12) Right Tackle 3.34 (27) Right End 3.57 (18)

The Chargers switched players at every position but center in 2013, and the results were favorable for the most part. However, it must be specified that the downturn in sacks, hits and hurries from 2012 to 2013 had as much to do with the passing game installed by Mike McCoy and Ken Whisenhunt as anything the front five did. The new Chargers coaching staff discarded the "vertical-or-bust" mindset of Norv Turner, and encouraged Philip Rivers to look for the hot route once in a while. Thus, as it's been with Peyton Manning and Drew Brees for years, Rivers started to make his line look better at times than it actually was.

Feeling a need for more power on that line, San Diego selected Alabama behemoth D.J. Fluker with the 11th overall pick in 2013. Fluker is not a fluid pass-blocker by any means—his kick step is clunky, and he will let speed rushers get past him on a regular basis. Were he protecting Rivers' blind side for any length of time in a seven-step drop offense, Rivers might be running for his life all over again. But as a run-blocker, Fluker came as advertised, using his size and wingspan to absolutely dominate defenders on a regular basis. He improved in his technique over the season, and while he has said that he can play just about anywhere on a line, he seems to be an ideal right tackle for this offense. Like Fluker, left tackle King Dunlap is an enormous man far better suited to slamming defenders back in the run game than picking up the finer points of pass blocking. No Eagles fan would have ever imagined the former seventh-round backup turning in such a strong season after signing with San Diego. We marked Dunlap with a blown block every 70.7 snaps, the best for any left tackle last year other than Anthony Collins and Andrew Whitworth of Cincinnati. However, neither Dunlap nor Fluker is very agile, and both can be outfoxed by stunts and advanced blitz concepts.

Jeromey Clary, the team's right tackle for the last several seasons, was moved inside to right guard by the Fluker selection and played reasonably well, though he may have been helped more than anyone by the new up-tempo offense. The Chargers selected Notre Dame guard Chris Watt in the third round and project him as Clary's replacement over time. Left guard Chad Rinehart played through injuries, excelling at the pull-blocks that Kris Dielman executed so well for recent Chargers teams. Center Nick Hardwick was considering retirement after another excellent year, but will come back for at least one more season.

Defensive Front Seven

			Overall								vs. Run					Pass Rush			
Defensive Line	**Age**	**Pos**	**G**	**Snaps**	**Plays**	**TmPct**	**Rk**	**Stop**	**Dfts**	**BTkl**	**Runs**	**St%**	**Rk**	**RuYd**	**Rk**	**Sack**	**Hit**	**Hur**	**Tips**
Corey Liuget	24	DE	16	713	44	5.7%	32	26	11	0	28	57%	84	3.8	83	5.5	9	12.0	2
Kendall Reyes	25	DE	16	710	36	4.7%	53	23	8	2	23	65%	74	3.6	80	5.0	3	14.5	1
Cam Thomas*	28	DT	16	473	25	3.2%	77	18	5	5	22	68%	70	1.5	18	0.0	0	5.0	1
Sean Lissemore	27	DE	15	210	24	3.3%	--	16	5	0	20	65%	--	2.6	--	2.0	1	2.5	0
Lawrence Guy	24	DE	12	45	23	4.0%	--	18	3	1	19	74%	--	2.6	--	0.0	3	2.0	4

			Overall								vs. Run					Pass Rush			
Edge Rushers	**Age**	**Pos**	**G**	**Snaps**	**Plays**	**TmPct**	**Rk**	**Stop**	**Dfts**	**BTkl**	**Runs**	**St%**	**Rk**	**RuYd**	**Rk**	**Sack**	**Hit**	**Hur**	**Tips**
Jarret Johnson	33	OLB	11	434	37	7.0%	18	32	7	2	25	84%	18	2.4	40	3.0	2	6.5	2
Thomas Keiser	25	OLB	12	396	23	4.0%	69	14	7	0	12	50%	77	4.2	76	4.5	3	8.0	1
Larry English	28	OLB	9	370	18	4.1%	65	15	5	1	13	85%	16	1.5	12	2.5	2	9.5	1
Tourek Williams	23	OLB	13	215	10	1.6%	--	4	1	3	7	43%	--	4.3	--	1.0	0	2.0	0

			Overall								Pass Rush			vs. Run					vs. Pass						
Linebackers	**Age**	**Pos**	**G**	**Snaps**	**Plays**	**TmPct**	**Rk**	**Stop**	**Dfts**	**BTkl**	**Sack**	**Hit**	**Hur**	**Runs**	**St%**	**Rk**	**RuYd**	**Rk**	**Tgts**	**Suc%**	**Rk**	**AdjYd**	**Rk**	**PD**	**Int**
Donald Butler	26	ILB	13	699	88	14.0%	36	36	10	6	0.5	0	4	48	48%	78	4.3	73	25	37%	66	6.9	46	3	1
Manti Te'o	23	ILB	13	524	65	10.3%	60	34	10	4	0.0	0	3	46	54%	72	3.7	54	22	66%	6	4.7	6	4	0
Reggie Walker	28	ILB	16	468	37	4.8%	82	20	10	5	3.0	4	8.5	20	50%	76	3.7	56	8	75%	--	4.8	--	0	0
Andrew Gachkar	26	ILB	16	166	24	3.1%	--	10	1	1	0.0	0	2	15	60%	--	3.3	--	3	34%	--	11.4	--	0	0
Bront Bird*	25	ILB	16	116	21	2.7%	--	10	1	0	0.0	0	0	18	50%	--	4.2	--	4	19%	--	6.3	--	0	0

Year	Yards	ALY	Rk	Power	Rk	Stuff	Rk	2nd Level	Rk	Open Field	Rk	Sacks	ASR	Rk	Short	Long
2011	4.38	4.32	25	75%	32	16%	28	1.12	10	0.79	19	32	6.5%	18	6	21
2012	3.81	3.80	7	59%	10	23%	7	1.18	15	0.54	8	38	7.0%	8	14	11
2013	4.46	4.45	31	73%	26	16%	27	1.39	30	0.55	11	35	6.9%	15	10	12
2013 ALY by direction:			*Left End 3.98 (24)*			*Left Tackle 4.28 (25)*			*Mid/Guard 4.61 (30)*			*Right Tackle 4.52 (25)*			*Right End 4.33 (27)*	

San Diego's defense regressed mightily last season, and that started up front. There was very little schematic variation, and injuries rendered the pass rush nearly invisible at times. Melvin Ingram, the second-year linebacker with star potential, missed the first 12 games of the 2013 season with a torn ACL. Veteran Dwight Freeney, acquired in the 2013 offseason to ostensibly provide some spark to a pass rush that was underwhelming the year before, missed all but the first four games of the season with a torn quadricep. Veteran left outside linebacker Jarrett Johnson was the best pass rusher left after that, but he too missed five games. At that point you're down to draft flop Larry English and unknowns like Thomas Keiser and Tourek Williams. What a mess. Things will be better this year, especially if Ingram can stay healthy. San Diego added Georgia Tech pass rusher Jeremiah Attaochu in the second round, and they hope he can play across from Ingram and move Freeney into a situational role, but it may take a while for Attaochu to get the hang of things at the next level. He's a tremendous athlete, but he's still learning how to play the run and how to drop back into coverage when necessary.

Donald Butler, who signed a seven-year, $48 million contract extension with $28 million guaranteed in February, was probably the team's best overall defensive player despite missing three games with a groin injury. Rookie Manti Te'o showed in the NFL what he displayed in college: though he has the ability to drop in coverage effectively, he's not an upper-tier run-stopper. Up in front, neither Corey Liuget nor Kendall Reyes was consistently strong against the run. (This in turn was a big reason why Butler and the other inside linebackers look poor in our run stats.) The Chargers used a fifth-round pick on Arkansas State's Ryan Carrethers with the idea that he can replace departed nose tackle Cam Thomas. The 6-foot-1, 337-pound Sun Belt star impressed general manager Tom Telesco with his play against bigger schools, and the hope is that he can man the point inside as others have not.

Defensive Secondary

			Overall								vs. Run					vs. Pass									
Secondary	Age	Pos	G	Snaps	Plays	TmPct	Rk	Stop	Dfts	BTkl	Runs	St%	Rk	RuYd	Rk	Tgts	Tgt%	Rk	Dist	Suc%	Rk	AdjYd	Rk	PD	Int
Eric Weddle	29	FS	16	992	112	14.5%	3	45	22	10	47	34%	53	6.1	24	44	9.9%	60	9.3	66%	10	6.2	22	7	2
Marcus Gilchrist	26	SS	16	986	81	10.5%	35	26	8	3	37	41%	36	6.0	23	23	5.3%	8	8.6	54%	43	6.4	27	5	2
Shareece Wright	27	CB	13	779	64	10.2%	16	23	8	6	12	42%	41	12.0	78	84	24.3%	68	14.1	38%	83	10.0	80	10	1
Richard Marshall	30	CB	16	624	67	8.7%	41	20	8	4	21	19%	76	8.0	54	51	18.2%	18	10.6	48%	65	8.0	57	4	0
Derek Cox*	28	CB	16	554	45	5.8%	78	13	4	3	5	0%	84	15.6	83	59	24.0%	65	13.1	46%	76	9.4	78	7	1
Johnny Patrick*	26	CB	13	474	36	5.7%	--	13	8	4	11	36%	--	9.0	--	37	17.3%	--	9.5	39%	--	9.8	--	2	1
Jahleel Addae	24	FS	16	372	31	4.0%	--	12	9	3	9	22%	--	9.6	--	10	6.1%	--	10.9	67%	--	6.8	--	3	0
Brandon Flowers	*28*	*CB*	*13*	*866*	*76*	*11.1%*	*9*	*23*	*11*	*3*	*9*	*44%*	*35*	*7.2*	*46*	*88*	*23.3%*	*62*	*11.9*	*47%*	*75*	*9.2*	*76*	*9*	*1*

Year	Pass D Rank	vs. #1 WR	Rk	vs. #2 WR	Rk	vs. Other WR	Rk	vs. TE	Rk	vs. RB	Rk
2011	31	32.5%	31	13.5%	23	2.1%	21	32.8%	31	-6.2%	11
2012	18	21.6%	27	-17.3%	5	-11.2%	8	-12.0%	5	23.4%	29
2013	31	24.7%	31	24.5%	32	3.4%	18	-5.1%	11	7.9%	22

The Chargers really needed two unexpected gifts if they wanted a shot at the Super Bowl this year, and they got one of them when they were able to pick Brandon Flowers up off the scrap heap. Unfortunately, the other is Peyton Manning being eaten by sharks.

Jettisoned from Kansas City because of contract issues and the Chiefs' newfound preference for bigger cornerbacks, Flowers fits well into a John Pagano scheme that has the outside pass defenders playing a lot of off coverage. Flowers has the hip turn and short-area flexibility to trail the best receivers on opposing teams on either side of the field (which he was tasked to do quite often), but he's not a true press boundary corner in the Darrelle Revis or Richard Sherman sense. At 5-foot-9 and 187 pounds, he will lose size battles on jump balls, and he can be beaten in a straight line by quicker outside guys—thus, the disconnect between a better-than-average player and some rather indifferent charting stats. True slot cornerbacks are tasked to do many different things—from option route recognition to covering bigger receivers and tight ends, to blitzes and run support. The Chiefs seemed to think the old way, which was that the slot was the place you put the pass defender you didn't quite know how to use.

The Chargers also tried to address their most pressing need in the first round of the draft by selecting TCU cornerback Jason Verrett. Some have questioned how much success Verrett can have as a 5-foot-10, 189-pound player in a league where larger press corners are now more coveted. The Chargers certainly don't seem fazed; in fact, their only cornerback who reaches six feet is the youngest of the Cromartie cousins, practice-squad scrub Marcus. General manager Tom Telesco, who spent 1998 through 2012 with the Colts franchise in different positions, has compared Verrett to safety Bob Sanders, who played far bigger than he was until injuries took him down. Verrett can play press very well, and his leaping ability makes him competitive against larger receivers. A torn labrum kept Verrett out of OTAs and may cost him part of training camp, and that's the short-term issue. The long-term issue is whether he has the attributes needed to be a true outside cornerback. If not, that's less a liability than it has ever been, since your average team actually plays more nickel than base. Nonetheless, dropping a first-round pick on a potential slot corner is still a bit suspect, even at this point in the NFL's evolution.

Only Pittsburgh's Ike Taylor and Dee Milliner of the New York Jets were targeted on a higher percentage of opponent passes than Shareece Wright, and that's certainly indicative that those opponents saw Wright as an easy mark. 2013 was the first season in which the four-year veteran became a starter of any note, and you could see the rough spots. Wright has decent speed in space and presses receivers at an average level, but he doesn't have exceptionally quick feet, and he's not "sticky" on routes requiring him to recover and reset quickly. Richard Marshall took over as the primary man opposite Wright after Derek Cox was benched, but at this point in his career, Marshall is far more a chase-and-tackle defender than any serious threat in coverage. The Chargers re-signed him to a one-year, vet-minimum deal, and the Flowers signing bumps him down to fourth on the depth chart.

Though this team is banking a lot on relatively unproven cornerbacks in 2014, at least Eric Weddle gives a level of security by playing at his normal level of excellence. From elite run support to deep coverage, Weddle has been as good as any free safety in the league over the last few seasons. The nice surprise in the defensive backfield (yes, there was one) was Marcus Gilchrist, who moved to strong safety after two seasons as the team's main slot cornerback. He played well enough to allow defensive coordinator John Pagano to use safety switches, and bring Weddle up into the box at certain times with relative impunity.

Special Teams

Year	DVOA	Rank	FG/XP	Rank	Net Kick	Rank	Kick Ret	Rank	Net Punt	Rank	Punt Ret	Rank	Hidden	Rank
2011	-1.6%	23	-0.4	17	-7.0	27	2.8	9	1.6	13	-5.0	22	-3.0	19
2012	3.0%	8	6.4	7	7.7	6	3.2	9	-4.9	22	2.4	11	2.8	9
2013	0.8%	15	3.4	11	-0.8	17	-2.2	19	7.4	7	-3.8	21	-0.1	15

Kicker Nick Novak was the star of San Diego's special teams, tying John Carney for the franchise record with 34 field goals. Novak missed just three in the regular season, and made three of four in the playoffs. Punter Mike Scifres had another good year, helping to demonstrate why you can't just judge punters on averages, whether gross or net. Scifres averaged 43.2 yards per punt, down 5.1 yards from his 2012 campaign. On the other hand, his average punt came from roughly the 33-yard line in 2012, but roughly the 39-yard line in 2013. Only three teams allowed fewer punt return yards than San Diego's 158, and the Chargers were the only team where three different players had at least 12 special-teams tackles: Seyi Ajirotutu, Darrell Stuckey, and Eric Weddle.

Rookie Keenan Allen led the Chargers in punt returns, somewhat odd given that Allen has never been known for his pure speed. Eddie Royal, who was also used in the role, is more of a standard punt returner. Of the kick returners on the roster (Danny Woodhead, Ronnie Brown, Lavelle Hawkins, and Fozzy Whittaker), Woodhead was the only one to rate above league average by our metrics, and that was just barely.

San Francisco 49ers

2013 Record: 12-4	**Total DVOA:** 17.4% (7th)	**2014 Mean Projection:** 9.0	**On the Clock (0-4):** 5%
Pythagorean Wins: 11.5 (4th)	**Offense:** 9.1% (8th)	**Postseason Odds:** 51.4%	**Mediocrity (5-7):** 19%
Snap-Weighted Age: 27.4 (2nd)	**Defense:** -4.6% (13th)	**Super Bowl Odds:** 8.7%	**Playoff Contender (8-10):** 48%
Average Opponent: 2.1% (9th)	**Special Teams:** 3.7% (7th)	**Proj. Avg. Opponent:** 2.8% (4th)	**Super Bowl Contender (11+):** 28%

2013: Close only counts in horseshoes and hand grenades.

2014: There are questions that suggest a lesser regular season, but the answers may come just in time for a Super Bowl run.

When Richard Sherman launched into a tirade against Michael Crabtree after the NFC Championship Game, and became the national celebrity and talking point for the two-week Super Bowl media cycle, it overshadowed the underlying play that decided the game. Once again, San Francisco had come within inches—in this case, a finger—of a victory in the playoffs, only to be denied.

A year earlier, Jim Harbaugh was incredulous after three straight incompletions at the goal line in Super Bowl XLVIII, including a potential defensive holding by Baltimore cornerback Jimmy Smith that went uncalled on the fourth-down pass to Crabtree.

Two years earlier, Kyle Williams fumbled a punt in overtime of the NFC Championship game, setting the Giants up for the winning field goal.

No team in NFL history has been so close to beating the Super Bowl champions in three straight seasons, but still losing every time. How differently would the legacy of this San Francisco team be with just a few more inches, slightly different bounces or calls, a few moments in time altered? If the 49ers had those plays go their way, we could be talking about them in the same vein as the New England Patriots of a decade ago.

If you believe that to be hyperbole, consider that there are only ten other teams in NFL history that have lost to the eventual title winner in three straight years in the playoffs (Table 1). None of them lost by smaller combined margins than Harbaugh's 49ers. San Francisco will hope to follow the footsteps of the 1954 Cleveland Browns, 1976 Oakland Raiders, and 2006 Indianapolis Colts, three of the four teams that came closest in smallest combined margin of defeat. All three teams were thought to be "incapable of winning the big one." All three won a championship on the fourth try, exorcising demons past with key wins along the way.

Back in the days when the postseason consisted of just one game, Cleveland had lost to Detroit in two straight NFL Championship contests. Matched up for a third straight year, the Browns clobbered the Lions 56-10. Oakland finally took out Pittsburgh in the middle of their dynasty run of the '70s, against what may have been the best version of the Steel Curtain defense. Indianapolis set the infamous Brady vs. Manning debates on their ear and destroyed the prewritten narratives, coming from down 21-3 to finally defeat the Patriots in the 2006 AFC Championship game.

To join these teams, the 49ers will have to exorcise their own demon: the team that is their mirror image in many ways, the Seattle Seahawks. It won't be easy. San Francisco faces the league's fourth toughest projected schedule according by DVOA. In addition to the division schedule, San Francisco draws the powerful AFC West and the well-rounded NFC East. By finishing second last year, they also get Chicago, a team we see improving, and New Orleans, the team we see as the clear class of the NFC South.

The 49ers will also be opening the new Levi's Stadium in 2014, after 43 seasons of playing in Candlestick Park. Surprising as it may sound, home-field advantage shows a "learning curve" in new stadiums. Past research[1] has shown that home-field advantage in a new stadium gets strongest in the *second* year. Teams that have opened the season in new stadiums over the last 20 years have gone only 10-10 in the stadium opener, and have their lowest home winning percentage in the first half-season in the new stadium (Table 2).

Yes, these records could be random variation, but there's also a rational explanation for why this may be a real phenomenon. Familiarity plays a role in home field advantage, and as the "fresh paint" smell wears off the new stadium, the home team gains comfort at a faster rate than opponents who visit

Table 1: Teams That Lost To Eventual Champions In Three Straight Postseasons

Team	Years	Combined Margin	Next Year
San Francisco 49ers	2011-2013	12	?????
Cleveland Browns	1951-1953	18	NFL CHAMPS
Oakland Raiders	1968-1970	24	Missed Playoffs
Indianapolis Colts	2003-2005	30	NFL CHAMPS
Oakland Raiders	1973-1975	34	NFL CHAMPS
Oakland Raiders	2000-2002	43	Missed Playoffs
Buffalo Bills	1990-1992	49	Lost Super Bowl
New York Giants	1961-1963	50	Missed Playoffs
Minnesota Vikings	1987-1989	60	Missed Playoffs
Houston Oilers	1978-1980	63	Missed Playoffs
Buffalo Bills	1991-1993	65	Missed Playoffs

1 http://www.pro-football-reference.com/blog/?p=320

Table 2. Team Records In First Two Years Of A New Stadium, 1994-2013

Games	W-L	Pct
Games 1-2	21-19	0.525
Games 3-4	23-17	0.575
Games 5-6	24-15-1	0.613
Games 7-8	24-16	0.600
Games 9-10	27-13	0.675
Games 11-12	26-13-1	0.663
Games 13-14	24-16	0.600
Games 15-16	27-13	0.675

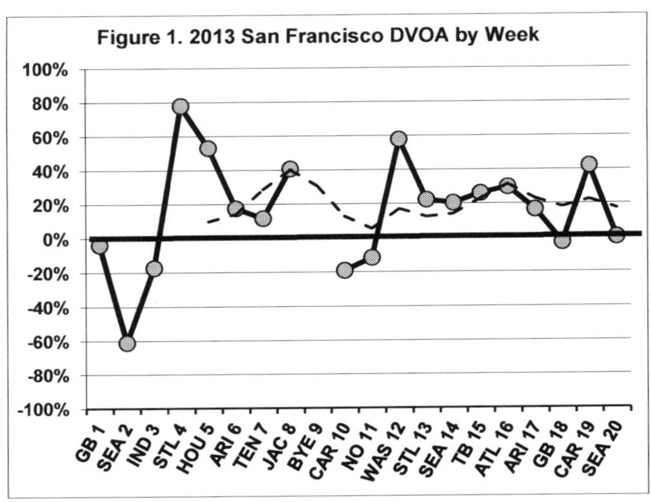

infrequently. The feel of the turf, the wind conditions that can be unique to each new design, the noise from the crowd—all of these can be factors that eventually work in the favor of the home team in a new stadium.

San Francisco has a much bigger issue to address early in the season, though, even while it also gets used to playing home games in a new venue for the first time since before Bill Walsh and Joe Montana. The linebacking corps has been the strength of the defense over the run to three consecutive NFC Championship games. And the play with the biggest impact on San Francisco's 2014 season may have already taken place in January, when All-Pro linebacker NaVorro Bowman tore his ACL and MCL while appearing to recover a fumble at the goal line against Seattle.

The timeline on Bowman's return is uncertain, though Jim Harbaugh said in February that realistically, "halfway through the season" was a good target for Bowman's return. Bowman himself reported that he was ahead of schedule in April, but such news following postseason surgeries is as frequent as reports that teams will "run the ball more" and "will find ways to get two talented backs on the field at the same time." We've seen some miraculously quick comebacks, most notably Adrian Peterson returning from his December knee injury to challenge Eric Dickerson's rushing record in 2012. Bowman returning by the start of the season, though, would be even more ambitious.

To play in the season opener at Dallas, Bowman would have to return in full game shape less than eight months after the initial knee injury. Bowman opening the season on the Physically Unable to Perform list, putting him out for at least the first six games, is the most likely scenario. Even a return to play after the Week 8 bye in October (following a meeting with Peyton Manning and the Broncos) would require Bowman to return in just over nine months. Adrian Peterson played in the Minnesota season opener in 2012 exactly eight and a half months after his knee injury.

Since the merger, only three inside linebackers have been named first-team All-Pro by the Associated Press three different times before age 26: NaVorro Bowman, Patrick Willis, and Ray Lewis. Playing next to Willis, Bowman was, if anything, underappreciated on a national scale until last season. When Willis missed two games with a groin injury last year, against St. Louis and Houston in Weeks 4 and 5, Bowman was everywhere.

Against St. Louis, the team was without not only Willis, but also Aldon Smith, who was placed on the non-football injury list following a series of off-the-field incidents that ultimately led to him entering alcohol rehabilitation. The team was coming off a pair of embarrassing performances in blowout losses, first in Seattle and then at home against Indianapolis. They allowed 11 points against St. Louis, and three against Houston. Against the Rams, Bowman led the team with two sacks, the only time he has gotten multiple sacks in a game in his career. Against the Texans, he led the team with 13 tackles as the defense had its best performance of the year.

Later in the season, it was Bowman who again came up with the key defensive play to clinch a playoff berth when the season was on the brink. It's easy to forget, in the aftermath of another playoff run through Green Bay and Carolina, just how close San Francisco was to missing the playoffs in late December. A loss to Atlanta would have made the final game at Arizona a showdown for a wild card spot against the surging Cardinals, who were coming off their shocking road win at Seattle. Atlanta had scored and recovered an onside kick (that slipped under Bowman's arms), and moved to San Francisco's 10-yard line with just over a minute remaining. Bowman snagged Matt Ryan's tipped pass that bounced off Harry Douglas, and raced 89 yards to guarantee a return to the playoffs.

From an emotional as well as physical standpoint, replacing Bowman will be a major challenge. When other teams have lost All-Pro caliber inside linebackers to injury, the biggest impact has been on second-level and open-field yards gained by opposing runners. Five other times in the last 15 years,

2014 49ers Schedule

Week	Opp.	Week	Opp.	Week	Opp.
1	at DAL	7	at DEN	13	SEA (Thu.)
2	CHI	8	BYE	14	at OAK
3	at ARI	9	STL	15	at SEA
4	PHI	10	at NO	16	SD (Sat.)
5	KC	11	at NYG	17	ARI
6	at STL (Mon.)	12	WAS		

Table 3: When Your All-Pro ILB is Injured

Player	Team	Year	RB Yds Per Carry		2nd Level Yd Rank		Open Field Yd Rank	
			Prev Yr	Injured Yr	Prev Yr	Injured Yr	Prev Yr	Injured Yr
Ray Lewis	BAL	2002	3.35	3.91	2	6	3	6
Brian Urlacher	CHI	2004	4.35	4.40	12	29	25	27
Ray Lewis	BAL	2005	3.62	3.91	9	8	4	21
Zach Thomas	MIA	2007	3.55	4.58	4	26	2	23
Jon Beason	CAR	2011	4.02	4.98	18	31	20	25
AVERAGE			**3.78**	**4.36**	**9**	**20**	**11**	**20**

an All-Pro caliber inside linebacker has missed at least seven games: Ray Lewis in 2002 and 2005, Brian Urlacher in 2004, Zach Thomas in 2007, and Jon Beason in 2011 (Table 3).

The 49ers have been very good at limiting big runs over the last three seasons, and the Bowman and Willis combination are a big reason for that. San Francisco ranked first preventing both second-level and open-field runs in 2011, top two in both categories in 2012, and sixth and second, respectively, last year. Over the same time period, the defense has ranked 31st, 16th, and 31st in percentage of runs that are stuffed behind the line.

Some of that is by design, with the linemen in the San Francisco 3-4 front controlling the blockers to allow Willis and Bowman to clean up and make tackles. It's a feature of many 3-4 defenses (Pittsburgh has also shown some tendency to limit big runs in recent years, at the expense of penetration and run stops for loss) but the splits with San Francisco have been at an extreme over the last three years.

Those other five teams that lost a star inside linebacker have seen a decline of roughly 10 spots in second-level and open-field yards. San Francisco does have one thing going for it, though: knowledge and planning because the injury was known before the offseason. Michael Wilhoite performed respectably last year when Willis was out, and will replace Bowman in the starting lineup. There are also a number of young linebackers behind Wilhoite, including second-year man Nick Moody, third-round pick Chris Borland, and undrafted free agent Shayne Skov.

The Bowman injury also comes at a time when the defense is getting younger in the secondary. San Francisco should be more athletic in the back end, but also working on cohesiveness. But while the defense has questions in both how it handles the Bowman injury, and how the new parts in the secondary blend together, the team hopes to offset any defensive struggles with a stronger, more versatile offense.

Michael Crabtree's Achilles injury was costly to the passing offense in 2013, and the young receivers failed to take advantage of the opportunity. 2012 first-round pick A.J. Jenkins was shipped to Kansas City in a garage sale swap meet deal, where San Francisco got fellow first-round bust Jon Baldwin. Baldwin, 2013 fourth-round pick Quinton Patton, and Kyle Williams managed to catch a total of 18 passes all season—fewer than Crabtree, despite the latter missing 11 games. The passing game was the football version of "Spahn and Sain and pray for rain," with Anquan Boldin playing the part of crafty lefthander Warren Spahn, Vernon Davis playing Johnny Sain, and the health of Crabtree's Achilles playing the part of rain.

Anquan Boldin was effectively one of the best sixth-round picks ever; that's all it cost San Francisco to add him when Baltimore no longer wanted to pay his $6 million salary. The Boldin/Davis duo accounted for 20 of San Francisco's 21 receiving touchdowns, an unheard of ratio for a pair of teammates. Boldin finished the regular season with 85 catches, Davis with 52 catches, and the team's third leading receiver was fullback Bruce Miller (25 catches), hardly someone who was going to keep defensive coordinators up at night (Table 4).

Table 4. Distribution of San Francisco Receptions in 2013

Player	Weeks 1-12 (11 games)	Weeks 13-20 (8 games)
Anquan Boldin	52	49
Michael Crabtree	--	34
Vernon Davis	38	19
Running Backs	17	10
Bruce Miller	16	9
Other TE	9	0
Other WR	25	6
Big Uglies	0	2

Includes playoffs

San Francisco finished fourth in passing offense DVOA thanks to formational diversity, running the ball frequently, and leaning heavily on Boldin. San Francisco was one of 16 teams since 1978 to have one wide receiver over 75 catches while no other wide receiver reached 30 catches (Table 5).

You don't have to go back very far to find a similar situation—the Chicago Bears went from a one-man show with Brandon Marshall to an explosive, versatile passing offense with the hire of Marc Trestman and the emergence of Alshon Jeffery. Boldin was also involved in another extreme split at the opposite end of his career, when he had 66 more catches than any other receiver on the roster as a rookie in Arizona in 2003. The next year, Arizona added Larry Fitzgerald, setting up one of the best receiving duos in the league.

Crabtree and Boldin have each had 85 catches in a season and now should be together all year. The team also added Stevie Johnson, who has been the leading receiver in Buffalo over the last four years. How will the increase in targets affect the team?

With Crabtree, Boldin, and Davis all in the lineup at the end of last year and in the postseason, Colin Kaepernick saw his completion percentage rise by 2.5 percent and his passing DVOA go from 9.8% in the first 11 games to 17.5% over the final eight games (including the playoffs). Those improve-

Table 5. One Wideout Don't Stop the Shows: Leading Receiver over 75 Catches with No Other Wide Receiver over 30

Team	Leading Receiver	Second Receiver
2012 Bears	Brandon Marshall (118)	Earl Bennett (29)
2001 Broncos	Rod Smith (113)	Eddie Kennison (15)
2003 Vikings	Randy Moss (111)	Nate Burleson (29)
1992 Packers	Sterling Sharpe (108)	Sanjay Beach (17)
2005 Panthers	Steve Smith (103)	Keary Colbert (25)
1991 Cowboys	Michael Irvin (93)	Alvin Harper (20)
1988 Jets	Al Toon (93)	Wesley Walker (26)
1989 Bills	Andre Reed (88)	Flip Johnson (25)
1988 Rams	Henry Ellard (86)	Aaron Cox (28)
2013 49ers	**Anquan Boldin (85)**	**Michael Crabtree (19)**
2005 Redskins	Santana Moss (84)	David Patten (22)
1983 Oilers	Tim Smith (83)	Mike Renfro (23)
2002 Giants	Amani Toomer (82)	Ike Hilliard (27)
2001 Lions	Johnnie Morton (77)	Larry Foster (22)
1989 Broncos	Vance Johnson (76)	Mark Jackson (28)
1997 Dolphins	OJ McDuffie (76)	Lamar Thomas (28)

ments came despite a struggling running game and an offensive line that was banged up by year's end, with three of the starters carrying injuries into the postseason even as they remained in the lineup.

We can expect that Michael Crabtree's targets will balance out with Boldin's, since Crabtree was just coming back from injury a year ago. Stevie Johnson will eat into some of the receptions as well, as the team *should* use more three-wide sets than it has in the past. This will likely leave Vernon Davis with better opportunities, but fewer of them. He should still be a prime red-zone target, but hitting 50 receptions again will be difficult. There's a reason Davis wants a new contract now rather than waiting a year.

So now that the 49ers have upgraded their receivers, how much more will they throw by design? They won't become the Greatest Show on Turf, as San Francisco has re-loaded with a stable of backs behind Frank Gore, but expect them to throw more than the 436 and 417 pass attempts from the last two seasons. Some of the increase may also be by necessity, and it will fall to Colin Kaepernick to maintain his efficiency while throwing more often. Early in the season, San Francisco will have to find its way defensively, and the offense may need to pick up the slack.

Tabbing San Francisco to be among the league's elite is as bland as a pair of Jim Harbaugh khakis, but this offseason the 49ers have been in the news a little too much for things that would fall in the dreaded "distraction" category. There were the Harbaugh-to-Cleveland trade rumors, which were likely started by individuals on their way out of that organization. That was coupled with talk that Trent Baalke and Harbaugh were at odds. Throw in the Aldon Smith airport fiasco, holdouts with veterans like Vernon Davis and Alex Boone, and numerous off-the-field incidents, and San Francisco led the league in offseason talking points.

These are the kinds of things that will be set upon with sharp quills by sportswriters if the season comes up a disappointment. If the 49ers contend for a title, they will mostly be forgotten in the archives, buried behind the next layer of search-engine fodder. The real questions are there—the age along the defensive front, an offensive line that declined late in the year, turnover in the secondary—that could be the true causes of a disappointing season. That said, this is as talented a roster as any in the league, top to bottom. The organization has drafted wisely (except at wide receiver, where it has now gone the "trade picks for veterans" route) and been among the NFL's best at working value in the draft. Redshirted talent gives the 49ers depth across the roster, and they are loaded at the "skill positions," something you would not have said at the start of the Harbaugh era. If the offense performs up to its apparently capabilities and Bowman is 100 percent healthy by the postseason, the fourth time around could prove charmed.

Jason Lisk

2013 49ers Stats by Week

Wk	vs.	W-L	PF	PA	YDF	YDA	TO	Total	Off	Def	ST
1	GB	W	34	28	494	385	+2	-4%	17%	19%	-2%
2	at SEA	L	3	29	207	290	-4	-61%	-51%	-5%	-15%
3	IND	L	7	27	254	336	-2	-17%	1%	15%	-4%
4	at STL	W	35	11	370	188	0	78%	33%	-40%	4%
5	HOU	W	34	3	284	313	+4	53%	19%	-29%	5%
6	ARI	W	32	20	387	403	+2	17%	10%	2%	10%
7	at TEN	W	31	17	349	368	+2	12%	23%	16%	5%
8	vs. JAC	W	42	10	398	318	0	41%	56%	11%	-5%
9	BYE										
10	CAR	L	9	10	151	250	0	-19%	-54%	-31%	4%
11	at NO	L	20	23	196	387	+2	-12%	-30%	-11%	8%
12	at WAS	W	27	6	304	190	0	58%	8%	-38%	12%
13	STL	W	23	13	338	312	0	22%	14%	-3%	6%
14	SEA	W	19	17	318	264	0	20%	17%	-1%	2%
15	at TB	W	33	14	376	183	+2	26%	7%	2%	21%
16	ATL	W	34	24	379	402	+2	30%	38%	10%	2%
17	at ARI	W	23	20	375	482	+2	16%	14%	4%	6%
18	at GB	W	23	20	381	281	-1	-3%	-6%	-1%	3%
19	at CAR	W	23	10	315	325	+2	42%	23%	-17%	2%
20	at SEA	L	17	23	308	308	-2	0%	-9%	-19%	-10%

Trends and Splits

	Offense	Rank	Defense	Rank
Total DVOA	9.1%	8	-4.6%	13
Unadjusted VOA	3.7%	14	-5.8%	9
Weighted Trend	9.4%	7	-5.3%	11
Variance	8.9%	25	3.8%	6
Average Opponent	-4.6%	3	-2.0%	24
Passing	31.8%	4	-2.1%	10
Rushing	2.3%	14	-8.1%	14
First Down	15.5%	6	10.3%	26
Second Down	-11.1%	22	-16.5%	5
Third Down	28.4%	5	-12.6%	7
First Half	11.8%	7	-13.0%	3
Second Half	6.2%	12	3.6%	19
Red Zone	15.9%	8	10.1%	21
Late and Close	14.3%	8	-2.5%	16

Five-Year Performance

Year	W-L	Pyth W	Est W	PF	PA	TO	Total	Rk	Off	Rk	Def	Rk	ST	Rk	Off AGL	Rk	Def AGL	Rk	Off Age	Rk	Def Age	Rk	ST Age	Rk
2009	8-8	9.5	7.1	280	390	-8	-1.2%	20	-14.1%	23	-14.0%	5	-1.1%	20	9.5	8	34.1	22	26.6	27	27.4	12	26.7	13
2010	6-10	6.8	6.9	305	346	-1	-11.2%	24	-11.1%	24	-1.4%	15	-1.5%	20	20.7	11	6.8	3	25.8	28	27.6	11	25.6	29
2011	13-3	12.3	10.8	380	229	+2	18.6%	6	-3.9%	18	-14.6%	3	7.8%	2	29.6	16	8.8	2	26.5	23	26.7	21	26.6	7
2012	11-4-1	11.4	12.5	397	273	+9	29.5%	4	16.5%	5	-14.4%	3	-1.5%	20	11.7	5	4.5	1	27.1	14	27.3	10	26.9	5
2013	12-4	11.5	10.6	406	272	+12	17.4%	7	9.1%	8	-4.6%	13	3.7%	7	36.9	17	47.3	26	27.8	5	27.4	9	26.9	4

2013 Performance Based on Most Common Personnel Groups

SF Offense					SF Offense vs. Opponents				SF Defense				SF Defense vs. Opponents			
Pers	Freq	Yds	DVOA	Run%	Pers	Freq	Yds	DVOA	Pers	Freq	Yds	DVOA	Pers	Freq	Yds	DVOA
21	26%	5.6	14.4%	48%	4-3-4	37%	5.8	17.7%	Nickel Even	48%	5.2	-9.4%	11	53%	5.7	11.7%
22	26%	5.3	7.8%	68%	3-4-4	29%	5.2	-2.6%	3-4-4	40%	4.4	-14.0%	12	19%	3.8	-36.0%
11	21%	6.0	16.8%	17%	Nickel Even	17%	6.3	26.8%	Dime+	6%	8.6	103.5%	21	10%	3.2	-39.2%
12	15%	5.5	10.7%	37%	Dime+	6%	6.2	27.1%	Nickel Odd	5%	6.9	34.4%	22	5%	5.3	5.2%
721	3%	2.9	18.4%	84%	Goal Line	4%	2.2	23.2%	4-4-3	1%	0.6	-26.1%	10	3%	6.4	9.2%
621	3%	5.3	19.1%	63%	Nickel Odd	3%	6.8	33.7%					02	3%	6.0	-31.6%
					4-4-3	3%	6.4	73.5%								

Strategic Tendencies

Run/Pass		Rk	Formation		Rk	Pass Rush		Rk	Secondary		Rk	Strategy		Rk
Runs, first half	42%	7	Form: Single Back	43%	32	Rush 3	11.7%	1	4 DB	40%	15	Play action	28%	5
Runs, first down	56%	3	Form: Empty Back	3%	26	Rush 4	68.8%	7	5 DB	53%	12	Avg Box (Off)	6.87	1
Runs, second-long	40%	5	Pers: 3+ WR	22%	32	Rush 5	17.1%	28	6+ DB	6%	17	Avg Box (Def)	6.07	32
Runs, power sit.	68%	3	Pers: 4+ WR	0%	27	Rush 6+	2.4%	32	CB by Sides	81%	11	Offensive Pace	30.71	18
Runs, behind 2H	31%	6	Pers: 2+ TE/6+ OL	52%	3	Sacks by LB	67.1%	4	DB Blitz	4%	32	Defensive Pace	30.94	29
Pass, ahead 2H	43%	25	Shotgun/Pistol	44%	28	Sacks by DB	0.0%	29	Hole in Zone	11%	13	Go for it on 4th	0.82	20

The 49ers continue to be *sui generis* when it comes to switching up personnel groupings. They were the only offense to use 11 personnel less than 30 percent of the time. Add in 12 personnel, which they used on 15 percent of plays, and for the second straight season they were the only offense to have four different personnel groups that were used on at least 15 percent of all plays. San Francisco was outstanding when it used extra offensive linemen, with 4.8 yards per play and 30.7% DVOA. The 49ers were the only team to use seven linemen on a regular basis. The 49ers recovered only four of their 13 fumbles on offense. Defenses generally like to blitz young, mobile quarterbacks with defensive backs—the quarterbacks who faced the most DB blitzes were Robert Griffin, Geno Smith, Mike Glennon, and Cam Newton—but for some reason Colin Kaepernick is a huge exception. Opponents only blitzed a defensive back on 8.2 percent of San Francisco pass plays. Only Drew Brees faced fewer DB blitzes. And like Brees, Kaepernick killed these blitzes, with 9.3 yards per pass. San Francisco's defense ranked second in the league in the first quarter (-32.7% DVOA), then 21st for the rest of the game (3.4% DVOA). The 49ers somehow had the worst defensive DVOA in the league against runs in the red zone, although they ranked 11th against passes in the red zone. To show how inconsistent this kind of thing can be, however, we'll note that in 2012 the 49ers ranked 26th in defense against passes in the red zone but second against runs. The 49ers ranked dead last in using big blitzes (six or more pass rushers) for the third straight season. However, on those rare occasions they do bring a big blitz, the 49ers are phenomenal. On 39 plays over the last three regular seasons, they've allowed just 3.5 yards per pass. For the second straight year, the 49ers faced the largest average box on offense and used the smallest average box on defense.

Passing

Player	DYAR	DVOA	Plays	NtYds	Avg	YAC	C%	TD	Int
C.Kaepernick	791	16.6%	456	2969	6.5	5.5	58.4%	21	7
B.Gabbert	*-429*	*-84.1%*	*98*	*410*	*4.2*	*6.6*	*48.8%*	*1*	*7*

Rushing

Player	DYAR	DVOA	Plays	Yds	Avg	TD	Fum	Suc
F.Gore	91	-0.8%	276	1134	4.1	9	3	42%
C.Kaepernick	91	11.8%	80	533	6.7	4	2	-
K.Hunter	16	-3.0%	78	364	4.7	3	1	36%
A.Dixon*	-13	-17.5%	28	56	2.0	2	0	39%
L.James	2	-3.2%	12	59	4.9	0	0	42%
B.Miller	-7	-23.9%	7	13	1.9	0	0	57%
B.Gabbert	*-8*	*-29.2%*	*9*	*32*	*3.6*	*0*	*0*	*-*

Receiving

Player	DYAR	DVOA	Plays	Ctch	Yds	Y/C	YAC	TD	C%
A.Boldin	386	25.8%	129	85	1179	13.9	5.0	7	66%
M.Crabtree	42	3.7%	33	19	284	14.9	7.2	1	58%
K.Williams*	-68	-46.8%	27	12	113	9.4	4.8	0	44%
M.Manningham*	-45	-38.8%	23	9	85	9.4	1.9	0	39%
J.Baldwin	-29	-55.4%	9	3	28	9.3	2.0	0	33%
S.Johnson	*-25*	*-15.6%*	*102*	*53*	*607*	*11.5*	*4.2*	*3*	*52%*
V.Davis	199	29.3%	84	52	850	16.3	5.1	13	62%
V.McDonald	-20	-23.8%	19	8	119	14.9	5.9	0	42%
B.Miller	41	5.2%	36	25	243	9.7	7.2	0	69%
F.Gore	-3	-16.3%	26	16	141	8.8	6.3	0	62%

Offensive Line

Player	Pos	Age	GS	Snaps	Pen	Sk	Pass	Run
Alex Boone	RG	27	16/16	990	8	2.0	15.5	4.0
Anthony Davis	RT	25	16/16	975	6	4.3	15.8	7.0
Jonathan Goodwin*	C	36	16/16	970	3	3.0	15.5	3.5
Joe Staley	LT	30	16/16	929	3	3.3	10.3	4.5
Mike Iupati	LG	27	12/12	694	3	2.8	15.8	3.0
Adam Snyder	G	32	16/4	362	3	2.5	8.0	2.0
Jonathan Martin	*LT*	*25*	*7/7*	*453*	*3*	*5.5*	*9.0*	*0.0*

Year	Yards	ALY	Rk	Power	Rk	Stuff	Rk	2nd Lev	Rk	Open Field	Rk	Sacks	ASR	Rk	Short	Long	F-Start	Cont.
2011	4.17	3.96	21	51%	29	20%	22	1.12	22	0.92	12	44	8.4%	25	16	13	28	43
2012	4.74	4.50	1	66%	12	17%	7	1.49	1	0.79	14	41	8.5%	29	4	26	13	48
2013	4.05	3.57	29	55%	28	24%	29	1.12	15	0.98	5	39	7.8%	22	9	18	19	39

2013 ALY by direction: Left End 3.00 (22) Left Tackle 3.35 (27) Mid/Guard 3.66 (25) Right Tackle 3.89 (17) Right End 3.49 (20)

Offensive line continuity has been a subtle factor in San Francisco's offensive versatility during the Jim Harbaugh era. Over the last three years, only seven players have started on the offensive line. Over the last two seasons, the quintet of Joe Staley, Mike Iupati, Jonathan Goodwin, Alex Boone, and Anthony Davis has made 156 of the 160 regular season starts. That continuity and chemistry will be tested this year, as the team let veteran center Goodwin leave (he later signed with New Orleans). Daniel Kilgore, a 2011 draft pick, is tabbed to replace him in the starting lineup, and the team also used a third-round pick on Marcus Martin of USC, one of the top-rated centers in the 2014 draft. Kilgore is described as a tenacious competitor and will seek to add some youth at the center position, and help the team rebound in runs up the middle. The 49ers' dropped from second to 25th in Adjusted Line Yards in runs up the middle last year, and dropped from 12th to 28th in converting short-yardage "Power" runs.

San Francisco has a reputation as a pounding running team. By volume, this is earned, as the team ranked third in rush attempts and 32nd in pass attempts last year. San Francisco also was ranked first in Adjusted Line Yards in 2012. But as 2013 progressed, the 49ers struggled to run the ball with consistent success. Bumps and bruises along the offensive line, even as players played through injuries, may have had an impact. Mike Iupati, who suffered a fractured ankle in the NFC Championship game, previously missed four games with a sprained MCL suffered in Week 11. Joe Staley went down with what looked like a serious knee injury two weeks later against the Rams, though he would return the following week and officially play in every game. Anthony Davis had offseason shoulder surgery, and revealed that the injury came during the Week 15 game against Tampa Bay.

We can see the effects of the injuries when we look at how the 49ers' running game declined in the second half of the season (Table 6). In the first eight games, San Francisco averaged 4.2 yards per rush from the running backs. Over the remainder of the season, the backs averaged 3.7 yards a carry, including 3.3 in the postseason. Runners were stuffed more often and converted in short yardage less often. These numbers will have to rebound as Iupati recovers from his ankle injury and Kilgore transitions at center, or San Francisco's days as a dominant running team may be over.

Table 6. San Francisco Running Game, Weeks 1-8 vs. Weeks 10-20

Weeks	RB Runs	RB Yards	ALY	Stuff	Power
Weeks 1-8	215	4.22	3.60	21%	73%
Weeks 10-19	251	3.71	3.46	27%	41%

Defensive Front Seven

			Overall								vs. Run					Pass Rush			
Defensive Line	**Age**	**Pos**	**G**	**Snaps**	**Plays**	**TmPct**	**Rk**	**Stop**	**Dfts**	**BTkl**	**Runs**	**St%**	**Rk**	**RuYd**	**Rk**	**Sack**	**Hit**	**Hur**	**Tips**
Justin Smith	35	DE	16	780	48	6.0%	30	37	14	1	41	73%	58	3.0	68	6.5	9	23.5	0
Ray McDonald	30	DE	14	642	38	5.4%	36	28	10	0	32	69%	68	3.1	74	3.5	4	11.5	1
Glenn Dorsey	29	DT	16	435	41	5.1%	40	34	3	1	39	82%	28	2.8	65	2.0	1	1.0	0
Tony Jerod-Eddie	24	DT	15	378	30	4.0%	--	20	4	0	24	58%	--	3.9	--	0.0	3	10.0	1
Demarcus Dobbs	27	DT	15	302	13	1.7%	--	8	3	0	10	60%	--	2.7	--	0.5	3	3.0	1

			Overall								vs. Run					Pass Rush			
Edge Rushers	**Age**	**Pos**	**G**	**Snaps**	**Plays**	**TmPct**	**Rk**	**Stop**	**Dfts**	**BTkl**	**Runs**	**St%**	**Rk**	**RuYd**	**Rk**	**Sack**	**Hit**	**Hur**	**Tips**
Ahmad Brooks	30	OLB	16	965	66	8.3%	8	51	15	4	44	75%	44	2.8	51	8.0	6	21.0	5
Aldon Smith	25	OLB	11	574	34	6.2%	27	28	13	3	20	85%	14	1.3	7	8.5	9	24.0	0
Dan Skuta	28	OLB	16	294	23	2.9%	--	16	6	1	15	73%	--	2.1	--	0.0	3	10.0	0
Corey Lemonier	23	OLB	16	276	13	1.6%	--	7	4	2	6	67%	--	2.0	--	1.0	2	10.5	1

			Overall								Pass Rush			vs. Run					vs. Pass						
Linebackers	**Age**	**Pos**	**G**	**Snaps**	**Plays**	**TmPct**	**Rk**	**Stop**	**Dfts**	**BTkl**	**Sack**	**Hit**	**Hur**	**Runs**	**St%**	**Rk**	**RuYd**	**Rk**	**Tgts**	**Suc%**	**Rk**	**AdjYd**	**Rk**	**PD**	**Int**
NaVorro Bowman	26	ILB	16	1040	151	18.9%	4	93	35	9	5.0	2	9	92	68%	28	2.8	22	45	63%	8	5.1	11	7	2
Patrick Willis	29	ILB	14	863	105	15.0%	26	58	24	5	3.0	2	3	52	60%	60	3.9	63	35	54%	33	7.9	61	1	0
Michael Wilhoite	28	ILB	16	164	20	2.5%	--	8	2	1	0.0	0	0	10	40%	--	6.0	--	7	51%	--	3.6	--	1	0

Year	Yards	ALY	Rk	Power	Rk	Stuff	Rk	2nd Level	Rk	Open Field	Rk	Sacks	ASR	Rk	Short	Long
2011	3.49	3.77	4	44%	1	15%	31	0.86	1	0.31	1	42	6.5%	17	15	17
2012	3.68	3.92	15	60%	17	19%	16	0.97	1	0.42	2	38	6.4%	17	16	10
2013	3.88	4.12	22	66%	18	14%	31	0.99	6	0.42	2	38	6.0%	29	9	14

2013 ALY by direction: Left End 3.36 (9) Left Tackle 4.06 (18) Mid/Guard 4.35 (29) Right Tackle 3.90 (17) Right End 3.18 (7)

The 49ers hope that no more bombs are dropped this offseason in regard to Aldon Smith. The talented pass rusher has shown questionable judgment on multiple occasions, and is at risk of a suspension. If he is out, Corey Lemonier and Dan Skuta will be pressed into the lineup at outside linebacker. The Earl of Lemonier is a competitive, versatile and fast player off the edge, though he does not have Smith's initial explosiveness; Skuta is a lunch-pail journeyman who would be seriously stretched as a starter.

Michael Wilhoite is the favorite to replace Navorro Bowman at inside linebacker until the All-Pro is healthy again. Wilhoite is a big run-stopper, but the team may have to use a committee approach to cover for his weaknesses. Vic Fangio was willing to put Bowman or Patrick Willis on slot receivers man-to-man, but there's no way Wilhoite is doing that. Nick Moody, an undersized sixth-round pick in his second season out of Florida State, will likely be on the field in passing situations. The team also used a third-round pick on Chris Borland (Wisconsin) and signed Shayne Skov (Stanford), and they will also get a chance to compete for snaps until Bowman returns. Borland projects as a run stopper who is instinctual and technically sound, but won't provide the sideline-to-sideline range of Bowman. Skov is a fiercely competitive and aggressive (sometimes overaggressive) local hero who went undrafted in part because of worries regarding his past knee surgeries.

The other position battle is at nose tackle, where Ian Williams returns from his broken ankle to compete with Glenn Dorsey, the former Chiefs first-round pick. Dorsey was a pleasant surprise at nose tackle last year, after several seasons underwhelming as a 3-4 defensive end in Kansas City. San Francisco only played a nose tackle on about 40 percent of the snaps last year, as depth behind Dorsey was a concern. With both Williams and Dorsey back, that percentage should go up, regardless of who the nominal starter is. The most underappreciated player on the line is Ray McDonald, who quietly goes about occupying blockers, and played through last season with a partially torn biceps for almost the entire year. As for the old man of the line, how much longer can Justin Smith continue? The veteran defensive end turns 35 years old in September, and while he no longer can replicate his dominant 2011 season, he is still a key part of the defense. The team invested in a potential replacement last year, when they spent a second-round pick and a "redshirt" season on Cornellius "Tank" Carradine. The aggressive Florida State product will be moving from a traditional 4-3 end position to five-technique in the 49ers' 3-4, much as Smith did when he came to San Francisco from Cincinnati.

Defensive Secondary

			Overall									vs. Run					vs. Pass									
Secondary	Age	Pos	G	Snaps	Plays	TmPct	Rk	Stop	Dfts	BTkl	Runs	St%	Rk	RuYd	Rk	Tgts	Tgt%	Rk	Dist	Suc%	Rk	AdjYd	Rk	PD	Int
Carlos Rogers*	33	CB	16	1046	55	6.9%	64	23	8	6	9	44%	35	5.2	16	83	18.0%	16	11.4	50%	58	7.8	48	8	2
Donte Whitner*	29	SS	16	1012	85	10.7%	32	30	12	7	28	32%	55	6.0	20	41	9.1%	54	13.7	62%	19	7.6	52	11	2
Eric Reid	23	FS	16	982	80	10.0%	37	29	12	10	25	32%	57	9.4	69	38	8.7%	51	12.0	67%	7	5.7	16	10	4
Tarell Brown*	29	CB	13	755	42	6.5%	71	16	8	4	6	33%	53	9.8	66	73	21.9%	49	12.2	50%	59	6.7	18	10	0
Tramaine Brock	26	CB	16	663	48	6.0%	76	17	13	0	0	0%	--	0.0	--	74	25.5%	76	13.7	54%	36	6.8	20	13	5
Antoine Bethea	*30*	*FS*	*16*	*1028*	*116*	*14.0%*	*5*	*40*	*19*	*6*	*65*	*40%*	*37*	*7.5*	*50*	*30*	*7.1%*	*25*	*13.3*	*41%*	*72*	*13.2*	*76*	*5*	*2*
Chris Cook	*27*	*CB*	*12*	*734*	*48*	*7.3%*	*58*	*15*	*5*	*7*	*11*	*36%*	*49*	*7.0*	*41*	*43*	*13.9%*	*2*	*12.0*	*35%*	*85*	*10.5*	*82*	*2*	*0*

Year	Pass D Rank	vs. #1 WR	Rk	vs. #2 WR	Rk	vs. Other WR	Rk	vs. TE	Rk	vs. RB	Rk
2011	5	-5.7%	7	-17.8%	6	-3.9%	17	-1.1%	6	2.1%	19
2012	6	-10.3%	10	-16.2%	7	2.1%	21	-9.5%	7	-17.0%	8
2013	10	-9.5%	11	-1.2%	14	-0.6%	14	-15.0%	8	-13.6%	7

No player expected to start in the San Francisco secondary this year had started a game for the franchise before 2013. Over the last two offseasons, the team has moved on from Dashon Goldson (to Tampa Bay before last season), Donte Whitner (Cleveland), Tarell Brown (Oakland), and Carlos Rogers (also signed with Oakland). Last year's first-round pick Eric Reid has gone from talented rookie to leader of the secondary in just a few months.

The team did add veteran safety Antoine Bethea from Indianapolis, and he will start opposite Reid while playing more of an strong safety role than he did with the Colts. Jimmie Ward, the first-round pick out of Northern Illinois, will also be in the safety mix and is expected to see the field as a nickel corner as well.

A year ago, Tramaine Brock was a fourth-year UDFA who had never started an NFL game and was stuck on the depth chart behind both starters as well as veteran Nnamdi Asomugha. By the time the playoffs arrived, he was the best cornerback on this roster. Brock had his coming out party against the Rams in Week 4, with two interceptions and a touchdown return, and by the end of the year was a stabilizing force at cornerback. The competition for the other starting spot would appear to be Chris Culliver's to lose. To this point, Culliver is better known for his off-the-field behavior, including controversial statements at the Super Bowl two years ago and an arrest earlier this offseason on felony weapons possession and hit and run charges. Even if he escapes punishment from Roger Goodell, Culliver is coming back from a knee injury, so his return to form is not guaranteed. Former Minnesota starter Chris Cook and journeyman Perrish Cox will also be competing for the job, and will hope to replicate Brock's rise up the depth chart. The opportunity is there, and the coaching staff has shown that name and previous rank does not matter. It will be interesting to see what the 49ers coaches can do with Cook, who came out with an odd set of numbers in last year's charting: he was targeted less than any starting cornerback other than Darrelle Revis despite being one of the worst corners in the league by all our metrics.

Special Teams

Year	DVOA	Rank	FG/XP	Rank	Net Kick	Rank	Kick Ret	Rank	Net Punt	Rank	Punt Ret	Rank	Hidden	Rank
2011	7.8%	2	4.7	7	6.4	6	4.8	3	13.1	4	10.0	3	-2.6	17
2012	-1.5%	20	-17.8	32	-2.6	23	-0.6	19	13.4	4	0.3	15	-2.0	21
2013	3.7%	7	5.9	6	10.0	3	-4.6	26	10.7	3	-3.6	20	2.0	12

Andy Lee was not named All-Pro last season, because Johnny Hekker was also very good and, by golly, sometimes it's nice to give someone else a turn. However, Lee still finished with a 48.2-yard gross punting average, and it was the seventh straight year where he ranked in the top five in the league in that category. Combine that with excellent coverage, and the 49ers ranked behind only St. Louis and New Orleans in net punt value. Phil Dawson discovered the fountain of youth between Cleveland and San Francisco, or perhaps is invigorated by playing on a contender after so many years with the Browns. The last three years, Dawson has been something that field-goal kickers rarely are—consistent, finishing sixth, fourth, and sixth in our placekicking metric. Dawson has always been average on gross kickoff distance but the 49ers' kick coverage was as phenomenal as their punt coverage last year. Four different players made at least 10 special-teams plays (tackles or assists): C.J. Spillman with 15, Michael Wilhoite with 13, and Kassim Osgood and Ray Ventrone with 10 apiece.

While the kicking game is in good hands, the return game has been an issue, declining steadily since Harbaugh's first year. LaMichael James was an improvement over Kyle Williams, but San Francisco still failed to produce many explosive plays. (Anthony Dixon had the longest return of the year, 47 yards in the second half of a blowout against Jacksonville, which sums up the situation nicely.) James has been unhappy this offseason and didn't appear at voluntary workouts, so while he is first in line for return duties again, don't rule out rookie Bruce Ellington, who has experience as a punt returner in college.

St. Louis Rams

2013 Record: 7-9	**Total DVOA:** 2.4% (14th)	**2014 Mean Projection:** 7.8 wins	**On the Clock (0-4):** 10%
Pythagorean Wins: 7.6 wins (17th)	**Offense:** -9.5% (22nd)	**Postseason Odds:** 29.7%	**Mediocrity (5-7):** 35%
Snap-Weighted Age: 25.4 (32nd)	**Defense:** -5.7% (11th)	**Super Bowl Odds:** 2.8%	**Playoff Contender (8-10):** 41%
Average Opponent: 6.2% (3rd)	**Special Teams:** 6.3% (4th)	**Proj. Avg. Opponent:** 2.6% (5th)	**Super Bowl Contender (11+):** 14%

2013: If you had to face this defensive line every day in practice, you would throw nothing but dumpoffs and short crosses too.

2014: Sam and Brian at the Last Chance Café.

The Rams have the best four-man defensive line in the NFL. They also have a quality linebacker corps. They are coursing with young talent at the offensive skill positions. From a name-and-potential standpoint, their offensive line should be very good. There is young talent in the secondary, and the pass rush has the power to absolve youthful sins by defensive backs. The Rams have a great young kicker and dangerous return men. Their head coach has a distinguished track record. Their uniforms are cool.

The Rams should be a very good team. Even with the Seahawks and 49ers blockading the top of the NFC West, the Rams should be where the Cardinals were a year ago: stomping their feet and demanding playoff entry with double-digit wins.

Yet something is missing. Quarterback was an obvious omission from the list above. Sam Bradford is young (he turns 27 in November) and gets paid like a franchise quarterback, but he is often injured and maddening to watch when healthy.

Bradford is an easy scapegoat for the Rams' slow development, but there is another likely culprit: offensive coordinator Brian Schottenheimer. Schottenheimer's Jets offenses never cracked the top ten in offensive DVOA. They only finished in the top half of the NFL in passing DVOA once: in 2006, Schottenheimer's first year as coordinator, with Eric Mangini giving him orders and Chad Pennington managing the huddle. Schottenheimer has posted positive DVOA once in the past seven years (he also managed a 0.0% figure once, but a Blutarsky joke would be mathematically misleading). As you probably know if you are familiar with the phrase "butt fumble," he also supervised the most direct downward trajectory of a quarterback prospect's development in recent memory.

Bradford or Schottenheimer? Chicken or egg? Sith Lord or dark apprentice? It does not matter, because Jeff Fisher is committed to both. Whoever was at fault in 2013, both coordinator and quarterback must solve a problem that is keeping the Rams from reaching their potential.

Rams passing statistics are a numerical quagmire. DVOA gave the passing game a positive grade (0.1%), though with a healthy curve for facing so many great-to-historic defenses: the Rams' non-adjusted passing DVOA was negative (-4.0%). The curve would have been more drastic if the Rams did not also face some of the *worst* pass defenses in the NFL, including the Cowboys and Falcons, two teams they could not move the ball against until garbage time. When you factor in other distortions, like penalties and the increased efficiency of passing games last year, the Rams ranked just 21st passing the ball—and that's after accounting for the unique circumstances their defense created.

A close look at the Rams' game-by-game passing DVOA shows that the team earned high scores almost exclusively in games in which the team took an early lead – often with a big boost from the defense – and threw the ball as infrequently as possible. In the Texans (103.1% passing DVOA), Colts (91.4%), and Saints games (89.2%), Bradford and Kellen Clemens attempted a TOTAL of 52 passes, completing 35 for 522 yards with seven touchdowns and no interceptions. The games were full of special-teams touchdowns and early scoring drives that began in opponents' territory after turnovers. It's rare for a team's passing DVOA to get a major boost from its defensive front four, but the Rams' pass rush is that good, and their passing game needed that much help.

Roll the game tape, and the Rams passing game looked well below any standard of "average." The first thing that becomes obvious is the sheer amount of micro-passing the team used. Bradford threw 262 passes. Only 34 of them were labeled as "deep" passes according to the play-by-play. That's roughly 13 percent. The average NFL quarterback throws "deep" passes a little over 18 percent of the time.

The five-percent difference does not convey just how short the Rams' short-passing game is, however. Bradford's average pass traveled 6.9 yards in the air. The average NFL pass travels 8.3 yards in the air. The average NFL quarterback throws 49 percent of his passes within five yards of the line of scrimmage, from screens to dumpoffs to shallow drags and hitches. Bradford threw within five yards of the line of scrimmage 58 percent of the time.

So Schottenheimer's offense is very short-pass heavy. Big deal. *Some* team has to be below average in the pass length statistics, right? And it's not like Tom Brady is Daryl Lamonica. The problem is that the Rams' short passing did not work very well. Bradford averaged 4.6 yards per attempt on those five-and-under dinks and dunks. The NFL average is 5.2. If you are curious, Kellen Clemens averaged 5.1. All of that short passing should result in an above-average completion rate, but Bradford was below league average (60.7 to 61.2), while Clemens was worse. The team ranked far below average in yards after catch on passes behind the line of scrimmage

2014 Rams Schedule

Week	Opp.	Week	Opp.	Week	Opp.
1	MIN	7	SEA	13	OAK
2	at TB	8	at KC	14	at WAS
3	DAL	9	at SF	15	ARI (Thu.)
4	BYE	10	at ARI	16	NYG
5	at PHI	11	DEN	17	at SEA
6	SF (Mon.)	12	at SD		

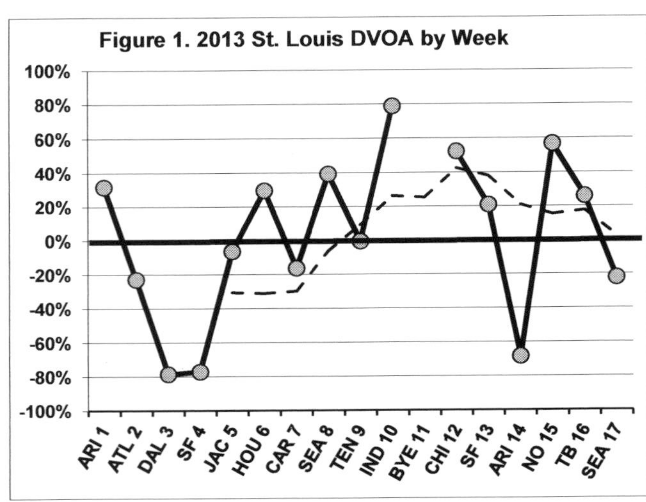

(7.5 vs. the league average of 8.7, 28th overall) and passes within five yards of the line (5.7 compared to an average of 6.2, 24th overall). The Rams threw shorter than most teams and did far less with those short throws.

To hammer home the shortness and predictability of the Rams offense: Bradford attempted just six "deep" passes in seven first quarters last year. Five of those passes were thrown 20 to 23 yards downfield, so they were hardly deep at all: the Rams never bothered to throw basic "stretch the field" bomb passes in their first few drives of the game. Instead, they offered defenses a steady diet of Schottenheimer specials: shallow crosses, play-action weirdness in the flat, tunnel screens to Tavon Austin, hitch routes, and other highly-engineered five-yard nonsense. Do you remember the old Warner Bros. cartoon about the factory that tears down an entire forest to create the perfect toothpick? That's what Schottenheimer's offense looked like last year.

Defenses knew what to expect. Bradford's first two interceptions of the year were pick-sixes by defensive linemen. Opponents dropped into zones, let Austin and other would-be playmakers catch drags, then tackled them for minimal gains. With zero big-play capability, the Rams had to execute-execute-execute down the field to score points. They were not up to the task. Young receivers dropped passes over the middle. Tight end Jared Cook, the alleged reliable veteran, fumbled in the open field and made other goofy mistakes. The Rams could clamp down when they got a lead (as in the Texans/Colts/Saints games), but they had a hard time getting leads. Bradford threw 44 passes when leading but 187 when trailing, skewing his (and the Rams') passing data with lots of meaningless fourth-quarter throws.

Was Schottenheimer restricting Bradford or protecting him with all of those four-yard tosses? Bradford's delivery was inconsistent, and his accuracy followed. Receivers had to reach in all directions for an alarming number of incredibly short passes. Deep passes, when they occurred, typically tailed toward the sidelines, and Bradford often threw late, as if he wasn't sure what an open downfield receiver looked like. By this point, Bradford should at least be at the Matthew Stafford stage of his career: funky mechanics, but a clear set of marketable quarterback skills. Instead, he looked like EJ Manuel last year, still getting comfortable with the basics of timing and accuracy.

Blaming Bradford for Schottenheimer or Schottenheimer for Bradford is immaterial as long as both remain together. There is a depressing chance that Bradford is damaged goods at this point: too many injuries, high-profile coordinators of dubious distinction (Josh McDaniels and Pat Shurmur also whispered in his ear), and bad habits may have sapped Bradford's potential. But there is no heir apparent on a roster that now features Shaun Hill as the backup and Gilbert Gottfried as the third-stringer. (Oops, that's SMU project Garret Gilbert, who won't be ready for anything anytime soon.) The Rams must make the best of things at quarterback and coordinator this year, then make decisions on a quarterback with a $13 million base salary in 2015 and a coordinator whose dad meant the world to Buddy Ryan's biological (Rex) and spiritual (Fisher) offspring.

The Rams reasoned in the offseason that the best way to improve their passing game was to improve the running game. General manager Les Stroud turned to Auburn to find lineman Greg Robinson and running back Tre Mason; suggesting that he should have grabbed Chip Kelly-meets-Joe Gibbs coordinator Scot Loeffler while he was there would be mean. Robinson is a pure run-blocker in the Jon Runyan mold who will begin his career at guard. Mason is a jackhammer between the tackles. The Rams running game was a major problem until Zac Stacy emerged late in the season, and the interior blocking contributed to the Schottenheimer-Bradford fear of slow-developing deep passes (guard Chris Williams was a mess), so Robinson and Mason fix legitimate problems. If the running game can creep past 3.0 yards per carry, the Mendoza Line for many of Bradford's starts, everyone benefits—though it is important to note that the running game will also improve if opposing safeties have to play deep, ever.

The Rams are also counting on some wide-receiver development. Poor Austin got stuck catching screen passes the whole defense saw coming early in last season, resulting in a bunch of six-catch, 30-yard stat lines. He had just started to flash his electrifying after-catch skills before getting hurting his ankle on a 56-yard end around late in the season. Stedman Bailey got lost in the crowd of young receivers last year but caught 16 of the 23 passes thrown to him in the final six games, consistently hauling in 10- to 15-yarders in an offense that treats such distances as suborbital flights. Chris Givens regressed badly last season as the theoretical deep threat, and both Brian Quick and Austin Pettis seemed confused about what they were supposed to do when not running shallow crossing routes, but the pure amount of talent here is much greater than it seems at first glance. With Robinson solidifying a retooled offensive line and Mason helping Stacy thump, perhaps Givens can provide some home runs, like he did in 2012. Maybe Austin will catch a screen and not face three waiting defenders. Maybe Kenny Britt, acquired quietly in the offseason, will get his mind right and challenge for a role.

Or perhaps Bradford and Schottenheimer have no chance of holding up their end of the bargain. Watch 2013 game film, whether Bradford or Clemens is under center, and you see an offense that looks uncoordinated. Receivers don't release off the line well or sell their routes when going deep. Quarterbacks barely look off safeties before searching for that checkdown option. The timing on short play-action passes looks like the sort of thing you see during July two-a-days. Jets fans reading this essay are nodding and/or shaking their heads. The Rams may be throwing offensive resources down a well.

The problem facing both coach and quarterback in 2014 is that this is not the AFC East four years ago. Great defense and a lumbering offense will not get anyone ten wins and a chance to stun Peyton Manning and Tom Brady in the playoffs. All those attributes will get the Rams in 2014 is another season circling .500. The Rams offense must play like one that features a veteran first-overall pick at quarterback, Pro Bowlers and top prospects on the offensive line, and a Who's Who of young skill position talent.

The Rams' front four has proven it belongs in conversations with the Seahawks and 49ers, and we have seen what Austin and the other receivers can do. Now that Robinson and Mason are here, there are no more excuses. Bradford won't get a real second chance with another team if he flops this year, and Schottenheimer is running out of Ryan scions in high places. If the Rams do not make the playoffs, they had better make sure they were clearly the Best Team Not to Make the Playoffs, a title NFC West teams may hold for the foreseeable future. Anything less will be an indictment on two men rapidly running out of benefits of the doubt.

Mike Tanier

2013 Rams Stats by Week

Wk	vs.	W-L	PF	PA	YDF	YDA	TO	Total	Off	Def	ST
1	ARI	W	27	24	366	390	0	32%	12%	-7%	12%
2	at ATL	L	24	31	421	393	-1	-23%	-1%	25%	4%
3	at DAL	L	7	31	232	396	0	-79%	-60%	24%	5%
4	SF	L	11	35	188	370	0	-77%	-52%	21%	-5%
5	JAC	W	34	20	351	363	+3	-6%	-2%	-6%	-11%
6	at HOU	W	38	13	216	420	+4	29%	22%	4%	12%
7	at CAR	L	15	30	317	282	-3	-16%	-16%	0%	-1%
8	SEA	L	9	14	339	135	-2	39%	-16%	-59%	-4%
9	TEN	L	21	28	363	363	0	-1%	4%	3%	-1%
10	at IND	W	38	8	372	406	+4	79%	-3%	-46%	36%
11	BYE										
12	CHI	W	42	21	406	424	+3	52%	36%	-4%	12%
13	at SF	L	13	23	312	338	0	21%	-1%	-11%	11%
14	at ARI	L	10	30	257	369	-1	-68%	-39%	31%	1%
15	NO	W	27	16	302	432	+3	57%	26%	-26%	5%
16	TB	W	23	13	277	170	0	26%	-14%	-31%	9%
17	at SEA	L	9	27	158	269	-2	-22%	-47%	-11%	14%

Trends and Splits

	Offense	Rank	Defense	Rank
Total DVOA	-9.5%	22	-5.7%	11
Unadjusted VOA	-13.1%	24	-4.1%	11
Weighted Trend	-5.8%	22	-12.4%	7
Variance	7.9%	22	6.4%	21
Average Opponent	-4.2%	4	1.7%	6
Passing	0.1%	21	4.7%	15
Rushing	-14.8%	28	-18.2%	3
First Down	-10.6%	25	-9.4%	9
Second Down	-13.0%	24	-1.6%	10
Third Down	-2.7%	16	-4.4%	13
First Half	-7.1%	22	-2.9%	12
Second Half	-12.0%	24	-8.1%	9
Red Zone	-8.5%	23	-29.2%	4
Late and Close	-3.4%	17	10.7%	26

Five-Year Performance

Year	W-L	Pyth W	Est W	PF	PA	TO	Total	Rk	Off	Rk	Def	Rk	ST	Rk	Off AGL	Rk	Def AGL	Rk	Off Age	Rk	Def Age	Rk	ST Age	Rk
2009	1-15	1.6	0.9	175	436	-13	-45.1%	31	-29.5%	32	17.2%	31	1.7%	11	38.4	27	36.3	23	26.8	24	26.2	27	25.5	28
2010	7-9	6.8	5.4	289	328	+5	-19.4%	28	-18.1%	30	2.1%	19	0.8%	14	47.1	32	9.7	4	25.7	29	26.8	17	26.1	19
2011	2-14	2.3	2.2	193	407	-5	-35.4%	32	-27.2%	32	3.4%	21	-4.8%	28	66.6	32	43.5	27	27.1	16	27.6	7	26.4	11
2012	7-8-1	6.6	8.2	299	348	-1	1.5%	15	-4.2%	21	-9.1%	7	-3.4%	26	28.0	16	8.3	3	26.3	23	26.3	24	25.5	29
2013	7-9	7.6	7.8	348	364	+8	2.4%	14	-9.5%	22	-5.7%	11	6.3%	4	26.7	10	22.3	10	26.1	28	25.0	31	25.0	30

2013 Performance Based on Most Common Personnel Groups

STL Offense					STL Offense vs. Opponents				STL Defense				STL Defense vs. Opponents			
Pers	Freq	Yds	DVOA	Run%	Pers	Freq	Yds	DVOA	Pers	Freq	Yds	DVOA	Pers	Freq	Yds	DVOA
11	42%	5.4	-0.4%	18%	Nickel Even	39%	5.0	-10.8%	4-3-4	47%	5.2	-6.6%	11	46%	6.1	0.8%
12	37%	5.4	-9.4%	56%	4-3-4	32%	5.6	-10.0%	Nickel Even	46%	5.8	-3.3%	12	16%	5.2	-16.0%
13	14%	4.4	-18.0%	73%	3-4-4	19%	4.6	-12.5%	Goal Line	2%	1.2	-29.3%	21	16%	5.8	-2.3%
10	2%	2.3	-82.5%	0%	Dime+	5%	6.5	20.3%	Dime+	2%	6.9	15.8%	22	8%	5.1	-9.7%
14	1%	1.3	-13.4%	60%	Nickel Odd	3%	7.9	68.0%	Nickel Odd	2%	12.2	6.5%	13	3%	3.6	-14.0%

Strategic Tendencies

Run/Pass		Rk	Formation		Rk	Pass Rush		Rk	Secondary		Rk	Strategy		Rk
Runs, first half	47%	2	Form: Single Back	57%	28	Rush 3	5.5%	18	4 DB	48%	8	Play action	22%	15
Runs, first down	54%	6	Form: Empty Back	7%	15	Rush 4	61.3%	17	5 DB	48%	17	Avg Box (Off)	6.45	7
Runs, second-long	31%	20	Pers: 3+ WR	46%	26	Rush 5	21.9%	19	6+ DB	2%	24	Avg Box (Def)	6.43	10
Runs, power sit.	46%	26	Pers: 4+ WR	3%	8	Rush 6+	11.3%	7	CB by Sides	84%	8	Offensive Pace	32.31	31
Runs, behind 2H	23%	27	Pers: 2+ TE/6+ OL	54%	2	Sacks by LB	9.4%	30	DB Blitz	9%	23	Defensive Pace	31.67	31
Pass, ahead 2H	41%	27	Shotgun/Pistol	41%	31	Sacks by DB	3.8%	23	Hole in Zone	16%	2	Go for it on 4th	0.83	19

The modern NFL, in a nutshell: St. Louis used shotgun formation on 41 percent of plays, the exact same rate as they used shotgun in 2012, but dropped from 21st in the NFL to 31st. The Rams dropped 30 passes, or 6.4 percent of all passes, more than any offense except Detroit. Meanwhile, their defense benefitted from only 17 opponent drops, the fewest in the league. The Rams might want to consider running outside a bit more often; they had only 8.3 percent of runs listed as "left end" or "right end," the lowest rate in the league. Despite using a first-round pick on a player whose skill set is tailored to wide receiver screens, the Rams used this play only 15 times, and gained just 2.3 yards per pass with -70.7% DVOA. The Rams recovered only five of their 15 fumbles on offense. The Rams' defense allowed a league-high 12.2 average yards after catch on passes thrown behind or at the line of scrimmage. St. Louis committed a league-high 32 penalties on kickoffs or punts, not counting delay of game; no other team was above 24. The Rams were also near the top of the league with 23 such penalties in 2012. Overall, the Rams were third in the league with 142 penalties after leading the league with 150 penalties the year before.

Passing

Player	DYAR	DVOA	Plays	NtYds	Avg	YAC	C%	TD	Int
S.Bradford	304	5.2%	277	1602	5.8	5.7	60.7%	14	4
K.Clemens*	60	-7.5%	262	1526	5.8	5.2	58.9%	8	7

Rushing

Player	DYAR	DVOA	Plays	Yds	Avg	TD	Fum	Suc
Z.Stacy	80	-0.7%	250	976	3.9	7	1	42%
D.Richardson	-34	-19.4%	69	215	3.1	0	0	42%
B.Cunningham	5	-5.7%	47	261	5.6	1	2	45%
K.Clemens*	-35	-52.9%	16	69	4.3	0	2	-
T.Austin	75	134.8%	9	151	16.8	1	0	-
S.Bradford	-25	-70.1%	8	39	4.9	0	1	-
I.Pead	-4	-21.2%	7	21	3.0	0	0	43%

Receiving

Player	DYAR	DVOA	Plays	Ctch	Yds	Y/C	YAC	TD	C%
C.Givens	-68	-22.8%	83	34	570	16.8	7.6	0	41%
T.Austin	-36	-19.4%	69	40	420	10.5	5.8	4	58%
A.Pettis	90	5.1%	63	38	399	10.5	3.1	4	60%
B.Quick	72	12.6%	34	18	304	16.9	5.8	2	53%
S.Bailey	36	7.5%	25	17	226	13.3	2.7	0	68%
K.Britt	*-101*	*-48.5%*	*35*	*11*	*96*	*8.7*	*1.2*	*0*	*31%*
J.Cook	58	2.8%	86	51	671	13.2	5.1	5	59%
L.Kendricks	3	-6.4%	46	32	258	8.1	3.4	4	70%
C.Harkey	13	2.2%	18	13	113	8.7	8.7	2	72%
Z.Stacy	-11	-19.7%	35	26	141	5.4	5.7	1	74%
D.Richardson	9	-3.6%	18	14	121	8.6	8.5	0	78%
I.Pead	8	-5.2%	15	11	78	7.1	6.5	0	73%
B.Cunningham	8	3.6%	10	6	59	9.8	10.2	0	60%

Offensive Line

Player	Pos	Age	GS	Snaps	Pen	Sk	Pass	Run
Chris Williams	LG	29	16/16	901	4	2.8	16.8	4.0
Jake Long	LT	29	15/15	851	5	6.8	13.3	6.0
Joseph Barksdale	RT	25	16/13	822	1	3.0	12.5	4.0
Scott Wells	C	33	12/12	738	4	1.3	3.3	1.0
Rodger Saffold	G/T	26	12/9	543	3	0.0	6.0	3.0
Harvey Dahl	RG	33	9/9	528	5	1.0	12.5	2.0
Shelley Smith	G	27	13/2	363	1	3.0	7.0	1.0
Tim Barnes	C	26	16/4	266	0	0.5	1.0	2.0
Davin Joseph	*RG*	*31*	*16/16*	*1009*	*6*	*2.0*	*20.0*	*7.5*

Year	Yards	ALY	Rk	Power	Rk	Stuff	Rk	2nd Lev	Rk	Open Field	Rk	Sacks	ASR	Rk	Short	Long	F-Start	Cont.
2011	4.22	3.75	30	48%	31	20%	20	1.25	10	0.72	22	55	9.1%	28	19	19	29	27
2012	4.30	4.08	14	63%	16	20%	21	1.26	11	0.76	16	35	6.2%	14	8	12	22	26
2013	3.95	3.95	12	58%	25	19%	13	1.05	20	0.68	16	36	6.8%	14	14	7	13	29

2013 ALY by direction: Left End 4.11 (11) Left Tackle 4.14 (11) Mid/Guard 3.88 (17) Right Tackle 4.10 (13) Right End 3.95 (12)

Scene: Rams adding protection for Sam Bradford. Take: Five... Action! The Rams have been trying to build a good offensive line for a long time, but draft flops (Hi, Jason Smith!) and injuries haven't allowed one to materialize. Jake Long was the free-agency prize last year, and while he was healthy enough to play 15 games before tearing his ACL, his level of play has declined after numerous injuries. He averaged a blown block every 44.0 snaps, which is on par with his 45.6 average in 2012 with Miami. That's a little below average for a left tackle. Long is expected to be ready to start by Week 1, and will line up next to second overall pick Greg Robinson. Sure, he's the future at tackle, but the Rams are determined to keep Robinson at left guard as a rookie. He's big and powerful, but his pass protection needs work. At run-heavy Auburn last year, Robinson only blocked for 273 pass plays (29.6 percent of his total snaps) and still allowed five knockdowns, eight pressures and four sacks, according to STATS LLC.

Rodger Saffold was the next draft pick the Rams made after taking Bradford first overall in 2010. Though once thought to be a franchise left tackle, injuries in 2011 and 2012 led to the team bringing in Long and moving Saffold to right tackle. Last year he moved to right guard; after one of the craziest stories of the offseason, it looks like that will be his new permanent home. The Rams looked to have lost Saffold in free agency when Oakland signed him to an absurd five-year deal worth $42.5 million. The move was heavily criticized, but days later the contract was nullified after results of a physical gave Oakland concerns about Saffold's shoulder. He returned to the Rams with a five-year deal worth a more reasonable $31.7 million. The Rams had "no concerns whatsoever" about Saffold's shoulder. OK, but can he actually stay healthy? Saffold hasn't played more than 12 games since his rookie season. Joe Barksdale, no relation to Avon, already made the Oakland-to-St. Louis trip in 2012 when the Raiders cut the third-round pick after just one season. He started 13 games last year and held his own at right tackle. Center Scott Wells enters his 11th season, but he's missed 13 games with injuries for the Rams the last two years. He's solid when he plays. Davin Joseph, once a Pro Bowl guard in Tampa Bay, was a strong depth addition to a line with durability issues.

Defensive Front Seven

			Overall								vs. Run					Pass Rush			
Defensive Line	**Age**	**Pos**	**G**	**Snaps**	**Plays**	**TmPct**	**Rk**	**Stop**	**Dfts**	**BTkl**	**Runs**	**St%**	**Rk**	**RuYd**	**Rk**	**Sack**	**Hit**	**Hur**	**Tips**
Michael Brockers	24	DT	16	792	45	5.3%	38	37	12	1	35	83%	27	2.6	60	5.5	6	8.0	0
Kendall Langford	28	DT	16	743	52	6.1%	29	43	15	2	41	83%	26	1.4	13	5.0	0	8.0	4
Jermelle Cudjo	28	DT	13	212	12	1.7%	--	10	1	0	10	80%	--	1.5	--	0.0	1	1.0	1

			Overall								vs. Run					Pass Rush			
Edge Rushers	**Age**	**Pos**	**G**	**Snaps**	**Plays**	**TmPct**	**Rk**	**Stop**	**Dfts**	**BTkl**	**Runs**	**St%**	**Rk**	**RuYd**	**Rk**	**Sack**	**Hit**	**Hur**	**Tips**
Chris Long	29	DE	16	839	41	4.8%	51	33	19	2	27	81%	23	1.8	17	8.5	5	20.8	2
Robert Quinn	24	DE	16	831	58	6.8%	21	48	33	2	37	76%	40	1.2	6	19.0	21	43.0	0
Eugene Sims	28	DE	16	385	28	3.3%	--	25	7	0	23	91%	--	2.3	--	2.0	5	6.8	1
William Hayes	29	DE	14	345	31	4.1%	--	24	13	2	18	78%	--	1.8	--	5.0	6	13.5	2

			Overall								Pass Rush			vs. Run					vs. Pass						
Linebackers	**Age**	**Pos**	**G**	**Snaps**	**Plays**	**TmPct**	**Rk**	**Stop**	**Dfts**	**BTkl**	**Sack**	**Hit**	**Hur**	**Runs**	**St%**	**Rk**	**RuYd**	**Rk**	**Tgts**	**Suc%**	**Rk**	**AdjYd**	**Rk**	**PD**	**Int**
James Laurinaitis	28	MLB	16	1055	124	14.5%	31	70	27	6	3.5	2	4	66	65%	44	3.5	51	47	48%	44	6.9	44	9	2
Alec Ogletree	23	OLB	16	1034	129	15.1%	25	73	34	13	1.5	0	8	58	69%	26	3.8	59	38	41%	61	7.3	54	5	1
Jo-Lonn Dunbar	29	OLB	12	419	39	6.1%	78	23	5	6	0.0	3	2	23	83%	3	1.9	5	9	18%	--	9.8	--	0	0

Year	Yards	ALY	Rk	Power	Rk	Stuff	Rk	2nd Level	Rk	Open Field	Rk	Sacks	ASR	Rk	Short	Long
2011	4.83	4.26	23	55%	8	18%	19	1.21	18	1.26	29	39	7.4%	9	17	16
2012	4.09	3.50	2	59%	13	25%	3	1.21	21	1.02	26	52	8.5%	3	18	24
2013	3.80	3.50	5	51%	4	27%	2	1.13	18	0.77	20	53	9.5%	1	20	17
2013 ALY by direction:			*Left End 3.20 (8)*			*Left Tackle 3.31 (4)*			*Mid/Guard 3.49 (6)*			*Right Tackle 3.76 (15)*			*Right End 3.68 (16)*	

Gregg Williams was hired to be the Rams' defensive coordinator in 2012, but served a year-long suspension for his role in the Saints bounty scandal. Two years later, he's finally reunited with pal Jeff Fisher, and he inherits an impressive collection of talent in the front seven. The defensive line features four players drafted no lower than 14th overall and still under the age of 30. Rookie defensive tackle Aaron Donald (Pittsburgh) is the latest to join the party, but he may not even start after Kendall Langford had a career year where he was just as impactful as Michael Brockers. Still, expect the undersized Donald to get plenty of pass-rushing snaps this year. Some scouts are worried about Donald's size (6-foot-1, 285 pounds), but Geno Atkins has fared quite well despite being only 6-foot-1 and 293 pounds.

The Rams' stars are their bookend rushers. Chris Long's picked up his production well the last few years, but he can't match the pass-rushing monster that Robert Quinn was on his way to All-Pro honors. Once upon a time, in the 2011 draft, Quinn was a bit overshadowed with Von Miller, Aldon Smith and J.J. Watt all picked before him. But last year, Quinn ranked second in the league in sacks (19.0), hurries (43.0), and quarterback knockdowns (36). He also led the league by drawing seven offensive holding penalties. Fisher had Jevon Kearse in Tennessee, but Quinn has surpassed the Freak at this point. He's a perfect fit for Williams, a Buddy Ryan disciple who has a history of aggressively applying pressure. William Hayes and Eugene Sims provide veteran depth. There's also a seventh-round pick you may have heard of named Michael Sam. A lot of fans have a lot of hopes riding on Sam's performance, but SackSEER is *very* pessimistic about him: he had very few sacks before his senior year, almost no passes defensed in college, and a terrible combine performance. With the depth chart deep at defensive end, Sam will need quite the preseason to make the final roster.

James Laurinaitis is known as the tackling machine in the middle, but rookie Alec Ogletree actually notched more tackles last season. Ogletree was a polarizing prospect in the draft community, but he certainly flashed at times with a 98-yard pick-six and six forced fumbles. He had just as many Defeats (34) as Luke Kuechly, and one more than Quinn. There were bad moments of course, such as 13 broken tackles (tied for fifth most) and struggles in coverage, but the Rams look to feature his athleticism more this year. In an injury-shortened season, Jo-Lonn Dunbar regressed from his solid 2012 debut with the Rams, but now he'll reunite with Williams who had him in New Orleans (2009-11).

With this athletic front seven, the Rams finished first in DVOA against tight ends in 2013, but in Fisher's two seasons, the pass defense has ranked 31st and 32nd in DVOA against running backs. Last year teams effectively used running back screens to avoid the pass rush and expose the linebackers, particularly Ogletree. With so many young defenders, especially in the secondary, Williams may want to be cautious in dialing up pressure. The other thing to watch out for is depth at linebacker: every player on the depth chart is an undrafted free agent in his first three seasons except for the three starters and a practice-squad scrub named Caleb McSurdy who was once a seventh-round pick.

Defensive Secondary

			Overall								vs. Run					vs. Pass									
Secondary	Age	Pos	G	Snaps	Plays	TmPct	Rk	Stop	Dfts	BTkl	Runs	St%	Rk	RuYd	Rk	Tgts	Tgt%	Rk	Dist	Suc%	Rk	AdjYd	Rk	PD	Int
Rodney McLeod	24	FS	16	1060	82	9.6%	44	28	15	8	34	29%	64	10.7	74	35	8.6%	47	12.6	65%	15	7.0	41	6	2
Janoris Jenkins	26	CB	16	1045	74	8.6%	42	32	9	8	13	54%	22	4.5	10	80	20.2%	34	12.0	45%	77	9.9	79	15	1
Trumaine Johnson	24	CB	16	871	77	9.0%	32	31	11	12	15	47%	32	6.1	27	73	22.1%	52	8.6	48%	66	7.1	34	10	3
T.J. McDonald	23	SS	10	650	57	10.7%	31	24	10	5	28	50%	21	5.0	13	20	8.1%	41	10.8	42%	70	8.5	58	4	1
Darian Stewart*	26	SS	13	567	39	5.6%	--	17	9	5	15	47%	--	5.3	--	13	6.0%	--	8.8	72%	--	3.3	--	5	0
Cortland Finnegan*	30	CB	7	361	28	7.5%	--	5	1	6	5	60%	--	7.2	--	29	20.8%	--	9.7	34%	--	9.2	--	1	1

Year	Pass D Rank	vs. #1 WR	Rk	vs. #2 WR	Rk	vs. Other WR	Rk	vs. TE	Rk	vs. RB	Rk
2011	15	8.3%	16	6.1%	18	8.5%	26	-11.3%	2	6.9%	22
2012	8	-17.3%	6	-7.7%	9	5.3%	23	5.4%	23	26.6%	31
2013	15	41.6%	32	-16.1%	5	0.6%	15	-41.6%	1	25.6%	32

Cortland Finnegan was released just two years into a five-year deal that was worth $50 million. Over the summer he called 2013 defensive coordinator Tim Walton's system "atrocious." Walton was fired, but atrocious is a fine word for Finnegan's play last year. He didn't have enough targets to qualify, but his Adjusted Success Rate would have been the second worst in the league. Trumaine Johnson fared a bit better in replacing Finnegan, and he joins Janoris Jenkins to give St. Louis a pair of third-year starting cornerbacks. Johnson needs to shore up his tackling; he had 12 broken tackles last year.

Jenkins is the star of the secondary, but he may have a little DeAngelo Hall syndrome going on, minus the attitude problems. That means when he's not making a big splash play, he's providing poor coverage. Jenkins flashed as a rookie with four defensive touchdowns, but he only had one interception returned for five yards last year while plummeting in Adjusted Success Rate (55th to 77th) and Adjusted Yards per Pass (33rd to 79th). Call it a sophomore slump if you want, but last year was a bad season for the young corner. Williams usually likes to play a lot of aggressive man coverage, which may suit Jenkins better. The Rams added Florida State cornerback Lamarcus Joyner with their second-round pick. He's small (5-foot-8), so his future may be covering the slot.

Rodney McLeod is a ho-hum safety with better coverage stats than expected, possibly due to the Rams getting roasted outside the numbers last year. He caught the only interception Josh McCown threw in 2013. Strong safety T.J. McDonald is the intriguing member of the secondary to watch. He missed six games as a rookie last year due to a broken leg, but he has Kam Chancellor-type size and could be the playmaking safety Williams has utilized successfully in the past (think Blaine Bishop and Sean Taylor). This secondary is young, especially when you consider the depth: after Joyner came three other defensive backs chosen on the final day of this year's draft. The standout in this trio is fourth-rounder Mo Alexander out of local Eureka High School, who comes back to his hometown after playing both linebacker and strong safety at Utah State.

Special Teams

Year	DVOA	Rank	FG/XP	Rank	Net Kick	Rank	Kick Ret	Rank	Net Punt	Rank	Punt Ret	Rank	Hidden	Rank
2011	-4.8%	28	-6.1	26	-0.3	19	-4.4	26	-14.8	31	1.6	13	-4.1	22
2012	-3.4%	26	1.0	16	1.3	14	-8.4	30	-2.3	18	-8.2	30	-1.4	20
2013	6.3%	4	1.4	16	12.6	1	-1.4	17	22.4	1	-3.5	19	11.1	4

We'll pretend the ghastly fake punt in the fourth quarter at Candlestick Park (Week 13) never happened, but otherwise it was a banner year for the Rams on special teams. Their dramatic improvement was keyed by strong legwork and top-notch coverage to lead the league in both kickoff and punt value. Kicker Greg Zuerlein became famous for his 13 attempts on field goals of 50-plus yards as a rookie. That number dropped to two last year, so his 26-of-28 field goal success was on par with his 2012 performance after adjusting for distance. His kickoffs did improve, though. Second-year punter Johnny Hekker was named a first-team All-Pro after setting an NFL single-season record with a net punting average of 44.2 yards. The Rams allowed a league-low 79 punt return yards. Rookie linebacker Ray Ray Armstrong paced the coverage teams with ten tackles.

Tavon Austin was expected to boost the return game, but the Rams were just average in that department. Just like how his biggest receptions came in Indianapolis, so too did Austin's longest punt return go 98 yards for a touchdown against the Colts. There was potential for more, but the return units endured an embarrassing number of penalties in the first five games of the season (as noted in the Strategic Tendencies section). Thanks to holding penalties, Austin lost an 84-yard punt return score against Dallas and a 49-yard return against Jacksonville. Returns are one of the easiest ways to get Austin the ball in space, and this is one area where the numbers didn't do him real justice last year. He'll be a danger to kick to this season.

Seattle Seahawks

2013 Record: 13-3	**Total DVOA:** 40.0% (1st)	**2014 Mean Projection:** 9.8 wins	**On the Clock (0-4):** 2%
Pythagorean Wins: 12.8 (1st)	**Offense:** 9.4% (7th)	**Postseason Odds:** 66.1%	**Mediocrity (5-7):** 11%
Snap-Weighted Age: 25.9 (30th)	**Defense:** -25.9% (1st)	**Super Bowl Odds:** 15.4%	**Playoff Contender (8-10):** 47%
Average Opponent: -0.4% (16th)	**Special Teams:** 4.7% (5th)	**Proj. Avg. Opponent:** 1.9% (9th)	**Super Bowl Contender (11+):** 39%

2013: Everything comes together for Pete Carroll's hand-crafted team.

2014: If they want to buck the odds and repeat as Super Bowl champs, the Seahawks will have to reinvent themselves... again.

"In men's sports no one ever talks about beauty or grace or the body. Men may profess their 'love' of sports, but that love must always be cast and enacted in the symbology [sic] of war: elimination vs. advance, hierarchy of rank and standing, obsessive statistics, technical analysis, tribal and/or nationalist fervor, uniforms, mass noise, banners, chest-thumping, face-painting, etc. For reasons that are not well understood, war's codes are safer for most of us than love's."

—*David Foster Wallace*

"Just because you make a mistake doesn't mean that you don't have all the good in you—for your future. People make mistakes all the time. We learn and grow. If there's patience and love and you care for people, you can work them through it, and they can find their greatest heights. I love that this message is part of our program, because it really needs to be part of a lot of programs."

—*Pete Carroll, right after Super Bowl XLVIII*

Since he came back to the NFL in 2010, Pete Carroll has played up his "Always Compete" mantra above all else. It's been the motto behind his and general manager John Schneider's whipsaw approach to personnel, especially in the early days. In that first season, Seattle engaged in 284 player transactions, and the team that won the Super Bowl in February had just two starters (center Max Unger and defensive tackle Brandon Mebane) from the 2009 campaign. The job that Carroll and Schneider have done in four seasons is singularly impressive; by hitting on so many low-round draft picks and undrafted players, the Seahawks have been in a position to spend their cap dollars wisely, and (perhaps more importantly) recover well when they make mistakes.

The love Carroll speaks of shows up as indulgence (in his reaction to his team's fairly breathtaking number of player suspensions for violations of the league's policies on performance-enhancing substances) and a buy-in attitude that now fills the roster after the coach has rifled through so many players to find the guys who get the message—by any means necessary. It's a unique operating system that works because Carroll understands from his days at USC how to motivate young athletes—and how to flip rosters every four years.

Now, coming into a season as defending NFL champions, the franchise will try to find a new iteration of the "Always Compete" credo, and inevitably discover that it's not quite as easy when you're already on top. No team since the 2005 Patriots has even won a playoff game the year after they won a Super Bowl, and the Pats from the year before are the last team to repeat as Super Bowl champs. That's the longest stretch of single Super Bowl winners in the game's history.

There are signs that the Seahawks may break that trend. For one, with an average AV-weighted age of 26.4 years per player, they are the youngest team ever to take the NFL title in the Super Bowl era.[1] The three next-youngest teams to even get to the big game—the 1971 Miami Dolphins (average age: 26.4 years), 1981 San Francisco 49ers (26.5 years), and 1974 Pittsburgh Steelers (26.6 years)—each had dynastic runs ahead of them. The fifth-youngest team was the 1996 Patriots, who Carroll inherited as head coach after they lost Super Bowl XXXI to the Green Bay Packers. Safe to say, Carroll's learned a few things from his mistakes back then. The 1992 Dallas Cowboys and the 1999 St. Louis Rams, by the way, tied for seventh on that list with an average age of 27 years. If you get there young, you've got a really good shot at going back.

The worrying points are tied up in the team's greatness to a degree. Consistently great defense is a hallmark of this Carroll era. Seattle went from fourth to first in defensive DVOA in 2013, so while there was already a lot in the tank, the 2013 squad played at an historic level. Literally. They're the seventh-best defense of the DVOA era, which currently stretches back to 1989. And the simple truth is, those historic defenses don't get better the next year (Table 1).

Carroll was the 49ers' defensive coordinator in 1995 and 1996; that was his stop between his failed tenures as head coach for the Jets and Patriots. The 1994 49ers won the Super Bowl with a -7.5% defensive DVOA, and Carroll's schematics made that defense even better in the following two seasons. (Marc Trestman, who presided over the Bears' defensive freefall in 2013, was the 49ers' offensive coordinator in both of those seasons, which proves that Mel Tucker, Chicago's current defensive coordinator, is no Pete Carroll.) Carroll saw that San

1 This is the age of the roster weighted by P-F-R's Approximate Value stat; since we only have snap data back to 2006, this is the best way to measure age of teams going back to the start of the Super Bowl era. For more, see this post by Chase Stuart: http://www.footballperspective.com/2013-av-adjusted-team-age/

2014 Seahawks Schedule

Week	Opp.	Week	Opp.	Week	Opp.
1	GB (Thu.)	7	at STL	13	at SF (Thu.)
2	at SD	8	at CAR	14	at PHI
3	DEN	9	OAK	15	SF
4	BYE	10	NYG	16	at ARI
5	at WAS (Mon.)	11	at KC	17	STL
6	DAL	12	ARI		

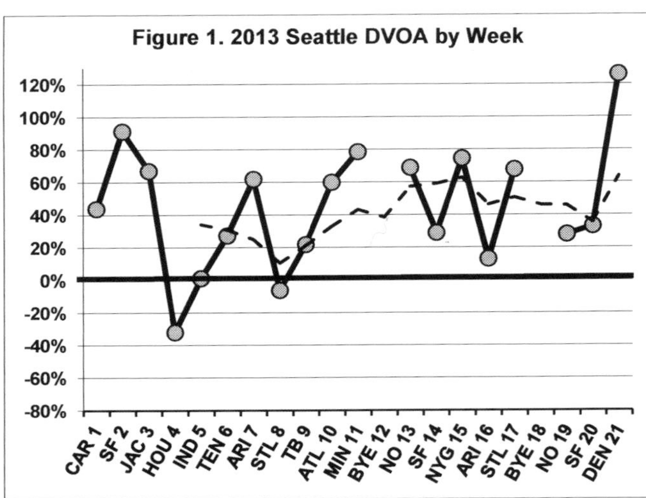

Francisco uptick despite the loss of Deion Sanders to Dallas in one of the NFL's first real big-money deals; he'll have no such problems now. Seattle signed its two most important defenders, Richard Sherman and Earl Thomas, to lucrative contract extensions in the offseason. The players who did depart, such as ends Red Bryant and Chris Clemons, are fairly easily replaced; Bryant's age and lack of conditioning started to show last year, and injuries relegated Clemons to the role of afterthought in 2013.

Which leaves one important contract to be done: Russell Wilson's. If the Seahawks are to repeat as Super Bowl champs despite the expected regression from their defense, it will be on Wilson to provide the difference. In the last two seasons, Wilson has attempted 800 passes in the regular season and another 130 in the postseason. In 2013 alone, Peyton Manning attempted 787 passes—a league-leading 659 in the regular season, and another 128 in three postseason games. No team has thrown fewer passes over the last two seasons than the Seahawks, which works if the defense and running game maintain historic levels of efficiency. If not, however, the margin for error becomes impossibly thin. The current Seahawks team is built to establish a lead through blunt force trauma and maintain that lead in the same way. In 2012, Seattle had one passing game over 300 yards, the loss to the Falcons in the divisional round of the playoffs. In 2013, they had three: the opener against the Panthers, the ridiculous 45-17 whitewash of the Jaguars in Week 3, and the Week 13 Monday night game against the Saints, when Wilson and the offense finally matched their own defense blow-for-blow in a 34-7 thrashing.

Table 1. Best Defensive DVOA Ever, 1989-2013, and Second-Year Regression

Year	Team	Year 1 DVOA	Year 2 DVOA	Regression
1991	Philadelphia Eagles	-42.4%	-18.1%	24.3%
2002	Tampa Bay Buccaneers	-31.8%	-17.6%	14.2%
2008	Pittsburgh Steelers	-29.0%	-4.6%	24.4%
2004	Buffalo Bills	-28.5%	8.6%	37.1%
2008	Baltimore Ravens	-27.8%	-14.2%	13.6%
2012	Chicago Bears	-26.7%	8.7%	35.4%
2013	Seattle Seahawks	-25.9%	—	—
2009	New York Jets	-25.5%	-10.9%	14.6%
2000	Tennessee Titans	-25.0%	10.3%	35.3%
2003	Baltimore Ravens	-25.0%	-19.9%	5.1%
1991	New Orleans Saints	-24.5%	-18.3%	6.2%
2000	Baltimore Ravens	-23.8%	-12.5%	11.3%
1995	San Francisco 49ers	-23.7%	-15.8%	7.9%
	AVERAGE	-27.8%	-8.7%	19.1%

Another 49ers team, the one that narrowly lost Super Bowl XLVII to the Baltimore Ravens at the end of the 2012 season, provides a paradigm to mirror. Colin Kaepernick's ability to create big plays through the air and on the ground—consistently or not—took an established team with a stellar defense and running game to a new level. One season later, Kaepernick has a seven-year, $129.7 million contract extension. There's a lot of funny money in there, as there is with all NFL contracts, but the point has been made—and it's now up to Wilson to make the same point.

Seattle's running game is already changing. No back has carried the ball more times over the last three seasons than Marshawn Lynch—334 carries per season, including the postseason. Lynch turned 28 in April, and though there are no obvious signs of decline that can't currently be explained away by Seattle's iffy offensive line, offensive coordinator Darrell Bevell caused quite a stir in early June when he intimated that the running back rotation was going to change... and soon.

"We are going to be running back by committee," Bevell said. "We really like what Christine Michael is doing right now ... with the quickness, the speed and the toughness he's shown. He's making great cuts. He has breakaway speed to finish a run and he has really quick moves in short areas."

Michael, the team's second-round pick in 2013, has the well-rounded skill set to become a franchise back over time in the right system, but what will happen to the Seattle offense if it gets caught between Lynch's decline and Michael's ascendency? One imagines that this would lead to a greatly increased role for Wilson.

Ben Roethlisberger provides a compelling comparison (Table 2). The 2005 Steelers won Super Bowl XL (and every Seahawks fan reading this chapter just choked all over again on that sentence) with their second-year quarterback as an adjunct factor to—guess what?—a dominant running game and an outstanding defense. Roethlisberger ranked seventh in the NFL in DYAR that season, but his role was still that of a somewhat rogue caretaker who could make plays with his arm and his feet. The reduction in DYAR in 2006 was as much a function of increased reps as anything else; it's a near-inevitability if the rest of the offense stays baseline. Roethlisberger's interception total shot up from nine to a league-leading 23; his yards per completion down from an NFL-best 14.2 to 12.5. And Pittsburgh's rushing attempts dropped from 549 to 469. It was the start of the Pittsburgh offense as a passing-heavy concern, and those types of drastic shifts usually take a little time. In 2007, Roethlisberger threw 32 touchdowns to 11 picks, and he was indeed a true difference-maker in his team's Super Bowl year.

The Seahawks would hope that Wilson's story doesn't turn out more like Griffin's, where the young quarterback is expected to do more without the right support system around him. Griffin was struggling with his famous knee injury to be sure, but the infrastructure of the offense was crumbling around him as well. To avoid a similar fate, the Seahawks selected two receivers in the draft—Colorado's Paul Richardson in the second round, and Alabama's Kevin Norwood in the fourth. Richardson is clearly a contingency plan for the seemingly inevitable Percy Harvin physical meltdown. Harvin missed all but 68 snaps in his first Seahawks season due to a hip injury, and his brief appearances indicated that had he been healthy all year, Seattle would have already opened up its passing game. Richardson is that same kind of smaller speedster, while Norwood is ostensibly the guy who can help with the team's red-zone issues by making tough catches in a lot of traffic. With Sidney Rice just about done and Golden Tate off to Detroit in free agency, it will be up to the kids to do a lot.

If the Seahawks are to move to more of an aerial attack, Wilson will have to make more definitive throws in the pocket. It's a primary reason he lasted until the third round of the 2012 draft—at 5-foot-11, many teams were scared that Wilson would not be able to create plays consistently because of the traffic in front of him. Like Michael Vick and Drew Brees before him, Wilson rolls out to create throwing lanes, and he's been prolific and successful in that regard. Last year, Wilson threw 91 actual passes outside the pocket, the most in the NFL, and he averaged a phenomenal 8.0 yards per pass, much higher than the NFL average of 5.9 yards. Encouragingly, Wilson has also been excellent when asked to stick and stay—once we account for sacks and scrambles, his DVOA ranked the same both in the pocket (35.0% DVOA, eighth) and out of the pocket (26.3%, eighth). But there could be a lot of weird residue in an extra 100 or so extra pass plays, especially if opposing defenses move their safeties back because they aren't as scared of their linebackers getting plowed over by Mr. Skittles.

Speaking of weird residue... Seattle's turnover magic from the second half of last season may be tough to replicate if the passing game is more expansive. In Week 9, Seattle had ones of its worst games of the year, somehow snagging a 27-24 win over Tampa Bay despite a turnover margin of minus-3. But that was pretty much it for turnovers the rest of the season. In the 10 remaining games, including the postseason, the Seahawks only turned the ball over five times. There were six games, including the Super Bowl, in which they didn't turn the ball over at all. Then again, they lost to the Arizona Cardinals at home (their first home loss in two seasons) despite Carson Palmer's four-pick day, and it is this loss that may explain why the Seahawks need to do things differently, risk be damned. Wilson completed 11 of 27 passes for 108 yards, one touchdown and one interception, and the Seattle offense was particularly impotent in the red zone. It was a problem overall: the 2013 Seahawks ranked 20th in red-zone DVOA, and 22nd in goal-to-go situations, despite the power running game. It's the fine balance between mistake-proofing one's entire team, and having enough explosive plays to dominate in multiple ways over time.

Even last November, Carroll seemed to be suggesting the offense move in another direction, one quite different than the "run the ball down their freakin' throats" philosophy he prefers to espouse.

"We're always committed to running the football because that's the formula we would like to exhibit, but you can't knock your head against the wall," he told the media. "When it ain't happening, it ain't happening. That's why we've always felt like we need to do what we have to do to get the game won. If it was a perfect world, we want to balance it out and make you have to defend it all, play everything off of the running game and make you have to defend the play [action] passes and the movement of the quarterback and all that."

Something's got to give in 2014. The Seahawks can continue to run (literally) with their old modus operandi, or they can hurdle themselves into what the NFL has become for most other teams over the last decade. If they stick with the former, they stand a serious chance of becoming an anachronistic footnote; yet another one-year wonder that couldn't adapt to the new realities. If they're able to make the shift intelligently, they've got as good a chance as any franchise over the last decade to break the streak that's been growing since the 2004 Patriots, and establish a legitimate dynasty.

It's simple. If Pete Carroll loves this team as much as he says he does, he'll let it go.

Doug Farrar

Table 2. Largest Year-to-Year Increase in Passing Attempts, 1989-2013

QB	First Year	Attempts	DYAR	Second Year	Attempts	DYAR	Attempts +/-	DYAR +/-
Robert Griffin III	2012	442	727	2013	611	-60	169	-787
Scott Mitchell	1994	459	28	1995	605	1520	146	1492
Ben Roethlisberger	2005	379	885	2006	523	623	144	-262
Matt Ryan	2008	434	1012	2009	570	701	136	-311
Steve Young	1994	511	1634	1995	644	1054	133	-580
Mark Sanchez	2009	393	-382	2010	525	234	132	616
Neil O'Donnell	1994	463	64	1995	592	679	129	615
Brett Favre	2003	473	654	2004	598	1284	125	630
Matt Hasselbeck	2001	462	-154	2002	587	938	125	1092
Joe Montana	1993	490	862	1994	615	724	125	-138

2013 Seahawks Stats by Week

Wk	vs.	W-L	PF	PA	YDF	YDA	TO	Total	Off	Def	ST
1	at CAR	W	12	7	370	253	+1	44%	26%	-6%	11%
2	SF	W	29	3	290	207	+4	91%	6%	-81%	5%
3	JAC	W	45	17	479	265	+1	67%	40%	-27%	-1%
4	at HOU	W	23	20	270	476	+1	-32%	-44%	-3%	9%
5	at IND	L	28	34	423	317	0	1%	15%	9%	-5%
6	TEN	W	20	13	404	223	0	27%	0%	-33%	-6%
7	at ARI	W	34	22	344	234	0	62%	19%	-40%	3%
8	at STL	W	14	9	135	339	+2	-6%	-39%	-27%	6%
9	TB	W	27	24	415	350	-3	22%	41%	35%	16%
10	at ATL	W	33	10	490	226	+1	60%	24%	-23%	12%
11	MIN	W	41	20	323	336	+4	78%	35%	-30%	13%
12	BYE										
13	NO	W	34	7	429	188	+1	69%	22%	-48%	-1%
14	at SF	L	17	19	264	318	0	29%	14%	-15%	-1%
15	at NYG	W	23	0	327	181	+4	74%	-3%	-66%	12%
16	ARI	L	10	17	192	307	+2	13%	-34%	-50%	-3%
17	STL	W	27	9	269	158	+2	68%	11%	-52%	5%
18	BYE										
19	NO	W	23	15	277	409	+1	28%	6%	-11%	10%
20	SF	W	23	17	308	308	+2	33%	-25%	-38%	20%
21	vs. DEN	W	43	8	341	306	+4	126%	34%	-65%	28%

Trends and Splits

	Offense	Rank	Defense	Rank
Total DVOA	9.4%	7	-25.9%	1
Unadjusted VOA	8.0%	9	-27.9%	1
Weighted Trend	8.7%	9	-30.0%	1
Variance	7.1%	18	8.3%	28
Average Opponent	-3.2%	9	-3.7%	31
Passing	27.4%	8	-34.2%	1
Rushing	6.4%	7	-15.2%	7
First Down	10.8%	9	-11.3%	8
Second Down	16.2%	5	-23.6%	1
Third Down	-3.9%	18	-55.6%	1
First Half	15.7%	5	-29.1%	1
Second Half	2.2%	16	-22.9%	2
Red Zone	-1.2%	20	-70.6%	1
Late and Close	-3.1%	16	-21.6%	4

Five-Year Performance

Year	W-L	Pyth W	Est W	PF	PA	TO	Total	Rk	Off	Rk	Def	Rk	ST	Rk	Off AGL	Rk	Def AGL	Rk	Off Age	Rk	Def Age	Rk	ST Age	Rk
2009	5-11	4.9	3.1	330	281	+9	-30.8%	29	-19.6%	27	12.0%	29	0.8%	15	44.3	29	30.9	19	27.5	13	27.2	17	27.1	4
2010	7-9	5.4	6.9	310	407	-9	-22.9%	30	-17.3%	29	12.0%	29	6.4%	2	34.3	24	27.2	20	27.8	11	27.6	10	26.4	14
2011	7-9	8.2	8.1	321	315	+8	-1.5%	19	-8.7%	22	-7.1%	10	0.2%	16	53.4	30	25.2	14	25.8	31	26.2	26	26.0	26
2012	11-5	12.5	13.0	412	245	+13	38.7%	1	18.5%	4	-14.5%	2	5.7%	3	14.8	6	15.0	6	25.9	27	25.6	31	26.0	18
2013	13-3	12.8	13.0	417	231	+20	40.0%	1	9.4%	7	-25.9%	1	4.7%	5	44.5	22	17.3	6	25.7	32	26.0	27	26.1	14

2013 Performance Based on Most Common Personnel Groups

SEA Offense					SEA Offense vs. Opponents				SEA Defense				SEA Defense vs. Opponents			
Pers	Freq	Yds	DVOA	Run%	Pers	Freq	Yds	DVOA	Pers	Freq	Yds	DVOA	Pers	Freq	Yds	DVOA
11	45%	5.8	18.4%	34%	Nickel Even	37%	6.0	20.0%	4-3-4	52%	4.7	-26.2%	11	39%	4.8	-28.7%
12	17%	6.6	24.3%	46%	4-3-4	24%	5.7	22.5%	Nickel Even	33%	4.8	-18.4%	12	23%	4.7	-28.5%
21	15%	4.8	0.0%	68%	3-4-4	20%	5.5	8.6%	Nickel Odd	6%	4.2	-54.5%	21	15%	6.3	10.3%
22	8%	4.7	2.2%	76%	Nickel Odd	9%	7.6	52.5%	3-4-4	5%	4.3	-9.1%	22	8%	3.2	-54.9%
10	5%	5.5	26.3%	43%	Dime+	6%	6.1	4.1%	Dime+	3%	4.1	-81.8%	13	5%	3.7	-46.0%

Strategic Tendencies

Run/Pass		Rk	Formation		Rk	Pass Rush		Rk	Secondary		Rk	Strategy		Rk
Runs, first half	43%	6	Form: Single Back	62%	22	Rush 3	7.0%	12	4 DB	57%	1	Play action	34%	1
Runs, first down	54%	4	Form: Empty Back	9%	8	Rush 4	65.1%	11	5 DB	40%	27	Avg Box (Off)	6.44	9
Runs, second-long	43%	4	Pers: 3+ WR	56%	17	Rush 5	23.1%	18	6+ DB	3%	21	Avg Box (Def)	6.44	9
Runs, power sit.	61%	9	Pers: 4+ WR	7%	3	Rush 6+	4.8%	27	CB by Sides	99%	2	Offensive Pace	31.49	26
Runs, behind 2H	31%	7	Pers: 2+ TE/6+ OL	30%	18	Sacks by LB	22.1%	20	DB Blitz	5%	31	Defensive Pace	31.85	32
Pass, ahead 2H	44%	22	Shotgun/Pistol	51%	25	Sacks by DB	2.3%	27	Hole in Zone	7%	25	Go for it on 4th	0.89	16

The Seahawks led the league in penalties, drawing 9.1 flags per game (including declined and offsetting). Historically, offensive penalties correlate with losing and defensive penalties do not… but the Seahawks are an exception, as they have ranked first or second in offensive penalties for the last three seasons. Seattle had the most right-handed passing game in the league, throwing to the right side on a league-leading 49 percent of passes with a league-low 16 percent of passes going to the middle of the field. It was a good strategy as the Seahawks had the league's best DVOA rating on passes to the right but ranked 30th on passes up the middle ahead of only Buffalo and Washington. Seattle was much better running from single-back formations (4.3 yards per carry, 9.7% DVOA) than from two-back formations (3.7 yards per carry, -15.1% DVOA). The Seahawks were the only team that ran more often than they passed on second downs. In his rookie year, Russell Wilson gained just 4.6 yards per pass when opponents blitzed a defensive back, the second lowest figure in the league. In his second year, Wilson gained 9.9 yards per pass against a DB blitz, second only to Philip Rivers. Despite the fact that opponents were constantly stuck passing to make up deficits, Seattle was one of only three defenses that faced shotgun on less than 50 percent of plays. It didn't matter much, as they had the best defensive DVOA in the league both on shotgun and standard under center plays. The Seattle pass rush pressured the quarterback 30 percent of the time when it brought just four men. No other team was above 23 percent. Overall, Seattle brought pressure on 34.4 percent of pass plays. Houston was second at 28.0 percent. Of course, even when they *didn't* bring pressure, the Seahawks ranked second with 1.5% DVOA and fourth with 6.7 yards allowed per pass.

Passing

Player	DYAR	DVOA	Plays	NtYds	Avg	YAC	C%	TD	Int
R.Wilson	770	15.6%	453	3070	6.8	5.7	64.0%	26	8
T.Jackson	83	81.9%	13	151	11.6	7.5	76.9%	1	0
T.Pryor	*-388*	*-31.6%*	*304*	*1542*	*5.1*	*5.8*	*58.0%*	*8*	*11*

Rushing

Player	DYAR	DVOA	Plays	Yds	Avg	TD	Fum	Suc
M.Lynch	185	5.9%	301	1265	4.2	12	3	48%
R.Wilson	134	23.3%	79	557	7.1	1	0	-
R.Turbin	-25	-17.0%	77	264	3.4	0	0	44%
C.Michael	14	10.6%	18	79	4.4	0	0	78%
T.Pryor	*105*	*16.1%*	*77*	*580*	*7.5*	*2*	*0*	*-*

Receiving

Player	DYAR	DVOA	Plays	Ctch	Yds	Y/C	YAC	TD	C%
G.Tate*	196	12.9%	100	66	920	13.9	7.6	5	66%
D.Baldwin	274	33.3%	73	50	778	15.6	4.6	5	68%
J.Kearse	116	26.2%	38	22	346	15.7	1.7	4	58%
S.Rice	8	-9.9%	35	15	233	15.5	1.3	3	43%
R.Lockette	27	41.3%	7	5	82	16.4	2.4	0	71%
Z.Miller	22	-1.0%	56	33	387	11.7	4.5	5	59%
L.Willson	48	18.2%	28	20	272	13.6	8.9	1	71%
M.Lynch	55	9.1%	44	36	316	8.8	7.9	2	82%
R.Turbin	-6	-24.2%	12	8	60	7.5	8.0	0	67%
D.Coleman	26	43.2%	8	8	62	7.8	5.8	1	100%

Offensive Line

Player	Pos	Age	GS	Snaps	Pen	Sk	Pass	Run	Player	Pos	Age	GS	Snaps	Pen	Sk	Pass	Run
J.R. Sweezy	RG	25	15/15	952	7	0.5	15.5	12.0	Breno Giacomini*	RT	29	9/9	534	6	2.5	15.0	5.0
Paul McQuistan	G/T	29	16/10	773	4	6.8	21.3	8.0	Michael Bowie	RT	23	9/8	523	2	3.3	15.3	4.0
James Carpenter	LG	25	16/10	760	6	1.8	10.8	10.0	Russell Okung	LT	27	8/8	425	7	2.0	10.0	0.0
Max Unger	C	28	13/13	753	3	1.0	7.5	6.5	Lemuel Jeanpierre	C	27	16/3	274	0	0.0	1.5	0.0

Year	Yards	ALY	Rk	Power	Rk	Stuff	Rk	2nd Lev	Rk	Open Field	Rk	Sacks	ASR	Rk	Short	Long	F-Start	Cont.
2011	4.12	4.01	19	73%	2	18%	10	1.11	26	0.72	24	50	8.3%	24	19	18	35	27
2012	4.83	4.42	4	70%	4	15%	1	1.42	2	0.94	8	33	7.2%	20	9	19	23	23
2013	4.03	4.05	9	49%	32	19%	15	1.17	13	0.59	23	44	9.6%	32	10	21	21	29

2013 ALY by direction: Left End 3.80 (12) Left Tackle 4.52 (7) Mid/Guard 3.81 (19) Right Tackle 4.14 (11) Right End 4.13 (8)

It's safe to say that the Seahawks won the Super Bowl despite their offensive line, not because of it. There's no question that Schneider and Carroll have missed when it comes to evaluating offensive line talent, both in the draft and free agency. Add that to offensive line coach Tom Cable and his habit of taking prospects at other positions and turning them into projects in his starting five, and you get exactly what we wrote about in last year's *Football Outsiders Almanac*: "an offensive line with two very good starters, two very bad ones, and a big question mark." And in 2013, even the two very good starters weren't bulletproof. Center Max Unger worked through an arm injury, a strained pectoral muscle, and a concussion, and missed three regular-season games. He moved from 9.5 blown blocks in 2012 to 14 in 2013 despite 224 fewer snaps. Left tackle Russell Okung played well when healthy, but missed eight games with a torn plantar plate in his foot. That left nothing but bad starters and question marks on Seattle's line for stretches of time. It worked because Russell Wilson is able to elude pressure and Marshawn Lynch seems oblivious to opposing defenders stacking the box against him most of the time, but it's a risky paradigm for long-term success.

When Okung was out, the Seahawks relied on Paul McQuistan, that most dangerous type of veteran—the guy who understands the system and wins the coaches over with his toughness, but can't compete consistently at an NFL level. Especially when tested at left tackle, McQuistan frequently found himself overmatched and overpowered. Fortunately, Okung came back in Week 11 and played with his usual quality through the playoff run. Breno Giacomini played much of the season at right tackle, but this spring he took his generally average play, and his predilection for penalties, off to the New York Jets. In his place, Seattle plans to immediately plug in second-round pick Justin Britt out of Missouri. The 6-foot-6, 325-pound Britt is the typically "gritty" player Cable likes, though he tends to get pushed back at times.

James Carpenter, selected in the first round of the 2011 draft as a right tackle, managed to transcend his injury-plagued NFL history to a degree after the team moved him to left guard. It's a better position for Carpenter, who has always struggled with protection on the edge. Right guard J.R. Sweezy, a defensive tackle at North Carolina State, is Cable's biggest project, and it shows. Though he's a powerful player in theory, Sweezy is still dealing with technique at his new position, and has a tendency to get owned at times as a result.

Defensive Front Seven

			Overall								vs. Run					Pass Rush			
Defensive Line	**Age**	**Pos**	**G**	**Snaps**	**Plays**	**TmPct**	**Rk**	**Stop**	**Dfts**	**BTkl**	**Runs**	**St%**	**Rk**	**RuYd**	**Rk**	**Sack**	**Hit**	**Hur**	**Tips**
Brandon Mebane	29	DT	16	531	46	5.8%	31	42	11	0	45	91%	8	1.0	3	0.0	7	14.0	1
Clinton McDonald*	27	DT	15	530	37	5.0%	44	33	14	1	25	92%	6	2.6	60	5.5	8	13.5	2
Tony McDaniel	29	DT	16	528	53	6.7%	21	39	9	3	49	73%	56	2.3	49	2.0	2	6.5	0
Kevin Williams	*34*	*DT*	*15*	*718*	*33*	*4.0%*	*64*	*27*	*10*	*3*	*23*	*78%*	*39*	*2.3*	*50*	*3.5*	*4*	*12.0*	*3*

			Overall								vs. Run					Pass Rush			
Edge Rushers	**Age**	**Pos**	**G**	**Snaps**	**Plays**	**TmPct**	**Rk**	**Stop**	**Dfts**	**BTkl**	**Runs**	**St%**	**Rk**	**RuYd**	**Rk**	**Sack**	**Hit**	**Hur**	**Tips**
Michael Bennett	29	DE	16	600	31	3.9%	70	30	16	2	22	95%	2	0.8	3	8.5	17	24.8	0
Chris Clemons*	33	DE	14	570	25	3.6%	72	14	8	3	17	41%	79	3.8	72	4.5	6	23.0	3
Cliff Avril	28	DE	15	551	24	3.2%	75	20	13	2	9	56%	74	4.9	78	8.0	9	29.3	4
Red Bryant*	30	DE	15	481	30	4.0%	68	26	6	3	26	85%	16	2.0	23	1.5	2	11.5	1

			Overall								Pass Rush			vs. Run					vs. Pass						
Linebackers	**Age**	**Pos**	**G**	**Snaps**	**Plays**	**TmPct**	**Rk**	**Stop**	**Dfts**	**BTkl**	**Sack**	**Hit**	**Hur**	**Runs**	**St%**	**Rk**	**RuYd**	**Rk**	**Tgts**	**Suc%**	**Rk**	**AdjYd**	**Rk**	**PD**	**Int**
Bobby Wagner	24	MLB	14	861	125	18.0%	8	76	16	3	5.0	3	4	71	68%	32	3.7	53	43	49%	42	5.9	18	5	2
K.J. Wright	25	OLB	13	738	84	13.1%	40	48	20	9	1.5	0	2.5	49	67%	34	3.3	36	40	38%	65	6.3	29	3	0
Bruce Irvin	27	OLB	12	499	42	7.1%	71	28	5	1	2.0	3	10	23	74%	12	3.8	57	16	71%	3	3.1	2	2	1
Malcolm Smith	25	OLB	15	482	53	7.1%	70	34	15	3	1.0	0	4	28	82%	4	1.3	2	22	60%	16	5.6	14	4	2

Year	Yards	ALY	Rk	Power	Rk	Stuff	Rk	2nd Level	Rk	Open Field	Rk	Sacks	ASR	Rk	Short	Long
2011	3.79	3.95	11	49%	4	20%	16	1.11	9	0.49	4	33	5.5%	28	17	12
2012	4.44	4.22	21	50%	3	18%	22	1.22	22	0.86	20	36	6.1%	21	15	14
2013	3.75	3.73	13	70%	24	21%	11	1.06	11	0.55	12	44	7.6%	7	20	14
2013 ALY by direction:			*Left End 2.50 (5)*			*Left Tackle 3.83 (12)*			*Mid/Guard 3.90 (15)*			*Right Tackle 3.40 (11)*			*Right End 4.15 (24)*	

Pete Carroll's over- and under-front defensive concepts reached their pinnacle in 2013, as Seattle sent wave after wave of freakishly athletic linemen at opponents. Nose tackle Brandon Mebane is the rock of the front line, and the only defensive starter whose tenure with Seattle predates the Carroll era. Seattle used Mebane in some interesting ways: as a two-gap nose tackle straight over center, as a one-tech shade tackle between the guard and center, and at a 45-degree angle to better penetrate blocking—the old "Stunt 4-3" the Steelers of the 1970s used with Joe Greene. In other schemes, Carroll pulled Mebane off the field and inserted Clinton McDonald and Tony McDaniel as matching tackles. And Michael Bennett, acquired from Tampa Bay, moved between end and tackle very impressively. McDonald signed a four-year deal with the Buccaneers this offseason, and Seattle signed Kevin Williams to a one-year deal to see what he has left in the tank. There's also a lot of buzz about Greg Scruggs, who put up two sacks in his rookie year of 2012 but missed the entire 2013 campaign due to a torn ACL, and the Seahawks hope to get something from 2013 draft picks Jordan Hill and Jesse Williams, both of whom were dealing with their own injuries.

The aforementioned Bennett was also effective at end—both as a pass-rusher and run-stopper, and free-agent acquisition Cliff Avril helped out as well. It was a good thing, because Chris Clemons, the former standout quarterback disruptor on that line, finally hit the age limit and saw his stats plummet as his body broke down. Clemons and Red Bryant, the former defensive tackle who current defensive coordinator Dan Quinn turned into a ginormous five-tech run-stopping end, both signed with Jacksonville, where they are reunited with former Seahawks defensive coordinator Gus Bradley. Kevin Williams could take some snaps at Bryant's old 5-tech end position, but otherwise, the depth here consists primarily of two rookies. Fourth-round pick Cassius Marsh doesn't score well in our SackSEER projection system, but that's in part because he's a hybrid player who kicked inside at UCLA when Anthony Barr would move up to defensive end. His ability to play multiple gaps has made him a Carroll favorite ever since the coach was trying to convince him to go to USC instead of UCLA. Jackson Jeffcoat, on the other hand, is a smaller, faster, and more specialized player who SackSEER absolutely adores. The son of former Cowboys defensive end Jim Jeffcoat had 13 sacks as a senior at Texas and won Big 12 Defensive Player of the Year, He also excelled in the combine drills that make up our "Explosion Index," making him the best undrafted prospect SackSEER has ever measured. His 91.3 percent rating is third in his class, tied with Barr behind only Khalil Mack and Jadeveon Clowney.

For all their success with specialists and unusual players, the Seahawks are still trying to figure out what to do with Bruce Irvin, their first-round pick in 2012. Irvin led all rookies in sacks with eight, but when Seattle made him a hybrid outside linebacker last year, Irvin looked lost for a while. It didn't help that he missed the first four games of the season due to his own league suspension for violating the NFL's PED policies (yes, this is still a trend). Irvin also had to learn to cover, and rush from different angles. There are no such issues with Bobby Wagner and K.J. Wright, who alternated between inside and outside roles depending on the scheme and did so with their usual consistency. The most interesting story of the linebacker corps was Malcolm Smith, who played for Carroll at USC and replaced Wright after a foot injury. Smith was playing well in coverage through the regular season and into the playoffs; this was a trend long before his pick-six in the Super Bowl. When Wright is healthy, he's the starter for sure, but Smith has proven himself worthy when it comes to overall reps.

Defensive Secondary

			Overall								vs. Run					vs. Pass									
Secondary	Age	Pos	G	Snaps	Plays	TmPct	Rk	Stop	Dfts	BTkl	Runs	St%	Rk	RuYd	Rk	Tgts	Tgt%	Rk	Dist	Suc%	Rk	AdjYd	Rk	PD	Int
Earl Thomas	25	FS	16	1008	109	13.8%	6	35	19	12	56	29%	66	7.8	56	30	7.3%	27	10.8	55%	41	6.9	39	8	5
Kam Chancellor	26	SS	16	1007	99	12.5%	18	50	13	6	57	58%	8	4.0	5	43	10.3%	63	7.2	62%	22	5.4	14	6	3
Richard Sherman	26	CB	16	980	64	8.1%	48	29	16	4	18	33%	53	10.6	69	65	16.0%	3	14.8	56%	29	7.7	46	14	8
Byron Maxwell	26	CB	16	482	37	4.7%	--	16	8	1	3	33%	--	2.3	--	44	22.0%	--	13.5	52%	--	6.6	--	12	4
Walter Thurmond*	27	CB	12	468	39	6.6%	--	21	11	3	7	29%	--	12.7	--	41	21.1%	--	6.7	60%	--	5.8	--	5	1
Brandon Browner*	30	CB	8	453	29	7.3%	57	16	7	1	3	33%	53	7.3	49	41	22.1%	51	13.7	57%	17	7.1	32	8	1
Phillip Adams	*26*	*CB*	*16*	*340*	*28*	*3.4%*	*--*	*10*	*1*	*5*	*10*	*40%*	*--*	*9.6*	*--*	*28*	*21.7%*	*--*	*12.0*	*51%*	*--*	*8.8*	*--*	*1*	*0*

Year	Pass D Rank	vs. #1 WR	Rk	vs. #2 WR	Rk	vs. Other WR	Rk	vs. TE	Rk	vs. RB	Rk
2011	8	-3.3%	10	-44.1%	1	-17.8%	11	2.0%	11	35.2%	32
2012	3	-37.5%	1	-7.4%	10	-6.0%	10	-1.6%	17	-9.3%	9
2013	1	-18.0%	4	-13.4%	7	-27.1%	3	-34.2%	3	-32.7%	1

Late in the Super Bowl, when Peyton Manning started overthrowing fades in order to avoid locking onto Seattle's defense in a blowout, you saw the conclusion of a season in which the Seahawks' secondary established itself as not only the best defensive backfield in the NFL, but perhaps the most effective and difference-making position group overall. This was despite the fact that Brandon Browner, one of its four starters at the beginning of the season, was waylaid by a combination of PED suspension and ineffective play. (He was actually benched against the Titans in October.) Browner doesn't have a lot of coverage subtleties; he was going to last as long as his trail speed did, and the fact that it might be gone is now Bill Belichick's problem. Seattle replaced Browner with Walter Thurmond and then Byron Maxwell when Thurmond had to serve a four-game suspension late in the year for (everyone say it together this time) a violation of the league's drug policy, and Maxwell became the most reliable fourth wheel over time. He was undressed a bit in the Super Bowl, but he's got the potential to keep pace with his battery mates. And that's saying something, because the other three guys in this secondary are pretty special.

Richard Sherman is the most well-known because of his mouth, but that active talk sometimes obscures just how good he really is. There is no better pure trail cornerback in the league—you throw a deep sideline route on him at your peril—and the thing that really sets him apart from "pure athletes" is the extent to which he studies film and improves as a player. In a Week 5 loss to the Colts, Sherman was exposed when asked to play bail coverage against Indy's trips and bunch formations. But by the end of the season, when asked to play off and at a more reactive angle, he used his footwork and recovery speed to lock receivers up as he does when he plays press in Seattle's base Cover-3 defense. Strong safety Kam Chancellor, who *should* have been Super Bowl MVP, absolutely destroyed Denver's short passing game as a "lurk" defender, often playing at linebacker depth and demolishing anyone fearless enough to run a slant. Chancellor is not yet a top-tier cover safety, but he's made strides in that department, and few defensive backs combine fundamentals with intimidation more consistently. With Walter Thurmond gone to the Giants, leading special-teams tackler Jeremy Lane has the inside track on the nickel spot.

But the best player in that secondary—and the best player on the team—is free safety Earl Thomas. There is no player in the league with more speed and range; even a cursory look at Thomas in an All-22 environment reveals an impressive number of "did he just do that?" plays. And though he will occasionally still overrun plays and miss tackles, Thomas (like Chancellor) has added fundamental understanding to his athleticism. Thomas has become the logical successor to Troy Polamalu and Ed Reed. Perhaps most encouraging (and most distressing to Seattle's opponents) is the fact that the team gave Thomas and Sherman lucrative extensions. As long as everyone stays healthy, there aren't many holes here.

Special Teams

Year	DVOA	Rank	FG/XP	Rank	Net Kick	Rank	Kick Ret	Rank	Net Punt	Rank	Punt Ret	Rank	Hidden	Rank
2011	0.2%	16	3.6	10	-2.0	24	1.9	12	-3.0	20	0.3	16	13.2	3
2012	5.7%	3	1.9	11	8.5	5	9.1	4	12.0	6	-3.0	19	-6.4	25
2013	4.7%	5	4.3	8	5.6	7	-3.8	22	10.4	4	7.2	6	-2.6	19

When Percy Harvin took the opening kickoff of the Super Bowl's second half 87 yards for a touchdown, it showed what the Seahawks hoped they would get from Harvin all season. Of course, that didn't happen due to Harvin's balky hip, but the team will hope for more and better in 2014. Harvin returned 114 kickoffs for 3,241 yards and five touchdowns during his four years in Minnesota, leading the league in return average twice. In Harvin's stead, kick returns were split along a committee, with 10 players taking at least one kick back. Seattle will also need a new punt returner to replace Golden Tate, who signed with Detroit. Look for Doug Baldwin, who got some of the money Seattle didn't want to give Tate, to take a lot of that slack.

Kicker Steven Hauschka tied for fifth in the league in field goal percentage, missing just two of 35 attempts. He also scored as the best kickoff artist according to our gross kickoff value over average metric, giving the Seahawks more than a touchdown worth of field position. Punter Jon Ryan had a decent season in 2013, but the real reason Seattle was so strong on punts was a coverage team that allowed an absolutely absurd 82 punt return yards *all season.*

Tampa Bay Buccaneers

2013 Record: 4-12	**Total DVOA:** -5.1% (19th)	**2014 Mean Projection:** 7.6 wins	**On the Clock (0-4):** 11%
Pythagorean Wins: 5.3 (28th)	**Offense:** -10.4% (24th)	**Postseason Odds:** 28.3%	**Mediocrity (5-7):** 37%
Snap-Weighted Age: 26.0 (28th)	**Defense:** -6.8% (8th)	**Super Bowl Odds:** 2.2%	**Playoff Contender (8-10):** 39%
Average Opponent: 9.5% (1st)	**Special Teams:** -1.5% (22nd)	**Proj. Avg. Opponent:** 0.5% (17th)	**Super Bowl Contender (11+):** 13%

2013: At one point, this was the strongest 0-8 team in NFL history, which Greg Schiano will surely stick on his resume.

2014: Could be meat, could be cake. It looks like... "meatcake."

History tells us that the Tampa Bay Buccaneers are a strong candidate to improve greatly in 2014. Here we have a team that played much better than its win-loss record last year, then put five years of chaos behind them by hiring a veteran coach known for his professionalism and leadership. Last year's quarterback, a raw rookie forced into action when the original starter was shockingly released, has been replaced by a veteran who finished 2013 as one of the highest-rated passers in the league. The Bucs have gone out of their way to supply that passer with the same type of big targets with which he had so much success last year. Their running back, so good as a rookie in 2012, should bounce back from an injury-riddled sophomore campaign. Their schedule, the toughest in the league a year ago, should be much closer to average. And they still have a handful of young players in the front seven who could shine for any team.

History also tells us that the Tampa Bay Buccaneers will struggle again in 2014. Their new quarterback is a 35-year-old journeyman who was playing in the UFL four years ago. They have also overhauled their offensive line, and they could have six new starters on offense alone. Only one wide receiver on the roster managed double digits in receptions last year. One year after they traded a first-round pick for an All-Pro cornerback, both the pick and the cornerback are gone forever. And coaching changes, even good ones, mean lots of turnover, which in the short term usually leads to lots of losses.

This is all a long way of saying that we have no idea what the Bucs are going to do this season. Their odds of winning the division are about as good as their odds of winning the first draft pick, which are about as good as their odds of finishing anywhere between those two extremes. There is nothing clear about their fate.

What is clear is that this team has a sense of stability and a long-term plan that it has lacked for half a decade now. For the first time in years, those in charge of player acquisition seem to be in sync with those in charge of player development and performance, and they have set in place a foundation for long-term success that has been missing in Tampa since the departure of Jon Gruden a few years ago.

This season, though, is a mystery. Every positive indicator around the Bucs is countered by an equally strong negative indicator. Let's go through them one at a time:

New Leadership

Positives: The pirate ship has been lost at sea since the Bucs fired Gruden in January of 2009. Raheem Morris managed to lose the roster in just three years, losing each of his last ten games, seven of them by more than 10 points. In stepped Greg Schiano, who called the Morris regime a "laughing-stock" in a meeting with season ticket holders last October. That same day, the 0-4 Bucs released Josh Freeman, who had been their starting quarterback just 11 days earlier. The Bucs then finished 4-12, losing their last three games by a combined margin of 98-44. If the Morris regime was a comedy, then Schiano's was a tragedy. Regardless, the theater is now over.

Lovie Smith, the man who once reached the Super Bowl with Rex Grossman as his quarterback, has taken over in Tampa Bay. Smith's tenure in Chicago was defined by his cool demeanor and level-headed nature. He coached some good teams and some bad teams, but he was never an embarrassment to the Bears or the city—which automatically makes him an upgrade for the Bucs. He's like the nice accountant you would want your sister to date after years of ne'er-do-wells and schemers.

Smith wasn't the only important hire for Tampa Bay. Also out is general manager Mark Dominik, the man who promoted Morris to head coach and hired Schiano to replace him. Dominik specialized in acquiring talented players who were bad fits for his coaches. In five years he drafted several potential starters who are now on other NFL rosters, including Roy Miller (Jaguars), E.J. Biggers (Redskins), Mike Williams (Bills), and Freeman, who was basically so messed up by Schiano's head games that he couldn't even keep a backup job with the Giants this offseason. Dominik also dismissed or traded Aqib Talib, LeGarrette Blount, and Michael Bennett, three key players on teams that reached last year's conference championships (and in Bennett's case, won the Super Bowl). His biggest move was the trade that brought Darrelle Revis to Florida, but that was a bad match from the start. Revis' greatest asset is his ability to shut down a receiver by himself, allowing safeties to lend help to other defenders in coverage. Schiano played Revis like he was any other corner: often with a safety over the top, or in zone coverage that wasted his man-to-man skills. The scheme also left lesser corners Johnthan Banks and Leonard Johnson vulnerable—a vulnerability opposing coaches were content to exploit over and over again.

2014 Buccaneers Schedule

Week	Opp.	Week	Opp.	Week	Opp.
1	CAR	7	BYE	13	CIN
2	STL	8	MIN	14	at DET
3	at ATL (Thu.)	9	at CLE	15	at CAR
4	at PIT	10	ATL	16	GB
5	at NO	11	at WAS	17	NO
6	BAL	12	at CHI		

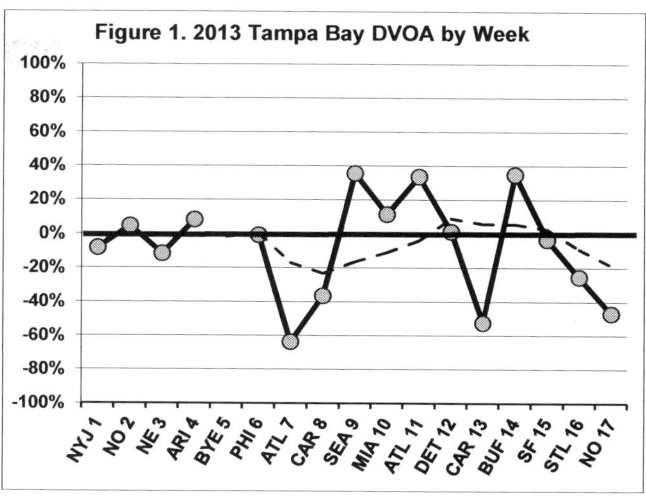

Tired of the left hand not knowing what the right was doing, the Bucs threw Dominik out along with Schiano. Into his place steps Jason Licht, formerly Vice President of Player Personnel in Arizona. It's already clear that Licht and Smith are on the same page. Smith's Chicago teams used a heavy dose of Tampa-2 zone coverage, and there was no point in paying Revis his $16 million salary for 2014 if the Bucs were going to play anything other than a steady diet of man-to-man. Revis' hefty contract made him untradeable, forcing Licht to bite the bullet and cut him loose with nothing in return. Licht then turned around and signed experienced zone corner Alterraun Verner for just $14 million in guaranteed money on a four-year deal. There's no question that the Revis trade was a disaster for the franchise, but there is also no question that the Verner acquisition demonstrates that Licht and Smith are working together to build a team from the ground up.

Negatives: All signs indicate that the Licht/Smith administration is a big improvement over its predecessors, but transition is always difficult. The new management team inherited a group full of players (like Revis) who were poor fits for their scheme, and it's going to take more than one offseason to find the kind of players they need. Verner aside, there are still plenty of questions in the secondary, and along the offensive line as well. Even if new linemen Anthony Collins and Evan Dietrich-Smith have the talent to stick as starters, it's going to take time for them to form cohesion with their teammates. These are the kind of growing pains all teams go through when they switch coaches, and that's why those changes should be avoided unless absolutely necessary—as they were for this team.

New Quarterback

Positives: Josh McCown just missed the record for lowest single-season interception rate by a few decimal points. He was also in the top ten for completion percentage, yards per pass, touchdown rate, sack rate, and NFL passer rating. And, if you've read this far, you'll be happy to hear he was fourth in DVOA and 13th in DYAR, in only five starts. By any statistical measure, this was one of the very best quarterbacks in football last season.

Negatives: Seriously, now. He's Josh McCown. This man entered the NFL 12 years ago, and almost all the evidence that he doesn't suck can be found in a six-game sample in the middle of last year. This is a man who has lost quarterback battles to Jake Plummer, Jeff Blake, Jon Kitna, Jake Delhomme, and Matt Moore. After a stint in the UFL, he failed to make the 49ers' roster in 2011 and started coaching high school. The Bears (and Lovie Smith) signed him later that season after Jay Cutler was injured. Over the next two seasons, the Bears waived him, re-signed him, let his contract expire, and re-signed him again until another Cutler injury gave him a shot at extended playing time last year, and he delivered in spades.

If you judge McCown by just those six games, there's no limit to how far he could take the Bucs this year. If you judge him by his full body of work, there's a good chance he won't be starting come December.

New Weapons

Positives: The Bucs entered the draft with one proven receiver in Vincent Jackson, one of the premier deep threats of this era, and that was it. So they doubled down in the draft, grabbing Texas A&M wide receiver Mike Evans with the seventh overall pick in the draft, then grabbing Washington tight end Austin Sefarian-Jenkins in the second round. In just two seasons with the Aggies, Evans twice went over a thousand yards receiving, and he led the SEC last year with a dozen touchdowns. Matt Waldman, who writes FO's *Futures* column, wasn't blown away by Evans' burst or route-running, but loved his physicality and downfield ability. In fact, before the draft, he compared Evans to Jackson. The new version of Playmaker Score found Evans to be a pretty typical first-round wideout prospect. Sefarian-Jenkins, meanwhile, won the Mackey Award in 2013. In three seasons with the Huskies, he averaged seven touchdowns and better than 600 yards a year, with 12.6 yards per reception. A former basketball player, he has the speed to run the full route tree and stretch the seams of a zone defense.

The Bucs also added Brandon Myers in free agency. Though Myers' athleticism won't be confused with Sefarian-Jenkins', he is a proven NFL receiver. He gained 522 yards and four touchdowns last year with the Giants, a year after gaining 806 yards and four touchdowns with the Raiders.

What all these players have in common is height. Jackson, Evans, and Sefarian-Jenkins are all 6-foot-5. Myers is 6-foot-4. Depth receivers like Chris Owusu (6-foot-0) and Skye Dawson (5-foot-9), along with running back Doug Martin

(5-foot-9), might bring that average down, but the point still stands: the Bucs are loaded with big downfield targets.

That's critical, because McCown made his name last year throwing to big downfield targets. His top receivers in Chicago, Brandon Marshall and Alshon Jeffery, each stand 6-foot-4, while tight end Martellus Bennett goes 6-foot-7. In an article on his site footballperspective.com, Chase Stuart weighted each NFL player by his total receiving yards and found that the average Bears receiver last year stood 75.9 inches. That wasn't just the tallest set of receivers in the league—it was the tallest since 1978. And if we throw out a handful of Eagles teams that had the 6-foot-8 Harold Carmichael catching Alley-Oops all day, the 2013 Bears had the tallest group of receivers since at least 1950.

McCown enjoyed his finest season by throwing passes to big receivers. The Bucs have done their best to replicate that success by grabbing every big receiver they could find.

Negatives: Very simply, this is a quite inexperienced group. Jackson has caught 52 touchdowns in his career; the rest of the roster has 25, combined, and eight of those were caught by Louis Murphy, a journeyman who had six receptions in 14 games for the Giants last year and is fighting for a spot at the bottom of the roster. Evans and Sefarian-Jenkins have talent, but they are raw, and rookies are almost never a safe bet to deliver right away. And if Jackson goes down with injury for an extended period of time, things could get real ugly, real fast.

O-Line Overhaul

Positives: The departures of left tackle Donald Penn, center Jeremy Zuttah, and right guard Davin Joseph could be a strong example of addition by subtraction. That's a total of nearly 70 blown blocks last season that the Bucs won't have to worry about in 2014. And it wasn't a one-year fluke, either. Despite the occasional big year from LeGarrette Blount or Doug Martin, Tampa Bay has struggled for years to produce consistent gains on the ground, ranking 22nd or worse in Adjusted Line Yards five seasons in a row now. Things had gotten stale, and it was time for new blood. So Licht went to work in free agency, signing Anthony Collins from Cincinnati and Evan Dietrich-Smith from Green Bay. If Carl Nicks can finally stay healthy, the 2014 Buccaneers line should be much more talented than last year's group.

Negatives: The projected starting lineup (Collins, Dietrich-Smith, Nicks, Demar Dotson, and, oh, let's say Jamon Meredith) played a total of 1,654 snaps for the Bucs last year. This is a ton of turnover for one season. This unit has gained talent, but lost continuity, which can be even more valuable to an offensive line's success. There will be struggles and breakdowns, especially early in the year.

The Revis Aftermath

Positives: Hmm. This is a tough one.

Well, we already established that Verner is a good fit for Smith's defense. Johnthan Banks was drafted in the second round in 2013 for a reason; the tall, versatile defender (he played both corner and safety in college) struggled as a rookie, but cornerback is one of the most difficult positions for rookies to play, and it's reasonable to expect significant improvement in his second season. Smith's Tampa-2 scheme should offer Banks and the other corners more support and protection, cutting down on big plays. Ideally, the corners will be able to make more plays knowing they have a safety helping them out.

Really, though, the biggest positive is that this deal is in the past, and the Bucs can move on.

Negatives: The first-round pick Tampa Bay lost in the Revis trade, the 13th overall choice in 2013, was used to take Sheldon Richardson. The next player drafted was Star Lotulelei. Desmond Trufant went less than a dozen picks later. What's done is done and those responsible have been sacked, but the damage caused by that trade is going to haunt this team for years.

From the front office to the quarterback to the receivers to the offensive line to the secondary, this is a team full of question marks, and teams like that usually fall short of the postseason. Smith, though, has taken teams to the promised land before, and he knows what kind of team he needs to get back. By his presence alone, he brings hope to Tampa Bay, and that's more than you could have said around these parts in years.

Vince Verhei

2013 Buccaneers Stats by Week

Wk	vs.	W-L	PF	PA	YDF	YDA	TO	Total	Off	Def	ST
1	at NYJ	L	17	18	250	304	0	-8%	-43%	-19%	16%
2	NO	L	14	16	273	371	0	5%	-20%	-33%	-9%
3	at NE	L	3	23	323	358	0	-12%	-9%	-7%	-10%
4	ARI	L	10	13	253	296	0	8%	-26%	-40%	-6%
5	BYE										
6	PHI	L	20	31	351	425	0	-1%	4%	16%	11%
7	at ATL	L	23	31	337	291	0	-64%	-31%	34%	1%
8	CAR	L	13	31	297	324	-1	-37%	-5%	27%	-5%
9	at SEA	L	24	27	350	415	+3	35%	62%	13%	-13%
10	MIA	W	22	19	264	213	0	11%	-7%	-5%	14%
11	ATL	W	41	28	410	420	+3	33%	29%	-12%	-7%
12	at DET	W	24	21	229	390	+5	1%	-12%	-29%	-15%
13	at CAR	L	6	27	206	426	0	-53%	-43%	8%	-2%
14	BUF	W	27	6	246	214	+3	35%	-41%	-66%	10%
15	SF	L	14	33	183	376	-2	-3%	8%	-6%	-18%
16	at STL	L	13	23	170	277	0	-25%	-33%	-9%	-1%
17	at NO	L	17	42	290	468	-1	-47%	-15%	43%	11%

Trends and Splits

	Offense	Rank	Defense	Rank
Total DVOA	-10.4%	24	-6.8%	8
Unadjusted VOA	-15.4%	28	-1.5%	15
Weighted Trend	-7.8%	23	-3.3%	12
Variance	7.8%	21	8.2%	27
Average Opponent	-4.8%	2	4.3%	3
Passing	-1.7%	22	-0.1%	11
Rushing	-11.2%	26	-14.9%	8
First Down	-0.5%	16	-19.4%	2
Second Down	-8.1%	19	0.1%	14
Third Down	-33.1%	31	8.3%	22
First Half	5.5%	13	-5.6%	8
Second Half	-28.6%	30	-8.1%	10
Red Zone	-6.0%	21	-9.9%	9
Late and Close	-39.3%	31	-4.6%	12

Five-Year Performance

Year	W-L	Pyth W	Est W	PF	PA	TO	Total	Rk	Off	Rk	Def	Rk	ST	Rk	Off AGL	Rk	Def AGL	Rk	Off Age	Rk	Def Age	Rk	ST Age	Rk
2009	3-13	3.7	4.8	244	400	-5	-23.8%	27	-19.3%	26	8.0%	25	3.5%	5	32.3	22	18.9	9	26.1	31	26.4	25	26.3	21
2010	10-6	8.7	8.4	341	318	+9	3.7%	12	8.0%	8	3.7%	23	-0.5%	18	22.9	14	37.9	25	25.6	31	25.9	27	25.4	30
2011	4-12	3.2	5.5	287	494	-16	-25.1%	30	-11.5%	26	14.2%	31	0.6%	14	17.1	6	34.3	20	26.0	30	25.6	31	25.3	31
2012	7-9	7.9	7.8	389	394	+3	-6.6%	20	0.6%	14	2.9%	20	-4.3%	27	26.7	14	30.1	18	26.4	22	25.6	30	25.7	24
2013	4-12	5.3	6.3	288	389	+10	-5.1%	19	-10.4%	24	-6.8%	8	-1.5%	22	76.6	31	9.9	1	27.0	16	25.0	32	26.2	11

2013 Performance Based on Most Common Personnel Groups

TB Offense					TB Offense vs. Opponents				TB Defense				TB Defense vs. Opponents			
Pers	Freq	Yds	DVOA	Run%	Pers	Freq	Yds	DVOA	Pers	Freq	Yds	DVOA	Pers	Freq	Yds	DVOA
11	51%	4.3	-9.8%	21%	Nickel Even	42%	4.1	-18.5%	Nickel Even	43%	6.5	2.1%	11	51%	6.4	2.0%
21	24%	5.7	-4.3%	63%	4-3-4	28%	5.8	3.5%	4-3-4	32%	4.7	-15.6%	12	19%	5.0	-16.6%
12	8%	4.6	-21.5%	37%	3-4-4	17%	4.9	-6.6%	Dime+	15%	5.9	0.2%	21	12%	5.7	0.8%
22	4%	5.3	6.1%	74%	Dime+	6%	4.8	-5.3%	Nickel Odd	5%	5.9	-17.4%	22	5%	4.6	3.2%
621	3%	2.4	6.3%	79%	Nickel Odd	5%	4.7	7.4%	3-4-4	4%	5.8	-29.2%	10	4%	5.3	-38.3%

Strategic Tendencies

Run/Pass		Rk	Formation		Rk	Pass Rush		Rk	Secondary		Rk	Strategy		Rk
Runs, first half	41%	12	Form: Single Back	64%	19	Rush 3	5.7%	17	4 DB	37%	18	Play action	19%	19
Runs, first down	51%	11	Form: Empty Back	3%	29	Rush 4	62.9%	14	5 DB	47%	18	Avg Box (Off)	6.42	11
Runs, second-long	45%	1	Pers: 3+ WR	54%	22	Rush 5	16.5%	29	6+ DB	15%	8	Avg Box (Def)	6.20	27
Runs, power sit.	45%	28	Pers: 4+ WR	0%	24	Rush 6+	15.0%	3	CB by Sides	56%	28	Offensive Pace	30.68	17
Runs, behind 2H	30%	9	Pers: 2+ TE/6+ OL	20%	29	Sacks by LB	31.4%	17	DB Blitz	15%	6	Defensive Pace	30.02	17
Pass, ahead 2H	43%	23	Shotgun/Pistol	43%	30	Sacks by DB	11.4%	10	Hole in Zone	13%	8	Go for it on 4th	1.32	5

The Bucs averaged just 3.9 average yards after catch, half a yard less than any other offense. Tampa Bay was outstanding when it used extra offensive linemen, with 4.9 yards per play and 32.6% DVOA. The Bucs were much better running from single-back formations (4.4 yards per carry, -2.6% DVOA) than from two-back formations (3.6 yards per carry, -19.7% DVOA). The Bucs ran on second-and-long (scrambles not included) a league-leading 45 percent of the time, and had 10.2% DVOA, second only to Philadelphia. Tampa Bay was one of the only two teams that didn't use a pistol formation all season. (New England was the other.) The Bucs almost never ran a screen pass, with only three wide receiver screens and 15 running back screens. When they did, it was horrible, with 1.1 yards per pass and -88.8% DVOA. When the Bucs blitzed, it seemed to work: we recorded pass pressure a league-leading 35 percent of the time when they sent five or more pass rushers. And yet, it didn't necessarily work: they still allowed 6.8 yards per play when blitzing, higher than the NFL average of 6.4 yards. The Bucs were in the top ten for using dime defenses last year, but that will change; Lovie Smith's Bears used dime on less than 0.5 percent of plays in both 2011 and 2012.

Passing

Player	DYAR	DVOA	Plays	NtYds	Avg	YAC	C%	TD	Int
M.Glennon	99	-7.7%	459	2260	4.9	3.7	59.8%	19	9
J.Freeman*	-95	-26.6%	103	540	5.2	5.1	45.7%	2	3
J.McCown	*659*	*32.1%*	*236*	*1786*	*7.6*	*5.6*	*66.7%*	*13*	*1*

Rushing

Player	DYAR	DVOA	Plays	Yds	Avg	TD	Fum	Suc
B.Rainey	-17	-12.0%	137	534	3.9	5	1	31%
D.Martin	-31	-14.9%	127	457	3.6	1	1	39%
M.James	59	14.6%	60	295	4.9	0	0	52%
B.Leonard*	5	-5.9%	47	182	3.9	0	0	43%
M.Glennon	-22	-45.6%	15	68	4.5	0	2	-
M.Hill*	-8	-38.5%	9	23	2.6	0	0	44%
J.McCown	*10*	*10.9%*	*9*	*70*	*7.8*	*1*	*1*	*-*

Receiving

Player	DYAR	DVOA	Plays	Ctch	Yds	Y/C	YAC	TD	C%
V.Jackson	122	-3.3%	161	79	1229	15.6	4.2	7	49%
T.Underwood*	133	23.6%	45	24	440	18.3	4.3	4	53%
M.Williams*	4	-11.4%	40	22	216	9.8	3.0	2	55%
K.Ogletree*	-18	-25.4%	20	8	70	8.8	2.6	1	40%
C.Owusu	-4	-15.6%	20	13	114	8.8	3.0	0	65%
E.Page	-6	-21.4%	9	4	68	17.0	5.3	0	44%
S.Dawson	-10	-28.1%	7	2	12	6.0	2.5	0	29%
L.Murphy	*-50*	*-61.2%*	*13*	*6*	*37*	*6.2*	*1.0*	*1*	*46%*
T.Wright	133	21.8%	75	54	571	10.6	2.6	5	72%
T.Crabtree	-5	-17.7%	7	4	21	5.3	3.3	1	57%
B.Myers	*7*	*-5.9%*	*75*	*47*	*522*	*11.1*	*3.6*	*4*	*63%*
B.Leonard*	2	-12.6%	37	29	179	6.2	5.3	0	78%
D.Martin	-45	-54.2%	24	12	66	5.5	4.8	0	50%
B.Rainey	-20	-35.6%	15	11	27	2.5	3.5	1	73%
E.Lorig*	-27	-43.6%	14	11	47	4.3	5.0	0	79%
M.James	-10	-30.5%	11	10	43	4.3	4.9	0	91%

Offensive Line

Player	Pos	Age	GS	Snaps	Pen	Sk	Pass	Run
Demar Dotson	RT	29	16/16	1034	4	3.0	16.0	4.0
Donald Penn*	LT	31	16/16	1032	5	8.5	21.5	6.0
Jeremy Zuttah*	C	28	16/16	1014	7	1.0	9.0	4.3
Davin Joseph*	RG	31	16/16	1009	6	2.0	20.0	7.5
Jamon Meredith	LG	28	16/8	475	6	0.5	7.0	5.5
Ted Larsen*	C/G	27	16/4	361	5	0.0	8.0	1.0
Gabe Carimi*	G/T	26	14/2	209	1	1.0	5.0	1.0
Carl Nicks	LG	31	2/2	145	1	0.5	2.5	0.8
Evan Dietrich-Smith	*C*	*28*	*16/16*	*1055*	*3*	*4.0*	*6.0*	*4.5*
Anthony Collins	*OT*	*29*	*15/7*	*578*	*1*	*0.5*	*3.0*	*1.5*
Oniel Cousins	*OT*	*30*	*16/4*	*311*	*4*	*0.0*	*9.5*	*3.0*

Year	Yards	ALY	Rk	Power	Rk	Stuff	Rk	2nd Lev	Rk	Open Field	Rk	Sacks	ASR	Rk	Short	Long	F-Start	Cont.
2011	4.32	3.96	22	65%	11	21%	26	1.23	12	0.79	19	32	6.2%	14	7	14	13	32
2012	4.50	4.09	13	60%	22	20%	22	1.19	15	1.09	5	26	4.8%	6	4	13	17	36
2013	4.00	3.63	27	59%	22	21%	22	1.12	16	0.77	13	47	7.7%	21	16	21	18	33

2013 ALY by direction: Left End 2.77 (26) Left Tackle 3.85 (16) Mid/Guard 3.93 (16) Right Tackle 3.56 (23) Right End 2.56 (31)

Between 2006 and 2008, Tampa Bay spent one first-round pick, two second-round picks, and a third-round pick on offensive linemen. Then they sat back and waited for that talent to develop. And they waited. And waited. They never really got the on-field production they were looking for, so now they have given up, cleaned house, and started over. They cut ties to the last of those linemen this offseason, treading Jeremy Zuttah to Baltimore and releasing Davin Joseph. Also departing is Donald Penn, an undrafted free agent who proved to be more reliable than any of his early-round peers. Penn has started every game since 2008, but he signed with Oakland.

The Bucs have also tried to build through free agency, signing Carl Nicks of the Saints to a $47.5 million contract in 2012. Nicks' tenure in Tampa Bay, though, has been ruined by a staph infection that limited him to seven games in 2012 and two in 2013. If he can get healthy, Nicks will return at left guard this year, if only because his contract makes him virtually un-cuttable. Also returning is Demar Dotson, a former undrafted free agent who has nailed down the right tackle position. The rest of the line will be filled by spare parts picked up cheap from other teams. Center Evan Dietrich-Smith spent three years on the Packers' bench before winning a starting role last year. Similarly, Anthony Collins spent six seasons as a spot starter for Cincinnati, impressing in limited duty. He was never able to nail down a first-string job, but he shined in 2013, with fewer blown blocks per snap than any other tackle. The right guard spot is a bit of a question mark. Patrick Omameh, an undrafted free agent out of Michigan, spent his rookie year on the practice squads in San Francisco and Tampa Bay. He has never played a regular-season game, but he was getting first-string snaps in June drills. Another candidate is Jamon Meredith, who spent time with the Bills, Lions, Giants, and Steelers before starting 20 games the last two seasons for the Buccaneers.

Defensive Front Seven

			Overall								vs. Run					Pass Rush			
Defensive Line	Age	Pos	G	Snaps	Plays	TmPct	Rk	Stop	Dfts	BTkl	Runs	St%	Rk	RuYd	Rk	Sack	Hit	Hur	Tips
Gerald McCoy	26	DT	16	963	54	6.5%	22	45	22	1	35	80%	34	2.0	36	9.5	13	40.0	4
Akeem Spence	23	DT	16	693	29	3.5%	73	20	8	1	25	76%	49	1.5	19	1.0	0	2.5	0
Clinton McDonald	*27*	*DT*	*15*	*530*	*37*	*5.0%*	*44*	*33*	*14*	*1*	*25*	*92%*	*6*	*2.6*	*60*	*5.5*	*8*	*13.5*	*2*

			Overall								vs. Run					Pass Rush			
Edge Rushers	Age	Pos	G	Snaps	Plays	TmPct	Rk	Stop	Dfts	BTkl	Runs	St%	Rk	RuYd	Rk	Sack	Hit	Hur	Tips
Adrian Clayborn	26	DE	16	932	65	7.9%	10	50	26	5	53	74%	48	1.6	14	5.5	9	26.5	0
Daniel Te'o-Nesheim*	27	DE	16	602	14	1.7%	79	13	4	2	13	92%	3	2.3	33	0.0	6	9.5	0
William Gholston	23	DE	12	312	34	5.5%	--	26	11	0	25	72%	--	2.2	--	2.0	2	3.0	3
Michael Johnson	*27*	*DE*	*15*	*906*	*65*	*8.3%*	*7*	*50*	*18*	*4*	*45*	*73%*	*49*	*2.5*	*42*	*3.5*	*20*	*26.5*	*7*

			Overall								Pass Rush			vs. Run					vs. Pass						
Linebackers	Age	Pos	G	Snaps	Plays	TmPct	Rk	Stop	Dfts	BTkl	Sack	Hit	Hur	Runs	St%	Rk	RuYd	Rk	Tgts	Suc%	Rk	AdjYd	Rk	PD	Int
Lavonte David	24	OLB	16	1022	154	18.7%	6	111	50	6	7.0	6	17.5	81	81%	5	2.1	6	52	58%	20	6.4	33	10	5
Mason Foster	25	MLB	15	770	98	12.7%	46	58	19	7	2.0	5	10.5	57	70%	21	3.1	27	27	39%	64	7.6	57	5	3
Dekoda Watson*	26	OLB	15	258	37	4.8%	--	21	8	1	2.0	3	4.5	22	68%	--	3.7	--	10	48%	--	6.3	--	1	1
Jonathan Casillas	27	OLB	12	197	27	4.4%	--	16	3	1	0.0	1	2	17	65%	--	3.2	--	6	51%	--	6.5	--	2	0

Year	Yards	ALY	Rk	Power	Rk	Stuff	Rk	2nd Level	Rk	Open Field	Rk	Sacks	ASR	Rk	Short	Long
2011	5.16	4.37	26	74%	31	23%	4	1.61	32	1.37	31	23	5.2%	30	13	6
2012	3.58	2.96	1	71%	27	33%	1	1.19	18	0.74	15	27	4.9%	31	10	8
2013	3.95	3.62	7	66%	17	24%	5	1.07	13	0.80	21	35	6.2%	25	14	11
2013 ALY by direction:			*Left End 3.07 (7)*			*Left Tackle 4.24 (24)*			*Mid/Guard 3.45 (4)*			*Right Tackle 4.35 (23)*			*Right End 3.37 (11)*	

Lavonte David's 49 Defeats was the best total for a linebacker in our database going back to 1996, breaking Ray Lewis' mark of 45 in 1999, and the second-best for all players behind J.J. Watt's 56 in 2012. That's mostly due to David's 17 tackles of running backs behind the line of scrimmage, but he also had eight third-down stops on running plays, eight more on third-down catches, and seven sacks (getting credit for a full Defeat on each of two half-sacks). In other words, he did a little bit of everything. And this wasn't a one-year fluke; David was fifth in the league with 30 Defeats as a rookie in 2012. He's the only player in the league with at least six sacks and six interceptions over the last two seasons. In short, he's one of the best young linebackers in the game and well deserving of his All-Pro recognition. At inside linebacker, Mason Foster has been an excellent hole-plugger in the running game but has been pulled off the field in nickel situations. However, Lovie Smith has said that Foster will be making on-field defensive calls this season, which implies he'll be taking a larger role on defense. In Chicago, Smith used base defense much more than the Bucs did last year (47 percent of plays in 2011, 46 percent in 2012—Tampa was at 38 percent), which means he'll need another starting linebacker. Jonathan Casillas, a sub player for three years in New Orleans and one year in Tampa Bay, is the only experienced option. The Bucs list six other linebackers on their roster, all undrafted, with a total of six NFL starts between them, all by Dane Fletcher, an end-backer who spent four seasons in New England.

Every great zone defense has had an interior lineman capable of generating pressure in a quarterback's face. The Steel Curtain Steelers had Joe Greene, the (original) Tampa-2 Bucs had Warren Sapp, and Lovie Smith's Bears had Tommie Harris, then Israel Idonije. Now, Smith comes to a Buccaneers team with the perfect player to fill that role in Gerald McCoy. McCoy had nine sacks last season, which tied for 26th and doesn't sound like the resume of a dominant rusher. However, only three of those 25 players with more sacks were defensive tackles like McCoy; the rest were perimeter players. Further, McCoy was also tied for 16th in hits, and third in the league in hurries. And now that the Bucs signed Clinton McDonald away from Seattle, McCoy won't be the only interior threat on the line. Don't count on McDonald to match his 2013 production though. In 37 games over his first three seasons, he failed to collect a sack. Tampa Bay traded up to take Akeem Spence in last year's draft, and the fourth-round rookie proved to be a solid two-down player next to McCoy.

On the outside, one defensive end spot will go to Michael Johnson, signed away from Cincinnati. Johnson's sack numbers last year were disappointing, but he was tied for third in passes tipped (it helps to be 6-foot-7), and he had 11.5 sacks in 2012. After Johnson, the Bucs have Adrian Clayborn and Da'Quan Bowers, the Brothers of Disappointment taken in the first two rounds of 2011. Clayborn has just 13.5 sacks over 35 games in his first three seasons, though he did lead all edge rushers last year with 19 Defeats in the running game. And he's certainly doing better than Bowers, who has only 5.5 sacks in his career and averaged less than 16 snaps per game last year before his season ended with a knee injury. "He's a good football player, but he needs to prove it right now," Smith told Rick Stroud of the *Tampa Bay Times*, adding that "A player like that should be able to excel in a defense like ours." Bowers then showed up out-of-shape for offseason workouts, putting his roster spot in jeopardy and opening a window for William Gholston, a fourth-round rookie who saw about two dozen snaps per game off the bench.

Defensive Secondary

			Overall								vs. Run					vs. Pass									
Secondary	Age	Pos	G	Snaps	Plays	TmPct	Rk	Stop	Dfts	BTkl	Runs	St%	Rk	RuYd	Rk	Tgts	Tgt%	Rk	Dist	Suc%	Rk	AdjYd	Rk	PD	Int
Darrelle Revis*	29	CB	16	948	61	7.4%	56	31	12	3	17	59%	10	5.1	14	50	13.4%	1	14.2	57%	22	6.4	11	11	2
Johnthan Banks	25	CB	16	940	60	7.3%	59	21	7	7	12	42%	41	9.8	64	69	18.8%	20	11.6	44%	79	8.8	70	4	3
Mark Barron	25	SS	14	834	95	13.2%	12	43	15	7	47	47%	26	6.9	36	31	9.5%	57	10.7	62%	20	6.5	28	8	2
Dashon Goldson	30	FS	13	807	78	11.6%	24	32	12	13	31	52%	19	7.1	42	24	7.4%	30	11.6	68%	6	6.9	37	8	1
Leonard Johnson	24	CB	16	691	69	8.4%	45	26	11	4	19	47%	31	4.8	12	55	20.2%	33	11.7	52%	45	8.5	67	7	1
Keith Tandy	25	FS/SS	16	441	40	4.8%	74	12	6	3	22	32%	58	7.6	52	26	15.1%	73	14.7	66%	8	4.2	6	3	3
Alterraun Verner	*26*	*CB*	*16*	*1003*	*79*	*9.5%*	*21*	*31*	*11*	*5*	*18*	*22%*	*71*	*6.8*	*39*	*72*	*17.5%*	*13*	*13.0*	*61%*	*8*	*7.2*	*36*	*23*	*5*
Mike Jenkins	*29*	*CB*	*15*	*903*	*70*	*9.1%*	*30*	*25*	*11*	*5*	*21*	*19%*	*76*	*8.0*	*54*	*68*	*19.9%*	*29*	*11.2*	*41%*	*82*	*8.7*	*69*	*6*	*2*
Major Wright	*26*	*SS*	*15*	*935*	*101*	*13.2%*	*10*	*27*	*8*	*8*	*58*	*38%*	*42*	*7.6*	*51*	*29*	*7.9%*	*40*	*14.1*	*29%*	*77*	*13.9*	*78*	*3*	*2*

Year	Pass D Rank	vs. #1 WR	Rk	vs. #2 WR	Rk	vs. Other WR	Rk	vs. TE	Rk	vs. RB	Rk
2011	30	-11.1%	5	56.6%	32	12.1%	28	6.4%	15	9.8%	24
2012	26	6.5%	21	6.7%	20	0.6%	18	12.8%	25	-1.5%	16
2013	11	-6.6%	13	-10.7%	8	20.6%	29	-7.4%	10	-19.5%	4

On the one hand, Darrelle Revis deserves credit for leading the league in lowest Target Percentage despite facing tough competition; he was covering the other team's top wideout on more than half of his targets. On the other hand, why bother throwing at Revis when you've got two other corners on the field each giving up more than 8.0 yards a pass? Regardless, Revis is out and Alterraun Verner is in. Verner comes from Tennessee, another defense that plays a lot of zone, so he should fit in well with Smith's scheme. He led the league in passes defensed last year, and has experience both split wide and in the slot. His charting numbers were quite good in 2013, but keep in mind that when Titans opponents targeted their top receivers, it was usually Jason McCourty in coverage (40 targets) and not Verner (14 targets). Johnthan Banks figures to start across from Verner. The former second-rounder is quite likely to improve in his second season; rookie cornerbacks usually struggle, and it often takes them two or three seasons to develop into quality starters. At nickelback, Mike Jenkins has more experience than Leonard Johnson, though not all of that experience is good. It speaks volumes that both Dallas and Oakland have let Jenkins walk away in consecutive years. Johnson, meanwhile, struggled as a rookie (58 percent Success Rate, 8.2 AdjYds), and then played even worse in his second season. In other words, expect No. 3 receivers to eat Tampa Bay alive again next season.

Mark Barron plays in the box as much as any safety in football. Our charters only listed him with six targets covering a wide receiver. Now he'll be asked to play a lot more deep zone in Lovie Smith's scheme, and his transition to that responsibility will go a long way in determining Tampa Bay's success this year. In some ways, Dashon Goldson's debut season with the Bucs was quite successful. He was top five in missed tackles, though, and too often he was unable to help the young corners on deep balls. The average deep pass gained 11.7 yards last year, but the 33 deep balls thrown at Banks and Johnson gained 15.5 yards apiece. Major Wright started 42 games for the Bears in the past three seasons, but he's clearly a backup here, joining Keith Tandy in a supporting role.

Special Teams

Year	DVOA	Rank	FG/XP	Rank	Net Kick	Rank	Kick Ret	Rank	Net Punt	Rank	Punt Ret	Rank	Hidden	Rank
2011	0.6%	14	7.5	4	1.1	17	0.7	15	4.5	11	-11.0	32	7.2	7
2012	-4.3%	27	1.9	12	1.7	12	-6.8	27	-15.1	30	-3.1	20	28.5	1
2013	-1.5%	22	-6.6	27	8.1	4	-7.2	31	-3.5	25	1.8	11	-7.9	26

The Bears finished sixth or better in special teams in each of Smith's last seven seasons in Chicago, including four seasons first overall. Obviously, the singular brilliance of Devin Hester had a lot to do with that, but three other players scored on kick returns under Smith, and the Bears were also often among the league leaders in field-goal and punting value. New Bucs special teams coordinator Kevin O'Dea spent four seasons in Chicago as an assistant to Dave Toub, who ran the Bears' special teams under Smith. In those four seasons, the Bears were first in our special teams ratings three times. However, this will be O'Dea's first season as the coordinator and not an assistant. Smith and O'Dea will have a lot of work to do, turning around a Bucs team that has finished in the top ten just once in the past 11 seasons.

Let's start with the positives. Michael Koenen was seventh in gross kickoff value last year, and the Bucs also had excellent coverage to finish fourth in net kickoff value. And... well, that's it. As a punter, Koenen has had negative value in each of the past three seasons, and the Bucs haven't had the same success covering punts that they have covering kickoffs. Koenen returns, so expect more of the same this year. Eric Page was the league's least valuable returner on kickoffs, thanks mainly to two fumbles in 22 returns. He was better on punt returns, but had a fumble there too. Page is still the primary returner entering camp, though you've got to figure that Jeff Demps (28.8-yard average on kickoff returns at Florida) will get a look here too.

Rian Lindell, the man responsible for that 27th place finish in field-goal kicking, was not re-signed after the season. Connor Barth kicked for the Bucs from 2009 to 2012, but missed last year with a torn Achilles tendon. The good news is that he's back. The bad news is that he has been a below-average kicker in his four-year Tampa Bay tenure. Pat Murray, a former punter and kicker for the Fordham Rams, was signed to compete with Barth.

Tennessee Titans

2013 Record: 7-9	**Total DVOA:** -6.1% (21st)	**2014 Mean Projection:** 7.7 wins	**On the Clock (0-4):** 11%
Pythagorean Wins: 7.5 (18th)	**Offense:** 1.4% (16th)	**Postseason Odds:** 33.8%	**Mediocrity (5-7):** 36%
Snap-Weighted Age: 26.7 (15th)	**Defense:** 4.2% (22nd)	**Super Bowl Odds:** 2.1%	**Playoff Contender (8-10):** 40%
Average Opponent: -2.3% (22nd)	**Special Teams:** -3.2% (26th)	**Proj. Avg. Opponent:** -5.1% (31st)	**Super Bowl Contender (11+):** 13%

2013: Definitely the last year Chris Johnson will ever predict a 2,000-yard season for himself in Tennessee. We think. Maybe.

2014: Definitely the last year we pretend Jake Locker can become a quality starting quarterback. We think. Maybe.

Culture change can happen quickly in the NFL if it is allowed to. No, this isn't the Michael Sam essay. We're talking about franchise culture, in both the front office and the locker room, and the transition of power from one custodian to the next. Take the Elway-managed Broncos, the Emery-ran Bears, or the Harbaugh 49ers. New management works to drill down on the issues they believe are holding the franchise back, and they work to fix these problems as quickly as possible.

The Tennessee Titans are the antithesis of those teams.

For years, Tennessee labored under the heavy hand of Bud Adams. In 2006, when the scouting staff wanted Jay Cutler, and the coaches wanted Matt Leinart, Adams broke the tie by decreeing Vince Young the selection. Adams wasn't quite Al Davis—he was second-class in both meddling and delusion—but he set the tone for the organization. Beat writers would pen what they thought Tennessee would do, then ultimately end their columns with some variation of "but, this really depends on what Bud thinks."

Adams passed away in the middle of the 2013 season, after years of increasing distance due to poor health and an unfortunate flipping the bird tale in 2009. The once-proud Titans team that contended in the early 2000s and had a brief resurgence in 2008 (without Young) had already shed their other power players. Jeff Fisher, Floyd Reese, and Mike Reinfeldt were gone. That left a rudderless organization that could only focus on one need at a time, handing in its draft cards while most of its free agents left. Mike Munchak would rail about the run game and they'd sign Delanie Walker, draft some offensive linemen, and call it an offseason. While Adams was still the strongest voice in the room, the overall vision of the franchise began to get blurry. When he died, the message became a full-fledged power vacuum.

The result is the roster you see in Tennessee today: an amalgamation of half-finished ideas that looks like a chameleon on the run. We jokingly decry the Titans as having no identity, but the best comedy has a little truth in it. Without a clear organizational ethos, it's hard to bunch players together in a way that makes sense. Say what you will about Jeff Fisher's idea of winning 19-10 in today's NFL… but it's an ethos.

New owner Tommy Smith, the son-in-law of Adams, has authorized the beginning of the cleanout. The Titans spent multiple seasons trying to create a line good enough for the mortal version of Chris Johnson to run through. They gave up on that and cut Johnson this offseason. The Titans often seemed ill-prepared and Mike Munchak fell on the sword. Kenny Britt couldn't have played the role of mercurial embattled wideout any better if he were auditioning for *Playmakers*. Tennessee finally stopped trying to make that work.

Enter Ken Whisenhunt and Ray Horton. Finally, it's time to demonstrate that the Titans are going in a new direction, right? Well, not exactly. The Titans spent the offseason prepping the middle of their defense for the shift to Horton's scheme, a 3-4 that relies on heavy pressure from the linebackers. Wesley Woodyard and Shaun Phillips came over from Denver to take care of one middle linebacker spot and provide situational pass pressure, respectively. Al Woods gives Tennessee a flexible defensive line piece.

But Tennessee didn't bring back their one core piece to hit the free-agent market: cornerback Alterraun Verner, who was a breakout star playing off-man coverage. Verner implied that some of former defensive coordinator Jerry Gray's motivational ploys to run more physically-gifted corners Tommie Campbell and Coty Sensabuagh ahead of him at times backfired, giving him reason to flee the Titans in the offseason. Tennessee didn't sign a cornerback to replace Verner. That should scare Titans fans, because that leaves the secondary looking very much like the unit Horton had in Cleveland last year. Except instead of Joe Haden, T.J. Ward, and assorted mid- to late-round picks who had proven nothing, the Titans have Jason McCourty, Michael Griffin, and assorted mid- to late-round picks that have proven nothing.

One thing that sticks out about Horton's defenses is that he has tended to play a very low amount of defensive backs (Table 1). He's played nickel packages somewhere between 44 and 47 percent of snaps in all three years that he's been an NFL defensive coordinator. But the passing league continues to evolve, and Horton's ranking in that category has gone from 13th-highest to 21st.

Table 1: Browns Defensive Changes under Horton

	2012	Rank	2013	Rank
Total DVOA	4.5%	22	8.2%	25
Third-down DVOA	-5.7%	10	33.9%	31
CB by Sides	80%	11	53%	31
5+ DB	56%	11	53%	24

2014 Titans Schedule

Week	Opp.	Week	Opp.	Week	Opp.
1	at KC	7	at WAS	13	at HOU
2	DAL	8	HOU	14	NYG
3	at CIN	9	BYE	15	NYJ
4	at IND	10	at BAL	16	at JAC (Thu.)
5	CLE	11	PIT	17	IND
6	JAC	12	at PHI		

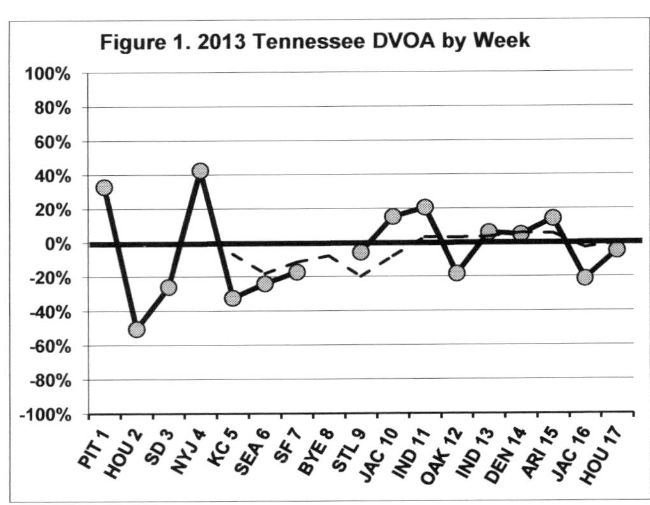

Horton's defenses have tended to rely on one dominant cornerback: first Patrick Peterson in Arizona, and then Joe Haden in Cleveland. That cornerback often roams around the formation, shadowing the opponent's most dangerous receiver. However, the play of the second, lesser, starting cornerback has often been the linchpin of the defense. In Arizona, both Richard Marshall (2011) and Greg Toler (2012) put up top-10 seasons by cornerback Success Rate with Horton. The Browns were balls-out spenders on defense in the 2013 offseason, reeling in Paul Kruger, Desmond Bryant, and Barkevious Mingo to accommodate his scheme. But even with Haden and T.J. Ward, the secondary was overmatched. Buster Skrine, nominal No. 2 cornerback, really struggled at times en route to finishing 39th in Adjusted Success Rate. Translate that to Tennessee: Jason McCourty may be up to taking on the Peterson/Haden mantle, but with Verner's departure, the rest of the corners are untested. Last year, the Browns spent a first-round pick and made $74 million in free-agent commitments almost exclusively on players to fit Horton's squad. The Browns still fell three spots in the defensive DVOA ratings because they couldn't cover anyone. The fact that Tennessee has let Verner walk does not inspire confidence that Horton can engineer a quick turnaround here. Just as with Horton's defense in Cleveland, there are hazy spots that stand out on the Tennessee depth chart—places where you can sort of see what the Titans are attempting to do, but question the way they're going about it.

As for the new head coach, Whisenhunt has a history of working with quarterbacks like Kurt Warner, Ben Roethlisberger, and Philip Rivers. This is an offensive mind that could conceivably do something to further the progress of the stalled-out Jake Locker—but Whisenhunt was never able to develop Leinart or the lower-tier projects that cluttered his final years in Arizona. We also don't understand why he replaced adequate backup quarterback Ryan Fitzpatrick with his ex-Chargers charge, Charlie Whitehurst. Whitehurst has started a grand total of four games in eight years in the NFL. For his career, he's been worth -301 DYAR with -39.2% DVOA. The backup quarterback doesn't seem like a big deal until you realize that Locker has missed 14 games over the past two seasons. A Locker injury and a quick cameo of realizing Whitehurst is awful might lead the Titans to the Zach Mettenberger Zone, formerly known as Skelton Street.

Whisenhunt learned from his time in San Diego that if you don't have much ability to stretch the field vertically, you better find a way to do so horizontally. The Chargers signed Danny Woodhead away from the Patriots and had him do just that. Woodhead's 284 receiving DYAR out of the backfield last year cracked the top-10 list for all running back seasons in the DVOA era. And while Woodhead is no Marshall Faulk or Darren Sproles, his ability as a receiving back is unquestionable. Woodhead is 17th all-time in receiving DYAR for a running back, despite more than 30 targets in a season only four times.

So Whisenhunt witnessed the effect Woodhead had on defenses and sought out a running back for the Titans who could add the same dimension. That's a smart idea. The only problem is that he picked Dexter McCluster as that back, and McCluster is one of the worst receivers to get regular playing time in recent memory. Based on our analysis, McCluster has averaged almost a yard less after the catch than we would otherwise expect given the types of passes he's catching. He posted a -16.0% DVOA on 84 targets last season, a -21.1% DVOA on 76 targets in 2012, and a -18.5% DVOA on 39 targets in 2010. It's true that because of the way baselines work for different positions, most running backs would end up with negative DVOA if we measured them as wide receivers. But then, McCluster also had poor receiving numbers when he was used much more as a running back: in 2011, he had a -12.6% DVOA on 63 targets. He also has 152 career rushes for 61 DYAR, but he's only carried the ball 20 times in the last two seasons. One could argue that McCluster is literally a zero-dimensional player. But he's fast, and he can catch a football even if he doesn't do anything after that, so the Titans rewarded him with a three-year deal with $4.5 million guaranteed.

Tennessee's other big offseason move was to bring in right tackle Michael Oher from Baltimore to replace mauler David Stewart, who retired after a down season. Oher was a fit insomuch as the Titans needed a right tackle and he was an available right tackle. But it was very peculiar that the Titans spent money on Oher, and then drafted Michigan's Taylor Lewan in the first round. For one thing, if they were considering drafting a tackle, why not spend free-agent money on a different position that could have used reinforcement? For another, if the plan is for Lewan to eventually replace the steady Michael Roos at left tackle, why sign Oher at all? The Titans are finally showing some foresight here, but on a team with as many holes as this one has, you would have to think the resources could've been allocated a little smarter.

We have the Titans with a mean projection near .500 this season, but that's more a function of the weak AFC South schedule they get to play than any real guarantee of effectiveness by us. They wouldn't rate as close to the playoffs in any other division or with any other schedule—four games against the Texans and Jaguars do a lot for their projected wins. If Locker does indeed get hurt—as has become a yearly occurrence—Tennessee will struggle to get anything done on offense, and the old Cardinals teams of yore that mixed adequate defense with a brutal offense will fly again.

If Locker does stay healthy, and plays to his established level, this squad has the potential to be a fun bridge team with little bits and pieces ripped from every philosophy embodying it. Elements of the 2013 Chargers offense mixed with the remnants of the Chris Johnson line, led by a quarterback with superior athleticism and shaky accuracy. The raw linebacker corps complied over the last few drafts, merged with the penetrating 3-4 Horton scheme that pressures the A-gap, led by one of the five best interior defenders in the league in Jurrell Casey. With reasonable quarterback play, this is a team that can squeeze out nine or ten wins in a bad division, en route to a hasty playoff exit.

It'll still be a bridge year. But maybe, at the end of that bridge, is something even more important: an actual focus on where the next bridge should be built.

Rivers McCown

2013 Titans Stats by Week

Wk	vs.	W-L	PF	PA	YDF	YDA	TO	Total	Off	Def	ST
1	at PIT	W	16	9	229	194	+2	33%	-12%	-37%	8%
2	at HOU	L	24	30	248	452	+2	-51%	-30%	12%	-9%
3	SD	W	20	17	452	277	+1	-26%	16%	24%	-18%
4	NYJ	W	38	13	322	330	+4	43%	23%	-14%	5%
5	KC	L	17	26	339	353	-1	-32%	-18%	-12%	-26%
6	at SEA	L	13	20	223	404	0	-24%	-16%	-4%	-12%
7	SF	L	17	31	368	349	-2	-17%	9%	17%	-9%
8	BYE										
9	at STL	W	28	21	363	363	0	-6%	16%	13%	-9%
10	JAC	L	27	29	362	214	-2	15%	-8%	-25%	-2%
11	IND	L	27	30	340	366	-1	20%	52%	26%	-5%
12	at OAK	W	23	19	426	353	+2	-18%	11%	22%	-7%
13	at IND	L	14	22	347	264	-3	6%	-28%	-31%	3%
14	at DEN	L	28	51	254	551	-2	5%	-6%	6%	17%
15	ARI	L	34	37	460	360	-3	14%	47%	29%	-4%
16	at JAC	W	20	16	346	289	0	-21%	-4%	15%	-2%
17	HOU	W	16	10	311	288	+3	-5%	-10%	12%	18%

Trends and Splits

	Offense	Rank	Defense	Rank
Total DVOA	1.4%	16	4.2%	22
Unadjusted VOA	3.0%	16	3.6%	22
Weighted Trend	4.5%	12	7.2%	21
Variance	5.7%	10	4.4%	10
Average Opponent	-0.3%	16	-3.1%	28
Passing	5.6%	19	6.8%	16
Rushing	2.8%	13	1.2%	25
First Down	0.0%	14	-1.9%	14
Second Down	-16.6%	28	14.9%	31
Third Down	30.0%	4	-0.9%	16
First Half	-3.3%	18	-0.5%	15
Second Half	6.0%	13	9.0%	22
Red Zone	27.3%	4	25.3%	27
Late and Close	-9.4%	21	7.4%	23

Five-Year Performance

Year	W-L	Pyth W	Est W	PF	PA	TO	Total	Rk	Off	Rk	Def	Rk	ST	Rk	Off AGL	Rk	Def AGL	Rk	Off Age	Rk	Def Age	Rk	ST Age	Rk
2009	8-8	6.7	7.9	354	402	-4	-6.6%	21	4.2%	15	9.1%	26	-1.7%	24	7.4	3	14.9	5	28.1	5	27.4	13	26.6	15
2010	6-10	8.5	8.6	356	339	-4	6.6%	11	-4.5%	20	-5.8%	8	5.3%	6	21.0	13	10.6	5	27.4	17	26.5	20	26.2	17
2011	9-7	8.2	8.3	325	317	+1	6.6%	13	0.6%	15	0.3%	15	6.3%	3	20.0	8	17.7	9	28.1	3	25.7	30	26.4	14
2012	6-10	4.6	3.3	330	471	-4	-29.4%	30	-20.5%	29	7.5%	25	-1.4%	19	49.9	26	14.6	5	27.7	9	25.3	32	26.0	15
2013	7-9	7.5	6.6	362	381	0	-6.1%	21	1.4%	16	4.2%	22	-3.2%	26	28.7	12	15.9	5	27.3	13	26.2	20	26.4	8

2013 Performance Based on Most Common Personnel Groups

TEN Offense					TEN Offense vs. Opponents				TEN Defense				TEN Defense vs. Opponents			
Pers	Freq	Yds	DVOA	Run%	Pers	Freq	Yds	DVOA	Pers	Freq	Yds	DVOA	Pers	Freq	Yds	DVOA
11	55%	6.2	18.6%	17%	Nickel Even	31%	5.6	11.0%	4-3-4	36%	5.4	0.6%	11	44%	5.7	1.6%
12	22%	4.1	-18.4%	58%	3-4-4	25%	4.6	-3.6%	Nickel Even	36%	5.8	10.1%	12	22%	5.5	1.6%
21	9%	4.8	4.8%	71%	4-3-4	18%	4.8	-15.5%	Dime+	12%	5.7	-9.7%	21	16%	5.8	4.9%
22	7%	5.6	12.4%	89%	Dime+	15%	7.0	45.4%	Nickel Odd	11%	6.6	23.6%	22	6%	4.1	-11.9%
13	3%	2.2	-55.9%	81%	Nickel Odd	9%	5.6	-0.2%	Goal Line	5%	2.3	-2.0%	10	3%	5.3	14.3%

Strategic Tendencies

Run/Pass		Rk	Formation		Rk	Pass Rush		Rk	Secondary		Rk	Strategy		Rk
Runs, first half	42%	9	Form: Single Back	66%	17	Rush 3	6.0%	16	4 DB	36%	19	Play action	13%	28
Runs, first down	53%	8	Form: Empty Back	8%	9	Rush 4	56.7%	25	5 DB	46%	22	Avg Box (Off)	6.35	17
Runs, second-long	34%	14	Pers: 3+ WR	56%	18	Rush 5	26.0%	14	6+ DB	12%	10	Avg Box (Def)	6.39	14
Runs, power sit.	43%	31	Pers: 4+ WR	1%	22	Rush 6+	11.3%	6	CB by Sides	78%	16	Offensive Pace	30.91	22
Runs, behind 2H	28%	15	Pers: 2+ TE/6+ OL	35%	12	Sacks by LB	16.7%	23	DB Blitz	7%	26	Defensive Pace	30.04	18
Pass, ahead 2H	40%	29	Shotgun/Pistol	53%	21	Sacks by DB	1.4%	28	Hole in Zone	13%	9	Go for it on 4th	0.94	14

The Titans have used "max protect" blocking very little over the last couple seasons, but don't expect that to change with Ken Whisenhunt taking over; the Chargers used max protect less often than any other offense in the league last year. The Titans offense fumbled 18 times but only lost five of them. For the third straight season, the Titans gave up much more yardage against runs from single-back formations (4.7 yards per carry) than against runs from two-back formations (3.3 yards per carry). The NFL averages were 4.2 and 3.9. The Titans were among the best teams in the league on both offense and defense when losing by more than a touchdown, but were mediocre or worse the rest of the time. Titans opponents dropped only 18 passes, the lowest figure in the AFC.

Passing

Player	DYAR	DVOA	Plays	NtYds	Avg	YAC	C%	TD	Int
R.Fitzpatrick*	179	-3.6%	369	2359	6.4	5.1	62.5%	14	12
J.Locker	69	-5.7%	199	1139	5.7	5.1	61.0%	8	4

Rushing

Player	DYAR	DVOA	Plays	Yds	Avg	TD	Fum	Suc
C.Johnson*	110	1.5%	279	1067	3.8	7	2	46%
S.Greene	61	8.9%	77	295	3.8	4	0	61%
J.Battle*	-8	-13.5%	36	142	3.9	1	0	33%
R.Fitzpatrick*	85	34.8%	35	232	6.6	3	0	-
J.Locker	32	20.7%	20	159	8.0	2	2	-
D.McCluster	*-25*	*-89.6%*	*8*	*5*	*0.6*	*0*	*0*	-

Receiving

Player	DYAR	DVOA	Plays	Ctch	Yds	Y/C	YAC	TD	C%
K.Wright	95	-3.7%	140	94	1085	11.5	5.9	2	67%
N.Washington	162	7.4%	104	58	919	15.8	4.0	3	56%
J.Hunter	30	-3.6%	42	18	354	19.7	5.1	4	43%
K.Britt*	-101	-48.5%	35	11	96	8.7	1.2	0	31%
D.Williams*	46	12.8%	23	15	178	11.9	3.1	0	65%
M.Preston	21	25.7%	7	5	37	7.4	0.8	2	71%
D.McCluster	*-22*	*-16.0%*	*83*	*53*	*511*	*9.6*	*4.9*	*2*	*64%*
D.Walker	38	-0.7%	86	60	571	9.5	2.9	6	70%
T.Thompson	-26	-55.9%	7	3	13	4.3	1.0	1	43%
C.Stevens	-34	-91.9%	6	2	5	2.5	1.5	0	33%
C.Johnson*	66	10.8%	52	42	351	8.4	9.4	4	81%
S.Greene	-7	-28.5%	7	6	39	6.5	10.2	0	86%
C.Mooney	-7	-34.1%	6	6	32	5.3	5.3	0	100%

Offensive Line

Player	Pos	Age	GS	Snaps	Pen	Sk	Pass	Run	Player	Pos	Age	GS	Snaps	Pen	Sk	Pass	Run
Michael Roos	LT	32	16/16	1075	3	4.0	19.8	4.5	Robert Turner*	C	30	6/6	394	4	0.0	6.0	2.0
Chance Warmack	RG	23	16/16	1075	5	6.5	19.3	12.5	Michael Otto*	OT	31	15/2	154	0	2.5	3.5	0.0
Andy Levitre	LG	28	16/16	1069	7	0.5	11.5	5.0	Byron Stingily	OT	26	5/2	140	0	2.0	3.0	1.5
David Stewart*	RT	32	12/12	800	3	4.5	20.8	4.0	Chris Spencer	C/G	32	16/1	120	1	0.0	0.0	0.0
Brian Schwenke	C	23	9/9	567	1	3.0	8.0	1.0	*Michael Oher*	*RT*	*28*	*16/16*	*1081*	*5*	*7.0*	*35.0*	*6.5*

Year	Yards	ALY	Rk	Power	Rk	Stuff	Rk	2nd Lev	Rk	Open Field	Rk	Sacks	ASR	Rk	Short	Long	F-Start	Cont.
2011	3.78	3.39	32	72%	3	24%	29	1.03	31	0.81	18	24	4.2%	2	11	10	12	39
2012	4.21	3.35	31	67%	11	24%	28	1.13	18	1.19	3	39	7.1%	19	13	13	17	28
2013	3.83	3.82	19	55%	29	20%	19	1.05	21	0.60	22	37	6.7%	12	14	13	9	29

2013 ALY by direction: Left End 4.79 (4) Left Tackle 3.76 (19) Mid/Guard 3.46 (29) Right Tackle 4.37 (5) Right End 4.47 (4)

The outside consensus on this unit would call it one with a lot of promise, perhaps the most of any position group on the team. Tennessee has invested a lot of draft capital on the line over the past few seasons, along with financial capital in a big deal for guard Andy Levitre. 2013's results were mixed. Levitre had a solid season, but a hip injury hampered him and he committed seven penalties. The injury prevented him from moving as fast as Tennessee would like, but he was still excellent in the run game at the line of scrimmage. Right guard Chance Warmack, selected in the first round of the 2013 draft, had more concrete issues. We charted him with more blown run blocks than any other offensive lineman in the league last season. He was much better as a pass blocker, but his mistakes tended to be big ones. Only Brian Winters of the Jets allowed more sacks as a pure interior lineman. Draftniks regarded Warmack as one of the most NFL-ready players in last year's class, so those numbers are troubling. Often, those types of players have hit their physical ceiling, so they have to get better mentally. At center, the Titans ditched Eugene Amano and Fernado Velasco, opening the year with Rob Turner. That was a mistake that Tennessee rectified as soon as possible. 2013 fourth-rounder Brian Schwenke stepped in at midseason, turning things around in a hurry up the middle—especially in the run game. He enters 2014 as the unquestioned starter. Schwnenke even showed typical center toughness by playing through a high-ankle sprain.

While the interior of the line is stable, the tackles are in flux. Long-time right tackle David Stewart retired after a subpar year. Tennessee responded with a free-agent signing and a first-round pick at the position. That level of investment seems puzzling, especially after you learn that the tackle they paid was Michael Oher. But with stalwart left tackle Michael Roos entering his thirties, Tennessee decided to try to get ahead of the curve. That may prevent a bloody position battle in the future, but it doesn't do much for them in 2014. Quinton Aaron's tape from *The Blind Side* is the best Oher tape we've seen since he was in college. Only Lamar Holmes and Mitchell Schwartz had more blown pass blocks than Oher did in 2013. Michigan's Taylor Lewan, the first-rounder in question, is an instant threat to Oher's job. Lewan was regarded as a high-floor, safe tackle selection … until Michigan police arraigned Lewan on assault charges after the draft. "A juvenile delinquent in the offseason," is how we imagine Harry Doyle would put that. Lewan denied the accusations, saying that he was "completely breaking things up." It likely won't be a long-term issue, but time off the field could keep him from beating out Oher for the job this season.

Defensive Front Seven

			Overall								vs. Run					Pass Rush			
Defensive Line	Age	Pos	G	Snaps	Plays	TmPct	Rk	Stop	Dfts	BTkl	Runs	St%	Rk	RuYd	Rk	Sack	Hit	Hur	Tips
Jurrell Casey	25	DT	15	870	57	7.3%	12	43	17	4	39	69%	66	3.2	76	10.5	5	14.0	2
Sammie Lee Hill	28	DT	13	383	30	4.5%	56	30	2	2	22	100%	1	1.6	25	0.0	0	2.0	5
Antonio Johnson	30	DT	16	380	23	2.8%	--	18	6	0	16	81%	--	1.7	--	3.0	1	4.0	0
Karl Klug	26	DT	16	317	15	1.8%	--	11	2	2	10	70%	--	2.1	--	2.0	2	7.0	2
Mike Martin	24	DT	13	235	15	2.2%	--	11	5	0	11	73%	--	2.6	--	1.0	1	0.0	0

			Overall								vs. Run					Pass Rush			
Edge Rushers	Age	Pos	G	Snaps	Plays	TmPct	Rk	Stop	Dfts	BTkl	Runs	St%	Rk	RuYd	Rk	Sack	Hit	Hur	Tips
Derrick Morgan	25	DE	15	796	34	4.4%	62	26	11	3	25	72%	51	2.2	27	6.0	17	19.0	2
Ropati Pitoitua	29	DE	16	576	48	5.8%	34	38	9	6	37	76%	40	1.9	21	4.0	1	6.0	4
Kamerion Wimbley	31	DE	16	352	9	1.1%	--	7	4	2	6	67%	--	2.8	--	3.0	3	11.0	0
Shaun Phillips	*33*	*DE*	*16*	*770*	*40*	*4.8%*	*53*	*32*	*19*	*4*	*19*	*68%*	*57*	*3.5*	*65*	*9.5*	*3*	*17.3*	*4*

			Overall								Pass Rush			vs. Run					vs. Pass						
Linebackers	Age	Pos	G	Snaps	Plays	TmPct	Rk	Stop	Dfts	BTkl	Sack	Hit	Hur	Runs	St%	Rk	RuYd	Rk	Tgts	Suc%	Rk	AdjYd	Rk	PD	Int
Zach Brown	25	OLB	16	756	94	11.3%	55	50	15	4	4.0	3	13	52	62%	55	5.3	80	38	48%	46	7.1	48	3	1
Akeem Ayers	25	OLB	16	722	53	6.4%	75	35	11	4	1.0	7	16	28	68%	30	2.6	19	28	57%	23	6.7	40	3	1
Moise Fokou	29	MLB	12	719	78	12.5%	47	33	13	7	1.0	2	6	44	55%	71	4.3	73	30	35%	69	10.8	71	0	0
Colin McCarthy	26	MLB	16	330	45	5.4%	--	25	6	9	0.0	0	2.5	32	56%	--	3.5	--	13	66%	--	4.8	--	1	1
Wesley Woodyard	*28*	*MLB*	*14*	*752*	*87*	*11.9%*	*50*	*52*	*18*	*2*	*2.0*	*6*	*9*	*44*	*66%*	*40*	*3.4*	*46*	*45*	*52%*	*39*	*6.2*	*27*	*4*	*1*

Year	Yards	ALY	Rk	Power	Rk	Stuff	Rk	2nd Level	Rk	Open Field	Rk	Sacks	ASR	Rk	Short	Long
2011	4.49	4.03	17	53%	6	22%	5	1.18	15	1.09	27	28	5.0%	31	13	12
2012	4.35	4.39	29	67%	24	20%	12	1.36	30	0.67	11	39	6.5%	13	16	9
2013	4.03	4.15	23	61%	12	17%	23	1.17	22	0.52	10	36	6.6%	20	11	11
2013 ALY by direction:			*Left End 4.05 (25)*			*Left Tackle 3.43 (6)*			*Mid/Guard 4.24 (27)*			*Right Tackle 4.11 (20)*			*Right End 5.16 (32)*	

Depth-chart syndrome means that fans will look at Tennessee's roster and argue over whether Derrick Morgan is a better fit at defensive end than he is at outside linebacker—or, at least, if he's better at their conceptual understanding of those positions. Here's what will happen: Tennessee will put its best interior pass rushers in a position to penetrate, put its best speed rushers on the outside, and ask its run-game players to hold multiple gaps. Let's not complicate things. Karl Klug isn't going to play two gaps because he's a "3-4 defensive lineman."

Jurrell Casey elevated his game with a phenomenal year in 2013. A pessimist's view would be to look at the ratio of sacks to hurries and worry that some regression may occur. But even without 10.5 sacks, he'll still be a force for offensive lines to reckon with inside. Tennessee rewarded Ropati Pitoitua with a three-year, $9.6 million deal for his work in the run game. He'll likely play end on run downs. And the Titans have a surplus of depth in the trenches. Klug (fifth-round pick in 2011), Mike Martin (third-round, 2012), Sammie Lee Hill (three-year, $11.4 million deal signed last offseason), Al Woods (two-year, $5 million deal this offseason), Da'Quan Jones (fourth-round pick this year), and Antonio Johnson (two-year deal signed this offseason) should give Horton plenty of pieces to mix-and-match this year. In fact, it's likely the Titans will be letting go of at least one decent rotation lineman at the end of training camp. The buzz word out of the Horton camp is "versatility." Most of these players can play anywhere along the line. The best penetrator of the bunch is Klug, who had seven sacks back in 2011, but according to the *Tennessean* he was on the roster bubble for the old regime.

Morgan is a fine ancillary pass rusher. The long-term trend is that Morgan racks up more hurries than sacks. Over the last three seasons, Morgan has 58 hurries to just 15 sacks. "Disruption equals production," was an axiom made famous by Rotoworld's Josh Norris this offseason, but it would be nice if Morgan actually finished the job more often. The average edge rusher has a ratio much closer to three hurries for every sack. Morgan will be learning the outside linebacker position this year, though he'll play end in some packages as well. The Titans signed Shaun Phillips to take over the other outside linebacker spot. Phillips is 33, but offers pass rush at a bargain price. Signing him was a masterstroke for a Titans front that needed more pressure, though we should note that all his sacks last season came with the Denver defense in nickel personnel. Akeem Ayers is a hard player to pin down. Some of his problems last season were the result of injuries, and he had surgeries to repair tendons in both of his knees after the year was over. The physical talent is there. He hasn't developed into the kind of rusher the Titans were hoping he would, though one sack undersells his pass-rush ability. His coverage numbers were good this year, but he wasn't especially fluid on tape. Ayers is an odd fit as a 3-4 outside linebacker given his lack of production as a pass rusher, but the Titans don't seem to have any plans to move him inside at this time. Kamerion Wimbley is no longer a starter, but could see some time at both end and linebacker.

Last year's middle linebackers were lacking, so Tennessee brought in Wesley Woodyard (ex-Broncos) in free agency. Speedy Zach Brown will likely move from the outside to handle the other inside spot. Brown was dismal in coverage last season and not much better against the run. Regardless, Brown still has the tools to be one of the better linebackers in the league. He's still a second-round pick going into his third season, and as a rookie he looked impressive in a smaller sample. Zaviar Gooden, a 2013 third-rounder from Missouri, could get a look here if Brown struggles. Colin McCarthy is also a candidate to see time, but tape, statistics, and common sense should keep that from happening.

Defensive Secondary

			Overall									vs. Run					vs. Pass									
Secondary	Age	Pos	G	Snaps	Plays	TmPct	Rk	Stop	Dfts	BTkl	Runs	St%	Rk	RuYd	Rk	Tgts	Tgt%	Rk	Dist	Suc%	Rk	AdjYd	Rk	PD	Int
Bernard Pollard	30	SS	16	1054	108	13.0%	13	49	23	7	43	53%	12	6.2	25	44	10.2%	62	9.4	63%	16	6.5	29	8	3
Jason McCourty	27	CB	16	1053	76	9.2%	28	30	15	4	9	44%	35	4.7	11	86	19.9%	31	12.3	56%	30	6.6	17	12	0
Alterraun Verner*	26	CB	16	1003	79	9.5%	21	31	11	5	18	22%	71	6.8	39	72	17.5%	13	13.0	61%	8	7.2	36	23	5
Michael Griffin	29	FS	14	898	85	11.7%	23	25	12	7	51	29%	64	7.3	48	23	6.1%	14	10.8	53%	44	6.1	21	4	1
Coty Sensabaugh	26	CB	14	493	33	4.5%	--	14	8	2	2	0%	--	13.0	--	42	20.5%	--	9.6	49%	--	6.9	--	5	0
George Wilson	33	SS	16	406	30	3.6%	--	13	5	2	16	38%	--	6.5	--	18	10.8%	--	7.7	50%	--	6.2	--	3	1

Year	Pass D Rank	vs. #1 WR	Rk	vs. #2 WR	Rk	vs. Other WR	Rk	vs. TE	Rk	vs. RB	Rk
2011	20	30.6%	29	-20.5%	3	-14.1%	14	29.6%	30	-6.2%	12
2012	19	24.3%	29	-13.5%	8	-5.4%	11	-5.5%	10	23.5%	30
2013	16	-13.2%	6	10.0%	23	-14.9%	7	8.6%	22	12.1%	26

Alterraun Verner this, Alterraun Verner that. Tampa Bay's new cornerback spent the season getting love from the football media for his advanced metrics. As you can see above, our metrics agree with the consensus: Verner had a hell of a year. But when it was time to cover Andre Johnson or Demaryius Thomas, the Titans called on stalwart Jason McCourty to take the task. When observers start listing the best cornerbacks in the NFL, McCourty is never in the discussion. But he's become an excellent one.

The task for Tennessee is to replace the departed Verner on the outside. It's a shame former defensive coordinator Jerry Gray couldn't be around to do the honors. Gray spent most of OTAs last year shuffling through bigger, less talented players on the outside in an attempt to make Verner a nickelback. Two of those players, Tommie Campbell and Coty Sensabaugh, will be in the mix for the starting role and at nickelback. Blidi Wreh-Wilson, who as a 2013 third-round pick out of Connecticut has the best pedigree of the three, is the other contender. Sensabaugh was the nickelback last season and should have the inside track for one of the spots. Wreh-Wilson notched 92 snaps last season—70 more than Campbell—and will get first crack at Verner's slot. If he succeeds, prepare for sports media to shorten his name to BW-W, then lengthen it to Buffalo Wild Wings. If he struggles, coaches will yell at him. Not about wings.

Bernard Pollard is a safety who was born 25 years too late. His aggressive, punishing style and instinctual playmaking would've made him a star in the '80s. But the era of two-receiver formations and limited concussion awareness is gone. Instead, we have a safety who can't cover one-on-one and commits a head-hunting penalty every other game. At least he's good for quote sheets and Bill Simmons memes. Michael Griffin is back to reprise his role as "disappointing safety who Madden has deemed 10 points better than reality," a position he's held in perpetuity. Expect broken tackles and mistakes on jumped routes. George Wilson is the veteran backup who also plays special teams. A job challenge may come from fourth-rounder Marqueston Huff (Wyoming). Huff played corner in his first three years in Laramie, so he could develop into the coverage safety that's currently not on this roster.

Special Teams

Year	DVOA	Rank	FG/XP	Rank	Net Kick	Rank	Kick Ret	Rank	Net Punt	Rank	Punt Ret	Rank	Hidden	Rank
2011	6.3%	3	13.7	2	1.1	16	4.1	6	9.4	7	3.4	10	7.5	6
2012	-1.4%	19	-4.6	25	-9.1	29	2.3	10	-13.1	27	17.8	1	2.4	11
2013	-3.2%	26	-1.8	22	-4.5	27	-1.3	16	0.6	18	-9.1	29	5.3	8

Former Pro Bowler Marc Mariani has been indisposed the last two years due to a horrifying broken leg in the 2012 preseason and a separated shoulder in 2013 training camp. So, Tennessee turned to Darius Reynaud on both kick and punt returns. That went well for one year, then terrible the next, so the Titans released Reynaud at midseason and he ended the year on the Jets. After brief flirtations with Devon Wylie and Damian Williams, the Titans relented and brought on Leon Washington. Washington has been one of the best return men of his era, and should help turn things around next season if he beats out Mariani for the job.

The other big change is the offseason release of long-time place kicker Rob Bironas. Bironas rebounded from a poor 2012, but it was more of a dead-cat bounce than a comeback. Mini-camp contestants for the job included Brazilian kicker Maikon Bonani, Washington's Travis Coons, and New Hampshire's Gregg Ogilve. We only made up one of those names. Let us know which one you thought it was. Ken Whisenhunt noted at OTAs that he thought "there will be opportunities potentially for veteran guys, too, if we feel like we need that." We feel like they might. Brett Kern returns as the punter: he's as unremarkable as it comes. Kern is routinely lousy in gross punt value (-10.7 Punt Pts+ last year, -13.1 in 2013), but Tennessee tends to have decent coverage teams.

Washington Controversies

2013 Record: 3-13	**Total DVOA:** -26.2% (29th)	**2014 Mean Projection:** 7.2 wins	**On the Clock (0-4):** 14%
Pythagorean Wins: 4.8 (30th)	**Offense:** -10.0% (23rd)	**Postseason Odds:** 22.4%	**Mediocrity (5-7):** 42%
Snap-Weighted Age: 27.4 (4th)	**Defense:** 4.2% (21st)	**Super Bowl Odds:** 1.3%	**Playoff Contender (8-10):** 34%
Average Opponent: 0.7% (12th)	**Special Teams:** -12.0% (32nd)	**Proj. Avg. Opponent:** -1.3% (22nd)	**Super Bowl Contender (11+):** 10%

2013: Your franchise quarterback and your mission end here.

2014: Can RG3 play in an RG3-4?

THE STORY SO FAR

You are Dan Snyder, the last passionate fan (and owner) of the Washington Redskins. You are the sole survivor of a sandstorm of mismanagement and public relations miscues that has forever ensnared any who would dare coach, work for, quarterback, or play for your franchise.

It is the year 2014, and 15 years have passed since Jack Kent Cooke relinquished control of one of the model franchises of the NFL to you. The other champions of the NFC East have risen and fallen, yet you have only four quick playoff exits to show for all your machinations. You have vowed to avenge the once-proud history and tradition of the Redskins. The rest of America would really rather you just change the name.

In the wake of the constant waves of coaches past, perpetual chaos befell a roster of highly-paid formerly good players and poorly-selected minimum wage hopefuls that had been poised to win eight games. Some factions which comprised this huge army, most notably the barbaric Shanaclan, began to fight with the others for control. This disorder quickly escalated into an all-out civil war, which allowed the Philadelphia Eagles to recover and launch a counter-offensive without huddling. Skillfully their leader, Chip Kelly, exploited the chaos and secured a swift and total victory over your beleaguered troops.

For seven months now, peace has reigned in the NFL. Under your direction, the once-ruined leg of Robert Griffin III has been thoroughly rebuilt and restored to its former glory, and the task of teaching a new generation of draft picks has been given to Jay Gruden, a promising coach from the outlands of Cincinnati. The new generation of Washington football players, all of whom were born around the last championship your franchise won, possess latent football skills. These skills must be nurtured and honed to perfection during their time on the field, so that they may teach and inspire future generations, thereby ensuring a competitive team in future years. Or at least that's the idea until you get bored and sign, we don't know… let's say Reshad Jones to a $29 million deal and let your own players walk.

Your attainment of the rank of NFL owner brought with it great rewards. Some, such as the ability to throw $25 million at Steve Spurrier and the undying contempt of all the local media you harass, could have been anticipated. Yet there have also been rewards which you could not have possibly foreseen. The discovery that within you lay the potential to alienate non-Washington fans was truly a revelation. Until now, alienating one's own fanbase was thought to be the ultimate range an owner could aspire to. Your discovery has inspired you to set out upon a new and previously unknown path in search of the wisdom and power that no NFL owner before you has ever possessed. In the name of your creator, the Lord Goodell, and for the greater glory of the NFL, you have vowed to reach the very pinnacle of Montgomery Burns perfection—to be so tone-deaf as to be despised by both the NFL landscape and America as a whole. To become the next Donald Sterling.

THE GAME RULES

For more than 15 years, ever since your arrival in the role of Washington owner, you have devoted yourself to developing further your belief that only you can be right (SMUGNESS) and your sheer ability to get past obstacles in your way (WILLPOWER). Before you begin this adventure, you need to measure how effective your training has been. To do this, roll a 10-sided die. The first number you roll in this way represents your SMUGNESS. Add 25 to the number you picked and write the total in the SMUGNESS section of your *Action Chart*. (A sample *Action Chart* is available below, but feel free to create your own.) When you fight with the press and your own coaches, your SMUGNESS will be pitted against that of your enemy. A high score in this section is therefore very desirable.

The second number that you roll represents your powers of WILLPOWER. Add 30 to this number and write the total in the WILLPOWER section of your *Action Chart*. If

Action Chart

Claude Items	Effect	Personnel	Effect
1		1	
2		2	
3		3	
4		4	
5		5	
6		6	
7		7	
8		8	
SMUGNESS:		WILLPOWER:	

2014 Redskins Schedule

Week	Opp.	Week	Opp.	Week	Opp.
1	at HOU	7	TEN	13	at IND
2	JAC	8	at DAL (Mon.)	14	STL
3	at PHI	9	at MIN	15	at NYG
4	NYG (Thu.)	10	BYE	16	PHI (Sat.)
5	SEA (Mon.)	11	TB	17	DAL
6	at ARI	12	at SF		

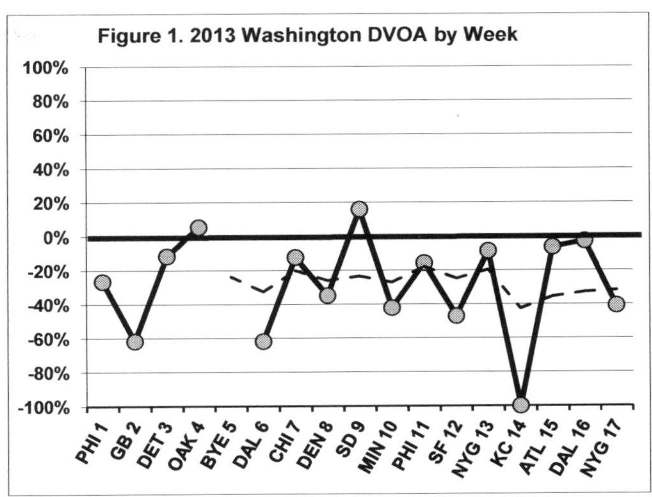

you are wounded by those who would dare question your vision, you will lose WILLPOWER points. If at any time your WILLPOWER score falls to zero, you will become a recluse like late-era Bud Adams and the adventure is over. Lost WILLPOWER points can be regained during the course of the adventure, but your number of WILLPOWER points cannot rise above the number you have when you start the adventure.

OWNER DISCIPLINES

Through the pursuit of new skills and the further development of your innate charm, you have set out upon a path of discovery that no other NFL owner has ever attempted with success. Your determination to become the next Donald Sterling by acquiring total proficiency in all seven of the NFL owner stereotypes is an awe-inspiring challenge.

In the years following your ascension to owner, you have reached the rank of NFL Owner Superior, which means that you have mastered up to four of the below stereotypes. It is up to you to choose which four stereotypes these are. Pick your four skills with care. The correct use of a discipline at the right time could make you money.

Grand Greedery—NFL owners with this skill have the amazing power to make bold cash grabs with no regard for how it affects the people around them. For instance, they could ban purses above a certain size from NFL stadiums, then sell approved plastic ones for $19.99 plus tax. Or, perhaps, become the first owner in the NFL to charge money to watch players work out. And for parking at the workouts.

Source-ry—No matter how great an NFL owner is at making money, sometimes he needs some good news planted about him in the public eye. With this skill, an NFL owner can rely on a high-placed source to defend him when things go wrong. For example, a writer could come up with a column about "the Dan Snyder you don't know," which paints him as a puppy-petting red-blooded American just trying to do the best that he can.

Privilegeship—An NFL owner with this skill is miraculously able to understand the plight of minorities while at the same time furthering his own business ventures. This skill will be extremely helpful on these adventures as Mr. Snyder deals with his unfortunately named football team. It will also help if, for instance, you try to tell Asian actors applying for a mascot job to "Emulate Charlie Chan."

Censority—With this skill, an NFL owner can cover up unfortunate truths. Don't like those signs talking about how you and Vinny Cerrato ruined football? Well, just take them away and give fans some nice appealing GEICO signs. Don't enjoy a certain paper's coverage of you? Just have your lawyers bully the paper with a threatened libel lawsuit.

Denseitude—NFL owners with this skill are miraculously unable to absorb any actual criticism of them, no matter how poignant or thoughtful it is. This skill will also enable an NFL owner to be much more effective at the idea of "letting bygones be bygones." After all, you started this Original Americans Foundation. You're giving Native Americans tractors. Why would anyone still hound you?

Moral Compassship—Sometimes an NFL owner will be forced to take action on something so disgusting that he may even feel some remorse about it. One could hypothetically sue a down-on-her-luck 73-year-old grandmother for not being able to keep up with her PSL payments. With this skill, the NFL owner will be able to prevent massive WILLPOWER losses that such guilt could provide by remembering to stay as true to his mission as he can.

Grand Marketeering—One of the great things about being an entrepreneur is being able to capture a market as it is developing. An NFL owner with this skill could, for instance, create a regular Washington football team hat with a red, white, and blue Pentagon stitched on the side in memoriam of the fifth anniversary of 9/11, declare that coaches are expected to wear them, and then sell them for $23.99. Use of this skill will enable an NFL owner to gather resources quickly.

EQUIPMENT

Before you set off on the long journey to Sterling-tude, you must outfit yourself and your team with provisions. Non-personnel items are handled by your bodyguard, Claude. (All bodyguards are named Claude.) Claude can only hold eight objects at a time.

You can take five things from the list below.

- Wylie's Elixir (Claude)—Restores four WILLPOWER points. There is enough for only one dose.
- Slightly used DeSean Jackson (Personnel)—Explosive deep-threat receiver with a history of getting fed up with his contract. It wouldn't be fair to call Jackson an Eagles deserter,

but it is peculiar that he was allowed to come into your possession. Is it a trap from the cunning Kelly, or does Jackson hold the key to opening up your offense?

- Fletcher's Whistle (Claude)—Blow this whistle and London Fletcher will un-retire and play middle linebacker. Item has more utility than you'd think given current state of Washington middle linebackers.
- Reed Doughty (Personnel)—Has no real use, but always seems to be on team.
- Ghave Spores (Claude)—When mixed with alchemy, can create powerful hazy cloud that makes spending a second-round pick on a rush linebacker when you already have Brian Orakpo and Ryan Kerrigan seem logical.
- Rocca's Medallion (Claude)—Replays all-22 film of all special teams plays against the Kansas City Chiefs. Boosts SMUGNESS by one point in battles of mentality, but may also make you believe 35-year-old Santana Moss can return punts.
- Frank Luntz focus groups (Personnel)—At least as effective at cornerback as Tracy Porter.
- Boombox that is permanently jammed on WTEM (Claude)—Healing waves of your own company-owned message can restore one WILLPOWER point on three separate occasions.
- Andre Roberts (Personnel)—If at first your Josh Morgan contract doesn't succeed, try, try again.
- Brandon Meriweather (Personnel)—Actively hurts team on football field, headhunts with no caution, and has shown no signs of being a good safety since 2008.

GOODELL'S WISDOM

Your mission to become the most reviled NFL owner of your day will be fraught with deadly dangers. The daunting spectacle of FedEx Field, where players can lose the function of a limb with one wrong twist on the enchanted grass, looms large over the proceedings.

You must do your best to juggle the competing missions of 1) making your team good while not knowing what makes a football team good and 2) earning the hatred of every sports fan on the planet, even those in Dallas. The return of Griffin's leg strength will help Washington, but given the quality of the defense and special teams, projections generally see the ability to rebound as limited to around seven or eight wins. If you can luck your way into the right combination of scrap-heap players and undrafted free agents, you just might deflect enough attention to pull off some amazing feats of greed.

Pick your four owner stereotypes with care, for a wise choice will enable you to complete the quest no matter how weak your initial SMUGNESS and WILLPOWER scores are.

You are Dan Snyder. You have the opportunity to read over your past and learn from your mistakes. You have the ability to recognize that your football decisions turn out really poorly and stay out of the way of the coaches and general managers you hire. Your team-name debacle could be easily transformed into a beautiful public relations coup with a graceful name change. You have the power to change all of these things.

You will forget all of this.

Rivers McCown

2013 Redskins Stats by Week

Wk	vs.	W-L	PF	PA	YDF	YDA	TO	Total	Off	Def	ST
1	PHI	L	27	33	382	443	-1	-27%	-1%	12%	-14%
2	at GB	L	20	38	422	580	0	-62%	15%	70%	-7%
3	DET	L	20	27	420	441	-1	-12%	-2%	11%	2%
4	at OAK	W	24	14	339	298	+2	5%	-4%	-33%	-23%
5	BYE										
6	at DAL	L	16	31	433	213	-1	-62%	-17%	-8%	-53%
7	CHI	W	45	41	499	359	0	-12%	28%	17%	-23%
8	at DEN	L	21	45	266	446	-1	-35%	-49%	-15%	0%
9	SD	W	30	24	500	410	+1	16%	13%	-8%	-6%
10	at MIN	L	27	34	433	307	+1	-42%	5%	34%	-13%
11	at PHI	L	16	24	427	402	-2	-16%	-2%	13%	-1%
12	SF	L	6	27	190	304	0	-47%	-47%	-5%	-5%
13	NYG	L	17	24	323	286	0	-9%	12%	21%	1%
14	KC	L	10	45	257	346	-1	-101%	-31%	18%	-52%
15	at ATL	L	26	27	476	243	-5	-6%	-25%	-23%	-4%
16	DAL	L	23	24	297	309	+1	-3%	-13%	-10%	1%
17	at NYG	L	6	20	251	278	-1	-41%	-62%	-16%	5%

Trends and Splits

	Offense	Rank	Defense	Rank
Total DVOA	-10.0%	23	4.2%	21
Unadjusted VOA	-7.6%	22	9.5%	24
Weighted Trend	-14.3%	27	-0.1%	17
Variance	6.6%	16	6.4%	22
Average Opponent	4.8%	31	5.5%	2
Passing	-13.9%	26	12.5%	22
Rushing	4.4%	9	-5.4%	17
First Down	-19.4%	28	14.4%	30
Second Down	1.0%	15	4.4%	22
Third Down	-8.8%	20	-17.3%	5
First Half	-9.1%	26	13.5%	30
Second Half	-10.8%	21	-5.1%	13
Red Zone	-21.2%	29	14.7%	24
Late and Close	-10.8%	22	-13.9%	8

Five-Year Performance

Year	W-L	Pyth W	Est W	PF	PA	TO	Total	Rk	Off	Rk	Def	Rk	ST	Rk	Off AGL	Rk	Def AGL	Rk	Off Age	Rk	Def Age	Rk	ST Age	Rk
2009	4-12	5.8	6.6	266	336	-11	-7.8%	22	-8.3%	21	-2.1%	12	-1.7%	23	55.0	31	20.2	11	28.0	7	28.0	3	27.7	1
2010	6-10	5.9	4.7	302	377	-4	-19.4%	28	-11.3%	25	5.8%	26	-2.3%	25	31.6	21	38.3	26	28.6	3	28.5	3	27.3	4
2011	5-11	5.7	6.3	288	367	-14	-7.0%	21	-7.0%	19	-1.2%	14	-1.2%	21	54.3	31	13.2	7	27.3	14	27.3	15	26.9	3
2012	10-6	9.2	9.8	436	388	+17	9.3%	9	15.3%	6	1.7%	17	-4.3%	28	34.8	20	48.8	26	26.1	26	27.8	5	27.1	3
2013	3-13	4.8	4.2	334	478	-8	-26.2%	29	-10.0%	23	4.2%	21	-12.0%	32	16.3	4	27.6	13	27.0	15	28.0	3	27.1	2

2013 Performance Based on Most Common Personnel Groups

WAS Offense					WAS Offense vs. Opponents				WAS Defense				WAS Defense vs. Opponents			
Pers	Freq	Yds	DVOA	Run%	Pers	Freq	Yds	DVOA	Pers	Freq	Yds	DVOA	Pers	Freq	Yds	DVOA
11	47%	5.5	-3.7%	15%	Nickel Even	33%	5.5	0.4%	3-4-4	44%	5.5	3.9%	11	56%	6.4	10.1%
12	28%	4.7	-20.1%	53%	4-3-4	29%	5.1	-11.4%	Nickel Even	42%	6.4	7.2%	12	17%	6.0	3.7%
21	15%	6.4	-3.3%	61%	3-4-4	20%	5.4	-11.9%	Dime+	7%	6.0	-17.1%	21	11%	4.6	-22.9%
22	4%	5.5	39.2%	78%	Dime+	9%	5.8	8.4%	Nickel Odd	5%	5.5	14.7%	22	6%	5.0	-0.1%
13	3%	6.7	40.0%	64%	Nickel Odd	7%	5.9	-13.9%	4-4-3	1%	0.8	55.1%	02	1%	2.9	-42.8%
									Goal Line	1%	-2.0	-118.0%				

Strategic Tendencies

Run/Pass		Rk	Formation		Rk	Pass Rush		Rk	Secondary		Rk	Strategy		Rk
Runs, first half	42%	11	Form: Single Back	61%	24	Rush 3	3.3%	24	4 DB	45%	11	Play action	27%	6
Runs, first down	45%	21	Form: Empty Back	6%	16	Rush 4	59.6%	20	5 DB	47%	20	Avg Box (Off)	6.42	12
Runs, second-long	34%	13	Pers: 3+ WR	49%	24	Rush 5	32.1%	2	6+ DB	7%	14	Avg Box (Def)	6.47	6
Runs, power sit.	61%	11	Pers: 4+ WR	2%	13	Rush 6+	4.9%	26	CB by Sides	53%	32	Offensive Pace	30.80	19
Runs, behind 2H	26%	20	Pers: 2+ TE/6+ OL	36%	9	Sacks by LB	75.0%	2	DB Blitz	12%	15	Defensive Pace	28.82	6
Pass, ahead 2H	47%	19	Shotgun/Pistol	73%	5	Sacks by DB	9.7%	13	Hole in Zone	14%	6	Go for it on 4th	0.96	12

His Name is Logan Paulsen Alert: Washington had the league's biggest gap between rushing from single-back formations (4.1 yards per carry, -11.7% DVOA) and rushing from two-back formations (4.9 yards per carry, 12.2% DVOA). With Robert Griffin hobbling, Washington's use of play action dropped by about one-third, due in part to fewer plays that started with a read-option fake. However, Griffin's injury didn't change the fact that Washington uses the pistol formation more than any other team in the league. They used it on 33.5 percent of plays; no other team was above 20 percent. Washington opponents blitzed with a defensive back on a league-leading 17.2 percent of pass plays. The Redskins defense just got destroyed by short passes, especially passes behind the line of scrimmage. They were average against passes thrown beyond the line of scrimmage, but only Philadelphia was worse against passes thrown before or at the line of scrimmage.

Passing

Player	DYAR	DVOA	Plays	NtYds	Avg	YAC	C%	TD	Int
R.Griffin	-60	-13.1%	495	2912	5.9	5.6	60.8%	16	12
K.Cousins	-314	-42.6%	160	820	5.1	4.0	52.9%	4	7

Rushing

Player	DYAR	DVOA	Plays	Yds	Avg	TD	Fum	Suc
A.Morris	121	2.0%	277	1278	4.6	8	6	48%
R.Griffin	42	-0.9%	81	485	6.0	0	3	-
R.Helu	48	8.5%	62	274	4.4	4	1	45%
D.Young	27	27.3%	12	41	3.4	3	0	58%

Receiving

Player	DYAR	DVOA	Plays	Ctch	Yds	Y/C	YAC	TD	C%
P.Garcon	104	-5.2%	181	113	1346	11.9	5.8	5	62%
S.Moss	-97	-28.3%	79	43	449	10.4	4.3	2	54%
L.Hankerson	46	-0.6%	50	30	375	12.5	4.4	3	60%
A.Robinson	9	-10.3%	46	18	365	20.3	4.8	2	39%
J.Morgan*	-4	-14.1%	35	22	227	10.3	5.2	0	63%
N.Williams	-47	-63.7%	11	3	15	5.0	0.3	0	27%
D.Jackson	*358*	*23.7%*	*125*	*82*	*1332*	*16.2*	*5.9*	*9*	*66%*
A.Roberts	*-15*	*-15.3%*	*76*	*43*	*471*	*11.0*	*2.6*	*2*	*57%*
J.Reed	98	19.5%	60	45	499	11.1	5.5	3	75%
L.Paulsen	-96	-36.4%	50	28	267	9.5	3.4	3	56%
F.Davis*	-43	-41.5%	18	7	70	10.0	3.0	1	39%
N.Paul	-11	-26.8%	8	4	51	12.8	5.5	0	50%
R.Helu	-3	-15.0%	42	31	254	8.2	6.1	0	74%
A.Morris	1	-12.0%	12	9	78	8.7	8.8	0	75%
D.Young	-1	-17.0%	9	4	71	17.8	10.0	1	44%

Offensive Line

Player	Pos	Age	GS	Snaps	Pen	Sk	Pass	Run	Player	Pos	Age	GS	Snaps	Pen	Sk	Pass	Run
Will Montgomery*	C	31	16/16	1144	9	3.0	10.5	4.0	Trent Williams	LT	26	16/16	1142	6	6.0	18.0	4.0
Chris Chester	RG	31	16/16	1143	6	2.0	23.5	6.0	Kory Lichtensteiger	LG	29	16/16	1126	4	2.0	15.5	6.0
Tyler Polumbus	RT	29	16/16	1143	1	6.0	30.5	5.5	*Shawn Lauvao*	*RG*	*27*	*11/11*	*741*	*3*	*4.5*	*16.5*	*5.0*

Year	Yards	ALY	Rk	Power	Rk	Stuff	Rk	2nd Lev	Rk	Open Field	Rk	Sacks	ASR	Rk	Short	Long	F-Start	Cont.
2011	4.19	4.21	10	62%	17	20%	19	1.19	15	0.67	25	41	6.5%	16	13	15	11	23
2012	4.72	4.24	8	58%	24	16%	3	1.40	5	0.85	13	33	7.8%	23	9	18	26	43
2013	4.51	3.75	23	76%	4	22%	28	1.29	5	0.95	7	43	7.6%	19	11	22	16	48

2013 ALY by direction: Left End 3.50 (17) Left Tackle 3.36 (26) Mid/Guard 4.27 (7) Right Tackle 4.12 (12) Right End 3.39 (21)

Trent Williams had another strong season, going to the Pro Bowl for the second year in a row. Umpire Roy Ellison, who was suspended a game for yelling obscenities at Williams, is likely the only person denigrating the Washington left tackle at this point. The line beyond Williams is much maligned, but there's only one sure personnel change: Will Montgomery was released and replaced by ex-Cleveland guard Shawn Lauvao. Our charters marked Montgomery down for fewer blown blocks than anyone on the Washington offensive line, but Montgomery also committed nine penalties, third among all the NFL's interior linemen. Of course, Lauvao isn't exactly a dramatic improvement—he's a solid run blocker, but he's had 15 or more blown pass blocks in each of the past three seasons. To accommodate Lauvao, Washington will move former college center Kory Lichtensteiger over from guard to man the middle.

The Skins brought in two third-round prospects, Nebraska guard Spencer Long and Virginia tackle Morgan Moses. An MCL tear ended Long's senior season, but early indications are that the team views him as a serious challenger to incumbent Chris Chester. Chester had a poor season in pass protection, but only blew seven pass blocks in 2012. Still, if his drop-off is age-related, it was smart of Washington to have Long ready. Moses is seen as more of a long-term project at right tackle, even if he was a mock draft darling towards the end of the process. The uninspiring Tyler Polumbus has long been capable of pouring gasoline on a fire blitz, but he was adequate at times last year. An ideal situation would probably see the changing of the guard (actually, the changing of the tackle) sometime towards the end of the season.

Defensive Front Seven

			Overall								vs. Run					Pass Rush			
Defensive Line	**Age**	**Pos**	**G**	**Snaps**	**Plays**	**TmPct**	**Rk**	**Stop**	**Dfts**	**BTkl**	**Runs**	**St%**	**Rk**	**RuYd**	**Rk**	**Sack**	**Hit**	**Hur**	**Tips**
Barry Cofield	30	DT	16	727	33	4.2%	59	27	11	2	27	78%	41	1.4	15	2.5	9	14.0	0
Kedric Golston	31	DE	16	466	21	2.7%	81	13	3	1	20	65%	76	1.9	34	0.0	1	10.0	0
Stephen Bowen	30	DE	10	416	20	4.1%	61	14	5	0	17	76%	46	1.6	23	0.0	3	5.0	2
Chris Baker	27	DT	15	410	27	3.7%	72	20	7	2	23	74%	54	1.7	26	1.0	5	7.5	1
Jarvis Jenkins	26	DE	12	330	22	3.7%	70	15	5	0	17	65%	77	3.1	72	2.0	0	2.0	0
Jason Hatcher	*32*	*DT*	*15*	*747*	*44*	*5.4%*	*35*	*38*	*24*	*2*	*28*	*86%*	*13*	*1.3*	*10*	*11.0*	*5*	*19.5*	*1*

			Overall								vs. Run					Pass Rush			
Edge Rushers	**Age**	**Pos**	**G**	**Snaps**	**Plays**	**TmPct**	**Rk**	**Stop**	**Dfts**	**BTkl**	**Runs**	**St%**	**Rk**	**RuYd**	**Rk**	**Sack**	**Hit**	**Hur**	**Tips**
Ryan Kerrigan	26	OLB	16	972	67	8.5%	5	46	23	5	40	65%	61	3.2	62	8.5	2	22.0	3
Brian Orakpo	28	OLB	15	812	64	8.7%	4	52	26	4	40	80%	27	2.4	39	10.0	8	26.0	1

			Overall								Pass Rush			vs. Run					vs. Pass						
Linebackers	**Age**	**Pos**	**G**	**Snaps**	**Plays**	**TmPct**	**Rk**	**Stop**	**Dfts**	**BTkl**	**Sack**	**Hit**	**Hur**	**Runs**	**St%**	**Rk**	**RuYd**	**Rk**	**Tgts**	**Suc%**	**Rk**	**AdjYd**	**Rk**	**PD**	**Int**
Perry Riley	26	ILB	16	987	120	15.2%	24	71	19	5	3.0	6	13	66	74%	11	3.0	26	38	64%	7	5.1	12	6	1
London Fletcher*	39	ILB	16	915	113	14.3%	32	54	15	9	2.0	1	3	70	56%	68	3.4	43	30	48%	45	7.0	47	2	0
Rob Jackson	29	ILB	12	185	16	2.7%	--	11	5	1	2.5	1	4	9	44%	--	3.8	--	1	100%	--	0.5	--	1	1
Akeem Jordan	*29*	*ILB*	*16*	*469*	*63*	*7.4%*	*68*	*36*	*5*	*1*	*0.0*	*0*	*0*	*50*	*64%*	*49*	*3.3*	*40*	*6*	*34%*	*--*	*7.1*	*--*	*0*	*0*
Darryl Sharpton	*26*	*ILB*	*15*	*718*	*88*	*12.2%*	*49*	*48*	*13*	*9*	*0.0*	*5*	*6.5*	*56*	*68%*	*30*	*3.4*	*44*	*34*	*33%*	*70*	*10.3*	*70*	*1*	*0*

Year	Yards	ALY	Rk	Power	Rk	Stuff	Rk	2nd Level	Rk	Open Field	Rk	Sacks	ASR	Rk	Short	Long
2011	4.26	4.19	22	54%	7	18%	21	1.14	12	0.76	15	41	7.4%	8	14	18
2012	4.35	4.08	17	79%	31	17%	26	1.19	16	0.86	19	32	5.9%	25	9	11
2013	4.02	3.58	6	68%	22	23%	6	1.18	25	0.82	22	36	7.0%	13	14	11

2013 ALY by direction: Left End 1.94 (3) — Left Tackle 4.33 (26) — Mid/Guard 3.91 (16) — Right Tackle 3.79 (16) — Right End 3.98 (20)

A lot went wrong in Washington last season, but one thing the Skins have nailed is the 1-2 punch of Brian Orakpo and Ryan Kerrigan at outside linebacker. Not only are they very effective pass rushers, but they also can hold their own whenever Jim Haslett's scheme requires them to drop into coverage. Orakpo and Kerrigan finished third and fourth in targets among edge rushers, and had Success Rates of 57 percent and 73 percent, respectively. That made it even more puzzling that the team spent its first selection in the draft (47th overall) on Stanford outside linebacker Trent Murphy. Murphy was described as a "try-hard" pass rusher by NFL Films' Greg Cosell, who charted Murphy's senior season and found that only two of his 15 sacks came from actually beating his blocker. Then again, the try-hard, good-effort tag was also applied to Kerrigan when he was coming out, and SackSEER likes Murphy not only for his sack totals but also for his excellent three-cone time and nine passes defensed in his last two seasons. With Orakpo on the franchise tag, this pick seems to be a pretty good sign that his days in Washington are numbered. Orakpo definitely has injury concerns, but it's strange that Washington is focusing on his problems amidst the rest of the roster's issues.

Inside linebacker can be classified as either barren or absolutely barren depending on what you think of Perry Riley. Riley received a three-year, $13 million deal to stay in Washington, where he'll hope to parlay his rapidly-disappearing youth into his first good season. At the very least, hits and hurries show he's an adequate A-gap blitzer. With London Fletcher finally retired, Washington turned to free agency again to pick up Houston castoff Darryl Sharpton, who, like Riley, also demonstrated an above-average ability to play neither the run nor the pass. Washington's best bet for a real solution at the position will be a quick maturation for 2012 fourth-rounder Keenan Robinson. Robinson has mostly played special teams at this point, but could slot in as a rangy "Mo" linebacker, though his zone coverage ability was questioned coming out of Texas.

On the defensive line, Jason Hatcher became this year's recipient of the Albert Haynesworth Memorial Batshit Insane Washington Free-Agent Contract. Hatcher, 32, is coming off an 11-sack season under the tutelage of one of the gurus of pass rush, Dallas defensive line coach Rod Marinelli. His previous season high was 4.5. Oh, and by the way, Hatcher is already set to undergo arthroscopic surgery and will miss part of training camp. And did we mention he's already 32? Hatcher is so old that he was a Top 25 Prospect in *Pro Football Prospectus 2008*. On the bright side, Washington can release him from his four-year, $27 million deal in 2016 and save $4.2 million towards their next awful purchase. Haslett's best line probably has Hatcher at right end and Barry Cofield at nose tackle. Left end is an open question mark. Jarvis Jenkins lost the first four games of 2013 to a PED suspension, and played poorly once he returned, but has the best track record on the line. Kedric Golston and Stephen Bowen are also options. Surprisingly, former nose tackle Chris Baker was first-team at OTAs.

Defensive Secondary

			Overall									vs. Run					vs. Pass									
Secondary	Age	Pos	G	Snaps	Plays	TmPct	Rk	Stop	Dfts	BTkl	Runs	St%	Rk	RuYd	Rk	Tgts	Tgt%	Rk	Dist	Suc%	Rk	AdjYd	Rk	PD	Int
DeAngelo Hall	31	CB	16	996	91	11.5%	4	35	16	13	22	32%	61	9.4	62	82	20.1%	32	11.2	49%	60	7.8	50	13	4
Josh Wilson*	29	CB	16	965	96	12.2%	1	41	19	13	34	56%	17	4.4	7	64	16.2%	4	11.0	49%	63	8.9	72	6	1
Brandon Meriweather	30	FS	13	736	72	11.2%	27	23	11	16	32	44%	30	5.8	18	20	6.7%	20	13.5	36%	74	9.6	65	3	2
David Amerson	23	CB	16	684	57	7.2%	60	23	11	7	10	50%	25	4.9	13	73	26.0%	79	10.7	56%	25	7.1	35	9	2
E.J. Biggers	27	CB	16	425	34	4.3%	--	11	6	7	12	58%	--	5.3	--	23	13.0%	--	11.9	40%	--	9.3	--	2	1
Reed Doughty*	32	SS	15	406	71	9.6%	43	35	6	10	53	58%	7	4.4	8	14	8.5%	44	9.6	55%	37	6.9	38	2	1
Bacarri Rambo	24	SS	11	334	38	7.0%	--	14	3	8	23	48%	--	6.3	--	9	6.6%	--	8.9	51%	--	7.4	--	0	0
Ryan Clark	*35*	*FS*	*16*	*1061*	*108*	*13.6%*	*7*	*34*	*9*	*9*	*66*	*45%*	*28*	*5.7*	*17*	*21*	*4.6%*	*4*	*15.8*	*46%*	*63*	*8.6*	*59*	*3*	*2*
Tracy Porter	*28*	*CB*	*16*	*985*	*79*	*9.7%*	*18*	*39*	*16*	*9*	*27*	*59%*	*8*	*3.8*	*4*	*78*	*20.9%*	*42*	*9.4*	*59%*	*13*	*7.1*	*31*	*12*	*2*

Year	Pass D Rank	vs. #1 WR	Rk	vs. #2 WR	Rk	vs. Other WR	Rk	vs. TE	Rk	vs. RB	Rk
2011	16	24.6%	25	-15.7%	9	-19.3%	10	23.7%	28	3.6%	20
2012	14	-3.1%	16	-3.3%	14	-17.5%	5	14.5%	27	-24.1%	4
2013	22	13.6%	27	-14.1%	6	12.9%	25	7.5%	21	5.1%	20

Ah, DeAngelo Hall, favorite whipping boy of Football Outsiders since the inception of the company. Has there ever been a corner more overrated for his combination of flashy plays, interception return touchdowns, and general inconsistency? Actually, we're here to give Hall some respect this year. Yes, we're surprised too. But given that Hall was moved all around the line of scrimmage, often shadowing top receivers like Dez Bryant and Calvin Johnson, the numbers above represent a sort of best-case scenario. A lot of corners would have completely cratered with the pressure Hall had to face last year, and instead he was just mildly below average.

As expected, second-rounder David Amerson spent the first half of the season battling his tendencies to read aggressively and forget about double moves. Amerson was picked on all year, even though he only played 67 percent of the snaps. OTA "Everything Is Awesome" Talk (term licensed from Mike Tanier[1]) had Washington coaches comparing Amerson to a young Aqib Talib. Amerson could eventually develop into a solid boundary corner, but nothing he's shown on the field so far would lead a rational observer to that conclusion. Journeyman Tracy Porter replaces journeyman Josh Wilson as the third corner. Porter had a nice Success Rate, but he's hardly a plug-and-forget player, especially on the upper third of the route tree.

Then there's safety. For some reason, Brandon Meriweather is penciled in as the starter. All he did last season was take poor angles, finish the season with the most broken tackles in the NFL, and head-hunt enough to earn a two-game suspension (eventually reduced on appeal). Ryan Clark would've been a fine signing for this secondary in 2008, but when someone is too old for even Pittsburgh's defense, that should be a neon warning sign for any who would dare pursue them. 2013 fourth-rounder Phillip Thomas missed the entire season with a Lisfranc injury, but the Fresno State All-American was a draftnik favorite coming out and ... well, if he can't beat out these two, that's a scary thought for his future. 2014 fourth-rounder Bashaud Breeland (Clemson) is seen as a possibility at corner or safety, but isn't expected to be an immediate contributor. Bacarri Rambo, the 2013 sixth-rounder with a great name, looks to be on the roster bubble heading into camp. There's no need to go on throwing more names on this tire fire: you know the direction.

1 https://www.youtube.com/watch?v=StTqXEQ2l-Y

Special Teams

Year	DVOA	Rank	FG/XP	Rank	Net Kick	Rank	Kick Ret	Rank	Net Punt	Rank	Punt Ret	Rank	Hidden	Rank
2011	-1.2%	21	-7.6	30	4.0	9	-5.1	27	8.8	8	-6.2	23	2.0	13
2012	-4.3%	28	1.2	14	0.6	15	-3.6	22	-13.8	29	-5.9	27	-9.0	28
2013	-12.0%	32	-2.5	23	-8.3	28	-6.4	29	-33.3	32	-9.4	30	-0.4	16

Washington's special teams broke the time-comedy barrier at least four separate occasions last season, en route to the finishing with the second lowest special teams DVOA since 1989. Dan Snyder remained focused on building the top of his roster rather than embracing depth, so this unit has for years been irrelevant at best. Washington hasn't finished above 21st in special teams DVOA since 2007.

The good news for Washington is that kicker Kai Forbath is healthy after a clash with Darklord Haakon, and he'll need to be to fend off seventh-rounder Zach Hocker (Arkansas). Washington spent on specialists Akeem Jordan and Adam Hayward to staunch the bleeding on coverage. The Skins also disposed of punter Sav Rocca, who had enough shanks last year to start a Renaissance Faire. Thus ends the good news. Washington enters training camp without an experienced NFL punter, leaving practice-squad refugees Robert Malone and Blake Clingan to duel for the job. Tight end Niles Paul, third wideout Andre Roberts, or the ageless Santana Moss are the main candidates for return duties. Washington special teams probably can't be as bad as they were in 2013, given the concept of regression and all (Table 1), but they still have plenty of question marks heading into training camp.

Table 1. Worst Special Teams DVOA, 1989-2013

YEAR	TEAM	ST DVOA	ST DVOA Y+1
2000	BUF	-15.4%	-5.0%
2013	WAS	-12.0%	---
1997	SEA	-11.1%	3.7%
2010	SD	-10.2%	-1.6%
2002	CIN	-9.4%	1.2%
1998	OAK	-9.3%	-4.9%
1997	CHI	-9.2%	2.7%
1992	TB	-9.2%	-1.1%
2004	STL	-9.0%	-4.7%
1993	MIN	-8.4%	-2.2%
1989	CIN	-7.9%	-2.4%
1995	PHI	-7.9%	-2.5%
2008	MIN	-7.9%	4.7%
AVERAGE		**-9.8%**	**-1.0%**

Quarterbacks

On the following pages, we provide the last three years' statistics for the top two quarterbacks on each team's depth chart, as well as a number of other quarterbacks who played significant time in 2013.

Each quarterback gets a projection from our KUBIAK fantasy football projection system, based on a complicated regression analysis that takes into account numerous variables including projected role, performance over the past two years, performance on third down vs. all downs, experience of the projected offensive line, historical comparables, collegiate stats, height, age, and strength of schedule.

It is difficult to accurately project statistics for a 162-game baseball season, but it is exponentially more difficult to accurately project statistics for a 16-game football season because of the small size of the data samples involved. With that in mind, we ask that you consider the listed projections not as a prediction of exact numbers, but the mean of a range of possible performances. What's important is not so much the exact number of yards and touchdowns we project, but whether or not we're projecting a given player to improve or decline. Along those same lines, rookie projections will not be as accurate as veteran projections due to lack of data.

Our quarterback projections look a bit different than our projections for the other skill positions. At running back and wide receiver, second-stringers see plenty of action, but, at quarterback, either a player starts or he does not start. We recognize that, when a starting quarterback gets injured in Week 8, you don't want to grab your *Football Outsiders Almanac* to find out if his backup is any good only to find that we've projected that the guy will throw 12 passes this year. Therefore, each year we project all quarterbacks to start all 16 games. If Tony Romo goes down in November, you can look up Brandon Weeden, divide the stats by 16, and get an idea of what we think he will do in an average week (and then, if you are a Dallas fan, pass out). There are full-season projections for the top two quarterbacks on all 32 depth charts.

The first line of each quarterback table contains biographical data—the player's name, height, weight, college, draft position, birth date, and age. Height and weight are the best data we could find; weight, of course, can fluctuate during the offseason. Age is very simple: the number of years between the player's birth year and 2014, but birthdate is provided if you want to figure out exact age.

Draft position gives draft year and round, with the overall pick number with which the player was taken in parentheses. In the sample table, it says that Matt Ryan was chosen in the first round of the 2008 NFL Draft, with the third overall pick. Undrafted free agents are listed as "FA" with the year they came into the league, even if they were only in training camp or on a practice squad.

To the far right of the first line is the player's Risk variable for fantasy football in 2014, which measures the likelihood of the player hitting his projection. The default rating for each player is Green. As the risk of a player failing to hit his projection rises, he's given a rating of Yellow or, in the worst cases, Red. The Risk variable is not only based on injury probability, but how a player's projection compares to his recent performance as well as our confidence (or lack thereof) in his offensive teammates. A few players with the strongest chances of surpassing their projections are given a Blue rating. Most players marked Blue will be backups with low projections, but a handful are starters or situational players who can be considered slightly better breakout candidates.

Next, we give the last three years of player stats. The majority of these statistics are passing numbers, although the final five columns on the right are the quarterback's rushing statistics.

The first few columns after the year and team the player played for are standard numbers: games and games started (**G/GS**), offensive **Snaps**, pass attempts (**Att**), pass completions (**Cmp**), completion percentage (**C%**), passing yards (**Yds**), passing touchdowns (**TD**). These numbers are official NFL totals and therefore include plays we leave out of our own metrics, such as clock-stopping spikes, and omit plays we include in our metrics, such as sacks and aborted snaps. (Other differences between official stats and Football Outsiders stats are described in the "Statistical Toolbox" introduction at the front of the book.)

The column for interceptions contains two numbers, representing the official NFL total for interceptions (**Int**) as well as our own metric for adjusted interceptions (**Adj**). For example, if you look at our sample table, Matt Ryan had 17 interceptions and 16 adjusted interceptions in 2013. Adjusted interceptions use game charting data to add dropped interceptions, plays where a defender most likely would have had an interception but couldn't hold onto the ball. Then we remove Hail Mary passes and interceptions thrown on fourth down when losing in the final two minutes of the game. We also remove "tipped interceptions," when a perfectly catchable ball deflected off the receiver's hands or chest and into the arms of a defender.

Matt Ryan Height: 6-4 Weight: 228 College: Boston College Draft: 2008/1 (3) Born: 17-May-1985 Age: 29 Risk: Green

Year	Team	G/GS	Snaps	Att	Comp	C%	Yds	TD	INT/Adj	FUM	ASR	NY/P	Rk	DVOA	Rk	DYAR	Rk	YAR	Runs	Yds	TD	DVOA	DYAR	QBR
2011	ATL	16/16	1062	566	347	61.3%	4177	29	12/11	5	5.3%	6.8	12	18.8%	7	1120	6	1204	37	84	2	19.8%	38	69.9
2012	ATL	16/16	1048	615	422	68.6%	4719	32	14/16	4	5.1%	7.0	4	16.5%	8	1196	5	1315	34	141	1	39.7%	54	74.8
2013	ATL	16/16	1065	651	439	67.4%	4515	26	17/16	5	5.9%	6.1	20	13.3%	9	1124	4	825	17	55	0	54.5%	23	61.1
2014	*ATL*			*632*	*415*	*65.8%*	*4492*	*26*	*17*	*5*		*6.2*		*3.4%*					*25*	*73*	*0*	*9.5%*		

2013: 53% Short 35% Mid 8% Deep 4% Bomb YAC: 4.8 (37) 2012: 51% Short 33% Mid 11% Deep 6% Bomb YAC: 4.9 (23)

Overall, adjusted interception rate is higher than standard interception rate, so most quarterbacks will have more adjusted interceptions than standard interceptions. On average, a quarterback will have one additional adjusted interception for every 120 pass attempts. Once this difference is accounted for, adjusted interceptions are a better predictor of next year's interception total than standard interceptions.

The next column is fumbles (**FUM**), which adds together all fumbles by this player, whether turned over to the defense or recovered by the offense (explained in the essay "Pregame Show"). Even though this fumble total is listed among the passing numbers, it includes all fumbles, including those on sacks, aborted snaps, and rushing attempts. By listing fumbles and interceptions next to one another, we're giving readers a general idea of how many total turnovers the player was responsible for.

Next comes Adjusted Sack Rate (**ASR**). This is the same statistic you'll find in the team chapters, only here it is specific to the individual quarterback. It represents sacks per pass play (total pass plays = pass attempts + sacks) adjusted based on down, distance, and strength of schedule. For reference, the NFL average was 6.7 percent in 2011, 6.5 percent in 2012, and 7.0 percent in 2013.

The next two columns are Net Yards per Pass (**NY/P**), a standard stat but a particularly good one, and the player's rank (**Rk**) in Net Yards per Pass for that season. Net Yards per Pass consists of passing yards minus yards lost on sacks, divided by total pass plays.

The five columns remaining in passing stats give our advanced metrics: **DVOA** (Defense-Adjusted Value Over Average), **DYAR** (Defense-Adjusted Yards Above Replacement), and **YAR** (Yards Above Replacement), along with the player's rank in both DVOA and DYAR. These metrics compare each quarterback's passing performance to league-average or replacement-level baselines based on the game situations that quarterback faced. DVOA and DYAR are also adjusted based on the opposing defense. The methods used to compute these numbers are described in detail in the "Statistical Toolbox" introduction at the front of the book. The important distinctions between them are:

- DVOA is a rate statistic, while DYAR is a cumulative statistic. Thus, a higher DVOA means more value per pass play, while a higher DYAR means more aggregate value over the entire season.
- Because DYAR is defense-adjusted and YAR is not, a player whose DYAR is higher than his YAR faced a harder-than-average schedule. A player whose DYAR is lower than his YAR faced an easier-than-average schedule.

To qualify for a ranking in Net Yards per Pass, passing DVOA, and passing DYAR in a given season, a quarterback must have had 100 pass plays in that season. 47 quarterbacks ranked for 2011, 39 quarterbacks ranked for 2012, and 45 quarterbacks ranked for 2013.

The final five columns contain rushing statistics, starting with **Runs**, rushing yards (**Yds**), and rushing touchdowns (**TD**). Once again, these are official NFL totals and include kneeldowns, which means you get to enjoy statistics such as Peyton Manning rushing 32 times for minus-31 yards. The final two columns give **DYAR** and **DVOA** for quarterback rushing, which are calculated separately from passing. Rankings for these statistics, as well as numbers that are not adjusted for defense (YAR and VOA) can be found on our website, FootballOutsiders.com.

The last number listed is the Total QBR metric from ESPN Stats & Information. Total QBR is based on the expected points added by the quarterback on each play, then adjusts the numbers to a scale of 0-100. There are five main differences between Total QBR and DVOA:

- Total QBR incorporates information from game charting, such as passes dropped or thrown away on purpose.
- Total QBR splits responsibility on plays between the quarterback, his receivers, and his blockers. Drops, for example, are more on the receiver, as are yards after the catch, and some sacks are more on the offensive line than others.
- Total QBR has a clutch factor which adds (or subtracts) value for quarterbacks who perform best (or worst) in high-leverage situations.
- Total QBR combines passing and rushing value into one number and differentiates between scrambles and planned runs.
- Total QBR is not adjusted for strength of opponent.

The italicized row of statistics for the 2014 season is our 2014 KUBIAK projection, as detailed above. Again, in the interest of producing meaningful statistics, all quarterbacks are projected to start a full 16-game season, regardless of the likelihood of them actually doing so.

The final line below the KUBIAK projection represents data from the Football Outsiders game charting project. First, we break down charted passes based on distance: **Short** (5 yards or less), **Mid** (6-15 yards), **Deep** (16-25 yards), and **Bomb** (26 or more yards). These numbers are based on distance in the air only and include both complete and incomplete passes. Passes thrown away or tipped at the line are not included, nor are passes on which the quarterback's arm was hit by a defender while in motion. We also give average yards after catch (**YAC**) with the Rank in parentheses for the 45 quarterbacks who qualify.

A number of third- and fourth-string quarterbacks are briefly discussed at the end of the chapter in a section we call "Going Deep."

Top 20 QB by Passing DYAR (Total Value), 2013

Rank	Player	Team	DYAR
1	Peyton Manning	DEN	2,475
2	Philip Rivers	SD	1,799
3	Drew Brees	NO	1,701
4	Matt Ryan	ATL	1,124
5	Nick Foles	PHI	1,011
6	Tom Brady	NE	979
7	Tony Romo	DAL	839
8	Colin Kaepernick	SF	791
9	Russell Wilson	SEA	770
10	Aaron Rodgers	GB	740
11	Ben Roethlisberger	PIT	724
12	Matthew Stafford	DET	690
13	Josh McCown	CHI	659
14	Andrew Luck	IND	650
15	Carson Palmer	ARI	547
16	Andy Dalton	CIN	541
17	Cam Newton	CAR	421
18	Jay Cutler	CHI	392
19	Sam Bradford	STL	304
20	Alex Smith	KC	262

Minimum 100 passes.

Top 20 QB by Passing DVOA (Value per Pass), 2013

Rank	Player	Team	DVOA
1	Peyton Manning	DEN	43.2%
2	Nick Foles	PHI	35.6%
3	Philip Rivers	SD	34.8%
4	Josh McCown	CHI	32.1%
5	Drew Brees	NO	26.9%
6	Aaron Rodgers	GB	25.4%
7	Colin Kaepernick	SF	16.6%
8	Russell Wilson	SEA	15.6%
9	Matt Ryan	ATL	13.3%
10	Tony Romo	DAL	11.5%
11	Tom Brady	NE	10.9%
12	Ben Roethlisberger	PIT	6.6%
13	Jay Cutler	CHI	5.5%
14	Sam Bradford	STL	5.2%
15	Matthew Stafford	DET	4.9%
16	Andrew Luck	IND	4.6%
17	Carson Palmer	ARI	2.7%
18	Andy Dalton	CIN	2.3%
19	Cam Newton	CAR	1.7%
20	Ryan Fitzpatrick	TEN	-3.6%

Minimum 100 passes.

Derek Anderson

Height: 6-6 Weight: 229 College: Oregon State Draft: 2005/6 (213) Born: 15-Jun-1983 Age: 31 Risk: Red

Year	Team	G/GS	Snaps	Att	Comp	C%	Yds	TD	INT/Adj	FUM	ASR	NY/P	Rk	DVOA	Rk	DYAR	Rk	YAR	Runs	Yds	TD	DVOA	DYAR	QBR
2011	CAR	2/0	11	0	0	0.0%	0	0	0/0	0	--	--	--	--	--	--	--	--	2	-2	0	--	--	--
2012	CAR	2/0	9	4	4	100.0%	58	0	0/0	0	1.4%	14.5	--	132.9%	--	47	--	48	0	0	0	--	--	91.6
2013	CAR	4/0	15	0	0	0.0%	0	0	0/0	0	--	--	--	--	--	--	--	--	5	0	0	27.7%	3	--
2014	*CAR*			*519*	*285*	*55.0%*	*3166*	*15*	*15*	*9*		*5.2*		*-14.5%*					*24*	*40*	*0*	*-14.2%*		

2012: 50% Short 50% Mid 0% Deep 0% Bomb YAC: 7.8 (--)

Anderson has been making more than $800,000 per season in Carolina to play about a dozen snaps a year. The Panthers, apparently impressed with his ability to kneel down at the end of blowouts, re-signed him this offseason to a two-year deal that actually raised his salary. This for a guy whose last regular-season touchdown came in an Arizona uniform, a three-yard strike to Larry Fitzgerald when the Cardinals were down by 25 points in the fourth quarter against Kansas City in November of 2010. Being a backup quarterback is just the best job in the world.

Matt Barkley

Height: 6-2 Weight: 230 College: USC Draft: 2013/4 (98) Born: 8-Sep-1990 Age: 24 Risk: Red

Year	Team	G/GS	Snaps	Att	Comp	C%	Yds	TD	INT/Adj	FUM	ASR	NY/P	Rk	DVOA	Rk	DYAR	Rk	YAR	Runs	Yds	TD	DVOA	DYAR	QBR
2013	PHI	3/0	76	49	30	61.2%	300	0	4/4	3	7.1%	5.3	--	-34.9%	--	-84	--	-96	2	-2	0	--	--	19.5
2014	*PHI*			*524*	*326*	*62.1%*	*3705*	*20*	*16*	*8*		*5.9*		*-0.6%*					*35*	*121*	*0*	*8.1%*		

2013: 41% Short 33% Mid 20% Deep 6% Bomb YAC: 2.9 (--)

The good: Barkley was only a rookie getting unexpected playing time in injury relief, so maybe he'll get better. The bad: Barkley had five turnovers on just 52 dropbacks. The ugly: Barkley's drive charts against the Cowboys and Giants must be seen to be believed.

- Interception
- Interception
- Interception
- Sack-fumble in red zone
- Incomplete on fourth-and-10
- Three-and-out punt
- Three-and-out punt
- Punt
- 5-yard pass on fourth-and-20
- Hail Mary interception

Blake Bortles Height: 6-4 Weight: 232 College: Central Florida Draft: 2014/1 (3) Born: 16-Dec-1991 Age: 23 Risk: Red

Year	Team	G/GS	Snaps	Att	Comp	C%	Yds	TD	INT/Adj	FUM	ASR	NY/P	Rk	DVOA	Rk	DYAR	Rk	YAR	Runs	Yds	TD	DVOA	DYAR	QBR
2014	*JAC*			*535*	*302*	*56.5%*	*3726*	*20*	*19*	*9*		*6.0*		*-11.4%*					*72*	*314*	*4*	*13.9%*		

Captain America to Johnny Manziel's Mighty Mouse, Blake Bortles fits the ideal physical stereotype of the quarterbacks of yore. Jacksonville liked him so much that they didn't even attempt a trade down from the No. 3 pick, so obviously they believe he can be an NFL star. Bortles has no crippling flaws, and he did some of his best work in the screen game that Jedd Fisch used plenty of last season. On the other hand, his conceptual knowledge of hybrid coverages is sub-par, and his footwork can be downright awkward at times. The plan is for Bortles to sit and learn for his first NFL season. Whether Chad Henne does well enough to let that happen is up for debate. Either way, expect the run on "BORTLES" license plates to wait for 2015.

Sam Bradford Height: 6-4 Weight: 236 College: Oklahoma Draft: 2010/1 (1) Born: 8-Nov-1987 Age: 27 Risk: Green

Year	Team	G/GS	Snaps	Att	Comp	C%	Yds	TD	INT/Adj	FUM	ASR	NY/P	Rk	DVOA	Rk	DYAR	Rk	YAR	Runs	Yds	TD	DVOA	DYAR	QBR
2011	STL	10/10	670	357	191	53.5%	2164	6	6/12	8	9.1%	4.9	41	-24.0%	38	-325	42	-374	18	26	0	-58.6%	-25	26.2
2012	STL	16/16	1034	551	328	59.5%	3702	21	13/12	7	6.3%	6.0	22	-0.8%	16	388	16	245	37	127	1	29.6%	42	50.3
2013	STL	7/7	450	262	159	60.7%	1687	14	4/5	3	6.0%	5.8	29	5.2%	14	304	19	387	15	31	0	-70.1%	-25	48.0
2014	*STL*			*548*	*334*	*60.9%*	*3727*	*19*	*13*	*7*		*6.1*		*-0.3%*					*26*	*59*	*0*	*-3.7%*		

2013: 58% Short 27% Mid 9% Deep 7% Bomb YAC: 5.7 (13) 2012: 51% Short 32% Mid 9% Deep 8% Bomb YAC: 4.7 (29)

The first rule of Sam Bradford is: *you do not talk about Sam Bradford.* Seriously, when was the last time a No. 1 overall pick generated as little discussion as Bradford? Steve Emtman, perhaps? Kenneth Sims? The Oklahoma section of his Wikipedia page is longer than the NFL section. No one cares if he's getting better, getting worse, recovering well from last October's ACL tear, or that he's already into the fifth year of his career. If Bradford had a six-star wanted level on *Grand Theft Auto III*, the tanks probably wouldn't even bother chasing him because he's just so damn insignificant.

The Rams have tried to build around Bradford. They've added offensive linemen, including Jake Long a year ago, but sack rate isn't really Bradford's problem. The Rams have drafted nine wide receivers in the first four rounds since 2008, but nothing seems to click in the St. Louis passing game. Tavon Austin was supposed to be a perfect fit for Bradford as a YAC demon, but the two got off to an embarrassing start: 198 yards on 46 targets (4.3 yards per pass). Bradford had 14 touchdown passes in seven games last year, but that's partly because the Rams didn't score a rushing touchdown until Week 9. He finally had a season with positive passing DVOA, but we're still waiting for evidence of anything more than an average quarterback with no media pulse.

Tom Brady Height: 6-4 Weight: 225 College: Michigan Draft: 2000/6 (199) Born: 3-Aug-1977 Age: 37 Risk: Yellow

Year	Team	G/GS	Snaps	Att	Comp	C%	Yds	TD	INT/Adj	FUM	ASR	NY/P	Rk	DVOA	Rk	DYAR	Rk	YAR	Runs	Yds	TD	DVOA	DYAR	QBR
2011	NE	16/16	1122	611	401	65.6%	5235	39	12/15	6	5.4%	7.9	2	35.3%	3	1994	3	1956	43	109	3	10.9%	57	73.0
2012	NE	16/16	1213	637	401	63.0%	4827	34	8/10	6	4.6%	7.0	5	35.1%	1	2035	1	1910	23	32	4	40.3%	56	77.7
2013	NE	16/16	1197	628	380	60.5%	4343	25	11/8	9	6.1%	6.2	19	10.9%	11	979	6	859	32	18	0	-19.4%	-5	61.1
2014	*NE*			*614*	*391*	*63.6%*	*4512*	*29*	*12*	*6*		*6.7*		*15.8%*					*34*	*8*	*0*	*-28.2%*		

2013: 47% Short 33% Mid 13% Deep 7% Bomb YAC: 5.3 (24) 2012: 41% Short 39% Mid 13% Deep 6% Bomb YAC: 5.5 (7)

It was a year of tremendous personal and professional change for the quarterback, who oversaw massive personnel changes before the season, as well as sizable shifts in offensive philosophy from week to week over the course of the year. Stripped of so many of the offensive options he had grown accustomed during recent seasons, there were times where he was easily flustered, and other times where he appeared overwhelmed as he was unable to jump start an occasionally sluggish New England offense. But at the same time, there were some truly great moments. He led five comeback wins, and his four-game stretch from November 3 through December 1 was as good as any series of games over the course of his career. Against the Steelers, Panthers, Broncos and Texans, Brady went 115-for-164 (70 percent) for 1,443 yards with 10 touchdowns and just two interceptions, good for 47.3% DVOA. By the end of the year, Brady was clearly back to his position as one of the top five quarterbacks in the league, and if age 37 didn't stop Peyton Manning, it's unlikely to stop Tom Brady either.

Drew Brees Height: 6-0 Weight: 209 College: Purdue Draft: 2001/2 (32) Born: 15-Jan-1979 Age: 35 Risk: Green

Year	Team	G/GS	Snaps	Att	Comp	C%	Yds	TD	INT/Adj	FUM	ASR	NY/P	Rk	DVOA	Rk	DYAR	Rk	YAR	Runs	Yds	TD	DVOA	DYAR	QBR
2011	NO	16/16	1110	657	468	71.2%	5476	46	14/17	1	4.5%	7.9	3	38.3%	2	2259	1	2363	21	86	1	30.5%	33	83.0
2012	NO	16/16	1095	670	422	63.0%	5177	43	19/23	6	4.9%	7.1	3	19.8%	5	1441	3	1397	15	5	1	34.2%	11	66.5
2013	NO	16/16	1110	650	446	68.6%	5162	39	12/14	5	5.3%	7.2	7	26.9%	5	1701	3	1550	35	52	3	33.6%	36	70.5
2014	*NO*			*636*	*422*	*66.3%*	*4926*	*38*	*14*	*5*		*6.9*		*21.3%*					*28*	*4*	*0*	*-24.3%*		

2013: 52% Short 30% Mid 10% Deep 8% Bomb YAC: 5.5 (20) 2012: 47% Short 35% Mid 10% Deep 8% Bomb YAC: 5.1 (15)

Even in this era of hyper-inflated passing numbers, Brees' statistics jump off the page. He has produced half of the eight 5,000-yard seasons in NFL history. Nobody else has more than one. He has thrown for 350 yards in a game 41 times, nine times more than anyone else. Our advanced metrics tend to slot him slightly below Peyton Manning and Tom Brady, but those three are the only men to rank in the top five in passing DYAR at least seven times. His 2013 season had its share of peaks and valleys, but the peaks were epic, and remember that few quarterbacks played a more difficult schedule. In six games against teams in the top 10 teams in pass defense DVOA (Seattle, Buffalo, Arizona, San Francisco, and Carolina twice), he completed 68 percent of his passes for 7.0 yards per attempt with 15 touchdowns and four picks. An easier schedule in 2014 (Goodbye, NFC West! Hello, NFC North!) should guarantee Brees another season in the early rounds of fantasy drafts across America.

Teddy Bridgewater Height: 6-2 Weight: 214 College: Louisville Draft: 2014/1 (32) Born: 10-Nov-1992 Age: 22 Risk: Red

Year	Team	G/GS	Snaps	Att	Comp	C%	Yds	TD	INT/Adj	FUM	ASR	NY/P	Rk	DVOA	Rk	DYAR	Rk	YAR	Runs	Yds	TD	DVOA	DYAR	QBR
2014	*MIN*			*510*	*293*	*57.5%*	*3538*	*18*	*18*	*9*		*6.1*		*-11.1%*					*54*	*122*	*2*	*-13.6%*		

Bridgewater and his glove are like KISS and their makeup. Bridgewater wore a glove for most of his career, but decided to take it off at the zaniest possible times: first in a Freezer Bowl game against the Cincinnati Bearcats, then at his Pro Day. He couldn't hit a pool from the diving board in the Cincy game, and his Pro Day has become the stuff of legend (tens of thousands will someday say they were there, and saw him try to shove a football in his own ear). When Norv Turner hosted Bridgewater for a pair of private workouts, he let Bridgewater keep his glove, and suddenly the quarterback (with a little coaching up) was his old accurate, comfortable self. As Dan Pompei wrote in the offseason, Turner more-or-less shrugged, figured a glove was good enough for Kurt Warner, and stopped worrying about the silly thing.

In other words, we have come to the point in 21st century Western Civilization where Norv Turner is a voice of reason. Have you melted down grandma's gold jewelry yet? Are you waiting for a more obvious sign of societal collapse? Don't come crying to the barbed-wire edge of our compound when it happens.

Jason Campbell Height: 6-5 Weight: 223 College: Auburn Draft: 2005/1 (25) Born: 31-Dec-1981 Age: 33 Risk: Green

Year	Team	G/GS	Snaps	Att	Comp	C%	Yds	TD	INT/Adj	FUM	ASR	NY/P	Rk	DVOA	Rk	DYAR	Rk	YAR	Runs	Yds	TD	DVOA	DYAR	QBR
2011	OAK	6/6	354	165	100	60.6%	1170	6	4/3	3	3.0%	6.8	15	19.8%	6	340	17	326	18	60	2	-19.1%	-6	55.1
2012	CHI	6/1	126	51	32	62.7%	265	2	2/2	2	9.9%	3.8	--	-50.2%	--	-129	--	-166	7	28	0	44.4%	9	23.5
2013	CLE	9/8	503	317	180	56.8%	2015	11	8/8	3	5.6%	5.8	28	-12.2%	30	-24	30	-80	14	107	0	34.0%	31	38.6
2014	*CIN*			*524*	*319*	*61.0%*	*3545*	*15*	*16*	*8*		*5.9*		*-7.5%*					*38*	*61*	*1*	*-13.6%*		

2013: 53% Short 31% Mid 10% Deep 6% Bomb YAC: 5.8 (8) 2012: 51% Short 35% Mid 6% Deep 8% Bomb YAC: 2.4 (–)

But for misfortune Campbell might have had a far better career. He's been saddled with revolving coaches, bad teams, and poor timing. Just when he appeared to be about to break out in Oakland, he was injured, and hasn't been the same since. Campbell has been reunited with his old Raiders coach, Hue Jackson, in Cincinnati, where he will serve as a veteran backup to Andy Dalton. If Dalton complains about the lashing he takes from fans and media for his playoff failures, Campbell will be there to remind him that it all could be much, much worse.

Derek Carr Height: 6-3 Weight: 220 College: Fresno St. Draft: 2014/2 (36) Born: 3/28/1991 Age: 23 Risk: Red

Year	Team	G/GS	Snaps	Att	Comp	C%	Yds	TD	INT/Adj	FUM	ASR	NY/P	Rk	DVOA	Rk	DYAR	Rk	YAR	Runs	Yds	TD	DVOA	DYAR	QBR
2014	*OAK*			*509*	*304*	*59.8%*	*3359*	*15*	*17*	*9*		*5.9*		*-17.2%*					*67*	*149*	*2*	*-16.3%*		

What do you do with a college quarterback who threw one-third of his passes at or behind the line of scrimmage and completed just 31 percent of his passes under pressure, while playing in a shotgun spread attack that rarely featured multiple reads? For one, the Oakland Raiders will not throw him immediately into the starting lineup, as it didn't take long for them to tell the media that drafting Carr did not mean he would be the starter in 2014. Why was he a second-round pick then? He has an excellent arm and a very good release, and it's easy to project him as an NFL starter if he improves some of those fundamentals and gets accustomed to the greater speed of the NFL game. Should injury or performance issues with Matt Schaub force him into the game, expect to see some pretty fade passes and yet another Oakland quarterback who lacks composure in the pocket.

Matt Cassel Height: 6-5 Weight: 230 College: USC Draft: 2005/7 (230) Born: 17-May-1982 Age: 32 Risk: Yellow

Year	Team	G/GS	Snaps	Att	Comp	C%	Yds	TD	INT/Adj	FUM	ASR	NY/P	Rk	DVOA	Rk	DYAR	Rk	YAR	Runs	Yds	TD	DVOA	DYAR	QBR
2011	KC	9/9	575	269	160	59.5%	1713	10	9/8	5	7.9%	5.5	34	-26.0%	39	-279	41	-169	25	99	0	13.5%	25	45.4
2012	KC	9/8	578	277	161	58.1%	1796	6	12/10	9	7.3%	5.8	27	-30.4%	36	-353	36	-275	27	145	1	17.8%	35	36.4
2013	MIN	9/6	459	254	153	60.2%	1807	11	9/10	3	6.1%	6.4	17	-5.9%	23	92	23	-7	18	57	1	5.2%	10	48.7
2014	*MIN*			*547*	*325*	*59.3%*	*3796*	*21*	*18*	*10*		*5.9*		*-9.3%*					*28*	*82*	*0*	*1.1%*		

2013: 47% Short 30% Mid 17% Deep 6% Bomb YAC: 5.2 (27) 2012: 41% Short 39% Mid 12% Deep 8% Bomb YAC: 4.9 (25)

Cassel attempted just six passes of 20+ yards (air length) in 122 attempts prior to the Week 14 Ravens game. He completed two, both of them in the fourth quarter of the Seahawks game while trailing by 28 points. In his final four starts, Cassel was 3-of-9 on 20+-yard passes, with completions of 22, 42, and 36 yards. Those aren't Aaron Rodgers deep splits, but it probably goes without saying that at least *trying* to nail a 30-yard deep pass or two before garbage time can do wonders for other aspects of the offense. Safeties, for example, might line up more than 18 inches from the line of scrimmage. The Eagles game, in particular, was evidence of what Cassel is still capable of when allowed to throw slants and seam routes like a real quarterback, not 24-7-365 screens and waggles. The Vikings are indicating that Cassel will perform caretaker starting duties while Teddy Bridgewater develops. Now that management-by-emergency has passed, he should just about be up to the task.

Jimmy Clausen Height: 6-3 Weight: 222 College: Notre Dame Draft: 2010/2 (48) Born: 21-Sep-1987 Age: 27 Risk: Red

Year	Team	G/GS	Snaps	Att	Comp	C%	Yds	TD	INT/Adj	FUM	ASR	NY/P	Rk	DVOA	Rk	DYAR	Rk	YAR	Runs	Yds	TD	DVOA	DYAR	QBR
2010	CAR	13/10	642	299	157	52.5%	1558	3	9/10	8	10.7%	4.1	45	-41.4%	44	-609	46	-613	23	57	0	-74.8%	-42	11.8
2014	*CHI*			*541*	*318*	*58.8%*	*3522*	*16*	*15*	*12*		*5.6*		*-5.5%*					*25*	*28*	*1*	*-16.6%*		

The year is 2010. Second-round rookie Jimmy Clausen throws three touchdowns and nine interceptions while going 1-9 as a starting quarterback for the Panthers. That same season, second-year passer Josh Freeman throws 25 touchdowns and six interceptions for a 10-6 Tampa Bay team; Vince Young, still only 27, throws 10 touchdowns and three interceptions in Tennessee; and a rookie in Denver named Tim Tebow throws five touchdowns and three picks with some fourth-quarter magic thrown in to tantalize Broncos fans. Here we are now, four years later, and Freeman, Young, and Tebow are unemployed, while Clausen has been earning a steady paycheck and living a controversy-free life. Granted, he hasn't thrown a regular-season pass since 2010, but then neither have any of the other backup quarterbacks on the Bears roster. Clausen has dropped back 125 times in the last three preseasons, completing 53 percent of his passes with 17 sacks and averaging 4.2 yards per play. Should Jay Cutler get injured this year (you know, like he did last year, and the year before that, and the year before that, and the year before that), Bears fans will get a chance to see what Clausen, Jordan Palmer, and David Fales can do. And maybe, just maybe, Josh Freeman's phone will ring.

Kellen Clemens Height: 6-2 Weight: 224 College: Oregon Draft: 2006/2 (49) Born: 6-Jun-1983 Age: 31 Risk: Red

Year	Team	G/GS	Snaps	Att	Comp	C%	Yds	TD	INT/Adj	FUM	ASR	NY/P	Rk	DVOA	Rk	DYAR	Rk	YAR	Runs	Yds	TD	DVOA	DYAR	QBR
2011	2TM	3/3	192	91	48	52.7%	546	2	1/1	2	9.7%	4.7	43	-11.9%	28	-5	28	-19	6	37	1	-3.0%	3	25.2
2012	STL	2/0	8	3	1	33.3%	39	0	1/0	1	1.0%	13.0	--	-207.0%	--	-62	--	-62	2	5	0	89.8%	5	1.6
2013	STL	10/9	554	242	142	58.7%	1673	8	7/9	7	7.7%	5.8	25	-7.5%	25	60	25	-133	23	64	0	-52.9%	-35	38.2
2014	*SD*			*549*	*345*	*62.8%*	*3608*	*15*	*16*	*10*		*5.7*		*-3.1%*					*35*	*36*	*2*	*-10.1%*		

2013: 49% Short 30% Mid 15% Deep 5% Bomb YAC: 5.2 (26) 2012: 0% Short 50% Mid 0% Deep 50% Bomb YAC: 1.0 (--)

A longtime Brian Schottenheimer disciple, Clemens succeeded in making B-Schott's short 'n' strange passing game even shorter and stranger. But Clemens was the quarterback of record for the Rams' three most noteworthy wins (Bears, Colts and Saints), so he earned a mini winner-sauce rep among those who judge quarterbacks by the final scores of games they did not watch. Instead of staying in Schottenheimer's spare bedroom and sparking a regrettable controversy with Sam Bradford, Clemens signed with the Chargers, who have always had a soft spot for career backups who can barely play. If there is an axis with Charlie Whitehurst on one side and Billy Volek on the other, Clemens rests right in the middle.

Kirk Cousins Height: 6-3 Weight: 214 College: Michigan State Draft: 2012/4 (102) Born: 19-Aug-1988 Age: 26 Risk: Red

Year	Team	G/GS	Snaps	Att	Comp	C%	Yds	TD	INT/Adj	FUM	ASR	NY/P	Rk	DVOA	Rk	DYAR	Rk	YAR	Runs	Yds	TD	DVOA	DYAR	QBR
2012	WAS	3/1	95	48	33	68.8%	466	4	3/3	1	8.2%	8.4	--	6.4%	--	59	--	55	3	22	0	74.5%	10	75.2
2013	WAS	5/3	238	155	81	52.3%	854	4	7/7	3	4.1%	5.1	43	-42.6%	45	-314	41	-300	4	14	0	-6.6%	1	26.5
2014	*WAS*			*621*	*381*	*61.3%*	*4187*	*20*	*16*	*13*		*5.9*		*-3.7%*					*41*	*76*	*0*	*-22.5%*		

2013: 42% Short 44% Mid 11% Deep 3% Bomb YAC: 4.0 (44) 2012: 41% Short 39% Mid 13% Deep 7% Bomb YAC: 5.8 (--)

With their season in the tank and Robert Griffin clearly struggling with the limitations of his leg injury, Washington turned to Cousins in December mostly in an attempt to boost his trade value. Look at the stat line above with us, and you'll learn that there's a reason nobody Kolb'ed themselves into trading assets for Cousins. Only Jim Miller and delusional 106.7 The Fan callers still think Cousins has a legitimate claim to the starting quarterback job at this point. He's an acceptable backup, and that's something this team may need with Griffin's injury history.

Jay Cutler Height: 6-3 Weight: 220 College: Vanderbilt Draft: 2006/1 (11) Born: 29-Apr-1983 Age: 31 Risk: Yellow

Year	Team	G/GS	Snaps	Att	Comp	C%	Yds	TD	INT/Adj	FUM	ASR	NY/P	Rk	DVOA	Rk	DYAR	Rk	YAR	Runs	Yds	TD	DVOA	DYAR	QBR
2011	CHI	10/10	615	314	182	58.0%	2319	13	7/9	7	7.4%	6.4	18	-3.5%	21	157	21	207	18	55	1	-14.5%	-1	55.9
2012	CHI	15/15	919	434	255	58.8%	3033	19	14/20	8	7.8%	5.9	24	-13.8%	27	-81	28	-42	41	233	0	96.2%	114	50.2
2013	CHI	11/11	636	355	224	63.1%	2621	19	12/13	4	6.0%	6.7	11	5.5%	13	392	18	423	23	118	0	58.4%	48	66.4
2014	*CHI*			*568*	*350*	*61.5%*	*4076*	*29*	*16*	*10*		*6.4*		*7.8%*					*46*	*82*	*2*	*-6.4%*		

2013: 48% Short 31% Mid 11% Deep 10% Bomb YAC: 4.1 (43) 2012: 39% Short 34% Mid 18% Deep 9% Bomb YAC: 4.5 (31)

Former Bears general manager Jerry Angelo trolled Cutler in February, just after Cutler signed his hefty new contract. "Has all the physical tools, but inconsistent in the clutch, mostly due to a lack of poise," Angelo said. Former executives make excellent trolls, and Angelo hit all the sweet spots with this one, working "clutch" and "poise" into one blurb. (He quickly dissed Cutler's field-reading ability as well.)

Angelo was working from an old script, though not an inaccurate one for those who buy into intangible/metaphysical scouting: in 2010 and 2011, Angelo's last seasons, Cutler threw seven touchdowns and nine interceptions in fourth quarters, and his other "clutch and poise" splits (like third down conversions) were not great. Then again, Cutler was getting sacked 52 times per year behind an almost purposely mismanaged offensive line, and that is the kind of thing that makes it hard to stay poised, or even standing.

Last season, Cutler threw nine touchdowns (with four interceptions) and completed 66.7 percent of his passes in the fourth quarter and demonstrated other signs of "clutch poisiness" or "poised clutchiness:" 4-of-6 passing on fourth downs, for example. That's not to buy into any intangible-laden argument, but to illustrate that giving a gifted quarterback a functional offensive line and a system that makes sense can work wonders on all of those invisible attributes. Cutler climbed into positive DVOA for the first time in his Bears career. His own maturity may well have played a role (parenthood does wonders), but the real source of improvement was addition by subtraction. No more Mike Martz, Mike Tice, enabler Lovie Smith, or J'Marcus Webb as default left tackle for life. Also, no more Jerry Angelo.

Andy Dalton Height: 6-2 Weight: 215 College: TCU Draft: 2011/2 (35) Born: 29-Oct-1987 Age: 27 Risk: Green

Year	Team	G/GS	Snaps	Att	Comp	C%	Yds	TD	INT/Adj	FUM	ASR	NY/P	Rk	DVOA	Rk	DYAR	Rk	YAR	Runs	Yds	TD	DVOA	DYAR	QBR
2011	CIN	16/16	1024	516	300	58.1%	3398	20	13/17	4	4.5%	6.0	23	5.6%	13	573	12	481	37	152	1	-14.6%	-4	49.8
2012	CIN	16/16	1025	528	329	62.3%	3669	27	16/19	8	8.5%	6.0	21	-5.9%	20	194	20	339	47	120	4	18.9%	53	48.9
2013	CIN	16/16	1117	586	363	61.9%	4293	33	20/21	4	5.2%	6.7	12	2.3%	18	541	16	612	61	183	2	13.0%	52	55.8
2014	*CIN*			*537*	*330*	*61.4%*	*3791*	*26*	*16*	*5*		*6.2*		*4.3%*					*47*	*113*	*2*	*1.2%*		

2013: 44% Short 35% Mid 12% Deep 8% Bomb YAC: 5.7 (9) 2012: 49% Short 31% Mid 12% Deep 8% Bomb YAC: 5.0 (17)

Dalton's deep passing ability gets plenty of criticism, but only Peyton Manning completed more passes targeted 20 or more yards downfield. Dalton was 31-of-86 with 14 touchdowns and five picks in that particular split, which can't all be explained away as A.J. Green making Red look good. If anything, Dalton targeted Green too often (180 times, 100 more than any other Bengal); 12 of his 20 interceptions were intended for his favorite target, with many of those either deflecting off Green's hands or the result of improper route-running (by the wideout's own admission).

Another place Dalton forced throws was the red zone. After not throwing any picks down deep in his first two years, he tossed six in 2013. Blowing off a run call at the one-yard line to audible into a fade to Green that resulted in a Baltimore interception was an emblematic (bad) decision. And familiarity bred contempt—the Ravens and Browns swiped ten of his passes in four games. Cincinnati split those contests, it should be noted, including the regular season finale against the Ravens, where Dalton threw four interceptions (including the one noted above) but the Bengals rolled by 17 points. It was a quintessential Dalton outing—highs leavened with unease, lows papered over by success.

A top-six fantasy quarterback a year ago, Dalton figures to regress in that area, both due to his own limitations and Cincy's stated intent to run the ball more in 2014. Owners in auction leagues will face a conundrum similar to that the Bengals face in "real life:" how much to pay for Dalton.

Chase Daniel Height: 6-0 Weight: 225 College: Missouri Draft: 2009/FA Born: 7-Oct-1986 Age: 28 Risk: Yellow

Year	Team	G/GS	Snaps	Att	Comp	C%	Yds	TD	INT/Adj	FUM	ASR	NY/P	Rk	DVOA	Rk	DYAR	Rk	YAR	Runs	Yds	TD	DVOA	DYAR	QBR
2011	NO	16/0	42	5	4	80.0%	29	0	0/0	0	-0.9%	5.8	--	15.4%	--	8	--	12	3	-3	0	--	--	21.5
2012	NO	16/0	13	1	1	100.0%	10	0	0/0	0	-2.1%	10.0	--	579.9%	--	34	--	36	3	17	0	108.0%	7	100.0
2013	KC	5/1	100	38	25	65.8%	248	1	1/1	0	4.7%	5.9	--	-13.6%	--	-6	--	22	14	52	0	47.0%	18	78.7
2014	*KC*			*529*	*319*	*60.3%*	*3484*	*19*	*15*	*11*		*5.7*		*-15.6%*					*76*	*220*	*1*	*-20.3%*		

2013: 75% Short 11% Mid 11% Deep 3% Bomb YAC: 5.9 (--) 2012: 100% Short 0% Mid 0% Deep 0% Bomb YAC: 5.0 (--)

People may have wondered why the Chiefs signed Daniel to a three-year, $10.5 million deal before the 2013 season, though Andy Reid's successful history with limited quarterbacks gave Daniel his best shot to overcome his own relatively short skill set. But the contract has voiding mechanisms which allow the team to get out of the deal if Daniel fails to throw for 2,000 yards and 12 touchdowns in any of those three seasons. Pretty safe bet there. This is what is known as "funny money" in the NFL, and with a $2.35 million base salary, Daniel could be on the outside looking in as soon as this September—especially with the decision to select Georgia's Aaron Murray in the fifth round of the 2014 draft.

Ryan Fitzpatrick Height: 6-2 Weight: 221 College: Harvard Draft: 2005/7 (250) Born: 24-Nov-1982 Age: 32 Risk: Yellow

Year	Team	G/GS	Snaps	Att	Comp	C%	Yds	TD	INT/Adj	FUM	ASR	NY/P	Rk	DVOA	Rk	DYAR	Rk	YAR	Runs	Yds	TD	DVOA	DYAR	QBR
2011	BUF	16/16	1011	569	353	62.0%	3832	24	23/22	7	3.7%	6.3	20	-6.3%	26	185	19	194	56	215	0	5.2%	38	50.5
2012	BUF	16/16	993	505	306	60.6%	3400	24	16/21	9	5.6%	6.1	20	-7.6%	23	120	23	161	48	197	1	0.5%	22	44.9
2013	TEN	11/9	680	350	217	62.0%	2454	14	12/13	9	5.8%	6.4	15	-3.6%	20	179	21	112	43	225	3	34.8%	85	55.4
2014	*HOU*			*577*	*343*	*59.5%*	*3730*	*23*	*22*	*8*		*5.6*		*-9.1%*					*52*	*219*	*2*	*21.1%*		

2013: 44% Short 37% Mid 11% Deep 8% Bomb YAC: 5.1 (28) 2012: 48% Short 36% Mid 10% Deep 6% Bomb YAC: 5.9 (3)

You've heard of the concept of a starter home? Fitzpatrick is the starter quarterback. More than happy to soak up games and show you the limitations of your system, can deliver downright adequate results at times, and will talk a good game in the locker room. A 3/1 in a decent, new-ish neighborhood. Bill O'Brien wouldn't trade up for Teddy Bridgewater or Johnny Manziel, because those high-risk ventures seemed a little risky. But after this season, he can look at what he learned from Fitzpatrick, and know that he can do so much better. Just like every other team that's seriously considered him for a starting job.

Joe Flacco Height: 6-6 Weight: 236 College: Delaware Draft: 2008/1 (18) Born: 16-Jan-1985 Age: 29 Risk: Green

Year	Team	G/GS	Snaps	Att	Comp	C%	Yds	TD	INT/Adj	FUM	ASR	NY/P	Rk	DVOA	Rk	DYAR	Rk	YAR	Runs	Yds	TD	DVOA	DYAR	QBR
2011	BAL	16/16	1077	542	312	57.6%	3610	20	12/20	11	5.6%	5.9	26	0.0%	18	413	14	389	39	88	1	19.3%	34	57.6
2012	BAL	16/16	1002	531	317	59.7%	3817	22	10/17	9	6.1%	6.3	18	-1.3%	17	358	17	403	32	22	3	-35.1%	-32	46.3
2013	BAL	16/16	1129	614	362	59.0%	3912	19	22/29	8	7.4%	5.4	40	-18.1%	35	-296	40	-242	27	131	1	37.4%	53	46.7
2014	*BAL*			*596*	*361*	*60.6%*	*3967*	*25*	*16*	*8*		*5.7*		*-2.5%*					*38*	*70*	*1*	*-10.5%*		

2013: 48% Short 28% Mid 13% Deep 10% Bomb YAC: 4.9 (35) 2012: 46% Short 31% Mid 12% Deep 12% Bomb YAC: 4.9 (21)

I'm a quarterback, I'm popular. My mom says I'm a catch, I'm popular. Flacco, ever the AFC's version of Eli Manning, was on top of the world last winter, but that changed once the season started. Is there any precedent for a quarterback following a Super Bowl win with inarguably the worst year of his career to that point? Sure, Ben Roethlisberger did it (without a helmet) in 2006 and he recovered just fine. Mark Rypien fell from grace in 1992 and kept getting worse, which isn't yet a huge concern for Flacco. Sometimes, life sucks and you have a down year. As you've probably gleaned from this book, there was a lot wrong with the Baltimore offense last season. Flacco's interception luck was bound to run out eventually, although it isn't like dropped interceptions suddenly turned into actual ones—the usual few dropped interceptions were still there. Nevertheless, in 2014 Flacco should rebound back to the same guy he's usually been. That's not the playoff hero, but the quarterback who completes 60 percent of his passes for upwards of 3,600 yards with about 20 touchdowns, a dozen picks and around 7.0 yards per attempt. Not sexy, not elite, but not losing games for the Ravens like the frequent struggles that consumed last season.

Matt Flynn Height: 6-2 Weight: 230 College: Louisiana State Draft: 2008/7 (209) Born: 20-Jun-1985 Age: 29 Risk: Green

Year	Team	G/GS	Snaps	Att	Comp	C%	Yds	TD	INT/Adj	FUM	ASR	NY/P	Rk	DVOA	Rk	DYAR	Rk	YAR	Runs	Yds	TD	DVOA	DYAR	QBR
2011	GB	5/1	113	49	33	67.3%	518	6	2/3	1	9.6%	9.2	--	47.3%	--	225	--	169	13	-6	1	20.9%	5	90.4
2012	SEA	3/0	37	9	5	55.6%	68	0	0/0	0	-3.2%	7.6	--	64.3%	--	27	--	15	4	-5	0	--	--	23.4
2013	3TM	7/5	394	200	124	62.0%	1392	8	5/7	7	11.8%	5.6	35	-24.5%	41	-196	39	-29	20	65	0	-69.0%	-41	19.4
2014	*GB*			*533*	*332*	*62.3%*	*3905*	*25*	*13*	*10*		*6.3*		*10.6%*					*32*	*114*	*2*	*18.5%*		

2013: 55% Short 28% Mid 10% Deep 7% Bomb YAC: 5.8 (7) 2012: 38% Short 38% Mid 13% Deep 13% Bomb YAC: 8.2 (--)

Look, some people are just destined to be Assistant Regional Distribution Manager for Hyundai of Central Iowa. It's their calling, their vocation. They may dream of moving up to manager, or transferring to the bright lights and high stakes of Indiana, but the results would be disastrous. They are maxed out making sure there are enough Elantras for the dealerships in Clive, and they do a fine job making sure those cars arrive in time for the Labor Day sales rush, but for heaven's sake, do not Peter Principle them into anything too taxing, like a leadership role in Oakland or Seattle, or even an emergency contractor position in upstate New York. Sometimes, happiness is not about achieving your goals but recognizing and embracing your limits.

In other words, the Packers fixed up that locker next to Aaron Rodgers just the way you like it, ol' buddy.

Nick Foles Height: 6-5 Weight: 243 College: Arizona Draft: 2012/3 (88) Born: 20-Jan-1989 Age: 25 Risk: Red

Year	Team	G/GS	Snaps	Att	Comp	C%	Yds	TD	INT/Adj	FUM	ASR	NY/P	Rk	DVOA	Rk	DYAR	Rk	YAR	Runs	Yds	TD	DVOA	DYAR	QBR
2012	PHI	7/6	453	265	161	60.8%	1699	6	5/11	8	8.2%	5.5	32	-20.4%	30	-166	30	-158	11	42	1	11.7%	11	43.1
2013	PHI	13/10	703	317	203	64.0%	2891	27	2/4	4	9.2%	7.9	2	35.6%	2	1011	5	1111	57	221	3	23.1%	72	69.0
2014	*PHI*			*519*	*336*	*64.6%*	*4003*	*27*	*8*	*11*		*6.8*		*13.9%*					*70*	*205*	*3*	*7.2%*		

2013: 49% Short 24% Mid 15% Deep 13% Bomb YAC: 6.8 (2) 2012: 49% Short 33% Mid 12% Deep 6% Bomb YAC: 5.2 (13)

What a difference a year and a new coach/scheme make. When he wasn't under pressure, Foles had the highest DVOA in the league (68.5%). After struggling to throw touchdowns as a rookie, Foles had the sixth-highest touchdown rate in a season since the 1970 merger (8.5 percent). His average touchdown pass traveled 17.4 yards in the air—highest in the league last year (minimum 10 touchdowns). The Eagles are known for throwing a lot of screens and getting YAC, but that wasn't the case with Foles' scoring strikes. He went deep and only 17.3 percent of the yards on his touchdowns were after the catch (third-lowest rate behind Jay Cutler and Matt Schaub). But that 27:2 touchdown-to-interception ratio is just dying to shrink this season. He might throw more touchdowns, but it will certainly take more attempts. He'll also naturally throw more interceptions. The list of single-season leaders in lowest interception percentage is filled with suspicious names and some greats, but all have one thing in common: a higher interception rate the next season.

Table 1: Lowest Interception Rate, 1960-2013

Rk	Quarterback	Year	Team	Pass	INT	INT%	Pass Y+1	INT Y+1	INT% Y+1	Increase
1	Damon Huard	2006	KC	244	1	0.41%	332	13	3.92%	3.51%
2	**Josh McCown**	**2013**	**CHI**	**224**	**1**	**0.45%**	-	-	-	-
3	**Nick Foles**	**2013**	**PHI**	**317**	**2**	**0.63%**	-	-	-	-
4	Tom Brady	2010	NE	492	4	0.81%	611	12	1.96%	1.15%
5	Steve DeBerg	1990	KC	444	4	0.90%	434	14	3.23%	2.32%
6	David Garrard	2007	JAC	325	3	0.92%	535	13	2.43%	1.51%
7	Alex Smith	2011	SF	445	5	1.12%	218	5	2.29%	1.17%
8	Steve Bartkowski	1983	ATL	432	5	1.16%	269	10	3.72%	2.56%
9	Neil O'Donnell	1998	CIN	343	4	1.17%	195	5	2.56%	1.40%
10	Jason Campbell	2008	WAS	506	6	1.19%	507	15	2.96%	1.77%
11	Brian Griese	2000	DEN	336	4	1.19%	451	19	4.21%	3.02%
12	Bart Starr	1966	GB	251	3	1.20%	210	17	8.10%	6.90%
13	Aaron Rodgers	2011	GB	502	6	1.20%	552	8	1.45%	0.25%
14	Jeff Garcia	2007	TB	327	4	1.22%	376	6	1.60%	0.37%
15	Seneca Wallace	2008	SEA	242	3	1.24%	120	2	1.67%	0.43%
	AVERAGE			**376**	**4.0**	**1.06%**	**370**	**10.7**	**2.89%**	**2.03%**

Minimum 200 attempts

Josh Freeman Height: 6-6 Weight: 248 College: Kansas State Draft: 2009/1 (17) Born: 13-Jan-1988 Age: 26 Risk: #N/A

Year	Team	G/GS	Snaps	Att	Comp	C%	Yds	TD	INT/Adj	FUM	ASR	NY/P	Rk	DVOA	Rk	DYAR	Rk	YAR	Runs	Yds	TD	DVOA	DYAR	QBR
2011	TB	15/15	942	551	346	62.8%	3592	16	22/22	8	6.1%	6.0	24	-13.7%	31	-96	34	-84	55	238	4	13.8%	70	44.0
2012	TB	16/16	1037	558	306	54.8%	4065	27	17/24	9	4.8%	6.7	11	-8.0%	24	118	24	204	39	139	0	3.7%	26	53.0
2013	2TM	4/4	260	147	63	42.9%	761	2	1/5	2	4.6%	4.5	45	-29.7%	42	-176	36	-208	5	20	0	-8.9%	0	18.9

2013: 34% Short 40% Mid 19% Deep 6% Bomb YAC: 4.9 (36) 2012: 42% Short 33% Mid 14% Deep 11% Bomb YAC: 5.4 (8)

Greg Schaino is a braying lunatic. We get that. But Freeman had the whiff of "doesn't get it" about him when Raheem Morris was in charge, too. It's hard to cut through all the conflicting stories—one minute Freeman was organizing team activities during the lockout, the next he was at the shooting range with his Desert Eagle when he is supposed to be rehabbing a hand injury—and things get a little explosive when questioning a black quarterback's work ethic. But Freeman never exactly spit shrapnel, and he plateaued hard in 2010, regressing steadily ever since except for a hot month in the middle of 2012. The fact that Schiano handled Freeman's demotion as cruelly and counterproductively as possible does not mean that there was nothing that had to be handled.

Blaine Gabbert Height: 6-4 Weight: 234 College: Missouri Draft: 2011/1 (10) Born: 15-Oct-1989 Age: 25 Risk: Blue

Year	Team	G/GS	Snaps	Att	Comp	C%	Yds	TD	INT/Adj	FUM	ASR	NY/P	Rk	DVOA	Rk	DYAR	Rk	YAR	Runs	Yds	TD	DVOA	DYAR	QBR
2011	JAC	15/14	910	413	210	50.8%	2214	12	11/17	13	9.1%	4.2	45	-46.5%	46	-1010	47	-897	48	98	0	-38.9%	-35	19.1
2012	JAC	10/10	515	278	162	58.3%	1662	9	6/6	5	6.9%	5.0	35	-25.3%	34	-268	32	-309	18	56	0	-6.8%	5	39.7
2013	JAC	3/3	159	86	42	48.8%	481	1	7/5	2	11.0%	4.2	--	-84.1%	--	-429	--	-480	9	32	0	-29.2%	-8	1.8
2014	*SF*			*480*	*277*	*57.7%*	*3216*	*15*	*20*	*8*		*5.6*		*-17.4%*					*34*	*25*	*0*	*-28.7%*		

2013: 49% Short 36% Mid 10% Deep 4% Bomb YAC: 6.6 (--) 2012: 49% Short 34% Mid 11% Deep 6% Bomb YAC: 4.3 (36)

A YouTube video surfaced before the season. It was called "Blaine Gabbert: Real American." Set to Hulk Hogan's theme song, the main chorus was "Blaine is a Real American/Damn straight the Jaguars are going to win." Sometimes, fan fiction is too unbelievable to even be fan fiction.

Gabbert ended the year with a spectacular -429 DYAR in just 98 passes. Combine that with his first two seasons, and you have the worst quarterback of the DVOA era (Table 2).

Table 2: Worst Quarterbacks in Career DYAR, 1989-2013

Player	Years	DYAR
Blaine Gabbert	3	-1,739
Ryan Leaf	3	-1,440
JaMarcus Russell	3	-1,204
Akili Smith	4	-1,126
David Carr	10	-1,106
Trent Dilfer	13	-1,031
Rick Mirer	8	-1,027
Chad Hutchinson	3	-976
Craig Whelihan	2	-966
John Skelton	3	-955

Gabbert was traded to the 49ers after the season, and Jim Harbaugh will try to tinker with Gabbert's process. Whatever he does, it can't hurt.

Jimmy Garoppolo Height: 6-2 Weight: 226 College: Eastern Illinois Draft: 2014/2 (62) Born: 11-Feb-1991 Age: 23 Risk: Yellow

Year	Team	G/GS	Snaps	Att	Comp	C%	Yds	TD	INT/Adj	FUM	ASR	NY/P	Rk	DVOA	Rk	DYAR	Rk	YAR	Runs	Yds	TD	DVOA	DYAR	QBR
2014	*NE*			*554*	*349*	*63.0%*	*4017*	*23*	*18*	*9*		*6.3*		*0.9%*					*42*	*83*	*1*	*-8.1%*		

Garoppolo got some quality reps at OTAs and minicamp, as Ryan Mallett had some excused absences over the course of the spring. As expected, he was a mixed bag, with some good and some bad. While the Mallett/Garoppolo positional battle will be scrutinized over the course of the season, it's important to note that Mallett is entering the final year of his rookie contract, and so when it comes to long-term possibilities, time is on Garoppolo's side. One optimistic note on Garoppolo—several offensive rookies noted this past spring that Garoppolo had taken a leadership role among the first-year players. (One report had him walking up to a fellow rookie, calling out plays and asking them about their responsibilities.) In addition, veterans noted that Garoppolo showed the same sort of command when he stepped in and led the huddle. That's a first step in what will be an extended learning curve.

Mike Glennon Height: 6-6 Weight: 218 College: North Carolina St. Draft: 2013/3 (73) Born: 12-Dec-1989 Age: 25 Risk: Red

Year	Team	G/GS	Snaps	Att	Comp	C%	Yds	TD	INT/Adj	FUM	ASR	NY/P	Rk	DVOA	Rk	DYAR	Rk	YAR	Runs	Yds	TD	DVOA	DYAR	QBR
2013	TB	13/13	842	416	247	59.4%	2608	19	9/11	7	8.3%	5.1	44	-7.7%	26	99	22	-73	27	37	0	-45.6%	-22	45.6
2014	*TB*			*539*	*328*	*60.9%*	*3320*	*20*	*16*	*9*		*5.1*		*-10.9%*					*23*	*59*	*1*	*-1.0%*		

2013: 43% Short 38% Mid 11% Deep 8% Bomb YAC: 3.7 (45)

My goodness, what a two-year ride it's been for Mike Glennon. Glennon led the ACC in interceptions in 2012, and the Long-Term Career Forecast (LCF) didn't like his odds of succeeding in the NFL. He was the third quarterback taken in the 2013 draft, theoretically a backup to Josh Freeman. Then Freeman went cuckoo and Glennon ended up starting, and in a bad situation he clearly outplayed EJ Manuel and Geno Smith, the two passers taken before him. His reward for this was a demotion back to the bench as the Bucs decided they would rather play a 35-year-old quarterback with 15 touchdowns in the past six seasons. Glennon's biggest issue is a tendency to run backwards under pressure—he took 14 sacks of 10 yards or more last year, tied with Cam Newton for most in the league—but that seems like a problem that can be fixed with experience and proper coaching. There's a good chance he'll wind up starting again before the year is out, especially if the Bucs fall out of the playoff race early.

Bruce Gradkowski Height: 6-1 Weight: 220 College: Toledo Draft: 2006/6 (194) Born: 27-Jan-1983 Age: 31 Risk: Yellow

Year	Team	G/GS	Snaps	Att	Comp	C%	Yds	TD	INT/Adj	FUM	ASR	NY/P	Rk	DVOA	Rk	DYAR	Rk	YAR	Runs	Yds	TD	DVOA	DYAR	QBR
2011	CIN	2/0	44	18	8	44.4%	109	1	1/2	0	5.2%	5.4	--	-58.4%	--	-51	--	-46	3	1	0	19.2%	2	24.5
2012	CIN	3/0	30	11	5	45.5%	65	0	0/0	1	0.0%	5.9	--	-14.9%	--	-3	--	-8	4	-2	0	--	--	54.7
2014	*PIT*			*545*	*323*	*59.1%*	*3579*	*19*	*14*	*9*		*5.7*		*-3.0%*					*41*	*93*	*1*	*-5.6%*		

2012: 44% Short 33% Mid 0% Deep 22% Bomb YAC: 1.0 (--)

By signing Gradkowski and drafting Landry Jones, the Steelers finally added youth to the backup quarterback position. Unexpectedly, Ben Roethlisberger played every snap for the first time in his career in 2013, but given his history, Gradkowski must be ready to play. Fittingly, the best and worst moments of his career have come at Heinz Field against the Steelers. As a rookie with Tampa Bay, he threw a career-high three interceptions in 2006 in a 20-3 loss. He also started a 31-0 loss for the 2008 Browns, completing 5-of-16 passes for 18 yards and two interceptions. His best moment came with the 2009 Raiders when Gradkowski became the first quarterback in NFL history to throw three go-ahead touchdown passes in the fourth quarter, including the game-winner with nine seconds left.

Robert Griffin Height: 6-2 Weight: 223 College: Baylor Draft: 2012/1 (2) Born: 12-Feb-1990 Age: 24 Risk: Red

Year	Team	G/GS	Snaps	Att	Comp	C%	Yds	TD	INT/Adj	FUM	ASR	NY/P	Rk	DVOA	Rk	DYAR	Rk	YAR	Runs	Yds	TD	DVOA	DYAR	QBR
2012	WAS	15/15	937	393	258	65.6%	3200	20	5/10	11	7.7%	7.0	7	16.6%	7	727	11	811	120	815	7	7.8%	109	73.2
2013	WAS	13/13	906	456	274	60.1%	3203	16	12/15	10	8.8%	6.0	22	-13.1%	31	-60	32	98	86	489	0	-0.9%	42	40.1
2014	*WAS*			*573*	*352*	*61.5%*	*4237*	*23*	*13*	*13*		*6.5*		*0.4%*					*104*	*462*	*3*	*-1.4%*		

2013: 47% Short 35% Mid 12% Deep 6% Bomb YAC: 5.6 (16) 2012: 47% Short 35% Mid 11% Deep 6% Bomb YAC: 5.6 (5)

There are easy player comments to write, and there are tough player comments to write. Griffin is a good example of the latter. Figuring out how to split up the Blame Pie for the Skins' offensive maladies in 2013 is an exercise in gut feelings. Griffin was clearly not over his ACL tear, and his mechanics were off to a comical extent at times. How much of that blame is on him, and how much of it is coming back from the injury too soon, is a sophisticated question. Then there's the Shanaclan offensive set up: did it fail because of Griffin's inability to run at his best, or were teams already figuring out a better way to defend it—or maybe a combination of both? It doesn't matter if you've scouted football for 30 years. You're going to have a hard time coming up with more than an opinion without the play calls and a lengthy history of Griffin's own thoughts on his comeback.

For what it's worth—and that can be very little sometimes, given the "Get Happy" vibes thrown out at minicamps and OTAs—Griffin has impressed Jay Gruden with both his mental and physical prowess early on. Gruden will try to make Griffin a pocket quarterback, and he has demonstrated success with that at Baylor. Whether it's smart to take away the read option that made Griffin so devastatingly effective in 2012 is a subject that probably demands a full essay rather than a player comment, but even if it reduces the injury risk slightly, that might be worth it. Griffin can be an upper-echelon pocket passer. If Gruden drags that out of him in year one, he should be on the short list for Coach of the Year.

Matt Hasselbeck Height: 6-4 Weight: 223 College: Boston College Draft: 1998/6 (187) Born: 25-Sep-1975 Age: 39 Risk: Red

Year	Team	G/GS	Snaps	Att	Comp	C%	Yds	TD	INT/Adj	FUM	ASR	NY/P	Rk	DVOA	Rk	DYAR	Rk	YAR	Runs	Yds	TD	DVOA	DYAR	QBR
2011	TEN	16/16	923	518	319	61.6%	3571	18	14/20	4	3.7%	6.4	19	0.6%	17	391	16	371	20	52	0	32.1%	21	58.8
2012	TEN	8/5	395	221	138	62.4%	1367	7	5/11	3	5.7%	5.4	33	-11.5%	26	-6	26	20	13	38	0	24.9%	9	46.0
2013	IND	3/0	23	12	7	58.3%	130	0	1/1	0	0.6%	10.8	--	-28.6%	--	-15	--	-9	2	-2	0	--	--	38.1
2014	*IND*			*553*	*327*	*59.2%*	*3643*	*24*	*15*	*6*		*5.7*		*-5.7%*					*29*	*45*	*1*	*-6.1%*		

2013: 40% Short 50% Mid 10% Deep 0% Bomb YAC: 12.9 (--) 2012: 50% Short 32% Mid 12% Deep 5% Bomb YAC: 4.1 (37)

Is Matt Hasselbeck the second-best quarterback in the AFC South right now? He outplayed Jake Locker when he was with the Titans, and could probably still out-accuracy him today. He can actually get past his first read without running for his life, so he's better than Ryan Fitzpatrick. He has actually had success in his career, unlike Chad Henne. Blake Bortles could be better—but is he better right now? Our main point is that life can be a cruel façade, especially if you root for a team in the AFC South besides the Colts.

Chad Henne Height: 6-2 Weight: 230 College: Michigan Draft: 2008/2 (57) Born: 2-Jul-1985 Age: 29 Risk: Red

Year	Team	G/GS	Snaps	Att	Comp	C%	Yds	TD	INT/Adj	FUM	ASR	NY/P	Rk	DVOA	Rk	DYAR	Rk	YAR	Runs	Yds	TD	DVOA	DYAR	QBR
2011	MIA	4/4	221	112	64	57.1%	868	4	4/4	1	8.9%	6.5	16	-2.7%	20	67	27	100	15	112	0	19.0%	20	63.2
2012	JAC	10/6	545	308	166	53.9%	2084	11	11/14	3	8.5%	5.7	29	-24.6%	33	-286	33	-171	19	64	1	-33.3%	-17	26.1
2013	JAC	15/13	897	503	305	60.6%	3241	13	14/21	2	7.4%	5.6	36	-13.9%	33	-94	34	-149	27	77	0	-39.9%	-37	31.9
2014	*JAC*			*575*	*349*	*60.8%*	*3786*	*17*	*16*	*6*		*5.5*		*-9.5%*					*35*	*71*	*1*	*-9.5%*		

2013: 53% Short 32% Mid 9% Deep 5% Bomb YAC: 5.9 (5) 2012: 39% Short 42% Mid 16% Deep 4% Bomb YAC: 5.1 (14)

Prior to joining the Jaguars, Chad Henne had accumulated DVOA ratings of -6.1%, 3.4%,1.0%, and -2.7% with the Dolphins. Since being brought in to overtake Blaine Gabbert with wave after wave of adequacy, he's posted DVOA ratings of -24.6% and -13.9%. It's very common for football talking heads to point out that the quarterback can raise everyone else's game, and to some extent it's true. However, the reverse is also true. A quarterback can't hide expansion-level talent, and that's the cross Henne has had to bear for the last two seasons. He led all quarterbacks by having 25 passes batted down at the line of scrimmage last year, seven more than second-place finisher Matthew Stafford. This is what happens when the interior of your offensive line has no business playing in the NFL. He probably didn't deserve the $4.5 million in guarantees he got from Jaguars on a two-year deal, but the Jacksonville staff loves Henne, and Henne should be a perfectly acceptable backup quarterback. Hopefully, Blake Bortles will eventually allow him to actually hold that job.

Shaun Hill Height: 6-5 Weight: 210 College: Maryland Draft: 2002/FA Born: 9-Jan-1980 Age: 35 Risk: Yellow

Year	Team	G/GS	Snaps	Att	Comp	C%	Yds	TD	INT/Adj	FUM	ASR	NY/P	Rk	DVOA	Rk	DYAR	Rk	YAR	Runs	Yds	TD	DVOA	DYAR	QBR
2011	DET	2/0	22	3	2	66.7%	33	0	0/0	0	-3.9%	11.0	--	134.1%	--	17	--	13	1	-1	0	--	--	79.6
2012	DET	1/0	19	13	10	76.9%	172	2	0/0	0	0.7%	14.3	--	136.4%	--	128	--	137	1	-1	0	-97.7%	-7	76.8
2013	DET	1/0	2	0	0	0.0%	0	0	0/0	0	--	--	--	--	--	--	--	--	2	-2	0	--	--	--
2014	*STL*			*526*	*346*	*65.7%*	*3226*	*15*	*15*	*6*		*5.1*		*-8.5%*					*23*	*55*	*0*	*-3.9%*		

2012: 42% Short 33% Mid 17% Deep 8% Bomb YAC: 4.7 (--)

Hill has made a career out of backing up No. 1 overall picks, but has more than held his own when called into action. He outperformed Alex Smith when they were in San Francisco, and he kept Detroit competitive in 2010 while Matthew Stafford was battling the "injury prone" tag a year before he emerged. Now Hill backs up Sam Bradford, another oft-injured No. 1 pick on a slow path of development. Not many backups, or starters for that matter, can boast a career touchdown-to-interception ratio of 1.78 like Hill.

Brian Hoyer Height: 6-2 Weight: 215 College: Michigan State Draft: 2009/FA Born: 13-Oct-1985 Age: 29 Risk: Red

Year	Team	G/GS	Snaps	Att	Comp	C%	Yds	TD	INT/Adj	FUM	ASR	NY/P	Rk	DVOA	Rk	DYAR	Rk	YAR	Runs	Yds	TD	DVOA	DYAR	QBR
2011	NE	3/0	12	1	1	100.0%	22	0	0/0	0	2.3%	22.0	--	215.0%	--	16	--	16	4	-3	0	--	--	96.0
2012	2TM	2/1	81	53	30	56.6%	330	1	2/2	1	7.2%	5.3	--	-26.5%	--	-60	--	-119	1	6	0	63.7%	5	37.7
2013	CLE	3/3	151	96	57	59.4%	615	5	3/4	0	7.1%	5.5	37	-10.4%	28	5	28	27	6	16	0	20.4%	4	47.5
2014	*CLE*			*588*	*365*	*62.0%*	*3898*	*16*	*18*	*7*		*5.8*		*-10.9%*					*42*	*46*	*1*	*-21.6%*		

2013: 49% Short 30% Mid 16% Deep 6% Bomb YAC: 5.5 (21) 2012: 42% Short 40% Mid 10% Deep 8% Bomb YAC: 3.1 (--)

In *The Color of Money,* Paul Newman as Fast Eddie Felson rues his forced retirement from pool hustling by saying, "It was over for me before it ever really got started." You'll forgive Hoyer for wincing in acknowledgment. A local kid who attended high school powerhouse St. Ignatius, Hoyer was the toast of Cleveland after leading the Browns to consecutive wins in his first two starts. Then he tore up his knee scrambling for a first down, and his magic carpet ride was over. Hoyer played less than nine quarters of mostly mediocre football last fall, but to hear the locals talk, he was Bernie Kosar reincarnate. He's supposedly the starter entering camp, but with the arrival of Sir John Football, Hoyer's career trajectory will almost certainly return to backup mode, unless Manziel also forgets to get out of bounds instead of taking a hit.

Tarvaris Jackson Height: 6-2 Weight: 226 College: Alabama State Draft: 2006/2 (64) Born: 21-Apr-1983 Age: 31 Risk: Red

Year	Team	G/GS	Snaps	Att	Comp	C%	Yds	TD	INT/Adj	FUM	ASR	NY/P	Rk	DVOA	Rk	DYAR	Rk	YAR	Runs	Yds	TD	DVOA	DYAR	QBR
2011	SEA	15/14	944	450	271	60.2%	3091	14	13/17	8	7.9%	5.7	30	-5.8%	25	165	20	61	40	180	1	-19.1%	-11	38.3
2012	BUF	0/0	0	0	0	0.0%	0	0	0/0	0	--	--	--	--	--	--	--	--	0	0	0	--	--	--
2013	SEA	3/0	39	13	10	76.9%	151	1	0/0	0	1.3%	11.6	--	81.9%	--	83	--	93	4	1	1	96.1%	9	89.0
2014	*SEA*			*459*	*280*	*60.9%*	*3002*	*13*	*12*	*9*		*5.7*		*-9.0%*					*59*	*172*	*2*	*-2.8%*		

2013: 46% Short 31% Mid 8% Deep 15% Bomb YAC: 7.5 (--)

Jackson signed a one-year, $1.25 million deal to stay in Seattle, and though his days as a prospective non-injury starter are gone, he fits what the Seahawks want to do in playing style and personality. Should Russell Wilson miss any time in 2014, Jackson can run around and make certain throws and keep a talented, balanced team at the .500 level, as he did with his 450 passing attempts the first time he was in Seattle. He doesn't have Wilson's acumen or potential, but he's a better-than-average option in a backup capacity.

Colin Kaepernick Height: 6-5 Weight: 233 College: Nevada Draft: 2011/2 (36) Born: 3-Nov-1987 Age: 27 Risk: Yellow

Year	Team	G/GS	Snaps	Att	Comp	C%	Yds	TD	INT/Adj	FUM	ASR	NY/P	Rk	DVOA	Rk	DYAR	Rk	YAR	Runs	Yds	TD	DVOA	DYAR	QBR
2011	SF	3/0	20	5	3	60.0%	35	0	0/0	0	0.0%	7.0	--	34.1%	--	14	--	17	2	-2	0	--	--	92.9
2012	SF	13/7	525	218	136	62.4%	1814	10	3/6	7	6.8%	7.2	2	25.8%	3	555	13	462	63	415	5	-1.5%	31	72.2
2013	SF	16/16	968	416	243	58.4%	3197	21	8/10	6	7.8%	6.5	13	16.6%	7	791	8	650	92	524	4	11.8%	91	68.6
2014	*SF*			*451*	*274*	*60.8%*	*3576*	*24*	*10*	*10*		*7.0*		*11.1%*					*91*	*422*	*6*	*25.2%*		

2013: 38% Short 39% Mid 16% Deep 6% Bomb YAC: 5.5 (22) 2012: 44% Short 32% Mid 16% Deep 8% Bomb YAC: 5.2 (11)

Kaepernick is a rare breath of fresh air at the quarterback position. And no, this is not referring to the tattoos, Beats by Dre, or Kaepernicking. When news of his contract extension initially came out, there were reports that he received the most guaranteed money ever. In actuality, the deal is favorable to San Francisco, paying Kaepernick as a top-10 quarterback rather than a top-five quarterback throughout his prime.

Kaepernick is a divisive figure, both in the press, and in the football community. Those that rave about his athletic ability and ability to throw the football downfield, and those that critique his consistency and ability to read the field and go through his progressions, are all correct. He is an elusive talent who is not fully formed as a pocket passer. Of course, this version of Kaepernick so far has been pretty good, finishing seventh and third in passing DVOA the last two seasons. 2014 is a big year, because Kaepernick won't have the excuses from last season when injuries and lack of depth at receiver affected him. If he doesn't progress as a passer this year, despite four quality options in the passing game, that's on him. His upside is pretty high this year, both when it comes to efficiency and when it comes to fantasy value.

Case Keenum Height: 6-2 Weight: 209 College: Houston Draft: 2012/FA Born: 17-Feb-1988 Age: 26 Risk: Yellow

Year	Team	G/GS	Snaps	Att	Comp	C%	Yds	TD	INT/Adj	FUM	ASR	NY/P	Rk	DVOA	Rk	DYAR	Rk	YAR	Runs	Yds	TD	DVOA	DYAR	QBR
2013	HOU	8/8	461	253	137	54.2%	1760	9	6/8	6	7.4%	5.8	26	-22.4%	39	-191	38	-201	14	72	1	23.8%	27	34.5
2014	*HOU*			*575*	*324*	*56.4%*	*3811*	*22*	*22*	*10*		*5.7*		*-9.1%*					*33*	*79*	*1*	*-1.6%*		

2013: 48% Short 33% Mid 8% Deep 10% Bomb YAC: 5.0 (33)

Keenum had a luck-inflated 23.6% DVOA after his first three starts, mostly because he hit on a few deep balls that came when he bought time scrambling. His deep-pass DVOA dropped from 119.8% in those weeks to -15.0% for the rest of the season. And since that was the only thing really keeping him afloat as a potential starting quarterback, he ... hold on a second. (Sees pass rush.) (Runs backwards 20 yards.) (Gets sacked anyway.)

Thaddeus Lewis Height: 6-2 Weight: 220 College: Duke Draft: 2010/FA Born: 19-Nov-1987 Age: 27 Risk: Red

Year	Team	G/GS	Snaps	Att	Comp	C%	Yds	TD	INT/Adj	FUM	ASR	NY/P	Rk	DVOA	Rk	DYAR	Rk	YAR	Runs	Yds	TD	DVOA	DYAR	QBR
2012	CLE	1/1	62	32	22	68.8%	204	1	1/1	0	8.4%	5.4	--	6.5%	--	42	--	46	1	3	0	-50.0%	-2	61.7
2013	BUF	6/5	356	157	93	59.2%	1092	4	3/4	7	9.6%	5.7	32	-18.7%	36	-84	33	-138	24	52	1	-60.3%	-47	24.1
2014	*BUF*			*473*	*289*	*61.0%*	*3243*	*16*	*15*	*12*		*5.9*		*-12.5%*					*65*	*190*	*2*	*-10.0%*		

2013: 46% Short 34% Mid 12% Deep 9% Bomb YAC: 5.1 (30) 2012: 38% Short 50% Mid 6% Deep 6% Bomb YAC: 2.8 (--)

The former undrafted free agent from Duke, who has bounced as a from St. Louis to Cleveland to Detroit to Buffalo like a mid-market commuter airliner, has apparently found something of a home with the Bills, as the apparent offseason retirement of Kevin Kolb means Lewis figures to now be No. 2 to EJ Manuel. In his first season with the Bills—with Manuel on the shelf for five games—he led the team to a pair of wins in five total starts, both of them coming against the Dolphins. One thing that could be working in his favor if he ends up playing in 2014 is the fact that he's reuniting with an old quarterback coach in Todd Downing, who came over from Detroit.

Jake Locker Height: 6-3 Weight: 231 College: Washington Draft: 2011/1 (8) Born: 15-Jun-1988 Age: 26 Risk: Yellow

Year	Team	G/GS	Snaps	Att	Comp	C%	Yds	TD	INT/Adj	FUM	ASR	NY/P	Rk	DVOA	Rk	DYAR	Rk	YAR	Runs	Yds	TD	DVOA	DYAR	QBR
2011	TEN	5/0	98	66	34	51.5%	542	4	0/1	0	8.3%	7.2	--	22.0%	--	143	--	172	8	56	1	61.4%	27	44.8
2012	TEN	11/11	595	314	177	56.4%	2176	10	11/13	4	8.2%	5.9	25	-23.6%	32	-265	31	-198	41	291	1	20.4%	54	44.5
2013	TEN	7/7	395	183	111	60.7%	1256	8	4/6	3	8.3%	5.8	27	-5.7%	22	69	24	130	24	155	2	20.7%	32	58.1
2014	*TEN*			*550*	*330*	*60.0%*	*3836*	*18*	*17*	*8*		*6.1*		*-3.3%*					*73*	*258*	*3*	*10.2%*		

2013: 38% Short 39% Mid 13% Deep 10% Bomb YAC: 5.1 (32) 2012: 40% Short 39% Mid 12% Deep 9% Bomb YAC: 4.7 (27)

Tennessee made the decision before the season to not pick up Locker's fifth-year option, meaning he enters 2014 playing for a new contract. There are many barriers in the way of him receiving one from the Titans. First, he has to actually play: he's missed 14 games since being named starter in 2012. The completion percentage finally bucked up above 60 percent, but it was hardly indicative of Locker playing well. Dowell Loggains' system provided lots of deep comeback and curl routes to account for the fact that Locker's timing on short-area throws is a bit off. Locker drops back like he's thinking through his entire knowledge of the play in real time. That process is then interrupted by his eyes letting him know that somebody is open, and could you please hurl the ball now? If *NFL Blitz* were an actual league, Locker would dominate in it. He's always seemed more comfortable in the two-minute drill—he had a 38.0% DVOA in the fourth quarter last season—when structure dies and he can just concentrate on playing football. Because of that, Locker probably has some Frank Reich comebacks in his back pocket once he actually becomes a backup. It shouldn't be too much longer.

Andrew Luck Height: 6-4 Weight: 234 College: Stanford Draft: 2012/1 (1) Born: 12-Mar-1989 Age: 25 Risk: Green

Year	Team	G/GS	Snaps	Att	Comp	C%	Yds	TD	INT/Adj	FUM	ASR	NY/P	Rk	DVOA	Rk	DYAR	Rk	YAR	Runs	Yds	TD	DVOA	DYAR	QBR
2012	IND	16/16	1169	627	339	54.1%	4374	23	18/30	15	6.8%	6.2	19	-5.1%	19	257	19	366	62	255	5	41.0%	123	65.2
2013	IND	16/16	1046	570	343	60.2%	3822	23	9/14	6	5.7%	6.0	23	4.6%	16	650	14	623	63	377	4	47.6%	151	62.0
2014	*IND*			*571*	*347*	*60.8%*	*4117*	*26*	*16*	*8*		*6.3*		*2.3%*					*67*	*170*	*3*	*16.5%*		

2013: 49% Short 30% Mid 13% Deep 7% Bomb YAC: 5.6 (15) 2012: 37% Short 38% Mid 17% Deep 8% Bomb YAC: 4.9 (24)

Andrew Luck is a witch. He completes two or three passes a game that only he and Aaron Rodgers can currently place right now. Game-winning drives are afterthoughts for him. He's downright Derek Jeter-esque when he has to step up, right down to the signature "there at the right time" moment he had when he ran a Donald Brown fumble into the end zone during the Wild Card game against the Chiefs. He was the best running back Indianapolis had at the end of the season. On raw talent, he's easily one of the best quarterbacks in the NFL.

And yet, Luck has been pretty streaky for two years now. He had halves against Houston, St. Louis, Jacksonville, and Arizona last year that were downright awful, to the point where even Andrew Luck couldn't rally the team in some cases. It's a tiny blemish on the face of one of the league's brightest stars, but it was noticeable. Luck should take another step forward in the advanced statistics this year, given that he'll throw to actual receivers this time. The question is: how high can the ceiling go?

Ryan Mallett Height: 6-7 Weight: 253 College: Arkansas Draft: 2011/3 (74) Born: 5-Jun-1988 Age: 26 Risk: Yellow

Year	Team	G/GS	Snaps	Att	Comp	C%	Yds	TD	INT/Adj	FUM	ASR	NY/P	Rk	DVOA	Rk	DYAR	Rk	YAR	Runs	Yds	TD	DVOA	DYAR	QBR
2012	NE	4/0	24	4	1	25.0%	17	0	1/0	0	-3.2%	4.3	--	-237.3%	--	-44	--	-46	8	-9	0	--	--	0.9
2014	*NE*			*561*	*348*	*61.9%*	*4072*	*25*	*18*	*9*		*6.2*		*-1.1%*					*27*	*48*	*0*	*-11.5%*		

2012: 50% Short 50% Mid 0% Deep 0% Bomb YAC: 19.0 (--)

Between the flap about whether or not Tom Brady is still an elite quarterback and the selection of Jimmy Garoppolo, Mallett became a bit of a forgotten man this past offseason. (Well, okay, except for the periodic brush fires about a potential trade to Houston.) In his three years with the Patriots, Mallett hasn't taken a significant snap in the regular season, but to his credit, he's done well to rehab a troubled image that dogged him coming out of college—on and off the record, the rest of the franchise says he's been a model teammate. With his rookie contract set to come to an end following the 2014 season, it will be interesting to see whether another team is going to give him a shot to start. It's hard to imagine him staying in New England now that Garoppolo is in the picture.

Eli Manning Height: 6-4 Weight: 218 College: Mississippi Draft: 2004/1 (1) Born: 3-Jan-1981 Age: 33 Risk: Green

Year	Team	G/GS	Snaps	Att	Comp	C%	Yds	TD	INT/Adj	FUM	ASR	NY/P	Rk	DVOA	Rk	DYAR	Rk	YAR	Runs	Yds	TD	DVOA	DYAR	QBR
2011	NYG	16/16	1075	589	359	61.0%	4933	29	16/17	8	5.0%	7.6	6	16.2%	9	1110	8	1136	35	15	1	-43.3%	-18	60.6
2012	NYG	16/16	1003	536	321	59.9%	3948	26	15/24	4	4.3%	6.8	9	9.0%	13	753	10	779	20	30	0	-40.5%	-15	68.9
2013	NYG	16/16	986	551	317	57.5%	3818	18	27/31	7	7.7%	6.0	21	-20.2%	38	-335	42	-202	18	36	0	-76.6%	-27	36.5
2014	*NYG*			*558*	*335*	*60.1%*	*3918*	*23*	*16*	*5*		*6.2*		*2.0%*					*27*	*39*	*0*	*-14.4%*		

2013: 40% Short 39% Mid 14% Deep 8% Bomb YAC: 4.6 (39) 2012: 38% Short 42% Mid 11% Deep 8% Bomb YAC: 4.3 (34)

Eli Manning has led the league in interceptions three different times in his career. If he does it one more time, he'll join a special quartet of quarterbacks who have done it four times: Vinny Testaverde, Norm Snead, Joe Namath, and George Blanda. The Giants have been able to take the bad with the good, which includes two Super Bowl rings and 25 fourth-quarter comebacks, the 11th most in NFL history. But with two consecutive down years, it's time to wonder if age has taken—and will continue to take—its toll on Manning. We've seen Brady, Brees, and older brother Peyton age gracefully, but non-Hall of Fame quarterbacks often fade at Manning's age. His completion percentage has dropped by at least one percent in each of the last three years; if that doesn't come to a stop in 2014, New York may need to address the quarterback position sooner than anyone expected.

Peyton Manning Height: 6-5 Weight: 230 College: Tennessee Draft: 1998/1 (1) Born: 24-Mar-1976 Age: 38 Risk: Yellow

Year	Team	G/GS	Snaps	Att	Comp	C%	Yds	TD	INT/Adj	FUM	ASR	NY/P	Rk	DVOA	Rk	DYAR	Rk	YAR	Runs	Yds	TD	DVOA	DYAR	QBR
2012	DEN	16/16	1111	583	400	68.6%	4659	37	11/14	2	4.2%	7.5	1	32.8%	2	1805	2	1956	23	6	0	-5.4%	2	82.4
2013	DEN	16/16	1156	659	450	68.3%	5477	55	10/12	10	3.4%	7.9	1	43.2%	1	2475	1	2674	32	-31	1	-110.6%	-30	82.9
2014	*DEN*			*615*	*417*	*67.8%*	*5085*	*41*	*12*	*5*		*7.9*		*33.7%*					*28*	*17*	*1*	*-18.2%*		

2013: 55% Short 26% Mid 13% Deep 6% Bomb YAC: 5.7 (10) 2012: 50% Short 31% Mid 12% Deep 7% Bomb YAC: 4.7 (28)

Outside of the arm-strength limitations *that game* in early February made painfully apparent, it is extremely difficult to find a flaw in Peyton Manning, Age-Defying Quarterbacking Machine. To put things in perspective: his DVOA splits on first downs, second downs, third and fourth downs, from the shotgun, under center, and in the red zone were all better than any other quarterback's total DVOA. His ability to check the Broncos in and out of the right play at the line of scrimmage is unparalleled, making the run game better than it would be otherwise and making him the least-pressured quarterback in the league. Outside of, again, *that game*, he was almost impossible to sack, thanks to that pressure recognition, phenomenal pocket movement for a not very mobile player, and a willingness to throw the ball away. He throws with phenomenal anticipation. He even picked up his first rushing touchdown since 2008, on an "I cannot believe that possibly worked" bootleg against the Cowboys. He almost certainly won't throw 55 touchdowns again, but unless the neck injury flares up, expect another year of quarterback greatness.

EJ Manuel Height: 6-5 Weight: 240 College: Florida State Draft: 2013/1 (16) Born: 19-Mar-1990 Age: 24 Risk: Green

Year	Team	G/GS	Snaps	Att	Comp	C%	Yds	TD	INT/Adj	FUM	ASR	NY/P	Rk	DVOA	Rk	DYAR	Rk	YAR	Runs	Yds	TD	DVOA	DYAR	QBR
2013	BUF	10/10	694	306	180	58.8%	1972	11	9/9	6	8.9%	5.5	38	-19.9%	37	-190	37	-87	53	186	2	11.0%	49	42.3
2014	*BUF*			*510*	*315*	*61.8%*	*3521*	*19*	*19*	*10*		*5.8*		*-9.8%*					*58*	*267*	*2*	*16.3%*		

2013: 52% Short 29% Mid 12% Deep 7% Bomb YAC: 5.1 (31)

What happened to the Bills over the course of the offseason represents a full-scale investment in not just the Buffalo offense, but Manuel in particular. Not going after one of the available quarterbacks in the upper reaches of the first round was one indication the Bills remain committed to Manuel. And two, there's the fact that Sammy Watkins (at the expense of multiple draft picks), Mike Williams and Bryce Brown were added to an offense that already has C.J. Spiller, Robert Woods and a good offensive line. For what it's worth, the coaching staff was wildly optimistic about his progress over the course of the offseason, with Doug Marrone saying in the spring that Manuel was in the "advanced stages" of the offensive scheme created by offensive coordinator Doug Hackett. There were times last year where he looked very impressive—nearly pulling off an upset of the Patriots in Buffalo in the season opener, as well as a last-second win over the Panthers the following week where he ended up with a career-best 296 yards. But there were also plenty of low points, including six of his 10 starts where he failed to hit 60 percent of his passes. (That included a December loss to the Bucs in Tampa where he threw four picks and completed barely 50 percent of his throws.) As general manager Doug Whaley noted in the days prior to the draft, "It's a quarterback-driven league," and for now, the Bills appear to be comfortable with Manuel behind the wheel.

Johnny Manziel Height: 6-0 Weight: 207 College: Texas A&M Draft: 2014/1 (22) Born: 6-Dec-1992 Age: 22 Risk: Red

Year	Team	G/GS	Snaps	Att	Comp	C%	Yds	TD	INT/Adj	FUM	ASR	NY/P	Rk	DVOA	Rk	DYAR	Rk	YAR	Runs	Yds	TD	DVOA	DYAR	QBR
2014				*508*	*289*	*56.9%*	*3534*	*18*	*18*	*10*		*6.1*		*-16.1%*					*120*	*682*	*7*	*23.4%*		

Texas A&M led the nation in Offensive F/+ in both of Manziel's years at the helm. His projection in our Long-Term Career Forecast was lower than most of the quarterbacks drafted this past spring mainly due to his propensity to run more than the others. The Browns sold more than 1,500 season tickets the day after drafting "Money Manziel," and he currently has the No. 1 selling jersey in the league. It is those last two metrics that matter right now, and will get Johnny on the field sooner rather than later. Only then will we truly get a handle on his ability to translate his unique game to the NFL. As we suspect is the case with all of you, we can't wait.

Josh McCown Height: 6-4 Weight: 215 College: Sam Houston St. Draft: 2002/3 (81) Born: 4-Jul-1979 Age: 35 Risk: Red

Year	Team	G/GS	Snaps	Att	Comp	C%	Yds	TD	INT/Adj	FUM	ASR	NY/P	Rk	DVOA	Rk	DYAR	Rk	YAR	Runs	Yds	TD	DVOA	DYAR	QBR
2011	CHI	3/2	137	55	35	63.6%	414	2	4/6	2	11.2%	6.0	--	-50.5%	--	-146	--	-110	12	68	0	12.2%	16	26.0
2013	CHI	8/5	421	224	149	66.5%	1829	13	1/3	3	4.8%	7.6	5	32.1%	4	659	13	773	13	69	1	10.9%	10	85.1
2014	*TB*			*542*	*335*	*61.8%*	*3719*	*20*	*19*	*7*		*6.0*		*-3.9%*					*27*	*99*	*1*	*15.0%*		

2013: 41% Short 42% Mid 12% Deep 5% Bomb YAC: 5.6 (17)

McCown and Damon Huard are the same person. Both are the better halves of quarterback brother tandems. Both enjoyed short dollops of early-career success that did not really fool anyone into thinking they were starters, then settled into roles as deep-bench backups. Huard reemerged at age 33 to throw eleven touchdowns and one interception as an emergency reliever for the Chiefs, and defense-oriented coach Herm Edwards overreacted by making him the starter for 2007. McCown finally climbed past Caleb Hanie and Jason Campbell for emergency relief duties at age 34 last year, throwing 13 touchdowns and one interception, four of the touchdowns in one game against a belly-flopping Cowboys defense. Defense-oriented coach Lovie Smith, who helped bury McCown behind the likes of Hanie two seasons ago, overreacted and signed McCown to be his new starter. Huard had a miserable follow-up year, and it helped choke off the development of Brodie Croyle, a mid-tier prospect with a post-college gift for falling into hard-luck circumstances. What the future holds for McCown and Mike Glennon is not clear. Or is it?

Luke McCown Height: 6-3 Weight: 208 College: Louisiana Tech Draft: 2004/4 (106) Born: 12-Jul-1981 Age: 33 Risk: Yellow

Year	Team	G/GS	Snaps	Att	Comp	C%	Yds	TD	INT/Adj	FUM	ASR	NY/P	Rk	DVOA	Rk	DYAR	Rk	YAR	Runs	Yds	TD	DVOA	DYAR	QBR
2011	JAC	4/2	131	56	30	53.6%	296	0	4/5	2	7.1%	4.3	--	-73.5%	--	-251	--	-274	7	23	0	32.9%	14	13.4
2012	ATL	2/0	10	0	0	0.0%	0	0	0/0	0	--	--	--	--	--	--	--	--	2	-3	0	--	--	--
2013	NO	16/0	16	1	0	0.0%	0	0	0/0	0	-5.4%	0.0	--	-89.2%	--	-3	--	-4	3	-4	0	--	--	85.1
2014	*NO*			*603*	*360*	*59.7%*	*4081*	*26*	*13*	*10*		*5.9*		*3.0%*					*28*	*25*	*1*	*-16.5%*		

McCown's lone pass attempt last season came on a fake field-goal attempt. If he is going to stick on an NFL roster for an 11th season (!), he'll need to win a camp battle with second-year player Ryan Griffin for the backup job behind Drew Brees. McCown admitted he was in a race, telling the *New Orleans Times-Picayune* that "Competition just helps you get better." He also said—and this is a real quote—"But the same thing, I'm trying to beat out Drew." That's adorable.

Matt McGloin Height: 6-1 Weight: 210 College: Penn State Draft: 2013/FA Born: 2-Dec-1989 Age: 25 Risk: Red

Year	Team	G/GS	Snaps	Att	Comp	C%	Yds	TD	INT/Adj	FUM	ASR	NY/P	Rk	DVOA	Rk	DYAR	Rk	YAR	Runs	Yds	TD	DVOA	DYAR	QBR
2013	OAK	7/6	378	211	118	55.9%	1547	8	8/10	4	3.1%	6.9	9	-11.9%	29	-11	29	62	11	27	0	21.1%	7	49.5
2014	*OAK*			*563*	*324*	*57.7%*	*3670*	*18*	*22*	*11*		*5.2*		*-25.4%*					*45*	*207*	*1*	*3.3%*		

2013: 45% Short 32% Mid 15% Deep 8% Bomb YAC: 5.5 (18)

To go from undrafted and fourth on the depth chart when training camp began to starting six games was quite an accomplishment for McGloin. The Raiders made it clear what they thought of his potential in the offseason, though, by acquiring Matt Schaub to be their 2014 starter and drafting Derek Carr in the second round to be their future starter. For all the success McGloin had in winning his first start, he is still an undersized player who had too many passes batted down at the line, is not particularly athletic, and does not have a great arm. When his decision-making fell apart late in the season, it was back to the bench. Carr reportedly passed him for the second-string job by June minicamp, so don't be surprised if he finds himself elsewhere in 2014. Wherever he plays this season, he will still have a great shot to be 2023's Josh McCown.

Matt Moore Height: 6-3 Weight: 202 College: Oregon State Draft: 2007/FA Born: 9-Aug-1984 Age: 30 Risk: Red

Year	Team	G/GS	Snaps	Att	Comp	C%	Yds	TD	INT/Adj	FUM	ASR	NY/P	Rk	DVOA	Rk	DYAR	Rk	YAR	Runs	Yds	TD	DVOA	DYAR	QBR
2011	MIA	13/12	774	347	210	60.5%	2497	16	9/12	13	9.0%	5.9	27	-5.7%	24	133	22	124	32	65	2	-34.9%	-21	54.5
2012	MIA	10/0	55	19	11	57.9%	131	1	0/0	0	9.7%	5.8	--	15.5%	--	40	--	31	5	-3	0	-110.2%	-4	59.7
2013	MIA	1/0	6	6	2	33.3%	53	0	2/2	1	-2.7%	8.8	--	-120.6%	--	-36	--	-45	0	0	0	--	--	1.3
2014	*MIA*			*534*	*314*	*58.9%*	*3125*	*14*	*16*	*11*		*4.9*		*-18.2%*					*31*	*42*	*2*	*-6.8%*		

2013: 17% Short 33% Mid 17% Deep 33% Bomb YAC: 6.5 (--) 2012: 44% Short 19% Mid 13% Deep 25% Bomb YAC: 2.5 (--)

Ryan Tannehill withstood last year's bruising up until Week 16 when Moore saw some action in the fourth quarter. His second play of the season was a 50-yard bomb to Brian Hartline on third-and-18, but he finished with two interceptions. He's a solid backup and if Miami hasn't solved the offensive line issues, he should always be on alert to step in and produce.

Cam Newton Height: 6-5 Weight: 248 College: Auburn Draft: 2011/1 (1) Born: 11-May-1989 Age: 25 Risk: Green

Year	Team	G/GS	Snaps	Att	Comp	C%	Yds	TD	INT/Adj	FUM	ASR	NY/P	Rk	DVOA	Rk	DYAR	Rk	YAR	Runs	Yds	TD	DVOA	DYAR	QBR
2011	CAR	16/16	1035	517	310	60.0%	4051	21	17/24	5	7.3%	6.9	10	0.8%	16	407	15	428	126	706	14	14.5%	188	56.2
2012	CAR	16/16	1019	485	280	57.7%	3869	19	12/15	14	7.6%	7.0	6	2.0%	15	422	14	422	127	741	8	11.3%	149	54.1
2013	CAR	16/16	1015	473	292	61.7%	3379	24	13/18	3	8.2%	5.9	24	1.7%	19	421	17	321	111	585	6	5.7%	102	56.2
2014	*CAR*			*480*	*306*	*63.8%*	*3210*	*18*	*12*	*7*		*5.7*		*-8.9%*					*115*	*626*	*6*	*19.2%*		

2013: 41% Short 39% Mid 12% Deep 8% Bomb YAC: 5.5 (19) 2012: 40% Short 37% Mid 16% Deep 8% Bomb YAC: 6.1 (1)

Newton hit the NFL like a lightning bolt in 2011, but in the following seasons, even as Carolina won a division title, other young quarterbacks have stolen the limelight. So let's take a moment and credit Newton for what he has already accomplished. His three-year total of 12,491 yards of total offense is the best start to a career in NFL history, and his 92 total touchdowns are second only to Dan Marino. And he has done all that with a corps of wide receivers so bad they basically all got fired at once (though, to be fair, it remains to be seen whether the new guys in Carolina will be any better). He perennially leads the league in "Houdini" plays where he breaks tackles to avoid sacks, but that's partly because he still has trouble progressing through his reads and often fails to recognize open receivers. Newton is still a few months younger than Nick Foles, a year younger than Russell Wilson, and two years younger than Colin Kaepernick, and for all his success, he is far from a finished product. His progression may have stalled somewhat (those first three seasons were remarkably similar), but Newton still has many years to develop. Ankle surgery threatened to keep Newton out of practices until July, but his rehab went better than expected and he threw in 7-on-7 drills in June OTAs.

Dan Orlovsky Height: 6-5 Weight: 230 College: Connecticut Draft: 2005/5 (145) Born: 18-Aug-1983 Age: 31 Risk: Green

Year	Team	G/GS	Snaps	Att	Comp	C%	Yds	TD	INT/Adj	FUM	ASR	NY/P	Rk	DVOA	Rk	DYAR	Rk	YAR	Runs	Yds	TD	DVOA	DYAR	QBR
2011	IND	8/5	364	193	122	63.2%	1201	6	4/4	7	6.9%	5.5	33	-2.2%	19	121	23	36	6	5	0	4.1%	1	49.9
2012	TB	1/0	12	7	4	57.1%	51	0	0/0	0	1.3%	7.3	--	0.4%	--	5	--	10	0	0	0	--	--	34.9
2013	TB	2/0	4	0	0	0.0%	0	0	0/0	0	--	--	--	--	--	--	--	--	0	0	0	--	--	--
2014	*DET*			*584*	*354*	*60.7%*	*3776*	*19*	*24*	*11*		*5.5*		*-13.5%*					*23*	*30*	*1*	*-13.1%*		

2012: 33% Short 33% Mid 33% Deep 0% Bomb YAC: 3.5 (--)

Orlovsky only saw the field for four snaps last season as a backup to Mike Glennon. The Lions signed him to replace Kellen Moore as Matthew Stafford's backup, but everyone involved knows that's a temporary move. Orlovsky was one of 25 players to take part in a "broadcast boot camp" with NFL Films, and he figures to line up in front of a camera rather than behind center in the not-too-distant future.

Kyle Orton Height: 6-4 Weight: 226 College: Purdue Draft: 2005/4 (106) Born: 14-Nov-1982 Age: 32 Risk: #N/A

Year	Team	G/GS	Snaps	Att	Comp	C%	Yds	TD	INT/Adj	FUM	ASR	NY/P	Rk	DVOA	Rk	DYAR	Rk	YAR	Runs	Yds	TD	DVOA	DYAR	QBR
2011	2TM	9/8	493	252	150	59.5%	1758	9	9/13	2	5.4%	6.4	17	-5.4%	23	97	25	170	11	13	0	4.9%	3	52.4
2012	DAL	1/0	11	10	9	90.0%	89	1	0/0	0	1.0%	8.9	--	110.7%	--	95	--	79	0	0	0	--	--	99.4
2013	DAL	3/1	78	51	33	64.7%	398	2	2/3	0	1.1%	7.8	--	4.0%	--	51	--	71	1	8	0	104.4%	7	37.3

2013: 46% Short 35% Mid 13% Deep 6% Bomb YAC: 6.7 (--) 2012: 50% Short 40% Mid 10% Deep 0% Bomb YAC: 2.7 (--)

For 58 minutes and 11 seconds of the Week 17 de facto playoff game against the Eagles, Orton did everything you could ask from a backup quarterback making his first start of the year in a huge spot. He kept the Cowboys in the game with 358 passing yards and didn't take a sack on 46 passes. But one field goal away from the postseason, disaster struck. Orton was picked off by Brandon Boykin on a poor pass and Dallas was done. The 31-year-old Orton, who was one of the best backup options in the league, skipped minicamp and contemplated retirement before Dallas released him in mid-July. He's not expected to continue his NFL career. With Brandon Weeden now backing up Tony Romo, the Cowboys only gain one year of youth, but lose one hell of a neckbeard.

Brock Osweiler Height: 6-7 Weight: 242 College: Arizona State Draft: 2012/2 (57) Born: 22-Nov-1990 Age: 24 Risk: Yellow

Year	Team	G/GS	Snaps	Att	Comp	C%	Yds	TD	INT/Adj	FUM	ASR	NY/P	Rk	DVOA	Rk	DYAR	Rk	YAR	Runs	Yds	TD	DVOA	DYAR	QBR
2012	DEN	5/0	33	4	2	50.0%	12	0	0/0	0	-1.5%	3.0	--	-1.4%	--	2	--	7	8	-13	0	--	--	10.4
2013	DEN	4/0	51	16	11	68.8%	95	0	0/0	0	11.3%	4.8	--	-8.5%	--	3	--	18	3	2	0	29.9%	3	43.3
2014	*DEN*			*537*	*329*	*61.3%*	*3707*	*23*	*18*	*9*		*5.8*		*-2.2%*					*23*	*59*	*1*	*4.5%*		

2013: 75% Short 13% Mid 6% Deep 6% Bomb YAC: 6.2 (--) 2012: 75% Short 25% Mid 0% Deep 0% Bomb YAC: 1.5 (--)

Since he plays behind the famously workaholic Peyton Manning, who demands every snap he can take in practice, it's hard to get a read on how Osweiler has developed heading into his third NFL season. The Broncos' offensive dominance meant he got into a couple games, but only one of his passing attempts to date has come with the Broncos holding less than a 31-point lead. (The Raiders had just scored to cut the lead to 34-7; the pass was called complete on the field, then reversed.)

Curtis Painter Height: 6-4 Weight: 230 College: Purdue Draft: 2009/6 (201) Born: 24-Jun-1985 Age: 29 Risk: Yellow

Year	Team	G/GS	Snaps	Att	Comp	C%	Yds	TD	INT/Adj	FUM	ASR	NY/P	Rk	DVOA	Rk	DYAR	Rk	YAR	Runs	Yds	TD	DVOA	DYAR	QBR
2011	IND	9/8	454	243	132	54.3%	1541	6	9/12	5	7.4%	5.5	32	-33.2%	44	-374	44	-312	17	107	0	10.3%	18	27.2
2013	NYG	3/0	40	16	8	50.0%	57	0	2/1	2	4.7%	3.0	--	-91.2%	--	-103	--	-117	3	-2	0	--	--	0.3
2014	*NYG*			*529*	*300*	*56.7%*	*3315*	*21*	*20*	*10*		*5.2*		*-17.9%*					*36*	*75*	*1*	*-10.2%*		

2013: 41% Short 41% Mid 18% Deep 0% Bomb YAC: 3.4 (--)

Painter had arthroscopic surgery on his right knee in the spring, presumably the result of the gruesome toll those 16 pass attempts took on him last year. The Giants signed then released Josh Freeman this offseason, which is either a good sign for Painter or a really, really bad sign for Freeman (or both). For now, Painter is just the clipboard holder in New York, the "break glass in case of emergency" quarterback in between the Eli Manning and the (Ryan Nassib? The team's next first-round pick at quarterback?) eras. His most notable contribution will be as part of the answer to the trivia question: who was the Colts quarterback in between Peyton Manning and Andrew Luck?

Carson Palmer Height: 6-5 Weight: 230 College: USC Draft: 2003/1 (1) Born: 27-Dec-1979 Age: 35 Risk: Green

Year	Team	G/GS	Snaps	Att	Comp	C%	Yds	TD	INT/Adj	FUM	ASR	NY/P	Rk	DVOA	Rk	DYAR	Rk	YAR	Runs	Yds	TD	DVOA	DYAR	QBR
2011	OAK	10/9	638	328	199	60.7%	2753	13	16/23	2	5.6%	7.7	5	2.5%	15	295	18	298	16	20	1	-32.1%	-16	59.7
2012	OAK	15/15	953	565	345	61.1%	4018	22	14/20	8	4.8%	6.5	16	-2.2%	18	340	18	447	18	36	1	17.1%	23	46.8
2013	ARI	16/16	1081	572	362	63.3%	4274	24	22/26	6	6.8%	6.5	14	2.7%	17	547	15	361	27	3	0	-30.4%	-3	51.9
2014	*ARI*			*565*	*358*	*63.3%*	*4070*	*21*	*14*	*7*		*6.3*		*6.9%*					*28*	*30*	*0*	*-34.9%*		

2013: 41% Short 36% Mid 15% Deep 8% Bomb YAC: 4.9 (34) 2012: 44% Short 37% Mid 13% Deep 6% Bomb YAC: 5.7 (4)

Watching Carson Palmer last year must have seemed like watching Johnny Unitas in his prime to Cardinals fans after the abyss that followed Kurt Warner's retirement. Palmer can still trust his arm too much, but with Michael Floyd and Larry Fitzgerald around, he has reason to take chances. Palmer threw nine of his 22 interceptions in three wins where the defense held opponents to 10 points or less (including four interceptions in the upset at Seattle). KUBIAK sees a regression in that interception total but expects the rest of Palmer's season to be similar in 2014.

Christian Ponder Height: 6-2 Weight: 229 College: Florida State Draft: 2011/1 (12) Born: 25-Feb-1988 Age: 26 Risk: Red

Year	Team	G/GS	Snaps	Att	Comp	C%	Yds	TD	INT/Adj	FUM	ASR	NY/P	Rk	DVOA	Rk	DYAR	Rk	YAR	Runs	Yds	TD	DVOA	DYAR	QBR
2011	MIN	11/10	574	291	158	54.3%	1853	13	13/17	6	10.5%	5.3	36	-31.5%	43	-404	45	-378	28	219	0	36.5%	59	30.0
2012	MIN	16/16	1032	483	300	62.1%	2935	18	12/19	7	6.5%	5.3	34	-6.1%	21	173	21	66	60	253	2	4.2%	36	51.7
2013	MIN	9/9	511	239	152	63.6%	1648	7	9/11	7	10.6%	5.7	31	-13.5%	32	-42	31	19	34	151	4	-32.3%	-31	51.2
2014	*MIN*			*524*	*313*	*59.7%*	*3525*	*19*	*19*	*12*		*5.5*		*-16.9%*					*57*	*271*	*2*	*12.0%*		

2013: 51% Short 26% Mid 14% Deep 9% Bomb YAC: 4.7 (38) 2012: 54% Short 32% Mid 10% Deep 5% Bomb YAC: 5.3 (9)

In fourth quarters last year, Ponder completed just 56.5 percent of his passes for a measly 4.7 yards per attempt, with no touchdowns, four interceptions, and five sacks in 67 dropbacks. That's the kind of stat split that causes a "not clutch" reputation and sends some head coaches to the airport in search of new starters, but there were extenuating circumstances. If the Vikings were leading in the fourth quarter, Bill Musgrave only fed Adrian Peterson to the pit vipers; if they were trailing, he switched to a pass-heavy game plan no one in the organization felt comfortable with. And, of course, Ponder is pretty bad in the first place, but the one thing he does not appear to lack is competitiveness and courage in tough situations.

Ponder probably has a future as a sparky backup off the bench; he has the legs, the holler guy personality, and just enough throwing ability to make it work. First, he must endure one more season as the Vikings' third option, one the team hopes to never turn to.

Terrelle Pryor Height: 6-6 Weight: 233 College: Ohio State Draft: 2011/3 (SUP) Born: 20-Jun-1989 Age: 25 Risk: Red

Year	Team	G/GS	Snaps	Att	Comp	C%	Yds	TD	INT/Adj	FUM	ASR	NY/P	Rk	DVOA	Rk	DYAR	Rk	YAR	Runs	Yds	TD	DVOA	DYAR	QBR
2011	OAK	1/0	0	0	0	0.0%	0	0	0/0	0	--	--	--	--	--	--	--	--	0	0	0	--	--	--
2012	OAK	3/1	69	30	14	46.7%	155	2	1/1	1	-0.1%	5.0	--	-9.1%	--	4	--	16	10	51	1	23.2%	22	59.7
2013	OAK	11/9	588	272	156	57.4%	1798	7	11/11	7	11.2%	5.3	41	-31.6%	43	-388	44	-398	83	576	2	16.1%	105	30.5
2014	*SEA*			*457*	*269*	*58.8%*	*3187*	*14*	*13*	*11*		*6.0*		*-12.2%*					*109*	*468*	*3*	*15.3%*		

2013: 47% Short 36% Mid 13% Deep 5% Bomb YAC: 5.8 (6) 2012: 37% Short 37% Mid 13% Deep 13% Bomb YAC: 2.1 (--)

We'll turn this over to Raiders general manager Reggie McKenzie: "With Terrelle, I thought he started out pretty good. He had the ups and downs, but I thought he did a good job going into [the season-opener against the Colts] and had a couple other pretty good plays throughout that game and a couple games to follow, but it was the inconsistency and making the decisions, whether to throw, whether to run, avoid and get rid of the ball, whatever it is, that needs to continue to improve. It didn't…it was too inconsistent there. … Terrelle has a ways to go with the decision making and timing of throwing guys open." Thanks to Reggie, and to Vic Tafur of the *San Francisco Chronicle* for the transcription.

Possibly the best pure runner at quarterback to enter the league since Michael Vick, thanks to his combination of size, athleticism, and movement, Pryor remains a tremendous work in progress as a passer. He relied too much on that mobility, especially rolling to his right, which let the Chiefs sack him 10 times in October. He throws a pretty good slant, but the weaknesses in his game let opponents squat on that. June reports after the trade to Seattle mentioned him having a breakthrough of sorts; for more on that, see Pryor's comment from last offseason after his work with quarterback guru Tom House about how he was "going in the right direction to be a pretty good quarterback who knows how to throw the ball."

Philip Rivers Height: 6-5 Weight: 228 College: North Carolina St. Draft: 2004/1 (4) Born: 8-Dec-1981 Age: 33 Risk: Yellow

Year	Team	G/GS	Snaps	Att	Comp	C%	Yds	TD	INT/Adj	FUM	ASR	NY/P	Rk	DVOA	Rk	DYAR	Rk	YAR	Runs	Yds	TD	DVOA	DYAR	QBR
2011	SD	16/16	1078	582	366	62.9%	4624	27	20/25	8	5.4%	7.2	7	17.0%	8	1117	7	1038	26	36	1	7.5%	14	63.4
2012	SD	16/16	1023	527	338	64.1%	3606	26	15/18	14	8.9%	5.7	30	-7.3%	22	138	22	124	27	40	0	-46.5%	-19	41.5
2013	SD	16/16	1100	544	378	69.5%	4478	32	11/13	3	5.9%	7.6	4	34.8%	3	1799	2	1884	28	72	0	-17.6%	-5	71.7
2014	*SD*			*564*	*373*	*66.1%*	*4414*	*30*	*12*	*6*		*7.0*		*21.7%*					*31*	*69*	*1*	*-3.5%*		

2013: 52% Short 29% Mid 13% Deep 5% Bomb YAC: 5.7 (14) 2012: 50% Short 32% Mid 10% Deep 8% Bomb YAC: 5.3 (10)

In one season, the discussion went from "Have we seen the best we'll ever see from Philip Rivers?" to "Is Philip Rivers one of the five best quarterbacks in football?" Funny what a scheme change will do, especially one that perfectly fits what Rivers can do—and what he shouldn't be doing under any circumstances. Rivers is one of the smartest and hardest-working NFL players at any position, but he's not functionally mobile at all, and his mechanical idiosyncrasies prevent him from throwing certain passes repeatably and consistently, especially under pressure. What new head coach Mike McCoy and new offensive coordinator Ken Whisenhunt did was to shorten the "error gaps" in Rivers' game—reduce the risky longer passes, shorten the longer drops that got him in trouble, and ask him to see the entire field with a hot route most of the time. It worked like a charm, and just as McCoy worked miracles (sorry) with Tim Tebow in Denver with the "first read open" concept, San Diego's new offense allowed Rivers to settle into drive-extending grooves. McCoy told The MMQB's Peter King in May 2013 that Rivers might complete 70 percent of his passes in the new system. Rivers came damned close at 69.5 percent, and it's worth noting that only four quarterbacks ever hit that mark in a season—Drew Brees (twice) and three guys groomed by Bill Walsh: Joe Montana, Steve Young, and Ken Anderson. What McCoy has done for Rivers is the rough equivalent of giving a fastballer a few necessary alternate pitches as his velocity starts to tank, and it ranks right up there with the most productive coach/quarterback combinations of the last couple decades.

Aaron Rodgers Height: 6-2 Weight: 223 College: California Draft: 2005/1 (24) Born: 2-Dec-1983 Age: 31 Risk: Green

Year	Team	G/GS	Snaps	Att	Comp	C%	Yds	TD	INT/Adj	FUM	ASR	NY/P	Rk	DVOA	Rk	DYAR	Rk	YAR	Runs	Yds	TD	DVOA	DYAR	QBR
2011	GB	15/15	919	502	343	68.3%	4643	45	6/4	3	7.2%	8.3	1	46.6%	1	2059	2	2121	60	257	3	18.7%	71	87.1
2012	GB	16/16	1069	552	371	67.2%	4295	39	8/11	7	8.7%	6.7	13	23.4%	4	1395	4	1276	54	259	2	30.6%	94	74.7
2013	GB	9/9	582	290	193	66.6%	2536	17	6/5	4	7.6%	7.8	3	25.4%	6	740	10	762	30	120	0	6.8%	23	68.7
2014	*GB*			*560*	*374*	*66.7%*	*4573*	*33*	*11*	*7*		*7.3*		*23.8%*					*53*	*194*	*2*	*16.3%*		

2013: 48% Short 30% Mid 14% Deep 8% Bomb YAC: 6.5 (3) 2012: 50% Short 33% Mid 11% Deep 6% Bomb YAC: 5.5 (6)

Rodgers was romantically linked in May to Olivia Munn, a former *Attack of the Show* cutie who now appears in HBO's *Thing You Don't Watch Because It Is Not Game of Thrones*. As recently as February, he was rumored to be snuggling up with *Gossip Girl* Jessica Szhor. And just weeks before that, Rodgers was allegedly gay, having just parted ways with personal assistant and roommate Kevin Lanflisi. According to *Us Weekly*, Taylor Swift was overheard giving Szhor relationship advice when Swift, Rodgers, and Szhor all went bowling together. The advice must not have stuck—or perhaps worked too well, as Swift changes boyfriends whenever she has a new single to promote—because Szhor and Rodgers soon parted, and Munn soon dumped *Robocop* actor Joel Kinnaman and was seen smooching with Rodgers. Szhor previously dated Chris Pine, who now dates Icelandic cutie Iris Bjork Johannesdottir, whose name is Icelandic for "John's daughter Iris, who dates Captain Kirk and wears a swan as a dress."

In other words, Rodgers is the best quarterback in the NFL right now and really should be dating actresses on the Amy Adams tier: she has been engaged for five years, but Rodgers could easily Favre that guy out of the picture for not making up his mind. For the record, Matt Flynn is married to Lacey Minchew, who had a small role in *Robosapien: Rebooted*. Kinnaman and Minchew would make a perfect robotic couple! The moral of this tale: Rodgers may not be Captain Kirk, and he may like to bowl with Taylor Swift, but he is emphatically NOT robosexual.

Ben Roethlisberger Height: 6-5 Weight: 240 College: Miami (Ohio) Draft: 2004/1 (11) Born: 2-Mar-1982 Age: 32 Risk: Yellow

Year	Team	G/GS	Snaps	Att	Comp	C%	Yds	TD	INT/Adj	FUM	ASR	NY/P	Rk	DVOA	Rk	DYAR	Rk	YAR	Runs	Yds	TD	DVOA	DYAR	QBR
2011	PIT	15/15	989	513	324	63.2%	4077	21	14/20	8	7.2%	6.9	11	13.4%	11	870	9	841	31	70	0	9.2%	18	62.7
2012	PIT	13/13	832	449	284	63.3%	3265	26	8/13	5	6.5%	6.5	15	13.2%	11	761	9	764	26	92	0	-6.2%	5	62.8
2013	PIT	16/16	1051	584	375	64.2%	4261	28	14/15	9	7.2%	6.4	16	6.6%	12	724	11	764	27	99	1	-41.5%	-26	54.3
2014	*PIT*			*567*	*368*	*64.9%*	*4362*	*27*	*12*	*7*		*6.8*		*16.6%*					*25*	*85*	*0*	*13.8%*		

2013: 48% Short 32% Mid 12% Deep 8% Bomb YAC: 5.4 (23) 2012: 46% Short 34% Mid 14% Deep 6% Bomb YAC: 5.2 (12)

In each of the last two seasons, Roethlisberger has averaged more passing yards per attempt in games he lost (7.54) than in games he won (6.97), which never happened in his first eight seasons. This hasn't happened to any primary quarterback in Pittsburgh since Neil O'Donnell in 1993. Yards per attempt usually correlates well with wins and losses. The Roethlisberger difference was less severe last year: 7.43 in eight losses, 7.13 in eight wins. Is this the outcome of Todd Haley's influence where the offense doesn't work as well if Roethlisberger's not getting rid of the ball quickly with short, timing passes? Roethlisberger also had the second lowest DVOA of his career in 2013, though it's hard to pinpoint that specifically to the loss of deep threat Mike Wallace.

As he's gotten older, Roethlisberger has decreased his sack rate with each offensive coordinator, but it's come with some sacrifice of the big play.

- Ken Whisenhunt (2004-06): 8.75 percent sack rate, 8.25 yards per attempt.
- Bruce Arians (2007-11): 8.61 percent sack rate, 7.92 yards per attempt.
- Todd Haley (2012-13): 6.52 percent sack rate, 7.29 yards per attempt.

Roethlisberger will be a free agent in 2016. Extension talks have been quiet, but if this offense is finally going to cater to him with more no-huddle and he takes fewer hits like the second half of last season, then that should make his (likely) final contract signing an amicable moment for both parties.

Tony Romo Height: 6-2 Weight: 219 College: Eastern Illinois Draft: 2003/FA Born: 21-Apr-1980 Age: 34 Risk: Yellow

Year	Team	G/GS	Snaps	Att	Comp	C%	Yds	TD	INT/Adj	FUM	ASR	NY/P	Rk	DVOA	Rk	DYAR	Rk	YAR	Runs	Yds	TD	DVOA	DYAR	QBR
2011	DAL	16/16	962	522	346	66.3%	4184	31	10/12	5	6.3%	7.2	8	26.8%	4	1344	4	1280	22	46	1	-18.0%	-4	69.5
2012	DAL	16/16	1089	648	425	65.6%	4903	28	19/25	5	5.9%	6.8	10	14.8%	10	1156	7	1036	30	49	1	-14.9%	-2	63.4
2013	DAL	15/15	919	535	342	63.9%	3828	31	10/10	4	6.7%	6.3	18	11.5%	10	839	7	898	20	38	0	44.3%	17	59.5
2014	*DAL*			*615*	*388*	*63.1%*	*4373*	*29*	*17*	*7*		*6.1*		*4.5%*					*33*	*47*	*1*	*-17.9%*		

2013: 48% Short 36% Mid 11% Deep 5% Bomb YAC: 5.2 (25) 2012: 45% Short 37% Mid 11% Deep 6% Bomb YAC: 4.6 (30)

Here's another perfect Romo stat: In his seven losses as a starter last year, Romo threw 17 touchdowns to three interceptions, but *everyone remembers all three interceptions* (late fourth-quarter picks against Denver and Green Bay). That's always the problem. Romo's mastered losing in memorable fashion so well that he overshadows his overall excellence in defeats that should be painting a clear picture that this franchise has much bigger problems. The Denver game inflates those numbers, but no quarterback since 1960 (minimum six losses or 100 attempts) had a touchdown-to-interception ratio better than 17:3 in losses. Romo's 2013 ranks up there with 2004 Daunte Culpepper and 2008 Philip Rivers as the best years if we look only at how a quarterback has played in losses. Those quarterbacks still made the playoffs at 8-8, but that hasn't been good enough for Dallas the last three years. One big area where Romo was actually subpar at last year: a -22.0% DVOA on third/fourth down. He had 28.0% DVOA on second down, so his drop to third down was bigger than every other qualifying quarterback except Matt Flynn.

Matt Ryan Height: 6-4 Weight: 228 College: Boston College Draft: 2008/1 (3) Born: 17-May-1985 Age: 29 Risk: Green

Year	Team	G/GS	Snaps	Att	Comp	C%	Yds	TD	INT/Adj	FUM	ASR	NY/P	Rk	DVOA	Rk	DYAR	Rk	YAR	Runs	Yds	TD	DVOA	DYAR	QBR
2011	ATL	16/16	1062	566	347	61.3%	4177	29	12/11	5	5.3%	6.8	12	18.8%	7	1120	6	1204	37	84	2	19.8%	38	69.9
2012	ATL	16/16	1048	615	422	68.6%	4719	32	14/16	4	5.1%	7.0	4	16.5%	8	1196	5	1315	34	141	1	39.7%	54	74.8
2013	ATL	16/16	1065	651	439	67.4%	4515	26	17/16	5	5.9%	6.1	20	13.3%	9	1124	4	825	17	55	0	54.5%	23	61.1
2014	*ATL*			*632*	*415*	*65.8%*	*4492*	*26*	*17*	*5*		*6.2*		*3.4%*					*25*	*73*	*0*	*9.5%*		

2013: 53% Short 35% Mid 8% Deep 4% Bomb YAC: 4.8 (37) 2012: 51% Short 33% Mid 11% Deep 6% Bomb YAC: 4.9 (23)

Table 3: Quarterbacks with Strongest Opponent Adjustment in a Season, 1989-2013

Player	Team	Year	DYAR	YAR	Difference
Tom Brady	NE	2009	2,021	1,649	372
Matt Ryan	ATL	2013	1,124	825	300
Sage Rosenfels	HOU	2007	550	277	272
Matthew Stafford	DET	2012	1,160	891	268
Vinny Testaverde	NYJ	2000	533	273	260
Peyton Manning	IND	2007	1,721	1,465	257
Kurt Warner	STL	2002	-95	-349	254
Matt Ryan	ATL	2009	702	458	244
Drew Brees	NO	2007	1,159	925	235
Chris Chandler	PHX	1991	-181	-411	230

This is what happens when you play the NFC West, the AFC East, and two games each against the Saints and Panthers. Ryan is the only quarterback in the top ten twice, but if we made this a top 20 we would see one more appearance each by Brady and Manning. Carson Palmer had three seasons in the top 25.

Once we account for opponent adjustments, Ryan finished in the top six in passing DYAR for the fourth straight season, and he did it with his top receiver on the shelf for two-thirds of the season, playing behind an offensive line so bad that up to four starters will be replaced this year. That's kind of a microcosm of Ryan's career. In the past four seasons, only the "big four" of Manning, Brady, Drew Brees, and Aaron Rodgers have more DYAR than Ryan, but you rarely hear his name discussed when people start to argue about great quarterbacks. That's partly because the Falcons haven't had much success in the playoffs, partly because difficult schedules have tended to suppress his numbers, and partly because he plays kind of a boring brand of football. Of the quarterbacks with at least 1,000 passes in the past four seasons, Ryan is significantly better than average in rates of completions, touchdowns, interceptions, and sacks, but his 10.9 yards per completion is lower than anyone except Sam Bradford and Christian Ponder. Ryan has proven he can win with that brand of dink-and-dunk football, but unless he changes his style or wins a few more playoff games, he's not likely to get the credit he deserves.

Mark Sanchez

Height: 6-2 Weight: 227 College: USC Draft: 2009/1 (5) Born: 11-Nov-1986 Age: 28 Risk: Yellow

Year	Team	G/GS	Snaps	Att	Comp	C%	Yds	TD	INT/Adj	FUM	ASR	NY/P	Rk	DVOA	Rk	DYAR	Rk	YAR	Runs	Yds	TD	DVOA	DYAR	QBR
2011	NYJ	16/16	1064	543	308	56.7%	3474	26	18/19	10	6.6%	5.6	31	-12.6%	29	-56	31	-13	37	103	6	-8.2%	7	36.0
2012	NYJ	15/15	938	453	246	54.3%	2883	13	18/21	10	6.9%	5.5	31	-29.4%	35	-593	39	-480	22	28	0	-85.4%	-67	25.8
2014	*PHI*			*520*	*338*	*65.1%*	*3727*	*19*	*15*	*6*		*6.1*		*-2.9%*					*27*	*33*	*0*	*-10.7%*		

A torn labrum in the preseason ended Mark Sanchez's season before it even started. He had shoulder surgery in October, and later had arthroscopic surgery on his knee. The good news is that he'll be fully healthy for the 2014 season. The bad news, at least for him, is that he probably won't have much to do. Sanchez is one of three former Pac-12 quarterbacks on Chip Kelly's roster, and he'll battle with Matt Barkley, the man who replaced Sanchez at USC, to back up Nick Foles. That's a battle Sanchez should be able to win. Whether Sanchez is a good fit for Kelly's offense is another matter. With the Jets, the biggest deficiencies in Sanchez's game were reading defenses and mid-area accuracy. Eagles fans better hope Foles stays healthy.

Matt Schaub

Height: 6-5 Weight: 235 College: Virginia Draft: 2004/3 (90) Born: 25-Jun-1981 Age: 33 Risk: Red

Year	Team	G/GS	Snaps	Att	Comp	C%	Yds	TD	INT/Adj	FUM	ASR	NY/P	Rk	DVOA	Rk	DYAR	Rk	YAR	Runs	Yds	TD	DVOA	DYAR	QBR
2011	HOU	10/10	677	292	178	61.0%	2479	15	6/6	3	5.6%	7.8	4	24.4%	5	701	10	690	15	9	2	9.7%	10	67.3
2012	HOU	16/16	1105	544	350	64.3%	4008	22	12/15	4	5.2%	6.7	12	7.5%	14	697	12	882	21	-9	0	-68.2%	-8	64.0
2013	HOU	10/8	610	358	219	61.2%	2310	10	14/19	2	6.1%	5.7	33	-16.2%	34	-123	35	-115	5	24	0	52.6%	9	37.3
2014	*OAK*			*572*	*366*	*64.0%*	*3862*	*18*	*17*	*6*		*5.8*		*-14.0%*					*28*	*17*	*0*	*-33.2%*		

2013: 47% Short 35% Mid 13% Deep 5% Bomb YAC: 4.2 (42) 2012: 48% Short 34% Mid 11% Deep 7% Bomb YAC: 5.0 (19)

Most of the Houston chapter was devoted to how badly Schaub unraveled, so check that out if you want the full ugly truth. The Oakland Raiders traded a sixth-round pick to acquire Schaub mostly out of the fear that Schaub would choose the Browns in free agency to work with Kyle Shanahan again. So that's a good sign for this marriage and another data point in "Reggie McKenzie Versus Evaluating Quarterbacks." In *Goldeneye* terms, Schaub used to have a PP7—he could string together about seven passes a game with enough mustard to make defenses respect his deep ball. Now he's got a Klobb, and the sound it makes is something like "blicketyblicketycheckdownblicketysailedoutofboundsblicketythirddownpassshortofthesticksblickety." Schaub ended David Carr's career as a starting quarterback when he took over in Houston in 2006. Derek Carr will be looking to return the favor, and it shouldn't take him more than 10 games.

Matt Simms Height: 6-3 Weight: 210 College: Tennessee Draft: 2012/FA Born: 27-Sep-1988 Age: 26 Risk: Red

Year	Team	G/GS	Snaps	Att	Comp	C%	Yds	TD	INT/Adj	FUM	ASR	NY/P	Rk	DVOA	Rk	DYAR	Rk	YAR	Runs	Yds	TD	DVOA	DYAR	QBR
2013	NYJ	3/0	66	31	16	51.6%	156	1	1/1	1	11.0%	3.8	--	-24.6%	--	-27	--	-52	5	37	0	-73.4%	-12	7.2
2014	*NYJ*			*508*	*263*	*51.7%*	*3373*	*20*	*25*	*9*		*5.2*		*-22.3%*					*38*	*133*	*1*	*-0.5%*		

2013: 43% Short 30% Mid 23% Deep 3% Bomb YAC: 4.1 (--)

Simms shined in the 2013 preseason, averaging 8.1 yards per attempt and posting a 104 passer rating over 75 attempts in three games. Once the regular season arrived, he came on in relief of Geno Smith in three ugly Jets losses, but generally didn't impress. By signing Michael Vick and drafting Tajh Boyd, it's clear that the Jets aren't comfortable turning over the reins to Simms. With a year in the system, he will have the edge on Boyd, but Simms is squarely on the roster bubble.

Alex Smith Height: 6-4 Weight: 212 College: Utah Draft: 2005/1 (1) Born: 7-May-1984 Age: 30 Risk: Yellow

Year	Team	G/GS	Snaps	Att	Comp	C%	Yds	TD	INT/Adj	FUM	ASR	NY/P	Rk	DVOA	Rk	DYAR	Rk	YAR	Runs	Yds	TD	DVOA	DYAR	QBR
2011	SF	16/16	1005	445	273	61.3%	3144	17	5/6	6	8.5%	5.8	29	3.3%	14	448	13	354	52	179	2	11.4%	38	47.3
2012	SF	10/9	484	218	153	70.2%	1737	13	5/5	3	9.7%	6.6	14	14.8%	9	418	15	365	31	132	0	26.0%	36	70.1
2013	KC	15/15	978	508	308	60.6%	3313	23	7/11	7	7.9%	5.7	30	-3.7%	21	262	20	416	76	431	1	18.7%	96	49.4
2014	*KC*			*522*	*330*	*63.2%*	*3458*	*19*	*12*	*10*		*5.7*		*-7.6%*					*58*	*246*	*2*	*3.6%*		

2013: 56% Short 27% Mid 12% Deep 5% Bomb YAC: 5.7 (11) 2012: 53% Short 33% Mid 7% Deep 6% Bomb YAC: 5.1 (16)

That Smith had his best season to date in his first season in Andy Reid's offense reportedly spurred the veteran quarterback to assume that it was time to get paid at the same level as the best in the business. Which is why, at press time, quarterback and team are no closer to a long-term extension. No franchise is eager to make the same mistake the Cardinals did with Kevin Kolb a few years back—to overpay an average quarterback because he excelled over a short period of time in a favorable Andy Reid system, and having suckered Rod Graves and Ken Whisenhunt in that trade, Reid knows that better than anyone. Reid has always had a way with athletically limited players at the position, and it wasn't as if Smith transcended his surroundings. As he did for Jim Harbaugh in 2011 and the first half of 2012, Smith proved that his best asset is a true understanding of his limitations. Kansas City's receiver corps is limited at best, so Smith leaned on Jamaal Charles as a receiver to a notable degree—Charles was the only NFL back last year who led his team in targets, catches, receiving yards, and receiving touchdowns. Smith is the right kind of quarterback for a team with a good line, an amazing running back, and a stellar defense, and he's been gifted with that troika over each of the last three seasons with two different teams. Smith has a base salary of $7.5 million in 2014, and if he plays at his average high level to date, that's about what he'll be worth in a comparative sense. It will get interesting for the Chiefs after that, when the time comes to think about either franchising Smith, setting a price that works for both sides in a long-term sense, or moving on to a younger and more physically gifted player.

Geno Smith Height: 6-3 Weight: 208 College: West Virginia Draft: 2013/2 (39) Born: 10-Oct-1990 Age: 24 Risk: Red

Year	Team	G/GS	Snaps	Att	Comp	C%	Yds	TD	INT/Adj	FUM	ASR	NY/P	Rk	DVOA	Rk	DYAR	Rk	YAR	Runs	Yds	TD	DVOA	DYAR	QBR
2013	NYJ	16/16	985	443	247	55.8%	3046	12	21/26	8	8.3%	5.6	34	-23.6%	40	-371	43	-434	72	366	6	9.5%	65	35.9
2014	*NYJ*			*485*	*285*	*58.8%*	*3285*	*18*	*18*	*10*		*5.9*		*-11.5%*					*61*	*315*	*3*	*30.1%*		

2013: 43% Short 35% Mid 13% Deep 9% Bomb YAC: 5.1 (29)

Geno Smith had a rough rookie season, but there were some positive developments. While Smith struggled overall, he was very effective in obvious passing situations. Among quarterbacks with at least 80 passes on third or fourth downs, Smith ranked 12th in passing DVOA. The effectiveness came despite the fact that Smith faced an average distance of 8.7 yards to go in those situations, the second-longest in the league (behind Brandon Weeden). Smith was also generally a much better passer in the shotgun (-16.0% DVOA) than not (-55.2%), which may explain his success on third downs.

You may be surprised to know that Smith also stood out in one traditional statistic: yards per completion. While we know that Smith posted an ugly completion percentage with lots of sacks and interceptions, the rookie ranked seventh in the league in yards per completion. Smith was aggressive in throwing the ball down field even as he struggled to adjust to the pro game. Eric Decker, who excelled as a deep threat last year, could be a perfect complement to Smith in 2014.

Matthew Stafford Height: 6-2 Weight: 225 College: Georgia Draft: 2009/1 (1) Born: 7-Feb-1988 Age: 26 Risk: Green

Year	Team	G/GS	Snaps	Att	Comp	C%	Yds	TD	INT/Adj	FUM	ASR	NY/P	Rk	DVOA	Rk	DYAR	Rk	YAR	Runs	Yds	TD	DVOA	DYAR	QBR
2011	DET	16/16	1082	663	421	63.5%	5038	41	16/25	5	5.9%	6.8	13	15.0%	10	1171	5	1312	22	78	0	-2.2%	7	64.4
2012	DET	16/16	1181	727	435	59.8%	4967	20	17/23	8	3.7%	6.3	17	12.2%	12	1160	6	891	35	126	4	0.9%	23	57.1
2013	DET	16/16	1125	634	371	58.5%	4650	29	19/27	12	4.5%	6.9	10	4.9%	15	690	12	838	37	69	2	-40.3%	-41	52.5
2014	*DET*			*642*	*388*	*60.4%*	*4637*	*30*	*20*	*6*		*6.2*		*2.1%*					*39*	*68*	*1*	*-8.1%*		

2013: 47% Short 32% Mid 15% Deep 7% Bomb YAC: 6.1 (4) 2012: 49% Short 29% Mid 15% Deep 6% Bomb YAC: 4.7 (26)

Did you notice Stafford's collapse over the second half of the season? It really jumps out at you when you look at his entire season month-by-month.

Month	G	DYAR	DVOA	Att	Comp	C%	Yds	Yd/At	TD	INT	Sacks	Rate
September (Weeks 1-4)	4	284	15.4%	156	100	64.1%	1262	8.09	7	3	3	96.2
October (Weeks 5-8)	4	369	18.3%	182	111	61.0%	1355	7.45	9	3	7	93.5
November (Weeks 10-13)	4	203	7.4%	162	85	52.5%	1208	7.46	11	8	4	78.9
December (Weeks 14-17)	4	-166	-29.8%	134	75	56.0%	825	6.16	2	5	9	63.8

Obviously, injuries to Calvin Johnson and others played a role in the decline. But while Stafford was going down with the ship, he should have been bailing with a much bigger bucket instead of spraying sidearmed interceptions all over the field. Stafford has both the talent and paycheck to elevate his team, not add a layer of ballast, and Jim Caldwell's most critical task will be providing body-and-mind upgrades to a quarterback who seems to have settled for middle-tier status. From a fantasy perspective, even an inconsistent, disappointing Stafford will produce 4,500 yards and a gob of touchdowns when climbing out of bed with the weapons he has and the system he plays in. From a wins-and-losses perspective, a lot of screw-tightening is required.

Drew Stanton Height: 6-3 Weight: 230 College: Michigan State Draft: 2007/2 (43) Born: 7-May-1984 Age: 30 Risk: Red

Year	Team	G/GS	Snaps	Att	Comp	C%	Yds	TD	INT/Adj	FUM	ASR	NY/P	Rk	DVOA	Rk	DYAR	Rk	YAR	Runs	Yds	TD	DVOA	DYAR	QBR
2010	DET	2	243	119	69	58.0%	780	4	3/4	2	5.4%	6.0	27	12.2%	12	174	24	84	18	113	1	20.5%	28	42.4
2014	*ARI*			*548*	*323*	*58.9%*	*3451*	*13*	*14*	*10*		*5.5*		*-10.6%*					*39*	*81*	*2*	*-7.5%*		

Remember those halcyon days of March 2013, when Bruce Arians was trying to convince everyone he was totally cool with the idea of Drew Stanton as his starting quarterback? Ah, nostalgia. Stanton is the very definition of a replacement-level quarterback and hasn't appeared in a game since 2010, but he'll stick around Arizona another year; you have to figure that if Carson Palmer were to get injured, Stanton would be much better prepared than Logan Thomas to replace him.

Ryan Tannehill Height: 6-4 Weight: 221 College: Texas A&M Draft: 2012/1 (8) Born: 27-Jul-1988 Age: 26 Risk: Yellow

Year	Team	G/GS	Snaps	Att	Comp	C%	Yds	TD	INT/Adj	FUM	ASR	NY/P	Rk	DVOA	Rk	DYAR	Rk	YAR	Runs	Yds	TD	DVOA	DYAR	QBR
2012	MIA	16/16	980	484	282	58.3%	3294	12	13/16	7	6.7%	5.9	23	-9.9%	25	39	25	86	49	211	2	-11.0%	2	50.4
2013	MIA	16/16	1020	588	355	60.4%	3913	24	17/26	9	8.7%	5.5	39	-9.8%	27	54	26	22	40	238	1	19.0%	46	45.8
2014	*MIA*			*557*	*345*	*61.9%*	*3724*	*23*	*16*	*9*		*5.4*		*-9.2%*					*42*	*162*	*2*	*11.5%*		

2013: 41% Short 42% Mid 10% Deep 7% Bomb YAC: 4.4 (41) 2012: 45% Short 38% Mid 10% Deep 7% Bomb YAC: 4.4 (32)

The struggling Tannehill-to-Mike Wallace connection did suffer some bad luck along the way. Tannehill was intercepted on a pass to Wallace on fourth-and-24 against the Patriots and again on fourth-and-28 against Tampa Bay (Darrelle Revis). The only other quarterback to have two interceptions on fourth-and-20 (or longer) since 1998 was Brett Favre in 2005. Defenders usually don't catch those balls, but that's the kind of luck Miami had on their deep connection last year.

Everyone knows about the 58 sacks, but Tannehill was only 31st out of 45 quarterbacks in frequency of pressure last year (22.3 percent of passes). That just means that when he was pressured, it was really effective. For proof, his DVOA under pressure was -119.9% compared to 34.5% without pressure—the sixth-largest difference in the league. Another area that's been a problem is third down. Tannehill posted a -27.3% DVOA on third/fourth down as a rookie and last year fell to -37.7%. Tannehill's managed his touchdowns and interceptions slightly better at home, which is not surprising, but the consistency in his workload through two seasons is fascinating. Tannehill has thrown 536 passes on the road and at home. He's completed 323 at home; 314 on the road. He's averaged 6.76 yards per attempt at home; 6.68 on the road. Miami will take the consistency, but there has to be improvement from Tannehill in year three.

Tyrod Taylor Height: 6-1 Weight: 216 College: Virginia Tech Draft: 2011/6 (180) Born: 3-Aug-1989 Age: 25 Risk: Yellow

Year	Team	G/GS	Snaps	Att	Comp	C%	Yds	TD	INT/Adj	FUM	ASR	NY/P	Rk	DVOA	Rk	DYAR	Rk	YAR	Runs	Yds	TD	DVOA	DYAR	QBR
2011	BAL	3/0	5	1	1	100.0%	18	0	0/0	0	65.9%	5.0	--	-40.3%	--	-4	--	0	1	2	0	-41.6%	-1	14.9
2012	BAL	6/0	92	29	17	58.6%	179	0	1/1	1	6.8%	4.7	--	-28.3%	--	-34	--	-56	14	73	1	13.8%	18	45.0
2013	BAL	3/0	21	5	1	20.0%	2	0	1/2	0	0.4%	0.4	--	-236.3%	--	-75	--	-75	8	64	0	26.2%	15	44.8
2014	*BAL*			*477*	*279*	*58.6%*	*2995*	*18*	*16*	*11*		*5.3*		*-23.2%*					*94*	*463*	*3*	*4.0%*		

2013: 60% Short 40% Mid 0% Deep 0% Bomb YAC: 1.0 (--) 2012: 52% Short 37% Mid 7% Deep 4% Bomb YAC: 4.7 (--)

Taylor's been a pretty good "Mr. August" for Baltimore, meaning he'll show some flashes every preseason (especially with his legs), but John Harbaugh doesn't want to see him in action once the real games start. Fortunately, Joe Flacco has been very durable and has started all 109 games (including the postseason) in his career. Taylor is going to start feeling some job pressure from sixth-round rookie Keith Wenning, who fits more of what Baltimore does with Flacco under center.

Scott Tolzien Height: 6-3 Weight: 205 College: Wisconsin Draft: 2011/FA Born: 9-Jan-1987 Age: 27 Risk: Green

Year	Team	G/GS	Snaps	Att	Comp	C%	Yds	TD	INT/Adj	FUM	ASR	NY/P	Rk	DVOA	Rk	DYAR	Rk	YAR	Runs	Yds	TD	DVOA	DYAR	QBR
2013	GB	3/2	158	90	55	61.1%	717	1	5/8	0	4.2%	7.6	--	-9.1%	--	13	--	19	5	55	1	117.5%	33	24.3
2014	*GB*			*532*	*338*	*63.5%*	*3894*	*20*	*16*	*9*		*6.5*		*2.9%*					*58*	*103*	*1*	*-14.6%*		

2013: 52% Short 27% Mid 13% Deep 8% Bomb YAC: 6.1 (--)

The Packers grabbed Tolzien off the waiver wire from San Francisco late in their "oops, no backup quarterback" comedy routine last September. Tolzien was in the huddle just two months later. He passes all the eyeball tests, with a decent arm and fine mobility, and he surprised the Eagles early in a November game before cycling through all of the pass plays he could execute with confidence. He began to melt against the Giants and got benched for his own psychological well-being against the Vikings. Tolzien is more gifted than Matt Flynn and could win the Packers primary backup job if given a real crack at it: under the ridiculous circumstances of last year, he handled himself pretty well.

Jeff Tuel Height: 6-3 Weight: 221 College: Washington State Draft: 2013/FA Born: 12-Feb-1991 Age: 23 Risk: Green

Year	Team	G/GS	Snaps	Att	Comp	C%	Yds	TD	INT/Adj	FUM	ASR	NY/P	Rk	DVOA	Rk	DYAR	Rk	YAR	Runs	Yds	TD	DVOA	DYAR	QBR
2013	BUF	2/1	111	59	26	44.1%	309	1	3/3	0	3.2%	5.0	--	-43.4%	--	-130	--	-152	3	17	0	-12.1%	0	9.6
2014	*BUF*			*484*	*243*	*50.3%*	*3020*	*16*	*24*	*9*		*5.1*		*-29.3%*					*45*	*175*	*0*	*-2.4%*		

2013: 37% Short 42% Mid 5% Deep 15% Bomb YAC: 5.9 (--)

An undrafted free agent who got his chance to start a game last year as part of Buffalo's 2013 quarterbacking carousel, the Washington State product figures to spend much of the 2014 season holding a clipboard behind EJ Manuel and Thad Lewis.

Michael Vick Height: 6-0 Weight: 215 College: Virginia Tech Draft: 2001/1 (1) Born: 26-Jun-1980 Age: 34 Risk: Red

Year	Team	G/GS	Snaps	Att	Comp	C%	Yds	TD	INT/Adj	FUM	ASR	NY/P	Rk	DVOA	Rk	DYAR	Rk	YAR	Runs	Yds	TD	DVOA	DYAR	QBR
2011	PHI	13/13	825	423	253	59.8%	3303	18	14/18	9	5.6%	7.1	9	10.8%	12	628	11	573	76	589	0	27.5%	131	64.7
2012	PHI	10/10	667	351	204	58.1%	2362	12	10/14	8	8.0%	5.8	28	-14.4%	28	-78	27	-108	62	332	1	-11.1%	3	45.8
2013	PHI	7/6	325	141	77	54.6%	1215	5	3/3	4	10.5%	7.2	6	-6.9%	24	40	27	49	36	306	2	70.0%	128	58.8
2014	*NYJ*			*472*	*272*	*57.7%*	*3384*	*17*	*17*	*11*		*6.0*		*-11.4%*					*74*	*454*	*1*	*10.3%*		

2013: 35% Short 34% Mid 23% Deep 8% Bomb YAC: 7.4 (1) 2012: 45% Short 36% Mid 12% Deep 7% Bomb YAC: 4.9 (20)

The highlights of Vick's 2013 season came in the first two weeks. He did well against a bad Washington team unprepared for Kelly's hyper-speed, zone-read attack, then he shredded the 32nd-ranked San Diego defense at home, although Philip Rivers put up more points. Cue the bad performances against better competition, the turnovers and the injuries. Nick Foles' breakout performance made Vick expendable in Philadelphia and he wound up with the Jets where the "open competition" at quarterback with Geno Smith has been one of the offseason's more agonizingly forced storylines.

In June, Vick took on the mantle of Pioneer Running Quarterback. "I was the guy who started it all," Vick told ESPN. "I revolutionized the game. I changed the way it was played in the NFL." Okay, now for the dose of reality. Running quarterbacks have existed for decades and Vick is showing his arrogance to superior players like Fran Tarkenton, Steve Young and Randall Cunningham by thinking he revolutionized anything. He could even put on tape of 1997 Kordell Stewart to see things he would later do.

Vick is the only player in NFL history to sign two contracts worth at least $100 million, and the return on investment could not have been worse. After signing with Atlanta in 2005 for 10 years and $130 million, Vick went 15-16 as a starter with 35 touchdowns and 26 interceptions before serving a prison sentence for his role in a dog-fighting organization. After a career season in 2010 with Philadelphia, the Eagles ponied up a six-year deal worth $100 million. Vick lasted three years and went 12-17 as a starter with 35 touchdowns and 27 interceptions. Revolutionary? Next Vick will tell us he knows how Joan of Arc felt.

Seneca Wallace Height: 5-11 Weight: 196 College: Iowa State Draft: 2003/4 (110) Born: 6-Aug-1980 Age: 34 Risk: #N/A

Year	Team	G/GS	Snaps	Att	Comp	C%	Yds	TD	INT/Adj	FUM	ASR	NY/P	Rk	DVOA	Rk	DYAR	Rk	YAR	Runs	Yds	TD	DVOA	DYAR	QBR
2011	CLE	6/3	190	107	55	51.4%	567	2	2/3	1	4.6%	4.8	42	-13.3%	30	-15	29	-89	7	70	0	53.4%	20	43.7
2013	GB	2/1	58	24	16	66.7%	139	0	1/1	0	15.2%	4.1	--	-54.2%	--	-75	--	-69	0	0	0	--	--	15.2

2013: 62% Short 33% Mid 5% Deep 0% Bomb YAC: 3.4 (--)

Wallace underwent abductor tendon surgery in January. The procedure took place in a white van. Wallace looked utterly toasted before getting injured last year; the days when he could scramble away from danger and get the football past the outstretched arms of defenders consistently are long behind him. His lasting contribution to human progress may have been as a harbinger of Russell Wilson, who taught the Pacific Northwest that a short-but-determined quarterback could be effective. The Seahawks just needed to find a much better one.

Brandon Weeden Height: 6-4 Weight: 221 College: Oklahoma State Draft: 2012/1 (22) Born: 14-Oct-1983 Age: 31 Risk: Yellow

Year	Team	G/GS	Snaps	Att	Comp	C%	Yds	TD	INT/Adj	FUM	ASR	NY/P	Rk	DVOA	Rk	DYAR	Rk	YAR	Runs	Yds	TD	DVOA	DYAR	QBR
2012	CLE	15/15	929	517	297	57.4%	3385	14	17/26	5	5.3%	5.8	26	-19.4%	29	-291	34	-210	27	111	0	8.0%	24	27.0
2013	CLE	8/5	452	267	141	52.8%	1731	9	9/11	6	9.7%	5.3	42	-36.1%	44	-443	45	-429	12	44	0	12.4%	11	24.7
2014	*DAL*			*596*	*388*	*65.1%*	*3901*	*21*	*18*	*10*		*5.2*		*-10.7%*					*26*	*54*	*0*	*-10.3%*		

2013: 47% Short 29% Mid 17% Deep 8% Bomb YAC: 4.5 (40) 2012: 53% Short 29% Mid 10% Deep 7% Bomb YAC: 6.0 (2)

The Mike Holmgren era in Cleveland was rife with bad judgment. Trading up to select a 28-year-old quarterback in the first round was the most unwise move of them all. Weeden followed a poor rookie season with an awful sophomore campaign that saw him benched, only to regain the gig through injury, just the thing for a team angling for a high draft pick. His -443 DYAR was dead last in the league among qualifying quarterbacks by a wide margin, and only Kirk Cousins had a worse DVOA. Mercifully cut by the Browns, Weeden will now take over for the retiring Kyle Orton as the backup in Dallas. His appearance in a game might be just the tonic for fans who needlessly carp about Tony Romo.

Charlie Whitehurst Height: 6-4 Weight: 220 College: Clemson Draft: 2006/3 (81) Born: 6-Aug-1982 Age: 32 Risk: Red

Year	Team	G/GS	Snaps	Att	Comp	C%	Yds	TD	INT/Adj	FUM	ASR	NY/P	Rk	DVOA	Rk	DYAR	Rk	YAR	Runs	Yds	TD	DVOA	DYAR	QBR
2011	SEA	3/2	100	56	27	48.2%	298	1	1/4	2	12.3%	4.0	--	-49.2%	--	-160	--	-138	4	13	0	-0.2%	2	17.9
2013	SD	2/0	12	0	0	0.0%	0	0	0/0	0	--	--	--	--	--	--	--	--	6	-5	0	--	--	--
2014	*TEN*			*536*	*312*	*58.1%*	*3560*	*16*	*18*	*11*		*5.6*		*-11.8%*					*33*	*68*	*1*	*-7.6%*		

How much is a quarterback whose previous team never allowed him to throw a pass worth? Apparently, up to $8 million over two seasons, or at least that's what Whitehurst is getting from the Titans after following last year's offensive coordinator Ken Whisenhunt to Tennessee. It was a curious move, considering that when he actually did start for Seattle in 2010 and 2011, two of the three games he finished featured a passing DVOA worse than -85.0%. Whisenhunt emphasized in June that Whitehurst is indeed the No.2 behind Jake Locker. Given Locker's injury history, we may get our first extended look at whether Whitehurst really is that bad.

Russell Wilson Height: 5-11 Weight: 204 College: Wisconsin Draft: 2012/3 (75) Born: 29-Nov-1988 Age: 26 Risk: Yellow

Year	Team	G/GS	Snaps	Att	Comp	C%	Yds	TD	INT/Adj	FUM	ASR	NY/P	Rk	DVOA	Rk	DYAR	Rk	YAR	Runs	Yds	TD	DVOA	DYAR	QBR
2012	SEA	16/16	979	393	252	64.1%	3118	26	10/12	10	7.4%	6.8	8	19.7%	6	872	8	741	94	489	4	22.3%	147	71.7
2013	SEA	16/16	973	407	257	63.1%	3357	26	9/9	10	9.8%	6.9	8	15.6%	8	770	9	699	96	539	1	23.3%	134	58.9
2014	*SEA*			*455*	*292*	*64.3%*	*3541*	*28*	*13*	*10*		*7.0*		*13.1%*					*91*	*421*	*2*	*1.4%*		

2013: 45% Short 31% Mid 14% Deep 10% Bomb YAC: 5.7 (12) 2012: 46% Short 32% Mid 12% Deep 9% Bomb YAC: 5.0 (18)

The question is not whether the Seahawks will expand Wilson's role and reps in 2014—they know they have to allow him to throw more passes and take more risks. The question is how Wilson can be used as a pure thrower in a paradigm that keeps him healthy. The one Seattle used in Wilson's first two seasons? That isn't it. In both 2012 and 2013, Wilson led the NFL in pass plays outside the pocket—163 in 2012 and 152 in 2013—and that's on a team that's thrown the fewest passes in the NFL over the last two seasons. Last season, only Terrelle Pryor (who's now one of Wilson's backups) had a higher percentage of out-of-pocket throws. What makes Wilson different than your garden variety run-around guy is that in his second season, he actually became more efficient in the pocket—a 35.0% DVOA in the pocket, and a 26.3% DVOA outside. Combining sacks and quarterback hits, Wilson was knocked down on 19.9 percent of pass plays last year; only Case Keenum and Thaddeus Lewis had higher rates. If you add 100 or so passing attempts in a new season into that soup, you begin to understand the need for better protection. Seattle is happy with its current guards for some unknown reason, and Wilson was set upon from the inside last season, so he'll have to provide his own survival mechanism with pocket awareness and movement.

So, when the Seahawks put more on Wilson's shoulders, will he be ready for that? The truly "elite" (ugh) NFL quarterbacks are consistently successful when forced to be exceptional. Last season, Wilson completed 78-of-132 passes on third or fourth down for 985 yards, with eight touchdowns and four interceptions (8.0% DVOA). In the fourth quarter, he was 45-of-73 for 635 yards, with seven touchdowns and five picks (9.6% DVOA). Not terrible, but not much better than average, and not what one would want from a quarterback who may command $20 million per year or more when he gets his next contract after the 2014 season. Wilson has the capacity to combine consistently explosive plays with mistake-proofing, but that process must begin now, and it must begin in the pocket.

The ideal would be Wilson's performance in the Super Bowl, when he went 7-of-9 for 82 yards and six first-down conversions on third or fourth down, completed all three deep passes he threw, and displayed an eerie composure in a game that has set many more experienced quarterbacks right on their butts.

T.J. Yates Height: 6-3 Weight: 195 College: North Carolina Draft: 2011/5 (152) Born: 28-May-1987 Age: 27 Risk: Green

Year	Team	G/GS	Snaps	Att	Comp	C%	Yds	TD	INT/Adj	FUM	ASR	NY/P	Rk	DVOA	Rk	DYAR	Rk	YAR	Runs	Yds	TD	DVOA	DYAR	QBR
2011	HOU	6/5	314	134	82	61.2%	949	3	3/3	4	11.1%	5.9	25	-19.7%	35	-81	32	-15	14	57	0	12.7%	10	45.8
2012	HOU	4/0	23	10	4	40.0%	38	0	1/1	3	8.6%	3.1	--	-128.3%	--	-85	--	-89	2	-1	1	56.0%	8	2.1
2013	HOU	3/0	50	22	15	68.2%	113	0	2/2	1	6.6%	4.4	--	-78.0%	--	-109	--	-112	1	0	0	--	--	12.2
2014	*ATL*			*587*	*349*	*59.5%*	*3616*	*16*	*21*	*12*		*5.2*		*-16.4%*					*41*	*76*	*1*	*-13.4%*		

2013: 60% Short 40% Mid 0% Deep 0% Bomb YAC: 3.0 (--) 2012: 67% Short 11% Mid 11% Deep 11% Bomb YAC: 7.3 (--)

"Ah yes, sonny, glad you came. Let me tell you the Football Fable about T.J. Yates."

"Grandpa, why can't we talk about someone more relevant?"

"Hush! The crowd turned on Matt Schaub, cheering torn ankle ligaments he suffered against the Rams in Week 7. He had been bad at football, you see. He threw several interceptions that were returned for touchdowns. Yates came in to relieve Schaub, got to the goal line, then threw a pick-six of his own. Texans fans finally had got what they wanted for weeks, only to learn that it wasn't really what they wanted."

"Grandpa, don't you have any stories about Johnny Manziel?"

"Not that I can share here."

GOING DEEP

McLeod Bethel-Thompson, SF: Bethel-Thompson's middle name is Baltazar, and as far as we can tell, no player named McLeod, or Baltazar, has ever appeared in a game in the NFL. He has been on three different rosters over the last three years, but has yet to make an appearance. I do beseech you, sir, have patience.

Tajh Boyd, NYJ: Over the last three years, Tajh Boyd and Derek Carr were the only two college quarterbacks to throw over 100 touchdowns. Boyd also ranked second to Carr in passing yards over that time frame, with 11,575 yards. Boyd was a fantastic college quarterback who guided Clemson to two Orange Bowls and a Chick-Fil-A Bowl victory over LSU. That doesn't mean very much in the NFL, and few teams know that fact quite like the Jets. Boyd carries the "winner" label but is short, looked slow at the combine, and does not possess a great arm. He's a good character guy and an ideal third quarterback. But with a training camp battle for the top quarterback spot, Boyd doesn't figure to get many snaps to show his worth this summer.

Tyler Bray, KC: Bray made a huge mistake coming out of Tennessee early after just one season as a starter, which sort of fits with the worries about his maturity that all the scouts had in the first place. He made the Chiefs as a UDFA, but Aaron Murray presumably takes his spot for this season.

Austin Davis, STL: Davis, now in his third year out of Southern Miss, has been hanging around the bottom of the Rams roster as the third-string quarterback but may lose his spot to sixth-round pick Garrett Gilbert.

Dominique Davis, FA: Davis played a lot in the 2013 preseason, dazzling defenses with an 8.2-yard average on 12 carries. Unfortunately, he only completed 53 percent of his 78 passes, for just 5.8 yards per throw. Those are numbers that get you fired, and sure enough the Falcons waived Davis this year after trading for T.J. Yates. Turns out that guys who lead Conference USA in interceptions twice don't make good NFL prospects. Who knew? (2013 stats: 5-for-7, 34 yards, 8 DYAR, 4.4% DVOA)

Pat Devlin, MIA: Devlin once held the Pennsylvania state high school record for career passing yards (8,162). That's rarely ever noteworthy, but Pennsylvania has an incredible lineage of great quarterbacks, including Joe Montana, Johnny Unitas, Dan Marino, Jim Kelly, Joe Namath, George Blanda and Rich Gannon. Devlin has yet to appear in a regular-season game, but the

Dolphins have kept the undrafted free agent for the last three seasons. He's rarely impressed in the preseason, but Miami must see something to keep him around this long.

Zac Dysert, DEN: The seventh-rounder showed enough so the Broncos were willing to keep him on the 53-man roster all season long, but not enough to make him active for a game. Behind Peyton Manning and Brock Osweiler, taking an NFL snap seems like a long way away for Dysert, whose collegiate game resembled that of fellow Miami (Ohio) quarterback Ben Roethsliberger, minus the arm strength and ability to avoid the rush.

David Fales, CHI: Fales, the Bears' sixth-round pick, produced a pair of seasons for San Jose State that looked nearly identical on the surface: 4,193 yards, 33 touchdowns, and nine interceptions in 2012, 4,189-33-13 in 2013. Dig deeper, and not only did Fales' interception rate go up, but his completion rate and yards per attempt went down; meanwhile, the Spartans went from 11-2 to 6-6 as they climbed from the WAC to the Mountain West Conference. Fales had the weakest arm of the Senior Bowl quarterbacks, with Jimmy Garoppolo barreling past him on the "small-program developmental quarterback" express train. Fales is accurate and has a quick, easy release, and you can picture Marc Trestman using some old-school West Coast Offense mojo on him, but the fact that he fades every time the level of competition increases is not an encouraging sign.

Garrett Gilbert, STL: The son of former San Diego backup Gale Gilbert improved his completion rate from 53 percent in 2012 to 67 percent in 2013 while cutting his interceptions in half. Do yourself a favor and search YouTube for his game-tying two-point conversion pass to help SMU force overtime with Rutgers in 2013.

Ryan Griffin, NO: Tulane's all-time leader in attempts and completions, Griffin threw a pair of touchdowns for New Orleans in the preseason, but failed to make the team and was signed to the taxi squad. The Rams wanted to sign him after Sam Bradford went down, but the Saints blocked the move by promoting him to the main roster, so clearly they see potential in the former Green Wave passer.

Rex Grossman, FA: Is this the untimely end of The Sex Cannon? There comes a point in every NFL player's life where news stories about him start following the "(TEAM X) not interested in (PLAYER Y)" template. Grossman has woken up in that world, and if Kyle Shanahan doesn't throw him a minimum backup contract bone, this could be it for Grossman.

Caleb Hanie, DAL: Hanie couldn't crack the Browns' December depth chart. Now he's in Dallas, along with fellow Cleveland washout Brandon Weeden, which makes JerryWorld the official Last Chance Saloon for NFL quarterbacks.

Josh Johnson, SF: With Jason Campbell and A.J. McCarron now in the quarterback room, Johnson was released by Cincinnati. It's a textbook case of the importance of relationships in the NFL. Johnson was a Jay Gruden disciple, while Campbell had his best performances in Oakland under incoming Bengals offensive coordinator Hue Jackson. Johnson signed in San Francisco; he has college ties with Jim Harbaugh, but Harbaugh already cut him once back before the 2012 season.

Landry Jones, PIT: Jones set school records at Oklahoma, but never won the Heisman Trophy like Jason White nor was he drafted in the first round like predecessor Sam Bradford. Many saw him a system quarterback fittingly drafted in the fourth round, but Landry was determined to be the best quarterback in the 2013 draft by former Colts general manager Bill Polian. Of course Polian had to cite being "a winner" in his analysis, which caused a pre-draft stir. On his memorable first snap of the preseason against the Giants, Jones ran into his running back on a handoff, leading to a fumble and safety, and quickly putting him on the path of being a NFL winner.

Kevin Kolb, FA: Still not cleared from a concussion he suffered in 2013, it appears that Kolb is going to call it a career after one season with the Bills. Regardless of what he does the rest of his life, perhaps the greatest achievement Kolb will take into retirement is the fact that prior to the 2011 season, Rod Graves and Ken Whisenhunt gave Kolb a five-year, $63.5 million extension to play for the Arizona Cardinals. Enjoy retirement while sleeping on a giant pile of money, Kevin.

Ryan Lindley, ARI: Arizona's 2012 quarterback disaster ended up forcing Lindley to play seven games as a sixth-round rookie; he threw 171 passes without a single touchdown and had -55.8% DVOA. Last year, he was a healthy inactive for 14 games, and then the Cardinals drafted Logan Thomas. Have you considered coaching?

A.J. McCarron, CIN: It stands to reason that when your girlfriend is Katherine Webb, your self-confidence is through the roof. That's the only way to explain McCarron's vision of himself as a first-round talent. His deep-ball throwing numbers were superb at Alabama (in his three years the Tide never finished lower than 12th in S&P+), and he was much more than a mere caretaker for a loaded college squad, but nevertheless, it would be a shock if Mr. Webb developed into anything more than an NFL backup. Over the last ten years, here are the top five quarterbacks chosen in the fourth round or later according to P-F-R's Approximate Value stat: Matt Cassel and Ryan Fitzpatrick (44), Kyle Orton (34), Derek Anderson (19), and Tyler Thigpen (10). In other words, Andy Dalton likely has little to worry about.

Colt McCoy, WAS: McCoy will go from Kaepernick insurance in San Francisco to RG3/Cousins insurance in Washington. Given what he did with Andy Dalton's limitations, you've got to figure that Jay Gruden could make McCoy useful if necessary, but Washington fans would rather not have to see that experiment.

Zach Mettenberger, TEN: A tall drink of water at 6-foot-5, Mettenberger had a breakout senior season at LSU on the backs of fellow draft picks Jarvis Landry and Odell Beckham. He fell to the sixth round due to a history of off-field concerns: he pleaded guilty to two sexual battery charges while at Georgia, and failed a drug test at the combine. Mettenberger has the tools to be an NFL quarterback. He'll need to improve his decision-making, both on and off the field, to become a starter.

Kellen Moore, DET: Skinny Steve Rogers from the start of the first Captain America movie: all heart and a body that looks like computer-generated emaciation. This is real life, unfortunately, so no one will arrive at Lions headquarters with Super Soldier Serum. Jim Caldwell will get a long look at Moore actually throwing passes in training camp and turn into either the Tommie Lee Jones general guy or Red Skull.

Aaron Murray, KC: Tony Dungy once insisted that Murray would be the top-rated quarterback had he come out for the 2013 draft, which makes one a bit more cautious when listening to Mr. Dungy's football analysis at any given time—at least, when it comes to quarterbacks. Not that Murray's a wasted draft pick or anything; he leaves the Bulldogs having set all kinds of SEC marks for quarterback productivity. His touchdown-to-interception ratio (121-41) is certainly encouraging, but Murray is more in the Alex Smith/Andy Dalton mode rather than a guy who blows up game tape as a real difference-maker. That Georgia finished fifth in Passing S&P+ in 2013 despite a multitude of WR injuries also speaks well for his future, especially with Andy Reid as his guide.

Ryan Nassib, NYG: Nassib is Brock Osweiler or Ryan Mallett, execpt with a Day Three pedigree. With 151 consecutive starts, Eli Manning has become the league's most durable quarterback, which relegates Nassib to clipboard duty for the foreseeable future. Nassib earned praise a year ago for his footwork, pocket presence, and quick release, but the true test will be whether he beats out Curtis Painter for the No. 2 job.

Brady Quinn, FA: Quinn is one of just seven quarterbacks in NFL history to start at least 20 games and lose at least 80 percent of his starts. He's joined by Ryan Leaf, Chuck Long, Jack Thompson, Blaine Gabbert, David Klingler, and Chris Weinke. Quinn spent time with the Seahawks, Jets, and Rams last year: in the process, he was released in favor of Tarvaris Jackson and David Garrard, and backed up Kellen Clemens in St. Louis. One of the LCF's big failures; sorry about that, folks.

Jordan Palmer, CHI: Carson's brother turned 30 in May and has made a career as a AAA quarterback: signed for camp, released before Labor Day, re-signed as a third stringer when a quarterback goes on IR. Not to be confused with Jordan Rodgers, though frankly it is okay if you do. We would like to thank the Bears for signing Jimmy Clausen so we didn't have to try to come up with a projection for Palmer as Jay Cutler's official backup.

Sean Renfree, ATL: Renfree started three years at Duke, so he has a lot of experience for a third-stringer. On the other hand, he never ranked higher than seventh in the ACC in yards per pass, which is why he's a third-stringer. He had 25 preseason throws in 2013 with no interceptions, but he averaged only 3.4 yards per pass.

Tom Savage, HOU: Let's start with the bad: Savage had a pedestrian NCAA career highlighted by two transfers, from Rutgers to Arizona and then to Pittsburgh. The Panthers finished just 61st in Passing S&P+. He has a disturbing proclivity to stick to his first reads. NCAA defensive backs were all over his routes. Then, there's the fact that the fast-rising quarterback at draft time almost always busts. Now, the good: he looks the part and has a cannon. Wow, one of those sections sure wound up shorter than the other, didn't it?

John Skelton, FA: There's a reason most fifth-round picks don't start 17 games in their first three seasons. Skelton went on a three-team 2013 tour following his Cardinals days. It wasn't exactly like a three-hour tour, but he did leave about three hours of impact on each team and his career is presumed missing.

Rusty Smith, FA: RUSTY SMITH GOING DEEP COMMENT TEMPLATE: Remind readers that Rusty Smith was the sole reason the 2010 Texans weren't regarded as the worst defense in modern history. Wonder why Rusty Smith still has a job with the Tita—wait, what? Another team signed him? Why? In fact, the Giants realized their mistake and cut him two weeks later.

Brad Sorensen, SD: Developmental quarterback, strong-armed pocket passer who operated out of the shotgun at Southern Utah. That's in the Big Sky Conference, for those wondering.

Ricky Stanzi, JAC: Remember all the Chiefs fans babbling about Stanzi when he was Kansas City's third-string quarterback in 2011 and 2012? Neither do they.

Alex Tanney, CLE: Why the Browns didn't let the trick-pass YouTube sensation play down the stretch last season is beyond us. The pride of Monmouth College and internet dreamers everywhere couldn't possibly have been worse than Brandon Weeden. Interested teams are asked to put receivers in moving cars so Tanney will have a better crack at hitting them in "stride."

Tyler Thigpen, CLE: Hey, look who's back after spending a year out of football! It's Herm Edwards' favorite quarterback *ever!* (The Herminator spent most of the "In-Game Decision Making" panel at the 2013 Sloan Sports Analytics Conference complaining about how hard it was to win games in Kansas City with Thigpen behind center.) We suppose Cleveland's decision to bring him in as the third quarterback makes some sense. His style was a bit of an evolutionary template for Johnny Manziel's game, much in the same way Space Invaders was an evolutionary template for Halo.

Logan Thomas, ARI: Like Sandor Clegane, Thomas is big, strong, and struggles with conceptual thinking under pressure. The 6-foot-5, 250-pound quarterback has awesome physical gifts, but can't feel pressure in the pocket and struggles with zone coverage. Bruce Arians clearly thinks this Virginia Tech alum is an unmolded ball of clay he can do something with, and Arizona grabbed him near the end of the fourth round.

Joe Webb, CAR: The Vikings, who were starved for quarterbacks last year but had plenty of receivers, gave up on their endless Webb-as-quarterback experiments, relegating him to fifth receiver status while Josh Freeman studied the playbook between series and Matt Cassel tried to rekindle a lost youth he never really possessed. The Panthers, set at quarterback with Cam Newton but so desperate at wide receiver that Mushin Muhammad could come out of retirement and start for them, are using Webb at quarterback. It's easy to think that Webb missed the opportunity to be a decent scrambling quarterback or capable slot receiver because he got stuck playing for organizations obsessed with doing everything in the most back-asswards possible way.

Keith Wenning, BAL: Baltimore's sixth-round pick was a very prolific passer at Ball State with 92 touchdowns and 11,402 yards; the Cardinals were 31st in Passing S&P+ despite the heavy opponent adjustments that come from playing in the MAC. He's more of a traditional backup for Joe Flacco than the athletic Tyrod Taylor. The Ravens haven't kept a No. 3 quarterback during the season since 2009 due to Flacco's durability, but Wenning has a shot to stick around or outright beat Taylor for the backup job.

Tyler Wilson, TEN: Wilson's craft is akin to a poker player trying to push out the blinds as a short-stacked all-in. In football terms: his brain wants his arm to hit throws that it can't make. Reggie McKenzie gave up on Wilson during the season after using a fourth-round pick on him, which means ... well, it may mean Reggie McKenzie isn't so good at this whole "finding a quarterback" thing. Wilson will battle Zach Mettenberger to back up Charlie Whitehurst, and since Wilson's only 6-foot-2, perhaps he should start taking the field in platform cleats to gain Ken Whisenhunt's attention.

Running Backs

In the following section we provide the last three years' statistics, as well as a 2014 KUBIAK projection, for every running back who either played a significant role in 2013 or is expected to do so in 2014.

The first line contains biographical data—each player's name, height, weight, college, draft position, birth date, and age. Height and weight are the best data we could find; weight, of course, can fluctuate during the offseason. **Age** is very simple, the number of years between the player's birth year and 2014, but birthdate is provided if you want to figure out exact age.

Draft position gives draft year and round, with the overall pick number with which the player was taken in parentheses. In the sample table, it says that LeSean McCoy was chosen in the 2009 NFL Draft in the second round with the 53rd overall pick. Undrafted free agents are listed as "FA" with the year they came into the league, even if they were only in training camp or on a practice squad.

To the far right of the first line is the player's Risk for fantasy football in 2014. As explained in the quarterback section, the standard is for players to be marked Green. Players with higher than normal risk are marked Yellow, and players with the highest risk are marked Red. Players who are most likely to match or surpass our forecast—primarily second- stringers with low projections—are marked Blue. Risk is not only based on injury probability, but how a player's projection compares to his recent performance as well as our confidence (or lack thereof) in his offensive teammates.

Next we give the last three years of player stats. First come games played and games started (**G/GS**). Games played is the official NFL total and may include games in which a player appeared on special teams, but did not carry the ball or catch a pass. We also have a total of offensive **Snaps** for each season. The next four columns are familiar: **Runs**, rushing yards (**Yds**), yards per rush (**Yd/R**) and rushing touchdowns (**TD**).

The entry for fumbles (**FUM**) includes all fumbles by this running back, no matter whether they were recovered by the offense or defense. Holding onto the ball is an identifiable skill; fumbling it so that your own offense can recover it is not. (For more on this issue, see the essay "Pregame Show" in the front of the book.) This entry combines fumbles on both carries and receptions.

The next five columns give our advanced metrics for rushing: **DVOA** (Defense-Adjusted Value Over Average), **DYAR** (Defense-Adjusted Yards Above Replacement), and **YAR** (Yards Above Replacement), along with the player's rank (**Rk**) in both **DVOA** and **DYAR**. These metrics compare every carry by the running back to a league-average baseline based on the game situations in which that running back carried the ball. DVOA and DYAR are also adjusted based on the opposing defense. The methods used to compute these numbers are described in detail in the "Statistical Toolbox" introduction in the front of the book. The important distinctions between them are:

- DVOA is a rate statistic, while DYAR is a cumulative statistic. Thus, a higher DVOA means more value per play, while a higher DYAR means more aggregate value over the entire season.
- Because DYAR is defense-adjusted and YAR is not, a player whose DYAR is higher than his YAR faced a harder-than-average schedule. A player whose DYAR is lower than his YAR faced an easier-than-average schedule.

To qualify for ranking in rushing DVOA and DYAR, a running back must have had 100 carries in that season. Last year, 47 running backs qualified to be ranked in these stats, compared to 42 backs in 2012 and 51 backs in 2011.

Success Rate (**Suc%**), listed along with rank, represents running back consistency as measured by successful running plays divided by total running plays. (The definition for success is explained in the "Statistical Toolbox" introduction in the front of the book.) A player with high DVOA and a low Success Rate mixes long runs with plays on which he was stuffed at or behind the line of scrimmage. A player with low DVOA and a high Success Rate generally gets the yards needed, but rarely gets more. The league-average Success Rate in 2013 was 46 percent. Success Rate is not adjusted for the defenses a player faced.

We also give a total of broken tackles (**BTkl**) according to the Football Outsiders game charting project. This total includes broken tackles on both runs and receptions.

The columns to the right of broken tackles give data for each running back as a pass receiver. Receptions (**Rec**) counts passes caught, while Passes (**Pass**) counts total passes thrown to this player, complete or incomplete. The next four columns list receiving yards (**Yds**), catch rate (**C%**), yards per catch (**Yd/C**), receiving touchdowns (**TD**), and average yards after the catch (**YAC**).

Our research has shown that receivers bear some responsi-

LeSean McCoy Height: 5-11 Weight: 198 College: Pittsburgh Draft: 2009/2 (53) Born: 12-Jul-1988 Age: 26 Risk: Yellow

Year	Team	G/GS	Snaps	Runs	Yds	Yd/R	TD	FUM	DVOA	Rk	DYAR	Rk	YAR	Suc%	Rk	BTkl	Rec	Pass	Yds	C%	Yd/C	TD	YAC	DVOA	Rk	DYAR	Rk
2011	PHI	15/15	867	273	1309	4.8	17	1	15.8%	4	304	1	262	51%	15	50	48	69	315	70%	6.6	3	8.1	-4.5%	32	38	27
2012	PHI	12/12	694	200	840	4.2	2	4	-12.6%	33	-34	35	7	48%	19	44	54	68	373	81%	6.9	3	8.9	9.2%	17	90	9
2013	PHI	16/16	873	314	1607	5.1	9	1	18.1%	3	341	1	321	52%	8	51	52	64	539	81%	10.4	2	11.3	23.8%	9	137	7
2014	*PHI*			*304*	*1440*	*4.7*	*11*	*2*	*10.7%*								*53*	*67*	*486*	*79%*	*9.2*	*3*		*28.9%*			

bility for incomplete passes, even though only their catches are tracked in official statistics. Catch rate represents receptions divided by all intended passes for this running back. The average NFL running back caught 74 percent of passes in 2013. Unfortunately, we don't have room to post the best and worst running backs in receiving plus-minus, but you'll find the top 10 and bottom 10 running backs in this metric listed in the statistical appendix.

Finally we have receiving DVOA and DYAR, which are entirely separate from rushing DVOA and DYAR. To qualify for ranking in receiving DVOA and DYAR, a running back must have 25 passes thrown to him in that season. There are 49 running backs ranked for 2013, 47 backs for 2012, and 51 backs for 2011. Numbers without opponent adjustment (YAR, and VOA) can be found on our website, FootballOutsiders.com.

The italicized row of statistics for the 2014 season is our 2014 KUBIAK projection based on a complicated regression analysis that takes into account numerous variables including projected role, performance over the past two years, projected team offense and defense, historical comparables, height, age, experience of the offensive line, and strength of schedule.

It is difficult to accurately project statistics for a 162-game baseball season, but it is exponentially more difficult to accurately project statistics for a 16-game football season. Consider the listed projections not as a prediction of exact numbers, but the mean of a range of possible performances. What's important is less the exact number of yards we project, and more which players are projected to improve or decline. Actual performance will vary from our projection less for veteran starters and more for rookies and third-stringers, for whom we must base our projections on much smaller career statistical samples. Touchdown numbers will vary more than yardage numbers.

There are three metrics tracked by ESPN Stats & Information which you will see mentioned in some player comments.

Top 20 RB by Rushing DYAR (Total Value), 2013

Rank	Player	Team	DYAR
1	LeSean McCoy	PHI	341
2	DeMarco Murray	DAL	295
3	Jamaal Charles	KC	247
4	Matt Forte	CHI	193
5	Marshawn Lynch	SEA	185
6	Knowshon Moreno	DEN	171
7	Rashad Jennings	OAK	164
8	Fred Jackson	BUF	163
9	Eddie Lacy	GB	160
10	Ryan Mathews	SD	141
11	Stevan Ridley	NE	135
12	DeAngelo Williams	CAR	126
13	Alfred Morris	WAS	121
14	Donald Brown	IND	117
15	Andre Ellington	ARI	117
16	LeGarrette Blount	NE	117
17	James Starks	GB	110
18	Chris Johnson	TEN	110
19	Tony Gerhart	MIN	105
20	Danny Woodhead	SD	104

Top 20 RB by Rushing DVOA (Value per Rush), 2013

Rank	Player	Team	DVOA
1	DeMarco Murray	DAL	24.0%
2	Donald Brown	IND	19.2%
3	LeSean McCoy	PHI	18.1%
4	Andre Ellington	ARI	17.5%
5	Rashad Jennings	OAK	15.8%
6	Danny Woodhead	SD	13.7%
7	Jamaal Charles	KC	13.7%
8	Arian Foster	HOU	11.4%
9	Stevan Ridley	NE	10.2%
10	LeGarrette Blount	NE	9.4%
11	Fred Jackson	BUF	9.1%
12	Mike Tolbert	CAR	9.0%
13	Knowshon Moreno	DEN	8.4%
14	Montee Ball	DEN	7.5%
15	Matt Forte	CHI	7.4%
16	DeAngelo Williams	CAR	7.2%
17	Marshawn Lynch	SEA	5.9%
18	Eddie Lacy	GB	5.3%
19	Ryan Mathews	SD	3.6%
20	Joique Bell	DET	2.0%

Minimum 100 carries.

Top 10 RB by Receiving DYAR (Total Value), 2013

Rank	Player	Team	DYAR
1	Danny Woodhead	SD	282
2	Joique Bell	DET	196
3	Knowshon Moreno	DEN	192
4	Darren Sproles	NO	174
5	Giovani Bernard	CIN	167
6	Shane Vereen	NE	151
7	LeSean McCoy	PHI	137
8	Jamaal Charles	KC	135
9	Pierre Thomas	NO	128
10	Andre Ellington	ARI	117

Top 10 RB by Receiving DVOA (Value per Pass), 2013

Rank	Player	Team	DVOA
1	Jason Snelling	ATL	46.2%
2	Danny Woodhead	SD	41.2%
3	Joique Bell	DET	40.3%
4	Knowshon Moreno	DEN	31.0%
5	Giovani Bernard	CIN	29.4%
6	Mike Tolbert	CAR	29.0%
7	Shane Vereen	NE	25.1%
8	Darren Sproles	NO	23.9%
9	LeSean McCoy	PHI	23.8%
10	Andre Ellington	ARI	22.3%

Minimum 25 passes.

ESPN tracks the number of defenders in the box for each snap, and tags each play as either "loaded" or "not loaded." A loaded box is when the defense has more players in the box than the offense has available blockers for running plays. Some player comments may reference how well a back performed in 2013 against loaded vs. not loaded formations, or how many average men in the box he faced.

ESPN also marks **yards after contact** for each play. In the end, we decided not to include this number in the player tables because most running backs are packed surprisingly close in this metric, and we need to do more research on how much these small differences between running backs matter. Last year, 45 of the 47 running backs with at least 100 carries averaged between 1.3 and 2.2 yards after contract on runs. The exceptions were Donald Brown (2.7 average yards after contact, but on just 101 carries) and Ray Rice (1.1 average yards after contact).

For many rookie running backs, we'll also include statistics from our college football arsenal, notably **POE** (Points Over Expected) and **Highlight Yards**. POE analyzes the output of college football running backs by comparing the expected EqPts value of every carry for a given ballcarrier (based on the quality of the rushing defense against which he's running) to the actual output. A positive POE indicates an above-average runner, with an average runner accruing exactly 0 POE. Highlight Yards are those yards not included in Adjusted Line Yards. So, for example, if a runner gains 12 yards in a given carry, and we attribute 7.0 of those yards to the line (the ALY formula gives the offensive line 100 percent credit for all yards gained between zero and four yards and 50 percent credit between five and 10), then the player's highlight yardage on the play is 5.0 yards. Highlight Yards are shown as an average per opportunity, which means Highlight Yards divided by the total number of carries that went over four yards. For more details on these stats, see the college football section of the book (p. 363).

Finally, in a section we call "Going Deep," we briefly discuss lower-round rookies, free-agent veterans, and practice-squad players who may play a role during the 2014 season or beyond.

C.J. Anderson Height: 5-8 Weight: 224 College: California Draft: 2013/FA Born: 2-Feb-1991 Age: 23 Risk: Yellow

Year	Team	G/GS	Snaps	Runs	Yds	Yd/R	TD	FUM	DVOA	Rk	DYAR	Rk	YAR	Suc%	Rk	BTkl	Rec	Pass	Yds	C%	Yd/C	TD	YAC	DVOA	Rk	DYAR	Rk
2013	DEN	5/0	21	7	38	5.4	0	0	53.0%	--	19	--	20	86%	--	1	0	1	0	0%	0.0	0	--	-91.1%	--	-5	--
2014	*DEN*			*73*	*329*	*4.5*	*3*	*1*	*4.2%*								*18*	*25*	*131*	*72%*	*7.3*	*1*		*-8.3%*			

A solid back at Cal, Anderson showed enough to make the Broncos as an undrafted rookie. While he lacks special qualities as a runner that could make him a feature back, a developing three-down skill set could make him a better bet than Ronnie Hillman for extra playing time should Montee Ball go down. They'll battle in camp for the official No. 2 job.

Dri Archer Height: 5-8 Weight: 173 College: Kent St. Draft: 2014/3 (97) Born: 8-Sep-1991 Age: 23 Risk: Green

Year	Team	G/GS	Snaps	Runs	Yds	Yd/R	TD	FUM	DVOA	Rk	DYAR	Rk	YAR	Suc%	Rk	BTkl	Rec	Pass	Yds	C%	Yd/C	TD	YAC	DVOA	Rk	DYAR	Rk
2014	*PIT*			*33*	*165*	*4.9*	*2*	*0*	*16.2%*								*21*	*28*	*182*	*75%*	*8.7*	*1*		*-1.5%*			

Todd Haley keeps trying to utilize a tiny ball of speed with very little success. He did this with Dexter McCluster (in Kansas City) and then Chris Rainey. Maybe Dri Archer, another running back/receiver hybrid who can also return kicks, will make the third time a charm. Archer's 4.26 forty-yard dash is the second fastest among running backs in combine history behind Chris Johnson (4.24). So he's really fast, but can he play in the NFL? He was nothing special at Kent State for two years, then ruled academically ineligible in 2011, but returned with a vengeance on his way to being named MAC Special Teams Player of the Year. With Le'Veon Bell and LeGarrette Blount being workhorses, there may not be many carries left for Archer, but the ideal plan for him would probably be around Darren Sproles' yearly usage levels: 50 runs, 70 catches and a lot of great returns. Kent State has already produced the all-time leader in kickoff return touchdowns (Josh Cribbs, who is tied with Leon Washington), but Archer won't be flying under the radar as a third-round pick.

Matt Asiata Height: 5-11 Weight: 220 College: Utah Draft: 2011/FA Born: 24-Jul-1987 Age: 27 Risk: Green

Year	Team	G/GS	Snaps	Runs	Yds	Yd/R	TD	FUM	DVOA	Rk	DYAR	Rk	YAR	Suc%	Rk	BTkl	Rec	Pass	Yds	C%	Yd/C	TD	YAC	DVOA	Rk	DYAR	Rk
2013	MIN	11/1	117	44	166	3.8	3	1	12.9%	--	41	--	24	55%	--	3	5	8	13	63%	2.6	0	4.4	-67.7%	--	-26	--
2014	*MIN*			*68*	*252*	*3.7*	*2*	*3*	*-15.4%*								*22*	*26*	*173*	*85%*	*7.8*	*0*		*11.0%*			

Asiata graduated from special-teamer to starter when Adrian Peterson and Toby Gerhart got injured. He grinded out a 30-51-3 stat line in the Eagles victory, though his afternoon was not as crazy as that line suggested: he carried 12 times while the Vikings nursed a healthy fourth-quarter lead. Asiata also ripped off a big run against the Lions in the season finale. Asiata can run and catch a little and block a lot, making him a contender for Gerhart's role, though he may be more valuable as a Norv Turner-style frequent-use fullback.

Edwin Baker

Height: 5-8 | Weight: 204 | College: Michigan State | Draft: 2012/7 (250) | Born: 1-Jun-1991 | Age: 23 | Risk: Green

Year	Team	G/GS	Snaps	Runs	Yds	Yd/R	TD	FUM	DVOA	Rk	DYAR	Rk	YAR	Suc%	Rk	BTkl	Rec	Pass	Yds	C%	Yd/C	TD	YAC	DVOA	Rk	DYAR	Rk
2013	CLE	3/2	97	43	171	4.0	2	0	13.1%	--	41	--	38	51%	--	4	8	9	57	89%	7.1	0	8.3	30.3%	--	23	--
2014	*CLE*			*27*	*100*	*3.7*	*0*	*1*	*-15.0%*								*11*	*18*	*68*	*61%*	*6.2*	*0*		*-17.1%*			

Baker was Cleveland's best back at season's end, showing good straight-line power and decent hands in the passing game. But with Ben Tate and Terrance West now in the Browns backfield, Baker figures to be cast back in to the journeyman role he was in before last December, unless injuries lash the depth chart.

Montee Ball

Height: 5-10 | Weight: 214 | College: Wisconsin | Draft: 2013/2 (58) | Born: 5-Dec-1990 | Age: 24 | Risk: Yellow

Year	Team	G/GS	Snaps	Runs	Yds	Yd/R	TD	FUM	DVOA	Rk	DYAR	Rk	YAR	Suc%	Rk	BTkl	Rec	Pass	Yds	C%	Yd/C	TD	YAC	DVOA	Rk	DYAR	Rk
2013	DEN	16/0	312	120	559	4.7	4	3	7.5%	14	86	21	89	54%	4	12	20	27	145	74%	7.3	0	7.0	-18.3%	41	-7	40
2014	*DEN*			*267*	*1214*	*4.6*	*9*	*4*	*2.8%*								*47*	*58*	*430*	*81%*	*9.1*	*2*		*29.9%*			

Ball earned increased playing time the second half of the season as he became more acclimated to the NFL game and the passing-game duties requested of him in the Denver offense. While in the lineup, he showcased younger, more explosive legs than Knowshon Moreno. This was apparent in Second-Level Yards, where he averaged 1.92 to Moreno's 1.18, and in Open-Field Yards, where his 1.38 doubled Moreno's 0.69. With Moreno's departure, Ball steps into the lead back role without a high-profile backup in place. His work last season and the Broncos' apparent lack of interest in adding a veteran back suggest he should be able to handle it, but that does not mean we won't have a "Goddammit, Montee!" video to amuse us next year.

Vick Ballard

Height: 5-10 | Weight: 219 | College: Mississippi State | Draft: 2012/5 (170) | Born: 16-Jul-1990 | Age: 24 | Risk: Green

Year	Team	G/GS	Snaps	Runs	Yds	Yd/R	TD	FUM	DVOA	Rk	DYAR	Rk	YAR	Suc%	Rk	BTkl	Rec	Pass	Yds	C%	Yd/C	TD	YAC	DVOA	Rk	DYAR	Rk
2012	IND	16/12	579	211	814	3.9	2	3	-7.4%	27	10	27	-10	48%	18	22	17	27	152	63%	8.9	1	6.9	10.7%	15	38	24
2013	IND	1/1	39	13	63	4.8	0	0	34.3%	--	22	--	18	46%	--	0	1	2	-5	50%	-5.0	0	-1.0	-131.0%	--	-18	--
2014	*IND*			*61*	*217*	*3.5*	*4*	*2*	*-6.4%*								*5*	*6*	*48*	*83%*	*9.5*	*0*		*19.6%*			

Ballard tore his ACL after Week 1 and was lost for the season. But since Trent Richardson decided not to Wally Pipp him, Ballard is still in the mix as he comes back from the injury. He was limited in OTAs but is expected to be full-go for training camp. Ballard received praise from the coaching staff for his small sample size of pass protection work last year, but he's better suited as a first- and second-down back.

Jackie Battle

Height: 6-2 | Weight: 238 | College: Houston | Draft: 2007/FA | Born: 1-Oct-1983 | Age: 31 | Risk: Red

Year	Team	G/GS	Snaps	Runs	Yds	Yd/R	TD	FUM	DVOA	Rk	DYAR	Rk	YAR	Suc%	Rk	BTkl	Rec	Pass	Yds	C%	Yd/C	TD	YAC	DVOA	Rk	DYAR	Rk
2011	KC	15/4	305	149	597	4.0	2	0	4.3%	16	76	22	78	44%	40	7	9	13	68	69%	7.6	0	8.8	-36.8%	--	-16	--
2012	SD	16/5	159	95	311	3.3	3	0	-23.8%	--	-67	--	-48	38%	--	3	15	15	108	100%	7.2	1	7.4	60.4%	--	63	--
2013	TEN	16/0	113	36	142	3.9	1	0	-13.5%	--	-8	--	-19	33%	--	5	4	5	36	80%	9.0	0	10.0	4.5%	--	4	--
2014	*TEN*			*36*	*138*	*3.8*	*1*	*1*	*-10.0%*								*7*	*9*	*47*	*78%*	*6.7*	*0*		*-1.1%*			

Every Jackie Battle carry in the history of the NFL has involved him plunging over the guard and trying to run over someone. Any broken tackles he incurs in the process are purely incidental. In Tennessee, he has found a team that, for some reason, values this skill set. Goal line carries aren't out of the question, but it'll take some injuries for him to get there.

Joique Bell

Height: 5-11 | Weight: 220 | College: Wayne State | Draft: 2010/FA | Born: 4-Aug-1986 | Age: 28 | Risk: Yellow

Year	Team	G/GS	Snaps	Runs	Yds	Yd/R	TD	FUM	DVOA	Rk	DYAR	Rk	YAR	Suc%	Rk	BTkl	Rec	Pass	Yds	C%	Yd/C	TD	YAC	DVOA	Rk	DYAR	Rk
2012	DET	16/0	381	82	414	5.0	3	1	12.6%	--	71	--	65	54%	--	20	52	69	485	75%	9.3	0	8.3	32.8%	3	193	2
2013	DET	16/4	547	166	650	3.9	8	4	2.0%	20	78	24	75	51%	10	24	53	69	547	77%	10.3	0	10.3	40.3%	3	196	2
2014	*DET*			*161*	*674*	*4.2*	*6*	*3*	*-3.5%*								*57*	*82*	*513*	*70%*	*9.0*	*1*		*6.4%*			

Bell was 7-of-12 converting goal-to-go carries for touchdowns last season. Reggie Bush was 2-of-6. Goal-to-go performance is somewhere between volatile and random, but given the choice between Bush and a 220-pound kid with tackle-breaking ability who bootstrapped his way through three practice squads and into a rotation, who would you select? Bell had two 20-carry games in December, and the Lions plan to give him and Bush roughly equal opportunities in 2014. Bell fumbled twice in the Eagles game and still saves his best receiving performances for when all hope is lost (10 catches in the sad-sack loss to the Giants, for example), so he is not exactly a perfect solution to the Lions' inconsistency in the running game. In other words, there is a difference between "more reliable than Reggie Bush" and "excellent," though Bell possesses enough special qualities to make him useful.

Le'Veon Bell Height: 6-1 Weight: 230 College: Michigan State Draft: 2013/2 (48) Born: 18-Feb-1992 Age: 22 Risk: Yellow

Year	Team	G/GS	Snaps	Runs	Yds	Yd/R	TD	FUM	DVOA	Rk	DYAR	Rk	YAR	Suc%	Rk	BTkl	Rec	Pass	Yds	C%	Yd/C	TD	YAC	DVOA	Rk	DYAR	Rk
2013	PIT	13/13	677	244	860	3.5	8	1	-7.0%	28	17	28	15	47%	23	21	45	65	399	68%	8.9	0	10.0	-5.9%	30	28	28
2014	*PIT*			*271*	*1163*	*4.3*	*10*	*2*	*3.5%*								*44*	*64*	*326*	*69%*	*7.4*	*1*		*-8.3%*			

Bell only averaged 3.52 yards per carry and ranked 28th in DVOA. That's in the range of Trent Richardson's rookie season (3.56 yards per carry and 34th in DVOA). So why is Bell not the walking punchline Richardson has become? Part of it is the eye test. On his first touchdown last year against Minnesota, Bell sidestepped a defender five yards behind the line of scrimmage, located his blocking, bounced the run to the outside, and had enough speed to finish with a dive for the end zone. The only tape of Richardson finding the hole might be the sex tape that TMZ reported last year, but no one wanted to buy that (literally). Bell also didn't have any offensive line continuity, didn't cost multiple first-round picks, and it's not like every other Pittsburgh back was wildly successful the way Colts not named Richardson were last year. Bell also appeared to improve down the stretch, averaging 4.01 yards per carry in his final five games with two of his best receiving efforts.

If Bell doesn't play better in 2014, his critics will come, but he's not T-Rich yet. Though with Haley and Mike Munchak coaching the offense, visions of Eddie George and Arizona Edgerrin James come to mind, meaning they will make sure Bell's the most respected sub-4.0 back in the NFL come hell or high water.

Giovani Bernard Height: 5-8 Weight: 202 College: North Carolina Draft: 2013/2 (37) Born: 22-Nov-1991 Age: 23 Risk: Green

Year	Team	G/GS	Snaps	Runs	Yds	Yd/R	TD	FUM	DVOA	Rk	DYAR	Rk	YAR	Suc%	Rk	BTkl	Rec	Pass	Yds	C%	Yd/C	TD	YAC	DVOA	Rk	DYAR	Rk
2013	CIN	16/0	614	170	695	4.1	5	1	-4.5%	27	28	27	69	48%	21	28	56	71	514	79%	9.2	3	9.4	29.4%	5	167	5
2014	*CIN*			*236*	*1041*	*4.4*	*7*	*2*	*3.0%*								*57*	*82*	*495*	*70%*	*8.7*	*1*		*5.0%*			

"Nat Gio" was specifically drafted to bring elusiveness and vapor trails to a running back group that resembled the sloth pen at the Cincinnati Zoo. Mission accomplished. His field-reversing, mind-blowing touchdown run against the Dolphins on national Thursday night broadcast was just the most visible of his spectacular plays. (Surprisingly, that was the only run by a Bengals back longer than 28 yards in 2013, as reflected by the team's near-bottom finishes in Second-Level and Open-Field Yards.) Perhaps more notable was Bernard's ability to push the pile—he seldom was knocked backwards and relished smashing into defenders expecting a juke. That may not bode well for a long-term career, but it makes him more likely to get the bulk of the team's carries in 2014. It helps that his pass blocking, a concern that *Hard Knocks* dwelled upon (for lack of much drama in Bengals camp), turned out to be excellent.

LeGarrette Blount Height: 6-0 Weight: 247 College: Oregon Draft: 2010/FA Born: 5-Dec-1986 Age: 28 Risk: Green

Year	Team	G/GS	Snaps	Runs	Yds	Yd/R	TD	FUM	DVOA	Rk	DYAR	Rk	YAR	Suc%	Rk	BTkl	Rec	Pass	Yds	C%	Yd/C	TD	YAC	DVOA	Rk	DYAR	Rk
2011	TB	14/14	392	184	781	4.2	5	5	0.6%	28	67	24	54	47%	23	30	15	25	148	60%	9.9	0	10.0	-45.2%	49	-43	49
2012	TB	13/0	92	41	151	3.7	2	0	-9.5%	--	-2	--	2	37%	--	2	1	2	2	50%	2.0	0	7.0	-102.8%	--	-11	--
2013	NE	16/7	286	153	772	5.0	7	3	9.4%	10	117	16	131	54%	3	17	2	5	38	40%	19.0	0	20.5	-5.0%	--	3	--
2014	*PIT*			*105*	*401*	*3.8*	*5*	*2*	*-6.1%*								*6*	*7*	*55*	*86%*	*9.1*	*0*		*21.2%*			

Blount was an afterthought following his 2012 season, but he rebounded with the Patriots. In Week 17 against Buffalo, he amassed 334 all-purpose yards. In his next game against the Colts in the playoffs, he rushed for 166 yards and four touchdowns. Consider Blount a case study in how far the league has come in viewing the expendability of running backs. In the past, Blount's late-season dominance would have earned him a spot on the team next year, but the Patriots have spent a decade running over the Bills and Colts with various backs. Free agency was quiet before the Steelers offered Blount a two-year deal for $3.85 million. The Steelers aren't well-versed in "going with the hot hand" in a committee approach. They'll push Bell with the most carries, but Blount should see his share of series and clock-killing runs. He is limited on third down as a receiving option.

Brandon Bolden Height: 5-11 Weight: 220 College: Mississippi Draft: 2012/FA Born: 26-Jan-1990 Age: 24 Risk: Blue

Year	Team	G/GS	Snaps	Runs	Yds	Yd/R	TD	FUM	DVOA	Rk	DYAR	Rk	YAR	Suc%	Rk	BTkl	Rec	Pass	Yds	C%	Yd/C	TD	YAC	DVOA	Rk	DYAR	Rk
2012	NE	10/0	99	56	274	4.9	2	0	12.8%	--	53	--	54	54%	--	5	2	2	11	100%	5.5	0	5.0	6.3%	--	2	--
2013	NE	12/2	266	55	271	4.9	3	0	13.1%	--	54	--	54	49%	--	5	21	29	152	72%	7.2	0	7.6	-14.6%	37	-1	37
2014	*NE*			*29*	*133*	*4.5*	*0*	*1*	*-0.9%*								*10*	*13*	*66*	*77%*	*6.6*	*1*		*0.5%*			

While the Patriots went outside their comfort zone a bit when it came to drafting Shane Vereen (second round) and Stevan Ridley (third round), Bolden follows in the tradition of BenJarvus Green-Ellis in that he's a UDFA who has found a home in New England. While he's not considered an elite back, he does a bunch of things well enough to be considered a valued, across-the-board backup. He's at a career crossroads now, and his original contract ends at the end of this season. The drafting of James White could mean he no longer has a role, especially if Bill Belichick wants to keep fullback James Develin around. But if the Patriots keep Bolden, and Vereen and Ridley depart as free agents following the 2014 season, there's an opportunity to take on a bigger role in the offense.

Ahmad Bradshaw Height: 5-11 Weight: 195 College: Marshall Draft: 2007/7 (250) Born: 19-Mar-1986 Age: 28 Risk: Green

Year	Team	G/GS	Snaps	Runs	Yds	Yd/R	TD	FUM	DVOA	Rk	DYAR	Rk	YAR	Suc%	Rk	BTkl	Rec	Pass	Yds	C%	Yd/C	TD	YAC	DVOA	Rk	DYAR	Rk
2011	NYG	12/9	488	171	659	3.9	9	1	2.5%	21	80	21	83	45%	32	21	34	44	267	77%	7.9	2	8.8	0.2%	27	31	32
2012	NYG	14/12	598	221	1015	4.6	6	3	15.8%	5	230	6	194	52%	8	14	23	31	245	74%	10.7	0	11.9	8.5%	18	35	25
2013	IND	3/2	102	41	186	4.5	2	0	9.3%	--	33	--	47	54%	--	3	7	8	42	88%	6.0	0	5.6	8.6%	--	10	--
2014	*IND*			*91*	*361*	*4.0*	*3*	*1*	*-2.2%*								*9*	*12*	*71*	*75%*	*7.9*	*0*		*2.3%*			

Every Ahmad Bradshaw carry is a mortality play. The runner must weigh his ability to cut and slash down the field against his body telling him it doesn't want to work that way. When the ability wins out, Bradshaw is a very effective back who mixes speed and power well. When Bradshaw's body wins out, he hits injured reserve and loses any chance of signing a decent contract. The league minimum was all it took to get Bradshaw back in the fold, and at that price, he's a decent risk for a team that lists an enigma at the top of the depth chart.

Andre Brown Height: 6-1 Weight: 196 College: North Carolina St. Draft: 2009/4 (129) Born: 30-Nov-1986 Age: 28 Risk: Green

Year	Team	G/GS	Snaps	Runs	Yds	Yd/R	TD	FUM	DVOA	Rk	DYAR	Rk	YAR	Suc%	Rk	BTkl	Rec	Pass	Yds	C%	Yd/C	TD	YAC	DVOA	Rk	DYAR	Rk
2012	NYG	10/2	222	73	385	5.3	8	0	45.6%	--	185	--	173	63%	--	4	12	17	86	71%	7.2	0	6.1	-17.3%	--	-3	--
2013	NYG	8/8	360	139	492	3.5	3	3	-16.3%	41	-44	41	-30	50%	15	8	20	29	103	69%	5.2	0	5.9	-46.7%	48	-49	48
2014	*HOU*			*51*	*226*	*4.4*	*0*	*2*	*-3.0%*								*8*	*12*	*59*	*67%*	*7.4*	*0*		*-7.3%*			

Brown may be the only back in the league who Darren McFadden would call injury-prone. Despite being in the league for five years, Brown has been limited to just 22 career games and 214 carries. Still, Brown is an effective player when healthy, a punishing runner who has some burst. Even last year, his 3.5 YPC average was still higher than the average of the other Giants running backs, so that number has more to do with his offensive line than Brown. In Houston, Brown won't be asked to be a goal-line back, but that was another area where Brown excelled during his time in New York. Brown turns 28 in December, so it's too late in his career to expect a breakout season; Texans fans just need to hope he stays healthy in the event Arian Foster misses some time due to injury.

Bryce Brown Height: 6-0 Weight: 220 College: Kansas State Draft: 2012/7 (229) Born: 14-May-1991 Age: 23 Risk: Green

Year	Team	G/GS	Snaps	Runs	Yds	Yd/R	TD	FUM	DVOA	Rk	DYAR	Rk	YAR	Suc%	Rk	BTkl	Rec	Pass	Yds	C%	Yd/C	TD	YAC	DVOA	Rk	DYAR	Rk
2012	PHI	16/4	334	115	564	4.9	4	4	-2.2%	23	29	24	29	39%	39	17	13	19	56	68%	4.3	0	7.0	-38.9%	--	-26	--
2013	PHI	16/1	194	75	314	4.2	2	0	-1.2%	--	23	--	12	48%	--	10	8	13	84	62%	10.5	0	11.8	8.7%	--	12	--
2014	*BUF*			*67*	*291*	*4.3*	*1*	*2*	*-4.5%*								*12*	*17*	*79*	*71%*	*6.6*	*0*		*-6.3%*			

Four big fumbles put a damper on some of the exciting things Brown did his rookie season. Last year he didn't fumble once, but his touches dropped from 136 to 83 under Chip Kelly. He was basically a non-factor until he rushed for 115 yards, including a 65-yard touchdown run, against a putrid Chicago defense in Week 16. Even in that game Brown wasn't used much until the Eagles led by 22-plus points in the fourth quarter. Then he played one snap in the playoffs. Brown was traded to Buffalo in May, meaning the Eagles are content with LeSean McCoy, Darren Sproles and Chris Polk. Buffalo has the duo of Fred Jackson and C.J. Spiller, so barring injuries at the top of the depth chart, Brown will have a hard time seeing the field much in 2014. But with Jackson getting ever older, he could have a big role in 2015.

Donald Brown Height: 5-11 Weight: 210 College: Connecticut Draft: 2009/1 (27) Born: 11-Apr-1987 Age: 27 Risk: Blue

Year	Team	G/GS	Snaps	Runs	Yds	Yd/R	TD	FUM	DVOA	Rk	DYAR	Rk	YAR	Suc%	Rk	BTkl	Rec	Pass	Yds	C%	Yd/C	TD	YAC	DVOA	Rk	DYAR	Rk
2011	IND	16/2	392	134	645	4.8	5	0	13.9%	5	119	15	101	37%	49	12	16	19	86	84%	5.4	0	5.9	-19.8%	--	-6	--
2012	IND	10/4	299	108	417	3.9	1	0	-9.8%	31	-5	31	-5	44%	30	5	9	13	93	69%	10.3	0	11.0	0.9%	--	11	--
2013	IND	16/5	373	102	537	5.3	6	0	19.2%	2	117	14	122	54%	2	17	27	36	214	78%	7.9	2	8.8	6.2%	19	44	22
2014	*SD*			*51*	*206*	*4.0*	*3*	*1*	*2.5%*								*16*	*22*	*124*	*73%*	*7.7*	*0*		*-0.6%*			

Finally, it was other teams saying "Goddammit, Donald," and not his quarterback. Brown's best season to date was buoyed by outstanding work in the shotgun, where he averaged 8.7 yards per attempt and led all runners with more than 12 carries by boasting a 74.8% DVOA on 30 totes. Brown moved on from the Colts in the offseason, joining the Chargers. That gives them *two* perpetually disappointing first-round backs who had surprisingly strong 2013 seasons. Danny Woodhead is locked in as the passing-down back, so how much is Brown going to play? We're sure the Chargers have some deeper plan here, but we can't suss out why they needed to guarantee Brown $4 million to enact it.

Ronnie Brown Height: 6-0 Weight: 233 College: Auburn Draft: 2005/1 (2) Born: 12-Dec-1981 Age: 33 Risk: #N/A

Year	Team	G/GS	Snaps	Runs	Yds	Yd/R	TD	FUM	DVOA	Rk	DYAR	Rk	YAR	Suc%	Rk	BTkl	Rec	Pass	Yds	C%	Yd/C	TD	YAC	DVOA	Rk	DYAR	Rk
2011	PHI	16/2	143	42	136	3.2	1	1	-14.9%	--	-12	--	-26	48%	--	1	0	2	0	0%	0.0	0	0.0	-96.9%	--	-10	--
2012	SD	14/1	354	46	220	4.8	0	0	10.2%	--	31	--	47	42%	--	10	49	60	371	83%	7.6	0	7.8	12.2%	13	79	10
2013	SD	16/0	149	45	157	3.5	1	0	-11.3%	--	-5	--	-9	36%	--	0	8	8	60	100%	7.5	0	6.9	37.6%	--	23	--

His career just didn't turn out as planned, did it? If you double Brown's stats for 2007 when he tore up his ACL at midseason, here's what you get as the most similar running backs through their first three years: William Andrews, Corey Dillon, DeMarco Murray, Thurman Thomas, Tony Collins, and Roger Craig. At least we'll always talk about Brown whenever the Wildcat comes up on *Top 10* or some other NFL Network program. Still unsigned as of press time.

Michael Bush Height: 6-1 Weight: 245 College: Louisville Draft: 2007/4 (100) Born: 16-Jun-1984 Age: 30 Risk: #N/A

Year	Team	G/GS	Snaps	Runs	Yds	Yd/R	TD	FUM	DVOA	Rk	DYAR	Rk	YAR	Suc%	Rk	BTkl	Rec	Pass	Yds	C%	Yd/C	TD	YAC	DVOA	Rk	DYAR	Rk
2011	OAK	16/9	724	256	977	3.8	7	1	-2.7%	33	65	26	45	45%	36	12	37	47	418	79%	11.3	1	8.6	44.8%	2	142	3
2012	CHI	13/1	248	114	411	3.6	5	1	4.5%	12	67	16	48	50%	12	5	9	11	83	82%	9.2	0	9.3	24.9%	--	23	--
2013	CHI	15/0	139	63	197	3.1	3	0	-27.3%	--	-56	--	-60	35%	--	7	4	8	48	50%	12.0	1	11.8	24.0%	--	15	--

Take away a 40-yard run against the Browns in Week 15, and Bush's yards per carry drop to 2.53. He carried 15 times for 14 yards in the red zone, including nine carries for minus-four yards and two touchdowns from the one-yard line, which is rather remarkable. Short-yardage backs are expected to generate at least one yard per rush, which is why Bush was still unsigned at press time, and Ka'Deem Carey was drafted as Matt Forte's stunt double.

Reggie Bush Height: 6-0 Weight: 200 College: USC Draft: 2006/1 (2) Born: 2-Mar-1985 Age: 29 Risk: Green

Year	Team	G/GS	Snaps	Runs	Yds	Yd/R	TD	FUM	DVOA	Rk	DYAR	Rk	YAR	Suc%	Rk	BTkl	Rec	Pass	Yds	C%	Yd/C	TD	YAC	DVOA	Rk	DYAR	Rk
2011	MIA	15/15	600	216	1086	5.0	6	4	-2.1%	30	51	32	91	44%	37	29	43	52	296	83%	6.9	1	6.9	-12.2%	40	5	41
2012	MIA	16/16	572	227	986	4.3	6	4	-8.3%	30	3	30	18	51%	10	24	35	51	292	69%	8.3	2	7.8	7.9%	19	54	17
2013	DET	14/14	610	223	1006	4.5	4	5	-7.8%	32	7	29	38	47%	24	22	54	80	506	68%	9.4	3	8.7	5.8%	20	94	13
2014	*DET*			*201*	*921*	*4.6*	*3*	*2*	*2.1%*								*57*	*83*	*450*	*69%*	*7.9*	*1*		*-6.7%*			

Another Bushtastic season. Bush continued his mid-career trend of hovering close to 1,000 rushing yards while giving DVOA plenty to quibble with: two of his three 100-yard games came against the defensively-dismantled Bears, he fumbled five times, provided zilch as a third-down rusher (just two carries), and so on. Bush still has all-purpose usefulness, but so does backup Joique Bell, who out DVOA'd him as both a rusher and receiver. The Lions plan something close to a 50-50 split between Bush and Bell, which may be as close to meritocracy they are willing to come in a season when Bush is making $4.5 million with bonuses.

Bush turned 29 in March, but do not expect him to follow the typical running back aging curve. Athletically, he is an outlier, and his performance variables for most of his career so far depended on ever-wavering focus and reliability, not twitch muscle mass. He could fall off the 1,000-yard train this season but reemerge two years later if both he and an employer get hungry at the same time. He is also a prime candidate to have a weird Herschel Walker ending to his career, hanging around as a return man for hire long after it seems like he should.

Travaris Cadet Height: 6-1 Weight: 210 College: Appalachian State Draft: 2012/FA Born: 1-Feb-1989 Age: 25 Risk: Red

Year	Team	G/GS	Snaps	Runs	Yds	Yd/R	TD	FUM	DVOA	Rk	DYAR	Rk	YAR	Suc%	Rk	BTkl	Rec	Pass	Yds	C%	Yd/C	TD	YAC	DVOA	Rk	DYAR	Rk
2012	NO	13/0	28	1	5	5.0	0	0	45.0%	--	2	--	2	100%	--	1	5	8	44	63%	8.8	0	10.8	4.9%	--	8	--
2013	NO	13/0	11	0	0	0.0	0	0	0.0%	--	0	--	0	--	--	0	2	2	5	100%	2.5	1	3.0	76.1%	--	11	--
2014	*NO*			*63*	*310*	*4.9*	*3*	*3*	*9.9%*								*45*	*67*	*400*	*67%*	*8.9*	*2*		*-11.6%*			

Cadet was New Orleans' primary kickoff returner in 2012, but the Saints used Darren Sproles more in that role last season. Sproles' departure leaves Cadet as the likely candidate to take over both kick and punt return duties (he did both at Appalachian State). He's also been practicing in Sproles' old role in the offense as the running back who runs a lot of routes, and Sean Payton has suggested he's a candidate to grab some of those snaps in the offense. At 6-foot-1, he certainly gives Drew Brees a much bigger target than Sproles did.

Ka'Deem Carey

Height: 5-9 Weight: 207 College: Arizona Draft: 2014/4 (117) Born: 30-Oct-1992 Age: 22 Risk: Green

Year	Team	G/GS	Snaps	Runs	Yds	Yd/R	TD	FUM	DVOA	Rk	DYAR	Rk	YAR	Suc%	Rk	BTkl	Rec	Pass	Yds	C%	Yd/C	TD	YAC	DVOA	Rk	DYAR	Rk
2014	*CHI*			*103*	*437*	*4.2*	*3*	*1*	*-2.3%*								*15*	*19*	*99*	*79%*	*6.6*	*1*		*-7.8%*			

Carey touched the ball 714 times in two seasons as the workhorse in Rich Rodriguez's read-option Arizona offense. He's a tough runner with good vision, but at 207 pounds with a skinny frame, Carey has absorbed an awful lot of inside punishment. Carey can do many of the things that Matt Forte does well—he has good hands, blocks with effort, and can use a stutter-step to create space up the middle—allowing him to do more as a committee back than plodding Michael Bush could do. It's also hard to talk about Carey without considering the ridiculously slow forty he ran at the combine, just 4.70 seconds. That works out to a miserable Speed Score of 84.8. Then again, Carey had an excellent 7.1 Highlight Yards per Opportunity in 2012 and then a reasonable 4.5 in 2013, so the few advanced metrics we do have for analyzing college running backs are split on the guy.

Jamaal Charles

Height: 5-11 Weight: 200 College: Texas Draft: 2008/3 (73) Born: 27-Dec-1986 Age: 28 Risk: Yellow

Year	Team	G/GS	Snaps	Runs	Yds	Yd/R	TD	FUM	DVOA	Rk	DYAR	Rk	YAR	Suc%	Rk	BTkl	Rec	Pass	Yds	C%	Yd/C	TD	YAC	DVOA	Rk	DYAR	Rk
2011	KC	2/1	34	12	83	6.9	0	1	-4.9%	--	2	--	6	50%	--	1	5	6	9	83%	1.8	1	-0.4	-29.7%	--	-5	--
2012	KC	16/15	577	285	1509	5.3	5	5	1.4%	17	109	12	158	46%	29	16	35	49	236	73%	6.7	1	7.3	-13.8%	32	0	32
2013	KC	15/15	845	259	1287	5.0	12	4	13.7%	7	247	3	258	51%	11	39	70	104	693	67%	9.9	7	9.4	8.5%	17	135	8
2014	*KC*			*267*	*1304*	*4.9*	*9*	*4*	*6.7%*								*70*	*91*	*549*	*77%*	*7.8*	*3*		*16.7%*			

Ladies and gentlemen, we'd like to re-introduce you to Mr. Jamaal Charles, also known as The Sum of Kansas City's Offense. The only back in the league last year to lead his team in targets, catches, receiving yards, and touchdowns, Charles was also the beneficiary of Andy Reid's gameplan for Alex Smith—check it down, and do so as often as possible. The fact that the Saints were the only team to throw more receiver screens than the Chiefs last year, detailed in the Kansas City chapter, doesn't even tell the whole story—New Orleans had 651 passing attempts to Kansas City's 546. Charles was Kansas City's leading red-zone receiver with 18 targets; he and tight end Anthony Fasano were the only Chiefs receivers with 10 or more targets to post a positive DVOA down past the 20. Oh, yeah—there's also the small matter of Charles' most productive rushing season since 2010, when he led the league in rushing DYAR and DVOA. He's not a third-down back per se (-25.1% DVOA on 22 third- and fourth-down carries), and nobody will ever mistake him for Marshawn Lynch between the guards (though he did score nine touchdowns on 17 goal-to-go carries), but these are relatively insignificant dings for a player who was as valuable to his team as any player in the league last season. If Alex Smith does get that fat new contract from the Chiefs, he should tithe at least half of it to his primary running back.

Tashard Choice

Height: 5-10 Weight: 215 College: Georgia Tech Draft: 2008/4 (122) Born: 20-Nov-1984 Age: 30 Risk: #N/A

Year	Team	G/GS	Snaps	Runs	Yds	Yd/R	TD	FUM	DVOA	Rk	DYAR	Rk	YAR	Suc%	Rk	BTkl	Rec	Pass	Yds	C%	Yd/C	TD	YAC	DVOA	Rk	DYAR	Rk
2011	3TM	13/1	229	57	152	2.7	1	3	-42.4%	--	-85	--	-96	36%	--	3	19	31	124	65%	6.5	0	8.0	-62.2%	51	-71	51
2012	BUF	12/0	124	47	193	4.1	1	0	3.2%	--	23	--	21	43%	--	4	4	9	9	44%	2.3	0	5.8	-101.9%	--	-45	--
2013	2TM	15/0	125	46	170	3.7	0	0	-4.0%	--	9	--	9	46%	--	3	5	9	15	56%	3.0	0	4.4	-51.9%	--	-16	--

Choice, who has now played for four different teams since the start of the 2011 season, has averaged just 3.5 yards per carry since 2010—including 3.6 yards per carry in 12 games last season with the Bills. (He ended the season with three games in Indy, primarily working in relief of Trent Richardson.) He will turn 30 this season, and is likely near the end of the road.

Benny Cunningham

Height: 5-10 Weight: 217 College: Middle Tennessee St. Draft: 2013/FA Born: 7-Jul-1990 Age: 24 Risk: Blue

Year	Team	G/GS	Snaps	Runs	Yds	Yd/R	TD	FUM	DVOA	Rk	DYAR	Rk	YAR	Suc%	Rk	BTkl	Rec	Pass	Yds	C%	Yd/C	TD	YAC	DVOA	Rk	DYAR	Rk
2013	STL	14/0	138	47	261	5.6	1	2	-5.7%	--	5	--	20	45%	--	6	6	10	59	60%	9.8	0	10.2	3.6%	--	8	--
2014	*STL*			*30*	*141*	*4.7*	*2*	*0*	*10.4%*								*9*	*11*	*69*	*82%*	*7.6*	*0*		*7.8%*			

Cunningham, an undrafted rookie from Middle Tennessee, carried 13 times for 109 yards against the Bears but 34 times for 152 yards against the rest of the NFL. Rushing against the Bears last year was like getting lucky in a brothel, and while Cunningham was also effective against the enigmatic Colts, the Rams were wise to hold off on the Benny Parade. Tre Mason and Zac Stacy should get the bulk of the carries this year, with Isaiah Pead as the theoretical third-down back, but Rams running-back committees shake out in unusual ways. See: Daryl Richardson's career.

Knile Davis Height: 5-11 Weight: 227 College: Arkansas Draft: 2013/3 (95) Born: 5-Oct-1991 Age: 23 Risk: Green

Year	Team	G/GS	Snaps	Runs	Yds	Yd/R	TD	FUM	DVOA	Rk	DYAR	Rk	YAR	Suc%	Rk	BTkl	Rec	Pass	Yds	C%	Yd/C	TD	YAC	DVOA	Rk	DYAR	Rk
2013	KC	16/1	170	70	242	3.5	4	2	-19.4%	--	-29	--	-15	34%	--	7	11	15	75	73%	6.8	0	8.3	-27.0%	--	-11	--
2014	*KC*			*50*	*201*	*4.0*	*2*	*2*	*-8.2%*								*16*	*21*	*114*	*76%*	*7.1*	*0*		*-0.1%*			

There are two things preventing Davis from becoming a major force in Kansas City's backfield in the 2014 season: the fractured fibula he suffered in the wild-card loss to the Colts, and the transcendent excellence of Jamaal Charles. And frankly, the fractured fibula (which didn't require surgery; Davis participated in OTAs) will be easier to get past. Still, it's tough to leave Davis on the bench, especially when he's so dynamic in short areas and power situations—he led the NFL among players with at least 10 red-zone carries with his 86.9% DVOA, and with his size/speed combination, it would be easy to imagine a scenario in which Davis is tasked more often to complement Charles' assets with his own. Of course, this would require a head coach and offensive play designer who runs a lot of two-back sets and calls running plays frequently, and Andy Reid is not that guy; only Detroit ranked lower in their percentage of formations with two or more backs than Kansas City's 27 percent. So, that's the third thing. In the interim, special teams coach Dave Toub says that the sky's the limit for Davis as a returner. Eventually, Davis will get his shot here or elsewhere, and he's got a good shot of making the most of it.

Lance Dunbar Height: 5-8 Weight: 191 College: North Texas Draft: 2012/FA Born: 25-Jan-1990 Age: 24 Risk: Blue

Year	Team	G/GS	Snaps	Runs	Yds	Yd/R	TD	FUM	DVOA	Rk	DYAR	Rk	YAR	Suc%	Rk	BTkl	Rec	Pass	Yds	C%	Yd/C	TD	YAC	DVOA	Rk	DYAR	Rk
2012	DAL	12/0	91	21	75	3.6	0	0	-13.9%	--	-5	--	-2	52%	--	2	6	12	33	50%	5.5	0	4.0	-41.4%	--	-20	--
2013	DAL	9/0	51	30	150	5.0	0	1	16.8%	--	31	--	22	60%	--	3	7	7	59	100%	8.4	0	8.7	-17.3%	--	-1	--
2014	*DAL*			*31*	*122*	*3.9*	*1*	*0*	*-10.9%*								*12*	*15*	*102*	*80%*	*8.5*	*0*		*11.6%*			

When Dallas remembers to run the ball, DeMarco Murray will still get the majority of carries, but Dunbar will battle Joseph Randle and Ryan Williams to be option No. 2. Dunbar had Dallas' longest run of 2013: a 45-yard scamper against Oakland where he made nearly half the defense miss him. That was also his last game of the season thanks to a knee injury. There's not much separating Dunbar and Randle. Murray has missed at least two games in all three of his seasons, so it's likely there will come a time when Dunbar's called upon to produce, but don't expect big things. Dunbar has his own laundry list of injury problems, he's only had 51 career carries, and he was taken off the kick return unit last year.

Jonathan Dwyer Height: 5-11 Weight: 229 College: Georgia Tech Draft: 2010/6 (188) Born: 26-Jul-1989 Age: 25 Risk: Green

Year	Team	G/GS	Snaps	Runs	Yds	Yd/R	TD	FUM	DVOA	Rk	DYAR	Rk	YAR	Suc%	Rk	BTkl	Rec	Pass	Yds	C%	Yd/C	TD	YAC	DVOA	Rk	DYAR	Rk
2011	PIT	7/0	28	16	123	7.7	0	0	8.8%	--	11	--	10	38%	--	2	1	1	6	100%	6.0	0	4.0	22.4%	--	1	--
2012	PIT	13/6	380	156	623	4.0	2	2	-18.0%	39	-60	38	-40	44%	31	29	18	25	106	72%	5.9	0	5.8	-8.2%	27	8	31
2013	PIT	15/0	138	49	197	4.0	0	0	-18.7%	--	-25	--	-8	47%	--	3	8	11	64	73%	8.0	0	6.4	8.5%	--	12	--
2014	*ARI*			*56*	*225*	*4.0*	*1*	*2*	*-10.0%*								*12*	*15*	*79*	*80%*	*6.5*	*0*		*1.1%*			

Dwyer did a lot of work in Pittsburgh to have a pretty forgettable four-year run. He was ineffective early and had to lose weight. He battled injuries, he had a few breakout 100-yard games in 2012, but he couldn't secure consistent playing time last year even with Le'Veon Bell injured to start the season. Unsurprisingly, Bruce Arians smuggled another Steelers player across Arizona state lines this offseason, but this will be even less notable than the Rashard Mendenhall move.

Andre Ellington Height: 5-9 Weight: 199 College: Clemson Draft: 2013/6 (187) Born: 3-Feb-1989 Age: 25 Risk: Yellow

Year	Team	G/GS	Snaps	Runs	Yds	Yd/R	TD	FUM	DVOA	Rk	DYAR	Rk	YAR	Suc%	Rk	BTkl	Rec	Pass	Yds	C%	Yd/C	TD	YAC	DVOA	Rk	DYAR	Rk
2013	ARI	15/1	405	118	652	5.5	3	1	17.5%	4	117	15	107	46%	30	28	39	57	371	68%	9.5	1	6.7	22.3%	10	117	10
2014	*ARI*			*234*	*1050*	*4.5*	*6*	*2*	*-0.1%*								*56*	*81*	*462*	*69%*	*8.3*	*1*		*-1.1%*			

Ellington averaged 5.53 yards per rush last year. The rest of the running backs on Arizona's roster averaged 3.16, primarily because the coaching staff gave 216 carries to the now-retired Rashard Mendenhall. Will Ellington be more Jerious Norwood (who had a high yards per carry in a limited role for years in Atlanta) or Jamaal Charles? The opportunity is there for a big season, so long as the coaching staff trusts him for 15 to 20 touches per game. Ellington averaged over 80 yards from scrimmage over the last eight games last year, and KUBIAK believes he is in line for a slight improvement on those numbers with Mendenhall gone.

Matt Forte Height: 6-2 Weight: 218 College: Tulane Draft: 2008/2 (44) Born: 10-Dec-1985 Age: 29 Risk: Green

Year	Team	G/GS	Snaps	Runs	Yds	Yd/R	TD	FUM	DVOA	Rk	DYAR	Rk	YAR	Suc%	Rk	BTkl	Rec	Pass	Yds	C%	Yd/C	TD	YAC	DVOA	Rk	DYAR	Rk
2011	CHI	12/12	564	203	997	4.9	3	2	-5.6%	40	24	38	64	45%	35	36	52	76	490	68%	9.4	1	8.0	-5.2%	34	35	28
2012	CHI	15/15	692	248	1094	4.4	5	2	3.1%	15	109	11	81	44%	32	15	44	60	340	73%	7.7	1	6.7	-1.1%	25	40	23
2013	CHI	16/16	928	289	1339	4.6	9	3	7.4%	15	193	4	191	47%	26	24	74	96	594	79%	8.0	3	6.8	8.5%	16	113	11
2014	*CHI*			*276*	*1250*	*4.5*	*9*	*2*	*6.4%*								*69*	*96*	*593*	*72%*	*8.6*	*2*		*5.7%*			

Exhibit B in the case against the Bears' offensive line and philosophy from 2010-2013; Exhibit A is Jay Cutler's sack totals. Running backs are not supposed to have their best statistical seasons when they are 28 years old, but Forte blossomed in a Goldilocks system that gave him decent blocking and plenty of opportunities as a rusher and receiver. Gone were the eight-carry, abandon-the-run efforts of the Mike Martz era and the 21-carry, 63-yard force feedings of the Mike Tice experience. Forte's role and production were dependable without being predictable, and he upgraded to four 20+-carry, 100+-yard efforts in December, when Josh McCown was under center or Jay Cutler was just back from injury.

If you know anything about running back aging patterns, you know that the good times are not likely to roll much longer for Forte. Marc Trestman is reasonable about carry totals and change-up rusher usage, so Forte's decline may be slower than typical backs approaching 30. At worst, his 2014 season may look like his 2010-12 seasons, which did not look bad until we saw what he is really capable of.

Arian Foster Height: 6-1 Weight: 225 College: Tennessee Draft: 2009/FA Born: 24-Aug-1986 Age: 28 Risk: Red

Year	Team	G/GS	Snaps	Runs	Yds	Yd/R	TD	FUM	DVOA	Rk	DYAR	Rk	YAR	Suc%	Rk	BTkl	Rec	Pass	Yds	C%	Yd/C	TD	YAC	DVOA	Rk	DYAR	Rk
2011	HOU	13/13	643	278	1224	4.4	10	5	2.3%	24	122	14	126	44%	39	32	53	73	617	74%	11.6	2	11.3	18.8%	15	127	4
2012	HOU	16/16	831	351	1424	4.1	15	3	-1.6%	20	105	13	139	47%	27	28	40	58	217	69%	5.4	2	6.9	-28.0%	41	-43	43
2013	HOU	8/8	327	121	542	4.5	1	0	11.4%	8	99	19	85	50%	16	9	22	35	183	63%	8.3	1	9.5	-9.2%	33	9	33
2014	*HOU*			*293*	*1297*	*4.4*	*7*	*3*	*1.6%*								*39*	*54*	*262*	*72%*	*6.7*	*2*		*-2.0%*			

Foster is a rarity in many ways. He overcame a middling college career to seize a starting NFL job. He actually carries a Twitter account that asks engaging questions rather than auto-posting "Rise and Grind" every morning. As he's gotten older, Foster has also become the rare back to get most of his yards purely on vision. Foster finished 38th in average Yards After Contact last season, sandwiched between speedy backs C.J. Spiller and Reggie Bush near the bottom of the list of qualifying backs.

Another reason Foster is rare is his contract: Foster and Ray Rice will probably be the last two running backs to carry a cap number over $8 million for a while. So far, they've both proven to be reasons why you don't give a back a big contract. Foster dealt with back and hamstring injuries in 2013, and his fantasy value will be boosted in Bill O'Brien's offense since he'll be catching more passes, but don't bet on him regaining star running back status. Though if he did, it'd certainly fit how unique his pattern has been.

Johnathan Franklin Height: 5-10 Weight: 205 College: UCLA Draft: 2013/4 (125) Born: 23-Oct-1989 Age: 25 Risk: #N/A

Year	Team	G/GS	Snaps	Runs	Yds	Yd/R	TD	FUM	DVOA	Rk	DYAR	Rk	YAR	Suc%	Rk	BTkl	Rec	Pass	Yds	C%	Yd/C	TD	YAC	DVOA	Rk	DYAR	Rk
2013	GB	11/0	62	19	107	5.6	1	2	12.2%	--	19	--	22	58%	--	5	4	5	30	80%	7.5	0	6.8	28.1%	--	15	--

A neck injury Franklin suffered while returning a kickoff against Minnesota in Week 12 will end his career before it really started. Would this be the case if Franklin had suffered this injury 30 years ago, before we knew all that we now know about concussions and other head and neck injuries? Perhaps he would have come back and had some kind of NFL career, giving him a lot more money and also a far worse quality of life upon retirement. Instead, Franklin will be able to move on and do something else and at least enjoy the rest of his life. And he's a man with plans: he was a political science major at UCLA and his stated goal is to become mayor of Los Angeles. In college, he interned with then-mayor Antonio Villaraigosa.

Devonta Freeman Height: 5-8 Weight: 206 College: Florida St. Draft: 2014/4 (103) Born: 15-Mar-1992 Age: 22 Risk: Yellow

Year	Team	G/GS	Snaps	Runs	Yds	Yd/R	TD	FUM	DVOA	Rk	DYAR	Rk	YAR	Suc%	Rk	BTkl	Rec	Pass	Yds	C%	Yd/C	TD	YAC	DVOA	Rk	DYAR	Rk
2014	*ATL*			*63*	*251*	*4.0*	*1*	*1*	*0.2%*								*21*	*33*	*165*	*60%*	*7.9*	*1*		*-11.9%*			

A fourth-round pick, Freeman ran for 14 touchdowns and 5.9 yards per carry (5.8 Highlight Yards per Opportunity) last year at Florida State, adding 278 receiving yards with an 88 percent catch rate. He's short and thick, with similar dimensions to a Maurice Jones-Drew. His Speed Score of 94.0 was below average, but the competition ahead of him in Atlanta is not the best.

Toby Gerhart Height: 6-0 Weight: 231 College: Stanford Draft: 2010/2 (51) Born: 18-Mar-1987 Age: 27 Risk: Yellow

Year	Team	G/GS	Snaps	Runs	Yds	Yd/R	TD	FUM	DVOA	Rk	DYAR	Rk	YAR	Suc%	Rk	BTkl	Rec	Pass	Yds	C%	Yd/C	TD	YAC	DVOA	Rk	DYAR	Rk
2011	MIN	16/5	387	109	531	4.9	1	1	5.4%	14	60	30	42	40%	47	11	23	28	190	82%	8.3	3	7.6	41.2%	3	84	10
2012	MIN	16/0	240	50	169	3.4	1	2	-26.0%	--	-34	--	-44	44%	--	4	20	27	155	74%	7.8	0	7.3	25.0%	6	55	16
2013	MIN	14/0	196	36	283	7.9	2	1	73.6%	--	105	--	102	50%	--	8	13	19	88	68%	6.8	0	6.4	10.7%	--	22	--
2014	*JAC*			*277*	*1177*	*4.2*	*6*	*4*	*-2.6%*								*38*	*52*	*260*	*73%*	*6.8*	*1*		*-7.3%*			

Vikings 2013 Offensive Mismanagement Exhibit Q: Gerhart carried the ball just four times in the Vikings first nine games, even though the team was afraid to throw downfield and Adrian Peterson certainly could have used the occasional breather. Gerhart resumed normal change-up duties when the Vikings abandoned all passing-game hope and was very effective against the Seahawks and Packers (15 carries for 158 yards, much of it admittedly in blowout time against the Seahawks). Gerhart took over for the injured Peterson against the Ravens, then promptly got hurt himself, leaving the Vikings with no choice but to start passing and discover they were not abysmally awful at doing so. The Jaguars envision a 20-30 touch role for Gerhart, which sounds hefty, but Gerhart is an excellent pass protector and pretty good outlet receiver in addition to a power runner, so he is worthy of some sort of multi-purpose role. And the Jaguars, frankly, don't have much else at running back.

Frank Gore Height: 5-9 Weight: 215 College: Miami Draft: 2005/3 (65) Born: 14-May-1983 Age: 31 Risk: Green

Year	Team	G/GS	Snaps	Runs	Yds	Yd/R	TD	FUM	DVOA	Rk	DYAR	Rk	YAR	Suc%	Rk	BTkl	Rec	Pass	Yds	C%	Yd/C	TD	YAC	DVOA	Rk	DYAR	Rk
2011	SF	16/15	687	282	1211	4.3	8	2	-10.0%	44	-17	47	3	42%	45	12	17	31	114	55%	6.7	0	6.0	-17.8%	45	-7	44
2012	SF	16/16	728	258	1214	4.7	8	3	17.4%	4	268	4	212	48%	17	27	28	36	234	78%	8.4	1	7.9	13.1%	12	50	18
2013	SF	16/16	745	276	1128	4.1	9	3	-0.8%	24	91	20	40	42%	38	15	16	26	141	62%	8.8	0	6.3	-16.3%	39	-3	39
2014	*SF*			*205*	*827*	*4.0*	*7*	*2*	*-3.5%*								*13*	*17*	*98*	*76%*	*7.5*	*0*		*3.7%*			

Frank Gore is the all-time leading rusher for the 49ers, which means a couple of things: he has been really good for a decade in the NFL after suffering two serious knee injuries in college, and he is hitting the twilight years in running back terms. Does he have one more good year at age 31? He had the lowest yards per carry (4.1) of his career and the fewest yards from scrimmage in a season since he was a rookie. But that was still enough to finish the season with the 17th-most rushing yards in NFL history for a 30-year-old running back. Over the last 10 games, he averaged only 3.65 yards a carry, and had two games (the finale against Arizona, and the championship game against Seattle) where he had 14 rushing yards.

He'll likely be in more of a platoon situation in 2014 with the likes of Kendall Hunter and rookie Carlos Hyde, where he gets more carries than the others while he remains productive, and while it may not be as good for fantasy owners, it can preserve him over the next couple of years.

BenJarvus Green-Ellis Height: 5-10 Weight: 219 College: Mississippi Draft: 2008/FA Born: 2-Jul-1985 Age: 29 Risk: Red

Year	Team	G/GS	Snaps	Runs	Yds	Yd/R	TD	FUM	DVOA	Rk	DYAR	Rk	YAR	Suc%	Rk	BTkl	Rec	Pass	Yds	C%	Yd/C	TD	YAC	DVOA	Rk	DYAR	Rk
2011	NE	16/6	392	181	667	3.7	11	0	3.9%	18	106	18	115	54%	6	10	9	13	159	69%	17.7	0	15.8	72.8%	--	64	--
2012	CIN	15/15	651	278	1094	3.9	6	3	-8.1%	29	6	29	22	48%	21	14	22	29	104	76%	4.7	0	4.1	-36.9%	44	-39	42
2013	CIN	16/16	464	220	756	3.4	7	2	-11.4%	37	-27	37	27	49%	18	17	4	8	22	50%	5.5	0	2.0	-61.0%	--	-20	--
2014	*CIN*			*46*	*194*	*4.2*	*2*	*0*	*3.7%*								*6*	*8*	*31*	*75%*	*5.2*	*0*		*-10.6%*			

The Law Firm began the season dominating what was supposed to be a split backfield, but as his limitations grew more pronounced vis-a-vis Gio Bernard's, the coaches belatedly evened things out. Bernard actually had two more touches than Green-Ellis by season's end. The downward trends on BJGE's numbers appear irreversible, and the Bengals spent a second-round pick on his replacement, Jeremy Hill. Green-Ellis is considered a pro's pro and is well-liked in the organization, but it's hard to see him entering the courtroom in an orange and black pinstriped suit come fall.

Shonn Greene Height: 6-0 Weight: 227 College: Iowa Draft: 2009/3 (65) Born: 21-Aug-1985 Age: 29 Risk: Green

Year	Team	G/GS	Snaps	Runs	Yds	Yd/R	TD	FUM	DVOA	Rk	DYAR	Rk	YAR	Suc%	Rk	BTkl	Rec	Pass	Yds	C%	Yd/C	TD	YAC	DVOA	Rk	DYAR	Rk
2011	NYJ	16/15	559	253	1054	4.2	6	1	2.2%	25	113	16	127	50%	16	13	30	41	211	73%	7.0	0	6.9	-8.5%	37	12	37
2012	NYJ	16/14	567	276	1063	3.9	8	5	-4.5%	24	49	22	84	52%	9	10	19	31	151	61%	7.9	0	6.9	-41.4%	45	-47	44
2013	TEN	11/0	155	77	295	3.8	4	0	8.9%	--	61	--	58	61%	--	3	6	7	39	86%	6.5	0	10.2	-28.5%	--	-7	--
2014	*TEN*			*142*	*563*	*4.0*	*3*	*1*	*-6.0%*								*13*	*20*	*98*	*65%*	*7.5*	*0*		*-10.7%*			

If fantasy football players decided to lift the template joke about (BLANK) being a pallbearer at their funeral, so they can let them down one last time, Greene would probably be one of their selections. But here we go again: the Tennessee depth chart is underwhelming, and there are reasons to doubt that Bishop Sankey will come in and be effective right away. Greene was miscast a bit as the Titans "power back." His goal-line success rates have actually tended to be very average over the last three years, and he doesn't have the same battering ram style that Jackie Battle does. As long as you can get past the fact that Greene has little upside as a receiver, he's a fine committee back. He's just also one without a defined strength that would really set him apart.

DuJuan Harris Height: 5-7 Weight: 197 College: Troy Draft: 2011/FA Born: 3-Sep-1988 Age: 26 Risk: Green

Year	Team	G/GS	Snaps	Runs	Yds	Yd/R	TD	FUM	DVOA	Rk	DYAR	Rk	YAR	Suc%	Rk	BTkl	Rec	Pass	Yds	C%	Yd/C	TD	YAC	DVOA	Rk	DYAR	Rk
2011	JAC	5/0	48	9	42	4.7	0	0	-2.6%	--	2	--	3	56%	--	1	1	2	4	50%	4.0	0	7.0	-78.5%	--	-7	--
2012	GB	4/2	68	34	157	4.6	2	0	31.1%	--	50	--	41	41%	--	3	2	2	17	100%	8.5	0	10.0	44.0%	--	7	--
2014	GB			76	358	4.7	1	2	1.3%								21	25	205	84%	9.8	1		24.9%			

A small all-purpose back who made a name for himself in the 2012 playoffs (164 total yards, two touchdowns in two games), Harris' 2013 season was ruined by a series of chronic knee ailments that extended from minicamp through the end of August, resulting in arthroscopic surgery and a trip to IR. There is room for a receiver-back behind Eddie Lacy and James Starks, especially now than Johnathan Franklin has been forced to retire. The Packers like to give their running backs second and third chances (check out Ryan Grant's career), so Harris should get a fair training camp opportunity.

Roy Helu Height: 5-11 Weight: 216 College: Nebraska Draft: 2011/4 (105) Born: 7-Dec-1988 Age: 26 Risk: Green

Year	Team	G/GS	Snaps	Runs	Yds	Yd/R	TD	FUM	DVOA	Rk	DYAR	Rk	YAR	Suc%	Rk	BTkl	Rec	Pass	Yds	C%	Yd/C	TD	YAC	DVOA	Rk	DYAR	Rk
2011	WAS	15/5	543	151	640	4.2	2	3	-4.6%	38	25	37	14	47%	24	14	49	59	379	83%	7.7	1	8.6	-0.8%	29	42	25
2012	WAS	3/0	44	2	2	1.0	0	0	-107.9%	--	-10	--	-9	0%	--	1	7	7	45	100%	6.4	0	6.7	14.8%	--	10	--
2013	WAS	16/0	526	62	274	4.4	4	2	8.5%	--	48	--	51	45%	--	9	31	42	251	74%	8.1	0	6.1	-15.0%	38	-3	38
2014	WAS			72	322	4.4	3	1	1.0%								38	51	289	75%	7.6	1		1.0%			

Helu's return from turf toe and Achilles tendon soreness in 2012 was a surprisingly effective one given his surroundings. Over his two healthy seasons, Helu has a weirdly pronounced split between his DVOA ratings on first and third down and his rating on second down. In 2011, it went 6.2%, -27.9%, 38.7% and in 2013 it went 40.9%, -44.4%, 16.8%. Possibly random variation, but still, really strange. There is some talk that Chris Thompson could push Helu for the third-down role, and that makes some sense as Helu isn't by any means a dominant pass catcher out of the backfield. Helu would be a nice lead back for a committee if his own durability weren't such an issue; alas, he'll have to settle for being a quality change-of-pace back.

Peyton Hillis Height: 6-0 Weight: 240 College: Arkansas Draft: 2008/7 (227) Born: 21-Jan-1986 Age: 28 Risk: Red

Year	Team	G/GS	Snaps	Runs	Yds	Yd/R	TD	FUM	DVOA	Rk	DYAR	Rk	YAR	Suc%	Rk	BTkl	Rec	Pass	Yds	C%	Yd/C	TD	YAC	DVOA	Rk	DYAR	Rk
2011	CLE	10/9	462	161	587	3.6	3	2	-1.7%	29	50	33	48	55%	4	4	22	34	130	65%	5.9	0	5.4	-37.4%	48	-43	48
2012	KC	13/2	210	85	309	3.6	1	2	-27.5%	--	-71	--	-42	40%	--	7	10	13	62	77%	6.2	0	7.4	-29.1%	--	-10	--
2013	NYG	7/1	202	73	247	3.4	2	2	-13.3%	--	-14	--	-20	49%	--	4	13	21	96	62%	7.4	0	7.9	-13.5%	--	0	--
2014	NYG			40	144	3.6	2	0	-8.8%								9	14	59	64%	6.6	0		-11.6%			

In retrospect, Hillis' 2010 season may be one of the greatest flukes in NFL history. Since then, the ex-*Madden* cover star has now had three straight seasons—with three different teams—where he's produced fewer than 3.65 yards per carry. Hillis had 61 catches in 2011, but just 63 in the other five seasons of his career. For some reason, the Giants brought him back, but the additions of Rashad Jennings (ex-Raiders) and Andre Williams (Boston College) have Hillis squarely on the roster bubble.

Jeremy Hill Height: 6-1 Weight: 233 College: LSU Draft: 2014/2 (55) Born: 10/20/1992 Age: 22 Risk: Green

Year	Team	G/GS	Snaps	Runs	Yds	Yd/R	TD	FUM	DVOA	Rk	DYAR	Rk	YAR	Suc%	Rk	BTkl	Rec	Pass	Yds	C%	Yd/C	TD	YAC	DVOA	Rk	DYAR	Rk
2014	CIN			100	416	4.1	4	1	-1.5%								19	23	163	83%	8.6	1		5.9%			

A surprising selection in the second round, Hill should supplant BenJarvus Green-Ellis as the power alternative to Gio Bernard in Cincy. His drafting shows the commitment the team has to improving the between-the-tackles run game. Hill has a tremendous blend of size, speed and vision (6.8 Highlight Yards per Opportunity in 2013), and is a good pass-catcher to boot (82 percent catch rate). He had some character concerns entering the draft, but wrote an impassioned letter to every team insisting that his checkered past was behind him. Even Vontaze Burfict didn't go that far.

Ronnie Hillman Height: 5-9 Weight: 200 College: San Diego State Draft: 2012/3 (67) Born: 14-Sep-1991 Age: 23 Risk: Blue

Year	Team	G/GS	Snaps	Runs	Yds	Yd/R	TD	FUM	DVOA	Rk	DYAR	Rk	YAR	Suc%	Rk	BTkl	Rec	Pass	Yds	C%	Yd/C	TD	YAC	DVOA	Rk	DYAR	Rk
2012	DEN	14/0	206	84	327	3.9	1	2	-15.7%	--	-24	--	-15	51%	--	3	10	12	62	83%	6.2	0	6.9	-17.0%	--	-2	--
2013	DEN	10/0	157	55	218	4.0	1	2	-6.9%	--	4	--	3	55%	--	2	12	14	119	86%	9.9	0	6.3	41.1%	--	45	--
2014	*DEN*			*64*	*261*	*4.1*	*2*	*1*	*-5.0%*								*19*	*22*	*140*	*86%*	*7.4*	*0*		*10.5%*			

Hillman's nominal dynamism as a quick-shift space runner has yet to translate into a positive DVOA, notwithstanding the very good success rate (which was in line with that of Denver's other backs). More importantly, he apparently remains an unfinished product when it comes to the blocking skills so important for a Peyton Manning back. He should still have a role as an occasional change of place player, but unless he improved a lot in the offseason, don't expect him to get a big workload or become the new lead back if Montee Ball goes down.

Kendall Hunter Height: 5-7 Weight: 199 College: Oklahoma State Draft: 2011/4 (115) Born: 16-Sep-1988 Age: 26 Risk: Green

Year	Team	G/GS	Snaps	Runs	Yds	Yd/R	TD	FUM	DVOA	Rk	DYAR	Rk	YAR	Suc%	Rk	BTkl	Rec	Pass	Yds	C%	Yd/C	TD	YAC	DVOA	Rk	DYAR	Rk
2011	SF	16/1	288	112	473	4.2	2	0	-6.5%	41	9	41	31	46%	30	7	16	26	195	62%	12.2	0	11.0	21.5%	10	50	22
2012	SF	11/0	170	72	371	5.2	2	0	29.1%	--	109	--	108	60%	--	5	9	12	60	75%	6.7	0	6.3	17.7%	--	21	--
2013	SF	16/0	189	78	358	4.6	3	1	-3.0%	--	16	--	2	36%	--	8	2	4	13	50%	6.5	0	8.0	-40.9%	--	-6	--
2014	*SF*			*69*	*301*	*4.4*	*3*	*2*	*0.5%*								*6*	*9*	*52*	*67%*	*8.7*	*0*		*2.5%*			

Hunter is kind of in purgatory in San Francisco, stuck between the veteran and all of the shiny new toys. He has averaged 4.6 yards a carry over the last three seasons serving as Frank Gore's backup. The four other backs since 1990 to have between 50 and 150 carries and average more than 4.1 yards per carry for three straight years at age 23 to 25: Charlie Garner (behind Ricky Watters), Jerious Norwood (behind Warrick Dunn), Michael Turner (behind LaDainian Tomlinson), and Pierre Thomas. Hunter was having a fine season in 2012 when it was ended by an Achilles injury, and was not quite as explosive in 2013. He's in the final year of his rookie contract, and could be playing for more touches elsewhere in 2014, with Carlos Hyde and Marcus Lattimore waiting behind Gore.

Carlos Hyde Height: 6-0 Weight: 230 College: Ohio St. Draft: 2014/2 (57) Born: 9/20/1991 Age: 23 Risk: Yellow

Year	Team	G/GS	Snaps	Runs	Yds	Yd/R	TD	FUM	DVOA	Rk	DYAR	Rk	YAR	Suc%	Rk	BTkl	Rec	Pass	Yds	C%	Yd/C	TD	YAC	DVOA	Rk	DYAR	Rk
2014	*SF*			*101*	*413*	*4.1*	*2*	*1*	*-11.2%*								*10*	*14*	*91*	*71%*	*9.1*	*0*		*4.1%*			

Hyde finished his Ohio State career with nine consecutive 100-yard rushing games, and 5.0 Highlight Yards per Opportunity is pretty good for a power back. He went into the draft as one of the backs most likely to make an immediate impact, but he will be part of a very crowded backfield in San Francisco. He should be part of a committee rotation in 2014 as the power back who can get carries to close out games, and is the most logical heir apparent to Frank Gore in 2015.

Mark Ingram Height: 5-11 Weight: 215 College: Alabama Draft: 2011/1 (28) Born: 21-Dec-1989 Age: 25 Risk: Blue

Year	Team	G/GS	Snaps	Runs	Yds	Yd/R	TD	FUM	DVOA	Rk	DYAR	Rk	YAR	Suc%	Rk	BTkl	Rec	Pass	Yds	C%	Yd/C	TD	YAC	DVOA	Rk	DYAR	Rk
2011	NO	10/4	215	122	474	3.9	5	1	2.3%	22	63	29	47	56%	3	9	11	13	46	85%	4.2	0	3.6	-27.1%	--	-11	--
2012	NO	16/5	266	156	602	3.9	5	0	0.8%	19	62	19	56	49%	15	13	6	10	29	60%	4.8	0	5.3	-45.4%	--	-21	--
2013	NO	11/3	168	78	386	4.9	1	0	4.6%	--	45	--	41	49%	--	15	7	11	68	64%	9.7	0	10.9	-5.4%	--	5	--
2014	*NO*			*84*	*326*	*3.9*	*1*	*3*	*-14.4%*								*9*	*11*	*93*	*82%*	*10.3*	*0*		*22.7%*			

The Saints seem to be losing confidence in Ingram. His carries per game have dropped from 12.2 as a rookie to 9.8 in 2012 to 7.1 last season. And though his rate stats jumped a bit last season, those are skewed by a 14-carry, 145-yard outing in Week 10 against a Dallas defense that was playing without Jason Hatcher. Take that game away and he fell below 4.0 yards per carry for the third straight year. Ingram was effective in the playoffs, gaining 146 yards on 28 carries against Philadelphia and Seattle, but a lost fumble against the Seahawks didn't do much to endear him to the coaching staff. The Saints declined to pick up the fifth year of his rookie contract, and the former first-round draft pick figures to be done in New Orleans after this season. It's probably best for everyone if the 2009 Heisman Trophy winner gets a fresh start somewhere else.

Chris Ivory Height: 6-0 Weight: 222 College: Tiffin Draft: 2010/FA Born: 22-Mar-1988 Age: 26 Risk: Green

Year	Team	G/GS	Snaps	Runs	Yds	Yd/R	TD	FUM	DVOA	Rk	DYAR	Rk	YAR	Suc%	Rk	BTkl	Rec	Pass	Yds	C%	Yd/C	TD	YAC	DVOA	Rk	DYAR	Rk
2011	NO	6/2	120	79	374	4.7	1	0	10.4%	--	64	--	74	58%	--	9	0	1	0	0%	0.0	0	0.0	-84.4%	--	-3	--
2012	NO	6/2	67	40	217	5.4	2	0	12.5%	--	33	--	34	48%	--	14	2	3	15	67%	7.5	0	14.0	-7.3%	--	1	--
2013	NYJ	15/6	331	182	833	4.6	3	2	-8.3%	33	2	33	38	44%	33	20	2	7	10	29%	5.0	0	4.0	-58.2%	--	-19	--
2014	*NYJ*			*120*	*562*	*4.7*	*2*	*2*	*3.6%*								*4*	*6*	*29*	*67%*	*7.3*	*0*		*-0.4%*			

After spending years in a crowded Saints backfield, Ivory was positioned to be the lead back with the Jets. But Bilal Powell stole the top job in training camp after Ivory was again slowed down by injuries. Ivory wound up playing well when healthy, however, and wound up leading New York in rushing. Despite recording just 182 carries, he was one of just four backs (Alfred Morris, LeSean McCoy, DeMarco Murray) with seven runs of 25+ yards last year. Injuries are always going to be a concern, but Ivory combines explosiveness with productive running when it counts (DVOA of 7.2% on third or fourth downs). He also ranked fourth in yards after first contact (2.1). Playing time will again be an issue in 2014 now that the Jets signed Chris Johnson. Ivory has only five career catches, and Johnson's edge in the passing game will likely leave Ivory on the bench for the majority of snaps.

Fred Jackson Height: 6-1 Weight: 215 College: Coe College Draft: 2007/FA Born: 20-Feb-1981 Age: 33 Risk: Red

Year	Team	G/GS	Snaps	Runs	Yds	Yd/R	TD	FUM	DVOA	Rk	DYAR	Rk	YAR	Suc%	Rk	BTkl	Rec	Pass	Yds	C%	Yd/C	TD	YAC	DVOA	Rk	DYAR	Rk
2011	BUF	10/10	567	170	934	5.5	6	2	13.7%	6	161	7	165	54%	7	33	39	50	442	78%	11.3	0	12.1	23.1%	9	97	9
2012	BUF	10/8	329	115	437	3.8	3	5	-14.3%	35	-27	32	-38	47%	26	19	34	42	217	81%	6.4	1	6.5	-8.4%	28	13	27
2013	BUF	16/6	663	206	890	4.3	9	3	9.1%	11	163	8	170	51%	9	27	47	66	387	71%	8.2	1	8.8	0.8%	23	52	20
2014	*BUF*			*163*	*731*	*4.5*	*6*	*2*	*3.4%*								*38*	*51*	*332*	*75%*	*8.7*	*1*		*10.4%*			

When healthy, Jackson is a perfectly capable back who has carved out a niche for himself in his seven seasons with the Bills as a steady and consistent presence between the tackles. He's had at least 170 carries, 890 yards and an average of 4.2 yards per carry in four of the last five seasons. But entering the final year of his contract—and with the recent pickup of Bryce Brown, which sparked awkward exchange on Twitter between Fred and DeSean Jackson, the latter of whom anointed Brown the "Day 1 starter"—there's a distinct feeling this could be the last year in Buffalo for Jackson. The Coe College alum, who turned 33 this offseason, said shortly after the 2013 season that he believes he can still play another three to four years. Given the fact that he fought through broken ribs and knee issues as a 32-year-old, that might be a long shot. If he does stay healthy and is still able to turn in a consistent performance when he does get his reps, it wouldn't be out of the realm to see Jackson try to take his act to a championship contender after the 2014 season as a part-time back in hopes of finishing a nice career on a high note.

Steven Jackson Height: 6-3 Weight: 229 College: Oregon State Draft: 2004/1 (24) Born: 22-Jul-1983 Age: 31 Risk: Green

Year	Team	G/GS	Snaps	Runs	Yds	Yd/R	TD	FUM	DVOA	Rk	DYAR	Rk	YAR	Suc%	Rk	BTkl	Rec	Pass	Yds	C%	Yd/C	TD	YAC	DVOA	Rk	DYAR	Rk
2011	STL	15/15	714	260	1145	4.4	5	2	-2.3%	31	64	27	67	39%	48	20	42	58	333	72%	7.9	1	7.4	0.2%	28	43	23
2012	STL	16/16	706	257	1042	4.1	4	0	5.3%	11	147	10	59	47%	28	21	38	53	321	72%	8.4	0	7.4	11.7%	14	72	12
2013	ATL	12/12	417	157	543	3.5	6	0	-8.8%	35	-2	35	-9	40%	40	15	33	49	191	67%	5.8	1	6.1	-26.0%	46	-36	47
2014	*ATL*			*187*	*781*	*4.2*	*4*	*1*	*-2.0%*								*36*	*50*	*267*	*72%*	*7.4*	*1*		*-2.7%*			

It turns out that replacing one aging runner with another is a bad move. Brought in last season to supplant Michael Turner, Jackson missed four games with a hamstring injury, and even when he was healthy he only carried the ball 13.1 times a game, his lowest rate since he backed up Marshall Faulk as a rookie. His first game in a Falcons uniform was a success, as he gained 77 yards on 11 carries against New Orleans, but he only topped a 4.0-yard average in two other games all season. The Falcons did little to acquire talent here, adding only fourth-round draftee Devonta Freeman, so Jackson seems likely to be Atlanta's top rusher again this year. That's not really a good thing. Jackson spent the bulk of his stellar career toiling away for a St. Louis club that was regularly one of the worst teams in the league. It would be great to see him contend for a Super Bowl in his final years, but things didn't work out that way.

Brandon Jacobs Height: 6-4 Weight: 264 College: Southern Illinois Draft: 2005/4 (110) Born: 6-Jul-1982 Age: 32 Risk: #N/A

Year	Team	G/GS	Snaps	Runs	Yds	Yd/R	TD	FUM	DVOA	Rk	DYAR	Rk	YAR	Suc%	Rk	BTkl	Rec	Pass	Yds	C%	Yd/C	TD	YAC	DVOA	Rk	DYAR	Rk
2011	NYG	14/6	297	152	571	3.8	7	3	-3.2%	35	35	34	29	49%	18	15	15	22	128	68%	8.5	1	7.9	1.0%	--	19	--
2012	SF	2/0	10	5	7	1.4	0	0	-35.1%	--	-5	--	-6	20%	--	0	0	--	0	--	0.0	0	--	--	--	--	--
2013	NYG	7/1	143	58	238	4.1	4	1	-0.2%	--	21	--	38	47%	--	6	2	7	13	29%	6.5	0	7.5	-41.3%	--	-9	--

It's nice to come home. Jacobs was able to put his awful San Francisco experience behind him with one more reasonable year for the Giants before retiring. He ends his career fourth on the Giants' all-time rushing yardage list. That sounds ridiculous, right? But as Mike Tanier points out in the updated Running Back Top Fives in *A Good Walkthrough Spoiled: The Best of Mike Tanier at Football Outsiders* (on sale now!), the Giants' storied history is filled with multi-position rusher-receiver types like Frank Gifford and Joe Morrison as well as "a gap from 1964 to 1984 when they might as well have been playing competitive backgammon." And so it goes Tiki Barner, Rodney Hampton, Joe Morris, and then Jacobs. He has two Super Bowl rings as well. This career will look a lot better in hindsight.

Mike James Height: 5-10 Weight: 223 College: Miami Draft: 2013/6 (189) Born: 13-Apr-1991 Age: 23 Risk: Red

Year	Team	G/GS	Snaps	Runs	Yds	Yd/R	TD	FUM	DVOA	Rk	DYAR	Rk	YAR	Suc%	Rk	BTkl	Rec	Pass	Yds	C%	Yd/C	TD	YAC	DVOA	Rk	DYAR	Rk
2013	TB	8/3	155	60	295	4.9	0	0	14.6%	--	59	--	54	52%	--	5	10	11	43	91%	4.3	0	4.9	-30.5%	--	-10	--
2014	*TB*			*71*	*321*	*4.5*	*1*	*2*	*-2.1%*								*16*	*19*	*135*	*84%*	*8.4*	*1*		*18.7%*			

When Doug Martin was injured in Week 6 against Atlanta, there was little indication that James would be anything special. He carried 14 times for 45 yards that week, and just 10 times for 39 yards a week later against Carolina. And then the winless Bucs traveled to Seattle and James went crazy, ripping the league's best defense for 158 yards on 28 carries and also throwing a touchdown pass as Tampa Bay took the Seahawks to overtime. He carried the ball only five more times (for 41 more yards!) before his own season ended with a fractured ankle. The Bucs added Charles Sims in the draft and expect Martin to be healthy again, which means James will likely have to win a camp battle with Bobby Rainey to keep his roster spot. If he is cut, he likely won't be unemployed for long.

Rashad Jennings Height: 6-1 Weight: 231 College: Liberty Draft: 2009/7 (250) Born: 26-Mar-1985 Age: 29 Risk: Yellow

Year	Team	G/GS	Snaps	Runs	Yds	Yd/R	TD	FUM	DVOA	Rk	DYAR	Rk	YAR	Suc%	Rk	BTkl	Rec	Pass	Yds	C%	Yd/C	TD	YAC	DVOA	Rk	DYAR	Rk
2011	JAC	0/0	0	0	0	0.0	0	--	--	--	--	--	--	--	--	--	0	--	0	--	0.0	0	--	--	--	--	--
2012	JAC	10/6	330	101	283	2.8	2	3	-31.8%	42	-97	41	-81	38%	40	15	19	26	130	73%	6.8	0	8.2	-22.6%	37	-11	37
2013	OAK	15/8	548	163	733	4.5	6	0	15.8%	5	164	7	158	47%	25	9	36	46	292	76%	8.1	0	8.7	3.3%	22	44	21
2014	*NYG*			*225*	*887*	*3.9*	*7*	*2*	*-4.7%*								*41*	*50*	*334*	*82%*	*8.2*	*1*		*15.2%*			

Jennings' direct, unsubtle game meshed well with the direct, unsubtle 2013 Raiders rushing offense, as it had with the Jaguars' similarly-schemed rushing offense. A (marginally) better offensive line and quarterback situation made for a much more productive overall season of mashing forward on gap plays and driving his legs for as many yards as he could get. There's not much of an explosive element to his game; the play where he stiff-armed Texans safety D.J. Swearinger in the hole and rumbled 80 yards was the second run of more than 28 yards in his career. Still, he has a three-down skill set and the Giants seem bullish on his prospects. General manager Jerry Reese referred to him as a bellcow type of back, and he could have a major role in New York this year. He's not young, but Fred Jackson showed us not that long ago that lightly-treaded older backs could have productive seasons at 29.

Chris Johnson Height: 5-11 Weight: 197 College: East Carolina Draft: 2008/1 (24) Born: 23-Sep-1985 Age: 29 Risk: Green

Year	Team	G/GS	Snaps	Runs	Yds	Yd/R	TD	FUM	DVOA	Rk	DYAR	Rk	YAR	Suc%	Rk	BTkl	Rec	Pass	Yds	C%	Yd/C	TD	YAC	DVOA	Rk	DYAR	Rk
2011	TEN	16/16	0	262	1047	4.0	4	3	-15.1%	49	-67	49	-51	41%	46	30	57	79	418	72%	7.3	0	5.9	-5.9%	35	33	29
2012	TEN	16/15	815	276	1243	4.5	6	4	-11.3%	32	-30	33	-6	41%	38	16	36	49	232	76%	6.4	0	6.5	-17.6%	35	-9	36
2013	TEN	16/16	798	279	1077	3.9	6	3	1.5%	22	110	17	75	46%	31	18	42	52	345	81%	8.2	4	9.4	10.8%	14	66	16
2014	*NYJ*			*173*	*765*	*4.4*	*6*	*1*	*6.0%*								*28*	*39*	*227*	*72%*	*8.1*	*1*		*5.8%*			

The theoretical Chris Johnson that Chris Johnson always talks about, the one that has rushed for 2,000 yards four seasons in a row and will do so again in New York this year, is a helluva back. The Chris Johnson of Reality is, instead, a decent committee speed back who is hurt by his limitations. Johnson has demonstrated poor vision for the last few seasons, his boom-and-bust style has produced fewer booms of late, and the less said about his blocking, the better.

Chris Johnson is a better back than his detractors would make him out to be. The problem is that early fantasy success and Johnson's habit of telling everyone from out-of-town reporters to house plants that he'll rush for 2,000 yards this season even though his offensive linemen are a sack of babies who are barely NFL-caliber have made Theoretical Chris Johnson an easy target for pushback. Real Johnson can help the Jets this season; just don't expect the Theoretical Johnson to walk through that door.

Dennis Johnson Height: 5-7 Weight: 193 College: Arkansas Draft: 2013/FA Born: 24-Feb-1990 Age: 24 Risk: Green

Year	Team	G/GS	Snaps	Runs	Yds	Yd/R	TD	FUM	DVOA	Rk	DYAR	Rk	YAR	Suc%	Rk	BTkl	Rec	Pass	Yds	C%	Yd/C	TD	YAC	DVOA	Rk	DYAR	Rk
2013	HOU	8/1	120	49	183	3.7	0	0	-12.8%	--	-10	--	-12	45%	--	2	8	12	46	67%	5.8	0	6.8	-39.3%	--	-18	--
2014	*HOU*			*34*	*150*	*4.4*	*0*	*1*	*-2.9%*								*15*	*18*	*121*	*83%*	*8.1*	*1*		*12.1%*			

A UDFA out of Arkansas, Johnson didn't break training camp with the Texans, but came over from Cleveland's practice squad after Arian Foster hit IR. Johnson is a decent zone runner; he's also supposed to be a very good receiver, able to run routes out of the slot as well as the backfield, though we certainly didn't see that in his performance a year ago. With Andre Brown in town to spell Foster on early downs, Johnson is facing an uphill battle with Bill O'Brien administration sixth-rounder Alfred Blue for his roster spot. The one saving grace of his situation is that neither Foster nor Brown was particularly healthy last season.

Maurice Jones-Drew Height: 5-8 Weight: 205 College: UCLA Draft: 2006/2 (60) Born: 23-Mar-1985 Age: 29 Risk: Green

Year	Team	G/GS	Snaps	Runs	Yds	Yd/R	TD	FUM	DVOA	Rk	DYAR	Rk	YAR	Suc%	Rk	BTkl	Rec	Pass	Yds	C%	Yd/C	TD	YAC	DVOA	Rk	DYAR	Rk
2011	JAC	16/16	780	343	1606	4.7	8	5	5.1%	15	197	3	199	49%	20	37	43	63	374	68%	8.7	3	9.3	2.2%	26	54	18
2012	JAC	6/5	240	86	414	4.8	1	1	-0.9%	--	27	--	42	48%	--	9	14	18	86	78%	6.1	1	5.1	5.8%	--	18	--
2013	JAC	15/15	647	234	803	3.4	5	1	-13.6%	38	-49	42	-66	37%	43	20	43	60	314	72%	7.3	0	7.7	-3.7%	28	32	27
2014	*OAK*			*120*	*516*	*4.3*	*4*	*2*	*-2.4%*								*31*	*44*	*179*	*70%*	*5.8*	*0*		*-14.7%*			

In a pre-camp interview, Jones-Drew admitted that he thought about retiring after the 2013 season. "Part of it was, just physically, I wasn't able to do some of the same things I'm used to doing," Jones-Drew admitted. He picked the closest NFL option to retirement when the Raiders came knocking in free agency, though it's hard to blame Jones-Drew (or any running back) for taking the money where it's offered. Jones-Drew will be fighting with Darren McFadden for the No. 1 job in Oakland, and has an edge in that he can take 20 carries without a bone on his person breaking. But the carries of a 29-year-old running back usually aren't pretty even on a loaded roster, and Oakland certainly won't offer the second part.

Felix Jones Height: 5-10 Weight: 207 College: Arkansas Draft: 2008/1 (22) Born: 8-May-1987 Age: 27 Risk: #N/A

Year	Team	G/GS	Snaps	Runs	Yds	Yd/R	TD	FUM	DVOA	Rk	DYAR	Rk	YAR	Suc%	Rk	BTkl	Rec	Pass	Yds	C%	Yd/C	TD	YAC	DVOA	Rk	DYAR	Rk
2011	DAL	12/8	355	127	575	4.5	1	4	-9.1%	43	-3	43	10	52%	10	14	33	44	221	75%	6.7	0	7.7	-2.6%	31	29	33
2012	DAL	16/7	381	111	402	3.6	3	1	-6.1%	25	11	26	28	49%	16	14	26	36	266	69%	10.2	2	9.0	45.1%	1	109	5
2013	PIT	16/2	150	48	184	3.8	0	1	-13.4%	--	-9	--	-5	40%	--	1	9	13	63	69%	7.0	0	4.8	-14.3%	--	0	--

Jerry Jones says Dallas was "proud to have [Felix Jones] with that No. 1 pick." The Eagles tried him out next and traded him three months later to Pittsburgh. He was expendable on offense once Le'Veon Bell returned healthy and most of Jones' contributions to Pittsburgh were on kick returns. In that role he was not nearly as explosive as his rookie year. That sentence is a summary of every Felix Jones season since 2010.

Eddie Lacy Height: 5-11 Weight: 231 College: Alabama Draft: 2013/2 (61) Born: 1-Jan-1990 Age: 25 Risk: Green

Year	Team	G/GS	Snaps	Runs	Yds	Yd/R	TD	FUM	DVOA	Rk	DYAR	Rk	YAR	Suc%	Rk	BTkl	Rec	Pass	Yds	C%	Yd/C	TD	YAC	DVOA	Rk	DYAR	Rk
2013	GB	15/15	680	284	1178	4.1	11	1	5.3%	18	160	9	171	46%	27	29	35	44	257	80%	7.3	0	8.9	-3.5%	27	26	29
2014	*GB*			*253*	*1117*	*4.4*	*10*	*2*	*3.3%*								*37*	*53*	*287*	*70%*	*7.8*	*1*		*1.1%*			

Lacy went through four distinct developmental stages during his eventful rookie season.

1) Clueless rookie who cannot find a hole or stay healthy (preseason through Redskins game).
2) Missing piece with the potential to play Terrell Davis to Aaron Rodgers' John Elway (first Lions through first Bears game).
3) Rented stump-grinder churning through 20 to 25 line plunges per week because the Packers had no quarterback (Eagles through Cowboys)
4) Nicked-up committee power back doing everything he could with limited touches (Steelers through playoffs).

Lacy was impressive enough in Stage 2 to excite fans, but too much of Stage 3 will limit him to Stage 4. In any case, the Packers are no longer at Square One at running back, which counts for something.

Marcus Lattimore Height: 5-11 Weight: 221 College: South Carolina Draft: 2013/4 (131) Born: 29-Oct-1991 Age: 23 Risk: Red

Year	Team	G/GS	Snaps	Runs	Yds	Yd/R	TD	FUM	DVOA	Rk	DYAR	Rk	YAR	Suc%	Rk	BTkl	Rec	Pass	Yds	C%	Yd/C	TD	YAC	DVOA	Rk	DYAR	Rk
2014	*SF*			*41*	*178*	*4.3*	*1*	*1*	*-4.9%*								*6*	*8*	*35*	*75%*	*5.8*	*0*		*-7.7%*			

Lattimore's redshirt season is over. After suffering a gruesome knee injury in October 2012, Lattimore went pro, and San Francisco saw value in using a fourth-round pick to potentially pick up a first-round talent a year later. He will be competing against Carlos Hyde and Kendall Hunter for touches behind Frank Gore. If he turns into the 21-year-old he was at South Carolina, then it will prove a wise investment. If not, there's no shortage of backs willing to make Lattimore waiver fodder.

Brian Leonard Height: 6-2 Weight: 226 College: Rutgers Draft: 2007/2 (52) Born: 3-Feb-1984 Age: 30 Risk: #N/A

Year	Team	G/GS	Snaps	Runs	Yds	Yd/R	TD	FUM	DVOA	Rk	DYAR	Rk	YAR	Suc%	Rk	BTkl	Rec	Pass	Yds	C%	Yd/C	TD	YAC	DVOA	Rk	DYAR	Rk
2011	CIN	13/0	231	17	85	5.0	0	0	18.5%	--	18	--	21	47%	--	4	22	31	210	71%	9.5	0	8.5	12.8%	18	43	24
2012	CIN	15/0	206	33	106	3.2	0	0	-11.1%	--	-4	--	-2	42%	--	2	11	15	67	73%	6.1	0	7.1	-41.3%	--	-23	--
2013	TB	16/1	291	47	182	3.9	0	0	-5.9%	--	5	--	24	43%	--	8	29	37	179	78%	6.2	0	5.3	-12.6%	35	2	35

A fullback and special-teamer (he played 181 snaps in the kicking game), Leonard carried the ball 20 times against Miami after Mike James hurt his ankle. Those 20 carries averaged a whopping 2.9 yards apiece, so the Bucs turned to Bobby Rainey as their primary runner and Leonard only collected 18 carries the rest of the year. There's not a lot of room for 30-year-old fullback/kick gunner types in the NFL, and Leonard's career appears to be over.

Marshawn Lynch Height: 5-11 Weight: 215 College: California Draft: 2007/1 (12) Born: 22-Apr-1986 Age: 28 Risk: Green

Year	Team	G/GS	Snaps	Runs	Yds	Yd/R	TD	FUM	DVOA	Rk	DYAR	Rk	YAR	Suc%	Rk	BTkl	Rec	Pass	Yds	C%	Yd/C	TD	YAC	DVOA	Rk	DYAR	Rk
2011	SEA	15/15	559	285	1204	4.2	12	3	8.9%	12	201	2	159	46%	27	34	28	41	212	68%	7.6	1	7.7	-7.1%	36	16	35
2012	SEA	16/15	675	315	1590	5.0	11	5	19.2%	3	361	2	267	50%	11	26	23	30	196	77%	8.5	1	8.8	13.2%	11	50	19
2013	SEA	16/16	710	301	1257	4.2	12	4	5.9%	17	185	5	146	48%	19	59	36	44	316	82%	8.8	2	7.9	9.1%	15	55	19
2014	*SEA*			*222*	*897*	*4.0*	*9*	*3*	*-4.4%*								*31*	*42*	*247*	*74%*	*8.0*	*1*		*4.8%*			

More than any offensive player on the team, Lynch has personified Seahawks head coach Pete Carroll's preference for toughness on both sides of the ball, and he's done so since the team stole him from the Bills in 2010 for a couple of low draft picks. However, though Lynch has exceeded even Carroll's positive expectations, it's clearly the franchise's current modus operandi to think about life with other running backs in charge. That came through when offensive coordinator Darrell Bevell spoke about a running back by committee in the offseason, and when the team balked at renegotiating the four-year, $31 million extension Lynch signed in 2012. Lynch's age, workload (nobody in the NFL has run the ball more over the last three seasons, and certainly nobody's done it more between the tackles and with all manner of defenders hanging all over him), and the ascension of younger backs Robert Turbin and Christine Michael seem to spell an imminent exit for the Beast Mode glory days, as does Lynch's $7.5 million base salary if he plays every game in 2015.

One thing's for sure—or, at least, one thing's been true up until now. If you stack the box against Lynch, it doesn't matter much. In 2013, he averaged 4.08 yards per carry against a loaded defensive box (defined as a scheme in which there are more defenders in the box than there are blockers) and 4.25 yards per carry against more standard defensive alignments. His Success Rate against stacked and non-stacked was the same—48 percent in both cases. Lynch has always been above-average (and sometimes transcendent) when it comes to running inside, but such backs always have a cruel expiration date. Lynch led the league in goal-line touchdowns with 10, and we'll see over time how much of that was specific talent and how much was general opportunity.

Doug Martin Height: 5-9 Weight: 223 College: Boise State Draft: 2012/1 (31) Born: 13-Jan-1989 Age: 25 Risk: Yellow

Year	Team	G/GS	Snaps	Runs	Yds	Yd/R	TD	FUM	DVOA	Rk	DYAR	Rk	YAR	Suc%	Rk	BTkl	Rec	Pass	Yds	C%	Yd/C	TD	YAC	DVOA	Rk	DYAR	Rk
2012	TB	16/16	821	319	1454	4.6	11	1	3.9%	14	155	9	204	48%	20	41	49	70	472	70%	9.6	1	8.9	3.1%	24	66	13
2013	TB	6/6	303	127	456	3.6	1	1	-14.9%	40	-31	38	-53	39%	41	6	12	24	66	50%	5.5	0	4.8	-54.2%	--	-45	--
2014	*TB*			*251*	*1046*	*4.2*	*7*	*3*	*-5.2%*								*42*	*60*	*340*	*70%*	*8.1*	*1*		*1.1%*			

Exhibit No. 7,583 in the case against ever drafting a running back in the first round: In the first seven weeks of the season, with Martin, Tampa Bay had a -21.2% offensive DVOA, and a -18.5% DVOA in rushing offense. After Martin tore his labrum against Atlanta, those numbers improved to -3.2% and -7.2%. That probably says more about the switch from Josh Freeman to Mike Glennon than it does about the switch from Martin to Mike James and Bobby Rainey, but it does show that you can field a productive offense with "just a guy" at running back. Martin is expected to be fully healed in training camp, but Tampa Bay's suddenly loaded backfield should probably knock him down a round or two in your fantasy draft.

Tre Mason Height: 5-8 Weight: 207 College: Auburn Draft: 2014/3 (75) Born: 8-Jun-1993 Age: 21 Risk: Green

Year	Team	G/GS	Snaps	Runs	Yds	Yd/R	TD	FUM	DVOA	Rk	DYAR	Rk	YAR	Suc%	Rk	BTkl	Rec	Pass	Yds	C%	Yd/C	TD	YAC	DVOA	Rk	DYAR	Rk
2014	*STL*			*107*	*465*	*4.4*	*4*	*1*	*-1.8%*								*20*	*31*	*140*	*65%*	*7.0*	*1*		*-13.8%*			

A compact between-the-tackles runner who got worked like a rented stump grinder for Auburn last year. Mason rushed 317 times for 1,816 yards and 23 touchdowns in the SEC, ending the season with a series of 25-45 carry punch-press efforts against the likes of Alabama and Missouri. Auburn's offense mixed Chip Kelly tactics with 1983 Redskins trim, so Mason lined up in a hurry-up shotgun set and ran a mix of zone plays, counters, and power sweeps, over and over again, from September through early January.

Mason uses his compact frame well as an interior runner, hit holes hard, can make quick cuts and knows when to bounce plays outside. He was barely used in the passing game and is an unpolished blocker. Mason can run away from linebackers and safeties in the open field but is no C.J. Spiller when he breaks free. A workload like the one Mason handled in 2013 would be a concern if he had been carrying 30 times per game for three years, but Mason shared duties with Onterio McCalebb and Michael Dyer early in his career. If anything, last season proved that he is durable, but not worn down. Mason looks a little like Frank Gore when slamming behind pulling linemen for five yards at a time, but Jeff Fisher may see him as more of an Eddie George.

Ryan Mathews Height: 6-0 Weight: 218 College: Fresno State Draft: 2010/1 (12) Born: 1-May-1987 Age: 27 Risk: Yellow

Year	Team	G/GS	Snaps	Runs	Yds	Yd/R	TD	FUM	DVOA	Rk	DYAR	Rk	YAR	Suc%	Rk	BTkl	Rec	Pass	Yds	C%	Yd/C	TD	YAC	DVOA	Rk	DYAR	Rk
2011	SD	14/14	520	222	1091	4.9	6	5	10.8%	10	171	6	134	50%	17	24	50	59	455	85%	9.1	0	8.7	25.4%	7	126	5
2012	SD	12/9	402	184	707	3.8	1	2	-7.7%	28	6	28	25	47%	23	17	39	57	252	68%	6.5	0	8.8	-15.4%	34	-5	34
2013	SD	16/14	472	285	1255	4.4	6	2	3.6%	19	141	10	120	49%	17	13	26	33	189	79%	7.3	1	7.3	19.9%	11	61	17
2014	*SD*			*253*	*1111*	*4.4*	*6*	*3*	*0.3%*								*26*	*36*	*205*	*72%*	*7.9*	*1*		*4.4%*			

It was a healthy and newly focused Mathews who turned in his best season to date in 2013. Playing in 16 games for the first time in his NFL career, and with the Chargers putting a greater emphasis on the run game in a higher-tempo offense, Mathews finally came close to living up to the promise the Chargers thought he had in 2010. He's always been a good runner after contact, and he increased his yards after contact from 366 to 501 last season. The primary difference, as it was for Philip Rivers, was that a new coaching staff simplified things for Mathews and allowed him to be the one-cut-and-go back he's supposed to be. And though the team signed Donald Brown, new offensive coordinator Frank Reich says that Mathews will still be the lead back. In the quicker offense Reich estimates the Chargers will be running, Mathews will have still more chances for two things—increased productivity, and increased injury risk. We'll see which way the ball bounces. It's a crucial season for Mathews, as he's on the final year of his rookie contract.

Dexter McCluster Height: 5-9 Weight: 172 College: Mississippi Draft: 2010/2 (36) Born: 26-Aug-1988 Age: 26 Risk: Yellow

Year	Team	G/GS	Snaps	Runs	Yds	Yd/R	TD	FUM	DVOA	Rk	DYAR	Rk	YAR	Suc%	Rk	BTkl	Rec	Pass	Yds	C%	Yd/C	TD	YAC	DVOA	Rk	DYAR	Rk
2011	KC	16/4	455	114	516	4.5	1	2	-2.3%	32	27	36	34	43%	41	11	46	63	328	75%	7.1	1	6.6	-12.3%	41	5	40
2012	KC	16/6	573	12	70	5.8	0	0	38.7%	--	42	--	42	--	0	0	52	76	452	68%	8.7	1	3.9	-21.1%	81	-34	79
2013	KC	15/6	581	8	5	0.6	0	0	-89.6%	--	-25	--	-27	--	0	6	53	83	511	64%	9.6	2	4.9	-16.0%	78	-22	76
2014	*TEN*			*31*	*134*	*4.3*	*1*	*0*	*-1.5%*								*40*	*55*	*359*	*73%*	*9.0*	*1*		*8.3%*			

McCluster made the Pro Bowl in 2013 after three seasons of relatively unimpressive production; offensive coordinator after offensive coordinator couldn't figure out how to best use his limited skill set until the team's new regime came in and decreed: "Let him return punts." McCluster led the NFL in punt returns, return yardage and return touchdowns, and he was a key cog in the Chiefs' top-ranked special teams unit. But Kansas City will replace him with Oregon rookie De'Anthony Thomas, while McCluster gets a shot in a satellite back role in Ken Whisenhunt's Titans offense. However, even satellite backs need to be able to take contact and keep moving, and that's never been McCluster's thing. Coach Whiz may find, as Andy Reid did, that his best attributes are tailored to special teams dominance. (Note: the 2011 stats and ranks above use running back baselines, while the 2012 and 2013 stats and ranks are for McCluster as a wide receiver.)

LeSean McCoy Height: 5-11 Weight: 198 College: Pittsburgh Draft: 2009/2 (53) Born: 12-Jul-1988 Age: 26 Risk: Yellow

Year	Team	G/GS	Snaps	Runs	Yds	Yd/R	TD	FUM	DVOA	Rk	DYAR	Rk	YAR	Suc%	Rk	BTkl	Rec	Pass	Yds	C%	Yd/C	TD	YAC	DVOA	Rk	DYAR	Rk
2011	PHI	15/15	867	273	1309	4.8	17	1	15.8%	4	304	1	262	51%	15	50	48	69	315	70%	6.6	3	8.1	-4.5%	32	38	27
2012	PHI	12/12	694	200	840	4.2	2	4	-12.6%	33	-34	35	7	48%	19	44	54	68	373	81%	6.9	3	8.9	9.2%	17	90	9
2013	PHI	16/16	873	314	1607	5.1	9	1	18.1%	3	341	1	321	52%	8	51	52	64	539	81%	10.4	2	11.3	23.8%	9	137	7
2014	*PHI*			*304*	*1440*	*4.7*	*11*	*2*	*10.7%*								*53*	*67*	*486*	*79%*	*9.2*	*3*		*28.9%*			

Shady's back, tell a friend. After a disappointing 2012 season, McCoy was at his best last year. His Success Rate was a career-best 52 percent and his consistency is the reason. McCoy's rushing DVOA by down could not have been any more consistent: 17.4% on first down, 19.4% on second down and 17.0% on third/fourth down. The zone read was a big help. McCoy had 214 zone-read runs for 1,144 yards (5.35 yards per carry)—more yards than any other team had using the zone read in 2013. On other runs, McCoy was still very good with 4.63 yards per carry. Having a healthy offensive line certainly helped McCoy's rebound season. According to ESPN Stats & Information, the Eagles averaged a league-best 3.6 yards before contact per rush. McCoy still managed the second most broken tackles in the league (51) and had his most prolific receiving season in addition to being the rushing champion.

Darren McFadden Height: 6-1 Weight: 211 College: Arkansas Draft: 2008/1 (4) Born: 27-Aug-1987 Age: 27 Risk: Red

Year	Team	G/GS	Snaps	Runs	Yds	Yd/R	TD	FUM	DVOA	Rk	DYAR	Rk	YAR	Suc%	Rk	BTkl	Rec	Pass	Yds	C%	Yd/C	TD	YAC	DVOA	Rk	DYAR	Rk
2011	OAK	7/7	279	113	614	5.4	4	1	11.6%	9	87	20	88	44%	38	12	19	23	154	83%	8.1	1	8.2	12.4%	--	33	--
2012	OAK	12/12	591	216	707	3.3	2	2	-26.7%	41	-153	42	-132	36%	41	14	42	64	258	69%	6.1	1	6.2	-36.7%	43	-82	47
2013	OAK	10/7	336	114	379	3.3	5	1	-17.0%	42	-38	40	-31	34%	46	6	17	25	108	68%	6.4	0	7.4	-8.8%	32	7	34
2014	*OAK*			*186*	*699*	*3.8*	*4*	*2*	*-11.9%*								*41*	*57*	*307*	*72%*	*7.5*	*0*		*-8.6%*			

At this point, a 16-game Darren McFadden seems about as chimerical as a team willing to take on the Tim Tebow Circus, so let's not even consider the possibility and just accept McFadden for what he is: an explosive straight-line runner who lacks the lateral agility and vision to be a top-level NFL back. He has morphed into a very boom-and-bust back dependent on the offensive line to create running room for him, a bit like fellow 2008 first-rounder Chris Johnson. Like Johnson, this leads to absurd statistics like a better DVOA (-2.1% v. -23.1%) against loaded boxes, because he won't find running room against non-loaded boxes anyway and has a better chance of breaking a big run against a loaded box. If the offensive line improves the way the Raiders hope it will, his style suggests he could be one of the biggest beneficiaries. After re-signing him to a one-year deal in the offseason, that's certainly what the Raiders are hoping.

Willis McGahee Height: 6-0 Weight: 228 College: Miami Draft: 2003/1 (23) Born: 21-Oct-1981 Age: 33 Risk: #N/A

Year	Team	G/GS	Snaps	Runs	Yds	Yd/R	TD	FUM	DVOA	Rk	DYAR	Rk	YAR	Suc%	Rk	BTkl	Rec	Pass	Yds	C%	Yd/C	TD	YAC	DVOA	Rk	DYAR	Rk
2011	DEN	15/14	458	249	1199	4.8	4	4	4.3%	17	131	12	117	47%	26	22	12	20	51	60%	4.3	1	4.3	-67.4%	--	-58	--
2012	DEN	10/9	393	167	731	4.4	4	5	-2.1%	22	49	23	79	58%	1	11	26	33	221	79%	8.5	0	9.0	7.2%	22	44	21
2013	CLE	12/6	265	138	377	2.7	2	1	-22.6%	45	-92	44	-98	46%	28	2	8	12	20	75%	2.5	0	1.9	-74.5%	--	-44	--

33-year old running backs coming off a season with 2.7 yards per carry don't generally receive contracts from CFL or Arena League teams, much less the NFL. Such is McGahee's lot. If this is indeed the end, he'll be remembered for his toughness, both on the field and in the rehab facility. His comeback from the horrific knee injury he suffered in the 2003 Fiesta Bowl to build an 11-year career remains McGahee's signal achievement.

Jerick McKinnon Height: 5-9 Weight: 209 College: Georgia Southern Draft: 2014/3 (96) Born: 5-Mar-1992 Age: 22 Risk: Blue

Year	Team	G/GS	Snaps	Runs	Yds	Yd/R	TD	FUM	DVOA	Rk	DYAR	Rk	YAR	Suc%	Rk	BTkl	Rec	Pass	Yds	C%	Yd/C	TD	YAC	DVOA	Rk	DYAR	Rk
2014	*MIN*			*38*	*184*	*4.8*	*0*	*1*	*2.1%*								*12*	*14*	*100*	*86%*	*8.3*	*1*		*12.4%*			

McKinnon was an option quarterback at Georgia Southern, but he showed at the Senior Bowl that he can transition quickly to running back. McKinnon is well built and does not shy away from contact like some option quarterbacks. He has good vision for inside rushing holes and blocking schemes: another attribute many conversion cases lack. McKinnon will get first dibs at Peterson changeup opportunities, with Matt Asiata serving more as a fullback and pass protector. Keeper leaguers should note that Peterson's cap number goes nuclear after his 30th birthday, so McKinnon may have a future as an every-down running back. Or, the way things go in Minnesota, as an emergency quarterback: the team also grabbed Northwestern's Kain Colter as a rookie free agent, so the Joe Webb dream remains very much alive.

Rashard Mendenhall Height: 5-10 Weight: 225 College: Illinois Draft: 2008/1 (23) Born: 19-Jun-1987 Age: 27 Risk: #N/A

Year	Team	G/GS	Snaps	Runs	Yds	Yd/R	TD	FUM	DVOA	Rk	DYAR	Rk	YAR	Suc%	Rk	BTkl	Rec	Pass	Yds	C%	Yd/C	TD	YAC	DVOA	Rk	DYAR	Rk
2011	PIT	15/15	458	228	928	4.1	9	1	2.3%	23	106	17	88	52%	11	34	18	28	154	64%	8.6	0	8.7	-4.7%	33	15	36
2012	PIT	6/4	104	51	182	3.6	0	3	-38.5%	--	-62	--	-55	43%	--	9	9	11	62	82%	6.9	1	10.9	22.7%	--	24	--
2013	ARI	15/15	459	217	687	3.2	8	4	-10.2%	36	-15	36	-66	42%	37	13	18	21	134	86%	7.4	0	8.7	21.3%	--	38	--

Mendenhall decided this spring that the world has more to offer than scuffling behind the Arizona offensive line for 3.2 yards per carry and the chance to constantly get whacked by guys like Patrick Willis and James Laurinaitis. After his retirement, he wrote an interesting piece for the Huffington Post about how "the business of entertainment" had changed the NFL. Mendenhall has a point that fans never understood his calm demeanor or his interests in art and literature. Which is why it is so weird that other parts of the piece came off like a parody of how 60-year-old guys talk about how great the NFL was back in the day. "When I came up, teammates fought together for wins and got respect for the fight. The player who gave the ball to the referee after a touchdown was commended; the one who played through injury was tough; the role of the blocking tight end was acknowledged; running backs who picked up blitzing linebackers showed heart; and the story of the game was told through the tape, and not the stats alone." Sorry, Rashard, those wonderful days when you were in high school and football was perfect were only ten years ago, and nothing was really different then. But we wish you good luck in your future endeavors, because you seem like an interesting dude when you aren't channeling Mike Ditka.

Christine Michael Height: 5-10 Weight: 220 College: Texas A&M Draft: 2013/2 (62) Born: 9-Nov-1990 Age: 24 Risk: Green

Year	Team	G/GS	Snaps	Runs	Yds	Yd/R	TD	FUM	DVOA	Rk	DYAR	Rk	YAR	Suc%	Rk	BTkl	Rec	Pass	Yds	C%	Yd/C	TD	YAC	DVOA	Rk	DYAR	Rk
2013	SEA	4/0	26	18	79	4.4	0	0	10.6%	--	14	--	17	78%	--	0	0	--	0	--	0.0	0	--	--	--	--	--
2014	*SEA*			*125*	*587*	*4.7*	*2*	*3*	*-2.2%*								*15*	*18*	*126*	*83%*	*8.4*	*0*		*13.9%*			

Michael fell into Kevin Sumlin's doghouse at Texas A&M, but the Seahawks still took him in the second round of the 2013 draft after they fell in love with his explosiveness and potential. It wasn't seen much in his first season because Marshawn Lynch had a bead on Seattle's RB1 position, but make no mistake—those in charge of Seattle's offense are still head over heels with what they think Michael can do over time. "We really like what Christine Michael is doing right now ... with the quickness, the speed and the toughness he's shown," offensive coordinator Darrell Bevell said in June. "He's making great cuts. He has breakaway speed to finish a run and he has really quick moves in short areas." Given Bevell's comments about a running back by committee, and the likelihood that Seattle will pass more, it becomes easy to project Michael moving closer to a role as Mr. Outside with Marshawn Lynch (and eventually, Robert Turbin) as Mr. Inside.

Lamar Miller Height: 5-11 Weight: 212 College: Miami Draft: 2012/4 (97) Born: 25-Apr-1991 Age: 23 Risk: Green

Year	Team	G/GS	Snaps	Runs	Yds	Yd/R	TD	FUM	DVOA	Rk	DYAR	Rk	YAR	Suc%	Rk	BTkl	Rec	Pass	Yds	C%	Yd/C	TD	YAC	DVOA	Rk	DYAR	Rk
2012	MIA	13/1	143	51	250	4.9	1	0	7.5%	--	35	--	48	55%	--	5	6	9	45	67%	7.5	0	6.7	-2.0%	--	6	--
2013	MIA	16/15	622	177	709	4.0	2	1	-7.7%	31	6	31	5	46%	29	16	26	35	170	74%	6.5	0	6.8	-7.9%	31	11	32
2014	*MIA*			*154*	*699*	*4.5*	*3*	*2*	*-0.9%*								*24*	*33*	*151*	*73%*	*6.3*	*1*		*-9.9%*			

Like with any of Miami's offensive players, we're interested to see what the perceived superior offensive line will do for Miller in 2014. Keeping in mind the line ranked 28th in Adjusted Line Yards, Miller's done little to distinguish himself in two years. He won the starting job last year, but he only ranked one spot ahead of teammate Daniel Thomas in DYAR and one spot behind in DVOA. He's a better receiver, but so is Knowshon Moreno, who joins the backfield this year. Miller's a speed back, so power situations aren't his strong suit. On third-and-short last year, he only converted two of six opportunities, but again, how much is this on the offensive line? The Dolphins were last in the league at converting on power-running plays (third or fourth down with 1-2 yards needed) no matter who carried the ball. Miller's 6.0 blown blocks tied for the ninth most among running backs. If healthy, Moreno may eat into Miller's carries. Moreno had 8.0 blown blocks himself. Rest now, Ryan Tannehill. Winter is coming.

Knowshon Moreno Height: 5-11 Weight: 200 College: Georgia Draft: 2009/1 (12) Born: 16-Jul-1987 Age: 27 Risk: Red

Year	Team	G/GS	Snaps	Runs	Yds	Yd/R	TD	FUM	DVOA	Rk	DYAR	Rk	YAR	Suc%	Rk	BTkl	Rec	Pass	Yds	C%	Yd/C	TD	YAC	DVOA	Rk	DYAR	Rk
2011	DEN	7/2	175	37	179	4.8	0	1	-16.0%	--	-9	--	-5	32%	--	7	11	15	101	73%	9.2	1	8.7	44.1%	--	37	--
2012	DEN	8/6	337	139	525	3.8	4	1	1.1%	18	56	20	67	56%	2	10	21	26	167	81%	8.0	0	6.0	25.3%	5	58	15
2013	DEN	16/15	703	241	1038	4.3	10	1	8.4%	13	171	6	199	50%	14	18	60	74	548	81%	9.1	3	7.9	31.0%	4	192	3
2014	*MIA*			*98*	*403*	*4.1*	*4*	*1*	*-2.0%*								*29*	*36*	*157*	*81%*	*5.4*	*1*		*-7.8%*			

His vision, patience, and three-down skill set made Moreno an extremely valuable player for the 2013 Broncos, highlighted by his 37-carry, 224-yard performance against the Patriots in Week 12 when he went blasting up the middle against injury fill-in tackles. That game notwithstanding, he seemed to wear down under the weight of the biggest workload of his career and rarely got more than what the offense gave him. The Dolphins were the only team to show serious interest in him in free agency, giving him a one-year deal for $3 million ($1.25 million guaranteed). He has the versatility to be their lead back, but after reporting to camp out of shape and undergoing knee surgery in late June that leaves him questionable for the start of camp, it seems likelier he'll be a third-down back.

Alfred Morris Height: 5-10 Weight: 219 College: Florida Atlantic Draft: 2012/6 (173) Born: 12-Dec-1988 Age: 26 Risk: Yellow

Year	Team	G/GS	Snaps	Runs	Yds	Yd/R	TD	FUM	DVOA	Rk	DYAR	Rk	YAR	Suc%	Rk	BTkl	Rec	Pass	Yds	C%	Yd/C	TD	YAC	DVOA	Rk	DYAR	Rk
2012	WAS	16/16	728	335	1613	4.8	13	4	10.3%	8	254	5	273	52%	7	27	11	16	77	69%	7.0	0	5.9	-14.6%	--	-1	--
2013	WAS	16/16	605	276	1275	4.6	7	6	2.0%	21	121	13	133	48%	20	24	9	12	78	75%	8.7	0	8.8	-12.0%	--	1	--
2014	*WAS*			*252*	*1155*	*4.6*	*9*	*3*	*1.3%*								*16*	*24*	*128*	*67%*	*8.0*	*0*		*-5.3%*			

As long as you aren't counting on Morris to deliver a PPR title to your fantasy team, he's a damn good running back. Offensive coordinator Sean McVay has already said that Washington will keep up the zone-blocking scheme, so there's little reason to be down on Morris heading into the year unless you're a true Lache Seastrunk believer. A decisive and agile back, Morris should also stand to benefit from Robert Griffin's improved health. The main change we're expecting is that Jay Gruden's scheme will probably move to a higher pass/run ratio, but that will also include more passes to running backs—maybe even Morris.

DeMarco Murray Height: 6-0 Weight: 213 College: Oklahoma Draft: 2011/3 (71) Born: 12-Feb-1988 Age: 26 Risk: Yellow

Year	Team	G/GS	Snaps	Runs	Yds	Yd/R	TD	FUM	DVOA	Rk	DYAR	Rk	YAR	Suc%	Rk	BTkl	Rec	Pass	Yds	C%	Yd/C	TD	YAC	DVOA	Rk	DYAR	Rk
2011	DAL	13/7	377	164	897	5.5	2	1	12.6%	7	149	11	162	58%	2	14	26	35	183	74%	7.0	0	8.6	-17.4%	44	-7	45
2012	DAL	10/0	466	161	663	4.1	4	4	1.7%	16	72	15	65	54%	5	26	34	42	247	83%	7.3	0	6.9	10.4%	16	60	14
2013	DAL	14/14	672	217	1121	5.2	9	3	24.0%	1	295	2	288	53%	6	35	53	66	350	80%	6.6	1	7.2	-3.5%	26	40	24
2014	*DAL*			*235*	*1081*	*4.6*	*9*	*3*	*4.2%*								*58*	*84*	*415*	*69%*	*7.1*	*2*		*-10.9%*			

Murray's best season was also his healthiest despite still missing two games. While he led the league in rushing DVOA, his season was not an example of consistency, though that's probably on the coaches' game plans as much as anything. Murray started stringing together great performances in November, but the season finale was a disappointment with 17 carries for 48 yards. Maybe if Dallas started that final drive with three Murray runs to get him to his magical mark of 20 carries, Kyle Orton wouldn't have thrown the season-ending interception and Dallas would have won the NFC East. Don't laugh. There are people who still believe Murray is the ultimate answer to Dallas' problems. The Cowboys are 11-0 when he has at least 20 rushing attempts. Long-time readers know the drill: winning leads to carries; not the other way around. When Murray has reached his 20th carry, Dallas either have a comfortable lead late in the game or are right within striking distance of a win. Murray's important to the offense, but not more important than Romo, Bryant, Smith, or Witten.

Chris Ogbonnaya Height: 6-0 Weight: 220 College: Texas Draft: 2009/7 (211) Born: 20-May-1986 Age: 28 Risk: Green

Year	Team	G/GS	Snaps	Runs	Yds	Yd/R	TD	FUM	DVOA	Rk	DYAR	Rk	YAR	Suc%	Rk	BTkl	Rec	Pass	Yds	C%	Yd/C	TD	YAC	DVOA	Rk	DYAR	Rk
2011	2TM	13/4	328	76	340	4.5	1	2	-4.9%	--	11	--	9	47%	--	8	23	31	165	74%	7.2	0	6.3	-9.4%	38	7	38
2012	CLE	15/1	152	8	30	3.8	0	1	-23.2%	--	-5	--	-5	50%	--	0	24	32	187	75%	7.8	0	8.7	-1.9%	26	23	26
2013	CLE	16/7	521	49	240	4.9	0	2	4.7%	--	29	--	35	53%	--	4	48	75	343	64%	7.1	2	6.0	-10.2%	34	14	31
2014	*CLE*			*28*	*113*	*4.1*	*0*	*1*	*-8.1%*								*35*	*58*	*276*	*60%*	*7.9*	*1*		*-11.7%*			

The Browns mostly used this one-time seventh-round draft choice of the Rams (sound familiar?) as a fullback last season, hoping to take advantage of Ogbonnaya's versatility. With pure fullback Ray Agnew in camp, Og appears to be a man without a country, and will slug it out with Edwin Baker for a roster spot.

Adrian Peterson Height: 6-2 Weight: 217 College: Oklahoma Draft: 2007/1 (7) Born: 21-Mar-1985 Age: 29 Risk: Yellow

Year	Team	G/GS	Snaps	Runs	Yds	Yd/R	TD	FUM	DVOA	Rk	DYAR	Rk	YAR	Suc%	Rk	BTkl	Rec	Pass	Yds	C%	Yd/C	TD	YAC	DVOA	Rk	DYAR	Rk
2011	MIN	12/12	498	208	970	4.7	12	1	10.4%	11	153	9	190	47%	25	26	18	23	139	78%	7.7	1	6.7	9.9%	--	28	--
2012	MIN	16/16	770	348	2097	6.0	12	4	24.9%	2	458	1	357	49%	14	44	40	51	217	78%	5.4	1	4.7	-14.9%	33	-3	33
2013	MIN	14/14	674	279	1266	4.5	10	5	-3.1%	26	60	25	135	44%	32	42	29	41	171	73%	5.9	1	5.5	-22.8%	45	-20	43
2014	*MIN*			*313*	*1418*	*4.5*	*12*	*8*	*1.9%*								*40*	*51*	*277*	*78%*	*6.9*	*1*		*-4.1%*			

Peterson underwent groin surgery in January and said that he was "about 80 percent" as of May. His cap numbers get stratospheric in the next two seasons, and Mike Freeman of Bleacher Report reported that this may be his last season with the Vikings. Add 29 years to $47 million (Peterson's cap number for 2015 to 2017), plus mounting old-rusher injuries, and you get a grim number for the greatest running back of this generation, and one of the five or six best ever.

If Peterson is really in his final days with the Vikings, then his legacy hangs in the balance. Peterson spurred two teams to playoff appearances that they had no business enjoying in 2008 and 2012. He extended Brett Favre's career by two years, one wonderful and one a four-month regret marathon. He had one of the greatest Conference Championship game performances in history, leading the Vikings to within a Favre interception and some Drew Brees overtime heroics of the Super Bowl. On the flip side, and through no fault of his own, Peterson was an enabler for an organization that took a wishful thinking approach to quarterback acquisition/development and married itself for too long to a Brad Childress-Leslie Frazier coaching regime whose bright ideas often began and ended with "feed Peterson."

All indicators but age and the groin injury suggest Peterson still has a lot left in the tank: his production after 20 carries in a game (4.9 yards per rush) and in short-yardage situations (the Vikings finished second in Power Success) demonstrate that there is some tread left on the tires. Mike Zimmer and Norv Turner will be less stubborn and strange about Peterson's touches, limiting the "everyone knows what's coming" situations. If Peterson carries the load and keeps the Vikings competitive during the transition to Teddy Bridgewater, providing a security blanket that allows the team to finally develop a franchise quarterback, it will be a worthy capstone to his Hall of Fame run in Minnesota. He took what could have been a bleak era and made it exciting, then paved the way for a brighter future. It's a legacy to be proud of.

Bernard Pierce Height: 6-0 Weight: 218 College: Temple Draft: 2012/3 (84) Born: 10-May-1991 Age: 23 Risk: Green

Year	Team	G/GS	Snaps	Runs	Yds	Yd/R	TD	FUM	DVOA	Rk	DYAR	Rk	YAR	Suc%	Rk	BTkl	Rec	Pass	Yds	C%	Yd/C	TD	YAC	DVOA	Rk	DYAR	Rk
2012	BAL	16/0	218	108	532	4.9	1	0	4.1%	13	54	21	52	47%	24	19	7	11	47	64%	6.7	0	6.1	1.8%	--	10	--
2013	BAL	16/1	398	152	436	2.9	2	0	-29.3%	47	-131	46	-125	38%	42	15	20	25	104	80%	5.2	0	5.7	-33.3%	47	-27	46
2014	*BAL*			*157*	*605*	*3.9*	*2*	*4*	*-15.5%*								*24*	*30*	*169*	*80%*	*7.0*	*0*		*1.3%*			

Baltimore fans are wondering if Pierce can erase last year and carry the load should Ray Rice face a lengthy suspension. Fantasy owners are scared to draft a guy who royally sucked, finishing dead last in DVOA. Maybe this will help everyone: Since 1989, running backs finishing last in rushing DVOA have averaged 86.5 carries for 344 yards the following season. Four of the 24 players did not play (three retired) and only Warrick Dunn rushed for 1,000 yards (2000). Nine players changed teams, including one of the very few successes (Garrison Hearst). Only seven players logged at least 100 carries the next season and on average they ranked 20th in DVOA. Rashad Jennings just had one of the best follow-up efforts (from 42nd to fifth in DVOA), but he also went from Jacksonville to Oakland. This doesn't sound good for Pierce, who also will never match Rice's receiving, but he is young and will have a few new starters on the offensive line. Still, this may be a year to stay away from Baltimore running backs in fantasy football.

Bilal Powell Height: 5-10 Weight: 205 College: Louisville Draft: 2011/4 (126) Born: 27-Oct-1988 Age: 26 Risk: Blue

Year	Team	G/GS	Snaps	Runs	Yds	Yd/R	TD	FUM	DVOA	Rk	DYAR	Rk	YAR	Suc%	Rk	BTkl	Rec	Pass	Yds	C%	Yd/C	TD	YAC	DVOA	Rk	DYAR	Rk
2011	NYJ	2/0	25	13	21	1.6	0	1	-115.1%	--	-54	--	-57	15%	--	0	1	1	7	100%	7.0	0	2.0	-22.8%	--	-1	--
2012	NYJ	14/2	397	110	437	4.0	4	0	5.6%	10	63	17	71	50%	13	9	17	36	140	47%	8.2	0	7.1	-24.7%	39	-22	40
2013	NYJ	16/11	618	176	697	4.0	1	1	-8.7%	34	-1	34	37	43%	35	13	36	57	272	63%	7.6	0	8.7	-20.2%	44	-20	44
2014	*NYJ*			*59*	*257*	*4.3*	*0*	*1*	*-3.7%*								*16*	*24*	*129*	*67%*	*8.1*	*0*		*-13.1%*			

Through four weeks, Powell was tied with Arian Foster for the conference lead in rushing yards. Over the final three months of the season, though, Powell gained just 405 yards on 3.7 yards per carry. More troublesome was an inability to gain yardage as a receiver. Among running backs with at least 40 targets—and not counting Marcel Reece, who is a fullback but also often lines up wide to run deeper routes—Powell had the worst catch rate last year at just 63 percent. Quite simply, he is a jack of all trades but master of none: he's a capable interior runner, a decent enough pass blocker, and able to handle a large workload. He'll also provide you with a few big plays from time to time. But he's eminently replaceable in the modern NFL where running backs grow on trees, and the addition of Chris Johnson moves Powell to third on the Jets depth chart.

Bobby Rainey Height: 5-7 Weight: 206 College: Western Kentucky Draft: 2012/FA Born: 16-Oct-1987 Age: 27 Risk: Green

Year	Team	G/GS	Snaps	Runs	Yds	Yd/R	TD	FUM	DVOA	Rk	DYAR	Rk	YAR	Suc%	Rk	BTkl	Rec	Pass	Yds	C%	Yd/C	TD	YAC	DVOA	Rk	DYAR	Rk
2013	2TM	15/6	326	150	566	3.8	5	1	-14.2%	39	-31	39	-43	31%	47	13	15	19	46	79%	3.1	1	4.5	-34.8%	--	-23	--
2014	*TB*			*27*	*132*	*4.8*	*2*	*1*	*14.7%*								*8*	*12*	*59*	*67%*	*7.3*	*1*		*-4.0%*			

Rainey's tenure in Cleveland produced 13 carries for 34 yards in six games before he was released. It says a lot about Rainey that Cleveland felt better going with Willis McGahee and Chris Ogbonnaya at running back, and remember that the Browns were 3-3 at the time and very much alive in the playoff race. He wound up in Tampa Bay, and after Doug Martin and Mike James were injured and Brian Leonard proved that he was still Brian Leonard, Rainey came up big against Atlanta, rambling for 163 yards on 30 carries. He added another big game against Buffalo in December (127 yards on 22 carries), but otherwise he averaged less than 3.0 yards per rush. Overall, Rainey was badly outplayed by Mike James last year, but there's talk that the Bucs might keep him over James this season. Honestly, the idea that any team would keep a guy who lost his job to Willis McGahee's corpse over Mike James is certifiably insane.

Joseph Randle Height: 6-0 Weight: 204 College: Oklahoma State Draft: 2013/5 (151) Born: 29-Dec-1991 Age: 23 Risk: Red

Year	Team	G/GS	Snaps	Runs	Yds	Yd/R	TD	FUM	DVOA	Rk	DYAR	Rk	YAR	Suc%	Rk	BTkl	Rec	Pass	Yds	C%	Yd/C	TD	YAC	DVOA	Rk	DYAR	Rk
2013	DAL	13/2	119	54	164	3.0	2	0	-8.1%	--	1	--	-9	44%	--	2	8	10	61	80%	7.6	0	7.6	-10.6%	--	2	--
2014	*DAL*			*54*	*194*	*3.6*	*1*	*2*	*-19.3%*								*17*	*22*	*114*	*77%*	*6.7*	*0*		*-3.2%*			

Randle was a bit of a workhorse for Oklahoma State, but he only managed 3.0 yards per carry last season while DeMarco Murray and Lance Dunbar were both over 5.0. He's fallen behind Dunbar on the depth chart, but he still has a good shot to make the roster. Dallas has brought in former Arizona back Ryan Williams, but he hasn't been able to stay healthy. Then again, being consistently injured seems to be a prerequisite for the Dallas backfield these days.

Marcel Reece Height: 6-3 Weight: 240 College: Washington Draft: 2008/FA Born: 23-Jun-1985 Age: 29 Risk: Green

Year	Team	G/GS	Snaps	Runs	Yds	Yd/R	TD	FUM	DVOA	Rk	DYAR	Rk	YAR	Suc%	Rk	BTkl	Rec	Pass	Yds	C%	Yd/C	TD	YAC	DVOA	Rk	DYAR	Rk
2011	OAK	12/6	333	17	112	6.6	0	1	45.2%	--	38	--	36	59%	--	5	27	36	301	75%	11.1	2	8.1	20.8%	11	72	14
2012	OAK	16/14	659	59	271	4.6	0	2	-6.9%	--	4	--	21	54%	--	15	52	73	496	71%	9.5	1	6.3	7.6%	21	90	8
2013	OAK	16/15	505	46	218	4.7	2	0	7.0%	--	31	--	21	39%	--	5	32	54	331	59%	10.3	2	7.1	-1.1%	24	38	25
2014	*OAK*			*40*	*168*	*4.2*	*2*	*2*	*2.3%*								*43*	*54*	*377*	*80%*	*8.8*	*1*		*12.2%*			

Reece's versatility earned him a contract extension at the beginning of the 2013 season and more questions about why he wasn't more involved in the offense. He would have been a great fullback for a 1980s-style West Coast offense, thanks to his ability to be productive as a ballcarrier, a receiver, and a lead blocker. The ability to line up in the slot gives him a bit more passing game versatility than, say, Tom Rathman, but it would be a pretty seamless fit. The problem is, while he can do a lot of different things, he's not great at any of them. Opposing defenses have to account for him and pay attention to where he lines up, including his ability to motion elsewhere. As long as they demonstrate that mindfulness, he won't necessarily do much. Thus the annual stories about his lack of involvement.

Ray Rice Height: 5-8 Weight: 199 College: Rutgers Draft: 2008/2 (55) Born: 22-Jan-1987 Age: 27 Risk: Red

Year	Team	G/GS	Snaps	Runs	Yds	Yd/R	TD	FUM	DVOA	Rk	DYAR	Rk	YAR	Suc%	Rk	BTkl	Rec	Pass	Yds	C%	Yd/C	TD	YAC	DVOA	Rk	DYAR	Rk
2011	BAL	16/16	819	291	1364	4.7	12	2	2.1%	26	129	13	108	45%	33	29	76	104	704	73%	9.3	3	8.7	28.1%	5	231	2
2012	BAL	16/16	811	257	1143	4.4	9	1	11.5%	7	205	7	193	44%	33	27	61	83	478	73%	7.8	1	7.7	-11.7%	31	10	28
2013	BAL	15/15	704	214	660	3.1	4	2	-27.9%	46	-169	47	-145	35%	45	9	58	73	321	79%	5.5	0	6.5	-19.1%	42	-21	45
2014	*BAL*			*176*	*598*	*3.4*	*5*	*2*	*-14.6%*								*44*	*63*	*325*	*70%*	*7.4*	*0*		*-11.3%*			

We know Rice was at his statistical worst last season in both rushing and receiving, but he even had the most blown blocks (12.3) of any running back. He just plain didn't pass the eye test as the player we have come to expect. Rice had 27 broken tackles in 2012, but that number dropped to nine last year, producing a lower rate than every back in the league except Willis McGahee. For his offseason troubles—something he has not had before—with his fiancée/wife, Rice could face a suspension in the neighborhood of 4-6 games, or whatever punishment Roger Goodell lands on with his "Jump to Conclusions" mat. The league's punishments have never been consistent, and neither is Rice anymore.

Daryl Richardson Height: 6-0 Weight: 192 College: Abilene Christian Draft: 2012/7 (252) Born: 12-Apr-1990 Age: 24 Risk: Green

Year	Team	G/GS	Snaps	Runs	Yds	Yd/R	TD	FUM	DVOA	Rk	DYAR	Rk	YAR	Suc%	Rk	BTkl	Rec	Pass	Yds	C%	Yd/C	TD	YAC	DVOA	Rk	DYAR	Rk
2012	STL	16/0	301	98	475	4.8	0	3	1.7%	--	40	--	7	42%	--	13	24	36	163	67%	6.8	0	7.6	-46.9%	47	-65	46
2013	STL	8/3	203	69	215	3.1	0	0	-19.4%	--	-34	--	-49	42%	--	4	14	18	121	78%	8.6	0	8.5	-3.6%	--	9	--
2014	*NYJ*			*32*	*133*	*4.2*	*0*	*1*	*-7.4%*								*17*	*23*	*94*	*74%*	*5.5*	*0*		*-13.4%*			

Richardson had a 56-yard run against the Redskins in his second NFL appearance back in 2012 and has been losing ground ever since. A few more productive change-up efforts behind Steven Jackson unraveled into a string of three-carry, five-yard outings due to some fumbles and the general offensive befuddlement that surrounds the Rams. Declared a "space player" in the 2013 offseason, Richardson somehow won a starting job as the featured Rams running back in camp, even though there is rarely any "space" between the tackles in a Brian Schottenheimer offense. Richardson kept his starting job for over a month despite a foot injury that sometimes flared up on his first carry of the game. After some 12-for-16 rushing days behind an awful line in a bad offense, Richardson lost his job to Zac Stacy and slowly faded into the land of inactives, posting two more of his three-carry specials on the way. Richardson is now with the Jets, who have lots of running backs who can carry the football three times per game, and several who can do even more.

Trent Richardson Height: 5-9 Weight: 228 College: Alabama Draft: 2012/1 (3) Born: 10-Jul-1991 Age: 23 Risk: Green

Year	Team	G/GS	Snaps	Runs	Yds	Yd/R	TD	FUM	DVOA	Rk	DYAR	Rk	YAR	Suc%	Rk	BTkl	Rec	Pass	Yds	C%	Yd/C	TD	YAC	DVOA	Rk	DYAR	Rk
2012	CLE	15/15	702	267	950	3.6	11	3	-13.3%	34	-51	37	-21	43%	36	31	51	70	367	73%	7.2	1	8.6	4.4%	23	73	11
2013	2TM	16/10	592	188	563	3.0	3	2	-22.2%	44	-108	45	-124	43%	36	24	35	52	316	67%	9.0	1	8.8	-2.6%	25	34	26
2014	*IND*			*195*	*759*	*3.9*	*5*	*1*	*-4.3%*								*42*	*58*	*342*	*72%*	*8.1*	*2*		*13.3%*			

As Fiona Grigson once sang, "I've been a bad, bad, GM/I've been careless with my first-round pick/and it's a sad, sad, world/when T-Rich can't rush for three yards a clip." Let's close the book on the Trent Richardson trade. There's no reason to pretend the Colts will ever see fair value from it. That doesn't mean Richardson can't become a respectable back. The recent running-back landscape is littered with first-round picks who took multiple years to figure it out or get healthy at the right time: Marshawn Lynch, Ryan Mathews, Donald Brown, Thomas Jones, Knowshon Moreno, Mark Ingram, etc. Richardson has the talent to join that list. He's just got to learn to trust what he sees rather than imagining that the interior of the Colts offensive line has collapsed and let three defenders into the backfield. They only do that every other play.

Stevan Ridley Height: 6-0 Weight: 223 College: LSU Draft: 2011/3 (73) Born: 27-Jan-1989 Age: 25 Risk: Green

Year	Team	G/GS	Snaps	Runs	Yds	Yd/R	TD	FUM	DVOA	Rk	DYAR	Rk	YAR	Suc%	Rk	BTkl	Rec	Pass	Yds	C%	Yd/C	TD	YAC	DVOA	Rk	DYAR	Rk
2011	NE	16/2	191	87	441	5.1	1	1	-0.1%	--	31	--	44	51%	--	10	3	5	13	60%	4.3	0	4.3	-45.6%	--	-9	--
2012	NE	16/12	549	290	1263	4.4	12	4	6.1%	9	192	8	191	55%	4	12	6	14	51	43%	8.5	0	7.8	-38.4%	--	-19	--
2013	NE	14/6	333	178	773	4.3	7	4	10.2%	9	135	11	133	52%	7	14	10	12	62	83%	6.2	0	5.7	-27.6%	--	-9	--
2014	*NE*			*194*	*842*	*4.3*	*9*	*3*	*2.2%*								*14*	*21*	*110*	*67%*	*7.8*	*1*		*-3.9%*			

At the start of the 2013 season, there was a real sense of optimism around Ridley for a few reasons, including the fact that he was on the cusp of rushing for 1,000 yards in back-to-back seasons, something no running back had ever done on a Bill Belichick-coached team. Then, the ball security issues that plagued him at the end of the 2012 season returned and he was yanked in and out of the lineup while LeGarrette Blount emerged as a battering ram for a suddenly resurgent ground game. Entering the final year of his rookie deal, and with Blount now in Pittsburgh, Ridley is the closest thing the Patriots have to a featured back—but if the ball security issues continue to persist, his spot is by no means secure.

Khiry Robinson Height: 6-0 Weight: 220 College: West Texas A&M Draft: 2013/FA Born: 28-Dec-1989 Age: 25 Risk: Red

Year	Team	G/GS	Snaps	Runs	Yds	Yd/R	TD	FUM	DVOA	Rk	DYAR	Rk	YAR	Suc%	Rk	BTkl	Rec	Pass	Yds	C%	Yd/C	TD	YAC	DVOA	Rk	DYAR	Rk
2013	NO	10/0	73	54	224	4.1	1	0	-11.9%	--	-7	--	4	41%	--	5	0	0	0	--	0.0	0	--	--	--	--	--
2014	*NO*			*106*	*454*	*4.3*	*2*	*4*	*-9.3%*								*6*	*7*	*53*	*85%*	*8.8*	*0*		*4.9%*			

Robinson became the eighth running back this century to carry the ball at least 50 times without catching a single pass. The last to do it, Chris Ivory in 2011, also played for the Saints. Sean Payton sure likes to keep a no-hands power back on the depth chart. Of course, that also describes Mark Ingram (356 career carries, 24 career receptions), which makes you wonder how long he and Robinson will last on the same roster. The Saints used Robinson more when games mattered most; he had 13 carries for 57 yards in the playoff loss to Seattle, his best game in either category all year. When word broke that Bill Parcells had called Payton and told him to use Robinson more, comparing him to Curtis Martin, Robinson's name began to pop up as a potential fantasy sleeper for 2014, but Payton has always used a committee approach for his running backs. Robinson's rise to prominence would just further muddy the waters.

Jacquizz Rodgers Height: 5-6 Weight: 196 College: Oregon State Draft: 2011/5 (145) Born: 6-Feb-1990 Age: 24 Risk: Yellow

Year	Team	G/GS	Snaps	Runs	Yds	Yd/R	TD	FUM	DVOA	Rk	DYAR	Rk	YAR	Suc%	Rk	BTkl	Rec	Pass	Yds	C%	Yd/C	TD	YAC	DVOA	Rk	DYAR	Rk
2011	ATL	16/0	316	57	205	3.6	1	1	-9.8%	--	-3	--	-3	46%	--	19	21	28	188	79%	9.0	1	6.5	32.5%	4	60	15
2012	ATL	16/0	464	94	362	3.9	1	0	-10.9%	--	-9	--	-12	38%	--	26	53	59	402	90%	7.6	1	8.2	26.1%	4	135	4
2013	ATL	15/4	435	96	332	3.5	2	1	-8.1%	--	2	--	-7	45%	--	16	52	62	341	84%	6.6	2	7.0	7.8%	18	72	15
2014	*ATL*			*104*	*402*	*3.8*	*2*	*1*	*-11.8%*								*53*	*62*	*450*	*85%*	*8.5*	*2*		*21.0%*			

When Steven Jackson missed four games with a hamstring injury, Rodgers got the first four starts of his career. His numbers in those four games: 47 carries, a 3.8-yard average, and a DVOA of 0.1%. He's shifty and hard to bring down, but he's had trouble translating that ability into big plays, with only two 20-yard runs in his career. In three years, he has basically been a replacement-level runner, and the Falcons may have drafted his replacement in fourth-rounder Devonta Freeman. Rodgers does have value as a receiver, and that's important for a quarterback who checks down as often as Matt Ryan does.

Bishop Sankey Height: 5-9 Weight: 209 College: Washington Draft: 2014/2 (54) Born: 9/15/1992 Age: 22 Risk: Yellow

Year	Team	G/GS	Snaps	Runs	Yds	Yd/R	TD	FUM	DVOA	Rk	DYAR	Rk	YAR	Suc%	Rk	BTkl	Rec	Pass	Yds	C%	Yd/C	TD	YAC	DVOA	Rk	DYAR	Rk
2014	*TEN*			*187*	*745*	*4.0*	*6*	*2*	*-6.4%*								*28*	*40*	*240*	*70%*	*8.6*	*1*		*-4.8%*			

Sankey has the physical talent to be one of the best backs in the league, but his status as first runner off the board was more about this class than his abilities. Sankey struggles to read the box beyond the line of scrimmage, and the Titans would be best-served letting him work on that or curbing their zone runs. Unfortunately, Tennessee's other options in the backfield include Shonn Greene and Jackie Battle, so Sankey will probably play right away and play early. The talent and opportunity are there for him to be a good fantasy football pick, but his conceptual understanding of the game may make him an early bust.

Charles Sims Height: 6-0 Weight: 214 College: West Virginia Draft: 2014/3 (69) Born: 9/19/1990 Age: 24 Risk: Yellow

Year	Team	G/GS	Snaps	Runs	Yds	Yd/R	TD	FUM	DVOA	Rk	DYAR	Rk	YAR	Suc%	Rk	BTkl	Rec	Pass	Yds	C%	Yd/C	TD	YAC	DVOA	Rk	DYAR	Rk
2014	*TB*			*67*	*288*	*4.3*	*1*	*1*	*-7.2%*								*27*	*34*	*250*	*79%*	*9.3*	*1*		*-6.1%*			

Sims only played one season at West Virginia, but he led the Big 12 last year in yards from scrimmage, adding 401 receiving yards (with an 82 percent catch rate) to 1,095 rushing yards (5.3 yards per carry and 6.5 Highlight Yards per Opportunity). His Speed Score of 106.3 was one of the top five among running backs at the combine this year. The Bucs took him in the third round, and though Bobby Rainey and Mike James had a lot of success last year, Sims could have the talent to pass them on the depth chart to back up Doug Martin—especially because his receiving talents should make him a standout third-down back.

Jason Snelling Height: 5-11 Weight: 235 College: Virginia Draft: 2007/7 (244) Born: 29-Dec-1983 Age: 31 Risk: #N/A

Year	Team	G/GS	Snaps	Runs	Yds	Yd/R	TD	FUM	DVOA	Rk	DYAR	Rk	YAR	Suc%	Rk	BTkl	Rec	Pass	Yds	C%	Yd/C	TD	YAC	DVOA	Rk	DYAR	Rk
2011	ATL	15/0	315	44	151	3.4	0	0	-22.9%	--	-25	--	-22	39%	--	8	26	32	179	81%	6.9	1	6.3	24.9%	8	60	16
2012	ATL	16/2	228	18	63	3.5	0	1	-19.6%	--	-9	--	-9	39%	--	7	31	35	203	89%	6.5	1	6.9	-8.8%	29	10	30
2013	ATL	14/1	226	44	164	3.7	1	0	1.2%	--	19	--	19	50%	--	10	29	33	216	85%	7.4	3	6.5	46.2%	1	109	12

Snelling did a little bit of everything in his Falcons career: running, receiving, blocking, and special teams, where he played 110 snaps last season. His retirement was a little surprising, but the Falcons don't use a particularly high number of two-back sets, and there are plenty of better options at running back. Well, maybe not in Atlanta, but in general.

C.J. Spiller Height: 5-11 Weight: 195 College: Clemson Draft: 2010/1 (9) Born: 15-Aug-1987 Age: 27 Risk: Green

Year	Team	G/GS	Snaps	Runs	Yds	Yd/R	TD	FUM	DVOA	Rk	DYAR	Rk	YAR	Suc%	Rk	BTkl	Rec	Pass	Yds	C%	Yd/C	TD	YAC	DVOA	Rk	DYAR	Rk
2011	BUF	16/11	462	107	561	5.2	4	2	6.4%	13	68	23	62	51%	13	17	39	54	269	74%	6.9	2	6.3	10.7%	21	80	11
2012	BUF	16/9	568	207	1244	6.0	6	3	27.6%	1	301	3	291	55%	3	34	43	57	459	75%	10.7	2	11.8	16.3%	9	91	7
2013	BUF	15/10	389	202	933	4.6	2	4	-17.8%	43	-70	43	-49	36%	44	18	33	40	185	83%	5.6	0	6.9	-17.8%	40	-8	41
2014	*BUF*			*200*	*913*	*4.6*	*4*	*3*	*-0.8%*								*45*	*59*	*437*	*76%*	*9.7*	*1*		*21.5%*			

This season looms as a key year for Spiller—he not only has the specter of last year's lackluster finish looming, but he also can opt out of his rookie deal at the end of 2014. There are still nagging questions about the Clemson product, who has been very good for an extended stretch, but never managed to put up the sort of consistent numbers that some believe he should be capable of posting. Ultimately, is he a good piece of an overall offensive puzzle—a back who can work as part of a group, in concert with others, providing depth and support as needed both as a runner and pass catcher? Or is he a potential offensive centerpiece, a truly special presence who deserves more touches, especially in the passing game?

Darren Sproles Height: 5-6 Weight: 181 College: Kansas State Draft: 2005/4 (130) Born: 20-Jun-1983 Age: 31 Risk: Green

Year	Team	G/GS	Snaps	Runs	Yds	Yd/R	TD	FUM	DVOA	Rk	DYAR	Rk	YAR	Suc%	Rk	BTkl	Rec	Pass	Yds	C%	Yd/C	TD	YAC	DVOA	Rk	DYAR	Rk
2011	NO	16/4	492	87	603	6.9	2	0	46.2%	--	193	--	194	53%	--	16	86	111	710	77%	8.3	7	8.3	25.8%	6	261	1
2012	NO	13/6	444	48	244	5.1	1	0	10.9%	--	34	--	25	44%	--	12	75	104	667	72%	8.9	7	8.9	21.5%	7	214	1
2013	NO	15/4	357	53	220	4.2	2	1	1.4%	--	21	--	25	49%	--	14	71	89	604	80%	8.5	2	7.3	23.9%	8	174	4
2014	*PHI*			*76*	*389*	*5.1*	*1*	*1*	*10.6%*								*66*	*89*	*510*	*74%*	*7.7*	*2*		*4.3%*			

The premier receiver out of the backfield of this generation—and sometimes, a premier receiver *not* out of the backfield (see Table 1, next page)—Sproles has finished among the top six running backs in receiving DYAR in each of the past six seasons, and has led the league in that category three times. Meanwhile, he has never carried the ball often enough to qualify for our rushing tables. There was talk that the Eagles might move him into the slot, but both Sproles and Chip Kelly insist he was brought in to play running back. The Eagles lean heavily on LeSean McCoy, limiting the opportunities for other runners, but they didn't trade for Sproles and then sign him to a two-year deal so he could sit on the bench.

Table 1. Top 10 Running Backs Lined Up as Wide Receivers, 2013

Player	Team	Wide	Slot	Total
Darren Sproles	NO	36	92	128
Andre Ellington	ARI	70	50	120
Reggie Bush	DET	52	61	113
Marcel Reece	OAK	32	77	109
Le'Veon Bell	PIT	25	57	82
Jamaal Charles	KC	48	11	59
Bruce Miller	SF	30	28	58
Danny Woodhead	SD	33	23	56
Chris Johnson	TEN	42	11	53
Shane Vereen	NE	37	10	47

Zac Stacy

Height: 5-8 Weight: 216 College: Vanderbilt Draft: 2013/5 (160) Born: 9-Apr-1991 Age: 23 Risk: Yellow

Year	Team	G/GS	Snaps	Runs	Yds	Yd/R	TD	FUM	DVOA	Rk	DYAR	Rk	YAR	Suc%	Rk	BTkl	Rec	Pass	Yds	C%	Yd/C	TD	YAC	DVOA	Rk	DYAR	Rk
2013	STL	14/12	566	250	973	3.9	7	1	-0.7%	23	80	23	55	42%	39	15	26	35	141	74%	5.4	1	5.7	-19.7%	43	-11	42
2014	*STL*			*234*	*884*	*3.8*	*8*	*2*	*-11.0%*								*30*	*45*	*196*	*67%*	*6.5*	*0*		*-19.0%*			

After getting buried on the bench for rookie cluelessness in camp, Stacy averaged 22.2 carries per game from Week 8 through the end of the season. He handled the workload well. He was a 61-carry battering ram in December wins against the Saints and Bucs, adding a little passing-game utility in other games and generally solving a severe running back problem that plagued the Rams in the first half of the season. But the Rams had enough draft choices to splurge at some positions, and if 33 carries up the middle is a part of a typical game plan, it pays to have two or more power runners. Tre Mason will likely overtake Stacy on the depth chart by the end of this season, but there are plenty of handoffs to go around and no really good contenders for the No. 2 role in St. Louis.

James Starks

Height: 6-2 Weight: 218 College: Buffalo Draft: 2010/6 (193) Born: 25-Feb-1986 Age: 28 Risk: Green

Year	Team	G/GS	Snaps	Runs	Yds	Yd/R	TD	FUM	DVOA	Rk	DYAR	Rk	YAR	Suc%	Rk	BTkl	Rec	Pass	Yds	C%	Yd/C	TD	YAC	DVOA	Rk	DYAR	Rk
2011	GB	13/2	431	133	578	4.3	1	2	-4.5%	37	22	39	6	49%	19	16	29	38	216	79%	7.4	0	9.3	6.7%	23	39	26
2012	GB	6/2	124	71	255	3.6	1	1	-4.3%	--	13	--	-3	51%	--	5	4	6	31	67%	7.8	0	10.5	-24.9%	--	-4	--
2013	GB	13/1	220	89	493	5.5	3	1	19.2%	--	110	--	130	54%	--	13	10	13	89	77%	8.9	1	10.9	38.0%	--	36	--
2014	*GB*			*55*	*246*	*4.5*	*2*	*2*	*4.7%*								*19*	*25*	*125*	*76%*	*6.6*	*0*		*-5.3%*			

Complementary running backs only look as good as the running backs they complement. Starks racked up his best numbers against desperate defenses: 20-132-1 against the Redskins, 11-88-0 in the finale against the Bears. But he was also excellent as an off-the-bench change up for Eddie Lacy, with a 25-yard touchdown in the first Bears game and 25- and 34-yard runs in two Vikings games, plus 47 yards of high Success-Rate grinding against the Steelers. It was roughly the same season Starks had in 2011, a little better than his 2012 season, but Lacy was far superior to Ryan Grant, Cedric Benson, and Alex Green. So instead of wondering why Starks could not do more, the Packers could make the most of what he did.

Jonathan Stewart

Height: 5-10 Weight: 235 College: Oregon Draft: 2008/1 (13) Born: 21-Mar-1987 Age: 27 Risk: Red

Year	Team	G/GS	Snaps	Runs	Yds	Yd/R	TD	FUM	DVOA	Rk	DYAR	Rk	YAR	Suc%	Rk	BTkl	Rec	Pass	Yds	C%	Yd/C	TD	YAC	DVOA	Rk	DYAR	Rk
2011	CAR	16/3	577	142	761	5.4	4	1	23.4%	2	194	4	178	53%	8	21	47	61	413	77%	8.8	1	10.3	19.1%	14	105	7
2012	CAR	9/6	312	93	336	3.6	1	2	-18.4%	--	-36	--	-55	42%	--	5	17	23	157	74%	9.2	1	10.5	15.0%	--	34	--
2013	CAR	6/1	110	48	180	3.8	0	1	-7.4%	--	2	--	1	48%	--	4	7	7	44	100%	6.3	0	6.0	30.1%	--	18	--
2014	*CAR*			*103*	*430*	*4.2*	*2*	*1*	*-3.6%*								*18*	*23*	*118*	*78%*	*6.6*	*0*		*0.3%*			

The annual decline in Stewart's carries since 2009 has been nearly linear. Every year, he carries the ball 30 or 40 times fewer than he did the season prior. Injuries and missed time have contributed to that pattern, but his 8.0 carries per game last season were a career low. Stewart's last two years have been ruined by ankle and knee problems, but he went into OTAs saying he was the healthiest he had been since his brilliant 2011 campaign. Given DeAngelo Williams' age, there is a chance for a bounceback season here. There's also a chance that Stewart's decline will continue and he'll somehow find a way to post negative carries.

Ben Tate Height: 5-11 Weight: 220 College: Auburn Draft: 2010/2 (58) Born: 21-Aug-1988 Age: 26 Risk: Green

Year	Team	G/GS	Snaps	Runs	Yds	Yd/R	TD	FUM	DVOA	Rk	DYAR	Rk	YAR	Suc%	Rk	BTkl	Rec	Pass	Yds	C%	Yd/C	TD	YAC	DVOA	Rk	DYAR	Rk
2011	HOU	15/2	328	175	942	5.4	4	4	12.5%	8	151	10	162	53%	9	19	13	19	98	68%	7.5	0	6.3	-2.7%	--	12	--
2012	HOU	11/0	143	65	279	4.3	2	1	-2.2%	--	18	--	33	49%	--	9	11	11	49	100%	4.5	0	3.6	-27.7%	--	-9	--
2013	HOU	14/7	481	181	771	4.3	4	5	-2.0%	25	50	26	51	51%	12	19	34	50	140	70%	4.1	0	4.7	-62.9%	49	-125	49
2014	*CLE*			*198*	*853*	*4.3*	*4*	*3*	*-2.1%*								*33*	*45*	*232*	*73%*	*7.0*	*0*		*-5.5%*			

If a generation of college players who would be running backs instead decide to play safety or linebacker, Tate's story will be an instrumental example of why. Drafted in the second round, Tate was supposed to be the bellcow that turned around Gary Kubiak's run game after Steve Slaton fell to injury. But Tate broke his ankle in the preseason, and Arian Foster proved to be better than the Texans had hoped. Instead, Tate spent two years as a backup, started half of a season with broken ribs after Foster hit IR, and found a cold market that led him to Cleveland for a paltry $1.5 million in guarantees. Tate is still only 25, and his downhill burst is enough to make him a potential top-15 back in the NFL. But between his inability to produce as a reciever, poor blocking, and vision that comes and goes, he's more of a head back in a committee than a 300-carry guy.

Stepfan Taylor Height: 5-9 Weight: 214 College: Stanford Draft: 2013/5 (140) Born: 9-Jun-1991 Age: 23 Risk: Red

Year	Team	G/GS	Snaps	Runs	Yds	Yd/R	TD	FUM	DVOA	Rk	DYAR	Rk	YAR	Suc%	Rk	BTkl	Rec	Pass	Yds	C%	Yd/C	TD	YAC	DVOA	Rk	DYAR	Rk
2013	ARI	16/0	131	36	115	3.2	0	0	-14.7%	--	-9	--	-11	39%	--	5	8	9	71	89%	8.9	0	7.5	-10.7%	--	2	--
2014	*ARI*			*105*	*431*	*4.1*	*2*	*1*	*-9.7%*								*24*	*28*	*204*	*86%*	*8.5*	*1*		*18.4%*			

Taylor only had one game last year with more than five carries, and he failed to impress against Atlanta. Still, he should have a larger role this year with Rashard Mendenhall no longer around. Taylor fills the power back role for Arizona opposite Andre Ellington, and has the potential to exceed his projection here if he is given red zone carries and becomes the dreaded touchdown vulture.

Daniel Thomas Height: 6-2 Weight: 228 College: Kansas State Draft: 2011/2 (62) Born: 29-Oct-1987 Age: 27 Risk: Red

Year	Team	G/GS	Snaps	Runs	Yds	Yd/R	TD	FUM	DVOA	Rk	DYAR	Rk	YAR	Suc%	Rk	BTkl	Rec	Pass	Yds	C%	Yd/C	TD	YAC	DVOA	Rk	DYAR	Rk
2011	MIA	13/2	367	165	581	3.5	0	2	-24.7%	50	-110	51	-100	42%	43	9	12	16	72	75%	6.0	1	5.3	11.8%	--	20	--
2012	MIA	12/0	323	91	325	3.6	4	3	-10.8%	--	-9	--	3	51%	--	13	15	22	156	68%	10.4	0	9.6	0.8%	--	14	--
2013	MIA	15/1	339	109	406	3.7	4	0	-7.7%	30	4	32	34	47%	22	14	15	17	63	88%	4.2	2	5.6	12.3%	--	27	--
2014	*MIA*			*112*	*440*	*3.9*	*3*	*2*	*-9.4%*								*16*	*20*	*97*	*80%*	*6.0*	*0*		*-4.4%*			

Consistent mediocrity thrives along the Miami offense. Thomas has had at least 90 carries in his first three seasons and he's never topped 3.75 yards per carry. That puts him on a list with just six other running backs since 1940: Karim Abdul-Jabbar, Keith Byars, Tucker Frederickson, Thomas Jones, Errict Rhett and Leonard Russell. Byars at least had receiving value and Jones turned things around, but the fake basketball player, Rhett and Russell notoriously led careers submerged under the league rushing average. Thomas may still be the best short-yardage runner in Miami, but there's no logical reason except "everyone else got hurt" to keep giving him 90-plus carries a season.

Pierre Thomas Height: 5-11 Weight: 210 College: Illinois Draft: 2007/FA Born: 18-Dec-1984 Age: 30 Risk: Green

Year	Team	G/GS	Snaps	Runs	Yds	Yd/R	TD	FUM	DVOA	Rk	DYAR	Rk	YAR	Suc%	Rk	BTkl	Rec	Pass	Yds	C%	Yd/C	TD	YAC	DVOA	Rk	DYAR	Rk
2011	NO	16/7	389	110	562	5.1	5	1	30.0%	1	180	5	180	61%	1	20	50	59	425	85%	8.5	1	9.4	16.2%	17	103	8
2012	NO	15/4	385	105	473	4.5	1	0	15.1%	6	97	14	80	53%	6	11	39	53	354	74%	9.1	1	9.3	18.7%	8	99	6
2013	NO	16/9	564	147	549	3.7	2	1	-7.6%	29	6	30	32	53%	5	16	77	84	513	92%	6.7	3	8.3	13.2%	13	128	9
2014	*NO*			*134*	*536*	*4.0*	*3*	*3*	*-7.6%*								*65*	*89*	*533*	*73%*	*8.2*	*2*		*8.8%*			

Thomas led all running backs in receptions last season, and though his advanced stats weren't quite that impressive, his newfound versatility may have saved his job. The Saints released a number of veterans this offseason in a salary purge, and Thomas has said he expected to join them. Instead, Darren Sproles was traded to the Eagles and Thomas stayed in town, though he did take a paycut in the process. With Sproles gone and Travaris Cadet unproven, Thomas enters camp as the most proven receiver (and blocker) in the Saints' backfield. That could mean more of a third-down role that would cut down on his carries and boost his receptions, which might bump him up to an RB2 in PPR leagues.

Jordan Todman Height: 5-9 Weight: 203 College: Connecticut Draft: 2011/6 (183) Born: 24-Feb-1990 Age: 24 Risk: Blue

Year	Team	G/GS	Snaps	Runs	Yds	Yd/R	TD	FUM	DVOA	Rk	DYAR	Rk	YAR	Suc%	Rk	BTkl	Rec	Pass	Yds	C%	Yd/C	TD	YAC	DVOA	Rk	DYAR	Rk
2012	JAC	1/0	7	3	8	2.7	0	0	-42.4%	--	-4	--	-5	33%	--	0	1	1	0	100%	0.0	0	3.0	-94.3%	--	-6	--
2013	JAC	16/2	263	76	256	3.4	2	0	-4.2%	--	13	--	6	37%	--	5	14	26	116	54%	8.3	1	6.9	-12.6%	36	2	36
2014	*JAC*			*45*	*163*	*3.6*	*1*	*1*	*-11.8%*								*15*	*20*	*92*	*75%*	*6.2*	*0*		*-9.3%*			

Todman showed good burst despite his poor offensive line, but helped the Jaguars more as a kick returner than as a runner. With Toby Gerhart in town, and Todman's pedestrian season as a receiver, it stands to reason that Todman will be purely a backup in 2013. For a practice squad signing, the Jaguars have found a pretty functional committee back. There are bigger problems on the Jacksonville roster, and the improved offensive line will help Todman should injury befall Gerhart.

Mike Tolbert Height: 5-9 Weight: 243 College: Coastal Carolina Draft: 2008/FA Born: 23-Nov-1985 Age: 29 Risk: Green

Year	Team	G/GS	Snaps	Runs	Yds	Yd/R	TD	FUM	DVOA	Rk	DYAR	Rk	YAR	Suc%	Rk	BTkl	Rec	Pass	Yds	C%	Yd/C	TD	YAC	DVOA	Rk	DYAR	Rk
2011	SD	15/1	484	121	490	4.0	8	2	-3.1%	34	30	35	49	48%	22	19	54	79	433	68%	8.0	2	8.0	-2.1%	30	54	19
2012	CAR	16/5	445	54	183	3.4	7	0	25.8%	--	103	--	106	65%	--	10	27	39	268	69%	9.9	0	10.2	7.7%	20	48	20
2013	CAR	16/13	599	101	361	3.6	5	0	9.0%	12	86	22	69	50%	13	11	27	32	184	84%	6.8	2	7.1	29.0%	6	77	14
2014	*CAR*			*60*	*207*	*3.4*	*3*	*1*	*-7.4%*								*30*	*38*	*196*	*79%*	*6.5*	*0*		*-0.8%*			

What we have here is a short-yardage specialist. Carolina running backs had 22 carries on "Power" downs last season, and Tolbert had 20 of them, with 14 conversions. (Cam Newton, if you're wondering, converted 16 of 20 "Power" runs.) Tolbert's average carry came with 6.8 yards to go for a first down, least for any runner with at least 100 carries. (Next lowest: Newton.) If Jonathan Stewart is as healthy as he claims, Tolbert's totals are likely to go down, but his short-yardage ability—plus value as a receiver, blocker, and special teamer (85 snaps last season)—ensure his spot on the roster.

Robert Turbin Height: 5-10 Weight: 222 College: Utah State Draft: 2012/4 (106) Born: 2-Dec-1989 Age: 25 Risk: Green

Year	Team	G/GS	Snaps	Runs	Yds	Yd/R	TD	FUM	DVOA	Rk	DYAR	Rk	YAR	Suc%	Rk	BTkl	Rec	Pass	Yds	C%	Yd/C	TD	YAC	DVOA	Rk	DYAR	Rk
2012	SEA	16/0	224	80	354	4.4	0	0	-5.2%	--	11	--	8	46%	--	7	19	23	181	83%	9.5	0	6.7	21.2%	--	48	--
2013	SEA	16/0	231	77	264	3.4	0	0	-17.0%	--	-25	--	-28	44%	--	4	8	12	60	67%	7.5	0	8.0	-24.2%	--	-6	--
2014	*SEA*			*62*	*272*	*4.4*	*1*	*2*	*-6.2%*								*12*	*15*	*95*	*80%*	*7.9*	*0*		*9.2%*			

Turbin and Christine Michael came to Seattle as virtually identical backs in some ways. Both measured in at 5-foot-10 and around 220 pounds at their scouting combines, Michael ran a 4.43 forty to Turbin's 4.42, and both have been waiting in the wings as Marshawn Lynch continues to define Seattle's running game—and, by proxy, Seattle's offense. That could easily change in 2014, given offensive coordinator Darrell Bevell's recent comments about a running back by committee approach, and while Michael is the more agile and explosive player, it's Turbin who has an extra year in the Seahawks' system under his belt—which makes him potentially more attractive to Pete Carroll when it comes to who gets more reps. Turbin has the edge in pass protection, which is especially crucial to the franchise as it looks to see just how much it can stack on Russell Wilson's shoulders. Bevell did mention in June that Turbin had several big plays in 2013 that were called back, including a 33-yard run to start the fourth quarter of the Super Bowl that was nixed by a holding call. So, as much as Michael may have more upside, it could be Turbin that's turned into the feature back in the short term of the post-Lynch landscape.

Shane Vereen Height: 5-10 Weight: 205 College: California Draft: 2011/2 (56) Born: 2-Mar-1989 Age: 25 Risk: Green

Year	Team	G/GS	Snaps	Runs	Yds	Yd/R	TD	FUM	DVOA	Rk	DYAR	Rk	YAR	Suc%	Rk	BTkl	Rec	Pass	Yds	C%	Yd/C	TD	YAC	DVOA	Rk	DYAR	Rk
2011	NE	5/0	26	15	57	3.8	1	0	-2.1%	--	4	--	1	40%	--	2	0	--	0	--	0.0	0	--	--	--	--	--
2012	NE	13/1	161	62	251	4.0	3	1	9.6%	--	47	--	52	52%	--	4	8	13	149	62%	18.6	1	17.5	69.6%	--	64	--
2013	NE	8/1	295	44	208	4.7	1	1	-5.0%	--	6	--	6	39%	--	11	47	69	427	68%	9.1	3	5.9	25.1%	7	151	6
2014	*NE*			*92*	*437*	*4.7*	*1*	*1*	*2.6%*								*66*	*92*	*536*	*72%*	*8.1*	*1*		*2.2%*			

Vereen suffered a wrist injury in the 2013 opener against the Bills, and was on the IR-DFR until mid-November. But even limited to eight games, he finished with 47 catches and 44 carries, just shy of the 50/50 mark last hit in New England by Kevin Faulk with 83 carries and 58 catches in 2008. A matchup nightmare as a receiver, his ability to operate in the slot or split wide can give opposing defensive coordinators ice cream headaches. He's fast enough to shake linebackers and bigger than many defensive backs. He's a dynamic offensive option, and if he can stay healthy for the course of a full season and avoid the occasionally ugly dropped pass, there's the chance he could veer dangerously close to Sprolesian territory.

Terrance West Height: 5-9 Weight: 225 College: Towson Draft: 2014/3 (94) Born: 1/28/1991 Age: 23 Risk: Yellow

Year	Team	G/GS	Snaps	Runs	Yds	Yd/R	TD	FUM	DVOA	Rk	DYAR	Rk	YAR	Suc%	Rk	BTkl	Rec	Pass	Yds	C%	Yd/C	TD	YAC	DVOA	Rk	DYAR	Rk
2014	*CLE*			*110*	*461*	*4.2*	*5*	*1*	*0.8%*								*19*	*24*	*173*	*79%*	*9.1*	*1*		*7.0%*			

Playing at tiny Towson in Maryland, West compiled eye-popping stats--over 2,500 yards rushing and 42 touchdowns just last season. He was the small-school equivalent of Carlos Hyde or Jeremy Hill, a banger with good vision and great quickness between the tackles. He should fit Kyle Shanahan's one-cut zone blocking scheme perfectly, and it wouldn't be a shock to see West supplant newly imported Ben Tate as Cleveland's lead back sooner rather than later. His action probably needs to come quickly--after 780 collegiate carries, West doesn't figure to accrue many years on his pro pension.

James White Height: 5-9 Weight: 204 College: Wisconsin Draft: 2014/4 (130) Born: 3-Feb-1992 Age: 22 Risk: Yellow

Year	Team	G/GS	Snaps	Runs	Yds	Yd/R	TD	FUM	DVOA	Rk	DYAR	Rk	YAR	Suc%	Rk	BTkl	Rec	Pass	Yds	C%	Yd/C	TD	YAC	DVOA	Rk	DYAR	Rk
2014	*NE*			*82*	*402*	*4.9*	*1*	*1*	*5.5%*								*35*	*50*	*316*	*70%*	*9.0*	*2*		*-1.1%*			

This fourth-round pick out of Wisconsin has a strong physical comparison to new teammate Shane Vereen. Both are 5-foot-10, while Vereen is listed as 200 pounds and White is at 194, and both demonstrated a nice ability to catch the ball out of the backfield as collegians. White had 73 catches as a collegian, including 39 last year, while Vereen had 74 at Cal. But when it comes to White's numbers, the stat that really jumps off the page is his fumbles, or lack thereof—he fumbled just twice in 754 career touches as a collegian. He figures to sit behind Vereen, Stevan Ridley and Brandon Bolden, but could find his way into the lineup sooner rather than later.

Fozzy Whittaker Height: 5-10 Weight: 202 College: Texas Draft: 2012/FA Born: 2-Feb-1989 Age: 25 Risk: #N/A

Year	Team	G/GS	Snaps	Runs	Yds	Yd/R	TD	FUM	DVOA	Rk	DYAR	Rk	YAR	Suc%	Rk	BTkl	Rec	Pass	Yds	C%	Yd/C	TD	YAC	DVOA	Rk	DYAR	Rk
2013	2TM	14/2	167	28	79	2.8	0	0	-25.2%	--	-17	--	-11	43%	--	1	21	35	155	60%	7.4	2	7.4	-5.5%	29	18	30

Cut by the Browns in March, Foswhitt Whittaker was about as obscure in an NFL context as Fozzy, wrestler Chris Jericho's band, was in heavy metal circles, and much more so than Fozzie the Bear was in the Muppets. Certainly Whitaker, roster filler who ended up with way too much playing time last year, never had a moment as sublime as Fozzie's answer to Kermit when told to "bear left." "Right, frog" was the reply. It was the furry hand puppet equivalent of an 80-yard touchdown run.

Andre Williams Height: 5-11 Weight: 230 College: Boston College Draft: 2014/4 (113) Born: 28-Aug-1992 Age: 22 Risk: Green

Year	Team	G/GS	Snaps	Runs	Yds	Yd/R	TD	FUM	DVOA	Rk	DYAR	Rk	YAR	Suc%	Rk	BTkl	Rec	Pass	Yds	C%	Yd/C	TD	YAC	DVOA	Rk	DYAR	Rk
2014	*NYG*			*71*	*278*	*3.9*	*2*	*1*	*-8.5%*								*13*	*17*	*124*	*76%*	*9.5*	*1*		*11.8%*			

Williams finished second in the nation in yards from scrimmage last year without catching a single pass. That's a remarkable feat that also tells you quite a bit about his game. Rashad Jennings is going to be New York's starter and third-down back, which means the change-ups will come on first and second down, and that in turn means opportunity for Williams. At Boston College, Williams was a dominant force in 2013, finishing fourth in the Heisman voting despite the Eagles being insignificant in the national picture. Of course, Williams forced himself into the national picture by rushing for 1,235 yards in one five-game stretch last fall, and he hit the 2,000-yard mark in his 11th game. He's a natural runner with great vision and a strong frame; he also managed to surprise some by running well at the combine. The Giants have a history of favoring big backs, and Williams certainly could turn into the next great workhorse. But he won't start until he improves his skills in the passing game.

DeAngelo Williams Height: 5-8 Weight: 210 College: Memphis Draft: 2006/1 (27) Born: 25-Apr-1983 Age: 31 Risk: Green

Year	Team	G/GS	Snaps	Runs	Yds	Yd/R	TD	FUM	DVOA	Rk	DYAR	Rk	YAR	Suc%	Rk	BTkl	Rec	Pass	Yds	C%	Yd/C	TD	YAC	DVOA	Rk	DYAR	Rk
2011	CAR	16/14	447	155	836	5.4	7	0	18.0%	3	158	8	147	46%	28	13	16	25	135	64%	8.4	0	9.8	5.9%	24	28	34
2012	CAR	16/10	417	173	737	4.3	5	2	-6.7%	26	14	25	19	48%	22	9	13	20	187	65%	14.4	2	16.4	38.9%	--	60	--
2013	CAR	15/15	470	201	843	4.2	3	3	7.2%	16	126	12	76	43%	34	17	26	36	333	72%	12.8	1	14.3	16.0%	12	57	18
2014	*CAR*			*174*	*753*	*4.3*	*4*	*1*	*-0.1%*								*18*	*23*	*135*	*78%*	*7.5*	*1*		*8.5%*			

Williams failed to score a touchdown on 17 carries inside the 10-yard line last year. This is nothing new. He had 12 carries inside the 10 in 2012, and only scored on one of them. Since 2010, he has scored only three touchdowns on 40 carries inside the 10. (For comparison's sake, Green Bay's Eddie Lacy scored 10 touchdowns on 25 carries inside the 10 as a rookie last year.) Goal-line stats oscillate wildly, so this kind of consistency really says something. What it says is that there are better goal-line options in Carolina, including the quarterback. A healthy Jonathan Stewart could also eat into Williams' playing time.

David Wilson Height: 5-10 Weight: 206 College: Virginia Tech Draft: 2012/1 (32) Born: 15-Jun-1991 Age: 23 Risk: Red

Year	Team	G/GS	Snaps	Runs	Yds	Yd/R	TD	FUM	DVOA	Rk	DYAR	Rk	YAR	Suc%	Rk	BTkl	Rec	Pass	Yds	C%	Yd/C	TD	YAC	DVOA	Rk	DYAR	Rk
2012	NYG	16/2	125	71	358	5.0	4	1	1.5%	--	30	--	29	39%	--	6	4	9	34	44%	8.5	1	3.5	-17.4%	--	-2	--
2013	NYG	5/4	111	44	146	3.3	1	2	-30.4%	--	-40	--	-42	45%	--	9	2	6	8	33%	4.0	0	5.5	-89.5%	--	-20	--
2014	*NYG*			*79*	*339*	*4.3*	*2*	*1*	*-0.8%*								*8*	*12*	*66*	*67%*	*8.2*	*0*		*-0.3%*			

Wilson suffered a serious neck injury in 2013 that may yet end his career. So far, Wilson has responded well to surgery and rehab, but until he's out on the field again, you might as well use a Magic 8 Ball to project Wilson's 2014 season. Even when healthy, Wilson needs to get over his fumble issues and re-learn how to take the sort of hits running backs face on a weekly basis. He may be the most talented back on the Giants roster, and he could still wind up leading the team in rushing as soon this season. The more likely result, though, is that the Giants ease him back slowly; with a suddenly-crowded backfield, the Giants would be wise to be very cautious with Wilson's development. If he returns, New York fans hope he can regain the explosiveness he had in 2012, when he led the NFL in kickoff return yardage and looked electric as a runner.

Danny Woodhead Height: 5-9 Weight: 200 College: Chadron State Draft: 2008/FA Born: 25-Jan-1985 Age: 29 Risk: Green

Year	Team	G/GS	Snaps	Runs	Yds	Yd/R	TD	FUM	DVOA	Rk	DYAR	Rk	YAR	Suc%	Rk	BTkl	Rec	Pass	Yds	C%	Yd/C	TD	YAC	DVOA	Rk	DYAR	Rk
2011	NE	15/4	367	77	351	4.6	1	0	22.6%	--	100	--	93	55%	--	3	18	31	157	58%	8.7	0	7.0	-10.9%	39	5	39
2012	NE	16/2	417	76	301	4.0	4	1	22.4%	--	101	--	75	55%	--	5	40	55	446	73%	11.2	3	9.3	35.9%	2	149	3
2013	SD	16/2	491	106	429	4.0	2	1	13.7%	6	104	18	105	60%	1	12	76	87	605	87%	8.0	6	6.1	41.2%	2	282	1
2014	*SD*			*87*	*337*	*3.9*	*3*	*1*	*-2.9%*								*72*	*93*	*627*	*77%*	*8.7*	*3*		*18.0%*			

One wonders how Boston sports analysts kept it together from 2010 through 2012, when Woodhead and Dustin Pedroia were in the same area: so much Gritty White Guy, so little time. Woodhead moved from Foxborough to San Diego for the 2013 season and made himself nearly as indispensable in short bursts as those who are mesmerized by short overachievers would insist. Woodhead was a very efficient first-down rusher, and he actually led the Chargers in red-zone targets as a receiver. Woodhead established career highs in catches and touchdowns in 2013, and head coach Mike McCoy clearly sees him as a satellite back in the Darren Sproles mold. Woodhead will never be mistaken for a No. 1 back, but he can play that role very well.

GOING DEEP

Joe Banyard, MIN: *Back at the Banyard, the Vikings need a runner. Back at the Banyard, last season was a bummer. Woo-ooo-ooo-ooo-oooh.* Boy, that Brian Wilson was a genius, wasn't he? The UTEP alum was practice-squad fodder before the Adrian Peterson-Toby Gerhart injuries, and to the practice squad he shall return with Peterson, Matt Asiata and Jerrick McKinnon ahead of him on the depth chart.

Kenjon Barner, CAR: Between rushes, receptions, kickoff returns and punt returns, Barner scored 50 touchdowns in his career at Oregon. In the Ducks' spread offense, however, he didn't do much blocking. So the Panthers effectively redshirted him, giving him only 10 total touches while he learned the fine art of the blitz pickup. DeAngelo Williams and Jonathan Stewart both return in Carolina, which likely means another season of limited opportunity for Barner, though Ted Ginn's departure at least opens a spot on special teams. (2013 stats: 6 carries for 7 yards, -14 DYAR, -67.2% DVOA; receiving stats: 2-for-3, 7 yards, -5 DYAR, -51.2% DVOA)

Alfred Blue, HOU: Blue has good size (6-foot-2, 218 pounds) and could factor in as a special-teams player for the Texans early. It's hard to see him getting a cut at this roster without significant improvement as a runner. He doesn't have a lot of burst (just 2.5 Highlight Yards per Opportunity) and Houston's running back depth chart is filled with could be/might be young runners such as Jonathan Grimes and Dennis Johnson.

Rex Burkhead, CIN: Burkhead only was active for a single game in 2013, but his role could well expand this year. His 4.6 yards per carry in the preseason showed promise, and he combines a bruising style with deceptive, long-striding speed.

Michael Cox, NYG: A seventh-round pick out of Massachusetts in 2013, Cox was never expected to contribute last season. But after a string of injuries at the position, Cox and newly-signed Peyton Hillis were the only healthy backs on the roster. He averaged two yards per carry, which basically made Hillis look like Jamaal Charles. (2013 stats: 22 carries for 43 yards, -27 DYAR, -41.3% DVOA; receiving stats: 3-for-3, 12 yards, -5 DYAR, -44.9% DVOA)

Isaiah Crowell, CLE: Crowell was an elite five-star recruit before getting booted out of the University of Georgia after multiple arrests. Has plenty of natural ability and tremendous vision but needs to lose the sense of entitlement that ruined his college career. If he straightens out his act, there's space at the bottom of the Cleveland depth chart.

Jeff Demps, TB: It has been two years now since we last really saw what Demps could do on a football field. Between running in the Olympics and World Championships and a groin injury that ended his 2013 season, Demps has only appeared in two NFL games, with just eight total touches. Now, he is healthy and fully committed to football, and Lovie Smith has talked about using him as a rusher, receiver, and returner. Almost certainly the fastest player in the league, Demps ran for 2,470 yards at Florida (averaging 6.7 yards per carry), and he's probably the scariest running back in Going Deep this year. (2013 stats: 3-for-3 as a receiver, 21 yards, 8 DYAR, 24.7% DVOA, one carry for 14 yards)

Anthony Dixon, BUF: "Jus flat outright salty right now WTF praying for more opportunities #FightBackMode," tweeted Dixon in mid-November after a loss to New Orleans where he carried the ball twice for seven yards and returned punts. "It jus sucks to have major skill and not allowed to show it wishing the hating would stop smh." Dixon signed with the Bills after the season, then watched the trade for Bryce Brown knock him down to fourth on the depth chart. WTF smh indeed, my friend. (2013 stats: 28 carries for 56 yards, 2 TDs, -13 DYAR, -17.5% DVOA; receiving stats: 3-for-3, 30 yards, 14 DYAR, 71.1% DVOA)

Tim Flanders, NO: Flanders ran for 1,430 yards at Sam Houston State in 2013, but only caught six passes. The Saints signed him after the draft because Sean Payton can never have too many power runners who can't catch.

Justin Forsett, BAL: Forsett is the textbook definition of a good third back. He offers some speed, some decisiveness, and can catch the ball out of the backfield. In Baltimore, he's reunited with Gary Kubiak, but probably won't make an impact as the Ravens try to rehabilitate Ray Rice and Bernard Pierce. (2013 stats: 6 carries for 31 yards, 7 DYAR, 20.8% DVOA; receiving stats: 15-for-16, 82 yards, -11 DYAR, 28.0% DVOA)

Tyler Gaffney, CAR: Oh good, another talented runner in Carolina. A bruiser of a runner at 6-foot-1, 221 pounds, Gaffney led the Pac-12 last year with 21 rushing touchdowns and finished third with 1,709 yards. The Panthers drafted the former Stanford Cardinal in the sixth round, perhaps impressed by his 108.3 Speed Score, third-best at the combine this year. The Panthers may be the deepest team in the league at this position, which should limit Gaffney's rookie playing time.

Mike Gillislee, MIA: Gillislee was born and went to high school in Deland, Florida. He played college football with the Florida Gators, finishing strong with 1,104 yards in 2012. He continued his Florida life when the Dolphins drafted him in the fifth round. Gillislee played 30 of his 38 snaps on special teams in 2013 and had six carries for 21 yards against the Jets. With Knowshon Moreno creating a crowded backfield in Miami, Gillislee will have to turn some heads on special teams in camp to keep a roster spot. (2013 stats: 6 carries for 21 yards, 8 DYAR, 29.1% DVOA)

Mike Goodson, FA: Goodson's career now seems destined to be a "what might have been" story. He flashed talent in Carolina, but couldn't stay healthy in Oakland or New York. His tenure with the Jets was forgettable: he was arrested on drug and serious gun charges in May, then tore his ACL and MCL in his second game with the team. He was cut by the Jets in June after failing to show up for mandatory minicamp, and then did not show up for a court appearance a week later on his drug and gun charges. Goodson faces up to ten years in prison if found guilty, and has bigger problems in life than finding a team to play for in 2014. (2013 stats: 7 carries for 61 yards, 16 DYAR, 60.0% DVOA; receiving stats: 2-for-3, 19 yards, 8 DYAR, 27.4% DVOA)

Ray Graham, FA: A short scatback out of Pittsburgh, Graham got four rushing attempts after the Texans packed it in for the 2013 season. He was released following the draft, and is currently unsigned. Graham has the speed to make a team, but not the body to take an NFL pounding for a full season. (2013 stats: 4 carries for 8 yards, -5 DYAR, -41.2% DVOA; receiving stats: 1-for-3, 12 yards, -5 DYAR, -41.5% DVOA)

Cyrus Gray, KC: Kansas City took Gray out of Texas A&M in the sixth round of the 2012 draft. This past January, he carried the ball twice for five yards after both Jamaal Charles and Knile Davis got knocked out of the playoff loss to Indianapolis. In between, Rotoworld did not post a single comment about Gray for 20 months. Do you know how hard it is for a backup running back on any active NFL roster to go unmentioned by a fantasy news website for *20 months*? (2013 stats: 9 carries for 24 yards, -2 DYAR, -14.6% DVOA; receiving stats: 7-for-10, 46 yards, 2 DYAR, -10.0% DVOA)

Alex Green, NYJ: The potential may still be there for Green, but the opportunity is not. After excelling at Hawaii, where he finished second in the country in yards per carry in 2010 and flashed strong receiving skills, Green's NFL career was derailed by an ACL injury in his rookie season. He was cut by the Packers, and failed to stand out with the Jets. Green is likely just camp fodder for now, but if injuries open a door, Green is a player to keep an eye on. (2013 stats: 11 carries for 35 yards, -5 DYAR, -17.5% DVOA; receiving stats: 2-for-2, 8 yards, -3 DYAR, -36.7% DVOA)

Marion Grice, SD: Grice averaged 5.7 yards per carry and 9.5 yards per reception in two years at Arizona State, with 4.5 Highlight Yards per Opportunity in 2013. Although he lasted until the sixth round, our own Matt Waldman ranked him fourth among this year's backs in his *Rookie Scouting Portfolio*, calling him "the best receiver from the backfield that I've seen since Shane Vereen."

Jonathan Grimes, HOU: Once Gary Kubiak was fired and the Texans started playing out the string, Grimes got heavy playing time. A 2012 UDFA from William and Mary, Grimes has bounced to the Jets and Jaguars as the Texans played the practice-squad dance with him. He's no Arian Foster, but he's a solid depth zone runner. (2013 stats: 21 carries for 73 yards, 1 TD, 27 DYAR, 21.7% DVOA; receiving stats: 6-for-6, 76 yards, 10 DYAR, 22.0% DVOA)

Dan Herron, IND: Herron, who is probably best remembered as one of the five suspended Ohio State players that sold autographs and memorabilia for money, has bounced between the Bengals and Colts rosters over the last two years as a reserve power back. He'll be battling 2014 UDFA Zurlon Tipton for that role this season. (2013 stats: 5 carries for 33 yards, 19 DYAR, 63.6% DVOA)

Michael Hill, GB: Hill ran for 2,168 yards and 16 touchdowns in 2012 at Missouri Western (go Griffons!), then spent last year bouncing on and off the rosters of the Packers and Bucs. Johnathan Franklin's career-ending neck injury opens a door for Hill to stick in Green Bay this season. (2013 stats: 9 carries for 23 yards, -8 DYAR, -38.5% DVOA; receiving stats: 2-for-2, 23 yards, 11 DYAR, 162.3% DVOA)

Stephen Houston, NE: The Patriots have managed to hit on a few undrafted free agents at running back over the last few years, including BenJarvus Green-Ellis, Brandon Bolden and Danny Woodhead (via the Jets). Like the Law Firm, Houston, who was fourth on Indiana's all-time rushing list with 25 rushing touchdowns, is a big banger who takes pride in grinding out tough yards. He was fundamentally signed with an eye towards 2015, since New England's three veteran backs all see their contracts end after this season. If only there was a way to keep him around doing nothing for a year (cough **injury** cough).

LaMichael James, SF: James is crowded out of the San Francisco backfield, and his only chance to contribute will likely be on special teams. He did show promise in that area, averaging over 26 yards per return on kicks while also outperforming Kyle Williams as the punt returner. (2013 stats: 12 carries for 59 yards, 2 DYAR, -3.2% DVOA; receiving stats: 2-for-3, 16 yards, 4 DYAR, 5.3% DVOA)

Storm Johnson, JAC: I'm your D.J. Chris "Champagne" Garnett and you're listening to "The Quiet Storm." [pushes button, thunder rumbling sound effect]. Right now we've got a potential third-down back for you. Catches the ball well out of the backfield, and he showed good vision in zone schemes at the University of Central Florida in hot and steamy Orlando. Passionate groans filling the air as he penetrates the A-gap. Ladies, the Jacksonville depth chart isn't hard to climb. [pushes button, thunder rumbling sound effect]

Deji Karim, FA: Unsigned as we went to press, Karim offers kick return skills and steady-but-unspectacular work carrying the ball. There are worse third-back skill sets to have. (2013 stats: 12 carries for 51 yards, 10 DYAR, 15.9% DVOA; receiving stats: 1-for-2, -1 yard, -8 DYAR, -98.2% DVOA)

Mikel Leshoure, DET: Leshoure spent 2013 in a rarely-used limbo: he was not injured but was rarely activated, appeared to be in the doghouse but was never in any specific trouble. The Lions did not want to dress him for games but were not keen on trading him, either. Nagging injuries slowed Leshoure for much of last offseason, and by the preseason coaches were so disinterested in him that he could barely get onto the field in games where UDFAs like Steven Miller were getting significant carries. Leshoure's inactivity is best chalked up to a combination of injuries, indifferent work habits, and limited usefulness: he is a one-dimensional power back with little receiving and no special-teams value. Leshoure started the Jim Caldwell era by missing some OTAs for personal reasons, so we can probably expect even more nothing in 2014.

Dion Lewis, CLE: The speedy former Pitt star broke his leg last preseason. While he was healing, his team signed a veteran free agent back and drafted another in the third round. That leaves third down duty for Lewis, who could be effective in the role if he's left his injury behind him. (2012 stats: 13 carries for 69 yards, 29 DYAR, 45.5% DVOA)

Latavius Murray, OAK: Murray at one point looked like the favorite to be Darren McFadden's backup, but a training camp ankle injury sent him to injured reserve before the season began. He will need to show he has regained his pre-injury burst to carve out a role in a more crowded Oakland backfield.

Isaiah Pead, STL: The absolute definition of a replacement-level running back, Pead is pretty useful on special teams and may be opting for the Fred McAfee career path. Check back in 12 years to see if it worked. (2013 stats: 7 carries for 21 yards, -4 DYAR, -21.2% DVOA; receiving stats: 11-for-15, 78 yards, 8 DYAR, -5.2% DVOA)

Cedric Peerman, CIN: A solid special-teamer and locker room favorite, Peerman provides quality depth, if not much more than that. (2013 stats: 8 carries for 17 yards, -12 DYAR, -55.5% DVOA)

Chris Polk, PHI: Polk went undrafted in 2012 due to injury concerns over his shoulder. He only had 15 offensive touches in 2013, but gained 159 yards and scored three touchdowns. He had a 38-yard touchdown run in the snow against Detroit and a 34-yard reception after he was left uncovered on a wheel route against Dallas. Neither play required a great effort from the running back, but he's in a favorable offense for his position. The trade of Bryce Brown opens up a good opportunity for Polk to back up LeSean McCoy since Darren Sproles is likely to have more receptions than carries. A handcuff to watch in your fantasy league. (2013 stats: 11 carries for 98 yards, 3 TDs, 64 DYAR, 120.4% DVOA; receiving stats: 4-for-5, 61 yards, 22 DYAR, 81.6% DVOA)

Chris Rainey, IND: Rainey was brought in at midseason because the Colts tired of David Reed's decision-making on kickoff returns. One broken Rainey leg later, they had to make another phone call. A Steelers cast-off who lost his spot after a battery charge, Rainey is fairly expendable and has zero fantasy relevance unless Ahmad Bradshaw and Vick Ballard go down again. He sure is fast, though.

Isaac Redman, FA: Redman had a distinctive running style of grinding out each carry like it was his last, but as he turns 30, he hopes just to have another NFL carry. Once a solid option in Pittsburgh's RBBC, Redman declined to -15.0% DVOA in 2012 and gained just 12 yards on 10 carries in 2013. After rookie Le'Veon Bell secured the starting job, Redman was released by the Steelers in October and remains a free agent. (2013 stats: 10 carries for 13 yards, -46 DYAR, -132.3% DVOA; receiving stats: 4-for-5, 14 yards, -9 DYAR, -40.3% DVOA)

Darius Reynaud, FA: Tennessee mistakenly tried to use Reynaud as a space player on offense, which was sort of like seeing an infant pretend a pine cone was a football. Reynaud also contributed some error-prone returner play, and was released and picked up by the Jets in December. He's unsigned as we go to press.

Theo Riddick, DET: Special-teams value matters, kids. Riddick leapt over Mikel Leshoure on the depth chart because of his versatility, ending the year with seven special teams tackles to go with uneventful appearances as the Lions No. 3 back. Riddick was a useful all-purpose back at Notre Dame and is enough like Joique Bell and Reggie Bush to play their roles in the offense, though not enough unlike Bell and Bush to carve out his own role. (2013 stats: 9 carries for 25 yards, 1 TD, 9 DYAR, 16.2% DVOA; receiving stats: 4-for-8, 26 yards, -4 DYAR, -22.0% DVOA)

Denard Robinson, JAC: Robinson actually did put great touch on his one throw of the season, a deep ball that Cecil Shorts dropped. Otherwise, the "offensive weapon" roster designation the Jaguars gave him remained purely theoretical. That was partially explained by nerve injury damage that Jacksonville felt hurt his ability to hold on to and carry the ball. Now that the Jaguars have brought in Toby Gerhart, Jedd Fisch is free to spend less time teaching Robinson professional techniques and more time designing wacky trick plays for him. (2013 stats: 20 carries for 64 yards, -61 DYAR, -86.1% DVOA)

Evan Royster, WAS: The lesson here may be that a great rushing DVOA in a small sample (45.7% DVOA with 5.9 yards per carry in 2011) means exactly as much going forward as nickel cornerback charting statistics. The Penn State bruiser is facing a roster crunch as Roy Helu has the second spot in hand and Jay Gruden wants a true scatback to make the team.

Bernard Scott, FA: The addition of rookie Giovani Bernard made Scott expendable in Cincinnati. He signed with Baltimore in October, but only saw limited action (13 snaps) for an offense that could not get Ray Rice and Bernard Pierce moving forward all season long. There wasn't even an option to put Scott at returner since Jacoby Jones is a superior player. Thus another 30-year-old roams the streets in No League for Old Backs. (2013 stats: 4 carries for 14 yards, -2 DYAR, -21.4% DVOA)

Da'Rel Scott, FA: Scott has been a scouting tease for years, courtesy of his unique size/speed combination and success at Maryland. Three years later, and Scott has just 98 career rushing yards. He was given his first real chance at the start of the 2013 season, as injuries to Andre Brown and David Wilson opened the door. As is wont to happen with Giants running backs, Scott suffered a hamstring injury trying to make it through that doorway, and was waived by the team in October. (2013 stats: 20 carries for 73 yards, -7 DYAR, -17.4% DVOA; receiving stats: 11-for-19, 102 yards, 1 TD, 26 DYAR, 13.7% DVOA)

Lache Seastrunk, WAS: An exciting and talented back with a litany of holes in his game. In the open field, Seastrunk can layer moves on bewildered defenders with ease (7.2 Highlight Yards per Opportunity in 2013). The problem is that he often doesn't get there. He's got some issues with patience and reading defenders, but the more surprising thing is that he was an awful receiving back at Baylor. He dropped 10 of 19 catchable targets. Then there's the matter of his subpar blocking. Seastrunk could well end up as a top-three back in this class when the retrospectives start. But it's easy to see why he lasted until the sixth round when you look at his game as a whole.

Kory Sheets, OAK: Sheets failed to find an NFL job coming out of Purdue in 2009. He returns to the NFL as the reigning Grey Cup MVP after helping lead Saskatchewan to the CFL title. If he is the more patient runner and better blocker he claims to be, he could end up the third back in Oakland's backfield. The presence of both Darren McFadden and Maurice Jones-Drew likely limits his snap count and upside, though.

Alfonso Smith, FA: Roster fodder in Arizona the last four years, now a free agent. Career probably over. (2013 stats: 18 carries for 54 yards, 1 TD, -16 DYAR, -27.5% DVOA; receiving stats: 10-for-13, 68 yards, 24 DYAR, 18.8% DVOA)

Antone Smith, ATL: Smith led the ACC in touchdowns in 2008, but in his first three NFL seasons, he had just one carry, and that went for a three-yard loss. His five carries in 2013 gained a whopping 145 yards (392.1% DVOA!), including a 50-yard touchdown against Tampa Bay and a 38-yard score against Buffalo. He became the seventh player in league history to top 100 yards on five or fewer carries; the other six all played wide receiver. Smith is still primarily a special-teamer (240 of his 265 snaps last year came on kicking plays), but he might be the league's most exciting fourth running back. (2013 stats: 5 carries for 145 yards, 2 TDs, 78 DYAR, 392.3% DVOA; receiving stats: 2-for-3, 10 yards, -2 DYAR, -32.0% DVOA)

LaRod Stephens-Howling, FA: Due to a lack of depth, Stephens-Howling had a great opportunity early last season to rack up touches as a third-down back and kick returner. However, just three quarters into the season opener he tore his ACL. The Steelers have since added other backs and Stephens-Howling remains a free agent. Someone looking for special-teams help may be the Pitt product's best shot at making a roster. (2013 stats: 6 carries for 19 yards, -6 DYAR, -40.5% DVOA; receiving stats: 2-for-3, 11 yards, -7 DYAR, -46.0% DVOA)

Lorenzo Taliaferro, BAL: Taliaferro scored 29 touchdowns in 2013 on his way to being named the Big South Conference Offensive Player of the Year at Coastal Carolina. The Ravens' sixth-round selection may have a sizeable rookie role depending on what happens to Ray Rice, but Taliaferro has his own issues to overcome. He was arrested in May for misdemeanor destruction of property and public intoxication.

Phillip Tanner, FA: Dallas is often criticized for not running the ball more, but Tanner has been a very inadequate option in his career with 56 carries for 149 yards (2.7 yards per carry), putting him below the "T-Rich Line" for running backs. He only gained 12 yards on nine carries last season and fell behind Joseph Randle and Lance Dunbar as alternatives to starter DeMarco Murray. (2013 stats: 9 carries for 12 yards, 1 TD, -19 DYAR, -53.1% DVOA; receiving stats: 3-for-4, 33 yards, 11 DYAR, 30.1% DVOA)

Marcus Thigpen, MIA: Not used to playing on offense, Thigpen had a 50-yard reception on a little dump pass against the Saints that was right up his alley: ball in his hands in the open field with only one man to beat. That man (Rafael Bush) did eventually stop him short of the end zone, but Thigpen—engineer of a return touchdown on both a punt and kickoff in 2012—remains Joe Philbin's return specialist despite a significant decline in performance. Thigpen averaged 12.2 yards per punt return and 27.4 yards per kick return in 2012, but those numbers respectively dipped to 7.8 and 22.5 in 2013. Thigpen also fumbled three times after just one in 2012. (2013 stats: 6 carries for 18 yards, -2 DYAR, -15.8% DVOA; receiving stats: 8-for-11, 97 yards, 1 TD, 48 DYAR, 66.2% DVOA)

De'Anthony Thomas, KC: With Dexter McCluster off to Tennessee, it could be up to Black Mamba to become Andy Reid's next satellite back. He was unable to participate in OTAs because of the league's dumb-assed semester rules, but running backs coach Eric Bieniemy certainly liked what he saw during the Chiefs' rookie minicamp. "I'll tell you one thing, he blew our socks off," Bieniemy said of Thomas in June. " Thomas was a Swiss Army tool in Oregon's offense, and he could add major value to a Kansas City return unit that already helped the Chiefs to the NFL's best overall special teams in 2013. Thomas has said that he's expecting to play every role he did at Oregon, but at 5-foot-9 and 174 pounds, he's best served just getting the ball in space. It's what the Chiefs tried to do with McCluster for years, and it never quite worked out.

Chris Thompson, WAS: This 2013 fifth-rounder out of Florida State in was the target of generous praise from new head coach Jay Gruden, who said he wanted to get Thompson some touches. Then the Redskins drafted Lache Seastrunk, who fills exactly the same niche. The lesson, as always, is to not believe a word any coach says to the media. Thompson's predilection to getting hurt doesn't help his chances of beating out Seastrunk for a roster spot.

Leon Washington, TEN: Leon Washington returns kicks. The Titans had this problem in 2013 where Darius Reynaud was really bad at returning kicks. Then they brought in other players, like Devon Wylie, who also couldn't return kicks. Then they noticed that one of the best kick returners of the last decade was available. Tennessee had much better returns with Washington on board. What's the most valuable thing you can do, kids? Own your niche.

James Wilder, CIN: Wilder has the DNA and the physical tools to be a pro, but needs to lower his pad level and knock off the off-field foolishness that crippled his draft status. Needs a standout camp to crack a crowded Bengals backfield.

Damien Williams, MIA: Our Speed Score metric came out very strange this season, with a couple undrafted free agents on top and one of the best-regarded prospects of the year, Ka'Deem Carey, near the bottom. Former Oklahoma back Williams was actually this year's Speed Score champion, running the combine forty in 4.45 seconds at 222 pounds for a score of 113.2. Williams is a technically sound one-cut runner with excellent acceleration, and his receiving and blocking skills are both better than usual for rookies. But he went undrafted because Bob Stoops kicked him off the team for unknown violations of team rules. Williams could make waves in Miami, especially if Knowshon Moreno can't get healthy.

Kerwynn Williams, SD: Williams is a passing-game mismatch waiting to happen, in the Darren Sproles mold. Unfortunately for him, the Chargers brought in Donald Brown to add to an already-loaded backfield, then drafted a player who duplicates Williams' key skill set, Marion Grice. Also, he's on a roster with Danny Woodhead, who has to be considered one of the best receiving backs in NFL history at this point. Don't be surprised if he resurfaces elsewhere after training camp.

Ryan Williams, DAL: Hey kids, here's another valuable lesson in "get paid while you can." Hopefully, Williams saved lots of money from the bonus he got with his second-round contract back in 2011. He blew out his knee as a rookie and tore up his shoulder in his second season, then spent his entire third season as a healthy scratch week after week. The Cardinals cut him in March, the Cowboys took a shot on him, and he'll compete with Joseph Randle to backup DeMarco Murray on early downs (with Lance Dunbar as the third-down back).

Cierre Wood, BAL: An undrafted free agent out of Notre Dame signed after the 2013 draft, Wood was released by the Texans following an "unspecified" (read: probably pot-related) violation of team rules. He signed a futures contract in Baltimore after the season. The talent to read the hole on zone plays is there for Wood, but the Baltimore depth chart is crowded and his offensive coordinator is the guy who kicked him off his last team. (2013 stats: 3 carries for 9 yards, 3 DYAR, 20.9% DVOA)

Wide Receivers

In the following two sections we provide the last three years' statistics, as well as a 2014 KUBIAK projection, for every wide receiver and tight end who either played a significant role in 2013 or is expected to do so in 2014.

The first line contains biographical data—each player's name, height, weight, college, draft position, birth date, and age. Height and weight are the best data we could find; weight, of course, can fluctuate during the off-season. **Age** is very simple, the number of years between the player's birth year and 2014, but birth date is provided if you want to figure out exact age.

Draft position gives draft year and round, with the overall pick number with which the player was taken in parentheses. In the sample table, it says that Eric Decker was chosen in the 2010 NFL Draft with the 87th overall pick in the third round. Undrafted free agents are listed as "FA" with the year they came into the league, even if they were only in training camp or on a practice squad.

To the far right of the first line is the player's Risk for fantasy football in 2014. As explained in the quarterback section, the standard is for players to be marked Green. Players with higher than normal risk are marked Yellow, and players with the highest risk are marked Red. Players who are most likely to match or surpass our forecast—primarily second- stringers with low projections—are marked Blue. Risk is not only based on injury probability, but how a player's projection compares to his recent performance as well as our confidence (or lack thereof) in his offensive teammates.

Next we give the last three years of player stats. Note that rushing stats are not included for receivers, but that any receiver with at least five carries last year will have his 2012 rushing stats appear in his team's chapter.

Next we give the last three years of player stats. First come games played and games started (**G/GS**). Games played represents the official NFL total and may include games in which a player appeared on special teams, but did not play wide receiver or tight end. We also have a total of offensive **Snaps** for each season. Receptions (**Rec**) counts passes caught, while Passes (**Pass**) counts passes thrown to this player, complete or incomplete. Receiving yards (**Yds**) is the official NFL total for each player.

Catch rate (**C%**) includes all passes listed in the official play-by-play with the given player as the intended receiver, even if those passes were listed by our game charters as "Thrown Away," "Tipped at Line," or "Quarterback Hit in Motion." The average NFL wide receiver has caught between 57 and 58 percent of passes over the last three seasons; tight ends caught between 63 and 64 percent of passes over the last three seasons.

Plus/minus (+/-) is a new metric that we introduced in *Football Outsiders Almanac 2010*. It estimates how many passes a receiver caught compared to what an average receiver would have caught, given the location of those passes. Unlike simple catch rate, plus/minus does not consider passes listed as "Thrown Away," "Tipped at Line," or "Quarterback Hit in Motion." Player performance is compared to a historical baseline of how often a pass is caught based on the pass distance, the distance required for a first down, and whether it is on the left, middle, or right side of the field. Note that plus/minus is not scaled to a player's target total.

Yards per catch (**Yd/C**) and receiving touchdowns (**TD**) are standard stats. Drops (**Drop**) list the number of dropped passes according to our game charting project. Our totals may differ from the drop totals kept by other organizations.

Next we list yards after catch (**YAC**), rank (**Rk**) in yards after catch, and **YAC+**. YAC+ is similar to plus-minus; it estimates how much YAC a receiver gained compared to what we would have expected from an average receiver catching passes of similar length in similar down-and-distance situations. This is imperfect—we don't specifically mark what route a player runs, and obviously a go route will have more YAC than a comeback—but it does a fairly good job of telling you if this receiver gets more or less YAC than other receivers with similar usage patterns. We also give a total of broken tackles (**BTkl**) according to the Football Outsiders game charting project.

The next five columns include our main advanced metrics for receiving: **DVOA** (Defense-Adjusted Value Over Average), **DYAR** (Defense-Adjusted Yards Above Replacement), and **YAR** (Yards Above Replacement), along with the player's rank in both DVOA and DYAR. These metrics compare every pass intended for a receiver and the results of that pass to a league-average baseline based on the game situations in which passes were thrown to that receiver. DVOA and DYAR are also adjusted based on the opposing defense and include Defensive Pass Interference yards on passes intended for that receiver. The methods used to compute these numbers are described in detail in the "Statistical Toolbox" introduction in the front of the book. The important distinctions between them are:

Eric Decker Height: 6-3 Weight: 217 College: Minnesota Draft: 2010/3 (87) Born: 15-Mar-1987 Age: 27 Risk: Red

Year	Team	G/GS	Snaps	Rec	Pass	Yds	C%	+/-	Yd/C	TD	Drop	YAC	Rk	YAC+	BTkl	DVOA	Rk	DYAR	Rk	YAR	Short	Mid	Deep	Bomb
2011	DEN	16/13	972	44	98	612	46%	-7.3	13.9	8	6	3.9	58	-1.3	1	-15.5%	76	-24	76	-40	30%	34%	16%	20%
2012	DEN	16/15	1048	85	123	1064	69%	+13.0	12.5	13	7	3.1	69	-0.7	3	27.2%	8	392	4	401	32%	45%	11%	12%
2013	DEN	16/16	1050	87	136	1288	64%	+4.3	14.8	11	7	4.3	58	-0.4	5	21.3%	12	381	4	382	35%	39%	17%	9%
2014	*NYJ*			*73*	*130*	*1025*	*56%*		*14.0*	*6*						*2.5%*								

• DVOA is a rate statistic, while DYAR is a cumulative statistic. Thus, a higher DVOA means more value per pass play, while a higher DYAR means more aggregate value over the entire season.

• Because DYAR is defense-adjusted and YAR is not, a player whose DYAR is higher than his YAR faced a harder-than-average schedule. A player whose DYAR is lower than his YAR faced an easier-than-average schedule.

To qualify for ranking in YAC, receiving DVOA, or receiving DYAR, a wide receiver must have had 50 passes thrown to him in that season. We ranked 90 wideouts in 2013, 86 wideouts in 2012, and 92 in 2011. Tight ends qualify with 25 targets in a given season; we ranked 51 tight ends in 2013, 49 tight ends in 2012, and 47 in 2011.

The final four columns break down pass length based on the Football Outsiders charting project. The categories are **Short** (5 yards or less), **Mid** (6-15 yards), **Deep** (16-25 yards), and **Bomb** (26 or more yards). These numbers are based on distance in the air only and include both complete and incomplete passes.

The italicized row of statistics for the 2014 season is our 2014 KUBIAK projection based on a complicated regression analysis that takes into account numerous variables including projected role, performance over the past two years, projected team offense and defense, projected quarterback statistics, historical comparables, height, age, and strength of schedule.

It is difficult to accurately project statistics for a 162-game baseball season, but it is exponentially more difficult to accurately project statistics for a 16-game football season. Consider the listed projections not as a prediction of exact numbers, but as the mean of a range of possible performances. What's important is less the exact number of yards we project, and more which players are projected to improve or decline. Actual performance will vary from our projection less for veteran starters and more for rookies and third-stringers, for whom we must base our projections on much smaller career statistical samples. Touchdown numbers will vary more than yardage numbers. Players facing suspension or recovering from injury have those missed games taken into account.

Note that the receiving totals for each team will add up to higher numbers than the projection for that team's starting quarterback, because we have done KUBIAK projections for more receivers than will actually make the final roster.

A few low-round rookies, guys listed at seventh on the depth chart, and players who are listed as wide receivers but really only play special teams are briefly discussed at the end of the chapter in a section we call "Going Deep."

Two notes regarding our advanced metrics: We cannot yet fully separate the performance of a receiver from the performance of his quarterback. Be aware that one will affect the other. In addition, these statistics measure only passes thrown to a receiver, not performance on plays when he is not thrown the ball, such as blocking and drawing double teams.

Top 20 WR by DYAR (Total Value), 2013

Rank	Player	Team	DYAR
1	Demaryius Thomas	DEN	430
2	Jordy Nelson	GB	402
3	Anquan Boldin	SF	386
4	Eric Decker	DEN	381
5	Antonio Brown	PIT	361
6	DeSean Jackson	PHI	358
7	Calvin Johnson	DET	347
8	Keenan Allen	SD	343
9	Josh Gordon	CLE	336
10	Brandon Marshall	CHI	284
11	Marvin Jones	CIN	279
12	Marques Colston	NO	276
13	Doug Baldwin	SEA	274
14	Alson Jeffery	CHI	248
15	Eddie Royal	SD	238
16	Jerricho Cotchery	PIT	235
17	Michael Floyd	ARI	220
18	Dez Bryant	DAL	215
19	Riley Cooper	PHI	212
20	A.J. Green	CIN	207

Top 20 WR by DVOA (Value per Pass), 2013

Rank	Player	Team	DVOA
1	Kenny Stills	NO	40.1%
2	Doug Baldwin	SEA	33.3%
3	Marvin Jones	CIN	32.4%
4	Eddie Royal	SD	31.6%
5	Keenan Allen	SD	28.2%
6	Jordy Nelson	GB	26.7%
7	Demaryius Thomas	DEN	26.5%
8	Jerricho Cotchery	PIT	26.2%
9	Anquan Boldin	SF	25.8%
10	DeSean Jackson	PHI	23.7%
11	Lance Moore	NO	22.1%
12	Eric Decker	DEN	21.3%
13	Riley Cooper	PHI	20.6%
14	Marques Colston	NO	19.5%
15	Antonio Brown	PIT	15.0%
16	Calvin Johnson	DET	14.9%
17	Josh Gordon	CLE	14.4%
18	Rod Streater	OAK	13.6%
19	Golden Tate	SEA	12.9%
20	Michael Floyd	ARI	12.9%

Minimum 50 passes.

Davante Adams Height: 6-1 Weight: 212 College: Fresno St. Draft: 2014/2 (53) Born: 12/24/1992 Age: 22 Risk: Red

Year	Team	G/GS	Snaps	Rec	Pass	Yds	C%	+/-	Yd/C	TD	Drop	YAC	Rk	YAC+	BTkl	DVOA	Rk	DYAR	Rk	YAR	Short	Mid	Deep	Bomb
2014	*GB*			*32*	*49*	*413*	*65%*		*12.9*	*2*						*8.0%*								

Smooth, skinny boundary-type receiver who was insanely productive catching passes from Derek Carr at Fresno State: 131 catches for 1,719 yards last season, with 24 touchdowns and a 75 percent catch rate. Adams has quick, nifty moves off the line, making him difficult to jam, and has a wide variety of double moves and adjustments in the open field. Add leaping ability and concentration, and you get the kind of sideline weapon Aaron Rodgers loves. Adams will have to settle for fourth receiver status as a rookie, but a) the Packers use their fourth receiver a lot and b) both Jordy Nelson and Randall Cobb are entering the contract cycle, so at least one job may soon open up.

Keenan Allen Height: 6-2 Weight: 206 College: California Draft: 2013/3 (76) Born: 27-Apr-1992 Age: 22 Risk: Red

Year	Team	G/GS	Snaps	Rec	Pass	Yds	C%	+/-	Yd/C	TD	Drop	YAC	Rk	YAC+	BTkl	DVOA	Rk	DYAR	Rk	YAR	Short	Mid	Deep	Bomb
2013	SD	15/14	946	71	104	1046	68%	+8.6	14.7	8	2	5.9	13	+1.5	10	28.2%	5	343	8	351	37%	43%	17%	3%
2014	*SD*			*80*	*125*	*1138*	*64%*		*14.2*	*7*						*12.0%*								

As Norman Mailer might say, statistics are nothing without their nuance. Many observers criticized Allen coming out of Cal as a limited possession receiver who might struggle to find a place as a lead dog in a vertical offense, and even we dinged him for a low Playmaker Score (which got better in the new version, but still isn't spectacular, 75.5 percent.) However, Allen turned out to be an indispensable target for Philip Rivers, especially in a passing game that featured more short throws and fewer deep drops. Limited receivers don't post 45.5% DVOA and a 68 percent catch rate on 41 third-down passes, and Allen's 6.7 yards after catch average matched what was seen on the field—that Allen is a determined player with excellent technique. Some will slight Allen because he doesn't have the upside of an A.J. Green or Julio Jones—ESPN did just that in the offseason—but that's missing the point. This is a third-round receiver who was debited in the draft because it was thought that he didn't have sufficient velocity to make plays, and he displayed nearly every possible compensatory attribute. You don't build championship teams with a couple of freakish athletes; you do it with players who fit a system and make everyone around them better. That's Allen's ultimate "upside," and it's why he'll continue to get heavy reps in this offense.

Danny Amendola Height: 5-11 Weight: 186 College: Texas Tech Draft: 2008/FA Born: 2-Nov-1985 Age: 29 Risk: Red

Year	Team	G/GS	Snaps	Rec	Pass	Yds	C%	+/-	Yd/C	TD	Drop	YAC	Rk	YAC+	BTkl	DVOA	Rk	DYAR	Rk	YAR	Short	Mid	Deep	Bomb
2011	STL	1/1	40	5	6	45	83%	+1.0	9.0	0	0	5.0	--	+0.4	0	12.9%	--	8	--	13	67%	33%	0%	0%
2012	STL	11/8	498	63	101	666	62%	+1.3	10.6	3	2	3.8	48	-0.7	4	-7.6%	67	80	45	10	52%	36%	4%	8%
2013	NE	12/6	571	54	83	633	65%	+0.9	11.7	2	4	4.7	43	-0.2	2	12.3%	21	163	27	116	45%	40%	9%	6%
2014	*NE*			*72*	*114*	*870*	*63%*		*12.1*	*6*						*5.8%*								

There were moments of real brilliance from Amendola last season; the Patriots don't beat the Bills in the regular season opener if he doesn't make multiple third-down receptions with the game on the line. But he was wildly underwhelming at times, and while Julian Edelman clearly earned respect from his quarterback throughout the year, there were times where Tom Brady clearly had no faith in Amendola. It wasn't just his groin injury; sometimes Brady had to motion him to the other side of the formation because he was lining up in the wrong place. After a really impressive 10-catch outing in a December loss to the Dolphins in South Florida, Amendola had just six catches over the final four games of the season—three in the last two regular-season games and three in the postseason. While Amendola's contract likely means he'll get another chance in 2014, he needs to build on the few positives from 2013 if he wants to remain a key part of the passing game in New England.

Miles Austin Height: 6-3 Weight: 215 College: Monmouth Draft: 2006/FA Born: 30-Jun-1984 Age: 30 Risk: Red

Year	Team	G/GS	Snaps	Rec	Pass	Yds	C%	+/-	Yd/C	TD	Drop	YAC	Rk	YAC+	BTkl	DVOA	Rk	DYAR	Rk	YAR	Short	Mid	Deep	Bomb
2011	DAL	10/10	553	43	73	579	59%	-0.4	13.5	7	2	4.7	32	+0.4	2	11.6%	28	125	41	154	31%	46%	17%	7%
2012	DAL	16/15	860	66	119	943	55%	-3.0	14.3	6	4	4.4	37	+0.1	6	3.3%	36	184	25	151	25%	43%	23%	9%
2013	DAL	11/8	524	24	49	244	49%	-6.8	10.2	0	3	4.2	--	-0.2	0	-25.9%	--	-51	--	-61	43%	48%	4%	4%
2014	*CLE*			*58*	*102*	*776*	*57%*		*13.4*	*5*						*-1.7%*								

What do you mean Miles Austin is 30 and well past his prime? Seems like just yesterday he was breaking out against the 2009 Chiefs. Age is a bastard, and so is the impact of injuries on a once promising career. Dallas released Austin to save $5.5 million this summer and no one will second guess this one. Austin caught 10 passes for just 72 yards in Week 1, and then had 14 catches the rest of the year. He was a non-factor and a litany of hamstring injuries has sapped his speed. His 10.2 yards per reception was easily the lowest of his career. Austin will try to rebound in Cleveland, which obviously worked great for Andre Rison, Donte Stallworth, Davone Bess, etc. His KUBIAK projection is high because the Browns really have nobody else to throw to except Jordan Cameron.

Tavon Austin Height: 5-8 Weight: 174 College: West Virgina Draft: 2013/1 (8) Born: 15-Mar-1991 Age: 23 Risk: Yellow

Year	Team	G/GS	Snaps	Rec	Pass	Yds	C%	+/-	Yd/C	TD	Drop	YAC	Rk	YAC+	BTkl	DVOA	Rk	DYAR	Rk	YAR	Short	Mid	Deep	Bomb
2013	STL	13/3	422	40	69	418	58%	-4.3	10.5	4	6	5.8	17	+0.2	7	-19.4%	81	-36	80	-38	54%	30%	7%	9%
2014	*STL*			*59*	*91*	*702*	*65%*		*11.9*	*3*						*3.0%*								

Brian Schottenheimer and speedy slot receivers don't mix. Coordinators love to claim that they will use Austin types "creatively," although it doesn't take much creativity to mix two screens and a reverse with various hitch routes and return duties, which is what these receivers inevitably end up doing. Schottenheimer lacks even that paint-by-numbers artistry, however. Screens to Austin involved Sam Bradford taking the snap and flicking the ball to Austin with nine teammates watching: window dressing like "play fakes" and "blocking" were not on the color palette. Austin also took a few handoffs between the tackles, which is creativity of a sort, we suppose. As an added bonus, the Rams had a habit of committing penalties on his longest returns early in the year.

Eventually, something finally shook loose, and Austin sprinted for 65 and 56 yard runs, caught a bona fide bomb for a touchdown, and produced some long returns. Unfortunately: a) the Colts defense was what "shook loose" in one of their existential quandary games, which provided many of the Austin highlights, and b) Austin injured himself at the end of one of the runs. The moral of the story is that some players are so talented that they can overcome their offensive coordinator, or will hurt themselves trying. Austin is one of them, and the Rams will be in shape when they find ten more.

Jason Avant Height: 6-0 Weight: 210 College: Michigan Draft: 2006/4 (109) Born: 20-Apr-1983 Age: 31 Risk: Red

Year	Team	G/GS	Snaps	Rec	Pass	Yds	C%	+/-	Yd/C	TD	Drop	YAC	Rk	YAC+	BTkl	DVOA	Rk	DYAR	Rk	YAR	Short	Mid	Deep	Bomb
2011	PHI	16/7	709	52	81	679	64%	+4.4	13.1	1	1	3.3	71	-0.8	1	2.5%	45	111	47	120	29%	51%	17%	3%
2012	PHI	14/6	656	53	77	648	70%	+7.3	12.2	0	0	2.7	76	-1.6	2	6.8%	28	137	33	118	33%	48%	16%	3%
2013	PHI	16/13	789	38	76	447	50%	-3.4	11.8	2	0	2.1	88	-2.2	1	-24.5%	85	-68	85	-55	26%	41%	24%	9%
2014	*CAR*			*37*	*61*	*425*	*61%*		*11.5*	*2*						*-4.4%*								

Did you think Jason Avant would last eight years in Philadelphia? The possession receiver known for his good hands apparently saw the writing on the wall that there wouldn't be a ninth. Avant was candid this summer about not seeing eye-to-eye with Chip Kelly on things like route running and route technique. "When they stop calling your number and guys start running some of the routes that you run—I knew from the beginning that I didn't fit his style of offense, in that I'm a crafty guy that gets open in an atypical way," Avant told the *Charlotte Observer*. Fortunately, the Panthers are welcoming receivers of all styles, ages, sizes and more. Avant was a decent signing to give Cam Newton another receiver who has actually, you know, caught a pass in the NFL.

Donnie Avery Height: 5-11 Weight: 183 College: Houston Draft: 2008/2 (33) Born: 12-Jun-1984 Age: 30 Risk: Green

Year	Team	G/GS	Snaps	Rec	Pass	Yds	C%	+/-	Yd/C	TD	Drop	YAC	Rk	YAC+	BTkl	DVOA	Rk	DYAR	Rk	YAR	Short	Mid	Deep	Bomb
2011	TEN	8/0	112	3	11	45	27%	-3.5	15.0	1	2	7.0	--	+3.2	0	-11.2%	--	5	--	-3	42%	33%	8%	17%
2012	IND	16/15	1025	60	125	781	48%	-8.0	13.0	3	6	3.5	63	-1.4	2	-19.1%	79	-75	83	-41	29%	42%	15%	14%
2013	KC	16/14	706	40	72	596	56%	-2.3	14.9	2	4	4.6	49	-0.0	3	-0.8%	52	68	54	72	44%	27%	11%	18%
2014	*KC*			*43*	*77*	*581*	*56%*		*13.5*	*4*						*-2.1%*								

World's Tallest Midget Department: Avery led the Chiefs' receivers in DVOA and finished just a few DYAR points behind Dwayne Bowe. He was especially effective on third and fourth down, where he posted a 53.6% DVOA. Avery's best game for the Chiefs came in Week 3, when he toasted the middle of Philadelphia's defense on slants, drags, and quick posts from the "X" and "Z" positions. Ideally, Avery would be a move-around guy and not a positional lead dog, but given what the Chiefs are holding at the receiver position overall, he may be pressed into service in places where he doesn't really belong. He's owed just $1.65 million in base salary in 2014, so any assumption that he could be released in favor of, say, A.J. Jenkins (as some have posited) is just a bit silly.

Stedman Bailey Height: 5-10 Weight: 193 College: West Virgina Draft: 2013/3 (92) Born: 11-Nov-1990 Age: 24 Risk: Yellow

Year	Team	G/GS	Snaps	Rec	Pass	Yds	C%	+/-	Yd/C	TD	Drop	YAC	Rk	YAC+	BTkl	DVOA	Rk	DYAR	Rk	YAR	Short	Mid	Deep	Bomb
2013	STL	16/2	188	17	25	226	68%	+3.3	13.3	0	0	2.7	--	-1.1	1	7.5%	--	36	--	33	33%	43%	24%	0%
2014	*STL*			*17*	*29*	*248*	*58%*		*15.0*	*1*						*3.8%*								

Bailey was the super-productive 100-catch complement to Tavon Austin at West Virginia, and led all receivers in the Class of 2013 in our Playmaker Score projections. As a rookie, he was lost in the shuffle of many talented young receivers with a minimal idea of what they were doing. Bailey came on strong with 15 receptions in his final five games, adding a 27-yard touchdown run on a reverse. Many of Bailey's receptions were short hitches in traffic, but since a) those routes make up about 80 percent of Brian Schottenheimer's passing playbook and b) the Rams have a need for a possession receiver, lots of short catches are not necessarily bad things. Bailey was also productive on special teams, and the depth chart in front of him is full of players who have learned fewer lessons over a longer period. Look for Bailey to push past some of the Brian Quick/Austin Pettis types whose scholarships are finally starting to lapse.

Doug Baldwin Height: 5-11 Weight: 189 College: Stanford Draft: 2011/FA Born: 21-Sep-1988 Age: 26 Risk: Green

Year	Team	G/GS	Snaps	Rec	Pass	Yds	C%	+/-	Yd/C	TD	Drop	YAC	Rk	YAC+	BTkl	DVOA	Rk	DYAR	Rk	YAR	Short	Mid	Deep	Bomb
2011	SEA	16/1	499	51	86	788	59%	-0.1	15.5	4	2	6.1	10	+1.0	5	14.5%	21	205	21	185	31%	38%	20%	11%
2012	SEA	14/4	434	29	50	366	58%	+0.1	12.6	3	3	2.7	77	-2.0	0	0.0%	47	45	58	38	33%	48%	9%	11%
2013	SEA	16/9	749	50	73	778	68%	+7.3	15.6	5	3	4.6	47	-0.2	2	33.3%	2	274	13	269	27%	45%	18%	11%
2014	*SEA*			*54*	*85*	*723*	*64%*		*13.4*	*5*						*5.4%*								

With all the talk about Percy Harvin and the departed Golden Tate and rookies Paul Richardson and Kevin Norwood, it's Baldwin—the undrafted free agent—who has become Seattle's most important receiver. It's hard to discern at times because he's always played in balanced or run-heavy offenses going back to his days at Stanford, but Baldwin has become a complete player over time. A slot receiver for the most part when he started out in the NFL, he became the team's most prolific deep receiver in 2013 with nine catches for 302 yards and two touchdowns on balls thrown at least 20 yards in the regular season, and the longest offensive play in Super Bowl XLVIII, when he toasted Champ Bailey for a 37-yard catch in the first quarter. It's this player who is the logical extension of the guy who became the first undrafted rookie in the Super Bowl era to lead his team in receptions and receiving yards back in 2011, not the one who followed that up with a tough sophomore season. The Seahawks agreed, signing Baldwin to a three-year, $13 million contract extension in May. Offensive coordinator Darrell Bevell has said that Baldwin will play more snaps in the "X" position in 2014, and if you believe that Seattle's passing offense will be more expansive, Baldwin could be taking off to a different level.

Cole Beasley Height: 5-8 Weight: 177 College: SMU Draft: 2012/FA Born: 26-Apr-1989 Age: 25 Risk: Yellow

Year	Team	G/GS	Snaps	Rec	Pass	Yds	C%	+/-	Yd/C	TD	Drop	YAC	Rk	YAC+	BTkl	DVOA	Rk	DYAR	Rk	YAR	Short	Mid	Deep	Bomb
2012	DAL	10/0	124	15	24	128	63%	-2.0	8.5	0	1	3.9	--	+0.1	1	-17.4%	--	-4	--	-6	67%	33%	0%	0%
2013	DAL	14/3	242	39	54	368	72%	+3.4	9.4	2	1	4.7	40	-0.3	3	1.5%	42	59	58	74	61%	37%	2%	0%
2014	*DAL*			*50*	*76*	*535*	*66%*		*10.7*	*2*						*-1.8%*								

Two years ago Beasley was already sick of the Wes Welker comparisons. "I get tired of it a little bit because I feel like I have a little bit more speed than Wes Welker does," said Beasley. Well, when teams keep finding these little guys to stick in the slot, feed them screens and ask them to do essentially everything Welker does, it's pretty hard not to make the comparison. If the shoe fits...

Beasley had 54 targets last year and only one traveled more than 10 yards in the air (a 17-yard pass he caught against the Saints). Whether he likes it or not, Beasley is Dallas' imitation of Welker, except he's even smaller at 5-foot-8. It might not seem like one inch makes a big difference—that's what she said—but the best wide receivers in NFL history under 69 inches are Tim Dwight and Stephen Baker. That's not encouraging.

Odell Beckham Height: 5-11 Weight: 198 College: LSU Draft: 2014/1 (12) Born: 5-Nov-1992 Age: 22 Risk: Red

Year	Team	G/GS	Snaps	Rec	Pass	Yds	C%	+/-	Yd/C	TD	Drop	YAC	Rk	YAC+	BTkl	DVOA	Rk	DYAR	Rk	YAR	Short	Mid	Deep	Bomb
2014	*NYG*			*47*	*85*	*639*	*55%*		*13.6*	*5*						*-1.4%*								

From 2004 to 2012, no LSU player gained 1,000 yards in a season, and that includes Dwayne Bowe, Brandon LaFell, Rueben Randle, and Devery Henderson. Then, in 2013, both Beckham and Jarvis Landry topped the 1,100 yard-mark as part of a revitalized Tigers passing attack manned by Zach Mettenberger. In New York, Beckham finds himself in a similar situation, teaming up with a talented receiving group (including Randle) and a strong-armed, classic pocket passer in Eli Manning. Some scouts viewed Beckham as a slot receiver because of his size and agility, but he's probably best suited as an outside receiver: in that respect, means landing with the Giants was a good fit, as Victor Cruz will be the slot man in three-receiver sets. Brandin Cooks is the only receiver in the Class of 2014 who ended up with a better Playmaker Projection than Beckham.

Kelvin Benjamin Height: 6-5 Weight: 240 College: Florida St. Draft: 2014/1 (28) Born: 5-Feb-1991 Age: 23 Risk: Red

Year	Team	G/GS	Snaps	Rec	Pass	Yds	C%	+/-	Yd/C	TD	Drop	YAC	Rk	YAC+	BTkl	DVOA	Rk	DYAR	Rk	YAR	Short	Mid	Deep	Bomb
2014	*CAR*			*51*	*93*	*733*	*55%*		*14.4*	*4*						*-2.8%*								

Benjamin played only two years at Florida State and enters the NFL with a massive amount of untapped potential. Not surprisingly, he stood out in early workouts as the most athletic receiver in Carolina, with several acrobatic catches. Also not surprisingly, his route-running was noticeably behind that of his new teammates. Benjamin led the ACC with 15 touchdown catches last year and averaged 18.7 yards per reception, though he was seventh in this draft class in Playmaker Rating. Given his inexperience, he may be the third wideout for Carolina this year, but you can expect to see him often on shot plays and red-zone passes. It could be a lot of fun if he takes off in the NFL. At a combined 12-foot-11 and 502 pounds, he and Cam Newton could be the biggest QB-WR combo you'll ever see.

Travis Benjamin Height: 5-10 Weight: 172 College: Miami Draft: 2012/4 (100) Born: 29-Dec-1989 Age: 25 Risk: Yellow

Year	Team	G/GS	Snaps	Rec	Pass	Yds	C%	+/-	Yd/C	TD	Drop	YAC	Rk	YAC+	BTkl	DVOA	Rk	DYAR	Rk	YAR	Short	Mid	Deep	Bomb
2012	CLE	14/3	297	18	37	298	49%	-2.2	16.6	2	1	3.6	--	+0.4	1	-1.5%	--	33	--	32	17%	47%	17%	19%
2013	CLE	8/3	143	5	13	105	38%	-1.8	21.0	0	1	12.0	--	+7.7	1	-8.3%	--	4	--	-2	23%	31%	23%	23%
2014	*CLE*			*32*	*57*	*509*	*56%*		*15.9*	*3*						*5.5%*								

Benjamin possesses what personnel types call a "dominant trait"—in his case, elite speed. A torn ACL suffered in late October makes said trait more recessive, but a lack of receivers in Cleveland may force him into the spotlight as the guy Johnny Manziel finds 25 yards downfield when he's scrambling around under pressure come December.

Earl Bennett Height: 5-11 Weight: 209 College: Vanderbilt Draft: 2008/3 (70) Born: 23-Mar-1987 Age: 27 Risk: #N/A

Year	Team	G/GS	Snaps	Rec	Pass	Yds	C%	+/-	Yd/C	TD	Drop	YAC	Rk	YAC+	BTkl	DVOA	Rk	DYAR	Rk	YAR	Short	Mid	Deep	Bomb
2011	CHI	11/4	442	24	43	381	56%	+2.0	15.9	1	0	5.2	--	+0.6	4	-1.4%	--	25	--	40	26%	37%	26%	11%
2012	CHI	12/4	417	29	49	375	59%	-3.4	12.9	2	1	6.4	10	+1.9	3	0.3%	45	60	55	54	38%	50%	8%	4%
2013	CHI	15/3	541	32	43	243	74%	+4.1	7.6	4	1	1.9	--	-3.0	3	-5.5%	--	25	--	39	50%	33%	14%	2%

Bennett has spent years slow-fading from the national consciousness after what appeared to be a breakout performance in 2009. His yardage totals have declined in each of the four seasons. After starting last season as a traditional slot receiver, Bennett's role became smaller and weirder; he frequently lined up in the backfield, and his two-catch 17-yard stat lines confused Pro Football Reference to the point where they listed him as the Bears' fullback. Cleveland signed him to be part of the group making up for Josh Gordon's suspension, and he looked so bad at OTAs that they cut him after just 33 days.

Davone Bess Height: 5-11 Weight: 193 College: Hawaii Draft: 2008/FA Born: 13-Sep-1985 Age: 29 Risk: #N/A

Year	Team	G/GS	Snaps	Rec	Pass	Yds	C%	+/-	Yd/C	TD	Drop	YAC	Rk	YAC+	BTkl	DVOA	Rk	DYAR	Rk	YAR	Short	Mid	Deep	Bomb
2011	MIA	16/4	551	51	86	537	59%	-0.2	10.5	3	2	4.5	36	-0.1	2	-24.5%	86	-111	89	-75	51%	34%	13%	3%
2012	MIA	13/13	738	61	105	778	58%	-0.7	12.8	1	4	4.1	42	+0.1	9	-3.7%	55	71	48	55	35%	44%	12%	8%
2013	CLE	14/3	533	42	86	362	49%	-14.4	8.6	2	9	3.5	73	-0.9	1	-32.3%	89	-135	89	-145	54%	40%	5%	1%

Struggled mightily with drops during the season; struggled mightily with social media and the penal code after it. Unsigned and seemingly unwanted.

Justin Blackmon Height: 6-1 Weight: 207 College: Oklahoma State Draft: 2012/1 (5) Born: 9-Jan-1990 Age: 24 Risk: #N/A

Year	Team	G/GS	Snaps	Rec	Pass	Yds	C%	+/-	Yd/C	TD	Drop	YAC	Rk	YAC+	BTkl	DVOA	Rk	DYAR	Rk	YAR	Short	Mid	Deep	Bomb
2012	JAC	16/14	963	64	132	865	48%	-12.7	13.5	5	8	4.4	36	+0.7	4	-15.0%	76	-4	75	-21	24%	55%	14%	7%
2013	JAC	4/4	247	29	48	415	60%	+0.4	14.3	1	1	7.6	--	+2.2	1	-4.2%	--	33	--	51	41%	43%	11%	4%

Justin Blackmon has an alcohol problem. He's going to be held on the roster, because it costs the Jaguars nothing and his contract years will roll over while he's suspended, but there is little chance of him playing professional football for the time being. That is a good thing. There's an allusion to be drawn to former NBA player Eddie Griffin, who fought the same demon and died behind the wheel. Blackmon's life is more important than his football career. Here's hoping he gets the help that he needs.

Anquan Boldin Height: 6-1 Weight: 218 College: Florida State Draft: 2003/2 (54) Born: 3-Oct-1980 Age: 34 Risk: Yellow

Year	Team	G/GS	Snaps	Rec	Pass	Yds	C%	+/-	Yd/C	TD	Drop	YAC	Rk	YAC+	BTkl	DVOA	Rk	DYAR	Rk	YAR	Short	Mid	Deep	Bomb
2011	BAL	14/14	879	57	106	887	54%	-4.2	15.6	3	4	3.9	56	-0.2	1	8.8%	34	226	16	172	13%	64%	16%	7%
2012	BAL	15/15	878	65	112	921	58%	+0.0	14.2	4	2	3.6	54	-0.7	5	3.4%	35	122	39	133	29%	47%	18%	7%
2013	SF	16/16	803	85	129	1179	66%	+9.9	13.9	7	4	5.0	30	+0.6	9	25.8%	9	386	3	409	30%	48%	20%	2%
2014	*SF*			*71*	*108*	*979*	*66%*		*13.8*	*8*						*16.0%*								

How great was that Boldin trade for San Francisco before last season? Baltimore was willing to part with him for peanuts in a cap move, believing the veteran receiver was no longer worth the cost, despite Boldin averaging 95 yards per game during the Ravens' Super Bowl run. After Michael Crabtree's Achilles injury, it was Boldin who became most of the San Francisco passing offense, and he finished with the seventh most yards all-time for a 33-year old-receiver. He started in the first game against Green Bay with over 200 yards, and he bookended it with the win at Arizona in the finale, where he was the focal point of the offense in the first half while San Francisco built a 17-0 lead. It was not just all about opportunity, as Boldin was one of the best receivers in the league and finished third in DYAR on a per-play basis. For what it's worth, 10 of the previous 15 wide receivers to have a 1,000-yard season at age 33 (since the league expanded to 16 games) duplicated it at age 34.

Current fantasy ADP ranks show that many people expect Michael Crabtree to take away a lot of Boldin's targets. We've seen the 49ers' numbers from the last few weeks of the season, and we think it's more likely that Colin Kaepernick throws more and gets guys like Bruce Miller involved less.

Dwayne Bowe Height: 6-2 Weight: 221 College: Louisiana State Draft: 2007/1 (23) Born: 21-Sep-1984 Age: 30 Risk: Green

Year	Team	G/GS	Snaps	Rec	Pass	Yds	C%	+/-	Yd/C	TD	Drop	YAC	Rk	YAC+	BTkl	DVOA	Rk	DYAR	Rk	YAR	Short	Mid	Deep	Bomb
2011	KC	16/14	905	81	141	1159	57%	+1.1	14.3	5	9	4.2	44	-0.2	11	-0.2%	51	166	28	165	26%	46%	21%	7%
2012	KC	13/12	739	59	114	801	52%	-2.5	13.6	3	4	4.0	43	+0.1	6	-4.1%	56	60	56	76	17%	54%	18%	11%
2013	KC	15/15	837	57	103	673	55%	-7.7	11.8	5	5	3.4	77	-0.6	6	-4.4%	61	71	52	76	33%	46%	19%	2%
2014	*KC*			*56*	*97*	*715*	*58%*		*12.8*	*7*						*1.2%*								

Bowe didn't look like the receiver we projected him to be last year until the wild card loss to the Colts, when Alex Smith kept peppering him with footballs as Kansas City's defense squandered a 38-10 third-quarter lead. Bowe was also slightly more productive in the second half of the season when Smith was slightly more daring with deep passes, but Bowe suffered just as much from the fact that Smith has an exceedingly low bar when it comes to deep balls, anyway. While Bowe is a pretty decent yards after catch guy who can win vertical battles, he's not a route-consistent receiver, which doesn't really make him an ideal No. 1 target for an Andy Reid offense. Bowe has had his share of consistency issues through the years, but he sounded nothing but positive as the Chiefs geared up for the 2014 season. "I'm moving good and I feel like I'm in the best shape of my life in these OTAs," Bowe said in June, adding that he's worked with trainers and nutritionists to drop down to 210 pounds. "The way they've been going, it's only going to get better." In a system with a more adventurous quarterback, perhaps. But Bowe will be tethered to Smith's limitations as much as his own, which has us projecting far more conservatively this time around.

Jarrett Boykin Height: 6-2 Weight: 218 College: Virginia Tech Draft: 2012/FA Born: 4-Nov-1989 Age: 25 Risk: Green

Year	Team	G/GS	Snaps	Rec	Pass	Yds	C%	+/-	Yd/C	TD	Drop	YAC	Rk	YAC+	BTkl	DVOA	Rk	DYAR	Rk	YAR	Short	Mid	Deep	Bomb
2012	GB	10/0	93	5	6	27	83%	+1.2	5.4	0	0	1.2	--	-2.8	0	-25.6%	--	-8	--	-6	50%	33%	0%	17%
2013	GB	16/8	663	49	83	681	59%	+3.2	13.9	3	3	5.2	26	+0.6	7	9.3%	23	146	32	138	36%	42%	12%	11%
2014	*GB*			*34*	*59*	*475*	*58%*		*14.0*	*4*						*5.1%*								

Boykin took over James Jones' old role—only 14 of his 83 targeted passes were listed as over the middle in play-by-play—with Jones pressed into more versatile duties to compensate for the losses of Randall Cobb and Jermichael Finley. Boykin looked like he had never even heard of Aaron Rodgers in his first start but came on suddenly; he caught 19 passes for 273 yards during the games in which Scott Tolzien threw passes, with 36-, 34-, and 52-yard receptions, a few of them beauties. Boykin is a high-effort blocker on screens and handoffs, has some niftiness after catching screens of his own, and has long speed and leaping ability when threatening the deep sidelines. He's what the Packers wanted Jones to be in 2009-2010, and he was a major reason why Jones was expendable. Cobb is back, and Davonte Adams will push for the deep sidelines role, but Boykin can do a lot of things to keep himself in the lineup and in Rodgers' crosshairs.

Kenny Britt Height: 6-3 Weight: 218 College: Rutgers Draft: 2009/1 (30) Born: 19-Sep-1988 Age: 26 Risk: Blue

Year	Team	G/GS	Snaps	Rec	Pass	Yds	C%	+/-	Yd/C	TD	Drop	YAC	Rk	YAC+	BTkl	DVOA	Rk	DYAR	Rk	YAR	Short	Mid	Deep	Bomb
2011	TEN	3/3	142	17	26	289	65%	+2.7	17.0	3	0	7.4	--	+2.1	5	34.6%	--	111	--	92	36%	32%	8%	24%
2012	TEN	14/11	600	45	90	589	50%	-4.8	13.1	4	7	2.8	74	-1.2	6	-23.7%	82	-46	81	-71	24%	48%	10%	17%
2013	TEN	12/3	299	11	35	96	31%	-9.2	8.7	0	5	1.2	--	-2.1	3	-48.5%	--	-101	--	-108	20%	46%	17%	17%
2014	*STL*			*14*	*28*	*190*	*50%*		*13.6*	*1*						*-11.3%*								

A mercurial talent. Britt dominated at times in both 2010 and 2012, but has not played at the same level since returning from a torn ACL. A defiant Britt informed reporters near the end of the season that he was "going to be a No.1 receiver somewhere else if I am not here next year, and that is guaranteed." Well, when you mix slower speed, a case of the drops, and off-field issues with the poor tape, you instead get a one-year prove-it deal with the Rams. Britt won't turn 26 until after the season starts, so if he's healthy, he still has a chance to play in this league for a while. He's got a ways to go to get back to his 2011 form, but this could be low risk, high reward.

Antonio Brown Height: 5-10 Weight: 186 College: Central Mighican Draft: 2010/6 (195) Born: 10-Jul-1988 Age: 26 Risk: Green

Year	Team	G/GS	Snaps	Rec	Pass	Yds	C%	+/-	Yd/C	TD	Drop	YAC	Rk	YAC+	BTkl	DVOA	Rk	DYAR	Rk	YAR	Short	Mid	Deep	Bomb
2011	PIT	16/3	608	69	124	1108	56%	-3.5	16.1	2	6	4.9	27	-0.0	2	9.4%	33	197	23	187	23%	42%	28%	7%
2012	PIT	13/10	652	66	106	787	63%	+3.9	11.9	5	3	5.3	21	-0.3	4	-1.9%	50	88	43	93	38%	38%	15%	9%
2013	PIT	16/14	954	110	167	1499	66%	+10.1	13.6	8	6	5.2	27	-0.2	15	15.0%	15	361	5	346	40%	35%	12%	13%
2014	*PIT*			*99*	*151*	*1343*	*66%*		*13.6*	*8*						*14.7%*								

You can take Bruce Arians out of Pittsburgh, but the bubble screen to Antonio Brown lives on. Brown's screen count since 2011 has gone from 11 to 23 to 30 last year. Overall, Brown caught more passes thrown behind the line of scrimmage than any other wide receiver with at least 70 catches last year, and he had the highest rate (25.5 percent) of his receptions coming on such plays. Brown's average gain from that depth level has been below the league average all three years, but it's still a better alternative to Pittsburgh's average running play. Still, last year proved Brown could do a lot more than catch short passes. He didn't need Mike Wallace to take the top off the defense to have an All-Pro caliber season at receiver and he provided solid value as a punt returner. Brown became the first receiver in NFL history to have at least five receptions and 50 receiving yards in all 16 games in a season. Maybe Dri Archer can take over the return duties and some of the short passes, allowing Brown to focus on perfecting his skills as a good short-to-intermediate route runner with the ability to make the occasional spectacular catch (check out video of the Chicago game sometime) down the field.

Marlon Brown Height: 6-4 Weight: 205 College: Georgia Draft: 2013/FA Born: 22-Apr-1991 Age: 23 Risk: Green

Year	Team	G/GS	Snaps	Rec	Pass	Yds	C%	+/-	Yd/C	TD	Drop	YAC	Rk	YAC+	BTkl	DVOA	Rk	DYAR	Rk	YAR	Short	Mid	Deep	Bomb
2013	BAL	14/12	791	49	83	524	59%	-2.4	10.7	7	2	4.8	35	+0.4	6	4.9%	31	117	41	106	44%	32%	16%	8%
2014	*BAL*			*14*	*24*	*174*	*58%*		*12.4*	*1*						*-2.9%*								

Brown surprised many people by becoming just the sixth undrafted rookie wideout to ever catch at least seven touchdowns. He didn't do it by being part of a great offense like Marc Boerigter (2002 Chiefs). He didn't have Dan Marino throwing the ball like Oronde Gadsden did (1998 Dolphins). Ken MacAfee (1954 Giants), Bill Groman (1960 Oilers) and Bobby Johnson (1984 Giants) are the others to do it, so it's hardly a predictor of a bright future. The Ravens threw passes of 21 or more yards to Brown 18 times, and connected on just one of them, though he did draw two pass interference penalties. Brown's strength and height do much more in the red zone where all seven of his touchdowns came. He easily led all Baltimore receivers with a 52.2% DVOA in the red zone.

However, if the Ravens are going to start Torrey Smith and Steve Smith, get back to Dennis Pitta in the red zone and favor the big-play ability of Jacoby Jones, then that leaves Brown as the fifth man, which usually doesn't bode well for targets and playing time. Brown reportedly had problems with drops in OTAs, which is unlikely to help his cause in improving on last season.

Mike Brown Height: 5-10 Weight: 200 College: Liberty Draft: 2012/FA Born: 9-Feb-1989 Age: 25 Risk: Blue

Year	Team	G/GS	Snaps	Rec	Pass	Yds	C%	+/-	Yd/C	TD	Drop	YAC	Rk	YAC+	BTkl	DVOA	Rk	DYAR	Rk	YAR	Short	Mid	Deep	Bomb
2012	JAC	2/1	13	0	1	0	0%	-0.7	0.0	0	1	0.0	--	--	0	-93.4%	--	-7	--	-7	0%	100%	0%	0%
2013	JAC	11/6	576	32	56	446	57%	+0.8	13.9	2	2	4.8	34	+0.6	3	-6.6%	65	27	68	21	37%	43%	8%	12%
2014	*JAC*			*9*	*20*	*90*	*45%*		*10.0*	*0*						*-34.3%*								

Caught in an influx of young receivers that were actually drafted, converted quarterback Brown will likely be battling for the fifth spot on the depth chart with waiver-claim scrubs such as Tandon Doss and Kerry Taylor. What's interesting is that Brown actually showed bursts of effectiveness last season—he notched a 10.7% DVOA over Weeks 5-7 before dealing with ankle and shoulder injuries in November and December. Should the rookies in front of him prove unready, Brown has a puncher's chance of turning in some good performances again.

Vincent Brown Height: 5-11 Weight: 184 College: San Diego State Draft: 2011/3 (82) Born: 25-Jan-1989 Age: 25 Risk: Yellow

Year	Team	G/GS	Snaps	Rec	Pass	Yds	C%	+/-	Yd/C	TD	Drop	YAC	Rk	YAC+	BTkl	DVOA	Rk	DYAR	Rk	YAR	Short	Mid	Deep	Bomb
2011	SD	14/4	336	19	40	329	48%	-1.1	17.3	2	1	4.1	--	-0.2	0	2.2%	--	45	--	50	18%	39%	21%	21%
2013	SD	16/12	918	41	69	472	59%	+4.4	11.5	1	1	2.3	87	-2.0	2	-4.1%	60	49	60	55	27%	40%	21%	11%
2014	*SD*			*42*	*70*	*597*	*60%*		*14.2*	*4*						*5.2%*								

Brown started just four games in his rookie year and missed the entire 2012 season due to injury, which made the former college star more like a rookie in 2013 than he would have liked. The upside is that the Chargers see his ... well, upside.

"I know he's been in the league for a couple years, but really, as far as heavy playing time, it was almost like a rookie year for him," general manager Tom Telesco said of Brown in January.. "[He's] definitely good moving forward. He's shown some promise. He finishes some tough catches downfield, and he's a good route runner, so we'll see where it goes."

Brown is also sloppy on certain routes, and you can see the effects of the time off in that regard. But the potential everybody saw at Brown's Senior Bowl and combine is still there—he'll just have to develop on a different curve, in a receiver rotation that starts to look more and more stacked.

Ryan Broyles Height: 5-10 Weight: 192 College: Oklahoma Draft: 2012/2 (54) Born: 9-Apr-1988 Age: 26 Risk: Green

Year	Team	G/GS	Snaps	Rec	Pass	Yds	C%	+/-	Yd/C	TD	Drop	YAC	Rk	YAC+	BTkl	DVOA	Rk	DYAR	Rk	YAR	Short	Mid	Deep	Bomb
2012	DET	10/3	278	22	32	310	69%	+2.7	14.1	2	3	6.9	--	+2.4	1	38.7%	--	140	--	117	57%	27%	7%	10%
2013	DET	6/3	187	8	14	85	57%	-1.0	10.6	0	2	4.8	--	+0.0	0	-23.0%	--	-11	--	-9	62%	8%	31%	0%
2014	*DET*			*28*	*49*	*351*	*57%*		*12.6*	*1*						*-5.8%*								

Broyles has now suffered two ACL tears and an Achilles tear in two NFL seasons. Jim Caldwell promises a "clean slate," and Broyles was cutting and jumping without incident before the draft, but you know how these things go. We all know what happened to the first-round receivers Matt Millen drafted before Calvin Johnson, but the Lions also drafted Titus Young and Broyles in back-to-back second rounds in 2011 and 2012. These gypsy curses sure do work in mysterious ways.

Dez Bryant Height: 6-2 Weight: 225 College: Oklahoma State Draft: 2010/1 (24) Born: 4-Nov-1988 Age: 26 Risk: Green

Year	Team	G/GS	Snaps	Rec	Pass	Yds	C%	+/-	Yd/C	TD	Drop	YAC	Rk	YAC+	BTkl	DVOA	Rk	DYAR	Rk	YAR	Short	Mid	Deep	Bomb
2011	DAL	15/13	765	63	103	928	61%	+4.1	14.7	9	3	4.8	29	+0.1	10	19.9%	14	246	14	249	26%	47%	16%	12%
2012	DAL	16/14	922	92	138	1282	67%	+9.0	13.9	12	9	4.9	30	+0.4	16	18.3%	17	392	3	352	34%	38%	14%	15%
2013	DAL	16/16	933	93	160	1233	58%	-1.7	13.3	13	6	5.7	18	+1.4	7	3.7%	33	215	18	242	32%	42%	17%	9%
2014	*DAL*			*97*	*152*	*1271*	*64%*		*13.1*	*12*						*14.3%*								

Bryant's caught 25 touchdowns over the last two seasons and his 2013 season was a clinic in how to play receiver in the red zone. He set a single-season record with nine touchdown grabs of one to five yards. The last player to have eight was Randy Moss in 2004. Bryant's caught a touchdown on 41.8 percent of his red-zone targets—the highest rate by any wide receiver since 1998.

Table 1. Highest Career WR Touchdown per Target Rate in Red Zone 1998-2013

Rk	Wide Receiver	Height	Pass	Rec	C%	Yards	TD	TD%	Rk	Wide Receiver	Height	Pass	Rec	C%	Yards	TD	TD%
1	Dez Bryant	6-2	55	35	63.6%	225	23	41.8%	11	Dwayne Bowe	6-2	88	43	48.9%	345	27	30.7%
2	Eric Decker	6-3	58	34	58.6%	276	22	37.9%	12	Terrell Owens	6-3	200	117	58.5%	838	61	30.5%
3	Joe Jurevicius	6-5	57	30	52.6%	241	21	36.8%	13	Calvin Johnson	6-5	122	54	44.3%	478	37	30.3%
4	Cris Carter	6-3	60	34	56.7%	231	22	36.7%	14	Jeremy Maclin	6-0	50	30	60.0%	223	15	30.0%
5	Roy Williams	6-4	78	38	48.7%	317	26	33.3%	15	Darrell Jackson	6-0	97	46	47.4%	342	29	29.9%
6	Wayne Chrebet	5-10	56	37	66.1%	318	18	32.1%	16	Demaryius Thomas	6-3	54	29	53.7%	233	16	29.6%
7	Marvin Harrison	6-0	185	112	60.5%	810	58	31.4%	17	Larry Fitzgerald	6-3	193	102	52.8%	680	57	29.5%
8	Marques Colston	6-4	142	87	61.3%	744	44	31.0%	18	Sidney Rice	6-4	61	33	54.1%	283	18	29.5%
9	Vincent Jackson	6-5	97	49	50.5%	423	30	30.9%	19	Anquan Boldin	6-1	133	80	60.2%	624	39	29.3%
10	Jordy Nelson	6-3	65	39	60.0%	289	20	30.8%	20	Antonio Freeman	6-1	62	34	54.8%	304	18	29.0%

Minimum 50 red-zone targets

If you're in the camp that thinks Jimmy Graham (40.8 percent) is a wide receiver, then Bryant has him beat too. Bryant has the ideal size and body control to be a dominant player at any depth level on the field, but his red-zone proficiency is a good indicator of more double-digit scoring seasons to come.

Martavis Bryant Height: 6-4 Weight: 211 College: Clemson Draft: 2014/4 (118) Born: 20-Dec-1991 Age: 23 Risk: Red

Year	Team	G/GS	Snaps	Rec	Pass	Yds	C%	+/-	Yd/C	TD	Drop	YAC	Rk	YAC+	BTkl	DVOA	Rk	DYAR	Rk	YAR	Short	Mid	Deep	Bomb
2014	*PIT*			*38*	*65*	*556*	*58%*		*14.6*	*4*						*7.3%*								

Hey look, it's a No. 2 receiver from a gimmicky offense where the No. 1 receiver was drafted much higher for his ability to gain yards after the catch! Otherwise, Bryant is nothing like last year's Stedman Bailey pick for the Rams. Bryant is a tall deep threat—he averaged 22.2 yards per reception at Clemson where he was mostly a one-year wonder in terms of significant production. Deep threats usually have a lousy catch rate, but Bryant caught 65 percent of his targets in 2013. He'll battle Markus Wheaton for playing time, but given Roethlisberger's height fetish, Bryant looks like a red-zone option and could even start over Wheaton at flanker opposite Antonio Brown.

Nate Burleson Height: 6-0 Weight: 192 College: Nevada Draft: 2003/3 (71) Born: 19-Aug-1981 Age: 33 Risk: Green

Year	Team	G/GS	Snaps	Rec	Pass	Yds	C%	+/-	Yd/C	TD	Drop	YAC	Rk	YAC+	BTkl	DVOA	Rk	DYAR	Rk	YAR	Short	Mid	Deep	Bomb
2011	DET	16/11	962	73	110	757	66%	-2.8	10.4	3	6	5.5	19	+0.5	12	-5.4%	59	31	62	73	64%	25%	8%	4%
2012	DET	6/5	356	27	43	240	63%	-0.1	8.9	2	0	3.1	--	-2.0	1	-14.0%	--	-24	--	4	51%	34%	12%	2%
2013	DET	9/8	496	39	54	461	72%	+2.9	11.8	1	3	5.5	20	+1.0	4	0.4%	46	56	59	65	54%	38%	6%	2%
2014	*CLE*			*45*	*81*	*557*	*56%*		*12.4*	*2*						*-5.6%*								

In Detroit, the reliable veteran slot receiver is the guy who crashes his car and fractures an arm during a pizza run. In Cleveland, the reliable veteran slot receiver is the guy who graduates from a pass-dropping spree to erratic airport behavior, so Burleson has huge shoes to fill as he replaces Davone Bess. Burleson re-aggravated his arm injury in a pre-draft minicamp, which is a pretty good start. Burleson has a knack for landing in hard-luck situations—he suffered through the dark days between Super Bowl runs in Seattle before becoming troupe leader for Detroit's Failure Scouts—so he should feel right at home in Jimmy Haslam's diesel-powered circus. Burleson can still beat underneath coverage and catch short passes when healthy, and look where it gets him.

Randall Cobb Height: 5-11 Weight: 190 College: Kentucky Draft: 2011/2 (64) Born: 22-Aug-1990 Age: 24 Risk: Red

Year	Team	G/GS	Snaps	Rec	Pass	Yds	C%	+/-	Yd/C	TD	Drop	YAC	Rk	YAC+	BTkl	DVOA	Rk	DYAR	Rk	YAR	Short	Mid	Deep	Bomb
2011	GB	15/0	274	25	31	375	81%	+4.2	15.0	1	2	7.5	--	+3.1	5	42.5%	--	121	--	133	35%	45%	19%	0%
2012	GB	15/8	631	80	104	954	77%	+11.3	11.9	8	8	5.7	18	-0.1	13	24.1%	9	357	6	303	55%	23%	20%	3%
2013	GB	6/4	333	31	47	433	66%	+4.8	14.0	4	1	5.6	--	+0.0	5	21.1%	--	121	--	105	43%	35%	15%	8%
2014	*GB*			*79*	*119*	*1084*	*66%*		*13.7*	*9*						*20.1%*								

Cobb returned from a broken leg in Week 17 to catch touchdown passes of 48 and seven yards, then caught 26- and 25-yard passes in the playoff loss to the 49ers; those were the only passes he was targeted for in those two games. He also replaced Micah Hyde on kickoffs, but that may not be worth the risk in non-playoff situations. Hyde's emergence makes Cobb an as-needed return man, Eddie Lacy has eliminated the need for those zany Cobb-as-shotgun-halfback draw plays, and Jarrett Boykin emerged as a worthy complement to Jordy Nelson. There are also lots of appealing rookies competing for depth positions. That means the Packers can use Cobb the way they want to, not in ways they have to, and there may not be a scarier slot receiver in the NFL, at least among players who are healthy enough to participate in non-Super Bowls.

Marques Colston Height: 6-4 Weight: 225 College: Hofstra Draft: 2006/7 (252) Born: 5-Jun-1983 Age: 31 Risk: Green

Year	Team	G/GS	Snaps	Rec	Pass	Yds	C%	+/-	Yd/C	TD	Drop	YAC	Rk	YAC+	BTkl	DVOA	Rk	DYAR	Rk	YAR	Short	Mid	Deep	Bomb
2011	NO	14/7	659	80	107	1143	75%	+16.0	14.3	8	3	3.2	76	-0.9	1	34.3%	5	430	5	444	22%	51%	20%	8%
2012	NO	16/13	832	83	130	1154	64%	+7.1	13.9	10	9	3.5	61	-0.1	1	19.7%	15	327	11	339	27%	56%	12%	5%
2013	NO	15/11	750	75	110	943	68%	+9.3	12.6	5	2	3.4	78	-0.6	4	19.5%	14	276	12	283	32%	47%	17%	4%
2014	*NO*			*68*	*102*	*910*	*67%*		*13.4*	*7*						*18.6%*								

Colston was bothered by a sore foot last year, which partially explains why he had his worst totals since 2008. He says he's healthy heading into training camp, but so is Brandin Cooks, and the 20th overall pick in this year's draft figures to get some of the passes that used to go Colston's way. Colston's days as a WR1 in fantasy football are probably over. Colston has publicly acknowledged that his contract makes him a likely salary-cap casualty a year or two down the road, but Drew Brees' favorite receiver should still have several productive seasons ahead, whether in New Orleans or elsewhere.

Brandin Cooks Height: 5-10 Weight: 189 College: Oregon St. Draft: 2014/1 (20) Born: 25-Sep-1993 Age: 21 Risk: Red

Year	Team	G/GS	Snaps	Rec	Pass	Yds	C%	+/-	Yd/C	TD	Drop	YAC	Rk	YAC+	BTkl	DVOA	Rk	DYAR	Rk	YAR	Short	Mid	Deep	Bomb
2014	*NO*			*58*	*84*	*729*	*69%*		*12.6*	*4*						*15.1%*								

Cooks led the Pac-12 with 17.2 yards per catch and 16 touchdowns, and led the nation with 1,730 yards, then ran a 4.33-second forty-yard dash at the Combine, so it's no surprise that he has the highest Playmaker Projection and Rating of any receiver in this draft class. Sean Payton has a history of getting the ball to rookie receivers (Marques Colston gained 1,038 yards in 2006, Reggie Bush 742 in 2006, Kenny Stills 641 yards last year), so he won't be shy about giving Cooks plenty of opportunity. Cooks enters camp as the fourth option behind Colston, Stills, and Jimmy Graham. He won't be the fourth option for very long.

Riley Cooper Height: 6-4 Weight: 222 College: Florida Draft: 2010/5 (159) Born: 9-Sep-1987 Age: 27 Risk: Yellow

Year	Team	G/GS	Snaps	Rec	Pass	Yds	C%	+/-	Yd/C	TD	Drop	YAC	Rk	YAC+	BTkl	DVOA	Rk	DYAR	Rk	YAR	Short	Mid	Deep	Bomb
2011	PHI	16/3	321	16	35	315	46%	+0.4	19.7	1	3	3.5	--	-1.4	1	-0.6%	--	23	--	33	10%	50%	20%	20%
2012	PHI	11/5	486	23	48	248	48%	-4.6	10.8	3	1	4.0	--	-0.3	2	-22.8%	--	-15	--	-25	27%	51%	16%	7%
2013	PHI	16/15	981	47	84	835	56%	+0.5	17.8	8	4	4.9	32	+0.1	4	20.6%	13	212	19	214	26%	37%	20%	18%
2014	*PHI*			*52*	*89*	*791*	*58%*		*15.2*	*6*						*9.9%*								

Cooper showed little promise in his first three seasons and last summer he was caught using a racial slur on video. That controversy had some thinking this guy played his last down in the NFL, but lo and behold, Cooper finished with a career season that earned him a five-year deal worth $25 million. That's reasonable money for a No. 2 receiver (not so much for a No. 3 if you believe in Jordan Matthews), but there are some red flags over his 2013 season. First, his production skyrocketed with the insertion of Foles into the starting lineup, but it did not sustain itself. Cooper had 53.8 percent of his yards and six of his eight touchdowns in Foles' first four starts. He only broke 60 yards twice in his last seven games and scored two touchdowns (including the playoffs). Then there's the eye test. Half of Cooper's touchdowns featured inexplicably poor coverage by bad defenses like Oakland and Green Bay, including a 63-yard bomb where the defender simply fell down. Cooper made his share of circus catches at times as well. Some players (Brandon Lloyd) can make a career out of that, but Cooper's track record is really limited and his sample of great games last year is also small.

Jerricho Cotchery Height: 6-1 Weight: 200 College: North Carolina St. Draft: 2004/4 (108) Born: 16-Jun-1982 Age: 32 Risk: Red

Year	Team	G/GS	Snaps	Rec	Pass	Yds	C%	+/-	Yd/C	TD	Drop	YAC	Rk	YAC+	BTkl	DVOA	Rk	DYAR	Rk	YAR	Short	Mid	Deep	Bomb
2011	PIT	13/0	277	16	31	237	55%	-0.7	14.8	2	1	4.1	--	+0.1	0	13.0%	--	57	--	51	20%	57%	23%	0%
2012	PIT	14/2	266	17	27	205	63%	+0.8	12.1	0	0	2.5	--	-1.2	0	2.8%	--	35	--	37	27%	46%	27%	0%
2013	PIT	16/6	635	46	76	602	61%	-0.8	13.1	10	3	4.7	41	+0.4	7	26.2%	8	235	16	214	32%	49%	14%	5%
2014	*CAR*			*52*	*86*	*586*	*60%*		*11.3*	*3*						*-5.2%*								

Cotchery's always been a receiver who gets more appreciation from fans than the national media. He was solid in Pittsburgh in a limited role, then when asked to do more last year, he responded with one of the more unexpected double-digit touchdown seasons in NFL history. He had seven touchdowns in his previous four seasons combined. All 10 last year were from within 20 yards, and Cotchery put up 62.3% DVOA in the red zone. Despite being 32 years old, he's looking at another significant role in Carolina due to the wholesale changes the Panthers have made at the position.

Michael Crabtree Height: 6-2 Weight: 215 College: Texas Tech Draft: 2009/1 (10) Born: 14-Sep-1987 Age: 27 Risk: Red

Year	Team	G/GS	Snaps	Rec	Pass	Yds	C%	+/-	Yd/C	TD	Drop	YAC	Rk	YAC+	BTkl	DVOA	Rk	DYAR	Rk	YAR	Short	Mid	Deep	Bomb
2011	SF	15/14	668	72	114	874	64%	+3.4	12.1	4	5	5.0	25	-0.2	10	5.2%	39	170	27	128	46%	29%	17%	8%
2012	SF	16/16	674	85	127	1105	68%	+6.4	13.0	9	5	6.5	9	+1.9	14	21.9%	13	334	10	336	53%	32%	12%	4%
2013	SF	5/5	237	19	33	284	58%	+1.8	14.9	1	1	7.2	--	+3.0	1	3.7%	--	42	--	42	38%	41%	14%	7%
2014	*SF*			*82*	*127*	*1229*	*65%*		*15.0*	*9*						*18.5%*								

In the 18 games that Michael Crabtree and Colin Kaepernick have started together, Crabtree has totaled 95 catches, 1367 yards, and nine touchdowns. Of course, those games have been spread out over multiple seasons and broken up by Kaepernick's time as the backup to Alex Smith and then Crabtree's Achilles injury. This is the year when we find out if those small sample sizes hold up for Crabtree. It is also the final year of Crabtree's rookie contract. If you believe in unicorns, fairy dust, and the power of the contract year, we'd suggest that your fantasy team rides Crabtree's coattails.

Victor Cruz Height: 6-1 Weight: 200 College: Massachusetts Draft: 2010/FA Born: 11-Nov-1986 Age: 28 Risk: Yellow

Year	Team	G/GS	Snaps	Rec	Pass	Yds	C%	+/-	Yd/C	TD	Drop	YAC	Rk	YAC+	BTkl	DVOA	Rk	DYAR	Rk	YAR	Short	Mid	Deep	Bomb
2011	NYG	16/7	747	82	129	1536	64%	+9.8	18.7	9	8	7.2	2	+2.6	11	31.4%	8	433	4	445	31%	41%	19%	9%
2012	NYG	16/16	902	86	143	1092	60%	+1.6	12.7	10	9	3.8	50	-0.1	6	1.2%	41	165	28	166	33%	48%	8%	11%
2013	NYG	14/12	785	73	121	998	60%	+2.4	13.7	4	3	3.4	76	-0.8	7	1.0%	44	133	35	172	25%	52%	12%	11%
2014	*NYG*			*86*	*144*	*1140*	*60%*		*13.3*	*8*						*5.9%*								

Sure, 2013 was a "down" year for Cruz, but it was a season where he increased both his yards per game and yards per catch averages. He remains a player who operates out of the slot on around 70 percent of his routes; that may have hurt his market value, but it makes him Eli Manning's most dependable weapon. New offensive coordinator Ben McAdoo got great slot production out of Randall Cobb and Jordy Nelson, so the switch in offensive schemes may wind up boosting Cruz's already impressive numbers. With Hakeem Nicks and Brandon Myers being replaced by unproven players, we expect Cruz to finish among the league leaders in both receptions and receiving yards in 2013.

Eric Decker Height: 6-3 Weight: 217 College: Minnesota Draft: 2010/3 (87) Born: 15-Mar-1987 Age: 27 Risk: Red

Year	Team	G/GS	Snaps	Rec	Pass	Yds	C%	+/-	Yd/C	TD	Drop	YAC	Rk	YAC+	BTkl	DVOA	Rk	DYAR	Rk	YAR	Short	Mid	Deep	Bomb
2011	DEN	16/13	972	44	98	612	46%	-7.3	13.9	8	6	3.9	58	-1.3	1	-15.5%	76	-24	76	-40	30%	34%	16%	20%
2012	DEN	16/15	1048	85	123	1064	69%	+13.0	12.5	13	7	3.1	69	-0.7	3	27.2%	8	392	4	401	32%	45%	11%	12%
2013	DEN	16/16	1050	87	136	1288	64%	+4.3	14.8	11	7	4.3	58	-0.4	5	21.3%	12	381	4	382	35%	39%	17%	9%
2014	*NYJ*			*73*	*130*	*1025*	*56%*		*14.0*	*6*						*2.5%*								

Decker is a very good outside receiver, doing his best work on intermediate routes. He does a good job of using his size and route-running skills to create separation from defensive backs and proved adept at winning one-on-one battles on jump balls and contested catches. We mentioned last year that Decker could easily be a No. 1 receiver on another team. Now he has his chance after signing a five-year, $36.25 million contract with the Jets. It could be quite a comedown after playing with Peyton Manning, especially as he may lack a standout quality that makes him a "true" No. 1 receiver. The Jets' quarterback (whether Michael Vick or Geno Smith) must give him the chance to win those one-on-one battles with his ball placement and willingness to throw the ball even when Decker may not appear open.

Aaron Dobson Height: 6-3 Weight: 210 College: Marshall Draft: 2013/2 (59) Born: 23-Jul-1991 Age: 23 Risk: Red

Year	Team	G/GS	Snaps	Rec	Pass	Yds	C%	+/-	Yd/C	TD	Drop	YAC	Rk	YAC+	BTkl	DVOA	Rk	DYAR	Rk	YAR	Short	Mid	Deep	Bomb
2013	NE	12/9	546	37	72	519	51%	-2.8	14.0	4	7	5.0	30	+0.9	2	-5.4%	63	46	62	41	22%	45%	18%	14%
2014	*NE*			*51*	*88*	*711*	*58%*		*13.9*	*6*						*5.3%*								

As overwhelmed and unsure as he appeared to be at times, Dobson had one of the best rookie seasons of any receiver under Tom Brady—at least statistically, he was as good as Deion Branch iwhen he had 43 catches for 489 yards and two touchdowns in 2002. Fair or not, what people will take away from his rookie year are the drops—he had three bad drops on national television in a September win over the Jets, and ended the year with seven. His offseason was thrown into doubt because of foot surgery, but he needs to assert himself this coming season. More will be expected of him in 2014, and will be interesting to see how he responds to the added pressure.

Tandon Doss Height: 6-3 Weight: 200 College: Indiana Draft: 2011/4 (123) Born: 22-Sep-1989 Age: 25 Risk: Blue

Year	Team	G/GS	Snaps	Rec	Pass	Yds	C%	+/-	Yd/C	TD	Drop	YAC	Rk	YAC+	BTkl	DVOA	Rk	DYAR	Rk	YAR	Short	Mid	Deep	Bomb
2011	BAL	6/0	30	0	2	0	0%	-1.2	0.0	0	0	0.0	--	+0.0	0	2.9%	--	1	--	4	0%	67%	0%	33%
2012	BAL	14/0	183	7	17	123	41%	-1.9	17.6	1	1	7.4	--	+3.1	0	5.3%	--	20	--	20	40%	33%	20%	7%
2013	BAL	15/2	298	19	36	305	53%	-2.7	16.1	0	3	4.5	--	-0.8	1	-6.6%	--	17	--	16	31%	44%	17%	8%
2014	*JAC*			*4*	*7*	*51*	*57%*		*12.7*	*0*						*-2.2%*								

Baltimore used a fourth-round pick on Doss in 2011, but three years of "potential deep threat" turned into little production and he's now with Jacksonville. Doss really only had two highlights last year. He had an 82-yard punt return touchdown against Houston, and the longest fourth-down conversion of the season: a 63-yard catch on fourth-and-21 against Green Bay. Of course it helps when the defensive back falls down behind you, but hey, that's a pretty nice conversion. Baltimore still has Jacoby Jones for punt returns and Torrey Smith for the deep ball, so Doss won't be missed one iota.

Harry Douglas Height: 5-11 Weight: 176 College: Louisville Draft: 2008/3 (84) Born: 16-Sep-1985 Age: 29 Risk: Green

Year	Team	G/GS	Snaps	Rec	Pass	Yds	C%	+/-	Yd/C	TD	Drop	YAC	Rk	YAC+	BTkl	DVOA	Rk	DYAR	Rk	YAR	Short	Mid	Deep	Bomb
2011	ATL	16/4	624	39	62	498	63%	+2.1	12.8	1	2	5.9	13	+0.9	1	-4.4%	57	33	61	37	44%	34%	15%	7%
2012	ATL	15/1	585	38	59	396	64%	+2.6	10.4	1	1	4.0	44	-1.0	3	-16.6%	77	-6	76	-4	52%	22%	20%	6%
2013	ATL	16/11	926	85	132	1067	64%	+1.0	12.6	2	7	6.0	9	+1.2	8	3.6%	34	171	26	147	48%	38%	8%	6%
2014	*ATL*			*65*	*105*	*799*	*62%*		*12.3*	*3*						*-0.8%*								

In 2013, injuries made Douglas a de facto replacement for Julio Jones. A year later, Douglas will serve as a de facto replacement for the retired Tony Gonzalez. That's a bit of an odd comparison—Douglas is six inches shorter and about 80 pounds lighter than Gonzo—but he'll run a lot of the same mid-length crossing routes that Gonzalez ran last year. Douglas caught fire in a five-game stretch in the middle of last season, averaging seven catches for 107 yards against Tampa Bay (twice), Arizona, Carolina, and Seattle. In the final five games of the year, though, those averages fell to five catches and 46.8 yards per game, with DYAR below replacement level every week. He's not really a starting-caliber receiver, and should fare much better this year as a third option behind Jones and Roddy White.

Kris Durham Height: 6-5 Weight: 216 College: Georgia Draft: 2011/4 (107) Born: 17-Mar-1988 Age: 26 Risk: Green

Year	Team	G/GS	Snaps	Rec	Pass	Yds	C%	+/-	Yd/C	TD	Drop	YAC	Rk	YAC+	BTkl	DVOA	Rk	DYAR	Rk	YAR	Short	Mid	Deep	Bomb
2011	SEA	3/0	32	3	4	30	75%	+0.6	10.0	0	0	1.0	--	-2.0	0	22.3%	--	13	--	10	0%	75%	25%	0%
2012	DET	4/3	218	8	21	125	38%	-2.4	15.6	1	1	3.1	--	-1.3	0	-15.2%	--	6	--	-12	19%	38%	33%	10%
2013	DET	16/13	936	38	85	490	45%	-9.7	12.9	2	7	3.2	79	-1.2	3	-18.5%	80	-39	81	-54	27%	44%	17%	12%
2014	*DET*			*13*	*27*	*181*	*48%*		*13.9*	*3*						*-10.5%*								

Each 2013 Lions player carries a little bit of failure within him, encoded in his mitochondrial DNA perhaps. Durham, knock-around roster filler for two seasons in Seattle and Detroit, bubbled up the depth chart after Nate Burleson's ill-fated pizza run, Ryan Broyles' annual debilitation, and Patrick Edwards' descent into vaporware. With Calvin Johnson banged up and getting octuple-teamed in early October, Durham was suddenly targeted 29 times in one three-game stretch, producing a semi-respectable 16 catches for 154 yards and a touchdown. This created a false sense that Durham was anything more than a role player, and he kept getting a few opportunities per game to catch three short passes. Durham could work his way open against No. 2 cornerbacks in single coverage but did not adjust well to the ball in the air, had unreliable hands, and was generally useless after the catch. The Lions never seemed to notice, and Durham kept getting opportunities even after Burleson returned. Golden Tate's presence moves Durham back down the depth chart where he belongs. As the fifth or sixth option in the passing game, he can do just enough to be helpful. (He's a good run blocker, for example.)

Julian Edelman Height: 6-0 Weight: 198 College: Kent State Draft: 2009/7 (232) Born: 22-May-1986 Age: 28 Risk: Green

Year	Team	G/GS	Snaps	Rec	Pass	Yds	C%	+/-	Yd/C	TD	Drop	YAC	Rk	YAC+	BTkl	DVOA	Rk	DYAR	Rk	YAR	Short	Mid	Deep	Bomb
2011	NE	13/0	117	4	8	34	50%	-0.7	8.5	0	0	2.3	--	-2.8	1	-61.3%	--	-30	--	-28	57%	29%	14%	0%
2012	NE	9/3	295	21	32	235	66%	-0.5	11.2	3	1	6.7	--	+0.5	3	10.3%	--	65	--	62	55%	32%	6%	6%
2013	NE	16/11	1021	105	151	1056	70%	+5.7	10.1	6	6	4.7	42	-0.8	11	4.3%	32	204	22	164	52%	29%	13%	6%
2014	*NE*			*78*	*114*	*866*	*68%*		*11.1*	*5*						*8.0%*								

Edelman was the first receiver in a New England uniform other than Wes Welker to finish a season with 100-plus catches since Troy Brown turned the trick in 2001. He was sturdy and dependable—and, for the first time in his career, you could actually refer to him as sturdy and dependable, because he finally stayed healthy for all 16 games. Now, the key is to build on that performance, and become a consistent and vital part of the passing game year after year. "Minitron" is a unique case in that he's a relative late-bloomer. He was a college quarterback, caught a combined 69 passes his first four years in the league, and then had 105 in 2013. History is littered with receivers who suddenly saw it all come together in their mid-20s, and would go on to relatively successful careers in their late 20s and early 30s, a group that includes Joe Horn, Donald Driver, Brown, and, to a lesser extent, Welker. Of course, there are others such as Albert Connell, Patrick Jeffers, and Marcus Robinson, all of whom had a one-year spike after a slow first few years in the league, then faded back into relative anonymity as one-year wonders. With Rob Gronkowski back and Danny Amendola (hopefully, maybe, who the heck knows) a little more healthy, we wouldn't expect him to be a 100-catch guy again in 2013. But if he can stay injury-free, he has a good chance to be part of the first group as opposed to the second group.

Mike Evans Height: 6-5 Weight: 231 College: Texas A&M Draft: 2014/1 (7) Born: 21-Aug-1993 Age: 21 Risk: Red

Year	Team	G/GS	Snaps	Rec	Pass	Yds	C%	+/-	Yd/C	TD	Drop	YAC	Rk	YAC+	BTkl	DVOA	Rk	DYAR	Rk	YAR	Short	Mid	Deep	Bomb
2014	*TB*			*48*	*88*	*675*	*55%*		*14.1*	*4*						*-3.7%*								

In a way, Evans embodies all trends of NFL wide receivers in 2014: they're getting bigger, and they're getting younger. Ten years ago, a receiver of Evans' size would have stood out. Now, he's just average height on his own team. Once, 21-year-old players would have been destined to spend some time on the bench "learning the game." In the last five years, though, 11 players that age have gone over 500 receiving yards in a season. Keenan Allen was 21 when he gained 1,046 yards last year. The Playmaker Score system dubs Evans "a pretty typical first-round wide receiver prospect." Mind you, most first-round wide receiver prospects turn out pretty good, so this isn't bad news at all. Evans gained 20.2 yards per catch with a 70 percent catch rate as the guy Johnny Football found after scrambling around for 15 seconds. A hamstring injury limited Evans' offseason workouts, but when healthy he spent time training with Brandon Marshall (another big wideout) and acknowledged that he needed to lose about 10 pounds to get back down to his playing weight of 230. Even with some baby fat, he figures to start in Tampa Bay, simply by virtue of not being Chris Owusu or Louis Murphy.

Larry Fitzgerald Height: 6-3 Weight: 225 College: Pittsburgh Draft: 2004/1 (3) Born: 31-Aug-1983 Age: 31 Risk: Green

Year	Team	G/GS	Snaps	Rec	Pass	Yds	C%	+/-	Yd/C	TD	Drop	YAC	Rk	YAC+	BTkl	DVOA	Rk	DYAR	Rk	YAR	Short	Mid	Deep	Bomb
2011	ARI	16/16	1013	80	154	1411	52%	-4.8	17.6	8	3	6.1	8	+1.5	8	9.4%	32	188	26	241	28%	33%	25%	13%
2012	ARI	16/16	1029	71	156	798	46%	-19.6	11.2	4	1	3.8	49	-0.3	8	-23.8%	83	-218	86	-186	38%	38%	18%	5%
2013	ARI	16/16	998	82	136	954	62%	+0.3	11.6	10	1	4.2	61	-0.9	6	-0.6%	49	132	36	152	37%	37%	20%	6%
2014	*ARI*			*84*	*135*	*1011*	*62%*		*12.0*	*8*						*4.8%*								

Fitzgerald's days as one of the league's most dominant receivers are likely over. He struggled through a lack of competent quarterback play in 2012, but his touchdown total rebounded with Carson Palmer throwing passes. However, despite playing all 16 games, he failed to reach 1,000 yards. Going forward, he is likely going to continue to provide value as a possession receiver and red zone machine. Consider that from age 26 to age 30, Fitzgerald had 420 catches, 5,392 yards, and 41 touchdowns. Cris Carter, at the same ages: 455 catches, 5,341 yards, and 44 touchdowns. And a list of the most similar wide receivers to Fitzgerald over a three-year span includes Isaac Bruce (2000-2002), Keenan McCardell (1997-1999), Steve Largent (1981-1983), and Art Monk (1986-1988).

Malcom Floyd Height: 6-5 Weight: 201 College: Wyoming Draft: 2004/FA Born: 8-Sep-1981 Age: 33 Risk: Yellow

Year	Team	G/GS	Snaps	Rec	Pass	Yds	C%	+/-	Yd/C	TD	Drop	YAC	Rk	YAC+	BTkl	DVOA	Rk	DYAR	Rk	YAR	Short	Mid	Deep	Bomb
2011	SD	12/9	513	43	70	856	61%	+7.5	19.9	5	1	4.2	46	-0.2	3	51.9%	2	339	7	345	12%	44%	31%	13%
2012	SD	14/14	845	56	84	814	67%	+10.2	14.5	5	1	1.8	86	-2.2	0	36.0%	3	281	15	303	16%	46%	26%	12%
2013	SD	2/2	88	6	11	149	55%	-0.5	24.8	0	0	2.0	--	-3.8	0	40.9%	--	47	--	45	25%	17%	50%	8%
2014	*SD*			*29*	*53*	*539*	*55%*		*18.6*	*3*						*19.3%*								

In Week 2 against the Eagles, Floyd was on the way to one of the best games of his career when his 2013 season came to a screeching—and scary—halt. He had caught five passes for 102 yards in the first half, but on the first play of the second half, Floyd took a quick post from Philip Rivers and was absolutely poleaxed by safety Nate Allen and linebacker DeMeco Ryans. He suffered a serious neck injury and was placed on injured reserve after several weeks of speculation. Floyd has been cleared by doctors to resume football activities for the 2014 season, and if he can maintain health, he's a good bet to get a lot of targets as a deep threat opposite Keenan Allen, who benefited most from Floyd's absence. Floyd still has good "get-up" speed and runs routes well enough to thrive in San Diego's new, more efficient passing game.

Michael Floyd Height: 6-3 Weight: 220 College: Notre Dame Draft: 2012/1 (13) Born: 27-Nov-1989 Age: 25 Risk: Green

Year	Team	G/GS	Snaps	Rec	Pass	Yds	C%	+/-	Yd/C	TD	Drop	YAC	Rk	YAC+	BTkl	DVOA	Rk	DYAR	Rk	YAR	Short	Mid	Deep	Bomb
2012	ARI	16/3	555	45	86	562	52%	-0.5	12.5	2	4	3.5	62	-0.9	4	-10.3%	71	-3	74	-20	24%	51%	11%	14%
2013	ARI	16/16	930	65	112	1041	58%	+3.5	16.0	5	4	4.3	57	-0.2	5	12.9%	20	220	17	229	18%	49%	20%	13%
2014	*ARI*			*67*	*113*	*985*	*59%*		*14.7*	*5*						*2.7%*								

Floyd had a three-game stretch in the second half of last year where he totaled 396 receiving yards on 18 catches. He has been the talk of OTAs and mini-camp, and big things are expected. He was used in a more vertical role over the second half of last year, averaging 19.6 yards per catch over the final 8 games, compared to 12.7 over the first eight games. Is that sizeable leap sustainable? Fitzgerald had 15 more catches than Floyd over the second half of the year, but the yards per catch difference was massive between the two.

Jacoby Ford Height: 5-9 Weight: 186 College: Clemson Draft: 2010/4 (108) Born: 27-Jul-1987 Age: 27 Risk: Yellow

Year	Team	G/GS	Snaps	Rec	Pass	Yds	C%	+/-	Yd/C	TD	Drop	YAC	Rk	YAC+	BTkl	DVOA	Rk	DYAR	Rk	YAR	Short	Mid	Deep	Bomb
2011	OAK	8/3	205	19	33	279	58%	-1.6	14.7	1	1	6.6	--	+2.1	3	-5.2%	--	-4	--	13	44%	41%	9%	6%
2013	OAK	14/1	278	13	24	99	54%	-2.7	7.6	0	0	5.6	--	-2.2	1	-56.5%	--	-78	--	-74	50%	29%	17%	4%
2014	*NYJ*			*22*	*40*	*280*	*55%*		*12.7*	*1*						*-7.6%*								

Remember back in 2010, when Ford looked like a future star after averaging almost 19 yards per catch and returning three kicks for touchdowns? He has spent the past three seasons as an oft-injured fourth/fifth receiver on a team lacking in quality receiving depth, showing only rare flashes of that sort of explosive play-making potential. He has a fresh start in New York with a similarly uncrowded depth chart, but think fourth receiver and kick returner until he shows a lot more growth in his game.

Pierre Garcon Height: 6-0 Weight: 210 College: Mount Union Draft: 2008/6 (205) Born: 8-Aug-1986 Age: 28 Risk: Yellow

Year	Team	G/GS	Snaps	Rec	Pass	Yds	C%	+/-	Yd/C	TD	Drop	YAC	Rk	YAC+	BTkl	DVOA	Rk	DYAR	Rk	YAR	Short	Mid	Deep	Bomb
2011	IND	16/16	937	70	134	947	52%	-2.1	13.5	6	4	5.1	24	+0.4	6	-16.8%	78	-36	78	-55	32%	41%	14%	13%
2012	WAS	10/10	394	44	68	633	66%	+1.0	14.4	4	4	7.1	5	+1.1	3	8.2%	26	131	35	131	36%	38%	21%	5%
2013	WAS	16/16	978	113	181	1346	62%	+0.2	11.9	5	6	5.8	15	+0.5	7	-5.2%	62	104	45	132	44%	36%	14%	6%
2014	*WAS*			*86*	*132*	*1086*	*65%*		*12.6*	*7*						*10.7%*								

Here's a rare player: someone who has done better after leaving Peyton Manning. Garcon will see his targets cut this season with DeSean Jackson in D.C., but that should help him be more efficient overall. He's gotten better at making contested catches over the years, and he was a threat on wideout screens in the Shanaclan offense. Jay Gruden loves those as well. The mass usage of Cover-3 around the Redskins should calm down a bit with Gruden's system, and Jackson will help lift the cover off defenses. There's nothing but good news for Garcon here, especially if Jordan Reed can stay healthy and occupy attention as well.

Brandon Gibson Height: 6-1 Weight: 210 College: Washington State Draft: 2009/6 (194) Born: 13-Aug-1987 Age: 27 Risk: Blue

Year	Team	G/GS	Snaps	Rec	Pass	Yds	C%	+/-	Yd/C	TD	Drop	YAC	Rk	YAC+	BTkl	DVOA	Rk	DYAR	Rk	YAR	Short	Mid	Deep	Bomb
2011	STL	15/9	591	36	71	431	51%	-3.7	12.0	1	7	2.9	80	-1.5	1	-11.0%	68	0	70	-5	29%	46%	15%	9%
2012	STL	16/13	761	51	82	691	62%	+8.5	13.5	5	4	2.2	84	-1.3	3	23.3%	11	214	21	204	23%	52%	17%	8%
2013	MIA	7/3	252	30	43	326	70%	+1.5	10.9	3	2	3.9	--	-0.4	3	16.3%	--	103	--	99	56%	35%	7%	2%
2014	*MIA*			*18*	*28*	*196*	*64%*		*10.9*	*0*						*-1.7%*								

From St. Louis to Miami, Gibson has spent his career on lifeless offenses, but the 2014 Dolphins should be the best collection of talent around him yet. Through seven games last year before he tore his patellar tendon, Gibson was one of four Miami receivers heavily clustered in a range of 29-35 catches for 326-438 yards. He easily had the best DVOA (16.3%) of the bunch. He'll have to battle for playing time with Rishard Matthews and rookie Jarvis Landry, but he's an adequate slot option.

Ted Ginn Height: 5-11 Weight: 178 College: Ohio State Draft: 2007/1 (9) Born: 12-Apr-1985 Age: 29 Risk: Red

Year	Team	G/GS	Snaps	Rec	Pass	Yds	C%	+/-	Yd/C	TD	Drop	YAC	Rk	YAC+	BTkl	DVOA	Rk	DYAR	Rk	YAR	Short	Mid	Deep	Bomb
2011	SF	14/3	351	19	33	220	58%	+0.4	11.6	0	5	2.3	--	-1.9	4	-10.2%	--	24	--	7	27%	60%	7%	7%
2012	SF	13/0	64	2	2	1	100%	+0.3	0.5	0	0	2.5	--	-6.7	0	-89.0%	--	-12	--	-13	100%	0%	0%	0%
2013	CAR	16/2	502	36	68	556	53%	-0.1	15.4	5	3	5.9	14	+0.8	2	0.3%	47	65	56	68	31%	42%	3%	24%
2014	*ARI*			*37*	*69*	*510*	*54%*		*13.8*	*2*						*-6.5%*								

Ginn will see a lot of action for Arizona, returning punts and kickoffs and playing third wideout behind Larry Fitzgerald and Michael Floyd. We'll see how long that lasts. For all his athletic ability, Ginn has never been productive on a per-target basis. He has been in the league for seven years now, and 2013 was the first time he cracked the top 50 in either DVOA or DYAR. The Cardinals will likely try to use his speed to stretch the defense, but as we discussed in the Carolina chapter, speed alone does not a deep threat make. Meanwhile, he hasn't been terribly effective as a returner, either. His career average on kickoff returns (23.7) is barely any better than the league average (23.4), and keep in mind that the league average includes things like pooch kicks and onside recoveries. He'll get a chance to play in Arizona because there are no obvious better options available, but the ceiling here looks pretty low.

Chris Givens Height: 5-11 Weight: 198 College: Wake Forest Draft: 2012/4 (96) Born: 6-Dec-1989 Age: 25 Risk: Yellow

Year	Team	G/GS	Snaps	Rec	Pass	Yds	C%	+/-	Yd/C	TD	Drop	YAC	Rk	YAC+	BTkl	DVOA	Rk	DYAR	Rk	YAR	Short	Mid	Deep	Bomb
2012	STL	15/12	615	42	80	698	53%	-4.5	16.6	3	4	6.6	7	+1.2	2	0.0%	48	80	44	52	37%	28%	9%	27%
2013	STL	16/13	779	34	83	569	41%	-9.2	16.7	0	3	7.6	3	+2.9	1	-22.8%	82	-68	84	-66	31%	33%	24%	12%
2014	*STL*			*45*	*89*	*690*	*51%*		*15.3*	*3*						*-6.3%*								

The Rams haven't had a 700-yard receiver since Torry Holt in 2008, after the final ashes of the Greatest Show on Turf were swept away. Givens showed a lot of promise as a fourth-round rookie with 698 receiving yards, but a lot of his deep-ball success came as the result of opportunities. On the surface, his two seasons look similar with a lack of big plays explaining the zero in the touchdown column for 2013. In both seasons Givens had 36 percent of his targets come on "deep" throws (at least 16 yards downfield), but last year's success rate was worse despite the throws actually being shorter. In 2012, Givens caught 10-of-28 deep passes (35.7 percent) with an average target depth of 33.8 yards. He had five catches on passes thrown at least 36 yards. In 2013, Givens only caught 7-of-29 deep passes (24.1 percent) with an average target depth of 25.1 yards. His two longest catches were 33 and 21 yards down the field. He also had two big drops and lost a fumble on one of his receptions. He's still the offense's deep threat, but his act could really use some more (reliable) tricks.

Marquise Goodwin Height: 5-9 Weight: 183 College: Texas Draft: 2013/3 (78) Born: 19-Nov-1990 Age: 24 Risk: Yellow

Year	Team	G/GS	Snaps	Rec	Pass	Yds	C%	+/-	Yd/C	TD	Drop	YAC	Rk	YAC+	BTkl	DVOA	Rk	DYAR	Rk	YAR	Short	Mid	Deep	Bomb
2013	BUF	12/1	313	17	32	283	53%	+1.3	16.6	3	0	2.8	--	-1.8	0	5.4%	--	47	--	47	18%	30%	15%	36%
2014	*BUF*			*22*	*42*	*349*	*52%*		*15.9*	*2*						*5.7%*								

The diminutive Goodwin has freakish speed and an ability to stretch the defense—his 16.6 yards per catch were best on the team—but has done little to inspire confidence when it comes to his route-running skills underneath. His 52 yards after the catch was the lowest total among any of the Buffalo pass catchers with at least 15 receptions. His speed and big-play abilities are an obvious asset, both in the passing game and on special teams (he had a pair of electric kick returns in the preseason). But if he wants to be a regular contributor at the NFL level, he needs to add some polish to his game.

Josh Gordon Height: 6-4 Weight: 220 College: Baylor Draft: 2012/2 (SUP) Born: 12-Apr-1991 Age: 23 Risk: Ultraviolet

Year	Team	G/GS	Snaps	Rec	Pass	Yds	C%	+/-	Yd/C	TD	Drop	YAC	Rk	YAC+	BTkl	DVOA	Rk	DYAR	Rk	YAR	Short	Mid	Deep	Bomb
2012	CLE	16/13	815	50	95	805	53%	-2.7	16.1	5	5	5.9	12	+1.5	2	-3.6%	54	64	53	79	34%	34%	15%	17%
2013	CLE	14/14	900	87	159	1646	55%	+1.8	18.9	9	10	7.3	4	+2.8	6	14.4%	17	336	9	321	25%	38%	23%	14%
2014				*42*	*80*	*721*	*53%*		*17.2*	*4*						*2.8%*								

Nearly half of Gordon's production—36 catches for 774 yards and five touchdowns—came in an insane four-game stretch around Thanksgiving, one that bumped up against heavily-rumored attempts by Cleveland to unload him on another team. In the short term, the Browns looked accidentally smart to hold off trading him; after Gordon's off-season implosion, the great month of play looked more like a long con by the mercurial wideout. Either way, the Browns have lost a game-changer on the outside to the sort of personal demons that led the team to consider trading him in the first place.

Gordon's punishment might have effects beyond the development of Johnny Manziel. Multiple reports stated the NFL was considering a revamp of its strict marijuana policy in the wake of Gordon's positive test. It did feel like misplaced justice when Gordon went down hard for something now legal in Colorado and Washington while Ray Rice became the umpteenth player to smack someone around and skate with far less consequence. Gordon's misfortune may prove a tipping point for the league to rethink its draconian approach to weed. Then again, after a July DUI arrest, maybe Gordon has made his own luck. The KUBIAK projection above represents an estimate of what he might do if Roger Goodell for some reason suspends him for only half the season.

T.J. Graham Height: 5-11 Weight: 188 College: North Carolina St. Draft: 2012/3 (69) Born: 27-Jul-1989 Age: 25 Risk: Green

Year	Team	G/GS	Snaps	Rec	Pass	Yds	C%	+/-	Yd/C	TD	Drop	YAC	Rk	YAC+	BTkl	DVOA	Rk	DYAR	Rk	YAR	Short	Mid	Deep	Bomb
2012	BUF	15/11	695	31	58	322	53%	-4.9	10.4	1	6	5.8	15	-0.0	1	-20.6%	80	-57	82	-43	52%	22%	5%	21%
2013	BUF	16/6	823	23	57	361	40%	-7.6	15.7	2	3	3.6	72	-1.0	4	-24.3%	83	-55	82	-58	25%	40%	5%	30%
2014	*BUF*			*25*	*45*	*289*	*56%*		*11.6*	*2*						*-7.2%*								

Entering his third season, the consensus among many in upstate New York is that Graham is on the roster bubble. He has shown neither the route-running skills of Robert Woods nor the game-breaking speed of Marquise Goodwin, and Sammy Watkins has pushed everyone one spot down the depth chart. If we use similarity scores to find the 10 most similar wide receivers over a two-year span and limit those guys to third-year players chosen in rounds one through four, we end up with an average of 19 catches for 272 yards and two touchdowns. But hey, one of those ten players is Jordy Nelson, so nothing is impossible!

A.J. Green Height: 6-4 Weight: 207 College: Georgia Draft: 2011/1 (4) Born: 31-Jul-1988 Age: 26 Risk: Green

Year	Team	G/GS	Snaps	Rec	Pass	Yds	C%	+/-	Yd/C	TD	Drop	YAC	Rk	YAC+	BTkl	DVOA	Rk	DYAR	Rk	YAR	Short	Mid	Deep	Bomb
2011	CIN	15/15	889	65	115	1057	57%	+3.7	16.3	7	2	4.1	50	-0.9	3	17.4%	17	272	12	276	30%	31%	18%	21%
2012	CIN	16/16	958	97	164	1350	59%	+4.9	13.9	11	8	3.9	47	-0.5	9	4.1%	33	205	22	233	34%	32%	15%	18%
2013	CIN	16/16	1055	98	178	1426	55%	-1.6	14.6	11	5	4.1	65	-0.6	7	1.9%	41	207	20	185	27%	44%	14%	15%
2014	*CIN*			*84*	*148*	*1217*	*57%*		*14.5*	*10*						*7.2%*								

While Cincy's two tight end schemes didn't result in explosive numbers for the tight ends, the set loosened defenses up for Green to dominate. He had 32 receptions, 17.4 yards per catch, and six touchdowns when the Bengals had two tight ends on the field. Good as they are, the numbers reflect an top-heavy tilt towards Adriel Jeremiah in the Bengals offense that is detrimental. Only Pierre Garcon and Andre Johnson had more targets than Green, but Washington and Houston are far less bountiful than Cincinnati in the playmaker department, starting with those two tight ends. It's hard to blame a team for wanting to get the ball as often as possible to such a physically gifted player, but Green's efficiency and catch rate figures declined as a result.

Green and his quarterback broke into the league together, and have worked very hard on their on-field chemistry. Yet far too often last year their miscommunication resulted in disaster. The sense that Andy Dalton defaulted to Green far too often, and that defenses were waiting for it, was tangible. Green remains an elite player, of course, but he has also now failed to impact three straight playoff games his team lost, including dropping a crucial would-be touchdown pass last January. An enormous contract extension is headed Green's way, but with the extra dough comes even higher expectations. He and Dalton have proven to be a top combination. Now they need to eliminate the mistakes and make big plays in big games.

Leonard Hankerson Height: 6-2 Weight: 209 College: Miami Draft: 2011/3 (79) Born: 7-May-1988 Age: 26 Risk: Red

Year	Team	G/GS	Snaps	Rec	Pass	Yds	C%	+/-	Yd/C	TD	Drop	YAC	Rk	YAC+	BTkl	DVOA	Rk	DYAR	Rk	YAR	Short	Mid	Deep	Bomb
2011	WAS	4/2	123	13	20	163	65%	+1.8	12.5	0	0	2.2	--	-2.1	0	1.4%	--	18	--	20	30%	40%	25%	5%
2012	WAS	16/5	573	38	57	543	67%	+3.8	14.3	3	4	3.9	45	-0.8	3	11.6%	21	129	37	128	32%	40%	14%	14%
2013	WAS	10/7	390	30	50	375	60%	+1.8	12.5	3	2	4.4	55	-0.0	1	-0.6%	50	46	61	72	40%	40%	20%	0%
2014	*WAS*			*16*	*29*	*174*	*55%*		*10.9*	*0*						*-14.7%*								

Coming off a torn ACL and LCL in 2013, Hankerson isn't expected to be ready for the start of the season. Can you be a post-hype sleeper in your fourth season? Hankerson has put up solid DVOA ratings in small sample sizes, but consistency is an issue he hasn't been able to shake. Heading into a contract season, he'd better find it fast if he has aims on being more than roster fodder.

Brian Hartline Height: 6-2 Weight: 195 College: Ohio State Draft: 2009/4 (108) Born: 22-Nov-1986 Age: 28 Risk: Yellow

Year	Team	G/GS	Snaps	Rec	Pass	Yds	C%	+/-	Yd/C	TD	Drop	YAC	Rk	YAC+	BTkl	DVOA	Rk	DYAR	Rk	YAR	Short	Mid	Deep	Bomb
2011	MIA	16/10	690	35	66	549	53%	+0.5	15.7	1	3	2.7	85	-2.0	0	11.9%	26	127	39	132	21%	44%	18%	18%
2012	MIA	16/15	893	74	131	1083	56%	+4.1	14.6	1	6	3.2	67	-0.7	3	0.6%	43	158	29	146	25%	50%	11%	14%
2013	MIA	16/15	907	76	133	1016	57%	-2.9	13.4	4	7	3.7	71	-0.3	6	-0.7%	51	123	38	135	26%	54%	14%	6%
2014	*MIA*			*69*	*120*	*929*	*58%*		*13.5*	*5*						*-1.8%*								

Hartline looks more like a Lowe's employee eager to get you a good deal on paint than a starting wide receiver in the NFL, but he's not a bad No. 2. He's one of only nine wide receivers to catch at least 70 passes for 1,000 yards in both 2012 and 2013. He doesn't pad his catches with screens, because Miami practically never calls any for him. He catches a lot of short sideline routes and slants. He can make tough catches (see his touchdown against the Steelers or the late grab against the Bengals in a comeback win). Miami almost has a Keyshawn Johnson-Wayne Chrebet Jets dynamic going on with Hartline and Mike Wallace. Hartline's the less-respected, less-paid player, but he works hard, he's just as productive, and he's had a higher DVOA the last two years. However, one area Hartline struggles with is scoring. Only 3.9 percent of his career receptions are touchdowns (fifth lowest in NFL history among wide receivers with at least 250 receptions).

Percy Harvin Height: 5-11 Weight: 192 College: Florida Draft: 2009/1 (22) Born: 28-May-1988 Age: 26 Risk: Red

Year	Team	G/GS	Snaps	Rec	Pass	Yds	C%	+/-	Yd/C	TD	Drop	YAC	Rk	YAC+	BTkl	DVOA	Rk	DYAR	Rk	YAR	Short	Mid	Deep	Bomb
2011	MIN	16/14	605	87	121	967	72%	+5.7	11.1	6	5	6.1	9	+0.3	6	3.6%	43	133	35	132	57%	30%	9%	4%
2012	MIN	9/8	420	62	86	677	73%	+2.2	10.9	3	0	8.5	1	+1.8	19	4.6%	31	194	24	148	67%	19%	12%	1%
2013	SEA	1/0	19	1	1	17	100%	+0.4	17.0	0	0	5.0	--	+1.7	0	102.4%	--	8	--	9	0%	100%	0%	0%
2014	*SEA*			*70*	*104*	*881*	*67%*		*12.6*	*7*						*12.8%*								

Harvin played just 68 snaps in his first Seattle season as a hip injury bedeviled him all year, but he certainly made the most of all those snaps he got in the Super Bowl. He took off for sweep runs of 30 and 15 yards while Denver's defense was busy over-focusing on Marshawn Lynch, and his 87-yard kick return to open the second half iced Seattle's first NFL championship. That's Harvin when he's healthy—a nearly unstoppable force of nature with otherworldly speed and agility. The other Harvin, and the one that's present just as much of the time, is the Harvin who leaves coaches and teammates talking about his amazing physical potential ... if only he could stay on the field. There's a reason the Seahawks took Colorado speedster Paul Richardson in the second round, and that reason is the number of plays Seattle clearly wanted to run with a healthy Harvin all year—deep posts, go routes, and sideline burners on play-action shot passes. If Harvin can stay healthy this time, all the better, but he's an ornament for this offense by virtue of his physical inconsistencies.

Andrew Hawkins Height: 5-7 Weight: 175 College: Toledo Draft: 2008/FA Born: 10-Mar-1986 Age: 28 Risk: Red

Year	Team	G/GS	Snaps	Rec	Pass	Yds	C%	+/-	Yd/C	TD	Drop	YAC	Rk	YAC+	BTkl	DVOA	Rk	DYAR	Rk	YAR	Short	Mid	Deep	Bomb
2011	CIN	13/0	174	23	34	263	68%	+0.9	11.4	0	0	6.3	--	+0.1	3	-2.8%	--	43	--	21	55%	33%	9%	3%
2012	CIN	14/2	518	51	80	533	64%	-2.2	10.5	4	4	6.7	6	+1.4	5	-9.2%	70	13	71	20	59%	26%	13%	1%
2013	CIN	8/0	118	12	18	199	67%	-0.1	16.6	0	2	11.3	--	+4.1	0	8.7%	--	31	--	30	53%	24%	18%	6%
2014	*CLE*			*55*	*83*	*745*	*66%*		*13.5*	*3*						*11.0%*								

The Bengals front office lowballed Baby Hawk's transition tag, allowing the Browns to swoop in and frontload a contract Cincinnati felt uncomfortable matching because it wanted to save the dough for A.J. Green's extension. A foot injury cost Hawkins half of last season, and the plethora of options in Cincy kept his numbers down after that. But Hawkins is among the league's best at evading tacklers in small spaces, and should bring some danger to Cleveland's screen and underneath passing attack.

Junior Hemingway Height: 6-1 Weight: 225 College: Michigan Draft: 2012/7 (238) Born: 27-Dec-1988 Age: 26 Risk: Yellow

Year	Team	G/GS	Snaps	Rec	Pass	Yds	C%	+/-	Yd/C	TD	Drop	YAC	Rk	YAC+	BTkl	DVOA	Rk	DYAR	Rk	YAR	Short	Mid	Deep	Bomb
2012	KC	1/0	0	0	0	0	--	--	--	0	0	--	--	--	0	--	--	--	--	--	--	--	--	--
2013	KC	16/2	312	13	19	125	68%	+1.5	9.6	2	0	1.9	--	-2.5	0	-22.9%	--	-15	--	-8	61%	17%	22%	0%
2014	*KC*			*28*	*45*	*342*	*62%*		*12.2*	*1*						*-3.7%*								

The Sports Xchange wittily called the Chiefs' 2012 draft one of the most literary in NFL history because it started with a Poe (Dontari) and ended with a Hemingway. And while Poe has firmly established himself in the Kansas City canon, Hemingway is still working to get published, in a manner of speaking. The 2012 Sugar Bowl MVP caught 34 passes for an impressive 20.6 yards per catch average in his final collegiate season, but he didn't have a single reception in his rookie season and had to wait until Donnie Avery suffered a concussion in 2013 for things to happen. He caught three passes against Denver to start his December, and ended that month with three receptions versus San Diego's porous defense. He finished his second season with two catches against the Colts in Kansas City's playoff loss, and he'll get a bigger shot in 2014 with the team's receiver corps in flux.

Darrius Heyward-Bey Height: 6-2 Weight: 210 College: Maryland Draft: 2009/1 (7) Born: 26-Feb-1987 Age: 27 Risk: Green

Year	Team	G/GS	Snaps	Rec	Pass	Yds	C%	+/-	Yd/C	TD	Drop	YAC	Rk	YAC+	BTkl	DVOA	Rk	DYAR	Rk	YAR	Short	Mid	Deep	Bomb
2011	OAK	15/14	795	64	115	975	56%	+2.1	15.2	4	7	3.9	55	-0.5	7	2.2%	46	95	50	124	23%	39%	24%	15%
2012	OAK	15/14	804	41	80	606	51%	-3.3	14.8	5	6	5.6	19	+1.5	11	-5.3%	59	31	66	45	22%	43%	20%	14%
2013	IND	16/11	603	29	64	309	45%	-7.4	10.7	1	6	4.5	50	-0.4	0	-24.5%	84	-63	83	-77	34%	43%	14%	9%
2014	*PIT*			*13*	*24*	*157*	*54%*		*12.1*	*1*						*-8.8%*								

Heyward-Bey escaped the Black Hole only to find that its qualities followed him to Indianapolis. Balls thrown in his direction tended to completely disappear, only to wind up on the ground a few seconds later. He was a Pep Hamilton staple early in the season because of his physicality and his ability to block outside. Hamilton, at one point, lamented that he wished Heyward-Bey's hands were "a little more consistent." That's the NFL equivalent of a Honda Odyssey owner wishing he could gun it to 60 in less than three seconds. Now in Pittsburgh, Heyward-Bey could receive a rushing attempt because Todd Haley is there and that means anything is possible.

Stephen Hill Height: 6-4 Weight: 215 College: Georgia Tech Draft: 2012/2 (43) Born: 25-Apr-1991 Age: 23 Risk: Yellow

Year	Team	G/GS	Snaps	Rec	Pass	Yds	C%	+/-	Yd/C	TD	Drop	YAC	Rk	YAC+	BTkl	DVOA	Rk	DYAR	Rk	YAR	Short	Mid	Deep	Bomb
2012	NYJ	11/8	412	21	47	252	45%	-2.8	12.0	3	4	1.5	--	-2.0	1	-15.4%	--	-19	--	-11	22%	50%	13%	15%
2013	NYJ	12/11	594	24	59	342	41%	-5.4	14.3	1	1	3.8	69	-1.1	1	-28.8%	88	-74	86	-81	31%	33%	13%	23%
2014	*NYJ*			*16*	*34*	*206*	*47%*		*12.9*	*2*						*-16.9%*								

Not only has Hill failed to adjust to the pro game, but the success of Alshon Jeffery—selected two picks later in the 2013 draft—has highlighted Hill's lack of development. Big, tall, and fast, Hill has even struggled in the areas where you might expect him to excel. He didn't catch a single one of his six red-zone targets; only Kenny Britt (also 0-for-6) failed to catch a red-zone pass while receiving more than three targets last year. And on 21 deep passes last year, Hill recorded just six receptions, while three of those passes turned into interceptions. The Jets like what they have seen out of David Nelson, added Jacoby Ford, and selected three receivers in the draft. It's now or never for Hill, but the smart money is on never.

T.Y. Hilton Height: 5-10 Weight: 183 College: Florida International Draft: 2012/3 (92) Born: 14-Nov-1989 Age: 25 Risk: Green

Year	Team	G/GS	Snaps	Rec	Pass	Yds	C%	+/-	Yd/C	TD	Drop	YAC	Rk	YAC+	BTkl	DVOA	Rk	DYAR	Rk	YAR	Short	Mid	Deep	Bomb
2012	IND	15/1	673	50	90	861	56%	-4.4	17.2	7	7	7.7	2	+2.0	6	10.7%	23	151	30	169	26%	43%	19%	11%
2013	IND	16/10	759	82	140	1083	60%	+0.1	13.2	5	5	4.8	39	-0.7	7	1.1%	43	155	29	152	36%	34%	17%	13%
2014	*IND*			*77*	*124*	*1058*	*62%*		*13.7*	*7*						*11.1%*								

There are a lot of nits to pick in T.Y. Hilton's skill set. He's not very physical, so he often needs an engineered clean release. He's not very elusive: the Colts had just a 38 percent Success Rate running screens with him. He's not going to win many jump balls. None of those matter because Hilton's double move is filthy. He accelerates so quickly on the turn that he can blow right past anyone who bites on it. Because his opponents have to respect that, he often gets a lot of room afforded to him underneath.

The targets may decrease this year with Hakeem Nicks in town and Reggie Wayne healthy, but Hilton is a credible weapon and can lift the top on any defense in the league.

Andre Holmes Height: 6-5 Weight: 206 College: Hillsdale Draft: 2011/FA Born: 16-Jun-1988 Age: 26 Risk: Red

Year	Team	G/GS	Snaps	Rec	Pass	Yds	C%	+/-	Yd/C	TD	Drop	YAC	Rk	YAC+	BTkl	DVOA	Rk	DYAR	Rk	YAR	Short	Mid	Deep	Bomb
2012	DAL	7/0	16	2	2	11	100%	+0.6	5.5	0	0	1.5	--	-3.6	0	17.9%	--	7	--	5	50%	50%	0%	0%
2013	OAK	10/4	380	25	52	431	48%	-3.6	17.2	1	4	4.4	51	+0.1	0	-2.1%	54	42	64	46	21%	42%	23%	15%
2014	*OAK*			*43*	*77*	*579*	*56%*		*13.5*	*3*						*-6.2%*								

The former Cowboys castoff worked his way through a PED suspension that cost him the first four games of the season and eventually into the starting lineup in Week 12. He became one of the prime beneficiaries from Matt McGloin's willingness to throw the ball, using his height to win jump balls and make contested catches. That and his consistency could be enough for him to keep the third receiver job, and he should win it outright if he can better translate his forty-yard dash speed to the field. Otherwise, he could remain a roster-fringe jump-ball specialist.

Santonio Holmes Height: 5-10 Weight: 185 College: Ohio State Draft: 2006/1 (25) Born: 3-Mar-1984 Age: 30 Risk: #N/A

Year	Team	G/GS	Snaps	Rec	Pass	Yds	C%	+/-	Yd/C	TD	Drop	YAC	Rk	YAC+	BTkl	DVOA	Rk	DYAR	Rk	YAR	Short	Mid	Deep	Bomb
2011	NYJ	16/16	988	51	101	564	50%	-6.7	11.1	8	5	3.7	64	-0.4	2	-8.6%	65	52	58	59	27%	47%	22%	5%
2012	NYJ	4/4	187	20	41	272	49%	-2.5	13.6	1	2	5.2	--	+0.5	0	-2.8%	--	-3	--	20	24%	49%	20%	7%
2013	NYJ	11/11	500	23	59	456	39%	-7.9	19.8	1	4	5.4	24	+0.9	0	-6.7%	66	27	66	8	16%	57%	18%	9%

While Holmes has shown flashes of the player he used to be over the past two seasons—a nine-catch game against Miami in 2012, a 154-yard performance against Buffalo last year—it appears as though the toxic wideout has reached the end of his NFL road. As of late July, Holmes remained unsigned, and it's safe to assume that Holmes' well-publicized issues in the Jets locker room are being held against him by the other 31 teams. Over the final four weeks of 2013, when Holmes was healthy and Geno Smith was playing some of his best football, Holmes was limited to just 10 catches for 130 yards. While he might be able to regain his old form if he's reunited with a franchise quarterback, the bet is no team with one of those is willing to sign Holmes.

DeAndre Hopkins Height: 6-1 Weight: 214 College: Clemson Draft: 2013/1 (27) Born: 6-Jun-1992 Age: 22 Risk: Green

Year	Team	G/GS	Snaps	Rec	Pass	Yds	C%	+/-	Yd/C	TD	Drop	YAC	Rk	YAC+	BTkl	DVOA	Rk	DYAR	Rk	YAR	Short	Mid	Deep	Bomb
2013	HOU	16/16	995	52	91	802	57%	+2.6	15.4	2	1	3.5	75	-1.1	1	6.9%	28	139	34	132	28%	38%	19%	15%
2014	*HOU*			*66*	*115*	*918*	*57%*		*13.9*	*7*						*4.5%*								

Gary Kubiak took one look at DeAndre Hopkins' ability to separate in short spaces and decided "hey, let's make this kid run all the clear out routes on the team." To be fair, Hopkins was benched at a point in the season for running the wrong route. But Hopkins is no Rueben Randle. Look for Bill O'Brien to involve Hopkins more in the offense, and look for the Texans to benefit from it if Ryan Fitzpatrick can throw with any accuracy.

Josh Huff Height: 5-11 Weight: 206 College: Oregon Draft: 2014/3 (86) Born: 10/14/1991 Age: 23 Risk: Red

Year	Team	G/GS	Snaps	Rec	Pass	Yds	C%	+/-	Yd/C	TD	Drop	YAC	Rk	YAC+	BTkl	DVOA	Rk	DYAR	Rk	YAR	Short	Mid	Deep	Bomb
2014	*PHI*			*24*	*46*	*345*	*52%*		*14.4*	*2*						*-5.3%*								

With Chip Kelly departed to Philadelphia, Huff broke the Oregon single-season record with 1,140 receiving yards in 2013, gaining 18.4 yards per catch with a 69 percent catch rate. Kelly grabbed him the third round, but general manager Howie Roseman was a big fan as well. "When we looked at the receiver board, he was just a guy we wanted, we wanted on this team because of his ability with the ball in his hands, his ability to separate, his toughness on special teams and his ability to return kicks," Roseman told ESPN.com. Playmaker Rating actually likes Huff (69.2 percent) a little more than second-round pick Jordan Matthews (61.6 percent).

Justin Hunter Height: 6-4 Weight: 196 College: Tennessee Draft: 2013/2 (34) Born: 20-Apr-1991 Age: 23 Risk: Red

Year	Team	G/GS	Snaps	Rec	Pass	Yds	C%	+/-	Yd/C	TD	Drop	YAC	Rk	YAC+	BTkl	DVOA	Rk	DYAR	Rk	YAR	Short	Mid	Deep	Bomb
2013	TEN	14/0	334	18	42	354	43%	-3.2	19.7	4	1	5.1	--	-0.1	2	-3.6%	--	30	--	45	12%	44%	17%	27%
2014	*TEN*			*48*	*88*	*709*	*55%*		*14.8*	*5*						*1.9%*								

Hunter is getting a lot of attention from fantasy magazines as a physically gifted wideout with a real opportunity for playing time. But this ignores the fact that Hunter played a very one-dimensional season last year. 25 of his 42 targets came on seam, corner, and post routes—the three vertical calls on the tree. He showed a lack of concentration on balls underneath, not attacking them out of the air. His route-running was pathetic to the point of actually skidding to a stop on some curls. Hunter has all the talent in the world, but he's no sure thing to bump his game up until he integrates actual techniques into his skill set.

DeSean Jackson Height: 5-9 Weight: 169 College: California Draft: 2008/2 (49) Born: 1-Dec-1986 Age: 28 Risk: Yellow

Year	Team	G/GS	Snaps	Rec	Pass	Yds	C%	+/-	Yd/C	TD	Drop	YAC	Rk	YAC+	BTkl	DVOA	Rk	DYAR	Rk	YAR	Short	Mid	Deep	Bomb
2011	PHI	15/15	847	58	104	961	56%	+3.9	16.6	4	10	3.9	54	-1.2	1	3.7%	42	159	29	148	25%	35%	18%	22%
2012	PHI	11/11	698	45	88	700	51%	+1.9	15.6	2	1	5.1	25	+0.7	8	-10.6%	72	42	61	14	21%	42%	17%	20%
2013	PHI	16/16	987	82	125	1332	66%	+12.2	16.2	9	4	5.9	12	+0.4	5	23.7%	10	358	6	374	36%	26%	22%	17%
2014	*WAS*			*66*	*127*	*1074*	*52%*		*16.3*	*6*						*3.3%*								

DeSean Jackson and Pierre Garcon both had career seasons in 2013. Both will be 28 this year. This is a most unusual pairing of young receivers. Garcon's already played two years with Robert Griffin III, but Jackson has been a more reliable player for his career. Does Jay Gruden really need to establish a No. 1 receiver, or can this be like the Greatest Show on Turf Rams with Isaac Bruce and Torry Holt both dominating? For fantasy purposes, Garcon seems like a safer bet in a PPR league, but Jackson has more big-play ability and touchdown value. Throw in Jordan Reed at tight end and the Redskins have quite the arsenal, but the limiting factor is just how well Griffin bounces back under a new coach and system. Keeping all of the talent happy on a consistent basis is harder than it sounds. Regression wise, Jackson and Garcon will probably both come down in production from last year, but how they work together is one of the top storylines to follow this season.

Vincent Jackson Height: 6-5 Weight: 241 College: Northern Colorado Draft: 2005/2 (61) Born: 14-Jan-1983 Age: 31 Risk: Yellow

Year	Team	G/GS	Snaps	Rec	Pass	Yds	C%	+/-	Yd/C	TD	Drop	YAC	Rk	YAC+	BTkl	DVOA	Rk	DYAR	Rk	YAR	Short	Mid	Deep	Bomb
2011	SD	16/16	955	60	115	1106	52%	+2.8	18.4	9	5	3.2	74	-1.4	4	16.2%	19	223	17	251	13%	38%	26%	23%
2012	TB	16/16	976	72	147	1384	49%	-2.6	19.2	8	3	5.0	27	+0.8	6	10.5%	24	224	20	288	12%	41%	25%	21%
2013	TB	16/16	968	78	161	1224	49%	-13.2	15.7	7	11	4.2	63	-0.2	5	-3.3%	57	122	39	138	21%	52%	13%	13%
2014	*TB*			*68*	*140*	*1085*	*49%*		*16.0*	*8*						*-2.2%*								

The two right-hand columns in that table tell you everything that was wrong with the Tampa Bay offense in 2013. Why would you take a top-level deep threat like Jackson and stop throwing him deep balls? Mike Williams saw a similar decline, so the answer might lie with Mike Glennon's performance as much as it does with the coaching staff, and that in turn might explain why the new regime was so desperate to bring in a veteran passer. If that's the case, Josh McCown might not have been the best choice. Only 17 percent of McCown's throws last year qualified as either Deep or Bomb passes. Regardless, Jackson isn't consistent enough to be an effective possession receiver. He finished second behind Brandon Marshall in drops, and led the league with 82 incomplete targets. The Bucs need to stop using Jackson to throw a series of jabs, and need to rely on him for occasional haymakers instead.

Alshon Jeffery Height: 6-3 Weight: 216 College: South Carolina Draft: 2012/2 (45) Born: 14-Feb-1990 Age: 24 Risk: Yellow

Year	Team	G/GS	Snaps	Rec	Pass	Yds	C%	+/-	Yd/C	TD	Drop	YAC	Rk	YAC+	BTkl	DVOA	Rk	DYAR	Rk	YAR	Short	Mid	Deep	Bomb
2012	CHI	10/6	431	24	48	367	50%	-1.7	15.3	3	1	2.7	--	-1.3	0	6.7%	--	97	--	77	15%	40%	21%	25%
2013	CHI	16/14	962	89	150	1421	59%	+7.1	16.0	7	6	4.7	44	-0.3	8	8.3%	26	248	14	255	26%	43%	17%	13%
2014	*CHI*			*78*	*138*	*1097*	*57%*		*14.1*	*7*						*4.9%*								

Sixteen carries are an awful lot for a wide receiver. All of Jeffery's runs were variations on the "jet sweep" type of reverse, and Marc Trestman called the play regularly: twice in three different games, three times in the Ravens monsoon bowl, and once in seven others. No other Bears wide receiver took a handoff, and the Bears did not use their No. 3 running back at all, so Jeffery's rushing production had an OCD quality to it. But Trestman was simply using the jet sweep the way other coaches now use the read option: as a tendency breaker and constraint play to keep the defense honest. Jeffery's last two rushes netted minus-10 yards, so Trestman clearly found the upper boundary of just how useful the receiver reverse is as an every-game strategy. Luckily, Jeffery has blossomed into a multi-dimensional No. 2 receiver, so he doesn't need a gimmick role to have a good time.

Greg Jennings Height: 5-11 Weight: 195 College: Western Michigan Draft: 2006/2 (52) Born: 21-Sep-1983 Age: 31 Risk: Yellow

Year	Team	G/GS	Snaps	Rec	Pass	Yds	C%	+/-	Yd/C	TD	Drop	YAC	Rk	YAC+	BTkl	DVOA	Rk	DYAR	Rk	YAR	Short	Mid	Deep	Bomb
2011	GB	13/13	642	67	101	949	66%	+8.4	14.2	9	2	4.1	49	-0.5	2	20.8%	13	302	9	309	28%	45%	19%	9%
2012	GB	8/5	416	36	62	366	58%	-1.7	10.2	4	2	4.6	35	+0.1	4	-5.2%	58	37	63	21	37%	44%	12%	7%
2013	MIN	15/15	742	68	105	804	65%	+4.7	11.8	4	3	5.0	29	+0.1	4	2.6%	38	127	37	112	39%	34%	18%	9%
2014	*MIN*			*57*	*101*	*751*	*56%*		*13.2*	*4*						*-3.6%*								

Jennings endured a midseason stretch, starting with the Josh Freeman Apocalypse against the Giants, where he caught 16-of-29 passes thrown to him for 153 yards and zero touchdowns in six games. He battled knee injuries, Achilles injuries, bad quarterbacks and insane gameplans through all of that stretch. He rebounded with 32 receptions in five December games, though he reverted to screen machine status for the final two games after solid possession-receiver efforts against the Ravens, Eagles, and Browns. So yes, that $45 million contract was a bad idea, and Jennings should have done far less chirping during the 2013 offseason, but a change of quarterbacks and philosophies could still work wonders. Jennings is most likely a No. 2 receiver at this point in his career, but he could be a productive one: Norv Turner has a history of using minor tweaks to get a second life out of veteran receivers.

Jerrel Jernigan Height: 5-9 Weight: 185 College: Troy Draft: 2011/3 (83) Born: 14-Jun-1989 Age: 25 Risk: Green

Year	Team	G/GS	Snaps	Rec	Pass	Yds	C%	+/-	Yd/C	TD	Drop	YAC	Rk	YAC+	BTkl	DVOA	Rk	DYAR	Rk	YAR	Short	Mid	Deep	Bomb
2011	NYG	8/0	14	0	2	0	0%	-1.2	0.0	0	0	0.0	--	0.0	0	-87.8%	--	-15	--	-14	50%	50%	0%	0%
2012	NYG	9/0	27	3	5	22	60%	-0.3	7.3	0	0	2.3	--	-1.6	0	-22.2%	--	-6	--	-5	60%	20%	20%	0%
2013	NYG	15/3	216	29	44	329	66%	+3.5	11.3	2	1	4.3	--	-0.7	6	0.0%	--	40	--	44	32%	49%	15%	5%
2014	*NYG*			*17*	*30*	*181*	*57%*		*10.6*	*0*						*-13.1%*								

For nearly three years, Jernigan was nothing but a tease. Then, during the final three weeks of the season, Jernigan had a mini-breakout, catching 19 passes for 237 yards and two touchdowns. Jernigan led the team with 27 targets in those games, a massive and impressive total considering he was still competing with Hakeem Nicks and Rueben Randle for attention (Victor Cruz missed the final two games of the year). That production prompted John Mara to call out the Giants coaching staff after the season, stating "I'm not sure why it took us three years to find out that Jerrel Jernigan can play." But perhaps the coaches were right for two-and-a-half years, and it took Jerrel Jernigan three years to find out that Jerrel Jernigan can play.

Andre Johnson Height: 6-3 Weight: 219 College: Miami Draft: 2003/1 (3) Born: 11-Jul-1981 Age: 33 Risk: Yellow

Year	Team	G/GS	Snaps	Rec	Pass	Yds	C%	+/-	Yd/C	TD	Drop	YAC	Rk	YAC+	BTkl	DVOA	Rk	DYAR	Rk	YAR	Short	Mid	Deep	Bomb
2011	HOU	7/7	335	33	51	492	65%	+3.9	14.9	2	3	4.2	47	-0.8	1	17.5%	16	142	33	127	31%	39%	16%	14%
2012	HOU	16/16	977	112	163	1598	69%	+13.3	14.3	4	7	4.9	29	+0.6	5	19.5%	16	461	2	464	31%	44%	13%	11%
2013	HOU	16/16	994	109	181	1407	60%	+2.6	12.9	5	5	3.7	70	-0.7	8	-2.3%	55	150	31	178	31%	45%	17%	8%
2014	*HOU*			*105*	*169*	*1283*	*62%*		*12.2*	*7*						*3.2%*								

Last season, Johnson was sentenced to run a bunch of curl routes and receive passes short of the sticks because Gary Kubiak either couldn't trust his quarterbacks or doesn't understand how football works. That artificially lowered his DVOA, despite the fact that he had one of the best receiving games of the season against the Colts in Week 9. Johnson is still one of the best receivers in the NFL, excelling against zone coverages where he always seems to know exactly where to settle down. He skipped OTAs, claiming that he didn't know "if this was the place for him." Well, a star wideout can only endure so much Schaubbing before he starts to ask questions. As long as he's on the field, Johnson is still one of the best wideouts in the game. Whether it's in Houston or elsewhere.

Calvin Johnson Height: 6-5 Weight: 239 College: Georgia Tech Draft: 2007/1 (2) Born: 25-Sep-1985 Age: 29 Risk: Yellow

Year	Team	G/GS	Snaps	Rec	Pass	Yds	C%	+/-	Yd/C	TD	Drop	YAC	Rk	YAC+	BTkl	DVOA	Rk	DYAR	Rk	YAR	Short	Mid	Deep	Bomb
2011	DET	16/16	1029	96	158	1681	61%	+9.5	17.5	16	3	5.1	21	+0.6	12	31.6%	7	535	1	572	25%	38%	18%	18%
2012	DET	16/16	1152	122	203	1964	60%	+9.5	16.1	5	8	4.1	40	+0.1	6	16.0%	19	488	1	459	26%	36%	27%	11%
2013	DET	14/14	877	84	156	1492	54%	+0.3	17.8	12	10	5.5	22	+1.2	6	14.9%	16	347	7	343	15%	46%	30%	9%
2014	*DET*			*97*	*171*	*1561*	*57%*		*16.1*	*11*						*11.9%*								

Knee and ankle injuries limited Megatron's play throughout last December, contributing a medium-sized pebble to the Lions' avalanche of awful. Megatron was also dealing with a chronic finger injury that dated back to 2012. That helps explain why he dropped two passes in the second Bears game, two more in the Ravens game, and a fourth-and-3 slant (thrown at roughly Mach-3 by Stafford, admittedly) against the Steelers. The Lions shut Megatron down in Week 17; give him back the two games he missed and something closer to his regular production in December, and Megatron may have come close to a 2,000-yard season.

Johnson had both knee and finger procedures in the offseason, and the arrivals of Jim Caldwell and Golden Tate should make for a more consistent Megatron: fewer 17-target games, but more consistent lines in his 7-115-1 sweet spot.

Darius Johnson Height: 5-10 Weight: 175 College: SMU Draft: 2013/FA Born: 22-Feb-1991 Age: 23 Risk: Yellow

Year	Team	G/GS	Snaps	Rec	Pass	Yds	C%	+/-	Yd/C	TD	Drop	YAC	Rk	YAC+	BTkl	DVOA	Rk	DYAR	Rk	YAR	Short	Mid	Deep	Bomb
2013	ATL	10/2	401	22	43	210	51%	-4.5	9.5	1	4	3.8	--	-1.4	1	-24.6%	--	-40	--	-50	37%	47%	7%	9%
2014	*ATL*			*20*	*34*	*250*	*59%*		*12.5*	*1*						*-3.4%*								

Since Drew Davis is sidelined for most of the preseason with a foot injury, Johnson figures to open the season as Atlanta's fourth wideout. Johnson only saw significant action in three games last year, collecting 27 total targets against the Cardinals, Bucs, and Saints. Those 27 balls produced just 12 catches for 125 yards. Johnson is too small to contribute on kicking plays (only 16 special-teams snaps last year) and on most teams, he would be a longshot to make the roster. In Atlanta, he could be one injury away from starting.

Steve Johnson Height: 6-2 Weight: 202 College: Kentucky Draft: 2008/7 (224) Born: 22-Jul-1986 Age: 28 Risk: Red

Year	Team	G/GS	Snaps	Rec	Pass	Yds	C%	+/-	Yd/C	TD	Drop	YAC	Rk	YAC+	BTkl	DVOA	Rk	DYAR	Rk	YAR	Short	Mid	Deep	Bomb
2011	BUF	16/16	918	76	134	1004	57%	-4.8	13.2	7	4	4.2	45	-0.1	5	-0.5%	52	117	44	134	34%	43%	19%	4%
2012	BUF	16/16	936	79	148	1046	53%	-6.7	13.2	6	5	4.6	33	+0.7	6	-4.7%	57	67	49	73	27%	53%	14%	6%
2013	BUF	12/12	701	52	102	597	52%	-9.1	11.5	3	8	4.2	60	-0.3	7	-15.6%	77	-25	78	-29	46%	39%	12%	4%
2014	*SF*			*27*	*56*	*395*	*48%*		*14.6*	*3*						*-9.7%*								

The decision to land Sammy Watkins in the draft and Mike Williams in a trade this past spring spelled the end of Johnson's time in Buffalo, and so it was not a surprise when he was dealt to the Niners for a conditional fourth-round pick in the 2015 draft that could become a third-round selection depending on Johnson's production. The receiver out of Kentucky perhaps distinguished himself as one of the best seventh-round picks in the history of the franchise, and certainly the most interesting. There were Twitter wars with God after dropping what would have been a game-winning touchdown, occasional beefs with guys like Aqib Talib and Plaxico Burress, messages scrawled on T-shirts underneath his uniform, and a burgeoning appreciation for some unique birthday cakes. (Google "Stevie Johnson" and "birthday cakes." If you're on a work computer, at that point, it's probably a good idea to clear your search history.) Along the way, he also had three consecutive seasons of 75-plus catches and 1,000-plus receiving yards with Ryan Fitzpatrick (and occasionally Trent Edwards) throwing him the ball. He became only the third receiver since the merger to put up three straight seasons between 1,000 and 1,100 receiving yards, joining Donald Driver and Derrick Mason.

If he's right, the mind reels at what sort of spice he'll be able to bring to the blood feud between San Francisco and Seattle. And he should excel at taking the top off the defense to give room underneath to Michael Crabtree and Anquan Boldin. But given that Jim Harbaugh has never really used three receivers in the San Francisco offense, we honestly have no clue what kind of statistical production Johnson is going to have.

Jacoby Jones Height: 6-3 Weight: 192 College: Lane Draft: 2007/3 (73) Born: 11-Jul-1984 Age: 30 Risk: Yellow

Year	Team	G/GS	Snaps	Rec	Pass	Yds	C%	+/-	Yd/C	TD	Drop	YAC	Rk	YAC+	BTkl	DVOA	Rk	DYAR	Rk	YAR	Short	Mid	Deep	Bomb
2011	HOU	16/10	793	31	64	512	50%	-0.5	16.5	2	1	4.4	40	-0.3	1	-4.2%	56	56	57	50	27%	27%	29%	17%
2012	BAL	16/3	426	30	55	406	55%	+1.2	13.5	1	1	2.8	75	-2.2	1	0.4%	44	37	64	51	32%	34%	14%	20%
2013	BAL	12/9	549	37	67	455	55%	+0.5	12.3	2	0	2.8	82	-1.4	0	-7.0%	67	30	65	15	30%	31%	20%	19%
2014	*BAL*			*37*	*65*	*487*	*57%*		*13.2*	*3*						*-1.4%*								

Fame's a little harder to obtain when safeties decide to cover the receiver and there's no postseason to become a hero. On the surface, Jones declined a bit on special teams and basically matched his 2012 receiving production in four fewer games. But the variation in his catch rate by down was fascinating: 54 percent on first down, 74 percent on second down and 35 percent on third/fourth down. The order of high to low was the same in 2012, but Jones' catch rate ranged more tightly from 44 percent to 60 percent. It's not like Jones has ever been considered a consistent receiver, but last year was especially erratic.

James Jones Height: 6-1 Weight: 208 College: San Jose State Draft: 2007/3 (78) Born: 31-Mar-1984 Age: 30 Risk: Red

Year	Team	G/GS	Snaps	Rec	Pass	Yds	C%	+/-	Yd/C	TD	Drop	YAC	Rk	YAC+	BTkl	DVOA	Rk	DYAR	Rk	YAR	Short	Mid	Deep	Bomb
2011	GB	16/0	487	38	55	635	69%	+4.4	16.7	7	4	7.1	3	+2.2	5	41.7%	3	220	18	221	39%	32%	16%	13%
2012	GB	16/16	1000	64	98	784	65%	+8.2	12.3	14	3	3.6	56	-0.4	2	22.6%	12	318	12	295	33%	45%	12%	11%
2013	GB	14/14	846	59	93	817	63%	+3.3	13.8	3	3	6.2	6	+1.1	8	2.1%	40	110	42	114	38%	37%	12%	13%
2014	*OAK*			*60*	*98*	*724*	*61%*		*12.1*	*4*						*-2.7%*								

Another alumnus of the A.J. Hawk Packers academy of slowly improving over the years, Jones took a small step backward in 2013 that was largely a result of quarterback turmoil. He is much more versatile than a few years ago, when he was one of the NFL's all-time champions at coming down with one foot inbounds after a catch. He remains almost exclusively a boundary receiver, but his inventory of slants and comeback-type routes has expanded. Jones was 4-of-9 on deep passes from Aaron Rodgers and a respectable 4-of-10 from Huey, Dewey, and Louie, a sign that he can help elevate a bad quarterback. That skill is about to come in really handy. Thirty-year old boundary receivers don't make great investments, but the Raiders may be banking on Jones' slow development cycle turning him into an All-Pro at age 40.

Julio Jones Height: 6-3 Weight: 220 College: Alabama Draft: 2011/1 (6) Born: 3-Feb-1989 Age: 25 Risk: Red

Year	Team	G/GS	Snaps	Rec	Pass	Yds	C%	+/-	Yd/C	TD	Drop	YAC	Rk	YAC+	BTkl	DVOA	Rk	DYAR	Rk	YAR	Short	Mid	Deep	Bomb
2011	ATL	13/13	705	54	95	959	57%	+1.2	17.8	8	4	7.5	1	+2.5	8	10.4%	30	110	48	158	33%	32%	20%	15%
2012	ATL	16/15	835	79	129	1198	61%	+5.2	15.2	10	8	5.9	13	+1.1	10	16.0%	20	340	9	320	38%	32%	17%	14%
2013	ATL	5/5	296	41	60	580	68%	+5.3	14.1	2	2	6.0	10	+0.3	4	0.4%	45	60	57	71	50%	21%	20%	9%
2014	*ATL*			*105*	*156*	*1363*	*67%*		*13.0*	*8*						*12.5%*								

Jones was on his way to a monster fantasy season before he injured his foot last year, ranking first or second in targets, receptions, and yards through the first five weeks of the year. With Jones, the Falcons' average offensive DVOA was 15.4%; without him, it fell to -1.5%. He was held out of OTAs, but was expected to be a full participant in training camp. The only man in the league with an 80-yard catch in each of the last three seasons, Jones is also a quality red-zone option; half of his career touchdowns have come inside the 20. In short, he's an automatic WR1, and a dark horse to finish atop the wide receiver rankings this year.

Marvin Jones Height: 6-2 Weight: 199 College: California Draft: 2012/5 (166) Born: 12-Mar-1990 Age: 24 Risk: Yellow

Year	Team	G/GS	Snaps	Rec	Pass	Yds	C%	+/-	Yd/C	TD	Drop	YAC	Rk	YAC+	BTkl	DVOA	Rk	DYAR	Rk	YAR	Short	Mid	Deep	Bomb
2012	CIN	11/5	354	18	32	201	56%	+0.3	11.2	1	1	1.9	--	-1.9	3	-2.1%	--	36	--	34	29%	42%	19%	10%
2013	CIN	16/3	542	51	80	712	64%	+4.2	14.0	10	3	4.4	53	-0.3	11	32.4%	3	279	11	269	24%	54%	14%	8%
2014	*CIN*			*60*	*101*	*768*	*59%*		*12.8*	*5*						*1.1%*								

Jones seized the No. 2 receiver role with both hands, and secured it tightly to his chest while getting both feet inbounds. It was Jones, not A.J. Green, who broke the franchise record for touchdown catches in a game, snagging four against the Jets in an October embarrassment of Gang Green. Jones' catch radius is huge, and he is tough and elusive as those broken tackles show. Expect his targets to climb as the Bengals stop force-feeding Green; while he might not get to ten touchdowns again, Jones is a worthy snag for your fantasy team.

Jermaine Kearse Height: 6-1 Weight: 209 College: Washington Draft: 2012/FA Born: 6-Feb-1990 Age: 24 Risk: Yellow

Year	Team	G/GS	Snaps	Rec	Pass	Yds	C%	+/-	Yd/C	TD	Drop	YAC	Rk	YAC+	BTkl	DVOA	Rk	DYAR	Rk	YAR	Short	Mid	Deep	Bomb
2012	SEA	7/1	80	3	7	31	43%	-0.4	10.3	0	2	0.3	--	-3.4	0	-22.9%	--	-1	--	-6	0%	50%	33%	17%
2013	SEA	15/5	469	22	38	346	58%	+1.5	15.7	4	3	1.7	--	-3.0	0	26.2%	--	116	--	108	16%	42%	24%	18%
2014	*SEA*			*17*	*32*	*280*	*53%*		*16.4*	*2*						*-1.6%*								

In May, the Seahawks became the first NFL team to send out a brochure to the agents of potential undrafted free agents, in which Pete Carroll was quoted as follows: "We wholeheartedly believe in competition in all aspects of our program, and the only way to compete is to show it on the field. We're dedicated to giving all of our players a look to find out who they are and what they're all about so we can field the best team possible."

A lot of coaches say this, but Carroll clearly believes it, and Kearse was one of eight such players contributing to the team in 2013, and one of two (Doug Baldwin was the other) who caught touchdown passes in the Super Bowl. Kearse finished near the top in DYAR and DVOA among receivers who were targeted 10 to 49 times. He was a feast-or-famine player last season, but with Golden Tate out the door, Kearse may get more looks as a slot receiver and in red-zone situations. No Seahawks receiver had more red zone opportunities in 2013 (Kearse tied with tight end Zach Miller), and the team likes his toughness in traffic. If either Percy Harvin gets injured again or Sidney Rice has to call it a career before the preseason ends, you'll want to double that KUBIAK projection.

Jeremy Kerley Height: 5-9 Weight: 188 College: TCU Draft: 2011/5 (153) Born: 3-May-1989 Age: 25 Risk: Green

Year	Team	G/GS	Snaps	Rec	Pass	Yds	C%	+/-	Yd/C	TD	Drop	YAC	Rk	YAC+	BTkl	DVOA	Rk	DYAR	Rk	YAR	Short	Mid	Deep	Bomb
2011	NYJ	14/1	308	29	47	314	62%	+2.6	10.8	1	2	3.4	--	-0.8	5	-10.9%	--	19	--	30	41%	39%	14%	7%
2012	NYJ	16/7	664	56	97	827	59%	+0.7	14.8	2	3	5.3	22	+0.4	4	-8.1%	69	14	70	42	42%	36%	14%	8%
2013	NYJ	12/8	567	43	72	523	60%	+1.3	12.2	3	0	4.1	64	-1.0	1	6.0%	29	97	46	95	37%	38%	20%	5%
2014	*NYJ*			*44*	*81*	*562*	*54%*		*12.8*	*2*						*-7.3%*								

Kerley had a very good year in 2012 but was mediocre on third downs; last year, his numbers took a hit, but he was very effective on third downs. He caught 21 of his 33 targets on third down in 2013, with 17 of those turning into first downs (the other four catches all came on third-and-17 or greater). He had the best DVOA of any Jets receiver in that situation, and was one of the main reasons Geno Smith was effective on third downs as a rookie. Kerley was banged up all season, making the injury report for not just for a nasty concussion suffered in Week 1, but with injuries to his finger, back, hamrstring, and elbow. The Jets drafted Jalen Saunders as insurance in the event of another injury-plagued year for Kerley, and Saunders could be the eventual replacement (Kerley is a free agent after this year). That makes 2014 a crucial season for a player who was considered one of the game's top slot receivers just one year ago.

Brandon LaFell Height: 6-3 Weight: 211 College: LSU Draft: 2010/3 (78) Born: 4-Nov-1986 Age: 28 Risk: Green

Year	Team	G/GS	Snaps	Rec	Pass	Yds	C%	+/-	Yd/C	TD	Drop	YAC	Rk	YAC+	BTkl	DVOA	Rk	DYAR	Rk	YAR	Short	Mid	Deep	Bomb
2011	CAR	16/6	689	36	56	613	64%	+4.4	17.0	3	1	6.5	5	+1.8	2	22.8%	11	156	30	147	26%	37%	28%	9%
2012	CAR	14/12	756	44	76	677	58%	-1.5	15.4	4	2	7.1	4	+2.2	4	2.8%	37	106	40	105	42%	32%	17%	8%
2013	CAR	16/16	907	49	85	627	58%	-2.2	12.8	5	6	5.2	25	+0.5	2	-6.2%	64	44	63	50	26%	44%	23%	7%
2014	*NE*			*14*	*26*	*181*	*54%*		*12.9*	*0*						*-7.6%*								

Bill Belichick has always loved versatile players, and he could find several different ways to use LaFell. The Panthers lined him up in the backfield for 18 plays last year, more than any wide receiver in the league; we also counted them using him at tight end 27 times. Panthers coach Ron Rivera dubbed LaFell the best blocking wideout in the league last October, and given the Patriots' depth chart at the two positions, he might see even more time playing off the tackle's hip this fall. LaFell is not a particularly good wide receiver, but he has a lot of value as a football player, and Belichick tends to get the most out of those kinds of guys.

For those curious, the rest of the wide receivers who were in the backfield at least 10 times are guys who are there to get the ball in space, not to block like LaFell. DeSean Jackson was second at 16, Dexter McCluster was third at 14, and then four receivers were tied at 10: Randall Cobb, Josh Morgan, Cordarrelle Patterson, and Ace Sanders.

Jarvis Landry Height: 5-11 Weight: 205 College: LSU Draft: 2014/2 (63) Born: 11/28/1992 Age: 22 Risk: Red

Year	Team	G/GS	Snaps	Rec	Pass	Yds	C%	+/-	Yd/C	TD	Drop	YAC	Rk	YAC+	BTkl	DVOA	Rk	DYAR	Rk	YAR	Short	Mid	Deep	Bomb
2014	*MIA*			*36*	*60*	*417*	*60%*		*11.6*	*3*						*-3.9%*								

The Dolphins had a salty relationship with wide receivers during Jeff Ireland's reign as general manager. In his departure they are still wildly throwing resources at the position, taking Landry out of LSU in the second round. Landry can play in the slot and outside for Miami. He's more of an intermediate route runner (lots of in-cuts and post routes) than a deep threat, but he can match a lot of what Miami gets from Brian Hartline and Brandon Gibson. Ryan Tannehill quickly fell in love with Landry's hands. "Some of the strongest hands I've seen ever since I've been playing football. He's a guy that's going to catch the ball if it's in his area. I've seen him already make some tough one-handed catches in practice," said Tannehill. Landry had only two drops in 2013. Reports from OTAs said Landry has progressed quickly and may pass Gibson on the depth chart by Week 1.

Cody Latimer Height: 6-6 Weight: 215 College: Indiana Draft: 2014/2 (56) Born: 10-Oct-1992 Age: 22 Risk: Red

Year	Team	G/GS	Snaps	Rec	Pass	Yds	C%	+/-	Yd/C	TD	Drop	YAC	Rk	YAC+	BTkl	DVOA	Rk	DYAR	Rk	YAR	Short	Mid	Deep	Bomb
2014	*DEN*			*28*	*47*	*422*	*60%*		*15.1*	*3*						*10.1%*								

An outstanding college receiver who averaged over 15 yards a catch while catching 66 percent of his targets as a senior, Latimer has excellent size and good speed, and the Broncos have told the media that they graded him as the best blocking receiver in the draft. John Elway's description of him as a "complete wide receiver" has an element of draft hyperbole, but he does slot nicely into the Eric Decker starting outside receiver role. That will most likely be in 2015, but he should have a more extensive role than last year's fourth receiver Andre Caldwell if he completes Peyton Manning Wide Receiver Boot Camp with the same zest he expressed before starting it.

Marqise Lee Height: 6-0 Weight: 192 College: USC Draft: 2014/2 (39) Born: 11/25/1991 Age: 23 Risk: Yellow

Year	Team	G/GS	Snaps	Rec	Pass	Yds	C%	+/-	Yd/C	TD	Drop	YAC	Rk	YAC+	BTkl	DVOA	Rk	DYAR	Rk	YAR	Short	Mid	Deep	Bomb
2014	*JAC*			*55*	*96*	*671*	*57%*		*12.2*	*4*						*-6.1%*								

Football moves pretty fast. If you have an off season, you might miss it. Lee would likely have been a top-five pick if he'd come out following a 2013 season where he desecrated the Pac-12 to the tune of 1,721 yards and 17 touchdowns. But he struggled with a left knee injury and the Matt Barkley Replacement Crew in 2013, thus enabling him to fall into the Jaguars' lap at No. 39. Lee should be an instant contributor in Jacksonville, and he's a good fit for their quick-strike offense. His catch rate and yards per catch actually increased in 2013 despite the injury. DVOA may not like him because of the poor supporting cast, but Lee will be the best young building block this offense has had in quite a while.

Greg Little Height: 6-2 Weight: 220 College: North Carolina Draft: 2011/2 (59) Born: 30-May-1989 Age: 25 Risk: Blue

Year	Team	G/GS	Snaps	Rec	Pass	Yds	C%	+/-	Yd/C	TD	Drop	YAC	Rk	YAC+	BTkl	DVOA	Rk	DYAR	Rk	YAR	Short	Mid	Deep	Bomb
2011	CLE	16/12	962	61	121	709	51%	-10.5	11.6	2	13	3.9	53	-0.5	13	-21.7%	84	-70	87	-104	47%	31%	14%	8%
2012	CLE	16/16	905	53	93	647	58%	-0.8	12.2	4	7	3.4	64	-0.9	5	-7.7%	68	45	59	35	38%	40%	16%	6%
2013	CLE	16/13	940	41	99	465	41%	-12.7	11.3	2	4	4.6	45	+0.1	5	-34.7%	90	-171	90	-197	34%	33%	23%	10%
2014	*OAK*			*8*	*14*	*74*	*57%*		*9.2*	*0*						*-24.0%*								

Even allowing for Cleveland's quarterback issues, Little got drastically worse in 2013. The Browns are desperate for receivers, but released Little in May anyway, which says it all. Little washed ashore in Oakland, so, you know. His former and new teams play this season, a fact Little Tweeted about upon signing: "October 26, 2014 is definitely circled beleedat." Little probably dropped the Sharpie he used to highlight the date on his calendar. Beleedat.

Brandon Lloyd Height: 6-0 Weight: 192 College: Illinois Draft: 2003/4 (124) Born: 5-Jul-1981 Age: 33 Risk: Green

Year	Team	G/GS	Snaps	Rec	Pass	Yds	C%	+/-	Yd/C	TD	Drop	YAC	Rk	YAC+	BTkl	DVOA	Rk	DYAR	Rk	YAR	Short	Mid	Deep	Bomb
2011	2TM	15/14	774	70	147	966	48%	-10.0	13.8	5	6	1.8	91	-2.6	0	-11.5%	69	-31	77	-15	14%	49%	24%	13%
2012	NE	16/15	1038	74	130	911	57%	+0.0	12.3	4	8	2.3	82	-1.6	2	1.8%	40	130	36	123	14%	55%	21%	10%
2014	*SF*			*7*	*14*	*90*	*50%*		*12.8*	*0*						*-14.2%*								

Brandon Lloyd is attempting a comeback after a year out of the NFL, after being released by New England. He will try to do so against long odds in San Francisco, the franchise that originally drafted him. How long ago was that? In his rookie year, Jeff Garcia was still throwing passes to Terrell Owens. He left after Alex Smith's rookie season in a trade to Washington. Jim Harbaugh was coaching the San Diego Toreros at the time.

Lloyd has often been equal parts talented and a head case, wearing out his welcome at five other stops in the NFL, and never lasting longer than the three years he spent in San Francisco. He might make the final roster but will probably not be a big factor. The Harbaugh 49ers have never used three receivers, so what on earth would they do with a fourth?

Jeremy Maclin Height: 6-0 Weight: 198 College: Missouri Draft: 2009/1 (19) Born: 11-May-1988 Age: 26 Risk: Green

Year	Team	G/GS	Snaps	Rec	Pass	Yds	C%	+/-	Yd/C	TD	Drop	YAC	Rk	YAC+	BTkl	DVOA	Rk	DYAR	Rk	YAR	Short	Mid	Deep	Bomb
2011	PHI	13/13	733	63	97	859	65%	+6.6	13.6	5	5	4.1	48	-0.5	1	12.6%	22	194	24	178	30%	40%	23%	8%
2012	PHI	15/15	974	69	121	857	56%	-5.2	12.4	7	5	3.8	51	-0.9	1	-6.5%	62	132	34	73	43%	33%	14%	10%
2014	*PHI*			*63*	*107*	*838*	*59%*		*13.3*	*6*						*3.8%*								

Even if Maclin sets some career highs this season, we should curtail the "Chip makes everyone better!" narrative, unless it's a really fantastic season. Maclin could break 1,000 yards for the first time in his career simpley because this is really the first time he's had to be the No. 1 receiver. Maclin, a first-round pick in 2009, kind of gets the Sam Bradford treatment: we don't talk about how good he is, if he's overrated, if he's overpaid, or if he's getting better or worse. We just don't talk much about Jeremy Maclin even after he does something like tearing his ACL last summer. Now he has his chance to shine and is playing on a one-year "prove it" deal worth $6 million. One great season and he'll likely get paid the big bucks, whether it's in Philadelphia or somewhere else. Perhaps working in his favor is the fact that Maclin's production perked up with Foles at quarterback in 2012. Foles is a better passer now and the system's better, so if there was ever a year to feel enthused over drafting Maclin to your fantasy team, this is the one.

Mario Manningham Height: 5-11 Weight: 181 College: Michigan Draft: 2008/3 (95) Born: 25-May-1986 Age: 28 Risk: Red

Year	Team	G/GS	Snaps	Rec	Pass	Yds	C%	+/-	Yd/C	TD	Drop	YAC	Rk	YAC+	BTkl	DVOA	Rk	DYAR	Rk	YAR	Short	Mid	Deep	Bomb
2011	NYG	12/10	587	39	77	523	51%	-0.4	13.4	4	3	2.7	83	-1.7	0	-5.1%	58	28	64	52	23%	36%	24%	17%
2012	SF	12/10	362	42	57	449	74%	+6.0	10.7	1	0	4.1	41	-0.5	9	-2.3%	52	36	65	50	41%	43%	7%	9%
2013	SF	6/3	148	9	23	85	39%	-3.6	9.4	0	1	1.9	--	-2.3	0	-38.8%	--	-45	--	-49	19%	62%	14%	5%
2014	*NYG*			*17*	*31*	*215*	*55%*		*12.7*	*1*						*-6.2%*								

Hey, look who's back in Jersey! Manningham will forever be a Giants legend for making a huge catch to help win Super Bowl XLVI, but he comes back with a left knee that's a total mess. He tore multiple ligaments in 2012 and was never quite able to come back right last year. It wouldn't be a surprise if he got healthy and caught a few balls for the Giants behind Victor Cruz and the LSU twins, but it also wouldn't be a surprise if he started the season on PUP and then quietly disappeared without ever seeing the field.

Brandon Marshall Height: 6-4 Weight: 229 College: UCF Draft: 2006/4 (119) Born: 23-Mar-1984 Age: 30 Risk: Yellow

Year	Team	G/GS	Snaps	Rec	Pass	Yds	C%	+/-	Yd/C	TD	Drop	YAC	Rk	YAC+	BTkl	DVOA	Rk	DYAR	Rk	YAR	Short	Mid	Deep	Bomb
2011	MIA	16/16	889	81	143	1214	57%	+1.4	15.0	6	10	3.8	61	-1.1	5	7.0%	36	191	25	218	33%	36%	15%	16%
2012	CHI	16/16	968	118	195	1508	61%	+8.8	12.8	11	9	2.9	72	-1.3	13	0.0%	46	267	16	205	27%	40%	22%	11%
2013	CHI	16/16	987	100	163	1295	61%	+4.7	13.0	12	12	2.8	83	-2.0	9	9.5%	22	284	10	291	26%	47%	14%	13%
2014	*CHI*			*94*	*151*	*1237*	*62%*		*13.2*	*11*						*15.3%*								

Marshall received a lucrative three-year extension in May as part of Phil Emery's Cirque du Soleil cap acrobatics. Marshall announced the deal on *The View*; moments later, to maintain the cosmic balance, Adam Schefter tweeted a Ree Drummond recipe for kale citrus salad.

Marshall, Wes Welker, and Andre Johnson are the only players in NFL history with five seasons with 100 or more receptions. Marshall barely made it, catching his 100th pass in the season finale against the Packers, and that's a good thing: Marshall's 194-target, 118-catch 2012 campaign was as much a testament to Mike Tice's stubbornness as Marshall's talent. Both Welker and Johnson have reputations for dependability, while Marshall is still thought of by many as a troublemaker. It's a label Marshall received because of a diagnosed (and now treated) mental illness, some high-profile personal problems, and an early-career run-in with Josh McDaniels in full Nero mode. Marshall hasn't missed a game since 2010, has cranked out 1,000-yard seasons since 2007, and has not made a prima donna peep despite years as almost comically overused offensive focal point for two different teams. Marshall may be one of the NFL's least-appreciated superstars, and it would be a shame if he never got to show what he could do in a playoff game. It's the next logical step after an offseason appearance on *The View.*

Keshawn Martin Height: 5-11 Weight: 194 College: Michigan State Draft: 2012/4 (121) Born: 15-Mar-1990 Age: 24 Risk: Green

Year	Team	G/GS	Snaps	Rec	Pass	Yds	C%	+/-	Yd/C	TD	Drop	YAC	Rk	YAC+	BTkl	DVOA	Rk	DYAR	Rk	YAR	Short	Mid	Deep	Bomb
2012	HOU	16/1	264	10	28	85	36%	-7.7	8.5	1	4	3.7	--	-2.1	2	-47.2%	--	-92	--	-82	54%	31%	12%	4%
2013	HOU	16/1	373	22	40	253	55%	-1.4	11.5	2	1	4.0	--	+0.0	3	-13.0%	--	-1	--	0	37%	54%	6%	3%
2014	*HOU*			*20*	*35*	*245*	*57%*		*12.2*	*2*						*-3.6%*								

The NFL equivalent of Ron Burgundy's *Anchorman* dog eating an entire wheel of cheese was Martin kicking a ball out of his own hands to gift the Jaguars a game-sealing interception in Week 11. Sometimes, blinding incompetence can be so impressive that there's no need to be mad. Martin and DeVier Posey are battling to be the No. 3 receiver for the Texans this season. Martin is the low-upside play of the two, as he has problems handling NFL physicality.

Jordan Matthews Height: 6-3 Weight: 212 College: Vanderbilt Draft: 2014/2 (42) Born: 7/16/1992 Age: 22 Risk: Red

Year	Team	G/GS	Snaps	Rec	Pass	Yds	C%	+/-	Yd/C	TD	Drop	YAC	Rk	YAC+	BTkl	DVOA	Rk	DYAR	Rk	YAR	Short	Mid	Deep	Bomb
2014	*PHI*			*41*	*72*	*620*	*57%*		*15.1*	*4*						*5.5%*								

Matthews left Vanderbilt with the most catches (262) and receiving yards (3,759) in SEC history. He has good measurables and was very productive with screen passes, which should make him a natural fit in Kelly's offense. So why only a second-round pick? One theory is that his screen reliance doesn't make him a complete receiver. His YAC on non-screens was subpar in 2013. However, that didn't stop Sammy Watkins from going fourth overall. Another theory is shaky hands. Matthews' 10 drops were the second most in college football last year. However, that reportedly wasn't an issue earlier in his career, and it's also something a young receiver can work on. Just look at the early career of Matthews' cousin Jerry Rice. Don't expect a dominant rookie season, but Matthews should be productive in filling the DeSean Jackson void.

Rishard Matthews Height: 6-0 Weight: 217 College: Nevada Draft: 2012/7 (227) Born: 12-Oct-1989 Age: 25 Risk: Green

Year	Team	G/GS	Snaps	Rec	Pass	Yds	C%	+/-	Yd/C	TD	Drop	YAC	Rk	YAC+	BTkl	DVOA	Rk	DYAR	Rk	YAR	Short	Mid	Deep	Bomb
2012	MIA	8/1	232	11	20	151	55%	+0.4	13.7	0	0	2.7	--	-1.4	0	-1.4%	--	20	--	25	28%	33%	33%	6%
2013	MIA	16/5	519	41	67	448	61%	+0.7	10.9	2	2	3.9	68	-0.6	0	-7.7%	68	27	67	43	38%	46%	14%	2%
2014	*MIA*			*19*	*30*	*187*	*63%*		*9.8*	*0*						*-9.5%*								

We noted last year that Matthews had a better Playmaker Score than the likes of T.Y. Hilton and Michael Floyd. He fell to the seventh round and did little as a rookie, but last season's injury to Brandon Gibson allowed him to make a good impression in the slot. Against Tampa Bay, Matthews stepped up with 11 catches for 120 yards and two touchdowns. He might be the most random player to have a game with that line since Kevin Curtis (2007) or Drew Bennett (2004), but that's rarely ever the performance of a random scrub. Watch his pair of 24-yard receptions against the Patriots (Week 15) and you'll see the talent that could help the Dolphins if given the opportunity this year.

Robert Meachem Height: 6-2 Weight: 210 College: Tennessee Draft: 2007/1 (27) Born: 28-Sep-1984 Age: 30 Risk: Green

Year	Team	G/GS	Snaps	Rec	Pass	Yds	C%	+/-	Yd/C	TD	Drop	YAC	Rk	YAC+	BTkl	DVOA	Rk	DYAR	Rk	YAR	Short	Mid	Deep	Bomb
2011	NO	16/8	742	40	60	620	67%	+6.6	15.5	6	3	2.6	87	-2.2	5	31.2%	9	227	15	218	27%	35%	18%	20%
2012	SD	15/3	398	14	32	207	44%	-3.9	14.8	2	1	2.4	--	-1.1	2	-12.3%	--	-10	--	-6	16%	47%	13%	25%
2013	NO	15/5	389	16	30	324	53%	+1.6	20.3	2	1	5.4	--	+0.9	2	15.7%	--	66	--	66	17%	41%	3%	38%
2014	*NO*			*10*	*21*	*186*	*48%*		*18.6*	*2*						*3.5%*								

Meachem has carved out a niche as a deep-ball specialist, a dying breed in today's NFL. His 38 percent "bomb rate" was the highest for any wideout in the last three seasons (minimum 32 targets), and he and Baltimore's Torrey Smith are the only to players in the league to top 20 percent in this category in each of the last three seasons. The youth of Kenny Stills and Brandin Cooks at wideout threatened to make Meachem expendable in New Orleans, but he was still taking first-team snaps by the end of minicamp, and his role as the designated "shot" guy seems secure for this season.

Denarius Moore Height: 6-0 Weight: 191 College: Tennessee Draft: 2011/5 (148) Born: 9-Dec-1988 Age: 26 Risk: Green

Year	Team	G/GS	Snaps	Rec	Pass	Yds	C%	+/-	Yd/C	TD	Drop	YAC	Rk	YAC+	BTkl	DVOA	Rk	DYAR	Rk	YAR	Short	Mid	Deep	Bomb
2011	OAK	13/10	609	33	76	618	43%	-3.7	18.7	5	5	3.8	59	-1.3	4	-1.6%	53	29	63	57	18%	36%	18%	28%
2012	OAK	15/15	793	51	114	741	45%	-12.6	14.5	7	6	5.0	26	+0.6	5	-12.4%	73	-33	78	-5	26%	38%	26%	10%
2013	OAK	13/10	590	46	86	695	53%	-2.9	15.1	5	4	5.6	19	+0.8	2	3.1%	35	107	43	113	30%	48%	16%	6%
2014	*OAK*			*36*	*65*	*494*	*55%*		*13.7*	*2*						*-6.5%*								

Moore burst onto the scene as a rookie in 2011 with explosive plays down the field, but the transition from deep threat to complete receiver never quite finished. The Raiders seem frustrated by his inconsistency, with offensive coordinator Greg Olson remarking last year about Moore's need for great maturity and head coach Dennis Allen indicating during this year's OTAs that "he's still got a lot of improvement that he's got to make," including working on the finer details of his game. No other receiver on the roster is as explosive as Moore, but the arrival of James Jones and development of Andre Holmes could push him from a starting spot to fourth on the depth chart without further improvement.

Lance Moore Height: 5-9 Weight: 177 College: Toledo Draft: 2005/FA Born: 31-Aug-1983 Age: 31 Risk: Yellow

Year	Team	G/GS	Snaps	Rec	Pass	Yds	C%	+/-	Yd/C	TD	Drop	YAC	Rk	YAC+	BTkl	DVOA	Rk	DYAR	Rk	YAR	Short	Mid	Deep	Bomb
2011	NO	14/7	415	52	73	627	71%	+6.3	12.1	8	2	3.0	79	-1.2	2	26.1%	10	260	13	254	36%	45%	14%	5%
2012	NO	15/7	608	65	104	1041	63%	+6.6	16.0	6	5	2.2	83	-1.9	0	31.2%	5	356	7	344	21%	46%	18%	15%
2013	NO	13/5	441	37	54	457	69%	+6.4	12.4	2	3	1.8	90	-2.2	0	22.1%	11	150	30	153	28%	50%	15%	7%
2014	*PIT*			*34*	*60*	*433*	*57%*		*12.7*	*2*						*-3.0%*								

This offseason the Steelers signed Moore and Darrius Heyward-Bey at wide receiver, which might be the greatest catch-rate disparity in the league. Moore's been a stellar slot receiver for the Saints, catching 66.9 percent of his targets. Heyward-Bey was a bust for Oakland and his career catch rate is only 46.7 percent. Moore should see plenty of slot action as he replaces Jerricho Cotchery, but don't expect him to replicate Cotchery's 10 touchdown catches in 2013. Moore already had his outlier scoring season when he caught 10 touchdowns in 2008.

Josh Morgan Height: 6-0 Weight: 219 College: Virginia Tech Draft: 2008/6 (174) Born: 20-Jun-1985 Age: 29 Risk: Green

Year	Team	G/GS	Snaps	Rec	Pass	Yds	C%	+/-	Yd/C	TD	Drop	YAC	Rk	YAC+	BTkl	DVOA	Rk	DYAR	Rk	YAR	Short	Mid	Deep	Bomb
2011	SF	5/5	237	15	20	220	75%	+2.7	14.7	1	0	6.4	--	+2.4	2	32.9%	--	74	--	83	37%	53%	11%	0%
2012	WAS	16/15	708	48	74	510	65%	-0.4	10.6	2	5	4.9	31	-0.1	7	-6.9%	65	17	68	39	41%	45%	8%	6%
2013	WAS	14/7	385	20	35	214	63%	+0.5	10.7	0	2	5.2	--	+0.2	1	-14.1%	--	-4	--	3	45%	39%	15%	0%
2014	*CHI*			*16*	*24*	*177*	*67%*		*11.1*	*1*						*7.2%*								

For $7.5 million in guarantees, Washington managed to grab 13 DYAR on 68 catches from Morgan. Morgan also resented the Shanaclan's attempt to bury him behind Leonard Hankerson, noting that "at the end of the day, you're not gonna piss on me and tell me it's raining." Morgan signed with the Bears for the veteran minimum, where he'll likely be used as a blocking receiver on screens and a third option if Marquess Wilson doesn't win the slot job. After an offseason arrest, Morgan's roster spot is not assured. Hopefully Marc Trestman has told him the source of the stream.

Joseph Morgan Height: 6-1 Weight: 184 College: Walsh Draft: 2012/FA Born: 23-Mar-1988 Age: 26 Risk: Green

Year	Team	G/GS	Snaps	Rec	Pass	Yds	C%	+/-	Yd/C	TD	Drop	YAC	Rk	YAC+	BTkl	DVOA	Rk	DYAR	Rk	YAR	Short	Mid	Deep	Bomb
2012	NO	14/4	382	10	21	379	48%	+2.5	37.9	3	1	8.7	--	+1.8	3	65.0%	--	135	--	131	11%	11%	11%	68%
2014	*NO*			*21*	*34*	*296*	*62%*		*14.1*	*2*						*9.2%*								

Morgan's tenure in New Orleans has been a mix of bad luck (season-ending knee injuries in 2011 and 2013), bad decisions (a DWI arrest after a trooper found him asleep at the wheel in May of 2013), and flashes of unique big-play ability (eight of his 10 career receptions have gained at least 27 yards). Still recovering from a torn ACL and meniscus, he sat out June drills, telling reporters he was at about 80 percent and hoped to be healthy by minicamp. Between his speed and his red flags,he's one of the most intriguing names to watch as roster cuts begin.

Santana Moss Height: 5-10 Weight: 185 College: Miami Draft: 2001/1 (16) Born: 1-Jun-1979 Age: 35 Risk: Red

Year	Team	G/GS	Snaps	Rec	Pass	Yds	C%	+/-	Yd/C	TD	Drop	YAC	Rk	YAC+	BTkl	DVOA	Rk	DYAR	Rk	YAR	Short	Mid	Deep	Bomb
2011	WAS	12/12	626	46	96	584	48%	-9.9	12.7	4	7	4.0	51	-1.1	4	-18.0%	81	-41	79	-26	43%	29%	18%	10%
2012	WAS	16/1	454	41	63	573	67%	+2.3	14.0	8	3	5.8	16	+0.5	5	11.6%	22	98	41	126	47%	35%	12%	7%
2013	WAS	16/1	550	42	79	452	54%	-7.4	10.8	2	6	4.3	59	-0.5	1	-28.3%	87	-97	87	-74	39%	47%	11%	3%
2014	*WAS*			*15*	*24*	*195*	*63%*		*13.0*	*0*						*7.0%*								

Santana Moss' draft selection pre-dates the release of the iPod. He's had a distinguished career—four 1,000-yard receiving seasons with the Jets and Skins is nothing to sneeze at—but he fits on an NFL roster like ... well, like an iPod fits on your Christmas list this year.

David Nelson Height: 6-5 Weight: 217 College: Florida Draft: 2010/FA Born: 7-Nov-1986 Age: 28 Risk: Red

Year	Team	G/GS	Snaps	Rec	Pass	Yds	C%	+/-	Yd/C	TD	Drop	YAC	Rk	YAC+	BTkl	DVOA	Rk	DYAR	Rk	YAR	Short	Mid	Deep	Bomb
2011	BUF	16/13	818	61	98	658	62%	-1.1	10.8	5	3	3.3	73	-1.0	4	1.2%	49	106	49	102	36%	50%	11%	3%
2012	BUF	1/1	28	2	5	31	40%	-1.3	15.5	0	0	5.0	--	+1.0	0	-4.0%	--	0	--	0	60%	20%	20%	0%
2013	NYJ	12/6	569	36	61	423	59%	+1.5	11.8	2	2	3.0	81	-1.3	1	2.4%	39	67	55	49	33%	40%	16%	12%
2014	*NYJ*			*28*	*52*	*344*	*54%*		*12.3*	*1*						*-10.3%*								

Nelson played almost exclusively in the slot during his time in Buffalo, but turned into one of New York's starting outside wideouts after he signed with the Jets in early October. At the time, Nelson was still recovering from surgery to repair his ACL that took place in September 2012. Nelson proved to be an effective blocker and wound up arguably becoming the team's best receiver by the end of the year. In December, Nelson led the team with 19 catches, 212 yards, and two touchdowns. It's difficult to tell how the Jets' depth chart is going to shake out after Eric Decker and Jeremy Kerley, but if he wins a job, Nelson should produce an effective season.

Jordy Nelson Height: 6-2 Weight: 217 College: Kansas State Draft: 2008/2 (36) Born: 31-May-1985 Age: 29 Risk: Green

Year	Team	G/GS	Snaps	Rec	Pass	Yds	C%	+/-	Yd/C	TD	Drop	YAC	Rk	YAC+	BTkl	DVOA	Rk	DYAR	Rk	YAR	Short	Mid	Deep	Bomb
2011	GB	16/9	609	68	96	1263	71%	+11.7	18.6	15	2	6.0	11	+1.2	7	52.9%	1	520	2	528	31%	40%	14%	14%
2012	GB	12/10	593	49	73	745	67%	+8.1	15.2	7	6	5.1	24	+1.2	3	30.8%	6	292	13	264	24%	54%	10%	13%
2013	GB	16/16	1083	85	127	1314	67%	+14.2	15.5	8	4	4.8	37	-0.1	11	26.7%	6	402	2	408	37%	33%	20%	10%
2014	*GB*			*73*	*112*	*1120*	*65%*		*15.3*	*9*						*24.2%*								

Nelson's catch rate from Aaron Rodgers was just below 70 percent (50 of 72). It was 64 percent (35 of 55) from the Three Kings of Disorient, which is simply remarkable. Randall Cobb was not available for those games, and James Jones was hurt for one of them, so Nelson had to do a little of everything: catch passes in the flat where Seneca Wallace could reach him, provide most of the big-pass capability, give Scott Tolzien an easy-to-find target, and every other role a receiver can play in a crisis. His numbers were practically indistinguishable from the ones he posts with Rodgers, which shows just how valuable Nelson is. Look for stat breakdowns like these to be part of Nelson's soon-to-start contract negotiations.

Hakeem Nicks Height: 6-3 Weight: 212 College: North Carolina Draft: 2009/1 (29) Born: 14-Jan-1988 Age: 26 Risk: Yellow

Year	Team	G/GS	Snaps	Rec	Pass	Yds	C%	+/-	Yd/C	TD	Drop	YAC	Rk	YAC+	BTkl	DVOA	Rk	DYAR	Rk	YAR	Short	Mid	Deep	Bomb
2011	NYG	15/15	951	76	133	1192	57%	+4.0	15.7	7	5	4.6	34	-0.1	5	12.5%	24	276	11	272	28%	33%	21%	18%
2012	NYG	13/11	668	53	100	692	53%	-2.6	13.1	3	3	3.7	52	-0.2	2	-5.9%	60	67	50	55	25%	51%	15%	9%
2013	NYG	15/15	833	56	101	896	55%	+1.5	16.0	0	7	4.8	38	+0.3	7	-2.4%	56	83	50	121	24%	47%	18%	12%
2014	*IND*			*43*	*79*	*569*	*54%*		*13.2*	*4*						*-2.6%*								

The Giants passing game was ugly in 2013 and Nicks failed to score a touchdown, which makes it easy to overlook that Nicks had a better year than you might recall. He posted his highest yards per catch average since his rookie year, and upped his yards per game production from 2012. The Giants let Nicks move on in the offseason, and no team was willing to roll the dice on Nicks on anything more than a one-year "prove-it" deal. Nicks has recovered from the nagging injuries that plagued his final two years in New York, but he's behind T.Y. Hilton and Reggie Wayne in the Colts' pecking order.

Kevin Ogletree Height: 6-2 Weight: 196 College: Virginia Draft: 2009/FA Born: 5-Dec-1987 Age: 27 Risk: #N/A

Year	Team	G/GS	Snaps	Rec	Pass	Yds	C%	+/-	Yd/C	TD	Drop	YAC	Rk	YAC+	BTkl	DVOA	Rk	DYAR	Rk	YAR	Short	Mid	Deep	Bomb
2011	DAL	14/1	267	15	26	164	58%	-0.7	10.9	0	0	4.3	--	-0.3	2	-18.5%	--	-8	--	-12	35%	50%	8%	8%
2012	DAL	15/1	453	32	55	436	58%	+0.5	13.6	4	3	2.6	78	-1.5	5	4.5%	32	92	42	78	19%	61%	11%	9%
2013	2TM	16/2	385	21	45	269	47%	-5.6	12.8	2	2	4.3	--	-0.1	2	-8.7%	--	14	--	6	33%	33%	22%	11%

In Week 1 of the 2012 season, Ogletree caught eight passes for 114 yards and two touchdowns against the Giants. It was a lot of fun that week watching fantasy football players who didn't remember the lessons of Frisman Jackson. Ogletree split last year between Tampa Bay and Detroit but is currently unsigned.

Chris Owusu Height: 6-2 Weight: 200 College: Stanford Draft: 2012/FA Born: 6-Jan-1990 Age: 25 Risk: Yellow

Year	Team	G/GS	Snaps	Rec	Pass	Yds	C%	+/-	Yd/C	TD	Drop	YAC	Rk	YAC+	BTkl	DVOA	Rk	DYAR	Rk	YAR	Short	Mid	Deep	Bomb
2012	TB	5/0	24	1	3	24	33%	-0.8	24.0	0	0	11.0	--	+8.5	1	-27.5%	--	-3	--	-2	33%	67%	0%	0%
2013	TB	9/4	263	13	20	114	65%	+0.3	8.8	0	0	3.0	--	-1.8	0	-15.6%	--	-4	--	-2	35%	40%	20%	5%
2014	*TB*			*31*	*55*	*353*	*56%*		*11.4*	*1*						*-12.6%*								

Owusu enters training camp with a small lead over Louis Murphy in the battle for the Bucs' slot receiver position. Owusu is fast—his 4.31-second forty-yard dash tied for the lead among receivers at the 2012 combine—but then, Murphy ran a 4.32-second forty in 2009. Murphy has more experience (121 career catches), but Owusu is three years younger. The two are very close in size. Neither has played much on special teams. It wouldn't be surprising to see them rotate throughout the season.

Cordarrelle Patterson Height: 6-2 Weight: 216 College: Tennessee Draft: 2013/1 (29) Born: 17-Mar-1991 Age: 23 Risk: Red

Year	Team	G/GS	Snaps	Rec	Pass	Yds	C%	+/-	Yd/C	TD	Drop	YAC	Rk	YAC+	BTkl	DVOA	Rk	DYAR	Rk	YAR	Short	Mid	Deep	Bomb
2013	MIN	16/6	436	45	77	469	58%	-2.5	10.4	4	3	6.1	8	-0.4	18	-12.0%	74	4	73	-3	49%	23%	15%	13%
2014	*MIN*			*71*	*119*	*1009*	*60%*		*14.2*	*7*						*6.2%*								

Patterson rushed for 33- and 50-yard touchdowns last year. The 50-yarder came in the season finale against the Lions on a broken reverse-option trick play. Patterson lined up as a pure I-formation halfback for the 33-yarder in a play that is part of a plain-brown-wrapper video sold in dirty bookstores as *The Humiliation of Chris Conte and the Bears Defense*. Patterson also caught 18 of the 21 screen or "smoke" passes thrown to him, dropping two, with one interception because Matt Cassel is just that amazing. He averaged eight yards per screen, but 79 of his 176 yards on such plays came in one Iditarod play against the Ravens on an ice sheet. Marry the constant screens to the backfield plays, and you can see that the Vikings dusted off the old Percy Harvin playbook, designed to get the ball into the hands of a playmaking receiver with minimal quarterback interference. Patterson is a very different player than Harvin, not as nimble but much more useful as a traditional every-down receiver, and one of the many items on the Vikings offensive agenda should be getting him the ball more regularly on old-fashioned forward passes.

Quinton Patton Height: 6-0 Weight: 204 College: Louisiana Tech Draft: 2013/4 (128) Born: 9-Aug-1990 Age: 24 Risk: Red

Year	Team	G/GS	Snaps	Rec	Pass	Yds	C%	+/-	Yd/C	TD	Drop	YAC	Rk	YAC+	BTkl	DVOA	Rk	DYAR	Rk	YAR	Short	Mid	Deep	Bomb
2013	SF	6/0	60	3	5	34	60%	-0.2	11.3	0	0	2.7	--	-3.6	0	-36.5%	--	-9	--	-11	40%	40%	20%	0%
2014	*SF*			*12*	*22*	*161*	*55%*		*13.4*	*0*						*-6.8%*								

The good news is that Quinton Patton was spending time with his quarterback this offseason. The bad news is that it was connected to a bizarre story out of Miami in April, where the authorities ultimately cleared Patton and Kaepernick of any wrongdoing in a sexual assault investigation. Patton will find it difficult to get in the news during the season, likely battling for the fourth receiver spot on an offense that has rarely gone with three in the past.

Austin Pettis Height: 6-3 Weight: 209 College: Boise State Draft: 2011/3 (78) Born: 7-May-1988 Age: 26 Risk: Red

Year	Team	G/GS	Snaps	Rec	Pass	Yds	C%	+/-	Yd/C	TD	Drop	YAC	Rk	YAC+	BTkl	DVOA	Rk	DYAR	Rk	YAR	Short	Mid	Deep	Bomb
2011	STL	12/3	346	27	48	256	56%	-0.9	9.5	0	3	3.5	--	-1.1	2	-22.5%	--	-47	--	-42	49%	40%	2%	9%
2012	STL	14/2	374	30	48	261	63%	+1.4	8.7	4	1	2.6	--	-1.5	1	0.6%	--	35	--	44	53%	33%	4%	9%
2013	STL	16/6	579	38	63	399	60%	+0.7	10.5	4	2	3.1	80	-1.1	1	5.1%	30	90	49	85	39%	40%	13%	8%
2014	*STL*			*51*	*80*	*557*	*64%*		*10.9*	*2*						*-3.5%*								

Can't possession receivers still get love too? Pettis doesn't have the draft status of Tavon Austin and Brian Quick. He doesn't have the big-play capability of Kenny Britt and Chris Givens. The Rams were also favoring Stedman Bailey down the stretch last season. It's a crowded depth chart, and the one advantage Pettis can claim is that Sam Bradford trusts him deep in the red zone. Inside the five-yard line since 2012, Bradford and Pettis have hooked up for seven touchdowns on eight passes. If only the Rams had this connection for the Week 8 goal-line stand by Seattle in a 14-9 loss…

DeVier Posey Height: 6-2 Weight: 211 College: Ohio State Draft: 2012/3 (68) Born: 15-Mar-1989 Age: 25 Risk: Green

Year	Team	G/GS	Snaps	Rec	Pass	Yds	C%	+/-	Yd/C	TD	Drop	YAC	Rk	YAC+	BTkl	DVOA	Rk	DYAR	Rk	YAR	Short	Mid	Deep	Bomb
2012	HOU	11/0	160	6	14	87	43%	-1.9	14.5	0	2	4.8	--	-0.4	1	-36.4%	--	-23	--	-20	38%	31%	15%	15%
2013	HOU	14/0	241	15	25	155	60%	+0.8	10.3	0	0	4.9	--	+0.1	2	-33.7%	--	-38	--	-40	55%	32%	5%	9%
2014	*HOU*			*18*	*33*	*197*	*55%*		*10.9*	*0*						*-15.2%*								

Posey was looking like a second-year leap candidate after catching a touchdown late in Houston's playoff loss to New England in 2012, but an Achilles tear sidelined him for part of the 2013 season. There wasn't much of a sample size for him to impress in, but as long as he's left the tear behind him, he has the physicality to be a problem for NFL defensive backs in the slot. His fantasy upside will be somewhat curbed by Bill O'Brien's tendency to favor 12 personnel.

Brian Quick Height: 6-4 Weight: 220 College: Appalachian State Draft: 2012/2 (33) Born: 5-Jun-1989 Age: 25 Risk: Green

Year	Team	G/GS	Snaps	Rec	Pass	Yds	C%	+/-	Yd/C	TD	Drop	YAC	Rk	YAC+	BTkl	DVOA	Rk	DYAR	Rk	YAR	Short	Mid	Deep	Bomb
2012	STL	15/1	182	11	27	156	41%	-4.0	14.2	2	3	2.1	--	-2.0	0	-25.0%	--	-33	--	-35	30%	37%	26%	7%
2013	STL	16/5	353	18	34	302	53%	-1.4	16.8	2	2	5.8	--	+1.3	3	12.6%	--	72	--	67	44%	29%	15%	12%
2014	*STL*			*10*	*19*	*122*	*53%*		*12.2*	*1*						*-12.3%*								

Quick was the first pick of the second round of the 2012 draft, but he's been a real disappointment with just 29 catches in 31 games. He improved his receiving metrics from his rookie season, but it's a marginal step compared to what some of his fellow classmates drafted after him have done—think T.Y. Hilton, Alshon Jeffery, Marvin Jones, Rueben Randle and teammate Chris Givens. Quick's scored four touchdowns on limited opportunities, but he should be further along by now. Brian Schottenheimer thinks Quick is the Rams' most improved player this offseason, but similar sentiments were shared about Austin Pettis last year. It's about production.

Rueben Randle Height: 6-3 Weight: 210 College: Louisiana State Draft: 2012/2 (63) Born: 7-May-1991 Age: 23 Risk: Red

Year	Team	G/GS	Snaps	Rec	Pass	Yds	C%	+/-	Yd/C	TD	Drop	YAC	Rk	YAC+	BTkl	DVOA	Rk	DYAR	Rk	YAR	Short	Mid	Deep	Bomb
2012	NYG	16/1	245	19	32	298	59%	-0.2	15.7	3	1	3.8	--	-1.0	2	16.3%	--	96	--	87	34%	44%	13%	9%
2013	NYG	16/3	578	41	79	611	52%	-2.1	14.9	6	4	4.8	36	+0.1	6	-1.5%	53	71	53	87	22%	39%	24%	15%
2014	*NYG*			*54*	*94*	*759*	*57%*		*14.1*	*5*						*3.5%*								

Perhaps no player on the Giants will benefit as much from the change at offensive coordinator as Randle. Coming out of LSU, Randle struggled to adapt to Kevin Gilbride's complex offense; he had several high-profile miscommunications with Eli Manning last year on audibles that led to incompletions or interceptions. Ben McAdoo's West Coast offense should be a good fit for Randle, who has already shown that he can be a playmaker when the ball is in his hands. In June, wide receivers coach Sean Ryan noted that Randle seemed "locked in" and more serious this year; while it's easy to expect every player in the NFL to give it their all 100 percent of the time, the truth is some players need to learn not just the pro game, but how to learn how to be a pro. If it took Randle a couple of years to learn that, Giants fans will forgive him, as long as it results in a breakout 2014 campaign.

Sidney Rice Height: 6-4 Weight: 200 College: South Carolina Draft: 2007/2 (44) Born: 1-Sep-1986 Age: 28 Risk: Red

Year	Team	G/GS	Snaps	Rec	Pass	Yds	C%	+/-	Yd/C	TD	Drop	YAC	Rk	YAC+	BTkl	DVOA	Rk	DYAR	Rk	YAR	Short	Mid	Deep	Bomb
2011	SEA	9/9	439	32	59	484	58%	+2.7	15.1	2	2	3.9	57	-1.5	1	-2.8%	55	86	53	51	21%	41%	10%	28%
2012	SEA	16/16	765	50	82	748	62%	+7.2	15.0	7	1	3.0	70	-1.4	1	29.7%	7	283	14	252	18%	51%	17%	13%
2013	SEA	8/6	331	15	35	231	43%	-2.6	15.4	3	1	1.3	--	-3.2	0	-9.9%	--	8	--	7	18%	38%	32%	12%
2014	*SEA*			*38*	*74*	*558*	*51%*		*14.7*	*4*						*-6.0%*								

Rice has played a full season only once in the three years since signing a $40 million contract with Seattle in 2011. It is also the only time he's done that in his NFL career. Rice is now at the point where he's been cut for salary cap reasons (as he was in February) and brought back at a much lower rate (as the Seahawks did with him two months later on a one-year, $1.4 million deal). Expectations should be tempered accordingly. Pete Carroll has said that he's not sure Rice will be ready for the start of the new season after he suffered an ACL tear in Week 8 of the 2013 campaign. He's still on the roster for two reasons—the coaches like the ways in which he mentors younger receivers, and he's a somewhat dynamic deep and red zone target when healthy. What that means in terms of production has everything to do with Rice's increasingly fragile physical state.

Paul Richardson Height: 6-0 Weight: 175 College: Colorado Draft: 2014/2 (45) Born: 4/13/1992 Age: 22 Risk: Red

Year	Team	G/GS	Snaps	Rec	Pass	Yds	C%	+/-	Yd/C	TD	Drop	YAC	Rk	YAC+	BTkl	DVOA	Rk	DYAR	Rk	YAR	Short	Mid	Deep	Bomb
2014	*SEA*			*26*	*48*	*342*	*54%*		*13.2*	*2*						*-12.7%*								

The Seahawks have a penchant for receivers who are productive in run-heavy, balanced, or basic offenses, which is understandable, given the team's schematic conceits. Richardson, who averaged 16.2 yards per catch and maintained a 60 percent catch rate as Colorado's No. 1 target in 2013, is just such a player. He managed to impress on all sorts of deep routes despite the fact that his offense wasn't exactly ... how shall we put this ... *evolved.* Richardson averaged an incredible 41.8 yards on his 21 collegiate touchdowns, and he'll be pressed into service as a deep threat as soon as possible. He showed what he could do on the first day of rookie minicamp, when he torched defensive back Eric Pinkins on a deep touchdown; Pinkins, who ran a 4.44 forty at his pro day, looked as if he was running in slow motion. As long as Seattle can protect his relatively slight frame, Richardson could give back big dividends, especially if Percy Harvin is felled by injury yet again.

Andre Roberts Height: 5-11 Weight: 195 College: The Citadel Draft: 2010/3 (88) Born: 9-Jan-1988 Age: 26 Risk: Green

Year	Team	G/GS	Snaps	Rec	Pass	Yds	C%	+/-	Yd/C	TD	Drop	YAC	Rk	YAC+	BTkl	DVOA	Rk	DYAR	Rk	YAR	Short	Mid	Deep	Bomb
2011	ARI	16/16	940	51	97	586	53%	-5.0	11.5	2	4	4.4	37	+0.2	5	-15.2%	75	-64	84	-37	37%	47%	11%	5%
2012	ARI	15/15	837	64	114	759	56%	-2.3	11.9	5	8	3.5	60	-0.4	3	-6.5%	63	12	72	25	36%	47%	13%	5%
2013	ARI	16/2	605	43	76	471	57%	-3.2	11.0	2	1	2.6	86	-2.3	2	-15.3%	76	-15	75	-5	31%	40%	17%	12%
2014	*WAS*			*39*	*67*	*500*	*58%*		*12.8*	*3*						*-0.6%*								

Roberts signed a four-year, $16 million deal to start opposite Pierre Garcon, then had to sit back and watch as DeSean Jackson stole his thunder and his job. Now he's going to be just the fourth option in the Washington passing game, but that spot should be safe. Behind Roberts is Santana Moss and then a bunch of not-yets and never-wases who might, sort of, possibly mean something.

Aldrick Robinson Height: 5-10 Weight: 182 College: SMU Draft: 2011/6 (178) Born: 11-Apr-1988 Age: 26 Risk: Yellow

Year	Team	G/GS	Snaps	Rec	Pass	Yds	C%	+/-	Yd/C	TD	Drop	YAC	Rk	YAC+	BTkl	DVOA	Rk	DYAR	Rk	YAR	Short	Mid	Deep	Bomb
2012	WAS	15/2	216	11	19	237	58%	+1.5	21.5	3	2	5.6	--	+0.8	1	51.4%	--	88	--	101	17%	44%	6%	33%
2013	WAS	16/1	407	18	46	365	39%	-6.7	20.3	2	3	4.8	--	+0.4	0	-10.3%	--	9	--	-3	11%	49%	16%	24%
2014	*WAS*			*14*	*25*	*271*	*56%*		*19.4*	*2*						*20.7%*								

Combine the shaky mechanics of post-injury Robert Griffin and the weak arm of Kirk Cousins with the deep-speed skill set of Aldrick Robinson and you get a fairly disappointing season. With Andre Roberts coming over from Arizona, Washington will be able to use Robinson more as a designated threat on play-action shot plays.

Allen Robinson Height: 6-2 Weight: 220 College: Penn St. Draft: 2014/2 (61) Born: 8/24/1993 Age: 21 Risk: Yellow

Year	Team	G/GS	Snaps	Rec	Pass	Yds	C%	+/-	Yd/C	TD	Drop	YAC	Rk	YAC+	BTkl	DVOA	Rk	DYAR	Rk	YAR	Short	Mid	Deep	Bomb
2014	*JAC*			*42*	*70*	*550*	*60%*		*13.1*	*2*						*-0.4%*								

This isn't a comparison that was made often in the lead-up to the draft, but Robinson reminds us a little of Justin Hunter. He's got the size and the speed to be a deep threat, but the physicality to win one-on-one balls comes and goes, and his route-running could also use improvement. Jacksonville loved throwing back-shoulder seam routes last year, and Robinson certainly has the radius to make that an effective part of his game going forward. Robinson can still be an effective situational reciever without improving, but to be a real contributor he'll need to refine his game in several areas.

Da'Rick Rogers Height: 6-2 Weight: 217 College: Tennessee Tech Draft: 2013/FA Born: 18-Jun-1991 Age: 23 Risk: Blue

Year	Team	G/GS	Snaps	Rec	Pass	Yds	C%	+/-	Yd/C	TD	Drop	YAC	Rk	YAC+	BTkl	DVOA	Rk	DYAR	Rk	YAR	Short	Mid	Deep	Bomb
2013	IND	5/3	205	14	23	192	61%	+0.2	13.7	2	2	8.4	--	+3.9	1	18.5%	--	60	--	50	30%	48%	4%	17%
2014	*IND*			*11*	*20*	*156*	*55%*		*14.2*	*2*						*2.0%*								

Pronounced "Derrick," to the great disappointment of all three people who remember ESPN's The Rick ad campaign. Rogers was regarded by some as a first-day NFL talent before he was forced to transfer from Tennessee to Tennessee Tech due to team rules violations. (Later, he admitted to failing three drug tests.) Rogers went undrafted, but bubbled up to the Colts active roster once they realized Darrius Heyward-Bey's hands are actually banana peels. He showed promise as an after-the-catch threat—his frame can take a pounding and he keeps the feet moving. His ability to make contested catches is iffy, but he's got some physical upside as a fourth receiver, and he doesn't flub the easy ones like DHB did.

Eddie Royal Height: 5-9 Weight: 184 College: Virginia Tech Draft: 2008/2 (42) Born: 21-May-1986 Age: 28 Risk: Green

Year	Team	G/GS	Snaps	Rec	Pass	Yds	C%	+/-	Yd/C	TD	Drop	YAC	Rk	YAC+	BTkl	DVOA	Rk	DYAR	Rk	YAR	Short	Mid	Deep	Bomb
2011	DEN	12/8	476	19	50	155	38%	-8.1	8.2	1	3	3.5	68	-1.8	2	-44.6%	92	-152	90	-148	33%	41%	13%	13%
2012	SD	10/2	272	23	44	234	52%	-4.4	10.2	1	0	3.9	--	-1.2	1	-22.7%	--	-56	--	-46	44%	42%	9%	5%
2013	SD	15/3	705	47	67	631	70%	+4.3	13.4	8	2	7.1	5	+1.6	4	31.6%	4	238	15	255	43%	28%	19%	10%
2014	*SD*			*31*	*51*	*410*	*61%*		*13.2*	*3*						*2.7%*								

After a first disappointing season in San Diego, Royal rebounded nicely in 2013 despite a toe injury that he played through most of the season. His career-high DVOA spoke to an efficiency that transferred to every down, and in the red zone, where he amassed a 33.5% DVOA on 14 targets. Still, Royal may have been on the roster bubble for 2014 before he restructured a contract that would have made him a $6 million cap hit. He'll be a better-than-average third or fourth option, depending on San Diego's receiver depth.

Ace Sanders Height: 5-7 Weight: 173 College: South Carolina Draft: 2013/4 (100) Born: 11-Nov-1991 Age: 23 Risk: Green

Year	Team	G/GS	Snaps	Rec	Pass	Yds	C%	+/-	Yd/C	TD	Drop	YAC	Rk	YAC+	BTkl	DVOA	Rk	DYAR	Rk	YAR	Short	Mid	Deep	Bomb
2013	JAC	15/4	600	51	86	484	59%	-2.1	9.5	1	4	5.8	16	-0.5	2	-28.0%	86	-99	88	-117	60%	28%	6%	6%
2014	*JAC*			*43*	*68*	*439*	*63%*		*10.2*	*1*						*-7.0%*								

Not to get too 1960s on you, but Sanders' best quality is his moxie. He's very deceptive running routes and tricked more than a few defenders underneath. Sanders has speed, but not much elusiveness in the open field. The Jaguars tried to use him as if he had the latter instead of just the former, and the results on the field were ugly. Sanders' upside is as an Antwaan Randle El-type receiver who can trick raw defenders in the slot and pull off four or five game-changing trick plays each year. He did complete a touchdown on his only throw of 2013.

Emmanuel Sanders Height: 5-11 Weight: 186 College: SMU Draft: 2010/3 (82) Born: 17-Mar-1987 Age: 27 Risk: Red

Year	Team	G/GS	Snaps	Rec	Pass	Yds	C%	+/-	Yd/C	TD	Drop	YAC	Rk	YAC+	BTkl	DVOA	Rk	DYAR	Rk	YAR	Short	Mid	Deep	Bomb
2011	PIT	11/0	339	22	43	288	51%	-2.7	13.1	2	0	5.8	--	+1.2	2	-7.7%	--	22	--	24	29%	38%	21%	12%
2012	PIT	16/7	721	44	74	626	59%	+1.0	14.2	1	4	4.8	32	+0.1	3	9.5%	25	124	38	121	36%	28%	30%	6%
2013	PIT	16/10	796	67	113	740	60%	-0.5	11.0	6	2	4.4	54	-0.9	7	-10.2%	71	22	69	-1	37%	35%	14%	15%
2014	*DEN*			*58*	*92*	*819*	*63%*		*14.1*	*5*						*12.2%*								

After the Patriots signed Sanders to an offer sheet last March, Pittsburgh could have had New England's third-round pick in the 2014 draft or matched the offer to retain him for one more year. The Steelers matched and Sanders had his most productive season in his biggest role yet. However, he left as an unrestricted free agent to Denver. So was it really worth it, Pittsburgh? In Denver, Sanders will get the Peyton Manning boost and should start in Eric Decker's spot. He likely won't be as productive as Decker with the deep ball or in the red zone, but Sanders is a smooth route-runner and he's faster. That's probably a fair trade-off come January in the AFC playoffs. We'll see how spoiled Manning has gotten with the size at receiver, but Sanders is more like a refurbished model of the Marvin Harrison/Reggie Wayne types that Manning spent most of his career throwing to.

Mohamed Sanu Height: 6-2 Weight: 211 College: Rutgers Draft: 2012/3 (83) Born: 22-Aug-1989 Age: 25 Risk: Green

Year	Team	G/GS	Snaps	Rec	Pass	Yds	C%	+/-	Yd/C	TD	Drop	YAC	Rk	YAC+	BTkl	DVOA	Rk	DYAR	Rk	YAR	Short	Mid	Deep	Bomb
2012	CIN	9/3	204	16	25	154	64%	+0.6	9.6	4	1	4.4	--	-0.8	0	13.8%	--	42	--	54	42%	50%	8%	0%
2013	CIN	16/14	749	47	78	455	60%	+1.2	9.7	2	6	5.4	23	+0.1	2	-10.0%	69	17	71	2	45%	33%	11%	11%
2014	*CIN*			*47*	*75*	*484*	*63%*		*10.3*	*2*						*-6.3%*								

Entering 2013, Sanu appeared to be closer to breaking out than fellow second-year man Marvin Jones, but he slid well behind Jones in production. Bengals wide receiver coach James Urban admitted the team didn't use Sanu properly last season, and with Andrew Hawkins gone, Sanu is a good bet to reappear as a featured element in the offense, particularly from the slot position. He will need to eliminate the drops to do so.

Cecil Shorts Height: 6-0 Weight: 200 College: Mount Union Draft: 2011/4 (114) Born: 22-Dec-1987 Age: 27 Risk: Yellow

Year	Team	G/GS	Snaps	Rec	Pass	Yds	C%	+/-	Yd/C	TD	Drop	YAC	Rk	YAC+	BTkl	DVOA	Rk	DYAR	Rk	YAR	Short	Mid	Deep	Bomb
2011	JAC	10/0	176	2	11	30	18%	-4.0	15.0	1	2	1.5	--	-2.6	0	-53.9%	--	-34	--	-37	18%	36%	18%	27%
2012	JAC	14/9	654	55	105	979	52%	-3.3	17.8	7	8	6.5	8	+2.7	9	5.2%	30	138	32	164	29%	39%	21%	11%
2013	JAC	13/13	759	66	125	777	53%	-5.5	11.8	3	7	4.2	62	-0.7	3	-16.3%	79	-36	79	-32	36%	36%	18%	10%
2014	*JAC*			*67*	*125*	*878*	*54%*		*13.1*	*6*						*-4.6%*								

The Jacksonville game plan for Shorts last year was to inundate him with back-shoulder routes. Those are harder balls to catch, and they wreaked havoc on Shorts' catch rate. He has the ability to make those catches, but making them consistently was a different matter (especially with Chad Henne and Blaine Gabbert throwing at him). Shorts' hands are an issue and they keep him from being an upper-echelon receiver, but he has the physicality to make tough catches and stay outside. Last season he was a No. 2 receiver that was asked to play No. 1 because of Justin Blackmon's alcohol woes, and it showed. Marquise Lee and Allen Robinson should help alleviate some of the pressure and let Shorts get back to his natural role.

Jerome Simpson Height: 6-2 Weight: 199 College: Coastal Carolina Draft: 2008/2 (46) Born: 4-Feb-1986 Age: 28 Risk: Green

Year	Team	G/GS	Snaps	Rec	Pass	Yds	C%	+/-	Yd/C	TD	Drop	YAC	Rk	YAC+	BTkl	DVOA	Rk	DYAR	Rk	YAR	Short	Mid	Deep	Bomb
2011	CIN	16/14	867	50	105	725	48%	-8.3	14.5	4	6	4.6	33	+0.4	3	-6.3%	63	57	56	30	24%	52%	13%	10%
2012	MIN	12/10	453	26	51	274	51%	-2.9	10.5	0	2	2.2	85	-2.1	2	-24.5%	84	-37	80	-58	24%	45%	18%	12%
2013	MIN	16/8	643	48	100	726	48%	-5.3	15.1	1	4	3.5	74	-1.1	2	-10.1%	70	20	70	-2	28%	35%	23%	14%
2014	*MIN*			*34*	*69*	*513*	*49%*		*15.1*	*3*						*-6.8%*								

Is there a more ridiculous role in all of sports than "Vikings deep-threat receiver?" Simpson caught 14 of the 36 deep passes thrown to him last year, for 458 yards and 12.5 yards per attempt. Remember that the NFL stat services classify a "deep" pass as 16 or more yards beyond the line of scrimmage. Nudge the slider up to 20 or more yards, and Simpson was 9-of-21 on the year: not terrible, but scant in both the targets and results department, especially when you examine the peripherals. Three of the deep passes to Simpson were intercepted. Two of the most productive completions (44 and 47 yards) came in the season opener, before the Vikings passing-game neurosis became a full-on syndrome; two of the others came against the smoldering ruins of the Bears defense.

Simpson squeezed a DUI arrest into this busy schedule, and he performed community service after the Vikings re-signed him to a one-year contract in the offseason. Simpson is responsible for one of the most famous single highlights of the last 20 years and remains a matchup problem as a run-and-jump player, but the one thing he was good at lined up exactly with the thing the Vikings were least likely to try to do. Simpson will compete with Jairus Wright for the No. 3 receiver spot, and with a new coaching regime in place, he may not win.

Steve Smith Height: 5-9 Weight: 185 College: Utah Draft: 2001/3 (74) Born: 12-May-1979 Age: 35 Risk: Yellow

Year	Team	G/GS	Snaps	Rec	Pass	Yds	C%	+/-	Yd/C	TD	Drop	YAC	Rk	YAC+	BTkl	DVOA	Rk	DYAR	Rk	YAR	Short	Mid	Deep	Bomb
2011	CAR	16/16	956	79	129	1394	61%	+3.4	17.6	7	7	5.8	14	+0.3	8	12.6%	23	285	10	246	30%	32%	23%	15%
2012	CAR	16/16	910	73	138	1174	53%	-2.6	16.1	4	8	3.7	53	-0.5	6	4.0%	34	171	27	161	18%	46%	26%	10%
2013	CAR	15/15	770	64	110	745	58%	-0.3	11.6	4	5	2.8	84	-1.7	12	-3.7%	58	74	51	80	27%	52%	13%	8%
2014	*BAL*			*61*	*106*	*712*	*58%*		*11.7*	*5*						*-4.9%*								

Smith is the greatest player in Carolina franchise history, and there's not much argument to be made for anyone else unless you're a member of Jordan Gross' immediate family. It wasn't always a rosy relationship, as a number of teammates with sore jaws (or, in Anthony Bright's case, a fractured orbital lobe) will tell you, but it was special, particularly in 2005 when he nearly dragged the team to the Super Bowl by himself. His advancing age and contract, though, meant he was no longer worth the headache, and the Panthers cut ties with him in March. He signed with the Ravens in part because they were so close to Charlotte, where his wife and children will remain. He promised "blood and guts" when the Ravens play the Panthers in September, then promptly got in a training camp fight with Lardarius Webb. Some things never change. Some things do, though. For the first time in more than a decade, Smith won't be counted on to carry a team's passing game by himself, as he'll be the No. 2 wideout behind Torrey Smith. Speaking of whom...

Torrey Smith Height: 6-1 Weight: 204 College: Maryland Draft: 2011/2 (58) Born: 26-Jan-1989 Age: 25 Risk: Yellow

Year	Team	G/GS	Snaps	Rec	Pass	Yds	C%	+/-	Yd/C	TD	Drop	YAC	Rk	YAC+	BTkl	DVOA	Rk	DYAR	Rk	YAR	Short	Mid	Deep	Bomb
2011	BAL	16/14	883	50	96	841	54%	+1.2	16.8	7	6	4.7	30	-0.3	2	11.6%	27	199	22	176	19%	34%	18%	29%
2012	BAL	16/16	919	49	110	855	45%	-5.9	17.4	8	5	4.6	34	+0.1	4	0.7%	42	143	31	132	21%	34%	15%	30%
2013	BAL	16/16	1099	65	137	1128	47%	-4.3	17.4	4	3	5.5	21	+0.7	2	0.0%	48	139	33	98	25%	32%	22%	21%
2014	*BAL*			*64*	*133*	*1046*	*48%*		*16.3*	*7*						*-1.7%*								

Smith had an odd season. He was heavily involved early with at least 85 yards in each of the first five games, but he only hit that mark once in the final 11 games. His targets dropped from 10.4 per game to 7.9, which really doesn't make sense since the running game never improved and other receivers didn't step up significantly. Smith had 604 more yards than Baltimore's next closest receiver—the biggest gap in franchise history.

Smith is clearly the team's deep threat and he was used that way again last year, which may mean Joe Flacco needs better protection to effectively use him. However, that's where things get even more interesting. In the first five games when Smith gained 49.3 percent of his season's yardage, Flacco was pressured on 25.5 percent of their targets. In the last 11 games when Smith wasn't very productive, Flacco was only pressured on 17.2 percent of Smith's targets. Smith's average target depth even decreased from 16.2 to 15.0 yards. In theory, a quarterback should throw better when he's not pressured and when it's a shorter pass, but that wasn't the case with Flacco to Smith in 2013.

More signs of Smith's verticality: He was only used on three screen passes and was one of four receivers to draw at least six pass interference penalties. Since he's a deep threat, you expect some inconsistency in Smith's production, but Baltimore has to get him more involved than he was in the last 11 games.

Kenny Stills Height: 6-0 Weight: 194 College: Oklahoma Draft: 2013/5 (144) Born: 22-Apr-1992 Age: 22 Risk: Red

Year	Team	G/GS	Snaps	Rec	Pass	Yds	C%	+/-	Yd/C	TD	Drop	YAC	Rk	YAC+	BTkl	DVOA	Rk	DYAR	Rk	YAR	Short	Mid	Deep	Bomb
2013	NO	16/10	689	32	51	641	65%	+6.4	20.0	5	1	6.2	7	+1.5	1	40.1%	1	206	21	218	31%	24%	22%	22%
2014	*NO*			*46*	*76*	*616*	*61%*		*13.4*	*5*						*6.8%*								

Stills led the league in DVOA, but he barely passed the 50-target threshold to qualify for our leaderboards. Other receivers to finish first in DVOA with just 50 to 60 targets include Tim Dwight, Dennis Northcutt, Anthony Gonzalez, J.J. Stokes, Devery Henderson, and Ricky Proehl, so let's not start work on Stills' bust for Canton just yet. Between the departure of Lance Moore and arrival of Brandin Cooks, Stills should again be the third receiver in New Orleans (fourth if you count Jimmy Graham), so his targets should still be limited, even in a pass-happy offense like Sean Payton's. If you've never seen his half-blond curly Mohawk, you should go do a quick image search before moving on to Rod Streater. It's phenomenal.

Rod Streater Height: 6-3 Weight: 200 College: Temple Draft: 2012/FA Born: 9-Feb-1988 Age: 26 Risk: Yellow

Year	Team	G/GS	Snaps	Rec	Pass	Yds	C%	+/-	Yd/C	TD	Drop	YAC	Rk	YAC+	BTkl	DVOA	Rk	DYAR	Rk	YAR	Short	Mid	Deep	Bomb
2012	OAK	16/2	580	39	75	584	52%	-3.1	15.0	3	4	3.6	57	-0.7	0	-1.9%	51	43	60	61	19%	53%	16%	11%
2013	OAK	16/14	748	60	100	888	61%	+4.4	14.8	4	4	5.1	28	+0.3	3	13.6%	18	204	23	203	31%	42%	17%	10%
2014	*OAK*			*56*	*96*	*760*	*58%*		*13.6*	*4*						*-2.5%*								

Streater is probably the Raiders' best success story in recent years, and not just because of his extensive community work and cookie-stealing Beats by Dre parody video. He earned a starting job and became a solid wide receiver by dint of effort, with wide receivers coach Ted Gilmore noting his self-motivation and desire to be great. He's still not a finished product, as he needs to continue to get stronger without losing his speed and has more work to do as a route-runner. The arrival of James Jones pushes him down to second man on the depth chart, but he should continue to start and play in all situations.

Golden Tate Height: 5-10 Weight: 199 College: Notre Dame Draft: 2010/2 (60) Born: 2-Aug-1988 Age: 26 Risk: Yellow

Year	Team	G/GS	Snaps	Rec	Pass	Yds	C%	+/-	Yd/C	TD	Drop	YAC	Rk	YAC+	BTkl	DVOA	Rk	DYAR	Rk	YAR	Short	Mid	Deep	Bomb
2011	SEA	16/5	526	35	60	382	62%	+2.8	10.9	3	0	4.5	35	-0.5	8	-14.4%	73	-10	74	-17	39%	39%	11%	11%
2012	SEA	15/15	715	45	70	688	69%	+7.6	15.3	7	2	5.9	11	+0.3	14	31.6%	4	245	19	249	41%	25%	10%	24%
2013	SEA	16/13	762	64	100	898	66%	+5.4	14.0	5	4	7.6	1	+2.0	23	12.9%	19	196	24	206	44%	30%	11%	14%
2014	*DET*			*55*	*93*	*807*	*59%*		*14.7*	*4*						*2.0%*								

It took Tate a while to get the hang of things in the NFL; he was benched for a time in his second season because he struggled to grasp the intricacies of route concepts at the next level. Of course, most NFL teams want their receivers to do more than what Tate did at Notre Dame, which was to leap as high as possible to grab all of Jimmy Clausen's errant air balls. But over time, Tate became a pretty estimable weapon as an outside and speed slot receiver. After Seattle's Super Bowl win, Tate said that he'd be happy to take a hometown discount to stay with the Seahawks, a notion that lasted exactly as long as it took the Lions to offer him a five-year, $31 million deal that Seattle was never going to match. In an offense that generally attempts twice the passes that his old one did, and with defenses strapped to Calvin Johnson on every play, we expect Tate to flourish. He certainly does, comparing his new role to that of Lance Moore's in New Orleans—which makes some sense, especially with former Saints assistant Joe Lombardi running Detroit's offense.

Kerry Taylor Height: 6-0 Weight: 200 College: Arizona State Draft: 2012/FA Born: 20-Feb-1989 Age: 25 Risk: Blue

Year	Team	G/GS	Snaps	Rec	Pass	Yds	C%	+/-	Yd/C	TD	Drop	YAC	Rk	YAC+	BTkl	DVOA	Rk	DYAR	Rk	YAR	Short	Mid	Deep	Bomb
2013	2TM	10/4	303	22	34	229	65%	+1.4	10.4	1	2	3.8	--	-1.1	1	-1.4%	--	30	--	27	26%	65%	10%	0%
2014	*JAC*			*4*	*7*	*42*	*57%*		*10.5*	*0*						*-12.7%*								

Kerry Taylor led the Jaguars in receiving in their meaningless Week 17 game against the Colts. With better health and an influx of rookies, Taylor is now no higher than sixth on the Jacksonville depth chart. Being sixth in the pecking order in Jacksonville is like being eighth in the pecking order somewhere else, which is a polite way of saying that Taylor probably has no real future in the league.

Demaryius Thomas Height: 6-3 Weight: 224 College: Georgia Tech Draft: 2010/1 (22) Born: 25-Dec-1987 Age: 27 Risk: Green

Year	Team	G/GS	Snaps	Rec	Pass	Yds	C%	+/-	Yd/C	TD	Drop	YAC	Rk	YAC+	BTkl	DVOA	Rk	DYAR	Rk	YAR	Short	Mid	Deep	Bomb
2011	DEN	11/5	533	32	70	551	46%	-2.2	17.2	4	3	3.5	67	-0.8	2	-5.6%	60	38	60	42	16%	51%	14%	19%
2012	DEN	16/16	1019	94	141	1434	67%	+10.3	15.3	10	6	5.7	17	+1.0	2	21.4%	14	354	8	401	42%	31%	12%	15%
2013	DEN	16/16	1106	92	142	1430	65%	+6.2	15.5	14	4	7.6	2	+2.5	8	26.5%	7	430	1	465	48%	24%	17%	11%
2014	*DEN*			*92*	*140*	*1376*	*66%*		*15.0*	*12*						*22.6%*								

Once upon a time, Demaryius Thomas was a fast, big-bodied guy who played for teams that ran the ball a lot and was asked mostly to block and run go routes. Then, Peyton Manning arrived and the lump of coal was revealed to be a diamond and a contender for the second-best wide receiver in the league behind Calvin Johnson. The Broncos used him extensively on wide receiver screens, and he averaged more yards per play than any other receiver in the league who was thrown at least five. (He caught 16 of 19 for 262 yards and four touchdowns.) Thomas has the speed to go vertically, the toughness to run inside breaking routes, the explosiveness to be productive running shallow crosses, and the route-running skill to get open on deep comebacks. Plus, he's a good enough blocker to be productive on run plays. There's no reason he should not be immensely productive again in 2014. Heading into the final year of his rookie deal, he should get an immense contract extension sooner rather than later.

Kenbrell Thompkins Height: 6-1 Weight: 196 College: Cincinnati Draft: 2013/FA Born: 17-Apr-1989 Age: 25 Risk: Yellow

Year	Team	G/GS	Snaps	Rec	Pass	Yds	C%	+/-	Yd/C	TD	Drop	YAC	Rk	YAC+	BTkl	DVOA	Rk	DYAR	Rk	YAR	Short	Mid	Deep	Bomb
2013	NE	12/8	574	32	70	466	46%	-10.5	14.6	4	5	4.3	56	-0.1	4	-11.9%	73	4	74	8	32%	43%	17%	7%
2014	*NE*			*22*	*40*	*340*	*55%*		*15.5*	*3*						*6.3%*								

Like the other rookie receivers, Thompkins had growing pains. There were more positive moments than negative ones, including a six-catch, 127-yard outing in a September win over the Steelers and the game-winning touchdown to beat the Saints in October. Yet at the same time, Thompkins had just nine catches after Week 7, and disappeared into the background down the stretch. Like Aaron Dobson (and to a lesser extent, Josh Boyce), Thompkins now needs to show progression and make improvements in his game in his second season. If Danny Amendola and Rob Gronkowski stay healthy, the targets are coming from Thompkins' total, not Dobson's.

Tiquan Underwood Height: 6-1 Weight: 184 College: Rutgers Draft: 2009/7 (253) Born: 17-Feb-1987 Age: 27 Risk: Green

Year	Team	G/GS	Snaps	Rec	Pass	Yds	C%	+/-	Yd/C	TD	Drop	YAC	Rk	YAC+	BTkl	DVOA	Rk	DYAR	Rk	YAR	Short	Mid	Deep	Bomb
2011	NE	6/0	87	3	6	30	50%	-0.5	10.0	0	1	2.0	--	-1.1	0	-19.2%	--	-3	--	-4	17%	50%	33%	0%
2012	TB	14/3	445	28	55	425	51%	-2.6	15.2	2	4	3.6	55	-0.2	1	-7.0%	66	4	73	28	18%	51%	22%	10%
2013	TB	12/7	563	24	45	440	53%	-0.8	18.3	4	3	4.3	--	+0.0	1	23.6%	--	133	--	126	24%	46%	22%	9%
2014	*CAR*			*10*	*17*	*128*	*59%*		*12.8*	*1*						*-3.8%*								

Underwood is most famous for having the best hairdo in the league, and for being cut the night before Super Bowl XLVI by the Patriots. He has actually been cut eight times in his career. Now, he is, at worst, the fourth receiver on the Panthers. He has struggled with drops throughout his career, but with a 4.31-second forty-yard dash, he might be able to solve Carolina's deep passing woes. He could also see time returning kicks or on other special teams duty.

Mike Wallace Height: 6-0 Weight: 199 College: Mississippi Draft: 2009/3 (84) Born: 1-Aug-1986 Age: 28 Risk: Red

Year	Team	G/GS	Snaps	Rec	Pass	Yds	C%	+/-	Yd/C	TD	Drop	YAC	Rk	YAC+	BTkl	DVOA	Rk	DYAR	Rk	YAR	Short	Mid	Deep	Bomb
2011	PIT	16/14	915	72	113	1193	64%	+6.4	16.6	8	6	6.5	7	+1.7	14	31.7%	6	383	6	377	35%	38%	8%	19%
2012	PIT	15/14	833	64	119	836	54%	-3.7	13.1	8	6	4.2	39	-0.8	4	-17.4%	78	-19	77	-25	33%	38%	12%	17%
2013	MIA	16/16	951	73	141	930	52%	-4.2	12.7	5	7	3.9	67	-0.9	5	-14.8%	75	-24	77	-37	26%	44%	9%	22%
2014	*MIA*			*74*	*137*	*963*	*54%*		*13.0*	*6*						*-6.2%*								

Since he exploded onto the scene in 2009, Wallace has ranked fourth, first, eighth, 78th and 75th in DVOA. That's an absurd decline, but it's one that started in the second half of 2011. Wallace was excellent at the start of that season, but in the last eight games (including a playoff clunker in Denver) he caught 28-of-60 targets for 351 yards. That's not far from the pace he kept in a disappointing 2012 campaign. He's been outplayed by Antonio Brown and Brian Hartline the last two years. His yards per catch have decreased four years in a row. Plain and simple, Wallace is a one-trick pony and the league has caught up to his dimension of great speed. Some better deep balls from Ryan Tannehill will help, but those glory days of 2010 when Wallace was legitimately the best deep threat in the game are moments lost in time, like tears in the rain.

Nate Washington Height: 6-1 Weight: 185 College: Tiffin Draft: 2005/FA Born: 28-Aug-1983 Age: 31 Risk: Yellow

Year	Team	G/GS	Snaps	Rec	Pass	Yds	C%	+/-	Yd/C	TD	Drop	YAC	Rk	YAC+	BTkl	DVOA	Rk	DYAR	Rk	YAR	Short	Mid	Deep	Bomb
2011	TEN	16/15	846	74	121	1023	61%	+3.7	13.8	7	6	4.3	42	-0.3	3	4.7%	41	218	19	194	41%	34%	16%	10%
2012	TEN	16/14	790	46	90	746	51%	-1.0	16.2	4	4	5.3	20	+1.1	3	-3.2%	53	66	51	70	26%	36%	26%	12%
2013	TEN	16/15	886	58	104	919	56%	+3.7	15.8	3	3	4.0	66	-0.4	3	7.4%	27	162	28	165	13%	58%	14%	15%
2014	*TEN*			*50*	*94*	*686*	*53%*		*13.7*	*4*						*-3.7%*								

Washington was a rumored release target all offseason, carrying a $4.8 million cap figure and leaving no dead money behind. Fortunately for Washington, the Titans didn't seem to have much of a plan to replace him. For good reason, too: they may need him to soak up targets given the uncertainty about Justin Hunter's leap to the next level. If there's one thing Washington has proven he can do over the past few seasons, it's that.

Sammy Watkins Height: 6-1 Weight: 211 College: Clemson Draft: 2014/1 (4) Born: 14-Jun-1993 Age: 21 Risk: Red

Year	Team	G/GS	Snaps	Rec	Pass	Yds	C%	+/-	Yd/C	TD	Drop	YAC	Rk	YAC+	BTkl	DVOA	Rk	DYAR	Rk	YAR	Short	Mid	Deep	Bomb
2014	*BUF*			*69*	*120*	*841*	*58%*		*12.2*	*5*						*-3.5%*								

As the fourth overall pick in this year's draft, Watkins will enter the NFL with great expectations. While his college resume—and his selection spot—certainly suggest he will have earned that level of respect, it's important to note that he's not the traditional highly drafted receiver. Instead, think of the 6-foot-1, 211-pounder as more of a shifty, elusive YAC weapon. Watkins gained 71.3 percent of his receiving yards after the catch at Clemson, which means his skill set is more comparable to Wes Welker or Percy Harvin than to Calvin Johnson or Andre Johnson. That's not to suggest that Watkins won't be able to be a tremendous asset in the Buffalo passing game. Instead, it's important to remember that he'll make most of his yardage on screens, hitches and working over the middle.

Reggie Wayne Height: 6-0 Weight: 198 College: Miami Draft: 2001/1 (30) Born: 17-Nov-1978 Age: 36 Risk: Green

Year	Team	G/GS	Snaps	Rec	Pass	Yds	C%	+/-	Yd/C	TD	Drop	YAC	Rk	YAC+	BTkl	DVOA	Rk	DYAR	Rk	YAR	Short	Mid	Deep	Bomb
2011	IND	16/16	969	75	131	960	57%	-1.2	12.8	4	3	3.7	63	-0.7	5	1.4%	48	153	32	125	26%	44%	23%	7%
2012	IND	16/15	1079	106	196	1355	55%	-1.7	12.8	5	7	3.4	65	-1.2	4	-6.8%	64	73	47	118	29%	44%	22%	4%
2013	IND	7/7	427	38	59	503	66%	+2.6	13.2	2	3	4.6	48	+0.1	5	8.6%	25	104	44	115	34%	40%	21%	5%
2014	*IND*			*64*	*110*	*845*	*58%*		*13.2*	*6*						*4.5%*								

Wayne is probably too famous for us to claim that he's on the Derrick Mason career path, but let's lay down the facts. As medical technology continues to advance, receivers are able to play at more advanced ages. When they do decline, though, the fall is often steep and sudden. Wayne was phenomenal when healthy in 2013, and more snaps in the slot helped his advanced numbers. He's also coming off a torn ACL and will turn 36 during the 2014 season. Rod Smith made the Pro Bowl at age 35, didn't get hurt at all, and could manage only 512 yards (in 16 starts) the next season. Mason had a 61-802-7 line at age 36, then managed 13 catches with two different teams on his 2011 farewell tour. It seems likely that Wayne will pick an extreme: either he'll be fully healthy and put up a fairly vintage Wayne season, or he'll crumble and wind up out of the league in 2015. The success of his comeback could very well mirror the success of the Colts this season.

Wes Welker Height: 5-9 Weight: 190 College: Texas Tech Draft: 2004/FA Born: 1-May-1981 Age: 33 Risk: Green

Year	Team	G/GS	Snaps	Rec	Pass	Yds	C%	+/-	Yd/C	TD	Drop	YAC	Rk	YAC+	BTkl	DVOA	Rk	DYAR	Rk	YAR	Short	Mid	Deep	Bomb
2011	NE	16/15	997	122	173	1569	71%	+10.9	12.9	9	6	5.8	15	+1.2	6	20.8%	12	445	3	469	46%	39%	11%	4%
2012	NE	16/12	1074	118	175	1354	67%	+5.1	11.5	6	12	5.8	14	+0.9	8	6.1%	29	251	18	231	46%	38%	10%	6%
2013	DEN	13/13	770	73	111	778	66%	+1.7	10.7	10	8	4.4	52	-0.4	7	9.3%	24	194	25	209	54%	28%	14%	5%
2014	*DEN*			*81*	*112*	*923*	*72%*		*11.4*	*8*						*19.0%*								

Just another season from the slot receiver extraordinaire. He was used almost exclusively in that spot in three-wide packages, running mostly short routes: the shallow crosses, jerk routes, and zone void sitdowns that have been a staple of his personal game since Miami and maybe even Texas Tech. He was particularly productive on third down; unlike Eric Decker or Demaryius Thomas, Welker posted a better DVOA rating there (21.4%) than he did on first and second downs (3.2% and 5.8%, respectively). Lack of production on deep passes as he continues to age will likely continue to keep his DVOA at modest overall levels, but as long as he can avoid injuries like the concussion that cost him a couple games in 2013, he has the lateral movement skills to keep running those same routes.

Griff Whalen Height: 5-11 Weight: 197 College: Stanford Draft: 2012/FA Born: 1-Mar-1990 Age: 24 Risk: Green

Year	Team	G/GS	Snaps	Rec	Pass	Yds	C%	+/-	Yd/C	TD	Drop	YAC	Rk	YAC+	BTkl	DVOA	Rk	DYAR	Rk	YAR	Short	Mid	Deep	Bomb
2013	IND	9/3	271	24	40	259	60%	-2.2	10.8	2	2	5.0	--	+0.5	3	-2.7%	--	32	--	30	51%	26%	23%	0%
2014	*IND*			*14*	*23*	*156*	*61%*		*11.2*	*0*						*-3.1%*								

Urban Dictionary defines a "griff" as a "large, testosterone-fueled, bear-like porn star." Hmmm, that description doesn't sound anything like Griff Whalen. Whalen mainly catches underneath routes out of bunch formations and then immediately falls down before anybody actually hurts him. He's a Stanford super ally of Andrew Luck's, but that may only get him back on the practice squad if Reggie Wayne and Hakeem Nicks stay healthy.

Markus Wheaton Height: 5-11 Weight: 189 College: Oregon Draft: 2013/3 (79) Born: 7-Feb-1991 Age: 23 Risk: Red

Year	Team	G/GS	Snaps	Rec	Pass	Yds	C%	+/-	Yd/C	TD	Drop	YAC	Rk	YAC+	BTkl	DVOA	Rk	DYAR	Rk	YAR	Short	Mid	Deep	Bomb
2013	PIT	12/1	159	6	13	64	46%	-1.4	10.7	0	0	6.0	--	+0.6	0	-30.5%	--	-18	--	-14	33%	42%	8%	17%
2014	*PIT*			*52*	*82*	*724*	*63%*		*13.9*	*4*						*10.5%*								

Pittsburgh's had great finds at wide receiver in the later rounds of the draft, so when Markus Wheaton went 79th overall in 2013, there were some expectations for him as the fourth receiver. All we got was 159 offensive snaps and six forgettable catches. Roethlisberger overthrew him five times on 13 targets. A broken finger slowed Wheaton's development, but if he can hold off Martavis Bryant, there's a spot for him in the starting lineup. His measurables are eerily close to Emmanuel Sanders, who had 740 yards and six scores last year. There may be more big-play potential with Bryant, but Wheaton safely fits the prototypical build of most recent Pittsburgh receivers.

Roddy White Height: 6-1 Weight: 201 College: Alabama-Birmingham Draft: 2005/1 (27) Born: 2-Nov-1981 Age: 33 Risk: Green

Year	Team	G/GS	Snaps	Rec	Pass	Yds	C%	+/-	Yd/C	TD	Drop	YAC	Rk	YAC+	BTkl	DVOA	Rk	DYAR	Rk	YAR	Short	Mid	Deep	Bomb
2011	ATL	16/16	1020	100	180	1296	56%	+1.6	13.0	8	16	3.6	65	-0.4	8	2.0%	47	211	20	223	24%	46%	21%	8%
2012	ATL	16/15	987	92	143	1351	64%	+10.5	14.7	7	3	3.5	59	-0.5	4	16.3%	18	360	5	360	28%	46%	17%	9%
2013	ATL	13/13	782	63	97	711	65%	+2.6	11.3	3	4	1.8	89	-2.3	0	2.7%	37	118	40	117	34%	45%	14%	6%
2014	*ATL*			*83*	*125*	*989*	*66%*		*11.9*	*6*						*8.4%*								

White failed to play 16 games last season for the first time in his career, missing games due to ankle and hamstring problems, and he has reached the age where nagging injuries are likely to be a constant. He's still capable of the occasional big-game explosion (witness his 10-catch, 143-yard outing against Buffalo, or his 12-catch, 141-yard performance against San Francisco), and he's still a dangerous deep threat, with 12 catches and a DPI for 326 yards on 20 deep passes last season. But he should no longer be counted on as a true No. 1 receiver, in either real or fantasy football.

Mike Williams Height: 6-2 Weight: 221 College: Syracuse Draft: 2010/4 (101) Born: 18-May-1987 Age: 27 Risk: Green

Year	Team	G/GS	Snaps	Rec	Pass	Yds	C%	+/-	Yd/C	TD	Drop	YAC	Rk	YAC+	BTkl	DVOA	Rk	DYAR	Rk	YAR	Short	Mid	Deep	Bomb
2011	TB	16/15	965	65	124	771	52%	-7.2	11.9	3	7	3.3	72	-1.3	5	-18.1%	82	-50	82	-63	31%	48%	15%	6%
2012	TB	16/16	898	63	126	996	50%	-3.9	15.8	9	4	5.1	23	+0.8	7	-1.4%	49	62	54	117	37%	28%	17%	19%
2013	TB	6/5	362	22	40	216	55%	-3.0	9.8	2	1	3.0	--	-1.6	1	-11.4%	--	4	--	8	32%	44%	17%	7%
2014	*BUF*			*35*	*57*	*418*	*61%*		*11.9*	*3*						*3.7%*								

After three good years, the Bucs signed Williams to a six-year, $40.5 million contract in July of 2013. For their money, they got six games, two touchdowns, one stab wound to Williams' thigh (inflicted by his own brother), one arrest on criminal mischief and trespassing charges, and assorted other off-field concerns. The new Tampa Bay regime of Jason Licht and Lovie Smith owed Williams no loyalty, and were all too happy to get rid of this headache, shipping him to Buffalo for a sixth-round pick before the draft. The Bills, for their part, chose not to put all their eggs in Williams' basket, and traded up in the draft for Sammy Watkins. With Watkins and Robert Woods holding down the top spots, and Marquise Goodwin coming on the field to run shot plays, Williams will battle T.J. Graham for the position of Buffalo's fourth receiver. Given his ocean of red flags and injury history—a gimpy hamstring knocked him out for ten games last year—there is speculation that he won't even be on the Buffalo roster come opening day.

Terrance Williams Height: 6-2 Weight: 208 College: Baylor Draft: 2013/3 (74) Born: 18-Sep-1989 Age: 25 Risk: Red

Year	Team	G/GS	Snaps	Rec	Pass	Yds	C%	+/-	Yd/C	TD	Drop	YAC	Rk	YAC+	BTkl	DVOA	Rk	DYAR	Rk	YAR	Short	Mid	Deep	Bomb
2013	DAL	16/8	677	44	75	736	60%	+1.9	16.7	5	2	4.6	46	-0.1	3	3.0%	36	92	48	128	28%	41%	16%	15%
2014	*DAL*			*62*	*103*	*880*	*60%*		*14.2*	*6*						*7.7%*								

The third-round rookie out of Baylor made Miles Austin expendable with his big-play ability. His rookie stat line is eerily similar to two past debuts by Dallas wide receivers. In 1986, Mike Sherrard had 41 receptions for 744 yards and five touchdowns. In 2002, Antonio Bryant had 44 receptions for 733 yards and six touchdowns. Things never got better in Dallas for Sherrard or Bryant, but Williams is in a better situation. If you're thinking Williams has the talent to make an Alshon Jeffery-type of leap in year two, just remember that he didn't finish his rookie year strong. In the last eight games he only caught 18 passes for 292 yards and one touchdown. He only went over 50 yards in Week 16, and that's only because of a 51-yard catch that came from outright embarassing coverage by Washington. Nonetheless, Tony Romo usually maximizes his wide receivers and Williams should see the third-most targets behind Dez Bryant and Jason Witten.

Marquess Wilson Height: 6-3 Weight: 194 College: Washington State Draft: 2013/7 (236) Born: 14-Sep-1992 Age: 22 Risk: Blue

Year	Team	G/GS	Snaps	Rec	Pass	Yds	C%	+/-	Yd/C	TD	Drop	YAC	Rk	YAC+	BTkl	DVOA	Rk	DYAR	Rk	YAR	Short	Mid	Deep	Bomb
2013	CHI	10/1	75	2	3	13	67%	+0.5	6.5	0	0	4.5	--	-2.7	3	-38.5%	--	-7	--	-5	33%	67%	0%	0%
2014	*CHI*			*29*	*49*	*435*	*59%*		*15.0*	*2*						*9.0%*								

An interesting prospect. Wilson is incredibly young—he does not turn 22 until mid-September—and spent most of last season as a never-used fourth receiver, catching a three-yard pass against the Redskins and a ten-yarder in the Packers season finale. He caught 23 touchdown passes in three seasons at Washington State and has the size-speed package to stick in the NFL. With only Josh Morgan, special teamer Eric Weems, and oft-injured journeyman Domenik Hixon ahead of him and behind the starters, Wilson could easily stick as the Bears' third or fourth receiver.

Robert Woods Height: 6-0 Weight: 201 College: USC Draft: 2013/2 (41) Born: 10-Apr-1992 Age: 22 Risk: Green

Year	Team	G/GS	Snaps	Rec	Pass	Yds	C%	+/-	Yd/C	TD	Drop	YAC	Rk	YAC+	BTkl	DVOA	Rk	DYAR	Rk	YAR	Short	Mid	Deep	Bomb
2013	BUF	14/14	910	40	85	587	47%	-6.0	14.7	3	2	2.8	85	-1.4	2	-11.7%	72	6	72	-6	19%	46%	23%	12%
2014	*BUF*			*43*	*76*	*575*	*57%*		*13.4*	*4*						*0.5%*								

As a rookie, Woods was part of an offense in transition, and while he had some impressive moments, it was a growth season. He didn't have a singular defining moment in 2013, but showed a nice chemistry with EJ Manuel, and ended up playing more snaps per game than any other Buffalo receiver. If Sammy Watkins develops into the serious threat that some believe he could become—and starts to draw the attention of opposing defenses—Woods could see some really nice opportunities in 2014.

Jarius Wright Height: 5-10 Weight: 182 College: Arkansas Draft: 2012/4 (118) Born: 25-Nov-1989 Age: 25 Risk: Green

Year	Team	G/GS	Snaps	Rec	Pass	Yds	C%	+/-	Yd/C	TD	Drop	YAC	Rk	YAC+	BTkl	DVOA	Rk	DYAR	Rk	YAR	Short	Mid	Deep	Bomb
2012	MIN	7/1	206	22	36	310	61%	-0.4	14.1	2	1	5.0	--	-0.0	4	4.4%	--	68	--	32	54%	23%	9%	14%
2013	MIN	16/3	417	26	43	434	60%	+3.4	16.7	3	1	4.5	--	-0.4	4	22.7%	--	117	--	109	30%	28%	30%	13%
2014	*MIN*			*17*	*33*	*225*	*52%*		*13.2*	*0*						*-11.8%*								

Wright generated a lot of buzz with 22 catches in the final seven games of 2012. The Vikings then shoved him down the depth chart in favor of Cordarrelle Patterson and Greg Jennings an completely forgot about him until late in the year, when he again provided pockets of promising production for an offense several dice short of Yahtzee. (He caught four passes for 95 yards against the Eagles and scored two touchdowns in a lost cause against the Seahawks.) Wright is a small receiver with a field-stretching game, making him a hybrid of slot-loving Jennings and deep threat-by-default Jerome Simpson. He could beat Simpson for the No. 3 role and even swipe some touches from Jennings if given the fair opportunity he was never given in 2013.

Kendall Wright Height: 5-10 Weight: 196 College: Baylor Draft: 2012/1 (20) Born: 12-Nov-1989 Age: 25 Risk: Yellow

Year	Team	G/GS	Snaps	Rec	Pass	Yds	C%	+/-	Yd/C	TD	Drop	YAC	Rk	YAC+	BTkl	DVOA	Rk	DYAR	Rk	YAR	Short	Mid	Deep	Bomb
2012	TEN	15/5	557	64	104	626	62%	-1.4	9.8	4	4	4.9	28	-0.4	8	-14.4%	75	15	69	-2	55%	34%	7%	3%
2013	TEN	16/12	808	94	140	1079	67%	+2.3	11.5	2	8	5.9	11	+0.6	14	-3.7%	59	95	47	96	49%	33%	13%	5%
2014	*TEN*			*89*	*139*	*1088*	*64%*		*12.2*	*6*						*5.4%*								

The table above notes that Kendall Wright had a 67 percent catch rate in 2013. Consider that he was catching passes from Ryan Fitzpatrick and Jake Locker, then recalibrate what you think of that number. Wright has phenomenal hands, and he's devastatingly effective in the screen game. He's also elusive enough in the open field to do some real damage after he catches the ball. Wright is especially good at bracing for contact to stay upright. Wright's spirit animal is a healthy Randall Cobb, and if he had better quarterback play, he'd easily be a top-10 fantasy wideout. Alas, he's stuck with more of Jake Locker, with an outside chance of Charlie Whitehurst. Ick.

GOING DEEP

Jared Abbrederis, GB: The Packers calmly selected one of each type of receiver in this year's receiver-deep draft. Davante Adams is from the James Jones school of sideline burners and leapers. Jeff Janis is a big, developmental possession target. Abbrederis is a slot gobbler over the middle. Abbrederis dominated Senior Bowl practices with his ability to get open short, catch passes in traffic, adjust to bad balls and throw his body around. He then posted a 4.50 forty at the Combine, promptly earning the "sneaky speed" label because his ancestors migrated to Europe, where their skin pigment gradually lightened to facilitate the production of Vitamin D during the Ice Age. Abbrederis has a Greg Jennings skill set and upside, but he is drawing comparisons to Jordy Nelson, whose ancestors also adapted to cold European climates that required heavy clothing by decreasing melanin production.

Seyi Ajirotutu, SD: Ajirotutu is basically the next Kassim Osgood, a kickoff/punt gunner who also catches a couple passes every year. He was tied for fourth in the league with 15 special-teams tackles last year and one of his three catches was a 26-yard touchdown to beat Kansas City with 31 seconds left in Week 12. That's a pretty nice catch to have if you're only going to get three. (2013 stats: 3-for-4, 64 yards, 1 TD, 39 DYAR, 140.3% DVOA)

Danario Alexander, FA: Alexander led the league with 41.6% DVOA in 2012, averaging 17.8 yards per catch (37 catches for 658 yards and seven touchdowns). Then he tore his right ACL in last year's preseason, and FOX has reported that an infection forced multiple surgeries. His left knee was already a mess. The most likely scenario: Alexander will sit out 2014, sign somewhere in 2015, fans of that team will get excited looking at his 2012 stats, and then Alexander will realize early on in training camp that his knees just can't take it.

Anthony Armstrong, CLE: The one-time Washington deep threat played with three different teams in 2012 and none in 2013, but the Browns have brought him in as part of their "throw everything at the wall and see what sticks" Josh Gordon-replacement policy.

Jonathan Baldwin, SF: Baldwin has 44 catches through his first three seasons, which ties him with "Big" Mike Williams in 122nd place among all first-round picks since 1970. That's not a good thing. One spot above, tied for 120th place, is Cordarelle Patterson—who has caught 45 passes in one season. (2013 stats: 3-for-9, 28 yards, -29 DYAR, -55.4% DVOA)

Arrelious Benn, PHI: It's now been six years since Benn was a 1,000-yard receiver at Illinois with Juice Williams at quarterback. It feels more like sixty years. The 39th pick in the 2010 draft, Benn was immediately overshadowed by Mike Williams, who Tampa Bay found in the fourth round that year. Benn has 862 receiving yards in the NFL and only 26 yards since 2012 thanks to multiple injuries, including a torn ACL last year with the Eagles. Just getting on the field this season would be an accomplishment.

Armon Binns, MIA: Binns missed all of 2013 after tearing his ACL and MCL in training camp. He caught 24 passes in 2012 (with only -18.7% DVOA), but the Dolphins already have five receivers virtually locked into a roster spot, so there may not be enough room for a possession receiver coming off a serious knee injury.

Geraldo Boldewijn, ATL: Boldewijn grew up in the Netherlands, played one year of high school football in the U.S., and earned a scholarship offer from Boise State. In his senior season with the Broncos, he caught 39 passes for 528 yards and two touchdowns. As a UDFA, he's a long-term size play, raw but 6-foot-4 and 220 pounds.

Alan Bonner, HOU: A sixth-round 2013 pick out of FCS Jacksonville State, Bonner went to IR before the season with a hamstring injury. The bottom of Houston's receiving corps is wide open, but Bonner was a pick of the previous regime and won't be guaranteed a spot by Bill O'Brien. He's supposedly a good special-teamer, which should help the cause.

Josh Boyce, NE: Because of an injury-shortened season—as well as some self-admitted struggles with the playbook—we're not quite sure what Boyce is at this stage. Is he Bethel Johnson for a new generation? Or was he simply the Patriots annual rookie redshirt, a role filled in the past by Shane Vereen and Benjamin Watson? Regardless, with the LeGarrette Blount Kick Return Experiment now done in New England, Boyce should get a chance to work as a return man. (2013 stats: 9-for-19, 121 yards, 9 DYAR, -6.9% DVOA)

LaVon Brazill, FA: Brazill actually showed decent play at times last season, especially against the Bengals in Week 14 and the Patriots in the Divisional Round. Then he went and got himself dinged for a third time by the league's substance abuse policy. That means a one-year automatic suspension, and the Colts told him to hit the road. (2013 stats: 12-for-27, 161 yards, 2 TDs, -37 DYAR, -30.2% DVOA)

Jaron Brown, ARI: Brown barely had 1,000 receiving yards at Clemson and was sixth on the roster in receptions his senior year, so when it comes to figuring out how on earth he made the Arizona roster as an undrafted free agent, your guess is as good as ours. (2013 stats: 11-for-18, 140 yards, 1 TD, 20 DYAR, 2.5% DVOA)

John Brown, ARI: Brown is a small (5-foot-10, 180-pound) receiver who runs a sub-4.4 forty, went to an unknown football school, and got drafted in the third round. Bruce Arians has been here before with T.Y. Hilton, but this time the school is even smaller: Division II Pittsburg State in Kansas instead of Florida International.

Justin Brown, PIT: The sixth-round rookie out of Oklahoma (by way of Penn State) spent the season on Pittsburgh's practice squad after showing very little in the preseason with six catches for 44 yards (7.3 yards per reception). Brown will likely compete with former teammate Derek Moye for the last wide receiver spot.

Stephen Burton, Retired: After two years with Minnesota and one with Jacksonville, this replacement-level receiver has been forced to retire due to concussion issues. And we literally mean replacement level: last year, he caught of 8-of-13 passes for 76 yards earning -1 DYAR with -13.2% DVOA.

Brice Butler, OAK: The seventh-round rookie started the season as the Raiders' No. 3 wide receiver. When success and productivity failed to follow, Butler virtually disappeared from the offense. In the last 10 games, he was a healthy inactive five times and played 29 total snaps in the five games he was active. That typically is not a recipe for additional playing time in your second season, especially in a deeper wide receiving corps. (2013 stats: 9-for-17, 103 yards, -19 DYAR, -28.1% DVOA)

Andre Caldwell, DEN: Caldwell finally caught a couple deep passes after spending most of his career in both Cincinnati and Denver catching short passes out of the slot. The Broncos thought enough of his play to bring him back for another two seasons, though at a salary that suggests he will once again be a rarely-used fifth receiver. (2013 stats: 16-for-29, 200 yards, 3 TDs, 35 DYAR, 2.0% DVOA)

Michael Campanaro, BAL: Baltimore has a deep depth chart at wide receiver, but there's not really a dedicated slot guy. That's what seventh-rounder Campanaro (Wake Forest) can be if given the chance. He had the smallest wingspan at the combine, but has all the traits you'd want in a slot receiver. He excels against zone coverage and could learn a lot from an undersized veteran like Steve Smith. Baltimore assistant general manager Eric DeCosta gloated about Campanaro in May, saying that the Ravens were "considering paying $5 million a year this year for a slot receiver in free agency. This guy is going to be that guy in two to three years."

Austin Collie, FA: Collie was on and off the Patriots' roster in 2013 because of personnel changes and injury, but showed up on the field at some surprisingly important times, including the AFC title game and the game-winning final drive against the Saints. He clearly earned the support of Tom Brady, which means he could be the "In case of emergency, break glass" veteran receiver the Patriots usually keep on speed dial, a role formerly filled by Deion Branch. (2013 stats: 6-for-11, 63 yards, 6 DYAR, -5.5% DVOA)

Josh Cooper, MIN: Cooper was thought to have great chemistry with Brandon Weeden, who was his collegiate quarterback at Oklahoma State. Alas, that was a science experiment that went drastically wrong at the pro level. Now with Minnesota, the former high-school kicker and college punt returner will try to stick as a special-teams ace. (2013 stats: 9-for-14, 60 yards, -17 DYAR, -28.4% DVOA)

Josh Cribbs, FA: Cribbs is in the discussion for greatest returner of all-time. No, he wasn't Devin Hester's equal when it came to punt returns, but he was a better kickoff returner (and, when not compared to Hester, a heckuva punt returner, too). Unfortunately, knee and shoulder injuries have left us talking more about Cribbs' past than his future. He was unsigned at the start of training camp, but it wouldn't be a surprise if a team signs him after losing a running back/receiver/kickoff returner/punt returner/Wildcat quarterback to injury. With the Jets, he didn't display the acceleration he had early in his career, but Cribbs still has the strength and vision to be an effective returner and slash player on offense. (2013 stats: only two receptions, but 13 carries for 55 yards, 12 DYAR, 16.6% DVOA)

Juron Criner, OAK: Criner finally made it off the bench at midseason, playing 63 snaps in Week 9 against the Eagles after being a healthy inactive for the first seven games. A shoulder injury sustained that game sent him to injured reserve. To earn more playing time in his third season, his improved practice habits will have to translate to better, more explosive movement on the field. (2013 stats: 3-for-8, 32 yards, -19 DYAR, -45.2% DVOA)

Drew Davis, ATL: Davis had 17 targets last season. Not surprisingly, only one of them came before Julio Jones' injury. Jones' return in 2014 means Davis will again be fighting for a roster spot, but he made the most of his limited opportunities last year and he also played 200 snaps on special teams. A foot injury knocked Davis out for six weeks in July and August and put him on the roster bubble. (2013 stats: 12-for-17, 216 yards, 2 TDs, 88 DYAR, 51.7% DVOA)

Skye Dawson, TB: An undersized burner, Dawson was one of the fastest 100-meter sprinters in the country coming out of high school, but he failed to translate that speed into any meaningful production at TCU, never gaining more than 543 yards from scrimmage in a season. He has spent the past two years bouncing off and on the Bucs' practice squad. Given the sorry nature of the Tampa Bay receiving corps, he should get plenty of chances to show his big-play potential in camp this summer.

Kevin Dorsey, GB: Dorsey redshirted on IR after the Packers took him out of Maryland in the seventh round of the 2013 draft. He has decent size and elusiveness in space, but has had problems separating from good coverage and holding on to the football.

Weston Dressler, KC: Dressler will try to succeed where Andy Fantuz failed a couple years ago with the Bears, going from CFL All-Star with the Saskatchewan Roughriders to NFL slot receiver. He's short (5-foot-8), scrappy, gritty, and hails from North Dakota, hitting pretty much all the "Wes Welker type" clichés. He also caught 70 passes for 1,011 yards and nine touchdowns last year, with 94 catches for 1,206 yards and 13 touchdowns the year before.

Marcus Easley, BUF: Easley has been about-to-happen as a wide receiver for a long time, and it ain't happening. Instead, he happened as a special-teams dynamo last year. Easley led the league with 23 special-teams tackles, and 21 of them were "return stops," ending an opposing return short of what we would consider average expectation. No other player had more than 15 of those.

Patrick Edwards, DET: Edwards 1) is the Houston receiver who slammed into a marching band vehicle in the end zone in a game against Marshall, the incident sparking brief concerns that the NCAA might not be 100% focused on the health and overall fulfillment of its scholar athletes, as the organization claims to be and as we all know really truly is; 2) came to Detroit as an undrafted rookie in 2012 and became a Designated Minicamp Superstar in 2013, with Nate Burleson predicting that he would be "a big-time player" for the Lions; 3) caught three passes on three targets for 30 yards in the season opener; 4) suffered a high ankle sprain in the second game of the season; 5) returned to suffer an 0-for-3 day as a deep threat against the Browns, with one pass getting intercepted, one tipped, and a third arriving too far inside for a clean catch; and 6) disappeared onto the practice squad forever as the Lions tinkered with Kevin Ogletree instead. The moral of the story: Patrick Edwards has terrible luck. (2013 stats: 5-for-11, 46 yards, -21 DYAR, -37.9% DVOA)

Bruce Ellington, SF: Fourth-round pick Ellington is a former basketball player at South Carolina, though at 5-foot-9, he doesn't follow the typical college basketball to NFL model that we have seen with so many prominent tight ends. Ellington should get some reps in the slot as a rookie, where he can utilize his speed and quickness and provide an element that other members of the more veteran 49ers receiving group cannot. He's a cousin of Cardinals running back Andre Ellington.

Quincy Enunwa, NYJ: The Jets carpet-bombed the wide receiver position in this year's draft; this Nebraska product was the third guy chronologically (sixth round, 208th overall) but is the first alphabetically. Enunwa had a 53 percent catch rate and 14.8 yards per catch as Nebraska's top target in 2013. He's a long-term project who has speed, strength, and athleticism, but also struggles to track the ball in the air.

Shaquelle Evans, NYJ: Evans is one of two players named Shaq chosen in this year's draft, evidence that the kids who were conceived around when Orlando made the NBA Finals are now reaching the age of college graduation. (Fifth-round Pittsburgh cornerback Shaquille Richardson is the other.) Evans averaged 15.1 yards per catch with a 58 percent catch rate as UCLA's No.

1 target in 2013, but he was probably an overdraft. NFL Draft Scout had him listed as "7-FA" even though the Jets took him in the fourth round, and he had just 10.1 percent Playmaker Rating, one of the five lowest among this year's drafted wide receivers.

Austin Franklin, STL: Here's our Playmaker Score sleeper for 2014, who went undrafted and signed with St. Louis. In 2012, he had 1,245 receiving yards and nine touchdowns for a New Mexico State team that in total had less than 3,000 passing yards and only 19 passing touchdowns.

Jeremy Gallon, NE: A mighty-mite return man and slot receiver who put up astounding numbers as a collegian, the Patriots took him in the seventh round out of Michigan. Over the last decade-plus, New England has done well at finding value in the seventh round (Julian Edelman, Matt Cassel, David Givens, Alfonzo Dennard and Tully Banta-Cain), and Gallon could be another nice late-round pickup. He broke Michigan records in 2013 for receiving yards in a single season (1,373 yards) and a single game (369 yards vs. Indiana). He also posted good numbers as a return man, compiling 589 yards on 27 kick returns in 2010, and 192 yards on 31 punt returns in 2011.

Clyde Gates, NYJ: Gates is really fast. As a receiver, his greatest strength is that he's really fast. He doesn't have good hands and is a poor route runner, but he's really fast. Gates is now ninth on the Jets depth chart, which is exactly as dismal as it sounds. As a returner, well, the Jets signed Josh Cribbs (during the season) and Jacoby Ford (after the season) after giving Gates the kickoff returner job to start the season. (2013 stats: 12-for-24, 122 yards, -43 DYAR, -36.2% DVOA)

Brittan Golden, ARI: Golden, a second-year UDFA out of West Texas A&M, had two huge catches in 2013. First, he burned Carlos Rogers for 53 yards on his first-ever NFL catch in Week 6. Then, he launched Arizona's upset of Seattle in Week 16 with a phenomenal 63-yard catch up the seam on the opening drive, beating Jeremy Lane and evading Kam Chancellor. That may do it for Brittan Golden career highlights, as the additions of John Brown and Ted Ginn leave very little room at the bottom of the Cardinals' depth chart. (2013 stats: 4-for-10, 136 yards, 16 DYAR, 9.4% DVOA)

Ryan Grant, WAS: Our Matt Waldman pegged Tulane's Grant as a prospect with "effort" problems—a receiver who had solid raw skills, but had technical issues that got worse when he was "off." The Washington depth chart is muddy at receiver, so if Grant figures it all out, he stands to benefit.

Cobi Hamilton, CIN: Hamilton spells his first name like former US Soccer mainstay Jones, not like the beef or the Black Mamba. He was taken with the sixth-round pick the Bengals got from the Patriots for Chad Ochocinco, then spent his whole rookie year on the practice squad. The Bengals like his size and precision route-running, but the Arkansas product is a dark horse to break through and crack the roster.

Chris Harper, GB: Proof the Seahawks make mistakes in places other than the offensive line, Harper couldn't make the Seattle roster as a fourth-round pick. The 49ers picked him up, clearly didn't learn any Seattle secrets from him, then tried to make him an H-back for a few weeks and gave up. He's apparently looked very good at Green Bay OTAs but there's really no room for him on this roster.

Dwayne Harris, DAL: If there's such a thing as an underrated special teams player, Dwayne Harris would be it. Last season he ranked fourth in punt return average (12.8) and second in kick return average (30.6) while also contributing as a gunner. On offense, he caught a game-winning touchdown against Minnesota. One might imagine him as a solid slot receiver worth a few screens a year, but Harris should probably stick to special teams and let someone like Cole Beasley handle those plays. Harris caught nine of his 14 targets, but he also had four drops. (2013 stats: 9-for-14, 80 yards, 2 TDs, 20 DYAR, 7.3% DVOA)

Matt Hazel, MIA: Hazel was Coastal Carolina's leading receiver the last three years and has the ability to play the slot and on the outside. NFL Network's Daniel Jeremiah thought he was one of the best picks the Dolphins made (sixth round, 190th overall), but roster spots are limited and the Dolphins are deep at receiver. Hazel may have to settle for the practice squad in year one.

Robert Herron, TB: Not every receiver in Tampa Bay is big. At 5-foot-10 and 187 pounds, Herron will have to make a living off his speed. (He ran a 4.48-second forty-yard dash at the Combine.) At Wyoming, he led the Mountain West Conference with 21.2 yards per catch in 2012, but that average plummeted last season. The Bucs are very thin at wideout and Herron will get a chance to make the roster as a sixth-round rookie, but he's far from a lock.

Devin Hester, ATL: Hester is finished as an offensive player but still dangerous as a return man. The Falcons' longest kickoff return of last season was 34 yards and longest punt return was 25 yards, so they need a jolt. Hester is one of six players in NFL history to average over 12 yards per punt return (75 returns to qualify). George McAfee, Jack Christiansen, Claude Gibson, Bill Dudley, and Ricky Upchurch are the others. If Upchurch is the only one you have heard of, it's because all the others retired at least 49 years ago.

Domenik Hixon, Retired: Just two years ago, Hixon gained more than 500 yards receiving for the Giants. He could barely get on the field last year for the Panthers, who were not exactly loaded at wide receiver, and retired after briefly signing with Chicago. (2013 stats: 7-for-9, 55 yards, 1 TD, 11 DYAR, 2.1% DVOA)

Chris Hogan, BUF: Dubbed "7-Eleven" by Reggie Bush a few years ago on *Hard Knocks*, the former Penn State lacrosse player has shown occasional flashes while in the slot in his two years in the league. (2013 stats: 10-for-17, 83 yards, -17 DYAR, -25.3% DVOA)

Jeff Janis, GB: A big fish in the Great Lakes Intercollegiate Athletic Conference, Saginaw Valley State's Janis proved he belonged at Senior Bowl week, catching a few passes in the game itself. Janis was a big-play bomber at the Division II level but projects as a possession receiver in the NFL. Janis has two rookie draftees and three productive veterans above him on the depth chart, but the Packers find room and developmental opportunities for players of Janis' skill set.

Lestar Jean, MIN: It's an annual rite of summer: CampStar Jean gets sleeper hype in the Texans receiving corps, sees a defensive back's shadow, and can't get open against it. He moved on to the Vikings after Bill O'Brien separated some chaff from the roster, so now he's Rick Spielman's chaff. (2013 stats: 4-for-8, 35 yards, -6 DYAR, -23.0% DVOA)

A.J. Jenkins, KC: Score one for our man Matt Waldman, who rated Jenkins at 36th among wide receivers in his 2012 *Rookie Scouting Portfolio*. The 49ers, remember, took Jenkins in the first round with the 30th overall pick—30th among *all players*, not just wide receivers. He's just never developed crisp route-running skills or figured out how to deal with press coverage. Maybe the Chiefs could spot him just against teams that play mostly zones, like the football version of a platoon outfielder who only faces lefties. (2013 stats: 8-for-17, 130 yards, -18 DYAR, -27.4% DVOA)

Damaris Johnson, PHI: Johnson went from playing a little bit of wide receiver in 2012 to almost none (53 snaps) under Chip Kelly last year. He did move up to being the primary kick returner, but had to share punt-returning duties with the now departed DeSean Jackson. With Darren Sproles, albeit a 31-year-old version, in Philadelphia now, Johnson may lose some more of his return duties.

T.J. Jones, DET: The Lions' sixth-round pick, Jones was a productive receiver and return man at Notre Dame: a good route runner with some niftiness but ordinary size and speed. The NFL Draft Scout profile points out that Jones has NFL bloodlines: the son of linebacker Andre Jones (two-year veteran), nephew of defensive end Philip Daniels (15-year veteran) and godson of wide receiver Raghib Ismail (nine-year veteran)." Read that last one carefully.

Tavarres King, CAR: A sixth-round pick for Denver last season, King caught five catches for 64 yards in the preseason. The Panthers signed him in October after the Broncos cut him off their practice squad, though he never made it into a regular-season game. King flashed big-play potential at Georgia (22.6 yards per catch and nine touchdowns in his senior season) and could make an impact, given the dire state of Carolina's receivers.

Ricardo Lockette, SEA: Lockette was the only member of the Seahawks' roster with previous Super Bowl experience going into February's big game, though that stat was a bit of a ringer—he didn't actually play any snaps in San Francisco's Super Bowl XLVII loss to the Ravens, though he was in the building. Lockette has circled around the league a few times, and Seattle keeps bringing him back—in 2013, he starred on special teams and ran a few quick routes. If he can ever get the hang of the full route tree, the Seahawks could have something there. (2013 stats: 5-for-7, 82 yards, 27 DYAR, 41.3% DVOA)

Jeff Maehl, PHI: Undrafted out of Oregon in 2011, Maehl was reunited with Chip Kelly last season when the Eagles traded offensive tackle Nate Menkin for him. At the 2011 combine, Maehl ran one of the fastest three-cone drills (6.42 seconds) in recent history. He saw little action with the Eagles, making his two most notable catches against Denver with the Eagles trailing 52-13 in the fourth quarter. His touchdown reception was just a little bubble screen. With two new rookies in town, it will be hard to find opportunities to contribute in 2014. (2013 stats: 4-for-9, 67 yards, 1 TD, 11 DYAR, 3.5% DVOA)

Marvin McNutt, CAR: Released by the Eagles in May and the Dolphins in August, McNutt was signed by the Panthers in October and saw the field for all of four snaps in a late-season game against Atlanta. So of course, he was one of the few receivers in Carolina who kept his job, though there's no guarantee he'll last till opening day.

Donte Moncrief, IND: Running a 4.34-second forty-yard dash is one way to get noticed when you are a 221-pound wideout. If you need a "veteran" narrative to apply here, it's that third-rounder Moncrief will do wonders for his career working with Reggie Wayne. Right now the Ole Miss speedster lacks route-running refinement. Indianapolis was the best possible place for him to end up. Don't expect to see much of him on the field this year unless injuries strike, but don't sleep on him in 2015.

Derek Moye, PIT: The Penn State product caught his first career target: a one-yard fade touchdown over Cincinnati's Leon Hall. Despite his 6-foot-5 height advantage and Ben Roethlisberger's fetish for tall receivers, Moye had just five more targets and one catch the rest of the season. The additions of Lance Moore, Darrius Heyward-Bey and Martavis Bryant will make it hard for Moye to make the roster again.

Louis Murphy, TB: Murphy is now on his fourth team in four years. At Florida, he showed ridiculous speed and questionable hands; that reputation has only been enforced after his time in Oakland and one-year pit stops with the Panthers and Giants. If you came to the Going Deep section of the book looking for trivia, you're in the right place. Of the 149 players in the NFL with at least 10 targets in each of the last three years, Murphy is the only player to catch fewer than half of his targets in each season. (2013 stats: 6-for-13, 37 yards, 1 TD, -50 DYAR, -61.2% DVOA)

Kevin Norwood, SEA: For all their success in 2013, the Seahawks' red-zone passing offense was nothing to write home about. They ranked 21st in DVOA in that category and 22nd in goal-to-go DVOA, with Zach Miller and Jermaine Kearse as the primary targets. Norwood, who scored seven receiving touchdowns on just 38 catches for the Crimson Tide last season, could help a lot in that department. "He's [got] a big strike zone, even bigger than 6-foot-2," Southeast area scout Jim Nagy said of Norwood after the Seahawks took him in the fourth round. "He's got a knack for high-pointing the ball."

Kassim Osgood, SF: If he makes the opening day roster this year, Osgood will tie Steve Tasker for most seasons playing as a "wide receiver" and finishing with 20 or fewer receptions, with 12 such seasons each. Osgood will likely not get prominent support from some media members for a spot in Canton, like Tasker has, but he has been a very good all-purpose special-teamer for a long time.

Eric Page, TB: An undrafted rookie out of Toledo, Page was the Bucs' primary kickoff and punt returner in 2013. He did OK on punts, but Tampa Bay's kickoff returns were among the league's worst. In college, he had three 1,000-yard receiving seasons, and returned five kicks for scores. He also ran for one touchdown and passed for four more, so there's certainly something to work with here. (2013 stats: 4-for-9, 68 yards, -6 DYAR, -21.4% DVOA)

Kealoha Pilares, CAR: Pilares has two receptions in his NFL career, both in 2012. That makes the him the only wideout on the Carolina roster who has ever caught a pass in a Panthers uniform. He missed the 2013 campaign with a torn ACL suffered in the final preseason game. Joe Person of the *Charlotte News & Observer* called Pilares "almost a lock to make the team," primarily because of his return ability—he scored a 101-yard touchdown on a kickoff return as a rookie in 2011.

Walter Powell, ARI: Maybe the Cardinals are just trying to screw with us by drafting two different non-FBS receivers this year. John Brown is the one who actually matters. Sixth-rounder Powell may be Murray State's all-time leading receiver, but he's not particularly tall or fast. Destined for the practice squad.

Michael Preston, TEN: Hailing out of powerhouse Heidelberg University, Preston saw field time due to injuries and caught two touchdowns in a ridiculous shootout against Arizona. The bottom of the Titans receiving depth chart is wide open, so he has a chance to stick as a fourth receiver. (2013 stats: 5-for-7, 37 yards, 2 TDs, 21 DYAR, 25.7% DVOA)

David Reed, SF: Reed opened the season as the main kick returner for the Colts, which is an amazing accomplishment for someone who returned kicks by closing his eyes and running as fast as he could. Now with the 49ers, he'll be battling Kassim Osgood and Devon Wylie for a chance as a bottom-of-the-roster special-teams "receiver."

Tevin Reese, SD: A San Diego seventh-round pick who played next to Kendall Wright and Terrance Williams at Baylor, Reese explodes off the line of scrimmage, has rare leaping ability, and desperately needs a sandwich. Or, at 5-foot-10 and only 163 pounds, like a hundred sandwiches. Averaged 22.8 yards per catch as a senior with a 58 percent catch rate.

Jeremy Ross, DET: The Packers waived Ross after he fumbled a kickoff return in September. The Lions gobbled him up, and it was one of their best moves of the season. Ross returned both a kickoff and a punt for touchdowns in the Eagles Snow Bowl, added a 50-yard punt return against the Giants, and took a pair of reverses 24 and 16 yards. There are not many footballs to go around in the passing game, but Ross is a perfect fit as a dollar-conscious double-duty return man. (2013 stats: 6-for-12, 67 yards, 1 TD, 6 DYAR, -6.8% DVOA)

Greg Salas, NYJ: Salas has played with Marty Mornhinweg in New York and Philadelphia, which gives him a leg up on some of the team's new additions. He's a longshot to make the roster, but is a solid route runner with decent hands. He is a cautionary tale of the danger of being a late-round pick. Salas did not play well as a rookie with the Rams, and then he got typecast as a late-round pick who couldn't make it with his first NFL team. A higher-round pick with a similar skill set would have been given more opportunities after an initial struggle; had Salas received that, he could have turned into a legitimate NFL receiver instead of constantly being on the roster bubble. (2013 stats: 8-for-13, 143 yards, 40 DYAR, 28.5% DVOA)

Dane Sanzenbacher, CIN: Jon Gruden turned him into the most notable Dane since Hamlet by screaming "SANZENBACHER" over and over during a dominant preseason performance on ESPN. With Andrew Hawkins gone upstate, Sanzenbacher has a chance to go from surname curio to regular contributor, and hear his name screamed from the heavens during the regular season. (2013 stats: 6-for-8, 61 yards, 13 DYAR, 9.2% DVOA)

Jalen Saunders, NYJ: The first receiver the Jets took this year (fourth round, 104th overall) is supposed to be fast with the ability to make guys miss, but then where was the yardage in college? After Saunders transferred from Fresno State, he averaged just 12.7 yards per catch over two seasons with Oklahoma, though he did have an absurd 82 percent catch rate as the Sooners' No. 3 target in 2012. Saunders is also teeny-tiny, just 5-foot-9 and 163 pounds.

Russell Shepard, TB: Shepard rarely saw the field at LSU, and with all due respect to one of college football's top programs, backups in college rarely accomplish much in the pros. Shepard had only 32 snaps on offense last year and never touched the ball, but he was fourth on the team in special-teams snaps and did force a fumble. That will help him hang onto the bottom of the Tampa Bay wide-receiver depth chart.

Matthew Slater, NE: A wide receiver in name only, Slater's speed and smarts have allowed him to become an absolutely vital part of New England's coverage teams. Still, he tends to be good for two or three targets per year.

Brad Smith, PHI: Smith was actually on Buffalo's injured reserve list last season before being released and signed by Philadelphia in November. He only played 20 snaps on offense, but Chip Kelly could find some interesting ways to get Smith touches. He has always been a jack-of-all-trades, doing everything from the Wildcat to wide receiver and return specialist. What Smith doesn't do is anything with great volume. He averages 3.0 touches per game in his career.

Rodney Smith, MIN: Smith is a 2013 UDFA out of Florida State hovering around the edges of the Vikings depth chart; his prime attributes are height (6-foot-5) and a willingness to play special teams.

Ryan Spadola, MIA: Undrafted out of Lehigh, Spadola had a 70-yard reception in the preseason for the Jets. He was released after 45 snaps with the team, only to be signed to rival Miami's practice squad. If the Jets didn't want him for their lowly receiving corps, then that might be a red flag, but he was dominant in the Patriot League and ran a very good forty (4.48 seconds) for someone in a possession receiver mold.

Brandon Stokley, Retired: In 2012 with Denver, Stokley caught 45-of-59 passes (76.3 percent) from Peyton Manning—one of the best catch rates on record. Returning to the team which drafted him, Baltimore, Stokley faced the Broncos in the 2013 season opener. On the third play of the game, Stokley caught a pass with no one within eight yards of him. He still came up two yards short of the first down on one of the slowest plays of the year, signifying it was about time for the 37-year-old slot receiver to hang up the cleats. Stokley did retire at season's end after a solid 15-year-career. (2013 stats: 13-for-21, 115 yards, -6 DYAR, -16.5% DVOA)

Devin Street, DAL: Street caught more passes at Pitt than Larry Fitzgerald, so there's an attention-grabber. Dez Bryant is the No. 1 target, Terrance Williams can be the deep threat, but there's a need for Street in the slot where his 6-foot-3 size can offer some mismatches the Cowboys will never get with the 5-foot-8 Cole Beasley. Without much else on the depth chart at receiver, Street should get ample opportunities to produce this season, which would put him ahead of schedule for where most thought he was as a fifth-round pick.

Julian Talley, NYG: The Giants signed Talley as a 2012 UDFA, hoping to strike gold twice with Massachusetts wide receivers. Talley was on the Giants' practice squad in 2012 and most of 2013, before getting a late December call up—ironically, after concussion issues ended Victor Cruz's season. His biggest asset may be a 41.5-inch vertical leap, but he's going to need to impress on special teams to earn a roster spot in 2014.

Brandon Tate, CIN: Despite wailing from the Cincinnati fans, Tate was re-signed to handle the primary return duties. As a receiver, Tate lacks precision and suddenness in his routes, making him a one-note weapon based on his speed, which isn't what it once was.

Deonte Thompson, BAL: Missing Anquan Boldin and tight end Dennis Pitta, Baltimore played a lot of different receivers last season, but Thompson trailed the pack of Torrey Smith, Marlon Brown, Jacoby Jones, Tandon Doss and Brandon Stokley. He had 50 receiving yards against Buffalo, but just 46 yards the rest of the season. With Steve Smith in town, Thompson will have to battle for the fifth receiver spot. (2013 stats: 10-for-19, 96 yards, 13 DYAR, -4.3% DVOA)

Nick Toon, NO: A fourth-round draft pick in 2012, Toon missed his entire rookie season with a foot injury, then spent most of 2013 as a healthy inactive. With Lance Moore gone, there is a spot available for Toon on the Saints roster if he can earn it. But clearly, it's put up or shut up time for the former Wisconsin Badger. (2013 stats: 4-for-12, 68 yards, -23 DYAR, -39.9% DVOA)

Bryan Walters, SEA: Walters' career "highlight" might be the fact that he was the guy the Seahawks brought up from the practice squad when Brandon Browner started serving his most recent suspension. He'll stay in the league as a special-teamer, and Pete Gogolak's status as the most prominent Cornell alum will be unthreatened... though friend of FO and fellow former Big Red Seth Payne would argue that as a kicker, Gogolak isn't the best representative, either. Well, there's always Kevin Boothe, we suppose...

Eric Weems, CHI: As the veteran replacement for Devin Hester, this all-purpose special-teamer has an incredibly important job in Chicago. It just does not involve catching passes. He's caught three of them in the last two seasons.

Ryan Whalen, CIN: Whalen is a poor man's Dane Sanzenbacher, which means unless there are several injuries he's a long shot for the Bengals roster.

Myles White, GB: A rookie free agent in 2013, White made the Packers roster because rookie free agents often make the Packers roster. He briefly climbed to No. 3 receiver status when James Jones and Randall Cobb were in various states of disability, catching five passes against the Vikings in Week 7. With Cobb back and three draftees vying for spots on the receiver depth chart, White faces a numbers crunch. (2013 stats: 9-for-12, 66 yards, -21 DYAR, -36.0% DVOA)

Damian Williams, MIA: Williams is a versatile receiver with experience both outside and in the slot, but he mysteriously fell out of favor with the Munchak administration. A violation of team rules that left him off the roster for the Arizona game could have been a factor. Now with the Dolphins, he's got a chance to stick at the bottom of the roster, but it would be better one if he played special teams. (2013 stats: 15-for-23, 178 yards, 46 DYAR, 12.8% DVOA)

Kyle Williams, KC: The Chiefs picked up Williams after the 49ers cut him halfway through last season, and in his first game with Kansas City, he promptly tore his left ACL for the second straight year. The Chiefs re-signed him in the offseason but he's a long shot to make the roster. (2013 stats: 12-for-27, 113 yards, -68 DYAR, -46.8% DVOA)

Nick Williams, WAS: Connecticut's Nick Williams signed with Washington as a 2013 UDFA. He didn't make final cuts, but stuck on the practice squad, and returned kicks after Chris Thompson hit IR. Being a part of the 2013 Washington special teams is not what you want on your resume going forward, especially when you're at the very bottom of the depth chart. (2013 stats: 3-for-11, 15 yards, -47 DYAR, -63.7% DVOA)

Stephen Williams, MIA: Williams has hung around as an UDFA out of Toledo since 2010, latching on to the end of rosters in Arizona, Seattle, and Jacksonville. Jacksonville released him after the draft, and the Dolphins swooped him up. You'd have to think if he was going to make an NFL impact it would've happened by now.

James Wright, CIN: The Matt Cassel of wideouts, Wright was drafted in the seventh round despite being stuck behind Odell Beckham and Jarvis Landry on LSU's depth chart. His future in Cincy is on special teams, where he was the Tigers' MVP in 2013.

Devon Wylie, SF: The Chiefs selected Wylie in the fourth round of the 2012 draft, but the John Dorsey/Andy Reid administration waived him to keep Chad Hall. He caught on with the Titans practice squad, was promoted as a kick returner after the Darius Reynaud experiment ended, and then subsequently let go. Wylie was highly-regarded as a slot fit by our Matt Waldman before he came out, but he's never really had an opportunity to show it. San Francisco's crowded depth chart at receiver is probably also not that place.

Tight Ends

Top 20 TE by DYAR (Total Value), 2013

Rank	Player	Team	DYAR
1	Jimmy Graham	NO	223
2	Julius Thomas	DEN	214
3	Vernon Davis	SF	199
4	Tony Gonzalez	ATL	135
5	Jason Witten	DAL	134
6	Tim Wright	TB	133
7	Ladarius Green	SD	113
8	Jeff Cumberland	NYJ	112
9	Jordan Cameron	CLE	99
10	Jordan Reed	WAS	98
11	Rob Gronkowski	NE	91
12	Brent Celek	PHI	89
13	Charles Clay	MIA	88
14	Greg Olsen	CAR	83
15	Jermichael Finley	GB	68
16	Martellus Bennett	CHI	65
17	Joseph Fauria	DET	64
18	Antonio Gates	SD	63
19	Mychal Rivera	OAK	60
20	Zach Ertz	PHI	60

Top 20 TE by DVOA (Value per Play), 2013

Rank	Player	Team	DVOA
1	Ladarius Green	SD	45.3%
2	Jeff Cumberland	NYJ	38.0%
3	Vernon Davis	SF	29.3%
4	Julius Thomas	DEN	27.0%
5	Jermichael Finley	GB	25.8%
6	Joseph Fauria	DET	24.2%
7	Jacob Tamme	DEN	23.7%
8	Tim Wright	TB	21.8%
9	Jordan Reed	WAS	19.5%
10	Brent Celek	PHI	18.3%
11	Luke Willson	SEA	18.2%
12	Jimmy Graham	NO	15.7%
13	Ryan Griffin	HOU	13.9%
14	Rob Gronkowski	NE	12.9%
15	Jason Witten	DAL	11.2%
16	Kellen Winslow	NYJ	9.9%
17	Zach Ertz	PHI	9.8%
18	Tony Gonzalez	ATL	8.7%
19	Mychal Rivera	OAK	8.1%
20	Charles Clay	MIA	6.0%

Minimum 25 passes.

Dwayne Allen Height: 6-3 Weight: 255 College: Clemson Draft: 2012/3 (64) Born: 24-Feb-1990 Age: 24 Risk: Yellow

Year	Team	G/GS	Snaps	Rec	Pass	Yds	C%	+/-	Yd/C	TD	Drop	YAC	Rk	YAC+	BTkl	DVOA	Rk	DYAR	Rk	YAR	Short	Mid	Deep	Bomb
2012	IND	16/16	905	45	66	521	68%	+1.7	11.6	3	2	5.4	9	+0.9	1	14.9%	9	67	15	86	47%	45%	3%	5%
2013	IND	1/1	30	1	2	20	50%	-0.1	20.0	1	0	5.0	--	+1.0	1	84.3%	--	12	--	14	0%	50%	50%	0%
2014	*IND*			*50*	*75*	*615*	*67%*	*--*	*12.3*	*6*						*20.9%*								

Allen's lone catch of the season was a beauty—a 20-yard touchdown reception where he demonstrated a lot of functional technique. A hip injury knocked him out for the rest of the season. His 2012 was very promising, and he was a plus as a blocker as well as a receiver. Seven months after surgery he was running at OTAs. If healthy, he could perform at a low-end fantasy TE1 level. Considering he'll be off the maps of most fantasy players, that should make him a tempting late-rounder.

Jace Amaro Height: 6-5 Weight: 265 College: Texas Tech Draft: 2014/2 (49) Born: 6/26/1992 Age: 22 Risk: Green

Year	Team	G/GS	Snaps	Rec	Pass	Yds	C%	+/-	Yd/C	TD	Drop	YAC	Rk	YAC+	BTkl	DVOA	Rk	DYAR	Rk	YAR	Short	Mid	Deep	Bomb
2014	*NYJ*			*29*	*49*	*341*	*59%*	*--*	*11.8*	*1*						*-1.1%*								

Amaro had a breakout performance against West Virginia in 2012, picking up 156 yards and a touchdown on five catches. But he suffered a lacerated spleen on a collision in the first half, causing him to miss most of the rest of his sophomore year. Then he came back with a vengeance for his junior season, and led the Big 12 in both receptions and receiving yards. Against Oklahoma State, Amaro caught 15 passes for 174 yards, one of six times he caught at least eight passes and gained 110 yards. Amaro struggled in OTAs with the Jets, and acknowledged to being overwhelmed by the speed of the pro game. But he's a huge target and has the strength to turn into a good blocker: his 28 reps in the bench press were the most of any FBS tight end at the combine.

Martellus Bennett Height: 6-6 Weight: 259 College: Texas A&M Draft: 2008/2 (61) Born: 10-Mar-1987 Age: 27 Risk: Green

Year	Team	G/GS	Snaps	Rec	Pass	Yds	C%	+/-	Yd/C	TD	Drop	YAC	Rk	YAC+	BTkl	DVOA	Rk	DYAR	Rk	YAR	Short	Mid	Deep	Bomb
2011	DAL	14/7	418	17	26	144	65%	+0.1	8.5	0	1	5.6	8	-0.5	1	-23.8%	41	-24	35	-16	65%	22%	9%	4%
2012	NYG	16/16	928	55	90	626	61%	-1.3	11.4	5	8	3.6	35	-0.9	3	4.6%	20	85	11	64	31%	48%	13%	9%
2013	CHI	16/15	951	65	94	759	69%	+5.9	11.7	5	5	5.7	11	+0.4	14	3.4%	23	65	16	59	51%	38%	7%	5%
2014	*CHI*			*62*	*93*	*749*	*67%*	*--*	*12.1*	*5*						*15.8%*								

The Black Unicorn has finally found a home. The Cowboys did not know what to do with him, the Giants are content to rent their tight ends a year at a time, but Marc Trestman found what he wanted: a solid blocker who can be split wide, stretch the seam, and basically eliminate the need for a slot receiver in most packages. Seven of Bennett's 11 receptions of 20+ yards came in the second half of the season, a sign that Bennett, Trestman, and the quarterbacks were growing more comfortable with one another.

Jordan Cameron Height: 6-5 Weight: 220 College: USC Draft: 2011/4 (102) Born: 7-Aug-1988 Age: 26 Risk: Yellow

Year	Team	G/GS	Snaps	Rec	Pass	Yds	C%	+/-	Yd/C	TD	Drop	YAC	Rk	YAC+	BTkl	DVOA	Rk	DYAR	Rk	YAR	Short	Mid	Deep	Bomb
2011	CLE	2/1	59	6	13	33	46%	-2.9	5.5	0	2	2.0	--	-2.2	0	-52.7%	--	-41	--	-51	50%	36%	14%	0%
2012	CLE	14/6	329	20	40	226	50%	+0.4	11.3	1	0	5.4	8	+1.1	1	-13.5%	39	-28	39	-30	48%	35%	10%	6%
2013	CLE	15/14	969	80	118	917	68%	+11.6	11.5	7	1	3.0	45	-1.6	0	5.6%	21	99	9	79	39%	40%	15%	6%
2014	*CLE*			*76*	*124*	*918*	*61%*	*--*	*12.1*	*5*						*0.4%*								

The former USC hoops player was frequently mistaken for Cameron Jordan of the Saints until he realized his potential as a mismatch nightmare last season under tight end whisperers Rob Chudzinski and Norv Turner. A concussion ended his season after 14 games but Cameron established himself as both an open-field and red-zone difference maker. Now he wants to get broken off, as the kids say. He fired his agent and is seeking a new contract. But Chud and Norv are gone, and the Browns may well wait until Cameron proves himself in Kyle Shanahan's system before paying or franchising him.

John Carlson Height: 6-4 Weight: 255 College: Notre Dame Draft: 2008/2 (38) Born: 12-May-1984 Age: 30 Risk: Yellow

Year	Team	G/GS	Snaps	Rec	Pass	Yds	C%	+/-	Yd/C	TD	Drop	YAC	Rk	YAC+	BTkl	DVOA	Rk	DYAR	Rk	YAR	Short	Mid	Deep	Bomb
2012	MIN	14/6	249	8	14	43	57%	-1.8	5.4	0	1	2.3	--	-2.9	0	-49.6%	--	-38	--	-44	50%	50%	0%	0%
2013	MIN	13/8	497	32	47	344	68%	+1.5	10.8	1	1	4.8	25	-0.6	1	-14.6%	47	-24	44	-11	47%	44%	9%	0%
2014	*ARI*			*33*	*46*	*269*	*72%*	*--*	*8.1*	*2*						*-6.4%*								

The Top Three Places to Live for a Notre Dame tight end: 1) Notre Dame. 2) Arizona, where Bruce Arians loves three-tight end sets and drafted Troy Niklas. 3) Minnesota, where the Vikings found multiple ways to get John Carlson and Kyle Rudolph on the field at the same time before both got injured. A concussion knocked Carlson out of action in 2013, but he still found his way from the third to the second-best location on our list! One year in Arizona, another playing third string behind Tyler Eifert in Cincinnati, and Carlson can call it a career.

Brent Celek Height: 6-4 Weight: 261 College: Cincinnati Draft: 2007/5 (162) Born: 25-Jan-1985 Age: 29 Risk: Green

Year	Team	G/GS	Snaps	Rec	Pass	Yds	C%	+/-	Yd/C	TD	Drop	YAC	Rk	YAC+	BTkl	DVOA	Rk	DYAR	Rk	YAR	Short	Mid	Deep	Bomb
2011	PHI	16/16	945	62	97	811	64%	-0.2	13.1	5	5	7.5	1	+1.8	8	2.6%	22	99	14	92	51%	29%	17%	2%
2012	PHI	15/14	861	57	87	684	66%	-0.1	12.0	1	8	5.4	10	+0.0	4	-12.8%	38	23	30	15	46%	36%	17%	1%
2013	PHI	16/15	845	32	51	502	63%	+0.7	15.7	6	3	8.8	5	+3.2	2	18.3%	10	89	12	100	52%	23%	21%	4%
2014	*PHI*			*40*	*61*	*422*	*66%*	*--*	*10.6*	*3*						*0.5%*								

We've deemed Celek a "boring" tight end in the past, so to spice things up, picture him strutting around the team facility with "Don't You (Forget About Me)" blasting as he defiantly fist-pumps the air. He took to heart your second-round selection of Zach Ertz, Chip Kelly. Maybe Ertz takes over this year, but last season, Celek was still the best tight end in Philadelphia. He had his highest DVOA since 2009 and his 15.7 yards-per-catch average was easily the highest of his career. He led Philadelphia's main receivers in DVOA on first-down passes (40.4%) with play action helping to produce four of his biggest gains of the season. Celek has the versatility to play in the slot and out wide, though Kelly was using Ertz out wide more last season. Even though Celek's best days are behind him, he can still be an effective and important part of this evolving offense.

Scott Chandler Height: 6-7 Weight: 270 College: Iowa Draft: 2007/4 (129) Born: 23-Jul-1985 Age: 29 Risk: Green

Year	Team	G/GS	Snaps	Rec	Pass	Yds	C%	+/-	Yd/C	TD	Drop	YAC	Rk	YAC+	BTkl	DVOA	Rk	DYAR	Rk	YAR	Short	Mid	Deep	Bomb
2011	BUF	14/9	523	38	46	389	83%	+8.2	10.2	6	0	4.0	31	-0.3	1	27.1%	4	112	10	116	57%	39%	5%	0%
2012	BUF	15/13	746	43	74	571	58%	-1.4	13.3	6	3	4.4	18	+0.6	0	1.2%	25	52	20	61	27%	57%	14%	1%
2013	BUF	16/7	918	53	81	655	65%	+3.6	12.4	2	4	5.2	15	+0.7	3	-1.3%	33	32	28	26	39%	44%	16%	1%
2014	*BUF*			*54*	*83*	*638*	*65%*	*--*	*11.8*	*4*						*11.8%*								

It was an odd offseason for the fairly reliable Chandler, who got a wildly lukewarm reception on the free-agent market. After finding little action, he returned to Buffalo for a two-year deal worth an average of just under $2.4 per season. The $1.2 million signing bonus is actually less than he made last year—despite the fact that he had a career-best (and team-best) 53 catches. A list of similar tight ends over a three-year span is much better than you might expect, starting with Heath Miller (2009-2011) before moving on to Bennie Cunningham (1980-1982), Jay Novacek (1989-1991), and Owen Daniels (2009-2011).

Dallas Clark Height: 6-3 Weight: 257 College: Iowa Draft: 2003/1 (24) Born: 12-Jun-1979 Age: 35 Risk: #N/A

Year	Team	G/GS	Snaps	Rec	Pass	Yds	C%	+/-	Yd/C	TD	Drop	YAC	Rk	YAC+	BTkl	DVOA	Rk	DYAR	Rk	YAR	Short	Mid	Deep	Bomb
2011	IND	11/10	544	34	65	352	52%	-9.4	10.4	2	9	4.4	27	-0.1	2	-25.4%	43	-61	44	-82	61%	34%	5%	0%
2012	TB	16/7	568	47	75	435	63%	-1.5	9.3	4	2	2.4	48	-1.6	1	-14.5%	40	-60	45	-19	43%	49%	7%	1%
2013	BAL	12/0	369	31	52	343	60%	-3.5	11.1	3	2	5.8	8	+1.4	1	-9.7%	40	-8	40	4	63%	29%	6%	2%

Clark retired in June after 11 seasons with the Colts, Buccaneers and Ravens. He's one of five tight ends in NFL history to reach 500 receptions, 5,000 receiving yards and 50 touchdown receptions. The others? Shannon Sharpe, Tony Gonzalez, Antonio Gates and Jason Witten. Clark wasn't the same caliber as those players, but his highlight reel will compare favorably. Just watch his third-down catch against the 2006 Ravens in the playoffs and ponder how he and Peyton Manning were able to make that connection against such great coverage.

Charles Clay Height: 6-3 Weight: 239 College: Tulsa Draft: 2011/6 (174) Born: 13-Feb-1989 Age: 25 Risk: Yellow

Year	Team	G/GS	Snaps	Rec	Pass	Yds	C%	+/-	Yd/C	TD	Drop	YAC	Rk	YAC+	BTkl	DVOA	Rk	DYAR	Rk	YAR	Short	Mid	Deep	Bomb
2011	MIA	14/9	395	16	25	233	64%	+1.1	14.6	3	2	5.0	50	-0.3	0	62.5%	1	119	6	124	48%	12%	28%	12%
2012	MIA	14/9	333	18	33	212	55%	-0.4	11.8	2	2	4.5	17	-1.1	1	-16.0%	41	-19	38	-14	50%	21%	25%	4%
2013	MIA	16/15	855	69	102	759	68%	+3.5	11.0	6	5	5.2	16	+0.5	13	6.0%	20	88	13	92	49%	40%	9%	2%
2014	*MIA*			*54*	*83*	*631*	*65%*	*--*	*11.7*	*5*						*5.5%*								

Dustin Keller's injury wasn't all bad news for the Dolphins. For all the things that went wrong with Miami's offense last year, the breakout season of Charles Clay, the human Swiss Army Knife, was a bright spot. We charted him with 90 appearances in the backfield, 36 plays split out wide, and 247 times he was flexed/in the slot. Miami moved him around everywhere and pretty much asked him to do everything but play quarterback. Maybe if he did, the Dolphins would have scored some points in Weeks 16-17. Among tight ends with at least 40 touches, only Martellus Bennett and Jermaine Gresham had a higher rate of broken tackles than Clay (17.1 percent). Clay's effort on a poorly thrown fourth-down bubble screen against the Patriots (Week 15) saved a game-winning drive. Miami's been spending mid-round picks on the position, but Clay, a sixth-round pick in 2011, is the answer at tight end. He doesn't have prototypical size, but that's why he can move around and do so many different things for Joe Philbin's offense.

Table 1. Top 10 Tight Ends Lined Up as Fullbacks, 2013

Player	Team	Snaps
Cory Harkey	STL	274
Michael Egnew	MIA	99
Gary Barnidge	CLE	91
Charles Clay	MIA	90
Logan Paulsen	WAS	89
Tyler Eifert	CIN	82
Richie Brockel	CAR	73
Jim Dray	ARI	73
Alex Smith	CIN	73
Bear Pascoe	NYG	72

Jared Cook Height: 6-6 Weight: 246 College: South Carolina Draft: 2009/3 (89) Born: 7-Apr-1987 Age: 27 Risk: Green

Year	Team	G/GS	Snaps	Rec	Pass	Yds	C%	+/-	Yd/C	TD	Drop	YAC	Rk	YAC+	BTkl	DVOA	Rk	DYAR	Rk	YAR	Short	Mid	Deep	Bomb
2011	TEN	16/5	601	49	81	759	60%	+4.2	15.5	3	1	5.7	7	+1.3	4	12.3%	16	99	13	90	30%	58%	9%	3%
2012	TEN	13/5	471	44	72	523	61%	+0.4	11.9	4	4	3.8	30	-0.5	3	-3.7%	33	9	34	13	45%	37%	12%	6%
2013	STL	16/13	718	51	86	671	59%	+0.5	13.2	5	6	5.1	19	+0.7	1	2.8%	24	58	21	65	39%	41%	16%	5%
2014	*STL*			*50*	*80*	*635*	*63%*	*--*	*12.7*	*4*						*9.8%*								

A maddening player for a maddening offense. Cook fumbled while running for a touchdown in the season opener and spent the rest of the season finding creative ways to frustrate, dropping six passes while showing his usual indifference to blocking, beating a jam, or breaking a tackle. Cook admitted at the end of last season that he was disappointed at his performance, and self-knowledge will go a long way toward seeing the back end of the loopy $35 million contract he signed. Cook is just as fast as the big-name tight ends and can catch the ball just as well when he is focused. His numbers will improve if the Rams offense sorts itself out or he helps sort it; there's a disturbing chance, however, that neither event will happen.

Jeff Cumberland Height: 6-4 Weight: 249 College: Illinois Draft: 2010/FA Born: 2-May-1987 Age: 27 Risk: Green

Year	Team	G/GS	Snaps	Rec	Pass	Yds	C%	+/-	Yd/C	TD	Drop	YAC	Rk	YAC+	BTkl	DVOA	Rk	DYAR	Rk	YAR	Short	Mid	Deep	Bomb
2011	NYJ	3/0	47	2	5	35	40%	-1.1	17.5	0	1	8.5	--	+0.9	0	-40.8%	--	-6	--	-9	40%	20%	40%	0%
2012	NYJ	15/12	592	29	53	359	55%	-4.1	12.4	3	3	3.9	29	-0.4	2	-8.5%	36	-12	37	-8	36%	36%	25%	4%
2013	NYJ	15/12	675	26	39	398	67%	+2.1	15.3	4	2	5.9	7	+0.9	3	38.0%	2	112	8	118	33%	36%	26%	5%
2014	*NYJ*			*29*	*50*	*374*	*58%*	*--*	*12.9*	*3*						*5.5%*								

How did Cumberland finish as the No. 2 tight end in DVOA? One reason was his efficiency on third downs, where he converted five of his eight opportunities, with two going for touchdowns. Cumberland spent the year as part of a committee, but only produced 11 catches for 134 yards and one touchdown in the four weeks when Kellen Winslow was suspended. He dealt with concussion injuries in the first half of the season, though, and perhaps those limited his play more than the team let on. He signed a three-year contract extension worth $5.7 million in March, so the team is interested in retaining him. But the drafting of Jace Amaro shows that the Jets view him as a role player and a capable blocker, not as a true difference maker at the position.

Owen Daniels Height: 6-3 Weight: 245 College: Wisconsin Draft: 2006/4 (98) Born: 9-Nov-1982 Age: 32 Risk: Green

Year	Team	G/GS	Snaps	Rec	Pass	Yds	C%	+/-	Yd/C	TD	Drop	YAC	Rk	YAC+	BTkl	DVOA	Rk	DYAR	Rk	YAR	Short	Mid	Deep	Bomb
2011	HOU	15/15	857	54	85	677	64%	+2.7	12.5	3	3	5.4	9	+1.1	1	14.4%	13	125	8	111	35%	51%	12%	3%
2012	HOU	15/14	864	62	104	716	60%	-3.4	11.5	6	5	5.0	13	+0.5	4	0.6%	27	33	26	52	43%	42%	11%	3%
2013	HOU	5/5	352	24	41	252	59%	-1.4	10.5	3	0	3.5	40	-1.1	2	-2.4%	34	14	35	4	42%	50%	8%	0%
2014	*BAL*			*43*	*66*	*468*	*65%*	*--*	*10.9*	*4*						*-0.1%*								

Houston had a pretty easy decision to make on Daniels once the season was over. They measured a $5.5 million cap savings against steadily declining performance, particularly in yards per reception. Daniels fled to Baltimore, where he'll be the No. 2 tight end and try to not be quite as washed up as Dallas Clark was last year.

Vernon Davis Height: 6-3 Weight: 250 College: Maryland Draft: 2006/1 (6) Born: 31-Jan-1984 Age: 30 Risk: Green

Year	Team	G/GS	Snaps	Rec	Pass	Yds	C%	+/-	Yd/C	TD	Drop	YAC	Rk	YAC+	BTkl	DVOA	Rk	DYAR	Rk	YAR	Short	Mid	Deep	Bomb
2011	SF	16/16	986	67	95	792	71%	+7.8	11.8	6	4	4.9	14	-0.1	8	4.4%	21	43	21	26	53%	23%	15%	10%
2012	SF	16/16	917	41	61	548	67%	+7.5	13.4	5	4	4.1	24	+0.2	6	17.5%	8	104	8	103	39%	30%	18%	13%
2013	SF	15/15	810	52	84	850	62%	+5.6	16.3	13	3	5.1	20	+0.2	3	29.3%	3	199	3	189	30%	34%	21%	15%
2014	*SF*			*55*	*84*	*788*	*65%*	*--*	*14.3*	*8*						*32.3%*								

Vernon Davis is threatening a holdout this summer, likely seeing the writing on the wall when it comes to his leverage. Last year, Davis was one of only two reliable options in the passing game along with Anquan Boldin. Once Michael Crabtree returned, he saw his targets drop, and the team will also have Stevie Johnson in the mix this year. By the way, only two tight ends have ever had double-digit touchdowns in consecutive seasons: Antonio Gates in 2004-2005, and Rob Gronkowski in 2010-2012.

Ed Dickson Height: 6-4 Weight: 249 College: Oregon Draft: 2010/3 (70) Born: 25-Jul-1987 Age: 27 Risk: Green

Year	Team	G/GS	Snaps	Rec	Pass	Yds	C%	+/-	Yd/C	TD	Drop	YAC	Rk	YAC+	BTkl	DVOA	Rk	DYAR	Rk	YAR	Short	Mid	Deep	Bomb
2011	BAL	16/16	939	54	89	528	61%	-0.4	9.8	5	6	2.9	45	-1.4	1	-1.3%	25	16	25	15	41%	38%	16%	5%
2012	BAL	13/11	538	21	33	225	64%	+1.3	10.7	0	1	4.0	28	-0.4	1	-5.8%	34	2	35	-6	52%	26%	16%	6%
2013	BAL	16/14	629	25	43	273	58%	-2.9	10.9	1	5	4.0	35	-0.6	1	-10.8%	41	-10	41	-2	41%	36%	20%	2%
2014	*CAR*			*30*	*45*	*284*	*67%*	*--*	*9.5*	*2*						*-7.4%*								

Dickson told the *Oregonian*, "I'm thinking Pro Bowl or bust for me" in Carolina this year. Obviously it's bust, because Greg Olsen is clearly the best tight end on the Panthers. Dickson also said he's going to bring his knowledge of how he got his ring in Baltimore, but that probably won't include physically bringing Jacoby Jones, Rahim Moore, or Dennis Pitta's superior hands to Carolina. Dickson couldn't get the job done in Baltimore last year. He dropped five passes on just 43 targets, including a tip that became an interception. If he sticks to blocking in Carolina, he should work out, but an injury to Olsen would be catastrophic for this receiving corps.

Eric Ebron Height: 6-4 Weight: 250 College: North Carolina Draft: 2014/1 (10) Born: 10-Apr-1993 Age: 21 Risk: Yellow

Year	Team	G/GS	Snaps	Rec	Pass	Yds	C%	+/-	Yd/C	TD	Drop	YAC	Rk	YAC+	BTkl	DVOA	Rk	DYAR	Rk	YAR	Short	Mid	Deep	Bomb
2014	*DET*			*54*	*92*	*665*	*59%*	*--*	*12.3*	*3*						*-3.1%*								

Ebron combines breathtaking speed, grace and agility, a huge catch circumference, and over-the-shoulder deep pass capability into one Jimmy Graham-like package. All that is missing from his receiving game is high-end concentration to make tough catches in traffic, and don't ask about the blocking, because no one cares. Ebron caught his share of bombs up the seam at North Carolina, but he was most dangerous when catching a shallow drag and turning upfield with two steps on all of the linebackers on underneath coverage. His ability to create in space will be a huge factor for the Lions, because Megatron and Golden Tate are going to create a lot of space.

Tyler Eifert Height: 6-6 Weight: 251 College: Notre Dame Draft: 2013/1 (21) Born: 8-Sep-1990 Age: 24 Risk: Yellow

Year	Team	G/GS	Snaps	Rec	Pass	Yds	C%	+/-	Yd/C	TD	Drop	YAC	Rk	YAC+	BTkl	DVOA	Rk	DYAR	Rk	YAR	Short	Mid	Deep	Bomb
2013	CIN	15/15	673	39	59	445	66%	+1.3	11.4	2	2	5.8	9	+1.2	6	-14.0%	45	-27	47	-6	54%	29%	13%	5%
2014	*CIN*			*59*	*92*	*718*	*64%*	*--*	*12.2*	*5*						*10.9%*								

Eifert didn't provide the spectacular rookie season some expected, but he was steady, and greatly improved as a blocker as the season went on until a neck injury sapped his final weeks. Eifert was limited in part by the surplus weaponry laying around in Jay Gruden's arsenal, and there didn't seem to be a coherent plan to deploy Eifert from game to game. Against the Lions Eifert went deep, boxed out his defender, and skied for a touchdown catch of deceptive simplicity. It was a play that spoke to his enormous skill set, and the Bengals would be wise to feature far more of it in Eifert's sophomore season.

Zach Ertz Height: 6-5 Weight: 249 College: Stanford Draft: 2013/2 (35) Born: 10-Nov-1990 Age: 24 Risk: Yellow

Year	Team	G/GS	Snaps	Rec	Pass	Yds	C%	+/-	Yd/C	TD	Drop	YAC	Rk	YAC+	BTkl	DVOA	Rk	DYAR	Rk	YAR	Short	Mid	Deep	Bomb
2013	PHI	16/3	450	36	56	469	64%	+3.3	13.0	4	2	4.4	30	-0.5	0	9.8%	17	60	20	71	34%	42%	17%	8%
2014	*PHI*			*56*	*83*	*675*	*67%*	*--*	*12.0*	*4*						*12.8%*								

Rookie tight ends are rarely prepared for instant stardom, but Ertz did outplay his projection a little bit last year. His best game was against Arizona, which actually doesn't tell us much since the Cardinals were fantasy gold for opposing tight ends. That's an example of good game-planning as Kelly really never pushed Ertz into a significant role last year. But that could change in a hurry. In May, Kelly was asked about replacing DeSean Jackson's production and his response to the *Philadelphia Inquirer* was "I think Zach can have a huge role." We agree, coach.

Gavin Escobar Height: 6-6 Weight: 254 College: San Diego State Draft: 2013/2 (47) Born: 3-Feb-1991 Age: 23 Risk: Green

Year	Team	G/GS	Snaps	Rec	Pass	Yds	C%	+/-	Yd/C	TD	Drop	YAC	Rk	YAC+	BTkl	DVOA	Rk	DYAR	Rk	YAR	Short	Mid	Deep	Bomb
2013	DAL	16/1	197	9	15	134	60%	-0.9	14.9	2	1	4.1	--	-0.4	1	24.8%	--	30	--	32	47%	33%	20%	0%
2014	*DAL*			*20*	*32*	*223*	*63%*	*--*	*11.1*	*2*						*-0.3%*								

After Jason Witten set a tight-end record with 110 receptions in 2012, the Cowboys thought using the 47th pick in the 2013 draft on tight end Gavin Escobar was the best course of action. Okay, but Escobar saw the field less often than blocking tight end James Hanna last year. On 15 targets, he did show some of his athletic receiving ability, catching two touchdowns (finishing one with a cartwheel into the end zone) and having the best DVOA of any tight end with 10-24 targets. He doesn't have the college basketball pedigree like some of his peers, but he fits into that receiver-first paradigm. Escobar may be the future for this offense, but his playing time this year will be predicated on how much he's improved as a blocker.

Anthony Fasano Height: 6-4 Weight: 255 College: Notre Dame Draft: 2006/2 (53) Born: 20-Apr-1984 Age: 30 Risk: Yellow

Year	Team	G/GS	Snaps	Rec	Pass	Yds	C%	+/-	Yd/C	TD	Drop	YAC	Rk	YAC+	BTkl	DVOA	Rk	DYAR	Rk	YAR	Short	Mid	Deep	Bomb
2011	MIA	15/15	899	32	54	451	59%	+3.8	14.1	5	0	3.1	43	-1.3	1	16.8%	8	70	18	85	34%	28%	34%	4%
2012	MIA	16/16	899	41	69	332	59%	-0.1	8.1	5	1	2.2	49	-1.7	2	-19.4%	44	-44	43	-38	51%	44%	5%	0%
2013	KC	9/9	503	23	33	200	70%	+1.3	8.7	3	2	3.2	44	-1.4	2	-12.7%	43	-12	42	5	45%	48%	0%	6%
2014	*KC*			*38*	*56*	*308*	*68%*	*--*	*8.1*	*3*						*-11.0%*								

The Chiefs signed Fasano to a four-year, $13 million deal before the 2013 season, hoping that he would be the stable and somewhat productive player he'd been through years in Miami. It didn't work out too well; Fasano missed seven games due to injury and posted a -34.1% DVOA on third down, which is not what you want from a 6-foot-4, 255-pound target whose speed is somewhere just north of your average offensive guard. It's likely that Fasano would have seen even fewer targets had Travis Kelce been healthy last season, and Fasano's continued production value probably has mostly to do with Alex Smith's limited arm and checkdown tendencies.

Joseph Fauria Height: 6-7 Weight: 255 College: UCLA Draft: 2013/FA Born: 16-Jan-1990 Age: 24 Risk: Green

Year	Team	G/GS	Snaps	Rec	Pass	Yds	C%	+/-	Yd/C	TD	Drop	YAC	Rk	YAC+	BTkl	DVOA	Rk	DYAR	Rk	YAR	Short	Mid	Deep	Bomb
2013	DET	16/2	303	18	30	207	60%	+0.9	11.5	7	0	2.9	46	-1.5	2	24.2%	6	64	17	65	34%	41%	17%	7%
2014	*DET*			*14*	*22*	*166*	*64%*	*--*	*11.8*	*4*						*13.0%*								

A three-touchdown game against the Browns gave Fauria fantasy buzz, and cute end-zone dancing gave him a week of *SportsCenter* fame. Then reality set in, and Fauria proved to be an ordinary second tight end, with perhaps a smidge more receiving talent than most. When Peter-Principled into the starting job by Brandon Pettigrew's ankle injury, Fauria proved he was a true Lions player by letting a fourth-quarter pass carom off his fingers and into the arms of a Giants defender for a pick-six. Eric Ebron's arrival relegates Fauria to No. 3 status, though he may see some action—especially in the red zone—in a system with lots of two-tight end packages.

Jermichael Finley Height: 6-4 Weight: 243 College: Texas Draft: 2008/3 (91) Born: 26-Mar-1987 Age: 27 Risk: #N/A

Year	Team	G/GS	Snaps	Rec	Pass	Yds	C%	+/-	Yd/C	TD	Drop	YAC	Rk	YAC+	BTkl	DVOA	Rk	DYAR	Rk	YAR	Short	Mid	Deep	Bomb
2011	GB	16/13	791	55	92	767	60%	+0.9	13.9	8	9	4.1	29	-0.3	1	18.3%	7	135	5	154	26%	45%	21%	8%
2012	GB	16/14	690	61	87	667	70%	+5.0	10.9	2	6	4.8	15	+0.1	8	7.0%	17	95	9	73	51%	33%	11%	5%
2013	GB	6/5	252	25	34	300	74%	+1.2	12.0	3	2	9.0	2	+3.2	9	25.8%	5	68	15	70	62%	24%	12%	3%

The fact that Jermichael Finley is still sitting on the open market as of press time makes it very clear that he has still not fully healed from the terrifying neck injury he suffered against Cleveland midway through last season. Finley has met with numerous teams this offseason, and their doctors keep saying no, even though the doctor who performed his surgery says that yes, Finley is ready to return to the field. That surgeon, Dr. Joseph Maroon, is based in Pittsburgh and does some work with the Steelers, so they certainly make the most sense for Finley. He's also personally expressed interest in returning to the Packers, but it looks like they want to see what they have with their current tight ends before making that choice.

Coby Fleener Height: 6-6 Weight: 247 College: Stanford Draft: 2012/2 (34) Born: 20-Sep-1988 Age: 26 Risk: Green

Year	Team	G/GS	Snaps	Rec	Pass	Yds	C%	+/-	Yd/C	TD	Drop	YAC	Rk	YAC+	BTkl	DVOA	Rk	DYAR	Rk	YAR	Short	Mid	Deep	Bomb
2012	IND	12/10	450	26	48	281	54%	-3.5	10.8	2	3	4.0	27	-0.1	0	-3.6%	32	-2	36	-10	56%	20%	20%	4%
2013	IND	16/12	815	52	87	608	60%	-2.3	11.7	4	1	4.9	23	+0.4	0	-11.3%	42	-24	45	-21	44%	40%	15%	1%
2014	*IND*			*42*	*70*	*506*	*60%*	*--*	*12.0*	*4*						*6.2%*								

You don't go in to the NFL draft hoping to land Just A Guy with the first pick of the second round, but here the Colts are. Fleener has shown no special traits as a receiver. Almost a third of his total receiving yards came on coverage busts. While he only had one drop, 11 of his passes were defensed and most of those were by trailing zone defenders Fleener didn't box out. When the Colts desperately needed a receiver to step up after Reggie Wayne went down for the season, Fleener did nothing even though the Colts expanded his role in the game plan. Forty-two of his targets were in Weeks 10-14, and he mustered a 45 percent Success Rate. Assuming Dwayne Allen is healthy this year, the target numbers should dip.

Antonio Gates Height: 6-4 Weight: 260 College: Kent State Draft: 2003/FA Born: 18-Jun-1980 Age: 34 Risk: Yellow

Year	Team	G/GS	Snaps	Rec	Pass	Yds	C%	+/-	Yd/C	TD	Drop	YAC	Rk	YAC+	BTkl	DVOA	Rk	DYAR	Rk	YAR	Short	Mid	Deep	Bomb
2011	SD	13/13	779	64	88	778	73%	+8.7	12.2	7	0	4.0	32	+0.0	2	29.8%	3	239	3	258	36%	48%	16%	1%
2012	SD	15/15	857	49	80	538	61%	+2.6	11.0	7	4	2.7	45	-1.4	1	4.6%	19	79	12	89	29%	51%	11%	9%
2013	SD	16/15	970	77	113	872	68%	+4.0	11.3	4	5	4.8	24	+0.3	8	0.7%	29	63	18	62	54%	36%	7%	3%
2014	*SD*			*65*	*99*	*731*	*66%*	*--*	*11.2*	*5*						*9.8%*								

One tight end was bound to benefit from San Diego's new quick-passing offense. Unfortunately for Gates, that man was Ladarius Green. The decline in Gates' game is obvious and inevitable at this point—the question is how much the Chargers can extract from a player who's simply not what he once was. The slight statistical uptick from 2012 was based primarily on early games against subpar pass defenses (Philly, Dallas, Oakland, Jacksonville, Washington). He trailed off in the second half of the season (as Rotoworld pointed out, Gates averaged 3.0 catches for 27.8 yards per game and scored one touchdown in San Diego's final eight games), and the 2014 schedule against the defenses of the NFC West and the AFC East doesn't figure to do him any favors.

Tony Gonzalez Height: 6-5 Weight: 251 College: California Draft: 1997/1 (13) Born: 27-Feb-1976 Age: 38 Risk: #N/A

Year	Team	G/GS	Snaps	Rec	Pass	Yds	C%	+/-	Yd/C	TD	Drop	YAC	Rk	YAC+	BTkl	DVOA	Rk	DYAR	Rk	YAR	Short	Mid	Deep	Bomb
2011	ATL	16/16	952	80	116	875	69%	+7.6	10.9	7	4	3.0	44	-0.9	8	15.7%	10	153	4	185	37%	49%	13%	1%
2012	ATL	16/16	964	93	124	930	75%	+13.3	10.0	8	4	2.7	46	-1.1	10	20.6%	7	286	1	258	37%	57%	6%	0%
2013	ATL	16/16	1003	83	121	859	69%	+8.3	10.3	8	3	2.7	48	-1.6	4	8.7%	18	135	4	137	32%	63%	5%	0%

How do you encapsulate Tony Gonzalez in a few hundred words? He finishes his career as the active leader in receptions, receiving yards, receiving touchdowns, total touchdowns, yards from scrimmage, games started, and two-point conversions. In his career, he played in more Pro Bowls than Ray Lewis or Reggie White, scored more touchdowns than Steve Largent or Don Hutson, gained more yards than Marvin Harrison or Cris Carter, and caught 223 more balls than anyone who ever played except Jerry Rice. He did all that as a tight end, and though the lines between positions are awfully blurry these days (last season, he lined up in the slot or out wide even more often than Jimmy Graham), we know that he often had to fight off linebackers or go across the middle of the field to get open. From 1999 to 2005—a time when Kansas City led the league in offensive DVOA three times and never ranked lower than seventh—Gonzalez caught 556 passes, more than double any of his teammates. He has also started a foundation dedicated to supporting sick children, and he once used the Heimlich Maneuver to save a man's life. For nearly two decades, he was everything you'd ever want in a football player on and off the field, and the NFL won't be as much fun without him.

Garrett Graham Height: 6-3 Weight: 243 College: Wisconsin Draft: 2010/4 (118) Born: 4-Aug-1986 Age: 28 Risk: Yellow

Year	Team	G/GS	Snaps	Rec	Pass	Yds	C%	+/-	Yd/C	TD	Drop	YAC	Rk	YAC+	BTkl	DVOA	Rk	DYAR	Rk	YAR	Short	Mid	Deep	Bomb
2011	HOU	7/0	19	1	2	24	50%	+0.4	24.0	0	0	8.0	--	+3.6	0	26.6%	--	5	--	4	0%	0%	100%	0%
2012	HOU	15/9	611	28	40	263	70%	+2.6	9.4	3	3	4.1	23	-0.8	1	6.8%	18	36	24	33	67%	19%	11%	3%
2013	HOU	13/11	772	49	89	545	55%	-6.1	11.1	5	4	4.2	33	-0.4	1	-21.3%	50	-84	50	-95	53%	35%	7%	5%
2014	*HOU*			*53*	*78*	*579*	*68%*	*--*	*10.9*	*4*						*7.5%*								

Graham was clearly stretched as a No. 1 tight end. In the first five games of the season, as the No. 2 tight end behind Owen Daniels, Graham had 15 DYAR and 2.9% DVOA, catching 71 percent of passes. After Daniels went on injured reserve, Graham had -99 DYAR and -29.2% DVOA in 11 games, with a 50 percent catch rate. As a fourth or fifth receiving option, Graham can be a credible receiver and take advantage of his skills. But he has no standout traits, the Texans drafted a blocking tight end in C.J. Fiedorowicz, and Ryan Fitzpatrick is slated to be the starting quarterback.

Jimmy Graham Height: 6-6 Weight: 260 College: Miami Draft: 2010/3 (95) Born: 24-Nov-1986 Age: 28 Risk: Yellow

Year	Team	G/GS	Snaps	Rec	Pass	Yds	C%	+/-	Yd/C	TD	Drop	YAC	Rk	YAC+	BTkl	DVOA	Rk	DYAR	Rk	YAR	Short	Mid	Deep	Bomb
2011	NO	16/11	798	99	149	1310	66%	+7.9	13.2	11	6	4.6	20	+0.1	8	16.0%	9	272	2	267	39%	40%	18%	3%
2012	NO	15/9	695	85	135	982	63%	-0.4	11.6	9	14	3.6	35	-0.6	4	2.7%	23	105	7	104	33%	52%	14%	1%
2013	NO	16/12	755	86	143	1215	60%	+5.1	14.1	16	4	4.7	26	+0.3	9	15.7%	12	223	1	212	36%	44%	11%	9%
2014	*NO*			*92*	*140*	*1202*	*66%*	*--*	*13.1*	*11*						*27.2%*								

Graham lined up as a wide receiver more often than any other tight end last season, but if we include plays where he lined up in the slot, he actually finished second behind Tony Gonzalez. Graham, though, was limited by a partially torn plantar fascia, and though he didn't miss any games, the Saints only used him sparingly. On a per-snap basis, Graham lined up wide or in the slot significantly more than Gonzalez or any other tight end (Table 2).

Table 2. Top 10 Tight Ends Lined Up as Wide Receivers, 2013

Player	Team	Wide	Slot	Total	Snaps	Pct
Tony Gonzalez	ATL	76	436	512	1003	51.0%
Jimmy Graham	NO	141	289	430	755	57.0%
Antonio Gates	SD	27	298	325	970	33.5%
Charles Clay	MIA	36	247	283	855	33.1%
Jared Cook	STL	71	209	280	718	39.0%
Greg Olsen	CAR	41	238	279	1001	27.9%
Jason Witten	DAL	14	263	277	984	28.2%
Jordan Cameron	CLE	14	251	265	969	27.3%
Vernon Davis	SF	56	167	223	810	27.5%
Martellus Bennett	CHI	38	184	222	951	23.3%

Regardless of the positional group to which you'd like to arbitrarily sort Graham, he remains a very special player. In the last three seasons, he leads all NFL players with 36 receiving touchdowns, while ranking fourth in receptions and eighth in receiving yards. Not surprisingly, he also leads the league in red zone targets (71) and scores (27) in the same timeframe. With a full offseason to heal, Graham should once again be the league's most dangerous weapon inside the 20.

Ladarius Green Height: 6-6 Weight: 237 College: Louisiana-Lafayette Draft: 2012/4 (110) Born: 27-Jan-1991 Age: 23 Risk: Green

Year	Team	G/GS	Snaps	Rec	Pass	Yds	C%	+/-	Yd/C	TD	Drop	YAC	Rk	YAC+	BTkl	DVOA	Rk	DYAR	Rk	YAR	Short	Mid	Deep	Bomb
2012	SD	4/1	37	4	4	56	100%	+1.1	14.0	0	0	10.5	--	+5.6	1	52.5%	--	10	--	11	100%	0%	0%	0%
2013	SD	16/10	365	17	30	376	57%	-0.1	22.1	3	1	9.8	1	+5.0	0	45.3%	1	113	7	109	23%	45%	26%	6%
2014	*SD*			*46*	*68*	*547*	*68%*	*--*	*11.9*	*4*						*10.7%*								

With limited targets last season, Green still proved that he has every attribute desired from the modern generation of receiving tight ends. He's quick enough to take a quick slant or drag route an extra 20 yards, big and tough enough to win a contested catch battle with the most aggressive safety, and route-savvy enough to benefit from the full palette of Mike McCoy's offensive designs. Everybody seems to believe that the third season will be the breakout one for Green, even Antonio Gates. All signs point to the future being now, and if Philip Rivers has Keenan Allen, Malcom Floyd, and Green as his primary receiving trio, San Diego's passing offense could improve estimably—especially at the quicker tempos promised by new offensive coordinator Frank Reich. Green will need to improve on his -24.5% red-zone DVOA, but he'll also get more than four red-zone targets to do so.

Jermaine Gresham Height: 6-5 Weight: 261 College: Oklahoma Draft: 2010/1 (21) Born: 16-Jun-1988 Age: 26 Risk: Green

Year	Team	G/GS	Snaps	Rec	Pass	Yds	C%	+/-	Yd/C	TD	Drop	YAC	Rk	YAC+	BTkl	DVOA	Rk	DYAR	Rk	YAR	Short	Mid	Deep	Bomb
2011	CIN	14/13	885	56	92	596	61%	-1.6	10.6	6	3	3.4	39	-1.6	3	-8.2%	30	18	24	-2	45%	40%	15%	0%
2012	CIN	16/15	1002	64	94	737	68%	+2.8	11.5	5	6	6.5	2	+1.3	6	3.2%	22	24	29	48	49%	37%	12%	2%
2013	CIN	14/14	891	46	67	458	69%	+1.3	10.0	4	3	5.8	10	-0.1	9	-18.5%	49	-47	49	-23	52%	30%	17%	0%
2014	*CIN*			*38*	*69*	*406*	*55%*	*--*	*10.7*	*2*						*-16.4%*								

The Bengals hoped the drafting of Tyler Eifert would set up a Patriots-esque double whammy at tight end, or at worst light a fire under the mercurial Gresham. But Gresham's 2013 was much like his previous three seasons, a mix of the spectacular with the mindless, great catches combined with untimely gaffes and dumb penalties. Gresham was flagged 11 times, easily the most of any skill position player, giving him 20 penalties in two seasons; he also fumbled three times. Gresham began the season by pancaking Geno Atkins during the Oklahoma Drill on a memorable *Hard Knocks* episode, but his blocking during the season was subpar. This isn't to say that the former first-rounder doesn't have use in this offense. But he is in the final year of his contract, and it will take some improvement for the Bengals to justify keeping him, especially with Eifert around.

Ryan Griffin Height: 6-6 Weight: 247 College: Connecticut Draft: 2013/6 (201) Born: 11-Jan-1990 Age: 24 Risk: Green

Year	Team	G/GS	Snaps	Rec	Pass	Yds	C%	+/-	Yd/C	TD	Drop	YAC	Rk	YAC+	BTkl	DVOA	Rk	DYAR	Rk	YAR	Short	Mid	Deep	Bomb
2013	HOU	15/8	362	19	28	244	68%	+2.1	12.8	1	0	5.2	17	+0.2	0	13.9%	13	38	26	43	50%	23%	15%	12%
2014	*HOU*			*25*	*38*	*262*	*66%*	*--*	*10.5*	*2*						*0.2%*								

Why not Griffin? He was one of the few Texans receivers to actually post good DVOA numbers last year in a lost season, and he can work the intermediate routes as a lower-rung option on a good offense. But with Garrett Graham re-signed and the Texans preferring the blocking of C.J. Fiedorowicz, his role on this team is unknown. It wouldn't be completely without merit for the Texans to give him a shot to beat out Graham for the move tight end role. On the pessimistic hand: it's a small sample size by a late-round pick, and *Family Guy* fatigue has set in to the point where we're all sick of Griffins.

Rob Gronkowski Height: 6-6 Weight: 264 College: Arizona Draft: 2010/2 (42) Born: 14-May-1989 Age: 25 Risk: Red

Year	Team	G/GS	Snaps	Rec	Pass	Yds	C%	+/-	Yd/C	TD	Drop	YAC	Rk	YAC+	BTkl	DVOA	Rk	DYAR	Rk	YAR	Short	Mid	Deep	Bomb
2011	NE	16/16	1092	90	125	1327	73%	+12.2	14.7	17	4	7.1	2	+2.1	13	46.2%	1	456	1	471	36%	43%	18%	3%
2012	NE	11/11	731	55	80	790	69%	+5.7	14.4	11	5	5.5	7	+1.1	2	41.2%	1	279	2	279	34%	45%	16%	5%
2013	NE	7/6	383	39	66	592	59%	-0.2	15.2	4	1	5.0	21	+1.0	4	12.9%	14	91	11	115	25%	45%	22%	7%
2014	*NE*			*73*	*113*	*1009*	*65%*	*--*	*13.8*	*11*						*31.9%*								

When it comes to the New England offense, Gronkowski's presence creates a sizable ripple effect. After starting the year on the sidelines, it took him a while to come around last year, but when he was truly healthy—pretty much the month of November—Gronkowski was his usual dominant self. Through Week 6, Tom Brady had targeted New England tight ends 15 times. In Week 7, his first game of the season, Gronkowski was targeted 17 times. In four games between Week 9 and Week 13, Gronk had 27 catches for 419 yards and four touchdowns, and was a game-changing presence for the New England offense. When he tore his ACL in Week 14, the Patriots shifted from a pass-first offense to a run-heavy game plan. (His absence wasn't the only reason New England changed, but it certainly wasn't a coincidence.) But while an ACL tear is a serious injury, there's actually less mystery about his health than there was last offseason, which should mean good things for the Patriots offense. Few players are as integral to the success or have a greater individual impact on their respective offensive scheme than Gronkowski.

Clay Harbor Height: 6-3 Weight: 252 College: Missouri State Draft: 2010/4 (125) Born: 2-Jul-1987 Age: 27 Risk: Green

Year	Team	G/GS	Snaps	Rec	Pass	Yds	C%	+/-	Yd/C	TD	Drop	YAC	Rk	YAC+	BTkl	DVOA	Rk	DYAR	Rk	YAR	Short	Mid	Deep	Bomb
2011	PHI	16/3	359	13	19	163	68%	+0.4	12.5	1	1	3.1	--	-1.4	2	17.0%	--	37	--	36	47%	21%	32%	0%
2012	PHI	14/9	340	25	39	186	64%	-1.2	7.4	2	2	2.8	44	-2.2	1	-37.2%	49	-66	47	-71	55%	39%	3%	3%
2013	JAC	16/7	358	24	35	292	69%	+3.8	12.2	2	0	5.3	14	+0.6	0	0.4%	30	18	34	15	35%	55%	6%	3%
2014	*JAC*			*25*	*44*	*241*	*57%*	*--*	*9.6*	*1*						*-20.7%*								

"Any Harbor in a storm," David Caldwell said to himself. So the Jaguars allowed Clay Harbor to showcase his replacement-level tight end skills for a half-season, going as far as to put him out wide on a few plays, and he outproduced many of their more-heralded receivers. Harbor lost playing time when Marcedes Lewis came back, but Jacksonville did re-up him after the season. Harbor's not a blocker, but he's a good enough receiver at tight end to play in a few packages.

Rob Housler Height: 6-6 Weight: 249 College: Florida Atlantic Draft: 2011/3 (69) Born: 17-Mar-1988 Age: 26 Risk: Red

Year	Team	G/GS	Snaps	Rec	Pass	Yds	C%	+/-	Yd/C	TD	Drop	YAC	Rk	YAC+	BTkl	DVOA	Rk	DYAR	Rk	YAR	Short	Mid	Deep	Bomb
2011	ARI	12/2	175	12	26	133	46%	-3.4	11.1	0	4	4.1	30	-0.5	2	-39.4%	47	-64	45	-58	29%	50%	17%	4%
2012	ARI	15/9	617	45	68	417	66%	+2.2	9.3	0	4	4.0	25	-0.5	6	-17.1%	43	-60	46	-41	51%	37%	11%	2%
2013	ARI	13/10	520	39	57	454	68%	+2.6	11.6	1	3	5.1	18	-0.4	1	0.8%	28	32	27	19	43%	34%	17%	5%
2014	*ARI*			*20*	*35*	*198*	*57%*	*--*	*9.9*	*1*						*-19.1%*								

It looks pretty clear that Housler has gradually improved since his rookie season, but that ends up meaning diddly-squat because Bruce Arians just isn't a big fan of his game. Most local reporters are projecting Housler as the fourth tight end on the depth chart, and why do you keep a guy like this as your fourth tight end? Maybe the Cardinals just cut him, although if you are a team like the Giants that needs a receiving tight end, you've got to figure Housler is worth sending Arizona a seventh-round pick or something.

Travis Kelce Height: 6-5 Weight: 255 College: Cincinnati Draft: 2013/3 (63) Born: 5-Oct-1989 Age: 25 Risk: Green

Year	Team	G/GS	Snaps	Rec	Pass	Yds	C%	+/-	Yd/C	TD	Drop	YAC	Rk	YAC+	BTkl	DVOA	Rk	DYAR	Rk	YAR	Short	Mid	Deep	Bomb
2013	KC	1/0	0	0	0	0	--	--	--	0	0	--	--	--	--	--	--	--	--	--	--	--	--	--
2014	*KC*			*39*	*65*	*429*	*60%*	*--*	*11.0*	*2*						*-7.6%*								

Kelce ranked fourth in the Big East in yards per reception with 16.0 in 2012, and it was hoped that he'd bring that same slot and flex production to Andy Reid's offense. Unfortunately, he suffered a knee injury in the preseason and underwent microfracture surgery in October. Since "microfracture" isn't quite the frightening word it used to be, it's possible that Kelce will see the field in 2014. He's not a total burner in the Jimmy Graham mold, but in an offense where the ostensible starting quarterback isn't going to test anyone downfield, Kelce has intriguing breakout potential—especially when you factor in the uncertain production of Kansas City's receivers.

Lance Kendricks Height: 6-3 Weight: 243 College: Wisconsin Draft: 2011/2 (47) Born: 30-Jan-1988 Age: 26 Risk: Green

Year	Team	G/GS	Snaps	Rec	Pass	Yds	C%	+/-	Yd/C	TD	Drop	YAC	Rk	YAC+	BTkl	DVOA	Rk	DYAR	Rk	YAR	Short	Mid	Deep	Bomb
2011	STL	10/1	609	28	58	352	48%	-7.4	12.6	0	4	6.6	3	+1.1	1	-26.8%	44	-82	46	-81	56%	25%	19%	0%
2012	STL	16/14	843	42	64	519	66%	+0.7	12.4	4	4	5.4	11	+0.9	3	13.0%	12	67	16	54	50%	35%	13%	2%
2013	STL	15/13	575	32	46	258	70%	+0.7	8.1	4	3	3.4	42	-1.4	1	-6.4%	38	3	38	0	72%	23%	5%	0%
2014	*STL*			*34*	*52*	*275*	*65%*	*--*	*8.1*	*2*						*-16.9%*								

Kendricks was progressing at a slow rate on a bad offense, but last year's arrival of Jared Cook stalled his production. Kendricks' 8.06 yards per reception was the second-lowest average among non-running backs with at least 30 receptions. He caught short passes, but couldn't generate yards after the catch to make a real impact. The Rams were second in the league in their frequency using two-tight end sets, but Kendricks is no higher than fifth on the imaginary chart of where this offense is looking to throw the ball.

Marcedes Lewis Height: 6-6 Weight: 255 College: UCLA Draft: 2006/1 (28) Born: 19-May-1984 Age: 30 Risk: Yellow

Year	Team	G/GS	Snaps	Rec	Pass	Yds	C%	+/-	Yd/C	TD	Drop	YAC	Rk	YAC+	BTkl	DVOA	Rk	DYAR	Rk	YAR	Short	Mid	Deep	Bomb
2011	JAC	15/15	799	39	85	460	46%	-9.5	11.8	0	4	3.9	33	-1.0	6	-35.5%	46	-166	47	-174	43%	34%	19%	4%
2012	JAC	16/15	830	52	77	540	68%	+1.6	10.4	4	5	4.7	16	-0.3	1	0.0%	28	21	31	31	50%	38%	12%	0%
2013	JAC	11/11	582	25	47	359	53%	-5.8	14.4	4	3	9.0	2	+4.0	8	-8.1%	39	-3	39	6	46%	41%	13%	0%
2014	*JAC*			*44*	*67*	*476*	*66%*	*--*	*10.8*	*4*						*7.2%*								

Coming off a breakout 2010 season, the Jaguars signed Lewis to a five-year, $34 million deal. Lewis has since played like an older version of the player he was from 2006-2009, mixing adequate numbers with a penchant for missing games. The fact that he is set to see year four of that contract is a testament to the wacky nature of the NFL salary cap over this time frame. Lewis was lucky enough to play in an uncapped year, then to play for a team with a need for a massive rebuilding program that has to hit a salary minimum. Can an adequate tight end be worth an $8.25 million cap number? Yes, if it's the only thing keeping your roster legal.

Vance McDonald Height: 6-4 Weight: 267 College: Rice Draft: 2013/2 (55) Born: 13-Jun-1990 Age: 24 Risk: Green

Year	Team	G/GS	Snaps	Rec	Pass	Yds	C%	+/-	Yd/C	TD	Drop	YAC	Rk	YAC+	BTkl	DVOA	Rk	DYAR	Rk	YAR	Short	Mid	Deep	Bomb
2013	SF	15/4	480	8	19	119	42%	-2.4	14.9	0	2	5.9	--	+1.2	1	-23.8%	--	-20	--	-27	41%	29%	18%	12%
2014	*SF*			*18*	*30*	*224*	*60%*	*--*	*12.4*	*1*						*-2.9%*								

McDonald was drafted as Delanie Walker's replacement in the second round last year, but while fellow rookies Zach Ertz, Tyler Eifert, and Jordan Reed showed promise as receivers, McDonald largely struggled, managing three drops while only making eight catches all year.

Sean McGrath Height: 6-5 Weight: 247 College: Henderson St. Draft: 2012/FA Born: 3-Dec-1987 Age: 27 Risk: Blue

Year	Team	G/GS	Snaps	Rec	Pass	Yds	C%	+/-	Yd/C	TD	Drop	YAC	Rk	YAC+	BTkl	DVOA	Rk	DYAR	Rk	YAR	Short	Mid	Deep	Bomb
2012	SEA	2/0	8	0	0	0	--	--	--	0	0	--	--	--	--	--	--	--	--	--	--	--	--	--
2013	KC	16/9	610	26	40	302	65%	+0.3	11.6	2	2	5.4	13	+0.8	1	1.0%	27	21	32	33	47%	34%	16%	3%
2014	*KC*			*12*	*19*	*107*	*63%*	*--*	*8.9*	*0*						*-17.1%*								

Forced into action after injuries depleted Kansas City's tight end rotation, McGrath performed decently enough, but he's best-known for what was certainly the NFL's best beard in 2013. McGrath shaved the furry beast in early 2014, promising on Twitter that the subsequent re-beard "shall rise from the ashes again, this time with ferocious girth that can't be matched." If McGrath doesn't make final cuts, which is a possibility, you can add McGrath to the list of mythical characters whose powers were stripped by unfortunate tonsorial decisions.

Heath Miller Height: 6-5 Weight: 256 College: Virginia Draft: 2005/1 (30) Born: 22-Oct-1982 Age: 32 Risk: Yellow

Year	Team	G/GS	Snaps	Rec	Pass	Yds	C%	+/-	Yd/C	TD	Drop	YAC	Rk	YAC+	BTkl	DVOA	Rk	DYAR	Rk	YAR	Short	Mid	Deep	Bomb
2011	PIT	16/16	1005	51	76	631	68%	+2.3	12.4	2	3	4.8	18	+0.1	3	13.6%	14	112	9	100	39%	47%	14%	0%
2012	PIT	15/15	994	71	101	816	70%	+5.2	11.5	8	3	4.8	14	+0.5	1	21.0%	6	165	4	172	50%	35%	14%	1%
2013	PIT	14/14	901	58	78	593	74%	+8.1	10.2	1	3	3.9	38	-0.9	3	-2.8%	35	23	29	22	53%	33%	11%	3%
2014	*PIT*			*57*	*79*	*637*	*72%*	*--*	*11.2*	*6*						*23.4%*								

While his age is becoming a factor at a position notorious for sudden declines, it's probably no coincidence Miller averaged a career-low 10.2 yards per reception after a serious knee injury late in 2012. The offense certainly missed Miller during a putrid start. He also cut his count of blown blocks in our game charting down from 14.0 in 2012 to 9.0 last year. What's unusual is that Miller only scored one touchdown, because he's known to be a favorite target for Roethlisberger in the red zone, where he's caught 37 of his 40 career touchdowns. Miller's eight red-zone targets were tied for the second fewest he's had in a season. A healthier Miller should be better in 2014, but the Steelers have to start searching for a long-term replacement.

Zach Miller Height: 6-5 Weight: 256 College: Arizona State Draft: 2007/2 (38) Born: 11-Dec-1985 Age: 29 Risk: Yellow

Year	Team	G/GS	Snaps	Rec	Pass	Yds	C%	+/-	Yd/C	TD	Drop	YAC	Rk	YAC+	BTkl	DVOA	Rk	DYAR	Rk	YAR	Short	Mid	Deep	Bomb
2011	SEA	15/15	852	25	44	233	57%	-0.9	9.3	0	3	3.2	42	-1.8	0	-25.0%	42	-40	39	-68	41%	38%	18%	3%
2012	SEA	16/15	850	38	53	396	72%	+6.2	10.4	3	1	3.4	40	-1.2	2	8.1%	15	47	23	50	53%	26%	21%	0%
2013	SEA	14/12	717	33	56	387	59%	-1.8	11.7	5	1	4.5	28	-0.5	3	-1.0%	32	22	30	13	55%	33%	10%	2%
2014	*SEA*			*42*	*59*	*453*	*71%*	*--*	*10.8*	*5*						*17.8%*								

The Seahawks will always use heavy two-tight end sets as long as Tom Cable is in the room and pounding the table very loudly for that concept, but one wonders if Miller might not be the odd man out in 2014 if the Seahawks stretch things out in the passing game. Never a new-breed player at the position—he's far more Jason Witten than Jimmy Graham—Miller has operated as a de facto third tackle through most of his time in Seattle, especially when the first two tackles were found to be lacking (which amounts to "whenever Russell Okung isn't on the field"). Last year, Miller found himself usurped in per-target production and efficiency by the younger Luke Willson, who has elements of the new wave of tight ends. In March, Miller reworked his current deal to cut his 2014 cap hit in half, and it wasn't out of the question that if he hadn't, he would have been gone. He's a good but unglamorous player in a spot where most teams are looking for flash these days.

Brandon Myers Height: 6-4 Weight: 250 College: Iowa Draft: 2009/6 (202) Born: 4-Sep-1985 Age: 29 Risk: Yellow

Year	Team	G/GS	Snaps	Rec	Pass	Yds	C%	+/-	Yd/C	TD	Drop	YAC	Rk	YAC+	BTkl	DVOA	Rk	DYAR	Rk	YAR	Short	Mid	Deep	Bomb
2011	OAK	16/7	398	16	27	151	59%	+0.1	9.4	0	1	3.4	37	-1.6	1	-35.0%	45	-48	41	-47	57%	26%	13%	4%
2012	OAK	16/16	1009	79	105	806	75%	+8.1	10.2	4	6	3.6	34	-1.0	2	10.7%	13	112	6	123	42%	50%	8%	0%
2013	NYG	16/14	848	47	75	522	63%	+0.4	11.1	4	2	3.6	39	-0.7	1	-5.9%	37	7	36	16	39%	44%	17%	0%
2014	*TB*			*48*	*73*	*485*	*66%*	*--*	*10.1*	*4*						*-2.0%*								

Myers is on his third team in three years, but the former sixth-round pick has carved out a solid career. Even though DVOA didn't love his production last year, it's hard to look good when your quarterback is constantly under duress and throwing eighty-bazillion interceptions. Myers has increased his yards per catch average every season of his career. The Bucs should make frequent use of the tight end position this year, and Myers, rookie Austin Seferian-Jenkins, and Tim Wright could all see significant action. While Myers won't sell many jerseys, he should prove to be a solid addition in Tampa Bay, and a more valuable NFL player than fantasy producer.

Troy Niklas Height: 6-6 Weight: 270 College: Notre Dame Draft: 2014/2 (52) Born: 9/18/1992 Age: 22 Risk: Yellow

Year	Team	G/GS	Snaps	Rec	Pass	Yds	C%	+/-	Yd/C	TD	Drop	YAC	Rk	YAC+	BTkl	DVOA	Rk	DYAR	Rk	YAR	Short	Mid	Deep	Bomb
2014	*ARI*			*28*	*43*	*297*	*65%*	*--*	*10.6*	*1*						*-5.9%*								

Niklas committed to Notre Dame as an offensive tackle prospect and then played linebacker as a freshman before switching to tight end. That kind of history has led Niklas to be promoted as the next Jason Witten, a tight end who is as strong a blocker as he is a receiver. Our college scouting writer Matt Waldman believes Niklas is a bit overrated as a blocker; the strength is there, but not the technique, and he particularly struggles sliding to block on screen passes. The height, athleticism, and catch radius are certainly there for him to be a useful receiver, though he doesn't have the seam speed of guys like Julius Thomas and Rob Gronkowski. Niklas broke his hand in OTAs but should be ready to play by Week 1.

Greg Olsen Height: 6-6 Weight: 254 College: Miami Draft: 2007/1 (31) Born: 11-Mar-1985 Age: 29 Risk: Green

Year	Team	G/GS	Snaps	Rec	Pass	Yds	C%	+/-	Yd/C	TD	Drop	YAC	Rk	YAC+	BTkl	DVOA	Rk	DYAR	Rk	YAR	Short	Mid	Deep	Bomb
2011	CAR	16/13	866	45	89	540	51%	-7.7	12.0	5	1	4.4	26	-0.3	0	-13.9%	34	-13	33	-46	27%	52%	15%	6%
2012	CAR	16/16	1005	69	104	843	66%	+6.7	12.2	5	2	3.5	38	-0.7	2	13.6%	10	157	5	147	30%	53%	12%	5%
2013	CAR	16/16	1001	73	111	816	66%	+7.7	11.2	6	5	4.5	29	-0.1	4	3.8%	22	83	14	65	39%	44%	13%	5%
2014	*CAR*			*70*	*107*	*761*	*65%*	*--*	*10.9*	*7*						*10.6%*								

Olsen arrived in Carolina in 2011, the same year as Cam Newton. Since then, only Steve Smith has more catches or receiving yards for the Panthers, and no player has more touchdown catches. With few other familiar faces on the field, Newton figures to lean on Olsen once again in 2014. The Panthers have said they will use more two-tight end sets this season (with their wide receivers, you would too), which could mean more favorable matchups for Olsen as well. On the other hand, he won't have a chance to pile up stats if the offense keeps punting, and that seems pretty likely this year.

Logan Paulsen Height: 6-5 Weight: 264 College: UCLA Draft: 2010/FA Born: 26-Feb-1987 Age: 27 Risk: Green

Year	Team	G/GS	Snaps	Rec	Pass	Yds	C%	+/-	Yd/C	TD	Drop	YAC	Rk	YAC+	BTkl	DVOA	Rk	DYAR	Rk	YAR	Short	Mid	Deep	Bomb
2011	WAS	16/6	358	11	19	138	58%	-0.1	12.5	0	0	5.6	--	+1.3	0	-4.6%	--	-15	--	-5	53%	35%	6%	6%
2012	WAS	16/10	675	25	36	308	69%	+1.8	12.3	1	2	4.4	20	+0.3	2	23.7%	4	69	14	76	37%	49%	11%	3%
2013	WAS	16/14	809	28	50	267	56%	-2.3	9.5	3	3	3.4	41	-1.2	1	-36.4%	51	-96	51	-100	56%	31%	11%	2%
2014	*WAS*			*15*	*23*	*138*	*65%*	*--*	*9.2*	*0*						*-13.0%*								

Fred Davis' career in Washington ended with a whimper. Jordan Reed missed time with concussions and other injuries. That meant that in-line blocker Paulsen became a key part of the Washington offense. The results are a good example of why you don't make plodding block-first tight ends a key part of your offense. Parked in a role more suitable for his talents, Paulsen should be more effective in 2014. If Reed gets hurt again, prepare for a lot of six-yard curls that end with Paulsen falling down as fast as he can.

Brandon Pettigrew Height: 6-6 Weight: 263 College: Oklahoma State Draft: 2009/1 (20) Born: 23-Feb-1985 Age: 29 Risk: Green

Year	Team	G/GS	Snaps	Rec	Pass	Yds	C%	+/-	Yd/C	TD	Drop	YAC	Rk	YAC+	BTkl	DVOA	Rk	DYAR	Rk	YAR	Short	Mid	Deep	Bomb
2011	DET	16/16	1043	83	126	777	66%	+1.9	9.4	5	6	3.7	35	-1.0	2	-12.4%	33	-53	43	-16	54%	34%	12%	0%
2012	DET	14/11	770	59	102	567	58%	-7.1	9.6	3	8	4.0	26	+0.1	1	-25.3%	45	-123	49	-126	55%	35%	9%	0%
2013	DET	14/14	888	41	63	416	65%	-0.2	10.1	2	3	4.6	27	-0.5	2	-16.6%	48	-37	48	-18	59%	25%	13%	3%
2014	*DET*			*38*	*56*	*393*	*68%*	*--*	*10.3*	*3*						*2.7%*								

In the fine Lions tradition, Pettigrew appeared to have turned the corner on a career of mild disappointments by midseason, with 15 catches for 149 yards on 16 targets during a three-game Packers-Bears-Browns stretch. He then began dropping passes and committing penalties, including two offensive pass interference fouls against the Bengals, making him just another Lions player looking for a hurdle to trip over. Pettigrew drew more blocking assignments in the second half of the season, largely because rookie LaAdrian Waddle was starting at right tackle and you don't want Reggie Bush doing too much pass protection. Pettigrew seems to think he will get more receiving opportunities now that he has a new four-year contract, but the arrival of Eric Ebron suggests otherwise. Pettigrew is a pricey No. 2 tight end, but that will be the Lions' base formation, and his blocking ability and matchup potential will keep him on the field, if not near the top of the stat sheet.

Dennis Pitta Height: 6-5 Weight: 245 College: BYU Draft: 2010/4 (114) Born: 29-Jun-1985 Age: 29 Risk: Red

Year	Team	G/GS	Snaps	Rec	Pass	Yds	C%	+/-	Yd/C	TD	Drop	YAC	Rk	YAC+	BTkl	DVOA	Rk	DYAR	Rk	YAR	Short	Mid	Deep	Bomb
2011	BAL	16/2	558	40	56	405	71%	+4.1	10.1	3	1	4.5	24	-0.5	3	12.4%	15	95	15	79	46%	41%	13%	0%
2012	BAL	16/5	639	61	94	669	65%	+1.2	11.0	7	3	4.1	22	-0.4	7	4.3%	21	51	21	68	43%	39%	10%	8%
2013	BAL	4/1	158	20	33	169	61%	-0.4	8.5	1	3	2.6	50	-1.8	0	-4.6%	36	6	37	-18	44%	44%	9%	3%
2014	*BAL*			*66*	*96*	*730*	*69%*	*--*	*11.1*	*7*						*14.8%*								

The impact of the singular loss of Pitta to the offense was exaggerated last season, but it was exacerbated by the trade of Anquan Boldin to San Francisco. Flacco didn't have a dependable target underneath and the replacement tight ends were not adequate. Still, even after Pitta returned from his offseason hip surgery, the offense was far from fixed. Pitta had solid DVOA numbers in 2011-12, a good Super Bowl run, and may have been peaking prior to 2013, but in his four games back he averaged 8.45 yards per reception and ranked 36th in DVOA, which still beat Dallas Clark (40th) and Ed Dickson (41st). With plenty of time to heal now, Pitta should get back to where he was in 2012.

Andrew Quarless Height: 6-5 Weight: 254 College: Penn State Draft: 2010/5 (154) Born: 6-Oct-1988 Age: 26 Risk: Green

Year	Team	G/GS	Snaps	Rec	Pass	Yds	C%	+/-	Yd/C	TD	Drop	YAC	Rk	YAC+	BTkl	DVOA	Rk	DYAR	Rk	YAR	Short	Mid	Deep	Bomb
2011	GB	10/2	195	3	4	36	75%	+0.3	12.0	0	0	6.3	--	+2.3	0	16.0%	--	7	--	7	75%	25%	0%	0%
2013	GB	16/10	693	32	53	312	60%	+0.6	9.8	2	2	4.3	32	+0.0	1	-14.4%	46	-25	46	-19	53%	38%	6%	2%
2014	*GB*			*28*	*44*	*279*	*64%*	*--*	*10.0*	*2*						*-5.8%*								

Quarless had identical six-catch, 66-yard, one touchdown performances in back-to-back games against the Falcons and Cowboys in Weeks 14 and 15. The 6-66 motiff may be a sign that Matt Flynn made a deal with the devil. Yep, he made a deal with the devil to become an adequate backup quarterback. That sounds like a Matt Flynn thing to do. If so, it was the second-worst quarterback contract in recent memory, just behind Colin Kaepernick's new deal.

Quarless will never be Jermichael Finley, but he should have a major role with the new-look Packers offense. The team now needs an in-line tight end and sometime H-back to block for Eddie Lacy more than it needs one more field-stretcher, and Quarless is handy at going from edge-sealing to lead blocking in the full-house formation to aiding and abetting the Matt Flynn Revelation.

Jordan Reed Height: 6-2 Weight: 236 College: Florida Draft: 2013/3 (85) Born: 3-Jul-1990 Age: 24 Risk: Yellow

Year	Team	G/GS	Snaps	Rec	Pass	Yds	C%	+/-	Yd/C	TD	Drop	YAC	Rk	YAC+	BTkl	DVOA	Rk	DYAR	Rk	YAR	Short	Mid	Deep	Bomb
2013	WAS	9/4	379	45	60	499	75%	+3.5	11.1	3	3	5.5	12	+0.5	2	19.5%	9	98	10	124	48%	45%	5%	2%
2014	*WAS*			*60*	*93*	*706*	*65%*	*--*	*11.8*	*6*						*12.4%*								

There aren't many players with the skill set that Jordan Reed possesses. He's physical enough to bully smaller corners in the slot, and he's fast enough to run past linebackers. He was wildly effective when healthy last season, and the only thing he didn't excel at was deep balls. But that was mostly because the Washington offense as a whole had problems creating those. Washington showed some confidence in Reed at the goal line, going as far as to single him outside against corners. The concussion that sat him for most of the second half of the season is cause for concern, but if Reed can stay healthy, he's the best bet for a "next Jimmy Graham" the NFL has.

Mychal Rivera Height: 6-3 Weight: 242 College: Tennessee Draft: 2013/6 (184) Born: 8-Sep-1990 Age: 24 Risk: Red

Year	Team	G/GS	Snaps	Rec	Pass	Yds	C%	+/-	Yd/C	TD	Drop	YAC	Rk	YAC+	BTkl	DVOA	Rk	DYAR	Rk	YAR	Short	Mid	Deep	Bomb
2013	OAK	16/3	592	38	60	407	63%	+2.5	10.7	4	4	2.4	51	-2.1	3	8.1%	19	60	19	57	42%	44%	11%	4%
2014	*OAK*			*41*	*68*	*445*	*60%*	*--*	*10.9*	*4*						*-6.0%*								

Staring at a pretty vacant depth chart, sixth-round rookie Rivera became the Raiders' primary pass-catching tight end because, well, somebody had to be. A move tight end with the ability to line up on the line, in the slot, and in the backfield, he has better agility than speed. Though a willing blocker, he was not a particularly good one and played mostly in passing situations. The depth chart is not any more crowded than it was last offseason. Given Matt Schaub's willingness, not to say eagerness, to throw to the tight end, Rivera should play a similar role in 2014 even if he may have been working behind David Ausberry in June minicamp.

Adrien Robinson Height: 6-4 Weight: 267 College: Cincinnati Draft: 2012/4 (127) Born: 23-Sep-1988 Age: 26 Risk: Yellow

Year	Team	G/GS	Snaps	Rec	Pass	Yds	C%	+/-	Yd/C	TD	Drop	YAC	Rk	YAC+	BTkl	DVOA	Rk	DYAR	Rk	YAR	Short	Mid	Deep	Bomb
2012	NYG	2/0	3	0	0	0	--	--	--	0	0	--	--	--	--	--	--	--	--	--	--	--	--	--
2013	NYG	1/0	0	0	0	0	--	--	--	0	0	--	--	--	--	--	--	--	--	--	--	--	--	--
2014	*NYG*			*30*	*47*	*330*	*64%*	*--*	*11.0*	*2*						*3.4%*								

The Giants are going bargain hunting at tight end this year, and Robinson is the prospect with the highest ceiling. He's yet to record a reception, but Robinson's natural athleticism led Jerry Reese to compare him to Jason Pierre-Paul after New York drafted him in 2012. Robinson has yet to show any signs of development in the NFL, and he failed to separate himself in OTAs and minicamp. Kevin M. Gilbride, the team's tight ends coach, noted that Robinson needed to improve his body control and blocking, and Robinson remains more project than product. Giants fans hope Robinson turns into the team's starter, but up until now, Robinson has done nothing but disappoint.

Richard Rodgers Height: 6-4 Weight: 257 College: California Draft: 2014/3 (98) Born: 1/22/1992 Age: 22 Risk: Red

Year	Team	G/GS	Snaps	Rec	Pass	Yds	C%	+/-	Yd/C	TD	Drop	YAC	Rk	YAC+	BTkl	DVOA	Rk	DYAR	Rk	YAR	Short	Mid	Deep	Bomb
2014	*GB*			*49*	*71*	*587*	*69%*	*--*	*12.0*	*3*						*16.2%*								

The pride of Worcester is a raw, hard-to-categorize prospect who falls somewhere between a slot receiver and an H-back. Rodgers played a lot of traditional in-line tight end at Cal, but he is undersized for the position in the NFL. His forty times were in the miserable 4.8 range, and it showed on the game tape: Rodgers could get deep on some linebackers but was easy to track down from behind. Rodgers was a fine positional blocker with a nasty cut block, but he is no bone-crusher and will have trouble sealing the edge on a power run. But sometimes, Ted Thompson sees things nobody else sees, and every bit of noise coming out of the Packers' OTAs seems to indicate that Rodgers is going directly into the starting lineup. The KUBIAK projection for a rookie receiver or tight end depends an awful lot on how good his quarterback is and, well, you know how good this guy's quarterback is.

Kyle Rudolph Height: 6-6 Weight: 265 College: Notre Dame Draft: 2011/2 (43) Born: 9-Nov-1989 Age: 25 Risk: Yellow

Year	Team	G/GS	Snaps	Rec	Pass	Yds	C%	+/-	Yd/C	TD	Drop	YAC	Rk	YAC+	BTkl	DVOA	Rk	DYAR	Rk	YAR	Short	Mid	Deep	Bomb
2011	MIN	8/1	486	26	39	249	67%	+2.5	9.6	3	1	3.4	40	-1.2	1	-4.6%	26	-1	30	6	53%	28%	19%	0%
2012	MIN	16/16	951	53	94	493	56%	-6.1	9.3	9	3	5.2	12	+0.2	4	-3.4%	31	64	17	8	53%	39%	7%	1%
2013	MIN	8/8	424	30	46	313	65%	+0.3	10.4	3	1	4.0	37	-0.7	6	-13.9%	44	-21	43	-13	44%	36%	20%	0%
2014	*MIN*			*75*	*119*	*847*	*63%*	*--*	*11.3*	*7*						*8.3%*								

Pointing to the exact moment when the Vikings offense went from depressing to insane is tricky. Most point to Josh Freeman's Monday night start, but Rudolph's foot injury took the Vikings into an even darker headspace. Rudolph was essentially the Vikings' slot receiver before the injury, giving the team a productive receiver and an extra blocker for their run-heavy offense. After the injury, the Vikings gave up passing over the middle (a big thing to give up when you have already abandoned the concept of going deep), while any creativity involving Adrian Peterson handoffs evaporated into a fog of off-tackle runs. Rudolph is back, and after Jordan Cameron's breakout season for the Browns in 2013, everyone is talking about how tight end friendly Norv Turner's system is again. The fact that Rudolph put up credible numbers in a passing-unfriendly offense last year suggests that Turner will again get undue right-place-and-time credit.

Austin Seferian-Jenkins Height: 6-5 Weight: 262 College: Washington Draft: 2014/2 (38) Born: 9/29/1992 Age: 22 Risk: Yellow

Year	Team	G/GS	Snaps	Rec	Pass	Yds	C%	+/-	Yd/C	TD	Drop	YAC	Rk	YAC+	BTkl	DVOA	Rk	DYAR	Rk	YAR	Short	Mid	Deep	Bomb
2014	*TB*			*35*	*56*	*373*	*63%*	*--*	*10.7*	*2*						*-2.2%*								

In three years as a starter at Washington, ASJ averaged 49 receptions, 613 yards, and seven touchdowns per season. His 36 catches and 450 yards in 2013 were actually career lows, but they were still good enough to win the Mackey Award as the nation's top collegiate tight end. That award has been an awfully good indicator of NFL success: prior winners include Aaron Hernandez (a very good football player before he started murdering people), Kellen Winslow, Dallas Clark, Heath Miller, Dwayne Allen, Marcedes Lewis, Tyler Eifert, and Fred Davis, plus long-lasting blocking specialists Daniel Graham and Matt Spaeth. Seferian-Jenkins has the athleticism to make leaping catches in traffic. (He grabbed 36 rebounds in only 122 minutes in his short basketball career with the Huskies.) February foot surgery limited him during minicamp, and then he was barred from any workouts until Washington's academic calendar ended in mid-June. Between that delay and the addition and the signing of Brandon Myers, Seferian-Jenkins might get off to a slow start this year, but he could be a good option come fantasy playoff time, and his long-term future is very bright.

Jacob Tamme Height: 6-3 Weight: 236 College: Kentucky Draft: 2008/4 (127) Born: 15-Mar-1985 Age: 29 Risk: Green

Year	Team	G/GS	Snaps	Rec	Pass	Yds	C%	+/-	Yd/C	TD	Drop	YAC	Rk	YAC+	BTkl	DVOA	Rk	DYAR	Rk	YAR	Short	Mid	Deep	Bomb
2011	IND	16/5	330	19	31	177	61%	-1.5	9.3	1	0	4.8	15	-0.3	1	-20.6%	40	-25	37	-33	73%	17%	10%	0%
2012	DEN	16/8	530	52	84	555	62%	+0.7	10.7	2	2	3.8	31	-0.3	1	-5.8%	35	18	32	34	43%	42%	15%	0%
2013	DEN	16/1	264	20	25	184	80%	+3.9	9.2	1	0	3.3	43	-0.7	1	23.7%	7	56	22	53	44%	48%	4%	4%
2014	*DEN*			*24*	*33*	*247*	*73%*	*--*	*10.3*	*2*						*9.3%*								

The emergence of Julius Thomas and the Broncos' regular use of 11 personnel relegated Tamme to more of a reserve role in 2013. His versatility gives him a place on the team—he played slot receiver in the games Wes Welker was injured, plus he led the Broncos in special-teams tackles—but don't expect an even-year increase in receiving production like he had in 2010 and 2012.

Julius Thomas Height: 6-5 Weight: 251 College: Portland State Draft: 2011/4 (129) Born: 27-Jun-1988 Age: 26 Risk: Green

Year	Team	G/GS	Snaps	Rec	Pass	Yds	C%	+/-	Yd/C	TD	Drop	YAC	Rk	YAC+	BTkl	DVOA	Rk	DYAR	Rk	YAR	Short	Mid	Deep	Bomb
2011	DEN	1/1	46	1	7	5	14%	-1.4	5.0	0	0	7.0	--	-1.9	0	-83.5%	--	-36	--	-37	25%	25%	25%	25%
2012	DEN	4/0	2	0	0	0	--	--	--	0	0	--	--	--	--	--	--	--	--	--	--	--	--	--
2013	DEN	14/14	901	65	90	788	72%	+6.0	12.1	12	3	6.2	6	+1.5	6	27.0%	4	214	2	214	58%	24%	18%	0%
2014	*DEN*			*77*	*107*	*932*	*72%*	*--*	*12.1*	*8*						*27.1%*								

For all the ballyhoo about basketball player-to-tight end conversion projects, there have not been too many high-profile success stories. Tony Gonzalez was an outstanding football player at Cal, so he doesn't really count. Antonio Gates does. Ditto Jimmy Graham. But they've been outnumbered by the Fendi Onobuns of the world. We were skeptical about Thomas' potential last offseason, simply because he was developing off the screen, on the practice fields at Dove Valley. Developing he was, though, and he burst onto the scene in Week 1 with 110 yards receiving and two touchdowns. That debut proved to be no fluke but instead the emergence of next standout vertical receiving tight end. In Week 1 and beyond, he displayed the speed to get past safeties and linebackers, plus that basketball background in using his body to create space for himself and make contested catches. Would he be as successful without Peyton Manning? Very likely not, but (a) that's true of basically offensive teammate of Manning's, and (b) we should not have to find out for sure until Peyton retires. He still has work to do on his blocking, but expect another season where he provides a key vertical stretch element to the Broncos' offense and excellent fantasy production.

Levine Toilolo Height: 6-8 Weight: 260 College: Stanford Draft: 2013/4 (133) Born: 30-Jul-1991 Age: 23 Risk: Red

Year	Team	G/GS	Snaps	Rec	Pass	Yds	C%	+/-	Yd/C	TD	Drop	YAC	Rk	YAC+	BTkl	DVOA	Rk	DYAR	Rk	YAR	Short	Mid	Deep	Bomb
2013	ATL	16/3	192	11	14	55	79%	+0.9	5.0	2	1	2.5	--	-2.5	0	-22.4%	--	-19	--	-19	73%	27%	0%	0%
2014	*ATL*			*33*	*45*	*349*	*73%*	*--*	*10.6*	*5*						*22.1%*								

No pressure, kid. You're just filling the shoes of the best guy ever to play your position. Actually, that's not entirely true. Tony Gonzalez was more slot receiver than tight end last season, and the Falcons have said that his targets will go to Harry Douglas this year while Toilolo puts his hand on the turf and focuses on blocking. On the other hand, he has had success as a receiver before. He caught 49 passes for 736 yards and 10 touchdowns his last two years at Stanford, even though he was playing behind Coby Fleener and Zach Ertz. It wouldn't be shocking to see him play a bigger role in the Atlanta offense by season's end.

Interesting digresson: The last time that an NFL team had to replace the greatest tight end of all-time, it used a first-round pick to fill the position. His name was Billy Joe Dupree, and the Cowboys took him 20th overall in the 1973 draft to replace Mike Ditka. He ended up giving the Cowboys an 11-year career, eight of them as a starter and three of them as a Pro Bowler.

Delanie Walker Height: 6-1 Weight: 241 College: Central Missouri Draft: 2006/6 (175) Born: 12-Aug-1984 Age: 30 Risk: Yellow

Year	Team	G/GS	Snaps	Rec	Pass	Yds	C%	+/-	Yd/C	TD	Drop	YAC	Rk	YAC+	BTkl	DVOA	Rk	DYAR	Rk	YAR	Short	Mid	Deep	Bomb
2011	SF	15/7	535	19	36	198	56%	-1.2	10.4	3	3	3.8	34	-1.6	3	-19.4%	39	-19	34	-31	61%	26%	6%	6%
2012	SF	16/4	570	21	39	344	54%	-0.8	16.4	3	7	2.7	47	-1.4	0	-2.8%	30	32	27	26	30%	35%	27%	8%
2013	TEN	15/11	762	60	86	571	70%	+6.8	9.5	6	4	2.9	47	-1.5	4	-0.7%	31	38	25	37	45%	36%	14%	5%
2014	*TEN*			*61*	*93*	*667*	*66%*	*--*	*10.9*	*4*						*5.6%*								

Versatility is the name of the game with Walker, who lined up all over the formation for the Titans last year. Walker isn't going to go to arbitration to figure out if he's a wideout or anything, but a good blocker that can play a solid underneath receiver is a valuable commodity in the NFL today. Walker's slow ramping up of yardage the last three years makes a similarity-score search interesting. The most similar three-year spans: Desmond Clark (2004-2006), Pete Holohan (1986-1988), and Freddie Jones (2001-2003).

Benjamin Watson Height: 6-3 Weight: 255 College: Duke Draft: 2004/1 (32) Born: 18-Dec-1980 Age: 34 Risk: Green

Year	Team	G/GS	Snaps	Rec	Pass	Yds	C%	+/-	Yd/C	TD	Drop	YAC	Rk	YAC+	BTkl	DVOA	Rk	DYAR	Rk	YAR	Short	Mid	Deep	Bomb
2011	CLE	13/11	662	37	71	410	52%	-7.5	11.1	2	4	5.2	12	+0.1	3	-17.0%	37	-42	40	-65	57%	31%	9%	3%
2012	CLE	16/14	853	49	81	501	60%	-2.9	10.2	3	0	4.4	19	+0.2	5	-12.8%	37	-37	42	-30	46%	45%	8%	1%
2013	NO	15/7	494	19	30	226	63%	+2.2	11.9	2	0	4.9	22	-0.0	0	2.5%	25	22	31	21	46%	25%	14%	14%
2014	*NO*			*25*	*43*	*276*	*58%*	*--*	*11.0*	*3*						*3.2%*								

Watson lined up 13 times in the backfield, 12 times split wide, and 19 times in the slot, but by and large he was a legitimate, good ol' fashioned in-line tight end. His per-target stats soared last season, perhaps because he was catching passes from Drew Brees instead of Colt McCoy and Brandon Weeden. Still, his totals were the lowest they had been in years, and they're unlikely to bounce back this season. It's not as if Brees is going to stop throwing to the Jimmy Grahams and Marques Colstons of the world.

Luke Willson Height: 6-5 Weight: 250 College: Rice Draft: 2013/5 (158) Born: 15-Jan-1990 Age: 24 Risk: Green

Year	Team	G/GS	Snaps	Rec	Pass	Yds	C%	+/-	Yd/C	TD	Drop	YAC	Rk	YAC+	BTkl	DVOA	Rk	DYAR	Rk	YAR	Short	Mid	Deep	Bomb
2013	SEA	16/7	404	20	28	272	71%	+2.5	13.6	1	1	8.9	4	+4.2	3	18.2%	11	48	24	43	64%	24%	8%	4%
2014	*SEA*			*25*	*34*	*253*	*74%*	*--*	*10.1*	*3*						*11.1%*								

In the narrow competition of "tight ends from Rice who were drafted by NFC West teams in 2013," Willson currently holds the edge over San Francisco's Vance McDonald, who caught eight passes to Willson's 20. And if Willson continues to improve his blocking, he could scoot ahead even further in this competition—and up Seattle's depth chart—in 2014. His most impressive game in his rookie campaign came against San Francisco in December, when he perhaps wanted to put forth the proposition that the 49ers took the wrong guy. That's open to debate, but as the Seahawks start to open up their offense, Willson is one to watch as a hybrid between the new wave of "big receiver" tight ends and the old school of bigger guys who could also block. The latter will be his ultimate key to more reps in the new season.

Kellen Winslow Height: 6-4 Weight: 254 College: Miami Draft: 2004/1 (6) Born: 21-Jul-1983 Age: 31 Risk: #N/A

Year	Team	G/GS	Snaps	Rec	Pass	Yds	C%	+/-	Yd/C	TD	Drop	YAC	Rk	YAC+	BTkl	DVOA	Rk	DYAR	Rk	YAR	Short	Mid	Deep	Bomb
2011	TB	16/15	822	75	120	763	63%	+2.6	10.2	2	4	3.4	38	-0.9	2	-15.4%	36	-50	42	-70	42%	48%	11%	0%
2012	NE	1/0	4	1	2	12	50%	-0.3	12.0	0	0	3.0	--	+1.1	0	-17.5%	--	0	--	-1	0%	100%	0%	0%
2013	NYJ	12/3	333	31	47	388	66%	+2.2	12.5	2	0	4.1	34	-0.3	2	9.9%	16	52	23	61	41%	48%	11%	0%

Winslow had a nice rebound season with the Jets and was a productive safety valve for his rookie quarterback in limited action. Of course, the biggest headlines Winslow made all year came in January, when he was arrested for possession of synthetic marijuana. Adding embarassment to arrest, Winslow told police he was looking for Boston Market after a woman called police alleging that Winsow was, um, going to market on himself. No team has touched him since, and it would be a surprise if he ever played another snap in the NFL.

Jason Witten Height: 6-6 Weight: 265 College: Tennessee Draft: 2003/3 (69) Born: 6-May-1982 Age: 32 Risk: Red

Year	Team	G/GS	Snaps	Rec	Pass	Yds	C%	+/-	Yd/C	TD	Drop	YAC	Rk	YAC+	BTkl	DVOA	Rk	DYAR	Rk	YAR	Short	Mid	Deep	Bomb
2011	DAL	16/16	1040	79	117	942	68%	+6.1	11.9	5	2	4.6	21	-0.0	11	5.9%	20	68	19	77	47%	38%	12%	3%
2012	DAL	16/16	1078	110	149	1039	74%	+14.2	9.4	3	7	2.8	42	-1.1	3	10.0%	14	192	3	147	43%	46%	10%	1%
2013	DAL	16/16	984	73	111	851	66%	-0.2	11.7	8	4	4.3	31	-0.2	7	11.2%	15	134	5	120	39%	44%	15%	2%
2014	*DAL*			*71*	*111*	*831*	*64%*	*--*	*11.7*	*7*						*15.0%*								

If there was any weakness in Witten's Hall of Fame resume, it would be his lack of touchdown receptions compared to his peers and past greats. But he boosted his total to 52 with eight last year (second most in his career). Dallas will likely try to get 2013 second-round pick Gavin Escobar more involved this year, but Witten's still a great target. His catches and yards dropped from previous seasons, but keep in mind Dallas ran the fewest offensive plays in the league. Witten might need to get more touches underneath to sustain longer drives that will keep that questionable Dallas defense rested and off the field.

Tim Wright Height: 6-3 Weight: 220 College: Rutgers Draft: 2013/FA Born: 7-Apr-1990 Age: 24 Risk: Blue

Year	Team	G/GS	Snaps	Rec	Pass	Yds	C%	+/-	Yd/C	TD	Drop	YAC	Rk	YAC+	BTkl	DVOA	Rk	DYAR	Rk	YAR	Short	Mid	Deep	Bomb
2013	TB	16/8	608	54	75	571	72%	+7.1	10.6	5	3	2.6	49	-1.9	0	21.8%	8	133	6	86	35%	53%	13%	0%
2014	*TB*			*18*	*25*	*178*	*72%*	*--*	*9.9*	*1*						*-1.6%*								

The top tight ends in Tampa Bay last season were supposed to be Luke Stocker and Tom Crabtree, but Stocker's season ended after two games with a hip injury, while Crabtree lasted until November before tearing his triceps. That left Wright in the starting lineup, and he stepped up in a big way, going over 75 yards receiving in games against Philadelphia, Detroit, and San Francisco. Still, there is a reason he went undrafted. The Bucs signed Brandon Myers in free agency and also drafted Austin Sefarian-Jenkins, meaning Wright will have to fight for a job at the bottom of the depth chart this year.

GOING DEEP

David Ausberry, OAK: Ausberry looked like the favorite to be the Raiders' starting tight end, but a training camp shoulder injury cost him the entire season. He needs to show continued development as a receiver and capable blocking, or else his status as presumptive starter will be confirmed as just a product of a depth chart lacking in any established names.

Jake Ballard, ARI: That whole "stash Ballard for a year" thing didn't quite work out for the Patriots, because in preseason games Ballard's knees looked like they were 200 years old. The Cardinals took a shot at him anyway at midseason and apparently Bruce Arians likes him more than Rob Housler, so he's likely to be Arizona's third tight end behind John Carlson and Troy Niklas—even though his knees are now 201 years old. (2013 stats: 7-for-9, 75 yards, 2 TDs, 31 DYAR, 38.3% DVOA)

Gary Barnidge, CLE: Barnidge co-runs global football clinics with close pal Breno Giacomini. He should be spending more time teaching young Nigerians the finer points of the drag route rather than catching NFL passes very soon, as Jim Dray will take all those snaps where he lined up at fullback (91 of them, third among tight ends). (2013 stats: 13-for-18, 127 yards, 2 TDs, -4 DYAR, -10.7% DVOA)

Rob Blanchflower, PIT: A seventh-round rookie tight end in Pittsburgh likely means a good, tough blocker, but a marginal receiver, and that's what Branchflower is. Stash this UMass alum on the back end of the roster, get him some special teams work, and he could be a serviceable replacement in 2015 when Matt Spaeth is a free agent.

Ted Bolser, WAS: Washington likely saw a lot of Niles Paul in Bolser when they grabbed him out of Indiana in the seventh round. He will be a plus on special teams and can catch the ball. He might not play much on offense until he irons out a few wrinkles in his game. He leads with his head too often while blocking, for one. But the Washington depth chart behind Jordan Reed is up for grabs.

Brandon Bostick, GB: All seven of Bostick's catches came in a five-game stretch from Weeks 10 through 14. He then broke a foot, and his slow recovery took him out of spring OTAs. Bostick has some seam-stretching capability, but there is a heck of a crowd forming on the Packers tight-end depth chart. (2013 stats: 7-for-14, 120 yards, 1 TD, -3 DYAR, -11.0% DVOA)

Richie Brockel, CAR: Officially a tight end, our charters spotted Brockel at fullback on a little more than a third of his 198 offensive snaps. He also played on 84 percent of Carolina's special-teams snaps, the third-highest rate of any player in the league. The Panthers do a fine job of maximizing Brockel's strengths (colliding into other men as violently as possible) and minimizing his weaknesses (carrying or catching a football).

Derek Carrier, SF: Carrier, who was promoted from the practice squad as a backup tight end in San Francisco last year, became the first player in the NFL from Beloit College since 1931. Back in the Roaring Twenties, Beloit provided the NFL names such as Pid Purdy, Boob Darling, and Mush Crawford. Beloit College: proof that nicknames aren't nearly as good as they used to be.

James Casey, PHI: After four seasons in Houston, Casey signed a three-year, $12 million deal with the Eagles. There was some talk that Chip Kelly would use the versatile Casey in two-tight end sets similar to the role Aaron Hernandez played in New England, though hopefully without having to alert the Attleboro police. When Zach Ertz was drafted in the second round, that plan essentially disappeared. Casey was featured on special teams and only caught three passes all season as the No. 3 tight end behind Ertz and Brent Celek. The Eagles used a three-tight end set on only nine plays last season, so Casey may continue being an expensive backup. (2013 stats: 3-for-6, 31 yards, -9 DYAR, -29.4% DVOA)

Garrett Celek, SF: Brent Celek's younger brother isn't much of a receiving threat at tight end, but has managed to stick around in San Francisco because of his blocking skills. If you play in a blocking fantasy league, he's a late-round sleeper. Also, if you play in a fantasy blocking league, seek help.

Orson Charles, CIN: Converted to fullback last preseason, Charles never won over skeptical position coach Hue Jackson, who is now the offensive coordinator. An offseason arrest makes his return to Cincy more unlikely. A return to his natural position could pay off elsewhere—he showed promise as a receiver during his rookie season.

Tom Crabtree, FA: Crabtree's first season in Tampa Bay was cut short due to a biceps injury, and Brandon Myers' arrival this year leaves one less spot available for a bottom-of-the-roster blocking tight end. He is similar in size and experience to Luke Stocker, and there was really no reason for the Bucs to keep both. (2013 stats: 4-for-7, 21 yards, 1 TD, -5 DYAR, -17.7% DVOA)

Justice Cunningham, STL: An unscientific top-five list of the best Mr. Irrelevant names ever: 5) Mort Landsberg (Steelers, 1941), 4) Ramzee Robinson (Lions, 2007), 3) Mike Snodgrass (Packers, 1962), 2) Tevita Ofahengaue (Cardinals, 2001), 1) Justice Cunningham (Colts, 2013). There, we found an NFL depth chart that Cunningham could top.

Fred Davis, FA: Titus Young probably had the worst calendar year of any NFL player this decade, but Davis tried to catch him by missing team meetings, getting suspended by the NFL for violating the substance abuse policy, and adding a DUI after the season. Two years ago, this man received the franchise tag. He's got a lot of amends to make before we even figure out how he'd fit with an NFL team again. (2013 stats: 7-for-18, 70 yards, 1 TD, -43 DYAR, -41.5% DVOA)

Kellen Davis, NYG: The Bears hoped that Davis would be a receiving tight end of a higher order, but that didn't pan out after five seasons in the Windy City. The Seahawks wanted him more as blocker, which he can do. Now signed by the Giants, Davis may be mismatched for his skill set again, given Big Blue's whiffs at the tight end position in recent years. (2013 stats: 3-for-4, 32 yards, 1 TD, 9 DYAR, 20.2% DVOA)

Dorin Dickerson, TEN: Dickerson suffered a concussion in the fourth quarter of the Lions' Week 16 game against the Giants but stayed on the field. In overtime, the H-back dropped a short pass and tried to block Justin Tuck by grabbing him around the ankles before admitting that he should report to coaches for protocols. "I mean, honestly, probably, after we leave here, I probably won't remember talking to you guys," Dickerson joked to reporters after the game. The concussion was the third of Dickerson's career, so there are obvious reasons why a fringe all-purpose sub would want to hide an injury that could take away his roster appeal. How a team reaches the point where it cannot cope with the loss of a woozy Dorin Dickerson against a mediocre opponent is another matter. The concussion protocols remain only as viable as coaches and players make them.

Larry Donnell, NYG: Never heard of Larry Donnell? The 6-foot-5 Grambling State product went undrafted in 2012 and has just three catches in two years. Donnell is not much of a receiver, but a roster spot may have been ensured when the Giants chose not to address this position in the draft. The Giants are hoping for a tight end to emerge, and it's more likely to be Adrien Robinson than Donnell, who can contribute at multiple positions and on special teams, but hasn't shown any ability to be a productive receiver in the NFL. Then again, neither has Robinson. (2013 stats: 3-for-6, 31 yards, -5 DYAR, -19.2% DVOA)

Jack Doyle, IND: Doyle is listed as a tight end, but was primarily a blocking fullback in the Pep Hamilton Establishing the Run parade. If Stanley Havili stays healthy, Doyle won't have much of an offensive role in Indy this year. (2013 stats: 5-for-7, 19 yards, -30 DYAR, -67.9% DVOA)

Jim Dray, CLE: Dray moved on after four years in Arizona and signed a three-year deal with Cleveland. He's a much better blocker than the tight ends who backed up Jordan Cameron a year ago, Gary Barnidge and MarQueis Gray. (2013 stats: 26-for-32, 215 yards, 2 TDs, 21 DYAR, 2.3% DVOA)

Joel Dreessen, FA: The emergence of Julius Thomas and the continued development of Virgil Green left the versatile but not standout Dreessen without a significant role in 2013. Cut right before press time. (2013 stats: 7-for-9, 47 yards, 1 TD, -5 DYAR, -14.2% DVOA)

Michael Egnew, MIA: It's been a disappointing two seasons for the 2012 third-round pick. After the horrific injury to Dustin Keller in the preseason, Egnew had an opportunity to step up, but finished the season with just seven receptions on 11 targets for 69 yards (-9 DYAR and -21.2% DVOA). The really strange thing is that the Dolphins keep using Egnew as a lead blocker, even though he was very specifically drafted as a receiving-first tight end from a collegiate spread offense at Missouri. Last year, Dolphins running backs had 64 carries with Egnew at fullback and averaged 2.7 yards per carry with 17 stuffs. They had 31 carries with Charles Clay at fullback and averaged 4.9 yards per carry with five stuffs.

Rhett Ellison, MIN: When Jim Kleinsasser retired, the Vikings took some of his genetic material to the cloning facility on planet Kamino and created an entire race of H-backs. The clones were not quite as good as Kleinsasser (a security feature to prevent an uprising consisting mostly of bootleg passes) except for one: Ellison, who was given Kleinsasser's old uniform number to symbolize his uniqueness. Ellison lurks quietly among the throngs of H-back clones on the Vikings fullback and tight-end depth charts, but if the team needs someone to catch a bootleg pass to force a tie against the Packers again, Ellison will be there. (2013 stats: 5-for-10, 61 yards, 1 TD, 3 DYAR, -3.1% DVOA)

Daniel Fells, NYG: Fells is generally more of an H-back than an in-line tight end. He didn't play in 2013 after the Patriots made him one of their final cuts, but the Giants signed him up to give him a try this offseason. The sad part is that, given the current state of the Giants' depth chart at the position, it's easy to imagine Fells starting multiple games for Big Blue this season. (2012 stats: 4-for-9, 85 yards, 10 DYAR, 16.8% DVOA)

C.J. Fiedorowicz, HOU: He's supposed to be Bill O'Brien's answer to Rob Gronkowski, but at this point this third-round pick from Iowa is a block-first tight end who can catch 4-5 balls a game. He's never going to threaten the defense after the catch, though he could develop into an intermediate receiver with some more work on his routes. In an ideal world, he turns into Heath Miller.

Chase Ford, MIN: Ford was activated from the Vikings practice squad when Kyle Rudolph got hurt last year, then started seeing offensive snaps when John Carlson turned the injured reserve into a Notre Dame tight end reunion. Ford caught a 37-yard pass against the Eagles and went 5-43-0 on seven targets in the season finale. The Vikings have an insatiable craving for tight ends and H-backs, so Ford is one of a throng. He will see few passes, but he could stick because a) he was useful on special teams; and b) the Vikings somehow wind up using all 25 of their H-backs every year. (2013 stats: 11-for-16, 133 yards, 6 DYAR, -1.2% DVOA)

Crockett Gillmore, BAL: With a name like Crockett Gillmore, you expect an '80s style wrestling heel from the south. He almost looks the part with his long hair, but Gillmore has a good shot to anonymously slip into the blocking tight end role with Dennis Pitta and Owen Daniels ahead of him as receivers. He has some catching ability, but at 6-foot-6, 260 pounds and experience at defensive end, Baltimore's third-round pick (out of Colorado State) going to earn his money in the trenches.

Chris Gragg, BUF: A seventh-round pick in 2013 who struggled to get playing time. He's shown an ability to get some separation with some nice speed, and could get an opportunity if Moeaki can't shake the injury woes that have dogged him as of late. (2013 stats: 5-for-7, 53 yards, 1 TD, 17 DYAR, 21.8% DVOA)

MarQueis Gray, CLE: Gray was a 6-foot-4, 255-pound college quarterback at Minnesota, which gives you an idea of his athleticism. He could prove a mismatch problem, but he blocks like a former quarterback as well. The Browns expect him to contribute after a bruise-filled rookie year.

Virgil Green, DEN: How do you manage a DVOA of -61.0% playing in an offense as prolific as Denver's last year? For one, make your routes short. Only one of Green's 12 targets came more than 5 yards downfield. Second, don't gain many yards after catch, like most receivers do on short passes. Third, don't post an exemplary catch rate. Green has the athleticism to be a more productive, more vertical receiver than he was in 2013 and is a willing blocker, but he's behind Julius Thomas and the Broncos spent most of their time in 2013 in 11 personnel. (2013 stats: 9-for-12, 45 yards, -44 DYAR, -61.0% DVOA)

James Hanna, DAL: With Jason Witten and Gavin Escobar stealing the spotlight by catching passes, someone has to do some blocking at tight end for Dallas. That falls to James Hanna, though he also lined up in the backfield at fullback 34 times. He also caught three more passes than the rookie Escobar, but that should change this season. (2013 stats: 12-for-15, 73 yards, -19 DYAR, -28.3% DVOA)

Cory Harkey, STL: While the Rams list Harkey as a tight end, he's really more of a fullback. Based on our count, he lined up in the backfield nearly three times as often as any other tight end in the league last year. The full table is in Charles Clay's comment. (2013 stats: 13-for-18, 113 yards, 2 TDs, 13 DYAR, 2.2% DVOA)

Ben Hartsock, FA: A partial history of Ben Hartsock's career, as told via player comments in *Pro Football Prospectus* and *Football Outsiders Almanac*:

2007: "He's an effective in-line blocker with acceptable hands and special-teams value."
2008: "Hartsock is a good blocker and special-teams player who can occasionally make plays as a receiver."
2009: "He blocks well enough to stick around as the third tight end, assuming the Falcons keep three."
2010: "[The Jets used Hartsock] to plow open holes for assorted running backs. He's good at that. Catching passes? Not so much."
2011: "[If] you need a second or third tight end for your goal-line sets, Hartsock might well be your guy."
2012: "He is milking the last drops of veteran special-teamer career value."
2013: "At what point do we just label him a mini-tackle and be done with it?"

Hartsock had zero targets in 13 games for Carolina last season, and now has 59 targets in 131 career games. Tyler Eifert had 59 targets as a rookie last year in Cincinnati. Hartsock's career stats: a 53 percent Catch Rate, 10.1 yards per catch, one touchdown, -72 DYAR, and a cumulative DVOA of -24.7%. Hartsock is still unsigned, but he has had a remarkably long career given his limited skill set, and we'll probably write about his good blocking and lousy hands again come 2015.

Josh Hill, NO: Hill lined up as an in-line tight end for 153 snaps last year, which doesn't sound like much, but it's nearly half of Jimmy Graham's total of 327. More importantly, Hill also played on more than two-thirds' of the Saints' special teams plays, and it's his performance there that will determine if he keeps his roster spot. (2013 stats: 6-for-10, 44 yards, 1 TD, -6 DYAR, -14.7% DVOA)

Michael Hoomanawanui, NE: "Hooman" won't make anyone forget about Rob Gronkowski, but he has distinguished himself as a relatively solid, dependable backup who can play multiple tight-end spots and rarely drops the ball whenever it's sent his way. (2013 stats: 12-for-19, 136 yards, 1 TD, 3 DYAR, -4.4% DVOA)

David Johnson, SD: A blocking tight end with 30 career targets in 52 games, Johnson missed the entire 2012 season due to a torn ACL and then played 75 snaps in 2013 before a left wrist injury placed him on injured reserve for the second year in a row. (2013 stats: 4-for-6, 70 yards, 18 DYAR, 41.8% DVOA)

Justin Jones, NE: Last year, the Patriots tried to utilize oversized UDFA Zach Sudfeld (6-foot-7, 253 pounds) as an under-the-radar possibility who could pick up some snaps in the absence of Rob Gronkowski. Sudfeld didn't make it past Halloween in Foxboro, cut before he caught a single regular-season pass. Jones (6-foot-8, 274 pounds) is this year's model. The East Carolina product has some impressive physical traits—as a collegian, he posted a 4 6.88-second three-cone drill and 38-inch vertical jump—but he's probably bound for the practice squad, especially if the Patriots land a veteran tight end who can help pick up the slack if/when Gronkowski goes down in 2014.

Dustin Keller, FA: Keller suffered a devastating injury last August during a preseason game with Miami. He tore his ACL, MCL, and PCL and dislocated his knee. He's been linked to the Patriots this offseason, but no deal is imminent and an injury this serious isn't exactly something easy to bounce back from. (2012 stats: 28-for-36, 317 yards, 2 TD, 76 DYAR, 26.4% DVOA)

Colt Lyerla, GB: Mark Bavaro meets Tony Montana. Lyerla quit the Oregon football team last season just a step ahead of John Law; he was arrested on cocaine possession a few days later, and his driver's license had already been revoked for multiple violations. Lyerla blocks well when his head and heart are in the game. He has soft hands, and forces defenders to gang tackle him in the open field. Obviously a risk-reward guy, Lyerla will draw Aaron Hernandez comparisons, because every kid who screws up with drugs in his early 20s ends up a murderer.

Arthur Lynch, MIA: A fifth-round pick out of Georgia, Lynch doesn't bring much to the party as a receiver. Some scouts weren't keen with his strength or quickness, but teams are always looking for a guy capable of blocking.

Jeron Mastrud, CHI: A willing blocker on an Oakland team with an anemic passing offense, a solid run game, and nothing established at his position, 2013 was likely the apex of Mastrud's NFL career. Signed with Chicago this offseason. (2013 stats: 6-for-13, 88 yards, -16 DYAR, -24.9% DVOA)

Anthony McCoy, SEA: It became a bit of a drinking game among Seattle sportswriters—take a shot later on for every pass McCoy dropped in practice. That game came to an end last season, when he went down with a torn Achilles tendon and missed the 2013 year. Re-signed by Seattle, McCoy will try once again to match his wavy concentration to his admittedly impressive physical skills. (2012 stats: 18-for-28, 291 yards, 3 TD, 90 DYAR, 35.5% DVOA)

Tony Moeaki, BUF: A wild card. If he can stay healthy, he could become a real presence in the Buffalo passing game. (He had 80 catches in two years with the Chiefs.) He's younger than expected starter Scott Chandler, and has considerably more upside as an athletic presence. But there have been head, knee, shoulder and back issues in his relatively brief NFL career. (2012 stats: 33-for-56, 453 yards, 1 TD, 49 DYAR, 7.1% DVOA)

Matthew Mulligan, CHI: A nice complementary player who signed with the Bears in the offseason, he gained his greatest fame in New England after his wife ordered a faux WWE championship belt from Hulk Hogan, and Hogan name-checked him in a promo video.

Danny Noble, FA: Noble caught a long play-action pass on fourth down when the Cardinals left him uncovered, scoring a touchdown. He also blocked defensive players sometimes. It's probably not a good sign for his future that the Jaguars released him, as there aren't many teams with a weaker depth chart at tight end. At least he got a cool highlight to show the kids, though.

Michael Palmer, PIT: Palmer mostly plays special teams (47 offensive snaps for a team with major injuries at tight end), much like fellow backup tight end David Paulson. Palmer is more of a blocker and the backup to Matt Spaeth while Paulson would be a better replacement for Heath Miller.

Bear Pascoe, ATL: Pascoe has been in the league for five years and has never caught three passes in a single regular-season game. His place on New York's roster showed us exactly how much time four catches and 33 yards in a Super Bowl could buy you: evidently, two more years. Pascoe may not be much of a receiver, but he's an above-average run blocker. In that light, he was a good addition to a Falcons team that ranked last in rushing attempts last year and is trying to get more physical on both sides of the ball. (2013 stats: 12-for-20, 81 yards, -54 DYAR, -52.0% DVOA)

Niles Paul, WAS: A converted wideout that was picked in the fifth round of the 2011 draft, Paul specializes in blocking and special teams work. Washington's depth chart is dangerously thin behind Jordan Reed, so if Reed's concussion problems re-emerge, we could wind up with more Niles in our life than we've had at any time since *Frasier* went off the air. (2013 stats: 4-for-8, 51 yards, -11 DYAR, -26.8% DVOA)

David Paulson, PIT: With Heath Miller and Matt Spaeth both injured early last season, Paulson was given ample opportunities to shine, but his lack of production only reminded the team how much they missed Miller. Once the Steelers were healthier at the position, Paulson's playing time on offense was marginalized. His last big play of the season was a 30-yard catch on a fake punt against the Packers. Paulson should continue to play a big part on special teams, but is more of an emergency tight end. (2013 stats: 6-for-10, 102 yards, -15 DYAR, -28.9% DVOA)

John Phillips, SD: Blocking specialist who tore his right ACL in December, unlikely to play this season. (2013 stats: 4-for-6, 30 yards, -15 DYAR, -42.9% DVOA)

Allen Reisner, MIN: Last year, Reisner more than doubled his career reception total, hauling in five whole receptions. Minnesota either realized that they missed his blocking, or they expect him to continue doubling his reception total every year until that means he's worthwhile. (It also helps that they didn't want to keep paying out John Carlson's bloated contract.) (2013 stats: 5-for-9, 40 yards, -22 DYAR, -48.4% DVOA)

Konrad Reuland, NYJ: Reuland struggled to find playing time with the Jets before a knee injury ended his season after Week 9. The former 49er offers little as a receiver, but is not a strong enough blocker to earn playing time even for a team that values blocking like New York. The 260-pound blocking tight end/H-back is close to becoming extinct; the 260-pounder who is a mediocre blocker never survived in the NFL.

Dante Rosario, CHI: The race for the Bears backup tight end job is wide open. Rosario, a backup tight end lifer, has the inside track; the rest of the gang is a Who's Who of Blockers for Kickoff Returns. Here's the thing: Marc Trestman shows zero interest in throwing passes to No. 2 tight ends, No. 4 receivers, backup running backs, or other peripheral players, so the winner of the backup sweepstakes will be lucky to double Rosario's one-catch 2013 production.

Weslye Saunders, IND: Saunders spent his offseason interning at SB Nation, where he wrote a column about how his combine experience coming out of college was a nightmare. The more he gets to block, the better. When the Colts were bereft of options last year, they actually threw at Saunders a few times. It wasn't pretty. (2013 stats: 4-for-11, 46 yards, -17 DYAR, -27.6% DVOA)

Tony Scheffler, FA: Scheffler squeezed three dropped passes into five games before suffering a concussion and getting released by the Lions as soon as he cleared protocols. That was overachieving by even Scheffler's lofty butter-fingered standards, as if after four seasons he was outright daring the Lions to admit they made a mistake and give up on him. (2013 stats: 7-for-12, 82 yards, -16 DYAR, -26.9% DVOA)

Dion Sims, MIA: He's an in-line tight end, but not nearly as versatile or productive as teammate Charles Clay. The Dolphins did ask Sims to line up in the slot at times with two of the rookie's six catches coming out of the slot. However, blocking alongside that battered offensive line made up most of Sims' rookie responsibilities. (2013 stats: 6-for-10, 32 yards, 1 TD, -12 DYAR, -22.0% DVOA)

Alex Smith, FA: Smith is a nine-year veteran of the league but his signature accolade is capturing the Madden Bowl title in back-to-back years. The former Tampa Bay Buc was brought to the Bengals by Jay Gruden as thanks for never going against the family; as such his future lies not in Cincy but D.C., if anywhere. (2013 stats: 3-for-6, 12 yards, 1 TD, -36 DYAR, -87.5% DVOA)

Lee Smith, BUF: Known more as a blocker, the chances in the passing game for this former Marshall standout are few and far between. He was probably one of the happier people in New York when the Bills passed on Eric Ebron this past spring, and brings depth and dependability at what should be the third tight spot for Buffalo. (2013 stats: 5-for-9, 78 yards, -4 DYAR, -13.7% DVOA)

Matt Spaeth, PIT: Spaeth is the consummate "can't really catch, but he'll make up for it by blocking" tight end. A disappointing third-round pick by the Steelers in 2007, Spaeth became another one of general manager Kevin Colbert's reclamation projects, returning to Pittsburgh after two seasons in Chicago. The return was delayed thanks to a Lisfranc injury that limited Spaeth to 132 snaps in 2013. Now healthy, Spaeth should return to his role as Heath Miller's primary backup.

Craig Stevens, TEN: Stevens, the patron saint of blocking tight ends, saw his snaps get cut in 2013 following the acquisition of Delanie Walker. It's nothing against Stevens' skill set—the Titans just ran fewer two-tight end sets. He's still the clear No. 2 on this depth chart, but don't expect fantasy relevance.

Luke Stocker, TB: Stocker's third season in Tampa Bay was cut short due to a hip injury, and Brandon Myers' arrival this year leaves one less spot available for a bottom-of-the-roster blocking tight end. He is similar in size and experience to Tom Crabtree, and there's really no reason for the Bucs to keep both. Yes, this comment was copy-and-pasted from Crabtree's. If there's any significant difference between the two, it is in age—Stocker is three years younger than Crabtree, and that might give him an edge in their competition.

Zach Sudfeld, NYJ: ~~With 900 yards and nine touchdowns, this Gronkowski clone was the Rookie of the Year and the fantasy steal of 2013. Please update this comment after season ends.~~ Sudfeld caught eight passes for 101 yards and a touchdown in the preseason and earned rave reviews in training camp with the Patriots. Then, in September, he failed to record a single catch with New England before mishandling an onside kick against Atlanta. He was promptly released by the Patriots. The Jets signed him but Sudfeld made little impact in his three months in New York. Still, there were reasons for the hype, and Sudfeld was a raw player coming out of Nevada and should be given time to grow. His unique measurables make it easy to see him as a potential nightmare, but first, Sudfeld needs to learn an NFL offense and improve as a run blocker. (2013 stats: 5-for-10, 63 yards, -10 DYAR, -20.1% DVOA)

Ryan Taylor, GB: Special-teamer and H-back, Taylor saw some action at tight end due to Jermichael Finley's injury last year. He's a helpful role player but the last guy the Packers want to see get more than one touch per month. (2013 stats: 6-for-9, 30 yards, -33 DYAR, -56.3% DVOA)

Taylor Thompson, TEN: If we ever made a Pro Day League for Teddy Bridgewater to struggle in, Taylor Thompson would be a star in it. He's tall (6-foot-6), fast (4.57 forty-yard dash time), and has done absolutely nothing of value for the Titans over the past two seasons. But at least he looked good doing it.

Brandon Williams, CAR: Williams briefly played for the Oregon Ducks before a diagnosis of spinal stenosis seemingly ended his football career. He spent some time on the basketball team at Portland Bible College (go Wildcats!) before further testing cleared him to play football again. The Panthers liked what they saw at a regional scouting combine in Seattle and gave him a deal, but his playing time as a rookie was limited to 91 snaps (only 26 of them on offense) in nine games. It's a great story and Williams is easy to cheer for, but he faces an uphill battle to make the team after Carolina added veterans Mike McNeill and Ed Dickson to back up Greg Olson.

D.J. Williams, NE: Williams won't play a sizable role for the Patriots in 2014, but he certainly won our hearts last year when, shortly after he was acquired, he said trying to pick up the Patriots' passing game was like trying to pick up "very attractive Hispanic lady."

Michael Williams, DET: A seventh-round pick last year, Williams bulked up from 270 pounds to 300 pounds and will try to stick with the Lions as a reserve tackle this year. Tony Scheffler tried to do the same thing but kept dropping the protein shakes.

2014 Kicker Projections

Listed below are the 2014 KUBIAK projections for kickers. Because of the inconsistency of field-goal percentage from year to year, kickers are projected almost entirely based on team forecasts, although a handful of individual factors do come into play:

• More experience leads to a slightly higher field-goal percentage in general, with the biggest jump between a kicker's rookie and sophomore seasons.

• Kickers with a better career field-goal percentage tend to get more attempts, although they are not necessarily more accurate.

• Field-goal percentage on kicks over 40 yards tends to regress to the mean.

Kickers are listed with their total fantasy points based on two different scoring systems. For Pts1, all field goals are worth three points. For Pts2, all field goals up to 39 yards are worth three points, field goals of 40-49 yards are worth four points, and field goals over 50 yards are worth five points. Kickers are also listed with a Risk of Green, Yellow, or Red, as explained in the introduction to the section on quarterbacks.

Note that field-goal totals below are rounded, but "fantasy points" are based on the actual projections, so the total may not exactly equal (FG * 3 + XP).

Fantasy Kicker Projections, 2014

Kicker	Team	FG	Pct	XP	Pts1	Pts2	Risk
Stephen Gostkowski	NE	35-40	88%	41	145	161	Green
Mason Crosby	GB	31-32	95%	50	141	156	Yellow
Matt Prater	DEN	25-28	90%	57	132	146	Green
Dan Bailey	DAL	31-35	89%	39	131	146	Yellow
Shayne Graham	NO	28-33	85%	47	130	143	Red
Nick Novak	SD	27-31	86%	46	128	141	Red
Robbie Gould	CHI	29-33	87%	41	127	142	Yellow
Blair Walsh	MIN	29-35	84%	38	126	142	Green
Mike Nugent	CIN	29-32	91%	40	126	140	Yellow
Adam Vinatieri	IND	27-33	82%	44	126	138	Green
Shaun Suisham	PIT	28-33	86%	43	125	138	Yellow
Jay Feely	ARI	31-35	88%	32	125	138	Yellow
Matt Bryant	ATL	29-32	90%	37	124	138	Yellow
Steven Hauschka	SEA	27-31	87%	42	124	136	Green
Justin Tucker	BAL	30-35	87%	33	122	140	Green
Nate Freese	DET	27-34	81%	42	122	134	Red
Nick Folk	NYJ	28-33	85%	36	122	134	Yellow
Ryan Succop	KC	29-34	86%	33	121	135	Green
Greg Zuerlein	STL	28-33	86%	36	118	135	Yellow
Phil Dawson	SF	25-29	86%	44	118	131	Green
Josh Brown	NYG	27-30	90%	37	117	130	Green
Graham Gano	CAR	26-31	85%	38	117	129	Red
Randy Bullock	HOU	26-31	84%	36	115	127	Green
Caleb Sturgis	MIA	25-30	84%	37	113	125	Red
Travis Coons	TEN	26-33	80%	36	113	124	Red
Sebastian Janikowski	OAK	28-32	89%	29	112	128	Yellow
Billy Cundiff	CLE	26-29	90%	35	112	124	Yellow
Connor Barth	TB	26-31	84%	33	111	124	Red
Alex Henery	PHI	22-27	82%	46	110	121	Green
Dustin Hopkins	BUF	25-30	84%	34	108	119	Red
Zach Hocker	WAS	23-29	78%	37	106	116	Red
Josh Scobee	JAC	25-29	87%	29	104	117	Yellow

Other kickers who may win jobs:							
Kicker	Team	FG	Pct	XP	Pts1	Pts2	Risk
Giorgio Tavecchio	DET	27-34	79%	42	122	134	Red
Derek Dimke	NO	27-32	84%	48	128	140	Red
Maikon Bonani	TEN	26-33	79%	36	114	127	Red
Kai Forbath	WAS	26-30	87%	37	115	127	Red

2014 Fantasy Defense Projections

Listed below are the 2014 KUBIAK projections for fantasy team defense. The projection method is discussed in an essay in Pro Football Prospectus 2006, the key conclusions of which were:

- Schedule strength is very important for projecting fantasy defense.
- Categories used for scoring in fantasy defense have no consistency from year-to-year whatsoever, with the exception of sacks and interceptions.

Fumble recoveries and defensive touchdowns are forecast solely based on the projected sacks and interceptions, rather than the team's totals in these categories from a year ago. This is why the 2014 projections may look very different from the fantasy defense values from the 2013 season. Safeties and shutouts are not common enough to have a significant effect on the projections. Team defenses are also projected with Risk factor of Green, Yellow, or Red; this is based on the team's projection compared to performance in recent seasons.

In addition to projection of separate categories, we also give an overall total based on our generic fantasy scoring formula: one point for a sack, two points for a fumble recovery or interception, and six points for a touchdown. Remember that certain teams (in particular San Francisco) will score better if your league also gives points for limiting opponents' scoring or yardage. Special teams touchdowns are listed separately and are not included in the fantasy scoring total listed.

Fantasy Team Defense Projections, 2014

Team	Fant Pts	Sack	Int	Fum Rec	Def TD	Risk	ST TD	Team	Fant Pts	Sack	Int	Fum Rec	Def TD	Risk	ST TD
CAR	128	47.7	17.0	10.8	4.2	Yellow	0.8	BAL	109	38.8	15.1	11.1	2.9	Yellow	0.9
SEA	128	43.1	20.0	11.8	3.6	Green	0.8	SF	108	38.7	17.1	9.1	2.8	Green	0.7
STL	125	48.8	16.1	12.3	3.3	Red	0.7	WAS	108	37.1	15.6	9.1	3.5	Yellow	0.8
DEN	121	44.2	18.6	10.8	3.0	Red	0.7	ARI	108	40.4	15.8	11.0	2.2	Yellow	0.5
BUF	119	44.5	16.9	11.8	2.9	Green	0.8	TEN	107	36.5	15.4	11.0	3.0	Red	0.6
NYJ	116	43.2	16.2	11.5	2.9	Yellow	0.9	GB	107	40.3	15.7	9.9	2.6	Yellow	0.7
NO	116	41.4	15.9	11.2	3.4	Red	0.9	CHI	104	34.6	16.8	10.1	2.6	Green	0.8
CIN	115	44.2	17.4	11.0	2.3	Yellow	0.6	TB	104	36.1	13.8	11.4	2.9	Yellow	0.8
NE	115	41.9	16.3	11.1	3.0	Green	0.7	DAL	103	30.3	15.2	12.6	2.9	Yellow	0.9
MIA	114	39.0	15.4	11.7	3.4	Red	0.8	SD	102	37.5	14.5	9.1	2.9	Red	0.9
DET	111	37.9	14.8	11.5	3.5	Yellow	0.9	CLE	100	35.5	14.6	9.6	2.7	Red	0.7
PHI	111	38.3	18.3	8.6	3.1	Green	0.7	OAK	100	38.6	13.7	10.5	2.2	Yellow	0.7
KC	111	39.9	16.0	10.4	3.0	Yellow	1.1	PIT	99	38.7	12.8	9.4	2.6	Red	0.9
HOU	111	39.8	14.7	11.6	3.0	Red	0.8	ATL	98	35.9	12.8	10.7	2.6	Yellow	1.4
NYG	110	37.2	16.3	11.3	2.9	Yellow	1.1	JAC	97	37.8	13.3	10.1	2.0	Yellow	0.9
MIN	109	37.6	15.3	11.8	2.9	Red	1.4	IND	93	34.9	13.3	9.0	2.2	Yellow	0.8

Projected Defensive Leaders, 2014

Solo Tackles			Total Tackles			Sacks			Interceptions		
Player	Team	Tkl	Player	Team	Tkl	Player	Team	Sacks	Player	Team	INT
P.Posluszny	JAC	113	L.Kuechly	CAR	160	R.Quinn	STL	12.1	R.Sherman	SEA	4.6
L.David	TB	105	V.Burfict	CIN	154	C.Jordan	NO	11.8	J.Byrd	NO	4.4
V.Burfict	CIN	102	L.David	TB	153	A.Smith	SF	11.5	D.Hall	WAS	3.7
L.Kuechly	CAR	101	P.Posluszny	JAC	148	C.Wake	MIA	11.4	E.Thomas	SEA	3.7
K.Dansby	CLE	98	J.Mayo	NE	146	Z.Ansah	DET	11.2	E.Reid	SF	3.5
D.Johnson	KC	97	J.Freeman	IND	133	J.J.Watt	HOU	11.2	A.Rolle	NYG	3.5
J.Mayo	NE	96	C.Lofton	NO	126	J.Peppers	GB	10.7	C.Bailey	NO	3.4
P.Willis	SF	94	K.Dansby	CLE	124	J.Allen	CHI	10.7	D.Milliner	NYJ	3.3
B.Church	DAL	90	B.Wagner	SEA	123	V.Miller	DEN	10.7	C.Godfrey	CAR	3.2
J.Laurinaitis	STL	89	C.Greenway	MIN	123	M.Williams	BUF	10.5	D.Rodgers-Cromartie	NYG	3.2
A.Ogletree	STL	88	D.Smith	BAL	120	E.Dumervil	BAL	10.4	S.Shields	GB	3.2
D.Ryans	PHI	88	L.Timmons	PIT	120	O.Vernon	MIA	10.4	T.Jennings	CHI	3.2

College Football Introduction and Statistical Toolbox

A college football season takes on a personality of its own as the 14 or so weeks of the regular season unfold. Sometimes it is marked by early upsets and late upstarts. Sometimes key injuries define the national title race. Sometimes the early-season favorites remain the favorites throughout.

When the first BCS standings of the season were unveiled in mid-October 2013, things seemed to be moving along as expected. Sure, there were surprises, both of the good (Missouri was 5-0 and fifth in the BCS) and bad (Florida was 4-3 and dropping like a rock) varieties, but the top spots belonged mostly to those projected to own the top spots: Alabama at No. 1, Oregon at No. 3, Ohio State at No. 4, Stanford at No. 6. Florida State was finally living up to its recruiting rankings, but that was only so much of a surprise.

Then a grenade named Auburn turned the season into one of the strangest and most thrilling on record. Led by new head coach and spread-to-run guru Gus Malzahn—their offensive coordinator during their 2010 national title run—the Tigers, 3-9 in 2012, started the season slowly, with narrow home wins over Washington State and Mississippi State and a loss at LSU. But beginning with a road upset of Texas A&M on October 19, their season began to take on a different look. They rocked Arkansas and Tennessee on the road and stood at 9-1 with two games left in the regular season. With home wins over Georgia (not a given) and Alabama (yeah, right), they could take the SEC West title.

Everything started out well against Georgia. Auburn took a 27-10 lead into halftime and increased the lead to 37-17 early in the fourth quarter. But a wounded Georgia team fought back, scoring three times in eight minutes to take a stunning 38-37 lead. Auburn quickly fell into a fourth-and-18 situation with just 36 seconds left, and quarterback Nick Marshall threw a prayer downfield toward receiver Ricardo Louis and two Georgia defenders; the two defenders ran into each other and deflected the ball into the air. Louis somehow found it over his left shoulder, reeled it in, and took it for a 73-yard score. Georgia actually managed to advance to the Auburn 20 as time expired, but the Tigers survived. It was the most miraculous finish of the season, and it remained that way for only seven days.

Alabama came to town, and Auburn's improbable run got even less probable. The game was tied at 21-21 heading into the fourth quarter, when Alabama's A.J. McCarron found Amari Cooper for a 99-yard bomb and the lead. Alabama quickly got the ball back with a chance to increase that lead, but Carl Lawson stuffed T.J. Yeldon on fourth-and-1 from the Auburn 13. Alabama got yet another chance, but Robenson Therezie blocked a Cade Foster field goal, Alabama's third miss of the day. With just 32 seconds remaining, Marshall ran left on what appeared to be an option keeper, then found Sammie Coates alone on the sideline for a 39-yard touchdown to tie the game.

With one second left and overtime imminent, Alabama lined up to try an unlikely 57-yard field goal. What's the worst that could happen, right? Adam Griffith's 57-yard attempt came up just short, and Chris Davis fielded it nine yards deep in his end zone...

...and returned it 109 yards for the game-winning score as time expired. What might be college football's most bitter, defining rivalry produced what might be college football's greatest ending.

The rest of the story barely matters at this point. Auburn survived a shootout with surprising Missouri in the SEC title game, then took a lead into the final seconds before falling to Florida State and Heisman winner Jameis Winston.

As with most recent years, offseason conversation has revolved around the potential changes that might one day be forced on the NCAA: Will student-athletes be granted a stipend to cover full cost of their school attendance (and which ones)? Will lawsuits regarding the sale of student-athletes' likenesses (with no extra money going to the athletes themsevles) succeed? In an era of increasing television money, what will college football – and college sports in general – look like 10 or 20 years from now?

The 2014 season, however, will forever represent the fruition of a different kind of change. At the end of the regular season, an appointed committee will choose four teams to play in the first ever College Football Playoff. The Rose Bowl and Sugar Bowl will host semifinal games on January 1, and AT&T Stadium, home of both the Dallas Cowboys and the Cotton Bowl, will host the championship on January 12. After more than four decades of debating, college football indeed has a playoff. It's a small one, but even small change is significant in a sport that is at once betrothed and chained to history and tradition.

Our history of analyzing college football at Football Outsiders is a bit shorter, but we have our own traditions. For 11 years, Brian Fremeau has been developing and enhancing the drive-based Fremeau Efficiency Index (FEI) and its companion statistics; for the last seven years, Bill Connelly's research has explored play-by-play data, developing measures of efficiency and explosiveness and creating his system, the S&P+ ratings. In January 2013, he began to include a drive component in the overall S&P+ numbers as well. Both systems are schedule-adjusted and effective in both evaluating teams and uncovering strengths and weaknesses. The combination of the two ratings, F/+, provides the best of both worlds.

The College Statistical Toolbox section that follows this introduction explains the methodology of FEI, S&P+, F/+, and other stats you will encounter in the college chapters of this book. There are similarities to Football Outsiders' NFL-based DVOA ratings in the combined approach, but college football presents a unique set of challenges different from the NFL. All football stats must be adjusted according to context, but how? If Team A and Team B do not play one another and don't share any common opponents, how can their stats be effectively compared? Should a team from the SEC or Big 12 be measured against that of an average team in its own conference, or an average FBS team? With nine years of full data, we are still only scratching the surface with these measures, but the recent progress has been both swift and exciting.

This book devotes a chapter to each of the five major conferences (they are no longer "BCS" conferences, as the BCS is no longer in existence), and a sixth chapter covering the best of the rest. The chapters provide a snapshot of each team's statistical profile in 2013 and projections for 2014, along with a summary of its keys to the upcoming season. Player and coaching personnel changes, offensive and defensive advantages and deficiencies, and schedule highlights and pitfalls are all discussed by our team of college football writers. The top prospects for the 2015 NFL draft are listed at the end of each team segment. An asterisk denotes a player who may or may not enter the draft as a junior eligible.

Each chapter concludes with a Win Probability table. For each of the 128 FBS teams, we project the likelihood of every possible regular-season record, conference and non-conference alike, and we've added division and overall conference championship likelihoods this year as well. We hope the Win Probability tables provide a broader understanding of our projections and the impact of strength of schedule on team records.

We've also produced the first College Football Playoff projections for the new era, the likelihood that each team will earn one of the four coveted spots in the inaugural playoff format. These projections are based not only on the win probabilities, but also schedule-strength factors we expect will weigh significantly in the selection committee's process.

By taking two different statistical approaches to reach one exciting series of answers to college football's most important questions, we feel we are at the forefront of the ongoing debates. Enjoy the college football section of *Football Outsiders Almanac 2014*, and join us at www.FootballOutsiders.com/college throughout the season.

College Statistics Toolbox

Regular readers of FootballOutsiders.com may be familiar with the FEI and Varsity Numbers columns and their respective stats published throughout the year. Others may be learning about our advanced approach to college football stats analysis for the first time by reading this book. In either case, this College Statistics Toolbox section is highly recommended reading before getting into the conference chapters. The stats that form the building blocks for F/+, FEI, and S&P+ are constantly being updated and refined.

Each team profile in the conference chapters begins with a statistical snapshot (defending BCS champion Florida State is presented here as a sample). Within each chapter, teams are organized by division (the final chapter lists all teams from 1 to 128) and Projected F/+ rank. The projected overall and conference records—rounded from the team's projected Mean Wins—are listed alongside the team name in the header. Estimates of offensive and defensive starters returning in 2014 were collected from team websites, spring media guides, and other reliable sources. All other stats and rankings provided in the team snapshot are explained below.

Drive-by-Drive Data

Fremeau Efficiency Index: Fremeau Efficiency Index (FEI) analysis begins with drive data instead of play-by-play data and is processed according to key principles. A team is rewarded for playing well against a strong opponent, win or lose, and is punished more severely for playing poorly against bad teams than it is rewarded for playing well against bad teams.

No. 1 Florida State Seminoles (12-0, 8-0)

2013: 14-0 (8-0) / F/+ #1 / FEI #1 / S&P+ #1 / Program F/+: #6					
2013 Offense			**2013 Defense**		
Offensive F/+	21.5%	3	Defensive F/+	25.7%	1
Offensive FEI	0.499	12	Defensive FEI	-0.653	5
Offensive S&P+	148.4	1	Defensive S&P+	161.9	1
Rushing S&P+	121.9	14	Rushing S&P+	138.1	4
Passing S&P+	156.7	1	Passing S&P+	142.4	4
Standard Downs S&P+	130.9	4	Standard Downs S&P+	147.2	2
Passing Downs S&P+	165.7	1	Passing Downs S&P+	125.3	12
2013 Special Teams			Special Teams F/+	2.0%	27
2014 Projections			SOS Rk	56	
Ret. Starters: 8 OFF, 5 DEF			Offensive F/+	14.5%	4
Proj. F/+	32.5%	1	Defensive F/+	17.9%	1
Mean Wins / Conf Wins	11.6 / 7.8		Conf. / Div. Title Odds	86.0% / 89.6%	

2013 Five Factors			
Efficiency	Off Success Rate+	130.4	2
	Def Success Rate+	128.3	3
	Total Efficiency	258.7	1
Explosiveness	Off IsoPPP+	116.9	6
	Def IsoPPP+	118.0	4
	Total Explosiveness	234.9	1
Field Position	Field Pos. Adv. (FPA)	0.562	2
Finishing Drives	Off Red Zone S&P+	139.0	2
	Def Red Zone S&P+	117.6	17
	Total Red Zone Rating	256.6	3
Turnovers	Turnover Margin	+17.0	2
	Exp. TO Margin	+6.1	23
	Difference	+10.9	5

To calculate FEI, the nearly 20,000 possessions in every season of major college football are filtered to eliminate first-half clock-kills and end-of-game garbage drives and scores. A scoring rate analysis of the remaining possessions then determines the baseline possession efficiency expectations against which each team is measured. Game Efficiency is the composite possession-by-possession efficiency of a team over the course of a game, a measurement of the success of its offensive, defensive, and special teams units' essential goals: to maximize the team's own scoring opportunities and to minimize those of its opponent. Finally, each team's FEI rating synthesizes its season-long Game Efficiency data, adjusted for the strength of its opposition; special emphasis is placed on quality performance against good teams, win or lose.

Offensive and Defensive FEI: Game Efficiency is a composite assessment of the possession-by-possession performance of team over the course of a game. In order to isolate the relative performance of the offense and defense, more factors are evaluated.

First, we ran a regression on the national scoring rates of tens of thousands of college football drives according to starting field position. The result represents the value of field position in terms of points expected to be scored by an average offense against an average defense—1.4 points per possession from its own 15-yard line, 2.1 points per possession from its own 40-yard line, and so on. These expected points are called Field Position Value (FPV).

Next, we ran a regression on the value of drive-ending field position according to national special teams scoring expectations. To determine the true national baseline for field-goal range, we took into account not only the 2200 field goals attempted annually, but also the 1400 punts kicked from opponent territory each year. In other words, if a team has an average field goal unit and a coach with an average penchant for risk-taking, the offensive value of reaching the opponent's 35-yard line is equal to the number of made field goals from that distance divided by the number of attempts plus the number of punts from that distance.

Touchdowns credit the offense with 6.96 points of drive-ending value, the value of a touchdown adjusted according to national point-after rates. Safeties have a drive-ending value of negative two points. All other offensive results are credited with a drive-ending value of zero.

Offensive efficiency is then calculated as the total drive-ending value earned by the offense divided by the sum of its offensive FPV over the course of the game. Defensive efficiency is calculated the same way using the opponent's offensive drive-ending value and FPV. Offensive and defensive efficiency are calibrated as a rating above or below zero—a good offense has a positive rating and a good defense has a negative one.

Offensive FEI and Defensive FEI are the opponent-adjusted values of offensive and defensive efficiency. As with FEI, the adjustments are weighted according to both the strength of the opponent and the relative significance of the result. Efficiency against a team's best competition is given more relevance weight in the formula.

Other offensive and defensive possession efficiency measures are defined as follows:

- Available yards are a function of the total yards earned divided by the total yards available based on starting field position.
- Explosive drives are possessions that average at least 10 yards per play.
- Methodical drives are possessions that last at least 10 plays.
- Value drives are possessions that begin on the offense's own side of midfield and reach the opponent's 30-yard line.

Field Position Advantage (FPA): FPA was developed in order to more accurately describe the management of field position over the course of a game. For each team, we calculate the sum of the FPV for each of its offensive series. Then, we add in a full touchdown value (6.96 points) for each non-offensive score earned by the team. (This accounts for the field-position value of special teams and defensive returns reaching the end zone versus tripping up at the one-yard line.) Special-teams turnovers and onside kicks surrendered have an FPV of zero. The sum of the FPV of every possession in the game for both teams represents the total field position at stake in the contest. FPA represents each given team's share of that total field position.

FPA is a description of which team controlled field position in the game and by how much. Two teams that face equal field position over the course of a game will each have an FPA of .500. Winning the field position battle is quite valuable. College football teams that play with an FPA over .500 win two-thirds of the time. Teams that play with an FPA over .600 win 90 percent of the time.

Play-by-Play Data

Success Rates: Our play-by-play analysis was introduced throughout the 2008 season in Bill Connelly's Varsity Numbers columns. Nearly one million plays over eight seasons in college football have been collected and evaluated to determine baselines for success for every situational down in a game. Similarly to DVOA, basic success rates are determined by national standards. The distinction for college football is in defining the standards of success. We use the following determination of a "successful" play:

- First down success = 50 percent of necessary yardage
- Second down success = 70 percent of necessary yardage
- Third/Fourth down success = 100 percent of necessary yardage

On a per play basis, these form the standards of efficiency for every offense in college football. Defensive success rates are based on preventing the same standards of achievement.

Equivalent Points and Points per Play: All yards are not created equal. A 10-yard gain from a team's own 15-yard line does not have the same value as a 10-yard gain that goes from the opponent's 10-yard line into the end zone. Based on expected scoring rates similar to FPV described above, we can calculate a point value for each play in a drive. Equivalent Points (EqPts) are calculated by subtracting the value of the resulting yard line from the initial yard line of a given play. This assigns credit to the yards that are most associated with scoring points, the end goal in any possession.

With EqPts, the game can be broken down and built back up again in a number of ways. With the addition of penalties, turnovers and special teams play, EqPts provides an accurate assessment of how a game was played on a play-by-play basis. We also use it to create a measure called Points per Play (PPP), representative of a team's or an individual player's explosiveness.

S&P: Like OPS (on-base percentage plus slugging average) in baseball, we created a measure that combines consistency with power. S&P represents a combination of efficiency (Success Rates) and explosiveness (Points per Play) to most accurately represent the effectiveness of a team or individual player.

A boom-or-bust running back may have a strong yards per carry average and PPP, but his low Success Rate will lower his S&P. A consistent running back that gains between four and six yards every play, on the other hand, will have a strong Success Rate but possibly low PPP. The best offenses in the country can maximize both efficiency and explosiveness on a down-by-down basis. Reciprocally, the best defenses can limit both.

S&P+: As with the FEI stats discussed above, context matters in college football. Adjustments are made to the S&P unadjusted data with a formula that takes into account a team's production, the quality of the opponent, and the quality of the opponent's opponent. To eliminate the noise of less-informative blowout stats, we filtered the play-by-play data to include only those that took place when the game was "close." This excludes plays where the score margin is larger than 28 points in the first quarter, 24 points in the second quarter, 21 points in the third quarter, or 16 points in the fourth quarter.

Beginning in 2013, we also factored in a drive efficiency measure that is calculated in a similar fashion to PPP, by comparing the expected value of a given drive (based on starting field position) to the actual value a team produces and adjusting it for the opponent at hand. The ability to finish drives is a singular skill that isn't perfectly encapsulated in a measure that only looks at play-by-play data.

The combination of the play-by-play and drive data gives us S&P+, a comprehensive measure that represents a team's efficiency and explosiveness as compared to all other teams in college football. S&P+ values are calibrated around an average rating of 100. An above-average team, offensively or defensively, will have an S&P+ rating greater than 100. A below-average team will have an S&P+ rating lower than 100. The "+" adjustment can be used for other components, as well, such as Success Rate+ and PPP+.

In the team capsules in each conference chapter, the S&P+ ratings are broken down further as follows:

- Rushing S&P+ includes only running plays, and unlike standard college statistics, does not include sacks.
- Passing S&P+ includes sacks and passing plays.
- Passing Downs S&P+ includes second-and-8 or more, third-and-5 or more, and fourth-and-5 or more. These divisions were determined based on raw S&P data showing a clear distinction in Success Rates as compared with Standard Downs.
- Standard Downs S&P+ includes all close-game plays not defined as Passing Downs.

These measures are all derived only from play-by-play data; drive efficiency data is only factored into the final, overall S&P+ figure.

Five Factors: In January 2014, Bill Connelly introduced a new set of concepts for analysis and debate within the realm of college football stats. At Football Study Hall, a college football stats site within the SB Nation network, he wrote the following: "Over time, I've come to realize that the sport comes down to five basic things, four of which you can mostly control. You make more big plays than your opponent, you stay on schedule, you tilt the field, you finish drives, and you fall on the ball. Explosiveness, efficiency, field position, finishing drives, and turnovers are the five factors to winning football games."

Unlike the Four Factors used by ESPN's Dean Oliver for discussion of basketball, these factors are heavily related to each other, and at press time, work to unpack each one is still ongoing. But for team tables in this section, we are including the following measures, which represent each of the five factors as currently constituted: Success Rate+ (the opponent-adjusted version of Success Rate), IsoPPP+ (an opponent-adjusted look at the average PPP gained only in successful plays), FPA (Brian Fremeau's Field Position Advantage measure), Red Zone S&P+, and Adjusted Turnover Margin (a comparison of a team's actual turnover margin to what would have been expected with neutral luck).

Highlight Yards: Highlight yards represent the yards gained by a runner outside of those credited to the offensive line through Adjusted Line Yards. The ALY formula, much like the same stat in the NFL, gives 100 percent credit to all yards gained between zero and four yards and 50 percent strength to yards between five and 10. If a runner gains 12 yards in a given carry, and we attribute 7.0 of those yards to the line, and the player's highlight yardage on the play is 5.0 yards. Beginning in 2013, we began calculating highlight yardage averages in a slightly different manner: Instead of dividing total highlight yardage by a player's overall number of carries, we divide it only by the number of carries that gain more than four yards; if a line is given all credit for gains smaller than that, then it makes sense to look at highlight averages only for the carries on which a runner got a chance to create a highlight.

Opportunity Rate: Opportunity Rate represents the percentage of a runner's carries that gained at least five yards. This gives us a look at a runner's (and his line's) consistency and efficiency to go along with the explosiveness measured by Highlight Yards.

Adjusted Score/Adjusted Points: Taking a team's single-game S&P+ for both offense and defense, and applying it to a normal distribution of points scored in a given season, can give us an interesting, descriptive look at a team's performance in a given game and season. Adjusting for pace and opponent, Adjusted Score asks the same question of every team in every game: if Team A had played a perfectly average opponent in a given game, how would they have fared? Adjusted Score allows us to look at in-season trends as well, since the week-to-week baseline is opponent-independent.

Combination Data

F/+: Introduced in *Football Outsiders Almanac 2009*, the F/+ measure combines FEI and S&P+. There is a clear distinction between the two individual approaches, and merging the two diminishes certain outliers caused by the quirks of each method. The resulting metric is both powerfully predictive and sensibly evaluative.

Program and Projected F/+: Relative to the pros, college football teams are much more consistent in year-to-year performance. Breakout seasons and catastrophic collapses certainly occur, but generally speaking, teams can be expected to play within a reasonable range of their baseline program expectations. The idea of a Football Outsiders program rating began with the introduction of Program FEI in *Pro Football Prospectus 2008* as a way to represent those individual baseline expectations.

As the strength of the F/+ system has been fortified with more seasons of full drive-by-drive and play-by-play data, the Program F/+ measure has emerged. Program F/+ is calculated from five years of FEI and S&P+ data. The result not only represents the status of each team's program power, but provides the first step in projecting future success.

The Projected F/+ found in the following chapters starts by combining Program F/+ (weighted more toward recent seasons) with measures of two-year recruiting success (using Rivals.com ratings for signees who actually ended up enrolling at each school) and offensive and defensive performance. We adjust that baseline with transition factors like returning offensive and defensive starters, talent lost to the NFL Draft, and disproportional success on passing downs. The result, Projected F/+, is a more accurate predictor of next-year success than any other data we have tested or used to date.

Strength of Schedule: Unlike other rating systems, our Strength of Schedule (SOS) calculation is not a simple average of the Projected FEI data of each team's opponents. Instead, it represents the likelihood that an elite team (typical top-five team) would win every game on the given schedule. The distinction is valid. For any elite team, playing No. 1 Florida State and No. 128 New Mexico State in a two-game stretch is certainly more difficult than playing No. 64 East Carolina and No. 65 Tennessee. An average rating might judge these schedules to be equal.

The likelihood of an undefeated season is calculated as the product of Projected Win Expectations (PWE) for each game on the schedule. PWEs are based on an assessment of five years of FEI data and the records of teams of varying strengths against one another. Roughly speaking, an elite team may have a 65 percent chance of defeating a team ranked No. 10, a 75 percent chance of defeating a team ranked No. 20, and a 90 percent chance of defeating a team ranked No. 40. Combined, the elite team has a 44 percent likelihood of defeating all three (0.65 x 0.75 x 0.90 = 0.439).

A lower SOS rating represents a lower likelihood of an elite team running the table, and thus a stronger schedule. For our calculations of FBS versus FCS games, with all due apologies to North Dakota State et al., the likelihood of victory is considered to be 100 percent.

Mean Wins and Win Probabilities: To project records for each team, we use Projected F/+ and PWE formulas to estimate the likelihood of victory for a given team in its individual games. The probabilities for winning each game are added together to represent the average number of wins the team is expected to tally over the course of its scheduled games. Potential conference championship games and bowl games are not included.

The projected records listed next to each team name in the conference chapters are rounded from the mean wins data listed in the team capsule. Mean Wins are not intended to represent projected outcomes of specific matchups; rather they are our most accurate forecast for the team's season as a whole. The correlation of mean projected wins to actual wins is 0.69 for all games, 0.61 for conference games.

The Win Probability tables that appear in each conference chapter are also based on the game-by-game PWE data for each team. The likelihood for each record is rounded to the nearest whole percent.

Brian Fremeau and Bill Connelly

Atlantic Coast Conference

Most power struggles follow a fairly predictable trajectory: king is deposed, successors battle to fill the vacuum, new king emerges from the contenders, etc., repeat as necessary. You know, you watch Game of Thrones. Only in the ACC version, the new king turns out to be the same as the old king, resurrected and omnipotent as ever. In retrospect, Florida State's re-ascension after a decade in the wilderness seems inevitable—who else in the conference has the resources, the personnel, the pedigree? In the end, of course it's Florida State.

But it's not as if the rest of the league didn't have its shot at the Seminoles' old crown. It just failed, repeatedly, to produce a worthy successor. From 2001-11, as FSU trudged through the decline of the Bowden era and the awkward transition to Jimbo Fisher, six different schools claimed at least one ACC championship, none of whom made any pretense to national relevance outside of the conference. In the same span, the ACC champion went 1-10 in BCS bowls, culminating in a series of blowouts that included in the most lopsided beating in BCS history in the 2012 Orange Bowl. In those years the conference earned a single top-10 finish in the AP poll.

Once the Seminole juggernaut was back up and running under Fisher, there wasn't even a pretender to stand in its way. The 2012 Noles ran roughshod, losing once in ACC play—by one point—en route to an otherwise uncontested title. (The Coastal Division contenders were so weak that not just one but two of them, Miami and North Carolina, turned down a shot at FSU in the championship game in favor of a self-imposed postseason ban to appease NCAA investigators; the honor fell instead to 6-6 Georgia Tech, which was promptly trounced.) In 2013, Florida State unleashed maximum destruction, obliterating conference opponents by 39 points per game; the only ostensible challenger, Clemson, was left scattered in tiny pieces across its own field in a 51-14 massacre that wasn't even that close. Before the BCS nail-biter against Auburn, only one other opponent (Boston College, a 48-34 victim in September) had come within four touchdowns of FSU. In our F/+ ratings, the Seminoles ranked No. 1 nationally on defense, No. 2 on offense and No. 1 overall by an historic margin: dating back to 2005, the first year in the F/+ database, the Seminoles' final score (+49.2%) is the fourth-best on record, behind only Alabama in 2011-12 and Florida in 2008. Meanwhile, the only other ACC outfit that managed to crack the top 25 was Clemson, at No. 16.

The gap in 2014 may be even wider. Across the conference, 11 teams will be breaking in new starters at quarterback, while Florida State plans to trot out the reigning Heisman winner. Including Jameis Winston, FSU has more players who arrived on campus with a five-star rating from the major recruiting sites (11) than the rest of the conference combined, just one reflection of its ongoing dominance in stockpiling talent. Like last year, the question where the ACC is concerned isn't so much the outcome at the top, but the margin. In that respect, the Seminoles are playing against history: no FBS program has pulled off back-to-back undefeated seasons since Nebraska in 1994-95. In the BCS era, a handful of defending champions came close—Miami in 2001-02, USC in 2004-05, Florida in 2008-09—only to watch the repeat slip away at the last moment. The arrival of a playoff format relieves some of the pressure of running the table, if only slightly, but for projection purposes we can take the 'Noles' presence in the "final four" for granted. From there, they're playing for posterity.

ATLANTIC DIVISION

No. 1 Florida State Seminoles (12-0, 8-0)

2013: 14-0 (8-0) / F/+ #1 / FEI #1 / S&P+ #1 / Program F/+: #6					
2013 Offense			**2013 Defense**		
Offensive F/+	21.5%	3	Defensive F/+	25.7%	1
Offensive FEI	0.499	12	Defensive FEI	-0.653	5
Offensive S&P+	148.4	1	Defensive S&P+	161.9	1
Rushing S&P+	121.9	14	Rushing S&P+	138.1	4
Passing S&P+	156.7	1	Passing S&P+	142.4	4
Standard Downs S&P+	130.9	4	Standard Downs S&P+	147.2	2
Passing Downs S&P+	165.7	1	Passing Downs S&P+	125.3	12
2013 Special Teams			Special Teams F/+	2.0%	27
2014 Projections			SOS Rk	56	
Ret. Starters: 8 OFF, 5 DEF			Offensive F/+	14.5%	4
Proj. F/+	32.5%	1	Defensive F/+	17.9%	1
Mean Wins / Conf Wins	11.6 / 7.8		Conf. / Div. Title Odds	86.0% / 89.6%	

2013 Five Factors			
Efficiency	Off Success Rate+	130.4	2
	Def Success Rate+	128.3	3
	Total Efficiency	258.7	1
Explosiveness	Off IsoPPP+	116.9	6
	Def IsoPPP+	118.0	4
	Total Explosiveness	234.9	1
Field Position	Field Pos. Adv. (FPA)	0.562	2
Finishing Drives	Off Red Zone S&P+	139.0	2
	Def Red Zone S&P+	117.6	17
	Total Red Zone Rating	256.6	3
Turnovers	Turnover Margin	+17.0	2
	Exp. TO Margin	+6.1	23
	Difference	+10.9	5

Maybe it would be more constructive at this point to examine the ways in which FSU is not an irresistible force destined to reduce every obstacle in its path to rubble. It will certainly be more succinct. Let's start with the defense, which lost six starters—four of them NFL draft picks—including last year's leading tackler, linebacker Telvin Smith, and All-Americans Timmy Jernigan and Lamarcus Joyner. The projected starting lineup on that side of the ball doesn't feature a single senior. Surely Jernigan's muscle will be missed in the middle of the defensive line? Who can replace Joyner's Polamaluvian range and versatility in the secondary? Who takes the place of wide receiver Kelvin Benjamin, a truly freakish talent even by Florida State standards? Raw as he may have been, Benjamin was arguably the best receiver in the nation over the last six weeks of the season, and he was the only Seminole drafted in the first round in April. And perish the thought, but what if Jameis Winston is injured, or suspended, or otherwise indisposed—even briefly—against this year's tougher schedule? The top backup in 2013, Jacob Coker, transferred to Alabama, leaving the nondescript sophomore Sean Maguire as the Seminoles' safety net.

So yes, if catastrophe strikes, the defending champs are potentially vulnerable. Otherwise, the deck is pretty well stacked. The ace, of course, is Winston, whose bona fides are well established. Aside from the most decorated quarterback in college football, though, the offense returns four other All-ACC picks (wide receiver Rashad Greene, tight end Nick O'Leary, tackle Cameron Erving and guard Tre' Jackson), all of whom are arguably the best in the nation at their respective positions entering their third year as full-time starters. Two other starters up front, Bobby Hart and Josue Matias, have 51 combined starts between them. The new tailback, converted safety Karlos Williams, has yet to start a game at either position, but looked so good last year in a part-time role (730 yards, 8.0 yards per carry, 7.5 highlight yards per opportunity, 11 TD) that he's already the top senior running back on most draft boards. Yet with blue-chip sophomore Ryan Green and five-star freshman Dalvin Cook in the pipeline, there's no guarantee Williams will remain the top running back on his own team.

On the other hand, the heavy attrition outlined above is much less concerning in context. Losses notwithstanding, FSU is still projected by both F/+ and S&P+ to repeat as the No. 1 overall defense in the nation. And why not? Last year's edition was forced to replace seven defensive starters from a top-five defense in 2012, and outperformed its predecessor with room to spare. Among the players we know about, juniors Mario Edwards Jr. and Eddie Goldman on the defensive line and P.J. Williams and Ronald Darby in the secondary are all on track for an early exit next spring, having firmly established themselves in the starting lineup as sophomores; were he eligible, sophomore free safety Jalen Ramsey would join that group after starting every game as a true freshman. Among the new faces—most notably sophomore defensive ends Chris Casher and DeMarcus Walker, sophomore strong safety Nate Andrews and a pack of second- and third-year linebackers—there is every reason to believe they'll follow the same track. Heck, even the special teams are loaded: Kicker Roberto Aguayo (21-of-22 on field goals) was a consensus All-American as a redshirt freshman, while true freshman Levonte "Kermit" Whitfield took a pair of kickoffs back for touchdowns en route to the best kick-return average in the nation. (The second of those touchdowns you'll recall from the fourth quarter of the BCS Championship Game.) Punting was a weak spot last year (116th in punt efficiency), but the Seminoles only had 30 non-garbage time punts on the season, fewest of any team in the nation.

Recent history tells us that no road to a repeat is that smooth, that faint cracks will appear in the surface ahead of the inevitable lapse. Fine. But as for the what, when and where, and especially the who, there are no answers in sight.

2015 Draft Prospects: DE Mario Edwards Jr. (1), OT Cameron Erving (1), QB Jameis Winston* (1), TE Nick O'Leary (1-2), CB P.J. Williams* (1-2), WR Rashad Greene (2), CB Ronald Darby* (2-3), DT Eddie Goldman* (2-3), G Tre' Jackson (2-3), RB Karlos Williams (3-4)*

No. 14 Clemson Tigers (9-3, 6-2)

2013: 11-2 (7-1) / F/+ #16 / FEI #22 / S&P+ #6 / Program F/+: #19					
2013 Offense			**2013 Defense**		
Offensive F/+	13.0%	19	Defensive F/+	14.0%	13
Offensive FEI	0.343	26	Defensive FEI	-0.422	17
Offensive S&P+	126.0	12	Defensive S&P+	130.7	12
Rushing S&P+	113.3	32	Rushing S&P+	123.8	12
Passing S&P+	132.8	10	Passing S&P+	121.2	17
Standard Downs S&P+	124.2	9	Standard Downs S&P+	120.7	13
Passing Downs S&P+	120.6	24	Passing Downs S&P+	120.7	18
2013 Special Teams			Special Teams F/+	-0.4%	78
2014 Projections			SOS Rk	7	
Ret. Starters: 4 OFF, 8 DEF			Offensive F/+	5.7%	33
Proj. F/+	16.0%	14	Defensive F/+	10.3%	13
Mean Wins / Conf Wins	8.9 / 6.1		Conf. / Div. Title Odds	4.5% / 6.4%	

2013 Five Factors			
Efficiency	Off Success Rate+	118.0	12
	Def Success Rate+	125.8	5
	Total Efficiency	243.8	2
Explosiveness	Off IsoPPP+	107.2	32
	Def IsoPPP+	91.4	107
	Total Explosiveness	198.6	74
Field Position	Field Pos. Adv. (FPA)	0.509	49
Finishing Drives	Off Red Zone S&P+	97.7	72
	Def Red Zone S&P+	121.4	11
	Total Red Zone Rating	219.1	25
Turnovers	Turnover Margin	+6.0	29
	Exp. TO Margin	+2.0	52
	Difference	+4.0	26

It didn't always feel this way at the time, thanks to the long shadow cast by Florida State in the same division, but at some point the last three years are going to be acknowledged as a kind of renaissance for Clemson football. Maybe even a golden era: from 2011-13, the Tigers won 32 games, spent 47 consecutive weeks in the national polls, spent 24 weeks in the top ten, and claimed their first conference championship since 1991, their first major bowl win since 1981, and their best finish in the AP poll since 1982. Contrary to its reputation for serial flopping in big games, Clemson was 7-5 in that span against ranked opponents, including wins over Auburn, Florida State, Virginia Tech (twice), LSU, Georgia and Ohio State. In the process, the university rewarded coach Dabo Swinney—and warded off would-be poachers—by making his staff as a whole the highest-paid in the nation outside of the SEC. After two decades on the fringe, from the outside the program looks as healthy as it's ever been.

Depending on how things go this fall, that appreciation may arrive very soon. It's no coincidence that the surge ran parallel to the tenure of the most prolific passer in ACC history, Tajh Boyd, the only constant in an offense that averaged 41 points per game over the past three seasons, ranking in the top 20 in Offensive F/+ in all three. (The only other teams that can make the latter claim are Alabama, Baylor, Oregon and Texas A&M.) When it came to highlight-reel talent, Boyd was often eclipsed by his favorite target, Sammy Watkins, but there is no mistaking the burden on senior quarterback Cole Stoudt to keep pace after an extended tour as Boyd's understudy. Obviously, there is no equivalent of Watkins among the returning wideouts, or anywhere else in college football, but there is depth: between junior Charone Peake, sophomores Mike Williams and Germone Hopper, and four incoming freshmen with four-star ratings from recruitniks, breakout candidates abound. Same goes for the tailbacks, and for a pair of new tackles, juniors Shaq Anthony and Isaiah Battle, both of whom have some starting experience under their belts. Stoudt, on the other hand, was not a highly regarded recruit four years ago and has only appeared in the meantime in mop-up roles. If the offense stalls in the season opener at Georgia, the presence of hyped freshman Deshaun Watson only increases the odds of a quick hook heading into the season-defining trip to Tallahassee three weeks later.

Even if the offense falters, the defense will remain dangerous. The front seven boasts nightmare potential exceeding even FSU's. As a team, Clemson led the nation in 2013 in total tackles for loss (123) and TFLs per game (9.5), and returns five players—defensive ends Vic Beasey, Corey Crawford and Shaq Lawson; defensive tackle Grady Jarrett; and linebacker Stephone Anthony—who were credited with at least ten TFLs apiece. In our S&P+ ratings, the Tigers ranked among the top 20 in every defensive category, finishing 12th overall, a great leap forward from the 2012 defense on all counts. (They also finished 13th in Defensive F/+, up from 51st in 2012, and led the nation by forcing three-and-outs on 46.4 percent of opponent drives) If a pair of untested second-year corners, MacKensie Alexander and Cordrea Tankersley, play up to expectations, for once the offense can afford to play it relatively close to the vest.

2015 Draft Prospects: DE/OLB Vic Beasley (1), ILB Stephone Anthony (2), DT Grady Jarrett (2), DE Corey Crawford (3-4), OLB Tony Steward (5-6).

No. 21 Louisville Cardinals (9-3, 6-2)

2013: 12-1 (7-1) / F/+ #12 / FEI #21 / S&P+ #5 / Program F/+: #39					
2013 Offense			**2013 Defense**		
Offensive F/+	11.8%	23	Defensive F/+	15.1%	10
Offensive FEI	0.361	25	Defensive FEI	-0.397	21
Offensive S&P+	119.7	18	Defensive S&P+	137.6	7
Rushing S&P+	108.6	42	Rushing S&P+	113.5	28
Passing S&P+	121.3	18	Passing S&P+	128.0	9
Standard Downs S&P+	117.0	19	Standard Downs S&P+	116.0	22
Passing Downs S&P+	113.7	38	Passing Downs S&P+	133.8	5
2013 Special Teams			Special Teams F/+	2.0%	28
2014 Projections			SOS Rk	29	
Ret. Starters: 8 OFF, 5 DEF			Offensive F/+	8.4%	19
Proj. F/+	13.8%	21	Defensive F/+	5.4%	33
Mean Wins / Conf Wins	9.0 / 5.7		Conf. / Div. Title Odds	2.6% / 4.0%	

2013 Five Factors			
Efficiency	Off Success Rate+	115.6	17
	Def Success Rate+	111.6	25
	Total Efficiency	227.1	15
Explosiveness	Off IsoPPP+	100.8	56
	Def IsoPPP+	108.5	25
	Total Explosiveness	209.4	34
Field Position	Field Pos. Adv. (FPA)	0.531	25
Finishing Drives	Off Red Zone S&P+	98.6	68
	Def Red Zone S&P+	116.9	18
	Total Red Zone Rating	215.6	29
Turnovers	Turnover Margin	+17.0	2
	Exp. TO Margin	+10.7	3
	Difference	+6.3	17

Rarely, if ever, has a school had the luxury of replacing the second-winningest coach in program history with the only guy who ranks ahead of him on the list, but then Bobby Petrino's career has never followed a conventional trajectory. In three decades in the business, Petrino has never remained in any one place longer than four years, including Louisville, where he won 41 games from 2003-06 with two conference championships—just good enough, as it turns out, to earn a repeat performance despite his infamous exits from Atlanta and Arkansas. Seven years after his first tour ended, he arrives from a one-year layover at Western Kentucky to find the place more or less as he left it. New conference notwithstanding, the 2013 Cardinals under Charlie Strong matched the school record for wins set by Petrino's last Louisville outfit in 2006, ranking 12th in overall F/+ and 15th in the final AP poll. Just as in 2006, the Cards came within a field goal of a perfect season, only to watch the coach who engineered that success use it as a springboard to a more high-profile job.

The other above-the-fold departure, of course, was Teddy Bridgewater, whose success here is hard to overstate: on a long list of prolific Louisville quarterbacks dating back to Johnny Unitas, Bridgewater had the most wins and was selected highest in the NFL draft. At the same time, though, it may be fairly easy to exaggerate the impact of his absence. In fact, the defense arguably took the bigger hit this offseason, losing three starters to the draft—two of them going ahead of Bridgewater in the first round—from a unit that quietly ranked No. 1 nationally with only 3.3 points per value drive allowed, second nationally in scoring defense, and tenth in Defensive F/+. Only four full-time starters from that unit return, none of them on the defensive line. (Senior defensive end Lorenzo Mauldin, a second-team All-ACC pick in 2013, is moving from end to outside linebacker in the transition from a 4-3 scheme to a 3-4.) By contrast, the offense returns eight starters, all in their fourth or fifth year in the program. Yes, the young quarterbacks vying to replace Bridgewater—sophomore Will Gardner and redshirt freshman Kyle Bolin—are blank slates. Given the experience around them, though, and Petrino's stellar track record with college passers, they're a better bet to keep the offense on course than the new faces on the other side.

2015 Draft Prospects: WR DeVante Parker (2-3), DE/OLB Lorenzo Mauldin (4-5), OT Jamon Brown (5-6), C Jake Smith (6-7), RB Dominique Brown (7-FA), RB Michael Dyer (7-FA).

No. 65 Syracuse Orange (5-7, 3-5)

2013: 7-6 (4-4) / F/+ #75 / FEI #86 / S&P+ #75 / Program F/+: #64					
2013 Offense			**2013 Defense**		
Offensive F/+	-5.6%	83	Defensive F/+	-0.3%	63
Offensive FEI	-0.205	87	Defensive FEI	-0.007	65
Offensive S&P+	93.9	75	Defensive S&P+	104.1	67
Rushing S&P+	113.2	33	Rushing S&P+	104.4	56
Passing S&P+	87.9	94	Passing S&P+	101.3	59
Standard Downs S&P+	107.3	42	Standard Downs S&P+	100.7	66
Passing Downs S&P+	84.6	102	Passing Downs S&P+	103.3	58
2013 Special Teams			Special Teams F/+	-0.3%	77
2014 Projections			SOS Rk	27	
Ret. Starters: 8 OFF, 7 DEF			Offensive F/+	-2.1%	79
Proj. F/+	-1.2%	65	Defensive F/+	0.9%	60
Mean Wins / Conf Wins	5.1 / 2.6		Conf. / Div. Title Odds	0.0% / 0.0%	

2013 Five Factors			
Efficiency	Off Success Rate+	99.4	66
	Def Success Rate+	99.7	54
	Total Efficiency	199.0	65
Explosiveness	Off IsoPPP+	94.1	92
	Def IsoPPP+	98.2	68
	Total Explosiveness	192.3	92
Field Position	Field Pos. Adv. (FPA)	0.498	64
Finishing Drives	Off Red Zone S&P+	111.0	24
	Def Red Zone S&P+	94.8	77
	Total Red Zone Rating	205.7	51
Turnovers	Turnover Margin	+2.0	48
	Exp. TO Margin	+1.9	56
	Difference	+0.1	55

Syracuse fans aren't about to start taking winning records for granted or anything. Before 2012-13, the Orange hadn't finished above .500 in consecutive seasons since 2000-01, a span that included six losing campaigns in a row and five last-place finishes in the Big East. Still, having done so now under two different head coaches, it's safe to say the proverbial bar has been raised—that is to say, it's emerged from its previous setting somewhere in the depths of Lake Erie. With junior Terrel Hunt entrenched at quarterback and seven starters back on defense (all of them seniors), a middling bowl appearance no longer qualifies as success, but as the bare minimum. Such is progress.

Offensively, Hunt is the key to sustaining that progress, and also a bit of a Rorschach test. On paper, last year's offense was dreadful, coming in 83rd nationally in Offensive F/+ and averaging just 15.5 points in ACC games, tied for dead last in the conference. On the other hand, the Orange rebounded from an 0-2 start to finish 7-4 with Hunt taking a majority of the snaps, good enough to make him the season MVP according to his teammates. He certainly looks the part at 6-foot-3, 215 pounds, and he has the tools athletically. The offense as a whole was dramatically better when defenses were forced to respect Hunt as a runner: according to S&P+, Syracuse ranked 42nd in efficiency on standard downs, compared to 101st on passing downs. (On an individual level, Hunt was sometimes able to function almost as a de facto tailback, averaging 60 yards rushing on 6.0 per carry in wins; in losses, that dropped to just 16 yards on 2.2 yards per carry.) Although he improved as a passer as the season wore on, in conference games Hunt finished with the worst efficiency rating among ACC starters (95.2), serving up eight interceptions to just three touchdowns.

The defense was a boom-or-bust affair, volunteering to serve as target practice for the likes of Northwestern (48 points), Clemson (49), Georgia Tech (56) and Florida State (59), while effectively clamping down on everyone else. (Among teams defeated by Syracuse, only Boston College topped 17 points.) The net effect, appropriately enough, was a unit that ranked 63rd in Defensive F/+, dead center among FBS programs. If that divide holds, the Orange are in for more long afternoons against Notre Dame, Louisville, FSU, and Clemson, all in a span of five weeks in September and mid-October. On either side of that gauntlet, though, Hunt should be able to remain in his comfort zone without having to worry about passing the team out of an ever-expanding hole.

2015 Draft Prospects: OLB Dyshawn Davis (3-4), OT Sean Hickey (3-4), SS Durrell Eskridge (4-5), WR Jarrod West (7-FA).

No. 70 N.C. State Wolfpack (6-6, 2-6)

2013: 3-9 (0-8) / F/+ #92 / FEI #98 / S&P+ #85 / Program F/+: #53						2013 Five Factors			
2013 Offense			2013 Defense				Off Success Rate+	91.5	87
Offensive F/+	-9.7%	100	Defensive F/+	-2.9%	77	Efficiency	Def Success Rate+	99.0	57
Offensive FEI	-0.349	103	Defensive FEI	0.121	80		Total Efficiency	190.5	89
Offensive S&P+	88.8	92	Defensive S&P+	103.6	70		Off IsoPPP+	101.9	50
Rushing S&P+	97.4	77	Rushing S&P+	89.3	99	Explosiveness	Def IsoPPP+	97.3	77
Passing S&P+	91.4	88	Passing S&P+	109.1	35		Total Explosiveness	199.2	73
Standard Downs S&P+	94.7	87	Standard Downs S&P+	99.3	71	Field Position	Field Pos. Adv. (FPA)	0.487	83
Passing Downs S&P+	93.3	80	Passing Downs S&P+	102.3	62		Off Red Zone S&P+	83.7	111
2013 Special Teams			Special Teams F/+	0.0%	68	Finishing Drives	Def Red Zone S&P+	82.1	114
2014 Projections			SOS Rk	25			Total Red Zone Rating	165.8	117
Ret. Starters: 7 OFF, 8 DEF			Offensive F/+	-5.7%	93		Turnover Margin	0.0	61
Proj. F/+	-2.6%	70	Defensive F/+	3.2%	46	Turnovers	Exp. TO Margin	-1.6	85
Mean Wins / Conf Wins	5.7 / 2.4		Conf. / Div. Title Odds	0.0% / 0.0%			Difference	+1.6	43

Listen, do we really need to dwell on the past here? Yes, 2013 ranks among the worst seasons in N.C. State history. Yes, the Wolfpack failed to win a conference game for the first time since 1959, all but one of the losses coming by double digits. No, they didn't place a single player on the postseason All-ACC team, even as "honorable mention." They were bad on defense (77th in Defensive F/+), worse on offense (100th in Offensive F/+) and died a slow, painful death in the red zone (which we'll get to in a moment). But let's focus on the positive! In 2014, the best quarterback on the roster is finally eligible, the offensive line is intact, and every position on the defense is manned by an upperclassman with starting experience. And let's face it: it would be almost impossible for things to get any worse.

First, the quarterback. After sitting out last year, Florida transfer Jacoby Brissett dominated the competition in the spring, and looks like the conference's most athletic quarterback this side of Jameis Winston. At 6-foot-4, 236 pounds, Brissett is certainly in the Winston mold physically, as evidenced by his sterling marks as a recruit in 2011. In front of him, the starting offensive line is no longer a ramshackle group with three untested sophomores on the interior, but rather a veteran group with a combined 71 career starts from tackle to tackle. One of those tackles, senior Rob Crisp, is a former five-star signee whose potential has been curbed by a bad back and a concussion that forced him to sit out last year as a medical redshirt. The lineup will also welcome back 2013 injury casualties at wide receiver (Bryan Underwood) and safety (Jarvis "Don't Call Me Jairus" Byrd), along with last year's leading rusher (Shadrach Thornton) and pass rusher (Art Norman).

Even if nothing else changed, however, the Wolfpack would still close some of last year's gap simply by regressing to the mean in the red zone. The Wolfpack were horrible at finishing drives, managing to put the ball in the end zone on just 43.6 percent of its trips inside the opposing 20-yard line; that rate ranked 123rd out of 125 FBS offenses. Meanwhile, the defense defied the odds by finishing 120th in red-zone defense, yielding 32 touchdowns in 40 opportunities (80 percent). Consider that six of N.C. State's nine losses last year came by margins between 14 and 18 points. All else being equal, if the red-zone math improves by as much as one additional touchdown and one additional stop per game, suddenly a few of those flops are nail-biters that can conceivably go the Wolfpack's way.

2015 Draft Prospects: None.

No. 74 Boston College Eagles (5-7, 2-6)

2013: 7-6 (4-4) / F/+ #65 / FEI #70 / S&P+ #61 / Program F/+: #58						2013 Five Factors			
2013 Offense			2013 Defense				Off Success Rate+	99.4	65
Offensive F/+	2.9%	49	Defensive F/+	-7.8%	92	Efficiency	Def Success Rate+	97.9	63
Offensive FEI	0.048	54	Defensive FEI	0.311	98		Total Efficiency	197.3	69
Offensive S&P+	108.2	43	Defensive S&P+	98.6	80		Off IsoPPP+	114.2	11
Rushing S&P+	113.7	31	Rushing S&P+	100.8	63	Explosiveness	Def IsoPPP+	97.9	73
Passing S&P+	108.5	41	Passing S&P+	99.4	66		Total Explosiveness	212.0	26
Standard Downs S&P+	119.6	15	Standard Downs S&P+	100.9	64	Field Position	Field Pos. Adv. (FPA)	0.491	77
Passing Downs S&P+	92.9	82	Passing Downs S&P+	97.6	79		Off Red Zone S&P+	97.9	71
2013 Special Teams			Special Teams F/+	2.7%	14	Finishing Drives	Def Red Zone S&P+	102.7	47
2014 Projections			SOS Rk	11			Total Red Zone Rating	200.6	61
Ret. Starters: 5 OFF, 6 DEF			Offensive F/+	-2.6%	81		Turnover Margin	+3.0	41
Proj. F/+	-3.7%	74	Defensive F/+	-1.1%	68	Turnovers	Exp. TO Margin	+8.2	13
Mean Wins / Conf Wins	4.7 / 2.0		Conf. / Div. Title Odds	0.0% / 0.0%			Difference	-5.2	104

Congratulations, Steve Addazio! In a single season on the job, you lifted Boston College from the ACC cellar into a bowl game, and got to enjoy the ride with BC's first Heisman finalist since Doug Flutie, to boot. Now comes the really fun part: starting over from scratch. Even without a single catch, running back Andre Williams accounted for 45.6 percent of the team's total yards from scrimmage, easily the highest individual share in the nation; subtract the production of wide receiver Alex Amidon, who accounted for another 22 percent, and two-thirds of last year's offensive production vanishes with just two players. Other departures include a four-year starter at quarterback (Chase Rettig); a trio of All-ACC picks at left tackle (Matt Patchan), linebacker (Kevin Pierre-Louis) and defensive end (Kasim Edebali); the leading tackler on defense (Steele Divitto); and an All-American kicker (Nate Freese) who connected on 26 consecutive field goal attempts going back to 2012. Sure, no problem, if we're talking about Florida State. At Boston College, those holes don't come with readymade refills.

Offensively, proven talent is in such short supply that Addazio went fishing over the winter for a quick fix, and came back with a pair of fifth-year transfers from Florida, quarterback Tyler Murphy and offensive tackle Ian Silberman. As Gators, Murphy and Silberman were both recruited to Gainesville by Addazio, then serving as Urban Meyer's offensive coordinator, and made a limited impact in 2013 as part-time starters. As Eagles, they wasted no time sewing up starting roles in the spring and figure to be cornerstones for the rebuilding offense. Otherwise, the only remotely recognizable name among the skill players is senior wide receiver Bobby Swigert, who had 249 receiving yards in 2012 but didn't see the field at all last year due to a lingering knee injury. The defense is in slightly better shape, experience-wise, thanks mainly to four returning starters in the secondary. But most of that experience came as part of a unit that ranked 92nd in Defensive F/+, and the most productive members of last year's front seven are all in NFL training camps.

2015 Draft Prospects: None.

No. 92 Wake Forest Demon Deacons (4-8, 1-7)

2013: 4-8 (2-6) / F/+ #81 / FEI #80 / S&P+ #81 / Program F/+: #83					
2013 Offense			**2013 Defense**		
Offensive F/+	-12.9%	112	Defensive F/+	4.5%	41
Offensive FEI	-0.402	111	Defensive FEI	-0.119	47
Offensive S&P+	79.8	111	Defensive S&P+	115.1	34
Rushing S&P+	79.2	117	Rushing S&P+	111.2	34
Passing S&P+	84.0	107	Passing S&P+	104.1	51
Standard Downs S&P+	87.8	106	Standard Downs S&P+	111.7	27
Passing Downs S&P+	73.0	120	Passing Downs S&P+	99.7	70
2013 Special Teams			Special Teams F/+	0.0%	69
2014 Projections			SOS Rk	16	
Ret. Starters: 5 OFF, 5 DEF			Offensive F/+	-12.7%	125
Proj. F/+	-8.2%	92	Defensive F/+	4.5%	36
Mean Wins / Conf Wins	3.8 / 1.3		Conf. / Div. Title Odds	0.0% / 0.0%	

2013 Five Factors			
Efficiency	Off Success Rate+	87.6	104
	Def Success Rate+	99.7	53
	Total Efficiency	187.3	94
Explosiveness	Off IsoPPP+	87.4	121
	Def IsoPPP+	114.4	9
	Total Explosiveness	201.8	60
Field Position	Field Pos. Adv. (FPA)	0.465	103
Finishing Drives	Off Red Zone S&P+	94.7	83
	Def Red Zone S&P+	116.4	19
	Total Red Zone Rating	211.0	40
Turnovers	Turnover Margin	-2.0	73
	Exp. TO Margin	+4.3	41
	Difference	-6.3	113

Jim Grobe spent 13 years at Wake Forest, building a resumé that included a conference championship, the highest poll finish in school history, a school record for wins (77), and five bowl games, as many as his predecessors in Winston-Salem had managed between them. At their best, from 2006-08, the Demon Deacons spent 18 weeks in the AP's top 25 and beat Florida State three years in a row. When he stepped down last December, Grobe boasted the best winning percentage over his entire tenure (.484) of any Wake coach since 1950. If there has ever been a better coach at Wake Forest, no one there is old enough to remember him. Still, in the end even Grobe had to admit he had been consumed by the Bermuda Triangle, conceding at his farewell press conference that "it's probably good for the program to have some new energy" after five consecutive losing seasons. Against opponents that finished above .500 in that span, the Deacons were 4-30.

In fact, "New Energy" is a fitting slogan for the lineup, too: besides the new coach, Dave Clawson, Wake returns the fewest full-time starters (eight) and fewest career starts across the roster (173) in the ACC. Really, though, what's to miss? Offensively, the departures include a quarterback, Tanner Price, who logged 46 career starts, and the most productive receiver in school history, Michael Campanaro, who was drafted in the seventh round. But the offense as a whole last year ranked 112th in Offensive F/+ after coming in 113th in 2012, finishing dead last in the conference in scoring in both seasons. Spring practice yielded no firm answers in the quarterback duel between junior Kevin Sousa and sophomore Tyler Cameron, and the top two tailbacks were converts from wide receiver (Orville Reynolds) and linebacker (Dominique Gibson), respectively; the top receiver, E.J. Scott, was a graduate transfer from Virginia. The defense is adjusting from a 3-4 scheme under the old staff to a 4-2-5 by converting a pair of linebackers, Desmond Floyd and Zachary "Ziggy" Allen, into defensive ends while praying that a pair of sub-260-pound tackles, Josh Banks and Johnny Garcia, can hold up on the interior. So the new part, they've got that down. We'll see how long the energy lasts after a cushy non-conference schedule gives way to back-to-back dates with Louisville and Florida State in the first two conference games.

2015 Draft Prospects: CB Merrill Noel (5-6), CB Kevin Johnson (6-7).

COASTAL DIVISION

No. 28 Virginia Tech Hokies (9-3, 6-2)

2013: 8-5 (5-3) / F/+ #27 / FEI #29 / S&P+ #21 / Program F/+: #18

2013 Offense			2013 Defense		
Offensive F/+	-5.9%	85	Defensive F/+	23.3%	3
Offensive FEI	-0.160	78	Defensive FEI	-0.696	4
Offensive S&P+	89.0	91	Defensive S&P+	147.7	3
Rushing S&P+	87.6	105	Rushing S&P+	134.0	5
Passing S&P+	99.5	65	Passing S&P+	144.8	2
Standard Downs S&P+	95.4	81	Standard Downs S&P+	147.0	3
Passing Downs S&P+	92.4	84	Passing Downs S&P+	129.0	8
2013 Special Teams			Special Teams F/+	-0.3%	75
2014 Projections			SOS Rk	62	
Ret. Starters: 9 OFF, 6 DEF			Offensive F/+	-5.5%	89
Proj. F/+	10.7%	28	Defensive F/+	16.3%	2
Mean Wins / Conf Wins	8.9 / 5.8		Conf. / Div. Title Odds	4.2% / 49.1%	

2013 Five Factors			
Efficiency	Off Success Rate+	91.1	89
	Def Success Rate+	137.3	2
	Total Efficiency	228.4	11
Explosiveness	Off IsoPPP+	103.6	43
	Def IsoPPP+	97.9	72
	Total Explosiveness	201.5	62
Field Position	Field Pos. Adv. (FPA)	0.493	72
Finishing Drives	Off Red Zone S&P+	83.8	110
	Def Red Zone S&P+	114.3	21
	Total Red Zone Rating	198.1	65
Turnovers	Turnover Margin	+7.0	23
	Exp. TO Margin	+6.0	24
	Difference	+1.0	50

Virginia Tech under Frank Beamer has always skewed a little too heavily toward the defense, so much so at this point that it kind of goes without saying. They've been calling it "Beamer Ball" for so long, it's almost redundant. (And anyway, shouldn't it really be "Foster Ball," after Beamer's longtime defensive coordinator, Bud Foster?) Even by Hokie standards, though, the divide in 2013 was less a reflection of philosophy than of borderline dysfunction: while the defense spent the entire season near the top of the charts, eventually finishing third in Defensive F/+, the offense languished, coming in at No. 85 after a dismal finale in the Sun Bowl. The chasm was the widest in the nation. On the scoreboard, it was worse—at 22.5 points per game, Tech ranked 100th in scoring, failing to reach 20 points in seven of 13 games. Although quarterback Logan Thomas left with school records for total yards and passing touchdowns in a career, he also served up more interceptions (39) than any active FBS quarterback with fewer than 1,300 attempts.

In Thomas' defense, the supporting cast was little more than window dressing. Despite the scorn he endured for falling short of his obvious potential, Thomas still accounted for a little over 70 percent of the team's total offense in 2012 and 2013, the highest individual share of the nation in both seasons. Whoever wins the quarterback duel between senior Mark Leal, sophomore Brenden Motley, and Texas Tech transfer Michael Brewer, he's almost certainly not going to be asked to assume that kind of burden. But if not the quarterback, then who? Tailback Trey Edmunds (675 rushing yards, 4.1 yards per carry, 5.5 highlight yards per opportunity) had his moments as a redshirt freshman, but ultimately averaged just 40.4 yards per game against ACC defenses and suffered a nasty broken leg in the regular-season finale; if he's not at full speed by fall, junior J.C. Coleman (284 yards, 3.4 yards per carry, 1.8 highlight yards per opportunity) has proven to be a part-time stopgap at best. Those guys will run behind an offensive line that was the worst in the conference at uprooting opposing fronts, ranking 109th in Adjusted Line Yards and 124th in Power Success Rate, with few prospects for dramatic improvement beyond regression to the mean. The receiving corps is intact, but far too ordinary to prop up another mediocre passer.

Again, the defense can be counted on to keep the bottom from falling out, if only by precedent—only one starter returns on the defensive line, and none among the linebackers. The front seven is being rebuilt around senior defensive tackle Luther Maddy, but the secondary is second to none. It boasts a pair of rising stars at the corners (sophomores Kendall Fuller and Brandon Facyson) backed by a pair of senior safeties (Detrick Bonner and Kyshoen Jarrett) with 56 career starts between them; along with departed cornerback Kyle Fuller, the same cast last year was second nationally in Defensive Passing S&P+. If these defenders have to clear that bar again to give the offense a chance, at least they're used to the altitude.

2015 Draft Prospects: SS Kyshoen Jarrett (3-4), DT Luther Maddy (4-5).

No. 38 North Carolina Tar Heels (8-4, 5-3)

2013: 7-6 (4-4) / F/+ #38 / FEI #43 / S&P+ #37 / Program F/+: #37						2013 Five Factors			
2013 Offense			2013 Defense			Efficiency	Off Success Rate+	107.7	35
Offensive F/+	6.8%	35	Defensive F/+	2.3%	49		Def Success Rate+	103.5	45
Offensive FEI	0.220	36	Defensive FEI	-0.055	59		Total Efficiency	211.2	37
Offensive S&P+	110.4	35	Defensive S&P+	111.4	39	Explosiveness	Off IsoPPP+	100.2	59
Rushing S&P+	99.0	71	Rushing S&P+	105.8	49		Def IsoPPP+	109.7	21
Passing S&P+	118.4	20	Passing S&P+	115.2	25		Total Explosiveness	209.8	31
Standard Downs S&P+	111.5	37	Standard Downs S&P+	106.1	43	Field Position	Field Pos. Adv. (FPA)	0.524	30
Passing Downs S&P+	105.2	50	Passing Downs S&P+	121.5	16	Finishing Drives	Off Red Zone S&P+	99.3	64
2013 Special Teams			Special Teams F/+	1.0%	48		Def Red Zone S&P+	113.3	22
2014 Projections			SOS Rk	60			Total Red Zone Rating	212.6	35
Ret. Starters: 8 OFF, 7 DEF			Offensive F/+	6.7%	28	Turnovers	Turnover Margin	+3.0	41
Proj. F/+	8.4%	38	Defensive F/+	1.7%	56		Exp. TO Margin	+5.8	28
Mean Wins / Conf Wins	7.5 / 4.7		Conf. / Div. Title Odds	1.0% / 16.4%			Difference	-2.8	80

For years now, North Carolina has been cast as a well-heeled underachiever on the brink of its big break. So leave it to UNC to put together a campaign that managed to generate the illusion of forward momentum while achieving nothing in particular: after a deflating 1-5 start in 2013, just salvaging a winning record with six wins in the final seven felt like tangible progress. Even more encouraging, the midseason turnaround coincided with the emergence of sophomore quarterback Marquise Williams, who proceeded to go 5-1 as a starter in place of injured senior Bryn Renner. In fact, out of 22 starters in the Belk Bowl, a 39-17 rout over Cincinnati, a dozen were freshmen or sophomores, a block that included Williams, three starters on the offensive line and a pair of true freshmen, running back T.J. Logan and wide receiver Ryan Switzer, who combined for 2,040 all-purpose yards on the season. (Switzer also tied the FBS record with five touchdowns as a punt returner, all in the final five games.) In a wide-open division with no obvious frontrunner, why not these Heels, why not now?

See how easy that is? If only actually getting over the hump was just a matter of optimism. Since 2009, Carolina has barely budged in the final F/+ rankings, landing somewhere between 36th and 46th five years in a row, under three different head coaches. Since 2008, it's 24-24 in ACC games, turning in consecutive records of 4-4, 4-4, 4-4, 3-5, 5-3 and 4-4. Is Marquise Williams the man to break the rut? Perhaps, but the jury is still very much out. The Tar Heels had limited big-play potential all year, ranking 85th nationally in explosive drives. Remove his record-breaking performance in November against an outmanned patsy, Old Dominion, and Williams' efficiency rating plummets from 141.5 (a slightly above-average number) to a very pedestrian 117.2. By the end of spring practice, he wasn't even the clear starter, having split first-team reps throughout with redshirt freshman Mitch Trubisky. Either way, the offense will be without its brightest star in 2013, tight end Eric Ebron, as well as All-ACC left tackle James Hurst, anchor of a front that led the conference in Adjusted Sack Rate; Hurst's likely replacement is a true freshman, Bentley Spain, who made a strong impression in the spring as an early enrollee. Two other early enrollees, running back Elijah Hood and CB M.J. Stewart, also look like immediate-impact types, promising once again that whatever happens this fall, the future is always bright.

2015 Draft Prospects: WR Quinshad Davis (3-4), CB Tim Scott (4), DE/OLB Norkeithus Otis (4-5), OLB Travis Hughes (7-FA).*

No. 40 Miami Hurricanes (7-5, 4-4)

2013: 9-4 (5-3) / F/+ #36 / FEI #42 / S&P+ #30 / Program F/+: #29						2013 Five Factors			
2013 Offense			2013 Defense			Efficiency	Off Success Rate+	121.0	8
Offensive F/+	17.3%	12	Defensive F/+	-7.6%	91		Def Success Rate+	91.7	95
Offensive FEI	0.473	14	Defensive FEI	0.268	92		Total Efficiency	212.8	34
Offensive S&P+	133.2	5	Defensive S&P+	95.9	89	Explosiveness	Off IsoPPP+	124.6	2
Rushing S&P+	125.9	11	Rushing S&P+	88.9	100		Def IsoPPP+	96.8	82
Passing S&P+	150.3	3	Passing S&P+	92.5	92		Total Explosiveness	221.4	10
Standard Downs S&P+	130.2	5	Standard Downs S&P+	96.5	85	Field Position	Field Pos. Adv. (FPA)	0.531	24
Passing Downs S&P+	154.7	2	Passing Downs S&P+	81.1	116	Finishing Drives	Off Red Zone S&P+	98.6	69
2013 Special Teams			Special Teams F/+	1.1%	42		Def Red Zone S&P+	99.1	64
2014 Projections			SOS Rk	24			Total Red Zone Rating	197.7	66
Ret. Starters: 6 OFF, 7 DEF			Offensive F/+	13.9%	7	Turnovers	Turnover Margin	+5.0	32
Proj. F/+	7.9%	40	Defensive F/+	-6.0%	98		Exp. TO Margin	+3.3	46
Mean Wins / Conf Wins	6.9 / 3.8		Conf. / Div. Title Odds	0.2% / 3.9%			Difference	+1.7	41

For a few weeks last October, if you glanced quickly enough and didn't ask too many questions, it was possible to get the impression that Miami was back—like, seriously back back, banging on the door of the penthouse where it resided for the better part of two decades. As of Halloween, the Hurricanes boasted a 7-0 record, an upset win over Florida, and a No. 7 ranking in the mainstream polls, their best standing there since 2005. The sprawling NCAA investigation that kept the Canes out of the postseason in 2011 and 2012 was finally resolved at midseason with no further bowl bans. The annual showdown with Florida State was hyped as a reprise of the old Miami-FSU classics with implicit national ramifications. By then, though, the cracks were already apparent in close calls against North Carolina and Wake Forest, and the Seminoles opened the floodgates. Beginning with the trip to Tallahassee, the Hurricanes dropped three straight by double digits, fell out of the polls altogether and came in for another beating in the long-awaited bowl game.

In hindsight, it's tempting to overplay the absence of dynamic running back Duke Johnson, who racked up nearly 1,400 all-purpose yards in eight games before breaking his ankle late in the loss to FSU, and to a lesser extent wide receiver Phillip Dorsett, who tore his MCL in mid-October. But the offense held up just fine down the stretch compared to the defense, which utterly collapsed, yielding 525 yards and 37 points per game over the final six; two opposing offenses in that span, Virginia Tech and Virginia, finished with season highs on both counts. The Canes were 26th in Defensive F/+ after seven weeks; by the end of the season, they had plummeted all the way to 91st. Not surprisingly, the official depth chart for the spring game in April listed multiple starters at eight positions—on the defensive line alone, coaches listed ten contenders as co-starters for four spots, and they will welcome two more with the arrival of juco transfer Michael Wyche and blue-chip freshman Chad Thomas. Aside from senior linebacker Denzel Perryman, a first-team All-ACC pick as a junior, the opening-night lineup against Louisville is anyone's guess.

The same might have been true for the starting quarterback as well, until senior Ryan Williams went down in the spring with a torn ACL. Now the job will almost certainly fall to redshirt freshman Kevin Olsen, a hyped 2013 recruit who inherits the spotlight from a long line of pretenders. Somehow, Miami hasn't had a quarterback drafted higher than the seventh round since Craig Erickson in 1992, or in any round since Ken Dorsey in 2003. Outgoing starter Stephen Morris did set a high bar in one respect, leaving with the school record for career passing yards; he also remained maddeningly erratic to the bitter end. If healthy, Johnson and sophomore wide receiver Stacy Coley (591 receiving yards, 17.9 yards per catch, 66 percent catch rate) are bona fide home-run threats, potentially as dangerous a one-two punch as Miami has boasted in a decade. But the line is replacing a pair of draft picks from a unit that ranked 10th in Adjusted Line Yards and 12th in Adjusted Sack Rate, and by now Miami fans know all too well the value of "potential."

2015 Draft Prospects: ILB Denzel Perryman (1), RB/KR Duke Johnson (2-3), DE Anthony Chickillo (4-5), OT Ereck Flowers* (4-5), WR Phillip Dorsett (5-6), G Jon Feliciano (6-7), CB Ladarius Gunter (6-7), TE Clive Walford (6-7).*

No. 43 Pittsburgh Panthers (8-4, 5-3)

2013: 7-6 (3-5) / F/+ #54 / FEI #52 / S&P+ #42 / Program F/+: #32					
2013 Offense			**2013 Defense**		
Offensive F/+	0.6%	58	Defensive F/+	5.4%	37
Offensive FEI	0.027	60	Defensive FEI	-0.141	44
Offensive S&P+	100.7	62	Defensive S&P+	117.4	28
Rushing S&P+	100.0	68	Rushing S&P+	122.5	15
Passing S&P+	101.3	61	Passing S&P+	113.6	30
Standard Downs S&P+	103.3	56	Standard Downs S&P+	118.1	19
Passing Downs S&P+	96.0	71	Passing Downs S&P+	117.2	29
2013 Special Teams			Special Teams F/+	-2.4%	103
2014 Projections			SOS Rk	86	
Ret. Starters: 7 OFF, 6 DEF			Offensive F/+	2.1%	49
Proj. F/+	6.2%	43	Defensive F/+	4.0%	41
Mean Wins / Conf Wins	8.0 / 4.6		Conf. / Div. Title Odds	0.8% / 17.1%	

2013 Five Factors			
Efficiency	Off Success Rate+	100.8	58
	Def Success Rate+	116.2	13
	Total Efficiency	217.0	26
Explosiveness	Off IsoPPP+	101.7	51
	Def IsoPPP+	98.9	64
	Total Explosiveness	200.6	66
Field Position	Field Pos. Adv. (FPA)	0.482	89
Finishing Drives	Off Red Zone S&P+	93.6	85
	Def Red Zone S&P+	121.6	10
	Total Red Zone Rating	215.2	30
Turnovers	Turnover Margin	-1.0	69
	Exp. TO Margin	+7.3	16
	Difference	-8.3	120

In its own way, Pitt is a marvel of consistency, falling somewhere on the scale between a zen master in search of perfect equilibrium and your dad sitting down for his morning bran flakes before schlepping off to the cubicle. Over the past four years, the Panthers are 24-24 against FBS opponents, turning in records of 7-5, 5-7, 6-6 and 6-6 under three different head coaches. In the same span, they're 15-14 in conference games, in two different conferences. Their per-game scoring average in all games in those seasons looks like this:

2010: 26.3 ppg (66th nationally)
2011: 24.2 ppg (83rd)
2012: 26.6 ppg (76th)
2013: 26.3 ppg (79th)

From 2010-12, they rang in the new year with three consecutive trips to the BBVA Compass Bowl. Under the current head coach, Paul Chryst, they've countered encouraging upsets over Virginia Tech in 2012 and Notre Dame in 2013, with depressing losses to Youngstown State, UConn and Navy. After ranking 24th in the final F/+ ratings in 2010, they've come in the last three seasons at 47th, 51st and 54th. They finished with turnover margin of plus-one or minus-one in three of the last four seasons. Year in, year out, Pitt is so lukewarm, so infuriatingly mediocre, it would almost command more respect by being consistently awful.

Last year, at least, the monotony was occasionally interrupted by hyper-productive defensive tackle Aaron Donald, who was rewarded handsomely on the postseason awards circuit for the time he spent in opposing backfields. But even the most decorated defender in the nation wasn't enough to move the needle in any discernible way beyond his own stat line: the defense as a whole didn't budge, moving from 45th in Defensive F/+ in 2012 to 37th in 2013, while yielding six more points per game. Offensively, the situation was worse, thanks largely to an offensive line that ranked 119th in Adjusted Sack Rate, leaving Tom "Sitting Duck" Savage to endure more sacks (43) than any other FBS quarterback. In that context, the promotion of sophomore guard Dorian Johnson, the most hyped signee in the 2013 recruiting class, into a full-time role may be better news for the new quarterback, sophomore Chad Voytik, than the presence of four returning starters. The 2013 recruiting class also produced a pair of breakout candidates in running back James Conner (799 rushing yards, 5.5 yards per carry, 5.2 highlight yards per opportunity) and wide receiver Tyler Boyd (1,174 receiving yards, 13.8 yards per catch, 71 percent catch rate), last year's leading rusher and receiver, respectively, as true freshmen. Again, though, unless Voytik is a revelation, the middle of the road beckons.

2015 Draft Prospects: FS Ray Vinopal (7-FA).

No. 45 Georgia Tech Yellow Jackets (7-5, 4-4)

2013: 7-6 (5-3) / F/+ #34 / FEI #35 / S&P+ #35 / Program F/+: #40					
2013 Offense			**2013 Defense**		
Offensive F/+	8.3%	31	Defensive F/+	1.5%	57
Offensive FEI	0.202	38	Defensive FEI	-0.100	51
Offensive S&P+	118.1	21	Defensive S&P+	104.0	68
Rushing S&P+	126.2	10	Rushing S&P+	105.2	54
Passing S&P+	106.0	48	Passing S&P+	92.5	93
Standard Downs S&P+	115.7	24	Standard Downs S&P+	96.7	84
Passing Downs S&P+	117.4	29	Passing Downs S&P+	97.9	76
2013 Special Teams			Special Teams F/+	2.2%	22
2014 Projections			SOS Rk	53	
Ret. Starters: 5 OFF, 5 DEF			Offensive F/+	7.7%	23
Proj. F/+	6.0%	45	Defensive F/+	-1.7%	72
Mean Wins / Conf Wins	6.9 / 3.9		Conf. / Div. Title Odds	0.3% / 7.2%	

2013 Five Factors			
Efficiency	Off Success Rate+	118.5	11
	Def Success Rate+	93.6	85
	Total Efficiency	212.1	35
Explosiveness	Off IsoPPP+	95.7	87
	Def IsoPPP+	100.6	56
	Total Explosiveness	196.4	79
Field Position	Field Pos. Adv. (FPA)	0.484	85
Finishing Drives	Off Red Zone S&P+	125.4	7
	Def Red Zone S&P+	72.8	124
	Total Red Zone Rating	198.2	64
Turnovers	Turnover Margin	-4.0	86
	Exp. TO Margin	-1.1	77
	Difference	-2.9	82

Just so we're clear here, you know Georgia Tech runs the triple option, right? Does this still require further clarification? Apparently so for quarterback Vad Lee, who—after three years on campus, the last as a full-time starter—explained to reporters in January that he was transferring from Tech because, in his words, "The triple option was never really my thing." Really? As opposed to what? Under old-school diehard Paul Johnson, the option is the only thing. From a sheer quantity standpoint, the Yellow Jackets have averaged upwards of 50 carries per game each of the last five seasons, rivaling the option schemes at Army and Navy as the most consistently ground-oriented attacks in the nation; rushing plays in that span have outnumbered passes roughly four to one. In terms of quality, Tech has managed to finish among the top dozen in both Offensive Rushing S&P+ and overall yards per carry each of the last three years, against defenses that have no doubt what's coming. The backfield is facing a significant overhaul in the absence of 2013's top three rushers, beginning with the new quarterback, Justin Thomas. But the specific personnel under Johnson has always been beside the point. Barring the unforeseen emergence of the next Demaryius Thomas to put some teeth in the dormant passing threat, the end result is boilerplate.

Unfortunately, the same can be said for the Tech defense, which has settled into a similarly narrow range of mediocrity: since 2009, the Jackets have ranked somewhere between 53rd and 70th in Defensive F/+ five years in a row, under three different coordinators. The 2013 edition had its moments, holding division rivals Duke, North Carolina, Virginia Tech and Pitt below 21 points apiece, and pitching a shutout against Syracuse. But it was also vulnerable in the secondary, coming in 93rd nationally in Defensive Passing S&P+. In six losses, opposing quarterbacks averaged 288 yards with a collective efficiency rating of 169.1. Some of that damage was mitigated by a solid pass rush, anchored by Jeremiah Attaochu, a second-round draft pick who racked up 28.5 sacks over the last three years. With Attaochu now in San Diego, the role of rush end will be played by junior Jabari Hunt-Days, who moved from middle linebacker to Attaochu's old position this spring. The secondary will also welcome the return of veteran safeties Isaiah Johnson and Jamal Golden from medical redshirts. Still, it's a relatively young group—besides Johnson, there's only one other senior starter, linebacker Quayshawn Nealy—and no individual member is on any scout's must-see list.

2015 Draft Prospects: G Shaquille Mason (5), OLB Quayshawn Nealy (5-6).

No. 48 Duke Blue Devils (7-5, 4-4)

2013: 10-4 (6-2) / F/+ #41 / FEI #33 / S&P+ #46 / Program F/+: #70					
2013 Offense			**2013 Defense**		
Offensive F/+	7.5%	33	Defensive F/+	-0.2%	62
Offensive FEI	0.274	32	Defensive FEI	0.026	70
Offensive S&P+	108.7	39	Defensive S&P+	107.4	53
Rushing S&P+	110.2	40	Rushing S&P+	95.5	82
Passing S&P+	113.1	30	Passing S&P+	103.6	53
Standard Downs S&P+	114.7	26	Standard Downs S&P+	96.8	83
Passing Downs S&P+	101.0	59	Passing Downs S&P+	111.8	37
2013 Special Teams			Special Teams F/+	1.2%	40
2014 Projections			SOS Rk	91	
Ret. Starters: 7 OFF, 8 DEF			Offensive F/+	8.3%	21
Proj. F/+	3.3%	48	Defensive F/+	-5.0%	91
Mean Wins / Conf Wins	7.4 / 3.8		Conf. / Div. Title Odds	0.2% / 6.2%	

2013 Five Factors			
Efficiency	Off Success Rate+	109.6	30
	Def Success Rate+	96.3	70
	Total Efficiency	205.9	50
Explosiveness	Off IsoPPP+	97.8	75
	Def IsoPPP+	107.5	29
	Total Explosiveness	205.4	45
Field Position	Field Pos. Adv. (FPA)	0.498	63
Finishing Drives	Off Red Zone S&P+	122.3	10
	Def Red Zone S&P+	91.3	85
	Total Red Zone Rating	213.6	32
Turnovers	Turnover Margin	+1.0	53
	Exp. TO Margin	+6.0	26
	Difference	-5.0	102

We'd love to pretend we saw the Blue Devils' championship run coming, but... well, you win some, you lose some. In fact, this space in last year's book looked at the Devils' unlikely run to a bowl bid in 2012 and scoffed: The "breakthrough" campaign had ended with five consecutive, lopsided losses, leaving them with the worst defense in the conference and a losing (6-7) record for the 18th year in a row. Our projection for 2013? A return to their default landing place in the Coastal Division cellar. (We weren't alone—a consensus of preseason magazines made the same call.) Instead, Duke turned the corner for real, upsetting Virginia Tech, Miami and North Carolina en route to an eight-game winning streak, a school record for wins and an outright division title. After narrowly missing a major stunner in the Chick-Fil-A Bowl, a wildly entertaining, 52-48 loss to Texas A&M, Duke landed in the final AP poll for the first time since 1961.

Given that record, a sixth-place projection in a division with no other obvious frontrunner might strike some readers as another diss. Certainly the talent level is no longer an excuse: in defiance of the annual recruiting rankings, league coaches voted six Duke players to the postseason All-ACC team last December, more than any other team except Florida State. Four of those headliners are back, including wide receiver Jamison Crowder (1,360 receiving yards, 12.6 yards per catch, 65 percent catch rate), who set a single-season ACC record for receptions (108) as a junior, and strong safety Jeremy Cash, an Ohio State transfer who racked up 124 tackles with four interceptions in his first year in the lineup. Accordingly, next spring's NFL draft is likely to feature at least as many Blue Devils as the last 15 drafts combined. Experience isn't in question, either: as a whole, the 2014 Devils have logged more career starts (319) than any other ACC roster.

Three factors account for the ongoing skepticism. First, this is still, you know, Duke: in part, the meh projection reflects the overall F/+ scores from 2009-12, when the Blue Devils ranked 68th, 78th, 75th and 81st, respectively. Secondly, despite their triumph in the standings, the Blue Devils actually finished fifth in the Coastal Division in F/+ last year, a reflection of just how razor-thin the margins in this division are. (The top five teams in the Coastal in 2013 all ranked between 27th and 41st nationally, and six teams are ranked within 20 spots of one another in our projections for 2014.) In ACC play, they yielded 75 yards more per game than they gained. And then there's the schedule, which sends them on the road for four of the first five conference games, including key swing dates against Miami, Georgia Tech and Pitt, followed by a trip to Syracuse. By the time Virginia Tech and North Carolina come to Durham in late November, the repeat bid will likely be hanging on by a thread, if it's still alive at all.

2015 Draft Prospects: G Laken Tomlinson (3), SS Jeremy Cash (3-4), TE Braxton Deaver (4-5), QB Anthony Boone (5-6), ILB Kelby Brown (5-6), WR Jamison Crowder (5-6).*

No. 67 Virginia Cavaliers (4-8, 2-6)

2013: 2-10 (0-8) / F/+ #79 / FEI #81 / S&P+ #76 / Program F/+: #78					
2013 Offense			**2013 Defense**		
Offensive F/+	-11.9%	108	Defensive F/+	4.6%	39
Offensive FEI	-0.378	108	Defensive FEI	-0.116	48
Offensive S&P+	82.1	107	Defensive S&P+	115.8	32
Rushing S&P+	95.1	86	Rushing S&P+	109.9	37
Passing S&P+	80.8	115	Passing S&P+	121.2	16
Standard Downs S&P+	92.9	94	Standard Downs S&P+	121.3	11
Passing Downs S&P+	78.6	114	Passing Downs S&P+	103.8	55
2013 Special Teams			Special Teams F/+	-0.4%	79
2014 Projections			SOS Rk	9	
Ret. Starters: 7 OFF, 10 DEF			Offensive F/+	-11.6%	121
Proj. F/+	-2.1%	67	Defensive F/+	9.5%	16
Mean Wins / Conf Wins	3.6 / 1.5		Conf. / Div. Title Odds	0.0% / 0.1%	

2013 Five Factors			
Efficiency	Off Success Rate+	90.6	92
	Def Success Rate+	119.1	10
	Total Efficiency	209.7	40
Explosiveness	Off IsoPPP+	87.5	119
	Def IsoPPP+	90.9	109
	Total Explosiveness	178.4	118
Field Position	Field Pos. Adv. (FPA)	0.462	108
Finishing Drives	Off Red Zone S&P+	92.3	90
	Def Red Zone S&P+	104.6	42
	Total Red Zone Rating	196.9	68
Turnovers	Turnover Margin	-5.0	93
	Exp. TO Margin	-5.0	106
	Difference	0.0	57

Against all odds, Mike London walked away from a crash landing in 2013 with his job intact, a minor miracle of self-preservation. In the era of multimillion-dollar salaries, how many coaches have survived into year five anywhere after overseeing three last-place finishes in the first four? Clearly, though, another reprieve is out of the question, and London knows it. Already, he's demoted the incumbent starter at quarterback, David Watford, in favor of sophomore Greyson Lambert. To cater to Lambert's strength as a pocket passer, coaches this spring promoted a pair of lanky outside targets, sophomores Keeon Johnson and Kyle Dockins, over the only proven wide receiver, diminutive senior Darius Jennings (340 receiving yards, 8.9 yards per catch, 51 percent catch rate). Defensively, the incoming recruiting class includes a pair of five-star headliners, defensive tackle Andrew Brown and safety Quin Blanding, who arrive with more advance hype than any previous London signee. Another touted recruit, Jamil Kamara, fits with the "bigger is better" theme at wide receiver. By betting on youth, London is hoping to close the talent gap between his roster—and it is now his roster, made up entirely of players who signed up to play for London—and the rest of the conference as quickly as possible. If it doesn't come together, his successor will thank him.

Although a calamity on the scale of 2013 certainly cannot be laid at the feet of a single player, it is hard to believe in retrospect that Watford survived the entire season as the starter—in the end, he came in dead last among regular ACC passers in efficiency rating (99.6) and interceptions (15), and the offense as a whole averaged just 17.1 points per game against FBS opponents. Not that Lambert was a revelation in an extended relief role over the last four games, by any means, but if he manages not to be the worst quarterback in the conference, he will be an upgrade. With running backs Kevin Parks (senior, 2,575 yards, 25 TD over the last three years) and Taquan "Smoke" Mizell (sophomore) behind him, he also has the basis for a reliable ground game capable of shouldering a larger share of the offense—even with Watford's struggles, the Cavaliers led the ACC in passes per game (42.2), largely out of necessity to keep pace in blowouts. On the other side, though, the defense wasn't as bad as the scoreboard suggests. Despite yielding the most points in the conference, Virginia wound up with respectable marks according to both Defensive F/+ (39th) and Defensive S&P+ (32nd), especially against the pass. On that front, the entire secondary returns intact, led by FBS interception leader Anthony Harris, and senior cornerback Demetrious Nicholson is back from a turf toe injury that cost him most of last season. Man for man, there is way too much potential here to justify the Cavs' status as perennial punching bags in such a middleweight division. But that's true for the other six teams, too, which have at least achieved a reliable mediocrity. From this vantage point, Virginia just plays the role too well to imagine it falling to anyone else.

2015 Draft Prospects: SS Anthony Harris (1-2), CB Demetrious Nicholson (5-6), RB Kevin Parks (5-6).

Matt Hinton

Projected Win Probabilities For ACC Teams

			Overall Wins													Conference Wins								
Div	**Conf**	**ACC Atlantic**	**12-0**	**11-1**	**10-2**	**9-3**	**8-4**	**7-5**	**6-6**	**5-7**	**4-8**	**3-9**	**2-10**	**1-11**	**0-12**	**8-0**	**7-1**	**6-2**	**5-3**	**4-4**	**3-5**	**2-6**	**1-7**	**0-8**
-	-	Boston College	-	-	-	-	1	5	18	31	29	13	2	1	-	-	-	-	1	7	22	36	27	7
6	5	Clemson	-	6	23	35	25	9	2	-	-	-	-	-	-	2	33	40	19	5	1	-	-	-
90	86	Florida State	67	28	5	-	-	-	-	-	-	-	-	-	-	80	19	1	-	-	-	-	-	-
4	3	Louisville	-	7	26	37	22	7	1	-	-	-	-	-	-	1	16	43	29	10	1	-	-	-
-	-	North Carolina State	-	-	-	1	6	19	32	28	12	2	-	-	-	-	-	-	2	11	30	37	17	3
-	-	Syracuse	-	-	-	-	3	11	22	28	22	11	3	-	-	-	-	1	5	17	32	30	13	2
-	-	Wake Forest	-	-	-	-	-	1	7	19	31	28	12	2	-	-	-	-	-	1	10	29	40	20
Div	**Conf**	**ACC Coastal**	**12-0**	**11-1**	**10-2**	**9-3**	**8-4**	**7-5**	**6-6**	**5-7**	**4-8**	**3-9**	**2-10**	**1-11**	**0-12**	**8-0**	**7-1**	**6-2**	**5-3**	**4-4**	**3-5**	**2-6**	**1-7**	**0-8**
6	-	Duke	-	1	6	16	26	27	17	6	1	-	-	-	-	-	1	8	20	30	26	12	3	-
7	-	Georgia Tech	-	-	2	9	21	29	24	12	3	-	-	-	-	-	2	9	22	31	24	10	2	-
4	-	Miami	-	-	2	9	21	28	23	12	4	1	-	-	-	-	1	6	20	32	26	12	3	-
17	1	North Carolina	-	1	7	17	26	25	16	6	2	-	-	-	-	1	6	19	30	26	13	4	1	-
17	1	Pittsburgh	-	3	11	23	28	21	10	3	1	-	-	-	-	1	6	19	29	26	14	4	1	-
-	-	Virginia	-	-	-	-	-	1	6	15	28	31	17	2	-	-	-	-	1	4	14	30	34	17
49	4	Virginia Tech	1	7	23	31	23	11	3	1	-	-	-	-	-	6	24	33	24	11	2	-	-	-

Big Ten Conference

Lest you forget, the Big Ten started all of this. The nation's first major football conference (unless you count the Ivy League) began this round of conference realignment drama—really, this was probably quite a few rounds—by kick-starting the Big Ten Network in 2007, then deciding it wanted to add schools to expand its (and its network's) reach. It added Nebraska, the Pac-10 tried to add half of the Big 12, the Big 12 ended up losing teams to those two conferences and the SEC (and taking teams from the Big East), the ACC jumped in and dealt the Big East a death blow, the SEC announced *its* own network, et cetera.

To get from 12 programs to 14, the conference is officially welcoming Maryland and Rutgers into the mix this fall. To some degree, it adds New York and Washington D.C. into the BTN's reach, which is good, but from a competitive standpoint, it's not exactly the SEC adding Texas A&M and Missouri or the ACC adding (sort of) Notre Dame.

In fact, the presence of Rutgers and Maryland will basically further the current defining characteristic of the Big Ten conference: lots of decent football with minimal elite play. Ohio State has gone 24-2 under Urban Meyer and will consistently be a national threat, and there are a few top-20 candidates. Michigan State surged beyond what even optimistic numbers thought could be achieved last year. Wisconsin is a steady top-20 program. Any minute now, Michigan's strong recruiting under Brady Hoke could magically turn the Wolverines back into Michigan™.

As a whole, though, there's a glut in the middle. This year's projections rank only one Big Ten team in the top ten but only one below 73rd. There are nine teams ranked between No. 12 and No. 52, and there should be all sorts of interesting battles among evenly matched teams from week to week. But unless Ohio State can find a pass defense, or Michigan State quarterback Connor Cook is ready to take another huge step forward, or Wisconsin can rebuild its defensive front seven on the fly, there might not be a national title contender in the bunch. All three have questions to answer, and all three are projected to lose two games, which would probably leave the Big Ten out of the playoff discussion.

There's nothing new about this, mind you. Since Ohio State won the 2002 national title, only two Big Ten teams have reached the BCS Championship: Ohio State in 2006 and 2007. Combined title game score: Opponent 79, Buckeyes 38. Granted, the College Football Playoff will help. Michigan State might have made it had the playoff existed last year, and Wisconsin probably would have made it in 2010. Plus, Ohio State was banned from the postseason in 2012, a year in which the Buckeyes went 12-0. So there will probably be chances on the horizon, but that only matters if you take advantage of them.

In 2014, however, there will be competition, and there will be high-level talent. Up to three Big Ten defensive linemen could go in the first round of next year's NFL Draft. Ohio State's Braxton Miller is returning to make another run at the Heisman and the title game. The electric Melvin Gordon of Wisconsin leads a bevy of excellent running backs that also includes Nebraska's Ameer Abdullah and Indiana's Tevin Coleman). Michigan State still has a few elite defenders, and while Maryland and Rutgers don't help the conference's perceptions overall, they do bring with them some blue-chip skill position talent and athleticism, particularly in the form of receivers Stefon Diggs (Maryland) and Leonte Carroo (Rutgers). There are plenty of reasons to follow the Big Ten this year, even if "finding national title contenders" might not be one of them.

EAST DIVISION

No. 8 Ohio State Buckeyes (10-2, 7-1)

2013: 12-2 (8-0) / F/+ #9 / FEI #13 / S&P+ #11 / Program F/+: #9					
2013 Offense			**2013 Defense**		
Offensive F/+	22.1%	2	Defensive F/+	3.9%	45
Offensive FEI	0.624	3	Defensive FEI	-0.148	42
Offensive S&P+	140.8	2	Defensive S&P+	110.3	42
Rushing S&P+	161.6	1	Rushing S&P+	103.4	58
Passing S&P+	121.6	17	Passing S&P+	101.2	61
Standard Downs S&P+	142.4	1	Standard Downs S&P+	97.7	79
Passing Downs S&P+	124.2	18	Passing Downs S&P+	108.2	42
2013 Special Teams			Special Teams F/+	3.9%	5
2014 Projections			SOS Rk	66	
Ret. Starters: 5 OFF, 7 DEF			Offensive F/+	12.9%	8
Proj. F/+	18.9%	8	Defensive F/+	6.0%	31
Mean Wins / Conf Wins	10.4 / 6.7		Conf. / Div. Title Odds	33.6% / 48.7%	

2013 Five Factors			
Efficiency	Off Success Rate+	137.3	1
	Def Success Rate+	97.5	66
	Total Efficiency	234.8	5
Explosiveness	Off IsoPPP+	102.1	49
	Def IsoPPP+	104.2	42
	Total Explosiveness	206.3	42
Field Position	Field Pos. Adv. (FPA)	0.550	8
Finishing Drives	Off Red Zone S&P+	140.9	1
	Def Red Zone S&P+	87.9	93
	Total Red Zone Rating	228.8	13
Turnovers	Turnover Margin	+5.0	32
	Exp. TO Margin	+8.6	11
	Difference	-3.6	90

It's pretty hard to win 24 straight games at a blue-blood school and come away with neither a conference title nor a spot in the national title game. But thanks to a 2012 postseason ban and a fateful trip to Indianapolis for the Big Ten championship game, Ohio State managed to do just that. After going 12-0 in 2012, the Buckeyes were deemed national title contenders despite potentially shaky numbers last fall. They almost lived up to the billing, but after a 12-0 start, they got beat up, 34-24, by Michigan State in Indianapolis, then dropped a 40-35 decision to Clemson in the Orange Bowl, one of the more delightful games of the season.

Heading into Year 3 in Columbus, then, Urban Meyer is 24-2 and ... disappointing? Maybe a little? Luke Fickell's defense was terribly frustrating last fall; it was incredibly young and projected to stumble a bit, but not to 45th in Defensive F/+, 58th in Rushing S&P+, and 61st in Passing S&P+. Ohio State allowed explosive drives on 15.7 percent of opponent possessions, 86th nationally and the fourth highest rate in the Big Ten. The secondary never gelled, and while the defensive front was aggressive and often successful—linebacker Ryan Shazier (a Pittsburgh first-round pick) had 23.5 tackles for loss, and the trio of ends Noah Spence and Joey Bosa and tackle Michael Bennett combined for 39 tackles for loss and 22 sacks—the glitches were costly and, in the end, just frequent enough to keep the Buckeyes from the BCS Championship game.

Shazier and defensive backs Bradley Roby and Corey Brown are all gone, which leaves Fickell to search for new playmakers in what were the shakiest areas of the defense. That said, the line should be outstanding. All four starters return up front, as does just about every backup. With experience comes consistency, and one has to figure the run defense will learn quite a bit from last year's breakdowns. The pass defense is still a serious question mark, however.

On offense, there aren't nearly as many questions, mainly because of Meyer's offensive background—aside from his final year at Florida, Meyer doesn't tend to oversee anything but elite offenses—and because of quarterback Braxton Miller. The senior from nearby Huber Heights will forever take too many sacks because of his penchant for playmaking, but he makes up for it with efficient passing (2,094 yards, 64 percent completion rate, 24 touchdowns, seven interceptions) and electric running (1,201 pre-sack rushing yards, 8.0 per carry, 8.4 highlight yards per opportunity). He is without Carlos Hyde this time around, but sophomores Dontre Wilson (small) and Ezekiel Elliott (medium) and senior Rod Smith (large) give him running backs in every possible size and style. Miller will need a new go-to receiver after the departure of Pitt Brown, but between Devin Smith, Evan Spencer, and tight end Jeff Heuerman, he has three reliable senior options.

Top 2015 draft prospects: DT Michael Bennett (1), DE Noah Spence (1-2), QB Braxton Miller (4-5), CB Doran Grant (4-5), WR Devin Smith (4-5), TE Jeff Heuerman (4-5).*

No. 12 Michigan State Spartans (10-2, 7-1)

2013: 13-1 (8-0) / F/+ #6 / FEI #8 / S&P+ #8 / Program F/+: #16

2013 Offense			2013 Defense		
Offensive F/+	4.8%	43	Defensive F/+	25.3%	2
Offensive FEI	0.267	33	Defensive FEI	-0.733	2
Offensive S&P+	98.3	64	Defensive S&P+	153.2	2
Rushing S&P+	97.1	78	Rushing S&P+	145.1	2
Passing S&P+	96.9	71	Passing S&P+	145.7	1
Standard Downs S&P+	88.2	103	Standard Downs S&P+	149.1	1
Passing Downs S&P+	116.4	32	Passing Downs S&P+	130.2	7
2013 Special Teams			Special Teams F/+	2.0%	29
2014 Projections			SOS Rk	35	
Ret. Starters: 7 OFF, 5 DEF			Offensive F/+	1.2%	58
Proj. F/+	17.4%	12	Defensive F/+	16.1%	4
Mean Wins / Conf Wins	9.8 / 6.6		Conf. / Div. Title Odds	27.7% / 42.4%	

2013 Five Factors			
Efficiency	Off Success Rate+	90.7	91
	Def Success Rate+	142.9	1
	Total Efficiency	233.7	6
Explosiveness	Off IsoPPP+	104.5	39
	Def IsoPPP+	97.7	74
	Total Explosiveness	202.2	57
Field Position	Field Pos. Adv. (FPA)	0.558	5
Finishing Drives	Off Red Zone S&P+	97.7	73
	Def Red Zone S&P+	123.8	7
	Total Red Zone Rating	221.5	21
Turnovers	Turnover Margin	+13.0	8
	Exp. TO Margin	+9.1	10
	Difference	+3.9	27

If only the College Football Playoff had come around one year earlier. There's a decent chance that Mark Dantonio's Michigan State Spartans could have secured a bid; they finished fourth in the final pre-bowl BCS standings, after all. The combination of a devastating, aggressive defense and an offense that, midway through the season, suddenly didn't stink was a devastating combination, one the Spartans rode to a Big Ten title and Rose Bowl victory.

It's a "strength gets weaker, weakness gets stronger" situation for State in 2014. The defense, so incredible a year ago—second in Defensive F/+, second in Rushing S&P+, first in Passing S&P+, first in value drive percentage —must replace a wealth of unique, dominant talent. Linebackers Denicos Allen and Max Bullough combined for 26 tackles for loss, seven sacks, and steady, jarring tackling. Darqueze Dennard was quite likely college football's best cornerback last fall. Safety Isaiah Lewis provided the kind of steady over-the-top help and run support.

Don't cry too much for Dantonio and defensive coordinator Pat Narduzzi, however. End Shilique Calhoun (14 tackles for loss, 7.5 sacks) is back. So are linebacker Taiwan Jones, end Marcus Rush, corner Trae Waynes, and plenty of other contributors from last fall's incredible run. A top-two finish in Defensive F/+ might not be likely this time around, but let's not pretend this will be a weak unit.

The offense isn't suddenly a threat to top the nation's rankings, either, but you will rarely see in-season improvement like what State engineered last year. Against their first three FBS opponents (Western Michigan, USF, and Notre Dame) the Spartans averaged 3.9 yards per play. The defense was more of a threat to score than the offense. But the staff showed faith in sophomore quarterback Connor Cook, and after completing just 28 of 59 passes for 209 yards in those three games, he figured things out. He completed 60 percent of his passes after October 1, averaged 13.0 yards per completion, and torched Ohio State for 304 yards and three scores in the Big Ten title game.

Three of Cook's four primary targets return, including Tony Lippett (613 receiving yards, 13.9 per catch, 67 percent catch rate) and Macgarrett Kings Jr. (509 receiving yards, 12.1 per catch, 60 percent catch rate), who were State's two best receivers late in the year. Despite this newfound passing success, however, the Spartans are still going to run as much as possible, and in Jeremy Langford, they return a steady, efficient back. Nick Hill and sophomore Delton Williams are potentially explosive change-of-pace backs as well. The efficient offense and strong special teams helped to create dramatic field position advantages for State, and even if the defense isn't quite as effective, that recipe might still be a winner in 2014.

Top 2015 draft prospects: DE Shilique Calhoun (1), CB Trae Waynes* (1-2), FS Kurtis Drummond (2-3), RB Jeremy Langford (3-4), DE Marcus Rush (6-7), P Mike Sadler (6-7).*

No. 27 Michigan Wolverines (8-4, 5-3)

2013: 7-6 (3-5) / F/+ #37 / FEI #36 / S&P+ #44 / Program F/+: #25						2013 Five Factors			
2013 Offense			**2013 Defense**						
Offensive F/+	5.3%	40	Defensive F/+	4.5%	40	Efficiency	Off Success Rate+	101.2	55
Offensive FEI	0.173	42	Defensive FEI	-0.201	37		Def Success Rate+	103.1	48
Offensive S&P+	108.2	44	Defensive S&P+	108.3	50		Total Efficiency	204.2	52
Rushing S&P+	97.6	75	Rushing S&P+	111.7	33	Explosiveness	Off IsoPPP+	115.4	10
Passing S&P+	117.1	25	Passing S&P+	103.6	54		Def IsoPPP+	103.3	43
Standard Downs S&P+	103.0	58	Standard Downs S&P+	107.9	39		Total Explosiveness	218.8	13
Passing Downs S&P+	115.8	33	Passing Downs S&P+	101.2	64	Field Position	Field Pos. Adv. (FPA)	0.497	65
2013 Special Teams			Special Teams F/+	0.3%	61	Finishing Drives	Off Red Zone S&P+	107.0	35
2014 Projections			SOS Rk	46			Def Red Zone S&P+	119.2	14
Ret. Starters: 6 OFF, 8 DEF			Offensive F/+	6.2%	31		Total Red Zone Rating	226.2	16
Proj. F/+	11.0%	27	Defensive F/+	4.8%	35	Turnovers	Turnover Margin	+5.0	32
Mean Wins / Conf Wins	8.2 / 5.2		Conf. / Div. Title Odds	3.1% / 6.9%			Exp. TO Margin	-3.1	90
							Difference	+8.1	11

The offensive line isn't going to get worse.

Of all the potential outcomes for Michigan in the 2014 season, that's about the only one we can say with any confidence. Yes, left tackle Taylor Lewan went to Tennessee in the first round of the NFL draft; remove the best player, and any unit could conceivably regress. But not this time. Michigan ranked 118th in Adjusted Line Yards and 112th in Adjusted Sack Rate in 2013. The line got quarterback Devin Gardner pressured constantly, ensured a steady series of second-and-9s, and eventually got offensive coordinator Al Borges fired. It could technically be this awful again in 2014 ... but it won't.

Michigan's running game ranked a generous 75th in Rushing S&P+ in 2013, inflated a bit by the athleticism and running ability of Gardner (2,960 passing yards, 60.3 percent completion rate, 34 sacks; 748 pre-sack rushing yards). Head coach Brady Hoke plucked offensive coordinator Doug Nussmeier away from Alabama, and assuming a sophomore-laden line indeed performs better than 2013's freshman-addled unit, Gardner could thrive. He is the dual threat Nussmeier didn't have at Alabama, and despite the loss of receiver Jeremy Gallon to the New England Patriots, he'll have a couple of pretty big, exciting weapons in Devin Funchess (748 receiving yards, 15.3 per catch, 53 percent catch rate) and Jehu Chesson.

When the offense failed in 2013, it failed almost instantaneously; the Wolverines went three-and-out or worse on 37.7 percent of their possessions (92nd nationally) and opponents enjoyed the eighth best average starting field position in the nation. But if done a few more favors, the Michigan defense should thrive. A relatively young, banged up secondary struggled at times, but it has playmakers in cornerback Raymon Taylor (73.5 tackles, 13 passes defensed) and nickelback Blake Countess (10 passes defensed) and a high-upside pass rusher in senior Frank Clark. The defensive tackle position has not lived up to its collective recruiting ranking of late, but in Jake Ryan and a host of other exciting athletes like James Ross III, Desmond Morgan, and Royce Jenkins-Stone, the Wolverines have a loaded linebacking corps.

Road trips to Notre Dame, Michigan State, Northwestern, and Ohio State should keep the win total tamped down, but it's hard to imagine this team being any worse than it was last season, and offensive line aside, it was still respectable then.

Top 2015 draft prospects: TE Devin Funchess (2-3), QB Devin Gardner (5-6), MLB Jake Ryan (2-3), CB Raymon Taylor (6-7), OLB Brennen Beyer (6-7).*

No. 42 Penn State Nittany Lions (7-5, 4-4)

2013: 7-5 (4-4) / F/+ #61 / FEI #65 / S&P+ #53 / Program F/+: #26						2013 Five Factors			
2013 Offense			**2013 Defense**				Off Success Rate+	94.4	81
Offensive F/+	-3.1%	72	Defensive F/+	6.2%	34	Efficiency	Def Success Rate+	114.1	20
Offensive FEI	-0.046	68	Defensive FEI	-0.148	43		Total Efficiency	208.6	43
Offensive S&P+	91.2	84	Defensive S&P+	120.0	23		Off IsoPPP+	91.3	106
Rushing S&P+	90.9	99	Rushing S&P+	130.2	8	Explosiveness	Def IsoPPP+	102.0	52
Passing S&P+	96.7	72	Passing S&P+	105.4	48		Total Explosiveness	193.4	89
Standard Downs S&P+	93.4	90	Standard Downs S&P+	117.6	21	Field Position	Field Pos. Adv. (FPA)	0.472	96
Passing Downs S&P+	93.9	79	Passing Downs S&P+	111.2	39		Off Red Zone S&P+	96.1	79
2013 Special Teams			Special Teams F/+	-3.1%	112	Finishing Drives	Def Red Zone S&P+	100.9	55
2014 Projections			SOS Rk	63			Total Red Zone Rating	197.0	67
Ret. Starters: 6 OFF, 7 DEF			Offensive F/+	-3.2%	84		Turnover Margin	-2.0	73
Proj. F/+	6.6%	42	Defensive F/+	9.8%	15	Turnovers	Exp. TO Margin	+1.6	59
Mean Wins / Conf Wins	7.3 / 4.2		Conf. / Div. Title Odds	0.5% / 1.7%			Difference	-3.6	89

It appears the worst might be over in Happy Valley. Destroyed by the worst NCAA punishment this side of SMU in the wake of the Jerry Sandusky sexual abuse conviction, Penn State has survived two years with crippling scholarship reductions and a postseason ban. Bill O'Brien led the post-Paterno Nittany Lions to a 15-9 record in two seasons, helping to weather attrition and recruiting reasonably well given the circumstances.

O'Brien left to become the Houston Texans' head coach in the offseason, but PSU made what appears to be a strong hire in his absence; James Franklin, the 42-year-old product of East Stroudsburg University and Neshaminy High School in Langhorne, takes over for O'Brien. Franklin spent the last three seasons raising Vanderbilt's profile significantly, and he brought a good portion of his staff with him from Nashville.

Expectations should still be rather modest in 2014, but with scholarship reductions getting dialed back, the light at the end of the tunnel is brighter than it was two summers ago.

Injuries will once again play a major role for this thin squad, but the first-string talent is rather impressive. Blue-chip sophomore quarterback Christian Hackenberg (2,955 passing yards, 59 percent completion rate, 20 touchdowns, 10 interceptions) survived as a true freshman and dominated in his season finale, producing four touchdowns and a 208.9 passer rating in an upset of Wisconsin. He'll be dealing with a new receiving corps after the departure of star wideout Allen Robinson (1,432 receiving yards, 14.8 per catch, 65 percent catch rate), who was basically the No. 1 and No. 2 target wrapped up in one. Running backs Zach Zwinak and Bill Belton add an efficiency component to the offense, though their explosiveness is lacking.

Linebacker Mike Hull and end C.J. Olaniyan combine to lead a defensive front seven that was sharp against the run in 2013, but while cornerback Jordan Lucas (4.5 tackles for loss, three interceptions, 13 passes broken up) and the secondary were exciting and aggressive, they got burned quite a bit, and the loss of two of the top three safeties probably won't help in that regard. Penn State can help itself with a renewed focus on special teams, as they were a miserable 117th in kickoff efficiency and 114th in kickoff return efficiency last year.

Top 2015 draft prospects: G Miles Dieffenbach (3-4), OLB Mike Hull (5-6), FS Adrian Amos (5-6), RB Bill Belton (6-7).

No. 50 Indiana Hoosiers (6-6, 3-5)

2013: 5-7 (3-5) / F/+ #56 / FEI #61 / S&P+ #47 / Program F/+: #87						2013 Five Factors			
2013 Offense			**2013 Defense**				Off Success Rate+	106.5	41
Offensive F/+	14.0%	16	Defensive F/+	-11.1%	106	Efficiency	Def Success Rate+	92.7	90
Offensive FEI	0.450	17	Defensive FEI	0.413	110		Total Efficiency	199.2	63
Offensive S&P+	121.5	16	Defensive S&P+	93.0	96		Off IsoPPP+	128.3	1
Rushing S&P+	126.6	9	Rushing S&P+	97.3	75	Explosiveness	Def IsoPPP+	97.0	80
Passing S&P+	117.9	21	Passing S&P+	89.6	100		Total Explosiveness	225.4	5
Standard Downs S&P+	120.2	14	Standard Downs S&P+	94.8	91	Field Position	Field Pos. Adv. (FPA)	0.501	61
Passing Downs S&P+	125.1	17	Passing Downs S&P+	89.6	91		Off Red Zone S&P+	103.9	43
2013 Special Teams			Special Teams F/+	-0.6%	84	Finishing Drives	Def Red Zone S&P+	107.7	34
2014 Projections			SOS Rk	42			Total Red Zone Rating	211.6	39
Ret. Starters: 8 OFF, 10 DEF			Offensive F/+	12.6%	9		Turnover Margin	-3.0	82
Proj. F/+	2.8%	50	Defensive F/+	-9.8%	112	Turnovers	Exp. TO Margin	+6.6	19
Mean Wins / Conf Wins	5.7 / 3.3		Conf. / Div. Title Odds	0.1% / 0.3%			Difference	-9.6	121

Kevin Wilson has been doing this offense thing for a while now. The Indiana head coach was an early spread offense innovator as Northwestern's offensive coordinator, then helped to set all sorts of records in the same role at Oklahoma. That he was able to craft an offense that ranked 16th in Offensive F/+ in his third year as Indiana's head coach should not be a surprise.

There's a little work to do in rebuilding a receiving corps that lost Cody Latimer to the Broncos and both Kofi Hughes and tight end Ted Bolser to the Redskins. But it's hard to worry too much about an offense that not only returns two experienced quarterbacks—Nate Sudfeld (2,523 passing yards, 21 touchdowns) and Tre Roberson (1,128 passing yards, 433 pre-sack rushing yards)—but also boasts perhaps the nation's most explosive running back, junior Tevin Coleman. Coleman rushed for 958 yards (7.3 per carry) and led the nation with an average of 12.0 highlight yards per opportunity. Get him to the second level of the defense, and he'll go a very long way. And a line that returns 10 players with starting experience (130 career starts) might be pretty good at getting him there.

So if Indiana had an explosive, exciting offense capable of keeping up in any shootout, how did the Hoosiers only go 5-7 last year? Defense, obviously. They ranked just 106th in Defensive F/+, which was the best ranking of the Wilson era but still clearly wasn't good enough. The Hoosiers allowed at least 6.1 yards per play in nine of 12 contests in 2013 (including seven of eight Big Ten games), and while they went undefeated when allowing fewer than 41 points, they only allowed fewer than 41 points five times.

New defensive coordinator Brian Knorr crafted an overachieving unit at Wake Forest in 2013, and he has some potential stars in veteran cornerback Tim Bennett (3.5 tackles for loss, 21 passes defensed) and big sophomore nose tackle Ralph Green III (6-foot-5, 325 pounds).

Indiana's recruiting has picked up under Wilson, but it's time for that to rub off on both sides of the ball.

Top 2015 draft prospects: CB Tim Bennett (6-7).

No. 52 Maryland Terrapins (5-7, 2-6)

2013: 7-6 (3-5) / F/+ #63 / FEI #71 / S&P+ #58 / Program F/+: #72					
2013 Offense			**2013 Defense**		
Offensive F/+	-3.6%	75	Defensive F/+	-0.3%	64
Offensive FEI	-0.208	88	Defensive FEI	0.016	68
Offensive S&P+	102.3	54	Defensive S&P+	106.1	58
Rushing S&P+	110.4	39	Rushing S&P+	106.9	42
Passing S&P+	110.9	33	Passing S&P+	99.9	64
Standard Downs S&P+	113.0	31	Standard Downs S&P+	108.9	35
Passing Downs S&P+	104.2	53	Passing Downs S&P+	94.6	84
2013 Special Teams			Special Teams F/+	2.6%	17
2014 Projections			SOS Rk	51	
Ret. Starters: 9 OFF, 9 DEF			Offensive F/+	-2.3%	80
Proj. F/+	1.9%	52	Defensive F/+	4.2%	39
Mean Wins / Conf Wins	5.0 / 2.2		Conf. / Div. Title Odds	0.0% / 0.0%	

2013 Five Factors			
Efficiency	Off Success Rate+	102.5	50
	Def Success Rate+	98.8	58
	Total Efficiency	201.2	57
Explosiveness	Off IsoPPP+	111.9	17
	Def IsoPPP+	102.6	48
	Total Explosiveness	214.5	19
Field Position	Field Pos. Adv. (FPA)	0.520	38
Finishing Drives	Off Red Zone S&P+	86.4	107
	Def Red Zone S&P+	104.6	41
	Total Red Zone Rating	191.0	84
Turnovers	Turnover Margin	-7.0	101
	Exp. TO Margin	-9.5	121
	Difference	+2.5	33

In 2012, head coach Randy Edsall's second season in College Park, Maryland lost every scholarship quarterback on the roster to injury but still managed to improve from 92nd in the F/+ rankings to 86th. In 2013, the Terps lost their two star receivers, the starting quarterback got hobbled again, and basically every linebacker missed time with injury; they improved again, this time to 63rd.

If the injury bug stops nibbling quite so much on the Terps, they could make some noise in their Big Ten debut. When healthy, quarterback C.J. Brown is a solid dual-threat, and he'll have a wealth of skill position options at his disposal.

Receivers Stefon Diggs and Deon Long are former blue-chip recruits who combined for 1,076 receiving yards (16.3 per catch, 59 percent catch rate) in just half of 2013 before each breaking bones. Levern Jacobs, Nigel King, and Amba Etta-Tawo are all underclassmen who stepped up in their absence. And Brandon Ross and Wes Brown, team rushing leaders in 2013 and 2012, respectively, are back as well. Two years of injuries have created a wealth of experience and depth the Terps will try to exploit. A healthy roster should find some consistency at the end of drives as well; the Terps ranked 113th nationally in points per value drive last season.

On defense, the front seven of coordinator Brian Stewart's 3-4 defense is loaded with playmakers, from end Andre Monroe to linebacker Matt Robinson. A glitchy secondary must be patched up, however. Corner Will Likely both made and allowed quite a few big plays as a freshman, and if the pass rush didn't get to opposing quarterbacks on passing downs, there was probably an open man to be found.

Top 2015 draft prospects: WR Stefon Diggs (2-3), OLB Matt Robinson (5-6), WR Deon Long (6-7), CB Jeremiah Johnson (6-7).*

No. 71 Rutgers Scarlet Knights (4-8, 1-7)

2013: 6-7 (3-5) / F/+ #91 / FEI #94 / S&P+ #94 / Program F/+: #56

2013 Offense			2013 Defense		
Offensive F/+	-7.1%	91	Defensive F/+	-8.5%	96
Offensive FEI	-0.226	90	Defensive FEI	0.314	99
Offensive S&P+	89.3	90	Defensive S&P+	95.8	91
Rushing S&P+	92.1	90	Rushing S&P+	116.9	22
Passing S&P+	92.9	84	Passing S&P+	90.4	99
Standard Downs S&P+	86.6	109	Standard Downs S&P+	103.7	52
Passing Downs S&P+	107.3	48	Passing Downs S&P+	89.8	90
2013 Special Teams			Special Teams F/+	3.3%	8
2014 Projections			SOS Rk	43	
Ret. Starters: 8 OFF, 9 DEF			Offensive F/+	-1.6%	75
Proj. F/+	-3.1%	71	Defensive F/+	-1.5%	70
Mean Wins / Conf Wins	3.7 / 1.4		Conf. / Div. Title Odds	0.0% / 0.0%	

2013 Five Factors			
Efficiency	Off Success Rate+	88.4	101
	Def Success Rate+	100.1	51
	Total Efficiency	188.5	92
Explosiveness	Off IsoPPP+	108.8	25
	Def IsoPPP+	96.5	84
	Total Explosiveness	205.3	46
Field Position	Field Pos. Adv. (FPA)	0.535	18
Finishing Drives	Off Red Zone S&P+	87.1	105
	Def Red Zone S&P+	85.0	103
	Total Red Zone Rating	172.0	109
Turnovers	Turnover Margin	-12.0	121
	Exp. TO Margin	+0.9	63
	Difference	-12.9	125

Rutgers was one of the most frustrating teams in the country to watch in 2013. It didn't take long to figure out that the Scarlet Knights had all sorts of athleticism. The offense featured running back Paul James (881 rushing yards, 5.6 per carry, 6.1 highlight yards per opportunity), big-play receiver Brandon Coleman (549 receiving yards, 15.7 per catch, 50 percent catch rate) and a host of young, exciting options: tight end Tyler Kroft (573 yards, 13.3 per catch, 62 percent), wide receiver Leonte Carroo (467 yards, 17.3 per catch, 53 percent), and the supremely raw Janarion Grant (two return touchdowns but only two receptions).

Rutgers had more speed and potential excitement than Rutgers is supposed to have. And the Scarlet Knights still ranked just 91st in Offensive F/+. Quarterback Gary Nova threw 14 interceptions and took 25 sacks while completing just 55 percent of his passes, James missed three games with injury, the offensive line struggled dramatically, and the whole never matched up with the sum of the parts.

Sans Coleman, these pieces all return in 2014. There's no excuse for anything but strong improvement.

Rutgers is used to having a frustrating offense, however. The reason the Knights fell from 9-4 in 2012 to 6-7 in 2013 is defense. After ranking in the Defensive F/+ top 20 in both 2011 and 2012, Rutgers fell to 96th last fall. The run defense was solid (and it should be again in 2014 with the return of tackle Darius Hamilton and all three starting linebackers), but an almost completely new secondary experienced even more growing pains than expected. Most of Rutgers' defensive two-deep returns in 2014; if there's talent to go with the newfound experience, we'll see it this fall.

Top 2015 draft prospects: G Kaleb Johnson (6-7), C Betim Bujari (6-7).

WEST DIVISION

No. 18 Wisconsin Badgers (10-2, 7-1)

2013: 9-4 (6-2) / F/+ #19 / FEI #19 / S&P+ #9 / Program F/+: #10

2013 Offense			2013 Defense		
Offensive F/+	9.5%	28	Defensive F/+	15.8%	9
Offensive FEI	0.286	31	Defensive FEI	-0.459	13
Offensive S&P+	116.2	24	Defensive S&P+	135.2	10
Rushing S&P+	129.3	5	Rushing S&P+	126.7	9
Passing S&P+	108.4	42	Passing S&P+	114.0	28
Standard Downs S&P+	119.5	16	Standard Downs S&P+	119.4	14
Passing Downs S&P+	115.2	35	Passing Downs S&P+	113.4	36
2013 Special Teams			Special Teams F/+	0.9%	50
2014 Projections			SOS Rk	73	
Ret. Starters: 6 OFF, 4 DEF			Offensive F/+	7.2%	25
Proj. F/+	14.5%	18	Defensive F/+	7.4%	25
Mean Wins / Conf Wins	9.9 / 6.7		Conf. / Div. Title Odds	23.4% / 58.9%	

2013 Five Factors			
Efficiency	Off Success Rate+	110.8	27
	Def Success Rate+	114.8	17
	Total Efficiency	225.5	17
Explosiveness	Off IsoPPP+	111.6	18
	Def IsoPPP+	106.9	34
	Total Explosiveness	218.5	14
Field Position	Field Pos. Adv. (FPA)	0.520	35
Finishing Drives	Off Red Zone S&P+	101.3	57
	Def Red Zone S&P+	108.8	28
	Total Red Zone Rating	210.1	42
Turnovers	Turnover Margin	+1.0	53
	Exp. TO Margin	+1.9	55
	Difference	-0.9	68

If Wisconsin ever remembers how to win close games, the sky's the limit. Since beating Utah State with help from a missed field goal in September 2012, the Badgers have lost eight consecutive games decided by one possession. That's a remarkable feat considering they're otherwise 15-1 in that span.

Gary Andersen's first year succeeding Bret Bielema in Madison didn't result in a fourth consecutive Rose Bowl bid, but it did finish with the Badgers in the F/+ top 20 for the fifth straight year. The Badgers have been the Big Ten's steadiest program of late, even if close games have not exactly been the cheese curds to their bratwurst.

In terms of personnel, the primary questions are on the defensive side of the ball. That's probably a good thing considering it's been a while since Andersen and defensive coordinator Dave Aranda have overseen a bad defense. In 2012, their Utah State defense ranked ninth in Defensive F/+, and their first stab at the 3-4 in Madison ranked the same in 2013. Still, they have a lot of pieces to replace in the front seven—almost all of them, in fact. Six of Wisconsin's seven starters up front in the Capital One Bowl were seniors, as were the two chief backups.

This defense is going to be well-coached no matter what and returns an active secondary led by junior safety Michael Caputo, sophomore corner Sojourn Shelton and junior corner Darius Hilary. But the Badgers are going to be extremely young up front, which could force a shift in identity considering run defense was their primary strength last year.

If the defense can avoid serious regression, the offense should pick up the slack and keep Wisconsin a top team. A very good line returns four starters and will be blocking for one of the nation's best running-back tandems. Melvin Gordon (1,609 rushing yards, 7.8 per carry, 7.1 highlight yards per opportunity) and Corey Clement (547 yards, 8.2 per carry, 7.7 highlight yards per opportunity) are back and should be more than capable of accounting for the loss of fellow back James White.

White's absence may be felt most in the passing game. Whoever wins the starting quarterback job—Joel Stave or fellow junior Tanner McEvoy, who looked good in the spring while Stave was out with injury—will be making do with a brand new set of targets. White caught 39 passes last year, as did tight end Jacob Pederson. But the biggest loss is that of Jared Abbrederis, who in three years as Wisconsin's go-to wideout caught 182 passes for 2,851 yards and 20 touchdowns. Wisconsin's top three returning wideouts combined for 26 catches, 290 yards, and no scores in 2013. Gordon and Clement are fantastic, but you do have to pass occasionally.

Top 2015 draft prospects: RB Melvin Gordon* (1-2), OT Rob Havenstein (4-5), C Dallas Lewallen (6-7).

No. 33 Iowa Hawkeyes (9-3, 6-2)

2013: 8-5 (5-3) / F/+ #29 / FEI #31 / S&P+ #25 / Program F/+: #27					
2013 Offense			**2013 Defense**		
Offensive F/+	0.5%	60	Defensive F/+	13.9%	14
Offensive FEI	0.080	52	Defensive FEI	-0.345	28
Offensive S&P+	95.8	70	Defensive S&P+	136.9	8
Rushing S&P+	99.3	70	Rushing S&P+	132.1	7
Passing S&P+	103.8	57	Passing S&P+	122.4	13
Standard Downs S&P+	99.8	65	Standard Downs S&P+	126.1	8
Passing Downs S&P+	100.4	62	Passing Downs S&P+	126.0	11
2013 Special Teams			Special Teams F/+	0.7%	52
2014 Projections			SOS Rk	95	
Ret. Starters: 8 OFF, 6 DEF			Offensive F/+	1.2%	59
Proj. F/+	10.3%	33	Defensive F/+	9.1%	17
Mean Wins / Conf Wins	9.4 / 6.0		Conf. / Div. Title Odds	10.0% / 33.5%	

2013 Five Factors			
Efficiency	Off Success Rate+	100.9	56
	Def Success Rate+	117.2	12
	Total Efficiency	218.1	24
Explosiveness	Off IsoPPP+	90.8	108
	Def IsoPPP+	115.1	8
	Total Explosiveness	206.0	44
Field Position	Field Pos. Adv. (FPA)	0.529	28
Finishing Drives	Off Red Zone S&P+	103.4	46
	Def Red Zone S&P+	104.4	43
	Total Red Zone Rating	207.8	46
Turnovers	Turnover Margin	-1.0	69
	Exp. TO Margin	+2.0	53
	Difference	-3.0	83

By almost any measure, Iowa had regressed for three straight years heading into 2013. The Hawkeyes had seen their record fall from 11-2 in 2009 to 8-5, to 7-6, to 4-8. Their F/+ ranking followed suit, dropping from 11th to 21st, then 46th, then 72nd.

Head coach Kirk Ferentz brought in a new offensive coordinator, former Texas playcaller Greg Davis, to turn a listless offense around; it wasn't spectacular, but mediocrity does count as improvement. Iowa ranked 60th in Offensive F/+ with an updated version of the run-first attack we've come to expect from the Hawkeyes. Big plays were minimal, but Iowa was better able to stay on schedule and avoid crippling turnovers.

With eight starters returning, including quarterback Jake Rudock, leading rusher Mark Weisman, and all-conference tackle Brandon Scherff, this fall's Iowa offense should look quite a bit like last fall's. The Hawkeyes probably won't be any more explosive, which is a hindrance, but in terms of creating field-position advantages and staying out of the defense's way, it should be more of the same from this unit in 2014.

The problem is that with losses on defense, the offense can't just hold steady; it has to improve. Last year's Iowa defense finally looked like the Iowa defense again, excellent at stopping both the run and pass despite some occasional leakiness on passing downs. A sturdy defensive line led by tackles Louis Trinca-Pasat (9.0 tackles for loss) and Carl Davis remains intact, but the best unit on the defense in 2013 was a linebacking corps that must replace all three starters. The backups barely played and are nearly complete unknowns, and while Iowa has made a habit of producing strong linebacker play, it's hard to imagine the defense avoiding a drop-off overall. Losing ball-hawking cornerback B.J. Lowery (three interceptions, 16 passes broken up, three forced fumbles) certainly won't help, either. But the easiest conference and overall schedule in the Big Ten gives Iowa an edge to overcoming those personnel losses.

Top 2015 draft prospects: OT Brandon Scherff (1), DT Carl Davis (1-2).

No. 41 Nebraska Cornhuskers (8-4, 5-3)

2013: 9-4 (5-3) / F/+ #39 / FEI #46 / S&P+ #54 / Program F/+: #21					
2013 Offense			**2013 Defense**		
Offensive F/+	0.4%	61	Defensive F/+	7.2%	32
Offensive FEI	-0.034	66	Defensive FEI	-0.358	26
Offensive S&P+	104.6	46	Defensive S&P+	106.6	55
Rushing S&P+	116.0	24	Rushing S&P+	95.3	84
Passing S&P+	101.5	60	Passing S&P+	106.9	41
Standard Downs S&P+	107.1	44	Standard Downs S&P+	96.1	88
Passing Downs S&P+	106.8	49	Passing Downs S&P+	117.9	25
2013 Special Teams			Special Teams F/+	1.5%	38
2014 Projections			SOS Rk	58	
Ret. Starters: 5 OFF, 6 DEF			Offensive F/+	-1.7%	76
Proj. F/+	7.0%	41	Defensive F/+	8.6%	19
Mean Wins / Conf Wins	7.7 / 4.6		Conf. / Div. Title Odds	1.2% / 5.4%	

2013 Five Factors			
Efficiency	Off Success Rate+	106.2	43
	Def Success Rate+	97.5	65
	Total Efficiency	203.7	54
Explosiveness	Off IsoPPP+	99.9	61
	Def IsoPPP+	102.3	51
	Total Explosiveness	202.2	56
Field Position	Field Pos. Adv. (FPA)	0.487	82
Finishing Drives	Off Red Zone S&P+	103.1	47
	Def Red Zone S&P+	109.6	25
	Total Red Zone Rating	212.7	34
Turnovers	Turnover Margin	-11.0	119
	Exp. TO Margin	-4.3	98
	Difference	-6.7	114

On the surface, it seems Nebraska is stuck in a *Groundhog Day* situation, reliving the same season over and over. The Huskers' offense cranks out rushing yards, the defense racks up the havoc stats, head coach Bo Pelini blows up on the sideline, and at the end of the year, Nebraska has four losses. They have gone either 9-4 or 10-4 in all six years of the Pelini era, setting a bar too high to get him fired but forever too low to meet fan expectations.

While the end result has remained the same, however, the components of each four-loss Nebraska team have changed rather drastically, and Pelini must feel like he's gathering sand by the handful in an attempt to break through. In 2009-10, the defense was among the best in the country, and the offense was mediocre at best. In 2011, the offense improved while the defense fell back into the 30s of the Defensive F/+ rankings. In 2012, both units improved and a consistently strong special teams unit fell apart. In 2013, special teams rebounded, and the offense was dinged by shaky quarterback play.

At first glance, it appears 2014 could resemble 2013. Sophomore Tommy Armstrong Jr. is the presumptive starting quarterback after filling in at times for injured Taylor Martinez last year. He's a decent runner and passer, and he'll get help from potential all-conference running back Ameer Abdullah (1,690 rushing yards, 6.0 per carry, 5.4 highlight yards per opportunity) in the backfield. The playcalling will be once again geared around avoiding obvious passing situations and riding Abdullah as far as he can take them.

The defense, meanwhile, should make another run at 100-plus tackles for loss. End Randy Gregory (16.0 tackles for loss, 9.5 sacks) is one of the nation's more celebrated returnees, but he and the rest of the front seven will have to come up big to account for the loss of quite a few defensive backs, including Stanley Jean-Baptiste (a second-round draft pick of the Saints) and Ciante Evans (10.5 tackles for loss, 10 passes defensed).

Top 2015 draft prospects: DE Randy Gregory (1), RB Ameer Abdullah (2-3), WR Kenny Bell (4-5), SS Corey Cooper (6-7).

No. 47 Northwestern Wildcats (7-5, 4-4)

2013: 5-7 (1-7) / F/+ #59 / FEI #60 / S&P+ #57 / Program F/+: #52					
2013 Offense			**2013 Defense**		
Offensive F/+	-2.1%	67	Defensive F/+	4.4%	42
Offensive FEI	-0.133	75	Defensive FEI	-0.216	36
Offensive S&P+	102.5	52	Defensive S&P+	106.4	56
Rushing S&P+	107.0	50	Rushing S&P+	104.1	57
Passing S&P+	109.7	35	Passing S&P+	97.8	73
Standard Downs S&P+	111.5	36	Standard Downs S&P+	101.2	63
Passing Downs S&P+	93.0	81	Passing Downs S&P+	99.0	71
2013 Special Teams			Special Teams F/+	-0.3%	72
2014 Projections			SOS Rk	65	
Ret. Starters: 10 OFF, 8 DEF			Offensive F/+	1.8%	52
Proj. F/+	3.7%	47	Defensive F/+	1.9%	55
Mean Wins / Conf Wins	6.6 / 3.9		Conf. / Div. Title Odds	0.3% / 1.9%	

2013 Five Factors			
Efficiency	Off Success Rate+	112.0	25
	Def Success Rate+	94.2	80
	Total Efficiency	206.2	49
Explosiveness	Off IsoPPP+	89.2	113
	Def IsoPPP+	109.0	22
	Total Explosiveness	198.3	75
Field Position	Field Pos. Adv. (FPA)	0.488	80
Finishing Drives	Off Red Zone S&P+	103.0	48
	Def Red Zone S&P+	106.9	37
	Total Red Zone Rating	209.9	44
Turnovers	Turnover Margin	+3.0	41
	Exp. TO Margin	+5.5	31
	Difference	-2.5	79

It almost seems too obvious to highlight Northwestern as some sort of breakthrough candidate in 2014. The Wildcats indeed broke through in 2012, reaching 10-3 and 29th in the F/+ rankings, but just about everything conceivable went wrong for them in 2013. One problem was injuries, as quarterback Kain Colter was banged up and star running back/return man Venric Mark (1,371 rushing yards, 12 touchdowns, and two punt return scores in 2012) missed most of the year. Another was tight-game misfortune. After going an unlikely 20-7 in games decided by one possession from 2007-10, then going

4-4 in such games in 2011-12, Northwestern went just 1-4 in 2013 and fell to 5-7 as a result. Field position was costly in each of their close losses, and the Wildcats dug themselves a deep hole too often: 27.5 percent of their drives started inside their own 20-yard line, 114th nationally. The snake-bitten season ended a five-year bowl streak.

In 2014, however, 18 starters return from a team that really was only a couple of plays away from a bowl game and, in theory, quite a few more wins. A healthy Mark will join senior Treyvon Green (738 rushing yards, 5.3 per carry, 5.5 highlight yards per opportunity) and sophomore Stephen Buckley in the backfield; both Green and Buckley got a chance to develop in Mark's absence, and the trio gets to run behind a line that ranked 23rd in Adjusted Line Yards and returns with its entire two-deep intact.

Meanwhile, senior quarterback Trevor Siemian gets four of his top five wideouts back, including seniors Tony Jones and Christian Jones, who combined for 1,284 receiving yards and a 69 percent catch rate last fall.

The bend-don't-break defense was a little bit glitchy against the pass a year ago but returns just about everybody of consequence. The backbone of the defense—tackle Chance Carter, middle linebacker Collin Ellis, and safeties Traveon Henry and Ibraheim Campbell—is talented and experienced, and ends Dean Lowry, Deonte Gibson, and Ifeadi Odenigbo combined for 13 sacks in 2013. Assuming no fallout from this offseason's union-related drama,[1] this team could not only reach projections and once again go bowling, but exceed projections.

Top 2015 draft prospects: C Brandon Vitabile (6-7), OLB Collin Ellis (6-7), SS Ibraheim Campbell (6-7).

No. 69 Minnesota Golden Gophers (5-7, 2-6)

2013: 8-5 (4-4) / F/+ #55 / FEI #55 / S&P+ #74 / Program F/+: #80					
2013 Offense			**2013 Defense**		
Offensive F/+	-3.2%	73	Defensive F/+	3.3%	47
Offensive FEI	-0.081	70	Defensive FEI	-0.181	39
Offensive S&P+	93.7	77	Defensive S&P+	104.5	65
Rushing S&P+	98.2	73	Rushing S&P+	96.3	79
Passing S&P+	98.1	67	Passing S&P+	105.4	47
Standard Downs S&P+	93.7	89	Standard Downs S&P+	98.3	76
Passing Downs S&P+	101.4	58	Passing Downs S&P+	104.1	53
2013 Special Teams			Special Teams F/+	2.8%	13
2014 Projections			SOS Rk	54	
Ret. Starters: 8 OFF, 6 DEF			Offensive F/+	-3.8%	86
Proj. F/+	-2.3%	69	Defensive F/+	1.5%	57
Mean Wins / Conf Wins	5.0 / 2.3		Conf. / Div. Title Odds	0.0% / 0.2%	

2013 Five Factors			
Efficiency	Off Success Rate+	96.9	71
	Def Success Rate+	97.9	64
	Total Efficiency	194.8	74
Explosiveness	Off IsoPPP+	94.6	91
	Def IsoPPP+	99.2	63
	Total Explosiveness	193.8	86
Field Position	Field Pos. Adv. (FPA)	0.523	32
Finishing Drives	Off Red Zone S&P+	102.2	51
	Def Red Zone S&P+	116.2	20
	Total Red Zone Rating	218.3	26
Turnovers	Turnover Margin	+3.0	41
	Exp. TO Margin	+5.0	35
	Difference	-2.0	74

There's nothing sexy about Jerry Kill's brand of football at Minnesota. The Golden Gophers run the ball early and often, play it safe more often than not, attempt to control the trenches, and stiffen defensively in the red zone. It is anything but innovative, but it probably isn't a coincidence that Minnesota has improved for two straight years under Kill.

Thanks to ho-hum recruiting and a retooled front seven, the F/+ projections are rather conservative with the Gophers in 2014, but if they can find some help for defensive ends Theiren Cockran and Alex Keith (combined: 15 tackles for loss, 9.5 sacks, four forced fumbles in 2013), they'll have a chance to improve for a third straight year. Tackles Ra'Shede Hageman (now with the NFL's Falcons) and Roland Johnson are gone, and Minnesota will be relatively inexperienced at linebacker, too. Eric Murray (10 passes defensed) is a potential star at cornerback, but there are questions up front.

On offense, Minnesota will quite possibly be even more run-heavy in 2014. Sophomore quarterback Mitch Leidner (619 passing yards, three touchdowns, and one interception; 477 pre-sack rushing yards) is the likely starter and will be joined at running back by not only David Cobb (1,202 rushing yards, 5.1 per carry, 5.7 highlight yards per opportunity) and big Rodrick Williams Jr., but also blue-chip freshman Jeff Jones, who chose the local Gophers over basically every program in the country. The receiving corps is littered with exciting sophomores, but the run will, as always, set the tone for the 2014 Gophers.

Top 2015 draft prospects: RB David Cobb (5-6).

---

1 The short version: Colter and others led an attempt by Northwestern athletes to form a union, and it was approved in the courts, which deemed the student-athletes employees of the university. For a longer version, visit http://bit.ly/NZh4Ut.

No. 73 Illinois Fighting Illini (5-7, 2-6)

2013: 4-8 (1-7) / F/+ #71 / FEI #77 / S&P+ #71 / Program F/+: #71

2013 Offense			2013 Defense		
Offensive F/+	5.7%	39	Defensive F/+	-10.0%	100
Offensive FEI	0.174	41	Defensive FEI	0.330	102
Offensive S&P+	109.5	37	Defensive S&P+	90.6	103
Rushing S&P+	112.7	35	Rushing S&P+	95.4	83
Passing S&P+	110.6	34	Passing S&P+	85.9	108
Standard Downs S&P+	116.5	22	Standard Downs S&P+	88.7	103
Passing Downs S&P+	103.3	55	Passing Downs S&P+	94.4	85
2013 Special Teams			Special Teams F/+	0.3%	58
2014 Projections			SOS Rk	48	
Ret. Starters: 6 OFF, 8 DEF			Offensive F/+	-1.2%	74
Proj. F/+	-3.6%	73	Defensive F/+	-2.4%	76
Mean Wins / Conf Wins	5.0 / 2.3		Conf. / Div. Title Odds	0.0% / 0.1%	

2013 Five Factors			
Efficiency	Off Success Rate+	107.0	36
	Def Success Rate+	94.1	83
	Total Efficiency	201.0	58
Explosiveness	Off IsoPPP+	112.4	15
	Def IsoPPP+	90.8	110
	Total Explosiveness	203.2	54
Field Position	Field Pos. Adv. (FPA)	0.472	97
Finishing Drives	Off Red Zone S&P+	105.3	40
	Def Red Zone S&P+	97.9	66
	Total Red Zone Rating	203.2	54
Turnovers	Turnover Margin	-10.0	115
	Exp. TO Margin	-4.7	102
	Difference	-5.3	106

Illinois has made a habit of drastic turnarounds—both good and bad—in recent years, rising or falling by an average of 41 spots in the F/+ rankings over the last eight seasons. Their No. 73 projection, just two spots behind last year's No. 71 ranking, appears sensible on paper, but the Fighting Illini have defied sense for most of the last decade.

If you're optimistic that another out-of-nowhere surge is in the works, you don't have to look hard for evidence. Oklahoma State transfer Wes Lunt takes over as quarterback for coordinator Bill Cubit's offense and has the kind of arm Cubit has rarely had a chance to work with through the years. He'll share the backfield with underrated, well-rounded junior running back Josh Ferguson (779 rushing yards, 5.5 per carry, 5.9 highlight yards per opportunity; 520 receiving yards, 83 percent catch rate). Plus, the defense should improve to some degree based solely on experience. Freshmen and sophomores littered the two-deep last year; they're now sophomores and juniors.

A pessimist, meanwhile, doesn't have to look hard for evidence either. The receiving corps is getting completely rebuilt, both lines were mediocre at best in 2013, and the only known playmakers on defense (end/linebacker Houston Bates and weakside linebacker Jonathan Brown) are gone. Plus, Lunt got himself into trouble at Oklahoma State by getting a little too aggressive with the ball; Cubit's often horizontal, spread-and-throw attack does not go deep that frequently—the Illini actually ranked 11th nationally in methodical drives, possessions that last at least 10 plays. This could end up a good thing—former starter Nathan Scheelhaase in no way had Lunt's arm—or Lunt could play Heroball a bit too much and end up on the bench.

Top 2015 draft prospects: none.

No. 104 Purdue Boilermakers (3-9, 1-7)

2013: 1-11 (0-8) / F/+ #114 / FEI #114 / S&P+ #112 / Program F/+: #86

2013 Offense			2013 Defense		
Offensive F/+	-14.6%	113	Defensive F/+	-11.5%	107
Offensive FEI	-0.437	113	Defensive FEI	0.424	111
Offensive S&P+	75.5	115	Defensive S&P+	92.3	99
Rushing S&P+	91.3	97	Rushing S&P+	97.1	76
Passing S&P+	85.1	102	Passing S&P+	97.6	76
Standard Downs S&P+	90.6	99	Standard Downs S&P+	100.2	67
Passing Downs S&P+	83.0	108	Passing Downs S&P+	92.6	87
2013 Special Teams			Special Teams F/+	-1.2%	91
2014 Projections			SOS Rk	67	
Ret. Starters: 7 OFF, 6 DEF			Offensive F/+	-6.3%	96
Proj. F/+	-12.0%	104	Defensive F/+	-5.7%	96
Mean Wins / Conf Wins	3.0 / 0.7		Conf. / Div. Title Odds	0.0% / 0.0%	

2013 Five Factors			
Efficiency	Off Success Rate+	91.0	90
	Def Success Rate+	90.1	99
	Total Efficiency	181.1	103
Explosiveness	Off IsoPPP+	93.2	97
	Def IsoPPP+	110.4	19
	Total Explosiveness	203.6	49
Field Position	Field Pos. Adv. (FPA)	0.463	107
Finishing Drives	Off Red Zone S&P+	91.5	93
	Def Red Zone S&P+	82.7	112
	Total Red Zone Rating	174.2	107
Turnovers	Turnover Margin	-2.0	73
	Exp. TO Margin	-4.8	104
	Difference	+2.8	31

It is almost incomprehensible how quickly Purdue became so bad. After ranking between 52nd and 76th in the F/+ rankings for six of the eight years between 2005 and 2008, and after returning to bowls in both 2011 and 2012 after a three-season absence, the Boilermakers plummeted in every possible way last fall. An already bad offense fell to 113th in Offensive F/+, and a decent defense sank to 107th in Defensive F/+. Sometimes you have to strip a house down to the studs in your first year as a head coach; now we'll see if second-year man Darrell Hazell knows how to build it back.

Hazell's second squad is not bereft of playmakers, but he could use a few more. Running back/utility man Akeem Hunt has proven adept and agile through the years, and one has to like where the pass-and-catch combination of sophomores Danny Etling (1,690 passing yards, 10 touchdowns, seven interceptions) and wideout DeAngelo Yancey (546 receiving yards, 17.1 yards per catch, 46 percent catch rate) could go in a year or two. But an offensive line that was already bad in 2013 gets younger in 2014, and Purdue graduated punter Cody Webster, the leg behind the nation's most efficient punt team last season.

Most of the known quantities in the defensive front seven are gone, too. Defensive end Ryan Russell has potential, and some highly touted younger players like linebacker Gelen Robinson and ends Antoine Miles and John Strauser could make an early impact. But it appears Purdue is at least one more year away from fielding a team that is worthy of some good attention.

Top 2015 draft prospects: TE Gabe Holmes (6-7).

Bill Connelly

Projected Win Probabilities For Big Ten Teams

			Overall Wins													Conference Wins								
Div	**Conf**	**Big Ten East**	**12-0**	**11-1**	**10-2**	**9-3**	**8-4**	**7-5**	**6-6**	**5-7**	**4-8**	**3-9**	**2-10**	**1-11**	**0-12**	**8-0**	**7-1**	**6-2**	**5-3**	**4-4**	**3-5**	**2-6**	**1-7**	**0-8**
-	-	Indiana	-	-	-	1	7	18	28	27	14	4	1	-	-	-	-	2	11	28	34	20	5	-
-	-	Maryland	-	-	-	1	3	10	21	28	23	11	3	-	-	-	-	-	2	10	25	35	23	5
7	3	Michigan	-	3	12	27	30	19	7	2	-	-	-	-	-	1	9	29	34	19	7	1	-	-
42	28	Michigan State	4	23	36	25	10	2	-	-	-	-	-	-	-	20	38	29	11	2	-	-	-	-
49	34	Ohio State	14	35	32	15	3	1	-	-	-	-	-	-	-	20	43	28	8	1	-	-	-	-
2	1	Penn State	-	1	5	14	26	27	18	7	2	-	-	-	-	-	2	11	26	31	21	8	1	-
-	-	Rutgers	-	-	-	-	-	2	8	17	29	28	14	2	-	-	-	-	-	3	12	29	37	19
Div	**Conf**	**Big Ten West**	**12-0**	**11-1**	**10-2**	**9-3**	**8-4**	**7-5**	**6-6**	**5-7**	**4-8**	**3-9**	**2-10**	**1-11**	**0-12**	**8-0**	**7-1**	**6-2**	**5-3**	**4-4**	**3-5**	**2-6**	**1-7**	**0-8**
-	-	Illinois	-	-	-	-	2	9	23	33	24	8	1	-	-	-	-	-	2	10	28	38	19	3
33	10	Iowa	4	16	28	27	16	7	2	-	-	-	-	-	-	9	27	33	21	8	2	-	-	-
-	-	Minnesota	-	-	-	-	2	9	22	32	25	8	2	-	-	-	-	-	2	10	27	37	21	3
6	1	Nebraska	-	1	6	20	30	26	13	3	1	-	-	-	-	-	3	16	35	32	12	2	-	-
2	-	Northwestern	-	-	2	6	17	27	26	15	6	1	-	-	-	-	1	9	21	31	25	11	2	-
-	-	Purdue	-	-	-	-	-	-	1	7	22	39	26	5	-	-	-	-	-	-	2	11	38	49
59	23	Wisconsin	7	26	35	23	8	1	-	-	-	-	-	-	-	22	41	27	9	1	-	-	-	-

Big 12 Conference

Before realignment, back when the Big 12 actually boasted twelve members, only two of them really seemed to matter. From 2000-09, Oklahoma and Texas claimed the conference championship eight times in ten years, racking up an absurd record of 130-17 (.884) against the rest of the league. In the same span, the Sooners and Longhorns played for six BCS championships, winning two, and combined for 15 top-ten finishes in the Associated Press poll. By contrast, after 2000, no other Big 12 program over the course of the decade landed in the top ten more than once. When simultaneous overtures from the Big Ten, Pac-10 and SEC in 2010 threatened to rip the Big 12 apart, no wonder it was the heavy hitters that decided it was worth salvaging.

Certainly no one at the time could have imagined the departures of Nebraska, Missouri and Texas A&M for greener pastures would somehow lead to greater *parity*. But here we are: since 2009, five different schools have worn the Big 12 crown in five consecutive seasons, the last three as the result of a traditional also-ran—Oklahoma State in 2011, Kansas State in 2012, Baylor in 2013—hitting an historic high note. Oklahoma, while remaining the league's most consistently competent outfit, has settled for the role of serial bridesmaid. Texas, despite entrenching its status as the most lucrative program in the sport, has stagnated on the field to the point of a booster revolt against coach Mack Brown. More so than in any other major conference, there is the sense here that any of the top six or seven teams is capable of a run in any given season—or at least of stopping one in its tracks on a given weekend.

Alas, parity comes with a cost. In the absence of an obvious kingpin, the Big 12 has been shut out of the BCS title game four years running, and very likely would have been shut out of a four-team playoff in three of those four seasons if the new playoff format had been in effect. (Oklahoma in 2010, K-State in 2012 and Baylor last year all ranked outside of the top four in both the final BCS standings and final regular-season AP poll; only Oklahoma State in 2011 would have been a no-brainer to make a four-team field.) This has not escaped commissioner Bob Bowlsby, who has leapt at every opportunity this offseason to tout the Big 12's round-robin conference schedule as the most legitimate format for crowning "one true champion"—a thinly veiled dig at the ACC, Big Ten and SEC, whose ranks have grown so large through expansion that teams in opposite divisions may go as long as seven years between head-to-head meetings. Does the playoff committee care? At this point, its priorities are a mystery; it may turn out that rewarding a conference championship in and of itself ranks high on the list. Just as likely, though, the egalitarian theme will only make the Big 12 champion that much easier for them to dismiss.

No. 6 Oklahoma Sooners (10-2, 8-1)

2013: 11-2 (7-2) / F/+ #20 / FEI #14 / S&P+ #24 / Program F/+: #4

2013 Offense			2013 Defense		
Offensive F/+	12.2%	21	Defensive F/+	10.9%	24
Offensive FEI	0.409	23	Defensive FEI	-0.443	15
Offensive S&P+	117.3	22	Defensive S&P+	115.4	33
Rushing S&P+	115.2	27	Rushing S&P+	97.6	72
Passing S&P+	111.6	32	Passing S&P+	117.9	21
Standard Downs S&P+	112.9	32	Standard Downs S&P+	105.0	47
Passing Downs S&P+	111.7	41	Passing Downs S&P+	114.9	33
2013 Special Teams			Special Teams F/+	1.6%	37
2014 Projections			SOS Rk	68	
Ret. Starters: 5 OFF, 9 DEF			Offensive F/+	6.0%	32
Proj. F/+	19.5%	6	Defensive F/+	13.5%	9
Mean Wins / Conf Wins	10.5 / 7.5		Conference Title Odds	54.0%	

2013 Five Factors			
Efficiency	Off Success Rate+	108.0	34
	Def Success Rate+	106.4	35
	Total Efficiency	214.4	31
Explosiveness	Off IsoPPP+	104.8	37
	Def IsoPPP+	98.7	66
	Total Explosiveness	203.5	50
Field Position	Field Pos. Adv. (FPA)	0.529	27
Finishing Drives	Off Red Zone S&P+	95.9	80
	Def Red Zone S&P+	118.3	16
	Total Red Zone Rating	214.2	31
Turnovers	Turnover Margin	+9.0	21
	Exp. TO Margin	+2.0	54
	Difference	+7.0	14

How do you solve a problem like Trevor Knight? When he was named Oklahoma's starting quarterback last summer, Knight was hailed as the Sooners' answer to Johnny Manziel: an undersized but elusive athlete who, as a redshirt freshman, would bring a running threat to the position that his pocket-bound predecessors, Sam Bradford and Landry Jones, never could. Instead, he struggled through his first start, an uninspiring win over Louisiana-Monroe, and was relegated to the bench by the end of his second, where he would remain until a string of nondescript appearances in November. By January, it was uncertain whether Knight would even see the field in the Sugar Bowl alongside co-starter Blake Bell, or whether there would still be a place for him the following morning on the 2014 depth chart.

So take a moment or two to consider that amid the summer buzz anointing Knight as a dark horse for the Heisman. Admittedly, if all you saw of Oklahoma's offense in 2013 was the New Year's ambush of Alabama, you could be forgiven for getting carried away. Against the most monolithically talented defense in the nation, Knight personally accounted for as many touchdowns (four) as the entire offense had managed in its three biggest regular-season games—against Texas, Baylor and Oklahoma State—combined, resulting in more points against 'Bama (45) than any opponent in the Nick Saban era. Based on that performance alone, Knight enters his sophomore season with even higher expectations than he faced last year as a freshman; meanwhile, Bell will close out his career as a converted tight end despite outperforming Knight on paper. (Even with Knight's star turn in the finale, he finished behind the "Belldozer" in terms of completion percentage, yards per pass, touchdown-to-interception ratio and overall efficiency.) The surrounding cast is as green as it is gifted, boasting high marks from the recruiting sites but only one skill player who has had significant playing time (junior wide receiver Sterling Shepard, who had 603 receiving yards with a 68 percent catch rate in 2013). Any one of a half-dozen incoming freshmen is liable to find himself in a starring role. (Most likely to succeed: freshman tailback Joe Mixon, who will start out behind another former five-star recruit, sophomore Keith Ford.) Still, as long as Knight is able to hold the spotlight, OU is a threat to light up every defense on the schedule.

As for their own defense, the Sooners are on more solid footing. Not that the 2013 edition didn't have its problems, ranking 72nd in Defensive Rushing S&P+ while yielding at least 30 points in five games. But that was an unusually young group—seven of the ten returning starters were freshmen or sophomores earning their first serious playing time last year—and it produced a pair of unlikely stars in defensive end Charles Tapper and linebacker Eric Striker. Both picked up All-Big 12 nods from league coaches as true sophomores, and both have first-round potential when they decide to make the leap. (Striker's stock in particular exploded after he registered three sacks against Alabama, including a forced fumble in the fourth quarter that put the upset on ice.) Not surprisingly, the Oklahoma defense was at its best on third-and-long, yielding a grand total of 35 first downs on 145 attempts (24.1 percent) with at least four yards to go. If the middle of the defensive line can stand its ground against the run, the pass rush should hold up its end on passing downs.

2015 Draft Prospects: OLB Eric Striker (1-2), DE Charles Tapper* (2), OT Daryl Williams (3-4), TE Blake Bell (6-7), OT Tyrus Thompson (7-FA).*

No. 15 Baylor Bears (10-2, 7-2)

2013: 11-2 (8-1) / F/+ #7 / FEI #11 / S&P+ #3 / Program F/+: #38					
2013 Offense			**2013 Defense**		
Offensive F/+	20.5%	4	Defensive F/+	10.7%	25
Offensive FEI	0.551	10	Defensive FEI	-0.355	27
Offensive S&P+	140.2	3	Defensive S&P+	122.2	21
Rushing S&P+	117.1	20	Rushing S&P+	109.6	38
Passing S&P+	152.7	2	Passing S&P+	111.5	34
Standard Downs S&P+	131.5	3	Standard Downs S&P+	109.8	31
Passing Downs S&P+	137.0	12	Passing Downs S&P+	117.6	28
2013 Special Teams			Special Teams F/+	-0.9%	88
2014 Projections			SOS Rk	52	
Ret. Starters: 5 OFF, 4 DEF			Offensive F/+	14.7%	3
Proj. F/+	15.9%	15	Defensive F/+	1.1%	58
Mean Wins / Conf Wins	9.6 / 6.7		Conference Title Odds	21.9%	

2013 Five Factors			
Efficiency	Off Success Rate+	119.4	9
	Def Success Rate+	112.4	23
	Total Efficiency	231.9	8
Explosiveness	Off IsoPPP+	118.1	3
	Def IsoPPP+	97.2	78
	Total Explosiveness	215.3	17
Field Position	Field Pos. Adv. (FPA)	0.541	14
Finishing Drives	Off Red Zone S&P+	127.6	5
	Def Red Zone S&P+	109.5	26
	Total Red Zone Rating	237.1	7
Turnovers	Turnover Margin	+13.0	8
	Exp. TO Margin	+7.0	18
	Difference	+6.0	19

OK, can we all agree now that the post-RG3 Bears are in no imminent danger of descending back into the primordial ooze that defined the program for nearly two decades prior to the dreadlocked messiah's arrival? Yes? Good. Now on to the really important business: keeping the pedal down against the rest of the league's upper crust.

In certain ways, Baylor pushed the throttle to the limit in 2013, finishing second in FBS history for total yards per game (618.2) and third for points (52.4) despite frequently applying the brakes in blowouts. In the S&P+ ratings, the offense also ranked among the top five nationally in both Passing and Drive Efficiency, and on Standard Downs. Still, somewhere in that barely perceptible gap between the record book and the advanced stats tables lies a crucial part of the story. After dispatching with the more flammable half of the schedule in September and October, the Bears found themselves leaning increasingly on their *defense* down the stretch. There were slow-starting wins over Oklahoma and Texas in Waco where the Sooners and Longhorns combined for 22 points, and a deceptively high-scoring victory at TCU where the defense returned two interceptions for touchdowns and set up another score with a fumble recovery at the TCU one-yard line. (Offensively, Baylor managed just 370 yards on 4.1 yards per play in Fort Worth, both season lows despite a 41-38 final score.) Baylor ranked 12th nationally in forcing three-and-outs (41.9 percent of opponent drives), the first time during the Briles era where the Bears ranked among the top 80 teams in that metric. On the two occasions when the defense could have used a little reciprocal help, against Oklahoma State in late November and Central Florida in the Fiesta Bowl, the offense sputtered in the first half and then spent the rest of both games trying in vain to close double-digit deficits. When the offense actually needed to respond in a back-and-forth, tit-for-tat shootout, it couldn't keep pace.

Again, big-picture statistical overkill should be no problem in 2014 given the return of prolific senior quarterback Bryce Petty and a receiving corps that offers proven production and up-and-coming talent in equal measure: seniors Antwan

Goodley and Levi Norwood combined for 2,206 yards (17.5 per catch, 70 percent catch rate) and 21 touchdowns as juniors, and the past two recruiting classes have yielded blue-chip signees in Robbie Rhodes, K.D. Cannon and Davion Hall. On the other side, though, the veteran core that orchestrated last year's defensive turnaround graduated en masse, leaving at least seven new starters to hold the line. Four of those fresh faces will belong to first- or second-year players in a totally revamped secondary. Most of the time, they'll be working with such a generous cushion on the scoreboard as to wreck the learning curve. The rest of the time, though, the margin for error offensively is that much steeper.

2015 Draft Prospects: OT Spencer Drango (1-2), QB Bryce Petty (1-2), WR Antwan Goodley (2-3), ILB Bryce Hager (4), WR Levi Norwood (4-5).*

No. 17 Oklahoma State Cowboys (8-4, 6-3)

2013: 10-3 (7-2) / F/+ #8 / FEI #9 / S&P+ #15 / Program F/+: #7					
2013 Offense			**2013 Defense**		
Offensive F/+	10.2%	26	Defensive F/+	20.4%	6
Offensive FEI	0.397	24	Defensive FEI	-0.717	3
Offensive S&P+	110.2	36	Defensive S&P+	133.2	11
Rushing S&P+	108.0	44	Rushing S&P+	120.0	17
Passing S&P+	117.1	24	Passing S&P+	123.8	12
Standard Downs S&P+	108.6	41	Standard Downs S&P+	117.8	20
Passing Downs S&P+	123.3	21	Passing Downs S&P+	128.9	9
2013 Special Teams			Special Teams F/+	-0.7%	85
2014 Projections			SOS Rk	8	
Ret. Starters: 5 OFF, 4 DEF			Offensive F/+	3.4%	41
Proj. F/+	15.6%	17	Defensive F/+	12.3%	11
Mean Wins / Conf Wins	8.3 / 6.3		Conference Title Odds	14.3%	

2013 Five Factors			
Efficiency	Off Success Rate+	110.9	26
	Def Success Rate+	114.3	18
	Total Efficiency	225.2	18
Explosiveness	Off IsoPPP+	104.5	38
	Def IsoPPP+	108.9	23
	Total Explosiveness	213.4	23
Field Position	Field Pos. Adv. (FPA)	0.535	19
Finishing Drives	Off Red Zone S&P+	118.4	15
	Def Red Zone S&P+	113.0	23
	Total Red Zone Rating	231.4	10
Turnovers	Turnover Margin	+15.0	5
	Exp. TO Margin	+10.7	4
	Difference	+4.3	25

Pretty much everything written about Oklahoma State since Mike "I'm a Man!" Gundy was promoted to head coach in 2005 has led with the offense, and we're not about to buck tradition here. But where to begin? Gundy's best teams, in 2010-11, were products of an up-tempo, spread passing attack that generated upwards of 44 points per game in both seasons. That number held in 2012 despite a downturn in the final record. By contrast, the 2013 edition was a mash-up that seemed to grasp for a new identity on a weekly basis, veering from the "Air Raid" to an emphasis on the read option and back again while shuffling personnel accordingly. At their best, the Cowboys were able to run just effectively enough to generate big plays off play-action in a 49-17 trouncing of Baylor, where senior quarterback Clint Chelf passed for 440 yards and three touchdowns on just 27 attempts. At worst, a nonexistent ground game led to chaos in an early loss at West Virginia, where sophomore J.W. Walsh completed just 20 of 47 passes with a pair of interceptions. Altogether, OSU fell from 12th nationally in Offensive F/+ in 2012 to 26th in 2013, and from 14th in Offensive S&P+ to 36th.

The fact that the win column defied that trajectory is a credit to Chelf, who grew into a steady hand after retaking the starting job from Walsh at midseason, and especially to the defense, which set a new high under Gundy by finishing sixth nationally in Defensive F/+. The defense also led the conference in takeaways, a big reason for a field-position advantage that had the Cowboys starting drives an average of 5.9 yards further downfield than their opponents.

As far as 2014 is concerned, though, it's back to the drawing board on both counts: eight of the top nine tacklers on defense are gone, as is Chelf, leaving Walsh all alone atop the depth chart. Tellingly, most of the optimism in spring was channeled toward junior-college transfer Tyreek Hill, who provided a badly needed spark in the backfield and the slot while moonlighting as an All-American sprinter on the OSU track team. But that says at least as much about the dearth of proven playmakers on both sides of the ball as it does about Hill himself. The really good news is that, following an opening-night slaughter at the hands of Florida State, the backloaded conference slate gives the new lineup two solid months to gel before running the November gauntlet of Kansas State, Texas, Baylor and Oklahoma.

2015 Draft Prospects: DT James Castleman (6-7).

No. 31 Kansas State Wildcats (7-5, 5-4)

2013: 8-5 (5-4) / F/+ #24 / FEI #25 / S&P+ #31 / Program F/+: #30					
2013 Offense			**2013 Defense**		
Offensive F/+	14.4%	14	Defensive F/+	4.4%	43
Offensive FEI	0.460	16	Defensive FEI	-0.230	35
Offensive S&P+	122.1	15	Defensive S&P+	105.2	61
Rushing S&P+	117.0	21	Rushing S&P+	95.0	86
Passing S&P+	128.9	11	Passing S&P+	106.4	42
Standard Downs S&P+	121.2	12	Standard Downs S&P+	99.5	70
Passing Downs S&P+	120.2	26	Passing Downs S&P+	105.1	51
2013 Special Teams			Special Teams F/+	1.8%	33
2014 Projections			SOS Rk	34	
Ret. Starters: 6 OFF, 4 DEF			Offensive F/+	9.7%	16
Proj. F/+	10.4%	31	Defensive F/+	0.7%	61
Mean Wins / Conf Wins	7.5 / 5.2		Conference Title Odds	3.7%	

2013 Five Factors			
Efficiency	Off Success Rate+	118.8	10
	Def Success Rate+	91.8	93
	Total Efficiency	210.6	38
Explosiveness	Off IsoPPP+	103.8	42
	Def IsoPPP+	116.3	6
	Total Explosiveness	220.1	11
Field Position	Field Pos. Adv. (FPA)	0.517	42
Finishing Drives	Off Red Zone S&P+	130.5	4
	Def Red Zone S&P+	95.2	76
	Total Red Zone Rating	225.7	17
Turnovers	Turnover Margin	0.0	61
	Exp. TO Margin	+7.9	14
	Difference	-7.9	119

Bill Snyder has always stalked the back roads to fill out a competitive roster, out of sheer necessity, but even by K-State standards the 2014 edition looks like the Island of Misfit Toys. Fully half of the projected starters arrived in Manhattan as junior-college transfers or walk-ons, a staggering number that anywhere else would portend certain doom. Here, the castoffs are proven commodities. Two of the former walk-ons, defensive end Ryan Mueller and center B.J. Finney, were first-team All-Big 12 picks last year as fourth-year juniors, while two others, linebacker Jonathan Truman and cornerback Randall Evans, have racked up well over 100 tackles apiece over the past two years. The starting quarterback, Jake Waters, is a product of the JUCO route, as are the three most touted signees in the incoming recruiting class, defensive tackle Terrell Clinkscales, linebacker D'vonta Derricott and offensive tackle Luke Hayes, all expected to take up immediate residence in the starting lineup. The resulting Kansas State squad is not necessarily the most *experienced* team in the league in terms of playing time—that distinction goes to Texas—but is certainly the least dependent on underclassmen.

It's also a team that rebounded last year from an 0-3 start in conference play to win five of its last six games, putting up at least 31 points in all six despite an ongoing *pas de deux* at quarterback that took the entire regular season to resolve. Theoretically, Waters and Daniel Sams complemented one another as the pocket passer and the "Wildcat" option, respectively, but the lines often blurred: although Waters attempted nearly five times as many passes, he also averaged 7.3 carries per game (not including sacks) to 11.5 for Sams, with six rushing touchdowns. And although Waters took the first snap in every game, it wasn't until late November that he managed to pull away as the true starter, cementing his status with a 271-yard, three-touchdown flourish against Michigan in the Buffalo Wild Wings Bowl. (Sams left the team in May after converting to wide receiver in spring practice.) The other star of the bowl game was All-Big 12 wide receiver Tyler Lockett (1,262 receiving yards, 15.6 per catch, 71 percent catch rate), who turned in his seventh 100-yard receiving game of the season, including 200-yard efforts against Texas and Oklahoma in regular-season losses. K-State will always try to be a run-first, option-oriented offense as long as Snyder is in charge, but it has also ranked among the top 20 teams in explosive drive percentage for two straight seasons. Barring an unexpected breakthrough by one of the new tailbacks, this particular attack is going to do most of its damage downfield.

2015 Draft Prospects: WR Tyler Lockett (3-4), C B.J. Finney (4-5), DE Ryan Mueller (6-7), G/T Cody Whitehair (6-7).

No. 34 Texas Longhorns (7-5, 5-4)

2013: 8-5 (7-2) / F/+ #35 / FEI #37 / S&P+ #48 / Program F/+: #22					
2013 Offense			**2013 Defense**		
Offensive F/+	4.1%	46	Defensive F/+	6.1%	35
Offensive FEI	0.166	43	Defensive FEI	-0.262	31
Offensive S&P+	103.6	49	Defensive S&P+	109.9	44
Rushing S&P+	99.3	69	Rushing S&P+	106.0	48
Passing S&P+	106.0	47	Passing S&P+	112.1	32
Standard Downs S&P+	104.7	54	Standard Downs S&P+	103.4	53
Passing Downs S&P+	98.9	63	Passing Downs S&P+	122.7	15
2013 Special Teams			Special Teams F/+	1.8%	31
2014 Projections			SOS Rk	39	
Ret. Starters: 6 OFF, 7 DEF			Offensive F/+	0.9%	61
Proj. F/+	9.1%	34	Defensive F/+	8.1%	22
Mean Wins / Conf Wins	6.7 / 4.9		Conference Title Odds	2.5%	

2013 Five Factors			
Efficiency	Off Success Rate+	100.2	62
	Def Success Rate+	105.3	40
	Total Efficiency	205.5	51
Explosiveness	Off IsoPPP+	99.2	66
	Def IsoPPP+	101.2	53
	Total Explosiveness	200.5	68
Field Position	Field Pos. Adv. (FPA)	0.501	62
Finishing Drives	Off Red Zone S&P+	96.3	78
	Def Red Zone S&P+	125.1	6
	Total Red Zone Rating	221.3	22
Turnovers	Turnover Margin	+4.0	38
	Exp. TO Margin	+5.6	29
	Difference	-1.6	70

Yes, Texas is one of the proverbial "dream jobs," a $100 million behemoth with its pick of talent in the most heavily recruited state in the union. But please understand if Charlie Strong is not suddenly feeling like the coach who has everything. In many respects, the roster he inherits in Austin hardly looks like an upgrade on the one he left at Louisville. True, regardless of the results on the field, Mack Brown never lost his mojo as the Pied Piper of the Plains, and the depth chart certainly does not lack for blue-chip potential. Yet for all that ostensible talent on hand, since 2010 the Longhorns have not placed a single offensive player on the All-Big 12 team, and have only heard one offensive player's name called in the past four NFL drafts. (That would be Bills wide receiver Marquise Goodwin, a former Olympian who turned more heads at the combine than he ever did as a part-time starter in Austin.) This year, Texas was shut out of the draft entirely for the first time since the Great Depression, while Strong's old team set a school record with three underclassmen taken in the first round.

Not that any of that figures to buy Strong much of a honeymoon. Man for man, UT's talent and depth is still the envy of the conference, and fans got a tantalizing glimpse of that potential last year in an out-of-nowhere trouncing of Oklahoma; from there, the Longhorns went on to a 6-0 start in Big 12 play and ultimately found themselves playing for the Big 12 title on the final Saturday of the season, even as the clamor over Brown's future reached a fever pitch. By that point, the Longhorns were playing without their starting quarterback (David Ash), top tailback (Johnathan Gray) and most experienced linebacker (Jordan Hicks), all of whom are expected back this fall from season-ending injuries.

Ash, in particular, remains the crucial wildcard. First, there's his health: in addition to the concussion that forced him into a medical redshirt in 2013, Ash was sidelined in the spring by a fractured foot, at least temporarily handing the keys to the offense to erratic sophomore Tyrone Swoopes. Even at full speed, though, Ash's 21 career starts have been more or less evenly split between brilliance, mediocrity, and disaster, often from week to week and occasionally from quarter to quarter. In theory, Ash's arm strength will open up the rest of the offense by stretching the field in a way his former replacement, the since-departed Case "Don't Call Me Colt" McCoy, rarely could. Better yet, it will work the other way around: with Gray and senior Malcolm Brown (combined: 1,684 rushing yards, 4.5 per carry, 4.3 highlight yards per opportunity), Ash has arguably the best individual backs in the conference at his disposal, and will find the going much easier downfield if they're able to push their combined production (129.5 yards per game in 2013, limited by Gray's injury) above the 150-yard mark.

2015 Draft Prospects: DT Malcom Brown (2-3), DE Cedric Reed (2-3), RB Malcolm Brown (3-4), CB Quandre Diggs (3-4), RB Johnathan Gray* (3-4), OLB Jordan Hicks (3-4), WR Jaxon Shipley (5-6), OLB Steve Edmund (6-7).*

No. 35 TCU Horned Frogs (8-4, 5-4)

2013: 4-8 (2-7) / F/+ #44 / FEI #50 / S&P+ #43 / Program F/+: #11

2013 Offense			2013 Defense		
Offensive F/+	-7.9%	94	Defensive F/+	14.5%	12
Offensive FEI	-0.258	95	Defensive FEI	-0.465	12
Offensive S&P+	88.8	93	Defensive S&P+	129.0	13
Rushing S&P+	85.3	110	Rushing S&P+	123.5	13
Passing S&P+	96.5	73	Passing S&P+	129.4	8
Standard Downs S&P+	94.6	88	Standard Downs S&P+	132.8	5
Passing Downs S&P+	89.3	91	Passing Downs S&P+	119.5	21
2013 Special Teams			Special Teams F/+	0.5%	55
2014 Projections			SOS Rk	55	
Ret. Starters: 7 OFF, 8 DEF			Offensive F/+	-6.1%	95
Proj. F/+	8.8%	35	Defensive F/+	15.0%	7
Mean Wins / Conf Wins	7.6 / 4.9		Conference Title Odds	3.1%	

2013 Five Factors			
Efficiency	Off Success Rate+	91.3	88
	Def Success Rate+	127.0	4
	Total Efficiency	218.3	23
Explosiveness	Off IsoPPP+	96.8	83
	Def IsoPPP+	98.2	69
	Total Explosiveness	195.0	84
Field Position	Field Pos. Adv. (FPA)	0.471	98
Finishing Drives	Off Red Zone S&P+	99.9	61
	Def Red Zone S&P+	139.5	4
	Total Red Zone Rating	239.4	6
Turnovers	Turnover Margin	-2.0	73
	Exp. TO Margin	-4.0	96
	Difference	+2.0	39

Gary Patterson is not accustomed to losing seasons; in his first 12 years in Fort Worth, he endured only one, in 2004. He certainly didn't pretend to be happy in 2013, when he punctuated a 4-8 debacle by publicly venting his frustration against Baylor coach Art Briles following a season-ending defeat. It was that kind of year: by mid-October, TCU had lost both its starting quarterback and its best defensive player for the rest of the season, setting the stage for the most dramatic swoon of Patterson's tenure with five losses in the last six games. (Even the lone victory in that span was an ugly one, a 21-17 nail-biter at Iowa State decided in the final minute.) In their entire seven-year stint in the Mountain West, the Horned Frogs lost a grand total of seven conference games, and they left in 2012 with a streak of 24 consecutive MWC wins and three straight league championships. In their first two years in the Big 12, they're 6-11 in conference play, and have yet to log two conference wins in a row.

Still, if you're determined to gamble on the latest dark horse taking its turn at the front of the Big 12 pack, the Frogs' candidacy is not out of the question. For one thing, they're not quite as in over their heads as the record suggests. Four of last year's losses came by a field goal or less, including close calls against Oklahoma, Kansas State and Baylor. In addition, the defense projects as the best in the conference in 2014 after ranking 12th nationally last year in Defensive F/+. Eight starters are back from that unit, including all-conference picks Chucky Hunter at defensive tackle and Sam Carter at strong safety, but *not* including defensive end Devonte Fields, a preseason All-American in 2013 who effectively missed the entire season due to a foot injury. In 2012, Fields wreaked so much havoc off the edge as a true freshman (10 sacks, 18.5 TFL) that Big 12 coaches named him Defensive Player of the Year. At full speed, he is a potential first-round talent.

Any still-lingering questions concern the offense, especially at quarterback. The incumbent is junior Trevone Boykin, a part-time starter over the last two years, who has also spent time playing wide receiver. The curveball is incoming Texas A&M transfer Matt Joeckel, younger brother to Luke Joeckel and former backup to Johnny Manziel. He already has a grasp of the "Air Raid" concepts being installed by the new co-offensive coordinators, Doug Meacham and Sonny Cumbie, and will be immediately eligible this fall as a grad student. In the best-case scenario, Joeckel asserts himself as the clear starter; Boykin thrives as a full-time wide receiver/Wildcat option; tailbacks B.J. Catalon and Kyle Hicks return from spring injuries at full speed; senior wideout Brandon Carter returns from a spring suspension in good standing; and former starting left tackle Tayo Fabuluje reasserts himself on the offensive line after leaving the team in 2013. Even if none of those scenarios pan out, though, the worst-case scenario will still be an improvement over an attack that ranked 88th in scoring and 94th in Offensive F/+.

2015 Draft Prospects: DE Devonte Fields (1-2), SS Sam Carter (3), DT Chucky Hunter (4-5), CB Kevin White (5-6).*

No. 46 Texas Tech Red Raiders (7-5, 4-5)

2013: 8-5 (4-5) / F/+ #43 / FEI #44 / S&P+ #45 / Program F/+: #47					
2013 Offense			**2013 Defense**		
Offensive F/+	12.3%	20	Defensive F/+	-0.9%	69
Offensive FEI	0.416	21	Defensive FEI	-0.034	62
Offensive S&P+	117.2	23	Defensive S&P+	99.2	78
Rushing S&P+	100.3	67	Rushing S&P+	87.1	107
Passing S&P+	116.4	26	Passing S&P+	105.5	46
Standard Downs S&P+	103.0	59	Standard Downs S&P+	99.5	69
Passing Downs S&P+	138.8	10	Passing Downs S&P+	91.3	88
2013 Special Teams			Special Teams F/+	-3.4%	116
2014 Projections			SOS Rk	50	
Ret. Starters: 8 OFF, 4 DEF			Offensive F/+	12.6%	11
Proj. F/+	5.8%	46	Defensive F/+	-6.8%	103
Mean Wins / Conf Wins	6.7 / 3.9		Conference Title Odds	0.6%	

2013 Five Factors			
Efficiency	Off Success Rate+	113.1	23
	Def Success Rate+	93.5	86
	Total Efficiency	206.6	48
Explosiveness	Off IsoPPP+	100.4	58
	Def IsoPPP+	103.0	46
	Total Explosiveness	203.4	51
Field Position	Field Pos. Adv. (FPA)	0.481	90
Finishing Drives	Off Red Zone S&P+	101.5	56
	Def Red Zone S&P+	97.3	69
	Total Red Zone Rating	198.8	63
Turnovers	Turnover Margin	-14.0	123
	Exp. TO Margin	-9.6	122
	Difference	-4.4	96

Last year, Tech fans embraced Kliff Kingsbury as enthusiastically as any new head coach in the nation, and for fairly obvious reasons. Barely a decade removed from his own stint as a record-breaking Red Raider quarterback, Kingsbury looks like Ryan Gosling, has an easy rapport with young players, and has no qualms about pushing the "Air Raid" philosophy he ran as a player to its limit. For the season, the Raiders ran more plays than any other FBS offense, nearly two-thirds of them calling for a true freshman quarterback to put the ball in the air. Superficially, that was all in sharp contrast to his older, more conservative predecessor, Tommy Tuberville. But the results followed the same deflating trajectory. In 2011, the Raiders moved to 5-2 with a major midseason upset of Oklahoma, only to drop their last five in lopsided fashion. In 2012, they lost four of their last five following a 6-1 start, prompting Tuberville's middle-of-the-night flight to Cincinnati. Sticking to the script, Kingsbury's Raiders rose even higher last fall, climbing to tenth in the Associated Press poll with a 7-0 record, and crashed even harder: they dropped their last five against the meat of the conference slate by an average margin of three touchdowns per game.

Unlike previous editions, though, at least the 2013 outfit was able to salvage some genuine optimism in a Holiday Bowl ambush of Arizona State, the kind of upset that lends itself easily to irrational exuberance over the offseason: if *that* team shows up in the fall, the sky is the limit. Nowhere is that more true than at quarterback, where true freshman Davis Webb delivered his best game by far against ASU (403 yards, 4 touchdowns, 183.0 passer rating) since taking over the starting job from fellow freshman Baker Mayfield at midseason. (Mayfield subsequently opted for a transfer to Oklahoma.) Despite the revolving door at quarterback, and the November swoon against the top half of the league, the offense as a whole managed to finish third in the conference in Offensive F/+, averaging 464 yards and 28 points per game even during the losing streak. In contrast to its aggressive reputation, Tech was actually the most methodical offense in the Big 12, with 21.7 percent of offensive drives lasting at least 10 plays. In 2012, that number was just 14.6 percent, 56th in the nation. Although they were second in the nation in passing yards per game, the Red Raiders were just 60th in yards per attempt (7.2).

Webb is now the unquestioned starter as a sophomore—he was literally the only quarterback on the roster in spring practice—and will have the benefit of last year's top two tailbacks (Kenny Williams and DeAndre Washington), a pair of diminutive but productive slot receivers (Jakeem Grant and Bradley Marquez), and four returning starters on the offensive line. On the other hand, he'll also be operating without last year's veteran safety blankets, Jace Amaro and Eric Ward, who hauled in more receptions between them (189) than any other pair of teammates in the nation. And there's still the perennial burden at Tech: the defense, which yielded an incredible 48.6 points per game during the five-game skid. Given that context, a mass exodus of eight starters is no great loss. Still, coaches were desperate enough for answers in the spring to audition their leading rusher, Kenny Williams, at outside linebacker, and they wound up listing him as a starter at the "Raider" position on the post-spring depth chart. If he winds up going both ways in the fall, or giving up offense altogether, it won't be an experiment so much as a Hail Mary.

2015 Draft Prospects: OT Le'Raven Clark (2-3), RB Kenny Williams (6-7).*

No. 60 West Virginia Mountaineers (4-8, 3-6)

2013: 4-8 (2-7) / F/+ #76 / FEI #66 / S&P+ #98 / Program F/+: #35					
2013 Offense			**2013 Defense**		
Offensive F/+	-7.2%	92	Defensive F/+	-0.4%	65
Offensive FEI	-0.200	86	Defensive FEI	-0.088	55
Offensive S&P+	86.8	97	Defensive S&P+	96.7	87
Rushing S&P+	85.6	109	Rushing S&P+	102.4	62
Passing S&P+	100.3	63	Passing S&P+	89.0	102
Standard Downs S&P+	97.2	75	Standard Downs S&P+	102.4	58
Passing Downs S&P+	92.1	85	Passing Downs S&P+	83.2	110
2013 Special Teams			Special Teams F/+	0.9%	49
2014 Projections			SOS Rk	15	
Ret. Starters: 7 OFF, 7 DEF			Offensive F/+	-1.9%	77
Proj. F/+	0.5%	60	Defensive F/+	2.4%	51
Mean Wins / Conf Wins	4.0 / 2.6		Conference Title Odds	0.0%	

2013 Five Factors			
Efficiency	Off Success Rate+	88.0	102
	Def Success Rate+	98.0	62
	Total Efficiency	186.0	98
Explosiveness	Off IsoPPP+	111.0	21
	Def IsoPPP+	91.6	105
	Total Explosiveness	202.6	55
Field Position	Field Pos. Adv. (FPA)	0.483	88
Finishing Drives	Off Red Zone S&P+	99.5	62
	Def Red Zone S&P+	96.7	71
	Total Red Zone Rating	196.2	70
Turnovers	Turnover Margin	-4.0	86
	Exp. TO Margin	-6.0	111
	Difference	+2.0	38

Three years and 38 games into the Dana Holgorsen administration, the prevailing theme in Morgantown is whiplash. In Holgorsen's first 18 games on the job, West Virginia claimed 15 wins, a conference championship, the most lopsided victory in BCS history and, briefly, a top-five ranking on the strength of a 5-0 start in 2012. Since then, the Mountaineers are 6-14 with a single victory over an opponent with a winning record, and rang out 2013 with back-to-back losses to the league doormats, Kansas and Iowa State. For the first time in his career, Holgorsen's bombs-away philosophy on offense couldn't be counted on to mask other problems, mainly because it *was* the problem: minus Geno Smith and his top three targets from 2012, WVU plummeted from 15th in Offensive F/+ to 92nd, the most dramatic offensive nose-dive in the nation.

It would be unfair to pin that entirely on the quarterbacks, especially considering that a) The ground game was the worst in the conference, ranking 108th in Offensive Rushing S&P+ behind an offensive line that ranked 113th in Adjusted Line Yards; and b) None of the three quarterbacks who saw the field lasted long enough to take a majority of the snaps for the season. The opening-day starter, Ford Childress, suffered a pectoral injury in the second game and went on the shelf for good after being rushed back for a 37-0 debacle against Maryland. (Childress was then suspended from the team in January and transferred to a junior college.) The next man in, Clint Trickett, played most of the season with a bum shoulder, and at least one game with a concussion. Given every opportunity to gain ground in the spring, however, neither Paul Millard, Skyler Howard, nor Logan Moore was able to supplant Trickett from the top of the depth chart, despite Trickett's absence from practice following shoulder surgery. How long he's able to stay there on his own merit in the fall—or remain standing on his own two feet—is anyone's guess.

Ironically, despite the departure of All-Big 12 tailback Charles Sims, the strength of this team is still in the backfield. Five other backs return with significant experience under their belts, most notably senior Dreamius Smith and sophomore Rushel Shell, a former five-star recruit who sat out last season after transferring from Pittsburgh. Shell offered a glimpse of that five-star potential when he was a true freshman at Pitt in 2012, with 157 yards on 6.8 per carry against Virginia Tech and 96 yards on 5.3 per carry against Louisville. But now he has the same problem as the other Mountaineer runners: their blockers. The numbers don't lie—even Sims, a third-round NFL draft pick, found no room to run against Big 12 defenses. Excluding sacks, West Virginia averaged 4.7 yards per carry in conference games, well below the NCAA average of 5.2 yards per carry. Between the quarterbacks and the front five, fulfilling whatever potential exists at the skill positions is an uphill battle.

2015 Draft Prospects: FS Karl Joseph (3-4), DE Shaquille Riddick (5-6), G Quinton Spain (5-6).*

No. 66 Iowa State Cyclones (4-8, 2-7)

2013: 3-9 (2-7) / F/+ #78 / FEI #72 / S&P+ #90 / Program F/+: #73

2013 Offense			2013 Defense		
Offensive F/+	-5.1%	81	Defensive F/+	-4.0%	81
Offensive FEI	-0.139	76	Defensive FEI	0.099	76
Offensive S&P+	90.4	88	Defensive S&P+	97.2	86
Rushing S&P+	100.5	66	Rushing S&P+	84.8	110
Passing S&P+	95.8	75	Passing S&P+	105.7	44
Standard Downs S&P+	99.6	68	Standard Downs S&P+	93.5	94
Passing Downs S&P+	94.8	77	Passing Downs S&P+	99.9	69
2013 Special Teams			Special Teams F/+	1.7%	34
2014 Projections			SOS Rk	44	
Ret. Starters: 8 OFF, 5 DEF			Offensive F/+	2.0%	50
Proj. F/+	-1.8%	66	Defensive F/+	-3.8%	86
Mean Wins / Conf Wins	4.0 / 2.3		Conference Title Odds	0.0%	

2013 Five Factors			
	Off Success Rate+	99.9	64
Efficiency	Def Success Rate+	94.0	84
	Total Efficiency	193.9	76
	Off IsoPPP+	93.3	95
Explosiveness	Def IsoPPP+	97.4	76
	Total Explosiveness	190.8	98
Field Position	Field Pos. Adv. (FPA)	0.494	69
	Off Red Zone S&P+	122.2	11
Finishing Drives	Def Red Zone S&P+	99.7	60
	Total Red Zone Rating	221.9	20
	Turnover Margin	-1.0	69
Turnovers	Exp. TO Margin	+5.3	33
	Difference	-6.3	112

When you're a century removed from your last conference championship, all success is relative—an upset here, a bowl bid there, the occasional moral victory against a traditional heavy hitter (just as long as you remember to dismiss the concept of moral victories at the postgame press conference.) Even by Iowa State standards, though, 2013 refused to lend itself to positive spin. An opening-night loss to an FCS team, Northern Iowa, was only a prelude to a seven-game losing streak in Big 12 play, four of those losses coming by at least 30 points. The Cyclones earned at least one first down on only 51 percent of their offensive possessions (third-worst in FBS). Defensively, the Cyclones yielded at least 42 points in six of their last eight games and turned in the worst Defensive F/+ score in the conference. If not for Kansas, the offense would have shared the distinction.

If there must be a silver lining, it was the late emergence of redshirt freshman quarterback Grant Rohach, who took over for sophomore Sam Richardson in November and closed with a pair of 300-yard, multiple-touchdown efforts in wins over Kansas and West Virginia. Not the most stringent competition, obviously, and Rohach's previous appearances—in losses to Oklahoma State, Kansas State, TCU and Oklahoma—were uninspiring to say the least. Still, he showed some semblance of growth in the role after Richardson began to founder. He also has the benefit of viable playmakers in running back Aaron Wimberly (778 yards from scrimmage in 2013), wide receiver Quenton Bundrage (673 receiving yards, 14.0 per catch, 53 percent catch rate) and tight end E.J. Bibbs (462 receiving yards, 11.8 per catch, 65 percent catch rate), not to mention the most touted ISU recruit in recent memory, wide receiver Allen Lazard. There are also six linemen up front who started at least eight games apiece last year due to the mixing and matching that resulted from multiple injuries. But the reality here, as always, is that the next time Iowa State matches firepower with the upper half of the league for more than a week or two at a time will be the first.

2015 Draft Prospects: TE E.J. Bibbs (3-4).

No. 102 Kansas Jayhawks (2-10, 1-8)

2013: 3-9 (1-8) / F/+ #101 / FEI #101 / S&P+ #111 / Program F/+: #105

2013 Offense			2013 Defense		
Offensive F/+	-18.5%	119	Defensive F/+	-0.5%	66
Offensive FEI	-0.583	119	Defensive FEI	-0.061	58
Offensive S&P+	71.4	121	Defensive S&P+	98.6	81
Rushing S&P+	91.5	93	Rushing S&P+	93.8	90
Passing S&P+	71.1	122	Passing S&P+	97.3	77
Standard Downs S&P+	85.7	112	Standard Downs S&P+	94.8	90
Passing Downs S&P+	74.2	119	Passing Downs S&P+	99.9	68
2013 Special Teams			Special Teams F/+	0.0%	67
2014 Projections			SOS Rk	37	
Ret. Starters: 7 OFF, 9 DEF			Offensive F/+	-14.8%	126
Proj. F/+	-10.9%	102	Defensive F/+	3.8%	43
Mean Wins / Conf Wins	2.4 / 0.7		Conference Title Odds	0.0%	

2013 Five Factors			
	Off Success Rate+	84.1	114
Efficiency	Def Success Rate+	94.3	77
	Total Efficiency	178.4	106
	Off IsoPPP+	89.5	112
Explosiveness	Def IsoPPP+	100.0	58
	Total Explosiveness	189.5	103
Field Position	Field Pos. Adv. (FPA)	0.486	84
	Off Red Zone S&P+	89.5	98
Finishing Drives	Def Red Zone S&P+	90.1	88
	Total Red Zone Rating	179.5	102
	Turnover Margin	+1.0	53
Turnovers	Exp. TO Margin	-1.1	78
	Difference	+2.1	36

Say what you will about Charlie Weis, and we know that you will, but give the man this: he knows how to read a blueprint. In this case, the architect is Weis' cross-state rival, Bill Snyder, who could not differ more by background, demeanor, or public persona, but who has excelled at a historically moribund program by building a pipeline for junior-college talent that richer programs tended to ignore. Accordingly, Weis' first full recruiting class at Kansas in 2013 featured 19 JUCO transfers, a staggering number even in Snyderian terms, six of whom took on a regular starting role last fall.

This year's incoming class includes eight more JUCO signees and a pair of transfers (ex-UCLA quarterback T.J. Milweard and ex-Florida tight end Kent Taylor), all in the name of purging the depth chart of the last remaining traces of Weis' doomed predecessor, Turner Gill. (Other refugees include two wide receivers: Justin McCay from Oklahoma and Nick Harwell, a two-time All-MAC pick at Miami of Ohio before sitting out last year under NCAA transfer rules.) Although Gill signees still make up nearly half of the starting lineup, in year three of the Weis administration the results are all his own.

So far, even the few signs of progress have come with an asterisk. Defensively, for example, the final F/+ rankings show clear improvement from horrendous (84th nationally in 2012) to merely bad (66th in 2013), reflecting the emergence of All-Big 12 linebacker Ben Heeney and safety Isaiah Johnson, the conference's Defensive Newcomer of the Year. Offensively, the situation was so dire that Kansas failed to reach 20 points in ten of 11 games against FBS competition. The lone exception was a late, 31-19 upset over West Virginia that snapped a 27-game conference losing streak behind a true freshman quarterback, Montell Cozart, making his first career start. Given Cozart's obvious limitations as a passer—in seven appearances altogether, he completed well below 40 percent of his attempts with zero touchdowns—his emergence as the "clear winner" of a four-way competition in the spring suggests a more option-friendly scheme than you might expect from a coach with Weis' NFL background. But regardless of the plan, there is nowhere to go but up.

2015 Draft Prospects: SS Isaiah Johnson (4), WR Nick Harwell (6-7).*

Matt Hinton

Projected Win Probabilities For Big 12 Teams

			Overall Wins													Conference Wins									
Div	Conf	Big 12	12-0	11-1	10-2	9-3	8-4	7-5	6-6	5-7	4-8	3-9	2-10	1-11	0-12	9-0	8-1	7-2	6-3	5-4	4-5	3-6	2-7	1-8	0-9
-	22	Baylor	4	19	33	27	13	3	1	-	-	-	-	-	-	4	20	33	27	12	3	1	-	-	-
-	-	Iowa State	-	-	-	-	-	2	10	21	30	25	10	2	-	-	-	-	-	3	12	27	34	20	4
-	-	Kansas	-	-	-	-	-	-	-	2	11	31	41	15	-	-	-	-	-	-	-	2	12	40	46
-	4	Kansas State	-	1	6	16	27	27	16	6	1	-	-	-	-	-	2	11	26	31	20	8	2	-	-
-	54	Oklahoma	18	35	29	14	3	1	-	-	-	-	-	-	-	19	35	29	13	3	1	-	-	-	-
-	13	Oklahoma State	-	3	13	29	31	18	5	1	-	-	-	-	-	2	13	29	32	18	5	1	-	-	-
-	3	TCU	-	1	7	18	28	25	14	6	1	-	-	-	-	-	2	10	22	30	24	10	2	-	-
-	3	Texas	-	-	2	8	19	27	24	14	5	1	-	-	-	-	1	9	21	31	25	11	2	-	-
-	1	Texas Tech	-	-	1	6	18	29	27	14	4	1	-	-	-	-	-	2	9	21	31	25	10	2	-
-	-	West Virginia	-	-	-	-	-	2	9	21	31	26	9	2	-	-	-	-	1	5	16	30	31	15	2

Pac-12 Conference

Each winter, in an annual courtship ritual on par with the theatrical nasal cavity of the hooded seal, ambitious schools with a fresh coaching vacancy approach Chris Petersen with outlandish displays of cash and autonomy to lure him from his niche at Boise State. Each winter, Petersen politely demurs. Texas A&M? UCLA? USC? Great opportunities, but… sorry, no. More money? Thanks, but no thanks. Another year, another jilted suitor: Since roughly 2006, when Petersen put Boise on the map in a ludicrous Fiesta Bowl upset over Oklahoma, such have been the rhythms of nature. Or so they were. Still, when Petersen finally took the bait last December, accepting a five-year deal from Washington to make him the Pac-12's highest-paid coach at an SEC-worthy $3.6 million per year, the timing felt right on both ends. After seven wildly successful campaigns in Boise—a span that included five top-10 finishes, two BCS wins and a No. 1 overall F/+ rating in 2010—the 2013 Broncos were the worst in Petersen's tenure, ranking 45th in F/+ with five losses. Meanwhile, conference realignment has settled into a tentative stasis and the window for upward mobility at have-not programs like BSU has been effectively slammed shut. For its part, Washington gets a coach who was actually more sought-after than the guy he's replacing, USC-bound Steve Sarkisian, just as the program is emerging from a decade-long stupor. Sarkisian laid a solid foundation over the unmourned burial ground of the Ty Willingham era, but ultimately came up short of returning Washington to its traditional perch in the Northwest, finishing 1-9 in his tenure against North Division heavies Oregon and Stanford. In fact, despite the Huskies' long-awaited return to the top 25 in 2013, all four losses came at the hands of teams that finished in the top 15 in overall F/+. Petersen, by contrast, arrives with proven big-game chops. In 2014, at least, he'll also have the most experienced roster in the league.

The power play in Seattle is another reflection of the escalating arms race across the Pac-12, fueled by an explosion in television money over the past three years. (Thanks to renegotiated deals with ESPN and FOX, the conference reported $334 million in total revenue for 2012-13, most of any conference, representing nearly a six-fold increase over the $59.5 million it took in during 2010-11; each school's share of the increased sum came to about $19.8 million, according to USA Today.) For most of this century, the league was derided as the "Pac-1," the one being USC during its run of seven consecutive championships under Pete Carroll; beginning with Chip Kelly's promotion to Oregon head coach in 2009, the Ducks replaced the Trojans in the penthouse. With the influx of money, though, every Pac-12 program has splurged on facilities and high-profile coaches in the name of keeping up with the Joneses, with the result that virtually every program has the veneer of an up-and-comer. At UCLA, Jim Mora has engineered a surprise South Division title in his first year, a top-15 finish in his second, and back-to-back wins over the cross-town rival, USC. At Arizona State, Todd Graham has as many wins in his first two seasons (18) as any new coach in ASU history. Arizona and Washington State placed their bets on a pair of established offensive innovators, Rich Rodriguez and Mike Leach, with respectable returns so far. Cal followed suit, enlisting Leach protégé Sonny Dykes to run the "Air Raid" in a newly refurbished stadium. Washington, having clawed its way out of oblivion on the field at last, overhauled its stadium in 2013, no doubt a selling point for Petersen. At the top of the standings, Oregon and Stanford hired from within to sustain their unprecedented success under Chip Kelly and Jim Harbaugh, while USC attempted to rekindle the flame by luring former Carroll assistants from the halcyon days—first Lane Kiffin, now Sarkisian. At the bottom, Colorado is just hoping for some semblance of stability under second-year boss Mike MacIntyre.

Across the league, the only teams that haven't changed head coaches since the end of the 2010 season are Oregon State (Mike Riley is entering year 14 in Corvallis) and Utah (Kyle Whittingham was promoted to succeed Urban Meyer in 2005), and the latter wasn't even a conference member until 2011. With each new hire, the salaries climb higher, and expectations follow suit. Eight Pac-12 schools finished in the F/+ top 25 last year, more than any other conference, including the SEC. Now, the prospect of Washington reentering the upper crust under Petersen only raises the stakes for everyone else: no matter how much money is coming in, the one resource that never expands is the number of available wins.

NORTH DIVISION

No. 3 Oregon Ducks (11-1, 8-1)

2013: 11-2 (7-2) / F/+ #5 / FEI #7 / S&P+ #10 / Program F/+: #2					
2013 Offense			**2013 Defense**		
Offensive F/+	20.0%	6	Defensive F/+	11.2%	22
Offensive FEI	0.612	4	Defensive FEI	-0.422	16
Offensive S&P+	133.0	7	Defensive S&P+	118.4	25
Rushing S&P+	137.2	3	Rushing S&P+	105.7	50
Passing S&P+	136.9	7	Passing S&P+	108.2	39
Standard Downs S&P+	130.1	6	Standard Downs S&P+	107.5	41
Passing Downs S&P+	148.1	5	Passing Downs S&P+	113.8	35
2013 Special Teams			Special Teams F/+	2.1%	26
2014 Projections			SOS Rk	49	
Ret. Starters: 9 OFF, 6 DEF			Offensive F/+	17.4%	1
Proj. F/+	24.5%	3	Defensive F/+	7.1%	26
Mean Wins / Conf Wins	10.7 / 7.9		Conf. / Div. Title Odds	53.8% / 73.2%	

2013 Five Factors			
Efficiency	Off Success Rate+	124.7	4
	Def Success Rate+	106.1	36
	Total Efficiency	230.8	10
Explosiveness	Off IsoPPP+	117.1	5
	Def IsoPPP+	108.5	26
	Total Explosiveness	225.6	4
Field Position	Field Pos. Adv. (FPA)	0.549	9
Finishing Drives	Off Red Zone S&P+	118.7	14
	Def Red Zone S&P+	97.5	68
	Total Red Zone Rating	216.2	28
Turnovers	Turnover Margin	+11.0	14
	Exp. TO Margin	+5.2	34
	Difference	+5.8	20

It took Oregon about a minute-and-a-half in 2013—the time elapsed from the opening kickoff to its first touchdown of the season—to vanquish any lingering doubts about the post-Chip Kelly gestalt. Right out of the gate, the Ducks were the Ducks: through October, they averaged 55.6 points per game and dispatched their first eight opponents by at least three touchdowns apiece, putting them back on track for the BCS title game. At season's end, they led the Pac-12 in scoring offense, total offense, Offensive F/+, and Offensive S&P+ for the fifth year in a row, all while deepening their indifference toward the concept of "ball control." (The 2013 edition was 124th out of 125 teams in time of possession, also the fifth year in a row Oregon has ranked 100th or worse in service of its up-tempo philosophy.) As Kelly's hand-picked successor, Mark Helfrich hit all the high notes.

In the meantime, though, the "same old Ducks" theme cut both ways. For the second year in a row, the championship push ended in November with a thud against the most physical, defensively-oriented opponent on the schedule. Stanford followed up a 17-14 upset in Eugene in 2012 with a methodical, 26-20 romp that wasn't nearly as close as the score suggests. (The Cardinal led 26-0 in the fourth quarter before conceding a cosmetic rally; even counting garbage time, Oregon limped out with its worst output for both rushing yards and total offense since 2009, in large part because the offense was on the field for less than 18 minutes.) For longtime Ducks skeptics, the blueprint was all too familiar. Under Kelly, all six Oregon losses from 2009-12 came at the hands of upper-crust opponents that went on to finish in the top ten in overall F/+, and the top 15 defensively—that is, against opponents with the muscle to clamp down on the line of scrimmage. Five of those six held Oregon's prolific ground game below 200 yards, a near-impossible feat for the Ducks' victims; four of them managed to hold Oregon below 20 points. Within the division, Stanford has claimed the crown by checking off both boxes in back-to-back seasons, adding insult to injury last year by pounding out 274 rushing yards of its own. Worse, the Ducks blew any chance of redemption two weeks later by yielding 304 yards on the ground in a shocking, 42-16 flop at Arizona, their most lopsided loss (and first at the hands of an unranked opponent) since 2008.

Naturally, the championship hype in 2014 revolves around hyper-efficient quarterback Marcus Mariota, as well it should. A two-time All-Pac-12 pick, Mariota might have been the first quarterback drafted in April if he had decided to leave school, and he will push Jameis Winston for the distinction in 2015. If there is any solace in the November slump, it's in the fact that Mariota was visibly struggling with a knee injury. Does any defense really stand a chance when he's at 100 percent? In context of the rivalry with Stanford, though, getting over the hump may hinge less on Mariota than on his offensive line, which returns essentially intact; between Hroniss Grasu, Tyler Johnstone, Jake Fisher, Hamani Stevens and Cameron Hunt, the front five boasts 108 career starts and at least three future pros. (The most senior member, Grasu, has delivered every non-garbage time snap over the past three years, making him the only starter left from the Ducks' last conference championship in 2011.) On paper, it looks like the most dominant line in the nation, coming off a season in which it fueled the offense as a whole by ranking fourth in both Adjusted Line Yards and Opportunity Rate. But it was well below average in short-yardage situations, ranking 83rd in Power Success Rate, and in the red zone, where Oregon uncharacteristically settled for a field goal or no points at all on two-thirds of its opportunities. (Two scoreless trips in the first half loomed especially large in the loss in Palo Alto.) And anyway, generically gaudy numbers here are taken for granted. More specifically, those running lanes have always been harder to come by against the likes of Stanford and Michigan State—the Spartans visit Eugene for a compelling non-conference test on September 6—and for a team with playoff ambitions it's those defenses that set the bar.

As for Oregon's own defense, it has generally held up its end of the up-tempo bargain better than its raw yardage numbers (and subsequent reputation) suggest. Under coordinator Nick Aliotti, the Ducks have ranked in the top 25 in Defensive F/+ each of the last five years, including top-10 finishes in 2010 and 2012. The 2013 edition faced more plays per game (80.2) than any FBS defense except Oklahoma State, but ranked seventh in yards per play allowed. Although Aliotti retired in December after 17 years on the job, his replacement, Don Pellum, has been on staff even longer—Pellum arrived as linebackers coach in 1993—and will run the same hybrid 4-3/3-4 scheme, which hinges on the versatility of the "drop" end position manned by senior Tony Washington. Athletically, the defense still lags behind the likes of Alabama and Florida State, a gap that was most evident against the run: Oregon ranked 50th in 2013 in Defensive Rushing S&P+ and looked especially overmatched in the losses to Stanford and Arizona. All three projected starters on the defensive line—DeForest Buckner, Arik Armstead and Alex Balducci—are former four- and five-star recruits entering their third year in the program, and must live up to the hype for the team to fulfill its potential.

2015 Draft Prospects: CB Ifo Ekpre-Olomu (1), QB Marcus Mariota (1), C Hroniss Grasu (2-3), OLB Derrick Malone (2-3), OT Tyler Johnstone* (3), DE/OLB Tony Washington (3-4), OT Jake Fisher (5-6).*

No. 4 Stanford Cardinal (10-2, 7-2)

2013: 11-3 (7-2) / F/+ #3 / FEI #2 / S&P+ #4 / Program F/+: #3					
2013 Offense			**2013 Defense**		
Offensive F/+	13.3%	18	Defensive F/+	21.6%	4
Offensive FEI	0.412	22	Defensive FEI	-0.742	1
Offensive S&P+	121.4	17	Defensive S&P+	136.3	9
Rushing S&P+	115.0	29	Rushing S&P+	132.3	6
Passing S&P+	135.0	9	Passing S&P+	129.6	7
Standard Downs S&P+	113.6	29	Standard Downs S&P+	135.9	4
Passing Downs S&P+	141.6	8	Passing Downs S&P+	120.2	20
2013 Special Teams			Special Teams F/+	5.1%	2
2014 Projections			SOS Rk	12	
Ret. Starters: 5 OFF, 6 DEF			Offensive F/+	6.6%	30
Proj. F/+	22.0%	4	Defensive F/+	15.4%	5
Mean Wins / Conf Wins	9.5 / 6.8		Conf. / Div. Title Odds	16.4% / 24.0%	

2013 Five Factors			
Efficiency	Off Success Rate+	116.4	15
	Def Success Rate+	115.4	16
	Total Efficiency	231.8	9
Explosiveness	Off IsoPPP+	106.3	34
	Def IsoPPP+	118.1	3
	Total Explosiveness	224.4	7
Field Position	Field Pos. Adv. (FPA)	0.561	3
Finishing Drives	Off Red Zone S&P+	101.7	54
	Def Red Zone S&P+	108.6	30
	Total Red Zone Rating	210.3	41
Turnovers	Turnover Margin	0.0	61
	Exp. TO Margin	+6.0	25
	Difference	-6.0	111

Stanford has surpassed Oregon as the conference standard-bearer by defining itself as the anti-Oregon, countering the Ducks' frenetic philosophy with a methodical, throwback mindset that puts a premium on owning the line of scrimmage. In the age of the spread, it's an improbably innovative niche: with a full assortment of "jumbo" sets, the Cardinal are able to exploit their strength in the trenches (literally) by embracing tight splits which deploy reserve linemen on a regular basis as oversized tight ends and fullbacks. At its best, the impression is of an elephantine army on an implacable march to the sea, 4.4 yards at a time. To that end, Stanford claimed the most run-oriented offense in the league in 2013, keeping the ball on the ground on nearly two-thirds of its total snaps. Individually, senior Tyler Gaffney was one of only two tailbacks nationally (along with Boston College's Andre Williams) to log more carries on the season himself (331) than his team attempted passes (311), and four offensive linemen were voted first- or second-team All-Pac-12 by league coaches. The Cardinal paired their ball-control offense with top-five rankings in defense, special teams, and field position, the first team since the 2008 Florida Gators to rank as highly in each of those three phases of the game.

At its worst, however, the Cro-Magnon attack can get bogged down for long stretches with no relief from the passing game. Although quarterback Kevin Hogan was generally efficient as a sophomore, and is more than capable of exploiting of run-occupied safeties on play-action—combined, top receivers Ty Montgomery, Devon Cajuste and Michael Rector averaged 19.7 yards per catch with 18 touchdowns—he was also less consistent than his steady reputation suggests. In nine games against opponents that finished with winning records, Hogan posted a very pedestrian efficiency rating of 130.0 (nearly 100 points below his rating against non-winning teams) with more interceptions in those games (eight) than touchdowns (six); in the late loss at USC, in particular, he was the goat, finishing 14-of-25 for 127 yards, zero touchdowns, and a pair of killer interceptions in the fourth quarter. Then again, in Hogan's defense, he was working without the safety blanket he enjoyed in 2012 from NFL-bound tight ends Zach Ertz and Levine Toilolo. In 2013, Cardinal tight ends combined for a grand total of 10 catches for 69 yards, one of the reasons they were increasingly replaced by bigger bodies as the year wore on. (The initial starter at tight end, Luke Kaumatule, was converted to defensive end at midseason; his successor in the lineup, Davis Dudchock, transferred to Vanderbilt, leaving a three-deep in the spring manned exclusively by redshirt freshmen.) On paper, the biggest concern offensively is replacing four decorated veterans from the line, but the roster is built specifically to do that: Two of the new starters up front, Kyle Murphy and Joshua Garnett, are former five-star recruits, as is the returning starter at left tackle, Andrus Peat. The real concern is finding a reliable, chain-moving target underneath to complement Montgomery and the other deep threats.

As with the offensive line, the mass exodus of all-conference headliners on defense is blunted both by a rising talent level across the board and a strong track record that precedes the most recent departures. Stanford has ranked among the top 20 nationally in Defensive F/+ four years in a row. It helps, despite the loss of 2012-13 leaders Trent Murphy, Shayne Skov, Ben Gardner and Ed Reynolds, that the seven returning starters on defense boast 149 career starts between them, and considerable pro potential in their own right. More than any combination of departing players, the most glaring loss over the winter was defensive coordinator Derek Mason, who left for the top job at Vanderbilt. As usual, Shaw stayed in-house for Mason's replacement by promoting outside linebackers coach Lance Anderson, the only other holdover from Jim Harbaugh's original Stanford staff in the dark days of 2007. And why not? After ranking fourth in Defensive F/+ last year under Mason, the 2014 edition is projected to finish fifth running the same scheme under Anderson. As long as continuity on the sideline translates into continuity in the standings, the Cardinal have every reason to embrace the status quo.

2015 Draft Prospects: OT Andrus Peat (1), WR Ty Montgomery (1-2), CB Alex Carter* (2-3), SS Jordan Richards (2-3), CB Wayne Lyons (3-4), DE/DT Henry Anderson (4-5), OLB James Vaughters (4-5), ILB A.J. Tarpley (6-7).*

No. 24 Washington Huskies (9-4, 5-4)

2013: 9-4 (5-4) / F/+ #18 / FEI #16 / S&P+ #23 / Program F/+: #48

2013 Offense			2013 Defense		
Offensive F/+	12.1%	22	Defensive F/+	11.8%	21
Offensive FEI	0.476	13	Defensive FEI	-0.384	24
Offensive S&P+	111.5	34	Defensive S&P+	124.4	20
Rushing S&P+	112.9	34	Rushing S&P+	109.5	39
Passing S&P+	109.2	38	Passing S&P+	131.2	6
Standard Downs S&P+	102.8	60	Standard Downs S&P+	114.7	26
Passing Downs S&P+	126.0	16	Passing Downs S&P+	138.3	4
2013 Special Teams			Special Teams F/+	2.4%	19
2014 Projections			SOS Rk	23	
Ret. Starters: 7 OFF, 5 DEF			Offensive F/+	7.9%	22
Proj. F/+	11.8%	24	Defensive F/+	3.9%	42
Mean Wins / Conf Wins	9.1 / 5.2		Conf. / Div. Title Odds	0.8% / 2.1%	

2013 Five Factors			
Efficiency	Off Success Rate+	108.9	31
	Def Success Rate+	112.9	21
	Total Efficiency	221.8	20
Explosiveness	Off IsoPPP+	101.1	54
	Def IsoPPP+	115.4	7
	Total Explosiveness	216.5	15
Field Position	Field Pos. Adv. (FPA)	0.518	41
Finishing Drives	Off Red Zone S&P+	117.4	16
	Def Red Zone S&P+	129.8	5
	Total Red Zone Rating	247.2	5
Turnovers	Turnover Margin	+7.0	23
	Exp. TO Margin	+9.4	7
	Difference	-2.4	76

Washington is still less than 25 years removed from a national championship, and less than 15 years removed from its last Rose Bowl, so there's no point in playing up a third-place finish in the division followed by a victory in the Fight Hunger Bowl as a season for the ages. On the other hand, there's no denying it was a crucial step forward in the face of rising expectations, either. The Huskies were in a rut: from 2010-12, they turned in identical 7-6 records three years in a row, good for 70th, 67th and 56th, respectively, in the overall F/+ rankings. That was fine at first, given the fresh memory of an 0-12 debacle in 2008, but it became increasingly frustrating as they failed to make any headway against the division heavies. In that context, 2013 was a victory over stagnation, resulting in Washington's best winning percentage since 2000 and best F/+ score (+26.3%, good for 18th nationally) since we started keeping track in 2005. For Steve Sarkisian, it was a culmination. For Chris Petersen, it's square one.

Offensively, the curve may not be as steep as would be suggested by the departures of last year's headliners, quarterback Keith Price and tailback Bishop Sankey. True, the offense was one of the most improved attacks anywhere, leading the overall turnaround with a leap from 63rd to 22nd in Offensive F/+. It was also among the most balanced, one of only five nationally to go over 3,000 yards both rushing and passing. Price left as the most efficient passer in school history over the course of his career, while Sankey set the school record for rushing yards in a season (1,870) in 2013. The Huskies also lost their leading receiver, Richard Smith, and huge tight end Austin Seferian-Jenkins, a perpetual mismatch and second-round draft pick. The exodus at the skill positions is offset in part by a fully intact offensive line that boasts more career starts (123) than any other front in the conference, as well as the return of senior wide receiver Kasen Williams (77 catches for 878 yards and six touchdowns in 2012) from a broken leg. And at any rate, the key that turns the lock is the new quarterback, Cyler Miles, a redshirt sophomore with prototype size (6-foot-4, 215 lbs) and athleticism and sky-high expectations to match. Miles missed spring practice over his role in an alleged assault following the Seahawks' victory in the Super Bowl, an incident that led to the dismissal of another former blue-chip recruit, wide receiver Damore'ea Stringfellow. But no charges were filed against Miles, who was reinstated in May with "Next Big Thing" status undiminished.

As with Stanford, specific personnel losses on defense—in this case, three senior starters from a secondary that ranked sixth in Defensive Passing S&P+—are overshadowed by the departure of the defensive coordinator, Justin Wilcox. In 2011, the year before Wilcox's arrival, Washington ranked 100th in Defensive F/+, yielding 35.9 points per game. In two subsequent years under Wilcox, the same unit improved to 37th in

Defensive F/+ in 2012 and 21st last year, when it allowed 22.8 points per game. They were especially strong in preventing costly big plays, ranking fifth nationally in opponent explosive drives (6.4 percent). The front seven returns intact from a dominant performance against BYU in the Fight Hunger Bowl, led by junior linebacker/safety/jack of all trades Shaq Thompson. (The new coaching staff was so intrigued by Thompson's versatility that they auditioned him at tailback in the spring, to rave reviews, albeit inconclusive ones in terms of whether he'll actually pull double duty in the fall.) The superlative pass defense in 2013 actually began up front, with the pass rush: As a team, the Huskies tied for fourth nationally with 41 sacks, all but two of them by players who remain on the two-deep. (They were 16th in Adjusted Sack Rate; not quite as amazing, but still very good.) Of course, those are the same players responsible for yielding 31 points to Stanford, 45 to Oregon, 53 to Arizona State and 41 to UCLA in their four biggest games, all losses. Still, barring a wave of injuries, a collapse by the new safeties, and/or a general rejection of new coordinator Pete Kwiatkowski, there's every reason to expect that gap to continue to close. But the Huskies still project to fall in line behind Stanford and Oregon, and a difficult cross-division swing against UCLA and Arizona in mid-November will keep them out of the conference title hunt.

2015 Draft Prospects: OLB/SS Shaq Thompson (2-3), WR Kasen Williams (2-3), DT Danny Shelton (3-4), DE Hau'oli Kikaha (5-6), DE/OLB Josh Shirley (7-FA).*

No. 37 Oregon State Beavers (7-5, 4-5)

2013: 7-6 (4-5) / F/+ #42 / FEI #38 / S&P+ #50 / Program F/+: #42

2013 Offense			**2013 Defense**		
Offensive F/+	6.5%	36	Defensive F/+	2.3%	50
Offensive FEI	0.188	39	Defensive FEI	-0.165	40
Offensive S&P+	111.8	33	Defensive S&P+	101.6	74
Rushing S&P+	108.1	43	Rushing S&P+	94.6	87
Passing S&P+	117.2	22	Passing S&P+	106.0	43
Standard Downs S&P+	122.9	11	Standard Downs S&P+	97.9	78
Passing Downs S&P+	110.2	44	Passing Downs S&P+	108.6	41
2013 Special Teams			Special Teams F/+	-0.3%	73
2014 Projections			SOS Rk	20	
Ret. Starters: 8 OFF, 6 DEF			Offensive F/+	7.6%	24
Proj. F/+	8.5%	37	Defensive F/+	0.9%	59
Mean Wins / Conf Wins	7.3 / 4.4		Conf. / Div. Title Odds	0.2% / 0.7%	

2013 Five Factors			
Efficiency	Off Success Rate+	116.6	14
	Def Success Rate+	99.5	55
	Total Efficiency	216.1	28
Explosiveness	Off IsoPPP+	104.0	40
	Def IsoPPP+	100.9	55
	Total Explosiveness	204.9	48
Field Position	Field Pos. Adv. (FPA)	0.536	17
Finishing Drives	Off Red Zone S&P+	110.6	26
	Def Red Zone S&P+	101.8	50
	Total Red Zone Rating	212.3	37
Turnovers	Turnover Margin	+3.0	41
	Exp. TO Margin	-8.0	118
	Difference	+11.0	4

Under Mike Riley, Oregon State has always been willing to adjust its personality to fit its personnel, and in 2013 that meant airing it out early and often—far more often, in fact, than in any other season in Riley's 14-year tenure. Which worked out fine, for a while: through seven games, OSU stood at 6-1, its only blemish coming in a 49-46 shootout against Eastern Washington on opening day. Over the course of the subsequent six-game winning streak, Oregon State averaged nearly 44 points per game while quarterback Sean Mannion emerged as the most prolific passer in the nation in terms of both yards and touchdowns. From there, the schedule sent the Beavers plummeting into oblivion. While Mannion continued to throw at a heavy clip, finishing with the single-season Pac-12 record for passing yards (4,662), the offense as a whole averaged just 21 points per game in a five-game skid against the league's upper crust, consecutive losses to Stanford, USC, Arizona State, Washington and Oregon. Mannion was picked off 11 times in that span, two of them going back for opponent touchdowns. Oregon State gained 36 points in scoring and field position value off of turnovers in its victories, and lost 24 points worth of field position on turnovers in its losses.

As a senior, Mannion will begin the season with more career attempts (1,385), yards (10,436) and interceptions (46) than any other active FBS quarterback. Philosophically, though, the veteran presence at quarterback may ultimately mean less than the absence of his favorite target, Brandin Cooks, a consensus All-American who left early to become a first-round draft pick. In terms of both quantity (168 targets, second among all FBS receivers) and quality (76.2 percent catch rate, second among receivers with at least 60 targets), Cooks was arguably the most valuable wideout in college football. (Our updated Playmaker Score gives him the highest rating of any of this year's shining NFL rookie wide receivers; see page 433.) Otherwise, the passing game tended to revolve around a nondescript cast of tight ends and running backs. In the former category, Connor Hamlett, Caleb Smith and Kellen Clute combined for 84 receptions, at 10.3 yards a pop; in the latter, Storm Woods and Terron Ward averaged 8.9 yards on 81 grabs. Between them, Woods and Ward have also racked up more than 2,300 yards and 30 touchdowns rushing over the past two years, which—given Mannion's overall inconsistency and the lack of an obvious successor to Cooks—should make them logical candidates to take over as the focal point of the offense. But that can't happen without a significant step forward by the offensive line, which ranked 83rd in Adjusted Line Yards, and was even worse (105th) on standard downs. If three new starters up front can't generate any additional room on the ground, the spotlight returns to Mannion.

2015 Draft Prospects: C/G Isaac Seumalo (2-3), QB Sean Mannion (3-4), CB Steven Nelson (3-4).*

No. 59 Washington State Cougars (4-8, 2-7)

2013: 6-7 (4-5) / F/+ #53 / FEI #56 / S&P+ #60 / Program F/+: #107

2013 Offense			2013 Defense		
Offensive F/+	1.5%	54	Defensive F/+	1.6%	54
Offensive FEI	0.047	55	Defensive FEI	-0.097	52
Offensive S&P+	102.7	51	Defensive S&P+	104.7	64
Rushing S&P+	106.7	51	Rushing S&P+	105.5	51
Passing S&P+	100.3	64	Passing S&P+	99.7	65
Standard Downs S&P+	98.7	71	Standard Downs S&P+	99.2	73
Passing Downs S&P+	123.0	22	Passing Downs S&P+	111.6	38
2013 Special Teams			Special Teams F/+	0.6%	53
2014 Projections			SOS Rk	19	
Ret. Starters: 8 OFF, 6 DEF			Offensive F/+	1.7%	54
Proj. F/+	0.5%	59	Defensive F/+	-1.2%	69
Mean Wins / Conf Wins	4.2 / 2.0		Conf. / Div. Title Odds	0.0% / 0.0%	

2013 Five Factors			
Efficiency	Off Success Rate+	108.6	32
	Def Success Rate+	100.0	52
	Total Efficiency	208.6	42
Explosiveness	Off IsoPPP+	97.6	77
	Def IsoPPP+	103.1	45
	Total Explosiveness	200.7	65
Field Position	Field Pos. Adv. (FPA)	0.484	86
Finishing Drives	Off Red Zone S&P+	114.9	19
	Def Red Zone S&P+	107.6	35
	Total Red Zone Rating	222.5	19
Turnovers	Turnover Margin	-5.0	93
	Exp. TO Margin	-6.5	112
	Difference	+1.5	44

At this point in his career, Mike Leach's own track record as a head coach—he's never led a team to a conference championship or a major bowl—pales in comparison to his influence over the handful of Leach disciples who have gone on to spread the gospel of the "Air Raid" from coast to coast. In his own obscure corner of the country, though, the mentor is still determined to set the template. For the second year in a row, Washington State was the pass-happiest offense in football in 2013, putting the ball in the air 58.2 times per game. Against Oregon, the Cougars set an FBS record (and infuriated the Ducks' coaches in a blowout) by launching 89 passes in a single night.

Nonetheless, the season as a whole—and that Oregon game especially—was a textbook reminder that throwing a lot bears little relationship to throwing well. Although now-senior quarterback Connor Halliday enjoyed far better protection last year than he had in 2012, and improved his efficiency overall, he also finished with more interceptions (22), fewer yards per attempt (6.4), and fewer yards per completion (10.2) than any other Pac-12 starter. Although nine different receivers came down with 25 receptions or more (all of whom are back in 2014), none of them ranked among the top 150 nationally for catch rate or yards per target. Unlike Leach's old teams at Texas Tech, which regularly ranked among the most productive offenses in the nation, the pedal-to-the-metal approach for Washington State yielded an attack that ranked just 54th in Offensive F/+, 64th in Offensive Passing S&P+, and 52nd in points per game. The Cougars were frustratingly inefficient, earning only 42 percent of available yards (87th nationally) and scoring only 4.6 points per value drive (92nd nationally).

Still, while that output is nothing to write home about for a reputed offensive guru, it marked a dramatic improvement in every respect from Leach's initial, underwhelming effort in Pullman in 2012. The defense didn't have as far to go to arrive in essentially the same place—it mirrored the offense by finishing 54th in Defensive F/+—and had lingering issues of its own, yielding well over 500 yards in six games. But the defense did deliver in the two upset wins that ultimately made the difference in lifting the Cougars from the cellar into a bowl game, holding USC to a single touchdown in September and Arizona to 17 points in November. (The offense's greatest triumph against a sentient opponent came a week later, when it dropped 578 yards on Utah to secure bowl eligibility for the first time in a decade, although the defense did its part there, too, by returning two interceptions for touchdowns in a 49-37 decision.) Arizona Cardinals' first-round pick Deone Bucannon is a glaring loss at safety. With six starters back among the front seven, though, the offense should not have to average 35 points per game just to break even.

2015 Draft Prospects: None.

No. 85 California Golden Bears (3-9, 1-8)

2013: 1-11 (0-9) / F/+ #103 / FEI #106 / S&P+ #102 / Program F/+: #75

2013 Offense			2013 Defense		
Offensive F/+	-6.7%	88	Defensive F/+	-10.0%	99
Offensive FEI	-0.211	89	Defensive FEI	0.323	101
Offensive S&P+	89.9	89	Defensive S&P+	90.1	104
Rushing S&P+	86.0	108	Rushing S&P+	105.3	53
Passing S&P+	97.1	70	Passing S&P+	87.4	105
Standard Downs S&P+	95.3	83	Standard Downs S&P+	99.2	72
Passing Downs S&P+	97.2	67	Passing Downs S&P+	84.2	106
2013 Special Teams			Special Teams F/+	-3.4%	116
2014 Projections			SOS Rk	22	
Ret. Starters: 8 OFF, 6 DEF			Offensive F/+	-0.8%	71
Proj. F/+	-6.0%	85	Defensive F/+	-5.3%	94
Mean Wins / Conf Wins	2.6 / 1.3		Conf. / Div. Title Odds	0.0% / 0.0%	

2013 Five Factors			
Efficiency	Off Success Rate+	90.4	94
	Def Success Rate+	104.4	44
	Total Efficiency	194.9	73
Explosiveness	Off IsoPPP+	109.5	22
	Def IsoPPP+	80.4	123
	Total Explosiveness	189.9	100
Field Position	Field Pos. Adv. (FPA)	0.413	125
Finishing Drives	Off Red Zone S&P+	84.5	109
	Def Red Zone S&P+	103.6	44
	Total Red Zone Rating	188.0	91
Turnovers	Turnover Margin	-15.0	124
	Exp. TO Margin	-12.9	125
	Difference	-2.1	75

If you sat down and wrote a script for the most depressing football season you could imagine, you could hardly do worse than Cal in 2013 without resorting to natural disaster, plague and/or a supervillain blowing up the entire stadium just when your special teams finally brings a kickoff back for a touchdown. Not that there was much room for disappointment: on the heels of a 3-9 debacle in 2012, the Bears were breaking in a new administration under first-year coach Sonny Dykes, as well as a mostly new starting lineup, the greenest in the conference by any measure. In August, Dykes doubled down on the youth movement by naming a true freshman, Jared Goff, as starting quarterback; by year's end, 17 other underclassmen had logged multiple starts as freshmen or sophomores. In part, that was due to the steady toll of injuries, which eventually claimed the seasons of six starters on defense and two more on the offensive line. And don't forget the schedule! The Baby Bears were thrown into the fire against the fourth-toughest slate in the nation according to FEI, featuring six opponents that finished in the F/+ top 25 and three others that played in bowl games. The result, predictably, was mass slaughter: ten losses by double digits, including a 41-24 loss at the hands of a fellow doormat, Colorado, and not even a brief hint of progress to carry into the offseason. The season finale, a 63-13 thrashing at Stanford, was the most lopsided defeat of the year.

So when anyone suggests Cal is destined to improve in 2014, take that in context: with this year's schedule another stacked deck, a realistic step forward means keeping a handful of games within reach in the fourth quarter and stealing an upset or two, at best. There is some optimism for Goff, who flashed a major-league arm en route to some meaninglessly inflated statistics; out of both design and necessity, Goff aired it out at such a furious rate (44.1 attempts per game) that he wound up with the single-season school record for passing yards on his final completion. In terms of efficiency, he was dead last among regular Pac-12 starters in passer rating, and the Bears ranked 69th in Passing S&P+. Still, his top four targets—Chris Harper, Bryce Treggs, Kenny Lawler and Darius Powe—all arrived in Berkeley as four-star recruits in 2012, and accounted for the vast majority of those yards last year as sophomores; with a year under their belt in Dykes' system, the passing game should evolve beyond last year's carpet-bombing mentality into something approximating an actual strength. All of the starters and would-be starters who missed time with injuries (defensive ends Brennan Scarlett and Sione Sina, tackle Mustafa Jalil, linebacker Hardy Nickerson, cornerback Stefan McClure and safety Avery Sebastian on defense; Chris Adcock and Matt Cochran on the offensive line) are expected back, with particularly high hopes for Nickerson as a redshirt sophomore. On paper, at least, the Bears have the look of a team that is going to come out of nowhere to ruin somebody's season. But for now, playing spoiler is as good as it gets.

2015 Draft Prospects: None.

SOUTH DIVISION

No. 10 USC Trojans (9-3, 7-2)

2013: 10-4 (6-3) / F/+ #11 / FEI #20 / S&P+ #13 / Program F/+: #20					
2013 Offense			**2013 Defense**		
Offensive F/+	6.5%	37	Defensive F/+	21.5%	5
Offensive FEI	0.314	28	Defensive FEI	-0.643	6
Offensive S&P+	101.4	59	Defensive S&P+	144.5	4
Rushing S&P+	111.3	38	Rushing S&P+	115.7	24
Passing S&P+	109.5	36	Passing S&P+	140.2	5
Standard Downs S&P+	111.6	35	Standard Downs S&P+	132.3	6
Passing Downs S&P+	105.1	51	Passing Downs S&P+	123.8	13
2013 Special Teams			Special Teams F/+	1.0%	46
2014 Projections			SOS Rk	30	
Ret. Starters: 7 OFF, 7 DEF			Offensive F/+	3.5%	40
Proj. F/+	17.6%	10	Defensive F/+	14.1%	8
Mean Wins / Conf Wins	9.2 / 6.6		Conf. / Div. Title Odds	15.8% / 48.7%	

2013 Five Factors			
Efficiency	Off Success Rate+	103.4	46
	Def Success Rate+	124.4	7
	Total Efficiency	227.8	12
Explosiveness	Off IsoPPP+	106.5	33
	Def IsoPPP+	107.1	33
	Total Explosiveness	213.6	22
Field Position	Field Pos. Adv. (FPA)	0.519	40
Finishing Drives	Off Red Zone S&P+	121.4	13
	Def Red Zone S&P+	102.7	46
	Total Red Zone Rating	224.1	18
Turnovers	Turnover Margin	+6.0	29
	Exp. TO Margin	+3.6	45
	Difference	+2.4	35

USC players had enough tact following Lane Kiffin's untimely demise as head coach to refrain from staging an impromptu parade through downtown L.A. with the marching band playing "Ding-Dong! The Witch Is Dead," but their response on the field wasn't far off. In their last eleven games under Kiffin, dating back to mid-2012, the Trojans were 4-7 with humiliating defeats in 2013 at the hands of Washington State and—the anvil that broke the camel's back—Arizona State. In nine subsequent games post-Kiffin, the same team rallied to go 7-2, including a November upset over the eventual Pac-12 champ, Stanford, and a 45-20 romp over Fresno State in the Las Vegas Bowl. (The former snapped a once-inconceivable four-game losing streak to the Cardinal, and spawned a movement to keep interim coach Ed Orgeron as the permanent boss despite his prominent role in the Kiffin regime and his own dismal record as a head coach at Ole Miss; wisely, athletic director Pat Haden took a longer view.) Suddenly the Trojans looked looser, almost recognizable from the "Pac-1" days. They settled on a quarterback, Cody Kessler, and led the conference in total defense. Left for dead in September, USC clawed its way back to 11th in overall

F/+ following the bowl game, its best finish since Pete Carroll's heyday in 2008.

On the rare occasion that anyone felt compelled to defend Kiffin, it was usually on the grounds that heavy scholarship restrictions, inherited from Carroll, had depleted the roster of its usual depth. But that argument never quite held up, for two reasons: one, a lengthy appeals process allowed USC to sign the full allotment of recruits in 2010 and 2011, classes that supplied the majority of last year's starting lineup; and two, the quality never dipped—based on composite rankings of every major recruiting site by 247Sports.com, the 2010, 2011 and 2012 classes were all regarded as the best incoming crop in the Pac-12 in those seasons, and among the top ten nationally. Among all Kiffin signees, nearly half (36 of 77) ranked among Rivals.com's top 100 prospects in their respective classes, regardless of position, including all three quarterbacks on the 2013 roster. Of 22 starters in Kiffin's final game, all but two (offensive linemen Marcus Martin and Chad Wheeler) came from that four- and five-star pool; 17 were in at least their third year in the program. Steve Sarkisian inherits a lineup that has not only played a lot of football—returning players have combined for 302 career starts—but remains the gold standard for raw talent west of the Mississippi.

Last year, that was more obvious on defense, which shook off the 62-point debacle at Arizona State to finish fifth nationally in Defensive F/+, allowing only 1.4 points per possession over the course of the season. With eight starters back and guaranteed-if-healthy draft picks on every level—Leonard Williams on the line, Hayes Pullard at linebacker, Josh Shaw in the secondary—the 2014 defense is on the short list to top that category. Still, a serious playoff run hinges on more consistency from the offense, and especially from the quarterback. But that's not necessarily a bad bet. As a sophomore, Kessler flourished following the coaching change, turning in an efficiency rating of 151.6 over the final nine games; across the conference, only Marcus Mariota turned in a better number (169.6) after the calendar turned to October. Although the ostensible headliner on offense, Marqise Lee, is now in the NFL, the Trojans actually return their leading receiver, junior Nelson Agholor (56 catches for 918 yards, six touchdowns), as well as junior tailbacks Tre Madden and Javorius "Buck" Allen, who combined for 1,477 yards on 5.4 yards per carry. Allen, who only entered the lineup in November after Madden was limited by a hamstring, went over 100 all-purpose yards in five of the last six games and was voted season MVP by his teammates for essentially a half-season's worth of work. The real question is the offensive line. Last year's unit never quite gelled, ranking 96th in Adjusted Sack Rate, and a combination of injuries, attrition and experimentation left Wheeler as the only constant in the spring, at left tackle. As always, there is no shortage of blue-chip options. It's just a matter of getting them in the right place and keeping them there long enough for the whole to match the sum of its parts.

2015 Draft Prospects: DE/DT Leonard Williams (1) ...WR Nelson Agholor* (1-2), CB Josh Shaw (2-3), TE Randall Telfer (3-4), ILB Hayes Pullard (4-5), G/T Aundrey Walker (4-5).*

No. 16 UCLA Bruins (8-4, 6-3)

2013: 10-3 (6-3) / F/+ #15 / FEI #12 / S&P+ #22 / Program F/+: #50					
2013 Offense			**2013 Defense**		
Offensive F/+	14.4%	15	Defensive F/+	10.9%	23
Offensive FEI	0.501	11	Defensive FEI	-0.417	18
Offensive S&P+	118.7	20	Defensive S&P+	117.6	27
Rushing S&P+	116.2	22	Rushing S&P+	106.3	44
Passing S&P+	119.9	19	Passing S&P+	117.5	22
Standard Downs S&P+	116.1	23	Standard Downs S&P+	108.6	36
Passing Downs S&P+	119.4	28	Passing Downs S&P+	121.1	17
2013 Special Teams			Special Teams F/+	2.5%	18
2014 Projections			SOS Rk	28	
Ret. Starters: 8 OFF, 8 DEF			Offensive F/+	9.4%	17
Proj. F/+	15.8%	16	Defensive F/+	6.4%	28
Mean Wins / Conf Wins	8.3 / 5.8		Conf. / Div. Title Odds	7.2% / 25.1%	

2013 Five Factors			
Efficiency	Off Success Rate+	116.9	13
	Def Success Rate+	98.5	59
	Total Efficiency	215.4	29
Explosiveness	Off IsoPPP+	98.7	69
	Def IsoPPP+	125.8	1
	Total Explosiveness	224.5	6
Field Position	Field Pos. Adv. (FPA)	0.530	26
Finishing Drives	Off Red Zone S&P+	114.2	21
	Def Red Zone S&P+	88.4	91
	Total Red Zone Rating	202.6	59
Turnovers	Turnover Margin	+10.0	19
	Exp. TO Margin	+4.8	37
	Difference	+5.2	24

Listen, reader, obviously you're the discerning type. You know your way around the preseason prediction scene. And of course you know we would never steer you wrong here. But be careful out there: absorb enough of the preseason chatter, and the next thing you know you're putting down a paycheck on UCLA making a dark-horse run to the playoffs. Or do the odds even look that dark? Elsewhere, the Bruins are unanimous favorites to take the Pac-12 South, and to land somewhere in the top ten nationally—a lot of love for a program that hasn't finished in the top ten since 1998, or anywhere in the final AP poll in 13 of 15 seasons since. One prominent pundit, Phil Steele, projected UCLA in his top five; another, Fox Sports' Tim Brando, has forecast the Bruins at No. 1.

In part, that's a testament to coach Jim Mora, who has more wins in his first two seasons (19) than any new coach in UCLA history. In bigger part, it's a testament to the forecasters' respect for junior quarterback Brett Hundley, a run/pass prototype in the EJ Manuel mold who passed on a possible first-round projection last winter to pad his college resumé. As a sophomore, Hundley accounted for just shy of two-thirds of UCLA's total offense, including a lion's share of the production on the ground; excluding sacks, he rushed for a team-best 970 yards, helping the ground game actually improve over 2012 in terms of yards per game, yards per carry and Rushing S&P+ despite the departure of All-American tailback Johnathan Franklin. (Hundley also led all Pac-12 rushers in Opportunity Rate, at 53.0 percent.) Defensively, the spotlight falls on sophomore Myles Jack, arguably the most impressive true freshman in the nation last year as both an All-Pac-12 linebacker (second team) and a part-time tailback when injuries depleted the backfield in November. In front of Jack, the Bruins have five-star potential on the defensive line in Eddie Vanderdoes, Ellis McCarthy, and Owa Odighizuwa; behind him, all four starters are back in the secondary. What's not to like? Short answer: the offensive line, a patchwork unit that wound up starting three true freshmen over the second half of the season, ranked 109th in Adjusted Sack Rate, and lost its best player, by far, in all-conference guard Xavier Su'a-Filo. The longer answer is that the offense as a whole looked like a liability against the league's upper crust, managing just 10 points against Stanford and 14 against Oregon and falling well short of 300 total yards in both games. Against Arizona State, a second-half rally couldn't overcome a lethargic first half in a loss that decided the division for ASU. For his part, Hundley was picked off five times in those three games with an efficiency rating of 120.2, more than 40 points below his rating in UCLA's wins, and none of his receivers ranked among the top 150 nationally for the season in yards per target. Against another relentless schedule—Texas, Arizona State and Oregon in the first six games, followed by Arizona, Washington, USC and Stanford in November—the bar for a playoff run is set way too high to expect such a leap. We estimate less than a 15 percent chance of UCLA escaping either of those two stretches unscathed, let alone both of them.

2015 Draft Prospects: QB Brett Hundley (1-2), ILB Eric Kendricks (3-4), G Malcolm Bunche (5-6), RB Jordon James (6-7), FS Anthony Jefferson (6-7), DE Owamagbe Odighizuwa (7-FA).*

No. 19 Arizona State Sun Devils (8-4, 6-3)

2013: 10-4 (8-1) / F/+ #13 / FEI #10 / S&P+ #16 / Program F/+: #33					
2013 Offense			**2013 Defense**		
Offensive F/+	17.7%	11	Defensive F/+	10.4%	26
Offensive FEI	0.597	6	Defensive FEI	-0.387	22
Offensive S&P+	124.6	14	Defensive S&P+	118.1	26
Rushing S&P+	123.2	13	Rushing S&P+	112.5	30
Passing S&P+	125.9	14	Passing S&P+	121.9	15
Standard Downs S&P+	117.6	18	Standard Downs S&P+	121.2	12
Passing Downs S&P+	137.5	11	Passing Downs S&P+	114.7	34
2013 Special Teams			Special Teams F/+	0.3%	60
2014 Projections			SOS Rk	32	
Ret. Starters: 7 OFF, 3 DEF			Offensive F/+	11.7%	12
Proj. F/+	14.2%	19	Defensive F/+	2.6%	50
Mean Wins / Conf Wins	8.2 / 5.5		Conf. / Div. Title Odds	5.0% / 19.7%	

2013 Five Factors			
Efficiency	Off Success Rate+	115.0	21
	Def Success Rate+	122.0	8
	Total Efficiency	237.0	4
Explosiveness	Off IsoPPP+	116.3	7
	Def IsoPPP+	91.2	108
	Total Explosiveness	207.4	39
Field Position	Field Pos. Adv. (FPA)	0.540	15
Finishing Drives	Off Red Zone S&P+	109.7	29
	Def Red Zone S&P+	85.8	99
	Total Red Zone Rating	195.6	72
Turnovers	Turnover Margin	+15.0	5
	Exp. TO Margin	+6.6	20
	Difference	+8.4	9

Stop the tape on Thanksgiving weekend, and the 2013 Sun Devils look like a team out for blood. At 10-2, Arizona State ended the regular season ranked fourth nationally in overall F/+. Half of those victories came at the expense of top-30 opponents—Wisconsin, USC, Washington, UCLA and Arizona, respectively—by an average margin of 18.8 points. With a 58-21 romp over Arizona, the Sun Devils had just clinched home field for the Pac-12 title game, where they were slight favorites to punch their ticket to the Rose Bowl against Stanford. Unfortunately, "pause" was not an option. In the postseason, ASU was brought to earth first by the Cardinal, in a 38-14 rout, and then by Texas Tech in the Holiday Bowl, a 37-23 upset that stood as arguably the most shocking result in a bowl season full of them. (The Raiders, who closed out their regular season by losing five straight by an average margin of 30 points, arrived as two-touchdown underdogs.)

Most of the credit for that success belongs to an offense that finished 11th nationally in Offensive F/+ and 10th in scoring, and that should production should hold steady. Senior quarterback Taylor Kelly (148.1 efficiency in 27 career starts) and junior wide receiver Jaelen Strong (75 catches for 1,122 yards, seven touchdowns in 2013) are the best pass-catch combo in the conference. Key departures at tailback and left tackle, respectively, will be blunted by a pair of proven commodities, D.J. Foster and Jamil Douglas. Meanwhile, juco transfer Eric Lauderdale is expected to add a second receiving threat that was sorely missing opposite Strong, while Auburn transfer Christian Westerman, a former five-star recruit, is set to inherit Douglas' old spot at left guard. The biggest goal for the offense will be to improve consistency, as last year Arizona State was 10th nationally in explosive drive production but 60th when it came to avoiding three-and-outs.

The defense is a much greater concern. Ten of last year's top dozen tacklers are gone, five of whom were first- or second-team All-Pac-12 picks by league coaches. The cornerbacks, in particular, are huge question mark following the graduation of both 2013 starters and the abrupt transfer of projected starter Rashad Wadood in June. In their place, the Devils will rely on a transfer from Pitt (Lloyd Carrington), a juco transfer who has yet to set foot on campus (Kweishi Brown), and—if worst comes to worst—a converted safety, Damarious Randall, in which case Randall's position on the back end would likely fall to one of several redshirt freshmen.

Beyond any personnel decisions, though, there's the burden of another unrelenting schedule, which stacks four of the conference's highest hurdles—UCLA, USC, Stanford and

Washington—in back-to-back-to-back-to-back games at midseason. Arizona State could easily be one of the top 15 or 20 teams in the nation and still hit November nursing a losing record, with Notre Dame and trips to Oregon State and Arizona still to go. (Unlike UCLA, which is facing the full brunt of the North Division's top half, ASU does catch a break by missing Oregon in the cross-division draw for the second year in a row.) The 2013 Devils were remarkably healthy in the regular season, but if the meat of the schedule amounts to a series of toss-ups, a few untimely absences could have a dramatic affect on the final record.

2015 Draft Prospects: WR Jaelen Strong (1-2), QB Taylor Kelly (3-4), G/T Jamil Douglas (7-FA).*

No. 36 Arizona Wildcats (7-5, 5-4)

2013: 8-5 (4-5) / F/+ #25 / FEI #26 / S&P+ #33 / Program F/+: #41						2013 Five Factors			
2013 Offense			**2013 Defense**			Efficiency	Off Success Rate+	115.2	19
Offensive F/+	10.4%	25	Defensive F/+	10.4%	27		Def Success Rate+	109.4	31
Offensive FEI	0.430	19	Defensive FEI	-0.404	19		Total Efficiency	224.6	19
Offensive S&P+	108.3	42	Defensive S&P+	116.3	31	Explosiveness	Off IsoPPP+	90.8	109
Rushing S&P+	120.3	15	Rushing S&P+	115.8	23		Def IsoPPP+	108.8	24
Passing S&P+	103.8	58	Passing S&P+	108.5	37		Total Explosiveness	199.6	70
Standard Downs S&P+	115.5	25	Standard Downs S&P+	111.0	29	Field Position	Field Pos. Adv. (FPA)	0.508	52
Passing Downs S&P+	98.0	64	Passing Downs S&P+	118.7	23	Finishing Drives	Off Red Zone S&P+	105.6	39
2013 Special Teams			Special Teams F/+	-2.7%	106		Def Red Zone S&P+	107.2	36
2014 Projections			SOS Rk	21			Total Red Zone Rating	212.8	33
Ret. Starters: 6 OFF, 6 DEF			Offensive F/+	5.7%	34	Turnovers	Turnover Margin	+4.0	38
Proj. F/+	8.8%	36	Defensive F/+	3.1%	48		Exp. TO Margin	-1.6	84
Mean Wins / Conf Wins	7.1 / 4.5		Conf. / Div. Title Odds	0.8% / 5.6%			Difference	+5.6	22

Arizona has never been a pipeline destination for blue-chip recruits, and despite Rich Rodriguez's best efforts, it isn't about to become one anytime soon. With a little patience, though, and a keen ear to the ground in the transfer market, Rodriguez has managed to turn his locker room into a kind of second-hand shop for the formerly hyped. As of early June, the Wildcats' roster includes eight players who began their careers as four-star signees in more high-profile settings, all but one of whom are eligible in 2014. (For some context: based on 247Sports' composite recruiting rankings, Rich Rod's first three classes at Arizona yielded just six four-star recruits between them, including four in the incoming class this fall.) The reclamation trend is most obvious at quarterback, where the spring competition revolved around refugees Jesse Scroggins (originally at USC), Connor Brewer (Texas) and Jerrard Randall (LSU), and at wide receiver, where sophomores DaVonte' Neal (Notre Dame) and Cayleb Jones (Texas) made inroads on the depth chart after sitting out 2013. Neal, especially, has the look of a breakout threat in the slot, no minor distinction at a position that already includes a pair of sophomore incumbents, Nate Phillips and Samajie Grant, who combined for 1,069 yards on 98 receptions as true freshmen. They'll be flanked on the outside by senior Austin Hill, a 2012 all-conference pick coming off a torn ACL that cost him all of 2013.

At his previous stops, Rodriguez was known as a spread-to-run evangelist, a theme that's been revived in Arizona due to the over-the-top success of departed running back Ka'Deem Carey. (Carey led the nation in rushing yards in 2012 and finished second last year, averaging just shy of 27 carries per game over both seasons.) But the "Spread 'n Shred" has not always been as one-dimensional as that reputation suggests; including sacks, the 2012 team actually passed slightly more often that it ran. Furthermore, the personnel this time around clearly lends itself to the air. There is no apparent heir to Carey's workhorse role in the backfield, the candidates at quarterback are all prototypical pocket types, and there is proven production at receiver with or without the influx of second-chance talent. On the other hand, four starters are back from a line that ranked second in the conference in Adjusted Line Yards, and Rodriguez has always found a way to make hay on the ground even if it takes a committee.

Now, for the part of the conversation where Michigan fans remind you that Rich Rod's track record on defense is a lot less reassuring. True, but the upgrade from year one to year two in Tucson was undeniable. After ranking 68th in Defensive F/+ in 2012, and 59th in Defensive Rushing S&P+, Arizona came in 27th overall and 23rd against the run last year, capping the turnaround by holding Boston College's Andre Williams—the only back nationally with more rushing yards than Carey—to 75 yards on just 2.9 yards per carry in the Independence Bowl. On the scoreboard, the 2012 Wildcats yielded 36 points or more eight times; in 2013, only twice. Size is still an issue for a three-man front: the new nose tackle, Dwight Melvin, is listed at 6-foot-1, 272 pounds, hardly ideal for absorbing double teams from blockers 20 to 30 pounds heavier. On the second level, though, seniors Tra'Mayne Bondurant and Jared Tevis have 52 career starts and 354 tackles between them in the hybrid OLB/SS roles, "Bandit" and "Spur," and as a true freshman last year, linebacker Scooby Wright (80 tackles, 9 TFLs) was the unexpected equal of senior tackle machines Jake Fisher and Marquis Flowers. Make no mistake, a projected regression to 48th in Defensive F/+ indicates this is still a decidedly middle-of-the-pack group. Still, at the very least it's no longer one that figures to put the burden on the offense to score 40 points on a weekly basis.

2015 Draft Prospects: WR Austin Hill (3-4), FS Tra'Mayne Bondurant (4), SS Jared Tevis (5-6), OT Mickey Baucus (7-FA), OT Fabbians Ebbele (7-FA).

No. 44 Utah Utes (5-7, 3-6)

2013: 5-7 (2-7) / F/+ #31 / FEI #30 / S&P+ #39 / Program F/+: #43					
2013 Offense			**2013 Defense**		
Offensive F/+	5.1%	42	Defensive F/+	7.3%	30
Offensive FEI	0.232	35	Defensive FEI	-0.241	34
Offensive S&P+	102.4	53	Defensive S&P+	117.1	29
Rushing S&P+	104.4	58	Rushing S&P+	121.9	16
Passing S&P+	108.9	40	Passing S&P+	112.7	31
Standard Downs S&P+	113.1	30	Standard Downs S&P+	115.3	24
Passing Downs S&P+	95.6	74	Passing Downs S&P+	115.2	31
2013 Special Teams			Special Teams F/+	1.5%	39
2014 Projections			SOS Rk	13	
Ret. Starters: 6 OFF, 5 DEF			Offensive F/+	-0.1%	70
Proj. F/+	6.0%	44	Defensive F/+	6.1%	30
Mean Wins / Conf Wins	5.2 / 3.2		Conf. / Div. Title Odds	0.1% / 0.9%	

2013 Five Factors			
Efficiency	Off Success Rate+	97.9	69
	Def Success Rate+	115.5	15
	Total Efficiency	213.3	33
Explosiveness	Off IsoPPP+	115.9	8
	Def IsoPPP+	96.5	83
	Total Explosiveness	212.4	25
Field Position	Field Pos. Adv. (FPA)	0.468	101
Finishing Drives	Off Red Zone S&P+	97.3	74
	Def Red Zone S&P+	110.5	24
	Total Red Zone Rating	207.7	48
Turnovers	Turnover Margin	-9.0	113
	Exp. TO Margin	+3.6	44
	Difference	-12.6	124

Utah finished 5-7 in 2012 and 5-7 again in 2013, so we're aware that predicting another 5-7 finish in 2014 probably looks like shooting fish in a barrel. But actually, from a projection standpoint, this team is a bona fide wild card. For starters, there is the status of junior quarterback Travis Wilson, whose sophomore season—and possibly his career—was cut short by the discovery of a damaged cranial artery last November. (He was cleared to play in early July.) As for the rest of the team, how do we accurately account for a sub-.500 outfit that was nevertheless good enough to A) upset Stanford, and B) build fourth-quarter leads in four of its seven losses? Even as the disappointments mounted, the Utes spent most of the season among the top 25 in overall F/+, eventually landing at No. 31—up 35 spots from 2012, and more than ten spots better than any other team with a losing record.

The disparity can be explained away by devastating turnovers, a total of 53.4 points in field position and scoring value forfeited over the course of the season. The value lost on turnovers in losses to Oregon State (-12.2), UCLA (-14.7), USC (-16.4), and Arizona State (-3.1) all exceeded Utah's scoring deficit in those games. If Utah had thrown one fewer interception in each of those four games—10 picks instead of 14 isn't too much to ask, is it?—they would have found themselves in the thick of the division race.

With Wilson or without, though, the buck stops with the lack of reliable firepower on offense. In Pac-12 games, the Utes ranked 11th in the conference in total offense (364.9 yards per game) and tenth in scoring (25.6 points per game), failing to top 27 points except in a pair of shootout losses. They also ranked 11th in plays covering at least 20 yards from scrimmage (36). On that front, senior wide receiver Dres Anderson (son of Flipper Anderson) is a legitimate deep threat, averaging 18.9 yards per catch with four touchdowns from 40 or longer. But Wilson can be erratic at any distance—at 56.1 percent, he was the only Pac-12 starter last year with a completion rate below 60 percent for the season, and he was picked off 16 times in nine games—and none of his would-be successors are going to scare opposing defenses with their arm strength. Without more from a perennially mediocre ground game, the defense is left with too little margin for error.

2015 Draft Prospects: WR Dres Anderson (4-5), SS/OLB Brian Blechen (6-7), DE Nate Orchard (7-FA), G Junior Salt (7-FA).

No. 98 Colorado Buffaloes (2-10, 1-8)

2013: 4-8 (1-8) / F/+ #95 / FEI #104 / S&P+ #101 / Program F/+: #109					
2013 Offense			**2013 Defense**		
Offensive F/+	-6.7%	87	Defensive F/+	-6.2%	88
Offensive FEI	-0.196	85	Defensive FEI	0.165	85
Offensive S&P+	88.7	94	Defensive S&P+	93.2	95
Rushing S&P+	79.9	116	Rushing S&P+	96.2	80
Passing S&P+	105.9	49	Passing S&P+	98.6	70
Standard Downs S&P+	97.0	76	Standard Downs S&P+	98.1	77
Passing Downs S&P+	92.8	83	Passing Downs S&P+	95.4	80
2013 Special Teams			Special Teams F/+	-1.9%	97
2014 Projections			SOS Rk	18	
Ret. Starters: 7 OFF, 8 DEF			Offensive F/+	-5.9%	94
Proj. F/+	-10.2%	98	Defensive F/+	-4.2%	88
Mean Wins / Conf Wins	2.5 / 0.6		Conf. / Div. Title Odds	0.0% / 0.0%	

2013 Five Factors			
Efficiency	Off Success Rate+	96.2	74
	Def Success Rate+	98.3	60
	Total Efficiency	194.6	75
Explosiveness	Off IsoPPP+	96.1	85
	Def IsoPPP+	95.7	90
	Total Explosiveness	191.8	96
Field Position	Field Pos. Adv. (FPA)	0.457	111
Finishing Drives	Off Red Zone S&P+	86.9	106
	Def Red Zone S&P+	107.8	33
	Total Red Zone Rating	194.7	76
Turnovers	Turnover Margin	-3.0	82
	Exp. TO Margin	+2.6	49
	Difference	-5.6	109

Colorado literally could not have been worse last year than it was in 2012, when its overall F/+ score ranked 124th out of 124 teams, and it did manage some inevitable, incremental progress relative to rock bottom. At 4-8, the Buffaloes avoided the humiliation of repeating as the absolute worst team in big-time college football, or even the worst in the Pac-12. (Thanks, Cal!) Beyond that distinction, though, any sense of forward momentum was superficial at best. Of the Buffs' four wins, two came against a pair of FCS patsies, Central Arkansas and Charleston Southern; a third came at the expense of the aforementioned Bears, who didn't come close to beating another FBS opponent. In its other eight conference games, Colorado was routinely obliterated, dropping seven of them by at least 22 points apiece; the average margin in those games, 29 points, was nearly identical to the scoring gap in 2012. Had they not been forced to cancel a September date with Fresno State due to wildfires—Charleston Southern was subsequently added as a de facto make-up game—it might have been impossible to tell the difference on paper at all.

Fortunately, no one made any pretense of expecting otherwise. 2013 was always going to be a transition year under a new head coach, Mike MacIntyre, and the learning curve was exacerbated by the promotion of a true freshman, Sefo Liufau, to starting quarterback at midseason. Elsewhere, true freshmen also led the team in rushing (Michael Adkins II) and tackles (Addison Gillam). Out of 36 returning players who logged at least one start last year, 18 were freshmen or sophomores. The one departure who will clearly be missed is wide receiver Paul Richardson, a second-round pick of the Seahawks who finished with more targets (139), catches (83) and yards (1,343) than any Pac-12 receiver who wasn't Brandin Cooks. Richardson also accounted for 19 of Colorado's 43 plays covering at least 20 yards from scrimmage, fewest of any offense in the conference, and Colorado surrendered nearly twice as many explosive drives (17.1 percent of opponent possessions) as they were producing themselves (9.4 percent). It's hard to imagine a scenario in which those numbers improve without him. If there's any hope of replacing Richardson's production on the whole, it will be the result of a committee approach requiring a half-dozen backs and receivers to pick up part of the slack in piecemeal fashion. Barring a huge, unforeseen leap forward by Liufau, that only gets them back to the first rung above the worst-case scenario, which still leaves a long climb ahead to escape the division cellar.

2015 Draft Prospects: CB Greg Henderson (6-7).

Matt Hinton

Projected Win Probabilities For Pac-12 Teams

			Overall Wins													Conference Wins									
Div	**Conf**	**Pac 12 North**	**12-0**	**11-1**	**10-2**	**9-3**	**8-4**	**7-5**	**6-6**	**5-7**	**4-8**	**3-9**	**2-10**	**1-11**	**0-12**	**9-0**	**8-1**	**7-2**	**6-3**	**5-4**	**4-5**	**3-6**	**2-7**	**1-8**	**0-9**
-	-	California	-	-	-	-	-	-	-	3	13	34	40	10	-	-	-	-	-	-	1	7	29	49	14
73	54	Oregon	24	39	26	9	2	-	-	-	-	-	-	-	-	30	41	22	6	1	-	-	-	-	-
1	-	Oregon State	-	-	3	12	27	32	19	6	1	-	-	-	-	-	-	3	14	30	33	16	4	-	-
24	16	Stanford	4	18	31	28	14	4	1	-	-	-	-	-	-	5	23	35	25	10	2	-	-	-	-
2	1	Washington*	-	2	11	25	30	21	9	2	-	-	-	-	-	-	3	12	27	31	20	6	1	-	-
-	-	Washington State	-	-	-	-	1	3	12	25	31	21	6	1	-	-	-	-	-	1	8	22	36	27	6
Div	**Conf**	**Pac 12 South**	**12-0**	**11-1**	**10-2**	**9-3**	**8-4**	**7-5**	**6-6**	**5-7**	**4-8**	**3-9**	**2-10**	**1-11**	**0-12**	**9-0**	**8-1**	**7-2**	**6-3**	**5-4**	**4-5**	**3-6**	**2-7**	**1-8**	**0-9**
6	1	Arizona	-	-	3	12	24	29	20	10	2	-	-	-	-	-	1	5	16	29	29	16	4	-	-
20	5	Arizona State	-	4	13	25	28	19	9	2	-	-	-	-	-	1	4	17	29	28	16	4	1	-	-
-	-	Colorado	-	-	-	-	-	-	-	3	13	32	35	15	2	-	-	-	-	-	-	1	10	38	51
25	7	UCLA	1	4	14	26	28	18	7	2	-	-	-	-	-	1	7	21	31	26	11	3	-	-	-
48	16	USC	2	12	28	30	19	7	2	-	-	-	-	-	-	3	18	34	29	13	3	-	-	-	-
1	-	Utah	-	-	-	1	3	12	24	30	21	8	1	-	-	-	-	-	2	11	25	34	22	6	-

**Washington will play 13 regular season games; for projected overall records, 12-0 means 13-0, 11-1 means 12-1, etc.*

Southeastern Conference

You might want to brace yourself for this: The SEC may not have been the best conference in the country last year.

Going by average F/+ ratings, the Pac-12 came out ahead of the SEC, plus-16.2 percent to plus-15.4 percent, for the title of FBS' Best Conference. (And before you go blaming No. 87 Arkansas and No. 97 Kentucky for dragging the SEC down, remember that the Pac-12 had No. 95 Colorado and No. 103 California.) The league that has defined itself as college football's most consistently strong circuit was certainly still very good, but defenses were younger and thinner than normal, and injuries struck down a few league offenses. It was all just enough to lend to the numbers a Pacific Coast bias.

And to top it off, the SEC's seven-year national title streak ended when Florida State knocked off Auburn in the final seconds of the final BCS Championship game.

Does this mean we're headed toward a golden age of conference parity in college football after a decade of Southern dominance? Yeah, probably not. While quite a few SEC teams must replace experienced quarterbacks and key offensive pieces, the defenses are once again seasoned and stacked. And when you combine that with further dominance on the recruiting side, you get some pretty powerful projections: four SEC teams in the top nine, six in the top 13, and 10 in the top 30.

Auburn and Texas A&M are projected ninth and 13th in the country ... and are expected to go 8-4. LSU stands at seventh and 9-3. No. 29 Mississippi State would be projected fifth in the Big Ten and ACC and fourth in the Big 12; the Bulldogs are sixth in the SEC West.

The SEC will be back in 2014, which is a strange thing to say because the SEC never actually went anywhere. And it will be defense-heavy, just as it was in basically every season B.J.F. (Before Johnny Football).

The story lines are almost as deep as the conference itself. Can 'Bama overcome turnover at quarterback and move past last season's rotten end? Is Auburn ready to make another title run considering last year's required two miracle finishes? Does depth trump star power for South Carolina? What the hell happened at Florida last year? Is there going to be anybody left in the Georgia secondary by the time the season begins? When does great recruiting turn into great results in College Station and Oxford? Is Anthony Jennings the man to lead a new LSU offense? What does Missouri do for an encore after last season's stunning run to 12 wins? No, seriously, what the hell happened at Florida last year? And while the league's quality wasn't at its highest-ever level, can the SEC possibly top the drama it created last season?

WEST DIVISION

No. 2 Alabama Crimson Tide (11-1, 7-1)

2013: 11-2 (7-1) / F/+ #2 / FEI #3 / S&P+ #2 / Program F/+: #1					
2013 Offense			**2013 Defense**		
Offensive F/+	17.8%	10	Defensive F/+	19.3%	7
Offensive FEI	0.551	9	Defensive FEI	-0.555	7
Offensive S&P+	128.7	10	Defensive S&P+	142.3	5
Rushing S&P+	127.8	6	Rushing S&P+	143.7	3
Passing S&P+	128.6	12	Passing S&P+	115.7	24
Standard Downs S&P+	123.2	10	Standard Downs S&P+	124.7	9
Passing Downs S&P+	142.0	7	Passing Downs S&P+	132.5	6
2013 Special Teams			Special Teams F/+	5.2%	1
2014 Projections			SOS Rk	45	
Ret. Starters: 7 OFF, 5 DEF			Offensive F/+	14.5%	5
Proj. F/+	29.9%	2	Defensive F/+	15.3%	6
Mean Wins / Conf Wins	11.3 / 7.3		Conf. / Div. Title Odds	66.3% / 83.3%	

2013 Five Factors			
Efficiency	Off Success Rate+	121.6	6
	Def Success Rate+	120.1	9
	Total Efficiency	241.7	3
Explosiveness	Off IsoPPP+	107.7	29
	Def IsoPPP+	111.8	16
	Total Explosiveness	219.6	12
Field Position	Field Pos. Adv. (FPA)	0.560	4
Finishing Drives	Off Red Zone S&P+	124.6	8
	Def Red Zone S&P+	122.8	9
	Total Red Zone Rating	247.5	4
Turnovers	Turnover Margin	+2.0	48
	Exp. TO Margin	+9.4	9
	Difference	-7.4	117

It's incredible how high the bar is set for Alabama. In 2013, Nick Saban's Crimson Tide ranked seventh in our defensive rankings, tenth in our offensive rankings, and first on special teams. On offense, they were sixth in Rushing S&P+, 12th in passing, 10th on standard downs, and seventh on passing downs. On defense, they were third in Rushing S&P+, ninth on standard downs and sixth on passing downs. They were fifth in Adjusted Line Yards on both sides of the ball. They finished in the F/+ top two for the fifth consecutive year. Fifth!

Ask a random Alabama fan or college football fan, however, and 2013 was not only a failure, but perhaps a rather significant one. Because of the flukiest of fluke endings against Auburn, and because of a poor first half against Oklahoma, the Crimson Tide lost two games for only the second time since 2008.

If you are really looking for a sign of Alabama's inevitable decline, we can't stop you, but ... it's not happening. Sure, the

Crimson Tide might have to again settle for being the second-best team in the country behind Florida State. And yes, there are plenty of questions to answer in Tuscaloosa, certainly more than in 2013. Can senior Blake Sims or Florida State transfer Jacob Coker take full command of the offense? Can the offensive line settle in after a second straight year of decent turnover? What new ideas might new offensive coordinator Lane Kiffin bring to the table, and will they be good ones? How much will the Tide miss impact linebackers C.J. Mosley and Adrian Hubbard? And can the already-shaky secondary gel without a pair of awesome safeties in Ha Ha Clinton-Dix and Vinnie Sunseri?

But take a quick glance at who's actually returning to last year's most explosive offense (29.3 percent of possessions averaged at least 10 yards per play), and your questions become less pressing. Alabama not only has T.J. Yeldon (1,235 yards, 6.0 per carry, 6.1 highlight yards per opportunity) at running back; the Tide also have Kenyan Drake, Jalston Fowler, and Sugar Bowl star Derrick Henry, whose combination of speed and size (9.3 highlight yards per opportunity at 235 pounds) is terrifying. They've still got all-world wideout Amari Cooper, who was banged up for much of last season. They've got blue-chip sophomore tight end O.J. Howard, who showed Ozzie Newsome flashes last fall. And despite the loss of Bills second-round pick Cyrus Kouandjio and second-team All-SEC pick Anthony Steen, they still return three starters from the offensive line.

On defense, both the pass rush and secondary will need upgrades. Nick Saban's Tide has never gone heavy after the passer but they have to do better than 2013, when they were a miserable 103rd in Adjusted Sack Rate. End A'Shawn Robinson (8 tackles for loss, 5.5 sacks) is a keeper, but he needs help. The secondary will benefit from greater depth and experience but could still be starting a converted wideout (Cyrus Jones) and a two-year reserve (Bradley Sylve) at cornerback.

Top 2015 draft prospects: SS Landon Collins (1), WR Amari Cooper* (1), RB T.J. Yeldon* (1-2), ILB Trey DePriest (2-3), DT Brandon Ivory (3-4), WR Christion Jones (3-4), G Arie Kouandjio (4-5).*

No. 7 LSU Tigers (9-3, 5-3)

2013: 10-3 (5-3) / F/+ #17 / FEI #15 / S&P+ #19 / Program F/+: #5					
2013 Offense			**2013 Defense**		
Offensive F/+	18.0%	9	Defensive F/+	5.6%	36
Offensive FEI	0.601	5	Defensive FEI	-0.199	38
Offensive S&P+	125.5	13	Defensive S&P+	113.0	35
Rushing S&P+	117.9	18	Rushing S&P+	109.0	40
Passing S&P+	135.5	8	Passing S&P+	118.4	20
Standard Downs S&P+	117.0	20	Standard Downs S&P+	111.1	28
Passing Downs S&P+	147.1	6	Passing Downs S&P+	120.5	19
2013 Special Teams			Special Teams F/+	2.9%	10
2014 Projections			SOS Rk	14	
Ret. Starters: 5 OFF, 7 DEF			Offensive F/+	10.0%	14
Proj. F/+	19.0%	7	Defensive F/+	8.9%	18
Mean Wins / Conf Wins	8.9 / 5.3		Conf. / Div. Title Odds	4.6% / 8.8%	

2013 Five Factors			
Efficiency	Off Success Rate+	115.2	20
	Def Success Rate+	104.5	42
	Total Efficiency	219.6	21
Explosiveness	Off IsoPPP+	115.9	9
	Def IsoPPP+	111.0	17
	Total Explosiveness	226.9	3
Field Position	Field Pos. Adv. (FPA)	0.507	53
Finishing Drives	Off Red Zone S&P+	109.2	31
	Def Red Zone S&P+	120.0	13
	Total Red Zone Rating	229.2	12
Turnovers	Turnover Margin	0.0	61
	Exp. TO Margin	+7.1	17
	Difference	-7.1	115

LSU was hit hard by NFL draft early entry this offseason. Jarvis Landry and Odell Beckham Jr., perhaps the best receiver tandem in the country (combined in 2013: 2,345 receiving yards, 17.2 per catch, 70 percent catch rate), both left Baton Rouge early. So did 1,400-yard rusher Jeremy Hill, two-year starting guard Trai Turner, and two defensive tackles (Ego Ferguson and Anthony Johnson) who combined for 12.5 tackles for loss a year ago. With these players returning for their respective senior seasons, Les Miles' Tigers would have been a national title contender. Instead, they will have to settle for leaning on great-as-always recruiting, a strong offensive line, and a potentially spectacular secondary, which should produce a mere top-10 team. Poor saps.

LSU's No. 7 projection is based mostly on the school's track record. The Bayou Bengals have simply been one of the most consistently stellar programs in the country, winning at least nine games in 12 of the last 14 seasons and finishing with a top-20 F/+ ranking in seven of the last nine. An inexperienced defense did slip a bit in 2013—the Tigers fell from sixth in Defensive F/+ to 36th—but most of the slippage was due to a slow start. Georgia and Mississippi State combined to average 7.0 yards per play and score 70 points in the fifth and sixth games of the season, but LSU dominated down the stretch. The Tigers held Texas A&M to 299 yards and 10 points, then squeezed Iowa for just 233 yards and 14 points.

The loss of Ferguson and Johnson will stunt the progress of what was a relatively inefficient run defense last year (53rd in Rushing Success Rate+), but the back seven of the defense is unimpeachable. Corners Jalen Mills and Tre'Davious White, a sophomore and freshman in 2013, respectively, held their own and combined for 6.5 tackles for loss, five interceptions, and 15 passes defensed. Strongside linebacker Kwon Alexander was a playmaker both close to (6.5 tackles for loss) and further from the line of scrimmage (four passes defensed). LSU ranked 20th in Passing S&P+ and could improve drastically with better health and experience.

As with so many teams in the SEC this year, there are more questions on offense than defense. Sophomore quarterback Anthony Jennings, who filled in for injured Zach Mettenberger late in 2013, is the likely starter. He showed decent pocket instincts and mobility in patches while getting thrown into the fire (11-of-26 for 158 yards with a touchdown and an interception against Arkansas and Iowa). But who will he be throwing to this fall? Landry, Beckham, Hill, and then-senior Kadron Boone combined for 75 percent of LSU's targets in 2013. The leading returning wideout, sophomore Travin Dural, caught seven passes.

The running game is less of a concern. LSU went four-deep at running back last fall, and while two are gone, Senior Terrence Magee (626 yards, 7.3 per carry, 8.7 highlight yards per opportunity) is a lightning rod and will be running behind a line that returns five players with starting experience (74 career starts), including senior tackle La'El Collins.

Top 2015 draft prospects: OT La'el Collins (1-2), CB Jalen Mills (2-3), RB Terrance Magee (5-6), DE Jermauria Rasco (6-7).*

No. 9 Auburn Tigers (8-4, 5-3)

2013: 12-2 (7-1) / F/+ #4 / FEI #4 / S&P+ #7 / Program F/+: #24					
2013 Offense			**2013 Defense**		
Offensive F/+	19.5%	7	Defensive F/+	12.3%	18
Offensive FEI	0.586	7	Defensive FEI	-0.475	10
Offensive S&P+	133.1	6	Defensive S&P+	118.6	24
Rushing S&P+	139.6	2	Rushing S&P+	110.0	36
Passing S&P+	123.1	16	Passing S&P+	118.7	19
Standard Downs S&P+	128.8	7	Standard Downs S&P+	104.7	49
Passing Downs S&P+	139.6	9	Passing Downs S&P+	140.4	3
2013 Special Teams			Special Teams F/+	3.3%	7
2014 Projections			SOS Rk	3	
Ret. Starters: 8 OFF, 6 DEF			Offensive F/+	14.4%	6
Proj. F/+	18.8%	9	Defensive F/+	4.4%	38
Mean Wins / Conf Wins	8.4 / 4.7		Conf. / Div. Title Odds	2.6% / 5.1%	

2013 Five Factors			
Efficiency	Off Success Rate+	122.8	5
	Def Success Rate+	110.4	27
	Total Efficiency	233.2	7
Explosiveness	Off IsoPPP+	112.0	16
	Def IsoPPP+	102.4	50
	Total Explosiveness	214.5	20
Field Position	Field Pos. Adv. (FPA)	0.516	44
Finishing Drives	Off Red Zone S&P+	126.1	6
	Def Red Zone S&P+	142.9	2
	Total Red Zone Rating	269.0	2
Turnovers	Turnover Margin	0.0	61
	Exp. TO Margin	+0.6	66
	Difference	-0.6	64

How does one get an appropriate read for what Auburn is capable of moving forward? The Tigers were incredibly lucky to get to 11-1 and win the West. They could have lost to Washington State and Mississippi State. They needed back-to-back miraculous finishes to beat Georgia (after blowing a huge lead) and Alabama. As well as we remember them playing at times, they still finished only fourth in the F/+ rankings. And now they are tasked with replacing star running back Tre Mason, dominant tackle Greg Robinson, defensive end Dee Ford, and cornerback/Alabama killer Chris Davis. Many are assuming the Tigers will be a top-five team again this fall, but have they earned that leap of faith?

At the same time, however ... did you see them play the last three games of the year? Did you see them rush for 358 yards per game and average 6.5 yards per play against three of the best defenses in the country (Florida State, Alabama, Missouri)? Did you see them nearly beat a Florida State team nobody else in the country could touch? Do you really see the Tigers regressing offensively, no matter who they lose, now that Gus Malzahn's incredible spread-to-run system has been fully implemented?

Whether you view Auburn as a national title contender once again, or whether you think the Tigers might have to settle for being one of many very good teams in the SEC West, probably depends on your view of the defense. It is loaded with former star recruits, from blue-chip sophomores Carl Lason (end) and Montravius Adams (tackle) up front, to juniors Cassanova McKinzy and Kris Frost at linebacker, to senior safeties Jermaine Whitehead and Robenson Therezie in the back. But Auburn's offense needed all those miracles in 2013, because the defense allowed 44.1 percent of opponent drives to cross the Tigers' 30-yard line, the 28th highest rate nationally.

Coordinator Ellis Johnson's unit did improve as the year progressed, but big plays were an issue even with Chris Davis at cornerback. And while the Tigers were outstanding at shutting down drives on passing downs (and stopping scoring opportunities short of the end zone), they often struggled to reach passing downs in the first place.

It may be difficult to know what to make of the defense, but one should just assume the offense will again dominate. Even with the reasonably slow start to the season, Auburn still ranked second in Rushing S&P+ and a respectable 16th in Passing S&P+. The Tigers dominated in the trenches and averaged 5.1 points per trip inside the opponent's 40, third in the country. This was a creative, powerful, devastating offense, and the reasons for that go beyond Mason and Robinson, who really were fantastic.

Quarterback Nick Marshall (1,976 passing yards, 1,193 presack rushing yards) returns and finds quite an arsenal at his disposal. He'll have Cameron Artis-Payne and Corey Grant (combined: 1,257 rushing yards, 8.0 per carry) beside him in the backfield, and he'll throw to a receiving corps that returns almost wholly intact. Plus, his line returns five players with starting experience (113 career starts). Yeah, this offense will be fantastic.

Top 2015 draft prospects: C Reese Dismukes (3-4), RB Corey Grant (3-4), DT Gabe Wright (3-4), FS Jermaine Whitehead (4-5), TE C.J. Uzomah (5-6).

No. 13 Texas A&M Aggies (8-4, 4-4)

2013: 9-4 (4-4) / F/+ #23 / FEI #24 / S&P+ #18 / Program F/+: #13					
2013 Offense			**2013 Defense**		
Offensive F/+	24.0%	1	Defensive F/+	-5.1%	86
Offensive FEI	0.738	1	Defensive FEI	0.193	87
Offensive S&P+	139.2	4	Defensive S&P+	100.3	76
Rushing S&P+	130.8	4	Rushing S&P+	97.0	77
Passing S&P+	143.1	4	Passing S&P+	101.1	62
Standard Downs S&P+	131.6	2	Standard Downs S&P+	99.9	68
Passing Downs S&P+	153.8	3	Passing Downs S&P+	98.0	75
2013 Special Teams			Special Teams F/+	2.3%	21
2014 Projections			SOS Rk	2	
Ret. Starters: 6 OFF, 9 DEF			Offensive F/+	17.4%	2
Proj. F/+	16.3%	13	Defensive F/+	-1.1%	67
Mean Wins / Conf Wins	8.1 / 4.1		Conf. / Div. Title Odds	0.5% / 1.2%	

2013 Five Factors			
Efficiency	Off Success Rate+	128.2	3
	Def Success Rate+	99.2	56
	Total Efficiency	227.4	14
Explosiveness	Off IsoPPP+	113.9	12
	Def IsoPPP+	96.2	87
	Total Explosiveness	210.1	29
Field Position	Field Pos. Adv. (FPA)	0.550	7
Finishing Drives	Off Red Zone S&P+	135.6	3
	Def Red Zone S&P+	99.4	62
	Total Red Zone Rating	235.0	8
Turnovers	Turnover Margin	+1.0	53
	Exp. TO Margin	+1.5	60
	Difference	-0.5	63

It looks to be a second straight transition year in College Station, both on the field and around it. As A&M continues to add on to Kyle Field—the goal, in the ongoing manhood measurement contest, is to make it bigger than Tennessee's Neyland Stadium by about 50 seats—head coach Kevin Sumlin continues to rebuild and supplement what he inherited.

Two years ago, the Aggies made the most perfect conference transition of all time. They hired a new coach, unleashed Johnny Manziel on the world, and went from 7-6 in the Big 12 to 11-2 in the SEC. But in 2013, with a rebuilding defense that was then blown apart by injuries (only one lineman and two linebackers played in all 13 games), they fell from third in the F/+ rankings to 23rd and needed a last-second win over Duke in the Chick-Fil-A Bowl to finish 9-4. The offense was spectacular despite nagging injury issues for Manziel, but the defense plummeted to 86th in Defensive F/+, struggling to generate any sort of push up front and putting too much pressure on the secondary to make plays.

The Aggies' defense returns basically everybody of consequence, so it should improve in 2014. A lot of young players got experience because of injuries, and a thin two-deep is now rather plump. Corners Deshazor Everett (senior) and De'Vante Harris (junior) are strong, and sophomore linebackers Shaan Washington and Darian Claiborne combined for 11 tackles for loss and 4.5 sacks in 2013. (Claiborne also proved a little reckless off the field, getting arrested for drug possession in December and for a noise violation in February.) And while the defensive line wasn't very good in 2013, it at least goes three-deep with experience. Defensive coordinator Mark Snyder, retained despite last year's struggles, should have quite a bit more to work with this fall.

The defense will have to improve, not only because it was an anchor last season, but because it will also need to account for some potential offensive regression. Tackle Jake Matthews (Atlanta), receiver Mike Evans (Tampa Bay), and Manziel (Cleveland) were all first-round draft picks. Throw in the loss of running back Ben Malena and two other key wideouts, and you've got a bit of a rebuilding project on your hands.

Of course, you probably shouldn't cry too hard for Sumlin and coordinator Jake Spavital. His offense still has an exciting set of junior running backs (Tra Carson, Trey Williams, and Brandon Williams combined for 1,005 yards, 6.1 per carry). It still has senior possession receiver Malcome Kennedy (658 receiving yards, 11.0 per catch, 71 percent catch rate) and a mass of highly touted sophomores (Ricky Seals-Jones, LaQuvionte Gonzalez, Edward Pope, Ja'Quay Williams, all of whom were four-star recruits). And despite losing a tackle to the top 10 of the draft for two straight years, it still has one of the nation's best offensive lines, this time led by senior tackle Cedric Ogbuehi.

Top 2015 draft prospects: OT Cedric Ogbuehi (1), CB Deshazor Everett (3-4), G Jarvis Harrison (6-7).

No. 23 Ole Miss Rebels (7-5, 4-4)

2013: 8-5 (3-5) / F/+ #28 / FEI #28 / S&P+ #29 / Program F/+: #46					
2013 Offense			**2013 Defense**		
Offensive F/+	5.3%	41	Defensive F/+	12.0%	20
Offensive FEI	0.216	37	Defensive FEI	-0.387	23
Offensive S&P+	104.5	47	Defensive S&P+	125.0	18
Rushing S&P+	104.7	55	Rushing S&P+	122.5	14
Passing S&P+	105.3	50	Passing S&P+	114.7	27
Standard Downs S&P+	97.0	77	Standard Downs S&P+	118.6	17
Passing Downs S&P+	121.8	23	Passing Downs S&P+	118.8	22
2013 Special Teams			Special Teams F/+	-1.2%	92
2014 Projections			SOS Rk	17	
Ret. Starters: 6 OFF, 9 DEF			Offensive F/+	0.0%	68
Proj. F/+	11.8%	23	Defensive F/+	11.8%	12
Mean Wins / Conf Wins	7.4 / 4.0		Conf. / Div. Title Odds	0.3% / 1.1%	

2013 Five Factors			
Efficiency	Off Success Rate+	100.3	61
	Def Success Rate+	107.6	34
	Total Efficiency	207.8	46
Explosiveness	Off IsoPPP+	102.4	48
	Def IsoPPP+	114.1	10
	Total Explosiveness	216.4	16
Field Position	Field Pos. Adv. (FPA)	0.488	79
Finishing Drives	Off Red Zone S&P+	106.7	37
	Def Red Zone S&P+	99.2	63
	Total Red Zone Rating	205.9	50
Turnovers	Turnover Margin	+1.0	53
	Exp. TO Margin	-5.3	108
	Difference	+6.3	18

Despite what Gus Malzahn and Auburn would have you believe, rebuilding takes a while. Even when you recruit like crazy, as Ole Miss head coach Hugh Freeze has done over the last two years, it takes a while to build depth and develop even the most exciting, precocious freshmen and sophomores. Freeze has laid some impressive groundwork in his two years in Oxford; he inherited a team that had gone 6-18 in its previous two seasons, and he immediately engineered back-to-back bowl campaigns. His Rebels beat Texas and LSU in 2013, and according to Rivals.com, he has inked the No. 7 (in 2013) and No. 19 (2014) classes in the country.

Nineteen four- and five-star recruits have signed for Ole Miss in the last two years, but again, it takes a while. Freeze's Rebels were young, exciting, and dreadfully inconsistent in 2013, and while the experience is growing, it appears there are just enough holes in 2014 to again hold the Rebels back.

Most of those holes are on the offensive side of the ball. A rather average line returns future All-American sophomore Laremy Tunsil at left tackle, but of the eight players who finished 2013 with starting experience, only three return. They'll be blocking for a pair of junior running backs, Jaylen Walton and I'Tavius Mathers, who are exciting but relatively inefficient. They combined for 1,095 rushing yards and 5.2 yards per carry, but only 36 percent of their carries gained five or more yards for just 5.7 highlight yards per opportunity.

Inefficiency was an issue all year for the Rebels. They ranked 10th nationally in avoiding three-and-outs (29.1 percent of possessions) but only 52nd in points per drive (2.3). The running game was all-or-nothing, and while there were some solid efficiency options in the passing game—sophomore wideout Laquon Treadwell, senior Vince Sanders, tight end Evan Engram, and Walton all caught at least 20 passes with a 70 percent catch rate—the best option was still Donte Moncrief, third-round pick of the Indianapolis Colts, who averaged 15.9 yards per catch with just a 53 percent catch rate. Treadwell, a former blue-chipper, caught 72 passes but averaged only 8.4 yards per catch. That quarterback Bo Wallace and Treadwell return is a good thing, but the duo needs to get the ball downfield more.

If the offense produces, the defense will make it pay off. Despite a rather undersized line, Ole Miss was 14th in Rushing S&P+ and sixth in Adjusted Line Yards in 2013. The line returns four of its top five tacklers, including sophomore blue-chipper Robert Nkemdiche (eight tackles for loss), along with speedy outside linebackers Serderius Bryant and Denzel Nkemdiche. The pass defense, meanwhile, was fantastic at limiting big plays thanks to the safety trio of Cody Prewitt, Tony Conner, and Trae Elston, who are all back.

Top 2015 draft prospects: FS Cody Prewitt (2-3), OLB C.J. Johnson (4-5), QB Bo Wallace (6-7).

No. 29 Mississippi State Bulldogs (8-4, 4-4)

2013: 7-6 (3-5) / F/+ #33 / FEI #32 / S&P+ #28 / Program F/+: #44

2013 Offense			2013 Defense		
Offensive F/+	2.9%	50	Defensive F/+	12.1%	19
Offensive FEI	0.121	46	Defensive FEI	-0.359	25
Offensive S&P+	102.2	56	Defensive S&P+	127.8	14
Rushing S&P+	105.4	53	Rushing S&P+	124.8	10
Passing S&P+	107.6	46	Passing S&P+	119.9	18
Standard Downs S&P+	105.1	53	Standard Downs S&P+	109.7	32
Passing Downs S&P+	110.2	43	Passing Downs S&P+	154.5	2
2013 Special Teams			Special Teams F/+	-2.4%	102
2014 Projections			SOS Rk	10	
Ret. Starters: 8 OFF, 8 DEF			Offensive F/+	0.6%	64
Proj. F/+	10.7%	29	Defensive F/+	10.1%	14
Mean Wins / Conf Wins	7.8 / 3.9		Conf. / Div. Title Odds	0.2% / 0.7%	

2013 Five Factors			
Efficiency	Off Success Rate+	103.0	47
	Def Success Rate+	116.0	14
	Total Efficiency	219.0	22
Explosiveness	Off IsoPPP+	102.9	47
	Def IsoPPP+	106.5	35
	Total Explosiveness	209.4	33
Field Position	Field Pos. Adv. (FPA)	0.513	46
Finishing Drives	Off Red Zone S&P+	101.0	58
	Def Red Zone S&P+	109.0	27
	Total Red Zone Rating	210.0	43
Turnovers	Turnover Margin	+7.0	23
	Exp. TO Margin	-4.9	105
	Difference	+11.9	3

Sometimes you're just trying to survive, and Mississippi State head coach Dan Mullen had a bit of a storm to weather in 2013. He engineered a top-15 finish and nine-win season in the brutal SEC West in 2010, just his second season in Starkville. The Bulldogs went 7-6 in 2011 and began 2012 with seven straight wins, but they hit a rough stretch that lasted well into a tough 2013. A backloaded 2012 schedule resulted in a 1-5 finish, and only tight wins over Bowling Green and Kentucky gave MSU a chance at a bowl when it was 4-6 with two games remaining last fall.

Three games later, the ship appears to have turned around. MSU beat Arkansas, came back to win the Egg Bowl in overtime, and then obliterated Rice in the Liberty Bowl. Now, with some ace recruits coming of age and a deep returning roster, the Bulldogs are projected to play at a top-30 level. Granted, with a top-15 projected schedule (for the sixth straight year) they're still projected sixth of seven teams in their loaded division, but good is good.

The defense dominated down the stretch, allowing a combined 54 points to Alabama, Arkansas, Ole Miss, and Rice and finishing 19th in Defensive F/+. It was impossible to run on the Bulldogs, and a bend-don't-break approach to pass defense worked pretty well most of the time. One has to assume a similar dynamic in 2014; a majority of MSU's front seven returns, including blue-chip sophomore tackle Chris Jones (7.0 tackles for loss) and junior linebacker Benardrick McKinney. MSU is huge up front and could take pressure off of a secondary that returns a pair of ball-hawking corners (Taveze Calhoun, Jamerson Love) but will be without its best playmaker, safety Nickoe Whitley, who graduated.

A sound defense could make up for what might still be a rather volatile offense. Virtually every wideout returns, including 2013 breakout star Jameon Lewis (923 receiving yards, 14.4 per catch, 63 percent catch rate), but the running game will be without both running back LaDarius Perkins and all-conference guard (and four-year starter) Gabe Jackson, both of whom ran out of eligibility. The team's ceiling will likely be set by junior quarterback Dak Prescott (1,940 passing yards; 897 pre-sack rushing yards), who battled injuries and alternated between dominant and shaky performances for most of the year. Against Rice, he was 17-for-28 for 283 yards and 78 rushing yards. Against Texas A&M, he rushed for 154 yards. And against LSU and South Carolina, he threw four interceptions.

Top 2015 draft prospects: CB Justin Cox (6-7), DT Kaleb Eulls (6-7).

No. 62 Arkansas Razorbacks (4-8, 1-7)

2013: 3-9 (0-8) / F/+ #87 / FEI #89 / S&P+ #80 / Program F/+: #31					
2013 Offense			**2013 Defense**		
Offensive F/+	-1.5%	65	Defensive F/+	-8.0%	94
Offensive FEI	-0.033	65	Defensive FEI	0.318	100
Offensive S&P+	96.8	67	Defensive S&P+	98.4	82
Rushing S&P+	115.1	28	Rushing S&P+	97.9	70
Passing S&P+	95.8	74	Passing S&P+	104.9	49
Standard Downs S&P+	99.1	69	Standard Downs S&P+	101.7	61
Passing Downs S&P+	113.0	40	Passing Downs S&P+	101.3	63
2013 Special Teams			Special Teams F/+	-0.6%	83
2014 Projections			SOS Rk		6
Ret. Starters: 7 OFF, 8 DEF			Offensive F/+	3.3%	42
Proj. F/+	0.2%	62	Defensive F/+	-3.1%	81
Mean Wins / Conf Wins	3.6 / 0.9		Conf. / Div. Title Odds	0.0% / 0.0%	

2013 Five Factors			
Efficiency	Off Success Rate+	103.0	48
	Def Success Rate+	94.3	78
	Total Efficiency	197.3	68
Explosiveness	Off IsoPPP+	96.0	86
	Def IsoPPP+	107.4	30
	Total Explosiveness	203.4	52
Field Position	Field Pos. Adv. (FPA)	0.469	100
Finishing Drives	Off Red Zone S&P+	108.0	32
	Def Red Zone S&P+	97.0	70
	Total Red Zone Rating	205.1	52
Turnovers	Turnover Margin	-9.0	113
	Exp. TO Margin	-3.8	94
	Difference	-5.2	103

The 2011 season seems like a long, long time ago for Arkansas fans. The Razorbacks capped that season with a Cotton Bowl win and a top-five poll ranking, and with head coach Bobby Petrino leading the way, they were a surefire top-10 team heading into 2012 as well. But then Petrino got into a motorcycle wreck and lied about having a female passenger with him aboard. He got fired, and Arkansas made the misguided decision to bring in a one-year caretaker, John L. Smith, to lead the way in 2012. They went 4-8 that year, then went 3-9 in Bret Bielema's first season last fall.

After three straight seasons in the F/+ top 25, the Hogs fell to 60th and then 87th over the last two years. And while the SEC is now the conference of sudden redemption—Auburn and Missouri went a combined 2-14 in conference play in 2012, then won their respective divisions the next year—it's hard to build up too much hope for that in Fayetteville.

That's not to say the Hogs won't be better, however. The running back duo of sophomore Alex Collins (1,026 yards, 5.4 per carry, 5.0 highlight yards per opportunity) and junior Jonathan Williams (900 yards, 6.0 per carry, 6.0 highlight yards per opportunity) might only get more effective, especially considering the line in front of them (which ranked 18th in Adjusted Line Yards) returns six players with starting experience, including two sophomores who were thrown into the fire last year.

Defensively, Arkansas is still well behind the curve. The Hogs could rush the passer in 2013, but that was about it, and now they must do so without ace pass rusher Chris Smith (11.5 tackles for loss, 8.5 sacks).

Top 2015 draft prospects: DE Trey Flowers (2-3), CB Tevin Mitchel (6-7).

EAST DIVISION

No. 5 South Carolina Gamecocks (10-2, 6-2)

2013: 11-2 (6-2) / F/+ #10 / FEI #6 / S&P+ #12 / Program F/+: #14					
2013 Offense			**2013 Defense**		
Offensive F/+	20.2%	5	Defensive F/+	12.9%	16
Offensive FEI	0.696	2	Defensive FEI	-0.468	11
Offensive S&P+	126.8	11	Defensive S&P+	122.0	22
Rushing S&P+	107.5	47	Rushing S&P+	110.4	35
Passing S&P+	140.8	6	Passing S&P+	122.2	14
Standard Downs S&P+	119.1	17	Standard Downs S&P+	122.2	10
Passing Downs S&P+	129.2	15	Passing Downs S&P+	103.6	57
2013 Special Teams			Special Teams F/+	-3.3%	114
2014 Projections			SOS Rk	33	
Ret. Starters: 8 OFF, 6 DEF			Offensive F/+	12.6%	10
Proj. F/+	20.2%	5	Defensive F/+	7.6%	23
Mean Wins / Conf Wins	9.7 / 6.2		Conf. / Div. Title Odds	15.2% / 50.6%	

2013 Five Factors			
Efficiency	Off Success Rate+	116.0	16
	Def Success Rate+	110.6	26
	Total Efficiency	226.5	16
Explosiveness	Off IsoPPP+	109.2	23
	Def IsoPPP+	105.9	38
	Total Explosiveness	215.1	18
Field Position	Field Pos. Adv. (FPA)	0.473	95
Finishing Drives	Off Red Zone S&P+	112.6	22
	Def Red Zone S&P+	106.6	38
	Total Red Zone Rating	219.2	24
Turnovers	Turnover Margin	+13.0	8
	Exp. TO Margin	+3.8	42
	Difference	+9.2	7

What's more important: depth or star power? In 2014, South Carolina has the former in abundance but must replace a good portion of the latter. Gone are NFL No. 1 overall pick Jadeveon Clowney, tackle Kelcy Quarles, and both starting cornerbacks (Victor Hampton and Jimmy Legree) on defense. Gone are quarterback Connor Shaw and go-to receiver Bruce Ellington from the offense. If you were to list the eight or nine best players from last season's South Carolina squad, those six would all probably make the list. They all had major roles to play in the Gamecocks' back-to-back-to-back 11-2, top-10 finishes.

But almost literally every other player from last year's team returns: every linebacker, every safety, every other receiver, every other defensive tackle, and all but one offensive lineman. Teams don't go 33-6 in a three-year span without outstanding depth, and that depth is projected to pay major dividends in 2014.

Passing was the primary strength of last year's South Carolina offense, and the combination of ultra-efficient quarterback Shaw (2,447 yards, 63 percent completion rate, 24 touchdowns, one solitary interception) and the underrated Ellington (775 receiving yards, 15.8 per catch, 70 percent catch rate) will be missed. But you don't get into the top 10 in passing because one guy caught 48 passes. Four other players caught at least 25 passes, including senior Damiere Byrd (575 yards, 17.4 per catch, 54 percent) and junior Shaq Roland (455 yards, 18.2 per catch, 63 percent). Plus, in two years of backing up the oft-injured Shaw, Dylan Thompson has thrown for 1,810 yards, 14 scores, and five picks. This team isn't starting from scratch here.

Any success in the aerial attack should open things up for tough running back Mike Davis; the junior rushed for 1,183 yards (5.8 per carry, 6.3 highlight yards per opportunity) and caught 34 passes for 342 yards. With six returning linemen with starting experience (97 career starts), including three-year starting guard A.J. Cann, South Carolina should be able to pull off the power game as well as anybody in the East. 23.2 percent of the Gamecocks' drives lasted at least 10 plays last year, fourth in the nation.

South Carolina's only real defensive weakness in 2014 was a bit of inefficiency and conservatism on passing downs. The Gamecocks were good at forcing a lot of passing downs with a top-10 defense on standard downs, however; if the reinforcements up front, led by tackle J.T. Surratt, can hold up, the linebacking corps can take it from there. South Carolina returns six exciting linebackers and all the safeties that were shuffled around constantly in 2013 (no safety played all 13 games). The star power on the edges—defensive end and cornerback—has absolutely dissipated, but it's easier to get over that when the backbone of the defense is sturdy.

By the end of September, Steve Spurrier's squad will have already played Texas A&M, East Carolina, Georgia, and Missouri, all at home. Start the season 5-0, and a trip to the SEC title game becomes highly likely.

Top 2015 draft prospects: RB Mike Davis (2-3), OT Brandon Shell* (2-3), G A.J. Cann (2-3), OT Corey Robinson (4-5), TE Rory Anderson (6-7).*

No. 11 Georgia Bulldogs (9-3, 6-2)

2013: 8-5 (5-3) / F/+ #22 / FEI #18 / S&P+ #17 / Program F/+: #17							2013 Five Factors			
2013 Offense			**2013 Defense**				Efficiency	Off Success Rate+	115.2	18
Offensive F/+	18.7%	8	Defensive F/+	3.5%	46			Def Success Rate+	112.2	24
Offensive FEI	0.567	8	Defensive FEI	-0.129	46			Total Efficiency	227.4	13
Offensive S&P+	131.2	8	Defensive S&P+	110.2	43		Explosiveness	Off IsoPPP+	111.3	20
Rushing S&P+	107.2	48	Rushing S&P+	118.5	20			Def IsoPPP+	99.6	61
Passing S&P+	140.9	5	Passing S&P+	108.6	36			Total Explosiveness	211.0	28
Standard Downs S&P+	121.0	13	Standard Downs S&P+	115.4	23		Field Position	Field Pos. Adv. (FPA)	0.480	91
Passing Downs S&P+	132.6	13	Passing Downs S&P+	107.8	44		Finishing Drives	Off Red Zone S&P+	123.3	9
2013 Special Teams			Special Teams F/+	0.1%	66			Def Red Zone S&P+	108.7	29
2014 Projections			SOS Rk	41				Total Red Zone Rating	232.0	9
Ret. Starters: 5 OFF, 10 DEF			Offensive F/+	10.0%	15		Turnovers	Turnover Margin	-7.0	101
Proj. F/+	17.4%	11	Defensive F/+	7.4%	24			Exp. TO Margin	-2.8	89
Mean Wins / Conf Wins	9.3 / 5.8		Conf. / Div. Title Odds	7.4% / 31.3%				Difference	-4.2	94

The last two years have been the ultimate tease for the Georgia Bulldogs. Mark Richt's squad finished 11-1 in the 2012 regular season and came within a batted pass and a few seconds of beating Alabama in the SEC Championship and reaching the national title game. Then, in 2013, the Dawgs lost every offensive star—literally every single one of them—to injury at one point or another, struggled with youth and inconsistency on defense, and still needed four losses by five or fewer points to miss another season of double-digit wins. They gave up 26.4 points in turnover value in five losses that came by a combined 32-point deficit. This is one of the healthiest, deepest programs in the country, but something always gets in the way.

So what might get in the way in 2014? Start with the fact that for the first time since 2009, the Dawgs will be starting a quarterback not named Aaron Murray in the season opener. Longtime backup Hutson Mason appears poised to hold the job this fall; he was decent down the stretch after Murray was lost with a knee injury (968 passing yards, 61 percent completion rate), but Murray was just so good for so long that it's hard to assume Mason will thrive at the same level.

Of course, this offense does return a number of other proven pieces. Because of the aforementioned injury crush, the Dawgs now have four different players who have spent time as their No. 1 receiver: Malcolm Mitchell, Chris Conley, Michael Bennett, and Justin Scott-Wesley. And in junior Todd Gurley, Georgia has the most punishing runner in college football. There's reason to question the line, which must replace three starters, but with reasonable health and perpetually underrated offensive coordinator Mike Bobo calling plays, it's hard to worry too much. The offense might hum with some random intramural flag football quarterback behind center.

A bigger concern in Athens is that the defense is still pretty young, and it's hard to find too much confidence in a secondary that suffered all sorts of deep breakdowns in 2013. Safeties Josh Harvey-Clemons and Tray Matthews were dismissed, corner Shaq Wiggins transferred, and exciting safety Quincy Mauger is still just a sophomore. So why might things be different in 2014? For starters, Richt hit a home run in stealing defensive coordinator Jeremy Pruitt from national champion Florida State. Not only did he prove world-class in his first year as a coordinator, but he's also a renowned defensive backs coach. Plus, the front seven returns most of last year's best playmakers, including senior end Ray Drew (eight tackles for loss, six sacks), senior inside linebackers Ramik Wilson and Amarlo Herrera (combined: 16 tackles for loss, 4.5 sacks, 10 passes defensed), and two fast, exciting outside lienbackers, Leonard Floyd and Jordan Jenkins (21.5 tackles for loss, 11.5 sacks). If the secondary can clean itself up a bit—certainly not a given—a defense that was stellar against the run could end up just plain stellar.

Top 2015 draft prospects: RB Todd Gurley (2), ILB Ramik Wilson (2-3), OLB Jordan Jenkins* (2-3), ILB Amarlo Herrera (4-5), C David Andrews (5-6), DE Ray Drew (5-6).*

No. 20 Missouri Tigers (8-4, 5-3)

2013: 12-2 (7-1) / F/+ #14 / FEI #5 / S&P+ #14 / Program F/+: #23					
2013 Offense			**2013 Defense**		
Offensive F/+	13.3%	17	Defensive F/+	15.1%	11
Offensive FEI	0.437	18	Defensive FEI	-0.529	8
Offensive S&P+	119.4	19	Defensive S&P+	126.0	17
Rushing S&P+	115.5	26	Rushing S&P+	113.6	27
Passing S&P+	117.2	23	Passing S&P+	124.6	11
Standard Downs S&P+	110.5	38	Standard Downs S&P+	118.8	15
Passing Downs S&P+	129.9	14	Passing Downs S&P+	117.8	26
2013 Special Teams			Special Teams F/+	0.1%	65
2014 Projections			SOS Rk	40	
Ret. Starters: 5 OFF, 4 DEF			Offensive F/+	5.4%	35
Proj. F/+	13.9%	20	Defensive F/+	8.5%	21
Mean Wins / Conf Wins	8.4 / 5.1		Conf. / Div. Title Odds	2.5% / 15.2%	

2013 Five Factors			
Efficiency	Off Success Rate+	106.7	40
	Def Success Rate+	109.6	30
	Total Efficiency	216.3	27
Explosiveness	Off IsoPPP+	112.4	14
	Def IsoPPP+	110.6	18
	Total Explosiveness	223.0	8
Field Position	Field Pos. Adv. (FPA)	0.533	21
Finishing Drives	Off Red Zone S&P+	121.5	12
	Def Red Zone S&P+	108.3	31
	Total Red Zone Rating	229.7	11
Turnovers	Turnover Margin	+16.0	4
	Exp. TO Margin	+5.8	27
	Difference	+10.2	6

Missouri hasn't made a habit of playing to expectations in recent seasons. *The Football Outsiders Almanac 2010* projected the Tigers to rank 38th and win eight games; they ranked 13th and won 10. The *Football Outsiders Almanac 2012* projected them 28th and 6-6; they ranked 58th and needed some close wins to even finish 5-7. Despite the shaky 2012, the *Football Outsiders Almanac 2013* projected them an ambitious 33rd and 7-5; they instead ranked 14th, went 12-2, and finished in the AP top five.

So when you see the Tigers projected at No. 20, assume either another top-five finish or a plummet out of the top 40.

At first glance, it seems pretty easy to assume the latter. Gary Pinkel must replace his starting quarterback (James Franklin), his starting running back (Henry Josey), his top three receivers (Dorial Green-Beckham, L'Damian Washington, and Marcus Lucas), a second-round left tackle (Justin Britt), one of the best defensive end duos in the country (Kony Ealy and Michael Sam), and an all-conference cornerback (E.J. Gaines), among others. For a program that doesn't swim in a pool of blue-chippers, that's an impossible amount of talent to lose in a single year.

Still, depth was the reason for Missouri's surge, and depth produced a new set of potential breakout stars for 2014. On defense, ends Markus Golden and Shane Ray (combined: 22 tackles for loss, 11 sacks) were fantastic complements to Ealy and Sam, and safety Braylon Webb (three interceptions, seven break-ups) has been a steady starter for parts of three seasons.

Sam and Ealy were fantastic against the run, but last year's top four defensive tackles return, and when that is combined with the return of five players with starting experience on the offensive line, it appears Mizzou might have a decent chance at replicating last year's solid numbers in the trenches (sixth in Adjusted Line Yards on offense, 24th on defense). And the return of backs Russell Hansbrough and Marcus Murphy (combined: 1,286 rushing yards, 6.2 per carry, 5.9 highlight yards per opportunity) means the Tigers will still be able to run the ball well.

The questions come in the passing game. Sophomore Maty Mauk mixed incredible play-making potential (1,071 passing yards, 15.8 per completion) with efficiency problems (51 percent completion rate) while spelling an injured Franklin in the middle of the season, but his receiving corps will be a mix of career role players and youngsters. Bud Sasser and Jimmie Hunt combined for 614 receiving yards last year (12.8 per catch, 61 percent catch rate), but the third leading wideout, Darius White, had just seven catches.

Top 2015 draft prospects: DE Markus Golden (1-2), T Mitch Morse (6-7).

No. 30 Florida Gators (7-5, 4-4)

2013: 4-8 (3-5) / F/+ #48 / FEI #49 / S&P+ #49 / Program F/+: #15					
2013 Offense			**2013 Defense**		
Offensive F/+	-8.9%	99	Defensive F/+	12.9%	17
Offensive FEI	-0.279	98	Defensive FEI	-0.403	20
Offensive S&P+	86.1	100	Defensive S&P+	127.3	15
Rushing S&P+	88.8	102	Rushing S&P+	115.4	25
Passing S&P+	93.1	83	Passing S&P+	144.6	3
Standard Downs S&P+	92.9	93	Standard Downs S&P+	118.8	16
Passing Downs S&P+	84.7	101	Passing Downs S&P+	161.2	1
2013 Special Teams			Special Teams F/+	2.2%	24
2014 Projections			SOS Rk	1	
Ret. Starters: 7 OFF, 7 DEF			Offensive F/+	-5.7%	92
Proj. F/+	10.5%	30	Defensive F/+	16.2%	3
Mean Wins / Conf Wins	6.9 / 3.9		Conf. / Div. Title Odds	0.3% / 2.8%	

2013 Five Factors			
Efficiency	Off Success Rate+	88.7	100
	Def Success Rate+	125.0	6
	Total Efficiency	213.8	32
Explosiveness	Off IsoPPP+	96.9	82
	Def IsoPPP+	105.3	39
	Total Explosiveness	202.1	58
Field Position	Field Pos. Adv. (FPA)	0.520	36
Finishing Drives	Off Red Zone S&P+	77.6	117
	Def Red Zone S&P+	142.9	3
	Total Red Zone Rating	220.5	23
Turnovers	Turnover Margin	-2.0	73
	Exp. TO Margin	-1.8	86
	Difference	-0.2	59

What the hell was that?

If the College Football Playoff had existed in 2012, Will Muschamp's Florida Gators may have scored a semifinal bid. They went 11-1 in the regular season and seemed to have an agreement in place with fans of Florida and/or aesthetically pleasing football: as long as we're winning, we can play as ugly as we want. The 2012 Gators were an entire team with the mindset of the running back who tries to run through defenders instead of around them. Florida chose defense over offense, toughness over finesse, and mean over pretty. Despite a Sugar Bowl loss to Louisville, it was clearly a success.

But in 2013, brilliantly ugly turned into plain old ugly. Murderball got murdered. The offense scuffled, lost its quarterback, imploded, and ended up blocking itself. The defense held out as long as it could but eventually succumbed to both injuries and offensive hopelessness. Muschamp's low-pace, grind-it-out style of football left minimal margin for error anyway—this team nearly lost to Jacksonville State, UL-Lafayette, and Missouri in 2012—so one swath of injuries was all it took to fall from 11 wins to four. The season finished with seven losses, including a 17-point home loss to Vanderbilt and a humiliating 26-20 defeat at the hands of injury-plagued FCS powerhouse Georgia Southern.

So what the hell happens now? To reestablish some semblance of offensive competence, Muschamp brought in Duke offensive coordinator Kurt Roper. Duke's offense combined spread elements with the balance and medium pace Muschamp probably feels most comfortable with, and if junior quarterback Jeff Driskel is healthy, he might have a decent catalyst. Driskel takes too many sacks in the name of making plays, but he's mobile and accurate. He'll have a decent go-to receiver in senior Quinton Dunbar (548 receiving yards, 14.1 per catch, 66 percent catch rate), and sophomore running back Kelvin Taylor (508 yards, 4.6 per carry, 4.6 highlight yards per opportunity) showed just enough glimpses of his father Fred's potential to build excitement. The line returns five players with 51 career starts, and hopefully this year they will remember to block guys from the other team.

If the offense produces anything, the defense will be fine. Muschamp knows what he's doing on that side of the ball. Sophomore corner Vernon Hargreaves III might already be the best in college football, and the front four is strong against both the run and the pass thanks to tackle Leon Orr and ends Dante Fowler Jr. and Jonathan Bullard. Plus, Florida's special teams have ranked in the top 25 every year since 2007.

Top 2015 draft prospects: DE Dante Fowler Jr. (1-2), TE Jake McGee (4-5), DT Leon Orr (6-7).*

No. 61 Vanderbilt Commodores (6-6, 2-6)

2013: 9-4 (4-4) / F/+ #50 / FEI #45 / S&P+ #64 / Program F/+: #60					
2013 Offense			**2013 Defense**		
Offensive F/+	1.4%	55	Defensive F/+	2.6%	48
Offensive FEI	0.130	45	Defensive FEI	-0.092	53
Offensive S&P+	95.3	71	Defensive S&P+	109.4	47
Rushing S&P+	87.6	104	Rushing S&P+	94.2	88
Passing S&P+	97.2	69	Passing S&P+	115.1	26
Standard Downs S&P+	98.4	73	Standard Downs S&P+	103.8	51
Passing Downs S&P+	77.4	115	Passing Downs S&P+	105.5	49
2013 Special Teams			Special Teams F/+	1.9%	30
2014 Projections			SOS Rk	47	
Ret. Starters: 7 OFF, 3 DEF			Offensive F/+	0.8%	63
Proj. F/+	0.4%	61	Defensive F/+	-0.4%	65
Mean Wins / Conf Wins	5.9 / 2.2		Conf. / Div. Title Odds	0.0% / 0.1%	

2013 Five Factors			
Efficiency	Off Success Rate+	96.5	73
	Def Success Rate+	94.1	82
	Total Efficiency	190.6	88
Explosiveness	Off IsoPPP+	88.0	118
	Def IsoPPP+	113.1	12
	Total Explosiveness	201.0	64
Field Position	Field Pos. Adv. (FPA)	0.502	60
Finishing Drives	Off Red Zone S&P+	102.0	52
	Def Red Zone S&P+	105.8	39
	Total Red Zone Rating	207.8	47
Turnovers	Turnover Margin	+7.0	23
	Exp. TO Margin	+14.7	1
	Difference	-7.7	118

In three years under head coach James Franklin, Vanderbilt accomplished more than it had in nearly half a century. The Commodores went to three bowl games from 2011-13 after going to just three from 1956-2010; they won two bowls after winning just two in their pre-Franklin history. They won 24 games in those three years after winning 25 from 2005-10. They finished ranked in the polls in both 2012 and 2013 after doing so just once ever (1948). They won SEC road games. They signed four-star recruits. Everything that happened in Nashville in this decade was mostly or completely without precedent.

Now Franklin's the head coach at Penn State, and Vandy is left to ask, what now?

The school made a sensible hire in replacing Franklin with a top assistant from another surging smart-kid school. Derek Mason, David Shaw's defensive coordinator at Stanford (and not Derrick Mason, the former Titans and Ravens receiver), takes over. The Cardinal defense, 103rd in Defensive F/+ the year before Mason was hired in Palo Alto, ranked in the top 20 in all three years under his control. He helped Stanford become the big, burly bully out West, and he will try to do the same for Vanderbilt ... eventually.

One has to assume he might need a rebuilding year to get situated. Vanderbilt will be without its primary (only?) weapons from last fall, receiver Jordan Matthews (1,477 receiving yards, an even 50 percent of Vandy's total in 2013) and all-conference tackle Wesley Johnson. Running backs Jerron Seymour and Brian Kimbrow will carry a huge load, that's for sure. The Commodores got a potential boost when former LSU quarterback Stephen Rivers elected to transfer to Vandy (he's eligible immediately), but they likely need more weapons than they actually have.

Meanwhile, a defense anchored by a great secondary in 2013

must replace all four starters in the backfield while getting acclimated to a move from a 4-3 to a 3-4. Junior Caleb Azubike (10 tackles for loss, four sacks) could be perfectly suited to play outside linebacker in this arrangement, but for most of the personnel, getting situated to this new scheme might take a while.

Top 2015 draft prospects: none.

No. 64 Tennessee Volunteers (4-8, 2-6)

2013: 5-7 (2-6) / F/+ #72 / FEI #74 / S&P+ #67 / Program F/+: #51					
2013 Offense			**2013 Defense**		
Offensive F/+	-6.8%	89	Defensive F/+	1.2%	58
Offensive FEI	-0.262	97	Defensive FEI	-0.018	64
Offensive S&P+	93.7	76	Defensive S&P+	109.6	46
Rushing S&P+	113.8	30	Rushing S&P+	97.4	74
Passing S&P+	89.2	92	Passing S&P+	117.5	23
Standard Downs S&P+	112.8	33	Standard Downs S&P+	107.9	40
Passing Downs S&P+	82.2	109	Passing Downs S&P+	103.1	59
2013 Special Teams			Special Teams F/+	0.4%	57
2014 Projections			SOS Rk	5	
Ret. Starters: 5 OFF, 5 DEF			Offensive F/+	-4.9%	88
Proj. F/+	-1.2%	64	Defensive F/+	3.7%	44
Mean Wins / Conf Wins	4.0 / 1.6		Conf. / Div. Title Odds	0.0% / 0.0%	

2013 Five Factors			
Efficiency	Off Success Rate+	102.0	52
	Def Success Rate+	106.0	37
	Total Efficiency	208.0	45
Explosiveness	Off IsoPPP+	99.5	65
	Def IsoPPP+	96.1	88
	Total Explosiveness	195.6	83
Field Position	Field Pos. Adv. (FPA)	0.520	34
Finishing Drives	Off Red Zone S&P+	102.8	50
	Def Red Zone S&P+	99.9	58
	Total Red Zone Rating	202.7	57
Turnovers	Turnover Margin	+1.0	53
	Exp. TO Margin	+1.6	58
	Difference	-0.6	66

Pressure and time. It's the geological logic behind Andy Dufresne's escape from Shawshank, and it's the only thing that will restore the Tennessee football program after a few years in the wilderness. After pushing out Phil Fulmer following a 5-7 campaign in 2008, the Vols have averaged just 5.6 wins per season and haven't attended a bowl since 2010's last-second loss to North Carolina in the Music City Bowl.

In the five years since Fulmer's demise, four different programs have won the SEC East, including one team (Missouri) that didn't even join the conference until 2012. Tennessee, meanwhile, has been stuck trying to creep over .500. Injuries and a back-loaded schedule contributed to a four-game losing streak and a 5-7 finish in 2013, and projections suggest it might take second-year coach Butch Jones another season, and perhaps another recruiting class, to get the ship steered in the right direction again.

It's a whole-versus-sum-of-parts situation on the offensive side of the ball. With a big, experienced line, some solid running backs, and one of the most high-upside receiving corps in the country, Tennessee ranked just 89th in Offensive F/+ last fall. Senior quarterback Justin Worley missed part of the season with injury, but the offense wasn't exactly high-flying before then. Sophomore Marquez North (496 receiving yards, 13.1 per catch, 62 percent catch rate) anchors a more experienced set of receivers, but the entire line is now getting rebuilt.

Actually, both lines are getting completely renovated. The top five tacklers from last year's defensive line are gone, including end Corey Miller (6.5 sacks) and man-mountain Daniel McCullers. With any pass rush whatsoever, the pass defense could be outstanding again—the secondary returns mostly intact—but opponents could once again run on the Vols at will.

Top 2015 draft prospects: ILB A.J. Johnson (2-3), OLB Curt Maggitt (6-7).

No. 77 Kentucky Wildcats (4-8, 1-7)

2013: 2-10 (0-8) / F/+ #97 / FEI #95 / S&P+ #93 / Program F/+: #84					
2013 Offense			**2013 Defense**		
Offensive F/+	-3.3%	74	Defensive F/+	-12.0%	109
Offensive FEI	-0.074	69	Defensive FEI	0.450	114
Offensive S&P+	92.9	81	Defensive S&P+	92.4	98
Rushing S&P+	104.8	54	Rushing S&P+	90.2	97
Passing S&P+	94.9	79	Passing S&P+	94.6	85
Standard Downs S&P+	105.3	52	Standard Downs S&P+	97.1	80
Passing Downs S&P+	89.0	92	Passing Downs S&P+	82.8	113
2013 Special Teams			Special Teams F/+	-0.8%	86
2014 Projections			SOS Rk	26	
Ret. Starters: 8 OFF, 8 DEF			Offensive F/+	1.6%	55
Proj. F/+	-4.9%	77	Defensive F/+	-6.5%	102
Mean Wins / Conf Wins	3.8 / 1.1		Conf. / Div. Title Odds	0.0% / 0.0%	

2013 Five Factors			
Efficiency	Off Success Rate+	95.0	79
	Def Success Rate+	91.1	98
	Total Efficiency	186.1	97
Explosiveness	Off IsoPPP+	107.3	31
	Def IsoPPP+	99.8	60
	Total Explosiveness	207.0	40
Field Position	Field Pos. Adv. (FPA)	0.466	102
Finishing Drives	Off Red Zone S&P+	110.9	25
	Def Red Zone S&P+	85.9	98
	Total Red Zone Rating	196.7	69
Turnovers	Turnover Margin	0.0	61
	Exp. TO Margin	-3.2	91
	Difference	+3.2	30

Mark Stoops has a career record of 2-10 as a head coach, but he's already received a contract extension at Kentucky. That's what happens when you ink the No. 22 recruiting class (according to 247 Sports) in your first full year on the job. With his Ohio ties and a charismatic staff, Stoops and the Wildcats outdid schools like Arizona State, Michigan State, Baylor, Oklahoma State, Wisconsin, Nebraska, and Missouri (combined record in 2013: 74-20) on the recruiting trail. Now they just have to wait until these prospects develop.

It probably won't happen in 2014, but the offense might begin to move pretty well. If a shaky line comes around with experience (74 career starts), redshirt junior quarterback Maxwell Smith (1,276 passing yards, 12.2 per completion, 57 percent completion rate, nine touchdowns, one interception) might be able to do some damage throwing to each of his top four returning receivers. Javess Blue (586 receiving yards, 13.6 per catch, 64 percent completion rate) became the go-to guy, but depth will be the real weapon here. Running back Jojo Kemp (482 rushing yards, 4.8 per carry, 4.2 highlight yards per opportunity) is the only returnee among last year's top five rushers, but he was rather efficient for a freshman.

The defense is still a work in progress. The pass rush could be excellent with the return of ends Alvin Dupree and Za'Darius Smith (combined: 16 tackles for loss, 13 sacks), but the pass rush was pretty good last year, too, and the defense still ranked below 109th in Defensive F/+. Experience is a strength, but that only matters if there's talent, too.

Top 2015 draft prospects: DE Alvin Dupree (3-4).

Bill Connelly

Projected Win Probabilities For SEC Teams

			Overall Wins													Conference Wins								
Div	Conf	SEC East	12-0	11-1	10-2	9-3	8-4	7-5	6-6	5-7	4-8	3-9	2-10	1-11	0-12	8-0	7-1	6-2	5-3	4-4	3-5	2-6	1-7	0-8
3	-	Florida	-	-	1	7	21	33	26	10	2	-	-	-	-	-	1	7	21	33	26	10	2	-
31	7	Georgia	3	14	29	30	17	6	1	-	-	-	-	-	-	4	22	36	27	9	2	-	-	-
-	-	Kentucky	-	-	-	-	-	1	4	18	36	31	9	1	-	-	-	-	-	1	5	22	43	29
15	3	Missouri	-	5	16	28	28	16	6	1	-	-	-	-	-	1	9	26	35	22	6	1	-	-
51	15	South Carolina	5	21	33	26	12	3	-	-	-	-	-	-	-	11	32	34	17	5	1	-	-	-
-	-	Tennessee	-	-	-	-	-	2	8	23	34	24	8	1	-	-	-	-	-	3	14	35	38	10
-	-	Vanderbilt	-	-	-	1	7	21	33	26	10	2	-	-	-	-	-	-	2	9	25	36	23	5
Div	**Conf**	**SEC West**	**12-0**	**11-1**	**10-2**	**9-3**	**8-4**	**7-5**	**6-6**	**5-7**	**4-8**	**3-9**	**2-10**	**1-11**	**0-12**	**8-0**	**7-1**	**6-2**	**5-3**	**4-4**	**3-5**	**2-6**	**1-7**	**0-8**
83	66	Alabama	46	39	13	2	-	-	-	-	-	-	-	-	-	47	39	12	2	-	-	-	-	-
-	-	Arkansas	-	-	-	-	-	1	4	14	31	34	15	1	-	-	-	-	-	-	4	16	40	40
5	3	Auburn	-	5	16	28	27	17	6	1	-	-	-	-	-	1	6	21	31	26	12	3	-	-
9	5	LSU	1	8	23	32	24	10	2	-	-	-	-	-	-	2	12	29	33	18	5	1	-	-
1	-	Mississippi	-	1	4	15	28	29	17	5	1	-	-	-	-	-	1	8	24	34	23	9	1	-
1	-	Mississippi State	-	1	6	19	33	28	11	2	-	-	-	-	-	-	1	6	21	35	27	9	1	-
1	1	Texas A&M	-	2	9	25	32	22	8	2	-	-	-	-	-	-	2	10	26	32	21	8	1	-

Independents, Group of Five

The College Football Playoff selection committee will be charged with identifying four teams to play for the ultimate prize this fall, and we don't know what consideration, if any, will be granted to the teams outside of the Big Five conferences. At least one of the champions of the SEC, ACC, Big Ten, Big 12, or Pac-12 will be on the outside looking in, and we anticipate that most of the arguments will revolve around the one-loss power conference teams at the top. Notre Dame's schedule will position the Irish favorably alongside Big Five conference contenders, but there's very little hope for the other 63 FBS programs not included in those leagues to squeeze into the four-team field.

The new era will grant a spot in a prestigious non-playoff bowl to the best team from among the American, Conference USA, Mountain West, Mid-American, and Sun Belt conferences, a "Group of Five" designation for a major bowl payday. A team from one of those conferences received a BCS bowl berth five times in the last five years, winning three of them. But one of those BCS bowl winners—TCU (2011 Rose Bowl over Wisconsin) —has since made the leap to a Big Five conference. The flag bearers of college football's second tier today include Central Florida (2014 Fiesta Bowl champion), Boise State (2007 and 2010 Fiesta Bowl champion), and independent BYU; very few others have any kind of national cache.

Our projection model for the College Football Playoff assumes that Big Five teams are going to get a significant benefit of the doubt from the selection committee. An undefeated season in Conference USA isn't likely to cut it, even if that team is the only undefeated one in the land. According to our projections, only Florida State, Alabama, and Oregon are more likely to go undefeated than the Thundering Herd of Marshall. But with the easiest schedule in football—historically easy, with zero opponents on their schedule ranked higher than 89th—an undefeated season at Marshall will only draw national attention if every game is a six- or seven-touchdown blowout.

That's not to say that the teams outside of the Big Five conferences don't matter, but their role in the playoffs will most likely be relegated to knocking other contenders out of the running. According to our projections, there is only a 3.6 percent chance that any of the six teams highlighted in this chapter will be ranked among the final four. Take Notre Dame out of the equation, and it drops to 1.7 percent. Even that feels too high.

No. 22 Notre Dame Fighting Irish (7-5)

2013: 9-4 / F/+ #26 / FEI #23 / S&P+ #34 / Program F/+: #12

2013 Offense			2013 Defense		
Offensive F/+	11.6%	24	Defensive F/+	6.4%	33
Offensive FEI	0.417	20	Defensive FEI	-0.293	30
Offensive S&P+	114.1	27	Defensive S&P+	108.6	48
Rushing S&P+	116.0	23	Rushing S&P+	105.1	55
Passing S&P+	123.1	15	Passing S&P+	104.1	50
Standard Downs S&P+	125.6	8	Standard Downs S&P+	101.8	59
Passing Downs S&P+	107.4	47	Passing Downs S&P+	110.0	40
2013 Special Teams			Special Teams F/+	-0.5%	82
2014 Projections			SOS Rk	4	
Ret. Starters: 6 OFF, 5 DEF			Offensive F/+	8.4%	20
Proj. F/+	12.6%	22	Defensive F/+	4.2%	40
Mean Wins / Conf Wins	7.3 / 0.0				

2013 Five Factors			
Efficiency	Off Success Rate+	112.8	24
	Def Success Rate+	94.9	76
	Total Efficiency	207.7	47
Explosiveness	Off IsoPPP+	111.4	19
	Def IsoPPP+	117.8	5
	Total Explosiveness	229.2	2
Field Position	Field Pos. Adv. (FPA)	0.483	87
Finishing Drives	Off Red Zone S&P+	95.5	82
	Def Red Zone S&P+	108.1	32
	Total Red Zone Rating	203.6	53
Turnovers	Turnover Margin	0.0	61
	Exp. TO Margin	+0.4	69
	Difference	-0.4	62

The Brian Kelly era enters year five at Notre Dame, a pivotal season in terms of program trajectory. The Fighting Irish followed up a 12-1 campaign in 2012 with a disappointing 9-4 performance last season. Lackluster losses (11 points at Michigan, seven points at Pittsburgh) outnumbered signature wins (17-13 over otherwise undefeated Michigan State counts, barely), and the ever-demanding fan base is restless again. The loss of significant starters to the NFL draft (eight total, including five in the first three rounds) lowers expectations somewhat this fall, but program stagnation won't make anyone happy. Win and win big, and oh yeah, get it done against one of the strongest schedules in the country.

The schedule-strength hurdle is the biggest factor holding back our projections for the Irish. Notre Dame will face five opponents ranked No. 21 or better according to F/+, and they'll take on two of three top-10 opponents on the road. There is an 86 percent chance the Irish will lose at least three times against Stanford, Florida State, Arizona State, Louisville, and USC—if our projections hold, of course. The last time we forecasted a brutal schedule for Notre Dame, several opponents never materialized as world-beaters, and the Irish took advantage with an undefeated regular season and an appearance in the BCS Championship game.

It just so happens that the quarterback for most of that magical 2012 season is back on campus this fall. Everett Golson served an academic suspension last year, but returns in 2014 as the presumed starter and potential superstar that can take the Brian Kelly offense to new heights. The most recent memories of Golson include a 62 percent completion rate and 1,033 yards in his final four starts, and he led the Irish with six rushing touchdowns in 2012 as well. The Irish running game is in great shape overall. They have a strong offensive line (No. 22 in Adjusted Line Yards, No. 2 in Adjusted Sack Rate), and a trio of running backs—efficient senior Cam McDaniel and dynamic sophomores Tarean Folston and Greg Bryant—who combined for 1,188 rushing yards a year ago (4.9 yards per carry, 3.8 highlight yards per opportunity). Golson's dual-threat capacity and Kelly's plans to finally push tempo could result in a significant bump in production from the offense, which has ranked in the top 25 by F/+ offensive efficiency in each of the last three years, but never higher than 35th nationally in total yardage or 49th nationally in scoring offense.

Extra points on the scoreboard may come in handy for a defense that has a few big holes to fill. The defensive line has to find new names to fill the enormous and talented shoes of Stephon Tuitt (Pittsburgh second-rounder) and Louis Nix III (Houston third-rounder). Senior defensive end Ishaq Williams has one more opportunity to make good on the five-star promise he brought to Notre Dame, and junior defensive tackle Sheldon Day can be a dominant pass rusher from the interior of the line. New defensive coordinator Brian VanGorder is expected to bring pressure from all over the field and will turn to sophomore linebacker Jaylon Smith (6.5 tackles for loss) to wreak havoc from a variety of pre-snap positions. The experienced secondary will feature three cornerbacks regularly—junior KeiVarae Russell, senior Matthias Farley, and senior Florida transfer Cody Riggs—and may leave them in one-on-one situations often to boost up a less reliable front seven. If the Irish wake up the defensive echoes from 2012 (No. 5 in points per drive allowed), they may find themselves in the playoff hunt.

2015 Draft Prospects: TE Ben Koyack (2-3), DE Ishaq Williams (4-5), WR DaVaris Daniels (4-5), DT Sheldon Day (4-5)*, CB KeiVarae Russell (4-5)*.*

No. 25 Central Florida Golden Knights (9-3, 7-1)

2013: 12-1 (8-0) / F/+ #21 / FEI #17 / S&P+ #20 / Program F/+: #36					
2013 Offense			**2013 Defense**		
Offensive F/+	16.4%	13	Defensive F/+	5.2%	38
Offensive FEI	0.467	15	Defensive FEI	-0.243	33
Offensive S&P+	130.1	9	Defensive S&P+	107.6	51
Rushing S&P+	126.9	7	Rushing S&P+	87.7	106
Passing S&P+	128.3	13	Passing S&P+	108.4	38
Standard Downs S&P+	116.8	21	Standard Downs S&P+	104.7	50
Passing Downs S&P+	152.4	4	Passing Downs S&P+	87.5	101
2013 Special Teams			Special Teams F/+	2.2%	23
2014 Projections			SOS Rk	79	
Ret. Starters: 6 OFF, 9 DEF			Offensive F/+	6.8%	27
Proj. F/+	11.6%	25	Defensive F/+	4.8%	34
Mean Wins / Conf Wins	9.4 / 6.8		Conference Title Odds	47.9%	

2013 Five Factors			
Efficiency	Off Success Rate+	121.5	7
	Def Success Rate+	96.4	69
	Total Efficiency	218.0	25
Explosiveness	Off IsoPPP+	108.2	26
	Def IsoPPP+	100.2	57
	Total Explosiveness	208.4	36
Field Position	Field Pos. Adv. (FPA)	0.520	37
Finishing Drives	Off Red Zone S&P+	104.6	41
	Def Red Zone S&P+	88.2	92
	Total Red Zone Rating	192.8	79
Turnovers	Turnover Margin	+5.0	32
	Exp. TO Margin	+8.4	12
	Difference	-3.4	85

Central Florida has only been playing major college football for 18 years, a program rising (unsteadily at times, but rising overall) since George O'Leary took charge a decade ago. It was less than a decade ago that the Knights went 0-11 in 2004. Last year, they capped off a 12-1 season with a Fiesta Bowl victory over Big 12 champion Baylor. In between, UCF claimed two Conference USA titles, each of which was immediately followed up with a losing season the following year. O'Leary now has back-to-back 10-win seasons under his belt and looks to keep the momentum going with an offense rebuilding in key spots.

Blake Bortles' move up I-4 to Jacksonville leaves a big hole in the center of the Knights' attack. Bortles was a two-year starter at UCF who connected on more than 65 percent of his passes and threw for 6,640 yards and 50 touchdowns in 2012 and 2013. UCF loses 1,000-yard rusher Storm Johnson and three offensive line starters as well, after ranking seventh in Rushing S&P+ and 11th in Adjusted Line Yards a year ago. The offense chewed up 60.4 percent of available yards last season (fourth in the nation) and scored 3.3 points per drive started inside their own 20-yard line (third).

Presumed new starting quarterback Justin Holman is a sophomore with a mere 14 career pass attempts, but at least he has a roster loaded with talented receivers to target. Three UCF receivers averaged more than 10 yards per target (seniors Rannell Hall and J.J. Worton plus junior Breshad Perriman) and UAB transfer Jackie Williams had more than 1,400 yards receiving in two seasons with the Blazers. If the rebuilt line can give Holman time to throw, he'll have options getting open downfield. Sophomore running back William Stanback (4.2 yards per carry) will get most of the carries out of the backfield; UCF has featured a different leading rusher in each of the last four seasons.

The defense brings back loads of experience and will only face one opponent (Missouri) that ranked among the top 25 in Offensive FEI last year. The strength of the defense is the secondary, led by senior strong safety Clayton Geathers (82 tackles, 12 passes defensed) and senior free safety Brandon

Alexander (three interceptions). Central Florida allowed only 7.4 percent of opponent drives to average at least 10 yards per play (11th best nationally). Junior defensive end Thomas Niles (four sacks, eight tackles for loss) anchors a defensive line that ranked fifth in stuff rate a year ago.

The schedule is front-loaded with four opponents ranked between No. 20 and No. 42 in the first seven weeks, and zero opponents ranked among the top 60 down the stretch. The Knights have a road test at Houston on October 2 that could decide the conference race, but this is a good candidate to get on a roll later in the year and potentially chase down a league title from behind.

2015 Draft Prospects: ILB Terrance Plummer (7-FA).

No. 26 Boise State Broncos (10-2, 7-1)

2013: 8-5 (6-2) / F/+ #45 / FEI #57 / S&P+ #38 / Program F/+: #8					
2013 Offense			**2013 Defense**		
Offensive F/+	3.9%	47	Defensive F/+	-1.5%	72
Offensive FEI	0.093	49	Defensive FEI	0.152	83
Offensive S&P+	108.7	40	Defensive S&P+	112.4	36
Rushing S&P+	107.6	46	Rushing S&P+	118.4	21
Passing S&P+	104.8	53	Passing S&P+	92.6	90
Standard Downs S&P+	107.1	43	Standard Downs S&P+	108.3	37
Passing Downs S&P+	104.0	54	Passing Downs S&P+	100.6	65
2013 Special Teams			Special Teams F/+	4.7%	3
2014 Projections			SOS Rk	102	
Ret. Starters: 7 OFF, 9 DEF			Offensive F/+	4.6%	36
Proj. F/+	11.0%	26	Defensive F/+	6.4%	29
Mean Wins / Conf Wins	10.2 / 7.3		Conf. / Div. Title Odds	65.8% / 81.1%	

2013 Five Factors			
Efficiency	Off Success Rate+	105.8	44
	Def Success Rate+	98.2	61
	Total Efficiency	204.0	53
Explosiveness	Off IsoPPP+	99.6	64
	Def IsoPPP+	112.3	15
	Total Explosiveness	212.0	27
Field Position	Field Pos. Adv. (FPA)	0.493	74
Finishing Drives	Off Red Zone S&P+	107.3	34
	Def Red Zone S&P+	119.0	15
	Total Red Zone Rating	226.4	15
Turnovers	Turnover Margin	+3.0	41
	Exp. TO Margin	+2.0	51
	Difference	+1.0	51

No program has celebrated victory more often over the last decade than Boise State, with a record of 106-18 (.855) against FBS opponents since the start of the 2004 season. The Broncos won at least 10 total games eight times in that span, earned a conference co-championship or outright title seven times, and played their way to two BCS bowl victories. Chris Petersen presided over almost all of that success, but the blow of his departure for Washington was softened a bit by the hire of new head coach Bryan Harsin, the offensive coordinator during both of Boise State's BCS bowl seasons. The Broncos bring a good mix of experience and young talent to the field this fall, and with a manageable schedule, they have the best projected opportunity to grab the "Group of Five" spot in 2014.

The Boise State offense will be at its most lethal on the ground this fall, if it can protect the football. Harsin's Arkansas State offense ran the ball on 61.2 percent of its plays last season and the Broncos have a workhorse in senior Jay Ajayi (1,425 yards, 5.7 yards per carry, 5.6 highlight yards per opportunity, eight games with 20 or more carries in 2013) to run early and often. Boise State was one of only four teams to rank among the top 20 in methodical drives (19.4 percent of possessions) and points per game (37.5) a year ago. The ground game was careless with the ball at times, however—13 fumbles lost on the year including four combined fumbles in costly losses to Fresno State and BYU (18.2 points of field position value surrendered on turnovers). Perhaps Harsin can make an impact on that front as well—his Red Wolves offense ranked seventh nationally in fewest turnovers lost last year (14).

The Broncos defense was not particularly efficient at getting opponents off the field in 2013 (89th in forcing three-and-outs, 88th in available yards), but they didn't get burned by big plays very often (fourth in explosive drives allowed) and the back seven returns all of its key contributors from a year ago. Junior cornerback Donte Deayon, senior cornerback Bryan Douglas, and junior safety Darian Thompson collected a total of 14 interceptions, but the Broncos' scheme allowed a high completion rate overall (64.6 percent, 90th in passing S&P+).

The Broncos special teams ranked third nationally in overall special teams efficiency, the fifth time they've finished among the top 10 in that metric in the last seven seasons. The schedule sets up nicely for a run to double-digit victories—after a neutral-site test against Ole Miss in the opener, the Broncos' three toughest remaining opponents (Fresno State, BYU, Utah State) all have to make a trip to Boise.

2015 Draft Prospects: None.

No. 32 BYU Cougars (9-3)

2013: 8-5 / F/+ #30 / FEI #27 / S&P+ #27 / Program F/+: #28					
2013 Offense			**2013 Defense**		
Offensive F/+	2.8%	51	Defensive F/+	13.8%	15
Offensive FEI	0.096	48	Defensive FEI	-0.459	14
Offensive S&P+	104.0	48	Defensive S&P+	126.7	16
Rushing S&P+	118.6	17	Rushing S&P+	124.1	11
Passing S&P+	97.7	68	Passing S&P+	111.9	33
Standard Downs S&P+	112.0	34	Standard Downs S&P+	118.4	18
Passing Downs S&P+	97.4	66	Passing Downs S&P+	116.6	30
2013 Special Teams			Special Teams F/+	-1.7%	95
2014 Projections			SOS Rk	77	
Ret. Starters: 8 OFF, 5 DEF			Offensive F/+	1.8%	53
Proj. F/+	10.4%	32	Defensive F/+	8.6%	20
Mean Wins / Conf Wins	9.0 / 0.0				

2013 Five Factors			
Efficiency	Off Success Rate+	100.6	59
	Def Success Rate+	114.2	19
	Total Efficiency	214.8	30
Explosiveness	Off IsoPPP+	108.2	27
	Def IsoPPP+	106.0	37
	Total Explosiveness	214.2	21
Field Position	Field Pos. Adv. (FPA)	0.505	57
Finishing Drives	Off Red Zone S&P+	103.8	45
	Def Red Zone S&P+	122.9	8
	Total Red Zone Rating	226.7	14
Turnovers	Turnover Margin	+2.0	48
	Exp. TO Margin	+5.0	36
	Difference	-3.0	84

The offseason can be unkind for some programs with attrition and injury, but the Cougars were dealt a blow at the ACC spring conference meetings held 2000 miles away from Provo, Utah. The ACC announced a new future scheduling policy that will require league teams to schedule one non-conference game annually against a "power" opponent, and BYU (23rd in all-time winning percentage against FBS opponents) was tossed into the non-power bucket. Potential marquee matchups may be harder to come by in the future, which raises the stakes for BYU to make a big statement this year. Road trips to UCF, Texas, and Boise State will each provide that opportunity.

BYU's biggest statements will be made up front with a roster loaded with offensive line experience. Junior right tackle Ryker Mathews and senior left guard Solomone Kafu have 36 career starts between them, and there are nine linemen on the roster who have started at least one game for the Cougars. BYU ranked 7th nationally in Adjusted Line Yards last year and could be even stronger this fall. That bodes well for junior quarterback Taysom Hill and junior running back Jamaal Williams, who combined for 2,806 yards and 17 touchdowns on the ground last season. Texas was on the wrong end of 441 of those yards from Hill and Williams last year, one of two games last season where BYU had more than 70 rushing attempts in a game. The passing attack is less reliable (53 percent completions, 68th in S&P+ passing) but when Hill finds a rhythm, defenses need to pick their poison.

BYU's defense will have new leadership following the departure of star linebacker Kyle Van Noy (Detroit second-rounder), but head coach Bronco Mendenhall has been solid for several years. The Cougars have ranked among the top 25 in available yards surrendered in each of the last four seasons, and they have consecutive top 10 rankings in points per value drive. Junior linebacker Alani Fua, and senior defensive backs Craig Bills and Robertson Daniel are the only returning starters who ranked among the top 10 in tackles for BYU in 2013. Several holes will be filled by upperclassmen returning from their Mormon missions, but there are enough question marks to be concerned about a modest drop-off in efficiency.

Look for field-position battles to swing games for the Cougars this fall. BYU started 23.5 percent of its possessions from inside its own 20-yard line (93rd nationally) and scored only 1.2 points per drive in those situations (82nd nationally).

2015 Draft Prospects: None.

No. 39 Houston Cougars (9-3, 6-2)

2013: 8-5 (5-3) / F/+ #46 / FEI #34 / S&P+ #52 / Program F/+: #45					
2013 Offense			**2013 Defense**		
Offensive F/+	-2.3%	68	Defensive F/+	7.9%	28
Offensive FEI	-0.129	74	Defensive FEI	-0.339	29
Offensive S&P+	101.5	58	Defensive S&P+	111.3	40
Rushing S&P+	107.8	45	Rushing S&P+	106.2	46
Passing S&P+	101.1	62	Passing S&P+	94.4	87
Standard Downs S&P+	106.2	49	Standard Downs S&P+	102.6	56
Passing Downs S&P+	102.0	56	Passing Downs S&P+	97.7	78
2013 Special Teams			Special Teams F/+	1.1%	43
2014 Projections			SOS Rk	100	
Ret. Starters: 8 OFF, 9 DEF			Offensive F/+	1.4%	57
Proj. F/+	8.2%	39	Defensive F/+	6.8%	27
Mean Wins / Conf Wins	9.4 / 6.3		Conference Title Odds	31.8%	

2013 Five Factors			
Efficiency	Off Success Rate+	94.4	82
	Def Success Rate+	97.5	67
	Total Efficiency	191.8	83
Explosiveness	Off IsoPPP+	117.7	4
	Def IsoPPP+	104.4	41
	Total Explosiveness	222.1	9
Field Position	Field Pos. Adv. (FPA)	0.547	10
Finishing Drives	Off Red Zone S&P+	93.5	86
	Def Red Zone S&P+	99.5	61
	Total Red Zone Rating	192.9	78
Turnovers	Turnover Margin	+25.0	1
	Exp. TO Margin	+3.8	43
	Difference	+21.2	1

Houston was a great example of a team in 2013 that wasn't particularly successful on a play-by-play basis, but found a way to win possessions anyway thanks to turnovers and field position. The Cougars defense ranked 87th in passing S&P+ and 62nd in overall S&P+ defense, but once opponents crossed into Houston territory their drives often sputtered and died (10th nationally in opponent points per value drive). Houston made a living on turnovers, with 43 takeaways and just 18 giveaways; that gave them an estimated 70.7 points worth of field position off turnovers on the year. The Houston offense started drives 4.6 yards further downfield on average than its opponents (15th nationally), equivalent to an extra 64-yard advantage in non-garbage time per game. Turnover luck—Houston recovered an unusual 63 percent of fumbles in 2013—is a bit of a red flag for our fall projections. But the Cougars play the lightest schedule of any projected top-50 team, and they have enough talent to challenge UCF for the American conference crown.

Sophomore quarterback John O'Korn threw more passes (446) than all but one other first-year player in the country last season, and only 10 of those fell in to the hands of his opponents. His accuracy (58.1 percent in 2013) may improve with a year of experience under his belt, and the big-play potential of his receiving corps is significant. Junior wide receiver Deontay Greenberry gained at least 20 yards on 19 receptions last year, and six went for 40 or more yards. Senior wideout Shane Ros is back in the lineup following a knee injury that sidelined him last fall, and could be another star (14.7 yards per reception in 2012). However, offensive efficiency plagued the boom-or-bust Cougars last year (97th in avoiding three-and-out), and an offensive line thin on experience could hold them back again in 2014.

The defensive front seven is loaded with experience and production. Houston tallied 31 sacks and 78 tackles for loss last year, and all but one of the players who chipped in to those totals is back on campus. Senior linebackers Derrick Mathews and Efrem Oliphant combined for 197 tackles, 25 tackles for loss, 9.5 sacks and five passes defensed a year ago. Houston was a bit susceptible to methodical drives (14.9 percent of opponent possessions, 72nd nationally), an area of focus for improvement that could in turn help the offense find a better rhythm.

2015 Draft Prospects: WR Deontay Greenberry (2-3).*

No. 49 Cincinnati Bearcats (8-4, 6-2)

2013: 9-4 (6-2) / F/+ #64 / FEI #54 / S&P+ #56 / Program F/+: #34						2013 Five Factors			
2013 Offense			**2013 Defense**				Off Success Rate+	100.0	63
Offensive F/+	2.3%	53	Defensive F/+	2.0%	52	Efficiency	Def Success Rate+	95.9	71
Offensive FEI	0.082	51	Defensive FEI	-0.090	54		Total Efficiency	196.0	70
Offensive S&P+	103.0	50	Defensive S&P+	106.7	54		Off IsoPPP+	100.1	60
Rushing S&P+	95.6	84	Rushing S&P+	103.2	60	Explosiveness	Def IsoPPP+	107.8	27
Passing S&P+	107.7	44	Passing S&P+	95.6	80		Total Explosiveness	207.9	37
Standard Downs S&P+	96.2	79	Standard Downs S&P+	105.5	46	Field Position	Field Pos. Adv. (FPA)	0.503	59
Passing Downs S&P+	120.5	25	Passing Downs S&P+	87.8	98		Off Red Zone S&P+	95.6	81
2013 Special Teams			Special Teams F/+	-5.7%	123	Finishing Drives	Def Red Zone S&P+	90.6	87
2014 Projections			SOS Rk	71			Total Red Zone Rating	186.2	94
Ret. Starters: 7 OFF, 6 DEF			Offensive F/+	2.7%	46		Turnover Margin	-7.0	101
Proj. F/+	3.0%	49	Defensive F/+	0.3%	62	Turnovers	Exp. TO Margin	+0.4	68
Mean Wins / Conf Wins	7.6 / 5.6		Conference Title Odds	14.1%			Difference	-7.4	116

A raw statistical view of the 2013 Cincinnati defense suggests this was one of the most impenetrable in college football. The Bearcats held seven opponents to 100 yards rushing or fewer, allowed only 34.7 percent of available yards (sixth best nationally) and forced three-and-outs on 44.4 percent of opponent drives (also sixth). But they played so few competent offenses (five ranked 104th or worse according to FEI), and an opponent-adjusted view of their performances was far less rosy. Cincinnati gave up an average of 35 points per game in losses against the only three top-50 offenses they faced last year. This year's team projects to have a similarly tough time handling the big dogs on the schedule (non-conference games against Ohio State and Miami), but could find itself in the American conference title chase simply due to the fact that they won't play league favorite UCF.

Quarterback play will be a key indicator of the kind of season Cincinnati is in store for right out the gate. Notre Dame transfer Gunner Kiel, a hyped recruit from three years ago, will finally take his first collegiate snap this fall. Kiel has a young offensive line, but a slew of experienced receivers and backs to target in the passing game. Junior wide receiver Shaq Washington was targeted 100 times last season and caught 77 percent of those passes for an average gain of 10.2 yards per reception. Remarkably, he only picked up one touchdown reception, a total that is sure to change with a more reliable passing game. Senior running backs Hosey Williams and Ralph David Abernathy IV shared the load with a combined 1,173 yards (4.7 per carry, 4.8 highlight yards per opportunity) and nine touchdowns on the ground.

The strength in the front seven comes off the edges—junior defensive end Silverberry Mouhon, senior defensive end Brad Harrah, and senior linebacker Nick Temple combined for 19 sacks and 36 tackles for loss last fall, leaders of a unit that ranked 14th in Adjusted Sack Rate on passing downs. Cincinnati is inexperienced elsewhere, so it is probably too much to ask that they leap forward on this side of the ball.

Again, the opposition should be weak enough that it may not matter.

What might matter most is cleaning up the terrible special teams performances from last season. The Bearcats had 10 games last season in which they lost value on special teams, and the kicking game in particular (124th nationally in field-goal efficiency, 7-of-17 on the year) did them no favors. Senior Tony Milano has 64 field goal attempts in the last three seasons, but his 64 percent career success rate wouldn't put him among the top 90 kickers last season.

2015 Draft Prospects: OT Eric Lefeld (4-5).

Brian Fremeau

Projected Win Probabilities For American Conference Teams

			Overall Wins													Conference Wins								
Div	Conf	American	12-0	11-1	10-2	9-3	8-4	7-5	6-6	5-7	4-8	3-9	2-10	1-11	0-12	8-0	7-1	6-2	5-3	4-4	3-5	2-6	1-7	0-8
-	48	Central Florida	3	16	30	29	16	5	1	-	-	-	-	-	-	23	42	26	8	1	-	-	-	-
-	14	Cincinnati	-	1	8	19	27	24	14	6	1	-	-	-	-	5	20	31	26	13	4	1	-	-
-	1	Connecticut	-	-	-	1	6	13	23	27	19	9	2	-	-	-	1	3	13	26	30	20	6	1
-	4	East Carolina	-	-	1	4	12	23	28	21	9	2	-	-	-	1	5	18	30	27	14	4	1	-
-	31	Houston	3	16	30	29	15	6	1	-	-	-	-	-	-	12	32	33	17	5	1	-	-	-
-	1	Memphis	-	-	-	-	3	10	21	28	23	12	3	-	-	-	-	3	11	24	30	22	9	1
-	-	SMU	-	-	-	-	-	1	5	13	24	28	20	8	1	-	-	1	6	18	31	29	13	2
-	-	South Florida	-	-	-	-	1	6	15	25	27	18	7	1	-	-	-	1	5	16	28	30	16	4
-	-	Temple	-	-	-	-	2	8	18	26	25	15	5	1	-	-	-	2	9	22	31	24	10	2
-	-	Tulane	-	-	-	-	1	3	9	20	29	25	11	2	-	-	-	-	3	14	28	32	19	4
-	1	Tulsa	-	-	-	2	6	17	26	25	16	6	2	-	-	-	1	6	18	30	28	14	3	-

Projected Win Probabilities For Conference USA Teams

			Overall Wins													Conference Wins								
Div	Conf	Conf USA East	12-0	11-1	10-2	9-3	8-4	7-5	6-6	5-7	4-8	3-9	2-10	1-11	0-12	8-0	7-1	6-2	5-3	4-4	3-5	2-6	1-7	0-8
5	2	Florida Atlantic	-	-	-	1	6	15	25	26	18	7	2	-	-	-	3	13	27	31	19	6	1	-
-	-	Florida International	-	-	-	-	-	2	8	21	32	27	10	-	-	-	-	-	2	8	20	32	28	10
79	54	Marshall	23	36	26	11	3	1	-	-	-	-	-	-	-	30	39	22	8	1	-	-	-	-
11	4	Middle Tennessee	-	-	1	6	16	26	26	17	7	1	-	-	-	1	9	23	31	23	10	3	-	-
-	-	Old Dominion	-	-	-	-	-	2	8	20	30	26	12	2	-	-	-	-	2	8	22	34	26	8
-	-	UAB	-	-	-	-	1	3	10	22	30	24	9	1	-	-	-	1	4	13	28	32	18	4
5	2	Western Kentucky	-	-	1	3	11	21	26	22	12	3	1	-	-	-	4	16	30	29	16	4	1	-
Div	Conf	Conf USA West	12-0	11-1	10-2	9-3	8-4	7-5	6-6	5-7	4-8	3-9	2-10	1-11	0-12	8-0	7-1	6-2	5-3	4-4	3-5	2-6	1-7	0-8
5	1	Louisiana Tech	-	-	-	-	3	9	20	28	24	12	4	-	-	-	1	8	19	28	26	14	4	-
36	14	North Texas	-	1	5	16	27	27	16	6	2	-	-	-	-	3	17	32	29	14	4	1	-	-
18	6	Rice	-	-	1	3	13	24	27	19	9	3	1	-	-	1	8	23	31	24	10	3	-	-
1	-	Southern Mississippi	-	-	-	-	1	6	16	28	28	16	4	1	-	-	-	1	7	19	31	28	12	2
1	-	UTEP	-	-	-	-	-	2	7	18	28	27	14	4	-	-	-	1	4	14	29	32	17	3
39	17	UTSA	-	-	2	10	23	29	22	10	3	1	-	-	-	5	21	32	26	13	3	-	-	-

Projected Win Probabilities For Independent Teams

			Overall Wins												
Div	Conf	Independents	12-0	11-1	10-2	9-3	8-4	7-5	6-6	5-7	4-8	3-9	2-10	1-11	0-12
-	-	Army	-	-	-	1	7	15	25	27	18	6	1	-	-
-	-	BYU	1	9	25	32	22	9	2	-	-	-	-	-	-
-	-	Navy	-	3	15	30	29	16	6	1	-	-	-	-	-
-	-	Notre Dame	-	-	4	14	27	28	18	7	2	-	-	-	-

Projected Win Probabilities For Mid-American Teams

			Overall Wins													Conference Wins								
Div	Conf	MAC East	12-0	11-1	10-2	9-3	8-4	7-5	6-6	5-7	4-8	3-9	2-10	1-11	0-12	8-0	7-1	6-2	5-3	4-4	3-5	2-6	1-7	0-8
3	-	Akron	-	-	-	-	1	7	19	32	28	11	2	-	-	-	-	4	15	32	32	15	2	-
71	36	Bowling Green	1	9	24	32	23	9	2	-	-	-	-	-	-	14	40	31	13	2	-	-	-	-
22	5	Buffalo	-	1	6	21	30	25	12	4	1	-	-	-	-	1	13	30	31	17	7	1	-	-
3	1	Kent State	-	-	-	1	4	13	25	28	19	8	2	-	-	-	1	6	22	36	25	9	1	-
-	-	Massachusetts	-	-	-	-	-	-	-	1	4	15	32	35	13	-	-	-	-	2	10	30	40	18
-	-	Miami (OH)	-	-	-	-	-	-	2	9	23	35	25	6	-	-	-	-	1	9	23	35	26	6
1	-	Ohio	-	-	-	1	4	12	23	28	21	9	2	-	-	-	-	3	11	24	31	22	8	1
Div	Conf	MAC West	12-0	11-1	10-2	9-3	8-4	7-5	6-6	5-7	4-8	3-9	2-10	1-11	0-12	8-0	7-1	6-2	5-3	4-4	3-5	2-6	1-7	0-8
6	3	Ball State	-	1	4	16	30	29	15	4	1	-	-	-	-	-	5	21	36	27	9	2	-	-
2	1	Central Michigan	-	-	1	5	12	23	28	20	9	2	-	-	-	-	1	9	26	34	21	8	1	-
-	-	Eastern Michigan	-	-	-	-	-	-	1	5	17	32	32	13	-	-	-	-	-	2	12	29	38	19
59	36	Northern Illinois	3	15	30	30	16	5	1	-	-	-	-	-	-	25	40	25	9	1	-	-	-	-
33	18	Toledo	-	3	13	26	30	19	8	1	-	-	-	-	-	10	33	35	17	4	1	-	-	-
-	-	Western Michigan	-	-	-	-	1	6	16	28	28	16	4	1	-	-	-	1	5	19	35	29	10	1

Projected Win Probabilities For Mountain West Teams

			Overall Wins													Conference Wins								
Div	Conf	MWC Mountain	12-0	11-1	10-2	9-3	8-4	7-5	6-6	5-7	4-8	3-9	2-10	1-11	0-12	8-0	7-1	6-2	5-3	4-4	3-5	2-6	1-7	0-8
-	-	Air Force	-	-	-	-	2	8	18	27	26	15	4	-	-	-	-	1	4	14	29	32	17	3
81	66	Boise State	12	32	32	17	6	1	-	-	-	-	-	-	-	47	38	13	2	-	-	-	-	-
2	1	Colorado State	-	-	2	6	17	26	25	16	6	2	-	-	-	-	2	9	25	33	22	8	1	-
-	-	New Mexico	-	-	-	-	-	-	3	9	23	31	24	7	3	-	-	-	-	3	15	31	35	16
17	10	Utah State*	-	2	12	25	29	20	10	2	-	-	-	-	-	4	27	38	23	7	1	-	-	-
-	-	Wyoming	-	-	-	-	-	2	9	21	30	25	11	2	-	-	-	-	4	14	29	32	17	4
Div	Conf	MWC West	12-0	11-1	10-2	9-3	8-4	7-5	6-6	5-7	4-8	3-9	2-10	1-11	0-12	8-0	7-1	6-2	5-3	4-4	3-5	2-6	1-7	0-8
52	15	Fresno State	-	-	4	15	29	29	16	6	1	-	-	-	-	3	21	37	27	10	2	-	-	-
2	-	Hawaii*	-	-	-	-	-	2	7	17	26	26	16	5	1	-	-	2	8	20	31	27	10	2
28	5	Nevada	-	-	2	8	19	27	24	14	5	1	-	-	-	1	9	23	30	23	11	3	-	-
12	2	San Diego State	-	-	-	4	14	29	29	17	6	1	-	-	-	-	2	12	30	32	17	6	1	-
5	1	San Jose State	-	-	-	1	4	11	22	28	22	10	2	-	-	-	1	6	18	30	27	14	4	-
1	-	UNLV*	-	-	-	-	-	2	10	21	31	25	10	1	-	-	-	1	7	18	31	29	12	2

**Utah State, Hawaii, and UNLV will play 13 regular season games; for projected overall records, 12-0 means 13-0, 11-1 means 12-1, etc.*

Projected Win Probabilities For Sun Belt Teams

			Overall Wins													Conference Wins								
Div	Conf	Sun Belt	12-0	11-1	10-2	9-3	8-4	7-5	6-6	5-7	4-8	3-9	2-10	1-11	0-12	8-0	7-1	6-2	5-3	4-4	3-5	2-6	1-7	0-8
-	-	Appalachian State	-	-	-	-	1	7	17	29	29	14	3	-	-	-	-	1	4	14	29	32	17	3
-	17	Arkansas State	-	-	3	11	24	29	21	10	2	-	-	-	-	3	17	33	28	14	4	1	-	-
-	-	Georgia Southern	-	-	-	-	-	3	10	23	30	23	9	2	-	-	-	2	10	22	30	24	10	2
-	-	Georgia State	-	-	-	-	-	1	7	19	31	28	12	2	-	-	-	1	4	15	31	32	14	3
-	1	Idaho	-	-	-	-	1	6	13	23	26	19	10	2	-	-	1	4	14	26	29	19	6	1
-	48	Louisiana Lafayette	-	2	16	32	29	15	5	1	-	-	-	-	-	17	34	30	14	4	1	-	-	-
-	7	Louisiana Monroe	-	-	-	1	6	17	27	26	16	6	1	-	-	1	9	23	31	23	10	3	-	-
-	-	New Mexico State	-	-	-	-	-	-	2	8	20	32	28	9	1	-	-	-	-	3	14	30	36	17
-	21	South Alabama	-	-	1	7	19	29	25	13	5	1	-	-	-	4	22	35	26	11	2	-	-	-
-	2	Texas State	-	-	-	1	4	12	24	29	20	8	2	-	-	-	1	9	21	31	25	11	2	-
-	4	Troy	-	-	-	3	13	24	29	20	9	2	-	-	-	-	4	17	31	29	15	4	-	-

NCAA Teams, No. 1 to No. 128

Rk	Team	Conf	Proj F/+	TMW	Rec	Conf	SOS	Rk	Play	Rk	Team	Conf	Proj F/+	TMW	Rec	Conf	SOS	Rk	Play
1	Florida State	ACC	0.325	11.6	12-0	8-0	0.337	56	73.4	56	Fresno State	MWC	0.009	7.4	7-5	6-2	0.444	69	0.0
2	Alabama	SEC	0.299	11.3	11-1	7-1	0.245	45	68.7	57	Marshall	Conf USA	0.006	10.6	11-1	7-1	0.946	128	1.0
3	Oregon	Pac-12	0.245	10.7	11-1	8-1	0.260	49	40.5	58	Navy	Ind-Navy	0.005	8.4	8-4	-	0.553	85	0.0
4	Stanford	Pac-12	0.220	9.5	10-2	7-2	0.087	12	27.9	59	Washington St.	Pac-12	0.005	4.2	4-8	2-7	0.125	19	0.0
5	South Carolina	SEC	0.202	9.7	10-2	6-2	0.196	33	12.1	60	West Virginia	Big 12	0.005	4.0	4-8	3-6	0.099	15	0.0
6	Oklahoma	Big 12	0.195	10.5	10-2	8-1	0.431	68	29.8	61	Vanderbilt	SEC	0.004	5.9	6-6	2-6	0.246	47	0.0
7	LSU	SEC	0.190	8.9	9-3	5-3	0.096	14	10.7	62	Arkansas	SEC	0.002	3.6	4-8	1-7	0.065	6	0.0
8	Ohio State	Big Ten	0.189	10.4	10-2	7-1	0.423	66	22.4	63	East Carolina	American	0.002	6.1	6-6	5-3	0.354	59	0.0
9	Auburn	SEC	0.188	8.4	8-4	5-3	0.043	3	12.5	64	Tennessee	SEC	-0.012	4.0	4-8	2-6	0.057	5	0.0
10	USC	Pac-12	0.176	9.2	9-3	7-2	0.180	30	5.8	65	Syracuse	ACC	-0.012	5.1	5-7	3-5	0.158	27	0.0
11	Georgia	SEC	0.174	9.3	9-3	6-2	0.216	41	5.8	66	Iowa State	Big 12	-0.018	4.0	4-8	2-7	0.240	44	0.0
12	Michigan State	Big Ten	0.174	9.8	10-2	7-1	0.203	35	16.7	67	Virginia	ACC	-0.021	3.6	4-8	2-6	0.069	9	0.0
13	Texas A&M	SEC	0.163	8.1	8-4	4-4	0.040	2	4.4	68	Nevada	MWC	-0.023	6.7	7-5	5-3	0.619	93	0.0
14	Clemson	ACC	0.160	8.9	9-3	6-2	0.069	7	11.5	69	Minnesota	Big Ten	-0.023	5.0	5-7	2-6	0.322	54	0.0
15	Baylor	Big 12	0.159	9.6	10-2	7-2	0.315	52	14.4	70	N.C. State	ACC	-0.026	5.7	6-6	2-6	0.150	25	0.0
16	UCLA	Pac-12	0.158	8.3	8-4	6-3	0.173	28	1.7	71	Rutgers	Big Ten	-0.031	3.7	4-8	1-7	0.230	43	0.0
17	Oklahoma St.	Big 12	0.156	8.3	8-4	6-3	0.069	8	7.1	72	UTSA	Conf USA	-0.036	7.0	7-5	6-2	0.551	83	0.0
18	Wisconsin	Big Ten	0.145	9.9	10-2	7-1	0.484	73	9.7	73	Illinois	Big Ten	-0.036	5.0	5-7	2-6	0.258	48	0.0
19	Arizona State	Pac-12	0.142	8.2	8-4	6-3	0.196	32	1.2	74	Boston College	ACC	-0.037	4.7	5-7	2-6	0.086	11	0.0
20	Missouri	SEC	0.139	8.4	8-4	5-3	0.212	40	1.2	75	Tulsa	American	-0.042	5.5	6-6	4-4	0.524	78	0.0
21	Louisville	ACC	0.138	9.0	9-3	6-2	0.174	29	5.1	76	La.-Lafayette	Sun Belt	-0.044	8.4	8-4	6-2	0.639	94	0.0
22	Notre Dame	Ind-ND	0.126	7.3	7-5	-	0.045	4	1.9	77	Kentucky	SEC	-0.049	3.8	4-8	1-7	0.156	26	0.0
23	Mississippi	SEC	0.118	7.4	7-5	4-4	0.106	17	0.4	78	Connecticut	American	-0.051	5.3	5-7	3-5	0.671	99	0.0
24	Washington	Pac-12	0.118	9.1	9-4	5-4	0.149	23	1.1	79	Temple	American	-0.055	4.7	5-7	3-5	0.588	88	0.0
25	Central Florida	American	0.116	9.4	9-3	7-1	0.532	79	0.3	80	North Texas	Conf USA	-0.056	7.4	7-5	5-3	0.790	114	0.0
26	Boise State	MWC	0.110	10.2	10-2	7-1	0.717	102	1.0	81	South Florida	American	-0.057	4.4	4-8	3-5	0.551	84	0.0
27	Michigan	Big Ten	0.110	8.2	8-4	5-3	0.246	46	1.1	82	Ball State	MAC	-0.057	7.5	7-5	5-3	0.752	105	0.0
28	Virginia Tech	ACC	0.107	8.9	9-3	6-2	0.392	62	1.2	83	SMU	American	-0.058	3.3	3-9	3-5	0.375	61	0.0
29	Mississippi St.	SEC	0.107	7.8	8-4	4-4	0.073	10	0.6	84	San Diego St.	MWC	-0.059	6.4	6-6	4-4	0.596	89	0.0
30	Florida	SEC	0.105	6.9	7-5	4-4	0.017	1	0.1	85	California	Pac-12	-0.060	2.6	3-9	1-8	0.146	22	0.0
31	Kansas State	Big 12	0.104	7.5	7-5	5-4	0.196	34	0.9	86	Colorado State	MWC	-0.065	6.5	7-5	4-4	0.777	111	0.0
32	BYU	Ind-BYU	0.104	9.0	9-3	-	0.515	77	0.1	87	Memphis	American	-0.066	4.9	5-7	3-5	0.487	74	0.0
33	Iowa	Big Ten	0.103	9.4	9-3	6-2	0.646	95	4.8	88	South Alabama	Sun Belt	-0.071	6.7	7-5	6-2	0.474	72	0.0
34	Texas	Big 12	0.091	6.7	7-5	5-4	0.210	39	0.3	89	Rice	Conf USA	-0.076	6.2	6-6	5-3	0.508	75	0.0
35	TCU	Big 12	0.088	7.6	8-4	5-4	0.323	55	0.8	90	San Jose State	MWC	-0.078	5.1	5-7	4-4	0.542	82	0.0
36	Arizona	Pac-12	0.088	7.1	7-5	5-4	0.142	21	0.1	91	W. Kentucky	Conf USA	-0.081	5.9	6-6	4-4	0.894	123	0.0
37	Oregon State	Pac-12	0.085	7.3	7-5	4-5	0.132	20	0.1	92	Wake Forest	ACC	-0.082	3.8	4-8	1-7	0.099	16	0.0
38	North Carolina	ACC	0.084	7.5	8-4	5-3	0.362	60	0.1	93	Tulane	American	-0.082	3.9	4-8	2-6	0.596	90	0.0
39	Houston	American	0.082	9.4	9-3	6-2	0.685	100	0.3	94	Florida Atlantic	Conf USA	-0.085	5.4	5-7	4-4	0.203	36	0.0
40	Miami	ACC	0.079	6.9	7-5	4-4	0.149	24	0.0	95	Arkansas State	Sun Belt	-0.088	7.1	7-5	6-2	0.832	119	0.0
41	Nebraska	Big Ten	0.070	7.7	8-4	5-3	0.341	58	0.2	96	Buffalo	MAC	-0.097	7.7	8-4	5-3	0.778	112	0.0
42	Penn State	Big Ten	0.066	7.3	7-5	4-4	0.393	63	0.2	97	Mid. Tennessee	Conf USA	-0.098	6.4	6-6	5-3	0.846	120	0.0
43	Pittsburgh	ACC	0.062	8.0	8-4	5-3	0.569	86	0.3	98	Colorado	Pac-12	-0.102	2.5	2-10	1-8	0.116	18	0.0
44	Utah	Pac-12	0.060	5.2	5-7	3-6	0.088	13	0.0	99	Hawaii	MWC	-0.105	4.6	5-8	3-5	0.759	108	0.0
45	Georgia Tech	ACC	0.060	6.9	7-5	4-4	0.321	53	0.0	100	C. Michigan	MAC	-0.107	6.2	6-6	4-4	0.895	124	0.0
46	Texas Tech	Big 12	0.058	6.7	7-5	4-5	0.271	50	0.1	101	Kent State	MAC	-0.108	5.2	5-7	4-4	0.532	80	0.0
47	Northwestern	Big Ten	0.037	6.6	7-5	4-4	0.417	65	0.0	102	Kansas	Big 12	-0.109	2.4	2-10	1-8	0.205	37	0.0
48	Duke	ACC	0.033	7.4	7-5	4-4	0.601	91	0.1	103	Army	Ind-Army	-0.117	5.4	5-7	-	0.456	70	0.0
49	Cincinnati	American	0.030	7.6	8-4	6-2	0.465	71	0.0	104	Purdue	Big Ten	-0.120	3.0	3-9	1-7	0.428	67	0.0
50	Indiana	Big Ten	0.028	5.7	6-6	3-5	0.227	42	0.0	105	UNLV	MWC	-0.122	4.0	4-9	3-5	0.584	97	0.0
51	Northern Illinois	MAC	0.019	9.4	9-3	7-1	0.873	122	0.1	106	Air Force	MWC	-0.126	4.7	5-7	2-6	0.830	118	0.0
52	Maryland	Big Ten	0.019	5.0	5-7	2-6	0.297	51	0.0	107	Louisiana Tech	Conf USA	-0.127	4.9	5-7	4-4	0.337	57	0.0
53	Bowling Green	MAC	0.013	8.9	9-3	7-1	0.671	98	0.0	108	Wyoming	MWC	-0.128	3.9	4-8	2-6	0.206	38	0.0
54	Toledo	MAC	0.011	8.2	8-4	6-2	0.752	106	0.0	109	UL-Monroe	Sun Belt	-0.131	5.5	6-6	5-3	0.395	64	0.0
55	Utah State	MWC	0.009	9.1	9-4	6-2	0.659	96	0.0	110	Ohio	MAC	-0.136	5.1	5-7	3-5	0.900	125	0.0

NCAA Teams, No. 1 to No. 128

Rk	Team	Conf	Proj F/+	TMW	Rec	Conf	SOS	Rk	Play	Rk	Team	Conf	Proj F/+	TMW	Rec	Conf	SOS	Rk	Play
111	Troy	Sun Belt	-0.137	6.2	6-6	5-3	0.606	92	0.0	120	Idaho	Sun Belt	-0.180	4.3	4-8	3-5	0.792	116	0.0
112	Southern Miss.	Conf USA	-0.147	4.6	5-7	3-5	0.191	31	0.0	121	Old Dominion	Conf USA	-0.193	3.9	4-8	2-6	0.921	126	0.0
113	Akron	MAC	-0.148	4.8	5-7	4-4	0.773	110	0.0	122	Appalachian St.	Sun Belt	-0.212	4.7	5-7	2-6	0.790	115	0.0
114	W. Michigan	MAC	-0.150	4.6	5-7	3-5	0.748	104	0.0	123	Ga. Southern	Sun Belt	-0.219	4.1	4-8	3-5	0.855	121	0.0
115	Texas State	Sun Belt	-0.161	5.2	5-7	4-4	0.938	127	0.0	124	E. Michigan	MAC	-0.222	2.7	3-9	1-7	0.509	76	0.0
116	UAB	Conf USA	-0.164	4.0	4-8	2-6	0.771	109	0.0	125	Miami (OH)	MAC	-0.224	3.1	3-9	2-6	0.722	103	0.0
117	New Mexico	MWC	-0.167	3.1	3-9	2-6	0.712	101	0.0	126	Georgia State	Sun Belt	-0.227	3.8	4-8	3-5	0.539	81	0.0
118	UTEP	Conf USA	-0.173	3.7	4-8	2-6	0.757	107	0.0	127	Massachusetts	MAC	-0.245	1.6	2-10	1-7	0.812	117	0.0
119	Florida Int'l	Conf USA	-0.178	4.0	4-8	2-6	0.779	113	0.0	128	New Mexico St.	Sun Belt	-0.268	3.0	3-9	2-6	0.573	87	0.0

Table 1. Top 2015 Draft Prospects from Other Schools

Name	Pos	School	Conf/Level	Proj Rnd
Christian Covington*	DT	Rice	Conference USA	1-2
Kyler Fackrell*	OLB	Utah State	Mountain West	2-3
Derron Smith	FS	Fresno State	Mountain West	2-3
Lorenzo Doss*	CB	Tulane	American	3-5
Justin Hardy	WR	East Carolina	American	3-5
Byron Jones	CB	Connecticut	American	3-5
Tyeler Davison	DT	Fresno State	Mountain West	4-5
Ty Sambrailo	OT	Colorado State	Mountain West	4-5
Chuckie Keeton	QB	Utah State	Mountain West	4-6
Junior Sylvestre	OLB	Toledo	MAC	4-6
Stephen Godbolt III	CB	Tennessee State	FCS	5-6
Andrew Manley	QB	Eastern Illinois	FCS	5-6
MyCole Pruitt	TE	Southern Illinois	FCS	5-6
Travis Raciti	DT	San Jose State	Mountain West	5-6
Zach Hodges	OLB	Harvard	FCS	5-7
Michael Orakpo	OLB	Texas State	Sun Belt	5-7
Lynden Trail	DE	Norfolk State	FCS	5-7
Dechane Durante	FS	Northern Illinois	MAC	6-7
Wes Saxton	TE	South Alabama	Sun Belt	6-7
D'Joun Smith	CB	Florida Atlantic	Conference USA	6-7

Playmaker Score v4.0

With the increased use of the passing game in both college and pro football alike, the task of sifting through the bevy of yearly draft prospects for the few players who will develop into legitimate NFL targets has never been more difficult or more important. Football Outsiders has attempted to do so through a series of evolving statistical models affectionately named Playmaker Score. This year, however, you may notice a different name now connected to Football Outsiders' projection system for college wide receivers. I'm Nathan Forster, the creator of SackSEER, which is a similar model used to identify likely successes and failures on defensive edge rushers. I've taken over the system from Vince Verhei and rebuilt it to have the same dual-output as SackSEER, with both a "Playmaker Projection" and a "Playmaker Rating."

Playmaker Projection projects a wide receiver prospect's average NFL regular-season receiving yards through the first five years of the player's career. Playmaker Projection incorporates the player's projected draft round per NFLDraftScout.com as an additional factor, in order to create a list of prospects that balances conventional wisdom with the factors identified by Playmaker Score. Playmaker Rating, on the other hand, uses the statistical trends identified by Playmaker only. Playmaker Rating is expressed in terms of the percentage of historical prospects that the player beats in terms of these statistical trends. So, for example, a Playmaker Rating of 75 percent would mean that the prospect is stronger than 75 percent of the prospects in our database based on the trends identified by Playmaker.

New Playmaker Score consists of the following elements:

- The wide receiver prospect's best or "peak" season for receiving yards per team attempt (i.e., a wide receiver with 1,000 receiving yards whose team passed 400 times would score a "2.50");
- The wide receiver prospect's peak season for receiving touchdowns per team attempt;
- The difference between the prospect's peak season for receiving touchdowns per team and the prospect's most recent season for receiving touchdowns per team attempt (this factor is simply "0" for a player whose peak season was his most recent season);
- The wide receiver's vertical jump from pre-draft workouts;
- A binary variable that rewards players who enter the draft as underclassmen and punishes those who exhaust their college eligibility;
- The wide receiver's college career yards per reception; and
- The wide receiver's rushing attempts per game during his peak season for receiving yards per team attempt.

In taking over Playmaker Score, I rebuilt it from the ground up in order to investigate some theories that were not covered in Vince's original research. Rebuilding the database with some speed, therefore, was of paramount importance, and the consequence of the quick rebuild was to jettison all non-FBS wide receiver prospects from Playmaker. The reasons for dropping FCS and Division II and III wide receivers are twofold: 1) comparing wide receiver numbers across such different competition levels likely will have consequences to the model that required additional care and analysis which we did not have the time to perform for the reboot, and 2) wide receiver statistics for sub-FBS schools do not exist in the same web spaces as FBS statistics, making the addition of each sub-FBS wide receiver much more work than adding his FBS counterparts. The upside, however, is that despite the loss of the sub-FBS wide receivers, we were still able to increase the size of the sample. Playmaker 3.0 was only built around wide receivers drafted from 2005–2009. New Playmaker Score includes all FBS wide receivers drafted from 1996–2011, creating a sample of 424 wide receivers.

The first two metrics for New Playmaker Score will be familiar to anyone who read about previous versions of Playmaker Score: yards per team passing attempt and touchdowns per team passing attempt. Specifically, Playmaker uses the prospect's best or "peak" seasons for these two metrics. As part of the rebuild, we attempted to create a metric that more holistically measured the quality of the wide receiver's college career by looking at multiple seasons. However, after looking at the data, it was pretty clear that this was exactly wrong way to look at wide receiver prospects. There are a surprising number of wide receivers who were "one-hit wonders" in college and parlayed that success into NFL stardom. Brandon Marshall, for example, had only 38 receptions for 479 yards and two touchdown receptions until his senior season, at which point he more than doubled his career output with 74 receptions for 1,195 yards and 11 touchdowns. Current 49ers wide receiver Stevie Johnson had only two FBS college seasons. In the first he had only 159 receiving yards, but in the second he had 1,041 receiving yards and 13 touchdowns. Indeed, I attempted to include various factors that measured the prospect's "second-best" season to provide some small punishment for players without consistent careers. However, these potential factors were not even close to being statistically significant and were almost laughably bad predictors of NFL performance.

One other methodological change that we considered was whether Playmaker should use the player's "peak" season or his final season. Differentiating between the two is difficult because, for a majority of wide receivers, their peak college seasons are their final seasons. However, what seemed to work best was to introduce a new factor that is simply the difference in touchdowns per team attempt between the peak season and the most recent season (we used receiving touchdowns, and not yards, because touchdowns are the stronger predictive factor). If the wide receiver has his peak season in his final season, the factor is simply zero. Historically, this factor ends up working out as roughly splitting the difference between the peak season and the final season. Thus, a wide receiver with a peak season of 12 touchdowns and a final season of six touchdowns would be treated like a wide receiver with a peak final season of nine touchdowns.

The wide receivers with large differences between their peak and final season touchdowns per team attempt have historically been a real boom-or-bust group. Some players who scored poorly on this metric were Andre' Davis, Limas Sweed, and Kevin Dyson, as well as a slew of late-round picks who looked like dynamos at some point in their college careers, but declined sharply and never worked out in the pros. Two important exceptions, however, are Dez Bryant and Torry Holt. Deion Sanders' interactions with Bryant and Bryant's failure to report the same resulted in a junior year "decline" for Bryant that had little to do with his talent. (We suppose it was just more proof that Deion Sanders can shut any receiver down.) Torry Holt, on the other hand, just had a weird ending to his college career; his receiving touchdowns dropped by nearly a third from his junior to senior year, but his receiving yards increased from 1,099 to 1,604.

The next new factor is whether the wide receiver prospect entered the draft as an underclassman. The fact that underclassmen outperform senior wide receivers is hardly surprising—players often enter the draft early only when they are likely to be high picks. What is surprising, however, is that the underclassmen factor is still highly statistically significant even after controlling for draft position.

There are a couple of reasons why college eligibility is an important metric. First, it controls for the structural advantage created by Playmaker's use of the player's "peak" seasons. As compared to a typical junior wide receiver prospect, senior wide receivers have an additional season to have that breakout year, and what's more, they're in a prime position to succeed given the physical maturity and football experience that goes with playing four years of college football. The underclassman factor quite sensibly downgrades senior wide receivers for this advantage.

Second, and perhaps more importantly, this factor rightly punishes wide receivers who do not mature quickly enough to become legitimate NFL prospects until just before their college eligibility runs out. Unlike other positions, such as quarterback, wide receiver prospects typically (and rightfully) have little interest in passing on the draft to help their college programs win the next bowl game. Accordingly, a receiver whose pre-senior draft prospects were too weak to coax him into the draft deserves skepticism, and Playmaker downgrades him accordingly.

Senior wide receivers who have succeeded at the next level tend to fall into one of the following categories: 1) played for a smaller FBS school, making it harder to garner the attention necessary to become a high pick early; 2) was a late entry to FBS-level pass catching due to junior college or a position switch; or 3) played at a time when few players declared early for the NFL Draft. The best drafted senior wide receivers drafted in the last ten years who played for AQ schools are Dwayne Bowe, Lee Evans, Roy Williams, Jordy Nelson, and Eric Decker, and that's where the list just about stops. Those are certainly decent players, but compare them to a similar list of players who came out during the same time period as underclassmen: Larry Fitzgerald, Calvin Johnson, A.J. Green, Anquan Boldin, Andre Johnson, Dez Bryant, and the list goes on.

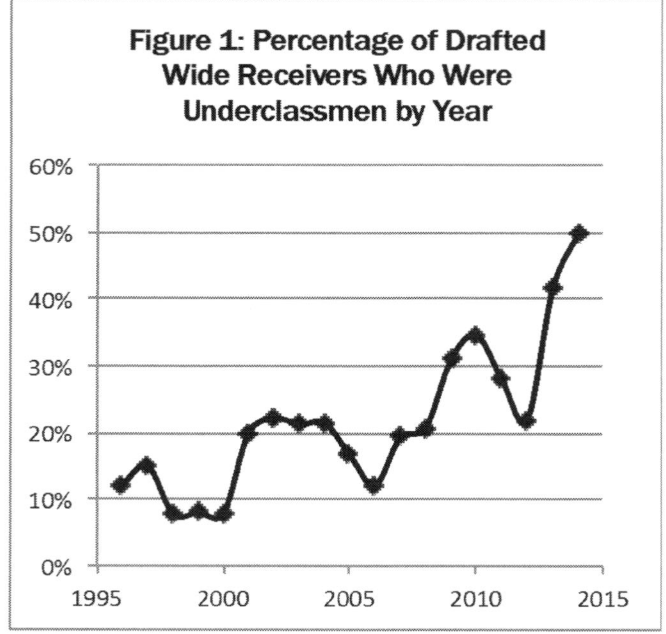

One trend to watch with this metric is the effect of the rookie wage scale on the incentives for wide receiver prospects to leave college early. The proportion of wide receivers who were drafted as underclassmen has increased over time (Figure 1). Only about 10 percent of wide receivers drafted were underclassmen in the mid-to-late '90s, but nearly half of modern day drafted wide receivers are underclassmen. It's hard to say how knowledge of this trend should factor into Playmaker, if at all. We could not come up with a good way to adjust for the surge in early entrants this year, but we might try to do so in the future.

The next factor, yards per reception, will be familiar to long-time followers of Playmaker Score. Big-play wide receivers in college, even if they lack a lot of touches, tend to translate well to the next level. Similarly, possession receivers in college rarely have a role in the NFL at all—with one important exception that leads to the next new factor for Playmaker Score.

The final new factor is the wide receiver's rushing attempts per game during his peak yards per team attempt season. Playmaker Score has been infamous for undershooting the pro prospects of gadget wide receiver/running back-type players. Based on the Playmaker Score rebuild, it appears that this defect can be corrected by including a factor for the wide receiver's usage in the running game.

There is considerable evidence in past data that a heavy workload in the running game can cause a college wide receiver's traditional statistics to be much more pedestrian than his talent might otherwise produce. First, these receivers almost always have unusually low yards per reception. Most likely, their yards per reception numbers are depressed by bubble screens and other "long handoff"-type passing plays that are unlikely to gain big yardage without an amazing play from the wide receiver. The relationship between rushing attempts and yards per reception is so close, in fact, that yards per reception is barely statistically significant without some adjustment for rushing attempts, but is highly statistically significant if such an adjustment is included.

Moreover, wide receivers with a lot of running attempts also tend to score lower in yards per team attempt and touchdowns per team attempt. There are a number of possible reasons for this phenomenon. Maybe rushing attempts cause additional fatigue, making wide receivers less effective when they're called on to perform their traditional function. Maybe coaches tend to reduce the number of snaps in the passing game for these wide receivers in order to give them a break, or even call passing plays that target other pass catchers in order to put less strain on their most versatile wideouts. Whatever the case, the data strongly suggests that an adjustment needs to be made before comparing wide receivers with rushing attempts to those who catch passes and do nothing else.

The rushing factor, as used in Playmaker Score, is designed to avoid giving too big of a bonus to those odd players who managed to accrue mammoth amounts of rushing attempts in college. There were a few players who spent a few seasons as a running back or a quarterback, and thus have outsized attempt numbers. By only using the rushes per game in the player's peak receiving season, Playmaker avoids giving a huge bump to players just because they used to play a different position. Essentially it asks, "How much were you running the ball when you saw the most use in the passing game?"

Incorporation of the rushing factor transforms some of Playmaker's past projections fairly radically. In particular, the old version of Playmaker looked at Percy Harvin as a likely bust, but the new version gives him one of the top projections ever. Percy Harvin only had 2.12 receiving yards per team attempt—more than a full receiving yard per team attempt less than nearly everyone else in the top 20. However, those numbers were extremely good for a player who was also averaging more than five rushing attempts per game during his peak receiving season. Two other interesting cases from last year's draft are Tavon Austin and Cordarrelle Patterson. Both players put up relatively anemic numbers in the passing game for top receiver prospects, but both were also used heavily in the running game. Austin in particular had 72 rushing attempts in his senior season. As a result, Playmaker has changed its mind on Austin and Patterson. Playmaker formerly thought that the two were likely busts, and it now thinks they are both fairly typical first-round prospects.

The final change to Playmaker is the way that it uses predraft workout data. The former version of Playmaker used the prospect's vertical jump and his ten-yard split from his forty-yard dash. For this version, we are keeping the vertical jump but leaving out the ten-yard split for a few reasons. First, ten-yard splits are hard to impossible to find for more than half of prospects in the database. The consequence of using the ten-yard split would be that we would use the forty-yard dash time to estimate the missing splits, which would make the ten-yard split factor mostly a forty-yard dash factor. Second, we are a little skeptical of ten-yard dash as a predictive metric because it does not seem to show up as an important factor for any other position. In short, if the ten-yard split is so important for wide receivers, why is it not important for running backs and edge rushers, positions where bursts in short areas are arguably more important? Also, as a related point, the ten-yard split showed up as barely statistically significant and was not statistically significant in two independent sets of data, meaning that it could possibly be the result of data dredging—the modeling problem that can occur when you look at so many factors that you are bound to stumble on one or more that are statistically significant due to chance. Finally, Alshon Jeffery and Keenan Allen, two prospects who have experienced a lot of success but are still too recent to add to the database, score poorly in this factor. Accordingly, it is likely that the fragile statistical significance of the ten-yard split will likely disappear in a few years once these players are added. Vertical jump remains a part of Playmaker Score. It's possible that in the future we could invent a more sophisticated combine metric that takes into account other drills, but for the time being, vertical jump will be fine. In any event, the vertical jump is the least important of Playmaker's factors so there is likely not too much that can be gained by additional meddling in combine data.

The previous version of Playmaker had an r-squared of 0.25, meaning that 25 percent of the variation for wide receiver success was accounted for by the model. New Playmaker Rating increases that r-squared to 0.345. New Playmaker Projection increases the r-squared to 0.434.

A list of the top 20 wide receivers from 1996-2011 by Playmaker Rating (Table 1) shows us that Playmaker Rating, despite being completely ignorant about draft position, rarely breaks too strongly from conventional wisdom. Except for two third-round picks and three second-round picks, the list is composed completely of players who were taken in the first round of the NFL Draft. Indeed, the most highly-rated fourth-rounder is Justin McCareins, Playmaker's 37th-highest ranked player.

Our list of the best Playmaker Ratings also shows us that even after improvement, the new Playmaker is far from perfect. The list in Table 1 includes future Hall of Famers like Randy Moss, Calvin Johnson, Marvin Harrison, and Larry Fitzgerald, but is nonetheless missing greats such as A.J. Green, Torry Holt, and Andre Johnson, whose Playmaker Ratings were respectable but not nearly as strong as their draft position and talent level warranted. There are also several clunkers in this list, most notably David Terrell and Charles Rogers. You can also probably add Stephen Hill to that list too; he would make the top ten if our list expanded to include the 2012 draft but already looks like a bust with the New York Jets.

Also, let's pause for a word about the mind-blowing awesomeness of Randy Moss. Randy Moss recorded 28 receiving touchdowns in his first year with the Marshall Thundering Herd. This accomplishment is all the more impressive considering that Marshall had only 31 passing touchdowns the whole season. So, yes, Randy Moss caught more than 90 percent of Marshall's passing touchdowns in 1997. Moss faced stronger competition in 1998, when Marshall moved up to FBS-level competition, but he also upgraded to a stronger quarterback in Chad Pennington. Moss's touchdown production dipped in 1998—from 28 to 26.

Another interesting list shows us the first-round picks with the worst Playmaker Ratings between 1996 and 2011 (Table 2). Reggie Wayne and Santana Moss are two of the most obvious misses by the new Playmaker Score, but it's not a coincidence that they both played for the University of Miami at the same time. The 2001 Hurricanes were loaded with NFL talent. They are the only team in the data set with two first-round wide receivers in the same draft, and the team also included tight end Jeremy Shockey and a very young Andre Johnson. Moss and Wayne each stole receptions from one another, and so it's unsurprising that they are both considerably underrated by Playmaker.

Wayne and Moss in particular prompted us to take a look at whether Playmaker should have an adjustment for players whose numbers might suffer from playing with another high-quality pass catcher. We tried to adjust for this by introducing a new metric that measured the draft capital used on other wide receivers that were on the same team as the prospect. In Wayne's case, he would receive a significant bump because he played at the same time as two other first-round wide receivers—Santana Moss and Andre Johnson. This factor did turn out to be statistically significant, but only barely so. Moreover, we had no way to apply this factor prospectively. For example, Reggie Wayne received a bump for playing with Andre Johnson, who would go on to be a high first-round prospect. However, if we were running Playmaker Score for Reggie Wayne when he entered the draft in 2001, we would have no way of knowing that Andre Johnson would be a first-round pick in 2003. So, at present, we have no good way to measure the "double prospect" effect, but it is something we might find a better way of adjusting for in the future.

All in all, it's best to keep in mind that Playmaker Score is not, and can never be, the be-all-end-all of wide receiver analysis. The numbers may be a good starting point in setting a baseline as to the strength of a wide receiver prospect, but the evaluator should not turn off his or her common sense.

With our introduction complete, let's take a look at the Class of 2014. Playmaker Score agrees with conventional wisdom that this year's draft is an exceptionally strong class for finding wide receiver talent. Indeed, Playmaker likes all of the receivers that were selected in the first round. However, according to Playmaker, the real strength of this wide receiver class is not the players on the top, but rather, its unprecedented depth. This year, there were 13 wide receivers drafted that have Playmaker Ratings of 80 percent or more. No other year since 1996 had more than eight such players.

Brandin Cooks, Oregon State
New Orleans (Round 1, Pick 20)
Playmaker Projection: 653 Yards
Playmaker Rating: 95.8%

The hype around Brandin Cooks grew tremendously during the past couple of weeks leading up to the Draft, and Playmaker believes that it is well-deserved. Cooks recorded 1,730 receiving yards his junior year, which is still a strong number even though the Oregon State Beavers dropped back to pass 625 times. Moreover, Cooks had 32 rushing attempts last year,

Table 1. Top 20 Wide Receivers by Playmaker Rating, 1996-2011

Player	Year	Rnd	Pick	College	Playmaker Projection	Playmaker Rating	Actual NFL Yards/ Season (through Y5 only)
Randy Moss	1998	1	21	Marshall	830	100.0%	1,349
Demaryius Thomas	2010	1	22	Georgia Tech	833	99.8%	863
Terry Glenn	1996	1	7	Ohio St.	801	99.5%	893
Larry Fitzgerald	2004	1	3	Pittsburgh	786	99.3%	1,195
Charles Rogers	2003	1	2	Michigan St.	772	99.1%	88
Calvin Johnson	2007	1	2	Georgia Tech	741	98.8%	1,174
Percy Harvin	2009	1	22	Florida	681	98.6%	664
Golden Tate	2010	2	60	Notre Dame	673	98.3%	510
Reidel Anthony	1997	1	16	Florida	659	98.1%	369
Dez Bryant	2010	1	24	Oklahoma St.	691	97.9%	958
David Terrell	2001	1	8	Michigan	705	97.6%	320
Nate Burleson	2003	3	71	Nevada	496	97.4%	535
Hakeem Nicks	2009	1	29	North Carolina	580	97.2%	924
Andre' Davis	2002	2	47	Virginia Tech	572	96.9%	323
Marvin Harrison	1996	1	19	Syracuse	643	96.7%	1,111
David Boston	1999	1	8	Ohio St.	689	96.5%	924
Santonio Holmes	2006	1	25	Ohio St.	676	96.2%	916
Koren Robinson	2001	1	9	North Carolina St.	662	96.0%	703
Antonio Bryant	2002	2	63	Pittsburgh	499	95.7%	605
Chris Henry	2005	3	83	West Virginia	487	95.5%	365

more than any other prospect in this class, suggesting that his receiving numbers would have been even higher had he not proven to be so versatile.

The knock on Cooks is his small-ish frame, but he is heavier than both DeSean Jackson and Steve Smith were when they were drafted, and we found no correlation between height and/or weight and a wide receiver underperforming or outperforming his draft position. A greater concern for Cooks is his inability to get off the line cleanly, as he reportedly has trouble with physical defenders, and NFL cornerbacks will be much more physical than those native to the pass-happy Pac-12.

Odell Beckham Jr., LSU
New York Giants (Round 1, Pick 12)
Playmaker Projection: 623 Yards
Playmaker Rating: 93.6%

If there was ever a wide receiver who could be considered a sure first-round pick and still fly under the radar, it would be Odell Beckham, Jr. Few talked much about Beckham before the draft because prospect lists typically ranked him behind Sammy Watkins, Mike Evans, and Marqise Lee. Beckham, however, is a legitimate prospect in his own right.

Beckham had 1,152 receiving yards and eight touchdowns as a junior, which does not seem impressive until you consider that LSU passed the ball only 326 times (and one of those pass attempts was Beckham's). As a result, Beckham actually outgunned his more highly regarded draftmates in yards per team attempt and touchdowns per team attempt last season (with the exception of Mike Evans, whom he tied in touchdowns per team attempt). Beckham also had a strong combine performance and had a high average yards per catch.

None of the non-Playmaker factors seem to militate against drafting Beckham either. Beckham's domination of his passing game is all the more impressive considering that he shared the field with fellow pro prospect Jarvis Landry, who likely vultured a number of Beckham's catches and touchdowns. LSU quarterback Zach Mettenberger was a sixth-round pick, not a Peyton Manning-level quarterback who could make a talent-poor wide receiver look as good as Beckham did in 2013. Beckham and Rueben Randle (86.1% Playmaker Rating, fourth amongst 2012 prospects) give the New York Giants an excellent pair of targets to partner with the superlative Victor Cruz.

Mike Evans, Texas A&M
Tampa Bay (Round 1, Pick 7)
Playmaker Projection: 573 Yards
Playmaker Rating: 86.4%

Mike Evans may have an unusual combination of size and speed, but according to the factors that Playmaker Score cares about, Evans is a pretty typical first-round wide receiver prospect. His numbers were good, but not in any universe that would invite Calvin Johnson or Randy Moss comparisons.

What is more interesting about Evans are the potential factors that might cause Playmaker to overrate or underrate him. Evans might arguably be overrated because he had the privilege of playing for Johnny Manziel, who completed nearly 70 percent of his passes last season and was a first-round pick in this year's draft. However, punishing wide receivers who had highly efficient quarterbacks does not seem to improve the model. Evans might arguably be underrated because, while Playmaker adjusts for underclassmen, Evans is really busting out early: he is a redshirt sophomore, rather than the more typical underclassman, who is a junior. Accordingly, the argument might be that Evans should get an extra bump in addition to the typical underclassman bump because he developed so quickly, and thus would have likely been even more dominant had he stayed in school for one more year. The limited amount of data, however, does not exactly support that conclusion. Larry Fitzgerald, effectively a redshirt sophomore when he entered the draft, has been truly excellent. Charles Rogers and Mike Williams, also effectively redshirt sophomores

Table 2. First-Round Picks with Lowest Playmaker Rating, 1996-2011

Player	Year	Rnd	Pick	College	Playmaker Projection	Playmaker Rating	Actual NFL Yards/ Season (through Y5 only)
Rae Carruth	1997	1	27	Colorado	420	70.7%	161
Keyshawn Johnson	1996	1	1	USC	508	69.5%	996
Yatil Green	1997	1	15	Miami	432	69.3%	47
Santana Moss	2001	1	16	Miami	490	67.4%	780
Mark Clayton	2005	1	22	Oklahoma	507	66.4%	623
Michael Jenkins	2004	1	29	Ohio St.	511	64.1%	474
Dwayne Bowe	2007	1	23	LSU	504	60.5%	985
Rod Gardner	2001	1	15	Clemson	364	57.7%	599
Reggie Wayne	2001	1	30	Miami	480	55.6%	833
Marcus Nash	1998	1	30	Tennessee	347	45.6%	15
R. Jay Soward	2000	1	29	USC	278	43.7%	30
Bryant Johnson	2003	1	17	Penn St.	360	37.8%	535
Travis Taylor	2000	1	10	Florida	416	34.5%	552
Kevin Dyson	1998	1	16	Utah	347	32.9%	462
Craig Davis	2007	1	30	LSU	277	24.3%	112

even though they may have technically been juniors when drafted, became humongous busts.[1]

Sammy Watkins, Clemson
Buffalo (Round 1, Pick 4)
Playmaker Projection: 558 Yards
Playmaker Rating: 83.1%

Sammy Watkins might be the most inscrutable prospect in this draft. Has Playmaker identified trends that expose Watkins as being slightly overrated? Or is Playmaker giving evaluators an opportunity to overthink a prospect whose tape verifies that he is the best wide receiver prospect since A.J. Green and Julio Jones—who, coincidentally, Playmaker also underestimated? (Green was at 83.9%, Jones at 88.2%.)

Watkins' 2013 numbers look good in the aggregate—1,464 yards and 12 touchdowns—but are somewhat less impressive when you discover that Clemson put the ball in the air nearly 500 times. On the one hand, surely some of Watkins' potential catches went to Martavis Bryant, who broke out with 828 receiving yards as a junior and was a fourth-round pick in this year's draft. On the other hand, Bryant's 22.2 yards per catch put Watkins' 14.1 yards per catch to shame, suggesting that maybe it wasn't the style of offense at Clemson that gave Watkins numbers more appropriate to a possession receiver. An examination of Watkins' quarterback situation is similarly unavailing. Tajh Boyd looked absolutely awful in pre-draft workouts and slipped all the way to the sixth round of the draft. However, given that most college quarterbacks do not even smell the end of the seventh round, it's perhaps being too charitable to Watkins to give him a bump just because his quarterback was a late-round prospect.

One caveat to add to Watkins' projection is that Playmaker Score uses his junior season but arguably should use his freshman season instead. Watkins was less prolific catching the ball as a freshman, but he had a many more rushing attempts. Thus, Watkins would have a stronger projection if his freshman year was used (615 yards, 88.9%) but his junior year is used because Playmaker is designed to use a player's top receiving season, not his top offensive season overall.

Watkins may indeed be very good. Watkins' Playmaker numbers are good, just not elite. However, you can add Playmaker to the chorus of voices who thinks that the Buffalo Bills were ill-advised to trade a future first-round pick to secure Watkins' services rather than standing pat and selecting Odell Beckham or Brandin Cooks.

Marqise Lee, USC
Jacksonville (Round 2, Pick 39)
Playmaker Projection: 530 Yards
Playmaker Rating: 90.6%

The most noteworthy factor for Marqise Lee is the difference between his production in his "peak" season and his production last year. As a sophomore, Lee recorded 1,721 receiving yards with 14 touchdowns and still managed to squeeze in 13 rushing attempts. That guy would undoubtedly be the strongest prospect in this class from a Playmaker perspective. However, that's not what teams are looking at here, as Lee crashed to Earth in a big way in 2013, recording only 791 receiving yards with four touchdowns.

On balance, Playmaker likes Lee, and the Playmaker Projection only places him behind Evans and Watkins because his draft stock slipped a bit in the eyes of draftniks before the draft. (NFL Draft Scout projected him as a "1–2" rather than a "1.") Lee does have some potentially legitimate excuses for a drop in his production—Lee nursed an injury in 2013 and had to transition from Matt Barkley to the green-behind-the-ears Cody Kessler. Furthermore, he likely lost significant targets to rising star Nelson Agholor, a likely first-round pick in next year's draft. Scouts have been pretty good at sorting out receivers who turn in poor performances in their final seasons. Dez Bryant and Torry Holt were first-round picks despite drops in their college production, but lesser talents who experienced production drops, such as Lee Mays and Eugene Baker, were allowed to drop to the later rounds. So the fact that Lee is still in relatively high regards with scouts could suggest that he may be closer to the guy who had 1,721 receiving yards than the one who had only 791.

POTENTIAL BUST ALERT

Kevin Norwood, Alabama
Seattle (Round 4, Pick 123)
Playmaker Projection: 115 Yards
Playmaker Rating: 17.2%

Picking a potential bust this year was difficult, given that Playmaker is fairly high on all of the FBS-level wide receivers who were drafted in the first three rounds. The best we could do is the Seattle Seahawks' selection of Kevin Norwood from Alabama in the fourth round. Playmaker's skepticism as to Norwood's prospects is no surprise given his stat line—Norwood's best season featured a rather pedestrian 568 yards and seven touchdowns. Those numbers are not quite as bad as they seem because Alabama only passed 365 times that year, but they still work out to a peak yards per team attempt of only 1.56 with no rushing attempts, which is worse than all of the wide receivers drafted this year, save for Detroit Lions sixth-round pick T.J. Jones.

Norwood's best excuse seems to be that he was potentially overshadowed by likely 2015 first-round pick Amari Cooper during his junior and senior years—when wide receiver prospects typically have their best seasons. However, it was not like Norwood was miles ahead of Alabama's No. 3 wide receivers either—he had just 30 more receiving yards than Kenny Bell in 2012 and just 34 more receiving yards than DeAndrew White in 2013. Norwood's selection may simply be a classic case of a team overvaluing middling players from

1 Why "effectively" redshirt sophomores? The NFL let Fitzgerald enter the draft because of an extra prep year. Rogers lost his freshman year of eligibility to Proposition 48 rules, while Williams of course tried to declare after his sophomore year and sat out his junior season. What's important for the comparison is that both players were three years out of high school but had only two years of playing experience.

strong football programs in the later rounds. And while you might be thinking "don't question the front office that just built a Super Bowl champion," last year the Seahawks used a fourth-round pick on Chris Harper (23.1% Playmaker Rating) and he couldn't make it through final roster cuts.

POTENTIAL SLEEPER

Austin Franklin, New Mexico State
St. Louis (Undrafted)
Playmaker Projection: 207 Yards
Playmaker Rating: 85.2%

Franklin weighs only 189 pounds and ran the forty-yard dash in just 4.56 seconds. Add that to the less than stellar competition that Franklin faced playing for New Mexico State, and you have a recipe for indifference from NFL teams. However, Franklin had a nice career statistically. During his best season, he had more than three yards for every team attempt and had a peak touchdown per attempt season that was nearly as good as Sammy Watkins'. Moreover, Franklin was also used as a running threat, averaging nearly a rushing attempt per game in his peak season and still managing a solid 15.2 yards per catch. Franklin went undrafted, but the St. Louis Rams made a smart move by adding Franklin as a free agent to a receiving corps that also includes two of last year's top three prospects by Playmaker, Stedman Bailey (96.2%) and Tavon Austin (85.9%).

What follows is a list of all of the FBS wide receivers who were drafted and their Playmaker Projections and Ratings, ordered by Playmaker Projection.

Nathan Forster

Table 3. Wide Receivers in 2014 Draft by Playmaker Projection

Name	Team	Round	Pick	College	Proj. Round	Projection	Rating
Brandin Cooks	NO	1	20	Oregon St.	1	653	95.8%
Odell Beckham Jr.	NYG	1	12	LSU	1	623	93.6%
Mike Evans	TB	1	7	Texas A&M	1	573	86.1%
Sammy Watkins	BUF	1	4	Clemson	1	558	82.6%
Marqise Lee	JAC	2	39	USC	1 - 2	530	90.8%
Allen Robinson	JAC	2	61	Penn St.	1 - 2	500	87.8%
Kelvin Benjamin	CAR	1	28	Florida St.	2	462	87.3%
Donte Moncrief	IND	3	90	Ole Miss	1 - 2	440	78.8%
Davante Adams	GB	2	53	Fresno St.	2 - 3	428	89.2%
Martavis Bryant	PIT	4	118	Clemson	2	410	83.1%
Paul Richardson	SEA	2	45	Colorado	3	386	88.0%
Cody Latimer	DEN	2	56	Indiana	2	380	74.1%
Jordan Matthews	PHI	2	42	Vanderbilt	2	363	62.1%
Bruce Ellington	SF	4	106	South Carolina	2 - 3	362	80.9%
Jarvis Landry	MIA	2	63	LSU	3 - 4	338	79.8%
Jared Abbrederis	GB	5	176	Oklahoma	3	246	42.1%
Josh Huff	PHI	3	86	Oregon	4 - 5	237	69.6%
Devin Street	DAL	5	146	Pittsburgh	4	160	36.5%
Robert Herron	TB	6	185	Wyoming	3 - 4	153	22.8%
Ryan Grant	WAS	5	142	Tulane	5	126	36.9%
Kevin Norwood	SEA	4	123	Alabama	4	115	17.2%
Jeremy Gallon	NE	7	244	Michigan	UDFA	109	61.9%
Jalen Saunders	NYJ	4	104	Fresno St. / Oklahoma	6 - 7	101	46.1%
Quincy Enunwa	NYJ	6	209	Nebraska	7 - UDFA	85	51.1%
Tevin Reese	SD	7	240	Baylor	7 - UDFA	80	55.5%
Mike Campanaro	BAL	7	218	Wake Forest	5	71	19.5%
Shaq Evans	NYJ	4	116	UCLA	7 - UDFA	29	27.5%
T.J. Jones	DET	6	189	Notre Dame	5 - 6	0	2.8%
James Wright	CIN	7	239	LSU	UDFA	0	0.0%

Rookie Projections

Football Outsiders has developed four different methods for forecasting the NFL success of highly-drafted players at various positions. Playmaker Score, our system for projecting wide receivers, has been upgraded this year and gets its own essay. Here is a rundown of the other three methods and what they say about the NFL's Class of 2014.

Quarterbacks: Long-Term Career Forecast

This is the system first introduced in *Pro Football Prospectus 2006*. It was originally created by David Lewin, now director of scouting for the Boston Celtics. We've changed the name from the "Lewin Career Forecast" because he keeps getting questions about college quarterbacks when he has bigger things to worry about, like who should be playing for the Maine Red Claws. The results of the 2014 LCF can be found in the Jacksonville chapter.

Running Backs: Speed Score

Speed Score was created by Bill Barnwell and introduced in *Pro Football Prospectus 2008*. The basic theory is simple: not all 40-yard dash times are created equal. A fast time means more from a bigger running back, and the range of 40 times for backs is so small that even a miniscule difference can be meaningful. The formula for Speed Score is:

(Weight x 200) / 40 time ^4

In general, you want a back chosen in the first couple rounds to be above 100. There's been some indication that Speed Score can be improved by also considering a couple of other things such as the three-cone drill; we're working on an updated version for next year.

In 2012 and 2013, the order of drafted running backs was somewhat close to the order of Speed Scores. This year, Speed Score seemed to bear absolutely no relationship to scouting reports. The top Speed Score came from Damien Williams of Oklahoma, who went undrafted. He ran a 4.45-second forty at 222 pounds for a Speed Score of 113.2. Jerick McKinnon, the former Georgia Southern option quarterback, finished second. He wasn't drafted until the end of the third round—and even that was earlier than expected. At the same time, no running back from the first three rounds had a terrible Speed Score.

We have listed the Speed Scores for all backs chosen in the first three rounds this year, as well as three backs drafted later with Speed Scores over 100 (Table 1).

Table 1: 2014 Draftees with Speed Score

Name	College	Team	Rnd	Pick	40 time	Weight	Speed Score
Bishop Sankey	Washington	TEN	2	54	4.49	209	102.8
Jeremy Hill	LSU	CIN	2	55	4.66	233	98.8
Carlos Hyde	Ohio St.	SF	2	57	4.66	230	97.5
Charles Sims	West Virginia	TB	3	69	4.48	214	106.3
Tre Mason	Auburn	STL	3	75	4.50	207	101.0
Terrance West	Towson	CLE	3	94	4.54	225	105.9
Jerick McKinnon	Ga. Southern	MIN	3	96	4.41	209	110.5
Dri Archer	Kent St.	PIT	3	97	4.26	173	105.1
Tyler Gaffney	Stanford	CAR	6	204	4.49	220	108.3
Andre Williams	Boston College	NYG	4	113	4.56	230	106.4
Lorenzo Taliaferro	Coastal Carolina	BAL	4	138	4.58	229	104.1

Edge Rushers: SackSEER

SackSEER is a method that projects sacks for edge rushers, including both 3-4 outside linebackers and 3-4 defensive ends, using the following criteria:

- An "explosion index" that measures the prospect's scores in the forty-yard dash, the vertical jump, and the broad jump in pre-draft workouts.
- Sacks per game, adjusted for factors such as early entry in the NFL Draft and position switches during college.
- Passes defensed per game.
- Missed games of NCAA eligibility due to academic problems, injuries, benchings, or suspensions.

SackSEER outputs two numbers. The first, SackSEER Rating, solely measures how high the prospect scores compared to players of the past. The second, SackSEER Projection, represents a forecast of sacks for the player's first five years in the NFL. It synthesizes metrics with conventional wisdom by adjusting based on the player's expected draft position (interestingly, not his actual draft position) based on pre-draft analysis at the site NFLDraftScout.com.

We have listed the SackSEER numbers for players drafted in the first two rounds of the 2014 draft, along with later-round picks (and one UDFA) with a high SackSEER rating (Table 2). Defensive ends drafted by 3-4 teams are not included. Linebackers drafted by 4-3 teams who will sometimes rush the passer (i.e. "Von Miller types") are included with an asterisk.

Table 2: 2014 Draftees with SackSEER

Name	College	Team	Rnd	Pick	SackSEER Projection	SackSEER Rating
Kahlil Mack*	Buffalo	OAK	1	5	38.9	98.1%
Anthony Barr*	UCLA	MIN	1	9	31.4	91.3%
Jadeveon Clowney	South Carolina	HOU	1	1	30.2	94.4%
Kony Ealy	Missouri	CAR	2	60	29.3	84.6%
Kyle Van Noy*	BYU	DET	2	40	27.3	71.0%
Trent Murphy	Stanford	WAS	2	47	25.8	91.0%
Jeremiah Attaochu	Georgia Tech	SD	2	50	16.8	64.1%
Marcus Smith	Louisville	PHI	1	26	16.3	57.0%
Dee Ford	Auburn	KC	1	23	16.3	30.0%
Demarcus Lawrence	Boise St.	DAL	2	34	12.0	36.0%
Carl Bradford	Arizona St.	GB	4	121	22.6	82.9%
Jackson Jeffcoat	Texas	SEA	UDFA	--	19.6	91.3%
Chris Smith	Arkansas	JAC	5	159	12.2	68.8%

Top 25 Prospects 2014

Here it is: Football Outsiders' eighth annual list of under-the-radar, lower-drafted prospects who could have a big impact on the NFL in the coming seasons. In the past, Rotoworld has referred to our Top 25 Prospects list as "an all-star team of waiver pickups" after we used it to promote young players such as Miles Austin, Jamaal Charles, and Arian Foster. We've also picked out defensive players who went on to have a big impact: our first list included Elvis Dumervil and Cortland Finnegan, while more recent lists have introduced readers to future stars such as Geno Atkins and Lardarius Webb. Of course we can't get them all right, but a lot of these are names you're going to want to know over the next few seasons.

For the uninitiated, this list is not like the prospect lists you read about in the world of baseball. Because the top prospects in college football are stars on national television before they get taken in the first round of the NFL Draft, there's not much utility in listing them here. Everyone knows who Sammy Watkins and Johnny Manziel are by this point. (Heck, your mom probably knows who Johnny Manziel is by this point.) Instead, we use a combination of statistics, scouting, measurables, context, and expected role to compile a list of under-the-radar players whom we expect to make an impact in the NFL, both in 2014 and beyond. To focus on these players, we limit the pool to guys who fit the following criteria:

- Drafted in the third round or later, or signed as an undrafted free agent.
- Entered the NFL between 2011 and 2013.
- Fewer than five career games started.
- Still on their initial contract with their current team (players who were cut and picked up elsewhere still qualify for the list)
- Age 26 or younger in 2014.

This year's list had more offensive line candidates than ever before, with a lot of lower-drafted and undrafted players getting set to move into the starting lineup in their second seasons. We also have two very strong tight ends and our usual collection of promising wide receivers and pass rushers. But this year's top player is a running back who lasted all the way until the seventh round last year, but might not even last until the third round of your fantasy draft this year.

1 Andre Ellington, RB, Cardinals

The Cardinals primarily used two running backs last year. One of them, veteran Rashard Mendenhall, averaged a dismal 3.2 yards per carry with -10.2% DVOA. But running behind the same line, seventh-round rookie Andre Ellington averaged 5.5 yards per carry with 17.5% DVOA. Now Mendenhall is gone and Ellington is the starter and a clear workhorse for the Cardinals. We were worried about Ellington coming into the NFL, since he ran the forty in 4.61 seconds at 199 pounds, leading to a Speed Score of just 88.1. However, he may have just been having a bad day; that time improved to 4.51 at his Pro Day, for a better Speed Score of 96.1. And he's certainly shown great speed getting to the edge so far in his NFL career; perhaps his speed just shows better running laterally instead of running straight ahead on a track with no blockers or defenders. Much like the similarly-sized Jamaal Charles, Ellington is a great receiver as well as runner. He can catch passes out of the backfield, but can also be split out wide or used on bubble screens. Last year he caught 39 passes for 371 yards, nearly ten yards per catch with 22.3% DVOA. Ellington's not going to average 5.5 yards per carry every season, but he's definitely a potential star in the making.

2 Travis Kelce, TE, Chiefs

Kelce, a third-round pick out of the University of Cincinnati, lost pretty much his entire rookie season to a knee injury, but he should be back on the field in time for this year's training camp. The Chiefs will start two tight ends, with Anthony Fasano as the more standard in-line tight end and Kelce moving all over the formation. Last year, our own Matt Waldman actually ranked Kelce above Tyler Eifert and Jordan Reed as the No. 1 tight end in his Rookie Scouting Portfolio. Make no mistake, Eifert and Reed are better receivers, but Kelce may be the superior all-around talent. He's a fantastic blocker who also shows great range of motion to block on the move as a fullback or H-back. That same fluid motion shows up as a receiver, along with great hands and the ability to get open in tight coverage and make hard breaks on routes.

3 Damontre Moore, DE, Giants

Moore had 12.5 sacks for Texas A&M in 2012, but was very slow adapting to his first year in the NFL. But the Giants got him on the field a lot more at the end of the year: Moore had just 34 total defensive snaps in the first 11 games of the season and then averaged 20 per game for the final five. Moore is quick off the edge and has long arms to ward off blocks, but he ended up dropping to the third round because of a mediocre combine performance. Yet despite the mediocre workouts, our SackSEER projection system (which does incorporate some combine drills) still thought he was an excellent prospect. He had the fourth highest SackSEER projection in the Class of 2013; we have him projected for 28 sacks through five seasons. Since he had zero as a rookie, he'll need to hit that in four seasons, but it really wouldn't be a surprise to see him do it. There's a real need for a good young pass rusher in New York; in fact, if Jason Pierre-Paul can't somehow find his lost 2011 form, there might be a real need for two of them.

4 Jordan Reed, TE, Redskins

There aren't many players with the skill set that Jordan Reed possesses. He's physical enough to bully smaller corners in the slot, and he's fast enough to run past linebackers. And while he didn't run a lot of deep routes as a rookie—just seven percent of intended passes went over 15 yards through the air—he has the speed to do so if Jay Gruden needs him to. Reed was fantastic as a rookie, and ended up tenth in our tight end DYAR numbers despite a concussion that ended his season after just ten games. But he's healthy again this year, and his quarterback should be healthier too, which can only help things. Kelce may be a slightly better overall prospect, but Reed is the more important name to know for fantasy leagues, especially this season.

5 Terron Armstead, OT, Saints

Armstead didn't get a lot of attention playing at Arkansas-Pine Bluff (Go, Golden Lions!), but he made a name for himself at the 2013 combine, leading all offensive line participants in the vertical leap and broad jump, while running a 4.71-second 40-yard dash that was the best for an O-line prospect in combine history. It's hard to judge linemen who play against competition like Langston and Tennessee State, and so nobody drafted Armstead until the Saints grabbed him 75th overall. The plan was to sit Armstead for a year, but he developed quickly enough that New Orleans promoted him into the starting lineup at left tackle in Week 16. The timing of the move speaks volumes: the Saints were 10-4, tied with Carolina for first place in the division, and Charles Brown, though not playing particularly well, was still healthy. (Imagine if we were talking about quarterbacks here, and a 10-4 team had benched its veteran passer for a third-round rookie in a game that might determine the division title. Skip Bayless might still be screaming.) Unfortunately, Armstead got his clock cleaned by Greg Hardy in that game—but he redeemed himself with strong play in Week 17 and in two postseason games. With a full offseason of first-string work under his belt, and a quarterback in Drew Brees who makes good linemen look great, Armstead figures to shine this year.

6 Marquess Wilson, WR, Bears

Look, kids, it's a tall (6-foot-3) receiver who excels at using his big body to win in tight coverage! The Bears don't have any guys like that, right? Actually, they have two guys like that currently starting, but Wilson will give them a third. Wilson's Playmaker Rating of 79.5 percent would rank him behind many of the receivers in this year's phenomenal rookie class, but it's still outstanding for a seventh-round pick and it ranked Wilson in the top ten for the Class of 2013. Plus, to make sure he was as strong as Brandon Marshall and Alshon Jeffrey, Wilson spent the offseason adding nearly 20 pounds in the weight room. We know that the Bears don't throw very much to their third receiver, but if either Marshall or Jeffrey suffers a major injury, it's fantasy stampede time.

7 Micah Hyde, DB, Packers

"Ready for anything at any position," is how an article at Packers.com described Hyde, and frankly, that's exactly what makes Hyde a great fit for Dom Capers' defense. Hyde played both cornerback and safety at Iowa. He's smart, instinctual, and has a strong burst, but he fell to the fifth round because he lacks top speed. Well, that lack of top speed didn't stop him from taking over both Green Bay return jobs by the end of the year. It didn't stop him from scoring a 93-yard punt return touchdown. And it doesn't tend to stop him from tracking down ballcarriers, as long as you aren't asking him to do something like cover Brandon Marshall on the outside. Hyde was primarily a nickel and dime cornerback as a rookie, but he's spent the offseason learning what Capers wants from his safeties as well. When Capers goes 2-4-5, that fifth defensive back can be doing all kinds of things: sometimes he's a nickelback covering a slot receiver, sometimes he's a strong safety in to stop the run, and sometimes he's a blitzer coming after the quarterback. This year, a lot of the time, that guy's going to be Micah Hyde.

8 William Gholston, DE, Buccaneers

The biggest knock on Gholston coming out of college was that the motor just wasn't always on. He's incredibly impressive physically—6-foot-6, 34-inch arms, excellent lateral movement—but only had 9.5 sacks in two years as a starter at Michigan State. However, it looks like things are going to be different in the NFL. Gholston flashed as a rookie, particularly near the end of season. In a Week 15 game against San Francisco, Gholston knocked down two passes and helped nail Frank Gore in the backfield on third-and-1. Now he gets to play for Lovie Smith, a well-regarded players' coach who is good at inspiring occasionally sluggish performers. Ex-Bears scout Greg Gabriel, writing for National Football Post, has gone on record predicting seven sacks and 50 tackles for Gholston in Smith's defense this season, though he's unlikely to put up numbers quite like that unless he can unexpectedly beat out Adrian Clayborn for a starting spot.

9 Markus Wheaton, WR, Steelers

It looked like this Oregon State product would slide right into Pittsburgh's No. 3 receiver spot after the Steelers took him in the third round of last year's draft. After all, with Emmanuel Sanders moving into the starting lineup, all Wheaton had to do was beat out veteran Jerricho Cotchery, who had only caught 33 passes in his first two seasons in Pittsburgh. Historically, the Steelers like to work rookies in slowly, so it wasn't a surprise when Cotchery still started the season ahead of Wheaton on the depth chart. But Wheaton never got that gradual move up in snap count because of two broken fingers suffered in Week 4, and he ended up with a lost rookie year while Cotchery somehow caught 10 touchdowns. Even when he did play, Ben Roethlisberger overthrew him five times on just 13 targets. Hopefully things are better with another training camp work of practices to work out their timing, because Wheaton may have been the most promising vertical receiver in the 2013 draft thanks to a combination of speed and ability to beat press coverage. With Sanders and Cotchery both elsewhere, the starting spot opposite Antonio Brown is Wheaton's to lose.

10 Knile Davis, RB, Chiefs

Our Speed Score metric looks at running back prospects based not only on speed but on weight, because a bigger back who is fast is generally better than a smaller back who is only slightly faster. Well, Knile Davis is the bigger back and the faster back. He weighed in at 227 pounds and ran the forty in 4.37 seconds at the 2013 combine, giving him a Speed Score of 124.5—the second highest of the past decade. Davis struggled a bit as a rookie, with just 3.5 yards per carry on 70 regular-season carries, but that's no reason to write him off. He'll get more of a chance to prove himself, as the Chiefs want to give Jamaal Charles a little more rest this season. But as a power back with 30 more pounds on him, Davis is more of a complement to Charles than a backup. The negatives on Davis? He's been injury prone, from the ankle injury that cost him his entire junior season at Arkansas to the leg fracture that knocked him out of last year's Wild Card game after he scored two touchdowns in relief of Charles. He's also never been able to solve his case of fumblitis, and he had two fumbles last year on just 81 touches.

11 John Hughes, DE, Browns

Hughes is a sturdy run-stopping 5-tech end on a team that certainly needs one. Ahtyba Rubin seems to be well-regarded around the league, but he's always come out poorly in our advanced run stats. Last year, Rubin made his average tackle on a running play after a gain of 3.1 yards, with a 63 percent Stop Rate. Hughes made his average tackle after a gain of 2.1 yards, with an 84 percent Stop Rate. As a bonus, he had six pass hurries, more than either Rubin or fellow backup Billy Winn. Hughes also enjoys meeting with his breakfast club before games, as well as road trips aboard planes, trains and automobiles.

12 Ray-Ray Armstrong, OLB, Rams

Armstrong came to the NFL after a very confusing college career. He played two seasons with the Miami Hurricanes as a safety, then was dismissed from the team, apparently for lying to officials during the Navin Shapiro investigation. Armstrong transferred to NAIA Faulkner University in Alabama, but when the NAIA declared him ineligible, he ended up spending the 2012 season as an assistant coach. He's a hard-hitter who was never strong in pass coverage, so a position switch upon entering the NFL made a lot of sense. He then led the Rams in special-teams tackles last year while learning the linebacker position. Gregg Williams likes to use safety/linebacker hybrids: that's how he planned to use Adam Archuleta in Washington, it's how he used Roman Harper in New Orleans, and it would be an interesting way to use Armstrong in St. Louis. However, Armstrong might just straight-out take over the strongside linebacker position, especially after veteran Jo-Lonn Dunbar went and got himself arrested in July. Let's be honest: the NFL would be a more fun place if at least one team had a starting linebacker named Ray-Ray.

13 Ryan Mallett, QB, Patriots

We put Mallett on this list in 2012 and 2013 and gosh darn it, we're putting him here in 2014 as well, because we're stubborn. And because, let's all be honest, there's a reason why we were hearing lots of Ryan Mallett trade rumors in April but no Ryan Nassib trade rumors, or Landry Jones trade rumors. Plenty of coaches still love his elite arm strength and his touch on the deep ball. The drafting of Jimmy Garoppolo means there's no way Mallett will be back with the Patriots in 2015, and some team somewhere is going to give him a shot at a starting job. Hopefully it will be a team with a good offensive line, because Mallett's biggest weakness is that he takes gobs and gobs of sacks.

14 Darrin Walls, CB, Jets

Walls, a third-year UDFA out of Notre Dame, is the man who replaced Dee Milliner last year when Rex Ryan benched the struggling rookie. He didn't play much in the second half of the year, but that's because the Jets finally just left Milliner in the lineup, not because Walls played poorly when he was on the field. Thirty targets aren't enough to make the rankings of our cornerback charting stats, but Walls would have ranked in the top half of the league with a 58 percent Adjusted Success Rate and in the top dozen with just 5.0 Adjusted Yards per Pass allowed. The Jets seem to view Walls as a special-teams player and backup, but there's a decent shot he ends up starting opposite Milliner this year. After all, the player the Jets brought in to replace Antonio Cromartie is Dmitri Patterson, who is 31, on his seventh team, and only played six games for the Dolphins last year.

15 Allen Bailey, DE, Chiefs

We'll fully admit that Bailey is just skirting the limits of being eligible for our list. He's a third-round pick going into his fourth season, and he has four career games started, which is our maximum. But as long as we're keeping to the rules, we definitely want to bring him to your attention, because he's likely to replace Tyson Jackson has Kansas City's starting left defensive end. He's gained 15-20 pounds this offseason to get over 300, which puts him in the same weight class as the players he is competing with for playing time (Mike DeVito, Vance Walker). It should also help him avoid getting pushed back on running plays; he made his average run tackle last year 3.3 yards downfield, one of the worst figures in the league for a defensive lineman.

16 Stedman Bailey, WR, Rams

On page 433 of this book, we present our updated version of Playmaker Score for projecting rookie wide receivers. Since 2004, only 13 wide receivers have scored a Playmaker Rating above 95 percent, making them the best of the best prospects. There are a couple of exceptions, but for the most part those players have become studs in the NFL: Larry Fitzgerald, Chris Henry, Santonio Holmes, Calvin Johnson, Percy Harvin, Hakeem Nicks, Demaryius Thomas, Golden Tate, Dez Bryant, Stephen Hill, Brandin Cooks… and Stedman Bailey. Stedman Bailey had 1,622 receiving yards and 25 touchdowns in his final year at West Virginia. He had all those yards and touchdowns even though he had to share the offense with Tavon Austin. Then again, that's also a sign that these two guys should work well together, which is good now that they're both on the Rams. It looked like Bailey was going to carry the late-season improvement of his rookie year into 2014 until he got handed a four-game suspension for violating PED policy. Still, the biggest worry for Bailey isn't the suspension. It's the possibility that poor quarterback play and constant confusion over what the Jets want to do on offense are the reasons Stephen Hill never blossomed. The Rams have the same problems right now, and when you look at that list of 13 receivers, Stephen Hill is clearly the worst-case scenario.

17 Robert Lester, SS, Panthers

Lester started 40 games at Alabama, winning three national titles and earning second-team honors on the 2012 All-SEC team. The NFL's own draft site tabbed Lester as a mid-round pick, but he surprisingly slipped out of the draft entirely. He signed with the Panthers, then made the jump from practice squad to NFL starter in one week when Carolina's secondary was ravaged with early-season injuries. He responded with interceptions in each of his first two games, and though he didn't stick in the starting lineup, he was a regular contributor the rest of the year. He has limited athleticism and speed, but he's a 225-pound thumper with good instincts and playmaking capacity; defensive coordinator Sean McDermott praised his ability to find the ball and make plays on it in the air.

18 Travaris Cadet, RB, Saints

Cadet is now in his third year as an undrafted free agent out of Appalachian State, primarily well-regarded for his abilities as a receiver. Do you know any head coaches down south who have a good track record with undrafted free-agent running backs? How about head coaches who like to use their running backs in the receiving game? Do you think Sean Payton might be the perfect head coach for a guy with Cadet's skill set? Now consider the fact that Darren Sproles has moved on to Philadelphia. Mark Ingram and Khiry Robinson certainly aren't going to be running Sproles' routes in the offense, and Payton likes to rotate backs and won't make Pierre Thomas any kind of workhorse. That leaves a big opening for Cadet. He has weaknesses as a runner, as he tends to run straight-up and lacks breakaway speed. But Sean Payton didn't become famous as an offensive innovator because he puts players in roles that emphasize their weaknesses.

19 Emmanuel Lamur, OLB, Bengals

Lamur was on our list last year after his strong rookie season in 2012. We praised him for his steady performance on special teams, his tackling in the open field, and his excellent pass coverage skills (he was a safety at Kansas State). Then he went and separated his shoulder in the fourth preseason game, ending his 2013 season. One year later, there's been even more excitement about Lamur coming out of Bengals OTAs, as he's put on extra muscle to improve his run-stopping abilities at linebacker. He's going to be the starting strongside linebacker, and should play all three downs alongside Vontaze Burfict, who like Lamur was an undrafted free agent.

20 Nickell Robey, CB, Bills

Robey, of course, has the perfect name for a nickelback, and his stats come with nickelback sample-size caveats. But he was outstanding last year as an undrafted rookie out of USC, finishing second among qualifying cornerbacks in our charting stats with a 68 percent Adjusted Success Rate, and 24th allowing 6.9 Adjusted Yards per Pass. The negatives on Robey's scouting report were much less about coverage and much more about trouble tackling or taking on blocks. When you combine those weaknesses with Robey's size (just 5-foot-7, 165 pounds), it means you have to use him in very specific ways. But as a rookie, he was put in a position that emphasized his strengths and delivered.

21 Ricky Wagner, OT, Ravens

After last year's debacle, the Ravens could really use some offensive linemen who excel at run blocking. Guess what? They have at least one. Wagner was a fifth-round pick last year out of Wisconsin, where the offensive linemen practically have "road-grader" tattooed on their foreheads. Last year, he played a couple snaps in each game in six-lineman packages, but now he will take over for Michael Oher at right tackle.

22 Chris Owusu, WR, Buccaneers

Owusu's 4.36-second forty-yard dash tied him with Stephen Hill and Travis Benjamin as the fastest wideouts at the 2012 combine. He hasn't done much in two years with the Bucs, who haven't even tried using his speed as a decoy; only one of his 20 targets last season was a "bomb" over 25 yards downfield. (In other news, Greg Schiano wasn't very good at getting the most out of his players.) Tampa Bay is woefully thin at receiver behind Vincent Jackson and first-round pick Mike Evans, and Owusu seems the favorite to win the third receiver job. Lovie Smith knows how to use guys with this kind of speed. Johnny Knox, who once ran the forty in 4.34 seconds, twice went over 700 yards and 18 yards per catch for Smith's Bears teams before a gruesome back injury against Seattle brought his career to a halt. Here's hoping that Owusu can match that production, and more importantly, that he can have better health.

23 Garrett Gilkey, G, Browns

The Browns took Gilkey out of Division II Chadron State in the seventh round of last year's draft. As expected from a Division II player, Gilkey was quite raw in his first NFL training camp. But he possesses prototypical size and strength along with surprising mobility (important in Kyle Shanahan's zone-blocking system) and a mean streak that sometimes runs over past the whistle. (He clashed with Browns nose tackle Phil Taylor repeatedly on one afternoon at OTAs this year.) The Browns are having a battle royal for their right guard spot, with veterans John Greco and Jason Pinkston as the leading contenders, but Gilkey could sneak out with a starting job.

24 Marquise Goodwin, WR, Bills

Marquise Goodwin is fast. He is super ridiculously fast. He ran a 4.27-second forty at the 2013 combine, the fastest time for any drafted wide receiver since Darrius Heyward-Bey. Goodwin is so fast that his college stats were terrible because the Texas Longhorns didn't have any quarterbacks who could actually get him the ball downfield. The Longhorns ended up giving him 34 carries over two seasons in order to try to get the ball in his hands, and he gained 371 yards on them. Last year, he averaged 16.6 yards on 17 catches and added a 31-yard gain on Defensive Pass Interference. In order to develop into a starter, he's going to have to learn how to beat man coverage on the rest of the route tree. But golly, he's fast.

25 Patrick Omameh, G, Buccaneers

Omameh went undrafted a year ago and signed to the 49ers' practice squad. Tampa Bay plucked him from there in mid-October, and while he never appeared in a game, the Bucs clearly had plans for him. He goes into this year's training camp in the lead for Tampa Bay's right guard position. The scouting reports on Omameh a year ago dinged him for sometimes being unable to finish blocks or move properly to the second level, but he's a consistent and powerful drive-blocker. His greatest attribute, however, is his intelligence. He was offered scholarships at MIT and Princeton before heading to Michigan, where he made Academic All-Big Ten. What can we say, we're suckers for a player with brains. Tune in next year when Kansas City's sixth-round pick Dr. Laurent Duvernay-Tardif[1] shows up on this list next to Baltimore fifth-rounder and budding mathematician John Urschel.

Honorable Mention

Kirk Cousins, QB, Redskins
Jayson DiManche, OLB, Bengals
Duron Harmon, SS, Patriots
DaVonte Holloman, OLB, Cownboys
Tim Lelito, C/G, Saints
Corey Lemonier, OLB, 49ers
Tharold Simon, CB, Seahawks
Dallas Thomas, G, Dolphins
Levine Toilolo, TE, Falcons
Blidi Wreh-Wilson, CB, Titans

Still Stuck on the Top 25 Prospects' PUP List

Marcus Lattimore, RB, 49ers

1 OK, technically he's not a doctor yet. Duvernay-Tardif will have one year of medical school left after his NFL and/or CFL career ends.

Fantasy Appendix

Here are the top 275 players according to the KUBIAK projection system, ranked by projected fantasy value (**FANT**) in 2014. We've used the following generic scoring system:

- 1 point for each 10 yards rushing, 10 yards receiving, or 20 yards passing
- 6 points for each rushing or receiving TD, 4 points for each passing TD
- -2 points for each interception or fumble lost
- 1 point for each extra point, 3 points for each field goal
- Team defense: 2 points for a fumble recovery, interception, or safety, 1 point for a sack, and 6 points for a touchdown.

These totals are then adjusted based on each player's listed **Risk** for 2014:

- Green: Standard risk, no change
- Yellow: Higher than normal risk, value dropped by 5 percent
- Red: Highest risk, value dropped by 10 percent
- Blue: Significantly lower than normal risk, value increased by 5 percent

Note that fantasy totals may not exactly equal these calculations, because each touchdown projection is not necessarily a round number. (For example, a quarterback listed with 2 rushing touchdowns may actually be projected with 2.4 rushing touchdowns, which will add 14 fantasy points to the player's total rather than 12.) Fantasy value does not include adjustments for week-to-week consistency,

Players are ranked in order based on marginal value of each player, the idea that you draft based on how many more points a player will score compared to the worst starting player at that position, not how many points a player scores overall. We've ranked players by value in a 12-team league working with three sets of rules:

- **Flex Rk:** starts 1 QB, 2 RB, 2 WR, 1 FLEX (RB/WR), 1 TE, 1 K, and 1 D.
- **3WR Rk:** starts 1 QB, 2 RB, 3 WR, 1 TE, 1 K, and 1 D.
- **PPR Rk:** starts 1 QB, 2 RB, 2 WR, 1 FLEX (RB/WR), 1 TE, 1 K, and 1 D. Also adds one point per reception to scoring.

The rankings also include half value for the first running back on the bench, and reduce the value of kickers and defenses to reflect the general drafting habits of fantasy football players. We urge you to draft using common sense, not a strict reading of these rankings.

A customizable spreadsheet featuring these projections is also available at FootballOutsiders.com for a $20 fee. This spreadsheet is updated based on injuries and changing forecasts of playing time during the preseason, and also has a version which includes individual defensive players.

Player	Team	Bye	Pos	Age	PaYd	PaTD	INT	Ru	RuYd	RuTD	Rec	RcYd	RcTD	FL	XP	FG	Fant	Risk	Flex Rk	3WR Rk	PPR Rk
LeSean McCoy	PHI	7	RB	26	0	0	0	304	1440	11	53	486	3	1	0	0	258	Yellow	1	1	2
Matt Forte	CHI	9	RB	29	0	0	0	276	1250	9	69	593	2	1	0	0	246	Green	2	2	1
Jamaal Charles	KC	6	RB	28	0	0	0	267	1304	9	70	549	3	2	0	0	241	Yellow	3	3	3
Adrian Peterson	MIN	10	RB	29	0	0	0	313	1418	12	40	277	1	4	0	0	223	Yellow	4	6	12
Calvin Johnson	DET	9	WR	29	0	0	0	0	0	0	97	1561	11	0	0	0	212	Yellow	5	4	4
Peyton Manning	DEN	4	QB	38	5085	41	12	28	17	1	0	0	0	3	0	0	373	Yellow	6	8	13
Montee Ball	DEN	4	RB	24	0	0	0	267	1214	9	47	430	2	2	0	0	210	Yellow	7	11	16
Jimmy Graham	NO	6	TE	28	0	0	0	0	0	0	92	1202	11	0	0	0	178	Yellow	8	9	7
Drew Brees	NO	6	QB	35	4926	38	14	28	4	0	0	0	0	2	0	0	369	Green	9	10	15
Demaryius Thomas	DEN	4	WR	27	0	0	0	0	0	0	92	1376	12	0	0	0	206	Green	10	5	5
Eddie Lacy	GB	9	RB	24	0	0	0	253	1117	10	37	287	1	1	0	0	202	Green	11	13	21
DeMarco Murray	DAL	11	RB	26	0	0	0	235	1081	9	58	415	2	1	0	0	200	Yellow	12	16	17
Le'Veon Bell	PIT	12	RB	22	0	0	0	271	1163	10	44	326	1	1	0	0	198	Yellow	13	18	20
Giovani Bernard	CIN	4	RB	23	0	0	0	236	1041	7	57	495	1	1	0	0	198	Green	14	19	18
Aaron Rodgers	GB	9	QB	31	4573	33	11	53	194	2	0	0	0	3	0	0	360	Green	15	15	19
Dez Bryant	DAL	11	WR	26	0	0	0	2	10	0	97	1271	12	0	0	0	197	Green	16	7	6
Antonio Brown	PIT	12	WR	26	0	0	0	5	29	0	99	1343	8	0	0	0	185	Green	17	12	8
A.J. Green	CIN	4	WR	26	0	0	0	0	0	0	84	1217	10	0	0	0	183	Green	18	14	10
Arian Foster	HOU	10	RB	28	0	0	0	293	1297	7	39	262	2	2	0	0	182	Red	19	22	37
Brandon Marshall	CHI	9	WR	30	0	0	0	0	0	0	94	1237	11	0	0	0	181	Yellow	20	17	9
Andre Ellington	ARI	4	RB	25	0	0	0	234	1050	6	56	462	1	1	0	0	180	Yellow	21	24	27
Rob Gronkowski	NE	10	TE	25	0	0	0	0	0	0	73	1009	11	0	0	0	148	Red	22	23	24
Doug Martin	TB	7	RB	25	0	0	0	251	1046	7	42	340	1	2	0	0	171	Yellow	23	28	40
Toby Gerhart	JAC	11	RB	27	0	0	0	277	1177	6	38	260	1	2	0	0	171	Yellow	24	29	44
Marshawn Lynch	SEA	4	RB	28	0	0	0	222	897	9	31	247	1	2	0	0	168	Green	25	32	54
Julius Thomas	DEN	4	TE	26	0	0	0	0	0	0	77	932	8	0	0	0	138	Green	26	27	22
Julio Jones	ATL	9	WR	25	0	0	0	2	9	0	105	1363	8	0	0	0	166	Red	27	20	11

Player	Team	Bye	Pos	Age	PaYd	PaTD	INT	Ru	RuYd	RuTD	Rec	RcYd	RcTD	FL	XP	FG	Fant	Risk	Flex Rk	3WR Rk	PPR Rk
Alfred Morris	WAS	10	RB	26	0	0	0	252	1155	9	16	128	0	2	0	0	166	Yellow	28	35	82
Ryan Mathews	SD	10	RB	27	0	0	0	253	1111	6	26	205	1	1	0	0	165	Yellow	29	37	65
Jordy Nelson	GB	9	WR	29	0	0	0	0	0	0	73	1120	9	0	0	0	164	Green	30	21	23
Reggie Bush	DET	9	RB	29	0	0	0	201	921	3	57	450	1	1	0	0	163	Green	31	39	33
C.J. Spiller	BUF	9	RB	27	0	0	0	200	913	4	45	437	1	2	0	0	161	Green	32	40	47
Andre Johnson	HOU	10	WR	33	0	0	0	0	0	0	105	1283	7	0	0	0	158	Yellow	33	25	14
Rashad Jennings	NYG	8	RB	29	0	0	0	225	887	7	41	334	1	1	0	0	156	Yellow	34	48	60
Michael Crabtree	SF	8	WR	27	0	0	0	0	0	0	82	1229	9	0	0	0	155	Red	35	26	28
Matthew Stafford	DET	9	QB	26	4637	30	20	39	68	1	0	0	0	3	0	0	317	Green	36	43	48
Joique Bell	DET	9	RB	28	0	0	0	161	674	6	57	513	1	1	0	0	153	Yellow	37	51	42
Vernon Davis	SF	8	TE	30	0	0	0	0	0	0	55	788	8	0	0	0	123	Green	38	47	53
Victor Cruz	NYG	8	WR	28	0	0	0	2	10	0	86	1140	8	0	0	0	152	Yellow	39	30	25
Randall Cobb	GB	9	WR	24	0	0	0	8	63	0	79	1084	9	0	0	0	150	Red	40	31	31
Larry Fitzgerald	ARI	4	WR	31	0	0	0	0	0	0	84	1011	8	0	0	0	149	Green	41	33	26
T.Y. Hilton	IND	10	WR	25	0	0	0	5	28	0	77	1058	7	0	0	0	148	Green	42	34	29
Trent Richardson	IND	10	RB	23	0	0	0	195	759	5	42	342	2	0	0	0	148	Green	43	58	66
Stevan Ridley	NE	10	RB	25	0	0	0	194	842	9	14	110	1	1	0	0	148	Green	44	59	117
Kyle Rudolph	MIN	10	TE	25	0	0	0	0	0	0	75	847	7	0	0	0	118	Yellow	45	55	38
Alshon Jeffery	CHI	9	WR	24	0	0	0	10	54	0	78	1097	7	0	0	0	147	Yellow	46	36	32
Vincent Jackson	TB	7	WR	31	0	0	0	0	0	0	68	1085	8	0	0	0	145	Yellow	47	38	41
Zac Stacy	STL	4	RB	23	0	0	0	234	884	8	30	196	0	1	0	0	145	Yellow	48	65	91
Greg Olsen	CAR	12	TE	29	0	0	0	0	0	0	70	761	7	0	0	0	115	Green	49	57	43
Pierre Garcon	WAS	10	WR	28	0	0	0	3	14	0	86	1086	7	0	0	0	142	Yellow	50	41	30
Chris Johnson	NYJ	11	RB	29	0	0	0	173	765	6	28	227	1	0	0	0	142	Green	51	68	98
Jordan Cameron	CLE	4	TE	26	0	0	0	0	0	0	76	918	5	0	0	0	112	Yellow	52	61	46
Andrew Luck	IND	10	QB	25	4117	26	16	67	170	3	0	0	0	4	0	0	304	Green	53	62	62
Colin Kaepernick	SF	8	QB	27	3576	24	10	91	422	6	0	0	0	5	0	0	304	Yellow	54	63	63
Philip Rivers	SD	10	QB	33	4414	30	12	31	69	1	0	0	0	3	0	0	304	Yellow	55	64	64
Jason Witten	DAL	11	TE	32	0	0	0	0	0	0	71	831	7	0	0	0	111	Red	56	66	56
Keenan Allen	SD	10	WR	22	0	0	0	4	39	0	80	1138	7	0	0	0	140	Red	57	42	39
Wes Welker	DEN	4	WR	33	0	0	0	3	17	0	81	923	8	0	0	0	138	Green	58	44	34
Cordarrelle Patterson	MIN	10	WR	23	0	0	0	14	91	1	71	1009	7	0	0	0	138	Red	59	45	50
DeSean Jackson	WAS	10	WR	28	0	0	0	3	14	0	66	1074	6	0	0	0	138	Yellow	60	46	52
Jacquizz Rodgers	ATL	9	RB	24	0	0	0	104	402	2	53	450	8	1	0	0	137	Yellow	61	76	69
Matt Ryan	ATL	9	QB	29	4492	26	17	25	73	0	0	0	0	2	0	0	298	Green	62	72	71
Stephen Gostkowski	NE	10	K	30	0	0	0	0	0	0	0	0	0	0	41	35	143	Green	63	69	78
Roddy White	ATL	9	WR	33	0	0	0	0	0	0	83	989	6	0	0	0	135	Green	64	49	36
Anquan Boldin	SF	8	WR	34	0	0	0	0	0	0	71	979	8	0	0	0	135	Yellow	65	50	49
Danny Woodhead	SD	10	RB	29	0	0	0	87	337	3	72	627	3	0	0	0	135	Green	66	77	45
Tom Brady	NE	10	QB	37	4512	29	12	34	8	0	0	0	0	3	0	0	297	Yellow	67	74	72
Cam Newton	CAR	12	QB	25	3210	18	12	115	626	6	0	0	0	4	0	0	297	Green	68	75	73
Marques Colston	NO	6	WR	31	0	0	0	0	0	0	68	910	7	0	0	0	134	Green	69	52	51
Kendall Wright	TEN	9	WR	25	0	0	0	2	9	0	89	1088	6	0	0	0	134	Yellow	70	53	35
Steven Jackson	ATL	9	RB	31	0	0	0	187	781	4	36	267	1	1	0	0	134	Green	71	78	99
Pierre Thomas	NO	6	RB	30	0	0	0	134	536	3	65	533	2	1	0	0	134	Green	72	79	55
Torrey Smith	BAL	11	WR	25	0	0	0	2	9	0	64	1046	6	0	0	0	133	Yellow	73	54	61
Frank Gore	SF	8	RB	31	0	0	0	205	827	7	13	98	0	1	0	0	133	Green	74	81	152
Robert Griffin	WAS	10	QB	24	4237	23	13	104	462	3	0	0	0	6	0	0	295	Red	75	80	79
Ben Tate	CLE	4	RB	26	0	0	0	198	853	4	33	232	0	1	0	0	132	Green	76	82	109
Martellus Bennett	CHI	9	TE	27	0	0	0	0	0	0	62	749	5	0	0	0	102	Green	77	86	70
DeAndre Hopkins	HOU	10	WR	22	0	0	0	2	10	0	66	918	7	0	0	0	131	Green	78	56	57
Dennis Pitta	BAL	11	TE	29	0	0	0	0	0	0	66	730	7	0	0	0	101	Red	79	89	75
Bishop Sankey	TEN	9	RB	22	0	0	0	187	745	6	28	240	1	1	0	0	130	Yellow	80	87	134
Seahawks D	SEA	4	D	--	0	0	0	0	0	0	0	0	0	0	0	0	115	Green	81	88	86
Antonio Gates	SD	10	TE	34	0	0	0	0	0	0	65	731	5	0	0	0	99	Yellow	82	91	76
Russell Wilson	SEA	4	QB	26	3541	28	13	91	421	2	0	0	0	5	0	0	291	Yellow	83	92	83
Michael Floyd	ARI	4	WR	25	0	0	0	2	10	0	67	985	5	0	0	0	128	Green	84	60	58
Fred Jackson	BUF	9	RB	33	0	0	0	163	731	6	38	332	1	1	0	0	128	Red	85	90	118
Jordan Reed	WAS	10	TE	24	0	0	0	0	0	0	60	706	6	0	0	0	98	Yellow	86	94	85
Ben Roethlisberger	PIT	12	QB	32	4362	27	12	25	85	0	0	0	0	4	0	0	289	Yellow	87	96	87
Nick Foles	PHI	7	QB	25	4003	27	8	70	205	3	0	0	0	5	0	0	289	Red	88	97	88
Mason Crosby	GB	9	K	30	0	0	0	0	0	0	0	0	0	0	50	31	132	Yellow	89	98	93
Eric Decker	NYJ	11	WR	27	0	0	0	0	0	0	73	1025	6	0	0	0	124	Red	90	67	67
Panthers D	CAR	12	D	--	0	0	0	0	0	0	0	0	0	0	0	0	110	Yellow	91	100	94
Tyler Eifert	CIN	4	TE	24	0	0	0	0	0	0	59	718	5	0	0	0	94	Yellow	92	103	92
Matt Prater	DEN	4	K	30	0	0	0	0	0	0	0	0	0	0	57	25	131	Green	93	101	97
Tony Romo	DAL	11	QB	34	4373	29	17	33	47	1	0	0	0	3	0	0	284	Yellow	94	107	95

Player	Team	Bye	Pos	Age	PaYd	PaTD	INT	Ru	RuYd	RuTD	Rec	RcYd	RcTD	FL	XP	FG	Fant	Risk	Flex Rk	3WR Rk	PPR Rk
Mike Wallace	MIA	5	WR	28	0	0	0	3	22	0	74	963	6	0	0	0	121	Red	95	70	68
Jeremy Maclin	PHI	7	WR	26	0	0	0	2	11	0	63	838	6	0	0	0	121	Green	96	71	74
Bills D	BUF	9	D	–	0	0	0	0	0	0	0	0	0	0	0	0	107	Green	97	106	100
Heath Miller	PIT	12	TE	32	0	0	0	0	0	0	57	637	6	0	0	0	91	Yellow	98	108	103
Percy Harvin	SEA	4	WR	26	0	0	0	8	50	0	70	881	7	0	0	0	120	Red	99	73	77
Dwayne Allen	IND	10	TE	24	0	0	0	0	0	0	50	615	6	0	0	0	89	Yellow	100	115	128
Jay Cutler	CHI	9	QB	31	4076	29	16	46	82	2	0	0	0	5	0	0	281	Yellow	101	116	101
Reggie Wayne	IND	10	WR	36	0	0	0	0	0	0	64	845	6	0	0	0	117	Green	102	83	80
Cecil Shorts	JAC	11	WR	27	0	0	0	2	8	0	67	878	6	0	0	0	117	Yellow	103	84	81
Julian Edelman	NE	10	WR	28	0	0	0	4	22	0	78	866	5	0	0	0	117	Green	104	85	59
Patriots D	NE	10	D	–	0	0	0	0	0	0	0	0	0	0	0	0	103	Green	105	114	110
Zach Ertz	PHI	7	TE	24	0	0	0	0	0	0	56	675	4	0	0	0	87	Yellow	106	123	112
Scott Chandler	BUF	9	TE	29	0	0	0	0	0	0	54	638	4	0	0	0	87	Green	107	124	111
Johnny Manziel	CLE	4	QB	22	3534	18	18	120	682	7	0	0	0	5	0	0	279	Red	108	125	106
DeAngelo Williams	CAR	12	RB	31	0	0	0	174	753	4	18	135	1	1	0	0	116	Green	109	102	171
Charles Clay	MIA	5	TE	25	0	0	0	0	0	0	54	631	5	0	0	0	86	Yellow	110	128	123
Delanie Walker	TEN	9	TE	30	0	0	0	0	0	0	61	667	4	0	0	0	86	Yellow	111	129	105
Jared Cook	STL	4	TE	27	0	0	0	0	0	0	50	635	4	0	0	0	86	Green	112	130	129
Andy Dalton	CIN	4	QB	27	3791	26	16	47	113	2	0	0	0	3	0	0	278	Green	113	131	107
Blair Walsh	MIN	10	K	24	0	0	0	0	0	0	0	0	0	0	38	29	123	Green	114	118	113
Adam Vinatieri	IND	10	K	42	0	0	0	0	0	0	0	0	0	0	44	27	123	Green	115	119	114
Rams D	STL	4	D	–	0	0	0	0	0	0	0	0	0	0	0	0	101	Red	116	122	115
Dan Bailey	DAL	11	K	26	0	0	0	0	0	0	0	0	0	0	39	31	122	Yellow	117	126	119
Steven Hauschka	SEA	4	K	29	0	0	0	0	0	0	0	0	0	0	42	27	122	Green	118	127	120
Brian Hartline	MIA	5	WR	28	0	0	0	0	0	0	69	929	5	0	0	0	113	Yellow	119	93	84
Jets D	NYJ	11	D	–	0	0	0	0	0	0	0	0	0	0	0	0	99	Yellow	120	132	121
Eagles D	PHI	7	D	–	0	0	0	0	0	0	0	0	0	0	0	0	99	Green	121	133	122
Justin Tucker	BAL	11	K	25	0	0	0	0	0	0	0	0	0	0	33	30	120	Green	122	134	124
Terrance Williams	DAL	11	WR	25	0	0	0	2	11	0	62	880	6	0	0	0	112	Red	123	95	102
Bengals D	CIN	4	D	–	0	0	0	0	0	0	0	0	0	0	0	0	98	Yellow	124	136	125
Broncos D	DEN	4	D	–	0	0	0	0	0	0	0	0	0	0	0	0	98	Red	125	137	126
Ryan Succop	KC	6	K	28	0	0	0	0	0	0	0	0	0	0	33	29	119	Green	126	138	130
Dwayne Bowe	KC	6	WR	30	0	0	0	0	0	0	56	715	7	0	0	0	111	Green	127	99	104
49ers D	SF	8	D	–	0	0	0	0	0	0	0	0	0	0	0	0	97	Green	128	139	131
Robbie Gould	CHI	9	K	32	0	0	0	0	0	0	0	0	0	0	41	29	118	Yellow	129	140	132
Eric Ebron	DET	9	TE	21	0	0	0	0	0	0	54	665	3	0	0	0	80	Yellow	130	153	141
Shaun Suisham	PIT	12	K	33	0	0	0	0	0	0	0	0	0	0	43	28	116	Yellow	131	146	135
Jay Feely	ARI	4	K	38	0	0	0	0	0	0	0	0	0	0	32	31	116	Yellow	132	147	136
Mike Nugent	CIN	4	K	32	0	0	0	0	0	0	0	0	0	0	40	29	116	Yellow	133	148	137
Phil Dawson	SF	8	K	39	0	0	0	0	0	0	0	0	0	0	44	25	116	Green	134	149	138
Riley Cooper	PHI	7	WR	27	0	0	0	0	0	0	52	791	6	0	0	0	108	Yellow	135	104	133
Danny Amendola	NE	10	WR	29	0	0	0	2	10	0	72	870	6	0	0	0	108	Red	136	105	90
Shane Vereen	NE	10	RB	25	0	0	0	92	437	1	66	536	1	1	0	0	108	Green	137	109	89
Darren McFadden	OAK	5	RB	27	0	0	0	186	699	4	41	307	0	1	0	0	108	Red	138	110	154
Giants D	NYG	8	D	–	0	0	0	0	0	0	0	0	0	0	0	0	94	Yellow	139	151	139
Lions D	DET	9	D	–	0	0	0	0	0	0	0	0	0	0	0	0	94	Yellow	140	152	140
Ladarius Green	SD	10	TE	23	0	0	0	0	0	0	46	547	4	0	0	0	76	Green	141	168	155
Darren Sproles	PHI	7	RB	31	0	0	0	76	389	1	66	510	2	0	0	0	105	Green	142	111	96
Ray Rice	BAL	11	RB	27	0	0	0	176	598	5	44	325	0	1	0	0	105	Red	143	112	157
Lamar Miller	MIA	5	RB	23	0	0	0	154	699	3	24	151	1	1	0	0	105	Green	144	113	188
Garrett Graham	HOU	10	TE	28	0	0	0	0	0	0	53	579	4	0	0	0	75	Yellow	145	169	149
Joe Flacco	BAL	11	QB	29	3967	25	16	38	70	1	0	0	0	4	0	0	266	Green	146	171	143
Sammy Watkins	BUF	9	WR	21	0	0	0	8	48	0	69	841	5	0	0	0	103	Red	147	117	108
Coby Fleener	IND	10	TE	26	0	0	0	0	0	0	42	506	4	0	0	0	73	Green	148	175	164
Emmanuel Sanders	DEN	4	WR	27	0	0	0	3	16	0	58	819	5	0	0	0	102	Red	149	120	142
Marvin Jones	CIN	4	WR	24	0	0	0	6	44	0	60	768	5	0	0	0	102	Yellow	150	121	127
Doug Baldwin	SEA	4	WR	26	0	0	0	2	9	0	54	723	5	0	0	0	99	Green	151	135	144
Zach Miller	SEA	4	TE	29	0	0	0	0	0	0	42	453	5	0	0	0	69	Yellow	152	184	179
Richard Rodgers	GB	9	TE	22	0	0	0	0	0	0	49	587	3	0	0	0	69	Red	153	185	166
Owen Daniels	BAL	11	TE	32	0	0	0	0	0	0	43	468	4	0	0	0	69	Green	154	186	169
Harry Douglas	ATL	9	WR	29	0	0	0	0	0	0	65	799	3	0	0	0	97	Green	155	141	116
Golden Tate	DET	9	WR	26	0	0	0	3	15	0	55	807	4	0	0	0	96	Yellow	156	144	146
Brandon Myers	TB	7	TE	29	0	0	0	0	0	0	48	485	4	0	0	0	66	Yellow	157	197	170
Rueben Randle	NYG	8	WR	23	0	0	0	3	17	0	54	759	5	0	0	0	95	Red	158	150	156
Rod Streater	OAK	5	WR	26	0	0	0	0	0	0	56	760	4	0	0	0	94	Yellow	159	154	150
Aaron Dobson	NE	10	WR	23	0	0	0	2	11	0	51	711	6	0	0	0	94	Red	160	155	161
Marcedes Lewis	JAC	11	TE	30	0	0	0	0	0	0	44	476	4	0	0	0	64	Yellow	161	203	190

Player	Team	Bye	Pos	Age	PaYd	PaTD	INT	Ru	RuYd	RuTD	Rec	RcYd	RcTD	FL	XP	FG	Fant	Risk	Flex Rk	3WR Rk	PPR Rk
Tavon Austin	STL	4	WR	23	0	0	0	12	90	0	59	702	3	0	0	0	93	Yellow	162	157	147
Steve Smith	BAL	11	WR	35	0	0	0	0	0	0	61	712	5	0	0	0	93	Yellow	163	158	145
Miles Austin	CLE	4	WR	30	0	0	0	0	0	0	58	776	5	0	0	0	93	Red	164	159	153
Marqise Lee	JAC	11	WR	23	0	0	0	6	35	0	59	721	4	0	0	0	93	Yellow	165	160	148
Greg Jennings	MIN	10	WR	31	0	0	0	0	0	0	57	751	4	0	0	0	92	Yellow	166	162	151
Maurice Jones-Drew	OAK	5	RB	29	0	0	0	120	516	4	31	179	0	1	0	0	92	Green	167	142	201
Carson Palmer	ARI	4	QB	35	4070	21	14	28	30	0	0	0	0	4	0	0	254	Green	168	214	158
Terrance West	CLE	4	RB	23	0	0	0	110	461	5	19	173	1	1	0	0	91	Yellow	169	143	229
Eli Manning	NYG	8	QB	33	3918	23	16	27	39	0	0	0	0	3	0	0	253	Green	170	219	159
Jake Locker	TEN	9	QB	26	3836	18	17	73	258	3	0	0	0	4	0	0	253	Yellow	171	220	160
Travaris Cadet	NO	6	RB	25	0	0	0	63	310	3	45	400	2	1	0	0	89	Red	172	145	189
Mychal Rivera	OAK	5	TE	24	0	0	0	0	0	0	41	445	4	0	0	0	59	Red	173	230	213
Chiefs D	KC	6	D	--	0	0	0	0	0	0	0	0	0	0	0	0	94	Yellow	174	209	172
Brandin Cooks	NO	6	WR	21	0	0	0	3	15	0	58	729	4	0	0	0	88	Red	175	172	162
Justin Hunter	TEN	9	WR	23	0	0	0	0	0	0	48	709	5	0	0	0	88	Red	176	173	184
Levine Toilolo	ATL	9	TE	23	0	0	0	0	0	0	36	349	5	0	0	0	58	Red	177	236	226
Brent Celek	PHI	7	TE	29	0	0	0	0	0	0	40	422	3	0	0	0	58	Green	178	237	209
Kelvin Benjamin	CAR	12	WR	23	0	0	0	6	37	0	51	733	4	0	0	0	87	Red	179	177	173
Ryan Fitzpatrick	HOU	10	QB	32	3730	23	22	52	219	2	0	0	0	4	0	0	249	Yellow	180	238	165
Josh Brown	NYG	8	K	35	0	0	0	0	0	0	0	0	0	0	37	27	115	Green	181	221	176
Matt Bryant	ATL	9	K	39	0	0	0	0	0	0	0	0	0	0	37	29	115	Yellow	182	222	177
Shayne Graham	NO	6	K	37	0	0	0	0	0	0	0	0	0	0	47	28	115	Red	183	223	178
Ravens D	BAL	11	D	--	0	0	0	0	0	0	0	0	0	0	0	0	93	Yellow	184	224	180
Saints D	NO	6	D	--	0	0	0	0	0	0	0	0	0	0	0	0	93	Red	185	225	181
Bears D	CHI	9	D	--	0	0	0	0	0	0	0	0	0	0	0	0	93	Green	186	226	182
Markus Wheaton	PIT	12	WR	23	0	0	0	4	24	0	52	724	4	0	0	0	86	Red	187	178	174
James Jones	OAK	5	WR	30	0	0	0	0	0	0	60	724	4	0	0	0	86	Red	188	179	163
Tre Mason	STL	4	RB	21	0	0	0	107	465	4	20	140	1	1	0	0	86	Green	189	156	236
Brandon Pettigrew	DET	9	TE	29	0	0	0	0	0	0	38	393	3	0	0	0	56	Green	190	245	217
Ryan Tannehill	MIA	5	QB	26	3724	23	16	42	162	2	0	0	0	4	0	0	248	Yellow	191	246	167
Andrew Hawkins	CLE	4	WR	28	0	0	0	3	16	0	55	745	3	0	0	0	85	Red	192	181	168
Nate Washington	TEN	9	WR	31	0	0	0	0	0	0	50	686	4	0	0	0	85	Yellow	193	182	175
Jeff Cumberland	NYJ	11	TE	27	0	0	0	0	0	0	29	374	3	0	0	0	55	Green	194	248	235
Travis Kelce	KC	6	TE	25	0	0	0	0	0	0	39	429	2	0	0	0	55	Green	195	249	218
Cardinals D	ARI	4	D	--	0	0	0	0	0	0	0	0	0	0	0	0	92	Yellow	196	231	185
Dolphins D	MIA	5	D	--	0	0	0	0	0	0	0	0	0	0	0	0	92	Red	197	232	186
Redskins D	WAS	10	D	--	0	0	0	0	0	0	0	0	0	0	0	0	92	Yellow	198	233	187
Josh Gordon (IF HE PLAYS)	CLE	4	WR	23	0	0	0	2	10	0	42	721	4	0	0	0	84	Red	199	183	202
Shonn Greene	TEN	9	RB	29	0	0	0	142	563	3	13	98	0	1	0	0	84	Green	200	161	247
Kenny Stills	NO	6	WR	22	0	0	0	3	19	0	46	616	5	0	0	0	83	Red	201	190	196
Jermaine Gresham	CIN	4	TE	26	0	0	0	0	0	0	38	406	2	0	0	0	53	Green	202	253	223
Nick Folk	NYJ	11	K	30	0	0	0	0	0	0	0	0	0	0	36	28	113	Yellow	203	239	191
Randy Bullock	HOU	10	K	25	0	0	0	0	0	0	0	0	0	0	36	26	113	Green	204	240	192
Nick Novak	SD	10	K	33	0	0	0	0	0	0	0	0	0	0	46	27	113	Red	205	241	193
Packers D	GB	9	D	--	0	0	0	0	0	0	0	0	0	0	0	0	91	Yellow	206	242	194
Chris Givens	STL	4	WR	25	0	0	0	3	15	0	45	690	3	0	0	0	82	Yellow	207	193	197
Odell Beckham	NYG	8	WR	22	0	0	0	4	22	0	47	639	5	0	0	0	82	Red	208	194	198
Bernard Pierce	BAL	11	RB	23	0	0	0	157	605	2	24	169	0	2	0	0	82	Green	209	163	237
Jeremy Hill	CIN	4	RB	22	0	0	0	100	416	4	19	163	1	1	0	0	82	Green	210	164	243
EJ Manuel	BUF	9	QB	24	3521	19	19	60	238	2	0	0	0	5	0	0	244	Green	211	255	183
Mike Evans	TB	7	WR	21	0	0	0	4	22	0	48	675	4	0	0	0	81	Red	212	196	199
Christine Michael	SEA	4	RB	24	0	0	0	125	587	2	15	126	0	2	0	0	80	Green	213	165	250
James White	NE	10	RB	22	0	0	0	82	402	1	35	316	2	0	0	0	80	Yellow	214	166	222
Robert Woods	BUF	9	WR	22	0	0	0	3	15	0	43	575	4	0	0	0	79	Green	215	201	203
Donnie Avery	KC	6	WR	30	0	0	0	2	9	0	43	581	4	0	0	0	79	Green	216	202	204
Roy Helu	WAS	10	RB	26	0	0	0	72	322	3	38	289	1	1	0	0	79	Green	217	167	216
Texans D	HOU	10	D	--	0	0	0	0	0	0	0	0	0	0	0	0	89	Red	218	254	200
Greg Zuerlein	STL	4	K	27	0	0	0	0	0	0	0	0	0	0	36	28	110	Yellow	219	257	205
Vikings D	MIN	10	D	--	0	0	0	0	0	0	0	0	0	0	0	0	88	Red	220	258	206
Cowboys D	DAL	11	D	--	0	0	0	0	0	0	0	0	0	0	0	0	88	Yellow	221	259	207
Bucs D	TB	7	D	--	0	0	0	0	0	0	0	0	0	0	0	0	88	Yellow	222	260	208
Jordan Matthews	PHI	7	WR	22	0	0	0	0	0	0	41	620	4	0	0	0	76	Red	223	215	224
Vincent Brown	SD	10	WR	25	0	0	0	2	17	0	42	597	4	0	0	0	76	Yellow	224	216	219
Knowshon Moreno	MIA	5	RB	27	0	0	0	98	403	4	29	157	1	0	0	0	76	Red	225	170	242
Sam Bradford	STL	4	QB	27	3727	19	13	26	59	0	0	0	0	3	0	0	238	Green	226	270	195
Benjamin Watson	NO	6	TE	34	0	0	0	0	0	0	25	276	3	0	0	0	45	Green	227	271	252
Alex Henery	PHI	7	K	27	0	0	0	0	0	0	0	0	0	0	46	22	109	Green	228	264	210

Player	Team	Bye	Pos	Age	PaYd	PaTD	INT	Ru	RuYd	RuTD	Rec	RcYd	RcTD	FL	XP	FG	Fant	Risk	Flex Rk	3WR Rk	PPR Rk
Titans D	TEN	9	D	--	0	0	0	0	0	0	0	0	0	0	0	0	87	Red	229	265	211
Allen Robinson	JAC	11	WR	21	0	0	0	3	18	0	47	625	3	0	0	0	74	Yellow	230	229	214
LeGarrette Blount	PIT	12	RB	28	0	0	0	105	401	5	6	55	1	1	0	0	74	Green	231	174	259
Austin Seferian-Jenkins	TB	7	TE	22	0	0	0	0	0	0	35	373	2	0	0	0	44	Yellow	232	272	245
Jarrett Boykin	GB	9	WR	25	0	0	0	0	0	0	34	475	4	0	0	0	73	Green	233	234	233
Hakeem Nicks	IND	10	WR	26	0	0	0	0	0	0	43	569	4	0	0	0	73	Yellow	234	235	221
Ka'Deem Carey	CHI	9	RB	22	0	0	0	103	437	3	15	99	1	1	0	0	73	Green	235	176	253
Nate Freese	DET	9	K	24	0	0	0	0	0	0	0	0	0	0	42	27	108	Red	236	268	215
Anthony Fasano	KC	6	TE	30	0	0	0	0	0	0	38	308	3	0	0	0	42	Yellow	237	273	244
Jeremy Kerley	NYJ	11	WR	25	0	0	0	3	11	0	44	562	2	0	0	0	71	Green	238	243	220
Sidney Rice	SEA	4	WR	28	0	0	0	0	0	0	38	558	4	0	0	0	71	Red	239	244	238
Martavis Bryant	PIT	12	WR	23	0	0	0	0	0	0	38	556	4	0	0	0	70	Red	240	247	239
Chris Ivory	NYJ	11	RB	26	0	0	0	120	562	2	4	29	0	1	0	0	70	Green	241	180	263
Alex Smith	KC	6	QB	30	3458	19	12	58	246	2	0	0	0	5	0	0	232	Yellow	242	275	212
Malcom Floyd	SD	10	WR	33	0	0	0	0	0	0	29	539	3	0	0	0	69	Yellow	243	250	248
Andre Holmes	OAK	5	WR	26	0	0	0	0	0	0	43	579	3	0	0	0	68	Red	244	251	234
Jerome Simpson	MIN	10	WR	28	0	0	0	0	0	0	34	513	3	0	0	0	68	Green	245	252	241
Falcons D	ATL	9	D	--	0	0	0	0	0	0	0	0	0	0	0	0	83	Yellow	246	274	227
Jerricho Cotchery	CAR	12	WR	32	0	0	0	0	0	0	52	586	3	0	0	0	66	Red	247	256	225
Marcel Reece	OAK	5	RB	29	0	0	0	40	168	2	43	377	1	1	0	0	66	Green	248	187	230
DuJuan Harris	GB	9	RB	26	0	0	0	76	358	1	21	205	1	1	0	0	66	Green	249	188	255
Stepfan Taylor	ARI	4	RB	23	0	0	0	105	431	2	24	204	1	1	0	0	66	Red	250	189	254
Nate Burleson	CLE	4	WR	33	0	0	0	0	0	0	45	557	2	0	0	0	65	Green	251	261	228
Andre Roberts	WAS	10	WR	26	0	0	0	2	9	0	39	500	3	0	0	0	65	Green	252	262	240
Travis Benjamin	CLE	4	WR	25	0	0	0	4	27	0	32	509	3	0	0	0	64	Yellow	253	263	249
C.J. Anderson	DEN	4	RB	23	0	0	0	73	329	3	18	131	1	1	0	0	64	Yellow	254	191	258
Denarius Moore	OAK	5	WR	26	0	0	0	2	8	0	36	494	2	0	0	0	63	Green	255	266	246
Daniel Thomas	MIA	5	RB	27	0	0	0	112	440	3	16	97	0	1	0	0	63	Red	256	192	260
Austin Pettis	STL	4	WR	26	0	0	0	0	0	0	51	557	2	0	0	0	62	Red	257	267	231
Ahmad Bradshaw	IND	10	RB	28	0	0	0	91	361	3	9	71	0	0	0	0	62	Green	258	195	266
Mohamed Sanu	CIN	4	WR	25	0	0	0	2	11	0	47	484	2	0	0	0	61	Green	259	269	232
Jonathan Stewart	CAR	12	RB	27	0	0	0	103	430	2	18	118	0	1	0	0	60	Red	260	198	261
Charles Sims	TB	7	RB	24	0	0	0	67	288	1	27	250	1	1	0	0	59	Yellow	261	199	256
Carlos Hyde	SF	8	RB	23	0	0	0	101	413	2	10	91	0	1	0	0	57	Yellow	262	200	268
Dexter McCluster	TEN	9	RB	26	0	0	0	31	134	1	40	359	1	0	0	0	56	Yellow	263	204	251
Mike Tolbert	CAR	12	RB	29	0	0	0	60	207	3	30	196	0	1	0	0	55	Green	264	205	257
Ronnie Hillman	DEN	4	RB	23	0	0	0	64	261	2	19	140	0	1	0	0	55	Blue	265	206	262
Dri Archer	PIT	12	RB	23	0	0	0	33	165	2	21	182	1	0	0	0	53	Green	266	207	264
Andre Williams	NYG	8	RB	22	0	0	0	71	278	2	13	124	1	0	0	0	53	Green	267	208	269
Khiry Robinson	NO	6	RB	25	0	0	0	106	454	2	6	53	0	2	0	0	52	Red	268	210	272
Donald Brown	SD	10	RB	27	0	0	0	51	206	3	16	124	0	0	0	0	52	Blue	269	211	267
Vick Ballard	IND	10	RB	24	0	0	0	61	217	4	5	48	0	1	0	0	51	Green	270	212	274
Matt Asiata	MIN	10	RB	27	0	0	0	68	252	2	22	173	0	1	0	0	51	Green	271	213	265
Mike James	TB	7	RB	23	0	0	0	71	321	1	16	135	1	1	0	0	50	Red	272	217	271
Kendall Hunter	SF	8	RB	26	0	0	0	69	301	3	6	52	0	1	0	0	49	Green	273	218	275
Mark Ingram	NO	6	RB	25	0	0	0	84	326	1	9	93	0	2	0	0	48	Blue	274	227	273
James Starks	GB	9	RB	28	0	0	0	55	246	2	19	125	0	1	0	0	47	Green	275	228	270

Statistical Appendix

Broken Tackles by Team, Offense

Rk	Team	Plays	Plays w/ BTkl	Pct	Total BTkl
1	SEA	958	93	9.7%	112
2	MIN	1012	77	7.6%	96
3	GB	1063	78	7.3%	97
4	PHI	1035	74	7.1%	85
5	CAR	987	70	7.1%	77
6	KC	1017	68	6.7%	77
7	PIT	1010	65	6.4%	70
8	DET	1092	70	6.4%	80
9	CIN	1078	68	6.3%	85
10	IND	1019	64	6.3%	72
11	NE	1127	69	6.1%	76
12	CHI	1001	60	6.0%	72
13	DAL	953	56	5.9%	67
14	BUF	1109	65	5.9%	72
15	ATL	1025	60	5.9%	67
16	NO	1060	62	5.8%	69
17	MIA	990	56	5.7%	64
18	TEN	1019	56	5.5%	64
19	NYG	989	54	5.5%	64
20	ARI	1028	56	5.4%	65
21	SF	949	51	5.4%	54
22	HOU	1091	56	5.1%	57
23	DEN	1141	56	4.9%	62
24	JAC	1021	49	4.8%	56
25	NYJ	1014	48	4.7%	58
26	SD	1057	48	4.5%	51
27	WAS	1103	49	4.4%	56
28	STL	961	40	4.2%	48
29	OAK	997	39	3.9%	45
30	TB	983	38	3.9%	43
31	BAL	1095	42	3.8%	45
32	CLE	1073	34	3.2%	38

Broken Tackles by Team, Defense

Rk	Team	Plays	Plays w/ BTkl	Pct	Total BTkl
1	BUF	1080	42	3.9%	49
2	KC	1065	42	3.9%	45
3	NE	1114	45	4.0%	46
4	DEN	1074	48	4.5%	52
5	NO	939	45	4.8%	48
6	PHI	1148	58	5.1%	67
7	NYG	1076	55	5.1%	62
8	SF	1015	52	5.1%	57
9	PIT	1031	53	5.1%	64
10	NYJ	1041	54	5.2%	64
11	IND	1021	54	5.3%	60
12	CIN	1038	55	5.3%	62
13	CLE	1093	58	5.3%	68
14	DET	969	52	5.4%	60
15	JAC	1076	58	5.4%	65
16	ARI	1037	56	5.4%	64
17	DAL	1085	59	5.4%	65
18	GB	1008	56	5.6%	61
19	SEA	990	58	5.9%	61
20	HOU	965	57	5.9%	74
21	TB	1009	61	6.0%	66
22	MIA	1090	66	6.1%	74
23	SD	956	59	6.2%	64
24	OAK	1019	63	6.2%	77
25	TEN	1015	63	6.2%	72
26	MIN	1119	70	6.3%	86
27	CAR	969	61	6.3%	73
28	BAL	1020	65	6.4%	76
29	STL	1012	73	7.2%	80
30	ATL	998	72	7.2%	83
31	CHI	1015	77	7.6%	95
32	WAS	970	85	8.8%	104

Top 20 Defenders, Broken Tackles

Rk	Player	Team	BTkl
1	B.Meriweather	WAS	16
2	C.Conte	CHI	15
3	C.Greenway	MIN	14
3	B.Ross	OAK	14
5	D.Goldson	TB	13
5	D.Hall	WAS	13
5	T.Jennings	CHI	13
5	L.Kuechly	CAR	13
5	A.Ogletree	STL	13
5	B.Skrine	CLE	13
5	J.Wilson	WAS	13
12	J.Ihedigbo	BAL	12
12	M.Jenkins	NO	12
12	T.Johnson	STL	12
12	S.Keo	HOU	12
12	M.Mitchell	CAR	12
12	E.Thomas	SEA	12
12	C.Woodson	OAK	12
19	B.Carr	DAL	11
19	M.Elam	BAL	11
19	W.Moore	ATL	11

Top 20 Defenders, Broken Tackle Rate

Rk	Player	Team	BTkl	Tkl	Rate	Rk	Player	Team	BTkl	Tkl	Rate
1	D.Harrison	NYJ	0	50	0.0%	11	S.Lee	DAL	2	86	2.3%
1	D.Poe	KC	0	47	0.0%	11	N.Suh	DET	1	43	2.3%
1	M.Cooper	KC	0	41	0.0%	13	B.Boykin	PHI	1	42	2.3%
1	C.Peters	ATL	0	40	0.0%	13	A.Jones	BAL	1	42	2.3%
5	B.Spikes	NE	1	68	1.4%	13	P.Sims	OAK	1	42	2.3%
6	A.Williams	BUF	1	63	1.6%	16	M.Brockers	STL	1	40	2.4%
7	M.Lawson	BUF	1	54	1.8%	16	G.McCoy	TB	1	40	2.4%
8	A.Jordan	KC	1	53	1.9%	16	S.Moore	OAK	1	40	2.4%
9	K.Williams	BUF	1	50	2.0%	16	R.Starks	MIA	1	40	2.4%
10	J.Robinson	MIN	1	47	2.1%	20	D.Hightower	NE	2	70	2.8%

Broken Tackles divided by Broken Tackles + Solo Tackles.
Special teams not included; min. 40 Solo Tackles

Bottom 20 Defenders, Broken Tackle Rate

Rk	Player	Team	BTkl	Tkl	Rate	Rk	Player	Team	BTkl	Tkl	Rate
1	B.Meriweather	WAS	16	62	20.5%	11	J.Evans	JAC	10	47	17.5%
2	B.Ross	OAK	14	58	19.4%	12	M.Mitchell	CAR	12	58	17.1%
3	T.Jennings	CHI	13	54	19.4%	13	C.Houston	DET	8	40	16.7%
4	S.Keo	HOU	12	53	18.5%	13	C.Conte	CHI	15	77	16.3%
5	C.McCarthy	TEN	9	40	18.4%	15	T.Johnson	STL	12	62	16.2%
6	D.Goldson	TB	13	58	18.3%	15	D.Hall	WAS	13	69	15.9%
7	M.Jenkins	NO	12	55	17.9%	17	L.Delmas	DET	10	55	15.4%
8	B.Skrine	CLE	13	60	17.8%	18	J.Wilson	WAS	13	72	15.3%
9	T.DeCoud	ATL	10	47	17.5%	18	M.Elam	BAL	11	61	15.3%
10	R.Doughty	WAS	10	47	17.5%	20	D.Milliner	NYJ	9	50	15.3%

Broken Tackles divided by Broken Tackles + Solo Tackles.
Special teams not included; min. 40 Solo Tackles

Most Broken Tackles, Running Backs

Rk	Player	Team	BTkl	Rk	Player	Team	BTkl
1	M.Lynch	SEA	59	10	A.Morris	WAS	24
2	L.McCoy	PHI	51	10	T.Richardson	2TM	24
3	A.Peterson	MIN	42	14	R.Bush	DET	22
4	J.Charles	KC	39	15	L.Bell	PIT	21
5	D.Murray	DAL	35	16	C.Ivory	NYJ	20
6	E.Lacy	GB	29	16	M.Jones-Drew	JAC	20
7	G.Bernard	CIN	28	16	B.Tate	HOU	20
7	A.Ellington	ARI	28	19	C.Johnson	TEN	18
9	F.Jackson	BUF	27	19	K.Moreno	DEN	18
10	J.Bell	DET	24	19	C.J.Spiller	BUF	18
10	M.Forte	CHI	24				

Most Broken Tackles, WR/TE

Rk	Player	Team	BTkl	Rk	Player	Team	BTkl
1	G.Tate	SEA	23	12	J.Finley	GB	9
2	C.Patterson	MIN	18	12	J.Graham	NO	9
3	A.Brown	PIT	15	12	J.Gresham	CIN	9
4	M.Bennett	CHI	14	12	B.Marshall	CHI	9
4	K.Wright	TEN	14	17	H.Douglas	ATL	8
6	C.Clay	MIA	13	17	A.Gates	SD	8
7	S.Smith	CAR	12	17	A.Jeffery	CHI	8
8	J.Edelman	NE	11	17	A.Johnson	HOU	8
8	M.Jones	CIN	11	17	J.Jones	GB	8
8	J.Nelson	GB	11	17	M.Lewis	JAC	8
11	K.Allen	SD	10	17	D.Thomas	DEN	8
12	A.Boldin	SF	9				

Most Broken Tackles, Quarterbacks

Rk	Player	Team	Behind LOS	Beyond LOS	BTkl	Rk	Player	Team	Behind LOS	Beyond LOS	BTkl
1	C.Newton	CAR	20	5	25	5	T.Pryor	OAK	5	4	9
2	R.Wilson	SEA	10	5	15	5	G.Smith	NYJ	5	4	9
3	B.Roethlisberger	PIT	12	0	12	8	R.Griffin	WAS	5	3	8
4	A.Luck	IND	8	2	10	8	M.Stafford	DET	6	2	8
5	C.Kaepernick	SF	7	2	9	10	J.Flacco	BAL	7	0	7

Best Broken Tackle Rate, Offensive Players (min. 80 touches)

Rk	Player	Team	BTkl	Touch	Rate	Rk	Player	Team	BTkl	Touch	Rate
1	A.Ellington	ARI	28	157	17.8%	11	A.Brown	PIT	15	117	12.8%
2	M.Ingram	NO	15	85	17.6%	12	G.Bernard	CIN	28	226	12.4%
3	M.Lynch	SEA	59	337	17.5%	13	S.Vereen	NE	11	91	12.1%
4	K.Wright	TEN	14	94	14.9%	14	B.Brown	PHI	10	83	12.0%
5	L.McCoy	PHI	51	366	13.9%	15	J.Charles	KC	39	329	11.9%
6	A.Peterson	MIN	42	308	13.6%	16	D.Sproles	NO	14	124	11.3%
7	D.Brown	IND	17	129	13.2%	16	D.Thomas	MIA	14	124	11.3%
8	J.Starks	GB	13	99	13.1%	18	L.Blount	NE	17	155	11.0%
9	D.Murray	DAL	35	270	13.0%	19	J.Bell	DET	24	219	11.0%
10	J.Nelson	GB	11	85	12.9%	20	C.Ivory	NYJ	20	184	10.9%

Top 20 Defenders, Passes Defensed

Rk	Player	Team	PD	Rk	Player	Team	PD
1	A.Verner	TEN	23	13	B.Boykin	PHI	15
2	B.Grimes	MIA	19	14	M.Cooper	KC	15
3	J.Haden	CLE	19	15	J.Jenkins	SL	15
4	L.McKelvin	BUF	19	16	R.Mathis	DET	15
5	L.Webb	BAL	19	17	J.Smith	BAL	15
6	S.Shields	GB	17	18	A.Talib	NE	15
7	B.Skrine	CLE	17	19	A.Ball	JAC	14
8	D.Trufant	ATL	17	20	A.Jones	CIN	14
9	K.Dansby	ARI	16	21	D.Rodgers-Cromartie	DEN	14
10	J.Joseph	HOU	16	22	R.Sherman	SEA	14
11	D.Milliner	NYJ	16	23	D.Smith	BAL	14
12	J.Powers	ARI	16				

Note: Based on the definition given in the Statistical Toolbox, not NFL totals.

Top 20 Defenders, Defeats

Rk	Player	Team	Dfts	Rk	Player	Team	Dfts
1	L.David	TB	50	11	S.Tulloch	DET	30
2	T.Davis	CAR	37	13	K.Alonso	BUF	28
3	N.Bowman	SF	35	14	D.Johnson	KC	27
3	J.J.Watt	HOU	35	14	J.Laurinaitis	STL	27
5	L.Kuechly	CAR	34	14	D.Levy	DET	27
5	A.Ogletree	STL	34	17	V.Burfict	CIN	26
7	R.Mathis	IND	33	17	A.Clayborn	TB	26
7	R.Quinn	STL	33	17	G.Hardy	CAR	26
9	D.Smith	BAL	32	17	B.Orakpo	WAS	26
10	K.Dansby	ARI	31	17	P.Posluszny	JAC	26
11	K.Burnett	OAK	30				

Top 20 Defenders, Run Tackles for Loss

Rk	Player	Team	RTFL	Rk	Player	Team	RTFL
1	A.Clayborn	TB	17	12	D.Johnson	KC	9
1	L.David	TB	17	12	B.Mebane	SEA	9
3	J.J.Watt	HOU	15	12	K.Williams	BUF	9
4	E.Henderson	MIN	13	17	Q.Coples	NYJ	8
5	A.Ogletree	SL	12	17	D.Dockett	ARI	8
5	R.Quinn	SL	12	17	D.Harrison	NYJ	8
7	L.Briggs	CHI	11	17	J.Hatcher	DAL	8
7	K.Burnett	OAK	11	17	C.Jones	NE	8
9	L.Kuechly	CAR	10	17	C.Lofton	NO	8
9	S.Richardson	NYJ	10	17	B.Spikes	NE	8
9	T.Ward	CLE	10	17	C.Thornton	PHI	8
12	K.Alonso	BUF	9	17	S.Tulloch	DET	8
12	C.Campbell	ARI	9	17	C.Wootton	CHI	8

Top 20 Defenders, Quarterback Hits

Rk	Player	Team	Hits	Rk	Player	Team	Hits
1	J.J.Watt	HOU	36	11	N.Suh	DET	15
2	R.Quinn	STL	21	14	C.Campbell	ARI	14
3	M.Johnson	CIN	20	14	M.Kiwanuka	NYG	14
4	C.Dunlap	CIN	18	16	N.Fairley	DET	13
5	J.Babin	JAC	17	16	C.Jordan	NO	13
5	M.Bennett	SEA	17	16	G.McCoy	TB	13
5	D.Morgan	TEN	17	19	D.Bryant	CLE	12
5	J.Worilds	PIT	17	19	J.Galette	NO	12
9	G.Hardy	CAR	16	19	C.Jones	NE	12
9	C.Wake	MIA	16	19	J.Tuck	NYG	12
11	J.Allen	MIN	15	19	K.Williams	BUF	12
11	Q.Coples	NYJ	15				

Top 20 Defenders, QB Knockdowns (Sacks + Hits)

Rk	Defender	Team	KD	Rk	Defender	Team	KD
1	J.J.Watt	HOU	47	10	J.Galette	NO	24
2	R.Quinn	STL	36	10	C.Jones	NE	24
3	G.Hardy	CAR	31	10	D.Morgan	TEN	24
4	M.Bennett	SEA	27	10	C.Wake	MIA	24
4	C.Dunlap	CIN	27	16	G.McCoy	TB	23
6	J.Allen	MIN	26	16	J.Tuck	NYG	23
6	J.Worilds	PIT	26	16	K.Williams	BUF	23
8	M.Johnson	CIN	25	19	R.Mathis	IND	22
8	C.Jordan	NO	25	20	M.Kiwanuka	NYG	21
10	J.Babin	JAC	24	20	N.Suh	DET	21
10	C.Campbell	ARI	24				

Full credit for whole and half sacks; includes sacks cancelled by penalty. Does not include strip sacks.

Top 20 Defenders, Hurries

Rk	Defender	Team	Hur	Rk	Defender	Team	Hur
1	B.Robison	MIN	46.5	11	T.Hali	KC	31.5
2	R.Quinn	STL	43.0	12	R.Ninkovich	NE	31.5
3	G.McCoy	TB	40.0	13	C.Avril	SEA	29.3
4	J.J.Watt	HOU	38.5	14	J.Allen	MIN	27.0
5	R.Mathis	IND	33.3	15	W.Young	DET	27.0
6	G.Hardy	CAR	33.0	16	A.Clayborn	TB	26.5
7	C.Jordan	NO	33.0	17	C.Johnson	CAR	26.5
8	C.Jones	NE	32.5	18	M.Johnson	CIN	26.5
9	J.Abraham	ARI	32.0	19	P.Kruger	CLE	26.5
10	J.Tuck	NYG	32.0	20	C.Wake	MIA	26.5

Top 12 Defenders, Drawing Offensive Holding Flags

Rk	Player	Team	Total	Pass	Run	Rk	Player	Team	Total	Pass	Run
1	R.Quinn	STL	7	7	0	5	K.Williams	BUF	5	4	1
1	T.Suggs	BAL	7	4	3	5	M.Wilkerson	NYJ	5	2	3
3	T.Hali	KC	6	5	1	5	B.Orakpo	WAS	5	4	1
3	C.Heyward	PIT	6	4	2	5	J.Casey	TEN	5	1	4
5	W.Mercilus	HOU	5	3	2	5	J.Allen	MIN	5	5	0
5	G.Hardy	CAR	5	4	1	5	R.Mathis	IND	5	5	0
5	K.Burnett	OAK	5	3	2						

Top 20 Quarterbacks, QB Hits

Rk	Player	Team	Hits	Rk	Player	Team	Hits
1	A.Luck	IND	87	12	C.Henne	JAC	46
2	C.Palmer	ARI	63	13	E.Manning	NYG	45
3	M.Ryan	ATL	60	14	J.Cutler	CHI	42
4	R.Wilson	SEA	54	15	R.Fitzpatrick	TEN	39
5	G.Smith	NYJ	50	16	C.Keenum	HOU	38
6	M.Stafford	DET	50	17	P.Manning	DEN	38
7	D.Brees	NO	48	18	B.Roethlisberger	PIT	38
8	R.Griffin	WAS	48	19	E.Manuel	BUF	37
9	T.Brady	NE	47	20	P.Rivers	SD	37
10	J.Flacco	BAL	47	21	B.Weeden	CLE	37
11	R.Tannehill	MIA	47				

Top 20 Quarterbacks, QB Knockdowns (Sacks + Hits)

Rk	Player	Team	Adj KD	Rk	Player	Team	Adj KD
1	A.Luck	IND	115	12	E.Manning	NYG	82
2	M.Ryan	ATL	103	13	B.Roethlisberger	PIT	76
3	R.Tannehill	MIA	101	14	M.Glennon	TB	71
4	C.Palmer	ARI	100	15	M.Stafford	DET	69
5	R.Wilson	SEA	96	16	A.Smith	KC	68
6	J.Flacco	BAL	92	17	P.Rivers	SD	67
7	G.Smith	NYJ	90	18	C.Newton	CAR	67
8	T.Brady	NE	86	19	E.Manuel	BUF	64
9	R.Griffin	WAS	84	20	B.Weeden	CLE	60
10	D.Brees	NO	83	21	C.Kaepernick	SF	60
11	C.Henne	JAC	83				

Includes sacks cancelled by penalties.
Does not include strip sacks or "self sacks" with no defender listed.

Top 10 Quarterbacks, Knockdowns per Pass

Rk	Player	Team	KD	Pct
1	T.Lewis	BUF	40	22.1%
2	C.Keenum	HOU	55	19.9%
3	R.Wilson	SEA	96	19.9%
4	B.Weeden	CLE	60	19.5%
5	M.Vick	PHI	31	18.9%
6	E.Manuel	BUF	64	17.9%
7	A.Luck	IND	115	17.9%
8	G.Smith	NYJ	90	17.8%
9	M.Flynn	3TM	40	17.0%
10	R.Griffin	WAS	84	16.5%

Min. 120 passes; includes passes cancelled by penalty

Bottom 10 Quarterbacks in Knockdowns per Pass

Rk	Player	Team	KD	Pct
1	M.McGloin	OAK	17	7.3%
2	A.Dalton	CIN	47	7.3%
2	P.Manning	DEN	53	7.4%
4	K.Cousins	WAS	14	8.6%
5	T.Romo	DAL	54	9.0%
6	M.Cassel	MIN	25	9.1%
7	M.Stafford	DET	69	10.2%
8	P.Rivers	SD	67	10.9%
9	A.Rodgers	GB	37	11.3%
10	D.Brees	NO	83	11.4%

Min. 120 passes; includes passes cancelled by penalty

Most Passes Tipped at Line, Quarterbacks

Rk	Player	Team	Total
1	C.Henne	JAC	25
2	M.Stafford	DET	18
3	A.Dalton	CIN	16
3	C.Kaepernick	SF	16
3	A.Luck	IND	16
6	A.Smith	KC	14
7	M.Cassel	MIN	13
7	P.Rivers	SD	13
7	M.Ryan	ATL	13
10	R.Griffin	WAS	12
10	C.Newton	CAR	12
10	C.Palmer	ARI	12

Most Passes Tipped at the Line, Defenders

Rk	Player	Team	Total
1	C.Barwin	PHI	8
1	S.Marks	JAC	8
3	J.Allen	MIN	7
3	M.Johnson	CIN	7
3	J.J.Watt	HOU	7
6	C.Campbell	ARI	6
6	C.Dunlap	CIN	6
6	C.Heyward	PIT	6
6	C.Wootton	CHI	6
10	A.Brooks	SF	5
10	S.Hill	TEN	5
10	M.Jackson	DEN	5
10	D.Poe	KC	5
10	P.Soliai	MIA	5

2013 Quarterbacks with and without Pass Pressure

Rank	Player	Team	Plays	Pct Pressure	DVOA with Pressure	Yds with Pressure	DVOA w/o Pressure	Yds w/o Pressure	DVOA Dif	Rank
1	P.Manning	DEN	688	14.8%	-93.4%	4.7	30.1%	8.6	-123.4%	29
2	A.Dalton	CIN	645	16.4%	-114.7%	1.2	27.4%	7.9	-142.2%	33
3	M.Stafford	DET	671	19.4%	-55.0%	4.4	22.5%	7.4	-77.5%	6
4	T.Brady	NE	680	20.3%	-96.3%	2.2	24.3%	7.4	-120.6%	27
5	M.Cassel	MIN	283	20.5%	-53.0%	2.9	17.2%	7.3	-70.1%	4
6	A.Smith	KC	601	21.1%	-67.1%	2.7	35.1%	6.8	-102.2%	20
7	M.Flynn	3TM	239	21.8%	-161.7%	0.1	35.8%	7.4	-197.5%	40
8	E.Manuel	BUF	369	22.0%	-53.5%	2.6	25.4%	6.5	-79.0%	8
9	P.Rivers	SD	601	22.0%	-69.0%	4.6	30.2%	8.6	-99.3%	17
10	T.Romo	DAL	585	22.1%	-78.1%	2.5	34.2%	7.4	-112.3%	24
11	A.Rodgers	GB	330	22.1%	-102.7%	2.0	63.7%	9.4	-166.4%	37
12	B.Roethlisberger	PIT	639	22.2%	-71.5%	3.8	25.3%	7.3	-96.8%	15
13	R.Tannehill	MIA	659	22.3%	-119.9%	1.1	34.5%	6.9	-154.4%	36
14	M.McGloin	OAK	224	22.3%	-34.3%	3.5	43.5%	8.3	-77.8%	7
15	D.Brees	NO	703	22.5%	-110.5%	2.9	37.1%	8.5	-147.6%	35
16	R.Fitzpatrick	TEN	398	23.1%	-50.9%	4.9	24.4%	7.0	-75.4%	5
17	C.Henne	JAC	556	23.7%	-51.8%	2.0	32.0%	6.7	-83.8%	11
18	C.Newton	CAR	557	24.2%	-70.1%	2.5	31.0%	7.4	-101.0%	19
19	J.Campbell	CLE	346	24.6%	-23.9%	4.0	17.4%	6.6	-41.2%	1
20	S.Bradford	STL	289	24.9%	-79.2%	2.3	41.9%	7.4	-121.2%	28
21	J.Flacco	BAL	690	25.1%	-66.8%	2.2	30.6%	7.0	-97.4%	16
22	N.Foles	PHI	366	25.7%	-59.8%	3.4	68.5%	9.5	-128.4%	30
23	J.McCown	CHI	245	25.7%	-9.7%	5.5	51.6%	8.4	-61.3%	3
24	C.Kaepernick	SF	507	26.0%	-64.4%	3.8	30.0%	7.9	-94.4%	14
25	J.Cutler	CHI	386	26.2%	-42.0%	4.9	11.4%	7.5	-53.4%	2
26	C.Palmer	ARI	632	26.6%	-125.8%	2.1	44.7%	8.3	-170.5%	38
27	J.Locker	TEN	214	27.1%	-55.6%	3.1	38.2%	7.4	-93.8%	13
28	A.Luck	IND	662	27.3%	-58.2%	3.6	33.6%	7.4	-91.9%	12
29	E.Manning	NYG	607	27.5%	-64.7%	2.1	38.9%	7.6	-103.6%	22
30	M.Schaub	HOU	388	27.8%	-64.2%	2.4	35.2%	7.1	-99.4%	18
31	B.Weeden	CLE	301	27.9%	-133.7%	0.9	37.8%	7.0	-171.6%	39
32	R.Griffin	WAS	533	28.0%	-57.4%	3.0	50.9%	7.2	-108.3%	23
33	C.Ponder	MIN	296	28.4%	-77.6%	2.4	41.9%	7.6	-119.5%	25
34	K.Clemens	STL	274	28.5%	-108.8%	2.8	33.7%	7.1	-142.5%	34
35	M.Ryan	ATL	712	28.7%	-75.8%	3.2	27.6%	7.4	-103.4%	21
36	G.Smith	NYJ	521	29.0%	-90.3%	2.2	42.0%	7.5	-132.2%	31
37	M.Glennon	TB	480	31.7%	-82.7%	1.5	37.3%	7.0	-120.0%	26
38	T.Pryor	OAK	338	34.3%	-50.8%	2.4	29.3%	7.2	-80.1%	9
39	R.Wilson	SEA	508	36.6%	-46.2%	4.9	37.1%	8.5	-83.3%	10
40	C.Keenum	HOU	276	37.7%	-78.5%	2.1	54.7%	8.1	-133.2%	32

Includes scrambles and Defensive Pass Interference. Does not include aborted snaps.
Minimum: 200 passes.

Top 20 Players, Passes Dropped

Rk	Player	Team	Total	Rk	Player	Team	Total
1	B.Marshall	CHI	12	10	E.Decker	DEN	7
2	V.Jackson	TB	11	10	A.Dobson	NE	7
3	J.Gordon	CLE	10	10	H.Douglas	ATL	7
4	D.Bess	CLE	9	10	K.Durham	DET	7
4	R.Bush	DET	9	10	B.Hartline	MIA	7
4	J.Charles	KC	9	10	H.Nicks	NYG	7
4	C.Johnson	DET	9	10	C.Shorts	JAC	7
8	S.Johnson	BUF	8	10	S.Vereen	NE	7
8	W.Welker	DEN	8	10	M.Wallace	MIA	7
10	L.Bell	PIT	7	10	K.Wright	TEN	7

Top 20 Players, Pct. Passes Dropped

Rk	Player	Team	Drops	Passes	Pct	Rk	Player	Team	Drops	Passes	Pct
1	K.Britt	TEN	5	35	14.3%	11	J.Charles	KC	9	104	8.7%
2	E.Dickson	BAL	5	43	11.6%	12	K.Durham	DET	7	85	8.2%
3	R.Bush	DET	9	80	11.3%	13	C.Ogbonnaya	CLE	6	75	8.0%
4	L.Bell	PIT	7	65	10.8%	14	S.Johnson	BUF	8	102	7.8%
5	D.Bess	CLE	9	86	10.5%	15	M.Sanu	CIN	6	78	7.7%
6	S.Vereen	NE	7	69	10.1%	16	S.Moss	WAS	6	79	7.6%
7	A.Dobson	NE	7	72	9.7%	17	F.Jackson	BUF	5	66	7.6%
8	D.Heyward-Bey	IND	6	64	9.4%	18	B.Marshall	CHI	12	163	7.4%
9	M.Reece	OAK	5	54	9.3%	19	J.Bell	DET	5	69	7.2%
10	T.Austin	STL	6	69	8.7%	20	W.Welker	DEN	8	111	7.2%

Min. five drops

Top 10 Teams, Pct Passes Dropped

Rk	Team	Drops	Passes	Pct
1	ARI	15	546	2.7%
2	HOU	16	575	2.8%
3	SD	15	514	2.9%
4	NO	18	615	2.9%
5	MIN	19	505	3.8%
6	BAL	23	589	3.9%
7	NYJ	18	443	4.1%
8	ATL	27	619	4.4%
9	GB	23	517	4.4%
10	PHI	21	469	4.5%

Bottom 10 Teams, Pct Passes Dropped

Rk	Team	Drops	Passes	Pct
23	TEN	27	507	5.3%
24	TB	27	480	5.6%
25	CHI	31	545	5.7%
26	CLE	36	622	5.8%
27	KC	30	510	5.9%
28	OAK	29	474	6.1%
29	BUF	31	502	6.2%
30	NE	38	605	6.3%
31	STL	30	471	6.4%
32	DET	46	592	7.8%

Top 20 Intended Receivers on Interceptions

Rk	Player	Team	Total	Rk	Player	Team	Total
1	A.J.Green	CIN	12	13	J.Graham	NO	6
2	V.Jackson	TB	10	13	H.Nicks	NYG	6
3	C.Johnson	DET	9	13	G.Jennings	GB	6
4	A.Johnson	HOU	8	13	C.Shorts	JAC	6
4	R.Randle	NYG	8	13	J.Simpson	MIN	6
4	M.Wallace	PIT	8	13	R.Streater	OAK	6
4	N.Washington	TEN	8	19	J.Cameron	CLE	5
8	H.Douglas	ATL	7	19	S.Hill	NYJ	5
8	L.Fitzgerald	ARI	7	19	S.Holmes	NYJ	5
8	M.Floyd	ARI	7	19	B.LaFell	CAR	5
8	P.Garcon	WAS	7	19	J.Nelson	GB	5
8	G.Little	CLE	7	19	E.Sanders	PIT	5

Top 10 Plus/Minus for Running Backs

Rk	Player	Team	Pass	+/-
1	D.Woodhead	SD	87	+12.5
2	P.Thomas	NO	84	+8.6
3	D.Sproles	NO	89	+5.6
4	J.Rodgers	ATL	62	+5.4
5	M.Tolbert	CAR	32	+4.3
6	M.Forte	CHI	96	+4.0
7	R.Jennings	OAK	46	+3.6
8	L.McCoy	PHI	64	+3.4
9	G.Bernard	CIN	71	+3.3
10	K.Moreno	DEN	74	+3.0

Min. 25 passes; plus/minus adjusted for passes tipped/thrown away.

Bottom 10 Plus/Minus for Running Backs

Rk	Player	Team	Pass	+/-
1	M.Reece	OAK	54	-7.1
2	B.Powell	NYJ	57	-5.9
3	J.Charles	KC	104	-5.7
4	C.Ogbonnaya	CLE	75	-5.5
5	T.Richardson	2TM	52	-4.7
6	F.Whittaker	2TM	35	-4.6
7	L.Bell	PIT	65	-4.1
8	R.Bush	DET	80	-3.9
9	F.Jackson	BUF	66	-3.7
10	A.Foster	HOU	35	-3.1

Min. 25 passes; plus/minus adjusted for passes tipped/thrown away.

Top 10 Plus/Minus for Wide Receivers

Rk	Player	Team	Pass	+/-
1	J.Nelson	GB	127	+14.2
2	D.Jackson	PHI	125	+12.2
3	A.Brown	PIT	167	+10.1
4	A.Boldin	SF	129	+9.9
5	M.Colston	NO	110	+9.3
6	K.Allen	SD	104	+8.6
7	D.Baldwin	SEA	73	+7.3
8	A.Jeffery	CHI	150	+7.1
9	K.Stills	NO	51	+6.4
10	L.Moore	NO	54	+6.4

Min. 50 passes; plus/minus adjusted for passes tipped/thrown away.

Bottom 10 Plus/Minus for Wide Receivers

Rk	Player	Team	Pass	+/-
1	D.Bess	CLE	86	-14.4
2	V.Jackson	TB	161	-13.2
3	G.Little	CLE	99	-12.7
4	K.Thompkins	NE	70	-10.5
5	K.Durham	DET	85	-9.7
6	C.Givens	STL	83	-9.2
7	S.Johnson	BUF	102	-9.1
8	S.Holmes	NYJ	59	-7.9
9	D.Bowe	KC	103	-7.7
10	T.J.Graham	BUF	57	-7.6

Min. 50 passes; plus/minus adjusted for passes tipped/thrown away.

Top 10 Plus/Minus for Tight Ends

Rk	Player	Team	Pass	+/-
1	J.Cameron	CLE	118	+11.6
2	T.Gonzalez	ATL	121	+8.3
3	H.Miller	PIT	78	+8.1
4	G.Olsen	CAR	111	+7.7
5	T.Wright	TB	75	+7.1
6	D.Walker	TEN	86	+6.8
7	J.Thomas	DEN	90	+6.0
8	M.Bennett	CHI	94	+5.9
9	V.Davis	SF	84	+5.6
10	J.Graham	NO	143	+5.1

Min. 25 passes; plus/minus adjusted for passes tipped/thrown away.

Bottom 10 Plus/Minus for Tight Ends

Rk	Player	Team	Pass	+/-
1	G.Graham	HOU	89	-6.1
2	M.Lewis	JAC	47	-5.8
3	D.Clark	BAL	52	-3.5
4	E.Dickson	BAL	43	-2.9
5	C.Fleener	IND	87	-2.3
6	L.Paulsen	WAS	50	-2.3
7	Z.Miller	SEA	56	-1.8
8	O.Daniels	HOU	41	-1.4
9	D.Pitta	BAL	33	-0.4
10	J.Witten	DAL	111	-0.2

Min. 25 passes; plus/minus adjusted for passes tipped/thrown away.

Top 20 First Downs/Touchdowns Allowed, Coverage

Rk	Player	Team	Total	Rk	Player	Team	Total
1	I.Taylor	PIT	46	12	C.Rogers	SF	34
2	B.Carr	DAL	44	12	L.Webb	BAL	34
3	S.Wright	SD	43	15	M.Cooper	KC	32
4	D.Hall	WAS	41	15	A.Cromartie	NYJ	32
5	J.Powers	ARI	40	15	B.Fletcher	PHI	32
6	C.Williams	PHI	39	15	S.Shields	GB	32
7	P.Amukamara	NYG	38	19	P.Peterson	ARI	31
8	B.Flowers	KC	37	20	K.Arrington	NE	30
8	B.Grimes	MIA	37	20	D.Butler	IND	30
10	C.Houston	DET	35	20	L.McKelvin	BUF	30
10	D.Milliner	NYJ	35	20	J.Smith	BAL	30
12	T.Jennings	CHI	34				

Includes Defensive Pass Interference.

Top 20 Passing Yards Allowed, Coverage

Rk	Player	Team	Yards	Rk	Player	Team	Yards
1	I.Taylor	PIT	1051	11	B.Flowers	KC	782
2	B.Carr	DAL	1017	12	T.Jennings	CHI	768
3	A.Cromartie	NYJ	1000	13	D.Hall	WAS	766
4	J.Powers	ARI	955	14	B.Grimes	MIA	756
5	S.Wright	SD	881	15	B.Fletcher	PHI	734
6	C.Houston	DET	879	16	J.Smith	BAL	708
7	J.Jenkins	STL	853	17	D.Milliner	NYJ	699
8	L.Webb	BAL	806	18	K.Jackson	HOU	696
9	C.Williams	PHI	794	19	A.Jones	CIN	681
10	M.Cooper	KC	794	20	P.Amukamara	NYG	672

Includes Defensive Pass Interference.

Fewest Yards After Catch Allowed, Coverage by Cornerbacks

Rk	Player	Team	YAC	Rk	Player	Team	YAC
1	J.Greer	NO	1.8	11	W.Gay	PIT	2.6
2	B.Browner	SEA	1.8	12	B.Fletcher	PHI	2.7
3	T.McBride	NYG	2.2	13	X.Rhodes	MIN	2.7
4	K.Lewis	NO	2.2	14	J.Joseph	HOU	2.7
5	K.Jackson	HOU	2.3	15	T.Brock	SF	2.8
6	T.Brown	SF	2.4	16	P.Amukamara	NYG	2.9
7	J.McCourty	TEN	2.4	17	L.McKelvin	BUF	3.0
8	J.Haden	CLE	2.5	18	J.Smith	BAL	3.1
9	A.Samuel	ATL	2.6	19	M.White	CAR	3.1
10	T.Mathieu	ARI	2.6	20	C.Munnerlyn	CAR	3.2

Min. 50 passes or 8 games started.

Most Yards After Catch Allowed, Coverage by Cornerbacks

Rk	Player	Team	YAC	Rk	Player	Team	YAC
1	A.Cromartie	NYJ	8.8	11	A.Talib	NE	5.4
2	M.Cooper	KC	7.8	12	S.Smith	KC	5.3
3	D.Rodgers-Cromartie	DEN	7.3	13	K.Arrington	NE	5.3
4	C.Houston	DET	7.2	14	D.Florence	CAR	5.2
5	W.Blackmon	JAC	6.8	15	B.Flowers	KC	5.2
6	R.McClain	ATL	6.7	16	V.Davis	IND	5.1
7	J.Jenkins	STL	6.0	17	M.Sherels	MIN	5.1
8	A.Jones	CIN	5.7	18	B.Carr	DAL	4.9
9	M.Claiborne	DAL	5.4	19	J.Banks	TB	4.8
10	J.Powers	ARI	5.4	20	T.Porter	OAK	4.8

Min. 50 passes or 8 games started.

Most Dropped Interceptions, 2013

Rk	Player	Team	Drops
1	D.Smith	BAL	4
2	D.House	GB	3
2	D.Milliner	NYJ	3
2	R.Sherman	SEA	3
5	22 players with		2

Most Dropped Interceptions, 2011-2013

Rk	Player	Team	Drops
1	T.Williams	GB	7
2	J.Haden	CLE	6
2	D.House	GB	6
2	J.McCourty	TEN	6
5	T.Newman	DAL/CIN	5
5	J.Sanford	MIN	5
5	D.Smith	JAC/BAL	5
8	A.Cromartie	NYJ	4
8	M.Giordano	OAK/STL	4
8	J.Greer	NO	4
8	T.Jennings	CHI	4
8	R.Marshall	ARI/MIA/SD	4
8	D.Rodgers-Cromartie	PHI/DEN	4
8	C.Rogers	SF	4
8	O.Scandrick	DAL	4
8	R.Sherman	SEA	4
8	C.Woodson	GB/OAK	4

Fewest Avg Yards on Run Tackle, Defensive Line or Edge Rusher

Rk	Player	Team	Tkl	Avg
1	B.Mebane	SEA	45	1.0
2	S.Lotulelei	CAR	35	1.0
3	C.Redding	IND	27	1.0
4	C.Matthews	GB	31	1.1
5	R.Quinn	STL	37	1.2
6	Q.Coples	NYJ	31	1.3
7	J.Hatcher	DAL	28	1.3
8	T.Knighton	DEN	27	1.3
9	K.Langford	STL	41	1.4
10	C.Campbell	ARI	47	1.4
11	B.Cofield	WAS	27	1.4
12	C.Wootton	CHI	29	1.4
13	A.Spence	TB	25	1.5
14	R.Starks	MIA	42	1.5
15	A.Clayborn	TB	53	1.6
16	D.Dockett	ARI	31	1.6
17	M.Wilkerson	NYJ	44	1.6
18	J.J.Watt	HOU	63	1.7
19	K.Williams	BUF	53	1.7
20	S.Marks	JAC	25	1.7

Min. 25 run tackles

Fewest Avg Yards on Run Tackle, Linebacker

Rk	Player	Team	Tkl	Avg
1	M.Smith	SEA	28	1.3
2	B.Cushing	HOU	36	1.8
3	L.Briggs	CHI	41	1.9
4	L.David	TB	81	2.1
5	K.Burnett	OAK	60	2.2
6	A.Moats	BUF	36	2.3
7	C.Robertson	CLE	42	2.3
8	D.Davis	NYJ	56	2.4
9	E.Henderson	MIN	71	2.4
10	J.Williams	NYG	25	2.4
11	D.Hawthorne	NO	59	2.5
12	S.Moore	OAK	31	2.5
13	K.Sheppard	IND	35	2.5
14	L.Timmons	PIT	75	2.5
15	J.Mays	HOU	49	2.5
16	C.Lofton	NO	74	2.5
17	B.Spikes	NE	72	2.6
18	A.Ayers	TEN	28	2.6
19	J.Bartu	ATL	52	2.7
20	K.Misi	MIA	38	2.7

Min. 25 run tackles

Fewest Avg Yards on Run Tackle, Defensive Back

Rk	Player	Team	Tkl	Avg
1	T.Porter	OAK	27	3.8
2	T.Ward	CLE	66	3.8
3	K.Chancellor	SEA	57	4.0
4	E.Berry	KC	32	4.3
5	J.Wilson	WAS	34	4.4
6	R.Mundy	NYG	42	4.4
7	R.Doughty	WAS	53	4.4
8	C.Munnerlyn	CAR	22	4.4
9	L.Delmas	DET	25	4.6
10	Y.Bell	ARI	38	4.8
11	D.Swearinger	HOU	38	4.9
12	D.Landry	NYJ	46	4.9
13	T.McDonald	STL	28	5.0
14	J.Ihedigbo	BAL	57	5.1
15	L.Webb	BAL	24	5.4
16	G.Quin	DET	30	5.4
17	H.Smith	MIN	26	5.7
18	R.Clark	PIT	66	5.7
19	B.Meriweather	WAS	32	5.8
20	D.Whitner	SF	28	6.0

Min. 20 run tackles

Top 20 Offensive Tackles, Blown Blocks

Rk	Player	Pos	Team	Sacks	All Pass	All Run	Total
1	L.Holmes	LT	ATL	10.0	37.5	4.0	41.5
1	M.Oher	RT	BAL	9.0	35.5	6.0	41.5
1	M.Schwartz	RT	CLE	7.0	35.0	6.5	41.5
4	L.Johnson	RT	PHI	9.0	34.0	5.0	39.0
5	J.Bushrod	LT	CHI	5.5	34.5	4.0	38.5
6	J.Mills	RT	CHI	2.0	34.0	3.0	37.0
7	T.Polumbus	RT	WAS	6.0	30.5	5.5	36.0
8	W.Beatty	LT	NYG	11.3	31.8	3.0	34.8
9	D.J.Fluker	RT	SD	5.5	30.0	4.5	34.5
10	B.Sowell	LT	ARI	9.0	29.0	5.0	34.0
11	E.Fisher	RT	KC	7.0	28.0	5.0	33.0
12	D.Barclay	RT	GB	7.5	25.0	7.0	32.0
13	M.Kalil	LT	MIN	5.5	22.5	8.0	30.5
14	D.Newton	RT	HOU	6.3	28.7	1.5	30.2
15	C.Brown	LT	NO	5.0	24.0	4.5	28.5
16	N.Solder	LT	NE	8.5	22.3	6.0	28.3
17	T.Clabo	RT	MIA	9.0	26.5	1.5	28.0
17	T.Smith	LT	DAL	3.0	21.5	6.5	28.0
19	C.Bradfield	LT	JAC	7.0	25.0	2.5	27.5
19	B.McKinnie	LT	2TM	10.5	19.5	8.0	27.5
19	D.Penn	LT	TB	8.5	21.5	6.0	27.5

Top 20 Interior Linemen, Blown Blocks

Rk	Player	Pos	Team	Sacks	All Pass	All Run	Total
1	M.McGlynn	RG	IND	3.0	29.7	3.5	33.2
2	W.Smith	LG	HOU	4.0	25.3	7.0	32.3
3	C.Warmack	RG	TEN	6.5	19.3	12.5	31.8
4	P.Fanaika	RG	ARI	5.5	20.5	10.0	30.5
4	T.Herremans	RG	PHI	3.5	27.5	3.0	30.5
6	C.Chester	RG	WAS	2.0	23.5	6.0	29.5
7	P.McQuistan	OL	SEA	6.8	21.3	8.0	29.3
8	H.Thornton	LG	IND	5.3	21.2	8.0	29.2
9	R.Wendell	C	NE	5.0	22.8	5.5	28.3
10	D.Joseph	RG	TB	2.0	20.0	7.5	27.5
10	J.R.Sweezy	RG	SEA	0.5	15.5	12.0	27.5
12	D.Diehl	RG	NYG	2.0	17.0	9.0	26.0
13	Z.Beadles	LG	DEN	1.0	20.8	4.0	24.8
14	M.Yanda	RG	BAL	2.5	17.0	7.0	24.0
15	J.Evans	RG	NO	1.5	17.0	6.5	23.5
15	P.Konz	C/G	ATL	6.5	16.5	7.0	23.5
17	B.Brooks	RG	HOU	2.8	18.3	5.0	23.3
18	R.Leary	LG	DAL	6.0	19.5	2.5	22.0
19	S.Lauvao	RG	CLE	4.5	16.5	5.0	21.5
19	K.Lichtensteiger	LG	WAS	2.0	15.5	6.0	21.5

Top 20 Offensive Tackles in Snaps per Blown Block

Rk	Player	Pos	Team	Sacks	All Pass	All Run	Total	Snaps	Snaps per BB
1	A.Collins	LT	CIN	0.5	3.0	1.5	4.5	578	128.4
2	C.Hilliard	RT	DET	0.0	4.5	1.0	5.5	452	82.2
3	A.Whitworth	LT	CIN	4.0	7.5	4.0	11.5	914	79.5
4	Z.Strief	RT	NO	3.0	12.5	1.0	13.5	1035	76.7
5	K.Dunlap	LT	SD	4.5	9.5	0.0	9.5	672	70.7
6	J.Thomas	LT	CLE	3.0	12.5	3.5	16.0	1106	69.1
7	J.Staley	LT	SF	3.3	10.3	4.5	14.8	929	62.6
8	B.Albert	LT	KC	3.5	9.5	3.0	12.5	775	62.0
8	T.Pashos	RT	OAK	5.0	11.5	0.0	11.5	713	62.0
10	D.Ferguson	LT	NYJ	4.5	14.5	3.0	17.5	1051	60.1
11	A.Pasztor	RT	JAC	5.5	11.5	2.0	13.5	790	58.5
12	D.Free	RT	DAL	2.5	15.0	3.0	18.0	997	55.4
13	C.Glenn	LT	BUF	1.5	15.5	6.0	21.5	1161	54.0
14	O.Franklin	RT	DEN	4.5	16.5	4.0	20.5	1092	53.3
15	E.Monroe	LT	2TM	4.5	16.5	3.0	19.5	1031	52.9
16	J.Gross	LT	CAR	5.0	15.0	4.0	19.0	1003	52.8
17	J.Trueblood	RT	ATL	1.5	10.0	2.0	12.0	628	52.3
18	T.Williams	LT	WAS	6.0	18.0	4.0	22.0	1142	51.9
19	D.Dotson	RT	TB	3.0	16.0	4.0	20.0	1034	51.7
20	E.Pears	RT	BUF	4.5	14.0	9.0	23.0	1161	50.5

Minimum: 400 snaps

Top 20 Interior Linemen in Snaps per Blown Block

Rk	Player	Pos	Team	Sacks	All Pass	All Run	Total	Snaps	Snaps per BB
1	D.Raiola	C	DET	0.0	3.0	1.0	4.0	1124	281.0
2	N.Hardwick	C	SD	0.0	3.0	1.0	4.0	1075	268.8
3	L.Vasquez	RG	DEN	0.0	2.3	3.0	5.3	1207	226.5
4	M.Pouncey	C	MIA	0.5	2.0	2.0	4.0	899	224.8
5	N.Mangold	C	NYJ	0.0	3.0	2.0	5.0	1049	209.8
6	E.Wood	C	BUF	0.0	4.5	2.0	6.5	1161	178.6
7	S.Wells	C	STL	1.3	3.3	1.0	4.3	738	170.3
8	S.Wisniewski	C	OAK	0.0	4.0	2.0	6.0	904	150.7
9	J.Sitton	LG	GB	0.5	6.5	1.3	7.8	1122	143.3
10	R.Hudson	C	KC	3.0	6.0	2.0	8.0	1006	125.8
11	J.Hawley	C	ATL	0.5	3.5	1.0	4.5	539	119.8
12	R.Kalil	C	CAR	2.5	6.5	2.0	8.5	1016	119.5
13	M.Slauson	LG	CHI	2.0	7.0	3.0	10.0	1057	105.7
14	C.Boling	LG	CIN	1.0	5.5	2.0	7.5	776	103.5
15	M.Brisiel	RG	OAK	0.0	6.5	2.0	8.5	871	102.5
16	A.Mack	C	CLE	0.5	8.5	2.5	11.0	1107	100.6
17	E.Dietrich-Smith	C	GB	4.0	6.0	4.5	10.5	1055	100.5
18	B.De La Puente	C	NO	2.0	9.0	3.5	12.5	1126	90.1
19	R.Foster	LG	PIT	1.0	9.0	1.0	10.0	842	84.2
20	C.Rinehart	LG	SD	1.0	7.0	1.0	8.0	669	83.6

Minimum: 400 snaps

Top 20 Non-Offensive Linemen, Blown Blocks

Rk	Player	Pos	Team	Sacks	All Pass	All Run	Total
1	L.Paulsen	TE	WAS	0.0	7.0	5.5	12.5
2	R.Rice	RB	BAL	3.8	12.3	0.0	12.3
3	A.Peterson	RB	MIN	2.0	12.0	0.0	12.0
4	J.Cumberland	TE	NYJ	0.5	6.5	5.0	11.5
4	M.Forte	RB	CHI	4.0	11.5	0.0	11.5
6	B.Celek	TE	PHI	0.0	6.0	5.0	11.0
7	M.Bennett	TE	CHI	1.5	4.5	6.0	10.5
7	A.Quarless	TE	GB	1.0	2.5	8.0	10.5
9	J.Collins	FB	NO	2.0	6.5	2.5	9.0
9	G.Graham	TE	HOU	1.0	3.0	6.0	9.0
9	H.Miller	TE	PIT	1.0	4.0	5.0	9.0
9	T.Richardson	RB	2TM	1.0	9.0	0.0	9.0
9	B.Watson	TE	NO	1.0	6.0	3.0	9.0
14	J.Dray	TE	ARI	1.5	4.5	4.0	8.5
15	R.Jennings	RB	OAK	0.0	8.0	0.0	8.0
15	K.Moreno	RB	DEN	0.5	8.0	0.0	8.0
15	J.Thomas	TE	DEN	0.5	2.0	6.0	8.0
18	L.Kendricks	TE	STL	1.0	2.5	5.0	7.5
18	Z.Miller	TE	SEA	1.0	4.5	3.0	7.5
18	C.Ogbonnaya	RB	CLE	3.5	7.0	0.5	7.5
18	G.Olsen	TE	CAR	0.5	1.5	6.0	7.5

Most False Starts, Offense

Rk	Player	Team	Pen
1	L.Holmes	ATL	9
2	E.Winston	ARI	8
3	J.Thomas	CLE	7
4	J.Troutman	SD	6
5	B.Albert	KC	5
5	K.Barnes	OAK	5
5	B.Brooks	HOU	5
5	J.Cameron	CLE	5
5	W.Colon	NYJ	5
5	D.Newton	HOU	5
11	M.Gilbert	PIT	4
11	M.Williams	TB	4
11	J.Gresham	CIN	4
11	T.Smith	BAL	4
11	B.Giacomini	SEA	4
11	T.Lang	GB	4
11	A.Gurode	OAK	4
11	D.Fluker	SD	4
11	D.Free	DAL	4
11	E.Fisher	KC	4
11	J.Jerry	MIA	4
11	A.Shipley	BAL	4
11	M.Yanda	BAL	4

Most Penalties, Offense

Rk	Player	Team	Pen	Yds
1	K.Barnes	OAK	13	65
1	D.Newton	HOU	13	45
3	E.Manning	NYG	12	99
3	C.Brown	NO	12	79
3	L.Holmes	ATL	12	65
6	J.Gresham	CIN	11	85
6	O.Franklin	DEN	11	80
6	D.Bakhtiari	GB	11	79
6	W.Colon	NYJ	11	73
6	J.Thomas	CLE	11	65
11	B.Albert	KC	10	65
11	E.Wood	BUF	10	60
11	D.Brees	NO	10	56
14	W.Montgomery	WAS	9	73
14	R.Wilson	SEA	9	70
14	W.Beatty	NYG	9	50
14	E.Winston	ARI	9	36
18	A.Q.Shipley	BAL	8	50
18	R.Leary	DAL	8	45
18	M.Gilbert	PIT	8	44
18	A.Boone	SF	8	44
18	L.Johnson	PHI	8	40
18	D.Free	DAL	8	40
18	C.Kaepernick	SF	8	35

Includes declined and offsetting, but not special teams.

Most Penalties, Defense

Rk	Player	Team	Pen	Yds
1	V.Burfict	CIN	14	150
2	T.Williams	GB	11	133
3	J.Jenkins	STL	10	113
3	M.Bennett	SEA	10	79
3	G.McCoy	TB	10	76
3	J.Babin	JAC	10	75
3	M.Wilkerson	NYJ	10	60
3	C.Long	STL	10	55
9	R.Sherman	SEA	9	124
9	K.Langford	STL	9	34
11	A.Cromartie	NYJ	8	110
11	A.Verner	TEN	8	83
11	N.Fairley	DET	8	80
11	A.Brooks	SF	8	75
11	A.Talib	NE	8	73
11	M.Jenkins	OAK	8	72
11	O.Scandrick	DAL	8	57
11	E.Dumervil	BAL	8	57
11	K.Vickerson	DEN	8	54
11	T.Johnson	STL	8	49
11	B.McCain	HOU	8	46
11	L.Houston	OAK	8	40
11	C.Munnerlyn	CAR	8	38

Includes declined and offsetting, but not special teams.

Top 10 Kickers, Gross Kickoff Value over Average

Rk	Player	Team	Kick Pts+	Net Pts+	Kicks
1	S.Hauschka	SEA	+7.9	+5.6	90
2	B.Cundiff	CLE	+6.8	+4.2	62
3	G.Gano	CAR	+5.0	+5.5	79
4	G.Zuerlein	STL	+3.9	+12.0	77
5	S.Gostkowski	NE	+3.9	+10.5	97
6	M.Prater	DEN	+3.1	-11.7	112
7	M.Koenen	TB	+2.2	+8.1	65
8	C.Sturgis	MIA	+2.1	+1.0	72
9	P.McAfee	IND	+2.1	+4.4	86
10	T.Morstead	NO	+1.5	-2.1	84

Min. 20 kickoffs; squibs and onside not included

Bottom 10 Kickers, Gross Kickoff Value over Average

Rk	Player	Team	Kick Pts+	Net Pts+	Kicks
1	A.Henery	PHI	-6.5	-12.5	86
2	S.Suisham	PIT	-6.4	-1.5	81
3	K.Forbath	WAS	-5.2	-9.1	51
4	R.Gould	CHI	-4.5	-4.2	79
5	M.Crosby	GB	-3.7	-2.2	52
6	N.Novak	SD	-3.5	-0.8	90
7	J.Feely	ARI	-2.7	-1.2	86
8	R.Bironas	TEN	-2.3	-3.3	73
9	P.Dawson	SF	-2.1	+11.1	89
10	M.Nugent	CIN	-1.9	-1.2	84

Min. 20 kickoffs; squibs and onside not included

Top 10 Punters, Gross Punt Value over Average

Rk	Player	Team	Punt Pts+	Net Pts+	Punts
1	B.Fields	MIA	+10.1	+9.4	85
2	S.Lechler	HOU	+8.2	-7.8	88
3	A.Lee	SF	+7.1	+10.7	79
4	T.Morstead	NO	+6.5	+11.1	61
5	B.Nortman	CAR	+6.3	+1.6	70
6	K.Huber	CIN	+5.4	+4.6	67
7	J.Hekker	STL	+5.0	+22.4	78
8	S.Weatherford	NYG	+4.6	-13.6	91
9	D.Jones	PHI	+4.4	+5.4	83
10	T.Masthay	GB	+4.4	+5.4	64

Min. 20 punts

Bottom 10 Punters, Gross Punt Value over Average

Rk	Player	Team	Punt Pts+	Net Pts+	Punts
1	B.Kern	TEN	-10.7	+0.6	81
2	B.Moorman	BUF	-9.8	-3.8	61
3	S.Rocca	WAS	-8.5	-33.3	85
4	Z.Mesko	PIT	-8.3	-10.2	34
5	J.Ryan	SEA	-7.5	+10.4	76
6	S.Lanning	CLE	-5.2	-1.9	85
7	M.McBriar	PIT	-4.9	-1.0	41
8	M.Koenen	TB	-4.1	-3.5	87
9	S.Powell	BUF	-2.6	-11.9	35
10	C.Jones	DAL	-1.9	-1.5	77

Min. 20 punts

Top 10 Kickoff Returners, Value over Average

Rk	Player	Team	Pts+	Returns
1	C.Patterson	MIN	+19.9	42
2	Q.Demps	KC	+14.8	33
3	J.Jones	BAL	+9.6	31
4	D.Harris	DAL	+8.6	28
5	K.Davis	KC	+6.5	10
6	L.Washington	2TM	+5.9	17
7	L.Blount	NE	+5.5	17
8	T.Holliday	DEN	+5.1	28
8	B.Tate	CIN	+3.7	35
10	J.Ross	2TM	+3.7	21

Min. eight returns

Bottom 10 Kick Returners, Value over Average

Rk	Player	Team	Pts+	Returns
1	E.Page	TB	-5.8	22
2	J.Arenas	ARI	-5.5	22
2	T.Jones	OAK	-5.5	26
4	M.Thigpen	MIA	-5.1	38
5	D.Reynaud	2TM	-3.4	18
6	G.Jenkins	OAK	-3.3	10
7	K.Martin	HOU	-3.0	36
8	J.Morgan	WAS	-2.9	12
9	D.Reed	IND	-2.5	24
10	J.Jernigan	NYG	-2.1	11

Min. eight returns

Top 10 Punt Returners, Value over Average

Rk	Player	Team	Pts+	Returns
1	D.McCluster	KC	+17.2	58
2	M.Sherels	MIN	+11.8	22
3	A.Brown	PIT	+11.8	32
4	T.Doss	BAL	+10.4	23
5	G.Tate	SEA	+8.8	51
6	J.Ross	2TM	+8.7	17
7	D.Hester	CHI	+6.5	18
8	M.Hyde	GB	+6.0	24
9	D.Harris	DAL	+5.5	20
10	J.Jones	BAL	+5.0	19

Min. eight returns

Bottom 10 Punt Returners, Value over Average

Rk	Player	Team	Pts+	Returns
1	L.McKelvin	BUF	-12.7	32
2	P.Peterson	ARI	-10.4	33
3	D.Sproles	NO	-4.8	29
4	M.Thigpen	MIA	-4.6	34
5	S.Moss	WAS	-4.4	18
6	K.Williams	SF	-4.2	12
7	A.Sanders	JAC	-3.9	25
8	J.Ford	OAK	-3.9	9
9	T.Holliday	DEN	-3.6	32
9	H.Douglas	ATL	-3.5	10

Min. eight returns

Top 20 Special Teams Plays

Rk	Player	Team	Plays	Rk	Player	Team	Plays
1	M.Easley	BUF	23	7	E.Lankster	NYJ	13
2	J.Bethel	ARI	21	7	J.Wendling	DET	13
3	N.Bellore	NYJ	17	7	M.Wilhoite	SF	13
4	S.Ajirotutu	SD	15	16	J.Bademosi	CLE	12
4	C.J.Spillman	SF	15	16	M.Herzlich	NYG	12
6	G.Wilson	TEN	14	16	J.Hull	WAS	12
7	N.Bradham	BUF	13	16	J.Lane	SEA	12
7	L.Dean	MIN	13	16	C.Peerman	CIN	12
7	J.DiManche	CIN	13	16	A.Sherman	KC	12
7	R.Golden	PIT	13	16	D.Stuckey	SD	12
7	D.House	GB	13	16	E.Weddle	SD	12
7	T.Jones	OAK	13				

Plays = tackles + assists; does not include onside or end-half squib kicks.

Top 10 Offenses, 3-and-out per drive

Rk	Team	Pct
1	SD	14.6%
2	DEN	16.1%
3	NE	19.4%
4	DET	19.7%
5	PHI	20.0%
6	HOU	20.5%
7	CHI	21.0%
8	GB	21.4%
9	ATL	21.7%
10	KC	21.9%

Bottom 10 Offenses, 3-and-out per drive

Rk	Team	Pct
23	MIA	24.9%
24	TB	25.0%
25	SF	25.4%
26	BUF	25.6%
27	PIT	26.2%
28	BAL	27.2%
29	NYJ	29.2%
30	STL	29.6%
31	NYG	29.6%
32	JAC	31.1%

Top 10 Offenses, avg LOS to start drive

Rk	Team	LOS
1	KC	32.7
2	SF	31.6
3	SEA	31.3
4	NE	29.7
5	PIT	29.3
6	CAR	29.2
7	DAL	29.1
8	BAL	29.0
9	MIN	28.4
10	ARI	28.3

Bottom 10 Offenses, avg LOS to start drive

Rk	Team	LOS
23	TB	26.9
23	NYG	26.9
25	BUF	26.7
25	OAK	26.7
27	ATL	26.2
28	CLE	26.1
28	STL	26.1
30	HOU	25.8
31	NYJ	25.6
32	WAS	25.4

Top 10 Defenses, 3-and-out per drive

Rk	Team	Pct
1	NO	29.4%
2	CIN	28.7%
3	SF	27.4%
4	HOU	27.3%
5	BAL	27.1%
6	DET	26.9%
7	CAR	26.7%
8	ARI	26.6%
9	CLE	25.9%
10	STL	25.8%

Bottom 10 Defenses, 3-and-out per drive

Rk	Team	Pct
23	GB	21.0%
24	NE	20.9%
24	NYJ	20.9%
26	ATL	20.7%
27	WAS	20.4%
27	SD	20.4%
29	TB	19.2%
30	PHI	18.9%
31	CHI	16.9%
32	DAL	16.3%

Top 10 Defenses, avg LOS to start drive

Rk	Team	LOS
1	KC	23.1
2	SD	23.7
3	NE	24.2
4	CAR	24.8
5	SF	25.3
6	SEA	25.9
7	IND	26.0
8	NO	26.3
9	STL	26.4
10	CHI	26.7

Bottom 10 Defenses, avg LOS to start drive

Rk	Team	LOS
23	CIN	29.4
24	MIN	29.5
25	PIT	30.1
26	NYJ	30.2
26	OAK	30.3
28	TB	30.4
29	CLE	30.7
30	NYG	30.9
31	BUF	31.1
32	WAS	31.7

Top 10 Offenses, Yards per drive

Rk	Team	Yds/Dr
1	SD	40.13
2	DEN	38.22
3	NO	36.58
4	GB	35.95
5	CHI	34.73
6	PHI	33.81
7	NE	33.70
8	DET	33.22
9	IND	32.91
10	ATL	32.13

Bottom 10 Offenses, Yards per drive

Rk	Team	Yds/Dr
23	CLE	28.04
24	HOU	27.41
25	OAK	27.32
26	BUF	26.70
27	MIA	26.23
28	NYJ	26.14
29	BAL	25.68
30	NYG	24.49
31	TB	24.14
32	JAC	24.11

Top 10 Offenses, Points per drive

Rk	Team	Pts/Dr
1	DEN	2.98
2	SD	2.46
3	NO	2.40
4	DAL	2.25
5	CHI	2.23
6	NE	2.21
7	GB	2.20
8	PHI	2.18
9	SEA	2.16
10	CAR	2.09

Bottom 10 Offenses, Points per drive

Rk	Team	Pts/Dr
23	OAK	1.56
24	WAS	1.54
25	BUF	1.53
26	BAL	1.47
27	TB	1.44
28	CLE	1.43
28	NYJ	1.43
30	NYG	1.37
31	HOU	1.30
32	JAC	1.19

Top 10 Defenses, Yards per drive

Rk	Team	Yds/Dr
1	BUF	25.78
2	ARI	26.01
3	SEA	26.14
4	CIN	26.32
5	BAL	26.58
6	SF	26.69
7	NYG	27.31
8	CAR	27.58
9	NO	27.68
10	CLE	28.11

Bottom 10 Defenses, Yards per drive

Rk	Team	Yds/Dr
23	OAK	31.95
24	STL	32.02
25	PHI	32.51
26	JAC	32.65
27	MIN	33.53
28	GB	33.99
29	ATL	35.85
30	SD	36.00
31	DAL	36.48
32	CHI	37.27

Top 10 Defenses, Points per drive

Rk	Team	Pts/Dr
1	SEA	1.22
2	CAR	1.38
3	CIN	1.41
4	SF	1.45
5	KC	1.51
6	ARI	1.57
7	BAL	1.61
8	NO	1.63
9	NYG	1.66
9	NE	1.66

Bottom 10 Defenses, Points per drive

Rk	Team	Pts/Dr
23	SD	2.02
24	TB	2.05
25	JAC	2.23
26	GB	2.24
27	OAK	2.26
28	WAS	2.30
29	MIN	2.31
29	DAL	2.31
31	CHI	2.44
32	ATL	2.47

Top 10 Offenses, Better DVOA with Shotgun

Rk	Team	% Plays Shotgun	DVOA Shot	DVOA Not	Yd/Play Shot	Yd/Play Not	DVOA Dif
1	PIT	56%	22.0%	-13.2%	6.2	4.6	35.2%
2	NO	48%	35.5%	0.7%	6.8	5.4	34.8%
3	ATL	60%	18.0%	-15.2%	6.1	4.5	33.1%
4	CHI	60%	26.3%	-3.6%	6.6	5.4	29.9%
5	TEN	53%	13.8%	-10.2%	6.2	4.3	23.9%
6	DEN	78%	39.0%	15.5%	6.8	5.7	23.5%
7	NYJ	68%	-7.4%	-29.3%	5.8	3.7	21.9%
8	SD	73%	29.2%	8.6%	6.7	4.6	20.6%
9	WAS	73%	-4.6%	-22.4%	5.6	4.6	17.8%
10	GB	62%	14.0%	0.9%	6.3	5.8	13.1%

Bottom 10 Offenses, Better DVOA with Shotgun

Rk	Team	% Plays Shotgun	DVOA Shot	DVOA Not	Yd/Play Shot	Yd/Play Not	DVOA Dif
23	MIA	68%	-1.7%	-1.8%	5.2	4.7	0.1%
24	ARI	38%	-2.7%	-2.2%	6.3	5.2	-0.5%
25	BUF	66%	-12.1%	-10.4%	5.1	4.9	-1.6%
26	KC	54%	2.0%	3.9%	5.4	5.4	-1.9%
27	HOU	53%	-23.2%	-14.9%	5.2	5.1	-8.3%
28	NE	45%	11.3%	19.8%	5.3	5.9	-8.6%
29	OAK	68%	-20.9%	-9.3%	5.4	5.4	-11.6%
30	CLE	59%	-20.2%	-7.9%	5.1	5.1	-12.3%
31	TB	43%	-19.8%	-4.5%	4.2	5.1	-15.3%
32	PHI	86%	19.8%	39.5%	6.5	6.5	-19.7%

Top 10 Defenses, Better DVOA vs. Shotgun

Rk	Team	% Plays Shotgun	DVOA Shot	DVOA Not	Yd/Play Shot	Yd/Play Not	DVOA Dif
1	BUF	54%	-28.3%	0.2%	4.9	5.2	-28.6%
2	IND	54%	-3.7%	5.6%	6.2	5.0	-9.3%
3	MIA	57%	-1.5%	6.6%	5.5	5.3	-8.2%
4	SEA	47%	-30.0%	-22.6%	4.9	4.5	-7.5%
5	CIN	69%	-13.7%	-10.5%	4.9	4.7	-3.2%
6	CAR	58%	-15.7%	-15.7%	5.0	5.1	0.0%
7	ARI	59%	-15.8%	-17.1%	5.3	4.6	1.2%
8	NO	60%	-4.9%	-7.1%	5.3	5.2	2.3%
9	NYG	62%	-10.5%	-12.8%	5.1	4.9	2.4%
10	JAC	50%	12.2%	9.8%	6.0	5.5	2.5%

Bottom 10 Defenses, Better DVOA vs. Shotgun

Rk	Team	% Plays Shotgun	DVOA Shot	DVOA Not	Yd/Play Shot	Yd/Play Not	DVOA Dif
23	WAS	65%	9.5%	-4.3%	6.3	5.2	13.9%
24	CHI	52%	16.0%	1.8%	6.8	5.7	14.2%
25	NYJ	52%	3.0%	-13.7%	5.8	4.7	16.7%
26	CLE	57%	16.1%	-1.0%	5.4	4.5	17.0%
27	TB	53%	2.9%	-16.2%	6.4	4.8	19.1%
28	HOU	50%	13.1%	-6.6%	6.2	4.8	19.7%
29	SF	57%	5.2%	-15.5%	5.6	4.4	20.7%
30	OAK	65%	18.2%	-2.5%	6.6	4.4	20.7%
31	PHI	65%	14.1%	-10.2%	6.3	4.2	24.3%
32	MIN	62%	23.9%	-8.7%	6.6	4.6	32.6%

Top 10 Offenses, Better DVOA with Play Action

Rk	Team	% PA	DVOA PA	DVOA No PA	Yd/Play PA	Yd/Play No PA	DVOA Dif
1	MIA	14%	50.0%	-0.9%	7.3	5.4	50.9%
2	BAL	13%	30.5%	-11.9%	8.2	5.4	42.4%
3	CLE	20%	25.6%	-15.0%	7.3	5.2	40.6%
4	SEA	34%	59.2%	19.4%	8.9	6.5	39.8%
5	DEN	25%	89.7%	53.4%	11.1	6.9	36.3%
6	SD	12%	81.2%	49.3%	9.5	7.5	31.9%
7	SF	28%	56.8%	28.6%	7.7	6.5	28.1%
8	CIN	19%	35.8%	9.8%	8.3	6.5	26.0%
9	DAL	13%	39.0%	14.5%	6.8	6.4	24.6%
10	OAK	26%	5.6%	-18.8%	7.7	5.6	24.4%

Bottom 10 Offenses, Better DVOA with Play Action

Rk	Team	% PA	DVOA PA	DVOA No PA	Yd/Play PA	Yd/Play No PA	DVOA Dif
23	KC	25%	11.4%	13.2%	6.2	5.9	-1.8%
24	WAS	27%	-13.0%	-8.2%	6.6	5.5	-4.8%
25	STL	22%	-5.6%	1.9%	8.2	5.3	-7.5%
26	BUF	16%	-17.9%	-10.1%	5.3	5.6	-7.8%
27	NO	24%	28.3%	40.8%	7.3	7.1	-12.5%
28	ATL	13%	5.3%	18.6%	6.3	6.2	-13.3%
29	TEN	13%	0.5%	15.9%	6.0	6.5	-15.4%
30	NYJ	21%	-20.9%	-3.7%	5.1	6.1	-17.2%
31	PIT	13%	4.1%	26.5%	7.4	6.4	-22.4%
32	CHI	20%	12.1%	36.4%	7.3	7.1	-24.3%

Top 10 Defenses, Better DVOA vs. Play Action

Rk	Team	% PA	DVOA PA	DVOA No PA	Yd/Play PA	Yd/Play No PA	DVOA Dif
1	CLE	21%	-9.5%	24.6%	5.8	5.8	-34.1%
2	DEN	21%	-4.7%	16.9%	6.1	6.5	-21.6%
3	PHI	17%	5.6%	21.0%	6.9	6.6	-15.5%
4	NE	17%	-0.8%	10.6%	6.2	6.3	-11.4%
5	MIN	24%	16.3%	27.3%	6.8	7.0	-10.9%
6	IND	21%	-2.7%	8.0%	6.7	6.5	-10.7%
7	ATL	25%	23.5%	27.5%	8.7	6.8	-3.9%
8	SEA	23%	-33.7%	-30.7%	5.3	5.2	-3.0%
9	CAR	19%	-16.1%	-14.1%	6.5	5.3	-1.9%
10	DAL	20%	22.0%	23.9%	8.1	6.8	-1.9%

Bottom 10 Defenses, Better DVOA vs. Play Action

Rk	Team	% PA	DVOA PA	DVOA No PA	Yd/Play PA	Yd/Play No PA	DVOA Dif
23	PIT	21%	24.8%	4.1%	8.5	5.4	20.7%
24	OAK	21%	41.5%	18.0%	8.9	6.6	23.5%
25	CHI	31%	24.1%	-0.7%	8.6	6.2	24.8%
26	STL	19%	25.0%	0.2%	7.8	6.5	24.8%
27	KC	13%	19.1%	-8.0%	8.3	6.1	27.0%
28	JAC	24%	45.7%	12.5%	8.6	6.4	33.2%
29	MIA	19%	31.3%	-6.4%	7.3	5.9	37.6%
30	BAL	22%	26.4%	-11.9%	8.3	5.8	38.3%
31	HOU	22%	48.7%	9.0%	8.6	6.0	39.7%
32	BUF	21%	19.2%	-32.9%	7.1	5.0	52.1%

2013 Defenses with and without Pass Pressure

Rank	Team	Plays	Pct Pressure	DVOA with Pressure	Yds with Pressure	DVOA w/o Pressure	Yds w/o Pressure	DVOA Dif	Rank	Rank
1	SEA	613	34.4%	-91.8%	2.4	1.5%	6.7	-93.3%	24	29
2	HOU	547	28.0%	-55.3%	3.7	48.0%	7.7	-103.3%	20	33
3	CAR	655	27.8%	-100.3%	1.5	18.5%	7.1	-118.8%	10	6
4	IND	619	27.6%	-61.6%	3.8	31.1%	7.6	-92.7%	25	27
5	ARI	699	27.6%	-92.9%	2.6	21.4%	6.9	-114.3%	12	4
6	BUF	639	27.2%	-78.4%	2.6	-0.3%	6.6	-78.1%	32	20
7	NO	581	26.7%	-95.5%	2.5	23.3%	6.9	-118.9%	9	40
8	TB	616	26.6%	-79.2%	3.3	34.7%	8.1	-114.0%	13	8
9	WAS	572	26.4%	-65.6%	2.9	38.0%	8.5	-103.5%	19	17
10	KC	679	25.9%	-72.3%	3.0	17.2%	7.5	-89.5%	26	11
11	DEN	696	25.9%	-71.7%	2.7	41.0%	7.7	-112.7%	16	19
12	STL	604	25.8%	-95.0%	2.4	39.5%	8.3	-134.5%	2	1
13	SF	648	25.6%	-98.3%	1.9	31.1%	7.2	-129.3%	4	28
14	MIA	651	24.9%	-97.5%	2.8	32.6%	7.3	-130.1%	3	16
15	BAL	616	24.8%	-75.1%	2.7	18.6%	7.5	-93.7%	23	30
16	OAK	616	24.7%	-61.3%	4.0	51.5%	8.0	-112.8%	15	3
17	MIN	715	24.6%	-37.5%	3.9	43.8%	7.9	-81.3%	30	14
18	DET	634	24.4%	-68.6%	3.8	36.0%	7.6	-104.6%	18	2
19	TEN	610	24.4%	-50.7%	3.9	28.5%	7.4	-79.2%	31	38
20	CLE	677	23.9%	-66.9%	2.3	41.8%	6.9	-108.7%	17	13
21	PHI	751	23.8%	-72.3%	2.7	45.6%	7.9	-117.8%	11	12
22	NE	663	23.2%	-83.8%	2.5	35.9%	7.4	-119.7%	8	22
23	NYG	665	22.7%	-69.8%	3.0	15.7%	6.7	-85.5%	27	18
24	JAC	622	22.7%	-77.4%	2.4	48.5%	8.3	-125.9%	6	39
25	PIT	631	22.3%	-80.3%	2.2	33.0%	7.1	-113.3%	14	23
26	SD	615	22.0%	-39.2%	3.5	44.5%	8.3	-83.7%	28	25
27	DAL	684	21.8%	-54.8%	4.0	45.4%	8.0	-100.2%	21	34
28	CIN	681	21.6%	-90.0%	1.3	7.0%	6.5	-97.0%	22	21
29	ATL	582	21.5%	-93.3%	2.2	58.2%	8.7	-151.5%	1	31
30	CHI	561	21.4%	-56.3%	4.0	25.3%	7.8	-81.7%	29	26
31	GB	607	21.3%	-79.9%	2.2	48.2%	8.2	-128.1%	5	9
32	NYJ	651	20.6%	-86.7%	2.4	33.5%	7.6	-120.1%	7	10
	NFL AVERAGE		**24.7%**	**-75.2%**	**2.8**	**32.6%**	**7.6**	**-107.9%**		**32**

Includes scrambles and Defensive Pass Interference. Does not include aborted snaps.

Author Bios

Editor-in-Chief and Statistician

Aaron Schatz is the creator of FootballOutsiders.com and the proprietary NFL statistics within *Football Outsiders Almanac*, including DVOA, DYAR, Adjusted Line Yards, and the KUBIAK fantasy football projections. He writes regularly for ESPN.com and *ESPN the Magazine*, and he has done custom research for a number of NFL teams. *The New York Times Magazine* has referred to him as "the Bill James of football." Before creating Football Outsiders, he was a radio disc jockey and spent three years tracking search trends online as the writer and producer of the Internet column "The Lycos 50." He has a B.A. in Economics from Brown University and lives in Framingham, Massachusetts. He promises that someday Bill Belichick will retire, the Patriots will be awful, and he will write very mean and nasty things about them.

Layout and Design

Vince Verhei has been a writer and editor for Football Outsiders since 2007. In addition to writing for *Football Outsiders Almanac 2014*, he did all layout and design on the book. During the season, he writes the "Quick Reads" column covering the best and worst players of each week according to Football Outsiders metrics. His writings have also appeared in *ESPN the Magazine* and in Maple Street Press publications, and he has done layout on a number of other books for Football Outsiders and for Prospectus Entertainment Ventures. His other night job is as a writer and podcast host for pro wrestling/MMA website Figurefouronline.com. He is a graduate of Western Washington University.

Contributors

Bill Connelly analyzes the ins and outs of college football play-by-play data in the weekly Football Outsiders column, "Varsity Numbers." He is also the College Sports Editor and Analytics Director for SB Nation, where he runs the college football blog Football Study Hall. His first book, *Study Hall: College Football, Its Stats and Its Stories*, was published in July 2013. He grew up a numbers and sports nerd in western Oklahoma, but now lives in Missouri with his wife, pets, and young daughter.

Doug Farrar has been a Seattleite for most of his adult life, so he has an affinity for underdog quarterbacks and marginally cursed NFL teams. He started writing for FO in 2006, held down the "Film Room" concept between the eras of Michael David Smith and Andy Benoit, and currently writes all kinds of NFL and draft stuff for *Sports Illustrated* and SI.com. He's also written for ESPN, Yahoo Sports, FOX Sports, the *Washington Post*, and the *Seattle Times*. Like many before him, Doug hopes to one day reach lowercase "dr. z" status.

Nathan Forster played wide receiver for his freshman football team, but unfortunately graduated before Matt Millen left the broadcast booth. He graduated with a B.A. in English from the University of Michigan and a J.D. from Boston College Law School, which naturally lead him to develop regression models that project the success of NFL Draft prospects. Nathan and his love-hate relationship with the Detroit Lions currently reside in the greater Boston area with his wife, Sarah, and daughter, Lily.

Brian Fremeau contributes the Fremeau Efficiency Index (FEI) and other college football stats, analysis, and data visualization design to FootballOutsiders.com, ESPN Insider, and Maple Street Press college football publications. He recently launched bcftoys.com, a personal archive of his stat analysis and graphics work. He lives in South Bend, Indiana, with his wife and daughter.

Tom Gower joined the writing staff in 2009 after being a game charter for three seasons. He co-writes our "Scramble for the Ball" column, and his work also appeared on ESPN.com. He has degrees from Georgetown University and the University of Chicago, whose football programs have combined for an Orange Bowl appearance and seven Big Ten titles but are still trying to find success after Pearl Harbor. When not practicing law in the Chicago area or writing for FO, he keeps a keen eye on Tennessee for the blog Total Titans.

Matt Hinton was the founding editor of Yahoo! Sports' college football blog, *Dr. Saturday, or: How I Learned to Stop Worrying and Love the BCS*, and has also written full-time for CBSSports.com and SB Nation.

Scott Kacsmar got his start in football analysis by creating the first standardized database of fourth-quarter comebacks and game-winning drives: two statistics that are increasingly used (and often mis-used) in NFL coverage. His first article appeared at the pro-football-reference blog in August 2009, indisputably crowning Dan Marino as the NFL's "Comeback King" and putting an end to John Elway and "The Myth of 47." Scott joined Football Nation in July 2011 and wrote the weekly Captain Comeback column for Cold, Hard Football Facts before moving over to Football Outsiders as assistant editor in August 2013. Scott has an Industrial Engineering degree from the University of Pittsburgh, which he wants his statistics professor to know has been very applicable to his football work. Contrary to belief, his interest in fourth-quarter comebacks was not the result of only wanting to do 25 percent of the work for 55 percent of the games.

Jason Lisk is a long-suffering Chiefs fan who grew up watching Deron Cherry and Bill Kenney, and cannot wait to see what DVOA says about the fluke 1986 playoff season. He lives in the Kansas City area with his wife Loree and four children. A reformed lawyer, he is the managing editor and lead NFL writer for the Big Lead, and previously wrote at the pro-football-reference blog.

Rivers McCown started charting games for Football Outsiders in 2007 on a lark and soon found himself engrossed in football writing, statistics, and the idea that Phil Simms was often wrong about things. A lifelong Houstonian by choice, he has built up a tolerance to humidity and bad football teams. Prior to joining Football Outsiders as an assistant editor, Rivers was Managing Editor for SB Nation Houston.

Since 2001, avowed football nerd and three-cone fetishist **Christopher Price** has covered Boston sports while simultaneously trying to make bow ties cool again. He's served as a contributor to ESPN.com, SI.com and Baseball America, as well as the *Boston Globe*, the *Washington Post*, the *Miami Herald*, *Rocky Mountain News*, and the *Cape Cod Times*. Since 2009, he's covered the NFL for WEEI.com, while also working as a co-host for WEEI's "NFL Sunday" and the "It Is What It Is" podcast. He's also authored three books, including *The Blueprint: How the New England Patriots Beat the System to Create the Last Great NFL Superpower*, which was named one of the five sports books of 2007 by *Sports Illustrated*. He's also written *Baseball by the Beach*, the definitive history of the Cape Cod Baseball League, as well as *New England Patriots: The Complete Illustrated History*. He lives outside of Boston with his wife and son, and spends way too much free time drinking coffee and searching for the end of the Internet.

Chase Stuart has written about football stats and history for over a decade. He now writes at his own site, FootballPerspective.com, after years of writing at Pro-Football-Reference.com. During the season, he contributes a weekly column for *The New York Times*. Even though he lives in Manhattan, we still like him. Chase made it nearly this entire paragraph without revealing that he is a self-loathing Jets fan, as if there were any other kind.

When **Mike Tanier** joined the Football Outsiders team in 2004, his biggest claim to fame was that he was (then college quarterback) Joe Flacco's calculus teacher. Since then, he has joined us on our journey through nine books, has been part of our FOX Sports and ESPN coverage, written for outlets as diverse as Rotoworld, *GQ*, *SI for Kids*, and *Maxim*, and spent three years writing the Sunday N.F.L. capsules (and much more) for *The New York Times*. He is now the NFL writer and designated sports comedian for Sports on Earth. A collection of his writing for our website, *A Good Walkthrough Spoiled: The Best of Mike Tanier at Football Outsiders* was published this spring; he has also written a book about the top athletes in Philadelphia history, *The Philly Fan's Code*. All that said, his biggest claim to fame remains that he was once Joe Flacco's calculus teacher.

Robert Weintraub bleeds orange, both because of his inexplicable passion for the Cincinnati Bengals (he grew up in suburban New York, not Ohio) and because of his alma mater, Syracuse University. Robert is a regular contributor to *The New York Times* and writes their college football previews. He also pens a media column for the *Columbia Journalism Review*, and writes for Sports on Earth, Slate, *The Guardian*, and many other media outlets. He has also written two books, *The Victory Season: World War II, The Homecoming, and the Birth of Baseball's Golden Age* and *The House That Ruth Built: A New Yankee Stadium, the First Championship, and the Redemption of 1923*. He lives with his family in Decatur, Georgia.

Acknowledgements

We want to thank all the Football Outsiders readers, all the people in the media who have helped to spread the word about our website and books, and all the people in the NFL who have shown interest in our work. A few specific acknowledgements:

- FO techmaster Steven Steinman, who is *still* working hard on the long-awaited FootballOutsiders.com back-end technical upgrade.
- J.J. Cooper for sack timing data.
- Mike Harris for help with the season simulation.
- Premium programmer Sean McCall, Excel macro master John Argentiero, and drive stats guru Jim Armstrong.
- FO writers who did not write for the book, including Cian Fahey, Mike Kurtz, Ben Muth, and Matt Waldman, plus the departed Mike Ridley.
- David Lewin, creator of the Long-Term Career Forecast (formerly the Lewin Career Forecast) and Jason McKinley, creator of O-Line Continuity Score.
- Jeremy Snyder, our incredibly prolific transcriber of old play-by-play gamebooks. (Stay tuned to FootballOutsiders.com for the unveiling of DVOA from the 1987 and 1988 seasons, sometime early next year.)
- Roland Beech of the Dallas Mavericks, formerly of Two-MinuteWarning.com, who came up with the original ideas behind our individual defensive stats.
- Our editors at ESPN.com and *ESPN the Magazine*, including Daniel Kaufman, Jeffrey Dooley, Michael Hume, and Ben Fawkes.
- Everybody at ESPN Stats & Information, for all the charting data and for listening to us when we suggested endless revisions to all the charting data.
- Bill Simmons, for constantly promoting us on his podcast, and Peter King, for lots of promotion on The MMQB.
- Chris Hoeltge at the NFL, for responding to our endless questions about specific items in the official play-by-play, and for collecting old gamebooks and making them available to us.
- All the friends we've made on coaching staffs and in front offices across the National Football League, who generally don't want to be mentioned by name. You know who you are.
- Our comrades in the revolution: Doug Drinen (creator of the indispensible pro-football-reference.com), Bill Barnwell (our long lost brother), Ben Alamar, Brian Burke, Neil Paine, Robert Mays, Kyle Wagner, and K.C. Joyner, plus the kids at Numberfire, the football guys from footballguys.com, and our friends at Prospectus Entertainment Ventures.
- Also, our scouting buddies, including Greg Bedard, Andy Benoit, Chris Brown, Greg Cosell, and Russ Lande.
- Joe Alread, who handles the special Football Outsiders cards in Madden Ultimate Team, and the other folks at EA Sports who make FO a part of the Madden universe.
- Interns who helped prepare data over the past year or for this book specifically, including Kurt Chipps, Thomas DeCaro, Greg Dorian, James Goldstein, Patrick Pascual, Andrew Potter, and Carl Yedor.
- All those who have volunteered their time and effort for the Football Outsiders game charting project, particularly those people who have been consistently charting for multiple seasons. Our regular charters last year included: Aimal Arsalla, Matthew Baumann, Chris Berney, Michael Bonner, Casey Boguslaw, Richard Chang, Kevin Clay, John DeVol, Jason Dooley, Michael Dunn, Dave DuPlantis, Robert Grebel, Willy Hu, Bo Hurley, Ajit Kirpekar, Bin Lee, Aaron Lindsey, Aaron McCurrie, Seth McDonald, Matt Morrow, David Neumann, Sander Philipse, Nate Richards, Michael Rutter, Augie Salick, Ken Schroeder, Navin Sharma, Ben St. Clair, Rob Stewart, Abe vander Bent, David Vesel, Matthew Weston, and Mark Wierichs. Weekly data collection was handled by Peter Koski.

Infinite gratitude goes to our families, for putting up with this silliness. Special 2014 thanks from Aaron to some very special friends who helped him get through the darkness of the past 10 months. They know who they are, and honestly, most of them will never see this anyway because they aren't football fans.

Follow Football Outsiders on Twitter

Follow the official account announcing new Football Outsiders articles at **@fboutsiders**. You can follow other FO writers at these Twitter addresses:

Bill Connelly: **@SBN_BillC**
J.J. Cooper: **@jjcoop36**
Cian Fahey: **@cianaf**
Brian Fremeau: **@bcfremeau**
Tom Gower: **@ThomasGower**
Matt Hinton: **@MattRHinton**
Scott Kacsmar: **@FO_ScottKacsmar**
Rivers McCown: **@FO_RiversMcCown**
Ben Muth: **@FO_WordofMuth**
Aaron Schatz: **@FO_ASchatz**
Vince Verhei: **@FO_VVerhei**
Matt Waldman: **@MattWaldman**
Robert Weintraub: **@robwein**

Plus, our special guests and returning all-stars for *Football Outsiders Almanac 2014*:

Doug Farrar: **@SC_DougFarrar**
Jason Lisk: **@JasonLisk**
Christopher Price: **@CPriceNFL**
Chase Stuart: **@fbgchase**
Mike Tanier: **@MikeTanier**

Made in the USA
Lexington, KY
11 August 2014

The World of Learning 1999

The World of Learning 1999

FORTY-NINTH EDITION

EUROPA PUBLICATIONS LIMITED

First published 1947
Forty-ninth Edition 1998

18 Bedford Square, London, WC1B 3JN, England

Australia
James Bennett Pty Ltd, 3 Narabang Way,
Belrose, NSW 2085, Australia

Japan
Maruzen Co Ltd, POB 5050, Tokyo International 100-31

ISBN 1 85743 049 2
ISSN 0084-2117

Library of Congress Catalog Card Number 47-30172

Typeset by UBL International and printed by Unwin Brothers Limited
The Gresham Press
Old Woking, Surrey

(Members of the MPG Information Division)

Bound by MPG Books Limited
Bodmin, Cornwall

(All members of the Martins Printing Group)

FOREWORD

We have once again tried to ensure that we include the latest possible information concerning entries in THE WORLD OF LEARNING. Every year a folder containing the previous year's proof is sent to each entry; continuous research in the world press and educational journals, as well as contact with official sources all over the world, supplements this method of revision.

We are always grateful to those individuals and organizations who help us to bring our information up to date with their prompt replies. We particularly emphasize the necessity for revised entries to be returned to us without delay, since important material may otherwise be held over until a later edition. Only by maintaining a strict timetable can the regular production of such a large work as THE WORLD OF LEARNING be assured.

We should like to point out that in the sections on Universities and Colleges our classification usually follows the practice of the country concerned. This in no way implies any official evaluation on our part. We suggest that readers who are interested in the matter of equivalences of institutions, degrees or diplomas, should correspond directly with the institution concerned, or with the national or international bodies set up for this purpose.

Many readers will be interested to know that from December 1999 a CD-ROM version of THE WORLD OF LEARNING will be available, enabling both individuals and institutions to be accessed according to the subjects in which they specialize and by geographic location. A prototype version of this CD-ROM, containing data from Germany and the United Kingdom, is available, free of charge, from the Editor of THE WORLD OF LEARNING, Europa Publications Ltd, 18 Bedford Square, London, WC1B 3JN, England (fax +44 171 580-3919; e-mail sales@europapublications.co.uk).

October 1998

CONTENTS

CONTENTS

CONTENTS

ABBREVIATIONS

AAAS — American Association for the Advancement of Science
Acad. — Academy; Academician
ACLS — American Council of Learned Societies
ACT — Australian Capital Territory
Admin. — Administrative, Administration
AFRC — Agricultural and Food Research Council
AIA — American Institute of Architects
AIChE — American Institute of Chemical Engineers
ALECSO — Arab League Educational, Cultural and Scientific Organization
Alta — Alberta
AP — Andhra Pradesh
ASCE — American Society of Civil Engineers
Asscn — Association
Assoc. — Associate
Asst — Assistant
ATC — Art Teacher's Certificate
Atty — Attorney
AUPELF — Association des Universités Partiellement ou Entièrement de Langue Française
Avv. — Avvocato (Advocate)

BA — Bachelor of Arts
BC — British Columbia
BILD — Bureau International de Liaison et de Documentation
Bldg — Building
Blvd — Boulevard
BMA — British Medical Association
BP — Boîte postale
Br. — Branch
BRGM — Bureau de Recherches Géologiques et Minières
Bro. — Brother
BSc — Bachelor of Science
B/TEC — Bachelor of Technology

c. — circa (approximately)
CAE — College of Advanced Education
CAR — Central African Republic
Ccl — Council
CEA — Commissariat à l'Energie Atomique
CEO — Chief Executive Officer
CERN — European Organization for Nuclear Research
CGIAR — Consultative Group on International Agricultural Research
Chair. — Chairman, Chairwoman, Chairperson
CIRAD — Centre de Coopération Internationale en Recherche Agronomique pour le Développement
Cmdr — Commander
CNAA — Council for National Academic Awards
CNR — Consiglio Nazionale delle Ricerche
CNRS — Centre National de la Recherche Scientifique
Co — Company; County
colln — Collection
Comm. — Commission
Commr — Commissioner
Conf. — Conference
Corpn — Corporation
Corresp. — Correspondent, Corresponding
CP — Case postale; Caixa postal
Cr — Contador
CSIRO — Commonwealth Scientific and Industrial Research Organization
CTFT — Centre Technique Forestier Tropical
Cttee — Committee

Del. — Delegate, delegation
Dept — Department
Deptl — Departmental
DES — Department of Education and Science
Dir — Director
Dist. — District
Dr — Doctor
Drs — Doctorandus (Netherlands higher degree)
DSIR — Department of Scientific and Industrial Research

E — East; Eastern
EC — European Community
ECOSOC — Economic and Social Council (UN)
ECSC — European Coal and Steel Community
EEC — European Economic Community
ENEA — Comitato Nazionale per la ricerca e lo sviluppo dell'Energia Nucleare e delle Energie Alternative
EngD — Doctor of Engineering
ESA — European Space Agency
ESCAP — Economic and Social Commission for Asia and the Pacific
esp. — especially
ESRC — Economic and Social Research Council
Est. — Established
ETH — Eidgenössische Technische Hochschule
Exec. — Executive

f. — founded
FAO — Food and Agriculture Organization
Fed. — Federation, Federal
fmr — former
Fr — Father
F.t.e. — Full-time equivalent (staff)

F.U.T. Federal University of Technology

Gen. General
Gov. Governor
Govt Government

HQ Headquarters
HE His Eminence; His (Her) Excellency
HM His (Her) Majesty
HND Higher National Diploma
Hon. Honourable; Honorary
HRH His (Her) Royal Highness

IAEA International Atomic Energy Agency
IAU International Astronomical Union
IBE International Bureau of Education
ICAR Indian Council of Agricultural Research
ICPHS International Council for Philosophy and Humanistic Studies
ICSU International Council of Scientific Unions
IEC International Electrotechnical Commission
IEMVT Institut d'Elevage et de Médecine Vétérinaire des Pays Tropicaux
IFAN Institut Fondamental d'Afrique Noire
IFREMER Institut Français de Recherche pour l'Exploitation de la Mer
IFLA International Federation of Library Associations and Institutions
IGU International Geographical Union
IICA Instituto Interamericano de Cooperación para la Agricultura
ILO International Labour Organization
IMU International Mathematical Union
Inc. Incorporated
incl. include(s), including
Ind. Independent
INFN Istituto Nazionale di Fisica Nucleare
INRA Institut National de la Recherche Agronomique
Instn Institution
Int. International
Ir Ingénieur (Engineer)
IRAT Institut de Recherches Agronomiques Tropicales et des Cultures Vivrières
IRC Institut de Recherches sur le Caoutchouc
IRCC Institut de Recherches du Café, du Cacao et autres plantes stimulantes
IRCT Institut de Recherches du Coton et des Textiles Exotiques
IRFA Institut de Recherches sur les Fruits et Agrumes
IRHO Institut de Recherches pour les Huiles et Oléagineux
ISME International Society for Music Education
ISO International Organization for Standardization
IUB International Union of Biochemistry
IUBS International Union of Biological Sciences
IUCr International Union of Crystallography
IUGG International Union of Geodesy and Geophysics
IUGS International Union of Geological Sciences
IUHPS International Union of the History and Philosophy of Science
IUIS International Union of Immunological Societies
IUMS International Union of Microbiological Societies
IUNS International Union of Nutritional Sciences
IUPAB International Union of Pure and Applied Biophysics
IUPAC International Union of Pure and Applied Chemistry
IUPAP International Union of Pure and Applied Physics
IUPHAR International Union of Pharmacology
IUPS International Union of Physiological Sciences
IUTAM International Union of Theoretical and Applied Mechanics

Jl Jalan (Indonesia, Malaysia)
JSC Joint Stock Company

m. million
MA Master of Arts
MAFF Ministry of Agriculture, Fisheries and Food
Man. Manager, Managing; Manitoba
Mem(s) Member(s)
Mgr Monseigneur; Monsignor; Magister (Master's degree)
Min. Minister; Ministry
MIT Massachusetts Institute of Technology
MRC Medical Research Council
MS Master of Science
MSc Master of Science

N North; Northern
NASA National Aeronautics and Space Administration
Nat. National
NB New Brunswick
ND North Dakota; National Diploma
NDD National Diploma in Dairying
NERC Natural Environment Research Council
NGO Non-Governmental Organization
NS Nova Scotia
NSW New South Wales
NUI National University of Ireland
NZ New Zealand

OAS Organization of American States
ODA Overseas Development Administration
OECD Organisation for Economic Co-operation and Development
OFS Orange Free State
OIC Organization of the Islamic Conference
On. Onorevole (Italian)

ABBREVIATIONS

ONERA	Office National d'Etudes et de Recherches Aérospatiales
Ont.	Ontario
Org.	Organization
OU	Open University
PCSIR	Pakistan Council of Scientific and Industrial Research
PEI	Prince Edward Island
PEN	Poets, Playwrights, Essayists, Editors and Novelists (Club)
PhD	Doctor of Philosophy
PMB	Private Mail Bag
POB	Post Office Box
Pres.	President
Prof.	Professor
Publ(s)	Publication(s)
q.v.	quod vide (which see)
Rep.	Representative; Represented
retd	retired
Rev.	Reverend
RIBA	Royal Institute of British Architects
RP	Révérend Père
Rt Hon.	Right Honourable
Rt Rev.	Right Reverend
S	South; Southern
SA	South Africa(n); South Australia
SDI	Selective Dissemination of Information
Sec.	Secretary
SERC	Science and Engineering Research Council
SHND	Scottish Higher National Diploma
SIPRI	Stockholm International Peace Research Institute
Soc.	Society
spec.	special
UK	United Kingdom
UN	United Nations
UNDP	United Nations Development Programme
UNESCO	United Nations Educational, Scientific and Cultural Organization
UNICEF	United Nations International Children's Emergency Fund
Univ.	University
UNRWA	United Nations Relief and Works Agency
UNU	United Nations University
UP	Uttar Pradesh (United Provinces)
URSI	Union Radio-Scientifique Internationale
USA	United States of America
USIS	United States Information Service
Vols	Volumes
W	West; Western
WA	Western Australia
WHO	World Health Organization

SPECIAL NOTE

Entries within the sections Learned Societies and Research Institutes are grouped under the following headings

GENERAL
AGRICULTURE, FISHERIES AND VETERINARY SCIENCE
ARCHITECTURE AND TOWN PLANNING
BIBLIOGRAPHY, LIBRARY SCIENCE AND MUSEOLOGY
ECONOMICS, LAW AND POLITICS
EDUCATION
FINE AND PERFORMING ARTS
HISTORY, GEOGRAPHY AND ARCHAEOLOGY
LANGUAGE AND LITERATURE
MEDICINE
NATURAL SCIENCES
- *General*
- *Biological Sciences*
- *Mathematical Sciences*
- *Physical Sciences*

PHILOSOPHY AND PSYCHOLOGY
RELIGION, SOCIOLOGY AND ANTHROPOLOGY
TECHNOLOGY

INTERNATIONAL SECTION

INTERNATIONAL

UNITED NATIONS EDUCATIONAL, SCIENTIFIC AND CULTURAL ORGANIZATION (UNESCO)

7 place de Fontenoy, 75352 Paris 07 SP, France
Telephone: 1-45-68-10-00
Telex: 204461
Fax: 1-45-67-16-90

UNESCO was established in 1946 'for the purpose of advancing, through the educational, scientific and cultural relations of the peoples of the world, the objectives of international peace and the common welfare of mankind'.

Functions

UNESCO's activities are funded through a regular budget provided by member states and also through other sources, particularly the UNDP.

International Intellectual Co-operation

UNESCO assists the interchange of experience, knowledge and ideas through a world network of specialists. Apart from the work of its professional staff, UNESCO co-operates regularly with the national associations and international federations of scientists, artists, writers and educators, some of which it helped to establish.

UNESCO convenes conferences and meetings, and co-ordinates international scientific efforts; it helps to standardize procedures of documentation and provides clearing house services; it offers fellowships; and it publishes a wide range of specialized works, including source books and works of reference.

UNESCO promotes various international agreements, including the Universal Copyright Convention and the World Cultural and Natural Heritage Convention, which member states are invited to accept.

Operational Assistance

UNESCO has established missions which advise governments, particularly in the developing member countries, in the planning of projects; and it appoints experts to assist in carrying them out. The projects are concerned with the teaching of functional literacy to workers in development undertakings; teacher training; establishing of libraries and documentation centres; provision of training for journalists, radio, television and film workers; improvement of scientific and technical education; training of planners in cultural development; and the international exchange of persons and information.

Promotion of Peace

UNESCO organizes various research efforts on racial problems, and is particularly concerned with prevention of discrimination in education, and improving access for women to education. It also promotes studies and research on conflicts and peace, violence and obstacles to disarmament, and the role of international law and organizations in building peace. It is stressed that human rights, peace and disarmament cannot be dealt with separately, as the observance of human rights is a prerequisite to peace and vice versa.

Member States

(June 1998)

Afghanistan
Albania
Algeria
Andorra
Angola
Antigua and Barbuda
Argentina
Armenia
Aruba (Associate Member)
Australia
Austria
Azerbaijan
Bahamas
Bahrain
Bangladesh
Barbados
Belarus
Belgium
Belize
Benin
Bhutan
Bolivia
Bosnia and Herzegovina
Botswana
Brazil
British Virgin Islands (Associate Member)
Bulgaria
Burkina Faso
Burundi
Cambodia
Cameroon
Canada
Cape Verde
Central African Republic
Chad
Chile
China, People's Republic
Colombia
Comoros
Congo, Democratic Republic
Congo, Republic
Cook Islands
Costa Rica
Côte d'Ivoire
Croatia
Cuba
Cyprus
Czech Republic
Denmark
Djibouti
Dominica
Dominican Republic
Ecuador
Egypt
El Salvador
Equatorial Guinea
Eritrea
Estonia
Ethiopia
Fiji
Finland
France
Gabon
Gambia
Georgia
Germany
Ghana
Greece
Grenada
Guatemala
Guinea
Guinea-Bissau
Guyana
Haiti
Honduras
Hungary
Iceland
India
Indonesia
Iran
Iraq
Ireland
Israel
Italy
Jamaica
Japan
Jordan
Kazakhstan
Kenya
Kiribati
Korea, Democratic People's Republic
Korea, Republic
Kuwait
Kyrgyzstan
Laos
Latvia
Lebanon
Lesotho
Liberia
Libya
Lithuania
Luxembourg
Macau (Associate Member)
Macedonia (former Yugoslav republic)
Madagascar
Malawi
Malaysia
Maldives
Mali
Malta
Marshall Islands
Mauritania
Mauritius
Mexico
Moldova
Monaco
Mongolia
Morocco
Mozambique
Myanmar
Namibia
Nauru
Nepal
Netherlands
Netherlands Antilles (Associate Member)
New Zealand
Nicaragua
Niger
Nigeria
Niue

Norway
Oman
Pakistan
Panama
Papua New Guinea
Paraguay
Peru
Philippines
Poland
Portugal
Qatar
Romania
Russia
Rwanda
St Christopher and Nevis
St Lucia
St Vincent and the Grenadines
Samoa
San Marino
São Tomé and Príncipe
Saudi Arabia
Senegal
Seychelles
Sierra Leone
Slovakia
Slovenia
Solomon Islands
Somalia
South Africa
Spain
Sri Lanka
Sudan
Suriname
Swaziland
Sweden
Switzerland
Syria
Tajikistan
Tanzania
Thailand
Togo
Tonga
Trinidad and Tobago
Tunisia
Turkey
Turkmenistan
Tuvalu
Uganda
Ukraine
United Arab Emirates
United Kingdom
Uruguay
Uzbekistan
Vanuatu
Venezuela
Viet Nam
Yemen
Yugoslavia
Zambia
Zimbabwe

Organization

GENERAL CONFERENCE

The supreme governing body of the Organization. Meets in ordinary session once in two years and is composed of representatives of the member states.

EXECUTIVE BOARD

Consists of 58 members. Prepares the programme to be submitted to the Conference and supervises its execution. Meets twice or sometimes three times a year.

SECRETARIAT

Director-General: FEDERICO MAYOR (Spain).

Director of the Executive Office: GEORGES MALEMPRÉ.

The Director-General has an international staff of some 2,500 civil servants. Of the professional staff (specialists in various disciplines and administrators), about two-thirds are away from headquarters on technical assistance missions to member states.

CO-OPERATING BODIES

In accordance with UNESCO's constitution, national commissions have been set up in most member states. These help to integrate work within the member states and the work of UNESCO.

UNESCO LIAISON OFFICES

Office for Liaison with United Nations: 2 United Nations Plaza, D.C. 2-0900, New York, NY 10017, USA; tel. (212) 963-5995; fax (212) 963-8014; e-mail UHNYO@unesco.org; Dir N. SIBAL.

UNESCO Liaison Office in Geneva: Villa des Feuillantines, Palais des Nations, CH-1211 Geneva, Switzerland.

UNESCO FIELD OFFICES

(See also under relevant country)

Africa: Luanda (Angola), Porto Novo (Benin), Ouagadougou (Burkina Faso), Bujumbura (Burundi), Yaoundé (Cameroon), Bangui (Central African Republic), Kinshasa (Democratic Republic of Congo), Brazzaville (Republic of Congo), Abidjan (Côte d'Ivoire), Addis Ababa (Ethiopia), Libreville (Gabon), Nairobi (Kenya), Maputo (Mozambique), Windhoek (Namibia), Lagos (Nigeria), Kigali (Rwanda), Dakar (Senegal), Pretoria (South Africa), Dar es Salaam (Tanzania), Lusaka (Zambia), Harare (Zimbabwe).

Arab States: Cairo (Egypt), Amman (Jordan), Beirut (Lebanon), Rabat (Morocco), Doha (Qatar), Tunis (Tunisia).

Asia and the Pacific: Dhaka (Bangladesh), Phnom Penh (Cambodia), Beijing (People's Republic of China), New Delhi (India), Jakarta (Indonesia), Tehran (Iran), Almaty (Kazakhstan), Kuala Lumpur (Malaysia), Kathmandu (Nepal), Islamabad (Pakistan), Apia (Samoa), Bangkok (Thailand), Tashkent (Uzbekistan).

Europe and North America: Sarajevo (Bosnia and Herzegovina), Quebec (Canada), Venice (Italy), Bucharest (Romania), Moscow (Russia).

Latin America and the Caribbean: Buenos Aires (Argentina), Bridgetown (Barbados), La Paz (Bolivia), Brasília (Brazil), Santiago de Chile (Chile), San José (Costa Rica), Havana (Cuba), Santo Domingo (Dominican Republic), Quito (Ecuador), San Salvador (El Salvador), Guatemala, Port-au-Prince (Haiti), Kingston (Jamaica), México (Mexico), Panama, Lima (Peru), Port-of-Spain (Trinidad and Tobago), Montevideo (Uruguay), Caracas (Venezuela).

Activities

EDUCATION

UNESCO has an overall policy of regarding education as a lifelong process. As an example, one implication is the increasing priority given to basic education for all, including early childhood care and development, primary education and adult education. This approach has been the guideline for many of the projects recently planned.

Each year expert missions are sent to member states on request to advise on all matters concerning education. They also help with programmes for training abroad, and UNESCO provides study fellowships; in these forms of assistance priority is given to the rural regions of developing member countries. The issues and problems involved in human resources development have been at the forefront of UNESCO's education programme since the Organization's foundation. Objectives include the eradication of illiteracy, universal primary education, secondary education reform, technical and vocational education, higher education, adult, non-formal and permanent education, population education, and education of women and girls. 1990 was 'International Literacy Year', in the course of which a world conference on 'Education for All' was held in Thailand. In addition to its regular programme budget, UNESCO's extra-budgetary sources include the World Bank, UNDP, UNFPA, UNICEF, etc.

NATURAL SCIENCES

UNESCO's activities under the programme The Sciences in the Service of Development aim to support and foster its member states' endeavours in higher education, advanced training and research in the natural sciences as well as in the application of these sciences to development, while at the same time attaching great importance to integrated and transdisiplinary approaches in its programmes. Activities in the natural sciences focus on the advancement, sharing and transfer of scientific and technological knowledge. At the same time, UNESCO continues to enhance human resources development and capacity building through fellowships, grants, workshops, and seminars, and has produced a number of training tools. At national level, upon request, UNESCO also assists member states in policy-making and planning in the field of science and technology generally, and by organizing training programmes in these fields.

At the international level, UNESCO has over the years set up various forms of intergovernmental co-operation concerned with the environmental sciences and research on natural resources.

The Man and Biosphere Programme (MAB) gives emphasis to the reinforcement of the World Network of Biosphere Reserves, which aims to reconcile the conservation of biodiversity, the quest for social and economic development and the maintenance of associated cultural values. The Man and the Biosphere Programme also promotes an interdisciplinary approach to solving land-use problems through research and training, covering topics such as arid-land crops, sacred sites, coastal regions, the Sahel-Sahara observatories and the biology and fertility of tropical soils.

The International Geological Correlation Programme (IGCP), networking in more than 150 countries, contributes to comparative studies in earth sciences, including the history of the earth and its geologial heritage. Geoscientific programmes have resulted in the production of thematic geological maps, postgraduate training, the application of remote sensing and geodata handling,and studies on climate change and industrial pollution. Guidelines and other awareness-building material on disaster prevention, preparedness and mitigation are also prepared.

The International Hydrological Programme (IHP) deals with the scientific aspects of water resources assessment and management; and the Intergovernmental Oceanographic Commission (IOC) (*q.v.*) promotes scientific investigation into the nature and resources of the oceans through the concerted action of its member states.

UNESCO provides the secretariat for the World Solar Programme (instituted in 1996) and has been designated lead agency for the Global Renewable Energy Education and Training Programme.

Major disciplinary programmes are promoted in the fields of physics (including support to the Abdus Salam Centre for Theoretical Physics), the chemical sciences, life sciences, including applied microbiology, mathematics, informatics, engineering sciences and new sources of energy.

SOCIAL AND HUMAN SCIENCES

UNESCO promotes teaching and research in the field of social and human sciences and encourages their application to a number of priority issues relating to education, development, urbanization, migration, youth, human rights, democracy and peace. The social sciences constitute a link between the Organization's two main functions: international intellectual co-operation leading to reflection on major problems, and action to solve these problems.

Among the Organization's subjects of research are the complex relations between demographic changes and socio-cultural transformation on a global scale; the ways in which societies react to global climatic and environmental change; and changes affecting women and families.

UNESCO's programme gives high priority to the problems of young people who are the first victims of unemployment, economic and social inequalities and the widening gap between developing and industrialized countries. Under the mobilizing project 'Youth shaping the Future', an International Youth Clearing House and Information Service was to be established in order to increase awareness among public and private decision-makers of the needs, aspirations and potential of young people.

The struggle against all forms of discrimination is a central part of the Organization's programme. It disseminates scientific information aimed at combating racial prejudice, works to improve the status of women and their access to education, and promotes equality between men and women.

CULTURE

In the field of cultural heritage, the programme concentrates on three major lines of action: activities designed to foster the world-wide application of three international conventions aiming at protecting and preserving cultural property and inserting it into the life of contemporary societies; operational activities such as international safeguarding campaigns designed to help member states to conserve and restore monuments and sites; activities designed to improve the quality of museum management, to train specialists, to disseminate information, such as the most up-to-date conservation methods and techniques, and to promote greater public awareness of the value of cultural heritage.

In addition to a new edition of the *History of the Scientific and Cultural Development of Mankind,* work is continuing on histories of Africa, Latin America, the Caribbean and the civilizations of Central Asia, as well as on a six-volume publication on the various aspects of Islamic culture. A 10-year programme for the collection and safeguarding of the non-physical heritage (oral traditions, traditional music, dance, medicine, etc.) was launched in 1988.

With respect to the cultural dimension of development, the programme includes continuing assistance to member states in the preparation and evaluation of cultural development policies, plans and projects and in the training of cultural development personnel. Proclaimed by the UN General Assembly in December 1986, the World Decade for Cultural Development was launched in January 1988 and was to end in 1997. The principal objectives of the Decade are: acknowledging the cultural dimension in development; asserting and enhancing cultural identities; broadening participation in cultural life; and promoting international cultural co-operation.

Following the approval by the General Conference of the Recommendation concerning the Status of the Artist, efforts are being made to encourage its systematic application in the member states. Particular attention is given to the promotion of music, dance, theatre, architecture, fine arts, design and arts and crafts, as well as the organization of interdisciplinary workshops and other experimental workshops related to the use of new technologies in artistic creation. To contribute to the mutual appreciation of cultures, UNESCO fosters, in the framework of the UNESCO Collection of Representative Works, translation and publication of literary masterpieces, publishes art albums, and produces and disseminates records, cassettes, audio-visual programmes and travelling art exhibitions.

UNESCO's programme for the promotion of books and reading includes activities for the development of book publishing, production and distribution infrastructures as well as for the training of personnel in all the book fields (including editing, layout and design, ad hoc management courses and courses at university level). A major thrust of the programme is aimed at reinforcing the development of reading at all levels of society (and especially that of children) through promotional activities, reading animation programmes, book weeks and book years.

COPYRIGHT

UNESCO's programme in the field of copyright consists of the following types of activities: (i) those aimed at heightening member states' awareness of the role played by copyright as a stimulant to intellectual creativity; (ii) the preparation of international instruments, the implementation of which is assured by the Secretariat (among these instruments should be cited the Universal Copyright Convention which, guaranteeing the minimal protection of authors, facilitates the circulation of intellectual and cultural materials); (iii) activities intended to ensure the adequacy of traditional laws vis-à-vis the means of reproduction and of successive diffusion made possible by the latest technological revolutions in the field of reprography, satellites, computers, cable television, cassettes and magnetic discs; (iv) the organization of individual or group training courses intended mainly for the nationals of developing countries; (v) activities to promote access to protected works; (vi) publications and a database on legislation for copyright specialists; (vii) production of a video to increase public awareness of the importance of copyright.

COMMUNICATION, INFORMATION AND INFORMATICS

UNESCO's Communication, Information and Informatics Programme is designed to encourage the free flow of ideas and to help reinforce communication, information and informatics capacities in developing countries. Its major innovation is the extension of the "free flow" principle to all forms of information contributing to the progress of societies, coupled with a comprehensive approach to challenges posed by the converging communication, information and informatics technologies.

Priorities in the area of communication include support for press freedom and the independence and pluralism of the media, reflection on their educational and cultural dimensions and efforts to reduce violence on the screen. A series of regional seminars on independence and pluralism of the media has resulted in the declarations and plans of action adopted by those fora being implemented in collaboration with professional media organizations. Furthermore, World Press Freedom Day, initiated by UNESCO in commemoration of the Windhoek Declaration, is celebrated every year on 3 May. UNESCO supports the Internatonal Freedom of Expression Exchange network (IFEX), which counts some 260 subscribers committed to protecting press freedom and the safety of journalists. The network of UNESCO Chairs in Communication (ORBICOM), which counts sixteen chairs in all regions of the world, provides an enlarged framework for co-operation among media practitioners, researchers and industries. UNESCO also supports the Global Network of Journalism Training (JOURNET) and the International Network of Women in the Media (WOMMED). The main operational arm of UNESCO's communication strategy, and a major funding channel, is the International Programme for the Development of Communication (IPDC) which focuses on strengthening news agencies, media training, community media and endogenous audiovisual production in developing countries. Since 1992, IPDC has given priority to projects in favour of independent and pluralist media. The Programme is governed by a Council of 39 member states.

The General Information Programme (PGI) pursues its efforts to promote international co-operation in the fields of libraries, archives and documentation, with emphasis on appropriate policies, in particular for the widest possible access to information in the public domain, and for methodologies and tools for information management. Among recent initiatives is the launching of the UNESCO Network of Associated Libraries (UNAL) which already includes some 300 members. The Memory of the World Programme aims at safeguarding the recorded memory of humanity, with a number of pilot projects under way in different countries. Furthermore, UNESCO organizes international aid campaigns in this field, such as the programme for the restoration of the National and University Library of Bosnia and Herzegovina. PGI's enlarged mandate covers trends and societal impacts of information technologies. The International Congress on Ethical, Legal and Societal Aspects of Digital Information (InfoEthics), held for the first time in Monte Carlo in March 1997, provided a forum for reflection and debate in this field.

UNESCO also supports the development of computer networking and the training of informatics specialists, through its Intergovernmental Informatics Programme (IIP). UNESCO-sponsored regional informatics networks—RINAF (Africa), RINAS (Arab States), RINSCA and RINSEAP (Asia/Pacific) and RINEE (Eastern Europe)—serve as test grounds for effective networking options, including links to the Internet.

PUBLICATIONS

UNESCO Courier: monthly illustrated journal devoted to the general interest of UNESCO; published in 32 languages.

UNESCO Sources: monthly, giving official information, records of meetings, reports, and articles on UNESCO's programme, etc.; English, French, Portuguese and Spanish.

Copyright Bulletin: quarterly review of special studies and documentation on the legislation in different countries, and on UNESCO's work on behalf of the harmonization of the various copyright laws; English, French, Spanish and Russian.

Museum: quarterly international review of museums and museology around the world; English, French, Spanish, Russian and Arabic.

International Social Science Journal: quarterly journal; English, French, Spanish, Arabic and Chinese.

Nature and Resources: quarterly review on environment and conservation; official bulletin of the Man and Biosphere Programme, the International Hydrological Programme and the International Geological Correlation Programme; English, French, Spanish, Russian.

Prospects: quarterly review on education; English, French, Spanish, Russian, Arabic and Chinese.

INTERNATIONAL INSTITUTE FOR EDUCATIONAL PLANNING (IIEP)

7–9 rue Eugène Delacroix, 75116 Paris, France

Telephone: 1-45-03-77-00
Fax: 1-40-72-83-66
E-mail: information@iiep.unesco.org

Established by UNESCO in 1963 to serve as a world centre for advanced training and research in educational planning. Its purpose is to help all member states of UNESCO in their social and economic development efforts, by enlarging the fund of knowledge about educational planning and the supply of competent experts in this field.

Legally and administratively a part of UNESCO, the Institute enjoys intellectual autonomy, and its policies and programme are controlled by its own Governing Board, under special statutes voted by the General Conference of UNESCO.

Chairman of Governing Board: Prof. LENNART WOHLGEMUTH.

Director: JACQUES HALLAK.

A catalogue of publications, listing 440 titles, is available on request.

INTERNATIONAL BUREAU OF EDUCATION (IBE)

CP 199, 1211 Geneva 20, Switzerland

Telephone: (22) 917-78-00
Telex: 415771
Fax: (22) 917-78-01
E-mail: doc.centre@ibe.unesco.org

Founded in 1925, the IBE became an intergovernmental organization in July 1929 and was incorporated into UNESCO in January 1969 as an international centre of comparative education.

COUNCIL

The Council of the IBE is composed of representatives of 28 member states designated by the General Conference of UNESCO.

Director: JACQUES HALLAK.

FUNCTIONS

International Conference on Education (irregular).

International Education Library: 120,000 vols; some 1,000 journals received regularly; 500,000 research reports on microfiche.

BUDGET

Financed from the budget of UNESCO.

PUBLICATIONS

Prospects, international comparative education review (quarterly).

Educational Innovation and Information (quarterly newsletter).

UNITED NATIONS UNIVERSITY

53—70, Jingumae 5-chome, Shibuya-ku, Tokyo 150, Japan

Telephone: (3) 3499-2811
Fax: (3) 3499-2828
E-mail: mbox@hq.unv.edu

(Office in Europe: c/o UNESCO, 1 rue Miollis, 75732 Paris Cedex 15, France; tel. (1) 45-68-30-08; telex 270602; fax 40-65-91-86)
(Office in North America: Room DC2-1462-70, United Nations, New York, NY 10017, USA; tel. (212) 963-6387; telex 422311; fax (212) 371-9454)

The University is an autonomous institution within the UN framework and is sponsored jointly by UN and UNESCO. It is guaranteed academic freedom by a charter approved by the General Assembly in 1973. Its work began in September 1975. The UNU is governed by a 24-mem. Council who are appointed by the Sec.-Gen. of the UN and the Dir-Gen. of UNESCO to serve for six years. They come from various regions of the world and have diverse academic backgrounds.

The UNU is funded by voluntary contributions from the govts of many countries, bilateral and multilateral development assistance agencies, foundations, and other public and private sources. The UNU receives no funds from the regular budget of the UN; contributions are made to the UNU Endowment Fund, which yields investment income, and to its operating funds, as well as to specific programmes and projects.

The UNU undertakes problem-oriented, multidisciplinary research on the problems of human survival, development and welfare that are the concern of the UN and its agencies, and works to strengthen research and training capabilities in developing countries. The programme covers the areas of peace and governance, development, environment, and science and technology. Although the UNU has no students or degree courses, it conducts various training activities in association with its programme and provides fellowships for post-graduate scientists and scholars from developing countries.

The research, training and dissemination activities of the UNU are carried out mainly through networks of collaborating institutions and individual scientists and scholars. These include associated institutions, which are universities and research institutes linked with the University under general agreements of co-operation. The programme is co-ordinated by the University Centre in Tokyo and by research and training centres and programmes (RTC/Ps) that are being established by the UNU to deal with long-term problems and needs. By 1997, eight RTC/Ps had been established: the UNU World Institute for Development Economics Research (UNU/WIDER) in Helsinki, Finland (1985); the UNU Institute for New Technologies (UNU/INTECH) in Maastricht, Netherlands (1990); the UNU International Institute for Software Technology (UNU/IIST) in Macau (1992); the UNU Institute for Natural Resources in Africa (UNU/INRA) in Accra, Ghana, with a mineral resources unit in Lusaka, Zambia (1990); the UNU Institute of Advanced Studies (UNU/IAS) in Tokyo, Japan (1996); the UNU Programme for Biotechnology in Latin America and the Caribbean (UNU/BIOLAC) in Caracas, Venezuela (1988); the UNU International Leadership Academy (UNU/ILA) in Amman, Jordan (1995); and the UNU International Network on Water, Environment and Health (UNU/INWEH) in Ontario, Canada (1996).

Rector: Prof. HANS J. A. VAN GINKEL.

Vice-Rector: Dr ABRAHAM BESRAT (acting).

Chairman of Council: Prof. JOSÉ JOAQUÍN BRUNNER RIED.

UNIVERSITY FOR PEACE

Apdo postal 138, Ciudad Colón, Costa Rica

Telephone: 2-49-10-72
Fax: 2-49-19-29

Founded 1980 by the UN but financially independent; will conduct academic research on all aspects of peace, including disarmament, conflict resolution and mediation, the relation between peace and development, and the effects on peace of migration and refugees; various int. and governmental institutions are collaborating with the university; library of 8,000 vols; first students were admitted in 1985.

Rector: Dr JAIME MONTALVO CORREA
Vice-Rector: Dr FRANCISCO BARAHONA RIERA

Number of teachers: 16
Number of students: 25

Publications: *Dialogue* (in Spanish and English), *Infopaz.*

INTERNATIONAL COUNCIL OF SCIENTIFIC UNIONS

International Council of Scientific Unions/Conseil international des unions scientifiques: 51 blvd de Montmorency, 75016 Paris, France; tel. 1-45-25-03-29; telex 645554; fax 1-42-88-94-31; ICSU was founded in 1931, succeeding the International Research Council founded in 1919, to co-ordinate international efforts in the different branches of science and its applications; to initiate the formation of international associations or unions deemed to be useful to the progress of science; to enter into relations with the governments of the countries adhering to the Council in order to promote investigations falling within the competence of the Council. Adhering organizations represent 95 countries and 25 international unions. In December 1946 an agreement was signed between UNESCO and ICSU recognizing the latter as the co-ordinating and representative body of international scientific unions; Pres. W. Arber; Vice-Pres D. A. Akyeampong, J. Palis; Sec.-Gen. H. Mooney; Treas. Y. Verhasselt; publs *ICSU Year Book*, *Science International* (quarterly).

UNION REPRESENTATIVES

IAU	J. Andersen
IUGG	P. J. Wyllie
URSI	T. B. A. Senior
IUPAC	A. E. Fischli
IUPAP	J. S. Nilsson
IGU	B. Messerli
IUBS	J.-C. Mounolou
IUHPS	R. Halleux
IUCr	P. Coppens
IUTAM	W. Schiehlen
IMU	S. Mori
IUBMB	Y. Anraku
IUPS	E. Weibel
IUGS	R. Brett
IUPAB	A. C. T. North
IUNS	B. A. Underwood
IUPHAR	S. Ebashi
IUIS	H. Metzger
IUMS	R. Mäkelä
IUPsyS	G. D'Ydewalle
IBRO	C. Belmonte
ISSS	W. E. H. Blum
IUAES	E. Sunderland
IUFoST	D. E. Hood
IUTOX	C. D. Klaassen

NATIONAL REPRESENTATIVES

S. Bauer	Austria
D. Ben Sari	Morocco
K. Birkenmajer	Poland
U. G. Cordani	Brazil
S. K. A. Danso	Ghana
J. Engelbrecht	Estonia
J. E. Fenstad	Norway
C. G. Gahmberg	Finland
F. Gros	France
H. Kleinkauf	Germany
A. McLaren	UK
M. K. Mahmoud	Egypt
I. M. Makarov	Russia
K. Mokhele	South Africa
H. Ohashi	Japan
G. I. Pearman	Australia
A. Peña	Mexico
Qian Yi	China
M. Rabin	Israel
C. N. R. Rao	India
F. S. Rowland	USA
I. Saavedra	Chile
J. Slotova	Czech Rep.
I. Smith	Canada
S. Wandiga	Kenya

UNIONS FEDERATED TO THE ICSU

International Astronomical Union/Union astronomique internationale: 98 bis blvd Arago, 75014 Paris, France; tel. (1) 43-25-83-58; fax (1) 43-25-26-16; f. 1919 to facilitate co-operation between the astronomers of various countries and to further the study of astronomy in all its branches; 60 affiliated countries, 8,500 individual mems; Pres. R. Kraft (USA); Gen. Sec. H. Rickman (Sweden); publs *Transactions of the International Astronomical Union and Symposia organized by the International Astronomical Union.*

International Geographical Union (IGU)/ Union géographique internationale: f. 1922 to encourage the study of problems relating to geography, to promote and co-ordinate research requiring international co-operation, and to organize international congresses and commissions; 83 mem. countries; Pres. Prof. Bruno Messerli (Switzerland); Sec.-Treas. Prof. E. Ehlers, Dept of Geography, University of Bonn, Meckenheimer Allee 166, 53115 Bonn, Germany; tel. (228) 739287; fax (228) 739272; e-mail secretariat@igu.bn.eunet.de; publ. *IGU Bulletin* (2 a year).

International Mathematical Union: Instituto de Matemática Pura e Aplicada, Estrada Dona Castorina 110, 22.460 Jardim Botânico, Rio de Janeiro, RJ, Brazil; tel. (21) 294-9032; fax (21) 512-4112; f. 1950 to promote international co-operation in mathematics; to support and assist the International Congress of Mathematicians and other international scientific meetings or conferences; to encourage and support other international mathematical activities considered likely to contribute to the development of mathematical science—pure, applied, or educational; 52 mem. countries; 2 commissions: Int. Comm. on Mathematical Instruction, Comm. for Development and Exchange; Joint Int. Comm. on the History of Mathematics, with the Int. Comm. on the History of Mathematics; Pres. Prof. J. L. Lions; Sec.-Gen. Prof. J. Palis.

International Union for Pure and Applied Biophysics: School of Biochemistry and Molecular Biology, The University of Leeds, Leeds LS2 9JT, England; tel. (113) 233 3023; fax (113) 233 3167; f. 1961 to organize international co-operation in biophysics and promote communication between biophysics and allied subjects, to encourage national co-operation between biophysical societies, and to contribute to the advancement of biophysical knowledge; mems: adhering bodies in 45 countries; Pres. D. A. D. Parry (New Zealand); Sec.-Gen. Prof. A. C. T. North (U.K.); publ. *Quarterly Reviews of Biophysics*.

International Union of Biochemistry and Molecular Biology: c/o Dr. F. Vella, 18 Leyden Crescent, Saskatoon, SK S7J 2S4, Canada; tel. (306) 374-1304; fax (306) 955-1314; e-mail f.vella@sk.simpatico.ca; f. 1955 (a) to encourage the continuance of a series of International Congresses and Conferences of Biochemistry and Molecular Biology, (b) to promote international co-ordination of research, discussion and publication, (c) to organize a permanent co-operation between the societies representing biochemistry in the adherent countries, and (d) to contribute to the advancement of biochemistry in all its international aspects; 46 adhering bodies, 15 assoc. adhering bodies, five assoc. organizations; Pres. Prof. W. J. Whelan (USA); Sec.-Gen. Dr. F. Vella (Canada) (acting); Treas. Prof. R. Brian Beechey (UK).

International Union of Biological Sciences/Union internationale des sciences biologiques: 51 blvd de Montmorency, 75016 Paris, France; tel. (1) 45-25-00-09; telex 645554; fax (1) 45-25-20-29; f. 1919 for the promotion of international co-operation in biology; 41 countries and 83 int. scientific organizations are represented; Exec. Dir Dr T. Younès; publs *Biology International—The IUBS News Magazine* (2 a year) and *Special Issues*.

International Union of Crystallography/ Union internationale de cristallographie: f. 1947 to promote international co-operation in crystallography; to contribute to the advancement of crystallography in all its aspects, including related topics concerning the non-crystalline states; to facilitate international standardization of methods, of units, of nomenclature and of symbols used in crystallography; and to form a focus for the relations of crystallography to other sciences; 40 mem. countries; 17 commissions; Pres. Prof. E. N. Baker (New Zealand); Gen. Sec. and Treas. Prof. S. Larsen (Denmark); Exec. Sec. M. H. Dacombe, 2 Abbey Square, Chester, CH1 2HU, England; tel. (1244) 345431; fax (1244) 344843; e-mail execsec@iucr.org; publs *Acta Crystallographica*, Section A (every 2 months), Section B (every 2 months), Section C (monthly), Section D (every 2 months), *Journal of Applied Crystallography* (every 2 months), *Journal of Synchrotron Radiation* (every 2 months), *International Tables for Crystallography, World Directory of Crystallographers*.

International Union of Geodesy and Geophysics/Union géodésique et géophysique internationale: C/o Bureau Gravimétrique International (Attn. Dr G. Balmino), Ave E. Belin 18, 31401 Toulouse Cedex 4, France; tel. 5-61-33-29-80; fax 5-61-25-30-98; f. 1919 to promote the study of problems relating to the form and physics of the earth; to initiate, facilitate and co-ordinate research into those problems of geodesy and geophysics which require international co-operation; to provide for discussion, comparison and publication. The Union is a federation of 7 associations representing Geodesy, Seismology and Physics of the Earth's Interior, Physical Sciences of the Ocean, Volcanology and Chemistry of the Earth's Interior, Hydrological Sciences, Meteorology and Atmospheric Physics, Geomagnetism and Aeronomy, which meet at the General Assemblies of the Union. In addition, there are Joint Committees of the various associations either among themselves or with other unions. The Union organizes scientific meetings and also sponsors various permanent services, the object of which is to collect, analyse and publish geophysical data; 76 mem. countries; Pres. P. J. Wyllie (USA); Vice-Pres. U. Shamir (Israel); Sec.-Gen. G. Balmino (France); publs *IUGG Year-book, IUGG Monographs* (irregular), *Proceedings of Assemblies*; in addition each member association has its own series of publs.

International Union of Geological Sciences/Union internationale des sciences géologiques: IUGS Secretariat, Geological Survey of Norway, Lade, POB 3006 Lade, 7002 Trondheim, Norway; tel. 73-92-15-00; fax 73-50-22-30; e-mail iugs.secretariat@ngu.no; f. 1961 as an offspring of the International Geological Congress; mems from 110 countries; Pres. Dr Robin Brett (USA); Vice-Pres. Dr Vilen A. Zharikov (Russia), Dr Liu Dunyi (People's Republic of China), Dr Francisco Hervé A. (Chile), Dr Gabor Gáal (Hungary), Dr Ian G. Speden (New Zealand), Dr Isaac Nyambok (Kenya), Dr Wissan al-Hashimi (Iraq); Sec.-Gen. Dr Attilio Carlo Boriani (Italy); publs *Episodes, International Geoscience Newsmagazine* (quarterly), Reviews or Annotated bibliographies on geological topics of current interest (irregular).

International Union of Immunological Societies (IUIS)/Union Internationale des Sociétés d'Immunologie: Lister Research Laboratories, University Dept of Surgery, Royal Infirmary, Lauriston Place, Edinburgh, EH3 9YW, Scotland, tel. (131) 536-3826; fax (131) 667-6190; 50 national and regional societies; Pres. Tomio Tada (Japan); Sec.-Gen. Prof. Keith James (UK).

International Union of Microbiological Societies (IUMS)/Union internationale des sociétés de microbiologie: Institut de Biologie Moléculaire et Cellulaire du CNRS, 15 rue Descartes, 67084 Strasbourg Cedex, France; tel. 3-88-41-70-22; fax 3-88-61-06-80; f. 1930; mems: 90 national societies; Sec.-Gen. Marc H. V. Van Regenmortel (France); publs *International Journal of Systematic Bacteriology* (quarterly), *The World Journal of Microbiology and Biotechnology* (every 2 months), *Archives of Virology* (every 2 months), *International Journal of Food Microbiology* (every 2 months), *Advances in Microbial Ecology* (annually), *Journal of Biological Standardisation* (quarterly).

International Union of Nutritional Sciences (IUNS)/Union Internationale des Sciences de la Nutrition: f. 1946 to study the science of nutrition and its applications; 64 corporate mems; Pres. Prof. A. Valyasevi (Thailand); Vice-Pres. Prof. A. A. Rérat (France), Prof. S. Berger (Poland), Dr Vinodini Reddy (India); Sec.-Gen. Prof. Dr J. G. A. J. Hautvast, c/o Dept of Human Nutrition, Agricultural Univ., Bomenweg 2, POB 8129, 6700 EV Wageningen, Netherlands; tel. (8370) 82589; fax (8370) 83342; Treas. Prof. E. Menden (Germany).

International Union of Pharmacology (IUPHAR)/Union Internationale de Pharmacologie: f. 1959 as section of Int. Union of Physiological Sciences, independent 1966; promotes international co-ordination of research, discussion, symposia, and publication in the field of pharmacology; co-operates with WHO in matters concerning drugs and drug research, and with related international unions; four-yearly international congresses; 52 national and 3 regional mem. socs; integral Division of Clinical Pharmacology and sections of Toxicology, Drug Metabolism and Gastrointestinal Pharmacology, which also arrange international meetings; Pres. T. Godfraind (Belgium); Sec.-Gen. W. C. Bowman, Dept of Physiology and Pharmacology, University of Strathclyde, Glasgow, G1 1XW, Scotland; tel. (141) 552-4400; fax (141) 552-2562.

International Union of Physiological Sciences: c/o S. Orsoni, LGN, Bâtiment CERVI, Hôpital de la Pitié Salpêtrière, 83 blvd de l'Hôpital, 75013 Paris, France; tel. 1-42-17-75-37; fax 1-42-17-75-75; e-mail Suorsoni@infobiogen.fr; f. 1953 to encourage the advancement of physiological sciences, to facilitate the dissemination of knowledge in the field of physiology, to promote the International Congresses of Physiology and such other meetings as may be useful for the advancement of physiological sciences; 54 mem. countries; Pres. Masao Ito (Japan); Sec.-Gen. Denis Noble (UK); publs *News in Physiological Sciences* (quarterly), *World Directory of Physiologists* (every 4 years).

International Union of Psychological Science/Union internationale de psychologie scientifique: f. 1951 at the 13th International Congress of Psychology (the first of which took place in 1889); congresses are held every four years; membership: 58 national societies or cttees of psychology; Pres. Kurt Pawlik (Germany); Sec.-Gen. Géry d'Ydewalle, Dept of Psychology, University of Leuven, 3000 Leuven, Belgium; tel. (16) 32-59-64; fax (16) 32-60-99.

International Union of Pure and Applied Chemistry (IUPAC)/Union internationale de chimie pure et appliquée: POB 13757, Research Triangle Park, NC 27709-3757, USA; tel. (919) 485-8700; fax (919) 485-8706; e-mail secretariat@iupac.org; f. 1919 to promote continuing co-operation among the chemists of the member countries; to study topics of international importance which require regulation, standardization or codification; to co-operate with other international organizations which deal with topics of a chemical nature; to contribute to the advancement of pure and applied chemistry in all its aspects; 45 mem. countries; Pres. J. Jortner (Israel); Sec.-Gen. E. D. Becker (USA); publs *Pure and Applied Chemistry* (monthly), *Chemistry International* (every 2 months).

International Union of Pure and Applied Physics (IUPAP)/Union internationale de physique pure et appliquée: f. 1922 to promote and encourage international co-operation in physics; 45 countries are affiliated; 19 international commissions; Pres. Prof. Y. Yamaguchi (INS); Sec.-Gen. Dr René Turlay, CEN Sacley, 91191 Gif-sur-Yvette Cedex, France; tel. 1-69-08-84-18; fax 1-69-08-76-36; publ. *IUPAP News Bulletin* (5 or 6 a year).

International Union of Radio Science/Union radio-scientifique internationale: c/o University of Ghent (INTEC), Sint-Pietersnieuwstraat 41, 9000 Ghent, Belgium; tel. 9-264.33.20; fax 9-264.42.88; e-mail heleu@intec.rug.ac.be; f. 1919; stimulates and co-ordinates research in the field of radio, telecommunication and electronic sciences, and facilitates the establishment of common radio measurement techniques and standards; there are 45 national committees; Pres. T. B. A. Senior (USA); Sec.-Gen. P. Lagasse (Belgium); publs *Proceedings of General Assemblies* (every 3 years), *Modern Radio Science* (every 3 years), *Review of Radio Science* (every 3 years), *The Radio Science Bulletin* (quarterly).

International Union of the History and Philosophy of Science: C/o Prof. Robert Halleux, 15 ave des Tilleuls, 4000 Liège, Belgium; tel. (4) 366-94-79; fax (4) 366-94-47; e-mail chst@ulg.ac.be; f. 1956; divisions of History of Science and of Logic, Methodology and Philosophy of Science; Sec.-Gen. Robert Halleux.

International Union of Theoretical and Applied Mechanics/Union Internationale de Mécanique Théorique et Appliquée: f. 1946 to form a link between persons and organizations engaged in scientific work (theoretical or experimental) in mechanics or in related sciences; to organize international meetings for subjects falling within this field; and to engage in other activities meant to promote the development of mechanics as a science; 49 mem. countries; the Union is directed by its General Assembly, which is composed of representatives of the organizations adhering and affiliated to the Union and of elected mems; Pres. Prof. Werner Schiehlen (Germany); Sec.-Gen. Prof. Michael A. Hayes, Mathematical Physics Dept, University College Dublin, Belfield, Dublin 4, Ireland; fax (1) 706-1172; e-mail iutam@ucd.ie; publs *Annual Report, Newsletter* (irregular).

COMMITTEES

Tasks which fall within the sphere of activities of two or more Unions have been undertaken by the following Scientific or Special Committees set up by the ICSU:

Committee on Capacity Building in Science (CCBS): f. 1993; aims to promote to the public and to decision-makers an understanding and appreciation of the proper role of science in modern society and to provide science education information to primary school teachers worldwide; Chair L. Lederman, CCBS, Fermilab, POB 500 m/s 105, Kirk and Pine Rds, Batavia, IL 60510-0500, USA; fax (630) 840-8752.

Committee on Data for Science and Technology (CODATA): f. 1966 by ICSU to improve the quality, reliability and accessibility of scientific data, including not only quantitative information on the properties and behaviour of matter, but also other experimental and observational data; 19 national and 15 scientific union mems; Pres. Prof. D. Abir (Israel); Secretariat: Phyllis Glaeser, 51 blvd de Montmorency, 75016 Paris, France; tel. (1) 4525-0496; telex 645554; fax (1) 42-88-14-66; publs *CODATA Newsletter* (quarterly), *International Compendium of Numerical Data Projects, International Conference Proceedings.*

Committee on Science and Technology in Developing Countries and International Biosciences Networks (COSTED-IBN): 24 Gandhi Mandap Rd, Madras 600025, India; tel. 4901367; fax 4914543; e-mail costed@giasmd01.vsnl.net.in; f. 1966 (reconstituted 1972, 1993) for the encouragement of science and technology in developing countries, the organization of meetings, seminars and symposia related to science teaching and natural resources, and the identification of problems of relevance to developing countries; 23 national mems; Chair. Dr Rodney Nichols (USA); Scientific Sec. Dr G. Thyagarajan (India); publ. *COSTED–IBN News* (3 a year).

Committee on Space Research (COSPAR): 51 blvd de Montmorency, 75016 Paris, France; tel. (1) 45-25-06-79; fax 40-50-98-27; f. 1958 to monitor the progress of all kinds of scientific investigations carried out with space vehicles, rockets and balloons; Pres. Prof. Dr Haerendel (Germany); Exec. Dir Prof. S. Grzedzielski; publs *COSPAR Information Bulletin* (3 a year), *International Reference Atmosphere Tables, COSPAR Directory of Organization and members* (every 2 years), *Proceedings of COSPAR Scientific Assemblies* (in *Advances in Space Research*), *Proceedings of COSPAR Colloquia* (in *COSPAR Colloquia Series*).

Scientific Committee on Antarctic Research (SCAR): f. 1958 by ICSU after the close of the International Geophysical Year to continue the promotion of international co-operation in scientific research in the Antarctic; mems: 24 countries; Pres. Prof. A. C. Rocha-Campos; Exec. Sec. Dr P. D. Clarkson, SCAR, c/o Scott Polar Research Institute, Cambridge, CB2 1ER, England; tel. (1223) 362061; fax (1223) 336549; e-mail execsec@scar.demon.co.uk; publ. *SCAR Bulletin* (quarterly).

Scientific Committee on Oceanic Research (SCOR): f. 1957 to further international scientific activity in all branches of oceanic research; scientific advisory body to UNESCO and to Intergovernmental Oceanographic Commission; mems: nominated mems by Cttees for Oceanic Research in 39 countries; rep. mems of affiliated organizations; invited mems by the exec. cttee; approx. 25 active working Groups, Cttees and Panels are investigating a broad range of oceanographic problems; Pres. Prof. J. G. Field (South Africa); Sec. Prof. B. Sundby (Canada); Exec. Dir Mrs E. Gross, Dept of Earth and Planetary Sciences, Johns Hopkins University, Baltimore, MD 21218, USA; tel. (410) 516-4070; fax (410) 516-4019; e-mail scor@jhu.edu; publ. *SCOR Proceedings* (irregular).

Scientific Committee on Problems of the Environment (SCOPE): 51 blvd de Montmorency, 75016 Paris, France; tel. 1-45-25-04-98; fax 1-42-88-14-66; e-mail scope@paris7.jussieu.fr; f. 1969; interdisciplinary research in environmental field; mems: 39 Nat. Cttees and 23 International Unions; Pres. Prof. Ph. Bourdeau (Belgium); publs *SCOPE Newsletter, SCOPE Reports.*

Scientific Committee on Solar-Terrestrial Physics (SCOSTEP): an Inter-Union

Commission f. 1966 by ICSU that became a Scientific Cttee in 1978 to promote and co-ordinate international interdisciplinary programmes in solar-terrestrial physics and to work with other ICSU bodies in the co-ordination of symposia in the field of solar-terrestrial physics; 300 mems; Pres. Prof. C. H. LIU (Taiwan); Sec. J. H. ALLEN (USA), C/o NOAA/NGDC, 325 Broadway, Boulder, CO 80303, USA; tel. (303) 497-7284; fax (303) 497-6513; e-mail jallen@ngdc.noaa.gov.

SERVICES AND INTER-UNION COMMISSIONS

Federation of Astronomical and Geophysical Data Analysis Services (FAGS): f. 1956; federates the following Permanent Services: International Earth Rotation Service, Bureau Gravimetrique International, International GPS Service for Geodynamics, International Center for Earth Tides, Permanent Service for Mean Sea Level, International Service of Geomagnetic Indices, Quarterly Bulletin of Solar Activity, International Space Environment Service, World Glacier Monitoring Service, Centre des Données Stellaires, Sunspot Index Data Center; Pres. Dr O. B. ANDERSEN; Sec. Prof. Dr H.-G. WENZEL, Geodätisches Institut, Universität Karlsruhe, Englerstr. 7, 76128 Karlsruhe, Germany; e-mail wenzel@gik.bau-verm.uni-karlsruhe.de.

Inter-Union Commission on Frequency Allocations for Radio Astronomy and Space Science (IUCAF): f. 1960 under auspices of URSI with representatives of URSI, IAU and COSPAR, to study the requirements for frequency bands and radio frequency protection for research in the fields of radio astronomy, earth exploration and space science, to make their requirements known to the appropriate frequency-allocation authorities; 10 mems; Chair. Dr W. A. BAAN, NAIC, Arecibo University, POB 995, Arecibo, PR 00613, Puerto Rico; tel. (809) 878-2612; fax (809) 878-1861.

INTERNATIONAL COUNCIL FOR PHILOSOPHY AND HUMANISTIC STUDIES

International Council for Philosophy and Humanistic Studies (ICPHS)/Conseil international de la philosophie et des sciences humaines: Secretariat: Maison de l'UNESCO, 1 rue Miollis, 75732 Paris Cedex 15, France; tel. 45-68-26-85; f. 1949 under the auspices of UNESCO to encourage respect for cultural autonomy by the comparative study of civilization, to contribute towards international understanding through a better knowledge of man, to develop international co-operation in philosophy, humanistic and kindred studies, to encourage the setting up of international organizations, to promote the dissemination of information in these fields, to sponsor works of learning, etc.; the Council is composed of 13 international non-governmental organizations listed below; these organizations represent 145 countries; in 1951 an agreement was signed between UNESCO and ICPHS recognizing the latter as the co-ordinating and representative body of organizations in the field of philosophy and humanistic studies; Pres. Prof. JULIO LABASTIDA MARTIN DEL CAMPO (Mexico); Sec.-Gen. Prof. JEAN BINGEN (Belgium); publs *Bulletin of Information* (every 2 years), *Diogenes* (quarterly).

UNIONS FEDERATED TO THE ICPHS

International Academic Union/Union académique internationale: Palais des Académies, 1 rue Ducale, 1000 Brussels, Belgium; tel. 550-22-00; fax 550-22-05; f. 1919 to promote international co-operation through collective research in philology, archaeology, history and social sciences; affiliated countries: Argentina, Australia, Austria, Belgium, Canada, China, Croatia, Czech Republic, Denmark, Egypt, Finland, France, Germany, Ghana, Greece, Hungary, India, Iran, Ireland, Israel, Italy, Japan, Repub. of Korea, Latvia, Luxembourg, Mexico, Morocco, The Netherlands, Norway, Poland, Portugal, Romania, Serbia, Slovakia, Slovenia, Spain, Sweden, Switzerland, Tunisia, Turkey, UK, USA; Pres. A. RONCAGLIA; Vice-Pres J. MONFRIN, M. CAVINESS; Admin. Secs PHILIPPE ROBERTS-JONES, JEAN-LUC DE PAEPE (Belgium); publs Dictionaries of International Law and Medieval Latin, *Monumenta Musicae Byzantinae*, Historical Documents concerning Japan, *Corpus Vasorum Antiquorum, Corpus Philosophorum, Corpus Vitrearum, Dictionnaire Pāli, Corpus des Troubadours*, etc.

International Association for the History of Religions/Association internationale pour l'histoire des religions: f. 1950 by the 7th International Congress for the Study of the History of Religions, to promote the study of the history of religions through the international collaboration of all scholars whose research has a bearing on the subject, to organize congresses and to stimulate the production of publications; 34 mem. countries; Pres. Prof. MICHAEL PYE; Gen. Sec. Prof. ARMIN W. GEERTZ, University of Aarhus, Main Building, 8000 Aarhus C, Denmark; publs *Numen* (3 a year), *Science of Religion* (2 a year).

International Committee of Historical Sciences/Comité international des sciences historiques: Ecole Normale Supérieure, 61 ave du Président Wilson, 94235 Cachan Cedex, France; tel. (1) 47-40-68-00; fax (1) 47-40-68-03; e-mail cish@ihtp-cnrs .ens-cachan.fr; f. 1926; int. congresses since 1900 to work for the advancement of historical sciences by means of international co-ordination; mems in 53 countries; general assembly every two or three years; Pres. IVAN T. BEREND (USA); Sec.-Gen. FRANÇOIS BÉDARIDA (France); publs Congress Reports, *Bulletin d'Information, Bibliographie Internationale des Sciences Historiques, World List of Historical Periodicals and Bibliographies, Histoire des Assemblées d'Etat, Répertoire des sources de l'Histoire des Mouvements Sociaux, Guia de las Personas que cultivan la Historia de America, Excerpta Historica Nordica, Bibliographie internationale de l'Humanisme et de la Renaissance, Bibliographie internationale de l'histoire des Universités, de l'histoire des villes, Guide international d'histoire urbaine, Bibliographie de l'histoire des routes maritimes*, etc.

International Committee for the History of Art/Comité international d'histoire de l'art: Secretariat: 13 rue de Seine, 75006 Paris, France; f. 1930 by the 12th International Congress on the History of Art, for collaboration in the scientific study of the history of art; mems in 31 countries; international congress every four years; international colloquium every year; Pres. Prof. RONALD DE LEEUW (Netherlands) Scientific Sec. PHILIPPE SÉNÉCHAL (France); Treas. and Admin. Sec. Prof. OSKAR BÄTSCHMANN (Switzerland); publs *Bulletin du CIHA, Bibliography of the History of Art* (quarterly).

International Congress of African Studies/Congrès International des Études Africaines: c/o Prof. Yusuf Fadhl Hassan, Vice-Chancellor, University of Khartoum, POB 321, Khartoum, Sudan; tel. 75100; f. 1900 to develop international co-operation in the field of African studies through periodic meetings and publications, to organize and promote research on an international basis and to serve as a body which shall encourage Africans to have a growing consciousness of their membership of the human race and to express themselves in all fields of human endeavour; Sec.-Gen. Prof. HURREIZ (Sudan); publ. *Proceedings* (in English and French).

International Federation for Modern Languages and Literatures/Fédération internationale des langues et littératures modernes: f. 1928 as the International Committee on Modern Literary History; changed to its present form in 1951; to establish permanent contact between historians of literature, to develop or perfect facilities for their work and to promote the study of the history of modern literature; 19 mem. associations, with mems in 92 countries; congress every three years; Pres. REGINALD AMONOO (Zimbabwe); Sec.-Gen. DAVID A. WELLS, Birkbeck College, Malet St, London WC1E 7HX, England; tel. (171) 631-6103; fax (171) 383-3729; publs *Acts of the Triennial Congresses.*

International Federation of Philosophical Societies/Fédération internationale des sociétés de philosophie: f. 1948 under the auspices of UNESCO, to encourage international co-operation in the field of philosophy, and to promote congresses, symposia and publications; 118 mem. societies from 50 countries and 28 international mem. societies; Pres. FRANCISCO MIRÓ QUESADA (Peru); Sec.-Gen. IOANNA KUÇURADI, Dept of Philosophy, Hacettepe University, Beytepe, Ankara, Turkey; tel. (312) 2351219; fax (312) 4410297; publs under the auspices of FISP: *Newsletter* (2 a year), *Proceedings of the International Congresses of Philosophy, An International Bibliography of Philosophy, Chroniques de Philosophie, Philosophers on their own work, Ideas Underlying Global Problems, Philosophy and Cultural Development*, etc.

International Federation of the Societies of Classical Studies/Fédération internationale des associations d'études classiques: c/o Prof. F. Paschoud, Chemin Aux-Folies 6, 1293 Bellevue, Switzerland; f. 1948 under the auspices of UNESCO to encourage research concerning the ancient civilizations of Greece and Rome; to group the main national associations so engaged; to ensure collaboration with relevant international organizations; mems: 79 societies in 44 countries; affiliated bodies include the International Society for Classical Bibliography, International Society for Classical Archaeology, International Society for Byzantine Studies, International Association for Greek and Latin Epigraphy, International Association of Papyrologists, Unione internazionale degli Istituti di Archaeologia, Storia e Storia dell'Arte in Roma, Société d'histoire des droits de l'antiquité, Comité international des Etudes mycéniennes, Association internationale des Etudes patristiques, etc.; Pres. Prof. C. J. CLASSEN (Germany); Sec. Prof. F. PASCHOUD (Switzerland); publs *L'Année Philologique, Thesaurus linguae Latinae* and other reference works.

International Musicological Society/Société internationale de musicologie: f. 1927 to promote musicological research, to encourage study in the field and to co-ordinate the work of musicologists throughout the world; 48 mem. countries, 1,500 mems; Pres. LÁSZLÓ SOMFAI (Hungary); Sec.-Gen. DOROTHEA BAUMANN, CP 1561, CH-4001 Basel, Switzerland; tel. (1) 923-10-22; fax (1) 923-10-27; e-mail imsba@swissonline.ch; publs *Acta Musicologica, Documenta Musicologica, Catalogus Musicus, International Repertory of Music Literature (RILM), International Repertory of Musical Iconography (RIDIM), International Inventory of Musical Sources (RISM), Répertoire International de la Presse Musicale (RIPM).*

International Permanent Committee of Linguists/Comité international permanent des linguistes: f. 1928 to work for the advancement of linguistics throughout the world and to encourage international co-operation in this field; 48 mem. countries and 2 international organizations; Pres. Prof. S. A. WURM (Australia); Sec.-Gen. Prof. P. G. J. VAN STERKENBURG, Instituut voor Nederlandse Lexicologie, Postbus 9515, 2300 RA Leiden, The Netherlands; tel. (71) 514-16-48; fax (71) 527-21-15; e-mail sterkenburg@rulxho.leidenuniv.nl; publ. *Linguistic Bibliography* (annually).

International Union of Anthropological and Ethnological Sciences: see under ISSC.

International Union of Oriental and Asian Studies/Union internationale des études orientales et asiatiques: f. 1951 as the International Union of Orientalists under the auspices of UNESCO, name changed 1973; to promote contacts between orientalists throughout the world, and to organize congresses, research and publications; 26 mem. countries; Pres. TATSURO YAMAMOTO; Sec.-Gen. GYÖRGY HAZAI, Közraktár u. 12/A, II/2, 1093 Budapest, Hungary; publs four oriental bibliographies, *Philologiae Turcicae Fundamenta, Materialien zum Sumerischen Lexikon, Sanskrit Dictionary, Corpus Inscriptionum Iranicarum, Linguistic Atlas of Iran, Matériels des parlers iraniens, Bibliographie Egyptologique,* etc.

International Union of Prehistoric and Protohistoric Sciences/Union internationale des sciences préhistoriques et protohistoriques: f. 1931 to promote congresses and scientific work in the fields of pre- and protohistory; 120 mem. countries; Pres. Prof. A. M. RADMILLI (Italy); Sec.-Gen. JEAN BOURGEOIS, Dept of Archaeology, University of Ghent, 2 Blandijnberg, B-9000 Ghent, Belgium; tel. (9) 264-41-11; fax (9) 264-41-73; e-mail uispp@ping.be; publs *Inventaria archaeologica, Archaeologia urbium,* etc.

INTERNATIONAL SOCIAL SCIENCE COUNCIL

International Social Science Council (ISSC)/Conseil International des Sciences Sociales: Maison de l'UNESCO, 1 rue Miollis, 75732 Paris Cedex 15, France; tel. 1-45-68-25-58; fax 1-45-66-76-03; e-mail issclak@unesco.org; f. 1952 for the advancement of the social sciences throughout the world and their application to the major problems of the world; and to spread co-operation at an international level between specialists in the social sciences. ISSC has a Standing Committee on Conceptual and Terminological Analysis (COCTA), est. in co-operation with IPSA and ISA, and Standing Committees on International Human Dimensions of Global Environmental Change Program (IHDP, cosponsored by ICSU), Comparative Research on Poverty (CROP) and Conflict Early Warning Systems (CEWS); 14 mem. assocs, 16 mem. orgs, 15 assoc. mems; Pres. E. ØYEN (Norway); Sec.-Gen. LESZEK A. KOSIŃSKI; publ. *ISSC Newsletter* (quarterly, in the *International Social Science Journal*).

ASSOCIATIONS FEDERATED TO THE ISSC

International Association of Legal Sciences/Association internationale des sciences juridiques: c/o ISSC, UNESCO, 1 rue Miollis, 75015 Paris, France; tel. (1) 45-68-25-58; fax (1) 43-06-87-98; f. 1950 to promote the mutual knowledge and understanding of nations and the increase of learning by encouraging throughout the world the study of foreign legal systems and the use of the comparative method in legal science. Governed by a President and an executive bureau of ten members known as the International Committee of Comparative Law; national committees in 46 countries; Pres. Prof. MARY ANN GLENDON (USA); Sec.-Gen. MEIR M. LEKER; Dir of Scientific Research Prof. P. SARCEVIĆ (Croatia).

International Economic Association/Association internationale des sciences économiques: 23 rue Campagne-Première, 75014 Paris, France; telex 264918, ext. 533; fax 1-42-79-92-16; f. 1949 to promote international collaboration for the advancement of economic knowledge and develop personal contacts between economists, and to encourage provision of means for the dissemination of economic knowledge; mem. associations in 57 countries; Pres. JACQUES DRÈZE (Belgium); Sec.-Gen. J.-P. FITOUSSI (France).

International Federation of Social Science Organizations/Fédération internationale des organisations de science sociale: C/o Treasurer's Office, 14 Via dei Laghi, 00198 Rome, Italy; f. 1979 to succeed the Conference of National Social Science Councils and Analogous Bodies (f. 1975) to encourage int. co-operation in the social sciences, to further the development of the social sciences, especially in the Third World, to further the exchange of information, ideas and experiences among its mems, to promote a more effective organization of research and teaching and the building of institutions in the social sciences; 22 mems; Pres. Prof. Dr CARMENCITA T. AGUILAR (Philippines); Sec.-Gen. Prof. J. BLAHOZ (Czech Republic); publs *Newsletter, International Directory of Social Science Organizations,* occasional papers.

International Geographical Union: see under ICSU.

International Institute of Administrative Sciences/Institut international des sciences administratives: 1 rue Defacqz, Bte 11, 1000 Brussels, Belgium; tel. (32-2) 5389165; fax (32-2) 5379702; e-mail iias@agoranet.be; f. 1930 for comparative examination of administrative experience in the various countries; research and programmes for improving administrative law and practices and for technical assistance; mems: 45 mem. states, 63 national sections, 11 int. governmental orgs, 75 corporate and individual members; library of 13,000 vols; consultative status with ECOSOC, ILO and UNESCO; international congresses; considers impact of new technologies on administration, management of multicultural societies, administration in transitional economies, administrative aspects of political transition, women in public administration, new regulations and new modes of control, implications of globalization and internationalization for national and local administration, interactions between NGOs and public administration, public administration and the social sectors, innovations in international administration; Pres. DAVID BROWN (Canada); Dir-Gen. TURKIA OULD DADDAH (Mauritania); publs *International Review of Administrative Sciences* (quarterly), *Newsletter (3 a year).*

International Law Association: Charles Clore House, 17 Russell Square, London, WC1B 5DR, England; tel. (171) 323-2978; fax (171) 323-3580; e-mail secretariat@ila-hq.org; f. 1873 for the study and advancement of international law, public and private, and the promotion of international understanding and goodwill; 50 regional branches worldwide; 4,200 mems, 25 international cttees; Pres. Prof. Judge BENGT BROMS (Finland); Chair. Exec. Council Lord SLYNN OF HADLEY (UK); Sec.-Gen. DAVID J. C. WYLD; publs reports of biennial conferences.

International Peace Research Association/Association internationale de recherche pour la paix: C/o Bjoern Moeller, Copenhagen Peace Research Institute, Fredericiagade 18, 1310 Copenhagen K, Denmark; f. 1964 to encourage the development of interdisciplinary research into the conditions of peace and the causes of war; mems in 93 countries: 1,050 individuals, 400 corporate, 10 national and regional asscns; Sec.-Gen. Bjoern Moeller (Denmark); publ. *IPRA Newsletter.*

International Political Science Association (IPSA)/Association Internationale de Science Politique: c/o Dept of Politics, University College Dublin, Belfield, Dublin 4, Ireland; tel. (1) 7068182; fax (1) 7061171; e-mail ipsa@ucd.ie; f. 1949; promotes internationally planned research and scholarly collaboration, organizes triennial world congresses, and provides documentary and reference services; mems: national asscns in 41 countries, 102 associates, 1,200 individuals; Pres. Prof. THEODORE J. LOWI (USA); Sec.-Gen. Prof. JOHN COAKLEY (Ireland); publs *Participation* (bulletin, 3 a year), *International Political Science Review* (quarterly), *International Political Science Abstracts* (every 2 months).

International Sociological Association/Association internationale de sociologie: Facultad CC. Políticas y Sociología, Universidad Complutense, 28223 Madrid, Spain; tel. (91) 352-76-50; fax (91) 352-49-45; e-mail isa@sis.ucm.es; f. 1949; aims to promote sociological research, to develop personal contacts among the sociologists of all countries and to ensure the exchange of sociological information; to attain its aims the ISA has established 50 research committees on a wide variety of sociological topics; holds World Congresses every four years; *c.* 3,500 individual, 150 collective mems; Pres. IMMANUEL WALLERSTEIN (USA); Exec. Sec. IZABELA BARLINSKA (Poland); publs *Current Sociology / Sociologie Contemporaine* (3 a year), *Sage Studies in International Sociology, ISA Bulletin, International Sociology* (quarterly).

International Studies Association: 324 Social Sciences, University of Arizona, Tucson, AZ 85721, USA; tel. (520) 621-7715; fax (520) 621-5780; e-mail isa@arizona.edu; f. 1959; professional society with multinational and multidisciplinary membership; 5,000 mems; Pres. JAMES CAPORASO; Exec. Dir THOMAS J. VOLGY; publs *International Studies Quarterly, International Studies Newsletter, International Studies Notes.*

International Union of Anthropological and Ethnological Sciences/Union internationale des sciences anthropologiques et ethnologiques: f. 1948 under the auspices of UNESCO to foster research and co-operation among anthropological and ethnological institutions; mems: 20 national, 80 institutional and over 200 individuals worldwide; also federated to ICPHS, ISSC and ICSU; Pres. Prof. VINSON H. SUTLIVE (USA); Sec.-Gen. Prof. E. SUNDERLAND, Univ. of Wales, Bangor, Gwynedd, LL57 2EF, Wales; tel. (1248) 353265; fax (1248) 355043; publ. *Newsletter* (3 a year).

International Union of Psychological Science: see under ICSU.

International Union for the Scientific Study of Population/Union internationale pour l'étude scientifique de la population: 34 rue des Augustins, B-4000 Liège, Belgium; tel. (4) 222-40-80; fax (4) 222-38-47; e-mail iussp@iussp.org; f. 1928, reconstituted 1947, to advance the progress of quantitative and qualitative demography as a science; mems: 1,900 scientists in 124 countries; Pres. JOSÉ A. DE CARVALHO (Brazil); Sec.-Gen. WOLFGANG LUTZ (Austria); Exec. Sec. J. VERRALL (UK); publs *Proceedings* (conferences and seminars), *IUSSP Newsletter, IUSSP papers,* etc.

World Association for Public Opinion Research/Association mondiale pour l'étude de l'opinion publique: c/o School of Journalism, University of North Carolina, CB 3365, Howell Hall, Chapel Hill, NC 27599-3365, USA; tel. (919) 962-4078; fax (919) 962-0620; f. 1947 to establish and promote contacts between persons in the field of survey research on opinions, attitudes and behaviour of people in the various countries of the world; to further the use of objective, scientific survey research in national and international affairs; mems: 500 individuals in 55 countries; Pres. Prof. Dr WOLFGANG DONSBACH (Germany); publ. *WAPOR Newsletter* (quarterly).

World Federation for Mental Health/Fédération Mondiale pour la Santé Mentale: 1021 Prince St, Alexandria, VA 22314 (USA); tel. (703) 838-7543; fax (703) 519-7648; e-mail wfmh@erols.com; f. 1948 to promote among all people and nations the highest possible standard of mental health in the broadest biological, medical, educational, and social aspects; to work with ECOSOC, UNESCO, the World Health Organization, and other agencies of the United Nations, in so far as they promote mental health; to help other voluntary associations in the improvement of mental health services; and to further the establishment of better human relations; 3,000 individual mems, 141 orgs, 135 affiliate orgs; Pres. MARTEN DE VRIES, (until September 1999), AHMED EL-AZAYEM (from September 1999); Sec.-Gen. E. B. BRODY (USA); publs *Newsletter* (quarterly), *Annual Report.*

AUTONOMOUS CENTRE OF ISSC

European Co-ordination Centre for Research and Documentation in Social Sciences/Centre Européen de Coordination de Recherche et de Documentation en Sciences Sociales: Grünangergasse 2, 1010 Vienna, Austria; tel. (222) 512-43-33; fax (222) 512-53-66-16; f. 1963 to promote research co-operation between East and West European countries; activities in all areas of social science: co-ordination of cross-national comparative projects, training social scientists, organization of conferences, programmes in social science information and documentation. Administered by a Board of Directors and a Permanent Secretariat; Pres. J. ARANGO (Spain); Dir. L. KIUZADJAN (CIS); publs *Vienna Centre Newsletter* (3 a year), *ECSSID Bulletin* (quarterly).

INTERNATIONAL ASSOCIATION OF UNIVERSITIES (IAU)

1 rue Miollis, 75732 Paris Cedex 15, France
Telephone: (1) 45-68-25-45
Telex: 270602
Fax: (1) 47-34-76-05
E-mail: iau@unesco.org

Founded 1950 to provide a centre of co-operation at the int. level among universities and similar institutions of higher education of all countries, as well as organizations in the field of higher education. Members: 650 universities and institutions of higher learning in 150 countries; 12 associate members (international and national university organizations).

Organization

GENERAL CONFERENCE

Composed of the full and associate members and meets every five years. Discusses topics of special importance for the future of university education, determines general policy and elects the President and members of the Administrative Board. Eleventh General Conference was to be held in Durban, South Africa, in 2000.

ADMINISTRATIVE BOARD

Composed of the President, 20 distinguished university leaders and the Secretary-General. Meets annually. Gives effect to decisions of the General Conference and supervises the activities of the International Universities Bureau.

President: Dr WATARU MORI, former President, University of Tokyo.

INTERNATIONAL UNIVERSITIES BUREAU

The IUB, created in 1949, provides the Permanent Secretariat for IAU. It is the principal instrument for the execution of the activities of IAU. Its main tasks include facilitating and promoting the exchange of information, experience and ideas, of students, teachers, researchers and administrators, and of publications and material for teaching and research.

Secretary-General: Dr FRANZ EBERHARD.

Principal Activities

Information

Under a formal Agreement with UNESCO, IAU operates at its International Universities Bureau a joint IAU/UNESCO Information Centre on Higher Education. The Centre holds 40,000 vols and a large collection of unpublished materials; it receives 300 specialized periodicals and has a collection of 4,000 calendars and catalogues of higher education institutions. The Centre has been fully computerized. There are two databases on higher education: one institutional (Hedata) and one bibliographical (Hedbib). The databases interlink with other national and international information centres and data networks. IAU acts as the co-ordinating agency for the World Academic Database (WAD).

Studies, Research and Meetings

IAU co-ordinates and carries out studies and research on issues of higher education and higher education policies which are either common to instns and systems worldwide, or where a comparative analysis of different situations and approaches appears particularly interesting. Conferences, symposia, colloquia, seminars, round tables and workshops provide an international forum for the discussion of topics of common concern to higher education leaders and specialists.

Co-operation

IAU provides an important clearing-house function to members for academic exchange and co-operation. IAU has adopted the Kyoto Declaration and Agenda 2000 for Sustainable Development to mobilize and support university co-operation.

SELECTED PUBLICATIONS

Higher Education Policy (English; quarterly).

IAU Newsletter (English and French; every 2 months).

International Handbook of Universities (English; every two years).

Issues in Higher Education (English; 3 or 4 a year).

World List of Universities and Other Institutions of Higher Education (English and French; every two years).

World Academic Database (CD-ROM; English and French; annually).

OTHER INTERNATIONAL ORGANIZATIONS

General

Academia Europaea: 31 Old Burlington St, London W1X 1LB, England; tel. (171) 734-5402; fax (171) 287-5115; e-mail acadeuro@compuserve.com; f. 1988; a free asscn of individual scholars working in Europe in all disciplines; aims to encourage European activities in scholarship and the undertaking of independent studies of important questions; holds meetings, symposia, study groups, etc.; 1,700 mems; Pres. STIG STRÖMHOLM; Exec. Sec. PETER COLYER; publ. *European Review* (quarterly).

Academia Scientiarum et Artium Europaea (European Academy of Sciences and Arts): Waagplatz 3, 5020 Salzburg, Austria; tel. (662) 84-13-45; fax (662) 84-13-43; f. 1990; promotes an overall view of the sciences and arts on a European level; 1,200 mems; Pres. FELIX UNGER; Vice-Pres NIKOLAUS LOBKOWICZ, RICARDO DIEZ-HOCHLEITNER; publs *Annales* (annually), *Litterae Academiae Scientiarum et Artium Europaeae* (quarterly).

Albert Einstein International Academy Foundation: c/o US Federal Bldg, 301 West Lexington St, Independence, MO 64050, USA; tel. (816) 833-0033; telex 3794273; fax (816) 833-2125; f. 1965 to promote literature, science, the fine arts and other fields of knowledge; bestows the Albert Einstein Medal and the honorary doctorate; conducts research on world peace, climate, ocean affairs and foreign affairs; affiliated with the Marquis Giuseppe Scicluna International University Foundation; Pres. Prof. Dr MARCEL DINGLI-ATTARD de' baroni INGUANEZ.

Agriculture and Veterinary Science

Food and Agriculture Organization of the United Nations/Organisation des Nations Unies pour l'Alimentation et l'Agriculture: Viale delle Terme di Caracalla, 00100 Rome, Italy; tel. 52251; telex 610181; fax 52253152; f. 1945 to raise level of nutrition and living standards, improve production and distribution of food and agricultural products and better the conditions of rural populations. The policy and budget are determined by the 174 mem. nations and 1 org. mem. (European Community) at the biennial Conference; the Conference elects a 49-mem. Council which is served by specialist cttees; there are 4,000 staff, 1,500 of whom are engaged in the Field Programme with 1,850 projects in 135 countries; there are three main sources of funding: regular contributions from mem. nations, used for financing the secretariat and Technical Co-operation Programmes; trust funds mainly provided by govts for use in FAO Field Programmes; and UNDP funding. FAO's main activities are centred around: improving production in all areas of agriculture, forestry and fisheries; promoting the conservation and management of plant and animal genetic resources; increasing investment in agriculture through irrigation, fertilizer, seed and other rural development schemes; collecting, analysing and disseminating information needed by govts and int. bodies; making available technical data through the FAO-co-ordinated AGRIS, CARIS and FAOSTAT computer-based int. information systems; working towards greater world food security by ensuring production of adequate food supplies, maximizing stability in the flow of supplies, and securing access to available supplies by those who need them; and by promoting rural development schemes. The interpretation and dissemination of information obtained from satellites to predict crop failure and locust migration is an illustration of FAO's GIEWS and ARTEMIS systems to monitor the world food situation. The FAO David Lubin Memorial Library holds 1 million vols and 7,000 periodicals; Dir-Gen. JACQUES DIOUF (Senegal); publs *The State of Food and Agriculture* (annually), *Unasylva, World Animal Review* (quarterly), *FAO Quarterly Bulletin of Statistics, Food and Agricultural Legislation* (every 6 months), *Rural Development* (annually), *FAO Documentation Current Bibliography* (monthly), *Plant Protection Bulletin, Yearbooks of Trade and Production in Agriculture, Forestry and Fisheries, Animal Health and Fertilizers, Commodity Review and Outlook.*

OTHER ORGANIZATIONS

CAB International (CABI): Wallingford, Oxon, OX10 8DE, England; tel. (1491) 832111; telex 847964; fax (1491) 833508; f. 1929; international intergovernmental organization which provides information and scientific and development services for agriculture and allied disciplines throughout the world; CABI Bioscience has centres in the UK, Kenya, Malaysia, Pakistan, Switzerland, and Trinidad and Tobago; owned by its 40 member govts; CAB Abstracts and CAB Health bibliographic databases, of research in agriculture, forestry, the environment, applied social sciences and aspects of human health, is accessible online or (from 1984 onwards) on CD-ROM; publs (i) Animal Science and Production: *Animal Breeding Abstracts* (monthly), *Dairy Science Abstracts* (monthly), *Nutrition Abstracts and Reviews, Series B – Livestock Feeds and Feeding* (monthly), *Pig News and Information* (quarterly), *Poultry Abstracts* (monthly), *Meat Focus International* (monthly); (ii) Veterinary Sciences and Parasitic Diseases: *Helminthological Abstracts* (monthly), *Index Veterinarius* (monthly), *Protozoological Abstracts* (monthly), *Review of Medical and Veterinary Entomology* (monthly), *Review of Medical and Veterinary Mycology* (quarterly), *Veterinary Bulletin* (monthly); (iii) Crop Science and Production: *Crop Physiology Abstracts* (monthly), *Field Crop Abstracts* (monthly), *Herbage Abstracts* (monthly), *Horticultural Abstracts* (monthly), *Irrigation and Drainage Abstracts* (quarterly), *Maize Abstracts* (every 2 months), *Ornamental Horticulture* (every 2 months), *Plant Breeding Abstracts* (monthly), *Plant Genetics Resources Abstracts* (quarterly), *Plant Growth Regulator Abstracts* (every 2 months), *Postharvest News and Information* (every 2 months), *Potato Abstracts* (every 2 months), *Rice Abstracts* (every 2 months), *Seed Abstracts* (monthly), *Soils and Fertilizers* (monthly), *Sorghum and Millets Abstracts* (every 2 months), *Soyabean Abstracts* (every 2 months), *Sugar Industry Abstracts* (every 2 months), *Wheat, Barley and Triticale Abstracts* (every 2 months); (iv) Forestry: *Agroforestry Abstracts* (quarterly), *Forest Products Abstracts* (every 2 months), *Forestry Abstracts* (monthly); (v) Crop Protection: *Biocontrol News and Information* (quarterly), *Nematological Abstracts* (quarterly), *Review of Agricultural Entomology* (monthly), *Review of Plant Pathology* (monthly), *Weed Abstracts* (monthly); (vi) Economics, Development and Sociology: *Leisure, Recreation and Tourism Abstracts* (quarterly), *Rural Development Abstracts* (quarterly), *World Agricultural Economics and Rural Sociology Abstracts* (monthly); (vii) Machinery and Buildings: *Agricultural Engineering Abstracts* (monthly); (viii) Human Nutrition: *Nutrition Abstracts and Reviews, Series A – Human and Experimental* (monthly); (ix) Biotechnology/Biodeterioration: *AgBiotech News and Information* (every 2 months), *Biodeterioration Abstracts* (quarterly), *Abstracts on Hygiene and Communicable Diseases* (monthly), *Aids Newsletter* (every 3 weeks), *Current Aids Literature* (monthly), *Public Health News* (monthly), *Tropical Diseases Bulletin* (monthly).

Constituent sectors:

CABI Biodiversity and Biosystematics: Bakeham Lane, Englefield Green, Egham, Surrey, TW20 9TY, England; tel. (1784) 470111; fax (1784) 470909; provides world services in Biosystematics and Molecular Biology, Biotechnology and the Utilization of Biodiversity, and Tropial Parasitic Diseases; Biosystematics Reference Collection (370,000 specimens) and Genetic Resources Collection (20,000 living fungi); identification of insects, mites, nematodes and fungi; library, and molecular and bacteriology facilities; training courses worldwide; Dir Dr W. M. HOMINICK; publs *Index of Fungi* (2 a year), *Mycological Papers* (irregular), *Phytopathological Papers* (irregular), *IMI Descriptions of Fungi* (2 sets of 10 twice a year), *Bibliography of Systematic Mycology* (2 a year), *Systema Ascomycetum* (with University of Umeå, 2 a year), *Mycopathologia* (with Kluwer Academic Publishers, quarterly).

CABI Biological Pest Management: Silwood Park, Buckhurst Rd, Ascot, Berks., SL5 7TA, England; tel. (1344) 872999; fax (1344) 875007; diagnosis and management of weed, insect, nematode and plant disease problems; Dir Dr J. K. WAAGE; publs *Biocontrol News and Information* (quarterly), *A Catalogue of the Parasites and Predators of Insect Pests,* technical bulletins and communications.

CABI Environment: Silwood Park, Buckhurst Rd, Ascot, Berks., SL5 7TA, England; tel. (1344) 872999; fax (1344) 875007; focuses on land use change and conservation ecology; Dir Prof. V. K. BROWN; publs *Bulletin of Entomological Research* (6 a year), *Distribution Map of Pests* (18 a year).

Commonwealth Forestry Association: Oxford Forestry Institute, South Parks Rd, Oxford, OX1 3RB, England; tel. (1865) 271037; fax (1865) 275074; e-mail cfa@plants.ox.ac.uk; f. 1921; 1,500 mems; publ. *Commonwealth Forestry Review* (quarterly).

Consultative Group on International Agricultural Research (CGIAR): 1818 H St, NW, Washington, DC 20433, USA; tel.

(202) 473-8951; fax (202) 473-8110; e-mail cgiar@cgnet.com; f. 1971; World Bank, FAO, UNEP and UNDP are co-sponsors; obtains financial support for international agricultural research programmes; 57 mems including governments, int. organizations and private foundations; Exec. Sec. ALEXANDER VON DER OSTEN.

Supports the following:

International Centre for Tropical Agriculture/Centro Internacional de Agricultura Tropical: Apdo aéreo 6713, Cali, Colombia; tel. (2) 4450000; telex 05769; fax (2) 4450073; f. 1967; research on cultivation of beans, cassava, rice and tropical fodder; library of 60,000 vols; 1,300 mems; Dir-Gen. GRANT M. SCOBIE; publs annual commodity research reports, periodic commodity newsletters, research monographs, conf. proceedings, etc.

International Maize and Wheat Improvement Center/Centro Internacional de Mejoramiento de Maíz y Trigo: Apdo 6-641, Lisboa 27, 06600 México, DF, Mexico; tel. (5) 726-9091; telex 1772023; fax (5) 726-7558; f. 1966; supported by Mexican Min. of Agriculture, various int. agencies, governments and private foundations; aims to improve maize and wheat research and production in the third world; promotes environmentally sound farming practices; 5 experimental stations in Mexico and 16 regional offices in Africa, Asia and South and Central America; library of 30,000 documents; Dir-Gen. Dr TIMOTHY REEVES; publs *Annual Reports*, bulletins, etc.

International Potato Center/Centro Internacional de la Papa: POB 1558, Lima, Peru; tel. (14) 36-6920; telex 25672; fax (14) 35-1570; f. 1971; non-profit institution dedicated to the increased and more sustainable use of potato, sweet potato and other roots and tubers in developing countries, and to the improved management of agricultural resources in mountain areas; regional offices in Lima, Nairobi, Tunis, Bogor and New Delhi; library of 10,300 vols, 400 journals, 12,850 reprints, 51,200 references; Dir-Gen. Dr HUBERT G. ZANDSTRA; publs *CIP Circular* (quarterly, in Spanish, English and French), *Annual Report* (in Spanish and English).

International Center for Agricultural Research in the Dry Areas (ICARDA): POB 5466, Aleppo, Syria; tel. (21) 213433; fax (21) 213490; e-mail ICARDA@cgnet.com; f. 1977; serves the entire developing world for the improvement of lentil, barley and faba bean; all dry-area developing countries for the improvement of on-farm water-use efficiency, rangeland and small-ruminant production; and West and Central Asia and North Africa for the improvement of bread and durum wheats, chickpea, and farming systems; library of 14,000 vols, 700 periodicals; Dir-Gen. Dr ADEL EL-BELTAGY; publs *RACHIS* (2 a year), *FABIS* (2 a year), *LENS* (2 a year), *ICARDA Caravan* (4 a year), *Annual Report.*

International Crops Research Institute for the Semi-Arid Tropics (ICRISAT): Patancheru, Andhra Pradesh 502 324, India; tel. (40) 596161; fax (40) 241239; e-mail icrisat@cgnet.com; f. 1972 as world centre for genetic improvement of sorghum, millets, pigeonpea, chickpea and groundnut, and for research on the management of resources in the world's semi-arid tropics; research covers all physical and socio-economic aspects of improving farming systems on un-irrigated land; Dir-Gen. SHAWKI M. BARGHOUTI (Jordan); publs *ICRISAT Report* (annually), *International Chickpea and Pigeonpea Newsletter* (annually), *International Arachis Newsletter* (annually), *International Sorghum and Millet Newsletter* (annually), Workshop Proceedings, Research and Information Bulletins.

International Food Policy Research Institute: 1200 Seventeenth St NW, Washington, DC 20036, USA; tel. (202) 862-5600; telex 440054; fax (202) 467-4439; f. 1975 to identify and analyse alternative national and international strategies for improving the food situation of the low-income countries; part of CGIAR *(q.v.)*; five divisions: Environment and Production Technology, Food Consumption and Nutrition, Markets and Structural Studies, Outreach, and Trade and Macroeconomics; library of 4,200 research reports, 3,000 monographs, 175 periodicals; Dir-Gen. PER PINSTRUP-ANDERSEN; publs research reports, abstracts, working papers, newsletters, etc.

International Livestock Research Institute: POB 30709, Nairobi, Kenya; tel. (2) 632311; fax (2) 631499; and POB 5689, Addis Ababa, Ethiopia; tel. (1) 613215; fax (1) 611892; f. 1995 as an interdisciplinary research, training and information centre to promote and improve livestock production worldwide; principal research units in Kenya and Ethiopia and field programmes in Ethiopia, Kenya, Niger and Nigeria; libraries of 37,500 vols, 32,000 microfiches, 1,800 periodicals; Dir-Gen. Dr HANK FITZHUGH; publs *Systems Studies Monographs, Bulletin, Annual Report,* progress and research reports, manuals, newsletters, bibliographies.

International Laboratory for Research on Animal Diseases (ILRAD): POB 30709, Nairobi, Kenya; tel. 632311; telex 22040; fax 631499; f. 1973; research programmes on control of trypanosomiasis and theileriosis; Dir Dr A. R. GRAY; publs *Annual Report, Annual Scientific Report, ILRAD Reports* (quarterly), *ILRAD Highlights* (annually).

International Plant Genetic Resources Institute: Via delle Sette Chiese 142, 00145 Rome, Italy; tel. 518921; fax 5750309; e-mail ipgri@cgnet.com; f. 1974; aims to further the collection, conservation and use of crop genetic resources worldwide and to stimulate research; Dir-Gen. Dr GEOFFREY HAWTIN; publs *Annual Report, Geneflow,* etc.

International Rice Research Institute: POB 933, 1099 Manila, Philippines; tel. (2) 845-0563; telex 40890; fax (2) 891-1292; e-mail postmaster@irri.cgnet.com; f. 1960; research on rice and rice-based cropping systems; library of 120,000 vols; Dir-Gen. Dr G. ROTHSCHILD; publs *Corporate Report* (annually), *Program Report* (annually), *Rice Literature Update* (3 a year), *IRRI Notes* (3 a year), *Rice Reporter* (3 a year), *Facts about Cooperation* (annually), *IRRI Hotline* (6–8 a year).

International Institute of Tropical Agriculture: Oyo Rd, PMB 5320, Ibadan, Nigeria; tel. (2) 241-2626; fax (2) 241-2221; e-mail iita@cgnet.com; f. 1967; mandate for agricultural research for tropical Africa; research stations in Nigeria, Benin, Cameroon, Côte d'Ivoire and Uganda; three main research divisions: resource and crop management, crop improvement, and plant health management; training programme for researchers in tropical agriculture; collaborative programmes in many African countries; library of 76,500 vols and in-house database of 105,500 records; Dir-Gen. LUKAS BRADER; publs *IITA Annual Report, IITA Research* (every 6 months).

West Africa Rice Development Association: 01 BP 2551, Bouake 01, Côte d'Ivoire; tel. (225) 63-45-14; telex 69138; fax (225) 63-47-14; e-mail warda@cgnet.com; f. 1970; mems: 17 West and Central African states; funds provided by CGIAR and mem. states; library of 15,000 vols, 1,400 periodicals; Dir-Gen. Dr KANAYO F. NWANZE; publs *Annual Report, Program Report*.

Dairy Society International (DSI)/Société internationale laitière: 7185 Ruritan Drive, Chambersburg, PA 17201, USA; f. 1946 to foster the extension of dairy and dairy industrial enterprise internationally through an interchange and dissemination of scientific, technological, economic, dietary and other relevant information and through a bringing together of persons and entities devoted thereto; organizer and sponsor of the first World Congress for Milk Utilisation; Pres. JAMES E. CLICK (USA); Vice-Pres. MITSUGI SATO (Japan); Man. Dir GEORGE W. WEIGOLD (USA); Sec. GORDON T. JEFFERS (USA); publs *DSI Report to Members, DSI Bulletin* (both approx. quarterly), *Market Frontier News, Dairy Situation Review* (every 2 months), and booklets on dairying in English and Spanish.

European Confederation of Agriculture/Confédération Européenne de l'Agriculture: 23–25 rue de la Science, Boîte 23, 1040 Brussels, Belgium; tel. (2) 230-43-80; fax (2) 230-46-77; e-mail cea@pophost.eunet.be; f. 1889 as International Confederation of Agriculture, re-formed in 1948 as European Confederation of Agriculture; represents the interests of European agriculture in the international field; 300 mems from 30 countries; Pres. HANS JONSSON (Sweden); publs *CEA Dialog,* publs on current technical, economic, social and cultural problems affecting European Agriculture, Annual Report on the General Assembly.

Inter-American Institute for Cooperation on Agriculture/Instituto Interamericano de Cooperación para la Agricultura: Apdo 55, 2200 Coronado, San José, Costa Rica; tel. (506) 229-02-22; telex 2144; fax (506) 2294741; f. 1942; a specialized agency of the inter-American system. Aims to stimulate, promote and support the efforts of the Member States to achieve agricultural development and rural well-being; offices in 29 of its 33 countries; Dir-Gen. Ing. Agr. CARLOS E. AQUINO G. (Dominican Republic); publ. *Turrialba* (quarterly).

International Association of Agricultural Economists/Conférence internationale des économistes agricoles: 1211 West 22nd St, Oak Brook, IL 60521, USA; f. 1929 to foster the application of the science of agricultural economics in the improvement of the economic and social conditions of rural people and their associated communities; to advance knowledge of agricultural processes and the economic organization of agriculture; and to facilitate communication and exchange of information among those concerned with rural welfare throughout the world; mems: 1,700 from 95 countries; Pres. ROBERT L. THOMPSON (USA); Vice-Pres. Programme JOACHIM VON BRAUN (Germany); Gen. Sec. and Treas. WALTER J. ARMBRUSTER (USA); publs *Proceedings of Conferences*.

International Association of Horticultural Producers/Association Internationale des Producteurs de l'Horticulture: Bezuidenhoutseweg 153, POB 93099, 2509 AB, The Hague, Netherlands; fax (31) 70-3477176; f. 1948 to represent through its professional member organizations the common interests of commercial horticultural producers by means of frequent meetings, regular publications, press notices, resolutions and addresses to governments and international authorities; mems: Australia, Austria, Belgium, Canada,

China, Colombia, Czechoslovakia, Denmark, Finland, Luxembourg, Netherlands, Norway, Poland, Spain, Sweden, Switzerland, UK, USA; Pres. O. KOCH; Gen. Sec. Dr J. B. M. ROTTEVEEL; publs numerous.

International Centre for Advanced Mediterranean Agronomic Studies: Secretariat: 11 rue Newton, 75116 Paris, France; tel. 153-23-91-00; fax 153-23-91-01; f. 1962 to provide a supplementary technical, economic and social education for graduates of the higher schools and faculties of agriculture in Mediterranean countries at a postgraduate level; to examine the international problems posed by rural development and regional planning; to develop methods of investigation in ecological topics; to contribute to the development of a spirit of international co-operation among agronomists and economists in Mediterranean countries; scholarships may be granted by the governing body; mems: Albania, Algeria, Egypt, France, Greece, Italy, Lebanon, Malta, Morocco, Portugal, Spain, Tunisia, Turkey, Yugoslavia; Chair. J. GODINHO AVO (Portugal); Sec.-Gen. ENZO CHIOCCIOLI (Italy); publ. *Options Méditerranéennes*.

The Centre comprises four institutes:

Mediterranean Agronomic Institute of Bari: courses on irrigation and drainage, soil conservation, pathology of Mediterranean fruit tree species; Dir COSIMO LACIRIGNOLA, Strada Provinciale per Ceglie, 70010 Valenzano, Bari, Italy; tel. (80) 7806-111; fax (80) 7806-206.

Mediterranean Agronomic Institute of Chania: courses on cultivation of vegetables and flowers under protective covering, Mediterranean forestry and range management, integrated rural development; Dir ALKINOOS NIKOLAIDIS, Alsyllion Agrokepion, POB 85, Chania TK 73100, Crete, Greece; tel. (821) 81-151; fax (821) 81-154.

Mediterranean Agronomic Institute of Montpellier: courses on economics and politics of the agricultural sector and food supplies, economics and agricultural policies, rural development and popularization; Dir GÉRARD GHERSI, 3191 route de Mende, BP 5056, 34033 Montpellier Cedex 1, France; tel. 4-67-04-60-00; fax 4-67-54-25-27.

Mediterranean Agronomic Institute of Zaragoza: courses on animal husbandry and rural environment, selection, nutrition and animal reproduction, agricultural and food products, marketing, pisciculture, rural environment, plant genetics; Dir MIGUEL VALLS ORTIZ, Apdo 202, Zaragoza, Spain; tel. (76) 57-60-13; fax (76) 57-63-77.

International Centre for Research in Agroforestry (ICRAF): POB 30677, Nairobi, Kenya; tel. (254-2) 521450; telex 22048; fax 521001; e-mail icraf@cgnet.com; f. 1977; to improve human welfare by alleviating poverty, increasing cash income, improving food and nutritional security, and enhancing environmental resilience in the tropics; Dir-Gen. Dr PEDRO A. SANCHEZ; publs *Agroforestry Systems, Agro-forestry Today* (quarterly), *Agroforestry Abstracts,* reviews, monographs, proceedings, etc.

International Commission for Food Industries/Commission internationale des industries agricoles et alimentaires: 16 rue Claude Bernard, 75005 Paris, France; tel. 1-43-31-30-36; fax 1-43-31-32-02; f. 1934 to develop international co-operation in promoting agricultural and food industries; to organize periodical international congresses and annual study sessions for agricultural and food industries; Sec.-Gen. GUY DARDENNE (France); publs *Food and Agriculture Industries Journal,* Proceedings of Congresses and Symposia.

International Commission of Agricultural Engineering: see under Engineering.

International Committee on Veterinary Gross Anatomical Nomenclature (ICVGAN)/Commission Internationale de la Nomenclature Macroanatomique Vétérinaire: Dept. of Veterinary Anatomy, University of Zürich, Winterthurerstr. 260, 8057 Zürich, Switzerland; f. 1957; 49 mems; Chair. Prof. JOSEF FREWEIN (Switzerland); Sec. Prof. HELMUT WAIBL (Germany); publs *Nomina Anatomica Veterinaria, Nomina Histologica, Nomina Embryologica Veterinaria.*

International Dairy Federation/Fédération internationale de laiterie: Square Vergote 41, 1030 Brussels, Belgium; tel. (2) 733-98-88; fax (2) 733-0413; e-mail info@fil-idf.org; f. 1903 to link all dairy associations in order to encourage the solution of scientific, technical and economic problems affecting the dairy industry; mems: national committees in 35 countries; Pres. J. J. KOZAK (USA); Sec.-Gen. E. HOPKIN (UK); publ. *Bulletin*.

International Federation of Agricultural Producers: 21 rue Chaptal, 75009 Paris, France; tel. (1) 45-26-05-53; fax 48-74-72-12; f. 1946 to represent, in the international field, the interests of agricultural producers, by laying the co-ordinated views of the national member organizations before any appropriate international body; to exchange information and ideas and help develop understanding of world problems and their effects upon agricultural producers; to encourage efficiency of production, processing, and marketing of agricultural products; 82 national farmers' organizations in 58 countries are represented in the Federation; Pres. GRAHAM BLIGHT (Australia); Sec.-Gen. DAVID KING; publs *IFAP Newsletter*, General Conference Reports, *Specialized Committee Reports, IFAP Monitoring.*

International Irrigation Management Institute: POB 2075, Colombo, Sri Lanka; tel. 867404; fax 866854; f. 1984; an autonomous, non-profit int. agricultural research and training institute; seeks to create sustainable increases in the productivity of irrigated agriculture within the overall context of water basins and the analysis of water resource systems as a whole; field offices in Pakistan, Colombia, Sri Lanka, Burkina Faso, Niger, Mexico; Dir-Gen. Dr DAVID SECKLER; publs newsletters.

International Organization for Biological Control of Noxious Animals and Plants (IOBC)/Organisation internationale de lutte biologique contre les animaux et les plantes nuisibles: Secretariat-General of IOBC Global Swiss Federal Research Station for Agronomy, POB 8046, Zürich, Switzerland; tel. (1) 377-72-35; fax (1) 377-72-01; f. 1956 to promote and co-ordinate research on biological and integrated control of pests and weeds; mems: public or private from over 50 countries; comprises regional sections based on biogeographical zones; Pres. Dr E. S. DELFOSSE (USA); Sec.-Gen. Dr F. BIGLER (Switzerland); publs *Entomophaga* (quarterly), *Bulletin* and Newsletters.

International Seed Testing Association/Association Internationale d'Essais de Semences: Reckenholz, POB 412, CH-8046 Zürich, Switzerland; tel. (1) 371-31-33; fax (1) 371-34-27; e-mail istach@iprolink.ch; f. 1924; aims to promote uniformity in the testing and judgment of seeds, through research and by organizing triennial congresses and periodical training courses; mems: 66 countries; Pres. SIMON COOPER (Scotland); Hon. Sec.-Treas. Prof. A. LOVATO (Italy); publs *Seed Science and Technology* (3 a year), *ISTA News Bulletin* (3 a year).

International Service for National Agricultural Research: POB 93375, 2509 AJ The Hague, The Netherlands; tel. (70) 3496100; telex 33746; fax (70) 3819677; e-mail isnar@cgnet.com; f. 1980 by Consultative Group on Int. Agricultural Research on basis of recommendations from an international task force; assists national governments in developing countries to organize and manage their agricultural research systems; non-profit, autonomous, non-political; funds from an informal group of *c.* 40 donor countries, banks, foundations, etc; runs training and communications programme in co-operation with developing countries; library of 24,000 vols; Dir-Gen. STEIN BIE; publ. *ISNAR Annual Report*.

International Society for Horticultural Science: Kardinaal Mercierlaan 92, 3001 Leuven, Belgium; tel. (16) 22-94-27; fax (16) 22-94-50; f. 1959; 3,500 mems; Pres. Prof. S. SANSAVINI; Exec. Dir J. VAN ASSCHE; publ. *Chronica Horticulturae, Acta Horticulturae*.

International Society for Tropical Crop Research and Development (ISTCRAD): C/o Prof. N. K. Nayar, Regional Agricultural Research Station, Pattambi 679306, Kerala, India; tel. (492) 612228; fax (487) 370019; f. 1990; provides a forum for interaction among scientists, progressive farmers and entrepreneurs; Sec.-Gen. Prof. N. K. NAYAR; publs *Scientific Journal* (quarterly), *News Bulletin* (quarterly).

International Society for Tropical Root Crops (ISTRC): C/o I.S.H.S., Englaan 1, 6703 ET Wageningen, Netherlands; tel. (8370) 21747; fax (8370) 21586; f. 1964; 300 mems; Pres. Dr S. K. HAHN; Sec. Ir H.H. VAN DER BORG; publ. *Newsletter* (annually).

International Society of Soil Science/Association Internationale de la Science du Sol/Internationale Bodenkundliche Gesellschaft: c/o Institute of Soil Science, University of Agricultural Sciences, Gregor-Mendel-Str. 33, 1180 Vienna, Austria; tel. (1) 3106026; fax (1) 3106027; e-mail isss@edv1.boku.ac.at; f. 1924 to promote soil science and its applications; mems: 7,200 individuals and 85 associations in 162 countries engaged in the study of soil sciences; Pres. Prof. Dr A. RUELLAN; Sec.-Gen. Prof. W. E. H. BLUM; publ. *Bulletin* (2 a year).

Standing Committee of the International Congress on Animal Reproduction/Comité permanent international du congrès de physiologie et pathologie de la reproduction animale: Dept of Animal Science, University of Sydney, NSW 2006, Australia; fax (2) 9351-3957; e-mail garethe@vetsci.su.oz.au; f. 1948; an international standing committee was appointed after the first congress in Milan in 1948; Pres. S. J. DIELEMAN (Netherlands); Sec.-Gen. Prof. G. EVANS (Australia).

International Union of Forestry Research Organizations/Union Internationale des Instituts de Recherches Forestières/Internationaler Verband Forstlicher Forschungsanstalten: Secretariat: Seckendorff-Gudent-Weg 8, 1131 Vienna, Austria; tel. (1) 877-01-51; fax (1) 877-93-55; f. 1892 for international co-operation in the various branches of forestry research and related fields; mems: 700 organizations in 115 countries (15,000 scientists), including forestry faculties, experimental stations, research institutions, etc.; Pres. Dr JEFFERY BURLEY (UK); Sec. Dipl. Ing. H. SCHMUTZENHOFER (Austria); publs *Annual Report,* Congress Proceedings, *IUFRO News* (quarterly), *IUFRO World Series,* scientific papers.

World Association for Animal Production: Via A. Torlonia 15A, 00161 Rome, Italy; tel. (6) 44238013; fax (6) 44241466; e-mail zoorec@rhnet.it; f. 1965; organizes a conference every 5 years; regional discussions;

mems: 17 societies (national and regional); Pres. Prof. In K. Han; Sec.-Gen. Prof. J. Boyazoglu; publ. *News Items* (2 a year).

World Veterinary Association/Association Mondiale Vétérinaire: Rosenlunds Allé 8, 2720 Valoese, Denmark; tel. 38-71-01-56; fax 38-71-03-22; f. 1863; mem. organizations in 80 countries, 20 assoc. mems; Pres. Dr A. T. Rantsios; Exec. Sec. Lars Holsaae; publs *World Veterinary Directory*, *Bulletin* (2 a year).

Arts

African Cultural Institute/Institut Culturel Africain: 13 ave du Président Bourguiba, POB 01, Dakar, Senegal; tel. (221) 25-04-11; f. 1971; scientific and cultural development, training of cultural action personnel and African cultural co-operation; mems: 19 African states; Regional Research and Documentation Centre for Cultural Development: see under Senegal; Dir-Gen. Alphonse Blague; publ. *ICA-Information* (quarterly).

Association for Commonwealth Literature and Language Studies: Dept. of English, University of Kelaniya, Kelaniya, Sri Lanka; tel. 856317; fax 521485; f. 1965 as an independent organization; encourages study in Commonwealth literatures and languages, including comparative studies, the relationship between literatures in English and indigenous literatures and languages, new kinds of English and use of mass media; holds triennial conferences and regional meetings; organizes visits and exchanges; collects source material and publishes creative, critical, historical and bibliographical material; 1,600 mems; Chair. Prof. D. C. R. A. Goonetilleke; Sec. Lakshmi de Silva; publ. *Bulletin*.

Commonwealth Association of Museums: POB 30192, Chinook Postal Outlet, Calgary, Alta T2H 2V9, Canada; tel. and fax (403) 938-3190; f. 1974; aims to maintain and strengthen links between members of the museum profession; encourages and assists members to obtain additional training and to attend appropriate conferences, seminars; collaborates with national and regional museum associations; national, institutional and individual mems in 30 countries; General Assembly every three years; Pres. Emmanuel N. Arinze; Sec.-Gen. Lois Irvine; publ. *Bulletin*.

Europa Nostra united with the International Castles Institute: 35 Lange Voorhout, 2514 EC The Hague, The Netherlands; tel. (31-70) 3560333; fax (31-70) 3617865; f. 1991 by merger of Europa Nostra and the International Castles Institute; pan-European organization for the protection of Europe's architectural and natural heritage; has an annual award scheme; 1,200 mems (organizations and individuals); Pres. HRH the Prince Consort of Denmark; Sec.-Gen. Antonio Marchini Camia.

European Cultural Foundation/Fondation Européenne de la Culture: Jan van Goyenkade 5, 1075 HN Amsterdam, The Netherlands; tel. (20) 676-02-22; fax (20) 675-22-31; e-mail ecsinfo@pi.net; f. 1954 as an ind., non-profit organization to promote cultural co-operation in Europe; develops new projects and programmes in priority areas; runs a grants programme related to its priorities; serves as a centre of a network of associated institutes for research and study in fields such as education, the media and the environment; 23 European national committees are active on behalf of the Foundation; the research network comprises the following: European Institute of Education and Social Policy, Paris; European Foundation Centre, Brussels; Association for Innovative Co-operation in Europe, Brussels; Institute for European Environmental Policy, Amsterdam, Madrid, London and Paris; Eurydice Central Unit of the Education Information Network in the European Communities, Brussels; European Institute for the Media, Düsseldorf; Fund for Central and East European Book Projects, Amsterdam; Inst. für die Wissenschaften vom Menschen, Vienna; Centre Européen de la Culture, Geneva; East-West Parliamentary Practice Project, Amsterdam; Pres. HRH Princess Margriet of the Netherlands; Sec.-Gen. Dr R. Stephan; publs *Annual Report*, *Newsletter*, *Annual Grants Report*, general information brochures.

European Society of Culture/Société Européenne de Culture: Dorsoduro 909, 30123 Venice, Italy; tel. (41) 5230210; fax (41) 5231033; f. 1950 to unite artists, poets, scientists, philosophers and others through mutual interests and friendship in order to safeguard and improve the conditions required for creative activity; mems: 2,000; library of 5,000 vols; Pres. Vincenzo Cappelletti (Italy); Premier Vice-Pres. Arrigo Levi (Italy); International Gen. Sec. Michelle Campagnolo-Bouvier (Italy); publ. *Comprendre* (irregular).

Fédération internationale des écrivains de langue française (FIDELF): 3492 rue Laval, Montreal, Que. H2X 3C8, Canada; tel. (514) 849-8540; f. 1982; 18 mem. asscns; Pres. Nouky Bataillard; Sec.-Gen. Bruno Roy.

International Amateur Theatre Association—Organization for Understanding and Education through Theatre: Vesterbrogade 175, 1800, FRB C, Copenhagen, Denmark; tel. 31-22-22-45; fax 33-25-25-53; e-mail aitaiata@post2.tele.dk; f. 1952; members in 70 states; composed of national centres; organizes international conferences, colloquia, seminars, workshops, festivals including world festival of amateur theatre (every 4 years); Pres. Thomas Hauger (Denmark); Admin. Tina M. Jakobsen; publs *Bulletin AITA / IATA*.

International Association of Applied Linguistics/Association Internationale de Linguistique Appliquée: f. 1964 to promote the application of linguistic theories to the solution of language and language-related problems in society; mems: *c.* 5,000; Pres. Christopher Candlin (Australia); Sec.-Gen. Andrew D. Cohen, ILASLL, 130 Klaeber Court, University of Minnesota, 320 16th Av SE, Minneapolis, MN 55455, USA; publ. *Review* (annually).

International Association of Art/Association internationale des arts plastiques: UNESCO House, 1 rue Miollis, 75015 Paris, France; tel. 45-68-26-55; fax 45-67-16-90; f. 1954; 81 national committees; Pres. Eduardo Arenillas.

International Association of Art Critics/Association Internationale des Critiques d'Art: 11 rue Berryer, 75008 Paris, France; tel. (1) 42-56-17-53; fax (1) 42-56-08-42; f. 1949 to promote international co-operation in the world of plastic arts (painting, sculpture, graphic arts, architecture); consultative status with UNESCO; 3,750 individuals and 72 National Sections; Pres. Kim Levin (USA); Sec.-Gen. Ramon Tio Bellido (France); publs *Newsletter AiCA*, *Annuaire AiCA*.

International Association of Literary Critics/Association Internationale des Critiques Littéraires: 38 rue du Faubourg-St-Jacques, 75014 Paris, France; tel. 1-40-51-33-00; telex 206963; fax 1-43-54-92-99; f. 1969; UNESCO consultative status B; organizes congresses, etc.; Pres. Robert André; publ. *Revue* (2 a year).

International Association of Museums of Arms and Military History (IAMAM)/Association internationale des musées d'armes et d'histoire militaire: Military Museum of Finland, Box 266, 00171 Helsinki, Finland; f. 1957; organization to establish contact between museums and other scientific institutions with collections of arms and armour, military equipment, uniforms, etc., which may be visited by the public; to promote the study of relevant groups of objects; triennial conferences; mems: 300 institutions in 51 countries; Pres. Claude Gaier (Belgium); Sec.-Gen. Bas Kist (Netherlands); publs *Repertory of Museums of Arms and Military History*, *Glossarium Armourum: Arma Defensiva*, *Triennial Reports*.

International Centre for Ancient and Modern Tapestry/Centre International de la Tapisserie Ancienne et Moderne: 4 ave Villamont, 1005 Lausanne, Switzerland; tel. 323-07-57; fax 323-07-21; f. 1961; documentation centre; organizes a biennial international exhibition of contemporary art in Lausanne and subsequently shown in other countries; library of 1,400 vols; Pres. Mayor of Lausanne; Exec. Sec. Philippe Jeanloz; publ. biennial exhibition catalogue.

International Centre for the Study of the Preservation and Restoration of Cultural Property (ICCROM): Via di San Michele 13, 00153 Rome, Italy; tel. (6) 585-531; fax (6) 5855-3349; e-mail iccrom@iccrom.org; f. 1959; inter-governmental org.; UNESCO Class A; assembles documentation and disseminates knowledge by way of publications and meetings; co-ordinates research, organizes training of specialists and short courses; offers technical advice; financed by 94 mem. countries; library of 55,000 items; int. documentation centre; Dir Marc Laenen; publs *Newsletter* (annually), *Index of Conservation Training* (periodically revised), *List of Acquisitions* of the Library (3 a year).

International Centre of Films for Children and Young People/Centre International du Film pour l'Enfance et la Jeunesse: 9 rue Bargue, 75015 Paris, France; tel. 40-56-00-67; f. 1957; research centre and clearing-house of information about entertainment films (cinema and television) for children all over the world; mems in 62 countries; Chair. Predrag Golubovic (Yugoslavia); Sec.-Gen. Lucien Galandrin; publs *News from ICFCYP*, *Young Cinema International*.

International Comparative Literature Association/Association internationale de littérature comparée: c/o Virgil Nemoianu, Catholic University of America, Washington, DC 20064, USA; f. 1954 to work for the development of the comparative study of literature; 6,000 mems (socs and individuals) in 65 countries; Pres. Gerald Gillespie (USA); Secs-Gen. Manfred Schmelling (Germany), Virgil Nemoianu (USA); publ. *ICLA Bulletin AILC* (2 a year), *Information AILC* (irregularly).

International Council for Film, Television and Audio-Visual Communication/Conseil International du Cinéma, de la Télévision et de la Communication audio-visuelle: 1 rue Miollis, 75732 Paris Cedex 15, France; tel. 1-45-68-25-56; fax 1-45-67-28-40; f. 1958 under auspices of UNESCO; seeks to provide a link of information and joint action between member-organizations, and to assist them in the international work they do in films and television; mems: 36 international associations and federations and 12 associates.

International Council of Graphic Design Associations (ICOGRADA): POB 398, London W11 4UG, England; tel. (171) 603-8494; fax (171) 371-6040; f. 1963 to raise the standards of graphic design and professional practice and the professional status of graphic designers; to collect and exchange information relating to graphic design; to organize exhibitions and congresses and to issue reports and surveys; mems: 54 associations in 37 countries; slide and book library at Design Museum, London; poster and records archives at Univ. of Reading, UK; Pres. GUY A. SCHOCKAERT; Sec.-Gen. MARY V. MULLIN; publ. *Message Board* (quarterly), *Faxnews* (monthly).

International Council of Museums (ICOM): Maison de l'UNESCO, 1 rue Miollis, 75732 Paris Cedex 15, France; tel. (1) 47-34-05-00; telex 204461; fax (1) 43-06-78-62; e-mail secretariat@icom.org; f. 1946; a professional organization, open to all members of the museum profession, set up to provide an appropriate organization to further international co-operation among museums, and to be the co-ordinating and representative international body furthering museum interests; in 116 countries an ICOM National Committee on international co-operation among museums has been organized, each as widely representative as possible of museum interests; maintains UNESCO-ICOM Museum Information Centre, a library and information service specializing in the field of museology and museum practice worldwide; there are 25 international committees and 12 international affiliated associations on specialized subjects; mems: 13,000 individual and institutional members from 147 countries; Pres. SAROJ GHOSE (India); Sec.-Gen. HARUS BRINKMAN; publs *ICOM News* (quarterly).

International Council on Monuments and Sites (ICOMOS)/Conseil international des monuments et des sites: 49–51 rue de la Fédération, 75015 Paris, France; tel. 1-45-67-67-70; fax 1-45-66-06-22; f. 1965 to promote the study and preservation of monuments and sites; to arouse and cultivate the interest of the authorities and people of every country in their monuments and sites and in their cultural heritage; to involve those public authorities, departments, institutions and individuals interested in the preservation and study of monuments and sites; Documentation Centre on preservation and restoration of monuments and sites: 14,000 vols, 350 periodicals, 9,000 slides; mems: 5,500, 92 national cttees, 18 int. cttees; Pres. ROLAND SILVA (Sri Lanka); Sec.-Gen. JEAN LOUIS LUXEN (Belgium); publ. *Icomos Newsletter*, *Icomos Scientific Journal*.

International Federation for Theatre Research/Fédération internationale pour la recherche théâtrale: f. 1955 by 21 countries at the International Conference on Theatre History, London; founded Istituto Internazionale per la Ricerca Teatrale, Casa Goldoni, Venice; international seminars in theatre history; Pres. ERIKA FISCHER-LICHTE; Joint Secs-Gen. Prof. J. M. LARRUE, Prof. MICHAEL J. ANDERSON; Flat 9, 118 Avenue Rd, London W3 8QG, England; publ. *Theatre Research International* (quarterly).

International Institute for Conservation of Historic and Artistic Works/Institut International pour la Conservation des Objets d'Art et d'Histoire: 6 Buckingham St, London, WC2N 6BA, England; tel. (171) 839-5975; fax (171) 976-1564; e-mail iicon@compuserve.com; f. 1950 to provide a permanent organization for co-ordinating and improving the knowledge, methods and working standards needed to protect and preserve precious materials of all kinds; publishes information on research into all processes connected with conservation, both scientific and technical, and on the development of those processes; mems: 3,200 individual, 475 institutional mems; Pres. JOHN WINTER; Sec.-Gen. DAVID BOMFORD; Exec. Sec. PERRY SMITH; publs *Studies in Conservation* (quarterly), *IIC Bulletin* (every 2 months), preprints of biennial international congresses.

International Literary and Artistic Association/Association littéraire et artistique internationale: C/o André Françon, 55 rue des Mathurins, 75000 Paris, France; tel. 1-47-42-58-46; f. 1878 at Congress of Paris, presided over by Victor Hugo. Objects: the protection of the rights and interests of writers and artists of all lands; extension of copyright conventions, etc.; the Association has national groups in Belgium, Canada, Denmark, Germany, Greece, Italy, Monaco, the Netherlands, Norway, Portugal, Sweden, Switzerland and Turkey, and members in Brazil, Luxembourg, Japan, Argentina, New Zealand, UK, USA; Pres. GEORGES KOUMANTOS; Perm. Sec. M. FRANÇON.

International Numismatic Commission/Commission internationale de numismatique: Dept of Coins and Medals, British Museum, London, WC1B 3DG, England; tel. (171) 323-8227; fax (171) 323-8171; e-mail aburnett@british-museum.ac.uk; f. 1927 to facilitate co-operation among individuals and institutions in the field of numismatics; mems: national organizations in 38 countries; Pres. A. BURNETT (UK); Sec. M. AMANDRY (France); publs *Compte rendu* (1 a year), *International Numismatic Newsletter* (2 a year).

International PEN (A World Association of Writers): 9–10 Charterhouse Bldgs, Goswell Rd, London, EC1M 7AT, England; tel. (171) 253-4308; fax (171) 253-5711; e-mail intpen@dircon.co.uk; f. 1921 by Mrs Dawson Scott under the presidency of John Galsworthy to promote co-operation between writers all over the world in the interests of literature, freedom of expression and international goodwill; 131 autonomous centres throughout the world, with total membership about 13,000; International Pres. HOMERO ARIDJIS; Int. Sec. ALEXANDRE BLOKH; publs *PEN International* (in English and French, with the assistance of UNESCO), various regional bulletins, etc.

International Pragmatics Association (IPrA): POB 33, 2018 Antwerp 11, Belgium; tel. and fax (3) 230-55-74; e-mail ipra@uia.ua.ac.be; f. 1986; aims to search for a framework for the discussion and comparison of results of research in all aspects of language use or functions of language, to stimulate the various fields of application, and to disseminate knowledge about pragmatic aspects of language; 1,400 individual mems; Research Center; Sec.-Gen. JEF VERSCHUEREN; publ. *Pragmatics* (quarterly).

International Robert Musil Society/Internationale Robert-Musil-Gesellschaft: 6600 Saarbrucken 11, St Johanner Stadtwald, Germany; f. 1974 under the patronage of Bruno Kreisky (Austria), to promote international co-operation in research and publications on Musil and editions of his writings; 55 founder mems from 25 countries; Pres. Prof. Dr MARIE-LOUISE ROTH (France); Secs.-Gen. Prof. Dr JACQUELINE MAGNOU, Dr ANNETTE DAIGGER (Germany); publ. *Musil-Forum* (annually).

International Theatre Institute/Institut international du théâtre: UNESCO, 1 rue Miollis, 75015 Paris, France; tel. (1) 45-68-26-50; fax (1) 45-66-50-40; f. 1948 to facilitate cultural exchanges and international understanding in the domain of the performing arts; conferences, publications; mems: 95 member nations; Pres. KIM JEONG OK (Republic of Korea); Sec.-Gen. ANDRÉ LOUIS PERINETTI; publ. *News* (3 a year).

International Union of Architects/Union internationale des architectes: 51 rue Raynouard, 75016 Paris, France; tel. 45-24-36-88; fax 45-24-02-78; f. 1948; mems in 106 countries; publ. *Lettre d'information* (monthly).

International Union of Non-Professional Cinema/Union internationale du cinéma non professionnel: f. 1937 to encourage development of art, techniques and critical judgment among amateurs, to facilitate contacts between national associations and to promote the exchange of films; mems: national federations in 35 countries; library of 500 films and videos; Sec.-Gen. ARIE DE JONG, Van Weerden Poelmanstr. 233, 6417 EM Heerlen, The Netherlands; tel. (45) 5660390; fax (45) 5660391; e-mail unica@knoware.nl.

Organization for Museums, Monuments and Sites of Africa/Organisation pour les Musées, les Monuments et les Sites d'Afrique: Centre for Museum Studies, PMB 2031, Jos, Plateau State, Nigeria; f. 1975; aims to foster the collection, study and conservation of the natural and cultural heritage of Africa; co-operation between member countries through seminars, workshops, conferences, etc., exchange of personnel, developing training facilities, and drawing up legislative and administrative measures; mems from 30 countries; Pres. Dr J. M. ESSOMBA (Cameroon); Sec.-Gen. K. A. MYLES (Ghana).

Society of African Culture: c/o Présence africaine, 25 bis rue des Ecoles, 75005 Paris, France; tel. (1) 43-54-13-74; fax (1) 43-25-96-67; f. 1956 to create unity and friendship among African scholars for the encouragement of their own cultures; mems from 22 countries; Pres. AIMÉ CESAIRE; Sec.-Gen. Mme CHRISTIANE DIOP; publ. *Présence Africaine* (quarterly).

World Academy of Art and Sciences: see under International—Science.

World Crafts Council: 19 Race Course Ave, Colombo 7, Sri Lanka; tel. (1) 69-5831; fax (1) 69-2554; f. 1964; a non-profit organization to maintain the status of crafts as a vital part of cultural life and to promote fellowship among the world's craftsmen; offers help and advice to craftsmen, consults with governments, nat. and int. institutions; mem. bodies in *c.* 90 countries; Pres. SIVA OBEYESEKERE (Sri Lanka); Sec.-Gen. HELMUT LUECKENHAUSEN (Australia).

Bibliography

Association for Health Information and Libraries in Africa: c/o WHO Regional Office for Africa, BP 6, Brazzaville, Congo; tel. 83-90-31; telex 5217; fax 83-94-00; f. 1984, name changed 1989; aims to promote co-operation among African health information centres and libraries, to enhance health information services and to develop an African Index Medicus; Pres. O. O. AKHIGBE (Nigeria); Sec. R. KAKEMBO (Uganda); publ. *AHILA Newsletter* (quarterly).

Association of Caribbean University, Research and Institutional Libraries: POB 23317, San Juan, Puerto Rico 00931; tel. (809) 764-0000; fax (809) 763-5685; f. 1969 to facilitate the development and use of libraries, archives and information services; identification, collection and preservation of information resources in support of intellectual and educational endeavours in the area; *c.* 200 mems; Pres. WILLAMAE JOHNSON (Bahamas); Exec. Sec. ONEIDA R. ORTIZ (Puerto Rico); publs *ACURIL Newsletter, Conference Proceedings*.

Commonwealth Library Association: POB 144, Mona, Kingston 7, Jamaica, West Indies; tel. 927-2123; fax 927-1926; f. 1972 to support and encourage library asscns in the Commonwealth; to forge and strengthen professional links between librarians; to promote the status and education of librarians and the reciprocal recognition of qualifications; to improve libraries; to initiate research projects designed to promote library provision and to further technical development of libraries in the Commonwealth; 52 mems incl. 40 national asscns, 130 affiliated mems; Pres. ELIZABETH WATSON; Exec. Sec. NORMA AMENU-KPODO; publ. *COMLA Newsletter* (3 a year).

European Association for Health Information and Libraries: 60 rue de la Concorde, 1050 Brussels, Belgium; tel. (2) 511-80-63; fax (2) 511-80-63; f. 1987, to bring together and represent health librarians and information officers in Europe; to promote co-operation between health libraries and documentation centres; 500 mems; Pres. ELISABETH HUSEM; Sec. TONY MCSEÀN; publs *Newsletter to European Health Librarians* (quarterly), *Proceedings of the EAHIL European Conference of Medical and Health Libraries* (every 2 years), *EAHIL Medical Libraries in Europe – A Directory.*

International Association for the Development of Documentation, Libraries and Archives in Africa: BP 375, Dakar, Senegal; tel. 24-09-54; f. 1957 to promote planning and organization of archives, libraries, documentation centres and museums in all African countries; Permanent Sec. EMMANUEL K. W. DADZIE.

International Association for Mass Communication Research/Association internationale des études et recherches sur l'information: POB 67006, 1060 JA Amsterdam, The Netherlands; premises at Aecherstijn, Baden Powellweg 109/111, 1069 LD Amsterdam, The Netherlands; tel. (20) 6101581; fax (20) 6104821; f. 1957 to disseminate information on teaching and research in mass media; to encourage research; to provide a forum for the exchange of information; to bring about improvements in communication practice, policy and research; and to encourage the improvement of training for journalism; over 1,000 mems in 63 countries; Pres. Prof. CEES HAMELINK (Netherlands).

International Association of Agricultural Information Specialists/Association Internationale des Spécialistes de l'Information Agricole: f. 1955 to promote, internationally and nationally, agricultural library science and documentation, as well as the professional interests of agricultural librarians and documentalists; over 800 mems, representing 80 countries; affiliated to the International Federation of Library Associations and to the Fédération Internationale de Documentation; Pres. Drs J. VAN DER BURG; Sec.-Treas. M. BELLAMY, CAB International, Wallingford, Oxon., OX10 8DE, England; publs *Quarterly Bulletin, World Directory of Agricultural Information Resource Centres.*

International Association of Bibliophiles/Association Internationale de Bibliophilie: C/o Bibliothèque Nationale de France, 58 rue Richelieu, 75084 Paris Cedex 02, France; f. 1963 to form a meeting point for bibliophiles from different countries, to organize conferences; international congresses every 2 years; 500 mems; Pres. ANTHONY R. A. HOBSON (UK); Sec.-Gen. JEAN-MARC CHATELAIN (France); publ. *Le Bulletin du Bibliophile.*

International Association of Law Libraries (IALL)/Association internationale des bibliothèques de droit: POB 5709, Washington, DC 20016-1309, USA; tel. (804) 924-3384; e-mail lbw@virginia.edu; f. 1959 to offer worldwide co-operation in the development of law libraries and the collection of legal documentation; mems: over 600 in 60 countries; Pres. LARRY B. WENGER (USA); Sec. BRITT S. M. KJÖLSTAD (Switzerland); publ. *International Journal of Legal Information* (3 a year), *IALL Messenger* (irregular).

International Association of Metropolitan City Libraries (INTAMEL): C/o CEO's office, Metropolitan Toronto Reference Library, 789 Yonge St, Toronto, Ont. M4W 2G8, Canada; tel. (416) 393-7215; fax (416) 393-7229; f. 1967 to encourage international co-operation between large city libraries, and in particular the exchange of books, exhibitions, staff and information and participation in the work of the International Federation of Library Associations; Pres. ANDREW MILLER (Scotland); Sec.-Treas. FRANCES SCHWENGER (Canada).

International Association of Music Libraries, Archives and Documentation Centres (IAML)/Association internationale des bibliothèques, archives et centres de documentation musicaux/ Internationale Vereinigung der Musikbibliotheken, Musikarchive und Musikdokumentationszentren: C/o Alison Hall, Cataloguing Dept, Carleton University, 1125 Colonel By Drive, Ottawa K1S 5B6, Canada; tel. (613) 520-2600 ext. 8150; fax (613) 520-3583; f. 1951 to facilitate co-operation between music libraries and information centres, compile music bibliographies, and to promote the professional training of music librarians and documentalists; national branches in 19 countries; mems in 42 countries; Pres. VESLEMÖY HEINTZ (Sweden); Sec.-Gen. ALISON HALL; publ. *Fontes artis musicae* (quarterly).

International Association of Technological University Libraries (IATUL)/Association internationale des bibliothèques d'universités polytechniques: C/o Chalmers University of Technology Library, 41296 Gothenburg, Sweden; tel. (31) 772-37-54; fax (31) 16-84-94; f. 1955 to promote co-operation between member libraries and conduct research on library problems; mems: 200 university libraries in 41 countries; Pres. Dr NANCY FJÄLLBRANT; Sec. SINIKKA KOSKIALA (Finland); publs *IATUL News*(quarterly), *IATUL Proceedings* (annually).

International Board on Books for Young People (IBBY): Nonnenweg 12, Postfach, 4003 Basel, Switzerland; tel. (61) 2722917; fax (61) 2722757; e-mail ibby@eye.ch; f. 1953 to support and unify those forces in all countries connected with children's book work; to encourage the production and distribution of good children's books especially in the developing countries; to promote scientific investigation into problems of juvenile books; to organize International Children's Book Day and a biennial international congress; to present the Hans Christian Andersen Award every two years to a living author and illustrator whose work is an outstanding contribution to juvenile literature, and the IBBY-Asahi Reading Promotion Award annually to an org. that has made a significant contribution to children's literature; mems: National Sections and individual mems in 60 countries; Pres. CARMEN DIANA DEARDEN (Venezuela); Exec. Dir Mrs LEENA MAISSEN (Switzerland); publs *Bookbird* (quarterly), *Congress Reports*, directories, booklists.

International Committee for Social Science Information and Documentation/ Comité international pour l'information et la documentation des sciences sociales: 410–412 Herengracht, 1017 BX Amsterdam, Netherlands; tel. (20) 622-5061; fax (20) 623-8374; f. 1950 to collect and disseminate information on documentation services in social sciences, help improve documentation, advise societies on problems of documentation and to draw up rules likely to improve the presentation of all documents; mems from international associations specializing in social sciences or in documentation, and from other specialized fields; Pres. KRISHNA G. TYAGI (India); Sec.-Gen. ARNAUD F. MARKS (Netherlands); publs *Newsletter, International Bibliography of the Social Sciences* (annually, four series), and occasional bibliographies, directories and reports.

International Council of Theological Library Associations/Conseil International des Associations de Bibliothèques de Théologie: Postfach 250104, 50517 Cologne, Germany; tel. (221) 3382-110; fax (221) 3382109; f. 1961; Pres. Dr A. GEUNS; Sec. Dr I. DUMKE.

International Council on Archives/Conseil international des archives: 60 rue des Francs-Bourgeois, 75003 Paris, France; tel. 1-40-27-63-06; fax 1-42-72-20-65; f. 1948; mems: 1,500 from 170 countries; Pres. WANG GANG; Sec.-Gen. Dr CHARLES KECSKEMÉTI (France); publs *Archivum* (annually), *Bulletin of the ICA* (2 a year), *Janus* (2 a year), and various regional and professional publications.

International Federation for Information and Documentation/Fédération internationale d'Information et de Documentation: POB 90402, 2509 LK, The Hague, Netherlands; tel. (70) 3140671; fax (70) 3140667; e-mail fid@python.konbib.nl; f. 1895 to promote, through international co-operation, research in and development of documentation, information science and information management, which includes organization, storage, retrieval, dissemination and evaluation of information in the fields of science, technology, social sciences, arts and humanities; contributes to the development and setting up of international networks of information systems; promotes and co-ordinates research and training in information science and encourages the establishment of information analysis and documentation systems; 68 national mems, 5 international mems, 350 institutional and personal mems in 70 countries; Pres. MARTHA B. STONE; publs *FID Bulletin* (6 a year), *International Forum on Information and Documentation* (quarterly), *Newsletter on Education and Training Programmes for Information Personnel* (quarterly), *FID Directory, Annual Report, Extensions and Corrections to the UDC* (annually).

International Federation of Film Archives/Fédération internationale des archives du film: 190 rue F. Merjay, 1180 Brussels, Belgium; tel. (2) 3430691; fax (2) 3437622; f. 1938 to encourage the creation of archives in all countries for the collection and conservation of the film heritage of each land; to facilitate co-operation and exchanges between these film archives; to promote public interest in the art of the cinema; to aid research in this field and to compile new documentation; conducts research; publishes manuals, etc.; holds annual congresses; 108 affiliates in 62 countries; Pres. MICHELLE AUBERT (France); Sr Administrator CHRISTIAN DIMITRIU (Belgium).

International Federation of Library Associations and Institutions (IFLA)/ Fédération Internationale des Associations de Bibliothécaires et des Bibliothèques: POB 95312, 2509 CH The Hague, Netherlands; tel. (70) 314-08-84; fax (70) 383-48-27; e-mail ifla.hq@ifla.nl; f. 1927; to promote international library co-operation in all fields of library activity, and to provide a representative body in matters of international interest; 1,550 mems in 144 countries; Pres. CHRISTINE DESCHAMPS (France); Sec.-Gen. LEO VOOGT (Netherlands); publs *IFLA*

Journal (6 a year), *International Cataloguing Bibliographic Control* (quarterly), *IFLA Directory, IFLA Professional Reports, IFLA Council Report.*

International Institute for Children's Literature and Reading Research/ Institut International de Littérature pour Enfants et de Recherches sur la Lecture: 1040 Vienna, Mayerhofgasse 6, Austria; tel. 505-28-31; fax 505-0359-17; e-mail kidlit@netway.at; f. 1965 as an international documentation and advisory centre of juvenile literature; promotes international research; arranges conferences and exhibitions; compiles recommendation lists; mems: individual and group members in 26 countries; Dir Mag. KARIN SOLLAT (Austria); publ. *1000 and 1 Buch* (6 a year) in co-operation with Ministry of Education and the Study and Information Centre for Children's and Juvenile Literature.

International Society for Knowledge Organization (ISKO): C/o Royal School of Librarianship, Birketinget 6, 2300 Copenhagen S, Denmark; tel. 31-58-60-66; fax 32-84-02-01; e-mail ISKO@db.dk; f. 1989 to promote research, development, and application of all methods for the organization of knowledge; gives advice on the construction, perfection and application of classification systems, thesauri, terminologies etc; organizes international conference every two years; 520 mems from 51 countries; Pres. Prof. HANNE ALBRECHTSEN; publs *Knowledge Organization* (quarterly), *ISKO News, Advances in Knowledge Organization* (irregularly), *Fortschritte in der Wissensorganisation* (irregularly), *Knowledge Organisation in Subject Areas 1994–* (irregularly).

International Translations Centre: Schuttersveld 2, 2611 WE Delft, The Netherlands; tel. (15) 2142242; fax (15) 2158535; f. 1961; an international awareness centre for published translations and translations made by industries and scientific institutes in the field of science and technology; produces *World Translations Index* data base (12 updates annually); edits *World Translations Index* (10 a year and annual cumulation), *Journals in Translation* (2 updates annually), *Five-Year Cumulations of World Index of Scientific Translations* (1967-71, 1972-76), *Nine-Year Cumulation World Transindex* (1977-85); provides information on the availability of translations; the Centre is managed by a board composed of representatives of 6 countries; Chair. Dr D. WOOD (UK); Dir Mrs M. RISSEEUW.

International Youth Library/Internationale Jugendbibliothek: Schloss Blutenburg, 81247 Munich, Germany; tel. (89) 891211-0; fax (89) 8117553; f. 1948; an associated project of UNESCO since 1953. Objects: to encourage int. exchange and co-operation in children's book publishing and research; to provide information and advice to students, teachers, publishers, etc.; to organize exhibitions; largest collection of int. children's literature in the world (500,000 vols in over 100 languages); Dir Dr BARBARA SCHARIOTH; publs Catalogues of various exhibitions, *Report* (2 a year), *White Ravens* (annually).

Ligue des Bibliothèques Européennes de Recherche (LIBER): c/o Prof. Dr H.-A. Koch, Universität Bremen, POB 330440, 28334 Bremen, Germany; tel. (421) 2183361; f. 1971 to establish close collaboration between the general research libraries of Europe, and national university libraries in particular; and to help in finding practical ways of improving the quality of the services these libraries provide; 320 mems; Pres. F. MICHAEL SMETHURST; publ. *European Research Library Co-operation* (quarterly).

Economics, Political Science and Sociology

International Labour Organisation (ILO): 4 route des Morillons, 1211 Geneva 22, Switzerland; fax (22) 799-85-78; e-mail pubvente@ilo.org; f. 1919, became Specialized Agency of UN in 1946; aims to build a code of international labour law and practice, is concerned with the safety, health and social security of workers and provides technical experts where needed by member countries; sets out to improve labour conditions, raise living standards and promote productive employment in all countries; library: see under Switzerland; mems: 173 countries; Dir-Gen. JUAN SOMAVIA; publs *International Labour Review, Official Bulletin, Bulletin of Labour Statistics, Yearbook of Labour Statistics, International Labour Documentation, World of Work,* studies, manuals and reports.

Associated institutions:

International Institute for Labour Studies: CP 6, 1211 Geneva 22, Switzerland; tel. (22) 799-61-28; fax (22) 799-85-42; f. 1960 by ILO; aims: to provide a global forum for interaction between business, labour, policy-makers and academics on emerging labour policy issues; to promote research networks on policy implications of changing relationships between labour, business and the State; to develop the research capacities of ministries of labour and employers' and workers' organizations; Chair. JUAN SOMAVIA (Dir-Gen., ILO); Dir PADMANABHA GOPINATH (Asst Dir-Gen., ILO).

International Training Centre of the ILO/Centre International de Formation de l'OIT: Corso Unità d'Italia 125, 10127 Turin, Italy; f. 1965 by International Labour Organisation to offer advanced training facilities for managers, trainers and trade union officials, and technical specialists from ILO mem. states; Chair. JUAN SOMAVIA (Dir-Gen., ILO); Dir FRANÇOIS TRÉMEAUD (Asst Dir-Gen., ILO).

OTHER ORGANIZATIONS

African Training and Research Centre in Administration for Development/Centre Africain de Formation et de Recherche Administratives pour le Développement (CAFRAD): Pavillon International, blvd Mohamed V, BP 310, Tangier, Morocco; tel. (9) 94-26-52; fax (9) 94-14-15; f. 1964 by agreement between Morocco and UNESCO; training of African senior civil servants; research into administrative problems in Africa, documentation or results, and the provision of a consultation service for governments and organizations in Africa; holds frequent seminars; mems: Algeria, Burkina Faso, Burundi, Cameroon, Central African Republic, Chad, Côte d'Ivoire, Dem. Rep. of Congo, Egypt, Gabon, Gambia, Ghana, Guinea, Guinea-Bissau, Liberia, Libya, Mali, Mauritania, Morocco, Niger, Nigeria, Sierra Leone, Somalia, Sudan, Togo, Tunisia; UNDP has provided assistance since 1971; Pres. H. E. MANSOURI MESSAOUD; Dir-Gen. Dr M. A. WALI; publs *African Administrative Studies* (2 a year), *CAFRAD News* (2 a year, English, French and Arabic), *African Administrative Studies* (2 a year, also in French), *Administrative Information Sources* (quarterly, also in French), *Index CAFRADIANA* (annually).

Association of International Accountants: South Bank Bldg, Kingsway, Team Valley, Gateshead, Tyne and Wear, NE11 0JS, England; tel. (191) 4824409; fax (191) 4825578; e-mail aia@a-i-a.org.uk; f. 1928; promotes and supports the advancement of the accountancy profession in all parts of the world; offers a professional qualification for company auditors; 18,000 mems and students; Chair. E. GILLESPIE; Chief Exec. J. R. A. TURNBULL; publ. *The International Accountant* (quarterly).

Association of Social Anthropologists of the Commonwealth: C/o The Royal Anthropological Institute, 50 Fitzroy St, London, W1P 5HS, England; tel. (71) 387-0455; f. 1946; 570 mems; Chair. Prof. P. CAPLAN; Hon. Sec. Prof. N. RAPPORT; publs *Newsletter* (annually), *ASA Annals, ASA Monographs, ASA Studies, ASA Essays, ASA Methods in Social Anthropology.*

Centre International des Civilisations Bantu: BP 770, Libreville, Gabon; tel. 73-96-50; telex 5689; fax 73-40-68; f. 1983; intergovernmental organization founded by 10 countries of the Bantu zone: Angola, CAR, Congo, Comoros, Gabon, Equatorial Guinea, Rwanda, São Tomé and Príncipe, Zaire, Zambia; research and documentation centre for the conservation and promotion of the cultural heritage of the Bantu peoples; activities in all fields of culture, science and education; 48 staff; an information centre is in the process of formation; library: 4,000 vols, and special collection of university theses (microfiche) on ten member states; Dir-Gen. VATOMENE KUKANDA; publs *Muntu* (2 a year), *CICIBA-Informations* (quarterly).

Econometric Society: Dept of Economics, Northwestern University, Evanston, IL 60208-2600, USA; tel. (847) 491-3615; f. 1930 to promote studies aimed at unification of the theoretical-quantitative and the empirical-quantitative approach to economic problems; 6,700 mems; Exec. Dir and Sec. JULIE P. GORDON (USA); Treas. ROBERT J. GORDON; publ. *Econometrica* (every 2 months).

Economic Development Institute of the World Bank: 1818 H St, NW, Washington, DC 20433, USA; tel. (202) 477-1234; telex 64145 (World Bank); fax (202) 676-0858; f. 1955; helps build development capacities and institutions by organizing training and discussion on issues connected with the management of economic development, and by assisting institutions in the developing world engaged in similar work; provides support for training institutions and technical assistance; prepares publications, a/v products and computer programs; Dir AMNON GOLAN.

European Association for Population Studies/Association Européenne pour l'Étude de la Population: POB 11676, 2502 AR The Hague, The Netherlands; tel. (70) 3565200; fax (70) 3647187; e-mail eaps@nidi.nl; f. 1983 to promote the study of population in Europe through fostering co-operation between persons interested or engaged in European population studies; mems: demographers and other population scientists from all European countries; Pres. GRAZIELLA CASELLI; Sec.-Gen. and Treas. NICO VAN NIMWEGEN; Exec. Sec. GYS BEETS; publs *European Journal of Population/Revue Européenne de Démographie, European Studies of Population.*

European Centre for Social Welfare Policy and Research: Berggasse 17, 1090 Vienna, Austria; tel. (1) 3194505-0; fax (1) 3194505-19; e-mail ec@euro.centre.org; non-profit autonomous intergovernmental organization affiliated to the United Nations; conducts research, and provides training and information, in the fields of welfare and social development; library of 4,500 vols; Exec. Dir Prof. Dr BERND MARIN; publ. *Eurosocial Reports Series* (in English, French and German).

European Foundation for Management Development (EFMD): 40 rue Washington, 1050 Brussels, Belgium; tel. (2) 648-03-85; fax (2) 646-07-68; e-mail info@efmd.be; f. 1971; provides forum for worldwide co-operation in management development; European Quality Initiative (EQUAL) project seeks int. co-operation in assessing quality in management education; mem. orgs (business schools, management centres, companies, consultancies) in 41 countries; Pres. GERARD VAN SCHAIK; Dir-Gen. BERNADETTE CONRATHS; publ. *Forum* (3 a year).

Futuribles International: 55 rue de Varenne, 75007 Paris, France; tel. (1) 42-22-63-10; fax 42-22-65-54; f. 1960; aims to act as an early-warning system to identify major trends and challenges of the future; to undertake research on current economic and social issues; to serve as a consulting group for futures studies and strategic planning; major fields of expertise: development strategies, and multi-disciplinary studies on economic, technological, social and cultural changes in industrialized countries; library and documentation system: 90,000 entries; Scientific Council: 41 mems from 15 countries; Pres. JACQUES LESOURNE; Exec. Dir HUGUES DE JOUVENEL (France); publs *Futuribles* (monthly), *Futuribles Info* (quarterly), *Futuribles Newsletter* (quarterly).

Institute for International Sociological Research: 20 rue Manin, 75019 Paris, France; tel. (1) 42-41-54-15; f. 1964; diplomatic and international affairs, social and political sciences, moral and behavioural sciences, arts and literature; 132 Life Fellows, 44 Assoc. Fellows; 14 research centres; Pres., Chair. Exec. Cttee and Dir-Gen. Consul Dr EDWARD S. ELLENBERG; publs *Diplomatic Observer* (monthly), *Newsletter, Bulletin* (quarterly), *Annual Report*, etc.

Affiliated institutes:

Academy of Diplomacy and International Affairs (ADIA)/Académie Diplomatique et des Affaires Internationales: C/o Institute for International Sociological Research, 20 rue Manin, 75019 Paris, France; f. 1972; 120 Life Fellows (elected) and unlimited mems; Pres. Consul Dr EDWARD S. ELLENBERG.

International Academy of Social and Moral Sciences, Arts and Letters (IASMAL)/Académie Internationale des Sciences Sociales et Morales, des Arts et des Lettres: C/o Institute for International Sociological Research, 20 rue Manin, 75019 Paris, France; f. 1972; 160 Life Fellows and unlimited mems; Pres. Consul Dr EDWARD S. ELLENBERG.

Inter-American Statistical Institute/Instituto Interamericano de Estadística: Balcarce 184 (of. 211), 1327 Buenos Aires, Argentina; tel. (1) 349-5777; fax (1) 349-5776; e-mail efabb@indec.mecon.ar; f. 1940; 238 mems; fosters statistical development in the Western Hemisphere; Pres. ENRIQUE DE ALBA (Mexico); Technical Sec. EVELIO O. FABBRONI; publs *Estadística* (2 a year), *Newsletter* (quarterly).

International African Institute (IAI)/Institut africain international: School of Oriental and African Studies, Thornhaugh St, Russell Square, London, WC1H 0XG, England; tel. (171) 323-6108; fax (171) 323-6118; f. 1926; facilitates the study of African societies and cultures and the dissemination of the results of that research; Chair. Prof. GEORGE CLEMENT BOND; Dir Prof. PAUL SPENCER; publs *Africa* (quarterly), *Africa Bibliography* (annually).

International Association for South-East European Studies/Association Internationale d'Etudes du Sud-Est Européen: 71268 Bucharest, Şos. Kiseleff 47; tel. (1) 222-54-09; fax (1) 223-30-63; f. 1963; 23 mem. countries; Pres. Prof. JAN KARAYANNOPOULOS (Greece); Sec.-Gen. Prof. RĂZVAN THEODORESCU; publ. *Bulletin* (1 a year).

International Association of Schools of Social Work (IASSW): C/o University of Southampton, Highfields, Southampton, SO17 1BJ, England; tel. (1703) 593054; fax (1703) 581156; e-mail ld@socsci.soton.ac.uk; f. 1928 to provide international leadership and encourage high standards in social work education; mems: 1,700 schools of social work in 90 countries and 35 national associations of schools; Pres. Dr LENA DOMINELLI (UK); publs *International Social Work* (quarterly), *Directory of Members, IASSW News*.

International Center for Monetary and Banking Studies/Centre International d'Etudes Monétaires et Bancaires: 11a ave de la Paix, 1202 Geneva, Switzerland; tel. (22) 734-95-48; fax (22) 733-38-53; f. 1973; independent, associated with the Graduate Institute of International Studies (*q.v.*); scientific study of international monetary, financial and banking issues; sponsors conferences, public lectures, organizes intensive executive courses for professionals in banking and finance; Dir Prof. HANS GENBERG; publ. *Center Papers / Cahiers du Centre*.

International Centre for Ethnic Studies: 554/1 Peradeniya Rd, Kandy, Sri Lanka; tel. (8) 234892; fax (8) 234892; f. 1982 to provide a clear institutional focus and identity for the study and understanding of the management of ethnic conflict; to stimulate cross-national comparative research in ethnic policy studies; library of 5,000 vols, special collections on ethnicity and women's issues; Exec. Dir K. M. DE SILVA (Sri Lanka); publ. *Ethnic Studies Report* (2 a year).

International Commission for the History of Representative and Parliamentary Institutions/Commission internationale pour l'histoire des assemblées d'états: Dept of History, 43–46 North Bailey, Durham, DH1 3EX, England; fax (191) 374-4754; f. 1936 to encourage research on the origin and history of representative and parliamentary institutions; mems: individuals in 40 countries; Pres. J. ROGISTER (UK); Sec. J. H. GREVER (USA); publs *Parliaments, Estates and Representation* (annually), occasional monographs.

International Council on Social Welfare/Conseil international de l'action sociale: C/o Sirpa Utriainen, 380 rue Saint-Antoine Ouest, Bureau 3200, Montreal, Qué. H2Y 3X7, Canada; f. 1928 to promote forms of social and economic development which aim to reduce poverty, hardship and vulnerability throughout the world, especially amongst disadvantaged people; mems: 72 committees and 20 international organizations; Pres. DIRK JARRÉ (Germany); Sec.-Gen. SIRPA UTRIAINEN (Canada); publs *International Social Work* (quarterly), *International Newsletter* (quarterly), *Proceedings of International Conferences on Social Welfare* (biennial), Regional Newsletters.

International Federation of Business and Professional Women/Fédération Internationale des Femmes de Carrières Libérales et Commerciales/Federación Internacional de Mujeres de Negocios y Profesionales: Studio 16, Cloisters House, Cloisters Business Centre, 8 Battersea Park Rd, London, SW8 4BG, England; tel. (171) 738-8323; fax (171) 622-8528; e-mail BPWI_HQ@compuserve.com; f. 1930; to promote the interests of business and professional women, and in particular to bring their specialized knowledge and skills to play a more effective part in the world government organizations; mems: over 250,000; Pres. SYLVIA G. PERRY; Dir TAMARA MARTINEZ; publ. *BPW News International* (monthly newsletter).

International Fiscal Association: World Trade Center, POB 30215, 3001 DE Rotterdam, Netherlands; tel. (10) 4052990; e-mail n.gensecr@ifa.nl; f. 1938; aims: to study and advance international and comparative law with regard to public finance and especially international and comparative fiscal law and the financial and economic aspects of taxation; mems: 9,500 in 90 countries, national branches in 47 countries; Pres. Prof. S. O. LODIN (Sweden); Sec.-Gen. J. F. SPIERDIJK (Netherlands); publs *Cahiers de Droit Fiscal International* (Studies on International Fiscal Law), *Yearbook of the International Fiscal Association, Congress Seminar Series*.

International Institute for Ligurian Studies/Istituto Internazionale di Studi Liguri: Museo Bicknell, Via Romana 39, 18012 Bordighera, Italy; tel. (184) 263601; fax (184) 266421; f. 1947 to conduct research on ancient monuments and regional traditions in the north-west arc of the Mediterranean; library of 82,000 vols; mems in France, Italy, Spain, Switzerland; Dir Prof. CARLO VARALDO (Italy).

International Institute of Philosophy (IIP)/Institut international de philosophie: 8 rue Jean-Calvin, 75005 Paris, France; tel. 1-43-36-39-11; f. 1937; aims: to clarify fundamental issues of contemporary philosophy in annual meetings, and, by several series of publications, to promote mutual understanding among thinkers of different traditions and cultural backgrounds; a maximum of 115 mems, considered eminent in their field, chosen from all countries and representing different tendencies, are elected; present mems: 100 in 39 countries; Pres. T. IMAMICHI (Japan); Sec.-Gen. P. AUBENQUE (France); publs *Bibliography of Philosophy* (quarterly), Proceedings of annual meetings, *Surveys (Chroniques)* of philosophy, *Philosophy and World Community* (series of texts in various languages), *Philosophical Problems Today*.

International Institute of Sociology/Institut International de Sociologie: C/o University of Kansas, Gerontology Center, 4089 Dole, Lawrence, KS 66045, USA; f. 1893 to further the study of sociology; mems: 300 representing 45 countries; Pres. ERWIN K. SCHEUCH (Germany); Gen. Sec./Treas. RHONDA J. V. MONTGOMERY (USA); publ. *Annales de l'Institut International de Sociologie / The Annals of the International Institute of Sociology*.

International Monetary Fund Institute: Washington, DC 20431, USA; tel. (202) 623-6660; fax (202) 623-6490; f. 1964 to provide specialist training in economic analysis and policy, statistics, public finance, and bank supervision, for officials of mem. countries; courses and seminars in Arabic, English, French and Spanish; library; Dir PATRICK DE FONTENAY; publ. *Courier*.

International Peace Academy: 777 United Nations Plaza, New York, NY 10017, USA; tel. (212) 687-4300; fax (212) 983-8246; f. 1970; acts as independent, non-partisan, international institution dedicated to promoting the prevention and settlement of armed conflicts between and within states; activities include: policy research, organizing symposia for policy-makers; conducting training seminars on peacemaking and peacekeeping; and public forum activities; Pres. OLARA A. OTUNNU; publs *IPA Newsletter, IPA Policy Briefing*.

International Society for Community Development: 54 Riverside Drive, New York, NY 10024, USA; f. 1962 to advance the understanding and application of community development principles and practices; mems: 500; Pres. GLEN LEET; publs Journals and Newsletter.

International Society for Ethnology and Folklore: f. 1964 to establish and maintain collaboration between specialists in folklore and ethnology; organizes commissions, symposia, congresses, etc.; affiliated to Int. Union of Anthropological and Ethnological Sciences and ICPHS; close links with International Folk Music Council and International Council of Museums; mems: 504; Pres. Prof. MIHAI POP (Romania), Inst. of Ethnology, Str. Nikos Beloiannis 25, Bucharest, Romania; Vice-Pres. Prof. J. CUISENIER, Prof. K. C. PEETERS and R. M. DORSON; publ. *Bulletin d'Informations SIEF* (annually).

International Society for the Study of Medieval Philosophy/Société Internationale pour l'Etude de la Philosophie Médiévale: c/o Institut supérieur de Philosophie, place du Cardinal Mercier 14, 1348 Louvain-la-Neuve, Belgium; tel. (10) 474807; fax (10) 478285; e-mail accademia .belgio@hella.stm.it; f. 1958 to promote the study of medieval thought and the collaboration between individuals and institutions concerned in this field; organizes international congresses every five years and annual colloquium between congresses; 568 mems in 35 countries; Pres. D. LUSCOMBE (UK); Sec. J. HAMESSE (Belgium); publ. *Bulletin de Philosophie Médiévale* (annually).

International Society for Third-Sector Research (ISTR): Johns Hopkins University, Wyman Park Building, 3400 N. Charles St, Baltimore, MD 21218-2688, USA; tel. (410) 516-4678; fax (410) 516-4870; e-mail istrmbd@jhunix.hcf.jhu.edu; f. 1992; encourages research relevant to nonprofit orgs, voluntarism and philanthropy; 540 mems; Pres. ANTONIN WAGNER (Switzerland); Exec. Dir MARGERY B. DANIELS; publs journal (4 a year), newsletter (4 a year).

International Society of Social Defence and Humane Criminal Policy/Société internationale de défense sociale pour une politique criminelle humaniste: c/o Centro nazionale di prevenzione e difesa sociale, Palazzo comunale delle scienze sociali, Piazza Castello 3, 20121 Milan, Italy; tel. (2) 86460714; fax (2) 72008431; e-mail Cnpds.Ispac@iol.it; f. 1946; non-governmental org. in consultative status with UN Economic and Social Council; the study of crime-related problems in the perspective of a system of reactions which, through prevention and resocialization of deviants, aims to protect the individuals and society at large; 350 mems; Pres. SIMONE ROZES (France); Sec.-Gen. EDMONDO BRUTI LIBERATI (Italy); Treas. LUCIANA MARSELLI MILNER (Italy); publ. *Cahiers de défense sociale* (annually, in English, Spanish and French).

Inter-Parliamentary Union: Place du Petit-Saconnex, CP 438, 1211 Geneva 19, Switzerland; tel. (22) 919-41-50; 414217; fax (22) 733-31-41; e-mail postbox@ mail.ipu.org; f. 1889 to promote contacts among members of the world's parliaments and unite them in common action for international peace and co-operation; studies political, economic, social, juridical, cultural and environmental problems of international significance, notably through conferences; promotes free and fair elections and provides assistance to representative assemblies; helps to solve cases of violation of parliamentarians' rights; promotes status of women in political life; gathers and disseminates information on parliamentary matters; world membership: 137 National Inter-Parliamentary Groups; Pres. of Inter-Parliamentary Council MIGUEL ANGEL MARTÍNEZ (Spain); Sec.-Gen. ANDERS B. JOHNNSSON (Sweden); publs *Inter-Parliamentary Bulletin* (2 a year), *Chronicle of Parliamentary Elections* (annually), *World Directory of Parliaments* (annually).

Italian–Latin American Institute: Piazza B. Cairoli 3, 00186 Rome, Italy; tel. (6) 59091; telex 614391; fax (6) 5914923; f. 1966 to develop and co-ordinate research and documentation on the problems, achievements and prospects of mem. countries in cultural, scientific, economic, technical and social fields; organizes meetings and promotes activities representative of the development process of Latin America in its social, economic, cultural and technical-scientific aspects; 21 mem. countries; library and documentation centre of 80,000 vols, 4,315 periodicals; Sec.-Gen. Amb. BERNARDINO OSIO; publs *Quaderni IILA, Quaderni IILA* (series *Economia, Scienza*).

Nordisk Institut for Asienstudier (Nordic Institute of Asian Studies): Leifsgade 33, 2300 Copenhagen S, Denmark; tel. 31-54-88-44; fax 32-96-25-30; e-mail sec@nias.ku.dk; f. 1967; non-profit org. funded through Nordic Council of Ministers; research and documentation centre for Asian studies within humanities and social sciences to promote research and publish books on Asia; library of 23,000 vols and 750 current journals; Chair. Prof. Dr KIRSTI KOCH CHRISTENSEN; Dir Prof. Dr THOMMY SVENSSON; publ. *NIASnytt / Nordic Newsletter of Asian Studies* (4 a year).

Organisation for Economic Co-operation and Development (OECD): 2 rue André-Pascal, 75775 Paris Cedex 16, France; tel. 1-45-24-82-00; telex 640048; fax 1-45-24-85-00; f. 1961; under the responsibility of three Committees (Scientific and Technological Policy, Education and Employment, Labour and Social Affairs), serviced by two Directorates (Science, Technology and Industry; Education, Employment, Labour and Social Affairs), OECD is concerned with the impact of science, technology, education and the changing pattern of employment structures on the balance of economic and social development of its 29 member countries (in Europe, North America and the Pacific area) and with the implications of technological development for the environment as well as with the broader aspects of policy to meet new social objectives; it seeks to co-ordinate its mems' economic and social policies, and aims at being informative, promotional and catalytic through surveys of the current situation, identification of tentative policies and the establishment of a statistical and methodological base in support of government decision making; serves as an international clearing-house for exchanges of information and provides a forum where experts and policy-makers can discuss common issues and benefit from mutual co-operation; special programmes include the Programme for Educational Building and the Centre for Educational Research and Innovation (*q.v.*); Sec.-Gen. DONALD J. JOHNSTON.

Pan-African Institute for Development/ Institut Pan-Africain pour le Développement: BP 4056, Douala, Cameroon; tel. 42-10-61; telex 6048; fax 42-43-35; f. 1965 for the training of African Development staff; supplies support services to development agencies; regional insts in Burkina Faso, Cameroon, Zambia; 4 libraries; Sec.-Gen. Prof. A. C. MONDJANAGNI; publs *Yearly Progress Report, PAID Report* (2 a year).

Society for International Development/ Société Internationale pour le Développement: Via Panisperna 207, 00184 Rome, Italy; tel. (6) 487-2172; fax (6) 487-2170; e-mail info@sidint.org; f. 1957; a global network of individuals and institutions concerned with development that is participative, pluralistic and sustainable; mobilizes and strengthens civil society groups by building partnerships among them and with other sectors; fosters local initiatives and new forms of social experimentation; 6,000 mems in 125 countries, with 77 local chapters; Pres. BOUTROS BOUTROS-GHALI; Sec.-Gen. ROBERTO SAVIO; publs *Development* (quarterly), *SID Annual Report, Bridges* (newsletter, 6 a year).

Statistical Institute for Asia and the Pacific: Akasaka POB 13, Tokyo 107-8691, Japan; tel. (3) 3357-8351; fax (3) 3356-8305; e-mail unsiap@po.iijnet.or.jp; f. 1970; subsidiary body of the Economic and Social Commission for Asia and the Pacific (ESCAP) to provide training in official statistics to govt statisticians in the Asia-Pacific region as recommended by resolution 75 (XXIII) of ESCAP; three courses a year: Practical Statistics (6 months), Automatic Data Processing for Trainers (2 months), Data Analysis and Interpretation of Statistics (2 months); also 'country courses' given at a country's request to deal with a specific subject; mems: 30 Fellows (Practical Statistics course), 20 Fellows (ADP Course), 10 Fellows (DAIS Course); library of 20,000 vols; Dir LAU KAK EN; publ. *Newsletter* (irregular).

Stockholm International Peace Research Institute (SIPRI): Frösunda, 169 70 Solna, Sweden; tel. (8) 6559700; fax (8) 6559733; e-mail sipri@sipri.se; f. 1966 for research into problems of peace and conflict with particular attention to the problems of disarmament and arms control; library of 26,000 vols; Dir Dr ADAM DANIEL ROTFELD (Poland); Chair. Prof. DANIEL TARSCHYS (Sweden); publ. *SIPRI Yearbook*.

United Nations Institute for Training and Research (UNITAR)/Institut des Nations Unies pour la formation et la recherche: Palais des Nations, 1211 Geneva 10, Switzerland; tel. (22) 798-58-50; fax (22) 733-13-83; f. 1965 as an autonomous body within the framework of the United Nations; it aims, by training and research, to enhance the effectiveness of the United Nations in achieving the major objectives of the Organization, in particular the maintenance of peace and security and the promotion of economic and social development; it conducts seminars for diplomats and others who work with the UN system and carries out training, either at UN headquarters or in the field, which has special relevance for developing countries; it conducts research into problems of concern to the UN system; Exec. Dir MARCEL A. BOISARD (Switzerland); publs over 50 titles in English and some in French, Spanish and Russian.

Vienna Institute for Development and Co-operation/Wiener Institut für Entwicklungsfragen und Zusammenarbeit: 1030 Vienna, Weyrgasse 5, Austria; tel. (222) 713-35-94; fax (222) 713-35-94-73; f. 1987 as successor to Vienna Institute for Development; aims to disseminate information on problems and achievements of developing countries by all possible means in order to convince the public or industrialized nations of the necessity to increase development aid and to strengthen international co-operation; research programmes; mems from 20 countries; Pres. FRANZ VRANITZKY (Austria); Dir ERICH ANDRLIK; publ. *Report* series.

World Council of Management/Conseil Mondial de Management: C/o Nederlandse Vereniging voor Management, Burg Feithplein 100, PB 266, 2270 AG Voorburg;

f. 1926, present name 1976; promotes scientific and professional management; research, education, training, development and practice; mem. organizations in 45 countries; Pres. ALBERTO KRYGIER (Venezuela); Sec. HERBERT MÜLLER (Germany); publ. *Newsletter*.

World Institute for Development Economics Research of the United Nations University (UNU/WIDER): Katajanokanlaituri 6B, 00160 Helsinki, Finland; tel. (9) 6159911; fax (9) 61599333; e-mail wider@wider.unu.edu; f. 1984; conducts policy-oriented research; main theme areas: the economics of transition in Eastern Europe and Asia; liberalization and development in sub-Saharan Africa; institutional and distributive issues; international financial and economic issues; global governance issues; Dir Prof. GIOVANNI ANDREA CORNIA.

World Intellectual Property Organization (WIPO): 34 chemin des Colombettes, 1211 Geneva 20, Switzerland; tel. (22) 338-9111; telex 412912; fax (22) 733-5428; e-mail wipo.mail@wipo.int; f. 1967; UN specialized agency for intergovernmental co-operation in industrial property (patents, rights in trademarks, industrial designs, etc.) and copyright and neighbouring rights (literary, musical and artistic works, films, records, etc.); promotes creative intellectual activity, and facilitates the transfer of technology, especially to and among developing countries; 169 mem. states; library of 23,000 vols; Dir-Gen. Dr KAMIL IDRIS; publs *Industrial Property and Copyright* (monthly), *WIPO Gazette of International Marks* (24 a year), *International Designs Bulletin* (monthly), *PCT Gazette* (weekly), *PCT Newsletter* (monthly), *Les appelations d'origine* (irregular), *Intellectual Property in Asia and the Pacific* (quarterly).

World Social Prospects Association/Association mondiale de prospective sociale: 5 route des Morillons, 1218 Grand-Saconnex, Geneva, Switzerland; tel. (22) 791-6187; telex 415730; fax (22) 791-0361; f. 1976 to encourage the study of the great issues emerging on the social horizon in the anticipation of establishing a new international order; to carry out and promote comparative research into the dynamic forces shaping the future of social policy; to discover social initiatives that could lead to a new international order; to formulate proposals that could influence decisions in economic and social policy; Sec.-Gen. ALBERT TÉVOÉDJRÉ.

World Society for Ekistics: c/o Athens Center of Ekistics, 24 Strat. Syndesmou St, 10673 Athens, Greece; tel. (1) 3623-216; fax (1) 3629-337; f. 1965; aims to promote the development of knowledge and ideas concerning human settlements by research and through publications, conferences, scholarships, etc.; to encourage the development and expansion of education in ekistics; to educate public opinion concerning ekistics; to recognize the benefits and necessity of an interdisciplinary approach to the needs of human settlements, and to promote and emphasize such an approach; 250 mems; Pres. WESLEY W. POSVAR (USA); Sec.-Gen.-Treas. PANAYIS PSOMOPOULOS.

Education

African and Mauritius Council on Higher Education/Conseil africain et mauricien de l'enseignement supérieur: BP 134, Ouagadougou, Burkina Faso; tel. 346-74; f. 1968 to ensure co-ordination between member states in the fields of higher education and research; mems: governments of 15 French-speaking African countries; Pres. DANIEL ABIBI; Sec.-Gen. HENRY VALERE KINIFFO.

African Association for Literacy and Adult Education: POB 50768, Finance House, 6th Floor, Loita St, Nairobi, Kenya; tel. 222391; telex 22096; f. 1984 to encourage and assist the formation and strengthening of adult education national asscns in mem. countries; runs training programmes, initiates and encourages research, publishes reports, etc., and acts as a clearing-house for information and documentation on all forms of adult education; 19 national asscns, 167 institutional mems, 867 individual mems, 30 assoc. mems; Chair. Dr ANTHONY SETS'ABI (Lesotho); Sec.-Gen. PAUL WANGOOLA (Uganda); publs *AALAE Newsletter* (3–4 a year), *Journal* (2 a year), reports of conferences, etc.

Agence Francophone pour l'Enseignement Supérieur et la Recherche: BP 400 Succ. Côte-des-Neiges, Montréal, Qué. H3S 2S7, Canada; tel. (514) 343-6630; telex 055 609 55; fax (514) 343-2107; f. 1961; aims: documentation, co-ordination, co-operation, exchange; 341 mems, 346 assoc. mems (B); Pres. MICHEL GERVAIS (Canada); Dir-Gen. MICHEL GUILLOU (France); publs *UREF-Actualités* (5 a year), *Universités* (quarterly).

Association for Teacher Education in Europe: 60 rue de la Concorde, 1050 Brussels, Belgium; tel. (2) 540-97-81; fax (2) 514-11-72; e-mail atee@euronet.be; f. 1976 to establish contacts between institutions for teacher education and those responsible for that education; arranges working groups, annual conference, etc.; undertakes consultancy work for European organizations; Pres. MIREIA MONTANÉ; Sec.-Gen. ISABEL GARCÍA; publs *Journal* (quarterly), *ATEE Newsletter* (quarterly), *Cahiers on Teacher Education*.

Association Montessori Internationale: Koninginneweg 161, 1075 CN Amsterdam, Netherlands; f. 1929 to propagate the ideals and educational methods of Dr Maria Montessori and to spread knowledge on child development without racial, religious or political prejudice; activities: supervises affiliated training courses for teachers in several countries; sponsors international congresses and study conferences on Montessori education; creates new training centres and offers affiliation to Montessori societies; Pres. G. J. PORTIELJE; Sec. R. MONTESSORI; publ. *Communications* (3 or 4 a year).

Association of African Universities/Association des Universités Africaines: POB 5744, Accra-North, Ghana; tel. (21) 774495; fax (21) 774821; e-mail secgen@aau.org; f. 1967 to collect, classify and disseminate information on higher education and research in Africa; to promote co-operation among African instns in training, research, community services and higher education policy, in curriculum development and in the determination of equivalence in academic degrees; to encourage increased contacts between mems and the int. academic world; to encourage the development and wide use of African languages and support training of univ. teachers and administrators to deal with problems in African education in general; mems: 142 university institutions in 43 African countries; Pres. Prof. ANDREW SIWELA (Zambia); Sec.-Gen. Prof. NARCISO MATOS (Mozambique); publs *Newsletter* (3 a year), *Handbook* (1 a year).

Association of American International Colleges and Universities: 27 place de l'Université, 13625 Aix-en-Provence, France; f. 1971 to promote co-operation among independent institutions offering international education in Europe and the Near East; 12 mem. univs and colleges; Pres. JULIA WATKINS; Sec.-Gen. DAVID WILSFORD.

Association of Arab Universities: POB 401, Jubeyha, Amman, Jordan; tel. 5345131; fax 5332994; e-mail secgen@aaru.edu.jo; f. 1964 to consolidate co-operation between Arab universities and institutions of higher education; mems: 140 universities; Sec.-Gen. Dr MARWAN R. KAMAL; publs *Bulletin* (annually), *Directory of Arab Universities, Directory of Teaching Staff of Arab Universities, Proceedings of Seminars*.

Association of Caribbean Universities and Research Institutes: POB 11532, Caparra Heights Station, San Juan, Puerto Rico 00922; f. 1968 to foster contact and collaboration between member universities and institutes; conferences, meetings, seminars, etc.; circulation of information through newsletters, bulletins; facilitates co-operation and the pooling of resources in research; encourages exchanges of staff and students; mems: 50 institutions; Sec.-Gen. GERARD LATORTUE; publ. *Caribbean Educational Bulletin* (quarterly).

Association of Commonwealth Universities: John Foster House, 36 Gordon Square, London, WC1H 0PF, England; tel. (171) 387-8572; fax (171) 387-2655; e-mail pubinf@acu.ac.uk; f. 1913; organizes major meetings of Commonwealth universities and their representatives, acts as a liaison office and general information centre on Commonwealth universities, through its appointments service provides a range of services to assist mem. universities in filling staff vacancies, hosts a management consultancy service, and provides secretariats for the Commonwealth Scholarship Commission in the United Kingdom and the Marshall Aid Commemoration Commission; it also administers the Commonwealth Foundation Medical Electives Bursaries, the Academic Exchange Fellowship, the *Times Higher Education Supplement* Academic Exchange Fellowship, the ACU Development Fellowships, the ODA Shared Scholarship Scheme, the T.H.B. Symons Fellowship, the Canada Memorial Foundation Scholarships, and the ACU/CHESS Women's Programme; library of 18,000 vols; mems: 463 universities and university colleges; Sec. Gen. Prof. M. G. GIBBONS; publs *Commonwealth Universities Yearbook, Postgraduate Study Abroad* series of Student Information Papers, Report of the Council of the ACU (all annually), *Awards for University Teachers and Research Workers, Awards for Postgraduate Study at Commonwealth Universities, Awards for University Administrators and Librarians, Awards for First Degree Study at Commonwealth Universities* (all every 2 years), *Who's Who of Commonwealth University Vice-Chancellors, Presidents and Rectors* (irregularly), *ACU Bulletin of Current Documentation* (5 a year, controlled circulation), *Appointments in Commonwealth Universities* (fortnightly).

Association of Eastern and Southern African Universities: c/o the Inter-University Council for East Africa, POB 7110, Kampala, Uganda; tel. (41) 256251; telex 61572; fax (41) 342007; f. 1984; regional co-operation in research, staff and student exchanges, external examiners, etc.; 30 mem. universities; Chair. Prof. G. S. ESHIWANI (Kenya); Exec. Sec. E. K. KIGOZI.

Association of European Universities/Association des universités européennes: 10 rue du Conseil Général, 1211 Geneva 4, Switzerland; tel. (22) 329-26-44; fax (22) 329-28-21; e-mail cre@uni2a.unige.ch; f. 1959 to provide a forum in which university leaders can discuss the strengths and weaknesses of the systems of higher education and research in Europe, as well as their common interests and problems, in order to determine likely areas for enhanced co-operation and academic improvement; mems: 500 institutions of higher education and research in 39 European countries; Pres. Prof. JOSEP BRICALL (Spain); Sec.-Gen. Dr ANDRIS BARBLAN (Switzerland); publs *CRE action, CRE info* (newsletter).

Association of Institutes for European Studies/Association des instituts d'études européennes: Institut Européen de l'Université de Genève, 2 rue Daniel-Colladon, 1204 Geneva, Switzerland; tel. (22) 7057850; fax (22) 7057852; f. 1951 to co-ordinate activities of member institutes in teaching and research, exchange information, provide a centre for documentation; 32 mem. institutes in nine countries; Pres. Prof. E. CEREXHE (Belgium); Sec.-Gen. Prof. DUSAN SIDJANSKI; publs *Annuaire, Nouvelles de l'AIEE.*

Association of Southeast Asian Institutions of Higher Learning: f. 1956 to promote the economic, cultural and social welfare of the people of Southeast Asia by means of educational co-operation and research programmes; to foster the cultivation of a sense of regional identity and interdependence and to co-operate with other regional and international organizations; serves as a clearinghouse for information, provides opportunities for discussion and recognizes distinctive academic achievements; mems: 150 institutions; Sec.-Gen. Dr NINNAT OLANVORAVUTH, Ratasastra Building, Chulalongkorn University, Henri Dunant Rd, Bangkok 10330, Thailand; tel. 2516966; fax 253-7909; publs *Newsletter, Handbook, Seminar Proceedings.*

Caribbean Regional Council for Adult Education: f. 1978 to promote and facilitate co-operation among national adult education organizations and agencies in non-Spanish-speaking territories of the region; to advocate awareness and recognition of the importance of adult education and to seek funding from governments and other sources; to hold conferences, seminars, training courses, etc.; to advise governments and other bodies on matters relating to adult education; library of 5,000 vols; Hon. Pres. Dr JOYCE ROBINSON; Chair. Dr CLAUDIA HARVEY; Exec. Sec.-Treas. Dr BRADLEY NILES, CARCAE, 3rd Ave, Belleville, St Michael, Barbados, West Indies; tel. (809) 429-2182; publs *Newsletter,* reports.

Centre for Educational Research and Innovation: c/o OECD, 75775 Paris Cedex 16, France; tel. 1-45-24-82-00; fax 1-45-24-90-98; f. 1968 to promote development of research in education, to encourage experiments in educational innovation and stimulate co-operation between mem. countries in research and development work on educational problems; projects under way deal with quality of schooling, including the curriculum and teacher training, education and new technologies, education for multi-cultural societies, the educational implications of changing work patterns, integration of disabled young people into education and work, school-based innovations, adult students in education, educational indicators and innovation exchange activities; Dir T. J. ALEXANDER; publs *Innovation in Education, Journal of Institutional Management in Higher Education* (3 a year).

Commonwealth Association of Polytechnics in Africa: c/o Kenya Polytechnic, POB 52428, Nairobi, Kenya; tel. 338156; telex 22529; fax (2) 338156; f. 1978 to provide a forum for exchange of professional ideas and practices in technical and business education and training, and to improve the content and methods of polytechnic teaching, to disseminate information through publications and workshops, and to create a data centre and reference library; 135 mem. polytechnics; library of 2,000 vols; Sec.-Gen. ELIFARA NGOMA; publs *CAPA Newsletter* (quarterly), *CAPA Journal of Technical Education and Training* (2 a year).

Commonwealth of Learning: Suite 600, 1285 West Broadway, Vancouver, BC, V6H 3X8, Canada; tel. (604) 775-8200; telex 04507508; fax (604) 775-8210; f. 1988 by Commonwealth Heads of Govt to promote co-operation among Commonwealth countries, utilizing distance education techniques, including communications technologies, to strengthen mem. countries' capacities in human resources development; works with colleges, universities and other institutions to increase access to opportunities for learning; Pres. and CEO Dato' Prof. GAJARAJ DHANARAJAN; publ. *Connections.*

Commonwealth Secretariat, Education Department, Human Resource Development Division: Marlborough House, Pall Mall, London, SW1Y 5HX, England; tel. (171) 747-6281; fax (171) 747-6287; encourages and supports educational consultation and co-operation between Commonwealth countries through conferences, seminars, workshops, meetings of experts, and training courses for educational personnel (with assistance from the Commonwealth Fund for Technical Co-operation); contributes to national educational development through studies of particular problems, handbooks, directories and training manuals, and by providing information on educational subjects; undertakes consultancies for govts on request; triennial conference of Ministers of Education; Dir (HRDD) Prof. STEPHEN A. MATLIN; publ. *Annual Report.*

Confederation of Central American Universities/Confederación Universitaria Centroamericana: Apdo 37-2060, Ciudad Universitaria Rodrigo Facio, San Pedro de Montes de Oca, San José, Costa Rica; tel. 225-27-44; fax 234-00-71; f. 1948; promotes regional co-operative initiatives in public higher education; promotes quality assurance and defends university autonomy and human rights in education; mems: Univ. of S. Carlos, Guatemala, Univ. College of Belize, Univ. of El Salvador, Univ. of Costa Rica, National Univ., Costa Rica, National Autonomous Univ. of Honduras, National Autonomous Univ. of Nicaragua-Managua, National Autonomous Univ. of Nicaragua-León, Univ. of Engineering, Nicaragua, Univ. of Panama; Pres. Dr LUIS GARITA (Costa Rica); Sec-Gen. Dr RICARDO SOL-ARRIAZA.

Conférence des Recteurs des Universités Africaines: BP 69, Brazzaville, Congo; f. 1976; aims to strengthen and develop inter-university co-operation in Africa; library of 20,000 vols and documentation centre; mems: 41; Pres. Mgr TSHIBANGU TSHISHIKU; Sec.-Gen. Prof. D. ABIBI.

Council for Cultural Co-operation: Council of Europe, 67075 Strasbourg Cedex, France; tel. 3-88-41-20-00; fax 3-88-41-27-50; f. 1962 to draw up and implement the educational and cultural programme of the Council of Europe; mems: 47 states; publs *Newsletter Education, European Heritage, EUDISED European Educational Research Yearbook.*

Education International (EI)/Internationale de l'Education (IE): 155 blvd Emile-Jacqmain 8è, 1210 Brussels, Belgium; tel. (2) 224-0611; fax (2) 224-0606; e-mail educint@infoboard.be; f. 1993 from the merger of the World Confederation of Organizations of the Teaching Profession (WCOTP/CMOPE) and the International Federation of Free Teachers' Unions (IFFTU/SPIE); to further the cause of organizations of teachers and education employees, promote status, interests and welfare of mems and defend their trade union and professional rights; to promote peace, democracy, social justice, equality and the application of the Universal Declaration on Human Rights through the development of education and the collective strength of teachers and education employees; mems: 284 national organizations in 149 countries; World Congress every three years; Pres. MARY HATWOOD FUTRELL (USA); Gen. Sec. FRED VAN LEEUWEN (Netherlands); publs *The EI Monthly Monitor, The Education International Quarterly Magazine* (both published in English, French and Spanish).

ERASMUS (European Community Action Scheme for the Mobility of University Students): 70 rue Montoyer, 1040 Brussels, Belgium; tel. (32) (2) 233-01-11; telex 63528; fax (32) (2) 233-01-50; f. 1987 by the Ccl of Ministers of the European Community; aims to encourage greater student and staff mobility throughout the EU and EFTA (European Free Trade Association) countries by means of the creation of a European University Network, the award of 'mobility' grants to students, arrangements for mutual recognition of qualifications and courses, and other supporting measures; publs *ERASMUS and Lingua Action II Directory* (annually), *Guidelines for Applicants,* etc.

European Association for the Education of Adults: Hotel d'Entitats, C/ Pere Vergés 1, 08020 Barcelona, Spain; tel. (3) 278-02-94; fax (3) 278-01-74; f. 1953 to encourage co-operation between adult education organizations on questions of methods, materials, and exchange of individuals, arranges study sessions and tours; offices in Barcelona (Spain), Brussels (Belgium), Helsinki (Finland) and Amersfoort (Netherlands); mems in 28 European countries and associate mems in America and Australia; Pres. P. FEDERIGHI; publ. *Newsletter.*

European Association of Distance Teaching Universities: Postbus 2960, 6401 DL Heerlen; tel. (45) 5762214; fax (45) 5741473; f. 1987; 18 mem. univs and 5 observer univs from 19 European countries; aims to promote higher distance education, to support bilateral and multilateral contacts between academic staff, to support co-operation in research, course development, course transfer and credit transfer, to develop new methods for higher distance education, and to organize common projects in co-operation with European authorities; European Open University Network (est. Jan. 1995) acts as executive arm and is responsbile for 60 EuroStudy Centres; Pres. Prof. J. M. BAÏSSUS; Sec.-Gen./Treas. P. HENDERIKX (Belgium).

European Documentation and Information System for Education (EUDISED): Council of Europe, 67075, Strasbourg Cedex, France; tel. 3-88-41-26-26; telex 870943; fax 3-88-41-27-06; e-mail michael.vorbeck@coe.fr; f. 1968 by the Ccl of Europe; two main components: a database containing abstracts in English, French or German on educational research in 34 European countries, and a multilingual thesaurus (European Education Thesaurus) available in 11 languages for indexing educational information; publs *European Yearbook of Educational Research,* reports.

European Institute of Education and Social Policy: Université Paris IX-Dauphine, 1 place du Maréchal de Lattre de Tassigny, 75116 Paris, France; tel. (1) 44-05-40-01; fax (1) 44-05-45-26; f. 1975 by the European Cultural Foundation, the European Commission, the International Council for Educational Development; its main purpose is the study of specific issues in education, employment and social policy; policy-oriented and research programmes and seminars undertaken for European governments, international organizations, universities, or regional and local bodies; Chair. PIERRE TABATONI; Dir JEAN-PIERRE JALLADE; publs *European Journal of Education* (quarterly in English), *Newsletter* (annually in English and French), reports, etc.

Fédération Internationale des Professeurs de Français/International Federation of Teachers of French: 1 ave Léon Journault, 92310 Sèvres, France; tel. 46-26-53-16; fax 46-26-81-69; f. 1969 to group together and assist teachers of French as a first or second language throughout the world; mems: 173 associations in 108 countries; Pres. ALAIN BRAUN (Belgium); Sec.-Gen. ANNIE MONNERIE-GOARIN (France); publs *Dialogues and Cultures* (annually), *L'Univers du Français: Lettre FIPF* (quarterly).

Higher Education and Research Committee: c/o Council of Europe, Higher Education Section, 67075 Strasbourg Cedex, France; tel. 3-88-41-20-00; fax 3-88-41-27-06; f. 1978 under the Council for Cultural Co-operation, set up within the Council of Europe by the signatories of the European Cultural Convention, to promote co-operation among European countries in the field of higher education and research; work programme: university policy, academic mobility (especially joint UNESCO-Council of Europe network of information centres on equivalences and mobility and a new joint convention on recognition); projects on access to higher education in Europe and legislative reform in higher education; mems: representatives of institutions of higher education and senior government officials from the 47 countries party to the European Cultural Convention; Chair. S. HALIMI (France); Sec. S. BERGAN.

Inter-American Council for Education, Science and Culture: General Secretariat of the Organization of American States, 1889 F St, NW, Washington, DC 20006, USA; f. 1970 as an organ of the OAS, replacing the Inter-American Cultural Council; aims: to promote friendly relations and mutual understanding among the people of the Americas through educational, scientific and cultural co-operation and exchange; to help prepare the inhabitants of member states to contribute fully to their progress; to stimulate intellectual and artistic expression and help protect, preserve and increase the cultural heritage; to recommend procedures for intensifying the integration of the countries' efforts and periodically to evaluate these efforts; mems: the 25 mems of OAS; Exec. Sec. ENRIQUE MARTÍN DEL CAMPO (Mexico).

Inter-American Organization for Higher Education/Organisation universitaire interaméricaine: Place Iberville IV, bureau 090, 2954 blvd Laurier, Sainte-Foy, Que. G1V 4T2, Canada; tel. (418) 650-1515; fax (418) 650-1519; e-mail secretariat@oui-iohe.qc.ca; f. 1980; inter-university co-operation and exchange; 360 mems; library of *c.* 1,500 vols; Pres. JUAN CARLOS ROMERO HICKS; Exec. Dir PIERRE VAN DER DONCKT; publs *Info OUI* (quarterly), *Inter-American Journal of University Management* (every 2 years).

International Association for Educational and Vocational Guidance/Association Internationale d'Orientation Scolaire et Professionnelle: f. 1951 to contribute to the development of vocational guidance and promote contact between persons associated with it; mems: 40,000 from 80 countries; Pres. Prof. JOSÉ FERREIRA MARQUES (Portugal); Sec.-Gen. LYN BARHAM, The Mount, 41 Rowden Hill, Chippenham, SN15 2AQ, England; publs *Bulletin—AIOSP* (2 a year), *Newsletter* (3 a year).

International Association for Educational and Vocational Information/ Association internationale d'information scolaire universitaire et professionnelle: 20 rue de l'Estrapade, 75005 Paris, France; f. 1956 to facilitate co-operation between national organizations concerned with supplying information to university and college students and secondary pupils and their parents, to compare methods and act as an international documentation centre, and to encourage the establishment of other national organizations; mems: national organizations in 30 countries; Pres. C. VIMONT (France); Vice-Pres. Dr LEVERKUS (Germany); M. KAWKA (Poland), M. AMARA (Tunisia), E. LAMA (Italy); Sec.-Gen. L. TODOROV (France); publ. *Informations universitaires et professionnelles internationales* (quarterly).

International Association for the Exchange of Students for Technical Experience (IAESTE): f. 1948 to organize exchange of students for on-the-job training; mems: 62 national committees; Gen. Sec. Dr A. SFEIR; Ecole des Mines de Nancy, BP 3672, 54096 Nancy Cedex, France; tel. 83-37-64-41; fax 83-57-97-94 (attn IAESTE); publs *Annual Report, Activity Report.*

International Association of Dental Students: c/o Dr P. A. Zillén, FDI World Dental Federation, 7 Carlisle St, London, W1V 5RG, England; tel. (171) 935-7852; fax (171) 486-0183; f. 1951 to promote international contact between dental students, to advance and stimulate their interest in the science and art of dentistry, to promote exchanges and international congresses; mems: 100,000 students in 23 countries; Pres. Dr VALENTINA STERJOVA (UK); Sec.-Gen. ROASANA HANKE (Puerto Rico); publs *IADS Newsletter, Bulletin* (quarterly), *Exchange Guide, Information Guide.*

International Baccalaureate Organisation (IBO): 15 route des Morillons, 1218 Grand-Saconnex/Geneva, Switzerland; tel. (22) 791-02-74; fax (22) 791-02-77; e-mail IBHQ@ibo.org; f. 1964; nonprofit foundation offering Diploma Programme for pre-university students, Middle Years Programme for students aged 11–16, and Primary Years Programme for ages 3–12; provides curriculum and assessment development, university entrance examination and teacher training; 800 participating schools in 95 countries; Dir-Gen. ROGER M. PEEL.

International Bureau of Education: see chapter on UNESCO.

International Centre for Agricultural Education (CIEA)/Internationales Studienzentrum für landwirtschaftliches Bildungswesen: Federal Office of Agriculture, CH-3003 Berne, Switzerland; tel. (31) 322-2619; fax (31) 322-2634; f. 1958; organizes international courses on vocational education and teaching in agriculture every two years; Dir (vacant).

International Council for Adult Education: 720 Bathurst St, Suite 500, Toronto, Ont. M5S 2R4, Canada; tel. (416) 588-1211; fax (416) 588-5725; e-mail icae@web.net; f.1973 to provide a network for international communication and information exchange; to encourage and stimulate the role of adult education in development; to strengthen research, training and organization of adult education, especially in developing countries; priority areas of work: women's education, environmental education, literacy, and peace and human rights; mems: 105 national and 7 regional organizations; Pres. LALITA RAMDAS; Exec. Dir THURAYA KHALIL-KHOURI (acting); publs *Convergence, ICAE News* (quarterly).

International Council for Open and Distance Education: Gjerdrums vei 12, 0486 Oslo 4, Norway; tel. 22-95-06-30; fax 22-95-07-19; e-mail icde@icde.no; f. 1938 as Int. Ccl for Correspondence Education, name changed 1982; dedicated to furthering the aims and methods of distance education throughout the world by promoting and funding research and scholarly publs, encouraging the formation of regional asscns, facilitating communications and information exchange, and organizing conferences and workshops; 7,000 mems in 120 countries; Pres. ARMANDO ROCHA TRINDADE (Portugal); Sec.-Gen. REIDAR ROLL; publ. *Open Praxis* (every 6 months).

International Federation of Catholic Universities/Fédération Internationale des Universités Catholiques (FIUC): C/o Institut Catholique, 21 rue d'Assas, 75270 Paris Cedex 06, France; tel. 1-44-39-52-26; fax 1-44-39-52-28; e-mail sgfiuc@club.internet.fr; f. 1949 to ensure a strong bond of mutual assistance among all Catholic universities in the search for truth to help to solve problems of growth and development, and to co-operate with other international organizations; 187 mems in 41 countries; Pres. ANDREW GONZALEZ (Philippines); Sec.-Gen. VINCENT HANSSENS (Belgium); publs *Idem Aliter* (3 a year), *Proceedings of General Assemblies*, reports, papers.

International Federation of University Women/Fédération internationale des femmes diplômées des universités: 8 rue de l'Ancien Port, Geneva, Switzerland; tel. (22) 731-2380; fax. (22) 738-0440; e-mail ifuw@iprolink.ch; f. 1919 to promote understanding and friendship between university women irrespective of race, nationality, religion or political opinions, to encourage international co-operation, to further the development of education, to represent university women in international organizations, to encourage the full application of their knowledge and skills to the problems which arise at all levels of public life and to encourage their participation in the solving of these problems; sponsors regional seminars; consultative status with the appropriate inter-governmental organizations; administers fellowships and study grants; provides assistance for university women in need; undertakes studies dealing with the status of women; affiliates in 68 countries with 182,000 mems; Pres. Dr ELIZABETH POSKITT (UK); Sec.-Gen. MURIELLE JOYE (Switzerland); publs *IFUW News* (monthly), occasional study papers, *Triennial Report.*

International Federation of Workers' Education Associations: c/o Histadrut, 93 Arlozorov St, Tel-Aviv 62098, Israel; tel. (3) 6917278; fax (3) 6962335; f. 1947 to promote co-operation between national non-government bodies concerned with adult and workers' education, through clearing-house services, exchange of information, publications, conferences, summer schools, etc.; 89 affiliated organizations; Pres. DAN GALLIN; Gen. Sec. AARON BARNEA; publ. *Workers' Education* (quarterly, in English, Spanish or French).

International Institute for Adult Education Methods: POB 19395/6194, Teheran, Iran; tel. (21) 205-0313; fax (21) 640-6940; f. 1986 by UNESCO and the Govt of Iran; collects, analyses and distributes information about methods and media used in continuing education programmes; arranges seminars; maintains documentation services and library on lifelong continuing education; Dir Dr GHOLAM ALI AFROOZ; publ. *Adult Education and Innovation* (2 a year).

International Institute for Educational Planning: see chapter on UNESCO.

International Phonetic Association (IPA): C/o J. H. Esling, Dept of Linguistics, University of Victoria, POB 3045, Victoria, BC V8W 3P4, Canada; tel. (250) 721-7424; fax (250) 721-7423; e-mail esling@uvic.ca; f. 1886 to promote the scientific study of phonetics and its applications; mems: 1,000; Pres. Dr J. J. Ohala (USA); Sec. Dr J. H. Esling; publ. *Journal of the International Phonetic Association* (2 a year).

International Reading Association: 800 Barksdale Rd, POB 8139, Newark, DE 19714-8139, USA; tel. (302) 731-1600; fax (302) 731-1057; f. 1956; aims to improve the quality of reading instruction through the study of the reading process and teaching techniques; to promote the lifetime reading habit and an awareness among all people of the impact of reading; and to promote the development of every reader's proficiency to the highest possible level; annual convention and biennial World Congress; 92,000 mems; library of 12,000 vols; Pres. Kathryn Ann Ransom; Exec. Dir Alan E. Farstrup; publs *The Reading Teacher*, *Journal of Adolescent and Adult Literature*, *Reading Research Quarterly*, *Lectura y Vida*, *Reading Today*.

International Schools Association (ISA): CIC Case 20, 1211 Geneva 20, Switzerland; f. 1951 to co-ordinate work in International Schools and promote their development; merged in 1968 with the Conference of Internationally-minded Schools (CIS) and now counts in its membership a number of selected national schools; member schools maintain the highest standards and accept pupils of all nationalities, irrespective of sex, race and creed; ISA carries out curriculum research; convenes annual Conferences on problems of curriculum and educational reform; has consultative status with UNESCO, UNICEF, UNHCR, UNEP and ECOSOC; mems: 85 schools throughout the world; Chair. James McLellan; publs *Educational Bulletin* and *Magazine* (3 a year).

International Society for Business Education/Société internationale pour l'enseignement commercial: 3550 Anderson St, Madison, WI 53704-2599, USA; tel. (608) 837-7518; fax (608) 834-1301; e-mail gkantin@madison.tec.wi.us; f. 1901 to organize international courses and congresses on business education; *c.* 2,000 mems organized in 19 national groups; Pres. Julie Ann Svenkerup (Norway); Gen. Sec. G. Lee Kantin (USA); publ. *International Review for Business Education*.

International Society for Education through Art (InSEA)/Société Internationale pour l'Education Artistique: f. 1951 to unite art teachers throughout the world, to exchange information and co-ordinate research into art education; a Category 'B' Society of UNESCO, being the non-governmental world organization for the study of art education, international congresses, exhibitions and other activities; *c.* 1,500 mems; Pres. Kit Grauer (Canada); Secs Peter Hermans, Diederik Schönau, POB 1109, 6801 BC Arnhem, Netherlands; fax (26) 3521202; e-mail insea@cito.nl; publ. *InSEA News* (3 a year).

International Union of Students/Union internationale des étudiants: POB 58, 17th November St, 1101 Prague 01, Czech Republic; tel. 2312812; telex 122858; fax 2316100; f. 1946 by World Student Congress in Prague; objects: to defend the rights and interests of students, to strive for peace, national independence, academic freedom and democratic education and to unite the student movement in furtherance of these objectives; activities include conferences, meetings, solidarity campaigns, relief projects, award of scholarships, travel and exchange, sports events, cultural projects, publicity and other activities in the furtherance of the Union's aims; mems: 99 full mem. countries, 25 consultative; Pres. Manish Tewari (India); Sec.-Gen. Mdeti Mpuru (South Africa); publs *World Student News*, *Newsletter*, *Democratization of Education*, various regional and other bulletins (quarterly).

International Young Christian Workers/Jeunesse ouvrière chrétienne internationale: 11 rue Plantin, 1070 Brussels, Belgium; tel. (2) 521-69-83; fax (2) 521-69-44; e-mail jociycw@skynet.be; f. 1925 to give social, economic and educational aid to the young worker; holds international councils; mems: national organizations in 60 countries; Pres. Helio A. Alves; Sec.-Gen. Dominador R. Olavere; publs *International Information* (2 a year), *Bulletin* (quarterly).

Islamic Educational, Scientific and Cultural Organization/Organisation Islamique pour l'Education, les Sciences et la Culture (ISESCO): Hay Mesk Al-Lail, Ave Attine-Hay Ryad, BP 2275-10104, Rabat, Morocco; tel. (7) 77-24-33; telex 326-45; fax (7) 77-74-59; f. 1982 under the aegis of the Islamic Conference Organization to strengthen co-operation between mem. states in the fields of education, culture and science; 42 mems; Islamic Data Bank service (BIDI); Dir-Gen. Dr Abdulaziz Othman Al-Twaijri; publs *ISESCO Bulletin* (quarterly), *Islam Today* (2 a year), *ISESCO Yearbook*, *ISESCO Triennial*.

Islamic Institute of Technology: Board Bazar, Gazipur, Dhaka, Bangladesh; tel. (2) 9800960; telex 642439; fax (2) 9800970; f. 1981; subsidiary of the Organization of the Islamic Conference; BSc, trade, vocational, postgraduate and instructor courses in fields of electrical, electronic and mechanical engineering and technical education; short courses in skill upgrading; technological research; library of 18,000 vols; 88 teachers, 1,000 students; Dir-Gen. Prof. Dr A. M. Patwari; publ. *News Bulletin* (1 a year).

Latin American Institute for Educational Communication/Instituto Latinoamericano de la Comunicación Educativa: Calle del Puente 45, Col. Ejidos de Huipulco, Del. Tlalpan, 14380 México, DF, Mexico; tel. (5) 728-65-00; fax (5) 594-96-83; f. 1956; supported by the Mexican Government to provide leadership in educational communication and technical assistance to mems; regional co-operation in research, experimentation, production and distribution of AV materials; produces and broadcasts educational television programmes; offers on-line educational services; training at the Center for Training and Advanced Studies on Educational Communication (CETEC); operates Center of AV Documentation for Latin America (CEDAL); 13 mem. countries; library of 34,000 vols; Dir-Gen. Lic. Guillermo Kelley Salinas; publ. *Tecnología y Comunicación Educativas* (quarterly).

Organisation of the Catholic Universities of Latin America/Organización de Universidades Católicas de América Latina (ODUCAL): f. 1953; aims to assist the cultural development of Latin America and to promote the activities of Catholic higher education in the region; mems: 34 Catholic universities in Argentina, Brazil, Colombia, Cuba, Ecuador, Mexico, Peru, Puerto Rico, and Venezuela; Pres. Juan Alejandro Tobias; Sec. Gen. Dr Eduardo Miras, Pontifical Catholic University of Buenos Aires, Juncal 1912, Buenos Aires, Argentina.

Organization of Ibero-American States for Education, Science and Culture/Organización de Estados Iberoamericanos para la Educación, la Ciencia y la Cultura (OEI): C/ Bravo Murillo 38, 28015 Madrid, Spain; tel. (91) 594-43-82; fax (91) 594-32-86; e-mail oeimad@oei.es; f. 1949 as Ibero-American Bureau of Education, name changed 1985; intergovernmental organization for educational, scientific and cultural co-operation within the Ibero-American countries; provides technical assistance to Ibero-American development systems in the above areas; provides information and documentation on the development of education, science and culture; encourages exchanges in these fields; organizes training courses; the General Assembly (at ministerial level) meets every four years; mems: govts of 20 Ibero-American countries; library of 8,000 vols, 500 periodicals; Sec.-Gen. (vacant).

Pax Romana: 15 rue du Grand-Bureau, CP 315, 1211 Geneva 24, Switzerland; tel. (22) 823-07-07; fax (22) 823-07-08; e-mail miicmica@paxromana.int.ch; f. 1921; two branches from 1947; the student branch—*International Movement of Catholic Students* (80 national federations); the graduate branch—*International Catholic Movement for Intellectual and Cultural Affairs* (60 national federations and 5 international professional federations); Pres. (IMCS) Roland Ranaivoarison; Sec.-Gen. (IMCS) Walter Prysthon; Pres. (ICMICA) Mary Mwingira; Sec.-Gen. (ICMICA) Anselmo Lee.; publs *Convergence*, *News / Nouvelles / Noticias* and national and professional federation publications.

Southeast Asian Ministers of Education Organization (SEAMEO): c/o SEAMES, Darakarn Bldg, 920 Sukhumvit Rd, Bangkok 10110, Thailand; tel. (66-2) 3910144; fax (66-2) 381-2587; f. 1965 to promote co-operation among the Southeast Asian nations through co-operative projects and programmes in education, science and culture; 15 regional centres; mems: Brunei, Cambodia, Indonesia, Laos, Malaysia, Myanmar, Philippines, Singapore, Thailand, Viet-Nam; associate mems: Australia, Canada, France, Germany, Netherlands, New Zealand; Pres. HE Pehin Orang Kaya Laila Wijaya Dato Haji Abdul Aziz Umar (Brunei); Dir Dr Suparak Racha-Intra; publs reports of conferences and seminars, annual reports, periodical (3 a year), technical publications, journals, bulletins, etc.

Unesco European Centre for Higher Education/Centre européen pour l'enseignement supérieur (CEPES): 39 str. Stirbei Voda, 70732 Bucharest, Romania; tel. (1) 613-08-39; fax (1) 312-35-67; e-mail cepes@cepes.ro; f. 1972; centre for policy development and the promotion of international higher education co-operation in Europe, North America and Israel; Secretariat of Joint Unesco/Council of Europe European Recognition Convention, and of the ENIC Network of Information Centres on Recognition and Mobility in Europe; Dir Lesley Wilson; publ. *Higher Education in Europe* (quarterly in English, French, Russian).

Unesco Institute for Education/Institut de l'Unesco pour l'Education/Unesco-Institut für Pädagogik: Feldbrunnenstr. 58, 20148 Hamburg, Germany; tel. (40) 448041-0; telex 2164146; fax (40) 4107723; e-mail uie@unesco.org; f. 1951 as an autonomous international research organization jointly sponsored by UNESCO, the Government of Germany and other funding agencies; its main concern is the content and quality of education in the framework of lifelong learning, with an emphasis on adult education, non-formal education and literacy; its main activities are research, diffusion, promotion, research-based training and documentation; a worldwide network for exchange of information on literacy; a research-oriented training programme; library of 55,000 vols, 300 periodicals; special collections: lifelong education, sample learning materials on literacy, post-literacy and continuing education from 120 countries; Dir Dr PAUL BÉLANGER (Canada); publs *International Review of Education* (every 2 months), *Newsletter* (annually).

Union of the Universities of Latin America/Unión de Universidades de América Latina: Secretariat: Apdo 70232, Ciudad Universitaria, 04510 México, DF, Mexico; tel. (5) 616-23-83; fax (5) 616-14-14; f. 1949 to link the Latin American universities and contribute to the cultural and academic integration of the regional nations; organizes General Assemblies and Conferences; permanent statistical work; library of 7,000 vols, 300 serials, records, microforms; mems: 167 universities in 21 countries; Pres. Dr JORGE BROVETTO CRUZ; Sec.-Gen. Dr ABELARDO VILLEGAS; publs *Revista Universidades* (2 a year), *Gaceta UDUAL* (quarterly), *Window* (6 a year), *Boletín UDUAL* (monthly), *Proceedings of Latin American Universities Conferences*.

World Association for Educational Research/Association Mondiale des Sciences de l'Education: Pedagogisch Laboratorium, Henri Dunantlaan 1, B-9000 Ghent, Belgium; tel. (9) 264-63-78; f. 1953, present title adopted 1977; aims: to encourage research in educational sciences by organizing congresses, issuing publications, the exchange of information, etc.; 660 individual mems in 50 countries; Pres. Prof. Dr W. MITTER; Gen. Sec. Prof. Dr M.-L. VAN HERREWEGHE (Belgium); publ. *Communicationes* (2 a year).

World Education Fellowship: 58 Dickens Rise, Chigwell, Essex, IG7 6NY, England; tel. (181) 281-7122; e-mail 106465.1075@compuserve.com; f. 1921 to promote the exchange and practice of progressive educational ideas in all parts of the world; sections and groups in 22 countries; Chair. CHRISTINE WYKES; Sec. GEORGE JOHN; publ. *The New Era in Education* (3 a year).

World Maritime University: POB 500, 201 24 Malmö, Sweden; tel. (40) 356300; fax (40) 128442; e-mail info@wmu.se; f. 1983 by the Int. Maritime Organization; offers postgraduate courses in various maritime disciplines, mainly for students from developing countries; 100 visiting professors, 200 students; library of 13,000 vols (special collections: UNCTAD and IMO depository); Rector KARL LAUBSTEIN; publs *Newsletter, Handbook*.

World Student Christian Federation (WSCF)/Fédération Universelle des Associations Chrétiennes d'Etudiants: c/o Centre Oecuménique, 5 route des Morillons, 1218 Grand-Saconnex (GE), Switzerland; tel. (22) 798-89-52; telex 415730; fax (22) 798-23-70; e-mail wscf@wcc-coe.org; f. 1895; an ecumenical student, university and secondary school organization with participants from all major Christian confessions; related groups in 100 countries; Chair. WONG WAI CHING (Hong Kong, acting); Co-Secs-Gen. CLARISSA BALAN-SYCIP (Philippines), KANGWA MABULUKI (Zambia); publs *WSCF Books, WSCF Dossier* (occasional), *Federation News* (quarterly), *WSCF Journal* (quarterly).

World Union of Jewish Students: POB 7914, 91077 Jerusalem, Israel; tel. (2) 5610133; fax (2) 5610741; e-mail wujs@jer1.co.il; f. 1924 to fight antisemitism and to act as an umbrella organization for national Jewish student bodies, organizes educational programmes, leadership training seminars, women's seminars and Project Areivim, a service programme for Diaspora communities; divided into six regions; organizes Congress every three years; mems: 51 national unions representing over 700,000 students; NGO mem. of UNESCO, youth affiliate of World Jewish Congress, mem. org. of World Zionist Organization; Chair. ILANIT SASSON MELCHIOR; publs *WUJS Leads, HERitage and HIStory* (Jewish student activist yearbook).

World University Service: 5 chemin des Iris, 1216 Geneva, Switzerland; tel. (22) 7988711; telex 415537; fax 798-0829; f. 1920; independent non-governmental organization composed of cttees of academics, students and staff in post-secondary institutions in 50 countries; finances and administers post-secondary scholarships for political refugees and those denied equal educational opportunities; supports community development programmes linking human and technical resources of universities to social and economic development; Pres. CALEB FUNDANGA (Zambia); Gen. Sec. XIMENA ERAZO (Chile) (acting); publs *WUS and Human Rights, Academic Freedom Report* (annually), reports on conferences, seminars and research.

Engineering and Technology

International Union of Technical Associations and Organizations/Union internationale des associations et organismes techniques (UATI): 1 rue Miollis, 75732 Paris Cedex 15, France; tel. (1) 45-68-27-70; fax (1) 43-06-29-27; e-mail uati@unesco.org; f. 1951; activities: working groups and cttees to identify, promote and co-ordinate actions of mem. asscns in areas of common interest, and to facilitate relations with international bodies, in particular UNESCO, UNIDO and ECOSOC; mems: 25 organizations; Pres. MICHEL SAILLARD (France); Sec.-Gen. CHARLES VAN BEGIN (Belgium); publ. *UATI Magazine* (2 a year).

MEMBER ORGANIZATIONS

International Association for Hydraulic Research/Association Internationale de Recherches Hydrauliques: c/o Delft Hydraulics, Rotterdamseweg 185, POB 177, 2600 MH Delft, Netherlands; tel. (15) 2858585; fax (15) 2858582; e-mail iahr@iahr.nl; f. 1935; 2,300 individual mems, 270 corporate mems; Sec.-Gen. Ir H. J. OVERBEEK (Netherlands); publs *Journal* (every 2 months, in English or French, and a summary in either language), *Bulletin, Proceedings of Biennial Congresses*.

International Commission of Agricultural Engineering/Commission Internationale du Génie Rural (CIGR): C/o Prof. Dr. P. Schulze Lammers, Institut für Landtechnik, Universität Bonn, Nussallee 5, 53115 Bonn, Germany; tel. (228) 73-23-89; fax (228) 73-25-96; e-mail ulp81a@ibm.rhrz.uni-bonn.de; f. 1930; application of soil and water sciences to agricultural engineering; conservation, irrigation, land improvement and reclamation; rural construction and equipment; agricultural machinery; distribution of electricity in rural areas and its application in the general energy context; scientific organization of agricultural work; food processing; mem. asscns from 30 countries, individual mems in 6 countries; Pres. O. KITANI (Japan); Sec.-Gen. Prof. Dr P. SCHULZE LAMMERS (Germany).

International Commission on Glass (ICG): c/o F. Nicoletti, Stazione Sperimentale del Vetro, Venezia-Murano, Via Briati 10, Italy; tel. (41) 739422; fax (41) 739420; f. 1933 in Venice to promote the dissemination of information on the art, history, science and technology of glass; mems: national societies in 27 countries; Pres. D. PYE (USA); Hon. Sec. F. NICOLETTI (Italy).

International Commission on Irrigation and Drainage/Commission Internationale des Irrigations et du Drainage: 48 Nyaya Marg, Chanakyapuri, New Delhi 110021, India; tel. 6116837; fax 6115962; e-mail icoiad@giasdlo1.vsnl.net.in; f. 1950; mems: 66 countries; Pres. ALY M. SHADY (Canada); Sec.-Gen. C. D. THATTE (India).

International Commission on Large Dams/Commission Internationale des Grands Barrages: 151 blvd Haussmann, 75008 Paris, France; tel. 1-40-42-68-24; fax 1-40-42-60-71; e-mail secretaire.general@icold-cigb.org; f. 1928; mems: national cttees in 80 countries; Sec.-Gen. JACQUES LECORNU; publs *ICOLD Congress Proceedings and Transactions* (every 3 years), *World Register of Dams*, technical bulletins.

International Committee of Foundry Technical Associations/Comité International des Associations Techniques de Fonderie: Konradstr. 9, CP 7190, 8023 Zürich, Switzerland; f. 1927 to bring together mem. associations in the technical field and promote their joint action in matters of common interest; congress every two years; mems: 36 national associations; Sec.-Gen. Dr J. GERSTER (Switzerland).

International Congress on Fracture (ICF): C/o Dr Masaki Kitagawa, Dept. of Research Planning and Administration, Research Institute, Ishikawajima-Harima Heavy Industries, 3-1-15 Toyoshu, Koto-ku, Tokyo 135, Japan; fax (3) 3534-3344; f. 1965; aims to foster research in the mechanics and phenomena of fracture, fatigue, and strength of materials; to promote co-operation among scientists in the field; holds Int. Conference every four years; 30 mem. organizations; Pres. Prof. JOHN KNOTT (UK); Sec.-Gen. Dr MASAKI KITAGAWA; publ. *Proceedings* (every 4 years).

International Dairy Federation: see under Agriculture.

International Federation of Automatic Control (IFAC)/Fédération Internationale de l'Automatique: IFAC Secretariat, Schlossplatz 12, A-2361 Laxenburg, Austria; tel. (2236) 71447; fax (2236) 72859; e-mail secr@ifac.co.at; f. 1957 to promote the science and technology of control in the broadest sense in all systems, e.g. engineering, physical, biological, social and economical, in both theory and application; mems: 49 national member organizations; Pres. Prof. YONG-ZAI LU (China); Sec. Dr G. HENCSEY (Hungary); publs *Automatica* (mainly selected papers of IFAC-sponsored symposia, monthly), *Control Engineering Practice* (6 a year), *IFAC Newsletter.*

International Gas Union/Union Internationale de l'Industrie du Gaz: C/o N.V. Nederlandse Gasunie, POB 19, 9700 MA Groningen, Netherlands; tel. (50) 21-29-99; fax (50) 25-59-51; f. 1931; 51 mems; Sec.-Gen. Dr J. F. MEEDER.

International Institute of Welding/Institut international de la soudure: BP 50362, 95942 Roissy CDG Cedex, France; tel. 1-49-90-36-08; fax 1-49-90-36-80; e-mail iiw@msn.com; f. 1948; mem societies in 40 countries; Pres. YUZURU FUJITA (Japan); Chief

Exec. MICHEL BRAMAT (France); publ. *Welding in the World* (every 2 months).

International Institution for Production Engineering Research/Collège international pour l'étude scientifique des techniques de production mécanique: 10 rue Mansart, 75009 Paris, France; tel. 1-45-26-21-80; fax 1-40-16-40-75; e-mail Cirp@lurpa .ens-cachan.fr; f. 1950; aims to promote by scientific research the study of mechanical processing of all solid materials including checks on efficiency and quality of work; 485 mems; Sec.-Gen. MICHEL VÉRON; publs *Annals* (2 vols, annually), *Proceedings of Manufacturing Systems Seminars* (annually), *Dictionaries of Production Engineering*.

International Measurement Confederation (IMEKO)/Confédération Internationale de la Mesure: POB 457, 1371 Budapest, Hungary; tel. 1531-562; telex 225792; fax 153-1406; f. 1958; promotes the int. exchange of scientific and technical information relating to developments in measuring techniques, instrument design and manufacture and in the application of instrumentation in scientific research and industry; promotes co-operation among scientists and engineers in the field, and with other int. organizations; organizes Congresses, symposia, etc.; 34 mem. organizations; Sec. Gen. T. KEMÉNY; publs *IMEKO Bulletin* (2 a year), *Measurement* (quarterly), proceedings of colloquia, symposia, etc.

International Union of Testing and Research Laboratories on Materials and Structures/Réunion Internationale des Laboratoires d'Essais et de Recherches sur les Matériaux et les Constructions (RILEM): 61 ave du Président-Wilson, 94235 Cachan Cedex, France; tel. (331) 47-40-23-97; fax (331) 47-40-01-13; e-mail sg@rilem .ens-cachan.fr; f. 1947; 850 mems; Pres. Dr J. BRESSON (France); Sec.-Gen. M. BRUSIN; publ. *Materials and Structures—Matériaux et Constructions* (10 a year).

Permanent International Association of Navigation Congresses/Association Internationale Permanente des Congrès de Navigation: Graaf de Ferraris, 11ème étage, Boîte 3, 156 blvd Emile Jacqmain, 1000 Brussels, Belgium; tel. (2) 553-71-60; fax (2) 553-71-55; e-mail navigation-aipcn-pianc@ tornado.be; f. 1885 to promote inland and ocean navigation by fostering and encouraging progress in the design, construction, improvement, maintenance and operation of inland and maritime waterways, ports, and of coastal areas for the benefit of mankind; mems: 2,098 individual mems, 548 corporate mems; Pres R. DE PAEPE; Sec.-Gen. C. VAN BEGIN; publs *PIANC Bulletin* (quarterly), *Papers of Congresses, Account of Proceedings of Congresses* (every 4 years), *Technical dictionary*, reports of Technical International Study Commissions and Working Groups.

World Energy Council (WEC)/Conseil Mondial de l'Energie (CME): 34 St James's St, London, SW1A 1HD, England; tel. (71) 930-3966; telex 264707; fax (71) 925-0452; f. 1924 in London as World Power Conference to consider the potential resources and all means of production, transportation, transformation and utilization of energy in all their aspects, and also to consider energy consumption in its overall relationship to the growth of economic activity; collects and publishes data; holds triennial congress; promotes regional symposia and technical studies; there are mem. committees in 98 countries; Pres. J. W. BAKER (UK); Chairman, Executive Assembly Dr G. OTT (Germany); Sec.-Gen. (vacant); publs *Journal* (every 6 months), *National Energy Data Profiles* (every 3 years), *World Survey of Energy Resources* (every 3 years).

World Road Association/Association Mondiale de la Route: La Grande Arche, Paroi Nord-Niveau 1, 92055 Paris la Défense Cedex 04, France; tel. (1) 47-96-81-21; fax (1) 49-00-02-02; e-mail piarc@pratique.fr; f. 1909 to help to promote a world network of roads; 1,640 mems; Pres. H. MITANI; Sec.-Gen. J. F. COSTE; publs *Bulletin, Dictionnaires Techniques Routiers, Rapports*.

OTHER ORGANIZATIONS

Arab Petroleum Training Institute: POB 6037, Al Tajeyat, Baghdad, Iraq; tel. (1) 5234100; telex 212728; fax (1) 5210526; f. 1979; training of high-level personnel in all aspects of the oil industry; 11 OAPEC mem. states; library of 5,000 vols, bibliographic and non-bibliographic data bases; Dir-Gen. Dr TAL'AT NAJEEB HATTAB.

Council of Academies of Engineering and Technological Sciences (CAETS): 2101 Constitution Ave NW, Room 306, Washington, DC 20418, USA; tel. (202) 334-3603; fax (202) 334-2290; e-mail caets@nae.edu; f. 1978 to promote the development of engineering and technology throughout the world and to provide an international forum for the discussion of technological and engineering issues; encourages int. engineering efforts in order to promote economic growth and social welfare; mems: 16 nat. instns; Pres. Sir DAVID DAVIES (UK); Vice-Pres. STEVEN N. ANASTASION (USA).

European Organisation for Civil Aviation Equipment (EUROCAE)/Organisation Européenne pour l'Equipement de l'Aviation Civile: 17 rue Hamelin, 75783 Paris Cedex 16, France; tel. (1) 45-05-71-88; telex 611045; fax (1) 45-53-03-93; f. 1963; the organization studies and advises on problems related to the application of equipment to aviation and prepares minimum performance specifications which administrations in Europe may use for approving equipment; 70 mems; Pres. J. P. LEPEYTRE; Sec.-Gen. F. GRIMAL.

European Society for Engineering Education, (SEFI): 60 rue de la Concorde, 1050 Brussels, Belgium; tel. (32) 2-540-97-70; fax (32) 2-540-97-15; e-mail sefi.come@euronet.be; f. 1973 to promote the quality of initial and continuing engineering education and to stimulate co-operation throughout Europe; organizes working groups, conferences and seminars; undertakes consultancy work for European organizations and industry; Pres. Dr W. SCHAUFELBERGER; Sec.-Gen. F. CÔME; publs *EJEE, SEFI News*, etc.

European Strategic Programme for Research and Development in Information Technology (ESPRIT): Directorate General XIII 'Telecommunications, Information, Industry and Innovation', Commission of the European Communities, 200 rue de la Loi, 1049 Brussels, Belgium; tel. 235-4477; telex 21877; fax 235-6461; main phase began 1984 and is due to run for 10 years; a collaborative research programme bringing together industrial and academic partners across the European Community; following annual calls for proposals, selected trans-national European consortia work on pre-competitive information technology R & D projects co-funded by the Community; Dir JEAN-MARIE CADIOU.

International Association for Bridge and Structural Engineering (IABSE)/Association Internationale des Ponts et Charpentes/Internationale Vereinigung für Brückenbau und Hochbau: Secretariat: ETH-Hönggerberg, 8093 Zürich, Switzerland; tel. (1) 633-26-47; fax (1) 371-21-31; e-mail secretariat@iabse.ethz.ch; f. 1929; aims: international co-operation among scientists, engineers and manufacturers; interchange of knowledge, ideas and the results of research work in the sphere of bridge and structural engineering in general, whether in steel, concrete or another material; mems: 4,200 from 100 countries; Pres. KLAUS OSTENFELD (Denmark); Exec. Dir ALAIN GOLAY; publs *Structural Engineering International* (quarterly), *IABSE Reports, IABSE Congress Reports, Structural Engineering Documents*.

International Association on Water Quality: Duchess House, 20 Masons Yard, Duke St, St James's, London, SW1Y 6BU, England; tel. (171) 839-8390; fax (171) 839-8299; e-mail iawq@compuserve.com; f. 1965 to encourage international communication, co-operative effort, and a maximum exchange of information on water pollution abatement and control, and water quality management; to sponsor regular international meetings; to provide a scientific medium for the publication of information on water pollution control and to shorten the time-lag between development of research and its application; mems: 53 national, 490 corporate, 5,860 individuals; Pres. Dr. T. M. KEINATH (USA); Exec. Dir A. MILBURN; publs *Water Research* (monthly), *Water Science and Technology* (24 issues a year), *Water Quality International* (6 a year), *Yearbook*.

International Cargo Handling Coordination Association (ICHCA): 71 Bondway, London, SW8 1SH, England; tel. (171) 793-1022; fax (171) 820-1703; f. 1952 to foster economy and efficiency in the movement of goods from origin to destination; mems: 2,000 from over 90 countries; Pres. GADI SASSOWER; Chief Exec. GERRY ASKHAM; publs *ICHCA News and Cargo Today* (6 a year including the ICHCA Cargo Management Information Service), *Who's Who in Cargo Handling, The ICHCA Buyers' Guide to Manufacturers* (annually), *The World of Cargo Handling* (annually), various occasional technical publications.

International Commission on Illumination/Commission Internationale de l'Eclairage: Kegelgasse 27, 1030 Vienna, Austria; tel. (1) 714-31-87-0; fax (1) 713-0838-18; e-mail ciecb@ping.at; f. 1900 as International Commission on Photometry, reorganized as CIE 1913; objects: to provide an international forum for the discussion of all matters relating to science, technology and art in the fields of light and lighting; to develop basic standards and procedures of metrology in the fields of light and lighting; to provide guidance in the application of basic principles and procedures to the development of international standards in the fields of light and lighting; to prepare and publish reports and standards; to maintain liaison and technical interaction with relevant international organizations; mems: 40 affiliated National Illumination Committees; Gen. Sec. C. HERMANN; publs *Comptes Rendus* of quadrennial plenary sessions, *International Lighting Vocabulary* in French, English, German and Russian, containing over 750 terms with definitions, *International standards for colorimetry, recommendations for colour rendering, colours of lights and surfaces for signalling, lighting of roads for motorized traffic and tunnel lighting*, technical committee reports, etc.

International Conference on Large High Voltage Electric Systems/Conférence Internationale des Grands Réseaux Electriques à Haute Tension (CIGRE): 21 rue d'Artois, 75008 Paris, France; tel. 1-53-89-12-90; fax 1-53-89-12-99; f. 1921; electrical aspects of electricity generation, sub-stations and transformer stations, high voltage electrical lines, interconnection of systems and their operation and protection; 4,000 mems; Pres. M. CHAMIA (Sweden); Sec.-Gen. M. HEROUARD

(France); publs *Electra* (every 2 months), *Session Proceedings* (every 2 years).

International Council for Building Research, Studies and Documentation/Conseil international du bâtiment pour la recherche, l'étude et la documentation: Kruisplein 25G, 3014 DB Rotterdam, Netherlands; tel. (10) 4110240; fax (10) 433-43-72; e-mail secretariat@cibworld.nl; f. 1953 to encourage and facilitate co-operation in building research, studies and documentation in all aspects; mems: 450 institutes and individuals in 70 countries; Pres. CH. SJÖSTRÖM; Sec.-Gen. Dr W. J. P. BAKENS; publs *Directory of Building Research and Development Organizations, CIB Congress and Symposium Proceedings,* newsletter (6 a year).

International Council for Scientific and Technical Information: 51 blvd de Montmorency, 75016 Paris, France; tel. 45-25-65-92; fax 42-15-12-62; f. 1952 as ICSU Abstracting Board, present name 1984; aims to increase accessibility to and awareness of scientific and technical information, and to foster communication and interaction among participants in the information transfer chain, in order to take advantage of the progress made independently by each information activity sector; 50 national and organizational mems in 11 countries; ICSTI is a Scientific Associate of ICSU; Pres. DAVID RUSSON (UK); Exec. Sec. MARTHE ORFUS.

International Electrotechnical Commission/Commission Electrotechnique Internationale: 3 rue de Varembé, 1211 Geneva 20, Switzerland; tel. (22) 919-0211; telex 414121; fax (22) 919-0300; e-mail info@iec.ch; f. 1906 to promote international co-operation in the electrotechnical industry; has originated a multilanguage vocabulary with more than 100,000 terms; originated the 'International System' (SI) of units of measurement; establishes worldwide standards for electrical and electronic equipment and installations; 53 national cttees; Pres. BERNARD H. FALK (USA); Gen. Sec. A. M. RAEBURN (UK); publs *Bulletin* (6 a year), *Annual Report*.

International Federation for Housing and Planning/Fédération internationale pour l'habitation, l'urbanisme et l'aménagement des territoires: Wassenaarseweg 43, 2596 CG The Hague, Netherlands; f. 1913 to promote throughout the world the study and practice of housing and regional, town and country planning, to secure higher standards of housing, the improvement of towns and cities and a better distribution of the population; Pres. IRENE WIESE-VON OFEN (Germany); Sec.-Gen. E. E. VAN HYLCKAMA VLIEG (Netherlands); publ. *Newsletter* (5 a year).

International Federation for Information Processing: C/o Plamen Nedkov, Hofstr. 3, 2361 Laxenburg, Austria; tel. (2236) 73616; fax (2236) 736169; f. 1960; UNESCO category B; aims to promote information science and technology by fostering int. co-operation in this field, stimulating research, development and the application of information processing in science and human activity, furthering the dissemination and exchange of information about the subject, and encouraging education in information processing; 46 mem. organizations representing 70 countries; publs *Computers in Industry, Computers and Security, Information Bulletin,* newsletters (quarterly).

International Federation of Automotive Engineering Societies/Fédération internationale des sociétés d'ingénieurs des techniques de l'automobile (FISITA): 1 Birdcage Walk, London, SW1H 9JJ, England; f. 1947 to promote the exchange of information between member societies, ensure standardization of techniques and terms, to publish research on technical and managerial problems and generally to encourage the technical development of mechanical transport; mem. organizations in 27 countries; Pres. Dr JACK SCHMIDT; Exec. Dir PETER THOMAS.

International Federation of Operational Research Societies (IFORS): Bldg 321, Tech. Univ. of Denmark, 2800 Lyngby, Denmark; tel. 45-25-34-10; fax 45-88-13-97; f. 1959; aims: the development of operational research as a unified science and its advancement in all nations of the world; mems: 44 national societies and 4 kindred societies; Pres. ANDRÉS WEINTRAUB (Chile); Sec. Mrs. HELLE WELLING; publs *International Abstracts in Operations Research Bulletin, International Transactions in Operational Research Bulletin*.

International Federation of Robotics: POB 5510, 114 85 Stockholm, Sweden; tel. (8) 782-08-00; fax (8) 660-33-78; f. 1987; 27 nat. mem. orgs; Chair. ERIC MITTELSTADT; Sec. BJÖRN WEICHBRODT; publ. *Newsletter* (quarterly).

International Federation of Surveyors/Fédération internationale des géomètres: C/o RICS, 12 Great George St, London, SW1P 3AD, England; tel. (171) 334-3796; fax (171) 334-3719; e-mail jwoolley@rics.org.uk; f. 1878; nine technical commissions; 73 national asscns are affiliated; Pres. PETER DALE (UK); Sec.-Gen. ROY SWANSTON (UK); publs Reports of Congresses, annual review and bulletins.

International Information Centre for Terminology (Infoterm): Simmeringer Hauptstr. 24, 1110 Vienna, Austria; tel. (1) 74040-441; fax (1) 74040-740; e-mail infopoint@infoterm.or.at; f. 1971 under UNESCO contract; affiliated with Austrian Standards Institute; works in liaison with Technical Cttee 37 'Terminology (Principles and Co-ordination)' of ISO; 7 permanent staff; library of 3,000 vols, 15,000 vocabulary standards; Dir CHRISTIAN GALINSKI; publs *Infoterm Newsletter* (quarterly), *BIT Biblio Term* (quarterly), *STT Standard Term* (quarterly), *TSH Terminology, Standardization and Harmonization* (quarterly), *TNN Term Net News* (quarterly), *Infoterm Series* (irregular).

International Institute of Communications: Tavistock House South, Tavistock Square, London, WC1H 9LF, England; tel. (171) 388-0671; fax (171) 380-0623; f. 1969 as Int. Broadcast Inst.; worldwide research and education on telecommunications, broadcasting and information technology; hosts seminars and annual conference; mems in over 70 countries; library of *c.* 15,000 items, *c.* 200 periodicals; Pres. HENRI PIGEAT (France); Exec. Dir ROGER HAYES; publ. *InterMedia* (every 2 months).

International Institute of Refrigeration/Institut International du Froid: 177 blvd Malesherbes, 75017 Paris, France; tel. 1-42-27-32-35; fax 1-47-63-17-98; e-mail iifiir@ibm.net; f. 1908; intergovernmental organization; object: the study of all technical, scientific and industrial questions concerning refrigeration systems, cryogenics, air conditioning, heat pumps and their applications; studies are undertaken, under the direction of a Scientific Council, by 10 Commissions; organizes congresses and seminars; large library, also computerized documentary data-base; provides bibliographical researches; mems: 57 countries and private or corporate associates; Dir L. LUCAS (France); publs *Bulletin of the IIR* (bibliographical, in French and English), *Proceedings of Meetings of Scientific and Technical Commissions, International Journal of Refrigeration*.

International Iron and Steel Institute (IISI)/Institut international du fer et de l'acier: 120 rue Col. Bourg, 1140 Brussels, Belgium; tel. (2) 702-89-00; telex 22639; fax (2) 702-88-99; e-mail steel@iisi.be; f. 1967 to promote the welfare and interests of the world's steel industries; to undertake research in all aspects of steel industries; to serve as a forum for exchange of knowledge and discussion of problems relating to steel industries; to collect, disseminate and maintain statistics and information; to serve as a liaison body between international and national steel organizations; mems in 50 countries; Sec.-Gen. LENHARD J. HOLSCHUH; publs *World Steel Statistics Monthly, Crude Steel Production Monthly, Iron Production Monthly, World Steel Bulletin* (3 a year), *Annual Conference Proceedings,* surveys and studies on various aspects of world steel.

International Organization for Standardization/Organisation internationale de normalisation: 1 rue de Varembé, CP 56, 1211 Geneva 20, Switzerland; tel. (41) (22) 749-01-11; telex 412205; fax (41) (22) 733-34-30; e-mail central@iso.ch; f. 1947 to promote the development of standardization and related activities in the world with a view to facilitating the international exchange of goods and services, and to developing mutual co-operation in the spheres of intellectual, scientific, technological and economic activity; 121 mems; Pres. LIEW MUN LEONG (Singapore); Sec.-Gen. L. D. EICHER; publs *ISO International Standards, ISO Memento* (annually), *ISO Catalogue* (annually), *ISO Bulletin* (monthly), *ISO 9000 News* (6 a year), *ISO General Information Brochure, ISO Standards Handbooks*.

International Society for Photogrammetry and Remote Sensing/Société internationale de Photogrammétrie et de Télédétection: f. 1910; research and information on the application of aerial and space photography and remote sensing to resource inventory, exploration and mapping; 82 mem. countries; Pres. Dr K. TORLEGÅRD (Sweden); Sec.-Gen. S. MURAI, Institute of Industrial Science, Univ. of Tokyo, 7-22-1 Roppongi, Minatoku, Tokyo 106, Japan; tel. (3) 3402-6231, ext. 2560; telex 2427317; publs *International Archives of Photogrammetry and Remote Sensing* (every 2 years), *Photogrammetry and Remote Sensing* (every 2 months).

International Society for Soil Mechanics and Geotechnical Engineering/Société internationale de mécanique des sols et de la géotechnique: Univ. Engineering Dept, Trumpington St, Cambridge, CB2 1PZ, England; tel. (1223) 355020; fax (1223) 359675; f. 1936; 70 mem. societies, *c.* 18,000 individual mems; Pres. Prof. KENJI ISHIHARA (Japan); Sec.-Gen. Dr R. H. G. PARRY (UK); publ. *ISSMGE News* (quarterly).

International Union of Public Transport/Union Internationale des Transports Publics (UITP)/Internationaler Verband für Öffentliches Verkehrswesen: 19 ave de l'Uruguay, 1000 Brussels, Belgium; tel. (2) 673-61-00; fax (2) 660-10-72; f. 1885 to study all problems related to the operation of public transportation; library of 25,000 vols; 1,700 mems; Pres. J.-P. BAILLY (France); Sec.-Gen. HANS RAT (Netherlands); publs *Public Transport International* (every 2 months), *Euroexpress, UITP express, UITP biblio-express* (6 a year), congress reports (every 2 years), bibliographies.

ITRI Ltd: Kingston Lane, Uxbridge, Middx, UB8 3PJ, England; tel. (1895) 272406; fax (1895) 251841; f. 1932; aims to maintain and extend the use and effectiveness of tin in modern technology; its work is directed to develop the use of tin and is based on scientific and technical study of the metal, its alloys and compounds, and of industrial processes which use tin or may provide future markets; there is an information centre in Brussels; Man. Dir R. BEDDER; publ. *Annual Report*.

Textile Institute, The: International Headquarters, 10 Blackfriars St, Manchester, M3 5DR, England; tel. (161) 834-8457; fax (161) 835-3087; f. 1910; Royal Charter 1925 and 1955; the international body for those concerned with any aspect of textiles and related industries; promotion of education and training, professional standards and exchange of information within the industry by means of publications, conferences, meetings and information services; 60 national and regional brs; 8,000 mems in 85 countries; library of 1,500 vols, 180 journals; Pres. S. ARGYROS; Gen. Sec. (vacant); publs *Journal* (quarterly), *Textile Horizons* (every 2 months), *Textiles* (quarterly), *Textile Progress* (quarterly).

Law

Hague Academy of International Law: Carnegieplein 2, 2517 KJ The Hague, The Netherlands; tel. (70) 3024242; f. 1923 as a centre of higher studies in international law (public and private) and cognate sciences, in order to facilitate a thorough and impartial examination of questions bearing on international juridical relations; Sec.-Gen. Prof. G. BURDEAU.

Associated centre:

Centre for Studies and Research in International Law and International Relations: The Hague; f. 1957; postdoctoral research courses in August and September after courses held by Academy; open only to participants who are highly qualified by intellectual maturity and experience (12 French-speaking, 12 English-speaking); library: use of Peace Palace Library.

Hague Conference on Private International Law/Conférence de La Haye de droit international privé: Scheveningseweg 6, 2517 KT The Hague, Netherlands; f. 1893 to work for the unification of the rules of private international law; mems: governments of Argentina, Australia, Austria, Belgium, Canada, Chile, China, Croatia, Cyprus, Czech Republic, Denmark, Egypt, Finland, France, Germany, Greece, Hungary, Ireland, Israel, Italy, Japan, Republic of Korea, Latvia, Luxembourg, former Yugoslav Republic of Macedonia, Malta, Mexico, Monaco, Morocco, Netherlands, Norway, Poland, Portugal, Romania, Slovak Republic, Slovenia, Spain, Suriname, Sweden, Switzerland, Turkey, UK, USA, Uruguay, Venezuela; Sec.-Gen. J. H. A. VAN LOON; publs *Actes* and *Documents* relating to each Session; various printed and mimeographed documents.

Institute of International Law/Institut de droit international: 'La Vague', 33 route de Suisse, 1297 Founex, Switzerland; tel. (22) 731-17-30; fax (22) 738-43-06; f. 1873 to promote the development of international law by endeavouring to formulate general principles in accordance with civilized ethical standards, and by giving assistance to genuine attempts at the gradual and progressive codification of international law; 132 mems and associates from all over the world; Sec.-Gen. Prof. CHRISTIAN DOMINICE; publs *Annuaire, Tableau général des Résolutions*.

Inter-American Bar Association: 1211 Connecticut Ave NW, Ste. 202, Washington, DC 20036, USA; tel. (202) 393-1217; fax (202) 393-1241; f. 1940; mems: bar associations and individual lawyers in 33 countries; Sec.-Gen. LOUIS G. FERRAND, Jr; publs *Newsletter* (quarterly), *Conference Proceedings*.

Intergovernmental Committee of the Universal Copyright Convention: UNESCO, 7 Place de Fontenoy, 75700 Paris, France; tel. 1-45-68-47-05; telex 204461; fax 1-45-68-55-89; f. 1952; studies the problems concerning the application and operation of the Universal Copyright Convention; makes preparation for periodic revisions of this Convention; mems: Algeria, Argentina, Australia, Austria, Cameroon, Chile, France, Greece, India, Israel, Japan, Mexico, Morocco, Portugal, Russia, UK and USA; Chair. GRACIELA H. PEIRETTI (Argentina).

International Association for Penal Law/Association internationale de droit pénal: Faculté de Droit, 12 place du Panthéon, 75005 Paris, France; f. 1924 to promote co-operation between those who, in different countries, are engaged in the study or practice of criminal law, to study crime, its causes and its cure, and to further the theoretical and practical development of international penal law; 800 mems; Pres. H. H. JESCHECK; Gen. Sec. M. CH. BASSIOUNI; publ. *Revue Internationale de Droit Pénal* (2 a year).

International Association for Philosophy of Law and Social Philosophy (IVR): C/o Univ. of Bologna, CIRFID, Via Zamboni 27/29, 40126 Bologna, Italy; tel. (51) 277211; fax (51) 260782; e-mail ivrmail@cirfid.unibo.it; f. 1909 for scientific research in philosophy of law and social philosophy at an international level; holds national and int. congresses every 2 years; 2,300 mems; national sections in 44 countries; Pres. E. PATTARO (Italy); Sec.-Gen. G. FINOCCHIARO (Italy); publs *IVR Newsletter* (2 a year), *Archiv für Rechts- und Sozial-philosophie* (quarterly).

International Association of Democratic Lawyers (IADL)/Association internationale des Juristes Démocrates: C/o Jitendra Sharma, 17 Lawyers' Chambers, Supreme Court, New Delhi 110001, India; fax (11) 6473145; f. 1946; aims to facilitate contacts and exchanges of view between lawyers and lawyers' associations and to foster understanding and goodwill; to work together to achieve the aims of the Charter of the United Nations; mems from 102 countries; in consultative status with UN Economic and Social Council and with UNESCO; Pres. (vacant); Sec.-Gen. JITENDRA SHARMA; publs *Revue Internationale de Droit Contemporain* (2 a year; also published in English and Spanish), *Bulletins*.

International Association of Lawyers/Union Internationale des Avocats: 25 rue du Jour, 75001 Paris, France; tel. (1) 45-08-82-34; fax (1) 45-08-82-31; e-mail 100771.2060@compuserve.com; f. 1927 to promote the independence and freedom of lawyers, and defend their ethical and material interests on an international level; to contribute to the development of an international order based on law; mems: 254 (collective), 3,000 (individual); Admin. Dir NATHALIE ALABERT BROUARD; publs *Juriste International, Newsletter*.

International Bar Association: 271 Regent St, London, W1R 7PA, England; tel. (171) 629-1206; fax (171) 409-0456; e-mail member@int-bar.org; f. 1947; membership comprises 173 national bar associations and law socs and 18,000 individual lawyers from 183 countries; Exec. Dir PAUL HODDINOTT; publs *International Bar News* (quarterly), *International Legal Practitioner* (quarterly), *International Business Lawyer* (11 a year), *Journal of Energy and Natural Resources Law* (quarterly).

International Bureau of Fiscal Documentation: Sarphatistraat 600, POB 20237, 1000 HE Amsterdam, The Netherlands; tel. (20) 626-77-26; fax (20) 622-86-58; an independent non-profit foundation; f. 1938 to supply information on fiscal law and its application; specialized library on international tax and investment legislation (26,000 vols); tax treaties database and European taxation database on CD-ROM, OECD database on floppy disks; Chief Exec. Prof. H. M. A. L. HAMAEKERS; publs *Bulletin for International Fiscal Documentation* (monthly), *European Taxation* (monthly review of European tax law), *International VAT Monitor*.

Attached Academy:

IBFD International Tax Academy: f. 1989 to provide education and training on international and comparative tax law through conferences, courses and traineeships; Technical Dir Prof. Dr W. G. KUIPER.

International Commission of Jurists/Commission internationale de juristes: BP 216, 81A ave de Châtelaine, 1219 Châtelaine/Geneva, Switzerland; tel. (22) 788-47-47; telex 418531; fax (22) 788-48-80; f. 1952 to promote and protect human rights, and to strengthen the Rule of Law in all its practical manifestations—institutions, legislation, procedures, etc.—and defend it through the mobilization of world legal opinion in cases of general and systematic violation of, or serious threat to, such principles of justice; library of 2,000 vols; Pres. Justice MICHAEL D. KIRBY; Sec.-Gen. ADAMA DIENG (Senegal); publs Special reports, *The Review* (2 a year), *ICJ Newsletter* (quarterly), *Yearbook of the Centre for the Independence of Judges and Lawyers, Attacks on Justice* (annually).

International Confederation of Societies of Authors and Composers/Confédération internationale des sociétés d'auteurs et compositeurs: 11 rue Kepler, 75116 Paris, France; f. 1926 to ensure more effective protection of the rights of authors and composers, to improve legislation on literary and artistic rights, and to organize research on problems concerning the rights of authors; participates in preparatory work for inter-governmental conferences on authors' rights; mem. societies in 90 countries; Pres. MARILYN BERGMAN; Sec.-Gen. JEAN-ALEXIS ZIEGLER; publ. *CISAC News*.

International Development Law Institute: Via di San Sebastianello 16, 00187 Rome, Italy; tel. (6) 6979261; telex 622381; fax (6) 6781946; e-mail idli@idli.org; f. 1983 for mid-career training and technical assistance, primarily for developing and transition country lawyers, legal advisers and judges; Rome-based courses and seminars in English and French address legal topics related to economic development and governance, including negotiation, int. contracting and economic law reform; also designs and organizes in-country training workshops on law-related economic development topics; library in process of formation; Dir L. MICHAEL HAGER.

International Federation for European Law/Fédération Internationale pour le Droit Européen (FIDE): Via Nicolò Tartaglia 5, 00197 Rome, Italy; fax 80-80-731; f. 1961 to advance studies on European law among members of the European Community by co-ordinating activities of member societies and by organizing regular colloquies on topical problems of European law; mems: 17 national associations; Pres. FRANCESCO CAPOTORII.

International Institute for the Unification of Private Law/Institut international pour l'unification du droit privé (Unidroit): Via Panisperna 28, 00184 Rome, Italy; tel. (6) 69941372; fax (6) 69941394; e-mail unidroit.rome@unidroit.org; f. 1926, to prepare for the establishment of uniform legislation, to prepare draft uniform laws and international conventions for adoption by diplomatic conferences, to prepare drafts of international agreements on private law, to undertake studies in comparative law, and to organise conferences and publish works on such subjects; meetings of organizations concerned with the unification of law; international congresses on private law; library of 230,000 vols; mems: governments of 58 countries; Pres. LUIGI FERRARI BRAVO (Italy): Sec.-Gen. WALTER RODINÒ (acting); publs *Uniform Law Review* (quarterly), *Digest of Legal Activities of International Organizations*.

International Institute of Space Law (IISL)/Institut International de Droit de l'Espace: f. 1959 at the XI Congress of the International Astronautical Federation; holds meetings, makes studies on juridical and sociological aspects of astronautics; publishes reports; makes awards; holds an annual Colloquium; mems: 386 individuals elected for life; Pres. Dr N. JASENTULIYANA (UN/Sri Lanka); Vice-Pres. Prof. Dr S. GOROVE (USA), V. S. VERESHCHETIN (CIS); Sec. TANJA L. MASSON-ZWAAN, IISL, 3-5 rue Mario-Nikis, 75015 Paris, France; tel. (1) 45-67-42-60; telex 205917; fax (1) 42-73-21-20; publ. *Proceedings of Colloquia*.

International Juridical Institute/Institut juridique international: Permanent Office for the Supply of Int. Legal Information, Spui 186, 2511 BW, The Hague, Netherlands; tel. (70) 346-0974; fax (70) 362-5235; e-mail iji@worldonline.nl; f. 1918 to supply information in connection with any matter of international interest, not being of a secret nature, respecting international, municipal and foreign law and the application thereof; Chair. Prof. A. V. M. STRUYCKEN; Sec. F. J. A. VAN DER VELDEN; Dir A. L. G. A. STILLE.

International Maritime Committee/Comité Maritime International: Markgravestraat 9, 2000 Antwerp, Belgium; tel. (3) 227-35-26; telex 31653; fax (3) 227-35-28; f. 1897 to contribute to the unification of maritime and commercial law, maritime customs, usages and practices; promotes the establishment of national associations of maritime law and co-operates with other international associations or organizations having the same object; work includes drafting of conventions on collisions at sea, salvage and assistance at sea, limitation of shipowners' liability, maritime mortgages, etc.; mems: associations in 51 countries; Pres. PATRICK GRIGGS (UK); Secs-Gen. Dr ALEXANDER VON ZIEGLER (Switzerland); publs *CMI News Letter, Year Book*.

World Jurist Association (WJA): Suite 202, 1000 Connecticut Ave NW, Washington, DC 20036, USA; tel. (202) 466-5428; telex 440456; fax (202) 452-8540; f. 1963 to promote the continued development of international law and world order; biennial world conferences, World Law Day, demonstration trials, research programmes and publications have contributed to the growth of law and legal institutions by focusing on matters of international concern; mems: lawyers, jurists and legal scholars in over 150 countries; Pres. Prof. VED P. NANDA (USA/India); Exec. Vice-Pres. MARGARETHA M. HENNEBERRY (USA); publs *World Jurist* (every 2 months), *Law / Technology* (quarterly), research reports and pamphlet series, etc.

Affiliated bodies:

World Association of Judges (WAJ): f. 1966 to mobilize judicial leaders on important transnational legal issues and to improve the administration of justice; over 23 cttees studying int. law; Pres. Prince BOLA AJIBOLA (Nigeria).

World Association of Lawyers (WAL): f. 1975 to develop transnational law and improve lawyers' expertise in related areas; over 100 committees studying the development of international law; Pres. JACK STREETER (USA).

World Association of Law Professors (WALP): f. 1975 to focus the attention of legal scholars and teachers on transnational legal issues, and improve scholarship and education in international legal matters, including training, practice, administration of justice, human rights, the environment and co-ordination of legal systems; Pres. SERAFIN V. GUINGONA (Philippines).

World Association of Center Associates (WACA): f. 1979 to mobilize interested individuals not in the legal profession to promote the objects of the WJA; Pres. PAOLO ASCANI (Italy).

Medicine and Public Health

World Health Organization/Organisation mondiale de la Santé: Ave Appia, 1211 Geneva 27, Switzerland; tel. 791-21-11; telex 415416; fax (22) 791-07-46; f. 1948. WHO, a specialized agency of the United Nations, is an inter-governmental agency charged under the terms of its constitution 'to act as the directing and co-ordinating authority on international health work'. WHO has proclaimed the goal of 'Health for all by the year 2000'—i.e. the attainment of a level of health that permits a socially and economically productive life. The Eighth General Programme of Work, covering the period 1990–95, is the second of three programmes that together will ensure continuing support to the 'Global Strategy for Health for All by the year 2000'. It emphasizes the importance of making optimal use of WHO's resources, in countries as well as at other organizational levels. This is to be achieved through sound resource management. WHO's limited regular budget resources are meant to support countries in strengthening their planning and managerial capacities to develop and carry out their strategies, build up their infrastructures and implement their technical programmes. The Eighth General Programme of Work defines 15 objectives and a number of targets as well as approaches for attaining these. Two general approaches corresponding to the Organization's main functions are especially emphasized: co-ordination and technical co-operation; 189 mem. states; library of 80,000 vols, 2,500 periodicals and 180,000 documents; Dir-Gen. Dr HIROSHI NAKAJIMA (Japan); publs *Bulletin* (WHO scientific papers, every 2 months), *International Digest of Health Legislation* (quarterly), *World Health Statistics Quarterly*, *World Health Forum* (quarterly), *World Health Statistics Annual*, *Weekly Epidemiological Record*, *Monograph Series*, *Technical Report Series*, *World Health* (intended for the general public, 6 a year).

OTHER ORGANIZATIONS

Council for International Organizations of Medical Sciences (CIOMS)/Conseil des organisations internationales des sciences médicales: Secretariat: c/o WHO, ave Appia, 1211 Geneva 27, Switzerland; tel. (22) 791-34-06; telex 415416; fax (22) 791-07-46; f. 1949 to facilitate and co-ordinate the activities of its members, to act as a co-ordinating centre between them and the national institutions, to maintain collaboration with the UN, to promote international activities in the field of medical sciences, to serve the scientific interests of the international biomedical community; 72 international associations, national academic and research councils in 30 countries; Pres. Dr JOHN H. BRYANT (USA); Sec.-Gen. Dr Z. BANKOWSKI (Switzerland); publs *Calendar of Congresses of Medical Sciences* (annually), *Proceedings of Round Table Conferences*, *Yearbook*, *International Nomenclature of Diseases*.

INTERNATIONAL MEMBERS OF CIOMS

FDI World Dental Federation/Fédération Dentaire Internationale: 7 Carlisle St, London, W1V 5RG, England; tel. (171) 935-7852; telex 21879; fax (171) 486-0183; f. 1900; 13,000 individual mems, 92 asscns in 83 countries; Pres. Dr HEINZ ERNI (Switzerland); Treas. Dr ARTHUR DUGONI (USA); Exec. Dir Dr P. A. ZILLÉN (Sweden); publs *Basic Facts*, *FDI World*, *International Dental Journal*, *Community Dental Health*, *European Journal of Prosthodontics and Restorative Dentistry*, *Gerodontology*, technical reports.

International Association for the Study of the Liver: f. 1958 to foster training of experts in hepatology; encourages research on the liver and its diseases and helps to facilitate prevention, recognition and treatment of liver and biliary tract diseases in the international community; Pres. Dr JOHN GOLLAN (USA); Sec./Treas. Prof. JUNE HALLIDAY, Queensland Institute of Medical Research, The Bancroft Centre, PO Royal Brisbane Hospital, Brisbane, Qld 4029, Australia.

International Association of Allergology and Clinical Immunology (IAACI): 611 East Wells St, Milwaukee, WI 53202, USA; tel. (414) 276-6445; fax (414) 272-6070; f. 1945 to further work in the educational, research and practical medical aspects of allergy diseases; mems: 20,000 from 42 national societies; publ. *Allergy & Clinical Immunology International News* (every 2 months).

International College of Surgeons, The/Collège International de Chirurgiens: 1516 Lake Shore Drive, Chicago, IL 60610, USA; tel. (312) 642-3555; fax (312) 787 1624; f. Geneva 1935, inc. Washington 1940; organized as a world-wide institution to advance the art and science of surgery by bringing together surgeons of all nations, without regard to nationality, creed or colour; through its Surgical Congresses, Research and Scholarship Project and Surgical Teams Project of volunteers to developing countries, an exchange of surgical knowledge is facilitated in the highest interest of patients; also operates the International Museum of Surgical Science located at HQ; *c.* 14,000 mems; Int. Pres. Prof. Dr

PEDRO A. RUBIO; Exec. Dir J. THOMAS VIALL; publ. *International Surgery* (quarterly).

International Council of Nurses: 3 place Jean-Marteau, 1201 Geneva, Switzerland; tel. (22) 908-01-00; fax (22) 908-01-01; f. 1899; federation of national nurses' asscns in 112 countries; Exec. Dir JUDITH A. OULTON; publ. *International Nursing Review*.

International Diabetes Federation/Fédération internationale du diabète: 1 rue Defacqz, 1000 Brussels, Belgium; tel. (2) 538-55-11; fax (2) 538-51-14; f. 1949; 151 member associations in 124 countries; holds triennial congresses; Pres. MARIA L. DE ALVA (Mexico); publs *IDF Bulletin*, (3 a year), *IDF Newsletter* (quarterly), *Triennial Report*.

International Federation of Clinical Neurophysiology/Fédération Internationale de Neurophysiologie Clinique: f. 1949 to attain the highest level of knowledge in the field of electro-encephalography and clinical neuro-physiology in all the countries of the world; 53 mem. organizations (nat. societies); Pres. Dr M. R. NUWER (USA); Sec. Dr HIROSHI SHIBASAKI, Dept. of Brain Pathophysiology, Faculty of Medicine, Kyoto University, Shogoin, Sakyo-ku, Kyoto 606-8507, Japan; tel. (75) 751-3601; fax (75) 751-3202; e-mail shib@kuhp.kyoto-u.ac.jp; publs *Electroencephalography and Clinical Neurophysiology* (monthly), *Evoked Potentials* (every 2 months), *EMG and Motor Control* (every 2 months).

International Federation of Oto-Rhino-Laryngological Societies/Fédération internationale des sociétés oto-rhino-laryngologiques: f. 1965; aims: to promote scientific and clinical research into oto-rhino-laryngology; to improve ear care in developing countries; to register educational programmes and promote co-operation; mems: from 98 countries and 10 international societies; Pres. Dr G. J. MCCAFFERTY (Australia); Sec.-Gen. P. ALBERTI; Secretariat: 7-221 Eaton N, 200 Elisabeth St, Toronto, Ont. M5G 2C4, Canada; tel. (416) 340-4190; fax (416) 340-4209; e-mail alberti@gpu.utcc.utototoronto.ca; publ. *IFOS Newsletter* (quarterly).

International Federation of Physical Medicine and Rehabilitation: f. 1950; international congresses every four years; mem. socs in 43 countries; Pres. Prof. R. OAKESHOTT (Australia); Sec. Prof. PETER DISLER, Essendon Hospital, Chester Street, Moonee Ponds, Melbourne, Vic. 3039, Australia; tel. (3) 9342-4509; fax (3) 9342-4617.

International Federation of Surgical Colleges/Fédération Internationale des Collèges de Chirurgie: Secretariat: La Panetière, 1279 Bogis-Bossey, Switzerland; tel. (22) 776-21-61; fax (22) 776-64-17; f. Stockholm 1958; object: the improvement and maintenance of the standards of surgery throughout the world, by establishment and maintenance of co-operation and interchange of medical and surgical information; encouragement of high standards of education, training and research in surgery and its allied sciences; mems: 57 national colleges or societies and 450 associates; Pres. Prof. J. TERBLANCHE; Sec. Prof. S. W. A. GUNN (Switzerland); publs *News Bulletin, The World Journal of Surgery*.

International League Against Rheumatism/Ligue internationale contre le Rhumatisme: C/o Dr John Sergent, Chief Medical Officer, Vanderbilt University, 3810A TVC, Nashville, TN 37232-5545, USA; fax (615) 343-6478; f. 1929 to promote international co-operation for the study and control of rheumatic diseases; to encourage the foundation of national leagues against rheumatism; to organize regular international congresses and to act as a connecting link between national leagues and international organizations; *c*. 13,000 mems; Pres. Dr ROBERTO ARINOVICHE (Chile); Sec.-Gen. Dr JOHN SERGENT (USA).

International Leprosy Association/Société internationale contre la lèpre: f. 1931 to promote international co-operation in work on leprosy; 1,200 mems; Pres. Dr YO YUASA; Sec. Dr PIETER FEENSTRA, Royal Tropical Institute, 135 Wibautstraat, 1097 DN Amsterdam, Netherlands; tel. (20) 6939-297; fax (20) 6680-823; publ. *International Journal of Leprosy and Other Mycobacterial Diseases* (quarterly).

International Pediatric Association/Association Internationale de Pédiatrie: Dept of Pediatrics (Room 4-8101), University of Rochester School of Medicine and Dentistry, 601 Elmwood Ave, Rochester, NY 14642-8777, USA; tel. (716) 275-0225; fax (716) 273-1038; f. 1912; holds regional and int. seminars and symposia; organizes int. paediatric congresses every 3 years; 161 mem. socs; Pres. Prof. MAMDOUH GABR (Egypt); Exec. Dir Dr ROBERT HAGGERTY (USA); publ. *International Child Health: A Digest of Current Information (quarterly)*.

International Rehabilitation Medicine Association: 1333 Moursund Ave, Houston, TX 77030, USA; tel. (713) 799-5086; fax (713) 799-5058; f. 1969; aims to educate and encourage governments and society to provide medical rehabilitation services to the handicapped (10% of the world's population); offers mems the opportunity to broaden their competence through formation of and participation in the activities of scientific sections geared to medicine and/or surgical specialities and/or specific interests; provides congresses on int. level, and speakers for local and national meetings; 1,900 mems; Pres. M. GRABOIS (USA); publ. *News and Views* (quarterly).

International Rhinologic Society: c/o Prof. P. A. R. Clement, ENT Dept, AZ-VUB, Laarbeeklaan 101, 1090 Brussels, Belgium; f. 1965; aims to create a central organization with which all national and regional societies of rhinology may be affiliated, organize int. congresses and courses of instruction, and stimulate study, research and scientific advancement in the field of rhinology and related sciences; national or regional society mems in 31 countries; Pres. Prof. Dr E. KERN (USA); Sec.-Treas. Prof. P. A. R. CLEMENT (Belgium); publs *Journal of Rhinology, American Journal of Rhinology*.

International Society of Audiology/Société Internationale d'Audiologie: f. 1952 to advance the study of audiology and protect human hearing; 300 individual mems; Pres. Prof. J. KANZAKI; Sec.-Gen. Dr J. VERSCHUURE, Dept ENT/Audiology, University Hospital Rotterdam, Dr Molewaterplein 40, 3015 GD Rotterdam, Netherlands; publ. *Audiology* (every 2 months).

International Society of Internal Medicine/Société internationale de médecine interne: f. 1948 to encourage research and education in internal medicine; to sponsor the International Congress of Internal Medicine every other year; mems: 42 national societies, 3,000 individuals from 54 countries; Pres. Prof. AKIHIRO IGATA (Japan); Sec.-Gen. Prof. R. A. STREULI, Regionalspital, 4900 Langenthal, Switzerland; tel. (62) 916-31-02; fax (62) 916-41-55; e-mail r.streuli@rsl.ch.

International Union Against Cancer/Union internationale contre le cancer: 3 rue du Conseil-Général, 1205 Geneva, Switzerland; tel. (22) 809-18-11; fax (22) 809-18-10; e-mail info@uicc.ch; f. 1933; a non-governmental ind. org. devoted solely to promoting on an international level the campaign against cancer in its research, therapeutic and preventive aspects; mems: 292 organizations in 89 countries; Pres. Dr NIGEL GRAY (Australia); Sec.-Gen. Dr GERALD P. MURPHY (USA); publs *UICC News* (quarterly), *International Journal of Cancer* (30 a year), *International Calendar of Meetings on Cancer* (2 a year).

Medical Women's International Association: Herbert-Lewin-Str. 1, 50931 Cologne, Germany; tel. (221) 4004558; fax (221) 4004557; e-mail MWIA@aol.com; f. 1919 to facilitate contacts between medical women and to encourage their co-operation in matters connected with international health problems; MWIA Congresses and General Assemblies every three years; mems: national associations in 46 countries, with 20,000 mems; Pres. Dr FLORENCE W. MANGUYU (Kenya); Sec.-Gen. Dr CAROLYN MOTZEL (Germany); publ. *MWIA Update* (3 a year).

World Federation for Medical Education: Faculty of Health Sciences, Københavns Universitet, Panum Institute, Blegdamsvej 3, 2200 Copenhagen N, Denmark; tel. 35-32-71-03; fax 35-32-70-70; e-mail wfme@adm.ku.dk; f. 1972 to promote and integrate the study and implementation of medical education world-wide; engaged on programme for worldwide reorientation of medical training; in non-governmental relations with WHO, UNICEF, UNESCO, UNDP and the World Bank; mems: 6 regional asscns on a global level; Pres. Dr HANS KARLE.

World Federation of Associations of Pediatric Surgeons: c/o Prof. J. Boix-Ochoa, Clinica Infantil 'Vall d'Hebron', Dpto de Cirugía Pediatrica, Fac. de Medicina, Univ. Autónoma, PO Valle de Hebron, s/n, 08035 Barcelona, Spain; f. 1974; 60 mem. asscns world-wide; Pres. S. CYWES (South Africa); Sec./Treas. Prof. J. BOIX-OCHOA.

World Federation of Neurology: f. 1957; 70 constituent national societies of neurology, representing 23,000 mems; Pres. Lord WALTON OF DETCHANT; Sec.-Treas.-Gen. Dr F. CLIFFORD ROSE, London Neurological Centre, 110 Harley Street, London, W1N 1AF, England; tel. (171) 935-3546; fax (171) 935-4172; publs *Journal of the Neurological Sciences, World Neurology* (quarterly).

World Heart Federation: 34 rue de l'Athénée, CP 117, 1211 Geneva 12, Switzerland; tel. (22) 347-67-55; fax (22) 347-10-28; e-mail worldheart@compuserve.com; f. 1978; aims to promote the study, prevention and relief of cardiovascular diseases through scientific and public education programmes and exchange of materials between its affiliated societies and foundations and with other agencies having related interests; organizes world congresses every four years; mems: 129 national, 6 continental, 3 individual; Pres. Dr TAK-FU TSE; Exec. Sec. MARIANNE BURLE DE FIGUEIREDO; publs *Heartbeat* (4 a year), *CVD Prevention* (4 a year).

World Medical Association/Association Médicale Mondiale: 28 ave des Alpes, BP 63, 01212 Ferney-Voltaire Cedex, France; tel. 4-50-40-75-75; fax 4-50-40-59-37; e-mail wma@iprolink.fr; f. 1947 to serve humanity by endeavouring to achieve the highest international standards in medical education, medical science, medical art and medical ethics, and health care for all people; the unit of membership is the national medical association; the association has established relations with UNESCO, WHO and other international bodies; six regions; mems: 68 nat. assocs; Pres. Dr D. H. JOHNSON (USA); Sec.-Gen. Dr D. HUMAN (South Africa); publ. *World Medical Journal*.

World Organization of Gastro-enterology/Organisation mondiale de gastro-entérologie (OMGE): f. 1935 to conduct research and contribute to the progress generally of the study of gastroenterology; mem. societies and groups in 68 countries; Pres. Prof. I. A. D. BOUCHIER; Sec.-Gen. Prof. MEINHARD CLASSEN, Dept of Internal Medicine, Technical University, Munich, Germany; fax (89) 41404871; publ. *Bulletin* (annually).

World Psychiatric Association/Association Mondiale de Psychiatrie: López-Ibor Clinic, Nueva Zelanda 44, 28035 Madrid, Spain; tel. 373-73-61; fax 316-27-49; f. 1961 at the 3rd World Congress of Psychiatry in Montreal; aims: the exchange, in all languages, of information concerning the problems of mental illness; the strengthening of relationships between psychiatrists in all countries; the establishment of working relations with WHO, UNESCO and other international organizations; the organization of World Psychiatric Congresses and of regional and inter-regional scientific meetings; mems: 99 national societies totalling 120,000 individual psychiatrists; Pres. FELICE LIEH MAK (Hong Kong); Sec.-Gen. JUAN J. LÓPEZ-IBOR, Jr (Spain).

ASSOCIATE MEMBERS OF CIOMS

American College of Chest Physicians: 3300 Dundee Road, Northbrook, IL 60062, USA; tel. (847) 498-1400; fax (847) 498-5460; f. 1935; postgraduate medical education; 15,000 mems; Exec. Vice-Pres. and CEO ALVIN LEVER; publ. *Chest* (monthly).

International Committee of Military Medicine/Comité international de médecine militaire: Hôpital Militaire, Liège, Belgium; tel. (4) 222-21-83; fax (4) 222-21-50; f. 1921 to promote world co-operation on questions of military medicine and to foster its international and humanitarian character; it also administers the International Military Medical Record Office (*Office International de Documentation de Médecine Militaire*), f. 1930; 93 countries are represented on the committee; Pres. Divr. Dr R. SCHLÖGEL (Austria); Sec.-Gen. Méd. Col J. SANABRIA (Belgium); publ. *Revue Internationale des Services de Santé des Forces Armées* (quarterly).

International Congress on Tropical Medicine and Malaria/Congrès International de Médecine Tropicale et de Paludisme: Congresses are held quinquennially; Sec.-Gen. Dr E. C. GARCIA, Institute of Public Health, University of the Philippines, POB EA-460, Manila, Philippines.

International Council on Alcohol and Addictions: CP 189, CH-1001 Lausanne, Switzerland; tel. (21) 320-98-65; fax (21) 320-98-17; e-mail icaa@pingnet.ch; f. 1907; aims to reduce and prevent the harmful effects of the use of alcohol and other drugs by the study of addiction problems and the development of programmes in this field, the study of concepts and methods of prevention, treatment and rehabilitation, and the dissemination of knowledge in the interests of public health and personal and social well-being; holds Int. Institute annually and Int. Congress every three or four years, symposia, study courses, training courses on substance abuse in developing countries, etc.; mems: 135 organizations, *c.* 500 individuals from 85 countries; library: special collection of *c.* 6,000 vols on drug dependence, *c.* 12,000 pamphlets, reprints, etc., 120 periodicals; Pres. I. AL-AWAJI; Exec. Dir Dr EVA TONGUE; publs *ICAA News* (quarterly), conference proceedings, reports, etc.

International Federation of Clinical Chemistry: f. 1952; mems: 63 national socs (*c.* 30,000 individuals); Pres. Prof. G. SIEST (France); Sec. Prof. O. ZINDER, Dept of Clinical Biochemistry, Rambam Medical Center, 31096 Haifa, Israel; fax (4) 542-409; publs *Journal* (every 2 months), *Annual Report*, recommendations and documents.

International Federation of Medical Students' Associations: C/o F. W. J. Hilhorst, Dept of Social Medicine, University of Amsterdam, Academic Medical Centre, POB 22700, 1100 DE Amsterdam, Netherlands; tel. (20) 566-53-66; fax (20) 697-23-16; e-mail gs@ifmsa.org; f. 1951 to serve medical students worldwide and to promote int. co-operation; organizes professional exchanges in preclinical and clinical fields of medicine; holds Gen. Assembly annually; 63 mem. asscns; Gen. Sec. F. W. J. HILHORST; publ. *Newsletter* (quarterly).

International Society of Blood Transfusion/Société Internationale de Transfusion Sanguine: National Directorate of NBTS, NWRHA, Gateway House, Piccadilly South, Manchester, M60 7LP, England; tel. (61) 236-2263; fax (61) 236-0519; f. 1937; mems: 2,080 in 108 countries; Pres. and acting Sec.-Gen. HAROLD GUNSON (UK); publs *Vox Sanguinis, Transfusion Today, World Directory of Blood Transfusion.*

Rehabilitation International—International Society for Rehabilitation of the Disabled/Société Internationale pour la Réadaptation des Handicapés: 25 E 21st St, New York, NY 10010, USA; tel. (212) 420-1500; telex 446412; fax (212) 505-0871; f. 1922; 118 mem. organizations in 80 countries; Pres. JOHN W. STOTT; Sec.-Gen. SUSAN PARKER; publ. *International Rehabilitation Review* (3 a year).

OTHER ORGANIZATIONS

African Medical and Research Foundation: Wilson Airport, POB 30125, Nairobi, Kenya; tel. (2) 501301; telex 23254; fax (2) 609518; e-mail amrefinf@africaonline.co.ke; f. 1957; independent, non-profit organization working to improve the health of people in Eastern Africa; funds from governmental and non-governmental aid agencies in Africa, Europe and North America, and private donors; official relations with WHO; activities: primary health care, training, teaching aids, health behaviour and education, airborne medicine, flying doctor service, medical radio communication, ground mobile medicine, emergency intervention in famine and other crises, research, consultancies; library of 6,000 vols, 122 periodicals; Chair. BETHUEL KIPLAGAT; Dir-Gen. JOHN BATTEN; publs *AMREF News* (quarterly), *AFYA* (quarterly), *Defender* (quarterly), *COBASHECA* (quarterly), *Helper* (quarterly), *HEN* (quarterly).

Association for Medical Education in Europe: University of Dundee, Tay Park House, 484 Perth Road, Dundee, DD2 1LR, Scotland; tel. (1382) 631967; fax (1382) 645748; e-mail p.m.lilley@dundee.ac.uk; f. 1972 to promote and integrate the study of medical education in the countries of Europe; mems: Asscns for Medical Education in most European countries; assoc. corporate mems in countries without Nat. Asscns; and individual mems; Pres. Dr J. NYSTRUP; Sec. Prof. R. M. HARDEN; publ. *Medical Teacher* (6 a year).

European Academy of Anaesthesiology: Strasbourg, France; f. 1978 to improve the standard of training, practice and research in anaesthesiology in Europe; 251 full mems, 190 assoc. mems; Pres. Prof. W. DICK (Germany); Sec. Prof. H. VAN AKEN; publ. *European Journal of Anaesthesiology*.

European Society of Cardiology: C/o The European Heart House, 2035 Route des Colles, Les Templiers, BP 179, 06903 Sophia Antipolis Cedex, France; tel. 4-92-94-76-00; fax 4-92-94-76-01; e-mail webmaster@escardio.org; f. 1950; aims to bring together societies of cardiology in all European countries, and to provide a common forum for working groups on subjects of common interest and for scientists and physicians interested in cardiology; 28,000 mems; Pres. LARS RYDÉN; publ. *The European Heart Journal* (monthly), *Cardiovascular Research* (monthly).

Inclusion International: 29 chaussée d'Ixelles, 393/32, 1050 Brussels, Belgium; tel. (2) 5027734; fax (2) 5022846; e-mail incluit@skynet.be; f. 1960 to promote the interests of the mentally handicapped without regard to nationality, race, religion, age, or degree of handicap; furthers co-operation between national bodies, organizes congresses and symposia; consultative status with UNESCO, UNICEF, WHO, ILO, ECOSOC and the Council of Europe; official relations with IIN, the Comm. of the European Communities and various other orgs; mems: 173 mem. socs in 109 countries; Pres. GERARD DON WILLS; Sec.-Gen. KLAUS LACHWITZ (Germany); publs Proceedings of Conferences, Symposia etc., brochures and pamphlets.

International Agency for Research on Cancer/Centre International de Recherche sur le Cancer: 150 cours Albert-Thomas, 69372 Lyon Cedex 08, France; tel. 4-72-73-84-85; telex 380023; fax 4-72-73-85-75; f. 1965 as an Agency of the World Health Organization; to promote international collaboration in cancer research; 16 mem. countries; library of 8,200 vols, 211 journals; Dir Dr P. KLEIHUES; publ. *Report* (every 2 years).

International Agency for the Prevention of Blindness/Organisation mondiale contre la cécité: Grosvenor Hall, Bolnore Rd, Haywards Heath, West Sussex, RH16 4BX, England; tel. and fax (1444) 458810; f. 1975; umbrella org. in official relationship with WHO; promotes the formation of national committees and programmes on prevention of blindness and the sharing of information; Pres. Dr R. PARARAJASEGARAM (UK); publ. *IAPB News* (every 6 months).

International Association for Child and Adolescent Psychiatry and Allied Professions/Association internationale de psychiatrie de l'enfant et de l'adolescent et de professions associées: Dept of Child and Adolescent Psychiatry, MAS, 21401, Malmö, Sweden; f. 1948 to promote the study, treatment, care and prevention of mental disorders and deficiencies of children, adolescents and their families by promoting research and practice through collaboration with allied professions; mems: national associations and individual membership in 39 countries; Sec.-Gen. KARI SCHLEIMER; publs Yearbooks, *Newsletter* (annually).

International Association for Radiation Research: f. 1962 to advance radiation research in the fields of physics, chemistry, biology and medicine; 3,246 mems; holds int. congress every four years; Pres. Dr J. J. BROERSE (Netherlands); Sec.-Treas. Dr E. M. FIELDEN, Medical Research Council, Harwell, Didcot, Oxon., OX11 0RD, England; tel. (1235) 834393; fax (1235) 834776; publ. *Proceedings of International Congresses*.

International Association of Agricultural Medicine and Rural Health/Association Internationale de Médecine

Agricole et de Santé Rurale: f. 1961 to study the problems of medicine in agriculture in all countries and to prevent the pestilences caused by the conditions of work in agriculture; mems: 500; Pres. Prof. JENÖ TÉNYI (Hungary); Sec.-Gen. Dr SHOSUI MATSUSHIMA (acting), Saku Central Hospital, 197 Usuda-machi, Minamisaku-Gun, Nagano 384-0301, Japan; tel. (267) 82-3131; fax (267) 82-9638; e-mail sakuchp@valley.or.jp.

International Association of Applied Psychology/Association internationale de psychologie appliquée: 21 Bonview Rd, Malvern, Vic. 3144, Australia; f. 1920, present title adopted in 1955; aims: to establish contacts between those carrying out scientific work on applied psychology, to promote research and the adoption of measures contributing to this work; mems: 2,000 in 80 countries; Pres. Prof. B. WILPERT (Germany); Sec.-Gen. Prof. M. C. KNOWLES (Australia); publ. *Applied Psychology: An International Review* (quarterly).

International Association of Asthmology/Association Internationale d'Asthmologie (INTERASMA): c/o Prof. F. B. Michel, Hôpital Aiguelongue, Ave du Major Flandre, 34059 Montpellier Cedex, France; tel. 67-54-54-47; fax 67-52-18-48; f. 1954 to advance medical knowledge of bronchial asthma and allied disorders; *c.* 1,000 mems in 52 countries; Pres. Prof. A. G. PALMA-CARLOS (Portugal); Sec. Dr G. SCHULTZE-WERNINGHAUS (Germany); publ. *News Bulletin* (every 4 months).

International Association of Environmental Mutagen Societies: C/o Prof. Paul Lohman, Medical Faculty, Leiden, University, Wassenaarse Weg 72, 2333 AL Leiden, Netherlands; tel. (71) 527-6150; fax (71) 522-1615; e-mail lohman@rullf2.medfac.leidenuniv.nl; f. 1973 for the stimulation of scientific activity and exchange of information by means of World Conference every 4 years; six mem. socs. (3,000 individuals); Pres. Dr M. WATERS (USA); Sec. Prof. PAUL LOHMAN (Netherlands).

International Association of Gerontology (IAG): C/o Gerontology Centre, Semmelweis Orvostudományi Egyetem, Rökk Szilárd u. 13, 1085 Budapest, Hungary; tel. (1) 269-9158; fax (1) 114-8476; f. 1950 to promote contacts between people and orgs interested in the study of gerontology and to organize meetings and congresses every 4 years; mems: 56 national societies and groups in 52 countries; Pres. Prof. Dr E. BEREGI (Hungary); Sec.-Gen. Dr I. GERGELY (Hungary); publ. *Newsletter* (2 a year).

International Association of Hydatidology/Asociación Internacional de Hidatidología: Florida 460, 3° piso, (1005) Buenos Aires, Argentina; tel. 322-3431 ext. 166; fax 325-8231; f. 1941; 650 mems in 40 countries; specialized library; Pres. Dr MIGUEL PÉREZ GALLARDO (Spain); Sec.-Gen. Prof. Dr RAÚL MARTÍN MENDY (Argentina); publs *Archivos Internacionales de la Hidatidosis* (every 4 years), *Boletín de Hidatidosis* (quarterly).

International Association of Oral and Maxillofacial Surgeons: Medical College of Virginia, Box 980410, MCV Station, Richmond, VA 23298-0410, USA; tel. (804) 828-8515; fax (804) 828-1753; f. 1963 to advance the science and art of oral and maxillofacial surgery; 3,000 mems; Exec. Dir. LASKIN (USA); publ. *International Journal of Oral Surgery* (every 2 months).

International Brain Research Organization (IBRO): 51 blvd de Montmorency, 75016 Paris, France; f. 1958 to assist all branches of neuroscience; 52,000 mems; Pres. Prof. D. P. PURPURA (USA); Sec.-Gen. Dr C. BELMONTE (Spain); publs *IBRO News, Neuroscience* (every 2 months).

International Cell Research Organisation/Organisation Internationale de Recherche sur la Cellule: c/o UNESCO, SC/BSC, 1 rue Miollis, 75015 Paris, France; f. 1962 to create, encourage and promote co-operation between scientists of different disciplines throughout the world for the advancement of fundamental knowledge of the cell, normal and abnormal; organizes international training courses and exchange of scientists, etc.; 500 mems; Chair. Dr E. CARAFOLI (Switzerland); Vice-Chair. Dr J. E. ALLENDE (Chile); Exec. Sec. Dr G. N. COHEN (France).

International Center of Information on Antibiotics: c/o Prof. M. WELSCH, Inst. de Pathologie, Université de Liège, Sart-Tilman, 4000 Liège, Belgium; f. 1961 to gather information on antibiotics and strains producing them; to establish contact with discovers of antibiotics with a view to obtaining samples and filing information; Dir Prof. M. WELSCH; Senior Scientist in Charge Dr L. DELCAMBE.

International Commission on Occupational Health/Commission Internationale de la Santé au Travail: f. 1906 to study new facts in the field of occupational health, to draw the attention of all responsible to the results of study and investigation in occupational health, and to organize meetings on national or international problems in this field; it has established 32 Scientific Cttees and three Scientific Working Groups dealing with specialized topics of occupational health; mems: 2,000 representatives from 121 countries; Pres. Prof. JEAN-FRANÇOIS CAILLARD (France); Sec.-Gen. Prof. J. JEYARATNAM, Dept of Community, Occupational and Family Medicine, Faculty of Medicine, MD3, National University of Singapore, Lower Kent Ridge Road, Singapore 119260; tel. 8744985; fax 7791489; publ. *Quarterly Newsletter*.

International Cystic Fibrosis Association: Av. Campanar 106 (6a), 46015 Valencia, Spain; tel. (6) 346-1414; fax (6) 349-4047; e-mail aramos.fq@vlc.servicom.es; f. 1964 to disseminate current information on cystic fibrosis in those areas of the world where the disease occurs and to stimulate participation of scientific and medical researchers to the end that the disease will be resolved; conducts annual medical symposia; mems: 51 national organizations; Pres. IAN A. THOMPSON; Sec. AISHA RAMOS.

International Epidemiological Association/Association Internationale d'Epidémiologie: C/o Dr Haroutune Armenian, 111 Market Place (Suite 840), Baltimore, MD 21202, USA; f. 1954; 2,000 mems in 100 countries; Pres. Dr RODOLFO SARACCI; Sec. Dr HAROUTUNE ARMENIAN; publ. *International Journal of Epidemiology* (every 2 months).

International Federation for Medical and Biological Engineering/Fédération Internationale du Génie Médical et Biologique: f. 1959 to promote international co-operation and communication among societies interested in life and engineering sciences; mem. orgs in 40 countries; Pres. Prof. FUMIHIKO KAJIYA (Japan); Sec.-Gen. Prof. Dr ir JOS A. E. SPAAN, University of Amsterdam, Faculty of Medicine, Dept of Medical Physics, AMC, Meibergdreef 15, 1105 AZ Amsterdam, Netherlands; tel. (20) 5665200; fax (20) 6917233; publs *Medical and Biological Engineering and Computing* (every 2 months), *Proceedings of International Conference on Medical and Biological Engineering* (every 3 years).

International Federation of Anatomists/Fédération internationale des associations d'anatomistes: Dept of Anatomy, Medical College of Ohio, POB 10008, Toledo, OH 43699-0008, USA; tel. (419) 381-4111; f. 1903; mems: 52 national and multinational associations; Pres. Prof. Dr LIBERATO J. A. DIDIO (USA); publs *Directory, Newsletter*, Proceedings of each Federative International Congress of Anatomy (every 4 or 5 years).

International Federation of Gynecology and Obstetrics/Fédération Internationale de Gynécologie et d'Obstétrique: 27 Sussex Place, Regent's Park, London, NW1 4RG, England; tel. (171) 723-2951; fax (171) 258-0737; f. 1954; assists and contributes to research in gynaecology and obstetrics; aims to facilitate the exchange of information and perfect methods of teaching; organizes international congresses; membership: national societies in 101 countries; Pres. Prof. M. SEPPÄLÄ (Finland); Sec.-Gen. Dr G. BENAGIANO (Italy); publ. *Journal*.

International Federation of Multiple Sclerosis Societies: 10 Heddon St, London, W1R 7LJ, England; tel. (171) 734-9120; fax (171) 287-2587; f. 1967 to co-ordinate and further the work of national multiple sclerosis organizations throughout the world, to stimulate and encourage scientific research in this and related neurological diseases, to collect and disseminate information and to provide counsel and active help in furthering the development of voluntary national multiple sclerosis organizations; Pres. JAMES R. CANTALUPO; publs *Federation Update, MS Management Magazine, MS Research in Progress*, etc.

International Federation of Ophthalmological Societies/Fédération Internationale des Sociétés d'Ophtalmologie: f. 1857; 75 national societies are affiliated; Pres. Prof. A. NAKAJIMA (Japan); Sec.-Gen. Dr BRUCE E. SPIVEY, Northwestern Healthcare, 980 N. Michigan Ave, Ste. 1500, Chicago, IL USA; tel. (312) 335-6035; fax (312) 335-6030.

International Federation of Physical Education/Fédération Internationale d'Education Physique: 4 Cleevecroft Ave, Bishops Cleeve, Cheltenham, Glos. GL52 4JZ, England; f. 1923; aims to develop national and international physical education and sport- for-all; organizes congresses and courses; mems in 116 countries; Pres. JOHN C. ANDREWS; Sec.-Gen. R. DECKER; publ. *FIEP Bulletin* (in English, French and Spanish; Portuguese edition from Brazil).

International Federation of Thermalism and Climatism/Fédération internationale du thermalisme et du climatisme: c/o Fédération Thermale Française, 16 rue de l'Estrapade, 75005 Paris, France; f. 1947; aims: promoting international collaboration in technical, economic and medical problems of thermalism and climatism; mems: 26 full mem. countries; Chair. Dr G. EBRARD; Gen.-Sec. CLAUDE OGAY.

International Hospital Federation/Fédération internationale des hôpitaux: 4 Abbot's Place, London, NW6 4NP, England; tel. (171) 372-7181; f. 1947; an independent organization supported by subscribing mems in *c.* 100 countries; aims to promote improvements in the planning and management of hospitals and health services through international conferences, field study courses, training courses, information services, publications and research projects; mems: national hospital and health service organizations, governmental and non-governmental, individuals from disciplines and occupations concerned with health services, and professional, commercial and industrial firms working in the health service field; Pres. W. M. DARLING (UK); Dir-Gen. Prof. PER-GUNNAR SVENSSON (Sweden); publs *World Hospitals* (3 a year; English with French and Spanish abstracts), *Hospital Management International* (annually), Health Services International Newsletter (quarterly; French and Spanish only), *Global Healthcare News Bulletin* (quarterly).

International Institute on Ageing: 117 St Paul's St, Valletta, VLT 07, Malta; tel. (356) 243045; fax (356) 230248; e-mail INIA@maltanet.net; f. 1988 by the UN; training in gerontology and geriatrics, social gerontology, income security, and physiotherapy; research and data collection, technical co-operation (advisory services, project design, planning and implementation of training programmes); library of 1,500 vols; Dir Prof. ANTHONY DE BONO; publ. *BOLD* (quarterly).

International League Against Epilepsy/ Ligue internationale contre l'Épilepsie: c/o Sec.-Gen., National Institute of Neurological Disorders and Stroke, NIH, Bld. 31, Rm 8A52, Bethesda, MD 20892, USA; f. 1909 to collect and disseminate information concerning epilepsy, to promote treatment of epileptic patients and to foster co-operation with other international institutions in similar fields; mems: national organizations (branches) and individuals in 42 countries; Pres. HARRY MEINARDI (The Netherlands); Sec.-Gen. ROGER J. PORTER (USA); publ. *Epilepsia* (every 2 months).

International Organization Against Trachoma/Organisation internationale contre le trachome: f. 1923 for the research and study of trachomatous conjunctivitis and ophthalmological tropical and sub-tropical diseases; Pres. Prof. GABRIEL COSCAS (France); Sec.-Gen. Prof. GEORGES CORNAND, La Bergère, Route de Grenoble, 05140 Aspres-sur-Buëch, France; publ. *Revue Internationale du Trachome* (quarterly).

International Psychoanalytical Association: 'Broomhills', Woodside Lane, London N12 8UD, England; tel. (181) 446-8324; fax (181) 445-4729; e-mail 100450.1362@compuserve.com; f. 1908 to hold meetings to define and promulgate the theory and teaching of psychoanalysis, to act as a forum for scientific discussions, to control and regulate training and to contribute to the interdisciplinary area which is common to the behavioural sciences; 9,500 mems; Pres. OTTO F. KERNBERG (USA); Sec. ROBERT L. TYSON (USA); publs *IPA Bulletin, Newsletter*.

International Radiation Protection Association: POB 662, 5600 AR Eindhoven, Netherlands; tel. (40) 473355; fax (40) 435020; f. 1966 to promote international contacts and co-operation among those engaged in health physics and radiation protection; to provide for discussion of the scientific and practical aspects of the protection of man and his environment from the hazards caused by ionizing and non-ionizing radiation, thereby facilitating the exploitation of radiation and nuclear energy for the benefit of mankind; 37 mem. socs, 16,000 individual mems; Scientific Associate of ICSU, official relations with WHO, ILO, IAEA, ICRP; Pres. C. B. MEINHOLD (USA); Sec.-Gen. Chr. J. HUYSKENS (Netherlands); publ. *IRPA Bulletin* (irregular).

International Scientific Council for Trypanosomiasis Research and Control/Conseil scientifique international de recherches sur les trypanosomiases et leur contrôle: Secretariat: OAU/STRC, Ports Authority Bldg, 26/28 Marina, PMB 2359, Lagos, Nigeria; tel. 2633430; fax 2636093; e-mail oaustrc.lagos@rcl.dircon.co.uk; f. 1949 to review the work on tsetse and trypanosomiasis problems carried out by the organizations and workers concerned in laboratories and in the field; to stimulate further research and discussion and to promote co-ordination between research workers and organizations in the different countries in Africa, and to provide a regular opportunity for the discussion of particular problems and for the exposition of new experiments and discoveries; Exec. Sec. Prof. JOHNSON A. EKPERE.

International Society for Cardiovascular Surgery/Société Internationale Cardiovasculaire: 13 Elm St, Manchester, MA 01944, USA; f. 1950 to stimulate research and to exchange ideas on an international basis at biennial conferences; mems: 2,000; Sec.-Gen. Dr MALCOLM O. PERRY (USA); publ. *Cardiovascular Surgery* (every 2 months).

International Society for Clinical Electrophysiology of Vision/Société Internationale d'Electrophysiologie Visuelle Clinique: Medical Physics Dept, Queen's Medical Centre, Nottingham, NG7 2UH, England; tel. (115) 970-9131; fax (115) 942-2745; e-mail Colin.Barber@Nottingham.ac.uk; f. 1958; 350 mems; Pres. Prof. E. ZRENNER; Sec.-Gen. Prof. COLIN BARBER; publs *Bibliographic Service, Documenta Ophthalmologica* (journal, 5 a year).

International Society of Art and Psychopathology/Société Internationale de Psychopathologie de l'Expression: Centre Hospitalier Ste Anne, 100 rue de la Santé, 75014 Paris, France; f. 1959 to bring together the various specialists interested in the problems of expression and artistic activities in connection with psychiatric, sociological and psychological research, as well as in the use of methods applied in fields other than that of mental illness; 625 mems; Pres. Dr ROUX (France); Sec.-Gen. Dr J. VERDEAU-PAILLÈS (France).

International Society of Criminology/ Société internationale de criminologie: 4-14 rue Ferrus, 75014 Paris, France; tel. (1) 45-88-00-23; fax (1) 45-89-40-76; f. 1938 to promote the development of the sciences in their application to the criminal phenomenon; library; 800 mems.; Pres. H.-J. KERNER (Germany); Sec.-Gen. G. PICCA (France); publ. *Annales Internationales de Criminologie*.

International Society of Haematology/ Société Internationale d'Hématologie: f. 1946 to promote and foster the exchange and diffusion of information and ideas relating to blood and blood-forming tissues throughout the world; to provide a forum for discussion of haematologic problems on an international scale and to encourage scientific investigation of these problems; to promote the advancement of haematology and its recognition as a branch of the biological sciences; to attempt to standardize on an international scale haematological methods and nomenclature; to promote a better understanding of the scientific basic principles of haematology among practitioners of haematology and physicians in general and to foster better understanding and a greater interest in clinical haematologic problems among scientific investigators in the field of haematology; Sec.-Gen. (Inter-American Division) Dr G. J. RUIZ-ARGÜELLES, Clínica Ruiz, Díaz Ordaz 808, 72530 Puebla, Mexico; (European and African Division) Dr E. KANSU, Institute of Oncology, Hacettepe University, 06100 Ankara, Turkey; (Asian-Pacific Division) Dr H. SAITO, First Department of Medicine, Nagoya University School of Medicine, Showa-ku, Nagoya 466, Japan.

International Society of Hypnosis: C/o Behavioural Medicine Unit, Austin and Repatriation Medical Centre, Repat Campus, Heidelberg West, Vic. 3081, Australia; tel. (3) 9496-4105; fax (3) 9496-4107; f. 1958 as an affiliate of the World Federation of Mental Health; to stimulate and improve professional research, to encourage co-operative relations among scientific disciplines with regard to the study and application of hypnosis; to bring together persons using hypnosis and set up standards for professional training and adequacy; Pres. Dr WALTER BONGARTZ (Germany); Sec.-Treas. ROBB STANLEY (Australia); publ. *Newsletter* (2 a year).

International Society of Lymphology: Dept of Surgery, 1501 North Campbell Ave, POB 245063, Tucson, AZ 85724-5063, USA; tel. (520) 626-6118; fax (520) 626-0822; e-mail lymph@u.arizona.edu; f. 1966 to further progress in lymphology and allied subjects; organizes international working groups, co-operates with other national and international organizations; international congresses and postgraduate courses; 400 mems; Pres. ETHEL FOLDI (Germany); Sec.-Gen. MARLYS WITTE (USA); publs *Lymphology* (quarterly), *Progress in Lymphology,* congress proceedings.

International Society of Neuropathology: f. 1972 to initiate and maintain permanent co-operation between national and regional societies of neuropathology, to foster links with other int. organizations in the same field, to initiate int. congresses, symposia, etc.; *c.* 2,500 mems; Pres. Prof. YNGVE OLSSON (Sweden); Sec.-Gen. Dr JANICE ANDERSON, Dept of Histopathology, Addenbrooke's Hospital, Hill's Road, Cambridge, CB2 2QQ, England; e-mail jrazo@cam.ac.uk.

International Society of Orthopaedic Surgery and Traumatology/Société internationale de chirurgie orthopédique et de traumatologie: 40 rue Washington, bte 9, 1050 Brussels, Belgium; tel. (2) 648-68-23; fax (2) 649-86-01; f. 1929 to contribute to the progress of science by the study of questions pertaining to orthopaedic surgery and traumatology; congresses are convened every three years; 113 mem. countries, 3,000 mems; Pres. C. SORBIE (Canada); Sec.-Gen. ANTHONY J. HALL (UK); publ. *International Orthopaedics* (every 2 months).

International Society of Radiology/Société Internationale de Radiologie: f. 1953 to develop and advance medical radiology by giving radiologists in different countries an opportunity of personally submitting their experiences, exchanging and discussing their ideas, and forming personal bonds with their colleagues; there are four permanent International Commissions: (*a*) on Radiological Protection (ICRP), (*b*) on Radiation Units and Measurements (ICRU), (*c*) on Rules and Regulations (ICRR), (*d*) on Radiological Education (ICRE); these Commissions meet during each Congress, held at four-yearly intervals; Pres. M. TUBIANA (France); Vice-Pres. L. TAN (Singapore); Gen. Sec.-Treas. Prof. W. A. FUCHS, Dept of Medical Radiology, University Hospital, 8091 Zürich, Switzerland; tel. (1) 255-29-00; fax (1) 255-44-43.

International Society of Surgery (ISS)/ Société Internationale de Chirurgie (SIC): Netzibodenstr. 34, POB 1527, 4133 Pratteln, Switzerland; tel. (61) 811-47-70; fax (61) 811-47-75; f. 1902; organizes congresses; 4,000 mems; Sec.-Gen. Prof. THOMAS RÜEDI; publ. *World Journal of Surgery* (monthly).

International Union against Sexually Transmitted Infections: 135 Hutt St, Adelaide, SA 5000, Australia; tel. (8) 8232-4511; fax (8) 82379-6145; e-mail iusti@ozemail.com.au; f. 1923; administrative and educational activities, public health, and technical aspects of sexually transmitted diseases and AIDS; 800 individual, 50 nat. and soc. mems; has consultative status with WHO; Pres. Dr M. A. WAUGH (UK); Sec.-Gen. Dr R. PHILPOT (Australia).

International Union against Tuberculosis and Lung Disease/Union internationale contre la tuberculose et les maladies respiratoires: 68 blvd Saint-Michel, 75006 Paris, France; tel. (1) 44-32-03-60; fax (1) 43-29-90-87; e-mail iuatldparis@compuserve.com; f. 1920 to co-ordinate the efforts of anti-tuberculosis associations, to promote programmes and research in tuberculosis control, chest diseases and community health, to co-operate in these respects with the World Health Organization, to promote international and regional conferences on the above subjects, to collect and disseminate relevant information, to assist in developing country programmes in co-operation with national associations; mems: associations in 165 countries; 3,000 individual mems; Chair. of Exec. Cttee Dr KJELL BJARTVEIT (Norway); Exec. Dir Dr N. BILLO (Switzerland); Treas. L.-J. DE VIEL CASTEL; publs *International Journal of Tuberculosis and Lung Disease* (monthly, in English), *Newsletter* (in English, French and Spanish).

International Union for Health Promotion and Education/Union internationale de Promotion de la Santé et d'Education pour la Santé: 2 rue Auguste Comte, 92170 Vanves, France; tel. (1) 46-45-00-59; fax (1) 46-45-00-45; f. 1951; mems: organizations in 21 countries, groups and individuals in 90 countries; Pres. S. HAGARD (UK); Exec. Dir M. C. LAMARRE (France); publ. *Promotion & Education / International Journal of Health Promotion and Education* (quarterly, in a trilingual edition in English, French and Spanish).

International Union of Physical and Engineering Sciences in Medicine: National Research Council, Rm. 393, Bldg M-55, Ottawa, Ont. K1A 0R8, Canada; tel. (613) 993-1686; telex 053-4143; fax (613) 954-2216; f. 1982; consists of two independent organizations: Int. Federation of Medical and Biological Engineering, Int. Asscn. of Medical Physics; is a Scientific Associate of ICSU; aims: to coordinate the combined Congresses of the two mem. organizations, to promote the welfare of nat. mem. organizations and individual scientists and technologists; to promote the development and dissemination of physical and engineering sciences in medicine and health care; Pres. Prof. ROBERT M. NEREM; Sec.-Gen. OREST Z. ROY.

International Union of Railway Medical Services/Union Internationale des Services Médicaux des Chemins de Fer: 85 rue de France, 1070 Brussels, Belgium; tel. (2) 525-25-50; f. 1948; 37 mems; Pres. Dr E. TARI (Hungary).

International Union of Therapeutics/Union Thérapeutique Internationale: f. 1934; 360 mems from 22 countries; Pres. Prof. A. PRADALIER (France), Hôpital Louis Mourier, 178 rue des Renouillers, 92700 Colombes, France; tel. 1-47-60-67-05; Gen. Sec. Prof. PH. LECHAT.

Pan-American Medical Association (PAMA): 263 West End Ave, New York, NY 10023, USA; f. 1925 to interchange medical knowledge and research among countries of the western hemisphere; to strengthen, through the medical profession, bonds of friendship among peoples of the western hemisphere; to hold Inter-American congresses; to send seminars to various American countries; to grant postgraduate scholarships to doctors of western hemisphere nations; mems: 6,000 in 38 countries; Pres. WILLIAM E. SORREL.

Permanent International Committee of Congresses of Comparative Pathology/Comité International Permanent des Congrès de Pathologie Comparée: c/o 4 rue Théodule-Ribot, 75017 Paris, France; tel. 622-53-19; f. 1912 to study social maladies of man, animals, and plants; mems: national committees; Pres. Prof. R. TRUHAUT (France); Sec. L. GROLLET (France); publ. *Revue de Pathologie comparée et de Médecine expérimentale.*

World Association of Societies of Anatomic and Clinical Pathology/Association Mondiale des Sociétés de Pathologie Anatomique et Clinique: f. 1947 (formerly International Society of Clinical Pathology) to improve health throughout the world by promoting the teaching and practice of all aspects of pathology/laboratory medicine; membership: 50 national associations; Pres. WILLIAM B. ZEILER (USA); Sec.-Gen. MIKIO MORI, Dept of Clinical Pathology, Koshigaya Hospital, Dokkyo University School of Medicine, 2-1-50 Minamikoshigaya, Koshigaya, Saitama 343, Japan; publ. *Newsletter* (2 a year).

World Association of Veterinary Microbiologists, Immunologists and Specialists in Infectious Diseases/Association Mondiale des Vétérinaires Microbiologistes, Immunologistes et Spécialistes des Maladies Infectieuses: Ecole Nationale Vétérinaire d'Alfort, 7 ave du Général de Gaulle, 94704 Maisons-Alfort Cedex, France; tel. 1-43-96-70-21; fax 1-43-96-70-22; f. 1967 to facilitate international contacts in the field of veterinary microbiologists, immunologists and specialists in infectious diseases; Pres. Prof. CH. PILET (France).

World Confederation for Physical Therapy: 4A Abbots Place, London, NW6 4NP, England; tel. (171) 328-5448; fax (171) 624-7579; f. 1951 to encourage improved standards of physical therapy in education and practice; to promote exchange of information between mem. orgs; to assist the development of informed public opinion regarding physical therapy; to co-operate with appropriate agencies of UN and national and international organizations; mems in 67 countries; Pres. D. P. G. TEAGER; Sec.-Gen. B. J. MYERS (UK); publs *Proceedings of Congresses, Monographs, Newsletter.*

World Council of Optometry: 1200 West Godfrey Ave, Fitch Hall, Philadelphia, PA 19141, USA; f. 1927; aims to co-ordinate efforts to provide a good standard of ophthalmic optical (optometric) care throughout the world; in pursuance of this object the WCO is active in providing a forum for exchange of ideas between different countries; a large part of its work is concerned with optometric education, and advice upon standards of qualification; the WCO also interests itself in legislation in relation to optometry throughout the world; mems: 70 orgs in 60 countries; Pres. ROLAND DES GROSEILLIERS (Canada); Exec. Dir ANTHONY F. DI STEFANO; publs *Reports, Interoptics, Optometric Syllabus and Teaching Guide, Model Optometry Act,* etc.

World Federation of Neurosurgical Societies/Fédération Mondiale des Sociétés de Neurochirurgie: f. 1957 to facilitate the exchange of knowledge and to encourage research; 53 mem. societies and affiliated organizations; Pres. ARMANDO BASSO, Neurocirugía, Universidad Buenos Aires, Ayacucho 1342, PB19, Buenos Aires 1111, Argentina; Sec. EDWARD R. LAWS, Jr (USA).

World Federation of Societies of Anaesthesiologists (WFSA)/Federación Mundial de Sociedades de Anestesiólogos/Weltverband der Anaesthesisten-Gesellschaften: 8th Floor, Imperial House, 15–19 Kingsway, London, WC2B 6TH, England; tel. (171) 836-5652; fax (171) 836-5616; e-mail wfsa@compuserve.com; f. 1955 to make available the highest standards of anaesthesia to all peoples of the world; mems: 108 nat. societies, 100,000 individuals; Pres. Prof. MICHAEL D. VICKERS (UK); Sec. Dr ANNEKE E. E. MEURSING (Netherlands); publs *World Anaesthesia* (3 a year in three languages), *Update in Anaesthesia* (2 a year in five languages), *Annual Report.*

Music

International Music Council (IMC)/Conseil international de la musique: UNESCO, 1 rue Miollis, 75732 Paris Cedex 15, France; tel. 1-45-68-25-50; telex 204461; fax 1-43-06-87-98; e-mail imc_cim@compuserve.com; f. 1949 under the auspices of UNESCO to foster the exchange of musicians, music (written and recorded), and information; to support contemporary composers, traditional music, and young professional musicians; to foster appreciation of music by the public; mems: 30 international non-governmental organizations, 65 national committees, 5 individual mems; Pres. FRANS DE RUITER (Netherlands); Sec.-Gen. GUY HUOT; publ. *Resonance* (quarterly).

MEMBERS OF IMC

European Festivals Association/Association européenne des festivals: 120B rue de Lausanne, 1202 Geneva, Switzerland; tel. (22) 7386873; fax (22) 7384012; e-mail geneva@eurofestivals.efa.ch; f. 1952 to maintain high artistic standards in festivals, widen the field of operation, organize joint propaganda and publicity; mems: 70 festivals in Austria, Belgium, Bulgaria, Croatia, Czech Republic, Finland, France, Germany, Great Britain, Greece, Hungary, Israel, Italy, Japan, Luxembourg, Former Yugoslav Republic of Macedonia, Mexico, Monaco, Netherlands, Norway, Poland, Portugal, Romania, Slovakia, Slovenia, Spain, Sweden, Switzerland, Turkey; Sec.-Gen. TAMÁS KLENJÁNSZKY; publ. *Festivals* (annually).

International Council for Traditional Music/Conseil international de la musique traditionelle: Department of Music, Columbia University, New York, NY 10027, USA; tel. (212) 678-0332; telex 220094; fax (212) 678-2513; f. 1947 (as Int. Folk Music Ccl) to further the preservation, study, practice and dissemination of traditional music (including dance) of all countries; affiliated to UNESCO; 1,400 mems; Pres. Dr ANTHONY SEEGER (USA); Sec.-Gen. Prof. DIETER CHRISTENSEN (USA); publs *Yearbook for Traditional Music, Bulletin* (2 a year), *Directory of Traditional Music* (every 2 years).

International Federation of Musicians/Fédération internationale des musiciens: 21 bis rue Victor Massé, 75009 Paris, France; tel. 1-45-26-31-23; fax 1-45-26-31-57; f. 1948 to promote and protect the interests of musicians in affiliated unions and to institute protective measures to safeguard musicians against the abuse of their performances; promotes the international exchange of musicians; makes agreements with other international organizations in the interest of member unions and of the profession; mems: 39 unions totalling 300,000 mems in 28 countries; Pres. JOHN MORTON (UK); Gen. Sec. JEAN VINCENT.

International Institute for Traditional Music/Internationales Institut für Traditionelle Musik: Winklerstr. 20, 14193 Berlin, Germany; tel. (30) 826-28-53; fax (30) 825-99-91; f. 1963; supported by the City of Berlin to promote, preserve and impart knowledge of musical traditions throughout the world (except Western art music); Annual Festival of Traditional Music; mems from 20 countries; Dir MAX PETER BAUMANN; publs *The World of Music* (3 a year), *Musikbogen* (in German), *Intercultural Music Studies*.

International Music Centre/Internationales Musikzentrum: Filmstadt Wien, Speisinger Str. 121–127, 1230 Vienna, Austria; tel. (1) 889-03-15; fax (1) 889-03-15-77; e-mail imz@magnet.at; f. 1961 for the promotion and dissemination of opera, dance, concert and music documentaries through the technical media (film, television, radio, gramophone); organizes congresses, seminars and screenings on music in the audiovisual media; organizes competitions to strengthen relations between composers, interpreters and directors, with particular emphasis on the promotion of the young generation; organizes Dance Screen and Opera Screen; mems: 200 Broadcasting Organizations and private production industries, 30 Associates; Pres. AVRIL MACRORY (UK); Sec.-Gen. FRANZ PATAY; publs *IMZ Reports, Catalogues, Music in the Media* (regular information in English, French and German).

International Musicological Society: see under International Council for Philosophy and Humanistic Studies.

International Research Institute for Media, Communication and Cultural Development (MEDIACULT): 1040 Vienna, Schönburgstr. 27/4, Austria; tel. (1) 504-13-16; fax (1) 504-13-164; f. 1969; library of 1,200 vols; Pres. K. PETER ETZKORN; Gen. Sec. ALFRED SMUDITS; publs *Newsletter* (in German, English and French).

International Society for Contemporary Music/Société internationale pour la musique contemporaine: c/o Henk Heuvelmans, Gaudeamus, Swammerdamstraat 38, 1091 RV Amsterdam, Netherlands; tel. (20) 694-73-49; fax (20) 694-72-58; e-mail iscm@xs4all.nl; f. 1922 to promote the development of contemporary music and to organize annual World Music Days; mem. organizations in 47 countries; Pres. ARNE MELLNÄS (Sweden); Sec.-Gen. HENK HEUVELMANS; publ. *World New Music Magazine* (1 a year).

International Society for Music Education: f. 1953 to stimulate music education as a part of general education and community life; organizes international conferences and seminars; co-operates with other international music organizations; acts as an advisory body to UNESCO; co-operates with organizations representing other fields of education; 1,650 mems; Pres. EINAR SOLBU; Sec.-Gen. JOAN THERENS, ICRME, University of Reading, Bulmershe Court, Reading, RG6 1HY, England; tel. and fax (118) 931-8846; publs *Reports of ISME Conferences and Seminars, International Journal of Music Education, ISME Newsletter*.

Jeunesses Musicales International: Palais des Beaux-Arts, 10 rue Royale, 1000 Brussels, Belgium; tel. (32) 2-5139774; fax (32) 2-5144755; e-mail fijm@arcadis.be; f. 1945 to enable young people to develop through music across all boundaries; runs a World Orchestra and a World Youth Choir; member organizations in 40 countries; Sec.-Gen. DAG FRANZEN (acting); publ. *Rapport Annuel de l'Assemblée Générale*.

World Federation of International Music Competitions/Fédération Mondiale des Concours Internationaux de Musique: 104 rue de Carouge, 1205 Geneva, Switzerland; tel. 321-36-20; fax 781-14-18; f. 1957; co-ordinates the activities of members and maintains links between them, arranges the calendar of competitions, helps competition-winners to get to know each other; 108 mem. competitions; Pres. RENATE RONNEFELD; Sec.-Gen. JACQUES HALDENWANG; publs annual programme of competitions.

OTHER ORGANIZATION

Répertoire International de Littérature Musicale (RILM)/International Repertory of Music Literature/Internationales Repertorium der Musikliteratur: RILM International Center, 33 West 42nd St, New York, NY 10036, USA; tel. (212) 642-2709; fax (212) 642-1973; f. 1966; autonomous body sponsored by International Association of Music Libraries, Archives and Documentation Centers, and International Musicological Society; research and gathering of bibliographic citations of all significant writing on music, from all nations, for online, printed and CD-ROM database; 63 mem. national cttees; library of 1,200 vols, 500 current music journals; Pres. BARRY S. BROOK; publ. *RILM Abstracts of Music Literature* (annually).

Science

Abdus Salam Centre for Theoretical Physics: Strada Costiera 11, 34014 Trieste, Italy; tel. (40) 2240111; telex 460392; fax (40) 224163; e-mail sci_info@ictp.trieste.it; f. 1964; sponsored by the International Atomic Energy Agency, UNESCO and the Italian govt.; work in condensed matter physics, physics of high and intermediate energies, mathematics, physics and energy (nonconventional energies), physics of the environment, physics of the living state, applied physics; library of 100,000 vols; Dir MIGUEL ANGEL VIRASORO (Argentina/Italy); publs *News* (quarterly), *Report of Scientific Activities* (annually).

African Academy of Sciences: POB 14798, Nairobi, Kenya; tel. (2) 884401; telex 25446; fax (2) 884406; f. 1985 to promote and foster the growth of the scientific community in Africa; activities: mobilization and strengthening of the African scientific community (includes the Network of African Scientific Institutions, profiles and databank of African scientists and instns, African Dissertation Internship Programme, assistance to regional orgs); research development and public policy; capacity building in science and technology; 111 Fellows; library of 1,500 vols; Pres. THOMAS R. ODHIAMBO (Kenya); Sec.-Gen. GIDEON B. A. OKELO (Kenya); publs *Discovery and Innovation* (quarterly), *Whydah* (quarterly), *African Journal on Medical Practice* (6 a year).

African Association for the Advancement of Science and Technology: c/o Prof. C. Kamala, KNAAS, POB 47288, Nairobi, Kenya; f. 1978; Sec. Prof. C. KAMALA.

African Association for Cartography and Remote Sensing/Organisation Africaine de Cartographie et Télédétection: BP 102, 16040 Hussein Dey, Algiers, Algeria; tel. (2) 77-79-38; telex 65474; fax (2) 77-79-34; f. 1988 to encourage the development of cartography and of remote sensing by satellite, organize conferences and other meetings, and promote the establishment of training institutions; co-ordinates four regional training centres, in Burkina Faso, Kenya, Nigeria and Tunisia; 24 mem. countries; Sec.-Gen. MUFTAH UNIS.

African Association of Science Editors: POB ST 125, Southerton, Harare, Zimbabwe; tel. (4) 621661; fax (4) 621670; f. 1985 to provide a forum for establishing and strengthening the profession and standards of scientific editing in Africa; promotes training programmes, communication and interchange of views; 160 mems; Chair. CYNTHIA SITHOLE; Sec. MAZVITA MADONDO; publ. *Bulletin* (quarterly).

African Oil Chemists' Society: 78 Hospital Rd, POB 678, Akure, Ondo State, Nigeria; tel. (34) 230183; fax (34) 231633; f. 1995; Pres. Dr MOUNIR HANNA ISKANDER; Sec.-Gen. Dr OLIVER ADESIOYE; publ. *AFOCS Journal* (4 a year).

Association for the Taxonomic Study of Tropical African Flora/Association pour l'Etude Taxonomique de la Flore d'Afrique Tropicale: National Botanic Garden of Belgium, Domein van Bouchout, 1860 Meise, Belgium; tel. (2) 269-39-05; fax (2) 270-15-67; e-mail j.rammeloo@br.fgov.be; f. 1950; *c.* 800 mems from 70 countries; Gen. Sec. Prof. Dr J. RAMMELOO; publs *AETFAT Bulletin* (annually), *Proceedings*.

Association of Information Dissemination Centers: c/o Secretariat, POB 8105, Athens, GA 30603, USA; tel. (706) 542-6820; f. 1968; independent organization with 100 centres representing industry, government and academia in the USA, Canada, Europe, Israel, Japan, India, South Africa and Australia; to promote applied technology of information storage and retrieval, and research and development for more efficient use of data bases; Pres. RANDALL MARCINKO; publ. *Newsletter* (2 a year).

BirdLife International: Wellbrook Court, Girton Rd, Cambridge, CB3 0NA, England; tel. (1223) 277318; fax (1223) 277200; e-mail birdlife@birdlife.org.uk; f. 1922; determines status of bird species throughout the world and compiles data on all endangered bird species; identifies conservation problems and priorities and runs a programme of field projects to address these priorities; partners and reps in 90 countries; Chair. Dr GERARD BERTRAND (USA); Dir and Chief Exec. Dr MICHAEL RANDS (UK); publs *World Birdwatch*, *Annual Report*.

Centre Naturopa: Council of Europe, 67075 Strasbourg Cedex, France; tel. 3-88-41-31-91; telex 870943; fax 88-41-27-15; f. 1967 by the Ccl of Europe to alert and inform public opinion on environmental problems; runs information campaigns; agencies in 40 member states; library of 5,000 vols, 250 journals; Head E. MORENO; publ. *Naturopa* (3 a year).

Charles Darwin Foundation for the Galapagos Isles/Fundación Charles Darwin para las Islas Galápagos: f. 1959 to organize and maintain the Charles Darwin Research Station in the Galapagos Islands and to advise the Government of Ecuador on scientific research and conservation in the archipelago; Pres. Dr CRAIG MACFARLAND (USA); Sec.-Gen. ALFREDO CARRASCO, Casilla 17-01-3891, Quito, Ecuador; tel. 244-803; fax 443-935; publ. *Noticias de Galápagos* (2 a year).

Circum-Pacific Council for Energy and Mineral Resources: c/o Michel T. Halbouty, 5100 Westheimer Rd, Houston, TX 77056, USA; tel. (713) 622-1130; fax (713) 622-5360; f. 1974 at the first Circum-Pacific Energy and Mineral Resources Conference, with the co-operation of 46 international geoscience organizations; sponsors conferences, meetings, research; supports and operates regional projects, including the Circum-Pacific Map Project, and international training schools; Chair. MICHEL T. HALBOUTY (USA); Map Project Chair. GEORGE GRYC (USA).

Commonwealth Geographical Bureau: c/o Prof. Victor Savage, Dept of Geography, National University of Singapore, 10 Kent Ridge Crescent, Singapore 119260; tel. 8743855; fax 7773091; f. 1968; encourages the development of geographical research and study, particularly in developing Commonwealth countries, through assistance to the profession; regional seminars, assistance for study visits; a board of management represents five regions: Asia, Africa, Americas, Australasia and Europe; Dir Prof. JOHN OVERTON (New Zealand); publ. *Newsletter* (annually).

Commonwealth Science Council: Commonwealth Secretariat, Marlborough House, Pall Mall, London, SW1Y 5HX, England; tel. (171) 839-3411; telex: 27678; fax: (171) 930-0827; e-mail comsci@gn.apc.org; f. 1975; an inter-governmental body, the Science and Technology Division of the Commonwealth Secretariat; seeks to increase the capability of Commonwealth countries to apply science and technology for social, economic and environmental development; conducts no in-house research, but provides support for putting into practice the results of research carried out by others and helps to produce knowledge required to solve developmental problems through research; programmes are: biological and genetic resources, renewable energy, water and mineral resources, advanced technologies; runs a fellowship scheme providing short-term placements at training programmes or research institutes in developing countries; runs a travel-grant scheme to help scientists from member countries attend scientific meetings; 7 professional staff; Sec. Dr U. O'D. TROTZ (Guyana); publs *Commonwealth Scientist* (4 a year), *Report* (every 2 years), reports, practical manuals.

Council for International Congresses of Entomology/Comité permanent des congrès internationaux d'entomologie: C/o Dr James H. Oliver, Institute of Arthropodology and Parasitology, Georgia Southern University, Landrum Box 8056, Statesboro, GA 30460-8056, USA; tel. (912) 681-5564; fax (912) 681-0559; e-mail joliver@gasou.edu; f. 1910 to act as a link between periodic congresses and to arrange the venue for each congress; the committee is also the entomology section of the International Union of Biological Sciences; Chair. Dr MAX WHITTEN (Philippines); Sec. Dr JAMES H. OLIVER (USA).

European Atomic Energy Community (Euratom): 200 rue de la Loi, 1049 Brussels, Belgium; tel. 235-11-11; based on a formal treaty signed in Rome in March 1957, at the same time as the treaty establishing the EEC. It aims to integrate the programmes of member states for the peaceful uses of atomic energy; since 1967 combined with the ECSC and EEC; Pres. of Comm. of the European Communities JACQUES SANTER.

European Centre for Medium-Range Weather Forecasts: Shinfield Park, Reading, Berks., RG2 9AX, England; tel. (118) 949-9000; telex 847908; fax (118) 986-9450; f. 1973; aims include the development of numerical methods for medium-range weather forecasting, the collection and storage of data, providing operational forecasts to the meteorological services of mem. states, and providing advanced training in numerical weather prediction; 18 mem. states; Dir Dr D. BURRIDGE.

European Geophysical Society: Postfach 49, Max-Planck-Str. 13, 37191 Katlenburg-Lindau, Germany; tel. (49) 5556-1440; fax (49) 5556-4709; e-mail egs@copernicus.org; f. 1971 for the study of the Earth and planetary sciences, to promote geophysics and planetary sciences in Europe and throughout the world and, in particular, young scientists in the geophysical disciplines; organizes annual General Assemblies, supports research projects, working groups and workshops/symposia organized by other orgs, etc; 3,000 mems; Pres. Prof. S. CLOETINGH (Netherlands); Exec. Sec. Dr ARNE K. RICHTER; publs *Annales Geophysicae, Newsletter, Geophysical Journal International* (jointly with the RAS and DGG), *Surveys in Geophysics, Hydrology and Earth System Sciences, Planetary and Space Science, Tectonics* (jointly with the AGU), *Journal of Geodynamics, Climate Dynamics, Nonlinear Processes in Geophysics, Physics and Chemistry of the Earth.*

European Institute of Environmental Cybernetics: Athens 162 32, Greece; f. 1970 to bring together scientists and scholars with cross-sectional background and research interests and to conduct multi-disciplinary educational and research activities studying the interactions between man and his environment (natural and technical); publs reports.

European Molecular Biology Laboratory: Postfach 10.2209, Meyerhofstr. 1, 69012 Heidelberg, Germany; tel. (6221) 3870; telex 461613; fax (6221) 387306; f. 1974; financed by 14 European states and Israel; basic research in molecular biology; outstations in Cambridge, Grenoble and Hamburg; library of *c.* 10,000 vols; Dir-Gen. FOTIS KATATOS; publs *Annual Report, Research Report.*

European Molecular Biology Organization (EMBO)/Organisation européenne de biologie moléculaire: Postfach 1022-40, 69012 Heidelberg, Germany; tel. (6221) 383-031; fax (6221) 384-879; f. 1964 to promote collaboration in the field of molecular biology; to award fellowships for training and research; 950 mems; Chair Prof. W. NEUPERT (Germany); Sec.-Gen. W. GEHRING (Switzerland); Exec. Dir Prof. F. GANNON; publ. *EMBO Journal* (24 a year).

European Organization for Nuclear Research (CERN)/Organisation européenne pour la recherche nucléaire: 1211 Geneva 23, Switzerland; tel. (22) 767-61-11; telex 419000; fax (22) 767-65-55; established 1954; mems: Austria, Belgium, Czech Republic, Denmark, Finland, France, Germany, Greece, Hungary, Italy, The Netherlands, Norway, Poland, Portugal, Slovakia, Spain, Sweden, Switzerland and United Kingdom; carries out and co-ordinates research on fundamental particles. Research is undertaken mostly by teams of visiting scientists who remain based at their parent institutions; in general the staff is drawn from the mem. states, but scientists from any country may be invited to spend a limited period at CERN; research is carried out with the aid of a proton synchrotron of 28 GeV (the PS), the super proton synchrotron (SPS) of 450 GeV and the 27 km LEP electron-positron collider; Pres. of the Council Dr H. ESCHELBACHER (Germany); Dir-Gen. Prof. LUCIANO MAIANI (Italy); publs *Annual Report* (in English and French), *CERN Courier* (monthly in English and French), scientific and technical reports, etc.

European Physical Society: 34 rue Marc Seguin, 68060 Mulhouse Cedex, France; f. 1968; aims to promote the advancement of physics in Europe and neighbouring countries by all suitable means; 36 nat. mem. organizations, 6,500 individual mems, 80 assoc. mems; Sec.-Gen. G. THOMAS; publs *Europhysics News* (every 2 months), *European Journal of Physics* (every 2 months).

European Science Foundation: 1 quai Lezay-Marnésia, 67080 Strasbourg Cedex, France; tel. 3-88-76-71-00; fax 3-88-37-05-32; f. 1974 to promote research in all branches of fundamental science and the humanities; to advance co-operation in European research; to examine and advise on research and science policy issues; to promote the mobility of research workers and the free flow of information and ideas; to facilitate co-operation in the planning and use of research facilities; to plan and manage collaborative research activities; mems: 60 nat. research funding agencies from 20 countries; Pres. Sir DAI REES (UK); Sec. Gen. E. BANDA (Spain); publs *Annual Report* (in English and French), *ESF Communications* (2 a year).

European Southern Observatory/ Organisation européenne pour des recherches astronomiques dans l'hémisphère austral: Karl Schwarzschild Str. 2, 85748 Garching b. München, Germany; tel. (89) 320060; telex 05-282820; f. 1962; aims: astronomical research in the southern hemisphere, construction and operation of an international observatory in Chile (see under Chile), fostering European co-operation in astronomy; mems: govts of Belgium, Denmark, Germany, France, Italy, The Netherlands, Sweden, Switzerland; Dir-Gen. Prof. Dr RICCARDO GIACCONI; publs *Annual Report, The Messenger*, reports.

European Space Agency: 8–10 rue Mario Nikis, 75738 Paris Cedex 15, France; tel. 53-69-76-54; telex 202746; fax 53-69-75-60; f. 1964, name changed 1975, to provide for, and to promote collaboration among European states in space research and technology and their space applications exclusively for peaceful purposes; provides scientific agencies of the member countries with the necessary technical facilities for the carrying out of space experiments, ranging from the study of the near terrestrial environment to that of stellar astronomy; also responsible for a European programme of application satellite projects, including telecommunications and meteorology, also for Spacelab and Ariane Launcher; supports the following establishments: European Space Research and Technology Centre (ESTEC) Noordwijk, Netherlands; European Space Operations Centre (ESOC), Darmstadt, Germany; European Space Research Institute (ESRIN), Frascati, Italy; European Astronaut Centre (EAC), Cologne, Germany; mems: Austria, Belgium, Denmark, Finland, France, Germany, Ireland, Italy, Netherlands, Norway, Spain, Sweden, Switzerland and UK; Canada is linked by a special co-operation agreement; library (ESTEC) of 42,000 vols, 1 million microfiche, 27,000 reports and standards; Dir-Gen. ANTONIO RODOTÀ (Italy); publs *Annual Reports, Bulletin, Journal, Earth Observation Quarterly, Reaching for the Skies* (all quarterly), *News and Views* (every 2 months), conference proceedings, scientific and technical reports.

Federation of Arab Scientific Research Councils: POB 13027, Baghdad, Iraq; tel. 8881709; telex 212466; f. 1976 to strengthen scientific and technological co-operation and co-ordination between Arab countries; holds conferences, seminars, workshops and training courses; publs Directory of Arab Scientific Research Institutions; 15 mem. countries; Sec.-Gen. Dr TAHA TAYIH AL-NAIMI; publs *Proceedings of Scientific Activities, Newsletter, Computer Research.*

Federation of Asian Scientific Academies and Societies (FASAS): c/o Indian National Science Academy, Bahadur Shah Zafar Marg, New Delhi 110002, India; tel. (11) 3232066; fax (11) 3235648; e-mail insa@giasdlo1.vsnl.net.in; f. 1984 to stimulate regional co-operation and promote national and regional self-reliance in science and technology by organizing meetings, training and research programs and encouraging exchange of scientists and information; 14 mems (national scientific academies and societies in Afghanistan, Australia, Bangladesh, People's Republic of China, India, Republic of Korea, Malaysia, Nepal, New Zealand, Pakistan, Philippines, Singapore, Sri Lanka, Thailand); Pres. Prof. C. S. DAYRIT (Philippines); Sec. Prof. INDIRA NATH (India).

Foundation for International Scientific Co-ordination/Fondation 'Pour la Science', Centre international de Synthèse: 12 rue Colbert, 75002 Paris, France; tel. (1) 42-97-50-68; fax (1) 42-97-46-46; e-mail synthese@filnet.fr; f. 1924; Founder HENRI BERR; Dirs MICHEL BLAY, ERIC BRIAN (France); publs *Revue de Synthèse, Revue d'Histoire des Sciences, Semaines de Synthèse, L'Evolution de l'Humanité.*

Institute of Mathematical Statistics: 3401 Investment Blvd 7, Hayward, CA 94545-3819, USA; tel. (510) 783-8141; fax (510) 783-4131; f. 1935; 4,000 mems; Pres. STEPHEN FIENBERG; Exec. Sec. KATHRYN ROEDER; publs *Annals of Probability, Annals of Statistics* (every 2 months), *Statistical Science, Annals of Applied Probability* (all quarterly), *IMS Bulletin* (every 2 months), *IMS Lecture Notes—Monograph Series, CBMS Regional Conference Series in Probability and Statistics.*

Intergovernmental Oceanographic Commission (IOC)/Commission Océanographique Intergouvernementale: c/o UNESCO, 1 rue Miollis, 75732 Paris Cedex 15, France; tel. 1-45-68-39-83; telex 204461; fax 1-45-68-58-10; f. 1960 to promote scientific investigation with a view to learning more about the nature and resources of the oceans, through the concerted action of its members; mems: 125 governments; Chair. GEOFFREY L. HOLLAND (Canada); Exec. Sec. Dr PATRICIO BERNAL (Chile); publs *Summary Reports of Sessions, IOC Technical Series, IOC Manuals and Guides, IOC Workshop Reports, IOC Training Course Reports* (irregular).

International Academy of Astronautics (IAA)/Académie Internationale d'Astronautique: BP 1268-16, 75766 Paris Cedex 15, France; tel. 47-23-82-15; fax 47-23-82-16; f. 1960; aims to foster the development of astronautics for peaceful purposes, recognizing individuals who have distinguished themselves in the field, and provides a programme through which mems can contribute to int. co-operation; liaises with national academies of science; developing a multilingual (20 languages) Data Base; maintains the following cttees: Space Sciences, Int. Space Plans and Policies, Life Sciences, Benefits to Society from Space Activities, Economics of Space Operations, Interstellar Space Exploration, Search for Extraterrestrial Intelligence, Safety and Rescue, Space and Environmental Change, History of Astronautics, Scientific Legal Liaison; mems: 975 from 56 countries; Pres. G. E. MUELLER (USA); Vice-Pres. H. CURIEN (France), M. YARYMOVYCH (USA), G. HAERENDEL (Germany), A. GRIGORIEV (CIS); Sec.-Gen. J. M. CONTANT (France); publs *Acta Astronautica* (12 issues a year), *Proceedings of Symposia.*

International Association for Cybernetics/Association internationale de cybernétique: Palais des Expositions, 2 ave Sugent Vrithoff, 5000 Namur, Belgium; tel. (81) 73-52-09; fax (81) 74-29-45; f. 1957 to ensure liaison between research workers engaged in various sectors of cybernetics, to promote the development of the science and of its applications and to disseminate information about it; mems: organizations, institutes, associations, industrial firms and individuals in 35 countries; Chair. J. RAMAEKERS (Belgium); publs *Cybernetica* (quarterly), *Newsletter* (quarterly), *Proceedings of the International Congresses on Cybernetics, Cybernetics, Work in Progress* (series).

International Association for Mathematics and Computers in Simulation/Association internationale pour les mathématiques et calculateurs en simulation: C/o Dept of Computer Science, Rutgers University, Brett Rd (Hill Center), New Brunswick, NJ 08903, USA; f. 1955 to further the study of general methods for modelling and computer simulation of dynamic systems; Pres. R. VICHNEVETSKY (USA); Sec.-Gen. J. ROBERT (Belgium); publs *Mathematics and Computers in Simulation, Applied Numerical Mathematics* (every 2 months).

International Association for Plant Physiology (IAPP): Food Science Australia, CSIRO, POB 52, North Ryde, NSW 1670, Australia; tel. (2) 9490-8333; telex 23407; fax (2) 9490-3107; e-mail douglas.graham@foodscience.afics.csiro.au; f. 1955 to promote the development of plant physiology at the international level, especially collaboration between developed and developing nations, through international congresses and symposia and by the publication of plant physiology matters and the promotion of co-operation between national and international associations and scientific journals; represents plant physiologists on the IUBS; mems: 40 national societies of plant physiology and related international groups; Pres. Prof. S. MIYACHI; Gen. Sec. Dr D. GRAHAM; publ. *Annual Newsletter.*

International Association for Plant Taxonomy/Association internationale pour la taxonomie végétale: Bureau for Plant Taxonomy and Nomenclature, Botanischer Garten und Botanisches Museum Berlin-Dahlem, Königin-Luise-Str. 6-8, 14191 Berlin, Germany; tel. (30) 8316010; fax (30) 83006218; f. 1950 to promote the development of plant taxonomy and encourage contacts between people and institutes interested in this work; mems: institutes and individuals in 87 countries; Pres. D. H. NICOLSON (USA); publs *Taxon* (quarterly), *Regnum vegetabile* (irregular).

International Association for the Physical Sciences of the Ocean (IAPSO)/Association internationale des Sciences physiques de l'Océan: POB 820440, Vicksburg, MS 39182-0440, USA; tel. (601) 634-2012; fax (601) 634-3433; f. 1919 to promote the study of scientific problems relating to the Oceans, chiefly in so far as such study may be carried out by the aid of mathematics, physics and chemistry; to initiate, facilitate and co-ordinate research; to provide for discussion, comparison and publication; mems: 81 mem. states; Pres. Dr ROBIN D. MUENCH (USA); Sec.-Gen. Dr FRED E. CAMFIELD (USA); publs *Publications Scientifiques* (irregularly), *Procès-Verbaux* (every 2–4 years).

International Association for Vegetation Science/Association Internationale pour l'Etude de la Végétation: f. 1937; aims for the development and unification of phytosociology; 1,300 mems; Pres. Prof. E. O. BOX (USA); Sec. Prof. Dr H. DIERSCHKE, 37073 Göttingen, Wilhelm-Weber-Str. 2, Germany; tel. (551) 395700; fax (551) 392287; e-mail hdiersc@gwdg.de; publs *Journal of Vegetation Science, Phytocoenologia.*

International Association of Biological Oceanography: f. 1966 to promote the study of the biology of the sea; part of IUBS (*q.v.*); Pres. Prof. J. F. GRASSLE (USA); Sec. Prof. J. B. L. MATTHEWS, Scottish Association for Marine Science, POB 3, Oban, Argyll, PA34 4AD, Scotland.

International Association of Geodesy/Association internationale de géodésie: University of Copenhagen, Dept of Geophysics, Juliane Maries Vej 30, 2100 Copenhagen O, Denmark; f. 1922 to promote the study of all scientific problems of geodesy and encourage geodetic research; to promote and co-ordinate international co-operation in this field; to publish results; a mem. asscn of IUGG; mems: national committees in 78 countries; Pres. Prof. K. P. SCHWARZ; Sec.-Gen. C. C. TSCHERNING; publs *Journal of Geodesy, Travaux de l'AIG, Publications spéciales.*

International Association of Geomagnetism and Aeronomy (IAGA)/Association internationale de géomagnétisme et d'aéronomie: f. 1919; aims: the study of magnetism and aeronomy of the earth and other bodies of the solar system and of the interplanetary medium and its interaction with these bodies; mems: the countries which adhere to the International Union of Geodesy and Geophysics are eligible as members; Pres. M. KONO (Japan); Sec.-Gen. J. A. JOSELYN, NOAA R/E/SE, 325 Broadway, Boulder, CO 80303-3328, USA; tel. (303) 497-5147; fax (303) 497-3645; publs *IAGA Bulletins* (irregular), *Geomagnetic Data* (annually), *IAGA News* (annually).

International Association of Hydrological Sciences: f. 1922; part of IUGG; aims to promote the study of hydrology, to provide means for discussion, comparison and publication of results of research, and the initiation and co-ordination of research that requires international co-operation; organizes general assemblies, symposia, etc.; 84 nat. cttees; Pres. Dr JOHN RODDA (UK); Sec.-Gen. Dr GORDON J. YOUNG, Wilfrid Laurier University, Dept of Geography, Waterloo, Ont. N2I 3C5, Canada; tel. (519) 884-1970 ext. 2387; fax (519) 846-0968; publs *Hydrological Sciences Journal* (every 2 months), *Newsletter* (3 a year), proceedings of symposia, etc.

International Association of Meteorology and Atmospheric Sciences (IAMAS)/Association Internationale de Météorologie et de Sciences de l'Atmosphère: f. 1919 to organize research symposia and co-ordinate research in atmospheric science fields; an Association of the International Union of Geodesy and Geophysics; Pres. Prof. R. DUCE (USA); Sec.-Gen. Prof. R. LIST, University of Toronto, Dept of Physics, Toronto, Ont. M5S 1A7, Canada; publ. *IAMAP Assembly Proceedings* (every 2 years).

International Association of Sedimentologists: f. 1952; 2,000 mems; Pres. Prof. M. E. TUCKER (UK); Sec.-Gen. Prof. Dr A. STRASSER, Institut de Géologie, Pérolles, 1700 Fribourg, Switzerland; tel. (26) 300-89-78; fax (26) 300-97-42; e-mail andreas.strasser@unifr.ch; publs *Sedimentology, Newsletter* (every 2 months).

International Association of Theoretical and Applied Limnology/Association internationale de Limnologie Théorique et Appliquée: Dept of Biological Sciences, University of Alabama, Tuscaloosa, AL 35487-0206, USA; tel. (205) 348-1793; fax (205) 348-1403; f. 1922; 3,100 mems; Pres. Prof. Dr CAROLYN BURNS (New Zealand); Gen. Sec. and Treas. Prof. ROBERT G. WETZEL (USA); publs *Verhandlungen, Mitteilungen.*

International Association of Volcanology and Chemistry of the Earth's Interior (IAVCEI)/Association Internationale de Volcanologie et de Chimie de l'Intérieur de la Terre: c/o R. W. Johnson, Australian Geological Survey Organisation, POB 378, Canberra, ACT 2601, Australia; tel. (6) 249-9377; fax (6) 249-9986; f. 1919 to promote scientific investigation and discussion on volcanology and in those aspects of petrology and geochemistry relating to the composition of the interior of the Earth; Pres. G. HEIKEN (USA); Sec.-Gen. R. W. JOHNSON (Australia); publs *Bulletin of Volcanology, Catalogue of the Active Volcanoes of the World, Proceedings in Volcanology.*

International Association of Wood Anatomists/Association Internationale des Anatomistes du Bois: c/o Projectgroep Herbarium, Heidelberglaan 2, 3584 CS Utrecht, Netherlands; tel. (30) 2532643; f. 1931 for the purpose of study, documentation and exchange of information on the anatomy of wood; 575 mems in 54 countries; Exec. Sec. REGIS B. MILLER; publ. *IAWA Journal* (quarterly).

International Astronautical Federation (IAF)/Fédération Internationale d'Astronautique: 3–5 rue Mario-Nikis, 75015 Paris, France; tel. (33-1) 45-67-42-60; fax (33-1) 42-73-21-20; e-mail iaf@wanadoo.fr; f. 1950 to foster the development of astronautics for peaceful purposes at national and international levels; the IAF created the International Academy of Astronautics (IAA), the International Institute of Space Law (IISL) (for information on these bodies, see elsewhere in this chapter), and committees on Activities and Membership; Allan D. Emil Award; Finances; Publications; Liaison with Int. Organizations and Developing Nations; Education; Student Activities; SYRE, Solar Sail; Astrodynamics; Earth Observations; Satellite Communications; Natural Disaster Reduction; Life Sciences; Microgravity Science and Processes; Space Exploration; Space Power; Space Propulsion; Space Transportation; Space Stations; Space Systems; Materials and Structures; annual student awards; mems: 137 national astronautical societies in 45 countries; Pres. K. DOETSCH (Canada); Vice-Pres M. G. CHANDRASEKHAR (India), J. FABIAN (USA), LIANG SI LI (China), H. MATSUO (Japan), M. ORRICO ALARCON (Mexico), J. C. POGGI (France), G. A. POPOV (Russia), H. J. RATH (Germany); Exec. Sec. C. GOURDET; publs *Proceedings* of Annual Congresses, *Symposia* and Working Group Reports.

International Atomic Energy Agency (IAEA): Vienna International Centre, POB 100, A-1400 Vienna, Austria; tel. (1) 2060; telex 112645; fax (1) 20607; e-mail Official.Mail@IAEA.org; the Statute of the Agency was unanimously approved by 80 nations meeting at the UN headquarters in New York on October 26th, 1956; mems: 127 states; the Board of Governors, consisting of 36 members designated or elected on a regional basis, carries out the functions of the Agency; aims: the contribution of atomic energy to peace, health and prosperity throughout the world; to provide materials, services, equipment and facilities; to foster the exchange of scientific and technical information on peaceful uses of atomic energy; to encourage the exchange and training of scientists and experts in the field of atomic energy; to establish health and safety standards and to prepare a comprehensive set of safety codes and guides covering all aspects of building and operating nuclear power plants; establishes safeguards against the military use of civil nuclear materials or equipment provided through the Agency and applies these safeguards in accordance with the Treaty on the Non-Proliferation of Nuclear Weapons, the Treaty for the Prohibition of Nuclear Weapons in Latin America, the Treaty for a Nuclear-Weapon-Free Zone in Africa, the Treaty for a Nuclear-Weapon-Free Zone in South-East Asia and the Treaty of the South Pacific Nuclear-Free Zone; joint library (with UNIDO and other UN organizations) of 80,000 vols, 708,000 technical reports in microfiche and hard copy, 3,569 current periodicals; 350 audiovisual items, 1.26m. documents; micro-card clearing-house; the International Nuclear Information System (INIS) provides world-wide coverage of literature on all aspects of peaceful uses of nuclear energy; it has become the first fully decentralized computer-based nuclear science abstracting service; the IAEA Energy and Economic Data Bank provides information on the world's energy situation and related economic parameters, based on data obtained from member states; Dir-Gen. Dr HANS BLIX (Sweden); publs *Nuclear Fusion* (monthly), *Atomic Energy Review, IAEA Bulletin, Meetings on Atomic Energy* (quarterly), *INIS Atomindex* (2 a month).

International Biometric Society, The (IBS)/Société internationale de biométrie: c/o Prof. E. Baráth, Chair of Statistics, 2103 Gödöllö, Hungary; tel. (28) 410694; fax (28) 430336; e-mail e_barath@gtk-f1.gau.hu; f. 1947; an international society for the advancement of quantitative biological science through the development of quantitative theories and the application, development and dissemination of effective mathematical and statistical techniques; the Society has 16 regional organizations and 17 national groups, is affiliated with the International Statistical Institute and the World Health Organization, and constitutes the section of Biometry of the International Union of Biological Sciences; mems: over 7,000 in more than 70 different countries; Pres. Prof. SUE WILSON (Australia); Gen. Sec. Prof. ELISABETH BARÁTH (Hungary); publ. *Biometrics* (quarterly); *Biometric Bulletin* (quarterly), *Journal of Agricultural, Biological and Environmental Statistics* (quarterly).

International Botanical Congress/Congrès International de Botanique: C/o Dr Peter Hoch, Missouri Botanical Garden, POB 299, St Louis, MO 63166-0299, USA; tel. (314) 577-5175; fax (314) 577-9589; e-mail ibc16@mobot.org; f. 1864 to inform botanists of recent progress in plant sciences; programme to cover nomenclature, metabolism and bioenergetics, developmental botany, genetics, breeding and biotechnology, structural botany, systematics and evolution, environmental botany.

International Bureau of Weights and Measures/Bureau International des Poids et Mesures: Pavillon de Breteuil, 92312 Sèvres Cedex, France; tel. (1) 45-07-70-70; fax (1) 45-34-20-21; f. 1875 for the preservation of standards of the International System of Units (SI) and world-wide unification of the units of measurement; determination of national standards; precision measurements in physics; establishment of the international atomic time scale; 48 member states; Pres. J. KOVALEVSKY (France); Sec. W. R. BLEVIN (Australia); Dir T. J. QUINN (UK); publs *Procès-Verbaux* (annually), *Sessions des neuf Comités consultatifs auprès du Comité International* (every few years for each committee), *Metrologia, Comptes Rendus des Conférences Générales* (every 4 years), monthly circular and annual report on atomic time.

International Centre of Insect Physiology and Ecology: POB 30772, Nairobi, Kenya; tel. (2) 802501; fax (2) 803360; f. 1970 to develop, through research, plant pest and human and animal disease management and control strategies, and to promote research and the conservation of arthropods; library of 7,500 vols, 3,500 vols bound periodicals, 200 periodicals; Dir Gen. Dr HANS RUDOLPH HERREN; publs *ICIPE Annual Report, Insect Science and Its Application.*

International Commission for Optics/Commission Internationale d'Optique: c/o Dr PIERRE CHAVEL, Institut d'Optique, BP 147, 91403 Orsay Cedex, France; tel. (1) 69-35-87-41; fax (1) 69-35-87-00; e-mail pierre.chavel@iota.u-psud.fr; f. 1948 to contribute on an international basis to the progress of theoretical and instrumental optics and its application, through conferences, colloquia, summer schools, etc., and to promote international agreement on nomenclature, specifications, etc.; 45 mem. countries; Pres. Prof. T. ASAKURA (Japan); Sec.-Gen. Dr P. CHAVEL (France).

International Commission for the Scientific Exploration of the Mediterranean Sea/Commission Internationale pour l'Exploration Scientifique de la Mer Méditerranée: 16 blvd de Suisse, MC-98000 Monaco; tel. 93-30-38-79; fax 92-16-11-95; f. 1919 for scientific exploration of the Mediterranean Sea, the study of physical and chemical oceanography, marine geology and geophysics, marine pollution, microbiology, biochemistry, plankton, benthos, lagoons, marine radioactivity, marine vertebrates, island biology, underwater exploration; 2,500 mems; 23 mem. countries; Pres. H.S.H. The Prince RAINIER OF MONACO; Dir-Gen. Prof. FRÉDÉRIC BRIAND; Sec.-Gen. Prof. FRANÇOIS DOUMENGE.

International Commission on Zoological Nomenclature/Commission internationale de nomenclature zoologique: c/o The Natural History Museum, Cromwell Rd, London, SW7 5BD, England; f. 1895; the Commission, formerly a standing organ of the International Zoological Congresses, now reports to the General Assembly of IUBS; the Commission has judicial powers to determine all matters relating to the interpretation of the *International Code of Zoological Nomenclature* and also plenary powers to suspend the operation of the *Code* where strict application would lead to confusion and instability of nomenclature; the Commission is responsible also for maintaining and developing the *Official Lists of Names in Zoology* and the *Official Indexes of Rejected and Invalid Names in Zoology;* Pres. Prof. A. MINELLI (Italy); Exec. Sec. Dr P. K. TUBBS (UK); publs *International Code of Zoological Nomenclature, Bulletin of Zoological Nomenclature, Official Lists and Indexes of Names and Works in Zoology.*

International Confederation for Thermal Analysis and Calorimetry (ICTAC): c/o Prof. M. E. Brown, Chemistry Dept, Rhodes University, Grahamstown 6140, South Africa; tel. (46) 6038254; fax (46) 6225109; e-mail chmb@warthog.ru.ac.za; f. 1968; 600 mems from 40 countries, 5,000 affiliate mems from 20 affiliated regional and national societies and groups; the confederation co-ordinates these groups and supplies information on their scientific activities; supports national regional seminars and symposia; holds a quadrennial international conference; Pres. Prof. E. L. CHARSLEY (UK); Sec. Prof. M. E. BROWN (South Africa); publ. *Newsletter* (every 6 months).

International Council for the Exploration of the Sea (ICES)/Conseil International pour l'Exploration de la Mer: Palægade 2–4, DK 1261, Copenhagen K, Denmark; tel. 33-15-42-25; fax 33-93-42-15; f. 1902 to promote and encourage research and investigations for the study of the sea, particularly those related to the living resources thereof; area of interest: the Atlantic Ocean and its adjacent seas, and primarily the North Atlantic; mems: governments of 19 countries; Gen. Sec. Prof. C. C. E. HOPKINS; publs *ICES Journal of Marine Science, ICES Marine Science Symposia, ICES Fisheries Statistics, ICES Techniques in Marine Environmental Sciences, ICES Cooperative Research Reports.*

International Earth Rotation Service: Paris Observatory, 61 Ave de l'Observatoire, 75014 Paris, France; f. 1988 to replace Int. Polar Motion Service and the earth-rotation section of the Int. Time Bureau; organized jointly by the IAU and IUGG; responsible for defining and maintaining a conventional terrestrial reference system based on observing stations that use the high-precision techniques of space geodesy; defining and maintaining a conventional celestial reference system based on extragalactic radio sources, and relating it to other celestial reference systems; determining the earth orientation parameters connecting these systems; organizing operational activities for observation and data analysis, collecting and archiving appropriate data and results, and disseminating the results; Dir of Central Bureau M. FEISSEL.

International Federation for Cell Biology/Fédération Internationale de Biologie Cellulaire: f. 1972; sponsors an int. congress every 4 years; Pres. Dr JUDIE WALTON; Sec.-Gen. Prof. IVAN CAMERON, Univ. of Texas Health Science Center at San Antonio, Dept of Cellular and Structural Biology, 7703 Floyd Curl Drive, San Antonio, TX 78284-7762, USA; publ. *Cell Biology International.*

International Federation of Societies for Electron Microscopy/Fédération Internationale des Sociétés de Microscopie Electronique: C/o Prof. D. Cockayne, Key Centre for Microscopy and Microanalysis, University of Sydney FO9, NSW 2006, Australia; tel. (2) 9351-2351; fax (2) 9351-7682; f. 1955; mems: representative organizations of 29 countries; Pres. Prof. A. MAUNSBACH; Sec. Prof. D. COCKAYNE.

International Food Information Service: IFIS Publishing, Lane End House, Shinfield, Reading, RG2 9BB, England; tel. (118) 988-3895; fax (118) 988-5065; e-mail ifis@ifis.org; IFIS GmbH, Bianca Schneider, C/o Deutsche Landwirtschafts-Gesellschaft eV, Eschborner Landstrasse 122, 60489 Frankfurt am Main, Germany; tel. (69) 24788308; fax (69) 24788114; f. 1968; governed by CAB International (UK), Institute of Food Technologists (USA), the Centrum voor Landbouwpublikaties en Landbouwdocumentatie (Netherlands) and the Bundesministerium für Landwirtschaft Ernährung und Forsten (represented by Deutsche Landwirtschafts-Gesellschaft eV) in Germany, for the promotion of education and research in food science and technology; Gen. Man. J. SELMAN; publs *Food Science and Technology Abstracts* (monthly in print, online, CD-ROM), *Food Science Profiles* (monthly in print and on diskette), *Viticulture and Enology Abstracts* (quarterly, in print and online).

International Foundation of the High-Altitude Research Stations, Jungfraujoch and Gornergrat/Fondation internationale des stations scientifiques du Jungfraujoch et du Gornergrat: 5 Sidlerstr, 3012 Bern, Switzerland; tel. (31) 631-4051; fax (31) 631-4405; f. 1931; Pres. Prof. H. DEBRUNNER.

International Genetics Federation: f. 1968 to encourage understanding, co-operation and friendship among geneticists of the world and to plan and support int. congresses of genetics; 37 mem. countries; Pres. Dr DEREK SMITH (UK); Sec. Dr ANTHONY GRIFFITHS, Botany Dept, UBC, 6270 University Blvd, Vancouver, BC V6T 1Z4, Canada; e-mail agriff@unixg.ubc.ca.

International Geological Congress/Congrès géologique international: 77–79 rue Claude Bernard, 75005 Paris, France; f. 1878 to contribute to the advancement of investigations relating to the study of the Earth and other planets, considered from theoretical and practical points of view; the congress is held every four years; Pres. V. Y. KHAIN; Sec.-Gen. (vacant); publs *Extended Abstracts, General Proceedings.*

International Glaciological Society: Lensfield Rd, Cambridge, CB2 1ER, England; tel. (1223) 355974; fax (1223) 336543; e-mail 100751.1667@compuserve.com; f. 1936 to stimulate interest in and encourage research into the scientific and technical problems of snow and ice in all countries; 800 mems; Pres. Dr N. MAENO (Japan); Vice-Pres Dr K. HUTTER (Germany), Dr T. H. JACKA (Australia); Sec.-Gen. C. S. L. OMMANNEY; publs *Journal of Glaciology* (3 a year), *Ice* (News Bulletin—3 a year), *Annals of Glaciology* (conference proceedings).

International Hydrographic Organization/Organisation hydrographique internationale: BP 445, 4 quai Antoine 1er, Monte Carlo, 98011 Monaco Cedex; tel. 93-10-81-00; telex 479164; fax 93-10-81-40; f. 1921 to establish a close and permanent association among the hydrographic offices of its mem. states; to co-ordinate the activities of these offices in order to render maritime navigation easier and safer; to obtain uniformity in nautical charts and documents; to encourage the adoption of the best methods of conducting hydrographic surveys and improvement in the theory and practice of hydrography; to encourage surveying in those areas where accurate charts are lacking; to encourage co-ordination of hydrographic surveys with relevant oceanographic activities and to provide for co-operation between the IHO and international organizations in the fields of maritime safety and oceanography; to extend and facilitate the application of oceanographic knowledge for the benefit of navigators; maintains computerized Tidal Data Bank; library of 750 vols, 100 periodicals, 26,000 charts published by member states; 63 member states; Directing Cttee: Rear-Adm. G. ANGRISANO (Italy, Pres.), Commodore N. GUY (South Africa), Commodore J. LEECH (Australia); publs *The International Hydrographic Review* (2 a year), *International Hydrographic Bulletin* (monthly), *Yearbook.*

International Institute for Applied Systems Analysis (IIASA): 2361 Laxenburg, Austria; tel. (2236) 807; fax (2236) 71313; e-mail inf@iiasa.ac.at; f. 1972 on the initiative of the USA and the USSR; non-governmental research organization; concerned with global environmental change, global economic and technological transition, and systems methods for the analysis of global change; mems: organizations from 15 countries; Chair. KURT KOMAREK (Austria); Dir Prof. GORDON J. F. MACDONALD (USA); publ. *Options* (4 a year).

International Institute of Seismology and Earthquake Engineering: Building Research Institute, Ministry of Construction, Government of Japan, 1 Tatehara, Tsukuba-shi, Ibaraki Prefecture 305-0802, Japan; tel. (298) 79-0678; fax (298) 64-6777; e-mail iisee@kenken.go.jp; f. 1962 to carry out training and research works on seismology and earthquake engineering for the purpose of fostering these research activities in the developing countries, and undertakes survey, research, guidance and analysis of information on earthquakes and their related matters; 15 mems; Dir HATSUKAZU MIZUNO; publs *Bulletin of IISEE* (annually), *Individual Study Report* (annually), *Year Book.*

International Mineralogical Association: f. 1958 to further international co-operation in the science of mineralogy; mems: national societies in many countries; Sec. Prof. S. S. HAFNER, Inst. of Mineralogy, Univ. of Marburg, 3550 Marburg, Germany; tel. (049-6421) 28-5617; telex 482372; publs *World Directories* (Mineralogists; Mineral Collections).

International Organisation of Legal Metrology/Organisation internationale de métrologie légale: 11 rue Turgot, 75009 Paris, France; tel. (1) 48-78-12-82; telex 234444; fax (1) 42-82-17-27; f. 1955 to serve as documentation and information centre on methods of verifying and checking measurements, to study ways of harmonization and to determine the general principles of legal metrology; mems: governments of 49 countries and 36 corresp. mems; Pres. K. BIRKELAND (Norway); Dir B. ATHANÉ; publs *Bulletin* (quarterly), *International Recommendations and Documents.*

International Ornithological Congress/Congrès International Ornithologique: c/o R. Nöhring, Zoologischer Garten, Hardenbergplatz 8, 1 Berlin 30, Germany; f. 1884; Pres. Prof. D. S. FARNER (USA); Sec.-Gen. R. NÖHRING (Germany).

International Palaeontological Association: N10, W8, Kita-ku, Sapporo 060, Japan; telex 932510; fax (11) 717-9394; f. 1933 following the meeting of the International Geological Congress; affiliated to the Int. Union of Geological Sciences and the Int. Union of Biological Sciences; meets every four years at International Geological Congress; mems: national organizations, research groups and ordinary mems; Pres. Prof. A. HALLAM (UK); Sec.-Gen. Dr M. KATO (Japan); publs *Lethaia, Directory of Palaeontologists of the World, IPA Fossil Collections of the World.*

International Society for Human and Animal Mycology (ISHAM)/Société Internationale de Mycologie Humaine et Animale: f. 1954 to encourage the practice and study of all aspects of medical and veterinary mycology; *c.* 990 mems from *c.* 74 countries; Pres. Prof. E. G. V. EVANS (UK); Gen.-Sec. Dr D. H. ELLIS, Mycology Unit, Women's and Children's Hospital, N. Adelaide, SA 5006, Australia; tel. (8) 8204-6459; fax (8) 8204-7589; e-mail dellis@mad.adelaide.edu.au; publs *Medical Mycology* (annually in 6 parts), *ISHAM Mycoses Newsletter* (2 a year).

International Society for Tropical Ecology: c/o Botany Dept, Banaras Hindu University, Varanasi 5, India; tel. (542) 317099; fax (542) 317074; f. 1956 to promote and develop the science of ecology in the tropics in the service of man; to publish a journal to aid ecologists in the tropics in communication of their findings; and to hold symposia from time to time to summarize the state of knowledge in particular of general fields of tropical ecology; mems: 500; Pres. Prof. HELMUT LIETH; Sec. Prof. J. S. SINGH; publ. *Tropical Ecology* (2 a year).

International Society of Biometeorology: f. 1956; aims: to unite all biometeorologists working in the fields of agricultural, botanical, cosmic, entomological, forestry, human, veterinary, zoological and other branches of biometeorology; mems: 265 individuals, nationals of 43 countries; Pres. Dr ANDRIS AULICIEMS; Sec. Dr. PAUL BEGGS, School of Earth Sciences, Macquarie University, Sydney, NSW 2109, Australia; tel. (2) 9850-8399; fax (2) 9850-8428; e-mail pbeggs@ocs1.ocs.mq.edu.au; publs *International Journal of Biometeorology* (quarterly), *Biometeorology* (Proceedings of Congresses), *Progress in Biometeorology, Biometeorology Bulletin.*

International Society of Cryptozoology: POB 43070, Tucson, AZ 85733, USA; tel. and fax (520) 884-8369; e-mail iscz@azstarnet.com; f. 1982 to serve as focal point for the investigation, analysis, publication, and discussion of all matters related to animals of unexpected form or size, or unexpected occurrence in time or space, and to encourage scientific examination of all evidence related to these matters; *c.* 800 mems; Pres. BERNARD HEUVELMANS (France); Sec. J. RICHARD GREENWELL (USA); publs *Cryptozoology* (annually), *The ISC Newsletter* (quarterly).

International Society of Development Biology: f. 1911 as International Institute of Embryology; aims to promote the study of developmental biology and to promote international co-operation among the investigators in this field; the Society is the Developmental Biology Section of the International Union of Biological Sciences (*q.v.*); mems: 900 personal, 7 corporate; Pres. Dr P. GRUSS (Germany); Sec.-Treas. Dr S. DE LAAT, Hubrecht Laboratory, Uppsalalaan 8, 3584 CT Utrecht, Netherlands; tel. (30) 510211; fax (30) 516464.

International Society of Electrochemistry: c/o Dr Otmar Dossenbach, Treasurer ISE, Postfach 475, 8501 Frauenfeld, Switzerland; tel. (1) 632-3044; fax (52) 722-4886; e-mail odossenbach@pingnet.ch; f. 1949 to promote the advance of electrochemical science and technology and to organize the free exchange of information in basic and applied electrochemistry; 1,100 mems in 50 countries; Sec.-Gen. Prof. Dr E. KÁLMÁR; Treasurer Dr O. DOSSENBACH; publ. *Electrochimica Acta.*

International Statistical Institute/ Institut international de statistique: Prinses Beatrixlaan 428, POB 950, 2270 AZ Voorburg, Netherlands; tel. (70) 337-5737; fax (70) 386-0025; f. 1885; an autonomous society devoted to the development and improvement of statistical methods and their application throughout the world; provides a forum for the int. exchange of knowledge between mems, and aims to mobilize mems' expertise to play an effective role in the practical solution of world problems; 10 hon. mems, 2,000 ordinary mems, 170 *ex-officio* mems, 70 corporate mems, 53 affiliated organizations; administers int. statistical education programme, incl. statistical education centre in Calcutta, and Indian Statistical Institute; conducts statistical research to undertake operational activities in the field of statistics which help to improve the data used in planning and policy formation, to the benefit of the countries concerned; to further integration of statistics and promote appropriate use of statistical methods in different socio-cultural settings; Pres. W. VAN ZWET (Netherlands); Sec.-Treas./Dir Permanent Office M. P. R. VAN DEN BROECKE; publs *International Statistical Review* (3 a year), *Bulletin* (proceedings of biennial sessions), *Statistical Theory and Method Abstracts* (quarterly), *ISI Newsletter* (3 a year), *Short Book Reviews* (3 a year).

International Table of Selected Constants/Tables Internationales de Constantes Sélectionnées: Université P. et M. Curie (Paris VI), Faculté des Sciences, Tour 13, 4 place Jussieu, 75252 Paris Cedex 05, France; f. 1909 to publish all the constants and numerical data concerning the pure and applied physico-chemical sciences; Pres. J.-M. FLAUD (France).

International Union for Quaternary Research (INQUA): f. 1928; field of activities: geology, geography, prehistory, palaeontology, palynology, pedology; Pres. Exec. Comm. Prof. S. C. PORTER; Sec.-Gen. Prof. S. HALDORSEN, Dept of Soil and Water Sciences, Agricultural University of Norway, POB 5028, 1432 AAS, Norway; tel. 64-94-82-52; fax 64-94-74-85; publs *Proceedings of Congresses, Quaternary International, Quaternary Perspective* (newsletter).

International Union for the Study of Social Insects/Union Internationale pour l'Etude des Insectes Sociaux: c/o P. E. Howse, Dept of Zoology, Univ. of Southampton, Southampton, England; f. 1951; mems: 500 individuals from 24 countries; Pres. Prof. C. D. MICHENER; Sec.-Gen. Dr P. E. HOWSE; publs *Insectes sociaux, Congress Proceedings,* etc.

International Union of Speleology/ Union Internationale de Spéléologie: f. 1965; karstology, speleology; 60 mem. countries; Pres. PAOLO FORTI (Italy), Via Zamboni 67, 40127 Bologna, Italy; Sec.-Gen. PAVEL BOSAK (Czech Republic); publs *Bulletin* (1 or 2 a year), *International Journal of Speleology* (annually), *Speleological Abstracts* (annually).

Joint Institute for Nuclear Research: Dubna, 141980 Moscow Region, Russia; tel. (09621) 65059; fax (09621) 65891; e-mail post@office.jinr.dubna.su; f. 1956; conducts studies on the structure of matter, high- and low-energy physics, condensed matter, heavy-ion and neutron physics; 18 member countries; maintains seven laboratories of the Joint Institute; library of 415,000 vols; Dir V. G. KADYSHEVSKY; publs *Journal of Elementary Particles and the Atomic Nucleus* (6 a year), *JINR Rapid Communications* (6 a year), *JINR News* (4 a year).

OECD Nuclear Energy Agency (NEA): Le Seine St-Germain, 12 blvd des Iles, 92130 Issy-les-Moulineaux, France; tel. 1-45-24-82-00; fax 1-45-24-11-10; f. 1958, name changed 1972; assesses the role of nuclear energy as a contributor to economic progress, and encourages co-operation between governments towards its safe development; encourages harmonization of governments' regulatory policies and practices in the nuclear field and co-operation on health and safety, radio-active waste management and nuclear third party liability; prepares forecasts of uranium resources, production and demand, and of developments in the nuclear fuel cycle; sponsors research and development projects jointly organized and operated by OECD countries; contributes to improved public understanding by publication of authoritative and impartial analyses and assessments on relevant questions; maintains NEA Data Bank for compilation and exchange of computer programmes and nuclear data (Issy-les-Moulineaux, France); mems: 27 countries; Dir-Gen. SAM THOMPSON (acting); publs *Annual Report, NEA Newsletter.*

Pacific Science Association/Association Scientifique du Pacifique: 1525 Bernice St, POB 17801, Honolulu, HI 96817, USA; tel. (808) 848-4139; fax (808) 847-8252; e-mail psa@bishop.bishop.hawaii.org; f. 1920 to co-operate in the study of scientific problems relating to the Pacific region; sponsors congresses and inter-congresses; mems: scientists and scientific institutions interested in the Pacific; Pres. Dr AKITO ARIMA (Japan); Exec. Sec. Dr L. G. ELDREDGE; publs *Information Bulletin, Congress Proceedings.*

Pan-American Institute of Geography and History/Instituto Panamericano de Geografía e Historia: Ex-Arzobispado 29, Col. Observatorio, Deleg. Miguel Hidalgo, 11860 México, DF, Mexico; tel. (905) 277-5888; fax (525) 271-6172; e-mail ipgh@laneta.apc.org; f. 1928; membership: the nations of the Organization of American States to encourage, co-ordinate and promote the study of cartography, geophysics, geography, history, anthropology, archaeology and other related scientific studies; library of 60,000 vols and 24,000 maps; periodicals collection of 54,000 vols; Pres. Dr NOE PINEDA PORTILLO (Honduras); Sec.-Gen. Ing. CARLOS CARVALLO YAÑEZ (Chile); publs *Revista de Historia de América, Revista Geográfica, Revista Cartográfica, Revista Folklore Americano, Revista Geofísica, Revista de Arqueología Americana, Boletín de Antropología Americana, Boletín Aéreo* (6 a year).

Third World Academy of Sciences: c/o Abdus Salam International Centre for Theoretical Physics, POB 586, Via Beirut 6, 34100 Trieste, Italy; tel. (39-40) 2240327; telex 460392; fax (39-40) 224559; e-mail twas@ictp.trieste.it; f. 1983 to give recognition and support to research carried out by scientists from developing countries, to facilitate their contacts and foster research for third-world development; awards prizes, research grants and fellowships to scientists working and living in third-world countries; 480 mems; Pres. Prof. JOSÉ I. VARGAS (Pakistan); Sec.-Gen. A. BADRAN (Jordan); Exec. Dir M. H. A. HASSAN (Sudan); publs *TWAS Newsletter* (quarterly), *TWAS Year Book,* reports, etc.

Wetlands International: 11 Marijkeweg, POB 7002, 6700 AC Wageningen, Netherlands; tel. (317) 474711; fax (317) 474712; f. 1954 to sustain and restore wetlands, their resources and biodiversity through worldwide research, information exchange and conservation activities; 48 mem. countries; Dir Dr MICHAEL MOSER; Head of Operations SIMON NASH.

World Academy of Art and Science: C/o Prof. Harlan Cleveland, 46891 Grissom St, Sterling, VA 20165, USA; tel. (703) 450-0428; fax (703) 450-0429; f. 1960; a forum for discussion of the social consequences and policy implications of knowledge; 471 Fellows in 62 countries; Pres. HARLAN CLEVELAND (USA); Vice-Pres. and Pres. of European Division Dr. HORACIO MENANO (Portugal); Vice-Pres. and Pres. of American Division Dr WALTER TRUETT ANDERSON; publs *WAAS Newsletter* (2 a year), Conference Reports, Occasional Papers.

World Conservation Union (IUCN)/ Union mondiale pour la nature (UICN): Rue Mauverney 28, 1196 Gland, Switzerland; tel. (22) 999-00-01; fax (22) 999-00-02; e-mail mail@hq.iucn.org; f. 1948 to influence, encourage and assist societies throughout the world to conserve the integrity and diversity of nature and to ensure that any use of natural resources is equitable and ecologically sustainable, and to guide the development of human communities towards ways of life that are both of good quality and in enduring harmony with other components of the biosphere; mems: governments of 73 states, 109 government agencies, 636 nat. non-governmental organizations, 58 int. non-governmental organizations and 37 affiliates, together representing 138 countries; Pres. YOLANDA KAKABADZE; Dir-Gen. DAVID McDOWELL; publs *World Conservation*, (in English, French and Spanish), *Red Data Book, World Conservation Strategy, Caring for the Earth.*

World Meteorological Organization/ Organisation Météorologique Mondiale: Secretariat: CP 2300, CH-1211 Geneva 2, Switzerland; tel. (41-22) 730-81-11; telex 414199; fax (41-22) 734-23-26; f. 1951; objects: world-wide co-operation in making meteorological, climatological, hydrological and related geophysical observations and in standardizing their publication; assists in training, research and technology transfer; furthers the application of meteorology to aviation, shipping, water problems and agriculture, environmental problems and to sustainable development; mems: 179 states and six territories maintaining their own meteorological or hydrometeorological services; constituent bodies: Congress, Executive Council, six regional associations, eight technical commissions; Pres. Dr J. W. ZILLMAN (Australia); Sec.-Gen. G. O. P. OBASI (Nigeria); publs Reports of meetings of constituent bodies, Regulations, Technical Manuals and Notes, *International Cloud Atlas, WMO Bulletin* (quarterly).

World Organisation of Systems and Cybernetics/Organisation Mondiale pour la Systémique et la Cybernétique: f. 1969 to act as clearing-house for all societies concerned with cybernetics, systems and allied subjects, to aim for the recognition of cybernetics as a bona fide science and to maintain liaison with other int. bodies; holds int. congresses every 3 years; organizes int. exhibitions; awards Norbert Wiener Memorial Gold Medal; mems: national and int. organizations in 33 countries, 27 hon. fellows; Pres. Prof. STAFFORD BEER; Dir.-Gen. Prof. ROBERT VALLÉE, 2 rue de Vouillé, 75015 Paris, France; tel. (33-1) 45-33-62-46; publs *Kybernetes, an International Journal of Cybernetics and Systems* (quarterly), congress proceedings, etc.

AFGHANISTAN

Learned Societies

GENERAL

Afghanistan Acadamy of Sciences: Sher Alikhan St, Kabul; tel. 20350; f. 1979; research in science, technology, humanities and culture; Central Library of 5,000 vols, Central Archives.

Research Institutes

GENERAL

Institute of Social Sciences: Kabul; attached to Afghanistan Acad. of Sciences; philosophy, economics, history, archaeology; Pres. Dr HAKIM HELALI; publs *Afghanistan* (quarterly in English, French and German), *Ariana* (quarterly in Pashtu and Dari).

LANGUAGE AND LITERATURE

Institute of Languages and Literature: Kabul; attached to Afghanistan Acad. of Sciences; linguistics, literature and folklore; study of Pashto and Dari languages, and Afghanistan dialects; publs *Kabul* (monthly, Pashtu), *Zayray* (weekly, Pashtu).

International Centre for Pashtu Studies: Kabul; attached to Afghanistan Acad. of Sciences; research, compilation and translation; publ. *Pashtu Quarterly*.

MEDICINE

Institute of Public Health: Ansari Wat, Kabul; f. 1962; public health training and research; govt reference laboratory; Dir Dr S. M. SADIQUE; publs *Afghan Journal of Public Health* (fortnightly), books and pamphlets.

NATURAL SCIENCES

General

Science Research Centre: Kabul; attached to Afghanistan Acad. of Sciences; institutes of botany, zoology, geology and chemistry, seismology, computer centre, plants museum and botanical garden.

Physical Sciences

Department of Geology and Mineral Survey: Ministry of Mines and Industries, Kabul; tel. 25848; f. 1955; research, mapping, prospecting and exploration; library of 8,300 vols; Pres. Dip. Eng. Haji MOHAMAD NAWZADI; publ. *Journal of Mines and Industries* (quarterly), maps and other reference works.

Libraries and Archives

Kabul

Kabul University Library: Kabul; tel. 42594; f. 1931; 250,000 vols; Dir Prof. ABDUL RASOUL RAHIN.

Library of the National Bank: Bank Millie Afghan, Ibn Sina Wat, Kabul; f. 1941; 5,600 vols; Dir A. AZIZ.

Library of the Press and Information Department: Sanaii Wat, Kabul; f. 1931; 28,000 vols and 800 MSS; Dir MOHAMMED SARWAR RONA.

Ministry of Education Library: Kabul; f. 1920; 30,000 vols; Chief Officer MOHAMAD QASEM HILAMAN; publ. *Erfan* (monthly journal in Pashtu and Dari).

Public Library: Charaii-i-Malik Asghar, Kabul; f. 1920; attached to Min. of Information and Culture; 60,000 vols, 433 MSS, 30 current periodicals; Dir MOHAMAD OMAR SEDDIQUI.

Women's Welfare Society Library: Kabul.

Museums and Art Galleries

Bamian

Bamian Museum: Bamian.

Ghazni

Ghazni Museum: Ghazni.

Herat

Herat Museum: Herat.

Kabul

Kabul Museum: Darul Aman, Kabul; tel. 42656; f. 1922; archaeology of the prehistoric, Greco-Roman, Buddhic and Islamic periods, coins, ethnography, Kushan art; Curator NAJIBULLA POPAL.

Kandahar

Kandahar Museum: Kandahar.

Maimana

Maimana Museum: Maimana.

Mazar-i-Sharif

Mazar-i-Sharif Museum: Mazar-i-Sharif.

Universities

POHANTOON-E-KABUL (Kabul University)

Jamal Mina, Kabul
Telephone: 40341
Founded 1932
Academic year: March to January
President: MAULAVI PIR MOHAMMAD ROHANI
Number of teachers: 462
Number of students: 9,334
Publication: *Natural Science and Social Science* (quarterly).

Faculties of Science, Languages and Literature, Agriculture, Economics, Journalism, Pharmacy, Veterinary Medicine, History and Philosophy, Education, Geosciences, and Fine Arts.

BAYAZID ROSHAN UNIVERSITY OF NANGARHAR

Jalalabad, Nangarhar
Founded 1962 from Medical Faculty of Kabul University, reorganized 1978
State control
Language of instruction: Pashtu

Faculties of medicine, engineering, agriculture and education.

HERAT UNIVERSITY

Herat
Telephone: 2001
Founded 1987
Rector: ABOBAKER RASHID
Librarian: SAID KHALLIL
Library of 2,000 vols
Number of teachers: 10
Number of students: 100

DEANS

Faculty of Language and Literature: M. SABBAH
Faculty of Agriculture: Prof. GH. RASSOL AMIRI

UNIVERSITY OF ISLAMIC STUDIES

Kabul
Founded 1988; in process of formation
Number of students: 450

Courses in Koranic exegesis, theology, logic, history of Islam, Arabic language, Islamic ethics.

Colleges

Institute of Agriculture: Kabul; f. 1924; veterinary medicine, forestry.

Institute of Arabic and Religious Study: Kabul. Other centres include: the Najmul-Madares, Nangrahar; the Jamé and Fakhrul Madares, Herat; the Asadia Madrasa, Mazar-i-Sharif; the Takharistan Madrasa, Kunduz; the Zahir Shahi Madrasa, Maimana.

Kabul Art School: Bibi Mahro, nr Kabul; music, painting and sculpture courses.

Kabul Polytechnic: Kabul; f. 1951; secondary level technical school; post-graduate engineering courses; departments of aviation, automotive-diesel, machine tools, building construction, civil and electrical-electronics technology; 50 staff; 450 students; library of 6,000 vols; Dir GHULAM SAKHI.

Kabul State Medical Institute: Kabul; f. 1978; 3,000 students.

School of Commerce: Kabul; f. 1943; banking, commercial law, economics, business administration, finance.

School of Mechanics: Kabul; for apprentice trainees.

ALBANIA

Learned Societies

GENERAL

Academy of Sciences: Tiranë; f. 1972; attached research institutes: see Research Institutes; 26 mems, 3 corresp. mems; Pres. SHABAN DEMIRAJ; Scientific Sec. EMIN RIZA; publs *Studia Albanica* (mainly in French, 2 a year), *Gjuha jonë* (Our Language, quarterly).

Komiteti Shqiptar për Marrëdhënie Kulturore me botën e jashtme (Albanian Committee for Cultural Relations Abroad): Tiranë; Pres. JORGO MELIKA.

LANGUAGE AND LITERATURE

Lidhja e Shkrimtarëve dhe e Artistëve të Shqipërisë (Union of Writers and Artists of Albania): Tiranë; f. 1957; 1,750 mems; Pres. DRITËRO AGOLLI; Secs NASI LERA, FEIM IBRAHIMI, PETRO KOKUSHTA; publs *Nëntori* (monthly Review), *Drita* (weekly journal), *Les Lettres Albanaises* (quarterly).

PEN Centre of Albania: C/o Union des Ecrivains, Tiranë; Pres. BESNIK MUSTAFAJ; Joint Secs PIRO MISHA, SABRI HAMITI.

NATURAL SCIENCES

Physical Sciences

Shoqata e Gjeologëve te Shqipërisë (Geologists' Association of Albania): Blloku 'Vasil Shanto', Tiranë; tel. 26597; f. 1989; 450 mems; Chair. ALEKSANDËR ÇINA; Sec.-Gen. ILIR ALLIU; publ. *Buletini i Shkencave Gjeologjike*.

Research Institutes

AGRICULTURE, FISHERIES AND VETERINARY SCIENCE

Instituti i Duhanit (Tobacco Institute): Cërrik; tel. (545) 2800; f. 1956; library of 1,000 vols; Dir BELUL GIXHARI; publ. *Bulletin des sciences de l'agriculture* (quarterly).

Instituti i Kërkimeve Bujqësore Lushnje (Lushnje Institute of Agricultural Research): Lushnje; f. 1952; focuses on cultivating new varieties of bread and durum wheat, cotton, sunflower and dry bean; library of 8,000 vols; Dir VLADIMIR MALO; publ. annual report.

Instituti i Kërkimeve Pyjore dhe Kullotave (Forest and Pasture Research Institute): Tiranë; f. 1992; Dir SPIRO KARADUMI.

Instituti i Kërkimeve të Foragjere (Forage Research Institute): Fushë-Krujë; tel. (42) 33354; f. 1973; Dir VASILLAQ DHIMA.

Instituti i Kërkimeve të Pemëve Frutore dhe Vreshtave (Institute of Fruit Growing and Vineyard Research): Tiranë; tel. 29704; f. 1984; library of 70 vols; Dir STEFAN GJOKA; publs *Pemëtaria, Bulletini i Shkencave Bujqësore*.

Instituti i Kërkimeve të Zooteknisë (Institute of Animal Husbandry Research): Laprake, Tiranë; tel. 23135; f. 1955; library of 1,900 vols; Dir MINA SPIRU.

Instituti i Kërkimeve Veterinare (Institute of Veterinary Research): Tiranë; f. 1928; Dir PETRO GJONI.

Instituti i Mbrojtjes Bimeve (Institute of Plant Protection Research): Durrës; tel. (52) 22182; telex 4209; fax (42) 27924; f. 1971; library of 1,800 vols; Dir Assoc. Prof. Dr FADIL GJATA.

Instituti i Msrit dhe i Orizit (Institute of Maize and Rice): Shkodër; tel. 3515; f. 1971; library of 7,000 vols; Dir Prof. HYSEN LAÇEJ; publ. *Science Bulletin* (quarterly).

Instituti i Perimeve dhe i Patates (Institute of Vegetables and Potatoes): Rr. Skënder Kosturi, Tiranë; tel. 26533; f. 1980; library of 6,000 vols; Dir MEVLUD HALLIDRI; publs *Bulletin of Agricultural Sciences, Bulletin of Vegetables and Potatoes, Bulletin of Vegetables*.

Instituti i Studimeve dhe i Projektimeve të Veprave të Kullimit dhe Ujitjes (Institute of Irrigation and Drainage Studies and Designs): Tiranë; f. 1970; Dir DHIMITËR VOGLI.

Instituti i Studimit të Tokave (Institute of Soil Studies): Tiranë; tel. 23278; fax 28367; f. 1971; library of 5,000 vols; Dir ALBERT DUBALI.

Instituti i Ullirit dhe i Agrumeve (Institute of Olives and Citrus Plants): 'Uji i Jtohtë,' Vlorë; tel. and fax (63) 23225; f. 1971; library of 500 vols; Dir Dr HAIRI ISMAILI; publ. *Bulletin*.

Stacioni i Mekanizimit të Bujqësisë (Agricultural Mechanization Station): Tiranë; f. 1971; Dir XHELAL SHKRETA; publ. *Mekanika Bujqësore* (irregular).

Stacioni i Panxharsheqerit (Sugar Beet Station): Korçë; tel. 2618; f. 1979; Dir NESTI TËROVA.

Stacioni i Studimeve dhe i Kërkimeve të Peshkimit (Fisheries Research): Durrës; f. 1960; Dir EQREM KAPIDANI.

ARCHITECTURE AND TOWN PLANNING

Instituti i Monumenteve të Kulturës (Institute of Cultural Monuments): Alqi Kondi 7, Tiranë; tel. 27511; f. 1965; research and restoration of ancient and medieval architecture, cultural buildings and artistic monuments; library of 7,100 vols; Dir VALTER SHTYLLA; publ. *Monumentet* (Monuments, 2 a year).

Instituti i Studimeve e Projektimeve Urbanistikë (Institute of Urban Planning and Design): Rr. M. Gjollesha Istn, Tiranë; tel. and fax (42) 23361; f. 1991; library of 400 vols; Dir GJERGJ KOTMILO.

ECONOMICS, LAW AND POLITICS

Instituti i Studimeve të Marrëdhënieve Ndërkombëtare (Institute of International Relations): Tiranë; tel. 29521; fax 32970; f. 1981; Dir SOKRAT PLAKA; publ. *Politika ndërkombëtare* (International Politics, quarterly).

EDUCATION

Instituti i Studimeve Pedagogjike (Institute of Pedagogical Studies): Rr. Naim Frashëri 37, Tiranë; tel. 22573; fax 25858; f. 1970; Dir LUAN HAJDARAGA; publs *Revista Pedagogjike* (quarterly), *Yllkat* (monthly), *Chemistry and Biology in School* (2 a year), *Mathematics and Physics in School* (2 a year), *Vocational Schools* (2 a year), *Social Materials in School* (2 a year), *Albanian Language and Literature in School* (2 a year), *Elementary School* (annually); *Nursery School 3–6* (annually), *Foreign Languages in School* (annually).

FINE AND PERFORMING ARTS

Qendra e Studimeve të Artit (Centre for Art Studies): Tiranë; f. 1984; attached to Acad. of Sciences; Dir. FERID HUDHRI.

HISTORY, GEOGRAPHY AND ARCHAEOLOGY

Instituti i Historisë (Institute of History): Rr. Naim Frashëri, Tiranë; tel. and fax (42) 25869; f. 1972; attached to Acad. of Sciences; library of 52,000 vols, 10,000 periodicals; Dir KASEM BIÇOKU; publ. *Studime Historike* (Study of History, 1 a year).

Instituti i Kërkimeve Arkeologjike (Institute of Archaeological Research): Tiranë; f. 1976; attached to Acad. of Sciences; Dir. NAMIK BODINAKU; publ. *Iliria* (Illyria, 2 a year, in Albanian and French).

Qendra e Kërkimeve Gjeografike (Centre for Geographical Research): Rr. M. Toptani 11, Tiranë; tel. and fax (42) 27985; f. 1987; attached to Acad. of Sciences; library of 3,000 vols; Dir Prof. Dr. ERGJIN SAMIMI; publ. *Studime Gjeografike* (Geographical Studies, 2 a year).

LANGUAGE AND LITERATURE

Instituti i Gjuhësisë dhe i Letërsisë (Institute of Language and Literature): Tiranë; f. 1972; attached to Acad. of Sciences; Dir BAHRI BECI; publ. *Studime Filologjike* (Study of Philology, quarterly).

MEDICINE

Instituti i Mjekësisë Popullore (Institute of Folk Medicine): Tiranë; tel. 23493; telex 4205; f. 1977; Dir Dr GËZIM BOCARI; publ. *Përmbledhje Studimesh* (Collections of Studies, irregular).

Instituti Kerkimor i Higjenës, Epidemiologjisë dhe i Prodhimeve Imunobiologjike (Research Institute of Hygiene, Epidemiology and Immunobiological Products): Tiranë; tel. 33553; f. 1969; Dir Dr AZMI DIBRA; publ. *Revista Mjekesore* (Medical magazine, every 2 months).

NATURAL SCIENCES

Biological Sciences

Instituti i Kërkimeve Biologjike (Institute of Biological Research): Tiranë; f. 1978; attached to Acad. of Sciences; Dir JANI VANGJELI; publ. *Vjetari i Punimeve Shkencore të QKB* (Annual Journal of the Scientific Work of QKB).

Mathematical Sciences

Instituti i Informatikës dhe i Matematikës së Aplikuar (Institute of Computer Science and Applied Mathematics): Tiranë; f. 1986; attached to Acad. of Sciences; Dir GUDAR BEQIRAJ; publ. *Informatika dhe Matematika Llogaritëse* (Computer Science and Computer Mathematics, irregular).

Physical Sciences

Instituti i Energjetikës (Institute of Energetics): Tiranë; f. 1982; Dir LLAZAR PAPAJORGJI.

Instituti i Fizikës Bërthamore (Institute of Nuclear Physics): Tiranë; f. 1971; attached to Acad. of Sciences; Dir ROBERT KUSHE; publ. *Punime të Institutit të Fizikës Bërthamore* (Works of the Institute of Nuclear Physics, irregular).

Instituti i Hidrometeorologjisë (Institute of Hydrometeorology): Tiranë; f. 1962; attached to Acad. of Sciences; Dir MIRON NURI; publs meteorological and hydrological bulletins (monthly and annually), *Studime Meteorologjike dhe Hidrologjike* (Meteorological and Hydrological Studies, irregular).

Instituti i Sizmologjise (Institute of Seismology): Tiranë; tel. and fax (42) 28274; e-mail betim@sizmo.tirana.al; f. 1993; attached to Acad. of Sciences; Dir Prof. Dr. BETIM MUÇO; publ. *Buletini Sizmologjik* (Seismological Bulletin, in Albanian and English, weekly, monthly, annually).

Instituti i Studimeve dhe Projektimeve të Gjeologjisë (Geological Research Institute): Blloku 'Vasil Shanto', Tiranë; tel. (42) 26597; f. 1962; library of 20,000 vols; Dir ALAUDIN KODRA; publ. *Buletini i Shkencave Gjeologjike* (quarterly).

RELIGION, SOCIOLOGY AND ANTHROPOLOGY

Instituti i Kulturës Popullore (Institute of Folk Culture): Rruga Kont Urani 3, Tiranë; tel. (42) 22323; fax (42) 23818; f. 1979; attached to Acad. of Sciences; Dir AGRON XHAGOLLI; publs *Etnografia Shqiptare* (Albanian Ethnography, irregular in French), *Kultura Popullore* (Popular Culture, 2 a year, annually in French), *Ceshtje te Folklorit Shqiptare* (Questions of Albanian Folklore).

TECHNOLOGY

Infraproject Consulting SH.p.K.: Rr. Sami Frasheri; Tiranë; tel. (42) 25206; fax (42) 28321; e-mail vguri@icc.al.eu.org; road, railway and waterway engineering; library of 900 vols; Dir-Gen. VEHIP GURI.

Instituti i Studimeve dhe i Projektimeve Gjeologjike të Naftës e të Gazit (Institute for Studies and Design of Oil and Gas Geology): Fier; f. 1965; Dir DRINI MEZINI; publ. *Buletini Nafta dhe Gazi* (2 a year, summaries in English).

Instituti i Studimeve dhe i Projektimeve Industriale (ISP Nr 4) (Institute of Industrial Project Studies and Design): Tiranë; tel. 22006; f. 1979; library of 2,250 vols; Dir MIHAL POGAÇE.

Instituti i Studimeve dhe i Projektimeve të Hidrocentraleve (Institute of Hydraulic Studies and Design): Tiranë; f. 1966; Dir EGON GJADRI.

Instituti i Studimeve dhe i Projektimeve të Metalurgjise (Institute for Metallurgical Studies and Designs): Elbasan; tel. (545) 5565; fax (545) 2121; f. 1978; metallurgy of iron, chrome, copper, nickel; library of 6,000 vols; Dir ALFRED MALKJA.

Instituti i Studimeve dhe i Projektimeve të Minierave (Mining Research Institute): Blloku 'Vasil Shanto', Tiranë; tel. 29445; f. 1983; library of 10,000 vols; Dir ENGJELL HOXHAJ; publ. *Buletini i Shkencave Minerare* (2 a year, summaries in English).

Instituti i Studimeve dhe i Projektimeve të Teknologjisë Kimike (Institute of Chemical Studies and Technological Design): Tiranë; f. 1981; Dir GASTOR AGALLIU.

Instituti i Studimeve dhe i Projektimeve të Teknologjisë Mekanike (Institute of Mechanical Technology Studies and Design): Tiranë; f. 1969; Dir ROBERT LAPERI.

Instituti i Studimeve dhe i Projektimeve Teknologjike të Mineraleve (Institute for Studies and Technology of Minerals): Tiranë; tel. 25582; f. 1979; mineral processing research; library of 1,480 vols; Dir JLIR LAKRORI.

Instituti i Studimeve dhe i Projektimeve Teknologjike të Naftës e të Gazit (Institute for Studies and Design of Oil and Gas Technology): Tiranë; f. 1981; Dir PERPARIM HOXHA; publ. *Nafta dhe Gazi* (Oil and Gas, every 2 months).

Instituti i Studimeve dhe i Teknologjisë Ndërtimit (Institute of Building Technology Studies): Tiranë; tel. and fax 23811; f. 1979; library of 1,500 vols; Dir Ing. MUHANEM DELIU.

Instituti i Studimeve dhe Projektimeve Mekanike (Mechanics Research Institute): Rruga 'Ferit Xajko', Tiranë; tel. 28543; f. 1970; library of 3,000 vols; Dir NEDIM KAMBO.

Instituti i Studimeve e Projektimeve Industria Ushqimore (Institute of the Food Industry): Rr. M. Gjollesha, Tiranë; tel. 26770; telex 4206; fax 26807; f. 1962; Dir KUJTIM BIÇAKU; publ. *Përmbledhje Studimesh* (Collections of Studies, irregular).

Laboratori i Kërkimeve Hidraulike (Laboratory of Hydraulic Research): Tiranë; f. 1968; attached to Acad. of Sciences; Dir LEFTER CANE; publ. *Kërkime dhe Studime Hidraulike* (Hydraulic Research and Studies, irregular).

Libraries and Archives

Durrës

Durrës Public Library: Durrës; tel. 22281; f. 1945; 180,462 vols; Dir PIRRO DOLLANI.

Elbasan

Elbasan Public Library: Elbasan; f. 1934; 284,000 vols.

Gjirokastër

Gjirokastër Public Library: Gjirokastër; 90,000 vols.

Korçë

Korçë Public Library: Korçë; f. 1938; 139,000 vols.

Shkodër

Shkodër Public Library: Shkodër; f. 1935; 250,000 vols.

Tiranë

Centre for Scientific and Technical Information and Documentation: Tiranë; f. 1981; attached to Cttee of Science and Technology; Dir AGIM NESHO; publ. *Buletin Analitik Ndërfushor dhe Fushor* (Interdisciplinary and Disciplinary Analytical Bulletin, irregular).

National Library: Tiranë; tel. and fax 23843; f. 1922; 1,000,000 vols; Dir NERMIN BASHA; publs *National Bibliography of Albanian Books* (quarterly), *National Bibliography of Albanian Periodicals* (monthly).

Scientific Library: Tiranë; f. 1972; attached to Acad. of Sciences; Dir NATASHA PANO.

State Central Archives: Tiranë; document conservation and research.

Museums and Art Galleries

Berat

Architecture Museum: Berat.

District Historical Museum: Berat; Dir LIMAN VAROSHI.

Ethnographic Museum: Berat.

'Onufri' Iconographic Museum: Berat; f. 1986; sited in the town's castle; exhibits include icons by the medieval painter, Onufri.

Durrës

Archaeological Museum: Durrës; f. 1951; exhibits representing life in ancient Durrës.

Ethnographic Museum: Durrës.

Museum of the Struggle for National Liberation: Durrës.

Elbasan

District Ethnographic Museum: Elbasan.

District Historical Museum: Elbasan.

Kristoforidhi, K., House-Museum: Elbasan; birth-place of the patriot and linguist; Dir LIMAN VAROSHI.

Museum of Education: Elbasan.

Museum of the Struggle for National Liberation: Elbasan.

Stafa, Q., House-Museum: Elbasan; birthplace of the national hero; Dir LIMAN VAROSHI.

Fier

Archaeological Museum: Fier; f. 1958; exhibits include archaeological items from the former town of Apollonia.

District Historical Museum: Fier; tel. 2583; f. 1948; Dir PETRIT MALUSHI.

Gjirokastër

Ethnographic Museum: Gjirokastër.

Museum of the Struggle for National Liberation: Gjirokastër.

National Renaissance Museum: Gjirokastër.

Rustemi, A., House-Museum: Gjirokastër.

Korçë

Ethnographic Museum: Korcë.

Fine Arts Gallery: Korçë.

Mio, V., House-Museum: Korçë; house where the painter worked; contains works of art by Mio.

Museum of Albanian Medieval Art: Korçë; f. 1981.

Museum of Education: Korçë; development of education in Albania.

Museum of the Struggle for National Liberation: Bulevard Repuplika, Korçë; tel. 2888; f. 1977; library of 400 vols.

National Renaissance Museum: Korçë.

Kruja

Scanderbeg Museum: Kruja; memorabilia of the nat. hero.

Përmet

District Historical Museum: Përmet.

Frashëri Brothers Museum: Përmet; birthplace of the brothers Frashëri.

Shkodër

District Historical Museum: Shkodër.

Gurakuqi, Luigi, House-Museum: Shkodër; house where the patriot lived.

Migjeni House-Museum: Shkodër; where the writer Migjeni lived.

National Exhibition of Popular Culture: Shkodër.

Pascha, Vaso, House-Museum: Shkodër; house where the patriot lived.

Tiranë

Albanian National Culture Museum: Tiranë; attached to the Institute of Nat. Culture; exhibits include agricultural tools of all periods, stock-breeding equipment, interiors and exteriors, household objects, textiles and customs, local crafts and ceramics up to the present day.

Fine Arts Gallery: Tiranë; Dir KSENOFON DILO.

National Museum of Archaeology: Tiranë; tel. 26541; telex 2214; f. 1948; attached to the Institute of Archaeology of the Acad. of Sciences; exhibits from prehistoric and historic times up to Middle Ages; responsible for archaeological museums at Durrës, Apollonia and Butrinti; library of 7,200 vols, film and photograph libraries; Curator ILIR GJIPALI; publ. *Illyria* (2 a year).

National Historical Museum: Skenderbe Square, Tiranë; tel. and fax 28389; f. 1981; Illyrian and Graeco-Roman artefacts, history of modern Albania; Dir VILSON KURI.

Natural Science Museum: Tiranë; attached to the Univ. of Tiranë; zoology, botany, geology.

Vlorë

District Historical Museum: Vlorë; tel. 2646; f. 1953; archaeology, history of art, history.

Independence Museum: Vlorë; tel. 2481; f. 1962; Chief Officer BASLUKIM FIFO.

Nushi Brothers Museum: Vuno, Vlorë.

Universities

FAN S. NOLI UNIVERSITY

Rr. Gjergj Kastrioti, Korçë

Telephone and fax: (824) 2230

Founded 1971 as Higher Agricultural Institute; present name and title 1992
State control
Language of instruction: English
Academic year: October to July

Rector: Asst Prof. Dr GJERGJI PENDAVINJI
Vice-Rector: Dr ROBERT DAMO
Chief Administrative Officer: PETRIKA PETRO
Librarian: IDA KANXHERI

Library of 22,000 vols
Number of teachers: 76
Number of students: 1,720 (incl. correspondence students)

Publication: *Bulletin*.

DEANS

Faculty of Agriculture: Dr EDMOND SPAHIU
Faculty of Economics: Dr ELFRIDA KOSTA
Faculty of Education: Dr PANDI NAPUCE

LUIGJ GURAKUQI UNIVERSITY OF SHKODËR

Shkodër

Telephone and fax: 3747

Founded 1991; based on former Instituti i Lartë Pedagogjik (Higher Pedagogical Institute), Shkodër (f. 1957)
State control
Academic year: September to July

Rector: Dr GJOVALIN KOLOMBI
Vice-Rector: ARTAN HAXHI
Registrar: SKENDER BILALI
Librarian: GEZIM VARFI

Number of teachers: 120
Number of students: 1,860
Publication: *Scientific Bulletin*.

DEANS

Faculty of Social Sciences: MIASER DIBRA
Faculty of Natural Sciences: FADIL GALIQI
Faculty of Education: VEHBI HOTI

UNIVERSITETI BUJQËSOR I TIRANËS (Agricultural University of Tiranë)

Kamzë, Tiranë

Telephone: 28201
Fax: 27804

Founded 1971
State control
Academic year: September to June

Rector: BESNIK GJONOGECAJ
Vice-Rector: VLADIMIR SPAHO

Library of 126,000 vols
Number of teachers: 230
Number of students: 2,300

Publications: *Buletini i Shkencave Bujqësore* (Bulletin of Agricultural Sciences, quarterly), faculty publs.

DEANS

Faculty of Agronomy: PELRIL RAMA
Faculty of Veterinary Science: DASHAMIR XHAXHIU
Faculty of Forestry: ANESTI POSTOLI
Faculty of Rural Economics: ARBEN VËRÇUNI

UNIVERSITETI I TIRANËS (University of Tiranë)

Tiranë

Telephone and fax: 28258
Telex: 2211

Founded 1957
Academic year: September to June

Rector: Dr HALIL SYKJA
Vice-Rector: SULEJMAN KODRA
Library Director: BEHAR SINANI

Library of 700,000 vols
Number of teachers: 750
Number of students: 8,755

Publications: *Buletini i Shkencave të Natyrës* (Natural Sciences, quarterly), *Buletini i Shkencave Mjekësore* (Medicine, quarterly), *Përmbledhje studimesh* (Collection of Studies, quarterly, with Institutes of Geological Research).

DEANS

Faculty of Natural Science: Prof. Dr REXHEP MEJDANI
Faculty of Medicine: Doc. KRISTO PANO
Faculty of Foreign Languages: Doc. AVNI XHELILI
Faculty of History and Linguistics: Dr PASKAL MILO
Faculty of Law: ZEF BROZI
Faculty of Economics: Dr KADRI XHULALI
Faculty of Philosophy and Sociology: Doc. LUAN PIRDENI
Faculty of Mechanics and Electronics: Dr GËZIM KARAPICI

Higher Institutes

Akademia e Arteve, Tiranë (Academy of Arts, Tiranë): Dëshmorët e Kombit St, Tiranë; tel. and fax (42) 25488; f. 1966; faculties of fine arts, music and drama; 120 teachers, 680 students; library of 40,000 vols; Rector Prof. GJERGJ ZHEJI.

ALGERIA

Learned Societies

GENERAL

El-Djazairia el-Mossilia: 1 rue Hamitouche, Algiers; f. 1930; cultural society, particularly concerned with Arab classical music; 452 mems; Pres. ALI BENMERABET; Sec.-Gen. ABDELHADI MERAOUBI.

HISTORY, GEOGRAPHY AND ARCHAEOLOGY

Société Archéologique du Département de Constantine (Constantine Archaeological Society): Musée Gustave Mercier, Constantine; f. 1852; 250 mems; library of 10,000 vols; Pres. Dr BAGHLI (acting); publ. *Recueil des Notices et Mémoires*.

Société Historique Algérienne (Algerian Historical Society): C/o Faculté des Lettres, Université d'Alger, Algiers; f. 1963; 600 mems; publ. *Revue d'Histoire et Civilisation du Maghreb*.

MEDICINE

Union Médicale Algérienne (Algerian Medical Association): 52 Blvd Mohamed V, Algiers; publ. *Algérie Médicale*.

Research Institutes

GENERAL

Organisme National de la Recherche Scientifique (National Bureau of Scientific Research): Route de Dély Ibrahim, Ben Aknoun, Algiers; main executive body for government policy; Dir (vacant).

Research centres:

Centre d'Etudes et de Recherche sur le Développement Régional, Annaba (CERDA) (Annaba Study and Research Centre for Regional Development): Université d'Annaba, Annaba; Dir M. AMIRI.

Centre d'Etudes et de Recherche sur le Développement Régional, Oran (CERDO) (Oran Study and Research Centre for Regional Development): Université d'Oran, Es-Senia, Oran; Dir M. TALEB.

Centre d'Etudes et de Recherches en Biologie Humaine et Animale (CERBHA) (Study and Research Centre for Human and Animal Biology): BP 9, Université des Sciences et de la Technologie Houari Boumédienne, Algiers; Dir K. BENLATRACHE.

Centre de Coordination des Etudes et des Recherches sur les Infrastructures, les Equipements du Ministère de l'Enseignement et de la Recherche Scientifique (Centre for the Co-ordination of Studies and Research on the Infrastructure and Facilities of the Ministry of Education and on Scientific Research): 1 rue Bachir Attar, Algiers; Dir A. GUEDIRI.

Centre d'Information Scientifique et Technique et de Transferts Technologiques (CISTTT) (Centre for Scientific and Technical Information and for Technological Transfer): BP 315, blvd Frantz Fanon, Algiers (Gare); Dir M. TIAR (acting).

Centre de Recherches Anthropologiques, Préhistoriques et Ethnographiques (CRAPE) (Centre for Anthropological, Prehistoric and Ethnographical Research): 3 blvd Franklin Roosevelt, Algiers; f. 1957; Dir M. BELKAID.

Centre de Recherches en Architecture et Urbanisme (CRAU) (Centre for Research in Architecture and Town Planning): BP 2, El-Harrach, Algiers; Dir AMEZIANE IKENE.

Centre de Recherches en Economie Appliquées (CREA) (Centre for Research in Applied Economics): 20 rue Mustapha Khallef, Ben Aknoun, Algiers; Dir ABDELATIF BENACHENHOU.

Centre de Recherches Océanographiques et des Pêches (CROP) (Centre for Oceanographic and Fisheries Research): Jetée Nord, Amirauté, Algiers; Dir RACHID SEMROUD.

Centre de Recherches sur les Ressources Biologiques Terrestres (CRBT) (Centre for Research on Biological Resources of the Land): 2 rue Didouche Mourad, Algiers; Dir (vacant).

Centre National d'Astronomie, d'Astrophysique et de Géophysique (CNAAG) (National Centre of Astronomy, Astrophysics and Geophysics): Observatoire de Bouzaréah, Algiers; Dir H. BENHALLOU.

Centre National d'Etudes et de Recherche en Energie Renouvelable (CRENO) (National Study and Research Centre for Renewable Energy): Observatoire de Bouzaréah, Algiers; Dir M. BOUADEF.

Centre National d'Etudes et de Recherches pour l'Aménagement du Territoire (CNERAT) (National Centre for Studies and Research in National and Regional Development): 3 rue Professor Vincent, Telemly, Algiers; Dir MESSAOUD TAIEB.

Centre National de Documentation et de Recherche en Pédagogie (CNDRP) (National Documentation and Research Centre for Education): Université d'Alger, 2 rue Didouche Mourad, Algiers; Dir M. D. CHABOU.

Centre National de Recherche sur les Zones Arides (CNRZA) (National Centre for Research on Arid Zones): Université d'Alger, 2 rue Didouche Mourad, Algiers; Dir N. BOUNAGA (acting).

Centre National de Recherches et d'Application des Géosciences (CRAG) (National Centre for Geoscientific Research and Application): 2 rue Didouche Mourad, Algiers; Dir R. ABDELHALIM.

Centre National de Traduction et de Terminologie Arabe (CNTTA) (National Centre for Arab Translation and Terminology): 3 blvd Franklin Roosevelt, Algiers; Dir A. MEZIANE.

Centre Universitaire de Recherches, d'Etudes et de Réalisations (CURER) (University Centre for Research, Study and Application): Université de Constantine, 54 rue Larbi Ben M'Hidi, Constantine; agriculture, forestry, energy resources; Dir FELLAH LAZHAR.

AGRICULTURE, FISHERIES AND VETERINARY SCIENCE

Institut National de la Recherche Agronomique (INRAA) (National Institute of Agronomic Research): 2 ave des Frères Ouadak, Belfort, El Harrach, Algiers; tel. 75-63-15; telex 64166; f. 1966; library of 6,500 vols; Dir M. BEKKOUCHE; publ. *Bulletin d'Agronomie Saharienne*.

Institut National de Recherche Forestière (National Institute of Forestry Research): Arboretum de Bainem, Algiers; tel. 79-72-96; telex 61407; fax 78-32-11; f. 1981; library of 4,000 vols; Dir FATEH DAHIEDINE; publ. *Annale de la recherche forestière*.

BIBLIOGRAPHY, LIBRARY SCIENCE AND MUSEOLOGY

Institut de Bibliothéconomie et des Sciences Documentaires (Institute of Library Economics and Documentation): Université d'Alger, 2 rue Didouche Mourad, Algiers; f. 1975.

HISTORY, GEOGRAPHY AND ARCHAEOLOGY

Centre National d'Etudes Historiques (National Centre for Historical Studies): Palais de la Culture, Plateau des Annassers, Kouba; tel. 58-68-95; f. 1973; historic and prehistoric studies; library of 35,000 vols; Dir M. SAOUDI; publ. *Madjallat et Tarikh* (every 2 months).

Institut National de Cartographie (National Institute of Cartography): 123 rue de Tripoli, BP 69, Hussein-Dey, Algiers; f. 1967; under trusteeship of Min. of Defence; Dir NADIR SAADI; publs maps (100 to 150 a year).

MEDICINE

Institut National d'Hygiène et de Sécurité (National Institute of Hygiene and Safety): Lotissement Meridja, Box 07, 42395 Saoula; f. 1972; research in the fields of hygiene and safety at work; library of 8,000 vols, 110 periodicals, 45,000 microfiches; Dir Gen. CHÉRIF SOUAMI; publ. *Revue Algérienne de Prévention* (quarterly).

Institut Pasteur d'Algérie (Pasteur Institute in Algeria): Rue du Dr Laveran, Algiers; tel. 65-88-60; telex 65337; fax 67-25-03; f. 1910; research and higher studies in microbiology, parasitology and immunology; preparation of vaccines and sera in conjunction with the health services of Algeria; library of 47,000 vols, 500 periodicals; Dir Prof. F. BOULAHBAL; publ. *Archives* (annually).

TECHNOLOGY

Commissariat aux Energies Nouvelles (Commission for New Sources of Energy): BP 1017, Algiers-Gare; tel. 61-14-18; telex 52245; f. 1983; research and development in the field of renewable sources of energy, including atomic, solar, wind and geothermal energy; includes centres for energy conversion and for nuclear and solar studies.

Office National de la Recherche Géologique et Minière (National Office of Geological and Mining Research): BP 102, Boumerdes, Algiers; tel. 81-96-81; telex 63486; f. 1883; library of 50,000 vols, periodicals, maps and aerial photographs; Dir MOHAND TAHAR BOUAROUDJ; publs *Bulletins, Mémoires, Cartes Géologiques, Notices explicatives*.

Libraries and Archives

Algiers

Archives Nationales d'Algérie (National Archives of Algeria): BP 61, Algiers-Gare; tel. (2) 54-21-60; fax (2) 54-16-16; Dir ABDELKRIM BADJADJA.

Bibliothèque de l'Université d'Alger (Library of the University of Algiers): 2 rue Didouche Mourad, Algiers; tel. 64-02-15; fax 61-31-44; f. 1880; 800,000 vols.

Bibliothèque Nationale (National Library): 1 ave Frantz Fanon, Algiers; tel. 63-06-32; f. 1835; 950,000 vols; spec. collns incl. Africa and the Maghreb; Dir MUHAMMAD AÏSSA-MOUSSA; publs *Bibliographie de l'Algérie* (2 a year), *Publications*, several collections in Arabic and French.

Section de Diffusion Scientifique et Technique du Centre Culturel Français d'Alger (Department for the Distribution of Scientific and Technical Information at the French Cultural Centre in Algiers): 7 rue du Médecin Capitaine Hassani Issad, 16000 Algiers; tel. 63-61-83; library of 25,000 vols, 350 periodicals; Dir MARC SAGAERT.

Constantine

Bibliothèque Municipale (Municipal Library): Hôtel de Ville, Constantine; f. 1895; 25,000 vols.

Museums and Art Galleries

Algiers

Direction du Patrimoine Culturel (Office of Cultural Heritage): Ministère de la Culture et du Tourisme, Kouba, Algiers; f. 1901; gen. admin. of museums, restoration, conservation and archaeological excavations; library of 8,000 vols, 300 periodicals; Dir Ş. A. BAGHLI; publ. *Bulletin d'Archéologie Algérienne* (annually).

Musée National des Antiquités (National Museum of Antiquities): Parc de la Liberté, Algiers; tel. 74-66-86; fax 74-74-71; f. 1897; library of 3,100 vols, 102 periodicals; Dir DRIAS LAKHDAR; publ. *Annales du Musée National des Antiquités*.

Musée National des Beaux Arts d'Alger (National Fine Arts Museum of Algiers): Place Dar-el-Salem, El-Hamma, Algiers; tel. 66-49-16; telex 65129; fax 66-20-54; f. 1930; library of 17,000 vols, 300 journal titles; Dir DALILA ORFALI; publ. *Revue* (1 a year).

Musée National du Bardo: 3 rue F. D. Roosevelt, Algiers; tel. 74-76-41; f. 1930; prehistory, ethnography; library of 500 vols; Dir TOUIL ABDELLALI; publs catalogues of collections.

Musée National du Djihad: El Madania, Algiers; tel. 65-34-88; f. 1983; contemporary history; publ. *Actes du Musée*.

Constantine

Musée de Cirta: Blvd de la République, Constantine; f. 1853; archaeology, art; library of 20,000 vols; Dir AHMED GUEDDOUDA; publ. *Recueil et Mémoires de la Société Archéologique de Constantine*.

Oran

Musée National Zabana: Blvd Zabana, Oran; tel. 34-37-81; telex 22590; f. 1935; prehistory, Roman and Punic archaeology, ethnography, zoology, geology, botany, sculpture and painting; Dir Dr MALKI NORDINE.

Sétif

Musée de Sétif: C/o Musée Marsa el-Kharez, BP 41, El-Kala; located at Sétif; f. 1991; Roman antiquities; Curator TAYEB HAFIANE.

Skikda

Musée de Skikda: Skikda; Punic and Roman antiquities, modern art.

Tlemcen

Musée de Tlemcen: Place Khemisti, 13000 Tlemcen; tel. (7) 26-55-06; Islamic art, minerals, botany, Numidian and Roman archaeology.

Universities

UNIVERSITÉ D'ALGER

2 rue Didouche Mourad, Algiers

Telephone: 64-69-70

Founded 1879 (reorganized 1909)

Languages of instruction: Arabic and French

State control

Academic year: September to June

Rector: AMAR SAKHRI

Vice-Rectors: S. BABA-AMEUR (Pedagogy), A. E. R. AZZI (Post-graduates and Scientific Research), RABAH KHIMA (Planning)

Librarian: ABDELLAH ABDI

Number of teachers: 1,400

Number of students: 32,000

UNIVERSITY INSTITUTES

Institut de Sciences juridiques et administratives: 11 Chemin Mokhtar Doudou ITFC, Ben-Aknoun; f. 1885; library of 60,000 vols, 500 periodicals; Dir Mr ZOUINA; publ. *Revue algérienne des sciences juridiques*.

Institut des Sciences Economiques: 2 rue Colonel Azzoug, Côte Rouge, Hussein Dey, Algiers; Dir DJILLALI DJELLATOU.

Institut des Sciences Politiques et Relations Internationales: 11 Chemin Mokhtar Doudou ITFC, Ben-Aknoun, Algiers; Dir Mr DEBÈCHE.

Institut de l'Information et de la Communication: 11 Chemin Mokhtar Doudou ITFC, Ben-Aknoun, Algiers; Dir Mr BEN-ZAOUI.

Institut de Langue et Littérature Arabes: 2 rue Didouche Mourad, Algiers; Dir Mr HADJAR.

Institut de Psychologie et Sciences de l'Education: c/o Ecole supérieure des transmissions, Bouzaréah, Algiers; Dir Mr LABOUDI.

Institut de Sociologie: c/o Ecole supérieure des transmissions, Bouzaréah, Algiers; Dir Mr GHALAMALLAH.

Institut d'Histoire: c/o Ecole supérieure des transmissions, Bouzaréah, Algiers; Dir Mr BEN-AMIRA.

Institut de Philosophie: c/o Ecole supérieure des transmissions, Bouzaréah, Algiers; Dir Mr ZEKKI.

Institut d'Archéologie: 2 rue Didouche Mourad, Algiers; Dir Mr BENGUERBA.

Institut des Langues Etrangères: c/o Ecole supérieure des transmissions, Bouzaréah, Algiers; Dir Mr HASSAINE.

Institut de Bibliothéconomie: f. 1975; EXEMEPS, Dely-Ibrahim, Algiers; Dir Mr TIAR.

Institut d'Interprétariat et traduction: 2 rue Didouche Mourad, Algiers; Dir AHMED ABBACHI.

Centre Intensif des Langues: 2 rue Didouche Mourad, Algiers; Dir Mr BOUCHAIB.

UNIVERSITÉ DES SCIENCES ET DE LA TECHNOLOGIE HOUARI BOUMEDIENNE

BP 32, El Alia, Bab Ezzouar, Algiers

Telephone: (2) 51-55-75

Fax: (2) 51-59-92

Founded 1974

Languages of instruction: Arabic, French

Academic year: September to June (2 semesters)

Rector: TAHA HOCINE ZERGUINI

Vice-Rectors: MALIKA DAHMANI, RABAH BAKOUR, SOLTANE LEBAILI

Secretary-General: RABAH BENGHANEM

Librarian: SAIDA BOUAOUNE

Number of teachers: 1,853

Number of students: 19,016

Publication: *Annales des Sciences et de la Technologie*.

DIRECTORS

Institute of Natural Sciences: RABEA SERIDJI
Institute of Chemistry: OUIZA CHERIFI
Institute of Mathematics: MOHAMED BENTARZI
Institute of Physics: EL KHIDER SI AHMED
Institute of Earth Sciences: MOULOUD IDRESS
Institute of Electronics: MOKHTAR ATTARI
Institute of Civil Engineering: MOHAMED CHABAAT
Institute of Mechanical Engineering: ABDELAZIZ ATTI
Institute of Industrial Engineering: RACHIDA MAACHI
Institute of Computer Science: HABIBA DRIESS
Institute of Higher Technical Studies: MOHAMED AREZKI BOUZEGHOUB

UNIVERSITÉ DE ANNABA

BP 12, El Hadjar, Annaba

Telephone: 87-89-07

Telex: 81847

Fax: 87-24-36

Founded 1975

State control

Languages of instruction: Arabic and French

Academic year: September to June

Rector: M. AMIR

Vice Rectors: A. ABDERRAHMANE (Postgraduate Studies and Research), M. T. LASKRI (Pedagogy), H. ZAOUI (Planning)

Chief Administrative Officer: S. ARABI

Librarian: B. FERAH

Number of teachers: 1,018

Number of students: 13,342

Publication: *Revue de l'Université*

DIRECTORS

Institute of Economic Sciences: B. NABET
Institute of Mines: D. MEHRI
Institute of Metallurgy: A. BOUCIF
Institute of Civil Engineering: F. HABITA
Institute of Mechanical Engineering: A. SKENDRAOUI
Institute of Electronics: B. DJEDDOU
Institute of Electrotechnics: A. MOUSSAOUI
Institute of Computer Sciences: M. MIZI
Institute of Physics: D. E. MEKKI
Institute of Chemistry: K. BERREZEG
Institute of Mathematics: N. FARFAR
Institute of Natural Sciences: M. GUELLATI
Institute of Social Sciences: A. BOUGUESSAS
Institute of Law and Administrative Sciences: A. DJEBELKHEIR
Institute of Languages and Arabic Literature: B. MOKNECHE
Institute of Foreign Languages: M. MANAA
Institute of Geology: B. BENLAKHLEF
Institute of Industrial Chemistry: M. OUCHEFOUN
Institute of Agro-Veterinary Sciences: Z. BOUZEBDA

Institute of Intensive Language Teaching: R. Mahmoudi
Institute of Communication Sciences: F. Bouguetta

UNIVERSITÉ DE BATNA

Ave Chahid Boukhlouf, 05000 Batna
Telephone: (4) 86-00-39
Fax: (4) 86-38-63
E-mail: unibat@ist.cerist.dz

Founded 1977 as Centre Universitaire de Batna

Rector: Mohamed Laabassi
Vice-Rectors: Mohamed Melizi, Ali Benzaid
Secretary-General: Rachid Merazguia

Library of 55,000 vols

Publications: *Revue des Sciences Sociales et Humaines* (2 a year), *Revue de l'I.E.E.A. Engineering* (2 a year).

Science and technology, humanities and social sciences, economics, agronomic and veterinary sciences, medicine, hydraulic and civil engineering.

UNIVERSITÉ DE BLIDA

Route de Soumaa Blida, BP 270, Blida
Telephone: (3) 41-10-00
Telex: 72970
Fax: (3) 41-78-13

Founded 1981 as Centre Universitaire de Blida

Rector: Zetili Noureddine
Vice-Rectors: Guend Abdelhani (Administration), Nader Salah (Teaching), Khelil Amara (Post-Graduate Affairs)

Number of teachers: 644
Number of students: 7,990

Publications: *Revue de l'Université.*

Departments of mechanics, aeronautics, electronics, industrial chemistry, architecture, civil engineering, agronomy, agricultural engineering, medicine, veterinary science, economics, mathematics, physics, law, social sciences, and language and literature.

UNIVERSITÉ DE BOUMERDES

Boumerdes
Founded 1981

CONSTITUENT INSTITUTES

Institut National des Hydrocarbures

Institut National de Productivité et Développement

Institut National des Industries Légères

Institut National de Génie Mécanique

Institut National d'Electricité et d'Electronique

Institut Algérien de Pétroléum

UNIVERSITÉ DE CONSTANTINE

Route d'Aïn El Bey, Constantine
Telephone: 69-73-85
Telex: 92436

Founded 1969
Languages of instruction: Arabic and French

Rector: Mourad Bensari
Vice-Rectors: Abdelhamid Djekoline (Teaching), Salah Eddine Bououd (Postgraduate Research), Mohamed Belakroum (Equipment, Orientation)
Secretary-General: Abdelkrim Benarab
Librarian: Noureddine Tachour

Library of 208,000 vols
Number of teachers: 1,770
Number of students: 22,000

Institutes of law and administration, Arabic, social sciences, psychology, biology, architecture and town planning, physics, chemistry, mathematics, earth sciences, economics, foreign languages, computer science, civil and mechanical engineering, agriculture and nutrition, veterinary science, technology, industrial chemistry, electronics, sociology, physical education, library science; also a pre-university centre and audio-visual department.

UNIVERSITÉ D'ORAN ES-SENIA

BP 1524, Es-Senia, Oran El-M'Naouer, Oran
Telephone: 41-69-54
Telex: 21493
Fax: 41-01-57

Founded 1965
State control
Languages of instruction: Arabic and French
Academic year: September to July (2 semesters)

Rector: Mohamed Abbou
Vice-Rector for Postgraduate Studies, Research and External Relations: Abdelbaki Benziane
Vice-Rector for Planning and Equipment: Abdelkader Bengueddach
Vice-Rector for Pedagogy and Registration: Mr Bentazi
Secretary-General: Abdelkader Bekkada
Librarian: Ahmed Ouramdane

Library of 200,000 vols
Number of teachers: 798
Number of students: 21,575

Publications: *Cahiers de Géographie de l'Ouest Algérien, Cahiers du Centre de Documentation des Sciences Humaines, Revue des Langues, Cahiers Mathématiques, Proceedings of the Research Unit in Social and Cultural Anthropology.*

DIRECTORS

Institute of Economics: Abdenasser Rouissat
Institute of Law and Administration: Eddine Bouzid
Institute of Foreign Languages: Rachida Yacine
Institute of History: Abdelaziz Hadri
Institute of Sociology: Ahmed Lalaoui
Institute of Earth Sciences: Aïssa Safa
Institute of Arabic Language and Literature: Laaradj Morceli
Institute of Library Studies: Bencherki Benmeziane
Institute of Computer Science: Bouziane Beldjilali
Institute of Psychology and Education: Ahmed Maarouf
Institute of Chemistry: Abdelkader Tayeb
Institute of Mathematics: Moussedek Remili
Institute of Physics: Abdeslem Mamoun
Institute of Commerce: Abderrahmane Lellou
Institute of Philosophy: Boukhari Hamana
Institute of Population Studies: Aïssa Delenda
IGLAEIL Institute: Mohamed Tayebi
Institute of Geography and Land Management: Tadj Bouchikhaoui
Institute of Natural Sciences: Zitouni Boutiba

UNIVERSITÉ DES SCIENCES ET DE LA TECHNOLOGIE D'ORAN

BP 1505, El M'naouer, Oran
Telephone and Fax: (6) 45-15-81
Telex: 22701

Founded 1975
Languages of instruction: Arabic and French
Academic year: September to July

Rector: Dr Mohamed Mebarki
Vice-Rectors: Fouad Taleb (Postgraduate Studies, Research and External Relations), Dahane Kadri (Teaching and Re-training), Mohamed Bensafi (Planning and Orientation)
Secretary-General: Ahmed Benziane
Librarian: Bachir Yakoubi

Number of teachers: 542
Number of students: 10,452

DIRECTORS

Institute of Architecture: Mounir Sariane
Institute of Industrial Chemistry: Mohamed Hadjel
Institute of Electronics: Nasr-Eddine Berrahed
Institute of Electrotechnics: Azzedine Bendiabdellah
Institute of Civil Engineering: Mabrouk Hamane
Institute of Marine Engineering: Omar Imine
Institute of Mechanical Engineering: Mohamed Tebbal
Institute of Hydraulics: Abdelkrim Khaldi
Institute of Computer Science: Mohamed Ayachi
Institute of Languages: Khadidja Maghraoui
Institute of Metallurgy: Mohamed Bellahouel
Department of Geology: Mohamed Belkharoubi

UNIVERSITÉ FERHAT ABBAS – SÉTIF

Route de Scipion, 19000 Sétif
Telephone: (5) 90-88-93
Telex: 86077
Fax (05) 90-38-79

Founded 1978
State control

Languages of instruction: Arabic and French
Academic year: September to June

President: Djafar Benachour
Vice-Presidents: Dr N. Haddaoui (Research and Graduate Studies), Dr A. Guechi (Undergraduate Studies), Dr A. Tachraft (Planning and Information)
Secretary-General: Ali Bensemcha
Librarian: Chérif Chidekh

Number of teachers: 594
Number of students: 12,700

DIRECTORS

Institut de Biologie: Rachid Gharzouli
Institut d'Electronique: S. Berretili
Institut de Chimie Industrielle: B. Djellouli
Institut d'Informatique: Samir Akrouf
Institut de Mécanique: Ahmed Manallah
Institut des Sciences Economiques: H. Sahraoui
Institut des Sciences Médicales: R. Talbi
Institut des Langues Etrangères: Abdelkrim Zeghad
Institut d'Architecture: Tahar Bellal
Institut d'Electrotechnique: Saad Belkhiat
Institut de Tronc-Commun et Technologie: Mabrouk Benkhedimallah
Institut de Mathématiques: Boubekeur Merouani
Institut de Physique: Abdelaziz Mansouri
Institut de Droit: M. Karmed
Institut des Lettres Arabes: Belkacem Nouicer
Institut de Génie Civil: M. Mimoun

UNIVERSITÉ ABOU BEKR BELKAID TLEMCEN

22 rue Abi Ayed Abdelkrim, Faubourg Pasteur, BP 119, 13000 Tlemcen
Telephone: (7) 20-09-22
Telex: 18971
Fax: (7) 20-41-89

Founded 1974 as Centre Universitaire de Tlemcen
State control (by Ministry of Higher Education and Scientific Research)
Languages of instruction: Arabic, French
Academic year: September to July
Rector: Zoubir Chaouche-Ramdane

Vice-Rectors: SIDI MOHAMMED BOUCHENAK-KHELLADI (External Relations), GHAOUTI MEKANCHA (Teaching), FOUAD GHOMARI (Planning)
Secretary-General: ABDELDJALIL SARI ALI

Librarian: NOUREDDINE HADJI
Library of 66,000 vols

Number of teachers: 514
Number of students: 9,989

PROFESSORS

Science:
BENYOUCEF, B., Energy Physics
BOUAMOUD, M., Atomic Physics
BENMOUANA, M., Nuclear Engineering
BOUCHERIF, A., Applied Mathematics
HADJIAT, M., Mathematics
TALEB BENDIAB, S. A., Chemistry
BABA AHMED, A., Physical Chemistry

Medicine:
ALLAL, M. R., Radiology
BENKALFAT, F. Z., Cardiology
HADJ ALLAL, F., Otorhinolarygology
BENKALFAT, M., General Surgery

Social Sciences and Humanities:
BOUCHENAK KHELLADI, S. M., Management
BELMOKADEM, M., Quantitative Technology
DERRAGUI, Z., Literature
BENDIABDALLAH, A., Management
SOUTI, M., Finance
KALFAT, C., Criminology
KAHLOULA, M., Private Law
DENDOUNI, H., Civil Law

DIRECTORS

Institute of Exact Sciences: ABDERRAHIM CHOUKCHOU BRAHAM
Institute of Arabic Language and Literature: MOHAMMED ABBAS
Institute of Electronics: FETHI TARIK BENDIMERAD
Institute of Civil Engineering: MUSTAPHA DJAFFOUR.
Institute of Hydraulics: ZINE EL ABIDINE CHERIF
Institute of Economics: MOHAMMED ZINE BARKA
Institute of Popular Culture: OKACHA CHAIF
Institute of Biology: KEBIR BOUCHERIT
Institute of Earth Sciences: MOHAMED EL KHAMIS BAGHLI
Institute of Forestry: RACHID BOUHRAOUA
Institute of Medical Sciences: FOUZI TALEB
Institute of Law and Administration: MOHAMMED BENAMAR
Institute of Foreign Languages: ZOUBIR DENDEN
Institute of Mechanical Engineering: FETHI METALSI-TANI
Institute for the Promotion of the Arabic Language and for Intensive Language Training: BOUMÉDIÈNE BENMOUSSAT

University Centres

Centre Universitaire de Mostaganem: BP 227, Mostaganem; tel. (6) 26-46-60; fax (6) 26-46-62; e-mail cumosta@elbahia.cerist.dz; f. 1977; science, technology, arts; library of 75,000 vols; Dir Dr M. MOUAICI.

Centre Universitaire de Sidi-Bel-Abbès: comprises nat. institutes of higher studies in computer science, biology, administration, electrical engineering, medicine.

Centre Universitaire de Tizi-Ouzou: f. 1975; depts of law and administration, Arab studies, sciences and engineering; 6,500 students.

CENTRE UNIVERSITAIRE DE TIARET

BP 78, 14000 Tiaret
Telephone: (7) 42-42-13
Fax: (7) 42-41-47
E.mail: cut@ist.cerist.dz

Founded 1980 as Institut National d'Enseignement Supérieur de Tiaret; re-founded 1992
Languages of instruction: Arabic and French
Director: NASSREDINE HADJ ZOUBIR
Vice-Director of Studies: AHMED BENAMARA
Vice-Director of Postgraduate Studies and Scientific Research: SAHUAOUI HADJ-ZIANE
Librarian: ABED MAKHLOUFI

Number of teachers: 213
Number of students: 5,100

HEADS OF INSTITUTES

Agronomy: A. OUFFAI
Veterinary Medicine: A. NIAR
Civil Engineering: M. SAHNOUNE
Mechanical Engineering: A. SASSI
Electronic Engineering: A. BENAYADA
Environment: A. KHALDI

HEADS OF DEPARTMENTS

Technology: A. BELBRAOUAT
Physics: A. BENMEDJADI
Economics: B. MADANI
Arabic Literature: B. BERKANE
Law: A. CHERIET
Biology: A. BOUDALIA

Colleges

Conservatoire Municipal de Musique et de Déclamation: 5 rue d'Igli, Oran; f. 1932; courses in music, dancing and dramatic art; 20 teachers, 500 students; Dir GILLES ACHACHE.

Conservatoire de Musique et de Déclamation: 2 blvd Ché Guévara, Algiers; f. 1920; library contains 6,800 vols; 82 teachers, 2,300 students; Dir-Gen. BACHETARZI MOHIEDDINE; Sec.-Gen. KADDOUR GUECHOUD.

Ecole Supérieure des Beaux-Arts: Blvd Krim Belkacem, Parc Zyriab, Algiers; tel. (2) 74-90-09; fax (2) 74-91-14; f. 1881; painting, sculpture, ceramics, design; library of 9,000 vols; 65 teachers, 350 students; Dir MOHAMMED DJEHICHE.

Ecole Nationale Polytechnique: BP 182, Ave Pasteur, El-Harrach, Algiers 10; tel. (2) 52-10-27; fax (2) 52-29-73; e-mail enp@ist.cerist.dz; f. 1962; graduate and undergraduate courses in civil engineering, electronic and electrical engineering, telecommunications, chemical engineering and petrochemistry, mechanical engineering, environmental engineering, hydraulic engineering, mining and metallurgy, industrial engineering; library of 40,000 vols; 300 teachers, 1,500 undergraduate, 500 graduate students; Dir Dr M. K. BERRAH; publ. *Algerian Journal of Technology* (French and English).

DEANS

Graduate School: Dr M. K. BERRAH
Undergraduate School: Dr A. BOUBAKEUR

Ecole Nationale Vétérinaire: BP 161, Ave Pasteur, El-Harrach, Algiers; tel. 52-47-81; fax 52-59-04; f. 1974; 60 teachers, 900 students; library of 8,000 vols, 40 periodicals; Dir A. OTHMANI.

Ecole Polytechnique d'Architecture et d'Urbanisme: BP 2, El Harrach; f. 1970; attached to the University of Algiers; 91 staff, 409 students; library of 2,120 vols, 362 periodicals; Dir M. MOKDAD.

Ecole Supérieure de Commerce d'Alger: BP 313, Rampe F. Chasseriau, Algiers; f. 1900, attached to the University of Algiers 1966; 4-year first degree courses; 34 teachers, 485 students.

Institut des Sciences Politiques et de l'Information: 11 Chemin Doudou Mokhtar, Ibn-Aknoun, Algiers; tel. (2) 781518; fax (2) 796641; f. 1948 as result of merger between Ecole Supérieure de Journalisme and Institut d'Etudes Politiques; attached to the University of Algiers; 100 teachers, 2,000 students; Dir Dr ISMAIL DEBECHE.

Institut des Techniques de Planification: Complexes des Instituts de Technologie, Chemin de la Touche, Hydra, Algiers.

Institut des Télécommunications: Es-Senia, Oran; f. 1971.

Institut Hydrométéorologique de Formation et de Recherches (IHFR): BP 7019, Seddikia, Oran; tel. 42-28-01; fax 42-13-12; f. 1970; 200 students; library of 15,000 vols; Dir A. LAGHA.

Institut National Agronomique: 1 ave Pasteur, Hacen-Badi, El-Harrach, Algiers; tel. 52-19-87; fax 52-35-47; f. 1905; 177 teachers, 2,212 students; library of 66,000 vols and 400 periodicals; Dir GUEZLANE ELOUARDI; publ. *Annales* (2 a year).

ANDORRA

Learned Societies

GENERAL

Amics de la Cultura (Friends of Culture): Plaça Co-Prínceps 4 bis, Despatx no. 1, Escaldes-Engordany.

Associació Cultural i Artística Els Esquirols (Els Esquirols Cultural and Arts Association): Sala Parroquial, Plaça de l'Església, La Massana.

Centre de Trobada de les Cultures Pirenenques: Edif. Prada Casadet, Prat de la Creu, Andorra la Vella; tel. 60768; fax 61998; f. 1983; attached to Comunitat de Treball dels Pirineus; database on the Pyrenees; Dir ELISENDA VIVES BALMAÑA.

Cercle de les Arts i de les Lletres (Arts and Letters Circle): Avda Carlemany 24, Escaldes-Engordany; tel. 21233; f. 1968; Pres. JOAN BURGUÉS MARTISELLA.

BIBLIOGRAPHY, LIBRARY SCIENCE AND MUSEOLOGY

International Council of Museums, Andorran National Committee: Patrimoni Cultural d'Andorra, Carretera de Bixessarri s/n, Aixovall; tel. 844141; fax 844343; f. 1988; Pres. MARTA PLANAS DE LA MAZA; Sec. MA. ÀNGELS RUF RIBA.

NATURAL SCIENCES

General

Societat Andorrana de Ciències (Andorra Scientific Society): Carrer Princep Benlloch 30 (3er pis), Andorra la Vella; tel. 829729; fax 852383; e-mail sac@andorra.ad; f. 1983; Pres. JOSEP VILANOVA; Sec. ANGELS MACH; publ. *El Sac* (monthly).

Biological Sciences

Associació per a la Defensa de la Natura (Association for Nature Conservation): Apartat de Correus Espanyols 96, Andorra la Vella; tel. 843248; fax 843868; e-mail adn@andorra.ad; f. 1986; 300 mems; Pres. SERGI RIBA; Sec. WIEBKE BERGER; publ. *Agüerola*.

Research Institutes

GENERAL

Institut d'Estudis Andorrans (Institute of Andorran Studies): Edif. Crédit Centre, C/ Bonaventura Armengol 6–8, Andorra la Vella; tel. 866585; fax 861229; e-mail iea@andorra.ad; f. 1976; Dir JORDI GUILLAMET.

Libraries and Archives

Andorra la Vella

Arxiu Històric Nacional (National Historic Archive): Prat de la Creu 8–12, Edif. Prada Casadet, Andorra la Vella; tel. 861889; fax 868645; e-mail sacultuna@andorra.ad; f. 1975; 200,000 documents; Head of Service SUSANNA VELA PALOMARES.

Biblioteca Nacional d'Andorra (Andorra National Library): Edif. Prada Casadet, Prat de la Creu, Andorra la Vella; tel. 828750; fax 829541; f. 1974; legal deposit; 45,000 vols, 100 periodicals; spec. colln on medieval history; Chief Librarian ANNA ARANA I MASSANA.

Canillo

Biblioteca Comunal de Canillo (Canillo Community Library): Comú de Canillo, Canillo; tel. 51888; f. 1988; 3,000 vols; Librarian DOLORS CALVÓ.

Encamp

Biblioteca Comunal d'Encamp (Encamp Community Library): Complex Socio-Cultural i Esportiu, Prat del Bau, Encamp; tel. 31080; fax 32034; f. 1980; 17,000 vols.

Escaldes-Engordany

Biblioteca del Centre Cultural d'Escaldes-Engordany (Library of the Escaldes-Engordany Cultural Centre): Passeig del Valira 9, Escaldes-Engordany; tel. 860729; fax 828959; f. 1972; 26,000 vols; Librarian ALEXIA CARRERAS SIRES.

La Massana

Biblioteca Comunal de la Massana (Massana Community Library): Cap del Carrer, La Massana; tel. 836920; fax 835834; f. 1990; library of 6,500 vols; Librarian NURIA PORQUERES.

Museums and Art Galleries

Andorra la Vella

Museu Filatèlic i Postal (Philatelic and Postal Museum): Casa de la Vall, Andorra la Vella; tel. 29129; f. 1986.

Encamp

Museu Nacional de l'Automòbil (National Motor Car Museum): Avda Co-Princep Episcopal 64, Encamp; tel. 32266; f. 1988; cars, motorbikes and bicycles from 1898 to 1950, components, miniature cars in porcelain and iron.

Escaldes-Engordany

Museu Viladomat: Avda Josep Viladomat s/n, Escaldes-Engordany; tel. and fax 829340; e-mail museuviladomat@andorra.ad; f. 1987; Curator GLORIA PUJOL.

Ordino

Museu Casa Areny de Plandolit: Ordino; tel. 36908; f. 1987; typical 17th-century house, with later alterations; furniture, porcelain, costumes, etc.

ANGOLA

Learned Societies

LANGUAGE AND LITERATURE

União dos Escritores Angolanos (Association of Angolan Writers): CP 2767-C, Luanda; tel. 322155; telex 3056; f. 1975; 75 mems; library of 2,000 vols; Sec.-Gen. LUANDINO VIEIRA; publs. *Lavra & Oficina* (monthly), *Criar* (quarterly).

Research Institutes

AGRICULTURE, FISHERIES AND VETERINARY SCIENCE

Centro de Investigação Científica Algodeira (Cotton Scientific Research Centre): Instituto do Algodão de Angola, Estação Experimental de Onga-Zanga, Catete; fibre technology laboratory, agricultural machinery station, crop irrigation station (Bombagem); library; Dir Eng. Agr. JOAQUIM RODRIGUES PEREIRA.

Instituto de Investigação Agronómica (Agronomic Research Institute): CP 406, Huambo; f. 1962; incorporates agrarian documentation centre; publs *Comunicações, Série Divulgação, Relatório Anual.*

Instituto de Investigação Veterinária (Institute for Veterinary Research): CP 405, Lubango; tel. 22094; f. 1965; Dir Dr A. M. POMBAL; publs *Relatório Anual, Acta Veterinaria-separatas* (annually).

MEDICINE

Instituto de Investigação Medica de Angola (Angola Medical Research Institute): Luanda; f. 1955.

NATURAL SCIENCES

Physical Sciences

Direcção Provincial dos Serviços de Geologia e Minas de Angola (Angolan Directorate of Geological and Mining Services): CP 1260-C, Luanda; f. 1914; geology, geological mapping and exploration of mineral deposits; library of 40,000 vols; Dir J. TRIGO MIRA; publs *Boletim, Memória, Carta Geológica de Angola.*

Libraries and Archives

Luanda

Arquivo Histórico Nacional (National Historical Archive): Rua Pedro Félix Machado 49, Luanda; tel. 334410; telex 4129; fax 323979; f. 1977; 20,000 vols, 3,000 periodicals; Dir ROSA CRUZ E SILVA; publs *Guias de Informação Documental para o Estudo da História de Angola.*

Biblioteca Municipal (Municipal Library): CP 1227, Luanda; tel. 392297; fax 33902; f. 1873; 30,000 vols; Librarian ANTONIO JOSÉ EMIDIO DE BRITO.

Biblioteca Nacional de Angola (National Library of Angola): Rua Comandante Jika, CP 2915, Luanda; tel. 322070; fax 323979; f. 1969; 84,000 vols; IFLA collection legal deposit, nat. deposit for UNESCO and FAO publs; Dir ALEXANDRA APARICIO.

Museums and Art Galleries

Luanda

Instituto Nacional do Patrimonio Cultural (National Institute for Cultural Heritage): CP 1267, Luanda; tel. 332575; telex 4129; national antiquities dept; Dir OSCAR GUIMARÃES.

Affiliated museums:

Museu Central das Forças Armadas (Central Museum of the Armed Forces): CP 1267, Luanda; Dir ARI DA COSTA.

Museu da Escravatura (Museum of Slavery): CP 1267, Luanda; Dir ANICETE DO AMARAL GOURGEL.

Museu do Dundu (Dundu Museum): CP 14, Chitato, Lunda Norte; ethnography; Dir FELIZARDO JESUS GURGEL.

Museu do Planalto Central (Museum of Planalto Central): CP 2066, Huambo; ethnography; Dir FRANCISCO XAVIER YAMBO.

Museo do Reino do Koongo (Museum of the Kingdom of Koongo): CP 49, Mbanza Koongo; history.

Museu Nacional de Antropologia (National Anthropology Museum): CP 2159, Luanda; tel. 337024; Dir MAMZAMBI VUVU FERNANDO.

Museu Nacional de Arqueologia (National Archaeology Museum): CP 79, Benguela; Dir JOAQUIM PAIS PINTO.

Museu Nacional de História Natural (National Museum of Natural History): CP 1267, Luanda; Dir MARIA MANUELA BATALHA VANDUNEM.

Museu Regional da Huila (Huila Regional Museum): CP 445, Lubango; ethnography; Dir JOSÉ FERREIRA.

Museu Regional de Cabinda (Cabinda Regional Museum): CP 283, Cabinda; ethnography; Dir TADEU DOMINGOS.

Museu Regional do Uige (Uige Regional Museum): CP 665, Uige; ethnography; Dir (vacant).

University

UNIVERSIDADE AGOSTINHO NETO

CP 815, Av. 4 de Fevereiro 7, 2° andar, Luanda

Telephone: 30517
Telex: 3076
Fax: 330520

Founded 1963
Language of instruction: Portuguese
Academic year: September to July

Rector: JOSÉ LUÍS GUERRA MARQUES
Vice-Rector: CASTRO PAULINO CAMARADA

Number of teachers: 423
Number of students: 6,290

DEANS

Faculty of Sciences: Dr ABILO ALVES FERNANDES
Faculty of Agriculture: Dr AMILCAR MATEUS DE OLIVEIRA SALUMBO
Faculty of Law: Dr ADERITO CORREIA
Faculty of Economics: Dr LAURINDA DE JESUS FERNANDES HOYGAARD
Faculty of Medicine: Dr PAULO ADÃO CAMPOS
Faculty of Engineering: CARLOS ALBERTO ABREU SERENO

AFFILIATED INSTITUTES

Instituto Superior de Ciências da Educação: CP 230, Lubango; tel. 20243; Dir Dr NARCISO DAMASIO DOS SANTOS BENEDITO.

Centro Nacional de Investigação Científica: Avda Revolução de Outubro, Luanda; tel. 350762; Coordinator Dr NANIZEYI KINDUDI ANDRÉ.

ANTIGUA AND BARBUDA

Learned Societies

BIBLIOGRAPHY, LIBRARY SCIENCE AND MUSEOLOGY

Library Association of Antigua and Barbuda: C/o Organization of Eastern Caribbean States, Economic Affairs Secretariat, Documentation Centre, POB 822, St John's, Antigua; tel. 462-3500; telex 2157; fax 462-1537; f. 1983; 40 mems; Pres. MOLIVAR SPENCER; Sec. TRACY SAMUEL.

Libraries and Archives

St John's

Antigua & Barbuda National Archives: Victoria Park, Factory Road, St John's, Antigua; tel. 462-4959; f. 1982; Dir MARJORIE GONSALVES.

Colleges

UNIVERSITY OF HEALTH SCIENCES ANTIGUA

POB 510, St John's, Antigua

Telephone: 1-809-463-1391

Founded 1982

President: Dr YELE AKANDE
Registrar: IVORY TAYLOR
Librarian: (vacant)
Dean, School of Medicine: Dr N. OLOWOPOPO
Library in process of formation
Number of teachers: 16
Number of students: 46

University of the West Indies School of Continuing Studies (Antigua and Barbuda): POB 142, St John's; tel. 462-1355; fax 462-2968; f. 1949; adult education courses, mainly: high school equivalency programmes, BSc in Management Studies, first year of BSc in Social Sciences, Cert. in Business Administration, in Education, in Public Administration, in Pre-School Education, in Professional (Administrative) Secretarial skills; also special programmes for women, summer courses for children, occasional seminars and workshops; 23 part-time tutors; *c.* 350 students; library of *c.* 7,000 vols; Resident Tutor Dr ERMINA OSOBA.

ARGENTINA

Learned Societies

AGRICULTURE, FISHERIES AND VETERINARY SCIENCE

Academia Nacional de Agronomía y Veterinaria (Academy of Agronomy and Veterinary Science): Avda Alvear 1711 (2°), 1014 Buenos Aires; tel. 812-4168; f. 1909; 69 mems; library of 3,000 vols; Pres. Dr NORBERTO RAS; Sec.-Gen. Dr ALBERTO CANO; *Anales* (annually).

Asociación Argentina de la Ciencia del Suelo (Argentine Association of Soil Science): J. R. de Velazco 847, 1414 Buenos Aires; tel. (1) 771-8968; fax (1) 322-3761; f. 1958; 800 mems; Pres. G. MOSCATELLI ; Sec. R. ALVAREZ; publs *Ciencia del Suelo* (2 a year), *Boletín* (3 a year).

Sociedad Rural Argentina (Argentine Agricultural Society): Florida 460, 1005 Buenos Aires; tel. (1) 322-0468; fax (1) 325-8231; f. 1866; 10,000 mems; library: see libraries; Pres. ENRIQUE C. CROTTO.

ARCHITECTURE AND TOWN PLANNING

Sociedad Central de Arquitectos (Architects' Association): Montevideo 938, 1019 Buenos Aires; tel. 812-3644; fax 813-6629; f. 1886; 8,500 mems; library of 9,200 vols, 90 periodical titles; Pres. Arq. JULIO KESELMAN; Sec. Arq. GUILLERMO MARENCO; publs *NoticiaSCA* (monthly), *Revista SCA* (6 a year).

BIBLIOGRAPHY, LIBRARY SCIENCE AND MUSEOLOGY

Asociación Argentina de Bibliotecas y Centros de Información Científicos y Técnicos (Argentine Association of Scientific and Technical Libraries and Information Centres): Santa Fé 1145, 1059 Buenos Aires; tel. 393-8406; f. 1937; 84 mems; Pres. ABILIO BASSETS; Tech. Sec. ERNESTO G. GIETZ; publ. *Union Catalogue of Scientific and Technical Publications*.

Asociación de Bibliotecarios Graduados de la República Argentina (ABGRA) (Association of Argentine Librarians): Tucumán 1424 (8° piso D), 1050 Buenos Aires; tel. (1) 373-0571; fax (1) 371-5269; e-mail postmaster@abgra.org.ar; f. 1953; 1,400 mems; Pres. ANA MARÍA PERUCHENA ZIMMERMANN; Sec.-Gen. ROSA EMMA MONFASANI; publ. *Revista REFERENCIAS*.

Comisión Nacional de Museos y de Monumentos y Lugares Históricos (National Commission for Museums and Historic Monuments and Sites): Avda de Mayo 556, Buenos Aires; tel. 331-6151; f. 1938; supervises museums and protects the national historical heritage; library; Pres. JORGE E. HARDOY; Gen. Sec. MATILDE I. ORUETA; publ. *Boletín*.

Comisión Nacional Protectora de Bibliotecas Populares (Commission for the Protection of Public Libraries): Ayacucho 1578, 1112 Buenos Aires; tel. 803-6545; f. 1870; Pres. Prof. DANIEL RÍOS; Sec. Prof. ANA T. DOBRA; publ. *Boletín*.

ECONOMICS, LAW AND POLITICS

Academia Nacional de Ciencias Económicas (National Academy of Economic Sciences): Avda Alvear 1790, 1014 Buenos Aires; tel. 813-2344; fax 813-2078; f. 1914; 35 mems; library of 13,500 vols; Pres. Dr ENRIQUE J. REIG; Sec. Dr LUIS GARCÍA MARTÍNEZ; publs *Anales* and special editions.

Academia Nacional de Ciencias Morales y Políticas (National Academy of Moral and Political Sciences): Avda Alvear 1711, PB, 1014 Buenos Aires; tel. 811-2049; f. 1938; 35 mems; library of 13,536 vols; Pres. Dr JORGE A. AJA ESPIL; Sec. Almte CARLOS A. SÁNCHEZ SAÑUDO; publ. *Anales*.

Academia Nacional de Derecho y Ciencias Sociales (National Academy of Law and Social Sciences): Avda Alvear 1711 (1°), 1014 Buenos Aires; tel. 821-3522; f. 1874; 25 mems; Pres. Dr SEGUNDO LINARES QUINTANA; Secs Dr A. G. PADILLA, L. MORENO; publ. *Anales*.

Academia Nacional de Derecho y Ciencias Sociales (Córdoba) (National Academy of Law and Social Sciences, Córdoba): Artigas 74, 5000 Córdoba; tel. and fax (51) 21-4929; e-mail acader@interactive.com.ar; f. 1941; 26 mems, 31 corresp. mems, 53 foreign mems; Pres. Dr LUIS MOISSET DE ESPANÉS; Sec. Dr RICARDO HARO; publs *Anales*, *Ediciones Academia*, *Cuaderno de Federalismo*, *Cuaderno de Historia*.

Colegio de Abogados de la Ciudad de Buenos Aires (Buenos Aires City Bar Association): Montevideo 640, 1019 Buenos Aires; tel. and fax (1) 371-2690; f. 1913; 1,600 mems; library of 45,000 vols; Pres. Dr OSCAR ALVARADO URIBURU; Sec. Dr URIEL F. O'FARRELL; publ. *Revista*.

FINE AND PERFORMING ARTS

Academia Nacional de Bellas Artes (National Academy of Fine Arts): Sánchez de Bustamante 2663, 1425 Buenos Aires; tel. (1) 802-2469; e-mail info@anba.com; f. 1936; 30 mems, 30 foreign corresp. mems; library of 3,000 vols; Pres. Prof. NELLY KIRGER DE PERAZZO; Sec.-Gen. Prof. ALEJANDRO PUENTE; publs *Monografías de Artistas Argentinos*, *Serie Estudios de Arte en la Argentina*, *Cuaderno Especial: 'Escenas del Campo Argentino' 1885–1900*, *Documentos de Arte Argentino*, *Documentos de Arte Colonial Sudamericano*, *Anuario*.

Fondo Nacional de las Artes (National Arts Foundation): Alsina 673, 1087 Buenos Aires; tel. (1) 343-1590; e-mail fnartes@satlink.com; f. 1958; promotes and supports the arts; library of 5,000 vols; Pres. AMALIA LACROZE DE FORTABAT; publs *Informativo*, *Anuario del Teatro Argentino*, *Bibliografía Argentina de Artes y Letras*.

HISTORY, GEOGRAPHY AND ARCHAEOLOGY

Academia Nacional de Geografía (National Academy of Geography): Avda Cabildo 381 (7° piso), 1426 Buenos Aires; tel. and fax (1) 771-3043; f. 1956; 30 mems; Pres. Ing. Mil. ROBERTO J. M. ARREDONDO; Sec. ANTONIO CORNEJO; publ. *Anales*.

Academia Nacional de la Historia (National Academy of History): Balcarce 139, 1064 Buenos Aires; tel. (1) 331-5147; fax (1) 331-4633; f. 1893; study of Argentinian and American history; 34 mems, 223 foreign corresp. mems; Pres. Dr VICTOR TAU ANZOATEGUI; Academic Sec. Dr MIGUEL ANGEL DE MARCO; publs *Boletín*, *Investigaciones y Ensayos*, papers and theses.

Instituto Bonaerense de Numismática y Antigüedades (Buenos Aires Institute of Numismatics and Antiquities): San Martín 336, 1004 Buenos Aires; tel. 49-2659; f. 1872; 107 mems; Pres. HUMBERTO F. BURZIO; publs *Boletín* and related works.

Junta de Historia Eclesiástica Argentina (Council of Argentine Ecclesiastical History): Reconquista 269, 1003 Buenos Aires; tel. 331-6239; f. 1942; 100 mems; Pres. Dr CARLOS MARIA GELLY Y OBES; Sec. ALBERTO S. J. DE PAULA; publ. *Revista Archivum* (annually), *Boletín*.

Sociedad Argentina de Estudios Geográficos (Argentine Society of Geographical Studies): Rodríguez Peña 158 (4° piso Dpto 7), 1020 Buenos Aires; tel. 40-2076; fax 382-3305; f. 1922; 4,000 mems; library of 12,000 vols; Pres. Dra SUSANA I. CURTO DE CASAS; Sec. Lic. ANALÍA S. CONTE; publs *Anales*, *GAEA Boletín*, *Geografía de la República Argentina*, *Serie Especial*, *Contribuciones Científicas*.

LANGUAGE AND LITERATURE

Academia Argentina de Letras (Argentine Academy of Letters): Sánchez de Bustamante 2663, 1425 Buenos Aires; tel. 802-3814; fax 802-8340; f. 1931; 24 mems, 53 corresp. mems; Pres. RAÚL H. CASTAGNINO; Sec.-Gen. RODOLFO MODERN; publs *Boletín* (quarterly), *Serie Estudios Lingüísticos y Filológicos*, *Serie de Clásicos Argentinos*, *Serie de Estudios Académicos*, *Serie de Discursos Académicos*, *Serie de Acuerdos acerca del Idioma*, *Boletín*, *Serie Homenajes*.

PEN Club Argentino—Centro Internacional de la Asociación PEN (International PEN Centre): Rivadavia 4060, 1205 Buenos Aires; f. 1930; 100 mems; Pres. MIGUEL A. OLIVERA; publ. *Boletín*.

Sociedad Argentina de Autores y Compositores de Música (SADAIC) (Argentine Society of Authors and Composers): Lavalle 1547, 1048 Buenos Aires; tel. (1) 374-2730; f. 1936; library of 4,000 vols, 13,000 music scores; Pres. ARIEL RAMIREZ; Cultural Dir EUGENIO INCHAUSTI; publs *Catálogos Bibliógráficos*.

Sociedad General de Autores de la Argentina (Argentores) (Argentine Society of Authors): J. A. Pacheco de Melo 1820, 1126 Buenos Aires; tel. 811-2582; f. 1910; 2,000 mems; library of 60,000 vols; Pres. ISAAC AISEMBERG; Sec. AUGUSTO GIUSTOZZI; publ. *Boletín* (4 a year).

MEDICINE

Academia Argentina de Cirugía (Argentine Academy of Surgery): Marcelo T. de Alvear 2415, 1122 Buenos Aires; tel. 925-3649; f. 1911; Pres. Dr E. ROBERTO VIDAL; Sec. Gen. JORGE SIVORI.

Academia de Ciencias Médicas: CC 130, 5000 Córdoba; f. 1975; 350 mems; Pres. Dr REMO BERGOGLIO; Sec. Dr JESÚS R. GIRAUDO.

Academia Nacional de Medicina (National Academy of Medicine): Las Heras 3092, 1425 Buenos Aires; tel. (1) 805-6890; fax (1) 806-6638; f. 1822; 35 mems; library of 50,000 vols; Pres. Acad. ARMANDO MACCAGNO; Sec.-Gen. Acad. OSCAR H. MORELLI; publ. *Boletín* (2 a year).

Asociación Argentina de Biología y Medicina Nuclear (Argentine Association for

Biology and Nuclear Medicine): Avda Santa Fé 1145, 1059 Buenos Aires; tel. 393-5682; f. 1963; 190 mems; Pres. Dr JUAN J. O'FARRELL; Sec. Dr CARLOS CAÑELLAS.

Asociación Argentina de Cirugía (Argentine Association of Surgery): Marcelo T. de Alvear 2415, 1122 Buenos Aires; tel. (1) 822-2905; fax (1) 822-6458; f. 1930; 4,000 mems; Pres. LUIS V. GUTIÉRREZ; Dir MARTIN MIHURA; publs *Revista Argentina de Cirugía* (8 a year), *Boletín Informativo* (fortnightly), *Anuario*.

Asociación Argentina de Farmacia y Bioquímica Industrial (Argentine Industrial Biochemistry and Pharmacy Association): Uruguay 469 (2° B), 1015 Buenos Aires; tel. (1) 373-8900; fax (1) 372-7389; f. 1952; 1,100 mems; library of 500 vols; Pres. Dr HUMBERTO TORRIANI; Sec. Dr RAÚL ALBERTO REVILLA; publs *Revista SAFYBI*, *Boletín Informativo* (3 a year).

Asociación Argentina de Ortopedia y Traumatología (Argentine Orthopaedic and Traumatology Association): Vicente López 1878, 1128 Buenos Aires; tel. (1) 803-2320; fax (1) 801-7703; f. 1936; 2,196 mems; library of 1,100 vols, 67 periodicals; Pres. Dr TRISTÁN MORENO; Sec. Dr GREGORIO M. ARENDAR; publ. *Revista* (6 a year).

Asociación Médica Argentina (Argentine Medical Association): Santa Fé 1171, 1059 Buenos Aires; tel. (1) 814-2182; fax (1) 814-0634; e-mail ama@datamar.com.ar; f. 1891; 51 br. asscns; library of 28,000 vols, 270,000 periodicals; Pres. ELÍAS HURTADO HOYO; Sec. MIGUEL FALASCO; publs *Revista* (4 a year), *Boletín Informativo* (monthly).

Asociación Odontológica Argentina (Argentine Dental Association): Junín 959, 1113 Buenos Aires; tel. (1) 961-6141; fax (1) 961-1110; f. 1896; includes postgraduate school for dentists; 8,000 mems; library of 7,200 vols, 11,300 periodicals; Pres. CARLOS A. SPIELBERG; Sec. GUILLERMO ROSSI; publ. *Revista*.

Asociación para la Lucha contra la Parálisis Infantil (Association for Combating Infantile Paralysis): Salguero 1639, 1425 Buenos Aires; tel. 84-1034; f. 1943; 30 mems; library of 3,000 vols; Pres. VERÓNICA S. M. DE BUSTO ; publ. *Memoria y Balance Anual*.

Federación Argentina de Asociaciones de Anestesiología (Argentine Federation of Anaesthesiology Associations): J.F. Aranguren 1323, 1405 Buenos Aires; tel. and fax 431-2463; f. 1970; 1,113 mems; Pres. Dr ALFREDO PAIRETTI; Admin. Sec. Dr ALFREDO CATTANEO; publs *Revista Argentina de Anestesiología*, *Boletín Informativo*.

Liga Argentina contra la Tuberculosis (Argentine Anti-Tuberculosis League): Santa Fé 4292, Buenos Aires; f. 1901; library of 140 series of periodicals; Pres. Dr RODOLFO CUCCHIANI ACEVEDO; Sec.-Gen. Dr GERMÁN QUINTELA NOVOA; publs *Revista Argentina del Tórax* (scientific), *La Doble Cruz* (popular).

Sociedad Argentina de Ciencias Fisiológicas (Argentine Society of Physiological Sciences): Solís 453, 1078 Buenos Aires; tel. 383-1110; fax 381-0323; f. 1950; 150 mems; library of 600 vols; Pres. Prof. Dr PEDRO ARAMENDÍA; Sec. Dr RICARDO A. QUINTEIRO; publ. *Acta Physiologica et Pharmacologica Latinoamericana*.

Sociedad Argentina de Ciencias Neurológicas, Psiquiátricas y Neuroquirúrgicas (Argentine Neurological, Neurosurgical and Psychiatric Society): Santa Fé 1171, 1059 Buenos Aires; tel. 41-1633; f. 1920; 400 mems; library of 35,000 vols; Pres. Prof. Dr DIEGO BRAGE; Sec. Prof. Dr CARLOS MÁRQUEZ; publ. *Revista* (monthly).

Sociedad Argentina de Dermatología (Argentine Society of Dermatology): B. Mitre 2517, 1039 Buenos Aires; tel. 48-9967; f. 1934; 600 mems; Pres. Dr SERGIO G. STRINGA; Sec.-Gen. Dr CARLOS BIANCHI.

Sociedad Argentina de Endocrinología y Metabolismo (Argentine Society of Endocrinology and Metabolism): Viamonte 2506 (1° 8), 1056 Buenos Aires; tel. (1) 963-7166; fax (1) 961-5106; f. 1941; 540 mems; Pres. Dr OSCAR LEVALLE; Sec. Dr HUGO BOQUETE; publ. *Revista* (4 a year).

Sociedad Argentina de Farmacología y Terapéutica (Argentine Society of Pharmacology and Therapeutics): Santa Fé 1171, 1059 Buenos Aires; tel. 41-1633; f. 1929; 100 mems; Pres. Prof. Dr MANUEL LITTER; Sec. Dr JOSÉ A. L. CHIESA.

Sociedad Argentina de Gastroenterología (Argentine Society of Gastroenterology): Santa Fé 1171, 1059 Buenos Aires; tel. 41-1633; f. 1927; 900 mems; Pres. Dr ERMAN E. CROSETTI; Sec.-Gen. Dr LEONARDO PINCHUK; publ. *Acta Gastroenterológica Latinoamericana*.

Sociedad Argentina de Gerontología y Geriatría (Argentine Gerontological and Geriatrics Society): French 2657, 1425 Buenos Aires; tel. (1) 805-1699; fax (1) 805-7051; e-mail sagg@connmed.com.ar; f. 1950; 1,500 mems; Pres. Dr HUGO ALBERTO SCHIFIS; Sec. Dr MIGUEL ANGEL ACANFORA; publ. *Revista Argentina de Gerontología y Geriatría* (6 a year), *Vivir en Plenitud* (6 a year).

Sociedad Argentina de Hematología (Argentine Society of Haematology): Avda Angel Gallardo 899, 1405 Buenos Aires; f. 1948; 350 mems; Pres. Dr GUILLERMO CARLOS VILASECA; Sec. Dr EDUARDO DIBAR.

Sociedad Argentina de Investigación Clínica (Argentine Society of Clinical Research): Instituto de Investigaciones Médicas, U.B.A., Donato Alvares 3150, 1427 Buenos Aires; tel. and fax 573-2619; f. 1960; 500 mems; Pres. BASILIO A. KOTSIAS; Sec. ADRIANA FRAGA; publ. *Medicina*.

Sociedad Argentina de Oftalmología (Argentine Ophthalmological Society): Santa Fé 1171, 1059 Buenos Aires; tel. 241-0392; f. 1920; 2,000 mems; Pres. Dr ROBERTO SAMPOALESI; Sec. Dr JOSÉ A. BADIA; publ. *Archivos de Oftalmología de Buenos Aires* (monthly).

Sociedad Argentina de Patología (Argentine Society of Pathology): Santa Fé 1171, 1059 Buenos Aires; tel. 41-1633; f. 1933; 220 mems; Pres. Dr ALBERTO SUNDBLAD; Sec. Dra MABEL POMAR DE GIL; publ. *Archivos*.

Sociedad Argentina de Pediatría (Argentine Paediatric Society): Coronel Díaz 1971, 1425 Buenos Aires; tel. 824-2063; f. 1911; 7,500 mems; library of 5,000 vols; Pres. Dr CARLOS A. GIANANTONIO; Sec. Dra MARÍA LUISA AGEITOS; publ. *Archivos Argentinos de Pediatría* (every 2 months).

Sociedad de Cirugía de Buenos Aires (Buenos Aires Surgical Society): Santa Fé 1171, 1059 Buenos Aires; tel. 44-0664; Pres. IVAN GOÑI MORENO; Sec.-Gen. GUILLERMO I. BELLEVILLE.

Sociedad de Psicología Médica, Psicoanálisis y Medicina Psicosomática (Society of Medical Psychology, Psychoanalysis and Psychosomatic Medicine): Avda Santa Fé 1171, 1059 Buenos Aires; tel. (1) 814-2182; f. 1939; 80 mems; Pres. Dr JOSÉ CUKIER; Sec. Dr A. STISMAN.

NATURAL SCIENCES

General

Academia Nacional de Ciencias de Buenos Aires (National Academy of Sciences of Buenos Aires): Avda Alvear 1711 (3° piso), 1014 Buenos Aires; tel. 41-3066; f. 1935; 35 mems; Pres. Ing. OSCAR A. QUIHILLALT; Sec. Dra AMALIA S. DE BÓRMIDA; publs *Anales*, *Escritos de Filosofía* (quarterly).

Academia Nacional de Ciencias de Córdoba (National Academy of Sciences of Córdoba): CC 36, Avda Vélez Sarsfield 229, 5000 Córdoba; tel. (51) 22-9687; fax (51) 24-4092; f. 1869; 35 mems; library of 50,205 vols, 900 periodicals; Pres. Dr ALBERTO P. MAIZTEGUI; Sec. ALFREDO COCUCCI; publs *Actas*, *Boletín*, *Miscelánea*.

Academia Nacional de Ciencias Exactas, Físicas y Naturales (National Academy of Exact, Physical and Natural Sciences): Avda Alvear 1711 (4°), 1014 Buenos Aires; tel. (1) 811-2998; fax (1) 811-6951; e-mail ancefn@interlink.com.ar; f. 1874; 38 full voting mems, 30 nat. corresp. mems, 59 foreign corresp. mems, 9 hon. mems; library of 550 collections of periodicals; Pres. Dr EDUARDO G. GROS; Sec.-Gen. Dr HUNER FANCHIOTTI; publs *Anales*, *Monografías*.

Asociación Argentina de Ciencias Naturales (Argentine Association of Natural Sciences): Avda Angel Gallardo 470, 1405 Buenos Aires; tel. 982-8370; f. 1912; 450 mems; Pres. JUAN CARLOS GIACCHI; Sec. Dra CRISTINA MARINONE; publ. *Physis*.

Asociación Argentina para el Progreso de las Ciencias (Association for the Advancement of Science): Avda Alvear 1711 (4° piso), 1014 Buenos Aires; tel. (1) 811-2998; fax (1) 811-6951; f. 1933; 200 mems, 15 assoc. mems; Pres. Dr EDUARDO HERNÁN CHARREAU; Sec. Dr AUGUSTO F. GARCÍA; publ. *Ciencia e Investigación*.

Sociedad Científica Argentina (Argentine Scientific Society): Avda Santa Fé 1145, 1059 Buenos Aires; tel. 393-8406; f. 1872; affiliations in Santa Fé, La Plata, San Juan; 698 mems; library of 80,337 vols; Pres. ARTURO OTAÑO SAHORES; publs *Anales* (annually), *Evolución de las Ciencias en la República Argentina*.

Biological Sciences

Asociación Argentina de Ecología (Argentine Association of Ecology): CC 1025, Correo Central, 5000 Córdoba; tel. (51) 22284 ext. 49; f. 1972; 600 mems; Pres. Dr RAÚL A. MONTENEGRO; publs *Ecology*, *Bulletin* (3 a year).

Asociación Argentina de Micología (Argentine Mycological Society): Universidad de Buenos Aires, Facultad de Medicina, Departamento de Microbiología, Paraguay 2155 (Piso 11), 1121 Buenos Aires; tel. (1) 962-7274; fax (1) 962-5404; e-mail micomuniz@connmed.com.ar; f. 1960; studies in medical and veterinary mycology, and mycotoxins; 150 mems; library; Pres. Dra CRISTINA IOVANNITTI; Sec. Dra ALICIA ARECHAVALA; publ. *Revista Argentina de Micología* (3 a year).

Asociación Paleontológica Argentina (Argentine Association of Palaeontology): Maipú 645 (1° piso), 1006 Buenos Aires; tel. and fax (1) 326-7463; e-mail secretaria@apa.inv.org.ar; f. 1955; 500 mems; Pres. Dr MIGUEL GRIFFIN; Sec. Dr PEDRO RAÚL GUTIÉRREZ; publ. *Ameghiniana* (quarterly).

Sociedad Argentina de Biología (Argentine Biological Society): Vuelta de Obligado 2490, 1428 Buenos Aires; tel. 783-2869; f. 1920; 180 mems; Pres. Dr JOSÉ RIMO BARAÑAO; Sec. Dr JUAN CARLOS CALVO; publ. *Revista* (2 a year).

Sociedad Argentina de Fisiología Vegetal (Argentine Society of Plant Physiology): Departamento de Agronomía, UNS, 8000 Bahía Blanca; tel. (91) 34775; fax (91) 21942; f. 1958; 260 mems; Pres. Dr GUSTAVO A. ORIOLI; Sec. Dr LUIS F. HERNANDEZ.

Sociedad Entomológica Argentina (SEA) (Argentine Entomological Society): Miguel Lillo 205, 4000 San Miguel de Tucumán;

f. 1925; 380 mems; library of 673 books, 485 periodicals; Pres. MERCEDEZ LIZARRALDE DE GROSSO; Sec. EDUARDO G. VIRLA; publ. *Revista de la Sociedad Entomológica Argentina*.

Mathematical Sciences

Unión Matemática Argentina (Argentine Mathematical Union): FAMAF, Ciudad Universitaria, 5000 Córdoba; tel. (51) 33-4051; fax (51) 33-4054; f. 1936; 600 mems; Pres. Dr JUAN A. TIRAO; Sec. Dr JORGE A. VARGAS; publ. *Revista*.

Physical Sciences

Asociación Argentina Amigos de la Astronomía (Argentine Association for the Friends of Astronomy): CC369, Correo Central, 1000 Buenos Aires; tel. and fax (1) 863-3366; e-mail postmaster@aaaa.edu.ar; f. 1929; maintains an observatory; 1,000 mems; library of 4,000 vols; Pres. GLORIA ROITMAN; publ. *Revista Astronómica*.

Asociación Argentina de Astronomía (Argentine Astronomy Association): Observatorio Astronómico, 1900 La Plata; tel. 27308; f. 1958; 120 mems; Pres. RAÚL COLOMB; Sec. HUGO LEVATO; publ. *Boletín* (annually).

Asociación Argentina de Geofísicos y Geodestas (Argentine Association of Geophysicists and Geodesists): CC 106, 1428 Buenos Aires; f. 1959; Pres. Dra MARÍA L. ALTINGER; Sec. Dra MARÍA C. POMPOSIELLO; publs reports of scientific meetings, *Geoacta* (annually), *Boletín* (3 a year).

Asociación Bioquímica Argentina (Argentine Biochemical Association): Venezuela 1823, 1096 Buenos Aires; tel. 38-2907; f. 1934.

Asociación Geológica Argentina (Argentine Geological Association): Maipú 645 (1° piso), 1006 Buenos Aires; tel. and fax (1) 325-3104; e-mail postmaster@aga.edu.ar; f. 1945; 1,750 mems; Pres. Dr A. C. RICCARDI; Sec. Dr S. DAMBORENEA; publ. *Revista* (quarterly).

Asociación Química Argentina (Argentine Chemical Association): Sánchez de Bustamante 1749, 1425 Buenos Aires; tel. and fax (1) 822-4886; f. 1912; 2,000 mems; library of 10,000 vols, 500 periodicals; Pres. MARCELO J. VERNENGO; Sec. Lic. GRACIELA F. DE WETZLER; publs *Anales de la Asociación Química Argentina* (Scientific), *Industria y Química* (Technical).

Centro Argentino de Espeleología (Argentine Centre of Speleological Studies): Avda de Mayo 651 (1° piso), 1428 Buenos Aires; tel. 331-6798; f. 1970; 60 mems; library of 250 vols; Pres. JULIO GOYÉN AGUADO; Sec. ROBERTO OSCAR BERMEJO; publ. *Las Brujas* (annually).

Grupo Argentino del Color (Argentine Colour Group): C/o Secretary of Research, School of Architecture, Buenos Aires University, Ciudad Universitaria, Pav. 3, 4th Floor, 1428 Buenos Aires; tel. and fax (1) 566-9328; e-mail postmast@semvis.fadu.uba.ar; f. 1979; study of colour science; 106 mems; Pres. Arch. JOSE LUIS CAIVANO; Sec. Lic. ANTONIO ALVAREZ; publ. *Boletín* (3 a year).

PHILOSOPHY AND PSYCHOLOGY

Sociedad Argentina de Psicología (Buenos Aires Psychological Society): Callao 435 (1° piso), 1022 Buenos Aires; tel. 432-3760; f. 1930; Pres. JUAN CUATRECASAS.

RELIGION, SOCIOLOGY AND ANTHROPOLOGY

Asociación Argentina de Estudios Americanos (Argentine Association of American Studies): Maipú 672, 1424 Buenos Aires; tel. 392-4971.

Sociedad Argentina de Antropología (Argentina Anthropological Society): Moreno 350, 1091 Buenos Aires; f. 1936; 255 mems; Pres. M. M. PODESTÁ; Sec. G. GURAIEB; publ. *Relaciones* (annually).

Sociedad Argentina de Sociología: Trejo 241, 5000 Córdoba; tel. 45901; f. 1950; Pres. Prof. ALFREDO POVIÑA; Sec.-Gen. Prof. ODORICO PIRES PINTO.

TECHNOLOGY

Asociación Argentina del Frío (Argentine Refrigeration Association): Avda Mayo 1123 (5° piso), 1085 Buenos Aires; tel. 381-7544; f. 1932; 178 mems; small library; Pres. Ing. ROBERTO RICARDO AGUILO; Sec. Ing. FLORENTINO ROSON RODRIGUEZ; publ. *Clima* (monthly).

Asociación Electrotécnica Argentina (Argentine Electrotechnical Association): Posadas 1659, 1112 Buenos Aires; tel. 804-3454; f. 1913; 2,000 mems; library of 2,500 vols; Pres. ERNESTO H. RODIL; publ. *Revista Electrotécnica*.

Centro Argentino de Ingenieros (Argentine Centre of Engineering): Cerrito 1250, 1010 Buenos Aires; tel. (1) 811-4961; fax (1) 812-0475; f. 1895; 10,231 mems; library of 11,000 vols; Pres. Ing. ROBERTO P. ECHARTE; publ. *Políticas de la Ingeniería*.

Federación Lanera Argentina (Argentine Wool Federation): Avda Paseo Colón 823, 1063 Buenos Aires; tel. (1) 300-7661; fax (1) 361-6517; f. 1929; concerned with all aspects of wool trade, from breeding to sales; 80 mems; Pres. JULIO AISENSTEIN; Sec. RICARDO VON GERSTENBERG; publs *Noticias Laneras* (Monday to Thursday), *Boletín Lanero* (Friday), *Argentine Wool Statistics* (monthly).

Research Institutes

GENERAL

Instituto Torcuato Di Tella: Miñones 2159/77, 1428 Buenos Aires; tel. (1) 783-8680; fax (1) 783-3061; f. 1958; promotes scientific research and artistic creativity on a nat. and int. scale; administers research centres and higher education institutions; postgraduate courses in economics, sociology and administration; library of 85,000 vols; Pres. GREGORIO KLIMOVSKY; Dir Dr ADOLFO CANITROT; publs annual report and research results.

AGRICULTURE, FISHERIES AND VETERINARY SCIENCE

Estación Experimental Agro-Industrial 'Obispo Colombres' ('Obispo Colombres' Agro-Industrial Experimental Research Station): CC 9, Las Talitas, 4101 Tucumán; tel. (81) 27-6561; fax (81) 27-6404; f. 1909; library of 8,000 books, 75,000 journal vols; Technical Dir Ing. Agr. GUILLERMO S. FADDA; publs *Revista Industrial y Agrícola de Tucumán* (quarterly), *Gacetilla Agro-Industrial, Miscelánea, Avance Agro-Industrial* (irregular).

Instituto Agrario Argentino de Cultura Rural (Argentine Agricultural Institute for Rural Education): Florida 460, 1005 Buenos Aires; tel. 392-2030; f. 1937; library of 2,000 vols; Dir Dr CORNELIO J. VIERA; Sec. MARÍA LUIS RIVAS; Technical Sec. EURIFUE ALFREDO VIVANA; publs *Reseñas Argentinas, Reseñas, Comunicados*.

Instituto de Edafología Agrícola (Institute of Agricultural Soil Science): Cerviño 3101, 1425 Buenos Aires; tel. 84-9623; f. 1944; library of 3,200 vols; Dir Ing. Agr. JORGE I. BELLATI; publs *Técnicas Apartados de Artículos Tiradas Internas, Suelos*.

Instituto Nacional de Tecnología Agropecuaria (INTA) (National Institute for Agricultural Technology): Rivadavia 1439, 1033 Buenos Aires; tel. 383-5095; telex 17518; fax 383-2024; f. 1956; 42 experimental stations, 13 research institutes; National Dir Ing. Agr. CARLOS TORRES; Pres. Ing. Agr. HÉCTOR HUERGO; publ. *Revista de Investigaciones Agropecuarias*.

Main research centre:

Centro Nacional de Investigación Agropecuaria (National Centre for Agricultural Research): CC 25, 1712 Castelar, Buenos Aires; tel. 621-1819; research in all aspects of farming; Dir Dr Vet. HUMBERTO CISALE.

Instituto Nacional de Vitivinicultura (National Vine Growing and Wine Producing Institute): San Martín 430, 5500 Mendoza; tel. (61) 49-6300; telex 55343; fax (61) 49-6306; f. 1959; library of 20,000 vols, 690 journals; Nat. Dir Lic. FELIX ROBERTO AGUINAED; publs *Estadística Vitivinícola* (annually), *Exportaciones Argentinas de Productos Vitivinícolas* (annually), *Revista Vinifera, Superficie de Vinos por Variedades Implatada en la República Argentina*.

ARCHITECTURE AND TOWN PLANNING

Instituto de Planeamiento Regional y Urbano (IPRU) (Regional and Urban Planning Institute): Calle Posadas 1265 (7° piso), 1011 Buenos Aires; fax 815-8673; f. 1952; Dir FERNANDO PASTOR; publs *Plan, Cuadernos de IPRU*.

BIBLIOGRAPHY, LIBRARY SCIENCE AND MUSEOLOGY

Centro de Documentación Bibliotecológica (Centre for Library Science Documentation): Universidad Nacional del Sur, Avda Alem 1253, 8000 Bahía Blanca; tel. (91) 28035; fax (91) 55-1447; f. 1962; teaching and research in library science; library of 2,980 vols, 332 periodicals; Chief Librarian MARTA IBARLUCEA DE RUIZ; publs *Bibliografía Bibliotecológica Argentina 1978–81, Documentación Bibliotecológica, Revista de Revistas*.

Instituto de Bibliografía del Ministerio de Educación de la Provincia de Buenos Aires (Bibliographical Institute of Ministry of Education of the Province of Buenos Aires): Calle 47 No. 510 (6° piso), 1900 La Plata; tel. 35915; Dir MARÍA DEL CARMEN CRESPI DE BUSTOS; publs *Bibliografía Argentina de Historia, Boletín de Información Bibliográfica*.

ECONOMICS, LAW AND POLITICS

Centro de Investigaciones Económicas: (Economic Research Centre): Instituto Torcuato Di Tella, Miñones 2159/77, 1428 Buenos Aires; tel. (1) 781-5014; fax (1) 786-2636; f. 1960; library of 85,000 vols; Dir ADOLFO CANITROT; publs *Documentos de Trabajo*.

Instituto de Desarrollo Económico y Social (Institute of Economic and Social Development): Aráoz 2838, Buenos Aires; tel. (1) 804-4949; fax (1) 804-5856; e-mail ides@clasco.edu.ar; f. 1960; library of 8,000 vols; Pres. ALFREDO MONZA; Dir JUAN CARLOS TORRE; publs *Desarrollo Económico, Revista de Ciencias Sociales* (quarterly).

Instituto Nacional de Estadística y Censos (National Institute of Statistics and Censuses): Avda Pte. Julio A. Roca 609, 1067 Buenos Aires; tel. (1) 349-9609; fax (1) 349-9601; e-mail ces@indec.mecon.ar; f. 1894; library of 30,000 vols; Dir Dr HÉCTOR MONTERO; publs *Estadística Mensual, Comercio Exterior Argentino* (annually), *Anuario Estadístico de la República Argentina* (annually).

Instituto para el Desarrollo de Empresarial en la Argentina (Institute for Management Development): Moreno 1850, 1094 Buenos Aires; tel. (1) 372-7667; fax (1) 49-6944; f. 1960; library of 10,000 vols, 50 periodicals; Dir RUBEN D. PUENTEDURA; publ. *IDEA*.

Instituto para la Integración de América Latina y el Caribe (Institute for Latin American and Caribbean Integration): Esmeralda 130 (pisos 16 y 17), Casilla 39, Suc. 1, 1401 Buenos Aires; tel. (1) 320-1850; fax (1) 320-1865; f. 1965 under auspices of Interamerican Development Bank; investigates all aspects of integration; Journals and Information Documentation Centre of 80,000 documents, 10,000 books, 50 journals; Dir JOSÉ M. PUPPO (acting); publs *Integración & Comercio (3 a year), Carta Mensual INTAL* (monthly).

FINE AND PERFORMING ARTS

Instituto Nacional de Estudios del Teatro (National Institute for the Study of the Theatre): Avda Córdoba 1199, 1055 Buenos Aires; tel. 46-8882; f. 1936; library of 16,000 vols, archives; also nat. theatre museum; Dir OSVALDO CALATAYUD; publ. *Boletín Informativo de Teatro* (monthly), *Revista Estudios de Teatro*, *Cuadernos de Divulgación*.

HISTORY, GEOGRAPHY AND ARCHAEOLOGY

Departamento de Estudios Históricos Navales (Department of Naval History Studies): Jefatura del Estado Mayor General de la Armada, Avda Almirante Brown 401, 1155 Buenos Aires; tel. 362-1248; f. 1957; Dir Capt. HUGO H. COLOMBOTTO; large number of publications, also paintings and medals.

Dirección Nacional del Antártico (National Antarctic Office): Cerrito 1248, 1010 Buenos Aires; tel. (1) 812-0071; fax (1) 812-3283; f. 1970; maintains Yubany station at King George Island, Antarctica; library of 15,000 vols, 1,500 charts; scientific colln; Dir Brig. JORGE EDUARD LEAL; publs *Contribuciones Científicas* (irregular), *Revista Antártica*, *Boletín del SCAR* (3 a year, Spanish edn of SCAR Bulletin).

Attached institute:

Instituto Antártico Argentino (Argentine Antarctic Institute): tel. (1) 812-1689; fax (1) 812-2039; f. 1951; Dir Dr CARLOS A. RINALDI.

Instituto Geográfico Militar (Military Geographical Institute): Avda Cabildo 381, 1426 Buenos Aires; tel. (1) 771-3031; fax (1) 776-1611; f. 1879; topographic survey of Argentina; Dir Col HORACIO ESTEBAN AVILA; publ. *Revista* (annually).

MEDICINE

Centro de Investigaciones Neurobiológicas 'Prof. Dr Christfried Jakob' (Christfried Jakob Centre for Neurobiological Research): Avenida Amancio Alcorta 1602, 1283 Buenos Aires; tel. and fax (1) 306-7314; e-mail postmaster@neubio.gov.ar; f. 1899; dependency of Min. of Public Health and Welfare; Dir Prof. Dr MARIO-FERNANDO CROCCO; publ. *Folia Neurobiológica Argentina*.

Instituto de Biología y Medicina Experimental (Institute of Biology and Experimental Medicine): Vuelta de Obligado 2490, 1428 Buenos Aires; tel. (1) 783-2869; fax (1) 786-2564; f. 1944; library of 15,000 vols; Dir Dr EDUARDO H. CHARREAU; publ. *Memoria* (annually).

Instituto de Investigaciones Médicas 'Alfredo Lanari' (Alfredo Lanari Institute of Medical Research): Avda Donato Alvarez 3150, 1427 Buenos Aires; tel. (1) 522-1438; f. 1957; clinical and basic medical research, teaching; library of 4,185 vols, 6,738 periodicals; Research Dir AQUILES J. RONCORONI.

Instituto Nacional de Microbiología (National Microbiological Institute): Avda Vélez Sarsfield 563, 1281 Buenos Aires; tel. 21-4115; f. 1916; library of 6,500 vols; Dir Dr ROBERTO HOSOKAWA.

NATURAL SCIENCES

General

Consejo Nacional de Investigaciones Científicas y Técnicas (CONICET) (National Council of Scientific and Technical Research): Avda Rivadavia 1917, 1033 Buenos Aires; tel. 953-3609; fax 953-4345; e-mail postmaster@conica.gov.ar; f. 1958; supports six regional research centres and 114 research institutes; maintains several scientific services; Pres. Dr ENRICO STEFANI.

Main research institutes:

Centro Argentino de Datos Oceanográficos (CEADO) (Argentine Centre of Oceanographic Data): Avda Montes de Oca 2124, 1271 Buenos Aires; tel. 303-2240; fax 303-2299; e-mail postmaster@ceado.edu.ar; Dir Capt. ADOLFO GIL VILLANUEVA.

Centro Argentino de Etnología Americana (CAEA) (Argentine Centre for American Ethnology): Avda de Mayo 1437 (1° piso Dpto. A), 1085 Buenos Aires; tel. (1) 381-1821; e-mail caea@caea.gov.ar; Dir Dr MARIO CALIFANO.

Centro Argentino de Primates (CAPRIM) (Argentine Primates Centre): San Cayetano CC 145, 3400 Corrientes; tel. and fax (783) 27790; e-mail ruiz@caprim.edu.ar; Dir Dr JULIO CÉSAR RUIZ.

Centro Austral de Investigaciones Científicas (CADIC) (Southern Centre for Scientific Research): Avda Malvinas Argentinas s/n, CC 92, Ruta Nacional n° 3, Barrio La Misión, Camino Lapataia, 9410 Ushuaia; tel. (901) 22310; fax (901) 30644; e-mail postmaster@cadica.edu.ar; f. 1975; biology, geology, archaeology, anthropology, hydrography, climatology; library of 1,000 vols; Dir Dr EDUARDO B. OLIVERO; publs *Boletín, Publicaciones especiales del CADIC, Contribuciones Científicas del CADIC*.

Centro de Diagnóstico e Investigaciones Veterinarias Formosa (CEDIVEF) (Formosa Centre of Veterinary Diagnosis and Research): Ruta Nacional n° 11, km. 1164, CC 292, 3600 Formosa; fax (717) 51334; Dir Dr CARLOS M. MONZON.

Centro de Ecofisiología Vegetal (CEVEG) (Centre for Plant Ecophysiology): Serrano 669 (5° y 6° piso), 1414 Buenos Aires, tel. and fax 856-7110; e-mail postmaster@ceveg.gov.ar; Dir Dr OSVALDO H. CASO.

Centro de Ecología Aplicada del Litoral (CECOAL) (Centre of Coastal Applied Ecology): Ruta Prov. No. 5, Km 2·5, CC 291, 3400 Corrientes; tel. (783) 54418; fax (783) 54421; Dir Prof. JUAN JOSÉ NEIFF.

Centro de Estudios e Investigaciones Laborales (CEIL) (Centre of Labour Study and Research): Corrientes 2470 (6° piso, of. 24 y 25), 1046 Buenos Aires; tel. and fax 952-5273; e-mail postmaster@ceil.edu.ar; f. 1971; Dir Dr JULIO CÉSAR NEFFA; publ. *Boletín – Serie Documentos*.

Centro de Estudios Farmacológicos y Botanicos (CEFYBO) (Centre for Pharmacological Studies and Botany): Serrano 669, 1414 Buenos Aires; tel. and fax 856-2751; e-mail postmaster@cefybo.edu.ar; f. 1975; Dirs Dra LEONOR STERIN DE BORDA, Dra MARÍA ANTONIETA DEL PERO.

Centro de Estudios Fotosintéticos y Bioquímicos (CEFOBI) (Centre for Studies in Photosynthesis and Biochemistry): Suipacha 531, 2000 Rosario; tel. (41) 37-1955; fax (41) 37-0044; e-mail rncefobi@arcride.edu.ar; f. 1976; Dir Dr RUBÉN H. VALLEJOS.

Centro de Investigación y Desarrollo en Criotecnología de Alimentos (CIDCA) (Research and Development Centre for Food Cryotechnology): Calles 47 y 116, C.C. 553, 1900 La Plata, Buenos Aires; tel. (21) 24-9287; fax (21) 25-4853; Dir Dra MARÍA C. AÑON.

Centro de Investigación y Desarrollo en Fermentaciones Industriales (CINDEFI) (Research and Development Centre for Industrial Fermentation): Calles 47 y 115, 1900 La Plata, Buenos Aires; tel. (21) 83-3794; fax 25-4533; e-mail voget@biol.unlp.edu.ar; Dir Dr RODOLFO J. ERTOLA.

Centro de Investigación y Desarrollo en Procesos Catalíticos (CINDECA) (Research and Development Centre for Catalytic Processes): Calle 47 N° 257, C.C. 59, 1900 La Plata, Buenos Aires; tel. (21) 21-1353; fax (21) 25-4277; e-mail cindeca@nahuel.biol.unlp.edu.ar; Dir Dr HORACIO J. THOMAS.

Centro de Investigación y Desarrollo en Tecnología de Pinturas (CIDEPINT) (Research and Development Centre for Paint Technology): Calle 52 a 121 y 122, 1900 La Plata, Buenos Aires; tel. (21) 21-6214; fax (21) 27-1537; e-mail cielsner@isis.unlp.edu.ar; Dir Dr VICENTE J. D. RASCIO.

Centro de Investigación y Estudios Ortopédicos y Traumatológicos (CINEOT) (Research and Study Centre for Orthopaedics and Traumatology): Potosí 4215, 1199 Buenos Aires; tel. 958-4011; fax 981-0991; e-mail cineot@impsat1.com.ar; Dir Dr DOMINGO L. MUSCOLO.

Centro de Investigaciónes en Antropología Filosófica y Cultural (CIAFIC) (Centre for Research in Philosophical and Cultural Anthropology): Juramento 142, 1609 Boulogne, Buenos Aires; premises at: Federico Lacroze 2100, 1426 Buenos Aires; tel. and fax 776-0913; e-mail postmaster@ciafic.edu.ar; Dir Dra LILA B. ARCHIDEO.

Centro de Investigaciónes en Recursos Geológicos (CIRGEO) (Centre for Research into Geological Resources): Ramírez de Velasco 847, 1414 Buenos Aires; tel. 772-9729; fax 771-3742; e-mail pompo@cirgeo.edu.ar; f. 1976; library of 6,000 vols, 90 periodicals; Dir Dr BERNABÉ J. QUARTINO.

Centro de Investigaciones Endocrinológicas (CEDIE) (Centre of Endocrinological Research): Gallo 1330, 1425 Buenos Aires; tel. 963-5931; fax 963-5930; e-mail master@fend.sld.arg; Dir Dr CÉSAR BERGADÁ.

Centro de Investigaciones Opticas (CIOP) (Centre for Optical Research): Camino Parque Centenario e/505 y 506, Gonnet, CC 124, 1900 La Plata, Buenos Aires; tel. (21) 84-0280; fax (21) 53-0189; e-mail postmaster@ciop.edu.ar; Dir Dr MARIO GALLARDO.

Centro de Investigaciónes sobre Regulación de Poblacion de Organismos Nocivos (CIRPON) (Centre for Research into Controlling Harmful Organisms): Pasaje Caseros 1050, C.C. 90, 4000 San Miguel de Tucumán; fax (81) 34-6940; e-mail postmaster@cirpon.untmre.edu.ar; Dir Dr ALBERTO A. P. FIDALGO.

Centro de Referencia para Lactobacilos (CERELA) (Reference Centre for Lactobacillus): Chacabuco 145, 4000 San Miguel de Tucumán; tel. and fax (81) 31-1720; e-mail crl@cerela.edu.ar; Dir Dra AÍDA A. P. DE RUIZ HOLGADO.

Centro de Tecnología en Recursos Minerales y Cerámica (CETMIC) (Technology Centre for Mineral and Ceramic Resources): CC 49, 1897 Gonnet, Buenos Aires; premises at: Camino Centenario y 506, 1897 Gonnet, Buenos Aires; tel. (21) 84-0247; fax (21) 71-0075; e-mail postmaster@cetmic.edu.ar; Dir Dr ENRIQUE PEREIRA.

Centro Experimental de la Vivienda Económica (CEVE) (Experimental Centre for Low-Cost Housing): Igualdad 3585, Villa Siburu, 5003 Córdoba; tel. and fax (51) 89-4442; e-mail postmaster@ceve.org.ar; Dir Arq. HORACIO BERRETTA.

Centro Nacional Patagónico (CNP) (National Patagónia Centre): Bv. Alte. Brown s/n, 9120 Puerto Madryn, Chubut; tel. (965) 51375; fax (965) 72885; e-mail postmaster@cenpat.edu.ar; Dir Dr ADAN E. PUCCI.

Instituto Argentino de Investigaciónes de las Zonas Aridas (IADIZA) (Argentine Institute for Arid Zones Research): Dr Adrián Ruiz Leal s/n, Parque Gral San Martín, 5500 Mendoza; fax (61) 287995; e-mail cricyt@planet.losandes.com.ar; f. 1974; Dir Ing. Agr. JUAN CARLOS GUEVARA (acting); publ. *Boletín Informativo*.

Instituto Argentino de Nivologia, Glaciologia y Ciencias Ambientales (IANIGLA) (Argentine Institute for Snow, Ice and Environmental Sciences): Dr Adrián Ruiz Leal s/n, Parque Gral San Martín, CC 131, 5500 Mendoza; tel. and fax 28-7029; e-mail cricyt@planet.losandes.com.ar; Dir Dr WOLFGANG VOLKHEIMER.

Instituto Argentino de Oceanografía (IADO) (Argentine Oceanographic Institute): Edificio E3, Complejo de la Carrindanga, Florida 4000, 8000 Bahía Blanca, Buenos Aires; tel. (91) 23555; fax 86-1112; e-mail postmaster@criba.edu.ar; f. 1969; Subdirector-in-Charge Dr JOSÉ KOSTADINOFF; publ. *Contribuciones Científicas IADO*.

Instituto Argentino de Radioastronomía (IAR) (Argentine Radioastronomy Institute): CC 5, 1894 Villa Elisa, La Plata, Buenos Aires; tel. (21) 87-0230; fax (21) 25-4909; e-mail postmaster.bajaja@irma.edu.ar; Dir Dr ESTEBAN BAJAJA.

Instituto de Botánica del Nordeste (IBONE) (Northeastern Institute of Botany): Sargento Cabral 2131, CC 209, 3400 Corrientes; tel. (783) 27309; fax (783) 27131; e-mail postmaster@unneib.edu.ar; Dir Ing. ANTONIO KRAPOVICKAS.

Instituto de Desarrollo Tecnológico para la Industria Química (INTEC) (Technological Development Institute of the Chemical Industry): Güemes 3450, 3000 Santa Fé; tel. (42) 55-9174; fax (42) 55-0944; e-mail director@intec.unl.edu.ar; Dir Dr ALBERTO E. CASSANO (acting).

Instituto de Geocronología y Geología Isotópica (INGEIS) (Institute of Isotope Geochronology and Geology): Pabellón INGEIS, Ciudad Universitaria, 1428 Buenos Aires; tel. 784-7798; fax 783-3024; e-mail postmaster@ingeis.uba.ar; Dir Dr ENRIQUE LINARES.

Instituto de Investigación de Productos Naturales, de Análisis y de Síntesis Orgánica (IPNAYS) (Institute for Research, Analysis and Organic Synthesis of Natural Products): Santiago del Estero 2829, 3000 Santa Fé; tel. (42) 55-3958; fax (42) 56-1146; e-mail rmalizia@fiqus.unl.edu.ar; Dir Ing. J. A. RETAMAR.

Instituto de Investigación Médica 'Mercedes y Martín Ferreyra' (INIMEC) (Mercedes and Martín Ferreyra Medical Research Institute): CC 389, 5000 Córdoba; premises at: Friuli 2434, Colinas de V. Sarfield, 5016 Cordoba; tel. (51) 68-1465; fax (51) 69-5163; e-mail lbeauge@immf.uncor.edu; Dir Dr LUISA BEAUGE.

Instituto de Investigaciones Bioquímicas (INIBIBB) (Biochemistry Research Institute): Edificio E3, Complejo de la Carrindanga, Florida 4000, 8000 Bahía Blanca, Buenos Aires; tel. (91) 26114; fax 86-1200; e-mail rtfjb1@criba.edu.ar; Dir Dr FRANCISCO J. BARRANTES.

Instituto de Investigaciónes en Catálisis y Petroquímica (INCAPE) (Catalysis and Petrochemistry Research Institute): Santiago del Estero 2654, 3000 Santa Fé; tel. (42) 53-3858; fax (42) 53-1068; e-mail parera@fiqus.unl.edu.ar; Dir Ing. JOSÉ M. PARERA.

Instituto de Investigaciones Estadísticas (INIE) (Statistical Research Institute): Av. Independencia 1900, CC 209, 4000 San Miguel de Tucumán; tel. (81) 36-4093; fax (81) 36-4105; e-mail postmaster@untiie.edu.ar; Dir Dr RAÚL P. MENTZ.

Instituto de Investigaciones Farmacológicas (ININFA) (Pharmacological Research Institute): Junín 956 (5° piso), 1113 Buenos Aires; tel. 961-6784; fax 963-8593; e-mail ininfa@huemul.ffyb.uba.ar; Dir Dra EDDA ADLER DE GRASCHINSKY.

Instituto de Investigaciones Geohistóricas (IIGHI) (Institute of Geohistorical Research): Av. Castelli 930, CC 438, 3500 Resistencia, Chaco; tel. (722) 27798; fax (722) 39983; e-mail postmaster@iighi.gov.ar; Dir Dr ERNESTO J. A. MAEDER.

Instituto de Limnología Dr Raul A. Ringuelet (ILPLA) (Limnology Institute): CC 712, 1900 La Plata, Buenos Aires; e-mail postmaster@ilpla.edu.ar; Dir Dr HUGO LOPEZ (acting).

Instituto de Matemática (INMABB) (Mathematics Institute): Avda Alem 1253, 8000 Bahía Blanca; tel. (91) 33382; fax (91) 55-1447; e-mail inmabb@arcriba.edu.ar; f. 1956; Dir Dra AURORA GERMANI.

Instituto de Mecánica Aplicada (IMA) (Institute of Applied Mechanics): Gorriti 43, 8000 Bahía Blanca; tel. (91) 45154; fax (91) 55-1447; e-mail ima@criba.edu.ar; Dir Dr PATRICIO A. A. LAURA.

Instituto de Neurobiología (IDNEU) (Neurobiology Institute): Serrano 669, 1414 Buenos Aires; tel. 855-7674; fax 856-7108; e-mail postmaster@fuacta.sld.ar; Dir Dr JUAN H. TRAMEZZANI.

Instituto Latinoamericano de Investigaciones Comparadas Oriente y Occidente (ILICOO) (Latin-American Institute for Comparative East-West Studies): Callao 853, 1023 Buenos Aires; tel. 811-2270; e-mail postmaster@uscsoc.edu.ar; f. 1973; library of 2,000 vols, 1,500 periodicals; Dir Prof. MARÍA M. TERREN; publ. *Oriente – Occidente*.

Instituto Multidisciplinario de Biología Celular (IMBICE) (Multidisciplinary Institute of Cellular Biology): Calle 525, e/10 y 11, CC 403, 1900 La Plata, Buenos Aires; tel. (21) 210112; fax (21) 25-3320; e-mail imbice@imbice.edu.ar; Dir Dr NÉSTOR O. BIANCHI.

Instituto Rosario de Investigaciónes en Ciencias de la Educación (IRICE) (Rosario Education Research Institute): Bv. 27 de Febrero 210 'bis', 2000 Rosario; tel. (41) 82-1769; fax (41) 82-1772; e-mail irice@ifir.ifir.edu.ar; Dir Dr NÉSTOR DIRECTORIO ROSELLI.

Fundación Miguel Lillo: Miguel Lillo 251, 4000 San Miguel de Tucumán; tel. and fax (81) 33-0868; f. 1931; scientific research in natural history; incl. institutes of Botany (Dir Lic. ANA MARÍA FRÍAS DE FERNANDEZ); Geology (Dir Dr CARLOS GONZALEZ) and Zoology (Dir Dr GUSTAVO SCROCCHI), Geobiological Information Centre of Northwest Argentina (135,000 documents, Dir. Prof. NATALIA SCHECHAJ), a natural history museum and cultural centre; Pres. Dr JORGE L. ROUGES; Dir Dr JOSÉ ANTONIO HAEDO ROSSI; publs *Genera et Species Plantarum Argentinarum, Genera et Species Animalium Argentinorum, Lilloa, Acta Zoologica Lilloana, Acta Geologica Lilloana, Opera Lilloana, Miscelánea, Serie Conservación de la Naturaleza, Extensión Científica y Cultural*.

Biological Sciences

Centro de Investigación de Biologia Marina (Marine Biology Research Centre): Hipólito Yrigoyen 3780, 1208 Buenos Aires; tel. 981-7934; f. 1960; library of 3,500 vols; Dir Dr OSCAR KÜHNEMANN; publs *Contribuciones Científicas, Contribuciones Técnicas*.

Centro de Investigaciones Pesqueras Bella Vista (Bella Vista Fisheries Research Centre): José Manuel Estrada 66, 3432 Bella Vista, Corrientes; tel. 42; f. 1954; library of 2,000 vols; Dir Lic. ALFREDO FORTUNY; publ. *Estadística pesquera Argentina* (annually).

Estación Hidrobiológica (Hydrobiology Station): 7631 Quequén, Buenos Aires; f. 1928; attached to 'B. Rivadavia' Argentine Museum of Natural Sciences; concerned especially with marine hydrobiology; Dir Prof. ENRIQUE BALECH; publ. *Trabajos de la Estación Hidrobiológica* (irregular).

Instituto de Botánica 'C. Spegazzini' (Botanical Institute): Calle 53 No. 477, 1900 La Plata, Buenos Aires; tel. (21) 21-9845; f. 1930; affiliated to the Museo de La Plata; mycological research; mycological collections from Argentina and all South America; Dir Prof. Dr ANGÉLICA M. ARAMBARRI; publs contributions to reviews, reprints.

Instituto de Botánica 'Darwinion' (Ch. Darwin Botanical Institute): Labardén 200, CC 22, 1642 San Isidro; tel. 743-4800; fax 747-4748; f. 1911; attached to the Academia Nacional de Ciencias Exactas, Físicas y Naturales and the Consejo Nacional de Investigaciones Científicas y Técnicas; research on vascular plants; library of 80,000 vols, 760 periodicals; herbarium; Dir Dr JUAN H. HUNZIKER; publs *Revista Darwiniana* (annually), *Hickenia* (irregular), *Taxonomic Research of Argentine Flora, Floras Regionales*.

Instituto Municipal de Botánica, Jardín Botánico 'Carlos Thays' (Municipal Botanical Institute, Carlos Thays Botanical Gardens): Sante Fé 3951, 1407 Buenos Aires; tel. 69-3954; f. 1898; library of 1,000 vols, 7,000 periodicals; Dir ANTONIO AMADO GARCÍA; publs *Index Seminum, Revista del Instituto de Botánica*.

Instituto Nacional de Investigación y Desarrollo Pesquero (National Institute for Fisheries Research and Development): Casilla 175, 7600 Mar del Plata; tel. (23) 86-0963; fax (23) 86-1830; e-mail postmaster@inidep.edu.ar; f. 1977; library of 3,400 vols, 750 periodicals; Dir Dr F. GEORGIADIS; publs *Revista, INIDEP Documento Científico, INIDEP Informe Técnico*.

Instituto Nacional de Limnología (National Institute of Limnology): José Maciá 1933, 3016 Santo Tomé, Santa Fé; tel. (42) 74-0723; fax (42) 75-0394; e-mail inali@arcride.edu.ar; f. 1962; library of 3,000 vols, 385 periodicals; Dir Prof. ELLY CORDIVIOLA DE YUAN.

Physical Sciences

Comisión Nacional de Energía Atómica (National Atomic Energy Commission): Avda del Libertador 8250, 1429 Buenos Aires; tel. (1) 704-1209; fax (1) 704-1154; f. 1950; govt agency; promotes and undertakes scientific and industrial research and applications of nuclear transmutations and reactions; research centres in Buenos Aires, Constituyentes, Ezeiza and Bariloche; library: see Libraries; Pres. Ing. EDUARDO SANTOS.

Comisión Nacional de Investigaciones Espaciales (CNIE) (National Commission for Space Research): Dorrego 4010, 1425 Buenos Aires; tel. 772-5474; telex 17511; f. 1960; carries out scientific and technological research into the peaceful use of space; library of 20,000 vols; Pres. GENARO MARIO SCIOLA; publ. *Informe Argentino de Actividades COSPAR* (annually).

Attached centres:

Centro de Investigaciones y Desarrollos Espaciales Mendoza (Mendoza Space Research and Development Centre): Observatorio Meteorológico Nacional, Parque Gral San Martín, 5500 Mendoza; tel. 24-7681; Dir Ing. OSVALDO A. PEINADO.

Centro del Teleobservación (Teleobservation Centre): Avda Libertador Gen. San Martín 1513, 1638 Vicente López; tel. 795-2689; f. 1977; Dir Com. Ing. RUBÉN HERNÁNDEZ.

Centro Espacial San Miguel—Observatorio Nacional de Física Cósmica (San Miguel Space Centre—National Cosmic Physics Observatory): Avda Mitre 3100, 1663 San Miguel; tel. 667-1272; f. 1935; library of 65,000 vols; Dir Ing. SIGFREDO PAGEL.

Instituto Argentino de Radioastronomía (Argentine Institute of Radioastronomy): Casilla de Correo 5, 1894 Villa Elisa; tel. and fax (21) 25-4909; f. 1963; library of 2000 vols, 100 periodicals; Dir Dr RAUL COLOMB; publ. *Contribuciones del Instituto*.

Observatorio Astronómico (Astronomic Observatory): Laprida 854, 5000 Córdoba; tel. (51) 40613; telex 51822; f. 1871; attached to the University of Córdoba; research and teaching; library of 5,000 vols; Dir Dr GUSTAVO J. CARRANZA; publs *Resultados, Reprints* (20 a year).

Observatorio Astronómico (Astronomic Observatory): Paseo del Bosque s/n, 1900 La Plata; tel. 21-7308; telex 31151; fax 21-1761; f. 1883; library of 25,000 vols, 500 periodicals; Dean Dr JUAN CARLOS FORTE.

Servicio Geológico Minero Argentino (Argentine Mining Geology Service): Avda Julio A. Roca 651 (10° piso), 1322 Buenos Aires; tel. (1) 349-3162; fax (1) 349-3160; attached to the State Secretariate of Mining of Min. of Economy; Exec. Sec. Dr ROBERTO PAGE; publs *Mapa geológico-económico de la República Argentina* (scale 1:200,000), *Mapa hidrogeológico de la República Argentina, Estadística Minera de la República Argentina*, etc.

Servicio Meteorológico Nacional (National Meteorological Service): 25 de Mayo 658, 1002 Buenos Aires; tel. (1) 312-4481; telex 27040; fax (1) 311-3968; f. 1872; library of 45,000 vols; Dir Com. RAMON AGUSTIN SONZINI; publs *Boletín informativo, Boletín climatológico*.

RELIGION, SOCIOLOGY AND ANTHROPOLOGY

Departamento de Estudios Etnográficos y Coloniales (Department of Ethnographical and Colonial Studies): Calle 25 de Mayo 1470, 3000 Santa Fé; tel. and fax (42) 59-5857; f. 1940; Dir Arq. LUIS MARIA CALVO.

Instituto Nacional de Antropología y Pensamiento Latinoamericano (National Institute of Anthropology and Latin American Thought): Calle 3 de Febrero 1378, 1426 Buenos Aires; tel. (1) 784-3371; fax (1) 784-3371; e-mail postmaster@bibapl.edu.ar; f. 1943; attached to the Secretariat for Culture at the President's Office; library of 15,000 vols, 1,600 periodicals; Dir Dra DIANA BOLANDI DE PERROT; publ. *Cuaderno*.

TECHNOLOGY

Instituto Argentino de Normalización (IRAM) (Argentine Standardization Institute): Chile 1192, 1098 Buenos Aires; tel. (1) 381-9754; f. 1935; library of 180,000 standards; Dir-Gen. Ing. JOSÉ LÓPEZ; publs *Nueva Dinámica* (4 a year), *Boletín IRAM* (monthly), *Catálogo General de Normas IRAM* (1 a year).

Instituto de Mecánica Aplicada y Estructuras (Institute of Structures and Applied Mechanics): Riobamba y Berutti, 2000 Rosario, Santa Fé; tel. (41) 25-6010; fax (41) 25-6207; f. 1963; library of 1,000 vols, 3,000 periodicals; Dir Ing. NOÉ NICOLÁS MATTANÓ.

Instituto Nacional de Tecnología Industrial (INTI) (National Institute of Industrial Technology): Avda Leandro N. Alem 1067 (7° piso), 1001 Buenos Aires; tel. 313-3013; telex 21859; fax 313-2130; f. 1957; library of 32,000 vols, 2,216 magazines, 105,000 standards; Pres. Eng. LEÓNIDAS J. F. MONTAÑA; publs *Boletín técnico* (irregular), *Dendroenergía* (2 a year), *Noticiteca* (quarterly).

Research institutes:

Centro de Investigación y Desarrollo en Construcciones (Centre for Construction Research and Development): Avda Gral Paz e/ Avda Albarellos 33/10, CC 157, 1650 San Martin, Buenos Aires; Dir Eng. R. LEONARDO CHECMAREW.

Centro de Investigación y Desarrollo en Física (Centre for Physics Research and Development): Avda Gral Paz e/ Avda de los Constituyentes y Avda Albarellos 3/44, CC 157, 1650 San Martin, Buenos Aires; fax (1) 713-4140; Dir Lic. GUSTAVO RANGUGNI.

Centro de Investigación en Tecnologías de Industrialización de Alimentos (Centre for Research on Technologies for the Industrialization of Food Production): Avda Gral Paz e/ Avda de los Constituyentes y Avda Albarellos 40, CC 157, 1650 San Martin, Buenos Aires; Dir Eng. GUILLERMO CAMBIAZZO.

Centro de Investigación de Tecnologías de Granos (Centre for Research on Technologies for the Industrialization of Grain Production): Avda Alte. Brown e/ Reconquista y Juan Jose Paso, 6500 Nueve de Julio, Buenos Aires; Dir Eng. NICOLÁS APRO.

Centro de Investigación y Desarrollo de Ingeniería Ambiental (Centre for Environmental Engineering Research and Development); Paseo Colón 850 (4 piso), 1063 Buenos Aires; tel. (1) 345-7541; fax (1) 331-5362; Dir Eng. LUIS A. DE TULIO.

Centro de Investigación y Desarrollo para el Uso Racional de la Energía (Centre for Research and Development for the Rational use of Energy): Avda Gral Paz e/ Avda de los Constituyentes y Avda Albarellos 5, CC 157, 1650 San Martin, Buenos Aires; Dir Eng. MARIO OGARA.

Centro de Investigación y Desarrollo de Métodos y Técnicas para Pequeñas y Medianas Empresas (Centre for Methods and Techniques Research and Development for Small and Medium-Size Industries): Avda Gral Paz e/ Avda de los Constituyentes y Avda Albarellos 12, CC 157, 1650 San Martin, Buenos Aires; Dir Eng. ROBERTO LÓPEZ.

Centro de Investigación de los Reglamentos Nacionales de Seguridad para Obras Civiles (Centre for Research for National Regulations on Civil Work Safety): Avda de los Immigrantes 1950 (Of. 22 y 24), 1104 Buenos Aires; Dir Eng. MARTA PARMIGIANI.

Centro de Investigación y Desarrollo sobre Contaminantes Especiales (Centre for Special Pollutants Research and Development): Avda Gral Paz e/ Avda de los Constituyentes y Avda Albarellos 38, CC 157, 1650 San Martin, Buenos Aires; tel. (1) 754-4074; fax (1) 753-5749; Dir Eng. ISABEL FRAGA.

Centro de Investigación y Desarrollo Textil (Centre for Textile Research and Development): Avda Gral Paz e/ Avda de los Constituyentes y Avda Albarellos 15, CC 157, 1650 San Martin, Buenos Aires; Dir Eng. PATRICIA MARINO.

Centro de Investigación y Desarrollo del Cuero (Centre for Leather Research and Development): Camino Centenario e/ 505 y 508, CC 6, 1897 Manuel Gonnet, Buenos Aires; tel. (21) 84-1876; fax (21) 84-0244; Dir Dr ALBERTO SOFÍA.

Centro de Investigación y Desarrollo de Carnes (Centre for Meat Research and Development): Avda Gral Paz e/ Avda de los Constituyentes y Avda Albarellos 47, CC 157, 1650 San Martin, Buenos Aires; Dir Eng. NÉLIDA PROLA.

Centro de Investigación y Desarrollo de Electrónica e Informática (Centre for Electronics and Computer Science Research and Development): Avda Gral Paz e/ Avda de los Constituyentes y Avda Albarellos 42, CC 157, 1650 San Martin, Buenos Aires; tel. (1) 754-4064; fax (1) 754-5194; Dir Eng. DANIEL LUPI.

Centro de Investigación y Desarrollo en Mecánica (Centre for Mechanics Research and Development): Avda Gral Paz e/ Avda de los Constituyentes y Avda Albarellos 9/46, CC 157, 1650 San Martin, Buenos Aires; tel. (1) 752-0818; fax (1) 754-5301; Dir Eng. MARIO QUINTEIRO.

Centro de Investigación y Desarrollo en Química y Petroquímica (Centre for Chemistry and Petrochemistry Research and Development): Avda Gral Paz e/ Avda de los Constituyentes y Avda Albarellos 38, CC 157, 1650 San Martin, Buenos Aires; Dir Lic. GRACIELA ENRIQUEZ.

Centro de Investigación y Asistencia Técnica a la Industria (Centre for Research and Technical Assistance to Industry): Avda Mitre y 20 de Junio, CC 548, 8336 Villa Regina, Rio Negro; tel. (941) 62810; Dir Eng. RODOLFO ARDENGHI.

Centro de Investigación de Celulosa y Papel (Centre for Cellulose and Paper Research): Avda Gral Paz e/ Avda de los Constituyentes y Avda Albarellos 15, CC 157, 1650 San Martin, Buenos Aires; Dir Eng. HUGO VELEZ.

Centro de Investigación y Desarrollo sobre Electrodeposición y Procesos Superficiales (Centre for Electroplating and Superficial Processes Research and Development): Avda Gral Paz e/ Avda de los Constituyentes y Avda Albarellos 46, CC 157, 1650 San Martin, Buenos Aires; Dir Eng. ALICIA NIÑO GÓMEZ.

Centro de Investigación y Desarrollo de la Industria de la Madera y Afines (Centre for the Wood Industry and Related Research and Development): Juana Gorriti 3520, 1708 Hurlingham, Buenos Aires; Dir Eng. GRACIELA RAMIREZ.

Centro de Investigación y Desarrollo de Envases y Embalajes (Centre for Packaging Research and Development): Avda Gral Paz e/ Avda de los Constituyentes y Avda Albarellos 48, CC 157, 1650 San Martin, Buenos Aires; Dir Eng. CARLOS LOMO.

Centro de Investigación y Desarrollo de Tecnológico de la Industria del Caucho (Centre for Research and Technological Development of the Rubber Industry): Avda Gral Paz e/ Avda de los Constituyentes y Avda Albarellos 10, CC 157, 1650 San Martin, Buenos Aires; Dir Lic. LILIANA REHAK.

Centro de Investigación y Desarrollo para la Industria Plástica (Centre for Research and Development for the Plastics Industry): Avda Gral Paz e/ Avda de los Constituyentes y Avda Albarellos 16, CC 157, 1650 San Martin, Buenos Aires; Dir Dr JUAN CARLOS LUCAS.

Libraries and Archives

Bahía Blanca

Asociación Bernardino Rivadavia—Biblioteca Popular (People's Library of the Bernardino Rivadavia Association): Avda Colón 31, 8000 Bahía Blanca; tel. (91) 27492; f. 1882; 119,265 vols; Pres. Prof. RAÚL OSCAR GOUARNALUSSE; Sec. MARÍA LUISA GASTAMINZA; publ. *Boletín Informativo* (quarterly).

Biblioteca Central de la Universidad Nacional del Sur (Central Library of the National University of the South): Avda Alem 1253, 8000 Bahía Blanca; tel. (91) 28035; telex 81712; fax (91) 55-1447; f. 1948; 164,000 vols, 7,293 periodicals; Chief Librarian MARTA IBARLUCEA DE ROIZ; publs *Memoria Anual, Ultimas Adquisiciones*.

Buenos Aires

Archivo General de la Nación (National Archives): Av. Leandro N. Alem 246, 1003 Buenos Aires; tel. (1) 331-5531; fax (1) 334-0065; f. 1821; Supervisor MIGUEL UNAMUNO; publ. *Revista* (annually).

Biblioteca Argentina para Ciegos (Argentine Library for the Blind): Lezica 3909, 1202 Buenos Aires; tel. and fax (1) 981-0137; f. 1924; talking books, 14,000 vols in Braille; Dir Dr MARIANO GODACHEVICH; publs *Burbujas, Hacia La Luz, Con Fundamento* (6 a year).

Biblioteca Central de la Armada (Central Library of the Navy): Estado Mayor General de la Armada, Calle Comodoro Py 2055 (3° piso), 1104 Buenos Aires; tel. 317-2039; f. 1914; 160,000 vols; 50 brs; Dir Capt. LUIS ALBERTO PONS; publ. *Revista de Publicaciones Navales*.

Biblioteca Central de la Universidad del Salvador 'Padre Guillermo Furlong' (Fr Guillermo Furlong Central Library of the University of the Saviour): Presidente Perón 1818, 1040 Buenos Aires; tel. 371-0422; e-mail uds-bibl@salvador.edu.ar; f. 1956; 55,000 vols; Dir LAURA MARTINO; publ. *Boletín Bibliográfico*.

Biblioteca de Arte (Art Library): Avda Libertador General San Martín 1473, 1425 Buenos Aires; tel. 803-0714; f. 1910; part of the Museo Nacional de Bellas Artes; visual arts; 40,000 vols; Dir RAQUEL EDELMAN.

Biblioteca del Servicio Geológico Minero Argentino (Library of the Argentine Mining Geology Service): Avda Julio A. Roca 651 (piso 9), 1322 Buenos Aires; tel. (1) 349-3200; fax (1) 349-3198; f. 1905; 150,000 vols, 45,000 pamphlets, 15,000 maps; Dir Lic. MARA JANITENS; publs *Boletines, Anales,* technical reports, statistics, maps, etc.

Biblioteca de la Sociedad Rural Argentina (Library of Argentine Agricultural Society): Florida 460, 1005 Buenos Aires; f. 1866; tel. (1) 322-3431; fax (1) 325-8231; 47,500 vols; Dir Dr VÍCTOR LUIS FUNES; publs *Anales de la Sociedad Rural Argentina* (quarterly), *Boletín, Memoria* (annually).

Biblioteca de Leprología 'Dr Enrique P. Fidanza' (Dr Enrique P. Fidanza Leprosy Library): Federación del Patronato del Enfermo de Lepra de la República Argentina, Beruti 2373/77, 1106 Buenos Aires; tel. 83-1815; f. 1930; 4,000 vols, 35,000 cards in its catalogues; museum of histopathology of skin; publ. *Temas de Leprología*.

Biblioteca del Banco Central de la República Argentina (Library of the Central Bank of the Republic of Argentina): San Martín 216, 1004 Buenos Aires; tel. (1) 348-3772; telex 24031; fax (1) 348-3771; f. 1935; 100,000 vols; Dir MARTA S. GUTIÉRREZ; publs *Boletín Estadístico* (monthly), *Boletín Monetario y Financiero* (4 a year), *Informe Anual del Presidente al Congreso* (1 a year), *Notas Técnicas* (irregular), *Documentos de Trabajo* (irregular), *Información de Entidades Financieras* (monthly).

Biblioteca del Bibliotecario 'Dr Augusto Raúl Cortazar' (Library of the Librarian Dr Augusto Raúl Cortazar): México 564, 1097 Buenos Aires; f. 1944; is a section of the Escuela Nacional de Bibliotecarios (Instituto Superior de Enseñanza); 2,500 vols; Dir RUBY A. ESCANDE.

Biblioteca del Congreso de la Nación (Library of the National Congress): Rivadavia 1850, 1033 Buenos Aires; tel. (1) 476-1641; fax (1) 954-1067; f. 1859; 2,000,000 vols; Dir DOMINGO A. BRAVI; publ. *Boletín*.

Biblioteca del Ministerio de Relaciones Exteriores y Culto (Ministry of Foreign Affairs and Religion Library): Arenales 761, 1061 Buenos Aires; tel. 41-1498; 50,000 vols; Dir HORACIO R. PIÑEYRO.

Biblioteca Nacional (National Library): Agüero 2502, 1425 Buenos Aires; tel. 806-6155; fax 807-0889; e-mail postmaster@siscor.bibnal.edu.ar; f. 1810; 2,000,000 vols, 46,177 MSS; Dir OSCAR SBARRA MITRE; publ. *La Biblioteca*.

Biblioteca Nacional de Aeronáutica (National Aeronautics Library): CC 3389, 1000 Buenos Aires; located at: Paraguay 748, 1057 Buenos Aires; tel. (1) 314-8061; fax (1) 314-1794; f. 1927; aeronautics, astronautics, aeronautical law; 50,000 vols; Chief Librarian ANGÉLICA A. LLORCA; publ. *Aeroespacio*.

Biblioteca Nacional de Maestros (National Library for Teachers): Pizzurno 953, 1020 Buenos Aires; tel. (1) 811-0275; fax (1) 811-0275; f. 1870; 150,000 vols; general reference and education; Dir Lic. GRACIELA PERRONE.

Biblioteca Nacional Militar (National Military Library): Santa Fé 750, 1059 Buenos Aires; tel. 311-4560; f. 1938; 150,000 vols; Librarian Cor. MARTÍN SUÁREZ.

Biblioteca Pública del Colegio de Escribanos (Library of the College of Notaries): Callao 1540, 1024 Buenos Aires; tel. and fax 807-1637; f. 1886; law and social science; 30,000 vols; Librarian ANA MARÍA DANZA; publs *Boletín Informativo, Revista del Notariado, Boletín de Legislación*.

Biblioteca Tornquist (Tornquist Library): Ernesto Tornquist & Cía Ltda, Bartolomé Mitre 559, 1036 Buenos Aires; tel. 33-4006; f. 1916; economics and social sciences; 55,000 vols; Dir JUAN JOSÉ GALLI.

Centro Argentino de Información Científica y Tecnológica (CAICYT) (Argentine Centre of Scientific and Technological Information): Moreno 431, 1091 Buenos Aires; tel. (1) 342-1777; fax (1) 342-1777; f. 1958; attached to Consejo Nacional de Investigaciones Científicas y Técnicas; Dir TITO SUTER.

Centro de Documentación e Información Internacional (International Centre of Documentation and Information): Dirección Nacional General de Cooperación Internacional, Ministerio de Cultura y Educación, Agüero 2502 (3° piso), 1425 Buenos Aires; f. 1959; publs of United Nations, Organization of American States, etc.; 5,000 vols; Dir FRANCISCO PIÑÓN.

Centro de Información de la Comisión Nacional de Energía Atómica (Information Centre of the National Atomic Energy Commission): Avda del Libertador 8250, 1429 Buenos Aires; tel. 701-9380; telex 23458; f. 1950; 36,700 vols, 450 current periodicals, 450,000 microcards and reports; Librarian ALEJANDRA NARDI; publs *Informes CNEA, Memoria CNEA*.

Centro de Información y Estadística Industrial (Centre for Industrial Information and Statistics): C/o INTI, Avda Leandro N. Alem 1067 (7° piso), 1101 Buenos Aires; attached to Instituto Nacional de Tecnología Industrial; Dir Ing. ALFREDO P. GALLIANO.

Dirección General de Bibliotecas Municipales (Public Libraries Administration): Calle Talcahuano 1261, 1014 Buenos Aires; tel. 811-9027; fax 811-0867; f. 1928; comprises 25 public municipal libraries in Buenos Aires with an aggregate of 350,000 vols; Dir-Gen. Prof. JOSEFINA DELGADO; publs *Cuadernos de Buenos Aires, Guía Cultural de Buenos Aires*.

Sistema de Bibliotecas y de Información, Universidad de Buenos Aires (Library and Information System of the University of Buenos Aires): Azcuénaga 280 (2° piso), 1029 Buenos Aires; tel. (1) 951-1366 ext. 500; fax (1) 952-6557; e-mail postmaster@sisbi.uba.ar; f. 1941; there are 17 constituent faculty libraries; Gen. Co-ordinator SUSANA SOTO.

Córdoba

Biblioteca de la Universidad Católica de Córdoba (Library of Córdoba Catholic University): Trejo 323, 5000 Córdoba; tel. 66024; f. 1956; 40,000 vols, 700 periodicals; Dir Dra ROSA HOFMANN DE BLANCO; publ. *Acta Scientifica* (irregular).

Biblioteca Mayor de la Universidad Nacional de Córdoba (Main Library of Córdoba National University): Calle Obispo Trejo 242 (1° piso), CC 63, 5000 Córdoba; tel. (51) 33-1072; fax (51) 33-1079; e-mail rbestani@sri.trejo.unc.edu.ar; f. 1613; 150,000 vols, 3,890 periodicals and pre-1860 newspapers; partial depository for UN publs; Dir Lic. ROSA M. BESTANI.

La Plata

Biblioteca de la Honorable Legislatura (Law Library): CC 101, 1900 La Plata; tel. 21-0081; 40,000 vols; Dir Dr RICARDO G. DELLA MOTTA.

Biblioteca de la Universidad Nacional de La Plata (Library of La Plata National University): Plaza Rocha 137, 1900 La Plata; tel. (21) 25-5004; telex 31151; fax (21) 25-5004; f. 1884; 450,000 vols, 5,000 periodicals; spec. collns incl. South American newspapers relating to the Independence movement, South American history and geography and first travels in South America; 60 br. libraries within the univ.; Dir CARLOS JOSÉ TEJO; publ. *Informaciones*.

Biblioteca del Ministerio de Gobierno de la Provincia de Buenos Aires (Library of the Buenos Aires Province Ministry of the Interior): Casa de Gobierno, 1900 La Plata; law, politics and economics; 20,000 vols.

Biblioteca y Centro de Documentación del Ministerio de Economía de la Provincia de Buenos Aires (Library and Documentation Centre of the Ministry of the Economy of the Province of Buenos Aires): Calle 8 entre 45 y 46 (piso 1 Of. 25), 1900 La Plata; tel. (21) 29-4400 ext. 4702; 13,800 vols; Dir (vacant); publs *Noticias de Economía* (6 a year), *Cuadernos de Economía* (6 a year).

Mendoza

Biblioteca Central de la Universidad Nacional de Cuyo (Central Library of the National University of Cuyo): CC 420, Centro Universitario, 5500 Mendoza; tel. 25-7463 ext. 2050; f. 1939; 120,000 vols; Dir Lic. JUAN GUILLERMO MILIA; publs *Boletín Bibliográfico, Cuadernos de la Biblioteca* (both irregular).

Biblioteca Pública General San Martín (General San Martín Public Library): Remedios Escalada de San Martín 1843, 5500 Mendoza; tel. 23-1674; f. 1822; 120,000 vols; special collections: local authors, children's books; Dir ANA MARIA GARCIA BUTTINI; publs *BAL* (Biblioteca de Autor Local, annually), *BIL* (Biblioteca Infanto/Juvenil, series expected to begin in 1991), *Versión* (annually), *Boletín Bibliográfico*.

Pergamino (Buenos Aires)

Biblioteca Pública Municipal 'Dr Joaquín Menéndez' (Dr Joaquín Menéndez Municipal Public Library): San Martín 838, 2700 Pergamino, Buenos Aires; f. 1901; 58,000 vols; Librarian ALICIA D. PARODI.

Resistencia

Centro de Información Bioagropecuaria y Forestal (CIBAGRO) (Bio-Farming and Forestry Information Centre): Dirección de Bibliotecas, Universidad Nacional del Nordeste, Avda Las Heras 727, 3500 Resistencia, Chaco; tel. and fax (722) 43742; f. 1976; 2,500 books, 2,800 pamphlets, 1,000 periodicals; special collections: FAO and other int. agricultural orgs; Dir JULIO E. ENCINAS; publs *Obras Nuevas en el Centro 'Ciencias Forestales', Obras Nuevas en el Centro 'Ciencias Agropecuarias', Ciencias Forestales – Bibliografía, Agronea, Bibliografía sobre El Quebracho, Bibliografía sobre El Picudo del Algodonero, Bibliografía Forestal Nacional* etc.

Forest Information Network for Latin America and the Caribbean (RIFALC): CIBAGRO, Dirección de Bibliotecas, Universidad Nacional del Nordeste, Avda Las Heras 727, 3500 Resistencia, Chaco; tel. and fax (722) 43742; f. 1985; co-ordinates and integrates at regional level the efforts made by individual networks, and makes accessible in each country all the information available; mems: 19 orgs in 12 countries; Exec. Sec JULIO E. ENCINAS; publ. *Boletín Informativo*.

Rosario

Biblioteca Argentina 'Dr Juan Alvarez' de la Municipalidad de Rosario (Dr Juan Alvarez Argentine Library of the Municipality of Rosario): Pte Roca 731, 2000 Rosario; tel. (41) 802-2538; fax (41) 80-2561; e-mail biblarg@rosario.gov.ar; f. 1912; 180,000 vols; Dir MARÍA DEL CARMEN D'ANGELO.

Biblioteca Pública 'Estanislao S. Zeballos' (Estanislao S. Zeballos Public Library): Bv. Oroño 1261, 2000 Rosario; tel. and fax (41) 26-4052 ext. 112; f. 1905; economics, accountancy, business studies, statistics; 111,000 vols; Dir BEATRIZ LODEZANO; publ. *Revista de la Facultad de Ciencias Económicas y Estadística* (irregular).

San Miguel (Buenos Aires)

Biblioteca de las Facultades de Filosofía y Teología S.I. (Library of the Faculties of Philosophy and Theology): Avda Mitre 3226, 1663 San Miguel, Buenos Aires; tel. (1) 455-7992; fax (1) 455-6442; e-mail gerardo@bibusv.edu.ar; f. 1931; central deposit library; 135,000 vols, 700 current periodicals; Librarian Prof. GERARDO LOSADA; publ. *Stromata* (quarterly).

Tucumán

Biblioteca Central de la Universidad Nacional de Tucumán (Central Library of the National University of Tucuman): Lamadrid 817, CC 167, 4000 Tucumán; tel. 31-0122; telex 61143; fax 31-1462; f. 1917; 110,000 vols; Dir Prof. GUILLERMO J. KREIBOHM; publs *Serie Ciencia de la Documentación, Boletín Bibliográfico, Colección del Sesquicentenario de la Independencia Argentina*.

Museums and Art Galleries

Buenos Aires

Museo Argentino de Ciencias Naturales 'Bernardino Rivadavia'—Instituto Nacional de Investigación de las Ciencias Naturales (Bernardino Rivadavia Argentine Museum of Natural Sciences—National Research Institute of Natural Sciences): Avda Angel Gallardo 470, Suc. 5, 1405 Buenos Aires; tel. 982-0306; fax 982-5243; f. 1823; zoology, botany, palaeontology, geology; library of 500,000 vols; Dir Dr WOLFGANG VOLKHEIMER; publs *Comunicaciones* and reviews on: Botanical Sciences, Geological Sciences, Zoological Sciences, Hydrobiology, Palaeontology, Entomology, Parasitology and Ecology; also pamphlets.

Museo de Armas de la Nación (National Arms Museum): Santa Fé 750, 1059 Buenos Aires; tel. 312-9774; f. 1904; library of 1,000 vols; Dir Cnl JULIO E. SOLDAINI.

Museo de Arte Hispanoamericano 'Isaac Fernández Blanco' (Isaac Fernández Blanco Museum of Spanish-American Art): Suipacha 1422, 1011 Buenos Aires; tel. 327-0183; f. 1947; 16th- to 19th-century Spanish- and Portuguese-American art, silver, furniture; library of 5,000 vols; Dir Arq. ALBERTO PETRINA.

Museo de Arte Moderno (Museum of Modern Art): Avda San Juan 350, 1147 Buenos Aires; tel. 361-1121; f. 1956; Latin American paintings, especially Argentine, and contemporary schools; Co-ordinator LAURA BUCCELLATO.

Museo de Bellas Artes de la Boca (Boca Fine Arts Museum): Pedro Mendoza 1835, 1169 Buenos Aires; tel. 21-1080; painting, sculpture, engravings, and maritime museum; Dir Dr GUILLERMO C. DE LA CANAL.

Museo de la Dirección Nacional del Antártico (Museum of the National Antarctic Administration): Angel Gallardo 470, 1405 Buenos Aires; tel. 812-7327; natural and physical sciences of the Antarctic; Dir Dr RICARDO CAPDEVILA.

Museo de la Policía Federal Argentina (Argentine Federal Police Museum): San Martín 353 (7° y 8° pisos), 1004 Buenos Aires; tel. 394-2017; f. 1899; Dir JOSÉ A. GUTIÉRREZ.

Museo Etnográfico 'Juan B. Ambrosetti' (Juan B. Ambrosetti Ethnographical Museum): Moreno 350, 1091 Buenos Aires; tel. and fax 331-7788; attached to the Faculty of Philosophy and Letters of the University of Buenos Aires; f. 1904; ethnography and archaeology of Argentina, the Americas, Africa, Asia and Oceania; library of 80,000 vols; Dir Dr JOSÉ ANTONIO PÉREZ GOLLÁN; publ. *Runa* (annually).

Museo Histórico de la Ciudad de Buenos Aires 'Brigadier-General Cornelio de Saavedra' (Brig.-Gen. Cornelio de Saavedra Historical Museum of the City of Buenos Aires): C. Larralde 6309, 1431 Buenos Aires; tel. 572-0746; f. 1942; library of 3,600 vols; Dir ALBERTO GABRIEL PIÑEIRO.

Museo Histórico Nacional (National History Museum): Defensa 1600, 1143 Buenos Aires; tel. (1) 307-4457; fax (1) 307-4457; f. 1889; library of 15,000 vols; Dir Dr ALFREDO I. BARBAGALLO.

Museo Histórico Sarmiento (Sarmiento History Museum): Cuba 2079, 1428 Buenos Aires; tel. (1) 783-7555; fax (1) 788-5157; f. 1938; library of 13,000 vols; Dir BEATRIZ ARTAZA DE GLEZER.

Museo Mitre (Mitre Museum): San Martín 336, 1004 Buenos Aires; tel. 394-7659; f. 1907; preserves the household of Gen. Bartolomé Mitre; antique maps, coins and medals; library of 66,621 vols on American history, geography and ethnology, archive of 80,000 historical documents; Dir Dr JORGE CARLOS MITRE.

Museo Municipal de Arte Español 'Enrique Larreta' (Enrique Larreta Municipal Museum of Spanish Art): Juramento 2291 y Obligado 2139, 1428 Buenos Aires; tel. (1) 784-4040; f. 1962; 13th- to 18th-century wood carvings, gilt objects and painted panels, paintings of Spanish School from 16th to 20th centuries, tapestries, furniture; library of 9,700 vols; Dir MERCEDES DI PAOLA DE PICOT.

Museo Nacional de Aeronáutica (National Museum of Aeronautics): Obligado 4550, 1425 Buenos Aires; tel. 773-0665; f. 1960; Dir Cdre SANTOS A. DOMINGUEZ KOCH (retd).

Museo Nacional de Arte Decorativo (National Museum of Decorative Art): Avda del Libertador 1902, 1425 Buenos Aires; tel. (1) 801-8248; fax 802-6606; f. 1937; furniture, sculpture, tapestries, European and South American works; library of 2,000 vols; Dir ALBERTO GUILLERMO BELLUCCI.

Museo Nacional de Arte Oriental (National Museum of Oriental Art): Avda del Libertador 1902 (1° piso), 1425 Buenos Aires; tel. and fax (1) 801-5988; f. 1966; Asian and African art; library of 1,500 books, 2,500 vols of periodicals; Dir Prof. OSVALDO SVANASCINI; publ. *Revista*.

Museo Nacional de Bellas Artes (National Museum of Fine Arts): Avda del Libertador 1473, 1425 Buenos Aires; tel. 803-0714; fax 803-4062; f. 1895; 19th- and 20th-century Argentine painting, American and European painting, classical painting and sculpture, pre-Colombian art; library of 50,000 vols, 200,000 booklets; Dir Arq. ALBERTO G. BELLUCCI.

Museo Naval de la Nación (National Museum of Naval History): Paseo Victorica 602, Tigre, 1648 Buenos Aires; tel. (1) 749-0608; f. 1892; library of 3,000 vols; Dir Capt. (retd) HORACIO MOLINA PICO.

Museo Numismático 'Dr José Evaristo Uriburu' (Dr José Evaristo Uriburo Numismatics Museum): Banco Central de la República Argentina, Calle San Martín 216, 1° piso, 1004 Buenos Aires; tel. 348-3882; fax 348-3699; f. 1935; Dir JOSÉ MARÍA AVILÉS.

Museo Social Argentino (Argentine Museum of Sociology): Avda Corrientes 1723, 1042 Buenos Aires; tel. 375-4601; fax 375-4600; f. 1911; library of 80,000 vols; Pres. Dr GUILLERMO GARBARINI ISLAS; publs *Foro Economico* (2 a year), *Foro Político* (3 a year).

Córdoba

Museo Botánico (Botanical Museum): Universidad Nacional de Córdoba, CC 495, 5000 Córdoba; tel. and fax (51) 33-2104; f. 1870; conducts research as a unit of Instituto Multidisciplinario de Biología Vegetal (run by CONICET and Universidad Nacional de Córdoba); library of 8,000 vols; Dir Ing. Agr. ARMANDO T. HUNZIKER; publs *Kurtziana* (annually), *Lorentzia* (irregular).

Museo Provincial de Bellas Artes 'Emilio A. Caraffa' (Emilio A. Caraffa Provincial

Museum of Fine Arts): Avda Hipólito Irigoyen 651, 5000 Córdoba; tel. 69-0786; f. 1916; Argentine and foreign paintings, sculptures, drawings and engravings; library and archive; Dir Lic. GRACIELA ELIZABETH PALELLA.

Museo Provincial de Ciencias Naturales 'Bartolomé Mitre' (Bartolomé Mitre Provincial Museum of Natural Sciences): Avda Hipólito Irigoyen 115, 5000 Córdoba; tel. 22-1428; f. 1919; geology, zoology, botany; library of 3,400 vols and periodicals; Dir MARTA CANO DE MARTIN.

Corrientes

Museo Histórico de Corrientes (Corrientes Historical Museum): Calle 9 de Julio 1044, 3400 Corrientes; f. 1929; history of Corrientes Province; library of 1,900 volumes; Dir MIGUEL FERNANDO GONZÁLEZ AZCOAGA; publ. *Boletín de Extensión Cultural*.

La Plata

Museo de La Plata (La Plata Museum): Paseo del Bosque s/n, 1900 La Plata; tel. (21) 39125; telex 31151; fax (21) 25-7527; f. 1884; anthropology, archaeology, geology, natural history (incl. palaeontological colln of Patagonian mammalia); library of 60,000 vols, 240,000 periodicals; Dir Dr EDGARDO O. ROLLERI; publs *Anales*, *Revista*, *Notas*, *Novedades*, *Obra del Centenario*, *Obra del Cincuentenario*, *Serie Técnica y Didáctica*.

Luján

Complejo Museografico 'Enrique Udaondo' (Enrique Udaondo Museographic Complex): Lezica y Torrezuri 917, 6700 Luján; tel. (323) 20245; f. 1923; comprises four museums: Museo Colonial e Histórico (history, archaeology, silver, paintings, furniture), Museo de Transportes (transport), Museo del Automóvil and Pabellón 'Belgrano' y Depósitos (vintage cars); Dir CARLOS A. SCANNAPIECO.

Mendoza

Museo de Ciencias Naturales y Antropológicas 'Juan Cornelio Moyano' (Juan Cornelio Moyano Museum of Anthropology and Natural Sciences): Extremo Sur del Lago, Parque General San Martín, 5500 Mendoza; tel. and fax (61) 28-7666; f. 1911; library of 18,900 vols on American and Argentine history; Asst Dir Prof. CLARA ABAL DE RUSSO; publ. *Boletín* (2 a year).

Paraná

Museo de Ciencias Naturales y Antropológicas 'Prof. Antonio Serrano' (Prof. Antonio Serrano Museum of Anthropology and Natural Sciences): CC 71, Avda Rivadavia 462, 3100 Paraná; tel. 31-2635; f. 1917; library of 35,000 vols; Dir Lic. CARLOS N. CERUTI; publs *Memorias*, research works.

Museo Histórico 'Martiniano Leguizamón' (Martiniano Leguizamón Historical Museum): Laprida y Buenos Aires, 3100 Paraná; tel. 12735; f. 1948; library of 27,000 vols; library and archive; Dir TERESA ROCHA.

Rosario

Museo Histórico Provincial de Rosario 'Dr Julio Marc' (Rosario Dr Julio Marc Provincial History Museum): Parque Independencia, 2000 Rosario; tel. 21-9678; f. 1939; library of 22,000 vols; Hon. Dir EUGENIO A. TRAVELLA.

Museo Municipal de Arte Decorativo 'Firma y Odilo Estevez' (Firma y Odilo Estevez Municipal Decorative Arts Museum): Santa Fé 748, 2000 Rosario; tel. and fax (41) 80-2547; e-mail museo@museoestevez.gov.ar; f. 1968; Curator P. A. SINOPOLI.

Museo Municipal de Bellas Artes 'Juan B. Castagnino' (Juan B. Castagnino Municipal Fine Arts Museum): Avda Pellegrini 2202, 2000 Rosario; tel. and fax 21-7310; f. 1937; library of 2,500 vols; Dir Prof. BERNARDO MIGUEL BALLESTEROS.

San Carlos de Bariloche

Museo de la Patagonia 'Dr Francisco P. Moreno' (Dr Francisco P. Moreno Museum of Patagonia): Centro Cívico, 8400 San Carlos de Bariloche, Río Negro; tel. (944) 22309; fax (944) 22309; e-mail museo@bariloche.com.ar; f. 1940; political history of Patagonia, ethnology, natural sciences, archaeology; library of 2,500 vols; Dir Lic. CECILIA GIRGENTI; publs *Antropología, Diversidad Cultural de la Argentina*.

Santa Fé

Museo de Bellas Artes 'Rosa Galisteo de Rodriguez' (Rosa Galisteo de Rodriguez Museum of Fine Arts): 4 de Enero 1510, 3000 Santa Fé; tel. and fax (42) 596142; f. 1922; contemporary Argentine and modern art; library of 4,200 vols; Dir Profa NYDIA DE IMPINI.

Museo Histórico Provincial de Santa Fé (Santa Fé Provincial Museum of History): San Martín 1490, 3000 Santa Fé; tel. (42) 59-3760; f. 1943; Dir Prof. ALICIA TALSKY DE RONCHI.

Museo Provincial de Ciencias Naturales 'Florentino Ameghino' (Florentino Ameghino Provincial Museum of Natural History): 1° Junta 2859, 3000 Santa Fé; tel. and fax (42) 52-3843; e-mail ameghino@magic.santafe.gov.ar; f. 1914; zoology, botany, geology, palaeobiology; public library of 40,000 vols; Dir Lic. CARLOS A. VIRASORO; publ. *Comunicaciones*.

Santiago del Estero

Museo Provincial de Arqueología 'Wagner' (Wagner Provincial Archaeological Museum): Calle Avellaneda, 4200 Santiago del Estero; tel. 1064; archaeology of Chaco-Santiagueno and later cultures; Dir OLIMPIA L. RIGHETTI.

Tandil

Museo Municipal de Bellas Artes de Tandil (Tandil Municipal Museum of Fine Arts): Chacabuco 357, 7000 Tandil; tel. 2000; f. 1920; paintings of Classical, Impressionist, Cubist and Modern schools; small library; Dir E. VALOR.

Ushuaia

Museo Territorial (Regional Museum): Maipú 174/177, 9410 Ushuaia, Tierra del Fuego; tel. and fax 21863; f. 1979; history and natural sciences; library of 5,000 vols; Dir OSCAR PABLO ZANOLA; publs *Museo Territorial*, *Programa Extremo Oriental del Archipiélago Fueguino*, *Arqueología de la Isla Grande de Tierra del Fuego*, *Raíces del Fin del Mundo* (3 a year).

Universities

There are three main categories of Universities in Argentina: National (or Federal), which are supported by the Federal Budget; Provincial (or State), supported by the Provincial Budgets, and Private Universities, created and supported entirely by private initiative, but authorized to function by the Ministry of Education.

National Universities

UNIVERSIDAD DE BUENOS AIRES

Calle Viamonte 430/444, 1053 Buenos Aires
Telephone: 312-5854
Fax: 311-0516

Founded 1821
Academic year: March to November

Rector: Dr OSCAR J. SHUBEROFF
Vice-Rector: Dr ALBERTO BOVERIS
Financial Director: CPN NÉLIDA MUFFATTI
Library Director: GUDELIA ARÁOZ

Number of teachers: 21,864
Number of students: 206,658

Library: see under Libraries

Publications: the faculties publish their own periodicals.

DEANS

Faculty of Law and Social Sciences (Avda Pte Figueroa Alcorta 2263): Dr ANDRÉS JOSÉ D'ALESSIO
Faculty of Economic Sciences (Avda Córdoba 2122): Dr RODOLFO PÉREZ
Faculty of Exact and Natural Sciences (Ciudad Universitaria, Pabellón 2, Núñez): Dr EDUARDO FRANCISCO RECONDO
Faculty of Architecture, Design and Town Planning (Ciudad Universitaria, Pabellón 3, Núñez): Arq. BERARDO DUJOVNE
Faculty of Philosophy and Letters: (Puan 470): Prof. LUIS AVELINO YANES
Faculty of Engineering (Paseo Colón 850): Ing. CARLOS ALBERTO RAFFO
Faculty of Medicine (Paraguay 2155): Dr LUIS NICOLÁS FERREIRA
Faculty of Agriculture (Avda San Martín 4453): Ing. Agr. GUILLERMO MARIO MURPHY
Faculty of Dentistry (M. T. de Alvear 2142): Dr JUAN ANTONIO PEZZA
Faculty of Pharmacy and Biochemistry (Junín 954): Dr D. ALBERTO ANTONIO BOVERIS
Faculty of Veterinary Sciences (Chorroarín 280): Med. Vet. SUSANA LAURA MIRANDE
Faculty of Psychology (Hipólito Irigoyen 3238/46): Lic. RAÚL COUREL
Faculty of Social Sciences (Marcelo T. de Alvear 2230): Lic. JUAN CARLOS PORTANTIERO

SELECTED AFFILIATED INSTITUTES

Escuela Superior de Comercio 'Carlos Pellegrini': Marcelo T. de Alvear 1851, 1122 Buenos Aires; tel. 812-1824; f. 1890; incorporated in the University of Buenos Aires 1912; six-year course in commercial education; Rector Dr ABRAHAM LEONARDO GAK.

Colegio Nacional de Buenos Aires: Bolívar 263, 1066 Buenos Aires; tel. 331-6777; Rector Dr. ENRIQUE GROISMAN.

Instituto de Investigaciones Médicas: see under Research Institutes.

Instituto de Oncología 'Angel H. Roffo': Avda San Martín 5481, 1417 Buenos Aires; tel. 503-4370; f. 1966; library of 3,000 vols, 180 periodicals; Dir Dr ALEJO A. L. CARUGATTI.

Instituto Modelo de Clínica Médica 'Luis Agote': Avda Córdoba 2351, 11° piso, Buenos Aires; tel. (1) 961-6001; Exec. Dir Dr FLORENTINO SANGUINETTI.

Instituto de Perfeccionamiento Médico-Quirúrgico 'Prof. Dr José María Jorge': Avda Córdoba 2351, 7° piso, Buenos Aires; tel. (1) 961-6001; Exec. Dir Dr FLORENTINO SANGUINETTI.

UNIVERSIDAD NACIONAL DE CATAMARCA

Esquiu 612, 4700 Catamarca

Telephone: (833) 2-4099
Fax: (833) 31200
E-mail: siuc@catam.unca.edu.ar

Founded 1972
Academic year: February to December

Rector: Agrim. JULIO LUIS SALERNO
Vice-Rector: Lic. ROLANDO E. CORONEL

Secretary-General: Ing. CARLOS RUBEN MICHAUD
Librarian: MARÍA EMILIA MARTÍNEZ

Number of teachers: 304
Number of students: 1,666

Publication: *Aportes*.

DEANS

Faculty of Agricultural Sciences: Ing. Agr. EDMUNDO JOSÉ A. AGUERO
Faculty of Economics and Administration: C. P. N. DANIEL EDUARDO TOLOZA
Faculty of Health Sciences: Dr JORGE DANIEL BRIZUELA DEL MORAL
Faculty of Technology and Applied Sciences: Agrim. FÉLIX RAMÓN DOERING
Faculty of Humanities: Lic. ROLANDO EDGARDO CORONEL
Faculty of Exact and Natural Sciences: Ing. Qco. BLANCA STELLA SOSA
School of Law: Dra IRMA DEL TRÁNSITO ROMERO NIEVA (Dir)
School of Archaeology: Lic. MÓNICA CATOGGIO DE ACOSTA (Dir)
Fray Mamerto Esquiu Higher School: Prof. HORTENCIA DURANTI DE ALVAREZ (Dir)

UNIVERSIDAD NACIONAL DEL CENTRO DE LA PROVINCIA DE BUENOS AIRES

General Pinto 399, 7000 Tandil
Telephone: (293) 21837
Fax: (293) 21608
E-mail: rector@rec.unicen.edu.ar

Founded 1974
State control
Academic year: February to December

Rector: Agrimensor CARLOS ALBERTO NICOLINI
Vice-Rector: Dr EDUARDO MIGUEZ.
Academic Secretary: Lic. SILVIA MARZORATTI
General Secretary: Ing. GILLERMO AMILCAR CORRES
Administrative Secretary: Cr JOSE LUIS BIANCHINI
Library Director: Prof. ZULEMA GRANDINETTI DE CAGLIOLO

Number of teachers: 1,585
Number of students: 7,000

Publications: *Anuario IEHS*, *Alternativas*.

DEANS

Faculty of Social Sciences: Lic. CRISTINA BACCIN
Faculty of Economics: Cr ROBERTO TASSARA
Faculty of Sciences: Dr GERY BIOUL
Faculty of Humanities: Lic. ALEJANDRO DILLON
Faculty of Engineering: Ing. EDUARDO F. IRASSAR
Faculty of Veterinary Science: Dr PEDRO STEFFAN
Faculty of Agricultural Sciences: Med. Vet. ARNALDO PISSANI
Faculty of Theatre: Dr CARLOS CATALANO

ATTACHED INSTITUTES

Instituto de Física de Materiales: Dir Dr RICARDO ROMERO.

Instituto de Física Arroyo Seco: Dir Dr HÉCTOR DI ROCCO.

Instituto de Sistemas Tandil: Dir Ing. JEAN PIERRE DESCHAMPS

UNIVERSIDAD NACIONAL DEL COMAHUE

Buenos Aires 1400, 8300 Neuquén
Telephone: (99) 49-0300
Fax: (99) 49-0351
E-mail: pbohosl@uncoma.edu.ar

Founded 1965
State control

Academic year: April to March

Rector: Lic. PABLO V. BOHOSLAVSKY
Vice-Rector: Ing. ARSENIO DELGADO
Academic Secretary: Prof. MARIA ELENA MARZOLLA
Chief Administrative Officer: Contador EDUARDO MUTCHINICK
Librarian: EUGENIA LUQUE

Number of teachers: 1,400
Number of students: 20,000

DEANS

Faculty of Agricultural Sciences: Ing. Agr. JORGE LUIS GIRARDIN
Faculty of Economics and Administration: Est. ESTELA AREVALO DE ACOSTA
Faculty of Education: Prof. MARIA E. MARZOLLA
Faculty of Engineering: Ing. RUBEN TABARROZZI
Faculty of Humanities: Dr CARLOS CALDERON
Higher School of Languages: Dr JOSÉ PASCULA MASULLO
Faculty of Law and Social Sciences: Lic. JUAN CARLOS BERGONZI
Faculty of Tourism: Lic. JOSÉ LUIS BOSCH
Bariloche Regional University Centre: Dr ERNESTO CRIVELLI
Zona Atlantica Regional University Centre: Ing. Agr. ROBERTO MARTÍNEZ

UNIVERSIDAD NACIONAL DE CÓRDOBA

Calle Obispo Trejo 242, 5000 Córdoba
Telephone: (51) 33-1072
Fax: (51) 33-1079

Founded 1613; charter received from Philip III of Spain 1622; fully established by Pope Urban VIII 1634; nationalized 1856
Academic year: February to December

Rector: Dr HUGO JURI
Vice-Rector: Arq. TOMÁS PARDINA
Secretary-General: Ing. RICARDO TORASSA
Librarian: Lic. ROSA M. BESTANI

Number of teachers: 6,918
Number of students: *c.* 82,000

Library: see Libraries

Publications: *Revista* and various faculty publs.

DEANS

Faculty of Architecture and Town Planning: Arq. MIGUEL ANGEL ROCA
Faculty of Agrarian Sciences: Ing. DANIEL DI GIUSTO
Faculty of Economics: Dr ROBERTO GIULIODORI
Faculty of Exact, Physical and Natural Sciences: Ing. JORGE GONZÁLEZ
Faculty of Medicine: Dr OSCAR H. JURI
Faculty of Chemical Sciences: Dr CARLOS DE PAULI
Faculty of Law and Social Sciences: Dra MARIA E. CAFFURE DE BATISTELLI
Faculty of Philosophy and Humanities: Dr HORACIO FASS
Faculty of Mathematics, Astronomy and Physics: Dr ALDO BRUNETTI
Faculty of Dentistry: Dr NAZARIO KUYUMLLIAM

DIRECTORS

Higher School of Languages: Lic. LEOPOLDO CHIZZINI MELO
'Manuel Belgrano' Higher School of Commerce: Prof. DELIA BELTRAN DE FERREYRA
Monserrat National College: Dr FERNANDO BEATO

UNIVERSIDAD NACIONAL DE CUYO

Centro Universitario, Parque General San Martín, 5500 Mendoza
Telephone: (61) 20-5115
Telex: 55267
Fax: (61) 23-3296

Founded 1939
State Control
Academic year: April to October

Rector: Ing. ARMANDO BERTRANOU
Vice-Rector: Lic. JOSÉ FRANCISCO MARTIN
Administrative Director: Cont. GERARDO ONTIVERO
Librarian: Lic. JUAN GUILLERMO MILIA

Library: see Libraries

Number of teachers: 4,794
Number of students: 22,000

Publication: *Boletín Oficial*.

DEANS

Faculty of Arts: Prof. ELIO ORTIZ
Faculty of Agricultural Sciences: Ing. JORGE TACCHINI
Faculty of Economics: Cont. RODOLFO SÍCOLI
Faculty of Medical Sciences: Dr ISAAC RIVERO
Faculty of Political and Social Sciences: Lic. CARLOS FINOCHIO
Faculty of Engineering: Ing. JUAN MANUEL GOMEZ
Faculty of Philosophy and Letters: Prof. MIGUEL VERSTRAETE
Faculty of Applied Science (Tirasso 300, 5600 San Rafael, Mendoza): Ing. ERNESTO MUÑOZ
Faculty of Law: Dr LUIS ABBIATI
Faculty of Dentistry: Dr ONOFRE CIPOLLA
Teacher Training College: MARÍA VICTORIA GOMEZ DE ERICE
Zona Sur: Dis. Ind. ADRIANA RUIZ

ATTACHED INSTITUTE

Centro Regional de Investigaciones Científicas y Tecnológicas (CRICYT): Calle Bajada del Cerro s/n, Parque General San Martín, Casilla de Correo 131, 5500 Mendoza; tel. (61) 28-8314; fax (61) 28-7370; Dir Dr RICARDO PAULINO DEI.

UNIVERSIDAD NACIONAL DE ENTRE RÍOS

Eva Perón 24/32, 3260 Concepción del Uruguay, Entre Ríos
Telephone: (442) 22108
Fax: (442) 25573

Founded 1973
State control
Academic year: April to March

Rector: Cont. CÉSAR GOTTFRIED
Vice-Rector: Psic. JUAN CARLOS ROQUEL
Director-General of Administration: Cont. PEDRO SANDOVAL
Academic Secretary: Prof. MARÍA ANGÉLICA G. F. DE MARCO
Library Dir: Prof. JORGE TITO MARTÍNEZ

Number of teachers: 1,219
Number of students: 8,000

Publications: *Guía de Carreras, Ciencia, Docencia y Tecnología* (3 a year).

CONSTITUENT INSTITUTIONS

Facultad de Ciencias de Educación (Education): Rivadavia 106, 3100 Paraná; Dean Prof. MARTHA BENEDETTO DE ALBORNOZ.

Facultad de Ciencias Económicas (Economics): Urquiza 52, 3100 Paraná; Dean Cont. JULIO CÉSAR YODICE.

Facultad de Ciencias Agropecuarias (Agrarian Sciences): Ruta Provincial 11, Km 13, 3114 Oro Verde; Dean Ing. FRANCISCO RAMÓN ETCHEVERS.

Facultad de Ciencias de la Administración (Administration): Alvear 1424, 3200 Concordia; Dean Cont. EDUARDO ASUETA.

Facultad de Ciencias de la Alimentación (Nutritional Sciences): Monseñor Tavella 1450, 3200 Concordia; Dean Ing. JORGE AMADO GERARD.

Facultad de Servicio Social (Social Services): La Rioja 6, Subsuelo, 3100 Paraná; Dean A. S. ALICIA MERCEDES GONZÁLEZ ALARCÓN.

Facultad de Bromatología (Bromatology): 25 de Mayo 709, POB 243, 2820 Gualeguaychú; Dean Lic. SUSANA NOVELLO DE METTLER.

Facultad de Ciencas de la Salud (Health Sciences): 8 de Junio 600, 3260 Concepción del Uruguay; Dean Dr JULIO SIMOVICH.

Facultad de Ingeniería (Engineering): Ruta Provincial 11, Km 13, 3114 Oro Verde; Dean Ing. AGUSTÍN CARPIO.

UNIVERSIDAD NACIONAL DE JUJUY

Avda Bolivia 1239, 4600 San Salvador de Jujuy
Telephone: (88) 221-500
Fax: (88) 221-507
E-mail: info@unju.edu.ar

Founded 1972
State control
Academic year: March to December

Rector: Ing. civil JORGE AUGUSTO VAN MESSEM
Vice-Rector: Lic. RUFINO ROJO MATEO
Secretary for Academic Affairs: Lic. JOSEFINA ROYO DE OVANDO
Secretary for Administrative Affairs: CPN MARCELO DAVID FICOSECO
Secretary for University Extension: Ing. qco JORGE ADERA
Secretary for Science and Technology: Dr SUSANA MURUAGA
Librarian: MARÍA E. CENTENO DE MARTÍNEZ

Library of 18,000 vols
Number of teachers: 700
Number of students: 6,000

DEANS

Faculty of Economics: CPN LILIÁN ABRAHAM DE MÉNDEZ
Faculty of Engineering: Ing. OSCAR GUILLERMO INSAUSTI
Faculty of Agriculture: Ing. Agr. ALBERTO RENÉ VIGIANI
Faculty of Humanities and Social Sciences: Lic. JOSÉ ALCALDE

ATTACHED RESEARCH INSTITUTES

Institute of Marine Biology: Dir Lic. MARTHA G. ARCE DE HAMITY
Institute of Geology and Mining: Dir Dra BEATRIZ COIRA

UNIVERSIDAD NACIONAL DE LA PAMPA

9 de Julio 149, 6300 Santa Rosa, La Pampa
Telephone: 3109, 3191

Founded 1958
Academic year: April to November

Rector: Dr MARCELO IVÁN AGUILAR
General Secretary: JUAN JOSÉ COSTA
Academic Secretary: Lic. LUIS MARÍA MORETE
Librarian: Lic. ATILIO DENOUARD

Number of teachers: 632
Number of students: 2,000

DEANS

Faculty of Economics: C. P. N. ROBERTO OSCAR VASSIA
Faculty of Human Sciences: Prof. JOSÉ RUFINO VILLARREAL
Faculty of Exact and Natural Sciences: Profa. NORA D. ANDRADA DE GUESALAGA
Faculty of Agronomy: Ing. Agr. GUILLERMO COVAS
Faculty of Veterinary Science: Dr RAÚL ANTONIO ALVAREZ

UNIVERSIDAD NACIONAL DE LA PATAGONIA SAN JUAN BOSCO

CC 786, Correo Central, 9000 Comodoro Rivadavia, Chubut
Telephone: (967) 33446
Fax: (967) 34442

Founded 1980 by merger of Universidad de la Patagonia San Juan Bosco and Universidad Nacional de la Patagonia
Academic year: February to December

Rector: Lic. ARTURO CANERO
Vice-Rector: Ing. ALDO LOPEZ GUIDI
Academic Secretary: Lic. EDUARDO BIBILONI
Librarian: MARIO D'ORTA

Number of teachers: 850
Number of students: 7,000
Library of 40,000 vols

Publications: *Universidad Abierta*‡ (irregular), *Naturalia Patagónica*‡ (quarterly).

DEANS

Faculty of Humanities and Social Sciences: Lic. DOLORES DEL CASTAÑO
Faculty of Engineering: Ing. ROBERTO AGUIRRE
Faculty of Natural Sciences: Lic. OMAR CESARIS
Faculty of Economics: Cr. JORGE STACCO

HEADS OF DEPARTMENTS

Faculty of Humanities and Social Sciences:
Education: Profa ELIZABETH GUGLIELMINO
History: Profa CRISTINA BARILE
Geography: Profa ANA BURCHERI
Literature: Prof. JOSÉ M. GUTIÉRREZ
Social Communication: Lic. LUIS SANDOVAL
Social Work: Prof. CELIA VICARI

Faculty of Natural Sciences:
Chemistry: Dra VILMA BALZARETTI
Geology: Geo. RAÚL GIACOSA
Human Biology: Ing. MÓNICA STRONATI
Biochemistry: Bioq. LAERTE MASSARI
Nursing: Enf. LIDIA BLANCO
Pharmacy: Phar. RITA CURDELAS

Faculty of Economics:
Economics: Lic. ESTER BADENAS
Law: Dra R. ROSALÍA DE ALCARO
Accounting: Cra RUDEL DE WALTER
Mathematics: Prof. ESTELA TOLOSA
Human Sciences: Lic. VIRGILIO ZAMPINI
Administration: Cra PATRICIA KENT

Faculty of Engineering:
Mathematics: Profa MARÍA GABINA ROMERO
Physics: Ing. MANUEL SCHAIGORODSKY
Industry: Ing. ENRIQUE ROST
Stability and Materials: Ing. JÚLIO CÉSAR MORA
Civil and Hydraulic Engineering: Ing. JUAN JOSÉ RAMÓN SERRA
Systems: C. C. PATRICIA UVIÑA
Surveying: Agr. CARLOS MISTÓ
Civil Engineering: Ing. JORGE HUBERMAN
Forestry Engineering: Ing. PEDRO ESTEBAN GUERRA

REGIONAL FACULTIES

Esquel: Alvear 1021, 3 piso, 9200 Esquel; tel. (945) 3729; Dir Lic. ROBERTO VIERA; forestry and economics.

Trelew: Faculty of Economics and Faculty of Humanities and Social Sciences, Fontana 488, 9100 Trelew; tel. (965) 31532; fax (965) 31276. Faculty of Engineering and Faculty of Natural Sciences, Belgrano 507, 9100 Trelew; tel. (965) 33305; Dir JUAN PÉREZ AMAT.

Puerto Madryn: Bv. Almirante Brown 3700, CC 164, 9120 Pto Madryn; tel. (965) 51024; Dir Dr MIGUEL A. HALLER; marine biology, computer science.

Ushuaia: CADIC, 9410 Ushuaia; tel. (901) 30892; Dir Dr OSCAR LOBO; tourism, computer science.

UNIVERSIDAD NACIONAL DE LA PLATA

Avda 7 No. 776, 1900 La Plata
Telephone: 21-5501
Telex: 31151
Fax: 30563

Founded 1905
Academic year: March to December

President: Dr ANGEL L. PLASTINO
Vice-President: Prof. Lic. ANGEL TELLO
Secretary-General: Ing. MARCELO RASTELLI

Librarian: Dr CARLOS TEJO
Library: see Libraries

Number of teachers: 6,300
Number of students: 50,000

Publications: *Revista de la Universidad*, faculty reviews.

DEANS

Faculty of Architecture and Town Planning: Arq. JORGE ALBERTO LOMBARDI
Faculty of Agriculture: Ing. GUILLERMO MIGUEL HANG
Faculty of Economic Sciences: (vacant)
Faculty of Engineering: Ing. LUIS JULIÁN LIMA
Faculty of Exact Sciences: Dr ENRIQUE PEREYRA
Faculty of Humanities and Education: Dr JOSÉ PANETTIERI
Faculty of Juridical and Social Sciences: RICARDO PABLO RECA
Faculty of Medical Sciences: Dr JAIME TRAJTENBERG
Faculty of Natural Sciences: Dr ISIDORO A. SCHALAMUCK
Faculty of Veterinary Sciences: Dr ALBERTO DIBBERN
Faculty of Dentistry: ALFREDO V. RICCIARDI
Faculty of Fine Arts: Prof. ROBERTO OSCAR ROLLIÉ
Faculty of Astronomy and Geophysics: Prof. CÉSAR AUGUSTO MONDINALLI

SELECTED AFFILIATED SCHOOLS AND INSTITUTES

Colegio Nacional 'Rafael Hernández' (National College): Avda 1 y 49, La Plata; Dir Prof. GRACIELA TERESA IBARRA.

Escuela Graduada 'Joaquín V. González' (Graduate School 'Joaquín V. González'): Calle 50 y 119, La Plata; Dir Prof. MARTHA S. BETTI DE MILICHIO.

Escuela Superior de Periodismo y Comunicación Social (School of Journalism): Avda 44 No 676, La Plata; Dir Lic. JORGE LUIS BERNETTI.

Escuela Práctica de Agricultura y Ganadería 'María Cruz y Manuel L. Inchausti' (School of Agriculture and Stockbreeding): Estación Valdés, 6660 25 de Mayo, Pca de Buenos Aires; Dir Dr RICARDO LUIS CABASSI.

Instituto de Física de Líquidos y Sistemas Biológicos: Calle 59 No 789, 1900 La Plata; tel. 47545; telex 31216; f. 1981; theoretical and applied research; 9 researchers; library of 582 vols, in process of formation; Dir Dr ANTONIO E. RODRÍGUEZ.

UNIVERSIDAD NACIONAL DE LA RIOJA

Avda Ortiz de Ocampo 1700, 5300 La Rioja
Telephone: (822) 25-910
Fax: (822) 28-836
E-mail: postmast@unlar.edu.ar

Founded 1972
State control

Rector: Dr ENRIQUE TELLO ROLDÁN
Vice-Rector: Ing. HECTOR LÓPEZ IZASA
Administrative Secretary: SANTIAGO ROMERO
Librarian: SILVIA DE LA FUENTE

Library of 23,000 vols
Number of students: 12,000

Faculties of economics, humanities and arts, social sciences, engineering.

UNIVERSIDAD NACIONAL DEL LITORAL

Blvd Pellegrini 2750, 3000 Santa Fé

Telephone: (42) 57-1110
Fax: (42) 57-1100
E-mail: dcopint@unl.edu.ar

Founded 1919
State control
Academic year: March to December

Rector: Arq. HUGO GUILLERMO STORERO
Vice-Rector: Ing. PEDRO MÁXIMO MANCINI
Secretary-General: Ing. MARIO DOMINGO BARLETTA
Administrative Secretary: RODOLFO M. R. ACANFORA GRECO
Librarian: MARISA PULIOTTI DE FERRARI

Number of teachers: 2,274
Number of students: 21,767

Publication: *Universidad* (2 a year).

DEANS

Faculty of Law and Social Sciences: Dr MARIANO T. CANDIOTI
Faculty of Chemical Engineering: Ing. PEDRO MÁXIMO MANCINI
Faculty of Economics: Cont. FRANCISCA SÁNCHEZ DE DUSSO
Faculty of Biochemistry and Biology: Bioq. EDUARDO RAMÓN VILLARREAL
Faculty of Agronomy and Veterinary Science: Ing. Agr. HUGO ARMANDO ERBETTA
Faculty of Architecture, Design and Town Planning: Arq. JULIO ALEJANDRO TALÍN
Faculty of Education: Prof. LEONOR JUANA CHENA
Faculty of Engineering and Hydrology: Ing. CRISTÓBAL VICENTE LOZECO

DIRECTORS

Dr Ramon Carrillo Higher School of Hygiene: Dr CARLOS PRONO
School of Agriculture, Stockbreeding and Farming: Ing. Agr. OSVALDO MARIO HERMANN
Institute of Technological Development for the Chemical Industry (INTEC): Dr ALBERTO ENRIQUE CASSANO
School of Food Science: Bioq. LUIS MARÍA NICKISH
Higher Institute of Music: Prof. MARIANO CABRAL MIGNO
Institute of Food Technology: Ing. JORGE HUGO DI PENTIMA
University School of Food Analysis: Ing. Qco. DANIEL MARCELO SCACCHI
Higher School of Industry: Ing. JORGE OSVALDO BASILICO

UNIVERSIDAD NACIONAL DE LOMAS DE ZAMORA

CC 95, 1832 Lomas de Zamora

Telephone: 283-0554
Fax: 283-0554

Founded 1972
State control

Chancellor: GUIDO DI TELLA
Rector: CARLOS ALBERTO PETIGNAT
Vice-Rector: PABLO MARTÍNEZ SAMECK
Secretary-General: NÉSTOR PAN
Librarian: MARIA LUISA ISHIKAWA

Number of teachers: 2,100
Number of students: 28,000

CONSTITUENT INSTITUTIONS

Faculty of Engineering and Agrarian Science: Ruta Provincial 4, Km. 2, 1836 Llavallol; Dean Ing. MARCELO YASKY.

Faculty of Economics: Ruta Provincial 4 y Juan XXIII, 1832 Lomas de Zamora; Dean Cdor. ROBERTO VAZQUEZ.

Faculty of Social Sciences: Ruta Provincial 4 y Juan XXIII, 1832 Lomas de Zamora; Dean Lic. HORACIO GEGUNDE.

Faculty of Law: Ruta Provincial 4 y Juan XXIII, 1832 Lomas de Zamora; Dean Dr PEDRO TOMA.

Faculty of Engineering: Ruta Provincial 4 y Juan XXIII, 1832 Lomas de Zamora; Dean Ing. OSCAR PASCAL.

UNIVERSIDAD NACIONAL DE LUJÁN

CC 221, 6700 Luján, Buenos Aires

Telephone: (323) 23171
Fax: 323-25795

Founded 1973
Academic year: February to December

Rector: Lic. ANTONIO F. LAPOLLA
Vice-Rector: Dr NORBERTO KRYMKIEWICZ
Registrar: Lic. MARCELO BUSALACCHI
Librarian: Lic. EDUARDO ZEISS

Number of teachers: 1,000
Number of students: 1,200

Publications: *Cuadernos de Economía Política, Cuadernos de Historia Regional.*

DEANS

Department of Education: Prof. HÉCTOR CUCUZZA
Department of Technology: Vef. JUAN TREGONING
Department of Social Sciences: Lic. AMALIA TESTA
Department of Basic Sciences: Dr JOSÉ AGUIRRE

UNIVERSIDAD NACIONAL DE MAR DEL PLATA

Juan Bautista Alberdi 2695, 7600 Mar del Plata, Pca de Buenos Aires

Telephone and fax: (23) 92-1705

Founded 1961
State control
Academic year: March to November

Rector: Ing. JORGE DOMINGO PETRILLO
Vice-Rector: Dr ARMANDO DANIEL ABRUZA
Secretary General (Planning and Institutional Development): Arq. ARIEL MAGNONI
Academic Secretary: Lic. MONICA VAN GOOL
Secretary for Extension: Prof. ADRIANA CORTES
Secretary for the University Community: Lic. PAULA PAZ
Secretary for Technological Development: Lic. OLGA DELLA VEDOVA
Secretary for Economics and Finance: C. P. JORGE HERRADA
Librarian: Lic. OSCAR FERNÁNDEZ

Number of teachers: 1,600
Number of students: 17,000

Publication: *Revista de Letras* (3 a year).

DEANS

Faculty of Architecture and Town Planning: Arq. MANUEL TORRES CANO
Faculty of Economics and Social Sciences: Cont. OTTORINO OSCAR MUCCI
Faculty of Engineering: Ing. MANUEL LORENZO GONZÁLEZ
Faculty of Humanities: Prof. CRISTINA ROSENTHAL
Faculty of Exact and Natural Sciences: Dr JULIO LUIS DEL RIO
Faculty of Agriculture: Ing. Agr. JOSÉ LUIS BODEGA
Faculty of Law: Dr LUIS PABLO SLAVIN
Faculty of Psychology: Lic MARIA CRISTINA DI DOMÉNICO
Faculty of Health Sciences and Social Services: Lic. GRISELDA SUSANA VICENS

DIRECTORS

Institute of Science and Materials Technology Research: Dr SUSANA ROSSO
Institute of Biological Research: Dr JORGE JULIAN SANCHEZ
Centre for Coastal and Quaternary Geology: Dir Lic. DANIEL MARTINEZ

UNIVERSIDAD NACIONAL DE MISIONES

Ruta 12 km. 7½, 3304 Estafeta Miguel Lanus, Posadas

Telephone: (752) 80916
Telex: 76197
Fax: (752) 80500

Founded 1973
State control
Academic year: February to December

Rector: Ing. LUIS ESTEBAN DELFREDERICO
Vice-Rector: Ing. JORGE CARLOS BETTAGLIO

Number of teachers: 900
Number of students: 8,800

Publications: *Revista, Boletín.*

DEANS

Faculty of Sciences: Ing. RAUL MARUCCI
Faculty of Economics: CPN JOSE LUIS LIBUTTI
Faculty of Humanities and Social Sciences: Prof. ANA MARÍA CAMBLONG
Faculty of Engineering: Ing. OSCAR EDUARDO PERRONE
Faculty of Arts: Prof. ADA SARTORI DE VENCHARUTTI
Faculty of Forestry: Ing. JUAN CARLOS MULARCZUK KOSARIK

UNIVERSIDAD NACIONAL DEL NORDESTE

25 de Mayo 868, 3400 Corrientes

Telephone: (783) 25060
Fax: (722) 25064

Founded 1957
Academic year: March to December

Rector: Dr ADOLFO DOMINGO TORRES
Vice-Rector: Prof. ANTONIO BADICAN MAHAVE
Secretaries-General: Arq. OSCAR V. VALDES (Academic Affairs); Dr HUGO A. PEIRETTI (Administration); Ing. Dr JORGE R. AVANZA (Science and Technology); Dr SERGIO M. FLINTA (Social Affairs); Dr LUCIANO R. FABRIS (University Extension); CPN GABRIEL E. OJEDA (Planning)
Librarian: Prof. ITALO JUAN L. METTINI

Number of teachers: 4,327
Number of students: 28,459

Publications: *Revista Nordeste, Cuadernos Serie Agro, Serie Medicina, Serie Planeamiento, Revista de la Facultad de Derecho, Revista de la Facultad de Ciencias Veterinarias.*

DEANS

Faculty of Engineering: Ing. MARIO BRUNO NATALINI
Faculty of Economics: CPN EDGARDO MARTÍN AYALA
Faculty of Humanities: Prof. ANA MARÍA FOSCHIATTI DE DELL'ORTO
Faculty of Architecture and Town Planning: Arq. HECTOR LUIS CABALLERO
Faculty of Natural Sciences and Surveying: Lic. MARÍA SILVIA AGUIRRE
Faculty of Law and Social and Political Sciences: Dr JORGE MARIÑO FAGES
Faculty of Medicine: Dr SAMUEL BLUVSTEIN
Faculty of Dentistry: Dr VÍCTOR MENDEZ
Faculty of Agricultural Sciences: Ing. Agr. LUIS AMADO MROGINSKY
Faculty of Veterinary Sciences: Dr ROBERTO A. JACOBO
Faculty of Agricultural Industries: Ing. MARÍA ALICIA JUDIS

DIRECTORS

Institute of Agrotechnology: Ing. CARLOS ENRIQUE TOMEI

Institute of Economics of Agriculture and Fishing: Ing. Agr. JULIO JORGE ESPERANZA
Institute of Administration of Agriculture and Fishing Business: Ing. Agr. ALBERTO DEZA
Institute of Regional Pathology: Dr JORGE O. GORODNER
Institute of Criminal Sciences: Lic. FRANCISCO CAMACHO
Patterns of Foreign Trade: C. P. N. JUAN CARLOS BARBAGALLO
Industrial Relations, Social Communication and Tourism: Prof. IRMA QUIJANO

UNIVERSIDAD NACIONAL DE RÍO CUARTO

Ruta Nacional 36 Km 601, 5800 Río Cuarto, Córdoba

Telephone: (51) 67-6200
Fax: (51) 68-0280

Founded 1971
State control
Academic year: February to December

Rector: Ing. Agr. MSc ALBERTO CANTERO GUTIÉRREZ
Vice-Rector: Dr JORGE DANIEL ANUNZIATA
Secretary-General: Ing. Agr. LEONIDAS CHOLAKY SOBARI
Academic Secretary: Ing. OSVALDO SIMONE
Science and Technology Secretary: Lic. MARIO CANTU
Extension and Development Secretary: Ing. Agr. VÍCTOR BECERRA
Economic Secretary: Lic. JOSÉ LUIS HERNÁNDEZ
Secretary for Technical Co-ordination and Services: Ing. OSCAR SPADA
Welfare Secretary: Prof. SERGIO CENTURION
Librarian: CRISTINA CH. DE FAUDA

Number of teachers: 1,281
Number of students: 8,525

Publications: *Revista*‡, *Serie Ciencias*‡, *Serie Extensión Rural*‡, *Serie Educación*‡, *Serie Divulgación Técnica Veterinaria*‡, etc.

DEANS

Faculty of Agriculture and Veterinary Science: Med. Vet. ANÍBAL BESSONE
Faculty of Exact, Physical, Chemical and Natural Sciences: Dr HÉCTOR FERNÁNDEZ
Faculty of Economics: Cr CARLOS MARCHESINI
Faculty of Humanities: Lic. ABELARDO BARRA RUATTA
Faculty of Engineering: Ing. DIEGO MOITRE

UNIVERSIDAD NACIONAL DE ROSARIO

Córdoba 1814, 2000 Rosario

Telephone: (41) 257146
Telex: 41817
Fax: (41) 259454
E-mail: jugalde@sede.unr.edu.ar

Founded 1968
State control
Academic year: April to November

Rector: Ing. RAÚL ARMANDO ARINO
Vice-Rector: Med. Vet. JOSÉ ARIEL UGALDE
Head of Administration: Dr CARLOS A. DULONG

Number of teachers: 5,741
Number of students: 54,319

DEANS

Faculty of Economic Sciences and Statistics: Cpn RICARDO SUÁREZ
Faculty of Medical Sciences: Dr JUAN MARIO MARRO
Faculty of Humanities and Arts: Dr HÉCTOR CARLOS VÁZQUEZ
Faculty of Law: Dr DANIEL A. ERBETTA
Faculty of Agricultural Sciences: Ing. Agr. LILIANA A. VERDURA
Faculty of Dentistry: Dr JUAN A. MIJOEVICH
Faculty of Biochemistry and Pharmacy: Dr MARÍA MÓNICA ELÍAS
Faculty of Architecture, Planning and Design: Arq. DANIEL E. VIDAL
Faculty of Exact Sciences, Engineering and Surveying: Ing. GREGORIO KROT
Faculty of Political Science and International Relations: Dr LUIS EDUARDO DÍAZ MOLANO
Faculty of Veterinary Sciences: Med. Vet. MIGUEL ÁNGEL PEDRANA
Faculty of Psychology: Dr ADELMO MANASSERI

UNIVERSIDAD NACIONAL DE SALTA

Buenos Aires 177, 4400 Salta

Telephone: (87) 31-1611
Telex: 65121
Fax: (87) 31-1611

Founded 1972

Rector: NARCISO RAMÓN GALLO
Vice-Rector: Ing. RAÚL PEDRO BELLOMO
General Secretary: JUAN HERIBERTO HERRERA
Academic Secretary: Prof. ELENA TERESA JOSÉ
Administrative Secretary: RAFAEL SEGUNDO ESTRADA

Library of 57,633 vols, 42,300 periodicals
Number of teachers: 1,390
Number of students: 12,399

DEANS

Faculty of Humanities: Lic. SONIA ALVAREZ DE TROGLIERO
Faculty of Health Sciences: MARÍA ISABEL LOZA DE CHÁVEZ
Faculty of Engineering: Ing. ELIO GONZO
Faculty of Economics, Juridical and Social Sciences: ROBERTO MARIO RODRÍGUEZ
Faculty of Natural Sciences: LUCIO LEONARDO YAZLLE
Faculty of Exact Sciences: ROBERTO GERMÁN OVEJERO

ATTACHED INSTITUTE

Consejo de Investigación (Research Council): Pres. Dr JOSÉ VIRAMONTE (acting).

UNIVERSIDAD NACIONAL DE SAN JUAN

Avda José Ignacio de la Roza 391(Este), 6° piso, 5400 San Juan

Telephone: (64) 214510
Telex: 59100
Fax: (64) 214586

Founded 1973
State control
Academic year: April to March

Rector: Ing. TULIO DEL BONO
Vice-Rector: Lic. PEDRO O. MALLEA
Admin. and Financial Sec.: Lic. ALEJANDRO LARREA
Librarian: RAÚL I. LOZADA

Number of teachers: 2,001
Number of students: 11,596

DEANS

Faculty of Engineering: Ing. ROBERTO ROMUALDO GOMEZ GUIRADO
Faculty of Architecture, Town Planning and Design: Arq. ROMEO BERNABÉ PLATERO
Faculty of Humanities, Philosophy and Arts: Prof. ZULMA LUCÍA CORZO
Faculty of Exact, Physical and Natural Sciences: Ing. JESÚS ABELARDO ROBLES
Faculty of Social Sciences: Lic. LUIS FRANCISCO MERITELLO

UNIVERSIDAD NACIONAL DE SAN LUIS

Lavalle 1189, 5700 San Luis

Telephone: 24689
Telex: 58125

Founded 1974
Academic year: March to December

Rector: Lic. ALBERTO F. PUCHMULLER
Vice-Rector: Lic. EDGARDO E. MONTINI
Librarian: MIGUEL A. LUCERO

Number of teachers: 255
Number of students: 8,500

DEANS

Faculty of Chemistry, Biochemistry and Pharmacy: Dr ROBERTO OLSINA
Faculty of Physical, Mathematical and Natural Sciences: Dr JULIO C. BENEGAS
Faculty of Education: Lic. NILDA E. PICCO DE BARBEITO
Faculty of Engineering and Business Administration (25 de Mayo 374, 5736 Villa Mercedes, San Luis): Ing. RAÚL A. MERINO

UNIVERSIDAD NACIONAL DE SANTIAGO DEL ESTERO

Avda Belgrano (S) 1912, 4200 Santiago del Estero

Telephone: (85) 222595
Telex: 64120

Founded 1973
Academic year: February to December

Rector: Dr HUMBERTO HERRERA
Vice-Rector: Geologo ARNALDO TENCHINI
Secretary-General: Ing. ANGEL EDUARDO LASBAINES
Librarian: JORGE LUJAN GEREZ

Library of 20,000 vols
Number of teachers: 400
Number of students: 2,960

Publication: *Cuadernos de la UNSE.*

DEANS

Faculty of Agriculture and Agricultural Industry: Ing. JOSÉ R. KOBILAÑSKY
Faculty of Science and Technology: Ing. CARLOS ALBERTO BONETTI
Faculty of Forestry: Ing. VICTORIO MARIOT
Faculty of Humanities: Lic. ROSA LUND DE SANTILLÁN

ATTACHED INSTITUTES

Centro de Tecnología Educativa: Lic. SARIFE ABDALA DE MACHIN
Centro Educativo Rural: Ing. LUIS E. LUQUE
Centro de Investigaciones Apícolas: Dr EDUARDO MARIO BIANCHI
Instituto de Control Biológico: Dr DANTE C. FIORENTINO
Instituto de Tecnología de la Madera: Ing. VÍCTOR RAÚL TABOADA
Instituto de Silvicultura y Manejo de Bosques: Ing. ANA MARÍA GIMÉNEZ DE BOLSÓN
Jardín Botánico: Ing. LUCAS DOMINGO ROIC
Instituto de Estudios para el Desarrollo Social: Lic. NATIVIDAD NASSIF DE GONZÁLEZ PÉREZ

UNIVERSIDAD NACIONAL DEL SUR

Avda Colón 80, 8000 Bahía Blanca

Telephone: (91) 24986
Telex: 012-2414
Fax: (91) 551443

Founded 1956
Academic year: February to December

Rector: Ing. CARLOS ENRIQUE MAYER
Vice-Rector: Ing. JORGE ANÍBAL REYES
Academic General Secretary: Ing. OSVALDO CURZIO
Scientific and Technological General Secretary: Dr ENRIQUE VALLES
Technical Administrative General Secretary: Ing. RODOLFO SERRALUNGA
Librarian: Lic. ATILIO PERALTA

Library: see Libraries
Number of teachers: 1,880
Number of students: 5,248

DIRECTORS

Department of Agriculture: Dr GUSTAVO ADOLFO ORIOLI
Department of Economics: Lic. RICARDO GUTIÉRREZ
Department of Biology: Lic. MARCELO ANTONIO SAGARDOY
Department of Administration: Cr ROBERTO MENGHINI
Department of Electrical Engineering: Ing. ALBERTO CARLOS ALVAREZ
Department of Physics: Lic. LUIS A. OCHOA
Department of Geography: Dr ROBERTO BUSTOS CARA
Department of Geology: Dr JUAN KROGER
Department of Humanities: Prof. GRACIELA FACCHINETTI DE ALVAREZ
Department of Engineering: Ing. RICARDO CASAL
Department of Mathematics: Dr MANUEL ABAD
Department of Chemistry and Chemical Engineering: Dr DANIEL E. DAMIANI

ATTACHED RESEARCH INSTITUTES

Instituto Argentino de Oceanografía: Avda Alem 53, Bahía Blanca; tel. 23555; run in conjunction with CONICET (*q.v.*); Dir Dr ADAN EDGARDO PUCCI.

Centro de Recursos Naturales Renovables de la Zona Semiarida: Altos del Barrio Palihue, Bahía Blanca; tel. 21127; Dir Dr OSVALDO FERNÁNDEZ.

Planta Piloto de Ingeniería Química: 12 de Octubre 1842, Bahía Blanca; tel. 33679; Dir Dr GUILLERMO CRAPISTE.

Instituto de Investigaciones Bioquímicas: Camino La Carrindanga, Km 7 (Edificio CRIBABB), Bahía Blanca; tel. 26114; Dir Dr FRANCISCO JOSÉ BARRANTES.

Instituto de Matemática: Avda Alem 1253, Bahía Blanca; tel. 25772, ext. 365; Dir Dr LUIZ MONTEIRO.

UNIVERSIDAD NACIONAL DE TUCUMÁN

Ayacucho 491, 4000 San Miguel de Tucumán

Telephone: (81) 24-7752
Telex: 61143
Fax: (81) 24-7772

Founded 1914
Language of Instruction: Spanish
Academic year: April to December

Rector: Dr CESAR ATILIO CATALAN
Vice-Rector: C.P.N. MARIO ALBERTO MARIGLIANO
Secretary, Administration: ANTONIO MARIO FORTUNA
Secretary, Academic Affairs: Ing. ANDRES E. ORTEGA
Secretary, Postgraduate Affairs: Prof. CLOTILDE YAPUR DE CACERES
Secretary, Science and Technology: Dr CARLOS FEDERICO KRISCHBAUM
Secretary, University Extension and Environment: Ing. Agr. ERNESTO ANTONIO GALLO

Library: see Libraries
Number of teachers: 3,545
Number of students: 34,329

Publications: *Memoria Anual*‡, faculty reviews, etc‡.

DEANS

Faculty of Exact Sciences and Technology: Ing. JUAN CARLOS REIMUNDIN
Faculty of Agriculture and Animal Husbandry: Ing. ALBERTO BRUNO ANDRADA
Faculty of Philosophy and Letters: Prof. LUIS MARCO BONANO
Faculty of Architecture and Town Planning: JUAN CARLOS DUFFY
Faculty of Biochemistry, Chemistry and Pharmacy: Dr LEOPOLDO SALES
Faculty of Economics: C. P. N. MARIO ALBERTO MARIGLIANO
Faculty of Medicine: Dra RITA WASERMAN DE CUNIO
Faculty of Dentistry: Dra ANA MARIA KERMES DE ABIB
Faculty of Law and Social Sciences: Dr LUIS RODOLFO ARGÜELLO
Faculty of Natural Sciences and Miguel Lillo Institute: Dr ALEJANDRO JOSÉ TOSELLI
Faculty of Fine Arts: Lic. CELIA AIZICZON DE FRANCO
Faculty of Psychology: Prof. MARIA LUISA ROSSI DE HERNANDEZ

UNIVERSIDAD TECNOLÓGICA NACIONAL

Sarmiento 440, 6° piso, 1347 Buenos Aires

Telephone: (1) 394-8075
Fax: (1) 322-0674

Founded 1959
Academic year: April to November

Rector: Ing. HECTOR C. BROTTO
Vice-Rector: Ing. BENITO POSSETTO
General Secretary: Ing. CARLOS FANTINI
Academic Secretary: Ing. CIRIO MURAD
Secretary for Technological Research: Ing. JORGE FERRANTES
Secretary for Student Affairs: Ing. RUBÉN SORO MARTÍNEZ
Secretary for University Extension: Ing. DANIEL FERRADAS
Secretary for Finance: Ing. CARLOS RAPP
Secretary for Institutional Relations: Prof. CARLOS RÍOS

Number of teachers: 16,185
Number of students: 70,087

Publication: *Boletín Informativo.*

REGIONAL FACULTIES

Avellaneda: Ing. Marconi 775, 1870 Avellaneda, Buenos Aires; mechanical, electrical and electronic engineering; Dean Ing. HÉCTOR R. GONZÁLEZ.

Bahía Blanca: 11 de Abril 461, 8000 Bahía Blanca, Buenos Aires; construction, electrical and mechanical engineering; Dean Ing. VICENTE EGIDI.

Buenos Aires: Medrano 951, 1179 Buenos Aires; textile, chemical, metallurgical, electronic, construction, electrical and mechanical systems analysis engineering; Dean Arq. LUIS A. DE MARCO.

Concepción del Uruguay: Ing. Pereyra 676, 3260 Concepción del Uruguay, Entre Ríos; electromechanical and construction engineering; Dean Ing. JUAN CARLOS PITER.

Córdoba: Uladíslao Frías s/n, 5000 Córdoba; chemical, metallurgical, mechanical, electronic and electrical engineering; Dean Ing. RUBÉN SORO MARTÍNEZ.

Delta: San Martín 1171, 2804 Campana, Buenos Aires; electrical, mechanical and chemical engineering; Dean Ing. GUSTAVO BAUER.

General Pacheco: Avda Irigoyen 2878, 1617 Gral Pacheco, Buenos Aires; mechanical engineering; Dean Ing. EUGENIO B. RICCIOLINI.

Haedo: París 532, 1707 Haedo, Buenos Aires; aeronautical engineering, electronics, mechanical engineering; Dean Ing. ELIO BIAGINI.

La Plata: Calle 60 esq. 124, 1900 La Plata, Buenos Aires; chemical, mechanical, electrical and construction engineering; Dean Ing. CARLOS FANTINI.

Mendoza: Rodríguez 273, 5500 Mendoza; construction, electromechanical, chemical, electronic engineering, systems analysis; Dean Ing. JULIO CÉSAR CLETO COBOS.

Paraná: Almafuerte 1033, 3100 Paraná, Entre Ríos; electromechanical and construction engineering; Dean Ing. RAÚL E. ARROYO.

Rafaela: Blvd Roca y Artigas, 2300 Rafaela, Santa Fe; electromechanical and construction engineering; Dean Ing. OSCAR DAVID.

Resistencia: French 414, 3500 Resistencia, Chaco; electromechanical engineering, systems analysis; Dean Ing. SEBASTIÁN VICENTE MARTÍN.

Río Grande: Belgrano 777, 9420 Río Grande, Tierra del Fuego; electronic and industrial engineering; Dean Ing. MARIO FERREIRA.

Rosario: Estanislao Zeballos 1341, 2000 Rosario, Santa Fé; electrical, mechanical, construction, chemical engineering and systems analysis; Dean Ing. DANIEL OSCAR BADÍA.

San Francisco: Av. Gral. Savio 501, 2400 Francisco, Córdoba; electromechanical engineering, electronics, information technology; Dean Ing. RAÚL C. ALBERTO.

San Nicolás: Colón 332, 2900 San Nicolás, Buenos Aires; electromechanical and metallurgical engineering; Dean Ing. NEORÉN P. FRANCO.

San Rafaél: Comandante Salas 370, 5600 San Rafaél, Mendoza; construction, electromechanical, chemical and civil engineering; Dean Ing. HORACIO P. PESSANO.

Santa Fé: Lavaise 610, 3000 Santa Fé; construction, electrical and mechanical engineering and systems analysis; Dean Ing. RICARDO O. SCHOLTUS.

Tucumán: Rivadavia 1050, 4000 San Miguel de Tucumán; construction, mechanical and civil engineering, information technology; Dean Ing. HUGO E. CELLERINO.

Villa María: Av. Universidad 450, Barrio Bello Horizonte, 5900 Villa María, Córdoba; mechanical and chemical engineering; Dean Ing. CARLOS R. RAPP.

ACADEMIC UNITS

Concordia: Salta 277, 3200 Concordia, Entre Ríos; construction and electromechanical engineering; Dir Ing. JOSÉ BOURREN.

Confluencia: Juan Manuel de Rosas y Juan Soufal, 8318 Plaza Huincul, Neuquén; electronic and chemical engineering; Dir Ing. SUSANA L. TARGHETTA DUR.

La Rioja: Facundo Quiroga y Beccar Varela, 5330 La Rioja; electromechanical engineering; Dir Dr MAURICIO KEJNER.

Rawson: Mitre 764, 9100 Rawson, Chubut; electromechanical and industrial engineering; Dir Ing. ERNESTO A. PASCUALICH.

Reconquista: Freyre 980, 3560 Reconquista, Santa Fé; electromechanical engineering; Dir Ing. OSVALDO DEL VALLE FATALA.

Río Gallegos: Maipú 53, 9400 Río Gallegos, Santa Cruz; electromechanical and industrial engineering; Dir Lic. SERGIO RAÚL RAGGI.

Trenque Lauquen: Villegas y Pereyra Rosas, 6400 Trenque Lauquen, Buenos Aires; electromechanical and construction engineering; Dir Ing. GUILLERMO A. GIL.

Venado Tuerto: Castelli 501, 2600 Venado Tuerto, Santa Fé; electromechanical and construction engineering; Dir Ing. ALFREDO ANÍBAL GUILLAUMET.

INSTITUTO UNIVERSITARIO AERONÁUTICO

Avda Fuerza Aérea, Km. 6½, 5103 Guarnicíon Aérea Córdoba

Telephone: (51) 65-3958
Fax: (51) 65-0765
E-mail: postmaster@inunae.edu.ar

Founded 1947
State control

Language of Instruction: Spanish
Academic year: February to December

Rector: Brig. (R) Raúl Juan Carlos Camussi
Vice-Rector (Academic): Lic. Héctor Oscar Benza
Vice-Rector (Distance Learning): Ing. Javier Etchegoyen
General Secretary: Ing. Pedro Emilio Murillo
Librarian: Marcela A. Ducasse

Library of 8,000 vols
Number of teachers: 174
Number of students: 1,234

DIRECTORS

Department of Aeronautical Engineering: Ing. Roque G. Hauser
Department of Electrical Engineering: Ing. José F. Nuñez
Department of Systems Engineering: Lic. Susana B. Barrionuevo de Bustos Acuña
Department of Business Management: Cont. Catalina Rosa Tinari
Department of Special Courses: Ing. Sergio Alfredo Medina
Department of Languages: Prof. Nicolás Erico German Andersen
Centre for Applied Research: Vicecomodoro Ladislao Mathe

Six-year courses for military personnel and civilians.

Private Universities

UNIVERSIDAD DEL ACONCAGUA

Catamarca 147, 5500 Mendoza

Telephone: (61) 232281
Fax: (61) 232281

Founded 1965
Academic year: April to October

Rector: Dr Osvaldo S. Caballero
Secretary-General: Oscar David Cerutti
Librarian: Haydee Torres Bousoño

Number of teachers: 451
Number of students: 2,150

DEANS

Faculty of Social Sciences and Administration: Dr Juan Farres Cavagnaro
Faculty of Economics and Commerce: Dr Rolando Galli Rey
Faculty of Psychology: Lic. Hugo Lupiañez
Faculty of Phono-audiology: Dr Gustavo Mauricio

UNIVERSIDAD ARGENTINA DE LA EMPRESA
(Argentine University of Administration Sciences)

Lima 717, 1073 Buenos Aires

Telephone: (1) 372-5454
Fax: (1) 381-3850
E-mail: mass@uade-1.satlink.net

Founded 1962
Academic year: March to December

Rector: Dr Cesar Marzagalli
Administrative Vice-Rector: Dr Aristides Jose Girosi (acting)
Academic Vice-Rector: Dr Aristides J. Girosi
Institutional Vice-Rector and Academic Secretary: Dr Norberto E. Fraga
Secretary for Student Affairs: Dra María Cristina Serrano
Librarian: Rodolfo Löhe

Library of 38,000 vols, 865 periodicals
Number of teachers: 706
Number of students: 14,400

Publications: *Cuadernos UADE*, *Estudios de Coyuntura* (monthly), *Entre Nosotros*.

DEANS AND DIRECTORS

Faculty of Economic Sciences: Dra Ana Maria Zaccai
Faculty of Business Administration: Dr Carlos Manuel Giménez
Faculty of Law and Social Sciences: Dra María Celia Marsili
Faculty of Agrarian Sciences: Ing. Agr. Alberto E. Etiennot
Faculty of Engineering: Ing. Domingo Emilio Ariagno
Faculty of Arts and Sciences: Arq. Frederico Ortiz

DEPARTMENTAL DIRECTORS

Administration and Business Organization: Dr Jose Peña
Social Sciences and Arts: Dr Enrique Timo
Marketing: Dr Hector Mario Bogo
Computing Systems and Methods: Dr Juan Carlos Ozores
Accounting and Taxation: Dr Juan Carlos Repila
Law: Dr Maria Celia Marsili
Economics: Dr Nestor Roque Suarez
Finance and Control: Dr Rodolfo Heriberto Apreda
Mathematics: Ing. Hector Micheloni
Human Resources: Dr Hector Jasminoy
Science and Technology: Ing. Ernesto Guillermo Bendinger
Languages: Prof. Virginia Antonello
Technology for Communications and Arts: Arq. Frederico Ortiz

ATTACHED INSTITUTES

Institute of Economics: Dir Dr Omar Chisari
Institute of Market Research: Dir Dr Paul Burone
Institute of Labor Studies: Dir Dr Daniel Funes de Rioja

UNIVERSIDAD ARGENTINA 'JOHN F. KENNEDY'

Calle Bartolomé Mitre 1411, 1037 Buenos Aires

Telephone: 476-4338
Fax: 476-2271

Founded 1961

Rector: Dr Miguel Herrera Figueroa
Vice-Rector: Dr Pedro R. David
Secretary-General: Ing. Miguel Herrera Filas

Library of 50,000 vols
Number of teachers: 1,800
Number of students: 10,000

HEADS OF DEPARTMENTS

Systems Analysis: Rodolfo Naveiro
Anthropology: Dr Luis Fernando Rivera
Architecture: Arq. Aldo de Lorenzi
Biology: Dr Aldo Imbriano
Building and Construction: Ing. M. Herrera Filas
Communications: Prof. Humberto Pacheco Milesi
Political Science: Prof. Luis M. Premoli
Demography and Tourism: Dr Raúl Gómez Fuentealba
Law: Dr José Alberto Vidal Díaz
Labour Studies: Dr Emilio Petrarca
Economics: Cont. Olver Benvenuto
Literature: Prof. María del Valle Romanelli
History: Dr Enrique de Gandia
Business Studies: Dr Francisco Risso Patrón
Mathematics: Ing. Miguel Herrera Filas
Development and Planning: Dr Miguel Herrera Figueroa
Criminology: Dr Horacio Maldonado
Education: Lic. Elisa Herren de David
Psychology: Dr Eleonora Zenequelli
Clinical Psychology: Dr Mario Coscio
Public Relations: Dr Juan Carlos Iglesias
Social Work: Julio Enrique Aparicio
Sociology: Dr Fernando Cuevillas
Chemistry: Dr Edmundo Savastano
Computer Studies: Carlos Vidal
Design: Julio César Abramof
Philosophy: Francisco García Bazán
Educational Psychology: Dr Mario Coscio
University Extension: Dra Cristina Herrera Filas

UNIVERSIDAD DE BELGRANO

Zabala 1837, 1426 Buenos Aires

Telephone: (1) 788-5400

Founded 1964
Private control
Academic year: March to November

Rector: Dr Avelino José Porto
Secretary for Legal and Technical Administration: Dr Eustaquio Castro
Secretary for Academic and Research Administration: Dr Omar Bravo
Secretary-General for Economics and Finance Administration: Prof. Aldo J. Pérez
Secretary for Institutional Administration: Arq. Juan José Bialet Salas
Librarian: Mercedes Patalano

Library of 75,000 vols
Number of teachers: 1,350
Number of students: 15,000

Publications: *Ideas en Ciencias Sociales* (quarterly), *Ideas en Arte y Tecnología* (quarterly), *La Ciudad* (2 a month), *Memorias* (annual).

DEANS

Faculty of Humanities: Dr Eva Muchinik
Faculty of Economics: Dr Adolfo Donadini
Faculty of Law and Social Sciences: Dr Eduardo Milberg
Faculty of Architecture and Urban Planning: Arq. Enrique Dimant
Faculty of Technology: Prof. Carlos Tomassino
Faculty of Agriculture: Ing. Marcelo Foulón
Faculty of Engineering: Ing. Marcelo Sobrevila
Faculty of Graduate Studies: Prof. Mario Serrafero
Faculty of Economics and International Commerce: Dr Carlos Cleri
Faculty of Languages and Foreign Studies: Prof. Aldo Blanco
Faculty of Distance Study: Prof. Mónica de Arteche

DIRECTORS

Centre of Advanced Studies for the Conservation of the Natural and Cultural Heritage: Arq. Jorge Gazzaneo
Centre of Far East Studies: (vacant)
Centre of Middle East Studies: Lic. Luis Giménez Gowland
Institute of Economic Studies: (vacant)
Institute of History: Dr Félix Luna
Institute of Psychology: Héctor Fernández Alvarez
Institute of Public Law: Dr Osvaldo Jesús Depaula
Institute of Strategic Studies: Gen. José Teófilo Goyret
Institute of Social Sciences: Dr Juan Carlos Agulla
Research Department: Dr Raúl E. Beranger

UNIVERSIDAD CAECE

Avda de Mayo 1400, 1085 Buenos Aires

Telephone: (1) 381-3229
Fax: (1) 381-6520

Founded 1967
Private control

Rector: Jorge E. Bosch
General Vice-Rector: Nicolás Patetta
Academic Vice-Rector: Roberto P. J. Hernández

Chief Administrative Officer: OLGA VILLAVERDE
University Librarian: SUSANA BUONO

Number of teachers: 300
Number of students: 2,000
Library of 9,000 vols

Publication: *Elementos de Matemática*‡.

HEADS OF DEPARTMENTS

Mathematics: ROBERTO P. J. HERNÁNDEZ
Education: MARTA L. LOCATELLI
Systems Analysis: ELENA I. GARCÍA
Biology: CLAUDIA AGUILAR

UNIVERSIDAD CATÓLICA ARGENTINA 'SANTA MARÍA DE LOS BUENOS AIRES'

Juncal 1912, 1116 Buenos Aires

Telephone: 812-1035

Founded 1958

Academic year: March to November

Rector: GUILLERMO PEDRO BLANCO
Vice-Rectors: Dr GERMÁN BIDART CAMPOS, Prof. JUAN CARLOS VÁZQUEZ
General Secretary: Lic. ANÍBAL CARLOS LUZURIAGA
Academic Secretary: Lic. ERNESTO JOSÉ PARSELIS
Administrative Secretary: GLORIA ALLO DE MARTÍNEZ

Number of teachers: 2,900
Number of students: 10,017

Publications: *Anuario, Universitas, El Derecho, Sapientia, Letras, Valores, Teología, Prudentia Iuris.*

DEANS

Faculty of Philosophy and Letters: Pbro. JOSÉ LUIS TORACA
Faculty of Law and Political Sciences: Dr ALFREDO DI PIETRO
Faculty of Economic and Social Sciences: Cr. MANUEL GONZÁLEZ ABAD
Faculty of Theology: Pbro. JUAN CARLOS MACCARONE
Faculty of Physical Sciences, Mathematics and Engineering: Ing. PEDRO ROSSIGNOLI
Faculty of Humanities and Education (Mendoza): Prof. ANA DEL CARMEN PIOVERA
Faculty of Arts and Music: Mtro ROBERTO CAAMAÑO DÍAZ
Faculty of Agriculture: Ing. PEDRO ROSSIGNOLI
Faculty of Economics (Mendoza): R. P. Dr JORGE MARTÍNEZ
Faculty of Law and Social Sciences (Rosario): Dr JOSÉ MARÍA MARTÍNEZ INFANTE
Faculty of Chemistry and Engineering (Rosario): Dr FRANCISCO CASIELLO

DIRECTORS

Institute of Culture: Ing. FLORENCIO ARNAUDO
Institute of Health Sciences: Dr ELADIO MASCÍAS
Institute of University Extension: Dr JULIO A. J. CARRILLO
Institute of Pre-University Studies: Lic. JORGE NÉSTOR ESPÓSITO
Institute of Spirituality and Pastoral Action: Pbro. JORGE MURIAS

UNIVERSIDAD CATÓLICA DE CÓRDOBA

Obispo Trejo 323, 5000 Córdoba

Telephone: (51) 23-5331
Fax: (51) 23-1937

Founded 1956
Academic year: February to December

Chancellor: Mgr RAÚL FRANCISCO PRIMATESTA, Cardinal Archbishop of Córdoba
Vice-Chancellor: R. P. ALVARO RESTREPO
Rector: Lic. ANDRÉS MARÍA JOSÉ SWINNEN
Vice-Rector for Development: (vacant)
Academic Vice-Rector: Ing. CARLOS LUIS DIAMANTI
Vice-Rector for Education: (vacant)
Vice-Rector for Economy: Cont. NÉSTOR D. GIRAUDO
Academic Secretary: Lic. JUAN SARDO
Librarian: (vacant)

Library: see Libraries
Number of teachers: 950
Number of students: 5,200

DEANS

Faculty of Architecture: Arq. BERNARDO MARCELO VILLASUSO
Faculty of Agriculture: Ing. Agr. OSCAR EDUARDO MELO
Faculty of Economics and Administration: Cont. ADOLFO MARTÍN GUSTAVO BERTOA
Faculty of Law and Social Sciences: Dr ARMANDO SEGUNDO ANDRUET
Faculty of Philosophy and Humanities: Dra. MÓNICA GEORINA LUQUE
Faculty of Engineering: Ing. JUAN GUILLERMO BOSCH
Faculty of Medicine: Dr ESTEBAN TRAKAL
Faculty of Chemical Sciences: Bioq. PABLO JOSÉ FERNÁNDEZ
Faculty of Political Sciences and International Relations: Dr JORGE EDMUNDO BARBARÁ
Institute of Administrative Sciences: Lic. JOSÉ ALEJANDRO BERNHARDT

UNIVERSIDAD CATÓLICA DE CUYO

Av. José Ignacio de la Roza 1516, Rivadavia, 5400 San Juan

Telephone: (64) 23-4689
Fax: (64) 232750
E-mail: catolica.cuyo@interredes.com.ar

Founded 1953

Rector: Dr PEDRO LUIS MARÍA MARTÍN
Vice-Rector: Dr ROBERTO O. BUSTAMANTE
Secretary-General: Dr MARIO ALBERTO HERRERO
Director of Library: EUGENIA CARRASCOSA DE YUNES

Library of 25,000 vols
Number of teachers: 408
Number of students: 3,072

Publications: *La Verdad, Cuadernos.*

DEANS

Faculty of Economics: Dr ANTONIO ORLANDO JUÁREZ
Faculty of Food Sciences: Lic. GRACIELA BEATRIZ MARTÍN DE ROCA
Faculty of Law and Social Sciences: Dr RAMÓN HÉCTOR MERCADO
Faculty of Philosophy and Humanities: Dra MARÍA ISABEL LARRAURI
Faculty of Social Sciences and Social Work 'Pío XII': Dr JULIO JOSÉ DE LA MOTA
Faculty of Health Sciences: Dr ARTURO ARABEL

UNIVERSIDAD CATÓLICA DE LA PLATA

Calle 13 No. 1227, 1900 La Plata

Telephone: (21) 34779

Founded 1968

Academic year: March to November

Grand Chancellor: Mons. Dr CARLOS GALAN
Rector: Cr CAYETANO A. LICCIARDO
General Secretary: Dr JORGE I. BENZRIHEN
General Secretary in charge of Colleges and Institutes: Prof. NANCY DI PIERO DE WARR
Librarian: GLADYS R. MARDUEL

Number of teachers: 635
Number of students: 3,000

Publication: *Revista*‡.

DEANS

Faculty of Architecture: Arq. CARLOS ALBERTO RUOTOLO
Faculty of Education: Prof. NANCY DI PIERO DE WARR
Faculty of Economics: Cr MARIO LUIS SZYCHOWSKI
Faculty of Social Sciences: Dr JORGE O. PERRINO
Faculty of Law: Dr JORGE O. PERRINO
Faculty of Applied Mathematics: Ing. EDUARDO FULCO
Department of Theology: Dir Pbro Ing. RUBEN A. GARINO

AFFILIATED COLLEGES AND INSTITUTE

Colegio San Miguel de Garicoits: Dir Prof. JOSE MARIA DELGADO ZURETTI.

Colegio Ministro Luis R. MacKay: Dir Prof. SILVIA LAPORTE.

Colegio José Manuel Estrada: Dir MONICA INES ROLANDELLI.

Instituto José Manuel Estrada: Rector Prof. NOEMI HILDA CARIONE.

UNIVERSIDAD CATÓLICA DE SALTA

Ciudad Universitaria, Campo Castañares, Casilla 18, 4400 Salta

Telephone: (87) 23-3270

Founded 1963
Academic year: March to December

Chancellor: Mons. MOISES JULIO BLANCHOUD
Rector: Dr PATRICIO GUSTAVO E. COLOMBO MURUA
Academic Vice-Rector: Pbro Dr JULIO RAÚL MÉNDEZ
Administrative Vice-Rector: Pbro NORMANDO JOAQUIN REQUENA
Secretary-General: Dra MARÍA ISABEL VIRGILI DE RODRÍGUEZ
Librarian: WARTHA ANSALDI DE VINANTE

Library of 31,000 vols
Number of teachers: 350
Number of students: 2,300

DEANS

Faculty of Arts and Sciences: Pbro CARLOS ESCOBAR SARAVIA
Faculty of Law: Dr LUIS MARTINEZ
Faculty of Engineering and Informatica: Ing. CARLOS TRUCCO
Faculty of Economics and Administration: Lic. BEATRIZ ELIDA RUBIO
Faculty of Architecture and Urban Planning: Arq. ROQUE GOMEZ
School of Social Service: A. S. LILIANA MARIN
School of Physical Education: Lic. DOLORES MEDINA BOUQUET
School of Tourism: Lic. MARIA ROSA DAGUERRE

UNIVERSIDAD CATÓLICA DE SANTA FÉ

Echagüe 7151, 3000 Santa Fé

Telephone and fax: (42) 60-3030
E-mail: postmaster@ucsfre.edu.ar

Founded 1957
Academic year: February to December

Grand Chancellor: Mons. EDGARDO GABRIEL STORNI
Rector: Arq. JOSÉ MARÍA PASSEGGI
Academic Vice-Rector: Lic. TOMÁS GUTIERREZ
Vice-Rector for Training: Pbro Lic. MARCELO MATEO
Secretary-General: Dra MARTA D. V. OLMOS
Library Director: Dr JUAN CARLOS P. BALLESTEROS

Number of teachers: 480
Number of students: 3,864

DEANS

Faculty of Law: Dr Ricardo Andrés Villa
Faculty of Economic Sciences: Cont. Luis Elio Bonino
Faculty of Philosophy: Prof. Daniel Vaschetto (acting)
Faculty of Social Communication: Lic. Carlos Tealdi
Faculty of Architecture: Arq. Ricardo María Rochetti
Faculty of Engineering, Geoecology and the Environment: Lic. Tomás Gutierrez
Faculty of Education: Dr Juan Carlos Pablo Ballesteros

UNIVERSIDAD CATÓLICA DE SANTIAGO DEL ESTERO

Avenida Alsina y Núñez de Prado, 4200 Santiago del Estero

Telephone: (85) 21-3820
Fax: (85) 21-9754

Founded 1960
Language of instruction: Spanish
Academic year: April to November

Grand Chancellor: Mons. Gerardo Eusebio Sueldo
Rector: Ing. Jorge Luis Feijóo
Administrative Director: Lic. María Élida Cerro de Ábalos
Librarian: Prof. Dr Matias Zuzec
Library of 19,000 vols

Number of teachers: 450
Number of students: 4,000

Publication: *Nuevas Propuestas*‡.

DEANS

Faculty of Politics, Social Sciences and Law: Abogada Maria Teresa Tenti de Volta
Faculty of Economics: Lic. Víctor Manuel Feijóo
Faculty of Education: Hna Lic. Liliana Badaloni
Faculty of Applied Mathematics: Ing. Octavio José Médici

PROFESSORS

Faculty of Politics, Social Sciences and Law:

Alegre, J. C., Agricultural and Mining Law
Argañaraz Orgaz, C., Administrative Law
Arguello, L. R., Roman Law
Arnedo, E., Private International Law
Auad, A., Social Philosophy
Benevole de Gauna, T., Legal Consultation
Bonacina, R. A., Introduction to Economics
Brizuela, N., General and Social Psychology
Brunello de Zurita, A., Civil Law
Castiglione, J. C., Philosophy of Law
Cerro, F. E., Theory of the State
Christensen, E., Finance and Financial Law
Haro de Surian, E., Economic Geography
Ledesma, A. E., Civil and Penal Procedural Law
Navarro, J. V., Penal Law
Paz, G. M., Civil Law
Paz, M. J., Commercial Law
Retamosa, J. R., History of Ideas and Political Institutions, History of the World, History of Argentina
Rigourd, C., Public Law
Rimini, J. C., Commercial Law
Salera, J. B., Sociology
Victoria, M. A., Agricultural and Mining Law
Zurita de González, M., Civil Law

Faculty of Economics:

Alegre, J. C., Bankruptcy Law
Bravo, W., Auditing
Chaya, H. N., Administration and Personnel
Coronel, J. C., Budgeting
Ferrero de Azar, A. M., Company Law
Marigliano, M., Business Organization
Marteleur, R., Introduction to Economics
Morellini, P. A., Accounting, Budget Sheet Analysis
Ostengo, H., Accounting
Pastorino, M. I., Statistics
Teruel, R., General Administration

Faculty of Education:

Castiglione, J. C., Theology
Gelid, T., General Sociology and Sociology of Education
Muhn, G., Vocational Orientation
Riera de Lucena, E., Philosophical Anthropology, Basic Epistemology
Sgoifo, M. del V., Psychology

Faculty of Applied Mathematics:

Coronel, J. C., Introduction to Mathematical Analysis
Korstanje, A. P., Operational Research
Martínez, E., Systems Evaluation
Pastorino, M. I., Numerical Methods
Trajtenberg, J. O., Introduction to Data Processing

UNIVERSIDAD DE CONCEPCIÓN DEL URUGUAY

8 de Junio 522, 3260 Concepción del Uruguay, Entre Ríos

Telephone: (442) 25606
Fax: (442) 27721

Founded 1971
Private control
Academic year: February to December

Rector: Dr Roberto Perinotto
Vice-Rector: Julio Cesar Vega
Chief Administrative Officer: Sra. Beatriz Merello
Chief Librarian: Prof. Rosa Murillo de Rousseaux

Library of 4,300 vols
Number of teachers: 222
Number of students: 850

Publication: *Ucurrencias*.

DEANS

Faculty of Agronomy: Ing. Carmen Blázquez
Faculty of Architecture: Arq. Cristina Bonus
Faculty of Economics: Cr. Marcelo Granillo

UNIVERSIDAD DE LA MARINA MERCANTE
(University of the Merchant Navy)

Billinghürst 376, 1174 Buenos Aires

Telephone: (1) 861-1130

Founded 1974
Private control
Academic year: March to December

President: Ing. Oscar Sonaglioni
Rector: Dr Jorge Luis Pera
Vice-Rector: Dr Ing. Oscar Sonaglioni
Executive Secretary: Prof. Edda Sartori
Secretary-General: Lic. Silvia Fabián de Etkin

Number of teachers: 130
Number of students: 951

DEANS

Faculty of Administration and Economics: Lic. Germàn A. Kraus
Faculty of Engineering: Ing. Francisco R. Agüera

UNIVERSIDAD DE MENDOZA

Avda Boulogne-sur-Mer 665, 5500 Mendoza

Telephone: 202017
Fax: 201100

Founded 1960
Language of instruction: Spanish
Academic year: March to November

Rector: Dr Juan C. Menghini
Vice-Rectors: Arq. Ricardo Perotti, Ing. Saturnino Leguizamón
Administrative Officer: Cont. Beatriz Rosa Celeste

Number of teachers: 372
Number of students: 3,638

Publications: *Idearium*‡, *Revista*‡, *Ideas*‡.

DEANS

Faculty of Law and Social Sciences: Dr Emilio Vázquez Viera
Faculty of Architecture and Town Planning: Arq. Ricardo Bekerman
Faculty of Engineering: Ing. José Luis Puliafito
Faculty of Health Sciences: (vacant)

DIRECTORS

Centre of Higher Research: Dr Juan C. Menghini
Institute of Private Law: Dr Luis E. Sarmiento García
Institute of Public Law: Dr Roberto Lavado
Institute of Practical Philosophy: Dr Nolberto Espinosa
Institute of Design: Aurelio Alvarez Campi
Institute of Scientific and Technical Studies and Research: Ing. Celeste d'Inca
Institute of Architectural and Urban Culture: Eliana Bormida
Institute of Architectural Technology: Mario Raina
Institute of Environmental, Urban and Regional Research: Ruth de Villareal
Institute of Environmental Studies: Dr Gerd K. Hartmann
Department of Telecommunications: Ing. Enrique Puliafito
Department of Digital Electronics: Ing. Raúl Funes
Department of Millimetric and Submillimetric Waves: Ing. Carlos Puliafito
Department of High-Frequency Electronics: Ing. José L. Puliafito
Department of Optoelectronics: Ing. José Quero
Department of Information Science: Ing. Salvador Navarría

UNIVERSIDAD DE MORÓN

Cabildo 134, 1708 Morón, Pcia de Buenos Aires

Telephone: (1) 483-1023
Fax: 627-8551
E-mail: postmaster@umocom.edu.ar

Founded 1960
Private control
Academic year: March to December

Rector: Dr Mario Armando Mena
Vice-Rector: Dr Albrané Horacio Malcervelli
Academic Secretary: Dr Eduardo Néstor Cozza
Administrative Secretary: Dr Mario Alberto Gayá
Library Director: Dr Graciela Susana Puente

Number of teachers: 2,200
Number of students: 15,000

DEANS AND DIRECTORS

Faculty of Law and Social Sciences: Dr Norberto Porto Lema
Faculty of Engineering: Ing. Horacio Lionetti
Faculty of Exact, Chemical and Natural Sciences: Dr Enrique Vandersluis
Faculty of Philosophy, Education and Humanities: Lic. Roberto Paterno
Faculty of Agronomy: Ing. Agr. Jorge Ottone
Faculty of Economics: Dr Jorge Raúl Lemos
Faculty of Architecture: Arq. Héctor P. Morales
Faculty of Tourism: Lic. Olga Villalba de Cesenj

Faculty of Technology, Computer and Communication Science: Ing. ROBERTO MANUEL IGARZA

UNIVERSIDAD DEL MUSEO SOCIAL ARGENTINO
(University of the Argentine Museum of Sociology)

Av. Corrientes 1723, 1042 Buenos Aires

Telephone: 375-4601
Fax 375-4600

Founded 1912

Rector: Dr GUILLERMO E. GARBARINI ISLAS
Librarian: Lic. GABRIEL MEDINA ERNST

DEANS

Faculty of Political, Juridical and Economic Sciences: Dr LUIS J. ZABALLA
Faculty of Information and Opinion Science: Lic. ADRIANA ADAMO
Faculty of Human Recovery Sciences: Lic. ESTELA SALAZAR
Faculty of Social Services: Dr GUSTAVO PINARD
School of Economics: Cont. ELBA FONT DE MALUGANI
University School of Translation: Lic. ALICIA BERMOLEN
Institute of Political Sciences: Dra MARTA BIAGI
Institute of Professional Training: Lic. MARIA E. PELLANDA

UNIVERSIDAD DEL NORTE SANTO TOMÁS DE AQUINO

9 de Julio 165, CC 32, 4000 San Miguel de Tucumán

Telephone: (81) 22-8805

Founded 1965
Academic year: April to November

Grand Chancellor: Fr. JUAN PABLO BERRA
Rector: Dr PEDRO WENCESLAO LOBO
Vice-Rector: Ing. JUAN CARLOS MUZZO
General Secretary: CPN EFRAIN OSCAR DAVID
Academic Secretary: Lic. ALEJANDRO SANCHO MIÑANO
Director of the Library: Prof. GUILLERMO KREIBHORN

Number of teachers: 642
Number of students: 3,738

DEANS

Faculty of Humanities: Lic. FRANCISCO JOSÉ TORRES NIETO
Faculty of Law and Social Sciences: Dr ROSENDO MATÍAS CARRACEDO
Faculty of Economics and Administration: CPN JUAN FÉLIX BANCHERO
Faculty of Engineering: Ing. JUAN ARISTIDES BALZARETTI
Faculty of Philosophy: Lic. JOSÉ ERNESTO PARSELIS
Faculty of Anthropology and Psychology: Lic. FRANCISCO J. TORRES NIETO (acting)
Graduate Department: Dr PEDRO WENCESLAO LOBO

ATTACHED INSTITUTES

University Centre in Concepción: Pres. Julio A. Roca 32, 4146 Concepción, Tucumán; Rectoral Delegate: Arq. EDUARDO E. KERN

Centre of Institutional Studies: Defensa 422, 1065 Buenos Aires; Dean: Fray RAFAEL CÚNSULO.

Centre of Institutional Studies in Tucumán: 9 de Julio 165, 4000 San Miguel de Tucumán; Moderator Dean Fray RAFAEL CÚNSULO.

Higher Institute of Social Work 'Juan XXIII': Laprida 390, 4000 San Miguel de Tucumán; Dir Mons. Dr LUIS LIBORIO RANDISI.

University Centre in Buenos Aires: Tucumán 1679, 5° piso, 1050 Buenos Aires; Dir Lic. ROBERTO ESTEVEZ.

Youth Institute: San Lorenzo 480, 1° piso, 4000 Tucumán; Dir Dra ANNA MARÍA FERRARI DE RAMBALDI.

Research Institute of Applied Science in Communications: Dir Lic. OTON MATIAS GRIMOLIZI.

Historical Research Institute 'Prof. Manuel García Soriano': Dir Fr Dr RUBÉN GONZÁLEZ.

UNIVERSIDAD NOTARIAL ARGENTINA
(Argentine University for Lawyers)

Avda 51 No. 435, 1900 La Plata

Telephone: (21) 21-9283
Fax: (21) 21-0552
E-mail: uninot@satlink.com

Founded 1964
Academic year: March to June, July to November

Chancellor: Not. JORGE F. DUMON
Rector: NÉSTOR O. PÉREZ LOZANO
Vice-Rector: Dr NORBERTO R. BENSEÑOR
General Director: Prof. ALICIA PALAIA
Librarian: Dra DORA C. TÁLICE DE SECO VILLALBA

Number of teachers: 150
Number of students: 2,300

Publications: *Cuadernos Notariales, Ediciones UNA*, monographs.

UNIVERSIDAD DEL SALVADOR
(University of the Saviour)

Viamonte 1856, 1056 Buenos Aires

Telephone: (1) 813-9630

Founded 1956

Academic year: January to December

Rector: Lic. JUAN ALEJANDRO TOBIAS
Academic Vice-Rector: Lic. JAVIER ALONSO HIDALGO
Vice-Rector (Economics): Dr ENRIQUE A. BETTA
Vice-Rector (Research and Development): Dr FERNANDO LUCERO SCHMIDT
Vice-Rector (Religious Training): Lic. JUAN ALEJANDRO TOBIAS (acting)
Secretary-General: Prof. PABLO GABRIEL VARELA
Librarian: Lic. LAURA MARTINO

Library: see under Libraries

Number of teachers: 2,800
Number of students: 16,500

Publications: *Anales, Signos, Bulletin of Number Theory and Related Topics.*

DEANS

Faculty of Law: Dr PRÁXEDES SAGASTA
Faculty of Philosophy: Lic. CELIA LYNCH PUEYRREDON
Faculty of Science and Technology: Ing. MIGUEL GUERRERO
Faculty of History and Arts: Dr JUAN C. LUCERO SCHMIDT
Faculty of Medicine: Dr ADOLFO LIZARRAGA
Faculty of Psychology: Dr CARLOS GUILLERMO VOSS
Faculty of Social Sciences: Lic. EDUARDO SUÁREZ
Faculty of Psychopedagogy: Prof. MARÍA I. OLIVER
Faculty of Educational Sciences and Social Communication: Prof. MARÍA MERCEDES TERREN
Faculty of Economics: Dr SERGIO GARCÍA
Faculty of Administration: Ing. AQUILINO LÓPEZ DIEZ
Faculty of Theology (in San Miguel): R. P. Lic. JOSÉ H. LUDY
Faculty of Philosophy (in San Miguel): R. P. Dr JORGE SEIBOLD

DIRECTORS

School of Theatre Arts: Prof. ALICE D. DE BEITÍA
School of Oriental Studies: Prof. LUISA ROSELL

Colleges

Escuela Nacional de Bibliotecarios: Avda Libertador 1602, 1425 Buenos Aires; tel. 801-0030.

Escuela Nacional de Educación Técnica 'Gral Ing. Enrique Mosconi': Calle Schreiber 892 Cutralco, 8318 Plaza Huincul, Neuquén; tel. (99) 63288; f. 1953; specializes in mechanical and petroleum engineering; 600 students; Dir Ing. ARMANDO PARIS.

Instituto Tecnológico de Buenos Aires: Avda Eduardo Madero 399, 1106 Buenos Aires; tel. (1) 314-7778; fax (1) 314-0270; e-mail postmaster@itba.edu.ar; f. 1959; private; 250 teachers, 1,523 students; library of 12,000 books; Rector Ing. ERNESTO MANUEL RUIZ; publs *Revista del Instituto Tecnológico de Buenos Aires, Boletín General, Acontecer.*

Schools of Art and Music

Conservatorio Municipal de Música 'Manuel de Falla': Sarmiento 1551, 1042 C.P., Buenos Aires; tel. (1) 371-5898; f. 1919; 3,000 mems; library of 8,000 scores and volumes; Dir AUGUSTO B. RATTENBACH.

Escuela Nacional de Arte Dramático (National School of Drama): French 3614, 1425 Buenos Aires; tel. 804-7970; f. 1924; 300 students; library of 4,200 vols; Rector CARLOS ALBARENGA.

Escuela Nacional de Bellas Artes 'Prilidiano Pueyrredón': Las Heras 1749, 1018 Buenos Aires; tel. 42-0657; f. 1878; depts of painting, engraving and sculpture; 373 students; library of 5,923 vols; Dir DOMINGO MAZZONE.

Escuela Nacional de Danzas: Esmeralda 285, 1035 Buenos Aires; tel. 45-5478; Rector Prof. GLADYS S. DE MUTTER.

Escuela Superior de Bellas Artes 'Ernesto de la Cárcova': Tristán Achaval Rodríguez 1701, 1107 Buenos Aires; tel. 361-5144; f. 1923; painting, sculpture, engraving and décors; museum of tracings; 156 staff; library of 4,500 vols; Rector Prof. EDUARDO A. AUDIVERT.

ARMENIA

Learned Societies

GENERAL

Armenian National Academy of Sciences: 375019 Yerevan, Pr. Marshala Bagramyana 24; tel. 52-70-31; telex: 243344; f. 1943; depts of Physical, Mathematical and Technological Sciences (Academician-Sec. YU. G. SHUKURYAN, Scientific Secs L. V. SIMONYAN, L. A. GRIGORYAN), Natural Sciences (Academician-Sec. E. S. GABRIELYAN, Scientific Sec. E. A. HOVHANESYAN), Humanities (Academician-Sec. G. KH. SARKISYAN, Scientific Sec. H. ZH. KOCHARYAN); research institutes attached to depts: see Research Institutes; 119 mems; Pres. F. T. SARKISYAN; Academician-Sec. V. B. BARKHUDARYAN; publs *Doklady* (Reports), *Izvestiya* (Bulletins: Mathematics, Mechanics, Physics, Engineering Sciences, Earth Sciences), *Astrofizika* (Astrophysics), *Neirokhimiya* (Neurochemistry), *Khimicheskii Zhurnal Armenii* (Chemical Journal of Armenia), *Biologicheskii Zhurnal Armenii* (Biological Journal of Armenia), *Vestnik Obshchestvennykh Nauk* (Herald of Social Sciences), *Meditsinskaya nauka Armenii* (Medical Science of Armenia), *Vestnik Khirurgii Armenii* (Herald of Armenian Surgery), *Istoriko-Filologicheskii Zhurnal* (Historical and Philological Journal), *Soobshcheniya Byurakanskoi Observatorii* (Reports of the Byurakan Astrophysical Observatory).

Research Institutes

AGRICULTURE, FISHERIES AND VETERINARY SCIENCE

Institute of Hydroponics Problems: 375082 Yerevan, Noragyugh 108; tel. (2) 56-51-62; e-mail mairap@hydro.nasgw.sci.am; f. 1947; attached to Armenian Nat. Acad. of Sciences; research for the cultivation of plants under soilless conditions; library of 9,000 vols; Dir S. K. MAIRAPETYAN; publ. *Communications of IHP* (1 a year).

Institute of Viticulture, Wine-making and Fruit-growing: 378312 Edmiadzinsky raion, Pos. Mertsavan; tel. 58-15-23.

BIBLIOGRAPHY, LIBRARY SCIENCE AND MUSEOLOGY

Institute of Ancient Manuscripts: 375009 Yerevan, Mashtots Ave 111; tel. 58-32-92; f. 1932; library of 100,000 vols; special collections: 16,800 MSS; Dir SEN AREVSHATIAN.

ECONOMICS, LAW AND POLITICS

Institute of Economics: 375001 Yerevan, Ul. Abovyana 15; tel. 58-19-71; attached to Armenian Nat. Acad. of Sciences; Dir M. KH. KOTANYAN.

HISTORY, GEOGRAPHY AND ARCHAEOLOGY

Institute of Archaeology and Ethnography: 375025 Yerevan, Charents 15; tel. (2) 55-68-96; f. 1959; attached to Armenian Nat. Acad. of Sciences; library of 8,500 vols; Dir A. A. KALANTARYAN.

Institute of History: 375019 Yerevan, Pr. Marshala Bagramyana 24G; tel. 52-92-63; attached to Armenian Nat. Acad. of Sciences; Dir G. A. AVETISYAN.

Institute of Oriental Studies: 375019 Yerevan, Pr. Marshala Bagramyana 24G; tel. 58-33-82; attached to Armenian Nat. Acad. of Sciences; Dir N. O. HOVHANESYAN.

LANGUAGE AND LITERATURE

Abegyan Institute of Literature: 375015 Yerevan, Ul. Grikora Lusavoricha 15; tel. 56-32-54; attached to Armenian Nat. Acad. of Sciences; Dir E. M. JERBASHYAN.

Acharyan Institute of Linguistics: 375001 Yerevan, Ul. Abovyana 15; tel. 56-53-37; attached to Armenian Nat. Acad. of Sciences; Dir G. B. JAUKYAN.

Institute of the Arts: 375019 Yerevan, Pr. Marshala Bagramyana 24G; tel. 58-37-02; attached to Armenian Nat. Acad. of Sciences; Dir L. H. HAKHVERDYAN.

MEDICINE

Armenian Institute of Spa Treatment and Physiotherapy: 375028 Yerevan, Ul. Bratev Orbeli 41; f. 1930; Dir Prof. G. AGADJANIAN; publ. *Transactions*.

Armenian Research Centre of Maternal and Child Health Care: 375002 Yerevan, Mesrop Mashtots Ave 22; tel. (2) 53-01-92; fax (2) 15-19-57; f. 1931; library of 25,000 vols; Dir Prof. K. B. AKUNTS.

Bedrosian, K., Yerevan Scientific Research Institute of Orthopaedics and Traumatology: Yerevan; f. 1945.

Research Centre for Epidemiology, Virology and Medical Parasitology: 375009 Yerevan, Ul. Gevorga Kochara 21A; tel. 56-21-02; Dir YU. T. ALEKSANYAN.

Research Centre for Surgery: Yerevan.

NATURAL SCIENCES

Biological Sciences

Bunlatyan Institute of Neurochemistry: 375044 Yerevan, Ul. Paruyra Sevaka 5/1; tel. 28-18-40; attached to Armenian Nat. Acad. of Sciences; Dir A. A. GALOYAN.

Centre for Ecological-Noosphere Studies: 375025 Yerevan, Charents 19; tel. 55-13-61; fax 58-02-54; e-mail ecocentr@pnas.sci.am; f. 1989; attached to Armenian Nat. Acad. of Sciences; Dir A. K. SAGATELYAN.

Institute of Botany and Botanical Garden: 375063 Yerevan, Avan; tel. 62-58-40; attached to Armenian Nat. Acad. of Sciences; Dir A. A. CHARCHOGLYAN.

Institute of Microbiology: 378510 Abovian; tel. (61) 2-16-22; fax (61) 2-32-40; e-mail microbio@pnas.sci.am; f. 1961; attached to Armenian Nat. Acad. of Sciences; library of 5,000 vols; Dir E. G. AFRIKYAN.

Institute of Molecular Biology: 375014 Yerevan, Hasratyan 7; tel. (2) 28-16-26; attached to Armenian Nat. Acad. of Sciences; Dir K. G. KARAGEUZYAN.

Institute of Zoology: 375044 Yerevan, Ul. Paruyra Sevaka 7; tel. 28-14-70; attached to Armenian Nat. Acad. of Sciences; Dir S. H. MOVSESYAN.

Orbeli Institute of Physiology: 375028 Yerevan, Orbeli Brothers 22; tel. (2) 27-04-41; attached to Armenian Nat. Acad. of Sciences; library of 4,000 books, 25,000 periodicals; Dir V. B. FANARDJYAN.

Sevan Institute of Hydroecology and Ichthyology: 378610 Sevan, Ul. Kirova 186; tel. 2-34-19; attached to Armenian Nat. Acad. of Sciences; Dir R. O. HOVHANESYAN.

Mathematical Sciences

Institute of Mathematics: 375019 Yerevan, Pr. Marshala Bagramyana 24B; tel. 52-47-91; attached to Armenian Nat. Acad. of Sciences; Dir A. A. TALALYAN.

Physical Sciences

Byurakan Astrophysical Observatory: 378433 Ashtarak raion, Byurakan; tel. 28-34-53; attached to Armenian Nat. Acad. of Sciences; Dir A. R. PETROSYAN.

Institute of Chemical Physics: 375004 Yerevan, Ul. Paruyra Sevaka 5/2; tel. 28-16-41; attached to Armenian Nat. Acad. of Sciences; Dir A. H. MANTASHYAN.

Institute of Fine Organic Chemistry: 375014 Yerevan, Pr. Azatutyana 26; tel. 28-83-34; attached to Armenian Nat. Acad. of Sciences; Dir B. T. GARIBJANYAN.

Institute of General and Inorganic Chemistry: 375051 Yerevan, Ul. Fioletova 11110; tel. 23-07-38; attached to Armenian Nat. Acad. of Sciences; Dir S. S. KARAKHANYAN.

Institute of Geology: 375019 Yerevan, Pr. Marshala Bagramyana 24A; tel. 52-44-26; attached to Armenian Nat. Acad. of Sciences; Dir R. J. DJERBASHYAN.

Institute of Geophysics and Engineering Seismology: 377501 Gjumry, Pr. Leningradyana 5; tel. (69) 3-12-61; fax (69) 3-38-40; attached to Armenian Nat. Acad. of Sciences; Dir S. M. HOVHANESYAN.

Institute of Organic Chemistry: 375094 Yerevan, Ul. Kamo 167A; tel. 28-35-21; attached to Armenian Nat. Acad. of Sciences; Dir SH. H. BADANYAN.

Research Institute of Radiophysical Measurements: 375014 Yerevan, Ul. Komitasa 49/4; tel. 23-49-90; Dir P. M. GERUNI.

Yerevan Physics Institute: 375036 Yerevan, Ul. Bratev Alikhanyan 2; tel. 34-15-00; fax 35-00-30; f. 1943; particle and nuclear physics; library of 10,000 vols; Dir R. L. MKRTCHYAN.

PHILOSOPHY AND PSYCHOLOGY

Institute of Philosophy and Law: 375010 Yerevan, Ul. Arami 44; tel. (2) 53-05-71; fax (2) 50-59-47; e-mail socio@arminco.com; attached to Armenian Nat. Acad. of Sciences; Dir G. A. POGOSYAN.

RELIGION, SOCIOLOGY AND ANTHROPOLOGY

Centre of Scientific Information on Social Sciences: 375019 Yerevan, Pr. Marshala Bagramyana 24D; tel. 58-72-02; attached to Armenian Nat. Acad. of Sciences; Dir. G. B. GARIBJANYAN.

Sociology Research Centre: 375010 Yerevan, Ul. Arami 44; tel. (2) 53-10-96; fax (2) 50-59-47; e-mail root@socio.arminco.com; attached to Armenian Nat. Acad. of Sciences; Dir G. A. POGOSYAN.

TECHNOLOGY

Institute for Physical Research: 378410, Ashtarak 2; tel. 28-81-50; attached to Armenian Nat. Acad. of Sciences; Dir E. S. Vardanyan.

Institute of Applied Problems in Physics: 375014 Yerevan, Ul. H. Nersesiana 25; tel. 24-58-96; attached to Armenian Nat. Acad. of Sciences; Dir. A. R. Mkrtchyan.

Institute of Mechanics: 375019 Yerevan, Pr. Marshala Bagramyana 24B; tel. 52-48-90; attached to Armenian Nat. Acad. of Sciences; Dir N. Agalovyan.

Institute of Problems in Informatics and Automation: 375044 Yerevan, Ul. Paruyra Sevaka 1; tel. 28-58-12; attached to Armenian Nat. Acad. of Sciences; Dir Yu. H. Shukurian.

Institute of Radiophysics and Electronics: 378410, Ashtarak 2, Alikhanyan Brothers 1; tel. (2) 28-78-50; e-mail irphe@arminco.com; f. 1960; library of 12,000 vols; attached to Armenian Nat. Acad. of Sciences; Dir R. M. Martirosyan.

Research Institute of Complex Electrical Equipment: 375006 Yerevan, Ul. Telmana 33; tel. 42-38-40; f. 1956; library of 14,600.

Research Institute of Electrical Engineering: 375056 Yerevan, 111 Norkskii massiv, 8-ya ul. 27; tel. 64-94-51; Dir K. A. Alikhanyan.

Special Experimental Construction Technological Institute: 377501 Gjumry, Ul. Leningradyana 5A; tel. 4-56-63; attached to Armenian Nat. Acad. of Sciences; Dir R. E. Sarkisyan.

Yerevan Mathematical Machines Research Institute: 375003 Yerevan, Ul. A. Akopyana 3; tel. 27-77-79; Dir A. E. Sarkisyan.

Libraries and Archives

Yerevan

Armenian Scientific and Technical Library: 375009 Yerevan, Moskovskaya ul. 35; 19,770,000 vols; Dir I. S. Akopyan.

Central Library of the Armenian Academy of Sciences: 375000 Yerevan, Ul. B. Musyana 24; tel. 57-73-10; f 1935; 2,200,000 vols; Dir G. N. Ovnan.

Matenadaran Institute of Ancient Armenian Manuscripts: Yerevan, Mashtots ave 111; tel. 58-32-92; f. 1920; incorporates research institute of Armenian textology and codicology; 17,000 Armenian MSS dating from 5th to 18th centuries, miniature paintings, 100,000 archival documents and works by Greek, Syrian, Persian, Arabic, Latin, Georgian and Ethiopian authors; Dir S. Arevshatian; publ. *Banber Matenadarani*.

National Library of Armenia: 375009 Yerevan, Teryan 72; tel. (2) 58-42-59; fax (39) 0-69-17; f. 1919; 6,114,000 vols; Dir Gevorg Ter-Vardanyan.

Yerevan State University Library: 375049 Yerevan, Ul. Mravyana 1; 1,500,000 vols; Dir V. S. Aslanian.

Museums and Art Galleries

Yerevan

Armenian State Historical Museum: Yerevan, Pl. Lenina; Dir M. S. Asratyan.

Armenian State Picture Gallery: 375010 Yerevan, Ul. Spandaryana 1; tel. 58-07-65; f. 1921; West European, Armenian, Russian and Oriental art; library of 10,330 vols; Dir A. Ter-Gabrielian.

Egishe Charents State Museum of Literature and Art: Yerevan, Aram St 1; f. 1921; history of Armenian literature (18th to 20th centuries), theatre, cinema and music; library of 84,526 vols, 862,252 MSS; Dir H. Bakchinyan; publs *Literary Inheritance, Guide Book*.

Geological Museum of the Institute of Geology: 375010 Yerevan, Ul. Aboyana 10; tel. 58-06-63; f. 1937; collection mainly from Armenia; Dir G. B. Mezhlumyan.

Yerevan Children's Picture Gallery: Yerevan, Ul. Aboviana 13; tel. 52-78-93; f. 1970; works of art by children of Armenian and other nationalities; Dir H. Ikitian.

Zoological Museum of the Institute of Zoology: 375044 Yerevan, Ul. P. Sevaka 7; tel. 28-15-02; Dir M. S. Adamyan.

University

YEREVAN STATE UNIVERSITY

375049 Yerevan, Alex Manoogian St 1

Telephone: (2) 55-46-29
Telex: 243388
Fax: (2) 15-10-87
E-mail: rector@ysu.am

Founded 1919
State control
Language of instruction: Armenian
Academic year: September to June

Rector: Radik M. Martirosian
Vice-Rectors: Edward Chubarian (Academic Affairs: Natural Sciences), Semion Hakhumian (Academic Affairs: Humanities), Rafael Matevosian (International Relations), Romen Sharkhatunian (Economic Development), Edward Kazarian (Education Development)
Director of Library: Vardges Aslanian

Numbers of teachers: 1,200
Number of students: 9,000

Publications: *Bulletin* (3 a year), *Transactions* (3 a year), *Yerevan University* (3 a year).

DEANS

Faculty of Mechanics: Vladimir Sarkisian
Faculty of Mathematics: Romen Shahbagian
Faculty of Physics: Yuri Chilingarian
Faculty of Radiophysics: Yuri Vardanian
Faculty of Chemistry: Aida Avetisian
Faculty of Biology: Misak Davtian
Faculty of Economics: Grigor Gharibian
Faculty of Geology: Marat Grigorian
Faculty of Geography: Lenvel Valesian
Faculty of Informatics and Applied Mathematics: Vladimir Yeghiazarian
Faculty of Armenian Philology: Vazgen Gabrielian
Faculty of Romanic-Germanic Philology: Karo Karapetian
Faculty of Russian Philology: Levon Mkrtchian
Faculty of Oriental Studies: Gurgen Melikian
Faculty of History: Babken Harutiunian
Faculty of Philosophy, Psychology and Sociology: Edward Margarian
Faculty of Law: Gagik Ghazinian
Faculty of Theology: Archbishop Shahe Ajemian
Teacher-Training Faculty: Hrachya Martirosian
Preparatory Faculty for Foreign Students: Leonard Shekian

Other Higher Educational Institutes

Armenian Agricultural Institute: 375009 Yerevan, Ul. Teryana 74; tel. 52-45-41; f. 1930; depts: agrochemistry and soil science; agronomy, fruit and vegetable growing, viticulture, plant protection, wine making, technology of preserving industry, mechanization, irrigation, economics and management, motor transport; 250 teachers; 4,000 students; library of 350,000 vols; extra-mural faculty; Rector M. A. Gülkhasian; publs *Scientific Works, Collection of Conference Scientific Reports, Agriculturist*.

State Engineering University of Armenia: 375009 Yerevan, Ul. Teryana 105; tel. 52-05-20; fax 15-10-68; f. 1930; faculties: machine-building, electrical engineering, power engineering, computer sciences, technical cybernetics, radiotechnical engineering, mining and geology, and transport; library of 667,000 vols; 1,100 teachers; 11,000 students; Rector Y. L. Sarkissian.

Yerevan Academy of National Economy: 375025 Yerevan, Ul. Abovyana 52; tel. 56-04-13; telex 411626; f. 1975; faculties of economic planning, finance and accounting, economics of labour and sociology, economics and organization of labour, economics of trade and commodities; 326 teachers; 5,600 students; publ. *Economics*.

Yerevan Institute of Architecture and Construction: Terian Str. 105, Yerevan 375009; tel. 580-177; fax 565-984; f. 1989; architecture, urban design, construction engineering, scientific research; 262 teachers; 3,200 students; library of 1,373,203 vols; Rector Arest G. Beglarian.

Yerevan Komitas State Conservatoire: 375009 Yerevan, Ul. Sayat-Novy 1; tel. 58-11-64; e-mail egc@arminco.com; f. 1926; piano, orchestral instruments, folk instruments, singing, choral conducting, composition, musicology; extra-mural dept; library of 43,000 vols.

Yerevan State Institute of Fine Arts: 375009 Yerevan, Ul. Isaakyana 36; tel. 56-07-26; f. 1944; faculties: fine arts, applied arts, history of art; library of 25,000 vols; Rector Aram E. Isabekyan.

Yerevan State Medical University: 375025 Yerevan, Ul. Korjun 2; tel. (2) 52-17-11; fax (2) 15-18-12; e-mail meduni@moon.yerphi.am; f. 1922; faculties of general medicine, stomatology, pharmacy, pediatrics, military medicine, sanitation and hygiene; library of 613,000 vols; 568 teachers; Rector V. P. Hakopian; publs *Mkhitar Heratsi* (4 a year), *Physician To Be* (weekly), Medical Science of Armenia (4 a year), *Actual and Fundamental Problems of Medicine* (2 a year).

Yerevan State Pedagogical Institute of Russian and Foreign Languages: 375051

Yerevan, per Pravdy; tel. 25-37-82; f. 1935; faculties of Russian language and literature, English, French, German; 240 teachers; 2,800 students; Rector IVETA ARAKELYAN.

Yerevan Zootechnical and Veterinary Institute: 375025 Yerevan, Ul. Nalbandyana 128; tel. 56-13-42; f. 1929; library of 210,000 vols; faculties of livestock management, veterinary science, technology of milk and dairy products, improvement of qualifications; 200 teachers; 2,900 students; Rector M. S. MELKONIAN; publ. *Trudy*.

AUSTRALIA

Learned Societies

GENERAL

Academy of the Social Sciences in Australia: GPO Box 1956, Canberra, ACT 2601; f. 1971; 301 Fellows; Pres. F. GALE; Exec. Dir Dr B. CLISSOLD; publs *Annual Report, Proceedings, Newsletter.*

Australian Academy of the Humanities: GPO Box 93, Canberra, ACT 2601; tel. (2) 6248-7744; fax (2) 6248-6287; f. 1969; language, literature, history, philosophy, fine arts; 311 Fellows, 52 Overseas and Hon. Fellows; Pres. Prof. M. CLUNIES ROSS; Hon. Sec. Prof. P. R. C. WEAVER; Exec. Dir Dr D. BENNETT; Int. Sec. DAVID MARR; publ. *Proceedings.*

AGRICULTURE, FISHERIES AND VETERINARY SCIENCE

Agriculture and Resource Management Council of Australia and New Zealand: Dept of Primary Industries and Energy, Barton, Canberra, ACT 2600; tel. (2) 6272-5216; fax (2) 6272-4772; f. 1992 to develop integrated and sustainable agricultural and land and water policies, strategies and practices; mems: Commonwealth, State, Territory and New Zealand ministers responsible for agriculture, soil conservation, water resources and rural adjustment; advised by a Standing Committee comprising heads of Commonwealth, State, Territory and New Zealand agencies responsible for agriculture, soil conservation and water resources, and representatives from CSIRO, Bureau of Meteorology and rural adjustment authorities; Sec. J. W. GRAHAM.

Australian Institute of Agricultural Science: 91 Rathdowne St, Carlton, Vic. 3053; tel. (3) 9662-1077; fax (3) 9662-2727; f. 1935; 2,500 mems; Exec. Dir SIMON L. FIELD; publ. *Agricultural Science* (every 2 months).

Australian Veterinary Association: POB 371, 134–136 Hampden Rd, Artarmon, NSW; f. 1921; professional association; 4,000 mems; Pres. W. SCANLON; Chief Exec. B. HORSFIELD; publ. *Australian Veterinary Journal* (monthly).

Dairy Industry Association of Australia Inc.: ADPF, 84 William St, Melbourne, Vic. 3000; tel. (3) 9642-8033; fax (3) 9642-8133; f. 1946; divisions in each State; 1,600 mems; Pres. M. SEURET; Sec. (vacant); publs *The Australian Journal of Dairy Technology* (2 a year), *Australian Dairy Foods* (6 a year).

ARCHITECTURE AND TOWN PLANNING

Australian Council of National Trusts: POB 1002, Civic Sq., ACT 2608; tel. (2) 6247-6766; fax (2) 6249-1395; e-mail acnt@spirit.com.au; f. 1965; Federal Council of the State and Territory National Trusts established for the conservation of lands and buildings of beauty or of national, historic, scientific, architectural or cultural interest and Aboriginal relics and wildlife; 80,000 mems of the National Trust movement; Exec. Officer ALAN GRAHAM.

Australian Institute of Quantity Surveyors: National Office, POB 301, Deakin West, ACT 2600; tel. (6) 282-2222; fax (6) 285-2427; f. 1971; 2,000 mems; Pres. PAUL LONSDALE; Gen. Man. TERRY SANDERS; publ. *The Building Economist* (quarterly).

Royal Australian Institute of Architects: 2A Mugga Way, Red Hill, Canberra, ACT; tel. (2) 6273-1548; fax (2) 6273-1953; inc. 1930; 8,500 mems; Chief Exec. MICHAEL PECK; Sec. NEIL EWART; publ. *Architecture Australia* (every 2 months), occasional newsletters, research papers, seminar and workshop papers, management and law notes.

Royal Australian Planning Institute Inc.: RAPI House, 615 Burwood Rd, Hawthorn, Vic. 3122; tel. (3) 9819-0728; fax (3) 9819-0676; f. 1951; professional asscn for town and regional planners; 3,300 mems; Pres. BARRIE MELOTTE; Sec./Treas. RICHARD N. HEAD; publs *Australian Planner* (quarterly), *National Office News* (6 a year).

BIBLIOGRAPHY, LIBRARY SCIENCE AND MUSEOLOGY

Australian Library and Information Association: POB E441, Kingston, ACT 2604; tel. (2) 6285-1877; e-mail enquiry@alia.org.au; f. 1937; 9,550 mems; Pres. JOHN SHIPP; Exec. Dir VIRGINIA WALSH; publs *Australian Library Journal* (quarterly), *inCite* (monthly).

Bibliographical Society of Australia and New Zealand: c/o Sec. Margaret Dent, Rare Books Librarian, National Library of Australia, Canberra, ACT 2600; f. 1969 to promote research in bibliography; 248 mems; Pres. W. D. THORN; publs *Bulletin* (quarterly), *Broadsheet* (3 or 4 a year), *Occasional Publications.*

Museums Australia, Inc.: c/o Nat. Dir, 24 Queens Parade, North Fitzroy, Vic. 3068; tel. (3) 9486-3399; fax (3) 9486-3788; e-mail manat@access.net.au; f. 1937 to promote museums to all levels of government and the community and to foster high standards in all aspects of museum management through research, policy formulation, publications and training; 2,000 mems; publ. *Museum National* (quarterly).

ECONOMICS, LAW AND POLITICS

Australasian Political Studies Association: Faculty of Arts, University of New England, Armidale, NSW 2350; tel. (67) 713407; f. 1952; Pres. ANDREW PARKIN; Hon. Sec. TOD MOORE; publs *Australian Journal of Political Science* (quarterly), *APSA Newsletter* (quarterly.

Australian Bar Association: Bar Association of Queensland, Level 5, Inns of Court, 107 North Quay, Brisbane, Qld 4000; tel. (7) 3236-2477; fax (7) 3236-1180; f. 1962 to advance the interests of barristers; to maintain and strengthen the position of the Bar, maintaining its independence and the rule of law; to maintain and improve standards of instruction and training of barristers; 3,440 mems; Pres. R. W. GOTTERSON; Sec. D. L. O'CONNOR.

Australian Institute of Credit Management: f. 1967 to provide a national and professional organization for credit managers and those engaged in the control of credit; holds conferences, discussions; maintains educational programmes at CAEs; *c.* 3,000 mems; divisions in all States; Pres. W. L. DUNCAN; Exec. Dir L. J. WILSON, POB 558, Artarmon, NSW 2064.

Australian Institute of International Affairs: 32 Thesiger Court, Deakin, ACT 2600; tel. (2) 6282-2133; fax (2) 6285-2334; f. 1933; 1,800 mems; brs in all States; Pres. Dr NEAL BLEWETT; Exec. Dir ROSS COTTRILL; publ. *Australian Journal of International Affairs* (3 a year).

Australian Institute of Management: 181 Fitzroy St, St. Kilda, Vic. 3182; tel. (3) 9534-8181; fax (3) 9534-5050; f. 1941; professional management association; information and training services; 30,000 professional mems, 7,500 corporate mems; divisions in all states; library of over 20,000 vols; publ. *National Management Today Magazine* (monthly).

Australian Institute of Valuers and Land Economists: 6 Campion St, Deakin, ACT 2600; tel. (6) 282-2411; fax: (06) 285-2194; f. 1926; professional body; 7,000 mems; Pres. ROBERT CONNOLLY; CEO BRIAN NYE; publ. *The Valuer and Land Economist* (quarterly).

Committee for Economic Development of Australia: CEDA House, 123 Lonsdale St, Level 1, Melbourne, Vic. 3000; tel. (3) 9662-3544; fax (3) 9663-7271; f. 1960 to develop discussion, research and interdisciplinary communication in the interests of the development of the national economy and the future of Australia; 965 Trustees and Associates; Pres. Dr W. W. J. UHLENBRUCH; Chief Exec. Dr J. P. NIEUWENHUYSEN.

Economic Society of Australia: c/o Prof. Steve Dowrick, Australian National University, Canberra, ACT 0200; tel. (2) 6249-3286; e-mail btrewin@coombs.anu.edu.au; f. 1925; 3,200 mems; brs in each State; Pres. R. G. GREGORY; Hon. Sec. P. ABELSON; publs *The Economic Record, Economic Papers.*

Institute of Municipal Management: POB 418, Level 1, 49–51 Stead Street, South Melbourne, Vic. 3205; tel. (3) 9645-9044; fax (3) 9690-1377; f. 1936; professional organization for city managers, town clerks and local authority chief executives; 3,000 mems; CEO (vacant); publ. *Local Government Management* (6 a year).

Institute of Public Affairs: 128/136 Jolimont Rd, Jolimont, Vic. 3002; tel. (3) 9654-7499; fax (3) 9650-7627; f. 1943; non-profit educational organization to study economic and industrial problems and to advance the cause of free enterprise in Australia; supported by 550 companies and 3,500 individuals; Chair. MICHAEL ROBINSON; Exec. Dir MIKE NAHAN; publs *IPA Review* (quarterly), *Backgrounder* (10 a year), *Current Issues* (5 a year).

Law Council of Australia: GPO Box 1989, Canberra, ACT 2601; premises at: 19 Torrens St, Braddon, ACT 2612; tel. (6) 247-3788; fax (6) 248-0639; f. 1933; 12 constituent bodies representing 30,000 mems; Pres. FABIAN DIXON; Sec.-Gen. PETER G. LEVY; publs *Australian Lawyer* (monthly), *Australian Legal Directory* (annually).

Law Society of New South Wales: 170 Phillip St, Sydney, NSW; tel. (2) 9926-0333; fax (2) 9231-5809; f. 1884; 15,500 mems; library of 32,000 vols; Sec. C. CAWLEY; publs *Law Society Journal* (11 a year), *Caveat* (irregular).

EDUCATION

Australian Association of Adult and Community Education: POB 308, Jamison

Centre, ACT 2614; tel. (6) 251-7933; fax (6) 251-7935; f. 1961; mem. of ICAE, ASPBAE, ICEA; co-ordinates and encourages adult and community education at national level; publishes educational books; lobbies govts and appropriate depts; holds national conferences, etc.; 700 mems, also corporate mems; Chair. Dr ROGER MORRIS; Exec. Dir. ALASTAIR CROMBIE; publs *Australian Journal of Adult and Community Education* (3 a year), *Adult Learning Australia* (6 a year).

Australian College of Education: 42 Geils Court, Deakin, ACT 2600; tel. (2) 6281-1677; f. 1959; an association of educators from every field of education throughout Australia; encourages professional advancement of its members and the national development of education; chapters in each state and territory; conducts national and chapter conferences, surveys and studies, etc.; 6,000 mems; Exec. Dir BEVERLEY J. POPE; publs *Unicorn, Education Review* (incl. *College National Review*, monthly), report of annual conference, chapter newsletters, etc.

Australian Research Council: GPO Box 9880, Canberra, ACT 2601; tel. (2) 6240-9837; fax (2) 6240-9869; f. 1965, present name 1988; responsible for the allocation of grants for research in the physical sciences, biological sciences, chemical sciences, earth sciences, applied sciences, social sciences and the humanities by individuals or research teams; 11 mems; Chair. Prof. VICKI SARA; publs annual reports.

Australian Vice-Chancellors' Committee: GPO Box 1142, Canberra, ACT 2601; f. 1920; consultative and advisory body for Australian university affairs; consists of Vice-Chancellors of Australian univs; 37 mems; Pres. Prof. JOHN NILAND (Vice-Chancellor, Univ. of New South Wales); Exec. Dir STUART HAMILTON; publs *Univation* (research newsletter, quarterly), *Occasional Papers, Information Summaries* (irregular).

Council of Adult Education: 256 Flinders St, Melbourne, Vic. 3000; tel. (3) 9652-0611; fax (3) 9654-6759; f. 1947; statutory body engaged in providing adult education and business training in Victoria; funded, in part, through the Govt of Vic.; library of 50,000 vols; Chair. PAUL HOY; Dir GRAHAM STEVENSON; publs *Program Guide* (5 a year), *Dialogue* (every 3 years, catalogue of book, film and music titles available for self-directed learning groups).

IDP Education Australia Ltd: GPO Box 2006, Canberra, ACT 2601; tel. (2) 6285-8222; fax (2) 6285-3036; f. 1969 as the Int. Development Program of Australian Universities and Colleges Ltd, renamed 1994; an independent company owned by the Australian Universities; seeks to promote Australian education and training services overseas; network offices in Jakarta, Singapore, Bangkok, Hong Kong, Seoul, Kuala Lumpur, Taipei, Manila, Mauritius, Beijing, Washington, Miami, Budapest, Ho Chi Minh City, Phnom Penh, Sydney, Port Moresby, Colombo, Madras, Bombay, Delhi, Johannesburg, Kiev and Budapest; Chief Exec. Dr D. G. BLIGHT; Gen. Man. W. L. STREAT; publs *Annual Report*, newsletters in Asia-Pacific languages.

FINE AND PERFORMING ARTS

Australia Council: 181 Lawson St, Redfern, NSW 2016; tel. (2) 9950-9000; fax (2) 9950-9111; e-mail mail@ozco.gov.au; f. 1968 as Australian Council for the Arts, present name 1975; aims to foster the development of the arts through the programmes of seven funds: Music, Dance, Theatre, New Media, Literature, Visual Arts/Craft, Community Cultural Development, and one board: Aboriginal and Torres Straits Islander Arts; library of 6,500 vols; Chair. MARGARET SEARES; publ. *Artforce* (quarterly).

Australian and New Zealand Association for Medieval and Renaissance Studies: c/o Dept of English, Sydney University, Sydney, NSW 2006; f. 1968; runs conferences every 2 years; 300 mems; Editor D. P. SPEED; publ. *Parergon*.

Musicological Society of Australia: GPO Box 2404, Canberra, ACT 2601; f. 1963; the advancement of musicology; *c*. 300 mems; Pres. SHIRLEY TREMBATH; Sec. ANNE-MARIE FORBES; publs *Musicology Australia* (annually), *Newsletter* (3 a year).

Royal Art Society of New South Wales: 25–27 Walker St, North Sydney, NSW 2060; f. 1880; for the promotion of high standards in Australian art; school for painting (beginners to Diploma RAS of NSW); 640 mems; Pres. RON STANNARD; Sec. CHRISTINE FEHER; publ. *Newsletter* (monthly).

Royal Queensland Art Society: Box 1602, GPO, Brisbane, Qld 4001; tel. 3831-3455; f. 1887; 850 mems; Sec. KAREN KANE.

Royal South Australian Society of Arts: Institute Bldg, 122 Kintore Ave, Adelaide, SA 5000; tel. (8) 8223-4704; f. 1856; 702 mems; Pres. ANDREW STEINER; Hon. Sec. PAUL GRISCTI; publ. *Kalori* (quarterly).

Victorian Artists' Society: 430 Albert St, East Melbourne, Vic. 3002; tel. (3) 9662-1484; fax (3) 9662-2343; f. 1870; 1,000 mems; four galleries and a studio; Pres. KATHLYN BALLARD; Sec. BEVERLEY SNELLING; publs *Newsletter, Annual Report, Gallery on Eastern Hill*.

HISTORY, GEOGRAPHY AND ARCHAEOLOGY

Australian Numismatic Society: PO Box R4, Royal Exchange, Sydney, NSW 2000; tel. (2) 9451-7896; f. 1913; promotes the study of coins, banknotes and medals with particular reference to Australasia and the Pacific region; monthly meetings in Sydney and Brisbane; 320 mems (incl. overseas); Pres. R. T. SELL; Sec. D. TOMS; publs *Report* (quarterly), *Journal* (every 2 years).

Geographical Society of New South Wales Inc.: POB 602, Gladesville, NSW 2111; tel. (2) 9817-3647; f. 1927; 500 mems; Hon. Sec. J. DODSON; publ. *Australian Geographer* (2 a year).

Mapping Sciences Institute, Australia: GPO Box 1817, Brisbane, Qld 4001; f. 1953; holds biennial conferences; mem. Int. Cartographic Asscn; 1,330 mems; Hon. Sec. K. H. SMITH; publ. *Cartography* (2 a year).

Royal Australian Historical Society: History House, 133 Macquarie St, Sydney, NSW 2000; tel. (2) 9247-8001; fax (2) 9247-7854; e-mail history@rahs.org.au; f. 1901; 2,000 mems; library of 20,000 items; Man. RALPH DERBIDGE; publs *Journal* (every 6 months), *History Magazine* (every 3 months).

Royal Geographical Society of Queensland, Inc.: 112 Brookes St, Fortitude Valley, Qld 4006; tel. (7) 3252-3856; fax (7) 3252-4986; e-mail rgsq@gil.com.au; f. 1885; 580 mems; 2,000 monographs; Pres. R. THWAITES; Sec. K. SMITH; publ. *Bulletin* (monthly).

Royal Historical Society of Queensland: POB 12057, Elizabeth St, Brisbane, Qld 4002; f. 1913; 600 mems; Welsby library; research; historical documents preserved and filed; photographic collection; costume collection and museum; Pres. MICHAEL WHITE; Gen. Secs HILARY FISHER, KIRSTIE MOAR; publs *Bulletin* (monthly), *Journal* (quarterly).

Royal Historical Society of Victoria: Royal Mint, 280 William St, Melbourne, Vic. 3000; tel. (3) 9670-1219; fax (3) 9670-1241; f. 1909; research; collection of historical material; exhibitions; 1,600 mems; library of 8,000 vols, MSS, photographs, paintings and prints; Pres. SUSAN PRIESTLEY; Exec. Officer KEVIN GATES; publs *Journal* (every 6 months), *History News* (monthly).

Royal Western Australian Historical Society: Stirling House, 49 Broadway, Nedlands, WA 6009; tel. (8) 9386-3841; fax (8) 9386-3309; f. 1926; museum and library; 1,000 mems; Exec. Officer (vacant); publs *Early Days* (annually), *Newsletter* (monthly).

Society of Australian Genealogists: Richmond Villa, 120 Kent St, Sydney, NSW 2000; tel. (2) 9247-3953; f. 1932; 7,500 mems; library of 20,000 vols; 1,000 microfilm reels, 1 m. names on microfiche, 40,000 photographs, 30,000 MSS; Pres. E. C. BEST; Exec. Officer H. E. GARNSEY; publ. *Descent* (quarterly).

LANGUAGE AND LITERATURE

Australasian and Pacific Society for Eighteenth-Century Studies: C/o Humanities Research Centre, Australian National University, ACT 0200; f. 1970; one of the sponsoring bodies of the David Nichol Smith Seminars; 80 mems; Pres. Prof. I. MCCALMAN.

Australian Society of Authors Ltd: POB 1566, Strawberry Hills, NSW 2012; tel. (2) 9318-0877; fax (2) 9318-0530; f. 1963, inc. 1980; 2,800 mems; Exec. Officer LYNNE SPENDER; publ. *The Australian Author* (quarterly).

English Association Sydney Inc.: English Dept, University of Sydney, Sydney, NSW 2006; f. 1923; 170 mems; Pres. Dr DEIRDRE COLEMAN; Hon. Sec. MARIE-LOUISE CLAFLIN; publ. *Southerly* (quarterly).

Fellowship of Australian Writers NSW Inc.: Box 488, Rozelle, NSW 2039; f. 1928; 3,500 national mems; brs in all states; Pres. BEVERLEY EARNSHAW; Sec. ALAN RUSSELL; publ. *Writers' Voice* (every 2 months).

PEN International (Sydney Centre): POB 153, Woollahra, NSW 2025; f. 1926; awards an annual fiction prize based on a competition open to all; 160 mems; Pres. STELLA WILKES; publ. *Newsletter* (quarterly).

MEDICINE

Australasian Association of Clinical Biochemists: POB 278, Mt Lawley, WA 6929; tel. (8) 9370-5224; fax (8) 9370-4409; f. 1961; e-mail office@aacb.asn.au; 1,400 mems; Pres. P. GARCIA-WEBB; Hon. Sec. J. GALLIGAN; publs *Clinical Biochemist Newsletter, Clinical Biochemist Reviews* (quarterly).

Australasian College of Dermatologists: 136 Pittwater Road, Gladesville, NSW 2111; tel. 9879-6177; fax 9816-1174; f. 1966; 280 mems; Pres. Dr W. A. LAND; Hon. Sec. Dr D. WONG; publ. *The Australasian Journal of Dermatology* (3 a year).

Australasian College of Sexual Health Physicians: Sydney Sexual Health Centre, POB 1614, Sydney, NSW 2001; tel. (2) 9382-7457; fax (2) 9382-7475; f. 1988; Pres. Dr I. DENHAM; Hon. Sec. Dr K. BROWN; publ. *Venereology*.

Australian Association of Neurologists: Royal Australasian College of Physicians, 145 Macquarie St, Sydney, NSW 2000, tel. (2) 9256-5443; fax (2) 9252-3310; f. 1950 to bring together clinical neurologists and scientific workers in the field of the nervous system and its diseases by such means as meetings, provision of special facilities and assistance in any publications on these matters; 450 mems; Pres. Dr WILLIAM CARROLL; Hon. Sec. Dr ALLAN KERMODE; publ. *Clinical and Experimental Neurology* (annually).

Australian Dental Association: 75 Lithgow St, St Leonards, POB 520, NSW 2065; tel.

(2) 906-4412; fax (2) 906-4676; f. 1928; 7,500 mems; Federal Pres. Dr PATRICK J. DALTON; Exec. Dir Dr ROBERT J. F. BUTLER; publs *News Bulletin, Australian Dental Journal.*

Australian Institute of Homoeopathy: POB 122, Roseville, NSW 2069; f. 1946; conducts a 3-year diploma course; Pres. ROGER DENNE; Hon. Sec. (vacant).

Australian Medical Association: 42 Macquarie Street, Barton, ACT 2600; tel. (2) 6270-5400; fax (2) 6270-5499; Sec.-Gen. WILLIAM COOTE; publs *Medical Journal of Australia, Australian Medicine.*

Australian Physiological and Pharmacological Society: tel. (3) 9905-2507; fax (3) 9905-2547; e-mail tony.luff@med.monash.edu.au; f. 1960 for the advancement of sciences of physiology and pharmacology; 550 mems; National Sec. Prof. A. R. LUFF, Dept Physiology, Monash University, Vic. 3168; publ. *Proceedings* (2 a year).

Australian Physiotherapy Association (NSW): POB 119, Concord, NSW 2137; tel. (2) 736-1122; fax (2) 736-2152; f. 1905; provides postgraduate courses and professional services; 3,000 mems; Pres. KAREN GINN; Exec. Dir LINDSAY A. CANE; publ. *NSW Physiotherapy Bulletin* (monthly).

Australian Society of Clinical Hypnotherapists: POB 471, Eastwood, NSW 2122; tel. (2) 9874-2776; fax (2) 9804-7149; f. 1974; to advance knowledge and practice of hypnosis and to maintain the highest ethical standards in its use; small library; *c.* 400 mems; Pres. ROBERT CARLON; Sec. ELIZABETH CARMEN; publ. *The Australian Journal of Clinical Hypnotherapy and Hypnosis* (2 a year).

Medical Foundation: Coppleson Institute, University of Sydney, Sydney, NSW 2006; tel. (2) 9351-7315; fax (2) 9351-4160; e-mail vharper@coppleson.usyd.edu.au; f. 1958 to raise funds for postgraduate medical education and research; awards Program Grants, grants-in-aid and postgraduate scholarships; Pres. P. I. BURROWS; Exec. Officer V. S. M. HARPER.

Optometrists Association Australia: POB 185, Carlton South, Vic. 3053; tel. (3) 9663-6833; fax (3) 9663-7478; f. 1918; promotes optometry and public education on vision care; 2,300 mems; Pres. JOHN DAVIS; Exec. Dir JOSEPH CHAKMAN; publs *Clinical and Experimental Optometry* (every 2 months), *Australian Optometry News* (monthly).

Royal Australasian College of Dental Surgeons: 64 Castlereagh St, Sydney, NSW 2000; tel. 9232-3800; fax 9221-8108; f. 1965; holds scientific meetings and administers examinations; 1,100 Fellows; Hon. Sec. K. H. WENDON; publ. *Annals.*

Royal Australasian College of Physicians: 145 Macquarie St, Sydney, NSW 2000; tel. (2) 9256-5444; fax (2) 9252-3310; f. 1938; charitable, educational and scientific activities; 70 Hon. Fellows, 7,000 Fellows; library of 30,000 vols; Ford Collection; Pres. Prof. R. SMALLWOOD (Vic.); Chief Exec. Officer D. W. SWINBOURNE (NSW); publ. *Australian and New Zealand Journal of Medicine* (every 2 months).

Royal Australasian College of Radiologists: Level 9, 51 Druitt St, Sydney, NSW 2000; tel. (2) 9264-3555; fax (2) 9264-7799; e-mail racr@racr.edu.au; f. 1935; 2,301 mems; CEO LES APOLONY ; publ. *Australasian Radiology.*

Royal Australasian College of Surgeons: Spring St, Melbourne, Vic. 3000; tel. (3) 9249-1200; fax (3) 9249-1219; e-mail surgeons.sec@hen.net.au; CEO P. H. CARTER; publ. *Australian and New Zealand Journal of Surgery* (monthly).

Royal Australian and New Zealand College of Psychiatrists: 309 La Trobe St, Melbourne, Vic. 3000; tel. (3) 9640-0646; fax (3) 9642-5652; f. 1963, present name 1976; 2,183 Fellows, 616 trainees; private library; Pres. Dr JANICE WILSON; Sec. Assoc. Prof. FIONA JUDD; publs *Australasian and New Zealand Journal of Psychiatry, Australasian Psychiatry.*

Royal Australian College of Ophthalmologists: 27 Commonwealth St, Sydney, NSW 2010; tel. (2) 9267-7006; fax (2) 9267-6534; f. 1969 (formerly Ophthalmological Society of Australia); 1,238 mems; Hon. Sec. Dr MICHAEL GIBLIN; publ. *Australian and New Zealand Journal of Ophthalmology* (quarterly).

Royal College of Nursing, Australia: 1 Napier Close, Deakin, ACT 2600; tel. (2) 6282-5633; fax (2) 6282-3565; e-mail canberra@rcna.org.au; f. 1949; 9,000 mems; aims to promote improvement in nursing practice through education and research; grants membership to graduates of approved courses; administers nat. scholarships and research grants; conducts policy and development programme, distance education programme; Exec. Dir ELIZABETH C. PERCIVAL; publs *Colnursa* (monthly), *Collegian* (quarterly), *Nursing Review* (monthly).

Royal College of Pathologists of Australasia: Durham Hall, 207 Albion St, Surry Hills, NSW 2010; f. 1956; 1,817 Fellows; Pres. Dr J. W. HAMER; Hon. Sec. Dr C. MACLEOD; publ. *Pathology.*

NATURAL SCIENCES

General

Australian Academy of Science: GPO Box 783, Canberra, ACT 2601; tel. (2) 6247-5777; fax (2) 6257-4620; e-mail eb@science.org.au; f. 1954; 300 Fellows; Pres. Prof. B. D. O. ANDERSON; Exec. Sec. P. VALLEE; Sec. (Physical Sciences) Prof. K. LAMBECK; Sec. (Biological Sciences) Prof. J. A. YOUNG; Sec. (Science Policy) Prof. J. W. WHITE; Foreign Sec. Prof. M. G. PITMAN; publs *Year Book, Records, Science and Industry Forum* reports.

Australian and New Zealand Association for the Advancement of Science (ANZAAS): POB 2816, Canberra, ACT 2601; f. 1886; 1,000 mems; Divisions in NSW, Vic., SA, WA, Tasmania, ACT and NT, also overseas mems; Sec. Brig. DON TIER; publ. *Search* (10 a year).

Australian Conservation Foundation: 340 Gore St, Fitzroy, Vic. 3065; tel. (3) 9416-1166; fax (3) 9416-0767; e-mail acflib@peg.apc.org; f. 1965; non-profit org. working for an ecologically sustainable society; 60,000 mems and supporters; library of 15,000 vols; Pres. Prof. DAVID YENCKEN; Dir JAMES DOWNEY; publs *Conservation News* (6 a year), *Habitat* (6 a year).

Federation of Australian Scientific and Technological Societies: POB 218, Deakin West, Canberra, ACT 2601; tel. (2) 6257-2891; fax (2) 6257-2897; e-mail fasts@anu.edu.au; f. 1985 to foster close relations between the scientific and technological societies in Australia and to take concerted action for promoting science and technology in Australia; 60 mem. socs; Pres. Prof. PETER CULLEN; Exec. Dir TOSS GASCOIGNE; publ. *FASTS Circular* (monthly).

Royal Society of New South Wales: 134 Herring Rd, North Ryde, POB 1525 Macquarie Centre, NSW 2113; tel. (2) 9887-4448; fax (2) 9887-4448; f. 1821; all fields of science; 305 mems; collection of monographs and periodicals relating to the history of Australian science, manuscripts of original research results; Pres. Dr D. J. O'CONNOR; Hon. Secs Dr M. LAKE, M. KRYSKO; publs *Journal and Proceedings* (2 a year), *Bulletin* (monthly).

Royal Society of Queensland: POB 21, St Lucia, Qld 4067; f. 1884; natural and applied sciences; 250 mems; library of 75,000 vols; Pres. Assoc. Prof. J. JELL; Hon. Sec. R. HARTY; publs *Proceedings* (annually), *Symposia, Newsletter* (monthly).

Royal Society of South Australia Inc.: South Australian Museum, North Terrace, Adelaide, SA 5000; tel. (8) 8223-5360; f. 1853; natural sciences; 350 mems; library of 17,000 vols, 400 periodicals; Pres. Dr T. C. R. WHITE; Hon. Sec. Dr OLE WIEBKIN; publs *Transactions, Regional Natural Histories* (occasional).

Royal Society of Tasmania: GPO Box 1166M, Hobart, Tas. 7001; tel. (3) 6235-0777; fax (3) 6234-7139; e-mail thorne@tassie.net.au; f. 1843; 480 mems; library of 38,000 vols; Pres. H. E. THE GOVERNOR; Hon. Sec. Dr JOHN G. THORNE; publ. *Papers and Proceedings.*

Royal Society of Victoria: 9 Victoria St, Melbourne, Vic. 3000; tel. (3) 9663-5259; fax (3) 9663-2301; f. 1854; 750 mems; library: large collection of scientific periodicals; Pres. Prof. H. H. BOLOTIN; Hon Sec. I. A. ENDERSBY; publ. *Proceedings* (2 a year).

Royal Society of Western Australia: Western Australian Museum, Perth, WA; fax (8) 9310-4929; f. 1913; to promote and foster science and counteract the effects of specialization; study of botany, zoology, geology and anthropology; 350 mems; Pres. Prof. M. JONES; Secs Dr M. LUND, V. HOBBS; publ. *Journal* (quarterly).

Biological Sciences

Australian Society for Fish Biology: CSIRO Division of Fisheries, GPO Box 1538, Hobart, Tas. 7001; f. 1971 to promote the study of fish and fisheries in Australia and provide a communications medium for Australian fish workers; 530 mems; Pres. Dr P. C. YOUNG; Sec. C. M. BULMAN; publ. *Newsletter* (2 a year).

Australian Society for Limnology: Museum of Victoria, 71 Victoria Crescent, Abbotsford, Vic. 3067; tel. (3) 9284-0218; fax (3) 9416-0475; e-mail rmarch@mov.vic.gov.au; f. 1961; 490 mems; Sec. Dr RICHARD MARCHANT; publs *Newsletter* (quarterly), *Special Publications* (approx. annually).

Australian Society for Microbiology Inc.: Unit 23, 20 Commercial Rd, Melbourne, Vic. 3004; tel. (3) 9867-8699; fax (3) 9867-8722; e-mail theasm@asm.auz.com; f. 1959; 3,200 mems; Pres. Assoc. Prof. JOHN FINLAY-JONES; Sec. Dr J. LANSER; publs *Microbiology Australia* (5 a year), *Recent Advances in Microbiology* (annually).

Australian Society for Parasitology: Secretariat, ACTS, GPO Box 2200, Canberra, ACT 2601; tel. (2) 6257-3299; fax (2) 6257-3256; f. 1964; all aspects of parasitology; 450 mems, 14 Fellows; publ. *International Journal for Parasitology* (8 a year).

Ecological Society of Australia Inc.: POB 1564, Canberra, ACT 2601; f. 1960 to promote the scientific study of plants and animals in relation to their environment, and publication of the results of research; to facilitate the exchange of ideas amongst ecologists; to promote the application of ecological principles to the development, utilization and conservation of Australian natural resources; to advise government and other agencies; to foster the reservation of natural areas for scientific and recreational purposes; 950 mems; Pres. Prof. J. B. KIRKPATRICK; Sec. Dr J. WHINAM; publs *Bulletin, Australian Journal of Ecology.*

Entomological Society of New South Wales: Entomology Dept, The Australian Museum, 6–8 College St, Sydney, NSW 2001; f. 1952; 194 mems; Pres. G. R. BROWN; Hon.

Sec. M. J. FLETCHER; publ. *General and Applied Entomology* (annually).

Entomological Society of Queensland: Entomology Dept, University of Queensland, St Lucia, Brisbane, Qld 4072; independent; f. 1923; 300 mems; Pres. Dr G. GORDH; Sec. Dr L. MUIR; publs *News Bulletin* (10 a year), *The Australian Entomologist* (3–4 a year).

Field Naturalists Club of Victoria: Locked Bag 3, Post Office, Blackburn, Vic. 3130; f. 1880; study of natural history and conservation of environment; 900 mems; Pres. Assoc. Prof. ROBERT WALLIS; publs *The Victorian Naturalist* (every 2 months), *Field Nats News* (monthly).

Malacological Society of Australasia: c/o Dept of Malacology, Australian Museum, 6-8 College St, Sydney, NSW 2000; tel. (2) 9320-6275; fax (2) 9320-6050; e-mail alisonm@msg.austmus.gov.au; f. 1955; *c.* 400 mems; Pres. Dr W. B. RUDMAN; Sec. A. MILLER; publs *Australasian Shell News* (quarterly), *Molluscan Research*.

Royal Australasian Ornithologists Union: 415 Riversdale Rd, Hawthorn East, Vic. 3123; tel. (3) 9882-2622; fax (3) 9882-2677; f. 1901; for conservation and scientific study of Australasian birds; extensive library; 5,000 mems; Pres. Prof. B. SNAPE; Sec. B. WILSON; publs *Wingspan*, *Emu*, *WA Bird Notes*, *NSW Bird Notes*, *VicGroup Newsletter* (quarterly).

Royal Zoological Society of New South Wales: POB 20, Mosman, NSW 2088; f. 1879; 1,500 mems; Pres. Dr CHRIS DICKMAN; Exec. Officer RONALD STRAHAN; publ. *Australian Zoologist* (2 a year).

Royal Zoological Society of South Australia: Frome Rd, Adelaide, SA; tel. (8) 8267-3255; fax (8) 8239-0637; f. 1878; maintains public Zoological Gardens and open-range park; 5,500 mems; library of 1,600 vols; Pres. Assoc. Prof. M. J. TYLER; Dir and Chief Exec. E. J. MCALISTER; publ. *Annual Report*.

Wildlife Preservation Society of Australia Inc.: POB 3428, Sydney, NSW 2001; f. 1909; occasional field excursions and lecture meetings; promotes overseas lecturers for Australia; 500 mems; Pres. VINCENT SERVENTY; Hon. Sec. SANDY JOHNSON; publ. *Australian Wildlife Newsletter* (quarterly).

Zoological Board of Victoria: POB 74, Parkville, Vic.; tel. (3) 9285-9300; fax (3) 9285-9330; f. 1937 as successor to Royal Zoological and Acclimatisation Society of Victoria (f. 1857); responsible for the management of the Royal Melbourne Zoological Gardens, Healesville Sanctuary and Victoria's Open Range Zoo at Werribee; 9 mems; Chair. D. K. HAYWARD; Chief Exec. Officer C. R. LARCOMBE.

Mathematical Sciences

Australian Mathematical Society, The: Dept of Mathematics, Univ. of Tasmania, GPO Box 252-37, Hobart, Tas. 7001; tel. (3) 6226-2442; fax (3) 6226-2867; f. 1956; 900 mems; Pres. Prof. A. J. VAN DER POORTEN; Sec. Prof. D. ELLIOTT; publs *Journal* (Series A and B), *Bulletin*, *Gazette*, *Lecture Series*.

Statistical Society of Australia Inc.: POB 85, Ainslie, ACT 2602; e-mail ss91@interact.net.au; f. 1959; 900 mems; Pres. Prof. D. NICHOLLS; Sec. N. WEBER; publs *The Australian Journal of Statistics* (4 a year), *Newsletter* (quarterly).

Physical Sciences

Astronomical Society of Australia: c/o School of Physics, University of Sydney, NSW 2006; tel. (2) 9351-3184; fax (2) 9351-7727; f. 1966; 350 mems; Pres. Dr R. W. CLAY; Secs Dr M. L. DULDIG, Dr J. W. O'BYRNE; publ. *Publications* (3 a year).

Astronomical Society of South Australia (Inc.): GPO Box 199, Adelaide, SA 5001; tel. 618-338-1231; f. 1892; 400 mems; library of 200 vols; Pres. PAUL ROGERS; Sec. P. A. ELLIN; publ. *The Bulletin* (monthly).

Astronomical Society of Tasmania Inc.: c/o M. GEORGE (Vice-Pres.), Queen Victoria Museum, Wellington St, Launceston, Tas. 7250; tel. (3) 6331-6777; fax (3) 6334-5230; e-mail peter@vision.net.au; f. 1934; 100 mems; Pres. R. COGHLAN; Sec. M. MULCAHY; publs *Bulletin* (every 2 months), *Annual Ephemeris for Tasmania*.

Astronomical Society of Victoria Inc.: Box 1059J, GPO Melbourne, Vic. 3001; f. 1922; 900 mems; library of 1,500 vols; Pres. P. VLAHOS; Sec. R. DAVIS; publs *Newsletter* (every 2 months), *Astronomical Yearbook*.

Australasian College of Physical Scientists and Engineers in Medicine: c/o Dept of Physical Sciences, Peter MacCallum Cancer Institute, Locked Bag 1, A'Beckett St, Melbourne, Vic. 3000; tel. (3) 9656-1253; fax (3) 9650-4870; e-mail jcoles@petermac.unimelb.edu.au; f. 1977 to promote the development of the physical sciences as applied to medicine, to facilitate the exchange of information and ideas among mems and others, to disseminate knowledge relating to physical sciences and their application to medicine; 160 corporate mems, 210 assoc. mems; Pres. Prof. B. ALLEN; Sec. Dr J. R. COLES; publ. *Australasian Physical and Engineering Sciences in Medicine* (quarterly).

Australian Acoustical Society: Professional Centre of Australia, Private Bag 1, Darlinghurst, NSW 2010; tel. (2) 9331-6920; fax (2) 9331-7296; e-mail watkinsd@melbpc.org.au; f. 1971; 420 mems; Pres. Dr GRAEME YATES; Gen. Sec. D. WATKINS; publ. *Acoustics Australia* (3 a year).

Australian Institute of Physics: 1/21 Vale Street, North Melbourne, Vic. 3051; tel. (3) 9326-6669; fax (3) 9328-2670; f. 1963; 2,500 mems; Pres. Prof. JOAN OITMAA; Hon. Sec. MOIRA WELCH; publ. *The Australian and New Zealand Physicist* (6 a year).

Geological Society of Australia: 706 Wynyard House, 301 George Street, Sydney, NSW 2000; tel. (2) 9290-2194; fax (2) 9290-2198; f. 1953; 3,200 mems; publs *Journal* (every 2 months), specialist group journals (irregular), *Meeting Abstracts* (irregular), *National Newsletter* (quarterly).

Royal Australian Chemical Institute: 1/21 Vale Street, North Melbourne, Vic. 3051; tel. (3) 9328-2033; fax (3) 9328-2670; f. 1917, inc. by Royal Charter 1932; it is both the qualifying body for professional chemists and a learned society which aims to promote the science and practice of chemistry in all its branches; 9,500 mems; Hon. Gen. Sec. Dr M. GALLAGHER; Exec. Dir Dr S. CUMMING; publ. *Chemistry in Australia* (monthly).

PHILOSOPHY AND PSYCHOLOGY

Australasian Association of Philosophy: Dept of Philosophy, University of New England, Armidale, NSW 2351; e-mail mtapper@philosophy.unimelb.edu.au; f. 1923; 400 mems; brs throughout Australia and New Zealand; Pres. MAX DEUTSCHER; Sec. MARION TAPPER; publ. *Australasian Journal of Philosophy* (quarterly).

Australian Psychological Society Ltd., The: POB 126, Carlton South, Vic. 3053; tel. (3) 9663-6166; fax (3) 9663-6177; f. 1966; 12,500 mems; Pres. BRUCE CROWE; Exec. Dir Dr ALISON GARTON; publs *Australian Journal of Psychology* (quarterly), *Australian Psychologist* (quarterly), *In-Psych* (every 2 months).

RELIGION, SOCIOLOGY AND ANTHROPOLOGY

Australian Sociological Association: Dept of Social Science and Social Work, Royal Melbourne Institute of Technology, GPO Box 2476V, Melbourne, Vic. 3001; f. 1963; aims to promote development of sociology in Australia; 550 mems; Pres. Dr SHARYN ROACH ANLEU; Sec. Dr HELEN MARSHALL; publ. *Australia and New Zealand Journal of Sociology* (3 a year).

TECHNOLOGY

Australasian Ceramic Society: c/o ANSTO, PMB1, Menai, NSW 2234; tel. (2) 9717-3477; fax (2) 9543-8205; e-mail dsp@ansto.gov.au; f. 1961; to promote ceramic science and technology for Australian industry and art; 400 mems; Fed. Pres. D. TAYLOR; Fed. Sec. Dr D. S. PERERA; publs *Journal*, *Newsbulletin*.

Australasian Institute of Mining and Metallurgy: Level 3, 15–31 Pelham St, Carlton, Vic. 3053; tel. (3) 9662-3166; fax (3) 9662-3662; f. 1893; incorporated by Royal Charter 1955; 8,500 mems; Pres. R. J. CARTER; CEO J. M. WEBBER; publs *The AusIMM Proceedings*, *The AusIMM Bulletin*, *Conference Series* and Monographs.

Australian Academy of Technological Sciences and Engineering: Ian McLennan House, 197 Royal Parade, Parkville, Vic. 3052; tel. (3) 9347-0622; fax (3) 9347-8237; e-mail atse@mail.enternet.com.au; f. 1976; 560 Fellows, 6 Hon. and 1 Royal Fellow; Pres. M. A. BESLEY; Hon. Sec. Prof. F. P. LARKINS; Administrator J. E. DUDINE; Exec. Officer Dr G. G. BROWN; publs *Annual Report*, *Annual Symposia Proceedings*, *Focus* (newsletter), *Climate Change Science: Current Understanding and Uncertainties*.

Australian Institute of Energy: POB 230, Wahroonga, NSW 2076; tel. and fax (2) 9983-9665; e-mail aie@tpgi.com.au; f. 1978; 1,500 mems; Pres. FREDERICK PHILLIPS; Sec. COLIN PAULSON; publ. *News Journal* (every 2 months).

Australian Institute of Food Science and Technology Ltd: 319, Noble Park, Vic. 3174; Pres. IAN EUSTACE; Exec. Sec. CHRISTINE HARFIELD.

Australian Institute of Nuclear Science and Engineering: PMB No. 1, Menai, NSW 2234; tel. (2) 9717-3376; fax (2) 9717-9268; f. 1958; consortium of Australian universities in partnership with the Australian Nuclear Science and Technology Organisation; aims to assist research and training in nuclear science and engineering and to make the facilities of the Lucas Heights Research Laboratories available to research staff and students from mem. institutions; projects in advanced materials, biomedicine, environmental science, applications of nuclear physics, nuclear technology and engineering; organizes Australian Numerical Simulation and Modelling Services and Australian Radioisotope Services; organizes conferences, awards postgraduate studentships and research grants; Scientific Sec. Dr DENNIS MATHER; publs *AINSE Activities*, *AINSE Annual Report*, *AINSE Conference Books*.

Australian Robotics and Automation Association Inc.: GPO Box 1527, Sydney, NSW 2001; tel (2) 9959-3239; fax (2) 9959-4632; e-mail michael@zip.com.au; f. 1981; Pres. ALEX ZELINSKY; Sec. MICHAEL KASSLER; publ. *Newsletter* (quarterly).

Chartered Institute of Transport in Australia: POB Q398, Queen Victoria P.O., Sydney 1230; tel. (2) 9264-6413; fax (2) 9267-1682; f. 1935; professional society concerned with all modes of transport; 2,600 mems in 17 sections throughout Australia and Papua

New Guinea; Exec. Dir K. L. DUNCAN; publs *CITIA News* (6 a year), *Australian Transport Review* (1 a year).

Institution of Engineers, Australia: 11 National Circuit, Barton, ACT 2600; tel. (6) 270-6555; fax (6) 273-1488; f. 1919; incorporates colleges of Biomedical Engineers, Chemical Engineers, Civil Engineers, Electrical Engineers, and Mechanical Engineers; 65,000 mems; Chief Exec. Dr JOHN WEBSTER; publs *Engineers Australia* (monthly), *Civil Engineers Australia* (monthly), *Engineering Times* (monthly), *Civil Engineering Transactions, Journal of Electrical and Electronics Engineering in Australia, Mechanical Engineering Transactions, Chemical Engineering in Australia, Multidisciplinary Engineering Transactions, Australian Geomechanics News, Conference Vols* (15 a year).

Institution of Surveyors, Australia: 27–29 Napier Close, Deakin, Canberra, ACT 2600; tel. (2) 6282-2282; fax (2) 6282-2576; e-mail isa@isaust.org.au; f. 1952; 3,620 mems; CEO JOHN D. CRICKMORE; publs *The Australian Surveyor* (quarterly), *Research Australasia* (2 a year).

Royal Aeronautical Society (Australian Division): POB 573, Mascot, NSW 2020; f. 1927; Pres. R. C. O'DAY; Hon. Sec. R. D. BARKLA.

Research Institutes

AGRICULTURE, FISHERIES AND VETERINARY SCIENCE

Department of Land and Water Conservation: GPO Box 39, Sydney, NSW 2001; tel. (2) 9228-6111; fax (2) 9228-6140; conservation and management of land and water resources; Dir-Gen. Dr R. SMITH.

EDUCATION

Australian Council for Educational Research Ltd, The: 19 Prospect Hill Rd (Private Bag 55), Camberwell, Vic. 3124; tel. (3) 9277-5555; fax (3) 9277-5500; f. 1930; independent; educational research and publishing; books for teachers at all levels, students, parents, psychologists, counsellors, administrators, curriculum writers; educational, psychological and personnel tests; Dir Prof. BARRY MCGAW; publs *Australian Journal of Education* (3 a year), *Australian Education Index* (quarterly), *Newsletter* (3 a year), *Bibliography of Education Theses in Australia* (annually), *Australian Journal of Career Development* (3 a year), *Australian Thesaurus of Education Descriptors* (annually).

National Centre for Vocational Education Research (NCVER) Ltd: 252 Kensington Rd, Leabrook, SA 5068; tel. (8) 8333-8400; fax (8) 8331-9211; e-mail ncver@ncver.edu.au; f. 1981 by the Australian State, Territory and Commonwealth Ministers responsible for Technical and Further Education to undertake Technical and Further Education research and development projects of national significance; Australian focal point for Asian and Pacific Skills Devt Information Network of ILO/APSDEP; library of 10,000 vols; National Vocational Education and Training Clearinghouse provides information on published documents about vocational education and training as well as research in progress; Chair. PETER KIRBY; Man. Dir CHRIS ROBINSON; publs *Annual Report, Australian and New Zealand Journal of Vocational Education Research* (2 a year), *Australian Training Review* (4 a year), *Vocational Education and Training Research Database* (4 a year).

HISTORY, GEOGRAPHY AND ARCHAEOLOGY

Tasmanian Historical Research Association: f. 1951; 400 mems; Chair. Dr STEFAN PETROW; Sec. J. E. SCRIVENER, POB 441, Sandy Bay, Tas. 7005; publ. *Papers and Proceedings* (quarterly).

MEDICINE

Australian Radiation Laboratory (Australian Department of Health): Lower Plenty Rd, Yallambie, Vic. 3085; f. 1929; tel. (3) 9433-2211; fax (3) 9432-1835; e-mail arl@arl.oz.au; research, development and scientific services in relation to the public health aspects of ionizing radiations and of microwave, laser and ultraviolet radiations, environmental radiation, mining and milling of radioactive ores, radiation dosimetry and quality assurance of radiopharmaceuticals; library of 3,000 vols; Dir. Dr K. H. LOKAN.

Australian Society for Medical Research: 145 Macquarie St, Sydney, NSW 2000; tel. (2) 9256-5450; fax (2) 9252-0294; e-mail asmr@world.net; f. 1961 to provide a forum for discussion of medical research across disciplinary boundaries, and to encourage recent graduates to consider research as a career; holds Nat. Scientific Conference; 1,400 mems; Admin Sec. CATHERINE WEST; publ. *Proceedings*.

Baker Medical Research Institute: Commercial Rd, Prahran, Vic. 3181; tel. (3) 9522-4333; fax (3) 9521-1362; f. 1926; basic, clinical and applied research on cardiovascular disease, physiology, pharmacology, endocrinology, molecular and cell biology; affiliated to WHO, Monash University, Alfred Hospital and including the Alfred-Baker Medical Unit (f. 1949); library of 15,000 vols; Pres. NORMAN O'BRYAN; Dir J. W. FUNDER; publs *Annual Report, Research*.

CSL Ltd.: 45 Poplar Road, Parkville, Vic. 3052; tel. (3) 9389-1911; fax (3) 9389-1434; f. 1916 for research, production and marketing of biologicals; Burnet Library of 8,500 vols; Man. Dir Dr B. MCNAMEE; publ. *Annual Report of Activities*.

Institute of Dental Research, The: United Dental Hospital, 2 Chalmers St, Sydney, NSW; tel. (2) 9282-0311; fax (2) 9282-0368; f. 1946; for research into biological problems relating to dental health; library of 9,500 vols; Dir Dr N. HUNTER (acting); publ. *Biennial Report*.

Institute of Medical and Veterinary Science: Frome Rd, Adelaide, SA 5000; tel. 8222-3000; fax 8222-3538; est. 1938 for purposes of research into diseases of human beings and animals, and to provide a diagnostic pathology service for the Royal Adelaide Hospital and for the State through 12 regional laboratories; teaching is provided for the Univ. of Adelaide Medical School; Chair. B. P. BURNS; Dir Dr B. J. KEARNEY; publ. *Annual Report*.

Kolling Institute of Medical Research: Royal North Shore Hospital of Sydney, St Leonards, NSW 2065; tel. (2) 926-7267; fax (2) 926-8484; f. 1930; research in allergic diseases, molecular genetics and growth factors; publ. *Biennial Report*.

Mental Health Research Institute of Victoria: Oak St, Parkville, Vic. 3052; tel. (3) 9388-1633; fax (3) 9387-5061; f. 1956; studies aspects of the nature and treatment of psychiatric illnesses with a particular emphasis on a neuroscience approach to Alzheimer's Disease and to the major psychoses, especially schizophrenia; library of *c.* 37,000 vols; Dir Prof. DAVID COPOLOV.

National Health and Medical Research Council: GPO Box 9848, Canberra, ACT 2601; tel. (2) 6289-1555; fax (2) 6289-7802; f. 1936 to advise on the achievement and maintenance of the highest practicable standards of individual and public health, and to foster research in the interests of improving those standards; Sec. B. WELLS; publs *Annual Report, Triennial Strategic Plan*.

National Vision Research Institute of Australia: 386 Cardigan St, Carlton, Melbourne, Vic. 3053; tel. (3) 9349-7480; fax (3) 9349-7473; f. 1972; basic, applied and clinical research into visual impairment, lens biochemistry, cataracts, presbyopia, methods of diagnosis and prevention; Chair. S. F. KALFF; Dir Assoc. Prof. R C. AUGUSTEYN; publs *Annual Report and Bulletin* (for members).

Queensland Institute of Medical Research: 300 Herston Rd, Brisbane, Qld 4029; f. 1945; research into medical problems important in the Australian and Asian Pacific region; current areas are tropical medicine, virology, oncology, cell biology, molecular biology, epidemiology, liver disease; library of 19,100 vols; Chair. of Council B. CARTER; Dir Prof. L. POWELL; publ. *Annual Report*.

Walter and Eliza Hall Institute of Medical Research, The: Post Office, Royal Melbourne Hospital, Vic. 3050; tel. (3) 9345-2555; fax (3) 9347-0852; f. 1916; research into cellular and molecular immunology, cancer, immunopathology and immunoparasitology, genome science and bioinformatics; 310 staff; library of 20,000 vols; Dir Prof. SUZANNE CORY; publ. *Report* (1 a year).

NATURAL SCIENCES

General

Commonwealth Scientific and Industrial Research Organisation (CSIRO): POB 225, Dickson, ACT 2602; tel. (2) 6276-6766; fax (2) 6276-6608; f. 1926; researches all fields of the physical and biological sciences except defence science, nuclear energy and clinical medicine; Sectors: Field Crops; Food Processing; Forestry, Wood and Paper Industries; Horticulture; Meat, Dairy and Aquaculture; Wool and Textiles; Biodiversity; Climate and Atmosphere; Land and Water; Marine; Information Technology and Telecommunications; Built Environment; Measurement Standards; Radio Astronomy; Services; Chemicals and Plastics; Integrated Manufactured Products; Pharmaceuticals and Human Health; Energy; Mineral Exploration and Mining; Mineral Processing and Metal Production; Petroleum; library: see Libraries and Archives; Chair. CHARLES ALLEN; Chief Exec. MALCOLM MCINTOSH; publs *Australian Journal of: Agricultural Research* (8 a year), *Botany* (every 2 months), *Chemistry* (monthly), *Experimental Agriculture* (every 2 months), *Marine and Freshwater Research* (every 2 months), *Physics* (every 2 months), *Plant Physiology* (every 2 months), *Soil Research* (every 2 months), *Zoology* (every 2 months); *Australian Systematic Botany* (quarterly), *Wildlife Research* (every 2 months), *Invertebrate Taxonomy* (every 2 months), *Reproduction, Fertility and Development* (every 2 months); *ECOS* (quarterly); *The Helix* (6 a year).

National Facility within CSIRO:

Australia Telescope: a radio telescope array consisting of six 22-m antennas at the Paul Wild Observatory, Narrabri, NSW, a 22-m antenna at Mopra, west of Coonabarabran, NSW, and a 64-m antenna near Parkes, NSW; Dir Prof. RON EKERS.

Biological Sciences

Australian Institute of Marine Science: PMB 3, Townsville, Qld 4810; tel. (77) 534211; fax (7) 4772-5852; f. 1972; carries out research in marine science emphasizing tropics; plus collaborative researchers and trainees; vessel fleet; library of 9,000 vols, 1,500 journals;

Dir Dr R. REICHERT; publs *Annual Report*, monographs, technical and data reports, etc.

Royal Botanic Gardens and National Herbarium of Victoria: Birdwood Ave, S. Yarra, Vic.; tel. (3) 9252-2300; fax (3) 9252-2350; e-mail rbg@rbgmelb.org.au; f. 1846; 36-ha (94-acre) garden with more than 10,000 different species and cultivars of Australian and exotic plants; herbarium of 1,000,000 specimens; library of 50,000 vols; also Royal Botanic Gardens, Cranbourne, for growing display and study of native Australian plants; Dir Dr PHILIP MOORS; Chief Botanist Prof. J. H. ROSS; publs *Guide, Muelleria*.

Royal Botanic Gardens Sydney: Mrs Macquaries Rd, Sydney, NSW 2000; tel. (2) 9231-8111; fax (2) 9231-8065; e-mail sads@rbgsyd.gov.au; f. 1816; 30-hectare living plant collection and herbarium of 1,000,000 specimens; library of 50,000 vols; Mount Tomah Botanic Garden for cool-climate plants; Mount Annan Botanic Garden for native plants; specialization in research on Australian native plants; Dir F. HOWARTH (acting); publs *Telopea, Cunninghamia, Seed List* (every 2 years).

Therapeutic Goods Administration Laboratories: GPO Box 100, Woden, ACT 2606; tel. (6) 232-8444; fax (6) 232-8659; f. 1958 as National Biological Standards Laboratories to ensure the quality, safety, efficacy and timely availability of therapeutic goods used in or exported from Australia; part of the Therapeutic Goods Administration, Dept of Human Sciences and Health; library of 30,000 vols and 5,000 microfiche; Dir Dr ELAINE WALKER; publ. *TGA Laboratory Information Bulletin* (every 6 months).

Mathematical Sciences

Australian Bureau of Statistics: PO Box 10, Belconnen, ACT 2616; tel. (6) 252-5000; fax (6) 251-6009; f. 1906; Australian Statistician W. MCLENNAN; library of 38,000 vols, 9,600 periodicals; publs *Yearbook Australia, Pocket Yearbook Australia,* and some 400 other titles listed in *Catalogue of ABS Publications*.

Physical Sciences

Australian Geological Survey Organisation (AGSO): GPO Box 378, Canberra, ACT 2601; tel. (2) 6249-9111; telex 62109; fax (2) 6249-9999; f. 1946 as Bureau of Mineral Resources, Geology and Geophysics (BMR) to develop a comprehensive, scientific understanding of the geology of Australia, its offshore area, and the Australian Antarctic Territory; to operate national geoscientific facilities such as the Australian Seismological Centre, and to contribute to national policy aims through int. geoscientific co-operation and overseas projects; library of 21,000 vols, 4,000 serials; Exec. Dir NEIL WILLIAMS; publs include *Bulletins, AGSO Journal of Australian Geology and Geophysics, Yearbook,* Records, Research Newsletter.

Australian Nuclear Science and Technology Organisation (ANSTO), Lucas Heights Research Laboratories: New Illawarra Rd, Lucas Heights, PMB 1, Menai, NSW 2234; tel. (2) 717-3111; telex 24562; fax (2) 543-5097; f. 1987 as successor to Australian Atomic Energy Commission (f. 1953); Australia's nat. nuclear org.; aims to bring the benefits of nuclear science and technology to industry, medicine and the community; research and devt programmes focusing on industrial and other applications of nuclear science, environmental science, advanced materials, biomedicine and health; operates nat. facilities, provides technical advice, aids training; library of 40,000 vols, 900,000 fiches; Chair. Prof. R. WARD-AMBLER; Exec. Dir Prof. H. GARNETT; publs *Annual Report*, scientific papers and reports.

Commonwealth of Australia Bureau of Meteorology: GPO Box 1289K, Melbourne, Vic. 3001; tel. (3) 9669-4000; telex 30601; fax (3) 9669-4699; f. 1908; regional offices in Perth, Adelaide, Brisbane, Sydney, Hobart, Darwin and Melbourne; library of 80,000 vols; Dir Dr J. W. ZILLMAN; publs daily weather bulletins and charts, monthly, seasonal and annual rainfall maps and statistical summaries, publications on special subjects, climatological reviews, *Australian Meteorological Magazine*.

Geological Survey of New South Wales: Dept of Mineral Resources, POB 536, St Leonards, NSW 2065; tel. (2) 9901-8300; fax (2) 9901-8256; f. 1874; advice on geology and mineral resources of NSW, incl. preparation of standard series geological, geophysical and metallogenic maps; research studies in tectonics, palaeontology, petrology and selected mineral commodities; Dir J. N. CRAMSIE; publs *Quarterly Notes, Geological Memoirs, Palaeontological Memoirs, Bulletins, Records, Mineral Resources, Mineral Industry, Geological and Metallogenic Maps* with notes, etc.

Geological Survey of Victoria: Dept of Natural Resources and Environment, POB 500, East Melbourne, Vic. 3002; tel. (3) 9412-5042; fax (3) 9412-5155; f. 1852; Man. TOM DICKSON; publs include Reports, Bulletins, Geological Maps, etc.

Geological Survey of Western Australia: Mineral House, 100 Plain St, East Perth, WA 6004; tel. (8) 9222-3333; fax (8) 9222-3633; f. 1888; 109 mems; library of 73,000 vols; Dir (vacant); publs *Bulletin, Mineral Resources Bulletin, Explanatory Notes* (1 : 250,000 maps), *Report Series, Memoirs*.

Mount Stromlo and Siding Spring Observatories: Private Bag, Weston Creek PO, ACT 2611; tel. (2) 6249-0266; fax (2) 6249-0233; e-mail director@mso.anu.edu.au; f. 1924 as Commonwealth Solar Observatory; research in astrophysics, incl. all phases of stellar, galactic and extra-galactic astronomy; transferred to Australian National University 1957; library of 17,000 vols; Dir Prof. J. R. MOULD.

Perth Observatory: Bickley, WA 6076; tel. (8) 9293-8255; fax (8) 9293-8138; f. 1896; positional astronomy, photometry, planetary observation and automated supernova search; library of 20,000 vols; museum and public tours; Govt Astronomer J. BIGGS; publ. *Communications* (irregular).

Queensland Department of Mines and Energy: GPO Box 194, Brisbane, Qld 4001; tel. (7) 3237-1435; fax (7) 3229-7770; f. 1874; geological mapping, sedimentary basin studies, metallogenic studies, biostratigraphy, geophysics, mineral, petroleum, coal and oil shale resources assessment, extractive industries and environmental management, land use planning, mining safety and technology, energy management, resource economics, computer and information services; library of 8,800 monographs, 27,000 reports, 1,000 serials, records, maps, map commentaries, guidebooks; Dir-Gen. Dr ROBERT DAY; publs *Annual Report, Minerals and Energy Review, Queensland Geology, DME Reviews, Records, Queensland Government Mining Journal* (monthly).

Riverview College Observatory: Lane Cove, NSW 2066; tel. (2) 882-8222; fax (2) 428-1734; f. 1908; meteorological observations, world-wide standard seismograph network station (1962); Dir LUKE TYLER.

South Australian Department of Mines and Energy Resources: 191 Greenhill Rd, Parkside, POB 151, Eastwood, SA 5063; tel. (8) 274-7500; fax (8) 272-7597; f. 1892; Geological Survey of South Australia, mining, energy and energy conservation, oil and gas; library of 25,000 vols (special coll. on early South Australian mining); Chief Exec. A. J. ANDREJEWSKIS; publs *Annual Report, Geological Survey Bulletin, MESA Journal* (quarterly), *Geological Survey Reports of Investigations*.

Tasmanian Geological Survey: c/o Mineral Resources Tasmania, POB 56, Rosny Park, Tasmania 7018; tel. (3) 6233-8333; fax (3) 6233-8338; e-mail klau@mrt.tas.gov.au; f. 1860; library of 2,500 monographs and 840 serials; Chief Geologist A. V. BROWN; publs *Geological Survey Bulletins, Geological Survey Record, Geological Survey Maps, Explanatory Reports*.

RELIGION, SOCIOLOGY AND ANTHROPOLOGY

Australian Institute of Aboriginal and Torres Strait Islander Studies: GPO Box 553, Canberra, ACT 2601; f. 1961; statutory body since 1964; provides funds, promotes research and publishes books on all aspects of Aboriginal and Torres Strait Islander studies, traditional and contemporary; library of 25,000 vols, 14,000 pamphlets; 18,000 hours of audio tapes, 8,000 MSS, 250,000 prints and colour slides, 7,000 hours of films and video tapes; Principal RUSSELL TAYLOR; publs *Australian Aboriginal Studies* (2 a year), *Annual Bibliography*, etc.

Australian Institute of Archaeology: Level 2, Centreway Arcade, 259 Collins St, Melbourne, Vic. 3000; tel. (3) 9650-3477; fax (3) 9654-2774; f. 1946 to investigate all discoveries and results which the Institute or any other organization shall publish, calculated to have bearing upon the authenticity, historicity, accuracy and inspiration of the Bible; teaching programmes and exhibitions on the ancient Near East and/or Biblical archaeology; library of 10,000 vols (special coll. on Palestinian, Egyptian and Mesopotamian archaeology) and museum (Ancient Times House, 116 Little Bourke St, Melbourne) with a collection of pottery and other artefacts of Biblical lands; Pres. Rev. Prof. A. M. HARMAN; Dir P. T. CROCKER; publ. *Buried History* (quarterly).

Australian Institute of Criminology: GPO Box 2994, Canberra, ACT 2601; tel. (2) 6260-9200; fax (2) 6260-9201; e-mail frontdesk@aic.gov.au; f. 1973; conducts criminology research, training courses, conferences and seminars, provides library and information services, publs results of research and other materials, and services the Criminology Research Council; library: see libraries; Dir Dr ADAM GRAYCAR; publs *Trends and Issues in Crime and Criminal Justice* (monthly), etc.

Elda Vaccari Collection of Multicultural Studies: Library, Victoria University of Technology, PO Box 14428, Melbourne Mail Centre, Melbourne, Vic. 3000; tel. (3) 9688-4809; fax (3) 9688-4920; e-mail mark=armstrong-roper@vut.edu.au; f. 1982 as Vaccari Italian Historical Trust; researches immigrant and minority groups in Australia; library of 10,000 vols; Librarian MARK ARMSTRONG-ROPER.

TECHNOLOGY

AMDEL: Stirling St, Thebarton, SA 5031; tel. (8) 8416-5200; telex 82520; fax (8) 8234-0355; f. 1960; analysis, testing, services in mineral engineering, chemical metallurgy, materials technology, mineralogy and petrology, process control instrument development, petroleum, geoanalysis, chemical analysis; offices and laboratories around Australia and New Zealand and representatives worldwide; 400 staff; Chair. of Board S. GERLACH; Man. Dir RAY F. DOUGHERTY; publ. *Annual Report*.

ARRB Transport Research Ltd: 500 Burwood Highway, Vermont South, Vic. 3133; tel. (3) 9881-1555; fax (3) 9887-8104; f. 1960;

research related to the design, planning, construction, maintenance and use of roads; library of *c.* 75,000 vols and journals; 125 staff; Exec. Dir I. R. JOHNSTON; Sec. R. BRENTNALL; publs *Road and Transport Research* (quarterly), *Proceedings of Biennial Conference, ARR Research Reports* (irregular), *INROADS database, ARRB Briefing, Special Reports* (irregular), *Annual Report, Internal Reports (AIR)* (irregular).

Defence Science and Technology Organisation: Anzac Park West Offices, Constitution Avenue, Canberra, ACT 2600; tel. (2) 6266-6661; fax (2) 6266-6320; attached to govt Dept of Defence; Dir-Gen. (Science Policy Development) Dr DAVID WYLLIE; Chief Defence Scientist Dr RICHARD BRABIN-SMITH.

Associated research laboratories:

Aeronautical Research Laboratories: 506 Lorimer St, Fishermens Bend, Vic. 3207; tel. (3) 647-7400; fax (3) 646-5584; f. 1939; incl. divisions of Air Operations, Guided Weapons, and Airframes and Engines; Dir WYNFORD CONNICK.

Electronics Research Laboratory: POB 1500, Salisbury, SA 5108; tel. (8) 259-5586; fax (8) 259-6567; f. 1949; incl.divisions of Information Technology, Electronic Warfare, and Communications; Dir SCOT ALLISON.

Materials Research Laboratories: POB 50, Ascot Vale, Vic. 3032; tel. (3) 246-8000; fax (3) 246-8001; f. 1917; incl. divisions of Ship Structures and Materials, Explosives Ordnance, and Maritime Operations; Dir DAVID HUMPHRIES.

Surveillance Research Laboratory: POB 1500, Salisbury, SA 5108; tel. (8) 259-5004; fax (8) 258-1369; includes divisions of High Frequency Radar, Microwave Radar, and Optoelectronics; Dir BOB RAMSAY.

IWS International Pty Ltd: Wool House, 369 Royal Parade, Parkville, Vic. 3052; tel. (3) 9341-9111; fax (3) 9341-9273; research and development and promotion arm of Australian wool industry; library of 4,000 monographs, 1,000 periodicals, 10,000 pamphlets and annual reports; Chair. A. MORRISON; Man. Dir A. KLOEDEN; publs *Annual Report*, etc.

Water Research Foundation of Australia: c/o Centre for Resource and Environmental Studies, Australian National University, Canberra, ACT 0200; tel. (2) 6249-0651; fax (2) 6249-0757; e-mail wrfa@cres.anu.edu.au; f. 1956; a non-profit research organization; research into the development, control, use and re-use of Australia's water resources; Hon. Sec. D. J. BEALE: publ. *Water and the Environment* (every 2 months).

Libraries and Archives

Australian Capital Territory

Australian Archives: POB 34, Dickson, ACT 2602; tel. (6) 209-3633; fax (6) 209-3931; archival authority of the Commonwealth since 1952; responsible for the management of Commonwealth records: survey, storage, preservation, retention or destruction, retrieval and access; provides information to the public on nature and location of Commonwealth records and on agencies and persons responsible for them; collections of documents, maps, plans, films, photographs, records, paintings, models, microforms and electronic records (487,522 shelf metres); holdings date from the early 19th century, but most date from Federation (1901), derived from a variety of sources; offices in Canberra, Darwin and all state capitals; library of 12,000 vols; Dir-Gen. G. E. NICHOLS; publ. *Annual Report*.

Australian Institute of Criminology, J. V. Barry Library: GPO Box 2944, Canberra, ACT 2601; tel. (2) 6260-9264; fax (2) 6260-9299; e-mail john.myrtle@aic.gov.au; f. 1974; material is collected in English in the fields of criminology, law, sociology and psychology; 25,000 monographs, 800 periodicals; articles and monographs of Australian criminological interest are indexed for *CINCH The Australian Criminology Database*, publicly available on the OZLINE network, also available on CD-ROM; *Australian Crime and Justice* on CD-ROM; Librarian JOHN MYRTLE.

Australian National University Library: Canberra, ACT 0200; fax (2) 6249-0734; f. 1948; 1,879,042 vols; focus on access to scholarly information via electronic sources and networks; Librarian C. R. STEELE.

Department of Employment, Education Training and Youth Affairs Library: GPO Box 9880, Canberra, ACT 2601; education, employment, unemployment, labour force economics, vocational training; 40,000 vols.

High Court of Australia Library: POB E435, Kingston, ACT 2604; tel. (2) 6270-6922; fax (2) 6273-2110; f. 1903; private library of the Justices of the Court and barristers appearing before it; 149,000 vols in Canberra; Librarian J. ELLIOTT.

IP Australia Library: Discovery House, POB 200, Woden, ACT 2606; tel. (2) 6283-2302; telex 61517; fax (2) 6282-5810; e-mail library@ipaustralia.gov.au; f. 1904; 14,000 vols, 1,000 periodicals; Australian and foreign patent specifications from all patent countries, science and technology and industrial property; Librarian ERIC POZZA.

National Library of Australia: Parkes Place, Canberra, ACT 2600; tel. (2) 6262-1111; telex 62100; fax (2) 6257-1703; e-mail www@nla.gov.au; f. 1901; reference and research library, online shared cataloguing system, the Australian Bibliographic Network; legal deposit library for Australian publications; important holdings of Australiana, including Petherick, Ferguson and Nan Kivell collections and Mathews Ornithological collection and of English literature, American history and publications in Asian languages; 2,500,000 vols, 66,000 current serial titles, 534,000 maps, 10,000 metres of manuscript material, 58,400 oral history tapes, 168,000 music scores, 43,000 pictures and prints, 559,000 photographs, 807,000 aerial photographs; Dir-Gen. WARREN HORTON; publs *Annual Report, National Library of Australia News* (monthly), *Australian Public Affairs Information Service* (monthly with annual cumulation).

University of Canberra Library: Bruce, ACT; f. 1968; *c.* 460,000 vols; *c.* 5,000 current serials; collection includes a/v material, access to electronic information services; Librarian LOIS V. JENNINGS.

New South Wales

Archives Office of New South Wales: 2 Globe St, The Rocks, Sydney, NSW 2000; tel. 9237-0200; fax 9237-0142; f. 1961; Principal Archivist D. J. CROSS.

Charles Sturt University – Division of Library Services: Private Bag 45, Bathurst, NSW 2795; tel. (2) 6338-4732; fax (2) 6338-4600; e-mail mmacpherson@csu.edu.au; 600,000 vols; libraries at Albury, Bathurst and Wagga Wagga; Exec. Dir MARGARET MACPHERSON.

City of Sydney Library: Town Hall Library, Sydney Square, off George St, Sydney, NSW 2000; tel. (2) 9265-9470; fax (2) 9267-8275; f. 1909; 2 brs.; 220,158 vols; 100 newspaper titles; provides Home Library Service for the housebound; Man. Library Services MARIANNE RAJKOVIC.

Macquarie University Library: NSW 2109; tel. (2) 9850-7539; fax (2) 9850-9236; e-mail mclean@library.mq.edu.au; f. 1964; 962,061 vols; University Librarian NEIL MCLEAN.

Newcastle Region Public Library: Cultural Centre, Laman St, Newcastle, NSW 2300; tel. (2) 4925-8300; fax (2) 4929-4157; f. 1948; 406,242 vols; 2,663 periodicals; 121 newspaper titles; special facilities: Information Works, Local Studies, Hunter Photo Bank, Earthquake Database; publs *Newcastle Morning Herald Index* (1861–84, annually), *Monographs* (irregular).

Parliamentary Library of New South Wales: Parliament House, Sydney, NSW 2000; tel. (2) 9230-2383; fax (2) 9231-1932; f. 1840; 180,000 vols; Chief Officer R. F. BRIAN; publs *Background Papers, Bills Digests, Briefing Papers*.

State Library of New South Wales: Macquarie St, Sydney, NSW 2000; tel. (2) 9273-1414; fax (2) 9273-1255; e-mail library@slnsw.gov.au; f. 1826; State legal deposit privileges; 4,000,000 items; special collections: Australiana, historical pictures, maps, MSS, of Australasia and the Pacific; State Librarian DAGMAR SCHMIDMAIER; publ. *LASIE* (4 a year).

University of New England Library: Armidale, NSW 2351; tel. (67) 73-2458; fax (67) 733273; f. 1954; 850,000 vols; special collections: Campbell Howard (Australian plays in manuscript), Gordon Athol Anderson (music), New England, Royal Society of New South Wales; Librarian K. G. SCHMUDE.

University of New South Wales Library: Sydney, NSW 2052; tel. (2) 9385-2615; fax (2) 9385-8002; e-mail information@unsw.edu.au; f. 1949; 2,000,000 items at Kensington and other centres; Principal Librarian MARIAN BATE.

University of Newcastle Library: Newcastle, NSW 2308; tel. (2) 4921-5848; fax (2) 4921-5833; f. 1965; 1,162,402 vols; Librarian BILL LINKLATER.

University of Sydney Library: University, Sydney, NSW 2006; tel. (2) 9351-2990; fax (2) 9351-2890; f. 1852; 4,400,000 vols; Librarian N. A. C. RADFORD.

Northern Territory

Northern Territory Library: Parliament House, POB 42, Darwin, NT 0801; tel. (8) 8999-7177; fax (8) 8999-6927; f. 1950 as Darwin Public Library; 118,000 monographs, 3,400 serials, 3,000 maps, 2,000 films/videos, 59,000 photographs, 6,000 microforms; includes the Northern Australia Collection (one copy of all types of library material dealing with North and Central Australia, and NT in particular); Dir LEA GILES-PETERS.

Queensland

Queensland Parliamentary Library: Parliamentary Annex, Alice St, Brisbane, Qld 4000; tel. (7) 3406-7199; fax (7) 3210-0172; f. 1860; information service to members of State Legislature; statistics, economics, politics, law and education; 120,000 vols; special collection: O'Donovan Collection of 19th-century literature; Librarian R. J. N. BANNENBERG; publ. *Queensland Parliamentary Handbook* (every 3 years).

State Library of Queensland: S. Bank, S. Brisbane, Qld; tel. (7) 3840-7666; fax (7) 3846-2421; f. 1896; 1,400,000 items; the state reference library, non-lending except for music scores and to libraries, groups and organizations; includes John Oxley Library of Queensland History and James Hardie Library of Australian Fine Arts; has library deposit privileges; State Librarian D. H. STEPHENS; publs *Queensland Government Publications* (monthly), *Directory of State and Public Lib-*

rary Services in Queensland: Statistical Bulletin (1 a year), *Access* (4 a year), *Newslib* (4 a year).

Supreme Court Library: George St, Brisbane, Qld; tel. (7) 3247-4373; fax (7) 3247-9233; e-mail aladin@cslqld.org.au; f. 1862; 155,000 vols; Librarian ALADIN RAHEMTULA; publs *Qld Legal Indexes, Qld Legal Indexes Consolidation, Qld Legal Indexes on Disk.*

University of Queensland Library: Qld 4072; tel. (7) 3365-6209; fax (7) 3365-7317; f. 1911; 1,800,000 vols; 633,000 microfiches; 37,000 audiovisual items; archive and manuscript collection, principally Australian literature; Librarian JANINE SCHMIDT.

South Australia

Flinders University Library: Bedford Park, SA 5042; tel. (8) 8201-2131; fax (8) 8201-2508; e-mail libinfo@flinders.edu.au; f. 1963; 1,040,000 vols; University Librarian W. T. CATIONS.

State Library of South Australia: North Terrace, GPO Box 419, Adelaide, SA 5001; tel. (8) 8207-7200; fax (8) 8207-7247; e-mail research@slsa.sa.gov.au; f. 1884; State general reference library and legal depository; online services including networked CD-ROMs; Bray Reference Library (400,000 vols, 21,000 serial titles, 6,000 current, 90,000 maps); Mortlock Library of South Australiana (62,000 vols, 12,000 serial titles, 8,000 current, Archival Collections of 3,500 metres); special collections include Children's Literature Research Collection (55,000 vols), Edwardes Collection of Shipping Photographs (8,000), Arbon-Le Maistre Collection of Shipping Photographs (70,000), Mountford-Sheard Collection of Aboriginal Ethnology, Thomas Hardy Wine Library (1,000 vols), Paul McGuire Maritime Library (3,000 vols), Rare Books Collection (92,000 vols), Royal Geographical Society of South Australia Library, Oral History Collection (1,500 cassette tapes), Pictorial Collection (55,500 images); supports 138 public libraries (1,500,000 vols); Dir ROBYN COLLINS; publs *Annual Report, Extra Extra* (4 a year).

University of Adelaide Library: University of Adelaide, Adelaide, SA 5005; tel. (8) 8303-5370; telex 89141; fax (8) 8303-4369; f. 1876; 2,000,000 items; Librarian RAY CHOATE.

University of South Australia Library: Joan Brewer Library, Underdale Campus, Holbrooks Road, Underdale, SA 5032; tel. (8) 8302-6611; fax (8) 8302-6756; David Murray Library, City East Campus, North Terrace, Adelaide, SA 5000; Levels Campus Library, The Levels, SA 5095; Thiele Library, Magill Campus, Lorne Avenue, Magill, SA 5072; City West Campus Library, North Terrace, Adelaide, SA 5000; Whyalla Campus Library, Nicolson Avenue, Whyalla Norrie, SA 5608; f. 1991; 1,000,000 vols; special collections include Oregon Collection of Theses in Physical Education & Sport, Australian Clearinghouse for Library & Information Science, Doris Taylor Collection on Ageing, Gavin Walkley collection on Architectural History; Clearinghouse in Australia for Adult Basic Education and Literacy; Librarian A. L. BUNDY.

Tasmania

State Library of Tasmania: 91 Murray St, Hobart, Tas. 7000; tel. (3) 6233-8011; fax (3) 6231-0927; e-mail slt_srl@e.c.c.tased.edu.au; f. 1849; 1,250,000 items; state deposit privileges; 49 brs, 3 bookmobiles and 6 reference and special collections; Dir R. A. COLLINS.

University of Tasmania Library: GPO Box 252C, Hobart, Tas. 7001; tel. (3) 6220-2223; fax (3) 6220-2878; f. 1892; 900,000 vols; Sandy Bay Campus libraries: Biomedical, Law, Morris Miller (social sciences and humanities), Science and Technology; Centre for the Arts Library, Hunter St, Hobart; Clinical Library, 43 Collins St, Hobart; Launceston Campus Library, Newnham, Launceston; special collections on Quakerism; houses the Royal Soc. of Tasmania Library.

Victoria

Commonwealth Scientific and Industrial Research Organisation, Information Services: 314 Albert St, East Melbourne, Vic. 3002; tel. (3) 418-7333; fax (3) 419-0459; publs and communicates science information in print, video and multimedia, and electronic databases; disseminates science and research information through CSIRO Library Network, search and inquiry services SEARCH PARTY; archival services for CSIRO research and records; Gen. Man. JINETTE DE GOOIJER.

La Trobe University Library: Bundoora, Vic. 3083; tel. (3) 479-2920; fax (3) 471-0993; f. 1964; 977,620 vols; special emphasis on Latin America, Health Sciences; Chief Librarian G. E. GOW; publs *Annual Report, Library Publications* (series).

Monash University Library: Clayton, Vic. 3168; tel. (3) 9905-2670; fax (3) 9905-2610; f. 1961; 2,500,000 vols, 17,800 periodicals; also libraries at Caulfield Campus, Caulfield East, Vic. 3145; Peninsula Campus, Frankston, Vic. 3199; Gippsland Campus, Churchill, Vic. 3842; and Berwick Campus, Berwick, Vic. 3806; Librarian E. LIM.

Parliament of Victoria Library: Parliament House, Spring St, Melbourne, Vic. 3002; tel. (3) 9651-8640; fax (3) 9650-9775; e-mail bruce.davidson@parliament.vic.gov.au; f. 1851; reference and research service for MPs and associated staff; statistics, economics, politics, law, government publs; Librarian B. J. DAVIDSON; publs *Victorian Parliamentary Handbook* (every 4 years), monographs.

Public Record Office of Victoria: POB 1156, South Melbourne, Vic. 3205; tel. (3) 9285-7930; fax (3) 9285-7953; f. 1973; 67,074 linear metres of public records; Keeper ROSS GIBBS; publs *Profile* (quarterly), *Proactive* (quarterly).

State Library of Victoria: 328 Swanston St, Melbourne, Vic. 3000; tel. (3) 669-9888; fax (3) 663-1480; f. 1854; the state general reference library and legal depository; 1,650,000 vols; special collections include La Trobe (Australiana) Collection, art, music and performing arts, Anderson Chess Collection, maps, manuscripts and pictures; CEO and State Librarian FRANCES AWCOCK; publs *La Trobe Library Journal* (2 a year), *Victorian Government Publications* (monthly).

University of Melbourne Library: Parkville, Vic. 3052; tel. (9) 344-5382; fax (9) 347-7243; f. 1855; 2,600,000 vols; Librarian HELEN HAYES.

Western Australia

Curtin University of Technology Library and Information Service: Kent St, Bentley, GPO Box U1987, Perth, WA 6001; tel. (8) 9351-7205; fax (8) 9351-2424; f. 1967; 390,526 vols, 11,917 current serial titles; Librarian VICKI WILLIAMSON.

Library and Information Service of Western Australia: Alexander Library Bldg, Perth Cultural Centre, Perth, WA 6000; tel. (8) 9427-3111; fax (8) 9427-3336; Reference and Information Services: 328,000 vols, 9,000 serial and newspaper titles, 35,000 music scores, 13,500 music recordings, 10,300 microfilm reels, 175 metres of microfiche; 6,200 community information database records, 8,300 videos, 8,300 16mm films; Public Library and Lending Services; provides stock and support services for 229 public libraries; 237,000 vols; State Archives: 8,300 metres of Government archives, 1,272 metres of private archives; J. S. Battye Library of West Australian History: f. 1887; legal deposit library of West Australian publs; 68,000 vols, 11,200 serial titles, 800 newspaper titles, 60,400 items of ephemera, 2,000 oral history transcripts, 114,200 pictures, 10,800 microfilm reels, 22,000 cartographic items, 2,400 State Film Archives titles; CEO and State Librarian Dr LYNN ALLEN; publs *Annual Report, Directory of Public Library Services* (1 a year), *Legal Deposit Publications in WA* (4 a year), *Statistical Bulletin for Public Libraries in Western Australia* (1 a year), *LISWA Newsletter* (6 a year).

University of Western Australia Library: Nedlands, WA 6907; tel. (8) 9380-2344; fax (8) 9380-1012; f. 1913; 1.1m. vols; Librarian JOHN ARFIELD.

Museums and Art Galleries

Australian Capital Territory

Australian War Memorial: GPO Box 345, Canberra, ACT 2601; tel. (2) 6243-4211; fax (2) 6243-4325; f. 1917; national war memorial, museum, research centre and art gallery illustrating and recording aspects of all wars in which the Armed Forces of Australia have been engaged; dioramas of historical battles, and a total collection of over 3.5m. items; works of art, relics, documentary and audiovisual records; library: books, serials, pamphlets, photographs, maps, film and sound recordings on military history; repository of operational records of Australian fighting units; Dir Maj.-Gen. STEVE GOWER; publ. *Wartime* (4 a year).

National Gallery of Australia: POB 1150, Canberra, ACT 2601; tel. (2) 6240-6411; telex 61500; fax (2) 6240-6529; f. 1975; the National Collection has 100,000 works of Australian and international art; Australian collection includes fine and decorative arts, folk art, commercial art, architecture and design; other collections include arts of Asia and Southeast Asia, Oceania, Africa and Pre-Columbian America, European art, also prints, drawings, illustrated books from 1800, photography; library of 85,000 monographs, 25,000 auction sales catalogues, 1,200 current serials, 47,000 microfiches, 700,000 ephemeral materials; Dir BRIAN P. KENNEDY; publs *Annual Report, Artonview.*

National Museum of Australia: POB 1901, Canberra, ACT 2601; tel. (2) 6208-5000; fax (2) 6208-5099; e-mail bookings@nma.gov.au; f. 1980; Australian history, Aboriginal and Torres Strait Island cultures, social history and environment; library of 1,500 vols, 25,000 monographs; Dir Dr WILLIAM JONAS; publ. *National Museum of Australia Annual Report.*

New South Wales

Art Gallery of New South Wales: Domain, Sydney, NSW; tel. (2) 9225-1700; fax (2) 9221-6226; f. 1874; representative collection of Australian art, Aboriginal and Melanesian art; collections of British 18th–20th-century art; European painting and sculpture (15th–20th century); Asian art, particularly Chinese and Japanese ceramics and Japanese painting; Australian, British and European prints and drawings; photography; Dir EDMUND CAPON; publs exhibition catalogues, guide, etc.

Australian Museum: 6 College St, Sydney, NSW 2000; tel. (2) 9320-6000; fax (2) 9320-6050; e-mail info1@amsg.austmus.gov.au; f. 1827; natural sciences, anthropology, palaeontology, mineralogy, biodiversity; Dir

D. J. G. GRIFFIN; library of 90,000 vols; publ. *Nature Australia* (4 a year).

Australian National Maritime Museum: GPO Box 5131, Sydney, NSW 2001; tel. (2) 9552-7777; fax (2) 9552-2318; f. 1985, open 1991; illustrates maritime history as exemplified by the Colonial Navies, the Royal Australian Navy, merchant shipping and trade, whaling and the fishing industry, explorers and mapmakers, immigration, the design and use of leisure and sporting craft and int. competition, surfing, surf life saving and the culture of the beach, and the maritime activities of the Aborigines; models, prints and drawings, glass plate negatives, uniforms, relics, full-size vessels; library of 12,000 vols and 750 serials; Dir Dr KEVIN FEWSTER; publs *Signals* (mems' magazine), *Annual Report*.

Macleay Museum: Univ. of Sydney, NSW 2006; tel. (2) 9351-2274; fax (2) 9351-5646; e-mail macleay@macleay.usyd.edu.au; collection started 1790, given to University 1888; entomology, zoology, ethnology, 19th-century scientific instruments; Australian photographs dating from 1850s; Dir VANESSA MACK.

Museum of Applied Arts and Sciences: POB K346, Haymarket, NSW 1238; tel. 9217-0111; fax 9217-0333; f. 1880; comprises Powerhouse Museum (decorative arts, social history, science and technology), Sydney Observatory astronomical museum; Dir TERENCE MEASHAM; publ. *Annual Report*.

Museum of Contemporary Art: Level 5, 140 George St, The Rocks, POB R1286, Sydney, NSW 2000; tel. (2) 9252-4033; fax (2) 9252-4361; f. 1989; Dir BERNICE MURPHY.

Nicholson Museum of Antiquities: Univ. of Sydney, Sydney, NSW 2006; tel. (2) 9351-2812; fax (2) 9351-4889; f. 1860; collection of Egyptian, Near Eastern Cypriot, European, Greek and Roman antiquities; Curator Prof. A. CAMBITOGLOU.

Shellshear, J. L., Museum of Comparative Anatomy and Physical Anthropology: Dept of Anatomy and Histology, Univ. of Sydney, Sydney, NSW 2006; f. 1958; comparative series of human skulls, skeletons, and marsupials; Curator Dr D. DONLON.

Wilson, J. T., Museum of Human Anatomy: Dept of Anatomy, Univ. of Sydney, NSW 2006; f. 1886; includes 1,000 dissected parts and cross-sections of the human body; Curator Prof. of Anatomy.

Queensland

Queensland Art Gallery: POB 3686, South Brisbane, Qld 4101; tel. (7) 3840-7303; fax (7) 3844-8865; f. 1895; State collection of Australian and foreign paintings, prints, drawings and photographs, sculpture and decorative arts; education and advisory services; library of 19,500 monographs, 400 serials, photographs, ephemeral material, catalogues; Dir DOUG HALL.

Queensland Herbarium: Meiers Rd, Indooroopilly, Qld 4068 (formerly Botanic Museum and Herbarium, f. 1874); tel. (7) 3896-9325; fax (7) 3896-9624; studies of flora and mapping of vegetation of Queensland, rare and threatened plant species, plant ecology, weeds, poisonous plants and economic botany; 575,000 specimens; library of 10,000 vols; Dir G. P. GUYMER; publs *Austrobaileya*, *Queensland Botany Bulletin*.

Queensland Museum: Cultural Centre, South Bank, South Brisbane, Qld 4101; tel. (7) 3840-7555; fax (7) 3846-1918; f. 1871; zoology, geology, history, ethnology, technology; library of 95,000 vols; Dir A. BARTHOLOMAI; publ. *Memoirs*.

South Australia

Art Gallery of South Australia, The: North Terrace, Adelaide, SA 5000; tel. (8) 8207-7000; fax (8) 8207-7070; f. 1881; comprehensive collection of Australian works of art, British and European painting, prints, drawings and sculpture 16th–20th centuries, English and European furniture, silver and glass; English, European and South East Asian ceramics and antiquities; changing temporary exhibitions; early S. Australian pictures; education services; Dir RON RADFORD; publs *Annual Report*, *Newsletter* (every 2 months), exhibition catalogues.

South Australian Museum: North Terrace, Adelaide, SA 5000; tel. (8) 8207-7500; fax (8) 8207-7430; f. 1856; anthropological, geological and zoological material mainly related to South Australia; the Australian ethnological collection is outstanding, and, for South and Central districts, the best in existence; education and advisory services; library of 45,000 vols; Dir Dr CHRIS ANDERSON; publ. *Records*.

Tasmania

Queen Victoria Museum and Art Gallery: Wellington St, Launceston, Tas.; tel. (3) 6331-6777; fax (3) 6334-5230; f. 1891; library of 7,000 vols; collections comprise pure and applied art, Tasmanian history, Tasmanian and general anthropology, Tasmanian botany, geology, palaeontology and zoology; Dir C. B. TASSELL; publs *Records*, *Annual Report*.

Tasmanian Museum and Art Gallery: 40 Macquarie St, Hobart, Tas. 7001 (GPO Box 1164-M); tel. (3) 6235-0777; fax (3) 6234-7139; f. 1852; art, natural and human history, applied science, with emphasis on Tasmania and Australia as a whole; includes Tasmanian Herbarium, coin collections, early photography, collections relating to the Aboriginal people of Tasmania; a branch museum (West Coast Pioneers' Memorial Museum) dealing with mining, at Zeehan; Dir P. SABINE; publs handbooks, exhibition catalogues, *Annual Report*.

Victoria

Museum of Victoria: 328 Swanston Walk, Melbourne, Vic. 3000; tel. (3) 9669-9997; fax (3) 9639-1090; fmrly National Museum of Victoria, f. 1854 and Science Museum of Victoria, f. 1870; exhibitions and collections in natural sciences and human studies, including social history and Australian and Pacific ethnology; Planetarium; Dir GRAHAM MORRIS.

Attached museum:

Scienceworks: 2 Booker St, Spotswood, Vic. 3015; tel. (3) 9392-4800; fax (3) 9392-4848; science and technology collection, exhibitions and inter-active displays.

National Gallery of Victoria: 180 St Kilda Rd, Melbourne, Vic.; tel. 9208-0222; fax 9208-0245; f. 1859; Old Masters and depts of Prints and Drawings, Modern European Art, Australian Art, Aboriginal and Oceanic Art, Decorative Art and Design, Asian Art, Antiquities, Photography, Pre-Columbian Art, Costume and Textiles; library of 35,000 vols, and slides; Dir Dr TIMOTHY POTTS; publs *Art Bulletin of Victoria*, catalogues.

Western Australia

Art Gallery of Western Australia: Perth Cultural Centre, Perth, WA 6000; tel. (8) 9492-6600; fax (8) 9492-6655; e-mail admin@artgallery.wa.gov.au; f. 1895; Aboriginal art, Australian and foreign paintings, sculpture, decorative arts and crafts; library of 16,000 vols; Dir ALAN R. DODGE; publ. *Annual Report*.

Western Australian Museum: Francis St, Perth, WA 6000; tel. 9328-4411; fax 9328-8686; f. 1891; natural history, archaeology, history, earth sciences, anthropology; library of 15,500 vols, 1,500 journal titles; Dir ANDREW REEVES; publs *Records*, *Records Supplements*, *Annual Report*.

Universities

UNIVERSITY OF ADELAIDE

SA 5005
Telephone: (8) 8303-4455
Telex: 89141
Fax: (8) 8224-0464

Founded 1874
Autonomous institution established by Act of Parliament
Academic year: March to December

Chancellor: W. F. SCAMMELL
Vice-Chancellor: Prof. MARY J. O'KANE
Deputy Vice-Chancellor (Academic): Prof. I. R. FALCONER
Deputy Vice-Chancellor (Research): (vacant)
Registrar: F. J. O'NEILL
Librarian: R. C. CHOATE

Number of full-time teachers: 900
Number of students: 14,000

Publications: *Research Report*, *Social Analysis* (every 6 months), *The Joseph Fisher Lecture in Commerce* (irregular), *Adelaide Law Review*, *Australian Economic Papers* (both every 6 months), *Australian Feminist Studies*, *Chinese Economy Research Unit Newsletter*, *Corporate and Business Law Journal*, *Labour Studies Briefing*, *Australian Journal of Social Research*, *Management Briefings* (3 a year).

DEANS

Faculty of Agricultural and Natural Resource Sciences: Prof. J. M. OADES (acting)
Faculty of Architecture and Urban Design: T. J. WILLIAMSON
Faculty of Arts: P. NURSEY-BRAY
Faculty of Dentistry: V. B. BURGESS
Faculty of Economics and Commerce: M. J. MEYLER
Faculty of Engineering: Prof. J. B AGNEW
Faculty of Law: Prof. R. J. FOWLER
Faculty of Mathematical and Computer Sciences: Prof. E. O. TUCK
Faculty of Medicine: Prof. D. B. FREWIN
Faculty of Performing Arts: Dr A. DONALDSON
Faculty of Science: Prof. I. KOTLARSKI
Graduate Studies: Dr D. R. LILJEGREN

PROFESSORS

Faculty of Agriculture and Natural Resource Sciences:

COVENTRY, D. R., Agronomy and Farming Systems
FINCHER, G. B., Plant Science
GRAHAM, R. D., Plant Science
HOJ, P., Viticulture
LEE, T., Oenology
OADES, J. M., Soil Science
PINNOCK, D. E., Crop Protection
POSSINGHAM, H. P., Environmental Science and Rangeland Management
SAMUEL, S. N., Agricultural Business
SCHMIDT, O., Crop Protection
SEDGLEY, M., Horticulture
SETCHELL, B. P., Animal Sciences
SMITH, S. E., Soil Science
SYMONS, R. H., Plant Science

Faculty of Architecture and Urban Design:

RADFORD, A. D.

Faculty of Arts:

BOUMELHA, P. A., English Language and Literature
HUGO, G. J., Geography
JAIN, P. C., Asian Studies
JOHN, I. D., Psychology
MCEACHERN, D., Politics
MUHLHAUSLER, P., Linguistics

PREST, W. R., History
SMOLICZ, J. J., Education
WATSON, A. J., Asian Studies
WEINER, J. F., Anthropology
WILLIAMS, M. A., Environmental Studies

Faculty of Dentistry:
PETERS, M. C.
SAMPSON, W. J.
SPENCER, A. J.
TOWNSEND, G. C.

Faculty of Economics and Commerce:
ANDERSON, K., Economics
HENDERSON, M. S., Commerce
MCDOUGALL, F. M., Graduate School of Management
PINCUS, J. J., Economics
POMFRET, R. W., Economics
SHERIDAN, K., Graduate School of Management
WALSH, C., Economics

Faculty of Engineering:
AGNEW, J. B., Chemical Engineering
BARTER, C. J., Computer Science
BOGNER, R. E., Electrical and Electronic Engineering
GRAY, D. A., Electrical Engineering
HENDERSON, I. D., Mechanical Engineering
LUXTON, R. E., Mechanical Engineering
WARNER, R. F., Civil Engineering

Faculty of Law:
BRADBROOK, A. J.
CHARLESWORTH, H. C.
DETMOLD, M. J.

Faculty of Mathematical and Computer Sciences:
CAREY, A. L., Pure Mathematics
COUTTS, R., Telecommunications
JARRETT, R. G., Statistics
TUCK, E. O., Applied Mathematics

Faculty of Medicine:
BARTER, P. J., Cardiology
BOCHNER, F., Clinical and Experimental Pharmacology
FREWIN, D. B., Clinical and Experimental Pharmacology
GOLDNEY, R. D., Psychiatry
HENNENBERG, M., Anatomy
HOROWITZ, M., Medicine
HOWIE, D. W., Orthopaedic Surgery and Trauma
JAMIESON, G. G., Surgery
JARRETT, D. B., Gerontology
JONES, N., Surgery
KOSKY, R. J., Child Psychiatry
MCFARLANE, A. C., Rehabilitation Psychiatry
MADDERN, G., Surgery
MARLEY, J. E., General Practice
MATTHEWS, C. D., Reproductive Medicine
PEARSON, A., Clinical Nursing
PILOWSKY, I., Psychiatry
PRIEDKALNS, J., Anatomy and Histology
ROBERTON, D. M., Paediatrics
ROBINSON, J. S., Obstetrics and Gynaecology
RUNCIMAN, W. B., Anaesthesia and Intensive Care
SHEARMAN, D. J. C., Medicine
THOMAS D. W., Paediatrics
VERNON-ROBERTS, B., Pathology
WORSLEY, A., Community Medicine
YOUNG, G. P., Medicine

Faculty of Science:
APPLEGATE, J. K., Petroleum Geology and Geophysics
BOWIE, J. H., Chemistry
BRUCE, M. I., Chemistry
BURRELL, C. J., Microbiology and Immunology
DAVIES, P. C. W., Physics and Mathematical Physics
FRAKES, L. A., Geology and Geophysics
GRIFFITHS, C. M., Petroleum Geology and Geophysics
LINCOLN, S. F., Chemistry
MCMILLEN, I. C., Physiology
MANNING, P. A., Microbiology and Immunology
MUNCH, J., Physics and Mathematical Physics
RATHJEN, P. D., Biochemistry
SAINT, R. B., Genetics
SMITH, F. A., Botany
THOMAS, A. W., Physics and Mathematical Physics
WISKICH, J. T., Botany
YPMA, P. J. M., Geology and Geophysics

ATTACHED RESEARCH INSTITUTE

Waite Agricultural Research Institute: Private Bag No. 1, Glen Osmond, SA 5064; f. 1924; Dir Prof. J. M. OADES (acting); publ. *Biennial Report*.

AFFILIATED RESIDENTIAL COLLEGES

St Mark's College Inc.: North Adelaide; f. 1924; number of students: 201.
Master: C. R. ASHWIN.

St Ann's College Inc.: North Adelaide; f. 1939; number of students: 154.
Principal: Dr R. BROOKS.

Aquinas College Inc.: North Adelaide; f. 1947; number of students: 160.
Rector: Fr T. OVERBERG.

Lincoln College Inc.: North Adelaide; f. 1951; number of students: 250.
Principal: Dr P. GUNN.

Kathleen Lumley College Inc.: North Adelaide; f. 1967; number of students (postgraduate): 72.
Master: Dr D. L. CLEMENTS.

**Roseworthy College, Inc.: Roseworthy; f. 1991; number of students: 275.
Principal: E. A. ALCOCK.**

AUSTRALIAN CATHOLIC UNIVERSITY

POB 968, North Sydney, NSW 2059
Telephone: (2) 9739-2929
Fax: (2) 9739-2905

Founded 1991 by amalgamation of Catholic College of Education Sydney, Institute of Catholic Education, Victoria, McAuley College, Brisbane and Signadou College, Canberra

Academic year: February to December

Chancellor: Cardinal EDWARD CLANCY
Pro-Chancellor: Br JULIAN MCDONALD
Vice-Chancellor: Prof. PETER W. SHEEHAN
Secretary: RICHARD DOYLE

Library of 463,139 vols
Number of teachers: 500
Number of students: 9,649

Publications: faculty handbooks, campus annual reports.

DEANS

Arts and Sciences: Prof. PETER CARPENTER
Education: Prof. MICHAEL DOYLE
Health Sciences: Prof. ELIZABETH CAMERON-TRAUB

AUSTRALIAN NATIONAL UNIVERSITY

Canberra, ACT 0200
Telephone: (2) 6249-5111
Telex: 62760
Fax: (2) 6248-9062

Founded 1946 for postgraduate research. Now consists of Institute of Advanced Studies (7 postgraduate research schools), The Faculties (all levels) and Institute of the Arts.

Academic year: March to December

Chancellor: Prof. T. BAURNE
Pro-Chancellor: P. M. GRIFFIN
Vice-Chancellor: Prof. R. D. TERRELL
Deputy Vice-Chancellor and Director, Institute of Advanced Studies: Prof. S. W. SERJEANTSON
Deputy Vice-Chancellor: Prof. M. E. POOLE
Academic Registrar: Dr A. C. B. DELVES
Secretary: W. R. WILLIAMS
Librarian: C. R. STEELE
Library: See under Libraries

Publications: *Annual Report, ANU Reporter.*

Institute of Advanced Studies: Chairman of the Board: Prof. B. L. KENNETT.

Number of academic staff: 725, including 10 professors
Number of postgraduate students: 902

Constituent Schools

Research School of Biological Sciences: Director: Prof. C. B. OSMOND

PROFESSORS

ANDREWS, T. J., Molecular Plant Physiology
FARQUHAR, G. D., Plant Environmental Biology
GIBBS, A. J., Molecular Evolution and Systematics
GIBSON, J. B., Molecular and Population Genetics
GUNNING, B. E. S., Plant Cell Biology
HORRIDGE, G. A., Visual Sciences
NAORA, H., Molecular Evolution and Systematics
ROLFE, B. G., Plant Microbe Interactions
SRINIVASAN, M. V., Visual Sciences

Research School of Chemistry: Dean: Prof. J. W. WHITE

PROFESSORS

BENNETT, M. A., Organic Chemistry
EVANS, D. J., Theoretical Chemistry
MANDER, L. N., Organic Chemistry
RADOM, L., Organic Chemistry
RAE, A. D., X-ray Crystallography
RICKARDS, R. W., Organic Chemistry
WHITE, J. W., Physical and Theoretical Chemistry

Research School of Earth Sciences: Director: Prof. D. H. GREEN

PROFESSORS

COMPSTON, W., Geochronology and Isotope Geochemistry
KENNETT, B. L. N., Seismology
LAMBECK, K., Geophysics
MCDOUGALL, I., Geochronology and Isotope Geochemistry

John Curtin School of Medical Research: Director: Prof. K. J. LAFFERTY

PROFESSORS

BLANDEN, R. V., Microbiology
BOARD, P. G., Molecular Medicine
COX, G. B., Membrane Biochemistry
DOE, W. F., Molecular Medicine
GAGE, P. W., Physiology
HENDRY, I. A., Developmental Neurobiology
LAFFERTY, K. J., Diabetics
LEVICK, W. R., Physiology
PARISH, C. R., Immunology and Cell Biology
REDMAN, S. J., Neuroscience
YOUNG, I. G., Biochemistry and Molecular Biology

Research School of Pacific and Asian Studies: Director: Prof. M. C. RICKLEFS

PROFESSORS

ANDERSON, A. J., Archaeology and Natural History
BALL, D. J., Strategic and Defence Studies
CHAPPELL, J. M. A., Biogeography and Geomorphology
DENOON, D. J. N., Pacific and Asian History

DIBB, P. D., Strategic and Defence Studies
DODGSON, M., MBA Programme
DRYSDALE, P. D., Australia–Japan Research Centre
DUNCAN, R. C., Development Studies
ELVIN, J. M. D., Pacific and Asian History
FOX, J. J., Anthropology
GARNAUT, R. G., Economics
HARRIS, S. F., International Relations
JONES, R. M., Archaeology and Natural History
KERKVLIET, B. J. T., Political and Social Change
LINGE, G. J. R., Human Geography
MCCORMACK, G. P., Pacific and Asian History
MCKIBBEN, W., Economics
MACK, A. J. R., International Relations
MORRIS-SUZUKI, T., Pacific and Asian History
NELSON, H. N., Pacific and Asian History
PAWLEY, A. K., Linguistics
REID, A. J. S., Pacific and Asian History
RICHARDSON, J. L., International Relations
STENING, B. W., MBA Programme
THAKUR, R. C., Peace Research Centre
WARD, R. G., Human Geography
WARR, P. G., Agricultural Economics

Research School of Information Sciences and Engineering: Director Prof. B. D. O. ANDERSON

PROFESSORS

ANDERSON, B. D. O., Systems Engineering
BITMEAD, R. R., Systems Engineering
BRENT, R. P., Computer Science
MEYER, R. K., Automated Reasoning Project

Research School of Physical Sciences and Engineering: Director: Prof. E. WEIGOLD

PROFESSORS

BAXTER, R. J., Theoretical Physics
DEWAR, R. L., Plasma Physics and Theoretical Physics
DRACOULIS, G. D., Nuclear Physics
HAMBERGER, S. M., Plasma Research
LUTHER-DAVIES, B., Laser Physics
MARCELJA, S., Applied Mathematics
MITCHELL, D. J., Optical Sciences Centre
MOORE, J. B., Systems Engineering
NINHAM, B. W., Applied Mathematics
OPHEL, J. R., Nuclear Physics
ROBSON, B. A., Theoretical Physics
SNYDER, A. W., Optical Sciences Centre
SPEAR, R. H., Nuclear Physics
WEIGOLD, E., Atomic and Molecular Physics
WILLIAMS, J. S., Electronic Materials Engineering

Research School of Social Sciences: Director: Prof. H. G. BRENNAN

PROFESSORS

BOURKE, P. F., History
BRAITHWAITE, J. B., Law
BRENNAN, H. G., Economics
CHAPMAN, B. J., Economic Policy
FINN, P. D., Law
GOODIN, R. E., Philosophy
GRANT, S. H., Economics
GREGORY, R. G., Economics
HIGMAN, B., History
HINDESS, B., Political Science
JACKSON, F. C., Philosophy
JONES, F. L., Sociology
JONES, G. W., Demography
MCDONALD, P. F., Demography
MCNICOLL, G. R., Demography
MEYER, R. K., Philosophy
NEAVE, M., Law
NELSON, H. N., History
PAGAN, A. R., Economics
PETTITT, P., Social and Political Theory
POPE, D., Economic History
RITCHIE, J. D., Australian Dictionary of Biography
SMITH, F. B., History
SNOOKS, G. D., Economic History
TROY, P. N., Urban Research
WAJEMAN, J., Sociology
WALSH, C., Federalism Research

Mount Stromlo and Siding Spring Observatories: Director: Prof. J. R. MOULD

PROFESSORS

DOPITA, M. A., Astronomy
FREEMAN, K. C., Astronomy
RODGERS, A. W., Astronomy

School of Mathematical Sciences: Dean: Prof. N. S. TRUDINGER

PROFESSORS

BAXTER, R. J., Mathematics
HALL, P. J., Statistics
HEYDE, C. C., Statistics
LEHRER, S. R., Statistics
OSBORNE, M. R., Advanced Computation
WILSON, S. R., Statistics

Faculties, The: Pro-Vice-Chancellor and Chairman of the Board: Prof. R. J. CAMPBELL

Number of academic staff: 482, including 45 professors
Number of students: 1,219 postgraduate, 7,397 undergraduate

DEANS

Faculty of Arts: Dr L. J. SAHA
Faculty of Asian Studies: Prof. A. C. MILNER
Faculty of Economics and Commerce: Dr D. F. NICHOLLS
Faculty of Law: Prof. T. D. CAMPBELL
Faculty of Science: Prof. R. M. PASHLEY
Faculty of Engineering and Information Technology: Prof. R. B. STANTON

PROFESSORS

Faculty of Arts:

AIKHENVALD, A. Y., Linguistics
ALTMAN, J. C., Aboriginal Economic Policy
CAMPBELL, R. J., Philosophy
CASTLES, F. G., Public Policy Program
CURTHOYS, A., History
DIXON, R. M. W., Linguistics
GREENHALGH, C. M. B., Art History
MCBRYDE, I., Prehistory
MARCEAU, J., Public Policy Centre
MERLAN, F. C., Anthropology
PIENEMANN, M., Modern European Languages
RAWSON, B. M., Classics
SAIKAI, A., Political Sciences
TENNANT, N. W., Philosophy
WARHURST, J. L., Political Science
WIERZBICKA, A. C., Linguistics
WRIGHT, I. R., English

Faculty of Asian Studies:

JENNER, W. J. F., Chinese
MILNER, A. C., SE Asian History

Faculty of Economics and Commerce:

CRAIG, R., Commerce
HEATHCOTE, C. R., Mathematical Statistics
NICHOLLS, D. F., Statistics

Faculty of Law:

CAMPBELL, T. D., Law
COPER, M. D., Law
DAVIS, J. L. R., Law
DISNEY, J. P., Law
GREIG, D. W., Law
GUNNINGHAM, N. A., Law
HAMBLEY, A. D., Law
PEARCE, D. C., Law
SWEENEY, M. D., Law
ZINES, L. R., Robert Garran Professor of Law

Faculty of Science:

ARCULUS, R. J., Geology
BACHOR, H.-A., Physics
BYRNE, D. G., Psychology
CHAPPELL, B. W., Geology
COCKBURN, A., Botany and Zoology
DAY, D. A., Biochemistry and Molecular Biology
ELESE, J. A., Chemistry
HALL, P. J., Centre for Mathematics and its Applications
HINDS, S., Physics and Theoretical Physics
HOWLETT, D. R., Geography
KANOWSKI, P. J., Forestry
PASHLEY, R. M., Chemistry
SANDERSON, R. J., Physics and Theoretical Physics
SELINGER, B. K., Chemistry
STANTON, R. B., Computer Science
TRUDINGER, N. S., Centre for Mathematics and its Applications
TURNER, J. C., Psychology
WASOON, R. J., Geography
WICKRAMASINGHE, D. T., Mathematics
WILLIAMS, J. F., Biochemistry and Molecular Biology
WILLIAMSON, D., Engineering Program

Institute of the Arts: Chairman of the Board: Prof. PETER KARMEL.

Number of academic staff: 87
Number of students: 664 undergraduate, 92 postgraduate

PROFESSORS

SITSKY, L., Composition
WILLIAMS, D., Visual Arts

SCHOOLS

Canberra School of Music: Dir W. HAWKEY (acting).

Australian Centre for Arts and Technology: Head D. WORRALL.

Canberra School of Art: Prof. D. WILLIAMS.

UNIVERSITY CENTRES

Centre for Resource and Environmental Studies: Dir Prof. H. A. NIX

Humanities Research Centre: Dir Prof. I. D. MCCALMAN.

National Health and Medical Research Council Social Psychiatry Research Unit: Dir Prof. A. S. HENDERSON.

Centre for Continuing Education: Dir Dr W. DONOVAN.

National Centre for Epidemiology and Public Health: Dir Prof. R. M. DOUGLAS.

Centre for Advanced Legal Studies in International and Public Law: Prof. J. H. P. DISNEY.

Centre for Information Science Research: Dir Prof. M. A. MCROBBIE.

Health Transition Centre: Dir Prof. J. C. CALDWELL.

Centre for Visual Science: Dir M. V. SRINIVASAN.

BOND UNIVERSITY

Gold Coast, Qld 4229

Telephone: (7) 5595-1111
Fax: (7) 5595-1140

Founded 1987
Private control
Academic year: January to December

Chancellor: Dr PAUL SCULLY-POWER
Vice-Chancellor: Prof. K. MOORES
Registrar: A. D. FINCH
Manager, Information Resources: E. WOODBERRY

Number of teachers: 153
Number of students: 1,700

Publications: *Bond Law Review, Bond Management Review, Revenue Law Journal, Bond Observer.*

DEANS

Business: Prof. R. BYRON
Humanities and Social Sciences: Prof. P. WILSON
Information Technology: Prof. G. GUPTA
Law: Prof. E. COLVIN

PROFESSORS

School of Business:

BYRON, R. P., Economics
CROUCH, A., Organizations and Management
FISHER, C.
GASTON, N., Economics
GOLDSWORHY, A., Leadership
MCTAGGART, D., Economics
MOORES, K., Accounting
SHARPLEY, C., Psychology
SHAW, J. B., Management

School of Humanities:

BOYLE, G., Psychology
MONTGOMERY, R., Psychology

School of Information Technology:

DE MESTRE, N.

School of Law:

ALLAN, D.
BOULLE, L.
COLVIN, E.
CORKERY, J.
EVERETT, D.
FARRAR, J.
HISCOCK, M.
WADE, J.

UNIVERSITY OF CANBERRA

POB 1, Belconnen, ACT 2616

Telephone: (2) 6201-5111
Fax: (2) 6201-5999

Founded 1990 from former Canberra CAE
Government control
Academic year: February to November (two semesters)

Chancellor: WENDY MCCARTHY
Vice-Chancellor: Prof. DON AITKIN
Deputy Vice-Chancellors: (vacant)
University Librarian: LOIS V. JENNINGS

Library: see Libraries
Number of teachers: 365 (full-time)
Number of students: 8,750

Publications: *Annual Report*, *Handbook* (annually), various information booklets and occasional publs.

DEANS

Faculty of Applied Science: Prof. A. CRIPPS
Faculty of Communication: Prof. P. PUTNIS
Faculty of Education: Prof. K. J. KENNEDY
Faculty of Environmental Design: Prof. E. BONOLLO
Faculty of Information Sciences and Engineering: Assoc. Prof. G. J. POLLARD
Faculty of Management: Assoc. Prof. J. C. MCMASTER

PROFESSORS

ANDREW, B., Accounting
BARTINIK, R., Mathematics
BONOLLO, E., Industrial Design
CARROLL, M. V., Psychology
CLARK, E., Law
CREAGH, D. C., Physics
CRIPPS, A., Health Sciences
CULLEN, P. W., Resource Science
EDWARDS, P. J., Electronics Engineering and Applied Physics
GERRITSEN, R., Local Government and Applied Policy
HALLIGAN, J., Public Administration
HARDING, A., Applied Economics and Social Policy
JAMES, J. A., Nursing
KEARNEY, R., Environmental Science
KENNEDY, K. J., Education
MANDLE, W. F., History
PEARSON, C., Cultural Heritage Conservation
PUTNIS, P., Communication
SHADDOCK, A. J., Special Education and Counselling
TAYLOR, K., Landscape Architecture
TAYLOR, P. J., Mathematics Education
TOMASIC, R., Law
WAGNER, M., Computing

CENTRAL QUEENSLAND UNIVERSITY

Rockhampton, Qld 4702

Telephone: (7) 4930-9777
Fax: (7) 4936-1361

Founded 1967 as Queensland Institute of Technology (Capricornia); became Capricornia Institute of Advanced Education in 1971; became University College of Central Queensland in 1990 and University of Central Queensland in 1992; present name 1994

Chancellor: Hon. Justice S. G. JONES
Vice-Chancellor: Prof. J. LAUCHLAN CHIPMAN
Deputy Vice-Chancellor: Prof. G. HANCOCK
Pro Vice-Chancellor (Research and Academic Development): (vacant)
Vice-Presidents: K. WINDOW (Administration), E. LAAKSO (Corporate Development)
Librarian: M. APPLETON (acting)

Number of teachers: 321
Number of students: 12,000

Publications: *Handbook, Annual Report.*

DEANS

Arts, Health and Sciences: Assoc. Prof. E. PAYNE
Business and Law: Prof. K. FAGG
Education and Creative Arts: Prof. L. BARTLETT
Engineering and Physical Systems: Prof. E. JANCAUSKAS
Informatics and Communication: D. CLAYTON (acting)

Campuses at Brisbane, Bundaberg, Emerald, Gladstone, Mackay, Melbourne, Rockhampton, Sydney.

CHARLES STURT UNIVERSITY

Chancellery, The Grange, Panorama Ave, Bathurst, NSW 2795

Telephone: (2) 6338-4200
Fax: (2) 6333-4833

Founded 1989 by amalgamation of Mitchell College of Advanced Education (f. 1951) and Riverina-Murray Inst. of Higher Education (f. 1947); campuses at Albury, Bathurst and Wagga Wagga.
Government control
Academic year: February to November

Chancellor: DAVID ASIMUS
Vice-Chancellor: Prof. CLIFF D. BLAKE
Deputy Vice-Chancellor (Academic): Prof. KATH BOWMER
Deputy Vice-Chancellor (Management Services): (vacant)
Secretary: Dr P. G. HODGSON
University Librarian: MARGARET H. MACPHERSON

Number of teachers: 550
Number of students: 24,500

Publications: *Handbook* (annually), *Annual Report, Times* (quarterly), *Billboard* (every 2 weeks), *Panorama* (quarterly).

DEANS

Faculty of Arts: Prof. R. CHAMBERS
Faculty of Commerce: Prof. J. HICKS
Faculty of Education: Prof. R. E. MEYENN
Faculty of Health Studies: Prof. D. A. BATTERSBY
Faculty of Science and Agriculture: Prof. J. E. PRATLEY

PROFESSORS

Faculty of Arts:

DOYLE, R., Social Work
GREEN, D. L., Art
MARCUS, J., Cultural Anthropology
MILLER, S., Social Philosophy
TULLOCH, J., Cultural Studies

Faculty of Commerce:

FATSEAS, V., Accounting
HEAZLEWOOD, C. T., Accounting and Finance
NOBLE, C. E., Economics

Faculty of Education:

BRAGGETT, E. J., Education

Faculty of Science and Agriculture:

BOSSOMAIER, T., Computer Systems
CORNISH, B. A., Computing
GREEN, D., Information Technology
MEYER, W., Irrigation
ROBERTSON, A., Environmental Science
WOLFE, T. C., Agriculture

Australian Graduate School of Police Management:

ROHL, T., (Executive Director)

Albury Campus

PO Box 789, Albury, NSW 2640

Telephone: (2) 6051-6800
Fax: (2) 6051-6629

Principal: Prof. BRYAN ROTHWELL

Bathurst Campus

Panorama Avenue, Bathurst, NSW 2795

Telephone: (2) 6338-4000
Fax: (2) 6331-9634

Principal: (vacant)

Wagga Wagga Campus

PO Box 588, Wagga Wagga, NSW 2678

Telephone: (2) 6933-2000
Fax: (2) 6933-2639

Principal: Prof. K. BOWMER

CURTIN UNIVERSITY OF TECHNOLOGY

GPO Box U1987, Perth, WA 6845

Telephone: (8) 9266-9266
Fax: (8) 9266-2255

Founded 1967, name changed from Western Australian Inst. of Technology in 1987
Academic year: February to November (two semesters)

Chancellor: HARRY PERKINS
Vice-Chancellor: Prof. LANCE TWOMEY
Senior Deputy Vice-Chancellor: Prof. LESLEY PARKER
Deputy Vice-Chancellor (Office of Teaching and Learning): Prof. IAN READ
Deputy Vice-Chancellor (Office of Curtin International): Prof. JOHN MILTON-SMITH
Executive Dean (Humanities): Assoc. Prof. WILL CHRISTENSEN (acting)
Executive Dean (Curtin Business School): Assoc. Prof. KEVIN MCKENNA (acting)
Executive Dean (Engineering and Science): Prof. RICHARD HORSLEY
Executive Dean (Health Sciences): Prof. CHARLES WATSON
Deputy Vice-Chancellor (Research and Development): Prof. PAUL ROSSITER
Executive Director (University Administration): PETER WALTON
University Librarian: VICKI WILLIAMSON

Number of teachers: 1,500
Number of students: 24,000

Publications: *University Handbook and Calendar, Annual Report, Research and Development Report,* etc.

DEANS

Faculty of Education: Dr G. DELLAR
Faculty of Engineering: Prof. T. SMITH
Faculty of Science: Prof. B. COLLINS

HEADS OF DEPARTMENTS

Centre for Aboriginal Studies: P. DUDGEON
Centre for International English: Prof. A. KIRKPATRICK
Department of Applied Physics: Dr I. BAILEY
Department of Computer Engineering: C. MAYNARD
Department of Computer Science: Prof. S. VENKATESH
Department of Dental Hygiene and Therapy: R. KENDELL
Department of Electrical Engineering: Dr B. LAWRANCE
Department of Electronic and Communication Engineering: Dr S. HO
Department of Environmental Health: R. PICKETT
Department of Epidemiology and Biostatistics: K. SAUER
Department of Exploration Geophysics: Assoc. Prof. N. UREN
Department of Health Information Management: B. POSTLE
Department of Health Policy and Management: Prof. D. BOLDY
Department of Health Promotion: Assoc. Prof. P. HOWAT
Department of Human Biology: Dr M. GARDINER
Department of Information Studies: K. SMITH
Department of Medical Imaging: T. KNIGHTS
Department of Minerals Engineering and Extractive Metallurgy: Prof. E. GRIMSEY
Department of Mining Engineering and Mine Surveying: Dr G. BAIRD
Department of Mineral Exploration and Mining Geology: Assoc. Prof. J. VAUGHAN
Department of Nutrition, Dietetics and Food Science: Assoc. Prof. S. ULIJASZEK
Graduate School of Business: Assoc. Prof. M. NOWAK
School of Accounting: J. NEILSON
School of Applied Chemistry: Prof. R. KAGI
School of Applied Geology: Assoc. Prof. S. WILDE
School of Architecture, Construction and Planning: Prof. L. HEGVOLD
School of Art: Assoc. Prof. E. SNELL
School of Biomedical Sciences: Dr R. DUNSTAN
School of Business Law: Assoc. Prof. D. YORKE
School of Chemical Engineering: Prof. T. SMITH
School of Civil Engineering: Prof. V. RANGAN
School of Communication and Cultural Studies: T. NICHOLLS
School of Computing: Prof. S. VENKATESH
School of Design: A. PRICE
School of Economics and Finance: Assoc. Prof. G. CROCKETT
School of Electrical and Computer Engineering: Prof. J. HULLETT
School of Environmental Biology: Prof. B. COLLINS
School of Information Systems: A. RUDRA (acting)
School of Management: Prof. L. SAVERY
School of Marketing: Assoc. Prof. R. RAMAESHAN
School of Mathematics and Statistics: Prof. L. CACCETTA
School of Mechanical Engineering: Dr K. TEH
School of Nursing: N. REES (acting)
School of Occupational Therapy: J. MILLSTEED
School of Pharmacy: Assoc. Prof. B. SUNDERLAND
School of Physical Science: Prof. B. O'CONNOR
School of Physiotherapy: Prof. J. COLE
School of Psychology: L. SMITH
School of Public Health: Prof. C. BINNS
School of Social Sciences and Asian Languages: Assoc. Prof. R. JONES
School of Social Work: Prof. R. HUGMAN
School of Speech and Hearing Science: Dr K. TAYLOR
School of Spatial Sciences: Prof. G. LODWICK

ATTACHED INSTITUTES

Muresk Institute of Agriculture: Northam, WA 6401; Dir Prof. M. McGREGOR.

Western Australian School of Mines: PMB 22, Kalgoorlie, WA 6430; f. 1902, coll. of univ. since 1969; Dir Prof. E. GRIMSEY.

Indian Ocean Centre: Dir Assoc. Prof. K. McPHERSON.

Research Institute for Cultural Heritage: Dir Prof. D. DOLAN.

Science and Mathematics Education Centre: Dir Prof. B. FRASER.

National Centre for Research into the Prevention of Drug Abuse: Dir T. STOCKWELL.

DEAKIN UNIVERSITY

Geelong, Vic. 3217; campuses: Burwood, Geelong, Rusden, Toorak, Warrnambool and Woolstores

Telephone: (3) 5227-1100
Fax: (3) 5227-2001

Founded 1974

Chancellor: J. B. LESLIE
Vice-Chancellor and President: Prof. G. WILSON
Deputy Vice-Chancellor and Vice-President (Academic): Prof. D. LE GREW
Pro Vice-Chancellor (Research): Prof. K. O'DEA
Pro Vice-Chancellor (Development): Prof. G. W. BEESON
Vice-President (Administration): R. H. ELLIOTT
Librarian: Prof. M. A. CAMERON

Library of 916,513 vols, 14,702 current periodical titles

Number of students: 30,191 (incl. 13,088 off-campus)

DEANS

Faculty of Arts: Prof. BRYAN TURNER
Faculty of Education: Prof. RICHARD BATES
Faculty of Health and Behavioural Sciences: Prof. LAWRENCE ST LEGER
Faculty of Management: Prof. PETER WOLNIZER
Faculty of Science and Technology: Prof. DAVID STOKES

HEADS OF SCHOOLS

Faculty of Arts:
- School of Australian and International Studies: Prof. JOAN BEAUMONT
- School of Languages, Interpreting and Translating: Prof. ADOLFO GENTILE
- School of Literary Communication Studies: Prof. CLARE BRADFORD
- School of Social Inquiry: Prof. ALLAN JOHNSTON
- School of Visual, Performing and Media Arts: Prof. BARBARA VAN ERNST

Faculty of Education:
- School of Social and Cultural Studies in Education: Prof. MARIE EMMITT
- School of Scientific and Development Studies in Education: Prof. MARJORY-DORE MARTIN

Faculty of Health and Behavioural Sciences:
- School of Human Movement: Prof. NEVILLE OWEN
- School of Nursing: Prof. CATHERINE TAYLOR
- School of Nutrition and Public Health: Assoc. Prof. RICHARD READ
- School of Psychology: Assoc. Prof. HILDE LOVEGROVE
- School of Studies in Disability: Prof. JOE GRAFFAM

Faculty of Management:
- Bowater School of Management and Marketing: Prof. MALCOM RIMMER
- School of Accounting and Finance: Prof. GARRY CARNEGIE
- School of Economics: Prof. PASQUALE SGRO
- School of Law: Prof. PHILIP CLARKE
- School of Management Information Systems: Prof. PETER JULIFF

Faculty of Science and Technology:
- School of Aquatic Science and Natural Resource Management: Prof. ROB WALLIS
- School of Architecture and Building: Assoc. Prof. NICK BEATTIE
- School of Biological and Chemical Sciences: Prof. RICHARD RUSSELL
- School of Computing and Mathematics: Prof. ANDRZEJ GOSCINSKI
- School of Engineering and Technology: Prof. LAWRIE BAKER

ATTACHED RESEARCH INSTITUTES

Australian Women's Research Centre: Dir Prof. ROBYN ROWLAND

Centre for Australian Studies: Dir Prof. DAVID WALKER

Centre for Citizenship and Human Rights: Dir Dr MICHAEL MUETZELFELDT

Centre for Research and Development in Interpreting and Translating: Dir Prof. ADOLFO GENTILE

Centre for Research in Cultural Communication: Dir Assoc. Prof. BRIAN EDWARDS

Centre for Research in Mathematics Education: Dirs Assoc. Prof. SUSIE GROVES, Assoc. Prof. IAN ROBOTTOM

Centre for the Body and Society: Dirs Dr LIZ ECKERMANN, NEVILLE MILLEN

Centre for the Study of Asia and Middle East: Dir Dr MARK McGILLIVRAY

Deakin Centre for Education and Change: Dirs Dr CHRIS BIGUM, JANE KENWAY

Sciences in Society Centre: Dirs Assoc. Prof. WADE CHAMBERS, Assoc. Prof. IRMLINE VEIT-BRAUSE

Taxation and Policy Research Institute: Dir Prof. RICK KREVER

EDITH COWAN UNIVERSITY

Pearson St, Churchlands, WA 6018

Telephone: (8) 9273-8333
Fax: (8) 9387-7095

Founded 1991
State control
Academic year: February to November (2 semesters)

Chancellor: Hon. Justice R. NICHOLSON
Vice-Chancellor: Prof. M. POOLE
Deputy Vice-Chancellors: Prof. B. LAWRENCE (Academic), Prof. L. STILL (Staffing)
Director, Student Administration: P. BAIMBRIDGE
Librarian: CHRISTOPHER MULDER

Number of teachers: 790
Number of students: 19,000

Publications: *Handbook* (annually), *Digest* (quarterly), *Quest* (quarterly), *Undergraduate Prospectus* (annually), *Research & Postgraduate Studies* (annually).

DEANS

Faculty of Arts: Assoc. Prof. E. JAGGARD
Faculty of Business: Assoc. Prof. G. SOUTAR
Faculty of Education: Prof. B. HARRISON
Faculty of Health and Human Sciences: Prof. R. UNDERWOOD

Faculty of Science, Technology and Engineering: Prof. P. GARNETT
Western Australian Academy of Performing Arts: Dr G. GIBBS

HEADS OF SCHOOL

Faculty of Arts:
- Language, Literature and Media Studies: Assoc. Prof. R. QUIN
- Social and Cultural Studies: Dr S. SAGGERS
- Kurongkurl Katitijn, School of Indigenous Australian Studies: Assoc. Prof. S. FORREST

Faculty of Business:
- Accounting: Prof. G. MONROE
- Business Economics and Finance: C. REYNOLDSON
- Business Law: W. CLAYDON
- Management: Assoc. Prof. A. BROWN
- Management Information Systems: S. BENSON
- Marketing and Tourism: R. GROVES

Faculty of Education:
- Arts and Humanities Education: Dr A. TAGGART
- Education and Social Enquiry: Dr R. CHADBOURNE
- Language Education: J. RIVALLAND
- Mathematics, Science and Technology Education: Assoc. Prof. D. GOODRUM
- Multimedia Learning Technologies: Assoc. Prof. G. RING

Faculty of Health and Human Sciences:
- Community Studies: Assoc. Prof. F. LOBO
- Health Studies: R. GAMBLE
- Nursing: B. JONES
- Psychology: L. PIKE

Faculty of Science, Technology and Engineering:
- Mathematics, Information Technology and Engineering: Prof. A. WATSON
- Physical and Life Sciences: Assoc. Prof. B. GIBSON

Western Australian Academy of Performing Arts:
- Conservatorium of Music: G. ASHTON
- Dramatic Arts: D. ORD
- Visual Arts: Dr N. WESTON

ATTACHED INSTITUTES

Centre for Applied Language Research: Head A. MCGREGOR.

Centre for Asian Communication, Media and Cultural Studies: Head Dr B. SHOESMITH.

Centre for Development Studies: Head N. HUDSON-RODD.

Centre for Disability, Research and Development: Head E. COCKS.

Centre for Ecosystem Management: Head Dr P. HORWITZ.

Centre for Human Genetics: Heads Prof. A. BITTLES, Dr L. KELAYDJIEVA.

Centre for Police Research: Head Dr. I. FROYLAND.

Centre for Research on Women: Head. A. GOLDFLAM.

Centre for Rural Health and Community Development: Dr S. AOUN.

Centre for Very High Speed Microelectronic Systems: Head Prof. K. ESHRAGHIAN.

Mathematics, Science and Technology Education Centre: Head Dr J. BANA.

Sport and Physical Activity Research Centre: Head Dr K. ALEXANDER.

Australian Institute for Research in Primary Mathematics Education: Head A. MCINTOSH.

Australian Institute of Security and Applied Technology: Head Dr A. LEAHY.

FLINDERS UNIVERSITY OF SOUTH AUSTRALIA

GPO Box 2100, Adelaide, SA 5001

Telephone: (8) 8201-3911
Fax: (8) 8201-3000

Founded 1966; previously established in 1963 as the University of Adelaide at Bedford Park; amalgamated in 1991 with Sturt Campus of South Australian College of Advanced Education
Academic year: March to November (2 semesters)

Chancellor: Sister D. F. JORDAN
Vice-Chancellor: Prof. I. CHUBB
Deputy Vice-Chancellor: Prof. A. EDWARDS
Pro-Vice-Chancellor: Prof. C. D. MARLIN
Director of Administration and Registrar: P. BAILIE
Librarian: W. T. CATIONS

Library: see Libraries
Number of teachers: 698
Number of students: 12,096

Publications: *Research Report* (annually), *Australian Economic Papers* (with University of Adelaide), *Bulletin of Labour* (quarterly).

HEADS OF FACULTY

Education, Humanities, Law and Theology: Prof. F. H. E. TRENT
Health Sciences: Prof. J. FINLAY-JONES
Science and Engineering: Dr J. RICE
Social Sciences: Dr J. G. BROWETT

PROFESSORS

ALPERS, J., Medicine
ANDERSON, J., Education
BARBER, J. G., Social Administration and Social Work
BARRITT, G. T., Medical Biochemistry
BAUM, F., Public Health
BERRY, M. N., Medical Biochemistry
BIRKETT, D. J., Clinical Pharmacology
BRADLEY, J., Clinical Immunology
BROWN, C. P., Asian Studies
BROWN, R., Special Education
BRUGGER, W., Politics
BURNS, M. E., Economics
BUTCHER, A. R., Speech Pathology
CLARE, J. M. R., Nursing
CORCORAN, S. A., Law
COSTA, M., Human Physiology
COSTER, D. J., Ophthalmology
CROCKER, A. D., Clinical Pharmacology
CURRIE, G., Philosophy
DARBYSHIRE, P., Nursing Practice
DOWNING, A. R., Engineering (Biomedical)
DUNN, S. V., Nursing
FEATHER, N. T., Psychology
FENNELL, T., French
FINLAY-JONES, J., Microbiology and Infectious Diseases
FINUCANE, P. M., Rehabilitation Aged and Extended Care
FORBES, D. K., Geography
FORSYTH, K. D., Paediatrics and Child Health
GIBBINS, I. L., Anatomy and Histology
GOLDSMITH, A. J., Legal Studies
GOODMAN, A. E., Biology
HALL, S. J., Biology
HASSAN, R. U., Sociology
HEARN, T. C., Orthopaedic Research
HENDERSON, D., Pathology
HOLTON, R. J., Sociology
KEIRSE, M., Obstetrics and Gynaecology
KOCH, G. A., Domiciliary Nursing
KALUCY, R. S., Psychiatry
LAWRANCE, W., Chemistry
LEONARD, D., Economics
MACKINNON, A. M., Telemedicine
MADDOCKS, I., Palliative Care
MARLIN, C. D., Computer Science
MARSHALL, V. R., Surgery
MCDONALD, J. M., Economics
MCDONALD, P. J., Microbiology and Infectious Diseases
MCMAHON, R., Commerce
MEGAW, J. V. S., Archaeology
MINERS, J. O., Environmental Health Unit
MORAN, W., Mathematics
MORLEY, A. A., Haematology
MORLEY, M. W., Drama
MURRAY, A. W., Biology
NICHOLAS, T. E., Human Physiology
PARKIN, A., Political and International Studies
PHILLIPS, G. D., Anaesthesia and Intensive Care
PHILLIPS, P., Medicine
PRAGER, R. H., Chemistry
RICHARDS, E. S., History
RYAN, L., Women's Studies Unit
SAGE, M. R., Diagnostic Radiology
SCHWERDTFEGER, P., Earth Sciences
SCOTT, G., Economics
SILAGY, C. A., Evidence-Based Care and General Practice
SKINNER, J., Pathology
SMYTH, J., Teacher Education
STEWART, A. J., Law
STORER, R., Physics
TOMCZAK, M., Earth Sciences
TOOULI, J., Surgery
TRENT, F. H., Education
WALKER, A., Northern Territory Clinical School
WHELDRAKE, J., Biological Sciences
WILSON, P., Psychology
WING, L. M. H., Medicine
WOODEN, M., Labour Studies
YOUNG, G. P., Gastroenterology

ATTACHED RESEARCH INSTITUTES

(The mailing address is that of the University)

Airborne Research Australia: Dir Assoc. Prof. J. M. HACKER.

Anti-Cancer Foundation South Australia: Dir I. YATES.

Australasian Cochrane Centre: Dir Prof. C. A. SILAGY.

Australian Institute of Nursing Research: Dir Prof. J. CLARE.

Flinders Cancer Centre: Dir Dr T. W. TILLEY (acting).

Centre for Applied Philosophy: Dir Dr I. A. HUNT.

Centre for Multimedia Educational Technology: Man. K. KNOX.

Centre for Research in the New Literatures in English: Dir Dr S. C. HARREX.

Centre for Development Studies: Dir Dr S. SCHECK.

Centre for Sensor Signal and Information Processing: Contact Dr M. BOTTEMA.

Centre for Neuroscience: Convenor Dr J. MORRIS.

Electronic Structure of Materials Centre: Dir Prof. P. TEUBNER.

Flinders Institute for Atmospheric and Marine Sciences: Dir Prof. M. TOMCZAK.

Flinders Institute for Signal and Image Analysis: Dir Prof. B. MORAN.

Flinders Institute of Public Policy and Management: Dir Prof. B. GUERIN.

Flinders University Institute of International Education: Dir Assoc. Prof. G. R. TEASDALE.

Institute for Australasian Geodynamics: Dir Dr F. CHAMALAUN.

National Centre for Education and Training on Addiction: Dir Assoc. Prof. S. ALLSOP.

National Institute of Labour Studies Inc.: Dir Prof. M. WOODEN (acting).

National Tidal Facility: Dir Dr W. SCHERER.

Institute for Australasian Geodynamics: Dir Dr F. J. CHAMALAUN.

Institute for the Study of Learning Difficulties: Dir Assoc. Prof. R. J. REES.

South Australian Centre for Economic Studies: Dir Prof. C. WALSH.

Centre for Multicultural Studies: Dir Assoc. Prof. R. J. HOLTON.

Liver Research Centre: Chair. and Co-Convenor Assoc. Prof. P. HALL.

Centre for Groundwater Studies: Dir Dr C. BARBER.

Pan Pacific Institute: Dir Assoc. Prof. D. A. DEBATS.

Centre for Health Advancement: Chair. Prof. C. A. SILAGY.

Centre for Scandinavian Studies: Dir Dr A. R. G. GRIFFITHS.

Flinders Institute for the Study of Teaching: Dir Prof. J. SMYTH.

Centre for Ageing Studies: Dir Prof. G. ANDREWS.

Centre for Plant Membrane Biology: Dir Prof. F. A. SMITH.

Lincoln Marine Science Centre: Operations Man. M. THOMAS.

Flinders Research Centre for Injury Studies: Dir Dr J. E. HARRISON.

National Police Research Unit: Dir R. HAMDORF.

GRIFFITH UNIVERSITY

Qld 4111

Telephone: (7) 3875-7111

Telex: 40362

Fax: (7) 3875-7965

(Griffith University Gold Coast Campus, PMB50, Gold Coast Mail Centre, Qld 4217; tel. (7) 5594-8800)

(Queensland Conservatorium of Music, Griffith University: POB 28, North Quay, Qld 4002; tel. (7) 3875-6111; fax (7) 3875-6262; f. 1957, became a college of Griffith University 1991)

(Queensland College of Art, Griffith University: POB 84, Morningside, Qld 4170; tel. (7) 3875-3111; fax (7) 3875-3199; f. 1881; became a college of Griffith University 1992)

Founded 1971, campuses at Nathan, Brisbane City, Mount Gravatt, Morningside, Logan and Gold Coast

State control

Academic year: February to June, July to November

Chancellor: The Hon. Mr Justice J. M. MACROSSAN

Vice-Chancellor: Prof. L. R. WEBB

Deputy Vice-Chancellor: (vacant)

Deputy Vice-Chancellor (Research): Prof. D. LINCOLN

Pro-Vice-Chancellor (Administration): COLIN MCANDREW

Pro-Vice-Chancellor (Arts, Teaching and Learning): Prof. J. WALTER

Pro-Vice-Chancellor (Business, Equity): Prof. MARGARET GARDNER

Pro-Vice-Chancellor (Information and International Services): Dr B. D. COOK

Pro-Vice-Chancellor (Science, Quality): Prof. M. C. STANDAGE

Pro-Vice-Chancellor (Health), Gold Coast University College: Prof. M. G. IRVING

Academic Registrar: Dr LYN HOLMAN

Provost and Director, Queensland Conservatorium of Music: Assoc. Prof. S. DE HAAN

Provost and Director, Queensland College of Art: Prof. I. HOWARD

Number of teachers: 1,010

Number of students: 19,668

Publications: *University Handbook, Annual Report and Research Report, Statistics* (annually).

DEANS

Faculty of Arts: Assoc. Prof. D. SAUNDERS

Faculty of Commerce and Management: Prof. P. BROSNAN

Faculty of Education: Prof. MARILYN MCMENIMAN

Faculty of Environmental Science: Prof. W. L. HOGARTH

Faculty of Health: Prof. J. G. O'GORMAN

Faculty of Law: Prof. SANDRA BERNS

Faculty of Science: Prof. W. MACGILLIVRAY

Faculty of Engineering: Prof. H. B. HARRISON

Faculty of International Business and Politics: Prof. D. LIM

Faculty of Information and Communication Technology: Prof. P. PRITCHARD

PROFESSORS

ARTHINGTON, A. H., Environmental Science
BAIN, J. D., Education
BAMBER, G., Graduate School of Management
BENNETT, F. A., Arts
BERNS, S., Law
BILLARD, L., Environmental Science
BROSNAN, P. A., Commerce and Management
BUCKLEY, R., Engineering
BUCKLEY, S. L., International Business and Politics
BULBECK, C., Arts
CATON, H. P., Arts
CONNELL, D. W., Environmental Science
DADDS, M. R., Health
DE HAAN, S. R., Music
DEWAR, J. K., Law
DROMEY, R. G., Information and Communication Technology
DUNLOP, M. J., Health
ELSON, R. E., International Business and Politics
FINNANE, M. J., Arts
FREEBODY, P. R., Education
GASS, G. C., Health
HAIRE, I. J., Arts
HALFORD, W. K., Health
HARRISON, H. B., Science and Technology
HODGSON, A., Commerce and Management
HOGARTH, W. L., Environmental Science
HOMEL, R. J., Humanities
HOWARD, I. G., Queensland College of Art
INGRAM, D., Arts
ISELIN, E. R., Commerce and Management
KELLOW, A. J., Environmental Science
KWON, O. Y., International Business and Politics
LIM, D. L., International Business and Politics
KITCHING, R. L., Environmental Science
KNIGHT, A. E., Science
LOO, Y.-C., Engineering
LOWE, I., Science
MACGILLIVRAY, W. R., Science
MACKERRAS, C. P., International Business and Politics
MCMENIMAN, M., Education
MCMURRAY, A., Health
MIA, L., Commerce and Management
MIZERSKI, R. W., Commerce and Management
MOORE, M. R., Environmental Science
MOREY, R., Commerce and Management
MOSS, D. M., Arts
MULLER, T. E., Commerce and Management
NAUGHTON, A. J., Commerce and Management
NESDALE, A. R., Commerce and Management
NICKLING, W. G., Environmental Science
NGUYEN, D. T., Commerce and Management
O'FAIRCHEALLAIGH, C., Commerce and Management
O'GORMAN, J. G., Health
PALIWAL, K., Science
PARKER, S. J., Law
PEGG, D. T., Science
POWER, D. J., Education
PRINGLE, R., Arts
PRITCHARD, P., Information and Communication Technology
QUINN, R. J., Science
RAMSDEN, P., Education
RYDER, P., Commerce and Management
SADLER, D. R., Education
SAMPFORD, C. J., Arts
SMITH, R. A., Education and the Arts
STEVENSON, J. C., Education
THIEL, D. V., Engineering
TOPOR, R. W., Information and Communication Technology
TUCKER, K., International Business and Politics
WELLER, P. M., Commerce and Management
WILLIS, R., Health

ACADEMIC FACULTIES AND THEIR CENTRES

Faculty of Environmental Science:

Air Quality Research Unit: Dir Assoc. Prof. R. SIMPSON

Centre for Catchment and In-Stream Research: Dir Assoc. Prof. A. H. ARTHINGTON

Centre for Environmental Risk Management and Policy: Dir Prof. A. KELLAU

Centre for Innovation and Research in Environmental Education: Dir Assoc. Prof. J. FIEN

Centre for Land Conservation: Dir Dr G. MCTAINSH

International Centre for Ecotourism Research: Dir Prof. R. BUCKLEY

Co-operative Research Centre for Tropical Rainforest, Ecology and Management: Dir Prof. R. KITCHING

Environmental Modelling and Research Unit: Dir Dr R. BRADDOCK

Waste Management Research Unit: Dir Dr D. MOY

Institute of Environment, Health and Development for the Asia-Pacific: Dr C. CHU

Faculty of International Business and Politics:

Australian Centre of the Asian Spatial Information and Analysis Network: Dir Assoc. Prof. L. CRISSMAN

Australian Centre for Korean Studies: Dir Prof. O. Y. KWON

Centre for Applied Linguistics and Languages: Dir Prof. D. E. INGRAM

Centre for the Study of Australia–Asia Relations: Dir BERNIE BISHOP

Key Centre for Asian Languages and Studies (with the University of Queensland): Co-Dir Prof. C. P. MACKERRAS

Taiwan Studies Unit: Dir Dr D. SCHAK

Unit for the Study of Religious Change and Consciousness: Dir Dr JULIA HOWELL

Faculty of Commerce and Management:

Applied and International Economic Research Unit: Dir Prof. T. NGUYEN

Centre for Australian Public Sector Management: Dir Prof. P. M. WELLER

Centre for Leisure Research: Dir Dr N. MCINTYRE

Centre for Research on Employment and Work: Dir Dr P. SHELDON

Centre for the Study of Organizational Process, Performance and Finance: Dir Assoc. Prof. P. SMITH

Centre for Tourism and Hotel Management Research: Dir Assoc. Prof. H. W. FAULKNER

Faculty of Education:

Centre for Applied Education: Dir D. JONES

Centre for Deafness Studies and Research: Dir Prof. D. POWER

Centre for Leadership and Management in Education: Dir Assoc. Prof. N. DEMPSTER

Centre for Learning and Work Research: Dir S. BILLETT

Centre for Literacy Education Research: Co-Dirs Prof. P. FREEBODY, Dr J. CUMMING

Centre for Movement Education and Research: Dir S. HAY

Griffith Institute for Higher Education: Dir Prof. P. RAMSDEN

Faculty of Environmental Science:
Centre for Strategic Human Services: Dir Dr N. BUYS
Neuropsychology Unit: Dir Dr D. SHUM
Faculty of Arts:
Centre for Crime Policy and Public Safety: Dir Dr M. HAURITZ
Australian Institute for Women's Research and Policy: Dir Prof. R. PRINGLE
Key Centre for Cultural and Media Policy: Dir Prof. T. BENNETT
National Institute for Law, Ethics and Public Affairs: Dir Assoc. Prof. W. HUDSON
Queensland Studies Centre: Dir Dr P. BUCKRIDGE
Unit for Contemporary German Thought: Dir Assoc. Prof. W. HUDSON
Unit for the Study of Comparative Criminal Justice History: Dir (vacant)
Faculty of Law:
Client-Centred Legal Practice Unit: Dirs M. LEBRUN, M. ROBERTSON
Intellectual Property Law Unit: Dirs S. MCVEIGH, B. SHERMAN
Law and the Family Research Unit: Dir Prof. J. DEWAR
Faculty of Health:
Australian Institute for Suicide Research and Prevention: Dir Assoc. Prof. J. O'GORMAN
Centre for Clinical Nursing and Health Studies: Dir (vacant)
Rotary District 9600 Centre for Cardiovascular Research: Dir J. HEDRICK
Queensland College of Art:
Centre for Design Excellence: Dir (vacant)
Visual Arts Research Unit: Dir Dr J. MCDOWALL
Faculty of Information and Communication Technology:
Australian Software Quality Research Institute: Dir Prof. G. R. DROMEY
Centre for Technology Management: Dir Dr R. FARR-WHARTON
Parallel Computing Unit: Dir Dr HONG SHEN
Co-operative Research Centre for Distributed Systems Technology: Dir M. D. BARBAGELLO (Univ. of Qld)
Faculty of Science:
Queensland Pharmaceutical Research Institute: Dir Prof. R. J. QUINN
Science Policy Research Centre: Dir Dr D. BURCH
Faculty of Engineering:
Space Industry Centre for Microwave Technology: Dir Prof. H. B. HARRISON
Graduate School of Management:
Centre for Strategic Change and Development: Dir Assoc. Prof. P. SMITH

JAMES COOK UNIVERSITY

Townsville, Qld 4811

Telephone: (7) 4781-4111
Fax: (7) 4779-6371

Founded 1970
Academic year: February to November

Chancellor: J. WILLIAMS
Deputy Chancellor: G. N. WHITMORE
Vice-Chancellor: Prof. B. P. MOULDEN
Registrar: R. E. GILLIVER
Librarian: J. W. MCKINLAY

Number of teachers: 428 full-time
Number of students: 9,650

Publications: *Annual Report, Academic Calendar, Year in Review, JCU Link* (annually), *Research Report* (every 2 years), *Campus News* (every 2 weeks).

EXECUTIVE DEANS

Faculty of Arts, Commerce and Economics: P. RYDER
Faculty of Health, Life and Molecular Sciences: I. WRONSKI
Faculty of Law and Education: R. MCTAGGART
Faculty of Science and Engineering: D. CLOSE
Faculty of Social Sciences: J. D. GREELEY

PROFESSORS

AYNSLEY, R. M., Tropical Architecture
BON, G., Music
BURNELL, J. N., Biochemistry
CARTER, R. M., Earth Sciences
CHOAT, J. H., Marine Biology
CLOSE, D. J., Mechanical Engineering
CROOK, S., Sociology
DAVIES, B., Education
DAVIS, D. F., Creative Arts
FAIRALL, P. A., Law
HASSALL, A. J., English
HAYES, B. A., Nursing
HERON, M. L., Physics
KAPFERER, B., Anthropology
LAWN, R. J., Tropical Crop Science
MARSH, H. D., Environmental Science
OLIVER, N. H. S., Economic Geology
PATTERSON, J. C., Environmental Engineering
PEARCE, P. L., Tourism
PIERCE, P. F., Australian Literature
SUMMERS, P. M., Tropical Veterinary Science
THORPE, R. M., Social Work

LA TROBE UNIVERSITY

Bundoora, Vic. 3083

Telephone: (3) 479-1111
Fax: (3) 478-5814

Founded 1964

Chancellor: Emeritus Prof. N. MILLIS
Vice-Chancellor: Prof. M. J. OSBORNE
Deputy Vice-Chancellor: Prof. G. H. MCDOWELL
Deputy Vice-Chancellor (Research): Prof. T. F. SMITH
Pro Vice-Chancellor (International): Prof. D. STOCKLEY
Pro Vice-Chancellor (Education Developments): Dr H. BATTEN
Pro Vice-Chancellor (Information Technology): Prof. E. R. SMITH
Pro Vice-Chancellor (Academic Programs and Access): Prof. S. BAMBRICK
Pro Vice-Chancellor (La Trobe Bendigo): Prof. L. A. KILMARTIN
Pro Vice-Chancellor (La Trobe Albury/Wodonga): T. KEATING
University Secretary: D. F. BISHOP
Chief Librarian: G. E. GOW

Number of teachers: 935
Number of students: 23,342

DEANS

Law and Management: Prof. G. C. O'BRIEN
Health Sciences: Prof. S. DUCKETT
Humanities and Social Sciences: Prof. G. C. DUNCAN
Science, Technology and Engineering: Prof. E. R. SMITH
Bendigo: Prof. L. A. KILMARTIN

PROFESSORS

AIKEN, M. E., Commerce
ALLEN, F. J., Archaeology
ALTMAN, D., Politics
ARNASON, J. P., Sociology and Anthropology
BECKER, N. G. Statistics
BENCH, R., Human Communication
BERNARD, C., Psychology
BLAKE, B. J., Linguistics
BOLAND, R. C., European Studies
BRANSON,, J. E., Education
CAHILL, L. W., Electronics Engineering
CAMILLERI, J., Politics
CATTRALL, R. W., Chemistry
CHANOCK, M., Law and Legal Studies
CHISHOLM, A. H., Agriculture
COUSENS, R., Agriculture
COX, D. R., Social Work
CROUCH, G., Tourism and Hospitality
CROZIER, R. H., Genetics and Human Variation
DILLON, T. S., Computer Science and Computer Engineering
DYSON, P., Physics
FITZGERALD, J. J., Asian Languages
FREADMAN, R. B., English
FROST, A. J., History
GATT-RUTTER, J. A., Italian Studies
GAUNTLETT, E., Hellenic Studies
GLEADOW, A. J., Earth Sciences
GRAVES, J. A. M., Genetics and Human Variation
HANDLEY, C., Human Biosciences
HOFFMAN, A., Genetics and Human Variation
HOOGENRAAD, N. J., Biochemistry
ISAAC, R. L., History
JAMES, J. E., Behavioural Health Sciences
JEFFREY, R., Politics
KAHN, J., Sociology and Anthropology
KELLEHEAR, S., Public Health
LAKE, M., History
LECKEY, R. C. G., Physics
LEDER, G., Education
LINDQUIST, B. I., Occupational Therapy
LUMLEY, J. M., Mothers' and Children's Health
MCDOWELL, G. H., Agriculture
MACY, J. M., Microbiology
MADDOCK, R. R., Economics
MILLS, T. M., Mathematics
MURPHY, P., Tourism and Hospitality
MURRAY, T. A., Archaeology
NAY, R. M., Nursing
O'MALLEY, P., Law and Legal Studies
PARISH, R. W., Botany
PERRY, A. R., Human Communication Science
PRATT, C., Psychological Sciences
PROSSER, M. T., Academic Development Unit
ROSENTHAL, D. A., Centre for Sexually Transmitted Diseases
SALMOND, J. A., History
SCOPES, R. K., Biochemistry
STEPHENSON, D., Zoology
SUGIMOTO, Y., Sociology and Anthropology
TAMIS, A., Hellenic Studies
THORNTON, M. R., Law and Legal Studies
WHITE, C. M., Graduate School of Management

MACQUARIE UNIVERSITY

Sydney, NSW 2109

Telephone: (2) 9850-7111
Fax: (2) 9850-7433

Founded 1964 (opened 1967)

Chancellor: MORRISH ALEXANDER BESLEY
Deputy Chancellor: His Hon. Dr J. F. LINCOLN
Vice-Chancellor: Prof. D. YERBURY
Deputy Vice-Chancellor (Academic): Prof. J. LOXTON
Deputy Vice-Chancellor (Research): Prof. PETER BERGQUIST
Deputy Vice-Chancellor (Administration): Prof. C. MARTIN
Registrar and Vice-Principal: B. J. SPENCER
Librarian: B. MITCHESON

Number of teachers: 775 (including 64 professors)
Number of students: 17,954

Publications: *Calendar, Annual Report, Research Report, Study at Macquarie* (all annually), *University News* (monthly).

HEADS OF SCHOOLS

School of Behavioural Sciences: Assoc. Prof. B. HESKETH (acting)
School of Biological Sciences: Assoc. Prof. J. M. GEBICKI
School of Chemistry: Assoc. Prof. B. D. BATTS
School of Earth Sciences: Assoc. Prof. D. C. RICH (acting)

School of Economic and Financial Studies: E. H. OLIVER
School of Education: Assoc. Prof. D. O'BRIEN
School of English and Linguistics: D. BLAIR
School of History, Philosophy and Politics: Dr L. FRAPPELL
School of Law: G. H. BOEHRINGER
School of Mathematics, Physics, Computing and Electronics: Prof. A. VAN DER POORTEN
School of Modern Languages: Prof. K. J. GOESCH
Institute of Early Childhood: J. WANGMANN

DIRECTORS OF INTERDISCIPLINARY CENTRES

Graduate School of the Environment: R. V. CARDEW
Graduate School of Management: Assoc. Prof. P. B. CAREY

PROFESSORS

BEATTIE, A. J., Biology
BERGQUIST, P. L., Biology
BLACKSHIELD, A. R., Law
CANDLIN, C. N., Linguistics
CANT, N., Chemistry
COLLINS, J., Psychology
COLTHEART, M., Psychology
COONEY, G. H., Teacher Education
COOPER, D. W., Biology
CROSS, A. G., Early Childhood Education
DAVIS, E., Management
DEUTSCHER, M. J., Philosophy
FAGAN, R. H., Human Geography
GIBBS, A. M., English and Cultural Studies
GILLIES, P. S., Business Law
GILMOUR, A. J., Environmental Studies
GILMOUR, P., Management
GLASER, S., Management
GOESCH, K. J., French
GOONERATNE, Y., English and Cultural Studies
GRAY, B. F., Chemistry
HAMILTON, A., Anthropology
HARRIS, C. K., Education
HARRISON, G. L., Accounting and Finance
HAYES, A. J., Early Childhood Studies
HENDERSON-SELLERS, A., Physical Geography
HEXT, J. B., Computing
HORNE, J., Economics
KANAWATI, N., Ancient History
KWIET, K., German
LOXTON, J., Mathematics
LIEU, S. N., History
LINDSAY, A. W., Management
MCNEIL, D. R., Statistics
MORE, E., Management
MURTAGH, B., Management
O'DONNELL, R. M., Economics
OFFEN, R. J., Information Technology
O'REILLY, S., Geology
ORR, B. J., Chemistry
PIPER, J. A., Physics
POLLARD, J. H., Actuarial Studies, Demography
RYAN, P. F., Business Law
SKELLERN, D. J., Electronics
SOLO, V., Statistics
SPILLANE, R. M., Management
SPRINGBORG, R., Politics
STREET, R., Mathematics
TALENT, J., Geology
TATZ, C. M., Politics
THROSBY, C. D., Economics
VAN DER POORTEN, A. J., Mathematics
VEEVERS, J., Geology
VERNON, R., Geology
WATERSON, D. B., Modern History
WENDEROTH, P. M., Psychology
WESTE, N. H., Microelectronic Systems
WESTOBY, M., Biology
WESTON, C. R., Management
WHELDALL, K., Special Education
WILLIAMS, K. L., Biology
YEATMAN, A., Sociology

UNIVERSITY OF MELBOURNE

Parkville, Vic. 3052
Telephone: (3) 9344-4000
Telex: 35185
Fax: (3) 9344-5104

Founded 1853 (opened 1855)
Autonomous institution established by Act of Parliament (Victoria) and financed mainly by the Commonwealth Government
Academic year: February to December

Chancellor: The Hon. Sir ALBERT EDWARD WOODWARD
Deputy Chancellors: N. G. CURRY, F. S. MARLES
Vice-Chancellor and Principal: Prof. ALAN GILBERT
Deputy Vice-Chancellors: Prof. C. B. SCHEDVIN (Academic), Prof. B. A. SHEEHAN (Resources), Prof. F. P. LARKINS (Research)
Assistant Vice-Chancellor: Prof. I. MORRISON (Information Technology)
Pro Vice-Chancellors: Prof. S. A. WALKER, Prof. T. W. HEALY
Registrar and Deputy Principal: J. B. POTTER
Academic Registrar: R. I. A. MARSHMAN
Librarian: H. M. HAYES

Number of teachers: 2,082
Number of students: 33,469

Publications: *Calendar* (microfiche), *Handbook, Research Report, Strategic Plan, Annual Report* (annually), *Gazette, The Melbourne Graduate Newsletter* (quarterly), *UniNews* (weekly).

DEANS

Institute of Land and Food Resources: Prof. L. FALVEY
Faculty of Architecture, Building and Planning: Prof. R. J. KING
Faculty of Arts: Prof. H. E. LE GRAND
Faculty of Economics and Commerce: Prof. R. A. WILLIAMS
Faculty of Education: Prof. K. C. LEE DOW
Faculty of Engineering: Prof. D. G. WOOD
Faculty of Law: Prof. B. M. L. CROMMELIN
Faculty of Medicine, Dentistry and Health Sciences: Prof. G. J. A. CLUNIE
Faculty of Music: Prof. W. A. BEBBINGTON
Faculty of Science: Prof. B. H. J. MCKELLAR
Faculty of Veterinary Science: Prof. I. W. CAPLE
Graduate Studies: Prof. B. EVANS

PROFESSORS AND HEADS OF DEPARTMENTS AND SCHOOLS

(H=non-professorial Head)

Faculty of Agriculture, Forestry and Horticulture:

CARY, J. W., Agriculture and Resource Management (H)
CHAPMAN, D. F., Agriculture and Resource Management
CONNOR, D. J., Agriculture (Agronomy)
EGAN, A. R., Agriculture
FALVEY, L., Agriculture
FERGUSON, I. S., Forest Science
VINDEN, P., Forest Industries
WHITE, R. E., Agriculture

Faculty of Architecture, Building and Planning:

BECK, D. H., Architecture
BRAWN, G. W., Architecture
FINCHER, R., Urban Planning
KING, R. J., Environmental Planning (H)
ROBINSON, J. R. W., Building

Faculty of Arts:

AUSTIN, P. K., Linguistics and Applied Linguistics
BUDIMAN, A., Indonesian
COADY, C. A. J., Philosophy
COALDRAKE, W. H., Japanese
DRYZEK, J., Political Science
DURING, S., English
ENRIGHT, N. J., Geography and Environmental Studies (H)
FREIBERG, A., Criminology
GALLIGAN, B. J., Political Science
GAUNTLETT, E., Language Studies (H)
GRIMSHAW, P. A., History
HOLM, D., Chinese
HOLMES, L. T., Political Science
HOME, R. W., History and Philosophy of Science
JACKSON, A. C., Social Work (H)
MACINTYRE, S. F., History
MARSHALL, D. R., Fine Arts (H)
MCPHEE, P. B., History
MEHIGAN, T., Germanic Studies and Russian (H)
NETTELBECK, C., French and Italian Studies
O'NEILL, T., Italian
RIDLEY, R., History
RUTHVEN, K. K., English Language and Literature
SCARLETT, B. F., Philosophy (H)
SEAR, F. B., Classics and Archaeology
STEELE, P. D., English
STEPHENS, A. R., German
WALLACE-CRABBE, C. K., English
WEBBER, M. J., Geography

Faculty of Economics and Commerce:

ABERNETHY, M. A., Managerial Accounting
CREEDY, J., Economics
DAVIS, K. T., Finance
DAWKINS, P. J., Applied Economic and Social Research
DEERY, S. J., Management and Industrial Relations
FREEBAIRN, J. W., Economics
HOUGHTON, K. A., Accounting
KNOX, D. M., Actuarial Studies
LLOYD, P. J., Economics
MCDONALD, I. M., Economics
NICHOLAS, S., Business Development and Corporate History
NICOL, R. E. G., Accounting
WILLIAMS, R. A., Econometrics

Faculty of Education:

CALDWELL, B. J., Education (Education Policy and Management)
CHRISTIE, F., Language, Literacy and Arts Education
GRIFFIN, P. E., Assessment
HILL, P., Education (Education Policy and Management)
LEE DOW, K. C., Education
MAGLEN, L. R., Vocational Education and Training
NIENHUYS, T. G. M., Early Childhood Studies (H)
POWLES, M. A., Centre for the Study of Higher Education
RABAN-BISBY, B., Early Childhood Studies
RICKARDS, F. W., Education (Learning, Assessment and Special Education)
STACEY, K. C., Science and Mathematics Education

Faculty of Engineering:

BOGER, D. V., Chemical Engineering
CHARTERS, W. W. S., Mechanical and Manufacturing Engineering
EVANS, R. J., Electrical Engineering
FRASER, C. S., Geomatics
GOOD, M. C., Mechanical and Manufacturing Engineering
HUTCHINSON, G. L., Civil and Environmental Engineering
KOTAGIRI, R., Computer Science
MCMAHON, T. A., Environmental Applied Hydrology
MAREELS, I. M. Y., Electrical Engineering
PERRY, A. E., Mechanical Engineering
STERLING, L. S., Computer Science
TUCKER, R. S., Electrical Engineering
VAN DEVENTER, J., Mineral and Process Engineering

WATSON, H. C., Mechanical and Manufacturing Engineering
WILLIAMSON, I. P., Geomatics

Faculty of Law:

COOPER, G. S., Taxation Law
CROMMELIN, B. M. L., Law
DAVIES, M. J., Law
LANHAM, D. J., Law
LUNTZ, H., Law
MCCORMACK, T. L. H., International Humanitarian Law
RAMSAY, I. M., Commercial Law
SAUNDERS, C. A., Law
SMITH, M. D. H., Asian Law
TILBURY, M., Law
WALKER, S. A., Law

Faculty of Medicine, Dentistry and Health Sciences:

ADAMS, J. MCK., Medical Biology
ALCORN, D., Anatomy
ALDRED, M. J., Dental Science
ANGUS, J. A., Pharmacology
CLARK, G. M., Otolaryngology
CLUNIE, G. J. A., Surgery
CONE-WESSON, B., Otolaryngology
CORY, S., Medical Biology
DENNERSTEIN, L., Public Health and Community Health
FARIS, I. B., Surgery
FURNESS, J. B., Anatomy
GRAHAM, K., Orthopaedic Surgery
HARDY, K. J., Surgery
HARRAP, S. B., Physiology
JOHNSTON, C. I., Medicine
KAYE, A. H., Surgery
LARKINS, R. G., Medicine
LOUIS, W. J., Clinical Pharmacology and Therapeutics
MCCLUSKY, J., Microbiology and Immunology
MCMEEKEN, J., Physiotherapy
MARTIN, T. J., Medicine
MASTERS, C. L., Pathology
MENDELSOHN, F. A. O., Medicine
MESSER, H. H., Restorative Dentistry
MESSER, L. J. B., Child Dental Health
MORGAN, T. O., Physiology
MORRISON, W. A., Surgery
NICHOLSON, G. C., Medicine
NICOLA, N., Medical Biology
PARKER, J. M., Postgraduate Nursing
PEACH, H. G., Public Health and Community Medicine
PEPPERELL, R. J., Obstetrics and Gynaecology
PHELAN, P. D., Paediatrics
PITTARD, A. J., Microbiology
REYNOLDS, E. C., Dental Science
SAWYER, W. H., Biochemistry
SCHREIBER, G. H., Biochemistry (Medical)
SINGH, B. S., Psychiatry
SMALLWOOD, R. A., Medicine
SMITH, P. J., Paediatrics
TAYLOR, H. R., Ophthalmology
THOMAS, R. J. S., Surgery
TREGEAR, G., Biochemistry
TRESS, B. M., Radiology
TRINDER, J. A., Psychology
WALES, R. J., Psychology
WEARING, A. J., Psychology
WILLIAMSON, R., Medical Genetics
WETTENHALL, R. E. H., Biochemistry
WILLIAMSON, R., Medical Genetics
WRIGHT, F. A. C., Preventive and Community Dentistry
YEOMANS, N. D., Medicine

Melbourne Business School:

DAINTY, P., Human Resources Management and Employee Relations
HARPER, I. R., International Finance
MANN, L., Organizational Behaviour and Decision Making
OFFICER, R. R., Finance
ROBERTSON, D. H., Practice of International Trade
ROSE, P. J. B., Commerce and Business Administration
SAMSON, D. A., Manufacturing Management
SINCLAIR, A. M. A., Management (Diversity and Change)
WEILL, P. D., Management (Information Systems)
WIDING, R. E., Retailing and Marketing
WILLIAMS, P. L., Management (Law and Economics)

Faculty of Music:

BEBBINGTON, W. A., Music
GRIFFITHS, J. A., Music

Faculty of Science:

BACIC, A., Botany
BROWN, T. C., Statistics
CAMERON, D. W., Organic Chemistry
CAMPBELL, G. D., Zoology
CHAN, D. Y. C., Mathematics
CLARKE, A. E., Botany
COLE, B. L., Optometry
GUTTMANN, A. J., Mathematics
HEALY, T. W., Physical Chemistry
HYNES, M. J., Genetics
KLEIN, A. G., Physics
KNOX, R. B., Botany
LADIGES, P. Y., Botany
LARKINS, F. P., Chemistry
MCKELLAR, B. H. J., Theoretical Physics
MCKENZIE, J. A., Genetics
MILLER, C. F., Mathematics
MORRISON, I., Information Systems
NUGENT, K. A., Physics
OPAT, G. I., Experimental Physics
PICKETT-HEAPS, J. D., Botany
PLIMER, I. R., Geology
RENFREE, M. B., Zoology
RUBINSTEIN, J. H., Mathematics
RUNNEGAR, B. N., Earth Sciences
THOMPSON, C. J., Mathematics
VITALE, M. R., Information Systems
WATTS, R. O., Chemistry
WEDD, A. G., Chemistry
WHITE, L. R., Mathematics

Faculty of Veterinary Science:

CAHILL, R. N. P., Veterinary Biology
CAPLE, I. W., Veterinary Medicine
SLOCOMBE, R. F., Veterinary Pathology
STUDDERT, V. P., Veterinary Clinical Science

School of the Victorian College of the Arts:

HULL, A. (H)

ASSOCIATED INSTITUTES

Austin Research Centre: Dir Prof. I. P. MCKENZIE.

Australian Artificial Intelligence Institute Ltd: Dir Dr M. P. GEORGEFF.

Australian Institute of Family Studies: Dir Dr H. MCGURK.

Australian Institute of Judicial Administration: Exec. Dir Prof. Assoc. G. J. REINHARDT.

Bionic Ear Institute: Dir Prof. G. M. CLARK.

Centre for International Research on Communication and Information Technologies: Dir Prof. J. BURKE.

Centre for the Study of Sexually Transmissible Diseases: Dir Dr D. ROSENTHAL.

CSIRO: Dir Dr D. NAIRN.

Hawthorn International Institute of Education Ltd: Dir Professorial Assoc. J. M. HEARN.

Howard Florey Institute of Experimental Physiology and Medicine: Dirs Prof. J. P. COGHLAN, Prof. F. A. O. MENDELSOHN.

Leo Cussen Institute: law; Exec. Dir E. LOFTUS.

Ludwig Institute for Cancer Research (Melbourne Tumour Biology Branch): Dir Prof. Assoc. A. W. BURGESS.

Macfarlane Burnet Centre for Medical Research Ltd: Dir Professorial Assoc. J. MILLS.

Marine and Freshwater Resources Institute: Dir Dr G. NEWMAN.

Melbourne College of Divinity: Dean H. J. PIDWELL.

Mental Health Research Institute of Victoria: Dir Professorial Assoc. D. COPOLOV.

Murdoch Institute for Research into Birth Defects Ltd: Scientific Dir Prof. R. WILLIAMSON.

Museum of Victoria: see under Museums.

National Ageing Research Institute Inc.: Dir Professorial Assoc. R. D. HELME.

National Vision Research Institute of Australia: see under Research Institutes.

Royal Botanic Gardens Melbourne: Dir Dr P. MOORS.

St Vincent's Institute of Medical Research: Dir Prof. T. J. MARTIN.

Skin and Cancer Foundation Inc.: Pres. J. M. BUTLER.

Tasman Institute Ltd and Tasman Area Pacific Pty Limited: Man. Dir Dr M. G. PORTER.

Turning Point Alcohol and Drug Centre Inc.: Dir M. HAMILTON.

Victorian College of Optometry: Dir Prof. B. L. COLE.

Victorian Institute of Forensic Pathology: Dir Prof. S. M. CORDNER.

Walter and Eliza Hall Institute of Medical Research: Dir Prof. S. CORY.

Zoological Board of Victoria: Dir C. R. LARCOMBE.

MONASH UNIVERSITY

Wellington Rd, Clayton, Vic. 3168
Telephone: (3) 9902-6000
Fax: (3) 9905-4007

Founded 1958 (opened 1961); amalgamated with Chisholm Institute of Technology and Gippsland Institute of Advanced Education 1990, and with Victorian College of Pharmacy 1992

Academic year: March to November

Chancellor: D. W. ROGERS
Vice-Chancellor: Prof. DAVID ROBINSON
Deputy Vice-Chancellors: Prof. P. LEP. DARVALL (Research and Development), Prof. J. E. MALONEY (International and Public Affairs), Prof. A. W. LINDSAY (Academic and Planning)
Pro Vice-Chancellor: Prof. J. WARREN
Librarian: Prof. E. LIM

Number of teachers: 1,703
Number of students: 42,044

Publications: *Annual Report, Eureka* (Annual Research Report), *VoiCe* (Schools Magazine), *Monash University Magazine, Monash University News, Monash Memo* (weekly).

DEANS

Faculty of Art and Design: Prof. J. K. REDMOND
Faculty of Arts: Prof. M. QUARTLY
Faculty of Business and Economics: Prof. J. RICKARD
Faculty of Information Technology: Prof. J. ROSENBERG
Faculty of Education: Prof. R. T. WHITE
Faculty of Engineering: Prof. M. L. BRISK
Faculty of Law: Prof. C. R. WILLIAMS
Faculty of Medicine: Prof. R. PORTER
Faculty of Science: Prof. R. W. DAVIES

Victorian College of Pharmacy: Prof. C. B. Chapman

PROFESSORS

Faculty of Art and Design:

Redmond, J. K., Industrial Design

Faculty of Arts:

Bigelow, J. C., Philosophy
Bouma, G. D., Sociology
Brown, T. C., Social Work
Caine, B., History
Clyne, M. G., Linguistics
Cokklin, C., Geography and Environmental Science
Davidson, A. B., Politics
Davison, G. J., History
Emy, H. V., Politics
Goldsworthy, D. J., Politics
Grosz, E. A., Critical and Cultural Studies
Hart, K. J., Comparative Literature and Cultural Studies
Jacobs, J. B., Asian Languages and Studies
Kartomi, M. J., Music
Kent, F. W., History
Kershaw, P. A., Geography and Environmental Science
Love, H. H. R., English
Mouer, R., Japanese Studies
Nelson, B., Romance Languages
Pargetter, R. J., Philosophy
Powell, J. M., Geography and Environmental Science
Probyn, C. T., English
Rickard, J. D., Australian Studies
Roberts, D. G. J., German Studies
Singer, P. A. D., Human Bioethics
Spearritt, P., Australian Studies
Ten, C. L., Philosophy
Thomson, P. J., German Studies
Threadgold, T. R., English

Faculty of Business and Economics:

Anderson, A. J., School of Business and Electronic Commerce, Gippsland
Barry, B. A., Management
Brown, R. L., Accounting and Finance
Chenhall, R. H., Accounting and Finance
Dixon, P. B., Policy Studies
FitzRoy, P. T., Marketing
Forsyth, P. J., Economics
Gabbott, T. M., Marketing
Griffin, G. D., Management
Hughes, O. E., Public Sector Management
King, M. L., Econometrics and Business Statistics
Ng, Y., Economics
Parmenter, B. R., Policy Studies
Peirson, C. G., Accounting and Finance
Powell, A. A. L., Econometrics and Business Statistics
Ratnatunga, J. T., Accounting and Finance
Richardson, J., Health Program Evaluation
Romano, C. A., Accounting and Finance
Russell, A. M., Business and Economics
Schroder, W. R., David Syme School of Business
Selby Smith, C., Management
Skully, M. T., Accounting and Finance
Snape, R. H., Economics
Sohal, A., Management
Tharenou, P., Management

Faculty of Information Technology:

Abramson, D., School of Computer Science and Software Engineering
Arnott, D. R., School of Information Management and Systems
Bignall, R., Gippsland School of Computing and Information Technology
Crossley, J. N., School of Computer Science and Software Engineering
Goldschlager, L. M., School of Computer Science and Software Engineering
Hurst, A. J., School of Computer Science and Software Engineering
Lim, E. H. T., School of Information Management and Systems
Schauder, D., School of Information Management and Systems
Schmidt, H. W., School of Computer Science and Software Engineering
Srinivasan, B., School of Computer Science and Software Engineering
Steele, P., Peninsula School of Computing and Information Technology
Willis, R. J., School of Business Systems

Faculty of Education:

Aspin, D. N.
Bishop, A. J.
Gunstone, R. F.
Rizvi, F. A.
White, R. T.

Faculty of Engineering:

Egan, G. K., Electrical and Computer Systems Engineering
Fenton, J. D., Mechanical Engineering
Grundy, P., Civil Engineering
Jarvis, J. R., Gippsland Campus
Jarvis, R. A., Electrical and Computer Systems Engineering
Johnston, R. E., Chemical Engineering
Jones, R., Mechanical Engineering
Mathew, J., Mechanical Engineering, Caulfield
Mathews, J., Chemical Engineering
Mein, R. G., CRC for Catchment Hydrology
Melbourne, W. H., Mechanical Engineering
Muddle, B. C., Materials Engineering
Sridhar, T., Chemical Engineering
Young, W., Civil Engineering, Caulfield

Faculty of Law:

Duggan, A. J.
Fox, R. G.
Lee, H. P.
Neave, M. A.
Ricketson, S.
Trindade, F. A.
Waller, P. L.

Faculty of Medicine:

Anderson, W. P., Physiology
Ashby, M., Palliative Care
Beart, P. M., Pharmacology
Burrows, R. F., Obstetrics and Gynaecology
Coppel, R. L., Microbiology
Cordner, S. M., Forensic Medicine
De Kretser, D. M., Reproduction and Development
Doherty, R. R., Paediatrics
Gibbs, C. L., Physiology
Goding, J. W., Pathology and Immunology
Goodchild, C. S., Anaesthesia
Harding, R., Physiology
Healy, D. L., Obstetrics and Gynaecology
Hearn, M. T. W., Biochemistry and Molecular Biology
Ho, F. C. S., Pathology and Immunology
Holdsworth, S. R., Medicine
Jarrott, B., Pharmacology
Keks, N. A., Psychological Medicine
Kola, I., Reproduction and Development
Kovacs, G. T., Obstetrics and Gynaecology
McNeil, J. J., Epidemiology and Preventive Medicine
Mitchell, C., Biochemistry and Molecular Biology
Mullen, P. E., Psychological Medicine
Murtagh, J., Community Medicine and General Practice
Nagley, P., Biochemistry and Molecular Biology
O'Brien, P. E., Surgery
O'Connor, D. W., Psychological Medicine
O'Dea, K., Medicine
O'Hehir, R. E., Medicine
Piterman, L., Community Medicine and General Practice
Proske, U., Physiology
Rodger, A., Radiation Oncology
Rood, J., Microbiology
Salem, H. H., Medicine
Smith, G. C., Psychological Medicine
Storey, E., Neurosciences
Strasser, R. P., Rural Health
Summers, R. J., Pharmacology
Taylor, G. S., Medical Education
Thomson, N. M., Medicine
Toh, B. H., Pathology and Immunology
Tonge, B. J., Psychological Medicine
Trounson, A. O., Early Human Development
Wahlqvist, M., Medicine
Walters, E. H., Medicine
Workman, G., Geriatric Medicine
Zimmet, P., Biochemistry and Molecular Biology

Faculty of Science:

Bond, A., Chemistry
Bradshaw, J. L., Psychology
Cas, R. A. F., Earth Sciences
Clayton, M., Ecology and Evolutionary Biology
Coleman, G. J. ,Psychology
Cull, J. P., Earth Sciences
Deacon, G. B., Chemistry
Dickson, R. S., Chemistry
Ecker, K., Mathematics
Grimshaw, R. H. J., Mathematics
Hall, W. D. M., Australian Crustal Research Centre
Hamill, J. D., Genetics and Developmental Biology
Hart, B. T., Chemistry
Irvine, D. R. F., Psychology
Jackson, W. R., Chemistry
Karoly, D. J., CRC for Southern Hemisphere Meteorology
Lake, P. S., Ecology and Evolutionary Biology
Lister, G. S., Earth Sciences
MacFarlane, D. R., Chemistry
Monaghan, J. J., Mathematics
Murray, K. S., Chemistry
Ng, K. T., Psychology
Pilbrow, J. R., Physics
Raston, C. L., Chemistry
Ross, D. G., Mathematics
Triggs, T. J., Psychology
Vickers-Rich, P., Earth Sciences, Ecology and Evolutionary Biology

Victorian College of Pharmacy:

Charman, W. N., Pharmaceutics
Reed, B. L., Biopharmaceutics
Stewart, P. J., Pharmaceutics
von Irzstein, M., Medical Chemistry

DIRECTORS

Accident Research Centre: Prof. A. P. Vulcan
Asian Business Research Unit: A. de Jonge
Australian APEC Studies Centre: A. Oxley
Australian Banking Research Unit: C. Viney
Australian Centre for Jewish Civilisation: Adjunct Prof. B. Rechter
Australian Centre for Retail Studies: A. D. Treadgold
Australian Crustal Research Centre: Prof. G. S. Lister
Australian Geodynamics Centre: G. Price
Australian Maritime Engineering Co-operative Research Centre: Dr S. M. Cannon
Australian Pulp and Paper Institute: Prof. R. E. Johnston
Centre for Advanced Materials Technology: Prof. B. C. Muddle
Centre for American Studies: Dr I. Mylchreest
Centre for Applied Mathematical Modelling: Prof. D. G. Ross
Centre for Applied Research and Development: Dr P. Edwards
Centre for Biomedical Engineering: Assoc. Prof. T. I. H. Brown
Centre for Bioprocess Technology: Prof. M. T. W. Hearn

Centre for Clinical Effectiveness: Dr F. Cicuttini
Centre for Comparative Literature and Cultural Studies: Dr C. G. Worth
Centre for Computational Mathematics: Prof. J. J. Monaghan
Centre for Drama and Theatre Studies: Assoc. Prof. P. H. Fitzpatrick
Centre for Dynamical Meteorology and Oceanography: R. H. J. Grimshaw
Centre for Early Childhood Research and Development: Assoc. Prof. A. Stonehouse
Centre for Early Human Development: Prof. A. O. Trounson
Centre of East Asian Studies: Prof. J. B. Jacobs
Centre for Electrical Power Engineering: Prof. R. E. Morrison
Centre for Electronic Commerce: Assoc. Prof. R. Bignall
Centre for European Studies: Prof. B. Nelson
Centre for Freshwater Ecology: Prof. P. Cullen
Centre for Geographical Information Systems: Assoc. Prof. J. A. Peterson
Centre for Gippsland Studies: M. Fletcher
Centre for Graduate Studies in Clinical Nursing: A. Nolan
Centre for Health Programme Evaluation: Prof. J. R. J. Richardson
Centre for Heart and Chest Research: Assoc. Prof. R. Harper
Centre for High Resolution Spectroscopy and Opto-Electronic Technology: Dr P. D. Godfrey
Centre for Higher Education Development: Prof. G. Webb
Centre for Human Bioethics: Dr H. Kuhse
Centre for Industrial Design: A. de Bono (acting)
Centre for Information Systems Practice: R. Sebo
Centre for Koorie Studies: M. Drysdale
Centre for Language and Learning: Assoc. Prof. L. G. Cairns
Centre for Machine Condition Monitoring: Prof. J. Mathew
Centre of Malaysian Studies: Prof. F. Rizvi
Centre for Migrant and Intercultural Studies: Dr G. Tsolidis
Centre for Multimedia and Hypermedia Research: Prof. J. Harris
Centre for Palynology and Palaeoecology: Prof. A. P. Kershaw
Centre for Police and Justice Studies: Assoc. Prof. A. E. Veno
Centre of Policy Studies and IMPACT Project: Prof. P. B. Dixon
Centre for Population and Urban Research: Dr R. J. Birrell
Centre for Research in Accounting and Finance: Prof. C. G. Pierson
Centre for Research in International Education: Prof. F. Rizvi
Centre for Rural Health: Prof. R. Strasser
Centre for Science, Mathematics and Technology Education: Prof. R. F. Gunstone
Centre of Applied and Professional Psychology: Dr G. J. Hyman
Centre of Medical Informatics: Assoc. Prof. B. Cesnik
Centre of South Asian Studies: Assoc. Prof. I. F. S. Copland
Centre of Southeast Asian Studies: Dr B. Hatley
Centre for Stress Management and Research: D. Guidara
Centre for Telecommunications and Information Engineering: Prof. G. K. Egan
Centre for Studies in Religion and Theology: Dr C. J. Mews
Centre for Women's Studies and Gender Research: Dr D. M. Cuthbert
Computer Centre: P. Annal
Co-operative Research Centre for Aerospace Structures: Prof. R. Jones
Co-operative Research Centre for Catchment Hydrology: Prof. R. G. Mein
Co-operative Research Centre for Hardwood Fibre and Paper Science: Prof. R. E. Johnston
Co-operative Research Centre for New Technologies for Power Generation from Low-Rank Coal: Prof. M. L. Brisk
Co-operative Research Centre for Polymers: Dr I. Dagley
Co-operative Research Centre for Southern Hemisphere Meteorology: Prof. D. Karoly
Dairy Process Engineering Centre: Dr R. S. Nicol
David Syme Taxation Research Unit: A. McNicol
David Syme Treasury Dealing Centre: K. G. Tant
Development Studies Centre: Dr S. Blackburn
Distance Education Centre: Prof. J. Harris
Elwyn Morey Child Study Centre: Dr L. Bartak.
Emerge Co-operative Multimedia Centre: Prof. G. K. Egan
Gippsland Centre for Environmental Science: Assoc. Prof. R. Hodges
Institute for Critical and Cultural Studies: Prof. E. Grosz
Institute of Public Health Research: (vacant)
Institute of Transport Studies, the Australian Key Centre in Transport Management, Monash: Prof. W. Young
Institute of Reproduction and Development: Prof. D. M. de Kretser
Intelligent Robotics Research Centre: Prof. R. A. Jarvis
Japanese Studies Centre: Dr A. Tokita
Koorie Research Centre: H. Curzon-Siggers
Krongold Centre for Exceptional Children: Dr L. Bartak
Language and Learning Unit: (vacant)
Language and Society Centre: Prof. M. G. Clyne
Language Unit: Assoc. Prof. U. Felix
Leadership Research Unit: Assoc. Prof. J. Sarros
Monash Asia Institute: Prof. J. McKay
Monash Centre for Environmental Management: F. G. H. Fisher
Monash Manufacturing and Industrial Engineering Centre: Dr J. W. H. Price
Monash Orientation Scheme for Aborigines: H. Curzon-Siggers
Monash Science Centre: Prof. P. Vickers-Rich
Monash University-ACER Centre for the Economics of Education and Training: Assoc. Prof. G. Burke
National Centre for Australian Studies: Prof. P. Spearritt
National Centre for Health Programme Evaluation: Prof. J. Richardson
National Key Centre in Industrial Relations: Prof. G. D. Griffin
Pearcey Centre: K. Hobbs (Exec. Officer)
Playbox Theatre Centre: A. Mellor
Professional Development Institute: M. Kupsch
Quality Management Research Unit: Prof. S. Amrik
Research Data Network Co-operative Research Centre: Prof. G. K. Egan
South Pacific Centre for School and Community Development: Dr A. Townsend
Timber Engineering Centre: Assoc. Prof. H. R. Milner
UNESCO Supported International Centre for Engineering Education: Assoc. Prof. Z. Pudlowski
Victorian Centre for Image Processing and Graphics: Dr R. T. Worley
Water Studies Centre: Prof. B. T. Hart

AFFILIATED INSTITUTIONS

Prince Henry's Institute of Medical Research: Monash Medical Centre, Level 4, Block E, 246 Clayton Road, Clayton, Vic. 3168; tel. (3) 9550-1111; Dir Prof. H. G. Burger.

Baker Medical Research Institute: Alfred Group of Hospitals, Commercial Road, Prahran, Vic. 3181; tel. (3) 9522-4333; Dir Prof. J. W. Funder.

Australian Centre for Contemporary Art Inc.: Dallas Brooks Drive, South Yarra, Vic. 3141; tel. (3) 9654-6422; Dir J. E. Duncan.

MacFarlane Burnet Centre for Medical Research: C/o Fairfield Hospital, Yarra Bend Road, Fairfield, Vic. 3078; tel. (3) 9280-2222; Dir Prof. J. Mills.

Mental Health Research Institute of Victoria: Locked Bag No. 11, Parkville, Vic. 3052; tel. (3) 9388-1633; Dir Prof. D. Copolov.

National Vision Research Institute of Australia: 386 Cardigan St, Carlton, Vic. 3053; tel. (3) 9347-4066; Dir Assoc. Prof. R. C. Augesteyn.

Leo Cussen Institute: 360 Little Bourke St, Melbourne, Vic. 3000; tel. (3) 9602-3111; Exec. Dir M. E. Loftus.

Mannix College: Wellington Road, Clayton, Vic. 3168; tel. (3) 9544-8895; Master Rev. D. P. Minns.

Catholic Theological College: Bayview Avenue, Clayton, Vic. 3168; tel. (3) 9543-1344; Master Rev. M. Coleridge.

Psychiatric Nursing Research Institute: Private Bag 3, Parkville, Vic. 3052; tel. (3) 9342-2333; Dir A. Benson.

Bureau of Meteorology: 150 Lonsdale St, Melbourne, Vic. 3000; tel. (3) 9669-4000; Dir J. W. Zillman.

Victorian Institute of Marine Sciences: Locked Bag 7, Collins St, E. P.O., Melbourne, Vic. 8003; tel. (3) 9412-7320; Dir G. Newman.

MURDOCH UNIVERSITY

Murdoch, WA 6150

Telephone: (8) 9360-6000
Fax: (8) 9310-7049

Founded: 1973; postgraduate courses began 1974; undergraduate courses began 1975
State control
Academic year: February to November

Chancellor: The Hon. Frederick Chaney
Vice-Chancellor: Prof. Steven Schwartz
Deputy Vice-Chancellor: Prof. Jeffrey Gawthorne
Pro Vice-Chancellor (Research): Assoc. Prof. Kateryna O. Longley
Pro Vice-Chancellor (International): Assoc. Prof. Lawrence R. Davidson
Pro Vice-Chancellor (Development): Assoc. Prof. Roger C. Lethbridge
Registrar: Richard N. MacWilliam
Director of Educational and Information Services: V. Nadanasabapathy

Number of teachers: 435
Number of students: 1,870 postgraduate, 8,867 undergraduate

Publications: *Annual Report, Synergy, Research Report, In Touch.*

DEANS

Division of Business, Information Technology and Law: Exec. Dean Prof. A. Davison
Division of Science: Exec. Dean Prof. T. Lyons
Division of Veterinary and Biomedical Sciences: Exec. Dean Prof. J. Yovich
Division of Social Sciences, Humanities and Education: Exec. Dean Assoc. Prof. T. Wright
School of Education: Assoc. Prof. S. Willis
School of Law: Prof. R. Simmonds
School of Engineering: Prof. P. Lee

PROFESSORS

Division of Business, Information Technology and Law:

ARMSTRONG, R. W., Marketing
BLAKENEY, M., Law
DAVISON, A. G., Accounting and Finance
MCLEOD, N. D. B., Law
NORRIS, W. K., Economics
PENDLETON, M. D., Law
SCOTT, I., Politics and Government
SIMMONDS, R., Law
ROBISON, R., South-East Asian Studies
THOMPSON, H. M., Economics

Division of Science:

BLOOM, W. R., Mathematics and Statistics
CARNEGIE, P., Biotechnology
DILWORTH, M. J., Microbiology and Biochemistry
GILES, R. G. F., Chemistry and Mineral Science
JAMES, I., Mathematics and Statistics
JONES, M. G. K., Plant Sciences
LYONS, T. J., Environmental Science
NICOL, M. J., Mineral Science
POTTER, I. C., Animal Biology
RITCHIE, I. M., Chemistry and Mineral Science
WEBB, J. M., Chemistry

Division of Veterinary and Biomedical Sciences:

PENHALE, W. J., Microbiology and Immunology
SWAN, R. A., Veterinary Clinical Studies
THOMPSON, A., Parasitology
WILCOX, G. E., Virology

Division of Social Sciences, Humanities and Education:

ANDRICH, D., Education
BALDOCK, C., Sociology
DE GARIS, B., History
FRODSHAM, J. D., English and Comparative Literature
HILL, B. V., Education
INNES, M., Psychology
NEWMAN, P., Science and Technology Policy
O'TOOLE, L. M., Communication Studies
RUTHROF, H. G., English and Comparative Literature

School of Engineering:

LEE, P. L., Instrumentation and Control Engineering
ROY, G., Software Engineering

DIRECTORS

A. J. Parker Co-operative Research Centre for Hydrometallurgy: Prof. I. RITCHIE
Asia-Pacific Centre for Human Rights and the Prevention of Ethnic Conflicts: Dr F. DE VARENNES
Asia-Pacific Intellectual Property Law Institute: Prof. M. PENDLETON
Asia Research Centre on Social, Political and Economic Change: Prof. R. ROBISON
Australian Co-operative Research Centre for Renewable Energy: M. THOMAS
Centre for Atomic, Molecular and Surface Physics (jointly with Univ. of Western Australia): Dr A. T. STELBOVICS, Prof. J. F. WILLIAMS
Centre for Curriculum and Professional Development: Assoc. Prof. S. GRUNDY
Centre for Federal and Regional Studies: Dr F. HARMAN
Centre for Labour Market Research: Dr T. STROMBECK (Curtin University of Technology)
Centre for Production Animal Research: Assoc. Prof. D. H. HAMPSON
Centre for Research in Culture and Communication: Dr T. O'REGAN
Centre for Research on Women: A. GOLDFLAM
Centre for Rhizobium Studies: Adjunct Assoc. Prof. J. HOWIESON
Co-operative Research Centre for Legumes in Mediterranean Agriculture: Prof. J. HAMBLIN (University of Western Australia)
Energy Research Institute: Dr T. PRYOR
Environmental Law and Policy Centre: Dr J. MUGAMBWA
Institute for Environmental Science: Assoc. Prof. G. HO
Institute for Molecular Genetics and Animal Disease: Prof. A. THOMPSON
Institute for Research in Safety and Transport: Assoc. Prof. L. R. HARTLEY
Institute for Science and Technology Policy: Prof. P. NEWMAN
Institute for Social Programme Evaluation: Prof. D. ANDRICH
Office of Continuing Veterinary Education: M. G. BREDHAUER
State Agricultural Biotechnology Centre: Prof. M. G. K. JONES

UNIVERSITY OF NEW ENGLAND

Armidale, NSW 2351

Telephone: (2) 6773-3333
Fax: (2) 6773-3122

Founded 1954; previously New England University College (f. 1938); Armidale College of Advanced Education amalgamated with the University in 1989
Commonwealth govt control
Academic year: February to November (2 semesters)

Chancellor: Dr P. J. O'SHANE
Deputy Chancellor: F. FISHER
Vice-Chancellor: Prof. I. MOSES
Deputy Vice-Chancellor: Prof. M. STODDART (Academic)
Pro Vice-Chancellor: Prof. R. GERBER (Research and International, acting)
Executive Director: G. DENNEHY (Business and Administration)
Secretary to Council: B. W. LANCASTER
Librarian: K. G. SCHMUDE

Library: see under Libraries

Number of teachers: 497
Number of students: 16,280

Publications: *Research Report, Smith's, Annual Report, Afterthoughts.*

DEANS

Faculty of Arts: Prof. W. G. MADDOX
Faculty of the Sciences: Prof. K. W. ENTWISTLE
Faculty of Economics, Business and Law: Prof. P. J. HUTCHINSON
Faculty of Education, Health and Professional Studies: Prof. R. GERBER

PROFESSORS

ATKINSON, A. T., Classics and History
BARKER, J. S. F., Animal Science
BYRNE, B. J., Psychology
CROFT, J. C. B., English, Communication and Theatre Studies
DANTHANARAYANA, W., Zoology
DAVIDSON, I., Geography, Planning, Archaeology and Palaeoanthropology
EGAN, A. F., Animal Science
FALKUS, M. E., Economic History
FORREST, P. R. H., Social Science
GOSSIP, C. J., Languages, Cultures and Linguistics
GRIFFITHS, W. E., Econometrics
HARMAN, G. S., Administration and Training
HEWISON, K. J., Social Science
HORSLEY, G. H. R., Classics and Ancient History
HUTCHINSON, P. J., Accounting and Financial Management
JARMAN, P. J., Ecosystem Management
KIERNANDER, A. R. D., English, Communication and Theatre
KINGHORN, B. P., Animal Science
MADDOX, W. G., Political Science
MAGNER, E. S., Law
MARTIN, P. R., Psychology
MAURER, O., Agricultural and Resource Economics/Marketing and Management
PIGGOTT, R. R., Agricultural and Resource Economics
PIGRAM, J. J. J., Centre for Water Policy Research
PRASADA RAO, D. S., Econometrics
RITCHIE, G. L. D., Chemistry
ROGERS, L. J., Zoology
ROHDE, K., Zoology
ROWE, J. B., Animal Science
TEATHER, D. C. B., Administration and Training
TREADGOLD, M. L., Economics
VAN LEEUWEN, J., Environmental Engineering
WALMSLEY, D. J., Geography, Planning, Archaeology and Palaeoanthropology

ATTACHED RESEARCH INSTITUTES

(The mailing address is that of the University, Armidale)

Agricultural Business Research Institute: Dir P. A. RICKARDS.

Animal Genetics and Breeding Unit: Dir Dr M. GODDARD.

Centre for Australian Language and Literature Studies (CALLS): Dir Dr R. J. MCDOUGALL.

Centre for Cognition Research in Learning and Teaching: Dir Assoc. Prof. J. E. PEGG.

Centre for Efficiency and Productivity Analysis: Dir Prof. D. S. PRASADA RAO.

Centre for Health Research and Development: Dir Assoc. Prof. K. A. PARTON.

Centre for Research in Aboriginal and Multicultural Studies: Dir Assoc. Prof. A.-K. ECKERMANN.

Centre for Local Government: Dir Assoc. Prof. V. E. WRIGHT.

Co-operative Research Centre for the Beef and Cattle Industry (Meat Quality): Dir Prof. B. BINDON.

Co-operative Research Centre for Premium Quality Wool: Dir Dr L. E. WARD.

Centre for Water Policy Research: Exec. Dir Assoc. Prof. J. J. J. PIGRAM.

Institute for Bioregional Resource Management: Dir D. J. BRUNCKHORST.

Institute of Biotechnology: Dir Dr B. ENTSCH.

Institute of Ecology: Dir Assoc. Prof. H. A. FORD.

Rural Development Centre: Exec. Dir R. A. STAYNER (acting).

UNE Asia Centre: Dir Prof. M. E. FALKUS.

UNIVERSITY OF NEW SOUTH WALES

Sydney, NSW 2052

Telephone: (2) 9385-1000
Telex: 26054
Fax: (2) 9385-2000

Founded 1948
Incorporated by Act of Parliament 1949
Academic year: February to November (2 sessions)

Chancellor: The Hon. Sir A. F. MASON
Vice-Chancellor and Principal: Prof. J. R. NILAND
Deputy Vice-Chancellors: Prof. A. J. WICKEN, Prof. C. J. D. FELL
Pro-Vice-Chancellor: Assoc. Prof. J. Y. MORRISON
Registrar and Deputy Principal: C. CONDOUS
Exec. Director, Business and Finance: C. M. LIDBURY
Director of Information Services and Deputy Principal: C. A. PAGE-HANIFY
Principal Librarian: MARIAN BATE
Number of teachers: 2,222

Number of students: 30,745

Publications: *Calendar* (annually), *Faculty Handbooks, Annual Report, UNSW Prospectus* (annually), *UNSW International Prospectus* (annually), *Uniken, Focus* (fortnightly), *Graduate Review* (2 a year).

DEANS

Faculty of Science and Technology: Prof. C. E. SUTHERLAND
Faculty of the Built Environment: Prof. C. T. WU
Faculty of Engineering: Prof. M. S. WAINWRIGHT
Faculty of Life Sciences: Prof. M. J. SLEIGH
Faculty of Arts and Social Sciences: Prof. J. E. INGLESON
Faculty of Commerce and Economics: Prof. R. A. LAYTON
Faculty of Medicine: Prof. S. B. DOWTON
Faculty of Law: Prof. P. M. REDMOND
Australian Graduate School of Management: Prof. P. DODD
University College: Prof. J. A. RICHARDS
Board of Studies in Science and Mathematics: Prof. C. E. SUTHERLAND
Board of Studies in Taxation: Prof. R. L. DEUTSCH
College of Fine Arts: Prof. K. B. REINHARD

PROFESSORS

AKGUN, F., Petroleum Engineering
ALBURY, W. R., Science and Technology
ALEXANDER, P. F., English
ANDERSON, E., Management
ANDREWS, J. G., Psychiatry
ARCHER, M., Biological Science
ARONSON, M. I., Law
ASHBURN, E., Art
ASHFORD, A. E., Botany
BALLINGER, J. A., Architecture
BARRY, P. H., Physiology
BAUME, P. E., Community Medicine
BELL, P. B., Media and Communications
BELL, R. J., History
BENNETT, M. J., Obstetrics and Gynaecology
BEWLEY, R. A., Econometrics
BIRKETT, W., Accounting
BLACK, D. S., Organic Chemistry
BLACK, J. A., Transport Engineering
BODE, H. H., Paediatrics
BOROWSKI, A., Social Work
BRODATY, H., Psychiatry
BROOKS, A. S., Law
BROOKS, P. M., Medicine
BROWN, D. B., Law
BUCKLE, K. A., Food Science and Technology
BURGESS, P. N., Law
BURKE, D. J., Neurology, Clinical Research
BYRNE, K. P., Applied Mechanics
CALVERT, G. D., Medicine
CARMICHAEL, D. G., Civil Engineering
CELLER, B. G., Electrical Engineering
CHAN, M. E., English
CHAPMAN, M., Obstetrics and Gynaecology
CHESTERMAN, C. N., Medicine, Pathology
CHESTERMAN, M., Law
CHISHOLM, D. J., Medicine, Metabolic Research
CHONG, B. H., Medicine
CHU, P. L., Electrical Engineering
CHUA, W. F., Accounting
CLARK, R. G., Experimental Physics
CLINCH, G. J., Management
COLLINS, R. R., Management
CONDREN, C. S., Political Science
COOPER, D. A., Medicine
COOPER, M., Education Management
CORONEO, M. T., Ophthalmology
COSTER, H., Biophysics
COWLING, M. G., Pure Mathematics
COX, P., Architecture
CROSS, J., Safety Engineering
CUTHBERT, R. A., Town Planning
DANCE, I. G., Inorganic Chemistry
DAVIES, D. J., Pathology
DAVIS, J. G. A., Management
DAWES, I. W., Genetics
DAWES, J., Physiology and Pharmacology
DAWSON, T. J., Zoology
DAY, R. O., Medicine, Clinical Pharmacology
DEANE, S. A., Surgery
DEUTSCH, R. L., Taxation
DICKSON, H. G., Rehabilitation, Aged and Extended Care
DODD, P., Management
DONALDSON, D. A., Management
DUNN, N. W., Biotechnology
DUNPHY, D. C., Management
DUNSMUIR, W., Statistics
DWYER, J. M., Medicine
EAGLESON, G. K., Management
EDMONDS, J. P., Medicine
EHRLICH, F., Rehabilitation, Aged and Extended Care
EISMAN, J. A., Medicine, Bone and Mineral Research
ELLIOTT, R. T., Education Studies
FANE, A. G., Chemical Engineering and Industrial Chemistry
FELL, C. J. D., Chemical Engineering and Industrial Chemistry
FELL, R., Civil Engineering
FINLAY-JONES, R. A., Psychiatry
FITZGERALD, S., Asia–Australia Studies
FLAMBAUM, V., Theoretical Physics
FLEET, G. H., Food Science and Technology
FLETCHER, C. A. J., Engineering
FOO, N. Y., Computer Science
FORGAS, J. P., Psychology
FORSTER, B. C., Geomatic Engineering
FOSTER, N. R., Chemical Engineering and Industrial Chemistry
FOX, B. J., Biological Science
FRENKEL, S. J., Management
GALVIN, J. M., Mining Engingeering
GANDEVIA, S. C., Medicine
GARNER, B. J., Geography
GAUDRY, G. A., Pure Mathematics
GECZY, C., Pathology
GIBB, D. B., Anaesthetics and Intensive Care, Physiology and Pharmacology
GILBERT, R. I., Civil Engineering
GILLAM, B. J., Psychology
GOVETT, G. J. S., Geology
GRAHAM, R., Medicine
GRAY, P. P., Biotechnology
GRAY, S. J., Asian Business and Language Studies
GRBICH, Y., Taxation
GREEN, M. A., Electronics
HAHN, E. J., Applied Mechanics
HALL, B. M., Medicine
HALL, R., Social Science and Policy
HALL, W. D., Drug and Alcohol Research
HAM, J. M., Surgery
HANEMAN, D., Physics
HARRIS, M. F., General Practice
HARRISON, G. A., Anaesthetics
HEBBLEWHITE, B. K., Mining Engineering
HELLESTRAND, G. R., Computer Science
HENRY, R. L., Paediatrics
HIBBERT, D. B., Analytical Chemistry
HILLER, J., Computer Science
HILLMAN, K. M., Anaesthetics and Intensive Care
HILMER, F. G., Management
HIRST, M. K., Management
HOLDEN, B. A., Optometry
HOLLINGTON, M. A., English
HOWE, R. F., Physical Chemistry
HOWES, L. G., Medicine, Physiology
HOWLETT, C. R., Pathology
INGLESON, J. E., History
JACK, R. C., Architecture
JEFFERY, D. R., Information Systems
JOHNSON, R., Spanish and Latin American Studies
JORDAN, R. J., Theatre Studies
KAEBERNIK, H., Industrial Technology and Management
KAKWANI, N. C., Statistics
KALDOR, J., Epidemiology
KEARSLEY, J. H., Surgery
KEHOE, E. J., Psychology
KEMP, M. C., Economics
KESSLER, C. S., Sociology
KHURANA, A. K., Petroleum Engineering
KING, R. J., Biological Science
KJELLEBERG, S., Microbiology
KOHN, R., Management
KOLLAR, L. P., Architecture
KRILIS, S. A., Medicine
KRYGIER, M. E. J., Law
LANG, J., Architecture
LAWRENCE, M. J., Information Systems
LAWRENCE, R. J., Social Work
LAWSON, J. S., Health Services Management
LAYTON, R. A., Marketing
LAZARUS, L., Medicine, Pathology
LEE, A., Medical Microbiology
LESLIE, L. M., Applied Mathematics
LLOYD, G. M., Philosophy
LORD, R. S. A., Surgery
LUMBERS, E. R., Physiology
MCCLOSKEY, D. I., Physiology, Medical Research
MCCONKEY, K. M., Psychology
MACDONALD, G. J., Medicine
MCLACHLAN, E. M., Physiology, Medical Research
MIDDLETON, J. H. F., Applied Mathematics
MIDGLEY, D. F., Management
MILBORROW, B. V., Biochemistry
MILFULL, J. R., German Studies
MILTON, B. E., Nuffield Prof. of Mechanical Engineering
MINDEL, A., Sexual Health Medicine
MORRIS, D. L., Surgery
MORRISON, G. L., Mechanical and Manufacturing Engineering
MORRISON, I. F., Electrical Engineering
NEILSON, D., Physics
NETTHEIM, R. G., Law
NEVILE, J. W., Economics
O'FARRELL, P. J., History
OITMAA, J., Physics
OLDROYD, D. R., History and Philosophy of Science
O'ROURKE, M. F., Medicine
O'SULLIVAN, W. J., Medical Biochemistry
PADDON-ROW, M. N., Chemistry
PAILTHORPE, M. T., Textile Technology
PALMER, G. R., Health Services Management
PARKER, G. B., Psychiatry
PATTERSON, C., Mechanical Engineering
PAXINOS, G., Psychology
PEARSON, M. N., History
PENNY, R., Clinical Immunology
PIGGOTT, J., Economics
PINCZEWOKI, W. V., Petroleum Engineering
PINSON, P. L., Art
POOLE, M. D., Surgery
POSTLE, R., Textile Physics
PUSEY, M., Sociology
QUINLAN, M., Industrial Relations
RAYWARD, W. B., Librarianship
REDMOND, P. M., Law
REES, N. W., Systems and Control
RIGBY, G. A., Electrical Engineering
ROBERTS, J., Geology
ROBERTS, J. H., Management
ROGERS, C., Applied Mathematics
ROGERS, P. L., Biotechnology
ROSSITER, J., Management
ROTEM, A., Medical Education
ROWE, M. J., Physiology
ROWLEY, S., Art History
ROXBOROUGH, F. F., Mining Engineering
RUSSELL, P., Medicine
SANDEMAN, D. C., Zoology
SCHINDHELM, K., Biomedical Engineering
SHARPE, I. G., Finance
SHINE, J., Biotechnology, Medicine, Neurobiology
SILOVE, D. M., Psychiatry
SIMNET, R., Accounting

Skyllas-Kazacos, M., Chemical Engineering and Industrial Chemistry
Sleigh, M., Biotechnology
Sloan, I. H., Applied Mathematics
Smith, T., Management
Sorrell, C. C., Ceramic Engineering
Stewart, B. W., Paediatrics, Children's Leukaemia and Cancer Research Centre
Storey, J. W. V., Physics
Sutherland, C. E., Mathematics
Sutherland, R. L., Medicine, Cancer Biology
Svensson, N. L., Mechanical Engineering
Sweller, J., Education
Thompson, P., Architecture
Torda, T. A. G., Anaesthetics and Intensive Care
Tracey, D. J., Anatomy
Trimm, D. L., Chemical Technology
Trinder, J. C., Surveying
Trotman, K. T., Accounting
Turner, D., Management
Uncles, M., Marketing
Valliappan, S., Geotechnical Engineering
Vinson T., Social Work
Wainwright, M. S., Chemical Engineering and Industrial Chemistry
Waite, T. D., Civil Engineering
Wakefield, D., Pathology
Walker, R. G., Accounting
Webster, I. W., Public Health
Weirick, J., Landscape Architecture
White, L., Paediatrics
Whittred, G., Management
Whitworth, J. A., Medicine
Wicken, A. J., Microbiology and Immunology
Winterton, G. G., Law
Wong, F. W. S., Obstetrics and Gynaecology
Wood, R., Management
Yetton, P., Management
Young, D. J., Materials Science and Engineering

ASSOCIATE COLLEGES

University College, Australian Defence Force Academy: Northcott Drive, Campbell, ACT 2601; tel. (2) 6268-8111; f. 1981 by agreement between the Commonwealth of Australia and the Univ. of NSW; degree courses started 1986; Rector Prof. H. P. Heseltine; Sec. T. R. Earle.

PROFESSORS

Arnold, J. F., Electrical Engineering
Bearman, R. J., Chemistry
Bennett, B. H., English
Cotton, J., Politics
Dennis, P. J., History
Duggins, R. K., Mechanical Engineering
Jackson, W. G., Chemistry
Kasper, W. E., Economics and Management
McLean, R. F., Geography
Newton, C. S., Computer Science
Pask, C., Mathematics
Richards, J. A., Electrical Engineering
Sammut, R. A., Mathematics
Young, I. R., Civil Engineering

Faculty of the College of Fine Arts: Selwyn St., Paddington, NSW 2021; Tel. (2) 9385-0888; f. 1990 following amalgamation of the City Art Institute and the University; Dean and Dir Prof. Kenneth B. Reinhard.

ASSOCIATED INSTITUTE

Australian Graduate School of Management: Sydney, NSW 2052; tel. (2) 9931-9200; f. 1975; postgraduate MBA and PhD courses, residential courses for executives; 42 faculty mems; library of 25,000 vols; Dir Prof. P. Dodd; publs *Australian Journal of Management, AGSM Working Paper Series*.

UNIVERSITY OF NEWCASTLE

University Drive, Callaghan, NSW 2308
Telephone: (49) 215000
Fax: (49) 216922

Founded 1965
State control
Academic year: March to November (2 semesters)

Chancellor: Ric Charlton
Vice-Chancellor: Prof. Roger Holmes
Deputy Vice-Chancellor: Prof. Brian English
Deputy Vice-Chancellor (Research): Prof. Ron MacDonald
Pro Vice-Chancellor (External Relations); Prof. Jenny Graham
Secretary and Registrar: Gem Cheong
Director, Central Coast Campus: Prof. Les Eastcott
Librarian: W. C. Linklater

Library: see under Libraries
Academic staff: 800
Number of students: 18,000

Publications: *Annual Report, Cetus* (annually), *Etcetera* (monthly).

DEANS

Faculty of Architecture: Prof. B. S. Maitland
Faculty of Art and Design: Prof. W. McKenna
Faculty of Arts and Social Science: Prof. J. Ramsland
Faculty of Economics and Commerce: Prof. A. Dobson
Faculty of Education: Prof. T. Lovat
Faculty of Engineering: Prof. A. W. Page
Faculty of Law: Prof. N. R. Rees
Faculty of Medicine and Health Science: Prof. R. Sanson-Fisher
Faculty of Music: Assoc. Prof. R. A. Constable
Faculty of Nursing: Prof. M. McMillan
Faculty of Science and Mathematics: Prof. D. C. Finlay

PROFESSORS

Faculty of Architecture:

Maitland, B. S., Architecture
McGeorge, W. D., Building

Faculty of Arts and Social Science:

Bryson, L. J., Sociology
Dutton, K. R., French
Emeljanow, V. E., Drama
English, B. A., Social Work
Frost, D. L., English
Hooker, C. A., Philosophy
Morton, L. D., Japanese
Ramsland, J. History
Tarrant, H. A. S., Classics

Faculty of Economics and Commerce:

Aisbett, J., Management
Bray, M., Management
Clarke, F. L., Accounting
Dobson, A. J., Biostatistics
Easton, S., Accounting and Finance
Graham, P., Management
Hughes, D. B., Economics
McFarlane, B. J., Economics
Winsen, J. K., Commerce

Faculty of Education:

Bourke, S. F., Education
Clements, M. A., Education
Laura, R. S., Education
Lovat, T., Education

Faculty of Engineering:

Antonia, R. A., Mechanical Engineering
Chambers, A. J., Mechanical Engineering
Eades, P. D., Computer Science
Fryer, J. G., Photogrammetry
Goodwin, G. C., Electrical Engineering
Jameson, G. J., Chemical Engineering
Kalma, J. D., Environmental Engineering
Ledwich, G., Power Engineering
Melchers, R. G., Civil Engineering
Murch, G. E., Materials Engineering
Page, A. W., Structural Clay Brickwork
Page, N. W., Mechanical Engineering
Roberts, A., Mechanical Engineering
Schröder, H., Microelectronics
Wall, T. G., Fuels and Combustion Engineering

Faculty of Law:

Bates, F. A., Law
Pengilley, W. J., Commercial Law
Rees, N. R., Law

Faculty of Medicine and Health Sciences:

Bogduk, N., Anatomy
Boura, A., Reproductive Medicine
Burns, G., Medical Biochemistry, Cancer Research
Burton, R. C., Surgical Science
Carr, V. J., Psychiatry
Christie, D. G. S., Environmental and Occupational Health
Clancy, R. L., Pathology
Cutfield, G., Anaesthesia and Intensive Care
Dunkley, P. R., Medical Biochemistry
Fletcher, P. J., Cardiovascular Medicine
Forbes, J. F., Surgical Oncology
Hamilton, J. D., Medicine
Heller, R. F., Community Medicine and Clinical Epidemiology
Henry, R. L., Paediatrics
Hensley, M. J., Medicine
Ravenscroft, P. J., Palliative Care
Reid, A. L. A., General Practice
Roberts, D. C. K., Nutrition and Dietetics
Sanson-Fisher, R. W., Behavioural Science in relation to Medicine
Smith, A. J., Clinical Pharmacology
Smith, R., Medicine
Spigelman, A., Surgical Science
Vimpani, G. V., Community, Child and Family Health
Walters, W. A. W., Reproductive Medicine
White, S. W., Human Physiology

Faculty of Music:

Constable R., Music

Faculty of Nursing:

Baker, H., Nursing
Madjar, I., Nursing
McMillan, M., Nursing
Stein, I., Nursing

Faculty of Science and Mathematics:

Colhoun, E. A., Geography
Cox, S., Geology
Finlay, D. C., Psychology
Fraser, B. J., Physics
King, M. G., Psychology
Lawrance, G. A., Chemistry
MacDonald, R. J., Physics
Raeburn, I. F., Mathematics
Wills, R. B. H., Food Technology

ATTACHED RESEARCH INSTITUTES

Cooperative Research Centre for Black Coal Utilisation: Dir Prof. R. J. MacDonald.

Cooperative Research Centre for Marsupial Conservation and Management: Head Dr M. Lin.

Australian Centre for Resources Engineering: Dir Emer. Prof. A. Roberts.

Centre for Clinical Epidemiology and Biostatistics: Dir Prof. R. Heller.

Centre for Health Law, Ethics and Policy: Dir Jo Cooper (acting).

Centre for Literary and Linguistic Computing: Dir Emer. Prof. J. Burrows.

Centre for Nursing Practice, Development and Research: Dir Prof. M. McMillan (acting).

Employment Studies Centre: Dir Dr R. Green.

Family Action Centre: Dir D. James

Institute for Bulk Materials Handling: Dir Emer. Prof. A. Roberts.

Institute of Coal Research: Dir Dr K. Moelle.

Institute of Industrial Economics: Dir B. Gibson.

Maternal Health Research Centre: Head Assoc. Prof. R. Smith.

Newcastle Legal Centre: Dir J. Boersig

Research Institute for Gender and Health: Dir Dr W. Brown

Special Education Centre: Dir Assoc. Prof. P. J. Foreman.

Special Research Centre for Industrial Control Science: Dir Prof. G. Goodwin.

NORTHERN TERRITORY UNIVERSITY

Darwin, NT 0909

Telephone: (8) 8946-6666
Fax: (8) 8927-0612

Founded 1989 from the merger of University College of the Northern Territory and the Darwin Institute of Technology
Federal control
Academic year: February to November

Chancellor: N. Giese
Vice-Chancellor: Prof. Ron McKay
Pro Vice-Chancellor (Vocational Education and Training and International): A. Barnaart
Pro Vice-Chancellor (Higher Education and Research): Assoc. Prof. C. Webb
Pro Vice-Chancellor (Administration and Registrar): Kevin Davis
Pro Vice-Chancellor (Information Resources): Alex Byrne

Number of academic staff: 400
Number of students: 11,000

DEANS

Aboriginal and Torres Strait Islander Studies: Assoc. Prof. I. Brown
Arts: Assoc. Prof. C. Healey
Business: Prof. N. Baydoun
Education: Assoc. Prof. B. Devlin
Foundation Studies: L. Skertchly
Industrial Education and Training: D. Kuhl
Law: Prof. N. Aughterson
Science: Prof. G. Hill
Technology: W. Jessup

UNIVERSITY OF QUEENSLAND

Qld 4072

Telephone: (7) 3365-1111
Telex: 40315
Fax: (7) 3365-1199

Founded 1910
Academic year: January to December (two semesters, and summer session)

Chancellor: Hon. Sir Llewellyn Edwards
Deputy Chancellor: Dr M. D. Mahoney
Vice-Chancellor: Prof. J. A. Hay
Senior Deputy Vice-Chancellor: Prof. E. T. Brown
Deputy Vice-Chancellor (Research): P. F. Greenfield
Pro Vice-Chancellor (Academic): Prof. T. J. Grigg
University Secretary and Registrar: D. Porter
Librarian: J. B. Schmidt

Library: see Libraries
Number of teachers: 1,407, including 153 professors
Number of students: 27,698

Publications: *University News, Annual Report*

EXECUTIVE DEANS

Faculty of Arts: Prof. A. G. Rix
Faculty of Biological and Chemical Sciences: Prof. M. McManus
Faculty of Business, Economics and Law: Prof. J. W. Longworth
Faculty of Engineering, Physical Sciences and Architecture: Prof. P. F. Greenfield
Faculty of Health Sciences: Prof. P. M. Brooks
Faculty of Natural Resources, Agriculture and Veterinary Science: Prof. C. J. Pearson
Faculty of Social and Behavioural Sciences: Prof. L. S. Rosenman

HEADS OF SCHOOL

School of Architecture and Planning: M. D. Keniger
School of Dentistry: Prof. G. J. Seymour
Graduate School of Education: Prof. A. Luke
School of Engineering: Prof. J. M. Simmons
School of Health and Rehabilitation Sciences: Prof. M. I. Bullock.
School of Information Technology: Prof. P. A. Bailes
School of Land and Food: Assoc. Prof. B. W. Norton
School of Law: Dr S. Ratnapala
School of Mathematics and Physical Sciences: Prof. J. A. Eccleston
Graduate School of Medicine: Prof. C. B. Campbell
School of Music: Dr P. K. Bracanin
School of Natural and Rural Systems Management: Assoc. Prof. R. Beeton
School of Pharmacy: Assoc. Prof. S. E. Tett
School of Psychology: Prof. S. H. Spence
School of Social Work and Social Policy: Prof. D. I. O'Connor
School of Veterinary Science and Animal Production: Prof. K. L. Hughes

PROFESSORS AND HEADS OF DEPARTMENTS

(H = Non-professorial Head of Dept)

Arts:

Almond, P. C., Studies in Religion
Bracanin, P. K., Music (H)
Christa, T. M., German Studies (H)
Crook, D. P., History
Cryle, P. M., Romance Languages
Frow, J. A., English
Gillies, M. G. W., Music
Jurgensen, M., German
Lattke, M. S., Studies in Religion
Louie, K., Chinese
Milns, R. D., Classics and Ancient History
Nuyen, A. T., Philosophy (H)
Pittam, J., English (H)
Priest, G. G., Philosophy
Rix, A. G., Japanese
Stuart-Fox, M., History (H)
Sussex, R. D., Language Teaching and Research
Tiffin, H. M., English
Turner, G., English
Watts, D., Classics and Ancient History (H)

Biological and Chemical Sciences:

Abernethy, A. B., Human Movement Studies
Adams, D. J., Physiology
Andrews, P. R., Drug Design and Development
Campbell, G. R., Anatomical Sciences
Campbell, J. H., Anatomical Sciences
Cooksley, W. G. E., Biochemistry
Cotton, J. D., Chemistry (H)
Craik, D. J., Drug Design and Development
De Jersey, J., Biochemistry
Dobson, C., Parasitology
Doddrell, D., Magnetic Resonance
Gordh, G., Entomology
Grigg, G. C., Zoology
Hume, D. A., Microbiology
Irwin, J. A. G., Botany
James, D. E., Physiology and Pharmacology
Jamieson, B. G. M., Zoology
Kirk, D., Human Movement Studies
Kitching, W., Chemistry
Lester, R. J. G., Parasitology
Mackenzie, J. S., Microbiology
MacKinnon, I. D. R., Microscopy and Microanalysis
Mattick, J. S., Molecular Biology
McManus, M. E., Pharmacology
O'Donnell, S. R., Physiology and Pharmacology
Pettigrew, J. D., Physiology and Pharmacology
Scott, K. J., Biochemistry
Waters, M., Physiology and Pharmacology
Wentrup, C., Organic Chemistry
Winzor, D. J., Biochemistry

Business, Economics and Law:

Anderson, D. K., Managerial Accounting
Callan, V. J., Management
Campbell, H. F., Economics
Craig-Smith, S. J., Hospitality, Tourism and Property Management
Finn, F. J., Finance
Fogg, A. S., Law
Foster, J., Economics
Kiel, G. C., Management
Moens, G. A., Law
Tisdell, C. A., Economics
Weber, R. A. G., Commerce
Wiltshire, K. W., Public Administration
Zimmer, I. R., Accounting

Engineering, Physical Sciences and Architecture:

Apelt, C. J., Civil Engineering
Bailes, P. A., Information Technology
Bracken, A. J., Mathematics
Bremhorst, K., Mechanical Engineering
Burrage, K., Computational Mathematics
Collerson, K. D., Earth Sciences
Darveniza, M., Electrical and Computer Engineering
Dimitrakopoulos, R. G., Mining Geology
Do, D. D., Chemical Engineering
Doddrell, D. M., Magnetic Resonance
Downs, T., Electrical and Computer Engineering
Drummond, P. D., Theoretical Physics
Dunlop, G. L., Materials Engineering
Eccleston, J. A., Statistics and Probability
Greenfield, P. F., Chemical Engineering
Hood, M., CRC for Mining Technology and Equipment
Johnson, N. W., Minerals Engineering
Kaplan, S. M., Information Technology
Keniger, M. D., Architecture (H)
Kitipornchai, S., Civil Engineering
Lister, A. M., Information Technology
Longstaff, I. D., Electrical and Computer Engineering
McDonald, G. T., Geographical Sciences and Planning
McKee, D. J., Minerals Engineering
Milburn, G. J., Physics
Murthy, D. N. P., Engineering and Operations Management
Napier-Munn, T. J., Minerals Processing
Orlowska, M. E., Information Technology
Playford, G., Earth Sciences
Pohl, J. H., Chemical Engineering
Rudolph, V., Chemical Engineering (H)
St John, D. H., Solidification Technology
Simmons, J. M., Engineering
Staples, J., Information Technology
Stimson, R. J., Australian Housing and Urban Research Institute
Street, A. P., Mathematics
Volker, R. E., Civil Engineering
Welsh, J., Information Technology
White, E. T., Chemical Engineering

Health Sciences:

Bartold, P. M., Dentistry
Batch, J. A., Paediatrics and Child Health
Black, M. E., Public Health
Boyd, A. W., Experimental Haematology
Bullock, M. I., Physiotherapy
Burns, Y. R., Physiotherapy (H)
Campbell, C. B., Medicine
Colditz, P. B., Perinatal Research
Crandon, A. J., Gynaecological Oncology
del Mar, C. B., General Practice

DONALD, K. J., Social and Preventive Medicine
DONNELLY, P. K., Surgery
FRAZER, I. H., Medicine
FREER, T. J., Dentistry
GARDINER, R. A., Surgery (H)
GEFFEN, L. B., Psychiatry
GORDON, R. D., Medicine
HANCOCK, J. F., Experimental Oncology
HAYS, R. B., General Practice and Rural Health
HIRST, L. W., Ophthalmology
HUMPHREY, M. D., Obstetrics and Gynaecology
HUNTER, E. M. M., Public Health
JASS, J. R., Pathology
JONES, I. S. C., Obstetrics and Gynaecology
JONES, R. D. M., Anaesthesiology and Intensive Care
KHOO, S. K., Obstetrics and Gynaecology
LA BROOY, J. T., Medicine
LAVIN, M. F., Molecular Oncology
MCCARTHY, S. T., Geriatric Medicine
MANDERSON, L., Tropical Health
MARSDEN, F. W., Orthopaedic Surgery
MOORE, M. R., National Research Centre for Environmental Toxicology
MURDOCH, B. E., Speech Pathology and Audiology
NURCOMBE, B., Child and Adolescent Psychiatry
PEARN, J. H., Paediatrics and Child Health
PEGG, S. P., Burns Surgery
PENDER, M. P., Medicine
POWELL, L. W., Medicine
RILEY, I. D., Tropical Health
ROBERTS, M. S., Clinical Pharmacology
SAUNDERS, J. B., Alcohol and Drug Studies
SEAWRIGHT, A. A., National Research Centre for Environmental Toxicology
SEYMOUR, G. J., Dentistry
SHEPHERD, R. W., Paediatrics and Child Health
STRONG, J., Occupational Therapy
STRONG, R. W., Surgery
TRIGGS, E. J., Pharmacy
WARD, B. G., Gynaecological Oncology
WEST, M. J., Cardiovascular Research
YELLOWLEES, P. M., Psychiatry

Natural Resources, Agriculture and Veterinary Science:

BELL, L. C., Agriculture
DE LACY, T. P., Environmental Policy
FROST, A. J., Veterinary Science
HEATH, T. J., Veterinary Science
HUGHES, K. L., Veterinary Science
LONGWORTH, J. W., Agricultural Economics
MOLL, E., Natural and Rural Systems Management
ROBINSON, W. F., Veterinary Science
SPRADBROW, P. B., Veterinary Science
TERNOUTH, J. H., Animal Production
WILLIAMS, R. R., Horticulture
WOODS, E., Agribusiness
YOUNG, B. A., Animal Production

Social and Behavioural Sciences:

ASHMAN, A. F., Education
BOREHAM, P. R., Government (H)
ELKINS, J., Education
GALLOIS, C., Psychology
GEFFEN, G. M., Psychology
HALFORD, G. S., Psychology
HENNINGHAM, J. P., Journalism
HOGG, M. A., Psychology
HUMPHREYS, M. S., Psychology
LUKE, A., Education
NAJMAN, J. M., Sociology
NOLLER, P., Psychology
O'CONNOR, D. I., Social Work (Direct Practice)
OEI, T. P. S., Psychology
RIGSBY, B. J., Anthropology
ROSENMAN, L. S., Social Work and Social Policy
SPENCE, S. H., Psychology

AFFILIATED RESIDENTIAL COLLEGES

Emmanuel College: Principal A. A. EDMONDS.

St. John's College: Warden Canon Dr J. L. MORGAN.

King's College: Master Rev. J. A. PATTON.

The Women's College: Principal Dr M. G. W. AITKEN.

St. Leo's College: Rector Very Rev. Fr W. UREN.

Duchesne College: Principal Sister G. BEHAN.

Union College: Warden P. E. FRASER.

Cromwell College: Principal Rev. Dr H. M. BEGBIE.

International House: Dir Dr N. HOLM.

Grace College: Principal Miss B. M. MORRISON.

ATTACHED RESEARCH INSTITUTES

(All at University of Queensland, Brisbane, unless noted otherwise)

Aboriginal Environments Research Centre: Dir Dr. P. C. MEMMOTT.

Advanced Computational Modelling Centre: Dir Prof. K. BURRAGE.

Advanced Wastewater Management Centre: Dir Dr J. KELLER.

Applied History Centre: Dir Dr R. M. FISHER.

Applied Population Research Unit: Dir Dr J. L. SKINNER.

Asian Business History Centre: Dr C. LAI.

Asian Studies Centre: Prof. K. LOUIE.

Assessment and Evaluation Research Unit: Dir G. S. MAXWELL.

Australasian Pig Institute: Dir A. KING.

Australian Centre for International and Tropical Health and Nutrition: Dir Prof. I. RILEY.

Australian Drama Studies Centre: Dir Dr V. E. KELLY.

Australian Equine Blood Typing Research Laboratory: Dir Dr T. K. BELL.

Australian Housing and Urban Research Institute: Dir Prof. R. J. STIMSON.

Australian Institute of Ethics and Professions: Dir Dr J. L. MORGAN.

Australian Institute of Foreign and Comparative Law: Dir Prof. G. A. MOENS.

Australian Key Centre in Land Information Studies: Dir Dr P. C. SHARMA.

Australian Seed and Propagation Technology Centre: Dir Dr D. TAY.

Australian Studies Centre: Dir Dr R. NILE.

Australian Tropical Dairy Institute: Dir Prof. T. COWAN.

Behaviour Research and Therapy Centre: Dirs Assoc. Prof. M. R. SANDERS, Dr R. YOUNG.

Brisbane Surface Analysis Facility: Dir Dr I. R. GENTLE.

Centre for Artificial Neural Networks and their Applications: Dir Prof. T. DOWNS.

Centre for Bacterial Diversity and Identification: Dir Dr. L. I. SLY.

Centre for Clinical and Experimental Therapeutics: Dir Dr A. JOHNSON.

Centre for Conservation Biology: Dir Dr C. MORITZ.

Centre for Democracy: Dir Assoc. Prof. G. M. STOKES.

Centre for Discrete Mathematics and Computing: Dir Prof. A. STREET.

Centre for Drug Design and Development: Dir Prof. P. R. ANDREWS.

Centre for General Practice: Dir Prof. C. B. DEL MAR.

Centre for Health Promotion and Cancer Prevention Research: Dir Assoc. Prof. J. B. LOWE.

Centre for Hypersonics: Dir Dr R. G. MORGAN.

Centre for Immunology and Cancer Research: Dir Prof. I. H. FRAZER.

Centre for Industrial and Applied Mathematics and Parallel Computing: Dir Prof. K. BURRAGE.

Centre for Information Technology Research: Dir Dr R. HENDY.

Centre for Integrated Resource Management: Exec. Dir Dr J. J. MOTT.

Centre for International Journalism: Dir Assoc. Prof. G. B. GRUNDY.

Centre for Language Teaching and Research: Dir Prof. R. D. SUSSEX.

Centre for Laser Science: Dir Prof. G. J. MILBURN.

Centre for Magnetic Resonance: Dir Prof. D. M. DODDRELL.

Centre for Microscopy and Microanalysis: Dir Prof. I. D. R. MACKINNON.

Centre for Mined Land Rehabilitation: Dir Dr D. MULLIGAN.

Centre for Molecular and Cellular Biology: Dir Prof J. S. MATTICK.

Centre for Organisational Psychology: Dir Prof. G. M. GEFFEN.

Centre for Pesticide Application and Safety: Dir N. WOODS.

Centre for Physical Activity and Sport Education: Dir Dr S. HOOPER.

Centre for Primary Health Care: Dir Assoc. Prof. R. BUSH.

Centre for Protein Structure, Function and Engineering: Dir Dr P. A. KROON.

Centre for Public Administration: Dir Prof. K. WILTSHIRE.

Centre for Research in Vascular Biology: Dir Dr J. H. CAMPBELL.

Centre for Research on Group Processes: Dir Dr M. HOGG.

Centre for Software Maintenance: Dir Prof. P. A. BAILES.

Centre for Statistics: Dir Prof. J. A. ECCLESTON.

Centre for Studies in Drug Disposition: Dirs Dr R. G. DICKINSON, Dr W. D. HOOPER.

Centre for Transmission Line Structures: Dir Prof. S. KITIPORNCHAI.

Centre for Waste Management and Environmental Quality: Dir Dr C. A. MITCHELL.

Centre of Applied Dynamical Systems, Mathematical Analysis and Probability: Dir P. M. DIAMOND.

Centre of National Research on Disability and Rehabilitation Medicine: Dir R. MCCLURE.

Cerebral and Sensory Functions Unit: Dir Dr P. J. SNOW.

Children's Nutrition Research Centre: Dir Prof. R. W. SHEPHERD.

Clinical Research Centre: Dir Prof. W. G. E. COOKSLEY.

Cognitive Psychophysiology Laboratory: Dirs Prof. G. M. GEFFEN, Prof. L. B. GEFFEN.

Communication Disability in Ageing Research Unit: Dir Dr L. E. WORRALL.

Computer Aided Process Engineering Centre: Dir Dr I. T. CAMERON.

Co-operative Research Centre for Alloy and Solidification Technology: Dir Prof. G. L. DUNLOP.

Co-operative Research Centre for Distributed Systems Technology: Dir D. BARBAGALLO.

Co-operative Research Centre for Mining Technology and Equipment: Moggill Rd, Pinjarra Hills, 4069; Dir Prof. M. HOOD.

Co-operative Research Centre for Sensor, Signal and Information Processing: Co-ordinator Prof. I. D. LONGSTAFF.

Co-operative Research Centre for Tropical Pest Management: Dir Dr G. A. NORTON.

Co-operative Research Centre for Tropical Plant Pathology: Dir Prof. J. A. G. IRWIN.

Co-operative Research Centre for Tropical Rainforest Ecology and Management: James Cook University, Cairns, 4870; Dir Prof. N. STORK.

Development Disability Unit: Dir Prof. N. LENNOX.

Endocrine Hypertension Research Unit: Dir Prof. R. D. GORDON.

Environmental Planning Research Unit: Dir Dr B. P. HOOPER.

Fred and Eleanor Schonell Special Educational Research Centre: Dir Prof. A. F. ASHMAN.

German/Australian Relations Research Unit: Dir Prof. M. JURGENSEN.

Heron Island Research Station: Heron Is., Qld 4680; Dir Dr I. D. WHITTINGTON.

International Relations and Asian Politics Research Unit: Dir Dr W. T. TOW.

Japanese Language Proficiency Unit: Dir P. M. DAVIDSON.

Joint Experimental Haematology Program: Chair. Prof. A. BOYD.

Joint Experimental Oncology Program: Chair. Prof. J. F. HANCOCK.

Joint Liver Program: Chair. Prof. L. W. POWELL.

Joint Program in Transplantation Biology: Chair. Prof. A. KELSO.

Julius Kruttschnitt Mineral Research Centre: Isles Rd, Indooroopilly, Queensland 4068; Dir Prof. T. J. NAPIER-MUNN.

Labour and Industry Research Unit: Dir Assoc. Prof. P. R. BOREHAM.

Materials Characterization and Processing Centre: Dir Dr M. E. MACKAY.

Media and Cultural Studies Centre: Dir Dr D. MARSHALL.

Minerals Industry Safety and Health Centre: Dir Prof. D. J. MCKEE.

Motor Speech Research Unit: Dir Assoc. Prof. B. E. MURDOCH.

National Heart Foundation Cardiovascular Research Unit: Dir Prof. M. J. WEST.

National Research Centre for Environmental Toxicology: Kessells Rd, Coopers Plains, 4108; Dir Prof. M. R. MOORE.

Neuroimmunology Research Unit: Dir Prof. M. P. PENDER.

Nutrition Program: Dir Dr G. C. MARKS.

Perinatal Research Centre: Dir Prof. P. COLDITZ.

Process and Environmental Analysis Centre: Dir K. DOBSON.

Psychology Clinic: Dir Assoc. Prof. M. R. SANDERS.

Queensland Alcohol and Drug Research Education Centre: Dir Dr A. ROCHE.

Queensland Poultry Research and Development Centre: Dir Dr D. J. FARRELL.

Queensland University Advanced Centre for Earthquake Studies: Dir Assoc. Prof. P. MORA.

Regional and Urban Economics Research Unit: Dir Prof. R. C. JENSEN.

Renal Research Unit: Dir Assoc. Prof. Z. H. ENDRE.

Research Data Network Co-operative Research Centre: Dir M. LLOYD.

Resources, Environmental and Development Research Unit in Economics: Dir Dr G. E. DOCWRA.

Rural Extension Centre: Dir Dr J. A. COUTTS.

School of Marine Science: Dir Assoc. Prof. J. G. GREENWOOD.

Sir Albert Sakzewski Virus Research Centre: Dir Assoc. Prof. E. J. GOWANS.

Sir James Foots Institute of Mineral Resources: Dir Prof. D. J. MCKEE.

Social and Economic Research Centre: Dir Prof. J. WESTERN.

Software Verification Research Centre: Dir Prof. J. STAPLES.

Technology Management Centre: Dir Assoc. Prof. T. HUNDLOE.

Tropical Health Program: Dir Prof. I. D. RILEY.

University of Queensland Archeological Services Unit: Dir Dr H. J. HALL.

University of Queensland Family Centre: Dir Prof. P. NOLLER.

Victorian Fiction Research Unit: Dir Dr B. E. GARLICK.

Vision, Touch and Hearing Research Centre: Dir Prof. J. D. PETTIGREW.

W. H. Bryan Mining Geology Research Unit: Dir Prof. R. DIMITRAKOPOULOS.

Women, Ideology and Culture Research Unit: Dir Assoc. Prof. C. FERRIER.

QUEENSLAND UNIVERSITY OF TECHNOLOGY

GPO Box 2434, Brisbane, Qld 4001

Telephone: (7) 3864-2111
Fax: (7) 3864-1510

Founded 1965; Brisbane CAE merged with the Univ. 1990
State control
Academic year: February to November

Chancellor: Dr C. HIRST
Vice-Chancellor: Prof. R. D. GIBSON
Deputy Vice-Chancellor: Prof. O. P. COALDRAKE
Pro Vice-Chancellor: Prof. H. J. CORDEROY (Research and Advancement)
Registrar: K. BAUMBER
Librarian: G. AUSTEN

Library of 635,000 vols
Number of students: 28,655

Publications: *Inside QUT*, Annual Report.

DEANS

Arts: Prof. R. SCOTT
Built Environment and Engineering: Prof. K. WALLACE (acting)
Business: Prof. T. GRIGG
Education: Prof. A. CUMMING
Health: Prof. K. J. BOWMAN
Information Technology: Prof. K. J. GOUGH
Law: Prof. D. G. GARDINER
Science: Prof. V. SARA

PROFESSORS

ARNOLD, N., Marketing and International Business
ASHBY, G., Early Childhood
BAMBER, G., Faculty Office (Business)
BOASHASH, B., Signal Processing Research Centre
BOULTON-LEWIS, G., Learning and Development
BOWMAN, K., Faculty Office (Health)
CAELLI, W., Data Communications
CARNEY, L., Optometry
CLARK, J., Data Communications
CLINTON, M., Nursing
COALDRAKE, P., Chancellery
COPE, M., Law
CORDEROY, J., PVC's Office (Research and Development)
CORONES, S., Law Research and Postgraduate Studies
CUMMING, A., Faculty Office (Education)
DALE, J., Life Science
DIEDERICH, J., Computing Science
DUNCAN, W., Law Research and Postgraduate Studies
EDWARDS, L., Accountancy
EMBELTON, G., Social Science
FISHER, D., Law Research and Postgraduate Studies
GARDINER, D., Faculty Office (Law)
GEORGE, G., Chemistry
GIBSON, D., Chancellery
GILBERT, C., Law
GOUGH, K., Faculty Office (Information Technology)
GRIGG, T., Faculty Office (Business)
HANSFORD, B., Professional Studies
HART, G., Nursing
HASTINGS, N., Mechanical, Manufacturing and Medical Engineering
HAZLEHURST, C., Humanities
HERINGTON, A., Life Science
HOLMES, S., Accountancy
KUBIK, K., Planning, Landscape Architecture and Survey
KYLE, N., Cultural and Policy Studies
LANKSHEAR, C., Languages and Literacy Education
LAVERY, P., Head of Academy Office
LAYTON, A., Economics and Finance
LIM, B., Architecture, Interior and Industrial Design
LITTLE, P., Accountancy
LONGLEY, D., Faculty of Information Technology
MCELWAIN, D., Mathematics
MOODY, M., Electrical and Electronic Systems Engineering
NORTON, R., Communication
OLDENBURG, B., Public Health
PAPAZOGLOU, M., Information Systems
PARKER, A., Human Movement Studies
PEARCY, M., Mechanical, Manufacturing and Medical Engineering
PETTITT, A., Mathematics
POPE, J., Physics
SARA, V., Faculty Office (Science)
SCOTT, R., Faculty Office (Arts)
SCOTT, W., Mechanical, Manufacturing and Medical Engineering
SHEEHAN, M., Social Science
SKITMORE, R., Construction Management
STIMSON, R., Faculty Office (Built Environment and Engineering)
THOMPSON, S., Economics and Finance
TROCKI, C., Humanities
TROUTBECK, R., Civil Engineering
WALLACE, K., Faculty Office (Built Environment and Engineering)
WONG, W., Mechanical, Manufacturing and Medical Engineering

ROYAL MELBOURNE INSTITUTE OF TECHNOLOGY

GPO Box 2476 V, Melbourne, Vic. 3001

Telephone: (3) 9662-0611
Fax: (3) 9663-2764

Founded 1887; university status 1992
Academic year: February to November

Chancellor: SAM SMORGON
Vice-Chancellor: Prof. DAVID BEANLAND
Deputy Vice-Chancellors: RUTH DUNKIN (Education and Training), Dr PETER FROST (Resources), Prof. DAVID WILMOTH (International), Prof. ANNE HENDERSON-SELLERS (Research and Development)
Pro Vice-Chancellors: BOB BANGAY (VET and Dir TAFE), Prof. HELEN PRAETZ (Higher Educational) (acting), Assoc. Prof. BOB GRAY (Academic Services and Equity), Prof. DAVID KNOWLES (Resource Projects), IAN PERMEZEL (Development)
Academic Registrar: JOHN HARTWELL
Librarian: ANDREW JEPHCOTT (acting)

Library of 1,221,500 vols
Number of teachers: 1,554
Number of students: 42,000

Publications: *Annual Report, Research Report* (annually), *RMIT Openline* (monthly).

DEANS

Faculty of Applied Science: Assoc. Prof. TERRY ROBERTS
Faculty of Art and Design: Prof. BILL GREGORY
Faculty of Business: Prof. JOHN JACKSON
Faculty of Biomedical and Health Sciences: Prof. DAVID STORY
Faculty of Education and Training: Prof. MARTIN COMTE (acting)
Faculty of Engineering: Prof. BILL CARROLL
Faculty of Environmental Design and Construction: Prof. LEON VAN SCHAIK
Faculty of Nursing: Prof. MARGARET BENNETT
Faculty of Social Sciences and Communication: Assoc. Prof. ERN REEDERS (acting)

ATTACHED CENTRES

Advanced Surface Processing Centre: Dir Prof. WILLIAM CARROLL.
Advanced Technology in Telecommunications Centre: Dir Prof. RICHARD HARRIS.
Applied and Nutritional Toxicology Centre: Dir Prof. JORMA AHOKAS.
Advanced Engineering Centre for Manufacturing (with Univ. of Melbourne, RMIT TAFE School of Mechanical Technology): Dir J. MARSHALL.
Applied Social Research Centre: Dir Assoc. Prof. ERICA HALLEBONE (acting).
Australian Housing and Urban Research Institute: Dir Prof. MIKE BERRY.
Centre in Finance: Dir JENNY DIGGLE (acting).
Collaborative Information Technology Research Institute: CEO Prof. PETER GERRAND.
CRC for Intelligent Decision Systems: Dir GRAHAME SMITH.
CRC for Polymer Blends: Dir Dr IAN DAGLEY.
Innovative and Service Management Centre: Dir MICHAEL FARIS (acting).
RMIT Centre for Remote Sensing and Geographic Information Systems: Dir ROD ALLAN (acting).
Key Centre for Knowledge Based Systems: Dir Prof. RON SACKS-DAVIS.
High Performance Computing Centre: Dir Prof. ANDREW JENNINGS.
Microelectronics and Materials Technology Centre: Dir Prof. MICHAEL AUSTIN.
Multimedia Database Systems, RMIT: Dir Prof. RON SACKS-DAVIS.
Polymer Technology Centre: Dir Prof. EDWARD KOSIER.
Rheology Centre: Dr Prof. SATI N. BHATTACHARYA.
Rheology and Materials Processing Centre: Dir Prof. SATI N. BHATTACHARYA.
Sir Lawrence Wackett Centre for Aerospace Design Technology: Dir Prof. LINCOLN WOOD.
Software Engineering Research Centre: Dir Prof. FERGUS O'BRIEN.

ATTACHED COLLEGE

RMIT College Penang: Dir Prof. BRIAN STODDART.

UNIVERSITY OF SOUTH AUSTRALIA

GPO Box 2471, Adelaide, SA 5001

Telephone: (8) 8302-6611
Telex: 82565
Fax: (8) 8302-2466

Founded 1991 by the merger of the South Australian Institute of Technology and three campuses of the South Australian College of Advanced Education; campuses at North Terrace, The Levels, Magill, Salisbury, Underdale and Whyalla

Autonomous (established by Act of Parliament)
Academic year: February to November

Chancellor: Dr BASIL HETZEL
Vice-Chancellor and President: Prof. DENISE BRADLEY
Deputy Vice-Chancellor and Vice-President: (vacant)
Registrar: ELIZABETH WATSON
Librarian: ALAN BUNDY

Libraries of 1,000,000 vols
Number of teachers: 1,025
Number of students: 24,325

Publications: *Annual Report, Calendar, New Outlook, News*.

DEANS

Faculty of Aboriginal and Islander Studies: Prof. COLIN BOURKE
Faculty of Art, Architecture and Design: Prof. PETER BURGESS
Faculty of Business and Management: Assoc. Prof. KEVIN O'BRIEN
Faculty of Education: Prof. KYM ADEY
Faculty of Engineering and the Environment: Prof. ERIC HOBSON
Faculty of Health and Biomedical Sciences: Prof. RUTH GRANT
Faculty of Humanities and Social Sciences: Dr MICHAEL ROWAN
Faculty of Information Technology: Prof. ROBERT NORTHCOTE
Faculty of Nursing: Prof. JAN PINCOMBE
Whyalla campus: JAMES HARVEY

HEADS OF SCHOOLS

Faculty of Aboriginal and Islander Studies:
- School of Aboriginal and Islander Administration: D. I. ROBERTS
- Aboriginal Research Institute: E. A. BOURKE

Faculty of Art, Architecture and Design:
- Louis Laybourne-Smith School of Architecture and Interior Design: Assoc. Prof. D. LANGMEAD
- School of Design: Assoc. Prof. G. KING
- South Australian School of Art: M. LYLE

Faculty of Business and Management:
- International Graduate School of Management: Prof. R. OXENBERRY
- School of Accounting: A. PEARCE
- School of Information Systems: T. ROBBINS-JONES
- School of Management: M. M. MAUGER
- School of Law and Legal Practice: Assoc. Prof. W. T. SARRE
- School of Economics, Finance and Property: G. M. PAGE

Faculty of Education:
- DeLissa Institute of Early Childhood and Family Studies: A. V. VEASE
- School of Education (Underdale campus): W. T. LUCAS
- School of Education (Magill/Salisbury campus): J. HARPER
- School of Studies in Education: W. LUCAS
- School of Physical Education, Exercise and Sports Studies: Assoc. Prof. K. I. NORTON
- School of Language and Literacy Education: Assoc. Prof. J. BURTON

Faculty of Engineering and the Environment:
- School of Engineering: Prof. S. PRIEST
- School of Environmental and Recreation Management: (vacant)
- School of Geoinformatics, Planning and Building: (vacant)

Faculty of Health and Biomedical Sciences:
- School of Chemical Technology: Assoc. Prof. D. E. MULCAHY
- School of Pharmacy and Medical Sciences: Prof. L. SANSOM
- School of Occupational Therapy: P. FARROW
- School of Medical Radiations: R. WINDLE
- School of Physiotherapy: Assoc. Prof. P. TROTT

Faculty of Humanities and Social Sciences:
- School of Communication and Information Studies: M. GALVIN
- School of Arts, Community Development and International Studies: A. SCARINO
- School of Psychology: Dr J. METZER
- School of Social Work and Social Policy: R. J. KENNEDY

Faculty of Information Technology:
- School of Computer and Information Science: J. F. RODDICK
- School of Mathematics: L. H. COLGAN
- School of Physics and Electronic Systems Engineering: (vacant)

Faculty of Nursing:
- School of Nursing (City East/Whyalla campus): A. LANGE
- School of Nursing Studies (Salisbury campus): M. WILLIAMS
- School of Nursing Studies (Underdale campus): P. MILLS.

ATTACHED INSTITUTES

Ian Wark Research Institute (technological research): Dir Prof. J. RALSTON.

Institute for Telecommunications Research: Dir Prof. MICHAEL MILLER.

Satellite Communications Research Centre: Prof. J. MILLER.

Mobile Communications Research Centre: Dr J. ASENSTORFER.

Telecommunications Systems Engineering Centre: Prof. J. BILLINGTON.

Defence Communications Research Centre: Prof. K. V. LEVER.

SOUTHERN CROSS UNIVERSITY

PO Box 157, Lismore, NSW 2480; campuses at Lismore and Coffs Harbour

Telephone: (2) 6620-3000
Fax: (2) 6622-1300

Founded 1993 from Northern Rivers and Coffs Harbour components of the University of New England

Academic year: February to November (2 semesters)

Vice-Chancellor: Prof. B. E. CONYNGHAM
Deputy Vice-Chancellor: Prof. A. R. HYLAND
Pro Vice-Chancellors: Prof. A. C. B. DELVES, Prof. L. Z. KLICH
Executive Director of Administration: M. H. MARSHALL
Executive Director of Information Services: Dr E. J. HANN

Number of teachers: 350
Number of students: 9,500

Publications: Newsletter (quarterly), *Annual Report*.

HEADS OF SCHOOL

School of Business: Dr D. T. O'BRIEN
School of Commerce and Management: R. H. K. SLOAN
School of Contemporary Arts: J. D. DAVIS
School of Education: L. J. REGAN
School of Exercise Science and Sport Management: Assoc. Prof. R. BRONKS
School of Humanities, Media and Asian Studies: H. WEARNE
School of Human Services: J. A. GRIFFITHS
School of Law and Justice: Assoc. Prof. B. FITZGERALD
School of Multimedia and Information Technology: Assoc. Prof. B. LO
School of Natural and Complementary Medicine: S. P. MYERS
School of Nursing and Health Care Practices: C. D. GAME
School of Resource Science and Management: Prof. P. SAENGER
School of Social and Workplace Development: M. A. WALLACE

School of Tourism and Hospitality Management: Prof. G. M. PROSSER
Graduate Research College: Prof. P. R. BAVERSTOCK
Graduate College of Management: (vacant)

PROFESSORS

CANTRELL, L. N., Humanities, Media and Asian Studies
CATTERAL, C., Resource Science and Management
COBB, P., Education
DAVIES, A. T., Co-operative Education (Dir)
GARTSIDE, D. F., Resource Science and Management
HARVEY, D. A., Commerce and Management
HAYDEN, M., Teaching and Learning Unit
HENRY, R. J., Plant Conservation Genetics
JACKSON, J. G., Law and Justice
MACLEOD, G. R., Technology in Learning and Teaching
MEREDITH, G., Business Administration
NECK, C., Business Administration
PEARSON, M., Humanities, Media and Asian Studies
PETERSON, R., Business Administration
SCOTT, D., Commerce and Management
SPECHT, R., Resource Science and Management
SPEEDY, S., Nursing and Health Care Practices
TAYLOR, B., Nursing and Health Care Practices
YEO, S. M. H., Law and Justice
ZANN, L. P., Resource Science and Management
ZUBER-SKERRITT, O., Graduate School of Management

UNIVERSITY OF SOUTHERN QUEENSLAND

Toowoomba, Qld 4350
Telephone: (7) 4631-2100
Fax: (7) 4631-2892

Founded 1992 (fmrly the University College of Southern Queensland, founded 1991 from the Darling Downs Institute of Advanced Education)
State control
Academic year: February to December

Chancellor: DONALD STEVENS
Vice-Chancellor: Prof. PETER SWANNELL
Deputy Vice-Chancellor: Prof. K. GOODWIN
Deputy Vice-Chancellor (Research and Advancement): Prof. M. MCKAY
Registrar: S. TANZER
Librarian: M. MCPHERSON

Library of 204,000 vols
Number of teachers: 340
Number of students: 18,956

Publications: *Handbook, Annual Report, Australasian Science, Pelangi.*

DEANS

Faculty of Arts: Assoc. Prof. M. FRENCH
Faculty of Business: Prof. A. BARNETT
Faculty of Commerce: Prof. R. J. COOMBES
Faculty of Education: Prof. N. K. ELLERTON
Faculty of Engineering and Surveying: Prof. D. WILSON
Faculty of Science: Dr H. AVEY

PROFESSORS

GRANT-THOMPSON, J., Engineering
LITTLER, C., Business
MCMILLEN, D., Arts
ROBERTS, B., Sciences
ROBERTS, T., Sciences
SMITH, R., Engineering
SUMMERS, J., Sciences
TAI, L., Commerce

ATTACHED CENTRE

Performance Centre: Dir Assoc. Prof. R. G. MCCART

SUNSHINE COAST UNIVERSITY COLLEGE

Locked Bag No. 4, Maroochydore South, Qld 4558; located at: Stringybark Rd and Sippy Downs Drive, Sippy Downs, Qld 4556
Telephone: (7) 5430-1234
Fax: (7) 5430-1111

Founded 1994

Vice-Chancellor: Prof. PAUL THOMAS

Number of students: 1,400

Degree courses in fields of business, arts and applied science.

SWINBURNE UNIVERSITY OF TECHNOLOGY

POB 218, Hawthorn, Vic. 3122; campuses at Hawthorn, Prahran and Lilydale
Telephone: (3) 9214-8000
Fax: (3) 9819-5454
E-mail: tgrigg@swin.edu.au

Founded 1908 as Eastern Suburbs Technical College; present name and status 1992
Federal (Higher Education) and State (TAFE) control
Academic year: March to November

Chancellor: R. PRATT
Vice-Chancellor: Prof. J. G. WALLACE
Deputy Vice-Chancellor: F. G. BANNON
Deputy Vice-Chancellor (Division of Higher Education, at Hawthorn and Prahran): Prof. I. C. GOULTER
Deputy Vice-Chancellor (Lilydale): Prof. B. VAN ERNST
Deputy Vice-Chancellor, Technical and Further Education (TAFE Division): V. SIMMONS
Registrar: Dr A. R. GRIGG
Librarian: F. HEGARTY

Library of 230,000 vols
Number of teachers: 410 (Higher Education), 344 (TAFE)
Number of students: 11,500 (Higher Education), 8,500 (TAFE)

Publications: handbooks, *Annual Report, Research Report.*

UNIVERSITY OF SYDNEY

Sydney, NSW 2006
Telephone: (2) 9351-2222

Founded 1850
Private control
Academic year: February to December

Chancellor: Emeritus Prof. Dame LEONIE KRAMER
Deputy Chancellor: D. A. KOK
Vice-Chancellor and Principal: Prof. GAVIN BROWN
Deputy Vice-Chancellors: Prof. K. ELTIS, Prof. J. KINNEAR, Prof. D. J. ANDERSON
Registrar: Dr WILLIAM ADAMS

Library: see under Libraries
Number of teachers: 2,494
Number of students: 33,727

Publications: *Annual Report, Research Report, Administrative Bulletin* (weekly), *The University of Sydney News* (weekly during semester), *The Gazette* (3 a year), *University of Sydney Archives Record* (irregular), etc.

DEANS

Faculty of Agriculture: L. W. BURGESS
Faculty of Architecture: G. MOORE
Faculty of Arts: B. CASS
Faculty of Dentistry: I. J. KLINEBERG
Faculty of Economics: T. WALTER (acting)
Faculty of Education: G. SHERINGTON
Faculty of Engineering: T. RAPER
Faculty of Health Sciences: M. KENDIG
Faculty of Law: J. WEBBER
Faculty of Medicine: S. R. LEEDER
Faculty of Nursing: L. RUSSELL
Faculty of Science: R. G. HEWITT
Faculty of Veterinary Science: D. R. FRASER

PROFESSORS

ADAM, C. M., Management
AITKEN, M. J., Finance
ALLEN, D. G., Physiology
APPS, P. F., Law
ARMITAGE, P., Behavioural and Social Sciences in Nursing
ARMITAGE, S., Nursing Practice
ASTOR, H., Law
AUSTIN-BROOS, D. J., Anthropology
BAKER, A. B., Anaesthesia
BANDLER, R. J., Anatomy and Histology
BARNETSON, R. ST. C., Dermatology
BASTEN, A., Immunology
BAXTER, R. C., Medicine
BENNETT, M. R., Physiology
BENRIMOJ, S. I., Pharmacy Practice
BEREND, N., Respiratory Medicine
BERRY, G., Public Health and Community Medicine
BEUMONT, P. J. V., Psychiatry
BILGER, R. W., Mechanical Engineering
BILLSON, F. A., Clinical Ophthalmology
BOAKES, R. A., Psychology
BOER, B. W., Environmental Law
BOKEY, E. L., Colorectal Surgery
BOYCE, P., Psychiatry
BOYD, A. E., Music
BRIDGES-WEBB, C., General Practice
BROE, G. A., Geriatric Medicine
BROWN, K. F., Pharmacy
BRYANT, R. W., Conservative Dentistry
BRYDEN, M. M., Veterinary Anatomy and Pathology
BURGESS, Agriculture
CAMPBELL, K. K., Philosophy
CARNEY, T. R., Law
CARSANIGA, G., Italian Studies
CARTER, J. P., Civil Engineering
CARTER, J. W., Law
CARTMILL, T. B., Paediatric Surgery
CASS, B., Sociology and Social Policy
CASTALDI, P. A., Medicine
CATERSON, I. D., Endocrinology
CHAMBERLAIN, M., Family and Community Health in Nursing
CHUDLEIGH, J., Orange Agricultural College
CLARKE, H. D. B., Asian Studies
CLUNIES ROSS, M. B., English
COCKAYNE, D. J. H., Electron Microscopy and Microanalysis
CODE, C., Speech Pathology
COLE, T. W., Electrical Engineering
COLLINS, R. E., Applied Physics
CONNELL, R. W., Social and Policy Studies in Education
COOK, D., Physiology
COSSART, Y. E., Infectious Diseases
COUSINS, M. J., Anaesthesia and Pain Management
CRAM, L. E., Astrophysics
CRASWELL, A. T., Accounting
CROWN, A. D., Semitic Studies
CURTHOYS, I., Psychology
CUTTANCE, P. F., Educational Psychology, Measurement and Technology
DAMPNEY, R., Physiology
DANCER, E. N., Mathematics and Statistics
DARENDELILER, M. A., Orthodontics
DAVIES, P. J., Geology and Geophysics
DAVIS, J., Astronomy
DEAN, R. T., Dir, Heart Research Institute
DELBRIDGE, L. W., Surgery
DEVERALL, B. J., Plant Pathology
DOMBERGER, S., Management
DREHER, B., Anatomy and Histology
DROEGE, P., Urban Design
DUNN, R. A., Sydney College of the Arts
DUNSTAN, H., Asian Studies
DURRANT-WHYTE, H., Mechanical and Mechatronic Engineering
EASTMAN, C. J., Clinical Professor (Medicine)
EBIED, R. Y., Semitic Studies

EGERTON, J. R., Animal Health
ELTIS, K. J., Education
FARRELL, G. C., Hepatic Medicine
FIELD, L. D., Chemistry (Organic Chemistry)
FISHER, M. MCD., Clinical Professor (Medicine)
FLETCHER, B. H., Australian History
FLETCHER, J. P., Surgery
FOLEY, W. A., Linguistics
FRASER, D. R., Animal Science
FRASER, I. S., Reproductive Medicine
FREEDMAN, B., Cardiology
GALLAGHER, N. D., Clinical Professor (Medicine)
GALLERY, E. D. M., Clinical Professor (Medicine)
GERO, J. S., Architectural and Design Science
GIBSON, W. P. R., Otolaryngology
GILBERT, G. L., Clinical Professor (Medicine)
GILBERT, R. G., Theoretical Chemistry
GILL, G. J., Government and Public Administration
GOULSTON, K. J., Medicine
GRAYCAR, R., Law
GREEN, J. R., Classical Archaeology
GROENEWEGEN, P. D., Economics
GYÖRY, A. Z., Medicine
HALES, J. R. S., Veterinary Clinical Sciences
HANCOCK, G. J., Steel Structures
HANDELSMAN, D. J., Medicine
HARLAND, D. J., Law
HARPER, C. G., Neuropathology
HARRIS, M. A., English Literature
HAYMET, A. D. J., Theoretical Chemistry
HAYNES, B., Chemical Engineering
HENDERSON-SMART, D. J., Perinatal Medicine
HENSHER, D. A., Graduate School of Business
HEWITT, R.
HIGGS, J., Physiotherapy
HILL, D., Electrical Engineering
HOGAN, W. P., Economics
HORVATH, J. S., Clinical Professor (Medicine)
HOUGHTON, C. R. S., Gynaecological Oncology
HUME, I. D., Biology
HUNT, N. H., Pathology
HUSBAND, A. J., Veterinary Pathology
IRWIG, L., Public Health and Community Medicine
JACKSON, M. W., Government and Public Administration
JANSEN, R. P. S., Clinical Professor (Medicine)
JEFFREYS, M. J., Modern Greek
JOHNSON, G. F. S., Psychiatry
JOHNSTON, G. A. R., Pharmacology
JONES, F. M., Nursing
KEFFORD, R. F., Medical Oncology
KELLY, D. T., Cardiology
KENDIG, H., Health Sciences
KENNEDY, I., Agricultural Chemistry and Soil Science
KERR, C. B., Preventive and Social Medicine
KINNEAR, J. F., Biological Sciences
KLINEBERG, I. J., Prosthetic Dentistry
KUCHEL, P. W., Biochemistry
LANSBURY, R. D., Industrial Relations
LARKUM, A. W. D., Biological Sciences
LAWLER, J., Nursing
LAWRENCE, J. R., Medicine
LAY, P., Chemistry
LEE, K. H., Classics
LEEDER, S. R., Public Health and Community Medicine
LEHRER, G. I., Mathematics and Statistics
LINDOY, L. F., Chemistry
LOUVIERE, J., Marketing
LUMBY, J., Clinical Nursing
LUSBY, R. J., Surgery
MACAULAY, T. G., Agricultural Economics
MCBRATNEY, A. B., Agricultural Chemistry and Soil Science
MCCALLUM, R. C., Industrial Law
MCCARTHY, W. H., Melanoma and Skin Oncology
MCINTOSH, R. A., Cereal Genetics and Cytogenetics
MCKENZIE, D., Physics
MCLEOD, J. G., Medicine and Neurology
MACLEOD, R. M., History
MCPHEDRAN, R. C., Physics (Electromagnetic Physics)
MAHER, M., Architectural and Design Science
MAI, Y.-W., Mechanical Engineering
MARKUS, G., Philosophy
MARSHALL, D. R., Plant Breeding
MARTIN, A. A., French
MARTIN, C. J., Surgery
MARTIN, P. M., Urban Horticulture
MASON, I. M., Geosciences
MATHER, L. E., Anaesthesia and Analgesia
MAY, J., Surgery
MEARES, R. A., Psychiatry
MELROSE, D. B., Theoretical Physics
MILLS, G., Economics
MINDEL, A., Sexual Health
MOORE, G., Architecture
MORRIS, J. G., Clinical Professor (Medicine)
NADE, S. M. L., Clinical Professor (Medicine)
NAPPER, D. H., Physical Chemistry
NUTBEAM, D., Public Health
PATTERSON, D. J., Biology
PESMAN, R.
PETRIE, J. G., Chemical Engineering
PHAN-THIEN, N., Mechanical Engineering
PHEGAN, C. S., Law
PHOON, W.-O., Occupational Health
POLLARD, J., Medicine
POTTS, D. T., Middle Eastern Archaeology
POULOS, H. G., Civil Engineering
PRETTY, S., Sydney Conservatorium of Music
PRICE, H., Philosophy
PRINCE, R. G. H., Chemical Engineering
QUINLAN, J. R., Computer Science
RAPER, J., Engineering
RASMUSSEN, H. H., Medicine
REED, V., Communication Disorders
REES, S. J., Social Work
REEVES, P. R., Microbiology
REID, B., Health Information Management
ROBINSON, B. G., Medicine (Endocrinology)
ROBINSON, J., Mathematical Statistics
ROMAGNOLI, J. A., Process Systems Engineering
ROSE, R. J., Veterinary Clinical Sciences
ROSENBERG, J., Computer Science
ROSS, D. L., Medicine
ROUFOGALIS, B. D., Pharmaceutical Chemistry
ROWE, P. B., Dir, Children's Medical Research Foundation
RUBIN, G., Public Health and Community Medicine
RUSSELL, P., Clinical Professor (Medicine)
RUSSELL, R. L., Nursing
SACHS, J. M., Teaching and Curriculum Studies
SADURSKI, W., Legal Philosophy
SAUNDERS, D. M., Obstetrics and Gynaecology
SCULTHORPE, P. J., Musical Composition
SEALE, J. P., Clinical Pharmacology
SEFTON, A. E., Physiology
SENETA, E., Mathematical Statistics
SHEARER, I. A., International Law
SHEIL, A. G. R., Surgery (Transplantation)
SHEPHERD, R. B., Physiotherapy
SHEPPARD, C. J. R., Physical Optics
SHERRINGTON, G. E., Education
SHINE, R., Evolutionary Biology
SIDDLE, D., Pro Vice-Chancellor (Research)
SILLENCE, D. O., Medical Genetics
SKURRAY, R. A., Biology (Genetics)
SMITH, D. S., Rehabilitation Medicine
SMITH, T., Art History and Theory
SORRELL, T. C., Clinical Infectious Diseases
SPATE, V. M., Contemporary Art
SPRINGBORG, P., Government and Public Administration
STAINTON, M. C., Family and Community Health in Nursing
STERNHELL, S., Organic Chemistry
STEVEN, G. P., Aeronautical Engineering
STEWART, J. H., Medicine
STONE, J., Anatomy
SULLIVAN, C. E., Medicine
SWAIN, M., Biomaterials Science
SWAN, P., Finance
TALLEY, N., Medicine
TANNER, R. I., Mechanical Engineering
TATTERSALL, M. H. N., Cancer Medicine
TAY, A. E.-S., Jurisprudence
TAYLOR, S., Accounting
TAYLOR, T. K. F., Orthopaedics and Traumatic Surgery
TAYLOR, W. C., Organic Chemistry
TEIWES, F. C., Chinese Politics
TENNANT, C. C., Psychiatry
TILLER, D. J., Clinical Professor (Medicine)
TOUYZ, S., Psychology
TRAHAIR, N. S., Civil Engineering
TRENT, R. J. A., Medical Molecular Genetics
TROMPF, G., Studies in Religion
TRUDINGER, B. J., Obstetrics and Gynaecology
TRUSWELL, A. S., Human Nutrition
TURTLE, J. R., Endocrinology
UNDERWOOD, A. J., Experimental Ecology
USHERWOOD, T., General Practice
UTHER, J. F. B., Clinical Professor (Medicine)
VANN, R. J., Law
VINCENT, P. C., Clinical Professor (Medicine)
WADDELL, E., Geosciences
WAKE, R. G., Biochemistry
WALKER, D. M., Oral Pathology
WALTER, T. S., Accounting
WATTS, G., Behavioural Sciences
WEBBER, G. P., Architecture
WEBBY, E. A., Australian Literature
WEISBROT, D., Law
WILDING, R. M., English and Australian Literature
WILSON, P. R., Applied Mathematics
WOODLAND, A. D., Econometrics
WOOLCOCK, A. J., Respiratory Medicine
WORSLEY, P. J., Indonesian and Malayan Studies
YAN, H., Electrical Engineering
YOUNG, J. A., Physiology
YUE, D. K., Medicine

ATTACHED COLLEGES

Orange Agricultural College: Principal Prof. J. W. CHUDLEIGH.

Sydney College of the Arts: Dir Prof. R. DUNN.

Sydney Conservatorium of Music: Principal Prof. S. E. PRETTY.

Graduate School of Business: Dir Prof. C. ADAM.

ATTACHED INSTITUTES

Accounting Research Centre
Ageing and Alzheimer's Disease Research and Education Institute
Australian Asia-Pacific Institute of Retail and Services Studies
Australian Centre and Network for Promoting Effective Healthcare
Australian Centre for Environmental Law
Australian Centre for Industrial Relations Research and Training
Australian Stuttering Research Centre
Centre for Asian and Pacific Law
Centre for Celtic Studies
Centre for Education and Research on Ageing
Centre for Health Economics Research and Evaluation
Centre for Lesbian and Gay Research
Centre for Medieval Studies
Centre for Microeconomic Policy Analysis
Centre for Nursing Research
Centre for Oral Health Research
Centre for Pain Management and Research
Centre for Peace and Conflict Studies
Centre for Performance Studies
Centre for Plain Legal Language
Centre for Research and Teaching in Civics
Centre for South Asian Studies
Centre for the Study and Treatment of Dieting Disorders
Centre for the Study of the History of Economic Thought

Centre for Values, Ethics and the Law in Medicine
Children's Centre
China Education Centre
Classical Languages Acquisition Research Centre
Competitive Tendering and Contracting Research Unit
Cumberland Health and Research Centre
Curriculum Development Centre
Education Technology Centre
European Studies Centre
Exercise Research Centre
Health Education Unit
Institute of Criminology
Micro-Economic Modelling Laboratory
Multicultural Research Centre
N.W.G. Macintosh Centre for Quaternary Dating
National Centre for Classification in Health
National Centre for Health Promotion
National Children's and Youth Law Centre
National Health and Medical Research Council Clinical Trials Centre
National Voice Centre (with Sydney Conservatorium of Music)
NOVAE Research Group
Nursing Professional Development Unit
Nursing Research Centre for Adaptation in Health and Illness
Power Institute of Fine Arts
Public Affairs Research Centre
Rehabilitation Research Centre
Save Sight and Eye Health Institute
Securities Industry Research Centre of Asia-Pacific
Sydney Institute for Biomedical Research
Sydney Nursing Research Centre
Teacher Education Centre
Teaching Resources and Textbooks Research Unit
Westmead Institutes of Health Research
WHO Collaborating Centre for Nursing
WHO Collaborating Centre for Rehabilitation
WHO Collaborating Centre in Health Promotion
Women's Studies Centre

UNIVERSITY OF TECHNOLOGY, SYDNEY

POB 123, Broadway, Sydney, NSW 2007

Telephone: (2) 9514-2000
Fax: (2) 9514-1551

Founded 1965 as NSW Institute of Technology; university status 1988
Academic year: February to December

Chancellor: Emeritus Prof. R. N. JOHNSON
Vice-Chancellor: Prof. A. J. D. BLAKE
Deputy Vice-Chancellor (Academic): Prof. B. C. LOW
Deputy Vice-Chancellor (Administration): R. KEMMIS
Pro-Vice-Chancellor (External Affairs): Prof. S. K. MUKHI
Pro-Vice-Chancellor (Research): Prof. L. JOHNSON
Registrar: Dr J. M. FITZGERALD

Librarian: S. V. O'CONNOR
Library of 700,000 vols
Number of teachers: 934
Number of students: 24,378

Publications: *Annual Report*, *Research Report* (1 a year).

DEANS

Faculty of Business: Prof. R. ROBERTSON
Faculty of Design, Architecture and Building: Assoc. Prof. G. CABAN
Faculty of Education: Prof. A. GONCZI
Faculty of Engineering: Prof. P. J. PARR
Faculty of Law: Prof. D. BARKER
Faculty of Mathematical and Computing Sciences: Assoc. Prof. M. FRY
Faculty of Nursing: Prof. J. F. WHITE
Faculty of Science: Prof. A. R. MOON
Faculty of Humanities and Social Sciences: Prof. E. JACKA
Institute for International Studies: Prof. D. S. G. GOODMAN
University Graduate School: Prof. M. BROWNE

ATTACHED RESEARCH INSTITUTES

Australian Centre for Independent Journalism: Dir ALAN KNIGHT.

Australian Co-operative Research Centre for Renewable Energy: Dir Prof. VIC RAMSDEN.

Australian Graduate School of Engineering Innovation: Dir Prof. PETER PARR.

Australian Legal Information Institute: Co-Dir ANDREW MOWBRAY.

Australian Technology Park, Sydney, Ltd: Project Dir Dr LESLEY JOHNSON.

Centre for Australian Community Organisations and Management: Dir Assoc. Prof. MARK LYONS.

Centre for Biomedical Technology: Dir Assoc. Prof. HUNG NGUYEN.

Centre for Dispute Resolution: Dir MARILYN SCOTT.

Centre for Ecotoxicology: Co-Dirs Prof. ROD BUCKNEY, Dr JOHN CHAPMAN.

Centre for Language and Literacy: Dir Dr MIKE BAYNHAM.

Centre for Learning and Teaching: Dir Assoc. Prof. KEITH TRIGWELL.

Centre for Local Government Education and Research: Dir Assoc. Prof. KEVIN SPROATS.

Centre for Materials Technology: Dir Prof. MICK WILSON.

Centre for Object Technology Applications and Research: Dir Assoc. Prof. JENNY EDWARDS.

Centre for Popular Education: Dir Assoc. Prof. GRIFF FOLEY.

Centre for Research and Education in the Arts: Dir ROSEMARY JOHNSTON.

Centre for Research on Provincial China: Dir Prof. D. S. G. GOODMAN.

Centre for Science Communication: Administrator Dr SUSANNAH ELLIOT.

Centre for Training and Development Services: Principal Consultant ANNE HALLARD.

Co-operative Research Centre for Aquaculture: Dir Dr PETER MONTAGUE.

Co-operative Research Centre for Cardiac Technology: Dir Prof. STEPHEN HUNYOR.

Co-operative Research Centre for Distributed Systems Technology: Dir Assoc. Prof. MICHAEL FRY.

Community Law and Research Centre: Dir PETER O'BRIEN.

Executive Development Unit: Dir KULJIT HUNJAN.

Institute for Coastal Resource Management: Dir Assoc. Prof. KEN BROWN.

Institute for Interactive Multimedia: Dir Assoc. Prof. SHIRLEY ALEXANDER.

Institute for Sustainable Futures: Dir Prof. MARK DIESENDORF.

International and Commercial Law Centre: Dir Prof. SAM BLAY.

National Centre for Groundwater Management: Dir Prof. MICHAEL J. KNIGHT.

Research Centre for Vocational Education and Training: Dir Prof. ROD MCDONALD.

Sydney Microwave Design Resources Centre: Dir Dr ANANDA M. SANAGAVARAPU.

UNIVERSITY OF TASMANIA

GPO Box 252-52, Hobart, Tas. 7001; POB 447, Burnie, Tas. 7320; and POB 1214, Launceston, Tas. 7250

Telephone: Hobart campus, (3) 6226-2999; Burnie campus (3) 6430-4949; Launceston campus, (3) 6324-1999
Fax: Hobart campus, (3) 6226-7871; Burnie campus (3) 6430-4950; Launceston campus, (3) 6324-3799

Founded 1991 by amalgamation of the University of Tasmania (f. 1890) and the Tasmanian State Institute of Technology
Academic year: February to November (two terms)

Chancellor: K. BOYER (acting)
Vice-Chancellor and Principal: Prof. D. MCNICOL
Deputy-Vice-Chancellor: Prof. R. LIDL
Pro-Vice-Chancellor (Research): Prof. A. R. GLENN (designate)
Pro-Vice-Chancellor (Information Services): Prof. A. H. J. SALE
Deputy Principal (Planning): C. J. CHAPMAN
Academic Registrar: C. P. CARSTENS
Librarian: V. ELLIOTT

Library: see under Libraries
Number of teachers: 800
Number of students: 12,600

Publications: *Calendar, Annual Report, Research Report, Law Review.*

DEANS

Faculty of Arts: Prof. M. J. WATERS
Faculty of Commerce and Law: Prof. P. J. DOWLING
Faculty of Education: Prof. W. R. MULFORD
Faculty of Health Science: Prof. A. CARMICHAEL
Faculty of Science and Engineering: Prof. P. HADDAD
Board of Graduate Studies by Research: Assoc. Prof. C. DENHOLM

PROFESSORS (at Hobart campus)

Faculty of Arts:

BENNETT, M. J., History and Classics
FROST, L., English and European Languages and Literatures
GARFIELD, J., Philosophy
SEDIVKA, J., Tasmanian Conservatorium of Music
WATERS, M. J., Sociology and Social Work

Faculty of Commerce and Law:

CHALMERS, D. R. C., Law
DEVEREUX, J., Law
GODFREY, J., Accounting and Finance
LEECH, S. A., Accounting and Finance
RAY, R., Economics
WARNER, C. A., Law

Faculty of Education:

HOGAN, D. J., Secondary and Postcompulsory Education

Faculty of Health Science:

BOYD, G. W., Clinical Sciences
CARMICHAEL, A., Women's and Children's Health
CLARK, M. G., Biochemistry
GOLDSMID, J. M., Pathology
HUNN, J. M., Surgery
KILPATRICK, D., Clinical Sciences
LISOWSKI, F. P., Anatomy and Physiology
MARSDEN, D. E., Women's and Children's Health
MULLER, H. K., Pathology
NICHOLLS, J. G., Anatomy and Physiology
SAUNDERS, N. R., Anatomy and Physiology

Faculty of Science and Engineering:

CANTY, A. J., Chemistry
CLARK, R. J., Agricultural Science
DAVIS, M. R., Civil and Mechanical Engineering
DELBOURGO, R., Physics

HADDAD, P. R., Chemistry
HILL, R. S., Plant Science
JOHNSON, C., Zoology
KIRKPATRICK, J. B., Geography and Environmental Studies
MCCULLOCH, P. M., Physics
MCMEEKIN, T. A., Agricultural Science
MURFET, I. C., Plant Science
NGUYEN, D. T., Electrical Engineering and Computer Science
PANKHURST, N., Aquaculture
REID, J. B., Plant Science

PROFESSORS (at Launceston campus)

Faculty of Commerce and Law:

DOWLING, P. J., Management
LIESCH, P. W. , Management

Faculty of Education:

BRAITHWAITE, R. J., Early Childhood and Primary Education
MULFORD, W. R., Secondary and Post Compulsory Education:
WILLIAMSON, J. C., Secondary and Post-Compulsory Education

Faculty of Arts:

MCGRATH, V. F., School of Art
MACKNIGHT, C. C., History and Classics

Faculty of Health Science:

MAGENNIS, M. P., Nursing
MOORHOUSE, C. P., Nursing
THOMSON, A. N., Community and Rural Health

Faculty of Science and Engineering:

ALEXANDER, P. W., Applied Science
CHOI, Y. J., Computing
OSBORN, A. W., Applied Science
WEBSTER, J. C., Architecture and Urban Design

ATTACHED INSTITUTES

(The mailing address is that of the Hobart campus unless indicated otherwise)

Menzies Centre for Population Health Research: Dir Prof. T. DWYER

Centre for Regional Economic Analysis: Dir Dr J. R. MADDEN

Special Research Centre for Ore Deposit Research: Dir Prof. R. R. LARGE

Molecular Biology Unit: Dir Prof. M. G. CLARK

Central Science Laboratory: Dir J. A. HUTTON

Centre for Furniture Design: Co-ordinator K. PERKINS

Centre for Citizenship and Education: Dir Prof. D. J. HOGAN

Centre for Tasmanian Historical Studies: Dir Prof. M. BENNETT

Cooperative Research Centre for Sustainable Production Forestry: Dir Prof. J. B. REID

Co-operative Research Centre for the Antarctic and Southern Ocean Environment: Dir Dr T. GIBSON

Centre for Legal Studies: Dir Prof. C. A. WARNER

Asia Centre: Dir Dr A. ROY

Institute of Antarctic and Southern Ocean Studies: Dir Prof. G. W. PALTRIDGE

Centre for Biodiversity and Evolutionary Biology: Dir Prof. R. HILL

Australian Clearinghouse for Youth Studies: Dir Assoc. Prof. C. DENHOLM

Strategic Research Centre for Environmental Accountability: Dir K. GIBSON

Centre for Public Management and Policy: Dir Dr W. RYAN

Centre for Research and Learning in Regional Australia: Dir Dr I. FALK

Tasmanian Institute of Agricultural Research: Dir Prof. R. CLARK

VICTORIA UNIVERSITY OF TECHNOLOGY

POB 14428, MCMC, Melbourne, Vic. 8001

Telephone: (3) 9688-4000
Fax: (3) 9689-4069

Founded 1990 by merger of Footscray Institute of Technology and the Western Institute: six campuses, at Footscray, Melton, St Albans, Werribee, Sunbury and Melbourne

Chancellor: PETER LAVER
Vice-Chancellor: Prof. JARLATH RONAYNE
Deputy Vice-Chancellors: Prof. PAUL CLARK, Prof. GABRIEL DONLEAVY (acting)
Pro-Vice-Chancellor (Technical and Further Education): Assoc. Prof. MICHAEL HAMERSTON
University Librarian: DOREEN PARKER

Number of teachers: 730
Number of students: 23,582

DEANS

Faculty of Arts: Prof. ROBERT PASCOE
Faculty of Business: Assoc. Prof. IAN ROBERTS (acting)
Faculty of Engineering and Science: Prof. ALBERT MCGILL
Faculty of Human Development: Prof. DAVID LAWSON

PROFESSORS

ADAMS, R., Pacific Studies
ANDERSON, R., Accounting
BECK, V., Engineering
BOOTH, D., Applied Physics
BRITZ, M., Bioprocessing
CARLSON, J., Exercise, Physiology and Sports Science
CLARK, C., Accounting
DONLEAVY, G., International Business, Law and Finance
EADE, R., Urban Studies
FAHEY, S., Asian Studies
FAIRCLOUGH, R., Biomedical Sciences
GABB, R., Higher Education Teaching and Learning
GEORGE, G., Accounting and Finance
KALAM, A., Electrical and Electronic Engineering
KEE, P., Asian Studies and Immigration
KING, B., Toursim
KYLE, S., Food Technology
LAWSON, D., Applied Physiology
LEUNG, C., Computer Sciences
MCGILL, A., Engineering
MATTHEWS, B., Australian Literature
MOORE, S., Psychology
PASCOE, R., History
PATIENCE, A., Political Science
PRIESTLY, I., Hospitality Systems
ROBERTS, I., Accounting
SEEDSMAN, T., Human Movement
SHAW, R., Hospitality and Tourism
SHEEHAN, P., Economics
SINCLAIR, J., Sociology of Communications
TOOMEY, R., Education
TROUT, G., Biological and Food Sciences
WILSON, J., Education
WILSON, K., Applied Economics
WORLAND, D., Industrial Relations

UNIVERSITY OF WESTERN AUSTRALIA

Nedlands, WA 6907

Telephone: (9) 380-3838
Fax: (9) 380-1075

Founded 1911
Academic year: February to October

Chancellor: The Hon. Justice G. A. KENNEDY
Pro-Chancellor: Prof. A. K. COHEN
Vice-Chancellor: Prof. D. M. SCHREUDER
Deputy Vice-Chancellor: Prof. A. D. ROBSON
Pro Vice-Chancellor (Research): Prof. M. N. BARBER
Registrar: M. R. ORR
Vice-Principal (Finance and Resources): M. L. GRIFFITH
Librarian: J. ARFIELD

Number of teachers: 971
Number of students: 14,055

Publications: *Annual Report, Calendar, UWA Leader* (fortnightly), *Uniview* (3 a year).

EXECUTIVE DEANS

Faculty of Agriculture: Prof. R. K. LINDNER
Faculty of Arts: Prof. E. J. JORY
Economics and Commerce, Education and Law Faculty Group: Prof. P. H. PORTER
Faculty of Engineering and Mathematical Sciences: Prof. B. H. BRADY
Faculty of Medicine and Dentistry: Prof. L. I. LANDAU
Faculty of Science: Prof. G. STEWART

PROFESSORS

ATKINS, C. A., Botany
ATTIKIOUZEL, Y., Electrical and Electronic Engineering
AYLMORE, L. A. G., Soil Science and Plant Nutrition
BADCOCK, D. R., Psychology
BADDELEY, A. J., Mathematics (Probability and Statistics)
BARTLETT, R. H., Law
BEAZLEY, L. D., Zoology
BEILIN, L. J., Medicine
BLANKSBY, B. A., Human Movement
BOAK, C. D., French Studies
BOSWORTH, A. B., Classics and Ancient History
BOSWORTH, R. J. B., History
BOWDLER, S., Archaeology
BRADSHAW, S. D., Zoology
BRENNAN, A. A., Philosophy
BROEZE, F. J. A., History
BROWN, P. R., Accounting
CHAPMAN, J. D., Education
CLEMENTS, K. W., Economics
COCKS, P. S., Agriculture (Plant Sciences)
CONSIDINE, J. A., Horticulture
CONSTABLE, I. J., Ophthalmology
CORDERY, J. L., Organizational and Labour Studies
CRAWFORD, P. M., History
DAVIS, T. M. E., Medicine
DAWKINS, R. L., Pathology
DODSON, J. R., Geography
EGGLETON, I. R. C., Accounting
ELLIOTT, B. C., Human Movement
ESTRIN, Y., Mechanical and Materials Engineering
ETHERINGTON, N. A., History
EWIN, R. E., Philosophy
FARAONE, L., Electrical and Electronic Engineering
FIGGIS, B. N., Inorganic Chemistry
FLETCHER, D. R., Surgery
FLICKER,L., Medicine
FÖRSTL, H., Psychogeriatrics
FRASER, H. D., English
GILKES, R. J., Soil Science and Plant Nutrition
GOLDIE, R. G., Pharmacology
GRAY, B. N., Applied Cancer Studies
GRIFFITHS, G., English
GROUNDS, M. D., Anatomy and Human Biology
GROVES, D. I., Geology and Geophysics
HALL, J. C., Surgery
HARDING, R. W., Law
HARTMANN, P. E., Biochemistry
HOLMAN, C. J. D., Public Health
HOOPER, B. J., Asian Studies
HOUSE, A. K., Surgery
HUMPAGE, W. D., Electrical Engineering
IFE, J. W., Social Work and Social Administration
IMBERGER, J., Environmental Engineering
IZAN, H. Y., Accounting and Finance
JABLENSKY, A. V., Psychiatry and Behavioural Science
JELINEK, G., Surgery

Kakulas, B. A., Neuropathology
Kamien, M., General Practice
Kaye, K. W., Urology
Kepert, D. L., Chemistry
Kirsner, K., Psychology
Klinken, S. P., Clinical Biochemistry
Lambers, H., Plant Sciences
Le Souëf, P. N., Paediatrics
Lindsay, D. R., Agriculture (Animal Science)
London, G. L., Architecture
Mastaglia, F. L., Neurology
McAleer, M., Economics
McCormick, P. G., Materials Engineering
McGeachie, J. K., Anatomy and Human Biology
McKelvey, R. S., Paediatrics and Child and Adolescent Psychiatry
MacLeod, C., Psychology
McShane, S., Management
Mees, A. I., Mathematics
Michael, C. A., Obstetrics and Gynaecology
Miller, P. W., Economics
Moleta, V. B., Italian
Mulvey, C., Industrial Relations
O'Donovan, J., Law
Papadimitriou, J. M., Pathology
Pate, J. S., Botany
Paterson, J. W., Clinical Pharmacology
Plowman, D. H., Management
Powell, C. M., Geology
Praeger, C. E., Mathematics
Randolph, M. F., Civil Engineering
Redgrave, T. G., Physiology
Reed, W. D., Medicine
Rhodes, G., Psychology
Robinson, B. W. S., Medicine
Rohl, J. S., Computer Science
Ronalds, B. F., Oil and Gas Engineering
Sargent, M. V., Chemistry
Shellam, G. R., Microbiology
Slee, R. C., Education
Stachowiak, G. W., Mechanical and Materials Engineering
Stanley, F. J., Paediatrics
Stannage, C. T., History
Stone, B. J., Mechanical Engineering
Taylor, R. R., Cardiology
Tonkin, J., European Languages
Tonkinson, R., Anthropology
Walters, M. N.-I., Pathology
White, R. S., English
Williams, J. F., Physics
Wood, D. J., Orthopaedics

UNIVERSITY OF WESTERN SYDNEY HAWKESBURY

Bourke St, Richmond, NSW 2753

Telephone: (45) 701333
Fax: (45) 783979

Founded 1989 (fmrly Hawkesbury Agricultural College, f. 1891)
Academic year: March to June, August to November

Chancellor: Sir Ian Turbott
Vice-Chancellor: Prof. Janice Reid
Deputy Vice-Chancellor and Chief Executive Officer: J. E. Clark
Registrar: N. J. S. Burnett
Head Librarian: A. Stevenson

Number of teachers: 245
Number of students: 5,000
Library of 113,000 vols

Publications: *Calendar* (annually), *Amaranth* (2 a year), *Research Report (annually), Annual Report.*

DEANS

Faculty of Agriculture and Horticulture: E. W. R. Barlow
Faculty of Health, Humanities and Social Ecology: M. Bickerton
Faculty of Management: R. Juchau
Faculty of Science and Technology: P. Baumgartner

UNIVERSITY OF WESTERN SYDNEY MACARTHUR

POB 555, Campbelltown, NSW 2560

Telephone: (2) 4620-3100
Fax: (2) 4628-1298
E-mail: l.leathley@uws.edu.au

Founded 1989 (fmrly Macarthur Institute of Higher Education)
Academic year: March to December

Deputy Vice-Chancellor and UWS Macarthur President: Prof. D. C. Barr
Registrar: R. A. Jackson
Librarian: J. L. O'Brien

Library of 310,000 vols
Number of teachers: 389
Number of students: 8,550

DEANS

Faculty of Arts and Social Science: Assoc. Prof. John O'Hara
Faculty of Business and Technology: Assoc. Prof. R. D. Alexander
Faculty of Education: Prof. D. Williams
Faculty of Health: Prof. J. McCallum
Faculty of Law: Prof. R. Woellner

UNIVERSITY OF WESTERN SYDNEY NEPEAN

POB 10, Kingswood, NSW 2747

Telephone: (2) 4736-0222
Fax: (2) 4736-0714

Founded 1989 (fmrly Nepean CAE)
State control
Academic year: February to November

UWS Deputy Vice-Chancellor and Nepean President: Prof. C. Duke
Pro-Vice-Chancellor (Academic): Prof. J. Falk
Pro-Vice-Chancellor (Research): Prof. T. Cairney
Registrar, Academic and Administrative Services Division: G. St Lawrence
Chief Librarian: K. Welsh

Library of 380,000 titles
Number of teachers: 354
Number of students: 12,500

Publications: *Research Matters, Nepean News & Prospector* (4 a year).

CHAIRS OF SCHOOL

Accounting: Alan Kilgore
Civic Engineering and Environment: Prof. Russel Bridge
Communication and Media: Conrad Zóg
Computing and Information Technology: Prof. Vijay Varadharajan
Contemporary Arts: Assoc. Prof. David Hull
Cultural Histories and Futures: Prof. Ian Ang
Design: Timothy Marshall
Economics and Finance: Brian Pinkstone
Employment Relations: Dennis Mortimer
Health and Nursing: Assoc. Prof. Helen Ledwidge
Law: Prof. Carolyn Sappideen
Learning Development and Early Education: Assoc. Prof. Alison Elliott
Lifelong Learning and Educational Change: Steven Wilson
Management: Prof. Alexander Kouzmin
Marketing, International Business and Asian Studies: Constant Cheng
Mechatronic, Computer and Electrical Engineering: Mahmood Nagrial
Quantitative Business Methods and Operations: Assoc. Prof. Rakesh Agrawal
Science: Assoc. Prof. Elizabeth Deane
Social, Community and Organizational Studies: Keith Bennett
Teaching and Educational Studies: Jillian Boyd
Centre of Astronomy: Assoc. Prof. Graeme White

PROFESSORS

Ang, I., Cultural Studies
Atherton, M. J., Music
Bailey, J., Educational Studies
Baumgart, N., Professional Studies (Education)
Bridge, R., Civil Engineering
Cairney, T., Education
Cooper, R., Economics
Duke, C., Life Long Learning
Dunk, A., Accounting and Finance
Dunsire, R., Visual Arts
Falk, J., Science and Technology Studies
Fung, E., Asian Studies
Garnett, J., Civic Engineering
Greenwood, J., Nursing
Holmes, C., Nursing (Mental Health)
Irwin, H., Humanities
Johnston, A. M., Health Studies
Kouzmin, A., Management and Administration (Commerce)
Leverett, P., Chemistry
Lucas, G., Electrical Engineering
Moore, P., Biological Sciences
Morris, R., Employment Relations
Nagy, S., Nursing (Paediatrics)
Roberts, B., Mechanical Automation Engineering
Sappideen, C., Law
Sappideen, R., Law
Valentine, T., Banking and Finance
Varadharajan, V., Computing
Walker, J., Curriculum Studies
Walkerdine, V., Critical Psychology
Wilkes, L., Nursing
Wilkinson, I., Marketing
Williams, P., Chemistry

RESEARCH CENTRES

Centre for Electrochemical Research and Analytical Technology (CERAT): Dir Assoc. Prof. S. Adeloju.

Women's Research Centre: Dir Dr C. Poynton.

Research Centre in Intercommunal Studies: Dir Prof. I. Ang.

UNIVERSITY OF WOLLONGONG

Northfields Ave, Wollongong, NSW 2522

Telephone: (2) 4221-3555
Fax: (2) 4221-3477

Founded 1961 as a College of the University of New South Wales; amalgamated with Wollongong Inst. of Education 1982
Academic year: March to November (two sessions), and a summer session from December to February

Chancellor: M. Codd
Vice-Chancellor and Principal: Prof. Gerard Sutton
Deputy Vice-Chancellor: Prof Peter Robinson
Pro-Vice-Chancellor (Academic): Prof. Christine Ewan
Pro-Vice-Chancellor (Research): Prof. William Lovegrove
Vice-Principal (Administration): David Rome
Vice-Principal (International): James Langridge
Librarian: F. McGregor

Number of academic staff: 1,590
Number of students: 12,619

Publications: *Annual Report, Research Report, University of Wollongong Outlook* (every 6 months), *Campus News* (weekly).

FACULTY DEANS

Faculty of Commerce: Prof. Gill Palmer
Faculty of Education: Assoc. Prof. John Patterson
Faculty of Science: Prof. Rob Norris
Faculty of Arts: (vacant)

Faculty of Creative Arts: Prof. SHARON BELL
Faculty of Engineering: Prof. BRENDON PARKER
Faculty of Health and Behaviourial Sciences: Prof. LEN STORLEIN
Faculty of Informatics: Prof. AH CHUNG TSOI
Faculty of Law: Prof. HELEN GAMBLE

PROFESSORS

Faculty of Arts:

BERN, J., Sociology
CASTLES, J. S., Centre for Multicultural Studies
WIELAND, J., English
WOLFERS, E., History and Politics

Faculty of Commerce:

BADHAM, R., Management
CASTLE, R., Economics
GAFFIKIN, M., Accounting and Finance
HOUGH, M., Management
JACKSON, D., Economics
JOHNSTONE, D., Accounting and Finance
LEWIS, D., Economics
LINSTEAD, S., Management
SCOTT, P., Marketing
SIM, A. B., Management
WINLEY, G., Business Systems

Faculty of Creative Arts:

BELL, S.

Faculty of Engineering:

ARNDT, G., Mechanical Engineering
ARNOLD, P., Mechanical Engineering
CHOWDHURY, R., Civil, Mining and Environmental Engineering
DUNNE, D., Materials Engineering
SCHMIDT, L., Civil, Mining and Environmental Engineering
SINGH, R., Civil, Mining and Environmental Engineering
TIEV, K., Mechanical Engineering
WEST, M., Mechanical Engineering

Faculty of Education:

FASANO, C.
GANNICOTT, K.
HEDBERG, J.

Faculty of Health and Behavioural Science:

BARRY, R., Psychology
CALVERT, G. D., Public Health and Nutrition
HOWE, P., Biomedical Science
STORLEIN, L., Biomedical Science

Faculty of Informatics:

ANIDO, G., Electrical, Computer and Telecommunications Engineering
BROADBRIDGE, P., Mathematics and Applied Statistics
COOK, C. D., Electrical, Computer and Telecommunications Engineering
COOPER, J., Information Technology and Computer Science
GRIFFITHS, D., Mathematics and Applied Statistics
SEBERRY, J., Information Technology and Computer Science

Faculty of Law:

FARRIER, D.
GAMBLE, H.
TSAMENYI, M.

Faculty of Science:

BREMNER, J., Chemistry
CHIVAS, A., Geosciences
FISHER, P., Physics
KANE-MAGUIRE, L., Chemistry
MORRISION, J., Environmental Science
NANSON, G., Geosciences
PYNE, S., Chemistry
WHELAN, R., Biological Sciences

Colleges

Ansto Training: Private Mail Bag 1, Menai, NSW 2233; tel. (2) 717-9430; telex 24562; fax (2) 717-9449; f. 1964; the training arm of the University of NSW and the Australian Nuclear Science and Technology Organisation; short courses in use of radioisotopes, radionuclides in medicine, radiation protection and occupational health and safety.

Australian Film, Television and Radio School: POB 126, North Ryde, NSW 2113; tel. (2) 9805-6611; fax (2) 9887-1030; f. 1973; library of 20,000 vols; 100 full-time, 3,000 part-time/short course students; courses: 1- and 2-year courses (postgraduate level), 7-month commercial radio course, short industry courses; Dir ROD BISHOP; Library Man. MICHELE BURTON; publ. *Media Information Australia*.

Australian Maritime College: POB 986, Launceston, Tas. 7250; tel. (3) 6335-4711; telex 58827; fax (3) 6326-6493; f. 1978; library of 35,000 vols; 75 teachers, 1,300 students: Principal N. OTWAY; Academic Registrar: J. HEWSON; Librarian C. NELSON; publs *Annual Report, Handbook, AMC News, Course Brochures*.

FACULTY DIRECTORS

Maritime Transport and Engineering: S. B. LEWARN
Fisheries and Marine Environment: C. BUXTON

National Art School: Forbes St, Darlinghurst, NSW 2010; tel. (2) 9339-8623; fax (2) 9339-8633; courses in fine arts, ceramics and fashion design; Dir BERNARD OLLIS.

National Institute of Dramatic Art: Sydney, NSW 2052; tel. (2) 9697-7600; fax (2) 9662-7415; f. 1958; degree and diploma courses; library of 28,000 vols, 55 periodicals; 150 full-time students, 5,000 part-time students in Open Program; Dir JOHN R. CLARK.

AUSTRIA

Learned Societies

GENERAL

Österreichische Akademie der Wissenschaften (Austrian Academy of Sciences): 1010 Vienna, Dr Ignaz Seipel-Platz 2; tel. (1) 51581; telex 0112628; fax (1) 5139541; f. 1847; sections of Mathematics and Natural Sciences (Sec. Dr GERHARD SCHADLER (acting)), Philosophy and Historical Sciences (Sec. Dr MARGARETE BIEDER (acting)); 152 mems, 445 corresp. mems, 14 hon. mems; attached research institutes: see Research Institutes; library: see Libraries and Archives; Pres. Prof. Dr WERNER WELZIG; Gen. Sec. Prof. Dr HERBERT MANG; Sec. Prof. Dr HERWIG FRIESINGER; publs *Almanach, Anzeiger math.-nat. Klasse, Anzeiger phil.-hist. Klasse, Sitzungsberichte math.-nat. Klasse Abt. I, II, Sitzungsberichte phil.-hist. Klasse, Denkschriften der Gesamtakademie, Denkschriften math.-nat. Klasse, Denkschriften phil.-hist. Klasse, Monatshefte für Chemie.*

AGRICULTURE, FISHERIES AND VETERINARY SCIENCE

Österreichische Gesellschaft der Tierärzte (Austrian Society of Veterinary Surgeons): 1210 Vienna, Josef-Baumanngasse 1; tel. and fax (1) 25077; e-mail sabine .schaefer@vu-wien.ac.at; f. 1919; 1,200 mems; Pres. Prof. Dr. A. HOLZMANN; Sec. Dr SABINE SCHÄFER; publ. *Wiener Tierärztliche Monatsschrift* (monthly).

ARCHITECTURE AND TOWN PLANNING

Österreichische Gesellschaft für Raumplanung (Austrian Society for Regional Planning): 1040 Vienna, Karlsplatz 13; tel. 588013380; Pres. Prof. Dr KLAUS SEMSROTH; publ. *Schriftenreihe* (irregular).

Österreichischer Ingenieur- und Architektenverein (Association of Austrian Engineers and Architects): 1010 Vienna, Eschenbachgasse 9; f. 1848; 4,000 mems; Pres. HELMUT HAINITZ; Gen. Sec. GEORG WIDTMANN; publ. *Österreichische Ingenieur- und Architekten-Zeitschrift* (monthly).

Zentralvereinigung der Architekten Österreichs-ZV (Central Association of Austrian Architects): 1010 Vienna, Salvatorgasse 10; tel. 5334429; f. 1907; 700 mems; Pres. Prof. EUGEN WÖRLE.

BIBLIOGRAPHY, LIBRARY SCIENCE AND MUSEOLOGY

Oberösterreichischer Musealverein—Gesellschaft für Landeskunde (Museums Association of Upper Austria): Linz, Landstr. 31, Ursulinenhof; tel. (732) 77-02-18; f. 1833; 1,200 mems; Chair. Dr GEORG HEILINGSETZER; publs *Jahrbuch, Beiträge zur Landeskunde von Oberösterreich, Schriftenreihe.*

Österreichische Gesellschaft für Dokumentation und Information (Austrian Society for Documentation and Information): C/o Termnet, 1110 Vienna, Simmeringer Hauptstr. 24; tel. (1) 74040280; fax (1) 74040281; e-mail oegdi@kermnet.at; f. 1951; 193 mems; Pres. GERHARD RICHTER; Exec. Sec. ROBERTA SCHWARZ; publs *Fakten Daten Zitate* (quarterly), *ÖGDI Aktuell.*

Vereinigung Österreichischer Bibliothekarinnen und Bibliothekare (Austrian Librarians Association): Rathaus, 1082 Vienna; tel. (1) 4000-84915; fax (1) 4000-7219; e-mail post@m09.magwien.gv.at; f. 1946; 1,100 mems; Pres. Dr Mag. H. WÜRTZ; publs *Biblos, Mitteilungen, Fakten-Daten-Zitate* (quarterly).

ECONOMICS, LAW AND POLITICS

Nationalökonomische Gesellschaft (Austrian Economics Association): Johannes Kepler Universität Linz, Abteilung für Wirtschaftspolitik, 4040 Linz; f. 1917; 240 mems; Chair. Prof. FRIEDRICH SCHNEIDER; Sec.-Gen. Doz. Dr RAINER BARTEL.

Österreichische Gesellschaft für Aussenpolitik und Internationale Beziehungen (Austrian Society for Foreign Policy and International Relations): 1010 Vienna, Hofburg, Schweizerhof/Brunnenstiege; f. 1958; 500 mems; Pres. Botschafter Dr WOLFGANG SCHALLENBERG; publ. *Österreichisches Jahrbuch für Internationale Politik* (annually).

Österreichische Gesellschaft für Kirchenrecht (Austrian Society for Ecclesiastical Law): 1010 Vienna, Freyung 6/2/4; tel. 5339861; fax 5351019; f. 1949; 200 mems; publ. *Österreichisches Archiv für Kirchenrecht.*

Österreichische Statistische Gesellschaft (Austrian Statistical Society): C/o Wirtschaftsuniversität, Institut für Statistik, 1090 Vienna, Augasse 2; tel. (1) 31336-4336; fax (1) 31336-711; e-mail oesg@ wu-wien.ac.at; f. 1951; 500 mems; Pres. Prof. Dr h.c. Dr P. HACKL; publ. *Österreichische Zeitschrift für Statistik* (irregular).

Wiener Juristische Gesellschaft (Vienna Legal Association): 1010 Vienna, Tuchlauben 13; tel. 534370; telex 613222216; fax 5332521; f. 1867; 600 mems; Pres. Prof. Dr WALTER BARFUSS.

EDUCATION

Österreichische Rektorenkonferenz (Standing Conference of Austrian Rectors): 1090 Vienna, Liechtensteinstrasse 22; tel. 31056560; fax 310565622; Pres. Prof. Dipl. Ing. Dr PETER SKALICKY; Sec.-Gen. Dr ANDREA HENZL.

Verband der Akademikerinnen Österreichs (Austrian Association of University Women): 1010 Vienna, Reitschulgasse 2; tel. (1) 5339080; f. 1922; promotes scientific and professional advancement of university women graduates; 650 mems; Pres. Dr RENATE HOREJSI; Sec. Mag. HEIDI ARINGER; publ. *VAÖ-Mitteilungen* (quarterly).

FINE AND PERFORMING ARTS

Bundesdenkmalamt (Federal Monuments Office): 1010 Vienna, Hofburg; tel. 53415; fax 53415252; f. 1850; protection and restoration of historical, artistic and cultural monuments; has control of excavations and art export; library of 35,000 vols; Pres. DI Dr WILHELM GEORG RIZZI; Curator Prof. Dr ERNST BACHER; publs *Österreichische Zeitschrift für Kunst und Denkmalpflege, Wiener Jahrbuch für Kunstgeschichte, Fundberichte aus Österreich, Dehio Handbuch, Die Kunstdenkmäler Österreichs, Österreichische-Kunsttopographie, Studien zur österreichischen Kunstgeschichte, Studien zu Denkmalschutz und Denkmalpflege, Corpus der mittelalterlichen Wandmalereien Österreichs, Corpus Vitrearum Medii Aevi Österreich.*

Gesellschaft der Musikfreunde in Wien (Society of Friends of Music in Vienna): 1010 Vienna, Bösendorferstr. 12; tel. (1) 5058681; fax (1) 5059409; f. 1812; organizes concerts; 11,000 mems; choir of 300 mems; library: see Libraries; collection of music, MSS, instruments etc.; Pres. Prof. Dr HORST HASCHEK; Gen. Sec. Dr THOMAS ANGYAN; publ. *Musikfreunde* (8 a year).

Internationale Franz Lehár-Gesellschaft (International Franz Lehár Society): 1160 Vienna, Neulerchenfelderstr. 3-7; f. 1949; Gen. Sec. Prof. EDUARD MACKU.

Johann Strauss-Gesellschaft Wien (Johann Strauss Society of Vienna): 1010 Vienna, Kleeblattgasse 9/9; tel. (1) 5339194; f. 1936; 300 mems; Pres. Prof. FRANZ MAILER; publ. *Wiener Bonbons* (quarterly).

Kunsthistorische Gesellschaft (Art History Society): 1090 Vienna, Spitalg. 2–4; tel. (1) 427741410; f. 1956; 200 mems; Dir Prof. Dr G SCHMIDT.

Künstlerhaus (Gesellschaft Bildender Künstler Österreichs) (Austrian Artists Asscn): 1010 Vienna, Karlsplatz 5; tel. 5879663; fax 5878736; f. 1861; 460 mems; Pres. Arch. DI MANFRED NEHRER.

Österreichische Gesellschaft für Filmwissenschaft, Kommunikations- und Medien Forschung (Austrian Society for Film Sciences, Research on Communications and Media): 1010 Vienna, Rauhensteingasse 5; tel. (222) 5129936; fax (222) 5135330; f. 1952; encouragement of scientific research for film and television; 196 mems; Pres. Prof. Dr GISELHER GUTTMANN; Gen. Sec. Dr JOSEF SCHUCHNIG; publs. *Filmkunst* (quarterly), *Mitteilungen* (4–6 a year), *Film / Video Manual* (2 a year).

Österreichische Gesellschaft für Kommunikationsfragen (Austrian Society of Communications): Institut für Kommunikationswissenschaft, Universität Salzburg, 5020 Salzburg, Rudolfskai 42; tel. (662) 80444150; fax (662) 80444190; e-mail oegk@sbg.ac.at; f. 1976; encourages co-operation between communication researchers and communication practitioners (journalists, mediaworkers); 480 mems; Sec. Gen. Dr GABRIELE SIEGERT; publ. *Medien Journal* (quarterly).

Österreichische Gesellschaft für Musik (Austrian Music Society): 1010 Vienna, Hanuschgasse 3; tel. 5123143; fax 5124299; f. 1964; library of 1,000 vols mainly on contemporary music, and records; Gen. Sec. Prof. Dr H. GOERTZ.

Österreichischer Komponistenbund (Association of Austrian Composers): 1031 Vienna, Baumannstr. 8–10; tel. and fax (1) 7147233; f. 1913; 414 mems; Pres. Prof. Mag. HEINRICH GATTERMEYER; Sec. BÄRBEL BEIER-NIENSTEDT.

Wiener Beethoven Gesellschaft (Vienna Beethoven Society): 1190 Vienna, Heiligenstadt, Probusgasse 6; tel. 3188215; f. 1954; 300 mems; Pres. Prof. ALEXANDER JENNER; publ. *Mitteilungsblatt der W.B.G.* (quarterly).

Wiener Konzerthausgesellschaft (Vienna Concert Hall Society): 1030 Vienna, Lothringerstr. 20; tel. 71246860; fax 7131709; e-mail mail@konzerthaus.at; f. 1913; 6,700 mems; Pres. Dr HARALD STURMINGER; Sec.-Gen. CHRISTOPH LIEBEN-SEUTTER; publ. *Konzerthaus Nachrichten* (8 a year).

Wiener Secession (Vienna Secessionist Group): Vienna I, Friedrichstr. 12; f. 1897; promotes art exhibitions in its own gallery and abroad; 150 mems; Pres. WERNER WÜRTINGER; publs numerous catalogues.

HISTORY, GEOGRAPHY AND ARCHAEOLOGY

Geschichtsverein für Kärnten (Historical Association of Carinthia): 9020 Klagenfurt, Museumgasse 2; tel. (463) 53630573; f. 1844; 2,300 mems; Dir Dr CLAUDIA FRÄSS-EHRFELD; Sec. Prof. Dr GERNOT PICCOTTINI; publs *Carinthia I* (annually), *Archiv für Väterlandische Geschichte und Topographie, Aus Forschung und Kunst*.

Heraldisch-Genealogische Gesellschaft 'Adler' ('Eagle' Heraldic and Genealogical Society): 1014 Vienna, Postfach 25, Haarhof 4A; f. 1870; 670 mems; library of 37,000 vols; Pres. Dr GEORG KUGLER; Sec.-Gen. Dr Baron ANDREAS CORNARO; publs *Jahrbuch, Zeitschrift* (quarterly).

Historische Landeskommission für Steiermark (Styrian Historical Land Commission): 8010 Graz, Karmeliterplatz 3/II; tel. (316) 8773015; f. 1892; 30 mems; Pres. W. KLASNIC; Sec. Prof. Dr OTHMAR PICKL; publs *Forschungen zur geschichtlichen Landeskunde der Steiermark, Veröffentlichungen, Arbeiten zur Quellenkunde, Quellen zur geschichtlichen Landeskunde der Steiermark, Forschungen und Darstellungen zur Geschichte des Steiermärkischen Landtages*.

Historischer Verein für Steiermark (Styrian Historical Association): 8010 Graz, Hamerlinggasse 3; tel. (316) 8772366; f. 1850; 1,400 mems; Chair. Prof. Dr GERHARD PFERSCHY; Sec. GERNOT FOURNIER; publs *Zeitschrift, Beiträge zur Erforschung Steirischer Geschichtsquellen, Blätter für Heimatkunde*.

Kommission für Neuere Geschichte Österreichs (Commission for Modern Austrian History): Institut für Geschichte Universität Salzburg, 5020 Salzburg; tel. (662) 80444776; fax (662) 8044413; e-mail franz.adlgasser@sbg.ac.at; f. 1900; 25 mems; Chair. Prof. Dr FRITZ FELLNER.

Orientalische Gesellschaft (Oriental Society): 1010 Vienna I, Universitätsstr. 7/V; f. 1952; Pres. Prof. Dr HERMANN HUNGER.

Österreichische Byzantinische Gesellschaft (Austrian Byzantine Society): 1010 Vienna, Postgasse 7–9; tel. 5120217; fax 5127023; f. 1946; 135 mems; Pres. Prof. Dr JOHANNES KODER; publ. *Mitteilungen aus der österreichischen Byzantinistik und Neogräzistik* (annually).

Österreichische Geographische Gesellschaft (Austrian Geographical Society): 1071 Vienna, Karl Schweighofer-Gasse 3; tel. and fax (1) 5237974; f. 1856; 1,355 mems; Pres. Dr INGRID KRETSCHMER; library: see Libraries; publ. *Mitteilungen* (annually).

Österreichische Gesellschaft für Archäologie (Austrian Archaeological Society): C/o Institut für Alte Geschichte, Altertumskunde und Epigraphik, Universität Wien, 1010 Vienna, Dr Karl Lueger-Ring I; f. 1972; 190 mems; Pres. Prof. Dr EKKEHARD WEBER; publ. *Römisches Österreich* (annually).

Österreichische Gesellschaft für Ur- und Frühgeschichte (Austrian Society for Pre- and Early History): 1190 Vienna, Franz-Klein-Gasse 1; tel. (1) 31352-373; f. 1950; 1,050 mems; Gen. Sec. Mag. ALEXANDRA KRENN-LEEB; publ. *Archäologie Österreichs* (2 a year).

Österreichische Numismatische Gesellschaft (Austrian Numismatic Society): 1010 Vienna, Burgring 5; tel. (1) 52524-383; fax (1) 52524-501; f. 1870; 400 mems; library of 5,000 vols; Pres. Ing. HELMUT HIRSCHBERG; Sec. Dr KARL SCHULZ; publs *Numismatische Zeitschrift* (irregular), *Mitteilungen* (every 2 months).

Verband Österreichischer Historiker und Geschichtsvereine (Union of Austrian Historical Associations): 1015 Vienna, Postfach 263; f. 1949; 130 mem. socs; Man. Vice-Pres. Prof. Dr LORENZ MIKOLETZKY; Gen. Sec. Dr ERWIN A. SCHMIDL; publ. *Veröffentlichungen*.

Verein für Geschichte der Stadt Wien (Association for the History of the City of Vienna): Wiener Stadt- und Landesarchiv, 1082 Vienna, Rathaus; tel. (1) 400084815; fax (1) 406896143; f. 1853; 1,592 mems; Chair. Prof. Dr FELIX CZEIKE; Sec. Dr KARL FISCHER; publs *Wiener Geschichtsblätter* (quarterly), *Jahrbuch, Forschungen und Beiträge zur Wiener Stadtgeschichte*.

LANGUAGE AND LITERATURE

Austria Esperantista Federacio (Austrian Esperanto Society): 1150 Vienna, Fünfhausgasse 16; tel. (1) 8934196; f. 1901; 500 mems; library of 1,500 vols, 1,000 pamphlets; Pres. Prof. Dr HANS MICHAEL MAITZEN; Gen. Sec. LEOPOLD PATEK; publs *Austria-Esperanto-Revuo, Esperanto-Servo* (quarterly).

Eranos Vindobonensis: Institut für Klassische Philologie, Universität, 1010 Vienna, Dr Karl Lueger-Ring 1; tel. (1) 4277-41916; f. 1885; philological society; 90 mems; Sec. Dr P. LORENZ.

Gesellschaft für Klassische Philologie in Innsbruck (Classical Philological Society of Innsbruck): Institut für Klassische Philologie, Universität Innsbruck, Innsbruck, Innrain 52; tel. (512) 5074082; fax (512) 5072982; f. 1958; 200 mems; Dir LAV SUBARIĆ; Sec. ANNA CHRISTOPH; publ. *Acta philologica Aenipontiana*.

Gesellschaft zur Förderung Slawistischer Studien (Society for Slavic Studies): 1180 Vienna, Teschnergasse 4/17; f. 1983; Dir AAGE HANSEN-LÖVE; publs *Wiener Slawistischer Almanach, Journal* (2 a year), monograph series (quarterly).

Österreichische Gesellschaft für Literatur (Austrian Literary Society): 1010 Vienna, Herrengasse 5; tel. 5338159; fax 5334067; f. 1961; Pres. MARIANNE GRUBER.

Wiener Goethe-Verein (Vienna Goethe Association): 1010 Vienna, Stallburggasse 2; f. 1878; 300 mems; library of 2,000 books; Pres. Prof. Dr HERBERT ZEMAN; publ. *Jahrbuch*.

Wiener Humanistische Gesellschaft: Institut für Klassische Philologie, Universität Wien, 1010 Vienna, Dr-Karl-Lueger-Ring 1; tel. (1) 4277-41917; fax (1) 4277-9419; e-mail kurt.smolak@univie.ac.at; f. 1947; philological society; 550 mems; Pres Prof. HEINRICH STREMITZER, Prof. KURT SMOLAK; Sec. Mag. MARGIT KAMPTNER; publ. *Wiener Humanistische Blätter*.

Wiener Sprachgesellschaft (Vienna Language Society): Institut für Sprachwissenschaft, Universität 1010 Vienna; f. 1947; 200 mems; Pres. Prof. H. SCHENDL; Sec. Dr H. CH. LUSCHÜTZKY; publ. *Die Sprache* (annually).

MEDICINE

Gesellschaft der Ärzte in Wien (Vienna Society of Physicians): 1096 Vienna, Postfach 147, Frankgasse 8; tel. (222) 4054777; fax (222) 4023090; f. 1837; 1,278 mems; library of 200,000 vols, 25,900 monographs; Pres. Prof. Dr W. HOLCZABEK; Secs Prof. Dr F. KUMMER, Prof. Dr P. AIGINGER; publ. *Wiener Klinische Wochenschrift*.

Gesellschaft der Chirurgen in Wien (Vienna Society of Surgeons): 1090 Vienna, Neues Allgemeines Krankenhaus; tel. (1) 40400; fax (1) 404004004; f. 1935; 137 mems; Dir Prof. Dr JOSEF KARNER; Sec. Prof. Dr BELA TELEKY.

Internationale Paracelsus-Gesellschaft: 5020 Salzburg, Ignaz-Harrer Strasse 79; f. 1950; 315 mems, 27 mem. asscns; Pres. Prof. Dr GERHART HARRER; Gen. Sec. GERTRAUD WEISS; publs *Salzburger Beiträge zur Paracelsusforschung, Parcelsus-Briefe*.

Österreichische Ärztegesellschaft für Psychotherapie (Austrian Medical Society of Psychotherapy): 1090 Vienna, Mariannengasse 10; f. 1950; Pres. Prof. V. E. FRANKL.

Österreichische Gesellschaft für Anästhesiologie, Reanimation und Intensivmedizin (Austrian Society of Anaesthesia, Resuscitation and Intensive Care Medicine): 1180 Vienna, Johann Nepomuk Vogl-Platz 1/1; tel. (1) 4064810; fax (1) 4064811; f. 1951; 1,154 mems; Pres. Prof. Dr A. F. HAMMERLE; Sec. Dr P. KRAFFT; publs *AINS, Newsletter*.

Österreichische Gesellschaft für Arbeitsmedizin (Austrian Society for Occupational Health): 6060 Hall in Tyrol, Arbeitsmedizinisches Zentrum; tel. 52237304; f. 1954; 350 mems; Pres. Doz. Dr EGMONT BAUMGARTNER; publ. *Jahresbericht*.

Österreichische Gesellschaft für Balneologie und Medizinische Klimatologie (Austrian Society for Balneology and Medical Climatology): C/o Institut für medizinische Physiologie der Universität Wien, 1090 Vienna, Schwarzspanierstr. 17; f. 1956; 136 mems; Pres. Dr W. MARKTL.

Österreichische Gesellschaft für Chirurgie (Austrian Society for Surgery): 1096 Vienna, Frankgasse 8; tel. (1) 4087920; fax (1) 4081328; f. 1958; includes the associated Austrian societies for Traumatology, Orthopaedic, Thoracic and Cardiac Surgery, Vascular Surgery, Neurosurgery, Obesity Surgery, Paediatric Surgery, Plastic, Aesthetic and Reconstructive Surgery, Ear, Nose and Head-and-Neck Surgery, Surgical Oncology, Osteosynthesis, Coloproctology, Hand Surgery, Surgical Research, Maxillo-Facial Surgery, Surgical Endocrinology, Minimal Invasive Surgery, Medical Videography; 4,350 mems; Sec. Prim. i. R. Prof. Dr K. DINSTL.

Österreichische Gesellschaft für Dermatologie und Venereologie (Austrian Dermatological and Venereological Society): 1090 Vienna, Alserstr. 4; Pres. Prof. Dr H. HINTNER; Sec. Prof. Dr J. AUBÖCK.

Österreichische Gesellschaft für Geriatrie und Gerontologie (Austrian Society for Geriatrics and Gerontology): Dept of Medicine, Krankenhaus Barmherzige Brüder, 1020 Vienna, Grosse Mohrengasse 9; f. 1955; 200 mems; library of 2,000 vols; Pres. Prof. Dr R. WILLVONSEDER; Sec. Prof. Dr MONIKA SKALICKY; publs *Scriptum Geriatricum* (annually), *Aktuelle Gerontologie* (monthly).

Österreichische Gesellschaft für Hals-, Nasen-, Ohrenheilkunde Kopf- und Halschirurgie (Austrian Society of ENT Science, Head and Neck Surgery): 1090 Vienna, Währingergurtel 18–20; tel. (222) 404003350; fax (222) 40400-3350; f. 1892; 640 mems; Pres. Prof. Dr K. EHRENBERGER; Gen. Sec. Prof. Dr K. ALBEGGER; publ. *Zeitschrift*.

Österreichische Gesellschaft für Innere Medizin (Austrian Society for Internal Medicine): Medizinische Universität Kliniken, Allgemeines Krankenhaus, 1090 Vienna, Währinger Gürtel 18–20; f. 1886; 400 mems; Dir Prof. Dr A. GANGL; publ. *Wiener Zeitschrift für Innere Medizin*.

Österreichische Gesellschaft für Kinder- und Jugendheilkunde (Austrian Society for Paediatrics): C/o Gottfr. v. Preyersches, Kinderspital, 1100 Vienna, Schrankenberggasse 31, f. 1962; 805 mems; Pres. Prof. Dr WALTER STÖGMANN; Sec. Prim. Dr FRANZ PAKY; publ. *Pädiatrie und Pädologie* (6 a year).

Österreichische Gesellschaft für Klinische Neurophysiologie (Austrian Clinical Neurophysiological Society): Institut für Neurophysiologie der Universität Wien, 1090 Vienna, Währingerstr. 17; f. 1954; 250 mems; Pres Prof. Dr B. MAMOLI, Prof. Dr G. BAUER, Prof. Dr E. DEISENHAMMER; Secs Prof. Dr G. LADURNER, Prof. Dr P. RAPPELSBERGER; publs *EEG/EMG, Thieme* (quarterly).

Österreichische Gesellschaft für Urologie (Austrian Society for Urology): C/o Urologie Universitätsklinik, 1090 Vienna IX, Währinger Gürtel 16–18; 338 mems; Pres. Prof. Dr H. MADERSBACHER.

Österreichische Gesellschaft zum Studium der Sterilität und Fertilität (Austrian Society for the Study of Sterility and Fertility): Universitäts-frauenklinik, 1090 Vienna, Spitalgasse 23; tel. (222) 404002851; Pres. Prof. Dr G. TSCHERNE; Sec. Prof. DDr J. C. HUBER.

Österreichische Ophthalmologische Gesellschaft (Austrian Ophthalmological Society): 1080 Vienna, Schlosselgasse 9; tel. (222) 4028540; fax (222) 4027935; f. 1955; 730 mems; library of 2,100 vols; Pres. Prim. Prof. Dr H. GNAD; Sec. Prim. Dr P. DROBEC; publ. *Spectrum der Augenheilkunde* (every 2 months).

Österreichische Röntgengesellschaft—Gesellschaft für Medizinische Radiologie und Nuklearmedizin (Austrian Radiography Society): 1090 Vienna, Rotenhausgasse 6; tel. (222) 4065222; f. 1946; 800 mems; Sec. Doz. Dr G. MOSTBECK; publ. *ÖRG- Mitteilungen* (quarterly).

Verein für Psychiatrie und Neurologie (Society for Psychiatry and Neurology): Neurologische Universitätsklinik, 1090 Vienna, Währingergurtel 18-20; f. 1868; Pres. Prof. Dr B. MAMOLI; Secs Doz. Dr W. LANG, Dr V. PASSWEG.

Wiener Medizinische Akademie für Ärztliche Fortbildung und Forschung (Vienna Academy of Postgraduate Medical Education and Research): 1090 Vienna, Alserstr. 4; tel. (222) 4051383-0; fax 4051383-23; f. 1896; Pres. Prof. Dr R. KOTZ; Secs Prof. Dr C. ZIELINSKI, Prof. Dr A. TUCHMANN.

NATURAL SCIENCES

General

Naturwissenschaftlicher Verein für Kärnten (Carinthian Association of Natural Sciences): 9020 Klagenfurt, Museumgasse 2; f. 1848; 1,300 mems; Pres. Dr HANS SAMPL; publs *Carinthia II* (annually with special issues), *Der Karinthin* (Mineralogy, Geology).

Biological Sciences

Österreichische Mykologische (Pilzkundliche) Gesellschaft (Austrian Mycological Society); 1030 Vienna, Rennweg 14; tel. 79794; fax 79794131; f. 1919; 300 mems; library of 1,000 vols; mycological herbarium collection; Pres. Prof. Dr M. MOSER; publs *Österreichische Zeitschrift für Pilzkunde, Austrian Journal of Mycology* (annually).

Zoologisch-Botanische Gesellschaft in Österreich (Zoological-Botanical Society of Austria): 1091 Vienna, Althanstr. 14, Postfach 287; f. 1851; 540 mems; Pres. Dr W. FIEDLER; Gen. Sec. Dr W. PUNZ; publs *Verhandlungen, Abhandlungen, Koleopterologische Rundschau.*

Mathematical Sciences

Mathematisch-Physikalische Gesellschaft in Innsbruck (Mathematics and Physics Society of Innsbruck): 6020 Innsbruck, Technikerstr. 25; tel. (512) 507-6211; fax (512) 507-2961; f. 1936; 112 mems; Chair. Assoc. Prof. Dr GERHARD GRÜBL.

Österreichische Mathematische Gesellschaft (Austrian Mathematical Society): Technische Universität, 1040 Vienna, Wiedner Hauptstr. 8–10; tel. (1) 588015454; f. 1904; 800 mems; Pres. Prof. Dr KARL SIGMUND; publ. *International Mathematical News* (3 a year).

Physical Sciences

Chemisch-Physikalische Gesellschaft in Wien (Vienna Chemico-Physical Society): 1090 Vienna, Strudlhofgasse 4; tel. 342630; telex 116222; f. 1869; 260 mems; Dir Prof. P. WEINZIERL; Sec. Doz. F. VESELY; publ. *Bulletin* (2 a year).

Gesellschaft Österreichischer Chemiker (Austrian Chemical Society): 1010 Vienna, Niebelungengasse 11/6; f. 1897; educational programme for professional advancement in chemistry; 2,500 mems, 3,000 mems in attached socs; Pres. DI Dr. WOLFGANG UNGER; Sec.-Gen. Dr FRANK A. BATTIG; publ. *Chemie—Das Österreichische Magazin für Wirtschaft und Wissenschaft.*

Österreichische Biochemische Gesellschaft (Austrian Biochemical Society): C/o Institut für Molekularbiologie, 5020 Salzburg, Billrothstrasse 11; tel. (662) 6396122; fax (662) 6396129; f. 1954; 825 mems; Pres. Prof. Dr G. KREIL; Sec. Dr M. GIMONA.

Österreichische Geologische Gesellschaft (Austrian Geological Society): Geologische Bundesanstalt, 1031 Vienna, Rasumofskygasse 23; tel. (1) 7125674; fax (1) 712567456; f. 1907; 700 mems; Pres. Prof. Dr E. WALLBRECHER; publ. *Mitteilungen.*

Österreichische Gesellschaft für Analytische Chemie (Austrian Society for Analytical Chemistry): C/o Prof. Dr W. Wegscheider, Institut für Allgemeine und Analytische Chemie, Montanuniversität Leoben, 8700 Leoben, Franz-Josef-Str. 18; tel. (3842) 402340; fax (3842) 402543; f. 1948; 400 mems; Dir Prof. Dr W. WEGSCHEIDER; Prof. Dr W. BUCHBERGER.

Österreichische Gesellschaft für Erdölwissenschaften (Austrian Society for Petroleum Sciences): 1031 Vienna, Erdbergstr. 72; tel. 7132348; telex 132138; f. 1960; 502 mems; Pres. Prof. Dipl.-Ing. Dr H. SCHINDLBAUER; Sec. (vacant); publs *Erdöl Erdgas Kohle*, scientific papers.

Österreichische Gesellschaft für Klinische Chemie (Austrian Society of Clinical Chemistry): 1090 Vienna, Währingerstr. 10; tel. (512) 5073503; fax (512) 5072865; e-mail oegkc@uibk.ac.at; f. 1968; 500 mems; Pres. Prof. Dr ERIKA ARTNER-DWORZAK; Sec. Doz. Dr HANS DIEPLINGER; publ. *Berichte der OGKC* (quarterly).

Österreichische Gesellschaft für Meteorologie (Austrian Meteorological Society): 1190 Vienna, Hohe Warte 38; tel. (1) 36026-2002; fax (1) 3691233; f. 1865; 225 mems; Pres. Prof. Dr HELGA KROMP-KOLB; Sec. Doz. Dr FRITZ NEUWIRTH; publ. *Wetter und Leben* (quarterly).

Österreichische Physikalische Gesellschaft (Austrian Physical Society): C/o Prof. Dr R. Dobrozemsky, Physics Dept, Österreichisches Forschungszentrum Seibersdorf, 2444 Seibersdorf; tel. (2254) 803137; f. 1950; 870 mems; Pres. Dipl.-Ing. H. LIST; Exec. Sec. Prof. Dr R. DOBROZEMSKY.

Österreichischer Astronomischer Verein (Austrian Astronomical Association): 1238 Vienna, Hasenwartgasse 32; tel. and fax (1) 8893541; e-mail astbuero@astronomisches-buero-wien.or.at; f. 1924; 1,500 mems; Pres. JOHANN ALBRECHT; Sec. HERMANN MUCKE; publs *Der Sternenbote, Österreichischer Himmelskalender, Seminarpapiere.*

PHILOSOPHY AND PSYCHOLOGY

Österreichische Gesellschaft für Parapsychologie und Grenzbereiche der Wissenschaften (Austrian Society for Parapsychology and Frontier Areas of Science): 1040 Vienna, Gusshausstr. 27; tel. (1) 4058335; e-mail peter.mulacz@blackbox.at; f. 1927; 220 mems; library of 1,200 vols; Pres. Asst Prof. Dr MANFRED KREMSER; Sec.-Gen. W. PETER MULACZ.

Philosophische Gesellschaft Wien (Philosophical Society of Vienna): 1010 Vienna, Universitätsstr. 7/2/2; f. 1954; 100 mems; Dir Prof. Dr HANS-DIETER KLEIN.

Sigmund Freud-Gesellschaft (Sigmund Freud Society): 1090 Vienna, Berggasse 19; tel. (1) 3191596; fax (1) 3170279; e-mail freud-museum@t0.or.at; f. 1968; history and application of psychoanalysis; 1,000 mems; library of 8,000 vols, 15,000 off-prints, 45 journals; archives; Sigmund Freud museum; Pres. Doz. Dr H. LEUPOLD-LÖWENTHAL; Vice-Pres. Prof. Dr E. WEINZIERL; publ. *Newsletter* (4 a year).

Wiener Psychoanalytische Vereinigung (Vienna Psychoanalytical Association): 1010 Vienna, Gonzagagasse 11; tel. (222) 5330767; f. 1908; 71 mems; Pres. Prim. Dr W. BURIAN; Sec. Dr LORE GRATZ-ERBLER.

RELIGION, SOCIOLOGY AND ANTHROPOLOGY

Anthropologische Gesellschaft in Wien (Vienna Anthropological Society): 1014 Vienna I, Burgring 7, Postfach 417; f. 1870; 335 mems; Pres. Prof. Dr KARL R. WERNHART; Sec. Dr ANTON KERN; publs *Mitteilungen, Anthropologische Forschungen, Ethnologische Forschungen, Prähistorische Forschungen, Volkskundliche Veröffentlichungen, Völkerkundliche Veröffentlichungen.*

Evangelische Akademie Wien (Evangelical Academy in Vienna): 1096 Vienna IX, Schwarzspanierstr. 13, Postfach 15; tel. 4080695; fax 408069533; f. 1955; Protestant adult education; documentation on church and society; Dir Dr THOMAS KROBATH.

Gesellschaft für die Geschichte des Protestantismus in Österreich (Society for History of Protestantism in Austria): 1090 Vienna, Rooseveltplatz 10; f. 1879; 300 mems; Chair. Prof. Dr GUSTAV REINGRABNER; publ. *Jahrbuch.*

Österreichische Ethnologische Gesellschaft (Austrian Ethnological Society): Museum für Völkerkunde, 1014 Vienna, Neue Hofburg; tel. 53430-519; f. 1957; 221 mems; Pres. Doz. Dr FERDINAND ANDERS; Sec. Mag. INGEBORG REISINGER; publ. *Wiener Völkerkundliche Mitteilungen* (annually).

Österreichische Gesellschaft für Soziologie (Austrian Sociological Society): Institut für Soziologie, 4040 Linz, Altenbergerstr. 69; tel. (732) 2468-242; fax (732) 2468-243; e-mail josef.gunz@jk.uni-linz.ac.at; f. 1950; Pres. Prof. JOSEF GUNZ; publs *ÖGS-Informationen, Österreichische Zeitschrift für Soziologie* (quarterly).

Verein für Landeskunde von Niederösterreich (Association for Regional Studies of Lower Austria): 1014 Vienna I, Herrengasse 11; tel. (222) 53110; f. 1864; 1,300 mems; Pres. Hofrat Prof. Dr H. RIEPL; Gen. Sec. Mag. WILLIBALD ROSNER; publs *Unsere Heimat* (quarterly), *Jahrbuch für Landeskunde von Niederösterreich, Forschungen zur Landeskunde von Niederösterreich.*

Verein für Volkskunde (Ethnographical Association): 1080 Vienna, Laudongasse 15–19; tel. (1) 4068905; fax (1) 4085342; f. 1894; 900 mems; Pres. Dir Dr KLAUS BEITL; Sec. Dr FRANZ GRIESHOFER; publs *Österreichische Zeitschrift für Volkskunde, Volkskunde in Österreich, Buchreihe der Österreichischen Zeitschrift für Volkskunde, Österreichische Volkskundliche Bibliographie,* also special publs.

Wiener Katholische Akademie (Vienna Catholic Academy): 1010 Vienna, Ebendorferstr. 8; tel. 4023917; f. 1945; seminars and lectures, scientific working groups, publications; 160 mems; library of 3,000 vols; Protector Erzbischof Cardinal Dr C. SCHÖNBORN; Gen. Sec. Dr E. MAIER; publ. *Schriften der Wiener Katholischen Akademie.*

TECHNOLOGY

Österreichische Gesellschaft für Artificial Intelligence (Austrian Association for Artificial Intelligence): 1014 Vienna, POB 177; tel. (1) 58801-4089; fax (1) 5040532; e-mail oegai@ai.univie.ac.at; f. 1981; 150 mems; Pres. SILVIA MIKSCH; publ. *ÖGAI-Journal* (quarterly).

Österreichische Gesellschaft für Vermessung und Geoinformation (Austrian Society for Surveying and Geological Information): 1025 Vienna, Schiffamtsgasse 1–3; tel. (1) 21176-3603; fax (1) 2167551; f. 1973; 700 mems; library of 3,000 vols; Pres. Dipl.-Ing. AUGUST HOCHWARTNER; Sec. Dipl.-Ing. GERT STEINKELLNER; publ. *Österreichische Zeitschrift für Vermessung und Geoinformation* (quarterly).

Österreichische Studiengesellschaft für Kybernetik (Austrian Society for Cybernetic Studies): 1010 Vienna I, Schottengasse 3; tel. 53532810; fax 5320652; e-mail sec@ai.univie.ac.at; f. 1969; 38 ord., 638 corresp. mems; Pres. Prof. Dr ROBERT TRAPPL; publs *Cybernetics and Systems: An International Journal* (8 a year), *Reports* (irregular).

Research Institutes

AGRICULTURE, FISHERIES AND VETERINARY SCIENCE

Bundesamt und Forschungszentrum für Landwirtschaft, Wien (Federal Office and Research Centre of Agriculture, Vienna): 1226 Vienna, Spargelfeldstr. 191, Postfach 400; tel. (1) 28816-0; fax (1) 28816-3107; e-mail bal.gump@computerhaus.at; f. 1869; library of 100,000 vols; Dir-Gen. Hofrat Dipl.-Ing. A. KÖCHL; publs *Pflanzenschutzberichte* (2 a year), *Pflanzenschutz* (quarterly), *Die Bodenkultur* (quarterly).

Bundesanstalt für Agrarwirtschaft (Federal Institute of Agricultural Economics): 1133 Vienna 13, Schweizertalstr. 36; tel. (1) 8773651; fax (1) 877365159; f. 1960; applied research; library of 42,000 vols, 350 periodicals; Dir HUBERT PFINGSTNER; publs *Monatsberichte* (monthly), *Schrifttum der Agrarwirtschaft* (every 2 months), *Schriftenreihe* (irregular), *Tätigkeitsbericht* (Report, annually).

Bundesanstalt für Alpenländische Landwirtschaft, Gumpenstein (Federal Research Institute for Agriculture in Alpine Regions, Gumpenstein): Steiermark, 8952 Irdning; tel. (3682) 22451; fax (3682) 2461488; f. 1947; library of 21,000 vols; Dir Dr KURT CHYTIL; publs *BAL-Sortenversuchsergebnisse, BAL-Veröffentlichungen, BAL-Berichte*.

Bundesanstalt für Veterinärmedizinische Untersuchungen (Federal Institute for Veterinary Research): 4021 Linz, Kudlichstr. 27; f. 1947; Dir Dr ERNST LAUERMANN.

Forstliche Bundesversuchsanstalt (Federal Forest Research Centre): 1131 Vienna, Seckendorff-Gudent-Weg 8; tel. 878380; fax 8775907; f. 1874; library of 43,000 vols; Dir FRIEDRICH RUHM; publs *Mitteilungen, FBVA-Berichte* (irregular), *Informationsdienst* (irregular), *Jahresbericht.*

Landesanstalt für Pflanzenzucht und Samenprüfung (National Establishment for Plant Cultivation and Seed Testing): 6074 Rinn, Tirol; tel. (5223) 78117; fax (5223) 78117-25; f. 1939; Dir Dipl.-Ing. K. HOLAUS; publ. *Trial-Report* (annually).

ARCHITECTURE AND TOWN PLANNING

Österreichisches Institut für Raumplanung (Austrian Institute for Regional Studies and Spatial Planning): 1011 Vienna I, Franz Josefs Kai 27; tel. (1) 5338747; fax (1) 5338747-66; e-mail oir@oir.or.at; f. 1957; library of 35,000 vols; Dir Mag. PETER SCHNEIDEWIND; publ. *RAUM* (quarterly).

BIBLIOGRAPHY, LIBRARY SCIENCE AND MUSEOLOGY

Österreichisches Institut für Bibliotheksforschung, Dokumentations und Informationswesen (Austrian Institute for Library Research, Documentation and Information): 1040 Vienna, Resselgasse 4; f. 1966; Chair. Dr J. WAWROSCH; Sec. Dr H. HRUSA; publ. *Biblos.*

ECONOMICS, LAW AND POLITICS

Forschungsstelle für Institutionellen Wandel und Europäische Integration (Research Unit for Institutional Change and European Integration): 1010 Vienna, Postgasse 7/1/2; tel. (1) 51581-565; fax (1) 51581-566; e-mail ice@oeaw.ac.at; f. 1998; attached to Austrian Acad. of Sciences; Dir Doz. Dr SONJA PUNTSCHER RIEKMANN.

Institut für Höhere Studien und Wissenschaftliche Forschung Wien (Vienna Institute for Advanced Studies and Scientific Research): 1060 Vienna, Stumpergasse 56; tel. (222) 59991; fax 5970635; f. 1963; postgraduate training and research in economics, finance, sociology and political science; library of 15,500 vols, 470 current periodicals; Dir Prof. BERNHARD FELDERER; publ. *Empirical Economics.*

Institut für Politische Wissenschaft (Institute for Political Science): 5020 Salzburg, Mönchsberg 2A; library of 9,500 vols; Dir Prof. Dr FRANZ-MARTIN SCHMÖLZ.

Institut für Sozialpolitik und Sozialreform (Institute for Social Politics and Social Reform): 1010 Vienna, Ebendorferstr. 6/IV; f. 1953; Pres. JOSEF STEURER; publ. *Gesellschaft und Politik.*

Österreichische Forschungsstiftung für Entwicklungshilfe (Austrian Foundation for Development Research): 1090 Vienna, Berggasse 7; tel. 3174010; fax 3174015; e-mail oefse.ga@magnet.at; f. 1967; documentation and information on development aid, developing countries and int. development, particularly relating to Austria; library of 22,000 vols, 250 periodicals; publs *Österreichische Entwicklungspolitik. Berichte-Analysen-Informationen* (annually); *Ausgewählte neue Literatur zur Entwicklungspolitik* (annotated bibliography, 2 a year).

Österreichisches Institut für Entwicklungshilfe und Technische Zusammenarbeit mit den Entwicklungsländern (Austrian Institute for Assistance and Technical Co-operation with the Developing Countries): 1010 Vienna, Wipplingerstr. 35; tel. 426504; f. 1963; projects for training of industrial training personnel; Pres Dr HANS IGLER, ERICH HOFSTETTER.

Österreichisches Institut für Wirtschaftsforschung (Austrian Institute of Economic Research): 1103 Vienna, Postfach 91; tel. 7982601; fax. 7989386; f. 1926; Dir Prof. Dr HELMUT KRAMER; publs *Monatsberichte* (monthly), *Empirica* (3 a year, with Austrian Economic Asscn), *Austrian Economic Quarterly.*

Österreichisches Meinungs- und Marktforschungsinstitut (Austrian Public Opinion and Market Research Institute): 1090 Vienna, Schlagergasse 6; Dir Dr F. KARMASIN.

Österreichisches Ost- und Südosteuropa-Institut (Austrian Institute of East and South-East European Studies): 1010 Vienna, Josefsplatz 6; tel. 5121895; fax 512189553; e-mail arnold.suppan@univie.ac.at; f. 1958; library of 33,000 vols, 2,400 (700 current) periodicals and documents; Chair. of Exec. Board Prof. Dr A. SUPPAN; Dir Doz. Dr WALTRAUD HEINDL; publs *Österreichische Osthefte* (quarterly), *Wiener Osteuropastudien, OSI-aktuell* (newsletter, irregular).

Österreichisches Statistisches Zentralamt (Austrian Central Statistical Office): 1033 Vienna, Hintere Zollamtsstr. 2B; tel. (1) 71128-0; fax (1) 71128-7728; f. 1829; library of 210,000 vols; Pres. Mag. ERICH BADER; publs *Statistisches Jahrbuch für die Republik Österreich* (annually), *Statistische Nachrichten* (monthly), etc.

Wirtschaftsförderungsinstitut der Wirtschaftskammer Österreich (Economic Promotion Institute of the Austrian Federal Chamber of Commerce): 1045 Vienna, Wiedner Hauptstr. 63; f. 1946; adult education, management and vocational training, public relations for Austrian economy, consulting service, trade fairs; Man. Dir Mag. STEFAN HLAWACEK; publs bulletins and brochures.

Zentrum für angewandte Politikforschung (Centre for Applied Political Research): 1030 Vienna, Reisnerstr. 40; tel. 7153780; fax 7153780/5410; e-mail zapol@ping.at; f. 1961; Dir Prof. Dr FRITZ PLASSER.

FINE AND PERFORMING ARTS

Abteilung Inventarisation und Denkmalforschung (Department of Art Research and Inventory): 1010 Vienna, Hofburg, Schweizerhof, Säulenstiege; affiliated to the Bundesdenkmalamt (see under Learned Societies); f. 1911; research and documentation on works of art in Austria; library of 22,000 vols; Chief Officer Dr ECKART VANCSA.

Gesellschaft für vergleichende Kunstforschung (Society of Comparative Art Research): 1090 Vienna, Universitätscampus AAKH, Spitalgasse 2 (Eingang Garnisongasse 13); tel. (1) 427741425; fax (1) 42779414; f. 1932; Sec.-Gen. Prof. Dr WALTER KRAUSE; publ. *Mitteilungen.*

Wiener Gesellschaft für Theaterforschung (Viennese Society for Theatre Research): 1010 Vienna, Hofburg, Batthyanystiege; tel. and fax (1) 5350590; f. 1944; Pres. Prof. Dr WOLFGANG GREISENEGGER; Gen. Sec. Dr OTTO G. SCHINDLER; publs *Jahrbuch, Theater in Österreich* (annually).

HISTORY, GEOGRAPHY AND ARCHAEOLOGY

Forschungsstelle für Archäologie (Research Unit for Archaeology): 1010 Vienna, Postgasse 7/4/1; attached to Austrian Acad. of Sciences; Dir Prof. Dr FRIEDRICH KRINZINGER.

Institut für Demographie (Institute of Demography): 1033 Vienna, Hintere Zollamstr. 2B; attached to Austrian Acad. of Sciences; Dir Dr RICHARD GIESSER.

Institut für Realienkunde des Mittelalters und der Frühen Neuzeit (Institute for Research into Austrian Daily Life and Material Culture in Medieval and Early Modern Times): 3500 Krems an der Donau, Körnermarkt 13; tel. (2732) 84793; fax (2732) 84793-1; e-mail imareal@oeaw.ac.at; f. 1969; attached to Austrian Acad. of Sciences; Dir Prof. Dr KARL BRUNNER.

LANGUAGE AND LITERATURE

Institut für Österreichische Dialekt- und Namenlexika (Institute for Lexicography of Austrian Dialects and Names): 1010 Vienna, Postgasse 7/2; attached to Austrian Acad. of Sciences; Dir Prof. Dr WERNER BAUER.

MEDICINE

Bundesstaatliche Anstalt für Experimentell-Pharmakologische und Balneologische Untersuchungen (Federal State Institute for Experimental Pharmacology and Balneology): 1090 Vienna, Währinger Str. 13A; tel. (1) 40480282; fax (1) 4027950; f. 1948; Dir Assoc. Prof. Dr H. PITTNER.

Institut for Biomedizinische Alternsforschung (Institute of Biomedical Research on Ageing): 6020 Innsbruck, Rennweg 10; attached to Austrian Acad. of Sciences; Dir Prof. Dr GEORG WICK.

NATURAL SCIENCES

General

Fonds zur Förderung der Wissenschaftlichen Forschung (Austrian Science Fund): 1040 Vienna, Weyringergasse 35; tel. (1) 50567400; fax (1) 5056739; f. 1967; all Austrian universities with their faculties, the art schools and the Austrian Academy of Sciences are represented, also delegates of non-univ. research instns and professional asscns; with the Austrian Industrial Research Fund, it forms *Österreichischer Forschungsförderungsrat* (Austrian Research Council), co-ordinating scientific, applied and industrial research and development and advising the Fed. and State govts on scientific matters; Pres Prof. Dr ARNOLD SCHMIDT, Prof. Dr WALTER KNAPP, Prof. Dr HERBERT MATIS; Sec. Gen. Dr EVA GLUCK.

Institut für Wissenschaft und Kunst (Institute for Science and Art): 1090 Vienna, Berggasse 17; tel. and fax 3174342; f. 1946; Gen. Sec. Dr HELGA KASCHL; publ. *Mitteilungen*.

Institut für Wissenschaftstheorie (Institute for the Philosophy of Science): Internationales Forschungszentrum, 5020 Salzburg, Mönchsberg 2; tel. (662) 842521; fax (662) 842521118; f. 1961; philosophy of science, foundations of logic, mathematics and ethics; library of 12,000 vols; Dir Prof. Dr PAUL WEINGARTNER; publ. *Forschungsgespräche* (irregular).

Biological Sciences

Biologische Station Neusiedler See (Biological Station Neusiedler See): Amt d. Burgenl. Landesregierung, Abt. 5, 7142 Illmitz; tel. (2175) 2328; fax (2175) 232810; e-mail biol.stat@netway.at; f. 1971; nature conservation, limnology; Dir Prof. Dr A. HERZIG; publ. BFB *(Biologisches Forschungsinstitut Burgenland)-Berichte* (irregular).

Institut für Biophysik und Röntgenstrukturforschung (Institute of Biophysics and X-Ray Structure Research): 8010 Graz, Steyrergasse 17; attached to Austrian Acad. of Sciences; Dir Prof. Dr PETER LAGGNER.

Institut für Botanik und Botanischer Garten der Universtät Wien (Institute of Botany and Botanical Garden of Vienna University): 1030 Vienna, Rennweg 14; tel. (1) 79794; fax (1) 79794131; f. 1754 (Garden) and 1844 (Institute); library of 40,000 vols; Dir Prof. Dr MICHAEL HESSE; publ. *Plant Systematics and Evolution* (5 vols a year).

Institut für Limnologie (Institute of Limnology): 5310 Mondsee, Gaisberg 116; attached to Austrian Acad. of Sciences; Dir Prof. Dr ARNOLD NAUWERCK.

Institut für Molekularbiologie (Institute of Molecular Biology): 5020 Salzburg, Billrothstr. 11; attached to Austrian Acad. of Sciences; Dir Prof. J. V. SMALL.

Physical Sciences

Atominstitut der Österreichischen Universitäten (Atomic Institute of the Austrian Universities): 1020 Vienna, Schüttelstr. 115; tel. (1) 727010; fax (1) 7289220; f. 1958; training of advanced students and basic research; Dirs Prof. Dr GERNOT EDER, Prof. Dr HELMUT RAUCH.

Forschungsstelle für Schallforschung (Research Unit for Sound Research): 1010 Vienna, Liebiggasse 5; attached to Austrian Acad. of Sciences; Dir Prof. Dr WERNER DEUTSCH.

Geologische Bundesanstalt (Geological Survey of Austria): 1031 Vienna, Rasumofskygasse 23, Postfach 127; tel. (1) 7125674-0; fax (1) 7125674-90; e-mail geolba@cc.geolba.ac.at; f. 1849; library of 245,000 vols, 43,000 geological maps, 9,000 aerial photographs, 11,000 archive items, 12,000 microforms; Dir Prof. Dr H. P. SCHÖNLAUB; publs *Jahrbuch, Abhandlungen, Archiv für Lagerstättenforschung, Berichte,* geological maps.

Hydrographisches Zentralbüro (Central Hydrographical Office): 1030 Vienna, Marxergasse 2; tel. (1) 71100-6942; fax (1) 71100-6851; f. 1893; library of 18,000 vols; Head Prof. F. NOBILIS; publs *Hydrographisches Jahrbuch von Österreich* (annually), *Beiträge zur Hydrographie Österreichs* (irregular), Mitteilungsblatt des Hydrographischen Dienstes in Österreich (annually), *Hydrologische Bibliographie von Österreich* (irregular).

Institut für Astronomie der Universität Innsbruck (Astronomy Institute of the University of Innsbruck): 6020 Innsbruck, Technikerstr. 25; tel. (512) 2185251; fax (512) 218-5252; f. 1904; library of 4,598 vols; Dir Prof. Dr J. PFLEIDERER; publ. *Mitteilungen* (irregular).

Institut für Astronomie der Universität Wien (Vienna University Observatory): 1180 Vienna, Türkenschanzstr. 17; tel. (222) 47068000; telex 133099; fax (222) 470680015; f. 1755; joined with L. Figl Observatory for Astrophysics; library of 98,000 vols; Head of Dept Dr PAUL JACKSON.

Associated body:

Figl Observatorium für Astrophysik (Figl Observatory for Astrophysics): 1180 Vienna, Türkenschanzstr. 17; St Corona at Schöpfl (Vienna forest); f. 1969.

Institut für Hochenergiephysik (Institute of High Energy Physics): 1050 Vienna, Nikolsdorfergasse 18; attached to Austrian Acad. of Sciences; Dir Prof. Dr WALTER MAJEROTTO.

Institut für Mittelenergiephysik (Institute of Medium Energy Physics): 1090 Vienna, Boltzmanngasse 3; attached to Austrian Acad. of Sciences; Dir Prof. Dr WOLFGANG BREUNLICH.

Institut für Weltraumforschung (Space Research Institute): 8010 Graz, Inffeldgasse 12; attached to Austrian Acad. of Sciences; Dir Prof. Dipl.-Ing. DDr WILLIBALD RIEDLER.

Kuffner-Sternwarte (Kuffner Observatory): 1160 Vienna, Johann-Staud-Str. 10; tel. (431) 9148130; fax (431) 914813031; e-mail admin@kuffner.ac.at; f. 1884; library of 500 vols; Dir PETER HABISON.

Ludwig Boltzmann Institut für Festkörperphysik (Ludwig Boltzmann Institute for Solid State Physics): 1060 Vienna VI, Kopernikusgasse 15; f. 1965; research into semiconductors, conducting polymers and high-temperature superconductors; Dir Prof. Dr KARLHEINZ SEEGER.

Österreichische Geodätische Kommission (Austrian Geodetic Commission): 1025 Vienna, Schiffamtsgasse 1–3; tel. (431) 21176-3201; fax (431) 21176-2224; f. 1863; Pres. Prof. Dr HANS SÜNKEL; Sec. Dr ERHARD ERKER; publ. *Geodätische Arbeiten Österreichs für die Internationale Erdmessung*.

Sonnenobservatorium Kanzelhöhe der Universität Graz (Kanzelhöhe Solar Observatory of the University of Graz): 9521 Treffen; tel. (4248) 27170; fax (4248) 4102; f. 1943; small library; Dir Dr A. HANSLMEIER; publ. *Mitteilungen* (irregular).

Sternwarte Kremsmünster (Kremsmünster Observatory): 4550 Kremsmünster; tel. and fax (7583) 5275235; e-mail sternwarte.kremsmuenster@telecom.at; f. 1748; library of 20,000 vols; Dir Mag. P. AMAND KRAML; publ. *Berichte des Anselm Desing Vereins* (irregular).

Umweltbundesamt (Federal Environment Agency): 1090 Vienna, Spittelauer Lände 5; tel. (1) 31304-0; fax (1) 31304-5400; e-mail umweltbundesamt@ubavie.gv.at; f. 1985; elaboration of scientific studies and basic data for fed. environmental protection policy in Austria; library of 20,000 vols, 300 periodicals; Dir Dr W. STRUWE.

Zentralanstalt für Meteorologie und Geodynamik (Central Institute for Meteorology and Geodynamics): 1191 Vienna, Hohe Warte 38; tel. (1) 36026; telex 131837; fax (1) 3691233; e-mail dion@zamg.ac.at; f. 1851; provides national weather service; acts in all fields of meteorology except aeronautical field; nat. body responsible for geophysics; library of 80,000 vols; Dir Prof. Dr PETER STEINHAUSER; publs yearbooks and bulletins.

PHILOSOPHY AND PSYCHOLOGY

Institut für Kultur- und Geistesgeschichte Asiens (Institute for the Cultural and Intellectual History of Asia): 1010 Vienna, Postgasse 7; attached to Austrian Acad. of Sciences; Dir Prof. Dr ERNST STEINKELLNER.

Konrad-Lorenz-Institut für Vergleichende Verhaltensforschung (Konrad Lorenz Institute of Comparative Behavioural Research): 1160 Vienna, Savoyenstr. 1A; attached to Austrian Acad. of Sciences; Dir Prof. Dr HANS WINKLER.

Psychotechnisches Institut Wien (Psychotechnical Institute, Vienna): 1190 Vienna, Vegagasse 4; tel. 341130; f. 1926; training of supervisors of all levels; library of 8,500 vols; Dir Hofrat Dr GUIDO HACKL; publ. *Mensch und Arbeit*.

RELIGION, SOCIOLOGY AND ANTHROPOLOGY

Institut für Kirchliche Sozialforschung (Institute of Socio-Religious Research): Vienna I, Grillparzerstr. 5; tel. (1) 4064284; fax (1) 4064284-18; f. 1952; library of 9,100 vols; Head Dr JUTTA SUMMER.

Institut für Kirchliche Zeitgeschichte (Institute for Contemporary Ecclesiastical History): 5020 Salzburg, Mönchsberg 2A; tel. (662) 842521161; fax (622) 84252118; f. 1961; library of 8,500 vols; Dir Doz. Dr ALFRED RINNERTHALER; publs *Hirtenbriefe aus Deutschland, Österreich und der Schweiz* (annually) and *Publikationen des Instituts für Kirchliche Zeitgeschichte*.

Institut für Religionswissenschaft und Theologie (Institute of Religious Knowledge and Theology): Salzburg, Mönchsberg 2A; tel. (662) 842521-141; fax (662) 842521-118; e-mail gglassnet@alpin.or.at; f. 1961; library of 10,000 vols; Dir Prof. DDr LUDGER BERNHARD.

Institut für Stadt und Regionalforschung (Institute of Urban and Regional Research): 1010 Vienna, Postgasse 7/1/2; attached to Austrian Acad. of Sciences; Dir Prof. Dr HEINZ FASSMANN.

TECHNOLOGY

Erich-Schmid-Institut für Materialwissenschaft (Erich Schmid Institute of Solid Material Sciences): 8700 Leoben, Jahnstr. 12; tel. (3842) 45511; fax (3842) 45512-16; e-mail fratzl@unileoben.ac.at; f. 1971; attached to Austrian Acad. of Sciences; Dir Prof. Dr PETER FRATZL.

Holzforschung Austria (Wood Research Austria): 1030 Vienna, Arsenal, Franz Grillstr. 7; tel. (1) 79826230; f. 1947; research institute of the Austrian Forest Products Research Society; library of 35,000 vols; Dir Prof. Dr WOLFGANG WINTER; publs *Holzforschung und Holzverwertung* (every 2 months), *Schrifttumskarteidienst der ÖGH* (2 a month).

Institut für Gewerbe- und Handwerksforschung (Institute for Small Business Research): 1040 Vienna, Gusshausstr. 8; tel. (222) 5059761; fax (222) 505976122; f. 1952; library of 2,500 vols; Pres. Prof. Dr J. H. PICHLER; Dirs Dr WALTER BORNETT, Mag. C. F. LETTMAYR; publ. *IfG-Mitteilungen* (2 a year).

Institut für Informationsverarbeitung (Institute of Information Processing): 1010 Vienna, Sonnenfelsg. 19; tel. (1) 51581326; fax (1) 5128901; f. 1972; attached to Austrian Acad. of Sciences; Dir Prof. Dr HARALD NIEDERREITER.

Institut für Technikfolgen-Abschätzung (Institute for Technology Assessment): 1010 Vienna, Postgasse 7; attached to Austrian Acad. of Sciences; Dir Prof. Dr GUNTHER TICHY.

Institut für Wasserbau und Hydrometrische Prüfung (Institute for Hydraulic Engineering and the Calibration of Hydrometrical Current-Meters): 1090 Vienna, Severingasse 7; tel. (1) 4026802-0; fax (1) 4026802-30; e-mail edv@iwb.bmlf.gv.at; f. 1913; attached to Federal Office of Water Resources Management; Dir Dipl.-Ing. Dr techn. M. HENGL.

Österreichisches Forschungsinstitut für Artificial Intelligence (Austrian Research Institute for Artificial Intelligence): 1010 Vienna, Schottengasse 3; tel. (1) 53532810; fax (1) 5320652; e-mail sec@ai.univie.ac.at; f. 1984; a research institute of the Austrian Soc. for Cybernetic Studies; library of 3,000 vols; Dir Prof. Dr ROBERT TRAPPL; publs *Applied Artificial Intelligence: An International Journal* (8 a year), *Technical Reports* (irregular).

Österreichisches Forschungsinstitut für Technikgeschichte (ÖFiT) am Technischen Museum für Industrie und Gewerbe in Wien (Austrian Research Institute for the History of Technology in Vienna): 1140 Vienna, Mariahilfer Str. 212; f. 1931; Pres. Hofrat Dipl.-Ing. Dr jr. FRANZ SKACEL.

Österreichisches Forschungszentrum Seibersdorf GmbH (Austrian Research Centre, Seibersdorf): 2444 Seibersdorf; tel. (2254) 7800; fax (2254) 74060; e-mail seibersdorf@arcs.ac.at; f. 1956; contract research and development in instrumentation and information technology, process and environmental technologies, engineering, life sciences and systems research; library of 15,500 vols; Dir Prof. Dr FRANZ LEBERL; publs OEFSZ Reports.

Österreichisches Giesserei-Institut (Austrian Foundry Institute): 8700 Leoben, Parkstr. 21; tel. (3842) 431010; fax (3842) 431011; f. 1952; library of 2,140 vols; Man. and Tech. Dir Dipl.-Ing. ANDREAS BÜHRIG-POLACZEK; publ. *Giesserei Rundschau*.

Österreichisches Normungsinstitut (ON) (Austrian Standards Institute): 1021 Vienna, Postfach 130, Heinestr. 38; tel. 21300; fax 21300-360; f. 1920; govt-supervised private institute for standardization in all fields; library of 1,000 vols, 30 periodicals, 600,000 foreign standards; Pres. Prof. Dr KARL KORINEK; Man. Dir Ing. Dr GERHARD HARTMANN; Chief Librarian MICHAELA GRAFF; publ. *CONNEX* (monthly).

Österreichisches Textil-Forschungsinstitut (Austrian Textile Research Institute): 1050 Vienna, Postfach 117, Spengergasse 20; tel. (1) 5442543; fax (1) 544254310; f. 1978; Dir Dipl.-Ing. Dr ERICH ZIPPEL.

Physikalisch-Technische Versuchsanstalt für Wärme- und Schalltechnik am Technologischen Gewerbemuseum (Physical-technical Institute for Research on Heat and Noise Technology at the Technological Industrial Museum): 1200 Vienna, Wexstr. 19–23; tel. (1) 33126411; telex 131824; fax (1) 3305925; Dir Ing. Mag. MATHIAS STANI.

Zentrum für Elektronenmikroskopie (Centre for Electron Microscopy): 8010 Graz, Steyrergasse 17; tel. (316) 825363; fax (316) 811596; f 1959; library of 2,000 vols; Pres. Prof. Dipl.-Ing. Dr h.c. HELMUT LIST; Dir Dr WOLFGANG GEYMAYER.

Libraries and Archives

Admont

Bibliothek der Benediktinerabtei (Library of the Benedictine Abbey): 8911 Admont; tel. (3613) 2312602; fax (3613) 2312320; f. 1074; 155,000 vols, 1,400 MSS, 530 incunabula; Dir Dr JOHANN TOMASCHEK.

Bregenz

Vorarlberger Landesarchiv (Vorarlberg Provincial Archives): 6901 Bregenz, Kirchstr. 28; tel. (5574) 5114510; fax (5574) 5114545; e-mail karl-heinz.burmeister@vlr.gv.at; f. 1898; Dir Hofrat Prof. DDr KARL HEINZ BURMEISTER; publ. *Zeitschrift Montfort* (quarterly).

Vorarlberger Landesbibliothek (Vorarlberg Provincial Library): 6901 Bregenz, Fluherstr. 4; tel. (5574) 5114410; fax (5574) 5114453; e-mail info.vlb@vlr.gv.at; f. 1977; 350,000 vols; Dir Dr HARALD WEIGEL.

Eisenstadt

Burgenländische Landesbibliothek (Burgenland Provincial Library): 7001 Eisenstadt, Freiheitsplatz 1, Landhaus; tel. (2682) 6002358; f. 1922; 100,000 vols; Dir Dr JOHANN SEEDOCH; publ *Burgenländische Landesbibliographie* (annually).

Burgenländisches Landesarchiv (Burgenland Provincial Archives): 7001 Eisenstadt, Freiheitsplatz 1, Landhaus; f. 1922; Dir Dr JOHANN SEEDOCH; publ. *Burgenländische Heimatblätter* (quarterly).

Graz

Steiermärkische Landesbibliothek (Styrian Federal State Library): Graz, Kalchberggasse 2; tel. (316) 80164600; fax (316) 80164633; f. 1811; 620,000 vols, 2,800 periodicals, 2,300 MSS; Dir Hofrat Dr J. F. DESPUT; publs *Arbeiten aus der Steiermärkischen Landesbibliothek* (irregular), *Steierische Bibliographie* (irregular), *Geschichte und Gegenwart* (quarterly).

Steiermärkisches Landesarchiv (Styrian Provincial Archives): 8010 Graz, Karmeliterplatz 3; tel. (316) 8772361; fax (316) 8772954; f. 1811; Dir Hofrat Doz. Dr WALTER BRUNNER; publs *Mitteilungen* (annually), *Veröffentlichungen, Styriaca* (irregular).

Universitätsbibliothek der Technischen Universität Graz (Technical University Library): 8010 Graz, Technikerstr. 4; tel. (316) 8736150; fax (316) 873-6671; e-mail bertha@tub.tu-graz.ac.at; f. 1875; 522,000 vols; Dir EVA BERTHA.

Universitätsbibliothek Graz (University Library, Graz): 8010 Graz, Universitätsplatz 3; tel. (316) 3803101; fax (316) 384987; e-mail sigrid.reinitzer@kfunigraz.ac.at; f. 1573; 2,600,000 vols, 10,500 periodicals, 2,203 MSS, 1,150 incunabula; Dir Dr SIGRID REINITZER; publs *Jahresbericht, Fachliche Benützungsanleitungen, Bibliographische Informationen, Schriftenreihe EDV-Projekt, News*.

Heiligenkreuz bei Baden

Stiftsarchiv des Zisterzienserstiftes (Cistercian Abbey Archives): Heiligenkreuz bei Baden; archives dating from the founding of the monastery in 1133; Archivist Dr ALBERICH STROMMER.

Innsbruck

Tiroler Landesarchiv (Tyrolese Provincial Archives): 6020 Innsbruck, Michael-Gaismair-Strasse 1; f. 13th century; records from 11th century; Dir Dr WERNER KÖFLER; publs *Tiroler Geschichtsquellen, Veröffentlichungen des Tiroler Landesarchivs* (irregular).

Universitätsbibliothek Innsbruck (University Library, Innsbruck): 6010 Innsbruck, Innrain 50; tel. (512) 5072401; fax (512) 5072864; f. 1746; 2,000,000 vols, 8,000 current periodicals, 1,100 MSS, 2,000 incunabula; Dir Dr WALTER NEUHAUSER.

Klagenfurt

Kärntner Landesarchiv (Carinthian Provincial Archives): 9020 Klagenfurt, St Ruprechter Str. 7; tel. (463) 56234; fax (463) 56234-20; f. 1904; Archivists Dr ALFRED OGRIS, Dr EVELYNE WEBERNIG, Dr WILHELM WADL, Dr WILHELM DEUER; publ. *Das Kärntner Landesarchiv* (annually).

Universitätsbibliothek Klagenfurt: 9020 Klagenfurt, Universitätsstr. 65–67; tel. (463) 2700253; f. 1775; 620,000 vols; Dir Dr MANFRED LUBE.

Klosterneuburg

Bibliothek des Augustiner-Chorherrenstiftes (Library of the Augustine Abbey): 3400 Klosterneuburg, Stiftsplatz 1; tel. (2243) 411-151; fax (2243) 82710; f. 1114; 240,000 vols, 1,250 MSS, 836 incunabula; Dir DDr FLORIDUS RÖHRIG.

Leoben

Universitätsbibliothek der Montanuniversität (Library of the Mining and Metallurgical University): 8700 Leoben, Franz-Josef-Str. 18; tel. (3842) 402576; fax (3842) 46380; e-mail jontes@unileoben.ac.at; f. 1840; 250,000 vols; Librarian Dr LIESELOTTE JONTES.

Linz

Bibliothek des Oberösterreichischen Landesmuseums (Library of the Upper Austrian Provincial Museum): 4010 Linz/Donau, Postfach 91, Museumstr. 14; e-mail mus-bibl@eunet.at; f. 1836; 130,000 vols; Librarian WALTRAUD FAISSNER.

Bundesstaatliche Studien-Bibliothek (Federal Public Library): 4020 Linz, Schillerplatz 2; f. 1774; 300,000 vols; Dir Dr KARL HAFNER.

Oberösterreichisches Landesarchiv (Upper Austrian Provincial Archives): 4020 Linz, Anzengruberstr. 19; tel. (732) 655523; fax (732) 6555234619; e-mail gerhart.marckhgott@ooe.gv.at; f. 1896; Dir Dr SIEGFRIED HAIDER; publs *Mitteilungen, Forschungen zur Geschichte Oberösterreichs, Beiträge zur Zeitgeschichte Oberösterreichs, Oberösterreicher, Quellen zur Geschichte Oberösterreichs* (all irregular).

Universitätsbibliothek der Universität Linz: 4040 Linz/Auhof; tel. (732) 2468; f. 1965; 580,000 vols, 2,500 periodicals; Dir Dr MONIKA SCHENK.

Melk

Bibliothek des Benediktinerklosters Melk in Niederösterreich (Library of the Melk Benedictine Monastery in Lower Austria): 3390 Stift Melk; fax (2752) 5231252; e-mail gglassner@alpin.or.at; 80,000 vols (mostly pre-19th-century), 1,800 codices, 750 incunabula.

Salzburg

Bibliothek der Benediktiner Erzabtei St Peter (Library of the Benedictine Abbey of St Peter): Salzburg, St Peter-Bezirk 1; tel. (662) 844576-58; fax (662) 844576-80; f. 700; 120,000 vols, 1,300 MSS, 923 incunabula; Dir Dr ADOLF HAHNL.

Landesarchiv Salzburg Salzburg Provincial Archives): 5010 Salzburg, Postfach 527; f. 1945; Dir Dr FRITZ KOLLER.

Universitätsbibliothek Salzburg (Salzburg University Library): 5010 Salzburg, Hofstallgasse 2–4; tel. (662) 842576; fax (662) 842576680; f. 1623; 750,000 vols, 1,100 MSS, 1,400 incunabula; Dir Hofrätin Dr CHRISTINE UNTERRAINER.

Sankt Florian

Bibliothek des Augustiner-Chorherrenstiftes (Library of the Augustine Canonical Foundation): 4490 St Florian; tel. (7224) 8902; f. 1071; 140,000 vols, 920 MSS, 800 incunabula; Dir Prof. DDr KARL REHBERGER.

Seckau

Bibliothek der Benediktinerabtei (Library of the Benedictine Abbey): 8732 Abteibibliothek Seckau; f. 1883; 160,000 vols; Dir Dr P. BENNO ROTH.

Vienna

Administrative Bibliothek und Österreichische Rechtsdokumentation im Bundeskanzleramt (Administrative Library and Law Documentation of the Chancellery): 1010 Vienna, Herrengasse 23; tel. (1) 531152708; fax (222) 531152707; f. 1849; 477,250 vols on jurisprudence, politics, economics, statutes, etc.; Dir Mag. HEIDEMARIE TERNYAK.

Archiv, Bibliothek und Sammlungen der Gesellschaft der Musikfreunde in Wien (Archives and Library of the Society of Friends of Music in Vienna): 1010 Vienna, Bösendorferstr 12; tel. (1) 5058681; fax (1) 505868166; f. 1812; 22,000 vols; 72,000 scores, historical material; Dir Dr OTTO BIBA.

Archiv der Universität Wien (Archives of the University of Vienna): 1010 Vienna, Postgasse 9; tel. 5131161; fax 5126911; f. 1708; records dating back to 13th century; Archivist Dr KURT MÜHLBERGER; publ. *Schriftenreihe*.

Archiv des Stiftes Schotten (Schotten Foundation Archives): 1010 Vienna, Freyung 6; f. 1155; archives of the Benedictine monastery; Archivist Abt Dr P. HEINRICH FERENCZY.

Bibliothek der Akademie der Bildenden Künste (Library of the Academy of Fine Arts): 1010 Vienna, Schillerplatz 3; tel. (222) 58816166; fax 58816227; f. 1773; 113,000 vols; Dir Dr ROBERT WAGNER; publs catalogues of exhibitions.

Bibliothek der Mechitharistenkongregation: 1070 Vienna, Mechitaristengasse 4; tel. 5236417; f. 1773; literature related to Armenia; 150,000 vols, 3,000 Armenian MSS, all current Armenian newspapers and periodicals; Dir P. VAHAN HOVAGIMIAN; publ. *Handes Amsorya* (annually).

Bibliothek der Österreichischen Akademie der Wissenschaften (Library of the Austrian Academy of Sciences): 1010 Vienna, Dr-Ignaz-Seipel-Platz 2; tel. (1) 5181262; fax (1) 51581256; e-mail bibliothek@oeaw.ac.at; f. 1847; 250,000 vols; Dir Doz. Dr CHRISTINE HARRAUER.

Bibliothek der Österreichischen Geographischen Gesellschaft (Library of the Austrian Geographical Society): 1071 Vienna, Karl Schweighofergasse 3; f. 1856; 21,000 vols; Librarian Dr PETER FRITZ.

Bibliothek der Veterinärmedizinischen Universität Wien (Library of Vienna Veterinary University): 1210 Vienna, Veterinärplatz 1; tel. (1) 25077-1414; fax (1) 25077-1490; f. 1767; 165,000 vols; Dir Dr GÜNTER OLENSKY.

Bibliothek der Wirtschaftskammer Wien (Vienna Chamber of Commerce Library): 1010 Vienna, Stubenring 8–10; tel. 51450370; fax 51450469; e-mail hpribyl@wkwien.wk.or.at; f. 1849; 190,000 vols; Dir Dr HERBERT PRIBYL.

Bibliothek des Bundesministeriums für Arbeit, Gesundheit und Soziales (Library of the Federal Ministry for Labour, Health and Social Affairs): 1010 Vienna, Stubenring 1; tel. (222) 711006143; fax (222) 7158258; e-mail internet.sektionl@bmags.gv.at; f. 1917; 150,000 vols; Dir ILGA ANNA KUBELA.

Bibliothek des Bundesministeriums für Finanzen (Library of the Ministry of Finance): 1015 Vienna, Himmelpfortgasse 4; tel. 514331247; fax 514331246; f. 1810; 280,000 vols; Librarian HEINZ RENNER.

Bibliothek des Bundesministeriums für Land- und Forstwirtschaft (Library of the Ministry of Agriculture and Forestry): 1012 Vienna, Stubenring 1; tel. (1) 71100; fax (1) 7103254; e-mail ingrid.saberi@bmlf.gv.at; f. 1868; 122,000 vols; Librarian Mag. INGRID SABERI.

Bibliothek des Bundesministeriums für Unterricht und Kulturelle Angelegenheiten und des Bundesministeriums für Wissenschaft und Verkehr (Library of the Federal Ministries of Education and Cultural Affairs and of Science and Transport): 1014 Vienna, Minoritenplatz 5; tel. (1) 531204302; telex 115532; fax (1) 53120-5172; f. 1849; 421,000 vols; history of Austrian science and pedagogy since 1848; colln of all state approved school books since 1848 and of annual secondary school programmes; admin. library of the Min. of Science and Transport; Dir (vacant); publs *Verzeichnis des Bücherzuwachses* (monthly), *Forschungspolitische Dokumentation* (quarterly), *EURODOC* (6 a year).

Bibliothek des Instituts für Österreichische Geschichtsforschung (Library of the Institute of Austrian Historical Research): 1010 Vienna, Dr Karl Lueger Ring 1; tel. 427727201; f. 1854; 65,000 vols; Librarian Dr MANFRED STOY; publ. *Verzeichnis der Zeitschriften des Instituts*.

Bibliothek des Österreichischen Patentamtes (Library of the Austrian Patents Office): 1014 Vienna, Kohlmarkt 8–10; tel. (1) 53424140; telex 136847; fax (1) 53424110; f. 1899; 375,000 vols; Dir Dr INGRID WEIDINGER; publs *Österreichisches Patentblatt, Österreichischer Markenanzeiger, Österreichischer Musteranzeiger, Österreichisches Gebrauchsmusterblatt, Patentschriften, Jahresbericht*.

Bibliothek des Österreichischen Staatsarchivs (Library of the Austrian State Archives): 1030 Vienna, Nottendorferg. 2; tel. 79540; history, military history; 400,000 vols; Dir Dr ADOLF GAISBAUER.

Bibliothek des Österreichischen Statistischen Zentralamtes (Library of the Austrian Central Statistical Office): 1033 Vienna, Postfach 9000; tel. (1) 71128-7814; fax (1) 7146251; f. 1829; 210,000 vols; Dir Dr ALOIS GEHART.

Bundesstaatliche Paedagogische Bibliothek beim Landesschulrat für Niederösterreich (Library of the Lower Austrian Education Authority): 1013 Vienna, Wipplingerstr. 28; tel. (1) 53414206; fax (1) 53414275; f. 1923; 160,000 vols, 460 periodicals; Dir Dr WILFRIED LANG.

Diözesanarchiv Wien (Vienna Diocesan Archives): Erzbischöflich Palais, 1010 Vienna, Wollzeile 2; tel. (1) 51552-3239; fax (1) 51552-3240; e-mail daw@magnet.at; f. 1936; history of archdiocese of Vienna and of parishes and convents in Vienna and Lower Austria; 30,000 vols, 700 periodicals, 4,000 documents and files; Dir Dr ANNEMARIE FENZL.

Dokumentations-Service der Österreichischen Bundesbahnen (Documentation Service of the Austrian Federal Railways): 1020 Vienna, Praterstern 3; tel. (1) 5800-33683; fax (1) 5800-25226; f. 1896; 130,000 vols; Librarian BRIGITTE ASSLER.

Fakultätsbibliothek für Rechtswissenschaften (Faculty Library of Legal Studies): 1010 Vienna, Schottenbastei 10–16; tel. (222) 401033315; fax (222) 5353217; f. 1922; 238,000 vols, 1,100 periodicals; Dir Dr UTE WASSERBURGER.

Hochschulbibliothek der Hochschule für Musik und darstellende Kunst in Wien (Library of the Vienna University for Music and Dramatic Art): 1030 Vienna, Lothringerstr. 18; f. 1909; 165,000 vols, 52,000 audiovisual media items; Bruno Walter Archive.

Niederösterreichische Landesbibliothek (Lower Austrian Provincial Library): 3109 Sankt Poelten, Landhausplatz 1; tel. (2742) 200-2847; e-mail post.k3@noel.gv.at; f. 1813; 196,000 vols; Dir Dr GEBHARD KOENIG.

Niederösterreichisches Landesarchiv (Lower Austrian Provincial Archives): 3100 St Pölten, Landhausplatz 1; tel. (2742) 2002044; fax (2742) 2006550; f. 16th century; 25,000 vols; Chief Archivist WHR Dr ANTON EGGENDORFER.

Österreichische Nationalbibliothek (Austrian National Library): 1015 Vienna, Josefsplatz 1; tel. (222) 53410; telex 112624; f. in 16th century; 2,700,000 books, 11,577 periodicals, 7,948 incunabula, 372,000 MSS, 113,000 vols of printed music, 48,500 music MSS, 243,900 maps, 193,000 papyri; Austrian literature archive, portrait colln and picture archive; International Esperanto Museum; Gen. Dir Dr JOHANN MARTE; publs *Ausstellungskatataloge, Jahresberichte* (annually), *Museion, Corpus Papyrorum Raineri, Mitteilungen aus der Papyrussammlung, Palatina-Nachrichten, Biblosschriften* (irreg.), *Biblios. Beiträge zu Buch, Bibliothek und Schrifttum* . Consists of nine collections and other departments.

Österreichisches Staatsarchiv (Austrian State Archives): 1030 Vienna, Nottendorfergasse 2; tel. (1) 79540; fax (1) 79540-109; f. 1945; Domestic, Court and State Archives, General Administrative Archives, Finance and Treasury Archives, War Archives, Archives of the Austrian Republic; Gen. Dir Prof. Dr LORENZ MIKOLETZKY; publ. *Mitteilungen* (annually).

Parlamentsbibliothek (Library of Parliament): 1017 Vienna, Dr Karl Renner-Ring 3; tel. (1) 40110-2285; fax (1) 40110-2825; f. 1869; 280,000 vols; Dir Dr ELISABETH DIETRICH-SCHULZ.

Sozialwissenschaftliche Studienbibliothek der Kammer für Arbeiter und Angestellte für Wien (Social Sciences Library of the Vienna Chamber of Labour): 1040 Vienna, Prinz Eugenstr. 20–22; tel. (222) 50165; fax (222) 501652229; f. 1922; 380,000 vols, 1,200 periodicals; Dir Dr HERWIG JOBST.

Städtische Büchereien der Gemeinde Wien (Municipal Libraries of Vienna): 1080 Vienna, Skodagasse 20; tel. 4000-84500; 1,300,000 vols, 55,000 audio media items; central library and 55 brs; Dir Dr FRANZ PASCHER.

Universitätsbibliothek Bodenkultur Wien (Library of the University of Agricultural Sciences, Vienna): 1190 Vienna, Peter-Jordanstr. 82; tel. (1) 47654-2060; fax (1) 47654-2092; e-mail 4205t3@edvl.boku.ac.at; f. 1872; 450,000 vols, 2,000 periodicals, 7,500 dissertations; Dir Dr WERNER HAINZ-SATOR.

Universitätsbibliothek der Technischen Universität Wien (Vienna University of Technology Library): 1040 Vienna, Resselgasse 4; tel. (1) 58801-5951; fax (1) 5868387; e-mail kub@nov5rv.ub.tuwien.ac.at; f. 1815; 1,070,000 vols; Dir Dr PETER KUBALEK.

Universitätsbibliothek der Wirtschaftsuniversität (Library of the University of Economics): 1090 Vienna, Augasse 2–6; tel. 313364990; fax 31336745; f. 1898; 704,952 vols; Dir Mag. Dkfm. GERTRAUD WEHRMANN.

Universitätsbibliothek Wien (Vienna University Library): Vienna I, Dr Karl Lueger Ring 1; tel. (1) 427715001; fax (1) 42779150; e-mail ilse.dosoudil@univie.ac.at; f. 1365; 5,300,000 vols; Dir Hofratin Dr ILSE DOSOUDIL.

Wiener Stadt- und Landesarchiv (Municipal Archives): 1082 Vienna, Felderstr. 1, Rathaus; tel. 400084808; records from 13th century; Dir Prof. Dr FERDINAND OPLL; publ. *Veröffentlichungen*.

Wiener Stadt- und Landesbibliothek (Vienna City and Provincial Library): 1082 Vienna, Rathaus; tel. (1) 400084915; fax (1) 40007219; f. 1856; 426,000 vols, 220,000 MSS, 65,000 musical items, 16,000 MSS musical items, 150,000 posters; Dir Mag. HERWIG WÜRTZ.

Zentralarchiv des Deutschen Ordens: 1010 Vienna, Singerstr. 7; tel. (222) 5137014; f. 1852; 9,000 vols; Archivist Dr BERNHARD DEMEL; numerous publications.

Zentralbibliothek für Physik in Wien (Central Library for Physics in Vienna): 1090 Vienna, Boltzmanngasse 5; tel. (1) 3190011; telex 116222; fax (1) 313673639; e-mail zb@pap.univie.ac.at; f. 1946; 307,000 vols, 2,800 periodicals, 1,120,000 microfiches; Dir Dr WOLFGANG KERBER.

Zentralbibliothek im Justizpalast (Central Library of the Palace of Justice): Vienna I, Museumstr. 12; tel. 52152-3351; fax 52152-3677; f. 1823; 102,664 vols; Dir WINFRIED KMENTA.

Zentrale Verwaltungsbibliothek und Dokumentation für Wirtschaft und Technik (Central Library for Economics and Technology): Bundesministerium für Wirtschaftliche Angelegenheiten, 1011 Vienna I, Stubenring 1; tel. 711005481; fax 7137995; f. 1850; 176,000 vols; Dir Mag. GERHARD GLASER.

Museums and Art Galleries

Bad Deutsch-Altenburg

Archäologisches Museum Carnuntinum (Carnuntinum Archaeological Museum): 2405 Bad Deutsch-Altenburg, Badgasse 40–46; tel. (2165) 62480; fax (2165) 64070; f. 1904; Roman archaeology; library of 12,000 vols; Curator Prof. Dr WERNER JOBST.

Bregenz

Vorarlberger Landesmuseum (Vorarlberg Provincial Museum): 6900 Bregenz, Kornmarkt; tel. (5574) 46050; fax 4605020; f. 1857; archaeology, art and folklore of the region; Dir Dr HELMUT SWOZILEK; publs *Jahrbuch, Schriften, Kataloge*.

Eggenburg

Krahuletz Museum: 3730 Eggenburg, Krahuletzplatz; colln f. 1866; geology, prehistory, ethnology; Pres. OTTO LAMATSCH; Curator WERNER VASICEK; publ. *Katalogreihe*.

Eisenstadt

Burgenländisches Landesmuseum (Burgenland Provincial Museum): 7000 Eisenstadt, Museumgasse 1–5; tel. (2682) 2652; f. 1926; archaeology, geology, history of art, natural history, ethnology, numismatics, astronomy, history of music; library of 31,000 vols; Dir Dr H. SCHMID; publs *Wissenschaftliche Arbeiten aus dem Burgenland, Burgenländische Heimatblätter* (quarterly), catalogues.

Graz

Steiermärkisches Landesmuseum Joanneum (Provincial Museum of Styria): 8010 Graz, Raubergasse 10; tel. (316) 80174700; f. 1811; history, natural history, art (exhibits housed on several sites); picture and sound archives; Dir Dr BARBARA KAISER.

Innsbruck

Kaiserliche Hofburg (Imperial Palace): 6020 Innsbruck, Rennweg 1; tel. (512) 587186; fax (512) 587186-13; Dir WALTRAUD SCHREILECHNER.

Kunsthistorische Sammlungen (Collections of Historical Art): 6020 Innsbruck, Schloss Ambras; tel. 348446; fax 361542; f. 1580; armour, furniture, pictures, sculpture; Curator Dr ALFRED AUER.

Museum im Zeughaus (Zeughaus Museum): 6020 Innsbruck, Zeughausgasse; tel. (512) 587439; fax (512) 587439-18; e-mail zeughaus@tiroler-landesmuseum.at; f. 1973; geology, history, technology; Pres. Prof. Dr JOSEF RIEDMANN; Curator Dr MEINRAD PIZZININI.

Tiroler Landesmuseum Ferdinandeum (Tyrol Provincial Museum): 6020 Innsbruck, Museumstr. 15; tel. (512) 59489; fax 5948988; f. 1823; ancient and early history, art; library of 150,000 vols; Dir Prof. Dr GERT AMMANN; publ. *Museum Report* (annually).

Tiroler Volkskunstmuseum (Tyrol Popular Art Museum): 6020 Innsbruck, Universitätsstr. 2; tel. 584302; f. 1929; local folk arts and crafts; library of 2,940 vols; Pres. FRITZ ASTL; Dir Dr HANS GSCHNITZER.

Klagenfurt

Botanischer Garten des Landes Kärnten (Botanical Garden of Carinthia): 9020 Klagenfurt, Prof.-Dr-Kahler-Platz 1; f. 1862; cultivation of central and southern Alpine flora; school and adult education in nature preservation; library of 200 vols; Dirs Dr GERFRIED H. LEUTE, ROBERT PASSEGGER.

Landesmuseum für Kärnten (Provincial Museum of Carinthia): 9021 Klagenfurt, Museumgasse 2; tel. (463) 53630552; f. 1844; history, natural history, art, folk arts and crafts; library of 120,000 vols; Dir Prof. Dr G. PICCOTTINI; publs *Carinthia I* (archaeology, history, history of art, and folklore), *Carinthia II* (science), *Archiv für Vaterländische Geschichte und Topographie, Kärntner Museumsschriften, Buchreihe, Kärntner Heimatleben*.

Krems

Museum Schloss Gobelsburg Österreichische Volkskunst (Gobelsburg Castle Museum of Austrian Folk Art): 3550 bei Krems (Niederösterreich); tel. (2734) 2422; fax (2734) 2422-20; f. 1966; under direction of Österreichisches Museum für Volkskunde; Dir MICHAEL MOOSBRUGGER.

Linz

Neue Galerie der Stadt Linz—Wolfgang Gurlitt Museum: 4040 Linz, Lentia 2000, Blütenstr. 15; tel. (732) 70703600; fax (732) 736190; f. 1947; paintings, drawings and sculptures of 19th and 20th centuries; library incl. 22,000 catalogues; Dir PETER BAUM.

Oberösterreichisches Landesmuseum (Regional Museum for Upper Austria): 4020 Linz, Museumstr. 14; tel. 774482; f. 1833; library of 120,000 vols; Dir Dr GUNTER DIMT; publs *Stapfia, Studien zur Kulturgeschichte von Oberösterreich*.

Salzburg

Carolino Augusteum Salzburger Museum für Kunst und Kulturgeschichte: 5020 Salzburg, Museumsplatz 6; tel. 841134; fax 84113410; f. 1834; prehistoric and Roman remains, art, coins, musical instruments, costumes, toys, peasants' art; library of 100,000 vols, archives; Dir Dr WOLFRAM MORATH.

Haus der Natur (Natural History Museum): Salzburg, Museumplatz 5; tel. (662) 842653; fax (662) 847905; e-mail hausdernatur@salzburg.co.at; f. 1924; zoology, botany, anthropology, geology; reptile zoo, aquarium, space hall; Dir Prof. Dr EBERHARD STÜBER.

Mozarteum: 5020 Salzburg, Schwarzstr. 26; tel. 88940-10; fax 882419; f. 1914 by 'Internationale Stiftung Mozarteum' concert rooms, a library of MSS, books and other Mozart memorabilia.

Mozarts Wohnhaus: Salzburg, Makartplatz 8; multivision 'Mozart and Salzburg'; the world of Mozart 1773–80; instruments from Mozart's time.

Residenzgalerie Salzburg: 5010 Salzburg, Residenzplatz 1; tel. (662) 840451; fax (662) 84045116; f. 1923; 16- to 19th-century European paintings; Dir Dr ROSWITHA JUFFINGER.

Schloss Hellbrunn (Hellbrunn Castle): 5020 Salzburg; tel. (662) 820003; fax (662) 82000331; furnished 17th-century castle, with water gardens, deer park and open-air theatre.

Stift Göttweig

Kunstsammlungen und Graphisches Kabinett Stift Göttweig (Stift Göttweig Museum of Graphic Art): 3511 Stift Göttweig, Post Furth; tel. (2732) 85581226; fax (2732) 85581266; graphic art from the 16th century to the present; library of 280,000 vols (history, law, theology, history of art, sciences), 1,110 MSS, 1,120 incunabula, 2,750 archives (1054–1900); Dir Doz. Dr P. GREGOR MARTIN LECHNER; publ. catalogue to accompany annual exhibitions.

Stillfried/March

Museum für Ur- und Frühgeschichte (Museum for Pre- and Early History): 2262 Stillfried/March (Niederösterreich); f. 1914; local archaeology and palaeontology; Dir GER-

HARD ANTL; publ. *Museumsnachrichten* (3–4 a year).

Vienna

Erzbischöfliches Dom- und Diözesanmuseum (Archiepiscopal Cathedral and Diocesan Museum): Vienna I, Stephansplatz 6; tel. 51552-3689; f. 1933; ecclesiastical art; Dir GERDA EDERNDORFER.

Galerie Graf Czernin (Count Czernin Art Gallery): Vienna VIII, Friedrich Schmidt Platz 4; f. 1800; paintings; Dir Count EUGEN CZERNIN; Curator Dr KARL TRAUTTMANSDORFF.

Gemäldegalerie der Akademie der Bildenden Künste in Wien (Vienna Academy of Fine Arts Gallery): 1010 Vienna, Schillerplatz 3; tel. (1) 58816225; fax (1) 5863346; f. 1822; 14th–20th-century paintings; Dir Dr RENATE TRNEK.

Graphische Sammlung Albertina (Albertina Graphic Art Collection): Vienna I, Augustinerstr. 1; f. 1769; prints, drawings, posters; library of 40,000 vols; Dir Univ. Prof. Dr KONRAD OBERHUBER.

Heeresgeschichtliches Museum (Military History Museum): Vienna III, Arsenal; tel. 795610; fax 7987555; f. 1891; exhibits dating from Thirty Years War to Second World War; library of 40,000 vols; Dir Dr MANFRIED RAUCHENSTEINER.

Historisches Museum der Stadt Wien (Historical Museum of the City of Vienna): 1040 Vienna, Karlsplatz; tel. (1) 5058747-84021; fax (1) 5058747-7201; f. 1887; local history from prehistoric times to the present; among many associated museums are premises once occupied by Beethoven, Haydn, Mozart, Schubert and Johann Strauss; Dir Hofrat Dr GÜNTER DÜRIEGL.

Josephinum: 1090 Vienna IX, Währinger Str. 25; f. 1785 as acad. for military surgeons; 18th-century wax anatomical collection, museum of the two Vienna Medical Schools and museum of medical endoscopy; library of 80,000 historical medical books; Dir Prof. Dr KARL HOLUBAR.

Kunsthistorisches Museum (Museum of Fine Arts): 1010 Vienna, Burgring 5; tel. (1) 52524-0; fax (1) 5232770; f. 1891 from Hapsburg Imperial collections; paintings, Egyptian and other antiquities, numismatics, armour, historical costume, plastics and handicrafts, musical instruments, secular and ecclesiastical relics of the Holy Roman Empire and the Hapsburg dynasty, state carriages (at Schönbrunn palace); library of 85,000 vols; Chief Dir Dr WILFRIED SEIPEL.

Kupferstichkabinett der Akademie der Bildenden Künste (Graphic Art Collection of the Academy of Fine Arts): 1010 Vienna, Makartgasse 3; tel. (1) 5813040; fax (1) 5813040-31; f. 1773; drawings, prints, photographs; library: see Libraries and Archives; Dir Dr ROBERT WAGNER; Curator Dr MONIKA KNOFLER.

Museum für Völkerkunde (Ethnological Museum): 1014 Vienna, Neue Hofburg, Ringstrassentrakt; tel. (1) 53430; fax (1) 5355320; f. 1876; ethnology of non-European peoples; library of 112,000 vols; Dir Dr PETER KANN; publs *Archiv für Völkerkunde* (annually), *Veröffentlichungen zum Archiv für Völkerkunde*.

Museum moderner Kunst Stiftung Ludwig Wien: 1030 Vienna, Arsenalstr. 1.

Comprises:

Palais Liechtenstein: 1090 Vienna, Fürstengasse 1; tel. 3176900; fax 3176901; Baroque palace containing 'modern classics', latest trends in modern art.

20er Haus (Museum of the 20th Century): 1030 Vienna, Schweizergarten; tel. 7996900; fax 7996901; f. 1962; modern art, sculpture garden.

Naturhistorisches Museum (Natural History Museum): 1014 Vienna I, Burgring 7; tel. (1) 52177; telex 134441; fax (1) 935254; f. 1748; geology, palaeontology, zoology, botany, anthropology, prehistory, speleology; library of 400,000 books; Dir Prof. Dr BERNHARD LÖTSCH; publ. *Annalen*.

Niederösterreichisches Landesmuseum (Provincial Museum of Lower Austria): 3109 St Pölten, Landhausplatz 1; tel. (2742) 200-5012; fax (2742) 200-5015; f. 1907; natural history, history of art (from baroque times onwards); many attached deptl museums are located in Lower Austria, incl. Haydn's birthplace at Rohrau; library of 10,000 vols; Dirs Dr ERICH STEINER, Dr. PETER ZAWREL; publs *Wissenschaftliche Mitteilungen*, catalogues. (The St Pölten site was not due to be opened to the public until 2002.)

Österreichische Galerie Belvedere (Austrian Gallery): 1037 Vienna, Postfach 134, Oberes and Unteres Belvedere, Prinz Eugenstr. 27; tel. (1) 79557; Austrian painting and sculpture from Middle Ages to present, foreign painting and sculpture of 19th and 20th centuries, spec. colln of sculpture by G. Ambrosi; Dir Dr GERBERT FRODL (acting); publ. *Belvedere*.

Österreichisches Gesellschafts- und Wirtschafts-Museum (Austrian Museum for Economics and Social Affairs): 1050 Vienna, Vogelsanggasse 36; tel. 5452551; fax 5453209; f. 1925; archives, maps, photographs; public library on 'Austria Yesterday and Today'; Dir JOSEF DOCEKAL; publ. *Österreichs Wirtschaft im Überblick* (annually).

Österreichisches Museum für angewandte Kunst (Austrian Museum of Applied Arts): 1010 Vienna, Stubenring 5; tel. (1) 711360; fax (1) 7131026; f. 1864; applied arts from Roman to modern times, oriental carpets, East Asian colln; library of 160,000 vols, 300 periodicals, 500,000 prints; Dir PETER NOEVER.

Österreichisches Museum für Volkskunde (Austrian Museum of Folk Life and Folk Art): 1080 Vienna, Laudongasse 15–19; tel. (1) 4068905; fax (1) 4085342; f. 1895; incl. nat. furniture colln and other spec. collns (housed on separate sites); Dir Dr FRANZ GRIESHOFER; publs *Veröffentlichungen, Raabser Märchen-Reihe, Kittseer Schriften zur Volkskunde,* catalogues.

Schloss Schönbrunn Kultur- und Betriebsges. m.b.H. (Schönbrunn Palace): 1130 Vienna, Schloss Schönbrunn; tel. 81113; fax 8121106; 18th-century fmr Imperial summer residence; baroque and botanical gardens; zoological garden built in 1752, aquarium; Dirs Dipl.-Ing. WOLFGANG KIPPES, Mag. FRANZ SATTLECKER.

Technisches Museum für Industrie und Gewerbe in Wien (Trade and Industrial Museum of Technology in Vienna:) 1140 Vienna, Mariahilferstr. 212; tel. (222) 9141610-0; fax (222) 9141610-4444; f. 1907; library of 40,000 vols; Dir Mag. PETER DONHAUSER; publ. *Blätter für Technikgeschichte* (annually).

Universities

(All institutions of higher education have university status)

DONAU-UNIVERSITÄT KREMS
(Danube University of Krems)

3500 Krems, Dr Karl-Dorrek-Str. 30
Telephone: (2732) 893
Fax: (2732) 4000
E-mail: info@donau-uni.ac.at

Founded 1995
State control
Languages of instruction: German, English
Academic year: October to June

Executive Board member: Dipl.-Ing. Dr techn INGELA BRUNER
Librarian: Dr JUDITH BAUER

Number of teachers: 400
Number of students: 418

PROFESSORS

FALKENHAGEN, D., Environmental and Medical Sciences
GOTTSCHLICH, M., Telecommunication, Information and Media
GUNTHER, J., Telecommunication, Information and Media
SCHUSTER, G., Environmental and Medical Sciences
STRAUBE, M., European Integration

KARL-FRANZENS-UNIVERSITÄT GRAZ
(Graz University)

8010 Graz, Universitätsplatz 3
Telephone: (316) 380-0
Fax: (316) 380-9140
E-mail: volion@email.kfunigraz.ac.at

Founded 1585
State control
Academic year: October to June (two terms)

Rector: Mag. Dr WOLF RAUCH
Pro-Rector: Dr HELMUT KONRAD
Chief Administrative Officer: HR. Dr M. SUPPANZ
Librarian: HRätin Dr SIGRID REINITZER

Library: see under Libraries
Number of teachers: 2,503
Number of students: 35,068

DEANS

Faculty of Catholic Theology: Dr MAXIMILIAN LIEBMANN
Faculty of Law: Dr GERNOT KOCHER
Faculty of Business Administration and Economics: DDr GERALD SCHÖPFER
Faculty of Medicine: Dr GERHARD PENDL
Faculty of Liberal Arts: Mag. Dr ARNO HELLER
Faculty of Science: Dr KURT IRGOLIC

PROFESSORS

Faculty of Catholic Theology:

ANGEL, H. F., Catechetics
HARNONCOURT, P., Liturgy
HIRNSPERGER, J., Canon Law
INHOFFEN, P., Moral Theology
JENSEN, A., History of Doctrine and Ecumenical Theology
KOLB, A., Philosophy
KÖRNER, B., Dogmatics
LARCHER, G., Fundamental Theology
LIEBMANN, M., Church History
MARBÖCK, J., Old Testament
WOSCHITZ, K., Bible Knowledge
ZEILINGER, F., New Testament
ZSIFKOVITS, V., Christian Sociology

Faculty of Law:

BRÜNNER, CH., Public Law
FUNK, B. CH., Public Law
GINTHER, K., International Law
HINTEREGGER, M., Civil Law
JELINEK, W., Civil Procedure, Private International Law, Agricultural Law
JUD, W., Commercial Law
KOCHER, G., History of Austrian Law
KOLLER, P., Philosophy of Law, Legal Theory, Sociology of Law
MANTL, W., Political Science and Constitutional Law
MARHOLD, F., Labour Law
NOVAK, R., Austrian Administrative Law

PICHLER, J., European Legal Development
POSCH, W., Civil Law
RUPPE, H. G., Financial Law
SCHICK, P., Criminal Law and Criminology
SCHILCHER, B., Private Law
SEILER, R., Criminal Law and Criminology
SIMOTTA, D., Civil Procedure
THÜR, G., Roman Law
WESENER, G., Roman Law
WÜNSCH, H., Commercial Law

Faculty of Business Administration and Economics:

ACHAM, K., Sociology
BAIGENT, N., Public Economy
BEINSEN, L., Political Economy
HALLER, M., Sociology
HÜLSMANN, J., Statistics, Econometry and Operations Research
KRAUS, H., Organization and Industrial Data Processing
KURZ, H. D., Political Economy
LIEBMANN, H. P., Marketing
MANDL, D., Business, Methodology of Economics
MANDL, G., Industrial Economics
RAUCH, W., Computer Science
SCHLEICHER, ST., Political Economy
SCHNEIDER, U., Industrial Economics
SCHÖPFER, G., Economic and Social History
STEINER, P., Industrial Economics
STREBEL, H., Business Administration
WAGENHOFER, A., Business Administration

Faculty of Medicine:

ANDERHUBER, F., Anatomy
DENK, H., Pathological Anatomy
DOHR, G., Histology and Embryology
FAULBORN, J., Ophthalmology
GELL, G., Medical Statistics
HARTUNG, H. P., Neurology
HÖLLWARTH, M., Paediatric Surgery
HUBMER, G., Urology
KENNER, T., Physiology
KERL, H., Venereal and Skin Diseases
KOSTNER, G., Medical Biochemistry
KREJS, G., Internal Medicine
KURZ, R., Paediatrics
LEINZINGER, E., Forensic Medicine
LIST, W., Anaesthesiology
MARTH, E., Hygiene
MISCHINGER, H. J., Surgery
MOSER, M., Oto-rhino-laryngology
NOACK, R., Social Medicine
PENDL, G., Neurosurgery
PESKAR, B., Pharmacology
PIERINGER, W., Medical Psychology and Psychotherapy
REIBNEGGER, G., Medical Chemistry
RIENMÜLLER, R., Radiology
SCHAUENSTEIN, K., Functional Pathology
SZYSZKOWITZ, R., Orthopaedic Surgery
TRITTHART, H., Medical Physics
WINDHAGER, E., Orthopaedics and Orthopaedic Surgery
WINTER, R., Midwifery and Gynaecology
ZAPOTOCZKY, J., Psychiatry

Faculty of Liberal Arts:

CSÁKY, M., Austrian History
EISMANN, W., Slavonic Philology
FILL, A., English Philology
FLOTZINGER, R., Musicology
GOLTSCHNIGG, D., German Philology
HÄRTEL, R., Medieval History
HELLER, A., American Studies
HELMICH, W., Roman Philology
HIEBEL, H., Austrian Literature and Theory of Literature
HÖRANDNER, E., Folklore
HOSSENFELDER, M., Philosophy
HURCH, B., General and Applied Linguistics
KAMITZ, R., Philosophy
KASER, K., South-East European History
KONRAD, H., Contemporary History
LENZ, W., Pedagogics
LORENZ, H. T., Archaeology of Art
MITTELBERGER, H., Comparative Linguistics
PIEPER, R., Economic and Social History
POCHAT, G., Art History
PORTMANN, P., German Philology
PRUNČ, E., Translation and Interpreting
RIEHLE, W., English Philology
SEEL, H., Pedagogics
SCHULZ-BUSCHHAUS, U., Romance Philology
SCHWOB, A., German Philology
SIMON, H., Romanic Philology
SUST, M., Sports Science
TOŠOVIĆ, B., Slavonic Philology
WALTER-KLINGENSTEIN, G., Modern History
WEILER, I., Pre-History
WOLF, W., English Philology

Faculty of Science:

ALBERT, D., Psychology
BLANZ, P., Botany
FLOR, P., Mathematics
HALTER-KOCH, F., Mathematics
HASLINGER, E., Pharmaceutical Chemistry
HEINRICH, G., Plant Anatomy and Physiology
HÖGENAUER, G., Microbiology
HOINKES, G., Mineralogy
HUBER, H., Psychology
IRGOLIC, K., Analytical Chemistry
JANOSCHEK, R., Theoretical Chemistry
KAPPEL, F., Mathematics
KARTNIG, TH., Pharmacognosy
KRATKY, CH., Physical Chemistry
KUNISCH, K., Mathematics
NETZER, F., Experimental Physics
PILLER, W., Geology and Palaeontology
REICH, L., Mathematics
ROEMER, H., Zoology
WAKONIGG, H., Geography
WALLBRECHER, E., Geology and Palaeontology

LEOPOLD-FRANZENS UNIVERSITÄT INNSBRUCK (Innsbruck University)

6020 Innsbruck, Innrain 52
Telephone: 507-0
Fax: 507-2800

Founded 1669

Rector: Prof. Dr CHRISTIAN SMEKAL
Pro-Rector: Prof. Dr HANS MOSER
Chief Administrative Officer: Dr iur. FRIEDRICH LUHAN
Librarian: Dr WALTER NEUHAUSER

Library: see Libraries
Number of teachers: 1,541
Number of students: 27,000

Publications: *Mitteilungsblatt* (irregular), *Vorlesungsverzeichnis* (every 6 months), Veröffentlichungen (irregular), *Veranstaltungskalender* (every 2 months).

DEANS

Faculty of Theology: Prof. Dr HERWIG BÜCHELE
Faculty of Law: Prof. Dr GUNTER H. ROTH
Faculty of Social and Economic Science: Prof. Dr FRIEDRICH ROITHMAYR
Faculty of Medicine: Prof. Dr PETER O. FRITSCH
Faculty of Arts: Prof Dr ELMAR KORNEXL
Faculty of Science: Prof. Dr SIGMAR BORTENSCHLAGER
Faculty of Construction Engineering and Architecture: Prof. Dr ERWIN KITTINGER

PROFESSORS

Faculty of Theology:

BÜCHELE, H., Christian Sociology
FISCHER, G., Old Testament Theology
HASITSCHKA, M., New Testament Theology
KRIEGBAUM, B., Church History
LEIBOLD, G., Christian Philosophy
LIES, L., Dogmatics
MUCK, O., Christian Philosophy
MÜHLSTEIGER, J., Church Law
NEUFELD, K., Fundamental Theology
ROTTER, H., Moral Theology
RUNGGALDIER, E., Philosophy
SCHAUPP, K., Pastoral Theology
SCHWAGER, R., Dogmatics
VASS, G., Dogmatics

Faculty of Law:

BERTEL, C., Austrian Penal Law and Criminology
BINDER, M., Labour Law and Social Law
DORALT, W., Financial Law
EBERT, K., History of German Law and Economy
ECCHER, B., Italian Law
FAISTENBERGER, C., Austrian Civil Law
HUMMER, W., International Law
KÖBLER, G., History of German Law and Economics
KÖNIG, B., Legal Procedure in Civil Law
LEISCHING, P., Church Law
MAYRHOFER, H., Civil Law
MORSCHER, S., Public Law
PERNTHALER, P., Constitutional and Administrative Law
RABER, F., Roman Law
REICHERT-FACILIDES, F., Foreign Law and Austrian Private Law
ROTH, G. H. Commercial Law
SPRUNG, R., Austrian Civil Court Procedure
WEBER, K., Public Law
WIMMER, N., Austrian Constitutional Law

Faculty of Social and Economic Science:

BRATSCHITSCH, R., Industrial Economics
CHEN, J. R., Economic Theory and Econometrics
HINTERHUBER, H., Industrial Economics
HOLUB, H. W., Political Economy
KAPPLER, E., Management
KAUFER, E., National Economy
LASKE, S., Industrial Economics
LEXA, H., Industrial Economics
MARINELL, G., Statistics
MOREL, J., Sociology
MÜHLBACHER, H., Industrial Economy
PELINKA, A., Political Science
ROITHMAYR, F., System Planning and Information Management
SCHREDELSEKER, K., Finance
SMEKAL, C., Financial Science
SOCHER, K., Political Economy
STREHL, F., Business Administration
VON WERLHOF, C., Political Science, Women's Studies and Research
WECK-HANNEMANN, H., Political Economy
WEIERMAIR, K., Industrial Economics

Faculty of Medicine:

AMBACH, W., Medical Physics
ANDERL, H., Plastic and Restorative Surgery
BARTSCH, G., Urology
BAUER, R., Orthopaedics
BECK, E., Traumatology
BENZER, H., Anaesthesiology and Intensive Care Medicine
BODNER, E., Surgery
DAPUNT, O., Gynaecology and Obstetrics
DEETJEN, P., Physiology
DIERICH, M., Hygiene
ENDRES, W., Paediatrics
FRITSCH, P., Dermatology
GAUSCH, K., Dental Medicine
GLOSSMANN, H., Biochemical Pharmacology
GÖTTINGER, W., Ophthalmology
GRUNICKE, H., Medical Chemistry
GSCHNITZER, F., Surgery
HINTERHUBER, H., Psychiatry
JASCHKE, W., Radiodiagnosis
LUKAS, P., Radiotherapy
MIKUZ, G., Pathological Anatomy
PATSCH, J., Internal Medicine
PAVELKA, M., Histology and Embryology
PFEIFFER, K. P., Biostatistics
PLATZER, W., Anatomy
POEWE, W., Neurology
RICCABONA, G., Nuclear Medicine
SCHEITHAUER, R., Forensic Medicine

SCHÜSSLER, G., Medical Psychology, Psychotherapy
STÖFFLER, G., Microbiology
THUMFART, W., Otorhinolaryngology
TWERDY, K., Neurosurgery
UTERMANN, G., Human Genetics
WACHTER, H., Medicinal and Analytical Chemistry
WICK, G., General and Experimental Pathology
WINKLER, H., Pharmacology

Faculty of Arts:
BICHLER, R., Ancient and Comparative History
DEPPERMANN, M., Comparative Literature
FETZ, F., Physical Education
HÄNDEL, P., Classical Philology
HIERDEIS, H., Pedagogics
KLEINKNECHT, R., Philosophy
KORNEXL, E., Physical Education
KRÖMER, W., Romance Philology
MARKUS, M., English Language and Literature
MASSER, A., Old German Language and Literature
MATHIS, F., Economic and Social History
MAZOHL-WALLNIG, B., Austrian History
MEID, W., Comparative Linguistics
MOSER, H., German Language and Medieval German Literature
MÜLLER-SALGET, K., New German Language and Literature
NAREDI-RAINER, P., Art History, Architectural Theory
OHNHEISTER, J., Slavonic Studies
PETZOLDT, L., European Ethnology
PLANGG, G., Romance Philology
RIEDMANN, J., History of the Middle Ages
RÖD, W., Philosophy
SCHEER, B., Modern English and American Literature
SCHEICHL, S., Austrian Comparative Literature
SEEBASS, T., Music
SPINDLER, K., Late Medieval and Modern Archeology, Urban Archeology
STEININGER, R., Current History
STRNAD, A., Modern History
WALDE, E., Classical Archaeology
WEISS, R., Pedagogics
WENSKUS, O., Classical Philology
ZACH, W., English Language and Literature

Faculty of Science:
ALBRECHT, R., Cybernetics and Numerical Mathematics
BISTER, K., Biochemistry
BOBLETER, O., Radio-chemistry
BONN, G., Analytical Chemistry
BORSDORF, A., Geography
BORTENSCHLAGER, S., Systematic Botany
BURGER, A., Pharmacognosy
GRUBER, J., Physical Chemistry
HEINISCH, G., Pharmaceutical Chemistry
HOCHMAIR, E., Applied Physics (Electronics)
KRÄUTLER, B., Organic Chemistry
KUHN, M., Meteorology and Geophysics
LARCHER, W., Botany
LIEDL, R., Mathematics
LOOS, O., Mathematics
MIRWALD. P., Mineralogy and Palaeontology
MOSTLER, H., Geology and Palaeontology
OBERST, U., Mathematics
PFLEIDERER, J., Astronomy
PHILIPPOU, A., Pharmacodynamics and Toxicology
PICHLER, H., Theoretical Meteorology
RIEGER, R., Zoology
RITTER, M., Psychology
ROTHLEITNER, J., Theoretical Physics
SCHWARZHANS, K. E., Inorganic and Analytical Chemistry
ZEILINGER, A., Neutron and Solid State Physics
ZOLLER, P., Theoretical Physics

Faculty of Construction Engineering and Architecture:
AXHAUSEN, K. W., Highway Engineering
CHESI, G., Geodesy and Photogrammetry
GIENCKE, V., Structural Engineering and Design
GRAEFE, R., Architecture and Preservation of Historic Monuments
HELMBERG, G., Mathematics
HOFSTETTER, G., Theory of Structures
INGERLE, K., Domestic and Industrial Sanitation
KITTINGER, E., Building Physics
KOLYMBAS, D., Geomechanics and Tunnel Engineering
KOPP, E., Railway Construction and Transport System
LACKNER, J., Painting, Design and Planning
LANGHOF, C., Town Planning
LESSMANN, H., Building Planning and Estimating
MOSER, K., Construction Statistics
SCHAUER, E., Building and Layout
SCHEUERLEIN, H., Hydraulic Engineering
SCHUËLLER, G., Mechanics
TSCHUPIK, J., Geometry
TSCHEMMERNEGG, F., Steel and Wood Constructions
WAUBKE, N. V., Instruction on Structural Materials and Materials Testing
WICKE, M., Reinforced Concrete Construction

AFFILIATED INSTITUTES

Arbeitskreis für Gleichbehandlungsfragen: 6020 Innsbruck, Technikerstrasse 13.

Universitätsarchiv: A-6020 Innsbruck, Innrain 52; f 1950.

Forschungsinstitut für Alpine Vorzeit: 6020 Innsbruck, Kaiser-Franz-Josef-Str. 12.

Forschungsinstitut für Hochgebirgsforschung in Obergurgl (Alpine Research Department of the University of Innsbruck in Obergurgl): A-6020 Innsbruck, Innrain 52; f. 1951.

Sportinstitut: A-6020 Innsbruck, Fürstenweg 185; f. 1959.

EDV-Zentrum (Computer Centre): A-6020 Innsbruck, Technikerstr. 13; f. 1971.

Forschungsinstitut für Alpenländische Land- und Forstwirtschaft (Dept of Alpine Agriculture and Forestry): A-6020 Innsbruck, Technikerstr. 13; f. 1977.

Forschungsinstitut 'Brenner-Archiv': A-6020 Innsbruck, Innrain 52, Neubau/VIII; f. 1979.

Forschungsinstitut für Textilchemie und Textilphysik: A-6850 Dornbirn, Höchsterstr. 73; f. 1982.

Senatsinstitut für Zwischenmenschliche Kommunikation: 6020 Innsbruck, Sillgasse 8; f. 1991.

Forschungsinstitut für Prophylaxe der Suchtkrankheiten: Krankenhaus Maria Ebene Frastanz, Vorarlberg; f. 1990.

UNIVERSITÄT KLAGENFURT (Klagenfurt University)

9020 Klagenfurt, Universitätsstr. 65-67

Telephone: (463) 2700
Fax: (463) 2700-103

Founded 1970
State control
Academic year: October to February, March to June

Rector: Prof. Dr WILLIBALD DÖRFLER
Vice-Rectors: Prof. Dr FRANZ KUNA, Prof. Dr GERHARD NEWEKLOWSKY, Dr NORBERT FREI
Chief Administrative Officer: Dr ARNULF LONGIN
Librarian: Dr MANFRED LUBE

Number of teachers: 520
Number of students: 5,500

Publication: *Verzeichnis der Lehrveranstaltungen und Personalstand* (catalogue, 2 a year).

DEANS

Faculty of Humanities: Prof. Dr KLAUS BOECKMANN
Faculty of Economics, Business Administration and Informatics: Prof. Dr HEINRICH C. MAYR

PROFESSORS

Faculty of Humanities:
ARNOLD, U., Philosophy
ASPETSBERGER, F., German Philology
BAMMÉ, A., Educational Science
BERGER, A., German Philology
BOECKMANN, K., Communications
BRANDSTETTER, A., German Philology
GSTETTNER, P., Educational Science
HEINTEL, P., Philosophy and Group Dynamics
HÖDL, G., Medieval History and Studies Related to History
HOVORKA, H., Special Educational Theory Relating to Disabilities
JAMES, A., English and American Studies
KLINGLER, J., Educational Theory
KUNA, F. M., English and American Studies
LARCHER, D., Educational Science
LÖSCHENKOHL, E., Psychology and Developmental Psychology
MAYERTHALER, W., General and Applied Philology
MELEZINEK, A., Teaching Methods
MENSCHIK, J., Educational Science
METER, H., Romance Studies
MITTERMEIR, R., Computer Science
MORITSCH, A., History of Southern and Eastern Europe
NEUHÄUSER, R., Slavic Studies
NEWEKLOWSKY, G., Slavic Studies
OTTOMEYER, K., Social Psychology
POHL, H.-D., General Philology
POSCH, P., Curriculum Studies
RUMPLER, H., Modern and Austrian History
SCHAUSBERGER, N., Modern Austrian History
VÖLKL, F., Educational Psychology
WANDRUSZKA, U., Romance Studies
ZIMA, P. V., General Comparative Literature

Faculty of Economics, Business Administration and Informatics:
BODENHÖFER, H.-J., Economics of Education
BÖSZÖRMÉNYI, L., Computer Science
DÖRFLER, W., Mathematics
EDER, J., Computer Science
FISCHER, R., Mathematics
FRIEDRICH, G., Computer Science
HORSTER, P., Computer Science
KALUZA, B., Business Administration
KELLERMANN, P., Sociology of Education
KOFLER, H., Business Administration
KROPFBERGER, D., Business Administration
MAYR, H., Computer Science
MITTERMEIR, R., Computer Science
MÜLLER, W., Mathematics
NADVORNIK, W., Business Administration
NECK, R., Business Administration
PILZ, J., Applied Statistics
REBHAHN, R., Law
RIECKMANN, H.-J., Business Administration
SAUBERER, M., Geography
SCHNEIDER, D., Business Administration
SEGER, M., Geography
STETTNER, H., Mathematics

ATTACHED INSTITUTE

Interuniversitäres Institut für Interdisziplinäre Forschung und Fortbildung: 9020 Klagenfurt, Sterneckstr. 15; tel. (463) 2700-754; fax (463) 2700-759; f. 1980; development of innovative research projects in such fields as man-machine relationship, preventive health policy, in-service teacher training;

Dir Prof. Dr ROLAND FISCHER; publ. *Perspektiven für Fernstudien*.

UNIVERSITÄT SALZBURG
(Salzburg University)

5020 Salzburg, Kapitelgasse 4

Telephone: (662) 8044-0

Fax: (0662) 8044214

E-mail: mailbox@sbg.ac.at

Founded 1622; closed 1810; College 1810–50, independent faculty of Catholic Theology 1850–1962; reconstituted 1962

State control

Academic year: October to end of June

Rector: Prof. Dr ADOLF HASLINGER

Pro-Rector: Prof. Dr EDGAR MORSCHER

Director: Dr ELISABETH HASLAUER

Librarian: Dr CHRISTINE UNTERRAINER

Library: see under Libraries

Number of teachers: 750

Number of students: 13,000

Publications: *Yearbook*, *University Prospectuses*.

DEANS

Faculty of Catholic Theology: Prof. Dr HEINRICH SCHMIDINGER

Faculty of Law: Prof. Dr OTTO TRIFFTERER

Faculty of Arts: Prof. Dr LEO TRUCHLAR

Faculty of Natural Science: Prof. Dr HELMUT RIEDL

PROFESSORS

Faculty of Catholic Theology:

- BACHL, G., Dogmatics
- BEILNER, W., New Testament Studies
- BUCHER, A., Catechism and Religious Education
- KÖHLER, W., Christian Philosophy and Psychology
- MÖDLHAMMER, J., Ecumenical Theology
- NIKOLASCH, F., Liturgy
- PAARHAMMER, J., Church Law
- PAUS, A., Epistemology and Religious Studies
- SCHLEINZER, F., Pastoral Theology
- SCHMIDINGER, H., Christian Philosophy
- WINKLER, G. B., Church History
- WOLBERT, W., Moral Theology

Faculty of Law:

- BERKA, W., General Theory of the State, Theory of Administration, Constitutional and Administrative Law
- BUSCHMANN, A., German Legal History, German Private and Civil Law
- GRILLBERGER, K., Industrial Law
- HACKL, K., Roman and Civil Law
- HAGEN, J., Sociology of Law
- HAMMER, R., Management
- HARRER, F., Civil and Commercial Law
- KARL, W., International Law
- KOJA, F., General Constitutional Law
- KOPPENSTEINER, H.-G., Austrian and International Commercial Law
- KYRER, A., Economics
- MAYER-MALY, TH., German and Austrian Private Law
- MIGSCH, E., Civil Law
- RAINER, J., Roman and Modern Private Law
- SCHÄFFER, H., Public Law
- SCHMOLLER, K., Austrian Criminal Law
- SCHUMACHER, W., International Commercial Law and Civil Law
- SCHWIMANN, M., International Civil Law
- STOLZLECHNER, H., Public Law
- TRIFFTERER, O., Austrian and International Criminal Law

Faculty of Arts:

- BETTEN, A., German
- BOTZ, G., History
- BRUCHER, G., History of Austrian Art
- DALFEN, J., Classical Philology
- DOPSCH, H., History
- EHMER, J., Modern History
- FABRIS, H., Journalism and Communications
- FELTEN, F., Classical Archaeology
- GOEBL, H., Romance Languages
- GRASSL, H., Ancient History
- GRÖSSING, S., Sport
- HAAS, H., Austrian History
- HAIDER, H., Linguistics
- HASLINGER, A., German
- JALKOTZY, S., Ancient History
- KLEIN, H. M., English
- KNOCHE, M., Journalism and Communications
- KOLMER, L., Medieval History and Historic Auxiliary Sciences
- KRONSTEINER, O., Slavic Languages
- KRUMM, V., Education
- KUON, P., Romance Philology
- MAYER, G., Slavic Languages
- MESSNER, D., Romance Languages
- MORSCHER, E., Philosophy
- MÜLLER, E., Physical Education
- MÜLLER, U., German
- PANAGL, O., Linguistics
- PATRY, J. L., Education
- PETERSMANN, G., Classical Philology
- PIEL, F., Medieval and Modern History of Art
- ROSSBACHER, K., German
- SCHMOLKE, M., Journalism and Communications
- STAGL, J., Sociology
- STENZL, J., Music Science
- TRUCHLAR, L., English
- WEINGARTNER, P., Philosophy
- ZAIC, F., English

Faculty of Natural Sciences:

- AMTHAUER, G., Geology
- BAUMANN, U., Psychology
- BENTRUP, F. W., Plant Physiology and Anatomy
- BREITENBACH, M., Molecular Genetics
- CLAUSEN, H., Systems Analysis
- CZIHAK, G., Genetics
- FÜRNKRANZ, D., Botany
- GERL, P., Mathematics
- HERMANN, A., Zoology
- NEUBAUER, F., Geology
- PERNER, J., Psychology
- PFALZGRAF, J., Computer Science
- RIEDL, H., Geography
- SCHWEIGER, F., Mathematics
- STADEL, CH., Geography
- STEINHÄUSLER, F., Biophysics
- STRACK, H.-B., Biochemistry
- WALLBOTT, H., Psychology
- WERNER, H., Sciences Education
- ZINTERHOF, P., Mathematics

Inter-faculty Institutes:

- CROLL, G., Music History of Salzburg
- FAUPEL, K., Political Science
- GACHOWETZ, H., Organizational Psychology
- HAUPTMANN, W., Criminal Psychology
- KOPPENSTEINER, H. G., European Law
- LAUBER, V., Political Science
- MAYER-MALY, TH., Energy Law, Law of Liechtenstein
- MIGSCH, E., Private Insurance Law
- MORSCHER, E., Philosophy, Technology, Economics
- ZINTERHOF, P., Software Technology

UNIVERSITÄT WIEN
(Vienna University)

1010 Vienna, Dr Karl Lueger-Ring 1

Telephone: (1) 4277-0

Fax: (1) 4277-9120

Founded 1365

Academic year: October to June

Rector: Prof. Dr WOLFGANG GREISENEGGER

Pro-Rector: (vacant)

Administrative Officer: Dr FRANZ SKACEL

Library: see under Libraries

Number of teachers: 3,415

Number of students: 86,015

DEANS

Faculty of Catholic Theology: Prof. Dr J. FIGL

Faculty of Protestant Theology: Prof. Dr G. REINGRABNER

Faculty of Law and Political Science: Prof. Dr P. PIELER

Faculty of Social Sciences and Economics: Prof. Dr P. GERLICH

Faculty of Medicine: Prof. Dr W. SCHÜTZ

Faculty of Philosophy: Prof. Dr N. BACHL

Faculty of Humanities: Prof. Dr F. RÖMER

Faculty of Natural Sciences: Prof. Dr W. FLEISCHHACKER

PROFESSORS

Faculty of Catholic Theology:

- AUF DER MAUR, H. J., Sacramental Theology and Liturgy
- BRAULIK, P. G., Old Testament and Biblical-Oriented Languages
- FIGL, J., Divinity
- FRANKL, K. H., Church History
- GABRIEL, I.
- KÜHSCHELM, R., Ethics and Social Sciences
- LANGER, W., Religious Education
- REIKERSTORFER, J., Fundamental Theology and Apologetics
- SUTTNER, E., Patrology and Eastern Churches
- VIRT, G., Moral Theology
- WEISMAYER, J., Dogmatics
- ZULEHNER, P., Pastoral Theology and Kerymetics

Faculty of Protestant Theology:

- ADAM, G., Religious Education
- HEINE, S., Practical Theology
- KÖRTNER, V., Systematic Theology
- REINGRABNER, G., Canon Law
- WAGNER, F., Systematic Theology
- WISENMEYER, W., Church History, Christian Archaeology, Sacred Art

Faculty of Law and Political Science

- AICHER, J., Commercial Law and Negotiable Instruments Law
- BÖHM, P., Civil Procedure
- BRAUNEDER, W., Legal History of Austria and Europe
- BURGSTALLER, M., Criminal Law and Criminology
- BYDLINSKI, F., Civil Law
- FENYVES, A., Civil Law
- FUCHS, H., Criminal Law and Procedure
- HAUSMANINGER, R., Roman Law
- HÖPFEL, F., Criminal Law and Procedure
- HOYER, H., Civil Law and International Private Law
- KORINEK, K., Austrian Constitutional and Administrative Law
- KOZIOL, H., Civil Law
- KREJCI, H., Commercial Law and Negotiable Instruments Law
- LUF, G., Philosophy of Law and Canon Law
- MAYER, H., Public Law
- NEUHOLD, H., International Law and Relations
- OGRIS, W., German Law and Austrian Constitutional and Administrative History
- ÖHLINGER, T., Public Law and Comparative Constitutional Law
- PIELER, P. E., Roman Law and History of Ancient Law
- POTZ, R., Canon Law
- RASCHAUER, B., Constitutional and Public Law
- RECHBERGER, W., Civil Procedure
- SCHRAMMEL, W., Labour Law and Social Law
- TOMANDL, T., Labour Law and Social Law
- WALTER , R., Public and Constitutional Law
- WELSER, R., Civil Law

Faculty of Social Sciences and Economics:

CLEMENZ, G., Economics
DIERKER, E., Economic Theory and Economic Policy
DOCKNER, E., Business Administration
FINSINGER, J., Business Administration
FISCHER, E., Business Administration
GERLICH, P., Political Science
HARING, G., Applied Informatics
HARTL, R., Business Administration
HEIDENBERGER, K., Business Administration
KARAGIANNIS, D., Economics and Informatics
LECHNER, E., Financial Law
MUELLER, D., Economics
NERMUTH, M., Economic Theory and Finance
OROSEL, G., Economics and Economic Theory
PFLUG, G., Computing
PÖTSCHER, B., Statistics
SCHACHERMAYER, W., Applied Mathematics and Statistics
SCHULZ, W., Sociology
STREISSLER, E., Economics, Econometrics and Economic History
TRAXLER, F., Sociology of Industry and Economics
VAN DER BELLEN, A., Economics
VETSCHERA, R., Business Administration
VINEK, G., Statistics and Applied Computer Science
WAGNER, U., Business Administration
WINCKLER, G., Economics and Economic Policy
ZECHNER, J., Business Administration
ZIMA, H., Applied Informatics

Faculty of Medicine:

BANTLEON, H.-P., Oral Surgery
BAUER, P., Medical Statistics
BERGMANN, H., Clinical Physics
BLOCK, L.-H., Internal Medicine (Pulmology)
DEECKE, L., Clinical Neurology
EHRENBERGER, K., Oto-rhino-laryngology
EWERS, R., Facial Surgery
FERCHER, A. F., Medical Physics
FIRBAS, W., Anatomy
FONATSCH, C., Biology
FREY, M., Plastic and Reconstructive Surgery
FREYLER, H., Ophthalmology
FRIEDRICH, M., Paediatric Neuropsychiatry
GANGL, A., Gastroenterology and Hepatology
GRUBER, H., Anatomy
HORCHER, E., Paediatric Surgery
HÖRL, W., Nephrology
HUBER, H., Internal Medicine
HUSSLEIN, P., Gynaecology and Obstetrics
JAKESZ, R., Surgery
KAFKA, A., Physiology
KASPER, S., Psychiatry
KERJASCHKI, D., Ultrasonic Pathology and Cell Biology
KNAPP, W., Immunology
KOTZ, R., Orthopaedics
KRESS, H. G., Anaesthesia
KUNZE, M., Social Medicine
LAGGNER, A., Emergency Medicine
LECHNER, K., Haematology
LEODOLTER, S., Gynaecology and Obstetrics
MARBERGER, M., Urology
MAURER, G., Internal Medicine (Cardiology)
MAYR, R., Anatomy
MAYR, W., Serology of Blood Groups
PETERLIK, M., General and Experimental Pathology
POLLAK, A., Paediatrics
POLTERAUER, P., Vascular Surgery
PÖTTER, R., Radiotherapy
RADASZICWICZ, T., Pathological Anatomy
ROTTER, M., Hygiene
RÜDIGER, H., Internal Medicine
SCHNEIDER, W., Molecular Genetics (Occupational Medicine)
SCHREINER, W., Medical Computer Science
SCHULTE-HERMANN, P., Experimental Toxicology
SCHÜTZ, W., Pharmacology
SMOLEN, J., Internal Medicine (Rheumatology)
SONNECK, G., Medical Psychology
SPERR, W., Dental Medicine
SPIECKERMANN, P., Physiology
STINGL, G., Dermatology
THOMA, H., Biomedical Technics
TRAPPL, R., Medical Cybernetics and Artificial Intelligence
URBANEK, R., Paediatrics
VECSEI, V., Accidental Surgery
WALDHÄUSL, W., Endocrinology
WATZEK, G., Dental Medicine
WINTERSBERGER, E., Medical Chemistry
WOLFF, K., Dermatology
WOLNER, E., Surgery
ZIMPFER, M., Anaesthesiology

Faculty of Philosophy:

BACHL, N., Physiology of Sports
BAHR, H. D., Philosophy
BAUER, A. T., Journalism and Communications
FISCHER, G., Psychological Methodology and Mathematical Psychology
FISCHER, H., Geography
GREISENEGGER, W., Theatre Arts
GRUBER, K. H., Educational and Comparative Paedagogics
GUTTMANN, G., General and Experimental Psychology
HATZE, H., Biomechanics of Sports
KLEIN, H.-D., Philosophy
KREISKY, H. E., Political Science
LANGENBUCHER, W. R., Journalism
LESER, N., Philosophy
OESER, E., Philosophy (Philosophy of Science)
OLECHOWSKI, R., Pedagogics
ROLLETT, B., Educational Psychology
SOBOTKA, R., Physical Education
WERNHART, K. R., Ethnology

Faculty of Humanities:

AMBROS, A. A., Arabic and Islamic Studies
ASH, M., Modern History
AVERINCEV, S., Slavic Literature
BACH, F., History of Arts
BESTERS-DILGER, J., Russian Studies
BIETAK, M., Egyptian Studies
BIRKHAN, H., Old and Middle High German Language and Literature
BORCHHARDT, J., Classical Archaeology
BOTZ, G., Modern History
CYFFER, N., African Studies
DE BEAUGRANDE, R., English and American Language and Literature
DIENST, H., Austrian History
DOBESCH, G., Roman History, Antiquities and Epigraphy
DÖNT, E., Classical Philology
DREKONJA, G., Non-European History
DRESSLER, W., General and Applied Linguistics
EBENBAUER, A., Old German Language and Literature
EICHNER, H., General and Indoeuropean Linguistics
FÖDERMAYR, F., Comparative Musicology
FRIESINGER, H., Prehistory
GRUBER, G., Musicology
HASELSTEINER, H., East Central European History
HASSAUER, F., Romance Philology
HÄUSLER, W., Austrian History
HEGER, H., Newer German Language and Literature
KASTOVSKY, D., English and American Language and Literature
KNITTLER, H., Economic and Social History
KODER, J., Byzantine Studies
KÖHBACH, M., Turkic Studies and Islamic Science
KOHLER, A., Modern History
KÖSTLIN, K., Folklore
KREMNITZ, G., Romance Philology
KRINZINGER, F., Classical Archaeology
KRUMM, H. J., German Language
LADSTÄTTER, O., Sinology
LINHART, S., Japanese Studies
LIPPERT, A., Prehistory
LORENZ, H., History of Art
MALECZEK, W., Medieval History and Auxiliary Sciences
MARTINO, A., Comparative Literature
METZELTIN, M., Romance Linguistics and Didactics
MIKLAS, H., Slavonic Studies
MITTERAUER, M., Economic and Social History
PASS, W., Musicology
PRIMMER, A., Classical Philology
REDEI, K., Finno-Ugric Studies
ROSENAUER, A., History of Medieval and Modern Art
RÖMER, F., Classical Philology
ROSSEL, S., Scandinavian Studies
SCHMIDT-DENGLER, W., Modern German Literature
SIEWERT, P., Greek History
SNELL-HORNBY, M., Translation Science
STEINKELLNER, E., Buddhism and Tibetology
STELZER, W., Medieval History and Auxiliary Sciences
STEMBERGER, G., Judaic Studies
WELZIG, W., History of Modern German Literature
WIESINGER, P., German Language and Early German Literature
WINCZER, P., Slavonic Literature
WODAK, R., Applied Linguistics
WOLFRAM, H., Medieval History and Auxiliary Sciences
ZACHARASIEWICZ, W., English and American Language and Literature
ZEMAN, H., Modern German Literature

Faculty of Natural Sciences:

BARTH, F., Zoology
BARTL, A., Theoretical Physics
BREGER, M., Astronomy
BRINKER, U., Organic Chemistry
BURIAN, K., Anatomy and Physiology of Plants
CIGLER, J., Mathematics
DICKERT, F., Analytical Chemistry
DITTAMI, J., Zoology
ELMADFA, I., Nutritional Science
FAUPL, P., Geology
FERGUSON, D., Palaeontology
FLEISCHHACKER, W., Pharmaceutical Chemistry
FRINGELI, U. P., Applied Physical Chemistry and Biophysical Chemistry
GRABHERR, G., Vegetation Ecology and Research in Nature Protection
GUTDEUTSCH, R., Geophysics
HANTEL, M., Theoretical Meteorology
HEISTRACHER, P., Pharmacodynamics and Toxicology
HEJTMANEK, J., Mathematics
KEPPLER, B., Inorganic Chemistry
KIESL, W., Geochemistry
KUBELKA, W., Pharmacognosy
KUTSCHERA, W., Nuclear Physics
LINDNER, W., Analytical Chemistry
LOSERT, V., Mathematics
MULZER, J., Organic Chemistry
NEUMAIER, A., Computer-oriented Mathematics
OLAJ, O., Chemical Physics
PAULUS, H., Zoology
PIETSCHMANN, H., Theoretical Physics
POPP, M., Chemical Physiology of Plants
RABEDER, G., Palaeontology and Palaeobiology
RICHTER, W., Mineralogy and Petrography
RUIS, H., Biochemistry
SCHIEMER, F., Zoology
SCHMIDT, K. W., Mathematics

SCHUSTER, P., Theoretical Chemistry
SCHWEIZER, D., Botany (Citology and Genetics)
SCHWEYEN, R., Genetics and Microbiology
SEIDLER, H., Human Biology
SIGMUND, K., Mathematics
STEINACKER, R., Meteorology and Geophysics
STEININGER, F., Biostratigraphy
STICKLER, R., Science of Materials
STUESSI, T., Botany
TILLMANNS, E., Mineralogy and Crystallography
VOGL, G., Physics
VON GABAIN, A., Microbiology
WEBER, M., Systematical Botany
WICHE, G., General Biochemistry
YNGUARSON, J., Theoretical Physics

TECHNISCHE UNIVERSITÄT GRAZ (Graz Technical University)

8010 Graz, Rechbauerstr. 12
Telephone: (316) 873-0
Fax: (316) 873-6009

Founded 1811

Rector: Dipl.-Ing Dr techn. IROLT KILLMANN
Chief Administrative Officer: Dr iur. FRIEDRICH AUER
Librarian: Dipl.-Ing. EVA BERTHA

Library: see Libraries
Number of teachers: 687
Number of students: 14,983

DEANS

Faculty of Architecture: Prof. Dipl.-Ing. FRANZ RIEPL
Faculty of Constructional Engineering: Prof. Dipl.-Ing. Dr techn. KLAUS RIESSBERGER
Faculty of Mechanical Engineering: Prof. Dipl.-Ing. Dr techn. ADOLF FRANK
Faculty of Electrical Engineering: Prof. Dipl.-Ing. Dr techn. MANFRED RENTMEISTER
Faculty of Natural Sciences: Prof. Mag. Dr HANS VOGLER

PROFESSORS

BAUER, U., Industrial Management
BEER, G., Building Statics
BERGMANN, H., Hydromechanics, Hydraulics and Hydrology
BESENHARD, O. J., Inorganic Chemical Technology
BRANDSTÄTTER, G., Applied Geodesy and Photogrammetry
BRUNNER, F. K., Geodesy
BURKARD, R., Mathematics
CELIGOJ, CH., Strength of Materials
CERJAK, H., Materials Science and Welding
CROSET, P. A., Construction and Design
DIETER, U., Mathematical Statistics
DOMENIG, G., Building and Domestic Architecture
DOURDOUMAS, N., Automatic Control
EGGER, H., Structural Design
FRANK, A., Manufacturing Technology
GAMERITH, H., Building and Design
GEYMAYER, H., Material Testing
GRAMPP, G., Physical Chemistry
GREINER, R., Timberwork and Elevation
GRIENGL, H., Organic Chemistry
HABERFELLNER, R., Management
HEIGERTH, G., Hydraulic Design and Water Resources Management
HUTTEN, H., Electro- and Biomedical Technology
JABERG, H., Hydraulic Turbo-machinery
JÄGER, H., Experimental Physics
JERICHA, H., Thermal Turbo-machinery
JÜRGENS, G., Machine Principles
KAHLERT, H., Solid State Physics
KECSKEMETHY, A., Theory of Machines
KNAPP, G., Analytical Chemistry
KUPELWIESER, H., Artistic Forms
LEBERL, F., Computer-aided Geometry and Graphics
LEOPOLD, H., Electronics
LUCAS, P., Software Technology
MAASS, W., Information Processing
MARR, R. J., Process Engineering
MAURER, H., Information Processing
MEUWISSEN, J.M.C., Building and Town Planning
MORITZ, H., Geodesy
MUHR, H.M., High Voltage Engineering
OSER, J., Materials Handling and Mechanical Engineering Design
PALTAUF, F., Biochemistry
PFANNHAUSER, W., Food Chemistry
PISCHINGER, R., Thermodynamics
PISCHL, R., Timberwork
POSCH, R., Applied Information Processing and Communications Technology
REETZ, B., Steam Engines
RENNER, H., Hydraulics, Agricultural and Industrial Water Construction
RENTMEISTER, M., Electrical Engineering
RICHTER, K., Electrical Engineering
RIEDLER, W., Information Methodology and Wave Propagation
RIEDMÜLLER, G., Geology, Petrography, Mineralogy
RIEPL, F., Country Planning and Architecture
RIESSBERGER, K., Railways
ROBRA, K. H., Biotechnology, Microbiology, Waste Products Technology
SCHUBERT, W., Rock Mechanics and Tunneling
SEMPRICH, S., Soil Mechanics and Foundation Engineering
SPAROWITZ, L., Concrete Construction
STADLER, G., Building
STARK, H., Pulp, Paper and Fibre Technology
STAUDINGER, G., Instrument Construction and Mechanical Techniques
STICKLER, H., Highway Engineering and Transportation
SÜNKEL, H., Theoretical Geodesy
TICHY, R., Mathematics
TUTSCHKE, W., Applied Mathematics
VOGLER, H., Geometry
VOSS, H., Biotechnology
WEISS, R., Computer Engineering
WILHELM, K., History of Art
WOHINZ, J., Industrial Management

TECHNISCHE UNIVERSITÄT WIEN (Vienna Technical University)

1040 Vienna, Karlsplatz 13
Telephone: (1) 58801
Telex: 131000
Fax: (1) 587-89-05

Founded 1815
State control
Academic year: October to June (two terms)

Rector: Prof. Dipl. Ing. Dr techn. PETER SKALICKY
Pro-Rector: Prof. Dipl.-Ing. Dr techn. FRIEDRICH MOSER
Chief Administrative Officer: Dr ERNST SCHRANZ
Librarian: Dr PETER KUBALEK

Library: see under Libraries
Number of teachers: 2,100
Number of students: 22,200

Publications: *Informationen, Schriftenreihe, Vorlesungs- und Personalverzeichnis, Mitteilungsblatt, TU-Aktuell.*

DEANS

Faculty of Regional Planning and Architecture: Prof. Dr EGON MATZNER
Faculty of Civil Engineering: Prof. DDr HERBERT MANG
Faculty of Mechanical Engineering: Prof. Dr HEINZ-BERND MATTHIAS
Faculty of Electrical Engineering: Prof. Dr ALEXANDER WEINMANN
Faculty of Technology and Natural Sciences: Prof. Dr HERBERT STACHELBERGER

PROFESSORS

Faculty of Civil Engineering:

BRANDL, H., Foundations
BRUNNER, P. H., Waste Management
DROBIR, H., Water Plant Construction, Navigable Waterways and Environmental Hydraulics
ENGEL, E., Railways and Traffic
GUTKNECHT, D., Hydraulic, Hydrology and Water Supply
JODL, H. G., Construction Practice and Methods
KNOFLACHER, H., Traffic Planning and Engineering
KROISS, H., Water Supply, Sewage Purification and Prevention of Water Pollution
LITZKA, J., Road Engineering and Maintenance
MAKOVEC, F., Geology
MANG, H., Elasticity and Strength
OBERNDORFER, W. J., Construction and Planning
OGRIS, H., Experimental Hydraulics
PAUSER, A., Structural Engineering
RAMBERGER, G., Steel Girder Construction
REIFFENSTUHL, H., Reinforced and Prestressed Concrete Structures
RUBIN, H., Structural Analysis
SCHNEIDER, U., Building Materials
SOMMER, D., Industrial Construction
ZIEGLER, F., Applied Mechanics

Faculty of Regional Planning and Architecture:

BÖKEMANN, D., Town and Country Planning
CERWENKA, P., Transport Systems Planning
DAHINDEN, J., Interior Decoration
FRANCK-OBERASPACH, G., Computer-aided Design and Planning Methods
GÖSCHL, R., Drawing and Painting
KRIER, R., Design
KUBELIK, M., History of Architecture and Historic Building Survey
LESAK, F., Model Construction
MATZNER, E., Finance and Infrastructure Policy
MOSER, F., Local Regional Planning
PUCHHAMMER, H., Structural Engineering for Architects
RICHTER, H., Structural Engineering for Architects
SCHWEIGHOFER, A., Building Construction and Design
STILES, R., Landscape Planning and Garden Architecture
WEBER, G., History of Art and Cultural Conservation
ZEHETNER, F., Public Law

Faculty of Electrical Engineering:

BONEK, E., High Frequency and Communications Technology
BRAUNER, G., Power Systems
DETTER, H., Precision Engineering
DIETRICH, D., Computer Technology
EIER, R., Data Processing
FASCHING, G., Materials used in Electrical Engineering
FRÖLICH, K., Switch Gear and High Voltage Technology
GORNIK, E., Solid State Electronics
JANSEN, P. J., Energy Industry
KLEINRATH, H., Electrical Machinery
MECKLENBRÄUKER, W., Low Frequency Technology
PASCHKE, F., General Electronics
PATZELT, R., Electrical Measuring Techniques
PRECHTL, A., Theory of Electrical Engineering
SCHMIDT, A., Quantum Electronics and Lasers
SELBERHERR, S., Software Technology for Microelectronic Systems
WEINMANN, A., Electrical Control, Navigation and Power Engineering

ZEICHEN, G., Flexible Automation

Faculty of Mechanical Engineering:

DESOYER, K., Mechanics
GRÖSEL, B., Handling and Transport Technology and General Design Engineering
HASELBACHER, H., Thermal Turbo-Machinery and Power Plants
JÖRGL, H. P., Machine- and Process-Engineering
KLUWICK, A., Hydrodynamics
KOPACEK, P., Handling Devices and Robotics
LENZ, H. P., Internal Combustion Vehicles
LINZER, W., Theory of Heat
MATTHIAS, H. B., Water-powered Machines and Pumps
RAMMERSTORFER, F., Light Engineering, Aeroplane Engineering
RINDER, L., Machine Parts
SCHNEIDER, W., Gas and Thermodynamics
SPRINGER, H., Machine Dynamics and Measurement
STEPAN, A., Industrial Business Management
STRAUBE, H., Materials and Material Testing
TROGER, H., Mechanics
VARGA, T., Welding
WESESLINDTNER, H., Computer Integrated Manufacturing
WOJDA, F., Business Management
ZEMAN, J., Pressure Vessel and Plant Technology

Faculty of Technology and Natural Sciences:

BARTH, W., Information Systems
BREITER, M., Electrochemistry
BRETTERBAUER, K., Geodesy
BROCKHAUS, M., Information Technology
BRÜCKL, E., Geophysics
DEISTLER, M., Economics
DUTTER, R., Technical Statistics
EBEL, H., Technical Physics
EDER, G., Nuclear Physics
FEICHTINGER, G., Business Research
FLEISSNER, P., Design and Assessment/Social Cybernetics
FRANK, A., Surveying and Geoinformation
FRISCH, H., Political Economics
GOTTLOB, G., Applied Informatics
GRASSERBAUER, M., Analytical Chemistry
GRUBER, P., Mathematical Analysis
GRÜNBACHER, H., Computer Engineering (VLSI-Design)
KAHMEN, H., General Geodesy
KELNHOFER, F., Cartography and Reproduction Technology
KERNER, K., Digital Analysis
KIRCHMAYR, H., Experimental Physics
KNÖZINGER, E., Physical Chemistry
KOPETZ, H., Software Technology
KRAUS, K., Photogrammetry
KROPATSCH, W., Design and Manufacturing
KUICH, W., Mathematical Logic and Computer Languages
KUMMER, W., Theoretical Physics
LANGER, H., Applied Analysis
LUX, B., Inorganic Chemical Technology
POTTMANN, A., Geometry
PREISINGER, A., Mineralogy, Crystallography and Structural Chemistry
RAUCH, H., Experimental Nuclear Physics
REVESZ, P., Theory of Probability
RÖHR, M., Biochemical Technology and Microbiology
SAUTER, F., Organic Chemistry
SCHILDT, G.-H., Automations Systems
SCHMIDT, A., Technical Procedures and Fuel Technology
SCHUBERT, U., Inorganic Chemistry
SKALICKY, P., Applied Physics
STACHEL, H., Geometry
STACHELBERGER, H., Botany, Technical Microscopy and Organic Raw Materials
STETTER, H., Numerical Mathematics
VIERTL, R., Applied Statistics and Information Science
WASHÜTTL, J., Food Technology
WEISS, R., Applied Mathematics
WINTER, H., General Physics
WOLFF, K., Actuarial Theory

UNIVERSITÄT FÜR BODENKULTUR WIEN
(University of Agricultural Sciences, Vienna)

1180 Vienna, Gregor Mendelstr. 33
Telephone: (1) 47654-0
Fax: (1) 4788115

Founded 1872
State control
Academic year: October to June

Rector: Prof. Dipl.-Ing. Dr LEOPOLD MÄRZ
Vice-Rectors: Dipl.-Ing. Dr HERBERT HAGER (Research), Prof. Mag. Dr WALTER SCHIEBEL (Continuing Education), Prof. Dr MANFRIED WELAN (Public Affairs), Prof. Dipl.-Ing. Dr WOLFGANG SAGL (Financial Affairs)
Registrar: Dr iur. ILONA GÄLZER
Librarian: Dr phil. WERNER HAINZ-SATOR

Library: see under Libraries
Number of teachers: 330, including 62 professors
Number of students: 8,000

Publications: *Die Bodenkultur, Zentralblatt für das gesamte Forstwesen* (quarterly), *Blick ins Land* (monthly), *Ökoenergie* (every 2 months).

PROFESSORS

Department of Agriculture:

BLUM, W. E. H., Soil Science
BOXBERGER, J., Agricultural Machinery and Operational Technology
FISCHER, J., Mechanical and Energy Engineering
GATTERBAUER, H., Agricultural Law
HAIGER, A., Livestock Breeding
HALBWACHS, G., Plant Anatomy and Physiology
HOFREITHER, M., Economics, Agricultural and Economic Policy
HOLZNER, W., Sociology and Ecology of Plants
HÜBL, E., Ecology and Sociology of Plants
JEZIK, K., Horticulture
LETTNER, F., Animal Nutrition
PIEBER, K., Fruit and Vegetable Production
RICHTER, H., Plant Anatomy and Physiology
RUCKENBAUER, P., Plant Breeding
SCHIEBEL, W., Agricultural Marketing and Nutritional Economics
SCHNEEBERGER, W., Agricultural Business Management
STEINER, H. M., Zoology, Anatomy and Physiology of Vertebrates
SWATONEK, F., Plant Protection
WEINDLMAYR, J., Plant Protection
WELAN, M., Law

Department of Forestry:

FÜHRER, E., Forest Entomology and Forest Protection
GLATZEL, G., Forest Soil Science, Nutrition and Site Classification
GLÜCK, P., Forestry Policy
GOSSOW, H., Wildlife Biology and Game Management
JÖBSTL, H., Forestry Economics
RESCH, H., Wood Technology
SAGL, W., Forestry Management and Forestry Economics
STERBA, H., Forest Mensuration, Growth and Yield Studies
TRZESNIOWSKI, A., Forest Engineering
WEINMEISTER, H., Watershed Engineering

Department of Civil Engineering and Water Management:

BERGMEISTER, K., Structural Engineering
BIFFL, W., Sanitary Engineering and Water Resources Protection
HABERL, R., Sanitary Engineering and Water Resources Protection
JUNGWIRTH, M., Hydrobiology, Fishery Management and Aquaculture
KASTANEK, F., Rural Water Management
LECHNER, P., Waste Management
NACHTNEBEL, H. P., Hydrology, Water Management and Hydraulics
NOWAK, W. G., Mathematics and Descriptive Geometry
RUPPERT, W., Mathematics
STANZEL-TSCHEGG, S., Physics
STRELEC, H., Statistics and Computer Science
WEBER, G., Regional Planning and Research
WEISS, E. H., Geology
ZAUSSINGER, A., Metrology

Department of Food Science and Biotechnology:

BERGHOFER, E., Food Science and Technology
FOISSY, H., Dairy Science and Agricultural Microbiology
GLÖSSL, J., Cell Biology
KATINGER, H., Technical Mycology and Biotechnological Assay Methods
KOSMA, P., Organic Chemistry
KULBE, K. D., Food Technology
MÄRZ, L., Biochemistry
SLEYTR, U. B., Ultrastructure Research
STINGEDER, G., Analytical Chemistry
ZENZ, H., Foodstuffs Processing and Quality Control

Department of Landscape Architecture and Planning:

KVARDA, W., Landscape Design
SCHACHT, H., Garden Architecture and Green-space Planning

ATTACHED RESEARCH CENTRES

Centre for Environmental Studies and Nature Conservation: Dir Prof. G. HALBWACHS.

Centre for Applied Genetics: Dir Prof. J. GLÖSSL.

Ultra Structures Research Centre: Dir Prof. U. SLEYTR.

JOHANNES KEPLER UNIVERSITÄT LINZ
(Linz University)

4040 Linz, Schloss-Auhof
Telephone: (732) 2468
Telex: 22323
Fax: 732-246810

Founded as College 1966, present name 1975
State control
Academic year: October to June

Rector: Prof. Dr FRANZ STREHL
Vice-Presidents: Prof. Dipl.-Ing. Dr HANS IRSCHIK (Research), Prof. Dr BRUNO BINDER (Science), Prof. Dr FRIEDRICH SCHNEIDER (Foreign Affairs)
Administrative Director: Hofrat Dr OTHMAR KÖCKINGER
Librarian: Oberrätin Dr MONIKA SCHENK

Library: see Libraries
Number of academic staff: 1,465
Number of students: 17,500

Publications: *Forschung und Lehre, Universitätsnachrichten* (6 a year), *Mitteilungsblatt der Universität* (weekly).

DEANS

Faculty of Law: Prof. Dr HERIBERT FRANZ KÖCK
Faculty of Social Sciences and Economics: Prof. Dr HELMUT SCHUSTER
Faculty of Technology and Natural Science: Prof. Dipl.-Ing. Dr HEINZ ENGL

PROFESSORS

Faculty of Law:

ACHATZ, M., Tax Law
APATHY, P., Roman Law

BINDER, B., Administrative Law
DOLINAR, H., Civil Procedure
FLOSZMANN, U., History of Austrian and German Law
HENGSTSCHLÄGER, J., Constitutional Law and Political Science
HOLZHAMMER, R., Civil Procedure
JABORNEGG, P., Commercial and Securities Law
KALB, H., Canon Law
KAROLLUS, M., Commercial Law
KEINERT, H., Commercial and Securities Law
KERSCHNER, F., Civil Law
KIENAPFEL, D., Criminal Law and Procedure
KLINGENBERG, G., Roman Law
KÖCK, H., International Law and Relations
MOOS, R., Criminal Law and Procedure
OBERNDORFER, P., Administrative Law
REISCHAUER, R., Civil Law
ROTTER, M., Public, European and International Law and Political Science
RUMMEL, P., Civil Law
SCHAMBECK, H., Public Law and Political Science
SPIELBÜCHLER, K., Civil Law
WIDDER, H., Public Law and Political Science

Faculty of Social Sciences and Economics:
ALTRICHTER, H., Education and Educational Psychology
ARDELT, R., Modern and Contemporary History
BÖHNISCH, W., Business Administration (Management)
BRANDSTÄTTER, H., Education and Educational Psychology
BRUNNER, J., Economics
DYK, I., Socio-politics
EULER, H. P., Sociology
GADENNE, V., Philosophy and Science Theory
HAFNER, R., Applied Statistics
HAKANSON, L., Business Administration (International Management)
HEINRICH, L. J., Information Engineering
HOLM, K., Sociology
KOHLER, W., National Economy
KROPF, R., Social and Economic History
LANDESMANN, M., National Economy
MALINSKY, A., Environmental Management in Business and Regional Policy
NIGSCH, O., Sociology
PERNSTEINER, H., Business Administration
PILS, M., Data Processing
PÖLL, G., Economics
POMBERGER, G., Software Engineering
REBER, G., Business Administration (Management and International Management Studies)
SANDGRUBER, R., Social and Economic History
SCHAUER, R., Business Administration (Public Administration and Non-Profit Organizations)
SCHNEIDER, F., Economics
SCHREFL, M., Data Engineering
SCHURER, B., Education and Educational Psychology
SCHUSTER, H., Economics
SERTL, W., Business Administration (Accountancy, Auditing, Business Taxation and Controllership)
SIXTL, F., Applied Statistics
STARY, C., Data Engineering
STIEGLER, H., Business Administration (Accountancy, Auditing, Business Taxation and Controllership)
VODRAZKA, K., Business Administration (Accountancy, Auditing, Business Taxation and Controllership)
WEIDENHOLZER, J., Socio-politics
WÜHRER, G., Business Administration (Marketing)
ZÄPFEL, G., Business Administration (Industrial and Production Economics)
ZAPOTOCZKY, K., Sociology

Faculty of Technology and Natural Sciences:
AMRHEIN, W., Power Electronics and Drive Technology
BÄUERLE, D., Applied Physics
BAUER, G., Semiconductor Physics
BERAN, H., Systems Engineering Sciences
BOLLER, H., Chemistry
BREMER, H., Robotics
BUCHBERGER, B., Mathematics
BUCHBERGER, W., Analytical Chemistry
CHROUST, G., Systems Engineering Sciences
COOPER, J. B., Mathematics
ENGL, H., Industrial Mathematics
FALK, H., Organic Chemistry
GITTLER, P., Fluid Dynamics and Thermal Processes
GRITZNER, G., Chemical Technology for Inorganic Substances
HAGELAUER, R., Systems Engineering Sciences
HEINRICH, H., Semiconductor Physics
IRSCHIK, H., Technical Mechanics
JANTSCH, W., Semiconductor Physics
KAPPEL, G., Computer Science
KLEMENT, E., Mathematics
KROTSCHEK, E., Theoretical Physics
LANGER, U., Mathematics
LERCH, R., Electronic Metrology
MARKOWICH, P., Mathematics
MÖSSENBÖCK, H., Computer Science
MÜHLBACHER, J., Systems Science
MÜHLHÄUSER, M., Computer Science
PICHLER, F., Systems Science
PILZ, G., Mathematics
RECHENBERG, P., Computer Science
SAMHABER, W., Process Engineering
SARICIFTCI, S., Physical Chemistry
SCHÄFFLER, F., Semiconductor Physics
SCHEIDL, R., Mechanical Engineering
SCHINDLER, H., Biophysics
SCHLACHER, K., Automatic Control and Electrical Drive
SCHLÖGLMANN, W., Teaching of Mathematics
SCHMIDT, H., Chemical Technology of Organic Materials
SOBCZAK, R., Physical Chemistry
THIM, H., Microelectronics
TITULAER, U., Theoretical Physics
TRAUNMÜLLER, R., Applied Computer Science
VOLKERT, J. J., Computer Science
WAGNER, R., Computer Science
WEIGEL, R., Communications and Information Enginnering
WEISS, P., Mathematics, Probability, Mathematical Statistics

WIRTSCHAFTSUNIVERSITÄT WIEN (Vienna University of Economics and Business Administration)

1090 Vienna, Augasse 2–6
Telephone: 313 36-0
Fax: 313 36-740

Founded 1898
State control
Languages of instruction: German and English
Academic year: October to June

Rector: Prof. Dr HANS ROBERT HANSEN
Vice-Rectors: Prof. Dr REINHARD MOSER, Prof. Dr CHRISTOPH BADELT, a.o. Prof. Dr GERLINDE MAUTNER, Prof. Dr JOSEF MAZANEC
Dean of Studies: Prof. Dr WOLFGANG KEMMETMÜLLER
Registrar: Dr THOMAS HERZOG
Librarian: HR Mag. GERTRAUD WEHRMANN

Library: see Libraries
Number of teachers: 344
Number of students: 22,000

Publication: *Journal für Betriebswirtschaft* (Journal for Business Administration, 6 a year).

PROFESSORS
ABELE, H., Economic Theory and Policy
ALEXANDER, R. J., English Language
BADELT, C., Social Policy
BAUER, L., Economic Theory and Policy
BERGMAN, E. M., Urban and Regional Studies
BERTL, R., Tax-oriented Business Management
BOGNER, ST., Department of Corporate Finance
BREUSS, F., Research Institute for European Affairs
BÜHLER, W., Bank Administration
CLEMENT, W., Economic Theory and Policy
DERFLINGER, G., Statistics
DORALT, P., Corporate Law
EDER, R., Foreign Trade and Development Economics
EGGER, A., Accounting and Auditing
ESCHENBACH, R., Business Management
FALLER, P., Transportation
FINK, G., Research Institute for European Affairs
FISCHER, M., Economic and Social Geography
GAREIS, R., Project Management
GASSNER, W., Tax Law
GRILLER, S., Research Institute for European Affairs
GRÜN, O., Business Organization and Materials Management
HACKL, P., Economic Statistics
HALLER, H., Constitutional and Administrative Law
HANSEN, H., Management and Computer Science
HOLOUBEK, M., Constitutional and Administrative Law
HRUBI, F., Theory of Education
JAMMERNEGG, W., Industrial Information Processing
JANKO, W., Information Processing and Information Economics
KASPER, H., General Management
KEMMETMÜLLER, W., Co-operatives
LANG, M., International Tax Law
LAURER, H. R., Constitutional and Administrative Law
LEDOLTER, J., Mathematical Methods of Statistics
LOISTL, O., Finance and Financial Markets
MATIS, H., Economic and Social History
MAYRHOFER, W., Business and Government Management
MAZANEC, J., Tourism
MIKL-HORKE, G., General Sociology and Economic Sociology
MOSER, R., International Business
MOSSER, A., Economic and Social History
MUGLER, J., Small Business
NOWOTNY, C., Civil, Commercial and Securities Law
NOWOTNY, E., Economic Theory and Policy
OBENAUS, W., English Language
OBERMANN, G., Public Finance
OTRUBA, H., Economic Theory and Policy
PANNY, W., Applied Computer Science
PFEIFFLE, H, Theory of Education
PICHLER, H., Economic Theory and Policy
PURCELL, H. D., English Language
RAINER, F., Romance Languages
RATHMAYR, R., Slavonic Languages
RILL, H., Constitutional and Administrative Law
RUNGGALDIER, U., Labour Law, Social Law
SANDNER, K., General Management
SCHAUER, M., Civil, Commercial and Securities Law
SCHEUCH, F., Marketing
SCHIFKO, P., Romance Languages
SCHLEGELMILCH, B., International Marketing and Management
SCHNEDLITZ, P., Retail Management
SCHNEIDER, W., Business Education
SCHÖPF, A., Public Finance
SCHUBERT, U., Environment and Economy

SCHUELEIN, J. A., General and Economic Sociology
SCHWEIGER, G., Advertising and Market Research
SEICHT, G., Industrial Management
STEINER, P., Corporate Finance
STRASSER, H., Experimental Methods of Mathematics and Statistics
STREMITZER, H., Insurance Management
TAUDES, A., Industrial Information Processing
TITSCHER, ST., General and Economic Sociology
TOPRITZHOFER, E., Operations Research
VOGEL, G., Technology and Commodity Economics
VON ECKARDSTEIN, D., Personnel Management
WALTHER, H., Employment Theory and Policy

MONTANUNIVERSITÄT LEOBEN
(University of Mining and Metallurgy, Leoben)

8700 Leoben, Franz-Josef Str. 18

Telephone: (3842) 402-0
Telex: 33322
Fax: (3842) 402-502

Founded 1840
Languages of instruction: German and English

Rector: Prof. Dr PETER PASCHEN
Administrator: Dr A. NEUBURG
Librarian: Dr LIESELOTTE JONTES

Library: see Libraries
Number of students: *c.* 2,500

PROFESSORS

BIEDERMANN, H., Economics, Industrial Management and Industrial Engineering
BÜHRIG-POLACZEK, A., Foundry Technology
CZUBIK, E., Mine Surveying, Subsidence Problems
DANZER, R., Ceramics
EBNER, F., Geology and Mineral Resources
FISCHER, D., Mechanics
FRATZL, P., Metal Physics
GAMSJÄGER, H., Physical Chemistry
GOD, CH., Heat Engineering, Industrial Furnace Engineering and Power Supply
GOLSER, J., Sublevel Construction
GRIMMER, K., Materials Handling
HARMUTH, H., Refractory Materials, Ceramics, Glass and Cement
HEINEMANN, Z., Reservoir Engineering
HIEBLER, H., Ferrous and Nonferrous Metallurgy
IMRICH, W., Applied Mathematics
JEGLITSCH, F., Physical Metallurgy and Material Testing
KEPPLINGER, W., Industrial Environmental Protection
KIRSCHENHOFER, P., Mathematics
KNEISSL, A., Metallography
KUCHAR, F., Physics
LANG, R., Plastics
LANGECKER, G., Plastics Technology
LEDERER, K., Chemistry of Plastics
LORBER, K., Decontamination
MAURITSCH, H., Geophysics
MILLAHN, K., Applied Geophysics
MILLHEIM, K. K., Petroleum Engineering
O'LEARY, P., Automation
SACHS, H., Applied Geometry
SCHWENZFEIER, W., Deformation Processing and Steel Mill Machineries
STEINER, H., Mineral Processing
VORTISCH, W., Applied Sedimentology
WAGNER, H., Mining Engineering
WEGSCHEIDER, F., General and Analytical Chemistry
WEISS, G., Electrical Engineering
WOERNDLE, R., Plastics
WOLFBAUER, J., Business Economics

VETERINÄRMEDIZINISCHE UNIVERSITÄT WIEN
(University of Veterinary Medicine, Vienna)

1210 Vienna, Veterinärplatz

Telephone: (1) 25077-0
Fax: (1) 25077-1090
E-mail: rektor@vu-wien.ac.at

Founded 1765
State control
Academic year: October to June

Rector: Prof Dr JOSEF LEIBETSEDER
Vice-Rector: Prof. Dr CHLODWIG FRANZ
Administrative Director: (vacant)

Library: see Libraries
Teaching staff: 174
Number of students: 2,700

Publication: *Wiener Tierärztliche Monatsschrift.*

PROFESSORS

ARNOLD, W., Wildlife Research and Ecology
AURICH, J. E., Obstetrics, Gynaecology and Andrology
BAMBERG, E., Biochemistry
BAUMGARTNER, W., Internal Medicine and Contagious Diseases of Ruminants and Swine
BREM, G., Animal Breeding and Genetics
BÖCK, P., Histology and Embryology
BRANDL, E., Milk Hygiene and Technology
EISENMENGER, E., Surgery and Ophthalmology
FRANZ, C., Botany and Food Science
GEMEINER, M., Medical Chemistry
GÜNZBURG, W., Virology
HOFECKER, G., Physiology
KÖNIG, H., Anatomy
KUTZER, E., Parasitology and Zoology
LUF, W., Nutrition
MAYRHOFER, E., Radiology
NOHL, H., Pharmacology and Toxicology
ROSENGARTEN, R., Bacteriology and Animal Hygiene
SMULDERS, F., Hygiene and Processing of Meat and Food Science
STANEK, CH., Orthopaedics in Ungulates
THALHAMMER, J. G., Internal Medicine of Solipeds and Small Animals
VASICEK, L., Poultry
WINDISCHBAUER, G., Medical Physics

AKADEMIE DER BILDENDEN KÜNSTE
(Academy of Fine Arts)

1010 Vienna, Schillerplatz 3

Telephone: 58-816
Fax: 587-7977

Founded 1692
State control
Academic year: October to June

Rector: Prof. CARL PRUSCHA
Pro-Rector: Prof. EDELBERT KÖB
Registrar: Mrs KASPAR
Librarian: Dr WAGNER

Library: see Libraries
Number of teachers: 190
Number of students: 672

PROFESSORS

BAATZ, W., Conservation and Technology
BAUER, U. M., Contemporary Art
BRAUER, A., Painting
DAMISCH, G., Graphic Arts
GIRONCOLI, B., Sculpture
GRAF, O., History of Art
HEMPEL, H., Space-Communication Hermeneutics
HIKADE, K., Painting
HOLLEGHA, W., Painting
HUNDERTWASSER, F., Painting
KÖB, E., Manual Arts and Crafts
LEHMDEN, A., Painting
MAIRINGER, F., Colour Science, Colour Chemistry and Material Science
MIKL, J., Nature Studies
ÖLZANT, F. X., Art of Making Medals and Small Sculptures
PEICHL, G., Architecture
PENTTILÄ, T., Architecture
PISTOLETTO, M., Sculpture
PRACHENSKY, M., Painting
PRUSCHA, C., Architecture and Research
SCHULZ, J., Textile Arts and Tapestry
WONDER, E., Stage Design
ZENS, H., Art Education and Science of Art
ZIESEL, W., Statics, Reinforced Concrete, Steel and Lightweight Structures

HOCHSCHULE FÜR ANGEWANDTE KUNST IN WIEN
(University of Applied Arts in Vienna)

1010 Vienna, Oskar Kokoschkaplatz 2

Telephone: (1) 71133
Fax: (1) 71133-222

Founded 1868

Rector: Prof. Dipl.-Ing. Dr RUDOLF BURGER
Academic Vice-Rector: Prof. ADOLF FROHNER
Administrative Vice-Rector: Dr HEINZ ADAMEK
Registrar: SENTA SCHWANDA
Librarian: Dr GABRIELE KOLLER

Library of 80,000 vols
Number of teachers: 250
Number of students: 1,100

Publications: exhibition catalogues (6–8 a year), *Studienführer, Prospect* (2 a year).

DEANS

Faculty of Architecture: Prof. Mag. arch. HANS HOLLEIN
Faculty of Fine Arts: Prof. ADOLF FROHNER
Faculty of Design: Prof. Dipl.-Ing. Dr techn. ALFRED VENDL
Faculty of Visual Communications: Prof. Mag. art. TINO ERBEN
Faculty of Art Education: Prof. Mag. art. ERNST W. BERANEK

HEADS OF DEPARTMENT

Faculty of Architecture:

- Master-Class for Architecture: Prof. Mag. arch. WILHELM HOLZBAUER
- Master-Class for Architecture: Prof. Mag. arch. HANS HOLLEIN
- Master-Class for Architecture (emphasis on interior design): Prof. WOLF DIETER PRIX
- Chair of Architectural History and Theory: Prof. Dr. FRIEDRICH ACHLEITNER
- Chair of Building Construction: Prof. Dipl.-Ing. ERNST MATEOVICS
- Chair of Statics: Prof. Dipl.-Ing. Dr techn. KLAUS BOLLINGER
- Chair of Building Technology: (vacant)
- Institute of Design: Prof. Mag. arch. HANS HOLLEIN
- Institute of Furniture Design and Interior Design: Prof. WOLF PRIX
- Institute of Urban Design: Prof. Mag. arch. WILHELM HOLZBAUER
- Institute of Model Construction: (vacant)

Faculty of Design

- Master-Class for Product Design: (vacant)
- Master-Class for Industrial Design: Prof. Mag. arch. PAOLO PIVA
- Master-Class for Fashion Design: Prof. JEAN-CHARLES DE CASTELBAJAC
- Master-Class for Product Design: Prof. RON ARAD
- Chair of Geometry: (vacant)
- Chair of Technical Chemistry: Prof Dr ALFRED VENDL
- Chair of History and Theory of Design: Prof. Arch. Dipl.-Ing. FRANÇOIS BURKHARDT
- Institute of Glass: (vacant)

Institute of Product Design: Prof. Mag. arch. PAOLO PIVA
Institute of Silicate Chemistry and Archaeometry: Prof. Dr ALFRED VENDL

Faculty of Visual Communications:
Master-Class for Graphic Arts: Prof. Mag. art. MARIO TERZIC
Master-Class for Graphic Arts: Prof. Mag. art. TINO ERBEN
Master-Class for Graphic Arts: Prof. WALTER LÜRZER
Master-Class for Scenography: Prof. Mag. art. BERNHARD KLEBER
Master-Class for Visual Media: Prof. PETER WEIBEL
Chair of Communication Theory: Prof. Dr rer. pol. MANFRED FASSLER
Chair of Artistic and Scientific Transfer: Prof. Dr CHRISTIAN REDER

Faculty of Fine Arts:
Master-Class for Painting: (vacant)
Master-Class for Painting: Prof. ADOLF FROHNER
Master-Class for Nude Drawing: Prof. OSWALD OBERHUBER
Master-Class for Painting, Movie Cartoon and Tapestry: Prof. Mag. CHRISTIAN ATTERSEE
Master-Class for Sculpture: (vacant)
Master-Class for Restoration and Conservation: Prof. HUBERT DIETRICH
Chair of Theory and Application of Graphics: (vacant)

Faculty of Art Education:
Master-Class for Art Teacher Education (Painting, Graphic Arts, Sculpture, Visual Media): (vacant)
Master-Class for Art Teacher Education (Painting, Graphic Arts, Sculpture, Visual Media): Prof. Dipl.-Ing. BERNHARD LEITNER
Master-Class for Art Teacher Education (Tectonics and Crafts): Prof. Mag. art. ERNST W. BERANEK
Master-Class for Art Teacher Education (Textile Design and Crafts): (vacant)
Chair of History of Culture and Civilization: Prof. Dr MANFRED WAGNER
Chair of History of Art: Prof. Dr PETER GORSEN
Chair of Philosophy: Prof. Dr RUDOLF BURGER
Institute of History and Theory of Costume: Prof. Dr MANFRED WAGNER
Institute for Museology: Prof. Dr phil. PETER GORSEN

HOCHSCHULE FÜR KÜNSTLERISCHE UND INDUSTRIELLE GESTALTUNG
(University of Art and Industrial Design)

4010 Linz, Hauptplatz 8

Telephone: (732) 7898
Fax: (732) 78-35-08

Founded 1947, present status 1973

Rector: Prof. Mag.art. WOLFGANG STIFTER
Vice-Rector: Prof. Arch. Dr WILFRIED POSCH
Chief Administrative Officer: Dr iur. CHRISTINE WINDSTEIGER
Librarian: JOHANNES VON WUNSCHHEIM

Library of 30,000 vols
Number of teachers: 90
Number of students: 500

HEADS OF DEPARTMENTS

Applied Graphic Arts: Prof. Mag. art. HELMUTH GSÖLLPOINTNER
Aesthetic Education: Prof. Mag. art. MARGARETA PETRASCHECK-PERSSON
Environmental Design: Prof. arch. Dr WILFRIED POSCH

HOCHSCHULE FÜR MUSIK UND DARSTELLENDE KUNST
(University of Music and Dramatic Art)

1030 Vienna III, Lothringerstr. 18

Telephone: 58-806

Founded 1812 as 'Conservatorium der Gesellschaft der Musikfreunde', nationalized 1909

Rector: Prof. ERWIN ORTNER
Vice-Rector: Prof. Dr GOTTFRIED SCHOLZ
Registrar: PETRA WEISSBERG
Library Director: Dr HELGA SCHOLZ

Number of teachers: 803
Number of students: 2,854

DEANS

Department of Theory, Composition and Orchestral Conducting: Prof. Mag. IVAN ERÖD
Department of Keyboard Instruments: Prof. HEINZ MEDJIMOREC
Department of String Instruments: Prof. WOLFGANG KLOS
Department of Wind and Percussion: Prof. Mag. CAROLE DAWN-REINHART
Department of Music Education: Prof. Mag. EWALD BREUNLICH
Department of Church Music: Prof. PETER PLAANYAVSKY
Department of Voice and Operatic Art: Prof. Mag. FRANZ DONNER
Department of Drama and Production: Prof. Dr NIKOLAUS WINDISCH-SPOERK
Department of Film and Television: Prof. WOLFGANG GLÜCK

AFFILIATED INSTITUTES

Institut für Volksmusikforschung: Head Prof. Dr. GERLINDE HAID.

Institut für Musiksoziologie: Head Prof. Dr IRMGARD BONTINCK.

Institut für Atem- und Stimmerziehung: Head (vacant)

Institut für Musiktheorie und Harmonikale Forschung: Head Prof. Dr MARIE-AGNES DITTRICH.

Institut für Elektroakustik und Experimentelle Musik: Head Prof. KLAUS P. SATTLER.

Institut für Organalogische Forschung und Dokumentation: Head Prof. Dr RUDOLF SCHOLZ.

Institut für Wiener Klangstil: Head Prof. HANS MARIA KNEIHS.

Institut für kirchenmusikalische Werkpraxis: Head Prof. ERWIN ORTNER.

Institut für Musikgeschichte: Head Prof. FRIEDRICH C. HELLER.

Institut für Musikanalytik: Head Prof. Dr GOTTFRIED SCHOLZ.

Institut für kulturmanagement: Head Prof. Mag. Dr WERNER HASITSCHKA.

Institut für Musikpädagogik: Head Prof. Mag. Dr FRANZ NIERMANN.

Arnold-Schönberg-Institut: Head Prof. Mag. Dr HARTMUT KRONES.

HOCHSCHULE FÜR MUSIK UND DARSTELLENDE KUNST IN GRAZ
(University of Music and Dramatic Arts in Graz)

8010 Graz, Leonhardstr. 15, POB 208

Telephone: (316) 389-0
Fax: (316) 322504

Founded 1963
State control
Language of instruction: German
Academic year: October to June

Rector: Prof. Dr OTTO KOLLERITSCH
Vice-Rector: Prof. WOLFGANG BOZIC
Chief Administrative Officer: Dr HERMANN BECKE
Librarian: Dr GÜNTER AMTMANN
Number of teachers: 102
Number of students: 1,541

DIRECTORS

Department of Theory and Composition: Prof. WOLFGANG BOZIC
Department of Keyboard Instruments: Prof. EUGEN JAKAB
Department of String Instruments: Prof. HEINZ IRMLER
Department of Wind and Percussion Instruments: Prof. PETER STRAUB
Department of Pedagogy: Prof. Mag. GERHARD WANKER
Department of Church Music: Prof. Mag. Dr FRANZ KARL PRASSL
Department of Singing, Choirleading and Stage Design: Prof. ANNEMARIE ZELLER
Department of Jazz: Prof. Mag. KARLHEINZ MIKLIN
Department of Drama: Prof. HERTA-K. BOROW-BUCHHAMMER

ATTACHED INSTITUTES

Institute of Ethnomusicology: Chair. Prof. Dr WOLFGANG SUPPAN
Institute of Musical Criticism and Aesthetical Research: Chair. Prof. Dr OTTO KOLLERITSCH
Institute of Performance Practice: Chair. Prof. Dr JOHANN TRUMMER
Institute of Jazz Research: Chair. Prof. Dr FRANZ KERSCHBAUMER
Institute of Electronic Music: Chair. Prof. Mag. GERD KÜHR

HOCHSCHULE FÜR MUSIK UND DARSTELLENDE KUNST 'MOZARTEUM' IN SALZBURG
('Mozarteum' University of Music and Dramatic Art in Salzburg)

5020 Salzburg, Mirabellplatz 1

Telephone: (662) 88908-0
Fax: (662) 872436

Founded 1841
State control
Academic year: October to June

Rector: Prof. Dr KLAUS AGER
Deputy Rector: Prof. Dr JOSEF WALLNIG
Administrative Officer: Dr ANNEMARIE LASSACHER-SANDMEIER
Librarian: Dr WERNER RAINER

Number of teachers: 458
Number of students: 1,700

Publication: *Jahresbericht.*

DIRECTORS

Department of Composition, Theory of Music and Conducting: Prof. Dr KARL WAGNER
Department of Keyboard Instruments: Prof. PETER LANG
Department of String Instruments: Prof. PAUL ROCZEK
Department of Wind and Percussion Instruments: Prof. EMIL RIEDER
Department of Music Education: Prof. Dr ALBERT HARTINGER
Department of Church Music: Prof. ALBERT ANGLBERGER
Department of Opera and Solo Singing: Prof. ROBERT PFLANZL
Department of Dramatic Art: Prof. WOLFGANG PILLINGER
Department of Art Education: Prof. RUDOLF ARNOLD
Department of Music Education (in Innsbruck): Prof. KURT HÜTTINGER
Department of Music and Movement Education: Prof. MARGARIDA PINTA DO AMARAL

ATTACHED INSTITUTES

Institute for Integrative Music Education and Polyaesthetic Education: Dir Prof. Dr WOLFGANG ROSCHER.

Institute for Musical Hermeneutics: Dir Prof. Dr SIEGFRIED MAUSER.

Institute for Music and Folklore: Dir Prof. Dr JOSEF SULZ.

Institute for Education and Research in Play and Games: Dir Prof. Dr GÜNTHER BAUER.

Richter Herf Institute for Research into the Basic Elements of Music: Dir Prof. Dr HORST-PETER HESSE.

Colleges of Technology

(in alphabetical order by town)

Höhere Technische Bundeslehranstalt Ferlach (Ferlach Federal College of Technology): 9170 Ferlach, Schulhausgasse 10; tel. (4227) 2331; fax (4227) 3866-37; f. 1878; arms technology, gunsmithery, machine tool construction, production engineering, engraving, gold- and silversmithery; 72 teachers, 600 students; library of 2,000 vols; Dir Dipl.-Ing. Dr HEINRICH JANSCHEK.

Höhere Technische Bundeslehranstalt (Federal College of Technology): 8013 Graz, Ortweingasse 4; tel. (316) 60-84; fax (316) 60-84-253; f. 1876; construction engineering, crafts, arts and design; 180 teachers, 1,500 students; Dir Dipl.-Ing. REINHOLD NEUMANN.

Höhere Technische Bundeslehr- und Versuchsanstalt (Federal College of Technology): 8051 Graz, Ibererstr. 15–21; tel. 6081-0; telex 684604; e-mail dion@htl-bulmegraz .ac.at; f. 1919; mechanical, electrical, communication and production engineering; 220 teachers; 1,750 students; Dir Dipl.-Ing. WOLFGANG GUGL.

Höhere Bundeslehranstalt und Bundesamt für Wein- und Obstbau (Federal College and Research Institute of Viticulture and Pomology): 3400 Klosterneuburg, POB 37, Wienerstr. 74; tel. (2243) 32159; fax: (02243) 26705; f. 1860; 31 teachers, 150 students; library of 30,000 vols; Dir Hofrat Univ.-Prof. Dipl.-Ing. Dr JOSEF WEISS; publ. *Mitteilungen Klosterneuburg* (every 2 months).

Höhere Technische Bundeslehranstalt (Federal College of Technology): 3500 Krems, Alauntalstr. 29; tel. (2732) 83190; f. 1942; architecture, building renovation, urban design, civil engineering, building, draftsmanship; 100 teachers, 670 students; library of 6,000 vols; Dir Dipl. Ing. Dr SCHÜLZ WERNER.

Berg- und Hüttenschule Leoben (Mining and Foundry Engineering College); 8700 Leoben, Max-Tendler-Str. 3; tel. (3842) 44888; fax (3842) 44888-3; e-mail htl.leoben@ unileoben.ac.at; f. 1865; trains foundry engineers; 23 teachers, 114 students; Dir Prof. Dipl.-Ing. HANS-WERNER STEINER (acting).

Höhere Technische Bundeslehranstalt Salzburg (Federal College of Engineering): 5022 Salzburg, Itzlinger Hauptstr. 30; tel. (662) 453610; fax (662) 453610-9; f. 1876; civil, electronic, electrical, mechanical and textile engineering; 200 teachers, 1,600 students; Dir Dipl. Ing. HELMUT WALTERS.

Höhere Technische Bundeslehranstalt Steyr (Federal College of Technology): 4400 Steyr, Schlüsselhofgasse 63; f. 1874; mechanical, motor vehicle, communication engineering and electronics; 110 teachers, 1,000 students; Dir Dipl.-Ing. Dr GOTTFRIED EHRENSTRASSER.

Höhere Bundeslehr- und Versuchsanstalt für Textilindustrie und Datenverarbeitung (Federal College of Textile Technology and Data Processing): 1050 Vienna, Spengergasse 20; tel. (1) 54-616-0; fax (1) 54-615-139; e-mail manager@ rohrpostfix.htl-tex.ac.at; f. 1758; 130 teachers, 1,300 students; Dir Dipl.-Ing. JOHANN HÖRDLER.

Höhere Graphische Bundes-Lehr- und Versuchsanstalt (Federal Training and Research Institute of Graphic Arts): 1140 Vienna, Leyserstr. 6; tel. (1) 9823914; fax (1) 9823914-111; f. 1888; photography, graphic design, reproduction and printing processes; library of 30,000 vols; 128 teachers, 700 students; Dir Hofrat Ing. Mag. WERNER SCHMIDMAYER.

Höhere Technische Bundeslehranstalt Wien I (Federal College of Technology): 1015 Vienna, Schellinggasse 13; tel. (222) 515-79-0; fax (222) 512-71-61; f. 1846; 240 teachers, 2,400 students; Pres. Oberstudienrat Dkfm. Mag. Ing. ALFONS WEICHSELBERGER; publ. *Jahresbericht.*

Höhere Technische Bundeslehr- und Versuchsanstalt (Federal College of Technology): 3340 Waidhofen an der Ybbs, Postfach 87; f. 1890; automation, electrical, mechanical and production engineering; 81 teachers, 746 students; Dir Dipl.-Ing. JOHANN DULLNIG.

Other Colleges

Diplomatische Akademie Wien (Diplomatic Academy of Vienna): 1040 Vienna, Favoritenstr. 15A; tel. (1) 5057272; fax (1) 5042265; e-mail diplomat@dakvienna.ac.at; f. 1754; diploma and Master of Advanced International Studies programmes prepare a maximum of 45 Austrian and foreign graduates annually for careers in diplomacy, international business and finance, international organizations and public administration; library of 35,000 vols, 330 newspapers in German, English, French, Spanish, Italian and Russian; Dir Dr P. LEIFER; publ. *Jahrbuch.*

Schools of Art and Music

Kärntner Landeskonservatorium (Carinthian Conservatory of Music): 9021 Klagenfurt, Miesstalerstr. 8; tel. (463) 511421; fax (463) 511421-85; f. 1931; 79 teachers, 750 students; library of 34,431 vols; Dir Prof. HANS-JÖRG SCHERR; publ. *Jahresbericht* (annual report).

Tiroler Landeskonservatorium (Tirol Conservatory of Music): 6020 Innsbruck, Paul-Hofhaimer-Gasse 6; tel. (512) 583447; fax (512) 583447-16; f. 1818; 69 teachers, 584 students; library of 100,000 vols and musical notes; Dir Prof. Mag. MICHAEL MAYR.

Konservatorium der Stadt Wien (Vienna Municipal Conservatory): 1010 Vienna, Johannesgasse 4A; tel. (222) 512-7747; fax (222) 512-7747/60; f. 1938; consists of Konservatorium (teaching staff 247; students 1,240), affiliated to it are 17 Musikschulen (teaching staff 301; students 4,215) and the Kindersingschule (teaching staff 36; students 2,836); Principal Prof. GERHARD TRACK; publ. *Fidelio* (5 a year).

Musikschule der Stadt Innsbruck: Innrain 5, 6020 Innsbruck; tel. (512) 585425; f. 1818; 70 teachers; 1,800 students; Dir H. GRUBER.

AZERBAIJAN

Learned Societies

GENERAL

Azerbaijan Academy of Sciences: 370601 Baku, Isteglal 10; depts of Physical-Engineering and Mathematical Sciences (Academician-Sec. F. G. MAKSUDOV, Learned Sec. I. I. O. SHEKINSKY), Chemical Sciences (Academician-Sec. S. D. MEKHTIEV (acting), Learned-Sec. E. SH. O. MAMEDOV), Earth Sciences (Academician-Sec. M. T. O. ABASOV, Learned Sec. E. S. O. GUSEINOV), Biological Sciences (Academician-Sec. D. A. R. O. ALIEV, Learned Sec. R. I. O. BABAEV), History, Economics, Philosophy and Law (Academician-Sec. A. M. O. ASLANOV, Learned Sec. I. M. KADIROV), Language, Literature and Art (Academician-Sec. B. A. NABIEV, Learned Sec. A. T. GASANOV); 39 mems, corresp. mems; attached research institutes: see Research Institutes; Pres. E. YU. SALAEV; Academician-Sec. A. A. K. NADIROV; Learned Sec. G. M. O. ALESKEROV; publs *Azerbaidzhanskii Khimicheskii Zhurnal* (Azerbaijan Chemical Journal), *Doklady* (Reports), *Izvestiya* (Bulletins: Physical Engineering and Mathematics, Earth Sciences and Oil, Biology Series, History, Philosophy and Law, Linguistics, Literature and Art, Economic Sciences), *Tsirkulyar Shemakhinskoi Astrofizicheskoi observatorii im. N. Tusi* (Newsletter of Shemakha Astrophysics Observatory), *Sovetskaya Tyurkologiya* (Soviet Turkology).

Attached societies:

Azerbaijan Biochemical Society: Baku; Chair. A. A. GASANOV.

Azerbaijan Genetics and Selection Society: Chair. I. K. ABDULLAEV.

Azerbaijan Mathematics Society: Baku 1, Isteglal 10; Chair. M. A. DZHAVADOV.

Azerbaijan Physical Society: 370143 Baku, Pr. Narimanova 33; Chair. Acad. G. M. ABDULLAEV.

Geographical Society of Azerbaijan: Chair. Prof. K. K. GYUL.

Helminthological Society: Baku; Chair. S. M. ASADOV.

Mineralogical Society: Baku; Chair. M. A. KASHKAI.

Palaeontological Society: Baku; Chair. K. A. ALIZADE.

Society of Physiologists and Pharmacologists: Baku; Chair. G. G. GASANOV.

Society of Soil Scientists: Baku; Chair. D. M. GUSEINOV.

Research Institutes

AGRICULTURE, FISHERIES AND VETERINARY SCIENCE

Agricultural Research Institute: 370098 Baku, Pos. Pirshagi, Sovkhoz No. 2; tel. 24-11-50.

Institute of Genetics and Selection: 370106 Baku, Pr. Lenina 159; tel. 62-94-44; attached to Azerbaijan Acad. of Sciences; Dir U. K. O. ALEKPEROV.

Institute of Soil Science and Agrochemistry: 370073 Baku, Ul. Krylova 5; attached to Azerbaijan Acad. of Sciences; Dir I. SH. O. ISKENDEROV.

Karaev, A. I., Institute of Physiology: 370100 Baku, Ul. Sharif-Zade 2; attached to Azerbaijan Acad. of Sciences; Dir G. G. GASANOV.

Research Institute for Plant Protection: Kirovabad, Ul. Fioletova 57; tel. 3-47-81.

ARCHITECTURE AND TOWN PLANNING

Institute of Architecture and Art: 370143 Baku, Pr. Narimanova 31; tel. 39-35-21; attached to Azerbaijan Acad. of Sciences; Dir. SH. G. FATULLAEV.

BIBLIOGRAPHY, LIBRARY SCIENCE AND MUSEOLOGY

Institute of Manuscripts: 370001 Baku, Istiglal 8; tel. 92-31-97; fax 93-30-66; f. 1950; attached to Azerbaijan Acad. of Sciences; library of 40,000 manuscripts, documents and books; Vice-Dir M. M. ADILOV; publs *Älyazmalar khäzinäsindä* (irregular), *Kechmishimizdän gälän säslär* (irregular).

ECONOMICS, LAW AND POLITICS

Institute of Economics: 370143 Baku, Pr. Narimanova 31; tel. 39-34-57; attached to Azerbaijan Acad. of Sciences; Dir A. A. MAKHMUDOV.

Institute of Philosophy and Law: 370143 Baku, Pr. Narimanova 31; tel. 39-37-28; attached to Azerbaijan Acad. of Sciences; Dir A. M. ASLANOV.

HISTORY, GEOGRAPHY AND ARCHAEOLOGY

Institute of Geography: 370145 Baku, Hüsein Javid St 31; tel. 38-29-00; f. 1945; attached to Azerbaijan Acad. of Sciences; library of 53,000 vols; Dir B. A. BUDGOV; publ. *Khabarlar* (2 a year).

Institute of History: 370143 Baku, Pr. Narimanova 31; tel. 39-36-15; attached to Azerbaijan Acad. of Sciences; Dir I. G. ALIEV.

Institute of Oriental Studies: 370143 Baku, Pr. H. Javida 31; tel. 38-87-55; attached to Azerbaijan Acad. of Sciences; Dir G. B. BAKHISHALIYEVA.

LANGUAGE AND LITERATURE

Nasimi Institute of Linguistics: 370143 Baku, Pr. Hussein Javid 31; tel. 39-35-71; f. 1932; attached to Azerbaijan Acad. of Sciences; library of 6,000 vols, 50 periodicals; Dir Prof. AGAMUSA AKHUNDOV; publ. *Turkology* (4 a year).

Nizami Institute of Literature: 370143 Baku, Pr. Narimanova 31; tel. 39-56-51; attached to Azerbaijan Acad. of Sciences; Dir YA. V. KARAEV.

MEDICINE

Azerbaijan Blood Transfusion Institute: Baku, Nagornaya ul. 23.

Azerbaijan Institute of Epidemiology, Microbiology and Hygiene: Baku, Ul. Gamalei 23.

Azerbaijan Institute of Orthopaedics and Restorative Surgery: Baku 5, Nagornaya 21.

Azerbaijan Institute of Roentgenology, Radiology and Oncology: 370012 Baku, Pr. Metbuat 31/63; tel. 32-57-95.

Azerbaijan Institute of Spa Treatment and Physiotherapy: Baku, Balakhanskoe shosse 3.

Azerbaijan Institute of Tuberculosis: Baku, Pr. Lenina 83.

Azerbaijan Research Institute of Ophthalmology: Baku, 6-ya Kommunisticheskaya ul. 5.

Research Institute of Gastroenterology: 370110 Baku, Leningradsky pr. 101; tel. 64-44-02; f. 1988; Dir B. A. AGAYEV; publ. *Actual Questions of Gastroenterology* (annually).

NATURAL SCIENCES

Biological Sciences

Botanical Garden: Baku, Patamdartskoe shosse 40; attached to Azerbaijan Acad. of Sciences; Dir U. M. AGAMIROV.

Institute of Zoology: 370602 Baku, Proezd 1128, Kvart. 504; tel. 39-73-71; attached to Azerbaijan Acad. of Sciences; Dir M. A. MUSAEV.

Komarov, V. L., Institute of Botany: 370073 Baku, Patamdartskoe shosse 40; tel. 39-32-30; attached to Azerbaijan Acad. of Sciences; Dir V. D. O GADZHIEV.

Mathematical Sciences

Institute of Mathematics and Mechanics: Baku, Ul. Agaeva 9, Kvartal 553; tel. 39-47-20; attached to Azerbaijan Acad. of Sciences; Dir F. G. MAKSUDOV.

Physical Sciences

Azerbaijan National Aerospace Agency: 370106 Baku, Pr. Azadlyg 159; tel. (12) 62-93-87; fax (12) 62-17-38; e-mail mekhtiev@anasa.baku.az; Dir Prof. Dr ARIF SH. MEKHTIEV.

Gubkin, I. M., Institute of Geology: 370143 Baku, Pr. Narimanova 29A; tel. 38-62-30; attached to Azerbaijan Acad. of Sciences; Dir A. A. M. ALIZADE.

Institute of Inorganic and Physical Chemistry: 370143 Baku, Pr. Narimanova 29; tel. 38-74-38; attached to Azerbaijan Acad. of Sciences; Dir R. G. K. O. RIZAEV.

Institute of Physics: 370143 Baku, Pr. Narimanova 33; tel. 38-76-46; attached to Azerbaijan Acad. of Sciences; Dir Acad. G. M. ABDULLAEV.

Shemakha Astro-Physical Observatory: Shemakha, Pos. Mamedalieva, Ul. Sverdlova 75; attached to Azerbaijan Acad. of Sciences; Dir G. F. SULTANOV.

TECHNOLOGY

Azerbaijan Electrical Engineering Research Institute: 370052 Baku, Ul. Aga Neimatula 44; telex 142166.

Azerbaijan Energy Research Institute: 370602 Baku, Pr. H. Zardabi 94; tel. 32-80-76; telex 142225; fax 98-13-68; f. 1941; library of 6,000 vols; Dir RAMAZANOV KERIM NAZIR OGLU; publ. *Transactions of the Azerbaijan Energy Research Institute* (annually).

Azerbaijan Research and Design Institute for Oil Engineering: 370603 Baku, Ul. Volodarskogo; telex 142188.

Gas Research and Design Institute: 370025 Baku, Ul. Barinova 23; tel. 67-43-12.

Institute of Additive Chemistry: 370603 Baku, Beyukshorskoe shosse, Kvart. 2062; tel. 67-65-33; f. 1965; attached to Azerbaijan Acad. of Sciences; additives to lubricants, fuels and cutting fluids; library of 9,000 vols; Dir V. M. FARZALIEV.

Institute of Chloro-Organic Synthesis: 373204 Sumgait, Samed Vargun ul. 124; attached to Azerbaijan Acad. of Sciences; Dir A. A. O. EFENDIEV.

Institute of Cybernetics: 370141 Baku, Ul. Agaeva 9, Kvartal 553; attached to Azerbaijan Acad. of Sciences; Dir T. A. ALIEV.

Institute of the Problems of Deep Oil and Gas Deposits: 370143 Baku, Pr. Narimanova 33; tel. 38-80-45; attached to Azerbaijan Acad. of Sciences; Dir M. T. ABASOV.

Institute of Theoretical Problems of Chemical Technology: 370143 Baku, Pr. Narimanova 29; tel. 38-77-56; attached to Azerbaijan Acad. of Sciences; Dir T. N. SHAKHTAKHTINSKII.

Mamedaliev, Yu. G., Institute of Petrochemical Processes: 370025 Baku, Ul. Telnova 30; tel. 66-61-50; attached to Azerbaijan Acad. of Sciences; Dir M. I. O. RUSTAMOV.

Oil Research and Design Institute (AzNIPIneft): 370033 Baku, Ul. Aga Neimatully 39; tel. 66-21-69.

Research and Design Institute for Oil Engineering: 370110 Baku, Ul. Inglab 57; telex 142212.

Research Institute of Oil Refineries: Baku 25, Telnovaya ul.; f. 1929; library of 80,000 vols; Dir V. S. ALIEV; publ. *Transactions* (annually).

Research Institute of Olefins: 370028 Baku, Komsomolskaya ul. 29; tel 66-04-17; Dir B. R. SEREBRYAKOV.

Research Institute of Photoelectronics: 370602 Baku, GSP; tel. 39-13-08; telex 142650; f. 1972; library of 1,095 vols; Dir Prof. SALAYEV ELDAR YUNIS OGLU.

Libraries and Archives

Baku

Akhundov, M. F., State Library of Azerbaijan: 370601 Baku, Ul. Khagani 29; tel. 93-40-03; f. 1923; 4,406,636 vols (incl. 1,300,294 periodicals), 26,723 sound recordings, 52,204 microforms; Dir L. YU. GAFUROVA; publs *Azerbaijan in Foreign Press, New Literature on Culture and Art, Information and Bibliographic Indexes*.

Azerbaijan Scientific and Technical Library: 330001 Baku, Ul. G. Gadzhieva 3; tel. 92-08-07; 9,000,000 vols; Dir G. D. MAMEDOV.

Baku State University Central Library: 370145 Baku, Ul. Z. Khalilova 23; tel. 39-08-58; fax 38-05-82; f. 1919; 2,000,000 vols; Librarian S. IBRAGIMOVA.

Central Library of the Azerbaijan Academy of Sciences: 370143 Baku, Pr. Narimanova 31; tel. 38-60-17; f. 1925; 2,500,000 books, periodicals and serials; Dir M. M. GASANOVA.

Museums and Art Galleries

Baku

Azerbaijan R. Mustafaev State Art Museum: Baku, Ul. Chkalova 9; Dir Z. M. KYAZIM.

Baku Museum of Education: 370001 Baku, Ul. Niazi 11; tel. (8922) 92-04-53; f. 1940; library of 52,000 vols; Dir T. Z. AHMEDZADE.

Museum of the History of Azerbaijan, of the Azerbaijan Academy of Sciences: 370005 Baku, Ul. Malygina 4; tel. 93-36-48; f. 1920; history of the Azerbaijanian people from ancient times; Dir P. A. AZIZBEKOVA; publ. *Trudy Muzeya Istorii Azerbaidzhana* (Activities of the Museum of the History of Azerbaijan).

Nizami Ganjari, State Museum of Azerbaijan Literature: 370001 Baku, Ul. Isteglal 53; tel. 92-18-64; f. 1939; history of Azerbaijan literature from ancient times to the present; Dir H. A. ALLAHYAROGLU; publ. *Works* (every 2-3 years).

State Museum Palace of Shirvan-Shakh: Baku, Zamkovaya Gora 76; tel. (12) 92-83-04; fax (12) 92-29-10; f. 1964; historical and architectural museum and national park; Dir DADASHEVA SEVDA.

Stepano-Kert

Stepano-Kert Museum of the History of Nagorno-Karabakh: Stepano-Kert, Ul. Gorkogo 4; history of the Armenian people of Arthakh.

Universities

AZERBAIJAN TECHNICAL UNIVERSITY

370602 Baku, H. Javid Ave 25

Telephone: 38-33-43
Fax: 38-32-80

Founded 1920
State control
Languges of instruction: Azerbaijani and Russian
Academic year: September to July

Rector: Prof. RAFFIG I. MEHDIEV
Vice-Rector for Student Affairs: Doc. RASIM J. BASHIRROV
Vice-Rector for Research and Development: Prof. ZARRIFA A. ISKENDERZADE
Vice-Rector for International Relations: Prof. AYAZ M. KENGERLI
Vice-Rector for Education: ALLAHVERDI O. ORUJOV
Vice-Rector for Administrative Affairs: RAFFIG H. KAZIMOV
Registrar: KHADIJJA FARZALLIYEVA
Librarian: NARINGUL A. KHALAFOVA

Library of 600,000 vols
Number of teachers: 884
Number of students: 6,463

Publications: *Ziyya* (monthly), *Research Works* (4 a year).

DEANS

Faculty of Automation and Computing Equipment: Doc. G. KHALILOV
Faculty of Electrical and Telecommunications Engineering: Doc. R. AKHADOV
Faculty of Machine-Building: Doc. A. M. HAJIYEV
Faculty of Automechanics: Doc. M. A. TALIBOV
Faculty of Metallurgy: Prof. B. Y. EYVAZOV
Faculty of Radio Engineering and Microelectronics: Doc. A. RAGIMOV
Faculty of Machine Sciences: Prof. M. H. HARIBOV
Faculty of Business and Management for the Engineering Industry: Doc. X. M. YAGUDOV
Faculty of Railway Transport: Doc. R. MAMMEDOV

PROFESSORS

Faculty of Automation and Computing Technology:

ABDULLAYEV, A. A., Industrial Electronics
ALIYEV, A. B., Applied Mathematics
BABAYEV, M. A., Automation
BAYRAMOV, K. T., Computers and Systems
HACHIYEV, C. A., Design and Manufacturing of Computers
HACHIYEV, M. A., Design and Manufacturing of Computers
JAFAROV, E. M., Automation
NOVRUZBEKOV, I., Applied Mathematics
RZAYEV, T. A., Design and Manufacturing of Computers
TALIBI, M. G., Industrial Electronics

Faculty of Machine-Building:

ABBASOV, V. A., Metal-Cutting Machines and Tools
ASTANOV, M., Mathematics
DUNYAMALIYEV, M., Mathematics
HUSSEYNOV, H. A., Automated Design Systems in Machinebuilding
HUSSEYNOV, S. O., Hydraulics and Hydraulic Machines
MIRZAJANOV, J. B., Machinebuilding Technology
NOVRUZOV, A., Mathematics
RUSTAMOV, M. I., Metal-Cutting Machines and Tools
SADYKHOV, R. J., Automated Design Systems in Machinebuilding

Faculty of Automechanics:

BILALOV, S. B., Internal Combustion Engine and Refrigeration Machines
EFENDIYEV, V. S., Internal Combustion Engine and Refrigeration Machines
HADIROV, N. B., Theoretical Mechanics
MAKHMUDOV, R. N., Theoretical Mechanics
MEHDIEV, R. I., Internal Combustion Engine and Refrigeration Machines
NAZIYEV, Y. M., Thermal Engineering and Heating Mechanisms
SHAKHVERDIYEV, A. H., Thermal Engineering and Heating Mechanisms
SHAMIYEV, F. H., Theoretical Mechanics
TAGIZADE, A. G., Organization of Transport and Traffic Flow

Faculty of Metallurgy:

ABBASOV, T. F., Physics
AMIROV, S. T., Construction Materials Technology, Powder Metallurgy and Corrosion
ASKAROV, K. A., Environment
BABAYEV, F. R., Chemistry
EYVAZOV, B. Y., Construction Materials Technology, Powder Metallurgy and Corrosion
GULIYEV, F. A., Industrial Ecology and Safety
HAMIDOV, R. S., Chemistry
HUSEYNOV, R. G., Construction Materials Technology, Powder Metallurgy and Corrosion
KHASAYEV, R. M., Industrial Ecology and Safety
MAMMEDOV, A. A., Industrial Ecology and Safety
RUSTAMOV, M. A., Chemistry
SHUKUROV, R. I., Metallurgy and Science of Metals

Faculty of Radio-Engineering and Microelectronics:

ABBILOV, CH. I., Microelectronics and Applied Physics
EFENDIYEV, C. A., Television and Radio Systems
EFENDIYEV, SH. M., Physics
ISKENDERZADE, Z. A., Microelectronics and Applied Physics
ISMIEV, E. G., Electrodynamics and High-Frequency Instruments
KENGERLI, U. S., General Theoretical Radio-Engineering
QOJAYEV, E., Physics

Faculty of Machine Sciences:

ABDULLAYEV, A. H., Lift Transport Machines
ALIZADE, R. I., Mechanical Theory
BABAYEV, E. P., Engineering Graphics
BAGIROV, SH. M., Mechanical Theory
GAFAROV, A. M., Metrology and Standardization
GARIBOV, M. H., Lift Transport Machines
HUBANOV, KH. I., Engineering Graphics
KENGERLI, A. M., Mechanical Theory
KHALILOV, A. M., Mechanical Theory
MAMMEDOV, N. R., Metrology and Standardization
MAMMEDOV, V. A., Mechanical Theory

Faculty of Business and Management for the Engineering Industry:

ABBASOV, M. A., History
ALIYEV, A. A., Theory of Economics
ALIYEV, A. H., Philosophy and Political Science
GARAYEV, S. N., History
GULIYEV, R. I., Theory of Economics
RAMAZANOV, F. F., Philosophy and Political Science
SAMEDZADE, SH. A., Management, Economics and Organization
TAGIYEV, A. M., Philosophy and Political Science

Faculty of Railway Transport:

AGAYEV, N. M., Technology and Safety of Machine Maintenance
BAGIROV, S. M., Automatics, Telemechanics and Communication on the Railway Transport System
MIRSALIMOV, V. M., Materials Resistance
SADYKHOV, A. M., Technology and Safety of Machine Maintenance

BAKU STATE UNIVERSITY

370145 Baku, Ul. Z. Khalilova 23
Telephone: 39-01-86
Fax: 38-05-82
Founded 1919
Rector: ALESKEROV MURTUZ NADJAF OGLU
Pro-Rectors: MARDANOV MISIR JUMA OGLU, ASKEROV BAKHRAM MEKHRALI OGLU, ASKEROV SHAHLAR, BAKHSHALIYEV TAHIR SHAMIR OGLU, ALIYEVA IFRAT SALIM GIZI
Librarian: S. IBRAGIMOVA
Library: see Libraries
Number of teachers: 1,275
Number of students: 12,390
Publications: *Vestnik Bakinskogo Universiteta: Fiziko - Matematicheskikh nauk, Estestvinnikh nauk, Gumanitarnikh nauk, Socialno - politicheskikh nauk,* (all quarterly).

Departments of journalism, philology, oriental studies, law, international law and international relations, library sciences, mathematics, applied mathematics, physics, chemistry, biology, geology and geography, philosophy and psychology, religion, commerce, preparatory studies.

Other Higher Educational Institutes

Azerbaijan Agricultural Institute: 374700 Kirovabad, Ul. Azizbekova 262; tel. 2-10-64; depts: agrochemistry and soil science, agronomy, fruit and vegetable growing, viticulture; animal husbandry, veterinary, silkworm breeding, mechanization, electrification, economics and management, accounting; library of 200,000 vols; Rector N. A. SAFAROV.

Azerbaijan N. Narimanov Medical Institute: 370022 Baku, Ul. Bakizkhanova 23; tel. 94-50-30; library of 203,000 vols.

Azerbaijan State Pedagogical Institute of Languages: 370055 Baku, Ul. Leitenanta Shmidta 60; tel. 96-51-53; f. 1959; faculties: Russian, English, French and German languages; Rector Dr A. S. ABDULLAEV; publ. *Scientific Proceedings* (quarterly).

Azerbaijan State Petroleum Academy: 370010 Baku, Pr. Azadlyg 20; tel. 93-45-57; telex 142195; f. 1920; faculties: oil and gas exploitation, power engineering, oil mechanical engineering, chemical technology, automation of production, engineering economics; 1,400 teachers; 14,600 students; library of 927,789 vols; brs in Sumgait and Mingechaur; Rector T. M. ALIEV; publ. *Oil and Gas Journal*.

Azerbaijan State University of Art: 370005 Baku, Ul. Mamedaliev 20; tel. 93-11-01; fax 98-61-25; f. 1945; 390 mems; library of 86,307 vols; Rector TEMUCHIN EFENDIYEV.

Uzeir Hajibeyov Baku Academy of Music: 370014 Baku, Shamsi Badalbeyli 98; tel. (12) 93-22-48; fax (12) 98-13-30; f. 1920; courses: piano, orchestral instruments, folk instruments, singing, choral conducting, composition, musicology; 290 lecturers; 630 students; library of 220,000 vols and 25,000 scores; Rector F. SH. BADALBEYLI.

Baku Civil Engineering Institute: 370073 Baku, Ul. Krylova 13; tel. 38-33-96; faculties: road building, construction technology; architecture, construction, irrigation and drainage, sanitary engineering.

Gyanzha Technological Institute: 374700 Gyanzha, pos. Kiraz; faculties: mechanics, technology of food production, technology of textile and light industry.

BAHAMAS

Learned Societies

GENERAL

Bahamas National Trust: POB N4105, Nassau; tel. 393-1317; fax 393-4978; e-mail bnt@bahamas.net.bs; f. 1958; preservation of buildings, wildlife and land of beauty or historic interest; 3,000 mems; Exec. Dir GARY E. LARSON; publs *Currents* (every 2 months), *The Bahamas Naturalist* (2 a year).

HISTORY, GEOGRAPHY AND ARCHAEOLOGY

Bahamas Historical Society: POB SS 6833, Nassau; f. 1959; 400 mems; Pres. Dr GAIL SAUNDERS; Corresp. Sec. JOLTON L. JOHNSON; publ. *Journal* (annually).

Libraries and Archives

Freeport

Sir Charles Hayward Public Lending Library: POB F40040, Freeport, Grand Bahama; f. 1966; 40,000 vols; Librarian ELAINE B. TALMA.

Nassau

College of the Bahamas Library: POB N4912, Nassau, tel. 323-7930; fax 326-7834; f. 1974; 70,000 vols; spec. collns incl. Caribbean dissertations; Dir WILLAMAE M. JOHNSON; publs *COBLA Journal, Library Informer.*

Nassau Public Library: POB N-3210, Nassau; f. 1837; 80,000 vols; Dir (vacant).

Public Records Office: Dept of Archives, POB SS-6341, Nassau; tel. 393-2175; fax 393-2855; e-mail archives@batelnet.bs; f. 1971; nat. archival depository; 2,689 linear feet of records; Dir Dr GAIL SAUNDERS; publ. *Preservum* (journal).

Ranfurly Out Island Library: POB N8350, Nassau.

Museums and Art Galleries

Nassau

Bahamia Museum: POB N1510, Nassau.

Colleges

University of the West Indies (Bahamas Office): POB N1184, Nassau; tel. 323-6593; fax 328-0622; f. 1965; Representative MATTHEW WILLIAM.

College of the Bahamas: POB N4912, Nassau; tel. 323-8550; fax 326-7834; f. 1974; 4-year college; gives associate degrees in arts, natural and social sciences, business, technology, nursing, teaching; offers Bachelor degrees in Banking and Finance, Management, Accounting, Nursing, Education; continuing education; 160 teachers, 3,463 students; library of 68,000 vols; Pres. Dr KEVA BETHEL; publs *College Forum* (2 a year), *COBLA Journal* (2 a year), *At Random* (annually).

BAHRAIN

Learned Societies

ECONOMICS, LAW AND POLITICS

Bahrain Bar Society: POB 5025, Manama; tel. 720566; fax 721219; f. 1977; 65 mems; Pres. ALI A. ALAYOOBI; publ. *Al Muhami*.

FINE AND PERFORMING ARTS

Bahrain Arts Society: POB 26264, Manama; tel. 590551; fax 594211; f. 1983; promotes fine arts of Bahrain nationally and internationally; includes a school of fine arts and art gallery, and the official photography club; 184 mems; small library; Pres. ALI AL-MAHMEED.

Bahrain Contemporary Art Association: POB 26232, Manama; tel. 728046; f. 1970; 60 mems; library of 250 vols; Pres. ABDUL KARIM AL-ORRAYED; publ. magazine.

HISTORY, GEOGRAPHY AND ARCHAEOLOGY

Bahrain Historical and Archaeological Society: POB 5087, Manama; tel. 727895; f. 1953; 143 mems; reference library; Pres. Dr ESSA AMIN; Hon. Sec. Dr KHALID KHALIFA AL-KHALIFA; publ. *Dilmun* (2 a year).

LANGUAGE AND LITERATURE

Bahrain Writers and Literators Association: POB 1010, Manama; f. 1969; 40 mems; library of 700 vols; Pres. ALI AL-SHARGAWI: Sec. FAREED RAMADAN.

MEDICINE

Bahrain Medical Society: POB 26136, Adliya; tel. 742666; fax 715559; f. 1972; 350 mems; library of 300 vols; Pres. Dr ALI MOHD MATAR; Gen. Sec. Dr FAISAL A. ALNASIR; publ. *Journal* (quarterly).

RELIGION, SOCIOLOGY AND ANTHROPOLOGY

Bahrain Society of Sociologists: POB 26488, Manama; tel. 727483; f. 1979; 65 mems; library of 423 vols; Pres. Dr AHMED AL-SHARYAN; Sec.-Gen. EBRAHIM ALALAWI.

Islamic Association: POB 22484, Manama; tel. 671788; fax 676718; f. 1979; teaches the Qur'an, Fiqh, Hadith, Sunnah; distributes zakat and donations; 200 mems; Pres. ABDULRAHMAN EBRAHIM ABDULSALAM.

TECHNOLOGY

Bahrain Information Technology Society: POB 26089, Manama; tel. 710018; fax 714732; e-mail bits@batelco.com.bh; f. 1981; 260 mems; Pres. MOHAMMED AHMED AL-AMER; publ. *BITS Update* (monthly).

Bahrain Society of Engineers: POB 835, Manama; tel. 727100; fax 729819; f. 1972; 980 mems; Pres. DHEYA A-AZIZ TOWFIQI; Sec. ISA JANAHI; publ. *Al-Mohandis* (quarterly).

Research Institutes

NATURAL SCIENCES

General

Bahrain Centre for Studies and Research: POB 496, Manama; tel. 754757; telex 9764; fax 754678; f. 1981; scientific study and research in all spheres; library of 9,000 vols, 300 periodicals; Sec.-Gen. Dr SALMAN RASHID AL-ZAYANI

Libraries and Archives

Isa Town

Manama Central Library: C/o Ministry of Education, POB 43, Manama; f. 1946; 155,000 vols, 150 periodicals, 1,475 cassettes; Dir MANSOOR MOHAMED SARHAN; publ. *Bahrain National Bibliography* (every 4 years).

University of Bahrain Libraries and Information Centre: POB 32038, Isa Town; tel. 449257; fax 449838; e-mail warwick@admin.uob.bh; 160,000 vols, 950 periodicals; Dir WARWICK PRICE.

Manama

Ahmed Al-Farsi Library (College of Health Sciences): POB 12, Manama; tel. 255555 ext. 5202; telex 8511; fax 242485; f. 1976; serves Min. of Health staff, also public and reference service; 29,000 vols, 545 periodicals, 375 audiovisual aids; Librarian Dr BRUCE M. MANZER.

Educational Documentation Library: POB 43, Manama; tel. 277702; telex 9094; fax 230610; f. 1975; part of Min. of Education; 18,931 vols, 215 periodicals, 300 files of documents; Chief Officer FAIQA SAEED AL-SALEH; publs *Educational Indicative Abstracts* (3 a year), *Educational Selective Articles* (every 2 months), *Educational Information Abstracts* (3 a year), *Educational Index of Arabic Periodicals*, *Educational Index of Foreign Periodicals*, *Educational Legislation Index*, *Acquisitions List* (monthly), *Bibliographical Lists* (annually).

Historical Documents Centre: POB 28882, Manama; tel. 664854; fax 651050; f. 1978; attached to the Crown Prince's Court; maintains historical documents and MSS on the history of Bahrain and the Gulf; library of 4,000 vols; Pres. SHAIKH ABDULLAH BIN KHALID AL-KHALIFA; Dir Dr ALI ABA-HUSSAIN; publ. *Al-Watheeka* (2 a year).

Museums and Art Galleries

Manama

Bahrain Museum: POB 43, Manama; f. 1970; archaeology, ethnography; Dir SHAIKHA HAYA AL-KHALIFA.

Universities

ARABIAN GULF UNIVERSITY

POB 26671, Manama

Telephone: 440044
Telex: 7319
Fax: 440002

Founded 1980 by the seven Gulf States

Languages of instruction: Arabic, English
Academic year: September to June

President: Dr IBRAHIM AL HASHEMI
Director of Administration and Financial Affairs: Dr RIYAD YOUSEF HAMZAH
Director of Student Affairs: Dr ISMAIL AL-MADANI
Registrar: Dr WAHIB AL-KHAJAH
Librarian: KHUSHNUD HASSAN

Number of teachers: 68
Number of students: 368

Publication: *AGU Annual Catalogue*

DEANS

College of Medicine: Prof. WILLEM LAMMERS
College of Applied Sciences: (vacant)
College of Education: Prof. FATHI ABD-EL RAHIM (acting)

PROFESSORS

AL-AAQIB, AR-R., Water Engineering, Energy
AL-ABADIN, M. Z., Physiology
AD-DIN, M. N., Microbiology
FULEIHAN, F., Internal Medicine
KHADER, M. H. A., Organic Chemistry
MATHUR, V., Pharmacology
NASSER, A. I., Mechanical Engineering
AL-QAISI, K. A., Botany, Algae
RAKHA, I., General Surgery, Orthopaedics
RAHIM, F. AS-A. A., Education and Psychology
ASH-SHAZALI, H., Paediatrics

UNIVERSITY OF BAHRAIN

POB 32038, Isa Town

Telephone: 682748
Telex: 9258
Fax: 681465

Founded 1986 by merger of University College of Arts, Science and Education, and Gulf Polytechnic
Autonomous control
Language of instruction: mainly Arabic
Academic year: September to June

Chairman of Board of Trustees: THE MINISTER OF EDUCATION
President: Dr IBRAHIM AL-HASHEMI
Vice-President for Academic Programmes and Research: Dr NIZAR AL-BAHARNA
Vice-President for Administration and Finance: Dr SAMIR FAKHRO
Vice-President for Planning and Community Service: Dr GEORGE NAJJAR
Registrar: Dr KHALID AL-KHALIFA
Director of Library and Information Services: WARWICK PRICE

Library: see Libraries
Number of teachers: 320
Number of students: 6,760

DEANS

College of Arts and Science: Dr HILAL AL-SHALJI
College of Business and Management: Dr GEORGE NAJJAR (acting)
College of Education: Dr ABBAS ADEBI
College of Engineering: Dr HANNA MAKHLOUF

HEADS OF DEPARTMENTS

College of Arts:
- Arabic and Islamic Studies: Dr IBRAHIM GHOLOOM
- English: Dr HUSSEIN DAIF
- General Studies: Dr BAQER AL-NAJJAR

College of Science:
- Biology: Dr JAMEEL ABDULLAH
- Chemistry: Dr SAID AL-ALAWI

Computer Science: Dr MANSOUR AL-A'ALI
Mathematics: Dr MOHAMMED ABDULLAH
Physics: Dr WAHIB AL-NASER

College of Business and Management:
Business and Management: Dr AMIN AL-AGHA
Continuing Management Education: Dr PARIS ANDREOU
Accounting: Dr JASIM ABDULLAH
Office Management: Dr ADEL AL-ALAWI
Economics: Dr KHALID ABDULLAH

College of Education:
Continuing Education: Dr KHALIL SHOBAR
Curricula and Teaching Methods: Dr HUSSEIN AL-SADEH
Education Technology: Dr MOHSIN AL-JAMLAN
Physical Education: Dr MOHAMMED AL-MOTAWA
Psychology: Dr MUSTAFA HEJAZI

College of Engineering:
Civil and Environmental Engineering: Dr BASHAR AHMEDI
Electrical Engineering and Computer Science: Dr ABDUL IMAM AL-SAMMAK
Mechanical and Chemical Engineering: Dr YOUSEF ABDEL GHAFFAR
Continuing Engineering Education: Dr FAYEZ FAWZI

Colleges

College of Health Sciences: POB 12, Ministry of Health, Bahrain; tel. 251360; telex 8511; fax 242485; f. 1976; library: see Libraries; 104 teachers; 503 students; Dean Dr FAISAL AL-HAMER; Registrar Dr AMAL AKLEH

CHAIRPERSONS OF DIVISIONS

Educational Development Centre: Dr LAMEA AL-TAHOO
Allied Health: Dr HASSAN JAROODI
Nursing: AMINA ABDULLA
Integrated Science: MUNA BUHAZZA
English: Dr MUHAMMAD YOUSIF

Hotel and Catering Training Centre: POB 22088, Manama; tel. 320191; telex 9134; fax: 332547; f. 1976; administered by the Ministry of Information; 2-year courses for school leavers, also in-service training; library of 10,000 vols; Dir ABDEL REHEEM AL-KHAJA.

BANGLADESH

Learned Societies

GENERAL

Society of Arts, Literature and Welfare: Society Park, K. C. Dey Rd, Chittagong; f. 1942; 500 mems; Gen. Sec. NESAR AHMED CHOWDHURY.

BIBLIOGRAPHY, LIBRARY SCIENCE AND MUSEOLOGY

Library Association of Bangladesh: C/o Institute of Library and Information Science, Bangladesh Central Public Library Bldg, Shahbagh, Ramna, Dhaka 1000; tel. 504269; f. 1956; runs courses in library and information sciences; Pres. M. SHAMSUL ISLAM KHAN; Gen. Sec. KH. FAZLUR RAHMAN; publs *Upatta* (newsletter in Bengali, (4 a year), *The Eastern Librarian* (2 a year).

ECONOMICS, LAW AND POLITICS

Bangladesh Bureau of Statistics: Building no. 8, Bangladesh Secretariat, Dhaka 1000; tel. 832274; f. 1971; collection, analysis and publication of statistics covering all sectors of the economy; 3,541 staff; Dir-Gen. WALIUL ISLAM; publs *Statistical Bulletin* (monthly), *Statistical Pocket Book* (annually), *Statistical Yearbook, Yearbook of Agricultural Statistics, Foreign Trade Statistics* (annually).

Bangladesh Economic Association: C/o Economics Dept, Dhaka University, Dhaka; f. 1958; Pres. Dr MAZHARUL HUQ; Sec. Dr S. R. BOSE.

EDUCATION

Association of Universities of Bangladesh: 28 Shyamolee, Dhaka 7; Sec. M. K. HUSSAIN SIRKAR.

LANGUAGE AND LITERATURE

Bangla Academy: Burdwan House, Dhaka 2; f. 1972; promotes culture and development of the Bengali language and literature; produces dictionaries, translates scientific and reference works into Bangla; library of 102,000 vols; Dir-Gen. Dr ASHRAF H. SIDDIQI; Sec. ABDUS SATTAR KHAN; publs *Research Journal, Science Journal* (quarterly, in Bangla), *Journal* (2 a year, in English), *Uttaradhikar* (literary, monthly), *Dhan Shaliker Desh* (juvenile, monthly).

MEDICINE

Bangladesh Medical Association: BMA House, 15/2 Topkhana Rd, Dhaka 2; f. 1971; 10,000 mems; library of 8,000 vols; Pres Dr M. A. MAJED; Sec.-Gen. Dr GAZI ABDUL HOQUE; publ. *Bangladesh Medical Journal* (quarterly).

NATURAL SCIENCES

General

Bangladesh Academy of Sciences: 3/8 Asad Ave, Mohammadpur, Dhaka 1207; tel. (2) 310425; f. 1973; 38 Fellows, 4 foreign Fellows; Pres. Dr S. D. CHAUDHURI; Sec. Prof. AMINUL ISLAM; publ. *Journal* (2 a year).

Biological Sciences

Zoological Society of Bangladesh: C/o Dept of Zoology, University of Dhaka, Dhaka 1000; tel. (2) 868333; e-mail zooldu@citecho.net; f. 1972; 806 mems; Pres. Prof. ALTAF HOSSAIN; Gen. Sec. Dr MOHD ISMAIL HOSSAIN; publs *Bangladesh Journal of Zoology* (2 a year), *Proceedings of National Conference* (every 2 years), *Bulletin* (irregular).

RELIGION, SOCIOLOGY AND ANTHROPOLOGY

Asiatic Society of Bangladesh: 5 Old Secretariat Rd (Nimtali), Ramna, Dhaka 1000; tel. (2) 9560500; f. 1952; study of Man and Nature of Asia; 1,400 mems; library of 7,595 vols, 500 Urdu and Persian MSS; Pres. Prof. WAKIL AHMED; Gen. Sec. Prof. AKMAL HUSSAIN; publ. *Journal*.

TECHNOLOGY

Institution of Engineers, Bangladesh: Ramna, Dhaka; f. 1948; 6,000 mems; library of 4,050 vols; Pres. Eng. S. M. AL-HUSAINY; Hon. Gen. Sec. Eng. MD ABUL QUASSEM; publs *Journal* (quarterly), *Engineering News* (monthly).

Research Institutes

GENERAL

Bangladesh Council of Scientific and Industrial Research: Mirpur Rd, Dhanmondi, Dhaka 5; tel. 505686; f. 1955; Chair. Prof. Dr S. S. M. A. KHORASANI; Sec. K. C. SIKDAR; publs *Bangladesh Journal of Scientific and Industrial Research, News Letter, Bijnaner Joyjattra, Purogami Bijnan*.

Attached research institutes:

BCSIR Laboratory, Dhaka: Dhaka; seven divisions: natural products; glass and ceramics; fibres and polymers; leather technology; physical instrumentation; analytical; industrial physics; Dir Dr MIR AMJAD ALI.

Institute of Food Science and Technology, Dhaka: Dhaka; seven divisions: technology of foodgrains; animal food products; plant food products; microbiology; food science and quality control; biochemistry and applied nutrition; industrial development; Dir Dr S. F. RUBBI.

Institute of Fuel Research and Development, Dhaka: Dhaka; seven divisions: solar energy; biomass and hydrocarbon research; combustion, application and pilot plant; Dir Dr M. EUSUF.

BCSIR Laboratory, Chittagong: Chittagong; four divisions: chemistry, botany, pharmacology, microbiology; Dir Dr M. MANZUR-I-KHUDA.

BCSIR Laboratory, Rajshahi: Rajshahi; four divisions: lac research; fats and oils; fibres; fruit processing and preservation; Dir Dr M. A. KHALEQUE.

AGRICULTURE, FISHERIES AND VETERINARY SCIENCE

Animal Husbandry Research Institute: Comilla; f. 1947; Prin. Scientific Officer SALIL KUMAR DHAR.

Bangladesh Jute Research Institute: Manik Miah Ave, Dhaka 1207; f. 1951; Dir-Gen. Dr MD A. ISLAM.

BIBLIOGRAPHY, LIBRARY SCIENCE AND MUSEOLOGY

Varendra Research Museum: Rajshahi; f. 1910; under control of University of Rajshahi; museum-based research instn; history, archaeology, anthropology, literature, art; library of 14,000 vols; museum colln; Dir Dr M. SAIFUDDIN CHOWDHURY; publ. *Journal* (annually).

ECONOMICS, LAW AND POLITICS

Bangladesh Institute of Development Studies: GPO Box 3854, E-17 Agargaon, Sher-e-Bangla Nagar, Dhaka 1207; tel. 9116159; fax 813023; e-mail bids@drik.bgd.toolnet.org; f. 1957; macroeconomics, agricultural, industrial and human resource development, population studies; library: see Libraries and Archives; Dir-Gen. ABU AHMED ABDULLAH; publs *Bangladesh Development Studies* (quarterly), *Bangladesh Unnayan Samikhha* (annually), Research Monograph Series, Research Report Series, *BIDS Library CAS Bulletin, Library Bulletin*.

MEDICINE

Institute of Epidemiology, Disease Control and Research (IEDCR): Mohakhali, Dhaka 1212; tel. (2) 608248; f. 1976; library of 4,000 vols; Dir MANINDRA CHOWDHURY.

International Centre for Diarrhoeal Disease Research, Bangladesh: GPO Box 128, Dhaka 1000; tel. (2) 871751; fax (2) 883116; e-mail msik@icddrb.org; f. 1960; funded by 45 countries and NGOs; library of 31,000 vols, 13,000 documents; Dir Prof. ROBERT M. SUSKIND; publs *Annual Report, Working Papers, Scientific Reports, Monographs, Glimpse* (newsletter, 4 a year), *Shasthya Sanglap* (newsletter in Bangla, 3 a year), *ICDDR, B News* (in English and Bangla, 4 a year), *Journal of Diarrhoeal Diseases Research* (4 a year), *DISC Bulletin* (fortnightly).

NATURAL SCIENCES

Physical Sciences

Geological Survey of Bangladesh: 153 Pioneer Rd, Segun bagicha, Dhaka 1000; tel. 406201; f. 1972; govt org. under Ministry of Energy and Mineral Resources; library of 7,000 vols, 97 journals; Dir-Gen. Dr MUJIBUR RAHMAN KHAN.

TECHNOLOGY

Bangladesh Atomic Energy Commission: POB 158, Dhaka 1000; tel. (2) 502600; telex 632203; f. 1973; library of 25,375 vols, 192 periodicals; Chair. Dr M. A. MANNAN; publs *Nuclear Science & Applications* (Series A: Biological Sciences, Series B: Physical Sciences).

Attached institutes:

Atomic Energy Research Establishment: Ganak Bari, Savar, POB 3787, Dhaka; consists of Institute of Nuclear Science and Technology, Institute of Computer Sciences, Institute of Electronics and Materials Science, Institute of Food and Radiation Biology, Institute of Nuclear Medicine.

Atomic Energy Centre: POB 164, Ramna, Dhaka 2; basic and applied research in physics, electronics and chemistry; library of 10,728 vols, 100 periodicals.

Libraries and Archives

Chittagong

Divisional Government Public Library: POB 771, K. C. Dey Rd, Chittagong; tel. (31) 611578; f. 1963; 51,000 vols, 93 periodicals; Senior Librarian MD. HARUNAR RASHID.

Dhaka

Bangladesh Central Public Library: 10 Kazi Nazrul Islam Ave, Shahbagh, Dhaka 1000; tel. 500819; f. 1958; 1,014,870 vols, 2,300 periodicals; spec. colln: depository for UNESCO publs; Dir A. F. M. BADIUR RAHMAN.

Bangladesh Institute of Development Studies Library and Documentation Centre: POB 3854, E-17, Agargaon, Sher-e-Bangla Nagar, Dhaka 1207; tel. 9118999; fax 813023; 100,000 printed items, 30,000 microfiches and microfilms; Chief Librarian NILUFAR AKHTER.

Bangladesh National Scientific and Technical Documentation Centre (BANSDOC): Dhanmondi, Dhaka 1205; tel. 507196; fax 860224; f. 1963; 16,000 books, 200 periodicals; Dir Dr MD. LUTFUR RAHMAN; publs *Bangladesh Science and Technology Abstracts* (annually), *National Catalogue of Scientific and Technological Periodicals of Bangladesh* (every 2 years), *Current Scientific and Technological Research Projects of Bangladesh* (every 2 years), *Report of the Survey of Research and Development Activities in Bangladesh* (every 2 years).

Directorate of Archives and Libraries: National Library Building, Sher-e-Bangla Nagar (Agargaon), Dhaka 1207; f. 1971; coordinating centre for archives and libraries at nat. level; Dir Dr SHARIF UDDIN AHMED.

Controls:

National Archives of Bangladesh: National Library Building, Sher-e-Bangla Nagar, Agargaon, Dhaka 1207; tel. 326572; f. 1973; 225,000 vols of records and documents, 3,500 books, 58 rolls of microfilm, 10,000 press clippings; Dir Dr SHARIF UDDIN AHMED; publs *Annual Reports 1973–84*, *Bulletin of Dissertations and Theses by Bangladeshi Scholars 1947–73*, *SWARBICA Journal Vol III*, etc.

National Library of Bangladesh: Sher-e-Bangla Nagar Agargaon, Dhaka 1207; tel. 326572; f. 1968; 1,000,000 books, 2,000 journals; Dir Dr SHARIF UDDIN AHMED; publs *Bangladesh National Bibliography*, *Articles Index*.

National Health Library: Mohakhali, Dhaka 12; tel. 603738; f. 1974; 12,000 vols, 15,000 journals; Chief Librarian ZAKIUDDIN AHMED.

University of Dhaka Library: Dhaka 1000; tel. (2) 505789; fax (2) 865583; f. 1921; 560,000 books and vols of periodicals, 30,000 MSS; Librarian Dr MD. SERAJUL ISLAM (acting).

Rajshahi

Rajshahi University Library: Rajshahi; tel. (721) 750666; fax (721) 750064; e-mail ru.phy@drik.bgd.toolnet.org; f. 1953; 274,000 vols, 550 journals; Administrator Prof. M. MOZAMMEL HAQUE.

Museums and Art Galleries

Dhaka

Balda Museum: Dhaka; f. 1927; art, archaeology; Superintendent MUHAMMAD HANNAN.

Bangladesh National Museum: POB 355, Shahbagh, Dhaka 2; tel. 500300; f. 1913; history, ethnography, art, natural history; library of 23,000 vols; Dir ENAMUL HAQUE; publs *Bangladesh Lalitkala*, *Annual Report*, *Catalogues*, *Buddhist and Brahmanical Iconography*, *Coins and Chronology of Independent Sultans of Bengal*, etc.

Universities

BANGABANDU SHIEKH MUJIB MEDICAL UNIVERSITY

POB 3048, Dhaka 1000

Founded 1965 as Institute of Postgraduate Medicine and Research; present name and status 1998

Vice-Chancellor: Prof. M. A. QUADERI

Pro Vice-Chancellors: MD. TAHIR, Prof. MAHMUD HASSAN

Chief Librarian: MD. SHAHADAT HUSSAIN

Library of 23,000 vols, 100 periodicals

BANGLADESH AGRICULTURAL UNIVERSITY

PO Agricultural University, Mymensingh
Telephone: (91) 55695
Fax: (91) 55810
E-mail: bau@drik.bgd.toolnet.org

Founded 1961
Autonomous control
Languages of instruction: English and Bengali
Academic year: July to June

Chancellor: Sheikh HASINA
Vice-Chancellor: Prof MUHAMMED HUSSAIN
Registrar: A. HANNAN KHAN
Public Relations and Publications Director: DEWAN RASHIDUL HASSAN
Librarian: ABDUL GAFUR DEWAN
Library of 168,000 vols.

Number of teachers: 404
Number of students: 4,537

Publications: *Bangladesh Journal of Agricultural Science*, *Bangladesh Journal of Animal Science*, *Bangladesh Journal of Horticulture* (2 a year), *Bangladesh Veterinary Journal*, *Bangladesh Journal of Agricultural Economics*, *Bangladesh Journal of Fisheries* (quarterly), *Bangladesh Journal of Aquaculture*, *Bangladesh Journal of Extension Education*, *Bangladesh Journal of Plant Pathology*, *Bangladesh Journal of Training and Development*, *Bangladesh Journal of Crop Science*, *Progressive Agriculture*, *Bangladesh Journal of Agricultural Engineering*, *The Bangladeshi Veterinarian*.

DEANS

Faculty of Agriculture: Prof. S. G. UDDIN
Faculty of Animal Husbandry: Prof. M. SADULLAH
Faculty of Veterinary Science: Prof. QUAMRUL HASSAN
Faculty of Agricultural Economics and Rural Sociology: Prof. M. A. SATTER MONDOL
Faculty of Agricultural Engineering and Technology: Prof. M. S. TALUKDER
Faculty of Fisheries: Prof. LUTFUN HUSSAIN

PROFESSORS

Veterinary Science:

AHMAD, M. U., Medicine
AHMED, J. U., Surgery and Obstetrics
AHMED, M., Anatomy and Histology
ALAM, M. G. S., Surgery and Obstetrics
ALI, M. R., Microbiology and Hygiene
AMIN, M. M., Microbiology and Hygiene
ANAM, M. K., Anatomy and Histology
AWAL, M., Pharmacology
BHUIYA, M. S., Agronomy
BAKI, M. A., Pathology
CHOWDHURY, K. A., Microbiology and Hygiene
DAS, P. M., Pathology
DEWAN, M. L., Pathology
HAQUE, M., Parasitology
HAQUE, S., Parasitology
HASAN, Q., Pharmacology
HOSSAIN, M. A., Surgery and Obstetrics
HOSSAIN, M. I., Pathology
HOSSAIN, M. I., Anatomy and Histology
HOSSAIN, W. I. M. A., Microbiology and Hygiene
ISLAM, A. W. M. S., Parasitology
ISLAM, K. S., Medicine
KARIM, M. J., Parasitology
KASEM, M. A., Anatomy and Histology
KHAN, M. A. B., Anatomy and Histology
KHAN, M. A. I., Pharmacology
MIAH, A. K. M., Anatomy and Histology
MONDAL, M. M. H., Parasitology
MUSTAFA, M., Pharmacology
MYRNUDDIN, M., Physiology
NOORUDDIN, M., Medicine
RAHMA, M., Physiology
RAHMAN, A., Medicine
RAHMAN, M. A., Microbiology and Hygiene
RAHMAN, M. A., Microbiology and Hygiene
RAHMAN, M. H., Parasitology
RAHMAN, M. M., Microbiology and Hygiene
RAHMAN, M. M., Microbiology and Hygiene
SAMAD, M. A., Medicine
SARKER, A. J., Microbiology and Hygiene
SEN, M. M., Medicine
SHAHJAHAN, M., Anatomy and Histology
SOBHAN, M. A., Pharmacology
UDDIN, M., Pathology

Agriculture:

AHMAD, K. N. U., Genetics and Plant Breeding
AHMAD, M. U., Plant Pathology
AHMED, M., Agronomy
AHMED, M., Entomology
ALAM, M. S. E., Genetics and Plant Breeding
ALI, M. M., Mathematics
ALI, M. S., Agricultural Chemistry
ASHRAFUZZAMAN, M. H., Plant Pathology
BHUIYAN, M. R. H., Biochemistry
CHOUDHURY, M. S. H., Horticulture
CHOUDHURY, M. Y., Agricultural Chemistry
FAROOQUE, A. M., Horticulture
GAFFAR, M. A., Agronomy
HALIM, A., Agricultural Extension Education
HANIF, M. A., Biochemistry
HAQUE, A., Agroforestry
HAQUE, M. A., Horticulture
HAQUE, M. M., Agricultural Extension Education
HAQUE, M. S., Soil Science
HAQUE, S. A., Soil Science
HAQUE, S. B., Entomology
HASHEM, M. A., Soil Science
HASSAN, L., Genetics and Plant Breeding
HOSSAIN, M., Entomology
HOSSAIN, M. A., Agroforestry
HOSSAIN, M. A., Biochemistry
HOSSAIN, M. A., Soil Science
HOSSAIN, M. M., Plant Pathology
HUSSAIN, S. M. A., Agronomy
IDRIS, M., Soil Science
ISHAQ, M., Agricultural Chemistry
ISLAM, B. N., Entomology
ISLAM, M. A., Agronomy
ISLAM, M. A., Genetics and Plant Breeding
ISLAM, M. M., Agricultural Extension Education

ISLAM, M. R., Soil Science
ISLAM, N., Agronomy
KAMAL, A. M. A., Agronomy
KARIM, A. S. M., Agricultural Extension Education
KARIM, M. A., Crop Botany
KARIM, M. M., Agronomy
KARIM, M. R., Entomology
KARIM, M. S., Chemistry
KARMAKER, R., Mathematics
KASEM, M. A., Agricultural Extension Education
KHAN, A. B., Entomology
KHAN, M. A. H., Crop Botany
KHAN, M. N. H., Agronomy
MAMUN, A. A., Agronomy
MASUD, A. R. M., Physics
MIAH, M. B., Plant Pathology
MIAN, M. M. H., Soil Science
MOMEN, A., Plant Pathology
MONDAL, A. G., Mathematics
MONDAL, M. F., Horticulture
MOTIN, M. A., Soil Science
MUHSI, A. A. A., Crop Botany
NEWAZ, M. A., Genetics and Plant Breeding
NEWAZ, N., Biochemistry
PATWARI, M. A. K., Genetics and Plant Breeding
QUDDUS, M. A., Genetics and Plant Breeding
RAHIM, M. A., Horticulture
RAHMAN, A. K. M. M., Entomology
RAHMAN, L., Genetics and Plant Breeding
RAHMAN, M. M., Genetics and Plant Breeding
RAHMAN, M. M., Soil Science
SAMAD, M. A., Agronomy
SARDER, M. M. A., Entomology
SARKER, A. U., Agronomy
SARKER, M. A. R., Agronomy
SATTER, M. A., Soil Science
SHAHJAHAN, M., Entomology
SHAMSUDDIN, A. K. M., Genetics and Plant Breeding
SHAMSUZZOHA, A. N. M., Agricultural Extension Education
SHARFUDDIN, A. F. M., Horticulture
SIDDIKA, A., Biochemistry
SIDDIQUE, M. A., Horticulture
TALUKDER, M. N., Agricultural Chemistry
UDDIN, M. Z., Soil Science
UDDIN, S. G., Biochemistry
WAHID-UZZAMAN, Agricultural Chemistry
WAZIUDDIN, M., Genetics and Plant Breeding
YUNUS, M., Agronomy

Animal Husbandry:

AHMED, S. U., Poultry Science
AKBAR, M. A., Animal Nutrition
ALAM, M. R., General Animal Science
ALI, A., Animal Breeding and Genetics
ALI, M. A., Poultry Science
ALI, S. Z., Animal Breeding and Genetics
BULBUL, S. M., Poultry Science
CHOWDHURY, S. D., Poultry Science
HAMID, M. A., Poultry Science
HAQUE, M. A., General Animal Science
HASNATH, M. A., Animal Breeding and Genetics
HASSAN, M. N., Dairy Science
HOSSAIN, S. M. I., Dairy Science
HOSSAIN, S. S., Animal Breeding and Genetics
HOWLIDER, M. A. R., Poultry Science
ISLAM, M. A., Dairy Science
ISLAM, M. M., Animal Nutrition
KHAN, A. S., Dairy Science
KHAN, M. T. UDDIN, Animal Nutrition
KHANDAKER, Z. H., Animal Nutrition
MANNAN, A. K. M., Dairy Science
MOKTARUZZAMAN, M., Dairy Science
RAHMAN, M. A., Poultry Science
REZA, A., Animal Nutrition
SADULLAH, M., General Animal Science
SAMAD, M. A., General Animal Science
SARKER, D. R. D., General Animal Science
TAREQ, A. M. M., Animal Nutrition
WADUD, A., Dairy Science
WAHID, M. A., Poultry Science

Agricultural Engineering and Technology:

AKHTARUZZAMAN, M., Farm Power and Machinery
BALA, B. K., Farm Power and Machinery
BEGUM, J. R. A., Food Technology and Rural Industries
BISWAS, M. R., Irrigation and Water Management
FAROOK, S. M., Farm Power and Machinery
HAQUE, M. M., Farm Power and Machinery
HAQUE, M. R., Irrigation and Water Management
HAQUE, Md. S., Food Technology and Rural Industries
HUSSAIN, A. A. MAINUL, Farm Power and Machinery
HUSSAIN, M. D., Farm Power and Machinery
HUSSAIN, M. M., Farm Power and Machinery
HUSSAIN, M. M., Farm Power and Machinery
ISLAM, MD. N., Food Technology and Rural Industries
KHAN, L. R., Irrigation and Water Management
KHAN, M. R., Irrigation and Water Management
MONAYEMDAD, M., Farm Structures
RAHMAN, K. S., Farm Structures
RASHID, M. A., Farm Structure
SARKER, M. R. I., Farm Power and Machinery
SATTER, M. A., Farm Power and Machinery
SHAMSUDDIN, M., Food Technology and Rural Industries
TALUKDER, M. S., Irrigation and Water Management
UDDIN, B. M., Food Technology and Rural Industries
ZIAUDDIN, A. T. M., Farm Power and Machinery

Agricultural Economics and Rural Sociology:

AHMED, A. R., Agricultural Statistics
AKBAR, M. A., Co-operation and Marketing
ALAM, M. F., Agricultural Finance
ALAM, S., Co-operation and Marketing
ALI, M. H., Co-operation and Marketing
ALI, R., Rural Sociology
BASAR, M. A., Agricultural Finance
CHOWDHURY, S. N. I., Agricultural Economics
HOSSAIN, M. I., Agricultural Statistics
HUSSAIN, A. M. M., Co-operation and Marketing
ISLAM, M. S., Agricultural Economics
KHAN, M. Z. A., Agricultural Statistics
MANDAL, A. S., Agricultural Economics
MIA, M. I. A., Co-operation and Marketing
MIAN, M. T. H., Agricultural Economics
MOLLA, M. A. R., Agricultural Economics
MURSHED, S. M. M., Agricultural Economics
RAHA, S. K., Co-operation and Marketing
RAHMAN, M. L., Agricultural Finance
RAHMAN, M. H., Agricultural Economics
RAHMAN, M. M., Agricultural Economics
RAHMAN, M. M., Agricultural Finance
SABUR, S. A., Co-operation and Marketing
TALUKDER, M. R. K., Agricultural Economics
ZAIM, W. M. H., Agricultural Economics
ZAMAN, M. A., Rural Sociology

Fisheries:

AHMED, G. U., Aquaculture
ALI, M. M., Aquaculture
CHANDRA, K. Z., Aquaculture
CHAKRABORTY, S. C., Fisheries Technology
CHOWDHURY, M. B. R., Aquaculture
DEWAN, S., Fisheries Management
HAQUE, M. S., Fisheries Management
HOSSEIN, M. A., Aquaculture
HUSSIN, L., Fisheries Biology and Genetics
ISLAM, M. AMINUL, Fisheries Biology and Genetics
ISLAM, M. ANWARUL, Aquaculture Genetics
ISLAM, M. NAZRUL, Fisheries Technology
KAMAL, M., Fisheries Technology
MIAN, M. Z. U., Aquaculture and Management
MOLLAH, M. F. A., Fisheries Biology and Genetics
RAHMAN, M. S., Fisheries Management
WAHAB, M. A., Aquaculture

DIRECTORS

Graduate Training Institute: Prof. M. HAZRAT ALI
Agricultural University Extension Centre: Prof. A. S. M. ZIAUL KARIM
Agricultural University Research System: Prof. M. MAHBUBUL KARIM

PRINCIPALS

Hazi Mohammad Danesh Krishi College: SADRUL AMIN
Portuakhali Krishi College: M. A. BARI
Bangladesh Agricultural Institute: Q. ZAMAN

BANGLADESH OPEN UNIVERSITY

Board Bazar, Gazipur 1704
Telephone: (2) 9800801
Fax: (2) 865750
E-mail: bou@driktap.tool.nl

Founded 1992
State control
Chancellor: Prime Minister of the People's Republic of Bangladesh
Vice-Chancellor: Prof. M. AMINUL ISLAM
Pro-Vice-Chancellor: Prof. R. I. SHARIF
Registrar: MD. MONZUR-E-KHODA TARAFDER
Librarian: MD. NAIMUL HAQUE

Library of 9,000 vols
Number of teachers: 52
Number of students: 80,000

DEANS

School of Education: Prof. M. SHAMSUL KABIR
Open School: Prof. MOHAMMAD ANWAR ALI
School of Social Science, Humanities and Language: Prof. Dr SHIREEN HUQ
School of Business: Prof. Dr ANWAR HOSSAIN
School of Science and Technology: Dr MOFIZ UDDIN AHMED
School of Agriculture and Rural Development: Prof. Dr A. H. M. FARUQUE

BANGLADESH UNIVERSITY OF ENGINEERING AND TECHNOLOGY

Ramna, Dhaka 1000
Telephone: 505171
Fax: 863026
E-mail: librarian.buet@drik.bgd.toolnet.org

State Control
Founded 1962
Languages of instruction: English and Bengali
Academic year: January to December

Chancellor: PRIME MINISTER OF THE PEOPLE'S REPUBLIC OF BANGLADESH
Vice-Chancellor: Prof. Dr IQBAL MAHMUD
Registrar: MOHAMMAD SHAHJAHAN
Librarian: MOHAMMAD ZAHIRUL ISLAM

Library of 120,954 vols
Number of teachers: 410
Number of students: 5,049

Publications: *Annual Report, Research Abstracts, Calendar, BUET Studies, departmental journals, etc.*

DEANS

Faculty of Architecture and Planning: Prof. FARUQUE AHMEDULLAH KHAN
Faculty of Engineering: Prof. Dr A. K. M. ABDUL QUADER
Faculty of Civil Engineering: Prof. Dr M. FEROZE AHMED
Faculty of Mechanical Engineering: Prof. Dr MD. MIZANUR RAHMAN

Faculty of Electrical and Electronic Engineering: Prof. Dr SAIFUL ISLAM

HEADS OF DEPARTMENTS

Architecture: Prof. KHALEDA RASHID
Chemistry: Prof. Dr MD. MONIMUL HUQUE
Chemical Engineering: Prof. Dr DIL AFROZA BEGUM
Civil Engineering: Prof. Dr MD. AZADUR RAHMAN
Computer Science and Engineering: Assoc. Prof. Dr MOHAMMAD KAYKOBAD
Electrical and Electronic Engineering: Prof. Dr MOHD. QAMRUL AHSAN
Industrial and Production Engineering: Prof. Dr M. ANWARUL AZIM
Mechanical Engineering: Prof. Dr AMALESH CHANDRA MANDAL
Metallurgical Engineering: Prof. Dr M. MOHAR ALI BEPARI
Water Resources Engineering: Prof. Dr MD. MIRJAHAN MIAH
Humanities: Asst Prof. MD. HABIBUR RAHMAN
Mathematics: Prof. Dr MD. ZAKERULLAH
Naval Architecture and Marine Engineering: Dr GAZI MD. KHALIL
Physics: Prof. Dr GIASUDDIN AHMAD
Urban and Regional Planning: Prof. Dr A. S. M. ABDUL QUIUM
Petroleum and Mineral Resources Engineering: Asst Prof. Dr MD. TAMIM

ATTACHED INSTITUTES

Institute of Appropriate Technology: Dir Prof. Dr MD. NAZRUL ISLAM.

Institute of Flood Control and Drainage Research: Dir Prof. Dr ABDUL FAZAL M. SALEH.

Computer Centre: Dir Prof. Dr A. B. M. SIDDIQUE HOSSAIN.

Centre for Energy Studies: Dir (vacant).

UNIVERSITY OF CHITTAGONG

University Post Office, Chittagong
Telephone: (31) 210133
Fax: (31) 210141

Founded 1966
Languages of instruction: Bengali and English
Academic year: July to June

Vice-Chancellor: Prof. ABDUL MANNAN
Pro Vice-Chancellor: Prof. MD. BADIUL ALAM
Registrar: Prof. S. M. MAHABUB-UL-HOQUE MAZUMDER
Librarian: MD. ANISUR RAHAMAN

Library of 14,430 vols
Number of teachers: 450
Number of students: 10,273

DEANS

Faculty of Arts: Prof. Dr MANIRUZZAMAN
Faculty of Commerce: Prof. Dr MD. FASIUL ALAM
Faculty of Law: Dr MD. SHAH ALAM
Faculty of Medicine: Prof. NURJAHAN BHUIYAN
Faculty of Science: Prof. Dr YUSUF SHARIF AHMED KHAN
Faculty of Social Science: Prof. Dr MD. ABDUL HAKIM

PROFESSORS

ADNAN, A. M. S., Economics
AHMED, G., Mathematics
AHMED, R., History
ALI, M. A., Chemistry
ANISUZZAMAN, M., Public Administration
AZAD, A. A., Bengali
BANU, H., Physics
BARUA, B. P., Political Science
BASIT, Q. A., Botany
BASHIRUDDIN, A. K. M., Fine Arts
BHUIYAN, A. L., Marine Biology
BHUIYAN, M. A., Physics
CHOWDHURY, A. F. H., Sociology
CHOWDHURY, A. J. M., Management
CHOWDHURY, S. H., Zoology
CHOWDHURY, S. R. I., Statistics
GHAFUR, M. A., Arabic and Persian
HOQUE, M., Economics
HOQUE, M. J., Accounting
HOSSAIN, M. D., Bengali
HOSSAIN, M. F., Mathematics
HUQ, M., Economics
HYDER, A. R. Z., Fine Arts
HYE, M. A., Accounting
ISLAM, J. N., Mathematical and Physical Sciences Centre
ISLAM, M. N., Physics
KHAN, A. A., Botany
KHAN, M. A. I., Accounting
KHAN, M. H., Islamic History and Culture
KHAN, M. S., Economics
KHAN, M. U. A., Islamic History and Culture
MANIRUZZAMAN, M., Bengali
MANNAN, M., Management
NABI, K. A., Accounting
NAG, A. B., Accounting
PRAMANIK, A. H., Economics
PRAMANIK, M. H. A., Physics
RAHMAN, M., History
RAHMAN, M. A., Forestry Institute
SALEH, M. A., Chemistry
SARAJUDDIN, Mrs A., History
SEN, A., Sociology
SHAMSUZZOHA, S., Management
ULLAH, A. K. M. B., Fine Arts
YUNUS, M., Management

There are 130 affiliated colleges.

ATTACHED INSTITUTES

Institute of Forestry: Chittagong; f. 1977; Dir M. K. BHUIYAN.

Institute of Marine Science: Chittagong; f. 1982; Dir M. A. QUADER

Research Centre for Mathematical and Physical Science: Chittagong; f 1988; Dir Prof. J. N. ISLAM.

UNIVERSITY OF DHAKA

Ramna, Dhaka
Telephone: (2) 9661900
Fax: (2) 865583

Founded 1921
State control
Languages of instruction: English and Bengali
Academic year: July to June (three terms)

Chancellor: PRESIDENT OF THE PEOPLE'S REPUBLIC OF BANGLADESH
Vice-Chancellor: Prof. A. K. A. CHOWDURY
Pro Vice-Chancellor: Prof. S. U. AHMED
Registrar: A. Z. SIKDER
Librarian: Dr M. S. ISLAM (acting)

Library: see Libraries
Number of teaching staff: 1,215
Number of students: 25,429

Publications: *Calendar, Annual Report, Dhaka University Studies* (2 a year), *Dhaka Viswa Vidyalaya Patrika* (3 a year), *Sahitya Patrika* (3 a year), *Dhaka Viswa Vidyalaya Barta* (4 a year).

DEANS

Faculty of Arts: Dr A. ISLAM
Faculty of Business Studies: M. M. U. KHAN
Faculty of Science: Dr M. S. CHOWDHURY
Faculty of Law: Dr M. E. BARI
Faculty of Medicine: Dr M. A. HADI
Faculty of Education: M. Z. RAHMAN
Faculty of Social Sciences: M. ASADUZZAMAN
Faculty of Biological Sciences: Dr M. S. HOSSAIN
Faculty of Pharmacy: Dr M. U. AHMED
Faculty of Post-graduate Medical Sciences and Research: Dr M. S. ALI

PROFESSORS

ABDULLAH, A. S. M., Accounting
ABDULLAH, M., Institute of Nutrition and Food Science
ABDULLAH, M., Persian and Urdu
ABRAR, C. R., International Relations
AFROZE, D., Psychology
AFSARUDDIN, M., Sociology
AHAD, S. A., Soil Science
AHMED, A., Economics
AHMED, A. H. M., Chemistry
AHMED, A. K. M. U., Economics
AHMED, A. T. A., Zoology
AHMED, A. U., Institute of Statistical Research and Training
AHMED, A. U., Political Science
AHMED, E., Political Science
AHMED, ETMINA, Chemistry
AHMED, F., Applied Physics and Electronics
AHMED, F., Economics
AHMED, H., Chemistry
AHMED, J. U., Finance and Banking
AHMED, K. U., Political Science
AHMED, M., Accounting
AHMED, M., Chemistry
AHMED, M., Economics
AHMED, M., Institute of Business Administration
AHMED, M., Pharmacy
AHMED, M., Physics
AHMED, M. F., Finance
AHMED, M. G., Chemistry
AHMED, N., Library and Information Science
AHMED, N., Arabic
AHMED, S., Economics
AHMED, S., Management
AHMED, S. A., Chemistry
AHMED, S. G., Public Administration
AHMED, S. U., History
AHMED, S. U., Management
AHMED, W., Bengali
AHSAN, R. M., Geography
AKHTER, S., Institute of Education and Research
AKHTERUZZAMAN, M., Botany
ALAM, A. H. M. M., Economics
ALAM, A. M. S., Chemistry
ALAM, F., English
ALAM, M. K., Soil Science
ALAM, M. M., Economics
ALI, M. ASHRAF, Institute of Education and Research
ALI, M. AZHAR, Institute of Education and Research
ALI, M. S., Mathematics
ALI, M. S., Physics
ALI, M. S., Zoology
ALI, S. H. J., Economics
ALI, S. M. K., Institute of Nutrition and Food Science
AMEEN, M., Zoology
AMIN, S., English
AMINUZZAMAN, S. M., Public Administration
ANAM, K., Soil Science
ANISUZZAMAN, Philosophy
ANISUZZAMAN, A. T. M., Bengali
ANOWAR, M. T., Mass Communication and Journalism
ARA, B. J., Institute of Modern Languages
AREFIN, H. K. S., Sociology
ASADUZZAMAN, M., Public Administration
AWAL, A. Z. M. I., History
AZAD, H., Bengali
AZAD, S. A. K., Marketing
AZIZ, A., Botany
BAHAR, M. H., Chemistry
BANU, H., Mathematics
BANU, N., Zoology
BANU, R., Pharmacy
BANU, S., Psychology
BANU, U. A. B. R. A., Political Science
BAQUEE, A. H. M. A., Geography and Environment
BAQUER, A. A. M., Management
BARI, M. E., Law

BARKAT, M. A., Economics
BARMAN, D. C., Political Science
BASET, K. A., Institute of Fine Arts
BASHAR, M. A., Zoology
BEGUM, A., Islamic History and Culture
BEGUM, A., Zoology
BEGUM, F., Sanskrit and Pali
BEGUM, H., Philosophy
BEGUM, H. A., Psychology
BEGUM, K., Institute of Education and Research
BEGUM, LUTFUNNESSA, Institute of Education and Research
BEGUM, Q. N., Physics
BEGUM, R., Psychology
BEGUM, Z. N. T., Botany
BEPARI, M. N. A., Political Science
BHATTACHARZEE, D. D., Management
BHUIYAN, M. A. R., Economics
BHUIYAN, M. A. W., Political Science
BHUIYAN, M. S., Political Science
BISWAS, N. C., Sanskrit and Pali
BISWAS, N. N., Bengali
CHAKMA, N. K., Philosophy
CHAKMA, P. B., Management
CHAKRABORTY, R. L., History
CHOWDHURY, A., Anthropology
CHOWDHURY, A. B. M. H. R., Islamic Studies
CHOWDHURY, A. F. S. I., English
CHOWDHURY, A. M., History
CHOWDHURY, A. M., Management
CHOWDHURY, A. Q., Institute of Fine Arts
CHOWDHURY, A. R., Law
CHOWDHURY, F., Mathematics
CHOWDHURY, H. U., Political Science
CHOWDHURY, I. G., Institute of Business Administration
CHOWDHURY, K. B. M. R., Biochemistry
CHOWDHURY, L. H., Public Administration
CHOWDHURY, M. A., Economics
CHOWDHURY, M. M., Political Science
CHOWDHURY, M. R., Mathematics
CHOWDHURY, M. S., Physics
CHOWDHURY, N., Political Science
CHOWDHURY, Q. A., Sociology
CHOWDHURY, R. A., Institute of Education and Research
CHOWDHURY, S. R., Institute of Fine Arts
ELAHI, S. F., Soil Science
FAIZ, S. M. A., Soil Science
FATTAH, Q. A., Botany
FERDOUS, N., Physics
GHOSH, S. N., Accounting
GOMES, B., Biochemistry
GUPTA, H. S., Physics
HABIBULLAH, M., Accounting
HADIUZZAMAN, S., Botany
HAIDER, A. F. M. Y., Physics
HALIM, M. A., International Relations
HAQ, M. R., International Relations
HAQUE, A. K. M. S., Statistics
HAQUE, K. B., Management
HAQUE, M., Geology
HAQUE, M., Institute of Education and Research
HAQUE, M. A., English
HAQUE, M. A., Geology
HAQUE, M. M., Botany
HAQUE, M. N., Law
HAQUE, M. S., Institute of Business Administration
HARUN, C. S. H., Political Science
HASAN, A., Applied Physics and Electronics
HASAN, C. M., Pharmacy
HASAN, M. A., Botany
HASAN, M. S., Anthropology
HASAN, P., Islamic History and Culture
HASAN, S. R., Marketing
HASHEM, A., Accounting
HASSAN, M. N., Institute of Nutrition and Food Sciences
HAYE, A. H. M. A., Institute of Modern Languages
HOSSAIN, A., Institute of Business Administration
HOSSAIN, A., International Relations
HOSSAIN, A. B. M. A., Psychology
HOSSAIN, K. M. Z., Zoology
HOSSAIN, M. A., Applied Chemistry and Chemical Technology
HOSSAIN, M. A., Biochemistry
HOSSAIN, M. A., Chemistry
HOSSAIN, M. A., Mathematics
HOSSAIN, M. A., Pharmacy
HOSSAIN, M. D., History
HOSSAIN, M. K., Finance
HOSSAIN, M. M., Mathematics
HOSSAIN, M. S., Geology
HOSSAIN, M. S., Physics
HOSSAIN, M. S., Soil Science
HOSSAIN, M. T., Physics
HOSSAIN, S., English
HOSSAIN, S., Library and Information Science
HOSSAIN, S. A., Bengali
HOSSAIN, S. A., History
HOSSAIN, S. A., Political Science
HOSSAIN, S. M., Accounting
HOSSAIN, S. M., Bengali
HOWLADER, M. M. A., Zoology
HOWLADER, S. R., Economics
HUQ, A. Q. M. F., Bengali
HUQ, A. T. M. Z., Economics
HUQ, D., Applied Chemistry and Chemical Technology
HUQ, K. M. H., English
HUQ, M., Institute of Fine Arts
HUQ, M., Psychology
HUQ, M. A. Q. L., Geography and Environment
HUQ, M. M., Public Administration
HUQ, S. M. I., Soil Science
HUQ, Z. S. M. M., Geography and Environment
IBRAHIM, M., Physics
IMAN, M. B., Geology
ISLAM, A., Philosophy
ISLAM, A. K. M. N., Botany
ISLAM, K. M. S., Library and Information Science
ISLAM, K. N., Philosophy
ISLAM, L. N., Biochemistry
ISLAM, M., Sociology
ISLAM, M. A., Geography and Environment
ISLAM, M. A., Mathematics
ISLAM, M. A., Statistics
ISLAM, M. H., Institute of Social Welfare
ISLAM, M. M., History
ISLAM, M. M., Management
ISLAM, M. N., Mathematics
ISLAM, M. N., Political Science
ISLAM, M. N., Sociology
ISLAM, M. N., Statistics
ISLAM, M. R., Bengali
ISLAM, M. S., Biochemistry
ISLAM, M. S., History
ISLAM, M. S., Management
ISLAM, N., Geography and Environment
ISLAM, S. M., English
ISLAM, T. S. A., Chemistry
JAFAR, M. A., Applied Physics and Electronics
JAHAN, K., Institute of Nutrition and Food Science
JAHAN, R., Psychology
JAHANGIR, B. K., Political Science
JAHANGIR, M., Institute of Modern Languages
JINNAH, M. A., Public Administration
KABIR, A., Bengali
KABIR, A., Zoology
KABIR, M. H., Institute of Statistical Research and Training
KABIR, R. H., Linguistics
KABIR, S. M. H., Zoology
KALAM, A., International Relations
KAMAL, A. H. A., History
KAMAL, B. A., Bengali
KAMAL, H. R., Institute of Social Welfare and Research
KARIM, R., Institute of Nutrition and Food Science
KARIM, S. F., Psychology
KARMAKAR, J. L., Botany
KARMAKAR, S. S., Management
KHAIR, A., Chemistry
KHALEQUE, A., Psychology
KHALID, A. B. M., Accounting
KHALILY, M. A. B., Finance and Banking
KHAN, A. F. M. K., Mathematics
KHAN, A. H., Chemistry
KHAN, A. K. M. K. R., Institute of Business Administration
KHAN, A. K. M. S. I., Microbiology
KHAN, A. M. M. A. U., Geography and Environment
KHAN, A. N. M. A. M., Arabic
KHAN, A. T. M. N. R., Bengali
KHAN, A. Z. M. N. A., Botany
KHAN, H., Biochemistry
KHAN, M. A. A., Management
KHAN, M. A. H., Institute of Fine Arts
KHAN, M. A. R., Finance and Banking
KHAN, M. H. R., Economics
KHAN, M. M., Accounting
KHAN, M. M., Public Administration
KHAN, M. N. H., Biochemistry
KHAN, M. R., Botany
KHAN, S., Institute of Education and Research
KHAN, S., Zoology
KHAN, S. A., Mass Communication and Journalism
KHAN, S. A., Sociology
KHAN, S. I., Psychology
KHAN, T. H., Soil Science
KHAN, Z. R., Public Administration
KHANDAKER, M., Botany
KHATUN, H., Institute of Education and Research
KHATUN, H., Islamic History and Culture
KHATUN, M., Bengali
KHATUN, R., Sociology
KHATUN, S., Arabic
KHATUN, S., Bengali
KHATUN, S., Institute of Education and Research
KHORASHANI, S. S. M. A., Applied Chemistry and Chemical Technology
KHUDA, B., Economics
LATIF, A. H., Institute of Education and Research
LATIFA, G. A., Zoology
MAHMOOD, A. B. M., History
MAHMOOD, A. J., Chemistry
MAHMUD, A. H. W., Economics
MAHMUD, I., Biochemistry
MAHMUD, S. H., Psychology
MAHMUDA, S., Bengali
MAHTAB, N., Public Administration
MAHTAB, R., Chemistry
MAJUMDER, A. R., Physics
MAJUMDER, K. A. B., Persian and Urdu
MAJUMDER, M. R. K., Applied Physics and Electronics
MALEK, M. A., Institute of Nutrition and Food Science
MALLICK, S. A., Statistics
MAMOON, M. K., History
MAMUN, M. A. A., Chemistry
MANNAN, A., Management
MANNAN, K. A. I. F. M., Physics
MANNAN, R. J., Chemistry
MATIN, A., Philosophy
MATIN, K. A., Institute of Statistical Research and Training
MATIN, M. A., Mathematics
MAZUMDER, M. R. K., Applied Physics and Electronics
MIAH, A. J., Chemistry
MIAH, A. J., Philosophy
MIAH, M. A., Management
MIAH, M. S., Institute of Education and Research
MINA, S., Finance
MOHAMMADULLAH, S., Soil Science
MOHSIN, K. M., History
MOLLA, M. G., Political Science
MOLLAH, M. S. H., Mathematics
MOLLAH, M. Y. A., Chemistry
MONDAL, P. C., Sanskrit and Pali
MONDAL, R., Soil Science

MONIRUZZAMAN, M., Bengali
MONIRUZZAMAN, T., Political Science
MOSHIHUZZAMAN, M., Chemistry
MORSHED, A. K. M., Bengali
MOSTAFA, M. G., Zoology
MOWLA, G., Institute of Nutrition and Food Science
MUNSHI, M. S. H., Political Science
MUSTOFA, A. I., Applied Chemistry and Chemical Technology
MUTTAQUI, M. A. I., Institute of Education and Research
NABI, M. R., Institute of Fine Arts
NABI, S. N., Chemistry
NAHAR, N., Chemistry
NAQUI, S. A., Sociology
NASIRUDDIN, M., Finance
NATH, L. M., Physics
NIZAMI, S. I., Institute of Fine Arts
NIZAMUDDIN, K., Geography and Environment
NURUDDIN, Q. A. I. M., Mass Communication and Journalism
OSMAN, B., Institute of Fine Arts
OSMANY, S. H., History
PASHA, N. A., Chemistry
PATWARY, A. B. M. M. I., Law
QADRI, S. S., Biochemistry
QUADER, M. A., Chemistry
QUASEM, M. A., Philosophy
QUDDUS, M. A., Marketing
QUDDUS, M. M. A., Zoology
RAB, A., Institute of Business Administration
RABBANI, K. S., Physics
RAFIQUE, S., Applied Physics and Electronics
RAHIM, K. A., Biochemistry
RAHMAN, A., Arabic
RAHMAN, A., Library and Information Science
RAHMAN, A., Physics
RAHMAN, A. F. M. A., Mathematics
RAHMAN, A. H. M. A., Political Science
RAHMAN, A. H. M. H., Finance
RAHMAN, A. H. M. M., Applied Chemistry and Chemical Technology
RAHMAN, A. K. M., Physics
RAHMAN, A. Z. M. A., Accounting
RAHMAN, B. W., Institute of Education and Research
RAHMAN, K. R., English
RAHMAN, M., Biochemistry
RAHMAN, M. A., Physics
RAHMAN, M. A., Political Science
RAHMAN, M. ANISUR, Psychology
RAHMAN, M. A., Psychology
RAHMAN, M. F., Zoology
RAHMAN, M. H., Sociology
RAHMAN, M. J., Applied Physics and Electronics
RAHMAN, M. K., Biochemistry
RAHMAN, M. L., Computer Science
RAHMAN, M. M., Chemistry
RAHMAN, M. M., Mathematics
RAHMAN, M. S., Bengali
RAHMAN, M. S., Institute of Education and Research
RAHMAN, M. S., Soil Science
RAHMAN, M. S., Statistics
RAHMAN, N., Institute of Business Administration
RAHMAN, N. N., Pharmacy
RAHMAN, P. I. S. M., Islamic History and Culture
RAHMAN, P. M. M., Institute of Statistical Research and Training
RAHMAN, Q. M. M., Institute of Statistical Research and Training
RAHMAN, R., Biochemistry
RAHMAN, S., Soil Science
RAHMAN, S. M. L., Bengali
RAHMAN, S. M. M., Finance
RAISUDDIN, A. N. M., Islamic Studies
RASHEED, K. B. S., Geography and Environment
RASHID, A. M. H., Physics
RASHID, H., Accounting
RASHID, M. A., Economics
RASHID, M. H., Political Science
RASHID, R. I. M. A., Physics
RAZZAQUE, A., Institute of Fine Arts
REZA, S. A. L., Economics
ROY, A. K., Physics
SAADUDDIN, K. A. M., Sociology
SAHA, M., Applied Chemistry and Chemical Technology
SALAMATULLAH, Q., Institute of Nutrition and Food Science
SALEH, M. A., Management
SALMA, U., Persian and Urdu
SAMAD, A., Geology
SARKER, A. Q., Physics
SARKER, N. J., Zoology
SARKER, N. R., Psychology
SARKER, S. U., Zoology
SATTER, M. A., Institute of Fine Arts
SATTER, M. A., Islamic Studies
SATTER, M. A., Mathematics
SEN, K., Statistics
SEN, R., Sociology
SHAFEE, A., Physics
SHAFEE, S., Physics
SHAFI, M., Zoology
SHAHA, S. K., Accounting
SHAHIDULLAH, A. K. M., Political Science
SHAHIDULLAH, A. M. M., Mathematics
SHAHIDULLAH, K., History
SHAHIDULLAH, S. M., Psychology
SHAHIDUZZAMAN, M., International Relations
SHAMIM, I., Sociology
SHAMSUDDOHA, M., English
SHARIF, M. R. I., Applied Physics and Electronics
SIDDIQ, A. F. M. A. B., Arabic
SIDDIQ, M. A. B., Arabic
SIDDIQUE, A. H., Management
SIDDIQUE, D., Physics
SUFI, G. B., Zoology
SUKLADAS, J. C., Accounting
SULTANA, R., Bengali
TALUKDER, R. B., Institute of Business Administration
YUSUF, H. K. M., Biochemistry
ZAFAR, M. A., Bengali
ZAMAN, N., English
ZAMAN, S. S., Institute of Education and Research
ZAMAN, Z., Zoology

CONSTITUENT COLLEGES

There are 35 constituent colleges.

INDEPENDENT UNIVERSITY, BANGLADESH

House 3, Road 10, Baridhara, Dhaka 1212
Telephone: (2) 9881681
Fax: (2) 883959
E-mail: info@iub-bd.edu

Founded 1992
Private control
Language of instruction: English
Academic year: August to May

Chancellor: President of the People's Republic of Bangladesh
President: Dr A. MAJEED KHAN
Rector: Prof. BAZLUL MOBIN CHOWDHURY
Registrar: Dr CYRIL D. MAYNARD
Librarian: MD. HOSSAM HAIDER CHOWDHURY (Senior Assistant Librarian)

Library of 7,000 vols
Number of teachers: 57
Number of students: 742

DIRECTORS OF SCHOOLS

School of Business: Dr BORHAN UDDIN
School of Communication: Prof. M. A. RAQIB
School of Environmental Science and Management: Prof. HAROUN-ER-RASHID
School of Liberal Arts and Science: Dr BAZLUL MOBIN CHOWDHURY
School of Graduate Study: Dr BORHAN UDDIN

ISLAMIC UNIVERSITY

Shantidanga-Dulalpur, Kushtia
Telephone: 4500
Founded 1980
Vice-Chancellor: Prof. INAMUL M. HOQUE
Registrar: K. M. ASHRAF HOSSAIN
Librarian: (vacant)
Library of 22,000 vols
Number of teachers: 65
Number of students: 1,500

DEANS

Faculty of Social Sciences: Dr M. MAMUN
Faculty of Theology and Islamic Studies: Prof. M. A. HAMID (acting)

JAHANGIRNAGAR UNIVERSITY

Savar, Dhaka
Telephone: 414079
Founded 1970
Languages of instruction: Bengali and English
Academic year: July to June (three terms)
Chancellor: PRESIDENT OF THE REPUBLIC
Vice-Chancellor: Prof. AMIRUL I. CHOWDHURY
Registrar: MOHAMED ALI
Librarian: Prof. MESBAHUDDIN AHMAD (acting)
Library of 61,341 vols, 150 periodicals
Number of teachers: 239
Number of students: 2,929
Publications: *Jahangirnagar Review* (annually), various departmental journals.

DEANS

Faculty of Arts and Humanities: Prof. MD. ENAMUL HUQ KHAN
Faculty of Social Sciences: MAFIZ UDDIN AHMED
Faculty of Mathematical and Physical Sciences: Prof. MD. ABU SAEED KHAN

HEADS OF DEPARTMENTS

Anthropology: Dr MOHAMMAD SHAH JALAL
Archaeology: Prof. BAZLUR RAHMAN KHAN (acting)
Bengali: U. H. M. SHAMSUN NAHAR
Business Studies: MAFIZ UDDIN AHMED (acting)
Chemistry: Dr MAHMOODA GHANI AHMED
Drama: MD. MOYEN UDDIN AHMED
Economics: Prof. ABDUL BAYES
Electronics: Prof. MD. IMAM UDDIN
English: SHAHEEN MAHBUBA MAHMOOD
Geography: Prof. SUBASH CHANDRA DAS
Geology: Dr DELWAR HOSSAIN
Government and Politics: Dr A. K. M. GOLAM HOSSAIN
History: Prof. MD. ENAMUL HAQ KHAN
Mathematics: Dr ANWARUL HAQUE SHARIF
Philosophy: ALI AHMED MALLICK
Physics: Prof. MD. MUNIRUZZAMAN
Statistics: Dr KANCHAN CHOWDHURY
Institute of Life Sciences: Dir Prof. A. B. M. ENAYET HOSSAIN
Botany: Dr ZAHED UDDIN MAHMOOD KHAN
Zoology: Dr MD. ABDULLAHEL BAQUI
Pharmacy: Prof. ABDUL GHANI

ATTACHED INSTITUTE

Institute of Computer and Information Technology: Dir Prof. M. KABIR.

KHULNA UNIVERSITY

Khulna 9208
Telephone: (41) 721791
Fax: (41) 731244
E-mail: ku@bdonline.com
Founded 1987
State control
Language of instruction: English
Vice-Chancellor: Prof. Dr S. M. NAZRUL ISLAM
Registrar: Dr S.M. ABU BAKAR

Librarian: MOKLESUR RAHMAN (Assistant Librarian)

Library of 20,000 vols

Number of teachers: 140

Number of students: 1,472

DEAN

School of Life Science: Prof. Dr MD. SAIFUDDIN SHAH

School of Science, Engineering and Technology: Prof. Dr MD. MOZAMMEL HUQ AZAD KHAN

School of Business Administration: Prof. Dr MD. KAYEMUDDIN

HEADS OF DISCIPLINE

Architecture: GOURI SHANKAR ROY

Computer Science and Engineering: Prof. Dr MD. MOZAMMEL HUQ AZAD KHAN

Urban and Rural Planning: MD. GHULAM MURTAZA

Forestry and Wood Technology: Prof. Dr MOHAMMAD ABDUR RAHMAN

Fisheries and Marine Resource Technology: Prof. Dr MD. SAIFUDDIN SHAH

Biotechnology: Dr KHONDOKER MOAZZEM HOSSAIN

Agrotechnology: MD. YASIN ALI

Business Administration: Prof. Dr MD. KAYEMUDDIN

Electronics and Communication Engineering: Prof. Dr MD. MOZAMMEL HUQ AZAD KHAN

Environmental Science: MD. SALEQUZZAMAN

Pharmacy: Dr MD. MOKADDEZ SARDER

UNIVERSITY OF RAJSHAHI

Rajshahi 6205

Telephone: (721) 750041

Fax: (721) 750064

E-mail: ru.phy@drik.bgd.toolnet.org

Founded 1953

Languages of instruction: English and Bengali

Academic year: July to June (three terms)

Chancellor: PRESIDENT OF THE PEOPLE'S REPUBLIC OF BANGLADESH

Vice-Chancellor: Prof. ABDUL KHALEQUE

Registrar: MUHAMMAD EUNUS (acting)

Librarian: (vacant)

Library: see Libraries

Number of teachers: 650

Number of students: 27,141 (university)

Publications: *Rajshahi University Studies* (annually), *Calendar* (every 2 years).

DEANS

Faculty of Arts: Prof. A. K. M. YAQUB ALI

Faculty of Social Science: Prof. MUHAMMAD MIZAM UDDIN

Faculty of Science: Prof. M. FAKHRUL ISLAM

Faculty of Life and Earth: Prof. M. ABDUL KHALEQUE

Faculty of Law: M. FAYEZ UDDIN

Faculty of Education: Prof. S. M. ENAMUL HAQUE

Faculty of Business Studies: M. SHAH NEWAJ ALI

Faculty of Medicine: Prof. M. M. SHAFIUR RAHMAN

PROFESSORS

Arts:

AHMED, K. M., Philosophy
AHMED, S., Islamic History and Culture
AHMED, W., History
ALAM, M. R., Philosophy
ALI, A. K. M. Y., Islamic History and Culture
ALI, M. S., History
ALI, M. W., History
ANOWAR, A., English
AWAL, M. A., Bengali
BARI, M. A., Islamic History and Culture
BEG, M. A., Bengali
CHOWDHURY, N. H., History
GHOSE, R. N., Philosophy
HAMID, M. A., Philosophy
HAQUE, K. S., Bengali
HASAN, M. A. D., English
HOQUE, K. M. A., Bengali
HUSSAIN, A. B. M., Islamic History and Culture
HUSSAIN, S., History
IBRAHIMI, M. S. A., Arabic
JAHAU, S., Bengali
JALIL, M. A., Bengali
KARIM, A. K. M. R., English
KHAN, M. A. A., Islamic History and Culture
KHONDKER, A. R., Bengali
MATIN, C. Z., Bengali
MIA, M. A. K., Bengali
MIA, M. M., Bengali
MOHIUDDIN, A. K. M., English
NAHAR, S., Islamic History and Culture
QAIYUM, M. N., History
RAHIM, M. A., History
RAHMAN, A. A., English
RAHMAN, A. F. M. S., History
RAHMAN, A. K. M. A., Bengali
RAHMAN, M. M., History
RAHMAN, M. M., Islamic History and Culture
RAHMAN, Q., Islamic History and Culture
SARKAR, M. S. A., Philosophy
SHAFI, M., History
SHAFIQULLAH, M., Islamic Studies
SHAHJAHAN, M., Philosophy
SHIBLY, A. H., History

Social Science:

AKBAR, M. A., Social Work
BHUIYAN, M. A. Q., Sociology
HABIB, A., Economics
HALIM, M. A., Social Work
HOSSAIN, K. T., Sociology
HUQ, M. A. F., Political Science
ISLAM, A. S. M. N., Social Work
ISLAM, T. S., Economics
KARIM, A. H. M. Z., Sociology
KHAN, F. R., Sociology
MIA, M. A. H., Economics
MIZANUDDIN, M., Sociology
MONDOL, M. S., Economics
MURSHED, G., Political Science
NATH, J., Sociology
RAHMAN, S., Public Administration
SADEQUE, M., Social Work
SAHA, S. K., Economics
SARKAR, P. C., Social Work
UDDIN, M. A., Economics

Science:

ABEDIN, S., Statistics
ABSAR, N., Biochemistry
AHMED, M., Mathematics
AHMED, N., Chemistry
AHMED, S., Chemistry
ALI, D. M., Mathematics
ALI, M. A., Chemistry
ALI, M. K., Population
ALI, M. U., Chemistry
ALI, M. Y., Chemistry
ALI, S. M. M., Applied Chemistry and Chemical Technology
ANSARI, A., Mathematics
BANU, K., Physics
BASAK, A. K., Physics
BEG, A. H., Mathematics
BHATTACHARJEE, S. K., Mathematics
BHATTACHARJEE, S. K., Statistics
BISWAS, R. K., Applied Chemistry and Chemical Technology
CHOUDHURY, G. M., Physics
DAS, B. K., Chemistry
DEVNATH, R. C., Applied Physics and Electronics
FARUKI, F. I., Applied Chemistry and Chemical Technology
HAKIM, M. O., Physics
HAQUE, M. E., Chemistry
HAQUE, M. E., Pharmacy
HAQUE, M. M., Physics
HOSSAIN, M. D., Applied Physics and Electronics
HOSSAIN, M. L., Chemistry
HOSSAIN, M. M., Applied Physics and Electronics
HUSSAIN, H. A., Statistics
ISLAM, A., Physics
ISLAM, A. K. M. A., Physics
ISLAM, G. S., Physics
ISLAM, M. A., Chemistry
ISLAM, M. F., Applied Chemistry and Chemical Technology
ISLAM, M. N., Chemistry
ISLAM, M. N., Physics
ISLAM, M. Q., Chemistry
ISLAM, M. S., Physics
ISLAM, M. S., Chemistry
ISLAM, M. W., Mathematics
ISLAM, S. N., Physics
KHAN, K. A., Applied Physics and Electronics
KHAN, M. A. R., Chemistry
KHAN, M. S. R., Applied Physics and Electronics
MAHTABWALI, S. Q. G., Physics
MAJUMDER, S., Mathematics
MIA, M. A. A., Applied Physics and Electronics
MIAH, M. A. J., Chemistry
MIAN, M. A. B., Statistics
MOLLAH, M. A. H., Applied Chemistry and Chemical Technology
MONDOL, M. A. S., Physics
MOSTAFA, M. G., Statistics
NOOR, A. S. A., Mathematics
PAUL, A. C., Mathematics
PAUL, S. C., Chemistry
QUAISUDDIN, M., Biochemistry
RAHMAN, M. A., Applied Chemistry and Chemical Technology
RAHMAN, M. B., Chemistry
RAHMAN, M. L., Chemistry
RAHMAN, M. Z., Mathematics
RAQUIBUZZAMAN, M., Applied Chemistry and Chemical Technology
RAZZAQUE, M. A., Statistics
SARKER, M. A. R., Applied Physics and Electronics
SATTAR, A., Mathematics
SATTAR, M. A., Chemistry
SATTAR, M. A., Statistics
SAYEED, M. A., Applied Chemistry and Chemical Engineering
SOBHAN, M.A., Applied Physics and Electronics
TARAFDER, M. T. H., Chemistry

Life and Earth:

AFSARUDDIN, M., Psychology
FARUK, T., Psychology
AHMED, A., Botany
AHMED, S. T., Geology and Mining
ALAM, M. S., Geography
ALAM, M. S., Botany
ALI, M. M., Zoology
ALI, M. S., Zoology
AMIN, M. N., Botany
ARA, S., Psychology
BHUIYAN, N. I. M. A. S., Zoology
FARUK, T., Psychology
GAUSUZZAMAN, M., Botany
HAQUE, M. E., Geography
HOQUE, A. B. M. Z., Psychology
HOQUE, M. M., Psychology
HOSSAIN, M. A., Zoology
HOSSAIN, M. M., Botany
ISLAM, A. K. M. R., Botany
ISLAM, M. B., Geology and Mining
JAHAN, M. S., Zoology
JOARDER, M. O. I., Genetics
JUNAID, M., Psychology

KABIB, M. G., Botany
KHALEQUE, M. A., Botany
KHALEQUZZAMAN, M., Zoology
KHAN, J. R., Geography
KUNDU, P. B., Botany
MANNAU, M. A., Zoology
MOEED, M. A., Psychology
MONDAL, A. K. M. S. H., Zoology
NADERUZZAMAN, A. T. M., Botany
NAHAR, S., Botany
PAUL, N. K., Botany
RAHMAN, A. S. M. S., Zoology
RAHMAN, M. A., Botany
RAHMAN, M. H., Geology and Mining
RAHMAN, M. H., Geology and Mining
RAHMAN, M. S., Botany
RAHMAN, M. S., Zoology
RAHMAN, M. S., Zoology
RAHMAN, S. M., Zoology
RUMI, S. R. A. Geography
SALAM, M. A., Zoology
SAMAD, A. G., Botany
SHAIKH, M. A. H., Geography
TAHA, M. A., Geography
WAHAB, M. A., Geography
ZAMAN, M., Botany
ZUBERI, M. I., Botany
ZUNAED, M., Psychology

Law:

HOSSAIN, M. M.
RAHMAN, M. H.
SIDDIQUE, M. A. B.
UDDIN, M. B.

Business Studies:

ANJUM, M. N., Management
DEY, M. M., Accounting
HAROON, M. A. A., Accounting
KHAN, M. A., Management
RAHMAN, M. A., Management
SAHA, A. C., Accounting

There are 241 affiliated colleges.

ATTACHED INSTITUTES

Institute of Bangladesh Studies: Dir MAHMUD SHAH QURESHI.

Institute of Biological Science: Dir K. A. M. SHAHADAT HOSSAIN MONDAL.

SHAHJALAL UNIVERSITY OF SCIENCE AND TECHNOLOGY

University P.O., Sylhet
Telephone: (821) 713491
Fax: (821) 715257

Founded 1987
State control
Languages of instruction: English, Bengali
Academic year: July to June

Chancellor: President of the People's Republic of Bangladesh
Vice-Chancellor: Prof. SYED MOHIB UDDIN AHMED
Pro-Vice-Chancellor: Prof. MD. HABIBUR RAHMAN
Registrar: JAMIL AHMED CHOWDHURY
Librarian: MD. ABDUL HAYEE SAMENI (Deputy Librarian)

Library of 11,000 vols
Number of teachers: 182
No of students: 2,170

DEANS

School of Applied Sciences and Technology: Prof. MD. ZAINAL ABEDIN
School of Physical Sciences: Prof. MD. HABIBUL AHSAN
School of Social Sciences: Prof. HABIBUR RAHMAN
School of Medical Science: Prof. GOLAM KIBRIA
School of Life Sciences: MD. EBRAHIM HOSSAIN (acting)

Colleges

Bangladesh Agricultural Research Institute: Joydebpur, Gazipur 1701; tel. 9332340; telex 64240; fax (2) 841678; e-mail dg@bari.bdmail.net; f. 1976; library of 24,000 vols, 185 periodicals; 3,006 staff (incl. college teachers); Dir-Gen. Dr M. A. MAZED; Senior Librarian A. B. M. FAZLUR RAHMAN.

Attached colleges:

Bangladesh Agricultural Institute: Sher-e-Bangla Nagar, Dhaka 1207; BSc course; 63 teachers; 686 students; Principal M. Q. ZAMAN.

Hazi Mohammad Danesh Krishi College: Basherhat, Dinajpur; BSc course; 54 teachers; 600 students; Principal MD. SADAT ULLAH.

Patuakhali Agricultural College: Dumki, Patuakhali; BSc course; 52 teachers; 560 students; Principal MD. SAFIUL ALAM.

Bangladesh College of Textile Technology: Tejgaon I/A, Dhaka 1208; tel. 604821; f. 1950; a constituent college of Dhaka Univ.; degree courses; 27 teachers; library of 8,535 vols; Principal Dr M. RAHMAN.

Chittagong Polytechnic Institute: Chittagong; f. 1962; 1,320 students.

Dhaka Polytechnic Institute: Tejgaon Industrial Area, Dhaka 8; f. 1955.

Institute of Leather Technology: Dhaka.

BARBADOS

Learned Societies

GENERAL

Caribbean Conservation Association: Savannah Lodge, Garrison, St Michael; tel. 426-5373; fax 429-8483; e-mail cca@caribsurf.com; f. 1967; independent, non-profit-making; preservation and development of the environment, and conservation of the cultural heritage in the Wider Caribbean; 509 mems; small library; Pres. PENELOPE HYNAM-ROACH; Exec. Dir GLENDA MEDINA.

BIBLIOGRAPHY, LIBRARY SCIENCE AND MUSEOLOGY

Library Association of Barbados: POB 827E, Bridgetown; f. 1968 to unite qualified librarians, archivists and information specialists, and all other persons engaged or interested in information management and dissemination in Barbados, and to provide opportunities for their meeting together; to promote the active development and maintenance of libraries in Barbados and to foster co-operation between them; to interest the general public in the library services available; 60 mems; Pres. SHIRLEY YEARWOOD; Sec. HAZELYN DEVONISH; publ. *Update* (irregular).

HISTORY, GEOGRAPHY AND ARCHAEOLOGY

Historical Society: see under Barbados Museum.

MEDICINE

Barbados Association of Medical Practitioners: BAMP Complex, Spring Garden, St Michael; f. 1973; 290 mems; Pres. Dr FRANK BISHOP; Gen. Sec. Dr CARLOS CHASE; publ. *BAMP Bulletin* (4 a year).

Barbados Pharmaceutical Society: POB 820 E., St Michael; f. 1948, inc. 1961; 155 mems; Pres. DELORES MORRIS; Sec. GEORGE ALLEYNE. Publ. *Pharmacy in Progress*.

Research Institutes

GENERAL

Bellairs Research Institute: St James; f. 1954; affiliated with McGill University, Canada; research and teaching in all aspects of tropical environments; library of 200 vols; Dir Dr WAYNE HUNTE.

Libraries and Archives

Bridgetown

Public Library: Coleridge St, Bridgetown; tel. 436-6081; fax 436-1501; f. 1847; an island-wide service is provided from the central library in Bridgetown by means of 7 brs, 6 centres, and a mobile service to 66 primary schools; acts as a national repository for legal deposit printed materials; 165,000 vols; special Barbadian and West Indian research collection; Dir JUDY BLACKMAN; publ. *National Bibliography of Barbados* (2 a year with annual cumulations).

University of the West Indies Main Library: POB 1334, Bridgetown; tel. 417-4444; telex 2257; fax 417-4460; e-mail gillme@caribsurf.com; f. 1963; 160,000 vols, special West Indies collection, UN, UNESCO and World Bank depository library; Librarian MICHAEL E. GILL; publ. *Guide to the Library* (irregular).

St Michael

Department of Archives: Black Rock, St Michael; tel. 425-1380; f. 1963; part of Min. of Education and Culture; 990.25 linear metres of archives, 2,366 books and pamphlets, 922 serials, 391 microfilm reels, 2,747 fiches, 220 sound recordings; Chief Archivist E. CHRISTINE MATTHEWS.

Museums and Art Galleries

St Ann's Garrison

Barbados Museum and Historical Society: St Ann's Garrison; tel. 427-0201; fax 429-5946; est. 1933; collections illustrating the island's geology, prehistory, history, natural history and marine life; European decorative arts; library; 1,000 mems; Pres. Dr T. CARMICHAEL; Dir H. ALISSANDRA CUMMINS; publs *Journal* (annually), *Newsletter* (quarterly).

University

UNIVERSITY OF THE WEST INDIES, CAVE HILL CAMPUS

POB 64, Bridgetown

Telephone: 417-4000

Fax: 425-1327

Founded 1963

Language of instruction: English

Private control

Academic year: September to May (2 terms)

One of the three campuses of the University of the West Indies, intended to serve Barbados, the Leeward and Windward Islands.

The teaching programme covers the humanities, education, law, science and technology, social sciences and clinical studies in medicine.

(See also under Jamaica and Trinidad)

Chancellor: Sir SHRIDATH RAMPHAL

Vice-Chancellor: Sir ALISTER MCINTYRE

Pro-Vice-Chancellor and Principal: Sir KEITH HUNTE

Registrar: ANDREW G. LEWIS

Librarian: MICHAEL GILL

Number of teachers: 266 (113 part-time)

Number of students: 3,568 (1,503 part-time)

DEANS

Faculty of Humanities: Prof. H. BECKLES

Faculty of Law: A. D. BURGESS

School of Clinical Medicine and Research: Prof. E. R. WALROND

Faculty of Science and Technology: Prof. G. E. MATHISON

Faculty of Social Sciences: Dr FARLEY BRATHWAITE

ATTACHED INSTITUTES

Institute of Social and Economic Research: Bridgetown; Dir Dr ANDREW DOWNES.

Caribbean Agricultural Research and Development Institute: Bridgetown; Head, Field Unit G. PROVERBS.

College

Barbados Community College: 'The Eyrie', Howell's Cross Rd, St Michael; tel. 426-2858; fax 429-5935; f. 1968; commerce, liberal arts, health sciences, fine arts, science, technology, Barbados Language Centre, Hospitality Institute, general and continuing education, computer studies, physical education; 104 full-time, 75 part-time teachers, 2,400 students; library of 27,000 vols; Principal NORMA J. I. HOLDER; Registrar SYDNEY O. ARTHUR.

BELARUS

Learned Societies

GENERAL

National Academy of Sciences of Belarus: 220072 Minsk, Pr. Skaryny 66; tel. (17) 284-18-01; fax (17) 239-31-63; e-mail academy@presidium.bas-net.by; f. 1929; depts of Physics, Mathematics and Informatics (Academician-Sec. N. M. Olekhnovich, Scientific Sec. G. A. Butkin), Physical and Technical Problems of Machine Building and Energetics (Academician-Sec. G. A. Anisovich, Scientific Sec. V. A. Gaiko), Chemical and Geological Sciences (Academician-Sec. I. I. Lishtvan, Scientific Sec. N. I. Plyushchevsky), Biological Sciences (Academician-Sec. A. G. Lobanok, Scientific Sec. V. A. Voinilo), Medical-Biological Sciences (Academician-Sec. V. N. Gurin, Scientific Sec. I. N. Semenenya), Humanities and Arts (Academician-Sec. A. I. Podluzhny, Scientific Sec. V. I. Levkovich); 76 academicians, 105 corresp. mems, 11 foreign mems, 1 hon. mem.; attached research institutes: see Research Institutes; library and archive: see Libraries and Archives; Pres. Aleksandr P. Voitovich; Chief Scientific Sec. Fyodor A. Lakhvich; publs *Doklady* (Reports, 6 a year), *Vestsi* (Bulletins: Physical-Technical Sciences, Biological Sciences, Physical-Mathematical Sciences, Humanities, Chemistry, 4 a year), *Differentsialnye Uravneniya* (Differential Equations, monthly), *Zhurnal Prikladnoi Spektroskopii* (Journal of Applied Spectroscopy, 6 a year), *Inzhenerno-Fizicheskii Zhurnal* (Engineering Physics Journal, 6 a year), *Trenie i Iznos* (Friction and Wear, 6 a year).

AGRICULTURE, FISHERIES AND VETERINARY SCIENCE

Academy of Agricultural Sciences of the Republic of Belarus: 220049 Minsk, Vul. Knorina 1; tel. (17) 266-06-17; fax (17) 268-80-83; depts of Economics (Academician-Sec. Vladimir G. Gusakov), Arable Farming and Plant Cultivation (Academician-Sec. Stanislav I. Grib), Animal Science and Veterinary Medicine (Academician-Sec. Ivan P. Sheiko), Mechanization and Energy (Vice-Academician-Sec. Alexandr V. Korotkevich); 19 academicians, 22 corresp. mems; attached research institutes: see Research Institutes; library: see Libraries and Archives; Pres. Vitaly S. Antonyuk; Chief Scientific Sec. Miroslav V. Yakubovsky; publ. newsletter (quarterly).

Research Institutes

AGRICULTURE, FISHERIES AND VETERINARY SCIENCE

Belarus Research and Technological Institute of Fisheries: 220115 Minsk, Vul. Stebeneva 22; tel. (17) 277-50-75; attached to Acad. of Agricultural Sciences of the Republic of Belarus; Dir Victor V. Konchits.

Belarus Research and Technological Institute of the Meat and Dairy Industry: 220075 Minsk, Partizansky trakt 10 km; tel. (17) 244-38-52; fax (17) 244-38-91; attached to Acad. of Agricultural Sciences of the Republic of Belarus; Dir Anatoly M. Dmitriev.

Belarus Research Institute for Land Reclamation and Grassland: 220040 Minsk, Vul. M. Bogdanovicha 153; tel. (17) 232-49-41; fax (17) 232-64-96; f. 1930; attached to Acad. of Agricultural Sciences of the Republic of Belarus; Dir Vladimir F. Karlovsky.

Belarus Research Institute for Potato Growing: 223013 Minsk raion, Pos. Samokhvalovichi, Vul. Kovaleva 2; tel. (17) 290-11-45; fax (17) 210-08-89; f. 1957; attached to Acad. of Agricultural Sciences of the Republic of Belarus; Dir Sergei A. Banadysev; publ. *Potato Growing* (1 a year).

Belarus Research Institute for Soil Science and Agrochemistry: 220108 Minsk, Vul. Kazintsa 62; tel. (17) 277-08-21; fax (17) 277-44-80; f. 1931; attached to Acad. of Agricultural Sciences of the Republic of Belarus; Dir Iosif M. Bogdevich.

Belarus Research Institute for the Mechanization of Agriculture: 220049 Minsk, Vul. Knorina 1; tel. (17) 266-02-91; fax (17) 266-27-75; attached to Acad. of Agricultural Sciences of the Republic of Belarus; Dir Igor S. Nagorsky.

Belarus Research Institute of Agricultural Economics and Information: 220108 Minsk, Vul. Kazintsa 103; tel. (17) 277-04-11; fax (17) 278-69-21; e-mail econinst@agr.ec.belpak.minsk.by; f. 1958; attached to Acad. of Agricultural Sciences of the Republic of Belarus; library of 20,000 vols; Dir Dr Vladimir G. Gusakov; publ. *Agroeconomika* (monthly).

Belarus Research Institute of Agricultural Radiology: 246050 Gomel, Vul. Fedyninskogo 16; tel. (23) 251-68-21; fax (23) 253-75-60; e-mail firs@biar.gomel.by; attached to Acad. of Agricultural Sciences of the Republic of Belarus; Dir Slava K. Firsakova.

Belarus Research Institute of Animal Production: 222160 Minsk raion, Zhodino, Vul. Frunze 11; tel. (1775) 3-34-26; fax (1775) 3-52-83; f. 1949; attached to Acad. of Agricultural Sciences of the Republic of Belarus; library of 68,000 vols; Dir Prof. Ivan P. Sheyko.

Belarus Research Institute of Arable Farming and Fodders: 222160 Minsk raion, Zhodino, Vul. Timiryazeva 1; tel. (17) 3-38-93; fax (17) 3-70-66; f. 1956; attached to Acad. of Agricultural Sciences of the Republic of Belarus; library of 66,000 vols; Dir Vladimir P. Samsonov.

Belarus Research Institute of Energetics and Electrification for Agriculture: 220024 Minsk, Vul. Stebeneva 20; tel. (17) 277-27-04; attached to Acad. of Agricultural Sciences of the Republic of Belarus; Dir Egor F. Sukhorukov.

Belarus Research Institute of Experimental Veterinary Medicine: 223020 Minsk raion, Pos. Kuntsevshchina; tel. and fax (17) 298-81-31; attached to Acad. of Agricultural Sciences of the Republic of Belarus; Dir Nikolai A. Kovalev.

Belarus Research Institute of Fruit Growing: 223013 Minsk raion, Pos. Samokhvalovichi; tel. (17) 290-11-40; attached to Acad. of Agricultural Sciences of the Republic of Belarus; Dir Vyacheslav A. Samus.

Belarus Research Institute of Plant Protection: 223011 Minsk raion, Pos. Priluki; tel. (17) 299-23-39; fax (17) 299-23-38; attached to Acad. of Agricultural Sciences of the Republic of Belarus; Dir Vilor F. Samersov.

Belarus Research Institute of Vegetable Crops: 220028 Minsk, Vul. Mayakovskogo 127; tel. (17) 221-37-11; attached to Acad. of Agricultural Sciences of the Republic of Belarus; Dir Gennady I. Ganush.

Central Research Institute of Utilization of Water Resources: Minsk, Vul. Slavinskaga 1.

Grodno Agricultural Research Institute: 231510 Grodno raion, Shchuchin, Akademicheskaya vul. 21; tel. and fax (1514) 2-19-58; attached to Acad. of Agricultural Sciences of the Republic of Belarus; Dir Pavel I. Zayats.

Institute of Forestry: 246654 Gomel, Praletarskaya vul. 71; tel. (23) 253-14-23; fax (23) 253-53-89; e-mail dvornik@fi.gomel.by; f. 1930; attached to Nat. Acad. of Sciences of Belarus; Dir Prof. Dr V. A. Ipatyev.

ARCHITECTURE AND TOWN PLANNING

Belarus State Research and Design Institute of Town Planning: Minsk, Kommunisticheskaya vul. 9.

ECONOMICS, LAW AND POLITICS

Central Research and Development Institute for Management and Control Engineering: 220033 Minsk, Partizansky pr. 2, Korpus 4; tel. 21-76-15; fax 21-75-04.

Economic Research Institute of the Ministry of the Economy: 220086 Minsk, Vul. Slavinskaga 1; tel. 64-02-78; fax 64-64-40; f. 1962; library of 51,425 vols.

Institute of Economics: 220072 Minsk, Vul. Surganava 1, Korpus 2; tel. (17) 284-24-43; fax (17) 284-07-16; e-mail fateyev@economics.bas-net.by; f. 1931; attached to Nat. Acad. of Sciences of Belarus; Dir Prof. Petr G. Nikitenko.

Institute of Philosophy and Law: 220072 Minsk, Vul. Surganava 1, Korpus 2; tel. (17) 284-18-63; fax (17) 284-29-25; f. 1931; attached to Nat. Acad. of Sciences of Belarus; Dir A. S. Maikhrovich.

Research Institute on Problems of Criminology and Forensic Expertise: 220600 Minsk, Gvardeiskaya vul. 7; tel. 26-72-79; fax 23-05-40; f. 1929; library of 1,000 vols; Dir I. S. Andreev; publ. *Problems of Criminology and Forensic Expertise* (annually).

EDUCATION

National Institute of Education: 220004 Minsk, Vul. Korolja 16; tel. (17) 220-59-09; fax (17) 220-56-35; e-mail nieby@Minsk.sovam.com; f.1990; library of 20,000 vols; Dir Dr Boris Kraiko; publ. *Adulcatsia i Wychawanne*.

HISTORY, GEOGRAPHY AND ARCHAEOLOGY

Institute of History: 220072 Minsk, Vul. Akademicheskaya 1; tel. and fax (17) 284-02-19; f. 1929; attached to Nat. Acad. of Sciences of Belarus; Dir M. P. Kostyuk.

LANGUAGE AND LITERATURE

Institute of Linguistics: 220072 Minsk, Vul. Surganava 1, Korpus 2; tel. 268-48-84; f. 1929;

attached to Nat. Acad. of Sciences of Belarus; Dir A. I. PODLUZHNYI.

Institute of Literature: 220072 Minsk, Pr. Skaryny 66; tel. (17) 268-58-86; f. 1931; attached to Nat. Acad. of Sciences of Belarus; Dir U. V. GNILOMEDOV.

MEDICINE

Alexandrov Research Institute of Oncology and Medical Radiology: 223052 Minsk, Pos. Lesnoy 2; tel. (17) 269-95-05; fax (17) 266-47-76; e-mail niiomr@niiomr.belpak.minsk.by; f. 1960; library of 14,000 vols, 55 periodicals; Dir EUGENE A. KOROTKEVICH; publ. *Topical Problems on Oncology and Medical Radiology* (1 a year).

Belarus Research Institute of Epidemiology and Microbiology: 220050 Minsk, Vul. K. Zetkina 4; tel. (17) 226-58-66; fax (17) 226-52-67; f. 1925; library of 9,000 vols; Dir Prof. LEONID P. TITOV.

Belarus Sanitary and Hygiene Research Institute: 220012 Minsk, Vul. Skaryny 8/47; tel. (17) 268-43-70; fax (17) 268-43-72; f.1927; library of 13,521 vols; Dir Dr VICTOR STELMACH.

Research Institute for Disability Assessment and Organization of Work of the Disabled: 220114 Minsk, Staroborisovsky trakt 24; tel. and fax (17) 264-25-08; f. 1974; library of 35,000 vols; Dir Prof. E. I. ZBOROVSKY.

Research Institute of Blood Transfusion: Minsk, Dolginovsky trakt 13.

Research Institute of Cardiology: 220036 Minsk, Vul. R. Lyuksemburga 110; tel. 56-07-69.

Research Institute of Maternity and Child Welfare: Minsk, Krasnoarmeiskaya vul. 34.

Research Institute of Neurology, Neurosurgery and Physiotherapy: 220061 Minsk, Vul. Filatova 9; tel. 46-40-88.

Research Institute of Oncology and Medical Radiology: Minsk raion, Pos. Lesnoi.

Research Institute of Pulmonology and Phthisiology: 223059 Minsk raion, Pos. Novinki; tel. (17) 37-25-60; fax (17) 37-15-21; e-mail pdv@tuber.belpak.minsk.by; f. 1923; library of 7,000 vols; Dirs V. BORSHCHEVSKY, O. KALECHITS; publ. annual report on research.

Research Institute of Traumatology and Orthopaedics: Minsk, Vul. Gorkogo 2.

Skin and Venereological Research Institute: Minsk, Prilukskaya vul. 46A.

NATURAL SCIENCES

Biological Sciences

Central Botanical Garden: 220012 Minsk, Vul. Surganava 2A; tel. 39-44-84; f. 1932; attached to Nat. Acad. of Sciences of Belarus; Dir YE. A. SIDOROVICH.

Institute of Biochemistry: 230017 Grodno, BLK-50; tel. (15) 233-78-35; fax (15) 233-41-21; e-mail nef@biochem.belpak.grodno.by; f. 1970; attached to Nat. Acad. of Sciences of Belarus; library of 40,000 vols; Dir Prof. LEONID NEFYODOV.

Institute of Bio-Organic Chemistry: 220141 Minsk, Zhodinskaya vul. 5; tel. 64-87-61; fax 63-67-72; f. 1974; attached to Nat. Acad. of Sciences of Belarus; Dir O. A. STRELCHENOK.

Institute of Experimental Botany: 220072 Minsk, Vul. Akademicheskaya 27; tel. 39-48-50; fax 20-91-25; f. 1931; attached to Nat. Acad. of Sciences of Belarus; Dir V. I. PARFENOV.

Institute of Genetics and Cytology: 220072 Minsk, Vul. Akademicheskaya 27; tel. (17) 284-18-48; fax (17) 284-19-17; e-mail igc@bas32.basnet.minsk.by; f. 1965; attached to Nat. Acad. of Sciences of Belarus; Dir Prof. N. A. KARTEL.

Institute of Microbiology: 220141 Minsk, Zhodinskaya vul. 2; tel. and fax (17) 264-47-66; f. 1975; attached to Nat. Acad. of Sciences of Belarus; Dir A. G. LOBANOK.

Institute of Photobiology: 220072 Minsk, Vul. Akademicheskaya 27; tel. (17) 284-17-49; fax (17) 284-23-59; e-mail volot@bas31.basnet.by; f. 1973; attached to Nat. Acad. of Sciences of Belarus; Dir I. D. VOLOTOVSKY.

Institute of Physiology: 220072 Minsk, Vul. Skaryny 28; tel. (17) 268-54-61; fax (17) 268-47-73; f. 1953; attached to Nat. Acad. of Sciences of Belarus; Dir V. N. GURIN.

Institute of Problems of Use and Ecology of Natural Resources: 220114 Minsk, Starabarisavskii trakt 10; tel. 64-26-31; fax 64-24-13; f. 1932; attached to Nat. Acad. of Sciences of Belarus; Dir I. I. LISHTVAN.

Institute of Radiobiology: 220141 Minsk, Vul. Akademika Kuprevicha 2; tel. and fax (17) 64-23-15; e-mail irb@radbio.bas-net.by; f. 1987; attached to Nat. Acad. of Sciences of Belarus; Dir YE. F. KONOPLYA.

Institute of Zoology: 220072 Minsk, Vul. Akademicheskaya 27; tel. (17) 22-84-21-89; fax (17) 22-84-10-36; e-mail 200@biobel.basnet.by; f. 1958; attached to Nat. Acad. of Sciences of Belarus; Dir M. M. PIKULIK.

Mathematical Sciences

Institute of Mathematics: 220072 Minsk, Vul. Surganava 11; tel. 39-47-01; fax 39-31-92; f. 1959; attached to Nat. Acad. of Sciences of Belarus; Dir I. V. GAISHUN.

Physical Sciences

Institute of Applied Optics: 212793 Mogilev, Vul. Bialynitskaga-Biruli 11; tel. and fax (22) 226-46-49; f. 1970; attached to Nat. Acad. of Sciences of Belarus; Dir V. P. REDKO.

Institute of General and Inorganic Chemistry: 220072 Minsk, Vul. Surganava 9; tel. (17) 284-27-03; fax (17) 284-27-03; e-mail secretar@igic.bas-net.by; f. 1959; attached to Nat. Acad. of Sciences of Belarus; Dir N. P. KRUTKO.

Institute of Geological Sciences: 220141 Minsk, Vul. Kuprevicha 7; tel. (17) 264-53-15; fax (17) 263-63-98; e-mail geology@ns.igs.ac.by; f. 1971; attached to Nat. Acad. of Sciences of Belarus; Dir A. V. MATVEYEV; publ. *Lithosphere* (2 a year).

Institute of Molecular and Atomic Physics: 220072 Minsk, Pr. Skaryny 70; tel. (17) 284-16-15; fax (17) 284-00-30; e-mail imafbel@imaph.bas-net.by; f. 1992; attached to Nat. Acad. of Sciences of Belarus; Dir V. I. ARKHIPENKO; publ. *Journal of Applied Spectroscopy.*

Institute of Physical-Organic Chemistry: 220072 Minsk, Vul. Surganava 13; tel. 39-50-49; fax 63-96-97; f. 1929; attached to Nat. Acad. of Sciences of Belarus; Dir V. S. SOLDATOV.

Institute of Physics: 220072 Minsk, Pr. Skaryny 70; tel. (17) 284-17-55; fax (17) 284-08-79; e-mail ifanbel@ifanbel.bas-net.by; f. 1955; attached to Nat. Acad. of Sciences of Belarus; Dir P. A. APANASEVICH.

Institute of Solid State and Semiconductor Physics: 220072 Minsk, Vul. P. Brovki 17; tel. (17) 284-15-58; fax (17) 284-08-88; e-mail ifttpanb@iftt.basnet.minsk.by; f. 1963; attached to Nat. Acad. of Sciences of Belarus; library of 72,000 items; Dir N. M. OLEKHNOVICH.

RELIGION, SOCIOLOGY AND ANTHROPOLOGY

Institute of Arts, Ethnography and Folklore: 220072 Minsk, Vul. Surganava 1, Korpus 2; tel. 39-59-21; f. 1957; attached to Nat. Acad. of Sciences of Belarus; Dir M. P. PILIPENKO.

Institute of Sociology: 220072 Minsk, Vul. Surganava 1, Korpus 2; tel. 39-48-65; fax 39-59-28; f. 1990; attached to Nat. Acad. of Sciences of Belarus; Dir E. M. BABOSOV.

TECHNOLOGY

Belarus Institute of Systems Analysis and Information Support in the Scientific and Technical Field: 220004 Minsk, Pr. Masherova 7; tel. (17) 226-74-98; fax (17) 223-35-40; Dir Dr OLEG I. GALINOVSKY.

Belarus Roads Research Institute: Minsk, Vul. Surganava 28.

Bely, V. A., Metal–Polymer Research Institute: 246652 Gomel, Vul. Kirava 32A; tel. (23) 255-10-42; fax (23) 252-53-62; e-mail plesk@polymer.gomel.by; f. 1969; attached to Nat. Acad. of Sciences of Belarus; library of 19,000 vols; Dir Prof. YU. M. PLESKACHEVSKY; publs *Friction and Wear* (6 a year), *Materials, Technologies, Tools* (4 a year).

Chemical-Technological Centre: 220141 Minsk, Zhodinskaya vul. 16; tel. and fax 63-19-23; f. 1993; attached to Nat. Acad. of Sciences of Belarus; Dir A. A. ERDMAN.

Engineering Centre for the Physics and Technology of Thin Films and Coatings 'Plazmoteg': 220141 Minsk, Vul. Zhodinskaya 1, Korpus 3: tel. 63-93-41; fax 63-59-20; f. 1990; attached to Nat. Acad. of Sciences of Belarus; Dir E. I. TOCHITSKY.

Institute of Applied Physics: 220072 Minsk, Vul. Akademicheskaya 16; tel. (17) 284-17-94; fax (17) 284-10-81; e-mail ipfanb@bas24.basnet.minsk.by; f. 1963; attached to Nat. Acad. of Sciences of Belarus; Dir P. P. PROKHORENKO.

Institute of Electronics: 220090 Minsk, Logoiiskii trakt 22; tel. 65-61-51; fax 65-25-11; f. 1973; attached to Nat. Acad. of Sciences of Belarus; Dir V. A. PILIPOVICH.

Institute of Energetics Problems: 220109 Minsk, Sosny; tel. 46-74-75; fax 46-76-15; f. 1991; attached to Nat. Acad. of Sciences of Belarus; Dir A. A. MIHALEVICH.

Institute of Engineering Cybernetics: 220012 Minsk, Vul. Surganava 6; tel. (17) 268-51-71; fax (17) 231-84-03; e-mail cic@newman.basnet.minsk.by; f. 1965; attached to Nat. Acad. of Sciences of Belarus; Dir V. S. TANAYEV.

Institute of Heat and Mass Transfer: 220072 Minsk, Vul. P. Brovki 15; tel. 30-51-36; fax 32-25-13; f. 1952; attached to Nat. Acad. of Sciences of Belarus; Dir O. G. MARTYNENKO.

Institute of Machine Reliability: 220072 Minsk, Vul. Akademicheskaya 12; tel. (17) 284-27-53; fax (17) 284-24-09; e-mail berest@bas25.basnet.minsk.by; f. 1971; attached to Nat. Acad. of Sciences of Belarus; Dir O. V. BERESTNEV.

Institute of Metal Technology: 212030 Mogilev, Vul. Bialynitskaga-Biruli 11; tel. 26-46-43; f. 1992; attached to Nat. Acad. of Sciences of Belarus; Dir G. A. ANISOVICH.

Institute of Radiative Physical-Chemical Problems: 220109 Minsk, Sosny; tel. 46-77-50; fax 46-76-15; e-mail rpcpi@irpcp.belpak.minsk.by; f. 1991; attached to Nat. Acad. of Sciences of Belarus; Dir L. I. SALNIKOV.

Institute of Radioecological Problems: 220109 Minsk, Sosny; tel. 246-72-53; fax 246-70-17; e-mail irep@sosny.basnet.minsk.by; f. 1991; attached to Nat. Acad. of Sciences of Belarus; Dir G. A. SHAROVAROV.

Institute of Technical Acoustics: 210717 Vitebsk, Pr. Lyudnikova 13; tel. (21) 25-41-89; fax (21) 24-39-53; e-mail lpm@ita.belpak.vitebsk.by; f. 1995; attached to Nat. Acad. of

Sciences of Belarus; library of 43,000 vols; Dir V. V. KLUBOVICH.

Non-Traditional Energetics and Energy-Saving Scientific and Engineering Centre: 220109 Minsk, Sosny; f. 1992; tel. 46-76-61; f. 1992; attached to Nat. Acad. of Sciences of Belarus; Dir V. N. YERMASHKEVICH.

Physical-Engineering Institute: 220141 Minsk, Zhodinskaya vul. 4; tel. 64-60-10; fax 63-76-93; attached to Nat. Acad. of Sciences of Belarus; Dir S. A. ASTAPCHIK.

Republican Scientific and Engineering Centre for Environmental Remote Sensing 'Ecomir': 220012 Minsk, Vul. Surganava 2; tel. (17) 268-53-60; fax (17) 239-31-71; f. 1990; attached to Nat. Acad. of Sciences of Belarus; Dir A. A. KOVALEV.

Research and Design-Technological Institute of Casting Production of the Automobile Industry: Minsk, Partizansky pr. 95.

Research Institute for the Industry of Primary Processing of Fibres: Minsk, Il. Mayakovskogo 127.

Research Institute for the Production of Food Products from the Potato: Minsk, Oranskaya vul. 6.

Research Institute of Building Materials: Minsk, Minina 23.

Research Institute of Microbiological Products: 220600 Minsk, GSP-29, Vul. Varvasheni 17; tel. (17) 234-31-58; fax (17) 234-32-06; f. 1972; Dir V. V. KARPENKO.

Scientific Centre for Problems of Machine Mechanics: 220072 Minsk, Vul. Skaryny 12; tel. 39-54-23; f. 1993; attached to Nat. Acad. of Sciences of Belarus; Dir M. S. VYSOTSKY.

Libraries and Archives

Minsk

Belarus Agricultural Library: 220108 Minsk, Vul. Kazintsa 88; tel. (17) 277-37-17; fax (17) 277-15-61; e-mail belal@belal .minsk.by; f. 1960; attached to Acad. of Agricultural Sciences of the Republic of Belarus; library of 300,000 vols; Dir VLADIMIR A. GOLUBEV.

Belarus State University Library: 220080 Minsk, Pr. Skaryny 4; tel. 20-71-79; f. 1921; 2,040,000 vols; Dir I. V. OREKHOVSKAYA.

Central Scientific Archive of the Academy of Sciences of Belarus: 220072 Minsk, Pr. Skaryny 66; tel. 39-52-87; fax 39-31-63; Head M. I. BELOV.

National Library of Belarus: 220636 Minsk, Chyrvonaarmeiskaya vul. 9; tel. (17) 227-54-63; fax (17) 29-24-94; e-mail sol@ nacbibl.minsk.by; f. 1922; 7,400,000 vols; Dir GALINA M. ALEJNIK; publs *Novyja Knigi* (monthly), *New Literature on the Culture and Art of Belarus* (monthly), *Chernobyl: Bibliographical Index* (2 a year), *Social Sciences* (monthly).

Republic of Belarus Scientific and Technical Library: 220004 Minsk, Masherova 7; tel. (17) 223-31-34; fax (17) 223-31-38; 22,100,000 vols (excl. patents); Dir G. I. PEKHOTA.

Yakub Kolas Central Scientific Library of the Academy of Sciences of Belarus: 220072 Minsk, Vul. Surganava 15; tel. 39-44-28; fax 66-18-91; f. 1925; 3,108,000 vols; Dir S. N. EMELYANOVA.

Museums and Art Galleries

Belovezhskaya Pushcha

'Belovezhskaya Pushcha' Museum: Brestskaya oblast, Belovezhskaya Pushcha; game preserve museum showing the work being done to preserve the European Bison, and to acclimatize other animals in this part of Belarus; Dir V. P. ZHUKOV.

Grodno

Grodno State Historical Museum: Grodno, Zamkovaya vul. 22; tel. 44-94-31; f. 1920; library of 35,000 vols; Dir E. A. SOLOVYOVA.

Minsk

Great Patriotic War Museum: 220030 Minsk, Pr. Skaryny 25A; f. 1943; Soviet Army's and partisans' war history from 1941 to 1945; library of 14,000 vols.

National Art Museum of the Republic of Belarus: 220030 Minsk, Vul. Lenina 20; f. 1939; nat. and foreign art; Dir VLADIMIR I. PROKOPTSOV.

National Museum of the History and Culture of Belarus: 220050 Minsk, Vul. K. Marksa 12; tel. and fax (17) 227-36-65; f.1957; history and local natural history; library of 20,000 vols; Dir I. P. ZAGRISHEV.

Universities

BELARUS STATE UNIVERSITY

220050 Minsk, Skaryny prospekt 4
Telephone: (17) 226-59-40
Fax: (17) 220-88-21

Founded 1921
State control
Languages of instruction: Belarusan and Russian
Academic year: September to June

Rector: A. V. KOZULIN
Vice-Rectors: P. I. BRIGADIN, U. A. ASTAPENKO, V. I. KORZIUK, S. K. RAHMANOV

Registrar: V. V. TKACH
Librarian: I. V. OREHOVSKAYA

Number of teachers: 5,000
Number of students: 13,000

Publications: *Vestnik BGU*, *Belarusskiy Universitet*.

DEANS

Faculty of Applied Mathematics: P. A. MANDRIK
Faculty of Biology: V. V. LYSAK
Faculty of Chemistry: G. A. BRANITSKY
Faculty of Geography: R. A. JMOIDIAK
Faculty of History: O. A. YANOVSKY
Faculty of Journalism: V. P. VOROBIOV
Faculty of Law: V. N. GODUNOV
Faculty of Mechanics and Mathematics: N. I. YURCHUK
Faculty of Philology: L. A. MURINA
Faculty of Philosophy and Economics: A. I. ZELENKOV
Faculty of Physics: V. M. ANISCHIK
Faculty of Radiophysics and Electronics: S. G. MULIARCHIK
Faculty of International Relations: A. V. SHARAPO

ATTACHED INSTITUTES

Institute of Applied Physics: Dir A. F. CHERNIAVSKY.

Institute of Nuclear Problems: Dir V. G. BARYSHEVSKY.

Institute of Physical-Chemical Problems: Dir O. A. IVASHKEVICH

GOMEL F. SKARYNA STATE UNIVERSITY

246699 Gomel, Sovetskaya ul. 104
Telephone: (23) 256-31-13
Fax: (23) 257-81-11

Founded 1969
State control
Language of instruction: Russian
Academic year: September to July

Rector: Prof. Dr L. A. SHEMETKOV
First Pro-Rector: Prof. Dr M. V. SELKIN
Pro-Rectors: Prof. Dr D. G. LIN, Dr A. P. KARMAZIN, Dr N. N. VOINOV

Library of 950,000 vols
Number of teachers: 550
Number of students: 7,000

Publications: *Belarusan Language*, *Problems in Algebra*.

Faculties of history, law, philology, mathematics, physics, biology, geology and geography, economics, physical training.

GRODNO STATE UNIVERSITY

230023 Grodno, Ul. Ozheshko 22

Telephone: 7-01-73

Founded 1978

Number of students: 6,200

Incorporates the former Grodna Pedagogical Institute, with faculties of history and education; philology, law, physics, mathematics.

Polytechnics

Belarus State Polytechnic Academy: 220027 Minsk, Skaryny pr. 65; tel. (17) 32-40-55; f. 1920; faculties: mechanics and technology, motor vehicles and tractors, power engineering, architecture, construction, instrument-making, robots and robot systems, road construction, economics and management; 2,643 teachers; 15,000 students; library of 2,035,737 vols; Rector Prof. Dr MIKHAIL I. DEMCHUK; publs *Vodnoe Khoziaistvo i gidrotekhnicheskoe stroitelstvo, Mashinostroenie, Metallurgiia*, etc.

Brest Polytechnic Institute: 220017 Brest, Moskovskaya ul. 267; tel. (16) 42-33-93; f. 1966; faculties: civil engineering, water supply and soil conservation, electronic and mechanical engineering, economics; 300 teachers; 3,000 students; library of 320,000 vols; Rector Prof. V. G. FYODOROV.

Gomel Polytechnic Institute: 246746 Gomel, Pr. Oktyabrya 48; tel. (23) 248-16-00; fax (23) 247-91-65; f. 1981; faculties: electrical engineering and automation, engineering, mechanical and technological engineering, economics; 4,141 students; Rector Prof. ALBERT S. SHAGINJAN.

Polotsk State University: 211440 Novopolotsk, Vul. Blokhina 29; fax (2144) 5-63-40; e-mail admin4@psu.vitebsk.by; f.1968; specialities: modern European languages, history, law, economics and production management, finance and credits, accounting and auditing, civil and industrial engineering, chemical technology, pipeline engineering, mechanical engineering, heating and ventilation, water supply and public health engineering, radio engineering, computer systems and networks, geodesy; 500 teachers; 4,000 students; library of 600,000 vols; Rector Prof. ERNST M. BABENKO.

Other Higher Educational Institutes

Belarus Academy of Arts: 220012 Minsk, Skaryny pr. 81; tel. (17) 232-15-42; fax (17) 232-20-41; f. 1945; faculties: theatre, arts, design; library of 81,000 vols; Rector V.P. SHARANGOVICH.

Belarus Academy of Music: 220030 Minsk, Internatsionalnaya ul. 30; tel. 27-49-42; fax 27-00-13; f. 1932; courses: piano, orchestral and folk instruments, conducting, singing, composition, pedagogics, musicology; 193 teachers; 885 students; library of 220,000 vols; Rector M. A. KOZINETS.

Belarus Agricultural Academy: 213410 Mogilev raion, Gorkii; tel. and fax (2233) 2-28-62; e-mail bsacad@user.unibel.by; f. 1840; faculties of agronomy, agroecology, bookkeeping, animal husbandry, economics, mechanization, land management and hydromelioration; 800 teachers; 11,000 students; library of 1,000,000 vols; Rector Prof. A. R. TSYGANOV; publ. collection of research works (annually).

Belarus Agricultural and Industrial University: 220068 Minsk, Skaryny pr. 99; tel. 64-47-71; fax 64-47-71; depts: mechanization, electrification, maintenance and repair; library of 415,000 vols; Rector Prof. L. S. GERASIMOVICH.

Belarus State Technological University: 220630 Minsk, Vul. Sverdlova 13A; tel. (17) 26-14-32; fax (17) 26-02-78; e-mail root@bgtu.minsk.by; f. 1930; faculties: chemistry technology and engineering, forestry management, forestry engineering and wood technology, organic substances technology, engineering and economics; 500 teachers; 5,500 students; library of 960,000 vols; Rector I. M. ZHARSKY.

Belarus State University of Economics: 220672 Minsk, Partizanskii pr. 26; tel. 49-30-68; fax 49-51-06; depts: commerce, management, banking, finance, accounting (for agriculture and trade), accounting (for industry), statistics, international economic relations; 10,000 students; library of 174,000 vols; Rector Prof. R. M. KARSEKO.

Belarus State University of Informatics and Radioelectronics: 220027 Minsk, Vul. Petrusya Brovki 6; tel. (17) 232-04-51; fax (17) 231-09-14; f. 1964; depts: radio engineering and electronics, computer systems and networks, telecommunication systems, information technology and control systems, computer-aided design, economics and enterprise management; library of 1,000,000 vols; Rector V. M. ILJIN; publ. *Proceedings* (annually).

Belarus State University of Transport: 246653 Gomel, Ul. Kirova 34; tel. (23) 252-57-13; fax (23) 255-41-96; f. 1953; faculties: traffic management, mechanical engineering, electrical engineering, construction, industrial and civil engineering, humanities; library of 650,000 vols; Rector V. P. YAROSHEVICH; publ. *Vestnik BelGUTa: Nauka i Transport* (quarterly).

Belarus University of Culture: 220001 Minsk, Rabkorovskii per. 17; tel. (17) 222-24-10; fax (17) 222-24-09; f. 1975; faculties: cultural studies, performing arts, library information systems; 400 teachers; library of 500,000 vols; Rector JADWIGA DOMINIKOVNA GRIGOROVICH.

Gomel Co-operative Institute: 246029 Gomel, Pr. Oktyabrya 52a; tel. (23) 48-17-07; fax (23) 47-80-68; f. 1964; faculties: economics and management, accounting and finance, commerce; 180 teachers; 4,700 students; library of 300,000 vols; Rector TAMARA SYROYEOL.

Grodno Agricultural Institute: 230600 Grodno, Ul. Tereshkovoi 28; tel. (15) 247-01-68; fax (15) 247-14-97; e-mail niwa@selhoz.belpak.grodno.by; f. 1951; depts: agronomy, animal husbandry, plant protection, economics; 186 teachers; 3,077 students; library of 297,000 vols; Rector W. K. PESTIS.

Grodno State Medical Institute: 230015 Grodno, Vul. Gorkogo 80; tel. (15) 233-03-65; fax (15) 233-53-41; e-mail indek@ggmi.belpak.grodno.by; f. 1958; library of 401,000 vols; 355 teachers; Rector Prof. D. A. MASLAKOV.

Minsk State Linguistic University: 220662 Minsk, Ul. Zakharova 21; tel. (17) 13-35-44; fax (17) 36-75-04; f. 1948; foreign language teacher and interpreter training; 535 teachers; 4,150 students; library of 700,000 books and periodicals; Rector NATALYA P. BARANOVA; publs *Methodology of Teaching Foreign Languages* (1 a year), *Studies in Romanic and Germanic Languages* (1 a year).

Minsk State Medical Institute: 220116 Minsk, Pr. Dzerzhinskogo 83; tel. (17) 271-94-24; fax (17) 272-61-97; e-mail rector@msmi.minsk.by; f. 1921; medical training; WHO collaborating centre for research; library of 560,000 vols; Rector Prof. P. BESPALCHUK.

Mogilev Mechanical Engineering Institute: 212005 Mogilev, Vul. Lenina 70; tel. 23-61-00; fax 22-58-21; e-mail mva@mmi.belpak.mogilev.by; f. 1961; faculties: electrotechnical, construction, machine-building, vehicle engineering, economics; 320 teachers; 4,071 students; library of 1,001,000 vols; Rector A. N. MAXIMENKO (acting).

Mogilev Technological Institute: 212027 Mogilev, Pr. Shmidta 3; tel. (222) 44-03-63; fax (222) 44-32-29; f. 1973; faculties: chemical and food technology, mechanics, technology; library of 500,000 vols; 234 teachers; 2,800 students; Rector E. I. CHIZHIK.

Vitebsk Medical Institute: 210602 Vitebsk, Pr. Frunze 27; tel. (21) 36-95-34; f. 1934; training of physicians and pharmacists; research programmes on genetics of parasitism, transplantation, infections in surgery, cardiovascular diseases, rehabilitation and Chernobyl; library of 392,000 vols; Rector A. N. KOSINET; publ. scientific medical report reviews (every 6 months).

Vitebsk State Academy of Veterinary Medicine: 210602 Vitebsk, Vul. 1-ya Dovatora 7/11; tel. (21) 25-41-62; fax (21) 37-02-84; e-mail vaum@belpak.vitebsk.by; 149 teachers; 2,750 students; library of 310,000 vols; Rector A. I. YATUSEVICH

Vitebsk State Technological University: 210028 Vitebsk, Moskovskii pr. 72; tel. 5-50-26; fax 5-90-00; f. 1965; faculties: mechanics and technology, economics and technology, design and technology; 273 teachers; 3,527 students; library of 304,000 vols; Rector V. S. BASHMETOV.

BELGIUM

Learned Societies

GENERAL

Académie Royale des Sciences, des Lettres et des Beaux-Arts de Belgique (Royal Academy of Science, Letters and Fine Arts of Belgium): Palais des Académies, 1 rue Ducale, 1000 Brussels; tel. (2) 550-22-11; fax (2) 550-22-05; f. 1772; divisions of Science (Dir JACQUES LAMBINON), Letters and Moral and Political Sciences (Dir PIERRE LEBRUN), Fine Arts (Dir EUGÉNIE DE KEYSER); 90 mems, 60 corresp. mems, 150 assoc. mems; library of 420,000 vols; Pres. JACQUES LAMBINON; Permanent Sec. PHILIPPE ROBERTS-JONES; publs *Bulletin* (monthly), *Memoirs*, *Year Book*, *Nouvelle Biographie Nationale* (2 a year).

Académie Royale des Sciences d'Outre-Mer/Koninklijke Academie voor Overzeese Wetenschappen (Royal Academy of Overseas Sciences): 1 rue Defacqz b. 3, 1000 Brussels; tel. (2) 538-02-11; fax (2) 539-23-53; f. 1928; the promotion of scientific knowledge of overseas areas, especially those with particular development problems; Perm. Sec. Prof. Y. VERHASSELT; 66 hon. mems, 50 mems, 34 hon. assocs, 49 assocs, 46 hon. corresps, 50 corresps; publs *Bulletin des Séances / Mededelingen der Zittingen*, *Mémoires / Verhandelingen*, *Recueils d'études historiques / Historische bijdragen*, *Biographie belge d'Outre-Mer / Belgische Overzeese Biografie*, *Actes Symposiums Annuels / Acta Jaarlijkse Symposia*.

Koninklijke Academie voor Wetenschappen, Letteren en Schone Kunsten van België (Royal Academy of Sciences, Letters and Fine Arts of Belgium): Paleis der Academiën, Hertogsstraat 1, 1000 Brussels; tel. (2) 550-23-23; fax (2) 550-23-25; f. 1938; divisions of Science (Dir Y. BRUYNSERAEDE), Letters and Moral and Political Sciences (Dir T. PEETERS), Fine Arts (Dir A. LAPORTE); 90 mems, 30 corresp. mems, 19 hon. mems, 150 foreign assoc. mems; library of 50,000 vols; Pres. Y. BRUYNSERAEDE; Permanent Sec. N. SCHAMP; publs *Academiae Analecta*, *Memoirs*, *Year Book*, *Iuris Scripta Historica*, *Collectanea Maritima*, *Fontes Historiae Artis Neerlandicae*, *Iusti Lipsi Epistolae*, *Collectanea Biblica et Religiosa Antiqua*, *Collectanea Hellenistica*.

Attached institute:

Commission Royale d'Histoire/Koninklijke Commissie voor Geschiedenis (Royal Historical Commission): Palais des Académies, 1 rue Ducale, 1000 Brussels; f. 1834; research, analysis and publication of written sources concerning the history of Belgium; Pres. A. GOOSE; Sec.-Treas. W. PREVENIER; publs *Chroniques et Documents inédits*, *Bulletin* (quarterly).

AGRICULTURE, FISHERIES AND VETERINARY SCIENCE

Alliance Agricole Belge: 23/25 rue de la Science, 1040 Brussels; tel. (2) 230-72-95; fax (2) 230-42-51; f. 1930; protects professional interests; 20,000 mems; Pres. L. MATHY; Sec.-Gen. ET. DE PAUL DE BARCHI-FONTAINE; publ. *Alliance Agricole* (weekly).

ARCHITECTURE AND TOWN PLANNING

Association Royale des Demeures Historiques de Belgique (Royal Association for Historic Buildings): 24 rue Vergote, 1200 Brussels; tel. (2) 735-09-65; fax (2) 735-99-12; f. 1934; Pres. Prince ALEXANDRE DE MERODE; publ. *La Maison d'Hier et d'Aujourd'hui* (quarterly).

Fédération Royale des Sociétés d'Architectes de Belgique: 537 blvd de Smet de Naeyer, Brussels 2; Sec.-Gen. E. DRAPS.

Société Belge des Urbanistes et Architectes Modernistes: 366 ave Brugmann, Brussels 18; f. 1919; Sec. L. OBIZINSKI.

Société Centrale d'Architecture de Belgique: Hôtel Ravenstein, 3 rue Ravenstein, 1000 Brussels; tel. (2) 511-34-92; f. 1872; promotion of architecture and town planning; 180 mems; library of *c*. 1,500 vols; Pres. WENLI KAO; Sec. MAURICE HEISTERCAMP; publ. *Bulletin mensuel* (monthly).

BIBLIOGRAPHY, LIBRARY SCIENCE AND MUSEOLOGY

Association Professionnelle des Bibliothécaires et Documentalistes: 7 rue des Marronniers, 5651 Thy-le-Château; tel. (71) 61-43-35; fax (71) 61-16-34; e-mail library .ipg@mail.interpac.be; f. 1975; 300 mems; Pres. JEAN-CLAUDE TREFOIS; Sec. ANGÉLIQUE MATTIOLI; publ. *Bloc-Notes* (4 a year).

Commission Belge de Bibliographie et de Bibliologie: 4 blvd de l'Empereur, 1000 Brussels; tel. (80) 51-04-64; fax (80) 51-04-65; e-mail chriverb@skynet.be; f. 1951; a sub-committee of UNESCO, studies methods of standardization of bibliography; 68 mems; Pres. C. F. VERBEKE; publs *Bibliographia Belgica*, *Coll.* (1 a year).

Service Belge des Echanges Internationaux: 4 blvd de l'Empereur, 1000 Brussels; tel. (2) 519-53-82; fax (2) 519-54-04; f. 1889; information, documentation, exchange and transmission; Dir J. MÉLARD.

Vereeniging der Antwerpsche Bibliophielen (Antwerp Association of Bibliophiles): Museum Plantin-Moretus, Vrijdagmarkt 22, 2000 Antwerp; tel. (3) 232-24-55; fax (3) 226-25-16; f. 1877; to increase knowledge of books, particularly in Belgium and the Netherlands; 420 mems; Pres. Prof. Dr L. VOET; Sec. Prof. Dr G. PERSOONS; publ. *De Gulden Passer* (annual).

Vereniging van Religieus-Wetenschappelijke Bibliothecarissen (Association of Theological Librarians): Minderbroederstraat 5, 3800 St Truiden; f. 1965; Pres. E. D'HONDT; Sec. K. VAN DE CASTEELE; publ. *V. R. B.-Informatie* (quarterly).

Vlaamse Museumvereniging (Flemish Museums Association): Plaatsnijdusstraat 2, 2000 Antwerp; tel. (3) 238-78-09; e-mail mwienen@kmska.be; f. 1968 to defend the interests of museums and museum personnel; 320 mems; Pres. F. VAN NOTEN; publs *Museumkatern* (4 a year), *VMV Nieuwsbrief*.

ECONOMICS, LAW AND POLITICS

European Economic Association: Université Catholique de Louvain, 34 voie du Roman Pays, 1348 Louvain-la-Neuve; tel. (10) 47-20-12; fax (10) 47-40-21; e-mail eea@core .ucl.ac.be; f. 1986 to contribute to the development and application of economics as a science in Europe, to improve communication and exchange between teachers, researchers and students in economics in the different European countries, to develop and sponsor co-operation between teaching instns of university level and research instns in Europe; organizes an annual congress (with 800 participants) and specialized summer schools; 1,800 mems; Pres. JEAN-JACQUES LAFFONT; Sec. HENRY TULKENS; publ. *European Economic Review* (9 a year).

Institut Belge de Droit Comparé: 14 rue Bosquet, 1060 Brussels; f. 1907; Pres. M. VAUTHIER, Hon. Pres. of the Conseil d'Etat; Sec. PAUL LANDRIEN; 400 mems; publ. *La Revue de Droit International et de Droit Comparé* (quarterly).

Institut Belge des Sciences Administratives/Belgisch Instituut voor Bestuurswetenschappen (Belgian Institute of Administrative Sciences): Voorlopig Bewindstraat 15, 1000 Brussels; f. 1936; Pres. W. LAMBRECHTS; studies and research in public administration, also studies questions submitted by the International Institute of Administrative Sciences; 150 mems; publ. *Administration publique* (quarterly and monthly).

Politologisch Instituut (Institute of Political Science): Van Evenstraat 2B, 3000 Leuven; tel. (16) 32-32-54; fax (16) 32-30-88; f. 1958; 600 mems; Pres. HELMUT GAUS; publs *Res Publica* (French, English, Dutch, 4 a year), *Belgian Political Yearbook* (Dutch, French, English).

Société Royale d'Economie Politique de Belgique (Royal Belgian Society of Political Economy): c/o CIFOP, 1B ave Gén. Michel, 6000 Charleroi; tel. (71) 32-73-94; fax (71) 32-86-76; f. 1855; for popularization and progress in political economy; 400 mems; Pres. RENÉ LAMY; Sec.-Gen. ALBERT SCHLEIPER; publ. *Comptes rendus des travaux* (5 or 6 a year).

Union Royale Belge pour les Pays d'Outre-Mer (UROME): 22 rue de Stassart, 1050 Brussels; f. 1912; 28 mems; Chair. PIERRE ANDRÉ.

EDUCATION

Conférence des Recteurs des Universités Belges: 5 rue d'Egmont, 1000 Brussels; tel. (2) 504-92-11; telex 25498; fax (2) 514-00-06; f. 1973; to study the problems of higher education and scientific research.

Attached bodies:

Conseil des Recteurs: 5 rue d'Egmont, 1000 Brussels; tel. (2) 504-92-11; telex 25498; fax (2) 514-00-06; e-mail kokkelkoren@cref.be; f. 1990 by rectors of French-speaking Belgian universities to study the problems of higher education and scientific research.

Conseil Interuniversitaire de la Communauté Française: C/o 5 rue d'Egmont, 1000 Brussels; f. 1980 to study the problems of higher education and scientific research in the French-speaking Belgian universities; Perm. Sec. ETIENNE LOECKX.

Vlaamse Interuniversitaire Raad: C/o 5 rue d'Egmont, 1000 Brussels; tel. (2) 512-91-10; fax (2) 512-29-96; f. 1976; promotes interuniversity co-operation; gives advice and proposals to the Minister of Education and Minister of Science Policy on behalf of the Dutch speaking Belgian universities; Dir. JEF VAN DER PERRE.

FINE AND PERFORMING ARTS

Association Belge de Photographie et de Cinématographie: 57 rue Claessens, 1020 Brussels; f. 1874; 130 mems; Pres. J. PEETERS; publ. *Informations* (monthly).

Société Belge de Musicologie (Belgian Society of Musicology): 30 rue de la Régence, 1000 Brussels; e-mail vanhulst@ulb.ac.be; f. 1946; encourages the study and progress of the science and history of music; 300 mems; Pres. R. WANGERMEE; Sec. H. VANHULST; publ. *Revue belge de Musicologie* (French, English, German and Flemish) (annually).

Société Royale des Beaux-Arts: 25 ave Jef. Lambeaux, Brussels; f. 1893; organizes exhibitions of paintings, sculpture and engravings in Brussels; Pres. Baron ALBERT HOUTART; Sec. (vacant); publs exhibition catalogues.

HISTORY, GEOGRAPHY AND ARCHAEOLOGY

Académie Royale d'Archéologie de Belgique/Koninklijke Academie voor Oudheidkunde van België (Royal Academy of Archaeology of Belgium): Musées Royaux d'Art et d'Histoire, 10 Parc du Cinquantenaire, 1000 Brussels; f. 1842; 60 mems, 40 corresp. mems; Pres. CLAUDINE LEMAIRE; Sec. CLAIRE DUMORTIER; publ. *Revue Belge d'Archéologie et d'Histoire de l'Art/Belgisch Tijdschrift voor Oudheidkunde en Kunstgeschiedenis* (annually).

Belgische Vereniging voor Aardrijkskundige Studies/Société Belge d'Etudes Géographiques (Belgian Society for Geographical Studies): W. de Croylaan 42, 3001 Heverlee (Leuven); tel. (16) 32-24-27; f. 1931; Pres. Y. VERHASSELT; Sec. H. VAN DER HAEGEN; centralizes and co-ordinates geographical research in Belgium; 400 mems; publ. *Bulletin/Tijdschrift* (2 a year).

Fondation Egyptologique Reine Elisabeth: Parc du Cinquantenaire 10, 1000 Brussels; tel. (2) 741-73-64; f. 1923 to encourage Egyptological and papyrological studies; 650 mems; library of 30,000 vols; Pres. Comte D'ARSCHOT; Dirs J. BINGEN, H. DE MEULENAERE; publs *Chronique d'Egypte, Bibliotheca Aegyptiaca, Monumenta Aegyptiaca, Papyrologica Bruxellensia, Bibliographie Papyrologique sur fiches*.

Institut Archéologique du Luxembourg: 13 rue des Martyrs, 6700 Arlon; tel. and fax (63) 22-12-36; f. 1847; Luxembourgeois museum covers prehistoric period, Belgian-Roman period, Frankish period; 800 mems; library of 50,000 vols; Pres ROGER PETIT; publs *Annales*, *Bulletin* (quarterly).

Institut Archéologique Liégeois: Musée Curtius, 13 quai de Maastricht, 4000 Liège; f. 1850; studies of history and archaeology and related sciences in the District of Liège; 450 mems, 40 corresps; Pres. HUBERT FRÈRE; Sec. B. DUMONT; publ. *Bulletin* (annually).

Institut Géographique National/Nationaal Geografisch Instituut: Abbaye de la Cambre 13, 1000 Brussels; tel. (2) 629-82-11; fax (2) 629-82-12; f. 1831; land surveying and cartography; 300 mems; library of 15,000 vols; Dir.-Gen. J. DE SMET; publ. *Catalog* (annually).

Société archéologique de Namur: Hôtel de Croix, 3 rue Saintraint, 5000 Namur; tel. and fax (81) 22-43-62; f. 1845; museum and library; *c.* 400 mems; Pres. C. DOUXCHAMPS-LEFEVRE; Sec. J. TOUSSAINT; publ. *Annales*.

Société Belge d'Études Byzantines: 4 blvd de l'Empereur, 1000 Brussels; tel. (9) 372-90-08; f. 1956; 75 mems; Pres. E. VOORDECKERS; Sec. J. DECLERCK; publ. *Byzantion, Revue internationale des études byzantines* (2 a year).

Société Royale Belge de Géographie: Laboratoire de géographie humaine, Campus de la Plaine ULB, Blvd du Triomphe, CP 246, 1050 Brussels; tel. (2) 650-50-73; fax (2) 650-50-92; f. 1876; 250 mems; library of 7,500 vols; Pres. J. P. GRIMMEAU; Sec.-Gen. J.-M. DECROLY; publ. *Revue Belge de Géographie* (quarterly).

Société Royale d'Archéologie de Bruxelles: 185 ave Winston Churchill, 1180 Brussels; tel. (2) 344-46-20; f. 1887; sections for archaeology proper, and the history of art; other collections in Musées Royaux d'Art et d'Histoire (*qv*); library of 20,000 vols; 450 mems; Pres. P. P. BONENFANTI; Sec.-Gen. A. VANRIE; Librarian R. LAURENT; publs *Bulletins, Annales*.

Société Royale de Numismatique de Belgique: Bibliothèque Royale, Cabinet des Médailles, 4 blvd de l'Empereur, 1000 Brussels; f. 1841; 50 full mems, 15 hon. mems, 112 national corresp. mems, 100 foreign corresp. mems; Pres. HUBERT FRÈRE; Secs FRANÇOIS DE CALLATAY, JOHAN VAN HEESCH; publ. *Revue Belge de Numismatique et de Sigillographie*.

LANGUAGE AND LITERATURE

Académie Royale de Langue et de Littérature Françaises (Royal Academy of French Language and Literature): Palais des Académies, 1 rue Ducale, 1000 Brussels; f. 1920; sections of Literature, Philology; 30 Belgian mems, 10 foreign mems; Dir RAYMOND TROUSSON; Permanent Sec. ANDRÉ GOOSSE; publs *Bulletin, Annuaire, Mémoires*.

Association des Ecrivains Belges de Langue Française (Association of Belgian Writers in the French Language): Maison Camille Lemonnier-Maison des Ecrivains, 150 chaussée de Wavre, 1050 Brussels; tel. and fax (2) 512-29-68; f. 1902; 500 mems; library of 11,000 vols; awards prizes for essays, poetry and prose; Camille Lemonnier museum; Pres. FRANCE BASTIA; Vice-Pres MARIE NICOLAÏ, EMILE KESTEMAN; publs *Nos Lettres* (10 a year), anthologies, bibliographies, etc.

International PEN Club, French-speaking Branch: f. 1922; 370 mems; Pres. GEORGES SION; Gen. Sec. HUGUETTE DE BROQUEVILLE, 10 ave des Cerfs, 1950 Kraainem; tel. and fax (2) 731-48-47.

International PEN Club, PEN-Centre Belgium: Dutch-speaking branch; f. 1935; 140 mems; Pres. Gov. MONIKA VAN PAEMEL; Gen. Sec. PAUL KOECK, Wiesbeek 41, 9255 Buggenhout; tel. (52) 35-11-18; fax (52) 35-11-19; publ. *PEN-Tijdingen* (quarterly).

Koninklijke Academie voor Nederlandse Taal- en Letterkunde (Royal Academy of Dutch Language and Literature): Koningstraat 18, 9000 Ghent; f. 1886; 30 mems, 4 hon. mems, 25 hon. foreign mems; library of 40,000 vols; Permanent Sec. G. DE SCHUTTER; publs *Jaarboek, Verslagen en Mededelingen* (3 a year).

Société Belge des Auteurs, Compositeurs et Editeurs (SABAM): 75–77 rue d'Arlon, Brussels 1040; tel. (2) 286-82-11; fax (2) 231-18-00; f. 1922; collection and distribution of copyrights; 25,000 mems; Pres. JACQUES LEDUC; Man. Dirs PAUL LOUKA, ROGER VAN RANSBEEK; Gen. Man. PETER VAN ROMPAEY; publ. *Bulletin trimestriel*.

Société d'Etudes Latines de Bruxelles (Brussels Society for Latin Studies): 6 rue du Palais St Jacques, 7500 Tournai; tel. and fax (69) 21-47-13; f. 1937; 750 mems; Pres. C. DEROUX; publs *Latomus* (quarterly), *Collection Latomus*.

Société de Langue et de Littérature Wallonnes (Society for Walloon Language and Literature): Université de Liège, 7 place du XX Août, 4000 Liège; tel. (86) 34-44-32, f. 1856; 400 mems; library (Bibliothèque des Dialectes de Wallonie, 8 Place des Carmes, 4000 Liège; tel. (41) 23-19-60, ext. 139; library of 20,000 vols; Pres. EMILE GILLIARD; Sec. V. GEORGE; publs *Wallonnes* (quarterly), *Dialectes de Wallonie* (annually), *Littérature dialectale d'aujourd'hui* (annually), *Mémoire Wallonne* (annually).

MEDICINE

Académie Royale de Médecine de Belgique (Royal Academy of Medicine of Belgium): Palais des Académies, 1 rue Ducale, 1000 Brussels; f. 1841; divisions of Biological Sciences, of Human Medicine, of Surgery and Obstetrics, of Microbiology, Parasitology, Immunology, Public Health and Forensic Medicine, of Pharmacy, of Veterinary Medicine; 80 mems, 37 corresp. mems, 12 hon. mems, 127 hon. foreign mems, 76 foreign corresp. mems; Pres. Prof. G. LEJEUNE; Permanent Sec. Prof. A. DE SCOVILLE; publ. *Bulletin et Mémoires* (monthly).

Association Belge de Santé Publique (Belgian Public Health Association): c/o Scientific Institute of Public Health, 14 rue Juliette Weytsman, 1050 Brussels; f. 1938; undertakes and promotes research in and outside Belgium; arranges Belgian participation in international conferences; 160 mems; Pres. Prof. Dr H. VAN OYEN; publ. *Archives de Santé Publique*.

Association Royale des Sociétés Scientifiques Médicales Belges: 138A ave Circulaire, 1180 Brussels; tel. (2) 374-51-58; fax (2) 374-96-28; f. 1945; 4,000 mems; Pres. Dr G. STALPAERT; Sec.-Gen. Dr P. DOR.

Koninklijke Academie voor Geneeskunde van België (Royal Academy of Medicine of Belgium): Paleis der Academiën, Hertogsstraat 1, 1000 Brussels; f. 1938; divisions of Anatomy, Physiology, Medical Physics and Chemistry, of Human Medicine, of Surgery and Obstetrics, of Hygiene and Forensic Medicine, of Pharmacy, of Veterinary Medicine; 50 mems, 18 corresp. mems, 2 hon. mems, 17 hon. foreign mems, 78 foreign corresp. mems; library: see Libraries and Archives; Pres. Prof. Dr A. KINT; Permanent Sec. Prof. Dr M. BOGAERT; publs *Proceedings, Year Book*.

Société Belge de Médecine Tropicale/Belgische Vereniging voor Tropische Geneeskunde: Nationalestraat 155, Antwerp; f. 1920; 24 hon. mems (Belgian and foreign), 66 assoc. mems, 85 titular mems, 394 corresp. mems; Sec. Prof. Dr B. GRYSEELS; publ. *Tropical Medicine and International Health* (monthly).

Société Belge d'Ophtalmologie, section francophone (Belgian Society of Ophthalmology, French-speaking section): 126 ave P. Hymans, 1200 Brussels; f. 1896; Sec. Prof. J. M. LEMAGNE; publ. *Bulletin* (quarterly).

NATURAL SCIENCES

General

Association pour la Promotion des Publications Scientifiques (APPS): 26 ave de l'Amarante, 1020 Brussels; tel. (2) 268-29-33; fax (2) 268-25-14; f. 1981; 80 mems and 20 assoc. mems; Pres. Dr J. C. BAUDET; publ. *Ingénieur et Industrie* (monthly).

Société Royale des Sciences de Liège (Royal Society of Sciences): 12 Grande Traverse, Sart Tilman B 37, 4000 Liège 1; tel. (4) 366-93-71; fax (4) 366-95-47; e-mail n.naa@ulg.ac.be; f. 1835; advancement of mathematical, physical, chemical, mineral and biological sciences; 200 mems; Pres. M. J. AGHION; Sec.-Gen. M. J. GODEAUX; publ. *Bulletin* (every 2 months).

Société Scientifique de Bruxelles: 61 rue de Bruxelles, 5000 Namur; tel. (81) 724464; fax (81) 724502; f. 1875; 140 mems; Pres. J. DELHALLE; Sec. C. COURTOY; publs *Revue des Questions Scientifiques* (quarterly).

Biological Sciences

Koninklijke Maatschappij voor Dierkunde van Antwerpen (Royal Zoological Society of Antwerp): 26 Koningin Astridplein, 2018 Antwerp; tel. (3) 202-45-40; fax (3) 231-00-18; f. 1843; Zoological and Botanical Gardens, Aquarium, Nature Reserve, Laboratories; educational and cultural services and scientific research; 32,000 mems; library of 34,000 vols; Dir F. J. DAMAN; publ. *Zoo* (quarterly, Dutch).

Naturalistes Belges, Les: 29 rue Vautier, 1000 Brussels; f. 1918; 1,000 mems; library of 5,000 vols; zoology, botany, geology, nature conservancy, etc; Pres. ALAIN QUINTART; publ. *Les Naturalistes Belges* (quarterly).

Société Belge de Biochimie et de Biologie Moléculaire/Belgische Vereniging voor Biochemie en Moleculaire Biologie (SBBBM/BVBMB): 75 ave Hippocrate, UCL-ICP 74.39, 1200 Brussels; tel. (2) 764-74-39; fax (2) 762-68-53; e-mail opperdoes@trop.ud.ac.be; f. 1951; 1,050 mems; Sec. FRED R. OPPERDOES.

Société Belge de Biologie: Europawijk, 2440 Geel; 110 mems; Sec. A. LEONARD.

Société royale belge d'Entomologie: 29 rue Vautier, 1040 Brussels; tel. (2) 627-42-96; fax (2) 646-44-33; f. 1855; 250 mems; library of 23,000 vols; Sec. G. COULON; publs *Bulletin et Annales* (quarterly), *Mémoires* (irregular), *Catalogue des Coléoptères de Belgique* (irregular).

Société Royale de Botanique de Belgique: Chaussée de Wavre 1850, 1160 Brussels; f. 1862; 350 mems; Pres. V. DEMOULIN; Sec. J. HOMÈS; publs *Bulletin* (2 a year), *Mémoires*.

Société Royale Zoologique de Belgique/Koninklijke Belgische Vereniging voor Dierkunde: 50 ave F. D. Roosevelt, 1050 Brussels; tel. (2) 650-22-63; fax (2) 650-22-31; e-mail jdeligne@resulb.ulb.ac.be; f. 1863; 400 mems; library of *c.* 1,500 periodicals; Pres. E. SCHOCKAERT; Sec. F. DE VREE; publ. *Belgian Journal of Zoology* (2 a year).

Mathematical Sciences

Conseil Supérieur de Statistique: 44 rue de Louvain, 1000 Brussels; tel. (2) 548-62-11; fax (2) 548-62-62; f. 1841; 36 mems; Pres. M. DESPONTIN; Sec. G. DUPONT.

Société Mathématique de Belgique/Belgisch Wiskundig Genootschap: ULB Campus Plaine, CP 218/01, Bd du Triomphe, 1050 Brussels; e-mail leroy@ulb.ac.be; f. 1921; 500 mems; Sec. JULES LEROY; publ. *Bulletin* (5 a year).

Physical Sciences

Geologica Belgica: 13 rue Jenner, 1000 Brussels; tel. (2) 627-04-10; fax (2) 647-73-59; f. 1887; 650 mems; Pres. M. STREEL; Sec. M. DUSAR; publ. *Geologica Belgica* (2 a year).

Koninklijk Sterrenkundig Genootschap van Antwerpen/Société Royale d'Astronomie d'Anvers (Royal Astronomical Society of Antwerp): Boerhaavestraat 94 b/1, 2008 Antwerp; f. 1905; dissemination, teaching and aid for the promotion of astronomy; 230 mems; Pres. WILLY DE KORT; Sec. Baron R. DE TERWANGNE; publ. *Rapport annuel*.

Société Astronomique de Liège (Liège Society of Astronomy): c/o Institut d'Astrophysique, 5 ave de Cointe, 4000 Liège; tel. (4) 253-35-90; telex 41264; fax (4) 252-74-74; f. 1938; brings together amateurs of astronomy, popularizes the science; 800 mems; library of 500 vols; Pres. A. LAUSBERG; Sec. L. PAUQUAY; publ. *Le Ciel* (monthly).

Société Géologique de Belgique (Belgian Geological Society): Université de Liège, 7 place du Vingt-Août, 4000 Liège; tel. (4) 366-53-95; fax (4) 366-56-36; e-mail a.anceau@ulg.ac.be; f. 1874; 458 mems; Pres. F. BOULEVAIN; Sec.-Gen. M. FAIRON-DEMARET; publ. *Annales* (2 a year).

Société Royale Belge d'Astronomie, de Météorologie et de Physique du Globe: 3 ave Circulaire, 1180 Brussels; tel. (2) 373-02-53; fax (2) 374-98-22; f. 1895; 800 mems; Sec. Gen. R. DEJAIFFE; publ. *Ciel et Terre* (every 2 months).

Société Royale de Chimie: ULB Campus Plaine, CP206-4, Blvd du Triomphe, 1050 Brussels; tel. (2) 650-52-08; fax (2) 650-51-84; e-mail src@ulb.ac.be; f. 1887; 1,000 mems; library at 48 ave Depage, Brussels; Pres. Prof. J. L. BREDAS; Gen. Sec. Prof. R. FUKS; publ. *Chimie Nouvelle* (quarterly).

PHILOSOPHY AND PSYCHOLOGY

Société Philosophique de Louvain: c/o Institut Supérieur de Philosophie, Collège Thomas More, 1348 Louvain-la-Neuve; tel. (10) 47-46-13; f. 1888; 225 mems; Pres. G. FLORIVAL; Sec. J. ETIENNE.

RELIGION, SOCIOLOGY AND ANTHROPOLOGY

Centre pour l'Etude des Problèmes du Monde Musulman Contemporain (Study Centre for Problems of the Contemporary Muslim World): 44 ave Jeanne, 1050 Brussels; tel. (2) 642-33-59; f. 1958; Dir Mme A. DESTREE; publs *Le Monde Musulman Contemporain—Initiations*.

Institut Belge des Hautes Etudes Chinoises: c/o Musées Royaux d'Art et d'Histoire, 10 parc du Cinquantenaire, 1000 Brussels; tel. (2) 741-73-77; fax (2) 733-77-35; f. 1929; Sinology and Buddhism; lectures, courses on Chinese art, history, painting and calligraphy; library of *c.* 60,000 vols; *c.* 300 mems; Pres. PIERRE WILLOCX; Scientific Dir JEAN-MARIE SIMONET; publ. *Mélanges Chinois et Bouddhiques* (every 2 years).

Ruusbroecgenootschap: Prinsstraat 13, 2000 Antwerp; tel. (3) 220-43-67; fax (3) 220-44-20; f. 1925; a society of mainly Flemish Jesuits engaged in spiritual studies of the Low Countries; since 1973 incorporated as Centrum voor Spiritualiteit of Universitaire Faculteiten Sint-Ignatius Antwerpen (*qv*); library of 115,000 vols (incl. *c.* 30,000 old and rare books), *c.* 500 MSS, *c.* 35,000 devotional prints; Dir G. DE BAERE; publs *Ons Geestelijk Erf* (quarterly), *Studiën en Tekstuitgaven van Ons Geestelijk Erf* (series).

Société des Bollandistes: 24 blvd St Michel, 1040 Brussels; fax (2) 739-33-32; e-mail socboll@kbr.be; f. at Antwerp in 1630, named after Bollandus, who died 1665; hagiography; its members are Belgian Jesuits engaged in the publication of the *Acta Sanctorum*, *Analecta Bollandiana* (2 a year) and *Subsidia Hagiographica* (a critical history of the Saints, with original sources or documents); library of 500,000 vols; Senior J. VAN DER STRAETEN.

Société Royale Belge d'Anthropologie et de Préhistoire: 29 rue Vautier, 1000 Brussels; tel. (2) 627-43-85; fax (2) 627-41-13; e-mail annehauzeur@kbinirsub.be; f. 1882; Pres. R. ORBAN; Sec.-Gen. A. HAUZEUR; 130 mems; publs *Anthropologie et Préhistoire* (annually), *Hominid Remains* (series).

TECHNOLOGY

Institut Belge de Normalisation (IBN) (Belgian Standards Institute): 29 ave de la Brabançonne, 1000 Brussels; tel. (2) 738-01-11; fax (2) 733-42-64; f. 1946; Belgian member of the International Organization for Standardization; 962 mems; Pres. F. SONCK; Dir-Gen. P. CROON; publs *Normes Belges, Revue IBN* (monthly), *Rapport annuel*.

Koninklijke Vlaamse Ingenieursvereniging (Royal Flemish Association of Engineers): KVIV Ingenieurshuis, Desguinlei 214, 2018 Antwerp; tel. (3) 216-09-96; fax (3) 216-06-89; f. 1928; 11,000 mems; Pres. Prof. Dr Ir W. VERSTRAETE; Sec.-Gen. Ir L. MONSEREZ; publs *Het Ingenieursblad* (monthly), *KVIV-Direkt* (fortnightly), *Journal A* (quarterly).

Société Belge de Photogrammétrie, de Télédétection et de Cartographie (Belgian Society for Photogrammetry, Remote Sensing and Cartography): C.A.E.-Tour Finances (Bte 38), 50 blvd du Jardin Botanique, 1010 Brussels; f. 1931; 163 mems; Pres. R. THONNARD; Sec. J. VAN HEMELRIJCK; publ. *Bulletin* (quarterly).

Société Royale Belge des Electriciens: C/o VUB-TW-ETEC, 2 Blvd de la Plaine, 1050 Brussels; tel. (2) 629-28-19; fax (2) 629-36-20; e-mail srbe-kbve@etec.2.uub.ac.be; f. 1884; 1,600 mems; Pres. X. VAN MERRIS; publ. *Revue E Tijdschrift* (quarterly).

Société Royale Belge des Ingénieurs et des Industriels: 3 rue Ravenstein, 1000 Brussels; tel. (2) 511-58-56; fax (2) 514-57-95; f. 1885; 2,000 mems; Pres. PIERRE KLEES; publ. *Bulletin Mensuel*.

Research Institutes

AGRICULTURE, FISHERIES AND VETERINARY SCIENCE

Centre d'Economie Agricole: WTC-3, 30 ave Simon Bolivar, 1000 Brussels; f. 1960; study and research in agricultural economics and rural sociology; Dir A. MOTTOULLE.

Centre de Recherches Agronomiques de Gembloux: 22 ave de la Faculté d'Agronomie, 5030 Gembloux; tel. (81) 61-19-55; fax (81) 61-49-41; f. 1872; agricultural research at 12 autonomous research units; Dir R. BISTON; publs *Rapport d'activité, Notes techniques*.

Centrum voor Onderzoek in Diergeneeskunde en Agrochemie/Centre d'Etude et de Recherches Vétérinaires et Agrochimiques (Veterinary and Agrochemical Research Centre): Groeselenberg 99, Ukkel, 1180 Brussels; tel. (2) 375-44-55; fax (2) 375-09-79; f. 1997; research sites in Brussels and Tervuren; Pres. and Dir Dr J. E. PEETERS; publ. *Activiteitsverlag / Rapport d'activite* (1 a year).

ECONOMICS, LAW AND POLITICS

Institut Royal des Relations Internationales: 65 rue Belliard, BR 4, 1040 Brussels; f. 1947; research in international relations, international economics, international politics and international law; specialized library containing 15,000 vols and 600 periodicals; archives; lectures and conferences are held; Exec. Dir M.-TH. BOCKSTAEL; publs *Studia Diplomatica* (every 2 months), *Internationale Spectator* (monthly).

FINE AND PERFORMING ARTS

Centre international d'étude de la peinture médiévale des bassins de l'Escaut et de la Meuse/Internationaal Studiecentrum voor de Middeleeuwse Schilderkunst in het Schelde- en in het Maasbekken (International Centre for the Study of Medieval Painting in the Schelde and Meuse Valleys): 1 Parc du Cinquantenaire, 1000 Brussels; tel. (2) 739-68-66; fax (2) 732-01-05; e-mail cyriel@kikirpa.be; f. 1950; research into 15th-century Flemish painting; 15 mems; library of 6,400 vols; Pres. H. Pauwels; Dir L. Masschelein; Scientific Secs C. Stroo, H. Mund; publs *Corpus de la Peinture des Pays-Bas Méridionaux et de la Principauté de Liège au 15e Siècle, Répertoire, Contributions*.

MEDICINE

Born-Bunge Research Foundation: Universiteitsplein 1, 2610 Wilrijk-Antwerp; tel. (3) 828-58-25; fax (3) 820-25-41; e-mail jjmneuro@uia.ac.be; f. 1963; research in neurological sciences and cardiology; Dir Dr J. J. Martin.

Fondation Médicale Reine Elisabeth: 3 ave J. J. Crocq, 1020 Brussels; tel. and fax (2) 478-35-56; supports medical research in the field of neurobiology through several Belgian university laboratories; Dir Prof. Th. de Barsy.

Institut Neurologique Belge: 152 rue de Linthout, Brussels 4; f. 1924; Pres. Comte Edouard d'Oultremont; publs *Acta Neurologica* and *Psychiatrica Belgica*.

Institut Pasteur: 642 rue Engeland, 1180 Brussels; tel. (2) 373-31-11; fax (2) 373-31-74; f. 1900; scientific research, analyses; Dir Jean Content; numerous publs.

NATURAL SCIENCES

General

Institut Royal des Sciences Naturelles de Belgique/Koninklijk Belgisch Instituut voor Natuurwetenschappen: 29 rue Vautier, 1000 Brussels; f. 1846; library: see Libraries; departments for vertebrates, invertebrates, palaeontology and biology, and general scientific services; Dir Dr D. Cahen; publs *Bulletins, Le Gerfaut/de Giervalk, Faune de Belgique, Documents de travail, Livrets-guide*.

Biological Sciences

Jardin Botanique National de Belgique/Nationale Plantentuin van België: Domein van Bouchout, 1860 Meise; tel. (2) 269-39-05; fax (2) 270-15-67; e-mail j.rammeloo@br.fgov.be; f. 1870; botanical taxonomy and geography, especially of African and European plants, including Cryptogams; gene bank of Phaseolinae; herbarium with over 2,000,000 specimens; library of *c.* 200,000 vols; Dir J. Rammeloo; publs *Bulletin* (2 a year), *Flore illustrée des champignons d'Afrique Centrale* (annually), *Dumortiera* (3 a year), *Flore d'Afrique Centrale, Distributiones plantarum africanarum, Icones mycologicae, Opera Botanica Belgica* (all irregularly).

Mathematical Sciences

Institut National de Statistique: 44 rue de Louvain, 1000 Brussels; tel. (2) 548-62-11; fax (2) 548-63-67; f. 1831; Dir-Gen. Claude Cheruy; publs *Bulletin de Statistique* (monthly), *Annuaire statistique de la Belgique*, etc.

Physical Sciences

Centre d'Etude de l'Energie Nucléaire/Studiecentrum voor Kernenergie: Boeretang 200, 2400 Mol; tel. (14) 33-21-11; fax (14) 31-50-21; f. 1952; nuclear R & D, reactor safety, fuel and materials irradiation, characterization and geological disposal of waste, decontamination and dismantling of facilities, radioprotection, nuclear services incl. irradiation in BR2 and post-irradiation examination; library of 32,000 vols, 500,000 reports; Dir-Gen. Paul Govaerts.

Institut d'Aéronomie Spatiale de Belgique: Ave Circulaire 3, 1180 Brussels; tel. (2) 374-27-28; fax (2) 374-84-23; f. 1964 to undertake research in aeronomy (physics and chemistry of atmosphere) from information gained from space vehicles; library of 3,000 vols and 150 periodicals; Dir Prof. Paul C. Simon; Sec. Marc Delancker; publs *Aeronomica Acta A* (research), *Aeronomica Acta F* (information).

Institut Royal Météorologique de Belgique: Ave Circulaire 3, 1180 Brussels; tel. (2) 373-05-02; telex 21315; fax (2) 375-12-59; reorganized 1913; departments for Climatology, Aerometry, Aerology, Applied Meteorology, Geophysics and Numerical Calculus; Dir Dr H. Malcorps; publs *Bulletin Quotidien du temps* (daily), *Observations climatologiques, Observations synoptiques, Observations géophysiques, Observations ionosphériques* (monthly), *Observations d'ozone* (quarterly), *Climatologie, Rayonnement solaire, Magnétisme terrestre, Marées terrestres à Dourbes, Hydrologie* (annually), *Publications de l'IRM* (series A and B) (occasional).

Observatoire Royal de Belgique/Koninklijke Sterrenwacht van Belgie: Ave Circulaire 3, 1180 Brussels; tel. (2) 373-02-11; telex 21565; fax (2) 374-98-22; f. 1826; fundamental astronomy, satellite positioning, time service, seismology, gravimetry, earth tides, celestial mechanics, astrometry, astrophysics, solar physics, radioastronomy; Dir Prof. P. Pâquet; publs *Annuaire, Bulletin Astronomique, Communications*.

PHILOSOPHY AND PSYCHOLOGY

Centre National de Recherches de Logique: 1 chemin d'Aristote, 1348 Louvain la Neuve; f. 1951; Pres. D. Batens; Sec.-Gen. J. de Greef; publ. *Logique et Analyse* (quarterly).

RELIGION, SOCIOLOGY AND ANTHROPOLOGY

Centre d'Etudes du Judaisme Contemporain de l'Institut de Sociologie de l'ULB (Centre for the study of Contemporary Judaism of the Sociology Institute of the ULB): 17 ave F.-D. Roosevelt, 1050 Brussels; tel. (2) 650-33-48; f. 1959; studies, publications and documentation on contemporary Jewry; library of 7,000 vols and 160 periodicals; Dir Willy Bok.

Centre d'Etudes et de Recherches Arabes: Université de l'Etat à Mons, 24 ave Champ de Mars, 7000 Mons; tel. (65) 37-36-15; telex 57764; fax (65) 84-06-31; e-mail h.safar@skynet.be; f. 1978; includes the dept of Arabic of the Ecole d'Interprètes Internationaux; teaching and research in Arabic language, culture, curriculum development in underdeveloped countries, immigration, international relations, transfer of technology and Euro-Arab dialogue; library of 2,000 vols; Dir Prof. H. Safar.

Centrum voor Interdisciplinair Antropologisch Onderzoek (Centre for Interdisciplinary Anthropological Research): Maria-Christinastraat 8, 3070 Kortenberg; f. 1967; Dir Kamel de Vos.

TECHNOLOGY

Institut Meurice (IIF–IMC–ISI): 1 ave Emile Gryzon, Anderlecht, 1070 Brussels; tel. (2) 526-73-00; fax (2) 526-73-01; f. 1892; research and training centre for industrial engineers in chemistry and biochemistry; Dir Dr Ir Patrick Dysseler.

Institut Scientifique de Service Public (ISSeP): Rue du Chéra 200, 4000 Liège; tel. (4) 252-71-50; fax (4) 252-46-65; f. 1990; applied research, development and demonstration relating to natural resources, the environment, technical and industrial security, solid fuels, radiocommunications in confined atmosphere; library of 11,000 vols; Gen. Man. M. de Waele.

Von Karman Institute for Fluid Dynamics: Chaussée de Waterloo 72, 1640 Rhode-St-Genese; tel. (2) 359-96-11; fax (2) 359-96-00; e-mail secretariat@vki.ac.be; f. 1956; multinational postgraduate teaching and research in aerodynamics, supported by the countries of NATO; depts of aeronautics/aerospace, turbomachinery, environmental fluid dynamics; library of 2,000 vols, 55,000 reports; Dir John F. Wendt; publs *Technical Notes, Lecture Series Notes*, etc.

Libraries and Archives

Antwerp

Archief en Museum voor het Vlaamse Cultuurleven (Archives and Museum of Flemish Culture): Minderbroedersstraat 22, 2000 Antwerp; tel. (3) 232-55-80; fax (3) 231-93-10; f. 1933; archives of Flemish literature, arts and politics; files and manuscripts can be seen on application; 55,000 vols, 50,000 files, 1,000,000 letters and MSS, 30,000 posters, 120,000 photographs; Dir R. Rennenberg.

Bibliotheek der Universitaire Faculteiten Sint-Ignatius: Prinsstraat 9, 2000 Antwerp; tel. (3) 220-49-96; fax (3) 220-44-37; e-mail ufsia@lib.ua.ac.be; f. 1852; 770,000 vols; Dir Th. Boeckx; Chief Librarian L. Simons.

Bibliotheek-Universitair Centrum: Middelheimlaan 1, 2020 Antwerp; tel. (3) 218-07-94; fax (3) 218-06-52; f. 1965; 175,000 vols; (Third World Development: Middelheimlaan 1, 2020 Antwerp; Science and Medicine: Groenenborgerlaan 171, 2020 Antwerp); Chief Librarian Dr B. Van Styvendaele.

Bibliotheek Universitaire Instelling Antwerpen: Universiteitsplein 1, 2610 Antwerp; tel. (3) 820-21-41; fax (3) 820-21-59; f. 1972; 400,000 vols; Dir J. Van Borm.

Rijksarchief te Antwerpen (Antwerp State Archives): Door Verstraetepl. 5, 2018 Antwerp; tel. and fax (3) 236-73-00; e-mail rijksarchief.antwerpen@skynet.be; documents from 12th to 20th century; Archivists H. Coppens, E. Houtman.

Stadsarchief (City Archives): Venusstraat 11, 2000 Antwerp; tel. (3) 206-94-11; fax (3) 206-94-10; f. 13th century; documents concerning the administration of Antwerp; history, genealogy, heraldry, cartography, sigillography; specialized library of 6,000 vols, 243 periodicals; Archivist Inge Schoups.

Stadsbibliotheek: Hendrik Conscienceplein 4, 2000 Antwerp; tel. (3) 206-87-10; fax (3) 206-87-75; e-mail sba@lib.ua.ac.be; f. 1481, reorganized 1834; Flemish and Dutch literature, history, humanities, local press; open to the public; 900,000 vols; Dir R. Rennenberg.

Arlon

Archives de l'Etat à Arlon: Parc des Expositions, 6700 Arlon; tel. and fax (63) 22-06-13; f. 1849; documents concerning the Province of Luxembourg from 12th to 20th century; 18 km shelving; library of 100,000 vols; Archivist P. Hannick; publs guides, inventories, exhibition catalogues, minutes of symposia.

Bruges

Rijksarchief te Brugge: Academiestraat 14, 8000, Bruges; tel. and fax (50) 337288; e-mail rijksarchief.brugge@skynet.be; documents on Western Flanders from 12th to 20th century; Archivist M. Nuyttens.

Brussels

Archives de la Ville de Bruxelles: 65 rue des Tanneurs, 1000 Brussels; tel. (2) 279-53-21; fax (2) 279-53-29; historical archives of the city of Brussels; reference library of 20,000 vols, 100 periodicals; Archivist Dr ARLETTE SMOLAR-MEYNART.

Archives du Centre public d'aide sociale de Bruxelles: 298A rue Haute, Brussels; archives concerning ancient hospices and places of refuge, 12th century to 1803, 1803–1925, 1925–1977; approx. 20,000 archives; 15,000 vols; Archivist Mme C. DICKSTEIN-BERNARD.

Archives Générales du Royaume: 2–4 rue de Ruysbroeck, 1000 Brussels; tel. (2) 513-76-80; fax (2) 513-76-81; f. 1815; 50 kms documents concerning the Low Countries, Belgium and Brabant from 11th–20th centuries; execution of legislation on Public Records; library of 60,000 vols; Gen. Archivist E. PERSOONS.

Includes:

Centre de recherches et d'études historiques de la seconde guerre mondiale: Résidence Palace, 155/B2 rue de la Loi, 1040 Brussels; tel. (2) 287-48-11; fax (2) 287-47-10; Dir J. GOTOVITCH.

Bibliothèque artistique, Académie Royale des Beaux-Arts: 144 rue du Midi, 1000 Brussels; tel. (2) 511-35-16; fax (2) 511-32-90; f. 1886; 16,000 vols, 400 rare books; Librarian MONIQUE DELEU.

Bibliothèque des Facultés Universitaires Saint-Louis: 43 blvd du Jardin Botanique, 1000 Brussels; tel. (2) 211-79-09; fax (2) 211-79-97; f. 1858; 210,000 vols; Librarians M.-C. MINGUET, N. PETIT.

Bibliothèque Centrale du Ministère de l'Education, de la Recherche et de la Formation (Communauté Française): 43 rue de Stassart, 1050 Brussels; f. 1879; contains vols on administration and law, all branches of science and pedagogy, educational books; 400,000 vols, 900 periodicals; open only to teachers and mems of French Dept; Dir J.-M. ANDRIN.

Bibliothèque d'Art Fondation Isabelle Errera, Ecole Nationale Supérieure des Arts Visuels: 21 abbaye de la Cambre, 1000 Brussels; f. 1926; 60,000 vols; Librarian RÉGINE CARPENTIER.

Bibliothèque de l'Institut Royal des Sciences Naturelles de Belgique: 29 rue Vautier, 1040 Brussels; f. 1846; 141,000 vols, 2,500 periodicals.

Bibliothèque, Documentation, Publications du Ministère de l'Emploi et du Travail: 51 rue Belliard, 1040 Brussels; tel. (2) 233-44-44; fax (2) 233-44-55; f. 1896 (since the foundation of the Board of Labour); specialized library of 80,000 vols, 500 periodicals on social sciences and labour relations; Dir J.-C. CASSIMONS.

Bibliothèque du Parlement: rue de la Loi 13, 1000 Brussels; f. 1831; 500,000 vols, 1,200 periodicals, collections on microfilms; Librarians ROLAND VAN NIEUWENBORGH, BERNARD VANSTEELANDT.

Bibliothèque Fonds Quetelet (Library of the Ministry of Economic Affairs): 6 rue de l'Industrie, 1000 Brussels; tel. (2) 506-60-54; fax (2) 502-84-25; f. 1841; 1,000,000 vols on statistics, economic and social sciences, 8,000 periodicals (3,000 current); open to the public; reference and computer-assisted bibliographic services; Chief Librarian E. VAN WESEMAEL; publs *Accroissements de la Bibliothèque* (monthly, in Dutch and French), selected bibliographies (monthly).

Bibliothèque Royale Albert 1er/Koninklijke Bibliotheek Albert I (The Belgian National Library): 4 blvd de l'Empereur, 1000 Brussels; tel. (2) 519-53-11; telex 21157; fax (2) 519-55-33; f. 1837; national depository library; 5,000,000 vols, 18,000 periodicals, 35,000 MSS, 35,000 rare printed books, 700,000 prints, 140,000 maps; 205,000 coins and medals; 10,000 records; Dir PIERRE COCKSHAW; publs *Bibliographie de Belgique/ Belgische Bibliografie* (monthly), *Bulletin de la Bibliothèque Royale* (quarterly), catalogues of collections and exhibitions, etc.

Bibliothèques de l'Université Libre de Bruxelles: 50 ave Franklin D. Roosevelt, 1050 Brussels; tel. (2) 650-23-78; fax (2) 650-41-86; f. 1846; 1,800,000 vols including periodicals and theses; Librarian JEAN-PIERRE DEVROEY.

Library of the European Commission: JECL 1/33, 200 rue de la Loi, 1049 Brussels; tel. (2) 295-29-76; telex 21877; fax (2) 296-11-49; e-mail biblio-library@dg10.cec.be; f. 1958; a central library linking a system of specialized library/documentation units; forms part of the EC's Directorate-General X (Information, Communication, Culture, Audiovisual); *c.* 400,000 vols and periodicals on European integration and European Union policies; also br. library in the Jean Monnet bldg in Luxembourg (tel. 4301-32808); Head NEVILLE KEERY.

NATO Library. Office of Information and Press: Office Nb 123, 1110 Brussels; tel. (2) 728-50-22; telex 23867; fax (2) 728-42-49; f. 1950; serves the int. staff, the Int. Military Staff and delegations; 40,000 vols, 700 periodicals; subject areas: politics, arms production, disarmament, economics, law, military science, strategy, int. orgs, applied science, technology, biography, current affairs; Dir ELIANE BAETENS; publs *Acquisitions List* (monthly), *Magazine Selection* (26 a year).

Service Fédéral d'Information/Federale Voorlichtingsdienst (Federal Information Service): Résidence Palace, 11e étage, 155 rue de la Loi, 1040 Brussels; tel. (2) 287-41-11; fax (2) 287-41-00; Information Centre: 54 blvd du Régent, 1000 Brussels; tel. (2) 514-08-00; fax (2) 512-51-25; e-mail fvdsfi@belgium.fgov.be; f. 1962; aims to make Belgium better known abroad with the help of information technology; collects documentation about Belgium's heritage and activities; provides information about Belgium, information and public relations programmes, audiovisual information, organizes exhibitions, etc.; Pres. JEAN-PIERRE HUBENS; Gen. Man. MIEKE VAN DEN BERGHE; publs *Faits / Feiten, Répertoire de l'Information / Repertorium van de Voorlichting*, etc.

SIST-DWTI (Scientific and Technical Information Service): 4 blvd de l'Empereur, 1000 Brussels; tel. (2) 519-56-40; fax (2) 519-56-45; e-mail stis@kbr.be; f. 1964; provides information in the fields of medicine, science and technology; focal point for library, documentation and information networks (national and international); Head of Unit Dr JEAN MOULIN.

Vrije Universiteit Brussel, Universiteitsbibliotheek: Pleinlaan 2, 1050 Brussels; tel. (2) 629-26-09; fax (2) 629-26-93; e-mail snamenw@vnet.3vub.ac.be; f. 1972; 420,000 vols; Librarian M. NAMENWIRTH.

Gembloux

Bibliothèque de la Faculté Universitaire des Sciences Agronomiques: 2 passage des Déportés, 5030 Gembloux; tel. (81) 62-21-02; fax (81) 61-45-44; e-mail pochet.b@fsagx.ac.be; f. 1860; 100,000 vols; Chief Librarian BERNARD POCHET; publs *Biotechnologies, Agronomie, Société et Environnement (BASE)* (quarterly).

Ghent

Bibliotheek van de Universiteit Gent: Rozier 9, 9000 Ghent; tel. (9) 264-38-51; fax (9) 264-38-52; e-mail guido.vanhooydonk@rug.ac.be; f. 1797/1817; 3,000,000 vols, 5,060 MSS; open to the public; Chief Librarian Prof. Dr G. VAN HOOYDONK; publs *Mededelingen van de Centrale Bibliotheek, Schatten van de Universiteitsbibliotheek, Bijdragen tot de Bibliotheekwetenschap, Uitgaven van de Centrale Bibliotheek.*

Leeszaal Faculteit Landbouwkundige en Toegepaste Biologische Wetenschappen (Reading room, Faculty of Agricultural and Applied Biological Sciences): Universiteit, Coupure links 653, 9000 Ghent; 65,000 vols.

Rijksarchief te Gent: Geraard de Duivelstraat 1, 9000 Ghent; tel. (9) 225-13-38; e-mail rijksarchief.gent@skynet.be; 7 km of documents mainly on Flanders from 9th to 20th centuries; Archivist WILLY BUNTINX.

Liège

Archives de l'Etat à Liège: 79 rue du Chera, 4000 Liège; tel. (41) 252-03-93; fax (41) 229-33-50; e-mail archives.liege@skynet.be; documents concerning the Liège district from 9th to 20th centuries; Archivist PAULETTE PIEYNS-RIGO.

Bibliothèque 'Chiroux-Croisiers': 8 place des Carmes, 4000 Liège; tel. (41) 23-19-60; fax (41) 23-20-62; general library, MSS, ancient works; 1,300,000 vols, local history, architecture, Walloon dialectology, *c.* 1,000 periodicals; Librarians B. DEMOULIN, J. P. ROUGE.

Bibliothèque de l'Institut Archéologique Liégeois: Musée Curtius, 13 quai de Maastricht, 4000 Liège; tel. (4) 221-94-04; fax (4) 221-94-32; f. 1850; archaeology, decorative arts; 27,000 vols (mostly periodicals); Librarian MONIQUE MERLAND; publ. *Bulletin de l'Institut Archéologique Liégeois* (annually).

Bibliothèques de l'Université: 1 place Cockerill, 4000 Liège; tel. (4) 366-52-06; fax (4) 366-57-02; e-mail joseph.denooz@ulg.ac.be; f. 1817; 2,600,000 vols and pamphlets (incl. 12,000 current serials and 6,000 MSS); open to the public; Chief Librarian Dr J. DENOOZ; publ. *Bibliotheca Universitatis Leodiensis.*

Louvain

Universiteitsbibliotheek-K.U. Leuven: Mgr Ladeuzeplein 21, 3000 Louvain; tel. (16) 32-46-60; fax (16) 32-46-16; f. 1425; 3,700,000 vols (70% in faculty and dept libraries), *c.* 1,000 MSS; Chief Librarian Prof. R. DEKEYSER.

Louvain-la-Neuve

Bibliothèques de l'Université Catholique de Louvain: C/o Bibliothèque générale et de Sciences humaines, Place Cardinal Mercier 31, 1348 Louvain-la-Neuve; tel. (10) 47-49-01; fax (10) 47-28-91; 2,000,000 vols; 9,000 current periodicals; Dir and Librarian J. GERMAIN.

Maredsous

Bibliothèque de l'Abbaye de Saint-Benoît: Maredsous, 5537 Denée; tel. (82) 69-82-11; fax (82) 69-83-21; f. 1872; books of learning, especially history and theology; 400,000 vols, 50,000 brochures; Chief Librarian Dom DANIEL MISONNE; publ. *Revue Bénédictine.*

Mechelen

Archief en Stadsbibliotheek: Goswin de Stassartstraat 145, 2800 Mechelen; tel. (15) 20-43-46; f. 1802; archives of the city of Malines (Mechelen) since the 13th century and the library of the Great Council of the Netherlands; Archivist H. INSTALLE; publs *Inventaire des Archives de la ville de Malines* (8 vols), *Catalogue méthodique de la Bibliothèque de Malines* (1 vol.).

Archives de l'Archevêché: Archevêché de Malines, de Merode straat 18, 2800 Mechelen; tel. (15) 29-84-21; f. 1825; archives from 12th to 20th centuries; some MSS and 1,000 books; also 1,200 files containing documents, 50,000 photographs, iconographs, souvenirs, etc; Archivist Drs A. JANS.

Mons

Archives de l'Etat: 23 place du Parc, 7000 Mons; archives date from 10th century to present day; library contains 25,000 vols; the buildings were badly damaged during the war and many records lost; at present there is rebuilding and the archives are being added to; the archives of the town of Mons are intact; there are also archives from the Abbeys and noble families of Hainaut; Keeper W. DE KEYZER.

Bibliothèque Centrale de la Faculté Polytechnique de Mons: Rue de Houdain, 7000 Mons; tel. (65) 37-40-10; fax (65) 37-30-68; e-mail biblio@fpms.fpms.ac.be; f. 1837; 39,500 vols; Chief Librarian NICOLE DELEBOIS-PONCIN.

Bibliothèque de l'Université de Mons-Hainaut: 2 rue Marguerite Bervoets, 7000 Mons; tel. (65) 37-30-50; telex 57764; fax (65) 37-30-54; f. 1797; reference and lending sections; rare and early books, local documents, periodicals and newspapers; 785,305 vols, 3,622 MSS and incunabula, maps, prints; Dir (vacant).

Namur

Archives de l'Etat à Namur: 45 rue d'Arquet, 5000 Namur; tel. (81) 22-34-98; fax (81) 22-34-98; f. 1848; documents concerning the County and Province of Namur from the 8th century; Archivist D. VAN OVERSTRAETEN.

Bibliothèque Universitaire Moretus Plantin: 19 rue Grandgagnage, 5000 Namur; tel. (81) 72-46-30; fax (81) 72-46-45; e-mail bump@fundp.ac.be; f. 1921; history of Western Europe, Classical, Roman and German philology, philosophy, law, economics, art, sciences; over 800,000 vols; special collection: rare books on natural sciences; Chief Librarian Prof. RENÉ NOËL; Sec. Y. WILQUET.

Sint Niklaas Waas

Bibliotheek voor Hedendaagse Dokumentatie (Library on Contemporary Documentation): Parklaan 2, 9100 Sint Niklaas Waas; tel. (3) 776-50-63; fax (3) 778-07-85; private political, social and economic library; *c.* 120,000 vols, 4,000 periodicals, 15,000 maps; special collections on governmental research, public administration; US govt documents depository collection; Librarian YVAN VAN GARSSE; publs *Bulletin* (monthly), *Governmental Publications Survey* (annually), Bibliographical Series (irreg.).

Ypres

Stedelijke Bibliotheek (Public Library): St-Jansstraat 7, 8900 Ypres; tel. (57) 20-22-00; fax (57) 20-23-79; e-mail ieper.pob@bib.vlaanderen.be; f. 1840; general interest; 80,000 vols, 350 periodicals; Librarian EDDY BARBRY.

Museums and Art Galleries

Antwerp

Etnografisch Museum: Suikerrui 19, 2000 Antwerp; tel. (3) 220-86-00; fax (3) 227-08-71; f. 1988; arts and crafts of pre-literate and non-European people; library of 7,000 vols; Dir JAN VAN ALPHEN; publ. *Bulletin van de Vrienden van het Etnografisch Museum Antwerpen*.

Koninklijk Museum voor Schone Kunsten (Royal Museum of Fine Arts): Leopold de Waelplein, 2000 Antwerp; tel. (3) 238-78-09; fax (3) 248-08-10; f. 1890; collections of Flemish Primitifs, early foreign schools, Rubens, 16th–17th-century Antwerp School, 17th-century Dutch School, works of Belgian artists of 19th and 20th centuries; important works of Leys, De Braekeleer, Ensor, Wouters, Smits, Magritte, Permeke; library of *c.* 35,000 vols; Dir Dr PAUL HUVENNE; publs *Jaarboek* (annually), *Museumkrant* (quarterly) and catalogues.

Kunsthistorische Musea (Art History Museums): Museum Mayer van den Bergh, Lange Gasthuisstraat 19, 2000 Antwerp; tel. (3) 232-42-37; Dir HANS NIEUWDORP.

Affiliated museums:

Rubenshuis (Rubens' House): Wapper 9–11, 2000 Antwerp; tel. (3) 232-47-51; f. 1946; reconstruction of Rubens' house and studio; original 17th-century portico and pavilion; paintings by P. P. Rubens, his collaborators and pupils; 17th-century furnishings; Asst Curator (vacant).

Rubenianum: Kolveniersstraat 20, 2000 Antwerp; tel. (3) 232-39-20; documentation centre for the study of 17th-century Flemish art; Asst Curator NORA DE POORTER; publ. *Corpus Rubenianum Ludwig Burchard*.

Openluchtmuseum voor Beeldhouwkunst Middelheim (Open-air Museum of Sculpture): Middelheimlaan 61, 2020 Antwerp; tel. (3) 827-15-34; f. 1950; important collection of contemporary sculpture, including Rodin, Maillol, Zadkine, Marini, Manzu, Gargallo, Moore, exhibited in a large park; exhibitions devoted to modern sculpture; Asst Curator M. MEEWIS.

Museum Smidt van Gelder: Belgiëlei 91, 2000 Antwerp; tel. (3) 239-06-52; f. 1950; famous collection of Chinese and European porcelains, Dutch 17th-century paintings, and of 18th-century French furniture; Asst Curator Miss CLARA VANDERHENST.

Museum Mayer van den Bergh: Lange Gasthuisstraat 19, 2000 Antwerp; tel. (3) 232-42-37; f. 1904; unique collection of paintings, including Breughel, Metsys, Aertsen, Mostaert, Bronzino, Heda, de Vos, and medieval sculpture, ivories, etc.; under the custody of a Board of Regents; Curator HANS NIEUWDORP.

Museum Vleeshuis: Vleeshouwersstraat 38, 2000 Antwerp; tel. (3) 233-64-04; f. 1913; archaeology, local history, Egyptian, Greek and Roman antiquities, numismatics, sculpture, applied art, ceramics, furniture, arms, posters, musical instruments; library of 15,000 vols; Asst Curator (vacant).

Museum Brouwershuis: Adriaan Brouwerstraat 20, 2000 Antwerp; tel. (3) 232-65-11; fax (3) 232-65-11; f. 1933; 16th-century installations for water-supply to breweries, rich council chamber; Curator F. DE NAVE.

Museum Plantin-Moretus: Vrijdagmarkt 22, 2000 Antwerp; tel. (3) 233-02-94; fax (3) 226-25-16; f. 1876; 16th–18th-century patrician house with ancient printing office and foundry, engravings on copper and wood; typography, drawings and pictures; illuminated MSS, library of 30,000 vols (15th to 18th centuries), archives; special collections: Max Horn Legacy, Ensemble Emile Verhaeren; Dir Dr FRANCINE DE NAVE.

Nationaal Scheepvaartmuseum (Steen) (National Maritime Museum): Steenplein 1, 2000 Antwerp; tel. (3) 232-08-50; fax (3) 227-13-38; e-mail scheepmus@antwerpen.be; f. 1952; maritime history, especially concerning Belgium; library of 43,000 vols; Asst Dir R. JALON.

Stedelijk Prentenkabinet: Vrijdagmarkt 23, 2000 Antwerp; f. 1938; 10,500 vols in library; ancient and modern collections of prints and drawings; Keeper Dr F. DE NOUE.

Volkskundemuseum: Gildekamersstraat 2–6, 2000 Antwerp; tel. (3) 220-86-66; fax (3) 220-83-68; f. 1907; folklore of the Flemish provinces, especially folk art and craft; library of 17,000 vols.

Bouillon

Musée Ducal 'Les Amis de Vieux Bouillon': Bouillon; tel. (61) 466839; f. 1947; archives, historical manuscripts and documents; archaeology, folklore; exhibition of the history of Godefroy de Bouillon; small library; Curator Mme CLÉMENT BODARD.

Bruges

Archeologisch Museum (Archaeological Museum): Mariastr. 36A, 8000 Bruges.

Arentshuis (Brangwynmuseum): Dijver 16, 8000 Bruges; tel. (50) 44-87-11; fax (50) 44-87-78; 18th-century manor house, contains a collection of lace and a permanent exhibition of works by Frank Brangwyn; Chief Curator Dr V. VERMEERSCH.

Groeningemuseum (Municipal Art Gallery): Dijver 12, 8000 Bruges; tel. (50) 44-87-11; fax (50) 44-87-78; Belgian and Dutch paintings from late medieval times to present; Chief Curator Dr V. VERMEERSCH.

Gruuthusemuseum: Dijver 17, 8000 Bruges; tel. (50) 44-87-11; fax (50) 44-87-78; municipal collection in the 15th-century Palace of the Lords of Gruuthuse; furniture, sculpture, ceramics, tapestries, metalwork, instruments; Chief Curator Dr V. VERMEERSCH.

Memling Museum: St John's Hospital, Mariastraat 38, 8000 Bruges; tel. (50) 44-87-11; fax (50) 44-87-78; f. *c.* 1150; paintings by Hans Memling and other artists, sculptures, furniture in 12th–14th-century hospital; 17th century pharmacy; Dir Dr H. LOBELLE-CALUWÉ.

Museum Onze-Lieve-Vrouw ter Potterie: Potterierei 79, 8000 Bruges; tel. (50) 44-87-11; fax (50) 44-87-78; old hospital f. 1276, museum and church; church ornaments, furniture, paintings, sculptures, 17th-century tapestries, etc.; Chief Curator Dr V. VERMEERSCH.

Stedelijk Museum voor Volkskunde (Municipal Museum of Folklore): Rolweg 40, 8000 Bruges; tel. (50) 33-00-44; fax (50) 44-87-78; f. 1973; popular art, 19th-century trades and crafts; Curator W. P. DEZUTTER.

Brussels

Koninklijk Museum voor Midden-Afrika/ Musée Royal de l'Afrique Centrale: Leuvensesteenweg 13, 3080 Tervuren, near Brussels; tel. (2) 769-52-11; fax (2) 767-02-42; f. 1897; large collections in the fields of prehistory, ethnography, native arts and crafts; geology, mineralogy, palaeontology; zoology (entomology, ornithology, mammals, reptiles, etc); history, economics; library of 100,000 vols; 37 scientific staff; Dir D. THYS VAN DEN AUDENAERDE; publs *Annales*, and miscellaneous publications.

Musée d'Ixelles: 71 rue Jean Van Volsem, Ixelles, 1050 Brussels; tel. (322) 511-90-84; fax (322) 647-66-72; f. 1892; ancient and modern masters, water-colours, drawings, engravings, sculptures, posters, etc.; works of Belgian and foreign schools, 15,000 vols (bibliography); Curator NICOLE D'HUART.

Musée Royal de l'Armée et d'Histoire Militaire: Parc du Cinquantenaire 3, 1000 Brussels; tel. (2) 733-98-24; fax (2) 734-54-21; e-mail piet.deguyse@cbit.rma.at.be; f. 1910; collection includes military history of Belgium from 10th century onwards; arms, uniforms, decorations, paintings, sculpture, maps, library of 450,000 vols and archives; Chief Curator P. LEFÈVRE; publs *Revue Belge d'Histoire Militaire / Belgisch Tijdschrift voor Militaire Geschiedenis* (quarterly), *AELR (Air et Espace, Lucht en Ruimtevaart) Militaria Belgica* (quarterly).

Musées Royaux d'Art et d'Histoire: 10 parc du Cinquantenaire, 1000 Brussels; tel. (2) 741-72-11; fax (2) 733-77-35; Dir Prof. Dr FRANCIS VAN NOTEN.

Include:

Musée du Cinquantenaire: 10 parc du Cinquantenaire, 1000 Brussels; tel. (2) 741-72-11; fax (2) 733-77-35; f. 1835; archaeology of Belgium, the Americas, Asia, the Pacific and North Africa, and of ancient Iran and the Near East, Egypt, Greece and Rome; European decorative arts; library of 100,000 vols; publ. *Art & Histoire / Kunst & Geschiedenis*.

Pavillon Chinois et Tour Japonaise: 44 ave Van Praet, 1020 Brussels; tel. and fax (2) 268-16-08; Chinese art, porcelain and furniture; Japanese architecture and decorative arts.

Porte de Hal/Hallepoort: Blvd du Midi, 1000 Brussels; tel. (2) 534-15-18; Brussels and European altar pieces. (Closed until 2000.)

Musée Instrumental: 17 Petit Sablon, 1000 Brussels; tel. (2) 511-35-95; fax (2) 512-85-75; musical instruments.

Pavillon Horta-Lambeaux: Parc du Cinquantenaire, 1000 Brussels; tel. (2) 741-72-11; fax (2) 733-77-35; marble relief of the Human Passions.

Musées Royaux des Beaux-Arts de Belgique: 9 rue du Musée, 1000 Brussels; tel. (2) 508-32-11; fax (2) 508-32-32; f. 1801; Brussels, medieval, Renaissance and modern pictures, drawings and sculpture; library of 200,000 vols; Chief Curator Dr ELIANE DE WILDE; publ. *Bulletin*.

Attached museums:

Musée d'Art Ancien: 3 rue de la Régence, 1000 Brussels; 15th–19th century paintings, drawings and sculpture.

Musée d'Art Moderne: 3 rue de la Régence, 1000 Brussels; 20th-century paintings, drawings and sculpture, temporary exhibitions.

Musée Constantin Meunier: 59 rue de l'Abbaye, 1000 Brussels; paintings, drawings and sculptures by Constantin Meunier, the artist's house and studio.

Musée Wiertz: 62 rue Vautier, 1000 Brussels; paintings by Antoine Wiertz; the artist's house and studio.

Museum Erasmus: 31 rue du Chapitre, 1070 Brussels; tel. (2) 521-13-83; fax (2) 527-12-69; e-mail erasmushuis.maisonerasme@skynet.be; f. 1932; documents, paintings, early editions and manuscripts relating to Erasmus and other Humanists of the 16th century; library of 3,000 vols; Curator A. VANAUTGAERDEN.

Ghent

Museum van Hedendaagse Kunst (Museum of Contemporary Art): Citadelpark, 9000 Ghent; tel. (9) 221-17-03; fax (9) 221-71-09; f. 1975; paintings, sculpture, drawings, etchings; library of 30,000 vols, 195 periodicals; Dir JAN HOET; publs catalogues.

Museum voor Schone Kunsten: Citadelpark, 9000 Ghent; tel. (9) 222-17-03; fax (9) 221-60-15; f. 1902; contains ancient and modern paintings, sculpture, tapestries, prints and drawings, icons; library; Dir ROBERT HOOZEE; publs catalogues.

Oudheidkundig Museum van de Stad Gent: Godshuizenlaan 2, 9000 Ghent; tel. (9) 225-11-06; fax (9) 233-34-59; f. 1833; prehistory, local history, applied arts, furniture, arms, numismatics, collection of Chinese art; Dir Dr A. VAN DEN KERKHOVE.

Liège

Collections artistiques de l'Université de Liège: 7 place du 20 août, 4000 Liège; tel. (4) 366-53-29; fax (4) 366-58-54; f. 1903; 30,000 prints and drawings, paintings of 15th and 16th centuries; modern Belgian paintings; 5,483 coins; collection of Zairian art and craft; Curator Dr JEAN-PATRICK DUCHESNE.

Musée d'Art Moderne et d'Art Contemporain: 3 parc de la Boverie, 4020 Liège; tel. (4) 343-04-03; fax (4) 344-19-07; f. 1981; modern paintings, sculptures and abstracts of the Belgian School, French and foreign masters; Curators FRANÇOISE DUMONT, FRANCINE DAWANS.

Musée de la Vie Wallonne: Cour des Mineurs, 4000 Liège; tel. (4) 223-60-94; fax (4) 221-10-35; f. 1912; varied collection covering south Belgium in the fields of ethnography, folklore, arts and crafts and history; 450,000 documents; library of 35,000 vols; Man. Dir NICOLE DONY; publ. *Enquêtes* (annually).

Musées d'Archéologie et d'Arts Décoratifs de Liège: Institut Archéologique Liégeois, 13 quai de Maastricht, 4000 Liège; tel. (4) 221-94-04; fax (4) 221-94-32; Curators ANN CHEVALIER, MARIE-CLAIRE GUEURY.

Include:

Musée Curtius: 13 quai de Maastricht, 4000 Liège; f. 1909; chief sections: prehistory, Romano-Belgian and Frankish, Liège coins, decorative arts (from the Middle Ages to the 19th century); Annexe: lapidary collection in Palais de Justice; the museum is the headquarters of the Archaeological Institute of Liège (*q.v.*).

Musée d'Ansembourg: 114 Féronstrée, 4000 Liège; f. 1905; collections of 18th-century decorative arts of Liège; reconstituted interiors.

Musée du Verre: 13 quai de Maastricht, 4000 Liège; f. 1959; all the main centres of production, from the earliest times to the 20th century, are represented.

Mariemont

Musée Royal et Domaine de Mariemont: 7140 Morlanwelz, Mariemont; tel. (64) 21-21-93; fax (64) 26-29-24; f. 1922; contains antiquities from Egypt, Greece, Rome, China, Japan; national archaeology; Tournai porcelain; bookbindings; library of 80,000 vols; Curator PATRICE DARTEVELLE; publ. *Les Cahiers de Mariemont* (annually).

Mechelen

Stadsmuseum: Hof van Busleyden-Fred. de Merodestraat 65–67, 2800 Mechelen; f. 1844; city museum; paintings, sculptures, history, etc.; section for contemporary painting and sculpture; Dir M. BAFCOP.

Verviers

Musée d'Archéologie: 42 rue des Raines, 4800 Verviers; f. 1959; history of art, archaeology, folklore, local history.

Musée de la Laine: 8 rue de Séroule, Verviers; f. 1985; history of wool-making before the industrial revolution of 1800.

Musée des Beaux-Arts: 17 rue Renier, 4800 Verviers; f. 1884; sculpture, paintings; ceramics of Europe and Asia; publ. *Guide du Visiteur.*

Universities

UNIVERSITEIT ANTWERPEN (University of Antwerp)

Ville La Chapelle, Beukenlaan 12–14, 2020 Antwerp

Telephone: (3) 827-38-64

Fax: (3) 827-13-06

Rector and President: Prof. Dr R. VERHEYEN

CONSTITUENT CAMPUSES

Universitair Centrum Antwerpen (Antwerp University Centre)

Groenenborgerlaan 171, 2020 Antwerp

Telephone: (3) 218-02-11
Fax: (3) 218-04-43

Founded 1852
Language of instruction: Dutch
State control
Academic year: October to July (two semesters)

Rector: Prof. Dr W. DECLEIR
Manager: Prof. Dr B. HEIJNEN
Librarian: Dr B. VAN STYVENDAELE

Library: see Libraries
Number of teachers: 135
Number of students: 3,100

Publication: *ALA – Africa Latin-America Asia.*

DEANS

Faculty of Applied Economic Sciences: Prof. Dr W. WINKELMANS
Faculty of Sciences: Prof. Dr A. VERSCHOREN
Faculty of Medicine: Prof. Dr D. SCHEUERMANN

PROFESSORS

ARICKX, F., Mathematics and Informatics
BRAEM, M., Dentistry
BRUTSAERT, D., Human Physiology
CALLEBAUT, M., Human Anatomy and Embryology
CAUBERGS, R., Botany
CRETEN, W., Physics
CUYVERS, L., International Economics
DE BRABANDER, A., Methodology
DE PELSMACKER, P., Marketing
DE SITTER, J., Informatics
DE WEIRDT, E., Finance
DECLEIR, W., General Biochemistry (animals)
DESSEYN, H., Inorganic Chemistry
DEVREESE, J., Applied Mathematics (Sciences)
DEWOLF, M., Biochemistry
D'HAESE, L., Economics of Development
ESMANS, E., Chemistry
HENDERICKX, E., Sociology
HILDERSON, H., Biochemistry
HOUVENAGHEL, A., General Physiology (animals)
HULSELMANS, J., General Zoology
KREMER, L., Applied Languages and Communication
LAGROU, A., Analytical Chemistry
LEMMENS, L., Physics
LOWEN, R., Applied Mathematics
MEEUSEN, W., Mathematics in Economics
RAMAN, E., Physics
RENARD, R., Economics of Development
REYNTJES, P., Governance and Development
SCHEUERMANN, D., Histology and Microscopic Anatomy
THEUNISSE, H., Accountancy
THIERS, G., Industrial Management
VAN BOGAERT, P., Electrobiology
VAN DEN BROECK, J., General Economics
VAN DER VEKEN, B., Chemistry
VAN DOREN, V., Physics
VAN DYCK, D., Physics
VAN LANDUYT, J., Physics and Solid State Physics
VAN LEUVEN, J., Theoretical Electricity
VAN TENDELOO, G., Physics
VERHEYEN, W., General Zoology
VERLUYTEN, S. P., Applied Languages and Communication
VERSCHOREN, A., Mathematics
WEYNS, A., Anatomy and Embryology of Domestic Animals
WINKELMANS, W., Transport Economics

ATTACHED INSTITUTES

Institute for Developing Countries: Middelheimlaan 1, 2020 Antwerp; f. 1920; lectures may be given here in languages other than Dutch; Pres. D. VAN DEN BULCKE.

Attached institute:

Institute for Administration Studies: Antwerp; Pres. D. VAN DEN BULCKE.

Universitaire Faculteiten Sint-Ignatius te Antwerpen

(St Ignatius University Faculty of Antwerp)

13 Prinsstraat, 2000 Antwerp

Telephone: (3) 220-41-11

Telex: 33599

Fax: (3) 220-44-20

Founded 1852

Language of instruction: mostly Dutch

Private control

Academic year: October to September

Rector: Prof. Dr C. REYNS

President of the General Assembly: Prof. F. VAN LOON

Chief Administrative Officer: R. VAN DER GOTEN

Treasurer: M. DECANCQ

Librarian: L. SIMONS

Library: see under Libraries

Number of teachers: 389

Number of students: 3,660

Publications: *Economisch en Sociaal Tijdschrift, Ons Geestelijk Erf, Bijdragen tot de Geschiedenis, Gezelliana, Economische Didaktiek, Weekblad voor Nederlandse Didaktiek, Info-Frans, CSB-Berichten.*

DEANS

Faculty of Law: J. VELAERS

Faculty of Philosophy and Letters: A. VANNESTE

Faculty of Political and Social Sciences: J. BREDA

Faculty of Applied Economic Sciences: A. VAN POECK

HEADS OF DEPARTMENTS

Philosophy and Religious Studies: J. TAELS

Languages and Literature: P. PELCKMANS

History: G. DEVOS

Law: H. VAN GOETHEM

Sociology and Social Politics: L. GOOSSENS

Economic and Social Research: J. PLASMANS

Industrial Economics: E. LAVEREN

Third World: S. MARYSSE

Study Centre for Technology, Energy and the Environment: A. VERBRUGGEN

AFFILIATED INSTITUTES

IPO UFSIA Management School: Kipdorp 19, 2000 Antwerp; Dir B. PODEVIN.

Instituut voor Didaktiek en Andragogiek-IDEA (Institute of Education): Prinsstraat 13, 2000 Antwerp; Pres. L. BRAECKMANS.

Dienst Informatica: Prinsstraat 10, 2000 Antwerp; Dir (vacant).

Centre for Business Administration (MBA): Prinsstraat 13, 2000 Antwerp; Dir D. VLOEBERGHS.

ICTL / Steunpunt voor Taal en Communicatie: Dir D. SANDRA.

Centrum voor Mexicaanse Studiën: Co-ordinator J. VAN HOUTTE.

Universitaire Instelling Antwerpen

Universiteitsplein 1, 2610 Antwerp (Wilrijk)

Telephone: (3) 820-20-20

Fax: (3) 820-22-49

Founded 1971

State control

Language of instruction: Dutch

President: M. VAN BOVEN

Rector: J. VAN STEENBERGE

Vice-President: E. VAN BUYNDER

Vice-Rector: F. VERBEURE

Librarian: J. VAN BORM

Library: see Libraries

Number of teachers: 245

Number of students: 3,200

Publications: *Research Topics University of Antwerp, Universiteit Antwerpen* (in co-operation with RUCA and UFSIA).

DEANS

Faculty of Sciences: R. VAN GRIEKEN

Faculty of Medicine and Pharmacy: D. SCHEUERMANN

Faculty of Philosophy and Letters: G. WILDEMEERSCH

Faculty of Law and Political and Social Sciences: Y. VANDEN BERGHE

HEADS OF DEPARTMENTS

Physics: J. DEVREESE

Mathematics and Computer Sciences: D. JANSSENS

Chemistry: E. VANSANT

Biochemistry: J. MERREGAERT

Biology: H. VAN ONCKELEN

Medicine: M. DE BROE

Pharmacy: A. HAEMERS

Germanic Languages and Literature: G. LERNOUT

Romance Languages and Literature: W. GEERTS

Law: A. VAN OEVELEN

Political and Social Sciences: H. MEULEMANS

Teacher Training: Fr DAEMS

ATTACHED RESEARCH INSTITUTES

Institute for Materials Sciences (IMS) (RUCA-UIA): Pres. J. VAN LANDUYT.

Institute of Environmental Studies: Pres. E. VANSANT.

KATHOLIEKE UNIVERSITEIT BRUSSEL

(Catholic University of Brussels)

Vrijheidslaan 17, 1081 Brussels

Telephone: (2) 412-42-11

Fax: (2) 412-42-00

Founded 1968; present name 1991; previously Universitaire Faculteiten Sint-Aloysius

Language of instruction: Dutch

Private control

Academic year: October to July

Rector: Prof. Dr C. MATHEEUSSEN

Librarian: E. DEFOORT

Library of 70,000 vols

Number of teachers: 51

Number of students: 800

DEANS

Department of Germanic Philology: D. DE VIN

Department of Law: M. VAN HOECKE

Department of Economic Sciences: I. VAN DE WOESTYNE

Department of History: E. DEFOORT

Department of Social and Political Sciences: J. SERVAES

Department of Philosophy: W. GOOSSENS

PROFESSORS

ACX, R., Bank and Credit Sciences

BECKERS, A., Psychology

BOON, H., General Introduction to Heuristics

BOUSSET, H., Dutch Literature

BRAEKMAN, W. L., English Literature

BREMS, H., History of Modern Dutch Literature

COSSEY, H., General and Social Psychology

DE CLERCQ, M., European Literature and Introduction to Modern Literature

DEFOORT, E., Modern French Texts

DEGADT, J., Economic Science and Social Statistics

DE GEEST, W. P. F., Dutch Linguistics

DE MARTELAERE, P., Philosophic Anthropology

DE MEYER, A., Communications Science

DE VIN, D., Dutch Literature

DONCKELS, R., Mathematics

GOOSSENS, W., Historic Introduction to Philosophy

GOTZEN, F., Introduction to Law

GRAUWEN, W. M., Medieval Latin Texts

HOOGHE, L., Politics

JANSSENS, J., History of Medieval Dutch Literature

JANSSENS, P., Modern Times

LINDEMANS, J.-F., Traditional Logics

LOOSVELDT, G., Methods and Techniques of Social Sciences

MATHEEUSSEN, C., Roman Law

MOOREN, L., History of Antiquity

MUYLLE, J., Art and Cultural History

NELDE, P. H., Germanic Linguistics

PERSOONS, A., Physics

PUTSEYS, Y., English Linguistics

RAYMAEKERS, E., Traffic Economics

SILVERANS, R., Natural Sciences

SMEYERS, J., Introduction to Germanic Philology

TACQ, J., Sociology

TAELS, J., Philosophy

VAN CAUWENBERGHE, E., Historic Methods and Medieval History

VAN DEN WIJNGAERT, M., History of Modern Times

VAN GORP, H., General Literary Science

VANHEMELRYCK, F., History of Modern Times

VAN HOECKE, M., Introduction to Law

VAN WINCKEL, F., Industrial Financing

VERAGHTERT, K., Modern Times

VERHOEVEN, J., Sociology

VERSTRAELEN, L., Mathematics

VERTONGHEN, R., Accountancy

UNIVERSITÉ LIBRE DE BRUXELLES

(Free University of Brussels)

50 ave Franklin Roosevelt, 1050 Brussels

Telephone: (2) 650-21-11

Fax: (2) 650-36-30

Founded 1834; became independent from the Vrije Universiteit Brussel in 1970

Language of instruction: French

Private control

Academic year: September to January, February to July

President: ROBERT TOLLET

Vice-President: FRANÇOISE PRÉVOT

Rector: JEAN-LOUIS VANHERWEGHEM

Secretary: CHRISTIAN DEJEAN

Librarian: JEAN-PIERRE DEVROEY

Library: see under Libraries

Number of teachers: 1,238

Number of students: 18,277

Publication: *Revue de l'Université.*

DEANS

Faculty of Philosophy and Letters: GUY HAARSCHER

Faculty of Law: XAVIER DIEUX

Faculty of Social, Political and Economic Sciences: JEAN-JACQUES HEIRWEGH

Faculty of Psychology and Education: JOSÉ JUNÇA DE MORAIS

Faculty of Sciences: GEORGES HUEZ

Faculty of Medicine: JEAN-PAUL DEGAUTE

Faculty of Applied Sciences: BERNARD LEDUC

INSTITUTES

Institute of Environmental Management and Development Planning: Dir CHRISTIAN VANDERMOTTEN

Institute of European Studies: Pres. ANDRÉ SAPIR

Institute of Labour: Pres. MATÉO ALALUF

Institute of Languages and Phonetics: Pres. JOSEPH VROMANS
Institute of Pharmacy: Pres. JEANINE FONTAINE FAMAEY
Institute of Physical Education and Physiotherapy: Pres. JACQUES DUCHATEAU
Institute of Statistics: Pres. PHILIPPE VINCKE
Institute for the Study of Religions and Secularism: Pres. HERVÉ HASQUIN
School of Public Health: Pres. RAPHAËL LAGASSE

ASSOCIATED INSTITUTES AND SCHOOLS

Ecole de Commerce Ernest Solvay (Ernest Solvay Business School): Pres. ANDRÉ FARBER.

Département d'Economie Appliquée (Applied Economics Department): 2 ave Paul Héger, 1050 Brussels; Dir PAUL KESTENS.

Ecole des Sciences Criminologiques Léon Cornil (Léon Cornil School of Criminology): Brussels; f. 1935; Pres. MARC PREUMONT.

Ecole d'Infirmières Annexée à l'Université (Nursing School attached to the University): Campus Erasme, 808 Route de Lennik, 1070 Brussels; Pres. M. VLAEMINCK.

Fondation Archéologique (Archaeological Foundation): Brussels; f. 1930; sculpture casts, photographs, slides and library; Pres. PIERRE BONENFANT.

Institut de Sociologie (Institute of Sociology): 44 ave Jeanne, 1050 Brussels; f. 1901; Dir JACQUES NAGELS.

Institut Jules Bordet (Jules Bordet Institute): 1 rue Héger-Bordet, 1000 Brussels; tel. (2) 538-28-20; diagnosis and treatment of tumours; Dir JAHNOS FRÜHLING.

Centre d'Etudes Canadiennes (Centre for Canadian Studies): Pres. RÉGINE KURGAN.

VRIJE UNIVERSITEIT BRUSSEL (Free University of Brussels)

Pleinlaan 2, 1050 Brussels

Telephone: (2) 629-21-11
Telex: 61051
Fax: (2) 629-22-82
E-mail: webmaster@vub.ac.be

Founded 1834; became independent from the Université Libre de Bruxelles in 1970
Languages of instruction: Dutch, English
Private control

President: R. VAN AERSCHOT
Rector: E. WITTE
Vice-Rectors: W. P. DE WILDE, P. GEERLINGS
Director-General: R. VANDEN BUSSCHE
Librarian: S. NAMENWIRTH

Number of teachers: 700
Number of students: 8,500

Publications: *VUB Magazine, Nieuw Tijdschrift van de VUB, VUB-Press.*

DEANS

Faculty of Philosophy and Letters: C. VAN DE VELDE
Faculty of Law: A. SPRUYT
Faculty of Science: J. LEMONNE
Faculty of Medicine: B. VAN CAMP
Faculty of Applied Science: J. TIBERGHIEN
Faculty of Social, Political and Economic Sciences: M. DESPONTIN
Faculty of Psychological and Educational Sciences: R. CLUYDTS
Faculty of Physical Education and Kinesiology: J. P. CLARIJS

CONSTITUENT COLLEGE

Vesalius College: Pleinlaan 2, 1050 Brussels; tel. (2) 629-28-22; fax (2) 629-36-37; f. 1987 in assn with Boston Univ.; degree courses in arts, sciences and engineering; language of instruction: English; Dean JEAN-PIERRE DEGRÈVE.

UNIVERSITEIT GENT (University of Ghent)

St.-Pietersnieuwstraat 25, 9000 Ghent

Telephone: (9) 264-30-67
Telex: 12754
Fax: (9) 264-35-97

Founded 1817
Language of instruction: Dutch
State control
Academic year: October to July (October–February, March–July)

Rector: J. WILLEMS
Vice-Rector: A. DE LEENHEER
Government Commissioner: Y. DE CLERCQ
Academic Administrator: R. HOOGEWIJS
Logistic Administrator: D. MANGELEER
Secretary of the Board: E. DE MEESTER

Library: see under Libraries

Number of teachers: 707
Number of students: 22,440

Publications: *Gent Universiteit,* and numerous departmental and faculty journals.

DEANS

Faculty of Arts and Philosophy: J.-P. VANDER MOTTEN
Faculty of Political and Social Sciences: E. DE BENS
Faculty of Law: H. BOCKEN
Faculty of Science: (vacant)
Faculty of Medicine: D. CLEMENT
Faculty of Engineering: E. NOLDUS
Faculty of Economics and Applied Economics: H. DE MAEGD
Faculty of Veterinary Medicine: A. DE KRUIF
Faculty of Psychology and Educational Sciences: P. COETSIER
Faculty of Agricultural and Applied Biological Sciences: A. HUYGHEBAERT
Faculty of Pharmaceutical Sciences: J.-P. REMON
School of Management: R. VAN DIERDONCK (Chair.)

PROFESSORS

Faculty of Arts and Philosophy:

BATENS, D., Logic and Philosophy of Science
DE MAEGD-SOËP, C., Russian Philology and Literature
DEVREKER, J., History of Antiquity
EVERAERT, J., Colonial History
HALLYN, F., French Literature
LAUREYS, G., Modern Scandinavian Languages
MILIS, L., Medieval History
MUSSCHOOT, A. M., Dutch Literature and Middle Dutch
PINXTEN, H., Anthropology
PREVENIER, W., Historic Methodology
VAN DAMME, F., Logic and Applied Epistemology
VAN EENOO, R., Modern History
WILLEMS, D., French Language

Faculty of Political and Social Sciences:

BRUTSAERT, H., Sociology
DE BENS, E., Communication Studies
GAUS, H., Political Science
PAGE, H., Population Studies and Social Science Research Methods
VAN HOOLAND, R., Management

Faculty of Law:

BOCKEN, H., Civil Law and Ecology Law
BOUCKAERT, B., General Legal Science
ERAUW, J., International Private Law
GERLO, J., Civil Law
MARESCEAU, M., European Law
MERCHIERS, Y., Commercial and Economic Law and Insurance Law
VAN MENSEL, A., Administrative Law, Law of the New States
WYMEERSCH, E., Commercial and Partnership Law

Faculty of Sciences:

CARDON, F., General and Experimental Physics
COOMANS, A., Zoology
CROMBEZ, G., Higher Analysis
DAMS, R., Analytical Chemistry
DE CLERCQ, P., Organic Chemistry
DELANGHE, R., Mathematical Analysis
GOETHALS, E., Organic Chemistry
GOMES, W., Physical Chemistry
HEYDE, K., Theoretical Physics
STOOPS, G., Mineralogy, Petrography and Micropedology
THAS, J., Geometry and Combinatorics
VANDEN BERGHE, G., Numerical Mathematics and Computer Science
VAN MONTAGU, M., Genetics

Faculty of Medicine:

BOGAERT, M., Pharmacodynamics and Therapy
CLEMENT, D., Internal Medicine
DE BACKER, G., Hygiene, Health and Safety in the Work Place
DE BOEVER, J., Prosthesis and Parodontology
DE HEMPTINNE, A., Normal and Pathological Physiology
DE HEMPTINNE, B., Surgery
DELAEY, J., Ophthalmology
DE REUCK, J., Neuropsychology
DERMAULT, L., Dentistry
ELEWAUT, A., Internal Medicine
LAMEIRE, N., Internal Medicine
LEROY, J., Childhood Diseases
PANNIER, J.-L., Human Biometrics
PAUWELS, R., Internal Medicine
ROELS, F., Pathological Anatomy
ROLLY, G., Anaesthesiology
VEYS, E., Internal Medicine

Faculty of Engineering:

BOUCIQUE, R., General Physics
BOUTE, R., Information Technology
BRUYLAND, I., Communication Technology
DE CALUWE, R., Computer Science
DE VYNCK, I., Technical Chemistry and Environmental Engineering
DEKONINCK, C., Machines
HOFFMAN, G., Information Technology
HOUBAERT, Y., Metallurgy and Materials Science
KULIASKO, F., Mathematical Analysis
LAGASSE, P., Acoustics and Optics
MARIN, G., Chemical Engineering
NOLDUS, E., Automation
PAUWELS, H., Electronics and Information Systems
VAN CAMPENHOUT, J., Electronics and Information Systems
VAN CAUWENBERGHE, A., Control Engineering and Automation
VANMASSENHOVE, F., Electrical Power Engineering
VERMEERSCH, CH., Town Building and Planning
WIEME, W., Physics
WILLEMS, J., Electricity

Faculty of Economics and Applied Economics:

DE MAEGD, H., General Economics
DE RIJCKE, J., Marketing
OOGHE, H., Industrial Financing
PAEMELEIRE, R., Management Information

Faculty of Veterinary Sciences:

DE MOOR, A., Animal Surgery
LAUWERS, H., Anatomy, Histology and Embryology of Domestic Animals
PENSAERT, M., Animal Virology and Immunology
VAN HOOF, J., Hygiene

Faculty of Psychological and Pedagogical Sciences:

CLAES, R., Personnel Management, Work and Organizational Psychology
COETSIER, P., Applied Psychology

De Clerck, K., Historical and Comparative Pedagogy
De Soete, G., Data Analysis
Denève, L., Personality Development
Faché, W., Youth Welfare and Mature Education
Quackelbeen, J., Applied Psychology
Van Oost, P., Interactional Psychology
Verhellen, E., Youth Welfare and Mature Education

Faculty of Agricultural Sciences:

Dejonckheere, W., Phytopharmaceutics
Demeyer, D., Animal Production
Huyghebaert, A., Food Chemistry and Food Microbiology
Lemeur, R., Applied Ecology and Environmental Biology
Martens, L., Agricultural Economics
Schamp, N., Organic Chemistry
Van Cleemput, O., Applied Analytical and Physical Chemistry
Vansteenkiste, G., Mathematics
Verhe, R., Organic Chemistry
Verstraete, W., General and Applied Microbial Ecology

Faculty of Pharmaceutical Sciences:

De Leenheer, A., Medical Biochemistry
Remon, J. P., Pharmaceutical Technology
Van den Bossche, W., Analysis of Medicine
Van Peteghem, C., Food Analysis

Vlerick School of Management:

Deschoolmeester, D., Seminar of Management and Information Systems
Van Dierdonck, D., Seminar of Management of Technology and Production Planning

UNIVERSITÉ DE LIÈGE
(University of Liège)

Place du 20-Août 7, 4000 Liège

Telephone: (4) 366-21-11
Fax: (4) 366-57-00

Founded 1817
Language of instruction: French
Academic year: October to September

Rector: W. Legros
Vice-Rector: B. Rentier
Administrator: L. Bragard

Library: see under Libraries
Number of teachers: 470
Number of students: 13,069

DEANS

Faculty of Philosophy and Letters: R. Leroy
Faculty of Psychology and Educational Sciences: Mme V. de Keyser
Faculty of Law: G. de Leval
Faculty of Economics, Business Administration and Social Sciences: B. Jurion
Faculty of Sciences: C. Houssier
Faculty of Medicine: J. Boniver
Faculty of Applied Sciences: J. Bozet
Faculty of Veterinary Medicine: P. Leroy

PROFESSORS WITH CHAIRS

Faculty of Philosophy and Letters:

Bajomee, D., Contemporary French Literature
Barrera Vidal, A., Special Methodology of Romance Languages, French and Spanish
Delbouille, P., French Stylistics and Analysis of Modern Authors
Desama, Cl., Economic and Social History
Dor, J., Medieval English Language and Literature
Dubois, J., Modern French Authors and Contemporary Literature
Jodogne, P., Italian Language and Literature
Joset, J., Spanish Language and Literature
Klinkenberg, J.-M., Rhetoric and Semiology
Kupper, J. L., History of the Middle Ages and Historical Geography
Leroy, R., Modern German Literature
Loicq, J., Roman History and Archaeology
Malaise, M., Oriental History and Philology
Massaut, J. P., Modern History
Michel, P., Modern English and American Literature
Motte, A., Moral Philosophy and History of Ancient Philosophy
Pastor, E., German Literature and Historical Philology
Somville, P., Aesthetics and Philosophy of Art
Theissen, S., Modern Dutch Philology
Wathelet, P., Greek Language, Literature and Civilization

Faculty of Psychology and Educational Sciences:

Born, M., Psychology of Criminality and Psycho-Social Development
Crahay, M., Experimental Education
De Keyser, Mme V., Business and Administrative Psychology
Fontaine, O., Psychology of Health, Behavioural Therapy Unit
Leclercq, D., Educational Technology
Rondal, J. A., Language Psychology
Van der Linden, M., Neuropsychology

Faculty of Law:

Beaufays, J., General and Regional Political Studies
Benoit-Moury, A., Commercial Law
De Leval, G., Civil Law
Delnoy, P., Civil Law and Juridical Methodology
Demaret, P., European Economic Law
François, L., General Theory of Law
Gothot, P., Comparative and International Law
Hansenne, J., Civil Law
Herbiet, M., Public and Administrative Law
Jamoulle, Mme M., Social Law
Kellens, G., Criminology
Lewalle, P., Public and Administrative Law
Melchior, M., Private International Law
Moreau-Margrève, Mme I., Civil Law
Pappalardo, A., European Competition Law
Scholsem, J. Cl., Public Law and Public Finance
Vanwijck-Alexandre, Mme M., Civil Law
Vigneron, R., Roman Law

Faculty of Economics, Business Administration and Social Sciences:

Bair, J., Mathematics in Economic and Management Sciences
Bawin-Legros, B., Sociology of the Family and General Sociology
Choffray, J.-M., Computing applied to Economics and Business
Crama, Y., Operational Research and Production Management
De Bruyn, C., Quantitative Management Methods
De Coster, M., Sociology
Dister, G., Management Sociology
Feld, S., Development Economics
Gazon, J., Economics
Jurion, B., Political Economy
Langaskens, Y., Economics
Michel, P. A., Financial Analysis
Minguet, A., Economics
Pestieau, P., Economic Science
Quaden, G., Political Economy and Economic Systems
Thiry, B., Political Economy and Applied Microeconomics

Faculty of Sciences:

Aghion, P., Vegetal Biochemistry
Beckers, J., Theoretical and Experimental Physics
Bernier, G., Vegetal Physiology
Cugnon, J., Theoretical Physics
Desreux, J. F., Inorganic Chemistry and Coordination Chemistry
De Wilde, M., Differential Geometry
Duchesne, J.-C., Petrology and Geochemistry
Evrard, R., Experimental Physics
Fransolet, A. M., Mineralogy
Frère, J. M., Enzymology Laboratory
Gerday, C., Biochemistry Laboratory
Gilles, R., Physiology
Goessens, G., Cell and Tissue Biology
Houssier, C. I., Macromolecular and Physical Chemistry
Jerome, R., Macromolecular Chemistry and Organic Materials
Lambinon, J., Vegetal Systematics and Geography
Lazlo, P., Organic Physical Chemistry
Lebon, G., Thermomechanics of Irreversible Phenomena
Lorquet, J., Physical Chemistry
Martial, J., Molecular Biology and Genetic Engineering
Matagne, R. F., Genetics of Micro-organisms
Merenne-Schoumaker, B., Economic Geography
Nihoul, J., Analytical Mechanics
Rentier, B., Basic Virology
Roubens, M., Statistics and Quantitative Management Methods
Ruwet, J.-C., Animal Ethology and Psychology
Schmets, J., Mathematics
Thonart, Ph., Microbiology
Thorez, J., Geology of Clays
Van de Vorst, A., Experimental Physics

Faculty of Medicine:

Angenot, L., Pharmacy
Boniver, J., Anatomy and Pathological Cytology
Dandrifosse, G., General Biochemistry and Physiology
Delarge, J., Pharmaceutical Chemistry
De Leval, J., Urology
Dresse, A., Pharmacology
Fillet, G., Haematology
Fisette, J., Topographical and Intestinal Human Anatomy
Foidart, J. M., General and Cellular Biology
Franck, G., Neurology
François, M., Stomatology
Gielen, J., Medical Chemistry
Hennen, G., Human and Pathological Biochemistry
Jacquet, N., Abdominal Surgery
Kulbertus, H., Medical Clinic
Lamy, M., Anaesthesiology
Lefebvre, P., Clinical Medicine
Lemaire, R., Surgery of Locomotor System
Limet, R., Cardiovascular Surgery
Moonen, G., Normal and Pathological Physiology
Pieron, M., Physical Education
Rorive, G., Nephrology
Senterre, J., Paediatrics
Stevenaert, A., Neurosurgery

Faculty of Applied Sciences:

Beckers, P.
Bozet, J., Mechanical Engineering
Cantraine, G., Electronics
Cescotto, S., Mechanics of Materials
Coheur, J. P., Iron and Steel Metallurgy
Dendal, J., Applied Acoustics
Destine, J., Microelectronics
Dimanche, F., Applied Geology
Dupagne, A., Methodology of Architectonic Composition
Essers, J. A., Aerodynamics
Etienne, J., Mathematics
Fawe, A., Telecommunications
Fleury, Cl., Aerospatial Structures
Fonder, G., Structural Mechanics
Geradin, M., Aeronautical Engineering
Germain, A., Industrial Chemistry
Hogge, M., Thermomechanics

LEBRUN, J., Thermodynamics, Nuclear Engineering
LEGROS, W., Electrical Engineering
LEJEUNE, A., Hydraulics
L'HOMME, G., Chemical Engineering
LITT, F. X., Applied Mathematics
MAQUOI, R., Mechanics of Materials, Stability of Structures
MARCHAL, J., Transport Systems and Shipbuilding
MONJOIE, A., Engineering and Hydrogeology
NGUYEN-DANG, H., Mechanics of the Rupture of Solid Bodies
PAVELLA, Mme M., Electrical Circuits
PETERS, F., Architecture
PIRARD, J. P., Applied Physical Chemistry
PIROTTE, P., Transport and Distribution of Electrical Energy
RIBBENS, D., Computer Science
RONDAL, J., Mechanics of Materials
VANDERSCHUEREN, H., Electrical Measurements
VAN MELLAERT, L., Automatics
WOLPER, P., Computer Science

Faculty of Veterinary Medicine:

ANSAY, M., Pharmacology and Treatment of Domestic Animals
COIGNOUL, F., Pathological Anatomy and Autopsies
DESSY-DOIZE, C., Histology, Embryology, Cytology
ECTORS, F., Obstetrics and Pathology
GODEAU, J. M., Biochemistry
HENROTEAUX, M., Semiology and Medical Treatment of Small Animals
LEROY, P., Information Science Applied to Animal Husbandry
LOMBA, F., Medical and Clinical Pathology
MAGHUIN-ROGISTER, G., Analysis of Foodstuffs derived from Animals
PASTORET, P. P., Virology and Immunology
VINDEVOGEL, H., Treatment of Birds, Food Hygiene

KATHOLIEKE UNIVERSITEIT LEUVEN
(Catholic University of Louvain)

Naamsestraat 22, 3000 Louvain
Telephone: (16) 32-40-10
Fax: (16) 32-40-14

Founded 1425 by Papal Bull
In 1970 the Katholieke Universiteit Leuven was officially split into two autonomous universities: the Katholieke Universiteit Leuven and the Université Catholique de Louvain
Languages of instruction: Dutch and English
Private control
Academic year: October to July

Rector: ANDRE OOSTERLINCK
Vice-Rector for Exact Sciences: GUIDO LANGOUCHE
Vice-Rector for Humanities: HERMAN DE DIJN
Vice-Rector for Biomedical Sciences: GUY MANNAERTS
Rector of Kortrijk Campus: MARCEL JONIAU
Librarian: R. DEKEYSER

Library: see Libraries
Number of teachers: 3,252
Number of students: 27,189

Publications: *Campuskrant, Jaarverslag, Programmaboek, Academische Agenda, Wegwijs,* and numerous scientific journals.

DEANS

Faculty of Theology: M. VERVENNE
Faculty of Canon Law: R. TORFS
Faculty of Law: J. HERBOTS
Faculty of Economics and Applied Economics: P. VANDEN ABEELE
Faculty of Social Sciences: F. LAMMERTYN
Faculty of Medicine: J. JANSSENS
Faculty of Arts: W. EVENEPOEL
Faculty of Psychology and Educational Sciences: R. VANDENBERGHE
Faculty of Science: L. VANQUICKENBORNE
Faculty of Engineering: J. BERLAMONT
Faculty of Agricultural and Applied Biological Sciences: R. SCHOONHEYDT
Faculty of Philosophy: C. STEEL
Faculty of Pharmaceutical Sciences: A. VERBRUGGEN
Faculty of Physical Education and Physiotherapy: J. PAUWELS

INTERFACULTY INSTITUTES

Catholic Documentation and Research Centre: Pres. J. DE MAEYER.

European Centre for Christian Ethics: Pres. H. DE DIJN.

Institute of Labour Studies: Pres. H. COSSEY.

Institute of Modern Languages: Pres. A. VAN AVERMAET.

UNIVERSITÉ CATHOLIQUE DE LOUVAIN
(Catholic University of Louvain)

Place de l'Université 1, 1348 Louvain-la-Neuve
Telephone: (10) 47-21-11
Telex: 59516
Fax: (10) 47-38-03

Founded 1425 by Papal Bull
Private control, became independent when the Katholieke Universiteit Leuven split into two autonomous universities in 1970
Language of instruction: French
Academic year: 2 terms (September to December, February to May)

Rector: M. CROCHET
Vice-Rectors: G. RINGLET, M. MOLITOR
General Administrator: A.-M. KUMPS
Librarian: J. GERMAIN

Library: see Libraries
Number of teachers: 1,260
Number of students: 20,517

Publications: *Bulletin des Amis de Louvain,* and various faculty and research reports, etc.

DEANS

Faculty of Theology: C. FOCANT
Higher Institute of Philosophy: TH. LUCAS
Faculty of Law: G. HORSMANS
Faculty of Economic, Political and Social Sciences: R. PEETERS
Faculty of Medicine: D. MOULIN
Faculty of Philosophy and Letters: M. MUND-DOPCHIE
Faculty of Psychology and Education: X. RENDERS
Faculty of Sciences: F. BORCEUX
Faculty of Applied Sciences: C. TRULLEMANS
Faculty of Agriculture: T. AVELLA-SHAW

HEADS OF DEPARTMENTS

Faculty of Law:

Private Law: J.-L. RENCHON
Public Law: F. DELPÉRÉE
Economic and Social Law: G. KEUTGEN
International Law: M. VERWILGHEN
Criminology and Penal Law: H. BOSLY

Faculty of Economic, Political and Social Sciences:

Political and Social Sciences: A. BASTENIER
Communication: M. LITS
Economics: P. DEHEZ
Administration and Business: A. DE BÉTHUNE
Population and Development Science: J.-M. WAUTELET

Faculty of Philosophy and Letters:

History: J. P. SOSSON
Greek, Latin and Oriental Studies: B. COULIE
Romance Studies: M. FRANCARD
Germanic Studies: S. GRANGER
Archaeology and History of Art: R. BRULET

Faculty of Psychology and Education:

Experimental Psychology: X. SERON
Clinical Psychology: E. BARUFFOL
Education Science: M. BONAMI

Faculty of Medicine:

Biochemistry and Cellular Biology: G. ROUSSEAU
Microbiology, Immunology and Genetics: G. CORNELIS
Physiology and Pharmacology: J. M. GILLIS
Morphology: J. RAHIER
Radiology: B. MALDAGUE
Internal Medicine: J. MELIN
Surgery: R. DETRY
Gynaecology, Obstetrics and Paediatrics: J.-P. BUTS
Neurology and Psychiatry: PH. VAN MEERBEECK
Dentistry and Stomatology: J. VREVEN
Pharmaceutics: R. K. VERBEECK
Physical Education and Rehabilitation: A. STORM
Public Health: F. ROGER FRANCE

Faculty of Sciences:

Mathematics: Y. FELIX
Physics: P. DEFRANCE
Chemistry: E. DE HOFFMANN
Biology: PH. VAN DEN BOSCH DE AGUILLAR
Geology and Geography: H. ZOLLER

Faculty of Applied Sciences:

Materials Science: J. P. ISSI
Architecture: A. DE HERDE
Electricity: P. SOBIESKI
Mechanics: R. KEUNINGS
Mathematical Engineering: G. BASTIN
Computer Engineering: E. MILGROM

Faculty of Agriculture:

Applied Chemistry and Bio-Industries: H. NAVEAU
Biology and Agricultural Production Department: H. MARAITE
Environmental Sciences and Rural Management Department: F. DEVILLEZ

PRESIDENTS OF INSTITUTES

Higher Institute of Religious Studies: A. HAQUIN

Institute of Labour Studies: A. SPINEUX

Institute for Developing Countries: J.-PH. PEEMANS

'Open' Faculty of Economic and Social Politics: G. LIENARD

Oriental Institute: B. COULIE

Institute of Family Studies and Sexology: P. SERVAIS

UNIVERSITÉ DE MONS-HAINAUT
(University of Mons)

20 place du Parc, 7000 Mons
Telephone: (65) 37-31-11
Fax: (65) 37-30-54
E-mail: martine.vanelslande@umh.ac.be

Founded 1965
Language of instruction: French
State control
Academic year: October to September

Rector: ALBERT LANDERCY
Vice-Rector: RONALD KRAMP
Administrator: J. QUENON
Librarian: (vacant)

Number of professors: 298
Number of students: 3,285

DEANS

Faculty of Sciences: PHILIPPE HERQUET
Faculty of Medicine: EMILE GODAUX

Faculty of Applied Economics: VICTOR VANDEVILLE
Faculty of Psycho-Educational Sciences: MARIE-THÉRÈSE ISAAC

PROFESSORS

ALEXANDRE, H., Biology and Embryology
BOFFA, M., Logic and Algebra
BOUGARD, J.-P., Historical Demography
BREDAS, J.-L., Chemistry of New Materials
COMBLÉDARJA, K., Accountancy and Finance
DAGONNIER, R., Physical Chemistry
DANG, N. N., Probability and Statistics
DE CONINCK, J., Molecular Modelling
DEFRAITEUR, R., Fiscal System
DE GOTTAL, P., Statistical Physics and Probability
DELFORGE, J., Physics and Technology
DEPOVER, CHR., Moulding Technology
DESMET, H., Social and Community Psychology
DHAENE, G., Applied Statistics
DONNAY-RICHELLE, J., Clinical Psychology
DOSIERE, M., Physics and Chemistry of Polymers
DUBOIS, P., Polymeric and Composite Materials
DUCHESNE, P.-Y., Anatomy
DUFOUR, P., Computer Sciences
DULIÈRE-CHAPELLE, J., History of Doctrines
DUPONT, P., Methodology and Formation
DUREZ-DEMAL, M., Management and Financial Analysis
ESCARMELLE, J.-F., Public Economy
FALMAGNE, P., Biological Chemistry
FINET, C., Mathematical Analysis
FORGES, G., Language Teaching
GILLIS, P., Experimental and Biological Physics
GOCZOL, J., Microeconomics and Marketing
GODAUX, E., Neurosciences
HARMEGNIES, B., Metrology in Psychology and Education
HECQ, M., Analytical and Inorganic Chemistry
HERQUET, P., Physics
HEUSON-STIENNON, J.-A., Histology
ISAAC-VANDEPUTTE, M.-T., Historical Bibliography
JANGOUX, M., Marine Biology
KRAMP, R., Physiology and Pharmacology
LANDERCY, A., Verbal Communication
LAUDE, L., Solid State Physics
LEBRUN-CARTON, C., Mathematics
LOWENTHAL, F., Cognitive Sciences
LUX, B., Company Management and Economics
MAGEROTTE, G., Education of the Handicapped
MAHY, B., Economic Analysis
MILLER, A., Biochemistry
MOREAU, M.-L., Linguistics
NOEL, G., Mathematical Analysis and Methodology
NUYTS, J., Theoretical and Mathematical Physics
PASSONE, S., Psychology
PLATTEN, J., General Chemistry
POURTOIS, J.-P., Psychosociology of Family and School Education
RADOUX, C., Mathematics and Numbers Theory
RASMONT, P., Zoology
SPILLEBOUDT-DETERCK, M., Finance
SPINDEL, P., Mechanics and Gravitation
STANDAERT, S., International Economic Analysis
TEGHEM-LORIS, J., Mathematics and Actuarial Science
THIRY, P., Management Information Science
TONDEUR, J.-J., Applied Physical Chemistry
VAN DAELE, A., Psychology of Labour
VANDEVILLE, V., Macroeconomic Theory
VAN HAVERBEKE, Y., Organic Chemistry
VAN PRAAG, P., Algebra and Algebraic Geometry
VANSNICK, J.-C., Quantitative Methods
VERHEVE, D., Chemical Technology

ATTACHED INSTITUTES

Ecole d'Interprètes Internationaux: Ave du Champ de Mars, 7000 Mons; Dir JEAN KLEIN.

Institut de Linguistique: 19 place du Parc, 7000 Mons; Dir BERNARD HARMEGNIES.

Centre de Didactique des Sciences: 8 ave Maistriau, 7000 Mons; Dir MICHEL WAUTELET.

Centre de Calcul et d'Informatique: 17 place Warocqué, 7000 Mons; Dir CHANTAL POIRET.

Service d'Instrumentation et de Techniques Audio-Visuelles (SITA): Ave du Champ de Mars, 7000 Mons; Dir ANDRÉ GODIN.

Institutions with University Status

FACULTÉ UNIVERSITAIRE DE THÉOLOGIE PROTESTANTE DE BRUXELLES/UNIVERSITAIRE FACULTEIT VOOR PROTESTANTSE GODGELEERDHEID TE BRUSSEL

40 rue des Bollandistes, 1040 Brussels

Telephone: (2) 735-67-46
Fax: (2) 735-47-31

Founded 1942; closed 1944–50
Languages of instruction: French and Dutch
Private control (United Protestant Church)

Rector: W. WILLEMS
Chairman of Administrative Board: C. PEETERS
Dean of Dutch-speaking Section: K. SMELIK
Dean of French-speaking Section: CH. LEJEUNE
Secretary: A. JOUÉ
Librarian: V. BOEVÉ

Library of 39,878 vols
Number of teachers: 26
Number of students: 110

Publications: *Programme et Horaire des Cours/Studiegids* (annually), *FACtualité/FACtualiteit* (quarterly), *Ad Veritatem* (quarterly), *Belgische Protestantse Biografieën/Biographies Protestantes Belges* (quarterly), *Analecía Bruxellensia* (annually).

PROFESSORS

French-speaking Section:

CHOPINEAU, J., Old Testament Studies and Hebrew
HORT, B., Dogmatics, History of Philosophy and Religious Philosophy
LEJEUNE, CH., New Testament Studies and Ethics
RAINOTTE, G., New Testament Greek
ROUVIÈRE, CHR., Practical Theology
WILLEMS, W., Church History and Methodology

Dutch-speaking Section:

DE LANGE, J., Practical Theology
REIJNEN, A. M., Ethics
SMELIK, K., Old Testament Studies, Hebrew
TOMSON, P., New Testament Studies, Greek
WIERSMA, J., Dogmatics, Philosophy
WILLEMS, W., Church History, History of Dogma and 16th-century History

FACULTÉ UNIVERSITAIRE DES SCIENCES AGRONOMIQUES DE GEMBLOUX

2 passage des Déportés, 5030 Gembloux

Telephone: (81) 622111
Fax: (81) 614544
E-mail: fsagx@fsagx.ac.be

Founded 1860, university status 1947
Language of instruction: French
State control

Rector: C. DEROANNE
Vice-Rector: J. RONDEUX
Dean: C. GASPAR
Secretary: R. PALM

Library: see under Libraries
Number of teachers: 52
Number of students: 1,000

Publication: *BASE* (4 a year).

PROFESSORS

BAUDOIN, J.-P., Phytotechnology of Tropical Zones
BERGANS, J., Rural Economy
BOCK, L., Soil Sciences
BODSON, M., General Horticulture
BURNY, A., Molecular Biology and Animal Physiology
CLAUSTRIAUX, J. J., Statistics and Data Processing
COPIN, A., Analytical Chemistry and Phytopharmacy
DAUTREBANDE, S., Agricultural Hydraulics
DEBOUCHE, C., Hydraulics and Topography
DELTOUR, J., Physics and Physical Chemistry
DELVINGT, W., Forestry
DEROANNE, C., Food Technology, Organic and Biological Chemistry
DESTAIN, M. F., Agricultural Machinery
DU JARDIN, P., Plant Biology
FALISSE, A., Phytotechnology of Temperate Zones
GASPAR, C., General and Applied Zoology
LAMBOTTE, J.-P., Mathematics
LEBAILLY, J.-P., General Economics
LEPOIVRE, P., Phytopathology
MALAISSE, F., Ecology
MARLIER, M., General and Organic Chemistry
PORTETELLE, D., Microbiology
RONDEUX, J., Forest Management and Economics
THEWIS, A., Stockbreeding
THONART, P., Bio-industries
VASEL, J.-L., Waste Water Treatment
VERBRUGGE, J.-P., Strength of Materials, Agricultural Engineering Constructions

FACULTÉ POLYTECHNIQUE DE MONS

Rue de Houdain, 7000 Mons

Telephone: (65) 37-41-11
Fax: (65) 37-42-00

Founded 1837

President of the Board: R. URBAIN
Rector: Prof. S. BOUCHER
Dean: Prof. C. CONTI

Library: see under Libraries
Number of teachers: 51
Number of students: 954

PROFESSORS

BARIGAND, M., General Chemistry and Electrochemistry
BARTHELEMY, J., Architecture
BERDAL, R., Civil Engineering
BERNARDO, J. P., Applied Mechanics
BLONDEAU, H., Computer Graphics
BLONDEL, M., Telecommunications
BOUCHER, S., Analytical Mechanics
BOUGARD, J., Thermodynamics
BOUQUEGNEAU, C., Fundamental and Modern Physics
BROCHE, C., Electrical Machines
BRUXELMANE, M., Chemical Engineering and Biochemistry
CHAPELLE, P., Electroacoustics
CHARLET, J. M., Geology
CONTI, C., Analytical Mechanics
CRAPPE, M., Industrial Applications of Electricity
CRAPPE, R., Electronics
DE HAAN, A., Physical Chemistry
GERIN, A., Electromagnetism

GUERLEMENT, G., Strength of Materials, Stability of Buildings
HANTON, J., Applied Mechanics
HEEMSKERK, J., Extractive Industries
HENRIETTE, J., Heat Transfer
JACOB-DULIERE, M., Metallurgy of Non-Ferrous Metals
JADOT, R., Thermodynamics
LAMBLIN, D., Strength of Materials, Stability of Buildings
LEDOCQ, J., Machine Design
LEICH, H., Signal Processing
LEROY, A., Machine Design, Mechanical Technology
LEROY, J., Electronics
LIBERT, G., Computer Science
MEUNIER, H., Heat Transfer
PETITJEAN, J. P., General Chemistry and Electrochemistry
PILATTE, A., Thermodynamics
PIRLOT, M., Mathematical Analysis, Algebra and Numerical Analysis
RIQUIER, Y., General Metallurgy, Iron and Steel Technology
ROBASZYNSKI, F., Geology
TEGHEM, J., Mathematical Analysis, Algebra and Numerical Analysis
TRECAT, J., Transport and Distribution of High-Voltage Electricity
VANCLEF, A., General Chemistry and Electrochemistry
VANDERSCHUREN, J., Chemical Engineering and Biochemistry

FACULTÉS UNIVERSITAIRES CATHOLIQUES DE MONS

Chaussée de Binche 151, 7000 Mons
Telephone: (65) 32-32-11
Institut Supérieur Commercial et Consulaire founded 1896; University founded 1965
Courses in economics, management science and political science
Language of instruction: French
Private control
Academic year: October to September
Rector: Prof. FRANZ JOMAUX
Vice-Rector: Prof. PATRICK SCARMURE
Number of teachers: 100
Number of students: 1,400

FACULTÉS UNIVERSITAIRES NOTRE-DAME DE LA PAIX

61 rue de Bruxelles, Namur
Telephone: (81) 72-41-11
Fax: (81) 72-50-37
E-mail: relations.exterieures@fundp.ac.be
Founded 1831
Language of instruction: French
Rector: M. GILBERT
Secretary: R. CAUDANO
Chief Librarian: R. NOËL
Library: see under Libraries
Number of teachers: 200
Number of students: 4,000
Publications: *Les Etudes Classiques* (quarterly), *Enjeux, Revue des Questions Scientifiques.*

DEANS

Faculty of Philosophy and Letters: M. PETERS
Faculty of Law: R. ROBAYE
Faculty of Economics, Social Sciences and Management: P. REDING
Faculty of Sciences: V. H. NGUYEN
Faculty of Medicine: A. PIRONT
Institute of Computer Science: J. FICHEFET

PROFESSORS

Faculty of Philosophy and Letters:
ALLARD, A., Classical Philology
BOSSE, A., German and Comparative Literature
BRACKELAIRE, J.-L., Psychology
BURNEZ, L., Prehistoric Art, Archaeology
DELABASTITA, D., English, General and Comparative Literature
DELCROIX, M., French Literature
DE RUYT, C., History of Ancient Art, Archaeology
GANTY, E., Modern Philosophy
GIOT, J., French Linguistics
HANTSON, A., English Language, Linguistics
ISEBAERT, L., Greek and Latin Linguistics
LEGROS, G., Romance Philology, Theory of Literature
LEIJNSE, E., Dutch, General and Comparative Literature
LENOIR, Y., History of Music
MARCHETTI, P., Classical Philology, Antiquity and Latin Authors
NOËL, R., Medieval History
PETERS, M., German Language, Linguistics
PHILIPPART, G., Medieval History
PIETERS, J., Logic, Philosophy of Language, Epistemology, Semiotics
POLET, J. C., French and Comparative Literature
RENARD, M.-F., Italian and Spanish Language
RIZZERIO, L., Ancient Philosophy
SAUVAGE, P., History of the 19th and 20th Centuries
VANDEN BEMDEN, Y., History of Post-Classical Art, Archaeology
WEISSHAUPT, J., Dutch Language, Linguistics
WYNANTS, P., History of Belgian Institutions

Faculty of Law:
BAUFAY, J., Philosophy, Metaphysics, Theology
BRACKELAIRE, J. L., Psychology
CHEFFERT, J. M., Micro-economic Analysis, Telecommunications Economy
COIPEL, N., Introduction to Legal Sources, Legal Methodology
COLSON, B., History of Contemporary Ideas and Institutions, Political Sociology
DIJON, X., Theology, Natural Law
DUCHESNE, P., Company Accountancy
DU JARDIN, J., Criminal Law
FIERENS, J., Methodology, Human Rights
HANOTIAU, B., Introduction to Private Law
POULLET, Y., Roman Law, Computer Law
ROBAYE, R., History of Private Law
THIRY, PH., General Theory of Knowledge
THUNIS, X., Law of the Obligations, Introduction to English Legal Terminology, Introduction to Common Law
VUYE, H., Constitutional Law, Dutch Legal Terminology
WERY, P., Fundamentals of Private Law
WODON, Q., International Economic Relations, Macro-economic Analysis
WYNANTS, B., Introduction to Sociology
WYNANTS, P., History of Public Law and Social Factors

Faculty of Economics, Social Sciences and Management:
BALAND, J.-M., Development Economics
BERTELS, K., Information Management
BODART, F., Management Information Systems
COIPEL, M., Commercial Law
DE COMBBRUGGHE DE PICQUENDAELE, A., International Trade Project Evaluation
DE MEESTER DE RAVESTEIN, J. C., Advanced Mathematics for Economists, Micro-economics
DESCHAMPS, R., Macro-economics
DULIEU, P., Public Enterprises
DUPLAT, J.-L., Fiscal Law
GEVERS, L., Micro-economics and Industrial Economics
GLEJSER, H., Econometrics, International and Interregional Economics
GREGOIRE, PH., Corporate Finance and Portfolio Management
GUILLAUME, M., Budgetary Control, Investment and Capital Expenditures
JACQUEMIN, J.-CH., International Trade, Methods of Economic Investigation
JACQUES, J.-M., Business Policy, International Strategy
JAUMOTTE, CH., Political Economy, Regional and Sectoral Economic Analysis
LEGRAND, M., Epistemology, Philosophical Anthropology
LESUISSE, R., Computer Science
LOUVEAUX, F., Mathematical Statistics, Mathematical Programming, Operations Research
MIGNOLET, M., Fiscal Policy and Business Strategies, Industrial Structures and Policies
NIZET, J., Sociology
PLATTEAU, J.-PH., Economic Development, Institutional Economics
PLATTEN, I., Finance and Financial Modelling
REDING, P., Money and Banking, Monetary Theory and Policy, International Monetary Economics
RIGAUX, N., Sociology
SCHEPENS, G., Operations Management, Management Information Systems
SNELDERS, H., Marketing
VAN GINDERACHTER, J., Regional Economic Policy
VAN WYMEERSCH, C., Managerial Finance, Business Forecasting, Accounting
WALLEMACQ, A., Human Resources Management
WERY, P., European Law, Common Law, Private Economic Law
WODON, Q., Public Management
WUIDAR, J., Mathematics
WYNANTS, P., History

Institute of Computer Science:
BERLEUR, J., Informatics and Sciences, Informatics and Rationality (Epistemological questions), Informatics and Society
BODART, F., Information Systems Design, Decision Support System, Man/Machine Interface
CARDINAEL, J. P., EDP Management
CAUDANO, R., Physics, Information Theory
CHERTON, C., Advanced Programming, Introduction to Informatics, Computer Architecture and Algorithms
DE KEYSER, V., Cognitive Psychology
DUBOIS, E., Software Engineering, Design of Distributed Systems, Requirements Engineering, Process Modelling
DUCHATEAU, CH., Construction of Algorithms
FICHEFET, J., Graph Theory, Linear Programming, Numerical Analysis, Operations Research, Multicriteria Decision Aid
GUILLAUME, M., Managerial Economics, Business Games
HAINAUT, J. L., Data Base Technology, Data Base Design
LE CHARLIER, B., Programming Methodology, Theory of Programming Languages
LESUISSE, R., Organization Design, Information Systems Strategies
LOBET-MARIS, C., Organization Theories, Psychological Aspects of Information Systems
NOIRHOMME-FRAITURE, M., Probabilities, Statistics, Stochastic Processes, Quantitative Methods relative to Performance
POULLET, Y., Computer Science and Law
RAMAEKERS, J., Operating Systems, Performance and Measurement of Computer Systems, Computer System Reliability and Security
SCHOBBENS, P.-Y., Artificial Intelligence Techniques, Software Specification and Proof, Artificial Intelligence in DSSs

van Bastelaer, Ph., Teleinformatics and Networks, Design of Distributed Systems

Faculty of Sciences:

André, J.-M., Quantum Chemistry
B'Nagy, J., Physical Chemistry, Spectroscopy
Blanquet, Gh., Molecular Infrared Spectroscopy and General Physics
Bodart, Fr., Experimental Physics, Atomic and Nuclear Physics
Callier, Fr., Differential and Integral Calculus, Graph Theory
Cardinael, G., Physics, Mathematics for Experimental Sciences, Electronics
Caudano, R., Solid State Physics and Medical Physics
Delhalle, J., Quantum Chemistry
Demortier, G., X-ray Physics and General Physics
Descy, J.-P., Ecology
Devos, P., Endocrinology and Zoology
Duchene, J., Philosophy of Science
Durant, F., Radiocrystallography and General Chemistry
Evrard, G., Radiocrystallography
Feytmans, E., Statistics, Molecular Biology
Giffroy, J.-M., Anatomy, Embryology and Ethology of Animals
Gillet, Cl., Theoretical Biotechnology
Gueur, H., Psychology
Hardy, A., Mathematics and Statistics
Henrard, J., Mathematics, Celestal Mechanics, Astronomy
Hevesi, L., Organic Chemistry
Khmelevskaja, G., Mathematics
Krief, A., Organic Chemistry
Lambert, D., Philosophy of Science
Lamberts, L., Analytical Chemistry
Lambin, P., Analytical Mechanics
Letesson, J. J., Microbiology, Immunology
Lucas, A., Theoretical Solid State Physics and Quantum Physics
Masereel, B., Pharmaceutical Sciences, Biochemistry and Cytology
Mengeot, J., Zoology
Micha, J.-Cl, Ecology
Nguyen, V. H., Differential and Integral Calculus, Optimization and Applied Mathematics
Orban-Ferauge, F., Geography, Cartography
Overlau, P., Mineralogy, Geology
Paquay, R., Animal Physiology
Pireaux, J.-J., Experimental Physics, Atomic and Molecular Physics
Pirson, P., Methodology of Chemistry
Raes, M., Biochemistry
Rasson, J.-P., Probabilities
Remacle, J., Biochemistry
Remon, M., Programming Statistics
Rousselet, D., Methodology of Biology
Schifflers, E., Probabilities, Statistics
Schneider, H., Methodology of Mathematics
Strodiot, J.-J., Optimization
Su, B. L., General Chemistry
Thill, G., Philosophy of Science
Thiran, J.-P., Numerical Analysis
Thiry, P., Solid State Physics
Toint, Ph., Algebra, Numerical Analysis
Van Cutsem, P., Biotechnology
Van den Haute, J., Genetics
Verbist, J., Physical Chemistry
Vercautern, D., General Chemistry, Kinetics, Physical Chemistry
Vigneron, J.-P., Solid State Physics

Faculty of Medicine:

Bosly, A., Immunology
Dulieu, J., Human Anatomy
Flamion, B., Physiology, Pharmacology
Goffinet, A., Special Physiology
Jadot, M., Human Biochemistry
Kolanowski, J., Endocrinology
Koulischer, L., Human Genetics
Leloup, R., Histology, Embryology
Mercier, M., Psychology and Medical Psychology
Piront, A., General Physiology
Poumay, Y., General Histology
Trigaux, J. P., Radiological Anatomy
Wattiaux-De Coninck, S., General Biochemistry
Zech, F., Microbiology

FACULTÉS UNIVERSITAIRES SAINT-LOUIS

43 blvd du Jardin Botanique, 1000 Brussels
Telephone: (2) 211-78-11
Fax: (2) 211-79-97
E-mail: webmaster@fusl.ac.be

Founded 1858
Language of instruction: French
Academic year: October to May

Rector: M. Van De Kerchove
Vice-Rector: J. P. Lambert

Library: see Libraries
Number of teachers: 82
Number of students: 1,200

DEANS

Faculty of Philosophy and Letters: J. Henderscheidt
Faculty of Law: P. Gerard
Faculty of Economic, Social and Political Sciences: A.-M. de Kerchove de Denterghem

PROFESSORS

Faculty of Philosophy and Letters:

Bousset, H., Dutch Authors and Literature
Braive, J., History
Brisart, R., Philosophy
Cauchies, J. M., History
Cheyns, A., Greek Philology and Authors
Cupers, J.-L., English Authors and Literature
De Ruyt, C., Ancient History and History of Art
Duchesne, J.-P., History of Art
Heiderscheidt, J., English Phonetics and Grammar
Jongen, R., German Phonetics and Grammar, Linguistics
Lenoble-Pinson, M., Modern French Grammar, Philology
Leonardy, E., German Literature
Loge, T., French Literature
Longree, D., Latin Philology
Maeschalck, M., Philosophy
Mattens, W., Dutch Grammar and Philology
Poucet, J., History of Greek and Latin Literature, and of Greek and Roman Institutions
Renard, M. C., French Authors, Modern Literatures, Italian and Spanish
Tihon, A., History
Tock, B. M., History
Willems, M., Medieval French Literature

Faculty of Law:

Cartuyvbis, Y., Introduction to Law
De Brouwer, J. L., Political Science
De Jemeppe, B., Dutch Language
De Thieux, A., Introduction to Law
Deville, A., Sociology
Dillens, A. M., Philosophy
Dumont, H., Public Law
Gerard, P., Introduction to Law
Hanard, G., Roman Law
Jacob, R., Private Law
Loriaux, C., English
Lory, J., Contemporary History, History of Thought
Mahieu, M., Introduction to Law
Nandrin, J. P., History
Ost, F., Introduction to Law
Robaye, R., Roman Law
Segers, M. J., Psychology
Strowel, A., Introduction to Law
Van de Kerchove, M., Introduction to Law
Van Gehuchten, P. P., Law
Wunsch, G., Political Economy

Faculty of Economic, Social and Political Sciences:

Bertrand, P., Physics
Callut, J. P., English Language
Citta-Vanthemsche, M., Mathematics
D'Aspremont Lynden, C., Philosophy and Social Sciences
de Kerchove de Denterghem, A. M., Economics
Deprins, D., Statistics
Deronge, Y., Accountancy
De Saint-Georges, P., Social Communication
de Stexhe, G., Philosophy and Ethics
Eich-Lerers, A., Accountancy
Everaert-Desmedt, N., Semiology
Franck, C., Political Science
Gillardin, J., Introduction to Law
Guerra, F., Accountancy
Hardy, A., Mathematics
Hubert, M., Sociology
Lambert, J. P., Economics
Leclercq, N. C., Civil Law
Loute, E., Mathematics and Computer Science
Marquet, J., Sociology
Mitchell, J., Economics
Rigaux, M.-F., Introduction to Law, Public Law
Servais, P., Economic and Social History
Simar, L., Statistics
Soete, J. L., Contemporary History
Sonveaux, E., Chemistry
Streydio, J. M., Physics
Strodiot, J. J., Mathematics
Tulkens, H., Political Economy
Van Campenhoudt, L., Sociology
Van Rillaer, J., Social and Industrial Psychology
Verhoeven, J., International Law
Wibaut, S., Political Economy
Witterwulghe, R., Political Economy

ATTACHED INSTITUTE

Ecole des Sciences Philosophiques et Religieuses: Brussels; f. 1925; Pres. M. J. Florence; 10 teachers; 230 students.

LIMBURGS UNIVERSITAIR CENTRUM

Universitaire Campus, Gebouw D, 3590 Diepenbeek
Telephone: (11) 26-81-11
Telex: 39948
Fax: (11) 26-81-99
E-mail: luc-rect@luc.ac.be

Founded 1971
Private control
State-aided

Chairman: M. Kelchtermans
Vice-Chairman: G. van Baelen
Rector: H. Martens
Vice-Rector: F. Dumortier
Permanent Secretary: W. Goetstouwers
Librarian: L. Egghe.

DEANS

Faculty of Applied Economics: R. Mercken
Faculty of Medicine: P. Steels
Faculty of Sciences: H. Callaert

HEADS OF DEPARTMENTS

Economics and Law: G. Heeren
Chemistry - Biology - Geology: J. Gelan
Human Sciences - Languages: R. M. Bruynooghe
Mathematics - Physics - Informatics: L. De Schepper
Basic Medical Sciences: K. J. Van Zwieten
Management: L. Peters

INSTITUTES OF THE UNIVERSITY

Expertise Centre for Digital Media: Dir E. FLERACKERS.

Institute for Materials Research: Dir L. STALS.

Centre for Environmental Sciences: Dir H. CLIJSTERS.

Institute of Social and Economic Sciences: Dir M. VAN HAEGENDOREN.

Limburg Institute for Applied Economic Research: Dir L. PEETERS.

Centre for Statistics: Dir G. MOLENBERGHS.

ATTACHED INSTITUTES

Dr L. Willems-Instituut v.z.w.: Dir J. RAUS.

WTCM: Scientific Consultant L. STALS.

University Level Institutions

COLLEGE OF EUROPE

Dijver 11, 8000 Bruges
Telephone: (50) 44-99-11
Fax: (50) 44-99-00
E-mail: info@coleurop.be

Founded 1949; institute of postgraduate European studies
Languages of instruction: English and French

President of Board of Trustees: JACQUES DELORS
Rector: O. VON DER GABLENTZ
Librarian: K. CLARA

Library of 100,000 vols
Number of teachers: 90
Number of students: 260

DIRECTORS

Department of Law: P. DEMARET
Department of Economics: P. C. PACLOUN
Department of Administration: D. MAHNCKE
Department of Development of Human Resources: R. GWYN
Programme of European General and Interdisciplinary Studies: R. PICHT

ÉCOLE DES HAUTES ÉTUDES COMMERCIALES

14 rue Louvrex, 4000 Liège
Telephone: (4) 232-72-11
Fax: (4) 232-72-40

Founded 1898
Language of instruction: French

President: M. HANSENNE
Director: M. DUBRU
Administrative Director: M. ALDENHOFF
Secretary-General: CH. HENNEGHIEN-ORBAN
Librarian: M. A. COLLARD-THOMAS

The library contains 12,000 vols
Number of teachers: 130
Number of students: 1,200

HEADS OF DEPARTMENTS

Accounting and Firm Management: J. MINSART
Applied Sciences: B. DE WOLF
Basic Courses: J. M. DUJARDIN
Computer Science in Management: M. J. TOUSSAINT
Economics: M. HERMANS
Languages: A. SPINETTE
Law: M. PARISSE
Marketing: J. P. BAEYENS
Quantitative and Managing Methods: L. ESCH

ECONOMISCHE HOGESCHOOL SINT-ALOYSIUS

Stormstraat 2 , 1000 Brussels
Telephone: (2) 210-12-11

Founded 1925
A university-level school of economics

Director: D. DE CEULAER

Number of teachers: 150

ERASMUSHOGESCHOOL-BRUSSEL

84 Trierstraat, 1040 Brussels
Telephone: (2) 230-12-60
Fax: (2) 230-99-90
E-mail: postmaster@erasmus.eunet.be

Founded 1991 by the amalgamation of the Administratieve en Economische Hogeschool (f. 1938) and the School for Translators and Interpreters (f. 1958)
Language of instruction: Dutch, but multilingual for postgraduate studies
Private control

Director-General and Delegate Administrator: H.-J. VERMEYLEN
Assistant Director: J. TERWECOREN

Publication: *Tijdschrift voor Bestuurswetenschappen en Publike Recht* (monthly), *Medium – Tijdschrift voor Toegepaste Taalwetenschap* (3 a year).

FACULTEIT VOOR VERGELIJKENDE GODSDIENSTWETENSCHAPPEN

(Faculty for Comparative Study of Religions)

Bist 164, 2610 Wilrijk-Antwerp
Telephone: (3) 830-51-58
Fax: (3) 825-26-73
E-mail: yuho@glo.be

Founded by Royal Decree in 1980
An international university level organization for the comparative study of religions
Languages of instruction: Dutch, English, German and French

Chairman of Board: JEREMY ROSEN
Rector: CHRISTIAAN J. G. VONCK
Dean: A. PEEL
Librarian: H. PEERLINCK

Publications: catalogue, *Acta Comparanda*.

H.E.C. SAINT-LOUIS

113 rue du Marais, 1000 Brussels
Telephone: (2) 219-27-03

Founded 1925

President: L. DELTOMBE
Director: J. VAN BESIEN

Library of 2,000 vols

Publication: *Bulletin des sommaires* (fortnightly).

Evening courses in commercial, management, marketing, information and financial sciences.

HANDELSHOGESCHOOL

Korte Nieuwstraat 33, 2000 Antwerp
Telephone: (3) 232-74-52
Fax: (3) 226-44-04
E-mail: directie@hha.be

Founded 1923

President: Dr F. CARRIJN
Librarian: S. DE LANDTSHEER

The library contains 25,000 vols
Number of teachers: 100
Number of students: 1,300

HAUTE ÉCOLE DE BRUXELLES

34 rue Joseph Hazard, 1180 Brussels
Telephone: (2) 340-12-95
Fax: (2) 347-52-64

President and Director: JEAN-MARIE VAN DER MEERSCHEN
Librarians: J. P. GAHIDE, O. GALMA

Library of 42,000 vols
Number of teachers: 162
Number of students: 1,900

Publication: *Équivalences* (2 a year).

DIRECTORS

Institute of Translating and Interpreting: GEORGES GUISLAIN
Institute of Teacher-Training: LUC BARBAY
Institute of Economics and Technology: MARIANNE COESSENS

HENRY VAN DE VELDE-INSTITUTE, ANTWERP

(Higher Institute of Architecture and Product Development)

Mutsaertstraat 31, 2000 Antwerp
Telephone: (3) 231-70-84
Fax: (3) 226-04-11

Founded 1663 by Teniers; independent 1952

Director: W. TOUBHANS
Administrator: H. MEES
Librarian: G. PERSOONS

Departments of architecture, interior design, urban development and physical planning, conservation of sites and monuments, building techniques, product development and design.

INSTITUT CATHOLIQUE DES HAUTES ÉTUDES COMMERCIALES

2 blvd Brand Whitlock, 1150 Brussels
Telephone: (2) 739-37-11

Founded 1934
Languages of instruction: French, Dutch and English

Rector: Prof. PIERRE DUPRIEZ
President: E. DAVIGNON
General Secretary: P. FLAHAUT
Librarian: M. VANDERHOEVEN-FLAHAUX

Library of 16,000 vols
Number of teachers: 116
Number of students: 1,600

Publication: *Reflets et Perspectives de la Vie Economique*.

HEADS OF DEPARTMENTS

Auditing: P. LURKIN
Commercial Engineering: G. JANNES
Finance: P. VAN NAMEN
Human Resources Management: C. DE BRIER
Information Science: J.-M. PONCELET
International Economics: E. CRACCO
Marketing: R. SAINTROND

ATTACHED SCHOOLS

Ecole Supérieure des Sciences Fiscales: 2 blvd Brand Whitlock, 1150 Brussels; f. 1958; library of 2,000 vols; 28 teachers; 200 students; Pres. Prof. P. DUPRIEZ; Librarian M.-C. SIBILLE-VAN GRIEKEN.

INSTITUT COOREMANS

11 place Anneessens, 1000 Brussels
Telephone: (2) 551-02-10
Fax: (2) 551-02-16

Founded 1911

Language of instruction: French (English for Accountancy and Finance Studies)

President: P. LAMBERT
Dean: L. COOREMANS

Number of teachers: 80
Number of students: 400

Courses at degree level in commerce and administration.

INSTITUT GRAMME LIÈGE INSTITUT SUPÉRIEUR INDUSTRIEL

28 quai du Condroz, 4031 Angleur (Liège)

Telephone: (4) 343-07-26
Fax: (4) 343-30-28

Founded 1906
Language of instruction: French

Director: JULES DUBOIS

Library of 11,528 vols
Number of teachers: 64
Number of students: 561

Courses in industrial engineering

Publications: *Nouvelles de l'Union Gramme* (quarterly), *Annuaire*.

INSTITUT SUPÉRIEUR D'ARCHITECTURE DE LA COMMUNAUTÉ FRANÇAISE — LA CAMBRE

19 place Eugène Flagey, 1050 Brussels

Telephone: (2) 640-96-96
Fax: (2) 647-46-55

Founded 1926
State control
Language of instruction: French

Director: Prof. MARCEL PESLEUX
Deputy Director: Dr GUY PILATE
Head of Academic Affairs: MARC GOSSE
Librarian: MARC BRUNFAUT

Library of 5,000 book titles

INSTITUT SUPÉRIEUR D'ARCHITECTURE INTERCOMMUNAL (ISAI)

Site Victor Horta, CP 248, Blvd du Triomphe, 1050 Brussels

Telephone: (2) 650-50-52

Founded 1711; now associated with Free University of Brussels and schools of architecture at Liège and Mons (ISAI)
Language of instruction: French

Director: GERARD VAN GOOLEN

Library of 30,000 vols
Number of teachers: 60
Number of students: 650

Publication: *I.S.A.Br.* (monthly).

Courses in architecture, urban design, restoration and heritage conservation.

KATHOLIEKE VLAAMSE HOGESCHOOL

Sint-Andriesstraat 2, 2000 Antwerp

Telephone: (3) 206-04-80
Fax: (3) 206-04-81
E-mail: kvh@kvh.be

Founded 1919

General Director: R. VAN LEUVEN
Deputy General Director: PH. MICHIELS
Librarian: G. HANEGREEFS

Library of 20,000 vols
Number of teachers: 150
Number of students: 1,700

HEADS OF DEPARTMENT

Translating and Interpreting: R. SINJAN
Psychology: J. DUYCK
Speech Therapy and Audiology: K. LAMBERS

PRINS LEOPOLD INSTITUUT VOOR TROPISCHE GENEESKUNDE/ INSTITUT DE MÉDECINE TROPICALE PRINCE LÉOPOLD

Nationalestraat 155, 2000 Antwerp

Telephone: (3) 247-66-66
Telex: 31648
Fax: (3) 216-14-31

Founded by Royal Decree in 1931
Languages of instruction: Dutch, French and English

President: C. PAULUS
Director: Prof. Dr B. GRYSEELS
Administrative Director: L. SCHUEREMANS
Librarian: G. ROELANTS

The library contains 30,000 books and 15,000 pamphlets
Number of teachers: 30

Publications: *Rapport Annuel* (Dutch, French and English), *Journal of Tropical Medicine and International Health*.

PROFESSORS

BRANDT, J., Helminthology
BUSCHER, PH., Serology
COLEBUNDERS, B., Clinical Services
COOSEMANS, M., Entomology
DE MUYNCK, A., Epidemiology
ELSEN, P., Entomology
GEERTS, S., Veterinary Pathology
KESTENS, L., Immunology
KUMAR, V., Tropical Veterinary Pathology
LAGA, M., Sexually-transmitted Diseases
LE RAY, D., Protozoology
PARENT, M., Tropical Paediatrics
PORTAELS, F., Microbiology
STROOBANT, A., Tropical Hygiene
SWINNE, D., Mycology
UNGER, J. P., Public Health
VAN DEN ENDE, J., Tropical Pathology
VAN DER GROEN, G., Virology
VAN DER STUYFT, P., Epidemiology
VAN GOMPEL, A., Tropical Pathology
VAN LERBERGHE, W., Public Health
VERHULST, A., Tropical Animal Production
WERY, M., Protozoology

ATTACHED INSTITUTE

Clinique Léopold II: Kronenburgstraat 43, 2000 Antwerp; forms an annexe to the Prins Leopold Instituut Voor Tropische Geneeskunde; treats patients from tropical countries and travellers; Dir Dr J. VAN DEN ENDE.

Colleges

Ecole Royale Militaire/Koninklijke Militaire School: 30 ave de la Renaissance, 1000 Brussels; tel. (2) 737-60-01; fax (2) 737-60-14; f. 1834; academic education of officers for Army, Navy, Air Force, Medical Service and Gendarmerie; languages of instruction: French and Dutch; 117 teachers, including 19 profs; 900 students; library of 100,000 vols; Commdt Maj.-Gen. P. GEORIS; Dir of Military Instruction Col BEM J. JOCKIN; Dir of Studies Prof. Ir JACQUES; Library Dir Cdt G. PEETERS.

PROFESSORS

ACHEROY, M. P. J., Electrical Engineering
BAUDOIN, Y., Applied Mathematics
BOURGOIS, R. A., Construction Engineering
CALLANT, A. A., Analytical Mechanics
CELENS, E., Armament and Ballistics
DE BISSCHOP, H., Chemistry
DECUYPERE, R. H., Applied Mechanics
DE VOS, L., History
GOBIN, M. A., Mathematics
JACQUES, R., Applied Mechanics
KALITVENTZEFF, B., General Chemistry
PASTYN, H. J., Mathematics and Operations Research
SCHWEICHER, E. J. P., Opto-electronics
STRUYS, W. R., Economics
THOMAS, FR., Law
VAN HAMME, J., Mathematics
VANDENPLAS, P. E. M., Physics and Director of the Laboratory of Plasma Physics
VLOEBERGHS, C., Telecommunications
WEYNANTS, R., Physics

Horeca en Sportinstituut Wemmel: Zijp 14–16, 1780 Wemmel; tel. (2) 456-01-01; Dir J. HUMBLET.

Institut des Hautes Études de Belgique: 44 ave Jeanne, 1050 Brussels; f. 1894; language of instruction: French; courses in natural sciences, mechanics, history, philosophy, arts and letters, economics, social and political sciences; Pres. S. HUYBERECHTS; Gen. Sec. G. SAMUEL.

ATTACHED SCHOOL

Ecole d'Ergologie: 50 ave F. D. Roosevelt, 1050 Brussels; f. 1925; Dir J. HOFMANS.

Institut Libre Marie Haps: 11 rue d'Arlon, 1050 Brussels; tel. (2) 511-92-92; fax (2) 511-98-37; f. 1919; two- and four-year courses for translators and interpreters; three-year courses in psychology and speech therapy; library of 12,000 vols; 154 teachers; 1,260 students; Dir B. DEVLAMMINCK; Sec.-Gen. B. QUOILIN-CLAUDE; Librarian M. VAN LIL; publ. *Le langage et l'homme* (3 a year).

Koninklijke Belgische Marine Academie/ Académie Royale de Marine de Belgique: Steenplein 1, 2000 Antwerp; tel. (3) 232-08-50; f. 1935; Pres CHRISTIAN KONINCKX; Sec.-Gen. LIONEL TRICOT; publs *Mededelingen, Communications* (annually).

Schools of Music, Art and Architecture

Académie Royale des Beaux-Arts de Bruxelles (Brussels Royal Academy of Fine Arts): 144 rue du Midi, 1000 Brussels; tel. (2) 511-04-91; f. 1711; drawing, painting, sculpture, decorative arts, interior decorating, illustration, publicity and engraving; library: see Libraries; Dir D. VIENNE.

Conservatoire Royal de Bruxelles/Koninklijk Conservatorium Brussel: 30 rue de la Régence, 1000 Brussels; f. 1832; *French section:* tel. (2) 511-04-27; 160 teachers; 850 students; Dir (vacant); *Flemish section:* tel. (2) 513-45-87; fax (2) 513-22-53; 200 teachers; 500 students; Dir A. VAN LYSEBETH; library of 1,000,000 vols; Librarian J. EECKELOO.

Conservatoire Royal de Musique de Liège: 14 rue Forgeur, Liège; tel. (4) 222-03-06; fax (4) 222-03-84; f. 1826; 80 professors; students taken from 15 years of age; all branches of music and theatre; Dir B. DEKAISE; Admin. Sec. CLAUDETTE VAN HOLSAET; Librarian PHILIPPE GILSON.

Conservatoire Royal de Musique de Mons: 7 rue de Nimy, 7000 Mons; tel. (65) 34-73-77; fax (65) 34-99-06; f. 1926; 420 students; library of 30,000 vols; Dir HENRI BARBIER.

Ecole Nationale Supérieure des Arts Visuels de la Cambre: Abbaye de La Cambre 21, 1050 Brussels; tel. (2) 648-96-19; f. 1926; library: see Libraries; *c.* 500 students; Dir FRANCE BOREL.

Hogeschool Antwerpen, Hoger Instituut voor Dramatische Kunst: Maarschalk Gérardstraat 4, 2000 Antwerp; tel. (3) 231-54-65; fax (3) 232-22-34; f. 1946; 4-year full-time academic education and professional training in theatre and related performing arts; Dir KAREL HERMANS.

Insas (Institut National Supérieur des Arts du Spectacle et Techniques de Diffusion): rue Thérésienne 8, 1000 Brussels; tel. (2) 511-92-86; fax (2) 511-02-79; e-mail insas@skynet.be; f. 1962 for advanced studies in dramatic art, cinema and broadcasting technique, including television; 3- and 4-year courses; Dir J. P. CASIMIR.

Koninklijk Vlaams Muziek Conservatorium van Antwerpen (Royal Flemish School of Music): Desguinlei 25, 2018 Antwerp; tel. (3) 244-18-00; fax (3) 238-90-17; f. 1898; library of 550,000 vols; 220 teachers, 375 students; Dir MICHAEL SCHECK; Admin. Sec. ROGER QUADFLIEG; Librarian MARIE THÉRÈSE BUYSSENS.

Nationaal Hoger Instituut en Koninklijke Academie voor Schone Kunsten-Antwerpen (National Higher Institute and Royal Academy of Fine Arts, Antwerp): Mutsaertstraat 31, 2000 Antwerp; tel. (3) 232-41-61; f. 1663; awards first and Master's degrees; 100 staff; library of 20,000 vols and prints, 250 periodicals; Dir G. GAUDAEN; Scientific Librarian Dr G. PERSOONS; publs catalogues of exhibits.

BELIZE

Learned Societies

BIBLIOGRAPHY, LIBRARY SCIENCE AND MUSEOLOGY

Belize Library Association: Central Library, Bliss Institute, POB 287, Belize City; tel. 7267; f. 1976; affiliated to IFLA and Commonwealth Library Asscn; close ties with national library service; aims to improve standards of library workers and libraries, and improve the cultural aspects of Belize; sponsors summer courses on library science, educational and cultural activities; 50 mems; Pres. H. W. YOUNG; Sec. R. T. HULSE; publ. *Bulletin* (quarterly).

Libraries and Archives

Belize City

Leo Bradley Library: Princess Margaret Drive, POB 287, Belize City; tel. (2) 34248; fax (2) 34246; f. 1935; nat. library service for Belize; incl. National Collection; 100,000 vols; 40 brs throughout Belize; Chief Librarian JOY YSAGUIRRE.

Belmopan

Belize Archives Department: 26/28 Unity Blvd, Belmopan; tel. 08-22247; fax 08-23140; e-mail archives@btl.net; f. 1965; 100,000 documents; Chief Archivist CHARLES A. GIBSON.

Colleges

Corozal Community College: POB 63, Corozal Town; tel. 04-22541; f. 1978 by merger of Fletcher College and St Francis Xavier College to form an ecumenical (Roman Catholic, Methodist, Anglican) college; 42 teachers; 680 students; four- and two-year courses in academic and commercial studies; Principal CARLOS CASTILLO.

University College of Belize: POB 990, Belize City; tel. (2) 32732; fax (2) 30255; e-mail acal@ucb.edu.bz; f. 1986; courses in fields of agriculture, business, medicine, law, social work, education, arts and sciences; library of *c.* 25,000 vols; Pres. Dr ANGEL E. CAL; publ. *UCB Journal of Belizean Affairs*.

University of the West Indies Extra-Mural Department: POB 229, University Centre, Belize City; tel. (2) 35320; fax (2) 32038; f. 1949; one resident and several part-time tutors; over 200 students; library of *c.* 10,000 vols; Resident Tutor JOSEPH O. PALACIO.

Wesley College: POB 543, 34 Yarborough Rd, Belize City; tel. (2) 77127; f. 1882; 4-year arts, science and commercial courses; 20 teachers; 336 students; library of 3,000 vols; Principal BRENDA J. ARMSTRONG.

BENIN

Research Institutes

GENERAL

Centre Régional de Recherche Sud-Bénin: Attogon; f. 1904; library of 2,000 vols and periodicals; Dir Dr J. DETONGNON.

Institut de Recherches Appliquées: BP 6, Porto Novo; f. 1942; library of 8,000 vols; Dir S. S. ADOTEVI; publ. *Etudes*.

AGRICULTURE, FISHERIES AND VETERINARY SCIENCE

Station de Recherches sur le Cocotier: Semé-Podji; coconut research; f. 1977; attached to IRHO (see entry under France); Dir HONORÉ TCHIBOZO.

Station de Recherches sur le Palmier à Huile: BP 1, Pobe; tel. 25-00-66; f. 1922; oil palm station; attached to Direction de la Recherche Agronomique/Ministère du Développement rural et l'Action coopérative (DRA/MDRAC); library of 70 vols, 54 reviews; Dir Dr MOÏSE HOUSSOU.

NATURAL SCIENCES

General

Institut Français de Recherche Scientifique pour le Développement en Coopération (ORSTOM): BP 390, Cotonou. (See main entry under France.)

TECHNOLOGY

Office Béninois de Recherches Géologiques et Minières: BP 249, Cotonou; tel. 31-03-09; fax 31-41-20; f. 1977; branch of Ministry of Industry, Trade and Tourism; library of 8,000 vols, 115 periodicals; Dir-Gen. IDRISSOU MARCOS.

Libraries and Archives

Porto Novo

Archives Nationales de la République du Bénin: BP 629, Porto Novo; tel. and fax 21-30-79; f. 1914; Dir ELISE PARAISO; publs *Bulletin* (annually), *Mémoire du Bénin* (4 a year).

Bibliothèque Nationale: BP 401, Porto Novo; tel. 212585; f. 1976; 35,000 vols; Dir H. N. AMOUSSOU.

Museums and Art Galleries

Abomey

Musée National d'Abomey: Abomey; Curator R.-PH. ASSOGBA.

Porto Novo

Musée National: c/o IRA, BP 6, Porto Novo; premises at Cotonou; Curator MARTIN AKABIAMU.

University

UNIVERSITÉ NATIONALE DU BÉNIN

Abomey-Calavi, BP 526, Cotonou
Telephone: (36) 00-74
Telex: 5010
Founded 1970
State control
Language of instruction: French
Academic year: October to July

Rector: Prof. KÉMOKO OSSÉNI BAGNAN
Vice-Rector: TAOFIKI W. AMINOU
Director of Administrative and Financial Affairs: ANOUROU AKPITI EPSE BOURAÏMA
Secretary-General: ROGER N'TIA
Librarian: PASCAL A. I. GANDAHO

Library of 40,000 vols
Number of teachers: 647
Number of students: 8,883

Publications: *UNB au Fil des Jours, Annuaire* and students' guide.

DEANS

Faculty of Scientific and Technical Studies: TIDJANI CHONIBARE
Faculty of Arts, Literature and Human Sciences: ALBERT NOUHOUAYI
Faculty of Health Sciences: CÉSAR AKPO
Faculty of Law, Economics and Politics: GÉRO FULBERT AMOUSSOUGA
Faculty of Agriculture: CLAUDE ADANDEDJAN

DIRECTORS

National School of Administration: LYDIE POGNON
National Institute of Economics: PAUL AGBOGBA
National Institute of Physical Education and Sport: SOUAÏBOU GOUDA
Teacher Training College: CHRISTIAN DOSSOU
Benin Centre for Foreign Languages: BIENVENU AKOHA
Regional Institute for Health Development Studies: PATHÉ DIALLO

BHUTAN

Libraries and Archives

Thimphu

National Library of Bhutan: Thimphu; tel. 22885; fax 22693; f. 1967, new building 1984; 1,600 vols of Tibetan MS and block-print books, 90,000 Tibetan books in other forms; 15,000 foreign (mainly English) books; Eastern branch: Kuenga Rabten, Tongsa, Thimphu; Dir SANGAY WANGCHUG (acting).

Thimphu Public Library: Thimphu; f. 1980; inc. the Jigme Dorji Wangchuk Library (f. 1978); UN depository library; 6,000 vols; Librarian Mrs TSHEWANG ZAM.

Museums and Art Galleries

Paro

National Museum: Ta Dzong, Paro; tel. (2) 29138; fax (2) 29103; opened to visitors in 1968; housed in seven-storey 17th-century fortress; gallery of paintings (Thankas), images, decorative art, arms, jewellery; copper, bronze, wood and bamboo objects; natural history of Bhutan; reference library with books on Northern Buddhism, Tibetology, museology, conservation and books on Bhutan; Dir Ven. MYNAK R. TULKU.

Colleges

National Institute of Education: Samtse; tel. (2) 65117; fax (2) 65104; f. 1968; three-year B.Ed. course, two-year certificate course, one-year postgraduate certificate course, five-year distance education course; academic year starts August; 247 students; library of 15,000 vols, 20 periodicals; Dir DORJEE TSHERING; Principal TSHEWANG CHHODEN WANGDI.

Royal Bhutan Polytechnic: Deothang; tel. 51146; f. 1974; three-year diploma courses in civil, mechanical and electrical engineering; library of 2,000 vols; Principal KEZANG CHADOR.

Royal Institute of Management: POB 416, Simtokha, Thimphu; tel. (2) 22873; fax (2) 24188; f. 1986; training courses for civil service and private sector at certificate, diploma and postgraduate diploma levels; graduate course; library of 5,000 vols, 80 periodicals; Dir KUNZANG WANGDI.

Incorporates:

Royal Commercial Institute: Thimphu; tel. 2610; f. 1977; Principal PABITRA KUMAR ROY.

Royal Accounts School: Thimphu.

Royal Technical Institute: Kharbandi; tel. 2317; fax 2171; five-year certificate courses for electricians, mechanics, motor mechanics; 48 graduates in 1986; Principal DAWA GYELTSHEN.

Sherubtse Degree College: PO Kanglung, Trashigang; tel. (4) 35100; fax (4) 35129; f. 1983; three-year honours degree courses in economics, English, geography, Dzongkha and commerce, and general degree courses in sciences; two-year pre-university course in science; language of instruction: English; 46 teachers, 484 students; library of 22,000 vols; Principal PEMA THINLEY; publ. *Sherub Doenme* (journal, in English, 2 a year).

Ugyen Wangchuck University: in process of formation.

BOLIVIA

Learned Societies

GENERAL

Academia Boliviana (Bolivian Academy): Casilla 4145, La Paz; f. 1927; Corresponding Academy of the Real Academia Española in Madrid; 26 mems; Dir Mons. JUAN QUIRÓS; Permanent Sec. CARLOS CASTAÑÓN BARRIENTOS; Pro-Sec. MARIO FRÍAS INFANTE; publ. *Revista*.

AGRICULTURE, FISHERIES AND VETERINARY SCIENCE

Sociedad Rural Boliviana (Agricultural Society): Casilla 786, Edif. El Condor piso 10, Of. 1005, La Paz; f. 1934; 30 assoc. mems; Pres. Ing. JOSÉ LUIS ARAMAYO V.; publs *IFAP News*, *El Surco, Cotar, Universitas*.

ARCHITECTURE AND TOWN PLANNING

Colegio de Arquitectos de Bolivia: Casilla 11876, La Paz; tel. 39-15-68; fax 39-15-68; f. 1940; architecture and town planning; 2,500 mems; library of 5,000 vols; Pres. FROILÁN CAVERO M.; Sec. JUAN C. BARRIENTOS M.; publs *Punku, Arquitectura y Ciudad, CDALP Informa*.

FINE AND PERFORMING ARTS

Círculo de Bellas Artes (Fine Arts Circle): Plaza Teatro, La Paz; f. 1912; Pres. ERNESTO PEÑARANDA.

HISTORY, GEOGRAPHY AND ARCHAEOLOGY

Academia Nacional de la Historia (National Academy of History): Avda Abel Iturralde 205, La Paz; f. 1929; 18 mems; Pres. Dr DAVID ALVESTEGUI; Sec.-Gen. Dr HUMBERTO VÁZQUEZ-MACHICADO.

Sociedad de Estudios Geográficos e Históricos (Geographical and Historical Society): Plaza 24 de Setiembre, Santa Cruz de la Sierra; f. 1903; Pres. Dr HERNANDO SANABRIA FERNÁNDEZ; Vice-Pres. Lic. PLÁCIDO MOLINA B.; Sec. AVELINO PEREDO; publ. *Boletín*.

Sociedad Geográfica de La Paz (La Paz Geographical Soc.): Casilla 1487, Edif. Santa Mónica, 13 Plaza Abaroa, La Paz; f. 1889; depts of pre-history, history, folklore, geography; 580 mems; Pres. Dr GREGORIO LOZA BALSA; publ. *Boletín* (2 a year).

Sociedad Geográfica y de Historia 'Potosí' (Geographical and Historical Society): Casilla 39, Potosí; tel. and fax (62) 2-27-77; f. 1905; 20 mems; library of 4,000 vols; Pres. Prof. ALFREDO TAPIA VARGS; Sec. WALTER ZAVAL; publ. *Boletín*.

Sociedad Geográfica y de Historia 'Sucre': Plaza 25 de Mayo, Sucre; f. 1887; 8 mems; library of 3,000 vols; Dir Dr JOAQUÍN GANTIER V.; publ. *Boletín*.

LANGUAGE AND LITERATURE

PEN Club de Bolivia–Centro Internacional de Escritores (International PEN Centre): Calle Goitia 17, Casilla 149, La Paz; f. 1931; 40 Bolivian mems, 7 from other South American countries; Pres. (vacant); Sec. YOLANDA BEDREGAL DE CÓNITZER.

MEDICINE

Ateneo de Medicina de Sucre (Athenaeum of Medicine): Sucre; Pres. Dr AGUSTÍN BENÁVIDES; Vice-Pres. Dr ABERTO MARTÍNEZ; Sec.-Gen. Dr ROMELIO A. SUBIETA.

Sociedad de Pediatría de Cochabamba (Paediatrics Soc.): Casilla 1429, Cochabamba; f. 1945; 14 mems; Pres. Dr JULIO CORRALES BADANI; Sec. Dr MOISÉS SEJAS.

NATURAL SCIENCES

General

Academia Nacional de Ciencias de Bolivia (Bolivian National Academy of Sciences): POB 5829, Avda 16 de Julio 1732, La Paz; tel. (2) 363990; fax (2) 379681; f. 1960; 42 mems; library of 8,000 vols; Pres. Dr CARLOS AGUIRRE BASTOS; Sec-Gen. Ing. ISMAEL MONTES DE OCA; Librarian Ing. ANTONIO SAAVEDRA; publs *Publicaciones* (irregular), *Boletín Informativo* (monthly), *Revista* (2 a year).

Physical Sciences

Sociedad Geológica Boliviana: Edif. Servicio Geológico de Bolivia, Calle Federico Zuazo-Esq., Reyes Ortiz 1673, Casilla 2729, La Paz; f. 1961; Pres. Ing. LORGIO RUIZ G.

TECHNOLOGY

Asociación de Ingenieros y Geólogos de Yacimientos Petrolíferos Fiscales Bolivianos (AIG—YPFB): Casilla 401, La Paz; f. 1959; 210 mems in 4 brs: La Paz, Camiri, Cochabamba, Santa Cruz; Pres. Ing. JUAN CARRASCO; publ. *Revista Técnica de Yacimientos Petrolíferos Fiscales Bolivianos* (quarterly).

Research Institutes

GENERAL

Institut Français de Recherche Scientifique pour le Développement en Coopération (ORSTOM): CP 9214, La Paz; tel. 357723; fax 391854; geology, hydrobiology, medical entomology, agronomy, nutrition, hydrology, climatology, social sciences; Dir Dr BERNARD POUYAUD. (See main entry under France.)

AGRICULTURE, FISHERIES AND VETERINARY SCIENCE

Instituto Boliviano de Tecnología Agropecuaria (IBTA): Edificio 'El Condor', Calle Batallón Colorados N° 24, Casilla 5783, La Paz; tel. 374289; fax 370883; f. 1975; 380 mems; library of 47,000 vols, 260 periodicals; Dir Ing. RAFAEL VERA; publ. *Boletín INFO-IBTA* (2 a month).

ECONOMICS, LAW AND POLITICS

Instituto Nacional de Estadística (National Institute of Statistics): Plaza Mario Guzmán Aspiazu 1, Casilla 612, La Paz; tel. 367444; telex 3505; fax 354230; f. 1936; national, economic and social statistics and censuses; library of 10,500 vols, 370 periodicals; Exec. Dir Lic. ROSA TALAVERAS; publs *IPC* (monthly), *Boletín de Cuentas Nacionales*.

HISTORY, GEOGRAPHY AND ARCHAEOLOGY

Instituto Geográfico Militar (Military Institute of Geography): Avda Saavedra 2303, Cuartel General, Miraflores, La Paz; tel. (2) 220513; fax (2) 228329; e-mail igm@chilepac.net; f. 1936; geodesy, nat. topographical survey Commandant Brig.-Gen. CARLOS BELMONTE CORDANO; publ. *Boletín Informativo*.

Instituto Nacional de Arqueología de Bolivia: Calle Tiwanaku 93, Casilla 20319, La Paz; tel. 329624; f. 1975; *c*. 26 mems; library of 6,000 vols; Dir CARLOS URQUIZO SOSSA; publ. *Arqueología Boliviana*.

LANGUAGE AND LITERATURE

Instituto Nacional de Estudios Lingüísticos (INEL): Junín 608, Casilla 7846, La Paz; f. 1965; part of *Instituto Nacional de Historia, Literatura y Antropología*; linguistic, social and educational research and teaching; specializations: Quechua and Aymara; library of 1,200 vols; Dir VITALIANO HUANCA TORREZ; publs specialized papers, *Yatiñataki, Notas y Noticias Lingüísticas* (monthly).

MEDICINE

Instituto de Cancerología 'Cupertino Arteaga': Hospital de Clínicas, Plaza de Libertad, Sucre; f. 1947; Dir Dr H. NUNEZ R.

Instituto Médico Sucre (Medical Inst.): San Alberto 8 y 10, Casilla 82, Sucre; f. 1895; 27 mems, 3 hon., and 130 corresponding; library of 8,000 vols, including *Flora Peruviensis* and 16th-century edition of *Aforismos de Hipocrates*, 6,000 pamphlets; research and production of vaccines and sera; Pres. Dr EZEQUIEL L. OSORIO; Sec. Dr JOSÉ AGUIRRE; Librarian Dr GUSTAVO VACA GUZMÁN; publ. *Revista* (quarterly).

Instituto Nacional de Medicina Nuclear: Casilla 5795, Calle M. Zubieta 1555, Miraflores, La Paz; tel. 356115; f. 1963; research into altitude physiology and physiopathology, clinical diagnosis with radioisotopes; postgraduate teaching; Dir LUIS F. BARRAGÁN M.

NATURAL SCIENCES

Physical Sciences

Observatorio San Calixto: Casilla 12656, La Paz; tel. (2) 356098; fax (2) 376805; e-mail adrake@datacom-bo.net; f. 1892; meteorology and seismology; library of 11,000 vols; Dir Dr LAWRENCE A. DRAKE.

Servicio Geológico de Bolivia: Federico Zuazo 1673, Casilla 2729, La Paz; tel. 322022; telex 363474; f. 1956 as a national department, reorganized 1965; 140 mems; 10 laboratories; library of *c*. 2,100 vols; Dir Ing. DANIEL HOWARD BARRÓN; publs geological maps and bulletins.

RELIGION, SOCIOLOGY AND ANTHROPOLOGY

Instituto de Sociología Boliviana (ISBO) (Inst. of Sociology): Apdo 215, Sucre; f. 1941; investigates economic, juridical and sociological problems; library of 15,000 vols; Dir TOMÁS LENZ B.; publ. *Revista del Instituto de Sociología Boliviana*.

TECHNOLOGY

Instituto Boliviano de Ciencia y Tecnología Nuclear: Avda 6 de Agosto 2905, Casilla 4821, La Paz; tel. (02) 356877; telex 2220; f 1983; Exec. Dir. Ing. JUAN CARLOS MÉNDEZ FERRY (acting).

Instituto Boliviano del Petróleo (IBP): Casilla 4722, La Paz; f. 1959 to support and co-ordinate scientific, technical and economic studies on the oil industry in Bolivia; 50 mems; library of 1,000 technical vols; Pres. Ing. JOSÉ PATIÑO; Gen. Sec. Ing. REYNALDO SALGUEIRO PABÓN; publs *Boletín, Manual de Signos Convencionales*.

Libraries and Archives

Cochabamba

Biblioteca Central Universitaria 'José Antonio Arze' (Universidad Mayor de San Simón): Avda Oquendo esq. Sucre, Casilla 992, Cochabamba; tel. (42) 31733; telex 6363; fax (42) 31691; f. 1930; 30,000 vols; Dir LUIS ALBERTO PONCE; publ. *Boletín Bibliográfico*.

La Paz

Biblioteca Central de la Universidad Mayor de San Andrés: CC 6548, La Paz; f. 1930; 121,000 vols; Dir Lic. ALBERTO CRESPO RODAS.

Biblioteca del Honorable Congreso Nacional (Congress Library): Calle Ayacucho esquina Mercado No. 308, La Paz; tel. (2) 314731; f. 1912; 22,000 vols; Dir VÍCTOR BERNAL SOLARES; Chief Librarian NELLY ARRAYA VASQUEZ; publ. *Reports of Congress*.

Biblioteca del Instituto Boliviano de Estudio y Acción Social: Avda Arce 2147, La Paz; special collections on social science, Boliviana, education and government documents; 12,000 vols; Dir ELENA PEDDLE.

Biblioteca del Ministerio de Relaciones Exteriores (Library of the Ministry of Foreign Affairs): Plaza Murillo, La Paz; f. 1930; 10,039 vols; private library; Dir Prof. PACÍFICO LUNA QUIJARRO.

Biblioteca Municipal 'Mariscal Andrés de Santa Cruz' (Municipal Library): Plaza del Estudiante, La Paz; tel. (2) 378477; f. 1838; 35,000 vols; Dir MARIA FEDAK KURPEL.

Centro Nacional de Documentación Científica y Tecnológica (Bolivian National Scientific and Technological Documentation Centre): CP 9357, Calle Ayacucho, La Paz; tel. (2) 359586; fax (2) 359491; f. 1967 to provide extensive information service for research and development; depository library for FAO, WHO and ILO; library of 9,800 vols; Dir RUBÉN VALLE VERA; publ. *Actualidades* (quarterly).

Potosí

Biblioteca Central Universitaria: Universidad Autónoma 'Tomás Frías', Casilla 54, Avda del Maestro, Potosí; tel. 27313; f. 1942; 43,796 vols, 1,471 periodicals; one central library, eight specialized libraries; Dir JULIA B. DE LÓPEZ; publs *Revista Orientación Pedagógica, Revista Científica, Revista de Ciencias*.

Biblioteca Municipal 'Ricardo Jaime Freires': Potosí; f. 1920; 30,000 vols; Dir LUIS E. HEREDIA.

Sucre

Biblioteca Central de la Universidad Mayor de San Francisco Xavier: Plaza 25 de Mayo, Apdo 212, Sucre; Dir AGAR PEÑARANDA.

Biblioteca y Archivo Nacional de Bolivia (Nat. Library and Archives): Calle Bolívar, Sucre; f. 1836; 150,000 vols; Dir GUNNAR MENDOZA.

Museums and Art Galleries

La Paz

Museo 'Casa de Murillo': Calle Jaén 790, La Paz; f. 1950; folk and colonial art; paintings, furniture, national costume, herb medicine and magic; Dir (vacant).

Museo Costumbrista: Parque Riosinhio, La Paz; f. 1979; history of La Paz.

Museo del Oro: Calle Jaén 777, Casilla 609, La Paz; f. 1983; pre-Columbian archaeology (especially gold and silver); Dir JOSÉ DE MESA.

Museo Nacional de Arqueología (National Museum): Calle Tihuanaco 93, Casilla oficial, La Paz; f. 1846, reinaugurated 1961; archaeological and ethnographical collections; Lake Titicaca district exhibits; Dir Lic. MAX PORTUGAL ORTIZ; publ. *Anales*.

Museo Nacional de Arte: Calle Socabaya esq. Calle Comercio, La Paz; tel. (2) 375016; fax (2) 371177; f. 1964; housed in 18th-century Baroque palace of Condes de Arana; colonial art, sculpture and modern art; Dir TERESA VILLEGAS DE ANEIVA.

Potosí

Museo Nacional de la Casa de Moneda de Potosí (Nat. Museum of the Potosí Mint): Casilla 39, Potosí; f. 1938; housed in 'Casa Real de la Moneda', the Royal Mint, founded 1542, now restored, said to be the most outstanding civic monument of the Colonial period in South America; colonial art, 18th-century wooden machinery, coins, historical archives, mineralogy, weapons, Indian ethnography, archaeology, modern art; Dir LUIS ALFONSO FERNÁNDEZ; publ. see under Sociedad Geográfica y de Historia de Potosí.

Sucre

Casa de la Libertad: Plaza Casilla Postal 101, 25 de Mayo (Mayor), Sucre; tel. 064-24200; fmrly Casa de la Independencia; historical collection concerned with Independence, including Bolivian Declaration of Independence; library of 4,000 vols, 1,000 maps; publ. *Memorias*.

Museo Charcas: Universidad Boliviana Mayor, Real y Pontificia de San Francisco Xavier, Bolívar 401, Apdo 212, Sucre; f. 1944; anthropological collection with pre-Inca archaeology; Dir JAIME URIOSTE ARANA; ethnographical and folklore collection: Dir ELIZABETH ROJAS TORO; colonial and modern art section, including Princesa de la Glorieta collection: Dir MANUEL GIMÉNEZ CARRAZANA; publ. *Boletín Antropológico*.

Universities

UNIVERSIDAD AUTÓNOMA 'GABRIEL RENÉ MORENO'

CP 702, Santa Cruz de la Sierra

Telephone: 3-342000
Fax: 3-342160

Founded 1879
State control
Language of instruction: Spanish
Academic year: March to December

Rector: Dr JERJES JUSTINIANO TALAVERA
Vice-rector: Dr SILVERIO MARQUEZ TAVERA
Secretary-General: Dr CARLOS HUGO MOLINA SAUCEDO
Librarian: CARMEN LOLA MATOS

Library of 40,000 vols
Number of teachers: 648
Number of students: 15,675

Publication: *'Universidad'*.

DEANS

Faculty of Technology: Ing. SERGIO JUSTINIANO
Faculty of Economics and Finance: Lic. HUMBERTO MUR
Faculty of Stockbreeding: Dr MIGUEL JUSTINIANO
Faculty of Law and Social Sciences: Dr HECTOR SANDOVAL
Faculty of Agriculture: Ing. ALFREDO PÉREZ
Polytechnic Faculty: Ing. ABSAEL CHÁVEZ
Polytechnic Faculty of Camiri: Lic. OMAR CABRERA

ATTACHED INSTITUTES

Postgraduate School: Dir Dr CARLOS GUZMÁN C.

'El Prado' Centre for Research and Production: Dir Dr ZACARIAS FLORES

'El Vallecito' Institute of Agricultural Research: Dir Ing. JAIME MAGNE

'El Remanso' Centre for Research and Production: Dir Ing. TEÓFILO SALGADO

UNIVERSIDAD AUTÓNOMA 'JUAN MISAEL SARACHO'

CP 51, Tarija

Telephone: 3110/11/12

Founded 1946
State control
Academic year begins March

Rector: Dr MARIO RIOS ARAOZ
Vice-Rector: Dr JORGE CASO REESE
Administrative Director: Lic. SATURNINO RIOS
Librarian: JUAN BALDIVIEZO

Number of teachers: 278
Number of students: 3,500

DEANS

Faculty of Law and Social Sciences: Dr ARIEL SIGLER V.
Faculty of Economics and Finance: Lic. JUAN CUEVAS A.
Faculty of Health Sciences: Dr LIONEL DARWICH C.
Faculty of Agriculture and Forestry: Ing. RAMIRO OLLER A.
Faculty of Sciences and Technology: Ing. GILBERTO FIENGO B.

UNIVERSIDAD AUTÓNOMA 'TOMÁS FRÍAS'

Casilla 36, Avda del Maestro, Potosí

Telephone: (62) 27300
Fax: (62) 26663

Founded 1892
State control
Academic year: April to November

Rector: Lic. ABDÓN SOZA YÁÑEZ
Vice-Rector: Ing. GERMÁN LIZARAZU PANTOJA
Chief Librarian: Dr CARLOS LOAYZA MENDIZABAL

Number of teachers: 380
Number of students: 7,551

Publication: *Vida Universitaria*.

DEANS

Faculty of Arts: Lic. LUIS TORRICO GAMARRA
Faculty of Economics, Finance and Administration: Lic. VALETÍN VIÑOLA QUINTANILLA
Faculty of Humanities and Social Sciences: Dr NESTOR GOITIA IRAHOLA
Faculty of Agriculture and Stockbreeding: Ing. AMILCAR MARISCAL CORTEZ
Faculty of Law: Dr JORGE QUILLAGUAMÁN SÁNCHEZ
Faculty of Engineering: Ing. ALBERTO SCHMIDT QUEZADA
Faculty of Mining: Ing. EDDY ROMAY MORALES

Faculty of Sciences: Lic. GONZALO POOL GARCÍA
Faculty of Geological Engineering: Ing. DANIEL HOWARD BARRÓN
Polytechnic: Téc. Sup. ENRIQUE ARROYO MAMANI

HEADS OF DEPARTMENTS

Law: Dr FÉLIX COLLAZOS MORALES
Social Work: Lic. YOLANDA MUÑOZ BURGOS
Linguistics and Language: Prof. LOURDES WAYLLACE GASPAR
Tourism: Lic. EDGAR VALDA MARTÍNEZ
Civil Construction: Ing. EDGAR SANGÜEZA FIGUEROA
Civil Engineering: Ing. ALFREDO ARANCIBIA CHAVEZ
Topography: Top. OMAR RIVERA ALVAREZ
Plastic Arts: Téc. Sup. JUÁN VILLARROEL SOLA
Musical Arts: Lic. MAGDALENA CAVERO GARNICA
Economics: Lic. OCTAVIO MARTÍNEZ CHURA
Auditing: Lic. VICTOR ANGEL SUBIETA
Business Management: Lic. AVELINO AIZA AVILA
Accountancy: Cr. JUÁN MEDINACELI LLANO
Accountancy (Tupiza Site): Lic. JOSÉ ANTONIO SURRIABLE BAREA
Mining: Ing. EPIFANIO MAMANI ALIZARES
Mathematics: Lic. OSCAR BARRIENTOS ENRIQUEZ
Physics: Lic. SANTIAGO MAMANI HUANACO
Chemistry: Ing. WILLY VARGAS ENRIQUEZ
Agricultural Engineering: Ing. RODOLFO PUCH CABRERA
Geology: Ing. HERNÁN CHUMACERO ENRIQUEZ
Automobile Engineering: Ing. MARIO SAAVEDRA MONTERO
Electricity: Téc. Sup. ZENOBIO SILES SOLIZ
Electronics: Egr HERNÁN ACEBEY OÑA
Mechanics: Téc. Sup. DULFREDO ZULETA SÁNCHEZ
Statistics: Lic. MARIO SOTO
Computing: Lic. ROSARIO VÁSQUEZ ARAUJO
Process Engineering: Ing. JORGE SOTELO
Nursing: Lic. ALCIRA MENESES CAMACHO
Veterinary Science and Zootechnics: Lic. WILBERT PEREIRA MAMANI

UNIVERSIDAD CATÓLICA BOLIVIANA

CP 4805, La Paz
Telephone: (2) 783148
Fax: (2) 786707
Founded 1966
Church control
Language of instruction: Spanish
Academic year: February to December
Chancellor: Mgr NINO MARZOLI
Rector: Dr LUIS ANTONIO BOZA FERNÁNDEZ
Administrative Vice-Rector: Lic. MARIO MORALES MARTINEZ
Academic Vice-Rector (La Paz): CARLOS MACHIADO S.
Academic Vice-Rector (Cochabamba): Dr HANS VAN DEN BERG
Academic Vice-Rector (Santa Cruz): Dr NABOR FERNANDO DURÁN SAUCEDO
Director (National Planning): RENÉ CALDERÓN JEMIO
Academic Secretary: Lic. ELIZABETH ALVAREZ R.
Librarian: RENÉ POPPE
Number of teachers: 778
Number of students: 11,000
Publications: *Busquedas* (every 6 months), *Universitas* (every 6 months).

HEADS OF DEPARTMENTS

La Paz Campus:

Business Administration: LUIS OCAMPO
Economics: MARCELA APARICIO DE GUZMÁN
Psychology: FELIX VIA ORELLANA
Communication Sciences: Dr RAÚL RIVADENEIRA PRADA
Law: Dr CARLOS ANTONIO MIRANDA GUMUCIO
Tourism: EDUARDO VILLARROEL
Accountancy: GABRIEL FUENTES
Systems Engineering: Ing. JOSÉ GIL I.
Architecture: GUSTAVO MEDEIROS
Postgraduate Studies: ALEJANDRO BLACUTT
Rural Studies Unit: Lic. HUGO OSSIO

Cochabamba Campus:

Communication Sciences: Dr GUSTAVO DEHEZA
Business Administration: Lic. CARLOS CALDERÓN
Systems Engineering: Dr OSCAR PINO
Industrial Engineering: Dr JUAN PABLO LEVY
Nursing: MARÍA ANGELES GONZALES
Philosophy: LUIS ALBERTO VACA
Theology: Dr HANS VAN DEN BERG, Lic. ALVARO RESTREPO
Religious Science: Dr EDWIN CLAROS
Law: Dr REMO DI NATALE
Education: JACQUELINE ROBLIN

Santa Cruz Campus:

Educational Psychology: WILMA FOREST
Religious Science: BERNARDITTA TAVAROZI
Agriculture: Dr DANTE INVERNIZZI
Business Studies: CARLOS CALDERÓN GUTIÉRREZ
Accountancy: RUBIN DORADO LEIGUE
Engineering, Systems Engineering and Industrial Engineering: CARLOS EDUARDO MIRANDA CARRASCO
Architecture: JORGE ROMERO PITTARI
Medicine: Dr ALFREDO ROMERO DÁVALOS
Education: JAVIER ARCE

ATTACHED INSTITUTES

Instituto de Investigaciones Socio-Económicas: Avda Hernando Siles 4737, CP 4805, La Paz; tel. (2) 784159; Dir Dr JUAN ANTONIO MORALES.

Instituto de Desarrollo Rural: Avda 14 de Septiembre 4807, Esq. Calle 2 (Obrajes), CP 4805, La Paz; tel. (2) 782222; Dir Lic. HUGO OSSIO.

Servicio de Capacitación en Radiodifusión para el Desarrollo: Avda Hernando Siles 4737, CP 4805, La Paz; Dir Lic. MARIOLA MATERNA.

UNIVERSIDAD MAYOR DE 'SAN ANDRÉS'

Casilla 4787, La Paz
Telephone: 359490
Fax: (591-2) 359491
Founded 1930
State control
Academic year: January to December
Rector: Ing. ANTONIO SAAVEDRA MUÑOZ
Vice-Rector: Dr GONZALO TABOADA LOPEZ
Administrative Director: Lic. EMILIO PÉREZ LARREA
Librarian: Lic. ELIANA MARTINEZ DE ASBUN
Library: see Libraries
Number of teachers: 2,266
Number of students: 37,109
Publications: *Boletín Tesis, Gaceta Universitaria, Memorias Universitarias.*

DEANS

Faculty of Architecture: Arq. DAVID BARRIENTOS ZAPATA
Faculty of Medicine: Dr BUDDY LAZO DE LA VEGA
Faculty of Social Sciences: Lic. TERESA MORENO
Faculty of Law and Political Science: Dr RAMIRO OTERO LUGONES
Faculty of Engineering: Ing. ADHEMAR DAROCA MORALES
Faculty of Pure and Natural Sciences: Lic. JUAN ANTONIO ALVARADO KIRIGIN
Faculty of Technology: Lic. LAURENTINO SALCEDO AGUIRRE
Faculty of Humanities and Education: Dr RENE CALDERÓN SORIA
Faculty of Pharmacy and Biochemistry: Dr OSWALDO TRIGO FREDERICKSEN
Faculty of Dentistry: Dra NELLY SANDOVAL DE MOLLINEDO
Faculty of Agronomy: Ing. PERCY BAPTISTA
Faculty of Geology: Ing. JOSÉ PONCE VILLAGOMEZ
Faculty of Economics and Finance: Lic. CARLOS CLAVIJO VARGAS

ATTACHED RESEARCH INSTITUTES

Instituto de Investigaciones Químicas: Ciudad Universitaria Calle 27 Cota Cota, Casilla 303, La Paz; tel. 792238; Dir Lic. LUIS MORALES ESCOBAR.

Instituto de Investigaciones Físicas: Ciudad Universitaria Calle 27 Cota Cota, Casilla 8635, La Paz; tel. 792622; Dir Lic. ALFONSO VELARDE.

Instituto de Ecología: Ciudad Universitaria Calle 27 Cota Cota, Casilla 20127, La Paz; tel. 7924416; Dir CECIL DE MORALES.

Instituto de Genética Humana: Avda Saavedra 2246, Facultad de Medicina Piso 11, La Paz; tel. 359613; Dir Dr JORGE OLIVARES PLAZA.

Instituto de Biología de la Altura: Avda Saavedra 2246, Facultad de Medicina, Piso 11, La Paz; tel. 376675; Dir Dr ENRIQUE VARGAS PACHECO.

Instituto de Investigaciones Históricas y Estudios Bolivianos: Avda 6 de Agosto 2080, La Paz; tel. 359602; Dir Lic. RAUL CALDERÓN GENIO.

Instituto de Hidráulica e Hidrología: Ciudad Universitaria Calle 27 Cota Cota, La Paz; tel. 795724; Dir Ing. FREDDY CAMACHO V.

Instituto de Ingenieria Sanitaria: Avda Villazón 1995, Pabellón 103, La Paz; tel. 359519; Dir Ing. JOSÉ DÍAZ BENAVENTE.

Instituto de Ensayo de Materiales: Avda Villazón 1995, Edificio Central, La Paz; tel. 359577; Dir Ing. MARIO TERAN.

Instituto de Investigaciones Económicas: Avda 6 de Agosto 2170, Edificio HOY, 5° Piso, La Paz; tel. 359618; Dir Lic. PABLO RAMOS SANCHEZ.

Instituto de Investigaciones Arquitectónicas: Calle Lisímaco Gutiérrez, Facultad de Arquitectura, La Paz; tel. 359568; Dir Arq. CRISTINA DAMM PEREIRA.

Centro de Investigaciones Geológicas: Ciudad Universitaria Calle 27 Cota Cota, La Paz; tel. 793392; Dir (vacant).

UNIVERSIDAD MAYOR DE SAN SIMON

Casilla 992, Cochabamba
Telephone: (42) 25512
Fax: (42) 32545
Founded 1832
Language of instruction: Spanish
State control
Academic year: February to December
Rector: Ing. ALBERTO RODRÍGUEZ MÉNDEZ
Vice-Rector: Lic. AUGUSTO ARGANDOÑA YÁÑEZ
Secretary-General: Ing. OSCAR ANTEZANA MENDOZA
Librarian: LUIS ALBERTO PONCE ARAUCO
Library: see Libraries
Number of teachers: 1,158
Number of students: 32,056
Publications: *Boletín Bibliográfico, Gaceta Médica, Revista de Agricultura, Boletín de Investigación, Búsqueda* (research in social sciences), *Los Tiempos* (weekly).

DEANS

Faculty of Law and Political Sciences: Dr EDDY FERNÁNDEZ GUTIÉRREZ
Faculty of Medicine: Dr LUIS QUIROGA MORENO
Faculty of Agriculture and Stockbreeding: Ing. FERNANDO QUITÓN DAZA
Faculty of Architecture: Arq. ROLANDO SALAMANCA CASTAÑOS
Faculty of Biochemistry and Pharmacy: Dr DEMETRIO DELGADILLO ARNEZ
Faculty of Dentistry: Dr VÍCTOR MORENO SORIA
Faculty of Sciences and Technology: Ing. FRANZ VARGAS LOAYZA

Faculty of Humanities and Education: Dr ROLANDO LÓPEZ HERBAS
Faculty of Economics and Sociology: Lic. RENÉ JALDÍN MEJÍA
Higher Technical School of Agriculture: Ing. RICARDO MUÑOZ RIVADENEYRA
Higher Technical School of Forestry: Ing. JULIO VARGAS MUÑOZ

HEADS OF DEPARTMENT

Faculty of Medicine:

Medicine: Dr RENÉ MEJÍA MENDOZA
Nursing: Lic. JUANA ANDRADE UGARTE

Faculty of Dentistry:

Dentistry: Dra MARTHA UZEDA SALGUERO

Faculty of Biochemistry and Pharmacy:

Pharmacy: Dra CARLOTA VELASCO CANELAS
Biochemistry: Dr JORGE AGUIRRE FERNÁNDEZ DE CÓRDOBA

Faculty of Economics and Sociology;

Economics: Lic. CRECENCIO ALBA PINTO
Auditing: Lic. RAÚL BALLÓN CURIONE
Business Administration: Lic. JAIME VÉLEZ OCAMPO
Sociology: Lic. RENÉ ANTEZANA ESCALERA

Faculty of Architecture

Design: Arq. JOAQUÍN BALDERRAMA BIRHUET
Technology: Arq. RUPERTO BECERRA ROZO
Social Sciences: Arq. FREDDY SURRIABRE GARCÍA

Faculty of Agriculture and Stockbreeding:

Veterinary Medicine: (vacant)
Crop Cultivation: (vacant)
Agricultural Engineering: (vacant)
Zootechnics: (vacant)

Faculty of Science and Technology:

Electrical Engineering: Ing. JAIME ORELLANA JIMÉNEZ
Industrial Engineering: Ing. GERARDO DOMÍNGUEZ GONZALES
Mechanical Engineering: Ing. WÁLTER GUTIÉRREZ MANCILLA
Civil Engineering: Ing. OSCAR ZABALAGA MONTAÑO
Chemistry: Lic. RONALD HOSSE SAHONERO
Biology: Lic. AMALIA ANTEZANA VALERA
Mathematics: Lic GUALBERTO CUPÉ CLEMENTE
Computing: Ing. JORGE ROCHA BARRENECHEA
Physics: Lic. NESTOR AVILÉS RÍOS

Faculty of Education Sciences and Humanities:

Psychology: Lic. TERESA MARZANA TÉLLEZ
Pedagogy: Lic. BÁRBARA OSSIO DE BARRIENTOS
Languages: Lic. MARÍA ESTHER CORTEZ LÓPEZ

RESEARCH INSTITUTES

Instituto de Estudios Sociales y Económicos: Dir Lic. IGOR IRIGOYEN HINOJOSA.
Instituto de Investigaciones de Arquitectura: Dir Arq. ADOLFO LEHM MALDONADO.
Centro de Estudios de Población: Dir ROSSEMARY SALAZAR.
Instituto de Investigación de la Facultad de Medicina: Dir Dr JOHNNY GUZMÁN V.
Instituto de Investigacíon de la Facultad de Ciencias Agrícolas y Pecuarias: Dir Ing. JOSÉ AMURRIO ROCHA.
Instituto de Investigaciones Jurídicas: Dir Dr AUGUSTO VILLARROEL TREVIÑO.
Centro Universitario de Medicina Tropical: Dir Dr JOSÉ HERNÁN BERMUDEZ PAREDES.
Centro de Estudios Superiores Universitarios: Dir Lic. FERNANDO MAYORGA UGARTE.

UNIVERSIDAD MAYOR, REAL Y PONTIFICIA DE SAN FRANCISCO XAVIER DE CHUQUISACA

Apdo 212, Sucre

Telephone: 23245

Founded 1624 by Papal Bull of Gregory XV dated 1621 and Royal Charter of Philip III, 1622

Autonomous control
Academic year: two semesters beginning March and August

Rector: Dr JORGE ZAMORA HERNÁNDEZ
Vice-Rector: Lic. FRANCISCO CAMACHO PUENTES
Administrative Officer: Lic. WÁLTER YAÑEZ FLORES
Librarian: Dr RONALD GANTIER LEMOINE

Number of teachers: 438
Number of students: 10,156

Publications: *Revista del Instituto de Sociología Boliviana, Archivos bolivianos de Medicina.*

DEANS

Faculty of Law, Political and Social Sciences: Dr RUFFO OROPEZA DELGADO
Faculty of Health Sciences: Dr ENRIQUE AZURDUY VACAFLOR
Faculty of Economics, Finance and Administration: Lic. MARCEL CIVERA GIL
Faculty of Humanities: Prof. GERMÁN PALACIOS CORS
Faculty of Technology: Ing. DANIEL ALVAREZ GANTIER
Faculty of Agriculture: Prof. ARMANDO GANTIER ALFARO
Polytechnic Institute: Ing. GERSON ANDRADE TABOADA

ATTACHED INSTITUTES

Instituto de Sociología Boliviana: Estudiantes esq. Junín, Sucre.

Instituto de Investigaciones Económicas: Grau 107, Sucre.

Instituto Experimental de Biología: Dalence 207, Sucre.

Instituto de Investigaciones Biológicas: Dalence 207, Sucre.

Instituto de Cancerología 'Cupertino Arteaga': Destacamento 111, No 1, Sucre.

Centro de Medicina Nuclear: Destacamento 111, No 1, Sucre.

Instituto de Anatomía Patológica: Destacamento 111, No 1, Sucre.

Instituto de Investigación Mal de Chagas: Colón final, Sucre.

Instituto de Investigaciones Tecnológicas: Regimiento Campos No 181, Sucre.

UNIVERSIDAD NACIONAL 'SIGLO XX'

CP 27, Llallagua
(Office in La Paz: CP 8721, La Paz)

Telephone: (052) 54385

Founded 1985

Rector: CIRILO JIMÉNEZ ALVAREZ
Vice-Rector: EDGAR F. VÁSQUEZ PALENQUE
Chief Administrative Officer: MARIO TÓRREZ MIRANDA
Librarian: FLAVIO FERNÁNDEZ MARISCAL
Academic Co-ordinator: VICENTE CÁCERES B.
Director-General for Research: DIÓGENES ROQUE T.
Director-General for Extension: EDGAR F. VÁSQUEZ P.

Number of teachers: 65
Number of students: 1,526

HEADS OF DEPARTMENTS

Health: RUTH FUENTES VENEROS
Mining and Metallurgy: WILLY FLORES O.
Communication: MARUJA SERRUDO
Political Training: EDGAR LIMA TÓRREZ
Languages: CRISTOBAL SOTO
Complementary Education: JOSÉ MORATÓ
Stockbreeding: JORGE PLAZA

UNIVERSIDAD TÉCNICA DE ORURO

CP 49, Avda 6 de Octubre 1209, Oruro

Telephone: (52) 50100
Fax: (52) 42215
E-mail: recuto%recuto@utonet.bo

Founded 1892
Autonomous control
Language of instruction: Spanish
Academic year: January to November

Rector: Ing. RUBÉN MEDINACELI ORTIZ
Vice-Rector: Lic. RAÚL ARIAS MURILLO
Administrative Director: Lic. VICTORIANO HUGO CANAVIRI CHÁNEZ
Librarian: SOFÍA A. ZUBIETA

Number of teachers: 487
Number of students: 10,403

Publications: *Revista Universitaria, Revista metalúrgica, Revista de Derecho, Revista de economía, Revista de Cultura Boliviana, Revista de Mecánica.*

DEANS

Faculty of Engineering: Ing. EDDY NISTTAHUZ GISBERT
Faculty of Agricultural Sciences: Ing. HARRY CARREÑO PEREYRA
Faculty of Legal, Political and Social Sciences: Dr VIDAL VILLARROEL VEGA
Faculty of Economics and Finance: Lic. ROLANDO MALDONADO ALFARO
University Polytechnic: HUMBERTO QUISPE GONZALES
Faculty of Architecture and Town Planning: Arq. RUBÉN URQUIOLA MURILLO

ATTACHED RESEARCH INSTITUTES

Institute of Economic Research
Institute of Social Research

UNIVERSIDAD TÉCNICA DEL BENI 'MARISCAL JOSÉ BALLIVIÁN'

Casilla de Correo 38, Trinidad, Beni

Telephone: 21590
Fax: 20236

Founded 1967
State control

Rector: Dr HERNAN MELGAR JUSTINIANO
Vice-Rector: Dr CARMELO APONTE VÉLEZ
Registrar: Ing. VIDAL CHÁVEZ PERALES
Librarian: LORGIA S. DE TANAKA

Library of 9,600 vols
Number of teachers: 155
Number of students: 1,039

Publications: *Boletines de los Institutos de Investigaciones, Socio-económicas, Ictícola del Beni, Investigaciones Forestales y de Defensa de la Amazonía.*

DEANS

Faculty of Stockbreeding: Dr PABLO MEMM DORADO

Faculty of Agriculture: Lic. CASTO PLAZA CUENCA

Faculty of Economics: RODOLFO ARTEAGA CÉSPEDES

AFFILIATED INSTITUTES

Instituto de Investigaciones Socio-económicas: Casilla 38, Trinidad, Beni; tel. 21566; Dir Lic. CARLOS NAVIA RIBERA.

Instituto de Investigaciones Icticolas del Beni: Casilla 38, Trinidad, Beni; tel. 21705; Dir Dr RENÉ VASQUEZ PÉREZ.

Instituto de Investigaciones Forestales y Defensa del Medio Ambiente de la Amazonia: Casilla 12, Riberalta, Beni; tel. 82484; Dir OSCAR LLANQUE.

Instituto Comercial Superior de la Nación: Campero 94, La Paz; tel. 373296; f. 1944; commercial and administrative training; 35 teachers; library of 6,132 vols; Dir Tte. ARMANDO DE PALACIOS; publ. *Mercurio* (annually).

Schools of Art and Music

Conservatorio Nacional de Música: CP 11226, Avda 6 de Agosto 2092, La Paz; tel. (2) 373297; fax (2) 361798; f. 1907; state control; 50 staff; library of 420 books, 3,900 scores; Dir ANTONIO ROBERTO BORDA.

Escuela Superior de Bellas Artes 'Hernando Siles': Calle Rosendo Gutiérrez 323, La Paz; tel. 371141; f. 1926; 18 teachers, 206 students; Dir ALBERTO MEDINA MENDIETA; Registrar WALLY DE MONTALBAN.

BOSNIA AND HERZEGOVINA

Learned Societies

BIBLIOGRAPHY, LIBRARY SCIENCE AND MUSEOLOGY

Društvo Bibliotekara BiH (Librarians' Society of Bosnia and Herzegovina): 71000 Sarajevo, Obala V. Stepe 42; tel. (071) 283-245; f. 1949; 450 mems; Pres. NEDA ĆUKAC; Sec. MIODRAG RAKIĆ; publ. *Bibliotekarstvo* (annually).

EDUCATION

Pedagoško Društvo BiH (Pedagogical Society of Bosnia and Herzegovina): 71000 Sarajevo, Djure Djakovića 4.

FINE AND PERFORMING ARTS

Muzička Omladina BiH (Bosnia and Herzegovina Society of Music Lovers and Young Musicians): Muzička akademija, 71000 Sarajevo, Svetozara Markovića 1; tel. (071) 25-007; f. 1958; organizes concerts, lectures, theatre events, exhibitions, film shows; 40,000 mems; library of 1,000 vols, record library of 1,000 items; Pres. KREŠIMIR BOŽIĆ; Sec. BORISLAV ĆURIĆ; publ. *Bulletin* (every 2 months).

Udruženje Muzičkih Umjetnika BiH (Association of Musicians of Bosnia and Herzegovina): 71000 Sarajevo, Sv Marko- vicá 1.

HISTORY, GEOGRAPHY AND ARCHAEOLOGY

Društvo Istoričara BiH (Historical Society of Bosnia and Herzegovina): Filozofski fakultet, 71000 Sarajevo, Račkog 1.

Geografsko Društvo BiH (Geographical Society of Bosnia and Herzegovina): Prirodno-matematički fakultet, 71000 Sarajevo, Vojvode Putnika 43A; f. 1947; 1,541 mems; Pres. Dr MILOŠ BJELOVITIĆ; Vice-Pres. Dr KREŠIMIR PAPIĆ; publs *Geografski pregled*, *Nastava geografije* (annually), *Geografski list* (5 a year).

MEDICINE

Društvo Ljekara BiH (Physicians' Society of Bosnia and Herzegovina): Zavod za zdravstvenu zaštitu BiH, 71000 Sarajevo, Maršala Tita 7.

NATURAL SCIENCES

General

Društvo Matematičara, Fizičara i Astronoma BiH (Society of Mathematicians, Physicists and Astronomers of Bosnia and Herzegovina): Prirodnomatematički fakultet, 71000 Sarajevo, Vojvode Putnika 43.

Research Institutes

LANGUAGE AND LITERATURE

Language Institute: 71000 Sarajevo, Hasana Kikića 12; tel. 39-817; f. 1973; library of 3,200 vols; Dir Dr NAILA VALJEVAC; publs *Književni jezik* (Literary Language, quarterly), *Radovi* (Works, annually), *Dijalektološki Zbornik* (Dialect Collection, irregular).

NATURAL SCIENCES

Physical Sciences

Institute of Meteorology: Sarajevo, Hadži Loje 4; f. 1891; Dir M. V. VEMIĆ.

TECHNOLOGY

Energoinvest-RO ITEN (Institute for Thermal and Nuclear Technology): Tvornička 3, Stup, 71000 Sarajevo; f. 1961; attached to Energoinvest co., Univ. of Sarajevo and Acad. of Bosnia and Herzegovina; research and development in the fields of thermal and nuclear technology; library of *c.* 6,000 vols, 100 periodicals; Dir Dr ALIJA LEKIĆ; publs *Energoinvest-Technology, Science, Engineering, MHD-Theory, Power Generation and Technology* (in Russian and English).

Libraries and Archives

Sarajevo

Gazi Husrevbegova biblioteka (Gazi Husrevbeg Library): Sarajevo, Hamdije Kreševljakovića 58; tel. (71) 658-143; fax (71) 205-525; f. 1537; oriental library; 60,000 vols, 11,000 Islamic MSS; Dir MUHAREM OMERDIĆ; Chief Librarian Dr MUSTAFA JAHIĆ; publs *Anali Gazi Husrevbegove biblioteke*, *Katalog arapskih, turskih i perzijskih rukopisa*.

Nacionalna i univerzitetska biblioteka Bosne i Hercegovine (National and University Library of Bosnia and Herzegovina): 71000 Sarajevo, Zmaja od Bosne 8B; tel. and fax (71) 533-204; f. 1945; 2,000,000 vols; copyright and deposit library; Head Dr ENES KUJUNDŽIĆ.

Zemaljski muzej Bosne i Hercegovine, Biblioteka (Bosnian and Herzegovinian National Museum Library): Sarajevo, Zmaja od Bosne 3; tel. and fax (71) 440-197; f. 1888; archaeology, ethnology and natural sciences; *c.* 200,000 vols; Chief Librarian OLGA LALEVIĆ.

Museums and Art Galleries

Banja Luka

Muzej Bosanske Krajine (Museum of Bosanska Krajina Region): 78000 Banja Luka, V. Karadžića b.b.; tel. (078) 35-486; f. 1930; regional museum for north-west Bosnia; depts of archaeology, history, ethnography, national revolution, workers' movement; library of 9,500 vols; Dir AHMET ĆEJVAN; publ. *Zbornik* (irregular).

Sarajevo

Umjetnička galerija Bosne i Hercegovine: 71000 Sarajevo, JNA 38; f. 1946; collections of modern art from Yugoslavia and Bosnia and Herzegovina; also ancient icons and art; library of 3,000 vols; Dir VEFIK HADŽISMAJLOVIĆ; publs catalogues.

Zemaljski Muzej Bosne i Hercegovine (Bosnian and Herzegovinian National Museum): Sarajevo, Zmaja od Bosne 3; tel. (71) 668-025; f. 1888; prehistoric, Roman, Greek and Medieval periods, ethnological, botanical, zoological, geological sections; botanical garden; library: see Libraries; Dir DJENANA BUTUROVIĆ; publs *Glasnik Zemaljskog muzeja*, *Arheologija*, *GZM–Etnologija*, *GZM–Prirodne nauke* (1 a year), *Wissenschaftliche Mitteilungen* (irregular).

Universities

UNIVERZITET U BANJOJ LUCI
(University of Banja Luka)

78000 Banja Luka, Trg srpskih vladara 2
Telephone: (78) 35-018
Fax: (78) 47-057

Founded 1975
State control
Academic year: October to August

Rector: Prof. Dr DRAGOLJUB MIRJANIĆ
Pro-Rectors: Prof. RADOSLAV GRUJIĆ, Prof. Dr STANKO STANIĆ
Chief Administrative Officer: VLADIMIR NIKOLIĆ
Librarian: PREDRAG LAZAREVIĆ

Number of teachers: 520
Number of students: 7,614

Publications: *Survey of Lectures* (annually), *Bulletin*.

DEANS

Faculty of Economics: Prof. Dr VLADISLAV DURASOVIĆ
Faculty of Law: Prof. Dr RAJKO KUZMANOVIĆ
Faculty of Electrical Engineering: Prof. Dr BRANKO DOKIĆ
Faculty of Mechanical Engineering: Prof. Dr ALEKSA BLAGOJEVIĆ
Faculty of Technology: Prof. Dr NEDELJKO ČEGAR
Faculty of Medicine: Prof. Dr LJILJANA HOTIĆ-ĆOVIČKOVIĆ
Faculty of Agriculture: Prof. Dr PETAR DURMAN
Faculty of Forestry: Prof. Dr RATKO ĆOMIĆ
Faculty of Philosophy: Prof. Dr MILAN VASIĆ
Faculty of Civil Engineering: Prof. Dr VLADIMIR LUKIĆ
Faculty of Mathematics and Natural Sciences: Prof. Dr ZDRAVKO MARIJANAC

ATTACHED INSTITUTE

Institute of Agriculture: Dir Dr VOJO MEJAKIĆ.

SVEUČILIŠTE U MOSTARU
(University of Mostar)

88000 Mostar, Trg hrvatskih velikana bb
Telephone: (88) 310-778
Fax: (88) 320-885

Founded 1977, present name 1992
State control
Academic year: September to August

Rector: Prof. Dr ZDENKO KORDIĆ
Pro-Rectors: Prof. Dr HRVOJE SOČE, Prof. Dr JAKOV PEHAR
General Secretary: MARINKO JURILJ
Librarian: SLAVICA JUKA

Number of teachers: 215
Number of students: 3,500

Publications: *Mostariensia* (2 a year), *Znanstveni glasnik* (2 a year).

DEANS

Law: Prof. Dr LJUBOMIR ZOVKO
Economics: Prof. Dr FRANO LJUBIĆ

Mechanical Engineering: Prof. Dr ANTE MIŠKOVIĆ
Civil Engineering: Prof. Dr MATO GOLUŽA
Education: Prof. Dr STOJAN VRLJIĆ
Agriculture: Prof. Dr MIROSLAV ARAPOVIĆ
Academy of Arts: Prof. Dr STIPE SIKIRICA

ATTACHED INSTITUTES

Institute of Agriculture: research and development in agriculture and agroeconomics; Dir Dr JAKOV PEHAR.
Institute of Economics: Dir Prof. Dr DANE KORDIĆ.
Institute of Mechanical Engineering: Dir Prof. Dr VOJISLAV VIŠEKRUNA.
Institute of Civil Engineering: Dir Prof. Dr HRVOJE SOČE.
Institute of Croatian Language, Literature and History: Dir Prof. Dr STOJAN VRLJIĆ.

UNIVERZITET U SARAJEVU
(University of Sarajevo)

71000 Sarajevo, Obala Kulina bana 7/II

Telephone: (71) 663-392
Fax: (71) 663-393

Founded 1949
Academic year: October to September
Rector: Prof. Dr NEDŽAD MULABEGOVIĆ
Vice-Rectors: Prof. Dr MUHAREM AVDISPAHIĆ, Prof. OSMAN-FARUK SIJARIĆ, Prof. Dr MILENKO VRANEŠIĆ, Prof. Dr SRETO TOMAŠEVIĆ
Secretary-General: BRANIMIR LJUBIČIĆ
Director, National and University Library: Dr ENES KUJUNDŽIĆ

Number of teachers: 1,391
Number of students: 12,000

Publications: *Bulletin* (quarterly), *Doctoral Dissertations – Summary* (annually).

DEANS

Faculty of Law: Prof. Dr KASIM BEGIĆ
Faculty of Economics: Prof. Dr BORIS TIHI
Faculty of Medicine: Prof. Dr NEDŽAD MULABEGOVIĆ
Faculty of Veterinary Sciences: Prof. Dr ZIJAH HADŽIOMEROVIĆ
Faculty of Philosophy: Prof. Dr IBRAHIM TEPIĆ
Faculty of Agriculture: Prof. Dr REFIK TELALBAŠIĆ
Faculty of Forestry: Prof. Dr VLADIMIR BEUS
Faculty of Civil Engineering: Prof. Dr MIRZA GOLOŠ
Faculty of Architecture: Prof. Dr MEHMED HRASNICA
Faculty of Mechanical Engineering: Prof. Dr EDHEM SEFEROVIĆ
Faculty of Mechanical Engineering in Zenica: Prof. Dr SAFET BRDAREVIĆ
Faculty of Mechanical Engineering in Bihać: Prof. Dr ISAK KARABEGOVIĆ
Faculty of Sciences: Prof Dr MUHAREM AVDISPAHIĆ
Faculty of Electrical Engineering: Prof. Dr ZIJO PAŠIĆ
Faculty of Metallurgy in Zenica: Prof. Dr ASIM KARLIĆ
Faculty of Political Sciences: Prof. Dr HALIM MULAIBRAHIMOVIĆ
Faculty of Physical Education: Prof. Dr MEHO SMAJIĆ
Faculty of Pharmacy: Prof. Dr SABIRA HADŽOVIĆ
Faculty of Transportation: Prof. Dr ŠEFKIJA ČEKIĆ
Faculty of Dentistry: Prof. Dr HAMID TAHMIŠČIJÁ
Faculty of Criminology: Prof. Dr IBRAHIM BAKIĆ
Academy of Fine Arts: SADUDIN MUSABEGOVIĆ
Academy of Dramatic Art: Prof. ADMIR GLAMOČAK
Academy of Music: Prof. FARUK SIJARIĆ
Teacher-Training Academy: Prof. Dr ZEHRA HUBIJAR
Teacher-Training Academy in Bihać: Prof. Dr. MEHMED ORUČEVIĆ
Teacher-Training Academy in Zenica: Prof. Dr MUHAMED ARNAUT

DIRECTORS

Institute of Architecture and Urbanization: Doc. MOMIR HRISAFOVIĆ
Institute of Control and Computer Sciences: Dr LJUBIŠA DRAGANOVIĆ
Institute of Biology: MILUTIN CVIJOVIĆ
Institute of Economics: SLOBODAN MAKSIMOVIĆ
Institute of Ergonomics: MIROSLAV JURIĆ
Institute of Oriental Research: Prof. Dr HASAN MURATOVIĆ
Institute of Protection of Works: SADIK BEGOVIĆ
Institute of Thermo-technics and Nuclear Technics: Dr ALIJA LEKIĆ
Institute of Welding: VELIZAR NIKOLIĆ
Electric Power Institute: Dr PREDRAG VUJOVIĆ
Institute of Organization and Economics: RADOJICA JOJIĆ

UNIVERZITET U TUZLI
(University of Tuzla)

75000 Tuzla, M. Fizovića-Fiska 6, POB 528

Telephone: (75) 252-061

Founded 1976

Rector: Prof. Dr SADIK LATIFAGIĆ
Vice-Rectors: Prof. Dr ŠEFIK MULABEGOVIĆ, Prof. Dr SLAVOLJUB PERDIJA
General Secretary: AIDA HODŽIĆ

Number of teachers: 425
Number of students: 5,000

DEANS

Faculty of Economics: MUHAMED PAMUKČIĆ
Faculty of Electrical and Mechanical Engineering: MIRZA KUŠLJUGIĆ
Faculty of Medicine: AHMED HALILBAŠIĆ
Faculty of Mining and Geology: TAIB OMERAGIĆ
Faculty of Technology: MAHMUT AHMETBAŠIĆ
Faculty of Philosophy: ENVER HALILOVIĆ
Faculty of Special Education: DŽEVDET SARAJLIĆ

BOTSWANA

Learned Societies

GENERAL

Botswana Society: POB 71, Gaborone; tel. 351500; fax 359321; f. 1968, in association with the National Museum and Art Gallery, to encourage knowledge and research on Botswana in all fields; 450 mems; Chair. G. W. MATENGE; Exec. Sec. D. DAMBE; publs *Botswana Notes and Records* (annually), Symposium proceedings, occasional papers, monographs.

BIBLIOGRAPHY, LIBRARY SCIENCE AND MUSEOLOGY

Botswana Library Association: POB 1310, Gaborone; tel. 355-2295; telex 2429; fax 357291; e-mail mbangiwa@noka.ub.bw; f. 1978; 60 mems; Chair. F. M. LAMUSSE; Sec. A. M. MBANGIWA; publ. *Journal, Botswana Journal of Library and Information Science* (2 a year).

Research Institutes

NATURAL SCIENCES

Physical Sciences

Geological Survey of Botswana: Private Bag 14, Lobatse; tel. 330327; telex 2293; f. 1948; library of 2,000 vols, 151 periodicals; Dir T. P. MACHACHA; publs annual reports, mineral resources reports, bulletins, etc.

Libraries and Archives

Gaborone

Botswana National Archives and Records Services: Khama Crescent, Government Enclave, POB 239, Gaborone; tel. 3601-000; telex 2994; fax 313584; f. 1967; central government, district, tribal, business and private archives from *c.* 1885; audio-visual and machine-readable archives; records management for central government, districts and Parastatal organizations; oral tradition programmes; educational programmes and exhibitions; library of 14,000 vols; Dir K. P. MAGOGWE; Senior Archivist C. T. NENGOMASHA; Librarian A. R. ADEKANMBI; publs *Annual Report, Archives Library Accessions List*.

Botswana National Library Service: Private Bag 0036, Gaborone; tel. 352288; fax 301149; f. 1968; nation-wide public library service; also acts as a national library (legal deposit); 221,931 vols; 21 branch libraries, two mobile; 201 book box service points; 55 village reading rooms; Dir BASAMIANG GAREBAKWENA; publs *Annual Report, National Bibliography of Botswana* (3 a year), *Quarterly Accessions List, Statistical Bulletin, Newsletter.*

Museums and Art Galleries

Gaborone

National Museum and Art Gallery: Independence Ave, Private Bag 00114, Gaborone; tel. 374616; f. 1968; provides, through dioramas and graphic displays, a visual education in the development of Man in Botswana; runs mobile education service for rural primary schools; repository for scientific collections relating to Botswana; National Herbarium contains 20,000 plant specimens; art gallery holds a collection of art of all races of Africa south of the Sahara, and exhibits works from any country; library of 5,000 vols and numerous journals; Dir T. L. MPULUBUSI; publs *The Zebra's Voice* (newsletter), *Botswana Notes and Records* (annually).

Mochudi

Phuthadikobo Museum: POB 367, Mochudi; tel. 377238; f. 1976; ethnography, photographic collections, conservation, community education; Dir PAT KOLLARS; publ. *Annual Report*.

University

UNIVERSITY OF BOTSWANA

Private Bag 0022, Gaborone
Telephone: Gaborone 351151
Telex: 2429
Fax: 356591
Founded 1976, present name 1982
State control
Language of instruction: English
Academic year: August to May
Vice-Chancellor: Prof. SHARON SIVERTS
Deputy Vice-Chancellor: Prof. M. J. MELAMU
Registrar: D. O. MOKGAUTSI
Librarian: H. K. RASEROKA
Number of teachers: 300
Number of students: 8,200
Publications: *Calendar* (annually), *Pula* (2 a year), *Annual Report*.

DEANS

Faculty of Social Sciences: Dr B. S. MGUNI
Faculty of Education: P. T. VANQA
Faculty of Humanities: Dr B. MOKOPAKGOSI
Faculty of Science: Prof. J. S. NKOMA
Faculty of Agriculture: Dr G. C. MREMA

HEADS OF DEPARTMENTS

Faculty of Social Sciences:
- Accounting: Dr S. E. NDZINGE
- Demography: Prof. S. K. GAISIE
- Economics: Prof. M. S. MUKRAS
- Law: Dr B. OTLHOGILE
- Political and Administrative Studies: Dr B. TSIE
- Social Work: Prof. M. HUTTON
- Sociology: Dr T. FAKO
- Statistics: Prof. S. K. SINHA

Faculty of Education:
- Educational Foundations: Dr A. F. NJABILI
- Department of Educational Technology: Dr S. R. PANDEY
- Department of Adult Education: Dr K. MOGOME NTSATSI
- Languages and Social Science Education: Dr R. KAPAALE
- Mathematics and Science Education: R. CHARAKUPA
- Nursing Education: Dr S. D. TLOU
- Physical Education, Health and Recreation: Prof. L. O. AMUSA

Faculty of Humanities:
- African Languages and Literature: N. MOTHIBATSELA
- English: Prof. F. MNTHALI
- French: Dr T. KITENGE-NGOY
- History: Prof. L. D. NGCONGCO
- Library Studies and Information: Prof. P. HAVARD-WILLIAMS
- Theology and Religious Studies: Rev. Dr J. N. AMANZE (acting)

Faculty of Science:
- Biology: Dr S. D. MPUCHANE
- Chemistry: Dr T. T. MOKOENA
- Environmental Sciences: Prof. R. M. K. SILITSHENA
- Geology: Dr M. WENDORFF
- Physics: Prof. K. R. S. DEVAN
- Mathematics: Prof. J. M. SALBANY
- Pre-entry Science: Dr M. MAWANDE

ATTACHED INSTITUTES

National Institute of Development and Cultural Research: Gaborone; Dir Prof. A. K. DATTA.

Centre for Continuing Studies: Gaborone; Dir A. K. DATTA.

Colleges

Botswana College of Agriculture: Private Bag 0027, Gaborone; tel. 328831; fax 328753; f. 1967; library of 2,600 vols; 85 teachers, 400 students; Principal E. J. KEMSLEY.

Botswana Institute of Administration and Commerce: POB 10026, Gaborone; tel. 356324; fax 359768; f. 1970; library of 7,000 vols; 73 teachers; Principal L. L. SEBINA; publ. *Newsletter* (4 a year).

Botswana Polytechnic: Private Bag 0061; Gaborone; tel. 352305; fax 352309; library of 13,000 vols; 120 teachers, 800 students; Principal A. KERTON; Registrar T. MOGKWATI.

HEADS OF DEPARTMENTS

Mechanical Engineering: D. JACKSON
Civil Engineering: H. PARAMESWAR
Electrical Engineering: D. DAWOOD
Technology and Education: M. KEWAGAMANG

Institute of Development Management: POB 1357, Gaborone; tel. 352371; telex 2429; fax 373144; f. 1974; management training in business management, education management, information management, administration of legal services; library of 8,000 vols (including special World Bank and SADCC collections); 25 teachers, 965 students; certificate courses; Regional Dir Dr M. DLAMIN.

BRAZIL

Learned Societies

GENERAL

Fundação Moinho Santista (Moinho Santista Foundation): Av. M.C. Aguiar 215, Bl. D, 7° andar, CEP 05804-905 São Paulo, SP; tel. (11) 3741-6832; fax (11) 3741-1288; f. 1955; to promote the advancement of science, letters and arts in Brazil by granting every year the Moinho Santista prizes and the Moinho Santista prizes for young people, consisting of the following: gold and silver medals, diploma of recognition for outstanding service in any of the scientific, literary or artistic fields, plus a sum of money; Chair. Prof. MIGUEL REALE; Exec. Sec. ROBERTA CORREIA.

Instituto 'Nami Jafet' para o Progresso da Ciência e Cultura ('Nami Jafet' Institute for the Advancement of Science and Culture): Rua Agostinho Gomes 1455, São Paulo, SP; f. 1961; awards annual prizes of 3,000 cruzados, a gold medal, diploma and scholarships; established in memory of the late industrialist Prof. Nami Jafet; Chair. of Consultative Council Prof. A. C. PACHECO E SILVA; Chair. of Bd of Dirs Prof. ALFREDO BUZAID; Exec. Sec. RONE AMORIN.

AGRICULTURE, FISHERIES AND VETERINARY SCIENCE

Associação Brasileira de Mecânica dos Solos (Brazilian Society for Soil Mechanics): CP 7141, 01064-970 São Paulo, SP; tel. and fax (11) 268-7325; f. 1950; 865 mems; Pres. Eng. SUSSUMU NIYAMA; Sec. MARCUS PACHECO; publ. *Solos e Rochas – Revista Brasileira de Geotecnia.*

Sociedade Nacional de Agricultura (National Agricultural Society): Av. General Justo 171, 20021-130 Rio de Janeiro, RJ; tel. (21) 533-0088; fax (21) 240-4189; f. 1897; 10,000 mems; library of 45,000 vols; Pres. OCTÁVIO MELLO ALVARENGA; Dir and 1st Sec. ELVO SANTORO; publs *A Lavoura* (every 2 months) and pamphlets.

BIBLIOGRAPHY, LIBRARY SCIENCE AND MUSEOLOGY

Associação dos Arquivistas Brasileiros: Rua da Candelária 9-sala 1.004, 20091-020 Rio de Janeiro, RJ; tel. and fax (21) 233-7142; f. 1971; co-operates with the Government, national and international organizations on all matters relating to archives and documentation; organizes national congresses, study courses, conferences, etc.; has achieved national legislation on archives; 800 mems; Pres. MARIZA BOTTINO; Sec. TANIA SOUZA PIMENTA; publs *Boletim* (quarterly), *Revista Arquivo e Administraçao.*

Federação Brasileira de Associações de Bibliotecários (FEBAB) (Brazilian Federation of Library Associations): Rua Avanhandava 40, conj. 110, 01306 São Paulo, SP; tel. (11) 257-99-79; f. 1959 to act for the regional library associations at a national level; to serve as a centre of documentation and bibliography for Brazil; biennial national congress; 27 mem. associations; Pres. JOÃO CARLOS GOMES RIBEIRO; Sec. Gen. WILMA ROSA; publs *Revista Brasileira de Biblioteconomia e Documentação, Boletim.*

ECONOMICS, LAW AND POLITICS

Academia Brasileira de Ciência da Administração (Brazilian Academy of Administration): Praia de Botafogo 190–12°, 22253-900 Rio de Janeiro, RJ; f. 1973; 40 mems; Pres. JORGE OSCAR DE MELLO FLORES; Vice-Pres. FANNY TCHAIKOWSKI.

Instituto Brasileiro de Economia (Brazilian Institute of Economics): Getúlio Vargas Foundation, CP 62-591, Rio de Janeiro, RJ; f. 1951; Chair. ANTÔNIO SALAZAR P. BRANDÃO; publs *Conjuntura Econômica* (monthly), *Revista Agroanalysis* (monthly).

Instituto dos Advogados Brasileiros (Institute of Brazilian Lawyers): Av. Marechal Câmara 210, 5° andar, Castelo, 20020-080 Rio de Janeiro, RJ; f. 1843; 1,141 mems; Pres. RICARDO CÉSAR PEREIRA LIRA; library: see Libraries; publ. *Revista.*

Instituto Municipal de Administração e Ciências Contábeis (Municipal Institute of Administration and Business Science): Parque Municipal, CP 1914, Belo Horizonte, MG; f. 1954; library of 33,000 vols; Pres. RAUL LOPES MURADAS.

EDUCATION

Associação de Educação Católica do Brasil (Assen for Catholic Education in Brazil): SBN Q01, Bloco H, Loja 40, 70040-000 Brasília, DF; tel. (61) 223-2947; fax (61) 226-3081; f. 1945; supervises 27 sections, with a total of 1,750 schools and seminaries; Pres. P. AGUSTÍN CASTEJÓN; publ. *Revista de Educação AEC, Cadernos de Educação.*

Conselho de Reitores das Universidades Brasileiras (Council of Brazilian University Rectors): SEUP/Norte, Quadra 516, Conj. D, Lote 09, 70770-535, Brasília, DF; tel. (61) 272-2960; fax (61) 274-4621; f. 1966; study of problems affecting higher education; 120 mems; library of 15,000 vols; Pres. JOSÉ CARLOS ALMEIDA DA SILVA; Gen. Sec. MARIA HELENA ALVES GARCIA; publs *Educação Brasileira, Estudos e Debates, Anais, Documentação Básica, Sistema de Informação das Universidades Brasileiras, Cadernos CRUB.*

Coordenação de Aperfeiçoamento de Pessoal de Nível Superior (Federal Agency for Postgraduate Education): Ministério da Educação e Cultura, Anexo I, 4° andar, CP 3540, 70047 Brasília, DF; tel. (61) 321-3200; telex (061) 2018; f. 1951; main objects are to deploy the human resources of graduate schools to help government and public enterprises, to give student grants, to evaluate and co-ordinate Master's and Doctor's courses; Dir-Gen. JOSÉ UBYRAJARA ALVES.

Fundação Carlos Chagas: CP 11478, Av. Prof. Francisco Morato 1565, 05513-900 São Paulo, SP; tel. (11) 813-4511; fax (11) 815-1059; e-mail fcc@fcc.org.br; f. 1964; activities in the fields of human resources and educational research; library of 23,000 vols; Pres. Prof. Dr RUBENS MURILLO MARQUES; Sec.-Gen. Prof. Dr NELSON FONTANA MARGARIDO; publs *Cadernos de Pesquisa* (quarterly), *Estudos em Avaliação Educacional* (2 a year).

Fundação de Desenvolvimento de Pessoal-Fundesp: Av. João Pessoa 5609, Damas, 60435 Fortaleza, CE; tel. (85) 292-1877; f. 1974; language courses; library of 6,128 vols; Pres. MARIA DO CARNO MAGALHÃES.

Fundação Getúlio Vargas: Praia de Botafogo 190, 22253-900 Rio de Janeiro, RJ; tel. (21) 536-9100; fax (21) 553-6372; f. 1944; technical, scientific, educational and philanthropic activities; includes 3 educational institutes; 385 mems in General Assembly; library of over 120,000 vols; Pres. Dr JORGE OSCAR DE MELLO FLÔRES; publs *Conjuntura Econômica* (monthly), *Correio da UNESCO* (monthly), *Revista de Administração de Empresas* (every 2 months), *Revista de Administração Pública,* (quarterly), *Revista Brasileira de Economia* (quarterly), *Agroanalysis* (monthly).

Instituto Brasileiro de Educação, Ciência e Cultura (IBECC) (Brazilian Institute of Education, Science and Culture): UNESCO National Commission, Av. Marechal Floriano 196, 3° andar, Palácio Itamaraty, 20080 Rio de Janeiro, RJ; tel. (21) 516-2458; telex 21047; fax (21) 516-2458; f. 1946; 60 mems; library of 2,500 vols; Pres. JOSÉ PELÚCIO FERREIRA; Exec. Sec. JOAQUIM CAETANO GENTIL NETO; publ. *Boletim.*

HISTORY, GEOGRAPHY AND ARCHAEOLOGY

Instituto Arqueológico, Histórico e Geográfico Pernambucano (Archaeological, Historical and Geographical Institute): Rua do Hospício 130, Recife, PE; f. 1862; library of 20,000 vols; 50 mems, 130 corresp. mems, 5 hon. mems; Pres. Dr JOSÉ ANTÔNIO GONSALVES DE MELO; First Sec. Prof. J. L. MOTA MENEZES; Librarian Prof. FERNANDA IVO NEVES; publ. *Revista.*

Instituto do Ceará (Ceará Institute): Rua Barão do Rio Branco 1594, 60025-061 Fortaleza, CE; tel. (85) 231-6152; fax (85) 254-4116; f. 1887; 40 mems; library of 40,000 vols; includes the following commissions: History, Manuscripts and Periodicals, Geography, Anthropology; Pres. PAULO AYRTON ARAUJO; Gen Sec. JOSÉ LIBERAL DE CASTRO; publs *Revista.*

Instituto Genealógico Brasileiro (Genealogical Institute): Rua Dr Zuquim 1525, São Paulo, SP; library of 972 vols; Pres. Colonel SALVADOR DE MOYA; Sec. Dr JORGE BUENO DE MIRANDA; publs *Anuário Genealógico Brasileiro, Anuário Genealógico Latino, Revista Genealógica Brasileira, Biblioteca Genealógica Brasileira, Biblioteca, Genealógica Latina, Indices Genealógicos Brasileiros, Subsídios Genealógicos.*

Instituto Geográfico e Histórico da Bahia (Bahia Geographical and Historical Institute): Av. 7 de Setembro 94 A, Piedade, 40060-001 Salvador, BA; tel. (71) 322-2453; fax (71) 321-4787; f. 1894; 300 mems; library of 35,000 vols; Pres. Profa CONSUELO PONDÉ DE SENA; Sec. Dr LAMARTINE DE ANDRADE LIMA; publ. *Revista* (annually).

Instituto Geográfico e Histórico do Amazonas (IGHA): Rua Bernardo Ramos 117, Manaus, AM; tel. 232-7077; f. 1917; 120 mems; library 45,158 vols; Pres. Dr ROBERIO DOS SANTOS PEREIRA BRAGA; Gen. Sec. Dr JOSÉ ROBERTO TADROS; Admin. Sec. JOSÉ GERALDO XAVIER DOS ANJOS; publs *Revista, Boletim.*

Instituto Geológico (Geological Institute): CP 8772, São Paulo, SP; f. 1886; library of 150,000 vols, periodicals and pamphlets; 50,000 maps; map collection, geological museum; Dir MARCIA MARIA N. PRESSINOTTI; publs *Boletim*, *Jornal*, reports, maps and monographs.

Instituto Histórico de Alagoas (Alagoas Historical Institute): Rua João Pessoa 382, 57000 Maceió, AL; f. 1869; 40 mems; library of 15,000 vols; Pres. Dr JOSÉ LAGES FILHO; Sec. Dr ABELARDO DUARTE; publ. *Revista*.

Instituto Histórico e Geográfico Brasileiro (Brazilian Historical and Geographical Institute): Av. Augusto Severo 8, 20021-040 Rio de Janeiro, RJ; f. 1838; library of 560,000 vols; archive of 110,000 documents; museum of 1,100 items; Pres. ARNO WEHLING; Sec. CYBELLE MOREIRA DE IPANEMA; publ. *Revista* (quarterly).

Instituto Histórico e Geográfico de Goiás (Historical and Geographical Institute): Rua 82, No 455, S. Sul, Goiânia; tel. 224-4622; f. 1933; 60 mems; library of 20,000 vols; rare collections of letters and newspapers; Dir Dr COLEMAR NATAL E SILVA; publs *Boletim* (quarterly), *Review* (annually).

Instituto Histórico e Geográfico de Santa Catarina (Santa Catarina Historical and Geographical Institute): Praça XV de Novembro/Palácio Cruz e Sousa, CP 1582, Florianópolis, SC; tel. (48) 221-3502; fax (48) 222-5111; f. 1896; 235 mems; library of 4,000 vols; Pres. Prof. Dr CARLOS HUMBERTO PEDERNEIRAS CORRÊA; Sec. Prof. JALI MEIRINHO; publs *Revista* (annually), *Anais*.

Instituto Histórico e Geográfico de São Paulo (São Paulo Historical and Geographical Institute): Rua Benjamim Constant 158, 01005-000 São Paulo, SP; f. 1894; library of 40,000 vols; Pres. HERNÂNI DONATO; Sec. MARIO SAVELLI; publ. *Revista*.

Instituto Histórico e Geográfico de Sergipe (Sergipe Historical and Geographical Institute): Rua de Itabaianinha 41, 49000 Aracajú; f. 1912; Pres. Prof. MARIA THETIS NUENS; publ. *Revista*.

Instituto Histórico e Geográfico do Espírito Santo (Historical and Geographical Institute): Av. República 374, CP 29020-620, Vitória; f. 1916; Pres. Prof. RENATO PACHECO; Gen. Sec. MIGUEL DEPES TALLON; publ. *Revista*.

Instituto Histórico e Geográfico do Maranhão (Maranhão Historical and Geographical Institute): Rua Santa Rita 230, 65000 São Luíz, MA; f. 1925; Pres. Dr JOSÉ RIBAMAR SEGUINS; Sec.-Gen. Dr FRANCISCO MARIALVA MONT'ALVERNE FROTA; publ. *Revista*.

Instituto Histórico e Geográfico do Pará (Pará Historical and Geographical Institute): Rua d'Aveiro-Cidade Irmã 62 (Antiga Thomazia Perdigão), CP 547, 66000 Belém; f. 1900; Pres. Dr JOSÉ RODRIGUES DA SILVEIRA NETTO; First Sec. Dr ALAÚDIO DE OLIVEIRA MELLO.

Instituto Histórico e Geográfico do Rio Grande do Norte (Rio Grande do Norte Historical and Geographical Institute): Rua da Conceição 622, 59000 Natal; f. 1902; library 50,000 vols; Pres. Dr ENÉLIO LIMA PETROVICH; Librarian OLAVO DE MEDEIROS FILHO; publ. *Revista*.

Instituto Histórico e Geográfico do Rio Grande do Sul (Rio Grande do Sul Historical and Geographical Institute): Rua Riachuelo 1317, 90010-271 Porto Alegre; tel. and fax (51) 224-3760; f. 1920; Pres. Dr SÉRGIO DA COSTA FRANCO; publ. *Revista*.

Instituto Histórico e Geográfico Paraíbano (Paraíba Historical and Geographical Institute): Rua Barão do Abiaí 64, CP 37, 58013-080 João Pessoa; f. 1905; library of 30,000 vols; 50 mems; 30 corresp.; Pres. LUIZ HUGO GUIMARÃES; Sec. DOMINGOS A. RIBEIRO; publ. *Revista*.

Instituto Histórico, Geográfico e Etnográfico Paranaense (Historical, Geographical, Ethnographic Institute of Paraná): Rua José Loureiro 43, 80000 Curitiba; f. 1900; Pres. Gen. LUÍZ CARLOS PEREIRA TOURINHO; Sec. NEY FERNANDO PERRACINI DE AZEVEDO; publ. *Boletim*.

Sociedade Brasileira de Cartografia: Av. Presidente Wilson 210, 7° andar, Centro, 20030-210 Rio de Janeiro, RJ; f. 1958; cartography, geodesy, surveying, photogrammetry and remote sensing; 1,500 mems; Pres. NEI ERLING; Sec. JOSÉ HENRIQUE DA SILVA; publs *Proceedings*, *Revista Brasileira de Cartografia*.

Sociedade Brasileira de Geografia (Brazilian Geographical Society): Praça da República 54, 1° andar, Rio de Janeiro, RJ; f. 1883; library of 13,712 vols; 284 mems; Pres. Prof. JURADYR DE CASTRO PIRES FERREIRA; Sec.-Gen. General HENRIQUE GUILHERME MULLER; publs *Boletim*, *Estante Paranista*.

LANGUAGE AND LITERATURE

Academia Amazonense de Letras (Amazonas Academy of Letters): Rua Ramos Ferreira 1009, Manaus, AM; f. 1918; Pres. DJALMA BATISTA; Sec. GENESINO BRAGA; Librarian MÁRIO YPIRANGA MONTEIRO; 40 mems; library of 3,500 vols; publ. *Revista*.

Academia Brasileira de Letras (Brazilian Academy of Letters): Av. Presidente Wilson 203, 20030 Rio de Janeiro, RJ; f. 1897; library of 50,000 vols; Pres. (vacant); Sec.-Gen. ABGAR RENAULT; Librarian BARBOSA LIMA SOBRINHO; publ. *Revista* (annals); preparing exhaustive *Dictionary of the Portuguese Language*; annual prizes awarded for best Brazilian works in prose, verse and drama.

Academia Cearense de Letras (Ceará Academy of Letters): Biblioteca, Rua São Paulo, 60000 Fortaleza, CE; f. 1894; 40 mems, 21 hon. mems; library of 10,000 vols; Pres. CLAUDIO MARTINS; Sec.-Gen. ITAMAR DE SANTIAGO ESPÍNDOLA; publ. *Revista*.

Academia de Letras da Bahia (Bahia Academy of Letters): Av. Joana Angélica 198, Nazaré, 40050 Salvador, BA; tel. (71) 243-7614; f. 1917; 40 mems, 19 corresponding in Brazil, 6 abroad; library of 10,000 vols; Pres. CLÁUDIO VEIGA; Vice-Pres. WILSON LINS; Sec. EDIVALDO M. BOAVENTURA; publ. *Revista* (annually).

Academia de Letras e Artes do Planalto (Planalto Academy of Arts and Letters): Rua do Santissimo Sacramento 32, 72800-000 Luziânia, GO; tel. (61) 621-1184; f. 1976; 30 mems; library of 8,000 vols; Pres. TEREZINHA DE JESUS RORIZ MACHADO.

Academia Mineira de Letras (Minas Gerais Academy of Letters): Rua da Bahia 1466, 30160 Belo Horizonte, MG; Pres. VIVALDI MOREIRA.

Academia Paraibana de Letras (Paraíba Academy of Letters): Rua Duque de Caxias 25, CP 334, 58000 João Pessoa, PB; f. 1941; 40 mems; Pres. AFONSO PEREIRA DA SILVA; Gen. Sec. AURÉLIO MORENO DE ALBUQUERQUE; publs *Revista*, *Boletim Informativo*, *Discursos e Ensaios*.

Academia Paulista de Letras (São Paulo Academy of Letters): Largo do Arouche 312, 01219 São Paulo, SP; f. 1909; 40 mems; library of 50,000 vols; Pres. ANTONIO A. S. AMORA; publ. *Revista*.

Academia Pernambucana de Letras (Pernambuco Academy of Letters): Av. Rui Barbosa 1596, Graças, 52050-000 Recife, PE; fax (81) 268-2211; f. 1901; library of 12,000 vols; 40 mems, unlimited number of hon. and corresp. mems in Brazil and abroad; Pres. LUIZ DE MAGALHAES MELO; Sec. Dr LUCILO VAREJÃO FILHO; publ. *Revista*.

Academia Piauiense de Letras (Piauí Academy of Letters): 64001-490 Teresina, PI; Pres. MANOEL PAULO NUNES; publ. *Revista*.

Academia Riograndense de Letras (Rio Grande Academy of Letters): Rua Cândido Silveira 43, Porto Alegre, RS; publ. *Revista*.

PEN Clube do Brasil—Associação Universal de Escritores (International PEN Centre): Praia do Flamengo 172, 10° andar, Rio de Janeiro, RJ; f. 1936; 106 mems; monthly free lectures; theatrical performances; Pres. Prof. MARCOS ALMIR MADEIRA; publs *Boletim*, novels, poetry.

Sociedade Brasileira de Autores Teatrais (Society of Playwrights): Av. Almirante Barroso 97, 3° andar, 20031-005 Rio de Janeiro, RJ; tel. (21) 240-7231; fax (21) 240-7431; f. 1917; non-profit making organization; 8,000 mems; library of 6,000 vols; Pres. CESAR VIEIRA; Communications Dir JOSÈ RENATO PÉCORA; publ. *Revista de Teatro* (quarterly).

MEDICINE

Academia de Medicina de São Paulo (Medical Academy of São Paulo): Rua Teodoro Sampaio 115, 2° andar, 05405 São Paulo, SP; tel. 853-9677; f. 1895 as Sociedade de Medicina e Cirurgia; Pres. Prof. RAUL MARINO JUNIOR; Gen. Sec. Prof. CLAUDIO COHEN.

Academia Nacional de Medicina (National Academy of Medicine): Av. General Justo 365 7°, CP 459, 20021-130 Rio de Janeiro, RJ; tel. (21) 262-1732; fax (21) 240-8673; f. 1829; 100 mems; library of 22,000 vols, 1,200 periodicals; Pres. RUBEM DAVID AZULAY; Sec.-Gen. JARBAS A. PORTO; publ. *Anais*.

Associação Bahiana de Medicina (Medical Society): Av. Sete de Setembro 48, 1°, Salvador, BA; f. 1894; Pres. Dr JOSÉ SILVEIRA; Sec.-Gen. Dr MENANDRO NOVÃES; publ. *Anais*.

Associação Brasileira de Farmacêuticos (Brazilian Pharmaceutical Association): Rua Andradas 96, 10°, ZC-25, Rio de Janeiro, RJ; fax (21) 263-0791; f. 1916; comprises the following Comms: *Econômica e Etica Farmacêutica* (Pharmaceutical Economics and Ethics); *Desenvolvimento Cultural* (Cultural Development); *Propaganda e Intercambio Associativo* (Propaganda and Exchange); *Legislação Comercial* (Commercial Legislation); *Legislação Sanitaria* (Sanitary Legislation); *Legislação Tributaria* (Tax Legislation); *Legislação de Marcas e Patentes* (Trade Marks and Patents); library; 950 mems, hon. and corresponding; Pres. LEILA DE MENDONÇA GARCIA; Vice-Pres. Prof. NUNO ÁLVARES PEREIRA; publ. *Revista Brasileira de Farmácia* (4 a year).

Associação Médica Brasileira (Brazilian Medical Association): Rua São Carlos do Pinhal 324, CP 8094, São Paulo; f. 1951; professional association; 35,000 mems; Pres. Dr PEDRO KASSAB; Sec.-Gen. Dr RADION SCHUELER BARBOZA; publs *Journal AMB* (weekly), *Boletim AMB* and *Revista AMB* (monthly), *Revista Brasileira de Ortopedia*, *Arquivos Brasileiros de Endocrinologia e Metabologia*, *Jornal Brasileira de Nefrologia*, *Anais Brasileiros de Geriatria e Gerontologia* (quarterly), *Revista Brasileira de Reumatologia* (every 2 months).

Associação Paulista de Medicina (São Paulo Medical Association): Av. Brigadeiro Luís Antônio 278, CP 2103, 01318-901 São Paulo; tel. (11) 232-3141; e-mail apm@apm.org.br; f. 1930; 22,000 active mems, 432 corresp. mems; Pres. Dr ELEUSES VIEIRA DE PAIVA; Scientific Dir Dr ÁLVARO NAGIB ATALLAH; publs *Revista Paulista de Medicina* (6 a year), *Jornal da APM* (monthly), *Revista Diagnóstico & Tratamento* (4 a year).

Sociedade Brasileira de Dermatologia (Brazilian Dermatological Society): CP 389, 20001-970 Rio de Janeiro, RJ; tel. (21) 253-

6747; f. 1912; 16 hon. mems, 56 corresponding mems, 3,800 mems; library of 4,000 vols, 200 periodicals; Sec.-Gen. Dr MARIA DE LOURDES VIEGAS; publ. *Anais Brasileiros de Dermatologia*.

Sociedade de Medicina de Alagoas (Alagoas Medical Society): Rua Barão de Anadia 5 (centro), CP 57025 Maceió, AL; tel. 223-3463; fax (82) 223-3463; f. 1917; 1,200 mems; library of 2,500 vols; Pres. Dr SERGIO TOLEDO BARBOSA; publs *Consulta, Boletim da SMA*.

Sociedade de Pediatria de Bahia (Paediatrics Society): Hospital Martagão Gesteira, Rua José Duarte 114, Salvador, BA; f. 1930; 200 mems; Pres. ELIEZER AUDÍFACE; publ. *Pediatria e Puericultura*.

NATURAL SCIENCES

General

Academia Brasileira de Ciências (Brazilian Academy of Sciences): Rua Anfilófio de Carvalho, 29, 20030-060 Rio de Janeiro, RJ; tel. (21) 220-4794; fax (21) 532-5807; e-mail abc@abc.org.br; f. 1916; 242 full mems, 123 assoc. mems, 132 foreign mems; Pres. EDUARDO MOACYR KRIEGER; Vice-Pres CARLOS EDUARDO ROCHA MIRANDA, RICARDO GATTASS; Sec.-Gen. LUIZ BEVILACQUA; publs *Anais*, *Revista Brasileira de Biologia*.

Sociedade Brasileira para o Progresso da Ciência (Brazilian Society for the Advancement of Science): Rua Maria Antonia 294, 4° andar, 01222-010 São Paulo, SP; tel. (11) 259-2766; fax (11) 3106-1002; e-mail diret@www.sbpcnet.org.br; f. 1948; 3,000 mems; Pres. SÉRGIO H. FERREIRA; Sec.-Gen. Prof. Dr ADEMAR FREIRE-MAIA; publs *Ciência e Cultura* (every 2 months), *Ciência Hoje* (every 2 months), *Jornal da Ciência* (fortnightly), *Revista Ciência Hoje das Crianças* (monthly).

Sociedade Científica de São Paulo (Scientific Society of São Paulo): CP 2679, São Paulo; f. 1939; library of 12,000 vols; departments: law, chemical technology, geology and mineralogy, astronomy, architecture, genealogy, philology, medicine, history and pre-history, topography; Pres. Dr GASTÃO F. DE ALMEIDA; Gen. Secs Prof. Dr R. F. MOREIRA, Dr M. F. DE ALMEIDA.

Biological Sciences

Sociedade Brasileira de Entomologia (Brazilian Entomological Society): CP 9063, 01065-970 São Paulo, SP; f. 1937; *c.* 500 mems; Pres. CARLOS RIBEIRO VILELA; Sec. PEDRO GNASPINI NETTO; publ. *Revista Brasileira de Entomologia* (quarterly).

Physical Sciences

Associação Brasileira de Química (Brazilian Chemical Association): Rua Alcindo Guanabara 24, Conj. 1601, CEP 20031-130, Rio de Janeiro, RJ; tel. (21) 262-1837; fax (21) 262-6044; f. 1922; affiliated to IUPAC; 3,000 mems; library of 3,000 vols; regional brs in Amazonas, Pará, Maranhão, Ceará, Rio Grande do Norte, Pernambuco, Paraíba, Bahia, Rio de Janeiro, São Paulo, Rio Grande do Sul and Brasília; Pres. HARRY SERRUYA; publs *Anais da Associação Brasileira de Química, Revista de Química Industrial*.

PHILOSOPHY AND PSYCHOLOGY

Sociedade Brasileira de Filosofia (Brazilian Philosophical Soc.): Praça da República 54, Rio de Janeiro, RJ; f. 1927; 80 mems, 8 hon., 5 Brazilian corresp., 12 foreign; Pres. Dr HERBERT CANABARRO REICHARDT; Sec.-Gen. Prof. ARNALDO CLARO DE SÃO THIAGO; publ. *Anais*.

RELIGION, SOCIOLOGY AND ANTHROPOLOGY

Comissão Nacional de Folclore (National Folklore Commission): Palácio Itamaraty, Av. Marechal Floriano 196, CEP 20080-002 Rio de Janeiro, RJ; fax (21) 516-2458; Dept of the Brazilian Institute of Education, Science and Culture (IBECC); Pres. ÁTICO VILAS BOAS DA MOTA; publ. *Boletim*.

TECHNOLOGY

Associação Brasileira de Metalurgia e Materiais (ABM) (Brazilian Metallurgy and Materials Society): Rua Antônio Comparato 218, 04605-030 São Paulo, SP; f. 1944; 5,500 mems; library of 5,000 vols, periodicals; Pres. SYLVIO N. COUTINHO; Vice-Pres. MARCUS J. A. TAMBASO; publ. *Metalurgia & Materiais* (monthly).

Associação de Engenharia Química (Society of Chemical Engineers): Conjunto das Químicas, Bloco 19, Cidade Universitária, São Paulo, SP; f. 1944; 500 mems; Pres. ALDO TONSO; Sec. UDO HUPFELD.

Research Institutes

AGRICULTURE, FISHERIES AND VETERINARY SCIENCE

Centro de Energia Nuclear na Agricultura (CENA) (Centre of Nuclear Energy in Agriculture): Univ. de São Paulo, Campus de Piracicaba, CP 96, 13400-970 Piracicaba, SP; tel. (19) 429-4600; telex (019) 1097; fax (19) 429-4610; f. 1966; 52 researchers; plant biochemistry, entomology, plant nutrition, radiogenetics, phytopathology, electron microscopy, soil fertility, soil physics, soil microbiology, animal nutrition, hydrology, radiochemistry, radiation protection, ecology, water pollution, genetic engineering; library of 9,000 vols and 366 periodicals; special collection: IAEA publs on life sciences; Dir Dr AUGUSTO TULMANN NETO; publs *Annual Report, Scientia Agrícola*.

Centro de Pesquisas Veterinárias 'Desidério Finamor' (Institute of Veterinary Research): CP 2076, 90001-970 Porto Alegre, RS; tel. (51) 4813711; fax (51) 4813337; f. 1949; research and training in all aspects of animal health; library of 1,400 vols; Dir Dr AUGUSTO CÉSAR DA CUNHA; publ. *Pesquisa Agropecuária Gaúcha*.

Empresa Brasileira de Pesquisa Agropecuária (EMBRAPA) (Brazilian Agricultural Research Enterprise): SAIN-Parque, CP 04-0315, 70770-901 Brasília, DF; telex (061) 1524; fax (61) 273-1041; f. 1972; attached to Ministry of Agriculture; controls agricultural research throughout the country; library of 20,000 vols; Pres. ALBERTO DUQUE PORTUGAL; publs *Pesquisa Agropecuaria Brasileira –PAB* (monthly), *Cadernos de Ciência e Tecnologia* (quarterly).

Research centres:

Centro de Pesquisa Agroflorestal da Amazônia Oriental: Travessa Dr Enéas Pinheiro s/n, Bairro do Marco, 66095-100 Belém, PA; tel. (91) 226-6622; telex 1210; fax (91) 226-6622; f. 1975.

Centro Nacional de Pesquisa de Florestas: Estrada da Ribeira km 111, CP 319, 83411-000 Colombo, PR; tel. (41) 766-1313; telex 30120; fax (41) 766-1692; f. 1978; forest research.

Centro de Pesquisa de Pecuária dos Campos sul Brasileiros: BR 153, km 141, Vila Industrial, Zona Rural, 96400-970 Bagé, RS; tel. (532) 42-4499; telex 2500; fax (532) 42-4395; f. 1975.

Centro de Pesquisa de Pecuária do Sudeste: Rodovia Washington Luiz km 234, 13560-970 São Carlos, SP; tel. (162) 72-7611; telex 2389; fax (162) 72-5774; f. 1975.

Centro Nacional de Pesquisa de Caprinos: Fazenda Três Lagoas/Estrada Sobral/Groaíras km 4, 62011-970 Sobral, CE; tel. (88) 612-1077; telex 2543; fax (88) 612-1132; e-mail Postmaster@cnpc.embrapa.br; f. 1975; research on goats.

Centro de Pesquisa Agropecuária dos Cerrados: BR 020 km 18, Rodovia Brasília/Fortaleza, 73301 Planaltina, DF; tel. (61) 389-1171; telex 1621; fax (61) 389-2953; f. 1975.

Centro Nacional de Recursos Genéticos e Biotecnologia: SAIN, Parque Rural (final W-3 Norte), CP 70602-000 Brasília, DF; tel. (61) 340-3500; telex 1022; fax (61) 340-3624; f. 1976.

Centro Nacional de Pesquisa de Hortaliças: BR 060 km 09, CP 218, 70359-970 Brasília, DF; tel. (61) 385-9000; fax (61) 556-5744; e-mail ruy@cnph.embrapa.br; f. 1975; vegetable research.

Centro Nacional de Pesquisa de Arroz e Feijão: Rodovia Gyn 12, km 10 (antiga Rod. Goiânia/Nerópolis), 74001-970 Goiânia, GO; tel. (62) 261-3459; telex 2241; fax (62) 261-3880; f. 1975; research on beans, cowpeas and rice.

Centro Nacional de Pesquisa de Gado de Leite: Rua Eugênio do Nascimento 610, Bairro Dom Bosco, 36038-330 Juiz de Fora, MG; tel. (32) 215-8550; telex 3157; fax (32) 215-8550; f. 1976; dairy research.

Centro de Pesquisa Agropecuária de Clima Temperado: BR 392 km 78, 9° Distrito de Pelotas, 96001-970 Pelotas, RS; tel. and fax (532) 21-2121; telex 2301; f. 1975; research on temperate fruit and vegetable crops and food technology.

Centro de Pesquisa Agroflorestal do Acre: Rodovia BR 364, km 14, 69901-180 Rio Branco, AC; tel. (68) 224-3931; telex 2589; fax (68) 224-4035; f. 1976.

Centro Nacional de Pesquisa de Suínos e Aves: BR 153, km 110, Vila Tamanduá, 89700-000 Concórdia, SC; tel. (49) 442-8555; fax (49) 442-8559; e-mail cnpsa@cnpsa.embrapa.br; f. 1975; research on pigs and poultry; library of 4,000 vols, 800 periodicals.

Centro Nacional de Pesquisa de Mandioca e Fruticultura Tropical: Rua EMBRAPA s/n, 44380-000 Cruz das Almas, BA; tel. (75) 721-2120; telex 2074; fax (75) 721-1118; f. 1975; research on pineapple, banana, citrus, mango, cassava.

Centro Nacional de Pesquisa de Milho e Sorgo: Rodovia MG 424, km 65; 35701-970, Sete Lagoas, MG; tel. (31) 779-1000; e-mail cnpms@cnpms.embrapa.br; f. 1975; research on maize and sorghum; library of 5,500 books, 65 periodicals; Head Dr ANTONIO FERNANDINO C. BAHIA F.

Centro de Pesquisa Agropecuária dos Tabuleiros Costeiros: Av. Beira Mar 3250, Praia 13 de Julho, 49025-040 Aracaju, SE; tel. (79) 231-9145; telex 2318; f. 1974.

Centro Nacional de Pesquisa de Uva e Vinho: Rua Livramento 515, 95700-000 Bento Gonçalves, RS; tel. (54) 252-2144; telex 3603; fax (54) 252-2792; f. 1975; research and development in viticulture and the wine industry.

Centro de Pesquisa Agroflorestal de Rondônia: BR 364, km 5.5, 78900-000 Porto Velho, RO; tel. and fax (69) 222-3857; telex 2258; f. 1975.

Centro de Pesquisa Agropecuária do Oeste: Rodovia Dourados/Caarapó, km 05,

79804-970 Dourados, MS; tel. (67) 421-5521; telex 2310; f. 1976.

Centro de Pesquisa Agroflorestal de Roraima: BR 174, km 08, Distrito Industrial, 69301-970 Boa Vista, RR; tel. (95) 224-9211; telex 2137; f. 1981.

Centro de Pesquisa Agroflorestal da Amazônia Ocidental: Rodovia AM-010 km 28, 69048-660 Manaus, AM; tel. (92) 233-5598; telex 2440; fax (92) 233-5336; f. 1975; rubber and oil palm research.

Centro Nacional de Pesquisa de Gado de Corte: Rodovia BR 262 km 04, 79106-000 Campo Grande, MS; tel. (67) 763-1030; telex 672153; fax (67) 763-1030; e-mail ainfo@cnpgc.embrapa.br; f. 1976; research on beef cattle.

Centro de Pesquisa Agropecuária do Pantanal: Rua 21 de Setembro 1880, 79320-900 Corumbá, MS; tel. (67) 231-1430; telex 7044; fax (67) 231-1430; research on beef cattle and pasture land.

Centro Nacional de Pesquisa de Soja: Rodovia Carlos João Strass (Londrina/Warta), Acesso Orlando Amaral, 86001-970 Londrina, PR; tel. (432) 20-4166; telex 2208; f. 1975; research on soya beans and sunflowers.

Centro de Pesquisa Agropecuária do Trópico Semi-Árido: BR 428 km 152, Zona Rural, 56300-000 Petrolina, PE; tel. (81) 961-4411; telex 0016; f. 1975.

Centro Nacional de Pesquisa de Algodão: Rua Osvaldo Cruz 1143, Centenário, 58107-720 Campina Grande, PB; tel. (83) 341-3608; telex 3213; f. 1975; research on cotton.

Centro Nacional de Pesquisa de Solos: Rua Jardim Botânico 1024, Gávea, 22460-000 Rio de Janeiro, RJ; tel. (21) 274-7897; telex 23824; fax (21) 274-5192; f. 1974; soil survey and conservation.

Centro Nacional de Pesquisa de Tecnologia Agroindustrial de Alimentos: Av. das Americas 29501, Guaratiba, 23020-470 Rio de Janeiro, RJ; tel. (21) 410-1350; telex 33267; fax (21) 410-1090; f. 1971; food science and technology centre.

Centro Nacional de Pesquisa de Trigo: BR 285 km 174, 99001-970 Passo Fundo, RS; tel. (54) 311-3444; telex 5319; fax (54) 311-3617; f. 1974; wheat research centre.

Serviço de Produção de Sementes Básicas: SAIN, Parque Rural, Av. W3 Norte (final), Ed. Sede EMBRAPA, 70770-901 Brasília, DF; tel. (61) 272-4241; telex 1738; fax (61) 347-9668; f. 1975; basic seed production service.

Centro Nacional de Pesquisa de Agrobiologia: Rodovia Rio/São Paulo km 47, Seropédica, 23851-970 Itaguaí, RJ; tel. and fax (21) 682-1230; telex 32723.

Centro de Pesquisa Agropecuária do Meio Norte: Avenida São Sebastião 2055, 64200 Parnaíba, PI; tel. (86) 322-1422; telex 2585.

Centro Nacional de Pesquisa de Monitoramento e Avaliaçao de Impacto Ambiéntal-CNPMA: Rodovia SP 340, km 127.5, Bairro Tanquinho Velho, 13820 Jaguariúna, SP; tel. (192) 97-1721; telex 2655; fax (192) 97-2202.

Centro de Pesquisa Agroflorestal do Amapá: Rodovia Juscelino Kubitschek, km 05, (Macapá/Fazendinha), 68902-280 Macapá, AP; tel. (96) 222-3551; telex 2399; fax (96) 223-3087.

Núcleo de Monitoramento Ambiental de Recursos Naturais por Satélite: Avenida Dr Júlio Soares de Arruda 803, Parque São Quirino, 13088-300 Campinas, SP; tel. (192) 52-5875; telex 7686; fax (192) 54-1100.

Centro Nacional de Pesquisa Tecnológica em Informática para a Agricultura: Rodovia D. Pedro I (SP 65), km 143.6, 13089-500 Campinas, SP; tel. (192) 40-1073; telex 7720; fax (192) 40-2007.

Centro Nacional de Pesquisa e Desenvolvimento de Instrumentação Agropecuária: Rua XV de Novembro 1452, Centro, 13560-970 São Carlos, SP; tel. (16) 274-2477; fax (16) 272-5958; e-mail postmaster@cnpdia.embrapa.br.

Centro Nacional de Pesquisa de Agroindústria Tropical (CNPAT): Rua dos Tabajaras 11, Praia de Iracema, Fortaleza, 60060-510 Ceará, CE; tel. (85) 231-7655; fax (85) 231-7762.

Instituto Agronômico (Institute of Agronomy): CP 28, 13020-902 Campinas, SP; tel. (19) 2315422; fax (19) 2314943; f. 1887; basic and applied research on plants, soils, environment, farming methods and agricultural machinery; Divisions: Biology, Experimental Stations, Agricultural Engineering, Food Plants, Industrial Plants, Soil; Technical Scientific Information Service; library of 164,378 vols; 20 experimental stations in the State of São Paulo; 248 research workers; exchange of specimens; Gen. Dir Dr Otávio Tisseli Filho; publs *Bragantia, O Agronômico,* bulletins and circulars.

Instituto Brasileiro do Meio Ambiente e dos Recursos Naturais Renováveis (IBAMA): (Brazilian Institute for the Environment and Renewable Natural Resources): SAIN Av. L4 Norte, 70800-200 Brasília, DF; tel. (61) 316-1205; fax (61) 226-5588; e-mail cnia@sede.ibama.gov.br; f. 1989; library of 40,000 vols; Pres. Eduardo de Souza Martins.

Instituto de Economia Agrícola (Agricultural Economics Institute): Av. Miguel Stefano 3900, Água Funda, CP 68029, 04301-903 São Paulo, SP; tel. (11) 577-0572; fax (11) 276-4062; e-mail iea@eu.ansp.br; f. 1968; affiliated to SP Secretariat of Agriculture and Provision; provides information for state and federal governments and other interested bodies; library of 50,000 vols, 1,500 periodicals; Dir Eng. Agr. Dr Paulo Edgard Nascimento de Toledo; publs *Agricultura em São Paulo, Informações Econômicas, Boletim Diário de Preços.*

Instituto de Zootecnia (Animal Husbandry Institute): Rua Heitor Penteado 56, CP 60, 13460 Nova Odessa, SP; tel. 66-1410; f. 1905; 116 staff; library of 10,710 vols, 1,610 periodicals; Dir-Gen. Dr Albino Luchiani Filho; publs *Boletim de Indústria Animal* (2 a year), *Zootecnia* (quarterly).

Instituto Florestal (Estado de São Paulo) (São Paulo State Forestry Institute): Rua do Horto 931, CP 1322, 01051 São Paulo, SP; tel. (11) 203-0122; telex 011-22877; f. 1896; 106 staff; library of 7,500 vols, 2,000 periodicals; Dir Helio Y. Ogawa; publs *Revista IF-Serie Registros.*

Serviço de Defesa Sanitária Vegetal (Plant Health Protection Service): Secretaria de Defesa Sanitária Vegetal, Ministério da Agricultura, Esplanada dos Ministérios, Bloco 8, Anexo 3° andar, Brasília, DF; tel. (61) 224-6543; telex (061) 1852; f. 1920; library of 5,000 vols, pamphlets and periodicals; Sec. Hélio Palma de Arruda; publs *Boletim Fitossanitário, Monografias.*

ECONOMICS, LAW AND POLITICS

Centro de Estatística e Informações (Statistics and Information Centre): Centro Administrativo da Bahia, Avenida 435 4a, 41750-300 Salvador, BA; tel. (71) 371-9665; fax (71) 371-9664; f. 1983; statistics, natural resources, economic indicators; library of 15,448 vols; Dir Renata Proserpio; publ. Bahia Análise e Dados (every 4 months).

EDUCATION

Instituto Nacional de Estudos e Pesquisas Educacionais (National Institute for Educational Research): CP 04662, Campus da Universidade de Brasília, Acesso Sul 70312 Brasília, DF; tel. (61) 347-6140; f. 1938; 130 mems; library of 50,000 vols, 985 periodicals; Dir Dr Og Roberto Doria; publs *Revista Brasileira de Estudos Pedagógicos, Bibliografia Brasileira de Educação, Em Aberto.*

HISTORY, GEOGRAPHY AND ARCHAEOLOGY

Fundação Instituto Brasileiro de Geografia e Estatística (Brazilian Institute of Geography and Statistics): Av. Franklin Roosevelt 166, 20021-120 Rio de Janeiro, RJ; f. 1936; produces and analyses statistical, geographical, cartographic, geodetic, demographic, socio-economic, natural resources and environmental information; Pres. Simon Schwartzman; publs *Revista Brasileira de Estatística, Anuário Estatístico do Brasil, Revista Brasileira de Geografia.*

MEDICINE

Centro de Pesquisa Básica, Instituto Nacional de Cancer: Praça Cruz Vermaelha 23, Rio de Janeiro, RJ; tel. (21) 292-4110; f. 1958; biochemistry, immunology, genetics, experimental pathology; 17 mems; Dir Dra Maria Aparecida Limongi Loures.

Fundacão Oswaldo Cruz (Oswaldo Cruz Foundation): Av. Brasil 4365, CP 926, 21045-900 Rio de Janeiro, RJ; tel. (21) 270-5141; telex 021-23239; fax (21) 260-6707; f. 1900; tropical medicine, infectious and parasitic diseases, public health; immunology, virology, entomology, epidemiology etc; library of 60,000 vols, 2,000 current periodicals; Pres. Dr Carlos Médicis Morel; publs *Memórias, Cadernos de Saúde Pública, História, Ciências, Saúde–Manguinhos.*

Instituto 'Adolfo Lutz': Av. Dr Arnaldo 355, Pacaembú, 01246-902 São Paulo, SP; f. 1892; fax (11) 853-3505; Central Laboratory of Public Health for the State of São Paulo; library of 50,000 vols, incl. periodicals; Dir.-Gen. Cristiano Corrêa de Azevedo Marques; publ. *Revista.*

Instituto 'Benjamin Constant' (Educational Institute for the Blind): Av. Pasteur 350/368, Urca, 22290-240 Rio de Janeiro, RJ; tel. (21) 2954498; fax (21) 2753745; f. 1854; the Institute took its present name from its third Director, Benjamin Constant (1869–89); braille and general library of 5,000 vols; Dir Prof. Carmelino Souza Vieira; publs in Braille, *Revista Brasileira para Cegos* (quarterly), *Pontinhos* (quarterly), *Revista Benjamin Constant.*

Instituto Brasileiro de Estudos e Pesquisas de Gastroenterologia (IBEPEGE): Rua Dr Seng 320, Bairro da Bela Vista, 01331-020 São Paulo; tel. (11) 288-2119; fax (11) 289-2768; f. 1963; study and research in gastroenterology, nutrition and psychosomatic medicine; postgraduate courses; library of 10,000 vols; Pres. Prof. José Fernandes Pontes; Vice-Pres. Dr José Vicente Martins Campos; publ. *Arquivos de Gastroenterologia* (quarterly).

Instituto Butantan (Butantan Institute): Av. Vital Brazil 1500, CP 65, 05504 São Paulo, SP; tel. (11) 813-7222; telex (011) 83325; fax (11) 815-1505; f. 1901; library of 72,826 vols, on ophiology and bio-medical sciences; famous snake farm; Public Health Institute for research and the production of vaccines, sera, etc.; also research in genetics, virology, pathology, etc.; Hospital Vital Brasil (snake, spider and scorpion accidents); Tech. Dir Prof. HISAKO GOWDO HIGASHI; publ. *Memórias* (annually).

Instituto de Saúde (Institute of Health): Av. Dr Eneas Carvalho de Aguiar 188, CP 8027, 01000 São Paulo; f. 1969; organization and supervision of study, research and activities in the fields of mother and child care, phthisiology, hansenology, dermatology, ophthalmology, nutrition and degenerative diseases; library: see Libraries; Dir-Gen. Dr EDMUR F. PASTORELO; publ. *Hansenologia Internationalis* (2 a year).

Instituto Evandro Chagas (MS-Fundação Nacional de Saúde): Av. Almirante Barroso 492, CP 1128, 66090-000 Belém, PA; tel. (91) 246-1022; fax (91) 226-1284; f. 1936; research in bacteriology, parasitology, pathology, virology, mycology, medical entomology, human ecology and environment; library of 50,000 vols, 134 current periodicals, 4,000 reprints; Dir Dr JORGE FERNANDO SOARES TRAVASSOS DA ROSA.

Instituto 'Oscar Freire' (Oscar Freire Institute): Rua Teodoro Sampaio 115, CP 05405-000, São Paulo, SP; f. 1918; for instruction and research in forensic medicine; assoc. with Univ. of São Paulo; library of 4,200 vols; Chair. Prof. Dr CLÁUDIO COHEN.

Instituto Pasteur: Av. Paulista 393, 01311 São Paulo, SP; tel. (11) 288-00-88; telex (11) 3134; f. 1903; practical measures and theoretical studies aimed at preventing rabies in humans; 15 staff; library of 904 vols and 1,083 periodicals; Technical Dir SOSTHENES VITAL DE KERBRIE.

Instituto 'Penido Burnier': Rua Dr Mascarenhas 249, POB 284, 13020-050 Campinas, SP; tel. (192) 32-5866; fax (192) 33-4492; f. 1920; a leading centre for clinical and surgical ophthalmological studies in South America; ophthalmology, otolaryngology, anaesthesiology; 70 staff; library of 11,585 vols; Chief Librarians Dr HILTON DE MELLO E OLIVEIRA, VANDA REGINA SILVA JUCÁ; publ. *Arquivos IPB* (2 a year).

NATURAL SCIENCES

General

Centro de Ciências, Letras e Artes (Science, Letters and Arts Centre): Rua Bernardino de Campos 989, CP 76, Campinas, SP; f. 1901; library of *c.* 30,000 vols; Pres. Dr JOÃO DE SOUSA COELHO; Gen. Sec. ARISTIDES DA COSTA VERDADE; Librarian G. ZINCK; publ. *Revista*; museum and art gallery attached.

Conselho Nacional de Desenvolvimento Científico e Tecnológico (National Council of Scientific and Technological Development): Av. W-3 Norte Quadra 507, Bl. B, 70740-905 Brasília, DF; tel. (61) 348-9400; telex (061) 1089; f. 1951; Pres. JOSÉ GALIZIA TUNDISI.

Institut Français de Recherche Scientifique pour le Développement en Coopération (ORSTOM): CP 7091, 71619-970 Brasília, DF; tel. (61) 248-5323; fax (61) 248-5378; e-mail orstom@apis.com.br; f. 1979; headquarters of the Brazilian delegation to Latin America; missions at various universities and research institutes; Delegate to Brazil MAURICE LOURD. (See main entry under France.)

Instituto Nacional de Pesquisas da Amazônia (National Research Institute for Amazonia): Alameda Cosme Ferreira Aleixo, 1756, CP 478, 69083 Manaus, AM; tel. (92) 643-3097; fax (92) 643-3095; e-mail ozorio@cr-am.rap.br; f. 1954; agronomics, biology, medicine, ecology, technology, forestry, and special projects; 1,003 staff; library of 48,000 items; herbarium; wood collection; Dir OZÓRIO JOSE DE MENEZES FONSECA; publ. *Acta Amazônica* (quarterly).

Biological Sciences

Campo de Santana: Praça da República, Rio de Janeiro, RJ; laid out 1870 by Auguste F. M. Glaziou, who collected 23,000 plants, including 700 trees; Herbário Glaziou forms the most noteworthy exhibit in the Botanical Division of the National Museum.

Centro de Pesquisa e Treinamento em Aqüicultura (CEPTA) (Research and Training Centre for Aquaculture): Rodovia Brigadeiro Faria Lima s/n, CP 64, Km 6.5, 13.630-970 Pirassununga, SP; telex 191803; fax (195) 65-1075; f. 1938; library of 2,171 vols; Dir JOSÉ AUGUSTO FERRAZ DE LIMA; publ. *Boletim Téc. do CEPTA*.

Departamento de Planejamento Ambiental (FEEMA) (Department of Enviromental Planning): Rua Fonseca Teles 121, 16°, 20940-200 Rio de Janeiro, RJ; f. 1975; library of 13,100 vols; Dir EDUARDO RODRIGUES.

Fundação Ezequiel Dias: Centro de Pesquisa e Desenvolvimento, CP 26, Rua Conde Pereira Carneiro 80, Gameleira, 30510-10 Belo Horizonte, MG; tel. (31) 332-2077 ext. 205; telex 392417; fax (31) 332-2534; f. 1907; attached to the Secretariat of Health and Public Welfare; health and welfare, biotechnology, immunology research; library; Superintendent Dr JOSÉ AGENOR ÁLVARES; Dir Prof. CARLOS RIBEIRO DINIZ.

Herbário 'Barbosa Rodrigues': Av. Marcos Konder 800, 88301-122 Itajaí, SC; f. 1942; botany of Southern Brazil, taxonomy, ecology; 123 mems; library of 5,500 vols; Dir VICTUS SCHLICKMANN ROETGER; publs *Sellowia*, *Flora Ilustrada Catarinense*.

Instituto Biológico (Biological Institute): Av. Cons. Rodrigues Alves 1252, 04014-002, São Paulo; tel. (11) 570-4234; fax (11) 570-9704; e-mail divulgacao@biologico.sp.gov.br; f. 1927; animal and plant protection; library of 13,000 vols, 105,000 periodicals; Dir-Gen. ZULEIDE ALVES RAMIRO; publs *Arquivos do Instituto Biológico* (2 a year), *O Biológico* (2 a year), *Boletim Técnico* (irregular).

Instituto de Botânica (Botanical Institute): CP 4005, 01061-970 São Paulo; tel. (11) 5584-6300; fax (11) 577-3678; f. 1938; library of 106,000 vols; herbarium of 320,000 plants; Dir Dr ADAUTO IVO MILANEZ; publs *Hoehnea* (2 a year), *Boletim* (irregular), *Flora da Ilha do Cardoso* (irregular).

Instituto de Pesquisas do Jardim Botânico do Rio de Janeiro: Rua Pacheco Leão 915, 22460-030, Rio de Janeiro, RJ; tel. (21) 511-0511; fax (21) 259-5041; f. 1808; attached to Min. of the Environment, Water Resources and Amazonia; botanical research in systematics, wood anatomy (7,148 samples and 17,000 microscope plates), cytomorphology and ecology; library of 15,000 vols, 50,000 periodicals, antiquarian collection of 3,000 vols; botanical garden with 7,800 species and 11,000 specimens; herbary with 350,000 samples; Dir SÉRGIO DE ALMEIDA BRUNI; publs *Arquivos, Rodriguésia, Estudos e Contribuições*.

Physical Sciences

Associação Internacional de Lunologia (International Association of Lunology): CP 322, Franca, São Paulo; f. 1969; to publish a review on lunar research carried out by all countries.

Centro Brasileiro de Pesquisas Físicas (Brazilian Centre for Physics Research): Rua Xavier Sigaud 150, 4° andar, Urca, 22290-180 Rio de Janeiro, RJ; tel. (21) 541-0337; telex 22563; fax (21) 541-2047; f. 1949; library of 18,951 vols, 811 periodicals; Dir AMÓS TROPER; publs *Notas de Físicas, Notas Técnicas, Ciência e Sociedade*.

Departamento Nacional da Produção Mineral (National Department of Mineral Production): Setor de Autarquias Norte, Quadra 1, Projeção E, Bloco B, Esplanada dos Ministérios, Brasília, DF; f. 1907; Dept of Ministry of Mines and Energy; Dir YVAN BARRETTO DE CARVALHO; publs *Boletim, Anuário Mineral Brasileiro, Avulso, Boletim de Preços, Balanço Mineral Brasileiro*.

Departamento Nacional de Meteorologia (Meteorological Office): Praça 15 de Novembro 2, 5° andar, 20010 Rio de Janeiro, RJ; f. 1921; library of 5,452 vols, pamphlets and periodicals; Dir JORGE CARLOS DE JESUS MARQUES; publs *Boletim Agroclimatológico, Boletim Climatológico, Boletim Técnico, Pesquisa Meteorológica*.

Laboratório de Análises (Analytical Laboratory): Av. Rodrigues Alves 81, 20081-250 Rio de Janeiro, RJ; tel. (21) 223-7743; f. 1889; covers organic, inorganic and pharmaceutical chemistry, biochemistry and materials; library of 4,000 vols; Dir Prof. MARCELO DE M. MOURA.

Observatório Nacional do Brasil (National Observatory): Rua General Bruce 586, 20921 Rio de Janeiro, RJ; tel. (21) 580-6087; f. 1827; library; astronomical and geophysical research programmes using 7 refractors, a Time Service at Rio de Janeiro and a Time Station at Brasília; operates 2 magnetic observatories; Dir SAYD JOSE CODINA LANDABERRY; Sec. SANDRA C. P. SILVA; publs *Efemérides Astronômicas* (annually), *Contribuições Científicas*.

PHILOSOPHY AND PSYCHOLOGY

Instituto Neo-Pitagórico (Neo-Pythagorean Institute): CP 1047, 80001-970 Curitiba, PR; located at: Templo das Musas, Rua Prof. Dario Vellozo 460, Vila Izabel, 80320-050 Curitiba, PR; tel. (41) 242-1840; f. 1909; courses in philosophy, history of religion, psychical research, theosophy, occultism, hierology, Pythagorean studies; 520 mems; library of 21,000 vols; Pres. Dr ROSALA GARZUZE; publs *A Lâmpada* (quarterly), *Circulares* (annually), *Biblioteca Neo-Pitagórica* (annually).

RELIGION, SOCIOLOGY AND ANTHROPOLOGY

Fundação Joaquim Nabuco: Av. 17 de Agosto 2187, Casa Forte, 52061-540 Recife, PE; tel. (81) 441-5500; telex 1180; fax (81) 441-5600; f. 1949; sociological, anthropological, economic, historical, political, educational, geographical, statistical and population studies about Brazil's north and north-east; 600 mems; specialized library of 60,238 vols and museum; Dir FERNANDO DE MELLO FREYRE; publs *Ciência & Trópico* (2 a year), *Cadernos de Estudos Sociais* (2 a year) and various reports and pamphlets.

TECHNOLOGY

Centro de Pesquisas e Desenvolvimento (CEPED) (Research and Development Centre): Rodovia BA 512, Km 0, CP 09, 42800-000 Camaçari, BA; tel. (71) 834-7300; telex 76-0339; fax (71) 832-2095; e-mail ceped@bahianet.com.br; f. 1969; research in agroindustrial and food technology, energy, chemistry and petro-chemistry, metallurgy, ores treatment, mineralogy, environmental engineering, building materials, quality control, materials testing, analysis; library of 26,702 vols; Dir Dr SYLVIO DE QUEIROS MATTOSO; publ. *Tecbahia* (3 a year).

Centro de Pesquisas e Desenvolvimento Leopoldo A. Miguez de Mello (PETROBRÁS) (PETROBRÁS Research and Development Centre): Ilha do Fundão, Quadra 7, CP 21949-900 Rio de Janeiro, RJ; tel. (21) 280-1101; telex 21-31219; fax (21)

598-6363; f. 1966; research into exploration, exploitation and refining of petroleum resources; 757 mems; specialized library of 35,000 vols, 520 current titles of periodicals; Gen. Man. ANTONIO SERGIO FRAGOMENI; publs *Boletim Técnico da PETROBRÁS* (quarterly), *Ciência-Tecnica-Petróleo, Boletim de Geociências da PETROBRÁS* (quarterly).

Comissão Nacional de Energia Nuclear (CNEN) (Commission for Nuclear Energy): Rua General Severiano 90, Botafogo, 22294-900 Rio de Janeiro, RJ; tel. (21) 295-9596; telex (021) 21280; f. 1956; supervisory nuclear agency, co-ordinates planning and financing of nuclear activities, promotes and executes research programmes, trains scientists and technicians; Pres. JOSÉ MANUO ESTEVES DOS SANTOS.

Attached institutes:

Instituto de Engenharia Nuclear (IEN) (Nuclear Engineering Institute): CP 2186, Rio de Janeiro, RJ; f. 1962; pure and applied research and development of uses of atomic energy, especially fast breeder reactors, instrumentation and control, cyclotron physics; Dir LUIZ ALBERTO ILHA ARRIETA.

Instituto de Radioproteção e Dosimetria (IRD) (Radiation Protection and Dosimetry Institute): CP 37025, Jacarepaguá, RJ; f. 1960; research and development of radiation protection and dosimetry methods and standards; finances users of radiation sources; trains in environmental radiological control of industry, medical and nuclear installations; Dir ELIANA AMARAL.

Instituto de Pesquisas Energéticas e Nucleares (IPEN) (Energetics and Nuclear Research Institute): CP 11049, São Paulo, SP; f. 1956; conducts pure and applied research in energy, mainly in nuclear sector; offers training courses; energy information centre; Dir CLAUDIO RODRIGUES.

Centro de Desenvolvimento da Tecnologia Nuclear (CDTN) (Nuclear Technology Development Centre): CP 2186, Rio de Janeiro, RJ; enviromental and atomic energy research.

Centro de Energia Nuclear na Agricultura (CENA): see under Agriculture.

Instituto Brasileiro de Petróleo (Brazilian Institute of Petroleum): Av. Rio Branco 156 (room 1035), Group 1035, 20043-900, Centro, Rio de Janeiro, RJ; tel. (21) 532-1610; fax (21) 220-1596; f. 1957; holds Brazilian standards for petroleum products and equipment; research in petroleum and petrochemical industries; mems: 146 companies; Pres. OTTO VICENTE PERRONE.

Instituto de Pesquisas Tecnológicas do Estado de São Paulo S.A. (IPT) (Institute for Technological Research of the State of São Paulo): Cidade Universitária Armando de Salles Oliveira, 05508-901 São Paulo, SP; tel. (11) 268-2211; fax (11) 819-5730; f. 1899, present name since 1934; non-profit making public corporation, owned by the State of São Paulo; has eight technical divisions: civil engineering; economy and systems engineering; geology; metallurgy; transport technology; mechanical and electrical engineering; forest products; chemistry; library of 76,000 vols, 44,000 periodicals, 150,000 industrial products catalogues, 1,000,000 technical standards; Dir MILTON DE ABREU CAMPANARIO; publs *IPT Noticias* (6 a year), *Interface* (monthly).

Instituto de Tecnologia do Paraná (Paraná Institute of Technology): Rua Algacyr Munhoz Mader 2400, 81310-020 Curitiba, PR; tel. (41) 346-3141; telex 33143; fax (41) 247-6788; f. 1940; research in all aspects of technology for the development of the state; produces vaccines; national and int. exchange with orgs in the same field; library of 8,000 vols, 1,054 periodicals; Dir/Pres. ALEXANDRE FONTANA BELTRÃO; publ. *Arquivo de Biologia e Tecnologia* (quarterly), *Boletim Técnico* (every 2 months).

Instituto Nacional de Pesquisas Espaciais (INPE) (National Institute for Space Research): Av. Dos Astronautas 1758, CP 515, 12227-010 São José dos Campos, SP; tel. (12) 345-6036; fax (12) 322-9285; f. 1961, renamed in 1971; astrophysics, solar physics, geomagnetism, ionosphere, upper atmosphere, medium and low atmosphere, plasma physics, basic meteorology, meteorological instrumentation, meteorological satellite services, meteorological applications, remote sensing for mineral resources, remote sensing for forestry and agronomic resources, remote sensing for sea resources, environmental analysis, image production, ground stations, control and tracking stations, structure and thermic control of space platforms, space telecommunications, energy supply, analogic and digital systems, orbital dynamics and control, payloads for space platforms, assembly, integration and tests of space platforms, qualification of components, units and systems for space applications, centre for satellite operation and missions, balloon launching centre, systems engineering, informatics, materials, combustion processes, sensors, space geodesy, human resources, technology transfer; library of 43,000 vols, microforms, CD-ROMs, microfilms and tapes, 1,600 periodicals, 21,000 specialized papers, 5,600 INPE reports, 5,400 maps; Dir Eng. MARCIO NOGUEIRA BARBOSA; publ. *Climanálise*.

Instituto Nacional de Tecnología (National Technological Institute): Av. Venezuela 82, 8° andar, 20081 Rio de Janeiro, RJ; tel. (21) 253-9422; telex 021-30056; f. 1922; research in chemical industry, chemistry of natural products, metallurgy, rubber and plastics, corrosion, pollution control, industrial design, energy conservation, computer-aided projects; *c.* 300 staff; library of 17,000 vols, 1,000 periodicals, 100,000 microfiches; Dir PAULO ROBERTO KRAHE; publs *Informativo do INT, Corrosão e Proteção Boletim Informativo* (Corrosion and Protection Bulletin), *Cadernos Técnicos INT* (Technical Books).

Instituto Tecnológico do Estado de Pernambuco (ITEP) (Technological Institute of the State of Pernambuco): Av. Prof. Luis Freire 700, Cidade Universitária, Recife, PE; tel. (81) 271-4399; fax (81) 271-4744; f. 1942; industrial research; library of 10,000 vols; Pres. JOSE FERNANDO THOMÉ JUCÁ; publ. *Revista Pernambucana de Tecnologia* (quarterly).

Libraries and Archives

Aracajú

Biblioteca Pública do Estado de Sergipe (Sergipe State Public Library): Aracajú, SE; f. 1851; Dir ALFREDO MONTES DE ARAÚJO PINTO; 153,750 vols, including periodicals.

Belém

Arquivo Público do Estado do Pará (Pará Public Archives): Rua Campos Sales, 273, 66019-050, Belém, PA; tel. (91) 241-9700; fax (91) 241-9097; f. 1901; 500 vols; special collection of 742 vols; Dir GERALDO MÁRTIRES COELHO; publ. *Anais do Arquivo Público do Pará* (every 2 years).

Biblioteca Central da Universidade Federal do Pará: Campus Universitário - Guamá, Setor Básico, 66075-970, Belém, PA; tel. (91) 229-2437; fax (91) 229-9677; f. 1962; 126,000 vols, 4,376 periodicals; Dir MARIA HILDA DE MEDEIROS GONDIM.

Biblioteca do Grêmio Literário e Comercial Português (Library of the Portuguese Literary and Commercial Union): Rua Senador Manuel Barata 237, Belém, PA; f. 1867; Sec. ANÍSIO DE SOARES TEIXEIRA; 29,568 vols; exchange service.

Belo Horizonte

Biblioteca Pública Estadual Luiz de Bessa (Public Library): Praça da Liberdade 21, 30140-010 Belo Horizonte, MG; tel. (31) 337-1265; fax (31) 269-1108; f. 1954; 280,000 vols, 5,124 vols of Braille, 300 talking books; 600 brs.

Universidade Federal de Minas Gerais, Biblioteca Universitária/Sistema de Bibliotecas da UFMG: 31270-901 Belo Horizonte, MG; tel. and fax (31) 499-4611; f. 1927; 613,000 vols, 6,000 maps, 14,763 rare works, 21,800 periodicals; collection of special documents; Librarian MARIA HELENA DE SÁ BARRETO.

Brasília

Biblioteca Central, Universidade de Brasília: Campus Universitário, Asa Norte, 70910 Brasília, DF; tel. (61) 348-2402; telex 1083; f. 1962; 530,292 vols, 7,864 periodicals; Dir Prof. ODILON PEREIRA DA SILVA.

Biblioteca Demonstrativa de Brasília FBN/minc (Public Library): Av. W/3 Sul, Entrequadras 506/507, 70350-580, Brasília, DF; tel. (61) 243-5682; fax (61) 243-3163; f. 1970; 92,000 vols, 2,400 periodicals on general subjects; also maps, microfilms, slides, pictures; Dir MARIA DA CONCEIÇÃO MOREIRA SALLES.

Biblioteca do Ministério da Justiça (Library of Ministry of Justice): Esplanada dos Ministérios, Ed. Sede Térreo, 70064-900 Brasília, DF; tel. (61) 218-3369; fax (61) 321-4797; e-mail biblioteca@mj.br; f. 1941; 130,000 vols, of which many are on law, economics, sociology, labour, and political science; very rare collection of laws of Portuguese colonial period; 6,000-vol. Goethe collection; Dir MARIA CRISTINA RODRIGUES SILVESTRE; publ. *Revista Arquivos do Ministério da Justiça*.

Biblioteca do Ministério das Relações Exteriores (Library of the Ministry of Foreign Affairs): Esplanada dos Ministérios, Anexo II, Térreo, 70170-900 Brasília, DF; tel. (61) 211-6359; telex (061) 1319; fax (61) 223-7362; f. 1906; 80,000 vols, including periodicals (history collection in Rio de Janeiro, *q.v.*); law, history, politics and economics; collection of UN documents; Chief Librarian MARIA SALETE CARVALHO REIS.

Biblioteca do Ministério do Trabalho (Library of Ministry of Labour): Esplanada dos Ministérios, Bloco 10, Anexo, Ala B, Térreo, 70059 Brasília, DF; tel. (61) 223 0211; f. 1871; 15,000 vols; 120 collections of newspapers; Librarian CLEUSA APARECIDA VALIN; publs *Emprego e Salário*, *Relação Anual de Informações Sociais, Boletim do SINE*.

Biblioteca do Senado Federal (Library of the Federal Senate): Praça dos Três Poderes, Palácio do Congresso (Anexo II – Térreo), 70165-900 Brasília, DF; tel. (61) 224-9784; fax (61) 311-1765; e-mail SSBIB@admass.senado .gov.br; f. 1826; specializes in social sciences, law, politics, public administration, legislation; also works on literature, history, geography, etc.; 150,000 vols; Dir SIMONE BASTOS VIEIRA; publs *Bibliografia Brasileira de Direito* (annually), *Dados Biográficos dos Senadores*.

Centro de Documentação e Informação da Câmara dos Deputados (Documentation and Information Centre of the House of Representatives): Palácio do Congresso Nacional, Praça dos Três Poderes, 70160-900 Brasília, DF; tel. (61) 318-6785; fax (61) 318-2171; f. 1971; 400,000 vols; 3,500 titles of periodicals; Dir SUELENA PINTO BANDEIRA; four divisions: (1) Archives (Dir GRANCINDA A. VASCONCELOS), (2) Legislative Studies (Dir DIRCE B. R. VIEIRA ALVES), (3) Library (f. 1866 at Rio de Janeiro, Dir MARLI ELIZABETH SCHREIBER), (4) Publications (Dir NELDA MENDONÇA RAULINO); Data Processing Section (Head ROBERTO ALEZINA BRAULE P. JÚNIOR); Technical Auxiliary Service (Reprography, Conservation and Restoration, Head CARLOS HENRIQUE OLIVEIRA P. FILHO); publs *Deputados Brasileiros* (every 4 years), *Anais da Câmara dos Deputados* (irregular), *Perfis Parlamentares* (irregular), *Constituição da República Federativa do Brasil, Regimento Interno da Câmera dos Deputados, Resoluções da Câmara dos Deputados* (irregular), *Legislação Interna* (irregular), Sumário de Periódicos (monthly), Alerta: o que há de novo na biblioteca (monthly).

Centro de Informações Bibliográficas em Educação: Ministério da Educação e do Desporto, Esplanada dos Ministérios, Bloco L, Térreo, 70047-900 Brasília DF, CP 08866; tel. (61) 214-8573; fax (61) 273-3233; f. 1981; 50,000 vols, 985 periodicals; specialized library on education; Dir GAETANO LO MONACO.

Coordenação Geral de Informação Documental Agrícola (CENAGRI) (National Centre of Agricultural Documentary Information): CP 02432, Ministério da Agricultura, Anexo I, Bl.B, Térreo e 1° andar, 70043-970 Brasília, DF; tel. (61) 218-2613; fax (61) 226-8190; f. 1974; central unit of National System of Agricultural Information and Documentation (SNIDA); responsible for establishing State libraries of agriculture in order to decentralize information sources; 50,000 vols, 7,032 serial titles, 216,000 microfiche documents; Co-ordinator CLAITON PIMENTEL; publs *Série Aptidão Agrícola das Terras, Série Estudos sobre o Desenvolvimento Agrícola, Série Levantamentos Bibliográficos, Bibliografia Brasileira de Agricultura, Banco de Bibliografias da América Latina e do Caribe, Bibliografias Agrícolas* (national series), *Bibliografias Agrícolas* (international series), *Thesaurus para Indexação / Recuperação da Literatura Agrícola Brasileira.*

Instituto Brasileiro de Informação em Ciência e Tecnologia (IBICT): SAS Quadra 05, Lote 06, Bloco H, 70070-000 Brasília, DF; fax (61) 226-2677; f. 1954 as IBBD, re-named 1976; co-ordinates scientific and technical information services throughout the country; provides technical assistance, and training; maintains the following databases available for public access, through the National Telecommunications Network: *ACERVO* (Library and Information Science, holds records from 1982 to present, updated daily), *EVENTOS* (current meetings, updated daily), *BEN* (directory of Brazilian institutions in science and technology, updated daily), *BPS* (Union Catalog of Serials Publications, updated daily), *TESES* (theses and dissertations from 1984 to present, updated daily), *FILMES* (Films and videos in science and technology from 1988 to present), *BASES* (directory of Brazilian databases from 1989), *EMPRESAS* (directory of software institutions), *CIENTE* (scientific and technological policy, updated daily); runs a postgraduate course in Information Science and a special course on scientific documentation; library of 205,000 vols; Dir JOSÉ RINCON FERREIRA; publs *Ciência da Informação* (3 a year), *Calendário de Eventos em Ciência e Tecnologia* (quarterly), *Qualidade & Produtividade: Eventos e Cursos* (quarterly), *Informativo IBICT* (every 2 months).

Curitiba

Biblioteca Central da Universidade Federal do Paraná (University of Paraná Library): CP 441, Rua Gen. Carneiro 370/80, 80001-970 Curitiba, PR; tel. (41) 264-5545; telex 415100; fax (41) 262-7784; f. 1956; 350,000 vols; 11 specialized libraries; Dir ELAYNE MARGARETH SCHLOGEL.

Biblioteca Pública do Paraná (Paraná Public Library): Rua Cândido Lopes 133, 80020-901 Curitiba, PR; tel. (41) 322-9800; fax (41) 225-6883; f. 1954; 416,000 vols, 6,000 periodicals; Dir MARILENE ZICARELLI MILARCH.

Florianópolis

Biblioteca Pública do Estado de Santa Catarina (Santa Catarina State Public Library): Rua Tenete Silveira 343, 88010 Florianópolis, SC; tel. (482) 22-1378; f. 1854; 60,000 vols; collections of rare books, Braille and talking books; Dir ISABELA SALUM FETT.

Fortaleza

Biblioteca Pública do Ceará (Ceará Public Library): Rua Solon Pinheiro 76, Fortaleza, CE; 15,000 vols; Librarian HILZANIR CALS DE ABREU.

Biblioteca Universitária da Universidade Federal do Ceará: Campus do Pici, CP 6025, Fortaleza, CE; tel. (85) 243-9506; fax (85) 243-9513; f. 1958, renamed 1982; 164,429 vols; Dir GABRIELITA CARRHÁ MACHADO.

João Pessôa

Biblioteca Pública do Estado da Paraíba (Paraíba Public Library): Av. General Osório 253, João Pessôa, PB; f. 1859; 10,000 vols; Dir GERALDO EMILIO PÔRTO.

Manaus

Biblioteca e Arquivo Público de Manaus (Manaus Public Library and Archives): Praça Pedro II 265, 69005 Manaus, AM; tel. (92) 232-3878; f. 1852; library of *c.* 3,000 vols; Dir Com. JUNOT C. FREDERICO; publ. *Arquivo do Amazonas.*

Niterói

Biblioteca Pública do Estado do Rio de Janeiro (Public Library of the State of Rio): Praça da República, Niterói, RJ; f. 1927; possesses rare early works, newspapers and valuable first editions; 80,000 vols, notably dictionaries, encyclopædias, reference books; Dir ALBERTINA FORTUNA BARROS.

Ouro Prêto

Biblioteca da Escola de Minas da Universidade Federal de Ouro Prêto (Library of the Ouro Prêto School of Mines): Praça Tiradentes 20, 35400-000 Ouro Prêto, MG; tel. (31) 551-1666; telex 312954; f. 1876; 50,000 vols, 1,900 periodicals; Dir MARIA DA GLÓRIA RIBEIRO SOARES ARAÚJO; publ. *Revista.*

Pelotas

Biblioteca Pública Pelotense (Public Library): Praça Coronel Pedro Osório 103, Pelotas, RS; tel. (532) 223856; f. 1875; 150,000 vols; museum, cultural exhibition; Pres. JOAQUIM SALVADOR COELHO PINHO.

Petrópolis

Biblioteca Municipal (Municipal Library): Petrópolis, RJ; f. 1871; Librarian MARIA HELENA DE AVELLAR PALMA; 100,000 vols; 2 branches.

Porto Alegre

Biblioteca Central da Universidade Federal do Rio Grande do Sul: CP 2303, 90001-970, Porto Alegre, RS; tel. (51) 316-3065; telex (051) 1055; fax (51) 227-3777; f. 1971; 32 branch libraries; 711,100 vols; Dir JANISE SILVA BORGES DA COSTA.

Biblioteca Pública do Estado do Rio Grande do Sul (Rio Grande do Sul State Public Library): Rue Riachuelo s/n, Porto Alegre, RS; f. 1871; 775,863 vols; Dir JULIANA VIANNA ROSA.

Recife

Biblioteca Central da Universidade Federal de Pernambuco: Av. dos Reitores s/n, Cidade Universitária, 50670-901 Recife, PE; fax (81) 271-8090; f. 1968; 405,291 vols (including all departmental libraries), 8,603 periodicals; a regional centre for the national bibliographic network organized by the Instituto Brasileiro de Informação em Ciência e Tecnologia (*q.v.*); Dir Profa ANA MARIA FERRACIN; publs *Sumários de Periódicos* (monthly), *BC-informa* (monthly).

Biblioteca Pública Estadual de Pernambuco (Pernambuco State Public Library): Recife, PE; f. 1852; 150,000 vols; Dir CLEA DUBEUX PINTO PIMENTEL.

Rio de Janeiro

Arquivo Nacional (National Archives): Rua Azeredo Coutinho 77, 20230-170 Rio de Janeiro, RJ; tel. (21) 252-2617; fax (21) 232-8430; f. 1838; specializes in history of Brazil, technique of archives and legislation; 26,000 vols, 8,000 periodicals; 45 shelf-km. of documents; Dir-Gen. JAIME ANTUNES DA SILVA; publs *BIBA, BIBAG, BBPO, Boletim, Revista Acervo.*

Biblioteca Bastos Tigre da Associação Brasileira de Imprensa (Library of Brazilian Press Association): Rua Araújo Porto Alegre 71, 12° andar, 20030 Rio de Janeiro, RJ; tel. 262-9822; f. 1911; 40,473 vols, 6,788 periodical titles; Dir AUGUSTO VILLAS-BÔAS.

Biblioteca da Sociedade Brasileira de Cultura Inglesa: CP 5215, Rua Raul Pompéia 231, 3° andar, Rio de Janeiro, RJ; tel. 287-0990 ext. 300; fax 267-6474; f. 1934; 3 brs; 34,000 vols; Head Librarian MARIA DE FÁTIMA BORGES GONÇALVES; publ. *Library News.*

Biblioteca do Centro Cultural Banco do Brasil (Library of the Banco do Brasil Cultural Centre): Rua Primeiro de Março 66, 5° andar, Centro, 20010-000 Rio de Janeiro, RJ; tel. (21) 216-0212; fax (21) 216-0216; f. 1931; social sciences, literature and arts; 100,000 vols; special collections: rare books, Brazilian music and folklore; Dir KLEUBER DE PAIVA PEREIRA.

Biblioteca do Exército (Army Library): Praça Duque de Caxias 25, Ala Marcillo Dias (3 and.), 20221-260 Rio de Janeiro; tel. (21) 253-7616; fax (21) 253-7535; f. 1881; 60,000 vols; general collections to supply cultural needs of the army; Dir Cel LUIZ PAULO MACEDO CARVALHO; publs *Revista A Defesa Nacional, Revista do Exército Brasileiro, Revista Militar de Ciência e Tecnologia* (4 a year).

Biblioteca do Instituto dos Advogados Brasileiros (Library of Lawyers' Institute): Av. Marechal Câmara 210, 5° andar, 20020-080 Rio de Janeiro, RJ; tel. (21) 240-3921; fax (21) 240-3173; f. 1843; 32,000 vols; Dir ROBERTO DE BASTOS LELIS.

Biblioteca do Ministério da Fazenda no Estado do Rio de Janeiro (Library of the Ministry of Finance of Rio de Janeiro State): Av. Pres. Antonio Carlos 375, sala 1238, 12° andar, 20020 Rio de Janeiro, RJ; tel. (21) 240-1120; f. 1943 by incorporation of various departmental libraries; 145,000 vols, 100 current periodicals; Librarian KATIA APARECIDA TEIXEIRA DE OLIVEIRA; publs *A Legislação Tributária no Brasil, Informe.*

Biblioteca do Ministério das Relações Exteriores no Rio de Janeiro (Library of the Ministry of Foreign Affairs in Rio de Janeiro): Av. Marechal Floriano 196, Centro 20080-002 Rio de Janeiro, RJ; tel. 253-5730; telex (021) 21761; f. 1906; history; 270,000 vols including periodicals; rare books; Dir SONIA DOYLE. (See also under Brasília.)

Biblioteca do Mosteiro de S. Bento (Library of the St Benedict Monastery): CP 2666,

20001-970 Rio de Janeiro, RJ; tel. (21) 291-7122; f. 1600; 125,000 vols; Librarian D. MIGUEL VEESER; also in the towns of São Paulo, Salvador (Bahia) and Olinda; publs *Pergunte e Responderemos, Liturgia e Vida*.

Biblioteca Nacional (National Library): Av. Rio Branco 219-39, 20040-008 Rio de Janeiro, RJ; tel. (21) 262-8255; fax (21) 220-4173; f. 1810, with 60,000 vols from the Real Biblioteca brought to Brazil by the Royal Family of Portugal in 1808; 8,500,000 documents; divided into two depts: Depto de Referência e Difusão and Depto de Processos Técnicos; special collections: Col. De Angelis (Brazilian and Paraguayan History), Col. Tereza Cristina Maria (donated by Imperator D. Pedro II, 1891), Col. Alexandre Rodrigues Ferreira (description with illustrations of travels in Amazônia by A. R. Ferreira, 1783–1792); Pres. EDUARDO PORTELLA; publs *Anais da Biblioteca Nacional, Brazilian Book Magazine*.

Biblioteca Popular do Leblon-Vinicius de Moraes: Av. Bartolomeu Mitre 1297, 22431-050, Rio de Janeiro, RJ; f. 1954; 8,000 vols; Dir MARIA ALICE AMARAL PATERNOT.

Biblioteca Pública do Estado do Rio de Janeiro: Av. Presidente Vargas 1261, 20071-004 Rio de Janeiro, RJ; tel. 224-6184; fax 252-6810; e-mail bperj@callnet.com.br.; f. 1873; attached to the State Office of Culture; 175,000 vols; Dir ANA LIGIA SILVA MEDEIROS.

Biblioteca Regional de Copacabana: Av. N.S. de Copacabana 702B, 3° andar, Rio de Janeiro, RJ; tel. (21) 237-8607; f. 1954; 29,706 vols; Dir ANA MARIA COSTA DESLANDES.

Fundação Casa de Rui Barbosa (Rui Barbosa Foundation): Rua S. Clemente 134, Botafogo, Rio de Janeiro, RJ; tel. (21) 537-0036; fax (21) 537-1114; f. 1930, became Foundation 1966; over 100,000 vols; includes a centre for research in law, philology and history, a centre of Brazilian literature (over 50,000 documents), a documentation centre, with a library, Rui Barbosa archive, a microfilm laboratory and a paper restoration laboratory; museum and auditorium; Pres. MARIO BROCKMANN MACHADO; Exec. Dir ROSA MARIA BARBOZA DEARAÚJO.

Fundação Instituto Brasileiro de Geografia e Estatística – Centro de Documentação e Disseminação de Informações, Divisão de Biblioteca e Acervos Especiais: Rua General Canabarro 706, térreo, 20271-201 Rio de Janeiro, RJ; fax (21) 569-2043 ext. 262; f. 1977; documentation and dissemination of research and studies in geoscience, environment, demography, social and economic indicators, national accounts, statistics; 48,000 vols, 2,105 periodicals, 20,000 maps, 115,000 photographs; Dir MARIA TERESA PASSOS BASTOS.

Serviço de Documentação da Marinha (Documentation Service of the Navy): Praça Barão de Ladário (Ilha das Cobras), Centro, 20091-000 Rio de Janeiro, RJ; tel. 233-9165; fax (21) 216-6716; f. 1802; maritime history of Brazil; includes a naval museum and archives; naval library of 110,000 vols; Dir JOSÉ CARLOS CARDOSO; publs *Revista Marítima Brasileira, Navigator,* and technical works.

Sistema de Bibliotecas e Informação da Universidade Federal do Rio de Janeiro (Library and Information System of the University of Rio de Janeiro): Av. Pasteur 250, Urca, 22295-900 Rio de Janeiro, RJ; tel. (21) 295-1595 ext. 119; fax (21) 295-1397; f. 1989; maintains National Catalogue of Periodicals; 1,000,000 vols, 40,000 periodicals; Dir MARIZA RUSSO.

Rio Grande

Biblioteca Rio-Grandense (Rio Grande Library): Rua General Osório 430, 96200-400 Rio Grande, RS; f. 1846; 400,000 vols, 7,600 maps; Pres. Dr JOÃO MARINONIO CARNEIRO LAGES; Dir Dr GILBERTO M. CENTENO CARDOSO.

Rio Negro

Biblioteca do Convento dos Franciscanos (Library of Franciscan Monastery): Rio Negro, PR; f. 1922; 20,000 vols; Sec. FREI ALFREDO SETÁRO.

Salvador

Biblioteca do Gabinete Português de Leitura (Portuguese Reading Room and Library): Praça da Piedade s/n, 40070-010, Salvador, BA; tel. 322-1580; fax 322-1299; 15,000 vols; Librarian AGNÚBIA OLIVEIRA.

Biblioteca Pública do Estado da Bahia (Bahia State Central Library): Rua Gen. Labatut 27, Barris-Salvador, BA; f. 1811, name changed 1984; 114,698 vols; Dir LÍDIA MARIA BASTISTA BRANDÃO.

Santos

Biblioteca da Sociedade Humanitária dos Empregados no Comércio de Santos (Library of Cultural Society of Commercial Employees): Praça José Bonifacio 59, 1° andar, CP 9, Santos, SP; tel. 34-2319; f. 1888; 20,494 vols; Librarian ANTONIO ODILON DO N. MORAES.

São José dos Campos

Biblioteca Pública 'Cassiano Ricardo' ('Cassiano Ricardo' Public Library): Rua Sebastião Humel 110, São José dos Campos, SP; tel. (123) 29-2000, ext. 3071; f. 1968; 49,300 vols and 8,500 periodicals; Dir ANA ELISABETE MARTINELLI GODINHO.

São Luis

Biblioteca Pública do Estado (Public State Library): Praça de Panteon, São Luis, MA; f. 1829; 38 mems; 45,000 vols; collections of more than 15,000 engravings, and newspapers dating back to 1821; Dir MARIA JOSÉ VAZ DOS SANTOS; Librarian ROBERTO TAMARA.

São Paulo

Arquivo do Estado de São Paulo (São Paulo State Archives): Rua Dona Antônia de Queirós 183, 01307 São Paulo, SP; tel. 256-3515; fax 257-7459; f. 1721; 50,000 vols; 8,000 vols of bound documents; 8,300 files of loose documents; State records, collections of rare books, MSS, periodicals, maps and plans; Dir Prof. NILO ODALIA; publs *Documentos Interessantes, Boletim Histórico e Informativo, Coleção de Monografias, Inventários e Testamentos*.

Biblioteca do Conservatório Dramático e Musical de São Paulo (Library of Academy of Music and Drama): Av. São João 269, São Paulo, SP; f. 1906; 30,000 vols; Dir Dr LUÍS CORRÊA FRAGOSO; Sec. JOSÉ RAYMUNDO LOBO.

Biblioteca do Instituto de Saúde (Health Institute Library): Av. Enéas Carvalho Aguiar 188, CP 8027, 01051 São Paulo, SP; f. 1969; 41,000 vols, valuable collection of works, reviews, maps on dermatology and Hansen's disease, and rare works dating from 1600; Librarian ASTRID B. WIESEL.

Biblioteca 'George Alexander' (George Alexander Library): Rua Itambé 45, São Paulo, SP; f. 1870 as Mackenzie Library, present name 1926; 150,000 vols (sections: central library, engineering, architecture, administration, economics, accountancy, law, technology, first degree); Dir ROSA CORRÊA; publ. *Boletim Bibliográfico* (annually).

Biblioteca Municipal Mário de Andrade (Municipal Library): Rua da Consolação 94, 01302-000 São Paulo, SP; tel. (11) 239-4384; fax (11) 239-3459; f. 1925; municipal library 344,000 vols and 11,000 journal titles; incorporates former Biblioteca Pública do Estado de São Paulo; specialized collections of 40,000 rare editions and MSS, 25,000 drawings and art books, 5,500 maps; microfilms, legislation and multi-media sections; Dir of Municipal Library MARLI MONTEIRO; publ. *Revista da Biblioteca Mário de Andrade*.

BIREME – Centro Latino-Americano e do Caribe de Informação em Ciências da Saúde (Latin American and Caribbean Health Science Information Centre): Rua Botucatu 862, CP 20381, 04023-901 São Paulo, SP; tel. (11) 549-2611; fax (11) 571-1919; f. 1967 under the auspices of the Pan American Health Organization to promote a regional network of health libraries and information centres; aims to index all health literature produced in the region; provides bibliographic searches, document delivery, training, etc.; 25,500 vols, 6,500 periodicals; Dir Dr CELIA RIBEIRO ZAHER; publ. *LILACS/CD-ROM* (3 a year).

Discoteca Oneyda Alvarenga: Centro Cultural São Paulo, Rua Vergueiro 1000, 01504-000 São Paulo, SP; tel. (11) 277-3611, ext. 244; fax (11) 277-3611, ext. 231; e-mail ccsp@eu.ansp.br; f. 1935; study and diffusion of Brazilian and international classical, folk and popular music; library of 42,000 vols of music scores and 8,300 books; collection of 74,000 records, 400 periodical titles; museum of folklore; Dir MARIA CRISTINA MAGALHÃES MARINHO.

Sistema Integrado de Bibliotecas da Universidade de São Paulo (São Paulo University Integrated Library System): Av. Prof. Luciano Gualberto, Trav. J, 374-1°andar, 05508-900 São Paulo, SP; tel. (11) 211-7448; fax (11) 815-2142; e-mail dtsibi@org.usp.br; f. 1981; 39 libraries, with 3,500,000 vols; Technical Dir ROSALY FÁVERO KRZYZANOWSKI.

Vitória

Biblioteca Estadual: Av. Pedro Palácios 76, Vitória, ES; f. 1855; 31,981 vols.

Biblioteca Municipal Vitória: Rua Barão Itapemirim 204, 1° andar, Vitória, ES; f. 1941; 12,859 vols.

Museums and Art Galleries

Belém

Museu Paraense Emílio Goeldi (Pará Museum): Av. Magalhães Barata 376, CP 399, 66017-970 Belém, PA; tel. (91) 249-1233; fax (91) 249-0466; e-mail postmaster@museu-goeldi.br; f. 1866; part of MCT/CNPq; natural history, archaeology, anthropology and ethnography of the Amazon region; zoological and botanical garden; library of 200,000 vols; collection of rare books; Dir ADÉLIA E. DE OLIVEIRA; publs *Boletim,* (four separate series on anthropology, botany, geology and zoology), *Guia*.

Belo Horizonte

Museu Histórico Abílio Barreto (Historical Museum): Rua Bernardo Mascarenhas s/n, B. Cidade Jardim, 30380-010 Belo Horizonte, MG; tel. (31) 296-3896; fax (31) 277-4800; f. 1943; local collection; special collections: original documentation of the Belo Horizonte Construction Commission, Minas Gerais provincial laws (1849–89); Dir ARNALDO AUGUSTO GODOY.

Campinas

Museu de História Natural (Natural History Museum): Rua Coronel Quirino 2, Bosque dos Jequitibás, Campinas, SP; tel. (192) 310555 ext. 372; f.1938; history, folklore and anthropology; Dir TEREZA CRISTINA SILVA MELLO BORGES.

Campo Grande

Museu Regional D. Bosco (D. Bosco Regional Museum): Rua Barão do Rio Branco 1885, CP 415, 79100 Campo Grande, MTS; f. 1951; ethnographic, shell and insect collections; Dir JOÃO FALCO.

Curitiba

Museu Paranaense (Paraná Museum): Praça Generoso Marques s/n, 80020-230 Curitiba, PR; tel. (41) 323-1411; fax (41) 222-5824; f. 1876; historical, ethnographical and archaeological collections; library of 6,000 vols and 2,200 periodicals; Dir JAYME ANTONIO CARDOSO; publs *Arquivos do Museu Paranaense, Nova Série*, and special papers.

Fortaleza

Museu do Ceará: Rua São Paulo 51, CEP 60030-100 Fortaleza, CE; historical collection.

Goiânia

Museu Estadual Prof. Zoroastro Artiaga (Goiás State Museum): Praça Cívica 13, Goiânia, GO; f. 1946; general collection; Dir Dr ELDER CAMARGO DE PASSOS.

Itu

Museu Republicano 'Convenção de Itu' (Itu Convention Republican Museum): Rua Barão de Itaim 67, 13300-000 Itu, SP; tel. and fax (11) 7823-0240; e-mail jonasouz@usp.br; f. 1923; historical; attached to Museu Paulista da Universidade de São Paulo (*q.v.*); library of 3,000 vols and 113 periodical titles; special collections: 22 journal titles, database 1870-1920, Prudente de Morais collection; archives, photographs; Curator Prof. JONAS SOARES DE SOUZA.

Macapá

Museu Territorial do Amapá (Amapá Territorial Museum): Fortaleza de S. José de Macapá, Macapá (Território do Amapá); f. 1948; zoology, archaeology, ethnography and numismatics; expeditions.

Olinda

Museu Regional de Olinda (Regional Museum of Olinda): Rua do Amparo 128, Olinda, PE; f. 1934; historic and regional art.

Ouro Preto

Museu da Inconfidência (History of Democratic Ideals and Culture): Praça Tiradentes 139, Ouro Preto, MG; tel. and fax (31) 551-1121; f. 1944; 18th- and 19th-century music MSS and works of art, documents related to Inconfidência Mineira, documents from the Notary Public's Office during the Colonial Period; library of 19,000 vols; Dir RUI MOURÃO; publ. *Anuário do Museu da Inconfidência*.

Museu Mineralógico da Escola de Minas (Mineralogical Museum of the School of Mines): Praça Tiradentes 20, 35400 Ouro Prêto, MG; tel. (31) 551-1100; telex 312954; fax (31) 551-1689; f. 1878; affiliated to the Universidade Federal de Ouro Prêto; Dir ANTÔNIO MARIA CLARET DE GOUVÊIA.

Petrópolis

Museu Imperial (Imperial Museum): Rua da Imperatriz 220, 25610-320 Petrópolis, RJ; tel. (242) 37-8000; fax (242) 37-8540; e-mail musimp@npoint.com.br; f. 1940; 11,024 period exhibits of Brazilian Empire (1808–89) and Petrópolis history, notably imperial regalia, jewels and apparel; special library on the history of Brazil 35,770 vols; historic archives of 100,000 MSS on Brazilian history in the 19th century; 4,000 photos, 500 maps and 700 iconographic items; Dir MARIA DE LOURDES PARREIRAS HORTA; publ. *Anuário*.

Porto Alegre

Museu de Arte do Rio Grande do Sul: Praça da Alfândega s/n 90010-150 Porto Alegre, RS; tel. (51) 227-2311; fax (51) 227-2311 ext. 37; f. 1954; art collection; art library of 2,500 vols; Dir PAULO CESAR BRASIL DO AMARAL; publs *Em Pauta* (monthly), *Jornal do MARGS* (monthly).

Museu 'Julio de Castilhos' (State Historical Museum): Rua Duque de Caxias 1205 e 1231, 90010-283 Porto Alegre, RS; tel. and fax (51) 221-3959; f. 1903; 10,100 exhibits of national history, including the 1835 Revolutionary period, the Paraguayan War, and collection of Indian pieces; armoury, antique furniture and slave pieces; library of 5,000 vols; Dir MIRIAM ALOISIO AVRUCH.

Recife

Museu do Estado de Pernambuco (State Museum): Av. Rui Barbosa 960, Graças, CEP 52050-000 Recife, PE; tel. 222-6694; fax 227-812; f. 1928; local history, paintings; library of 2,000 vols, 110 periodicals; Dir TEREZA COSTA REGO.

Rio de Janeiro

Museu Carpológico do Jardim Botânico do Rio de Janeiro (Museum of Carpology of the Botanical Garden): Rua Pacheco Leão 915, 22460-030 Rio de Janeiro, RJ; tel. and fax (21) 511-2749; f. 1915; specializes in botany; collection of 6,200 fruits; Dir Dra NILDA MARQUETE.

Museu da Fauna (Wildlife Museum): Quinta da Boa Vista, São Cristónão, Rio de Janeiro, RJ; tel. 2280556; f. 1939; collections include vertebrates, mammals, birds, butterflies and reptiles from the principal regions of Brazil; part of Tijuca National Park; scientific expeditions; publ. *Monograph*.

Museu da República (Museum of the Republic): Rua do Catete 153, 22220-000 Rio de Janeiro, RJ; tel. (21) 265-9747; fax (21) 285-6320; e-mail musrepublica@ax.ibase.org.br; f. 1960; sited in Catete Palace, built 1858–67, fmr seat of Government; exhibits of items belonging to former Presidents; special collections: history of Brazil, historical archive with 85,000 photographs and documents; library of 10,000 vols; Dir ANELISE PACHECO.

Museu da Secção de Tecnologia do Serviço Florestal do Ministério da Agricultura (Museum of the Technological Department of the Forestry Service —Ministry of Agriculture): Rua Major Rubéns Vaz 122, Gávea, Rio de Janeiro, RJ; f. 1938; specializes in wood technology; contains 7,000 samples of wood from Brazil and other countries; display of forestry products and hand-made wood objects; Dir Dr NEARCH AZEVEDO DA SILVEIRA; publs *Arquivos do Serviço Florestal, Revista Florestal e Rodriguésia*.

Museu de Arte Moderna do Rio de Janeiro (Museum of Modern Art): Av. Infante Dom Henrique 85, 20021 Rio de Janeiro, RJ; f. 1948; library of 25,000 vols; collections representing different countries; exhibitions, courses, films; Pres. M. F. DO NASCIMENTO BRITO.

Museu de Ciências da Terra, Departamento Nacional da Produção Mineral (Earth Sciences Museum, National Department of Mineral Production at the Ministry of Mines and Energy): Av. Pasteur 404, 2° andar, Praia Vermelha, 22290-240 Rio de Janeiro, RJ; tel. (21) 295-7596; fax (21) 295-3895; f. 1907; collection of fossils, minerals, rocks, gems, ore minerals and meteorites from Brazil and other countries; Dir PAULO ROBERTO DE MELLO.

Museu do Índio (Museum of the Indian): Rua das Palmeiras 55, Botafogo, 22270-070 Rio de Janeiro, RJ; tel. (21) 286-2097; fax (21) 286-8899; e-mail museudoindio@ax.apc.org.br; f. 1953; ethnology, ethnohistory, museology, linguistics, documentation; conducts research into Indian societies and cultures; library of 28,000 vols; scientific archives (documents, photographs, films and music); Chair. JOSÉ CARLOS LEVINHO; publs *Boletim*, *Museo Vivo*.

Museu do Instituto Histórico e Geográfico Brasileiro (Museum of the Brazilian Historical and Geographical Institute): Av. Augusto Severo 8, 20021-040 Rio de Janeiro, RJ; f. 1838; history, geography and ethnography collection.

Museu e Arquivo Histórico do Centro Cultural Banco do Brasil (Museum and Historical Archives of the Banco do Brasil Cultural Centre): Rua Primeiro de Março 66, Centro, 20010-000 Rio de Janeiro, RJ; tel. (21) 216-0620; fax (21) 263-6314; f. 1955; collection of banknotes and coins from Brazil and other countries, documents relating to the economic history of Brazil and to the Banco do Brasil; library: see Libraries; Dir KLEUBER DE PAIVA PEREIRA.

Museu Histórico da Cidade do Rio de Janeiro (Historical Museum of the City): Estrada Santa Marinha, s/n, Parque da Cidade, Gávea, 22451 Rio de Janeiro, RJ; f. 1934; art and history of the City; library of 4,000 vols; Dir BEATRIZ DE VICQ CARVALHO.

Museu Histórico Nacional (National Historical Museum): Praça Marechal Ancora s/n, 20021 Rio de Janeiro, RJ; tel. (21) 240-9529; fax (21) 220-6290; e-mail aguedes@visualnet.com.br; f. 1922; collections of coins, medals, ceramics, weapons, furniture, prints, paintings, besides historical exhibits; organizes courses in museology, national history, arts; library of 50,000 vols, historical archive; Dir VERA LÚCIA BOTTREL TOSTES; publs guides, catalogues, etc.

Museu Nacional (National Museum): Quinta da Boa Vista, Rio de Janeiro, RJ; tel. (21) 254-4320; f. 1818; departments: anthropology, botany, entomology, geology and palaeontology, invertebrates and vertebrates; 4,000,000 specimens; library of 443,000 vols; one of the most important natural history museums in South America; Dir JANIRA MARTINS COSTA; publs *Arquivos, Boletins, Manuais, Publicações Avulsas*, guides, catalogues, pamphlets, etc.

Museu Nacional de Belas Artes (National Museum of Fine Arts): Av. Rio Branco 199, Rio de Janeiro, RJ; tel. 240-9869; f. 1937; collections of Brazilian and European paintings and sculpture; graphic arts and furniture; primitive art, numismatics, posters, photographs; exhibitions and educational services; library of 12,000 vols; Dir Prof. HELOISA A. LUSTOSA; publs *Boletim*, catalogues, monographs.

Museus Raymundo Ottoni de Castro Maya: R. Murtinho Nobre 93, 20241-050 Santa Teresa, Rio de Janeiro, RJ; tel. (21) 224-8524; fax (21) 507-1932; e-mail c.maya01@visualnet.com.br; f. 1962 by Raymundo Ottoni de Castro Maya, now run by the Ministry of Culture; two museums: Museu da Chácara do Céu (modern Brazilian and European art, Chinese pottery and sculpture, Luso-Brazilian furniture etc.) and Museu do Açude (17th- to 19th-century Portuguese tiles and sculpture, Luso-Brazilian furniture etc. in 19th-century manor house); library of *c.* 2,000 vols; Dir VERA DE ALENCAR.

Rio Grande

Museu Oceanográfico 'Prof. Eliézer de C. Rios' (Oceanographic Museum): CP 379, 96200-970, Rio Grande, RS; tel. (532) 32-34-96; fax (532) 32-96-33; f. 1953; attached to Univ. of Rio Grande; oceanography, ichthyology, malacology, mammalogy; large shell collection, cetaceans collection; library; Dir Oc. Ms. LAURO BARCELLOS.

Sabará

Museu do Ouro (Gold Museum): Rua da Intendência, 34500 Sabará, MG; tel. and fax (31) 671-1848; f. 1945; museum housed in a building dated 1730; sections: technical, historical, artistic; antique methods of gold mining and smelting; gold ingots, 18th-century silverware, 18th-century furniture and typical handicrafts of the mining districts; library of 3,000 vols, 35,000 documents; Dir SELMA MELO MIRANDA.

Salvador

Museu de Arte Antiga, Instituto Feminino da Bahia (Early Art Museum: Bahia Women's College): Rua Monsenhor Flaviano 2, Salvador, BA; f. 1933; collections of religious art, Brazilian art and feminine apparel; also the Museu de Arte Popular; f. 1929; gold, silver, jewellery, clothing, weapons; Dir HENRIQUETA MARTINS CATHARINO.

Museu de Arte da Bahia (Bahia Art Museum): Av. 7 de Setembro 2340, Vitória, Salvador, BA; f. 1918; library of 8,000 vols; 9,209 exhibits; general collection, with emphasis given to art, particularly Bahian Colonial art; Dir LUIZ JASMIN; publ. *Publicações do Museu*.

São Paulo

Museu de Arqueologia e Etnologia da Universidade de São Paulo: Av. Prof. Almeida Prado 1466, CEP 05508-900 São Paulo, SP; tel. (11) 818-4978; fax (11) 818-5042; f. 1964; 88 staff; library of 16,000 vols, 2,000 periodical titles; Dir Dr ADILSON AVANSI DE ABREU; publs *Revista do Museu de Arqueologia e Etnologia* (annually), *Sumários de Periódicos* (6 a year).

Museu de Arte Contemporânea da Universidade de São Paulo (Contemporary Art Museum of São Paulo University): Rua da Reitoria 160, CEP 05508-900 São Paulo, SP; tel. (11) 818-3538; fax (11) 212-0218; f. 1963; a permanent exhibition of international and Brazilian plastic arts; library of 6,000 vols, 30,000 catalogues, 20,500 slides, 4,000 posters; Dir Prof. Dr JOSÉ TEIXEIRA COELHO; publ. *MAC Revista*.

Museu de Arte de São Paulo: Av. Paulista 1578, 01310-200 São Paulo, SP; tel. 251-5644; fax 284-0574; f. 1947; classical and modern paintings, Italian, Spanish, Dutch, Flemish, and French schools; also representative works by Portinari and Lasar Segall; departments of theatre, music, cinema, art history, exhibitions, printing, photography and education; Dir JULIO NEVES.

Museu de Arte Sacra: Av. Tiradentes 676, CEP 01102-Luz, São Paulo, SP; tel. 227-7694; f. 1970, formerly Museu da Curia Metropolitana; sacred art, furniture, numismatics, paintings, silverware, jewellery, textiles, etc.; specialized library of 3,400 vols; Dir Eng. Dr JOÃO MARINO.

Museu de Zoologia, Universidade de São Paulo (Museum of Zoology, University of São Paulo): Av. Nazaré 481, CP 42694, 04299-970 São Paulo, SP; formerly Departamento de Zoologia da Secretaria de Agricultura do Estado de São Paulo; f. 1939; 7,000,000 specimens of neotropical and world fauna; library of 73,000 vols; Dir M. T. U. RODRIGUES; publs *Arquivos de Zoologia, Papeis Avulsos de Zoologia*.

Museu Florestal 'Octávio Vecchi' (Forestry Museum): Rua do Horto 931, Bairro Horto Florestal, CEP 02377-000, São Paulo, SP; tel. 952-8555; fax (11) 204-8067; f.1931; a dependency of the Forestry Institute of the Sec. of State for Environment; forestry and forest technology, collections of local timber; Dir DALMO DIPPOLD VILAR.

Museu Paulista da Universidade de São Paulo (São Paulo University Museum): Parque da Independência s/n, Ipiranga, CP 42503, 04299-970 São Paulo, SP; tel. (11) 215-4588; fax (11) 215-4588(-2050); f. 1895; history, material culture, historical and numismatic specimens; also collections of furniture and stamps; library of 25,000 vols, 2,300 periodical titles; Dir JOSÉ SEBASTIÃO WITTER; publs *Anais, Cadernos*.

Pinacoteca do Estado de São Paulo (State Art Museum): Av. Tiradentes 141–Luz, 01101-010 São Paulo, SP; tel. (11) 227-6329; fax (11) 228-9637; f. 1905; Brazilian art from 19th century to the present; temporary and permanent exhibitions, workshops, lectures, international meetings; specialized library of 1,906 vols, 3,100 exhibition catalogues; Exec. Dir EMANOEL ARAÚJO; publ. *Catalogue*.

Terezina

Museu do Piauí: Praça Marechal Deodoro, 64000 Terezina, PI; tel. 2226027; f. 1980; historical, cultural and artistic exhibitions; Dir SELMA DUARTE FERREIRA; publ. *Boletim*.

Vitória

Museu Solar Monjardim: Av. P. Müller, Jucutuquara, Vitória, ES; f. 1939 as State Museum; inc. Jan. 1967 to Federal Univ.; history, sacred art, furniture, porcelain, paintings, arms, books, silverware and photographs; publ. *Boletim* (weekly).

Universities

UNIVERSIDADE FEDERAL DO ACRE

CP 500, Campus Universitario, BR 364, Km 04, 69900 Rio Branco, Acre

Telephone: (68) 226-1160
Telex: (68) 2532

Founded 1971

Rector: SANSÃO RIBEIRO DE SOUSA
Librarian: VALCI AUGUSTINHO

Library of 46,000 vols
Number of teachers: 274
Number of students: 2,013

DIRECTORS

Law: ANA ROSA BAYMA AZEVEDO
Economics: VICENTE ABREU NETO
Education: JOAQUIM LOPES DA CRUZ FILHO
Language and Literature: LINDA BARBARY MESQUITA
Geography: MARIA DAS DORES SILVA LUSTOSA
History: PEDRO MARTINELLO
Mathematics and Statistics: AROLDO CARDOSO CAMPOS
Social Sciences and Philosophy: PEDRO VICENTE COSTA SOBRINHO
Health Sciences: PASCOAL TORRES MUNIZ
Natural Sciences: MAURO LUIZ ALDRIGUE
Physical Education: WALTER FÉLIX DE SOUZA
Technology of Civil Construction: JAIR VICENTE MANOEL
Agrarian Science: JOSÉ DE RIBAMAR TORRES DA SILVA

UNIVERSIDADE FEDERAL DE ALAGOAS

Campus A. C. Simões, BR/101 norte, Km 14, Cidade Universitária 570810 Maceió, AL

Telephone: (82) 241–6141
Telex: (82) 2307

Founded 1961

State (Federal) control
Language of instruction: Portuguese
Academic year: March to December (two semesters)

Rector: Profa. DELZA LEITE GOES GITAI
Vice-Rector: Prof. JOSÉ M. MALTA LESSA
Chief, Rector's Office: Prof. ELIAS PASSOS TENÓRIO
Pro-Rector (Academic Affairs): Prof. EDUARDO ALMEIDA SILVA
Pro-Rector (Community Affairs): Prof. WILD SILVA
Pro-Rector (Planning Affairs): Prof. JOÃO FERREIRA AZEVEDO
Pro-Rector (Postgraduate and Research Affairs): Prof. MANOEL M. RAMALHO AZEVEDO

Number of teachers: 907
Number of students: 6,128

Publication: *Boletim da UFAL*.

DEANS

Centre of Exact and Natural Sciences: Prof. EDMILSON DE VASCONCELOS PONTES
Centre of Human Sciences, Letters and Arts: Profa. GEORGETTE CASTRO DE ALMEIDA
Centre of Biological Sciences: Profa DELZA LEITE GITAI
Centre of Technology: Prof. REINALDO MARINHO
Centre of Health Sciences: Prof. ÚLPIO PAULO DE MIRANDA
Centre of Agrarian Sciences: Prof. PAULO GALINDO MARTINS
Centre of Applied Social Sciences: Prof. JAIR GALVÃO FREIRE

UNIVERSIDADE DO AMAZONAS

Av. Gen. Rodrigo Otávio Jordão Ramos 3000, Campus Universitário, 69077-000 Aleixo

Telephone: (92) 644-2244
Telex: 92-2554
Fax: (92) 644-1620

Founded 1962

Federal control
Academic year: March to December

Rector: Dr NELSON ABRAHIM FRAIJI
Vice-Rector: Prof. HÉLVIO NEVES GUERRA
Sub-Rectors: Prof. BRUCE PATRICK OSBORNE (Academic Affairs), Profa LUIZA MARIA BESSA REBELO (Planning), Prof. EMERSON PIRES DE SOUZA (Administrative Affairs), Prof. HINDENBERG ORTOGOITH DA FROTA (Research and Graduate Affairs), Profa ARMINDA RACHEL MOURÃO DIEDERICHS (Community Affairs), Profa ZEINA REBOUÇAS CORRÊA THOMÉ (Extension Services)
Librarian: SOL ABTBOL MACHADO

Number of teachers: 850
Number of students: 12,756

Publications: *Relatório de Atividades, Boletim Estatístico, Orçamento Programa, Catálogo de Teses, Boletim Bibliográfico, Plano Diretor, Caderno de Humanidades e Ciências Sociais,* etc.

DIRECTORS

Institute of Exact Sciences: Prof. EVERARDO LIMA MAIA
Institute of Human Sciences and Literature: Prof. GEDEÃO TIMÓTEO AMORIM
Institute of Technology: Prof. JORGE ANDRADE FILHO
Faculty of Social Studies: Prof. ROSALVO MACHADO BENTES
Faculty of Health Sciences: Prof. MENA BARRETO SEGADILHA FRANÇA
Faculty of Law: Prof. JOÃO DOS SANTOS PEREIRA BRAGA
Centre for Environmental Sciences: Prof. NELITON MARQUES DA SILVA
Computer Centre: Prof. ADEMAR MAURO TEIXEIRA
Centre for Arts: Prof. RAIMUNDO NONATO PEREIRA

UNIVERSIDADE FEDERAL DA BAHIA

Palácio da Reitoria, Rua Augusto Viana s/n, Canela, 40170-290 Salvador, BA
Telephone: (71) 245-2811
Telex: 1978
Fax: (71) 245-2460

Founded 1946
State control

Rector: LUIZ FELIPE PERET SERPA
Vice-Rector: MARIA GLEIDE SANTOS BARRETO
Administrative Officer: NICE AMERICANO DA COSTA
Secretary-General: JUSSARA BARBARA MARTINS PINHEIRO
Librarian: Prof. NIDIA MARIA LIENERT LUBISCO

Libraries: one central and 35 departmental libraries, 492,000 vols
Number of teachers: 1,812
Number of students: 16,836

Publications: *Universitas,* various faculty and institute publications.

DIRECTORS

Faculty of Architecture: GUIVALDO BITTENCOURT BAPTISTA
Faculty of Communication: ANTONIO ALBINO CANELAS RUBIM
Faculty of Economics: PAULO REBOUÇAS BRANDÃO
Faculty of Law: ANTÔNIO CARLOS ARAÚJO DE OLIVEIRA
Faculty of Medicine: THOMAS RODRIGUES PORTO DA CRUZ
Faculty of Dentistry: JAIRO DINIZ
Faculty of Education: IRACY PICANÇO
Faculty of Pharmacy: MARIA DE NAZARETH VIANA
Faculty of Philosophy and Humanities: TEREZA ARAGÃO
Polytechnic School: MAERBAL BITTENCOURT MARINHO
School of Fine Arts: JUAREZ MARIALVA TITO MARTINS PARAÍSO
School of Librarianship: MARIA JOSÉ RABELO DE FREITAS
School of Nursing: NEUZA DIAS ANDRADE AZEVEDO
School of Administration: REGINALDO SOUZA SANTOS
School of Agriculture: JOELITO DE OLIVEIRA RESENDE
School of Veterinary Medicine: LUCIANO JOSÉ COSTA FIGUEREDO
School of Dietetics: EDILEUZA NUNES GAUDENZI
School of Music: ALDA DE JESUS OLIVEIRA
School of Dance: SILVIA CRISTINA GAMA LOBO
School of Theatre: Prof. CARLOS ALBERTO CARDOSO NASCIMENTO
Institute of Mathematics: ADELMO RIBEIRO DE JESUS
Institute of Physics: AURINO RIBEIRO FILHO
Institute of Chemistry: LAFAIETE ALMEIDA CARDOSO
Institute of Biology: JACY LINS E SILVA FRANCO
Institute of Geology: DÉLIO JOSÉ FERRAZ PINHEIRO
Institute of Letters: AURÉLIO GONÇALVES DE LACERDA
Institute of Health Sciences: Prof. LUIZ CÉSAR DANTAS NASCIMENTO
Institute of Community Health: NAOMAR DE ALMEIDA FILHO
Human Resources Centre: TANIA MARIA DE ALMEIDA FRANCO
Data Processing Centre: DIONICARLOS VASCONCELOS
Centre of Afro-Oriental Studies: JEFFERSON BACELLAR
Centre of Bahian Studies: FERNANDO PERES
Centre of Inter-disciplinary Studies for Public Services: MARGARIDA ANDRADE BRANDÃO
University Hospital: ANTONIO CARLOS LEMOS
Maternity Hospital: NÉLIA MARIA DOURADA L. BRITO

UNIVERSIDADE REGIONAL DE BLUMENAU

Rua Antônio da Veiga 140, CP 1507, 89010-971 Blumenau, SC
Telephone: (47) 321-0200
Telex: 473-302
Fax: (47) 322-8818

Founded 1968

Under control of the Fundação Universidade Regional de Blumenau
Language of instruction: Portuguese
Academic year: January to December

Rector: Prof. MÉRCIO JACOBSEN
Vice-Rector: Prof. EGON JOSÉ SCHRAMM
Pro-Rectors: Prof. CARLOS XAVIER SCHRAMM (Administration), Profa MARLI MARIA SCHRAMM (Teaching), Prof. EDELBERTO LUIZ REINEHR (Research and Postgraduate Studies), Prof. JOSÉ CARLOS GRANDO (Extension and Community Relations)
Librarian: NESSI DAVINA LENZI CRISTELLI

Library of 290,000 vols
Number of teachers: 648
Number of students: 12,902

Publication: *Revista de Divulgação Cultural, Dynamis – Revista Tecno-Científica.*

DIRECTORS

Centre of Applied Social Sciences: Prof. SAUL ALCIDES SGROTT
Centre of Human Sciences and Communication: Prof. VITOR BAZANELLA
Centre of Exact and Natural Sciences: Prof. DAVID HÜLSE
Technology Centre: Profa Dra ELISETE TERNES PEREIRA
Education Centre: Prof. ALMERINDO BRANCHER
Legal Studies Centre: Prof. Dr JOÃO JOSÉ LEAL
Health Sciences Centre: Prof. RUI RIZZO

ATTACHED RESEARCH INSTITUTES

Institute of Social Research: Dir Prof. VILMAR JOSÉ TOMIO.

Institute of Technological Research: Dir Prof. EDÉSIO LUIZ SIMIONATTO.

Institute of Environmental Research: Dir Profa BEATE FRANK.

UNIVERSIDADE DE BRASÍLIA

Campus Universitário Asa Norte, CEP 70910-900 Brasília, DF
Telephone: (61) 348-2022
Fax: (61) 272-1053

Founded 1961; inaugurated 1962

Under the control of the Fundação Universidade de Brasília
Language of instruction: Portuguese
Academic year of two terms: March to June, August to November

Rector: Prof. ANTONIO IBAÑEZ RUIZ
Vice-Rector: Prof. EDUARDO FLÁVIO OLIVEIRA QUEIROZ
Dean of Graduate Studies and Research: Prof. JOÃO DA ROCHA HIRSON
Dean of Administration and Finance: Prof. MARIA LUIZA FALCÃO
Dean of Extension: Prof. JOÃO CARLOS TEATINI DE SOUZA CLÍMACO
Dean of Undergraduate Studies: Prof. ANTONIO CARLOS PEDROSA
Dean of Community Affairs: CONCEIÇÃO ZOTTA LOPES
Central Library Director: Prof. ODILON PEREIRA DA SILVA

Library: see Libraries
Number of teachers: 1,299
Number of students: 10,400

Publication: *Revista Humanidades* (quarterly).

DIRECTORS AND HEADS OF DEPARTMENTS

Institute of Exact Sciences: ANTONIO MOZAR MARTINS MONTEIRO
- Physics: MARCO ANTONIO AMATO
- Mathematics: ROBERTO OSCAR GANDULFO
- Chemistry: MARÇAL DE OLIVEIRA NETO
- Statistics: JOSÉ ÂNGELO BELLONI
- Computer Science: RENATO DA VEIGA GUADAGNIN

Institute of Biological Sciences: WALDENOR BARBOSA DA CRUZ
- Cell Biology: CESAR MARTIUS DE SÁ
- Genetics and Morphology: ZULMIRA GUERRERO MARQUES
- Physiological Sciences: ANTONIO SEBBEN
- Ecology: MUNDAYATAN HARIDASAN
- Phytopathology: FRANCISCO PEREIRA CUPERTINO
- Botany: LINDA STYER CALDAS

Institute of Human Sciences: CELESTINO PIRES
- Economics: AÉRCIO DA CUNHA
- Sociology: LAURA MARIA GOULART DUARTE
- Anthropology: LUIS ROBERTO C. DE OLIVEIRA
- Social Services: MARIA CILENE M. SALES DOS SANTOS
- Philosophy: JOÃO PEDRO MENDES
- Geography: LEONOR FERREIRA BERTONI
- History: JOSÉ FLÁVIO SOMBRA SARAIVA

Institute of Literature: DIANA BERNARDES
- Linguistics, Classical and Vernacular Languages: ENILDE LEITE DE JESUS FAUSTICH
- Literary Theory and Literature: DANILO PINTO LOBO
- Foreign Languages and Translation: GILBERTO ANTUNES CHOUVET

Institute of Arts: GRACE M. MACHADO DE FREITAS
- Scenic Arts: SILVIA ADRIANA DAVINI DE RIBEIRO
- Visual Arts: FERNANDO ROCHA DUARTE
- Music: GABRIEL SALGADO DOS SANTOS

Institute of Geosciences: MARIA DO PERPETUO SOCORRO ADUSUMILLI
- Mineralogy and Petrology: JOSÉ CARUSO MORESCO DANNI
- General and Applied Geology: JOÃO WILLY CORREA ROSA
- Geochemistry and Mineral Resources: BHASKARA RAO ADUSUMILLI
- Seismological Observatory: JOSÉ A. VIVAS VELOSO

Institute of Psychology: TIMOTHY MARTINS MULHOLLAND
- Clinical Psychology: ANNICK ROSIERS FONSECA
- Basic Psychological Processes: JOÃO CLÁUDIO TODOROV
- Child Psychology and Developmental Psychology: SANDRA FRANCESCA C. DE ALMEIDA
- Social and Occupational Psychology: HARMUT GUNTHER

Institute of Architecture and Town Planning: FRANK ALGOT EUGEN SVENSSON
- Architecture: ERICO PAULO SIEGMAR WEIDLE
- Town Planning: RICARDO LIBANEZ FARRET

Faculty of Technology: LUIZ AFONSO BERMUDEZ
- Agricultural Engineering: ANTONIO CARLOS DOS SANTOS
- Civil Engineering: MARCELO DA CUNHA MORAES
- Electrical Engineering: IVAN MARQUES DE TOLEDO CAMARGO
- Mechanical Engineering: ALDO FOAO DE SOUZA
- Forestry Engineering: JOSÉ WAGNER BORGES MACHADO

Faculty of Health Sciences: JOSIMAR MATA DE FARIAS FRANÇA
- Collective Medicine: IVONETTE SANTIAGO DE ALMEIDA
- Surgery: ANDRÉ LUIZ VIANNA
- Paediatrics: MARINICE COUTINHO M. JOAQUIM
- Pathology: ALBINO VERÇOSA DE MAGALHÃES
- Nursing: MARIA APARECIDA GUSSI

Gynaecology and Obstetrics: ELENICE MARIA FERRAZ
Morphology: MARIA LUCIA DA S. TEIXEIRA
Nutrition: BETHSÁIDA DE ABREU S. PEREIRA
Odontology: JORGE ALBERTO C. PORTILHO
Physical Education: OSMAR RIEHL
Clinical Medicine: LUCY GOMES VIANNA

Faculty of Applied Social Studies: MURILO BASTOS DA CUNHA
Management and Accounting: JORGE FERNANDO VALENTE DE PINHO
Information and Documentation Science: JAIME ROBREDO
Political Science and International Relations: LUIZ PEDONE
Law: CARLOS F. MATHIAS DE SOUZA

Faculty of Education: MARIA ROSA ABREU DE MAGALHÃES
Theory and Basic Education: BERNADO KIPNINS (acting)
Methods and Techniques: MARIA ROSA ABREU DE MAGALHÃES
Planning and Administration: ROGÉRIO DE ANDRADE CÓRDOVA

Faculty of Communications: SÉRGIO DAYRELL PORTO
Audio-visual Communication and Publicity: UBIRAJARA SILVA
Journalism: JOSÉ SALOMÃO DAVID AMORIM (acting)

UNIVERSIDADE 'BRAZ CUBAS'

Av. Francisco Rodrigues Filho 1233 CP 511, 08730 Mogi das Cruzes, SP

Telephone: (11) 469-6444
Telex: (11) 39267

Founded 1940, university status 1986
Private control
Language of instruction: Portuguese
Academic year: February to June, August to December

Rector: Prof. MAURÍCIO CHERMANN
Pro-Rectors: Dr JACKS GRINBERG (Teaching, Research and Extension), Dr BENEDICTO LAPORTE VIEIRA DA MOTTA (Finance), Dr ISRAEL ALVES DOS SANTOS (Administration), ISAAC GRINBERG (Community), Dr SAUL GRINBERG (Planning)
Secretary-General: PÉRCIO CHAMMA JUNIOR
Librarian: JANDIRA MARIA COUTINHO

Library of 97,000 vols
Number of teachers: 512
Number of students: 10,494

DIRECTORS

Centre for Applied Social Studies: Dr MARCO ANTONIO RODRIGUES NAHUM
Centre for Exact and Technological Sciences: Dr BENEDITO LUIZ FRANCO
Centre for Human Sciences, Literature and Education: Prof. DILSON DEL BEM

COURSE CO-ORDINATORS

Law: Profa MARCIA D. NIGRO CONCEIÇÃO
Executive Bilingual Secretarial and Communication: FRANCISCO J. AROUCHE ORNELLAS
Economics, Administration and Accountancy: Prof. JAIR GONÇALVES DA CUNHA
Basic and Natural Sciences: Prof. PIO TORRE FLORES
Architecture and Town Planning: Prof. CIRO FELICE PIRONDI
Human Sciences: Prof. CESAR BILITARDO
Postgraduate Courses: JARBAS VARGAS NASCIMENTO
Engineering and Technology: Prof. PIO TORRE FLORES
Odontology: Prof. TADAAKI ANDO

PONTIFÍCIA UNIVERSIDADE CATÓLICA DE CAMPINAS

CP 317, Rua Marechal Deodoro 1099, 13020-904 Campinas, SP

Telephone: (19) 756-7000
Telex: 191806
Fax: (19) 256-8477
E-mail: reitoria@zeus.puccamp.br

Founded 1941
Private control
Academic year: March to December

Chancellor: Dom GILBERTO PEREIRA LOPES, Archbishop of Campinas
Rector: Prof. Pe. JOSÉ BENEDITO DE ALMEIDA DAVID
Vice-Rector for Academic Affairs: Prof. CARLOS DE AQUINO PEREIRA
Vice-Rector for Administrative Affairs: Prof. JOSÉ FRANCISCO B. VEIGA SILVA
Secretary-General: Prof. MARCEL DANTAS DE CAMPOS
Librarian: ROSA MARIA VIVONA B. OLIVEIRA

Number of teachers: 1,103
Number of students: 19,893

Publications: *Notícia Bibliográfica e Histórica, Reflexão, Revista 'Letras', Revista Jurídica, Revista Estudos de Psicologia, Revista Comunicarte, Revista de Nutrição, Revista BIOIKOS, Revista 'Ciências da Saúde', TransInformação, Oculum.*

DIRECTORS

Faculty of Architecture and Town Planning: Prof. WILSON RIBEIRO SANTOS JÚNIOR
Faculty of Librarianship: Profa EDILZE BONAVITA MARTINS MENDES
Faculty of Economic and Administrative Sciences: Prof. JOSÉ HOMERO ADABO
Faculty of Medicine: Prof. ROQUE JOSÉ BALBO
Faculty of Technology: Prof. PAULO ROBERTO DE QUEIROZ GUIMARÃES
Faculty of Law: Prof. FRANCISCO VICENTE ROSSI
Faculty of Education: Profa. MARIA ROSA CAVALHEIRO MARAFON
Faculty of Physical Education: Profa. MARIA CESARINA GÂNDARA B. SANTOS
Faculty of Nursing: Profa SANDRA DE SOUZA LIMA ROCHA
Faculty of Dentistry: Prof. THOMAZ WASSAL
Faculty of Social Service: Profa MARIA THEREZINHA C. MARQUES
Institute of Arts and Communications: Profa ZELINDA FAVERO GERVÁSIO
Institute of Computer Studies: Profa. ANGELA DE MENDONÇA ENGELBRECHT
Institute of Biological Sciences: Prof. NELSON EUGÊNIO LAUER
Institute of Exact Sciences: Prof. TADEU FERNANDES DE CARVALHO
Institute of Philosophy: Prof. PAULO DE TARSO GOMES
Institute of Human Sciences: Profa JULEUSA MARIA THEODORO TURRA
Institute of Literature: Profa MARIA DE FÁTIMA SILVA AMARANTE
Institute of Psychology: Profa MARIA FERNANDA M. BARRETO
Institute of Theology and Religious Studies: Prof. Pe. JOSÉ ARLINDO DE NADAI

UNIVERSIDADE ESTADUAL DE CAMPINAS

Cidade Universitária 'Zeferino Vaz', 13083-970 Campinas, SP

Telephone: (19) 239-3746
Fax: (19) 788-7160
E-mail: mohamed@rei.unicamp.br

Founded 1966
State control
Academic year: March to June, August to December

Rector: Prof. Dr HERMANO TAVARES
Vice-Rector: Prof. Dr FERNANDO GALEMBECK
Dean for Research: Prof. Dr IVAN EMÍLIO CHAMBOULEYRON
Dean for University Development: Prof. Dr LUIS CARLOS GUEDES PINTO
Dean for Undergraduate Studies: Prof. Dr ANGÊLO LUIZ CORTELAZZO
Dean for Graduate Studies: Prof. Dr JOSÉ CLAÚDIO GEROMEL
Dean for Extension and Community Matters: Prof. Dr JOÃO WANDERLEY GERALDI
Secretary-General: MIRIADES JANOTI
Librarian: LEILA M. ZERLOTTI MERCADANTE

Number of teachers: 2,200
Number of students: 19,401

DIRECTORS

Institute of Fine Arts: Profa Dra REGINA MÜLLER
Institute of Biology: Prof. Dr ARICIO XAVIER LINHARES
Institute of Philosophy and Humanities: Prof. Dr PAULO CELSO MICELI
'Gleb Wataghin' Institute of Physics: Prof. Dr ELIERMES ARRAES MENESES
Institute of Language Studies: Profa Dra RAQUEL SALEK FIAD
Institute of Mathematics, Statistics and Computer Science: Prof. Dr WALDIR ALVES RODRIGUES JUNIOR
Institute of Chemistry: Prof. Dr OSWALDO LUIZ ALVES
Institute of Geosciences: Prof. Dr NEWTON MÜLLER PEREIRA
Institute of Economics: Prof. Dr GERALDO DI GIOVANNI
Institute of Computer Science: Prof. Dr TOMAS KOWALTOWSKI
School of Medical Sciences: Prof. Dr FERNANDO FERREIRA COSTA
School of Education: Prof. Dr LUIZ CARLOS DE FREITAS
School of Agricultural Engineering: Prof. Dr JOÃO DOMINGOS BIAGI
School of Food Engineering: Prof. Dr JOSÉ LUIZ PEREIRA
School of Mechanical Engineering: Prof. Dr ANTÔNIO CELSO F. DE ARRUDA
School of Civil Engineering: Prof. Dr DIRCEU BRASIL VIEIRA
School of Electrical Engineering: Prof. Dr WAGNER CARADORI DO AMARAL
School of Chemical Engineering: Profa Dra MARIA REGINA WOLF MACIEL
School of Dentistry: Prof. Dr JOSÉ RANALI
School of Physical Education: Prof. Dr PEDRO JOSÉ WINTERSTEIN
Technology Centre: Prof. CARLOS ALFREDO DE CAMPOS
Computer Centre: Prof. Dr HANS KURT EDMUND LIESENBERG

UNIVERSIDADE DE CAXIAS DO SUL

CP 1352, Rua Francisco Getúlio Vargas 1130, Bairro Petrópolis, 95070-560 Caxias do Sul, RS

Telephone: (54) 212-1133
Fax: (54) 212-1049
E-mail: ucs@ucs01.ucs.anrs.br

Founded 1967
Academic year: March to July, August to December
Private control
Language of instruction: Portuguese

Rector: Prof. RUY PAULETTI
Vice-Rector: Prof. LUIZ ANTONIO RIZZON
Pro-Rectors: Prof. LUIZ ANTONIO RIZZON (Undergraduates), Profa OLGA MARIA PERAZZOLO (Postgraduates), Prof. ARMANDO ANTONIO SACHET (Extension and University Relations), Prof. ENESTOR JOSÉ DALLEGRAVE (Administration), Prof. JOSÉ CARLOS KÖCHE (Planning)

Chief Librarian: Lígia Gonçalves Hesseln
Number of teachers: 1,153
Number of students: 19,197
Publications: *Revista Chronos, Caderno da Editora da Universidade de Caxias do Sul, Boletim Atos e Fatos, Guia Acadêmico, Jornal Multicampi e Cadernos de Pesquisa.*

DIRECTORS AND HEADS OF DEPARTMENTS

Centre of Science and Technology: Dir Prof. Alexandre Viecelli
  Department of Mechanical Engineering: Prof. Paulo Roberto Linzmaier
  Department of Chemical Engineering: Prof. Luiz Antonio Rezende Muniz
  Department of Physics and Chemistry: Prof. Marcos Luiz Andreazza
  Department of Mathematics, Statistics and Computation: Profa. Helena Maria Lüdke
  Department of Computer Science: Profa. Maria de F. Weber do Prado
Centre of Humanities and Arts: Dir Prof. Olivar Maximino Mattia
  Department of Languages: Prof. Normélio Zanotto
  Department of Arts: Profa. Guadalupe Bolzani
  Department of History and Geography: Profa. Heloisa Délia Eberle Bergamaschi
  Department of Sociology: Profa. Ramone Mincato
  Department of Psychology: Profa Siloe Pereira
  Department of Communication: Maurício José Moraes
  Campus 8: Dir Profa Ana Mery Sehbe de Carli
Centre of Applied Social Studies: Dir Prof. Nelson Goulart Ramos
  Department of Juridical Science: Prof. Itamar Luis Franca
  Department of Economics: Lodonha M. Portela Coimbra Soares
  Department of Accountancy: Prof. Renato Francisco Toigo
  Department of Business Administration: Prof. Julio Paulo Duso
Centre of Biological Sciences and Health: Dir Prof. Celso Piccoli Coelho
  Department of Biological Science: Prof. Germano Roberto Schüür
  Department of Nursing: Profa Nilva Lucia Rech Stedile
  Department of Clinical Surgery: Prof. Wilson Paloschi Spiandorello
  Department of Clinical Medicine: Prof. Petrônio Fagundes de Oliveira Filho
  Department of Physical Education: Prof. Paulo Eugênio Gedoz de Carvalho
  Department of Biomedical Sciences: Prof. Valter Teixeira da Motta
Centre of Philosophy and Education: Dir Profa Corina Michielon Dotti
  Department of Education: Prof. José Dario Perondi
  Department of Philosophy: Prof. Décio Osmar Bombassaro
University Campus of the Winery Region: Dir Prof. Pedro Ernesto Gasperin
Department of Humanities, Social Sciences and Languages: Profa Bernardete S. Caprara
Department of Exact and Natural Sciences: Profa Laci Maria Francio
Department of Economic and Administrative Sciences: Prof. Roberto José Possamai
University Campus of Vacaria: Dir Prof. Nelson Francisco Benvenutti
Department of Social Studies and Communication: Prof. Homero Francisco Peixoto Camargo
Department of Education: Profa Clenia Maria Zanela
College of Farroupilha: Dir Prof. Raul Bampi
College of Guaporé: Dir Prof. R ui Bresolin
College of Nova Prata: Dir Prof. José Reovaldo Oltramari
College of Veranópolis: Dir Prof. José Reovaldo Oltramari
College of Hotel Management of Canela: Dir Prof. Gilberto Bonatto
School of Technical Studies of Caxias do Sul: Dir Profa Ana C. Possap Cesa

UNIVERSIDADE ESTADUAL DO CEARÁ

Campus do Itaperi, Av. Paranjana 1700, 60740-000 Fortaleza, CE
Telephone: (85) 245-2611
Fax: (85) 292-4299
E-mail: coopint@uece.br
Founded 1975
State control
Academic year: March to June, August to December
Rector: Prof. Dr Manassés Claudino Fonteles
Vice-Rector: Prof. Francisco de Assis Moura Araripe
Registrar: Prof. Dr Fábio Perdigão Vasconcelos
Librarian: Ângela Maria Pinho de Barros
Library of 60,338 vols, 586 periodicals
Number of teachers: 1,071
Number of students: 11,970
Publication: *Revista Lumen Ad Viam.*

DEANS

Health Science Centre: Prof. Antônio de Pádua Velença da Silva
Science and Technology Centre: Prof. Raimundo Santiago dos Santos
Applied Social Studies Centre: Prof. Gedyr Lírio Almeida
Humanities Centre: Prof. João Nogueira Mota Morais
Veterinary College: Prof. José Mário Girão Abreu
Faculty of Education, Sciences and Arts at Iguatu: Profa Maria Auxiliadora Benedine O. Bezerra
Faculty of Education, Sciences and Arts of the Central Interior: Profa Fátima Maria Leitão Araújo
Faculty of Philosophy 'Dom Aureliano Matos': Prof. Arnobio Santiago de Freitas
Faculty of Education at Crateús: Profa Elda Maria de Freire Maciel
Faculty of Education at Itapipoca: Prof. João Batista Carvalho Nunes
Centre for Education, Science and Technology at Sertão dos Inhamuns: Prof. João Álcimo Viana Lima
Advanced Campus at Baturite: Prof. Rômulo Mascarenhas dos Santos Júnior
Advanced Campus at Senador Pompeu: Profa Cleide Maria dos Santos Amorin
Advanced Campus at Pentecoste: Prof. Manoel Lopes Martins
Centre for Continuing and Distance Education: Profa Lúcia Helena Fonseca Grangeiro

HEADS OF DEPARTMENTS

Health Sciences Centre:
  Department of Nutrition: Profa Ana Maria MacDowell Costa
  Department of Biology: Prof. Luiz Menezes de Arruda
  Department of Nursing: Profa Maria Eurides de Castro
  Department of Physiology: Profa Lia Magalhães Almeida Silva
  Department of Physical Education: Prof. Eduardo Humberto Garcia Ellery
  Department of Public Health: Profa Clayre Anne Holanda Veras
Applied Social Studies Centre:
  Department of Accountancy: Prof. Artur Linhares Mendes
  Department of Economics: Prof. Francisco das Chagas Gouveia
  Department of Law: Prof. Márcio Malveira de Queiroz
  Department of Administration: Profa Anahid Boyadjian de Miranda Soares
  Department of Foundations of Education: Profa Bernardete Cândido Furtado
  Department of Education, Methods and Techniques: Profa Selma Maia de Oliveira
  Department of Methods and Techniques of Social Work: Prof. Paulo Roberto de Aguiar Lopes
Humanities Centre:
  Department of Portuguese Language: Prof. Rosilmar Alves dos Santos
  Department of Foreign Languages: Prof. Francisco Lúcio Cabral Pinheiro
  Department of Social Sciences: Prof. Belisa Maria Veloso Holanda
  Department of Arts: Profa Maria José Benevides Di Calvacanti
  Department of Philosophy: Prof. Adauto Lopes da Silva Filho
  Department of History: Prof. Francisco Agileu de Lima Gadelha
  Department of Psychology: Profa Sandra Maria Muniz Rebouças
Sciences and Technology Centre:
  Department of Statistics and Computation: Profa Roberta Sousa Pontes
  Department of Mathematics: Prof. Luciano Moura Cavalcante
  Department of Physics and Chemistry: Prof. Paulo Auber Rouquayrol
  Department of Geo-Science: Prof. Antônio de Oliveira Gomes Neto
Veterinary College:
  Department of Animal Production and Rural Extension: Prof. José Eduardo Cabral Maia
  Department of Veterinary Medicine: Prof. Olacílio Lopes de Souza
Faculty of Education, Sciences and Arts at Iguatu:
  Department of Education: Profa Liduina Maria Duarte dos Reis
Faculty of Education at Itapipoca:
  Department of Education and Arts: Profa Maria Romelia dos Santos
Faculty of Education, Sciences and Arts of the Central Interior:
  Department of Humanities: Profa Fátima Maria Leitão Araújo
  Department of Natural Sciences: Jose Maildo Nunes
Faculty of Philosophy 'Dom Aureliano Matos':
  Department of Geosciences: Profa Francisca Maria do Oliveira
  Department of Education: Profa Maria do Socorro Holanda
  Department of Arts: Prof. Jose Mendes de Andrade
  Department of Social Sciences: Francisco Edberto Jorge

UNIVERSIDADE FEDERAL DO CEARÁ

Av. da Universidade, 2853 Benfica, 60020-181 Fortaleza, CE
Telephone: (85) 281-3011
Fax: (85) 281-5383
Founded 1955
Rector: Prof. Roberto Cláudio Frota Bezerra
Administrative Officer: Vera Maria Bezerra Rae
Librarian: Norma Helena Pinheiro de Almeida

Number of teachers: 1,452
Number of students: 11,924

Publications: *Catálogo Anual,* various department publications.

HEADS OF DEPARTMENTS

Sciences Centre:

Mathematics: JOSÉ OTHON DANTAS LOPES
Statistics: Profa ELIANA MIRANDA SAMPAIO
Physics: Prof. FRANCISCO ERIVAN DE ABREU MELO
Chemistry: Prof. NILO DE MORAES BRITTO FILHO
Geography: Prof. ANTÔNIO JEOVAH DE ANDRADE MEIRELES
Geology: Prof. FRANCISCO MARQUES JÚNIOR
Biology: Profa MARIA APARECIDA OLIVEIRA ALVES
Computer Sciences: Profa LUCY VIDAL SILVA

Humanities Centre:

Social Sciences: Prof. CÉSAR BARREIRA
Social Communications: Profa OLGA MARIA RIBEIRO GUEDES
History: Prof. PEDRO AIRTON QUEIROZ LIMA
Letters: Profa COEMA ESCÓRCIO DE ATHAYDE DAMASCENO

Technology Centre:

Civil Engineering: Prof. JOSÉ ADEMAR GONDIM VASCONCELOS
Mechanical Engineering: Prof. CARLOS ANDRÉ DIAS BEZERRA
Electrical Engineering: Prof. FERNANDO LUIZ MARCELO ANTUNES
Architecture and Town Planning: Profa MARGARIDA JÚLIA FARIAS DE SALLES ANDRADE

Agricultural and Food Sciences Centre:

Agronomy: Prof. PAULO TEODORO DE CASTRO
Fisheries: Prof. LUÍS PESSOA DE ARAÚJO
Domestic Science: Profa ELISA MARIA MAIA GOMES
Food Technology: Prof. ANTÔNIO CLÁUDIO LIMA GUIMARÃES

Health Sciences:

Medicine: Prof. ELIAS GEOVANI BOUTALA SALOMÃO
Dentistry: Prof. FRANCISCO BESSA NOGUEIRA
Pharmacy: Profa VERBENA LIMA VALE

Faculty of Economics, Management and Accounting: Profa MARIA DA GLÓRIA ARRAIS PETER
Faculty of Education: Prof. OZIR TESSER
Faculty of Law: Prof. ÁLVARO MELO FILHO

UNIVERSIDADE CATÓLICA DOM BOSCO

Campus Universitário, Av. Tamandaré 6000, CP 801, 79002-905 Campo Grande, MS
Telephone: (67) 721-2040
Fax: (67) 382-4039

Founded 1993 from Faculdades Unidas Católicas de Mato Grosso

Rector: Pe. JOSÉ MARINONI

Library of 175,000 vols
Number of teachers: 217

Publications: *Jornal UCDB* (monthly), *Revista Koembá Pytã* (2 a year), *Revista do Direito* (every 2 months).

Faculties of Philosophy, Science and Literature, Law, Economics, Accounting and Administration, Social Work.

UNIVERSIDADE FEDERAL DO ESPÍRITO SANTO

Campus Universitário, Av. Fernando Ferrari, Goiabeiras, 29060-900 Vitória, ES
Telephone: (27) 335-2222
Fax: (27) 335-2244

Founded as State University in 1954, as Federal University in 1961
Federal control
Language of instruction: Portuguese
Academic year: March to July, August to December

Rector: JOSÉ WEBER FREIRE MACEDO
Vice-Rector: RUBENS SERGIO RASSELI
Registrar: ELIANA MARA BORTOLONI FRIZERA
Librarian: ANGELA MARIA BECALLI

Number of teachers: 1,036
Number of students: 10,187

Publications: *Dados Estatísticos, Revista de Cultura da UFES, Caderno de Pesquisa da UFES, RCP — Revista Universo Pedagógico, Jornal Laboratório, Revista de História, Primeira Mão, Revista Você da Secretaria de Cultura da UFES, Revista Sofia do Departamento de Filosofia, Journal UFES.*

DIRECTORS

Agricultural and Animal Husbandry Centre: JOSÉ AUGUSTO TEIXEIRA DO AMARAL
Arts Centre: KLEBER PERINI FRIZZERA
Biomedical Centre: WILSON MÁRIO ZANOTTI
Education Centre: MARIA JOSÉ CAMPOS RODRIGUES
General Studies Centre: LUIZ MÁRIO CÓ, SANTINHO FERREIRA DE SOUZA
Law and Economic Sciences Centre: ANA MARIA PETRONETO SERPA
Physical Education and Sports Centre: JOSÉ CHRISTOFARI FRADE
Technology Centre: EDSON BAPTISTA
Exact Sciences Centre: MARIA JOSÉ SCHWARTZ FERREIRA

HEADS OF DEPARTMENTS

Agricultural Engineering: ROSEMBERGUE BRAGANÇA
Phytotechnics: JOSÉ CARLOS LOPES
Animal Husbandry and Agricultural Economics: ARY CAETANO GONÇALVES MACEDO
Architecture and Urban Planning: MARCO ANTONIO C. ROMANELLI
Industrial and Decorative Arts: MARCIA BRAGA CAPOVILLA ALVES
Artistic Formation: ROSANA LUCIA PASTE
Technical-Artistic Foundations: MARCIA JARDIM CALGARO
Physiological Sciences: ADÉRCIO JOÃO MARQUEZINI
Clinical Surgery: JOHNSON JOAQUIM GOUVEA
Clinical Medicine: AYRTON GOMES DA FONSECA FILHO
Clinical Odontology: ARMELINDO ROLDI
Nursing: ANGELA MARIA DE CASTRO SIMÕES
Gynaecology and Obstetrics: LUIZ CLÁUDIO FRANCA
Specialized Medicine: ADELSON JOÃO DA CUNHA
Social Medicine: DÉCIO NEVES DA CUNHA FILHO
Morphology: GILTON COUTINHO BARROS
Pathology: JOSÉ BENEDITO MALTA VAREJÃO
Dental Prosthesis: JOÃO HELVÉCIO XAVIER PINTO
Administration: REGINA MARIA MONTEIRO
Library Management: MARIA DE FÁTIMA BARRETO
Accountancy Sciences: GERALDO ANTONIO M. DE OLIVEIRA
Social Communication: RUTH DE CÁSSIA DOS REIS
Law: GERALDO VIEIRA SIMÕES FILHO
Economics: PEDRO JOSÉ MANSUR
Social Service: MARIA MADALENA DO NASCIMENTO SARTIM
Sports: OG GARCIA NEGRÃO
Gymnastics: VALTER BRACHT
Biology: CELSO OLIVEIRA AZEVEDO
Social Sciences: LUIS MURAMATSU
Statistics: MARIA ANGELICA F. DE OLIVEIRA
Philosophy: ANACLETO RODGRIGUES DA SILVA
Physics and Chemistry: REINALDO CENTODUCATTE
Geosciences: JARA DE ALMEIDA
History: GILVAN VENTURA DA SILVA
Languages and Literature: WALKYRIA PUPPIM
Mathematics: STANDARD SILVA
Psychology: ELIZABETH MARIA ANDRADE ARAGÃO
Administration and Student Supervision: ANA LUCIA BAPTISTA ROCHA
Didactics and Practice of Teaching: MARIA JOSÉ CAMPOS RODRIGUES
Foundations of Education and Educational Orientation: IZABEL CRISTINA NOVÃES
Electrical Engineering: EDSON PEREIRA CARDOSO
Industrial Engineering and Computer Science: MARIA CHRISTINA PEDROSA VALLI
Mechanical Engineering: OSWALDO PAIVA ALMEIDA FILHO
Structures and Buildings: JOSÉ MARIA RODRIGUES NICOLAU
Hydraulics and Sanitation: ALEXANDRE JOSÉ SERAFIM
Transport: MARCO ANTONIO BARBOZA DA SILVA

ATTACHED INSTITUTES

Institute of Technology: Superintendent ANNIBAL EWALD MARTINS.

Institute of Dental Medicine: Superintendent RANULFO GIANORDOLI NETO.

UNIVERSIDADE ESTADUAL DE FEIRA DE SANTANA

BR 116, Km 3, Campus Universitário, 44031-460 Feira de Santana, Bahia
Telephone: (75) 224-1521
Telex: 75-2403
Fax: (75) 224-2284

Founded 1976
State control
Language of instruction: Portuguese
Academic year: March to July, August to December

Rector: JOSUÉ DA SILVA MELLO
Vice-Rector: JOAQUIM PONDÉ FILHO
Academic Pro-Rector: ANACI BISPO PAIM
Administrative Pro-Rector: EUTÍMIO DE OLIVEIRA ALMEIDA
Academic Director: ANTÔNIO RAIMUNDO BASTOS MELO
Administrative Director: ROBERTO GOMES DA SILVA NETO
Financial Director: GILDINCE LIMA FERREIRA
Director of Student Affairs: ANTONIO ROBERTO SEIXAS DA CRUZ
Librarian: VERA VILENE FERREIRA NUNES

Library of 72,700 vols
Number of teachers: 508
Number of students: 4,253

Publication: *Sitientibus* (2 a year), *Intercampus.*

HEADS OF DEPARTMENT

Letters and Arts: RUBENS EDSON ALVES PEREIRA
Applied Social Sciences: JORGE JESUS ALMEIDA
Biological Sciences: CLEIDE MÉRCIA SOARES PEREIRA
Exact Sciences: INÁCIO DE SOUZA FADIGAS
Technology: GENIVAL CORREIA DE SOUZA
Human Sciences and Philosophy: MARIA LÚCIA CINTRA BARRETO
Health: DENICE VITÓRIA DE BRITO
Education: EUNICE FREITAS FERREIRA

UNIVERSIDADE FEDERAL FLUMINENSE

Rua Miguel de Frias 9, Icaraí, 24220-000 Niterói, RJ
Telephone: (21) 717-0860
Telex: (21) 32076
Fax: (21) 620-4553
E-mail: garaai@vm.uff.br

Founded 1960 as Federal University of State of Rio de Janeiro, present title 1960
Academic year: March to July, August to December

Rector: LUIZ PEDRO ANTUNES
Vice-Rector: FABIANO DA COSTA CARVALHO

Pro-Rector (Academic Affairs): MARIA HELENA DA SILVA PAES FARIA
Pro-Rector (Extension): AYDIL DE CARVALHO PREIS
Pro-Rector (Research and Postgraduate): MARCOS MOREIRA BRAGA
Pro-Rector (Planning): WALTER PINHO DA SILVA FILHO
Chief Administrative Officer: ALDERICO MENDONÇA FILHO
Librarian: JOÃO CARLOS GOMES RIBEIRO

Libraries with 492,000 vols
Number of teachers: 2,637
Number of students: 23,982 undergraduates; 2,068 postgraduates

Publications: *Revista da Faculdade de Educação, Revista de Ciências Médicas.*

DIRECTORS

General Studies Centre: ESTHER HERMES LUCK
Institute of Arts and Social Communications: ANA MARIA LOPES PEREIRA
Institute of Biology: LUIZ ANTÔNIO BOTELHO ANDRADE
Institute of Human Sciences and Philosophy: HUMBERTO FERNANDES MACHADO
Institute of Physics: PAULO ROBERTO SILVEIRA GOMES
Institute of Language and Literature: LAURA CAVALCANTI PADILHA
Institute of Mathematics: LUIZ ANTONIO DOS SANTOS CRUZ
Institute of Chemistry: LEONOR REISE DE ALMEIDA
Institute of Earth Sciences: WALTER RONALDO NUNES
Institute of Biomedical Science: ALEXANDRE SAMPAIO DE MARTINO
Applied Social Studies Centre: RAUL DE ALBUQUERQUE FILHO
Institute of Law: MARIA ARAIR PINTO PAIVA
Institute of Economics and Administration: ALBERTO SANTOS LIMA FILHO
Institute of Education: MARIA FELISBERTA BAPTISTA TRINDADE
School of Social Service: MARIA AUXILIADORA DA COSTA SIMÃO
Department of Social Service (Campos): GERALDA FREIRE BELLO DE CAMPOS

Nilo Peçanha Agricultural School: FERNANDO GONÇALVES DA CRUZ, Jr

Ildefonso Bastos Technical Agricultural School: JOSÉ BASTOS CAVICHINI

Medical Sciences Centre: JOSÉ CELESTINO BICALHO DE FIGEIREDO
School of Nursing: CARLOS ALBERTO MENDES
School of Pharmacy: ANTONIO CARLOS CARRERA FREITAS
School of Medicine: JOSÉ CARLOS CARRARO EDUARDO
School of Veterinary Science: MARIO AUGUSTO RONCONI
School of Dentistry: RAUL FERES MONTE ALTO FILHO
Rodolfo Albino University Laboratory: CARLOS DE CASTRO PEREIRA JORGE
School of Nutrition: STELA MARIA PEREIRA DE GREGÓRIO

Veterinary Experimental Centre (Iguaba): ADEMIL DE SOUZA PINTO
Technology Centre: HEITOR LUIZ SALLES SOARES DE MOURA
School of Engineering: JOSÉ JAIRO ARAÚJO DE SOUZA
School of Architecture and Town Planning: PEDRO ALFREDO MORAES LENTINO
School of Industrial Metallurgy: ANTONIO FONTANA

UNIVERSIDADE DE FORTALEZA

CP 1258, Av. Washington Soares 1321, Edson Queiroz Block, 60811-341 Fortaleza, CE

Telephone: (85) 273-2833
Telex: (85) 3701
Fax: (85) 273-1667

Founded 1973

Private control (Fundação Edson Queiroz)

Chancellor: AIRTON JOSÉ VIDAL QUEIROZ
Rector: Prof. ANTONIO COLAÇO MARTINS
Librarian: LEONILHA BRASILEIRO DE OLIVEIRA

Library of 87,453 vols
Number of teachers: 601
Number of students: 11,076

ATTACHED CENTRES

Administrative Sciences Centre: 81 Rua da Paz, Apto 100, Meireles, 60165-180 Fortazela, CE; Dir Prof. JOSÉ MARTÔNIO ALVES COELHO.

CCS: Rua Paschoal de Castro Alves 350/401, 600155-420 Fortaleza, CE; Dir Profa FÁTIMA MARIA FERNANDES VERAS.

Human Sciences Centre: 626 Léa Pompeu St, 60821-490 Fortaleza, CE; Dir Prof. JOSÉ BATISTA DE LIMA.

Technological Sciences Centre: 758 Prof. Heráclito St, 60155-440 Fortaleza, CE; Dir Profa NISE SANFORD FRAGA.

UNIVERSIDADE GAMA FILHO

Rua Manoel Vitorino 625, Piedade, 20748-900 Rio de Janeiro, RJ

Telephone: (21) 269-7272
Fax: (21) 591-4448

Founded 1972

Private control
Language of instruction: Portuguese
Academic year: February to June, August to December

Chancellor: Prof. Dr PAULO GAMA FILHO
Vice-Chancellors: Prof. Ms PAULO CESAR GAMA FILHO; Prof. LUIZ ALFREDO GAMA FILHO
Rector: Prof. Ms SÉRGIO DE MORAES DIAS
Vice-Rectors: Dr MANOEL JOSÉ GOMES TUBINO (Academic); Prof. SÉRGIO DE MORAES DIAS (Planning and Co-ordination); Prof. PERALVA DE MIRANDA DELGADO (Community); Prof. AYRTON LUIZ GONÇALVES (Development); Prof. PREDUÊNCIO FERREIRA (Administrative)
Secretary General: Dra MARIA CECÍLIA NUNES AMARANTE
Librarian: Profa LÚCIA BEATRIZ R. T. PARANHOS DE OLIVEIRA

Library of 146,000 vols; 130,000 periodicals
Number of teachers: 1,080
Number of students: 15,500

Publications: *Artus* (every 6 months), *Ciência* (every 6 months), *Ciência Humana* (every 6 months), *Ciência Social* (every 6 months).

DEANS

Sciences and Technology Centre: Prof. SÉRGIO FLORES DA SILVA
Biological and Health Sciences Centre: Prof. JOAQUIM JOSÉ DO AMARAL CASTELLÕES
Social Sciences Centre: Prof. HENRIQUE LUÍS ARIENTE
Human Sciences Centre: Profa PAULINA CELI GAMA DE CARVALHO

ATTACHED INSTITUTES

Instituto de Pesquisas Gonzaga da Gama Filho: Rio de Janeiro; Admin. Dir Prof. UBIRAJARA PEÇANHA ALVES; Scientific Dir Prof. JOÃO CARLOS DE OLIVEIRA TÓRTORA.

Instituto de Estudos de Linguas Estrangeiras: Rio de Janeiro; Co-ordinator REGINA LUCIA MORAES MARIN.

UNIVERSIDADE CATÓLICA DE GOIÁS

Av. Universitária 1440, Sector Universitário, CP 86, 74605-010 Goiânia, GO

Telephone: (62) 227-1188
Fax: (62) 224-3617

Founded 1959
Private control
Academic year: March to July, August to December

Chancellor: Father JOSÉ PEREIRA DE MARIA
Rector: Profa CLÉLIA BRANDÃO ALVARENGA CRAVEIRO
Vice-Rector for Academic Affairs: Prof. ANTONIO CAPPI
Vice-Rector for Research and Graduate Studies: Prof. RODOLFO PETRELLI
Vice-Rector for Administrative Affairs: Prof. MARISVALDO C. AMADO
Vice-Rector for Community and Student Affairs: Prof. ANDERSON L. DA SILVEIRA
Registrar: ROSIVAL B. LAGARES
Librarian: DANIEL RODRIGUES BARBOSA

Number of professors: 830
Number of students: 13,150

Publications: *Estudos* (quarterly), *Flash* (weekly), *Momento* (weekly).

DIRECTORS

Languages: Profa REGINA LÚCIA DE A. E NOGUEIRA
History, Geography and Social Sciences: Profa MARIA AMÉLIA G. DE ALENCAR
Law: Prof. ARNO REIS
Social Services: Profa MARIA JOSÉ DE F. VIANA
Philosophy and Theology: Prof. DARCY CORDEIRO
Education: Profa ELIANA STEIN
Nursing: Profa MARLENE MARIA DE C. SALUM
Biomedical Sciences: Prof. SERGIO ANTÔNIO MACHADO
Engineering: Prof. ARGEMIRO ANTÔNIO F. MENDONÇA
Architecture: Prof. FERNANDO CARLOS RABELO
Mathematics and Physics: Prof. HÉLIO CORRÊA DA SILVA
Psychology: Prof. MARCIO DE QUEIROZ BARRETO
Speech Pathology: Profa SILVIA M. RAMOS
Economics: Prof. LUIZ CARLOS DE C. COELHO
Accounting: Prof. NAZARENO ROCHA JÚNIOR
Business Administration: Prof. CELSO ORLANDO ROSA
Computer Science: Prof. JOSÉ ROLDÃO G. BARBOSA
Zootechnics: Prof. ROBERTO DE CAMARGO WASCHECK
Biology: Prof. JOSÉ WELLINGTON G. DA S. LEMOS

ATTACHED INSTITUTES

Institute of Prehistory and Anthropology: Dir Prof. JEZUS M. DE ATAÍDES.

Centre for Biological Studies and Research: Dir Prof. HELDER LÚCIO R. SILVA.

Sub-humid Tropics Institute: Dir Prof. ALTAIR SALES BARBOSA.

UNIVERSIDADE FEDERAL DE GOIÁS

CP 131, Campus Samambaia, Km 7, 74000-970 Goiânia, GO

Telephone: (62) 205-1777
Telex: (62) 2206
Fax: (62) 205-1327

Founded 1960

Rector: Prof. ARY MONTEIRO DO ESPÍRITO SANTO
Pro-Rectors: Profa ELIANA FRANÇA CARNEIRO (Undergraduates), Adm. IVOLEIDE M. DE CASTRO E SOUZA (Administration and Finance), Prof. VALTER CASSETI (Research and Postgraduate), Profa MARIA TEREZA L. DA FONSECA (Extension), Profa IARA BARRETO (Community Affairs)
Librarian: CLAUDIA OLIVEIRA DE M. BUENO

Number of teachers: 1,114
Number of students: 12,384

Publications: *Boletim do Pessoal* (monthly), *Anais da Escola de Agronomia e Veterinária* (annually), *Anais da Universidade* (2 a year), *Inter-Ação, Revista Goiana de Artes* (2 a year), *Revista da Faculdade de Direito* (2 a year),

Boletim Estatístico (2 a year), *Revista Goiana de Medicina* (quarterly), *Revista de Patologia Tropical* (quarterly), *Letras em Revista* (2 a year), *Ciências Humanas em Revista* (2 a year), *Cerrado* (2 a year)

DIRECTORS

Faculty of Law: Prof. MAURO DE FREITAS CORREA
Faculty of Education: WALDERÊS NUNES LOUREIRO
Faculty of Medicine: Profa ELEUSE M. DE BRITO GUIMARÃES
Faculty of Pharmacy: Prof. JAIR SEBASTIÃO G. DE OLIVEIRA
Faculty of Dentistry: Prof. MARCOS ROCHAEL
Faculty of Engineering: Prof. PAULO CESAR MIRANDA
Faculty of Nursing and Nutrition: MILCA SEVERINO PEREIRA
School of Agronomy: Prof. LÁZARO EURÍPEDES XAVIER
School of Veterinary Science: Prof. HÉLIO LOUREDO DA SILVA
Institute of Mathematics and Physics: Profa ILKA DE A. MOREIRA
Institute of Tropical Pathology: Profa DULCINEIRA MARIA BARBOSA CAMPOS
Institute of Biological Sciences: Prof. CARLOS ALBERTO TANEZINI
Institute of Chemistry and Geosciences: Prof. CELSO MACHADO
Institute of Arts: Profa MIRIAM DA COSTA MANSO MOREIRA DE MENDONÇA
Institute of Human Sciences and Literature: FRANCISCO ITAMI CAMPOS
School of Physical Education: Prof. ANTONIO CELSO FERREIRA FONSECA

HEADS OF DEPARTMENTS

School of Engineering:

Construction: OSWALDO CASCUDO MATOS
Hydraulics and Sanitation: Prof. EDWARD BONFIM DE SOUZA
Structural Engineering: Prof. NEWTON DE CASTRO
Electronics: Profa GISELE GUIMARÃES
Electrical Engineering: EMILSON ROCHA DE OLIVEIRA

Institute of Human Sciences and Literature:

History: Profa WALDINICE MARIA DO NASCIMENTO
Social Sciences: Profa DALVA M. BORGES DE L. D. DE SOUZA
Philosophy: JOSÉ NICOLAU HECK
Social Communication: FRANCISCO EDUARDO P. PIERRE
Letters: Prof. AGOSTINHO POTENCIANO DE SOUZA

Faculty of Pharmacy:

Pharmaceutical Technology: Prof. JAIRO DE SOUSA SANTOS
Clinical Analysis, Toxicology and Bromatology: JAIR SEBASTIÃO G. OLIVEIRA

Institute of Biological Sciences:

Anatomy: Prof. PAULO ROBERTO DE SOUZA
General Biology: JESUINO ANDRIOLO
Biochemistry and Biophysics: MARIA DE LOURDES BRESEGHELO
Botany: Prof. JOSÉ ÂNGELO RIZZO
Physiology, Pharmacology: Prof. ITAMAR DOS SANTOS PONTES
Histology and Embryology: Prof. ALVARO JOSÉ DO AMARAL MATEUS

Faculty of Medicine:

Surgery: Prof. LUIS CARLOS GOMES
Clinical Medicine: Prof. AUGUSTO SAMPAIO TEIXEIRA
Gynaecology and Obstetrics: Prof. OSVALDO DE ALENCAR ARRAES
Ophthalmology: Prof. ELIEZER FERREIRA DA COSTA
Otorhinolaryngology: Prof. JOÃO SEBBA NETO
Orthopaedics: Prof. EDEGMAR NUNES COSTA
Paediatrics and Puericulture: Prof. SAULO GUIMARÃES DE SOUZA
Pathology: Prof. BENVINDO BEERRA GERAIS
Psychiatry and Forensic Medicine: Prof. ABRÃO MARQUES DA SILVA
Radiology: Prof. WALSIR FAGANELO FIORI
Experimental Surgery: Prof. DJALMA RODRIGUES DE SOUSA

Faculty of Nursing and Nutrition:

Nursing: Profa MARIA DAS GRAÇAS N. DE OLIVEIRA
Nutrition: Profa MARIA MARGARETH VELOSO N. CABRAL

Faculty of Dentistry:

Oral Medicine: Prof. EDSON VIVAS DE REZENDE
Oral Rehabilitation: Prof. LUIZ HERNANI DE CARVALHO
Social Dentistry: Prof. DISNEI ALVES DA CUNHA
Polyclinic: Profa ENILZA MARIA MENDONÇA

Institute of Arts:

Theory and Applied Arts: Profa MARIA IGNES DE GRANDI MÜLLER
Plastic Arts: Prof. ORLANDO FERREIRA CASTRO
Vocal: Profa MARIA LÚCIA MASCARENHAS RORIZ
Figurative Arts: ÂNGELOS ANDRÉ KTENAS
Complementary Subjects: Profa EVANY DIAS FONSECA
Keyboard and Percussion Instruments: Profa VITÓRIA HELENA MAIA A. MARTINS

Institute of Tropical Pathology:

Immunology, Pathology: Profa REGINA BEATRIZ BEVILACQUA
Public Health: Profa IONIZETE GARCIA DA SILVA
Tropical Medicine: Prof. PAULO CÉZAR BORGES
Microbiology: Profa MARCIA ALVES VASCONCELOS RODRIGUES
Parasitology: Profa JULIETA MACHADO PACO

Institute of Chemistry and Geoscience:

Geography: Profa ZELINDA FANUCH DE MENDONÇA
Topography and Geodesy: (vacant)
Geology: (vacant)
Analytical Chemistry: Profa MARIA GISELDA DE OLIVEIRA TAVARES
Organic Chemistry: Prof. ALBERTO E. FINOTTI
General and Inorganic Chemistry: Profa CAROLINA MARIA GOETZ

Institute of Mathematics and Physics:

Mathematics: Profa GISELE DE ARAÚJO PRATEADO GUSMÃO
Statistics and Informatics: Profa NADIR MACHADO GONÇALVES
Physics: Prof. ANTONIO CARLOS DE FARIA

Faculty of Education:

Teaching Practice: Profa DINALVA LOPES COSTA TEIXEIRA
Education: Profa MINDE BADAUY DE MENEZES
Applied Studies: Profa NANCY ESPERANÇA LOPES

Faculty of Law:

Basic Law: Prof. CARLOS ALBERTO GUIMARÃES
Private Law: Prof. JOSÉ BEZERRA COSTAS
Criminal Law: Prof. BYRON SEABRA GUIMARÃES
Complementary Studies: Prof. LUIZ CARLOS P. ARRUDA
Civil and Labour Law: Prof. ALBERTO ABINAGEM

School of Agronomy:

Agriculture: Prof. DOMINGOS TIVERON FILHO
Horticulture: Profa IRAIDES FERNANDES CARNEIRO
Rural Economy: Prof. DORIVAL GOMES GERALDINE
Agricultural Engineering: Prof. ILDEU MATIAS DO NASCIMENTO
Food Technology: Profa HENRIQUETA MERCON VIEIRA ROLIM
Plant Hygiene: Profa VALQUÍRIA DA ROCHA SANTOS VELOSO

School of Veterinary Medicine:

Clinics: Prof. ARY DA SILVA RODRIGUES
Preventive Medicine: Prof. CARLOS STUART CORONEL PALMA
Pathology: Prof. JOÃO MAURÍCIO LUCAS GORDO
Animal Husbandry: Prof. CARLOS ALBERTO XAVIER BEZERRA

UNIVERSIDADE DE ITAÚNA

Rua Capitão Vicente 10, CP 100, 35680 Itaúna, MG

Telephone: 241-2375

Founded 1965

Private control
Academic year: March to July, August to December

Rector: GUARACY DE CASTRO NOGUEIRA
Executive Director: JOSÉ W. TEIXEIRA DE MELO
Librarian: MARIA DA CONCEIÇÃO APARECIDA CARVALHO CARRILHO

Number of teachers: 200
Number of students: 2,154

Publications: *Odonto-Itaúna, Cadernos de Extensão*.

DIRECTORS

Faculty of Dentistry: JAIR RASO
Faculty of Engineering: FRANCISCO JOSÉ DE CASTRO BIANCHI
Faculty of Law: GERALDO DOS SANTOS
Faculty of Philosophy, Sciences, Languages and Social Sciences: ANNA ALVES VIERA DOS REIS
Faculty of Economics: RAIMUNDO DA SILVA RABELLO

UNIVERSIDADE FEDERAL DE JUIZ DE FORA

Rua Benjamin Constant 790, Centro, 36015-400 Juiz de Fora, MG

Telephone: (32) 215-5966
Fax: (32) 231-1998
E-mail: foreign@propesq.ufjf.br

Founded 1960

Federal control
Language of instruction: Portuguese
Academic year: March to July, August to December

Rector: Prof. RENÊ GONÇALVES DE MATOS
Vice-Rector: Prof. CARLOS ALBERTO TARCHI CRIVELLARI
Pro-Rectors: MURILO CESAR MENDES GARCIA (Administration), Profa SONIA MARIA ROCHA HECKERT (Community Affairs), Prof. LUIZ ANTONIO VALLE ARANTES (Planning and Development), Profa MARLENE CALIL NETTO (Teaching), Profa MARIA MARGARIDA MARTINS SALOMÃO (Research)
Registrar: Profa MARIA HELENA BRAGA
Librarian: LEOPOLDINA LEONOR FAGUNDES MUNIZ

Number of teachers: 1,020
Number of students: 9,977

Publications: *Revista do Hospital Universitário* (quarterly), *Boletim do Centro de Biologia da Reprodução* (annually), *Boletim do Instituto de Ciências Biológicas* (annually), *Locus* (annually), *Educacão em Foco* (2 a year), *Ética e Filosofia Política* (2 a year), *Revista do Instituto de Ciências Exatas* (annually), *Revista Eletrônica de História do Brasil* (2 a year).

DIRECTORS

Faculty of Medicine: Prof. JOSÉ OLINDO D. FERREIRA
Faculty of Dentistry: Prof. HENRIQUE DUQUE M. C. FILHO
Faculty of Economics and Administration: Profa MARIA ISABEL DA SILVA AZEVEDO

Faculty of Pharmacy and Biochemistry: Profa MIRIAM APARECIDA PINTO VILELA
Faculty of Engineering: Prof. JÚLIO CÉSAR DA SILVA PORTELA
Faculty of Law: Prof. JOSÉ ANTÔNIO CÚGULA GUEDES
Faculty of Education: Prof. MANOEL PALÁCIOS DA P. E. MELO
Faculty of Social Services: Profa SANDRA A. HALLACK
Faculty of Physical Education: Prof. PAULO ROBERTO BASSOLI
Faculty of Social Communication: Prof. JOSÉ LUIZ RODRIGUES
Faculty of Nursing: Prof. MARLI SALVADOR
Institute of Biological Sciences: Prof. JOÃO B. PICININI TEIXEIRA
Institute of Human Sciences and Letters: Profa TEREZINHA MARIA SCHER PEREIRA
Institute of Exact Sciences: Prof. EMANOEL DE CASTRO ANTUNES FELÍCIO

UNIVERSIDADE ESTADUAL DE LONDRINA

CP 6001, Campus Universitário, 86051-970 Londrina, PR
Telephone: (43) 371-4000
Telex: (043) 256
Fax: (43) 328-4440

Founded 1971

Language of instruction: Portuguese
Academic year: February to December

Rector: Prof. JACKSON PROENÇA TESTA
Vice-Rector: NITIS JACON DE ARAÚJO MOREIRA
Secretary-General: Prof. ITAICY WAGNER MENDONÇA
Librarian: Profa SONIA MARIA MARQUEZ DE OLIVEIRA

Library of 109,000 vols, 3,934 periodicals, 5,320 (vols) pamphlets
Number of teachers: 1,473
Number of students: 11,704

Publications: *Boletim Informativo BC* (monthly), *Temática: estudos de administração* (termly), *Boletim do CCH* (termly), *Boletim de Geografia* (irregular), *Semina* (termly), *Notícia* (weekly) and various departmental publs.

DEANS

Centre of Letters and Human Sciences: Profa ANA CLEIDE CHIAROTTI CESÁRIO
Centre of Biological Sciences: Prof. ANTONIO CARLOS ZORATO
Centre of Exact Sciences: Prof. MILTON FACCIONE
Centre of Applied Social Studies: Prof. MAURO ONIVALDO TICIANELLI
Centre of Health Sciences: Prof. PEDRO ALEJANDRO GORDAN
Centre of Education, Communication and Arts: Profa NÁDINA APARECIDA MORENO
Centre of Agrarian Sciences: Prof. ERNST ECKEHARDT MÜLLER
Centre of Physical Education: Prof. DÉCIO BARBOSA DE SOUZA
Centre of Technology and Urbanism: Prof. ANTONIO CARLOS ZANI

HEADS OF DEPARTMENTS

Centre of Biological Sciences:

General Biology: LEDA MARIA KOELBLINGER SODRÉ DE LIMA
Animal and Plant Biology: MOACYR EURÍPEDES MEDRI
General Pathology: Profa ODETE LIMA PIMENTA DE OLIVEIRA
Anatomy: Profa MARILINDA VIEIRA DA COSTA
Histology: NEILA RECANELLO ARREBOLA PEREIRA
General Psychology and Behaviour Analysis: MAURA ALVES NUNES GONGORA
Basic Psychology and Psychoanalysis: LUCIA HELENA TIOSSO MORETTI
Social and Institutional Psychology: SEBASTIÃO OVÍDIO GONÇALVES
Physiological Sciences: ELEONORA ELÍSIA ABRA BLANCO

Centre of Letters and Human Sciences:

History: JAIRO QUEIROZ PACHECO
Philosophy: MARIA CRISTINA DE OLIVEIRA ESPÍNOLA
Social Sciences: Profa DEISE MAIA
Modern and Foreign Languages: CLEIDE MADALENA CORDEIRO CAMARGO
Classical and Vernacular Languages: ESTHER GOMES DE OLIVEIRA

Centre of Health Sciences:

General Medicine: Prof. MARCOS CESAR BARROS DE ALMEIDA CAMARGO
Surgery: Prof. ANTONIO MARCOS ARNULF FRAGA
Mother and Child Care and Community Sciences: ELISABETE DE FÁTIMA P. DE ALMEIDA NUNES
Nursing: ELMA MATHIAS DESSUNTI
Applied Pathology and Legal Medicine: APARECIDA DE LOURDES PERIN ALVARENGA
Restorative Dentistry: JORGE AUGUSTO CESAR
Oral Medicine and Odontopaediatrics: DAVID WILSON AHYUB
Physiotherapy: EDSON LOPES LAUADO

Centre of Education, Communication and Arts:

Education: LEONI MARIA PADILHA HENNING
Communication: WALDYR GUTIERREZ FORTES
Arts: CLARICE BRENAN ALVARES
Library Science: IVONE GUERREIRO DI CHIARA

Centre of Applied Social Sciences:

Private Law: Prof. JOSÉ ALVARES DELFINO
Public Law: JOSÉ ALMEIDA LEÃO
Economy: CARLOS ROBERTO FERREIRA
Accounting Sciences: CÉLIO VILAR REIS
Business Administration: FERNANDO ANTONIO PRADO GIMENEZ
Social Services: Profa SANDRA DA CRUZ PERDISÃO DOMICIANO

Centre of Exact Sciences:

Mathematics: ANTONIO CARLOS MASTINE
Applied Mathematics: Prof. JOÃO BATISTA MARTINS
Physics: Prof. MARCOS DE CASTRO FALLEIROS
Chemistry: Profa MARIA CRISTINA SOLCI
Geosciences: Prof. JAIME DE OLIVEIRA
Biochemistry: LÚCIA HELENA MENDONÇA VARGAS
Computer Science: Profa MARIA ANGÉLICA OLIVEIRA CAMARGO BRUNETTO

Centre of Agrarian Sciences:

Agronomy: LÚCIA SADAYO ASSARI TAKAHASHI
Veterinary Science: Prof. NEY CARLOS REICHERT NETTO
Preventive Veterinary Medicine: Prof. ITALMAR TEODORICO NAVARRO
Stockbreeding: IVONE YURIKA MIZUBUTI
Food and Drug Technology: Prof. RAUL JORGE HERNAN CASTRO GOMEZ

Centre of Technology and Town Planning:

Structures: JORGE BOUNASSAR FILHO
Civil Engineering: PAULO ROBERTO DE OLIVEIRA
Architecture and Town Planning: HUMBERTO TETSUYA YAMAKI

Centre of Physical Education:

Gymnastics, Recreation and Dance: PEDRO LANARO FILHO
Individual and Collective Sports: LUIZ CLAUDIO REEBURG STANGANÉLLI
Fundamentals of Physical Education: JUSY FERRAZ RAMON

UNIVERSIDADE MACKENZIE

Rua Itambé 45, Higienópolis, São Paulo, SP
Telephone: 256-6611
Founded 1952
Private control
Academic year: March to June, August to December

President: Dr ATHOS VIEIRA DE ANDRADE
Rector: Prof. Dr AURORA C. G. ALBANESE
Pro-Rector: Prof. Dr CLAUDIO SALVADOR LEMBO
Secretary-General: Prof. NELSON CALLEGARI

Number of teachers: 121
Number of students: 14,022

Publications: *O Picareta, Revista Mackenzie, Jornal Análise, Horacinho, Oráculo, Perfil Mackenzie.*

DIRECTORS

School of Engineering: Prof. MARCEL MENDES
School of Architecture and Town Planning: Prof. WALTER SARAIVA KNEESE
School of Letters and Education: Profa MARIA LUCIA MARCONDES CARVALHO VASCONCELOS
School of Economics, Administration and Accounting: Prof. HAMILTON MENEZES FISCINA
School of Law: Prof. FRANCISCO LÉO MUNARI
School of Technology: Prof. OSNY RODRIGUES
School of Sciences: Profa ANA MARIA PORTO CASTANHEIRA
School of Arts and Communication: Profa MARCIA CRISTINA GONÇALVES DE OLIVEIRA

UNIVERSIDADE FEDERAL DO MARANHÃO

Campus Universitário Bacanga, Prédio Marechal Castelo Branco, 65080-420 São Luís, MA
Telephone: (98) 217-8001
Telex: 098-2214
Fax: (98) 222-3186

Founded 1966

Federal control
Academic year: March to June, August to December

Rector: ALDY MELLO DE ARAÚJO
Vice-Rector: REGINA CELI MIRANDA REIS LUNA
Pro-Rectors: RAIMUNDO NONATO PALHANO SILVA (Administration); SEBASTIÃO MOREIRA DUARTE (Post-graduates and Research); MARIA DA PAZ PORTO MACEDO COSTA (Extension and Student Affairs); CERES COSTAS FERNANDES VAZ DOS SANTOS (Undergraduates)
Librarian: MARIA DA GRAÇA MONTEIRO FONTOURA

Number of teachers: 867
Number of students: 8,895

DIRECTORS

Centre of Health Sciences: JAMILE ALVES DE OLIVEIRA
Centre of Basic Studies: SEBASTIÃO BARBOSA CAVALCANTI FILHO
Centre of Social Sciences: RUBEM RODRIGUES FERRO
Centre of Technology: PEDRO JAFAR BERNIZ

COURSE CO-ORDINATORS

Centre of Health Sciences:

Medicine: ROSE MARIE DE JESUS J. C. GOMES
Pharmacy: SANDRA MARIA JANSEN CUTRIM CORRÊA
Dentistry: MARIA CELESTE DE MESQUITA AGUIAR
Nursing: NAIR PORTELA SILVA COUTINHO
Physical Education and Sports Technology: WALDECY DAS DORES VIEIRA VALE
Biological Sciences: SILMA REGINA PEREIRA MARTINS

Centre of Basic Studies:

Philosophy: MARIA DE FÁTIMA GARCÊS TEIXEIRA
Psychology: LOIDE CÉLIA DE BRITO
Geography: JOSÉ RIBAMAR TROVÃO

Literature: MARCUS VINÍCIUS MAGALHÃES CATNUDA
Arts: ALDO DE JESUS MUNIZ LEITE
Tourism: MARIA DO SOCORRO ARAÚJO

Centre of Social Sciences:

Librarianship: JOANA RITA VILAS BOAS MUALEM
Accountancy: RAIMUNDO NONATO SERRA CAMPOS FILHO
Economics: ELIZEU SERRA DE ARAÚJO
Social Communication: ADEILCE GOMES DE AZEVEDO
Law: VALÉRIA MARIA PINHEIRO MONTENEGRO
Social Service: ANA MARIA SANTANA NEIVA COSTA
Practical Art: IVALBERTO CASTRO CAMPOS
Social Sciences: LÚCIA HELENA FERNANDES DE SABOIA
Teaching: LUCINETE MARQUES LIMA
Hotel Management: JOSÉ MARIA GOMES DE AGUIAR

Centre of Technology:

Industrial Chemistry: PEDRO EURICO NOLETO CRUZ
Electrical Engineering: MANUEL LEONEL DA COSTA NETO
Computer Science: JORGE HENRIQUE MARQUES CARACAS
Industrial Design: PAULO SERGIO LAGO DE CARVALHO
Mathematics: ABINAEL ASCENÇÃO RIBEIRO
Chemistry: MARIA DA GRAÇA SILVA NUNES
Physics: RAIMUNDO ANTONIO DA SILVA SANTOS

FUNDAÇÃO UNIVERSIDADE ESTADUAL DE MARINGÁ

Av. Colombo 5790, Zona 7, 87020-900 Maringá, PR

Telephone: (44) 226-2727
Fax: (44) 222-2754
E-mail: fadec@wnet.com.br

Founded 1970

Academic year: March to December

Rector: LUIZ ANTONIO DE SOUZA
Vice-Rector: NEUSA ALTOÉ
Pro-Rectors: JOÃO DIRCEU NOGUEIRA CARVALHO (Administration), SILVIA INES CONEGLIAN CARRILHO DE VASCONCELOS (Teaching), CELSO SOUZA (Extension and Culture), MILTON MIRANDA DE ARAÚJO (Human Resources and Community Affairs), ERIVELTO GOULART (Research and Postgraduates)
Librarian: ANA MARIA MARQUEZINI ALVARENGA

Number of teachers: 1,287
Number of students: 9,804

Publications: *Unimar, Unimar Jurídica, Universidade e Sociedade, Boletim de Geografia, Revista de Educação Física, Revista Apontamentos, Cadernos de Administração, Revista Enfoque-Reflexão Contábil, A Economia em Revista, Revista Tecnológica, Jornal Alfabetizando, Caderno da Semana de Geografia, Revista Diálogos, Caderno de METEP, Revista de Psicologia.*

DIRECTORS

Socio-Economic Studies Centre: JOSÉ ROBERTO PINHEIRO DE MELO
Humanities and Arts Centre: ROMILDA MARINS CORREA
Biological Sciences Centre: SANDRA REGINA STÁBILLE
Health Sciences Centre: MARIA JOSÉ SCOCHI
Exact Sciences Centre: LUIZ ROBERTO EVANGELISTA
Technology Centre: MAURO ANTONIO DA SILVA SÁ RAVAGNANI
Agricultural Sciences Centre: GERALDO TADEU DOS SANTOS

HEADS OF DEPARTMENTS

Humanities and Arts Centre:

Geography: JOSÉ CANDIDO STEVAUX
Arts and Letters: JULIANO TAMANINI
Social Sciences: CELENE TONELLA
Education: JORGE CANTOS
Psychology: MARIA TERESA CLARO GONZAGA
Principle of Education: LIZETE SHIZUE BOMURA MACIEL
History: ALBERTO GAWRYSZEWSKI

Socio-Economic Studies Centre:

Private and Procedural Law: FABÍOLA VILELLA MACHADO
Public Law: FAUSTINO FRANCISCO DE SOUZA
Economics: REINALDO CONSONI
Business Administration: LUIZ TATTO
Accountancy: MÁRIO LONARDONI

Biological Sciences Centre:

Biology: ISMAR SEBASTIÃO MOSCHETA
Cellular Biology: VERONICA ELIZA P. VICENTINI
Biochemistry: SÉRGIO PAULO SEVERO DE S. DINIZ
Morphophysiological Sciences: DIÓGENES SANCHES

Health Sciences Centre:

Clinical Analysis: RICARDO ALBERTO MOLITERNO
Medicine: JOSÉ CARLOS DA SILVA
Odontology: ANDRES JOSÉ TUMANG
Physical Education: LUIZ ANTONIO PEREIRA DA SILVA
Nursing: VALMIR RYCHETA CORREIA
Pharmacy and Pharmacology: ROBERTO BARBOSA BAZOTTE

Agricultural Sciences Centre:

Animal Husbandry: ANTONIO CLAUDIO FURLAN
Agronomy: SUELI SATO MARTINS

Exact Sciences:

Chemistry: JONES SOARES
Mathematics: JULIO SANTIAGO PRATES FILHO
Physics: ANTONIO JOSÉ PALANGANA
Statistics: MARGARETH CIZUKA TOYAMA UDO

Technology Centre:

Civil Engineering: LUIZ DOMINGOS MORENO DE CARVALHO
Computer Science: WESLEY ROMÃO
Chemical Engineering: MARCELINO LUIZ GIMENES

DIRECTORS

Centre for the Integration of Children and Adolescents: CLEUZA LUCENA
Languages Institute: CRISTINA MORAES
Applied Psychology Centre: MARIA JOSÉ SARAIVA RIBEIRO
Data Processing Centre: DILVO PAUPITZ

UNIVERSIDADE FEDERAL DE MATO GROSSO

Av. Fernando Corrêa da Costa s/n, 78060-900 Cuiabá, MT

Telephone: (65) 315-8301
Telex: (65) 1371
Fax: (65) 361-1119

Founded 1970

Rector: Profa LUZIA GUIMARÃES
Administrative Officer: Profa NEUSA SOUZA DOURADO

Number of teachers: 1,167
Number of students: 9,195

Faculties of agrarian sciences, biological and health sciences, literature and human sciences, social sciences, exact sciences and technology.

FUNDAÇÃO UNIVERSIDADE FEDERAL DE MATO GROSSO DO SUL

CP 649, Cidade Universitária, 79100 Campo Grande, MT

Telephone: (67) 387-3833
Telex: (67) 2331

Founded 1970

Centres of biology, general studies, physical education, computer studies, education. Campuses in Corumbá, Aquidaúana, Dourados, Três Lagoas.

PONTIFICIA UNIVERSIDADE CATÓLICA DE MINAS GERAIS

Av. Dom José Gaspar 500, CP 2686, 30535-610 Belo Horizonte, MG

Telephone: (31) 319-1144
Fax: (31) 319-1225

Founded 1958

Chancellor: Dom SERAFIM FERNANDES DE ARAÚJO
Rector: Fr GERALDO MAGELA TEIXEIRA
Chief Executive Officer: JOSÉ TARCÍSIO AMORIM
Executive Co-ordinator: FÁBIO HORÁCIO PEREIRA
Chief Librarian: Profa ROSANGELA VASSALE DE CASTRO

Number of teachers: 854
Number of students: 17,655

HEADS OF DEPARTMENT

Polytechnic Institute: Dir HELOÍSA HELENA VIEIRA MACHADO

Civil Engineering: MARCUS SOARES NUNES
Electrical Engineering: EDERSON BUSTAMANTE
Electronic and Telecommunication Engineering: FLÁVIO MAURÍCIO DE SOUZA
Mechanical Engineering: RÔMULO ALBERTINI RIGUEIRA

Institute of Humanities: Dir AUDEMARO TARANTO GOULART

Education: GISLAINE MARIA DE CARVALHO
Philosophy and Theology: SÍLVIA MARIA CONTALDO DE LARA
History: MARIA MASCARENHAS DE ANDRADE
Geography: IONE MENDES MALTA
Portuguese and English: VERA LÚCIA FELÍCIO PEREIRA

Institute of Biological and Health Sciences: Dir UBIRATAN BARROS DE MELO

Dentistry: FÉLIX DE ARAÚJO SOUZA
Biological Sciences: EUGÊNIO BATISTA LEITE
Nursing: TEMA MACIEL SILVA

Institute of Informatics: Dir CARLOS BARRETO RIBAS

Computer Science: JOSÉ WILSON DA COSTA

Other Departments:

Psychology: ANA LÚCIA ANDRADE MARÇOLA (Dir)
Business Administration: MARIA LUIZA PROENÇA DOYLE
Accounting: OSCAR LOPES DA SILVA
Economics: PAULO SÉRGIO MARTINS ALVES
Social Communication: SANDRA MARIA DE FREITAS
Social Work: MARIA EULÁLIA MOREIRA
Sociology: GILMAR ROCHA
Mathematics and Statistics: JONAS LACHINI
Physics and Chemistry: MOZART SILVÉRIO SOARES
Continuing Education: JOSÉ MÁRCIO DE CASTRO (Dir)
Architecture and Urbanism: CLÁUDIO LISTHER MARQUES BAHIA

Faculty of Law: Dir JOSÉ CARLOS PIMENTA

AFFILIATED FOUNDATION

Fundação Dom Cabral: Rua Bernardo Guimarães 3071, CP 30140-083, Belo Horizonte, MG; tel. (31) 275-3466; telex (31) 2503; fax

(31) 275-1558; f. 1976; Dean Prof. EMERSON DE ALMEIDA.

UNIVERSIDADE FEDERAL DE MINAS GERAIS

Av. Antônio Carlos, 6627, Campus Pampulha 31270-010, CP 1621, Belo Horizonte, MG

Telephone: (31) 499-4125
Telex: (31) 2308
Fax: (31) 499-4130
E-mail: gabinete@reitoria.ufmg.br

Founded 1927
Governmental control
Language of instruction: Portuguese
Academic year: February to December

Rector: Prof. TOMAZ AROLDO DA MOTA SANTOS
Vice-Rector: Prof. JACYNTHO JOSÉ LINS BRANDÃO
Vice-Chancellors: Prof. ANTÔNIO MARIA CLARET TÔRRES (Administration), Prof. WALDEMAR SERVILHA (Planning), Profa LUCÍLIA DE ALMEIDA NEVES DELGADO (Undergraduate), Profa DORILA PILO VELOSO (Research), Prof. EVANDRO JOSÉ LEMOS DA CUNHA (Extension), Prof. DIRCEU BARTOLOMEU GRECO (Postgraduate)
Director of Libraries: MARIA HELENA DE SÁ BARRETO

Libraries of 522,100 vols, 19,400 periodicals
Number of teachers: 2,527
Number of students: 21,691

Publications: *Revista Brasileira de Estudos Políticos, Arquivos da Escola de Veterinária da UFMG, Estudos Germânicos, Barroco, Kriterion,* etc.

DIRECTORS

Fine Arts: Prof. JOSÉ ADOLFO MOURA
Literature: Profa ROSÂNGELA BORGES LIMA
Music: Prof. MAURIÍCIO FREIRE GARCIA
Philosophy and Human Sciences: Profa MAGDA MARIA BELLO DE ALMEIDA NEVES
Biological Sciences: Prof. RAMON MOREIRA COSENZA
Exact Sciences: Prof. ALFREDO GONTIJO DE OLIVEIRA
Geo-Sciences: Prof. MARCOS ROBERTO MOREIRA RIBEIRO
Architecture: Profa MARIA LÚCIA MALARD
Librarianship: Profa VERA LUCIA FURST GONÇALVES DE ABREU
Economic Sciences: Prof. ANTÔNIO CARLOS FERREIRA CARVALHO
Law: Prof. ALOÍZIO GONZAGA ANDRADE ARAÚJO
Education: Prof. NEIDSON RODRIGUES
Physical Education: Profa ROSA BELMA AFONSO VIOTTI
Nursing: Profa MARIA JOSÉ CABRAL GRILLO CALDEIRA BRANT
Engineering: Prof. AÉCIO FREITAS LIRA
Medicine: Prof. EDISON JOSÉ CORRÊA
Dentistry: Prof. RENATO DURVAL MARTINS
Veterinary Sciences: Prof. JONAS CARLOS CAMPOS PEREIRA
Pharmacy: Prof. HOMERO JACKSON DE JESUS LOPES

AFFILIATED INSTITUTES

Centre for Development and Regional Planning: Rua Curitiba 832, Belo Horizonte, MG; Dir Prof. JOSÉ ALBERTO MAGNO DE CARVALHO.
Astronomical Observatory: Dir Prof. RENATO LAS CASAS.
Institute of Technology and Agriculture: Dir Prof. GUALTER PEREIRA OLIVEIRA.

UNIVERSIDADE DE MOGI DAS CRUZES

CP 411, 08701-970 Mogi das Cruzes, SP; located at: Av. Dr Cândido Xavier de Almeida Souza 200, 08780-911 Mogi das Cruzes, SP

Telephone: (11) 4796-7000
Fax: (11) 4798-7198

Founded 1973
Private control

Chancellor: Prof MANOEL BEZERRA DE MELO
Vice-Chancellor: Profa MARIA COELI BEZERRA DE MELO
Rector: Prof. Dr ROBERTO LEAL LOBO E SILVA FILHO
Vice-Rector: Profa MARIA BEATRIZ DE CARVALHO MELO
Pro-Rectors: Prof. JOSÉ ROBERTO DRUGOWICH DE FELÍCIO (Administrative), Prof. Dr OSCAR HIPÓLITO (Academic)
General Secretary: Profa VERA LÚCIA PEREIRA DE LIMA
Librarian: REJANE PEREIRA DA SILVA GONÇALVES

Library of 97,000 vols
Number of teachers: 814
Number of students: 14,392

Publications: *Antena Ligada, Revista UMC, UMC em Notícias.*

DEANS

Human Sciences: Prof. Dr JOSÉ ÊNIO CASALECCHI
Science and Technology: Prof. JOSÉ CARLOS MORILLA
Biomedical Sciences and Sports Sciences: Prof. Dr DALMO DE SOUZA AMORIM

CO-ORDINATORS

Computer Sciences: TATUO NAKANISHI
Architecture and Town Planning: Profa Dra GILDA COLLET BRUNA
Chemical Engineering and Chemistry: Prof. GERSON UNGER DE OLIVEIRA
Mechanical Engineering: Prof. Dr GLAUCO AUGUSTO DE PAULA CAURIN
Electrical Engineering: Prof. MITSUO NITTA
Civil Engineering: Prof. Dr FRANCISCO DE ASSIS SOUZA DANTAS
Mathematics: Prof. Dr PAULO FERREIRA DA SILVA PORTO JUNIOR
Biological Sciences: Prof. Dr LUIZ ROBERTO NUNES
Biomedicine: Prof. JOSÉ EDUARDO CAVALCANTE TEIXEIRA
Dentistry: Profa ZILDA MARIA MUSSOLINO
Phonoaudiology: Profa DENISE DE OLIVEIRA TEIXEIRA
Medicine: Prof. ANTONIO YOITI SAKOTANI
Psychology: Profa MIRLENE MARIA MATIAS SIQUEIRA
Nutrition: Profa Dra SUSANA FONSECA DA SILVEIRA
Physiotherapy: Prof. Dr CESAR AUGUSTO CALONEGO
Pharmacy: Prof. JOSÉ JORGE NETO
Nursing: Profa Dra MARIA ROMANA FRIENDLANDER
Physical Education: Profa Dra MARA LUCY DOMPIETRO RUIZ DENADAI
Human Sciences: Prof. JORGE NAGLE
Social Communications: Prof. JOSÉ CARLOS ARONCHI
Economics, Accountancy and Administration: Prof. HÉLIO BENEDITO COSTA
Literature, Pedagogy, History and Arts: Profa Dra CLEIDE MARLY NÉBIAS
Law: Prof. CARLOS AURÉLIO MOTA DE SOUZA

UNIVERSIDADE REGIONAL DO NOROESTE DO ESTADO DO RIO GRANDE DO SUL

CP 560, Rua São Francisco 501, Bairro São Geraldo, 98700-000 Ijuí, Rio Grande do Sul

Telephone: (55) 332-7100
Fax: (55) 332-9100
E-mail: reitoria@main.unijui.tche.br

Founded 1985
Private control (Fundação de Integração, Desenvolvimento e Educação do Noroeste do Estado)
Language of instruction: Portuguese
Academic year: March to February (2 semesters)

Rector: Prof. Dr WALTER FRANTZ
Vice-Rectors: ERONITA SILVA BARCELOS, DILSON TRENNEPOHL, SÉRGIO LUIS ALLEBRANDT
Academic Secretary: TANIA MARIA LUCCHESE
Librarian: KENIA M. BERNINI

Library of 106,000 vols
Number of teachers: 569
Number of students: 8,465

Publication: *Contexto & Educação* (4 a year), *Espaço da Escola* (quarterly), *Município e Saúde* (2 a year), *Direito em Debate* (annually), *Ciência e Ambiente* (2 a year), *Educação, Subjetividade e Poder* (2 a year), *Humanidades em Revista* (2 a year).

HEADS OF DEPARTMENT

Administration: ENISE BARTH TEIXEIRA
Law: DARCÍSIO CORRÊA
Economics and Accountancy: JOSÉ VALDEMIR MUENCHEN
Teaching: JOSÉ MARIA NODARI
Philosophy and Psychology: LALA NODAR
Literature and Arts: BRANCA CABEDA E. MOELLWALD
Sciences: BERNADETE AZAMBUJA
Nursing, Obstetrics and Nutrition: TEREZINHA WEILLER
Biology and Chemistry: MIRNA LUDWIG
Agronomy: ARLINDO J. PRESTES DE LIMA
Technology: MARCOS CÉSAR CARDOSO CARRARD
Physics, Statistics and Mathematics: TÂMIA MICHEL PEREIRA

UNIVERSIDADE FEDERAL DE OURO PRÊTO

Rua Diogo de Vasconcelos 122, 35400-000 Ouro Prêto, MG

Telephone: (31) 551-1211
Telex: (31) 2954
Fax: (31) 551-1689

Founded 1969
State control

Rector: RENATO GODINHO NAVARRO
Vice-Rector: DIRCEU DO NASCIMENTO
Chief Administrative Officer: ELIDO BONOMO
Librarian: JUSSARA SANTOS SILVA

Number of teachers: 336
Number of students: 2,068

Publications: *Revista da Escola de Minas, Revista de Historia, Jornal da UFOP, Jornal Revirarte.*

CONSTITUENT INSTITUTES

School of Mining: Praça Tiradentes 20, 35400-000 Ouro Prêto, MG; f. 1876; courses in civil engineering, mining, geology, metallurgy; Dean ANTONIO GOMES DE ARAUJO.

School of Pharmacy: Rua Costa Sena 171, 35 400-000 Ouro Prêto, MG; f. 1839; courses in pharmacy, nutrition; Dean JOÃO DE MIRANDA CASTRO.

Institute of Human and Social Sciences: Rua do Seminário, 35420-000 Mariana, MG; f. 1979; courses in history, literature; Dean M. M. BRANDÃO.

Institute of Exact and Biological Sciences: Campus Universitario, Morro do Cruzeiro, 35400-000 Ouro Prêto, MG; f. 1982; courses in computer science; Dean MARCONE JAMILSON FREITAS SOUZA.

Institute of Arts and Culture: Rua Corornel Alves 55, 35400-000 Ouro Prêto, MG; f. 1981; Dean ANA MARIA DE ALMEIDA.

UNIVERSIDADE FEDERAL DO PARÁ

Av. Augusto Corrêa s/n, Campus Universitário, Bairro do Guamá, 66075-970 Belém, PA

Telephone: (91) 211-2121
Fax: (91) 211-1734

Founded 1957
Federal control
Academic year: March to December
Language of instruction: Portuguese

Rector: Prof. Dr CRISTOVAM WANDERLEY PICANÇO DINIZ
Vice-Rector: Profa TELMA DE CARVALHO LOBO
Central Library Administrator: MARIA DAS GRAÇAS DA SILVA PENA

Number of professors: 2,179
Number of students: 28,492

Publications: *Cadernos do Centro de Filosofia e Ciências Humanas, MOARA, Ver a Educação, Cadernos de Pós-Graduação em Direito da UFPA, Revista do Tecnológico, Revista do Centro do Ciências Jurídicas, Humanitas, Revista do Centro Sócio-Econômico.*

DIRECTORS

Exact and Natural Sciences Centre: Prof. RENATO BORGES GUERRA
Biology Centre: Profa SETSUKO NORO DOS SANTOS
Philosophy and Human Sciences Centre: Prof. JOSÉ ALVES DE SOUZA JÚNIOR
Arts and Literature Centre: (vacant)
Health Science Centre: Prof. Dr CLÁUDIO JOSÉ DIAS KLAUTAU
Technology Centre: Profa VERA MARIA NOBRE BRÁZ
Socio-Economic Centre: Prof. MARIO NAZARENO NORONHA FARIA E SOUZA
Education Centre: Profa ANA MARIA ORLANDINA TANCREDI CARVALHO
Geosciences Centre: Prof. MARCONDES LIMA DA COSTA
Law Sciences Centre: Prof. JOÃO BATISTA KLAUTAU LEÃO

UNIVERSIDADE ESTADUAL DA PARAÍBA

CP 791, Av. Mar. Floriano Peixoto 718, 58100-001 Campina Grande, PB

Telephone: (83) 341-3300
Telex: (83) 3226
Fax: (83) 341-4509

Founded 1966
Municipal control
Language of instruction: Portuguese
Academic year: March to December

Rector: ITAN PEREIRA DA SILVA
Vice-Rector: JOSÉ BENJAMIN PEREIRA FILHO
General Secretary: CLEÓMENES LOIOLA CAMINHA
Librarian: IVONETE ALMEIDA GALDINO

Library of 65,000 vols
Number of teachers: 650
Number of students: 10,000

Publications: *Catálogo Geral* (annually), *Roteiro, Informativo UEPB.*

DIRECTORS

Agricultural College 'Assis Chateaubriand': JOSÉ PAULO DE AMORIM FARIAZ
Faculty of Sciences and Technology: GIVANILDO GONÇALVES DE FARIAS
Faculty of Physical Education: SIDELENE GONSAGA DE MELO
Faculty of Physiotherapy: LÍDIA MARIA ALBUQUERQUE MARQUES
Faculty of Nursing: JOSEFA JOSETE DA SILVA SANTOS
Faculty of Pharmacy and Biology: LUIZA MARIA BARRETO DA SILVEIRA
Faculty of Odontology: CARLTON FERREIRA NÓBREGA
Faculty of Psychology: GUTEMBERG GERMANO BARBOSA
Faculty of Administration and Accounting: FRANCISCO LUIZ DE OLIVEIRA
Faculty of Social Communication: SIMÃO ARRUDA
Faculty of Law: HARRISON ALEXANDRE TARGINO
Faculty of Education, Letters and Social Sciences: ZÉLIA MARIA PEREIRA FERNANDES
Faculty of Social Work: MARIA JOSÉ DA COSTA SILVA
Faculty of Philosophy, Sciences and Letters: TANIA PORPINO MARINHO DO NASCIMENTO
School of Agricultural Engineering, Catolé do Rocha: PEDRO FERREIRA NETO

UNIVERSIDADE FEDERAL DA PARAÍBA

Campus Universitário, 58059-900 João Pessoa, PB

Telephone: (83) 216-7200
Telex: (083) 2187
Fax: (83) 225-1901

Founded 1955
Academic year: March to June, August to December
Language of instruction: Portuguese

Rector: JÁDER NUNES DE OLIVEIRA
Vice-Rector: MARCOS ANTÔNIO GONÇALVES BRASILEIRO
Registrar: SILVIO JOSÉ ROSSI
Librarian: BABINE NEIVA DE G. RIBEIRO

Number of teachers: 2,930
Number of students: 21,758

Publications: *Boletim de Serviços* (monthly), *Relatório Geral, Catálogo de Extensão* (annually), *Catálogo de Graduação, Catálogo de Post-Graduação, Revista CCS* (quarterly).

DIRECTORS

Campus I—João Pessoa: 58059-900 João Pessoa, PB; tel. (83) 216-7200

Health Sciences: ZORAIDE MARGARET BEZERRA LINS
Applied Social Sciences: JOSÉ EDINALDO DE LIMA
Human Sciences, Letters and Arts: MARIA YARA CAMPOS MATOS
Education: ANEDITE ALMEIDA DE FREITAS
Exact and Natural Sciences: BENEDITO ROGÉRIO VASCONCELOS ARAGÃO
Technology: ORLANDO DE CAVALCANTI VILLAR FILHO
Law: MARIA DO LIVRAMENTO BEZERRA

Campus II—Campina Grande: 58109-000 Campina Grande, PB; tel. (83) 310-1463

Sciences and Technology: BENEDITO GUIMARÃES AGUIAR NETO
Human Sciences: MARIA CRISTINA DE MELO MARIN
Biological Sciences and Health: VILMA LÚCIA FONSECA MENDOZA

Campus III—Areia: 58397-000 Areia, PB; tel. (83) 362-2218

Agricultural Sciences: ALBERÍCIO PEREIRA DE ANDRADE

Campus IV—Bananeiras: 58220-000 Bananeiras, PB; tel. (83) 363-2621

Technologist Training Centre: ROBERTO GERMANO COSTA

Campus V—Cajazeiras: 58900-000 Cajazeiras, PB; tel. (83) 531-3046

Teacher Training Centre: JOSÉ MARIA GURGEL

Campus VI—Sousa: 58800-970 Sousa, PB; tel. (83) 521-1363

Law and Social Sciences: MOZART GONÇALVES DA SILVA

Campus VII—Patos: 58700-970 Patos, PB; tel. (83) 421-3397

Veterinary and Rural Technology: JACOB SILVA SOUTO

PONTIFICIA UNIVERSIDADE CATÓLICA DO PARANÁ

Curitiba Campus

Rua Imaculada Conceição 1155: Prado Velho, 80215-901 Curitiba, PR

Telephone: (41) 330-1515
Fax: (41) 332-5588
E-mail: postmaster@pucpr.br

Founded 1959
Private control
Academic year: March to December (two semesters)

Grand Chancellor: PEDRO FEDALTO, Archbishop of Curitiba
Rector: CLEMENTE IVO JULIATTO
Vice-Rector: Dr JOSÉ GERALDO LOPES DE NORONHA
Administrative Pro-Rector: Prof. ARAMIS DEMETERCO
Academic Pro-Rector: SÉRGIO RICARDO SCHNEIDER
Community Pro-Rector: ADILSON MORAES SEIXAS
Pro-Rector for Planning and Development: JOÃO OLEYNIK
Pro-Rector for Graduate Studies, Research and Extension Services: ROBERTO BORGES FRANÇA
Registrar: OSVALDO ULYSSES MAZAY
Library Director: Profa NEUZA APARECIDA RAMOS

Number of teachers: 1,065
Number of students: 16,028

Publications: *Estudos de Biologia* (2 a year), *Psicologia Argumento* (annually), *Vida Universitária* (monthly), *Revista de Filosofia* (annually), *Revista Acadêmica* (2 a year), *Revista de Fisioterapia* (2 a year), *Revista 'Círculo de Estudos'* (annually), *Estudos Jurídicos* (annually), *PUC-PR em Dados* (annually).

DEANS

Centre for Humanities and Theological Studies: MARIA IGNEZ MARINS
Centre for Judicial and Social Sciences: ALVACIR ALFREDO NICZ
Centre for Exact and Technological Sciences: FLÁVIO BORTOLOZZI
Centre for Biological and Health Sciences: ALBERTO ACCIOLY VEIGA
Centre for Agronomy and Environmental Sciences: SYLVIO PELLICO NETO
Centre of Applied Social Sciences: SÉRGIO PEREIRA LOBO

HEADS OF DEPARTMENTS

Education: PATRÍCIA LUPION TORRES
Philosophy: SÉRGIO DE ANGELIS
Theology: ANTÔNIO QUIRINO DE OLIVEIRA
Physical Education: FANI TEREZINHA LOPES VIERA
Languages: MARIA IGNEZ MARINS
Law: ALVACIR ALFREDO NICZ
Social Sciences: MARIA OLGA MATTAR
Social Work: MARIA BERNADETE M. P. RODRIGO
Social Communication: CELINA DO ROCIO PAZ ALVETTI
Mathematics: ROMUALDO WANDRESEN
Industrial Design: JOSÉ LUIZ CASELLA
Civil Engineering: LUIS RUSSO NETO
Architecture and Town Planning: SILVIANE ROSI MÜLLER
Computer Science: CELSO ANTÔNIO ALVES KAESTNER

Computer Engineering: Marco Antônio Masoller Eleutério
Mechanical Engineering: Ronaldo Mayrhofer
Electrical Engineering: Júlio César Nievola
Management Information Systems (Bachelor Degree): Manoel Camilo de Oliveira Penna Neto
Industrial Chemistry and Chemical Engineering: Alsedo Leprevost
Psychology: Regina Celina Cruz
Nursing: Maria Leda Vieira
Medicine: Alberto Accioly Veiga
Dentistry: Monir Tacla
Physiotherapy: Jorge Tamaki
Speech Therapy and Audiology: Leomara de Araújo B. G. dos Santos
Biology: Rubens Viana
Pharmacy and Biochemistry: Antonio Carlos Mira
Food Engineering: Álvaro César C. do Amarante
Religious Studies: Dagmar Haj Mussi
Brazilian Studies and Citizenship: Antonio Celso Mendes

ATTACHED INSTITUTES

Institute of Psychology: Dir Marilita Bertassoni da Silva.

Institute of Speech Therapy and Audiology: Dir Profa Elaine Abreu Setim.

Institute of Research and Technical Studies: Dir Cesar Zanchi Daher.

Institute of Environmental Health: Dir Carlos Mello Garcias.

Model Law Office: Dir Profa Eloete Camilli Oliveira.

Graduate Institute of Business Administration: Dir Marcos Mueller Schlemm.

São José dos Pinhais Campus

Seminário dos Sagrados Corações, BR 376, Km 14, 83010-500 São José dos Pinhais, Paraná

Telephone: (41) 283-4434
Fax: (41) 382-1223
Director: Prof. Sergio Pereira Lobo

HEADS OF DEPARTMENTS

Accounting: Orivaldo João Busarelo
Law: Noel Sanways
Business Administration: Sérgio Lobo
Economics: Carlos Alberto Reinchen de Souza Miranda
Religious Studies: Zélia Kopacheski
Management Information Systems: Cláudio de Oliveira
Sports and Recreation: Vilma Sueli Jentsch
Agronomy: Sylvio Pellico Neto
Veterinary Medicine: Dorei Brandão
Zootechnics: Sílvio Degasperi
Brazilian Studies and Citizenship: Valério Hoerner

UNIVERSIDADE FEDERAL DO PARANÁ

Rua 15 de Novembro 1299, CP 441, 80060-000 Curitiba, PR

Telephone: (41) 362-3038
Telex: (41) 5100
Fax: (41) 264-2243

Founded 1912

Rector: José Henrique de Faria
Vice-Rector: Mário Portugal Pederneiras
Chief Administrative Officer: Benedito Gomes Barboza
Librarian: Regina Maria de Campos Rocha

Libraries: see Libraries
Number of teachers: 1,888
Number of students: 23,165

Publications: *Acta Biológica Paranaense, Boletim Administrativo, Nerítica, Floresta, Letras,* etc.

DIRECTORS

Agriculture: Eleutério Dallazem
Biological Sciences: Waldemiro Gremski
Exact Sciences: Antonio José de Nardi
Humanities, Letters and Arts: Cesar Augusto Ramos
Health Sciences: José Roberto Carazzani
Applied Social Sciences: Zaki Akel Sobrinho
Education: Suely Carta Cardoso
Technology: José Alfredo Brenner
Law: Joaquim Roberto Munhoz de Mello

UNIVERSIDADE DE PASSO FUNDO

Bairro São José, CP 611, 99001-970 Passo Fundo, RS

Telephone: (54) 316-8103
Fax: (54) 311-1307

Founded 1968
Private control
Academic year: March to November (two semesters)

Rector: Elydo Alcides Guareschi
Academic Vice-Rector: Lorivan Fisch de Figueiredo
Administrative Vice-Rector: Prof. Ilmo Santos
Research and Extension Vice-Rector: Tania M. K. Rösing
Registrar: Prof. Luis de Cesaro
Librarian: Wlademir Pinto

Number of teachers: 839
Number of students: 11,409

Publications: Academic Guide, *Jornal Universitário,* faculty reviews.

DIRECTORS

School of Education: Prof. Selina Maria Dal Moro
School of Physical Education: Prof. Carlos Ricardo Schlemmer
School of Economics and Administration: Prof. Acioly Rösing
School of Law: Prof. Luiz J. Nogueira de Azevedo
School of Engineering: Prof. Luiz Fernando Prestes
School of Agronomy: Prof. Walter Boller
School of Dentistry: Prof. Rui Getúlio Soares
School of Medicine: Prof. Luiz Sérgio de Moura Fragomeni
Institute of Philosophy and Humanities: Prof. Telisa Graeff
Institute of Biological Sciences: Prof. Lorena Geib
Institute of Exact and Geosciences: Prof. Geraldo Hallwass
Institute of Arts: Profa Maria C. de Britto Ramos

UNIVERSIDADE CATÓLICA DE PELOTAS

Rua Félix da Cunha 412, CP 402, 96010-000 Pelotas, RS

Telephone: (532) 22-1555
Fax: (532) 25-3195
E-mail: ucpel@phoenix.ucpel.tche.br

Founded 1960
Private control
Language of instruction: Portuguese
Academic year: March to June, August to November

Chancellor: Dom Jayme Henrique Chemello
Rector: Prof. Teófilo Alves Galvão
Pro-Rectors: Prof. Osmar Schaefer (Academic), Prof. Rolf Hilmar Lichtnow (Administrative)
Librarian: Cristiane de Freitas Chim Yser

Library of 65,000 vols
Number of teachers: 530
Number of students: 6,360

DIRECTORS

School of Engineering and Architecture: Prof. Paulo Guterres
School of Computer Science: Prof. Francisco de Paula Marques Rodrigues
School of Psychology: Prof. Ricardo Azevedo da Silva
School of Medicine: Profa Dra Elizabeth Zerwes
School of Pharmacy and Biochemistry: Profa Maria Regina Soares Lopes
School of Education: Profa Clarisse Siqueira Coelho
School of Social Services: Profa Adelina Baldissera
School of Social Communication: Prof. Cilon Dias Rodriguez
School of Law: Prof. Rubens Bellora
School of Economics and Business: Prof. Ademir Pinto Geissler

ATTACHED INSTITUTES

Higher Institute of Philosophy: Dir Prof. Egon Afonso Michels
Higher Institute of Theology: Dir Pe. Danilo Silveira Porto
Institute of Religious Culture: Dir Pe. Flávio Martinez de Oliveira

UNIVERSIDADE FEDERAL DE PELOTAS

Campus Universitário, 96010-900 Pelotas, RS

Telephone: 21-20-33, 21-06-64
Fax 21-50-23

Founded 1883 as Universidade Federal Rural do Rio Grande do Sul; present name 1969

Rector: Prof. Antonio Cesar Gonçalves Borges
Vice-Rector: Prof. Daniel Souza Soares Rassier
Pro-Rectors: Flávio Chevarria Nogueira (Administrative), Antonio Leonel da Silva Cunha (Development Planning), Profa Inguelore Scheunemann de Souza (Graduates), Prof. Francisco Elifalete Xavier (Culture), Prof. Alci Enimar Loek (Postgraduates)

Number of teachers: 800
Number of students: 5,500

Publication: *Boletim Administrativo da Reitoria.*

DIRECTORS

Faculty of Agronomy: Prof. José Carlos Fachinello
Faculty of Veterinary Studies: Prof. Alexandre da Rocha Gonçalves
Faculty of Law: Prof. José Luiz Marasco Cavalheiro Leite
Faculty of Dentistry: Prof. Alcebiades Nunes Barbosa
Faculty of Medicine: Prof. Dercio José Zerwes
Faculty of Domestic Science: Profa Maria da Graça Gomes Ramos
School of Physical Education: Prof. Enio Araújo Pereira
Faculty of Education: Prof. Gomercindo Ghiggi
Conservatory of Music: Affonso Celso Costa Júnior
Institute of Letters and Arts: Profa Maria de Lourdes Valente Reyes
Institute of Humanities: Prof. Sidney Gonçalves Vieira
Institute of Physics and Mathematics: Prof. Élio Paulo Zonta
Institute of Chemistry and Geosciences: Prof. Sérgio Luiz dos Santos Nascimento
Institute of Biology: Prof. Tasso Faraco de Azevedo
Institute of Sociology and Politics: Profa Neusa Regina Soares Recondo
Agricultural Technology Team: Prof. Odeli Zanchet
Faculty of Meteorology: Profa Maria Helena de Carvalho

Faculty of Architecture and Planning: Prof. Rogério Gutierrez Filho
Faculty of Nutrition: Profa Marilda Borges Neutzling
Faculty of Agricultural Engineering: Prof. Mário José Milman
Faculty of Nursing and Obstetrics: Profa Elodi dos Santos

UNIVERSIDADE CATÓLICA DE PERNAMBUCO

Rua do Príncipe 526, Boa Vista, 50050-900 Recife, PE

Telephone: (81) 216-4000
Fax: (81) 231-1842

Founded 1951
Private control
Academic year: February to December (two semesters)

Chancellor: Ferdinand Azevedo
Rector: Fr Theodoro Paulo Severino Peters
Pro-Rectors: Erhard Cholewa (Academic), Altamir Soares de Paula (Administrative), Walter James Conlan Júnior (Community Relations)
Registrar: Ferdinando Pereira Rêgo
Librarian: Rosilda Miranda da Silva

Number of teachers: 632
Number of students: 13,326

Publication: *Symposium.*

DEANS

Centre for Social Sciences: Profa Miriam de Sá Pereira
Centre for Sciences and Technology: Prof. Reginaldo Lourenço da Silva
Centre for Theology and Human Sciences: Prof. Junot Cornélio Matos

HEADS OF DEPARTMENTS

Centre for Theology and Human Sciences:
- Department of Theology: Fr Jacques Trudel
- Department of Philosophy: Prof. Karl-Heinz Efken
- Department of Education: Profa Maria Lúcia Cavalcanti Galindo
- Department of Psychology: Profa Edilene Freire de Queiroz
- Department of Language and Literature: Profa Rachel de Hollanda Costa
- Department of History: Profa Maria José Pinheiro

Centre for Sciences and Technology:
- Department of Mathematics: Prof. Nivaldo Pinheiro da Silva
- Department of Physics: Prof. Augusto Otávio Galvão de Lima
- Department of Chemistry: Prof. Antônio Helder Parente
- Department of Statistics and Information Science: Prof. Jessé Gomes de Oliveira
- Department of Engineering: Prof. Jarbas de Souza Corrêa
- Department of Biology: Prof. Bento Ferreira de Carvalho

Centre for Social Sciences:
- Department of Law: Prof. João Poluca de Araújo
- Department of Sociology: Profa Davina Maria Guimarães Barros
- Department of Economics and Administration: Prof. Cícero Barbosa da Silva Filho
- Department of Social Communication: Prof. Carlos Augusto Pacheco Benevides
- Department of Geography: Prof. Luiz Ernani de Saboia Campos

UNIVERSIDADE FEDERAL DE PERNAMBUCO

Av. Prof. Moraes Rego 1235, Cidade Universitária, 50670-901 Recife, PE

Telephone: (81) 271-8000
Fax: (81) 271-8029

Founded 1946
Academic year: March to December

Rector: Prof. Mozart Neves Ramos
Pro-Rector for Research and Postgraduate Affairs: Prof. Paulo Roberto Freire Cunha
Pro-Rector for Planning and General Co-ordination: Prof. Hermino Ramos de Souza
Pro-Rector for Administration: Prof. José Francisco Ribeiro Filho
Pro-Rector for Community Affairs: Prof. Washington Luiz Martins da Silva
Pro-Rector for Cultural Affairs and Scientific Exchange: Profa Célia Maria Medicis Maranhão Campos
Pro-Rector for Academic Affairs: Prof. Josenildo dos Santos

Library: see Libraries
Number of teachers: 1,654
Number of students: 16,123

Publication: *Boletim Oficial.*

DIRECTORS OF CENTRES AND HEADS OF DEPARTMENTS

Centre of Arts and Communication: Dir Profa Gilda Maria Lins de Araújo
- Art Theory and Artistic Expression: Prof. João Denys Araújo Leite
- Architecture and City Planning: Prof. Antenor Vieira de Melo Filho
- Social Communication: Prof. Luiz Anastácio Momesso
- Letters: Prof. Lourival de Holanda Barros
- Design: Profa Iolanda Andrade Campos Almeida
- Librarianship: Profa Sílvia Cortez Silva
- Music: Prof. Edson Magalhães Bandeira de Mello

Centre of Exact and Natural Sciences: Dir Prof. Cid Bartolomeu de Araújo
- Physics: Prof. Celso Pinto de Melo
- Mathematics: Prof. Sóstenes Lins
- Statistics: Profa Jacira G. Carvalho da Rocha
- Chemistry: Prof. Alfredo Mayall Simas
- Computing: Profa Ana Carolina Brandão Salgado

Centre of Biological Sciences: Dir Profa Ana Maria Santos Cabral
- Anatomy: Prof. Alexandre M. Bittencourt
- Histology and Embryology: Profa Maria Odete de Vasconcelos
- Biochemistry: Profa Elizabeth Alves de Oliveira
- Biophysics and Radiobiology: Prof. Romildo de Albuquerque Nogueira
- Physiology and Pharmacology: Profa Maria Luiza Martins Alessio
- Genetics: Prof. Paulo Paes de Andrade
- Mycology: Profa Elza Áurea de Luna A. Lima
- Biology of Species: Profa Angela Maria Isidro de Farias
- Antibiotics: Profa Silene Carneiro do Nascimento
- Botany: Prof. José Vicente da Silva

Centre of Philosophy and Humanities: Dir Prof. Antonio Jorge de Siqueira
- Philosophy: Profa Solange Araújo de França
- History: Prof. Marc Jay Hoffnagel
- Social Sciences: Profa Maria Auxiliadora Ferraz de Sá
- Psychology: Profa Elizabete Maranhão de Miranda
- Geography: Profa Aldemir Dantas Barbosa

Education Centre: Dir Prof. João Francisco de Souza
- Socio-Philosophic Bases of Education: Prof. Ricardo Swain Aléssio
- Psychology and Educational Orientation: Profa Cleide Peixoto de Oliveira
- School Administration and Educational Planning: Prof. Jorge Expedito de Gusmão Lopes
- Teaching Methods and Techniques: Profa Telma Santa Clara Cordeiro

Centre of Applied Social Sciences: Dir Profa Anita Aline Albuquerque Costa
- Administrative Sciences: Prof. Pedro Lincoln Carneiro Leão de Mattos
- Accountancy: Prof Gutembergue Leal de Mesquita
- Economics: Prof. Augusto César Santos
- Social Service: Profa Miriam Damasceno Padilha

Centre of Health Sciences: Dir Prof. Gilson Edmar Gonçalves da Silva
- Mother and Child Health: Prof. João Sabino de Lima Pinho Neto
- Clinical Medicine: Prof. Ênio Torreão Soares Castellar
- Surgery: Prof. Renato Dornelas Câmara Neto
- Tropical Medicine: Profa Vera Magalhães
- Neuro-Psychiatry: Prof. José Francisco de Albuquerque
- Pathology: Prof. Nicodemos Teles de Pontes Filho
- Social Medicine: Prof. Rogerio Dubosselard Zimmermann
- Pharmacy: Profa Miracy Muniz de Albuquerque
- Clinical and Preventive Odontology: Prof. Ranilson Amorim
- Prosthesis and Orofacial Surgery: Prof. Adolfo José Cabral
- Nutrition: Profa Florisbela de Arruda C. S. Campos
- Nursing: Profa Vânia Pinheiro Ramos
- Physical Education: Prof. Nairton Sakur de Azevedo
- Physiotherapy and Occupational Therapy: Profa Armèle Dornelas de Andrade

Technology Centre: Dir Prof. Armaro Henrique Pessoa Lins
- Cartographical Engineering: Prof. Francisco Jaime Bezerra Mendonça
- Civil Engineering: Prof. Manoel Sylvio Carneiro Campello Netto
- Electrical Engineering and Potential Systems: Prof. Elto Marques Luna
- Mechanical Engineering: Prof. José Laurêncio Accioly Filho
- Mining Engineering: Prof. José carlos da Silva Oliveira
- Chemical Engineering and Industrial Chemistry: Prof. Augusto Knoechelmann
- Geology: Prof. Edmilson Santos de Lima
- Nuclear Energy: Prof. Carlos Alberto Brayner de Oliveira Lira
- Oceanography: Prof. Fernando Antonio do Nascimento Feitosa
- Electronics and Systems: Prof. Mauro Rodrigues dos Santos

Centre of Juridical Sciences (Faculty of Law): Dir Prof. José Souto Maior Borges
- General and Procedural Law: Profa Dalva Rodrigues Bezerra de Almeida
- Public Law: Prof. Ricardo José da Costa Pinto Neto
- General Theory of Law and Private Law: Profa Vera Regina de Cravo Barros Della Santa

UNIVERSIDADE FEDERAL RURAL DE PERNAMBUCO

CP 2071, Rua D. Manuel de Medeiros s/n, Dois Irmãos, 52171-900 Recife, PE

Telephone: (81) 441-2600
Telex: (81) 1195

Founded 1912

Federal control
Language of instruction: Portuguese

Rector: Emídio Cantídio de Oliveira Filho
Vice-Rector: Tânia Maria Muniz de Arruda Falcão
Administrative Officer: Walderi Ribeiro

Librarian: NANCI DE OLIVEIRA TOLEDO

Library of 42,000 vols
Number of teachers: 398
Number of students: 5,175

Publications: *Caderno Ômega* (irregular), *Anais* (annually).

HEADS OF DEPARTMENTS

Agronomy: CLODOALDO JOSÉ DA ANUNCIAÇÃO FILHO
Veterinary Medicine: TOMOE NODA SAUKAS
Animal Husbandry: LUIZ GONZAGA DA PAZ
Fishery: ISABEL CRISTINA DE SÁ MARINHO
Education: FRANCISCO FERREIRA DA ROCHA
Domestic Science: CARLA SUELY VITA BEZERRA SANTIAGO
Physics and Mathematics: ALEXANDRE JOSÉ DE MEDEIROS
Chemistry: MARTHA MARIA ANDRADE PESSOA
Biology: MARCELO DE ATAÍDE SILVA
Morphology: ARMANDO JOSÉ RIBEIRO SAMICO
Letters and Humanities: EXPEDITO BANDEIRA DE ARAÚJO
Rural Technology: CLARIVALDO GERMANO DA COSTA
'Dom Agostinho Ikas' Grade 2 College: RICARDO WAGNER DE GUIMARÃES ROCHA

FUNDAÇÃO UNIVERSIDADE DE PERNAMBUCO

Av. Agamenon Magalhães, s/n, Santo Amaro, 50100-010 Recife, PE

Telephone: (81) 421-3111
Telex: (081) 2310
Fax: (81) 224-4623

Founded 1965

President: Prof. HINDENBURG T. LEMOS
Vice-President: Prof. GUSTAVO A. M. TRINDADE HENRIQUES
Rector: Prof. JÚLIO FERNANDO PESSOA CORREIA
Vice-Rector: Prof. EMANUEL DIAS DE OLIVEIRA E SILVA
Administrative Pro-Rector: Prof. ANDRÉ JORGE DE BARROS E SILVA
Pro-Rector (Postgraduate, Research and Extension): Prof. ANTONIO GILDO PAES GALINDO
Pro-Rector (Planning): Prof. CARLOS MAGNO PADILHA CURSINO
Pro-Rector (Undergraduates): Prof. VALDEMAR VIEIRA DE MELO
Librarian: LÍDIA PONTUAL

Library of 8,000 vols, 8,302 periodicals (390 titles)
Number of teachers: 879
Number of students: 10,968 undergraduate, 350 postgraduate, 610 extension

DIRECTORS

Faculty of Medicine: Prof. JOSÉ GUIDO CORREIA DE ARAÚJO
Faculty of Administrative Sciences: Prof. ARANDI MACIEL CAMPELO
Faculty of Dentistry: Prof. JOSÉ RICARDO DIAS PEREIRA
School of Nursing: Profa KÁTIA REJANE VERGUEIRO CÉSAR
School of Physical Education: Prof. RENATO MEDEIROS DE MORAES
Polytechnic: Prof. ARMANDO CARNEIRO P. REGO FILHO
Institute of Biological Sciences: Prof. CARLOS ROBERTO DA SILVA
Oswaldo Cruz University Hospital: Dr ÊNIO LUSTOSA CANTARELLI
Amaury de Medeiros Integrated Health Centre: Dr ARINALDO VASCONCELOS DE ALENCAR
Faculty of Teacher Training (in Garanhuns): Prof. LUIZ TENÓRIO DE CARVALHO
Faculty of Teacher Training (in Petrolina): Prof. JOAQUIM SILVA E SANTANA
Faculty of Teacher Training (in Nazaré da Mata): Prof. LUIZ INTERAMINENSE

UNIVERSIDADE CATÓLICA DE PETRÓPOLIS

Rua Benjamin Constant 213, Centro, CP 90944, 25621-970 Petrópolis, RJ

Telephone: (24) 237-5062
Fax: (24) 242-7747
E-mail: eitoria@risc.ucp.br

Founded 1961
Private control
Academic year: February to June, August to December

Rector: Profa MARIA DA GLÓRIA RANGEL SAMPAIO FERNANDES
Vice-Rector: Prof. Dr GETÚLIO CHEHAB
Chief Administrative Officer: Prof. PEDRO RUBENS PANTOLA DE CARVALHO
Registrar: LUIZ HERIQUE SCHAEFFER
Librarian: MARIA DAS NEVES FRANCA LEITE KRÜGER

Number of teachers: 266
Number of students: 3,390

Publications: *Informativo UCP* (6 a year), *Revista UCP* (3 a year) and *O Communitário* (monthly).

DIRECTORS

Faculty of Law: Prof. LINDOLPHO DE MORAES MARINHO
Faculty of Economics, Accounting and Administration: Prof. CELSO PERMÍNIO SCHIMID
Faculty of Education: Profa SANDRA TEREZA LA CAVA DE ALMEIDA AMADO
School of Engineering: Prof. RICARDO GRECHI PACHECO
School of Rehabilitation: Prof. GERSON DE AGUIAR LOUREIRO
Institute of Theology, Philosophy and Human Science: Prof. ALFREDO AUGUSTO GARCIA QUESADA
Institute of Exact and Natural Sciences: Prof. GUILHERME CRISTÓVÃO NICODEMUS
Institute of Arts and Communication: Profa RUTH M. RANGEL SAMPAIO FERNANDES
Rehabilitation School: Prof. GERSON DE AGUIAR LOUREIRO

UNIVERSIDADE FEDERAL DO PIAUÍ

Campus Universitário, Bairro Ininga, 64050 Teresina, PI

Telephone: (86) 232-1212
Telex: (86) 2271
Fax: (86) 232-2812

Founded 1968
Controlled by the Fundação Universidade Federal do Piauí
Academic year: March to June, August to November

Rector: CHARLES CARVALHO CAMILO DA SILVEIRA
Vice-Rector: (vacant)
Administrative Director: FRANCISCO JOACY SAMPAIO
Librarian: MARGARETH DE LUCENA MARTINS LIMA

Library of 88,617 vols
Number of teachers: 1,104
Number of students: 11,612

Publication: *Notícias da FUFPI* (monthly).

DIRECTORS

Health Sciences: NATHAN PORTELLA NUNES
Natural Sciences: ANTONIO MACEDO SANTANA
Human Sciences and Letters: JOSÉ DE RIBAMAR FREITAS
Educational Sciences: MARIANO DA SILVA NETO
Technology: RAFAEL V. DO REGO MONTEIRO
Agrarian Sciences: ANTONIO M. G. E ALMENDRA CASTELO BRANCO FILHO

HEADS OF DEPARTMENTS

Health Sciences:
- Specialized Medicine: WILTON MENDES DA SILVA
- Community Medicine: ANTONIO J. CASTRO AGUIAR
- General Clinic: ANTÔNIO DE DEUS FILHO
- Pathological and Clinical Dentistry: JOSÉ RESENDE LEITE
- Restorative Dentistry: CANDIDA FORTES DA COSTA MENESES
- Nursing: MARIA HELENA BARROS DE ARAÚJO LUZ
- Physical Education: CONRADO NOGUEIRA BARROS
- Mother and Child Care: TERESINHA DAS GRAÇAS DE OLIVEIRA FORTES

Natural Sciences:
- Mathematics: MARIO LUCIO DA COSTA FERREIRA
- Physics: MÔNICA M. MACHADA R. N. CASTRO
- Chemistry: JOSÉ A. DANTAS LAGES
- Biology: ROSA MARIA DA SILVA ARAÚJO
- Biomedical Sciences: ANA ZÉLIA CORREIA L. C. BRANCO

Human Sciences and Letters:
- Law: PEDRO DE ALCÂNTARA FERREIRA TEIXEIRA
- Social Sciences: MAURINO MEDEIROS DE SANTANA
- Letters: CATARINA DE SENA S. MENDES DA COSTA
- Geography and History: MARIA DO SOCORRO ALMEIDA WAQUIM
- Philosophy: FRANCISCA MENDES DE SOUSA
- Administration and Economics: PRETEXTATO S. Q. GOMES DE OLIVEIRA MELLO

Educational Sciences:
- Educational Foundations: CONCEIÇÃO DE MARIA BOAVISTA DE OLIVEIRA
- Methods and Techniques of Teaching: LEONTINA P. LOPES DE MENDONÇA
- Practical Arts: MARIA DE JESUS SILVA
- Artistic Education: MÁRCIA ALVES SEMENTE

Technology:
- Civil Construction: AMAURI RIBEIRO BARBOSA
- Structures: MARIA DE LOURDES TEIXEIRA MOREIRA
- Transportation: ANTÔNIO DE ABREU LOPES
- Hydrology and Applied Geology: JOSE GERALDO DE OLIVEIRA FERRO

Agrarian Sciences:
- Agricultural Engineering and Soil Science: ADEODATO ARI CAVALCANTE SALVIANO
- Phytotechnology: FRANCISCO RODRIGUES LEAL
- Zootechnology: MARIA DE NAZARÉ BONA DE ALENCAR ARARIPE
- Agricultural Planning and Policy: VICENTE PAULO GOMES
- Veterinary Morphology: MARIA ACELINA MARTINS DE CARVALHO
- Veterinary and Surgery Clinic: ANTONIO FRANCISCO DE SOUSA

UNIVERSIDADE METODISTA DE PIRACICABA

Rua Rangel Pestana 762, CP 68, 13400-901 Piracicaba, SP

Telephone: (19) 422-1515
Fax: (19) 422-2500
E-mail: unimep@unimep.br

Founded 1975
Private control
Language of instruction: Portuguese
Academic year: March to June, August to December

President: ALMIR DE SOUZA MAIA
Administrative Vice-President: GUSTAVO JACQUES DIAS ALVIM
Academic Vice-President: ELY ESER BARRETO CÉSAR
Registrar: IRENE DE CARVALHO MACÊDO JARDIM

Librarian: Regina Fraceto

Library of 146,000 vols

Number of teachers: 550

Number of students: 12,000

Publications: *Revista de Ciência e Tecnologia, Impulso, Revista Brasileira de Educação Especial.*

DIRECTORS

Centre of Applied Sciences: Prof. Dorgival Henrique

Centre of Biological and Health Sciences: Profa Gislaine Cecília de Oliveira Cerveny

Centre of Exact Sciences: Prof. Waldo Luis de Lucca

Centre of Philosophy and Theology: Prof. Sérgio Marcus Pinto Lopes

Centre of Human Sciences: Profa Maria Cecília Carareto Ferreira

Centre of Technology: Prof. José Antônio Arantes Salles

Graduate Studies: Co-ordinator: Prof. Davi Ferreira Barros

UNIVERSIDADE ESTADUAL DE PONTA GROSSA

Praça Santos Andrade s/n, CP 992-993, 84010 Ponta Grossa, PR

Telephone: (422) 25-2121

Telex: (422) 242

Fax: (422) 23-7708

Founded 1970

Academic year: March to June, August to November

Rector: João Carlos Gomes

Vice-Rector: Roberto Frederico Merhy

Pro-Rectors: Ireneu Czepula (Administrative Affairs), Carlos Luciano Sant'Ana Vargas (Undergraduates), Leide Mara Schmidt (Research and Post-Graduates), Wolfgang João Meyer (Extension and Cultural Affairs)

Librarian: Maria E. Madalosso Ramos

Number of teachers: 597

Number of students: 6,929

Publications: *Revista Uniletras, Catálogo Geral, Cadernos Universitários, CAC Informativo, Relatório de Atividades, UEPG.*

DIRECTORS

Sector of Applied Social Sciences: Prof. Nelson Osternack Postiglione

Sector of Exact and Natural Sciences: Prof. José Carlos Borsato

Sector of Letters and Human Sciences: Prof. Lauro Franchin

Sector of Biological Sciences and Health: Prof. Carlos Henrique Franke

Sector of Agriculture Science and Technology: Prof. Altair Justino

HEADS OF DEPARTMENTS

Mathematics and Statistics: Prof. José Dárcio Glapinski

Physics: Prof. Cirineu Foltran

Chemistry: Jesuan Henrique Ruppel

Geosciences: Eraldo Medeiros

Engineering: Italo Sérgio Grande

Phytotechnology: Áurea Tomoko Matsumoto

Zootechnics and Food Technology: Maria Aparecida da Fonseca Martins

Computer Science: Paulo Sérgio Lopes de Souza

General Biology: Marco Antonio Jimenes Basso

Odontology: Zeno Baroncini Filho

Pharmaceutical Sciences: Profa Mirian Schwab

Clinical and Toxicological Analysis: Prof. Paulo Roberto Favero

Education: Ninfa Merli Zambrycki Peltack

Economics: Edu de Oliveira

Administration: Nadir Laidane

Accounting: Diva Brecailo Abib

Law: Adelângela de Arruda Moura

History: Hélcio de Oliveira Ladeira

Modern Foreign Languages: Jeane Silvane Eckert

Vernacular Languages (Languages and Corresponding Literatures): Norberto Jacob Ceccato

Teaching Methods: Hermínia Bugeste Marinho

Social Service: Liza Mass

Physical Education: Prof. Fausi Aziz Chagury

Communication: Edgard Cesar Melech

Soil Science and Agricultural Engineering: Valter Schultz

ATTACHED INSTITUTE

Agricultural College 'Augusto Ribas': Rua Nabuco de Araújo s/n; Dir Rolf Guenther Hatschbach Loose.

FUNDAÇÃO UNIVERSIDADE DO RIO GRANDE

Rua Eng. Alfredo Huch 475, CP 474, 96201-900 Rio Grande, RS

Telephone: (532) 329900

Fax: (532) 323346

Founded 1969

State control

Language of instruction: Portuguese

Academic year: March to November

Rector: Prof. Carlos Rodolfo Brandão Hartmann

Vice-Rector: Prof. Vicente Mariano Pias

Chief Administrative Officer: Eng. Carlos Kalikowski Weska

Librarian: Maria da Conceição de Lima Hohmann

Library of 75,000 vols

Number of teachers: 647

Number of students: 4,722

HEADS OF DEPARTMENTS

Mathematics: Prof. Nélson Lopes Duarte Filho

Physics: Prof. Carlos Alberto Eiras Garcia

Chemistry: Prof. Sérgio Mendonça Giesta

Geosciences: Prof. Helem Maria Vieira

Literature and Arts: Prof. Cláudio Gabiatti

Economics: Prof. José Vanderlei Silva Borba

Juridical Sciences: Prof. João Moreno Pomar

Materials and Construction: Prof. Humberto Camargo Piccoli

Librarianship and History: Prof. Henriqueta Graciela Dorfmann de Cuartas

Education and Behavioural Sciences: Profa Dorilda Grolli

Oceanography: Prof. Luiz Carlos Krug

Surgery: Prof. Nilo Cardoso Dora

Mother and Child Health: Prof. Antonio Samir Bertaco

Internal Medicine: Prof. Luis Suarez Halty

Morphology and Biological Sciences: Prof. João Renan Silva de Freitas

Physiology: Prof. Fernando Amarante Silva

Pathology: Prof. Ivo Gomes de Mattos

UNIVERSIDADE FEDERAL DO RIO GRANDE DO NORTE

Campus Universitário s/n, Lagoa Nova, CP 59072-970 Natal, RN

Telephone: (84) 231-1266

Telex: (84) 2296

Fax: (84) 231-4467

Founded 1958

Federal control

Language of instruction: Portuguese

Academic year: March to June, August to November

Rector: Geraldo dos Santos Queiroz

Vice-Rector: João Felipe da Trindade

Librarian: Profa Ligia de Araújo Alvos

Number of teachers: 1,760

Number of students: 16,226

DIRECTORS

Centre for Exact Sciences: Prof. Óton Anselmo de Oliveira

Centre for Humanities, Letters and Arts: Prof. Geraldo de Magela Fernandes

Centre for Technology: Luis Pedro de Araújo

Centre for Applied Social Sciences: Profa Celoa Maria Rocha Ribeiro

Centre for Biological Sciences: Prof. Carlos José de Lima

Centre for Health Sciences: Prof. Carlos dos Santos Fonseca

UNIVERSIDADE REGIONAL DO RIO GRANDE DO NORTE

Rua Almino Afonso 478, Centro, CP 70, 59610-210 Mossoro, RN

Telephone: (84) 321-4997

Fax: (84) 317-4323

Founded 1968

State control

Rector: Prof. José Walter da Fonsêca

Chief Administrative Officer: Profa Mariana Neuman Vidal da Costa

Librarian: Elvira Fernandes de Araújo

Number of teachers: 400

Number of students: 5,300

Publications: *Expressão* (2 a year), *Contexto* (2 a year), *Terra e Sal* (2 a year).

DEANS

Faculty of Economic Science: Prof. Olismar Mederios Lima

Faculty of Social Service: Profa Wálbia Maria Carlos de Araújo Leite

Faculty of Arts: Prof. Gilberto de Oliveira Silva

Faculty of Education: Profa Francisca Glaudionora da Silveira

Faculty of Philosophy and Social Science: Profa Helenita Castro Soares

Faculty of Nursing: Profa Maria José de Carvalho

Faculty of Natural and Physical Science: Prof. Francisco Valdomiro de Morais

Faculty of Law: Profa Maria Hélderi Queiróz Diógenes Negreiros

Faculty of Physical Education: Prof. José Eustáquio de Morais

PONTIFÍCIA UNIVERSIDADE CATÓLICA DO RIO GRANDE DO SUL

Av. Ipiranga 6681, CP 1429, 90619-900 Porto Alegre, RS

Telephone: (51) 320-3501

Fax: (51) 339-1564

E-mail: gabreit@tauros.pucrs.br

Founded 1948

Private control

Academic year: March to December

Chancellor: Dom Altamiro Rossato

President: Prof. Norberto Francisco Rauch

Vice-President: Prof. Dr Joaquim Clotet

Head of Administration: Prof. Paulo Alberto Galia

Librarian: Prof. César Augusto Mazzillo

Number of teachers: 1,892

Number of students: 24,087

Publications: *Veritas* (4 a year), *Letras de Hoje* (4 a year), *Teocomunicação* (4 a year), *Anuário* (1 a year), *Mundo Jovem* (monthly), *Estudos Ibero-Americanos* (2 a year), *Direito e Justiça* (2 a year) *PUCRS Informação* (monthly), *Agenda PUCRS* (monthly), *Odontociência* (2 a year), *Psico* (2 a year), *Educação* (2 a year), *Analise* (2 a year), *Brasil* (2 a year), *Biociências* (2 a year), *Revista de Medicina da PUCRS* (4 a year), *Hífen* (2 a year), *Revista da FAMECOS* (2 a year).

DIRECTORS

Faculty of Education: Prof. ARMANDO LUÍZ BORTOLINI
Faculty of Economics and Political Sciences: Prof. JORGE ALBERTO FRANZONI
Faculty of Law: Prof. CARLOS ALBERTO ALLGAYER
Faculty of Medicine: Prof. Dr LUIZ CARLOS BODANESE
Faculty of Nursing: Prof. BEATRIZ SEBBEN OJEDA
Faculty of Pharmacy: Prof. SÉRGIO DE MEDA LAMB
Faculty of Dentistry: Prof. RAPHAEL ONORINO CARLOS LORO
Faculty of Social Communications Media: Prof. JERÔNIMO CARLOS SANTOS BRAGA
Faculty of Social Service: Prof. JAIRO MELO ARAÚJO
Institute of Psychology: Prof. CELITO FRANCISCO MENGARDA
Institute of Philosophy and Humanities: Prof. THADEU WEBER
Polytechnic School: Prof. EDUARDO GIUGLIANI
Institute of Physics: Prof. ANTÔNIO DIAS NUNES
Institute of Mathematics: Prof. ALAYDES SANT'ANNA BIANCHI
Institute of Chemistry: Prof. TIZIANO DALLA ROSA
Institute of Biosciences: Prof. CLARICE PRADE CARVALHO
Institute of Theology: Prof. Pe. GERALDO LUIZ BORGES HACKMAN
Institute of Literature and Arts: Prof. MAINAR LONGHI
Faculty of Zootechnics, Veterinary Science and Agronomy (Uruguaiana campus): Prof. RUI LUIZ CADORIN
Faculty of Accountancy, Administration and Computer Science (Uruguaiana campus): Prof. CLEITON TAMBELLINI BORGES
Faculty of Philosophy, Sciences and Letters (Uruguaiana campus): Prof. MARIA DE LOURDES SOUZA VILLELA
Institute of Computer Science: Prof. IÁRA TEREZINHA PEREIRA CLÁUDIO
Institute of Aeronautical Sciences: Prof. MARIA REGINA DE MORAES XAUSA
Faculty of Law (Uruguaiana campus): Prof. ROBERTO DURO GICK
Faculty of Architecture and Urbanization: Prof. IVAN GILBERTO BORGES MIZOGUCHI

UNIVERSIDADE FEDERAL DO RIO GRANDE DO SUL

Av. Paulo Gama 110, 90046-900 Porto Alegre, RS

Telephone: (51) 316-3601
Fax: (51) 316-3973
E-mail: relinter@vortex.ufrgs.br

Founded 1934
Federal control
Language of instruction: Portuguese
Academic year: March to November (2 semesters)

Rector: Prof. WRANA MARIA PANIZZI
Vice-Rector: Prof. NILTON RODRIGUES PAIM
Pro-Rectors: JOSÉ CARLOS FERRAZ HENNEMANN (Graduate Studies), MARIA DA GRAÇA KRIEGER (Research), LORENA HOLZMANN DA SILVA (Undergraduate Studies), LUIS ROBERTO DA SILVA (Administration), CHRISTOPH BERNASIUK (General Services), LUIZ FERNANDO COELHO DE SOUZA (Extension), MARIA BEATRIZ GALARRAGA (University Community), MARIA ALICE LAHORGUE (Planning)
Registrar: MARIA RIBEIRO TEODORO
Librarian: VELEIDA ANA BLANK

Number of teachers: 2,212
Number of students: 16,720 undergraduates, 3,923 graduates

DIRECTORS

Faculty of Economic Sciences: OTILIA BEATRIZ KROEFF CARRION
Faculty of Medicine: PEDRO GUS
Faculty of Architecture: ELVAN SILVA
Faculty of Dentistry: JOÃO JORGE DINIZ BARBACHAN
Faculty of Agriculture: SÉRGIO NICOLAIEWSKY
Faculty of Pharmacy: ELFRIDES EVA SCHAPOVAL
Faculty of Veterinary Medicine: CARLOS MARCOS B. DE OLIVEIRA
Faculty of Education: MÉRION CAMPOS BORDAS
Faculty of Librarianship and Communication: RICARDO SCHNEIDERS DA SILVA
Faculty of Law: EDUARDO KROEFF MACHADO CARRION
School of Engineering: JARBAS MILITITSKY
School of Physical Education: ANTONIO CARLOS S. GUIMARÃES
School of Nursing: IDA XAVIER
School of Management: CARLOS ALBERTO M. CALLEGARO
Institute of Arts: SANDRA JAMARDO DANI
Institute of Biological Sciences: ELOY JULIUS GARCIA
Institute of Chemistry: DIMITRIUS SAMIOS
Institute of Food Technology: ISA BEATRIZ NOLL
Institute of Geological Sciences: RICARDO N. AYUP ZOUAIN
Institute of Hydraulic Research: RAUL DORFMAN
Institute of Literature: MARIA CRISTINA L. FERREIRA
Institute of Mathematics: ARON TAITELBAUM
Institute of Philosophy and Humanities: JOSÉ VICENTE TAVARES DOS SANTOS
Institute of Physics: DARCY DILLENBURG
Institute of Computer Science: ROBERTO TOM PRICE
Institute of Basic Health Sciences: MOACIR WAJNER
Institute of Psychology: LUIZ OSVALDO LEITE

ATTACHED RESEARCH CENTRES

Ecology Centre: Dir ALBANO SCHWARTZBOLD
Technology Centre: Dir IVAN GUERRA MACHADO
Biotechnology Centre: Dir JOÃO ANTONIO P. HENRIQUES
Olympic Centre: Dir ALBERTO RAMOS BISCHOFF
Veterinary Hospital: Dir ANDRÉ LUIZ DE ARAÚJO ROCHA
Remote Sensing Centre: Dir RICARDO DUCATTI
Astronomical Laboratory: Dir HORACIO DOTTORI
Experimental Agronomic Station: Dir LUIS CANICIO LOCH
Management Research Centre: Dir LUIZ ANTÔNIO SLONGO
Economics Research Centre: Dir FERNANDO FERRARI FILHO
Coastal and Oceanic Geological Research Centre: Dir IRAN CARLOS S. CORREA
Coastal, Limnological and Oceanic Research Centre: Dir JOÃO CARLOS COIMBRA
Computer Centre: Dir JUSSARA ISSA MUSSE
National Supercomputer Centre: Dir DENISE GRUENE EWALD

PONTIFÍCIA UNIVERSIDADE CATÓLICA DO RIO DE JANEIRO

Rua Marquês de São Vicente 225, Gávea, 22453-900 Rio de Janeiro, RJ

Telephone: (21) 274-4547

Founded 1941
Private control
Academic year: March to July, August to December

Grand Chancellor: His Eminence D. EUGÉNIO DE ARAÚJO SALES, The Cardinal Archbishop of Rio de Janeiro
Registrar: PATRICIA ESPOSEL CARNEIRO DE MESQUITA
Librarian: Dra ELDA MULHOLLAND

Library of 460,000 vols, 5,500 periodicals
Number of teachers: 1,060
Number of students: 13,843

Publication: *Anuário.*

DEANS

Social Sciences Centre: Prof. LUIZ ROBERTO DE AZEVEDO CUNHA
Theology and Human Sciences Centre: Profa ENEIDA DO REGO M. BONFIM
Technical and Scientific Centre: Prof. LUIZ CARLOS SCAVARDA DO CARMO
Medical Centre: Prof. Dr FRANCISCO DE PAULA AMARANTE NETO

HEADS OF DEPARTMENTS

Theology and Human Sciences Centre:
- Theology: Prof. Pe. MANOEL BOUZON GARCIA
- Philosophy: Prof. EDGARD JOSÉ JORGE FILHO
- Education: Profa SONIA KRAMER
- Psychology: Profa MARIA EUCHARES DE SENNA MOTTA
- Literature: Profa LILIANA CABRAL BASTOS
- Arts: Profa VERA DAMAZIO

Social Sciences Centre:
- History and Geography: Prof. MARCO ANTONIO VILLELA PAMPLONA
- Sociology and Political Science: Prof. EDUARDO DE VASCONCELOS RAPOSO
- Economics: Prof. GUSTAVO MAURICIO GONZAGA
- Law: Prof. Dr FRANCISCO MAURO DIAS
- Communications: Profa ANGELUCCIA HARBERT
- Social Work: Profa LUIZA HELENA NUNES ERMEL
- Business Administration: Prof. JOSÉ CARLOS SARDINHA

Technical and Scientific Centre:
- Mathematics: Prof. Pe. PAUL ALEXANDER SCHWEITZER
- Physics: Prof. ENIO FROTA DA SILVEIRA
- Chemistry: Profa ANGELA DE LUCA R. WAGENER
- Computer Science: Prof. ARNDT VON STAA
- Civil Engineering: Prof. PEDRICTO ROCHA FILHO
- Electrical Engineering: Prof. MARCOS AZEVEDO DA SILVEIRA
- Mechanical Engineering: Prof. LUIS FERNANDO ALZUQUIR AZEVEDO
- Metallurgical Engineering: Prof. EDUARDO BROCCHI
- Industrial Engineering: Prof. LEONARDO JUNQUEIRA LUSTOSA

DIRECTORS OF ATTACHED INSTITUTES

Institute of International Relations: Profa SONIA DE CAMARGO
Centre for Telecommunications Research: Prof. LUIZ COSTA DA SILVA
Rio Data Centre (Computer Centre): Prof. JOSÉ RAIMUNDO LOPES DE OLIVEIRA
Dentistry Institute (Post-graduate): Dr RICARDO GUIMARÃES FISCHER
Post-graduate Medical School: Prof. Dr PAULO NIEMEYER FILHO
Technological Institute: Prof. SÉRGIO LEAL BRAGA

UNIVERSIDADE DO ESTADO DO RIO DE JANEIRO

Rua São Francisco Xavier 524, Maracanã, 20550-013 Rio de Janeiro, RJ

Telephone: (21) 587-7100
Fax: (21) 591-4803
E-mail: comuns@uerj.br

Founded 1950
State control
Language of instruction: Portuguese
Academic year: March to December (two semesters)

Chancellor: MARCELLO ALENCAR
Rector: Prof. ANTONIO CELSO ALVES PEREIRA
Vice-Rector: Prof. NILCÉA FREIRE
Pro-Vice-Chancellors: Prof. RICARDO VIEIRALVES DE CASTRO (Graduate), Prof. REINALDO GUIMA-

RÃES (Postgraduate and Research), Profa MARIA THEREZINHA NÓBREGA DA SILVA (Culture and Extension)

General Administrative Director: RUBENS SILVA E SILVA

Librarian: SILVIA MARIA GAGO DA COSTA

Number of teachers: 2,005
Number of students: 17,615

Publications: *Cadernos de Antropologia da Imagem, Geo UERJ, Espaço e Cultura, Qfwfq, Logos, Em Pauta, Revista de Enfermagem da UERJ, Matraga, Revista do Centro de Estudos da Faculdade de Odontologia da UERJ* (all 2 a year).

SECTOR DIRECTORS AND DEANS

Bio-medical Centre: Prof. ELLEN MARCIA PERES
- Faculty of Medicine: Prof. JOSÉ AUGUSTO FERNANDES QUADRA
- Faculty of Dentistry: Prof. MILTON SANTOS JABUR
- Faculty of Nursing: Profa VERA RODRIGUES OLIVEIRA ANDRADE
- Institute of Biology: Prof. ELIZEU FAGUNDES DE CARVALHO
- Institute of Social Medicine: Prof. RICARDO TAVARES
- Institute of Nutrition: Profa MARCIA VERONICA DE S. V. BELLA

Education and Humanities Centre: Prof. JOSÉ RICARDO DA SILVA ROSA
- Faculty of Education: Prof. ISAC JOÃO DE VASCONCELLOS
- Institute of Letters: Prof. CLAUDIO CEZAR HENRIQUES
- Institute of Physical Education and Sport: JOÃO GONZAGA DE OLIVEIRA
- Institute of Psychology: Prof. SOLANGE DE OLIVEIRA SOUTO

Faculty of Social Communication: Prof. RICARDO FERREIRA FREITAS

'Fernando Rodrigues da Silveira' Training College: Profa MARICÉLIA BISPO

Technology and Science Centre: Prof. MAURÍCIO JOSÉ FERRARI REY
- Faculty of Engineering: Prof. NIVAL NUNES DE ALMEIDA
- Institute of Mathematics and Statistics: Profa MARINILZA BRUNO DE CARVALHO
- Institute of Geosciences: Profa ANA LÚCIA TRAVASSOS ROMANO
- Faculty of Physics: Prof. JADER BERNUZZI MARTINS
- Institute of Chemistry: Prof. ILTON JORNADA
- Faculty of Geology: Prof. RUI ALBERTO AZEVEDO DOS SANTOS

Higher School of Industrial Design: Prof. FRANK ANTHONY BARRAL DODD

Social Science Centre: Prof. JOSÉ FLAVIO PESSOA DE BARROS
- Faculty of Law: Prof. ANTONIO CELSO ALVES PEREIRA
- Faculty of Economics: Prof. RALPH MIGUEL ZERKOUVISKY
- Faculty of Administration and Finance: Prof. DOMÊNICO MANDARINO
- Faculty of Social Service: Profa ROSANGELA NAIR DE C. BARBOSA
- Institute of Philosophy and Human Sciences: Prof. LUIZ EDMUNDO TAVARES

UNIVERSIDADE FEDERAL DO RIO DE JANEIRO

Av. Brig. Trompowski s/n, Prédio da Reitoria (2° andar), 21949.900 Rio de Janeiro, RJ

Telephone: (21) 560-7491
Fax: (21) 260-7750
E-mail: scri@reitoria.ufrj.br

Founded 1920
State control

Rector: Prof. PAULO ALCANTARA GOMES

Vice-Rector: Prof. JOSÉ HENRIQUE VILHENA DE PAIVA

Secretary-General: Dr IVAN RODRIGUES DA SILVA

Director of Central Library: MARIZA RUSSO

42 faculty libraries

Number of teachers: 3,580
Number of students: 40,000

Publications: *Anais, Boletim*.

DEANS AND DIRECTORS

Mathematics and Natural Sciences Centre: Prof. MARCO ANTONIO FRANÇA FARIA
- Institute of Physics: Prof. CARLOS ALBERTO ARAGÃO DE CARVALHO FILHO
- Institute of Geosciences: Prof. JORGE SOARES MARQUES
- Institute of Mathematics: Prof. LUIS PAULO VIEIRA BRAGA
- Institute of Chemistry: Prof. ROBERTO MARCHIORI
- Computer Science Centre: Prof. EDUARDO PAES
- Valongo Observatory: Profa HELOÍSA MARIA BOECHAT ROBERTY

Literature and Arts Centre: Prof. CARLOS ANTONIO KALIL TANNUS
- Faculty of Architecture and Town Planning: Profa MARIA ANGELA DIAS ELIAS
- Faculty of Literature: Prof. EDIONE TRINDADE DE AZEVEDO
- School of Fine Arts: Prof. VICTORINO DE OLIVEIRA NETO
- School of Music: Dir Prof. JOSÉ ALVES DA SILVA

Centre of Philosophy and Human Sciences: Prof. CARLOS ALBERTO MESSEDER PEREIRA
- Faculty of Education: Profa MARLENE DE CARVALHO
- School of Communications: Prof. ANDRE DE SOUZA PARENTE
- School of Social Services: Profa MARIA DURVALINA FERNANDES BASTOS
- Institute of Philosophy and Social Sciences: Profa NEYDE THEML
- Institute of Psychology: Profa MARIA INÁCIA D'AVILLA NETTO
- School of Teacher Training: Prof. MOACYR BARRETO DA SILVA JUNIOR

Technology Centre: Prof. OSCAR ACSELRAD
- School of Engineering: Prof. HELOI JOSÉ FERNANDES MOURA
- School of Chemistry: Prof. CARLOS AUGUSTO GUIMARÃES PERLINGEIRO
- Institute of Macromolecules: Prof. AÍLTON DE SOUZA GOMES
- Coordination of Graduate Programmes in Engineering: Prof. SEGEN FARID ESTEFEN

Law and Economic Sciences Centre: Prof. CARLOS LESSA
- Faculty of Law: Prof. AYRTON DA COSTA PAIVA
- Faculty of Business Administration and Accounting: Prof. CARLOS ALBERTO BESSA
- Institute of Economics: Prof. JOÃO CARLOS FERRAZ
- Institute of Research, Regional and Town Planning: Prof. HERMES MAGALHÃES TAVARES
- Graduate School of Business Administration: Prof. AGRÍCOLA DE SOUZA BETHLEM

Health Sciences Centre: Profa VERA LUCIA RABELO DE CASTRO HALFOUN
- Institute of Biomedical Sciences: Prof. ANÍBAL GIL LOPES
- School of Nursing: Profa IVONE EVANGELISTA CABRAL
- Faculty of Pharmacy: Prof. JOSÉ CARLOS DA SILVA LIMA
- Faculty of Medicine: Profa SYLVIA DA SILVEIRA DE MELLO VARGAS
- Institute of Microbiology: Prof. SÉRGIO EDUARDO LONGO FRANCALANZZA
- Institute of Nutrition: Profa REJANE ANDRÉA RAMALHO NUNES DA SILVA
- Faculty of Dentistry: Prof. NÉLIO VICTOR DE OLIVEIRA
- School of Physical Education and Sport: Prof. JOSÉ MAURICIO CAPINASSO
- Institute of Biology: Prof. SERGIO LUIS COSTA BONECKER
- Institute of Biological and Health Sciences: Prof. ANIBAL GIL LOPES
- Institute of Biophysics: Prof. ANTONIO CARLOS CAMPOS DE CARVALHO
- Institute of Gynaecology: Prof. PASCHOAL MARTINI SIMÕES
- Institute of Neurology: Prof. GIANNI MAURELIO TEMPONI
- Institute of Psychiatry: Prof. JOÃO FERREIRA DA SILVA FILHO
- Institute of Child Care and Education: Prof. LUÍS AFONSO HENRIQUE MARIZ
- Institute of Thoracic Diseases: Prof. ALFREDO RISSON PEYNEAU
- Maternity School Hospital: Prof. JOFFRE AMIM JUNIOR
- Clementino Fraga Filho University Hospital: Prof. AMANCIO PAULINO
- São Francisco de Assis School Hospital: Profa SONIA REGINA CARVALHAL GOMES
- Technology Education Institute for Health: Profa ELIANA CLÁUDIA DE OTERO RIBEIRO
- Institute of Natural Product Research: Prof. ANTONIO JORGE RIBEIRO DA SILVA
- Community Health Study Centre: Profa DIANA MAUL DE CARVALHO

Forum for Science and Culture: Profa MYRIAN DAVELSBERG

UNIVERSIDADE FEDERAL RURAL DO RIO DE JANEIRO

Km. 47, Antiga Rio São Paulo, 23851-970 Seropédica, RJ

Telephone: (55-021) 682-1210
Telex: 021-34411
Fax: (21) 682-1220

Founded 1910 as Escola Superior de Agronomia e Medicina Veterinária
Federal control
Language of instruction: Portuguese
Academic year: March to June, August to December (two semesters)

Rector: MANLIO SILVESTRE FERNANDES
Vice-Rector: JOSÉ CARLOS NETTO FERREIRA
Chief Administrative Officer: DAYSE SENNA DE SOUZA CARDOSO
Librarian: VERA LUCIA RATTON FIGUEIREDO

Library of 47,898 vols

Number of teachers: 619
Number of students: 4,035

Publications: *Revista Universidade Rural—Ciências da Vida* series (2 a year), *Ciências Humanas* series (2 a year), *Ciências Exatas e da Terra* series (2 a year).

DIRECTORS

Institute of Agronomy: CLARINDO ALDO LOPES
Institute of Biology: CARLOS LUIZ MASSARD
Institute of Pure Sciences: LUCIO VITTORIO IANNARELLA
Institute of Humanities: ANA LUIZA BARBOSA DA COSTÁ VEIGA
Institute of Education: ANTÔNIO ADOLFO GARBOCCI BRUNO
Institute of Forestry: WALDEMIR JOÃO HORA
Institute of Technology: REGINA CÉLIA LOPES ARAÚJO
Institute of Animal Husbandry: JOSÉ PAULO DE OLIVEIRA

FUNDAÇÃO UNIVERSIDADE FEDERAL DE RONDÔNIA

BR 364 Km 9.5, Campus Universitário, José Ribeiro Filho

Telephone: (69) 216-8500
Fax: (69) 216-8506

Founded 1982
Federal govt control

Academic year: March to December

Rector: Prof. OSMAR SIENA
Vice-Rector: NEIDE YOHOKO MIYAKAWA
Administrative Pro-rector: FRANCISCO PAULO DUARTE
Librarian: CLEIDE MARIA DE MEDEIROS

Number of teachers: 240
Number of students: 3,208

Faculties of Education (depts of Letters, Geography, Mathematics, Physical Education, Teaching), Social Sciences (depts of Business Administration, Accounting, Economics, Law), Health Sciences (Nursing, Psychology).

UNIVERSIDADE DO SAGRADO CORAÇÃO

Rua Irmã Arminda 10–50, 17044-160 Bauru, SP
Telephone: (14) 235-7000
Fax: (14) 235-7325
E-mail: secretariareitoria@usc.br

Founded 1953
Private control

Rector: Dra Ir JACINTA TUROLO GARCIA
Vice-Rector: Ir MARISABEL LEITE
Secretary-General: LÚCIA HELENA PEREIRA DA SILVA
Librarian: VALÉRIA MARIA CAMPANERI

Library of 83,000 vols
Number of teachers: 301
Number of students: 5,218

Publications: *Revista Mimesis, Revista Salusvita, Boletim Cultural, Cadernos de Divulgação Cultural.*

PROFESSORS

BASTOS TENTOR, S., Education
CASATI ALVARES, L., Odontology
DOMINGUES, M., Social Sciences
DUARTE DE SOUZA, C., Biological Sciences
GARCIA DE MORAIS, A., Literature
MATIOLI, M. C., Law
MAZONI, J. R., Social Sciences
MILANI, M. E., Literature
MONTEIRO BRANCO FOLKIS, G., Literature
TUROLO GARCIA, J., Philosophy

UNIVERSIDADE CATÓLICA DO SALVADOR

Praça Ana Nery s/n, Largo da Palma Mouraria, 40040-020 Salvador, BA
Telephone: (71) 321-1753
Fax: (71) 322-4331

Founded 1961
Private control
Languages of instruction: Portuguese, French, English

Chancellor: Cardinal Dom LUCAS MOREIRA NEVES
Rector: Dr JOSÉ CARLOS ALMEIDA DA SILVA
Vice-Rector: LILIANA MERCURI ALMEIDA
Librarian: SONIA RODRIGUES

Number of teachers: 690
Number of students: 12,000

DIRECTORS

Faculty of Education: Profa ITALVA SIMÕES
School of Social Services: Profa EMILIA NORONHA LYRA
School of Business Administration: Prof. HUGO BELEUS
Faculty of Law: Prof. THOMAS BACELLAR
Faculty of Philosophy and Human Sciences: Prof. JURANDYR OLIVEIRA
Faculty of Nursing: Profa MARGARIDA MACHADO
Institute of Sciences: Profa LYGIA PARAGUASSU
Institute of Theology: Pe. ADEMAR DANTOS DE SOUZA
School of Engineering: Prof. LUIZ GONZAGA MARQUES
Institute of Letters: Profa TEREZA CHIANCA
Institute of Music: Profa LEDA MARGARIDA DE SOUZA
Institute of Mathematics: NILTON CRUZ
Faculty of Economics: (vacant)
Faculty of Accountancy: (vacant)
School of Physical Education: (vacant)

UNIVERSIDADE DO ESTADO DE SANTA CATARINA

Campus Universitário, Av. Madre Benvenuta 2007, CP D-34, Itacorubi, 88035-001 Florianópolis, SC
Fax: (48) 334-6000
E-mail: r4sl@pobox.udesc.br

Founded 1965
State control
Language of instruction: Portuguese
Academic year: March to June, August to December

Rector: RAIMUNDO ZUMBLICK
Chief Administrative Officer: PIO CAMPOS FILHO
Chief Academic Officer: SANDRA M. SALLES
Librarian: NOÊMA SCHOFFEN PRADO

Library of 75,838 vols
Number of teachers: 402
Number of students: 10,000

Publications: *Boletim do Centro de Artes, CCII News, Jornal da UDESC.*

DIRECTORS

Faculty of Education: OSNI DE BIASI
Business School: OSVALDO MOMM
Faculty of Engineering (Joinville): WESLEY MASTERSON BELO DE ABREU
School of Physical Education: IVAIR DE LUCCA
School of Agronomics and Veterinary Medicine (Lages): ADEMIR MONDADORI
School of Fine Arts: VERA REGINA COLLAÇO

UNIVERSIDADE FEDERAL DE SANTA CATARINA

Campus Universitário, CP 476, 88040-900 Trindade (Florianópolis), SC
Telephone: (482) 31-9000
Telex: (0482) 240
Fax: (482) 34-4069

Founded 1960
Public control
Language of instruction: Portuguese
Academic year: March to June, August to November

Rector: Prof. ANTÔNIO DIOMÁRIO DE QUEIRÓZ
Vice-Rector: Profa NILCÉA LEMOS PEDANDRÉ
Chief Administrative Officer: Prof. FELÍCIO WESSLING MARGOTTI
Librarian: BEL. MARIA GHIZONI DEL RIO

Number of teachers: 1,604
Number of students: 17,000

Publications: *Sequência, Travessia, Ciências Humanas, Ciências da Saúde, Ilha do Desterro, Perspectiva, Geosul, Biotemas.*

DEANS

Agrarian Sciences Centre: Prof. MÁRIO LUIZ VINCENZI
Engineering and Technology Centre: Profa ANA MARIA DE MATTOS JULIANO
Bio-Medical Sciences Centre: Prof. LUMAR VALMOR BERTOLI
Social and Economic Sciences Centre: Prof. ADEMAR ARCÂNGELO CIRIMBELLI
Education Centre: Prof. VALPI COSTA
Physical Education Centre: Prof. JOEL CARDOSO
Communication Centre: Prof. JOSÉ ARNO SCHEIDT
Physics and Mathematics Centre: Prof. WILSON ERBS
Biological Sciences Centre: Prof. CÂNDIDO GERALDO FREITAS
Philosophy and Social Sciences Centre: Prof. MARCOS RIBEIRO FERREIRA
Law Sciences Centre: Prof. ROGÉRIO STOETERAU

UNIVERSIDADE SANTA CECÍLIA

Rua Osvaldo Cruz 255, 11045-100 Santos, SP
Telephone: (13) 221-3242
Fax: (13) 232-4010
E-mail: scecilia@usc.stcecilia.br

Founded 1961
Private control
Academic year: February to December

Chancellor: Dr MILTON TEIXEIRA
President: Dra LÚCIA M. TEIXEIRA FURLANI
Vice-President: Profa MARIA CECÍLIA P. TEIXEIRA
Rector: Dra SÍLVIA A. TEIXEIRA PENTEADO
Academic Pro-Rector: Profa ZULEIKA DE A. SENGER GONÇALVES
Administrative Pro-Rector: Dr MARCELO PIRILO TEIXEIRA
Community Pro-Rector: Prof. AQUELINO J. VASQUES
Pro-Rector for University Development: Profa EMÍLIA MARIA PIRILLO
General-Secretary: WALDIR GRAÇA
Chief Librarian: ANA MARIA RACCIOPI SILVEIRA

Library of 84,000 vols
Number of teachers: 640
Number of students: 13,000

Publications: *Ceciliana, Revista de Estudo.*

COORDINATORS

Campus Santa Cecília:
- Profa LÚCIA MARIA TEIXEIRA FURLANI
- Profa MARIA CECÍLIA TEIXEIRA
- Dr MARCELO TEIXEIRA

Campus Bandeirante I:
- Profa ROSINHA GARCIA DE SIQUEIRA VIEGAS

Campus Bandeirante II:
- Profa CARMEN LÚCIA TABOADA DE CARVALHO

DEANS

Faculty of Arts and Communication: Prof. A. J. VASQUES
Faculty of Sciences and Technology: Prof. R. PATELLA
Faculty of Industrial Engineering: Eng. A. E. P. FIGUEIREDO
Faculty of Civil Engineering: Eng. A DE SALLES PENTEADO
Faculty of Dentistry: Dr R. G. DE SIQUEIRA VIEGAS
Faculty of Education and Human Sciences: Prof. C. M. BAFFA
Faculty of Commercial and Administrative Sciences: Prof. A. PORTO PIRES
Faculty of Chemical Engineering: Eng. A. DE SALLES PENTEADO
Faculty of Physical Education: Prof. V. A. TABOADA DE CARVALHO RAPHAELLI
Faculty of Dance: Prof. L. RACCINI
Faculty of Law: Dr R. MEHANNA KHAMIS

UNIVERSIDADE FEDERAL DE SANTA MARIA

Faixa de Camobi, Km 9, Edif. da Adm. Central, 97119-900 Santa Maria, RS
Telephone: (55) 226-1616
Telex: (55) 2230
Fax: (55) 226-1975

Founded 1960
Federal (Government) control
Academic year: March to December (two semesters)

Rector: Prof. ODILON ANTÔNIO MARCUZZO DO CANTO
Vice-Rector: Prof. ANTÔNIO ADALBERTO BRUM SIQUEIRA
Pro-Rectors:
- Postgraduate and Research: Prof. ALFRÂNIO ALMIR RIGHES

Undergraduate: Prof. ÉRICO ANTÔNIO LOPES HENN
Student Affairs: Profa ALDEMA MENINE TRINDADE
Extension: Prof. ALCENO ANTÔNIO FERRI
Planning: Prof. JOSÉ MARIA DIAS PEREIRA
Administration: Prof. MARCO ANTÔNIO DE OLIVEIRA FLORES

Administrative Officer: LUIZ ANTÔNIO ANTUNES PEREIRA
Librarian: MARISA SEVERO CORRÊA

Library of 80,000 vols
Number of teachers: 1,322
Number of students: 10,131

Publications: *Relatório Geral, Catálogo Geral, Catálogo Ementário,* etc.

DIRECTORS OF CENTRES

Technology: Profa NILZA ZAMPIERI
Arts and Letters: Prof. ROBSON PEREIRA GONÇALVES
Rural Sciences: Prof. JOSÉ OSVALDO JARDIM FILHO
Education: Prof. RICARDO ROSSATO
Health Sciences: Prof. CLÓVIS SILVA LIMA
Social and Human Sciences: Prof. JOSÉ ODIM DEGRANDI
Natural and Exact Sciences: Profa MARIA EMÍLIA CAMARGO

ATTACHED INSTITUTES

Faculty of Nursing: Av. Presidente Vargas 2777, 97100 Santa Maria, RS; Dir Ir. NOEMI LUNARDI.

Faculty of Philosophy, Sciences and Letters: Rua Andradas 1614, 97100 Santa Maria, RS; Dir Profa MARIA A. MARQUES.

UNIVERSIDADE FEDERAL DE SÃO CARLOS

Rodovia Washington Luiz, Km 235, CP 676, 13565-905 São Carlos, SP

Telephone: (16) 260-8111
Fax: (16) 261-2081

Founded 1970
Federal control
Language of instruction: Portuguese
Academic year: March to December

Chancellor: PAULO RENATO DE SOUZA
Rector: Dr JOSÉ RUBENS REBELATTO
Vice-Rector: Dr OSWALDO BAPTISTA DUARTE FILHO
Chief Administrative Officer: Dr JOÃO CARLOS PEDRAZZANI
Librarian: LOURDES DE SOUZA MORAES

Number of teachers: 635
Number of students: 6,222

DIRECTORS

Institute of Sciences and Technology: Dr JOÃO SERGIO CORDEIRO
Institute of Education and Human Sciences: Dr JULIO CESAR COELHO DE ROSE
Institute of Biological and Health Sciences: Dr SÉRGIO EDUARDO DE ANDRADE PEREZ
Institute of Agricultural Sciences: Dr RUBSMAR STOLF

HEADS OF DEPARTMENTS

Sciences and Technology:
Computer Science: Dr ANTONIO FRANCISCO DO PRADO
Statistics: Dr CARLOS ALBERTO RIBEIRO DINIZ
Materials Engineering: Dr CLAUDIO SHYNTI KIMINAMI
Chemical Engineering: Dr CLÁUDIO ALBERTO TORRES SUAZO
Production Engineering: Dr OSWALDO MÁRIO SERRA TRUZZI
Civil Engineering: Dr JOSÉ FRANCISCO PONTES ASSUMPÇÃO
Physics: Dr HAMILTON VIANA DA SILVEIRA
Mathematics: Dr NÉLIO BALDIN
Chemistry: Dr MILTON DUFFLES CAPELATTO

Education and Human Sciences:
Psychology: Dra MARIA BENEDITA LIMA PARDO
Social Sciences: Dr MAURÍCIO OTÁVIO MENDONÇA JORGE
Education: Dr POTIGUARA ACÁCIO PEREIRA
Philosophy and Methodology of Science: Dr JOSÉ ANTONIO DAMASIO ABIB
Teaching Methodology: Dra MARIA WALDENEZ DE OLIVEIRA
Spanish and English: DENISE DE PAULA MARTINS DE ABREU E LIMA
Arts: Dra TELMA LUZIA PEGORELLI OLIVIERI
Information Science: ELIZABETH MÁRCIA MARTUCCI

Biological and Health Sciences:
Ecology and Evolutionary Biology: Dr CRISTIANO DOS SANTOS NETO
Health Sciences: Dr ANTONIO SÉRGIO SPANÓ SEIXAS
Nursing: Dra ELISETE SILVA PEDRAZZANI
Physiotherapy: Dra ROSANA MATTIOLI
Occupational Therapy: Dra MARINA SILVEIRA PALHARES
Genetics and Evolution: Dr ORLANDO MOREIRA FILHO
Physiological Sciences: Dra MARISA NARCISO FERNANDES
Botany: Dr ARMANDO AUGUSTO HENRIQUES VIEIRA
Hydrobiology: Dr ALBERTO CARVALHO PERET
Physical Education: Profa ANA CLAUDIA GARCIA DE OLIVEIRA DUARTE

Agricultural Sciences:
Agroindustrial Technology and Rural Development: OCTÁVIO ANTONIO VALSECHI
Natural Resources and Environmental Safety: Dr VICTÓRIO L. FURLANI NETO
Vegetal Biotechnology: Dr ANTONIO ISMAEL BASSINELLO

UNIVERSIDADE DE SÃO FRANCISCO

Av. São Francisco de Assis 218, CP 163, 12900-000 Bragança Paulista, SP

Telephone: (11) 7844-8000
Fax: (11) 7844-1825
E-mail: webmaster@usf.com.br

Founded 1976, university status 1985
Private control
Language of instruction: Portuguese
Academic year: February to December

Chancellor: Fr. CAETANO FERRARI
Rector: Fr. CONSTÂNCIO NOGARA
Vice-Rector: Fr. FÁBIO PANINI
Pro-Rectors: Profa ACÁCIA AP. ANGELI DOS SANTOS (Undergraduate), Profa MARIA APARECIDA BARBOSA MARQUES (Research, Postgraduate and Extension), ANTÔNIO CARLOS DE ALMEIDA (Community), Prof. GILBERTO LUIS MORAES SELBER (Administrative)
General Secretary: Prof. JOSÉ ENIO TRIERVAILER
Librarian: IVANI BENASSI

Library of 132,000 vols, 1,200 periodicals

Number of teachers: 821
Number of students: 17,561

Publications: *Informativo USF* (monthly), *Semeando* (monthly), *Cadernos do IFAN* (4 a year), *InformIPPEX* (monthly), *Anais do Encontro de Iniciação Científica e Pesquisadores* (1 a year), various faculty journals.

DIRECTORS

Câmpus de Bragança Paulista: Av. São Francisco de Assis 218, CP 163, 12900-000 Bragança Paulista, SP
Faculty of Pharmacy: Prof. EDSON RODRIGUES
Faculty of Medicine: Prof. SÉRGIO LUIZ MARTIN NARDY
Faculty of Law: Prof. JOSÉ NICOLA JANNUZZI
Faculty of Economics and Administration: Profa HILDA MARIA C. BARROSO BRAGA
Faculty of Philosophy, Sciences and Literature: Prof. MIGUEL HENRIQUE RUSSO
Faculty of Dentistry: Prof. ROSSINE AMORIM MACIEL

Câmpus de Itatiba: Rua Alexandre Rodrigues Barbosa 45, 13251-900 Itatiba, SP
Faculty of Engineering: Prof. WERNER MERTZIG
Faculty of Human Sciences: Profa CARMEM BEATRIZ RODRIGUES FABRIANI
Faculty of Administrative and Exact Sciences: Prof. FÁBIO ALEXANDRE GAION CASOTTI

Câmpus de São Paulo: Rua Hannemann 352, Pari, 03031-040 São Paulo, SP
Faculty of Education and Social Sciences: Prof. MARINO ANTONIO SEHNEN
Faculty of Business and Administration: Prof. LUIZ MAURÍCIO DE ANDRADE DA SILVA
Faculty of Law: Prof. MARLON WANDER MACHADO

ATTACHED INSTITUTES

Franciscan Institute of Anthropology: Dir Fr ORLANDO BERNARDI.

Institute for Graduate Research and Extension: Dir Profa JOSIANE MARIA DE FREITAS TONELOTTO.

UNIVERSIDADE DE SÃO PAULO

Cidade Universitária, CP 3751, 05508-900 São Paulo, SP

Telephone: (11) 818-4244
Fax: (11) 815-5665

Founded 1934
State control
Academic year: March to November

Rector: Prof. Dr JACQUES MARCOVITCH
Vice-Rector: Prof. Dr. ADOLPHO JOSÉ MELFI
Pro-Rector for Graduate Studies: Profa Dra ADA PELLEGRINI GRINOVER
Pro-Rector for Postgraduate Studies: Prof. Dr HÉCTOR FRANCISCO TERENZI
Pro-Rector for Culture and University Extension: Prof. Dr ADILSON AVANSI DE ABREU
Pro-Rector for Research: Prof. Dr HERNAN CHAIMOVICH GURALNIK
Secretary: Profa Dra LOR CURY

Library: see Libraries
Number of teachers: 4,953
Number of students: 61,128

Publications: many faculty and institute reviews.

DEANS

Faculty of Law: Prof. Dr ÁLVARO VILLAÇA AZEVEDO
Faculty of Medicine: Prof. Dr MARCELLO MARCONDES MACHADO
Faculty of Philosophy, Literature and Human Sciences: Prof. Dr JOÃO BAPTISTA BORGES PEREIRA
Faculty of Pharmaceutical Sciences: Prof. Dr SEIZI OGA
Faculty of Dentistry: Prof. Dr JOSÉ FORTUNATO FERREIRA SANTOS
Faculty of Veterinary Medicine and Zootechnics: Prof. Dr JOÃO PALERMO NETO
Faculty of Public Health: Prof. Dr JAIR LÍCIO FERREIRA SANTOS
Faculty of Architecture and Town Planning: Prof. Dr JULIO ROBERTO KATINSKY
Faculty of Medicine (Ribeirão Prêto): Prof. Dr MICHEL PIERRE LISON
Faculty of Dentistry (Bauru): Prof. Dr AYMAR PAVARINI
Faculty of Education: Profa Dra MYRIAM KRASILCHIK
School of Communication and Arts: Prof. Dr TUPÃ GOMES CORRÊA
Polytechnic School: Prof. Dr ANTONIO MARCOS DE AGUIRRA MASSOLA

'Luiz de Queiroz' Higher School of Agriculture: Prof. Dr Evaristo Marzabal Neves
School of Nursing: Profa Dra Paulina Kurcgant
School of Nursing (Ribeirão Prêto): Profa Dra Isabel Amélia Costa Mendes
School of Engineering (São Carlos): Prof. Dr Jurandyr Povinelli
School of Physical Education: Prof. Dr José Geraldo Massucato
Institute of Bio-sciences: Prof. Dr João Stenghel Morgante
Institute of Biomedical Sciences: Profa Dra Magda Maria Sales Carneiro Sampaio
Institute of Physics: Prof. Dr Silvio Roberto de Azevedo Salinas
Institute of Geophysics and Astronomy: Prof. Dr Oswaldo Massambani
Institute of Mathematics and Statistics: Prof. Dr Sian Wun Song
Institute of Chemistry: Prof. Dr Paulo Sergio Santos
Institute of Psychology: Prof. Dr Lino de Macedo
Institute of Geosciences: Prof. Dr Adilson Carvalho
Institute of Mathematical Sciences and Computing Systems (São Carlos): Prof. Dr Hildebrando Munhoz Rodrigues
Institute of Physics (São Carlos): Profa Dra Yvonne Primerano Mascarenhas
Institute of Oceanography: Prof. Dr Rolf Roland Weber
Institute of Chemistry (São Carlos): Prof. Dr Ernesto Rafael Gonzalez
Faculty of Pharmaceutical Sciences (Ribeirão Prêto): Profa Dra Suely Vilela
Faculty of Dentistry (Ribeirão Prêto): Prof. Dr Wanderley Ferreira da Costa
Faculty of Economics and Administration: Prof. Dr Denisard Cneio de Oliveira Alves
Faculty of Philosophy, Sciences and Literature (Ribeirão Prêto): Prof. Dr José Aparecido da Silva
Faculty of Animal Husbandry and Food Engineering (Pirassununga): Dir Prof. Dr Marcus Antonio Zanetti

ATTACHED INSTITUTES

Institute of Advanced Studies: Dir Prof. Dr Alfredo Bosi.

Institute of Electrical Engineering and Energy: Dir Prof. Dr Carlos Américo Morato de Andrade.

Centre of Marine Biology: Dir Prof. Dr José Carlos de Freitas.

Centre of Nuclear Energy Applied in Agriculture: Dir Prof. Dr Augusto Tulmann Neto.

Institute of Brazilian Studies: Dir Profa Dra Marta Rossetti Batista.

UNIVERSIDADE ESTADUAL PAULISTA 'JULIO DE MESQUITA FILHO'

Alameda Santos 647, Cerqueira Cesar, 01419-901 São Paulo, SP

Telephone: (11) 252-0233
Telex: 1119001
Fax: (11) 252-0201

Founded 1976, incorporating previous existing Faculties in São Paulo State

State control

Academic year: March to November

Rector: Prof. Dr Antonio Manoel dos Santos Silva
Vice-Rector: Prof. Dr Luís Roberto de Toledo Ramalho
Head of Administration: Prof. Dr Widsney Alves Ferreira
Secretary-General: Profa Dra Maria Lourdes Mariotto Haidar
Librarian: Glaura M. Oliveira Barbosa de Almeida

Number of teachers: 3,400
Number of students: 26,842

Publications: various faculty publs

DEANS AND DIRECTORS

Araçatuba Campus: Rua José Bonifácio 1193, 16015-050 Araçatuba, CP 533; tel. (186) 23-2120; fax (186) 22-2638
Faculty of Dentistry: 136 teachers, 593 students; Dir Prof. Dr João Cesar Bedran de Castro

Araraquara Campus: Pres. Prof. Dr Welingtom Dinelli

Faculty of Pharmaceutical Sciences: Rod. Araraquara – Jaú km 1, 14801-902 Araraquara, CP 331; tel. (162) 32-0200; fax (162) 22-0073; 69 teachers, 461 students; Dir Prof. Dr Paulo Eduardo de Toledo Salgado
Faculty of Dentistry: Rua Humaitá 1680, 14801-903 Araraquara; tel. (162) 32-1233; fax (162) 22-4823; 96 teachers, 465 students; Dir Prof. Dr Welingtom Dinelli
Faculty of Sciences and Letters: Estrada Araraquara—Jaú Km 1, 14800-901 Araraquara; tel. (162) 32-0444; fax (162) 32-0698; 187 teachers, 2,238 students; Dir Prof. Dr Claudio Benedito Gomide de Souza
Institute of Chemistry: Rua Prof. Francisco Degne s/n, Bairro do Quitandinha, 14800-900 Araraquara, CP 355; tel. (162) 32-2022; fax (162) 22-7932; 72 teachers, 559 students; Dir Prof. Dr José Roberto Ernandes

Assis Campus: Av. Dom Antônio s/n, 19800-000 Assis; tel. (183) 22-2933; fax (183) 22-5743
Faculty of Sciences and Letters: 164 teachers, 1,714 students; Dir Prof. Dr Antonio Quelce Salgado

Bauru Campus: Av. Luiz Edmundo Carrijo Coube s/n, 17033-360 Bauru; tel. (142) 30-2111; telex 142312; fax (142) 34-4470; Pres. Profa Dra Cleide Santos Costa Biancardi
Faculty of Architecture, Arts and Communication: 119 teachers, 1,755 students; Dir Profa Dra Cleide Santos Costa Biancardi
Faculty of Sciences: 175 teachers, 1,025 students; Dir Prof. Dr José Misael Ferreira do Vale
Faculty of Engineering and Technology: 96 teachers, 1,011 students; Dir Prof. Dr Edwin Avolio

Botucatu Campus: Distrito Rubião Junior s/n, 18610-000 Botucatu; tel. (149) 21-2121; fax (149) 22-3199; Pres. Elias José Simon
Faculty of Agricultural Sciences: Fazenda Experimental Lageado, 18603-970 Botucatu; 102 teachers, 956 students; Dir Prof. Dr Elias José Simon
Faculty of Medicine: Distrito Rubião Junior s/n, 18618-000 Botucatu; tel. (149) 21-2121; fax (149) 22-0421; 253 teachers, 1,193 students; Dir Prof. Dr Paulo Eduardo de Abreu Machado
Faculty of Veterinary Medicine and Animal Husbandry: Distrito Rubião Junior s/n, 18618-000 Botucatu; tel. (149) 21-2121; fax (149) 21-2343; 81 teachers, 572 students; Dir Profa Dra Eunice Oba
Institute of Biosciences: Distrito Rubião Junior s/n, 18618-000 Botucatu; tel. (149) 21-2121; fax (149) 21-3744; 160 teachers, 546 students; Dir Profa Dra Sheila Zambello de Pinho

Franca Campus: Rua Major Claudiano 1488, 14400-690 Franca; tel. (16) 722-6222; fax (16) 723-6645
Faculty of History, Law and Social Service: 104 teachers, 1,419 students; Dir Profa Dra Neide Aparecida de Souza Lehfeld

Guaratinguetá Campus: Av. Dr Ariberto Pereira da Cunha 333, 12500-000 Guaratinguetá; tel. (125) 22-2800; fax (125) 32-2466
Faculty of Engineering: 133 teachers, 1,111 students; Dir Prof. Dr Fernando Augusto S. Marins

Ilha Solteira Campus: Av. Brasil Centro 56, Município de Pereira Barreto, 15378-000 Ilha Solteira; tel. (187) 62-3113; fax (187) 62-2735
Faculty of Engineering: 196 teachers, 957 students; Dir Prof. Dr Orivaldo Arf

Jaboticabal Campus: Rodovia Carlos Tonnani Km 5, 14870-000 Jaboticabal; tel. (163) 23-2500; fax (163) 22-4275
Faculty of Agrarian and Veterinary Sciences: 237 teachers, 1,506 students; Dir Prof. Dr Julio César Durigan

Marília Campus: Av. Hygino Muzzi Filho 737, Campus Universitário, 17525-900 Marilia; tel. (144) 33-1844; fax (144) 22-4797
Faculty of Philosophy and Sciences: 148 teachers, 1,449 students; Dir Prof. Dr Antonio Geraldo de Aguiar

Presidente Prudente Campus: Rua Roberto Simonsen 305, 19060-900 Presidente Prudente, CP 957; tel. (182) 21-5388; fax (182) 33-2227
Faculty of Sciences and Technology: 210 teachers, 1,930 students; Dir Prof. Dr Alvanir de Figueiredo

Rio Claro Campus: Pres. Prof. Dr Marcos Aurélio F. de Oliveira
Institute of Bio-Sciences: Av. 24A, 1515, 13500-900 Rio Claro; tel. (195) 34-0244; fax (195) 34-0009; 123 teachers, 1,289 students; Dir Prof. Dr Osvaldo Aulino da Silva
Institute of Geo-Sciences and Exact Sciences: Rua Dez 2527, 13500-230 Rio Claro; tel. (195) 34-0122; 148 teachers, 1,321 students; Dir Prof. Dr Silvio Carlos Bray

São José dos Campos Campus: Av. Eng. Francisco José Longo 777, 12245-000 São José dos Campos, CP 314; tel. (123) 21-8166; fax (123) 21-2036
Faculty of Dentistry: 92 teachers, 265 students; Dir Prof. Dr José Eduardo Junho de Araújo

São José de Rio Prêto Campus: Rua Cristovão Colombo 2265, 15054-000 São José do Rio Prêto; tel. (172) 24-4966; fax (172) 24-8692
Institute of Bio-Sciences, Letters and Exact Sciences: 189 teachers, 1,740 students; Dir Prof. Dr Wilson Maurício Tadini

São Paulo Campus (I): Rua Dom Luiz Lasagna 400, Ipiranga, 04266-030 São Paulo; tel. (11) 274-4733; fax (11) 215-1371
Institute of Arts: 65 teachers, 580 students; Dir Profa Dra Regina Coeli G. de Souza Pinto

São Paulo Campus (II): Rua Pamplona 145, 01405-900 São Paulo, tel. (11) 251-5155
Theoretical Physics Institute: 26 teachers, 58 students; Dir Prof. Dr José Geraldo Pereira

COMPLEMENTARY UNITS

'Paula Souza' State Centre for Technology: Praça Coronel Fernando Prestes 74, 01124-060 São Paulo; tel. (11) 228-0126; fax (11) 228-0123; Dir Prof. Elias Horani

Aquaculture Centre: Rodovia Carlos Tonanni km 5, 14870-000 Jaboticabal, SP; tel. and fax (16) 323-2100; Dir Profa Dra Elisabeth Criscuolo Urbinati

Centre for Teaching and Research on the São Paulo Coast: Praça Infante Dom Henrique s/n, 11330-205 São Vicente, SP; tel. (13)

469-7682; fax (13) 469-7374; Dir Prof. Dr ANTONIO JOÃO CANCIAN

Centre for the Study of Venom and Venomous Animals (CEVAP): Distrito de Rubião Junior s/n, CP 577, 18610-000 Botucatu, SP; tel. and fax 821-3963; Dir Prof. Dr CARLOS ALBERTO DE MAGALHÃES LOPES

Centre for Environmental Studies (CEA): Av. 24-A 1515, 13500-900 Rio Claro, SP; tel. (19) 534-7298; fax (19) 534-2358; Dir Prof. Dr JOÃO ANTONIO GALBIATTI

Centre for Education and Cultural Radio and Television: Av. Eng. Luiz Edmundo Carrijo Coube s/n, 17033-360 Bauru, SP; tel. (14) 230-3608; fax (14) 230-3649; Dir Prof. Dr CIRO ANTONIO ROSOLEM

Institute of Meteorological Research (IPMet): Av. Eng Luiz Edmundo Carrijo Coube s/n, 17033-360 Bauru, SP; tel. (14) 230-3608; fax (14) 230-3649; Dir Prof. LUIZ ROBERTO TROVATI

Centre for Tropical Roots (CERAT): Fazenda Experimental Lageado, CP 237, 18603-970 Botucatu, SP; tel. (14) 821-3883; fax (14) 821-3438; Dir Profa Dra MARNEY PASCOLI CEREDA

AFFILIATED FACULTIES

Faculty of Technology of São Paulo: Praça Coronel Fernando Prestes 30, 01124-060 São Paulo; tel. (11) 225-0366; fax (11) 229-5481; 345 teachers, 4,969 students; Dir Profa HELENA GEMIGNANI PETEROSSI

Faculty of Technology of Sorocaba: Av. Eng. Carlos Reinaldo Mendes 2015, 18103-280 Sorocaba; tel. (152) 31-2124; fax (152) 32-1083; 72 teachers, 1,228 students; Dir Prof. Dr ANTONIO CARLOS DE OLIVEIRA

Faculty of Technology of Americana: Av. Nossa Senhora de Fátima 567, 13465-000 Americana; tel (0149) 61-7049; fax (149) 61-3026; 44 teachers, 516 students; Dir Prof. Dr MARCO ANTONIO SICCHIROLI LAVRADOR

Faculty of Technology of Baixada Santista: Av. Bartolomeu de Gusmão 110, 11045-908 Santos; tel. (132) 27-6015; fax (132) 27-6003; 26 teachers, 462 students; Dir Prof. GERSON PRANDO

Faculty of Technology of Jahu: Rua Frei Galvão s/n, 17212-650, Jaú; tel. (146) 22-8533; fax (146) 22-8280; 32 teachers, 301 students; Dir Profa Dra VERA LUCIA SILVA CAMARGO

Faculty of Technology of São Paulo – Extension in Ourinhos: Av. do Contorno s/n, Campus Universitário, 19900-000 Ourinhos SP; tel. (143) 22-3152; fax (143) 23-1486; 21 teachers, 413 students; Co-ordinator Dr PAULO HENRIQUE CHÍXARO.

Faculty of Technology of Guaratinguetá: Praça Conselheiro Rodrigues Alves 48, 12500-000 Guaratinguetá, SP; tel. (125) 32-5110; 5 teachers, 30 students; Dir Prof. JOSÉ MANOEL S. NEVES.

Faculty of Technology of Indaiatuba; Rua Pedro Gonçalves 477, 13330-000 Indaiatuba, SP; tel. (192) 75-9091; 4 teachers, 40 students; Dir Prof. JOSÉ ROBERTO B. DE SOUZA.

Faculty of Technology of Taquaritinga: Rua Francisco Valzacchi 51, 15900-000 Taquaritinga, SP; tel. (162) 52-5250; fax (162) 52-5251; 18 teachers, 435 students; Dir Prof. ANTONIO MANUEL DA ROCHA RIBEIRO.

PONTIFÍCIA UNIVERSIDADE CATÓLICA DE SÃO PAULO

Rua Monte Alegre 984, Perdizes, 05014-001 São Paulo, SP

Telephone: (11) 873-3011
Fax: (11) 624-920

Private control
Founded 1946

Academic year: March to December (two semesters)

Grand Chancellor: Dom PAULO EVARISTO ARNS, Cardinal Archbishop of São Paulo
Rector: Prof. Dr ANTONIO CARLOS CARUSO RONCA
Vice-Rector for Administration: ADHEMAR APPARECIDO DE CAROLI
Vice-Rector for Academic Affairs: Prof. FERNANDE JOSÉ DE ALMEIDA
Vice-Rector for Community Affairs: Prof. AMÉRICO DE PAULA E SILVA
General Secretary: Dr JOSÉ FELICIANO FERREIRA DA ROSA AQUINO
Librarian: ANA MARIA RAPASSI

Number of teachers: 2,204
Number of students: 15,713 (first semester), 15,883 (second semester)

DIRECTORS AND DEANS

Centre of Law, Economics and Administration: Profa MARIA ANGÉLICA BORGES
- Faculty of Law: Profa ELIZABETH NAZAR CARRAZZA
- Faculty of Economics and Administration: Prof. ANTONIO VICO MAÑAS

Centre of Humanities: Prof. ADEMIR ALVES DA SILVA
- Faculty of Psychology: Profa ANA MERCÊS BAHIA BOCK
- Faculty of Communications and Philosophy: Profa MARISIS ARANHA CAMARGO
- Faculty of Social Service: Profa MARIANGELA BELFIORE WANDERLEY
- Faculty of Social Sciences: Profa HELENA RIBEIRO WHITAKER SOBRAL

Centre of Mathematical, Physical and Technological Sciences: Profa TANIA MARIA MENDONÇA CAMPOS
- Faculty of Mathematical and Physical Sciences: Prof. JOSÉ HENRIQUE MENDES TARCIA

Centre of Education: Profa YVONNE ALVARENGA G. KHOURI
- Faculty of Education: Profa MARIA ANITA VIVIANE

Centre of Biological and Medical Sciences: Prof. HUDSON HUBNER FRANÇA
- Faculty of Biological Sciences: Profa MARIA ELISA ZULIANI MALUF
- Faculty of Medical Sciences: Prof. GLADSTON OLIVEIRA MACHADO

UNIVERSIDADE FEDERAL DE SERGIPE

Cidade Universitária, Rosa Elze, 49100-000 São Cristóvão, SE

Telephone: (79) 241-2848
Telex: (79) 2189
Fax: (79) 241-3995

Founded 1967

Federal control
Language of instruction: Portuguese
Academic year: March to June, August to December

Rector: Prof. LUIZ HERMÍNIO DE AGUIAR OLIVEIRA
Vice-Rector: Prof. JOSÉ PAULINO DA SILVA
President of Council: Dr LUIZ GARCIA
Librarian: JUSTINO ALVES LIMA

Number of teachers: 448
Number of students: 5,908

Publications: *Revista* (irregular), *Jornal* (fortnightly), *Relatório Anual de Atividades*.

DIRECTORS

Centre of Biological Sciences and Health: Rua Claudio Batista, Bairro Sanatório, Aracaju, Sergipe; Prof. Dr ANTONIO CESAR CABRAL DE OLIVEIRA
Centre of Applied Social Sciences: Prof. NAPOLEÃO DOS SANTOS QUEIROZ
Centre of Education and Humanities: Prof. LUIZ ALBERTO DOS SANTOS
Centre of Exact Sciences and Technology: Prof. JOSÉ AIRTON DOS SANTOS

HEADS OF DEPARTMENTS

Centre of Biological Sciences and Health:
- Biology: Profa MARIA HELENA ZUCON
- Surgery: Profa SÔNIA OLIVEIRA LIMA
- Physical Education: Prof. FERNANDO SANTOS OLIVEIRA
- Nursing and Nutrition: Profa LINDETE AMORIM SANTOS
- Physiology: Prof. ANTONIO EDILSON DO NASCIMENTO
- Internal Medicine: Prof. JOSÉ MARIA RODRIGUES SANTOS
- Morphology: Prof. GILENO DE SÁ CARDOSO
- Odontology: Prof. FERNANDO SANTOS VASCONCELOS
- Community Health: Prof. ANTÔNIO SAMARONE DE SANTANA

Centre of Applied Social Sciences:
- Administration: Prof. NAPOLEÃO DOS SANTOS QUEIROZ
- Law: Profa ARLENE PEREIRA CHAGAS
- Economics: Prof. JOSÉ MANUEL PINTO ALVIDOS
- Social Services: Profa TEREZINHA LEMOS S. DE ARAÚJO
- Accountancy: Prof. CARLOS AUGUSTO DOS SANTOS

Centre of Education and Humanities:
- Education: Profa ANTONIA GONÇALVES MAYNARD DIAS
- Geography: Prof. AGAMENON GUIMARÃES DE OLIVEIRA
- Philosophy and History: Profa LENALDA ANDRADE SANTOS
- Letters: Prof. JOSÉ COSTA ALMEIDA
- Psychology: Prof. JOSÉ CARLOS TOURINHO E SILVA
- Social Sciences: Prof. NADIA FRAGA VILLAS BOAS

Centre of Exact Sciences and Technology:
- Civil Engineering: Prof. JOÃO GALO DOS SANTOS AMARAL
- Chemical Engineering: Prof. EMERALDINO CASALI
- Statistics and Information: Profa YVONETE LOPES DE OLIVEIRA
- Mathematics: Prof. JOSÉ AIRTON BATISTA
- Physics: Prof. JOSÉ FERNANDES DE LIMA
- Chemistry: Prof. MARCIONILO DE MELO LOPES NETO

UNIVERSIDADE DE TAUBATÉ

Rua 4 de Março 432, 12020-270 Taubaté, SP

Telephone: (12) 232-7555
Fax: (12) 232-7660

Founded 1976
Municipal control
Academic year: March to June, August to November

Rector: Prof. Dr NIVALDO ZÖLLNER
Vice-Rector: Prof. CELSO FERRO
Pro-Rectors: Prof. PAULO GUAYCURÚ SAN-MARTIN (Economics and Finance), Profa MARIA JOSÉ MILHAREZI ABUD (Undergraduates), Profa VANDA APARECIDA VÁRZEA CURSINO (Extension), Profa MARIA JÚLIA FERREIRA XAVIER RIBEIRO (Research and Postgraduate Studies), Prof. WANDERLEY ANTONIO ANGARANO (Administration)
Secretary General: JOSÉ LUIZ RIBEIRO DO VALLE
Chief Librarian: HENNY PETERSEN FRANÇA

Library of 195,000 vols
Number of teachers: 820
Number of students: 12,538

Publication: *Taubaté*.

HEADS OF DEPARTMENTS

Biological Sciences and Health:
- Medicine: Prof. JOSÉ CARLOS DE CARVALHO
- Biology: Prof. SÉRGIO DE MOURA ARAÚJO
- Nursing and Obstetrics: Profa CARMEN LÚCIA S. PUPIO
- Psychology: Profa CRISTIANA M. ESPER BERTHOUD
- Clinical Psychology: Profa MARIA DE FÁTIMA C. D. FERREIRA
- Dentistry: Prof. GILSON SERRA NOGUEIRA
- Physical Education: Prof. SÉRGIO LUIZ QUERIDO
- Agronomy: Prof. VICENTE DE JESUS CARVALHO

Human Sciences and Literature:
- Social Communication: Prof. JOSÉ FELÍCIO GOUSSAIN MURADE
- Law: Prof. WILLIAM BENY BLOCK TELLES ALVES
- Social Work: Profa MARIA CÉLIA C. MINAMISAKO
- Social Science and Literature: Prof. GILIO GIACOMOZZI
- Economics, Accounting and Administration: Prof. ORLANDINO ROBERTO PEREIRA FILHO
- Education: Profa MÉRCIA APARECIDA DA CUNHA OLIVEIRA

Sciences and Technology:
- Architecture and Town Planning: Prof. JOSÉ ROBERTO NAVES SILVA
- Civil Engineering: Prof. JOSÉ CARLOS SIMÕES FLORENÇANO
- Electrical Engineering: Prof. JOÃO BOSCO GUAYCURÚ BISCARDI
- Mechanical Engineering: Prof. SEBASTIÃO CARDOSO
- Mathematics and Physics: Prof. REINALDO GOMES ALVARENGA
- Data Processing: Prof. JOSÉ ALBERTO FERNANDES FERREIRA

UNIVERSIDADE FEDERAL DE UBERLÂNDIA

Av. Engenheiro Diniz 1178, CP 593, 38401-136 Uberlândia, MG

Telephone: (34) 239-4810
Fax: (34) 235-0099

Founded 1969

Academic year: February to June, August to December

Rector: Prof. GLADSTONE RODRIGUES DA CUNHA FILHO
Vice-Rector: Prof. GILBERTO ARANTES CARRIJO
Pro-Rectors: Prof. RENATO ALVES PEREIRA (Planning and Administration), Prof. OSVALDO FREITAS DE JESUS (Education), Prof. HUMBERTO EUSTÁQUIO COELHO (Research and Postgraduates), Prof. WALDENOR BARROS MORAES FILHO (Extension, Culture and Student Affairs), EDNA PEREIRA ALVIM DE SOUSA (Human Resources)
Secretary-General: ELAINE DA SILVEIRA MAGALI
Librarian: ELZA MARIA PENA F. COSENZA

Library of 132,000 vols, 5,200 periodicals
Number of teachers: 1,209
Number of students: 12,432

Publications: *Economia e Ensaios, Letras & Letras, Educação e Filosofia, Sociedade e Natureza, Veterinária e Notícias, Revista do CEBIM, Revista do CETEC, Revista do Direito, Ciência e Engenharia, Ensino em Revista.*

HEADS OF COURSES

Centre of Biomedical Sciences: Dir Prof. SEBASTIÃO RODRIGUES FERREIRA FILHO
- Physical Education: Prof. ROBERTO JOSÉ TENÓRIO LIRA
- Biology: Profa ANA MARIA COELHO CAVALHO
- Medicine: Prof. EDUARDO ANTÔNIO ANDRADE
- Veterinary Medicine: Prof. MARCOS SILVA
- Odontology: Prof. CARLOS JOSÉ SOARES
- Agronomy: Prof. ELIAS NASCENTES BORGES
- Immunology and Applied Parasitology: Prof. ERNESTO AKIO TAKETOMI
- Post-graduate Genetics and Biochemistry: Prof. WARWICK ESTEVAM KERR
- Post-graduate Clinical Medicine: Prof. RENATO ENRIQUE SOLOGUREN ACHÁ

Centre of Exact Sciences and Technology: Dir Prof. ARQUIMEDES DIÓGENES CILONI
- Mathematics: Prof. MÁRCIO JOSÉ HORTA DANTAS
- Civil Engineering: Profa ILCE OLIVEIRA CAMPOS
- Electrical Engineering: Prof. KEIDE MATUMOTO
- Electrical Engineering (Postgraduate): Prof. DARIZON ALVES DE ANDRADE
- Chemical Engineering: Prof. ALVIMAR FERREIRA NASCIMENTO
- Mechanical Engineering: Prof. OROSIMBO ANDRADE A. REGO
- Mechanical Engineering (Postgraduate): Prof. ÁLISSON ROCHA MACHADO
- Chemistry: Profa EFIGÊNIA AMORIM
- Computer Science: Profa MÁRCIA APARECIDA FERNANDES
- Chemical Engineering (Master's): Prof. ELOÍZIO JÚLIO RIBEIRO
- Physics: Prof. ANTONIO TADEU LINO

Centre of Humanities and Arts: Dir Prof. LUIZ GONZAGA BARBOSA PIRES
- Arts: Profa HELIANA OMETTO NARDIM
- Music: Profa CÍNTIA THAÍS MORATO LOPES
- Decorative Arts: Profa MARIA LOURDES PEREIRA FONESCA
- Administration: Prof. FRANCISCO JOSÉ WANDERLEI OSTERNE
- Economics: Prof. PAULO ANTÔNIO DE OLIVEIRA GOMES
- Law: Profa APARECIDA MONTEIRO DE FRANÇA
- Geography: Prof. JÚLIO CÉSAR LIMA RAMIREZ
- History: Profa CHRISTINA SILVA ROQUETE LOPREATO
- Letters: Profa MARIA CRISTINA MARTINS
- Education: Profa HELENICE CAMARGOS VIANA DINIZ
- Education (Master's): Prof. JEFFERSON ILDEFONSO DA SILVA
- Psychology: Profa MARCIONILA RODRIGUES DA SILVA BRITO
- Accountancy: Prof. JOÃO BATISTA MENDES
- Law Internships: Prof. ANTÔNIO CAIXETA RIBEIRO
- Philosophy: Prof. ALEXANDRE GUIMARÃES TADEU SOARES
- Social Sciences: Prof. ANTÔNIO RICARDO MICHELOTO
- Languages: Prof. EVANDRO SILVA MARTINS
- Development Economics: Prof. ANTÔNIO CÉSAR ORTEGA

UNIVERSIDADE DO VALE DO RIO DOS SINOS

Av. Unisinos 950, CP 275, 93022-000 São Leopoldo, RS

Telephone: (51) 590-3333
Fax: (51) 592-1035
E-mail: wolf@helios.unisinos.tche.br

Founded 1969
Private control
Language of instruction: Portuguese
Academic year: March to July, August to December

President: Prof. Dr ALOYSIO BOHNEN
Vice-President: P. EGYDIO EDUARDO SCHNEIDER
Pro-Presidents: P. EGYDIO EDUARDO SCHNEIDER (Development), Prof. EMI MARIA SANTINI SAFT (Undergraduate Studies and Research), Prof. CÉLIO PEDRO WOLFARTH (Administration), Prof. VICENTE DE PAULO OLIVEIRA SANT'ANNA (Community and Extension), Prof. TARCILLO LAWISCH (Head of President's Office)
Registrar: Prof. JOSÉ MARCULANO
Library Director: P. Dr LODOMILO AUGUSTO MALLIMANN

Library of 388,000 books and periodicals
Number of teachers: 907
Number of students: 22,789

Publications: *Pesquisas, Estudos Leopoldenses, Acta Biologica Leopoldensia, Estudos Tecnológicos (Geologia, Arquitetura, Engenharia), Acta Geologica Leopoldensia, Perspectiva Econômica, Estudos Jurídicos, Scientia, Verso e Reverso, História e Estória das Palavras, Palavra Como/Vida, UNISINOS em Revista, Jornal UNISINOS.*

DEANS

Human Sciences: Prof. BENNO JOÃO LERMEN
Health Sciences: Prof. CORNÉLIA HULDA VOLKART
Communication Sciences: Prof. PEDRO GILBERTO GOMES
Law: Prof. FLORIANO MILLER NETTO
Economics: Prof. ENIO ERNI KLEIN
Exact Sciences: Prof. ARETÊ PORCÚNCULA DE ÁVILA
Technological Sciences: Prof. SILVIA COSTA DUTRA

ATTACHED INSTITUTES

Centre for Documentation and Research (Population and Family): Dr ROQUE LAUSCHNER.
Institute Anchietano for Research: Dr PEDRO IGNÁCIO SCHMITZ.
Institute for Research into Planarians: Dr JOSEF HAUSER.
Languages Institute: Prof. MIRYAM SPONCHIADO CELARO.

UNIVERSIDADE FEDERAL DE VIÇOSA

Av. P.H. Rolfs s/n, 36571-000 Viçosa, MG

Telephone: (31) 899-2103
Fax: (31) 899-2203
E-mail: reitoria@mail.ufv.br

Founded 1926; formerly Universidade Rural do Estado de Minas Gerais
State control
Language of instruction: Portuguese
Academic year: March to June, August to November

Rector: Prof. LUIZ SÉRGIO SARAIVA
Vice-Rector: Prof. CARLOS SIGUEYUKI SEDIYAMA
Pro-Rectors: Profa MAGDALA ALENCAR TEIXEIRA (Research and Postgraduate), Prof. JOÃO CARLOS PEREIRA DA SILVA (Undergraduate), Prof. FLAVIO ARAUJO COUTO (Extension and Culture), Prof. WALMER FARONI (Community Affairs), Prof. ANTONIO SANTANA FERRAZ (Administration), Prof. ANTONIO LUIZ DE LIMA (Planning and Budget)
Chief Administrative Officer: Prof. VICENTE DE PAULA LELIS
Director of Library: DORIS MAGNA DE AVELAR OLIVEIRA

Number of teachers: 761
Number of students: 7,715 (incl. 778 at high school level)

Publications: *Revista Ceres* (6 a year), *Boletim Técnico de Extensão, Revista Brasileira de Armazenamento, Revista da Sociedade Brasileira de Zootecnia* (6 a year), *Revista Oikos* (2 a year), *Revista Árvore* (4 a year), *Revista de Educação Física* (2 a year), *Revista Seiva, Revista de Engenharia na Agricultura* (monthly), *Boletim de Economia Rural* (6 a year), *Revista Gláuks* (2 a year), *Jornal da UFV* (monthly), *UFV – Debate* (2 a year).

DEANS

Agricultural Sciences Centre: Prof. FERNANDO DA COSTA BAÊTA
Human Sciences and Liberal Arts Centre: Prof. PAULO SHIKAZU TOMA

Engineering and Technological Sciences Centre: Prof. JOSÉ CARLOS BOHNENBERGER
Biological and Health Sciences Centre: Prof. MARCELO JOSE VILELA

HEADS OF DEPARTMENTS

Agricultural Sciences Centre:
- Agricultural Economics: Prof. ERLY CARDOSO TEIXEIRA
- Agricultural Engineering: Prof. ANTÔNIO ALVES SOARES
- Agronomy: Prof. GERALDO ANTÔNIO DE ANDRADE ARAÚJO
- Forestry Engineering: Prof. AMAURY PAULO DE SOUZA
- Phytopathology: Profa ROSÂNGELA D'ARC DE LIMA OLIVEIRA
- Soil Science: Prof. LUIZ EDUARDO FERREIRA FONTES
- Animal Science: AUGUSTO CÉSAR DE QUEIRÓZ

Biological and Health Sciences Centre:
- Animal Biology: Prof. PAULO SÉRGIO FIÚZA FERREIRA
- Biochemistry and Molecular Biology: Profa MARIA GORETI DE ALMEIDA OLIVEIRA
- General Biology: Prof. MARCOS RIBEIRO FURTADO
- Plant Biology: Prof. MARCO ANTÔNIO OLIVA CANO
- Physical Education: Prof. ADILSON OSÉS
- Nutrition and Health: Profa MARILENE PINHEIRO EUCLYDES
- Microbiology: Prof. ARNALDO CHAER BORGES
- Veterinary Medicine: Prof. RICARDO JUNQUEIRA DEL CARLO

Engineering and Technological Sciences:
- Civil Engineering: Prof. ANTÔNIO SIMÕES SILVA
- Physics: ORLANDO PINHEIRO DA FONESCA RODRIGUES
- Computer Science: Prof. LUIZ CARLOS DE ABREU ALBUQUERQUE
- Architecture: Prof. ANTONIO CLÉBER GONÇALVES TIBIRIÇÁ
- Mathematics: Prof. ANTÔNIO JOSÉ MACIEL
- Chemistry: Prof. BENJAMIN GONÇALVES MILAGRES
- Food Technology: Prof. FREDERICO JOSÉ VIEIRA PASSOS

Human Sciences and Liberal Arts Centre:
- Business Administration: Prof. ADRIEL RODRIGUES DE OLIVEIRA
- Economics: Profa ROSA MARIA OLIVERA FONTES
- Home Economics: Profa AURORA RIBEIRO DE GOICOCHEA
- Education: Prof. WILLER ARAÚJO BARBOSA.
- Languages and Fine Arts: Prof. EUSTÁQUIO MARCONCINI BINI
- Law: Prof. DANIEL AMIN FERRAZ

Colleges

GENERAL

Associação de Ensino Unificado do Distrito Federal: SEP/SUL, Eq. 704/904, Conjunto A, 70390-045 Brasília, DF; tel. (61) 321-3838; fax (61) 223-7195; f. 1967; controls Instituto de Ciências Sociais; courses in accountancy, administration, economics, education and law; 290 teachers; library of 42,000 vols; Pres. REZENDE RIBEIRO DE REZENDE.

Centro de Ensino Unificado de Brasília: EQN 707/9, Brasília, DF; f. 1968; controls Faculdade de Direito do Distrito Federal, Faculdade de Filosofia, Ciências e Letras do Distrito Federal, Faculdade de Ciências Econômicas, Contábeis e Administrativas do Distrito Federal; 8,229 students; library of 22,000 vols; Pres. Dr ALBERTO PÉRES; publ. *Universitas* (quarterly).

Faculdades Oswaldo Cruz: Rua Brigadeiro Galvão 564, 540, São Paulo; tel. 825-4266; f. 1967; library of 26,400 vols; 278 teachers; 4,320 students; Dir. CARLOS EDUARDO QUIRINO SIMÕES DE AMORIM; Librarian YÁDIA SIQUEIRA PEQUENO.

Comprises:

Faculdade de Ciências Farmacêuticas e Bioquímicas: courses in pharmacy and biochemistry; Dir Profa MARIA A. POURCHET CAMPOS.

Escola Superior de Química: courses in industrial chemistry, engineering; Dir Prof. NELSON C. F. BONETTO.

Faculdade de Ciências Econômicas, Contábeis e Administrativas: courses in economics, accountancy and management; Dir Prof. Dr HIRONDEL S. LUDERS.

Faculdade de Filosofia, Ciências e Letras: courses in chemistry, physics, mathematics, Portuguese; Dir Prof. MIGUEL TABET.

Federação de Escolas Superiores: Rua Cobre 200, 30000 Belo Horizonte, MG; f. 1967; controlled by the Fundação Mineira de Educação e Cultura; courses in psychology, education, civil engineering, business administration; 203 professors; 2,691 students; library of 25,000 vols; Pres. HÉLIO LOPES.

Fundação Valeparaibana de Ensino: Praça Cândido Dias Castejón 116, 12245 São José dos Campos, SP; tel. (123) 22-2355; f. 1963; Pres. Dr BAPTISTA GARGIONE FILHO.

Controls the following:

Faculdades Integradas de São José dos Campos: São José dos Campos; SP; 206 teachers; library of 53,000 vols; Dir Gen. JOÃO LUIZ TEIXEIRA PINTO.

Courses are offered by the following faculties:

Faculdade de Ciências Humanas: f. 1967; 48 teachers; 1,130 students; Dir IVONNE TESSIN WEIS.

Faculdade de Ciências Exatas e Tecnologia: f. 1968; 90 teachers; 800 students; Dir LUIZ ANTONIO PEDROSO DE MORAIS.

Faculdade de Ciências Sociais Aplicadas: f. 1952; 68 teachers; 1,560 students; Dir FRANCISCO JOSÉ DE CASTRO PIMENTEL.

Instituição 'Moura Lacerda': Rua Padre Euclides 995, Ribeirão Prêto, SP; tel. 636-1010; f. 1923; consists of the Faculdade de Ciências Econômicas de Ribeirão Prêto, the Instituto Politécnico de Ribeirão Prêto, the Faculdade de Filosofia, Ciências e Letras de Ribeirão Prêto, the Faculdade de Arquitetura e Urbanismo de Ribeirão Prêto, the Faculdade de Educação Física de Jaboticabal, also two teacher training colleges and a music conservatoire; library of 50,000 vols; Pres. Dr OSCAR LUIS DE MOURA LACERDA.

BIBLIOGRAPHY AND LIBRARY SCIENCE

Curso de Biblioteconomia e Documentação: Rua Xavier Sigaud 290, URCA, Rio de Janeiro; f. 1911; certificate and diploma courses in library science and documentation; Dir Prof. DÉA SANTOS DE ARAÚJO COUTINHO AMADEO.

Escola de Biblioteconomia e Documentação de São Carlos: Rua São Sebastião 2828, 13560-230 São Carlos, SP; tel. and fax (162) 72-1325; f. 1959; 12 professors; 40 students; library of 11,000 vols; Dir MARIA CHRISTINA DE A. NOGUEIRA; publ. *Biblio . . . Que?*.

ECONOMICS, POLITICAL SCIENCE, SOCIOLOGY

Escola de Administração de Emprêsas de São Paulo da Fundação Getúlio Vargas: Av. 9 de Julho 2029, 01313-902 São Paulo, SP; tel. 281-7700; fax (11) 284-17-89; e-mail stempfer@eaesp.fgvsp.br; f. 1954; business and public administration; library of 70,000 books, 1,200 periodicals; 250 teachers, 4,616 students; Dir ALAIN F. STEMPFER; publs *Revista de Administração de Emprêsas, Relatórios de Pesquisa.*

Universidade de Santa Cruz do Sul: Av. Independência 2293, CP 236, Santa Cruz do Sul, RS; tel. (51) 713-1633; fax (51) 713-1011; f. 1964; courses in accountancy; library of 26,000 vols; Course Co-ordinator Profa MÁRCIA ROSANE FREY.

Faculdade de Ciências Econômicas do Sul de Minas: Av. Pres. Tancredo de A. Neves 55, CP 37500, Itajubá, MG; f. 1965; Dir HÉCTOR GUSTAVO ARANGO.

Faculdade de Ciências Econômicas e Administrativas de Santo André: Av. Príncipe de Gales 821, CP 247, Santo André, SP; tel. (11) 449-3093; fax (11) 440-2048; f. 1954; supported by the Fundação Santo André; library of 19,340 vols; Dir Prof. CARLOS VIEIRA.

Faculdade de Ciências Econômicas e Administrativas de Taubaté: Rua Visconde do Rio Branco 210, Taubaté, SP; f. 1961; courses in accounting, economics and business administration; Dir Dr ULISSES VIEIRA.

Faculdade de Ciências Políticas e Econômicas de Cruz Alta: Rua Andrade Neves 308, Cruz Alta, RS; f. 1955; independent; library of 4,605 vols; Dir DARIO SILVEIRA NETTO.

Faculdade Estadual de Ciências Econômicas de Apucarana: Rodovia do Café, BR 376-Km 3, CP 98, 86800 Apucarana, PR; f. 1959; state school; Dir Prof. ADRIANO CORRÊA.

Instituto Rio Branco: Anexo II do Palácio Itamaraty, Ministério das Relações Exteriores, 70170-900 Brasília, DF; tel. 211-6194; telex 61-1311; fax 322-8355; f. 1945; official Brazilian Diplomatic Academy; 2-year graduate courses; also courses for foreign students; Dir Min. ANDRE MATTOSO MAIA AMADO; publ. *Yearbook*.

Instituto Universitário de Pesquisas do Rio de Janeiro: Rua da Matriz 82, Botafogo, 22260-100, Rio de Janeiro, RJ; tel. (21) 537-8020; fax (21) 286-7146; f. 1963; research and graduate training in sociology and political science; 18 teachers; library of 20,000 vols; Dir RENATO LESSA; publs *Dados* (3 a year), *Indice de Ciências Sociais* (2 a year), *Série Estudos* (monthly), *Cadernos de Conjuntura* (irregular).

LAW

Faculdade de Direito Cândido Mendes: Praça 15 de Novembro 101, Rio de Janeiro, RJ: f. 1953; courses in law, sociology and economics; library of 10,000 vols; Dir Prof. CÂNDIDO MENDES DE ALMEIDA; publ. *Dados*.

Faculdade de Direito de Caruarú: Av. Portugal s/n, 55100 Caruarú, PE; f. 1959; library of 6,027 vols; Dir Prof. LUÍZ PINTO FERREIRA; publ. *Revista*.

Faculdade de Direito de São Bernardo do Campo: Rua Java 425, Jardim do Mar, CP 180, 09750-650 São Bernardo do Campo, SP; f. 1964; library of 20,000 vols; Dir DIOGNES GASPARINI.

Faculdade de Direito de Sorocaba: Rua Dra. Ursulina Lopes Torres 123, 18100 Sorocaba, SP; f. 1957; library of 10,000 vols; Dir Dr HELIO ROSA BALDY; publ. *Revista*.

MEDICINE

Escola de Farmácia e Odontologia de Alfenas: Rua Gabriel Monteiro da Silva 714, 37130-000 Alfenas, MG; tel. (35) 299-1000; fax (35) 299-1063; f. 1914; graduate courses in dentistry, biochemical and applied pharmacy, general nursing and obstetrics; 119 teachers;

library of 16,059 vols; Dean Prof. JOÃO BATISTA MAGALHÃES; publ. *Journal*.

Universidade Federal de São Paulo: Rua Botucatú 740, 04023-062 São Paulo; tel. (11) 549-7699; fax (11) 549-2127; e-mail unifesp@ epm.br; f. 1933 (formerly Escola Paulista de Medicina); medicine, biomedical sciences, nursing, phonoaudiology and ophthalmic technology; library of 19,000 vols, 2,600 journals; 675 teachers, 4,150 students; Dean Dr HELIO EGYDIO NOGUEIRA; publs *Jornal da Paulista* (monthly), *Revista do Hospital São Paulo* (6 a year), *A Folha Médica* (6 a year).

Faculdade de Ciências Médicas de Pernambuco: Hospital Escola Oswaldo Cruz, Rua Arnóbio Marques 310, Santo Amaro, Recife, PE; tel. (81) 421-1761; f. 1950; supported by the Fundação do Ensino Superior de Pernambuco; 165 teachers; library of 22,763 vols; Dir Prof. JOSÉ GUIDO CORRÊA DE ARAÚJO.

Faculdade de Medicina do Triângulo Mineiro: Rua Frei Paulino 30, 38025-180 Uberaba, MG; f. 1953; Dir Prof. VALDEMAR HIAL.

Faculdade de Odontologia de Lins: Rua Tenente Florêncio Pupo Neto 300, CP 118, 16400 Lins, SP; f. 1954; independent; Dir NICÁCIO GARCIA HERNANDES; publ. *Revista da Faculdade de Odontologia de Lins*.

Faculdade de Odontologia, Universidade de Passo Fundo: Rua Teixeira Soares 817, 99010-080 Passo Fundo, RS; tel. (54) 311-1177; fax (54) 311-1307; f. 1961; dentistry; 44 teachers; 310 students; Dean Dr RUI GETÚLIO SOARES

Faculdade de Odontologia de Pernambuco: CP 1536, Av. Gral. Newton Cavalcanti 1650, Caramajibe, São Lourenço da Mata, PE; f. 1957; supported by the Fundação da Ensino Superior de Pernambuco; undergraduate and postgraduate courses; 32 teachers, 243 students; Dir Prof. EDRIZIO BARBOSA PINTO.

Faculdade de Odontologia do Triângulo Mineiro: Av. Guilherme Ferreira 217, CP 93, 38100 Uberaba, MG; f. 1947; four-year graduate course in Dentistry; library of 3,500 vols; Dir Prof. JAYME SOARES BILHARINHO NETTO; Sec. Dr ANDRÉ LUÍZ MARTINS COIMBRA.

Fundação Faculdade Federal de Ciências Médicas de Porto Alegre: Rua Sarmento Leite 245, 90050-170 Porto Alegre, RS; tel. 26-79-13; telex (051) 3080; f. 1953; library of 9,000 vols; 211 teachers; Dir Prof. OSCAR BELMIRO MANOEL MAY PEREIRA; publ. *Pesquisa Médica*.

PHILOSOPHY, ARTS AND LITERATURE

Faculdade de Filosofia, Ciências e Letras de Ouro Fino: Rodovia MG 290, Km 59, Ouro Fino, CP 38, MG; f. 1972; run by Associação Sul Mineira de Educação e Cultura; 23 teachers, 1,437 students; library of 8,306 vols, 3,522 periodicals; Pres. Prof. GUILHERME BERNARDES; publ. *Signum*.

Faculdades Salesianas – Unidade de Ensino de Lorens: Rua Dom Bosco 284, CP 41, 12600-000 Lorena, SP; f. 1985; courses in psychology, history, geography, education, law, philosophy and sciences; library of 60,000 vols; Dir Pe. DILSON PASSOS JUNIOR; Sec. GETULINO DO ESPÍRITO SANTO MACIEL; publ. *Revista*.

TECHNICAL

Escola de Engenharia de Lins: Av. Nicolau Zarvos 1925, CP 103, 16400-000 Lins, SP; tel. (145) 22-2300; fax (145) 22-2300; f. 1961; departments of civil and electrical engineering, attached faculties of informatics and of Social Services; 50 teachers, 650 students; Pres. EDGAR PAULO PASTORELLO; Dir of Engineering Prof. BERNARDO LUIZ COSTAS FUMIÓ.

ATTACHED INSTITUTE

Faculdade de Informática de Lins: f. 1986; department of data processing technology; 25 teachers; 280 students; Dir of Data Processing Profa MARIA EMILCE FERREIRA VILLELA PASTORELLO.

Escola de Engenharia de Taubaté: Av. Marechal Deodoro 605, Taubaté, SP; f. 1962; courses in civil, mechanical and electrical engineering; library of 6,000 vols; Dir Eng. ADOLFO FERNANDES ARAÚJO.

Escola de Engenharia Mauá: Estrada das Lágrimas 2035, CEP 09580-900, São Caetano do Sul, SP; tel. (11) 741-3000; fax (11) 741-3041; e-mail maua@eu.ansp.br; f. 1961; civil, electrical, mechanical, metallurgical, industrial, sanitary, chemical and food engineering, packaging technology; library of 50,000 vols; 240 teachers; 3,800 students; Dir OTAVIO DE MATTOS SILVARES.

Escola Federal de Engenharia de Itajubá: Campus Prof. José Rodrigues Seabra, Av. BPS 1303, 37500-000 Itajubá, MG; tel. (35) 629-1124; fax (35) 622-3596; f. 1913; undergraduate and postgraduate courses in electrical and mechanical engineering; 141 teachers, 1,620 students; library of 21,000 vols; Dir Prof. JOSÉ CARLOS GOULART DE SIQUEIRA; publ. *Pesquisa e Desenvolvimento Tecnológico* (quarterly).

Escola Superior de Desenho Industrial: Rua Evaristo da Veiga 95, Rio de Janeiro 20031-040; tel. and fax (21) 240-1890; f. 1962; state school, affiliated to Univ. do Estado do Rio de Janeiro; courses in product and graphic design; 34 teachers, 160 students; Dir FRANK BARRAL.

Faculdade de Ciências Agrárias do Pará: CP 917, 66077-530 Belém, PA; tel. (91) 246-2233; fax (91) 226-3814; f. 1951; agronomical, forestal and veterinary studies; 131 teachers, 1,696 students; library of 17,000 vols, 1,343 periodicals; Dir Eng. Forestal PAULO LUIZ CONTENTE DE BARROS; publs *Boletim, O Trimestre*.

Faculdade de Ciências de Barretos: Av. Prof. Roberto Frade Monte 389, CP 16, 14783-266 Barretos, SP; tel. (173) 22-6411; fax (173) 22-6205; f. 1969; physics, mathematics, chemistry and food engineering and processing; library of 13,300 vols; Principal LUIZA MARIA PIERINI MACHADO.

Faculdade de Engenharia de Barretos: Av. Prof. Roberto Frade Monte 389, CP 16, 14783-226 Barretos, SP; tel. (173) 22-6411; fax (173) 22-6205; f. 1965; part of the Fundação Educacional de Barretos; civil and electrical engineering; library of 14,000 vols; Principal Eng. Prof. ROBERTO PINHEIRO GATSIOS.

Instituto Militar de Engenharia: Praça Gen. Tibúrcio 80, Praia Vermelha, 22290-270 Rio de Janeiro, RJ; tel. (21) 295-8146; telex (021) 38089; fax (21) 275-9047; f. 1792, present name 1959; undergraduate, master's and doctoral courses in sciences and engineering; 200 teachers; 500 students; library of 20,000 vols; Dir JOSÉ CARLOS ALBANO DO AMARANTE.

Instituto Nacional de Telecomunicações de Santa Rita do Sapucaí (INATEL): Av. João de Camargo 510, CP 05, Santa Rita do Sapucaí, MG; tel. (35) 471-9200; fax (35) 471-9314; e-mail informa@inatel.br; f. 1965; electrical engineering (electronics and telecommunications); library of 13,000 vols; Dir Prof. PEDRO SERGIO MONTI.

Instituto Tecnológico de Aeronáutica: Praça Mal. do Ar Eduardo Gomes 50, Vila das Acácias, 12228-900, São José dos Campos, SP; tel. (12) 340-5800; fax (12) 341-3500; e-mail euclides@adm.ita.cta.br; f. 1950; divisions of Electronic Engineering, Aeronautical Engineering, Mechanical Engineering, Civil and Basic Engineering, Computer Science; 130 teachers, 800 students; library of 90,000 vols and reports, 135,000 microforms, 2,000 periodicals; Rector Prof. Dr EUCLIDES CARVALHO FERNANDES; Dean Prof. Dr CLÁUDIO JORGE PINTO ALVES; Admin. Officer Dr NEHEMIAS LIMA LACERDA; publ. *Theasaurus Aeroespacial, Produção Técnico-científica, Revista, Boletim Informativo*.

Instituto Tecnológico e Científico 'Roberto Rios' (INTEC): Av. Prof. Roberto Frade Monte 389, 14780 Barretos, SP; f. 1981; soil physics, solar energy, apiculture, civil and electrical engineering; Dir WANDERLEY MAURO DIB.

Schools of Art and Music

Centro de Letras e Artes da UNI-RIO: Av. Pasteur 436, Urca, 22290-240 Rio de Janeiro, RJ; tel. (21) 295-2548; fax (21) 295-1043; f. 1969; four-year course in theatre and music, Masters course in theatre and Brazilian music; 96 teachers, 850 students; library of 25,000 vols, 7,000 scores, 3,000 records; Dean EDIR EVANGELISTA GANDRA; Dirs AUSONIA BERNARDES MONTEIRO, NEREIDA DE ASSIS NOGUEIA DE MOURA RANGEL.

Conservatório Brasileiro de Música: Av. Graça Aranha 57, 12°, Rio de Janeiro; tel. (21) 240-5431; fax (21) 240-6131; f. 1936; undergraduate and postgraduate courses; library of 6,000 vols; Dir-Gen. MARINA H. LORENZO FERNANDEZ SILVA; publ. *Revista Pesquisa e Música*.

Conservatório Dramático e Musical de São Paulo: Av. São João 269, São Paulo; f. 1906; library of 30,000 vols; Dir Dr ALONSO A. DA FONSECA (acting).

Escola de Artes Visuais (School of Visual Arts): Rua Jardim Botânico 414, Parque Lage, 22461 Rio de Janeiro, RJ; f. 1950; linked administratively to the State Department of Culture; courses in painting, engraving, ceramics, paper-making, photography, sculpture, drawing; library of 5,500 vols; 40 teachers, 1,200 students; Dir LUIZ ALPHONSUS DE GUIMARAENS.

Escola de Comunicações e Artes: Av. Prof. Lúcio M. Rodrigues 443, Cidade Universitária, 05508-900 São Paulo; tel. 818-4066; e-mail rebeca@edu.usp.br; f. 1967; undergraduate and postgraduate training given; mass communication, library and information science, journalism, public relations, film, radio, television, the arts, theatre courses, music, advertising, tourism, publishing; library of 28,000 vols, 1,600 periodical titles, 6,000 records, 10,000 slides, 900 video tapes, 6,000 art exhibition catalogues, 250 films, 3,200 theses, 2,300 photographs, etc; Librarian BÁRBARA JÚLIA M. LEITÃO BISCARO.

Escola de Música e Belas Artes do Paraná: Rua Emiliano Perneta 179, 80000 Curitiba, PR; f. 1948; library of 2,350 vols, also tapes, records; musical instruments, singing, plastic arts; Dir LILIAN M. SCHEEL.

Escola de Música da Universidade Federal do Rio de Janeiro: Rua do Passeio 98, Lapa, 20021-290 Rio de Janeiro, RJ; tel. (21) 240-1391; fax (21) 240-1591; f. 1848; 77 teachers; 478 students; library (f. 1855), 100,000 vols of music; museum of 90 antique instruments; Dir Prof. JOSÉ ALVES; Librarian DOLORES BRANDÃO DE OLIVEIRA; publ. *Revista Brasileira de Música* (irregular).

Attached to the school:

Centro de Pesquisas Folclóricas: f. 1943; Dir Prof. SAMUEL MELLO ARAÚJO, Jr.; collections of traditional music on records.

Faculdade de Belas Artes de São Paulo: 76 A. Alvim Dr., São Paulo; tel. 229-9422; f. 1925; architecture, town planning, industrial arts and design, painting, sculpture, etc.;

130 teachers; library of 10,000 vols; Dir PAULO ANTONIO GOMES CARDIM.

Faculdade de Música Mãe de Deus: Av. São Paulo 651, CP 106, 86100 Londrina, PR; f. 1965; library of 2,650 vols; Dir Profa. THEODOLINDA GERTRUDES MORO; publ. *Fôlha de Londrina*.

Faculdade Santa Marcelina – (FASM): Rua Dr Emílio Ribas 89, 05006-020 Perdizes, SP; tel. (11) 826-9700; fax (11) 826-9700 ext. 209; e-mail diretoria@fasm.com.br; f. 1929; music, musical instruments, singing, composition, artistic education, plastic arts, design, fashion design, electric-acoustic music; 99 teachers; library of 48,000 vols; Pres. FERNANDA MARTELLINI; Dir ÂNGELA RIVERO.

Fundação Armando Alvares Penteado: Rua Alagoas 903, 10242 São Paulo; tel. 826-4233; f. 1947; 1,120 teachers, 12,000 students; Pres. LUCIA C. PINTO DE SOUZA.

Instituto de Letras e Artes: Rua Marechal Floriano 179, 96015-440 Pelotas, RS; fax (532) 22-4318; f. 1971; institute of the Universidade Federal de Pelotas; degree courses in plastic arts, music, literature and culture; 60 teachers; Dir MARIA DE LOURDES VALENTE REYES.

BRUNEI

Research Institutes

AGRICULTURE, FISHERIES AND VETERINARY SCIENCE

Research and Development Division, Department of Agriculture: Ministry of Industry and Primary Resources, Brunei Darussalam; Head of Division Haji INSANUL BAKTI BIN ABDUL AZIZ.

HISTORY, GEOGRAPHY AND ARCHAEOLOGY

Brunei History Centre: f. 1982; government dept under the Ministry of Culture, Youth and Sports; research on Brunei's history; genealogy and history of the Royal Family and Sultans; publs *Pusaka* (Heritage) (every 6 months), *Darussalam* (The Abode of the Peace) (annual).

Libraries and Archives

Bandar Seri Begawan

Language and Literature Bureau Library: Jalan Elizabeth II, Bandar Seri Begawan; tel. (2) 235501; f. 1961; reference and lending facilities open to the public; 300,000 vols in Malay and English; one central and 4 full-time brs; 5 mobile units; Chief Librarian Hj. ABU BAKAR BIN Hj. ZAINAL; publs *Accessions List*, indexes.

Museums and Art Galleries

Bandar Seri Begawan

Brunei Museum: Kota Batu, Bandar Seri Begawan 2018; tel. (2) 244545; fax (2) 242727; f. 1965; ethnographical, historical, archaeological and natural history collections; reference library of 10,000 vols, Borneo collection of 2,000 vols, 38,000 local publs; Brunei National Archives; legal depository for Brunei; Dir PG Hj. HASHIM PG Hj. MOHD JADID (acting); publ. *Brunei Museum Journal* (monthly).

Constitutional History Gallery: Jalan Sultan, Bandar Seri Begawan 2085; tel. 238362; fax 242727; f. 1984; Dir PG HAJI HASHIM BIN PG Haji MOHD JADID (acting).

Malay Technology Museum: Kota Batu, Bandar Seri Begawan BD 1510; tel. (2) 242861; fax (2) 242727; f. 1988; ethnography of Brunei Darussalam; Dir PG Hj. HASHIM PG Hj. MOHD JADID.

Royal Regalia Gallery: Jalan Sultan, Bandar Seri Begawan BS 8610; tel. (2) 238358; fax (2) 242727; f. 1992; Dir PG Haji HASHIM BIN PG Haji MOHD JADID.

University

UNIVERSITY OF BRUNEI DARUSSALAM

Tungku Link, Gadong BE 1410
Telephone: (2) 249001
Fax: (2) 249003

Founded 1985; the Sultan Hassanal Bolkiah Teachers' College was integrated into the University in 1988

State control

Languages of instruction: Malay and English

Academic year: August to May (two semesters)

Chancellor: HM Sultan Haji HASSANAL BOLKIAH MUIZZADDIN WADDAULAH

Vice-Chancellor: Pehin Dato ABU BUKAR APONG

Assistant Vice-Chancellor: Haji ABD LATIF Haji IBRAHIM

Registrar and Secretary: JANIN ERIH

Chief Librarian: Dr OLI MOHAMMED BIN ABDUL HAMID

Library of 250,000 vols

Number of teachers: 295

Number of students: 1,520

Publication: *Ungkayah* (4 a year).

DEANS

Faculty of Arts and Social Science: Dr K. U. SIRINANDA

Sultan Hassanal Bolkiah Institute of Education: Prof. SIM WONG KOOI

Faculty of Management and Administrative Studies: Dr SHAFRUDDIN HASHIM

Faculty of Science: Dr D. S. EDWARDS

Faculty of Islamic Studies: Dr Hj. MAGHFUR USMAN

Academy of Brunei Studies: Haji ISMAIL Haji DURAMAN (Dir)

Colleges

Institut Teknologi Brunei: POB 2909, Bandar Seri Begawan 1929; tel. 330427; telex 2557; f. 1986; library of 25,000 vols; 50 teachers; 200 students; B/TEC HND and HNC courses; Dir Haji ABU HANIFAH BIN Haji MOHD SALLEH; Registrar Haji MOHAMMAD BIN Haji HIDUP; Librarian PUSPARAINI BTE Haji THANI.

HEADS OF DEPARTMENTS

Business and Management: RAMACHANDRAN NAIR

Computing and Information Systems: Haji AWANG YUSSOF BIN Haji AWANG MOHAMMAD

Electrical and Electronic Engineering: DERYK MCNEILL

Civil Engineering: TERENCE WILLIAM MANSFIELD

Mechanical Engineering: Dr FAQIR GUL

Jefri Bolkiah College of Engineering: POB 63, Kuala Belait; 6000; f. 1970; craft and technical courses; 78 staff, 350 students; Principal AZAHARAINI BIN Haji MOHD JAMIL.

Seri Begawan Religious Teachers' College: Bandar Seri Begawan.

Sultan Saiful Rijal Technical College: POB 914, Simpang 125, Jalan Muara, Brunei Darussalam.

There are Adult Education Centres attached to colleges and schools.

BULGARIA

Learned Societies

GENERAL

Bulgarian Academy of Sciences: 1040 Sofia, 15 Noemvri 1; tel. (2) 8-41-41; fax (2) 88-04-48; f. 1869; 45 academicians, 84 corresp. mems, 76 foreign mems; attached research institutes: see Research Institutes; library: see Libraries and Archives; Pres. Prof. Dr IVAN YUKHNOVSKI; Gen. Scientific Sec. Prof. NAUM YAKIMOV; Scientific Secs Prof. ANGEL BALTOV, Prof. STEFAN DASKALOV, Prof. ATANAS ATANASSOV, Assoc. Prof. STEFAN HADZHITODOROV, Assoc. Prof. ALEKSANDAR VAVREK, Assoc. Prof. ALEXANDER POPOV, Assoc. Prof. DIMITAR SIRAKOV; publs *Spisanie na Bălgarskata Akademija na Naukite* (Review of the Bulgarian Academy of Sciences), *Dokladi na Bălgarskata Akademija na Naukite* (Reports), *Teoretichna i Prilozhna Mehanika* (Theoretical and Applied Mechanics), *Tehnicheska Misăl* (Technical Thought), *Fiziko-matematichesko Spisanie* (Physical-Mathematical Review), *Priroda* (Nature) and many others.

Union of Scientists in Bulgaria: 1504 Sofia, Oborishte 35; tel. 944-11-57; fax 944-15-90; f. 1944; 4,000 mems; Pres. Prof. I. MATEV; Sec.-Gen. Prof. K. GABROVSKI; publ. *Nauka* (every 2 months).

AGRICULTURE, FISHERIES AND VETERINARY SCIENCE

Bulgarian Soil Society: 1080 Sofia, Shose Bankia 7, POB 1369; tel. 2-52-71; telex 22701; f. 1959; Pres. Prof. T. BOYADZHIEV; Sec. Prof. Dr. R. DILKOVA.

Scientific and Technical Union of Specialists in Agriculture: 1000 Sofia, G. Rakovski 108; tel. 87-65-13; telex 22185; fax 87-93-60; f. 1965; Pres. Prof. NIKOLA TOMOV; Sec. DIMITAR RADULOV; publ. *Buletin Vnedreni Novosti*.

ARCHITECTURE AND TOWN PLANNING

Union of Architects in Bulgaria: 1504 Sofia, Krakra 11; tel. 44-26-73; telex 23569; fax 946-08-00; f. 1965; 4,500 mems; library of 3,000 vols; Pres. Prof. EVLOGI TSVETKOV; publs *Architectura, Arch & Art Borse*.

ECONOMICS, LAW AND POLITICS

Bulgarian Association of Criminology: 1000 Sofia, Vitosha 2; tel. 87-47-51; f. 1986; Pres. Assoc. Prof. Y. BOYADZHIEVA.

Bulgarian Association of International Law: 1680 Sofia, Belite brezi bl. 6; tel. and fax (2) 59-80-92; f. 1962; 50 mems; Pres. A. JANKOV; Sec. Dr M. GANEV; publ. *Trudove po Mezhdunarodno Pravo*.

Union of Economists: 1000 Sofia, G. Rakovski 108; tel. 80-55-75; f. 1968; Pres. R. GEORGIEV; Sec. I. POPOV; publ. *Bjuletin*.

FINE AND PERFORMING ARTS

Union of Bulgarian Actors: 1000 Sofia, Narodno Sabranie 12; tel. 87-07-25; fax 88-33-01; f. 1919; Pres. STEFAN ILIEV; publ. *Teatăr*.

Union of Bulgarian Artists: 1504 Sofia, Shipka 6; tel. 44-61-15; fax 946-02-12; f. 1893; Pres. L. ZIDAROV; publs *Promishlena Estetika, Dekorativno Izkustvo*.

Union of Bulgarian Composers: 1000 Sofia, Iv. Vazov 2; tel. 88-15-60; fax 87-43-78; f. 1947; 207 mems; library of 25,280 vols; Pres. Prof. V. CHUCHKOV; publ. *Muzika – Vchera, Dnes* (monthly).

Union of Bulgarian Film Makers: 1504 Sofia, Dondukov 67; tel. and fax (2) 946-10-69; f. 1934; 1,006 mems; Pres. P. A. VASSEV; publ. *Kino* (6 a year).

HISTORY, GEOGRAPHY AND ARCHAEOLOGY

Bulgarian Geographical Society: 1000 Sofia, Tsar Osvoboditel 15; tel. (2) 46-43-10; fax (2) 44-64-87; f. 1918; Pres. Prof. P.V. PETROV; Sec. L. TSANKOVA; publs *Geografija, Geoecologija, Geografijata Dnes*.

Union of Numismatic Societies: Veliko Tarnovo; tel. (62) 2-37-72; f. 1964; 11,000 mems; Pres. H. KHARITONOV; Sec. Dr L. BOJILOV; publ. *Revue Numismatica* (quarterly).

LANGUAGE AND LITERATURE

Balkanmedia Association: 1407 Sofia, Luibotran 96; tel. 81-42-56; fax 87-16-98; f. 1990; ind. non-profit org. for mass media and communication culture in the Balkan countries; 36 assoc. mems (from all Balkan countries); Pres. ROSEN MILEV; publ. *Balkanmedia*.

Bulgarian Philologists' Society: 1000 Sofia, Moskovska 13; tel. 80-33-11; f. 1977; Pres. Prof. S. HADZHIKOSEV; publ. *Ezik i literatura* (6 a year).

Bulgarian Translators' Union: 1000 Sofia, Graf Ignatiev 16, POB 161; tel. (2) 981-09-60; f. 1974; Pres. L. PAUNOVA; publs *Panorama, News Bulletin*.

Society of Aesthetes and Art and Literary Critics: 1000 Sofia, Krakra 21; f. 1970; Pres. (vacant); Sec. Prof. K. GORANOV.

Union of Bulgarian Journalists: 1000 Sofia, Graf Ignatiev 4; tel. 87-27-73; telex 22635; fax 88-30-47; f. 1944; 5,500 mems; Pres. A. ANGELOV; publs *Pogled, Bălgarski zhurnalist*.

Union of Bulgarian Writers: 1000 Sofia, A. Kanchev 5; tel. 89-83-46; fax 88-06-85; f. 1913; 483 mems; Pres. N. HAITOV; publs *Bulgarian Writer, Letopisi, Plamăk*, Slavejche, Savremennik.

MEDICINE

Bulgarian Society of Neurosciences: 1431 Sofia, Zdrave 2; tel. 51-86-23; fax 51-87-83; f. 1987; Pres. Prof. V. OVCHAROV.

Bulgarian Society of Parasitology: 1113 Sofia, Acad. G. Bonchev bl. 25; tel. 713-23-74; f. 1965; Pres. Prof. O. POLIAKOVA-KRASTEVA.

Bulgarian Society of Sports Medicine and Kinesitherapy: Dept of Sports Medicine, National Sports Academy, 1000 Sofia, Gurgulyat 1; tel. (2) 88-30-64; f. 1953; 200 mems; Pres. Prof. Dr MARIA TOTEVA; Sec. Dr TODOR TODOROV; publ. *Sport i Nauka* (monthly).

Union of Scientific Medical Societies in Bulgaria: 1431 Sofia, D. Nestorov 15, Hygiene Centre, 12th Floor, Room 19; tel. and fax (2) 59-50-32; f. 1968; 12,000 mems, 64 mem. socs; Pres. Prof. Dr N. NACHEV; publ. *Modern Medicine* (quarterly).

NATURAL SCIENCES

Biological Sciences

Bulgarian Botanical Society: 1113 Sofia, Acad. G. Bonchev bl. 23; tel. 72-06-85; fax 71-90-32; f. 1923; Pres. (vacant); Sec. M. ANCHEV.

Bulgarian Society of Natural History: 1164 Sofia, D. Zankov 8; tel. 66-65-94; f. 1896; 1,000 mems; Pres. Prof. D. VODENICHAROV; Sec. S. DIMITROVA; publ. *Priroda i Znanie* (10 a year).

Mathematical Sciences

Union of Bulgarian Mathematicians: 1113 Sofia, Acad. G. Bonchev bl. 8; tel. (2) 73-80-76; fax (2) 971-36-49; e-mail smb@math.acad.bg; f. 1977; Pres. Dr CH. LOZANOV; Sec. S. GROZDEV; publ. *Mathematics and Mathematical Education* (annually).

Physical Sciences

Bulgarian Geological Society: 1000 Sofia, Moskovska 6, POB 228; tel. 87-24-50; e-mail vtvuchev@geology.acad.bg; f. 1925; 460 mems; library of 21,000 vols; Pres. Prof. V. VUCHEV; Sec. G. AIDAMLIISKI; publ. *Review* (3 a year).

Union of Physicists in Bulgaria: 1126 Sofia, J. Bourchier 5; tel. 62-76-60; f. 1971; Pres. Prof. I. LALOV; Sec. Prof. M. VELEVA; publ. *Bulgarian Journal of Physics*.

PHILOSOPHY AND PSYCHOLOGY

Bulgarian Pedagogical Society: 1547 Sofia, Shipchenski prohod 69A; tel. (2) 72-08-93; f. 1975; Pres. Prof. G. BIZHKOV.

Bulgarian Philosophical Association: 1000 Sofia, Lege 5; tel. and fax (2) 981-42-80; f. 1968; 320 mems; Pres. Prof. IVAN KALCHEV; Sec. R. KRIKORIAN; publ. *Filosofski Forum*.

Society of Bulgarian Psychologists: 1606 Sofia, Liulin Planina 14, POB 1333; tel. 54-12-95; f. 1969; Pres. Prof. D. GRADEV; Sec. ZH. BALEV; publ. *Balgarsko Spisanie po Psikhologija*.

RELIGION, SOCIOLOGY AND ANTHROPOLOGY

Bulgarian Sociological Association: 1000 Sofia, Lege 5; tel. (2) 88-40-35; fax (2) 52-24-07; f. 1959; Pres. Prof. Dr PETAR-EMIL MITEV; Sec. M. MIRCHEV.

TECHNOLOGY

Bulgarian Astronautical Society: 1113 Sofia, Akad. G. Bonchev 3, Tsentralna laboratoria po slanchevo-zemni vazdeistvia; tel. (2) 70-02-29; f. 1957; 600 mems; library of 500 vols; Pres. Prof. D. MISHEV; Scientific Sec. Prof. A. SIMEONOV.

Federation of Scientific and Technical Unions in Bulgaria: 1000 Sofia, G. Rakovski 108; tel. (2) 89-83-79; telex 22185; fax (2) 987-93-60; f. 1893; Pres. Prof. V. GANOVSKI; publs *No, Nauka i Obshestvo*.

Scientific and Technical Union of Civil Engineering: 1000 Sofia, G. Rakovski 108; tel. 88-46-78; telex 22185; fax 87-93-60; f. 1965; Pres. Dr K. KOSEV; Sec. M. RUSEVA; publs *Stroitelstvo, Stroitel 2000*.

Scientific and Technical Union of Energetics: 1000 Sofia, G. Rakovski 108; tel. 88-41-58; telex 22185; fax 87-93-60; f. 1965; Pres.

Prof. L. PETKANCHIN; Sec. Eng. D. TOMOV; publ. *Energetika*.

Scientific and Technical Union of Forestry: 1000 Sofia, G. Rakovski 108; tel. 88-36-83; fax 87-93-60; f. 1965; Pres. I. KOSTOV; Sec. S. SAVOV; publs *Dărvoobrabotvashta i mebelna Promislenost*, *Celuloza i Hartija*.

Scientific and Technical Union of Mechanical Engineering: 1000 Sofia, G. Rakovski 108; tel. (2) 987-72-90; fax (2) 80-23-65; f. 1965; Pres. Prof. ALEXANDER SKORDEV; Sec. D. DAMJANOV; publ. *Mashinostroene*.

Scientific and Technical Union of Mining, Geology and Metallurgy: 1000 Sofia, G. Rakovski 108; tel. 87-57-27; fax 87-93-60; f. 1965; Pres. Prof. V. STOYANOV; Sec. V. GENEVSKI; publs *Văglishta*, *Rudodobiv*, *Metalurgija*.

Scientific and Technical Union of Textiles, Clothing and Leather: 1000 Sofia, G. Rakovski 108; tel. 88-16-41; fax 87-93-60; f. 1965; Pres. Prof. E. KANTCHEV; Sec. I. MECHEV; publs *Tekstilna Promishlenost*, *Kozhi i Obuvki*.

Scientific and Technical Union of the Food Industry: 1000 Sofia, G. Rakovski 108; tel. 87-47-44; fax 87-93-60; f. 1965; Pres. K. KLYAMOV; Sec. A. CHUDOMIROV; publ. *Hranitelna promishlenost*.

Scientific and Technical Union of Transport: 1000 Sofia, G. Rakovski 108; tel. 87-23-71; fax 87-93-60; f. 1965; Pres. S. KOTOV; Sec. ST. GAIDAROV; publs *Zelezopăten Transport*, *Patishta*.

Scientific and Technical Union of Water Development: 1000 Sofia, G. Rakovski 108; tel. 88-53-03; fax 87-93-60; f. 1965; Pres. Prof. E. MONEV; Sec. M. SJAROVA; publ. *Vodno delo*.

Union of Chemists in Bulgaria: 1000 Sofia, G. Rakovski 108; tel. 87-58-12; telex 22185; fax 87-93-60; f. 1901; Pres. G. BLIZNAKOV; Sec. S. DZHALEV; publ. *Himija i Industrija*.

Union of Electronic and Electrical Engineering and Communications: 1000 Sofia, G. Rakovski 108; tel. 87-99-67; telex 22185; fax 87-93-60; f. 1965; Pres. D. MICHEV; publ. *Elektrotekhnika i Elektronika*.

Union of Surveyors and Land Managers: 1000 Sofia, G. Rakovski 108; tel. (2) 89-83-79; telex 22185; fax (2) 87-93-60; f. 1937; Pres. Prof. Dr Ing. G. MILEV; Sec. ST. BOGDANOV; publ. *Geodesija, Kartografija i Zemeustrojstvo* (6 a year).

Research Institutes

AGRICULTURE, FISHERIES AND VETERINARY SCIENCE

Barley Research Institute: 8400 Karnobat; tel. 27-31; telex 83621; fax (559) 58-47; f. 1925; library of 17,000 vols; Dir Assoc. Prof. I. MIHOV.

Canning Research Institute: 4000 Plovdiv, V. Aprilov 154; tel. (32) 5-58-04; fax (32) 55-22-86; e-mail canri@main.infotel.bg; f. 1962; library of 19,000 vols; Dir PAVLINA PARASKOVA.

Central Veterinary Research Institute 'Prof. G. Pavlov': 1606 Sofia, P. Slavejkov 15; tel. (2) 52-12-77; fax (2) 54-29-25; f. 1901; Dir Prof. SV. MARTINOV.

Cotton and Durum Wheat Research Institute: 6200 Chirpan; tel. (416) 23-45; fax (416) 31-33; f. 1925; library of 16,000 vols; Dir CHOCHO K. LALEV.

Dairy Research Institute: 3700 Vidin; tel. 2-32-04; telex 36441; fax 3-46-32; f. 1959; library of 8,000 vols; Dir A. KOZHEV; publs *Dairy Abstracts Bulletin* (monthly), *Advanced Experience* (2 a year).

Fisheries Industry Institute: 8000 Burgas, Industrialna 3; tel. (56) 4-48-92; fax (56) 4-03-31; f. 1965; Dir Dr ZH. NECHEV.

Forage Institute: 5800 Pleven, I. Vazov 89; tel. (64) 2-34-74; telex 34440; fax (64) 3-85-28; f. 1955; Dir Prof. T. ZHELIAZKOV.

Forestry Research Institute: 1756 Sofia, Kl. Ohridski 132; tel. (2) 62-20-52; fax (2) 62-29-65; f. 1928; attached to Bulgarian Acad. of Sciences; library of 38,000 vols; Dir Prof. Dr IVAN RAEV; publs *Forestry Science* (quarterly), *Silva Balcanica* (2 a year).

Freshwater Fisheries Research Institute: 4003 Plovdiv, V. Levski 248; tel. (32) 55-60-33; fax (32) 55-39-24; f. 1978; Dir G. GROZEV.

Fruit-Growing Research Institute: 4004 Plovdiv, Ostromila 12; tel. (32) 77-13-49; telex 44609; fax (32) 77-08-08; f. 1950; Dir Prof. D. DIMITROV.

Institute for the Control of Foot and Mouth Disease and Dangerous Infections: 8800 Sliven, Trakia 75; tel. (44) 2-20-39; fax (44) 2-26-42; f. 1974; Dir R. KASABOV.

Institute of Agricultural Economics: 1618 Sofia, Tsar Boris III 136; tel. 56-28-08; telex 24427; fax 56-28-05; f. 1935; library of 29,463 vols; Dir Prof. R. TRENDAFILOV.

Institute of Animal Science: 2232 Kostinbrod (Sofia District); tel. (729) 32-91-64; telex 23335; f. 1947; library of 25,200 vols; Dir Prof. H. STANCHEV.

Institute of Cattle and Sheep Breeding: 6000 Stara Zagora; tel. (42) 4-10-76; fax (42) 4-71-48; f. 1942; Dir Prof. H. SARTMANDZHIEV.

Institute of Fisheries: 9000 Varna, Primorski 4; tel. (52) 23-18-52; fax (52) 25-78-76; f. 1932; library of 23,000 vols; Dir Dr P. KOLAROV.

Institute of Fruit Growing: 2500 Kyustendil; tel. (78) 2-75-32; fax (78) 2-74-11; f. 1929; library of 9,000 vols; Dir Assoc. Prof. Dr DIMITAR DOMOZETOV.

Institute of Grains and Feed Industry: 2232 Kostinbrod 2; tel. and fax (729) 87-12-93; f. 1965; library of 9,050 vols, 132 periodicals; Dir M. MACHEV.

Institute of Introduction and Plant Genetic Resources: 4122 Sadovo (Plovdiv District); tel. (32) 22-51; fax (32) 493-00-26; f. 1977; library of 30,000 vols; Dir Dr R. KOEVA.

Institute of Soya Bean Growing: 5200 Pavlikeni, POB 8; tel. (610) 22-75; telex 66505; fax (610) 25-41; f. 1925; Dir Assoc. Prof. G. TONCHEV.

Institute of the Mechanization and Electrification of Agriculture: 1331 Sofia, Shose Bankya 3; tel. 2-52-41; telex 22805; fax 24-78-42; f. 1949; library of 22,000 vols; Dir Prof. YORDAN PANAYOTOV.

Institute of the Sugar Industry and Bioproducts: 5100 Gorna Orjahovica; tel. (618) 4-18-80; fax (618) 4-05-65; f. 1963; library of 10,600 vols; Dir K. TODOROVA.

Institute of the Wine Industry: 1618 Sofia, Tsar Boris III 134; tel. 55-40-21; telex 22466; fax 55-60-25; f. 1951; Dir K. FARTSOV.

Institute of Upland Stockbreeding and Agriculture: 5600 Trojan, V. Devski 281; tel. (670) 2-28-60; fax (670) 2-30-32; f. 1978; Dir P. DONCHEV.

Institute of Viticulture and Oenology: 5800 Pleven, Kala tepe 1; tel. (64) 2-21-61; fax (64) 2-64-70; f. 1902; Dir Prof. P. ABRASHEVA.

Institute of Water Problems: 1113 Sofia, Acad. G. Bonchev bl. 1; tel. (2) 72-25-72; fax (2) 72-25-77; e-mail santur@bgcict.acad.bg; f. 1960; attached to Bulgarian Acad. of Sciences; Dir Prof. O. SANTURDZHIAN.

Institute of Wheat and Sunflower 'Dobroudja': 9520 General Toshevo (Dobrich District); tel. (58) 2-74-54; telex 74595; fax (58) 2-63-64; f. 1940; library of 32,000 vols; Dir Prof. Dr PETER IVANOV.

Maize Research Institute: 3230 Knezha; tel. (9132) 21-63; fax (9132) 27-11; f. 1924; Dir Assoc. K. ANGELOV.

'Maritsa' Vegetable Crops Research Institute: 4003 Plovdiv, Brezovsko shose 32 (kl. 3), PK 20; tel. (32) 55-12-27; telex 44525; fax (32) 65-01-77; e-mail izk@main.infotel.bg; f. 1930; library of 20,000 vols; Dir Prof. Dr IVAN B. PORYAZOV.

'N. Pushkarov' Soil Science and Agroecology Research Institute: 1080 Sofia, Shose Bankja 7; tel. 2-52-71; telex 22701; fax 24-89-37; f. 1947; Dir Prof. V. VALEV.

'Obraztsov Chiflik' Institute of Agriculture and Seed Science: 7007 Ruse; tel. and fax 22-58-98; f. 1905; Dir Dr DIMITAR RUSEV.

Plant Protection Institute: 2230 Kostinbrod, POB 238; tel. (721) 20-70; fax (721) 20-71; e-mail nevena@bis.cit.bg; f. 1935; Dir Asst Prof. Dr NIKOLA ATANASOV.

Regional Veterinary Institute: 4000 Plovdiv, Nezavisimost III; tel. (32) 26-08-68; fax (32) 22-33-67; f. 1936; library of 10,000 vols; Dir D. ARNAUDOV.

Regional Veterinary Institute: 5000 Veliko Tărnovo, Slavjanska 5; tel. and fax 2-16-69; telex 66726; f. 1932; library of 11,840 vols; Dir Assoc. Prof. V. RADOSLAVOV.

Regional Veterinary Research Institute and Centre: 6000 Stara Zagora, Slavyanska 58; tel. (42) 2-67-32; fax (42) 2-31-15; f. 1931; Dir Assoc. Prof. N. NIKOLOV.

Research Institute for Irrigation, Drainage and Hydraulic Engineering: 1618 Sofia, Tsar Boris III 136; tel. (2) 56-30-01; telex 23446; fax (2) 55-41-58; e-mail riidhe@bgcict.acad.bg; f. 1953; library of 18,000 vols; Dir Asst Prof. Dr PLAMEN PETKOV; publ. *Proceedings* (every 3 years).

Research Institute for Roses, Aromatic and Medicinal Plants: 6100 Kazanlak, Bul. Osvobojdenie 49; tel. (431) 2-20-39; fax (431) 4-10-83; f. 1907; library of 3,600 vols; Dir Dr GEORGE CHAUSHEV.

Scientific and Production Enterprise with Sugar Beet Research Institute 'Prof. Ivan Ivanov': 9747 Carev Brod (Shumen District); tel. (54) 5-51-02; fax (54) 5-69-06; f. 1926; Dir Assoc. Prof. S. KRASTEV.

Scientific and Production Institute for Veterinary Preparations: 3000 Vraca; tel. 4-94-81; telex 33538; fax 4-75-30; f. 1942; library of 5,000 vols; Dir Dr NINO NINOV.

Scientific Research Institute of Pig Breeding: 9700 Shumen; tel. 6-02-41; fax 6-28-32; f. 1955; 130 mems; library of 10,900 vols; Dir A. STOIKOV; publs *Zhivotnovadni Nauki*, *Genetica i selectija*.

Tobacco and Tobacco Products Institute: 4108 Plovdiv; tel. (32) 67-23-64; telex 66402; fax 77-51-56; f. 1944; library of 40,000 vols; Dir Dr ELENA APOSTOLOVA; publ. *Bulgarian Tobacco* (every 2 months).

Veterinary Institute of Immunology Ltd: 1360 Sofia, Bakareno shose 1; tel. (2) 26-31-70; fax (2) 26-24-85; f. 1942; Pres. Prof. Dr STEFANOV.

ARCHITECTURE AND TOWN PLANNING

Centre for Architectural Studies: 1113 Sofia, Acad. G. Bonchev bl. 1; tel. 72-46-20; f. 1949; attached to Bulgarian Acad. of Sciences; Dir Assoc. Prof. K. BOYADZHIEV.

National Centre for Regional Development and Housing Policy: 1000 Sofia, Alabin 14–16; tel. (2) 980-03-08; fax (2) 980-03-12; f. 1960; library of 9,000 vols; Dir-Gen.

Dr V. GANIZOV; publ. *Series for the Municipalities* (every 2 months).

ECONOMICS, LAW AND POLITICS

Institute of Economics: 1000 Sofia, Aksakov 3; tel. 87-30-15; fax 88-21-08; e-mail ineco@iki.acad.bg; f. 1949; attached to Bulgarian Acad. of Sciences; Dir Prof. ALEXANDER DIMITROV; publ. *Ikonomicheska Misăl*.

Institute of Law Science: 1000 Sofia, Serdika 4; tel. (2) 987-97-85; f. 1948; attached to Bulgarian Acad. of Sciences; Dir Assoc. Prof. TS. KAMENOVA.

Research Institute of Forensic Science and Criminology: 1000 Sofia, POB 934; tel. 82-47-51; fax 87-82-10; Dir Prof. K. BOBEV; publ. *News Bulletin*.

EDUCATION

National Centre for Education: 1113 Sofia, Tsarigradsko shose 125 bl. 5; tel. 71-72-24; fax 70-20-62; f. 1992; library of 80,000 vols; publ. *Strategies for Policy in Science and Education*.

Research Institute of Suggestology: 1000 Sofia, A. Kanchev 5; tel. (2) 981-44-64; f. 1992; Dir R. NONCHEVA.

FINE AND PERFORMING ARTS

Institute of Art Studies: 1504 Sofia, Krakra 21; tel. (2) 44-24-14; f.1949; attached to Bulgarian Acad. of Sciences; Dir Assoc. Prof. E. TONCHEVA.

HISTORY, GEOGRAPHY AND ARCHAEOLOGY

Archaeological Institute and Museum: 1000 Sofia, Saborna 2; tel. 88-14-73; fax 88-24-05; f. 1921 (Institute), 1879 (Museum); attached to Bulgarian Acad. of Sciences; Dir Prof. I. YURUKOVA.

Institute of Balkan Studies: 1000 Sofia, Moskovska 45; tel. (2) 87-49-79; fax (2) 980-62-97; f. 1963; attached to Bulgarian Acad. of Sciences; library of 27,000 vols; Dir Assoc. Prof. A. GARABEDYAN; publ. *Études Balkaniques* (4 a year).

Institute of Demography: 1114 Sofia, Akad. G. Bonchev bl. 6 (Et. 6); tel. (2) 70-53-03; f. 1982; attached to Bulgarian Acad. of Sciences; Dir Assoc. Prof. E. KHRISTOV; publ. *Naselenie*.

Institute of Geography: 1113 Sofia, Acad. G. Bonchev bl. 3; tel. and fax (2) 70-02-04; f. 1950; attached to Bulgarian Acad. of Sciences; library of 17,000 vols; Dir Assoc. Prof. G. GESHEV: publ. *Problems of Geography* (4 a year).

Institute of History: 1113 Sofia, Shipchenski prohod 52 bl. 17; tel. 70-16-34; fax 70-21-91; f. 1947; attached to Bulgarian Acad. of Sciences; Dir Prof. G. MARKOV.

Institute of Thracian Studies: 1000 Sofia, Moskovska 13; tel. (2) 80-35-43; fax (2) 81-89-66; f. 1972; attached to Bulgarian Acad. of Sciences; library of 6,000 vols; Dir Assoc. Prof. KIRIL JORDANOV; publ. *Orpheus* (journal, 1 a year).

LANGUAGE AND LITERATURE

Institute for Literature: 1113 Sofia, Shipchenski prohod 52 bl. 17; tel. 70-18-30; f. 1948; attached to Bulgarian Acad. of Sciences; Dir Assoc. Prof. S. KOZHUHAROV.

Institute for the Bulgarian Language: 1113 Sofia, Shipchenski prohod 52 bl. 17; tel. 72-23-02; f. 1942; attached to Bulgarian Acad. of Sciences; Dir Assoc. Prof. Y. BALTOVA.

MEDICINE

Centre of Physiotherapy and Rehabilitation: 1618 Sofia, Ovcha kupel 2B; tel. 56-28-24; fax 55-30-23; f. 1949; Dir Assoc. Prof. P. NIKOLOVA; publ. *Journal*.

Clinical Centre for Haemodialysis: 1431 Sofia, G. Sofijski 1; tel. 54-07-40; telex 23668; fax 51-73-43; f. 1967; Dir Prof. ZDRAVKO KIRIAKOV.

Clinical Centre of Gastroenterology: 1527 Sofia, Bialo More 8; tel. (2) 434-45-13; fax (2) 44-31-14; f. 1959; Dir Prof. A. MENDIZOVA.

Institute of Obstetrics and Gynaecology: 1431 Sofia, Zdrave 2; tel. (2) 51-72-42; fax (2) 51-70-92; f. 1976; library of 2,000 vols; Dir Assoc. Prof. AL. YARAKOV; publ. *Problems of Obstetrics and Gynaecology* (annually).

National Centre of Cardiovascular Diseases: 1309 Sofia, Miko Papo 65; tel. 22-31-34; fax 22-31-28; f. 1972; Dir Prof. I. TOMOV.

National Centre of Clinical and Transfusional Haematology: 1756 Sofia-Dărvenica, Plovdivsko pole 6; tel. and fax 72-25-92; f. 1948; Dir Prof. T. MESHKOV.

National Centre of Hygiene, Medical Ecology and Nutrition: 1431 Sofia, Bul. D. Nestorov 15; tel. (2) 59-10-11; telex 22712; fax (2) 958-12-77; f. 1995; library of 32,000 vols; Dir Assoc. Prof. TODOR POPOV; publs *Problems of Hygiene* (annually), *Official Bulletin* (annually).

National Centre of Radiobiology and Radiation Protection: 1756 Sofia, Kl. Ohridski 132; tel. 62-60-36; fax 62-10-59; f. 1991; Dir Prof. G. VASILIEV.

National Drug Institute: 1504 Sofia, Bul. Yanko Sakazov 26; tel. 44-65-66; fax 44-26-97; f. 1949; registration, analysis and control of drugs; Dir Dr JASMINA MIRCHEVA.

National Oncological Centre: 1756 Sofia, Plovdivsko Pole 6; tel. (2) 72-06-54; fax (2) 72-06-51; f. 1952; library of 22,000 vols; Dir Prof. I. CHERNOZEMSKI; publ. *Oncology* (4 a year).

'Pirogov' Emergency Medical Institute: 1606 Sofia, Makedonija 21; tel. (2) 52-10-77; fax (2) 52-17-17; f. 1965; Dir Prof. E. TAKOV.

Research Institute of Infectious and Parasitic Diseases: 1504 Sofia, Yanko Sakazov 26; tel. (2) 4-34-71; fax (2) 44-22-60; f. 1972; Dir Prof. B. PETRUNOV; publ. *Problems of Infectious and Parasitic Diseases*.

State Institute of Endocrinology and Gerontology: 1303 Sofia, Dame Gruev 6; tel. (2) 87-71-01; fax (2) 87-41-45; f. 1972; Dir Prof. B. LOZANOV.

NATURAL SCIENCES

Biological Sciences

Central Laboratory of General Ecology: 1113 Sofia, Gagarin 2; tel. (2) 73-61-37; fax (2) 70-54-98; e-mail ecolab@bgcict.acad.bg; f. 1956; attached to Bulgarian Acad. of Sciences; library of 8,000 vols; Dir Assoc. Prof. Dr GEORGI HIEBAUM.

Centre for Biomedical Engineering: 1113 Sofia, Acad. G. Bonchev bl. 105; tel. 70-03-26; fax 72-37-87; f. 1979; attached to Bulgarian Acad. of Sciences; Dir Prof. Dr I. DASKALOV.

Institute of Biophysics: 1113 Sofia, Acad. G. Bonchev bl. 21; tel. (2) 971-22-64; fax (2) 971-24-93; f. 1967; attached to Bulgarian Acad. of Sciences; Dir Prof. K. BOEV.

Institute of Botany: 1113 Sofia, Acad. G. Bonchev bl. 23; tel. 72-09-51; fax 71-90-32; e-mail botinst@iph.bio.acad.bg; f. 1889; attached to Bulgarian Acad. of Sciences; Dir Prof. E. PALAMAREV.

Institute of Experimental Morphology and Anthropology: 1113 Sofia, Acad. G. Bonchev bl. 25; tel. (2) 70-65-47; fax (2) 71-90-07; f. 1953; attached to Bulgarian Acad. of Sciences; Dir Prof. J. JORDANOV.

Institute of Experimental Pathology and Parasitology: 1113 Sofia, Acad. G. Bonchev bl. 25; tel. 72-24-26; fax 71-01-17; f. 1948; attached to Bulgarian Acad. of Sciences; Dir Prof. O. POLYAKOVA-KRASTEVA.

Institute of Genetics: 1113 Sofia, Plovdivsko shose 13 km, POB 96; tel. 75-90-41; fax 75-70-87; f. 1940; attached to Bulgarian Acad. of Sciences; Dir Assoc. Prof. B. DIMITROV.

Institute of Microbiology: 1113 Sofia, Acad. G. Bonchev bl. 26; tel. 70-10-81; fax 70-01-09; f. 1947; attached to Bulgarian Acad. of Sciences; Dir Prof. A. GALABOV.

Institute of Molecular Biology: 1113 Sofia, Acad. G. Bonchev bl. 21; tel. and fax (2) 72-35-07; e-mail grs@obzor.bio21.acad.bg; f. 1960; attached to Bulgarian Acad. of Sciences; library of 5,000 vols; Dir Prof. G. RUSEV.

Institute of Physiology: 1113 Sofia, Acad. G. Bonchev bl. 23; tel. 71-91-08; fax 71-91-09; f. 1947; attached to Bulgarian Acad. of Sciences; Dir Prof. R. RADOMIROV.

Institute of the Biology and Immunology of the Reproduction and Development of Organisms: 1784 Sofia, Carigradsko shose 73; tel. 72-00-18; fax 72-00-22; f. 1939; attached to Bulgarian Acad. of Sciences; Dir Prof. I. KEKHAYOV.

Institute of Zoology: 1000 Sofia, Tsar Osvoboditel 1; tel. (2) 988-51-15; fax (2) 88-28-97; e-mail zoology@bgcict.acad.bg; f. 1889; attached to Bulgarian Acad. of Sciences; Dir Prof. V. GOLEMANSKY.

'Methodi Popov' Institute of Plant Physiology: 1113 Sofia, Acad. G. Bonchev bl. 21; tel. 72-84-80; fax 73-99-52; f. 1948; attached to Bulgarian Acad. of Sciences; Dir Prof. E. KARANOV.

Mathematical Sciences

Institute of Mathematics and Informatics: 1113 Sofia, Acad. G. Bonchev bl. 8; tel. (2) 70-10-72; fax (2) 971-36-49; e-mail director@math.acad.bg; f. 1947; attached to Bulgarian Acad. of Sciences; Dir Prof. N. YANEV; publ. *Serdica* (4 a year).

Physical Sciences

Central Laboratory of Electrochemical Power Sources: 1113 Sofia, Acad. G. Bonchev bl. 10; tel. (2) 72-25-43; fax (2) 72-25-44; e-mail stoynov@sf.cit.bg; f. 1967; attached to Bulgarian Acad. of Sciences; Dir Prof. Z. STOINOV.

Central Laboratory of Geodesy: 1113 Sofia, Acad. G. Bonchev bl. 1; tel. (2) 72-08-41; fax (2) 72-08-41; 41; f. 1956; attached to Bulgarian Acad. of Sciences; Dir Assoc. Prof. V. KOTSEV.

Central Laboratory of Optical Storage and the Processing of Information: 1113 Sofia, Acad. G. Bonchev bl. 101; tel. 71-00-18; fax 71-91-65; f. 1975; attached to Bulgarian Acad. of Sciences; Dir Assoc. Prof. V. SAYNOV.

Central Laboratory of Photoprocesses: 1113 Sofia, Acad. G. Bonchev bl. 109; tel. (2) 72-00-73; fax (2) 72-24-65; e-mail clf@clf.acad.bg; f. 1967; attached to Bulgarian Acad. of Sciences; Dir Assoc. Prof. I. KONSTANTINOV.

Central Laboratory of Solar Energy and New Energy Sources: 1784 Sofia, Carigradsko shose 72; tel. 75-40-16; fax 75-40-16; f. 1977; attached to Bulgarian Acad. of Sciences; Dir Assoc. Prof. P. VITANOV.

Geological Institute 'Acad. Str. Dimitrov': 1113 Sofia, Acad. G. Bonchev bl. 24; tel. (2) 72-35-63; fax (2) 72-46-38; f. 1947; attached to Bulgarian Acad. of Sciences; library of 73,000 vols; Dir Prof. H. HRISCHEV; publs *Geologica Balcanica* (quarterly), *Review of the Bulgarian Geological Society* (3 a year).

Institute of Catalysis: 1113 Sofia, Acad. G. Bonchev bl. 11; tel. and fax 75-61-16; e-mail icpetrov@bgearn.acad.bg; f. 1983; attached to Bulgarian Acad. of Sciences; Dir Prof. L. A. PETROV.

Institute of General and Inorganic Chemistry: 1113 Sofia, Acad. G. Bonchev bl. 11; tel. 72-48-01; fax 70-50-24; f. 1960; attached to Bulgarian Acad. of Sciences; Dir Prof. Dr P. PESHEV.

Institute of Geophysics: 1113 Sofia, Acad. G. Bonchev bl. 3: tel. 971-26-77; telex 22632; fax 70-02-26; f. 1960; attached to Bulgarian Acad. of Sciences; Dir Prof. G. MILOSHEV.

Institute of Mechanics and Biomechanics: 1113 Sofia, Acad. G. Bonchev bl. 4; tel. (2) 71-71-86; telex 22628; fax (2) 70-74-98; e-mail imbm@imech.imbm.acad.bg; f. 1977; attached to Bulgarian Acad. of Sciences; library of 5,000 vols; Dir Assoc. Prof. E. MANOACH; publ. *Journal of Theoretical and Applied Mechanics*.

Institute of Nuclear Research and Nuclear Energy: 1784 Sofia, Carigradsko shose 72; tel. (2) 74-31; fax (2) 975-36-19; e-mail inrne@inrne.acad.bg; f. 1972; attached to Bulgarian Acad. of Sciences; Dir Prof. I. STAMENOV; publ. *Proceedings of the International School on Nuclear Physics*.

Institute of Oceanology: 9000 Varna, Kv. Asparuhovo 40, POB 152; tel. (52) 77-45-49; fax (52) 77-42-56; f. 1973; attached to Bulgarian Acad. of Sciences; Dir Assoc. Prof. A. KONSULEV.

Institute of Organic Chemistry with Centre of Phytochemistry: 1113 Sofia, Acad. G. Bonchev bl. 9; tel. 72-48-17; fax 70-02-25; f. 1960; attached to Bulgarian Acad. of Sciences; Dir Prof. YU. STEFANOVSKI.

Institute of Physical Chemistry: 1113 Sofia, Acad. G. Bonchev bl. 11; tel. 72-75-50; fax 971-26-88; f. 1958; attached to Bulgarian Acad. of Sciences; Dir Prof. H. NANEV.

Institute of Polymers: 1113 Sofia, Acad. G. Bonchev bl. 103-A; tel. 70-73-77; fax 70-75-23; e-mail instpoly@mail.polymer.acad.bg; f. 1973; attached to Bulgarian Acad. of Sciences; Dir Prof. I. SCHOPOV.

Institute of Solid State Physics: 1784 Sofia, Carigradsko shose 72; tel. 77-34-92; telex 23561; fax 975-36-32; f. 1972; attached to Bulgarian Acad. of Sciences; Dir Prof. N. KIROV.

Institute of Space Research: 1000 Sofia, Moskovska 6; tel. (2) 88-35-03; fax (2) 981-33-47; f. 1973; attached to Bulgarian Acad. of Sciences; Dir Dr PETAR GETZOV; publ. *Aerospace Research in Bulgaria* (1 a year).

National Astronomical Observatory – Rozhen: 4700 Smoljan, POB 136; tel. and fax (3021) 3-56; attached to Bulgarian Acad. of Sciences.

National Institute of Hydrology and Meteorology: 1184 Sofia, Carigradsko shose 66; tel. (2) 975-39-96; telex 22490; fax (2) 88-44-94; f. 1954; attached to Bulgarian Acad. of Sciences; Dir Assoc. Prof. V. SHAROV; publ. *Problemi na meteorologia i hidrologia*.

Solar Terrestrial Influences Laboratory: 1113 Sofia, Acad. G. Bonchev bl. 3; tel. 70-02-29; fax 70-01-78; f. 1990; attached to Bulgarian Acad. of Sciences; Dir Prof. D. MISHEV.

PHILOSOPHY AND PSYCHOLOGY

Institute of Philosophical Research: 1000 Sofia, Patriarh Evtimij 6; tel. 88-18-41; f. 1945; attached to Bulgarian Acad. of Sciences; Dir Prof. V. PRODANOV.

Institute of Psychology: 1113 Sofia, Akad. G. Bonchev bl. 6 (Et. 5); tel. (2) 70-32-17; f. 1972; attached to Bulgarian Acad. of Sciences; Dir Assoc. Prof. V. RUSINOVA.

RELIGION, SOCIOLOGY AND ANTHROPOLOGY

Ethnographic Institute: 1000 Sofia, Moskovska 6A; tel. (2) 987-41-91; f. 1947; attached to Bulgarian Acad. of Sciences; Dir Assoc. Prof. R. POPOV.

Institute of Folklore: 1113 Sofia, Acad. G. Bonchev bl. 6; tel. (2) 713-30-11; f. 1972; attached to Bulgarian Acad. of Sciences; library of 4,200 vols, 73 periodicals; Dir Assoc. Prof. MILA SANTOVA; publ. *Bulgarian Folklore* (4 a year).

Institute of Sociology: 1000 Sofia, Moskovska 13A; tel. (2) 980-90-86; fax (2) 980-58-95; e-mail banis@bgcict.acad.bg; f. 1968; attached to Bulgarian Acad. of Sciences; Dir Prof. G. FOTEV; publs *Sociological Problems* (4 a year), *Sociological Review* (6 a year).

TECHNOLOGY

Central Laboratory of Applied Physics: 4000 Plovdiv, Rodopi 59; tel. (32) 23-51-19; telex 44374; fax (32) 22-28-10; f. 1979; attached to Bulgarian Acad. of Sciences; Dir R. KAKANAKOV.

Central Laboratory of Mechatronics and Instrumentation: 1113 Sofia, Acad. G. Bonchev bl. 2; tel. 72-35-71; fax 71-01-64; f. 1990; attached to Bulgarian Acad. of Sciences; Dir Assoc. Prof. B. STOJANOV.

Central Laboratory of Mineralogy and Crystallography: 1000 Sofia, Rakovski 92; tel. 87-24-50; fax 88-49-79; e-mail mincryst.@bgcict.acad.bg; f. 1977; attached to Bulgarian Acad. of Sciences; Dir Assoc. Prof. N. ZIDAROV.

Central Laboratory of Physical and Chemical Mechanics: 1113 Sofia, Acad. G. Bonchev bl. 1; tel. (2) 71-81-82; fax (2) 70-34-33; e-mail clphchm@bgearn.acad.bg; f. 1972; attached to Bulgarian Acad. of Sciences; Dir Prof. G. ZACHARIEV; publ. *Physico-Chemical Mechanics* (2 a year).

Central Laboratory of Seismic Mechanics and Earthquake Engineering: 1113 Sofia, Acad. G. Bonchev bl. 3; tel. and fax (2) 971-24-07; e-mail ltzenov@geophys.acad.bg; f. 1982; attached to Bulgarian Acad. of Sciences; Dir. Prof. Dr LUDMIL TZENOV.

Institute of Applied Cybernetics: 1784 Sofia, Carigradsko shose 125 bl. 2; tel. 72-01-32; telex 22836; fax 70-04-78; f. 1990; attached to Bulgarian Acad. of Sciences; Dir Prof. Dr LUDMIL TZENOV.

Institute of Computer and Communication Systems: 1113 Sofia, Acad. G. Bonchev bl. 2; tel. (2) 71-90-97; fax (2) 72-39-05; e-mail fenerdjiev@iccs.acad.bg; f.1990; attached to Bulgarian Acad. of Sciences; Dir Assoc. Prof. LUBOMIR FENERDZHIEV.

Institute of Control and Systems Research: 1113 Sofia, Acad. G. Bonchev bl. 2; tel. (2) 73-28-45; fax (2) 73-28-45; f. 1982; attached to Bulgarian Acad. of Sciences; Dir Prof. Y. ZAPRIANOV.

Institute of Electronics: 1784 Sofia, Carigradsko shose 72; tel. 75-00-77; telex 23561; fax 975-32-01; f. 1963; attached to Bulgarian Acad. of Sciences; Dir Prof. P. ATANASOV.

Institute of Engineering Chemistry: 1113 Sofia, Acad. G. Bonchev bl. 103; tel. 70-42-49; fax 70-75-23; e-mail ichemeng.@bgean .acad.bg; f. 1972; attached to Bulgarian Acad. of Sciences; Dir Prof. V. BESHKOV.

Institute of Information Communication and Automation Systems: 1574 Sofia, Shipchenski prohod 69; tel. 71-00-44; telex 23745; fax 70-61-53; f. 1987; Dir I. DIKOV; publ. *News in Telecommunications*.

Institute of Information Technology: 1113 Sofia, Acad. G. Bonchev bl. 29A; tel. 72-04-97; telex 22836; fax 72-04-97; f. 1990; attached to Bulgarian Acad. of Sciences; Dir Assoc. Prof. V. VASILEV.

Institute of Laser Technology: 1326 Sofia, Galichitsa 33A; tel. 68-89-13; fax 68-89-13; f. 1980; Dir Assoc. Prof. I. KHRISTOV.

Institute of Metal Science: 1574 Sofia, Shipchenski prohod 67; tel. (2) 971-32-19; fax (2) 70-32-07; f. 1967; attached to Bulgarian Acad. of Sciences; Dir Prof. Y. ARSOV.

ISOMATIC Labs Ltd: 1797 Sofia, Bul. Universiada 4; tel. (2) 77-45-96; fax (2) 975-30-32; e-mail isomatic@isomatic.com; f. 1992; robotics, electronics; Dir Assoc. Prof. G. NACHEV.

Technological Institute of Agricultural Engineering: 7005 Ruse, A. Getsov 106; tel. 4-19-21; telex 62453; fax 5-93-82; f. 1962; Dir G. NIKOLOV.

Libraries and Archives

Burgas

'P. K. Yavorov' Regional Library: 8000 Burgas, A. Bogoridi 21; tel. (56) 4-27-53; f. 1888; 542,781 vols; Dir K. KHRUSANOVA.

Plovdiv

Ivan Vazov National Library: 4000 Plovdiv, Avksentii Veleshki 17; tel. 22-29-15; f. 1879; 1,660,000 vols, 3,000 periodical titles, 892 MSS, 4,134 incunabula; Dir RADKA KOLEVA; publ. *Plovdivski Kraj* (1 a year).

Ruse

Regional Library: 7000 Ruse, D. Korsakov 1; tel. 22-24-30; fax 22-23-49; f. 1888; 685,000 vols; Dir Z. KALINOVA.

Shumen

Public Library: 9700 Shumen, Slaviansky 19; tel. 5-70-93; f. 1922; 684,000 vols; Dir Z. KUKUSHKOVA.

Sofia

Central Agricultural Library: 1113 Sofia, Tsarigradsko shose 125 bl. 1; tel. 70-91-68; f. 1961; 504,000 vols; Dir M. GRUEVA.

Central Library of Sofia: 1000 Sofia, Slaveikov 4; tel. 80-22-34; fax 88-22-36; f. 1886; 938,000 vols; Dir NADEZHDA ALEKSANDROVA.

Central Library of the Bulgarian Academy of Sciences: 1040 Sofia, 15 Noemvri 1; tel. (2) 87-89-66; fax (2) 80-31-27; e-mail banlib@bgcict.acad.bg; f. 1869; 1,835,000 vols; 48 affiliated institute libraries; Dir Assoc. Prof. Dr D. KRASTEV.

Central Library of the Higher Technical Institutes: 1421 Sofia, Bul. Dragan Tzankov 2; tel. 66-52-74; fax 65-68-63; e-mail lib@uacg .acad.bg; f. 1942; science and technology; 605,000 vols; Dir A. TODOROVA.

Central Medical Library: 1431 Sofia, G. Sofijski 1; tel. and fax 52-31-71; e-mail medlib@medun.acad.bg; f. 1919; 542,000 vols; 25 affiliated libraries; Dir P. DABCHEV; publ. *Abstracts of Bulgarian Scientific Medical Literature*.

Central State Archive: 1000 Sofia, Moskovska 5; tel. 80-19-21; fax 980-14-43; 110,000 files, documenting the activities of state instns, political parties, state and private companies and enterprises, from the mid 19th century to recent times; personal papers of eminent Bulgarians; Dir G. CHERNEV.

Central Technological Library: 1125 Sofia, G. M. Dimitrov 50; tel. 70-29-35; telex 22404; fax 71-01-57; e-mail ctb@nacid.acad.bg; f. 1962; 4,922,000 vols and materials; Dir M. PAREVA.

Centre for European Studies: 1125 Sofia, G. M. DIMITROV 52A; tel. and fax (2) 971-24-

11; f. 1990; European Documentation Centre receiving all official publs of EC; Dir I. SHIKOVA; publ. *Europa* (monthly).

Centre for Scientific, Technical and Economic Information (at the Agricultural Academy): 1113 Sofia, Tsarigradsko shose 125 bl 1; tel. 70-30-58; f. 1961; Dir V. YOVEV.

General Department of Archives at the Council of Ministers: 1000 Sofia, Moskovska 5; tel. (2) 987-91-71; fax (2) 980-14-43; administers one central and 27 regional archives; library of 34,000 vols, 130 periodicals; Dir P. KOLEV; publs *Izvestiya na darzavnite arhivi* (2 a year); *Arhiven pregled* (4 a year).

National Centre for Information and Documentation (at the Ministry of Industry): 1125 Sofia, Dr G. M. Dimitrov 52A; tel. 71-92-03; fax 71-01-57; e-mail nacid@mcr1.poptel.org.uk; f. 1993; 4,650,000 vols; Gen. Dir J. KHLEBAROV; publ. *Scientific and Technical Publications in Bulgaria* (quarterly, in English).

National Centre of Health Information: 1431 Sofia, D. Nestorov 15; tel. 958-19-32; telex 22134; fax 59-01-47; f. 1976; Dir KH. GRIVA; publ. *Zdraveopazvane*.

St Cyril and St Methodius National Library: 1504 Sofia, V. Levski 88; tel. 88-28-11; fax 43-54-95; e-mail nbkm@bgcict.acad.bg; f. 1878; 2,465,457 books and periodicals, 5,486 MSS, 2,856 old and rare publs, 277,000 maps, prints and portraits, 81,000 scores and gramophone records, 287,348 patents and standards, 3,020,926 archival documents; archive of Bulgarian printed material; nat. information centre in the field of social admin., science and culture; research institute in library science, bibliography and bibliology; Dir Dr KIRIL TOPALOV; publs 17 information periodicals incl. 8 bulletins forming the current nat. bibliography.

St Kliment Ohridsky University of Sofia Library: 1504 Sofia, Tsar Osvoboditel 15; tel. 44-37-19; fax 46-71-70; f. 1888; 1,700,000 vols; Dir Prof. ZH. STOYANOV.

Scientific Archives of the Bulgarian Academy of Sciences: 1040 Sofia, 15 Noemvri 1; tel. (2) 88-40-46; fax (2) 981-66-29; e-mail banlib@bgcict.acad.bg; f. 1947; MSS and 110,000 scientific dossiers; Head TODOR BAKALOV.

Stara Zagora

Regional Library: 6000 Stara Zagora, Tsar Kalojan 50; tel. 4-81-31; e-mail library-sz@mbox.digsys.bg; f. 1955; 410,000 vols; Dir D. DUNCHEVA.

Varna

'Pencho Slaveykov' Public Library: 9010 Varna, Slivnitsa 34; tel. 22-33-51; fax 22-33-51; 773,000 vols; Dir L. STOYANOVA.

Veliko Tărnovo

Regional Library: 5000 Veliko Tărnovo, I. Boteva 2; tel. 2-02-08; f. 1922; 552,760 vols; Dir D. MINCHEV.

Museums and Art Galleries

Blagoevgrad

Regional Cultural and Historical Heritage Management Board: 2700 Blagoevgrad, Rila 1; tel. and fax (73) 2-90-20; f. 1951; controls several museums in fields of archaeology, history, ethnography, natural history and fine arts; library of 17,000 vols; Dir K. GRANCHAROVA.

Burgas

Historical Museum: 8000 Burgas, Slavjanska 69; tel. (56) 4-02-93; f. 1948; Dir TS. DRAZHEVA; publ. *Izvestija*.

Dobrich

Literary Museum of Jordan Jovkov: 9300 Dobrich; tel. 2-81-59; f. 1968; literature and theatre art (life and creative work of Jovkov, Dora Gabe, the actress Adriana Budevska, the ballet-master Anastas Petrov and the artist Petar Dachev); Curator K. MITEVA.

Regional Museum of History: 9300 Dobrich, Gen. Gurko 4; tel. (58) 2-82-13; fax (58) 2-82-56; f. 1953; library of 20,000 vols; Dir B. S. VASILEV; publ. *Dobrudja* (annually).

Haskovo

Regional Museum of History: 6300 Haskovo, Pl. Svoboda; tel. 3-20-67; f. 1952; Dir G. GRAMATIKOV.

Kalofer

Khristo Botev Museum: 4370 Kalofer, Khr. Botev 5; tel. 22-71; f. 1945; birth-place of the poet, revolutionary and fighter against Ottoman rule; Dir A. NIKOLOVA.

Karlovo

Vassil Levski Museum: 4300 Karlovo, Gen. Kartsov 61; tel. 34-89; f. 1937; birth-place of the founder of the Revolutionary Committee for the liberation of Bulgaria from Ottoman rule; Dir D. CHAUSHEVA.

Kazanlăk

Sipka-Buzludza National Park Museum: 6100 Kazanlăk, P. R. Slavejkov 8; tel. 2-24-95; f. 1956; monuments connected with the liberation of Bulgaria from Ottoman rule; Dir I. KHRISTOV.

Lovech

Regional Museum of History: 5500 Lovech, Pl. T. Kirkova; tel. 2-62-59; f. 1895; Dir I. LALEV.

Montana

Regional Museum of History: 3400 Montana, Tsar Boris III 2; tel. 2-84-81; fax 2-25-36; f. 1953; Dir U. DERAKCHIISKA.

Pazardzhik

Regional Museum of History: 4400 Pazardzhik, Pl. K. Velichkov 15; tel. 2-81-13; f. 1923; library of 11,000 vols; Dir D. MITREV; publ. *Bulletin des Musées de la Bulgarie du Sud*.

Stanislav Dospevsky Art Gallery: 4400 Pazardzhik, Pl. K. Velichkov 15; tel. 2-71-52; f. 1963; Dir NEICHEV.

Pernik

Regional Museum of History: 2300 Pernik, Fizkulturna 2; tel. 31-18; f. 1954; Dir O. ASPROV.

Pleven

Regional Museum of History: 5800 Pleven, Stojan Zaimov 3; tel. 2-26-91; f. 1903; library of 21,000 vols; Dir MIKHAIL GRANCHAROV; publ. *Museum Studies in North-Western Bulgaria* (monthly).

Plovdiv

Ethnographical Museum: 4000 Plovdiv, Dr Chomakov 2; tel. 22-62-04; f. 1945; Dir A. YANKOV.

Natural Science Museum: 4000 Plovdiv, Chr. G. Danov 34; tel. 22-30-96; f. 1955; library of 8,720 vols; Dir I. BASAMAKOV; publ. *Izvestija na Muzeite ot Juzna Balgaria* (Bulletin of the Museums of Southern Bulgaria) (annually, with English abstracts, French or English summaries).

Regional Museum of Archaeology: 4000 Plovdiv, Pl. Săedinenie 1; tel. 23-17-60; f. 1882; library of 12,000 vols; Dir M. BOSPACHIEVA; publ. *Pulpudeva*.

Regional Museum of History: 4000 Plovdiv, Pl. Săedinenie 1; tel. 26-99-55; f. 1948; Dir S. SHIVACHEV.

State Gallery of Fine Arts: 4000 Plovdiv, Saborna 14A; tel. (32) 26-37-90; f. 1952; Dir KRASIMIR LINKOV.

Rila

Rila Monastery National Museum: 2643 Rilski Monastir (Sofia District); tel. (93714) 22-08; f. 1961; Bulgarian art and architecture during the Ottoman period, Bulgarian history and history of the monastery; Dir P. MITEV.

Ruse

Regional Museum of History: 7000 Ruse, Kniaz A. Batemberg 3; tel. 23-61-15; f. 1904; library of 13,800 vols; Dir R. GANCHEV; publ. *Izvestija*.

Shumen

Regional Museum of History: 9700 Shumen, Slavjanski 17; f. 1904; Dir D. LECHEV.

Sofia

Dimitr Blagoev Museum: 1606 Sofia, L. Koshut 34; tel. 52-31-45; f. 1948; house of the founder of the Bulgarian Social-Democratic Party, containing documents and personal effects; Dir. R. RUSSEV.

Boyana Church National Museum: 1616 Sofia, Boiansko ezero 3; tel. 68-53-04; f. 1947; medieval orthodox painting; Dir M. TRIFONOVA.

Georgi Dimitrov National Museum: 1303 Sofia, Opălchenska 66; tel. 32-01-49; f. 1951; Dir VERA DICHEVA.

Ivan Vazov Museum: 1000 Sofia, I. Vazov 10; tel. 88-12-70; f. 1926; house in which the Bulgarian poet lived; Curator I. BACHEVA.

Museum of Sofia's History: 1000 Sofia, Exarh Yossif 27; tel. and fax (2) 83-15-26; f. 1952; library of 16,000 vols; Dir E. BOJADZIEVA.

National Archaeological Museum: 1000 Sofia, Saborna 2; tel. and fax 88-24-06; f. 1892; Dir M. VAKLINOVA.

National Art Gallery: 1000 Sofia, Pl. Knyaza Batemberga 1; tel. 980-33-20; f. 1948; revivalist and modern Bulgarian art; br. in St Alexander Nevsky Cathedral (icons and medieval ecclesiastical art); Dir Dr R. MARINSKA.

National Ethnographical Museum: 1000 Sofia, Moskovska 6A; tel. 988-19-74; fax 81-40-38; f. 1906; library of 22,221 vols; Dir N. TENEVA; publ. *Bulgarian Ethnology*.

National Gallery of Decorative Arts: 1000 Sofia, Vasil Levsky 56; tel. and fax (2) 65-41-72; f. 1976; works from the 1950s to the present; library of 2,000 vols; Dir ZDRAVKO MAVRODIEV.

National Museum of Literature: 1000 Sofia, G. Rakovski 138; tel. 988-24-93; Dir DZH. KAMENOV.

National Museum of Ecclesiastical History and Archaeology: 1000 Sofia, Pl. Sv. Nedelya 19; tel. 89-01-15; Dir N. KHADZHIEV.

National Museum of History: 1000 Sofia, Vitosha 2; tel. 88-41-60; fax 88-32-84; f. 1973; Dir B. DIMITROV.

National Museum of Military History: 1463 Sofia, Gen. Skobelev 23; tel. 52-15-96; f. 1916; library of 6,100 vols; br. in Varna; Dir P. YOTOV.

National Natural History Museum: 1000 Sofia, Tsar Osvoboditel 1; tel. 988-51-15; fax 88-28-97; f. 1889; library of 7,200 vols; Dir

Assoc. Prof. P. BERON; publ. *Historia naturalis bulgarica* (annually).

National Polytechnical Museum: 1303 Sofia, Opalchenska 66; tel. 31-80-18; f. 1968; science and technology; library of 10,000 vols; Dir A. VALCHEV; publs *Annual of the National Polytechnical Museum, Technitartché*.

Sopot

Ivan Vazov Museum: 4330 Sopot; tel. 20-70; f. 1935; birth-place of the writer; Dir C. NEDELCHEVA.

Stara Zagora

Regional Museum of History: 6000 Stara Zagora, Graf Ignatiev 11; tel. 2-39-31; f. 1907; Dir H. BUJUKLIEV.

Trjavna

Museum of Wood Carving and Icon Paintings: 5350 Trjavna, Pl. Kapitan Nikola 7; tel. 22-78; f. 1963; Dir TSVETAN KOLEV.

Trojan

Museum of Folk Craft and Applied Arts: 5600 Trojan, Pl. Vazrashdane; tel. 2-20-62; f. 1962; library of 2,700 vols; Dir T. TOTEVSKI; publ. *Cultural and Historical Inheritance of Trojan Region*.

Varna

Regional Museum of History: 9000 Varna, Osmy 8, Primorski polk 41; tel. (52) 23-73-44; f. 1906; library of 24,000 vols; br. open-air museums: Roman Baths, Aladzha Monastery, 'Stone Forest' National Park; Dir A. MINCHEV; publ. *Izvestija*.

Veliko Tărnovo

National Museum of Architecture: 5000 Veliko Tărnovo, Ivan Vazov 35, POB 281; tel. 3-05-87; f. 1979; library of 4,600 vols; Man. Dir T. TEOPHILOV.

Regional Museum of History: 5000 Veliko Tărnovo, Nikola Pikolo 2; tel. 2-02-56; fax 3-69-54; f. 1871; library of 10,000 vols; Dir P. PENKOV; publ. *Bulletin* (1 a year).

Vidin

Regional Museum of History: 3700 Vidin, S. Veliki 13; tel. 2-44-21; f. 1910; library of 8,500 vols; Dir A. BANOVA.

Vratsa

Regional Museum of History: 3000 Vratsa, Pl. Hr. Boteva 2; tel. 2-03-73; f. 1952; Dir I. RAJKINSKY.

Universities

SOFIISKI UNIVERSITET 'SVETI KLIMENT OHRIDSKY' (St Kliment Ohridsky University of Sofia)

1504 Sofia, Tsar Osvoboditel 15

Telephone: (2) 85-81

Telex: 23296

Fax: (2) 46-35-89

Founded 1888 as High School; granted charter 1909

State control

Academic year: September to June (two terms)

Rector: Prof. Dr I. LALOV

Pro-Rectors: Prof. Dr P. BONCHEV; Prof. Dr N. MARTINOV, Prof. Dr G. BAKALOV, Prof. Dr G. PETKANOV, Assoc. Prof. E. DRAGANOVA, Assoc. Prof. I. ZHELEV, Assoc. Prof. D. IVANOV

Director of International Relations: N. VULKANOVA

Secretary: R. STANIMIROVA

Director of Library: Prof. ZH. STOYANOV

Library: see under Libraries

Number of teachers: 1,608

Number of students: 25,454

Publication: *Godishnik*.

DEANS

Faculty of Philosophy: Assoc. Prof. V. STEFANOV
Faculty of History: Prof. Dr G. BAKALOV
Faculty of Pedagogy: Prof. Dr M. ANDREEV.
Faculty of Slavonic Philology: Prof. Dr B. BIOLCHEV
Faculty of Classical and Modern Philology: Assoc. Prof. M. PENCHEVA
Faculty of Mathematics and Information Science: Prof. Dr E. HOROSOV
Faculty of Physics: Prof. Dr N. NIKOLOV
Faculty of Chemistry: Prof. Dr N. PETSEV
Faculty of Biology: Prof. Dr K. RALCHEV
Faculty of Geology and Geography: Prof. D. TOPLIISKI
Faculty of Law: Assoc. Prof. D. KRUSANOV
Faculty of Journalism: Prof. Dr V. DIMITROV
Faculty of Primary and Pre-School Education: Prof. G. BIZHKOV
Faculty of Theology: Prof. Dr I. DENEV
Faculty of Economics: Assoc. Prof. G. CHOBANOV

PROFESSORS

Faculty of Philosophy:
ALEKSANDROV, P., History of Psychology
ANDONOV, A., Philosophy
ANGUSHEV, G., Abnormal Developmental Psychology
BOYADZHIEV, T., History of Philosophy
DESEV, L., Social Psychology
DINEV, V., Philosophical Anthropology
FOL, A., History of Culture
GENCHEV, N., History of Culture
GERGOVA, A., Book Science
GINEV, V., Theory of Culture
GRADEV, D., Social Psychology
KARASIMEONOV, G., Political Science
KRUMOV, K., Social Psychology
MIHAILOVSKA, E., Sociology
MITEV, P.-E., Political Science
NESHEV, K., Ethics
PETKOV, K., Sociology
RADEV, R., History of Philosophy
SIVILOV, L., Epistemology
STEFANOV, I. I., Sociology
VASILEV, N., Philosophy
VENEDIKOV, Y., Sociology
ZNEPOLOSKY, I., Theory of Culture

Faculty of History:
BAKALOV, G., Byzantine History
DIMITROV, I., Bulgarian History
DRAGANOV, D., Modern History
GEORGIEV, V., Bulgarian History
GEORGIEVA, I., Ethnography
GETOV, L., Archaeology
GYUZELEV, V., Bulgarian History
ILIEV, I., Modern History
LALKOV, M., Modern History
NAUMOV, G., Bulgarian History
NIKOLOV, J., Mediaeval History
OGNYANOV, L., Bulgarian History
PANTEV, A., Modern History
POPOV, D., Ancient History and Thracian Studies
SEMKOV, M., Modern History
TACHEVA, M., Ancient History and Thracian Studies
TRIFONOV, S., Modern History

Faculty of Pedagogy:
ANDREEV, M., Didactics
BOYCHEVA, V., History of Pedagogy
DIMITROV, L., Theory of Education
PAVLOV, D., Didactics
STOYANOV, P., History of Pedagogy
VASILEV, D., Didactics

Faculty of Slavonic Philology:
BIOLCHEV, B., Slavonic Literature
BOEVA, L., Russian Literature
BOYADZHIEV, T., Bulgarian Language
BOYADZHIEV, Z., Linguistics
BRESINSKI, S., Bulgarian Language
BUNDZHALOVA, B., Russian Language
BUYUKLIEV, I., Slavonic Linguistics
CHERVENKOVA, I., Russian Language
CHOLAKOV, Z., Bulgarian Literature
DIMCHEV, K., Teaching Methods of Bulgarian Language and Literature
DOBREV, I., Studies on Cyril and Methodius
GEORGIEV, N., Theory of Literature
HADZHIKOSEV, S., Theory of Literature
MINCHEVA, A., Studies on Cyril and Methodius
NITSOLOVA, R., Bulgarian Language
PASHOV, P., Bulgarian Language
PAVLOV, I., Slavonic Literature
PAVLOVA, R., Russian Language
POPIVANOV, I., Theory of Literature
POPOVA, V., Bulgarian Language
RADEVA, V., Bulgarian Language
TROEV, P., Russian Literature
VASILEV, M., Bulgarian Literature
VIDENOV, M., Bulgarian Language
YANEV, S., Bulgarian Literature
YOTOV, T., Russian Language

Faculty of Classical and Modern Philology:
ALEKSIEVA, B., English Philology
BOEV, E., Eastern Languages
BOGDANOV, B., Classical Philology
BOYADZHIEV, D., Classical Philology
DAKOVA, N., German Philology
DELIIVANOVA, B., German Philology
GALABOV, P., Romance Philology
KANCHEV, I., Ibero-Romance Philology
PARASHKEVOV, B., German Philology
PETKOV, P., German Philology
SHURBANOV, A., English Philology

Faculty of Mathematics and Information Science:
BOYANOV, B., Numerical Analysis and Algorithms
DENCHEV, R., Complex Analysis and Topology
GENCHEV, T., Differential Equations
HADZHIIVANOV, N., Education in Mathematics and Computer Sciences
HOROSOV, E., Differential Equations
HRISTOV, E., Complex Analysis and Topology
LILOV, L., Analytical Mechanics
MARKOV, K., Continuous Media Mechanics
POPIVANOV, N., Differential Equations
SKORDEV, D., Mathematical Logic and Applications
STANILOV, G., Education in Mathematics and Computer Sciences
TROYANSKI, S., Mathematical Analysis
ZAPRYANOV, Z., Continuous Media Mechanics

Faculty of Physics:
APOSTOLOV, A., Solid State Physics
DENCHOV, G., Geophysics
DINEV, S., Quantum Electronics
GEORGIEV, G., Quantum Electronics
ILIEV, M., Condensed Matter Physics
IVANOV, G., Astronomy
KAMENOV, P., Nuclear Physics and Energetics
KUTSAROV, S., Electronics
LALOV, I., Condensed Matter Physics
LUKYANOV, A., Nuclear Physics and Energetics
MARTINOV, N., Condensed Matter Physics
MATEEV, M., Theoretical Physics
NIKOLOV, N., Plasma Physics
PANCHEV, S., Meteorology and Geophysics
POPOV, A., Semiconductor Physics
SALTIEV, S., Quantum Electronics
SLAVOV, B., Quantum and Nuclear Physics
ZAHARIEV, Z., Theoretical Physics
ZHELYASKOV, I., Plasma Physics

Faculty of Chemistry:
ALEKSANDROV, S., Analytical Chemistry
BONCHEV, P., Analytical Chemistry
BUDUROV, S., Inorganic Chemical Technology

DOBREV, A., Organic Chemical Technology
FAKIROV, S., Organic Chemical Technology
GALABOV, B., Organic Chemical Technology
IVANOV, I., Physical Chemistry
KALCHEVA, B., Organic Chemical Technology
KOSTADINOV, K., Inorganic Chemical Technology
LAZAROV, D., Inorganic Chemical Technology
MARKOV, P., Organic Chemistry
PANAYOTOV, I., Physical Chemistry
PETROV, B., Organic Chemical Technology
PETSEV, N., Organic Chemistry
PLATIKANOV, D., Physical Chemistry
RADOEV, B., Physical Chemistry
TOSHEV, B., Physical Chemistry

Faculty of Biology:

BOZHILOVA, E., Botany
IVANOVA, I., Plant Physiology
KIMENOV, G., Plant Physiology
KOLEV, D., Biochemistry
MARGARITOV, N., Hydrobiology and Ichthyology
MINKOV, I., Human and Animal Physiology
TEMNISKOVA, D., Botany
VLAHOV, S., General and Industrial Microbiology

Faculty of Geology and Geography:

BACHVAROV, M., Geography of Tourism
BRESKOVSKA, V., Mineralogy, Petrology and Economic Geology
ESKENAZI, G., Mineralogy, Petrology and Economic Geology
KANCHEV, D., Economic Geography
MANDOV, G., Geology and Palaeontology
PETROV, P., Geography
SHISHKOV, G., Geology and Palaeontology

Faculty of Law:

BOYCHEV, G., Theory of State Law
GERDZHIKOV, O., Civil Law
MIHAYLOV, D., Criminal Law
PAVLOVA, M., Civil Law
PETKANOV, G., Finance Law
POPOV, P., Civil Law
SREDKOVA, K., Civil Law
STOYCHEV, S., Constitutional and Administrative Law
TSANKOVA, TS., Civil Law
TSEKOV, TS., Criminal Law
ZAHAROV, V., Theory of State Law
ZIDAROVA, I., International Law

Faculty of Journalism:

DIMITROV, V., Radio Journalism
KARAIVANOVA, P., Journalism
PANAYOTOV, F., History of Journalism
SEMOV, M., Theory of Journalism

Faculty of Primary and Pre-School Education:

BALTADZHIEVA, A., Special Education
BIZHKOV, G., Primary Education
DOBREV, Z., Special Education
KOLEV, J., Primary Education
PETROV, P., Primary Education
RADEVA, B., Anatomy
TSVETKOV, D., Primary Education
ZDRAVKOVA, S., Primary Education

Faculty of Theology:

DENEV, I., Practical Theology
HUBANCHEV, A., Christian Philosophy
KIROV, T., Moral Theology
KOEV, T., Dogmatics
MADZHUROV, N., Christian Philosophy
POPTODOROV, R., Canon Law
SHIVAROV, N., Old Testament Studies
SLAVOV, S., Old Testament Studies
STOYANOV, H., Church History

Faculty of Economics:

BEHAR, H., History of Economics
SERGIENKO, R., General Economic Theory

ATTACHED RESEARCH CENTRES

Centre for Ancient Languages and Civilizations: Dir (vacant).

Ivan Duichev Centre for Slavic and Byzantine Studies: Dir Prof. A. DZHUROVA.

PLOVDIVSKI UNIVERSITET 'PAISII HILENDARSKI' ('Paisii Hilendarski' University of Plovdiv)

4000 Plovdiv, Tsar Asen 24
Telephone: (32) 23-86-61
Telex: 44251
Fax: (32) 23-50-49
E-mail: interrel@ulccw.uni-plovdiv.bg

Founded 1961 from 'Paisij Hilendarski' Higher Pedagogical Institute, Plovdiv; university status 1972

Rector: Prof. O. SAPAREV
Vice-Rectors: Prof. L. FUTEKOV, Prof. I. KUTSAROV, Assoc. Prof. D. MITEV
Registrar: D. BOIKOV
Librarian: R. PANOVA

Number of teachers: 450
Number of students: 15,000

Publications: *Nauchni Trudove*.

DEANS

Faculty of Mathematics: Assoc. Prof. G. ZLATANOV
Faculty of Chemistry: Assoc. Prof. G. ANDREEV
Faculty of Biology: Prof. B. GRUEV
Faculty of Physics: Prof. N. BALABANOV
Faculty of Philology: Assoc. Prof. I. CHOBANOV
Faculty of Pedagogics: Assoc. Prof. P. RADEV
Faculty of Public Professions: Prof. G. BACHVAROV
Faculty of Economics: Assoc. Prof. M. MIHAILOVA
Faculty of Law: Assoc. Prof. T. KAMENOVA

PROFESSORS

ANGELOV, P., Zoology
ATANASOV, A., Theoretical Physics
BALABANOV, N., Nuclear Physics
DIMITROV, R., Technology of Inorganic Chemistry
FUTEKOV, L., Analytical Chemistry
IVANOV, A., Microbiology
IVANOV, S., Technology of Organic Chemistry
KUTSAROV, I., Morphology of Modern Bulgarian Language
MINKOV, I., Plant Physiology
MOLLOV, T., Algebra
VELCHEV, N., Physics of Dielectrics

VELIKO TĂRNOVSKI UNIVERSITET 'KIRIL I METODII' (Cyril and Methodius University of Veliko Tărnovo)

5000 Veliko Tărnovo, T. Tarnovski 2
Telephone: (62) 26-11
Fax: (62) 28-023

Founded 1971 from 'Kiril i Metodii' Higher Pedagogical Institute

Rector: Assoc. Prof. I. STOYANOV
Pro-Rectors: Prof. P. TODOROV, Assoc. Prof. N. DONCHEVA, Assoc. Prof. P. KHRISTOV
Administrative Officer: O. BOZANOV
Librarian: ST. GALIZOVA

Number of teachers: 470
Number of students: 6,600

AMERICAN UNIVERSITY IN BULGARIA

2700 Blagoevgrad
Telephone: 2-09-51
Fax: 2-06-03

Founded 1991
Private control
Language of instruction: English
Academic year: August to May

President: JULIA WATKINS
Provost: BARRY CHAMBERS
Registrar: EVELINA TERZIEVA

Number of teachers: 40 full-time, 20 part-time
Number of students: 650

CHAIRS OF ACADEMIC DIVISIONS

Sciences: Assoc. Prof. IVAN GOCHEV
Social Sciences: Asst Prof. KIRSTA GLENN
Arts and Humanities: Asst Prof. VERNON PEDERSEN

BA degree; majors in business administration, applied economics, computer science, English, history, journalism and mass communication, political science and international relations, south-eastern European studies.

Technical Universities and Higher Institutes

(in alphabetical order by town)

BURGAS PROF. ASSEN ZLATAROV UNIVERSITY

8010 Burgas, Prof. Jakimov 1
Telephone: 66-01-19
Telex: 83689
Fax: 68-61-41

Founded 1963 (until 1992, Higher Institute of Chemical Technology; until 1995, Burgas University of Technology)
State control
Language of instruction: English
Academic year: September to July

Rector: Prof. NIKOLAI RALEV
Vice-Rectors: Prof. PETKO PETKOV (Education), Prof. TODOR ORESHKOV (Research), Prof. RADOSTIN KUTSAROV (International Relations)
Registrar: IVAN MARKOV
Librarian: KOSTADINKA MURGOVA

Library of 160,000 vols
Number of teachers: 351
Number of students: 5,300

Publication: *Godishnik*.

DEANS

Faculty of Organic Chemistry: Prof. G. KOSTOV
Faculty of Inorganic Chemistry: Prof. IVAN NENOV
Faculty of Business and Economics: Prof. Z. DICHEV
Faculty of Humanities: Prof. T. OYKOVA
Faculty of Engineering: Prof. ST. PETROV
Faculty of Education: Prof. T. HADZHIPETROV
Technical College: Prof. PETKO BARZOV
College of Tourism: Prof. BRATOY KOPRINAROV
College of Medicine: Prof. MIMI STOYCHEVA

HEADS OF DEPARTMENTS

Organic Chemistry:

Organic Chemistry: Prof. D. ALEXSIEV
Oil Technology: Prof. D. MINKOV
Polymer Technology: Prof. T. GEORGIEV
Biotechnology: Prof. BL. SHOPOVA
Organic Synthesis Technology: Prof. K. KURTEV
Central Research Laboratory: Prof. K. MARKOVA

Inorganic Chemistry:

Analytical Chemistry: Prof. E. POPOVA
Physical Chemistry: Prof. OV. MEKENYAN
Water Technology: Prof. T. PANAYOTOVA
Silicate Technology: Prof. B. BOGDANOV
Inorganic Substances: Prof. Z. KIROVA-YORDANOVA

Business and Economics:

Economics and Industrial Management: Prof. M. VALCHEVA

Marketing and Management: Prof. T. STOINOV
Mathematics: Prof. IV. DORCHEV
Industrial Technology: Prof. A. DIMOV
Economics and Management of Tourism: Prof. ST. NEYCHEV
Physical Education and Sport: Prof. M. UZUNOVA

Humanities:

Inorganic Chemistry: Prof. K. DAVARSKI
Bulgarian Language: G. PETROVA
Foreign Languages: A. FRANSAZOVA
Physics: Prof. A. PETRAKIEV
Pedagogics and Methodology of Education: V. SHIVACHEVA
Social Sciences: Prof. P. PEEVA

Engineering:

Fundamentals of Chemical Technology: Prof. A. DIMOV
Chemical Engineering: Prof. CHR. KARAGYOZOV
Mechanics: Prof. D. DIMITROVA
Environmental Protection: Prof. M. DIMOVA
Theory and Science of Materials: Prof. G. DENEV

ATTACHED INSTITUTES

Foreign Students Training Section: Dir Prof. R. KUTSAROV.

Postgraduate Qualifications Department: Dir Prof. R. KUTSAROV.

Research Section: Prof. T. ORESHKOV.

TECHNICAL UNIVERSITY, GABROVO

5300 Gabrovo, Hadzhi Dimităr 4

Telephone: (66) 2-19-31
Telex: 67513
Fax: (66) 24856

Founded 1964 as Higher Mechanical and Electrical Engineering Institute of Gabrovo; adopted present name 1990
Academic year: September to July

Rector: Prof. P. STOYANOV
Vice-Rectors: Prof. P. CHANTROV, Assoc. Prof. I. NEMIGENCHEV, Assoc. Prof. SV. SIMEONOV
Registrar: D. PETROV

Number of teachers: 272
Number of students: 5,285

DEANS

Faculty of Machine-Building and Instrument-Building: Assoc. Prof. K. KIROV
Faculty of Electrotechnics and Electronics: Assoc. Prof. D. PETROV
Faculty of Engineering Economics: Assoc. Prof. P. GANCHEV

HIGHER INSTITUTE OF FOOD AND FLAVOUR INDUSTRIES

4000 Plovdiv, Maritza 26

Telephone: (32) 44-00-05
Fax: (32) 44-01-02
E-mail: vihvp@plovdiv.integ.bg

Founded as an independent institute 1953
State control
Academic year: October to July

Rector: Prof. S. DANCHEV
Vice-Rectors: Prof. S. DICHEV, Assoc. Prof. A. NESTOROV
Registrar: T. KUZMANOV
Librarian: V. GESHEVA

Number of teachers: 225
Number of students: 2,040 (full-time), 1,100 (part-time)

Publication: *Nauchni Trudove*.

DEANS

Technological Faculty: Assoc. Prof. G. SOMOV
Technical Faculty: Assoc. Prof. S. VASILEV

PROFESSORS

ANDREEV, A., Technology of Milk Industry
BABEV, D., Technology of Sugar
BALDZIEV, D., Technology of Grain Processing
BALTADZIEVA, M., Technology of Milk Products
BOSHKOV, L., Technology of Sugar
DANCHEV, S., Technology of Meat Products
DICHEV, S., Refrigeration
GENCHEV, L., Technology of Fruit and Vegetable Canning
GEORGIEV, S., Technology of Tobacco and Tobacco Products
KAROVA, E., Microbiology
KHADZHIISKI, TS., Technology of Vegetable Oils
KONAREV, A., Organization and Management
KRACHANOV, H., Organic Chemistry
KUPENOV, L., Microbiology
LOMEV, M., Technology of Grain Processing and Fodder
MURGOV, I., Microbiology
OBRETENOV, T., Organic Chemistry
PEEV, P., Economics of Public Catering
POPOV, I., Automation of Production
STAMOV, S., Technology, Organization and Design in Public Catering
TANCHEV, S., Technology of Canning
VANGELOV, A., Technology of Bread-making and Pasta Products
ZLATEV, T., Ecology

AGRICULTURAL UNIVERSITY PLOVDIV

4000 Plovdiv, D. Mendeleev 12

Telephone: (32) 2-34-98
Telex: 44405
Fax: (32) 23-31-57
E-mail: info@au-plovdiv.bg

Founded 1945
State control
Academic year: September to June

Rector: Assoc. Prof. Dr G. MOSKOV
Pro-Rectors: Prof. R. ANGELOVA, Prof. A. POPOV, Assoc. Prof. G. PEPELYANKOV
Chief Administrative Officer: P. TOROZOV
Chief Librarian: E. ANASTASOVA

Number of teachers: 218
Number of students: 2,652

Publication: *Scientific Works* (4 a year).

DEANS

Faculty of Agronomy: Prof. Dr KH. GORASTEV
Faculty of Horticulture: Assoc. Prof. N. ALEXIEV
Faculty of Plant and Soil Protection: Prof. S. KAROV
Faculty of Tropical and Sub-tropical Farming: Assoc. Prof. Dr KH. BONCHEV
Faculty of Agricultural Economics: Prof. K. MURGOV
Free Faculty: Assoc. Prof. Dr G. RACHOVSKI

PROFESSORS

ANGELOVA, R., Entomology
ATANASSOV, I., Ecology
BABRIKOV, D., Viticulture
BABRIKOVA, T., Entomology
BRAIKOV, D., Viticulture
CIRKOV, J., Microbiology
DIMITROV, Z., Land Improvement
GORASTEV, KH., Plant Genetics and Breeding
GORBANOV, S., Agrochemistry
HARIZANOV, A., Entomology
KAROV, S., Phytopathology
KOLEV, K., Agricultural Engineering
KOSTOVA, Z., Animal Husbandry
KRASTEV, A., Tropical and Sub-tropical Animal Husbandry
MATEV, J., Agrochemistry
MIKHAILOV, M., Agricultural Economics
MITOV, P., Fruit Growing
MURGOV, K., Agroinformatics
NAKOV, B., Phytopathology
PANDELIEV, S., Viticulture
PETKOVA, S., Plant Genetics and Breeding
POPOV, A., Phytopathology
POPOV, D., Agricultural Engineering
POPOVA, M., Botany
SENGALEVICH, G., Agroecology
SMIRNOVA, V., Agricultural Organization
SPASOV, V., Crop Farming
TERZIISKI, D., Botany

HIGHER MEDICAL INSTITUTE

4000 Plovdiv, V. Aprilov 15A

Telephone: (32) 44-38-39
Fax: (32) 44-21-94

Founded 1945
Academic year: September to May (two terms)

Rector: Prof. AT. DZHURDZHEV

DEANS

Faculty of Medicine: Assoc. Prof. P. UCHIKOV
Faculty of Dentistry: Assoc. Prof. ST. VLADIMIROV

ANGEL KANCHEV UNIVERSITY OF RUSE

7017 Ruse, Studentska 8

Telephone: (82) 45-10-92
Telex: 62462
Fax: (82) 45-51-45

Founded 1954 as Institute of Mechanization and Electrification of Agriculture; became Angel Kanchev Higher Technical School 1982 and Angel Kanchev Technical University of Ruse 1990; present name 1995
State control
Academic year: September to July

Rector: Assoc. Prof. B. TOMOV
Vice-Rectors: Assoc. Prof. ZH. NIKOLOV, Prof. K. ANDONOV, Assoc. Prof. P. STAMATOV
Chief Administrative Officer: Assoc. Prof. ML. TRIFONOV
Librarian: E. LEKHOVA

Library of 306,641 vols
Number of teachers: 535
Number of students: 6,408

Publication: *Nauchni Trudove*.

DEANS

Faculty of Agricultural Machinery and Mechanization of Farming: Assoc. Prof. Y. DOCHEV
Faculty of Mechanical and Manufacturing Engineering: Assoc. Prof. ST. VICHEV
Faculty of Electrical Engineering, Electronics and Automation: Assoc. Prof. ST. KAZANDZHIEV
Faculty of Automation: Assoc. Prof. T. TOTEV
Faculty of Business and Management: Assoc. Prof. V. PENCHEV
Faculty of Education: Assoc. Prof. SV. BILCHEV
Faculty of Law: Assoc. Prof. L. DACHEV
Faculty of Kinesitherapy: Prof. Dr K. KOZHUKHAROV

PROFESSORS

ANDONOV, K., Mechanization and Electrification of Stock-Breeding and Livestock Farming
ANDREEV, D., Machine Elements
DASKALOV, DZH., Agriculture
DIMITROV, I., Machine Elements
ENCHEV, K., Theory of Mechanisms
GRADINAROV, A., Casting
GUZGULOV, G., Hydro-engineering
ILIEV, L., Internal Combustion Engines
ILIEV, V., Automation
KANEV, M., Material Science and Technology of Metals
KOZHUKHAROV, K., Kinesitherapy
KUMDZHIEV, KHR., Mechanics
LYUBENOV, SL., Motor Cars and Tractors
MARINOV, KH., Theory of Mechanics
MINCHEV, N., Law
MITKOV, A., Agriculture

NEDEV, I., Bulgarian Philology
NENOV, P., Machine Elements
PAPAZOV, K., Economics
PARASHKEVOV, I., Mechanization and Electrification of Agriculture
POPOV, G., Metal Forming
SIMEONOV, D., Motor Cars and Lorries
VASILIEV, K., Mechanization and Electrification of Agriculture
VELCHEV, S., Machine-Tools
VITLIEMOV, V., Technology of Mechanical Engineering

'KONSTANTIN PRESLAVSKI' UNIVERSITY

9712 Shumen
Telephone: (54) 6-31-51
Telex: 73421
Fax: (54) 6-31-71
Founded 1971
Rector: Prof. T. TOTEV
Publication: *Godishnik*.

UNIVERSITY OF ARCHITECTURE, CIVIL ENGINEERING AND GEODESY

1421 Sofia, H. Smirnenski 1
Telephone: (2) 6-33-21
Telex: 23574
Fax: (2) 963-17-96
E-mail: aceint@uacg.acad.bg
Founded 1942 (until 1990, Higher Institute of Architecture and Civil Engineering)
State control
Academic year: September to June
Rector: Prof. I. PAPAZCHEV
Vice-Rectors: Prof. T. GANEV, Prof. B. DIMITROV, Assoc. Prof. V. TROEVA
Registrar: L. SKRIMOVA
Librarian: A. TODOROVA
Library of 450,000 vols
Number of teachers: 435
Number of students: 4,000

DEANS

Faculty of Structural Engineering: Assoc. Prof. T. VASSILEV
Faculty of Hydrotechnics: Assoc. Prof. R. NIKOLAEVA
Faculty of Geodesy: Assoc. Prof. P. PENEV
Faculty of Architecture: Assoc. Prof. M. RILSKI
Faculty of Transport Engineering: Prof. N. KOSSEV

PROFESSORS

Faculty of Structural Engineering:

BANKOV, B., Building Mechanics
DARAKCHIEV, B., Building Materials
DIMITROV, B., Reinforced Concrete Structures
DRAGANOV, N., Steel, Timber and Plastic Structures
GANEV, T., Building Mechanics
IVANCHEV, I., Reinforced Concrete Structures
JANCHULEV, A., Organization and Economics of Construction
KARAMANSKI, T., Building Mechanics
KATOV, P., Building Technology and Mechanization
KIROV, N., Building Technology and Mechanization
MINEV, M., Reinforced Concrete Structures
MIRONOV, K., Construction Safety
PAMUKCHIEV, S., Reinforced Concrete Structures
PETKOV, J., Building Technology and Mechanization
RANGELOV, R., Building Mechanics
SAKAREV, I., Organization and Economics of Construction
SOTIROV, P., Steel, Timber and Plastic Structures
STAJKOV, P., Steel, Timber and Plastic Structures
TEPAVICHAROV, A., Building Mechanics
TRANKA, K., Reinforced Concrete Structures
VENKOV, L., Steel, Timber and Plastic Structures

Faculty of Hydrotechnics:

ALEXANDROV, V., Theoretical Mechanics
BOITCHEV, S., Water Supply
GIRGINOV, T., Water Supply
IVANOV, S., Water Supply
KAZAKOV, B., Hydraulics and Hydrology
KISHKILOV, M., Theoretical Mechanics
KISLJAKOV, S., Theoretical Mechanics
KJURKCHIEV, R., Theoretical Mechanics
KOLEV, P., Theoretical Mechanics
MALENOV, R., Technical Mechanics
MARINOV, E., Hydraulics and Hydrology
MLADENOV, K., Theoretical Mechanics
PAPAZCHEV, I., Hydrotechnics
PETKOV, P., Water Supply
POPOV, A., Irrigation and Drainage
STEFANOV, I., Theoretical Mechanics
TOSHEV, S., Physics

Faculty of Geodesy:

DASKALOVA, M., Geodesy
DIMITROV, D., Surveying
MARINOV, M., Photogrammetry
STOINOV, V., Geodesy
TOMOVA, P., Surveying
VALEV, G., Geodesy

Faculty of Architecture:

KALAIDZHIEV, I., Interior Design
KRASTEV, T., History of Architecture
MIRIANOV, M., Housing Construction
NIKIFOROV, I., Town Planning
PAPAGALOV, G., History of Architecture
POPOV, S., Public Building
PRAMATAROV, I., Drawing
SIVREV, L., Industrial Building
STARCHEV, V., Drawing and Modelling
TSVETKOV, E., Interior Design

Faculty of Transport Engineering:

ETIMOV, T., Geotechnics
GICHEV, T., Mathematics
KOSEV, N., Geotechnics
KRASTILOV, I., Geotechnics
SABEV, M., Railway Engineering
TODOROV, T., Road Engineering
TOTEV, J., Railway Engineering

UNIVERSITY OF CHEMICAL TECHNOLOGY AND METALLURGY

1756 Sofia, bul. Kliment Ohridski 8
Telephone: (2) 68-15-13
Fax: (2) 68-54-88
Founded as a state university 1953
State control
Academic year: September to July
Rector: Prof. Dr KAMEN VELEV
Vice-Rector for Research and International Co-operation: Prof. Dr PETER NOVAKOV
Vice-Rector for Education: Assoc. Prof. K. MUTAFCHIEVA
Chief Administrative Officer: Assoc. Prof. ASSEN PETKOV
Librarian: EUGENIA GANCHEVA
Library of 66,000 vols
Number of teachers: 321
Number of students: 3,521
Publication: *Godishnik* (1 a year).

DEANS

Faculty of Organic Technology and Chemical Engineering: Assoc. Prof. ST. VELEVA
Faculty of Inorganic Technology and Automation of Industry: Assoc. Prof. CH. BOYADZHIEVA
Faculty of Metallurgy: Assoc. Prof. NIKOLA AKHMAKOV
Faculty of Liberal Professions, Postgraduate Studies and Co-ordination of Colleges integrated with the University: Assoc. Prof. IVAN DOSEV

PROFESSORS

Faculty of Inorganic Technology and Automation of Industry:

BOZADJIEV, P., Technology of Inorganic Compounds
DIMITRIEV, Y., Silicate Technology
GRANCHAROV, I., Technology of Inorganic Compounds
GUROV, R., Economics
HADJIISKY, M., Automation of Industry
ILCHEVA, L., Analytical Chemistry
KARADAKOV, B., Analytical Chemistry
KASABOV, I., Silicate Technology
PEEV, G., Chemical Technology and Materials for Microelectronics
SAMUNEVA, B., Silicate Technology
SHISHKOV, D., Technology of Inorganic Compounds
STAVRAKEVA, D., Silicate Technology
STOYANOV, S., Automation of Industry
VELEV, K., Automation of Industry
VUCHKOV, I., Automation of Industry
YONCHEV, H., Automation of Industry

Faculty of Organic Technology and Chemical Engineering:

ALEXIEV, B., Biotechnology
ASSENOV, A., Chemical Engineering
DIMITROV, R., General Chemical Technology
DJAGAROVA, E., Chemical Technology of Rubber
DRAGANOVA, R., Chemical Technology of Wood
GEORGIEVA, M., Technology of Plastics
HARDALOV, I., Textile Finishing and Man-Made Fibres
IVANOV, I. M., Biotechnology
KRASTEVA, M., Biotechnology
LITOVSKI, Z., Chemical Technology of Wood
MATEVA, R., Technology of Plastics
MINCHEV, A., Chemical Engineering
MONDESHKA, D., Organic Chemistry
NATOV, M., Technology of Plastics
NATOVA, L., Technology of Plastics
NOVAKOV, P., Technology of Plastics
SOKOLOVA, E., Physical Chemistry
VASILEVA, S., Technology of Plastics

Faculty of Metallurgy:

AVRAMOV, A., Ferrous Metallurgy
BAKARDJIEV, P., Non-ferrous Metallurgy
DEVENSKI, P., Physics
DRAKALIJSKI, B., Ferrous Metallurgy
HARALAMPIEV, G., Non-ferrous Metallurgy
KANAZIRSKI, H., Physics
KAROLEVA, V., Non-ferrous Metallurgy
MANEVA, M., Inorganic Chemistry
POPOV, K., Mechanical Science
POPOVA, M., Mechanical Science
VODENICHAROV, H., Physics
ZAYACHKI, V., Physics

UNIVERSITY OF FORESTRY

1756 Sofia, Kl. Ohridski 10
Telephone: (2) 9-19-07
Fax: (2) 62-28-30
Founded as an independent institute 1953
State control
Academic year: September to June (two terms)
Rector: Prof. Dr DIMITAR KOLAROV
Pro-Rectors: Prof. CH. SHECHTOV, Assoc. Prof. D. GEORGIEV
Registrar: (vacant)
Librarian: R. KRINTCHEVA
Number of teachers: 202
Number of students: 1,500
Publications: *Forest Ideas, Nauchni Trudove*.

DEANS

Faculty of Forestry: Assoc. Prof. K. LIUBENOV
Faculty of Forestry Industry: Assoc. Prof. B. DINKOV
Faculty of Ecology and Landscape Architecture: Assoc. Prof. EK. PAVLOVA
Faculty of Veterinary Medicine: Prof. G. KOVACHEV
Faculty of Agronomy: Assoc. Prof. G. TRENCHEV
Faculty of Industrial Management: Assoc. Prof. IV. YOVKOV
Faculty of Extramural and Postgraduate Studies: Assoc. Prof. I. VASILEVA

PROFESSORS

ASPARUCHOV, K., Harvesting Machinery and Technology
DIMITROV, E., Basis of Forestry
DJALKOV, N., Dendrology
GENCHEVA, S., Ecology and Conservation, Soil Science
GRIGOROV, P., Sawing of Timber
KAVALOV, A., Furniture Technology
KOLAROV, D., Plant Physiology
KOVACHEV, G., Veterinary Medicine
KULELIEV, J., Planting Trees and Flowers
KYUCHUKOV, G., Furniture Construction
MICHOV, I., Forest Mensuration
PUCHALEV, B., Organization and Planting in Landscape Architecture
RAICHEV, A., Thermodynamics, Heat and Mass Transfer
SHECHTOV, CH., Automation of Technological Processes
SHKTILYANOVA, EL., Floriculture
VIDELOV, H., Hydrothermal Treatment of Wood
YOROVA, K., Soil Science
YOSIFOV, N., Particle-Board Technology

ATTACHED INSTITUTE

Balkan Centre of Study and Research in Ecology and Environmental Protection: Dir Assoc. Prof. I. DOMBALOV.

MEDICAL UNIVERSITY

1431 Sofia, D. Nestorov 15
Telephone: 59-00-52
Fax: 59-40-94

Founded 1972, as the Academy of Medicine, by the integration of the former Higher Medical Institute and the medical research institutes; present name and status 1995
State control
Academic year: September to June

Rector: Prof. DIMITAR DZEROV
Pro-Rectors: Prof. NIKOLA POLIKHRONOV (Education), Prof. IVAN ASENOV (International Relations and Research), Prof. IVAN MENDIZOV (Medical Affairs)
Chief Administrative Officer: KHRISTO ANACHKOV
Librarian: Dr DABCHEV

Number of teachers: 1,561
Number of students: 4,802

Publications: *Acta Medica Bulgarica* (quarterly) and 12 specialized publs.

DEANS

Faculty of Medicine: Prof. I. SMILOV
Faculty of Pharmacy: Prof. R. SHEKERDZIISKY
Faculty of Stomatology: Assoc. Prof. N. ATANASOV
Free Faculty: Assoc. Prof. N. VRABCHEV
Faculty of Nursing: Assoc. Prof. K. YURUKOVA

UNIVERSITY OF MINING AND GEOLOGY

1100 Sofia, Darvenica
Telephone: 6-25-81
Fax 62-10-42

Founded 1953

Academic year: October to June (two terms)
Rector: Prof. K. KOVACHEV
Pro-Rectors: Prof. M. MATEEV, Assoc. Prof. V. KOVACHEV, Prof. B. BOZHINOV
Registrar: S. IVANOV
Scientific Information Department: D. KOSTOVA
Librarian: K. DRAGANOVA

Number of teachers: 298
Number of students: 2,217

Publication: *Godishnik* (annually).

DEANS

Faculty of Mining Electromechanics: Assoc. Prof. A. KUZMANOV
Faculty of Mining Technology: Assoc. Prof. V. IVANOV
Faculty of Geological Prospecting: Assoc. Prof. S. BAKARDIEV
Faculty of Public Professions: Assoc. Prof. V. ANGELOVA

PROFESSORS

Faculty of Mining Electromechanics:
GEGOV, E., Automation of Mining
KOSEV, T., Mechanical Engineering
MATEEV, M., Mechanization of Mining
MENTESHEV, M., Mine Electrification
OBRESHKOV, D., Theory of Mechanisms
PANOV, V., Electrical Engineering
PENEV, A., Mechanization of Mining
TSVETKOV, H., Mechanization of Mining
VASILEV, V., Mechanization of Mining

Faculty of Mining Technology:
ARNAUDOV, B., Mining Engineering
BOZHINOV, B., Mining Engineering
CHESHANKOV, L., Mine Construction and Geodesy
DIMOV, I., Technical Mechanics
DRAGANOV, L., Mine Construction
HADZHIEV, P., Mineral Processing
HRISTOV, S., Mining Engineering
KAMENOV, I., Chemistry
KLISURANOV, G., Mineral Processing
KOLEV, K., Rock Mechanics
KOVACHEV, K., Mineral Processing
LAZAROV, S., Drilling and Blasting
MAJDRAKOV, M., Mine Construction and Geodesy
MIRCHEV, M., Mine Construction and Geodesy
NIKOLAEV, N., Rock Mechanics
PARLAPANSKI, M., Chemistry
STEFANOV, D., Mining Engineering
STOEV, S., Mineral Processing
STOEVA, P., Mining Engineering
STOJANOV, D., Mining Engineering

Faculty of Geological Prospecting:
GALABOV, M., Hydrogeology and Engineering Geology
IVANOVA, V., Applied Geophysics
MARINOV, T., Mineralogy and Petrology
POPOV, P., Economic Geology
STOYNOVA, M., Mineralogy and Petrology

TECHNICAL UNIVERSITY, SOFIA

1156 Sofia, Studentski grad 'Hristo Botev'
Telephone: (2) 62-30-73
Telex: 22575
Fax: (2) 68-32-15

Founded 1945

Rector: Prof. D. DIMITROV
Pro-Rectors: Prof. G. MANDICHEV, Prof. KHR. PETROV, Prof. V. ZHIVKOV
Sec.-Gen.: V. DIMITROV
Librarian: V. PATIOVA

Library: see under Libraries
Number of teachers: 1,097
Number of students: 14,258

Publication: *Izvestija*.

DEANS

Faculty of Electronics and Electronic Technologies: Assoc. Prof. R. IVANOV
Faculty of Communications and Communication Technologies: Assoc. Prof. E. ALTIMIRSKY
Faculty of Electrical Engineering: Assoc. Prof. K. ZAKHARINOV
Faculty of Computer Science and Technology: Assoc. Prof. KH. OSKAR
Faculty of Machine Technology: Assoc. Prof. A. DIKOV
Faculty of Mechanical Engineering: Prof. K. DONEV
Faculty of Power Engineering and Power Machines: Prof. K. SHUSHULOV
Faculty of Automation: Prof. G. GATEV
Faculty of Transport: Assoc. Prof. B. BELNIKOLOVSKY
Faculty of Management: Prof. G. TSVETKOV
Open Faculty: Assoc. Prof. T. ATANASOV

ATTACHED CENTRES

Centre for Applied Mathematics: Prof. B. CHESHANKOV
Centre of Physical Education and Sports: Assoc. Prof. I. BOZOV
Centre of Physics: Prof. N. ANDREEV

UNIVERSITY OF NATIONAL AND WORLD ECONOMICS

1156 Sofia, Studentski grad 'Hristo Botev'
Telephone: (2) 62521
Telex: 22040
Fax: (2) 689029

Founded 1920

Rector: Prof. K. MIRKOVICH
Pro-Rectors: Prof. V. STOYANOV, Prof. H. KOZHUKHAROV, Prof. N. NIKOLOV, Assoc. Prof. T. KANALIEV
Chief Administrative Officer: P. KIOSEV
Librarian: S. TSENOVA

Library of 428,000 vols
Number of teachers: 525
Number of students: 27,600

Publications: *Trudove*, *Informacionen bjuletin*, *Alternativi*, *Ikonomist*.

DEANS

Agro-Industrial Faculty: Prof. I. GROZEV
Faculty of Commerce & Transport: Prof. L. MUTAFCHIEV
Faculty of Economic Information: Assoc. Prof. TODOR KANALIEV.
Faculty of General Economics: Prof. K. MIRKOVICH
Faculty of International Economic Relations: Assoc. Prof. B. BOEVA
Faculty of Business: Assoc. Prof. G. KALUSHEV
Faculty of Infrastructure: Prof. M. GENESHKY
Dean's Office for Foreign Students and Postgraduate Students: Assoc. Prof. V. VARBANOV

PROFESSORS

Agro-Industrial Faculty:
ANACHKOV, V., Agrarian Economics
ATANASOV, P., Agrarian Economics
CHOLEV, J., Agrarian Economics
DINOV, D., Agrarian Economics
DOCHEV, I., Industrial Economics
GEORGIEV, T., Agrarian Economics
GROZEV, I., Agrarian Economics
KALOJANOV, A., Agrarian Economics
KOVACHEVA, Z., Industrial Economics
LENKOV, L., Agrarian Economics
MISHEV, V., Agrarian Economics
MONOV, I., Agrarian Economics
NIKOV, M., Agrarian Economics
PETKOV, P., Agrarian Economics
POPOV, T., Agrarian Economics
SHTONOV, D., Agrarian Economics
VALEV, G., Industrial Technology
ZAHARIEV, Z., Agrarian Economics
ZLATANOV, Z., Industrial Economics

Faculty of Commerce and Transport:
- ALEKSANDROV, K., Home Trade
- ANDREEV, A., Science of Commodities
- KRASTEV, K., Regional Economics
- MUTAFCHIEV, L., Transport Economics

Faculty of Economic Information:
- AJKOV, S., Information Processing
- BACHVAROV, A., Information Processing
- BALEVSKI, D., Statistics
- DINEV, M., General and Specialized Control
- DUSHANOV, I., Accounting
- GANEV, A., Information Processing
- PARVULOV, B., Theory of Management
- PERGELOV, K., Accounting and Book-keeping
- RAJCHINOV, I., Mathematics
- SAJKOVA, I., Statistics
- TOTEV, T., Accounting
- VAKLIEV, G., Accounting and Book-keeping
- VELICHKOVA, N., Statistics

Faculty of General Economics:
- ANGELOV, T., Planning
- BEROV, L., History of Economic Doctrines
- BONEV, S., Planning
- HRISTOV, M., Finance
- ILIEV, I., Planning
- KOSTOV, I., Political Economy
- LJUBIKOV, T., Planning
- MINKOV, M., Sociology
- MIRKOVICH, K., Political Economy
- NAUMOV, N., Labour Economics
- PACEV, T., Sociology
- PETROV, G., Finance
- SAVOV, S., Political Economy
- SHOPOV, D., Labour Economics
- VELIKOV, N., Political Economy

Faculty of International Economic Relations:
- ANANIEVA, N., International Relations
- DANAILOV, D., Organization and Management of Foreign Trade
- DIMITROV, D., International Law
- IVANOV, I., International Law
- KARAKASHEVA, L., Organization and Management of Foreign Trade
- PETROV, M., International Economic Relations
- SAVOV, M., International Economic Relations
- STOIMENOV, M., International Monetary and Financial Relations

THRACIAN UNIVERSITY

6000 Stara Zagora, Students' Campus

Telephone: (42) 28-09

Fax: (42) 74-11

E-mail: post@uzvm.uzvm.bg

Founded 1995, following merger of Higher Institute of Animal Sciences and Veterinary Medicine and Higher Institute of Medicine

State control

Languages of instruction: Bulgarian, English

Academic year: September to July

Rector: Prof. Dr IVAN BOZHKOV

Pro-Rectors: Prof. Dr B. TODOROV (Teaching), Prof. Dr A. ATANASSOV (Research), Prof. Dr G. KAITAZOV (Administration and Finance)

Supervisor of Administration: Assoc. Prof. A. STOYANOV

Librarian: I. DEMIREVA

Library of 300,000 vols

Number of teachers: 650

Number of students: 4,800

DEANS

Faculty of Agriculture: Assoc. Prof. SVETLIN TANCHEV

Faculty of Veterinary Medicine: Prof. Dr L. GEORGIEV

Faculty of Medicine: Prof. Dr CHR. CHUCHKOV

In-service Teacher Training Institute: Assoc. A. KARAGYOZOV (Dir)

Medical College, Stara Zagora: Dr K. KOSTOV (Dir)

Medical College, Haskovo: Dr I. RUSSEVA (Dir)

Medical College, Sliven: M. NADEVA (Dir)

Technical College, Yambol: (vacant)

HEADS OF DEPARTMENT

Faculty of Agriculture:
- Agricultural Economics: Assoc. Prof. I. GEORGIEV
- Agricultural Management: Prof. V. STANKOV
- Agricultural Engineering and Farm Buildings: Prof. M. SPASOV
- Animal Genetics and Breeding: Prof. G. NIKOLOV
- Animal Hygiene: Assoc. Prof. D. DIMANOV
- Animal Nutrition: Prof. N. TODOROV
- Animal Physiology: Prof. A. PETKOV
- Biochemistry: Prof. O. PETKOVA
- Biology and Special Animals: Assoc. Prof. M. STOEVA
- Cattle Husbandry: Prof. I. KARABALIEV
- Foreign Languages: N. TANEVA
- Horse Breeding: Assoc. Prof. A. BARZEV
- Mathematics and Physics: Assoc. Prof. G. BOYCHEV
- Microbiology and Milk Processing: Prof. I. PEICHEVSKI
- Morphology of Farm Animals: Assoc. Prof. ST. TENEV
- Pig Production: Assoc. Prof. V. KATSAROV
- Plant Science: Assoc. Prof. D. PAVLOV
- Poultry Production: Prof. G. KAYTAZOV
- Reproduction: Assoc. Prof. IV. MANOLOV
- Sheep Production: Prof. S. TYANKOV
- Social Science: Assoc. Prof. ST. PASHOV
- Special Branches: Assoc. Prof. P. NENCHEV
- Farmers' College: Dir Assoc. Prof. D. PAVLOV

Faculty of Veterinary Medicine
- Anatomy of Domestic Animals: Assoc. Prof. S. GADZHEV
- Biochemistry: Prof. CH. POPOV
- Cytology, Histology and Embryology: Assoc. Prof. S. VITANOV
- Epizootology and Infectious Diseases: Assoc. Prof. P. IVANOV
- Foreign Languages: N. TANEVA
- General and Organic Chemistry: Assoc. Prof. S. CHERVENKOV
- Genetics and Private Breeding: Prof. IV. YOTOVA
- Hygiene and Control of Foodstuffs: Prof. L. GEORGIEV
- Internal Medicine: Prof. CHR. GEORGIEV
- Obstetrics and Gynaecology: Prof. S. TSOLOV
- Organization of the Veterinary Service: Prof. I. BOZHKOV
- Parasitology: Prof. D. GEORGIEVA
- Pathological Anatomy: Prof. A. ANGELOV
- Pathological Physiology: (vacant)
- Physical Education and Sports: T. GURGURIEV
- Pharmacology and Toxicology: Prof. D. PASHOV
- Principles of Animal Husbandry: Prof. TS. NENOV
- Radiobiology and Radioecology: Assoc. Prof. P. GEORGIEV
- Surgery: Assoc. Prof. ZH. FILIPOV
- Veterinary Microbiology, Virology and Immunology: Assoc. Prof. K. KOLEV
- Veterinary Physiology with Endocrinology: Assoc. Prof. Y. ILIEV
- Zoohygiene and Animal Nutrition: Prof. N. NETSOV

Faculty of Medicine:
- Anaesthesiology and Reanimation: Assoc. Prof. Dr ZH. KARAKOLEV
- Anatomy: Prof. Dr CHR. CHUCHKOV
- Catastrophe Medicine: Assoc. Prof. Dr V. POPZAKHARIEVA
- Chemistry and Biochemistry: Assoc. Prof. B. CHEMISHEV
- Clinical Laboratory: Assoc. Prof. Dr V. LAZAROVA
- Dermatology and Venereology: Assoc. Prof. P. GARDEV
- General Medicine: Assoc. Prof. Dr V. POPZAHARIEVA
- Forensic Medicine: Assoc. Prof. Dr M. GROZEVA
- General and Operational Surgery: Prof. Dr A. ATANASOV
- Hygiene and Professional Diseases: Assoc. Prof. Dr R. DELIRADEVA
- Internal Diseases: Prof. Dr ST. MANTOV
- Microbiology and Epidemiology: Assoc. Prof. Dr P. SOTIROVA
- Molecular Biology and Immunology: Assoc. Prof. ZH. ZHELEV
- Neurology: Assoc. Prof. I. MANCHEV
- Centre for Neurosurgery: Dr P. VALKANOV
- Obstetrics and Gynaecology: Prof. Dr B. ATANASOV
- Ophthalmology: Assoc. Prof. Dr E. FILIPOV
- Orthopaedics and Traumatology: Assoc. Prof. Dr G. PROICHEV
- Oto-rhino-laryngology: Assoc. Prof. Dr P. DIMOV
- Paediatrics: Assoc. Prof. Dr P. CHAKUROVA
- Pathological Anatomy: Prof. Dr GR. VELEV
- Pathophysiology: (vacant)
- Pharmacology: Assoc. Prof. Dr V. SPASSOV
- Physics: IVAN TANEV
- Physiology: (vacant)
- Physiotherapy, Rehabilitation and Remedial Gym: Assoc. Prof. M. BELCHEV
- Propadeutics of Internal Diseases: Assoc. Prof. Y. VULKOV
- Roentgenology and Radiology: Assoc. Prof. Dr VLAHOV
- Social Medicine: (vacant)
- Special Surgery: Assoc. Prof. Dr A. ANDREEV
- Surgery Diseases: Prof. Dr G. DIMITROV
- University Hospital: Dr ZH. KARAKOLEV (Dir)
- Urology: Assoc. Prof. AT. UZUNOV

D. TSENOV ACADEMY OF ECONOMICS

5250 Svishtov, Em. Chakarov 2

Telephone: (631) 2-27-22

Telex: 66684

Fax: (631) 2-34-72

E-mail: uircomm@comm.uni-svishtov.bg

Founded 1936 as D. A. Tsenov Higher School of Commerce; became Higher School of Economics and Social Studies in 1948; reorganized in 1952/53; became D. Tsenov Economic University in 1990; present name 1995

State control

Academic year: September to July

Rector: Assoc. Prof. A. DAMIANOV

Vice-Rectors: Assoc. Prof. Dr N. PAVLOV, Assoc. Prof. Dr P. KANEV, Assoc. Prof. Dr G. GERGANOV, Assoc. Prof. Dr L. KIREV

Chief Administrative Officer: V. TANEV

Librarian: S. LALEV

Library of 211,000 vols

Number of teachers: 196

Number of students: 11,618

Publications: *Economic World Library* (6 a year), *Narodnostopanski Arhiv* (quarterly), *Biznes – Upravlenie* (quarterly).

DEANS

Faculty of Accounting: Assoc. Prof. Dr G. BATASHKI

Faculty of Finance: Assoc. Prof. Dr R. LILOVA

Faculty of Industry and Trade: Assoc. Prof. Dr V. PETROV

Faculty of Management and Marketing: Assoc. Prof. Dr S. TONKOVA

Open Faculty: Assoc. Prof. Dr N. GEORGIEV

PROFESSORS

- CHONOV, N., Economics
- DAMIANOV, D., Accounting
- DIMITROV, M., Accounting
- DRAGANOV, H., Insurance
- KANEV, M., Economics

MOINOV, M., Informatics
PANAIOTOV, D., Strategic Planning
RADKOV, R., Finance
SLAVEV, S., Regional Economics

HIGHER MEDICAL INSTITUTE

Varna 9000 Varna, M. Drinov 55

Telephone: 22-54-22
Telex: 77464

Founded 1961
Academic year: October to June (two terms)

Rector: Assoc. Prof. D. KAMBUROV

VARNA UNIVERSITY OF ECONOMICS

9002 Varna, Bul. Kniaz Boris I 77

Telephone: 2-13-51
Fax: 23-56-80
E-mail: rector@mail.mt-mt.bg

Founded 1920
State control
Academic year: September to June

Rector: Prof. Dr KALIYU DONEV
Pro-Rectors: Assoc. Prof. BOJKO ATANASOV, Assoc. Prof. NIKOLA BAKALOV, Assoc. Prof. DIMITAR RADILOV
Registrar: Dr S. IVANOV
Librarian: Mag. T. TSANEVA

Library of 265,000 vols
Number of teachers: 268
Number of students: 10,880

Publications: *Godishnik, Izvestya.*

DEANS

Faculty of Business Administration: Assoc. Prof. V. DJAMBAZHOV
Faculty of Computer Science: Prof. D. DOCHEV
Faculty of Finance and Accounting: Assoc. Prof. G. TODOROV
Faculty of Management: Assoc. Prof. E. TODOROVA
Faculty of Law: Assoc. Prof. Dr P. TSANKOV
Faculty of World Economics: Assoc. Prof. I. ILIEV

PROFESSORS

DIMITROV, G., Economics of Building
DOCHEV, D., Mathematics
DONEV, K., Auditing
GENOV, G., Accountancy
JOSIFOV, N., Law
ILIEV, P., Computer Sciences
KOTSEV, T., Finance and Credit
KOVACHEV, Z., Economics
LICHEV, I., Management
MIKHAILOV, P., Economics
MINCHEV, S., Organic Chemistry
PEKHLIVANOV, V., Finance
SALOVA, N., Economics and Organization of Trade
STANKOV, B., Law

TECHNICAL UNIVERSITY

9010 Varna, Kv. Levski, POB 10

Telephone: 30-24-44
Telex: 77401
Fax: 30-27-71

Founded 1962 as Higher Institute of Electrical and Mechanical Engineering; adopted present name in 1990

Rector: Prof. ASSEN NEDEV
Pro-Rectors: Assoc. Prof. G. DISHLIEV, Assoc. Prof. ST. BARUDOV, Assoc. Prof. T. PAZVANTOV
Registrar: DIMITAR DIMITRAKIEV
Librarian: M. ATANASOVA

Library of 285,000 vols
Number of teachers: 493
Number of students: 7,775

Publication: *Godishnik*.

DEANS

Faculty of Machine Technologies: Assoc. Prof. N. NICOV
Faculty of Mechanical Engineering: Assoc. Prof. N. MINTCHEV
Faculty of Shipbuilding: Prof. P. KOLEV
Faculty of Electrical Engineering: Assoc. Prof. L. DIMITROV
Faculty of Electronics: Assoc. Prof. D. YUDOV
Faculty of Computer Science and Automatics: Assoc. Prof. V. STANTCHEV
Faculty of Liberal Arts: Assoc. Prof. MITKOV
Faculty of Ecology and Environmental Protection: Prof. C. CHOMAKOV
Faculty of Law: Assoc. Prof. N. KEMANOV

PROFESSORS

BAKARDZHIEV, I., Metal Science
CHOMAKOV, CH., Biology
DIMITROV, D., Electrical Apparatus
DIMITROV, D., Law
DONCHEV, D., Electrical Machines
HRISTOV, H., Radiotechnics
JOSIFOV, R., Ship Energetic Machines and Mechanics
KOLEV, P., Ship Design
KOLEV, S., Production Automation
MARINOV, M., Electrical Equipment of Industry and Water Transport
MILANOV, ZY., Law
MINCHEV, N., Theory of Machines and Mechanisms
MITKOV, V., Law
NEDEV, A., Ship Power Units
NEDYALKOV, S., Biology
PANTEV, N., Control Systems
RACHEV, M., Machine Tools and Equipment
RAYKOV, R., Law
SERAFIMOV, M., Internal Combustion Engines
SEVASTIAKEV, V., Internal Combustion Engines

Schools of Art and Music

ACADEMY OF MUSIC AND DANCE

4025 Plovdiv, T. Samodumov 2

Telephone: 22-83-11
Fax: 23-16-68

Founded 1972

Rector: Prof. G. KANEV
Pro-Rectors: Prof. N. TODOROV, Prof. P. LUKANOV
Secretary-General (Manager): I. MATANSKI
Librarian: R. PENEVA

Number of teachers: 98
Number of students: 880

'PANCHO VLADIGEROV' STATE ACADEMY OF MUSIC

1505 Sofia, E. Georgiev 94

Telephone: (2) 47-01-81
Fax: (2) 46-36-77

Founded 1904; became Conservatoire 1954 and Academy 1995

Rector: Prof. G. KOSTOV
Pro-Rectors: Prof. I. EFTIMOV, Prof. S. SHOPOVA, Prof. P. GERDZHIKOV, Prof. N. NIKOLOV
Registrar: A. ANASTASOV
Librarian: E. PETKOVA

Number of teachers: 220
Number of students: 995

Publication: *Godishnik*.

DEANS

Faculty of Musical Theory, Composition and Conducting: Prof. AL. TEKELIEV
Faculty of Instrumentation: Prof. D. MOMCHILOV
Faculty of Vocal Studies: Prof. P. GERDZHIKOV
Dean for Foreign Students: Prof. N. NIKOLOV

'KRĂSTJU SARAFOV' NATIONAL ACADEMY FOR THEATRE AND FILM ARTS

1000 Sofia, G. Rakovski 108A

Telephone: (2) 987-98-62
Fax: (2) 89-73-89

Founded 1948

Rector: Prof. H. ROUKOV
Pro-Rectors: Prof. V. DIMITROV, Prof. B. MATANOV, Assoc. Prof. S. TANKOVSKA, Prof. S. LASAROV
Registrar: I. ALEKSANDROV
Librarian: R. DJACHKA

Number of teachers: 204
Number of students: 499

NATIONAL ACADEMY OF ARTS

1000 Sofia, Shipka 1

Telephone: (2) 88-17-01
Fax: (2) 87-33-28

First founded 1896; reorganized as an institute 1954, as an academy 1991

Rector: Prof. O. SHOSHEV
Pro-Rectors: Assoc. Prof. L. CHEKHLAROV, Assoc. Prof. I. ENEVA, Assoc. Prof. Z. STOYANOV
Registrar: S. GADZHEVA
Librarian: D. DIUKMEGCHIEVA

Number of teachers: 111
Number of students: 828

DEANS

Faculty of Fine Arts: Assoc. Prof. ST. STOYANOV
Faculty of Applied Arts: Prof. G. GRIGOROV

BURKINA FASO

Research Institutes

GENERAL

Centre National de la Recherche Scientifique et Technologique: BP 7047, Ouagadougou; tel. 33-23-94; fax 30-50-03; f. 1950, 1968 incorporated into Ministère de l'Education Nationale, 1978 into Ministère de l'Enseignement Supérieur et de la Recherche Scientifique; basic and applied research in humanities, social sciences, natural sciences, agriculture, energy, medicine; library of 20,000 vols; 102 researchers; Dir-Gen. MICHEL P. SEDOGO; publs *Science et Technique* (2 a year), *CNRST-Information* (every 2 months), *Euréka,* (quarterly).

Institut Français de Recherche Scientifique pour le Développement en Coopération, Centre ORSTOM à Ouagadougou: BP 182, Ouagadougou 01; tel. 306737; fax 310385; hydrology, geography, agronomy, botany, medical entomology, economics, demography, anthropology, pedology, ethnology, geology, sociology; library; Dir GEORGES GRANDIN.

Institut Français de Recherche Scientifique pour le Développement en Coopération (ORSTOM): BP 171, Bobo-Dioulasso 01; tel. 97-12-69; fax 97-09-42; f. 1947; medical entomology, human geography, ecology, malariology; library of 1,200 vols, 30 current periodicals; Dir J. L. DEVINEAU. (See main entry under France.)

AGRICULTURE, FISHERIES AND VETERINARY SCIENCE

Centre de Recherches sur les Trypanosomoses Animales, IEMVT et CCE: BP 454, Bobo-Dioulasso 01; tel. 97-20-53; telex 8227; fax 97-23-20; f. 1972; vector-transmitted diseases of cattle; library of 950 vols; Dir SAYDIL M. TOURE; publ. *Rapport d'activité* (annually).

CIRAD – Forêt: BP 1759, Ouagadougou 01; tel. 33-40-98; fax 30-76-17; f. 1963; research in silviculture, agroforestry and tree-breeding; Head of Mission DENIS DEPOMMIER.

Institut de l'Environnement et de Recherches Agricoles: BP 7192, Ouagadougou 03; tel. 34-02-69; fax 34-02-71; e-mail sereme@burkina.coraf.bf; f. 1978; research on production systems, sorghum, millet and maize, oil-bearing plants, tubers, market gardening, animal products, forest products, rice, soil fertilization and machinery, cotton; library of 2,500 vols, 2,500 documents; Dir PACO SEREME.

EDUCATION

Institut Pédagogique du Burkina: BP 7043, Ouagadougou; tel. 33-63-63; f. 1976 by the Ministry of National Education, for the development of methods and courses in primary education; library of 16,000 vols (Min. of Education Library); 150 staff; Dir Gen. JUSTINE TAPSOBA; publ. *Action, Réflexion et Culture* (8 a year).

MEDICINE

Organisation de Coordination et de Coopération pour la lutte contre les Grandes Endémies (OCCGE): 01 BP 153, Bobo-Dioulasso 01; tel. 97-01-01; fax 97-00-99; e-mail sg@pegase.occge.bf; f. 1960 to combat endemic and transmitted diseases and malnutrition; conducts research and trains medical workers; mem. states: Benin, Burkina Faso, Côte d'Ivoire, Mali, Mauritania, Niger, Senegal and Togo; library of 2,200 vols, 40 current periodicals, 10,000 technical documents, 10 special collections; Sec.-Gen. ABDOULAYE AG RHALY; publs *Bulletin bibliographique mensuel*, *Bulletin OCCGE – Informations* (3 a year).

TECHNOLOGY

Bureau de Recherches Géologiques et Minières (BRGM): BP 86, Ouagadougou; tel. 33-50-42; telex 5267. (See main entry under France.)

Libraries and Archives

Ouagadougou

Centre National des Archives: Présidence du Faso, BP 7030, Ouagadougou; tel. 33-61-96; telex 5221; fax 31-49-26; f. 1970; Dir DIDIER E. OUEDRAOGO.

University

UNIVERSITÉ DE OUAGADOUGOU

BP 7021, Ouagadougou

Telephone: 30-70-64

Telex: 5270

Founded 1969, university status 1974

Academic year: October to June

State control

Language of instruction: French

Rector: FILIGA MICHEL SAWADOGO

Vice-Rector: SITA GUINKO

Secretary-General: SOULEYMANE OUEDRAOGO

Librarian: MAÏMOUNA SANOKO

Library of 70,000 vols

Number of teachers: 390

Number of students: 10,000

Publications: *Cahiers du Centre d'Etudes, de Documentation et de Recherches Economiques et Sociales* (quarterly), *Revue burkinabé de Droit* (2 a year), *Annales* (2 a year).

DEANS

Faculty of Science and Technology: Prof. LAYA SAWADOGO

Faculty of Health Sciences: Prof. B. ROBERT SOUDRE

Faculty of Languages, Letters, Arts, Humanities and Social Sciences: ALBERT OUEDRAOGO

Faculty of Law and Politics: KOURITA SANDWIDI

Faculty of Economics and Management Sciences: Prof. KIMSEYINGA SAWADOGO

Colleges

Centre d'Etudes Economiques et Sociales d'Afrique Occidentale: BP 305, Bobo-Dioulasso; tel. 97-10-17; fax 97-08-02; e-mail cesao.bobo@fasonet.bf; f. 1960; areas of study include the enhancement of rural orgs on an institutional level, the promotion of women, faith and humanity, community health, administration of the development of rural communities, environment and land administration, savings and investments in rural areas, development projects; 16 staff; library of 14,000 vols and 77 periodicals; Dir ROSALIE OUOBA; publ. *Construire Ensemble* (every 2 months).

Ecole Inter-Etats d'Ingénieurs de l'Equipement Rural: BP 7023, Ouagadougou 03; tel. 30-20-53; telex 5266; fax 31-27-24; f. 1968 by governments of 14 francophone African states; 3-year postgraduate diploma course; hydraulics, civil engineering, refrigeration technology, sanitary engineering; Dir MICHEL GUINAUDEAU.

BURUNDI

Research Institutes

AGRICULTURE, FISHERIES AND VETERINARY SCIENCE

Institut des Sciences Agronomiques du Burundi: BP 795, Bujumbura; tel. 223390; telex 5147; fax 225798; f. 1962; agronomical research and farm management; library of 11,500 vols, 120 periodicals; Dir-Gen. Dr JEAN NDIKURANA.

MEDICINE

Laboratoire Médicale: Bujumbura; devoted to clinical analyses and physio-pathological research nutritional studies.

NATURAL SCIENCES

Physical Sciences

Centre National d'Hydrométéorologie: Bujumbura; Dir E. KAYENGAYENGE.

TECHNOLOGY

Direction Générale de la Géologie et des Mines: Ministère de l'Energie et des Mines, BP 745, Bujumbura; tel. 22278; telex 5182; fax 23538; Dir-Gen. Dr AUDACE NTUNGICIMPAYE.

Libraries and Archives

Bujumbura

Bibliothèque de l'Université: BP 1320, Bujumbura; f. 1961; tel. 222857; 192,000 vols, 554 periodicals; Chief Librarian THARLISSE NSABIMANA.

Bibliothèque Publique: Bujumbura; 26,000 vols.

Museums and Art Galleries

Bujumbura

Musée Vivant de Bujumbura: BP 1095, Bujumbura; tel. 26852; f. 1977; part of Centre de Civilisation Burundaise attached to Ministry of Youth, Sport and Culture; reflects the life of the Burundi people in all its aspects; includes a reptile house, aquarium, aviary, traditional Rugo dwelling, open-air theatre, fishing museum, botanical garden, herpetology centre, musical pavilion, and crafts village; Dir EMMANUEL NIRAGIRA.

Gitega

Musée National de Gitega: BP 110, Gitega; tel. (040) 2359; f. 1955; history, ethnography, arts, folk traditions; library in process of formation (100 vols); Curator J. MAPFARAKORA.

University

UNIVERSITÉ DU BURUNDI

BP 1550, Bujumbura
Telephone: (2) 3288
Founded 1960, present name 1980
Academic year: October to September
President of the Administrative Council: P. NZINAHORA
Rector: Prof. LUC RUKINGAMA
Vice-Rector: Prof. THARCISSE NSABIMANA
Academic Director: LIN NDAYIPFUKAMIYE
Research Director: PHILIPPE NTAHOMBAYE
Librarian: VENANT BUSHUBIJE
Number of teachers: 239
Number of students: 2,749
Publications: *Revue de l'Université* (quarterly), *Le Flambeau* (annually), *Le Héraut* (every 2 months), *Actes de la Semaine de l'Université* (annually), *Actes de la Conférence des Universités des Etats Membres de la CEPGL* (annually).

DEANS

Faculty of Letters and Humanities: HENRI BOYI
Faculty of Economic and Administrative Sciences: DÉO NGENDAKUMANA
Faculty of Sciences: THÉODORE MUBAMBA
Faculty of Law: GERVAIS GATUNANGE
Faculty of Medicine: EVARISTE NDABANEZE
Faculty of Psychology and Education: GABRIEL NTUNAGUZA
Faculty of Agriculture: PONTIEN NDABANEZE
Faculty of Applied Sciences: THÉOPHILE NDIKUMANA

DIRECTORS

Higher Technical Institute: THÉOPHILE NDIKUMANA
Institute of Physical Education and Sports: THARCISSE NIYONZIMA
Institute of Education: DOMITIEN NIZIGIYIMANA

Colleges

Centre Social et Éducatif: Bujumbura; f. 1957; courses in crafts, photography, mechanics; 75 students.

Ecole Supérieure de Commerce du Burundi: BP 1440, Bujumbura; tel. (2) 4520; telex 5166; f. 1982; 304 students; library of 1,200 vols; Dir PIERRE NZEYIMANA.

Institut Supérieur d'Agriculture: BP 35, Gitega; tel. (040) 2335; telex 5147; f. 1983; under Min. of Nat. Education; courses in tropical agriculture, stockbreeding, agricultural engineering, food technology; 213 students; Dir (vacant); publ. *Revue des Techniques Agricoles Tropicales* (2 a year).

Institut Supérieur de Techniciens de l'Aménagement et de l'Urbanisme: BP 2720, Bujumbura; tel. (2) 3694; telex 5048; f. 1983; under the Min. of Public Works and Urban Development; 103 students; library of 863 vols; Dir SALVATOR NAHIMANA.

Lycée Technique: Bujumbura; f. 1949; training apprentices, craftsmen and professional workers; four workshops: mechanics, masonry, carpentry, electrical assembling; 450 students.

CAMEROON

Research Institutes

GENERAL

Institut des Sciences Humaines: Yaoundé; f. 1979; part of Min. of Higher Education; Dir W. NDONGKO.

Institut Français de Recherche Scientifique pour le Développement en Coopération (ORSTOM): Représentation ORSTOM, BP 1857, Yaoundé; tel. 20-15-08; fax 20-18-54; pedology, sedimentology, hydrology, ecology, medical entomology, cell biology, demography, linguistics, geography, anthropology, ornithology, sociology; Representative MICHEL MOLINIER. (See main entry under France.)

Instituts du Ministère de l'Enseignement Supérieur: BP 1457, Yaoundé; tel. 27-29-83; 5 university institutes and 5 research institutes; soil science, hydrology, nutrition, psycho-sociology, demography, economics, geography, archaeology, botany and vegetal biology, and medical entomology; Sec.-Gen. PIERRE OWONO ATEBA; publs *Revue Science et Technique* (quarterly, in 3 series: agriculture, health sciences, human sciences), *Annales* (quarterly, in 4 series: languages and literature, human sciences, law, economics).

AGRICULTURE, FISHERIES AND VETERINARY SCIENCE

Centre des Recherches Forestières de Nkolbisson: BP 2102, Yaoundé; tel. 23-26-44; f. 1980; forestry research; 170 staff (14 researchers); Dir A. M. MAINO; publ. *Rapport Annuel.*

Institut de la Recherche Agronomique: BP 2123, Yaoundé; tel. 23-26-44; telex 1140; f. 1979; part of Ministry of Higher Education; agriculture, agronomy, phytopathology, entomology, pedology, botany; 6 research centres, 16 stations; 314 staff; library of 2,600 vols, 2,500 brochures, 450 periodicals; Dir Dr J.-A. AYUK-TAKEM; publs *Science et Technique (Series Sciences agronomiques et zootechniques)* (quarterly), *Mémoires et Travaux de l'IRA*, *Rapport Annuel.*

Institut de Recherches pour les Huiles et Oléagineux (IRHO): BP 243, Douala; f. 1949; Dir J. N. REGAUD. (See main entry under France.)

Institut des Recherches Zootechniques et Vétérinaires (IRZV): BP 1457, Yaoundé; tel. 23-24-86; telex 8418; fax 23-24-86; f. 1974; part of Min. of Higher Education; research on livestock, fisheries and wildlife, and environment; library of 1,800 vols, 358 periodicals; Dir Dr JOHN TANLAKA BANSER; publ. *Science and Technology Review.*

BIBLIOGRAPHY, LIBRARY SCIENCE AND MUSEOLOGY

Centre Régional pour la Promotion du Livre en Afrique de l'UNESCO (CREPLA)/UNESCO Regional Book Development Centre for Africa South of the Sahara: POB 1646, Yaoundé; f. 1962.

ECONOMICS, LAW AND POLITICS

Institut de Formation et de Recherche Démographiques: BP 1556, Yaoundé; tel. 22-24-71; telex 8441; fax 22-67-93; f. 1972 with the co-operation of the UN; ECA Executing Agency; training and research on demographic phenomena and their links with economic and social factors; library of 15,000 vols; Dir AKOTO ELIWO; publ. *Annales* (3 a year).

Institut des Relations Internationales du Cameroun (IRIC): BP 1637, Yaoundé; tel. and fax 31-03-05; f. 1971 by the Federal Government, the Carnegie Endowment for International Peace, the Swiss Division for Technical Co-operation and others; a bi-lingual, postgraduate institute for education, training and research in diplomacy and international studies, attached to the university; library of 15,000 vols; Dir Dr LISETTE ELOMO NTONGA; Sec.-Gen. Dr JEAN-EMMANUEL PONDI.

EDUCATION

Centre National d'Education: Yaoundé; f. 1979; part of Min. of Higher Education; Dir E. BEBEY.

HISTORY, GEOGRAPHY AND ARCHAEOLOGY

Institut Géographique National: BP 157, Ave Mgr.-Vogt, Yaoundé; f. 1945; survey office; Dir J. L. LE FLOCH.

LANGUAGE AND LITERATURE

Centre Régional de Recherche et de Documentation sur les Traditions Orales et pour le Développement des Langues Africaines (CERDOTOLA): BP 479, Yaoundé; tel. 23-05-46; f. 1978; research on African languages, oral literature, traditional music; 20 mem. countries; library in process of formation; Exec. Sec. SOUNDJOCK-SOUNDJOCK; publs linguistic atlases, literary collections.

MEDICINE

Institut de Recherches Médicales et d'Etudes des Plantes Médicinales: Yaoundé; tel. 23-13-61; telex 8418; f. 1979; 250 staff; library of *c.* 1,000 vols, 50 periodicals; Dir A. ABONDO; publs *Science et Technique* (series *Sciences Médicales*), *Cahiers.*

Laboratoire Interdépartemental: BP 4046, Douala; attached to the Ministry of Health; research on hygiene and public health matters.

NATURAL SCIENCES

Physical Sciences

Direction de la Météorologie Nationale: 33 rue Ivy, BP 186, Douala; tel. and fax. 42-16-35; telex 5097; f. 1934; Dir EMMANUEL EKOKO ETOUMANN; publs *RCM: Résumé climatologique mensuel*, *Résumé mensuel du Temps* (both monthly), *Annales climatologiques* (irregular), *Bulletin agrométéorologique décadaire.*

TECHNOLOGY

Compagnie Française pour le Développement des Fibres Textiles (CFDT): BP 1699, Douala; brs at Garoua, Maroua, Mora, Touboro and Kaele; textile research.

Institut de Recherches Géologiques et Minières: POB 4110, Yaoundé; tel. and fax 21-03-16; f. 1979; Dir GEORGES E. EKODECK.

Libraries and Archives

Yaoundé

Archives Nationales: BP 1053, Yaoundé; f. 1952; conserves and classifies all documents relating to the Republic; library of 15,000 vols; Dir EMERANT MBON MEKOMPOMB.

Bibliothèque Nationale du Cameroun: BP 1053, Yaoundé; 64,000 vols.

Museums and Art Galleries

Bamenda

International Museum and Library—Akum: POB 389, Bamenda, Northwest Province; f. 1948; local and foreign artefacts of interest to researchers and students of sociology, anthropology and archaeology; brasswork, paintings, beaded work, clay figures, animal skins, masks, postage stamps, iron work, sculpture, stools, traditional costumes, films and books; Curator PETER S. ATANGA.

Universities and University Centres

UNIVERSITÉ CATHOLIQUE DE L'AFRIQUE CENTRALE

BP 11628, Yaoundé

Telephone: 23-74-00

Fax: 23-74-02

Founded 1989

Language of instruction: French

Rector: Père BARTHÉLEMY NYOM

First Vice-Rector: Père DENIS MAUGENEST

Second Vice-Rector: Abbé JEAN-PIERRE ELELAGHE NZE

Secretary-General: Dinh ALFRED MANDENGUE

Librarian: Père JOSEPH BOUTE

Library of 28,000 vols

Number of teachers: 150

Number of students: 770

Publication: les cahiers de l'U.C.A.C. (1 a year)

DEANS

Faculty of Theology: Père LAURENT MPONGO

Faculty of Social Sciences and Administration: Père BERNARD CHANDON-MOËT

Faculty of Philosophy: Père CLAUDE PAIRAULT

DIRECTORS

Dept of Canon Law: Père ALFRED NOTHUM

School of Nursing: RENÉE GEOFFRAY

UNIVERSITY OF BUEA

POB 63, Buea

Telephone: 32-21-34

Telex: 5155

Fax: 32-22-72

Founded 1977 (opened 1986) as Buea University Centre; present name and status 1992

State control

Languages of instruction: English, French and Spanish
Academic year: September to June

Chancellor: Dr PETER AGBOR TABI
Pro-Chancellor: Prof. VICTOR ANOMAH NGU
Vice-Chancellor: Dr DOROTHY L. NJEUMA
Deputy Vice-Chancellor: Prof. SAMMY BEBAN CHUMBOW
Registrar: Dr HERBERT NGANJO ENDELEY

Number of teachers: 93 full-time, 115 part-time
Number of students: 3,300

Publications: *Epasa Moto* (annually), *Newsletter* (quarterly).

DEANS

Faculty of Arts: Prof. MARTIN Z. NJEUMA
Faculty of Science: Dr VINCENT TITANJI
Faculty of Social and Management Sciences: Prof. SAMMY BEBAN CHUMBOW
Faculty of Health Sciences: Dr THEODOSA MCMOLI (Vice-Dean)
Faculty of Education: Dr LYDIA LUMA (acting)

CONSTITUENT INSTITUTE

Advanced School of Translators and Interpreters (ASTI): Dir Dr ETIENNE ZÉ AMVELA.

UNIVERSITÉ DE YAOUNDÉ I

BP 337, Yaoundé

Telephone: 22-07-44
Telex: 8384
Fax: 22-13-20

Founded 1962
State control
Languages of instruction: English and French
Academic year: October to July

Rector: PETER AGBOR TABI
Vice-Rector: NOAH NGAMNUENG
Secretary-General: ANDRÉ MARIE NTSOBE NDJOH
Librarian: PETER CHATEH

Library of 90,000 vols
Number of teachers: 875
Number of students: 41,000

Publications: *Guide Bibliographique du Monde Noir, Annales, Revues.*

DEANS

Faculty of Law and Economics: PAUL GÉRARD POUGOUE
Faculty of Arts: PIERRE NGIJOL NGIJOL
Faculty of Science: ROBERT ROUX

DIRECTORS

Ecole Normale Supérieure: JEAN TABI MANGA
Institut des Relations Internationales: PETER AGBOR TABI
Ecole Nationale Supérieure Polytechnique: PAUL VERMANDE
Centre Universitaire des Sciences de la Santé: PIERRE CARTERET
Ecole Supérieure des Sciences et Techniques de l'Information et de la Communication: JACQUES FAME NDONGO

HEADS OF DEPARTMENTS

Faculty of Arts:

Negro-African Literature: PIERRE NGIJOL NGIJOL
African Languages and Linguistics: SAMMY CHUMBOW BEBAN
Geography: JEAN LOUIS DONGMO
Philosophy: ANTOINE MANGA BIHINA
English: PAUL NKAD MBANGWANA
Sociology: JEAN MFOULOU
History: MARTIN Z. NJEUMA
French: ANDRÉ MARIE NTSOBE NDJOH
German: ALEXANDRE KUMA NDOUMBE III
Spanish: DOMINIQUE AKOA

Faculty of Law and Economics:

Private Law (French): STANISLAS MELONE
Private Law (English): PETER Y. NTAMARK
Public Law: JOSEPH MARIE BIPOUN WOUM
Economics: SAMUEL NGONGANG

Faculty of Science:

Biochemistry: FÉLICITÉ MBIAPO
Physics: HANDT BISSECK
Animal Biology and Physiology: THOMAS NJINE
Computer Science: MAURICE TCHUENTE
Mathematics: FRANCIS CAGNAC
Earth Sciences: SAMUEL-MARTIN ENO-BELINGA
Inorganic Chemistry: ROLAND WANDJI
Organic Chemistry: LUC SONDENGAM
Plant Biology and Physiology: ROGER ATANGANA ETEME

Ecole Normale Supérieure:

Philosophy: CHARLES NDIMI
French: JEAN TABI MANGA
English: PETER ABETY
Languages: JOSEPH MBASSI
History and Geography: MARTIN NTONE KONO
Education: LYDIA LUMA EWENYE
Mathematics: NORBERT NOUTCHEGUEME
Physics: SAMUEL MBOM ABANE
Biology: GUY TSALA NDZOMO
Chemistry: PAUL HELL

Ecole National Supérieure Polytechnique:

Civil Engineering and Town Planning: AMOS FOUDJET
Electrical Engineering: SYLVESTER KWANKAM YUNKAP
Mathematics: AWONO ONANA
Mechanics: ERNEST KAPTOUOM
Physics and Chemistry: DANIEL HARRAN

Centre Universitaire des Sciences de la Santé:

Biomedical Sciences: MICHEL ASONGANYI TAZOACHA
Clinical Sciences: PAUL KOUEKE
Public Health: (vacant)

Ecole Supérieure des Sciences et Techniques de l'Information et de la Communication:

Television: TJADE EONE
Communication: (vacant)
General: FRANCIS WETE
Press: FERDINAND CHINDJI KOULEU
Radio: EMMANUEL TATAH MENTAN

UNIVERSITÉ DE YAOUNDÉ II

BP 1365, Yaoundé

Telephone: 23-65-53
Fax: 23-65-54

Rector: Prof. EPHRAÏM NGWAFOR
Secretary-General: NICOLE C. NDOKO

UNIVERSITÉ DE DOUALA

BP 2701, Douala

Telephone: 42-82-53
Telex: 6140
Fax: 42-00-50

Founded 1977
State control
Languages of instruction: French and English
Academic year: October to July

Rector: Prof. THÉOPHILE NGANDO MPONDO
Deputy Rector: Prof. ROGER GABRIEL NLEP
Secretary-General: ABRAHAM ZOUA-HOULI
Librarian: JEREMIE NSANGOU

Number of teachers: 140
Number of students: 6,500

Publications: *Revue de Sciences Economiques et de Management* (quarterly), *Technologie et Développement* (every 2 years), *Arts Review* (1 a year).

CONSTITUENT INSTITUTES

Ecole Normale Supérieure de l'Enseignement Technique: BP 1872, Douala; Dir Dr NDEH NTOMAMBANG NINGO.

Ecole Supérieure des Sciences Economiques et Commerciales: BP 1931, Douala; Dir Dr ROBERT BILONGO.

Institut Universitaire de Technologie: BP 8698, Douala; Dir Dr AWONO ONANA.

Faculté des Sciences: BP 24157, Douala; Dean Prof. THÉOPHILE NGANDO MPONDO.

Faculté des Lettres et des Sciences Humaines: BP 3132, Douala; Dean Prof. SYLVESTRE BOUELET IVAHA.

Faculté des Sciences Economiques et de Gestion Appliquée: BP 4032, Douala; Dean Prof. BLAISE MUKOKO.

Faculté des Sciences Juridiques et Politiques: BP 4982, Douala; Dean Dr LEKENE DONFACK.

UNIVERSITÉ DE DSCHANG

POB 96, Dschang

Telephone and fax: 45-13-81

Founded 1977
State control
Languages of instruction: French and English
Academic year: October to July

Rector: Prof. MAURICE TCHUENTE
Vice-Rector: Dr NJIKAM NJIFUTIE
Secretary-General: Prof. GUY TSALA NDZOMO
Librarian: MARTIN TCHINDA

Number of teachers: 215
Number of students: 4,200

DEANS

Faculty of Arts, Letters and Social Sciences: Prof. MARTIN KUETE
Faculty of Law and Political Science: Prof. PAUL GERARD POUGOUE
Faculty of Economics and Management Sciences: Prof. FRANÇOIS KAMAJOU
Faculty of Sciences: Prof. FOYERE JOHNSON AYAFOR
Faculty of Agriculture: Prof. ABINA FRANÇOIS TCHALA

UNIVERSITÉ DE NGAOUNDÉRÉ

BP 454, Ngaoundéré

Telephone: 25-27-60
Telex: 7645
Fax: 25-16-82

Founded 1977, opened 1982
State control
Languages of instruction: French and English
Academic year: September to June

Rector: Prof. JOSEPH NOAH NGAVENG
Vice-Rector: (vacant)
Secretary-General: Dr FRANÇOIS-XAVIER ETOA

Library of 10,000 vols
Number of teachers: 116
Number of students: 1,300

DEANS

Faculty of Arts and Humanities: Prof. J. LOUIS NDONGMO.
Faculty of Law and Political Science: (vacant)
National Higher School of Agriculture and Industry: Prof. P. PARROT

Colleges

Ecole Nationale d'Administration et de Magistrature: BP 1180, Yaoundé; f. 1959; training for public administration; library of *c.* 11,000 vols; 10 full-time, 75 part-time teachers, 500 students; Dir. V. MOUTTAPA.

Institut d'Administration des Entreprises: BP 337, Yaoundé; 150 students; Dir G. NDJIEUNDE.

CANADA

Learned Societies

GENERAL

Académie des lettres du Québec: 3460 rue McTavish, Montréal, Qué. H3A 1X9; tel. 398-7409; f. 1944 (frmly Académie canadienne-française); for the promotion of the French language and culture in Canada; 36 chairs; Pres. JEAN-PIERRE DUQUETTE; Sec. JEAN ROYER; publ. *Les Ecrits* (3 a year).

Canadian Council for International Co-operation/Conseil canadien pour la coopération internationale: 1 Nicholas St, Suite 300, Ottawa, Ont. K1N 7B7; tel. (613) 247-7007; fax (613) 241-5302; f. 1968 (formerly Overseas Institute of Canada, f. 1961); co-ordination centre for voluntary agencies working in international development; 115 mems; Chair. CAMERON CHARLEBOIS; Pres. and CEO BETTY PLEWES; publs *Newsletter* (6 a year), *Directory of Canadian NGOs*.

Royal Canadian Academy of Arts: 401 Richmond St West (Suite 375), Toronto, Ont. M5V 3A8; tel. (416) 408-2718; f. 1880; visual arts; Pres. ERNEST ANNAU.

Royal Canadian Institute: 196 Carlton St, Toronto, Ont. M5A 2K8; tel. (416) 928-2096; f. 1849, aims to increase public understanding of science; 800 mems; Pres. Dr GEORGE VANDERKUUR.

Royal Society of Canada: 225 Metcalfe St (Suite 308), Ottawa, Ont. K2P 1P9; tel. (613) 991-6990; fax (613) 991-6996; e-mail adminrsc@rsc.ca; f. 1882; academies: Academy I (Lettres et Sciences Humaines), Academy II (Humanities and Social Sciences), Academy III (Science); 1,495 Fellows, 4 Hon. Fellows; Pres. JEAN-PIERRE WALLOT; Hon. Sec. PATRICIA SMART; publs *Transactions* (1 a year), *Proceedings* (1 a year), *Présentations* (1 a year).

AGRICULTURE, FISHERIES AND VETERINARY SCIENCE

Agricultural Institute of Canada: Suite 1112, 141 Laurier Ave. West, Ottawa, Ont. K1P 5J3; tel. (613) 232-9459; fax (613) 594-5190; f. 1920 to organize and unite all workers in scientific and technical agriculture and to serve as a medium where progressive ideas for improvements in agricultural education, investigation, publicity and extension work can be discussed and recommended for adoption; represents 6,500 scientists and agrologists, publs *Canadian Journal of Plant Science*, *Canadian Journal of Soil Science*, *Canadian Journal of Animal Science* (all quarterly).

Canadian Forestry Association: 185 Somerset St West, Suite 203, Ottawa, Ont. K2P 0J2; tel. (613) 232-1815; fax (613) 232-4210; f. 1900; 9 provincial asscns with a membership of 6,000; educational and other programmes designed to encourage better understanding of forests and related resources, and to encourage their wise use and sustainable development; Pres. IVAN BALENOVIC; publs *Forest Forum* (2 a year), *Proceedings* of conferences, etc.

Canadian Society of Animal Science: c/o Agricultural Institute of Canada, Suite 1112, 141 Laurier Ave W, Ottawa, Ont. K1P 5J3; tel. (613) 232-9459; fax (613) 594-5190; part of the Agricultural Institute of Canada (*q.v.*); f. 1925 to provide opportunities for discussion of problems, improvement and co-ordination of research, extension and teaching and to encourage publication of scientific and educational material relating to animal and poultry industries; holds annual meetings, produces occasional papers and presents awards to members; c. 550 mems; Pres. V. STEVENS; Sec.-Treas. R. G. ROTTER; publs *Canadian Journal of Animal Science* (quarterly), *CSAS Newsletter* (quarterly, mems only).

Canadian Veterinary Medical Association/Association Canadienne des Médecins Vétérinaires: 339 Booth St, Ottawa, Ont. K1R 7K1; tel. (613) 236-1162; fax (613) 236-9681; f. 1948; 4,000 mems; publs *Canadian Journal of Veterinary Research* (quarterly), *Canadian Veterinary Journal* (monthly).

ARCHITECTURE AND TOWN PLANNING

Canadian Society of Landscape Architects/Association des Architectes Paysagistes du Canada: POB 870, Station B, Ottawa, Ont. K1P 5P9; tel. (613) 253-4938; fax (613) 253-5585; e-mail csla@escape.ca; f. 1934; 1,100 mems, a federation of seven component asscns; Exec. Dir L. R. PATERSON; publ. *CSLA Bulletin* (quarterly).

Royal Architectural Institute of Canada: 55 Murray St, Suite 330, Ottawa, Ont. K1N 5M3; f. 1908; 3,500 mems; Exec. Dir TIMOTHY KEHOE.

BIBLIOGRAPHY, LIBRARY SCIENCE AND MUSEOLOGY

ASTED (Association pour l'avancement des sciences et des techniques de la documentation) Inc. (Association for the advancement of documentation sciences and techniques): 3414 ave du Parc, Bureau 202, Montréal, Qué. H2X 2H5; tel. (514) 281-5012; fax (514) 281-8219; f. 1973; a professional organization of libraries, librarians and library technicians; 700 mems; Pres. JOANNE COURNOYER; Exec. Dir LOUIS CABRAL; publs *Documentation et bibliothèques* (quarterly), *Nouvelles de l'ASTED*.

Bibliographical Society of Canada: POB 575, Postal Station P, Toronto, Ont. M5S 2T1; e-mail dondertman@library.utoronto.ca; f. 1946; 500 mems; Pres. ANNE YANDLE; Sec. ANNE DONDERTMAN; publs *Papers / Cahiers*, *Bulletin* (2 a year).

Canadian Association of Law Libraries: PO Box 1570, 190 Railway St, Kingston, Ont. K7L 5C8; tel. (613) 531-9338; fax (613) 531-0626; f. 1961 to promote law librarianship, to develop and increase the usefulness of Canadian law libraries, and to foster a spirit of co-operation among them, to provide a forum for meetings and to co-operate with other similar orgs; Pres. SUZAN A. HEBDITCH; publ. *CALL Newsletter* (5 a year).

Canadian Library Association: 200 Elgin St (Suite 602), Ottawa, Ont. K2P 1L5; tel. (613) 232-9625; fax (613) 563-9895; f. 1946; 5,000 mems; Pres. PAUL WHITNEY; Exec. Dir KAREN ADAMS.

Canadian Museums Association/Association des musées canadiens: 280 Metcalfe, Suite 400, Ottawa, Ont. K2P 1R7; tel. (613) 567-0099; fax (613) 233-5438; f. 1947; advancement of public museums and art galleries services; 1,500 mems; Exec. Dir JOHN G. MCAVITY; publs *Muse* (quarterly), *Museogramme* (6 a year).

ECONOMICS, LAW AND POLITICS

Canadian Bar Association: 902-50 O'Connor St, Ottawa, Ont. K1P 6LZ; tel. (613) 237-2925; fax (613) 237-0185; f. 1914 to promote the administration of justice and uniformity of legislation throughout Canada; to encourage a high standing of legal education, training and ethics; 34,000 mems; Pres. GORDON PROUDFOOT; publs *The National*, *The Canadian Bar Review*.

Canadian Council for European Affairs/Conseil Canadien des Affaires Européennes: c/o Dept of Political Studies, 9 Campus Drive, University of Saskatchewan, Saskatoon, S7N 5A5; tel. (306) 966-5231; fax (306) 966-5250; f. 1980; independent; aims to foster constructive interaction among those sections of Canadian society which share or could develop an interest in European affairs (universities, federal and provincial governments, private sector, etc.); Chair. ELDON P. BLACK; Gen. Dir Prof. H. J. MICHELMANN; publ. *Journal of European Integration*.

Canadian Economics Association: f. 1967; Pres. Prof. P. HOWITT; Sec.-Treas. Prof. C. GREEN, c/o Dept of Economics, McGill University, Montréal, Qué.; publs *Canadian Journal of Economics / Revue Canadienne d'Economique, Canadian Public Policy / Analyse de Politique*.

Canadian Institute of Chartered Accountants, The: 277 Wellington St W, Toronto, Ont. M5V 3H2; tel. (416) 977-3222; fax (416) 977-8585; f. 1902; professional and examining body; 58,544 mems; Chair. R. G. GAGE; Pres. M. H. RAYNER; publ. *CA Magazine* (monthly).

Canadian Institute of International Affairs: Glendon Hall, Glendon College, 2275 Bayview Ave, Toronto, Ont. M4N 3M5; tel. (416) 979-1851; fax (416) 979-8575; e-mail mailbox@ciia.org; f. 1928; 1,400 mems in 15 brs; library of 8,000 vols; Chair. PETER G. WHITE; Pres. and CEO ALAN SULLIVAN; publs *Behind the Headlines*†, *International Journal*†, *Contemporary Affairs* (1 a year), *Annual Report*, *Choix* (irregular) and special research projects.

Canadian Political Science Association/Association canadienne de science politique: Suite 205, 1 Stewart St, Ottawa, Ont. K1N 6H7; f. 1913; Pres. DONALD SAVOIE; Exec. Sec. MICHELLE HOPKINS; publs *Canadian Journal of Political Science*, *Bulletin* (newsletter), *Annual Meeting / Congrès annuel* (microfiched collection of annual conference papers).

EDUCATION

Association internationale de pédagogie universitaire: Service pédagogique, Université de Montréal, CP 6128, Suc. A, Montréal, Qué. H3C 3J7; tel. (514) 343-7087; fax (514) 343-2107; f. 1979 for the promotion of research and development in the field of teaching and higher education; 800 mems; Sec.-Gen. JEAN-MARIE VAN DER MAREN; publ. *Pédagogiques* (2 a year).

Association of Universities and Colleges of Canada: 350 Albert St, Suite 600, Ottawa, Ont. K1R 1B1; tel. (613) 563-1236; fax (613)

563-9745; e-mail info@aucc.ca; f. 1911; promotes the interests of higher education; 90 univ. mems; Pres. ROBERT J. GIROUX; Chair. Dr PAUL DAVENPORT; publs *Directory of Canadian Universities* (1 a year), *University Affairs* (10 a year), *Universities Telephone Directory* (annually); all published in English and French.

Canadian Bureau for International Education/Bureau canadien de l'éducation internationale: 220 Laurier Ave W, Suite 1100, Ottawa, Ont. K1P 5Z9; tel. (613) 237-4820; telex 053-3255; fax (613) 237-1073; f. 1966 to promote international development and intercultural understanding through a broad range of educational activities in Canada and abroad; 3 divisions: Membership and Corporate Relations, Client Services and Trade Promotion, Centre for Central and Eastern Europe; library of 300 vols and journals; 110 institutional mems; Chair. GEORGE IVANY; Pres. JAMES W. FOX; publs *Canadian Internationalist* (4 a year), *Annual Report*, *International Students' Handbook, National Report on International Students in Canada* (every 2 years), etc.

Canadian Education Association/Association canadienne d'éducation: 252 Bloor St W, Suite 8-200, Toronto, Ont. M5S 1V5; tel. (416) 924-7721; fax (416) 924-3188; f. 1891; 600 mems; Exec. Dir PENNY MILTON; publs *Education Canada* (2 or 3 a year), *Newsletter* (8 a year), *Bulletin* (French, 8 a year), *CEA Handbook / Ki-es-Ki* (annually).

Canadian Society for the Study of Education: 260 Dalhousie St (Suite 204), Ottawa, Ont. K1N 7E4; tel. (613) 230-3532; fax (613) 230-2746; e-mail csse@csse.ca; f. 1972; to enhance educational research in Canada; 1,000 mems; Admin. TIM G. HOWARD; publ. *Canadian Journal of Education* (quarterly).

FINE AND PERFORMING ARTS

Canada Council/Conseil des Arts du Canada: POB 1047, 350 Albert St, Ottawa, Ont. K1P 5V8; tel. (613) 566-4365; fax (613) 566-4390; f. 1957; the Council provides grants and services to professional Canadian artists and arts organizations; maintains secretariat for Canadian Commission for UNESCO; administers Killam Program of prizes and fellowships to Canadian research scholars, and recognizes achievement through a number of prizes, including Governor General's Literary Awards, Molson Prizes and Glenn Gould Prize; 90% state-funded; 11 mems; Chair. DONNA SCOTT; Vice-Chair. FRANÇOIS COLBERT; publ. *Annual Report*.

Canadian Film Institute: 2 Daly, Ottawa, Ont. K1N 6E2; tel. (613) 232-6727; fax (613) 232-6315; f. 1935 to encourage and promote the study, appreciation and use of motion pictures and television in Canada; division of Cinémathèque Canada; operates CFI Film Library, renting 6,500 educational films and videos; cinema; Canadian Centre for Films on Art; hosts Ottawa International Animation Festival; Pres. SERGE LOSIQUE.

Canadian Music Centre: 20 St Joseph St, Toronto, Ont. M4Y 1J9; tel. (416) 961-6601; fax (416) 961-7198; f. 1959; for the collection and promotion, in Canada and abroad, of music by Canadian composers; collection of 14,000 scores; produces Canadian concert recordings (Centre-discs); Exec. Dir SIMONE AUGER; publ. list of acquisitions (annually).

Sculptors' Society of Canada: 40 Armadale Ave, Toronto M6S 3W8; f. 1928; Pres. MAY MARX.

Society of Composers, Authors and Music Publishers of Canada (SOCAN): 41 Valleybrook Drive, Don Mills, Ont. M3B 2S6; tel. (416) 445-8700; fax (416) 445-7108; e-mail socan@socan.ca; f. 1990; performing right soc.; Gen. Man. MICHAEL ROCK; publ. *Words & Music / Paroles & Musique* (11 a year).

Visual Arts Ontario: 439 Wellington St W, 3rd Floor, Toronto, Ont. M5V 1E7; f. 1973; federation of professional artists; 3,600 mems; Exec. Dir HENNIE L. WOLFF.

HISTORY, GEOGRAPHY AND ARCHAEOLOGY

Antiquarian and Numismatic Society of Montreal (Château Ramezay Museum)/ Société d'Archéologie et de Numismatique de Montréal (Musée du Château Ramezay): 280 Notre Dame St E, Montréal, Qué. H2Y 1C5; tel. (514) 861-7182; fax (514) 861-8317; f. 1862; 150 mems; library of 8,000 books; Dir ANDRÉ J. DELISLE; Sec. SUZANNE LALUMIÈRE; publs archaeological reports.

Canadian Association of Geographers: Burnside Hall, McGill Univ, 805 Sherbrooke St W, Montréal, Qué. H3A 2K6; tel. (514) 398-4946; fax (514) 398-7437; f. 1951; 1,400 mems; Pres. Prof. IAIN WALLACE; Sec.-Treas. Prof. PETER FOGGIN; publs *The Canadian Geographer (quarterly), The CAG Newsletter* (6 a year), *The Directory* (annually).

Canadian Historical Association/Société historique du Canada: 395 Wellington St, Ottawa, Ont. K1A 0N3; tel. (613) 233-7885; fax (613) 567-3110; e-mail cha-she@archives.ca; f. 1922, to encourage historical research and public interest in history; 2,000 mems; Sec. (English) DONALD WRIGHT; Sec. (French) BÉATRICE CRAIG; publs *Journal of the CHA / Revue de la SHC, Historical Booklets, Bulletin, Register of Dissertations, Canada's Ethnic Groups* (series).

Genealogical Association of Nova Scotia: POB 641, Stn M, Halifax, NS B3J 2T3; f. 1982; *c.* 1,300 mems; Pres. KAREN MACKAY; publ. *The Nova Scotia Genealogist* (3 a year), *Directory of Members and Surname Interests* (annually).

Genealogical Institute of the Maritimes: POB 3142, Halifax South Postal Stn, Halifax, NS B3J 3H5; f. 1983; accreditation of professional researchers; 44 mems; Pres. LOIS K. YORKE; Registrar VIRGINIA CLARK; publ. *Annual Report*.

Institut d'histoire de l'Amérique française: 261 Bloomfield Ave, Montréal, Qué. H2V 3R6; tel. (514) 278-2232; f. 1947; independent institution; 900 mems; library of over 15,000 vols, 3,500 documents; Pres. JOANNE BURGESS; Sec. DENIS GOULET; publ. *Revue d'histoire de l'Amérique française* (quarterly).

Ontario Historical Society: 34 Parkview Ave, Willowdale, Ont. M2N 3Y2; tel. (416) 226-9011; fax (416) 226-2740; f. 1888; 3,000 mems; 300 affiliated societies; Exec. Dir DOROTHY DUNCAN; publs *Ontario History, OHS Bulletin* (5 a year).

Royal Canadian Geographical Society, The: 39 McArthur Ave, Vanier, Ont. K1L 8L7; tel. (613) 745-4629; fax (613) 744-0947; f. 1929; 260,000 mems; Pres. D. A. ST-ONGE; publ. *Canadian Geographic* (every 2 months).

Royal Nova Scotia Historical Society: 1643 Chestnut St, Halifax, NS B3H 3T3; f. 1878; history, biography, social studies of provincial past; 350 mems; Pres. ROBERT N. BÉRARD; Sec. R. BARBOUR; publ. *Collections* (irregular).

Société Généalogique Canadienne Française: Case postale 335, Place d'Armes, Montréal, Qué. H2Y 3H1; tel. (514) 729-8366; fax (514) 729-1180; f. 1943; studies and publications on the origins and history of French Canadian families since 1615; library of *c.* 5,000 vols, and over 3,000,000 cards on marriages; 4,000 mems; Pres. NORMAND ROBERT; publ. *Mémoires* (quarterly).

Waterloo Historical Society: C/o Kitchener Public Library, 85 Queen St N, Kitchener, Ont. N2H 2H1; f. 1912; local history; collection at Kitchener Public Library, Ont.; Sec. BOB WILDFONG; publ. annual volume containing articles on regional history.

LANGUAGE AND LITERATURE

Canadian Authors Association: Box 419, Campbellford, Ont. K0L 1L0; tel. (705) 653-0323; fax (705) 653-0593; e-mail canauth@redden.on.ca; f. 1921; 900 mems; administers awards; annual conference; workshops and seminars; Pres. MURPHY SHEWCHUK; publs *Canadian Author* (quarterly), *The Canadian Writer's Guide* (irregular).

Canadian Linguistic Association/Association canadienne de linguistique: Dept of Linguistics, Memorial University of Newfoundland, St John's, Nfld A1B 3X9; f. 1954 to advance the study of linguistics, languages in Canada; 731 mems; Pres. DENIS BOUCHARD; Sec.-Treas. JIM BLACK; publ. *The Canadian Journal of Linguistics / La Revue Canadienne de Linguistique* (quarterly).

PEN International, Centre québécois: 1195 rue Sherbrooke Ouest, Montréal, Qué. H3A 1H9; f. 1982; international literary association; 125 mems; Pres. JEANNE DENERS; Sec. STÉPHANE STAPINSKY.

MEDICINE

Academy of Medicine: c/o Fudger Library, Toronto Hospital (Bell Wing, 9th Floor), 585 University Ave, Toronto, Ont. M5G 2C4; tel. (416) 340-3259; e-mail btrojan@torhosp.toronto.on.ca; f. 1907; 2,200 fellows; sections of medicine, surgery, paediatrics, pathology, obstetrics and gynaecology, ophthalmology, otolaryngology, anaesthesia, haematology and gastrointestinal diseases, preventive medicine, cancer, neurological sciences, urology, dermatology, cardiovascular sciences, orthopaedic surgery, history of medicine, aviation, space and underwater medicine, medical archaeology and anthropology; library of 100,000 vols; Contact B. TROJAN; publ. *Bulletin*.

Canadian Association of Anatomy, Neurobiology and Cell Biology: c/o Dr B. W. C. ROSSER, Dept of Anatomy and Cell Biology/Medicine, University of Saskatchewan, 107 Wiggins Road, A315 H.Sc. Saskatoon, Sask. S7N 5E5; f. 1956; 188 mems; Pres. Dr P. HASSE; Sec. Dr B. W. C. ROSSER.

Canadian Association of Optometrists: 234 Argyle Ave, Ottawa, Ont. K2P 1B9; tel. (613) 235-7924; fax (613) 235-2025; f. 1948; Pres. Dr DOUGLAS COTÉ; Dir-Gen. MICHAEL J. DICOLA; publ. *The Canadian Journal of Optometry / La Revue Canadienne d'Optométrie* (quarterly).

Canadian Dental Association: 1815 Alta Vista Drive, Ottawa, Ont. K1G 3Y6; tel. (613) 523-1770; fax (613) 523-7736; f. 1902; Exec. Dir A. JARDINE NEILSON; publ. *Journal*.

Canadian Lung Association: 1900 City Park Drive, Suite 508, Gloucester, Ont. K1J 1A3; tel. (613) 747-6776; fax (613) 747-7430; f. 1900; medical sections: Canadian Thoracic Society, Canadian Nurses' Respiratory Society, Canadian Physiotherapy Cardio-Respiratory Society; Pres. and CEO MARGO CRAIG GARRISON.

Canadian Medical Association: 1867 Alta Vista Drive, Ottawa, Ont. K1G 3Y6; tel. (613) 731-9331; fax (613) 523-0937; f. 1867; 45,000 mems; Sec.-Gen. Dr LÉO-PAUL LANDRY; publs *Canadian Medical Association Journal, Canadian Journal of Surgery, CMA News, Strategy, Clinical and Investigative Medicine, Canadian Association of Radiologists Journal, Canadian Journal of Respiratory Therapy,*

Mediscan, Cancer Prevention and Control, Journal of Psychiatry and Neuroscience.

Canadian Paediatric Society (Société canadienne de pédiatrie): 100–2204 Walkley Road, Ottawa, Ont. K1G 4G8; tel. (613) 526-9397; fax (613) 526-3332; e-mail info@cps.ca; f. 1923; 2,000 mems; Pres. Dr EMMETT FRANCOEUR; Exec. Vice-Pres. Dr VICTOR MARCHESSAULT; publ. *Paediatrics and Child Health* (6 a year).

Canadian Pharmacists Association, Inc.: 1785 Alta Vista Drive, Ottawa, Ont. K1G 3Y6; f. 1907; 10,500 mems; Exec. Dir L. C. FEVANG; publs *Compendium of Pharmaceuticals and Specialties* (English and French edns, annually), *Nonprescription Drug Reference for Health Professionals* (English only, every 4 years), *Compendium of Non Prescription Products* (English only, annually), *Therapeutic Choices* (English only).

Canadian Physiological Society: f. 1936; 536 mems; Pres. Dr F. RICHMOND; Sec. Dr A. M. J. BUCHAN, Dept. of Physiology, University of British Columbia, Vancouver, BC V6T 1Z3; tel. (604) 822-2083; fax (604) 822-6048; publs *The Canadian Journal of Physiology and Pharmacology* (monthly), *Physiology Canada* (2 a year).

Canadian Psychiatric Association/ Association des psychiatres du Canada: 441 MacLaren Street, Suite 260, Ottawa, Ont. K2P 2H3; tel. (613) 234-2815; fax (613) 234-9857; e-mail cpa@medical.org; f. 1951 to promote research into psychiatric disorders and foster high standards of professional practice; 2,600 mems; Pres. Dr PIERRE BEAUSÉJOUR; Chief Exec. Officer ALEX SAUNDERS; publs. *The Canadian Journal of Psychiatry* (10 a year), *Bulletin* (every 2 months).

Canadian Public Health Association: 1565 Carling Ave, Suite 400, Ottawa, Ont. K1Z 8R1; tel. (613) 725-3769; fax (613) 725-9826; f. 1910; 2,000 mems; Pres. JOHN HASTINGS; CEO GERALD H. DAFOE; publ. *Canadian Journal of Public Health* (every 2 months).

Canadian Society for Nutritional Sciences: c/o Dr T. GLANVILLE, Mount St. Vincent University, Halifax, NS B3M 2J6; f. 1957 to extend knowledge of nutrition by research, discussion of research reports, and exchange of information; 340 mems; Pres. Dr D. FITZPATRICK; Sec. Dr T. GLANVILLE; publ. *Nutrition / Forum de Nutrition* (2 a year).

Pharmacological Society of Canada: f. 1956; 320 mems; Pres. Dr KHEM JHAMANDAS; Sec. Dr BRIAN BENNETT, Dept of Pharmacology and Toxicology, Queen's University, Kingston, Ont. K7L 3N6; tel. (613) 545-6473; fax (613) 545-6412; e-mail bennett@post.queensu.ca; publ. *Canadian Journal of Physiology and Pharmacology.*

Royal College of Physicians and Surgeons of Canada: 774 Echo Drive, Ottawa, Ont. K1S 5N8; tel. (613) 730-8177; fax (613) 730-8830; f. 1929; 31,000 mems; accredits postgraduate medical residency programmes; acts as examining body to certify medical, surgical and laboratory specialists; offers a maintenance of competence programme; Pres. Dr LUC DESCHÊNES; publ. *Annals* (8 a year).

NATURAL SCIENCES

General

Association Canadienne-Française pour l'Avancement des Sciences: 425 rue De La Gauchetière Est, Montréal, Qué. H2L 2M7; tel. (514) 849-0045; fax (514) 849-5558; f. 1923; 45 societies as mems; a federation of French-Canadian learned societies; aims to popularize science by means of lectures, meetings, awards, publications; Exec. Dir FRANÇOISE BRAUN; publs *Annales* (annually), *Interface* (every 2 months), *Les Cahiers de l'Acfas* (3–4 a year).

Nova Scotian Institute of Science: Science Services, Killam Library, Dalhousie University, Halifax, NS B3H 4H8; tel. (902) 494-2384; f. 1862; monthly lecture series; 300 mems; Pres. Dr SHERRY NIVEN; Sec. CAROLYN BIRD; publ. *Proceedings* (1 a year).

Biological Sciences

Canadian Phytopathological Society: f. 1929; 500 mems; Pres. Dr RON HOWARD; Sec. Dr B. OTRYSKO, MAPAQ 'Les Buissons', CP 455, Les Buissons, Qué. G0H 1H0; tel. (418) 567-2235; fax (418) 567-8791; publs *News* (quarterly), *Canadian Journal of Plant Pathology* (quarterly).

Canadian Society for Cellular and Molecular Biology: Centre de recherche, Hôtel-Dieu de Québec, 11 Côte du Palais, Quebec, Que. G1R 2J6; f. 1966; 400 mems; Pres. N. MARCEAU; Sec. C. CASS; publ. *Bulletin* (3 a year).

Canadian Society for Immunology: C/o Immunology Research Group, University of Calgary, 2500 University Drive NW, Calgary, Alta T2N 1N4; tel. (403) 492-0712; fax (403) 439-3439; f. 1966; 400 mems; Pres. Dr JOHN REYNOLDS; Sec.-Treas. Dr DONNA CHOW; publ. *Bulletin* (irregular).

Canadian Society of Microbiologists/Société Canadienne des Microbiologistes: CSM Secretariat, 1200E Prince of Wales Drive, Ottawa, Ont. K2C 1M9; tel. (613) 723-7233; f. 1951; 500 mems; Pres. Dr D. SPROTT; Sec.-Treas. Dr A. FRASER; publs *CSM Newsletter* (3 a year), *Programme & Abstracts* (annually).

Cercles des Jeunes Naturalistes: 4101 Sherbrooke est, Suite 124, Montréal, Qué. H1X 2B2; tel. (514) 252-3023; telex 05-829647; f. 1931; 3,000 mems; Pres. Gen. GERTRUDE DE CHAMPLAIN; Dir ELISE TOUSIGNANT; publs *Feuillets du Naturaliste, Tracts CJN, Série Le Naturaliste, Série l'Évolution, Guide de Sensibilisation aux Sciences de la Nature, Nouvelles CJN* (monthly), *Hibou* (monthly).

Entomological Society of Canada: 393 Winston Ave, Ottawa, Ont. K2A 1Y8; tel. (613) 725-2619; fax (613) 725-9349; e-mail entsoc .can@sympatico.ca; f. 1868; 600 mems: 800 subscribers; 7 affiliated regional societies; Pres. HUGH DANKS; Sec. R. WEST; publs *The Canadian Entomologist* (every 2 months), *Bulletin*.

Genetics Society of Canada/Société de Génétique du Canada: Suite 1112, 141 Laurier Avenue West, Ottawa, Ont. K1P 5J3; tel. (613) 232-9459; fax (613) 594-5190; f. 1956; 425 mems; Pres. ROSS HODGETTS; Sec. BARBARA SPYROPOULOS; publs. *Bulletin* (quarterly), *Genome* (6 a year), *Chromosoma*, *Annual Reviews*.

Manitoba Naturalists Society: 401–63 Albert St, Winnipeg, Man. R3B 1G4; tel. (204) 943-9029; f. 1920; 1,500 mems; Pres. WES TRETIAK; Exec. Dir HERTA GUDAUSKAS.

Société de Protection des Plantes du Québec: f. 1908; 225 mems; Pres. RICHARD BELANGER; Sec. L. TARTIER, Station de recherches agricoles, CP 480, Saint-Hyacinthe, Qué. J2S 7B8; publs *Echos phytosanitaires* (quarterly), *Phytoprotection* (3 a year).

Société linnéenne du Québec: 650 Graham-Bell (Bureau 400), Sainte-Foy, Qué. G1N 4H5; tel. (418) 683-2432; fax (418) 683-2893; f. 1929; 800 mems; natural history; Pres. DANIEL BANVILLE; Dir AGATHE SAVARD; publ. *Le Linnéen* (quarterly).

Vancouver Natural History Society: POB 3021, Vancouver, BC V6B 3X5; tel. (604) 738-3177; f. 1918; 1,100 mems; aims to promote interest in nature, conservation of natural resources, protection of endangered species and ecosystems; Pres. JEREMY GORDON; publ. *Discovery* (quarterly).

Mathematical Sciences

Canadian Mathematical Society/Société mathématique du Canada: 577 King Edward, Ottawa, Ont. K1N 6N5; tel. (613) 562-5702; fax (613) 565-1539; f. 1945, inc. 1979; promotes mathematics in Canada at all educational levels; 1,100 mems; Pres. Dr KATHERINE HEINRICH; Exec. Dir and Sec. Dr G. P. WRIGHT; publs *Canadian Mathematical Bulletin* (quarterly), *Canadian Journal of Mathematics* (every 2 months), *CMS Notes* (9 a year), *Crux Mathematicorum* (10 a year).

Physical Sciences

Canadian Association of Physicists/ Association canadienne des physiciens et physiciennes: McDonald Bldg (Suite 112), 150 Louis Pasteur, Ottawa, Ont. K1N 6N5; tel. (613) 562-5614; fax (613) 562-5615; f. 1945; 2,000 mems; Pres. P. S. VINCETT; Exec. Dir. F. M. FORD; publ. *Physics in Canada* (every 2 months).

Canadian Meteorological and Oceanographic Society/Société Canadienne de Météorologie et d'Océanographie: McDonald Bldg (Suite 112), 150 Louis Pasteur, Ottawa, Ont. K1N 6N5; tel. (613) 562-5616; fax (613) 562-5615; f. 1977; 1,000 mems; Pres. Dr MICHEL BÉLAND; Exec. Dir Dr NEIL CAMPBELL; publs *Atmosphere-Ocean* (quarterly), *CMOS Bulletin SCMO* (every 2 months), *Congress Program and Abstracts* (annually).

Canadian Society of Biochemistry, Molecular and Cellular Biology/Société Canadienne de Biochimie et de Biologie Moléculaire et Cellulaire: c/o Dr E. R. Tustanoff, Dept of Biochemistry, University of Western Ontario, London, Ont. N6A 5C1; tel. (519) 471-1961; fax (519) 661-3175; e-mail etustan@julian.uwo.ca; f. 1958; 1,000 mems; Pres. Dr J. WEINER; Sec. Dr E. R. TUSTANOFF; publ. *Bulletin* (1 a year).

Canadian Society of Petroleum Geologists: 505, 206–7th Ave SW, Calgary, Alta T2P 0W7; tel. (403) 264-5610; fax (403) 264-5898; e-mail cspg@cspg.org; f. 1927; 3,200 mems; Business Man. TIM HOWARD; Office Man. DEANNA WATKINS; publ. *Bulletin of Canadian Petroleum Geology* (quarterly).

Chemical Institute of Canada: 130 Slater St, Suite 550, Ottawa, Ont. K1P 6E2; tel. (613) 232-6252; fax (613) 232-5862; e-mail cic_adm@fox.nstn.ca; f. 1945; 27 local sections, 16 subject divisions, 116 student chapters and 3 constituent societies—Canadian Society for Chemical Engineering, the Canadian Society for Chemical Technology and the Canadian Society for Chemistry; Exec. Dir (vacant); official publs *Canadian Chemical News* (10 a year), *The Canadian Journal of Chemical Engineering* (every 2 months).

Geological Association of Canada: Dept of Earth Sciences, Memorial University of Newfoundland, St John's, Nfld A1B 3X5; tel. (709) 737-7660; fax (709) 737-2532; f. 1947 to advance the science of geology and related fields of study and to promote a better understanding thereof throughout Canada; 3,000 mems; Pres. HUGH MILLER; Sec.-Treas. RICHARD HISCOTT; publs *Geoscience Canada* (quarterly), *Geolog* (4 a year).

Royal Astronomical Society of Canada: 136 Dupont St, Toronto, Ont. M5R 1V2; tel. (416) 924-7973; fax (416) 924-2911; e-mail rasc@rasc.ca; f. 1890; 23 centres; 3,000 mems; Nat. Sec. Capt. RAYMOND AUCLAIR; publs *Journal* (every 2 months), *Observers' Handbook* (annually).

Society of Chemical Industry (Canadian Section): c/o D. W. W. KIRKWOOD, Praxair

Canada Inc., 1 City Centre Drive, Suite 1200, Mississauga, Ont. L5B 1M2; tel. (905) 803-1703; fax (905) 803-1696; f. 1902; fosters contact between chemical industry, universities and govt; rewards achievement in industry and universities; promotes international contact; 150 mems; Chair. BRIAN MCCARRY.

Spectroscopy Society of Canada/Société de Spectroscopie du Canada: c/o Treasurer, ANA H. DELGADO, POB 332, Stn A, Ottawa, Ont. K1N 8V3; f. 1957; 350 mems; provides the annual Herzberg Award, the Barringer Research Award and an award to the Youth Science Foundation; Pres. Dr MICHAEL W. HINDS; publ. *Canadian Journal of Analytical Sciences and Spectroscopy*.

PHILOSOPHY AND PSYCHOLOGY

Canadian Philosophical Association/Association canadienne de philosophie: POB 450, Stn A, Ottawa, Ont. K1N 6N5; tel. (613) 569-0506; fax (613) 569-2081; e-mail saubin@aix1.uottawa.ca; f. 1958 to promote philosophical scholarship in Canada and to represent Canadian philosophers; 800 mems; Administrator SYLVIE AUBIN; publ. *Dialogue* (French/English, quarterly).

Canadian Psychological Association/Société Canadienne de Psychologie: 151 Slater St, Suite 205, Ottawa, Ont. K1P 5H3; tel. (613) 237-2144; fax (613) 237-1674; f. 1939 to promote psychological research and the practical applications of psychology in Canada; 4,000 mems; Pres. Dr JANEL GAUTHIER; publs *Canadian Journal of Experimental Psychology, Canadian Psychology, Canadian Journal of Behavioral Science, Psynopsis* (all quarterly).

RELIGION, SOCIOLOGY AND ANTHROPOLOGY

Association for the Advancement of Scandinavian Studies in Canada (AASSC): Dept of History, Memorial University, St John's, Nfld A1C 5S7; tel. (709) 737-8418; fax (709) 737-2164; f. 1982; 180 mems; Pres. Dr CHRISTOPHER ENGLISH; Sec. DAISY NEIJMANN; publ. *Newsbulletin* (every 6 months), *Scandinavian-Canadian Studies* (annually).

Canadian Association of African Studies/Association Canadienne des Etudes Africaines: c/o Innis College, 2 Sussex Ave, Toronto, Ont. M5S 1J5; tel. (416) 978-7789; fax 978-5503; f. 1970; 310 mems; promotion of the study of Africa in Canada; aims to improve the Canadian public's knowledge and awareness of Africa; provides a link between Canadian and African scholarly and scientific communities; publs *Canadian Journal of African Studies / Revue Canadienne des Etudes Africaines* (3 a year), *Newsletter / Bulletin* (3 a year).

Canadian Association of Latin American Studies/Association Canadienne des Etudes Latino-Américaines: c/o Prof. Antonio Urrello, Sec.-Treas. CALAS/ACELA, Dept of Hispanic Studies, Univ. of British Columbia, Vancouver, BC V6T 1W5; f. 1969; 200 mems; Pres. J. C. M. OGELSBY; Vice-Pres. CLAUDE MORIN; publs *North South / Nord Sud / Norte Sur, Canadian Journal of Latin American Studies* (2 a year), *Newsletter* (quarterly), *Directory of Canadian Scholars and Universities interested in Latin American Studies*.

Canadian Society of Biblical Studies: c/o Dept of Religion and Culture, Wilfrid Laurier University, Waterloo, Ont. N2L 5T8; e-mail mdesjard@mach1.wlu.ca; f. 1933; the promotion of scholarship in Biblical studies; 287 mems; Pres. D. FRAIKIN; Exec. Sec. M. DESJARDINS; publs *Newsletter for Ugaritic Studies, Newsletter for Targum Studies* (2 a year), *Bulletin* (annually).

TECHNOLOGY

Canadian Academy of Engineering/Académie canadienne du génie: 130 Albert St, Suite 1414, Ottawa, Ont. K1P 5G4; tel. (613) 235-9056; fax (613) 235-6861; e-mail acadeng@ccpe.ca; f. 1987; assesses the changing needs of Canada and the technical resources that can be applied to them and sponsors programmes to meet these needs; provides independent and expert advice on matters of national importance concerning engineering; highlights exceptional engineering achievements; works by co-operation with national and international bodies; 220 mems; Pres. JOHN H. DINSMORE; Exec. Dir PIERRE A. H. FRANCHE; publ. *Newsletter* (quarterly).

Canadian Aeronautics and Space Institute: 130 Slater, Suite 818, Ottawa, Ont. K1P 6E2; tel. (613) 234-0191; fax (613) 234-9039; f. 1954; 2,000 mems; Pres. R. KIND; Exec. Dir I. ROSS; publs *Canadian Aeronautics and Space Journal* (quarterly), *Canadian Journal of Remote Sensing* (quarterly).

Canadian Council of Professional Engineers: Suite 401, 116 Albert St, Ottawa, Ont. K1P 5G3; tel. (613) 232-2474; fax (613) 230-5759; f. 1936; co-ordinating body for 12 Provincial and Territorial Licensing Bodies; total membership of constituent associations 160,000; Pres. WENDY RYAN-BACON (acting).

Canadian Electrical Association: Suite 1600, 1 Westmount Square, Montréal, Qué. H3Z 2P9; tel. (514) 937-6181; fax (514) 937-6498; f. 1891; represents Canada's electric utility industry; 35 corporate utilities, 38 corporate manufacturers, 109 assoc. cos, 2,500 individual mems; Pres. H. R. KONOW; Sec. I. M. PHILLIPS; publs *Reports* (various), *Electricity* (annually), *Connections* (10 a year).

Canadian Institute of Mining, Metallurgy and Petroleum: Xerox Tower, Suite 1210, 3400 de Maisonneuve Blvd West, Montréal, Qué. H3Z 3B8; tel. (514) 939-2710; fax (514) 939-2714; f. 1898; 10,500 mems; Exec. Dir Y. JACQUES; publs *Bulletin* (10 a year), *CIM Directory* (annually), *Journal of Canadian Petroleum Technology* (10 a year).

Engineering Institute of Canada, The: 1980 Ogilvie Rd, POB 27078, RPO Gloucester CTR, Gloucester, Ont. K1J 9L9; tel. (613) 742-5185; fax (613) 742-5189; f. 1887; 16,000 mems and 5 mem. socs; Pres. RAY BENSON; Exec. Dir MICHAEL BOZOZUK.

Research Institutes

GENERAL

Alberta Research Council: 250 Karl Clark Rd, Edmonton, Alta T6N 1E4; tel. (403) 450-5111; fax (403) 450-5333; f. 1921; promotes technology development and application, conducts applied research and provides expert advice, technical information and scientific infrastructure; has wide range of scientific, engineering and technological capabilities in agriculture, biotechnology, energy, environment, forestry, information technology and manufacturing; library of 39,500 vols, 3,500 reports, 500 current periodicals; Man. Dir and CEO JOHN R. MCDOUGALL; publs *R & D Newsletter* (every 2 months), *Annual Report*.

British Columbia Research Inc. (BCRI): 3650 Wesbrook Mall, Vancouver, BC V6S 2L2; tel. (604) 224-4331; fax (604) 224-0540; f. 1944; private organization, deriving 80% of revenue from private sector contracts; conducts technological research in fields of applied biology, applied chemistry, engineering-physics; Exec. Chair. Dr HUGH WYNNE-EDWARDS; Pres. and CEO JOHN C. ANDERSON.

InNOVAcorp: 101 Research Drive, Woodside Industrial Park, POB 790, Dartmouth, NS B2Y 3Z7; tel. (902) 424-8670; fax (902) 424-4679; e-mail corpcomm@innovacorp.ns.ca; f. 1995; library of 20,000 vols; assists firms based in Nova Scotia to develop and market products, particularly in the fields of life sciences, advanced engineering, information technology and oceans technology; CEO R. F. MCCURDY; publ. *Annual Report, Progress Report* (4 a year).

National Research Council of Canada/Conseil national de recherches Canada: Ottawa, Ont. K1A 0R6; tel. (613) 993-9101; fax (613) 952-9696; f. 1916; integrated science and technology agency of the federal govt; provides scientific and technological information through Canada Institute for Scientific and Technical Information and industrial support through Industrial Research Assistance Program; research carried out by 17 research institutes linked to 5 technology groups: biotechnology, construction, information and telecommunications technologies, manufacturing technologies and infrastructure technologies; Pres. Dr ARTHUR J. CARTY; publs. *Biochemistry and Cell Biology, Environmental Reviews, Genome, Canadian Geotechnical Journal, Canadian Journals of Botany, Chemistry, Physics, Microbiology, Fisheries and Aquatic Sciences, Genetics and Cytology, Physiology and Pharmacology, Zoology, Forest Research, Civil Engineering, Earth Sciences, Computational Intelligence*.

North-South Institute: 55 Murray St, Suite 200, Ottawa, Ont. K1N 5M3; tel. (613) 241-3535; fax (613) 241-7435; f. 1976; policy-relevant research on issues of relations between industrialized and developing countries; library of 8,000 vols, 300 periodical titles; Pres. Dr ROY CULPEPER; publ. *Review*.

ORTECH Corporation: Sheridan Park, Mississauga, Ont. L5K 1B3; tel. (905) 822-4111; fax (905) 823-1446; f. 1928; contract research for industry and govt in areas of energy, environment, materials, products, processes transportation systems and resources; Pres. R. WOODLAND; Sec. B. T. PORTER; library of 10,000 vols; publ. *Annual Report*.

RPC (Research and Productivity Council): 921 College Hill Rd, Fredericton, NB E3B 6Z9; tel. (506) 452-1212; fax (506) 452-1395; e-mail vjackson@rpc.unb.ca; f. 1962; professional and technical services to help industry develop new products and innovative solutions to operating problems; departments include Engineering Materials and Diagnostics, Inorganic Analytical Services, Food, Fisheries and Aquaculture, Chemical and Biotechnical Services, Product Innovation, and Process and Environmental Technology; information centre with 21,000 vols, 250 periodicals, inter-library loan services, access to on-line databases; Exec. Dir Dr P. LEWELL; publ. *Annual Report*.

Saskatchewan Research Council: 15 Innovation Blvd, Saskatoon, Sask. S7N 2X8; tel. (306) 933-5400; fax (306) 933-7446; f. 1947; assists science and technology in the Province through research in chemistry, geology, environmental sciences, industrial management and engineering, and technology transfer; library (Information Services) of 25,000 vols, 3,100 in-house publs and 400 periodicals; Pres. R. WOODWARD; publ. *SRC News* (irregular).

AGRICULTURE, FISHERIES AND VETERINARY SCIENCE

Canadian Forest Service: Ottawa, Ont. K1A 0E5; f. 1899; forest production, tree improvement, forest statistics and the environmental aspects of forestry; supports the Forest Engineering Research Institute of

Canada; also supports research at Canadian forestry schools; Asst Dep. Minister Dr YVAN HARDY; publs *Annual State of Canada's Forests, CFS Research Notes, Information Reports Digest, Forestry Technical Reports, Research Centre Information Information Reports*.

Research establishments:

Pacific Forestry Centre: 506 West Burnside Rd, Victoria, BC V8Z 1M5; Dir-Gen. C. WINGET.

Northern Forestry Centre: 5320 122nd St, Edmonton, Alta T6H 3S5; Dir-Gen. B. CASE.

Great Lakes Forestry Centre: Box 490, 1219 Queen St East, Sault Ste Marie, Ont. P6A 5M7; Dir-Gen. E. KONDO.

Laurentian Forestry Centre: Box 3800, 1055 du P.E.P.S., Ste-Foy, Qué. G1V 4C7; Dir-Gen. N. LAFRENIÈRE.

Maritimes Forestry Service: Box 4000, Fredericton, NB E3B 5P7; Dir-Gen. H. OLDHAM.

Dominion Arboretum: Bldg 72, Central Experimental Farm, Ottawa, Ont. K1A 0C6; tel. (613) 995-3700; fax (613) 992-7909; f. 1886; part of Agriculture Canada; evaluation of woody plants for cold hardiness and adaptability; display area of 35 ha; special living collections; Dir Dr H. DAVIDSON.

MEDICINE

Cancer Care Ontario: 620 University Ave, Suite 1500, Toronto, Ont. M5G 2L7; tel. (416) 971-9800; fax (416) 971-6888; f. 1943; prevention, diagnosis, treatment, supportive care, education and research in cancer; Pres./CEO Dr C. H. HOLLENBERG; publ. *Cancer Care*.

Dentistry Canada Fund: 1815 Alta Vista Drive, Ottawa, Ont. K1G 3Y6; tel. (613) 731-0493; fax (613) 523-7489; f. 1902.

Medical Research Council of Canada: 5th Floor, Tower B, Holland Cross, Ottawa, Ont. K1A 0W9; tel. (613) 941-2672; fax (613) 954-1800; f. 1969; function is to fund, assist and promote basic, applied and clinical research in Canada in the health sciences; Pres. Dr HENRY FRIESEN; publs (English and French) *MRC Newsletter* (quarterly), *Report of the President* (annually), *Grants and Awards Guide* (annually).

National Cancer Institute of Canada: Suite 200, 10 Alcorn Ave, Toronto, Ont. M4V 3B1; tel. (416) 961-7223; fax (416) 961-4189; f. 1947; grant-awarding agency; Pres. Dr JAMES TILL; Exec. Dir Dr ROBERT A. PHILLIPS; publs *Annual Report, Annual Scientific Report, NCIC Update, NCIC CBCRI Breast Cancer Bulletin*.

NATURAL SCIENCES

General

Arctic Institute of North America: Library Tower, University of Calgary, 2500 University Drive, NW, Calgary, Alta T2N 1N4; tel. (403) 220-7515; fax (403) 282-4609; f. 1945, became inst. of Univ. of Calgary 1979; multidisciplinary research on physical, biological and social sciences; 300 fellows, 2,100 mems; library of 40,000 vols; Exec. Dir MICHAEL P. ROBINSON; publs *Arctic* (quarterly), occasional monographs.

International Development Research Centre: POB 8500, Ottawa, Ont. K1G 3H9; tel. (613) 236-6163; telex 053-3753; fax (613) 238-7230; f. 1970 by Act of the Canadian Parliament; to support research in the developing regions of the world in the fields of environment and natural resources; information sciences and systems; health science; social science; training and research utilization; library of 60,000 vols, 5,000 serials, 1,000 pamphlets and annual reports; Pres. (vacant); Sec. ROBERT AUGER; publs annual report, *IDRC Reports* (quarterly).

Natural Sciences and Engineering Research Council of Canada: 350 Albert St, Ottawa, Ont. K1A 1H5; tel. (613) 995-5992; f. 1978; a crown corporation of the federal Government reporting to Parliament through the Minister of Industry; supports both basic university research through research grants and project research through partnerships of universities with industry, as well as the advanced training of highly qualified people in both areas; Pres. T. BRZUSTOWSKI; publs *NSERC Researcher's Guide, NSERC Scholarships and Fellowships Guide, Visiting Fellowships in Canadian Government Laboratories, Contact* (newsletter).

Biological Sciences

Huntsman Marine Science Centre: Brandy Cove, St Andrews, NB E0G 2X0; tel. (506) 529-1200; fax (506) 529-1212; f. 1969 with the co-operation of universities and the federal government; mems include 9 Canadian universities, Fisheries and Oceans Canada, National Research Council of Canada, the New Brunswick Depts of Education and of Fisheries and Aquaculture, corporations, organizations and individuals; research and teaching in marine sciences and coastal biology; marine education courses for elementary, high school and university groups; Centre includes a public aquarium with local flora and fauna, and the Atlantic Reference Centre which houses a zoological and botanical museum reference collection; Dir Dr JOHN H. ALLEN; publ. *Marine Science News* (2 a year).

Jardin botanique de Montréal: 4101 Sherbrooke St East, Montréal, Qué. H1X 2B2; tel. (514) 872-1400; fax (514) 872-3765; f. 1931; affiliated botanic and horticultural societies; library of 18,000 vols, 500 periodicals; Asst Dir GILLES VINCENT; publs *Quatre-temps* (Amis du Jardin botanique) (quarterly), *Index Seminum* (annually).

Physical Sciences

Algonquin Radio Observatory: Lake Traverse, Ont.; operated by the National Research Council; includes 150 ft-diameter radiotelescope completed in 1966.

David Dunlap Observatory of the University of Toronto: 123 Hillsview Drive, Richmond Hill, Ont. L4C 1T3; tel. (905) 884-2112; fax (905) 884-2672; f. 1935; 50 mems; library of 30,000 vols; Dir E. R. SEAQUIST.

Dominion Astrophysical Observatory: 5071 West Saanich Rd, Victoria, BC V8X 4M6; f. 1918; part of Nat. Research Ccl Herzberg Inst. of Astrophysics; 70 mems; library of 20,000 vols; Dir J. E. HESSER.

Geological Survey of Canada: 601 Booth St, Ottawa, Ont. K1A 0E8; tel. (613) 996-3919; fax (613) 943-8742; f. 1842; part of Natural Resources Canada; regional centres in Dartmouth, NS, Calgary, Alta, Vancouver and Sidney, BC, Sainte-Foy, Que.; geological, geophysical and geochemical research; studies in marine geology, surficial geology and quaternary research; mineral and energy resource studies; studies of Appalachian, Cordilleran and Inuitian orogens, sedimentary basins, and geology of the Canadian Shield; manages geoscience component of National Library of Canada (400,000 vols, 4,000 journals, 350,000 maps); major cartographic service; extensive publication programme for geological and geophysical maps and reports; Asst Deputy Minister Dr MARC DENIS EVERELL.

Toronto Biomedical NMR Centre: Department of Medical Genetics, University of Toronto Medical Sciences Building, Toronto, Ont. M5S 1A8; f. 1970; a national centre for high field NMR spectroscopy servicing industry, universities and the Government; Dir Dr A. A. GREY.

RELIGION, SOCIOLOGY AND ANTHROPOLOGY

Humanities and Social Sciences Federation of Canada: Suite 415, 151 Slater St, Ottawa, Ont. K1P 5H3; tel. (613) 238-6112; fax (613) 238-6114; Exec. Dir MARCEL LAUZIÈRE; publs *Annual Report, Bulletin* (4 a year).

International Center for Research on Language Planning/Centre international de recherche en aménagement linguistique: Pavillon De Koninck, Cité Universitaire, Sainte-Foy, Qué. G1K 7P4; tel. (418) 656-3232; f. 1967; basic research on language planning, description of oral and written Quebec French, new information technologies, learning of a second language; 19 researchers, 80 graduate students, 4 staff; library of 6,000 vols, 50 periodicals; Exec. Dir D. DESHAIES.

Social Sciences and Humanities Research Council of Canada/Conseil de recherches en sciences humaines du Canada: 350 Albert St, Box 1610, Ottawa, Ont. K1P 6G4; tel. (613) 992-0691; fax (613) 992-1787; e-mail z-info@sshrc.ca; f. 1977 to promote research and advanced training in the social sciences and humanities; offers grants for basic and applied research; doctoral and postdoctoral fellowships; scholarly publishing journals and conferences; Pres. Dr MARC RENAUD.

TECHNOLOGY

Atomic Energy of Canada, Ltd (AECL): 2251 Speakman Drive, Mississauga, Ont. L5K 1B2; tel. (905) 823-9040; fax (905) 823-6120; f. 1952; development of economic nuclear power, scientific research and development in the nuclear energy field, and marketing of nuclear reactors; Chair. R. F. NIXON; Pres. and CEO R. MORDEN.

Attached laboratories:

AECL Research, Chalk River Laboratories: Chalk River, Ont. K0J 1J0; f. 1944; nuclear reactors (NRU, NRX, Pool Test Reactor and ZED-2), Tandem Accelerating Super Conducting Cyclotron, equipment for nuclear research and engineering development.

AECL Research, Whiteshell Laboratories: Pinawa, Man. R0E 1L0; f. 1960; I-10/1 Accelerator, Underground Research Laboratory, equipment for nuclear research and engineering development.

BC Advanced Systems Institute: 450-1122 Mainland St, Vancouver, BC V6B 5L1; tel. (604) 689-0551; fax (604) 689-4198; f. 1986; promotes research and development in high technology areas such as microelectronics and artificial intelligence; Chair. BARRY JINKS; Exec. Dir BRENT SAUDER.

Canada Centre for Inland Waters/Centre canadien des eaux intérieures: 867 Lakeshore Rd, POB 5050, Burlington, Ont. L7R 4A6; tel. (905) 336-4981; fax (905) 336-6444; f. 1967; a joint freshwater research complex of the Depts of Environment and Fisheries and Oceans; freshwater environmental and fisheries research and monitoring; 600 mems; co-operative management by committee of institutional directors.

Attached research institutes:

National Water Research Institute: 867 Lakeshore Rd, POB 5050, Burlington, Ont. L7R 4A6; under Dept of Environment; aquatic ecology, physical dynamics of water, hydraulics of waves, measurements of chemical and microbiological pollutants and toxic chemicals in freshwater ecosystems, etc.; 245 mems; library of 25,000 vols, 20,000 reports, 1,800 journals; Exec. Dir Dr JOHN CAREY; publs *NWRI Contributions*.

Bayfield Institute: 867 Lakeshore Rd, POB 5050, Burlington, Ont. L7R 4A6; under Dept of Fisheries and Oceans; comprises: Great Lakes Laboratory for Fisheries and Aquatic Sciences; Fisheries and Habitat Management; Canadian Hydrographic Service; Small Craft Harbours branch; and support for shipping. Together with the Freshwater Research Institute in Winnipeg, it provides the federal Fisheries and Oceans programme for the Central and Arctic Region.

Forintek Canada Corp.: Head Office and Western Laboratory, 2665 East Mall, Vancouver, BC V6T 1W5; tel. (604) 224-3221; fax (604) 222-5690; Eastern Laboratory, 319 rue Franquet, Sainte-Foy, Qué. G1P 4R4; f. 1979 (formerly Eastern and Western Forest Products Laboratories of Forestry Canada); solid wood products research; Pres. I. A. DE LA ROCHE; Corp. Sec. P. K. P. CHAU; publ. annual report.

Institute for Aerospace Studies: 4925 Dufferin St, Toronto, Ont. M3H 5T6; tel. (416) 667-7700; f. 1949; part of the Univ. of Toronto; undergraduate and graduate studies; research in aerospace science and engineering, and associated fields; serves industrial research and development needs in government and industry; facilities for experimental and computational research; library of 80,000 vols; Dir Prof. A. A. HAASZ; publs *Progress Report* (annually), series of technical notes, reviews and reports.

Pulp and Paper Research Institute of Canada: 570 Blvd St-Jean, Pointe Claire, Qué. H9R 3J9; tel. (514) 630-4100; fax (514) 630-4134; f. 1925; pulp and paper research, contract research and technical services; postgraduate training programme in co-operation with McGill University and University of British Columbia; library of 20,000 vols; Pres. J. D. WRIGHT; Sec. C. D. DOUCET; publ. *Annual Report*.

Libraries and Archives

Alberta

Calgary Public Library: 616 Macleod Trail SE, Calgary, Alta T2G 2M2; fax (403) 237-5393; 1,730,709 items; 16 brs; special section on petroleum; Dir GERRY MEEK.

City of Edmonton Archives: 10440 108th Ave, Edmonton, Alta T5H 3Z9; tel. (403) 496-8710; f. 1971; reference library of 10,000 vols, also MSS, newspapers, slides, city records, photographs and maps of the city; Man. BRUCE IBSEN.

Edmonton Public Library: 7 Sir Winston Churchill Square, Edmonton, Alta T5J 2V4; fax (403) 496-7097; f. 1913; 14 brs; 1,200,000 vols, 215,000 audio-visual items; Librarian LINDA C. COOK.

Glenbow Library and Archives: 130 9th Ave SE, Calgary, Alta T2G 0P3; tel. (403) 268-4204; fax (403) 232-6569; f. 1955; 80,000 vols, 700,000 photographs and a large collection of manuscript materials, chiefly on Western and Northern Canada.

Legislature Library: 216 Legislature Bldg, 10800 97th Ave, Edmonton, Alta T5K 2B6; tel. (403) 427-2473; fax (403) 427-6016; e-mail lbuhr@assembly.ab.ca; f. 1906; parliamentary library of 228,700 vols and documents; Librarian L. R. BUHR; publs *Directory of Alberta Government Libraries* (2 a year), *New Books in the Library*, *Selected Periodical Articles List* (11 a year), *Library Handbook* (12 a year).

Parkland Regional Library: 5404-56 Ave, Lacombe, Alta T4L 1G1; tel. (403) 782-3850; fax (403) 782-4650; f. 1959; serves 145 school and public library service points; Dir PATRICIA SILVER.

Provincial Archives of Alberta: 12845 102nd Ave, Edmonton, Alta T5N 0M6; tel. (403) 427-1750; fax (403) 427-4646; f. 1963; collections of non-current govt records, private papers, church records, municipal records, photos, taped interviews, films, videotapes and maps pertaining to the history of Alberta; special collection of Western Canadiana, local histories and archival literature (10,000 vols); thematic and recent accession exhibitions; Provincial Archivist Dr SANDRA M. THOMSON; publs *Information Leaflets, Occasional Papers, Publication Series*.

University of Alberta Library: Edmonton, Alta T6G 2J8; tel. (403) 492-3790; fax (403) 492-8302; f. 1909; 3,535,738 vols, 2,384,919 government publications, 18,665 current serials and periodicals, 3,083,888 microforms; Dir E. INGLES; publ. *Library Editions* (2 a year).

University of Calgary Library: 2500 University Drive NW, Calgary, Alta T2N 1N4; tel. (403) 220-5953; fax (403) 282-1218; f. 1966; 6,868,000 items (1,996,272 vols incl. government publs, 3,201,917 microforms, also pamphlets, audio-visual materials, maps, aerial photographs), 930 metres of archives, Canadian Authors' Manuscripts Colln; Dir YVONNE HINKS (acting).

British Columbia

British Columbia Archives: 655 Belleville St, Victoria, BC V8V 1X4; tel. (250) 387-1952; fax (250) 387-2072; f. 1893; 71,000 items of printed material, 7,000 linear metres of MSS and government records, 5,000,000 photographs, 9,000 paintings, 35,000 maps, charts and architectural plans, 25,000 hours of sound recordings, 4,000 cans of moving images; Provincial Archivist GARY A. MITCHELL (acting).

Fraser Valley Regional Library: Headquarters: 34589 Delair Rd, Abbotsford, BC V2S 5Y1; tel. (604) 859-7141; f. 1930; 22 brs; 733,000 vols, 10,000 talking books; Chief Admin. Officer JEAN DIRKSEN.

Public Library InterLINK: 110–6545 Bonsor Ave, Burnaby, BC V5H 1H3; tel. (604)437-8441; fax (604) 430-8595; f. 1994; a federation of 15 autonomous public libraries sharing resources and services and providing open access to all member libraries to all area residents; special services: taped books for the visually impaired (37,000 vols), multilingual books, staff training videotapes, children's educational videotapes; Office Administrator RITA AVIGDOR.

Greater Victoria Public Library: 735 Broughton St, Victoria, BC, V8W 3H2; tel. (250) 382-7241; fax (250) 382-7125; f. 1864; 771,000 vols, 75,000 audio-visual items, 1,500 periodicals; Chief Librarian SANDRA ANDERSON.

Legislative Library: Victoria, BC V8V 1X4; tel. (250) 387-6510; fax (250) 356-1373; f. 1893; 500,000 vols; Dir JOAN A. BARTON.

Simon Fraser University, W.A.C. Bennett Library: Burnaby, BC V5A 1S6; tel. (604) 291-4658; fax (604) 291-3023; f. 1965; 1,214,111 vols, 937,181 microforms; Librarian T. C. DOBB.

University of British Columbia Library: Vancouver, BC V6T 1Z1; tel. (604) 822-3871; fax (604) 822-3893; f. 1915; 14 brs; 3,600,000 vols, 4,600,000 microforms; Librarian CATHERINE QUINLAN.

Vancouver Island Regional Library: Headquarters: 6250 Hammond Bay Rd, Box 3333, Nanaimo, BC V9R 5N3; tel. (250) 758-4697; fax (250) 758-2482; e-mail virl@island.net; f. 1936; 36 brs; 1,143,000 vols; Exec. Dir PENNY GRANT.

Vancouver Public Library: 350 West Georgia St, Vancouver, BC V6B 6B1; tel. (604) 331-3600; fax (604) 331-4080; e-mail vplboard@vpl.vancouver.bc.ca; f. 1887; 2,000,000 vols; 21 brs; Dir MADELEINE AALTO.

Vancouver School of Theology Library: 6050 Chancellor Blvd, Vancouver, BC V6T 1X3; tel. (604) 822-9430; fax (604) 822-9212; e-mail geraldt@unixg.ubc.ca; f. 1971; 80,000 vols; Librarian GERALD TURNBULL (acting).

Manitoba

Manitoba Culture, Heritage and Citizenship: Public Library Services: Unit 200, 1525 1st St, Brandon, Man. R7A 7A1; tel. (204) 726-6590; fax (204) 726-6868; e-mail pls@chc.gov.mb.ca; f. 1972; 136,000 vols, 4,000 government publs, 1,464 films, 2,950 talking books, 3,081 video tapes; 30 book deposit stations; Dir SYLVIA NICHOLSON; publs *Manitoba Public Library Statistics* (every 2 years), *Directory of Libraries in Manitoba* (every 2 years), *Public Library Services Newsletter* (5 a year).

Manitoba Justice Great Library: 331-408 York Ave, Winnipeg, Man. R3C 0P9; tel. (204) 945-1958; fax (204) 948-2138; f. 1877; 50,000 vols; Librarian R. GARTH NIVEN.

Manitoba Legislative Library: 200 Vaughan St, Main floor, Winnipeg, Man. R3C 1T5; tel. (204) 945-4330; fax (204) 948-2008; e-mail legislative_library@chc.gov.mb.ca; f. 1870; 1.4m. items; special collections: Canadian, Western Canadian and Manitoba history, economics, political and social sciences, urban, rural and ethnic language newspapers of Manitoba, government publications; Legislative Librarian SUSAN BISHOP; publs *Selected New Titles* (monthly), *Monthly Checklist of Manitoba Government Publications, Memo for Members*.

Provincial Archives of Manitoba: 200 Vaughan St, Winnipeg, MB R3C 1T5; tel. (204) 945-3971; fax (204) 948-2008; f. 1884; 5,000 linear ft private MSS, 36,000 linear ft Manitoba government records, 7,500 linear ft Hudson's Bay Co Archives records, 120,000 architectural drawings, 1,000,000 photographs, 32,000 maps, 300 paintings, 5,300 prints and drawings, 2,200 sound records; special collections: Red River Settlement and Red River Disturbance, Lieut-Governors' papers, Winnipeg General Strike, Canadian Airways Ltd, Archives of the Ecclesiastical Province of Rupert's Land, records of local govts and school divisions; Provincial Archivist PETER J. BOWER.

University of Manitoba Libraries: Winnipeg, Man. R3T 2N2; tel. (204) 474-9881; fax (204) 474-7583; f. 1877; collections supporting 15 faculties and 5 schools; special collections: Slavic, Icelandic; 2,000,000 vols, 507,000 government publications, 157,500 other print items (maps, performance music, text book collection, etc.), 1,108,000 microforms, 31,000 audio-visual items, 12,500 serial titles; Dir CAROLYNNE PRESSER.

New Brunswick

Bell, R. P., Library: Mount Allison University, 49 York St, Sackville, NB E4L 1C6; tel. (506) 364-2562; f. 1840; 330,000 vols; 425,000 microforms, 234,000 documents; Librarian SARA LOCHHEAD.

Bibliothèque Champlain (Université de Moncton): Moncton, NB E1A 3E9; tel. (506) 858-4012; fax (506) 858-4086; f. 1965; general academic collections; 518,000 vols, 1,799 current periodicals and 392,788 microfiches; Head Librarian PIERRE LAFRANCE.

Harriet Irving Library: University of New Brunswick, POB 7500, Fredericton, NB E3B 5H5; tel. (506) 453-4740; fax (506) 453-4595; f. 1790; 1,067,621 vols and 2,091,893 (equivalent vols) microforms; Librarian JOHN D. TESKEY.

Legislative Library: Box 6000, Fredericton, NB E3B 5H1; tel. (506) 453-2338; fax (506) 444-5889; f. 1841; 35,000 vols; Librarian ERIC L. SWANICK.

Provincial Archives of New Brunswick: POB 6000, Fredericton, NB E3B 5H1; tel. (506) 453-2122; fax (506) 453-3288; e-mail provarch@gov.nb.ca; f. 1968; 25,000 ft of govt and private textual documents, 250,000 photographs, 300,000 cartographic and architectural documents, 4,600 hours audio recordings, 1,800 video tapes and films, 60,000 microfiches, 14,000 reels microfilm; Provincial Archivist MARION BEYEA.

Newfoundland

Provincial Archives of Newfoundland and Labrador: Colonial Bldg, St John's, Nfld A1C 2C9; tel. (709) 729-3065; fax (709) 729-0578; f. 1960; Provincial Archivist SHELLEY M. SMITH.

Provincial Public Libraries Service: Arts and Culture Centre, St John's, Nfld A1B 3A3; tel. (709) 737-3964; fax (709) 737-3009; f. 1934; 1,148,327 vols; special collection of Newfoundland history and newspapers; Provincial Dir DAVID GALE.

Provincial Resource Library: Arts and Culture Centre, St John's, Nfld A1B 3A3; tel. (709) 737-3752; fax (709) 737-2660; f. 1934; Newfoundland Collection open to the public; back-up resource library for the provincial system; 181,604 vols (incl. Newfoundland Collection); Man. CHARLES CAMERON.

Queen Elizabeth II Library: Memorial University of Newfoundland, St John's, Nfld A1B 3Y1; tel. (709) 737-7428; fax (709) 737-2153; f. 1925; 1,983,000 vols, 2,540,000 microform units; Librarian RICHARD H. ELLIS.

Nova Scotia

Angus L. Macdonald Library: St Francis Xavier University, Box 5000, Antigonish, NS B2G 2W5; tel. (902) 867-2267; fax (902) 867-5153; 700,000 vols; special collection: Celtic history, literature and language; Librarian RITA CAMPBELL; publ. *The Antigonish Review* (quarterly).

Dalhousie University Library System: Halifax, NS B3H 4H8; 1,756,000 vols; University Librarian WILLIAM R. MAES.

Halifax Regional Library: 60 Alderney Drive, Dartmouth, NS B2Y 4P8; tel. (902) 490-5744; f. 1996; 992,000 vols, 62 microfilms, 92,454 audio-visual items; 4,854 periodical subscriptions, 79,698 periodicals; CEO JUDITH HARE.

Nova Scotia Archives and Records Management: 6016 University Ave, Halifax, NS B3H 1W4; tel. (902) 424-6060; fax (902) 424-0628; e-mail nsarm@gov.ns.ca; f. 1857; provincial govt records; family, political, personal and business papers; maps, plans, charts; photographs, paintings; microfilmed files of leading newspapers; film, television and sound archives; research library of about 50,000 vols; Provincial Archivist BRIAN SPEIRS.

Nova Scotia Legislative Library: Province House, Halifax, NS B3J 2P8; fax (902) 424-0574; f. 1862; Nova Scotiana Collection; 170,000 vols; Librarian MARGARET MURPHY; publ. *Publications of the Province of Nova Scotia* (monthly and annually).

Vaughan Memorial Library, Acadia University: Wolfville, NS; tel. (902) 585-1249; fax (902) 585-1073; f. 1843; 1,000,000 vols and govt documents; Librarian LORRAINE MCQUEEN.

Ontario

Canada Institute for Scientific and Technical Information (CISTI): Montreal Rd, Ottawa, Ont. K1A 0S2; tel. (613) 993-1600; operated by National Research Council of Canada; f. 1974, fmrly National Science Library; focal point of a national scientific and technical information network; resources of over 50,000 serial titles are made available through loan, copies and consultation; information services include operation of a national computerized current awareness service (InfoAlert), an online table of contents service (Swet Scan), Customized Literature Search Service providing custom bibliographies on requested topics, MEDLARS co-ordinator for Canada; Dir. Gen. BERNARD DUMOUCHEL (acting).

Canada–Natural Resources Canada, Headquarters Library: 580 Booth St, Ottawa, Ont. K1A 0E4; tel. (613) 996-8282; fax (613) 992-7211; f. 1958; 65,000 vols and bound periodicals, 3,000 reports; mineral and energy economics, policy, taxation, legislation and statistics, energy conservation; Dir S. E. HENRY.

Canadian Agriculture Library: Sir John Carling Bldg, Agriculture and Agri-Food Canada, Ottawa, Ont. K1A 0C5; tel. (613) 759-7068; fax (613) 759-6643; f. 1910; 1,000,000 vols, 22,200 serials; specializes in agriculture, biology, biochemistry, plant science, entomology, veterinary medicine, food sciences, economics; serves 28 field libraries; Dir V. G. DESROCHES.

Canadian Postal Archives: 344 Wellington St, Ottawa, Ont. K1A 0N3; tel. (613) 992-3744; f. 1971; Chief CIMON MORIN.

Carleton University Library: 1125 Colonel By Drive, Ottawa, Ont. K1S 5B6; tel. (613) 520-2735; fax (613) 520-2750; f. 1948; 1,664,000 vols, 10,487 serials subscriptions, 1,348,465 items (microforms, maps, a/v); Librarian MARTIN FOSS; publ. *Library News* (irregular).

Departmental Library, Indian and Northern Affairs Canada: Ottawa, Ont. K1A 0H4; tel. (819) 997-0811; fax (819) 953-5491; f. 1966; 52,000 unique titles, 100,600 vols, 20,000 bound periodicals, 2,000 rare books, 3,500 government documents, 3,000 microfilm reels, incl. records relating to Indian Affairs; service to Native people, researchers, libraries; Chief Librarian JULIA FINN.

Earth Sciences Information Centre: 601 Booth St, Ottawa, Ont. K1A 0E8; tel. (613) 996-3919; telex 053 3117; fax (613) 943-8742; f. 1842; component of Natural Resources Canada; interlibrary loans, on-line retrospective searching; 400,000 vols, 260,000 geological maps; Head of ESIC Services BEVERLY CHEN (acting); publ. *List of Translations* (irregular).

Hamilton Public Library: 55 York Blvd, POB 2700, Station A, Hamilton, Ont. L8N 4E4; tel. (905) 546-3200; telex 061-8602; fax (905) 546-3202; f. 1889; special collections of local history, Canadiana to 1950, govt documents; 1,492,467 vols and 1,876 periodicals; 9 br. libraries; 2 bookmobiles; CEO KEN ROBERTS.

Library of Parliament: Ottawa, Ont. K1A 0A9; tel (613) 995-1166; fax (613) 992-1269; f. 1867; 378,889 vols in integrated systems, 510,000 microforms; Parl. Librarian RICHARD PARÉ; publs *Quorum* (daily, during session), *Articles* (weekly during session), *Guide to Library Services, Current Issue Reviews* (monthly), *Background Papers, Annual Report*, bibliographies, etc.

Library of the Pontifical Institute of Mediaeval Studies: 113 St Joseph St, Toronto, Ont. M5S 1J4; tel. (416) 926-7146; e-mail suma@vax.library.utoronto.ca; f. 1929; 96,000 vols, 230 periodicals, 10,000 folios of MSS on photostats, 250,000 folios of MSS on microfilm; Librarian Rev. JAMES K. FARGE.

London Public Library: 305 Queens Ave, London, Ont. N6B 3L7; tel. (519) 661-4600; fax (519) 663-5396; f. 1894; 1,027,000 vols, 92,400 non-book materials; CEO REED E. OSBORNE.

McMaster University Libraries: 1280 Main St West, Hamilton, Ont. L8S 4L6; tel. (905) 525-9140; fax (416) 546-0625; f. 1887; 1,760,000 vols, 1,423,000 microform items, 175,000 non-print items, 3,600 linear metres archival material; contains among others Vera Brittain archives, Bertrand Russell archives and 18th-century collection; Librarian GRAHAM R. HILL; publs *Library Research News*, *Russell: The Journal of the Bertrand Russell Archives*.

Metropolitan Toronto Reference Library: 789 Yonge St, Toronto, Ont. M4W 2G8; tel. (416) 393-7000; f. 1967; Canada's largest public reference library; services to other libraries in its area; 1,500,079 vols and periodicals; specialized depts: Consumer Health Information Service, Video/Picture Collection, Special Collections, Genealogy/Maps Centre, Performing Arts, Language Learning, Newspapers and Periodicals, Business, Main Reference and IntelliSearch; CEO FRANCES SCHWENGER; publs *Annual Report*, *MTRL News*, etc.

National Archives of Canada: 395 Wellington St, Ottawa, Ont. K1A 0N3; tel. (613) 995-5138; f. 1872; depository of public records and historical material; photographs, MSS, maps, pictures, sound tapes and film, books and pamphlets; computer-generated records; Dir JEAN-PIERRE WALLOT; publs *The Archivist / L'Archiviste* (2 a year), *Annual Report, General Guide Series*.

National Defence Headquarters Library: 101 Colonel By Drive, Ottawa, Ont. K1A 0K2; tel. (613) 996-0831; fax (613) 995-8176; f. 1903; library services, inter-library loans, information retrieval; 30,000 vols incl. military Canadiana; Librarian P. GREIG.

National Library of Canada/Bibliothèque nationale du Canada: 395 Wellington St, Ottawa, Ont. K1A 0N4; tel. (613) 995-9481; fax (613) 943-1112; e-mail reference@nlc-bnc.ca; f. 1953; 16,000,000 items; special collections: Canadian materials (govt publs, MSS, newspapers, periodicals, monographs, sound recordings, microforms and educational kits), children's literature, music, native rights, rare books, rare Hebraica and Judaica; National Librarian MARIANNE SCOTT; publs *Canadiana,* national bibliography (monthly, annual cumulations), *Canadian Thesis – Thèses Canadiennes (microfiche), National Library News – Nouvelles de la Bibliothèque Nationale* (monthly), *Annual Report, Publications Catalogue* (annually), *Union List of Canadian Newspapers* (microfiche), *Union List of Serials in the Social Sciences and Humanities* (microfiche).

North York Public Library: 5120 Yonge Street, North York, Ont. M2N 5N9; tel. (416) 395-5500; fax (416) 395-5542; f. 1950; 2,383,000 vols; special collections: Judaica, Canada, Native People's Collection, West Indian/Black Heritage Collection, urban affairs; CEO JOSEPHINE BRYANT; publ. *New Notes* (every 2 months).

Ontario Legislative Library: Legislative Bldg, Queen's Park, Toronto, Ont. M7A 1A9; tel. (416) 325-3939; fax (416) 325-3909; f. 1867; 95,229 vols of monographs; Exec. Dir MARY E. DICKERSON; publs *Periodical Contents, Selected*

New Titles (monthly), *Status of Bills Report, Toronto Press Today, Provincial Press.*

Ottawa City Archives: 174 Stanley Ave, Ottawa, Ont. K1M 1P1; tel. (613) 742-5014; fax (613) 742-5113; f. 1976; repository of public records of civic administration and other historical material; special collections: genealogy, heraldry, local railroad history; City Archivist LOUISE ROY-BROCHU.

Ottawa Public Library: 120 Metcalfe St, Ottawa, Ont.; tel. (613) 236-0301; fax (613) 567-4013; e-mail clubbb@opl.ottawa.on.ca; f. 1906; 1,092,000 vols; Chief Librarian B. CLUBB.

Queen's University Library: Kingston, Ont. K7L 5C4; tel. (613) 545-2519; f. 1842; 1,946,198 vols, 3,092,933 other items; Chief Librarian PAUL WIENS.

Supreme Court of Canada Library: 301 Wellington St, Ottawa, Ont. K1A 0J1; tel. (613) 996-8120; fax (613) 952-2832; e-mail library@scc-csc.gc.ca; 175,000 vols; Dir F. D. TEEPLE.

Toronto Public Library: 281 Front St E., Toronto, Ont. M5A 4L2; tel. (416) 393-7500; fax (416) 393-7782; f. 1883; 2,000,000 vols; 33 brs; Osborne Collection of Early Children's Books, Merril Collection for Science Fiction, Speculation and Fantasy; CEO GABRIELE LUNDEEN; publ. *What's On* (6 a year).

University of Ottawa Library Network: 65 University St, Ottawa, Ont. K1N 9A5; tel. (613) 562-5883; fax (613) 562-5195; f. 1848; 1,475,000 vols, 1,417,000 microforms, 766,000 govt documents, 663,000 non-book materials, 9,000 periodicals; University Chief Librarian RICHARD GREENE.

University of Toronto Libraries: Toronto, Ont. M5S 1A5; tel. (416) 978-5093; fax (416) 978-7653; f. 1891; 8,487,000 vols, 4,395,000 microforms, 986,000 other non-book items (maps, sound recordings, audio-visual, manuscript titles, aerial photographs, etc.); 44,574 serials; Chief Librarian CAROLE MOORE.

University of Trinity College Library: 6 Hoskin Ave, Toronto, Ont. M5S 1H8; tel. (416) 978-2653; fax (416) 978-2797; f. 1851; 130,000 vols; special collections: Strachan Collection, SPCK Collection; Librarian Mrs L. CORMAN.

University of Waterloo Library: Waterloo, Ont. N2L 3G1; tel. (519) 885-1211; telex 069-55259; fax (519) 747-4606; f. 1957; 1,703,916 vols, 1,806,400 microfiches, 6,344 periodicals, 4,491 records and tapes; University Librarian MURRAY C. SHEPHERD; publs *Bibliography* (irregular), *Occasional Paper* series (irregular), *Technical Paper* series (irregular).

University of Western Ontario Library System: London, Ont. N6A 3K7; tel. (519) 679-2111; fax (519) 661-3911; f. 1878; 2,221,000 vols; 3,314,000 microforms; 1,199,000 other items; 15,000 serials; Dir of Libraries CATHERINE QUINLAN.

Victoria University Library: 71 Queen's Park Crescent East, Toronto, Ont. M5S 1K7; tel. (416) 585-4472; fax (416) 585-4591; e-mail viclib@chass.utoronto.ca; 250,000 vols; special collections: humanities (general), religions and theology, S. T. Coleridge, V. Woolf/Bloomsbury/Hogarth Press, Tennyson, Wesleyana, Northrop Frye, E. J. Pratt; George Baxter (books and prints), 19th-century Canadian Poetry, French and French-Canadian Literature (Rièse collection); folklore; Librarian ROBERT C. BRANDEIS.

Prince Edward Island

Confederation Centre Public Library: Box 7000, Charlottetown, PEI C1A 8G8; tel. (902) 368-4642; fax (902) 368-4652; e-mail ccpl@gov.pe.ca; f. 1773; 72,000 vols; Librarian DON SCOTT.

Prince Edward Island Provincial Library: POB 7500, Morell, PEI C0A 1S0; est. 1933; 310,000 vols in regional system of 23 rural and town public libraries; Dir of Archives and Libraries HARRY HOLMAN.

Public Archives and Records Office: POB 1000, Charlottetown, PEI; tel. (902) 368-4290; fax (902) 368-6327; f. 1964; Provincial Archivist HARRY T. HOLMAN.

Québec

Archives Nationales du Québec: 1210 ave du Séminaire, CP 10450, Sainte-Foy, Qué. G1V 4N1; tel. (418) 644-3906; f. 1920; 37,365 vols; regional centres at Hull, Trois-Rivières, Montréal, Chicoutimi, Sherbrooke, Rouyn-Noranda, Rimouski; Sept-Iles; public administration, politics, history, etc.; Archivist ROBERT GARON.

Bibliothèque de l'Assemblée nationale du Québec: Edifice Pamphile-Lemay, Québec, Qué. G1A 1A5; tel. (418) 643-4408; fax (418) 646-3207; e-mail bibliotheque@assnat.qc.ca; f. 1802; law and legislation, political science, parliamentary procedure, history; 928,000 vols; Chief Librarian GASTON BERNIER; publs *Bulletin* (quarterly), *Journal des débats: index* (irregular), *Débats de l'Assemblée législative 1867–1962* (irregular), *Rapport Annuel* (annually).

Bibliothèque de l'Université Laval: Cité Universitaire, Québec, Qué. G1K 7P4; tel. (418) 656-3344; fax (418) 656-7897; f. 1852; 3,476,000 vols, 13,655 periodicals, 12,900 films, 125,500 maps; Dir CLAUDE BONNELLY; publ. *Répertoire des vedettes-matière*.

Bibliothèque de Montréal: 1210 Sherbrooke Est, Montréal, Qué. H2L 1L9; tel. (514) 872-5171; fax (514) 872-1626; f. 1902; 2,102,600 vols, of which 51,700 books, 20,757 pamphlets, 43,900 pictures and photographs, 1,547 maps, 3,035 slides and 99,200 microforms relate to Canada and Canadian history; 23 brs, 1 sound-recording library and 1 bookmobile; Dir JACQUES PANNETON.

Bibliothèque de Théologie (Facultés de Théologie et de Philosophie de la Compagnie de Jésus): 5605 ave Decelles, Montréal, Qué. H3T 1W4; tel. (514) 737-1465; f. 1882; 195,000 vols; books from 16th, 17th and 18th centuries, Canadiana; Dir C.-R. NADEAU.

Bibliothèque du Barreau de Montréal (Library of the Bar of Montreal): Palais de Justice, 17e étage 1, rue Notre-Dame est, Montréal, Qué. H2Y 1B6; tel. (514) 866-2057; fax (514) 879-8592; f. 1828; 75,000 vols; Librarian CÉLINE AMNOTTE.

Bibliothèque Nationale du Québec: 2275 rue Holt, Montréal, Qué. H2G 3H1; tel. (514) 873-1100; fax (514) 873-4310; f. 1967 (absorbed Bibliothèque Saint-Sulpice); 325,276 titles of printed books, 36,971 periodicals, 825 linear metres of private records and archives, 8,678 old and rare books, 45,298 maps and atlases, 110,940 sheets of music; Pres./Dir-Gen. PHILIPPE SAUVAGEAU; publs *Bibliographie du Québec* (printed and machine readable, monthly), *Point de Repère (Index analytique d'articles de périodiques québécois et étrangers)* (every 2 months).

Bibliothèques de l'Université de Montréal: CP 6128, Succursale Centre-ville, Montréal, Qué. H3C 3J7; tel. (514) 343-6905; fax (514) 343-6457; f. 1928; 2,518,000 vols, 15,673 current periodicals, 1,477,300 microforms, 161,950 audiovisual documents; Dir of Libraries Mme A. JOFFE-NICODÈME.

Concordia University Libraries: 1455 de Maisonneuve Blvd West, Montréal, Qué. H3G 1M8; tel. (514) 848-7780; fax (514) 848-2882; f. 1974; 2,730,000 vols; Dir W. CURRAN.

Fraser-Hickson Institute, Montreal (Free Library): 4855 Kensington Ave, Montréal, Qué. H3X 3S6; tel. (514) 489-5301; fax (514) 489-5302; e-mail frahick@cam.org; f. 1870; over 150,000 vols; collection and archives of Institut Canadien of Montréal; Librarian FRANCES W. ACKERMAN; publ. *Annual Report, Newsletter.*

McGill University Libraries: 3459 McTavish St, Montréal, Qué. H3A 1Y1; tel. (514) 398-4734; fax (514) 398-7184; f. 1855; 16 libraries, 2.8 million vols, 16,406 current periodicals, 1,347,565 microtexts, 831,845 govt documents; Dir FRANCES GROEN.

Osler Library: McGill University, McIntyre Medical Sciences Bldg, 3655 Drummond St, Montréal, Qué. H3G 1Y6; tel. (514) 398-4475 ext. 094163; fax (514) 398-5747; f. 1929; history of medicine and allied sciences; 50,000 vols; Librarian JUNE SCHACHTER; publ. *Newsletter*.

Saskatchewan

Regina Public Library: POB 2311, Regina, Sask. S4P 3Z5; tel. (306) 777-6000; fax (306) 352-5550; f. 1908; 9 brs; 765,000 vols; Library Dir KEN JENSEN; publs *Community Information Catalogue, Regina Public Library Film Catalogue*.

Saskatchewan Legislative Reference Library: 234 Legislative Bldg, Regina, Sask. S4S 0B3; tel. (306) 787-2276; fax (306) 787-1772; f. 1878; 33,592 vols, 177,000 govt publs (paper), 161,700 fiches; social sciences, law and history; noted for its collection of government documents and Western Canadiana; Legislative Librarian Mrs MARIAN J. POWELL; publ. *Checklist of Saskatchewan Government Publications* (monthly).

Saskatchewan Provincial Library: 1352 Winnipeg St, Regina, Sask.; tel. (306) 787-2972; fax (306) 787-2029; f. 1953; co-ordinates library services in the province; 1,004,860 vols, specializing in library science, multilingual books, talking books, research resource materials including govt publs, bibliography; Provincial Librarian M. WOODS; publ. *Annual Report.*

Saskatoon Public Library System: 311 23rd St East, Saskatoon, Sask. S7K 0J6; tel. (306) 975-7558; fax (306) 975-7542; f. 1913; 7 brs, 1 booktrailer; 629,000 vols, 8,400 records, 28,000 audio-cassettes, 25,000 videos, 25,000 compact discs, 904 current periodical titles; local history room; Dir of Libraries ZENON ZUZAK; publ. *Preface* (4 a year).

University of Saskatchewan Libraries: 3 Campus Drive, Saskatoon, Sask. S7N 5A4; tel. (306) 966-5927; fax (306) 966-5932; f. 1909; main library and 7 brs; 1.6m. print vols, 8,500 current journals, 2.7m. items on microform, 471,764 govt documents and pamphlets, Russell Green music MSS, Adam Shortt collection of Canadiana, Conrad Aiken Collection of Published Works; Dir of Libraries F. WINTER.

Wapiti Regional Library: 145 12th St East, Prince Albert, Sask. S6V 1B7; tel. (306) 764-0712; fax (306) 922-1516; e-mail kpope@panet.pa.sk.ca; f. 1950; 54 brs; 448,000 vols; Dir KITTY POPE.

Museums and Art Galleries

Alberta

Banff Park Museum: Box 900, Banff, Alta T0L 0C0; tel. (403) 762-1558; fax (403) 762-1565; original museum f. 1895; natural and human history of the park.

Department of Earth and Atmospheric Sciences Museum, University of Alberta:

Edmonton, Alta; f. 1912; geology, meteorites, mineralogy, vertebrate palaeontology, stratigraphy; Curators D. G. W. SMITH (Minerals and Meteorites), R. C. FOX (Vertebrate Palaeontology), B. JONES (Invertebrate Palaeontology).

Edmonton Art Gallery, The: 2 Sir Winston Churchill Square, Edmonton, Alta T5J 2C1; tel. (403) 422-6223; fax (403) 426-3105; f. 1924; Canadian and international paintings, sculpture and photography; courses in art education; exhibitions; library of 10,000 vols, periodicals on art and education, 16,466 slides and prints; Exec. Dir VINCENT J. VARGA.

Glenbow Museum: 130 9th Ave SE, Calgary, Alta; tel. (403) 268-4100; fax (403) 265-9769; e-mail glenbow@glenbow.org; f. 1966; western Canadian and foreign cultural history, ethnology, military history, mineralogy and art; library of 100,000 vols, archives of 1,250,000 photos and negatives; Pres. Dr ROBERT R. JANES; Chair. Board of Governors ROBERT G. PETERS; publ. *Glenbow Magazine* (2 a year).

Luxton Museum: 1 Birch Ave (Box 850), Banff, Alta; tel. and fax (403) 762-2388; f. 1953; promotes education and awareness of the Northern Plains and Rockies Indian; natural history exhibits; owned and operated by Buffalo Nations Cultural Society; Pres. HAROLD HEALY.

Medicine Hat Museum and Art Gallery: 1302 Bomford Crescent, Medicine Hat, Alta; tel. (403) 527-6266; f. 1967; cultural and natural history, palaeontology, and primitive peoples representative of SE Alberta; art gallery; monthly exhibits by Canadian and international artists.

Provincial Museum of Alberta: 12845 102nd Ave, Edmonton, Alta T5N 0M6; tel. (403) 453-9100; fax (403) 454-6629; f. 1963; Alberta history, geology, natural history; Dir Dr PHILIP H. R. STEPNEY; publs *Museum Notes, Occasional Papers, Exhibition Catalogues* and leaflets.

Royal Tyrrell Museum of Palaeontology: Box 7500, Drumheller, Alta T0J 0Y0; tel. (403) 823-7707; fax (403) 823-7131; e-mail rtmp@dns.magtech.ab.ca; f. 1985; collection, research, display and interpretation of fossils as evidence for history of life, with emphasis on famous dinosaur fauna of Alberta; resource management, vertebrate and invertebrate palaeontology, taphonomy, palynology, sedimentology, stratigraphy, preparation, illustration, administration; library of 50,000 vols, special biographical collection on Joseph Burr Tyrrell; 110,000 catalogued fossil specimens; field station in Dinosaur Provincial Park; UNESCO World Heritage Site; Dir BRUCE G. NAYLOR.

British Columbia

Helmcken House Museum: 10 Elliott St Square, Victoria, BC V8V 1W1; (mailing address: John D. Adams, Heritage Properties Branch, Parliament Bldgs, Victoria, BC V8V 1X4); tel. (604) 356-1040; fax (604) 387-5129; four rooms in house built in 1852; historic medical collection; maintained by Heritage Properties Branch; Supervisor JOHN D. ADAMS.

Museum of Northern British Columbia: 100 1st Ave West, POB 669, Prince Rupert, BC; tel. (250) 624-3207; fax (250) 627-8009; f. 1924; exhibits cover 10,000 years of human habitation, incl. First Nations culture, local pioneer history and natural history; library of 800 vols (50 rare); Dir ROBIN WEBER; Curator SUSAN MARSDEN; publ. *Curator's Log*.

Pacific Space Centre Society: 1100 Chestnut St, Vancouver, BC V6J 3J9; tel. (604) 738-7827; fax (604) 736-5665; f. 1988; administers the Pacific Space Centre, H. R. MacMillan Planetarium and Gordon Southam Observatory; multimedia astronomy shows, laser shows, exhibitions, Observatory activities, lectures, etc.; 3,500 mems; publ. *Starry Messenger* (quarterly).

Royal British Columbia Museum: POB 9815 Stn Prov. Govt, Victoria, BC V8W 9W2; tel. (250) 387-3701; fax (250) 356-8197; f. 1886; contains reference collections and exhibits pertaining to natural history and human history of BC; library of 30,000 vols; CEO BILL BARKLEY; publs *Heritage Records, Handbooks, Discovery.*

Vancouver Art Gallery: 750 Hornby St, Vancouver, BC V6Z 2H7; tel. (604) 662-4700; fax (604) 682-1086; f. 1931; paintings, sculpture, graphics, photography, video; int. contemporary paintings and graphics with emphasis on BC artists; Emily Carr Collection; modern American prints; British watercolours; 18th-20th-century British paintings; library of 25,000 vols; Dir ALF BOGUSKY; publ. *Members' Calendar* (4 a year).

Vancouver Maritime Museum: 1905 Ogden Ave, Vancouver, BC V6J 1A3; tel. (604) 257-8300; fax (604) 737-2621; e-mail jpdvmm@aol.com; f. 1958; maritime history, local and international heritage vessels, RCMP *St Roch* Arctic patrol vessel, school programmes, lectures and summer festivals; library of 10,000 vols; Dir JIM DELGADO; publ. *Signals* (quarterly).

Manitoba

Manitoba Museum of Man and Nature: 190 Rupert Ave, Winnipeg, Man. R3B 0N2; tel. (204) 956-2830; fax (204) 942-3679; e-mail info@museummannature.mb.ca; f. 1965; human and natural history of Manitoba; planetarium; 'Touch the Universe' interactive science centre; library of *c.*26,000 vols; Exec. Dir JOANNE V. DICOSIMO; publ. *Happenings* (every 2 months).

Winnipeg Art Gallery: 300 Memorial Blvd, Winnipeg, Man. R3C 1V1; tel. (204) 786-6641; fax (204) 788-4998; f. 1912; exhibitions, lectures, films, performing arts, education programmes; library of 18,000 vols; Dir MICHEL V. CHEFF.

New Brunswick

Beaverbook Art Gallery: POB 605, Fredericton, NB E3B 5A6; tel. (506) 458-8545; fax (506) 459-7450; e-mail bag@fundy.net; f. 1959; medieval and Renaissance furniture, tapestries, paintings; 18th-, 19th- and 20th-century English and continental paintings; 19th- and 20th-century Canadian paintings; 18th- and 19th-century English porcelain; English sculptures; lectures, films, children's art classes, travelling exhibitions and guided tours, etc.; Dir IAN G. LUMSDEN; publs *Tableau* (3 a year), *Annual Report*.

Fort Beauséjour National Historic Site: 111 Fort Beauséjour Loop Rd, Aulac, NB E4L 2W5; tel. (506) 364-5080; fax (506) 536-4399; e-mail fort_beausejour@pch.gc.ca; f. 1926; exhibit areas, restored ruins and guide services.

Miramichi Natural History Museum: 149 Wellington St, Miramichi, NB E1N 1L7; fax (506) 773-7905; f. 1880; Pres. WALTER J. BROWN.

New Brunswick Museum: 277 Douglas Ave, Saint John, NB E2K 1E5; tel. (506) 643-2300; f. 1842; archives, library, fine art, decorative art, natural science and history; bookshop specializing in New Brunswick books; Dir Dr FRANK MILLIGAN.

York-Sunbury Historical Society Museum: POB 1312, Fredericton, NB E3B 5C8; tel. (506) 455-6041; f. 1932; domestic and military exhibits, temporary exhibitions of New Brunswick fine art and craft; Curator KELLY MCKAY.

Newfoundland

Newfoundland Museum: 285 Duckworth St, St John's, Nfld; tel. (709) 729-2329; fax (709) 729-2179; e-mail bransom@confed_dom.confed_po; f. 1887; archaeology, ethnology, marine, natural, native peoples, human and military history; publ. *Notes series.*

Subsidiary museums:

Mary March Regional Museum: Grand Falls–Windsor, Nfld; tel. (709) 489-9331; fax (709) 292-4526.

Southern Newfoundland Seamen's Museum: Grand Bank, Nfld; tel. (709) 832-1484; fax (709) 832-2053.

Nova Scotia

Art Gallery of Nova Scotia: 1723 Hollis St, POB 2262, Halifax, NS B3J 3C8; f. 1975; paintings, drawings, sculpture, prints, collection of Nova Scotia folk art; Dir BERNARD RIORDON.

Fort Anne National Historic Site and Museum: Annapolis Royal, NS B0S 1A0; tel. (902) 532-2397; fax (902) 532-2232; Area Superintendent LILLIAN STEWART.

Fortress of Louisbourg National Historic Site: POB 160, Louisbourg, NS B0A 1M0; tel. (902) 733-2280; reconstruction and restoration project, including 18th-century period rooms and museum complex; archives and library collections of 18th-century French and North American colonial material; District Dir CAROL WHITFIELD.

Maritime Museum of the Atlantic: 1675 Lower Water St, Halifax, NS B3J 1S3; tel. (902) 424-7490; fax (902) 424-0612; f. 1982; naval and merchant shipping history; small boat collection.

Nova Scotia Museum of Natural History: 1747 Summer St, Halifax, NS B3H 3A6; tel. (902) 424-7370; fax (902) 424-0560; f. 1868; collections, research and exhibits relating to natural history and archaeology of NS; 22 br. museums throughout NS; Dir D. L. BURLESON.

Ontario

Art Gallery of Hamilton: 123 King St West, Hamilton, Ont. L8P 4S8; tel. (905) 527-6610; fax (905) 577-6940; f. 1914; 7,500 works, mainly Canadian paintings, sculpture and graphics; also art from the USA, Britain and other European countries; exhibitions, workshops and lectures; library of 3,000 vols; Dir ROBERT RIDGE; publ. *Insights* (quarterly).

Art Gallery of Ontario: 317 Dundas St W, Toronto, Ont. M5T 1G4; tel. (416) 979-6648; fax (416) 979-6646; e-mail director@ago.net; f. 1900; European and North American art, 15th century to contemporary; Inuit in all media; Henry Moore; research; library of 100,000 vols; Dir MAXWELL L. ANDERSON; Chief Curator MATTHEW TEITELBAUM; publs *MJ* (4 a year), *Annual Report*, exhibition catalogues.

Canadian Museum of Nature: 240 McLeod St at Metcalfe, POB 3443 Stn D, Ottawa, Ont. K1P 6P4; tel. (613) 566-4700; fax (613) 364-4021; research and collections in the areas of evolution, mineralogy, botany, zoology and palaeobiology; houses National Herbarium, the Canadian Centre for Biodiversity, the Biological Survey of Canada and the Centre for Traditional Knowledge; Pres. JOANNE DICOSIMO; publ. *Global Biodiversity* (4 a year).

Collingwood Museum: POB 556, Memorial Park, St Paul St, Collingwood, Ont. L9Y 4B2; tel. (705) 445-4811; fax (705) 445-9004; e-mail cm-chin@georgian.net; f. 1904; display, programming, research, special events; Dir/Curator TRACY MARSH; publ. *On Track* (quarterly).

Dundurn Castle: York Blvd, Hamilton, Ont. L8R 3H1; tel. (905) 546-2872; fax (905) 546-2875; former home of Sir Allan MacNab,

Prime Minister of United Province of Canada 1854–56, built 1834, restored 1967; guided tours, special exhibits, period demonstrations; Curator WILLIAM NESBITT.

Jordan Historical Museum of the Twenty: 3802 Main St, Jordan, Ont. L0R 1S0; tel. (905) 562-5242; fax (905) 562-7786; f. 1953; a collection illustrating life in the Twenty Mile Creek area after 1776; Curator HELEN BOOTH.

London Regional Art and Historical Museums: 421 Ridout St N, London, Ont. N6A 5H4; tel. (519) 672-4580; f. 1940; paintings, prints, drawings, sculptures; 25,000 historical artifacts; Dir TED FRASER.

Marine Museum of Upper Canada: Exhibition Place, Toronto, Ont. M6K 3C3; tel. (416) 392-1765; fax (416) 392-1767; f. 1959; operated by the Toronto Historical Board; preserves and interprets the marine history of Toronto, Toronto Harbour and Lake Ontario; collections include 1932 steam tug *Ned Hanlan* in dry dock; Curator JOHN SUMMERS.

National Arts Centre: 53 Elgin St, Box 1534, Station B, Ottawa, Ont. K1P 5W1; tel. (613) 996-5051; fax (613) 996-9578; opened 1969; opera, theatre, studio, workshops, restaurant and reception halls; 700 performances a year; resident 46-piece orchestra; produces theatre, dance and music performances in French and English; Chair. JEAN THÉRÈSE RILEY; publs *Annual Report*, *Calendar* (monthly).

National Gallery of Canada: 380 Sussex Drive, Ottawa, Ont. K1N 9N4; tel. (613) 990-1985; fax (613) 993-4385; f. 1880; Old Masters; modern European, American and Canadian paintings and sculpture; world's foremost collection of Canadian art; prints, drawings, photographs and Inuit art; decorative arts; library of 77,000 vols; also includes Canadian Museum of Contemporary Photography; Dir PIERRE THÉBERGE.

National Museum of Science and Technology Corporation: 1867 St Laurent Blvd, Ottawa, Ont.; tel. (613) 991-3044; fax (613) 990-3654; e-mail scitech@nmstc.ca; f. 1967; shows Canada's role in science and technology through displays such as: steam locomotives, vintage cars, cycles, carriages, household appliances, computers, communications and space technology, model ships, and through experiments, demonstrations, special exhibitions and educational programmes and an evening astronomy programme; the Corporation also includes the National Aviation Museum and the Agriculture Museum; Dir Dr GENEVIEVE SAINTE-MARIE; publs *Calendar of Events* (3 a year), *Material History Review* (2 a year), *Sky News* (6 a year).

Ontario Science Centre: 770 Don Mills Rd, North York, Ont. M3C 1T3; tel. (416) 429-4100; fax (416) 696-3124; f. 1965; over 800 exhibits in all fields of science and technology; library of 12,000 vols.

Queen's University Museums: Miller Hall, Union St, Kingston, Ont. K7L 3N6; geology dept, tel. (613) 545-6767, f. 1901, Curator M. H. BADHAM; biology dept, f. 1880, Curator A. A. CROWDER; anatomy dept, f. 1854, Curator Dr M. G. JONEJA.

Royal Ontario Museum: 100 Queen's Park, Toronto, Ont. M5S 2C6; tel. (416) 586-8000; fax (416) 586-5863; e-mail info@rom.on.ca; f. 1912; worldwide art, archaeology, geology and natural history, modern Canadian life; library of 150,000 vols; Far Eastern Library 20,000 vols; Dir LINDSAY SHARP; publs *Annual Report, Life Sciences Occasional Papers, Rotunda* (quarterly), etc.

Has attached:

McLaughlin Planetarium: 100 Queen's Park, Toronto, Ont. M5S 2C6; f. 1968; Head Dr T. CLARKE.

George R. Gardiner Museum of Ceramic Art: 111 Queen's Park, Toronto, Ont. M5S 2C7; f. 1984.

Stephen Leacock Museum: Old Brewery Bay, 50 Museum Rd, Orillia, Ont.; f. 1957; summer home, correspondence, manuscripts, personal effects of Stephen Butler Leacock 1869–1944; Curator DAPHNE MAINPRIZE.

Tom Thomson Memorial Art Gallery: 840 1st Ave West, Owen Sound, Ont. N4K 4K4; tel. (519) 376-1932; fax (519) 376-3037; e-mail ttm-chin@bmts.com; f. 1967; Tom Thomson paintings, memorabilia; changing exhibitions of historic and contemporary art; Dir BRIAN MEEHAN; publ. *Newsletter* (4 a year).

Upper Canada Village: R.R. 1, Morrisburg, Ont. K0C 1X0; tel. (613) 543-3704; fax (613) 543-2847; opened 1961; living historical site; 45 restored buildings portraying a rural community *c.* 1865; archives/library of 5,000 vols; special collection of 19th-century business records from Eastern Ontario; Man. B. HUGHES.

Prince Edward Island

Confederation Centre Art Gallery and Museum: 145 Richmond St, Charlottetown, PEI C1A 1J1; tel. (902) 628-6111; fax (902) 566-4648; f. 1964; national collection of 15,000 19th- and 20th- century Canadian art: paintings, drawings, prints, sculpture and photography; Harris Collection (paintings, drawings, MSS and records of Robert Harris, 1849–1919); temporary exhibitions on historical research and the contemporary artist; Dir TERRY GRAFF; publ. *ArtsAtlantic*.

Québec

Biodôme de Montréal: 4777 ave Pierre-de-Coubertin, Montréal, Qué. H1V 1B3; tel. (514) 868-3000; fax (514) 868-3065; e-mail biodome@ville.montreal.qc.ca; f. 1992; natural science museum; Dir JEAN-PIERRE DOYON.

Canadian Centre for Architecture: 1920 rue Baile, Montréal, Québec, H3H 2S6; tel. (514) 939-7000; fax (514) 939-7020; f. 1979 as a non-profit organization, recognized as a museum in 1989; study centre and museum to research and make known the significance of architecture through study programmes, exhibitions, publications, seminars, lectures and internships; library of 165,000 vols, 20,000 master drawings and prints, 50,000 photographs, important architectural archives; Pres. and Dir PHYLLIS LAMBERT.

Canadian Museum of Civilization: 100 Laurier St, POB 3100, Station B, Hull, Qué. J8X 4H2; tel. (819) 776-7000; fax (819) 776-8300; f. 1967; archaeology, physical anthropology, ethnology, linguistics, folk culture studies, history of Canada; study collections open to qualified researchers; incl. Archaeological Survey of Canada, Canadian Centre for Folk Culture Studies, Canadian War Museum, Canadian Ethnology Service, Canadian Postal Museum, Canadian Children's Museum and other elements; library of 50,000 vols accessible to public; Pres. and CEO Dr GEORGE F. MACDONALD.

Insectarium de Montréal: 4581 rue Sherbrooke Est, Montréal, Qué. H1X 2B2; tel. (514) 872-1400; fax (514) 872-0662; f. 1990; collection of 150,000 insects; Dir GUY BÉLAIR.

McCord Museum of Canadian History, The: 690 Sherbrooke St West, Montréal, Qué. H3A 1E9; tel. (514) 398-7100; fax (514) 398-5045; f. 1921; museum of Canadian social history with collections of Canadian ethnology, paintings, drawings, prints, costumes, decorative arts, toys, documents; Notman Photographic Archives containing 700,000 glass plates and prints; Exec. Dir Dr VICTORIA DICKERSON.

Montréal Museum of Fine Arts: 1379 and 1380 Sherbrooke St West, Montréal, Qué. H3G 2T9; tel. (514) 285-1600; fax (514) 844-6042; e-mail webmaster@mbamtl.org; f. 1860; library of over 90,000 vols and, slide library; permanent collection of paintings (European and Canadian), sculptures, decorative arts and drawings; guided tours, lectures, etc.; Pres. BERNARD LAMARRE; Dir GUY COGEVAL; publs. *Collage* (4 a year), calendar (2 a year), catalogues.

Musée d'art contemporain de Montréal: 185 St Catherine St West, Montréal, Qué. H2X 3X5; tel. (514) 847-6212; fax (514) 847-6291; f. 1964; exhibits contemporary Québec and international art; organizes multimedia events, art videos, art workshops, lectures, etc.; library of 37,221 vols and exhibition catalogues, 713 periodicals, 42,913 slides, 36,514 microfiches, 483 videos, 285 audio cassettes, 11,193 document files on artists, styles, movements, etc., and complete archives of Paul-Emile Borduas; Dir-Gen. MARCEL BRISEBOIS.

Musée de l'Amérique française: 9 rue de l'Université, CP 460, Hauteville, Qué. G1R 4R7; tel. (418) 692-2843; fax (418) 692-5206; f. 1983; art and history of French North America; Dir ROLAND ARPIN.

Musée du Québec: Parc des Champs de Bataille, Québec, Qué. G1R 5H3; f. 1933; beaux-arts; Dir Dr JOHN R. PORTER.

Planétarium de Montréal: 1000 rue Saint-Jacques Ouest, Montréal, Qué. H3C 1G7; tel. (514) 872-4530; fax (514) 872-8102; f. 1966; astronomy, meteorite collection; Dir PIERRE LACOMBE.

Redpath Museum: 859 Sherbrooke St West, Montréal, Qué. H3A 2K6; tel. (514) 398-4087; fax (514) 398-3185; f. 1882; natural history, geology, mineralogy, paleontology, anthropology, herpetology, vertebrate and invertebrate zoology; Dir GRAHAM BELL.

Saskatchewan

MacKenzie Art Gallery: 3475 Albert St, Regina, Sask. S4S 6X6; tel. (306) 522-4242; fax (306) 569-8191; f. 1936; permanent collection of Canadian historical and contemporary art, 19th- and 20th-century international art, permanent collection displays and travelling exhibitions; public programmes; Resource Centre of 3,500 vols; Dir (vacant); publ. *Vista* (quarterly).

Mendel Art Gallery and Civic Conservatory (Saskatoon Gallery and Conservatory Corporation): 950 Spadina Crescent East, POB 569, Saskatoon, Sask. S7K 3L6; tel. (306) 975-7610; fax (306) 975-7670; e-mail mendel@mendel.saskatoon.sk.ca; f. 1964; Canadian and international art, exhibitions, permanent collection; library of 10,000 vols; Dir (vacant); publ. *Folio* (6 a year).

Musée Ukraina Museum: Box 1003, Saskatoon, Sask. S7K 3M4; located at: 202 Ave M South, Saskatoon, Sask. S7M 2K4; tel. (306) 244-4212; f. 1953; ethnographic collections representing the spiritual, material and folkloric culture of Ukraine; Dir EMELIA PANAMAROFF.

Prince Albert Historical Museum: C/o Prince Albert Historical Society, 10 River St East, Prince Albert, Sask. S6V 8A9; tel. (306) 764-2992; f. 1923; run by Prince Albert Historical Society; local historical exhibits, early settlement, pioneers, Indian life, etc.; archives and photographic collection available for research; Pres. F. R. SERJEANT.

Royal Saskatchewan Museum: Wascana Park, Regina, Sask.; tel. (306) 787-2815; fax (306) 787-2820; f. 1906; Earth Sciences Gallery depicts 2.5 billion years of Saskatchewan's geological history; First Nations Gallery traces 12,000 years of aboriginal history and culture; Paleo Pit interactive gallery; Megamunch, a roaring robotic Tyrannosaurus rex; Dir DAVID BARON (acting).

Saskatchewan Western Development Museum: 2935 Melville St, Saskatoon, Sask. S7J 5A6; tel. (306) 934-1400; fax (306) 934-4467; f. 1949; brs at North Battleford, Moose Jaw, Saskatoon, and Yorkton; collection associated with the settlement of the Canadian West; agricultural machinery, early transport and household items; annual summer shows; George Shepherd Library of 15,000 historical vols; Exec. Dir DAVID KLATT; publ. *Sparks off the Anvil* (8 a year).

Universities and Colleges

ACADIA UNIVERSITY

Wolfville, NS B0P 1X0

Telephone: (902) 585-2201

Founded 1838

Provincial control

Language of instruction: English

Academic year: September to April

Chancellor: A. IRVING

President and Vice-Chancellor: Dr K. K. OGILVIE

Academic Vice-President: Dr M. LEITER

Vice-President for Administration: H. D. AUSTIN

Registrar: J. CAYFORD

Librarian: L. MCQUEEN

Library: see Libraries

Number of teachers: 260 full-time, including 80 professors

Number of students: 3,500 (full-time)

DEANS

Faculty of Arts: T. REGAN

Faculty of Pure and Applied Sciences: Dr G. DABORN (acting)

Faculty of Management and Education: W. MCLEOD

Faculty of Theology: A. D. MACRAE

PROFESSORS

ADAMS, G. C., English
ADAMSON, A.
ALLEN PETERS, J., Nutrition
ASHLEY, T. R.
BARR, S. M., Geology
BAWTREE, M., English
BEDINGFIELD, E. W., Recreation and Physical Education
BISHOP, R. L., Physics
CABILIO, P., Mathematics
CAMERON, B. W., Geology
CHEN, M. Y. T., Sociology
CHIPMAN, F. H., Mathematics
COLWELL, J., Geology
CONLEY, M. W., Political Science
CONNOR, J., Economics
CONRAD, M. R., History
DABORN, G. R., Biology
DADSWELL, M., Biology
DAVIES, G., English
DAVIES, J. E., Economics
DAVIES, R. A., English
DICK, A. J., Chemistry
EBERBACH, E., Computer Science
FISHER, S. F., Music
FOSTER, J., Education
GENEST, M., Psychology
GRUND, M. S., Biology
HERMAN, T. B., Biology
HOBSON, P., Economics
JOHNSON, E. M., Nutrition
KRANE, R. V., Psychology
LATTA, B., Physics
LEITER, M. P., Psychology
LEWIS, R. C., English
LOOKER, E. D., Sociology
MCLEOD, W., Physical Education
MATTHEWS, B., History
MITCHELL, L. A., Business
MOODY, B. M., History
MOUSSA, H., Economics
MULDNER, T., Computer Science
MACLATCHY, C. S., Physics
MACRAE, A. D., Theology
NESS, G., Physical Education
NORTHEY, A. D., German
OGILVIE, K. K., Chemistry
OLIVER, L., Computer Science
O'NEILL, P. T. H., Psychology
PARATTE, H. D., French
PEACH, M. E., Chemistry
PETERS, J. A., Home Economics
PYRCZ, G. E., Political Science
RAESIDE, R. P., Geology
REGAN, T., Sociology
RIDDLE, P. H., Music
ROSCOE, J. M., Chemistry
ROSCOE, S., Chemistry
SACOUMAN, R. J., Sociology
SCHUMACHER, D., Mathematics
SMITH, P., Biology
SMYTH, D. E., English
STEWART, I., Political Science
STILES, D. A., Chemistry
TAYLOR, M. A., Mathematics
THOMPSON, R. H., English
TOEWS, D. P., Biology
TOMEK, I., Computer Science
TOWNLEY, P., Economics
TRITES, A. A., Theology
TUGWELL, M., Economics
VAN DER KLOET, S. P., Biology
VAN WAGONER, N. A., Geology
VEINOTTLE, D., Theology
VERSTRAETE, B. C., Classics
WILSON, R. S., Theology
WINTER, J., Economics
YOUNG, A. R., English
ZINCK, E. E., Chemistry

AFFILIATED COLLEGE

Acadia Divinity College: Wolfville; f. 1968; on campus; under direction of Atlantic United Baptist Convention; degrees granted by the University; Principal A. D. MACRAE.

UNIVERSITY OF ALBERTA

Edmonton, Alta T6G 2M7

Telephone: (403) 492-3113

Fax: (403) 492-7172

Founded 1906

Provincial control

Language of instruction: English (Faculté Saint-Jean: French)

Academic year: September to August

Chancellor: L. HOLE

President and Vice-Chancellor: Dr R. D. FRASER

Vice-President (Academic): D. R. OWRAM

Vice-President (Finance and Administration): G. HARRIS

Vice-President (Research and External Affairs): R. S. SMITH (acting)

Associate Vice-President and Registrar: B. J. SILZER

Associate Vice-President (Learning Support Systems) and Director of Libraries: E. INGLES

Library: see Libraries

Number of teachers: 1,600

Number of students: 25,842 full-time; 3,994 part-time

Publications: *The New Trail* (quarterly), *Folio* (2 a month), *Report of the Governors of the University of Alberta* (annually), *Calendar* (annually).

DEANS AND DIRECTORS

Faculty of Arts: P. D. CLEMENTS

Faculty of Engineering: D. T. LYNCH

Faculty of Medicine and Oral Health Sciences: D. L. J. TYRELL

Faculty of Agriculture & Forestry and Home Economics: I. N. MORRISON

Faculty of Law: L. N. KLAR

Faculty of Education: L. S. BEAUCHAMP

Faculty of Pharmacy and Pharmaceutical Science: R. E. MOSKALYK

Faculty of Science: R. E. PETER

Faculty of Graduate Studies and Research: M. R. GRAY

Faculty of Business: M. PERCY

School of Library and Information Studies: A. SCHRADER

Faculty of Physical Education and Recreation: H. A. QUINNEY

Faculty of Nursing: M. J. WOOD

Faculty of Rehabilitation Medicine: A. M. COOK

Faculté St-Jean: C. TARDIFF

School of Native Studies: J. DEMPSEY

Faculty of Extension: D. R. GARRISON

AFFILIATED COLLEGES

North American Baptist College: 11525-23 Ave, Edmonton, Alta T6J 4T3; affiliated since 1988; offers first-year courses in liberal arts; Pres. Dr P. SIEWERT.

St Joseph's College: Edmonton, Alta T6G 2J5; affiliated 1926; Roman Catholic; courses in philosophy and Christian theology; Pres G. T. SMITH.

St Stephen's College: Edmonton, Alta T6G 2J6; affiliated 1909; theological school of United Church of Canada; offers its own courses to degree level and certain courses open to students of the University; Principal C. LEVAN.

UNIVERSITY RESEARCH INSTITUTES AND CENTRES

Alberta Centre for Gerontology: Dir Dr L. LIU (acting).

Alberta Law Reform Institute: Dir Prof. PETER J. M. LOWN.

Alberta Microelectronic Centre: Pres. and CEO C. LUMB.

Applied Mathematics Institute: Dir Dr T. BRYANT MOODIE.

Canadian Centre for the Development of Instructional Computing: Dir M. W. PETRUK.

Canadian Circumpolar Institute (CCI): Dir Dr C. HICKEY.

Canadian Co-ordinating Centre for Cardiovascular Research and VIGOUR: Nat. Co-ordinator P. W. ARMSTRONG.

Canadian Institute of Ukrainian Studies: Dir Dr Z. E. KOHUT.

Centre for Advanced Study in Theoretical Psychology; Dir Dr L. P. MOS.

Centre for Constitutional Studies: Dir B. P. ELMAN.

Centre for Criminological Research: Co-ordinator Dr L. KENNEDY.

Centre for Experimental Sociology: Dir Dr W. DAVID PIERCE.

Centre for International Business Studies: Dir Dr J. CHAMBERS.

Centre for International Education and Development: Dir S. H. TOH.

Centre for Mathematics, Science and Technology Education: Dir Dr H. KASS.

Centre for Research in Applied Measurement and Evaluation: Dir W. T. ROGERS.

Centre for Research in Child Development: Dir Dr G. GISANZ.

Centre for Research for Teacher Education and Development: Dir Dr J. D. CLANDININ.

Centre for Studies in Clinical Education: Dir Dr P. Hagler
Centre for Subatomic Research: Dir Dr J. L. Pinfold.
C-FER Technologies Inc.: Pres. and CEO Dr P. R. Jamieson.
Developmental Disabilities Centre: Dir Dr R. Sobsey.
Devonian Botanic Garden: Dir Dr Dale Vitt.
Health Law Institute: Chair. Morris M. Litman.
Institute of Geophysics, Meteorology and Space Physics: Dir Dr M. E. Evans.
Institute of Pharmaco-Economics: Board Chair. D. F. Mazankowski.
International Ombudsman Institute: Dir Diane Callan.
Peter Jacyk Centre for Ukrainian Historical Research: Dir Dr F. E. Sysyn.
Population Research Laboratory: Dir J. Murphy.
Prairie Centre of Excellence for Research on Immigration and Integration: Dir S. M. Abu-Laban.
Rehabilitation Research Centre: Dr S. Warren.
Research Institute for Comparative Literature: Dir Prof. Milan V. Dimic.
Surgical-Medical Research Institute: Dir Dr Ray V. Rajotte.
Telecommunications Research Laboratories (TRLabs): President and CEO H. Glenn Rainbird.
Theoretical Physics Institute: Dir W. Rozmus.
Water Resources Centre: Dir Dr David Chanasyk.
Western Centre for Economic Research: Dir Dr Edward J. Chambers.

ATHABASCA UNIVERSITY

Box 10,000, Athabasca, Alta T9S 1A1
Telephone: (403) 675-6200
Fax: (403) 675-6145

Founded 1970
Provincial control
'Open' university providing undergraduate and masters-level courses for adult, non-residential students
Language of instruction: English
Continuous admission and registration

Chairman, Governing Council: D. Aberg
President: D. A. M. X. Abrioux
Vice-President (Academic): Alan Davis
Vice-President (Finance): A. Nutt
Registrar: Joan Fraser
Librarian: S. Schafer (acting)

Number of teachers: 81 full-time, 174 part-time
Number of students: 10,534

Publications: *Annual Report, Calendar* (annually).

DIRECTORS

Centre of Community Studies: Bruce Spencer
Centre of Computer Information Systems and Mathematics: Peter Holt
Centre of Distance Education: Bob Spencer
Centre of Economics, Industrial Relations and Organizational Studies: John Newark
Centre of Global and Social Analysis: Jeremy Mouat
Centre of Innovative Management: Stephen Murgatroyd
Centre of Information and Communication Studies: Andy Woudstra
Centre of Language and Literature: Joe Pivato
Centre of Nursing and Health Studies: Roberta Carey
Centre of Psychology: Lyle Grant
Centre of Natural and Human Science: Dietmar Kennepohl
Centre of State and Legal Studies: Andy Khan

AUGUSTANA UNIVERSITY COLLEGE

4901–46 Ave, Camrose, Alta T4V 2R3
Telephone: (403) 679-1100
Fax: (403) 679-1159

Founded 1910; independent status 1987 (frmly Camrose Lutheran College)
Private (Evangelical Lutheran Church) liberal arts college
Language of instruction: English
Academic year: September to May

President: Richard L. Husfloen
Academic Dean: David W. Dahle
Registrar: Raymond T. Blacklock
Librarian: Nancy E. Goebel

Number of teachers: 55
Number of students: 803

CHAIRPERSONS OF DIVISIONS

Biology and Chemistry: Neil C. Haave
Fine Arts: Milton R. Schlosser
History, Sociology and Political Studies: Roger I. Epp
Humanities: Paul W. Harland
Interdisciplinary Studies: Kieran M. Bonner
Modern Languages: Kim I. Fordham
Physical Education: Yvonne M. Becker
Physics and Mathematical Sciences: William W. Hackborn
Psychology, Economics and Geography: Timothy W. Parker

BISHOP'S UNIVERSITY

Lennoxville, Que. J1M 1Z7
Telephone: (819) 822-9600
Fax: (819) 822-9661

Founded 1843, constituted a university by Royal Charter 1853
Language of instruction: English
Part of provincially supported system of higher education
Academic year: September to May (two terms)

Chancellor: Alex K. Paterson
Vice-Chancellor and Principal: Janyne M. Hodder
Vice-Principal: Robert D. Cook
Vice-Principal, Administration: Jean-Luc Grégoire
Registrar and Sec.-Gen.: Ann Montgomery
Librarian: (vacant)

Number of teachers: 118 full-time
Number of students: 1,850

DEANS

Business Administration: S. Barlow
Humanities: R. Forrest
Natural Science and Mathematics: A. Dean
Social Sciences: A. Johnson
Graduate School of Education: N. Ferguson

BRANDON UNIVERSITY

Brandon, Man. R7A 6A9
Telephone: (204) 728-9520
Fax: (204) 726-4573

Founded 1899; gained full autonomy July 1967
Public control
Language of instruction: English
Academic year: September to April

Chancellor: K. Kavanagh
President and Vice-Chancellor: C. D. Anderson
Registrar: D. Bower
Librarian: R. Foley

Number of teachers: 170
Number of students: 2,800 (full- and part-time)

Publications: *Annual Report, Alumni News* (quarterly), *Canadian Journal of Native Studies, Abstracts of Native Studies, Cross Cultural Psychology Bulletin,* Calendars of several faculties.

DEANS AND DIRECTORS

Faculty of Arts: Dr R. Florida
Faculty of Science: Dr R. Smith
Faculty of Education: Dr R. Common
School of Music: Dr G. Carruthers
General Studies: G. Coates
School of Health Studies: Dr L. Ross

HEADS OF DEPARTMENT

Faculty of Arts:
- Business Administration: Prof. R. Playter
- Drama: Prof. J. Forsythe
- Economics: Prof. J. Dolecki
- English: Dr R. Kramer
- Fine Arts: Prof. C. Cutschall
- History: Dr J. Naylor
- Languages: Dr M. Finke
- Native Studies: Dr S. Corrigan
- Philosophy: Prof. P. Gosselin
- Political Science: Dr L. Liu
- Religion: Dr E. Milton
- Sociology and Anthropology: Dr W. Dehaney

Faculty of Science:
- Botany: Dr W. Paton
- Chemistry: Dr C. Belke
- Geography: Dr E. Haque
- Geology: Dr L. Quinn
- Mathematics and Computer Science: Dr J. Williams
- Physics and Astronomy: Dr R. Dong
- Psychology: Prof. D. Oleson
- Zoology: Dr J. Hare

Faculty of Education:
- Administration and Education Services: Dr A. Novak
- Education in Humanities: Dr T. MacNeill
- Education in Mathematics and Sciences: Dr G. Neufeld
- Physical Education and Recreation: Dr N. Stanley
- Psychology and Foundations of Education: Dr L. Frost

School of Music:
- General Programme: Dr A. Bower
- Applied Programme: Prof. A. Ehnes
- Music and Education: Prof. S. Pimental

UNIVERSITY OF BRITISH COLUMBIA

Vancouver, BC V6T 1Z1
Telephone: (604) 822-2211
Fax: (604) 822-5785

Founded 1908

Chancellor: W. L. Sauder
President and Vice-Chancellor: Martha C. Piper
Vice-Presidents: D. R. Birch (Academic and Provost), T. Sumner (Administration and Finance), P. W. Ufford (External Affairs), B. H. Bressler (Research), M. M. Klawe (Student and Academic Services)
Registrar: R. A. Spencer
Librarian: R. J. Patrick

Number of teachers: 1,870
Number of students: 31,331

Publications: *University Calendar* (winter and summer), *Canadian Literature, Pacific Affairs, BC Studies, The Canadian Yearbook of International Law, BC Asian Review, UBC Law Review, The Canadian Journal of Family Law.*

DEANS

Faculty of Agricultural Sciences: J. F. Richards
Faculty of Applied Science: A. Meisen
Faculty of Arts: M. P. Marchak

Faculty of Commerce and Business Administration: M. A. GOLDBERG
Faculty of Dentistry: E. H. K. YEN
Faculty of Education: N. M. SHEEHAN
Faculty of Forestry: C. S. BINKLEY
Faculty of Graduate Studies: J. R. GRACE
Faculty of Law: C. L. SMITH
Faculty of Medicine: M. J. HOLLENBERG
Faculty of Pharmaceutical Sciences: J. H. MCNEILL
Faculty of Science: B. C. MCBRIDE

DIRECTORS OF SCHOOLS

School of Architecture: S. HIRSHEN
School of Audiology and Speech Science: Prof. JUDITH R. JOHNSTON
School of Community and Regional Planning: Prof. W. E. REES
School of Family and Nutritional Sciences: Prof. MARGARET ARCUS
School of Human Kinetics: Prof. M. E. HOUSTON
School of Library, Archival and Information Studies: Prof. K. HAYCOCK
School of Music: JESSE READ
School of Nursing: Prof. KATHARYN A. MAY
School of Rehabilitation Sciences: Prof. A. BELCASTRO
School of Social Work: ELAINE STOLAR

PROFESSORS

ABBOTT, F. S., Pharmaceutical Sciences
ABBOUD, R. T., Medicine
ADAM-MOODLEY, K., Educational Studies
ADAMS, R. A., Mathematics
AFFLECK, I. K., Physics
AKLUJKAR, A. N., Asian Studies
ALBERT, D. J., Psychology
ALDEN, L., Psychology
ALDERSON, S. A., Creative Writing
ALLAN, J. A. B., Counselling Psychology
ALLDRITT, K., English
ALLEN, R. C., Economics
AMES, M. M., Anthropology
AMIT, R., Entrepreneurship and Venture Capital
AMUNDSON, N. E., Counselling Psychology
ANDERSEN, R. J., Chemistry and Oceanography
ANDERSON, D. L., Civil Engineering
ANDERSON, J. M. A., Nursing
APPLEGARTH, D. A., Paediatrics
ARCUS, M. E., Family and Nutritional Sciences
ARLIN, M. N., Educational Psychology and Special Education
ARLIN, P. K., Educational Psychology and Special Education
ARTIBISE, A. F. J., Community and Regional Planning
ASCHER, U. M., Computer Science
ASTELL, C. R., Biochemistry and Molecular Biology
ATKINS, D. R., Commerce and Business Administration
AUBKE, F., Chemistry
AULD, E. G., Physics
AUMAN, J. R., Geophysics and Astronomy
AUTOR, A. P., Pathology and Laboratory Medicine
AXELSON, J. E., Pharmaceutical Sciences
AXEN, D. A., Physics
BAIMBRIDGE, K. G., Physiology
BAIRD, P. A., Medical Genetics
BALLARD, T. M., Forest Resources Management, Soil Science
BALZARINI, D. A., Physics
BARER, M. L., Health Care and Epidemiology
BARLOW, M. T., Mathematics
BARMAN, J., Educational Studies
BARNES, T. J., Geography
BARR, S. I., Family and Nutritional Sciences
BARRETT, A. A., Classics
BARRETT, J. D., Wood Science
BASKERVILLE, G., Forest Resources Management
BEAMES, R. M., Animal Science
BEATTIE, B. L., Medicine
BELCASTRO, A., Rehabilitation Sciences
BELLWARD, G. D. B., Pharmaceutical Sciences
BENBASAT, I., Management Information Systems
BENEDET, J. L., Obstetrics and Gynaecology
BENGUEREL, A.-P., Audiology and Speech Sciences
BENJAMIN, W. E., Music
BENNETT, I., Clinical Dental Sciences
BERGER, J. D., Zoology
BERGERSEN, B., Physics
BERINBAUM, M. C., Music
BERT, J. L., Chemical Engineering
BEVAN, D. R., Anaesthesia
BHAGAVATULA, S. S. R., Pharmacology and Therapeutics
BINKLEY, C. S., Forest Resources Management
BIRCH, D. R., Educational Studies
BLACK, T. A., Soil Science
BLACKORBY, C., Economics
BLADES, M. W., Chemistry
BLAIR, R., Animal Science
BLAKE, D. E., Political Science
BLAKE, R. W., Zoology
BLOM, J., Law
BLUMAN, G. W., Mathematics
BOARDMAN, A. E., Commerce and Business Administration
BOHM, B. A., Botany
BOOTH, K. S., Computer Science
BOOTHROYD, P., Community and Regional Planning
BORGEN, W. A., Counselling Psychology
BOSHIER, R., Educational Studies
BOWEN, B. D., Chemical Engineering
BOWIE, W. R., Medicine
BOYD, D. W., Mathematics
BOYD, M. A., Clinical Dental Sciences
BOYLE, C., Law
BRADLEY, P. G., Economics
BRAGG, P. D., Biochemistry and Molecular Biology
BRANDER, J. A., International Business and Public Policy
BRANION, R. M. R., Chemical Engineering
BRAYER, G. D., Biochemistry and Molecular Biology
BREE, A. V., Chemistry
BREEN, D. H., History
BRESSLER, B. H., Anatomy
BREWER, J. H., Physics
BRIMACOMBE, J. K., Metals and Materials Engineering
BRION, C. E., Chemistry
BROCK, H. W., Zoology
BROOKS, D. E., Pathology and Chemistry
BRUMELLE, S. L., Commerce and Business Administration
BRUNETTE, D. M., Oral Biology
BUCHAN, A. M. J., Physiology
BUI, A. T., Mathematics
BUNNELL, F. L., Forest Sciences
BURES, D. J., Mathematics
BURHENNE, H. J., Radiology
BURNELL, E. E., Chemistry
BURNS, P. T., Law
BURT, H. M., Pharmaceutical Sciences
BURY, K. V., Mechanical Engineering
BUSTIN, R. M., Earth and Ocean Sciences
BUTLER, G. G., Music
BYRNE, P. M., Civil Engineering
CALISAL, S. M., Mechanical Engineering
CALNE, D. B., Medicine
CALVERT, S. E., Oceanography
CAMPANELLA, R. G., Civil Engineering
CANDIDO, E. P. M., Biochemistry and Molecular Biology
CAROLAN, J. F., Physics
CARRELL, J. B., Mathematics
CARTER, J. E., Paediatrics
CASSELMAN, W. A., Mathematics
CASWELL, J. O., Fine Arts
CAVALIER-SMITH, T., Botany
CHALMERS, F. G., Curriculum Studies
CHANDLER, M. J., Psychology
CHANG, Y., Sociology
CHASE, R. L., Geological Sciences and Oceanography
CHATMAN, S. G., Music
CHERCHAS, D. B., Mechanical Engineering
CHIARENZA, M., Hispanic and Italian Studies
CHIENG, S. T., Bio-Resource Engineering
CHONG, D. P., Chemistry
CHOW, A. W. C., Medicine
CHRISTENSEN, C., Social Work
CHURCH, M., Geography
CHURG, A. M., Pathology and Laboratory Medicine
CLARKE, G. K. C., Earth and Ocean Sciences
CLEATOR, I. G. M., Surgery
CLEMENT, D. B., Family Practice, Human Kinetics
CLOWES, R. M., Earth and Ocean Sciences
COCHRAN, L. R., Counselling Psychology
COLE, R. J., Architecture
COMISAROW, M. B., Chemistry
COOMBS, J. R., Educational Studies
COOP, J. A., Music
COOPERBERG, P., Radiology
COREN, S., Psychology
CRADDOCK, M. K., Physics
CRAGG, J. G., Economics
CRAIG, K. D., Psychology
CROWHURST, M., Language Education
CULHAM, J. A. G., Radiology
CULLEN, W. R., Chemistry
CULLIS, P. R., Biochemistry and Molecular Biology
CURAT, H., French
CURZON, F. L., Physics
CYNADER, M. S., Ophthalmology
CZAYKOWSKI, B., Russian
DANIELSON, D. R., English
DANIELSON, P., Philosophy
DAVIDSON, A. G. F., Paediatrics
DAVIES, E. M., Nursing
DAVIES, J. E., Microbiology and Immunology
DAVIS, H. C., Community and Regional Planning
DAVISON, A. J., Kinesiology
DAWES, A. A., Music
DAWSON, A. B., English
DE JONG, P., Commerce and Business Administration
DENNIS, P. P., Biochemistry and Molecular Biology
DESAI, I. D., Family and Nutritional Sciences
DE SILVA, C. W., Mechanical Engineering
DEVEREUX, M. B., Economics
DEWREEDE, R. E., Botany
DEXTER, A. S., Commerce and Business Administration
DIAMOND, J., Pharmaceutical Sciences
DIEWERT, W. E., Economics
DIMMICK, J. E., Pathology and Laboratory Medicine
DOLPHIN, D. H., Chemistry
DOMMEL, H. W., Electrical Engineering
DONALDSON, D., Oral Medical and Surgical Sciences
DONALDSON, D. J., Economics
DONALDSON, R. W., Electrical Engineering
DORCEY, A. H. J., Community and Regional Planning
DOUGLAS, D., Chemistry
DOUGLAS, M. J., Anaesthesia
DOUGLAS, R. R., Mathematics
DUKE, M. S., Asian Studies
DUMONT, G. A. M., Electrical Engineering
DUNCAN, C. P., Orthopaedics
DURBACH, E., Theatre
DUTTON, D. G., Psychology
DYBIKOWSKI, J. C., Philosophy
EATON, G. W., Horticulture
EVANS, E., Pathology and Laboratory Medicine
EAVES, A. C. E., Medicine, Pathology and Laboratory Medicine
EAVES, C. J., Medical Genetics
EISEN, A. A., Medicine
EL-KASSABY, Y. A., Forest Sciences
ELDRIDGE, J. E., Physics
ELKINS, D. J., Political Science

ELLIOT, R. M., Law
ELLIOTT, B., Sociology
ELLIS, B. E., Plant Science, Soil Science
ELLIS, R. M., Earth and Ocean Sciences
EMERMAN, J. T., Anatomy
EPSTEIN, J. B., Oral Medical and Surgical Sciences
ERICKSON, G., Curriculum Studies
ERICSON, R. V., Sociology, Law
ESWARAN, M., Economics
EVANS, E., Pathology and Laboratory Medicine, Physics
EVANS, R. G., Economics
EVANS, R. L., Mechanical Engineering
FAHLMAN, G. G., Geophysics and Astronomy
FANKHAUSER, J. L., Music
FARRELL, K., Paediatrics
FARQUHAR, K. B., Law
FEAVER, G. A., Political Science
FELDMAN, J. S., Mathematics
FELTHAM, G. A., Accounting
FERGUSON, A. C., Paediatrics
FERRIS, J. A. J., Pathology and Laboratory Medicine
FIBIGER, H. C., Psychiatry
FINE, S. H., Psychiatry
FINLEY, R. J., Surgery
FINN, W. D. L., Civil Engineering
FISHER, D., Educational Studies
FLEETHAM, J. A., Medicine
FLEMING, D. G., Chemistry
FLETCHER, W. K., Geological Sciences
FLORES, R. M., Hispanic and Italian Studies
FORBES, J. D., Commerce and Business Administration
FOSCHI, M. S., Sociology
FOSCHI, R. O., Civil Engineering
FOSTER, J. W., English
FOURNIER, A., Computer Science
FOURNIER, J. J. F., Mathematics
FRANKS, I. M., Human Kinetics
FREEMAN, D. S., Social Work
FREEMAN, H. J., Medicine
FREI, A., Mathematics
FRIEDMAN, J. M., Medical Genetics
FRIESEN, J. D., Counselling Psychology
FROESE, V., Language Education
FROHLICH, J., Pathology and Laboratory Medicine
FROST, P. J., Organizational Behaviour
FRUIN, W. M., History
FRYZUK, M. D., Chemistry
FYFE, C. A., Pathology and Laboratory Medicine, Chemistry
GANDERS, F. R., Botany
GARTSHORE, I. S., Mechanical Engineering
GASKELL, J., Educational Studies
GERRY, M. C. L., Chemistry
GHOUSSOUB, N., Mathematics
GILBERT, J. H. V., Audiology and Speech Sciences
GILLIAM, S., Pathology and Laboratory Medicine
GLASS, A. D. M., Botany
GLOBE, A. V., English
GODIN, D. V., Pharmacology and Therapeutics
GODOLPHIN, W. J., Pathology and Laboratory Medicine
GODWIN, C. I., Geological Sciences
GOELMAN, H., Language Education
GOLD, A. V., Physics
GOLDBERG, M. A., Urban Land Policy
GOLDIE, J. H., Medicine
GOMEL, V., Obstetrics and Gynaecology
GOOD, G., English
GORN, G. J., Consumer Behaviour
GORZALKA, B., Psychology
GOSLINE, J. M., Zoology
GRACE, J. R., Chemical Engineering
GRACE, S. E., English
GRAF, P., Psychology
GRANIRER, E. E., Mathematics
GRANOT, D., Management
GRANOT, F., Management Science
GRANTHAM, P. R., Family Practice
GREEN, B. R., Botany
GREEN, L. W., Health Care and Epidemiology
GREENWOOD, P. E., Mathematics
GREGORY, D. J., Geography
GREGORY, P. C., Physics
GRIFFITH, W. S., Educational Studies
GRIFFITHS, A. J. F., Botany
GRIGLIATTI, T. A., Zoology
GUILBAUT, S., Fine Arts
GUNEW, S., English
GUPPY, N., Sociology
HAERING, R. R., Physics
HAGLER, R. A., Library, Archival and Information Studies
HAKSTIAN, A. R., Psychology
HALEY, D., Forest Resources Management
HALL, J. G., Medical Genetics, Paediatrics
HALL, K. J. F., Civil Engineering
HALL, R. J., Film
HANCOCK, R. E. W., Microbiology and Immunology
HANNAM, A. G., Oral Biology
HARDWICK, D. F., Pathology and Laboratory Medicine
HARDWICK, W. G., Geography
HARDING, P. E., Classics
HARDY, W. N., Physics
HARE, R. D., Psychology
HARRIS, R. C., Geography
HARRIS, S. R., Rehabilitation Sciences
HARRISON, P. J., Botany and Oceanography
HASINOFF, M. D., Physics
HAUSSMANN, U. G., Mathematics
HAWBOLT, E. B., Metals and Materials Engineering
HAYCOCK, K., Library, Archival and Information Studies
HAYDEN, M. R., Medical Genetics
HEAD, I., Political Science and Law
HEALEY, M. C., Community and Regional Planning, Oceanography
HEAVER, T. D., Transportation
HEINKEL, R. L., Finance
HELLIWELL, J. F., Economics
HENDRICKS, K., Economics
HERBERT, C., Family Practice
HERRING, F. G., Chemistry
HERTZMAN, C., Health Care and Epidemiology
HEYWOOD, J. G., Mathematics
HICKLING, M. A., Law
HIGHTOWER, H. C., Community and Regional Planning
HILL, A., Paediatrics
HILL, P. G., Mechanical Engineering
HIRSHEN, S., Architecture
HO, S. P. S., Economics
HOCHACHKA, P. W., Zoology
HODGSON, R. G., French
HOGARTH, J., Law
HOGG, J. C., Pathology and Laboratory Medicine
HOLL, F. B., Plant Science
HOLLENBERG, M. J., Anatomy and Ophthalmology
HOLM, D. G., Zoology
HOLSTI, K. J., Political Science
HOUSTON, M. E., Human Kinetics
HO YUEN, B., Obstetrics and Gynaecology
HUDSON, J. B., Pathology and Laboratory Medicine
HUGHES, G. C., Botany
HUNDERT, E. J., History
HUTTON, S. G., Mechanical Engineering
INGRAM, D., Linguistics
INNIS, S. M., Paediatrics
IQBAL, M., Mechanical Engineering
ISAACSON, M., Civil Engineering
ITO, M. R., Electrical Engineering
JACKSON, M. A., Law
JACKSON, R. H., Political Science
JAMES, B. R., Chemistry
JASTAK, T., Oral Medical and Surgical Sciences
JOB, B. L., Political Science
JOE, H., Statistics
JOHNSON, L. M., English
JOHNSON, R. R., Physics
JOHNSTON, J. R., Audiology and Speech Sciences
JOHNSTON, R. G. C., Political Science
JOLLIFFE, P. A., Plant Science
JONES, D. R., Zoology
JONES, G., Physics
JULL, E. V., Electrical Engineering
JURILOFF, D. M., Medical Genetics
KAHN, S. E., Counselling Psychology
KALOUSEK, D., Pathology and Laboratory Medicine
KASSIS, H. E., Classics
KATZ, S., Pharmaceutical Sciences
KEHOE, J. W., Curriculum Studies
KERR, C. R., Medicine
KESHET, L., Mathematics
KESSELMAN, J. R., Economics
KIEFFER, S. W., Geological Sciences
KIEFL, R., Physics and Astronomy
KILBURN, D. G., Microbiology and Immunology
KIM, S. U., Medicine
KIMMINS, J. P., Forest Sciences
KINKADE, M. D., Linguistics
KIRKPATRICK, D. G., Computer Science
KLAWE, M. M., Computer Science
KLEIN, M. C., Family Practice
KLINKA, K., Forestry Sciences
KOTWAL, A., Economics
KOZAK, A., Forest Resources Management
KRAUS, A., Finance
KREBS, C. J., Zoology
KRELL, R., Psychiatry
KRÖLLER, E.-M., English
KRYSTAL, G., Pathology and Laboratory Medicine
KUBICEK, R. V., History
KUTNEY, J. P., Chemistry
LABRIE, E. R., English
LAM, K. Y., Mathematics
LAM, S., Medicine
LAQUIAN, A. A., Community and Regional Planning
LARY, D., History
LASKOWSKI, J. S., Mining and Mineral Process Engineering
LASZLO, C. A., Electrical Engineering
LAVKULICH, L. M., Soil Science
LAWRENCE, P. D., Electrical Engineering
LEBLOND, P. H., Oceanography
LEDSOME, J. R., Physiology
LEE, C.- Y. G., Obstetrics and Gynaecology
LEE, S.- S., Educational Psychology and Special Education
LEGZDINS, P., Chemistry
LEICHTER, J., Family and Nutritional Sciences
LENTLE, B. C., Radiology
LEUNG, C. S. K., Electrical Engineering
LEUNG, P. C. K., Obstetrics and Gynaecology
LEVI, M. D., International Finance
LEVY, J., Microbiology and Immunology
LEWIS, A. G., Oceanography and Zoology
LEY, D. F., Geography
LI, D. K., Radiology
LIDDLE, P. F., Psychiatry
LILEY, N. R., Zoology
LIM, C. J., Chemical Engineering
LINDEN, W., Psychology
LIRENMAN, D. S., Paediatrics
LIVESLEY, W. J., Psychiatry
LO, K. V., Bio-Resource Engineering
LOCKITCH, G., Pathology and Laboratory Medicine
LOEFFLER, P., Theatre
LONG, B., Counselling Psychology
LOWE, A. A., Clinical Dental Sciences
LUFT, E., Mathematics
LYSTER, D. M., Pharmaceutical Sciences
MCBRIDE, B. C., Oral Biology, Microbiology and Immunology
MCCLEAN, A. J., Law
MCCLUNG, D. M., Civil Engineering, Geography
MCCOMB, P. F., Obstetrics and Gynaecology
MACCRIMMON, K. R., Management
MACCRIMMON, M. L. T., Law
MCCUTCHEON, W. H., Physics

MACDONALD, J. L., Mathematics
MCDONALD, M., Philosophy
MACDOUGALL, D. J., Law
MCEACHERN, J.-A., French
MACENTEE, M. I., Clinical Dental Sciences
MCERLANE, K. M. J., Pharmaceutical Sciences
MACFARLANE, J. K., Surgery
MCGILLIVRAY, B. C., Medical Genetics
MACGILLIVRAY, R. T. A., Biochemistry and Molecular Biology
MACGREGOR, R., Curriculum Studies
MCGEE, T. G., Geography
MCGRAW, R. W., Orthopaedics
MCINTOSH, C. H. C., Physiology
MACINTYRE, J. M., Law
MCKENZIE, D. C., Family Practice, Human Kinetics
MACKIE, G. A., Biochemistry and Molecular Biology
MACKWORTH, A. K., Computer Science
MCLEAN, D., Dermatology
MCLEAN, J. A., Forest Sciences
MCLEAN, P. D., Psychiatry
MACLEOD, K. M., Pharmaceutical Sciences
MCMANUS, B., Pathology and Laboratory Medicine
MCMASTER, W. R., Medical Genetics
MCMILLAN, J. M., Physics
MCNEILL, J. H., Pharmacology and Toxicology
MCPHAIL, J. D., Zoology
MCWHIRTER, G., Creative Writing
MAGER, D. I., Medical Genetics
MAGIL, A. B., Pathology and Laboratory Medicine
MANCINI, G. B. J., Medicine
MARCHAK, M. P., Sociology
MARTIN, P. W., Physics
MATHIAS, R. G., Health Care and Epidemiology
MATSON, R. G., Archaeology
MAUK, A. G., Biochemistry and Molecular Biology
MAVINIC, D. S., Civil Engineering
MAY, K. A., Nursing
MAZE, J. R., Botany
MEADOWCROFT, T. R., Metals and Materials Engineering
MEASDAY, D. F., Physics
MEISEN, A., Chemical Engineering
MERER, A. J., Chemistry
MERIVALE, P., English
MEYER, J., Physics
MIDDLETON, P. J., Pathology and Laboratory Medicine
MILLER, R. C., Jr, Microbiology and Immunology
MILSOM, W. K., Zoology
MINDESS, S., Civil Engineering
MITCHELL, A., Metals and Materials Engineering
MITCHELL, K. A. R., Chemistry
MIURA, R. M., Mathematics
MIZGALA, H. F., Medicine
MOHAN, B. A., Language Education
MOLDAY, R. S., Biochemistry and Molecular Biology
MONEY, T., Chemistry
MOON, Y. S., Obstetrics and Gynaecology
MORNIN, J. E. W., Germanic Studies
MORRISON, B. J., Health Care and Epidemiology
MORRISON, M. D., Surgery
MULAR, A. L., Mining and Mineral Process Engineering
MÜLLER, N. L., Radiology
MUNRO, G. R., Economics
MURRAY, D., Medicine
MURTHA, P. A., Forest Resources Management, Soil Science
MYERS, J. H., Zoology, Plant Science
NADEL, I. B., English
NAGATANI, K., Economics
NAKAMURA, M., Commerce and Business Administration
NAMKOONG, G., Forest Sciences
NAVIN, F. P. D., Civil Engineering
NEHER, P. A., Economics
NEILL, W. E., Zoology
NELEMS, B., Surgery
NEW, W. H., English
NEWMAN, D. E., Radiology
NG, A. K., Physics
NORMAN, M. G., Pathology and Laboratory Medicine
OGRYZLO, E. A., Chemistry
OKE, T. R., Geography
OLDENBURG, D. W., Earth and Ocean Sciences
OLOMAN, C. W., Chemical Engineering
ORVIG, C. E. R., Chemistry
OSTROW, D., Medicine
OUM, T. H., Business Administration
OVALLE, W. K., Jr, Anatomy
OVERMYER, D. L., Asian Studies
OWEN, D. A., Pathology and Laboratory Medicine
OZIER, I., Physics
PACHECO, A., Hispanic and Italian Studies
PAGE, S. S. , Mathematics
PALATY, V., Anatomy
PANG, C. C. Y., Pharmacology and Therapeutics
PARÉ, P. D., Medicine
PARSONS, R. R., Physics
PASZNER, L., Wood Science
PATERSON, D. G., Economics
PATERSON, R. K., Law
PATEY, G. N., Chemistry
PATTON, T. E., Philosophy
PATY, D. W., Medicine
PAULY, D., Zoology
PAVLICH, D. J., Law
PEARSE, P. H., Forest Resources Management
PEARSON, J. A., Physiology
PEARSON, R. J., Archaeology
PEDERSEN, T. F., Oceanography
PEDERSON, R. A., Physiology
PENDAKUR, V. S., Community and Regional Planning
PENFOLD, P. S., Psychiatry
PERKINS, E. A., Mathematics
PERKS, A. M., Zoology
PERLMAN, D., Family and Nutritional Sciences
PETERSEN, K., Germanic Studies
PETKAU, A. J., Statistics
PETTY, R. E., Paediatrics
PHILLIPS, A. G., Psychology
PHILLIPS, J. E., Zoology
PIERS, E., Chemistry
PINCOCK, R. E., Chemistry
PINDER, C. C., Commerce and Business Administration
PINEL, J. P. J., Psychology
PIPPENGER, N., Computer Science
PIRIE, S., Curriculum Studies
PITCHER, T. J., Zoology
PODLECKI, A. J., Classics
POLING, G. W., Mining and Mineral Process Engineering
POLLAY, R. W., Commerce and Business Administration
POON, P. Y., Radiology
POWELL, G. E., English
PRATT, G., Geography
PRICE, C., Oral Medical and Surgical Sciences
PRIOR, J. C., Medicine
PRITCHARD, H., Pathology and Laboratory Medicine
PUE, W. W., Law
PUIL, E., Pharmacology and Therapeutics
PULFREY, D. L., Electrical Engineering
PUTERMAN, M. L., Management
QUAMME, G. A., Medicine
QUARTERMAIN, P. A., English
QUASTEL, D. M. J., Pharmacology and Therapeutics
QUAYLE, M., Architecture
QUEYRANNE, M., Commerce and Business Administration
QUICK, M. C., Civil Engineering
RABKIN, S., Medicine
RACHMAN, S. J., Psychology
RAMSEY, H., Mechanical Engineering
RANDALL, D. J., Zoology
RAOUL, V., French
RASTALL, P., Physics
RATNER, R. S., Sociology
RAY, A. J., History
REDISH, A., Economics
REES, W. E., Community and Regional Planning
REINER, N. E., Medicine
RESNICK, P., Political Science
REYNOLDS, W., Educational Psychology and Special Education
RICHARDS, J. F., Food Science
RICHER, H. B., Geophysics and Astronomy
RICOU, L. R., English
RIDDELL, W. C., Economics
RITLAND, K., Forest Sciences
ROAD, J., Medicine
ROBINSON, J. B., Geography
ROBITAILLE, D. F., Curriculum Studies
ROGERS, R. G., Music
ROLFSEN, D. P., Mathematics
ROOTMAN, J., Ophthalmology, Pathology and Laboratory Medicine
ROSE, A. M., Medical Genetics
ROSEN, L. M., Mathematics
ROSENGARTEN, H. J., English
RUBENSON, K., Educational Studies
RUDDICK, J. N. R., Wood Science
RUNECKLES, V. C., Plant Science
RURAK, D. W., Obstetrics and Gynaecology
RUSSELL, A. D., Civil Engineering
RUSSELL, J., Classics
RUSSELL, J. A., Psychology
RUSSELL, S. O., Civil Engineering
SACKS, S. L., Medicine
SADDLER, J. N., Wood Science
SALCUDEAN, M. E., Mechanical Engineering
SAMARASEKERA, I. V., Metals and Materials Engineering
SAMS, J. R., Chemistry
SANDERS, D. E., Law
SANDOR, G. G. S., Paediatrics
SANDY, G. N., Classics
SARKONAK, R., French
SAVITT, S. F., Philosophy
SCHECHTER, M. T., Health Care and Epidemiology
SCHEFFER, J. R., Chemistry
SCHEIFELE, D. W., Paediatrics
SCHELLENBERG, R. R., Medicine
SCHMIDT, J. D., Asian Studies
SCHRACK, G. F., Electrical Engineering
SCHRADER, J. W., Medicine
SCHREIER, H. E., Soil Science
SCHULZER, M., Statistics, Medicine
SCHUTZ, R. W., Human Kinetics
SCHWAB, B., Commerce and Business Administration
SCHWARZ, D. W. F., Surgery
SCHWERDTFEGER, C. F., Physics
SCUDDER, G. G. E., Zoology
SEELIG, M. Y., Community and Regional Planning
SEMENOFF, G. W., Physics
SEYMOUR, B. R., Mathematics
SHAPIRO, J. E., Language Education
SHEARER, R. A., Economics
SHEEHAN, N. M., Social and Educational Studies
SHEPPARD, A. F., Law
SHERRILL, J. M., Curriculum Studies
SHIZGAL, B., Chemistry
SIEMENS, A. H., Geography
SILVERMAN, M., Anthropology
SILVERMAN, R., Music
SIMMONS, P. A., Library, Archival and Information Studies
SIMUNIC, D. A., Accounting
SINCLAIR, A. J., Geological Sciences
SINCLAIR, A. R. E., Zoology
SINCLAIR, J. G., Pharmacology and Toxicology
SINEL, A. A., History
SJERVE, D. K., Mathematics
SKALA, J. P., Paediatrics
SKARSGARD, L. D., Physics
SLADE, M. E., Economics

SLAYMAKER, H. O., Geography
SLONECKER, C. E., Anatomy
SMITH, C. L., Law
SMITH, J. A., Pathology and Laboratory Medicine
SMITH, J. L., Geological Sciences
SMITH, J. N. M., Zoology
SMITH, M., Biochemistry and Molecular Biology
SMITH, P. L., Geological Sciences
SNIDER, R. F., Chemistry
SOUDACK, A., Electrical Engineering
SPEERT, D. P., Paediatrics
SPENCER, B., Trade Policy
SPIEGELMAN, G. B., Microbiology and Immunology
SRIVASTAVA, K. D., Electrical Engineering
STANBURY, W. T., Regulation and Competition Policy
STANICK, G., Music
STANWOOD, P. G., English
STEEVES, J. D., Zoology
STEIGER, J. H., Psychology
STEIN, H. B., Medicine
STEINBRECHER, U., Medicine
STENBERG, P. A., Germanic Studies
STEYN, D. G., Geography
STIEMER, S. F., Civil Engineering
STIVER, G. H., Medicine
STORR, A., Chemistry
STRANGWAY, D. W., Geological Sciences, and Geophysics and Astronomy
STRINGER, D., Radiology
STRONG-BOAG, V., Educational Studies
STULL, R., Geography
SUEDFELD, P., Psychology
SULLIVAN, S. D., Classics
SUTHERLAND, J. N., Educational Studies
SUTTER, M. C., Pharmacology and Therapeutics
SUZUKI, D., Zoology
TAKASHIMA, K.-I., Asian Studies
TAKEI, F., Pathology and Laboratory Medicine
TAUNTON, J. E., Family Practice, Human Kinetics
TAYLOR, F. J. R., Botany and Oceanography
TAYLOR, I. E. P., Botany
TAYLOR, P. J., Obstetrics and Gynaecology
TEES, R. C., Psychology
TEH, H. S., Microbiology and Immunology
TENNANT, P. R., Political Science
THOMPSON, D. W., Chemical Engineering
THOMPSON, J. R., Animal Science
THOMPSON, M. E., Industrial Relations
THOMPSON, R. C., Chemistry
TIEDJE, T., Electrical Engineering and Physics
TINGLE, A. J., Paediatrics and Pathology
TODD, M. E., Anatomy
TODD, R. B., Classics
TONKIN, R. S., Paediatrics
TROMANS, D., Metals and Materials Engineering
TROTTER, J., Chemistry
TSURUTA, K., Asian Studies
TULLEY, W. A., History
TURKINGTON, R. A., Botany
TURNER, C. J. G., Hispanic and Italian Studies
TURRELL, B. G., Physics
TYERS, G. F. O., Surgery
TZE, W. J., Paediatrics
UHLER, R. S., Economics
UITTO, V. V.-J., Oral Biology
ULRYCH, T. J., Earth and Ocean Sciences
UNDERHILL, A. B., Physics
UNGER, R. W., History
UNGERLEIDER, C., Social and Educational Studies
UNRUH, W. G., Physics
URRELLO, A., Hispanic and Italian Studies
VAID, Y. P., Civil Engineering
VAN BREEMEN, C., Pharmacology and Therapeutics
VAN DER KAMP, B. J., Forest Sciences
VAN KOOTEN, G. C., Forest Resources Management
VARAH, J. M., Computer Science
VAUGHAN, H., Mechanical Engineering
VERTINSKY, I. B., International Business Studies
VERTINSKY, P. A., Educational Studies
VINCENT, S., Psychiatry
VOGL, A. W., Anatomy
VOGT, E. W., Physics
WALES, T. J., Economics
WALKER, D. C., Chemistry
WALKER, G. A. H., Geophysics and Astronomy
WALKER, L. J., Psychology
WALKER, M. J. A., Pharmacology and Therapeutics
WALKER, R., Curriculum Studies
WALL, J. D., Fine Arts
WALLACE, M. D., Political Science
WALSH, J. B., Mathematics
WALTERS, C. J., Zoology
WAND, Y., Management Information Systems
WARD, L. M., Psychology
WARD, R. K., Electrical Engineering
WARD, W. P., History
WARREN, R. A. J., Microbiology and Immunology
WASSERMAN, J., English, Theatre
WATKINSON, A. P., Chemical Engineering
WEBBER, W. A., Anatomy
WEDEPOHL, L. M., Electrical Engineering
WEEKS, G., Microbiology and Immunology
WEETMAN, G. F., Forest Sciences
WEHRUNG, D. A., Commerce and Business Administration
WEILER, J. M. P., Law
WEILER, L. S., Chemistry
WEINBERG, C. B., Marketing
WEINBERG, J., Anatomy
WEIR, M. L., English
WEISS, N., Physics
WERKER, J., Psychology
WESTWICK, R., Mathematics
WESTWOOD, M. J., Counselling Psychology
WEYMARK, J. A., Economics
WHITE, B. L., Physics
WHITE, K. J., Economics
WHITTAKER, E., Anthropology
WIELAND, G. R., English
WIGGINS, J., Psychology
WILKIE, D. M., Psychology
WILLIAMS, D. LL., Physics
WILLIAMS, E. H., Classics
WILLIAMS, J. T., Commerce and Business Administration
WILLINSKY, J., Language Education
WILLMS, J. D., Educational Studies
WILSON, J. D., Educational Studies
WINDSOR-LISCOMBE, R., Fine Arts
WINKLER, E. R., Philosophy
WISENTHAL, J. L., English
WITHERS, S. G., Chemistry
WONG, D. H. W., Anaesthesia
WONG, P. K. H., Paediatrics
WONG, R., Psychology
WOOD, S., Medical Genetics
WOODHAM, R. J., Computer Science
WOODSIDE, A. B., History
WRIGHT, J. L., Pathology and Laboratory Medicine
WYNN, G. C., Geography
YELLOWLEY, I., Mechanical Engineering
YEN, E. H. K., Clinical Dental Sciences
YEUNG, M.-W., Medicine
YOUNG, R. A., Counselling Psychology
YUILLE, J. C., Psychology
ZACHER, M. W., Political Science
ZIDEK, J. V., Statistics
ZIEMBA, W. T., Management Science
ZIS, A., Psychiatry

THEOLOGICAL COLLEGES

Carey Hall: 5920 Iona Drive, Vancouver, BC V6T 1J6; tel. 224-4308; Baptist; Principal Dr B. F. STELCK.

Regent College: 5800 University Boulevard, Vancouver, BC V6T 2E4; tel. 224-3245; transdenominational; Pres. Dr W. C. WRIGHT, Jr.

St Andrew's Hall: 6040 Iona Drive, Vancouver, BC V6T 2E8; tel. (604) 822-9720; Presbyterian; Dean Rev. B. J. FRASER.

St Mark's College: 5935 Iona Drive, Vancouver, BC V6T 1J7; tel. 224-3311; Roman Catholic; Principal Rev. T. J. HANRAHAN.

Vancouver School of Theology: 6000 Iona Drive, Vancouver, BC V6T 1L4; tel. (604) 228-9031; fax (604) 228-0189; an ecumenical school of theology, incorporated 1971; continues work of the Anglican Theological College of BC and Union College of BC; provides theological education for laymen, for future clergy and for graduates in theology; Principal Rev. WILLIAM J. PHILLIPS.

BROCK UNIVERSITY

Merrittville Highway, St Catharines, Ont. L2S 3A1

Telephone: (905) 688-5550
Fax: (905) 688-2789

Founded 1964
Provincial control
Academic year: September to April
Language of instruction: English

Chancellor: R. WELCH
President and Vice-Chancellor: D. ATKINSON
Registrar: L. R. ARIANO
Vice-President Administration: T. B. VARCOE
Vice-President Academic: R. T. BOAK
Librarian: J. HOGAN

Library of 1,000,000 items
Number of teachers: 450
Number of students: 10,500

Publications: *Calendar* (annually) *Surgite* (quarterly)

DEANS

Humanities: J. SIVELL
Social Sciences: W. WEBSTER
Science and Mathematics: W. CADE
Education: (vacant)
Business: M. KUSY
Physical Education and Recreation: R. KERR

HEADS OF DEPARTMENTS

Applied Language Studies: G. H. IRONS
Biological Sciences: A. CASTLE
Business:
  Accounting and Finance: (vacant)
  Business Economics: J. KUSHNER
  Management, Marketing and Human Resources: C. SALES
Canadian Studies: J. KOUSTAS
Chemistry: J. M. MILLER
Child Studies: C. BLAIS
Classics: N. D. ROBERTSON
Computer Science: J. RADUE
Computing and Business: D. HUGHES
Earth Sciences: G. FINN
Economics: W. VELOCE
Education:
  Continuing Studies: R. CHODZINSKI
  Graduate and Undergraduate Studies: C. REYNOLDS
  Pre-service Education: L. FAST
English: A. A. SOMERVILLE
Environmental Studies:
  Environmental Economics: D. P. DUPONT
  Environmental Policy: J. MIDDLETON
  Environmental Science: F. M. MCCARTHY
Film Studies, Dramatic and Visual Arts: P. FELDMAN
French, Italian and Spanish: L. A. ROSMARIN
Geography: J. MENZIES
Germanic and Slavic Studies: D. MACRAE
Health Studies: (vacant)
History: J. A. SAINSBURY
International Studies: J. SIVELL
Labour Studies: D. G. GLENDAY
Liberal Studies: W. MATHIE
Mathematics: H. E. BELL
Music: H. LOEWEN

Philosophy: R. R. SINGH
Physical Education:
Physical Education: N. MURRAY
Athletic Services: R. M. DAVIS
Physics: F. S. RAZAVI
Politics: N. BAXTER-MOORE
Psychology: N. DECOURVILLE
Recreation and Leisure Studies: J. LARSEN
Sociology: W. WATSON
Sport Management: R. KERR
Women's Studies: M. CONNOLLY

UNIVERSITY OF CALGARY

2500 University Drive NW, Calgary, Alta T2N 1N4

Telephone: (403) 220-5110
Telex: 038-21545
Fax: (403) 282-7298

Founded in 1945 as a branch of the University of Alberta, gained full autonomy 1966

Language of instruction: English

Academic year: 1 July to 30 June (four sessions)

Chancellor: M. A. MCCAIG
President and Vice-Chancellor: TERRENCE WHITE
Vice-President (Academic) and Provost: R. B. BOND
Vice-President (Finance and Services): G. K. WINTER
Vice-President (Research): C. H. LANGFORD
Registrar: G. J. KRIVY
Director of Libraries: (vacant)

Number of teachers (full-time): 1,228 including 517 professors

Number of students: 19,714 full-time, 4,023 part-time

Publications: *The University Calendars, Annual Report, Canadian Journal of Law and Society* (all 1 a year), *Canadian and International Education* (2 a year), *Canadian Ethnic Studies, Classical Views – Echos du monde classique, Journal of Child and Youth Care, Journal of Comparative Family Studies, Journal of Educational Thought* (all 3 a year), *Calgary Alumni, Abstracts of English Studies, Arctic Journal* (Arctic Inst. of North America), *Ariel: review of international English literature, Canadian Journal of Philosophy* (all 4 a year), *International Journal of Man-Machine Studies* (monthly), *University Gazette* (weekly), Canadian Energy Research Institute publs (irregular), *The Gauntlet* (student newspaper).

DEANS

Faculty of Continuing Education: T. P. KEENAN
Faculty of Education: I. S. WINCHESTER
Faculty of Engineering: S. C. WIRASINGHE
Faculty of Environmental Design: R. J. D. PAGE
Faculty of Fine Arts: M. YACOWAR
Faculty of General Studies: M. J. MCMORDIE
Faculty of Graduate Studies: B. R. GAINES
Faculty of Humanities: H. JOLDERSHA (acting)
Faculty of Law: M. I. WYLIE
Faculty of Management: P. M. MAHER
Faculty of Medicine: D. G. GALL
Faculty of Nursing: C. ROGERS (acting)
Faculty of Physical Education: W. L. VEALE
Faculty of Science: B. J. MOORMAN
Faculty of Social Sciences: S. J. RANDALL
Faculty of Social Work: R. J. THOMLINSON

PROFESSORS

ABRA, J. C., Psychology
ADAMS, M. E., Medicine
ADDINGTON, D. E. N., Psychiatry
AFXENTIOU, P. C., Economics
AGGARWALA, B. D., Mathematics and Statistics
ARBOLEDA-FLOREZ, J. E., Psychiatry
ARCHER, C. I., History
ARCHER, K. A., Political Science
ARNATT, R. A., Art
ATKINSON, M. H., Medicine
AUER, R. N., Clinical Neurosciences and Pathology
AUSTIN, C. D., Social Work
BACK, T. G., Chemistry
BAKAL, D. A., Psychology
BANKES, N. D., Law
BARCLAY, R. M. R., Biological Sciences
BARKER, P. A., Psychiatry and Paediatrics
BARRY, D., Political Science
BASKETT, H. K., Continuing Education
BAUMBER, J. S., Medical Physiology and Office of Medical Education
BAZETT-JONES, D. P., Anatomy
BECKER, W. J., Clinical Neurosciences and Medicine
BEHIE, L. A., Chemical and Petroleum Engineering
BELENKIE, I., Medicine
BELIK, J., Paediatrics
BELL, A. G., Medicine
BELL, D. M., Music
BENEDIKTSON, H., Pathology
BENN, M. H., Chemistry
BENNETT, S., English
BERCUSON, D. J., History
BERSHAD, D. L., Art
BHARADWAJ, B. B., Surgery
BIDDLE, F. G., Paediatrics and Medical Biochemistry
BINDING, P. A., Mathematics and Statistics
BIRSS, V. I., Chemistry
BISHNOI, P. R., Chemical and Petroleum Engineering
BISZTRICZKY, T., Mathematics and Statistics
BLAND, B. H., Psychology
BOND, R. B., English
BOORMAN, P. M., Chemistry
BOS, L. P., Mathematics and Statistics
BRADLEY, J., Computer Science
BRANNIGAN, A., Sociology
BROWDER, L. W., Biological Sciences
BROWN, C. A., Law
BROWN, R. J., Geology and Geophysics
BROWNELL, A. K. W., Clinical Neurosciences and Medicine
BRUCE, C. J., Economics
BRUTON, L. T., Electrical and Computer Engineering
BSHOUTY, N. H., Computer Science
BULLOCH, A. G. M., Medical Physiology
BURGESS, K. R., Programme of Dance
BURKE, M. D., Mathematics and Statistics
BUSS, H. M., English
CAHOON, A. R., Management
CAIRNS, K. V., Faculty of Education
CAMERON, E., Art
CAMPBELL, G. W., French, Italian and Spanish
CAMPBELL, N. R. C., Medicine
CANNON, M. E., Geomatics Engineering
CAVEY, M. J., Biological Sciences
CERI, H., Biological Sciences
CHAN, W.-C., Electrical and Computer Engineering
CHANG, K.-W., Mathematics and Statistics
CHAPMAN, M. A., Geomatics Engineering
CHINNAPPA, C. C., Biological Sciences
CHIVERS, T., Chemistry
CHOKSY, L. D., Music
CHRISMAN, J. J., Management
CHUA, J. H., Management
CLARK, A. W., Pathology and Clinical Neurosciences
CLARK, P. D., Chemistry
COELHO, V. A., Music
COLIJN, A. W., Computer Science
COLLINS, D. G., Physical Education
COLLINS, J. R., Mathematics and Statistics
COOK, E.-D., Linguistics
COOK, F. A., Geology and Geophysics
COOPER, F. B., Political Science
CORENBLUM, B., Medicine
COUCH, W. E., Mathematics and Statistics
CRAMER, E. C., Music
CROMWELL, L. D., Art
CROPP, M. J., Greek, Latin and Ancient History
CRUSE, P. J. E., Surgery
CURRY, B., Pathology and Clinical Neurosciences
DAIS, E. E., Law
DAVID, N. C., Archaeology
DAVIES, J. M., Anaesthesia
DAVIES, W. K. D., Geography
DAVIS, R. C., English
DAVISON, J. S., Medical Physiology
DAY, R. L., Civil Engineering
DEACON, P. G., Art
DELONG, K. G., Music
DEWAR, M. J., Greek, Latin and Ancient History
DICKIN, J. P., General Studies
DOBSON, K. S., Psychology
DONCKERWOLCKE, R., Paediatrics and Medicine
DRAPER, D. L, Geography
DRURY, S. B., Political Science
DUCKWORTH, K., Geology and Geophysics
DUFF, H. J., Medicine
DUGAN, J. S., Drama
DUGGAN, M. A., Pathology and Obstetrics and Gynaecology
EAGLE, C. J., Anaesthesia
EDWARDS, M. V., Music
EGGERMONT, J. J., Psychology
EINSIEDEL, E. F., Communications Studies
ELFORD, R. W., Family Medicine
EMES, C. G., Physical Education
ENGLE, J. M., Music
ENNS, E. G., Mathematics and Statistics
EPSTEIN, M., Mechanical Engineering
ESLINGER, L. M., Religious Studies
FATTOUCHE, M. T., Electrical and Computer Engineering
FAUVEL, O. R., Mechanical Engineering
FEASBY, T. E., Clinical Neurosciences
FERRIS, J. R., History
FEWELL, J. E., Obstetrics and Gynaecology, Paediatrics and Medical Physiology
FICK, G. H., Community Health
FIELD, L. L., Paediatrics
FLANAGAN, T. E., Political Science
FORD, G. T., Medicine
FOREMAN, C. L., Music
FOUTS, G. T., Psychology
FRANCIS, R. D., History
FRANK, A. W., Sociology
FRANK, C. B., Surgery
FRANKLIN, S. E., Geography
FRENCH, R. J., Physiology
FRIDERES, J. S., Sociology
FRIESEN, J. W., Educational Policy and Administrative Studies
FRITZLER, M. J., Medicine and Medical Biochemistry
FUJITA, D. J., Medical Biochemistry
GABOR, P. A., Social Work
GAINES, B. R., Computer Science
GALL, D. G., Paediatrics and Medicine
GANDHI, R. S., Sociology
GEDAMU, L., Biological Sciences
GETZ, D. P., Management
GHALI, A., Civil Engineering
GHENT, E. D., Geology and Geophysics
GIBBINS, R., Political Science
GILES, W. R., Medical Physiology and Medicine
GILL, M. J., Medicine
GILLIS, A. M., Medicine
GIOVINETTO, M. B., Geography
GOLDENBERG, S., Sociology
GONZALEZ, A., Geography
GORDON, C. J., Curriculum and Instruction
GORDON, D. V., Economics
GORDON, T. M., Geology and Geophysics
GOREN, H. J., Medical Biochemistry
GORESKY, G. V., Anaesthesia and Paediatrics
GREEN, F. H. Y., Pathology
GREENBERG, S., Computer Science
GRIFFITH, B. E., Education
GRINNELL, R. M., Social Work
GU, J., Electrical Engineering
GU, P., Mechanical Engineering
GUPTA, A., Management

GUZIE, T. W., Educational Policy and Administrative Studies
HALL, J. S., Art
HANLEY, D. A., Medicine
HANNAH, R. S., Anatomy
HARASYM, P. H., Office of Medical Education
HARASYMIW, B., Political Science
HART, D. A., Microbiology and Infectious Diseases, Medicine
HARTMAN, F. T., Civil Engineering
HASLETT, J. W., Electrical and Computer Engineering
HAWES, M. R., Physical Education
HAWKES, R. B., Anatomy
HEBERT, Y. M., Curriculum and Instruction
HECKEL, W., Latin and Ancient History
HEIDEMANN, R. A., Chemical and Petroleum Engineering
HEINTZ, J. W., Philosophy
HERWIG, H. H., History
HERZOG, W., Physical Education
HEXHAM, I. R., Religious Studies
HEYMAN, R. D., Educational Policy and Administrative Studies
HIEBERT, B. A., Educational Psychology
HILLER, H. H., Sociology
HOGAN, D. B., Medicine and Clinical Neurosciences and Community Health Sciences
HOLLENBERG, M. D., Pharmacology and Therapeutics
HUBER, R. E., Biological Sciences
HUDSON, H. C., Social Work
HUGHES, M. E., Law
HULL, R. D., Medicine
HULLIGER, M., Clinical Neurosciences and Medical Physiology
HURKA, T. M., Philosophy
HUSHLAK, G. M., Art
HUTCHEON, I. E., Geology and Geophysics
HWANG, W. S., Pathology
IATROU, K., Medical Biochemistry
ISMAEL, J. S., Social Work
ISMAEL, T. Y., Political Science
JACKSON, R. C., Physical Education
JADAVJI, T., Microbiology and Infectious Diseases and Paediatrics
JAMIESON, W., Environmental Design
JARRELL, J. F., Obstetrics and Gynaecology
JAVIDAN, M., Management
JEJE, A. A., Chemical and Petroleum Engineering
JENNETT, P. A., Office of Medical Education and Community Health Sciences
JOHNSON, D. P., Mathematics and Statistics
JOHNSON, E. A., Biological Sciences
JOHNSTON, R. H., Electrical and Computer Engineering
JONES, D. C., Educational Policy and Administrative Studies
JONES, V. J., Management
JORDAN, W. S., Music
JORGENSEN, J. L., Management
JOSHI, R. C., Civil Engineering
JOY, M. M., Religious Studies
KALER, K. V. I., Electrical and Computer Engineering
KAPLAN, B. J., Paediatrics
KARIM, G. A., Mechanical Engineering
KATZENBERG, M. A., Archaeology
KAWAMURA, L. S., Religious Studies
KEAY, B. A., Chemistry
KEENAN, T. P., Continuing Education
KEITH, R. C., Political Science
KENDALL, E. J. M., Computer Science
KENTFIELD, J. A. C., Mechanical Engineering
KERR, W. A., Economics
KERTZER, J. M., English
KINSELLA, T. D., Medicine
KIRBY, M. R., Environmental Design
KLASSEN, J., Pathology and Medicine
KLINE, D. W., Psychology
KNAFLA, L. A., History
KNOLL, P. J., Law
KNOPFF, R., Political Science
KOOPMANS, H. S., Medical Physiology
KOSTYNIUK, R. P., Art
KRAUSE, F. F., Geology and Geophysics
KURTZ, S. M., Education
KWOK, S., Physics and Astronomy
KYDD, R. A., Chemistry
LACHAPELLE, G. J., Geomatics Engineering
LAFRENIÈRE, R., Surgery
LAING, W. J. H., Art
LANGFORD, C. H., Chemistry
LAWTON, D. C., Geology and Geophysics
LEAHY, D. A., Physics and Astronomy
LEBLANC, F. E., Surgery and Clinical Neurosciences
LEE, E., History
LEE, P. W. K., Microbiology and Infectious Diseases
LEE, T. G., Environmental Design
LEVIN, G. J., Music
LEVY, J. C., Law
LEWKONIA, R. M., Medicine and Office of Medical Education and Paediatrics
LI, A. K. F., Educational Psychology
LICKER, P. S., Management
LOOV, R. E., Civil Engineering
LORSCHEIDER, F. L., Medical Physiology
LOUIE, T. J., Medicine, Microbiology and Infectious Diseases
LOVE, E. J., Community Health Sciences, Obstetrics and Gynaecology
LOWRY, R. B., Paediatrics and Community Health Sciences
LUCAS, A. R., Law
LUCIER, G. E., Medical Physiology and Office of Medical Education
LUKASIEWICZ, S. A., Mechanical Engineering
LUKOWIAK, K., Medical Physiology
LUPART, L. L., Educational Psychology
LUPRI, E., Sociology
MACCANNELL, K. L., Pharmacology and Therapeutics, and Medicine
MACINTOSH, B. R., Kinesiology
MACINTOSH, J. J., Philosophy
MACVICAR, B. A., Medical Physiology
MAHER, P. M., Management
MAHONEY, K. E., Law
MALTBY, J. R., Anaesthesia
MANDIN, H., Medicine
MANSELL, R. L., Economics
MAO, X., Mechanical Engineering
MARTIN, C. B., Philosophy
MARTIN, R. H., Paediatrics
MARTIN, S. L., Law
MASH, E. J., Psychology
MATHEWS, T., Physics and Astronomy
MATTHEWS, P. L., Archaeology
MATO, D., Art
MCCALLUM, P. M., English
MCCAULEY, F. E. R., Biological Sciences
MCCONNELL, C. S., Art
MCCULLOUGH, D. T., Drama
MCDOUGALL, D., Educational Psychology and Teacher Education and Supervision
MCGHEE, J. D., Medical Biochemistry
MCGILLIS, R. F., English
MCMILLAN, D. D., Paediatrics
MCMORDIE, M. J., Environmental Design and General Studies
MCMULLAN, W. E., Management
MCRAE, R. N., Economics
MEDDINGS, J. B., Medicine
MEHROTRA, A. K., Chemical and Petroleum Engineering
MEYNELL, H. A., Religious Studies
MILONE, E. F., Physics and Astronomy
MITCHELL, I., Paediatrics
MITCHELL, L. B., Medicine
MOKKELBOST, P. B., Management
MOLLIN, R. A., Mathematics and Statistics
MOLONEY, M. M., Biological Sciences
MOORE, G. J., Medical Biochemistry
MOORE, R. G., Chemical and Petroleum Engineering
MORRALL, J. F., Civil Engineering
MORTON, F. L., Political Science
MUELLER, J. H., Educational Psychology
MUNRO, M. C., Management
MURPHREE, J. S., Physics and Astronomy
MUZIK, I., Civil Engineering
MYLES, S. T., Surgery and Clinical Neurosciences
NEU, D. E., Management
NEUFELDT, A. H., Education
NEUFELDT, R. W., Religious Studies
NEWSTED, P. R., Management
NICHOLLS, J. W., Geology and Geophysics
NICHOLSON, W. K., Mathematics and Statistics
NIGG, B. M., Physical Education
NKEMDIRIM, L. C., Geography
NORRIE, D. H., Mechanical Engineering
NOSAL, M., Mathematics and Statistics
OLSON, M. E., Microbiology and Infectious Diseases
O'REILLY, R. R., Educational Policy and Administrative Studies
OSBORN, G. D., Geology and Geophysics
OSLER, M. J., History
PAGE, R. J. D., Environmental Design
PALIWODA, S. J., Management
PARSONS, H. G., Paediatrics
PATTISON, D. R. M., Geology and Geophysics
PAUL, R., Chemistry
PINEO, G. F., Medicine
PITTMAN, Q. J., Medical Physiology
POEWE, K. O., Anthropology
POLZER, J., Art
PONAK, A. M., Management
PONTING, J. R., Sociology
POON, M.-C., Medicine and Paediatrics
PRESHAW, R. M., Surgery
PRUDEN, B. B., Chemical and Petroleum Engineering
PRUSINKIEWICZ, P., Computer Science
RABIN, H. R., Microbiology, Infectious Diseases and Medicine
RAFFERTY, N. S., Law
RAMRAJ, V. J., English
RANDALL, S. J., History
RANGAYYAN, R. M., Electrical and Computer Engineering
RAO, N. D., Electrical and Computer Engineering
RASPORICH, B. J., General Studies
RATTNER, J. B., Anatomy and Medical Biochemistry
RAUK, A., Chemistry
RAY, D. I., Political Science
READER, G. T., Mechanical Engineering
REID, D. M., Biological Sciences
REMMERS, J. E., Medicine, Medical Physiology
RENDALL, J. A., Law
REVEL, R. D., Environmental Design
REWCASTLE, N. B., Pathology and Clinical Neurosciences
REYNOLDS, J. D., Medical Physiology and Medicine
RIPPIN, A. L., Religious Studies
RITCHIE, J. R. B., Management
ROBERTS, D. A., Curriculum and Instruction
ROBERTSON, D. I., Pathology, Obstetrics and Gynaecology
ROBERTSON, S. E., Educational Psychology
ROBINSON, M. P., Arctic Institute of North America
ROGERS, T. B. H., Psychology
ROKNE, J. G., Computer Science
ROMNEY, D. M., Educational Psychology
RORSTAD, O. P., Medicine
ROSS, W. A., Environmental Design
ROTH, S. H., Pharmacology and Therapeutics, and Anaesthesia
ROTHERY, M. A., Social Work
ROWNEY, J. I. A., Management
ROWSE, J. G., Economics
RUETHER, B. A., Medicine
RUSSELL, A. P., Biological Sciences
SAINSBURY, R. S., Psychology
SAMUELS, M. T., Educational Psychology
SANDALS, L. H., Educational Psychology
SANDHAM, J. D., Medicine and Anaesthesia
SAUER, N., Mathematics and Statistics
SAUNDERS, I. B., Continuing Education
SAUVE, R. S., Paediatrics, Community Health Sciences

SCHACHAR, N. S., Surgery
SCHMIEL, R. C., Classics
SCHNELL, R. L., Educational Policy and Administrative Studies
SCHNETKAMP, P. P. M., Medical Biochemistry
SCHRYVERS, A. B., Microbiology and Infectious Diseases
SCHULTZ, G. A., Medical Biochemistry
SCHULZ, R. A., Management
SCHURCH, F. S., Medical Physiology, Medicine
SCHWARZ, K.-P., Geomatics Engineering
SCOTT, R. B., Paediatrics
SERLETIS, A., Economics
SEVERSON, D. L., Pharmacology and Therapeutics
SHAFFER, E. A., Medicine
SHAPIRO, B. L., Education
SHAW, M. L. G., Computer Science
SHAW, W. J. D., Mechanical Engineering
SHELDON, R. S., Medicine
SHRIVE, N. G., Civil Engineering
SICK, G. A., Management
SIDERIS, I. M. G., Geomatics Engineering
SILVER, E. A., Management
SILVERMAN, E., General Studies
SIMONY, P. S., Geology and Geophysics
SMITH, D. D. B., History
SMITH, D. G., Geography
SMITH, E. R., Medicine and Medical Physiology
SMITH, M. R., Electrical and Computer Engineering
SNIATYCHI, J., Mathematics and Statistics
SNYDER, F. F., Paediatrics, Medical Biochemistry
SOKOL, P. A., Microbiology and Diseases
SORENSEN, T. S., Chemistry
SPENCER, R. J., Geology and Geophysics
SREENIVASAN, S. R., Physics and Astronomy
STAINTON, M. C., Nursing
STAM, H. J., Psychology
STAUM, M. S., History
STEBBINS, R. A., Sociology
STELL, W. K., Anatomy and Surgery
STEWART, R. R., Geology and Geophysics
STOCKING, J. R., Art
STONE-BLACKBURN, S. B., English
STRATTON, S. B. C., English
STUART, G. C. E., Obstetrics and Gynaecology, Oncology
SUTHERLAND, G. R., Clinical Neurosciences
SUTHERLAND, L. R., Medicine and Community Health Sciences
SVRCEK, W. Y., Chemical and Petroleum Engineering
SWADDLE, T. W., Chemistry
TANNEY, B. L., Psychiatry
TARAS, D., General Studies
TAYLOR, A. R., Physics and Astronomy
TEMPLE, W. J., Surgery
TER KEURS, H. E. D., Medicine and Medical Physiology
TESKY, W. F., Geomatics Engineering
THOMLINSON, B. J., Social Work
THOMLISON, R. J., Social Work
THOMPSON, D. A. R., Environmental Design
TOEWS, J. A., Psychiatry
TOMM, K. M., Psychiatry
TORRENCE, R. J., Mathematics and Statistics
TRAVERS, T. H. E., History
TREBBLE, M. A., Chemical and Petroleum Engineering
TRIGGLE, C. R., Pharmacology and Therapeutics
TURNER, L. E., Electrical and Computer Engineering
TUTTY, L. M., Social Work
TYBERG, J. V., Medicine and Medical Physiology
UNGER, B. W., Computer Science
VAN DE SANDE, J. H., Medical Biochemistry
VAN HERK, A., English
VAN ROSENDAAL, G. M. A., Medicine
VARADARAJAN, K., Mathematics and Statistics
VEALE, W. L., Medical Physiology and Physical Education
VICKERS, J. N., Physical Education
VINOGRADOV, O., Mechanical Engineering
VIOLATO, C., Educational Psychology, Teacher Education and Supervision
VOGEL, H. J., Biological Sciences
VOORDOUW, G., Biological Sciences
VREDENBURG, H., Management
WAH, F. J., English
WAISMAN, D. M., Medical Biochemistry
WALBANK, M. B., Greek, Latin and Ancient History
WALKER, D. C., French, Italian and Spanish
WALL, A. J., French, Latin and Spanish
WALL, R. J., English
WALLACE, J. L., Medical Physiology
WALSH, M. P., Medical Biochemistry
WANNER, R. A., Sociology
WARDEN, W. T., International Centre
WARE, R. X., Philosophy
WARNICA, J. W., Medicine
WATERS, N. M., Geography
WEBSTER, D. R., Environmental Design
WEISS, S., Anatomy
WEST, M. L., Psychology
WESTRA, H. J., Greek, Latin and Ancient History
WHITELAW, W. A., Medicine
WIERZBA, I., Mechanical Engineering
WIESER, H., Chemistry
WILKENS, J. L., Biological Sciences
WILLIAMS, R., Psychiatry
WILMAN, E. A., Economics
WIRASINGHE, S. C., Civil Engineering
WITTEN, I. H., Computer Sciences
WONG, N. C. W., Medicine
WOODROW, P., Art
WOODROW, R. E., Mathematics and Statistics
WOODS, D. E., Microbiology and Infectious Diseases
WRIGHT, L. M., Nursing
WYSE, D. G., Medicine, Pharmacology and Therapeutics
WYVILL, B. L. M., Computer Science
YACOWAR, M., Fine Arts
YEAGER, H. L., Chemistry
YEUNG, E. C. J., Biological Sciences
YOON, J. W., Microbiology and Infectious Diseases and Paediatrics
ZACHARIAH, M., Educational Policy and Administrative Studies
ZANZOTTO, L., Civil Engineering
ZEKULIN, N. G. A., Germanic, Slavic and East Asian Studies
ZERNICKE, R. F., Surgery
ZIEGLER, T., Chemistry
ZVENGROWSKI, P. D., Mathematics and Statistics
ZWIERS, H., Medical Physiology and Medical Biochemistry

ATTACHED RESEARCH INSTITUTES

(The mailing address is that of the University itself)

Arctic Institute of North America: see under Research Institutes.

Calgary Institute for the Humanities: Dir J. KELLEY.

Centre for Gifted Education.

Environmental Research Centre: Dir G. A. YARRANTON.

Institute for Space Research.

Institute for Transportation Studies: Chair. N. M. WATERS.

UNIVERSITY COLLEGE OF CAPE BRETON

POB 5300, Sydney, NS B1P 6L2

Telephone: (902) 563-1330
Fax: (902) 563-1371

Founded 1951
State control
Language of instruction: English
Academic year: September to April

Chancellor: JOHN MCLENNAN
President and Vice-Chancellor: Dr JACQUELYN SCOTT
Executive Vice-President: RAYMOND IVANY
Controller: GORDON WALKER
Registrar: GRAHAM SHEPPARD
Librarian: PENELOPE MARSHALL

Library of 331,000 vols, 800 periodicals
Number of teachers: 172 full-time, 66 part-time
Number of students: 3,068 full-time, 529 part-time

Publication: *Express* (every 2 weeks).

DEANS

School of Arts and Letters: THOMAS RENDALL
School of Business: STEPHEN KAVANAGH
School of Community Studies: J. ARTHUR TUCKER
School of Science and Technology: STEPHEN MANLEY
Extension and Community Affairs: JANE LEWIS (acting)

CHAIRS OF DEPARTMENTS

Languages and Letters: HAROLD BARRATT
History and Fine Art: MARY K. MACLEOD
Philosophy and Religious Studies: RODERICK NICHOLLS
Financial and Information Management: ALEXIS MANLEY
Organizational Management: EDWARD GRIMM
Specialist Business Studies: ANNE MACDOUGALL
Communication: CAROL CORBIN
Culture, Heritage and Leisure Studies: TERRY MACLEAN
Politics, Government and Public Administration: BRIAN HOWE
Problem-Centred Studies: NICOLE CLAENER
Social Science and Practice: ROBERT CAMPBELL
Engineering: HUBERT CHIASSON
Physical and Applied Sciences: WILLIAM WISEMAN
Behavioural and Life Sciences: WILLIAM CLEMENS
Trades: WINSTON INGRAHAM

ATTACHED RESEARCH INSTITUTES

(The mailing address is that of the University College)

Bras d'Or Institute: Sydney, NS; f. 1972 to stimulate research, development and enquiry relevant to Cape Breton Island, particularly the Bras d'Or Lakes.

Tompkins Institute for Human Values and Technology: Sydney, NS; f. 1974; investigates the impact of technological change on Cape Breton society; Dir Dr GREGORY MACLEOD.

Beaton Institute of Cape Breton Studies: Sydney, NS; repository of Cape Breton social, economic, political and cultural history; Dir Dr ROBERT MORGAN.

CARLETON UNIVERSITY

1125 Colonel By Drive, Ottawa, Ont. K1S 5B6

Telephone: (613) 520-2600
Telex: 053-4232
Fax: (613) 520-3847

Founded 1942
Provincial control
Language of instruction: English
Academic year: September to May

Chancellor: ARTHUR KROEGER
President and Vice-Chancellor: Dr RICHARD VAN LOON
Vice-President (Academic): Dr STUART ADAM
Vice-President (Finance and Administration): DUNCAN WATT

Vice-President (Research and External): JOHN APSIMON
Assistant Vice-President (Enrolment Management): SUSAN GOTTHEIL
Librarian: MARTIN FOSS

Library: *see* Libraries
Number of full-time teachers: 684
Number of students: 17,541

Publications: *Calendars* (Undergraduate, Graduate, Summer School, Extension), *The President's Report, The University Report, Research and Studies, The Charlatan* (weekly), *This Week at Carleton* (weekly).

DEANS

Faculty of Arts and Social Science: WILLIAM JONES
Faculty of Public Affairs and Management: ALLAN MASLOVE
Faculty of Science: PETER WATSON
Faculty of Engineering: MALCOLM BIBBY
Faculty of Graduate Studies and Research: ROGER BLOCKLEY

CHAIRS AND DIRECTORS

Faculty of Arts and Social Science:
- Art History: R. MESLEY
- Canadian Studies: J. RAMISCH
- Centre for Applied Language Studies: I. PRINGLE
- English Language and Literature: R. LOVEJOY
- French: D. SMITH
- Geography: M. SMITH
- History: G. GOODWIN
- Humanities: P. EMBERLEY
- Interdisciplinary Studies: J. A. BROOK
- Philosophy: J. LEYDEN
- Psychology: K. MATHESON (acting)
- Sociology and Anthropology: J. CHEVALIER
- Studies in Art and Culture: B. GILLINGHAM (acting)
- Women's Studies: KATHERINE ARNUP

Faculty of Public Affairs and Management:
- Business: V. KUMAR
- Central/East European and Russian-area Studies: J. DEBARDELEBEN
- Economics: D. MCFETRIDGE
- International Affairs: M. A. MOLOT
- Journalism and Communication: C. DORNAN
- Law: T. B. DAWSON
- Political Economy: W. CLEMENT
- Political Science: G. WILLIAMS
- Public Administration: F. ABELE
- Social Work: A. MOSCOVITCH

Faculty of Science:
- Biochemistry: J. SINCLAIR
- Biology: I. LAMBERT
- Chemistry: G. BUCHANAN
- Computer Science: E. KRANAKIS
- Earth Sciences R. TAYLOR
- Mathematics and Statistics: K. WILLIAMS
- Neuroscience: J. KELLY
- Physics: J. C. ARMITAGE

Faculty of Engineering:
- Architecture: B. GIANNI
- Civil and Environmental Engineering: J. L. HUMAR
- Electronics: J. S. WIGHT
- Industrial Design: M. DE LEEUW
- Mechanical and Aerospace Engineering: R. BELL
- Systems and Computer Engineering: R. GOUBRAN

CONCORDIA UNIVERSITY

1455 de Maisonneuve Blvd West, Montréal, Qué. H3G 1M8 (Sir George Williams Campus)
7141 Sherbrooke St West, Montréal, Qué. H4B 1R6 (Loyola Campus)
Telephone: (514) 848-2424
Fax: (514) 848-3494

Founded 1974 by merger of Sir George Williams University (established 1948) and Loyola College (incorporated 1899)
Provincial control
Language of instruction: English
Academic year: May to April

Chancellor: E. MOLSON
Rector and Vice-Chancellor: Prof. FREDERICK H. LOWEY
Provost and Vice-Rector, Research: J. LIGHTSTONE
Vice-Rector, Institutional Relations: M. DANIS
Vice-Rector, Services: C. EMOND
Secretary-General: B. GAUDET
Registrar: L. PRENDERGAST
Director of Libraries: K. R. BONIN

Library: see Libraries
Number of teachers: 822 full-time, 1,068 part-time
Number of students: 24,353

Publications: *The Thursday Report, Annual Report, Concordia University Magazine.*

DEANS

Faculty of Arts and Science: M. SINGER
Faculty of Commerce and Administration: M. ANVARI
Faculty of Engineering and Computer Science: N. ESMAIL
Faculty of Fine Arts: C. JACKSON
School of Graduate Studies and Research: C. BÉDARD

HEADS OF DEPARTMENTS

Faculty of Arts and Science:
- Applied Social Science: M. TAYLOR
- Biology: R. ROY
- Chemistry and Biochemistry: J. A. CAPOBIANCO
- Classics, Modern Languages and Linguistics: A. TEFFETELLER
- Communication Studies: M. ALLOR
- Economics: I. IRVINE
- Education: R. SCHMID
- English: G. SHEPS
- Exercise Science: B. KILGOUR
- French Studies: L. LEQUIN
- Geography: P. THORNTON
- Geology: D. FROST
- History: M. SINGER
- Journalism: E. RAUDSEPP
- Leisure Studies: D. DICKS
- Library Studies: M. GIGUÈRE
- Mathematics and Statistics: J. HILLEL
- Philosophy: M. CLARKE
- Physics: D. CHEEKE
- Political Science: H. HABIB
- Psychology: W. BUKOWSKI
- Religion: M. OPPENHEIM
- Sociology and Anthropology: D. HOWES
- Teaching of English as a Second Language: P. ACHESON
- Theological Studies: P. BRIGHT

Faculty of Commerce and Administration:
- Accountancy: M. IBRAHIM
- Decision Sciences and Management Information Systems: J. ETEZADI
- Finance: A. BRODT
- Management: R. MOLZ
- Marketing: Z. GIDENGIL

Faculty of Engineering and Computer Science:
- Building Studies: P. P. FAZIO
- Civil Engineering: S. RIZKALLA
- Computer Science: C. LAM
- Electrical and Computer Engineering: J. C. GIGUÈRE
- Mechanical Engineering: V. HOA

Faculty of Fine Arts:
- Art Education: A. FAIRCHILD
- Art History: C. MACKENZIE
- Art Therapy: L. PETERSON
- Cinema: P. RIST
- Contemporary Dance: S. PANET-RAYMOND
- Design Art: G. GARVEY
- Interdisciplinary Studies: N. WAGNER
- Music: M. CORWIN
- Studio Arts: P. COUSINEAU
- Studio Art (Graduate Programme): A. DUTKEWYCH
- Theatre: E. MONGERSON

HEADS OF UNITS WITHIN FACULTY OF ARTS AND SCIENCE

Interdisciplinary Studies: M. SANTATERESA (adviser)
Liberal Arts College: E. FIDLER
Lonergan University College: W. P. BYERS
School of Community and Public Affairs: M. MENDELL
Science and Human Affairs: S. SHEETS-PYENSON
Science College: G. SZAMOSI
Simone de Beauvoir Institute and Women's Studies: C. MAILLÉ
Urban Studies: J. ZACHARIAS

DIRECTORS

Applied Psychology Centre: D. STACK
Canadian Picosecond Laser Flash Photolysis Centre: N. SERPONE
Centre for Building Studies: P. P. FAZIO
Centre for Community and Ethnic Studies: E. GAVAKI
Centre for Continuing Education: R. J. DIUBALDO
Centre for Human Relations and Community Studies: K. DALFEN
Centre for Industrial Control: R. M. H. CHENG
Centre for Research in Human Development: D. GOLD
Centre for Signal Processing and Communications: T. LE-NGOC
Centre for Studies in Behavioural Neurobiology: J. STEWART
Centre for the Study of Classroom Processes: P. ABRAMI
Concordia Centre for Broadcasting Studies: H. FINK
Concordia Centre for Composites: S. V. HOA
Concordia Centre for Pattern Recognition and Machine Intelligence: C. Y. SUEN
Concordia Centre for Small Business and Entrepreneurial Studies: A. IBRAHIM
Concordia Computer-Aided Vehicle Engineering: S. RAKHEJA
Concordia Pharmaceutical Management Centre: K. L. MCGOWN
Conservatory of Cinematographic Art: S. LOSIQUE
Learning Development: R. A. SMITH
Montreal Institute for Genocide Studies: K. JONASSOHN
Off-Campus and Distance Learning: R. J. DIUBALDO
Science Industrial Research Unit: R. PATTERSON
Treasury Management Centre: M. ANVARI

(In conjunction with l'Université du Québec à Montréal)

Interuniversity Centre for Religious Studies: G. MENARD

(In conjunction with Laval and McGill Universities)

Interuniversity Centre for Algebraic Computation: H. KISILEVSKY

DALHOUSIE UNIVERSITY

Halifax, NS B3H 4H6
Telephone: (902) 494-2450
Fax: (902) 494-1630
E-mail: registrar@dal.ca

Founded 1818; amalgamated with Technical University of Nova Scotia 1997

Private control
Language of instruction: English
Academic year: September to August

Chancellor: Sir GRAHAM DAY
President and Vice-Chancellor: THOMAS D. TRAVES
Vice-Presidents: S. SCULLY (Academic and Research), B. G. MASON (Finance and Administration), E. A. MCKEE (Student Services), D. GODSOE (Development and Alumni Affairs), R. FOURNIER (Associate Vice-President Research and International Relations)
Registrar: G. E. CURRI
Librarian: W. MAES

Library: see Libraries
Number of teachers: 891 full- and part-time
Number of students: 12,369 full- and part-time

DEANS

Faculty of Arts and Social Sciences: V. THIESSEN (acting)
Faculty of Science: P. J. C. RYALL (acting)
Faculty of Law: D. RUSSELL
Faculty of Medicine: J. RUEDY
Faculty of Dentistry: W. A. MACINNIS
Faculty of Graduate Studies: P. J. RICKETTS
Faculty of Health Professions: L. MCINTYRE
Faculty of Management: P. ROSSON
Faculty of Architecture: T. EMODI (acting)
Faculty of Engineering: A. BELL
Faculty of Computer Science: J. SLONIM

PROFESSORS

Faculty of Arts and Social Sciences:

ANDREWS, A. B., Theatre
APOSTLE, R., Sociology and Social Anthropology
ATHERTON, J. P., Classics (King's) (Chair)
AUCOIN, P. C., Political Science
BAKVIS, H., Political Science
BARKOW, J. H., Sociology and Social Anthropology
BAXTER, J., English (Chair)
BEDNARSKI, H. E., French
BINKLEY, M., Sociology and Social Anthropology
BISHOP, M., French
BOARDMAN, R., Political Science
BROWN, J. E., French
BURNS, S., Philosophy
CAMERON, D. M., Political Science (Chair)
CAMPBELL, R. M., Philosophy (Chair)
CLAIRMONT, D. H., Sociology and Social Anthropology
CROSS, M. S., History
CROWLEY, J. E., History
CURRAN, J., German (acting Chair)
DE MEO, P., French (Chair)
FARRELL, D., Music
FAULKNER, C. T., Comparative Religion
FREIDRICH, R., Classics
FURROW, M. M., English
GAEDE, F. W., German
GESNER, B. E., French
GORDON, W. T., French
HANKEY, W., Classics (King's)
HANLON, G., History
HUEBERT, R. M., English
JIMENES, M., Spanish (Chair)
KEMP, W. H., Music (Chair) (King's)
KIRK, J. M., Spanish
MACFARLANE, S. N., Political Science
MARTIN, R., Philosophy (Chair)
MIDDLEMISS, D., Political Science
MONK, P., English
MORGAN, J. G., Sociology and Anthropology (Chair)
O'BRIEN, History (Chair)
OORE, I., French
PARPART, J., History and International Development Studies
PEREIRA, N. G. O., History and Russian (Chair, Russian)
PERINA, P., Theatre
RAVINDRA, R., Comparative Religion (Chair)
RUIZ SALVADOR, A., Spanish
RUNTE, H. R., French
SCHOTCH, P., Philosophy
SCHROEDER, D., Music
SCHWARZ, H. G., German
SHAW, T. M., Political Science
SHERWIN, S., Philosophy
STAIRS, D. W., Political Science
STARNES, C. J., Classics (King's)
STOKES, L. D., History
TETREAULT, R., English
THIESSEN, V., Sociology and Social Anthropology
TRAVES, T., History
WAINWRIGHT, J. A., English and Canadian Studies
WATERSON, K., French
WINHAM, G. R., Political Science
WOOLF, D., History

Faculty of Science:

ARNOLD D. R., Chemistry
AUE, W. A., Chemistry
BEAUMONT, C., Oceanography
BLACKFORD, B. L., Physics
BOWEN, A. J., Oceanography (Chair)
BOYD, C. M., Oceanography
BOYD, R. J., Chemistry (Chair)
BRADFIELD, F. M., Economics
BROWN, R. E., Psychology (Chair)
BROWN, R. G., Biology
BURFORD, N., Chemistry
CALKIN, M., Physics
CAMERON, T. S., Chemistry
CHATT, A., Chemistry
CHYLEK, P., Oceanography and Physics
CLARKE, D. B., Earth Sciences
CLEMENTS, J., Mathematics, Statistics and Computing Science
COLEY, A., Mathematics, Statistics and Computer Science
CONNOLLY, J. F., Psychology
COXON, J. A., Chemistry
CROLL, R., Psychology
CULLEN, J., Oceanography
DAHN, J. R., Chemistry and Physics
DASGUPTA, S., Economics
DUNHAM, P. J., Psychology
DUNLAP, R., Physics
FENTRESS, C. J., Psychology
FIELD, C. A., Mathematics, Statistics and Computing Science
FILLMORE, P. A., Mathematics, Statistics and Computing Science
FORREST, T. P., Chemistry
FOURNIER, R. O., Oceanography
FREEDMAN, W., Biology and Resource and Environment Studies
GABOR, G., Mathematics, Statistics and Computing Science
GELDART, D. J. W., Physics
GIBLING, M. R., Earth Sciences
GRANT, J., Oceanography
GRINDLEY, B., Chemistry
GROSSERT, J. S., Chemistry
GRUNENFELDER, L., Mathematics, Statistics and Computing Science
GUPTA, R. P., Mathematics, Statistics and Computing Science (Chair)
HALL, B. K., Biology
HALL, J. M., Earth Sciences
HAMILTON, D. C., Mathematics, Statistics and Computing Science
HAY, A., Oceanography
JAMIESON, R. A., Earth Sciences
JERICHO, M. H., Physics
KAMRA, O. P., Biology
KEAST, P., Mathematics, Statistics and Computing Science
KIANG, D. B. I., Physics (Chair)
KIMMINS, W. C., Biology (Dean)
KLEIN, E., Economics
KLEIN, R. M., Psychology
KREUZER, H. J., Physics
KUTCHER, S., Psychology
KWAK, J. C., Chemistry
LANE, P. A., Biology
LANGSTROTH, G. F. O., Physics
LEE, R., Biology
LESSER, B., Economics (Chair)
LEWIS, M., Oceanography
LOLORDO, V. M., Psychology
LOUDEN, K. E., Oceanography
LYONS, R., Psychology
MACKINNON, J. C., Engineering
MACRAE, T., Biology
MCALLISTER, R. I., Economics
MCGRATH, P. J., Psychology
MARFELS, C. T., Economics
MEINERTZHAGEN, I. A., Psychology
MILLS, E. L., Oceanography
MITCHELL, D. E., Psychology
MOORE, C. L., Psychology (Chair)
MOORE, R. M., Oceanography
MYERS, R. A., Biology
NOWAKOWSKI, R., Mathematics, Statistics and Computing Science
NUGENT, S. T., Engineering
O'DOR R. K., Biology
OSBERG, L. S., Economics
PACEY, P. D., Chemistry
PARÉ, R., Mathematics, Statistics & Computing Science
PATON, B. E., Physics
PATRIQUIN, D. G., Biology
PHILLIPS, D., Psychology
PHIPPS, S. A., Economics
PINCOCK, J. A., Chemistry
RADJAVI, H., Mathematics, Statistics and Computing Science
RAMALEY, L., Chemistry
RAO, U. L. G., Economics
REYNOLDS, P. H., Earth Sciences and Physics
ROBERTSON, H., Psychology
ROBINSON, P. T., Earth Sciences
RUDDICK, B., Oceanography
RUSAK, B., Psychology
RYALL, P., Earth Sciences (Chair)
SCHEIBLING, R., Biology
SCOTT, D., Earth Sciences
SEMBA, K., Psychology
SHAW, S., Psychology
SIMPSON, A. M., Physics (Chair)
STEPHENS, R. W., Chemistry
STEWART, P. N., Mathematics, Statistics and Computing Science
STROINK, G., Physics
SUTHERLAND, W. R., Mathematics, Statistics and Computing Science
TAN, K. K., Mathematics, Statistics and Computing Science
THOMPSON, A. C., Mathematics, Statistics and Computing Science
WASYLISHEN, R. E., Chemistry
WHITE, M. A., Chemistry and Physics
WHITEHEAD, H., Biology
WILLISON, J. H. M., Biology (Chair)
WOOD, R. J., Mathematics, Statistics and Computing Science
WRIGH, J. M., Biology
YOON, M., Psychology
ZENTILLI, M., Earth Sciences
ZOUROS, E., Biology

Faculty of Law:

ARCHIBALD, B.
BLACK, V.
CHRISTIE, I.
DEVLIN, R.
GIRARD, P. V.
KAISER, A.
KINDRED, H. M.
MACKAY, A. W.
O'BRIEN, H. L.
THOMAS, P.
THOMPSON, D. A. R.
THORNHILL, E. M. A.
TRAKMAN, L. E.
VANDERZWAGG, D.
WILDSMITH, B. H.
WOODMAN, F. L.

Faculty of Medicine:

ALLEN, A., Paediatrics
ANDERSON, R., Microbiology and Immunology
ARMOUR, J. A., Physiology and Biophysics
ATTIA, E., Otolaryngology (Head)
AWAD, S. A., Urology (Head)
BASKETT, T., Obstetrics and Gynaecology
BELITSKY, P., Urology
BITTER-SUERMANN, H., Surgery
BORTOLUSSI, R., Paediatrics
BRADLEY, B. W. D., Medicine
BRECKENRIDGE, W. C., Biochemistry (Head)
BROWN, M., Community Health and Epidemiology
BUTT, J. C., Pathology
CAMERON, I., Family Medicine
CAMFIELD, C., Paediatrics (acting Head)
CAMFIELD, P. R., Paediatrics
CARR, R. I., Medicine
CHANDLER, B. M., Medicine
CHESLEY, A. E., Urology
COOK, H. W., Paediatrics
COONAN, T., Anaesthesia (Head)
CROCKER, J. F. S., Paediatrics
CROLL, R. P., Physiology and Biophysics
CURRIE, R. W., Anatomy and Neurobiology
DICKSON, D. H., Anatomy and Neurobiology
DOANE, B. K., Psychiatry
DOLPHIN, P. J., Biochemistry
DOOLITTLE, W. F., Biochemistry
DOWNIE, J. W., Pharmacology
FERNANDEZ, L. A. V., Medicine
FERRIER, G. R., Pharmacology
FINE, A., Physiology and Biophysics
FINLEY, J. P., Paediatrics
FOX, R. A., Medicine
FRASER, D. B., Radiology (Head)
FRENCH, A. S., Physiology and Biophysics (Head)
GARDNER, M. J., Medicine
GASS, D. A., Family Medicine
GRANTMYRE, E. B., Diagnostic Radiology
GRAY, J. D., Medicine and Pharmacology
GRAY, M. W., Biochemistry
GUERNSEY, D. L., Pathology, Physiology and Biophysics
HALPERIN, S., Paediatrics
HANDA, S. P., Medicine
HANLY, J. G., Medicine
HELLEINER, C. W., Biochemistry
HIRSCH, D., Medicine
HOFFMAN, P., Microbiology and Immunology
HOLNESS, R. O., Surgery
HOPE, C. E., Anaesthesia
HOPKINS, D. A., Anatomy and Neurobiology (Head)
HORACEK, B. M., Physiology and Biophysics
HORACKOVA, M., Physiology and Biophysics
HUNDMAN, J. C., Surgery
ISSERKUTZ, T. B., Paediatrics
JAMESON, C. G.
JANIGAN, D., Oral and Maxillofacial Surgery
JOHNSTON, G. C., Microbiology and Immunology (Head)
JOHNSTONE, D. E., Medicine
KENNY, N. P., Paediatrics
KHANNA, V., Medicine
KIRBY, R. L., Medicine
KLASSEN, G. A., Physiology, Biophysics and Medicine
KUTCHER, S., Psychiatry (Head)
LAIDLAW, T., Division of Medical Education
LANGLEY, G. R., Medicine
LAZIER, C. B., Biochemistry
LEBLANC, R. P., Ophthalmology (Head)
LEE, S. H., Microbiology and Immunology
LEE, T., Microbiology and Immunology
LEIGHTON, A. H., Community Health and Epidemiology
LISTON, R. M., Obstetrics and Gynaecology
LUTHER, E. R., Obstetrics and Gynaecology
MACDONALD, A. S., Surgery
MCDONALD, T. F., Physiology and Biophysics
MCGRATH, P. J., Paediatrics and Psychiatry
MACLACHLAN, R., Family Medicine (Head)
MACLEAN, D., Community Health and Epidemiology (Head)
MACLEOD, A. J., Medicine
MACSWEEN, J. M., Medicine
MAHONY, D. E., Microbiology and Immunology
MALATJALIAN, D. A., Pathology
MANN, K. V., Division of Medical Education
MARRIE, T. J. J., Medicine
MAUDSLEY, R., Division of Medical Education
MEINERTZHAGEN, I., Microbiology and Immunology
MOGER, W. H., Physiology and Biophysics
MOSS, M. A., Pathology (Head)
MUNRO, A., Psychiatry
MURPHY, D. A., Surgery
MURPHY, J., Psychiatry
MURRAY, T. J., Medicine
NEUMANN, P. E., Anatomy and Neurobiology
NORMAN, R., Urology
NOVOTNY, G. M., Otolaryngology
OULTON, M. R., Obstetrics/Gynaecology
PALMER, F. B. St. C., Biochemistry
PARKHILL, W. S., Surgery
PEDDLE, L. J., Obstetrics and Gynaecology (Head)
PELZER, D., Physiology and Biophysics
PHILLIPS, D., Psychology and Otolaryngology
POWELL, C., Medicine (acting Head)
PURDEY, R. A., Medicine
RAMSEY, M., Ophthalmology
RASMUSSON, D., Physiology and Biophysics
RENTON, K. W., Pharmacology
RITTMASTER, R., Medicine
ROBERTSON, H. A., Pharmacology (Head)
ROWDEN, G., Pathology
ROZEE, K., Microbiology and Immunology
RUEDY, J. (Dean)
RUSACK, B., Psychiatry
RUSSEL, D. W., Biochemistry
RUTHERFORD, J., Anatomy and Neurobiology
SALISBURY, S., Medicine
SANGALANG, V. E., Pathology
SAWYNOK, J., Pharmacology
SCHLECH, W., Medicine
SEMBA, K., Anatomy and Neurobiology
SINGER, R. A., Biochemistry
STANISH, W. D.
STEWART, M. J., Community Health and Epidemiology
STEWART, R. D., Anaesthesia
STOLTZ, D. B., Microbiology and Immunology
STONE, R. M., Surgery (Head)
STUTTARD, C., Microbiology and Immunology
TONKS, R. S., Medicine
VAN VELZEN, Pathology
VOHRA, M. D., Pharmacology
WALLACE, C. J. A., Biochemistry
WASSERSUG, R. J., Anatomy and Neurobiology
WHITE, F., Community Health and Epidemiology
WHITE, T. D., Pharmacology
WILKINSON, M., Physiology, Biophysics, Obstetrics and Gynaecology
WILLIAMS, C. N., Medicine
WOLF, H. K., Physiology and Biophysics
WRIGHT, J. R., Pathology
WRITER, W. D. R., Anaesthesia
WRIXON, W., Obstetrics and Gynaecology
YABSLEY, R. H., Surgery
YORK, S., Medicine
ZAYID, I., Pathology

Faculty of Dentistry:

BRAYTON, S. M.
BUTT, School of Dental Hygiene (Director)
CHAYTOR, D., Dental Clinical Sciences
COHEN, M., Oral and Maxillofacial Science
HARSONYI, B. B.
ISMAIL, A., Dental Clinical Sciences (Chair)
JONES, D. W., Applied Oral Sciences (Chair)
LONEY, R.
LOVELY, F., Oral and Maxillofacial Science
MACDONALD, K., Director of Continuing Education
PRECIOUS, D. S., Oral Maxillofacial Science (Chair)
SUTOW, E. J., Applied Oral Sciences
SYKORA, O. P.

Faculty of Health Professions:

College of Pharmacy:

CHANDLER, R. F. (Director)
SKETRIS, I.
YEUNG, P. K. F., Pharmacy
YUNG, D. K.

School of Recreation, Physical and Health Education:

HOLT, L. E.
KEDDY, B.
LYONS, R. F.
MCKRIDES, L.
SINGLETON, J.
YOUNG, A. J.

Maritime School of Social Work:

CARLSON, R. W.
DROVER, G.
WIEN, F. C.

School of Nursing:

KEDDY, B. A.
RITCHIE, J. A.

School of Occupational Therapy:

O'SHEA, B. J.
TOWNSEND, E. (Director)

School of Physiotherapy:

EGAN, D. A.
MAKRIDES, L. (Director)
TURNBULL, G. I.
WALKER, J. M.

School of Human Communication Disorders:

GREEN, W. R.
YANG, E.

School of Health Services Administration:

COHEN, M. M., Jr
NESTMAN, L.

Faculty of Management:

ROSSON, P. J. (Dean)

School of Business Administration:

BROOKS, M. R.
FOOLADI, I.
KLAPSTEIN, R. E. (Director)
MACLEAN, L. C.
MCNIVEN, J. D.
MEALISA, L. W.
SANKAR, Y.
SCHELLINCK, D. A.

School of Resource and Environmental Studies:

COHEN, F. G.
WOOD, S. (Director)

School of Library and Information Studies:

AMEY, L. J.
DYKSTRA LYNCH, M.

School of Public Administration:

AUCOIN, P. C.
BAKVIS, H.
BROWN, M. P.
MCNIVEN, J. D.
POEL, D. H.
SULLIVAN, K.
TRAVES, T.

Henson College of Public Affairs and Continuing Education:

BENOIT, J.
FRASER, L.
MACMILLAN, J. R.
MORRISSEY, M. (Dean)
NOVACK, J.

ATTACHED INSTITUTES

Atlantic Research Centre: Dir Dr H. W. Cook.

Centre for Foreign Policy Studies: Dir Dr T. M. Shaw.

Trace Analysis Research Centre: Dir Dr L. Ramaley.

Centre for African Studies: Dir Dr J. L. Parpart.

Centre for International Business Studies: Dir Dr M. R. Brooks.

Atlantic Institute of Criminology: Dir Dr D. Clairmont.

Atlantic Region Magnetic Resonance Centre: Dir D. L. Hooper.

Centre for Marine Geology: Dir D. B. Scott.

Lester Pearson International Institute: Dir P. Rodee.

Oceans Institute of Canada: (vacant).

Dalhousie Health Law Institute: Dir J. Downie.

Neuroscience Institute: Exec. Dir Dr R. E. Brown.

Atlantic Health Promotion Research Centre: Dir Dr R. Lyons.

Atlantic Industrial Research Institute: Dir G. P. Wilson.

Canadian Institute of Fisheries Technology: Dir T. A. Gill.

Centre for Marine Vessel Development and Research: Dir C. C. Hsiung.

Centre for Water Resource Studies: Dir D. H. Waller.

Nova Scotia CAD/CAM Centre: Dir A. A. Mufti.

Vehicle Safety Research Team: Dir C. R. Baird.

Minerals Engineering Centre: Dir W. F. Calley.

COLLÈGE DOMINICAIN DE PHILOSOPHIE ET DE THÉOLOGIE

96 Empress Ave, Ottawa, Ont. K1R 7G3

Telephone: (613) 233-5696
Fax: (613) 233-6064

Founded 1909 as 'Studium Generale' of Order of Friars Preachers in Canada; present name 1967
Private control
Language of instruction: French

Chancellor: Thomas R. Potvin
President and Regent of Studies: Michel Gourgues
Vice-President and Vice-Regent of Studies: Gabor Csepregi
Master of Studies and Registrar: M.-T. Nadeau
Secretary-Treasurer: Jean-Jacques Robillard
Librarian: D. Regimbald

Library of 120,000 vols, 500 periodicals
Number of teachers: 22
Number of students: 81 full-time, 373 part-time

DEANS

Institute of Pastoral Theology: J.-L. Larochelle
Faculty of Theology: Y.-D. Gelinas
Department of Philosophy: G. Csepregi

UNIVERSITY OF GUELPH

Guelph, Ont. N1G 2W1

Telephone: (519) 824-4120
Fax: (519) 766-9481 (for undergraduate studies); (519) 766-0843 (for graduate studies)

Founded 1964 from Ontario Agricultural College, Ontario Veterinary College and Macdonald Institute, formerly affiliated to the University of Toronto
Private/Provincial control
Language of instruction: English
Three semester system

Chancellor: L. M. Alexander
President and Vice-Chancellor: Mordechai Rozanski
Vice-President (Academic): J. L. Campbell
Vice-President (Finance and Administration): Nancy Sullivan
Vice-President (Research): Larry Milligan
Vice-President (University Affairs and Development): J. D. Mabley
Registrar: C. Cunningham
Librarian: M. Ridley

Library of over 2.5 million vols
Number of teachers: 750
Number of students: 14,000

Publications: *Graduate Calendar*, *Undergraduate Calendar*, *President's Report*.

DEANS

Ontario Agricultural College: R. J. McLaughlin
Ontario Veterinary College: A. H. Meek
College of Biological Science: R. Sheath
College of Family and Consumer Studies: M. Nightingale
College of Arts: C. J. Stewart
College of Social Science: D. B. Knight
College of Physical and Engineering Science: R. McCrindle
Faculty of Graduate Studies: A. J. Summerlee
Faculty of Environmental Sciences: M. R. Moss

CHAIRS AND DIRECTORS OF DEPARTMENTS AND SCHOOLS

Barclay, J. K., Human Biology and Nutritional Sciences
Butler, D. G., Clinical Studies
Calvert, B., Philosophy
Christofides, L. N., Economics
Clarke, A., Microbiology
Cyr, M., Fine Art and Music
Fitzgibbon, J. E., School of Rural Planning and Development
Gibbins, A. M., Animal and Poultry Science
Gillespie, T. J., Land Resource Science
Goddard, J., Chemistry and Biochemistry (acting)
Hebert, P., Zoology
Hinch, R., Sociology and Anthropology
Hume, D. J., Crop Science
Jeffrey, K. R., Physics
Joseph, A. E., Geography
Leatherland, J., Biomedical Sciences
Linders, J., Computing and Information Science
Manning, G., Literatures and Performance Studies in English (acting)
Mancuso, M., Political Studies
Martin, S. W., Population Medicine
Matthews, M. L., Psychology
Meilke, K. D., Agricultural Economics and Business (acting)
Mokanski, J. P., Mathematics and Statistics
Otten, L., School of Engineering
Peterson, R. L., Botany
Pletsch, D., Rural Extension Studies
Reiche, E. G., History
Rothstein, S., Molecular Biology and Genetics
Sears, M. K., Environmental Biology
Shewen, P. E., Pathobiology
Shute, J. C. M, Centre for International Programs
Sullivan, J. A., Horticultural Science (acting)
Taylor, J. R., Landscape Architecture
Thomas, A., Languages and Literatures (acting)
Wall, M. J., Consumer Studies
Walsh, J., School of Hotel and Food Administration (acting)
Woolcott, D. M., Family Studies
Yada, R. Y., Food Science (acting)

UNIVERSITY OF KING'S COLLEGE

Halifax, NS B3H 2A1

Telephone: (902) 422-1271
Fax: (902) 423-3357
E-mail: admissions@ukings.ns.ca

Founded 1789 by United Empire Loyalists; granted Royal Charter 1802; entered into association with Dalhousie University 1923
Language of instruction: English
Academic year: September to May

Chancellor: J. T. Eyton
President and Vice-Chancellor: C. J. Starnes
Vice-President: A. M. Johnston
Registrar: P. M. Robertson
Bursar: G. G. Smith
Librarian: H. Drake Petersen

Number of professors: 30
Number of students: 853

Publication: *Calendar* (annually).

PROFESSORS

Atherton, J. P., Classics
Bishop, M., French
Brown, J., French
Burns, S. A. M., Philosophy
Cobden, M., Journalism
Edwards, E., Contemporary Studies Programme (Dir)
Hankey, W. J., Classics
Kemp, W. H., Music
Kimber, S., School of Journalism (Dir)
Robertson, N. G., Foundation Year Programme (Dir)
Roper, H., Foundation Year Programme, Humanities and Social Sciences
Starnes, C. J., Classics
Steffen, D., Humanities and Social Sciences

LAKEHEAD UNIVERSITY

Oliver Rd, Thunder Bay, Ont. P7B 5E1

Telephone: (807) 343-8110
Fax: (807) 343-8023

Founded 1965; previously established as Lakehead College of Arts, Science and Technology, 1956, and Lakehead Technical Institute, 1946
Academic year: September to April; Spring and Summer sessions

Chancellor: Lois M. Wilson
President: Robert G. Rosehart
Registrar: Pentti A. Paularinne
Librarian: Anne Deighton

Number of teachers: 261
Number of students: 5,572 full-time, 1,253 part-time

DEANS

Arts and Science: James H. Gellert
Business Administration: Bahram Dadgostar
Education: J. David Bates
Engineering: J. Gary Locker
Forestry: David Euler
Director of Graduate Studies and Research: Connie H. Nelson

HEADS OF DEPARTMENTS

Anthropology: J. S. Hamilton
Biology: A. D. Macdonald
Chemistry: D. E. Orr
Economics: W. B. Jankowski
English: M. Richardson
Geography: B. J. Lorch
Geology: M. Kehnlenbeck
History: A. E. Epp
Indigenous Learning: A. Ernest Epp
Kinesiology: Ronald S. Lappage

Languages: W. Emil Dolphin
Library and Information Studies: M. Maclean
Mathematical Sciences: J. Griffith
Music: A. Carastathis
Nursing: L. S. McDougall
Outdoor Recreation, Parks and Tourism: T. W. Stevens
Philosophy: R. E. Maundrell
Physics: M. Hawton
Political Science: Pradip Sarbadhikari
Psychology: J. L. Jamieson
Social Work: S. Taylor
Sociology: R. Ruiperez
Visual Arts: A. Clarke

LAURENTIAN UNIVERSITY OF SUDBURY

Ramsey Lake Rd, Sudbury, Ont. P3E 2C6
Telephone: (705) 675-1151
Fax: (705) 675-4812

Founded 1960

Provincially-assisted, non-denominational

Teaching is in French and English, certain departments offering parallel courses in both languages

President: Geoffrey Tesson
Vice-President (Administration): Ron Chrysler
Vice-President (Academic): Hermann Falter
Executive Director, University Advancement: Joyce Garnett
Registrar: Ron Smith
Director of Library: Lionel Bonin
Director, Centre for Continuing Education: Denis Mayer
Director, Division of Physical Education: S. Knox
Director, Graduate Studies and Research: Frank Smith

Number of teachers: 291
Number of students: 4,274 full-time, 1,863 part-time winter session

Publications: *Laurentian Journal*, *Gazette*.

DEANS

Humanities and Social Sciences: R. Segsworth
Sciences and Professions: J. Mount

CHAIRS OF DEPARTMENT

Behavioural Neuroscience: M. Persinger
Biology: G. Ferroni
Chemistry and Biochemistry: W. Rank
Classical Studies: A. Kurke
Commerce and Administration: H. Blanco
Earth Science: R. James
Economics: E. Willauer
Education: E. Gignac-Pharaud
Engineering: P. Lindon
English: J. Riddell
Environmental Earth Science: D. Pearson
Ethics Studies: B. Aitken
Film Studies: R. Schell
Folklore: J.-P. Pichette
French: A. Raguigui
Geography: J. P. Martin
History: R. M. Bray
Human Development: J. H. Lewko
Human Kinetics: M. Guay
Law and Justice: C. Neff
Liberal Science: N. I. Robb
Mathematics and Computer Science: B. Adams
Midwifery: H. Botlard
Modern Languages: C. Stos
Music: C. Leonard
Native Human Services: H. Nabigon
Native Studies: R. Spielmann
Nursing: J. Pomerleau
Philosophy: P. Simpson
Physics and Astronomy: N. I. Robb
Political Science: O. Croci
Psychology: E. Levin
Religious Studies: G. MacQueen
Social Work: J. M. Bélanger
Sociology and Anthropology: D. Dennie
Sports Administration: G. Zorbas
Theatre Arts: V. Senyk
Translators and Interpreters: R. Henry
Women's Studies: A. Levan

CONSTITUENT INSTITUTIONS

Algoma University College: 1520 Queen St E, Sault Ste Marie, Ont. P6A 2G4; Pres. J. D. Lawson; Registrar R. McCutcheon.

Collège Universitaire de Hearst: Hearst, Ont. P0L 1N0; f. 1952; Rector R. Tremblay; Registrar J. Doucet.

FEDERATED UNIVERSITIES

University of Sudbury: Ramsey Lake Rd, Sudbury, Ont. P3E 2C6 (conducted by the Jesuit Fathers); f. 1957; Pres. J. Monet; Registrar L. Beaupré.

Huntington University: Ramsey Lake Rd, Sudbury, Ont. P3E 2C6 (related to United Church of Canada); f. 1960; Pres.-Principal K. G. MacQueen; Registrar D. Joblin.

Thorneloe University: Ramsey Lake Rd, Sudbury, Ont. P3E 2C6; Provost D. Thompson; Registrar Margaret Kechnie.

UNIVERSITÉ LAVAL

Cité Universitaire, Québec, Qué. G1K 7P4
Telephone: (418) 656-2131
Telex: 051-31621
Fax: (418) 656-2809

Founded 1852; Royal Charter signed December 1852, Pontifical Charter 1876, Provincial Charter 1970

Language of instruction: French
Academic year: September to January, January to May, May to August

Rector: F. Tavenas
Vice-Rectors: Jacques Racine (Executive); J. Faille (Assistant Executive); J. Samson (Human Resources); C. Godbout (Academic); L. Milot (Academic); L. Filliou (Research); M. Trudel (Development)
Secretary-General: A. Côte
Director of Undergraduate Curriculums: G. Kirouac
Director of Continuing Education: (vacant)
Registrar: R. Tremblay
Director of Communications: M. Héroux
Librarian: Claude Bonnelly

Library: see Libraries
Number of teachers: 1,665
Number of students: 22,479 full-time, 9,610 part-time

Publications: *Université Laval—Rapport* (annually), *Renseignements généraux, Aide financière, Guide de l'admission, Statistiques, Gazette officielle* (monthly, on Internet), *Au fil des Événements* (University gazette, weekly), *Répertoires des cours, Répertoires des programmes, Règlements d'études*.

DEANS AND DIRECTORS

Faculty of Agriculture and Food Sciences: André Gosselin
Faculty of Architecture, Planning and Visual Arts: Takashi Nakajima
Faculty of Dentistry: Diane Lachapelle (acting)
Faculty of Education: Jean-Claude Gagnon
Faculty of Forestry and Geomatics: C. Godbout
Faculty of Law: André C. Côté
Faculty of Letters: Jacques Desautels
Faculty of Medicine: L. Larochelle
Faculty of Philosophy: J. M. Narbonne
Faculty of Sciences and Engineering: A. Cardinal
Faculty of Social Sciences: L. Darveau-Fournier
Faculty of Theology: R.-M. Roberge
School of Actuarial Science: A. Prémont
Faculty of Music: R. Ringuette
Faculty of Nursing: E. Côté
Faculty of Pharmacy: G. Barbeau
School of Psychology: Robert Rousseau
School of Social Work: L. Tessier

PROFESSORS

Faculty of Agriculture and Food Sciences:

Amiot, J., Food Science
Antoun, H., Soil Science
Asselin, A., Plant Science
Beaudry, M., Human Nutrition
Benhamou, N., Plant Science
Boudreau, A., Food Science
Cailler, M., Soil Science
Calkins, P., Rural Economy
Carel, M., Rural Economy
Castaigne, F., Food Science
Cescas, M. P., Soil Science
Charest, P.-M., Plant Science
Dansereau, B., Plant Science
De La Noue, J., Science and Food Technology
Desilets, D., Rural Economy
Despres, J.-P., Food Science
Dion, P., Plant Science
Dube, P.-A., Plant Science
Dufour, J. C., Rural Economics
Dufour, J.-J., Animal Science
Duhaine, G.
Dumais, B., Rural Economics
Gauthier, R., Plant Science
Gendron, G., Plant Science
Ghersi, G., Rural Economics
Gosselin, A., Plant Science
Gouin, D.
Goulet, J., Food Science
Jacques, H., Food Science
Karam, A., Soil Science
Lacroix, C., Food Science
Lagacé, R., Rural Engineering
Laverdière, M.-R., Soil Science
Leroux, G., Plant Science
Levallois, R., Rural Economy
Marquis, A., Soil Science
Martin, F.
Morisset, M., Rural Economics
Paquin, P., Food Science
Parent, L. E., Soil Science
Picard, G., Food Science
Romain, R.
Savoie, L., Human Nutrition
Seoane, J. R., Animal Science
Simard, R. E., Food Science
Sirard, M.-A., Animal Science
St-Laurent, G., Animal Science
St-Louis, R., Rural Economics
St-Pierre, C. A., Plant Science
Tessier, S., Soil Science
Thériault, R., Rural Engineering
Trudel, M.-J., Plant Science
Turgeon-O'Brien, H., Human Nutrition
Wampach, J.-P., Rural Economics
Zee, J., Human Nutrition

Faculty of Architecture, Planning and Visual Arts:

Baker, J., Architecture
Bourque, P.-N., Architecture
Clibbon, P. B., Planning
Cossette, M. A., Visual Arts
Dubé, C., Planning
Dumas, A., Visual Arts
Fréchette, P., Planning
Guertin, P. S., Architecture
Jampen, P., Architecture
Jean, M., Visual Arts
Labbé, M., Visual Arts
Larochelle, P.-P., Architecture
Migneron, J.-G., Architecture
Nakajima, T., Architecture
Noppen, L., Architecture
Simard, C. A., Visual Arts
Usheff, A., Visual Arts
Villeneuve, P., Planning

Faculty of Dentistry:

BERNARD, C.
DUFOUR, L.
FOURNIER, A.
GAGNON, P.
GOULET, J.-P.
LACHAPELLE, D.
LAFLÈCHE, R.
LANDRY, R. G.
MARANDA, G.
MORAND, M.-A.
MORENCY, R.
MOUTON, C.
OUELLET, R.
PANUEBON, Y.
PERUSSE, R.
PROULX, M.
ROY, S.
TRAHAN, L.
TURCOTTE, J.-Y.
VALOIS, A.

Faculty of Education:

ARRIOLA-SOCOL, M., Counselling and Guidance
BAILLARGEON, M., Psychopedagogy
BARD, C., Physical Education
BEAUDOUX, C., School Administration
BELANGER, P.-W., School Administration
BERNIER, J.-J., Educational Measurement and Evaluation
BERTRAND, R., Educational Measurement and Evaluation
BHUSHAN, V., Educational Measurement and Evaluation
BOISCLAIR, A., Psychopedagogy
BOUCHARD, C., Physical Education
BOUCHARD, P., School Administration
BOULAY, M. R., Physical Education
BRIEN, R., Educational Technology
BRUNELLE, J., Physical Education
CLOUTIER, R., School Administration
COOK, B., Didactics
CÔTÉ, R., Psychopedagogy
DEBLOIS, C., School Administration
DESHAIES, G., Counselling and Guidance
DESHARNAIS, R., Physical Education
DESHAUTELS, J., Didactics
DESROSIERS, P., Physical Education
DIAMBOMBA, M., School Administration
DROLET, J.-L., Counselling and Guidance
DROUIN, D., Physical Education
DUPUIS, F.-A., Educational Measurement and Evaluation
FAHMY, P., Counselling and Guidance
FLEURY, J.-M., Educational Technology
FLEURY, M., Physical Education
GAGNON, J.-C., Didactics
GAULIN, C., Didactics
GAUTHIER, C.
GIASSON, J., Didactics
GIRARD, R., Educational Measurement and Evaluation
GODBOUT, P., Physical Education
LAGASSE, P. P., Physical Education
LAPOINTE, J. J., Educational Technology
LAVILLE, C., Didactics
LEAHEY, J., Counselling and Guidance
LEDUC, A., Psychopedagogy
LEGAULT, M.
LEMIRE, G., Didactics
MARCOTTE, G., Physical Education
MARCOUX, Y., Counselling and Guidance
MARTON, P., Educational Technology
MOISSET, J.-J., School Administration
MONETTE, M., Counselling and Guidance
MORENCY, C., Counselling and Guidance
MORIN, L., School Administration
MOUETTE, M.
MURA, R., Didactics
NADEAU, M.-A., Educational Measurement and Evaluation
OUELLET, R., School Administration
PÉPIN, Y., Counselling and Guidance
PERRON, M., Psychopedagogy
PLANTE, J., Educational Measurement and Evaluation
RIVERIN-SIMARD, D., Counselling and Guidance
ROBERT, B., Didactics
ROBERT, M., School Administration
ST-LAURENT, L., Psychopedagogy
SAINTE-MARIE, J., Educational Technology
SCALLON, G., Educational Measurement and Evaluation
SIMARD, C., Physical Education
SPAIN, A., Counselling and Guidance
TOUSIGNANT, M., Physical Education
TREMBLAY, A., Physical Education
TROTTIER, C., School Administration
VOYER, J. P., Educational Measurement and Evaluation

Faculty of Forestry and Geomatics:

BEAUDOIN, M., Wood and Forest Sciences
BÉDARD, Y., Geomatics
BÉLANGER, J., Wood and Forest Sciences
BÉLANGER, L., Wood and Forest Sciences
BELLEFLEUR, P., Wood and Forest Sciences
CAMIRÉ, C., Wood and Forest Sciences
CHEVALIER, J.-J., Geomatics
DESSUREAULT, M., Wood and Forest Sciences
FORTIN, Y., Wood and Forest Sciences
GAGNON, P., Geomatics
GAGNON, P.-A., Geomatics
GOLD, C., Geomatics
JOBIN, J., Geomatics
LALONDE, M., Wood and Forest Sciences
LOWELL, K., Wood and Forest Sciences
PICHÉ, Y., Wood and Forest Sciences
PINEAU, M., Wood and Forest Sciences
PLAMONDON, A. P., Wood and Forest Sciences
POLIQUIN, J., Wood and Forest Sciences
RIEDL, B., Wood and Forest Sciences
THIBEAULT, J.-R., Wood and Forest Sciences
THOMSON, K., Geomatics

Faculty of Law:

ANTAKI, N.
ARBOUR, M.
BELLEAU, C.
BELLEY, J.-G.
BERNIER, I.
BRUN, H.
CÔTE, A. C.
COTE-HARPER, G.
CRÊTE, R.
DAMÉ-CASTELLI, M.
DELEURY, E.
DESLAURIERS, J.
DUPLE, N.
FERLAND, D.
FRENETTE, F.
GARANT, P.
GARDNER, D.
GIGUÈRE, M.
GIROUX, L.
GOULET, J.
LAREAU, A.
LEMIEUX, D.
LEMIEUX, P.
L'HEUREUX, J.
L'HEUREUX, N.
MANGANAS, A.
NABHAN, V.
NORMAND, S.
OTIS, G.
POUDRIER-LEBEL, L.
PRUJINER, A.
ROBINSON, A.
ROUSSEAU, G.
ROYER, J. C.
SAMSON, C.
TREMBLAY, G.
VERGE, P.

Faculty of Letters:

ALLARD, M., Geography
AUGER, P., Languages and Linguistics
BABY, F., Literature
BEAUCHAMP, M., Information and Communication
BÉGIN, Y., Geography
BELANGER, M., Literature
BELANGER, R., History
BERGERON, C., History
BERNIER, J., Geography
BERNIER, J., History
BERTHIAUME, A., Literature
BOISCLAIR, M.-N., History
BOIVIN, A., Literature
BOULANGER, J.-C., Languages and Linguistics
BOURQUE, P.-A., Literature
BUREAU, C., Languages and Linguistics
BUREAU, L., Geography
CARANI, M., History
CAULIER, B., History
COSSETTE, J. C., Information and Communication
COURVILLE, S., Geography
DAGENAIS, B., Information and Communication
DAVIAULT, A., Literature
DE BONVILLE, J., Information and Communication
DE GUISE, J., Information and Communication
DE KONINCK, R., Geography
DE LA GARDE, R., Information and Communication
DENIS, P.-Y., Geography
DESAUTELS, J., Literature
DESHAIES, D., Languages and Linguistics
DIONNE, J. C., Geography
DOLAN, C., History
DUBERGER, J., History
DUFFLEY, P., Languages and Linguistics
DUPONT, J.-C., History
EMOND, M., Literature
FAITELSON-WEISER, S., Languages and Linguistics
FILION, L., Geography
FINETTE, L., Literature
FORTIN, M., History
GAGNÉ, M., Literature
GAUTHIER, G., Information and Communication
GIRARD, G., Literature
GIROUX, H., History
GREIF, H.-J., Literature
GUILBERT, L., History
HAMERS, J. F., Languages and Linguistics
HÉBERT, C., Literature
HERMON, E., History
HIRTLE, W. H., Languages and Linguistics
HUFTY, A., Geography
HULBERT, F. M. L., Geography
HUMMEL, K., Languages and Linguistics
HUOT, D., Languages and Linguistics
HUOT-LEMONNIER, F., Languages and Linguistics
JOLY, R., Literature
JONES, R. A., History
JUNEAU, M., Languages and Linguistics
KAREL, D., History
KOSS, B. J., History
LAMBERT, F., Literature
LAPOINTE, M., History
LAROCHE, M., Literature
LAURENCE, G., Information and Communication
LAVOIE, R., History
LEBEL, J.-G., Language and Linguistics
LEBLANC, A., Literature
LEMIEUX, J., Information and Communication
LESAGE, R., Language and Linguistics
LÉTOURNEAU, J., History
LOUDER, D. R., Geography
LOWE, R., Languages and Linguistics
MALONEY, G., Literature
MANIET, A., Languages and Linguistics
MANNING, A., Languages and Linguistics
MARTIN, P., Languages and Linguistics
MATHIEU, J., History
MENEY, L., Language and Linguistics
MEPHAM, M., Languages and Linguistics

MIGEOTTE, L., History
MILOT, L., Literature
MOISAN, J.-C., Literature
MOUSSETTE, M., History
NADEAU, V., Literature
NAKOS, O., Languages and Linguistics
OUELLET, R., Literature
OUELLON, C., Language and Linguistics
PAGE, M., Literature
PAQUETTE, G., Information and Communication
PAQUETTE, J.-M., Literature
PAQUOT, A., Languages and Linguistics
PARADIS, C., Languages and Linguistics
PELLETIER, E., Literature
PERELLI-CONTOS, I., Literature
PIETTE, C., History
POIRIER, C., Languages and Linguistics
PONTBRIAND, J.-N., Literature
PORTER, J. R., History
POULIN, J.-C., History
RASPA, A., Literature
RATCLIFFE, B. M., History
RAVENEAU, J. L., Geography
REISNER, T.-A., Literature
RITCHOT, G., Geography
RIVET, J., Information and Communication
ROBITAILLE, B., Geography
ROBY, Y., History
ROCHETTE, C. E., Languages and Linguistics
ROSS, L., Information and Communication
ROUFFIGNAT, J., Geography
SABOR, P., Literature
SAINT JACQUES, D., Literature
SAINT YVES, M., Geography
SANFAÇON, A., History
SANFAÇON, R., History
SAUVAGEAU, F., Information and Communication
SEGAL, A., History
SIMARD, J., History
STRYCKMAN, P., Information and Communication
TETU, M., Literature
TETU DE LABSADE, F., Literature
THERIAULT, M., Geography
TREMBLAY, G., Geography
TREMBLAY, J.-L., Languages and Linguistics
TURGEON, L., History
VALLIÈRES, M., History
VINCENT, D., Languages and Linguistics
WADDEL, E., Geography
WILLETT, G., Information and Communication

Faculty of Medicine:

ACKERMANN, H.-W., Microbiology
ALLEN, T., Family Medicine
AUDETTE, M., Microbiology
BARDEN, N., Physiology
BEAUCHAMP, D., Microbiology
BEAULIEU, A., Medicine
BEDARD, P., Pharmacology
BÉLANGER, A., Physiology
BÉLANGER, A. Y., Rehabilitation
BÉLANGER, L., Biochemistry
BELLEAU, R., Medicine
BERGERON, M. G., Microbiology
BERNARD, L. E., Medicine
BERNARD, P.-M., Medicine
BERNATCHEZ, J.-P., Psychiatry
BLONDEAU, F., Family Medicine
BORGEAT, P., Physiology
BOUCHARD, J.-P., Medicine
BOULET, L.-P., Medicine
BRAILOVSKY, C. A., Biochemistry
BRISSON, J., Social and Preventive Medicine
BRODEUR, B., Microbiology
BUKOWIECKI, L. J., Physiology
CABANAC, M., Physiology
CARETTE, S., Medicine
CLOUTIER, R., Clinical Surgery
CORMIER, Y., Medicine
CÔTÉ, C., Rehabilitation
COUTURE, J., Surgery
DE KONINCK, M., Social and Preventive Medicine
DELAGE, C., Pathology
DERY, P., Paediatrics
DESCHENES, L., Clinical Surgery
DESCHÊNES, M., Physiology
DESHAIES, Y., Physiology
DESLAURIERS, J., Clinical Surgery
DESMEULES, H., Anaesthesia
DESMEULES, M., Medicine
DINH, B. L., Biochemistry
DIONNE, L., Surgery
DORVAL, J., Paediatrics
DUBE, J.-Y., Medicine
DUMESNIL, J.-G., Medicine
DURAND, P.-J., Social and Preventive Medicine
DUSSAULT, J. H., Medicine
FILION, M., Physiology
FOREST, J.-C., Biochemistry
FORTIER, M.-A., Obstetrics and Gynaecology
FOURNIER, L., Anaesthesia
FRADET, Y., Clinical Surgery
FRENETTE, J., Medicine
GAGNE, R., Medicine
GAGNON, D., Pharmacology
GAUDREAU, J., Family Medicine
GLENN, J., Biochemistry
GOSSELIN, C., Surgery
GRANTHAM, H., Psychiatry
GROSE, J.-H., Medicine
GUAY,R., Microbiology
GUIDOIN, R., Surgery
HANCOCK, R., Biochemistry
HUOT, J., Pharmacology
JOBIN, F., Medicine
JOBIN, L., Medicine
JOUANOVIC, S.-M., Anatomy
JULIEN, P., Medicine
LABERGE, C., Medicine
LABRIE, F., Physiology
LAGACÉ, R., Pathology
LALANNE, M., Biochemistry
LAMARCHE, P.-A., Social and Preventive Medicine
LAMBERT, R. D., Obstetrics and Gynaecology
LANDRY, J., Medicine
LATULIPPE, L., Medicine
LAVIOLETTE, L., Medicine
LEBEL, M., Medicine
LEBLOND, P., Medicine
LECLERE, H., Medicine
LELIÈVRE, M., Paediatrics
LEMAY, A., Obstetrics and Gynaecology
LETARTE, R., Microbiology
LÉVESQUE, R., Microbiology
MAHEUX, R., Obstetrics and Gynaecology
MALOUIN, F., Rehabilitation
MARCEAU, F., Medicine
MARCEAU, N., Medicine
MARCEAU, P., Surgery
MARCHAND, R., Anatomy
MARCOURT, S., Social and Preventive Medicine
MARQUIS, Y., Medicine
MEYER, F., Social and Preventive Medicine
MIRAULT, M.-E., Medicine
MONTGRAIN, N., Psychiatry
MORIN, Y., Medicine
MOSS, T., Biochemistry
MOUTQUIN, J.-M., Obstetrics and Gynaecology
MURTHY, M.-R.-V., Biochemistry
NACCACHE, P.-H., Medicine
NADEAU, A., Medicine
PAGE, M., Biochemistry
PARENT, A., Anatomy
PELLETIER, G., Medicine
PELLETIER, G.-H., Physiology
PHILIPPE, E., Physiology
POIRIER, G., Biochemistry
POMERLEAU, G., Psychiatry
POTVIN, P., Physiology
POUBELLE, P., Medicine
RICHARD, D., Physiology
RICHARDS, C. L., Rehabilitation
RIOUX, F., Medicine
RIOUX, F., Pharmacology
RIOUX, J. E., Obstetrics and Gynaecology
ROCHON, J., Medicine
ROULEAU, J., Medicine
ROUSSEAU, A., Ophthalmology
ROY, M., Obstetrics and Gynaecology
ROY, P.-E., Pathology
RUIZ-CARRILLO, A., Biochemistry
SAUCIER, G., Clinical Medicine
STERIADE, M., Physiology
SZOTO, F., Paediatrics
TANGUAY, R., Medicine
TETREAULT, S., Rehabilitation
TETU, B., Pathology
TREMBLAY, J.-P., Anatomy
TREMBLAY, R., Medicine
TURCOTTE, F., Medicine
TURGEON, J., Medicine
VERRET, S., Medicine
VIENS, P., Medicine
WARREN, Y., Medicine

Faculty of Philosophy:

BOSS, G.
BOUCHARD, G.
CUNNINGHAM, H.-P.
DE KONINCK, T.
KNEE, P.
PELLETIER, Y.
VALOIS, R.

Faculty of Sciences and Engineering:

AIT-KADI, A., Chemical Engineering
AIT-KADI, D., Mechanical Engineering
AMIOT, P. L., Physics
ANDERSON, W. A., Biology
ANGERS, D., Electrical Engineering
ANGERS, R., Metallurgy
ARDOUIN, P., Computer and Information Science
ARSENAULT, H. H., Physics
AUPETIT, B., Mathematics
BARBEAU, C., Chemistry
BARIL, M., Physics
BARRETTE, C., Biology
BAZUIN, G., Chemistry
BEAULIEU, D., Civil Engineering
BÉDARD, G., Physics
BÉDARD, J.-H., Biology
BÉLANGER, P. A., Physics
BELLEMARRE, G., Biochemistry
BERGERON, J., Computer and Information Sciences
BERUBE, M. A., Geology
BORRA, E. F., Physics
BOULET, M.-M., Computer and Information Sciences
BOURGET, E., Biology
BOURQUE, C., Mechanical Engineering
BOURQUE, P. A., Geology
BOVET, J., Biology
BURNELL, R.-H., Chemistry
CANONNE, P., Chemistry
CAPERAA, P., Mathematics
CARDINAL, A., Biology
CARDOU, A., Mechanical Engineering
CASSIDY, C., Mathematics
CHAGNON, J. Y., Geology
CHÊNEVERT, R., Chemistry
CHIN, S. L., Physics
CLOUTIER, C., Biology
CLOUTIER, L., Mechanical Engineering
COTE, A.-G., Civil Engineering
CÔTÉ, R., Mathematics and Statistics
DE KONINCK, J. M., Mathematics
DELISLE, G. Y., Electrical Engineering
DESLAURIERS, N., Biochemistry
DESROCHERS, P., Mechanical Engineering
DICKINSON, J., Mechanical Engineering
DODSON, J., Biology
DUBE, L. J., Physics
DUGUAY, M.-A., Electrical Engineering
DUVAL, A., Biology
FAFARD, M., Civil Engineering
FAUCHER, G., Mechanical Engineering
FISET, M., Mining and Metallurgy

FORTIN, M., Mathematics
FREI, G. H., Mathematics
FRENETTE, M., Civil Engineering
GAGNE, S., Electrical Engineering
GAKWAYA, A., Mechanical Engineering
GALIBOIS, A., Mining and Metallurgy
GAMACHE, A., Computer Sciences
GANGULY, U. S., Electrical Engineering
GELINAS, P. J., Geology
GENEST, C., Mathematics
GERVAIS, J.-J., Mathematics
GHALI, E., Mining and Metallurgy
GIROUX, Y.-M., Civil Engineering
GOSSELIN, C., Mechanical Engineering
GOSSELIN, C., Mechanical Engineering
GUDERLEY, H., Biology
GUILLOT, M., Mechanical Engineering
HABASHI, F., Mining and Metallurgy
HARDY, E., Physics
HEBERT, R., Geology
HENGARTNER, W., Mathematics
HIMMELMAN, J., Biology
HODGSON, B. R., Mathematics
HO-KIM, Q., Physics
HODOUIN, D., Mining and Metallurgy
HUOT, J., Biology
HUOT, L., Biology
HUYNH, H. T., Electrical Engineering
ISHAQ, M., Mathematics
KALIAGUINE, S., Chemical Engineering
KNYSTAUTAS, E., Physics
KONRAD, J.-M., Civil Engineering
KRETSCHMER, D., Mechanical Engineering
KRISHNADEV, M., Mining and Metallurgy
KROEGER, H., Physics
LACHANCE, L., Civil Engineering
LACROIX, N., Mathematics
LANGLOIS, J.-M., Biology
LAPOINTE, J., Biochemistry
LAROCHELLE, J., Biology
LARZILLIÈRE, M., Physics
LAURENT, R., Geology
LECOURS, M., Electrical Engineering
LEDUY, A., Chemical Engineering
LEGENDRE, L., Biology
LE HUY, H., Electrical Engineering
LELOUCHE, R., Computer Sciences
LEMIEUX, C., Biochemistry
LEMIEUX, G., Biochemistry
LÉONARD, J., Chemistry
LEROUEIL, S., Civil Engineering
LESSARD, P., Civil Engineering
LESSARD, R. A., Physics
LÉVESQUE, C., Mathematics
LOCAT, J., Geology
LOCONG, L., Computer Sciences
MARCHAND, P. D., Computer Sciences
MARLEAU, L., Physics
MASSE, J.-C., Mathematics
MATHIEU, P., Physics
MAYRAND, D., Biochemistry
MCNEIL, J. N., Biology
METHOT, J.-C., Chemical Engineering
MICHEL, B., Civil Engineering
MOREAU, J. R., Chemical Engineering
MOREAU, P., Biochemistry
MORIN, H.-G., Mathematics
MORISSET, P., Biology
MOULIN, B., Computer Sciences
NGUYEN, N. D., Mechanical Engineering
OUELLET, Y., Civil Engineering
PALLOTTA, D., Biology
PAYETTE, S., Biology
PERRON, J.-M., Biology
PEZOLET, M., Chemistry
PHILIPPIN, G., Mathematics
PICARD, A., Civil Engineering
PICHÉ, M., Physics
PIERRE, R., Mathematics
PIGEON, M., Civil Engineering
PINEAUET, S., Physics
POMERLEAU, A., Electrical Engineering
POUSSART, D., Electrical Engineering
PREMONT, A., Mathematics
PRUD'HOMME, R., Chemistry
RANSFORD, T.-J., Mathematics
RICHARD, M. J., Mechanical Engineering
RIVEST, L.-P., Mathematics
ROBERGE, M.-M., Physics
ROBERT, J.-L., Civil Engineering
ROCHELEAU, M., Geology
ROY, C., Chemical Engineering
ROY, D., Physics
ROY, J. R., Physics
ROY, M., Civil Engineering
ROY, P.-H., Biochemistry
ROY, R., Physics
SAINT ARNAUD, R., Electrical Engineering
ST PIERRE, C., Physics
SAVOIE, R., Chemistry
SEGUIN, M. K., Geology
SERODES, J.-B., Civil Engineering
TANGUY, D., Chemical Engineering
TARASIEWICZ, S., Mechanical Engineering
TAVENAS, F., Civil Engineering
TÊTU, M.
THEODORESCU, R., Mathematics
THIBAULT, J., Chemical Engineering
TRAN, D. K., Electrical Engineering
TREMBLAY, R., Mining and Metallurgy
TREMBLAY, R., Physics
TURCOTTE, J., Chemistry
TURMEL, M., Biochemistry
VADEBONCOEUR, C., Biochemistry
VAN NESTE, A., Mining and Metallurgy
VERRETTE, J.-L., Civil Engineering
VIAROUGE, P., Electrical Engineering
VINCENT, W. F., Biology
VO-DAI, T., Computer Sciences

Faculty of Social Sciences:

ACHOUR, D., Administration
ARCAND, B., Anthropology
ARELLANO CUEVA, R., Marketing
AUDET, M., Management
AUTIN, C., Economics
AYOUB, A., Economics
BACCIGALUPO, A., Political Science
BARITEAU, C., Anthropology
BEAUCHAMP, C., Sociology
BÉDARD, J., Accounting
BEGIN, C., Management
BÉLANGER, G., Economics
BÉLANGER, L., Industrial Relations
BÉLANGER, M., Management
BÉLIVEAU, D., Marketing
BELLEHUMEUR, A., Economics
BERGERON, F., Management Information Systems
BERNARD, J.-T., Economics
BERNIER, G., Finance
BERNIER, J., Industrial Relations
BHERER, H., Management
BILLETTE, A., Sociology
BLOUIN, R., Industrial Relations
BOCTOR, F. F., Operations and Decision Systems
BOIVIN, J., Industrial Relations
BOULARD, R., Industrial Relations
BRETON, Y., Anthropology
CARRIER, C.-A., Economics
CHALIFOUX, J.-J., Anthropology
CHAREST, G., Finance
CHAREST, P. F., Anthropology
COSSET, J.-C., Finance
COUILLARD, M.-A., Anthropology
COULOMBE, D., Accounting
CRÊTE, J., Political Science
DAGENAIS, H., Anthropology
D'AMBOISE, G., Management
D'AVIGNON, G. R., Operations and Decision Systems
DECALUWE, B., Economics
DELAGE, D., Sociology
DESCHENES, J.-P., Industrial Relations
DES ROSIERS, F., Administration
DIONNE, P., Management
DOMINIQUE, C. R., Economics
DORAIS, L.-J., Anthropology
DUMAIS, A., Sociology
ELBAZ, M., Anthropology
FORTIN, A., Sociology
FORTIN, B., Economics
FRECHETTE, P., Economics
GAGNON, J. M., Finance
GAGNON, N., Sociology
GARNIER, B., Management
GASCON, A., Operations and Decision Systems
GASSE, Y., Management
GAUDET, G., Economics
GENDRON, M., Finance
GENEST, S., Anthropology
GINGRAS, L., Management Information System (MIS)
GOSSELIN, G., Political Science
GRISÉ, J., Management
HERVOUET, G., Political Science
HUDON, R., Political Science
HUNG, N. M., Economics
IMBEAU, L., Political Science
KETTANI, O., Operations and Decision Systems
KHOURY, N., Finance
LABRECQUE, M.-F., Anthropology
LAFLAMME, G., Industrial Relations
LAFOREST, G., Political Science
LANDRY, M., Management Information System (MIS)
LANDRY, R., Political Science
LANGLOIS, S., Sociology
LAROCQUE, A., Industrial Relations
LEBLANC, G., Economics
LEE-GOSSELIN, H., Management
LEFRANÇOIS, P., Operations and Decision Systems
LEGAULT, A., Political Science
LEGAULT, M., Accounting
LEMIEUX, V., Political Science
LESSARD, M.-A., Sociology
LETARTE, P.-A., Administration
MACE, G., Political Science
MARTEL, A., Operations and Decision Systems
MARTEL, J.-M., Operations and Decision Systems
MASSON, C., Economics
MERCIER, J., Political Science
MERCURE, D., Sociology
MOFFET, D., Finance
MONTREUIL, B., Operations and Decision Systems
MORIN, F., Industrial Relations
NADEAU, R., Operations and Decision Systems
NEMNI, M., Political Science
ORAL, M., Operations and Decision Systems
OUELLET, G., Management
PAINCHAUD, P., Political Science
PARÉ, P.-V., Accounting
PELLETIER, R., Political Science
PETROF, J. V., Marketing
PILOU, L., Anthropology
POULIN, D., Management
PRICE, W. L., Operations and Decision Systems
QUESNEL, L., Political Science
RAHN, R. J., Operations and Decision Systems
RIGAUX-BRICMONT, B., Marketing
SAILLANT, F., Anthropology
SAINT PIERRE, J., Finance
SALADIN-D'ANGLURE, B., Anthropology
SAMSON, L., Economics
SANTERRE, R., Anthropology
SCHMITZ, N., Anthropology
SCHWARZ, A., Sociology
SCHWIMMER, E., Anthropology
SEROR, ANN C., Management
SEXTON, J., Industrial Relations
SIMARD, J.-J., Sociology
SIMONIS, Y., Anthropology
SURET, J.-M., Finance
THWAITES, J., Industrial Relations
TREMBLAY, D., Accounting
TRUCHON, M., Economics
TRUDEL, F., Anthropology
TURMEL, A., Sociology

URBANO, H., Sociology
VALLERAND, J.-P.-M., Management
VEILLETTE, D., Sociology
VERNA, G., Management
VEZINA, P., Accounting
VINET, A., Industrial Relations
WAYLAND, D.-G., Management
ZYLBERBERG, J., Political Science

Faculty of Theology:
AUBERT, M.
BRODEUR, R.
CHENARD, G.
FILTEAU, J.-C.
GAUDETTE, P.
GERVAIS, M.
GIGUÈRE, H.
LANGEVIN, P. E.
LEMIEUX, R.
PELCHAT, M.
POIRIER, P.-H.
RACINE, J.
RICHARD, J.
ROBERGE, M.
ROBERGE , R. M.
ROBITAILLE, L.
VIAU, M.

School of Actuarial Science:
FAILLE, J.
PREMONT, A.

Faculty of Music:
BIOT, B.
BLANCHET, U.
BOUCHARD, A.
FISCHER, F.
GAGNON, A.
MASSON-BOURQUE, C.
MATHIEU, L.
MENARD, R.
MOREL, F.
PARE-TOUSIGNANT, E.
POIRIER, L.
RINGUETTE, R.
SIMARD, G.
STUBER, U.
TEREBESI, G.

Faculty of Nursing:
BLONDEAU, D.
CHALIFOUR, J.
GENDRON, C.
GODIN, G.
HAGAN, L.
O'NEIL, M.
ROUSSEAU, N.

Faculty of Pharmacy:
BARBEAU, G.
BEAULAC-BAILLARGEON, L.
BELANGER, P. M.
CASTONGUAY, A.
DI PAOLO-CHENEVERT, T.
DUMAS, J.
GRÉGOIRE, J.-P.
GRENIER, D.
LABRECQUE, G.
LEBLANC, P. P.

School of Psychology:
BACHELOR, A.
BOISVERT, J.-M.
BOIVIN, M.
CLOUTIER, R.
DE GRACE, G. R.
DORÉ, F.-Y.
EVERETT, J.
FORTIN, C.
GAUTHIER, J.
GUAY, J.
JOSHI, P.
KIROUAC, G.
LADOUCEUR, R.
LAVALLÉE, M.
LAVOIE, F.
LORANGER, M.
MORIN, P.-C.
PEPIN, M.
PICHE, C.
PLÉCHATY, M.
POCREAU, J.-B.
RENAUD, A.
ROUSSEAU, R.
SABOURIN, S.
SAINT-YVES, A.
TESSIER, R.
VÉZINA, J.

School of Social Work:
AUCLAIR, R.
BEAUDOIN, A. L.
BELIVEAU, G.
BILODEAU, G.
CAREY-BELANGER, E.
CÔTÉ, C.
DARVEAU-FOURNIER, L.
DORE, G.
DOUCET, L.
FORTIN, D.
GENDRON, J.-L.
HURTUBISE, Y.
LINDSAY, J.
OUELLET, F.
OUELLET, H.
POULIN, M.
SIMARD, M.
TROTTIER, G.
VACHON, J.
VEZINA, A.

ATTACHED RESEARCH INSTITUTES

Centre d'études nordiques: Université Laval, Québec G1K 7P4; Dir SERGE PAYETTE.

Groupe de recherche en écologie buccale: Université Laval, Québec G1K 7P4; Dir DENIS MAYRAND.

RESEARCH CENTRES

Centre d'études sur la langue, les arts et les traditions populaires des francophones d'Amérique du Nord: Dir LAURIER TURGEON.

Centre de recherche sur les propriétés des interfaces et la catalyse: Dir DENIS ROY.

Centre de recherche en science et ingénierie des macromolécules: Dir ROBERT E. PRUD'HOMME.

Centre interuniversitaire en calcul mathématique algébrique: Dir CLAUDE LÉVESQUE.

Centre interuniversitaire d'études québécoises: Dir SERGE COURVILLE.

Centre interuniversitaire sur le saumon atlantique: Dir JULIAN DOBSON.

Centre international de recherche en aménagement linguistique: Dir CONRAD OUELLON.

Centre d'optique, photonique et laser: Dir MICHEL TÊTU.

Centre de recherche en biologie forestière: Dir JEAN BOUSQUET.

Centre de recherche en cancérologie: Dir LUC BÉLANGER.

Centre de recherche en littérature québécoise: Dir DENIS SAINT-JACQUES.

Centre de recherche en géomatique: Dir KEITH THOMSON.

Centre de recherche en horticulture: Dir SERGE YELLE.

Centre de recherche en infectologie: Dir MICHEL BERGERON.

Centre de recherche interuniversitaire sur le béton: Dir MICHEL PIGEON.

Centre de recherche en neurobiologie: Dir MICHEL FILION.

Centre de recherche en rhumatologie et en immunologie: Dir PIERRE BORGEAT.

Groupe interdisciplinaire de recherche en éléments finis: Dir MICHEL FORTIN.

Groupe interuniversitaire de recherches océanographiques du Québec: Dir LOUIS FORTIER.

Centre de recherche en biologie de la reproduction: Dir MARC-ANDRÉ SIRARD.

Groupe de recherche en économie de l'énergie et des ressources naturelles: Dir DENIS BOLDUC.

Groupe de recherche sur l'inadaptation psychosociale chez l'enfant: Dir RÉJEAN TESSIER.

Laboratoire de recherche en endocrinologie moléculaire: Dir FERNAND LABRIE.

Observatoire du Mont Mégantic: Dir JEAN-RENÉ ROY.

Centre de recherche en sciences et technologie du lait: Dir CHRISTOPHE LACROIX.

UNIVERSITY OF LETHBRIDGE

4401 University Drive, Lethbridge, Alta T1K 3M4

Telephone: (403) 320-5700
Fax: (403) 329-5159
E-mail: inquiries@uleth.ca

Founded 1967
Provincial control
Language of instruction: English
Academic year: September to April (2 semesters), also summer sessions

Chancellor: ROBERT HIRONAKA
President: HOWARD TENNANT
Vice-President: SEAMUS O'SHEA
Registrar: LESLIE LAVERS
Chief Librarian: JUDY HEAD

Number of teachers: 248 full-time
Number of students: 5,361
Library of 498,000 vols

Publications: *Annual Calendar, Annual Report of the Board of Governors*.

DEANS

Faculty of Arts and Science: B. D. DUA
Faculty of Education: L. WALKER
Faculty of Management: A. DASTMALCHIAN
School of Nursing: U. RIDLEY
School of Fine Arts: C. SKINNER

McGILL UNIVERSITY

845 Sherbrooke St West, Montréal, Qué. H3A 2T5

Telephone: (514) 398-4455
Fax: (514) 398-3594

Founded 1821 by legacy of Hon. James McGill
Provincial control
Language of instruction: English
Academic year: September to May (two terms)

Chancellor: GRETTA CHAMBERS
Principal and Vice-Chancellor: B. J. SHAPIRO
Vice-Principal (Academic): T. H. CHAN
Vice-Principal (Administration and Finance): P. HEAPHY
Vice-Principal (Macdonald Campus) D. J. BUSZARD (acting)
Vice-Principal (Information Systems and Technology): B. PENNYCOOK
Vice-Principal (Research): P. BÉLANGER
Vice-Principal (Development and Alumni Relations): D. DRUMMOND
Secretary-General: V. LEES
Registrar and Director of Admissions: M. JOHANSEN
Director of Libraries: F. K. GROEN

Library: see Libraries
Number of teachers: 21,063 (full-time and part-time)
Number of students: 29,369 (full-time and part-time)

Publications: *McGill Reporter* (fortnightly), *Annual Report*, *Announcements*, *McGill Journal of Education* (quarterly).

DEANS

Faculty of Agricultural and Environmental Sciences: D. J. BUSZARD
Faculty of Arts: C. MILLER
Faculty of Dentistry: J. LUND
Faculty of Education: A. E. WALL
Faculty of Engineering: J. M. DEALY
Faculty of Graduate Studies and Research: P. BÉLANGER
Faculty of Law: S. TOOPE
Faculty of Management: W. CROWSTON
Faculty of Medicine: A. FUKS
Faculty of Music: R. LAWTON
Faculty of Religious Studies: B. B. LEVY
Faculty of Science: A. SHAVER
Dean of Students: R. JUKIER
Dean—Continuing Education: M. YALOVSKY

DIRECTORS OF SCHOOLS

Architecture: D. COVO
Communication Sciences and Disorders: R. MAYBERRY
Computer Science: D. THERIEN
Dietetics and Human Nutrition: P. JONES
Graduate School of Library and Information Studies: J. A. LARGE
Nursing: L. GOTTLIEB
Physical and Occupational Therapy: S. WOOD-DAUPHINEE
Social Work: W. S. ROWE
Urban Planning: J. M. WOLFE

CHAIRS OF DEPARTMENTS

Faculty of Agricultural and Environmental Sciences:

Agricultural Economics: P. THOMASSIN
Agricultural and Biosystems Engineering: G. S. V. RAGHAVAN
Animal Science: K. F. NG-KWAI-HANG
Food Science and Agricultural Chemistry: I. ALLI
Natural Resource Sciences: D. J. LEWIS
Plant Science: K. STEWART

Faculty of Arts:

Anthropology: D. W. ATWOOD
Art History: H. BÖKER
Classics: M. J. SILVERTHORNE
East Asian Studies: R. YATES
Economics: C. GREEN
English: G. WIHL
French Language and Literature: J.-C. MORISOT
German Studies: P. M. DALY
Hispanic Studies: D. A. BORUCHOFF
History: G. TEOY
Italian: M. PREDELLI
Jewish Studies: E. ORENSTEIN
Linguistics: M. PARADIS
Philosophy: D. F. NORTON
Political Science: H. MEADWELL
Russian and Slavic Studies: P. M. AUSTIN
Sociology: J. HALL

Centre for Continuing Education:

Education: R. KEYSERLINGK
General Studies: M. YALOVSKY (acting)
Languages and Translation: J. ARCHIBALD
Career and Management Studies: R. ELEY

Faculty of Education:

Culture and Values in Education: D. SMITH
Educational and Counselling Psychology: B. M. SHORE
Educational Studies: J. WOLFORTH
Physical Education: G. REID
Second Language Education: M. H. MAGUIRE

Faculty of Engineering:

Chemical Engineering: R. MUNZ
Civil Engineering and Applied Mechanics: R. JAPP
Electrical Engineering: N. C. RUMIN
Mechanical Engineering: S. J. PRICE
Mining and Metallurgical Engineering: G. DEMOPOULOS

Faculty of Medicine:

Anatomy and Cell Biology: J. J. M. BERGERON
Anaesthesia: F. CARLI
Biochemistry: P. E. BRANTON
Biomedical Engineering: G. R. E. KEARNEY
Epidemiology and Biostatistics: G. THÉRIAULT
Family Medicine: L. NASMITH
Human Genetics: L. PINSKY
Social Studies of Medicine: G. WEISZ
Medicine: D. GOLTZMAN
Microbiology and Immunology: M. DUBOW
Neurology and Neurosurgery: J. ANTEL
Obstetrics and Gynaecology: S. L. TAN
Occupational Health: G. THÉRIAULT
Oncology: B. LEYLAND-JONES
Ophthalmology: M. N. BURNIER
Otolaryngology: M. D. SCHLOSS
Paediatrics: H. GUYDA
Pathology: R. P. MICHEL
Pharmacology and Therapeutics: A. C. CUELLO
Physiology: A. SCHRIER
Psychiatry: J. PARIS
Radiation Oncology: C. R. FREEMAN
Radiology, Diagnostic: M. ATRI (acting)
Surgery: D. MULDER

Faculty of Music:

Performance: E. PLAWUTSKY
Theory: B. MINORGAN

Faculty of Science:

Atmospheric and Oceanic Sciences: J. DEROME
Biology: D. KRAMER
Chemistry: I. BUTLER
Earth and Planetary Sciences: A. E. WILLIAMS-JONES
Geography: T. R. MOORE
Mathematics and Statistics: G. SCHMIDT
Physics: J. BARRETTE
Psychology: N. WHITE

INCORPORATED COLLEGES AND CAMPUSES

Macdonald Campus: Ste Anne de Bellevue, Qué. H9X 1C0; site of the Faculty of Agricultural and Environmental Sciences and School of Dietetics and Human Nutrition.

Royal Victoria College: Montréal; non-teaching; provides residential accommodation for women students; Warden F. TRACY.

AFFILIATED BODIES

Montreal Diocesan Theological College: 3473 University St, Montréal, Qué. H3A 2A8; Principal J. SIMONS.

Presbyterian College: 3495 University St, Montréal, Qué. H3A 2A8; Principal W. J. KLEMPA.

United Theological College: 3521 University St, Montréal, Qué. H3A 2A9; Principal P. GOLDBERGER.

ATTACHED RESEARCH INSTITUTES AND ADDITIONAL FACILITIES

Biological and Medical Sciences

Aerospace Medical Research Unit: Dir D. G. D. WATT.

McGill Aids Centre: Dir M. WAINBERG.

McGill Centre for Studies in Aging: Dir J. POIRIER.

Allan Memorial Institute: Dir H. GUTTMAN.

Anesthesia Research Department: Dir K. KRNJEVIC.

Animal Resources Centre: Dir R. H. LATT.

Artificial Cells and Organs Research Centre: Dir T. M. S. CHANG.

Avian Science and Conservation Centre: Dir D. M. BIRD.

Bellairs Research Institute, Barbados, W.I.: Dir W. HUNTE.

Sheldon Biotechnology Centre: Dir H. P. G. BENNETT.

McGill Basic Cancer Research Centre: Dir C. P. STANNERS.

McGill Centre for Clinical Immunobiology and Transplantation: Dir R. D. GUTTMANN.

Centre for Continuing Medical Education: Dir L. SNELL.

Dairy Herd Analysis Service: Dir B. FARMER.

Dairy Research Group: Coordinator K. F. NG KWAI HANG.

Centre for Research on Endocrine Mechanisms: Dir Y. PAREL.

Farm Management and Technology Program: Dir M. COUTURE.

Gault Estate and Mont St. Hilaire Biosphere Reserve: Dir M. LECHOWICZ.

The McGill Centre for the Study of Host Resistance: Dir E. SKAMENE.

The McGill University Herbarium: Curator M. J. WATERWAY.

Limnology Research Centre: Dir J. KALFF.

Lyman Entomological Museum: Dir G. HSIUNG.

Macdonald Campus Farm: Dir L. BAKER.

Centre for Medical Education: Dir V. PATEL.

Medical Physics Unit: Dir E. B. PODGORSAK.

Montreal Neurological Institute: Dir R. MURPHY.

Centre for Nonlinear Dynamics in Physiology and Medicine: Dir M. MACKEY.

Morgan Arboretum: Dir E. R. THOMPSON.

Centre for Research in Neuroscience: Dir A. J. AGUAYO.

McGill Nutrition and Food Science Centre: Dir E. B. MARLISS.

Institute of Parasitology: Dir M. E. SCOTT.

Plasma Technology Research Centre: Dir R. MUNZ.

McGill University Phytotron: Dir M. J. LEICHOWICZ.

Redpath Museum: Dir G. BELL.

McGill Centre for the Study of Reproduction: Dir R. FAROOKHI.

Schefferville Sub-Arctic Research Station: Dir W. POLLARD.

McGill Centre for Tropical Diseases: Dir J. D. MACLEAN.

Humanities and Social Sciences

Institute and Centre of Air and Space Law: Dir M. MILDE.

Anthropology of Development Program: Dir L. BOSSEN.

Faculty of Arts Computer Services: Dir A. MASI.

McGill Institute for the Study of Canada: Dir D. MORTON.

McGill Cognitive Science Centre: Dir V. L. PATEL.

Graduate Program in Communications: Dir W. STRAW (acting).

Institute of Comparative Law: Dir H. P. GLENN.

Centre for Developing Area Studies: Dir R. BOYD.

Dobson Centre for Entrepreneurial Studies: Dir P. R. JOHNSON.

English and French Language Centre: Dir H. POULIN-MIGNAULT.

Centre for East Asian Studies Research: Dir R. D. S. YATES.

Centre for Applied Family Studies: Dir W. ROWE (acting).

Centre for International Management Studies: Dir W. B. CROWSTON.

Office of International Research: Dir D. Conway.

Institute of Islamic Studies: Dir A. U. Turgay.

Learning Centre of Quebec: Dir W. J. Smith.

McGill Executive Institute: Dir J. A. Duff.

McGill Management Sciences Research Centre: S. Li.

McCord Museum of Canadian History: Exec. Dir C. Benoit.

McGill Centre for Medicine, Ethics and Law: Exec. Dir B. Robaire.

McGill Conservatory of Music: Dir K. Woodman.

Minimum Cost Housing Group: Dir V. Bhatt.

Centre for Northern Studies and Research: Dir W. H. Pollard.

Power Corps International: Dir W. Crowston.

Québec Research Centre of Private and Comparative Law: Dir N. Kasirer.

Québec Studies Program: Dir A. Gagnon.

McGill Centre for Society, Technology and Development: Dir J. G. Galaty.

Centre for the Study of Regulated Industries: Dir R. Janda.

Centre for Strategy Studies in Organizations: Dir J. Jorgensen.

McGill Summer Studies: Dir V. Pasztor.

Centre for University Teaching and Learning: Dir C. B. Weston.

McGill Centre for Research and Teaching on Women: Dir S. Mulay.

Office of Technology Transfer: Dir A. Navarre.

Centre for Educational Leadership: Dir S. Sklar.

Centre for Research on Canadian Cultural Industries and Institutions: Dir W. Straw.

Office of Research in Educational Policy: Dir W. J. Straw.

Physical Sciences and Engineering

Canadian Centre for Automation and Robotics in Mining: Dir F. Hassani.

Brace Research Institute: Dir M. R. Kamal.

Centre for Climate and Global Change Research: Dir N. Roulet.

Centre for Drainage Studies: Dir R. S. Broughton.

Foster Radiation Laboratory: Dir J. Barrette.

Geotechnical Research Centre: Dir R. D. Japp.

McGill High Energy Physics Group: Dir D. Stairs.

Centre for Intelligent Machines: Dir M. D. Levine.

Co-operative Centre for Research in Mesometeorology: Dir I. Zawadzki.

McGill Metals Processing Centre: Dirs R. I. L. Guthrie, J. J. Jonas.

Mining Engineering Program: Dir M. Scoble.

Centre for the Physics of Materials: Dir M. J. Zuckermann.

Polymer McGill: Coordinator A. Eisenberg.

McGill Pulp and Paper Research Centre: Dir T. G. M. Van de Ven.

J. Stewart Marshall Radar Weather Observatory: Dir I. Zawadzki.

McMASTER UNIVERSITY

Hamilton, Ont. L8S 4L8
Telephone: (905) 525-9140
Telex: 061-8347
Fax: 527-0100

Established in Toronto 1887, moved to Hamilton 1930
Private control
Language of instruction: English
Academic year: September to April

Chancellor: J. H. Taylor
President and Vice-Chancellor: Prof. Peter J. George
Provost and Vice-President (Academic): A. C. Heidebrecht
Vice-President (Research): R. F. Childs
Vice-President (Administration): A. L. Darling
Vice-President (Health Sciences): J. Bienenstock
Registrar: S. Porter
Librarian: G. R. Hill

Library: see Libraries
Number of teachers: 1,025 full-time
Number of students: 17,775 full- and part-time

Publications: *Staff Directory* (annually), *Calendars* (annually), *Year I Handbook* (annually), *McMaster Times*, *McMaster University Library Research News*, *Journal of the Bertrand Russell Archives* (quarterly), *The Research Bulletin* (monthly), *The Courier* (every 2 weeks).

DEANS

School of Business: W. G. Truscott
Faculty of Humanities: E. Simpson
Faculty of Health Sciences: J. Bienenstock
Faculty of Social Sciences: J. A. Johnson
Faculty of Science: R. H. McNutt
Faculty of Engineering: M. Shoukri
Graduate Studies: J. Weaver
Principal of the Divinity College: W. H. Brackney

CHAIRMEN OF DEPARTMENTS

Anaesthesia: D. H. Morison
Anthropology: E. V. Glanville
Art and Art History: H. Galloway
Arts and Science Programme: B. M. Ferrier
Biochemistry: G. Gerber
Biology: B. N. White
Biomedical Sciences: A. K. Ball (acting)
Chemical Engineering: P. E. Wood
Chemistry: B. E. McCarry
Civil Engineering: A. Ghobarah
Classics: K. M. Dunbabin
Clinical Epidemiology and Biostatistics: G. Browman
Computer Science and Systems: P. J. Ryan
Drama: B. S. Pocknell
Economics: A. Harrison
Electrical and Computer Engineering: D. R. Conn
Engineering Physics: W. J. Garland
English: B. John
Family Medicine: R. G. McAuley
French: M. Jeay
Geography: S. M. Taylor
Geology: W. A. Morris
History: R. H. Johnston
Kinesiology: D. G. Sale
Materials Science and Engineering: M. B. Ives
Mathematics and Statistics: E. T. Sawyer
Mechanical Engineering: M. Elbestawi
Medicine: J. Cairns
Modern Languages: N. Kolesnikoff (acting)
Music: P. Rapoport (acting)
Nursing: C. Byrne
Obstetrics and Gynaecology: R. Burrows (acting)
Occupational Therapy: P. Salvatori
Paediatrics: F. J. Holland
Pathology: J. Gauldie
Philosophy: W. Waluchow
Physics: D. W. L. Sprung
Physiotherapy: C. Gowland
Political Science: K. R. Nossal
Psychiatry: R. Joffe
Psychology: G. Smith
Radiology: G. W. Stevenson
Religious Studies: D. R. Kinsley
Social Work: J. E. MacIntyre
Sociology: C. H. Levitt
Surgery: R. Hansebout

PROFESSORS

Faculty of Business:

Abad, P., Management Science
Adams, R. J., Industrial Relations
Agarwal, N. C., Human Resources
Banting, P. M., Marketing
Chan, M. W. L., Finance and Business Economics
Cooper, R. G., Marketing
Gaa, J. C., Accounting
Jain, H. C., Human Resources and Labour Relations
Krinsky, I., Human Resources
Kwan, C. C. Y., Finance
Love, R. F., Management Science
Mittenburg, G. J., Production and Management Science
Mountain, D. C., Finance and Business Economics
Muller, T. E., Marketing
Parlar, M., Management Science
Rose, J. B., Industrial Relations
Ross, R. E., Marketing
Steiner, G., Management Science
Truscott, W. G., Production and Management Science
Wesolowsky, G. O., Production and Management Science

Faculty of Humanities:

Alsop, J. D., History
Aziz, M., English
Ballstadt, C. P., English
Bayard, C., French
Bishop, A. G., English
Blewett, D. L., English
Braswell-Means, L. A., English
Brennan, A. S., English
Browning, J. D., Hispanic Studies
Cain, T. H., English
Cassels, A., History
Cioran, S. D., Russian
Coldwell, J., English
Cro, S., Italian
Dunbabin, K. M. D., Classics
Ferns, J., English
Fritz, P. S., History
Geagan, D. J., History, Classics
Griffin, N., Philosophy
Hammond, A. D., Drama
Jeay, M., French
John, B., English
Johnston, R. H., History
Jones, H., Classics
King, J. W., English
Kolesnikoff, N., Russian
Levenstein, H., History
Madison, G. B., Philosophy
Maginnis, H. B. J., Art and Art History
Morgan, O. R., French
Morton, R. E., English
Murgatroyd, P., Classics
Petrie, G., Drama, English
Rempel, R. A., History
Roebuck, W. G., English
Rouben, C., French
Russo, D. J., History
Simpson, J. E., Philosophy
Slater, W. J., Classics
Smyrniw, W., Russian
Teuscher, G., German
Thomas, G., Russian
Vince, R. W., Drama, English
Walker, A., Music
Weaver, J. C., History
Wood, C., English

Faculty of Health Sciences:

Adam, K. S., Psychiatry
Adams, D. W., Psychiatry
Alexopoulou, I., Pathology
Ali, M. A. M., Pathology
Ananthanarayanan, V. S., Biochemistry
Andrew, M., Paediatrics
Atkinson, S. A., Paediatrics
Bacchetti, S., Pathology

BAR-OR, O., Paediatrics
BARR, R. D., Paediatrics
BARTOLUCCI, G., Psychiatry
BAUMANN, A., Nursing
BECKINGHAM, A. C., Nursing
BELBECK, L. W., Pathology
BIENENSTOCK, J., Pathology
BLAJCHMAN, M. A., Pathology
BLUMBERG, P., Family Medicine
BRAIN, M. C., Medicine
BRANDA, L. A., Biochemistry
BROWMAN, G. P., Medicine, Clinical Epidemiology and Biostatistics
BROWNE, R. M., Nursing
BUCHANAN, M. R., Pathology
BUCHANAN, W. W., Medicine
BUTLER, R. G., Biomedical Sciences
CAIRNS, J. A., Medicine
CHAMBERS, L. W., Clinical Epidemiology and Biostatistics
CHAN, W. W., Biochemistry
CHANG, P. L., Paediatrics
CHERNESKY, M. A., Paediatrics
CHUI, D. H. K., Pathology
CHURCHILL, D. N., Medicine
CLARK, D. A., Medicine
COATES, G., Radiology
COHEN, G. S., Family Medicine
COHEN, M., Family Medicine
COLLINS, J. A., Obstetrics and Gynaecology
COLLINS, S. M., Medicine
CRANKSHAW, D. J., Obstetrics and Gynaecology
CROOK, J. M., Nursing
CUNNINGHAM, C. E., Psychiatry
DAWSON, D. F. L., Psychiatry
DENBURG, J. A., Medicine
DENT, P. B., Paediatrics
DESA, D. J., Pathology
DEVLIN, M. C., Obstetrics and Gynaecology
DIXON, A. S., Family Medicine
DOLOVICH, J., Paediatrics
DWYER, D. E., Medicine
EPAND, R. M., Biochemistry
EVANS, C. E., Family Medicine
FALLEN, E. L., Medicine
FEIGHTNER, J. W., Family Medicine
FERRIER, B. M., Biochemistry
FINLAYSON, M. A. J., Psychiatry
FIRNAU, G., Radiology
FORREST, J. B., Anaesthesia
FOX-THRELKELD, J. E. T., Nursing
FREEMAN, K. B., Biochemistry
FRENCH, S. E., School of Nursing
GAFNI, A., Clinical Epidemiology and Biostatistics
GARNETT, E. S., Radiology
GAULDIE, J., Pathology
GENT, M., Clinical Epidemiology and Biostatistics
GERBER, G. E., Biochemistry
GHOSH, H. P., Biochemistry
GILBERT, J. R., Family Medicine
GOLDSMITH, C. H., Clinical Epidemiology and Biostatistics
GRAHAM, F. L., Biology
GROVER, A. K., Biomedical Sciences
GROVES, D. J., Pathology
GUPTA, R. N., Pathology
GUPTA, R. S., Biochemistry
GUYATT, G. H., Clinical Epidemiology and Biostatistics
HANSEBOUT, R. R., Surgery
HARGREAVE, F. E., Medicine
HASLAM, R. J., Pathology
HASSELL, J. A., Biochemistry, Biology and Pathology
HATTON, M. W. C., Pathology
HAYNES, R. B., Clinical Epidemiology and Biostatistics
HEGGTVEIT, H. A., Pathology
HEIGENHAUSER, G. J. F., Medicine
HEWSON, J. R., Anaesthesia
HILL, R. E., Pathology
HIRSH, J., Medicine
HOLLAND, F. J., Paediatrics
HUNT, R. H., Medicine
ISSENMAN, R. M., Paediatrics
KAY, J. M., Pathology
KELTON, J. G., Pathology and Medicine
KILLIAN, K. J., Medicine
KINGSTONE, E., Psychiatry
KRISTOFFERSON, M. W., Psychiatry
KWAN, C. Y., Biomedical Sciences
LAMONT, J. A., Obstetrics and Gynaecology
LAMONT, K. G., Obstetrics and Gynaecology
LEE, R. M. K., Anaesthesia
LEVINE, M. N., Medicine
LOCK, C. J. L., Chemistry
LOMAS, J., Clinical Epidemiology and Biostatistics
LUDWIN, D., Medicine
MANDELL, L. A., Medicine
MARTIN, R. F., Surgery
MCAULEY, R. G., Family Medicine
MCBRIDE, J. A., Pathology
MACLEOD, R. J., Psychiatry
MACLEOD, S. M., Clinical Epidemiology and Biostatistics
MCCOMAS, A. J., Biomedical Sciences and Medicine
MCCULLOCH, P. B., Medicine
MCDERMOTT, M. R., Pathology
MCFARLANE, A. H., Psychiatry
MACPHERSON, A. S., Psychiatry, Clinical Epidemiology and Biostasis
MCQUEEN, M. J., Pathology
MISHRA, R. K., Psychiatry
MOHIDE, P. T., Obstetrics and Gynaecology
MOORE, C. A., Family Medicine
MORISON, D. H., Anaesthesia
MORSE, J. L. C., Medicine
MOUDGIL, G. C., Anaesthesia
MUGGAH, H. F., Obstetrics and Gynaecology
MUIR, D. C. F., Medicine
NEAME, P. B., Pathology
NEUFELD, V. R., Medicine
NIEBOER, E., Biochemistry
NILES, L. P., Biomedical Sciences
NORMAN, G. R., Clinical Epidemiology and Biostatistics and Family Medicine
O'BYRNE, P. M., Medicine
OFFORD, D. R., Psychiatry
OFOSU, F. A., Pathology
ORR, W., Pathology
PAI, M. K. R., Paediatrics
PARKER, K. R., Family Medicine
PATTERSON, C. J. S., Medicine
POWLES, A. C. P., Medicine
PREVEC, L. A., Biology
RANGACHARI, P. K., Medicine
RATHBONE, M. P., Biomedical Sciences
RATHBONE, R. L., Pathology
REGOECZI, E. L., Pathology
RICHARDSON, H., Pathology
RIDDELL, R. H., Pathology
ROBERTS, R. S., Clinical Epidemiology and Biostatistics
ROLAND, C. G., Family Medicine
ROSENBAUM, P. L., Paediatrics
ROSENFELD, J. M., Pathology
ROSENTHAL, D., Medicine
ROSENTHAL, K. L., Pathology
SACKETT, D. L., Clinical Epidemiology and Biostatistics
SAIGAL, S., Paediatrics
SARGEANT, E. J., Obstetrics and Gynaecology
SAXENA, B. M., Psychiatry
SCHATZ, S., Surgery
SEARS, M. R., Medicine
SEGGIE, J. A. L., Biomedical Sciences and Psychiatry
SEIDELMAN, W. E., Family Medicine
SHANNON, H. S., Clinical Epidemiology and Biostatistics
SHRAGGE, B. W., Surgery
SIMON, G. T., Pathology
SINCLAIR, J. C., Paediatrics
SINGAL, D. P., Pathology
SMILEY, J. R., Pathology
SMITH, E. K. M., Medicine
SOMERS, S., Radiology
STEINER, M., Psychiatry
STEVENSON, G. W., Radiology
STODDART, G. L., Clinical Epidemiology and Biostatistics
STREINER, D. L., Psychiatry, Clinical Epidemiology and Biostasis
SWEENEY, G. D., Medicine
SZECHTMAN, H., Biomedical Sciences
TANSER, P. H., Medicine
TARNOPOLSKY, A., Psychiatry
TAYLOR, D. W., Clinical Epidemiology and Biostatistics
TAYLOR, S. M., Geography
THOMAS, E. J., Surgery
THORNLEY, J. H., Pathology
TOMKINS, D. J., Paediatrics
TUNKS, E. R., Psychiatry
TURPIE, A. G. G., Medicine
UNDERDOWN, B. J., Pathology
UPTON, A. R. M., Medicine
VAN DER SPUY, H. I. J., Psychiatry
VERMA, D. K., Family Medicine
VIVIANI, G. R., Surgery
WAKEFIELD, J. S., Family Medicine
WALKER, I. R., Medicine
WALKER, W. H. C., Pathology
WALTER, S. D., Clinical Epidemiology and Biostatistics
WATTS, J. L., Paediatrics
WAY, R. C. K., Paediatrics
WEBBER, C. E., Radiology
WEITZ, J. I., Medicine
WHELAN, D., Paediatrics
WHITE, N. F., Psychiatry
WILLAN, A. R., Clinical Epidemiology and Biostatistics
WILSON, B. C., Radiology
WILSON, D. M. C., Family Medicine
WILSON, W. M., Paediatrics
WITELSON, S. F., Psychiatry
WOODWARD, C. A., Clinical Epidemiology and Biostatistics
YOUNGLAI, E. V., Obstetrics and Gynaecology and Pathology
YUSUF, S., Medicine

Faculty of Social Sciences:

AHMAD, S., Economics
ATKINSON, M. M., Political Science
BROWNING, M. J., Economics
BUNTING, B. T., Geography
BURBIDGE, J. B., Economics
CHAN, K. S., Economics
CHANDLER, W. M., Political Science
COLARUSSO, J. J., Anthropology
COLEMAN, W. D., Political Science
COOPER, M. D., Anthropology
COUNTS, D. R., Anthropology
CUNEO, C. J., Sociology
DAVIES, J. A., Geography
DENTON, F. T., Economics
DRAKE, J. J., Geography
ELLIOTT, D., Kinesiology
EYLES, J. E., Geography
FEENY, D. H., Economics
FEIT, H. A., Anthropology
FORD, D. C., Geography
GLANVILLE, E. V., Anthropology
GOLDSTEIN, M. N., Political Science
GRANOFF, P., Religious Studies
HAAS, J., Sociology
HALL, F. L., Geography
HALLPIKE, C. R., Anthropology
HARRISON, A. J., Economics
HOWARD, R. E., Sociology
JACEK, H. J., Political Science
JOHNSON, J. A., Economics
JONES, S. R. G., Economics
KING, L. J., Geography
KINSLEY, D. R., Religious Studies
KUBURSI, A. A., Economics
KUHN, P. J., Economics
LEVITT, C. H., Sociology
LEWCHUK, W. A., Economics
LEWIS, T. J., Political Science
LIAW, K.-L., Geography

MacDougall, J. D., Kinesiology
Magee, L. J., Economics
Matthews, D. R., Sociology
McCann, S. B., Geography
Mendelson, A., Religious Studies
Mestelman, S., Economics
Noble, W. C., Anthropology
Nossal, K. R., Political Science
Oksanen, E. H., Economics
Osborne, M. J., Economics
Papageorgiou, Y. Y., Economics and Geography
Potichnyj, P. J., Political Science
Preston, R. J., Anthropology
Pritchard, R. M., Psychology
Robb, A. L., Economics
Robertson, J., Religious Studies
Rodman, W. L., Anthropology
Rosenthal, C., Gerontology and Sociology
Rouse, W. R., Geography
Sale, D., Kinesiology
Saunders, S. R., Anthropology
Scarth, W. M., Economics
Shaffir, W., Sociology
Shinohara, K., Religious Studies
Spencer, B. G., Economics
Sproule-Jones, M., Political Science
Starkes, J., Kinesiology
Stein, M. B., Political Science
Stubbs, R., Political Science
Taylor, S. M., Geography
Veall, M. R., Economics
Walters, V., Sociology
Watt, M. S., Social Work
Williams, J. R., Economics
Woo, M-K., Geography
Younger, P., Religious Studies

Faculty of Science:

Allan, L. G., Psychology
Ananthanarayanan, V. S., Biochemistry
Bader, R. F. W., Chemistry
Bain, A., Chemistry
Ballik, E. A., Engineering Physics and Physics
Begg, I. M., Psychology
Bell, R. A., Chemistry
Berlinsky, A. J., Physics and Astronomy
Bhaduri, R. K., Physics and Astronomy
Billigheimer, C. E., Mathematics and Statistics
Branda, L. A., Biochemistry
Brooks, L. R., Psychology
Brown, I. D., Physics and Astronomy
Bunting, B. T., Geography
Burke, D. G., Physics and Astronomy
Cameron, J. A., Physics and Astronomy
Carbotte, J. P., Physics and Astronomy
Carment, D. W., Psychology
Chadam, J. M., Mathematics and Statistics
Chan, W. W., Biochemistry
Chettle, D. R., Physics and Astronomy
Childs, R. F., Chemistry
Choe, T. H., Mathematics and Statistics
Clarke, W. B., Physics and Astronomy
Clifford, P. M., Geology
Collins, M. F., Physics and Astronomy
Crocket, J. H., Geology
Csima, J., Mathematics and Statistics
Daly, M. A., Psychology
Datars, W. R., Physics and Astronomy
Davies, J. A., Geography
Davison, T. M. K., Mathematics and Statistics
Dawson, P. T., Chemistry
de Catanzaro, D., Psychology
Dickin, A., Geology
Drake, J. J., Geography
Epand, R. M., Biochemistry
Eyles, J. D., Geography
Ferrier, B. M., Biochemistry
Ford, D. C., Geography
Freeman, K. B., Biochemistry
Galef, B. G., Psychology
Gerber, G. E., Biochemistry
Ghosh, H. P., Biochemistry
Goodings, D. A., Physics and Astronomy
Graham, F. L., Biology
Greedan, J., Chemistry
Grundy, H. D., Geology
Gupta, R. S., Biochemistry
Hall, F. L., Geography and Civil Engineering and Engineering Mechanics
Hambleton, I., Mathematics and Statistics
Harms, A. A., Physics and Astronomy
Harris, R. S., Geography
Harris, W. E., Physics and Astronomy
Hassell, J. A., Biochemistry, Biology and Pathology
Heinig, H. P., Mathematics and Statistics
Hileman, O. E., Chemistry
Hitchcock, A. P., Chemistry
Hoppe, F. M., Mathematics and Statistics
Humphreys, D. A., Chemistry
Husain, T., Mathematics and Statistics
Jacoby, L. L., Psychology
Kenney-Wallace, G. A., Chemistry and Physics
King, L. J., Geography
Kolster, M., Mathematics and Statistics
Kramer, J. R., Geology
Laposa, J. D., Chemistry
Lauer, P. E., Computer Science and Systems
Leigh, W. J., Chemistry
Levy, B. A., Psychology
Liaw, K.-L., Geography
Link, S. W., Psychology
Lock, C. J. L., Chemistry
Lott, J. N. A., Biology
McCann, S. B., Geography
McDonald, D. G., Biology
MacDonald, G. M., Geography
MacDonald, P. D., Mathematics and Statistics
McGlinchey, M. J., Chemistry
McNutt, R. H., Geology
Maurer, D. Mc D., Psychology
Middleton, G. V., Geology
Min-oo, M., Mathematics and Statistics
Mohanty, S. G., Mathematics and Statistics
Moore, G., Mathematics and Statistics
Morrison, G. R., Psychology
Morton, R. A., Biology
Müller, B. J. W., Mathematics and Statistics
Nicas, A. J., Mathematics and Statistics
Nieboer, E., Biochemistry
Nogami, Y., Physics and Astronomy
Nurse, C. A., Biology
O'Donnell, M. J., Biology
Papageorgiou, G. J., Geography and Economics
Platt, J. R., Psychology
Prestwich, W. V., Physics and Astronomy
Prevec, L. A., Biology
Pritchard, R. M., Psychology
Pudritz, R. E., Physics and Astronomy
Rachubinski, R., Biochemistry
Racine, R. J., Psychology
Rainbow, A. J., Biology
Riehm, C. R., Mathematics and Statistics
Risk, M. J., Geology
Roberts, L. E., Psychology
Rosa, A., Mathematics and Statistics
Rouse, W. R., Geography
Ryan, P. J., Computer Science and Systems
Santry, D. P., Chemistry
Sawyer, E. T., Mathematics and Statistics
Schrobilgen, G. J., Chemistry
Schwarcz, H. P., Geology
Siegel, S., Psychology
Singh, R. S., Biology
Smith, G. K., Psychology
Smyth, W. F., Computer Science and Systems
Snaith, V. P., Mathematics and Statistics
Sorger, G. J., Biology
Sprung, D. W. L., Physics and Astronomy
Stager, C. V., Physics and Astronomy
Stewart, J. D., Mathematics and Statistics
Sutherland, P. G., Physics and Astronomy
Takahashi, I., Biology
Taylor, D. W., Physics and Astronomy
Taylor, S. M., Geography
Terlouw, J. K., Chemistry
Tiku, M. L., Mathematics and Statistics
Timusk, T., Physics and Astronomy
Waddington, J. C., Physics and Astronomy
Walker, R. G., Geology
Walton, D., Physics and Astronomy
Wang, M. Y.-K., Mathematics and Statistics
Warkentin, J., Chemistry
Weingarten, H., Psychology
Werstiuk, N. H., Chemistry
White, B. N., Biology
Woo, M. K., Geography
Wood, C. M., Biology
Yip, P. C.-Y., Mathematics and Statistics

Faculty of Engineering:

Alden, R. T. H., Electrical and Computer Engineering
Baird, M. H. I., Chemical Engineering
Ballik, E. A., Engineering Physics and Physics
Bandler, J. W., Electrical and Computer Engineering
Brash, J. L., Chemical Engineering and Pathology
Carter, C. R., Electrical and Computer Engineering
Chang, J.-S., Engineering Physics
Conn, D. R., Electrical and Computer Engineering
Crowe, C. M., Chemical Engineering
Dokainish, M. A., Mechanical Engineering
Drysdale, R. G., Civil Engineering
Elbestawi, M., Mechanical Engineering
Embury, J. D., Materials Science and Engineering
Feuerstein, I. A., Chemical Engineering
Findlay, R. D., Electrical and Computer Engineering
Ghobarah, A., Civil Engineering
Hall, F. L., Civil Engineering and Geography
Harms, A. A., Engineering Physics
Haykin, S. S., Electrical and Computer Engineering
Heidebrecht, A. C., Civil Engineering
Irons, G. A., Materials Science and Engineering
Ives, M. B., Materials Science and Engineering
Johari, G. P., Materials Science and Engineering
Judd, R. L., Mechanical Engineering
Kay, D. A. R., Materials Science and Engineering
Keech, G. L., Computer Science and Systems
Korol, R. M., Civil Engineering
Latto, B., Mechanical Engineering
Lauer, P. E., Computer Science and Systems
Litva, J., Electrical and Computer Engineering
Lu, W.-K., Materials Science and Engineering
MacGregor, J. F., Chemical Engineering
Marlin, T. E., Chemical Engineering
Mirza, F. A., Civil Engineering
Murphy, K. L., Civil Engineering
Nicholson, P. S., Materials Science and Engineering
Parnas, D. L., Electrical and Computer Engineering
Pelton, R. H., Chemical Engineering
Pietruszczak, S., Civil Engineering
Purdy, G. R., Materials Science and Engineering
Reilly, J. P., Electrical and Computer Engineering
Round, G. F., Mechanical Engineering
Ryan, P. J., Computer Science and Systems
Shoukri, M., Mechanical Engineering
Simmons, J. G., Engineering Physics
Sowerby, R., Mechanical Engineering

SZABADOS, B., Electrical and Computer Engineering
TAYLOR, P. A., Chemical Engineering
THOMPSON, D. A., Engineering Physics
TSO, W. K., Civil Engineering
VLACHOPOULOS, J., Chemical Engineering
WEATHERLY, G. C., Materials Science and Engineering
WEAVER, D. S., Mechanical Engineering
WILKINSON, D. S., Materials Science and Engineering
WONG, K. M., Electrical and Computer Engineering
WOOD, P. E., Chemical Engineering
WOODS, D. R., Chemical Engineering

Divinity College:

BELLOUS, J. E., Christian Ministries
BRACKNEY, W. H., Historical Theology
DEKAR, P. R., Christian History
FRASER, R. B., Field Education
HOBBS, T. R., Old Testament and Hebrew
HORNSELL, M. J. A., Old Testament and Hebrew
KERSTAN, R. J., Preaching and Communication
LONGENECKER, R. N., New Testament
PINNOCK, C. H., Systematic Theology
ROOK, J. T., New Testament and Greek
ROXBURGH, A. J., Christian Ministries

ATTACHED RESEARCH INSTITUTES

McMaster Institute for Energy Studies: Hamilton; f. 1980 to encourage communication between researchers in different fields of energy study; Dir Dr M. L. KLIMAN; publ. *Newsletter* (3 a year).

Office of Gerontological Studies: Hamilton; f. 1979; a multidisciplinary unit to promote and develop research and educational programmes on aging; Dir Dr E. RYAN.

Institute for Materials Research: Hamilton; research in the chemistry, engineering, metallurgy and physics of solid materials is supplemented through this multidisciplinary unit; principal areas: lattice dynamics, kinetics and diffusion, mechanical properties, microelectric and electro-optic devices, optical materials, phase transformations, thermodynamics, radiation damage, structure determination, surfaces and catalysis; Dir Dr A. J. BERLINSKY.

Institute of Polymer Production Technology: Hamilton; provides a facility and environment in which University staff and technical personnel from industry can do research and development on process technology for polymer production; Dir Dr A. E. HAMIELEC.

Communications Research Laboratory: Hamilton; provides experimental facilities for research in signal processing; Dir JOHN LITVA.

Centre for Health Economics and Policy Analysis: Hamilton; research, consultation, education, liaison; organizes conferences, etc.; publishes health policy commentaries and research reports; Co-ordinator Dr J. LOMAS.

Institute for Molecular Biology and Biotechnology: Hamilton; research, teaching, development of links with industry; Dir Dr J. A. HASSELL.

Educational Centre for Aging and Health: Hamilton; encourage gerontological input in educational programmes and the exchange of data; Dir Dr A. S. MACPHERSON.

Centre for Electrophotonic Materials and Devices: Hamilton; research and development; Dir Dr D. A. THOMPSON.

Centre for Flexible Manufacturing Research and Development: Hamilton; technological solutions to automation problems; test bed for prototypes, etc.; Dir Dr E. H. ELMARAGHY.

R. Samuel McLaughlin Centre for Gerontological Health Research: Hamilton; research, training and promotion of health and preventive care for the elderly; organizes conferences; publishes reports; Dir Dr L. W. CHAMBERS.

McMaster International: Hamilton; co-ordinates institutional international activities; provides leadership in international education and research, and in the provision of professional services by McMaster personnel to the global community; includes Centre for International Health; Dir Dr G. A. WARNER.

Centre for International Health: Hamilton; f. 1989 to facilitate and promote international health activities with the Faculty of Health Sciences, through education and project development; a clearing house and liaison centre for international health in collaboration with McMaster International; Dir Dr V. R. NEUFELD.

Institute of Environment and Health: Hamilton; research, health surveys and health assessments, identification and evaluation of hazards, development of preventive policies and strategies and of educational programmes; participation in community-based environment and health initiatives; conducts workshops and seminars; Dir Dr S. M. TAYLOR.

Centre for Peace Studies: Hamilton; research, graduate and undergraduate courses, seminars, lectures, conferences and other projects in the area of international peace; Dir Dr D. G. MACQUEEN.

UNIVERSITY OF MANITOBA

Winnipeg, Man. R3T 2N2
Telephone: (204) 474-8880
Fax: (204) 474-7536

Founded 1877
Language of instruction: English
Academic year: September to April (two terms)

Chancellor: ARTHUR MAURO
President and Vice-Chancellor: Dr EMÖKE SZATHMÁRY
Vice-President (Administration): MICHAEL W. MCADAM
Vice-President (Academic) and Provost: Dr JAMES S. GARDNER
Vice-President (Research): JOANNE KESELMAN
Vice-Provost (Academic Programs): R. A. LOBDELL (acting)
Vice-Provost (Academic Staff): K. C. OGDEN
Vice-Provost (Student Affairs): Dr D. MORPHY
Director of Libraries: C. PRESSER

Number of teachers: 1,141
Number of students: 16,238 full-time, 4,845 part-time

DEANS

Faculty of Agricultural and Food Sciences: J. ELLIOT
Faculty of Architecture: M. G. COX
Faculty of Arts: R. CURRIE
Faculty of Dentistry: R. C. BAKER (acting)
Faculty of Education: R. F. MAGSINO
Faculty of Engineering: D. H. SHIELDS
Faculty of Graduate Studies: F. DE TORO
Faculty of Human Ecology: R. BERRY
Faculty of Law: E. A. BRAID
Faculty of Management: J. L. GRAY
Faculty of Medicine: N. ANTHONISEN
Faculty of Nursing: J. BEATON
Faculty of Pharmacy: K. W. HINDMARSH
Faculty of Physical Education and Recreation Studies: D. W. HRYCAIKO
Faculty of Science: J. JAMIESON
Faculty of Social Work: D. FUCHS

DIRECTORS

School of Agriculture: D. FLATEN
School of Art: D. AMUNDSON
School of Dental Hygiene: E. BROWNSTONE
School of Medical Rehabilitation: B. LOVERIDGE (Overall Dir), ANN D. BOOTH (Occupational Therapy), A. FERNANDO (Physical Therapy)
School of Music: R. B. WEDGEWOOD
Continuing Education Division: B. LEVIN
Natural Resources Institute: S. SIMONOVIC

PROFESSORS

Faculty of Agricultural and Food Sciences:

BALLANCE, G. M., Plant Science
BOYD, M. S., Agricultural Economics and Farm Management
BRITTON, M. G., Biosystems Engineering
CAMPBELL, L. D., Animal Science
DRONZEK, B. L., Plant Science
ELLIOT, J. I., Animal Science
FAMINOW, M. D., Agricultural Economics and Farm Management
GALLOWAY, T. D., Entomology
GOH, T. B., Soil Science
GUENTER, W., Animal Science
HILL, R. D., Plant Science
HOLLEY, R. A., Food Science
HOLLIDAY, N. J., Entomology
JAYAS, D. S., Biosystems Engineering
KRAFT, D. F., Agricultural Economics and Farm Management
MACKAY, P. A., Entomology
MACMILLAN, J. A., Agricultural Economics and Farm Management
MCVETTY, P. B. E., Plant Science
MARQUARDT, R. R., Animal Science
MUIR, W. E., Biosystems Engineering
OLESON, B. T., Agricultural Economics and Farm Management
PALMER, C. E., Plant Science
PRITCHARD, M. K., Plant Science
RACZ, G. J., Soil Science
REMPHREY, W. R., Plant Science
RIMMER, S. R., Plant Science
ROUGHLEY, R. E., Entomology
SCARTH, R., Plant Science
SHAYKEWICH, C. F., Soil Science
VEIRA, D. M., Animal Science
WITTENBERG, K. M., Animal Science

Faculty of Architecture:

CARVALHO, M. E., City Planning
COX, M. G., Interior Design
FONSECA, R., Environmental Design, Architecture
FULLER, G. R., Interior Design
MACDONALD, R. I., Environmental Design
NELSON, C. R., Jr, Landscape Architecture
NEWBURY, R., Landscape Architecture
RATTRAY, A. E., Landscape Architecture
THOMSEN, C. H., Landscape Architecture
VEITCH, R. M., Interior Design
WELCH, J. D., Environmental Design

Faculty of Arts:

ADAIR, J. G., Psychology
ALBAS, D. C., Sociology
ANNA, T. E., History
ARNASON, D. E., English
BAILEY, P. C., History
BOLDT, E. D., Sociology
BRIERLEY, J. S., Geography
BUMSTED, J. M., History
BUTEUX, P. E., Political Studies
CAMERON, N. E., Economics
CARROLL, F. M., History
CATCHPOLE, A. J. W., Geography
COOLEY, D. O., English
CURRIE, R. F., Sociology
DEAN, J. M., Economics
EATON, W. O., Psychology
FERGUSON, B. G., History
FINLAY, J. L., History
FINNEGAN, R. E., English
FORTIER, P., French, Spanish and Italian
FRIESEN, G. A., History
GARDNER, J. S., Geography
GERUS, O. W., History
GONICK, C. W., Economics
GORDON, A. L., French, Spanish and Italian

GORDON, D. K., French, Spanish and Italian
GRISLIS, E., Religion
HALLI, S. S., Sociology
HELLER, H., History
HINZ, E. J., English
HUM, D., Economics
JANISSE, M. P., Psychology
JOHNSON, C. G., English
JOUBERT, A., French, Spanish and Italian
JUDD, E. R., Anthropology
KENDLE, J. E., History
KERR, I. J., History
KESELMAN, H. J., Psychology
KINNEAR, E. M., History
KINNEAR, M. S. R., History
KLOSTERMAIER, K. K., Religion
KOULACK, D., Psychology
KWONG, J., Sociology
LEBOW, M. D., Psychology
LEVENTHAL, L. Y., Psychology
LINDEN, E. W., Sociology
LOBDELL, R. A., Economics
LOXLEY, J., Economics
MCCANCE, D., Religion
MCCARTHY, D. J., Philosophy
MARTIN, D. G., Psychology
MARTIN, G. L., Psychology
MOULTON, E. C., History
NAHIR, M., Linguistics
NICHOLS, J. D., Linguistics
NICKELS, J. B., Psychology
NORTON, W., Geography
OAKES, J. E., Native Studies
O'KELL, R. P., English
PEAR, J. J., Psychology
PERRY, R. P., Psychology
PHILLIPS, P. A., Economics
RAMU, G. N., Sociology
REA, J. E., History
REMPEL, H., Economics
ROBERTS, L., Sociology
RUBENSTEIN, H., Anthropology
SANDIFORD, K. A. P., History
SCHAFER, A. M., Philosophy
SCHLUDERMANN, E. H., Psychology
SCHLUDERMANN, S., Psychology
SEGALL, A., Sociology
SHEPHARD, A. H., Psychology
SHKANDRIJ, M., German and Slavic Studies
SIMPSON, W., Economics
SINGER, M., Psychology
SMIL, V., Geography
SMITH, G. C., Geography
SPRAGUE, D. N., History
STACKHOUSE, J., Jr, Religion
STAMBROOK, F. G., History
STEIMAN, L. B., History
SZATHMÁRY, J. E., Anthropology
TAIT, R. W., Psychology
TAVUCHIS, N., Sociology
THOMAS, P. G., Political Studies
TODD, D., Geography
TOLES, G. E., English
TOWNSEND, J. B., Anthropology
VADNEY, T. E., History
WATERMAN, Rev. A. M. C., Economics
WEIL, H. S., English
WIEST, R. E., Anthropology
WILLIAMS, D. L., English
WILSON, L. M., Psychology
WOLF, K., Icelandic
WOLFART, H. C., Linguistics
WORTLEY, J. T., History

Faculty of Dentistry:

BOWDEN, G. H. W.
DAWES, C.
FLEMING, N.
HAMILTON, I. R.
KARIM, A. C.
LAVELLE, C. L. B.
LOVE, W. B.
SCHAFER, A.
SCHWARTZ, A.
SCOTT, J. E.
SINGER, D. L.
SUZUKI, M.
WILTSHIRE, W.

Faculty of Education:

BARTELL, R., Educational Administration, Foundations and Psychology
BRUNO-JOFRÉ, R., Educational Administration, Foundations and Psychology
CAP, O., Curriculum (Mathematics and Natural Sciences)
CLIFTON, R. A., Postsecondary Studies, Educational Administration, Foundations and Psychology
FREEZE, D. R., Educational Administration, Foundations and Psychology
GREGOR, A. D., Postsecondary Studies, Educational Administration, Foundations and Psychology
GRUNAU, H. H., Curriculum (Mathematics and Natural Sciences)
HARVEY, D. A., Curriculum (Mathematics and Natural Sciences)
HLYNKA, L. D., Curriculum (Mathematics and Natural Sciences)
JANSSON, L. C., Curriculum (Mathematics and Natural Sciences)
JENKINSON, D. H., Curriculum (Humanities and Social Sciences)
KESELMAN, J. C., Postsecondary Studies, Educational Administration, Foundations and Psychology
LEVIN, B., Educational Administration, Foundations and Psychology
LONG, J. C., Educational Administration, Foundations and Psychology
MADAK, P., Curriculum (Mathematics and Natural Sciences)
MAGSINO, R., Educational Administration, Foundations and Psychology
MORPHY, D. R., Postsecondary Studies
PERRY, R. P., Postsecondary Studies
POONWASSIE, D., Educational Administration, Foundations and Psychology
POROZNY, G. H. J., Curriculum (Mathematics and Natural Sciences)
RAMPAUL, W., Educational Administration, Foundations and Psychology
RIFFEL, J. A., Educational Administration, Foundations and Psychology
ROBERTS, L. W., Postsecondary Studies
SCHULZ, W. E., Educational Administration, Foundations and Psychology
SEIFERT, K. L., Educational Administration, Foundations and Psychology
STAPLETON, J. J., Educational Administration, Foundations and Psychology
STINNER, A. O., Curriculum (Mathematics and Natural Sciences)
STRAW, S. B., Curriculum (Humanities and Social Sciences)
YOUNG, J. C., Educational Administration, Foundations and Psychology
ZAKALUK, B. L., Curriculum (Humanities and Social Sciences)

Faculty of Engineering:

ALFA, A. S., Mechanical and Industrial
AZAD, R. S., Mechanical and Industrial
BALAKRISHNAN, S., Mechanical and Industrial
BASSIM, M. N., Mechanical and Industrial
BURN, D. H., Civil and Geological
CAHOON, J. R., Mechanical and Industrial
CARD, H. C., Electrical and Computer
CHATURVEDI, M. C., Mechanical and Industrial
CIRIC, I. M. R., Electrical and Computer
CLAYTON, A., Civil and Geological
GOLE, A. M., Electrical and Computer
GRAHAM, J., Civil and Geological
KINSNER, W., Electrical and Computer
LAJTAI, E. Z., Civil and Geological
LEHN, W., Electrical and Computer
MARTENS, G. O., Electrical and Computer
MCLAREN, P. G., Electrical and Computer
MCLEOD, R. D., Electrical and Computer
MENZIES, R. W., Electrical and Computer
OLESZKIEWICZ, J. A., Civil and Geological
ONYSHKO, S., Electrical and Computer
PEDRYCZ, W., Electrical and Computer
PINKNEY, R. B., Civil and Geological
POLYZOIS, D., Civil and Geological
POPPLEWELL, N., Mechanical and Industrial
RAGHUVEER, M. R., Electrical and Computer
RAJAPAKSE, R. K. N. D., Civil and Geological
RIZKALLA, S. H., Civil and Geological
RUTH, D. W., Mechanical and Industrial
SEBAK, A., Electrical and Computer
SHAFAI, L., Electrical and Computer
SHAH, A. H., Civil and Geological
SHIELDS, D. H., Civil and Geological
SHWEDYK, E., Electrical and Computer
SIMONOVIC, S. P., Civil and Geological
SOLIMAN, H. M., Mechanical and Industrial
STIMPSON, B., Civil and Geological
STRONG, D., Mechanical and Industrial
THOMSON, D. J., Electrical and Computer
THORNTON-TRUMP, A. B., Mechanical and Industrial
VENDA, V., Mechanical and Industrial
YUNIK, M., Electrical and Computer

Faculty of Human Ecology:

BERRY, R. E., Family Studies
BIRD, R. P., Foods and Nutrition
BOND, J. B., Family Studies
FITZPATRICK, D., Foods and Nutrition
HARVEY, C. D. H., Family Studies

Faculty of Law:

ANDERSON, D. T.
BALDWIN, J.
BRAID, E. A.
DEUTSCHER, D.
EDWARDS, C. H. C.
ESAU, A.
GUTH, D. J.
HARVEY, D. A. C.
IRVINE, J. C.
LONDON, J.
NEMIROFF, G.
NEPON, M. B.
OSBORNE, P. H.
PENNER, R.
SCHWARTZ, B. P.
SNEIDERMAN, B.
STUESSER, L.
VINCENT, L.

Faculty of Management:

BARTELL, M., Business Administration
BECTOR, C. R., Business Administration
BHATT, S. K., Business Administration
BRUNING, E. R., Marketing
BRUNING, N. S., Business Administration
ELIAS, N. S., Accounting and Finance
FROHLICH, N., Business Administration
GOOD, W. S., Marketing
GOULD, L. I., Accounting and Finance
GRAY, J. L., Business Administration
HILTON, M. W., Accounting and Finance
HOGAN, T. P., Business Administration
MCCALLUM, J. S., Accounting and Finance
NOTZ, W. W., Business Administration
OWEN, B. E., Business Administration
STARKE, F. A., Business Administration

Faculty of Medicine:

ADAMSON, I. Y. R., Pathology
ALGUACIL-GARCIA, A., Pathology
ANGEL, A., Medicine and Physiology
ANTHONISEN, N., Medicine
AOKI, F. Y., Continuing Medical Education, Medical Microbiology, Medicine, Pharmacology and Therapeutics
ARNETT, J. L., Clinical Health Psychology and Continuing Medical Education
BAKER, S., Medicine
BARAGAR, F., Medicine
BARAKAT, , Psychiatry
BARAL, E., Medicine, Radiology
BARWINSKY, J., Cardiothoracic Surgery
BEAZLEY, G. G., Family Medicine
BEBCHUK, W., Psychiatry
BECKER, A., Paediatrics and Child Health

Begleiter, A., Medicine, Pharmacology and Therapeutics
Berczi, I., Immunology
Biehl, D., Obstetrics, Gynaecology and Reproductive Sciences
Biehl, D. C., Continuing Medical Education
Biehl, D. R., Anaesthesia
Blakley, B., Otolaryngology
Blanchard, R. J. W., Surgery
Booth, F., Paediatrics and Child Health
Bose, D., Anaesthesia, Medicine, Pharmacology and Therapeutics
Bose, R., Pharmacology and Therapeutics
Bowden, G. H., Medical Microbiology
Bowman, D.M., Medicine
Bowman, J. M., Paediatrics and Child Health
Bowman, W. D., Paediatrics and Child Health
Brandes, L. J., Medicine, Pharmacology and Therapeutics
Bristow, G. K., Anaesthesia
Brownell, E. G., Medicine
Brunham, R. C., Medical Microbiology, Medicine, Obstetrics, Gynaecology and Reproductive Sciences
Bruni, J. E., Human Anatomy and Cell Science
Burns, C. M., General Surgery
Carr, I., Pathology
Carter, S. A., Medicine and Physiology
Casior, O., Paediatrics and Child Health
Cattini, P., Physiology
Chernick, V., Paediatrics and Child Health
Choy, P. C., Biochemistry and Molecular Biology
Chudley, A. E., Continuing Medical Education, Human Genetics, Paediatrics and Child Health
Craig, D. B., Anaesthesia
Cristante, L., Surgery
Cuddy, T. E., Medicine
Cumming, G. R., Paediatrics and Child Health
Dakshinamurti, K., Biochemistry and Molecular Biology
Danzinger, R. G., General Surgery
Davie, J. R., Biochemistry and Molecular Biology
Dean, H., Paediatrics and Child Health
Dhalla, N., Physiology
Donen, N., Anaesthesia, Continuing Medical Education
Downs, A. R., General Surgery
Dubo, H. I. C., Medicine
Duke, P. C., Anaesthesia
Evans, J. A., Community Health Sciences, Human Genetics, Paediatrics and Child Health
Ferguson, C. A., Paediatrics and Child Health
Fine, A., Medicine
Foerster, J., Medicine
Gartner, J., Immunology, Pathology
Geiger, J., Pharmacology and Therapeutics
Gerrard, J. M., Paediatrics and Child Health
Glavin, G., Pharmacology and Therapeutics
Gordon, R., Radiology
Greenberg, A. H., Human Genetics, Immunology, Paediatrics and Child Health, Physiology
Greenberg, C. R., Human Genetics, Paediatrics and Child Health
Grewar, D. A. I., Family Medicine, Paediatrics and Child Health
Hall, P. F., Obstetrics, Gynaecology and Reproductive Sciences
Hamerton, J. L., Paediatrics and Child Health
Hammond, G., Medicine
Hammond, G. W., Medical Microbiology
Harding, G., Medicine
Harding, G. M., Medical Microbiology
Harvey, D. A., Community Health Sciences
Hassard, T. H., Community Health Sciences
Havens, B., Community Health Sciences
Hay Glass, K. T., Immunology
Hershfield, E. A., Community Health Sciences
Hershfield, E. S., Medicine
Hill, N. C., Neurosurgery
Hoeschen, R., Medicine
Hogan, T. P., Community Health Sciences
Horne, J. M., Community Health Sciences
Hudson, R., Anaesthesia
Hughes, K. R., Physiology
Ireland, D. J., Otolaryngology
Israels, L., Medicine
Jay, F. T., Medical Microbiology
Jeffery, J., Medicine
Jordan, L. M., Physiology
Kanfer, J. N., Biochemistry and Molecular Biology
Katz, P., Psychiatry
Kaufert, J. M., Community Health Sciences
Kaufert, P. A., Community Health Services
Kaufman, B. J., Medicine
Kirk, B. W., Medicine
Kirk, P. J., Family Medicine
Kirkpatrick, J. R., Continuing Medical Education, General Surgery
Krepart, G. V., Obstetrics, Gynaecology and Reproductive Sciences
Kroeger, E. A., Physiology
Kryger, M., Medicine
LaBella, F. S., Pharmacology and Therapeutics
Lautt, W. W., Pharmacology and Therapeutics
LeJohn, H. B., Human Genetics
Lertzman, M., Continuing Medical Education, Medicine
Levi, C. S., Radiology
Levitt, M., Medicine
Light, B., Medicine
Light, R. B., Medical Microbiology
Lindsay, W., Surgery
Longstaffe, S., Paediatrics and Child Health
Lyons, E. A., Radiology, Obstetrics, Gynaecology and Reproductive Sciences
McAlpine, P. J., Human Genetics, Paediatrics and Child Health
McCarthy, D. S., Medicine
McCoshen, J. A., Obstetrics, Gynaecology and Reproductive Sciences
McCrea, D. A., Physiology
McCullough, D. W., Continuing Medical Education, Otolaryngology
MacEwan, D., Community Health Sciences
McKenzie, J. K., Medicine, Pharmacology and Therapeutics
Markesteyn, P., Pathology
Martin, R. M., Clinical Health Psychology
Minuk, G. Y., Medicine, Pharmacology and Therapeutics
Moffatt, M. E., Community Health Services, Paediatrics and Child Health
Moore, K. L., Human Anatomy and Cell Science
Murphy, L. C., Biochemistry and Molecular Biology, Medicine
Murphy, L. J., Medicine and Physiology
Mutch, A., Anaesthesia
Nagy, J. I., Physiology
Naimark, A., Physiology
Nance, D. M., Pathology
Nicole, L. E., Medical Microbiology
Nicolle, L., Medicine
Oen, K., Paediatrics and Child Health
Olweny, C., Medicine
O'Neil, J. D., Community Health Sciences
Ong, B. Y., Anaesthesia
Oppenheimer, L., General Surgery
Orr, F. W., Pathology
Pagtakhan, R. D., Paediatrics and Child Health
Panagia, V., Human Anatomy and Cell Science, Physiology
Paraskevas, F., Immunology and Medicine
Paraskevas, M., Pathology
Parkinson, D., Neurosurgery
Pasterkamp, H., Paediatrics and Child Health
Paterson, J. A., Human Anatomy and Cell Science
Peeling, J., Pharmacology and Therapeutics
Peeling, W. J., Radiology
Penner, B., Medicine
Penner, S. B., Pharmacology and Therapeutics
Persaud, T. V. N., Human Anatomy and Cell Science, Obstetrics, Gynaecology and Reproductive Sciences, Paediatrics and Child Health
Pettigrew, N., Pathology
Pierce, G. N., Physiology
Pillay, N., Medicine
Plummer, F. A., Medical Microbiology, Medicine
Postl, B., Community Health Sciences, Paediatrics and Child Health
Postuma, R., General Surgery
Ramsey, E., Surgery
Reed, M. H., Continuing Medical Education, Paediatrics and Child Health, Radiology
Rennie, W., Orthopaedic Surgery
Riese, K. T., General Surgery and Otolaryngology
Rigatto, H., Paediatrics and Child Health, Obstetrics, Gynaecology and Reproductive Sciences
Ronald, A. R., Community Health Sciences, Medical Microbiology, Medicine
Roos, L. L., Community Health Sciences
Roos, N. P., Community Health Sciences
Ross, R. T., Medicine
Roy, R., Clinical Health Psychology
Rubin, J. A., Otolaryngology
Rush, D., Medicine
Sabbadini, E., Immunology
Schacter, B., Medicine
Schipper, H., Medicine
Schroeder, M., Paediatrics and Child Health
Sehon, A., Immunology
Seshia, M. M. K., Obstetrics, Gynaecology and Reproductive Sciences, Paediatrics and Child Health
Shapiro, E., Community Health Sciences
Shiu, R. P. C., Physiology
Shojania, A. M., Medicine, Paediatrics and Child Health, Pathology
Simons, F. E. R., Immunology, Paediatrics and Child Health
Simons, K., Paediatrics and Child Health
Singal, P. K., Physiology
Sitar, D., Medicine, Pharmacology and Therapeutics
Smyth, D. D., Continuing Medical Education, Pharmacology and Therapeutics
Smythe, D., Medicine
Sneiderman, B. M., Community Health Sciences
Stanwick, R. S., Community Health Sciences
Stephens, N. L., Physiology
Stevens, F. C., Biochemistry and Molecular Biology
Stranc, M. F., Plastic Surgery
Sutherland, J. B., Radiology
Szathmary, E. J. E., Human Genetics
Tenenbein, M., Community Health Sciences, Medicine, Pharmacology and Therapeutics, Paediatrics and Child Health
Thliveris, J. A., Human Anatomy and Cell Science
Thomson, I., Anaesthesia
Unruh, H. W., Surgery
Vriend, J., Human Anatomy and Cell Science
Wade, J., Community Health Sciences
Warren, C. P. W., Continuing Medical Education, Medicine

WARRINGTON, R. J., Immunology and Medicine
WILKINS, J. A., Immunology, Medicine, Medical Microbiology
WILLIAMS, T., Medical Microbiology, Paediatrics and Child Health
WOODS, R. A., Human Genetics
WRIGHT, J. A., Biochemistry and Molecular Biology
WROGEMANN, K., Biochemistry and Molecular Biology, Human Genetics
YASSI, A., Community Health Sciences
YOUNES, M., Medicine
YOUNG, T. K., Community Health Sciences

Natural Resources Institute:

BERKES, F.
SIMNOVIC, S. P.

Faculty of Nursing:

BEATON, J. I.
DEGNER, L. F.

Faculty of Pharmacy:

BRIGGS, C. J.
HASINOFF, B.
HINDMARSH, K. W.
SIMONS, K. J.
STEELE, J. W.
TEMPLETON, J. F.

Faculty of Physical Education and Recreation Studies:

ALEXANDER, M. J. L.
DAHLGREN, W. J.
HARPER, J.
HRYCAIKO, D. W.
JANZEN, H. F.
JOHNS, D. P.
READY, A. E.
SEARLE, M.

Faculty of Science:

AITCHISON, P. W., Applied Mathematics
ARNASON, A. N., Computer Science
AYRES, L. D., Geological Sciences
BALDWIN, W. G., Chemistry
BARBER, R. C., Physics and Astronomy
BATTEN, L. M., Mathematics
BELL, M. G., Mathematics
BERRY, T. G., Applied Mathematics
BIRCHALL, J., Physics and Astronomy
BOOTH, J. T., Botany
BREWSTER, J. F., Statistics
BUTLER, M., Microbiology
CERNY, P., Geological Sciences
CHAN, L. K., Statistics
CHARLTON, J. L., Chemistry
CHENG, S. W., Statistics
CHOW, A., Chemistry
CLARK, G. S., Geological Sciences
COHEN, A., Applied Mathematics
COLLENS, R. J., Computer Science
DAVISON, N. E., Physics and Astronomy
DICK, T. A., Zoology
DOOB, M., Mathematics
DUCKWORTH, H. W., Chemistry
EALES, J. G., Zoology
ELIAS, R. J., Geological Sciences
EVANS, R. M., Zoology
FALK, W., Physics and Astronomy
FU, J. C., Statistics
GERHARD, J. A., Mathematics
GHAHRAMANI, F., Mathematics
GRATZER, G., Mathematics
GUO, B., Applied Mathematics
GUPTA, C. K., Mathematics
GUPTA, N. D., Mathematics
HALDEN, N. M., Geological Sciences
HAWTHORNE, F. C., Geological Sciences
HOSKINS, J. A., Computer Science
HOSKINS, W. D., Applied Mathematics
HRUSKA, F. E., Chemistry
HUEBNER, E., Zoology
HUNTER, N. R., Chemistry
JAMIESON, J. C., Chemistry
JANZEN, A. F., Chemistry
KELLY, D., Mathematics
KENKEL, N. C., Botany
KING, P. R., Computer Science
KLASSEN, G. R., Microbiology
KOCAY, W. L., Computer Science
KOCHERLAKOTA, K., Statistics
KOCHERLAKOTA, S., Statistics
KRAUSE, G., Mathematics
LAKSER, H., Mathematics
LAST, W. M., Geological Sciences
LAZNICKA, P., Geological Sciences
LÉJOHN, H. B., Microbiology
LOEWEN, P. C., Microbiology
LOLY, P. D., Physics and Astronomy
MACARTHUR, R. A., Zoology
MCCLURE, J. P., Mathematics
MCKINNON, D. M., Chemistry
MACPHERSON, B. D., Statistics
MAEBA, P. Y., Microbiology
MEEK, D. S., Computer Science
MENDELSOHN, N. S., Mathematics
MOON, W., Geological Sciences
MORRISH, A. H., Physics and Astronomy
OSBORN, T. A., Physics and Astronomy
PADMANABHAN, R., Mathematics
PAGE, J. H., Physics and Astronomy
PARAMESWARAN, M. R., Mathematics
PLATT, C., Mathematics
PUNTER, D., Botany
QUACKENBUSH, R. W., Mathematics
RAYBURN, M. C., Mathematics
RIEWE, R. R., Zoology
ROBINSON, G. G. C., Botany, Environmental Science Program
ROSHKO, R. M., Physics and Astronomy
SAMANTA, M., Statistics
SCHAEFER, T., Chemistry
SCUSE, D. H., Computer Science
SEALY, S. G., Zoology
SECCO, A. S., Chemistry
SHARMA, K. S., Physics and Astronomy
SHIVAKUMAR, P. N., Applied Mathematics
SICHLER, J., Mathematics
SOUTHERN, B. W., Physics and Astronomy
STANTON, R. G., Computer Science
STEWART, J. M., Botany
STEWART, K. W., Zoology
SUZUKI, I., Microbiology
SVENNE, J. P., Physics and Astronomy
TABISZ, G. C., Physics and Astronomy
TELLER, J. C., Geological Sciences
THOMAS, R. S. D., Applied Mathematics
TRIM, D. W., Applied Mathematics
VAIL, J. M., Physics and Astronomy
VANCAESEELE, L. A., Botany
VAN OERS, W. T. H., Physics and Astronomy
VAN REES, G. H. J., Computer Science
WALLACE, R., Chemistry
WALTON, D. J., Computer Science
WESTMORE, J. B., Chemistry
WIENS, T. J., Zoology
WILLIAMS, G., Physics and Astronomy
WILLIAMS, H. C., Computer Science
WILLIAMS, J. J., Applied Mathematics
WOODS, R. G., Mathematics
WRIGHT, J. A., Microbiology

Faculty of Social Work:

FUCHS, D. M.
GALAWAY, B.
ROY, R.
TRUTE, B.

School of Art:

AMUNDSON, D. O.
BAKER, M. C.
FLYNN, R. K.
HIGGINS, S. B.
MCMILLAN, D. S.
PURA, W. P.
SAKOWSKI, R. C.
SCOTT, C. W.

School of Dental Hygiene:

AOKI, F. Y.
BORDEN, S. M.
BOWDEN, G. H. W.
DAWES, C.
HAMILTON, I. R.
LAVELLE, C. L. B.
PRUTHI, V. K.
SINGER, D. L.
WRIGHT, J. N.
ZEBROWSKI, E. J.

School of Medical Rehabilitation:

LOVERIDGE, B.

School of Music:

ENGBRECHT, H.
KEAHEY, D. J.
KEAHEY, T. H.
WEDGEWOOD, R.

Continuing Education Division:

LEVIN, B.

Counselling Service:

EIDE, L. J.
WALKER, L. J.

Division of Occupational Therapy:

COOPER, J. E.

Division of Physical Therapy:

LOVERIDGE, B.

ATTACHED INSTITUTE

Natural Resources Institute Dir Prof. S. SIMONOVIC

AFFILIATED COLLEGES

St Andrew's College: 29 Dysart Rd, Winnipeg, Man. R3T 2M7; tel. (204) 474-8900; fax (204) 474-8895; f. 1964 (Ukrainian Orthodox Church); Principal R. YERENIUK.

St Boniface College: 200 Cathedral Ave, St Boniface, Man. R2H 0H7; tel. (204) 233-0210; f. 1818 (Roman Catholic); Rector P. RUEST.

St John's College: 400 Dysart Road, Winnipeg, Man. R3T 2M5; tel. (204) 474-8363; fax (204) 261-1215; f. 1849 (Anglican); Warden and Vice-Chancellor Dr J. HOSKINS (acting).

St Paul's College: 430 Dysart Rd, Winnipeg, Man. R3T 2M6; tel. (204) 474-8575; f. 1926 (Roman Catholic); Rector J. J. STAPLETON.

University College: 500 Dysart Rd, Winnipeg, Man. R3T 2M8; tel. (204) 474-9126; Provost G. WALZ.

MEMORIAL UNIVERSITY OF NEWFOUNDLAND

POB 4200, Elizabeth Ave, St John's, Nfld A1C 5S7

Telephone: (709) 737-8000
Telex: 016-4101
Fax: (709) 737-4569

Founded 1925 by Provincial Government as Memorial University College, university status 1949

Academic year: September to August (three terms)

Language of instruction: English

Chancellor: J. CROSBIE
President and Vice-Chancellor: A. MAY
Vice-Presidents:
Academic and Pro Vice-Chancellor: J. TUINMAN
Administration: W. W. THISTLE
Research: K. KEOUGH
Principal, Sir Wilfred Grenfell College: K. BINDON
Registrar: G. W. COLLINS
Librarian: R. ELLIS

Number of teachers: 1,367
Number of students: 17,226

Publications: *Culture and Tradition, Regional Language Studies* (both annually), *Canadian folklore canadien, Labour / Le Travail* (both 2 a year), *Newfoundland Quarterly* (quarterly), *Luminus* (3 a year), *Gazette* (fortnightly), *Communicator* (quarterly), *Échos du Monde Classique / Classical Views* (3 a year).

DEANS AND DIRECTORS

Office of Student Affairs and Services: W. E. Ludlow
Faculty of Arts: T. Murphy
Faculty of Business Administration: W. Blake
Faculty of Science: A. Law
Faculty of Education: T. Piper
Faculty of Engineering and Applied Science: R. Seshadri
Faculty of Medicine: M. I. Bowmer
School of Continuing Education: D. Whalen (acting)
School of Graduate Studies: G. Kealey
School of Nursing: M. Lamb
School of Physical Education and Athletics: W. Redden
School of Social Work: J. Pennell
School of Music: M. Volk
School of Pharmacy: G. Duncan

PROFESSORS

Adamec, R. E., Psychology
Adams, G. B., Medicine
Adams, R. J., Psychology
Aksu, A. E., Earth Sciences
Allderice, P., Medicine, Cytogenetics
Andersen, R. R., Anthropology
Andrews, F. E., Philosophy
Bajzak, D., Engineering
Baksh, I. J., Education
Bal, A. K., Biology
Barker, W. W., English
Barnes, J. G., Business Administration
Bartels, D., Sir Wilfred Grenfell College (Anthropology, Sociology)
Barth, R. T., Business Administration
Bass, D. W., Mathematics and Statistics
Bassler, G. P., History
Bear, J. C., Medicine (Genetics)
Bell, D. N., Religious Studies
Bella, L., Social Work
Bieger, D., Medicine (Pharmacology)
Bindon, K., Sir Wilfred Grenfell College (History)
Bishop, N. B., French and Spanish
Booth, P. I., Mathematics and Statistics
Booton, M., Engineering
Bose, N., Engineering
Bowmer, I. M., Medicine
Briggs, J. L., Anthropology
Brooker, M. H., Chemistry
Brosnan, J. T., Biochemistry and Medicine
Brosnan, M. E., Biochemistry and Medicine
Bruce, I. A. F., Classics and History
Bruce-Lockhart, M., Engineering
Brunner, H., Mathematics and Statistics
Bubenik, V., Linguistics
Buchanan, R., English
Bulcock, J. W., Education
Burford, G., Social Work (Assoc. Dir)
Burnell, J., Chemistry
Burry, J. H., Mathematics
Burton, D., Biology
Butrica, J., Classics
Cake, L. J., Sir Wilfred Grenfell College (Psychology)
Canning, P., Education
Chadwick, A., French and Spanish
Chandra, R. K., Medicine (Paediatric Research)
Cherwinski, W. J., History
Chittal, S. M., Medicine
Clark, R. J., Classics
Clarke, S. A., Linguistics
Close, D. W., Political Science
Clouter, M. J., Physics
Colbo, M. H., Biology
Collins, M. A. J., Biology
Cooper, A. R., Medicine (Pathology)
Corbett, D. R., Medicine
Coyne, J. M., Sir William Grenfell College (Visual Arts)
Craske, B., Psychology
Crellin, J. K., Medicine (History and Physiology)
Crim, L. W., Ocean Sciences Centre (Biology)
Crocker, R. K., Education
Curtis, F. A., Engineering
Davidson, W. S., Biochemistry
Deibel, D. R., Ocean Studies Centre
den Otter, A. A., History
Doyle, C. P., Education
Duguid, N. J. D., Medicine
Duncan, G., Pharmacy
Dunne, J. T., Medicine (Obstetrics and Gynaecology)
Eddy, R. H., Mathematics and Statistics
Edstrom, H. W., Medicine (Respirology)
English, C. J. B., History
Evans, S. M., Sir Wilfred Grenfell College (Geography)
Facey-Crowther, D., History
Faseruk, A. J., Business Administration
Fernandez, D., Medicine (Pathology)
Fischer, L., History
Fletcher, G.L., Ocean Sciences Centre (Biology)
Fowler, A., Sir Wilfred Grenfell College (English)
Friel, J. K., Biochemistry
Gale, J. E., Earth Sciences
Gardner, P. G., English
Garlie, N. W., Education
Gaskill, H. S., Mathematics
Gien, L. T., Nursing
Gien, T. T., Physics
Gillard, P., Computer Science
Gogan, N. J., Chemistry
Goodaire, E. G., Mathematics and Statistics
Gordon, R., Biology
Graham, D. E., French and Spanish
Greatbatch, R. J., Physics
Green, J. M., Biology
Greenlee, J. G. C., Sir Wilfred Grenfell College (History)
Gregory, B., Chemistry
Gunther, G., Sir Wilfred Grenfell College (Mathematics and Statistics)
Haddara, M. M. R., Engineering
Hadley, N. H., Education
Haedrich, R. L., Ocean Sciences Centre (Biology)
Haegert, D. G., Medicine (Pathology)
Hall, J., Earth Sciences
Hannah, T. E., Psychology
Hansen, P. A., Medicine
Harger-Grinling, V. A., French and Spanish
Harley, C. A., Psychology
Harnett, J. D., Medicine
Harper, J., Earth Sciences
Harris, P. F., Philosophy
Hawkin, D. J., Religious Studies
Hawkins, F. R., Social Work
Heath, P. R., Mathematics and Statistics
Herzberg, G. R., Biochemistry and Medicine
Heughan, C., Medicine (Surgery)
Higgs, C., Physical Education
Hiller, J. K., History
Hiscott, R. N., Earth Sciences
Hodych, J. P., Earth Sciences
House, J. D., Sociology
Howe, M. L., Psychology
Hulan, H., Biochemistry
Hurley, G. W., Counselling Centre
Husain, T., Engineering
Inglis, G. B., Anthropology
Ingram, D. W., Medicine
Ives, E. J., Medicine (Paediatrics)
Jablonski, C. R., Chemistry
Jacobs, J. D., Geography
Jeffrey, G. H., Education
Jespers, E., Mathematics and Statistics
Jones, G. P., English
Jones, K. C., Sir Wilfred Grenfell College (Visual Arts)
Jordaan, I. J., Ocean Engineering
Ke, P. J., Biochemistry
Kealey, G. S., History
Kelleher, R. R., Education
Kennedy, J. C., Anthropology
Khan, R. A., Biology
Kimberley, M. D., Social Work
King, A. F., Earth Sciences
King, E. H., English
King, F. G., Medicine
Kozma, A., Psychology, Nursing and Medicine
Kufeldt, K., Social Work
Kwan, A., Medicine (Surgery)
Lai, T. T. L., Philosophy
Lal, M., Mathematics
Larson, D. J., Biology
Law, A., Computer Science
Lee, C. I. C., Mathematics and Statistics
Lemelin, J.-M., French and Spanish
Leyton, E. H., Anthropology
Liddell, A., Psychology
Lines, L. R., Earth Sciences
Loader, C. E., Chemistry
Loomis, C. W., Pharmacy
Lucas, C. R., Chemistry
Ludlow, W. E., Student Affairs and Services (Education)
Machin, W. D., Chemistry
McKim, W. D., Psychology
Macleod, M. K., History
McManamon, P. J., Medicine (Radiology)
Malpas, J. G., Earth Sciences
Malsbury, C., Psychology and Medicine
Mannion, J. J., Geography
Manson, H., Medicine (Anaesthesia)
Maroun, F., Medicine (Neurosurgery)
Marshall, W. H., Medicine (Immunology)
Martin, A. M., Biochemistry
Martin, J. R., Medicine
Marzouk, H. M., Engineering
Mathieson, G., Medicine (Pathology)
Maxwell, D. V., Philosophy
May, J. D., Economics
Meja, V., Sociology
Michalak, T. I., Medicine
Michalski, C. J., Medicine (Molecular Biology)
Miller, E., English
Miller, H. G., Assoc. Exec. Dir of Marine Institute
Molgaard, J., Engineering
Montevecchi, W. A., Psychology
Murphy, T. M., Religious Studies
Murray, P. M., Medicine
Narayanaswami, P. P., Mathematics and Statistics
Narvaez, P., Folklore
Nesbit, W. C., Education
Netten, J. E., Education
Neuman, R. S., Medicine (Pharmacology)
Newton, M. C., Sir Wilfred Grenfell College (Religious Studies)
Nichol, D. W., English
Norris, S. P., Education
Nurse, D., Linguistics
O'Dea, S., English
Ommer, R. E., History
Overton, J., Sociology
Paddock, H. J., Linguistics
Parfrey, P. S., Medicine
Parmenter, M. M., Mathematics and Statistics
Pastore, R. T., History
Patel, T. R., Biology
Pater, A., Medicine (Molecular Biology)
Patey, P., Medicine (Family Practice)
Payton, B. W., Medicine (Physiology)
Pennell, J., Social Work
Penney, C. G. B., Psychology
Peters, H., English
Peterson, C. L., Psychology
Phillips, L. M., Education
Pickup, P. G., Chemistry
Pierson, S. O., History
Piper, T., Education
Pocius, G., Folklore
Porter, M. B., Sociology
Pryse-Phillips, W., Medicine (Neurology)
Quaicoe, J. E., Engineering
Quinlan, G. M., Earth Sciences
Rabinowitz, F. M., Psychology
Rahimtula, A. D., Biochemistry and Medicine
Rahman, M. D., Engineering
Ralph, E. K., Chemistry

RAYNER-CANHAM, G., Sir Wilfred Grenfell College (Chemistry)
REDDY, E. J., Medicine
REDDY, S. P., Physics
REVUSKY, B. T., Psychology
REVUSKY, S. H., Psychology
RICH, N. H., Physics
RIVERS, C. J. S., Earth Sciences
ROBINSON, J., Engineering
ROCHESTER, M. G., Earth Sciences
ROLLMAN, H., Religious Studies
ROMPKEY, R. G., English
ROSE, G., Marine Institute
ROSENBERG, N., Folklore
ROSKIN, R. R., Business Administration
ROSS, A. S., Psychology
ROY, N., Economics
RYAN, S., History
SABIN, G. C. W., Engineering
SACHDEV, P., Social Work
SAHA, S., Business Administration
SCHNEIDER, D. C., Ocean Sciences Centre
SCHRANK, B., English
SCHRANK, W. E., Economics
SCHWARTZ, R. D., Sociology
SCOTT, J. A., Philosophy
SCOTT, T. M., Medicine (Anatomy)
SEGOVIA, J., Social and Preventive Medicine
SESHADRI, R., Engineering
SEXTY, R. W., Business Administration
SHAHIDI, F., Biochemistry
SHARAN, A. M., Engineering
SHARP, J. J., Engineering
SHAWYER, B. L. R., Mathematics and Statistics
SHERRICK, M. F., Psychology
SINCLAIR, P. R., Sociology
SINGH, A., Education
SINGH, S. P., Mathematics
SINHA, B. P., Engineering
SKIPTON, M. D., Business Administration
SMITH, F. R., Chemistry
SMITH, P., Folklore
SMITH, W. G., Engineering
SNELLEN, J. W., Medicine (Applied Physiology)
SOOKLAL, L. R., Business Administration
STAVELEY, M., Geography
STEELE, D. H., Biology
STEELE, V. J., Biology
STEFFLER, J. E., Sir Wilfred Grenfell College (English)
STEIN, A. R., Chemistry
STEVENS, K., Education
STEWART, D. B., Business Administration
STOREY, K. J., Geography
SUMMERS, D., Mathematics and Statistics
SUTRADHAR, B. C., Mathematics and Statistics
SWAMIDAS, A. S. J., Engineering
TANNER, A., Anthropology
THOMPSON, L. K., Chemistry
THOMPSON, R. J., Ocean Sciences Centre
TREMAINE, P. R., Chemistry
TRESLAN, D. L., Education
TSEGA, E., Medicine
TSOA, E., Economics
TUCK, J. A., Anthropology
VASDEV, S. C., Medicine
VENKATESAN, R., Engineering
VEYSOGLU, R., Economics
VICKERS, D. F., History
VIDYASANKAR, K., Computer Science
VIRGO, B., Pharmacy and Medicine
VIRMANI, S., Medicine
WALLEY, R. L., Medicine (Obstetrics and Gynaecology)
WATSON, B. B., Mathematics
WEST, R., Pharmacy and Medicine
WHITE, R. W., Geography
WHITMORE, M. D., Physics
WHITTAKER, J., Classics
WILLIAMS, E. R., Mathematics
WILLIAMS, H., Earth Sciences
WILLIAMS, S. H., Earth Sciences
WILTON, D. H. C., Earth Sciences
WITHEY, M. J., Business Administration
WOLINETZ, S. B., Political Science
WOOD, C., Geography
WRIGHT, E. S., Medicine (Surgery)
WRIGHT, J. A., Earth Sciences
WROBLEWSKI, J. S., Ocean Sciences Centre (Physics)
YOUNG, D. C., Medicine (Obstetrics and Gynaecology)
ZUBEREK, W. M., Computer Science

ATTACHED INSTITUTES

Art Gallery: Dir P. GRATTAN.

Botanical Garden: Dir W. NICHOLS.

Centre for Newfoundland Studies: Head A. HART.

Harlow Campus: Chair., Dean's Harlow Co-ordinating Committee D. TRESLAN.

Institut Frecker: Dir A. THAREAU.

Marine Institute: Exec. Dir L. O'REILLY.

Maritime History Archive: Curator H. WAREHAM.

Queen's College: Provost Rev. B. MORGAN.

Sir Wilfred Grenfell College: Principal K. BINDON.

ATTACHED RESEARCH INSTITUTES

(The mailing address is that of the University itself)

Archaeology Unit: Chair. J. A. TUCK.

Canadian Centre for Fisheries Innovation: Dir A. O'REILLY.

Canadian Centre for International Fisheries Training and Development: International Liaison Officer A. B. DICKINSON.

Cartographic Laboratory: Dir C. H. WOOD.

Centre for Cold Ocean Resources Engineering: Pres/CEO J. WHITTICK.

Centre for Computer-Aided Engineering: Man. D. PRESS.

Centre for Earth Resources Research: Dir G. QUINLAN (acting).

Centre for International Business: Dir B. WINSOR.

Centre for Management Development: Dir G. ROWE.

Centre for Material Culture Studies: Dirs S. O'DEA, G. POCIUS.

Centre for Offshore and Remote Medicine: Dir H. MANSON.

Continuing Engineering Education: Dir (vacant).

English Language Research Centre: Co-ordinator W. KIRWIN.

Folklore and Language Archive: Dir M. LOVELACE.

Geographical Information and Digital Analysis Laboratory: Dir A. SIMMS.

Institute of Social and Economic Research: Research Dir J. TUCK.

Labrador Institute of Northern Studies: Dir D. WILTON (acting).

Maritime Studies Research Unit: Chair. D. VICKERS.

Ocean Engineering Research Centre: Dir N. BOSE.

Ocean Sciences Centre: Dir L. CRIM.

P. J. Gardiner Institute for Small Business: Dir W. KING.

Seabright Corporation Ltd: Pres/CEO D. KING.

Telemedicine Centre: Dir JANICE COOPER (acting).

Telemedicine and Educational Technology Resources Agency: Co-Dir R. HYDE.

UNIVERSITÉ DE MONCTON

Moncton, NB E1A 3E9
Telephone: (506) 858-4000
Telex: 014-2653
Fax: (506) 858-4585
E-mail: registrariat@umoncton.ca

Founded 1864 as St Joseph's University, name changed 1963

Language of instruction: French
Private control
Academic year: September to April
Campuses also in Edmundston (Saint-Louis-Maillet) and Shippagan

Chancellor: ANTONINE MAILLET
Rector: JEAN-BERNARD ROBICHAUD
Vice-Rectors (Campuses): ARMAND CARON (Shippagan); Edmundston: (vacant)
Vice-Rectors: FERNAND LANDRY (Human Resources and Administration)
Secretary-General: SIMONNE RAINVILLE (acting)
Librarian: GILLES CHIASSON

Number of teachers: 405 full-time, 236 part-time

Number of students: 4,755 full-time, 1,664 part-time

Publications: *La Revue, Annuaire général, Répertoire de l'Université de Moncton.*

Moncton Campus

DEANS

Faculty of Administration: G. WYBOUW
Faculty of Arts: Z. CHIASSON
Faculty of Education: R. LANDRY
Faculty of Higher Studies and Research: T. VO-VAN
Faculty of Sciences: V. MALLET
Faculty of Social Sciences: I. MCKEE-ALLAIN

DIRECTORS

School of Law: M. DOUCET
School of Nutrition and Home Economics: L. VILLALON
School of Nursing: M. TRUDEAU
School of Engineering: S. YACOUT
School of Physical Education: H. COUTURIER

HEADS OF DEPARTMENTS AND SCHOOLS

Faculty of Administration:
- Accounting: E. MCGRAW
- Administration: C. LE BLANC

Faculty of Arts:
- Dramatic Art: L. LEMIEUX
- English: T. QUIGLEY
- French Studies: G. CHEVALIER
- History and Geography: G. BEAULIEU
- Music: R. VAUTOUR
- Translation and Languages: M. GUISSET
- Visual Arts: G. CLERMONT
- Philosophy and Religions: D. LAMONTAGNE

Faculty of Education:
- Learning and Teaching: T. LEBLANC
- Physical Education: H. COUTURIER
- School Guidance and Educational Administration: R. DESJARDINS

Faculty of Sciences:
- Biology: J. NUCKLE
- Chemistry: C. BOURQUE
- Computer Science: J. ALMHANA
- Mathematics: T. PHAM-GIA
- Physics: F. WEIL

Faculty of Social Sciences:
- Economics: (vacant)
- Political Science: R. OUELLETTE
- Psychology: T. RETFALVI
- Social Service: M. LAFOREST
- Sociology: M. MUJICA
- Public Administration: G. BOUCHARD

Edmundston Campus

DIRECTORS

Academic Services: J.-G. POITRAS
Arts and Letters: B. BEAULIEU
Business Administration: P. ALBERT
Education: C. CARRIER
Human Sciences: A. LECLERC
Sciences: L. FRENETTE
School of Forestry: R. BARRY
School of Nursing: F. MARQUIS

Shippagan Campus

DIRECTORS

Administration and Secretarial Sciences: R. DUGUAY
Arts and Human Sciences: G. D'SOUZA
Sciences: D. HÉTU

ATTACHED RESEARCH INSTITUTES

Centre d'études acadiennes: Dir M. BASQUE.

Centre d'études du vieillissement: Dir D. POIRIER.

Centre de recherche en linguistique appliquée: Dir C. PHILIPPONNEAU.

Centre de recherche en sciences de l'environnement: Dir A. BOGHEN.

Centre de ressources pédagogiques: Dir B. BOUDREAU.

Centre de traduction et de terminologie juridiques: Dir G. SNOW.

Institut canadien de recherche sur le développement régional: Dir D. SAVOIE.

Microelectronics-microelectronique Concept + Inc.: (vacant).

Centre de génie éolien: Dir D. VO-NGOC.

Centre de technologie manufacturière: Dir C. MAILLET.

Centre de documentation et d'études madawaskayennes: Dir M. THÉRIAULT.

Centre de recherches sur les aliments: Dir A. CORMIER.

Institut de leadership: (vacant).

Centre de recherche et de développement en éducation: Dir R. ALLARD.

Centre assomption de recherche de développement en entrepreneuriat: Dir P. J. BLANCHARD.

Centre de commercialisation internationale: Dir M. ZEITOUN.

Centre de recherche en conversion d'énergie: Dir S. SAMI.

Centre international de la common law en français: Dir (vacant).

Centre de conservation des sols et de l'eau de l'Est du Canada: Dir L. OUELLETTE.

Centre pour l'innovation scientifique et technologie dans l'industrie: Dir J.-G. HACHÉ.

Centre de recherche de la tourbe: Dir J.-Y. DAIGLE.

Centre de recherche de produit marin: Dir R. RIOUX.

Centre multimédia appliqué: Dir R. GERVAIS.

Chaire d'études coopératives: (vacant).

Centre international pour le développement de l'inforoute en français: Dir J. NADEAU.

UNIVERSITÉ DE MONTRÉAL

CP 6128, Succursale Centre-ville, Montreal, Que. H3C 3J7

Telephone: (514) 343-6111
Fax: 343-5976

Founded 1878
Language of instruction: French
Private control

Chancellor: ANDRÉ BISSON
Rector: ROBERT LACROIX
Vice-Rectors: CLAIRE MCNICOLL, ALAIN CAILLÉ, FRANÇOIS DUCHESNEAU, PATRICK ROBERT, MICHEL TRAHAN
Secretary-General: MICHEL LESPÉRANCE
Registrar: FERNAND BOUCHER
Director of Finances: ANDRÉ RACETTE
Librarian: Mme ARLETTE JOFFE-NICODÈME

Library: see Libraries
Number of teachers: 1,901
Number of students: 46,636

Publications: *Cahiers d'histoire, Cahiers du Centre d'études de l'Asie de l'Est, Cinémas, CIRCUIT* (North American 20th-century music), *Collection Tiré à part* (School of Industrial Relations), *L'Actualité économique, Criminologie, Études françaises, Revue des sciences de l'éducation, Revue juridique Thémis, Géographie physique et Quaternaire, Le Médecin vétérinaire du Québec, META, Journal des traducteurs, Sociologie et sociétés, Gestion, La Gazette des Sciences mathématiques du Québec, Paragraphes, Théologiques, Surfaces.*

DEANS

Faculty of Graduate Studies: L. MAHEU
Faculty of Theology: J.-M. CHARRON
Faculty of Law: C. FABIEN
Faculty of Medicine: P. VINAY
Faculty of Arts and Sciences: M. MATHIEU
Faculty of Dental Medicine: J. TURGEON
Faculty of Pharmacy: R. GOYER
Faculty of Environment Design: M. GARIÉPY
Faculty of Music: R. POIRIER
Faculty of Nursing: S. KÉROUAC
Faculty of Education Sciences: G. PAINCHAUD
Faculty of Veterinary Medicine: R. S. ROY
Faculty of Continuing Education: R. LEROUX

PROFESSORS

Faculty of Education Sciences:

Department of Curriculum and Instruction

BARRET, G.
BEER-TOKER, M.
BIBEAU, G.
GAGNÉ, G.
LEMOYNE, G.
PAINCHAUD, G.
PARET, M.-C.
PIERRE, R.
RETALLACK-LAMBERT, N.
SAINT-JACQUES, D.
TARRAB, E.
THÉRIEN, M.
VAN GRUNDERBEECK, N.

Department of Education and Educational Administration Studies

AJAR, D.
BOURGEAULT, G.
BRASSARD, A.
BRUNET, L.
CHARLAND, J.-P.
CHENÉ, A.
CRESPO, M.
DUPUIS, P.
JOFFE-NICODÈME, A.
LAMONTAGNE, J.
LESSARD, C.
OLLIVIER, É.
PELLETIER, G.
TRAHAN, M.
VAN DER MAREN, J.-M.

Department of Psychopedagogy and Andragogy

COMEAU, M.
DUFRESNE-TASSÉ, C.
FOURNIER, É.
GAUDREAU, J.
LÉVESQUE, M.
TREMBLAY, N.

Faculty of Environmental Design:

School of Architecture

BARACS, J.
DALIBARD, J.
DAVIDSON, C. H.
MARSAN, J.-C.
PARISEL, C.

School of Landscape Architecture

CINQ-MARS, I.
JACOBS, P.
LAFARGUE, B.
POULLAOUEC-GONIDEC, P.
ROUTABOULE, D.

School of Industrial Design

CAMOUS, R.
FINDELI, A.

Institute of Urbanism

BARCELO, M.
BOISVERT, M.
CARDINAL, A.
GARIÉPY, M.
HAMEL, P.
LESSARD, M.
MCNEIL, J.
PARENTEAU, R.
PARIS, J.
SOKOLOFF, B.
TRÉPANIER, M.-O.

Faculty of Theology:

DUHAIME, J.
GENEST, O.
LAPOINTE, G.
NADEAU, J.-G.
PARENT, R.
PETIT, J.-C.

Faculty of Law:

BICH, M.-F.
BOHÉMIER, A.
BRILLON, Y.
BRISSON, J.-M.
BROSSARD, J.
CHEVRETTE, F.
CIOTOLA, P.
CÔTÉ, P.-A.
CÔTÉ, P. P.
DUMONT, H.
FABIEN, C.
FRÉMONT, J.
GAGNON, J.-D.
HÉLEINE, F.
HÉTU, J.
KNOPPERS, B.
LABRÈCHE, D.
LAJOIE, A.
LAMONTAGNE, D.-C.
LLUELLES, D.
MACKAAY, E.
MOLINARI, P. A.
OUELLETTE, M.
OUELLETTE, Y.
PINARD, D.
POPOVICI, A.
RIGALDIES, F.
TALPIS, J.
TREMBLAY, A.
TRUDEL, P.
TURP, D.
VIAU, L.
WOEHRLING, J.

Faculty of Medicine:

Department of Anaesthesia

DONATI, F.

Department of Biochemistry

BOILEAU, G.
BOUVIER, M.
BRAKIER-GINGRAS, L.
BRISSON, N.
CEDERGREN, R. J.
CRINE, P.
DAIGNEAULT, R.
GINGRAS, G.
LANG, F. B.
MAMET-BRATLEY, M.
MORAIS, R.
SKUP, D.
SYGUSCH, J.

School of Rehabilitation

ARSENAULT, B.
CHAPMAN, C. E.
DUTIL, E.
FERLAND, F.
GRAVEL, D.
WEISS-LAMBROU, R.

Department of Occupational and Environmental Health

CARRIER, G.
CHAKRABARTI, S. K.
GÉRIN, M.
VIAUD, C.

Department of Health Administration

BÉLAND, F.

Champagne, F.
Contandriopoulos, A.-P.
Dussault, G.
Tilquin, C.

Department of Medicine

Ayoub, J.
Beauregard, H.
Bichet, D.
Bradley, E., (Ted)
Brazeau, P.
Butterworth, R.
Cardinal, J.
Dagenais, G. R.
D'Amour, P.
Delespesse, G.
Gougoux, A.
Grassino, A.
Hamet, P.
Huet, P.-M.
Jolivet, J.
Laplante, L.
Lecours, A. R.
Le Lorier, J.
Malo, J.-L.
Marleau, D.
Martel-Pelletier, J.
Matte, R.
Nadeau, R.
Nattel, S.
Pelletier, J.-P.
Perreault, C.
Poitras, P.
Rouleau, J.-L.
St-Hilaire, J.-M.
Sénécal, J.-L.
Vinay, P.

Department of Microbiology and Immunology

Auger, P.
Joly, J.
Menezes, J.
Montplaisir, S.
Morisset, R.
Sekaly, R.-P.

Department of Nutrition

Delise, H.
Houde-Nadeau, M.
Ledoux, M.
Levy, E.
Prentki, M.
Rasio, E.
Serri, O.
Simard-Mavrikakis, S.
van de Werve, G.

Department of Obstetrics and Gynaecology

Bélisle, S.
Drouin, P.
Fugère, P.
Lefebvre, Y.

Department of Paediatrics

Bard, H.
Collu, R.
Dallaire, L.
Davignon, A.
Fouron, J.-C.
Frappier, J.-Y.
Gagnan-Brunette, M.
Gauthier-Chouinard, M.
Labuda, D.
Lacroix, J.
Melançon, S. B.
Morin, C. L.
Rasquin-Weber, A.-M.
Robitaille, P. O.
Rousseau, E.
Seidman, E. G.
Teasdale, F.
van Vliet, G.
Weber, M.
Wilkins, J.

Department of Pathology and Cellular Biology

Babaï, F.
Bendayan, M.
Chartrand, P.
Dumont, A.
Giroux, L.
Kessous, A.
Latour, J.-G.
Messier, P.-E.
Michaud, J.
Royal, A.
Schürch, W.
Simard, R.

Department of Pharmacology

Cardinal, R.
de Léan, A.
Du Souich, P.
Élie, R.
Gascon-Barré, M.
Larochelle, P.
Lavoie, P.-A.
Momparler, R.
Sharkawi, M.
Yousef, I.

Department of Physiology

Bergeron, M.
Berteloot, A.
Billette, J.
Castellucci, V.
Couture, R.
de Champlain, J.
Descarries, L.
Drew, T. B.
Dykes, R. W.
Feldman, A. G.
Gulrajani, R.
Imbach, A.
Kalaska, J.
Lamarre, Y.
Lavallée, M.
LeBlanc, A.-R.
Maestracci, D.
Reader, T. A.
Roberge, F. A.
Rossignol, S.
Sauvé, R.
Smith, A. M.

Department of Preventive and Social Medicine

Brodeur, J.-M.
Dassa, C.
Laberge-Nadeau, C.
Lambert, J.
Levy, R.
Maheux, B.
Philippe, P.
Pineault, R.
Séguin, L.

Department of Psychiatry

Amyot, A.
Borgeat, F.
Chouinard, G.
Gauthier, Y.
Grunberg, F.
Lalonde, P.
Lamontagne, Y.
Lemay, M.-L.
Monday, J.
Montplaisir, J. Y.
Saucier, J.-F.
Weisstub, D. N.

Department of Radiology, Radio-Oncology and Nuclear Medicine

Lafortune, M.

Department of Surgery

Bernard, D.
Blanchard, H.
Chartrand, C.
Corman, J.
Daloze, P.
Duranceau, A.
Girard, R.
Lavoie, P.
Molina-Negro, P.
Perreault, J.-P.
Rivard, C.-H.
Robidoux, A.
Smeesters, C.
Tassé, D.

School of Speech Pathology and Audiology

Gagné, J.-P.
Getty, L.
Joanette, Y.

Faculty of Arts and Sciences:

Department of Philosophy

Bodeüs, R.
Duchesneau, F.
Gauthier, Y.
Gravel, P.
Grondin, J.
Lagueux, M.
Le Blanc, C.
Lepage, F.
Lévesque, C.
Piché, C.
Roy, J.

Department of Classical and Medieval Studies

Fasciano, D.

Department of Psychology

Bordeleau, Y.
Bouchard, M.-A.
Caouette, C.
Claes, M.
Comeau, J.
Cossette-Ricard, M.
Delorme, A.
Dubé, L.
Favreau, O.
Fortin, A.
Granger, L.
Haccoun, R.
Hodgins, S.
Kiely, M. C.
Lasry, J.-C.
Lassonde, M.
Lecomte, C.
Lepore, F.
Mathieu, M.
Morval, J.
Pagé, M.
Peretz, I.
Perron, J.
Ptito, M.
Robert, M.
Roskies, E.
Sabourin, M.
Savoie, A.
Stravynski, A.
Strobel, M.
Tétreau, B.
Tremblay, R. E.
Tziner, A.
Vikis-Freibergs, V.
Wright, J.
Zavalloni, M.

School of Educational Psychology

Charlebois, P.
Gagnon, C.
Larivée, S.
LeBlanc, M.
Van Gijseghem, H.
Vitaro, F.

Department of English Studies

Bochner, J.
Kinsley, W. B.
Martin, R. K.

Department of French Studies

Dupriez, B.
Gauvin, L.
Godin, J. C.
Hébert, F.
Laflèche, G.
Larose, J.
Léonard, M.
Melançon, R.
Nepveu, P.
Pierssens, M.

Department of Geography

BRYANT, C. R.
CAVAYAS, F.
COFFEY, W.
COMTOIS, P.,
FOGGIN, P. M.
GANGLOFF, P.
GRAY, J. T.
MANZAGOL, C.
MAROIS, C.
RICHARD, P. J. H.
ROY, A. G.
SINGH, B.
THOUEZ, J.-P.

Department of History

ANGERS, D.
BOGLIONI, P.
DICKINSON, J. A.
DUROCHER, R.
KEEL, O.
LAVALLÉE, L.
LÉTOURNEAU, P.
LUSIGNAN, S.
MORIN, C.
PERREAULT, J. Y.
RABKIN, Y.
RAMIREZ, B.
ROUILLARD, J.
SUTTO, C.

Department of History of Art

DE MOURA SOBRAL, L.
DUBREUIL, N.
GAGNON, F.-M.
GAUDREAULT, A.
KRAUSZ, P.
LAFRAMBOISE, A.
LAROUCHE, M.
LHOTE, J.-F.
MARSOLAIS, G.
NAUBERT-RISER, C.
TOUSIGNANT, S.
TRUDEL, J.

Department of Linguistics and Translation

CONNORS, K.
CORMIER, M. C.
FORD, A.
GÉMAR, J.-C.
HOSINGTON, B.
JAREMA-ARVANITAKIS, G.
KITTREDGE, R.
MEL'ČUK, I. A.
MÉNARD, N.
MORIN, J.-Y.
MORIN, Y.-C.
REIGHARD, J.
ST-PIERRE, P.
SCHULZE-BUSACKER, E.
SINGH, R.

Department of Chemistry

BEAUCHAMP, A. L.
BERTRAND, M.
BRISSE, F.
D'AMBOISE, M.
DUGAS, H.
DUROCHER, G.
HANESSIAN, S.
HUBERT, J.
PRUD'HOMME, J.
SALAHUB, D.
ST-JACQUES, M.
WUEST, J. D.

Department of Comparative Literature

CHANADY, A.
GUÉDON, J. C.
KRYSINSKI, W.
MOSER, W.

Department of Literature and Modern Languages

BOUCHARD, J.
CARRASCO, F.
GÜRTTLER, K. R.
RÄKEL, H.-H.

Department of Biology

ALI, M. A.
ANCTIL, M.
BARON, G.
BOUCHARD, A.
BROUILLET, L.
BRUNEL, P.
CABANA, T.
CAPPADOCIA, M.
CARIGNAN, R.
CHUNG, Y. S.
DE LUCA, V.
HARPER, P.-P.
JOLICOEUR, P.
LEGENDRE, P.
MCNEIL, R.
MOLOTCHNIKOFF, S.
PINEL-ALLOUL, B.
SAINI, H. S.
SIMON, J.-P.

Department of Geology

BOUCHARD, M. A.
BROOKS, C.
HOFMANN, H.
HUBERT, C.
MAMET, B. L.
MARTIGNOLE, J.
TRZCIENSKI, W. E.

Department of Computing Sciences and Operational Research

BRASSARD, G.
BRATLEY, P.
CERNY, E.
FERLAND, J. A.
FLORIAN, M.
FRASSON, C.
GECSEI, J.
GENDREAU, M.
LAPALME, G.
L'ÉCUYER, P.
LUSTMAN, F.
MARCOTTE, P.
MCKENZIE, P.
NGUYEN, S.
STEWART, N.
VAUCHER, J.

Department of Mathematics and Statistics

ARMINJON, P.
BÉLAIR, J.
BENABDALLAH, K.
BRUNET, R.
CLÉROUX, R.
DELFOUR, M.
DUCHARME, G.
GAUTHIER, P.
GAUTRIN, H.-F.
GIRI, N. C.
GIROUX, A.
JOFFE, A.
LEPAGE, Y.
LESSARD, S.
MAAG, U.
NGO, V. Q.
PATERA, J.
RAHMAN, Q. I.
REYES, G.
ROSENBERG, I.
ROUSSEAU, C.
ROY, R.
SABIDUSSI, G.
SAINT-AUBIN, Y.
SANKOFF, D.
SCHLOMIUK, D.
TARDIF, S.
TURGEON, J.
WINTERNITZ, P.
YATRACOS, Y.
ZAIDMAN, S.

Department of Physics

BASTIEN, P.
BEAUDET, G.
BREBNER, J.
CARIGNAN, C.
COCHRANE, R. W.
DEL BIANCO, W.
DEMERS, S.
FONTAINE, G.
GOULARD, B.
JÉRÉMIE, H.
LAPRADE, R.
LÉPINE, Y.
LEROY, C.
LESSARD, L.
LETOURNEUX, J.
LEWIS, L.
MICHAUD, G.
MOFFAT, A.
MOISAN, M.
MONARO, S.
PEARSON, M.
ROY, G.
TARAS, P.
TEICHMANN, J.
VINET, L.
WESEMAEL, F.
ZACEK, V.

Department of Anthropology

BEAUCAGE, P.
BERNIER, B.
BIBEAU, G.
CHAPAIS, B.
CLERMONT, N.
MEINTEL, D.
MULLER, J.-C.
PANDOLFI, M.
PARADIS, L. I.
SAVARD, R.
SMITH, P.
THIBAULT, P.
TOLSTOY, P.
VERDON, M.

Department of Communication

BOUDON, P.
CARON, A. H.
GIROUX, L.
LAFRANCE, A. A.
MÉAR, A.
RABOY, M.

School of Library and Information Sciences

BERTRAND-GASTALDY, S.
COUTURE, C.
DESCHATELETS, G.
LAJEUNESSE, M.

School of Criminology

BROCHU, S.
BRODEUR, J.-P.
CUSSON, M.
LANDREVILLE, P.
NORMANDEAU, A.
TRÉPANIER, J.

Department of Demography

LAPIERRE-ADAMCYK, E.
PICHÉ, V.

Department of Economics

BOYER, M.
BRONSARD, C.
DUDLEY, L.
DUFOUR, J.-M.
GAUDET, G.
GAUDRY, M. J. I.
LACROIX, R.
MARTENS, A.
MARTIN, F.
MONTMARQUETTE, C.
PERRON, P.
PROULX, P.-P.
TREMBLAY, R.
VAILLANCOURT, F.

School of Industrial Relations

BROSSARD, M.
COUSINEAU, J.-M.
DOLAN, S.
GUÉRIN, G.
RAINVILLE, J.-M.
SIMARD, M.
TRUDEAU, G.

Department of Politics

BÉLANGER, A.-J.
BERNIER, G.
BLAIS, A.
BOISMENU, G.

BOUTHILLIER, G.
CLOUTIER, É.
DION, S.
FAUCHER, P.
FORTMANN, M.
GOW, J. I.
JENSON, J.
KORANY, B.
MONIÈRE, D.
SOLDATOS, P.

Department of Sociology

BERNARD, P.
FOURNIER, M.
GAGNON, G.
HOULE, G.
JUTEAU, D.
LAURIN, N.
MAHEU, L.
RACINE, L.
RENAUD, J.
RENAUD, M.
ROCHER, G.
SALES, A.
VAILLANCOURT, J.-G.
VANDYCKE, R.

School of Social Work

BERNIER, D.
CHAMBERLAND, C.
GROULX, L. H.
LEGAULT, G.
MAYER, R.
PANET-RAYMOND, J.
PÂQUET-DEEHY, A.
RINFRET-RAYNOR, M.
RONDEAU, G.
ZUNIGA, R.

Faculty of Dental Medicine:

Department of Dental Prosthesis

BALTAJIAN, H.
BOUDRIAS, P.
DESAUTELS, P.
HÉLIE, P.
LAMARCHE, C.
LEMIAN, L.
PRÉVOST, A.
TACHÉ, R.

Department of Oral Health

ALBERT, G.
BOURASSA, M.
CHARLAND, R.
JULIEN, M.
KANDELMAN, D.
LAVIGNE, G.
MASSEREDJIAN, V.
REMISE, C.
SHAPIRO, A.
TURGEON, J.
WECHSLER, M.

Department of Stomatology

DEMIRJIAN, A.
DONOHUE, W. B.
DUNCAN, G.
DUPUIS, R.
DUQUETTE, P.
FOREST, D.
LEMAY, H.
MASCRÈS, C.
MICHAUD, M.
NANCI, A.

Faculty of Pharmacy:

ADAM, A.
BESNER, J.-G.
BISAILLON, S.
GAGNÉ, J.
GOYER, R.
MCMULLEN, J.-N.
ONG, H.
VARIN, F.
YAMAGUCHI, N.

Faculty of Music:

BELKIN, A.
DURAND, M.
EVANGELISTA, J.
GUERTIN, M.
LEFEBVRE, M.-T.
LEROUX, R.
MANNY, G.
MASINO, R.
NATTIEZ, J.-J.
POIRIER, R.
SMOJE, D.
VAILLANCOURT, L.

Faculty of Veterinary Medicine:

Department of Clinical Sciences

BLAIS, D.
BONNEAU, N. H.
BRETON, L.
CÉCYRE, A.
CHALIFOUX, A.
COUTURE, Y.
D'ALLAIRE, S.
DI FRUSCIA, R.
LAMOTHE, P.
LAROUCHE, Y.
MARCOUX, M.
MARTINEAU, G.-P.
PARADIS, M.
VAILLANCOURT, D.
VRINS, A.

Department of Pathology and Microbiology

BIGRAS-POULIN, M.
DROLET, R.
ELAZHARY, Y.
FAIRBROTHER, J. M.
FONTAINE, M.
HIGGINS, R.
JACQUES, M.
LALLIER, R.
LARIVIÈRE, S.
MITTAL, K. R.
MORIN, M.
ROY, R. S.
SILIM, A. N.

Department of Veterinary Biomedicine

BARRETTE, D.
BISAILLON, A.
DALLAIRE, A.
DEROTH, L.
GOFF, A. K.
LARIVIÈRE, N.
MURPHY, B. D.
TREMBLAY, A.

Faculty of Nursing:

BERGERON, F.
DUQUETTE, A.
FORTIN, F.
GAGNON, L.
GOULET, C.
GRENIER, R.
KÉROUAC, S.
REIDY, M.
RICARD, N.

Department of Physical Education:

ALAIN, C.
ALLARD, P.
GAGNON, M.
GARDINER, P.
LABERGE, S.
LAVOIE, J.-M.
LÉGER, L.
PÉRONNET, F.
PROTEAU, L.
SHEEDY, A.

School of Optometry:

BEAULNE, C.
LOVASIK, J. V.
SIMONET, P.

AFFILIATED INSTITUTIONS

Ecole Polytechnique: 2500 ch. de Polytechnique, Montreal; tel. (514) 340-4711; f. 1873; Dir RÉJEAN PLAMONDON.

Ecole des Hautes Etudes Commerciales: 3000, ch. de la Côte-Sainte-Catherine, Montreal, Que. H3T 2A7; tel. (514) 340-6000; f. 1907; Dir JEAN-MARIE TOULOUSE.

MOUNT ALLISON UNIVERSITY

Sackville, NB E0A 3C0

Telephone: 364-2275
Fax: 364-2216

Founded 1840
Private control
Language of instruction: English
Academic year: September to May

Chancellor: HAROLD PURDY CRAWFORD
President and Vice-Chancellor: IAN D. C. NEWBOULD
Vice-President (Academic): WILLIAM DRIEDZIC
Vice-President (Administration and Finance): D. J. STEWART
Dean of Arts: KATHRYN HAMER
Dean of Science: (vacant)
Dean of Social Science: PATRICK BAKER
Registrar: L. A. OWEN
Librarian: S. LOCHHEAD

Number of teachers: 125
Number of students: 2,200

Publications: *President's Report* (annually), *Mount Allison Record* (quarterly alumni production), *Mount Allison News Letter*.

PROFESSORS

AIKEN, R., Biology
BAERLOCHER, F. J., Biology
BAKER, C., Mathematics
BAKER, P., Anthropology
BEATTIE, M., Mathematics
BEATTIE, R., Mathematics
BEATTY, D. P., History
BOGAARD, P., Philosophy
BURKE, R., Fine Arts
CALKINS, R. W., English
CODE, J., Music
DEBENEDETTI, G., Economics
DEKSTER, B., Mathematics
DRIEDZIC, W., Biology
EDWARDS, P., French
ELLARD, B., Music
ENNALS, P., Geography
FANCY, A. B., French
GANN, A., French
GODFREY, W. G., History
GODIN, J.-G., Biology
GRANT, D., Chemistry
GRANT, M. C., Religious Studies
HAMER, K., French
HAMMOCK, J., Music
HAMMOCK, V., Fine Arts
HANNAH, G., Engineering
HAWKES, R., Physics
HOLOWNIA, T., Fine Arts
IRELAND, R., Biology
JOERGER, T., German
LANGLER, R., Chemistry
MACMILLAN, C., English
MARK, J., Music
MILLER, B. A., Mathematics
MILLER, M., Music
MOSSMAN, D., Geoscience
NEWBOULD, I., History
READ, J. F., Chemistry
REINSBOROUGH, V. C., Chemistry
ROSEBRUGH, R., Mathematics
SEALY, R., Mathematics
STANTON, J., History
STANWAY, R. A., Philosophy
STARK, J., Music
STORM, C., Psychology
THOMPSON, R. G., Biology
TREASH, G., Philosophy
TUCKER, M., Political Science
VARMA, P., Engineering
VOGAN, N., Music
WEHRELL, R., Commerce
WEISS, J., Spanish
WELCH, C., Philosophy
WELCH, L., French

NON-PROFESSORIAL HEADS OF DEPARTMENTS

COHEN, I., Classics
FLEMING, B., Sociology/Anthropology
GOODRICH, E., History
STRAIN, F., Economics

MOUNT SAINT VINCENT UNIVERSITY

Halifax, NS B3M 2J6

Telephone: (902) 457-6788
Fax: (902) 445-3960

Founded 1925
Language of instruction: English
Academic year: September to April, two summer sessions

Chancellor: MARY LOUISE BRINK
President and Vice-Chancellor: Dr SHEILA A. BROWN
Registrar: J. LYNNE THERIAULT
Academic Vice-President: Dr JUDITH WOODSWORTH
Administrative Vice-President: (vacant)
University Librarian: LILLIAN BELTAOS

Number of teachers: 151 full-time, 81 part-time
Number of students: 3,800

Publications: *The Connection* (monthly), *Folia Montana, Atlantis* (quarterly).

DEANS

Humanities and Sciences: Dr DAVID FURROW
Professional Studies: Dr ROSEMARIE SAMPSON
Student Affairs: Dr CAROL HILL

HEADS OF DEPARTMENTS

Biology: Dr BARBARA RAO
Business Administration and Tourism and Hospitality Management: NED KELLEHER
Chemistry: Dr MARGIE JAMES
Child and Youth Study: Dr KIM KIENAPPLE
Economics: Dr WENDY CORNWALL
Education: Dr MARY CROWLEY
English: Dr SUSAN DRAIN
Fine Arts: Dr JOSETTE DELEAS
Gerontology: Dr JANICE KEEFE
History: Dr FRANCES EARLY
Human Ecology: Dr THERESA GLANVILLE
Information Management: BARBARA CASEY
Mathematics: Dr TINA HARRIOTT
Modern Languages: Dr MARIE-LUCIE TARPENT
Philosophy: Dr PIERRE PAYER
Political Studies/Canadian Studies: Dr MICHAEL MACMILLAN
Psychology: Dr JEN MCLAREN
Public Relations: Dr MARIE RILEY
Religious Studies: Dr JACQUES GOULET
Sociology/Anthropology: Dr NORMAN OKIHIRO
Speech and Drama: PATRICK O'NEILL
Women's Studies: Dr PAT BAKER

ATTACHED INSTITUTE

Institute for the Study of Women: (vacant).

UNIVERSITY OF NEW BRUNSWICK

POB 4400, Fredericton, NB E3B 5A3

Telephone: (506) 453-4666
Fax: (506) 453-4599

Established 1785

Provincial control
Language of instruction: English
Academic year: September to May

Chancellor: FREDRIK S. EATON
President and Vice-Chancellor: ELIZABETH PARR-JOHNSTON
Vice-President (Academic): L. VISENTIN
Vice-President (Finance and Administration): J. F. O'SULLIVAN
Vice-President (Research and International Co-operation): J. D. MCLAUGHLIN
Vice-President (Saint John Campus): F. C. MINER
Comptroller: D. V. MURRAY
Secretary: S. STROPLE
Registrar: DEANNE DENNISON
Director (Development and Public Relations): SUSAN MONTAGUE
Librarian: J. TESKEY

Number of teachers: 632
Number of students: 9,782 full-time, 2,533 part-time

Publications: *Undergraduate Calendar, Summer School Calendar, Graduate Studies Calendar, Freshman Bulletin, Fiddlehead* (short stories and poetry, quarterly), *Acadiensis,* a historical journal of the Atlantic provinces (2 a year), *Research Inventory* (annually), *Studies in Canadian Literature* (3 a year), *International Fiction Review* (2 a year).

DEANS

Faculty of Administration: F. SIMYAR
Faculty of Arts: P. C. KENT
Faculty of Computer Science: W. D. WASSON
Faculty of Education: H. COWAN (acting)
Faculty of Engineering: W. FAIG
Faculty of Forestry and Environmental Management: E. W. ROBAK (acting)
Faculty of Science: I. UNGER
Faculty of Law: ANNE LA FOREST
Faculty of Nursing: PENELOPE ERICSON
Faculty of Kinesiology: T. HAGGERTY
School of Graduate Studies: J. SEXSMITH (acting)

Saint John Campus:
Faculty of Arts: K. COATES
Faculty of Business: E. PIKE (acting)
Faculty of Science, Applied Science and Engineering: C. K. TOMPKINS

PROFESSORS AND HEADS OF DEPARTMENT

(H = Head of Dept)

(Fredericton Campus):

Faculty of Administration:

ARCELUS, F. J.
ASKANAS, W.
DUPLESSIS, D.
EISELT, H. A.
GRONDIN, D.
KABADI, S.
LIN, E. Y.-H.
NAIR, K. P. K.
NASIEROWSKI, W.
RAHIM, M. A.
RASHID, M.
SCHAEFER, N. V.
SHARMA, B.
SIMYAR, F.
SMITH, A.
SRINIVASAN, G.
STABER, U.
STOREY, R. G.
TOLLIVER, J.
TRENHOLM, B.

Faculty of Arts:

ALLEN, J. G., Political Science (non-Professorial H)
AUSTIN, D., English
BRANDER, J. R. G., Economics
BROWN, A., French
BUCKNER, P. A., History
BYERS, E. S., Psychology
CAMERON, A. B., English
CAMERON, C. A., Psychology
CAMPBELL, G., History
CICHOCKI, W., French (H)
CLARK, D. A., Psychology
COCKBURN, R. H., English
COOK, B., Economics (H)
CUPPLES, B. W., Philosophy
DALTON, W. G., Anthropology
DICKSON, S., German and Russian (non-professorial H)
DICKSON, V., Economics
DONALDSON, A. W., Psychology
EPPERT, F., German and Russian
FIELDS, D. L., Psychology
FORBES, E. R., History
FRANK, D., History
GAIR, W. R., English
GRONDIN, C. R., Political Science
HARRISON, D., Sociology
HIEW, C. C., Psychology
HORNOSTY, J. M., Sociology
KENT, P. C., History
KEPROS, P. G., Psychology
KERR, W., Classics and Ancient History (non-professorial H, acting)
KLINCK, A., English
KONISHI, H., Classics and Ancient History
LARMER, R., Philosophy
LAUTARD, E. H., Sociology
LEBLANC, D., French
LEMIRE, B., History
MACDONALD, R. C., Philosophy (non-professorial H)
MACDONELL, A. J., Sociology
MACGILL, N. W., Philosophy
MCDONNELL, P. M., Psychology
MCGAW, R. L., Economics
MIKAELIAN, H. H., Psychology
MILLER, A., Psychology
MILLS, M. J., Classics and Ancient History
MILNE, W., Economics
MILNER, M., History
MULLALY, E. J., English
MURRAY, J., Classics and Ancient History
MURRELL, D., Economics
MYATT, A. E., Economics
NASON-CLARK, N., Sociology
NICKI, R. M., Psychology
PASSARIS, C. E., Economics
PATTERSON, S. E., History
PLOUDE, R. J., English (H)
POOL, G. R., Anthropology
POYATOS, F., Spanish (H)
REHORICK, D. A., Sociology
REZUN, M., Political Science
RICHARDSON, C. J., Sociology (H)
ROBBINS, W. J. R., English
ROBINSON, G. B., Psychology
ROWCROFT, J. E., Economics
SCHERF, K., English
SEPHTON, P. S., Economics
SHYU, L. N., History
SMITH, S. A., History
SPINNER, B., Psychology (H)
STOPPARD, J. M., Psychology
THOMPSON, D. G., History (H)
TRYPHONOPOULOS, D., English
TURNER, R. S., History
VAN DEN HOONAARD, W. C., Sociology
VIAU, R., French
WAITE, G. K., History
WIBER, M., Anthropology (H)

Faculty of Computer Science:

AUSTIN, T. A.
BHAVSAR, V. C.
COOPER, R. H.
DEDOUREK, J. M.
FELLOWS, D. M.
FRITZ, J.
GUJAR, U. G.
HORTON, J. D.
JOHNSON, L. F.
KURZ, B. J.
MACNEIL, D. G.
WARE, C.
WASSON, W. D.

Faculty of Education:

ALLEN, P., Adult and Vocational Education (non-professorial H)
BERRY, K., Educational Foundations
BEZEAU, L., Educational Foundations
BURGE, E., Adult and Vocational Education
CAINE, D., Curriculum and Instruction
CASHION, M., Educational Foundations (H)
CLARKE, G. M., Curriculum and Instruction
COOPER, T. G., Curriculum and Instruction
CROLL, J. C., Educational Foundations

EDWARDS, V., Curriculum and Instruction
ESTABROOKS, G., Student Teaching (non-professorial H)
HUGHES, A. S., Curriculum and Instruction
LEAVITT, R., Curriculum and Instruction (H)
LEBLANC, D. R., Adult and Vocational Education
LONDON, J. D., Curriculum and Instruction
LOWE, A., Adult and Vocational Education
MCFADDEN, C. P., Curriculum and Instruction
MACKERACHER, D., Adult and Vocational Education
NASON, P. N., Curriculum and Instruction
OTT, H. W., Educational Foundations
PAUL, L., Curriculum and Instruction
PAZIENZA, J., Curriculum and Instruction
RADFORD, K., Curriculum and Instruction
REHORICK, S., Curriculum and Instruction
SEARS, A., Curriculum and Instruction
SMALL, M. S., Curriculum and Instruction
SMITH, T. M., Adult and Vocational Education
SOUCY, D. A., Curriculum and Instruction
STEWART, J., Educational Foundations
STIRLING, M. L., Curriculum and Instruction
SULLIVAN, V., Adult and Vocational Education
TAYLOR, B. W., Educational Foundations
WHITEFORD, G., Curriculum and Instruction
WILLMS, J. D., Educational Foundations

Faculty of Engineering:

BIDEN, E., Mechanical Engineering
BISSON, B. G., Civil Engineering
BONHAM, D. J., Mechanical Engineering
BRAY, D. I., Civil Engineering (H)
BREMNER, T. W., Civil Engineering
BURGESS, J. P., Electrical Engineering
CHAPLIN, R. A., Chemical Engineering
CHRISTIAN, J., Civil Engineering
CHRZANOWSKI, A. J., Geodesy and Geomatics Engineering
COUTURIER, M., Chemical Engineering (H)
DAVIES, H. G., Mechanical Engineering (H)
DAWE, J. L., Civil Engineering
DIDUCH, C., Electrical Engineering
DORAISWAMI, R., Electrical Engineering
DOUGLAS, R. A., Civil Engineering
FAIG, W., Geodesy and Geomatics Engineering
FRIZE, M., Electrical Engineering
HILL, E. F., Electrical Engineering
HUSSEIN, E., Mechanical Engineering
INNES, J. D., Civil Engineering
IRCHA, M. C., Civil Engineering
KLEUSBERG, A., Geodesy and Geomatics Engineering (H)
LANGLEY, R. B., Geodesy and Geomatics Engineering
LEE, Y. C., Geodesy and Geomatics
LEWIS, J. E., Electrical Engineering (H)
LIN, K. C., Civil Engineering
LISTER, D., Chemical Engineering
LUKE, D. M., Electrical Engineering
MAYER, L., Geodesy and Geomatics Engineering
MCLAUGHLIN, J. D., Geodesy and Geomatics Engineering
MORELAND, C., Chemical Engineering
NARRAWAY, J. J., Electrical Engineering
PARKER, P. A., Electrical Engineering
ROGERS, R. J., Mechanical Engineering
SCOTT, D. G., Mechanical Engineering
SHARAF, A. M. M., Electrical Engineering
SOUSA, A. C. M., Mechanical Engineering
TAYLOR, J. H., Electrical Engineering
TRANQUILLA, J. M., Electrical Engineering
VALSANGKAR, A. J., Civil Engineering
VAN HEININGEN, A., Chemical Engineering
VANICEK, P., Geodesy and Geomatics Engineering
VENART, J. E. S., Mechanical Engineering
WELLS, D. E., Geodesy and Geomatics Engineering

Faculty of Forestry and Environmental Management:

ARP, P. A.
DOUGLAS, R. A.
JORDAN, G.
KEPPIE, D. M.
MENG, C.-H.
METHVEN, I.
QUIRING, D. T. W.
RICKARDS, E. J.
ROBAK, E. W.
ROBERTS, M. R.
SAVIDGE, R.
SCHNEIDER, M. H.
SHORT, C. A.
SMITH, I.

Faculty of Science:

BACHINSKI, D. J., Geology
BANERJEE, P. K., Mathematics and Statistics
BARCLAY, D. W., Mathematics and Statistics
BOTTOMLEY, F., Chemistry
BOUWER, I. Z., Mathematics and Statistics
BROSTER, B., Geology
CASHION, P. J., Biology
CHERNOFF, W. W., Mathematics and Statistics
COOMBS, D. H., Biology
COWAN, F. B. M., Biology
CWYNAR, L., Biology
DIAMOND, A., Biology
DILWORTH, T. G., Biology (H)
DUNN, T., Geology
GEGENBERG, J., Mathematics and Statistics
GREIN, F., Chemistry
IRELAND, K. F., Mathematics and Statistics
KEPPIE, D. M., Biology (also under Faculty of Forestry and Environmental Management)
LEES, R. M., Physics
LESTER, J. A., Mathematics and Statistics
LINTON, C., Physics
LYNCH, W. H., Biology
MAILER, C., Physics
MASON, G. R., Mathematics and Statistics
MATTAR, S., Chemistry
MONSON, B. R., Mathematics and Statistics
MUREIKA, R. A., Mathematics and Statistics
PASSMORE, J., Chemistry
PICKERILL, R. K., Geology
RIDING, R. T., Biology
ROSS, S., Physics
ROSS, W. R., Physics
SEABROOK, W. D., Biology
SHARP, A. R., Physics (H)
SINGH, K., Mathematics and Statistics
SIVASUBRAMANIAN, P., Biology
SMALL, R. D., Mathematics and Statistics
SPRAY, J., Geology
SULLIVAN, D., Mathematics and Statistics
THAKKAR, A., Chemistry (H)
THOMPSON, J. H., Mathematics and Statistics (H)
TIMOTHY, J. G., Physics
TINGLEY, D., Mathematics and Statistics
TUPPER, B. O. J., Mathematics and Statistics
TURNER, T. R., Mathematics and Statistics
UNGER, I., Chemistry
VAN DER LINDE, J., Physics
WHITE, J. C., Geology (H)
WHITTAKER, J. R., Biology
WIGGS, A. J., Biology
WILLIAMS, P. F., Geology
YOO, B. Y., Biology
ZAIDI, H. R., Physics

Faculty of Law:

BELL, D. G.
BIRD, R. W.
BLADON, G. L.
BRUCE, B. D.
DORE, K. J.
FLEMING, D. J.
HUGHES, P.
KUTTNER, T. S.
LAFOREST, A.
MACLAUCHLAN, H. W.
MCEVOY, J. P.
TOWNSEND, D.
VEITCH, E.
WALSH, C.
WILLIAMSON, J. R.

Faculty of Nursing:

ERICSON, P.
GETTY, G.
GIBSON, C.
GILBEY, V. J. U.
LEWIS, K.
OUELLET, L.
RUSH, K. L.
STORR, G.
WIGGINS, N.
WUEST, J.

Faculty of Kinesiology:

HAGGERTY, T. R.
PATON, G. A.
SEXSMITH, J.
STEVENSON, C. L.
WRIGHT, P. H.

(Saint John Campus):

Faculty of Arts:

BRADLEY, M. T., Psychology
CHANTELOUP, R., Social Science
COATES, K. S., History and Politics
CONDON, A. G., History and Politics
DONNELLY, F., History and Politics (H)
GENDREAU, P., Psychology
KABIR, M., Social Science (H)
NOBLE, J. E., Humanities and Languages (H, acting)
PONS-RIDLER, S., Humanities and Languages
RIDLER, N. B., Social Science
SMITH, M. E., Humanities and Languages
STEWART-ROBERTSON, J. C., Humanities and Languages
TAUKULIS, H., Psychology (H)
TONER, P., History and Politics
WILSON, A., Psychology (H)

Faculty of Business:

CHALYKOFF, J.
DAVIS, C. H.
DAVIS, G.
GILBERT, E.
MINER, F. C.
PIKE, E.
ROUMI, E.
STERNICZUK, H.
WANG, S.
WONG, J.

Faculty of Science, Applied Science and Engineering:

BECKETT, B. A., Physical Sciences
BUCHANAN, J., Nursing (non-professorial H, acting)
COTTER, G. T., Engineering (H)
GAREY, L. E., Mathematics, Statistics and Computer Science
GUPTA, R. D., Mathematics, Statistics and Computer Science
HALCROW, K., Biology (H)
HAMDAN, M., Mathematics, Statistics and Computer Science (non-professorial H)
KAMEL, M. T., Mathematics, Statistics and Computer Science
KAYSER, M., Physical Sciences
LEUNG, C.-H., Physical Sciences
LOGAN, A., Physical Sciences (H)
MACDONALD, B., Biology
NUGENT, L., Nursing (H)
PRASAD, R. C., Engineering
TERHUNE, J. M., Biology

FEDERATED UNIVERSITY

St Thomas University: Fredericton, NB; f. 1910; Pres: DANIEL O'BRIEN.

UNIVERSITY OF NORTHERN BRITISH COLUMBIA

3333 University Way, Prince George, BC V2N 4Z9

Telephone: (250) 960-5555
Fax: (250) 960-5528

Founded 1990; full opening September 1994
Language of instruction: English
Academic year: September to April (two semesters)

Chancellor: Dr K. George Pedersen
President/Vice-Chancellor: Dr Charles Jago
Vice-President, Academic: Dr Deborah Poff
Associate Vice-President, Student Services, and Registrar: R. Alex Reed
Librarian: Neil Campbell

Number of teachers: 150 (f.t.e.)
Number of students: 2,200 (f.t.e.)

DEANS

College of Arts, Social and Health Sciences: Dr Robin Fisher
College of Science and Management: Dr Lee Keener (acting)

NOVA SCOTIA AGRICULTURAL COLLEGE

Truro, NS B2N 5E3

Telephone: (902) 893-6600
Fax: (902) 895-5529
E-mail: reg_info@www.nsac.ns.ca

Founded 1905
Under the direction of the Nova Scotia Department of Agriculture and Marketing

Principal: H. G. Coffin
Vice-Principal Academic: E. B. Burnside
Vice-Principal Administration: B. M. MacDonald
Registrar: T. Dolhanty
Librarian: B. R. Waddell

Library of *c.* 19,000 vols
Number of teachers: 69
Number of students: 900

Publications: *NSAC College Calendar.*

HEADS OF DEPARTMENTS

Agricultural Engineering: J. D. Cunningham
Animal Science: M. Anderson
Economics and Business Management: S. G. Russell
Environmental Sciences: A. R. Olson
Mathematics, Physics and Humanities: C. T. Madigan
Plant Science: J. Nowak

NOVA SCOTIA COLLEGE OF ART AND DESIGN

5163 Duke St, Halifax, NS B3J 3J6

Telephone: (902) 494-8129
Fax: (902) 425-2420

Founded 1887

President: Alice Mansell
Vice-President (Academic): Jill Grant
Library Director: Ilga Leja

Library of 30,000 vols, 220 art periodicals, 125,000 colour slides
Number of teachers: 43
Number of students: 550 full-time, 70 part-time

Fine art studios in painting, sculpture, printmaking, ceramics, weaving, video, film, wood and metal working, textiles, jewellery, photography; digital media programmes in communication design, environmental design and art history.

UNIVERSITY OF OTTAWA

550 Cumberland St, POB 450 Stn A, Ottawa, Ont. K1N 6N5

Telephone: (613) 562-5800
Fax: (613) 562-5103

Founded 1848
Languages of instruction: French and English, almost generally in parallel courses
Control: independent, Provincially assisted
Academic year: September to August (undergraduate 2 semesters, graduate 3 terms)

Chancellor: Huguette Labelle
Rector: Marcel Hamelin
Vice-Rectors:
- (Academic): Gilles G. Patry
- (University Relations and Development): Jean-Michel Beillard
- (Resources): Carole Workman
- (Research): Howard Alper

Registrar: Henri Wong
Secretary-General: Pierre-Yves Boucher
Head Librarian: Richard Greene

Library: see under Libraries
Number of teachers: 1,071 full-time, 485 part-time
Number of students: 16,323 full-time, 6,372 part-time

Publications: *University of Ottawa Gazette* (2 a month), *Tabaret, La Rotonde, The Fulcrum,* Calendars of the several faculties.

DEANS

Faculty of Medicine: Peter Walker
Faculty of Health Sciences: Denise Alcock
Faculty of Law:
- Civil Law: Louis Perret
- Common Law: Sandra Rodgers

Faculty of Science: Christian Detellier
Faculty of Engineering: Tyseer Aboulnasr
Faculty of Arts: David Staines
Faculty of Social Sciences: Caroline Andrew
Faculty of Education: Johanne Bourdages
Faculty of Administration: Jean-Louis Malouin
School of Graduate Studies and Research: Joseph De Koninck

HEADS OF FACULTY UNITS

Faculty of Administration:
- Programmes: David Zussman

Faculty of Arts:
- Classics and Religious Studies: Peter Beyer
- Communication: Sherry Ferguson
- English: Keith Wilson
- Geography: Antoni Lewkowicz
- History: Jean-Guy Daigle
- Lettres françaises: Nicole Bourbonnais
- Linguistics: Paul Hirschbuhler
- Modern Languages and Literatures: Richard Sokoloski
- Music: Ingemar Korjus
- Philosophy: Guy Lafrance
- Theatre: Margaret Coderre-Williams
- Visual Arts: Olivier Asselin
- School of Translation and Interpretation: Geneviève Mareschal
- Second Language Institute: Robert Courchêne

Faculty of Education:
- Graduate Programmes: Renée Forgette-Giroux
- Teacher Education Section (Anglophone Sector): Sharon Cook
- Teacher Education Section (Francophone Sector): Raynald Lacasse

Faculty of Engineering:
- School of Information Technology and Engineering: Emil Petriu
- Chemical Engineering: Vladimir Hornof
- Civil Engineering: Vinod K. Garga
- Mechanical Engineering: William Hallett
- Engineering Management Programme: Dan Necsulescu

Faculty of Health Sciences:
- School of Human Kinetics: Roger Gauthier
- School of Nursing: Betty Cragg
- School of Rehabilitation Sciences: Andrée Durieux-Smith

Faculty of Medicine:
- Anaesthesia: Dennis Reid
- Biochemistry, Microbiology and Immunology: Jo-Anne Dillon
- Cellular and Molecular Medicine: Kenneth Marshall (acting)
- Epidemiology and Community Medicine: Ian McDowell
- Family Medicine: Nicholas Busing
- Medicine: Peter Tugwell
- Obstetrics & Gynaecology: Carl Nimrod
- Ophthalmology: Bruce Jackson
- Oto-rhino-laryngology: Paul Odell
- Paediatrics: Robert G. Peterson
- Pathology and Laboratory Medicine: Vital Montpetit (acting)
- Psychiatry: Jacques Bradwejn
- Radiology: Ian Hammond
- Surgery: Hartley Stern

Faculty of Science:
- Biology: David Brown
- Chemistry: Barry Morrow
- Earth Sciences: Ian Clark
- Mathematics and Statistics: Wulf Rossman
- Physics: Bela Joos (acting)

Faculty of Social Sciences:
- School of Psychology: Richard Clément
- School of Social Work: Roland Lecomte
- Criminology: Daniel dos Santos
- Economics: Giles Grenier
- Leisure Studies: Jean-Claude Pageot
- Political Science: Douglas Moggach
- Sociology: Ann Denis

PROFESSORS

Faculty of Medicine:
- Adam, J. E., Medicine
- Allen, J. D., Ophthalmology
- Altosaar, I., Biochemistry, Microbiology and Immunology
- Anderson, P. J., Biochemistry, Microbiology and Immunology
- Aye, M. T., Medicine: Haematology
- Baird, M. G., Medicine: Cardiology
- Bakish, D., Psychiatry
- Benzie, R. J., Obstetrics and Gynaecology
- Bernatchez-Lemaire, I., Cellular and Molecular Medicine
- Birnboim, H. C., Medicine
- Biro, G. P., Cellular and Molecular Medicine
- Broughton, R. J., Medicine: Neurology, Cellular and Molecular Medicine
- Burns, B. F., Pathology and Laboratory Medicine
- Busing, N., Family Medicine
- Cameron, W., Medicine
- Campbell, J. S., Pathology and Laboratory Medicine
- Chan, A. C., Biochemistry, Microbiology and Immunology
- Christie-Seely, J., Family Medicine
- Copestake, G. G., Radiology
- Dales, R. B., Medicine: Internal
- Davies, R., Medicine: Cardiology
- de Bold, A. J., Pathology and Laboratory Medicine
- DesGroseilliers, J. P., Dermatology
- Don, C. J., Radiology
- Drouin, J., Medicine
- Dunscombe, P., Radiology
- Feldman, W., Epidemiology and Community Medicine, Paediatrics
- Forster, J. M., Family Medicine
- Franks, D., Pathology and Laboratory Medicine
- Freeman, J., Surgery
- Fryer, J. N., Cellular and Molecular Medicine
- Garber, G., Medicine
- Garner, P. R., Obstetrics and Gynaecology
- Gelfand, T., History of Medicine

Gibb, W., Obstetrics and Gynaecology, Cellular and Molecular Medicine
Gosselin, J.-Y., Psychiatry
Hakim, A. M., Medicine
Hammond, I. D, Radiology
Heick, H., Biochemistry, Microbiology and Immunology, and Paediatrics
Hendelman, W., Cellular and Molecular Medicine
Higginson, L. A. J., Medicine: Cardiology
Hill, D. P., Pathology and Laboratory Medicine
Himms-Hagen, J., Biochemistry, Microbiology and Immunology
Hodder, R., Medicine: Internal
Huebsch, L., Medicine
Humphreys, P., Paediatrics
Hunter, A. G. W., Paediatrics
Jackson, W. B., Ophthalmology
Kacew, S., Cellular and Molecular Medicine
Karsh, J., Medicine
Keon, W. J., Surgery
Koranyi, E. K., Psychiatry
Korneluk, R., Paediatrics, Biochemistry, Microbiology and Immunology
Krantis, A., Cellular and Molecular Medicine
Lalonde, A., Obstetrics and Gynaecology
Lapierre, Y. D., Cellular and Molecular Medicine/ Psychiatry
Lau, D. C. W., Medicine
Laupacis, A., Medicine
Leader, A., Obstetrics and Gynaecology
Leenen, F., Medicine, Cellular and Molecular Medicine
Lemaire, S., Cellular and Molecular Medicine
Levine, D. Z., Medicine, Cellular and Molecular Medicine
MacDonald, N. E., Paediatrics, Microbiology and Immunology
McDowell, I. W., Epidemiology and Community Medicine
McBurney, M. W., Medicine
McKendry, R. J. R., Rheumatology
McLaine, P., Paediatrics
McPherson, R., Medicine: Endocrinology
Maler, L., Cellular and Molecular Medicine
Maroun, J., Medicine
Marshall, K. C., Cellular and Molecular Medicine
Mikhael, N. Z., Pathology and Laboratory Medicine
Milne, R., Pathology and Laboratory Medicine, Biochemistry
Montpetit, V. J. A., Pathology and Laboratory Medicine
Nair, R. C., Epidemiology and Community Medicine
Nathan, H., Anaesthesia
Nelson, R. F., Neurology
Nimrod, C. A., Obstetrics and Gynaecology
Ooi, T. C., Medicine: Endocrinology
Parry, D. J., Cellular and Molecular Medicine
Perez, E. L., Psychiatry
Peterson, L. M., Cellular and Molecular Medicine/Paediatrics
Peterson, R. G., Paediatrics/Cellular and Molecular Medicine
Pivik, R., Psychiatry
Raaphorst, G. P., Radiology
Rakusan, K. J., Physiology
Ravindran, A. V., Psychiatry
Reid, D., Anaesthesia
Rock, G., Cellular and Molecular Medicine
Rubin, S. Z., Surgery
Sattar, S. A., Biochemistry, Microbiology and Immunology
Seely, J. F., Medicine
Simeon, J. G., Psychiatry
Spasoff, R. A., Epidemiology and Community Medicine
Spence, J. E. H., Obstetrics and Gynaecology
Staines, W., Anatomy and Neurobiology
Stern, H. S., Surgery
Tanphaichitr, N., Obstetrics and Gynaecology
Thomas, R., Family Medicine
Todd, T. R., Surgery
Tremblay, P. C., Obstetrics and Gynaecology
Trifaro, J.-M., Pharmacology
Trites, R. L., Psychiatry
Tsang, B. K., Obstetrics and Gynaecology
Tuana, B., Cellular and Molecular Medicine
Tugwell, P. S. L., Medicine, Epidemiology and Community Medicine
Turnbull, J., Medicine
Vlad, P., Medicine: Cardiology
Walker, R., Paediatrics
Watters, J., Surgery
Wells, G., Medicine
Williamson, D. G., Biochemistry, Microbiology and Immunology
Wilson, A., Psychiatry
Yazdi, H., Pathology and Laboratory Medicine

Faculty of Health Sciences:

School of Human Kinetics:

Gauthier, R. R.
Hansen, H.
Harvey, J.
Orlick, T. D.
Ross, S.
Salmela, J. H.
Soucie, D.
Thoden, J. S.

School of Nursing:

Alcock, D.
Fothergill-Bourbonnais, F.
Hinds, C.
O'Connor, A.
Ross, M.

School of Rehabilitation Sciences:

Davis, H. L.
Durieux-Smith, A.

Faculty of Law:

Civil Law Section:

Archambault, J.-D.
Bisson, A.-F.
Boivin, M.
Braen, A.
Caparros, E.
de Montigny, Y.
Duplessis, Y.
Emanuelli, C.
Grondin, R.
Jodouin, A.
Lacasse, J.-P.
Larouche, A.
Morin, M.
Pelletier, B.
Perret, L. M. H.
Proulx, D.
Vincelette, D.

Common Law Section:

Adams, G. W.
Granger, C.
Jackman, M.
Krishna, V.
Magnet, J. E.
McRae, D. M.
Morse, B. W.
Paciocco, D. M.
Payne, J. D.
Ratushny, E. J.
Rodgers, S.
Sheehy, E.
Sullivan, R.
Zweibel, E.

Faculty of Science:

Alper, H., Chemistry
Alvo, M., Mathematics and Statistics
Anderson, P. J., Biochemistry
Armstrong, J. B., Biology
Arnason, J. T., Biology
Bishop, D. M., Chemistry
Bonen, L., Biology
Brown, D. L., Biology
Burgess, W. D., Mathematics and Statistics
Castonguay, C., Mathematics and Statistics
Closs, M. P., Mathematics and Statistics
Currie, D., Biology
Deo, C. M., Mathematics and Statistics
Detellier, C. G., Chemistry
Dixon, O. A., Earth Sciences
Durst, T., Chemistry
Fallis, A. G., Chemistry
Fenwick, J. C., Biology
Fortin, E., Physics
Fowler, A., Earth Sciences
French, H. M., Earth Sciences
Gambarott, S., Chemistry
Handelman, D. E., Mathematics and Statistics
Hattori, K., Earth Sciences
Hickey, D. A., Biology
Hodgson, R. J. W., Physics
Ivanoff, G. B., Mathematics and Statistics
Joos, B., Physics
Kaplan, H., Chemistry
Keddy, P. A., Biology
Logan, B. A., Physics
McDonald, D. R., Mathematics and Statistics
Moon, T. W., Biology
Morrow, B. A., Chemistry
Neher, E., Mathematics and Statistics
Perry, S. F., Biology
Philogène, B. J. R., Biology
Racine, M. L., Mathematics and Statistics
Rancourt, D., Physics
Rossman, W., Mathematics and Statistics
Roy, R., Chemistry
Scott, P. J., Mathematics and Statistics
Slater, G., Physics
Song, A. K. S., Physics
Stadnik, Z., Physics
Vaillancourt, R., Mathematics and Statistics
Veizer, J., Earth Sciences

Faculty of Arts:

Babe, R. E., Communication
Barbier, J. A., History
Behiels, M. D., History
Berthiaume, P., French Literature
Brisset, A., Translation and Interpretation
Carlson, D., English
Choquette, R., Religious Studies
Clayton, J. D., Russian
Cohen, L., Visual Arts
Cornaire, C., Second Language Learning
D'Allaire, M., History
Davis, D. F., History
De Bruyn, F., English
Delisle, J., Translation and Interpretation
Dennis, N. R., Spanish
Donskov, A., Russian
Egervari, T., Theatre
Ferguson, S., Communication
Ferris, I., English
Floyd, C., Music
Folkart, B., Translation and Interpretation
French, H. M., Geography
Fry, P. F., Visual Arts
Gaffield, C. M., History
Gajewski, K., Geography
Gellman, S., Music
Geurtz, M.-A., Geography
Goldenberg, N., Religious Studies
Goodluck, H., Linguistics
Grise, Y., French Literature
Imbert, P. L., French Literature
Jennings, L. C., History
Johnson, P. G., Geography
Koerner, E. F. K., Linguistics
Kunstmann, P. M. F., French Literature
Labelle, N., Music
La Bossière, C. R., English Literature
Lafrance, L. G., Philosophy
Langlois, A., Geography
Lapierre, A., Linguistics

Lauriol, B., Geography
LeBlanc, R., Centre for Second Language Learning
Le Moine, R., French Literature
Lepage, Y. G., French Literature
Lugg, A. M., Philosophy
Lynch, G., English
McCormick, P. J., Philosophy/English
Major, J.-L., French Literature
Major, R., French Literature
Makaryk, I. R., English
Manganiello, D., English
Mayne, S., English
Merkley, P., Music
Moss, J., English
Munoz-Liceras, J., Spanish
Patel, P., Linguistics
Piva, M., History
Ploegaerts, L. H. A., Geography
Poplack, S., Linguistics
Pummer, R. E., Classics and Religious Studies
Reid, L., Visual Arts
Rivero, M. L., Linguistics
Roberts, R. P., Translation and Interpretation
Ruano de la Haza, J. M., Spanish
Savard, P., History
Sbrocchi, L. G., Italian
Scully, J. P. E., Philosophy
St-Jacques, R. C., English
Staines, D. M., English
Tavernier-Courbin, J. M., English
Vandendorpe, C., French Literature
Von Maltzahn, N., English
Wellar, B. S., Geography
Wesche, M. B., Centre for Second Language Learning
Wilson, K. G., English
Yardley, J. C., Classics and Religious Studies

Faculty of Social Sciences:

Alschuler, L. R., Political Science
Andrew, C. P., Political Science
Axline, W. A., Political Science
Bodkin, R. G., Economics
Cellard, A., Criminology
Chossudovsky, M., Economics
Crabbe, P., Economics
Crelinsten, R., Criminology
da Rosa, V. M. P., Sociology
D'Costa, R. B., Sociology
Denis, A. B., Sociology
Gabor, T., Criminology
Grenier, G., Economics
Havet, J. L., Sociology
Laplante, J., Criminology
Laux, J. K., Political Science
Lavoie, M., Economics
Los, M. J., Criminology
Mellos, K., Political Science
Miguelez, R. J., Sociology
Moggach, D., Political Science
Murphy, R. J., Sociology
Pires, A., Criminology
Poulin, R., Sociology
Roberts, J., Criminology
Seccareccia, M. Economics
Thériault, J. Y., Sociology
Waller, I., Criminology

School of Psychology:

Campbell, K. B.
Cappeliez, P.
Clement, R.
de Koninck, J.-M.
Edwards, H. P.
Firestone, P.
Fouriezos, G.
Girodo, M.
Hunsley, J.
Johnson, S.
McCarrey, M.
McInnis, C. E.
Merali, Z.
Mook, B.
Piccinin, S.
Ritchie, P.
Sarrazin, G.
Stelmack, R. M.
Tougas, F.
Vaillancourt, R.

School of Social Work:

Lecomte, R.
St-Amand, N.

Faculty of Engineering:

Adamowski, K., Civil Engineering
Bruneau, M., Civil Engineering
Cheng, S.-C., Mechanical Engineering
Dhillon, B. S., Mechanical Engineering
Droste, R. L., Civil Engineering
Duvnjak, Z., Chemical Engineering
Evgin, E., Civil Engineering
Fahim, A. E., Mechanical Engineering
Flanagan, R. C., Mechanical Engineering
Gardner, N. J., Civil Engineering
Garga, V. K., Civil Engineering
Haddad, Y. M., Mechanical Engineering
Hallett, W. L. H., Mechanical Engineering
Hornof, V. Chemical Engineering
Kennedy, K. J., Civil Engineering
McLean, D. D., Chemical Engineering
Mitsoulis, E., Chemical Engineering
Munro, M. B., Mechanical Engineering
Neale, G. H., Chemical Engineering
Necsulescu, D.-S., Mechanical Engineering
Redekop, D., Mechanical Engineering
Saatcioglu, M., Civil Engineering
Tanaka, H., Engineering
Tavoularis, S., Mechanical Engineering
Townsend, D. R., Civil Engineering

School of Information Technology and Engineering:

Aboulnasr, T.
Ahmed, N. U.
Bochmann, G. V.
Cheung, T.-Y.
Georganas, N. D.
Ionescu, D.
Karmouch, A.
Krieger, M.
Logrippo, L.
Matwin, S. J.
Petriu, E.
Probert, R. L.
Rival, I.
Ural, H.
Yongacoglu, A. M.

Faculty of Education:

Bordeleau, L.-G.
Calve, P.
Cazabon, B.
Cook, S.
Cousins, B.
Fortin, J.-C.
Gagne, E.
Giroux, A.
Herry, Y.
Jefferson, A. L.
Laveault, D.
Leblanc, R.
Leroux, J. A.
Michaud, J. P.
Poirier, P.
Rancourt, R.
Taylor, M.

Faculty of Administration:

Ahmed, S. A.
Calvet, A. L.
Doutriaux, J.
Gandhi, D. K.
Guiot, J. M.
Henault, G. M.
Henin, C. G.
Islam, N.
Jabes, J.
Lane, D.
Manga, P.
Nash, J. C.
Paquet, G.
Perrakis, S.
Sidney, J. B.
Subbarao, A. V.
Wright, D. J.
Zeghal, D.
Zussman, D.

FEDERATED UNIVERSITY

Saint Paul University: 223 Main St, Ottawa K1S 1C4; Rector Rev. Prof. Dale Schlitt.

DEANS

Faculty of Theology: (vacant)
Faculty of Canon Law: Rev. Roch Pagé
Faculty of Pastoral, Mission and Communication Studies: Jean-Guy Goulet

PROFESSORS

Faculty of Theology:

Coyle, J. K.
Dumais, Rev. M.
Hardy, R. P.
Hurtubise, Rev. P.
Laberge, Rev. L.
Melchin, K.
Michaud, Rev. J.-P.
Pambrun, J.
Peelman, Rev. A.
Provencher, Rev. M. N.
Van den Hengel, Rev. J.
Vogels, Rev. W.

Faculty of Canon Law:

Mendonça, Rev. A
Morrisey, Rev. F. G.
Page, R.
Woestman, Rev. W. H.

Faculty of Pastoral, Mission and Communication Studies:

Daviau, P.
Dubé-Socqué, C. (H)
Lapointe, Rev. E. (H)
Rigby, P.
Roberge, Rev. M.
Tremblay, J.-P. (H)
Turcotte, P.-A.

UNIVERSITY OF PRINCE EDWARD ISLAND

550 University Ave, Charlottetown, PEI C1A 4P3

Telephone: 566-0439
Fax: 566-0795

Founded 1969 by merger of St Dunstan's University (f. 1855) and Prince of Wales College (f. 1834)

Academic year: September to May (two semesters)

Chancellor: Norman Webster
President and Vice-Chancellor: Elizabeth Epperley
Vice-President, Academic Support: John Crossley
Vice-President, Finance and Facilities: Neil Henry
Registrar: John R. DeGrace
Chief Librarian: Dan Savage

Library: see Libraries
Number of teachers: 180 full-time
Number of students: 2,444

DEANS

Arts: Philip Smith
Business Administration: J. Joseph Revell
Science: Roger Gordon
Education: Vianne Timmons
Nursing: Sheila Dresen
Veterinary Medicine: Lawrence Heider

DEPARTMENTAL HEADS

Anatomy/Physiology (Veterinary Medicine): William Ireland (acting)

Biology: Christopher Lacroix
Business Administration: J. Joseph Revell
Canadian Studies: James Sentance
Chemistry: Robert Haines
Classics: David Buck
Companion Animals (Veterinary Medicine): Brian Hill
Economics: Mian Ali
Education: Vianne Timmons
Engineering: Donald Gillis
English: Colman O'Hare
Fine Arts: Janos Fedak
Health Management (Veterinary Medicine): Timothy Ogilvie
History: Andrew Robb
Home Economics: Debbie MacLellan
Mathematics and Computer Science: Wayne Cutcliffe
Modern Languages: Lothar Zimmermann
Music: Alan Reesor
Nursing: Margaret Munro
Pathology/Microbiology (Veterinary Medicine): Frederick Markham
Philosophy: Verner Smitheram
Physics: Douglas Dahn
Political Studies: David Milne (acting)
Psychology: Cathy Ryan
Religious Studies: David Morrison
Sociology/Anthropology: Satadal Dasgupta

UNIVERSITÉ DU QUÉBEC

2875 Blvd Laurier, Sainte-Foy, Qué. G1V 2M3

Telephone: (418) 657-3551
Telex: 051-31623
Fax: (418) 657-2132

Founded 1968
Language of instruction: French

President: Pierre Lucier
Vice-President (Administration and Finance): M. Leclerc
Secretary-General: M. Quimper
Director of Public Relations: (vacant)
Librarian: (vacant)

Library (network) of 2,340,000 vols
Number of students: 33,152 full-time, 42,523 part-time

Publications: *Réseau* (monthly), *Rapport annuel, Inventaire de la recherche subventionnée et commanditée* (annually).

CONSTITUENT INSTITUTIONS

Université du Québéc en Abitibi-Témiscamingue

445 blvd de l'Université, Rouyn-Noranda, Qué. J9X 5E4

Telephone: (819) 762-2922
Fax: (819) 797-4727

Founded 1981 as Centre d'etudes universitaires, name changed 1984

Rector: Jules Arsenault
Vice-Rectors: Roger Claux (Teaching and Research), L. Bergeron (Resources)
Registrar: N. Murphy
Director of Services: N. Murphy
Secretary-General: J. Turgeon
Librarian: A. Béland

Library of 201,000 items
Number of teachers: 75
Number of students: 911 full-time, 1,932 part-time

HEADS OF DEPARTMENTS

Management Sciences: Johanne Jean
Applied Sciences: François Godard
Education: J.-P. Marquis
Social and Health Sciences: Sarah Shilder
Human Behavioural Science: Jean Caron

Université du Québec à Chicoutimi

555 blvd de l'Université, Chicoutimi, Qué. G7H 2B1

Telephone: (418) 545-5004
Telex: 051-36108
Fax: (418) 545-5012

Founded 1969
State control
Language of instruction: French
Academic year: September to April

Rector: B. Angers
Secretary-General: M. Côté
Registrar: R. Gagnon
Librarian: G. Caron

Library of 336,000 items
Number of teachers: 222
Number of students: 3,480 full-time, 3,621 part-time

HEADS OF DEPARTMENTS

Education Sciences: C. Bouchard
Economic and Administrative Sciences: A. Courtemanche
Human Sciences: M.-A. Morency
Basic Sciences: C. Cholette
Applied Sciences: M. Bouchard
Religious Sciences and Ethics: C. Ménard
Arts and Letters: F. Roy
Computer Science and Mathematics: A. Tremblay

Université du Québec à Hull

CP 1250, Succursale 'B', Hull, Qué. J8X 3X7

Telephone: (819) 595-3900
Fax: (819) 595-3924

Founded 1970
Language of instruction: French
Academic year: September to June

Rector: Francis R. Whyte
Secretary-General: M. Bondu-Deschênes
Registrar: M. Bonoy
Librarian: M. Légère

Library of 209,844 items
Number of teachers: 130
Number of students: 2,037 full-time, 2,729 part-time

Publication: *L'Uniscope* (2 a month).

DIRECTORS OF DEPARTMENTS

Accountancy: G. Poirier
Administration: F. Rancourt
Education: A. Boulet
Computer Science: W. J. Bock
Social Work: L. Fréchette
Psychoeducation: D. Pelletier
Health Sciences: M. Séguin
Industrial Relations: A. Beaucage

Université du Québec à Montréal

CP 8888, Succ. Centre-ville, Montréal, Qué. H3C 3P8

Telephone: (514) 987-3000
Fax: (514) 987-3009

Founded 1969

Rector: Paule Leduc
Vice-Rectors: Louise Dandurand (Strategic and Financial Planning and General Secretary), Lynn Drapeau (Academics and Research), Alain Dufour (Human Resources and Administrative Affairs), Paule Leduc (acting) (Partnership and External Affairs), Michel Robillard (Academic Services and Technological Development)
Registrar: Ygal Leibu
Librarian: Jean-Pierre Côté

Library of 2,388,000 vols
Number of teachers: 903
Number of students: 18,406 full-time, 18,989 part-time

HEADS OF DEPARTMENTS

Accountancy: A. Naciri
Administration: D. Desbiens
Plastic Arts: C. Mongrain
Chemistry: P. Pichet
Communications: E. Carontini
Computing: G. Gauthier
Dance: M. Epoque
Design: J. P. Hardenne
History of Art: C. Hould
Literature: M. Nevert
Geography: J. Carriere
History: J.-C. Robert
Kinanthropology: J. Boucher
Law: D. Desmarais
Linguistics: C. Germain
Mathematics: R. V. Anderson
Music: C. Dauphin
Philosophy: R. Nadeau
Physics: E. Boridi
Psychology: J. Belanger
Biology: J. Lafond
Earth Sciences: M. Lamothe
Education: M. Turgeon
Economics: Y. Fauvel
Political Sciences: T. Hentsch
Religion: M.-A. Roy
Sexology: J.-J. Levy
Social Work: H. Duval
Sociology: P. Drouilly
Theatre: M. Laporte
Urban and Touristic Studies: L.-N. Tellier

Université du Québec à Rimouski

300 Allée des Ursulines, Rimouski, Qué. G5L 3A1

Telephone: (418) 723-1986
Fax: (418) 724-1525
E-mail: uqar@uqar.uquebec.ca

Founded 1969
State control
Academic year: September to April (2 semesters)

Rector: Pierre Couture
Vice-Rectors: Michel Ringuet (Teaching and Research), J.-N. Thériault (Administration and Human Resources)
Secretary-General: M. Bourassa
Librarian: Gaston Dumont

Library of 334,600 items
Number of teachers: 172
Number of students: 2,100 full-time; 2,300 part-time

Publications: *UQAR-Info* (6 a year), *Rapport annuel* (1 a year).

HEADS OF DEPARTMENTS

Letters: T. Paquin
Economics and Business Studies: L. Gosselin
Biology and Health Sciences: D. Rajotte
Oceanography: S. DeMora
Education Sciences: P. Côté
Religion and Ethics: M. Dumais
Human Sciences: P. Bruneau
Mathematics, Computer and Engineering: M. Lavoie

ATTACHED CENTRE

Oceanography Centre: Dir V. Koutitonsky.

Université du Québec à Trois-Rivières

3351 blvd des Forges, CP 500, Trois-Rivières, Qué. G9A 5H7

Telephone: (819) 376-5047
Telex: 051-3488
Fax: (819) 376-5012

Founded 1969
Provincial control
Academic year: September to April

Rector: J.-A. Plamondon

Vice-Rectors: A. THIBAULT (Teaching and Research), R. FILLION (Administration and Finance)
Vice-Rector and Secretary-General: A. BROUSSEAU
Registrar: M. CÔTÉ
Librarian: M. JACOB

Library of 500,000 items
Number of teachers: 344
Number of students: 6,020 full-time, 5,211 part-time

Publication: *En Tête.*

HEADS OF DEPARTMENTS

Chemistry-Biology: A. MAIRE
Engineering: J. PARENT
Mathematics and Computer Science: A. PARADIS
Accounting: D. MCMAHON
Administration and Economics: B. VERMOT-DESROCHES
Education: B. BALMER
Human Sciences: G. MASSÉ
Theology: A. TURMEL
French: G. ROUSSEAU
Philosophy: J. NAUD
Physics: G. M. LEFEBVRE
Psychology: R. ASSELIN
Physical Education: M.-A. GILBERT
Health Sciences: M. RAJIC
Arts: M. POISSON
Leisure Sciences: G. PRONOVOST
Modern Languages: R. SERRANO
Pulp and Paper: H.-C. LAVALLÉE
Quebec Studies: N. SÉGUIN

Ecole Nationale d'Administration Publique: 945 rue Wolfe, Sainte-Foy, Qué. G1V 3J9; tel. (418) 657-2485; fax (418) 657-2620; f. 1969; 59 teachers; 1,143 students; library of 90,000 vols; Dir-Gen. PIERRE DE CELLES.

Ecole de Technologie Supérieure: 4750 Ave Henri-Julien, Montréal, Qué. H2T 2C8; tel. (514) 289-8800; f. 1974; 69 teachers; 1,256 full-time, 1,156 part-time students; library of 30,000 items; Dir-Gen. ROBERT L. PAPINEAU.

Institut Armand-Frappier: 531 blvd des Prairies, CP 100, Laval, Qué. H7N 1B7; tel. (514) 687-5010; f. 1938; microbiological research; graduate studies programme, production of vaccines and diagnostic products; 36 teachers; 55 full-time, 71 part-time students; library of 9,768 vols; Dir-Gen. C. PICHETTE.

Institut National de la Recherche Scientifique: Tour de la Cité, 2600 blvd Laurier, bureau 640, CP 7500, Sainte-Foy, Qué. G1V 4C7; tel. (418) 654-2500; f. 1969; 127 teachers; 250 full-time, 337 part-time students; library of 18,968 vols; Dir-Gen. ALAIN SOUCY.

Télé-université: Tour de la Cité, 2600 blvd Laurier, 7e étage, Québec, Qué. G1V 4V9; tel. (418) 657-2262; f. 1972; distant-study programmes; 35 teachers; 258 full-time, 5,458 part-time students; library of 11,985 vols; Dir-Gen. A. MARREC.

QUEEN'S UNIVERSITY AT KINGSTON

Kingston, Ont. K7L 3N6
Telephone: (613) 545-2000
Fax: (613) 545-6300

Founded 1841
Language of instruction: English
Academic year: September to May (two terms)

Chancellor: PETER LOUGHEED
Rector: IAN MICHAEL
Vice-Chancellor and Principal: Dr W. C. LEGGETT
Vice-Principal (Academic): Dr D. TURPIN
Vice-Principal (Research): Dr S. FORTIER
Vice-Principal (Health Sciences): Dr B. T. SMITH
Vice-Principal (Operations and Finance): Dr J. S. COWAN
Vice-Principal (Advancement): F. M. CAMPBELL
Registrar: JO-ANNE BECHTHOLD
Chief Librarian: PAUL WIENS

Number of teachers: 1,158
Number of students: 16,538

Publications: *Queen's Gazette, Douglas Library Notes, Golden Words, Queen's Quarterly, Queen's Review, Queen's Journal.*

DEANS

Faculty of Applied Science: T. J. HARRIS
Faculty of Arts and Sciences: R. A. SILVERMAN
Faculty of Education: R. B. UPITIS
Faculty of Health Sciences: B. T. SMITH
Faculty of Law: D. CARTER
School of Business: M. NORTHEY
School of Graduate Studies and Research: R. J. ANDERSON

PROFESSORS

(Some staff teach in more than one faculty)

Faculty of Applied Science:

AITKEN, G. J. M., Electrical and Computer Engineering
ANDERSON, R. J., Mechanical Engineering
ARCHIBALD, J. F., Mining Engineering
BACON, D. W., Chemical Engineering
BAYOUMI, M. M., Electrical and Computer Engineering
BEAULIEU, N. C., Electrical and Computer Engineering
BIRK, A. M., Mechanical Engineering
BOYD, J. D., Materials and Metallurgical Engineering
BRYANT, J. T., Mechanical Engineering
CAMERON, J., Materials and Metallurgical Engineering
CAMPBELL, T. I., Civil Engineering
CARTLEDGE, J. C., Electrical and Computer Engineering
DAUGULIS, A. J., Chemical Engineering
FAIRMAN, F. W., Electrical and Computer Engineering
GRANDMAISON, E. W., Chemical Engineering
HALL, K., Civil Engineering
HAMACHER, V. C., Electrical and Computer Engineering
HARRIS, T. J., Chemical Engineering
HOPE, B. B., Civil Engineering
JESWIET, J., Mechanical Engineering
JORDAN, M. P., Mechanical Engineering
KAMPHUIS, J. W., Civil Engineering
KORENBERG, M., Electrical and Computer Engineering
KRSTIC, V. D., Materials and Metallurgical Engineering
MCLANE, P. J., Electrical and Computer Engineering
MITCHELL, R. J., Civil Engineering
MOUFTAH, H. T., Electrical and Computer Engineering
MULVENNA, C. A., Mechanical Engineering
OOSTHUIZEN, P. H., Mechanical Engineering
PICKLES, C. A., Materials and Metallurgical Engineering
POLLARD, A., Mechanical Engineering
ROSE, K., Civil Engineering
SAIMOTO, S., Materials and Metallurgical Engineering
SEN, P. C., Electrical and Computer Engineering
SMALL, C. F., Mechanical Engineering
SURGENOR, B. W., Mechanical Engineering
TAVARES, S. E., Electrical and Computer Engineering
TURCKE, D. J., Civil Engineering
VAN DALEN, K., Civil Engineering
WATT, W. E., Civil Engineering
WEVERS, H. W., Mechanical Engineering
WILSON, K. C., Civil Engineering
WYSS, U. P., Mechanical Engineering
YEN, W.-T.
YEVICK, D. O., Electrical and Computer Engineering

Faculty of Arts and Science:

AARSSEN, L. W., Biology
AKENSON, D. H., History
AKL, S. G., Computing and Information Science
ANTLIFF, R. M., Art
ATHERTON, D. L., Physics
BAIRD, M. C., Chemistry
BAKER, W. E., Chemistry
BANTING, K. G., Politics
BEACH, C. M., Economics
BECKE, A. D., Chemistry
BERMAN, B. J., Politics
BERNHARDT, D., Economics
BERRY, J. W., Psychology
BICKENBACH, J. E., Philosophy
BLY, P. A., Spanish and Italian
BOADWAY, R. W., Economics
BOAG, P. T., Biology
BOGOYAVLENSKIJ, O. I., Mathematics and Statistics
BROWN, R. S., Chemistry
BURKE, F., Film
CALLE-GRUBER, M., French
CAMPBELL, H. E. A., Mathematics and Statistics
CARMICHAEL, D. M., Geological Sciences
CARMICHAEL, H. L., Economics
CASTEL, B., Physics
CHRISTIANSON, P., History
CLARK, A. H., Geology
CLARK, G., English
COLWELL, F. S., English
CONAGHAN, C. M., Politics
CORDY, J. R., Computing and Information Science
COURCHÊNE, T. J., Economics
CRAWFORD, R. G., Computing and Information Science
CRUSH, J., Geography
CUDDY, L. L., Psychology
DALRYMPLE, R. W., Geology
DAVIDSON, R., Economics
DE CAEN, D. J. P., Mathematics and Statistics
DIXON, J. M., Geology
DONALD, M. W., Psychology
DUNCAN, M. J., Physics
DU PREY, P. D., Art
ELTIS, D., History
ERDAHL, R. M., Mathematics and Statistics
ERRINGTON, E. J., History
FINLAYSON, J., English
FISHER, A., Music
FLATTERS, F. R., Economics
FLETCHER, R., Physics
FORTIER, S., Chemistry
FOX, M. A., Philosophy
FROST, B. J., Psychology
GEKOSKI, W. L., Psychology
GERAMITA, A. V., Mathematics and Statistics
GILBERT, R. E., Geography
GLASGOW, J., Computing and Information Science
GOHEEN, P. G., Geography
GREGORY, A. W., Economics
GREGORY, D. A., Mathematics and Statistics
GUNN, J. A. W., Politics
HAGEL, D. K., Classics
HAGLUND, D. G., Politics
HAMILTON, R., Sociology
HAMM, J.-J. N., French
HANES, D. A., Physics
HANSEN, K. J., History
HARMSEN, R., Biology
HARRISON, J. P., Physics
HARTWICK, J. M., Economics
HELMSTAEDT, H., Geology
HENRIKSEN, R. N., Physics
HERZBERG, A. M., Mathematics and Statistics
HEYWOOD, J. C., Art
HIRSCHORN, R. M., Mathematics and Statistics
HODSON, P. V., Biology

HOLDEN, R. R.,Psychology
HOLMES, J., Geography
HUNTER, B. K., Chemistry
JAMES, N. P., Geology
JEEVES, A. H., History
JOHNSTONE, I. P., Physics
JONKER, L. B., Mathematics and Statistics
KALIN, R., Psychology
KANI, E., Mathematics and Statistics
KEANE, D. R., Music
KILPATRICK, R. S., Classics
KNAPPER, C., Psychology
KNOX, V. J., Psychology
KOBAYASHI, A., Women's Studies
KYSTER, T. K., Geology
LAKE, K. W., Physics
LAYZELL, D. B., Biology
LEDERMAN, S., Psychology
LEGGETT, W. C., Biology
LEIGHTON, S. R., Philosophy
LELE, J. K., Politics
LESLIE, J. R., Physics
LESLIE, P. M., Politics
LEVISON, M., Computing and Information Science
LEWIS, F. D., Economics
LINDSAY, R. C. L., Psychology
LOBB, R. E., English
LOCK, F. P., English
LOGAN, G. M., English
LOVELL, W. G., Geography
LYON, D., Sociology
MACARTNEY, D. H., Chemistry
MACEWEN, G. H., Computing and Information Science
MACKENZIE, B. W., Geology
MACKINNON, J. G., Economics
MACLACHLAN, D. L. C., Philosophy
MACLEAN, A. W., Psychology
MACLEOD, A. M., Philosophy
MACLEOD, I. A., Computing and Information Science
MALCOLMSON, R. W., History
MANUTH, V., Art
MARSHALL, W. L., Psychology
MCCAUGHEY, J. H., Geography
MCCOWAN, J. D., Chemistry
MCCREADY, W. D., History
MCDONALD, A. B., Physics
MCINNIS, R. M., Economics
MCLATCHIE, W., Physics
MCTAVISH, J. D., Art
MEWHORT, D., Psychology
MILNE, F., Economics
MINGO, J. A., Mathematics and Statistics
MONKMAN, L. G., English
MONTGOMERIE, R. D., Biology
MOORE, E. G., Geography
MORRIS, G. P., Biology
MUIR, D. W., Psychology
MURTY, M. R. P., Mathematics and Statistics
NARBONNE, G. M., Geology
NATANSOHN, A. L., Chemistry
NORRIS, A. R., Chemistry
O'NEILL, P. J., German
ORZECH, M., Mathematics and Statistics
OSBORNE, B. S., Geography
OVERALL, C. D., Philosophy
PAGE, S. C., Politics
PALMER, B. D., History
PEARCE, G. R. F., Sociology
PEARCE, T. H., Geology
PENTLAND, C. C., Politics
PERLIN, G. C., Politics
PETERS, R. D., Psychology
PIKE, R. M., Sociology
PLANT, R. L., Drama
PRACHOWNY, M. F. J., Economics
PRADO, C. G., Philosophy
PRICE, R. A., Geology
PRITCHARD, J., History
QUINSEY, V. L., Psychology
REEVE, W. C., German
RIDDELL, J. B., Geography
ROBERTS, L. G., Mathematics and Statistics
ROBERTSON, B. C., Physics
ROBERTSON, R. J., Biology
ROBERTSON, R. M., Biology
ROSENBERG, M. W., Geography
SACCO, V. F., Sociology
SANDOR, M. A., History
SAYER, M., Physics
SCHROEDER, F. M., Classics
SILVERMAN, R. A., Sociology
SKILLICORN, D. B., Computing and Information Science
SMITH, G. S., History
SMITH, G. W., Economics
SMOL, J., Biology
SNIDER, D. L., Sociology
SPARKS, G. R., Economics
STAYER, J. M., History
STEGEMANN, K., Economics
STEVENSON, J. M., Physical and Health Education
STEWART, J. D., Art
STONE, J. A., Chemistry
STOTT, M. J., Physics
SWAINSON, D., History
SZAREK, W. A., Chemistry
TAYLOR, D. R., Physics
TAYLOR, P. D., Mathematics and Statistics
TENNENT, R. D., Computing and Information Science
THOMSON, C. J., Geology
TINLINE, R. R., Geography
TULCHINSKY, G., History
TURPIN, D. B., Biology
USHER, D., Economics
VANLOON, G. W., Chemistry
VERNER, J. H., Mathematics and Statistics
VERNET, M., French
WALKER, V. K., Biology
WAN, J. K. S., Chemistry
WARDLAW, D. M., Chemistry
WARE, R., Economics
WEISMAN, R. G., Psychology
WIEBE, M. G., English
WOLFE, L. A., Physical and Health Education
WRIGHT, A. C., Russian
YOUNG, P. G., Biology
YUI, N., Mathematics and Statistics
ZAMBLE, E., Psychology
ZAREMBA, E., Physics
ZUK, I. B., Education
ZUREIK, E. T., Sociology

Faculty of Education:

KIRBY, J. R.
MUNBY, A. H.
O'FARRELL, L.
RUSSELL, T.
UPITIS, R. B.
WILSON, R. J.

Faculty of Health Sciences:

ANASTASSIADES, T. P., Medicine
ANDERSON, J. E., Family Medicine
ANDREW, R. D., Anatomy and Cell Biology
ASTON, W. P., Microbiology and Immunology
BIRTWHISTLE, R. V., Family Medicine
BOEGMAN, R. J., Pharmacology and Toxicology
BRIEN, J. F., Pharmacology and Toxicology
BURGGRAF, G. W., Medicine
BURKE, S. O., School of Nursing
CARSTENS, E. B., Microbiology and Immunology
CHAPLER, C. K., Physiology
CLARK, A. F., Biochemistry
COLE, S. P. C., Pathology
COTE, G. P., Biochemistry
CRUESS, A. F., Ophthalmology
DA COSTA, L. R., Medicine
DAGNONE, L. E., Emergency Medicine
DAVIES, P. L., Biochemistry
DEELEY, R. G., Pathology
DELISLE, G. J., Microbiology and Immunology
DINICOLA, V. F., Psychiatry
DUFFIN, J. M., Health Sciences
DUNCAN, P. G., Anaesthesia
DWOSH, I. L., Medicine
EISENHAUER, E. A., Radoncology
ELCE, J. S., Biochemistry
ELLIOTT, B. E., Pathology
FERGUSON, A. V., Physiology
FISHER, J. T., Physiology
FLYNN, T. G., Biochemistry
FORD, P. M., Medicine
FORKERT, P. G., Anatomy and Cell Biology
FROESE, A. B., Anaesthesia
GILES, A. R., Pathology
GORWILL, R. H., Obstetrics and Gynaecology
GROLL, A., Medicine
HALL, S. F., Otolaryngology
HEATON, J. P. W., Urology
HOLDEN, J. J. A., Psychiatry
HUCKER, S. J., Psychiatry
HUDSON, R. W., Medicine
JACKSON, A. C., Medicine
JARRELL, K. F. J., Microbiology and Immunology
JHAMANDAS, K., Pharmacology and Toxicology
JONEJA, M. G., Anatomy and Cell Biology
JONES, G., Biochemistry
KISILEVSKY, R., Pathology
KROPINSKI, A. M., Microbiology and Immunology
LAMB, M. W., School of Nursing
LAWSON, J. S., Psychiatry
LEES, R. E. M., Community Health and Epidemiology
LILLICRAP, D. P., Pathology
LOEB, G. E., Biomedical Engineering and Physiology
LOWE, J. A., Obstetrics and Gynaecology
LUDWIN, S. K., Pathology
MCCREARY, B., Psychiatry
MAK, A. S., Biochemistry
MANLEY, P. N., Pathology
MASSEY, T. E., Pharmacology and Toxicology
MILNE, B., Anaesthesia
MORALES, A., Urology
MUNT, P. W., Medicine
NAKATSU, K., Pharmacology and Toxicology
NESHEIM, M. E., Biochemistry
NOLAN, R. L., Diagnostic Radiology
O'CONNOR, H. M., Emergency Medicine
OLNEY, S. J., Rehabilitation Therapy
PANG, S. C., Anatomy and Cell Biology
PATER, J. L., Community Health and Epidemiology
PATERSON, W. G., Medicine
PROSS, H. F., Microbiology and Immunology
RACZ, W. J., Pharmacology and Toxicology
RAPTIS, L. H., Microbiology and Immunology
REID, R. L., Obstetrics and Gynaecology
REIFEL, C., Anatomy and Cell Biology
RICHMOND, F. J., Physiology
RIOPELLE, R. J., Medicine
ROSE, P. K., Physiology
SHANKS, G. L., Rehabilitation Medicine
SHIN, S. H., Physiology
SHORTT, S. E. D., Community Health and Epidemiology
SIMON, J. B., Medicine
SINGER, M. A., Medicine
SMITH, B. T., Paediatrics
SPENCER, J. H., Biochemistry
STERNS, E. E., Surgery
SURRIDGE, D. H. C., Psychiatry
SZEWCZUK, M. R., Microbiology and Immunology
WALKER, D. M. C., Emergency Medicine
WEAVER, D. F., Medicine
WHERRETT, B. A., Paediatrics
WIGLE, R. D., Medicine
WILSON, C. R, Family Medicine

Faculty of Law:

ADELL, B. L.
ALEXANDROWICZ, G. W.
BAER, M. G.
BALA, N. C.
CARTER, D. D.
CHEN, T.-P.

DELISLE, R. J.
EASSON, A. J.
GALLOWAY, J. D. C.
LAHEY, K. A.
LAWFORD, H. J.
MAGNUSSON, D. N.
MANSON, A. S.
MARSHALL, D. S.
MULLAN, D. J.
SADINSKY, S.
STUART, D. R.
WEISBERG, M. A.
WHYTE, J. D.

School of Business:

ANDERSON, D. L.
ARNOLD, S. J.
BARLING, J. I.
BURNS, R. N.
COOPER, W. H.
DAUB, M. A. C.
DOWNIE, B. M.
GALLUPE, R. B.
GORDON, J. R. M.
JOHNSON, L. D.
MCKEEN, J. D.
MORGAN, I. G.
NEAVE, E. H.
NIGHTINGALE, D. V.
NORTHEY, M. E.
PETERSEN, E. R.
RICHARDSON, A. J.
RICHARDSON, P. R.
RUTENBERG, D. P.
TAYLOR, A. J.
THORNTON, D. B.
TURNBULL, S. M.

School of Policy Studies:

LEISS, W.
WILLIAMS, T. R.

School of Urban and Regional Planning:

LEUNG, H. L.
QADEER, M. A.
SKABURSKIS, A.

AFFILIATED COLLEGE

Queen's Theological College: Kingston; f. 1841; Principal Rev. H. E. LLEWELLYN.

REDEEMER COLLEGE

777 Garner Rd East, Ancaster, Ont. L9K 1J4
Telephone: (905) 648-2131
Fax: (905) 648-2134
E-mail: adm@redeemer.on.ca

Founded 1976, present name 1980, university status 1982
Committed to the advancement of Reformed Christian education in all academic disciplines
Language of instruction: English
Private control
Academic year: September to May

President: Dr JUSTIN COOPER
Vice-President (Academic): Dr ELAINE BOTHA
Vice-President (Administration and Finance): BILL VAN STAALDUINEN
Registrar: MARIAN RYKS-SZELEKOVSZKY
Librarian: JANNY EIKELBOOM

Library of 100,000 items
Number of teachers: 37
Number of students: 498

FACULTY DIVISION HEADS

Foundations: JACOB ELLENS
Literature and Arts: DOUGLAS LONEY
Natural Sciences: GARY CHIANG
Social Sciences: SUSAN VAN WEELDEN

UNIVERSITY OF REGINA

Regina, Sask. S4S 0A2
Telephone: 585-4111
Telex: (230) 961-000

Founded 1974 (previously Regina Campus, University of Saskatchewan)
State control
Language of instruction: English
Academic year: September to June (2 terms, plus spring and summer sessions)

Chancellor: V. L. PETRY
Vice-Chancellor and President: D. O. WELLS
Vice-President (Academic): D. L. COMMON
Vice-President (Admin.) and Controller: D. BARNARD
University Secretary: R. R. ROBINSON
Registrar: G. MEEHAN
Librarian: W. MAES

Number of teachers: 442
Number of students: 7,953 full-time, 3,260 part-time

Publications: *Wascana Review* (2 a year), *General Calendar* (annually), *Graduate Studies Calendar* (every 2 years), *UR Quality Bulletin* (every 2 months), *Carillon* (monthly), *The Third Degree* (annually).

DEANS

Administration: G. GARVEN
Arts: K. M. KNUTTILA
Education: M. TYMCHAK
Engineering: A. CHAKMA
Fine Arts: M. RUSHTON
Graduate Studies and Research: L. R. SYMES
Physical Activity Studies: R. NILSON
Science: K. DENFORD
Social Work: S. MCKAY

PROFESSORS

ALFANO, D. P., Psychology
ANTROBUS, P., Psychology
ASHTON, N. W., Biology
AUSTIN, B. J., Administration
BALE, D. J., Education
BARNARD, D., Computer Science
BEATTIE, D. L., Economics
BERGBUSCH, M. L. T., English
BERTOLDI, E., Philosophy
BESHARA, R. L., Administration
BESSAI, F., Education
BHOLE, S. D., Engineering
BINDA, P. L., Geology
BLASS, K. G., Chemistry
BRENNAN, J. W., History
BROWN, L. A., Political Science
CATANIA, P. J., Engineering
CHAKMA, A., Engineering
CHAMBERLAIN, J. S., English
CHANADY, A. A., History
CHANDLER, W. D., Chemistry
CHAPCO, W., Biology
CHERLAND, M., Education
CHOW, S. L., Psychology
CLARK, D. J., Physical Activity Studies
COLEMAN, R. A., Physics
COLLIER, K. D., Social Work
COMMON, D. L., Education
CONWAY, J. F., Sociology and Social Studies
COOKE, W. B. H., Engineering
COWIN, J. L., Visual Arts
CULLIMORE, D. R., Biology
DALSIN, B. R., History
DE VLIEGER, D., Political Science
DENFORD, K. D., Biology
DRIEDGER, O. H., Social Work
DUDGEON, P., Administration
FISHER, J. C., Mathematics
FULLER, G. A., Systems Engineering
GEAR, J. R., Chemistry
GILLIGAN, B. C., Mathematics
GINGRICH, P. A., Sociology and Social Studies
GRAY, G. E., Education
HANOWSKI, A. J., Social Work
HANSON, D., Mathematics
HARDING, J., Human Justice
HART, E. P., Education
HEIN, L. I., University Extension
HEMINGWAY, P., Education
HORDERN, R., Religious Studies
HOWARD, W. J., English
HURLBERT, E. L., Education
ITO, J. K., Administration
JOHNSON, K. E., Chemistry
JULE, L., Education
KATZ, R., Social Work
KAUL, S. K., Mathematics
KELLN, R. A., Chemistry and Biochemistry
KELLY, A. K., Economics
KENNY, S. D., History
KESTEN, C. A., Education
KNUTTILA, K. M., Sociology and Social Studies
KOH, E. L., Mathematics
KOS, J. F., Physics
KOZEY, L. M., Education
KRENTZ, A. A., Philosophy
KRENTZ, C. D., Education
KWON, O. Y., Administration
KYBETT, B. D., Chemistry
LALONDE, A. N., History
LANG, H. R., Education
LEE, D. G., Chemistry
LEESON, H. A., Political Science
LEWIS, E. L., Music
LEWRY, J. F., Geology
LOBAUGH, H. B., Music
LOLOS, G. J., Physics
MACDONALD, B. F., English
MAGNESON, H. W., Social Work
MAGUIRE, R. B., Computer Science
MARISI, P., Education
MARSHALL, G. J., Philosophy
MASLANY, G. W., Social Work
MATHIE, E. L., Physics
MCCARTHY, S., English
MCCULLOCH, R. G., Physical Activity Studies
MCGOVERN, K. L., Philosophy
MCLAREN, R. I., Administration
MISSKEY, W. J., Systems Engineering
MITCHELL, K. R., English
MOORE, R. J., Psychology
MUIR, W. R., Psychology
MURRAY, D. C., English
MUTHUCHIDAMBARAM, S. P., Administration
NICHOLLS, E. A., Physical Activity Studies
NICOL, C. J., Economics
OPSETH, A. L., Engineering
PALMER, R. J. F., Systems Engineering
PAPINI, G. A., Physics
PARSLOW, G. R., Geology
PAUL, A. H., Geography
PETRACEK, R. S., Education
PITSULA, J. M., History
PRENDERGAST, G. M., Theatre
RAINEY, B. E., French
RAUM, J. R., Music
ROBERTS, J. K., Political Science
ROBERTSON, B. E., Physics
RUDDICK, N., English
RUMMENS, F. H. A., Chemistry
RYSTEPHANICK, R. G., Physics
SANKARAN, S., Administration
SATO, D., Mathematics
SAXTON, L. V., Computer Science
SCARFE, B. L., Economics
SCHLICHTMANN, H. G., Geography
SCHUDEL, T. M., Music
SEABORNE, A. A., Geography
SECOY, D. M., Biology
SHARMA, S., Systems Engineering
SMOLLETT, E. W., Anthropology
SRINIVAS, K. M., Administration
STAHL, W. A., Sociology
STARK, C., Psychology
STEWART, J. D., Education
STIRLING, R. M., Sociology and Social Studies
SURES, J. J., Visual Arts
SWALES, R. J. W., History
SYMES, L. R., Computer Science
SZABADOS, B., Philosophy
TAYLOR, M. M., Education
TOMKINS, R. J., Mathematics
TURTLE, J. P., Administration
TYMCHAK, M. J., Education
VANDENBERGHE, D. G., Systems Engineering
VIRARAGHAVAN, T., Systems Engineering

WEISBART, M., Biology
WELLS, D. O., Physics
WESTON, H. O., Mathematics
WONG, S. K. M., Computer Science
YAKEL, N. C., Education
ZIARKO, W., Computer Science

FEDERATED COLLEGES

Campion College: Regina, Sask. S4S 0A2; f. 1917; Pres. Rev. J. SCHNER.

Luther College: Regina, Sask. S4S 0A2; f. 1913; Pres. R. HORDERN.

Saskatchewan Indian Federated College: Regina, Sask. S4S 0A2; f. 1975; Pres. E. HAMPTON.

ATTACHED INSTITUTES

Canadian Plains Research Center: Regina; Exec. Dir D. GAUTHIER.

Centre for Advanced Systems: Dir M. WONG.

Development Institute of Saskatchewan: Regina; Dir G. PARSONS.

Energy Research Unit: Regina; Dir B. D. KYBETT.

Asia Pacific Management Institute: Regina; Dir J. CARLSON.

Language Institute: Dir A. LALONDE.

Prairie Justice Research: Dir R. SCHRIML.

Regina Water Research Institute: Dir D. R. CULLIMORE.

Sample Survey and Data Bank Unit: Chair. P. SMITH.

Saskatchewan Instructional Development and Research Unit of the Faculty of Education: Dir C. D. KRENTZ.

Social Administration Research Unit: Dir D. BROAD.

ROYAL MILITARY COLLEGE OF CANADA

Kingston, Ont. K7K 5L0

Telephone: (613) 541-6000
Fax: (613) 542-3565

Founded 1876
Languages of instruction: English and French
Academic year: September to December (fall term); January to May (winter term)

Chancellor and President: The Minister of National Defence
Commandant: Brig.-Gen. J. C. A. EMOND
Principal and Director of Studies: B. J. PLANT
Registrar: M. LABBÉ
Director of Cadets: Lt-Col J. M. M. HAINSE
Director of Administration: Lt-Col J. A. G. LANGLOIS
Chief Librarian: S. O. ALEXANDER

Library of 380,000 vols
Number of teachers: 174
Number of students: 865 (760 undergraduate, 105 graduate)

DEANS AND CHAIRMEN OF DIVISIONS

Arts: R. G. HAYCOCK
Science: A. J. BARRETT
Engineering: A. Y. CHIKHANI
Graduate Studies and Research: R. D. WEIR
Academic Services: P. E. ALLARD

PROFESSORS

AKHRAS, G., Civil Engineering
AL-KHALILI, D., Electrical Engineering
ALLARD, P. E., Electrical Engineering
AMPHLETT, J. C., Chemistry
ANTAR, Y., Electrical Engineering
ARSENAULT, G. P., Chemistry
BARDON, M. F., Mechanical Engineering
BARRETT, A. J., Mathematics
BATHURST, R. J., Civil Engineering
BENESCH, R., Mathematics
BINHAMMER, H. H. F., Economics
BONESS, R. J., Mechanical Engineering
BONIN, H. W., Chemical Engineering
BONNYCASTLE, S., English
BOUTILIER, J. A., History
BRIMBERG, J., Business Administration
BROUGHTON, M. B., Electrical Engineering
BUSSIERES, P., Mechanical Engineering
CHAN, Y. T., Electrical Engineering
CHAUDHRY, M. L., Mathematics
CHIKHANI, A. Y., Electrical Engineering
COULTER, D. M., Mechanical Engineering
DREIZIGER, N. A. F., History
DUNNETT, P., Political and Economic Science
EDER, W. E., Mechanical Engineering
ERRINGTON, J., History
EVANS, M. J. B., Chemistry
FAROOQ, M., Electrical Engineering
FAUREAU, F. R., Physics
FERGUSON, R. J., Mechanical Engineering
FJARLIE, E. J., Mechanical Engineering
FURTER, W. F., Chemical Engineering
GERVAIS, R., Mathematics
HAYCOCK, R. G., History
ION, A., History
JARRETT, P. M., Civil Engineering
JENKINS, A. L., Engineering Management
KIRK, D. W., Civil Engineering
LABONTE, G., Mathematics
LACHAINE, A. R., Physics
LAPLANTE, J. P., Chemistry
MCBRIDE, S. L., Physics
MAILET, L., Military Psychology and Leadership
MANN, R. F., Chemical Engineering
MOFFATT, W. C., Mechanical Engineering
MONGEAU, B., Electrical Engineering
MUKHERJEE, B. K., Physics
NEILSON, K. E., History
PARKER, G. L., English
POTTIER, R. H., Chemistry
RACEY, T. J., Physics
RANGANATHAN, S., Mathematics
ROBERGE, P. R., Chemistry
ROCHON, P., Physics
SCHURER, R. J., Physics
SEGUIN, G., Electrical Engineering
SHEPARD, C. O., Electrical Engineering
SHOUCRI, R. M., Mathematics
SIMMS, B. W., Engineering Management
SOKOLSKY, J. J., Political Science
SRI, P. S., English
ST PIERRE, A., Business Administration
THOMPSON, W. T., Chemical Engineering
TORRIE, G. M., Mathematics
TREDDENICK, J. M., Economics
VINCENT, T. B., English
WEIR, R. D., Chemical Engineering
WHITEHORN, A. J., Political Science
WIEDERICK, H. D., Physics
WILMOT, M., Mathematics
WILSON, J. D., Electrical Engineering
WRIGHT, L. S., Physics

ATTACHED INSTITUTES

Applied Military Science: Dir Col R. L. AITKEN.

Language Centre (Second Languages): Dir K. D. JENSEN.

RYERSON POLYTECHNIC UNIVERSITY

350 Victoria St, Toronto, Ont. M5B 2K3

Telephone: (416) 979-5000

Founded 1963; until 1993 Ryerson Polytechnical Institute
Provincial control
Language of instruction: English
Academic year: September to May

Chancellor: D. CROMBIE
President and Vice-Chancellor: C. LAJEUNESSE
Vice-Presidents: D. R. MOCK (Academic), L. GRAYSON (Administration), M. DEWSON (Faculty and Staff Affairs)
Registrar: K. ALNWICK
Chief Librarian: R. MALINSKI

Number of teachers: 570
Number of students: 12,139 (full-time), 1,649 (part-time), 42,000 registrations (Continuing Education)

Publications: *Annual Report*, *Forum*, *The Ryerson Magazine*.

DEANS

Applied Arts: I. LEVINE
Arts: E. ASPEVIG
Business: S. HEATH
Community Services: J. SANDYS
Engineering and Applied Science: D. NORTHWOOD
Continuing Education: M. BOOTH

HEADS OF DEPARTMENTS/SCHOOLS

Applied Arts:
- Business and Technical Communication: Dr D. P. WHITE
- School of Fashion: J. FULLER
- School of Graphic Communications Management: M. BLACK
- School of Interior Design: L. KELLY
- School of Journalism: P. RUSH (acting)
- Film and Photography: B. DAMUDE
- School of Radio and Television Arts: R. GARDNER
- Theatre School: S. BLACK

Arts:
- Economics: D. RAJAGOPAL
- English: M. MORRISS
- French: J.-P. CHAVY
- Applied Geography: P. COPPACK
- History: A. WARQO
- Philosophy: E. M. HARLOW
- Politics: Dr C. CASSIDY
- Psychology: I. ENGEL
- Sociology: M. POMERANCE

Business:
- School of Business Management: M. MAYO
- School of Hospitality and Tourism Management: I. DEVINE
- Administration and Information Management: D. HO

Community Services:
- School of Child and Youth Care: F. HARE
- School of Early Childhood Education: J. POLLARD
- School of Environmental Health: B. CLARENCE
- School of Health Services Management: P. GAMBLE
- School of Nutrition, Consumer and Family Studies: P. JENSEN
- School of Nursing: S. WILLIAMS
- School of Social Work: E. S. MESBUR
- School of Urban and Regional Planning: B. MOORE MILROY

Community Services/Continuing Education:
- Midwifery: V. VAN WAGNER

Engineering and Applied Science:
- Mechanical Engineering: M. A. ROSEN (Chair.), D. NAYLOR (Dir)
- Mathematics, Physics and Computer Science: Dr C. ALEXOPOULOS
- Architectural Science and Landscape Architecture: M. C. MILLER
- Applied Chemical and Biological Sciences: Dr D. NARANJIT
- School of Civil Engineering: R. SALVAS
- Electrical Engineering: Dr M. ZEYTINOGLU
- School of Computer Science: J. D. GRIMSHAW, A. LAN
- School of Aerospace Engineering: M. A. ROSEN (Chair.), J. LEA (Dir)
- School of Chemical Engineering: Dr A. LOHI
- School of Industrial Engineering: M. A. ROSEN (Chair.), F. STEWART (Dir)

ATTACHED INSTITUTIONS

Centre for Entrepreneurship Education and Research: Dir B. ORSER

Centre for the Study of Commercial Activity: Dir K. JONES

Centre for Tourism Studies: Dir M. HALLE

ST FRANCIS XAVIER UNIVERSITY

POB 5000, Antigonish, NS B2G 2W5

Telephone: (902) 863-3300

Founded 1853

Language of instruction: English

Academic year: September to May

Chancellor: Most Rev. COLIN CAMPBELL

President: Dr SEAN E. RILEY

Academic Vice-President: H. A. GILLIS

Administrative Vice-President: J. T. LANGLEY

Director of University Extension: T. WEBB

Director of Coady International Institute: M. COYLE

Registrar: C. M. DUNCAN

Librarian: R. CAMPBELL

Library: see Libraries

Number of teachers: 190, including 63 professors

Number of students: 3,376

Publications: *Xavieran Weekly, Xavieran Annual, Antigonish Review* (literary).

DEANS

Arts: R. JOHNSON

Science: E. MCALDUFF

Dean of Students: J. MACDONALD

Admissions Officer: R. A. SEPTON (acting)

PROFESSORS

AALTO, S., Mathematics, Statistics and Computer Science
BECK, J., Chemistry
BERRIDGE, J., Religious Studies
BIGELOW, A., Psychology
BROOKS, G. P., Psychology
BUNBURY, D. L., Chemistry
CURRIE, S., English
DAVIS, A., Sociology and Anthropology
DEN HEYER, K., Psychology
DOSSA, S. A., Political Science
DUNCAN, C. M., Business Administration
EDWARDS, J., Psychology
EL-SHEIKH, S., Economics
GALLANT, C. D., Mathematics, Statistics and Computer Science
GALLANT, L., Business Administration
GALLANT, M., Human Kinetics
GARBARY, D., Biology
GERRIETS, M., Economics
GILLEN, M., Adult Education
GILLIS, A., Nursing
GILLIS, H. A., Chemistry
HARGREAVES, J., Music
HARRISON, J. F., Political Science
HENKE, P., Psychology
HOGAN, M. P., History
HOLLOWAY, S., Political Science
HUNTER, D., Physics
JACKSON, W., Sociology and Anthropology
JAN, N., Physics
JOHNSON, R. W., Psychology
JOSHI, Y. N., Physics
MCALDUFF, E., Chemistry
MACDONALD, B., Religious Studies
MACDONALD, M. Y., Religious Studies
MACEACHERN, A., Mathematics, Statistics and Computer Science
MCFARLAND, J. M., Human Kinetics
MACFARLANE, E., Nursing
MACINNES, D., Sociology and Anthropology
MACKINNON, N., History
MACKINNON, R. J., Information Systems
MADDEN, R. F., Business Administration
MARSHALL, W. S., Biology
MENSCH, J., Philosophy
MILNER, P., English
MURPHY, J. B., Geology
MUTIMER, B. T. P., Human Kinetics
NASH, R., Sociology and Anthropology
NEWSOME, G. E., Biology
NILSEN, K., Celtic Studies
O'BRIEN, K., English
O'DONNELL, J., Music
PALEPU, R., Chemistry
PHILLIPS, P., History
PINK, D., Physics
QUINN, J., Mathematics, Statistics and Computer Science
QUINN, W. R., Engineering
RASMUSSEN, R., Human Kinetics
SCHUEGRAF, E. J., Mathematics, Statistics and Computer Science
SEYMOUR, N., Biology
SMITH, D., English
SMITH-PALMER, T., Chemistry
STEINITZ, M. O., Physics
STOUFFER, A. P., History
TAYLOR, J., English
WALSH, P., English
WOOD, D., English
WRIGHT, E., Psychology

ATTACHED INSTITUTE

Coady International Institute: POB 5000, Antigonish, NS B2G 2W5; tel. (902) 867-3961; f. 1959; runs leadership and organization development programs with peoples of Third World countries; diploma and certificate courses in Canada, also training courses and projects overseas; library of 7,000 vols, 90 periodicals; Dir M. COYLE; publs *Newsletter* (2 a year), project reports.

UNIVERSITÉ SAINTE-ANNE

Pointe-de-l'Église, NS B0W 1M0

Telephone: (902) 769-2114

Fax: (902) 769-2930

E-mail: admission@ustanne.ednet.ns.ca

Founded 1890

Language of instruction: French

Academic year: September to April

Chancellor: LOUIS R. COMEAU

President: Dr HARLEY D'ENTREMONT

Vice-President (Academic): IAN RICHMOND

Registrar: Dr GERALD C. BOUDREAU

Librarian: MILDRED COMEAU-SAVOIE

Library of 84,000 vols

Number of teachers: 37

Number of students: 400

Publications: *Calendar, La Revue Sainte-Anne* (annually).

HEADS OF DEPARTMENTS

Commerce: CAROLINE THÉRIAULT
Education: Dr JOSEPH DICKS
English: Dr JAMES QUINLAN
Extension: NADINE BELLIVEAU
French: Dr JEAN WILSON
Humanities: Dr ANDREAS BUSS
Science: Dr NABIL ABBOUD
French Immersion: LISETTE TARDIF

ATTACHED INSTITUTES

Acadian Research Center: Dir Dr NEIL BOUCHER.

Provincial Resources Center: Dir JEAN-LOUIS ROBICHAUD.

Centre de littérature jeunesse: Dir Dr YVES CORMIER.

Centre Jodrey: Dir RONNIE ROBICHAUD.

SAINT MARY'S UNIVERSITY

Robie St, Halifax, NS B3H 3C3

Telephone: (902) 420-5582

Fax: (902) 420-5151

Founded 1802

Chancellor: (vacant)

Vice-Chancellor: Rev. OWEN CONNELLY

President: KENNETH L. OZMON

Vice-President (Administration): GABRIELLE MORRISON

Vice-President (Academic and Research): J. COLIN DODDS

Registrar: ELIZABETH A. CHARD

Librarian: RASHID TAYYEB (acting)

Number of teachers: 384

Number of full-time students: 5,100

Number of part-time students: 2,151

DEANS

Dean of Arts: MICHAEL J. LARSEN
Dean of Education: MICHAEL J. LARSEN (acting)
Dean of Science: DAVID RICHARDSON
Dean of Commerce: PAUL DIXON

PROFESSORS

AMIRKHALKHAI, D., Economics
ARYA, P. L., Economics
BARRETT, G., Sociology
BOWLBY, P., Religious Studies
BOYLE, W. P., Engineering
BRUCE, D., Psychology
BYRNE, C. J., English, Irish Studies
CARRIGAN, D. O., History
CATANO, V. M., Psychology
CHAMARD, J. C., Management
CHARLES, A., Finance
CHENG, T., Accounting
CHESLEY, G. R., Accounting
CHRISTIANSEN-RUFFMAN, L., Sociology
CONE, D., Biology
CONNELLY, P., Sociology and International Development Studies
COSPER, R., Sociology
DAR, A., Economics
DARLEY, J., Psychology
DAS, H., Management
DAVIS, S., Anthropology
DAY, E. E. D., Geography
DOAK, E. J., Economics
DODDS, J. C.
DOSTAL, J., Geology
ELSON, C., Chemistry
ERICKSON, P. A., Anthropology
FARRELL, A., Modern Languages and Classics
FITZGERALD, P., Management
FLIKEID, K., Modern Languages and Classics
GINSBURG, J., Chemistry
HAIGH, E., History
HARTNELL, B., Mathematics
HARVEY, A., Economics
HILL, K., Psychology
HOWELL, C. D., History and Atlantic Canada Studies
KATZ, W., English
KIANG, M.-J., Mathematics and Computing Science
KONAPASKY, R., Psychology
KRUSE, R. L., Mathematics
LANDES, R., Political Science
LARSEN, M. J., English
LEE, E., Finance
LENZER, I., Psychology
MCCALLA, R., Geography
MACDONALD, M., Economics and Women's Studies
MACDONALD, R. A., English
MCGEE, H., Anthropology
MACKINNON, K., English
MCMULLEN, J., Sociology
MILLS, A., Management
MILLWARD, H., Geography
MITCHELL, G., Astronomy
MORRISON, J. H., History and Asian Studies
MUKHOPADHYAY, A. K., Economics
OVERINGTON, M., Sociology
OZMON, K. L., Psychology
PENDSE, S., Management
PE-PIPER, G., Geology
REID, J. G., History, Atlantic Canada Studies
RICHARDSON, D. H. S., Biology
SASTRY, V., Engineering
SCHWIND, H., Management

SIDDIQUI, Q., Geology
SWINGLER, D., Engineering
TARNAWSKI, V., Engineering
THOMAS, G., English
TOBIN, V., Classics
TURNER, D. G., Astronomy and Physics
TWOMEY, R. J., History
VAUGHAN, K., Chemistry
VELTMEYER, H., Sociology, International Development Studies
WALDRON, J., Geology
WHALEN, T., English
WILES, M., Biology
YOUNG, G. F. W., History

UNIVERSITY OF SASKATCHEWAN

105 Administration Place, Saskatoon, Sask. S7N 5A2

Telephone: (306) 966-6766
Fax: (306) 966-6730
E-mail: registrar@usask.ca

Founded 1907; two-campus institution 1967 (Saskatoon and Regina). Legislation was passed in 1974 creating two separate Universities.

State control
Language of instruction: English
Academic year: September to August

Chancellor: M. L. MCKERCHER
President and Vice-Chancellor: J. W. G. IVANY
Vice-President (Academic): M. ATKINSON
Vice-President (Finance and Administration): A. J. WHITWORTH
University Secretary: R. I. MACLEAN
Registrar: K. M. SMITH
Librarian: F. WINTER

Number of teachers: 929
Number of students: 17,468

Publication: *Calendar* (1 a year).

DEANS

College of Agriculture: J. W. B. STEWART
College of Arts and Science: (vacant)
College of Commerce: V. L. PEARSON
College of Dentistry: R. E. MCDERMOTT
College of Education: K. G. JACKNICKE
College of Engineering: F. BERRUTI
College of Graduate Studies and Research: G. KACHANOSKI
College of Law: R. P. MACKINNON
College of Medicine: D. R. POPKIN
College of Nursing: Y. M. R. BROWN
College of Pharmacy: (vacant)
College of Physical Education: R. A. FAULKNER
College of Veterinary Medicine: A. LIVINGSTON

DIRECTORS

School of Physical Therapy: E. HARRISON

PROFESSORS AND HEADS OF DEPARTMENT

(H = Head of Dept)

ABD-EL-BARR, M. H., Computational Science
ADAMS, G. P., Veterinary Anatomy
AIKENHEAD, G. S., Curriculum Studies
AKKERMAN, A., Geography
ALI, S. K., Oncology
ALTMAN, M., Economics (H)
ANDERSON, A. B., Sociology
ANDERSON, D. W., Soil Science
ANGEL, J. F., Biochemistry (H)
ARCHIBOLD, O. W., Geography
ARMITAGE, G. R., Oncology
ARMSTRONG, K. R., Herd Medicine and Theriogenology (H)
AXWORTHY, C. S., Law
BABIUK, L. A. B., Veterinary Biology
BAILEY, J. V., Veterinary Anaesthesiology, Radiology and Surgery
BAKER, R. J., Crop Science and Plant Ecology
BALA, R. M., Medicine
BARANSKI, A. S., Chemistry
BARBER, E. M., Agricultural and Bioresource Engineering (H)
BARBER, S. M., Veterinary Anaesthesiology, Radiology and Surgery
BARBOUR, S. L., Civil Engineering
BARNETT, D. C., Curriculum Studies
BARR, W., Geography (H)
BARRON, F. L., Native Studies
BARTH, A. D., Herd Medicine and Theriogenology
BASINGER, J. F., Geological Sciences (H)
BASRAN, G. S., Sociology
BAXTER, G. C., Accounting
BECK, R. G., Economics
BELL, K. T. M., Art and Art History
BELL, L. S., Art and Art History (H)
BERGSTROM, J. C., Physics and Engineering Physics
BERMAN, S., Mathematics and Statistics
BERNHARDSON, C. S., Psychology
BERRUTI, F., Chemical Engineering
BESANT, R. W., Mechanical Engineering
BETTANY, J. R., Soil Science
BIDWELL, P. M., English (H)
BIETENHOLZ, P. G., History
BILLINTON, R., Electrical Engineering
BILSON, R. E., Law
BLACKBURN, J. L., Pharmacy
BLACKSHAW, S. L., Psychiatry
BLAKLEY, B. R., Veterinary Physiological Sciences
BLOCKA, K. L. N., Medicine
BOCTOR, M. A., Medicine
BOLARIA, B. S., Sociology
BOND, D. J., French
BONE, R. M., Geography
BORTOLOTTI, G. R., Biology
BOULTON, A. A., Psychiatry
BOWEN, R. C., Psychiatry (H)
BOYD, C. W., Management and Marketing (H)
BOYD, Rev. J. I., English
BRENNAN, W. J., Accounting
BRETSCHER, P., Microbiology
BRISTOL, F., Herd Medicine and Theriogenology
BROOKE, J. A., Mathematics and Statistics
BROWN, F. B., Curriculum Studies
BROWN, M., Psychology
BROWN, Y. M. R., Nursing
BROWNE, P. J., Mathematics and Statistics
BUGLASS, R. B., Law
BUNT, R. B., Computer Science
BURKE, R. C., Accounting
BURKHOLDER, G. D., Anatomy and Cell Biology (H)
BURNELL, P., Classics (H)
BURTON, R. T., Mechanical Engineering
BUTLER, R. S., Herd Medicine and Theriogenology
CALDER, R. L., English
CALDWELL, D. E., Applied Microbiology and Food Science
CAMPBELL, J., Psychology
CAPLAN, H. S., Physics and Engineering Physics (H)
CARD, R. T., Medicine
CARLSEN, S. A., Oncology
CARLSON, R. A., Educational Foundations
CARPENTER, D. C., English
CARSON, A. B., Mathematics and Statistics
CASSIDY, R. M., Chemistry
CHAPPELL, E. W., Surgery
CHRISTENSEN, D. A., Animal and Poultry Science (H)
CLARK, D. H., Law
CLASSEN, H. L., Animal and Poultry Science
CLAYTON, H. M., Veterinary Anatomy
CLEIN, L. J., Surgery
COCHRANE, D. B., Educational Foundations
COCKCROFT, D. W., Medicine
COHEN, R. D. H., Animal and Poultry Science
COLLINS, M., Educational Foundations
CONWAY, J. B., Psychology
COOKE, J. E., Computer Science
COOPER-STEPHENSON, K. D., Law
CORRIGAN, K., Philosophy
COTTON, D. J., Medicine (H)
COURTNEY, J. C., Political Studies
CRONE, L. A., Anaesthesia
CROSSLEY, D. J., Philosophy (H)
CUJEC, B., Medicine
CUMING, R. C. C., Law
CUSHMAN, D. O., Economics
D'ARCY, C., Psychiatry
DART, J., Management and Marketing
DAVIS, B. A., Psychiatry
DAYTON, E., Philosophy
DE COTEAU, W. E., Medicine
DE JONG, E., Soil Science
DELBAERE, L. T. J., Biochemistry
DENG, S. L., Management and Marketing
DENHAM, W. P., English
DENIS, W. B., Sociology
DESAUTELS, M., Physiology
DEUTSCHER, T. B., History
DEVINE, M. D., Crop Science and Plant Ecology (H)
DEVON, R. M., Oral Biology
DHAND, H., Curriculum Studies
DHINGRA, H. L., Finance and Management Science
DICKINSON, H. D., Sociology
DIMMOCK, J. R., Pharmacy
DODDS, D. E., Electrical Engineering
DONAT, J. R. , Medicine
DOOLEY, P. C., Economics
DOSMAN, J. A., Medicine
DOUCETTE, J. R., Anatomy and Cell Biology
DURDEN, D. A., Psychiatry
DYCK, L. E., Psychiatry
DYCK, R. F., Medicine
EAGER, D. L., Computer Science (H)
ECKROTH, M., Music
EDELL, F., Drama
EDOUARD, J. L., Community Health and Epidemiology
ELLIS, J. A., Veterinary Microbiology
ERVIN, A. M., Anthropology and Archaeology
ESMAIL, M. N., Chemical Engineering
EVERED, M. D., Physiology (H)
EWING, G. H., Oncology
FARROW, C. S., Veterinary Anaesthesiology, Radiology and Surgery
FAULKNER, R. A., Physical Education
FERGUSON, J. G., Veterinary Anaesthiology, Radiology and Surgery
FINDLAY, L. M., English
FISCHER, D. G., Psychology
FISHER, R., Psychology
FLANNIGAN, R., Law
FLOOD, P. F., Veterinary Anatomy (H)
FORSYTH, G. W., Veterinary Physiological Sciences
FORSYTH, L., French
FOWKE, L. C., Biology (H)
FOWLER, J. D., Veterinary Anaesthesiology, Radiology and Surgery
FOWLER-KERRY, S. E., Nursing
FREDLUND, D. G., Civil Engineering
FULTON, M. E., Agricultural Economics
FUNG, K. I., Geography
FURTAN, W. H., Agricultural Economics
GAMBELL, T. J., Curriculum Studies
GANDER, R. E., Electrical Engineering
GENDZWILL, D. J., Geological Sciences
GERMIDA, J. J., Soil Science
GILES, K. L., Horticultural Science
GILLIES, J. A., Agricultural and Bioresource Engineering
GILLOTT, C., Biology
GILMOUR, T. H. J., Biology
GINGELL, S. A. R., English
GORDON, J. R., Veterinary Microbiology
GORECKI, D. K. J., Pharmacy
GRAHAM, B. L., Medicine
GRANT, P. R., Psychology
GRASSMANN, W. K., Computer Science
GREER, J. E., Computer Science
GRESCHNER, D., Law
GRIFFITH, G. J., Mathematics and Statistics
GULLICKSON, G., Music (H)
GUPTA, M. M., Mechanical Engineering
GUPTA, V. S., Veterinary Physiological Sciences
GUSTHART, J. L., Physical Education

HABBICK, B. F., Community Care and Epidemiology
HADER, W. J., Rehabilitation Medicine (H)
HADERLEIN, K. G. J., Modern Languages
HAIG, T. H. B., Surgery
HAIGH, J. C., Herd Medicine and Theriogenology
HAIGHT, K. R., Family Medicine
HAINES, D. M., Veterinary Microbiology
HAINES, L. P., Education of Exceptional Children
HAJNAL, Z., Geological Sciences
HAMILTON, D. L., Veterinary Physiological Sciences (H)
HAMILTON, W. P. C., Art and Art History
HANDY, J., History
HARDING, A. J., English
HARMS, V. L., Biology
HARRIS, R. L., English
HARVEY, B. L., Horticulture Science (H)
HAUG, M. D., Civil Engineering
HAWES, E. M., Pharmacy
HAYDEN, J. M., History
HAYES, S. J., Microbiology
HEBER, L., Nursing
HENDERSON, J. R., English
HERMAN, R. J., Pharmacology
HERTZ, L., Pharmacology
HERTZ, P. B., Mechanical Engineering
HICKIE, R. A., Pharmacology
HILL, G. A., Chemical Engineering
HIROSE, A., Physics and Engineering Physics
HOEPPNER, V. H., Medicine
HOLM, F. A., Crop Science and Plant Ecology
HOOVER, J. N., Diagnostic and Surgical Sciences
HOPE, J. A., Curriculum Studies
HOSAIN, M. U., Civil Engineering
HOUSE, C. L., Music
HOWE, E. C., Economics
HUANG, P. M., Soil Science
HUBBARD, J. W., Pharmacy
HUGHES, G. R., Crop Science and Plant Ecology
HULL, P. R., Medicine
HURST, T. S., Medicine
ILLERBRUN, D. W., Education of Exceptional Children (H)
INGLEDEW, W. M., Applied Microbiology and Food Science
IRVINE, J. D., Family Medicine
IRVINE, V. B., Accounting
ISH, D., Law
IVANY, J. W. G., Curriculum Studies
IVERSEN, J. O., Veterinary Microbiology
JACKNICKE, K. G., Curriculum Studies
JANA, S., Crop Science and Plant Ecology
JANZEN, E. D., Herd Medicine and Theriogenology
JOHNSON, D. H., Medicine
JOHNSON, H. C., History
JOHNSTON, G. H. F., Surgery
JONES, G. A., Applied Microbiology and Food Science
JULIEN, J., French (H)
JUORIO, A. V., Psychiatry
JUURLINK, B. H. J., Anatomy and Cell Biology
KACHANOSKI, R. G., Soil Science
KALRA, J., Pathology (H)
KASAP, S. O., Electrical Engineering
KASIAN, G. F., Paediatrics
KEEGAN, D. L., Psychiatry
KEIL, J. M., Computer Science
KEITH, R. G., Surgery (H)
KELLY, I. W., Educational Psychology
KENT, C. A., History
KERR, D. C., English
KHACHATOURIANS, G. G., Applied Microbiology and Food Science
KHANDELWAL, R. L., Biochemistry
KING, J., Biology
KLOSE, R. E., Music
KOKKINIDIS, L., Psychology
KOMIYAMA, K., Oral Biology (H)
KONCHAK, P. A., Community and Paediatric Dentistry (H)
KORCHINSKI, E. D., Family Medicine
KRAUSE, A. E., Electrical Engineering
KRISTJANSON, L. F., Economics
KULSHRESHTHA, S. N., Agricultural Economics
KUSHWAHA, R. L., Agricultural and Bioresource Engineering
LAARVELD, B., Animal and Poultry Science (H)
LACALLI, T. C., Biology
LAING, G. P., Nursing
LAL, K., Economics
LANIGAN, D. T., Diagnostic and Surgical Sciences
LATSHAW, W. K., Veterinary Anatomy
LEE, G. E., Agricultural Economics
LEE, J. S., Biochemistry
LEE, M. H., Finance and Management Science
LEHMKUHL, D. M., Biology
LEIGHTON, F. A., Veterinary Pathology (H)
LEONG, C. K., Education of Exceptional Children
LESZCZYNSKI, J., Rehabilitation Medicine
LI, P. S., Sociology
LINDSAY, R. M., Accounting (H)
LINDSAY, W. D., Accounting
LINWOOD, M. E., Nursing
LIVINGSTON, A., Veterinary Physiological Sciences
LLEWELLYN, E. J., Physics and Engineering Physics
LOEWY, J., Medical Imaging (H)
LOH, L. C., Microbiology
LONEY, R. W., Restorative and Prosthetic Dentistry
LONG, R. J., Industrial Relations and Organizational Behaviour
LOPTSON, P. J., Philosophy
LOW, N. H., Applied Microbiology and Food Science
LOWRY, N., Paediatrics
LUCAS, R. F., Economics
LUKIE, B. E., Medicine
LYONS, J. E., Educational Foundations
MCCALLA, G. I., Computational Science
MCCLEMENTS, J., Physical Education
MCCONNELL, J. G., Geography
MCCONNELL, W. H., Law
MCCROSKY, C. D., Computer Science
MCDERMOTT, R. E., Community and Paediatric Dentistry
MACDONALD, D. G., Chemical Engineering
MACDONALD, M. B., Nursing
MCDUFFIE, N. M., Physiology
MCKAY, G., Pharmacy
MCKAY, R., Surgery
MACKENZIE, P. T., Philosophy
MCKERCHER, R. B., Soil Science
MACKINNON, R. P., Law
MCLENNAN, B. D., Biochemistry
MCMEEKIN, J. D., Medicine
MCMULLEN, L. M., Psychology (H)
MCNEILL, J. R. J., Pharmacology (H)
MAGINNES, E. A., Horticulture Science
MAJEWSKI, M., Chemistry
MALE, D. H., Mechanical Engineering
MANNS, J. G., Veterinary Physiological Sciences
MANSON, A. H., Physics and Engineering Physics
MAPLETOFT, R. J., Herd Medicine and Theriogenology
MARKEN, R. N. G., English
MARSHALL, M. A., Mathematics and Statistics
MARTIN, J. R., Mathematics and Statistics
MARTZ, L. W., Geography
MASSEY, K. L., Pathology
MATHESON, T. J., English
MATHUR, B. J., Nursing
MATTHEWS, P. C., Psychiatry
MERRIAM, J. B., Geological Sciences
MESSIER, F., Biology
MEYER, D., Anthropology and Archaeology
MEZEY, P. G., Chemistry
MICHELMANN, H. J., Political Studies
MIKET, M. J., Mathematics and Statistics
MILLER, J. R., History
MILLS, J. A., Psychology
MIQUELON, D., History
MIRWALD, R. L., Physical Education
MISANCHUK, E. R., Extension
MISRA, V., Veterinary Microbiology
MORRIS, G. B., Educational Psychology
MOSS, G. M., Extension
MOULDING, M. B., Restorative and Prosthetic Dentistry (H)
NAYLOR, J. M., Veterinary Internal Medicine
NEAL, B. R., Biology
NEUFELD, E, Computer Science
NORMAN, K. E., Law
NORUM, D. I., Agricultural and Bioresource Engineering
OLES, R. D., Oral Biology
OLIPHANT, L. W., Veterinary Anatomy
PACKOTA, G. V., Diagnostic and Surgical Sciences (H)
PATO, M. D., Biochemistry
PAULSON, K. V., Physics and Engineering Physics
PAWLOVICH, W., Educational Psychology (H)
PENG, D.-Y., Chemical Engineering
PENNOCK, D. J., Soil Science
PETRIE, L., Veterinary Internal Medicine
PFEIFER, K., Philosophy
PHARR, J. W., Veterinary Anaesthesiology, Radiology and Surgery
PIERSON, R. A., Obstetrics and Gynaecology
PINILLA, J. C., Surgery
POLLEY, L. R., Veterinary Microbiology (H)
POMEDLI, M. M., Philosophy
POOLER, J. A., Geography
POPKIN, D. R., Obstetrics and Gynaecology
PORTER, J. M., Political Studies
POST, K., Veterinary Internal Medicine (H)
POSTLETHWAITE, J., Chemical Engineering (H)
PROCTOR, L. F., Curriculum Studies
PUFAHL, D. E., Civil Engineering (H)
PYWELL, R. E., Physics and Engineering Physics
QUAIL, J. W., Chemistry
QUALTIERE, L. F., Microbiology (H)
QUIGLEY, T. L., Law
RADOSTITS, O. M., Veterinary Internal Medicine
RAE, D. I., Nursing
RAJPUT, A. H., Medicine
RAMSAY, M. A., Biology
RANDHAWA, B. S., Educational Psychology
RANGACHARYULU, C., Physics and Engineering Physics
RANK, G. H., Biology
RATZ, A. E., Modern Languages
RAWLINGS, N. C., Veterinary Physiological Sciences
REDMANN, R. E., Crop Science and Plant Ecology
REEDER, B. A., Community Health and Epidemiology
REEVES, M. J., Geological Sciences
RELKE, D., Women's and Gender Studies (H)
REMILLARD, A. J., Pharmacy
RENAUT, R. W., Geological Sciences
RENIHAN, P. J., Educational Administration (H)
REZANSOFF, T., Civil Engineering
REZKALLAH, K. S., Mechanical Engineering
RHODES, C. S., Herd Medicine and Theriogenology
RIBBLE, C. S., Herd Medicine and Theriogenology
RICHARDSON, J. S., Pharmacology
RIDDELL, C., Veterinary Pathology
RINGNESS, C. O., Art and Art History
RIPLEY, E. A., Crop Science and Plant Ecology
ROBINSON, S. D., Curriculum Studies
ROHANI, S., Chemical Engineering
ROMANCHUK, K. G., Ophthalmology (H)
ROMO, J. T., Crop Science and Plant Ecology
ROSAASEN, K. A., Agricultural Economics
ROSENBERG, A. M., Paediatrics (H)
RUBIN, S. I., Veterinary Internal Medicine
RUSSELL, R., Sociology
RYAN, A. G., Curriculum Studies
SACKNEY, L. E., Educational Administration
SAINI, G. L., Mathematics and Statistics

ST LOUIS, L. V., Economics
SAKLOFSKE, D. H., Educational Psychology
SALEH, F. A., Management and Marketing (H)
SALT, J. E., Electrical Engineering
SANCHE, R. P., Education of Exceptional Children
SANKARAN, K., Paediatrics
SARGENT, C. M., Mechanical Engineering
SARJEANT, W. A. S., Geological Sciences
SARKAR, A. K., Management and Marketing
SASS, R., Industrial Relations and Organizational Behaviour
SAWATZKY, J. E., Nursing
SAWHNEY, V. K., Biology
SCHARF, M. P., Educational Administration
SCHISSEL, B., Sociology
SCHMUTZ, S. M., Animal and Poultry Science
SCHOENAU, G. J., Mechanical Engineering (H)
SCHONEY, R. A., Agricultural Economics
SCHWIER, R. A., Curriculum Studies
SCISSONS, E. H., Extension
SCOLES, G. J., Crop Science and Plant Ecology
SCOTT, R. I., English
SEARCY, G. P., Veterinary Pathology
SEMCHUK, K. M., Nursing
SEMPLE, R. K., Geography
SENIOR, N. M., French
SHARGOOL, P. D., Biochemistry
SHARMA, R. K., Pathology
SHEARD, J. W., Biology
SHERIDAN, D. P., Medicine
SHIN, Y. M., Physics and Engineering Physics
SHUAIB, A., Medicine
SIBLEY, J. T., Medicine
SIDHU, T. S., Electrical Engineering
SIMPSON, G. M., Crop Science and Plant Ecology
SINGH, R. R., Mathematics and Statistics
SINHA, B. M., Religious Studies (H)
SISODIA, C. S., Veterinary Physiological Sciences
SKOPIK, D. M., Physics and Engineering Physics
SLIGHTS, C. W., English
SLIGHTS, W. W. E., English
SMART, M., Veterinary Internal Medicine
SMITH, B. L., Nursing
SMITH, D. E., Political Studies
SMITH, R. J. F., Biology
SMITH, S. G., Family Medicine
SOFKO, G. J., Physics and Engineering Physics
SOKALSKI, A. A., French
SOKHANSANJ, S., Agricultural and Bioresource Engineering
SOLEM, R. J., Music
SPAFFORD, D. S., Political Studies
SPARKS, G. A., Civil Engineering
SPINK, K. S., Physical Education
SPOONER, H. J., Medical Education
SPRIGGS, J., Agricultural Economics
SPRIGINGS, E. J. C., Physical Education
STABLER, J. C., Agricultural Economics (H)
STAUFFER, M. R., Geological Sciences
STEEVES, J. S., Political Studies
STEPHANSON, R. A., English
STEPHEN, A. M., Nutrition and Dietetics
STEPHENSON, J. W., Mathematics and Statistics
STEWART, J. W. B., Soil Science
STEWART, L., History
STOICHEFF, R. P., English
STOLTE, W. J., Civil Engineering
STOREY, G. G., Agricultural Economics
SULAKHE, P. V., Physiology
SULAKHE-HEMMINGS, S. J., Physiology
SUTHERLAND, R. G., Chemistry (H)
SUVEGES, L. G., Pharmacy
SWAN, P. M., History
SZYSZKOWSKI, W., Mechanical Engineering
TABEL, H., Veterinary Microbiology (H)
TAKAYA, K., Electrical Engineering
TAN, L. K. T., Community Health and Epidemiology (H)
TAYLOR, K. F., Mathematics and Statistics
TAYLOR, S. M., Veterinary Internal Medicine
TEPLITSKY, P. E., Restorative and Prosthetic Dentistry
THACKER, P. A., Animal and Poultry Science
THOMPSON, C. A., English
THOMPSON, D. G., Extension
THOMPSON, J. R., Sociology
THORNHILL, J. A., Physiology
TOMUSIAK, E. L., Physics and Engineering Physics
TOUGH, F., Native Studies
TOWNSEND, H. G. G., Veterinary Internal Medicine
TREMBLAY, J. P., Computer Science
TURNELL, R. W., Obstetrics and Gynaecology (H)
TYLER, R. T., Applied Microbiology and Food Science (H)
TYMCHATYN, E. D., Mathematics and Statistics
TYRRELL, M. J., Paediatrics
UKRAINETZ, P. R., Mechanical Engineering
VAN HESTEREN, F., Educational Psychology
VERMA, S. P., Electrical Engineering
VERRALL, R. E., Chemistry
VICQ, J. G., Accounting
VON BAEYER, C. L., Psychology
WACKER, G., Electrical Engineering
WAGNER, P. S., Nursing
WAGNER, R. M. K., Extension
WAISER, W. A., History (H)
WAKIL, S. P., Sociology
WALDRAM, J. B., Native Studies
WALKER, E. G., Anthropology and Archaeology (H)
WALLACE, S. M., Pharmacy
WALTZ, W. L., Chemistry
WALZ, W., Physiology
WARD, D. E., Chemistry
WARRINGTON, R. C., Biochemistry
WASON-ELLAM, L., Curriculum Studies
WATSON, L. G., Mechanical Engineering
WAYGOOD, E. B., Biochemistry
WEST, N. H., Physiology
WETZEL, K. W., Industrial Relations and Organizational Behaviour
WHITE, D. F., Oncology (H)
WHITE, G. N., Family Medicine (H)
WHITING, S. J., Nutrition and Dietetics (H)
WICKETT, R. E. Y., Educational Foundations (H)
WILKINSON, A. A., Medical Imaging
WILLIAMSON, R. G., Anthropology and Archaeology
WILSON, T. W., Pharmacology
WISHART, T. B., Psychology
WITTLIN, C. J., French
WOBESER, G. A., Veterinary Pathology
WONG, A. T., Extension
WOOD, H. C., Electrical Engineering (H)
WOODHOUSE, E., Educational Foundations
WOROBETZ, L. J., Medicine
WOTHERSPOON, T. L., Sociology (H)
YANG, H. Y., Computer Science
YANNACOPOULOS, S., Mechanical Engineering
YIP, R. W., Anaesthesia (H)
YONG-HING, K., Surgery
YU, P. H., Psychiatry
ZEMORE, R. W., Psychology
ZICHY, F. A., English
ZIOLA, B., Microbiology

FEDERATED COLLEGE

St Thomas More College: 1437 College Drive, Saskatoon, Sask. S7N 0W6; Pres. J. R. THOMPSON.

JUNIOR COLLEGE

St Peter's College: Box 10, Munster, Sask. S0K 2Y0; Dir A. V. SARETSKY.

AFFILIATED COLLEGES

Central Pentecostal College: 1303 Jackson Ave, Saskatoon, Sask. S7H 2M9; Pres. Rev. R. KADYSCHUK (acting).

College of Emmanuel and St. Chad: 1337 College Drive, Saskatoon, Sask. S7N 0W6; Principal Rev. C. W. CHRISTENSEN.

Lutheran Theological Seminary: 114 Seminary Crescent, Saskatoon, Sask. S7N 0X3; Pres. Rev. R. W. NOSTBAKKEN.

St. Andrew's College: 1121 College Drive, Saskatoon, Sask. S7N 0W3; Co-Pres Dr M. G. BOURGEOIS, Rev. C. A. CARON.

UNIVERSITÉ DE SHERBROOKE

2500 Blvd de l'Université, Sherbrooke, Que. J1K 2R1

Telephone: (819) 821-7000
Telex: 05836149
Fax (819) 821-7966

Founded 1954
Private control
Language of instruction: French
Academic year: September to May

Chancellor: H. E. Mgr JEAN-MARIE FORTIER, Catholic Archbishop of Sherbrooke
Rector: PIERRE REID
Vice-Rector (Studies): JEAN-PIERRE KESTEMAN
Vice-Rector (Research): ALAIN CAILLÉ
Vice-Rector (Administration): DANIEL HADE
Vice-Rector (Personnel and Students): TREFFLÉ MICHAUD
Vice-Rector (Public Relations): JEAN COMTOIS
Secretary-General: MICHEL POIRIER
Registrar: JEAN-PIERRE BERTRAND
Librarian: JULES CHASSÉ

Library of 1,676,000 vols
Number of teachers: 650 full-time, 1,100 part-time
Number of students: 11,843 full-time, 10,255 part-time

DEANS

Faculty of Administration: J. INGHAM
Faculty of Letters and Human Sciences: N. WENER
Faculty of Law: N. RATTI
Faculty of Medicine: M. BARON
Faculty of Science: P.-Y. LEDUC
Faculty of Applied Science: Y. VAN HOENACKER
Faculty of Theology, Ethics and Philosophy: J. F. MALHERBE
Faculty of Education: D. LAFOREST
Faculty of Physical and Sport Education: J. SARRASIN
School of Music: M. WIDNER

PROFESSORS

Faculty of Administration:

Accountancy

BEAUCHESNE, A.
COMTOIS, J.
GODBOUT, R.
JOLIN, M.
LEMIEUX, P.
MENARD, P.
MORIN, R.
MORIN, R. J.
NOËL, R.

Finance

BEN-AMOR, A.
GARANT, J.-P.
GARNIER, G.
GUERIN, F.
PAGE, J. P.
PRÉFONTAINE, J.
PREZEAU, C.

Management

BERGERON, J.-L.
COUPAL, M.
LAFLAMME, M.
LEONARD, H.
PETIT, A.
PRÉVOST, P.
ROBIDOUX, J.
ROY, A. F.
TURCOTTE, P.

Marketing

Boivin, Y.
D'Astous, A.
Valence, G.

Quantitative Methods

Bastin, E.
Beaudoin, P.-H.
Ingham, J.
Maltais, G.
Theoret, A.

Faculty of Letters and Human Sciences:

Economics

Ascah, L.-G.
Bastien, R.
Dauphin, R.
Hanel, P.
Larin, G.-N.
Pelletier, G.-R.
Roy, G.
Wener, N

Geography and Remote Sensing

Bonn, F.
Choquette, R.
Dubois, J.-M.
Gagnon, R.
Gwyn, H.
Morin, D.
Nadeau, R.
Paquette, R.
Poulin, A.
Pouliot, M.

Human Sciences

Blais, M.
Chaput, B.
Chotard, J.-R.
De Bujanda, J.-M.
Dumont, M.
Gagnon, M.
Giroux, L.
Lachance, A.-L.
Laperrière, G.
Legault, G.
Luc, L.
Valcke, L.
Vandal, G.

Letters and Communications

Beauchemin, N.
Bonenfant, J.
Dupuis, H.
Forest, J.
Giguère, R.
Giroux, R.
Hébert, P.
Jones, D.-G.
Leard, J.-M.
Malus, A.
Martel, P.
Michon, J.
Painchaud, L.
Sirois, A.
Sutherland, R.
Theoret, M.
Tremblay, R.
Vinet, M. T.

Psychology

Charbonneau, Cl.
Leclerc, G.
L'Ecuyer, R.
Normandeau, A.
Payette, M.
St-Arnaud, Y.

Social Service

Alary, J.
Lefrançois, R.
Malavoy, M.

Faculty of Law:

Anctil, J.
Bergeron, J.-G.
Blache, P.
Boisclair, Cl.
Charron, C.
Codère, D.
Dubé, J.-L.
Dubé, M.
Gagnon, J.
Kouri, R.-P.
Lavoie, J.-M.
Melanson, J.
Patenaude, P.
Pepin, R.
Philips-Nootens, S.
Poirier, M. Z.
Ratti, N.
Tétrault, R.

Faculty of Education:

Special Education

Hade, D.
Lefebvre, R.
Otis, R.
Poulin, G.
Rheault, M.
Tardif, J.

Pre-School and Primary Education

Lafontaine, L.
Martel, G.
Roy, G.-R.
Thérien, L.

Counselling and School Administration

Dupont, P.
Laflamme, Cl.
Limoges, J.
Marceau, D.
Masse, D.
Reid, A.

Pedagogy

Cormier, R. A.
Harvey, V.
Hivon, R.
Robidas, G.
Scholer, M.
Serre, F.
Stringer, G.

Faculty of Physical Education and Sport:

Bissonnette, R.
Cuerrier, J.-P.
Demers, P. J.
Deshaies, P.
Gauthier, P.
Lemieux, G.-B.
Nadeau, M.
Nadon, R.
Ouellet, J.-G.
Quenneville, G.
Roy, R.
Royer, D.
Therrien, R.
Vanden-Abeele, J.

Faculty of Medicine:

Anatomy and Cellular Biology

Brière, N.
Calvert, R.
Menard, D.
Nemirovsky, M.-S.
Nigam, V.-N.

Anaesthesia

Lamarche, Y.
Tétreault, J. P.

Biochemistry

Bastin, M.
De Médicis, M.-E.
Dupuis, G.
Gibson, D.
Grant, A.
Lehoux, J.-G.
Tan, L.

Biophysics and Physiology

Payet, M. D.
Ruiz-Petrich, E.
Schanne, O.
Seufert, W. D.

Cardiovascular and Thoracic Surgery

Teijeira, F. J.

General Surgery

Devroede, G.
Rioux, A.

Orthopaedic Surgery

Des Marchais, J. E.

Medicine

Baron, M., Internal Medicine
Beaudry, R., Gastroenterology
Begin, R., Pneumology
Bellabarba, D., Endocrinology
Bénard, B., Endocrinology
Côté, M., Cardiology
Dumais, B., Cardiology
Haddad, H., Gastroenterology
Longpré, B., Haematology
Lussier, A., Rheumatology
Marcoux, J.-A., Infectious Diseases
Ménard, D. B., Gastroenterology
Ménard, H., Rheumatology
Montambault, P., Nephrology
Nawar, T., Nephrology
Pépin, J.-M., Internal Medicine
Pigeon, G., Nephrology
Plante, A., Internal Medicine
Plante, G.-E., Nephrology
Reiher, J., Neurology
Rochon, M., Haematology
Rouleau, J. L., Cardiology
Tétreault, L., Internal Medicine

Family Medicine

Bernier, R.
Caux, R.
Grand'maison, P.

Nuclear Medicine and Radiobiology

Jay-Gerin, J.-P.
Sanche, L.
Van Lier, J.

Microbiology

Bourgaux, D.
Bourgaux, P.
Thirion, J.-P.
Weber, J.

Obstetrics and Gynaecology

Ainmelk, Y.
Blouin, D.
Gagner, R.

Ophthalmology

Brunette, J.-R.

Oto-rhino-laryngology

Charlin, B.

Pathology

Coté, R. A.
Lamarche, J.
Madarnas, P.
Massé, S.

Paediatrics

Bureau, M. A.
Langlois, L.
Lemieux, B.
Paré, C.
Rola-Pleszczynski, M.

Pharmacology

Escher, E.
Regoli, G.
Sirois, P.

Diagnostic Radiology

Brazeau-Lamontagne, L.
Schmutz, G.

Nursing Sciences

Chartier, L.
Lalancette, D.

Community Health

Béland, R.
Iglesias, R.
Vobecky, J.
Vobecky, J. S.

Faculty of Sciences:

Biology

BEAUDOIN, A.
BEAUMONT, G.
BÉCHARD, P.
BERGERON, J.-M.
CYR, A.
LEBEL, D.
MATTON, P.
MORISSET, J.-A.
O'NEIL, L.-C
ROBIN, J.

Chemistry

BANDRAUK, A. D.
BROWN, G. M.
CABANA, A.
DESLONGCHAMPS, P.
GIGUÈRE, J.
JERUMANIS, S.
JOLICOEUR, C.
LESSARD, J.
MÉNARD, H.
MICHEL, A.
PELLETIER, G.-E.
RUEST, L.

Mathematics and Computer Science

ALLARD, J.
BAZINET, J.
BELLEY, J.-M.
BOUCHER, C.
BRISEBOIS, M.
COLIN, B.
CONSTANTIN, J.
COURTEAU, B.
CUSTEAU, G.
DUBEAU, F.
DUBOIS, J.
FOURNIER, G.
GIROUX, G.
HAGUEL, J.
KRELL, M.
LEDUC, P.-Y.
MORALES, P.
SAINT-DENIS, R.
SAMSON, J.-P.

Physics

AUBIN, M.
BANVILLE, M.
CAILLÉ, A.
CARLONE, C.
CARON, L. G.
JANDL, S.
LEMIEUX, A.
SIMARD, P.-A.
TREMBLAY, A. M.

Faculty of Applied Sciences:

Chemical Engineering

BOULOS, M.
BROADBENT, A. D.
CHORNET, E.
DEKEE, D.
GRAVELLE, D.
JONES, P.
THÉRIEN, N.

Civil Engineering

AITCIN, P.-C.
BALLIVY, G.
BRUNELLE, P.-E.
GALLEZ, B.
JOHNS, K. C.
LAHOUD, A.
LEFEBVRE, D.
LEFEBVRE, G. A.
LEMIEUX, P.
LUPIEN, C.
MORIN, J.-P.
NARASIAH, S. K.
NEALE, K. W.
ROHAN, K.

Electrical Engineering and Computer Engineering

ADOUL, J.-P.
AUBÉ, G.
BÉLAND, B.
BOUTIN, N.
DALLE, D.
DELISLE, J.
DENIS, G.
DUVAL, F.
GOULET, R.
LEROUX, A.
MORISSETTE, S.
RICHARD, S.
THIBAULT, R.

Mechanical Engineering

BOURASSA, P.-A.
GALANIS, N.
LANEVILLE, A.
MASSOUD, M.
MERCADIER, Y.
NICOLAS, J.
PROULX, D.
ROY, C.
VAN HOENACKER, Y.

Faculty of Theology, Ethics and Philosophy:

BÉDARD, A.
BOISVERT, L.
MELANÇON, L.
OUELLET, F.
RACINE, L.
VACHON, L.
VAILLANCOURT, R.

SIMON FRASER UNIVERSITY

Burnaby, BC V5A 1S6
Telephone: (604) 291-3111
Fax: (604) 291-4969

Founded 1963
Provincial control
Language of instruction: English
Academic year: September to August (3 semesters)

Chancellor: J. SEGAL
President: J. O. STUBBS
Vice-President (Academic) and Provost: D. P. GAGAN
Vice-President (Simon Fraser University for Harbour Centre, and Continuing Studies): J. BLANEY
Vice-President (Finance and Administration): R. WARD
Vice-President (Research) and Dean of Graduate Studies: B. P. CLAYMAN
Registrar: W. R. HEATH
Librarian: T. C. DOBB

Number of teachers: 618 (faculty status)
Number of students: 18,252

Publications: *Undergraduate / Graduate Calendar, Summit* (annually), *West Coast Line, Computational Intelligence, Contact: Review for French Teachers, International Historical Review, Afterthoughts* (all quarterly), *Simon Fraser News* (fortnightly), *The Peak* (weekly), *Alumni Journal,* faculty publs.

DEANS

Faculty of Applied Sciences: R. G. MARTENIUK
Faculty of Arts: J. T. PIERCE
Faculty of Business Administration: J. H. WATERHOUSE
Faculty of Science: C. H. W. JONES
Faculty of Education: R. BARROW

PROFESSORS AND HEADS OF DEPARTMENTS

(H = Non-professorial Head of Dept)

Faculty of Applied Sciences:

Communication

ANDERSON, R. S.
GRUNEAU, R.
HARASIM, L. M.
HEYER, P.
KLINE, S.
LEWIS, B.
LEWIS, B.
LORIMER, R. M.
TRUAX, B. D.
WALLS, J. W.
WILDEN, A.

Computing Science

AIT-KACI, H.
BHATTACHARYA, B. K.
BURTON, F. W.
CALVERT, T. W.
DAHL, V.
FUNT, B. V.
HAN, J. W.
HELL, P.
HOBSON, R. F.
KAMEDA, T.
LIESTMAN, A. L. (H)
LUK, W. S.
PETERS, J. G.
WEINKAM, J. J.

Engineering Science

BIRD, J. S.
CALVERT, T. W.
CAVERS, J. K.
DEEN, M. J.
DILL, J. C.
GRUVER, W. A.
HARDY, R. H. S.
HOBSON, R. F.
LEUNG, A. M.
RAWICZ, A. H.
STAPLETON, S. P.
SYRZYCKI, M.

Kinesiology

BANISTER, E. W.
BAWA, P. N. S.
BHAKTHAN, N. M. G.
CALVERT, T. W.
CHAPMAN, A. E.
DAVISON, A. J.
DICKINSON, J.
GOODMAN, D.
HOFFER, J. A.
MARTENIUK, R. G.
MEKJAVIC, I.
MORRISON, J. B.
ROSIN, M.
TIBBITS, G.
WEINBERG, H.

Resource and Environmental Management Programme

DAY, J. C.
KNETSCH, J. L.
NEWBURY, B.
PETERMAN, R. M.

Faculty of Arts:

Archaeology

BURLEY, D. V.
FLADMARK, K. R.
GALDIKAS, B. M. F.
HAYDEN, B. D.
NANCE, J. D.
NELSON, D. E.

School for the Contemporary Arts

ALOI, S. A.
DIAMOND, M.
GARLAND, I.
MACINTYRE
TRUAX, B. D.
UNDERHILL, O.

Criminology

BOYD, N. T.
BRANTINGHAM, P. J.
BRANTINGHAM, P. L.
CORRADO, R. R.
GRIFFITHS, C. T.
JACKSON, M. A.
LOWMAN, J.
MENZIES, R. J.
VERDUN-JONES, S. N.

Economics

BOLAND, L. A.
CHANT, J. F.

DE VORTZ, D. J.
DEAN, J. W.
DOW, G.
EASTON, S. T.
EATON, B. C.
GLOBERMAN, S.
GRAUER, R. R.
GRUBEL, H. G.
HARRIS, R. G.
HOLMES, R. A.
JONES, R. A.
KENNEDY, P. E.
KHAN, M. H.
KNETSCH, J. L.
LEBOWITZ, M. A.
LIPSEY, R. G.
MAKI, D. R.
MUNRO, J. M.
OLEWITER, N. D.
SPINDLER, Z. A.

English

BLACK, S. A.
BOWERING, G.
COE, R. M.
DELANY, P.
DELANY, S.
DJWA, S.
GERSON, C.
HARDEN, E. F.
MEZEI, K.
MIKI, R. A.
PAGE, M.
RUDRUM, A.
STEIG, M.
STOUCK, D.
STURROCK, J.
ZASLOVE, J.

French

FAUQUENOY, M. C.
MERLER, G.

Geography

BAILEY, W. G.
HAYTER, R.
HICKIN, E. J.
PIERCE, J. T. (H)
POIKER, T. K.
ROBERTS, M. C.
WONG, S. T.

Gerontology

GUTMAN, G.

History

BOYER, R. E.
CLEVELAND, W. L.
COLE, D. L.
DAY, C. R.
DEBO, R. K.
DUTTON, P. E.
FELLMAN, M. D.
GAGAN, D. P.
HUTCHINSON, J. F.
INGRAM, E. R.
JOHNSTON, H. J. M.
KITCHEN, J. M.
LITTLE, J. I.
NEWTON, R. C.
STEWART, M. L.
STUBBS, J. O.

Humanities

DUGUID, S. (H)
DUTTON, P. E.
KIRSCHNER, T. J.
ZASLOVE, J.

Latin American Studies

ESCUDERO, M. (H)

Linguistics

GERDTS, D. B.
HAMMERLY, H.
LINCOLN, N. J.
ROBERTS, E. W.
SAUNDERS, R.

Philosophy

DAVIS, S.
JENNINGS, R. E.
SWARTZ, N. M.
TIETZ, J. H. (H)

Political Science

CIRIA, A.
COHEN, L. J.
COHEN, M. G.
COHN, T. H.
COVELL, M. A.
MCBRIDE, S.
ROSS, D. A.
WARWICK, P. V.

Psychology

ALEXANDER, B. K.
CRAWFORD, C. B.
KIMBALL, M.
KREBS, D. L.
MACFARLAND, C. G.
MARCIA, J. E.
MODIGLIANI, V.
OGLOFF, J R. P.
PARANJPE, A. C.
ROESCH, R. M.
STRAYER, J. N.
WEBSTER, C. D.
WHITTLESEA, B. W. A.

Sociology and Anthropology

ADAM, H.
DYCK, N.
GEE, E.
KENNY, M.
WYLLIE, R. W.

Spanish

GÓMEZ-MORIANA, A. (H)

Women's Studies

COHEN, M. G.
KIMBALL, M. M.
STEWART, M. L.
WENDELL, S.

Faculty of Business Administration:

CHOO, E. U.
FINLAY, D. R.
GRAUER, R. R.
HOLMES, R. A.
LOVE, C. E.
MCSHANE, S. L.
MAUSER, G. A.
MEREDITH, L. N.
PINFIELD, L. T.
SCHONER, B.
SHAPIRO, D. M.
SHAPIRO, S. J.
TJOSVOLD, D.
TUNG, R. L.
VINING, A. R.
WATERHOUSE, J. H.
WEDLEY, W. C.
WEXLER, M. N.
WYCKHAM, R. G.
ZAICHKOWSKY, J. L.

Faculty of Education:

BAILIN, S.
BARROW, R.
COLEMAN, P. E. F.
DAWSON, A. J.
DECASTELL, S. C.
EGAN, K.
GRIMMETT, P. P.
MANLEY-CASIMIR, M.
MARTIN, J.
OBADIA, A. A.
WIDEEN, M. F.
WINNE, P. H.
WONG, B. Y. L.

Faculty of Science:

Biological Sciences

ALBRIGHT, L. J.
BAILLIE, D. L.
BECKENBACH, A. T.
BORDEN, J. H.
BRANDHORST, B. P.
COOKE, F.
DILL, L. M.
DRUEHL, L. D.
FARRELL, A. P.
LAW, F. C. P.
MACKAUER, J. P. M.
MATHEWES, R. W.
MCKEOWN, B. A.
PUNJA, Z.K.
RAHE, J. E.
ROITBERG, B. D.
SMITH, M. J.
SRIVASTAVA, L. M.
VERBEEK, N. A. M.
WEBSTER, J. M.
WINSTON, M. L.
YDENBERG, R. C.

Chemistry

CUSHLEY, R. J.
D'AURIA, J. D.
EINSTEIN, F. W. B.
GAY, I. D.
JONES, C. H. W.
KORTELING, R. G.
MALLI, G. L.
OEHLSCHLAGER, A. C.
PERCIVAL, P. W.
PINTO, B. M.
POMEROY, R. K.
RICHARDS, W. R.
SLESSOR, K. N.
SUTTON, D.

Earth Sciences

ROBERTS, M. C. (H)

Mathematics and Statistics

ALSPACH, B. R.
BERGGREN, J. L.
BORWEIN, P. B.
BROWN, T. C.
DAS, A.
GRAHAM, G. A. C.
HEINRICH, K.
HELL, P.
LACHLAN, A. H.
LOCKHART, R. A.
REILLY, N. R.
ROUTLEDGE, R. D.
RUSSELL, R. D.
SHEN, C. Y.
THOMASON, S. K.
THOMSON, B. S.

Physics

ARROTT, A. S.
BALLENTINE, L. E.
BOAL, D. H.
CLAYMAN, B. P.
COLBOW, K.
CROZIER, E. D.
CURZON, A. E.
ENNS, R. H.
FRINDT, R. F.
HÄUSSER, O. F.
HEINRICH, B.
HUNTLEY, D. J.
IRWIN, J. C.
KIRCZENOW, G.
PLISCHKE, M.
THEWALT, M. L. W.
VISWANATHAN, K. S.
WORTIS, M.

ATTACHED INSTITUTES

(The mailing address is that of the University itself)

Institute for Aquaculture Research: Dir C. H. W. JONES.

Institute for Applied Algorithms and Optimization: Dir A. L. LIESTMAN.

Western Canadian Universities Marine Biological Station: f. 1969; Dir Dr A. N. SPENCER.

Behavioural Ecology Research Group: f. 1989; Dir L. M. DILL.

Institute for Business and Innovation Studies; Dir M. LIPSETT.

W. J. VanDusen BC Business Studies Institute: f. 1982; Dir S. SHAPIRO.

Canadian Centre for Studies in Publishing: f. 1987; Dir R. M. LORIMER.

Institute for Canadian Urban Research Studies: Dir P. L. BRANTINGHAM.

Chemical Ecology Research Group: f. 1981; Dir Dr J. BORDEN.

Community Economic Development Centre: Dir J. PIERCE.

Laboratory for Computer and Communications Research: f. 1982; Dir Dr T. KAMEDA.

International Centre for Criminal Law Reform and Criminal Justice Policy: f. 1991; Exec. Dir D. C. PRÉFONTAINE.

Institute for Studies in Criminal Justice Policy: f. 1980; Dir M.A. JACKSON.

Criminology Research Centre: f. 1978; Dir W. GLACKMAN.

Centre for Education, Law and Society: f. 1984; Co-Dirs M. MANLEY-CASIMIR, W. CASSIDY.

Environment Science Research Institute: f. 1991; Dir T. N. BELL (acting).

Centre for Experimental and Constructive Mathematics: Dir J. BORWEIN.

Institute of Fisheries Analysis: f. 1980; Dir T. HEAPS.

Feminist Institute for Studies on Law and Society: f. 1990; Dir D. CHUNN.

Gerontology Research Centre: f. 1982; Dir Dr G. GUTMAN.

Institute of Governance Studies: Dir P. J. SMITH.

Institute of Human Factors and Interface Technology: Dir D. WEEKS.

Centre for Human Independence Engineering: Dir A. RAWICZ.

Institute for the Humanities: Dir Dr J. ZASLOVE.

Centre for Image and Sound Research: Exec. Dir J. BIZZOCHI.

Centre for Labour Studies: Dir Dr T. NESBIT.

David Lam Centre for International Communication: f. 1989; Dir J. W. WALLS.

Logic Programming and Functional Programming Group: f. 1990; Dir V. DAHL.

Mental Health, Law and Policy Institute: f. 1991; Dir R. ROESCH.

Institute of Micromachine and Microfabrication Research: Dir A. M. LEUNG.

Institute of Molecular Biology and Biochemistry: Dir Dr B. P. BRANDHORST.

Centre for Policy Research on Science and Technology: Dir P. ANDERSON.

Institute for Quaternary Research: f. 1984; Dir Dr M. C. ROBERTS.

Dr Frank Linville Institute in Sensory Research: f. 1986; Dir Dr K. COLBOW.

Centre for Systems Science: Dir Dr B. FUNT.

Institute for Studies in Teacher Education: Dir Dr M. F. WIDEEN.

Centre for Tourism Policy and Research: Dir P. W. WILLIAMS.

Tri-University Meson Facility (TRIUMF): Dir A. ASTBURY.

UNIVERSITY OF TORONTO

215 Huron St, Toronto, Ont. M5S 1A1
Telephone: (416) 978-2011
Telex: 06218915
Fax: (416) 978-5702

Founded 1827
Language of instruction: English
Provincially supported, assisted by private funds
Academic year: September to May (May to August, summer session)

Chancellor: ROSE WOLFE
President: ROBERT PRICHARD
Vice-President and Provost: A. S. S. SEDRA
Vice-President, Administration and Human Resources: M. G. FINLAYSON
Vice-President, Development and University Relations: J. S. DELLANDREA
Vice-President, Research and International Relations: H. M. MUNROE-BLUM
Chief Librarian: CAROLE MOORE

Library: see Libraries
Number of teachers: 3,362, including 1,122 professors
Number of students: total 55,024

Publications: *Calendars, Undergraduate Admission Handbook, Bulletin, The Graduate, President's Report.*

DEANS AND DIRECTORS

Faculty of Arts and Science: D. DEWEES (acting)
Faculty of Medicine: A. ABERMAN
Faculty of Applied Science and Engineering: M. E. CHARLES
Faculty of Forestry: R. B. BRYAN
Faculty of Dentistry: B. SESSLE
Faculty of Pharmacy: D. G. PERRIER
Faculty of Law: R. J. DANIELS
Faculty of Music: R. FALCK (acting)
Faculty of Education: M. FULLAN
Faculty of Physical and Health Education: B. KIDD
Faculty of Social Work: W. SHERA
Faculty of Nursing: D. M. P. PRINGLE
Faculty of Library and Information Sciences: L. HOWARTH (acting)
Faculty of Management: (vacant)
Faculty of Graduate Studies: J. S. COHEN
Faculty of Continuing Studies: M. C. BARRIE
Faculty of Architecture and Landscape Architecture: A. EARDLEY

PROFESSORS

N.B.—In the following list staff members of colleges are indicated thus: Erindale Coll. (E), New Coll. (N), St Michael's Coll. (M), Scarborough Coll. (S), Trinity Coll. (T), University Coll. (C), Victoria Univ. (V)

Faculty of Arts and Science:

ABOUHAIDAR, M. G., Botany
ABRAMOVICH, R. S., Psychology (E)
ACCINELLI, R. D., History
ADAMOWSKI, T. H., English
AIVAZIAN, V. A., Economics (E)
AKCOGLU, M. A., Mathematics
ALDERSON SMITH, G. A., Anthropology
ALLEN, P. R., English
ALLOWAY, T. M., Psychology (E)
ANDERSON, G. J., Economics (E)
ANDERSON, G. M., Geology
ANDERSON, J. B., Botany (E)
ANDREW, E. G., Social Sciences (S)
ANDREWS, D. F., Statistics
ARROWOOD, A. J., Psychology
ARTHUR, J. G., Mathematics
ASTER, S., History (E)
BAECKER, R. M., Computer Science
BAILEY, R. C., Physics
BAIRD, J., English (C)
BALDUS, B., Sociology
BALL, P. W., Botany (E)
BAND, L. E., Geography
BARBEAU, E. J., Mathematics
BARKER, J. S., Political Science
BARNES, C. J., Slavic Languages and Literature
BARNES, M. A., Paediatrics
BARNES, T. D., Classics
BARRETT, F. M., Zoology
BARRETT, S. C. H., Botany
BASHKEVIN, S., Political Science
BASSILI, J. N., Psychology (S)
BECK, R. L., Classics (E)
BEDFORD, C. H., Slavic Languages and Literatures
BEINER, R. S., Political Science (E)
BENTLEY, G. E., English
BERGER, C. C., History
BERGER, J., Zoology
BERKOWITZ, M. K., Economics
BERMAN, O., Social Sciences (S)
BERMAN, W. C., History
BERRY, R. A., Economics (S)
BERTRAND-JENNINGS, C. L., Humanities (S)
BIEDERMAN, G. B., Psychology (S)
BIERSTONE, E., Mathematics
BINNICK, R. I., Linguistics (S)
BIRD, R. M., Economics
BIRNBAUM, E., Mid East and Islamic Studies
BISZTRAY, G., Slavic Languages and Literature
BLACKBURN, J. R., Mid East and Islamic Studies
BLANCHARD, P. H., History
BLAND, J. S., Mathematics (E)
BLISS, J. M., History
BLOOM, T., Mathematics
BOLTON, C. T., Astronomy
BOONSTRA, R., Life Sciences (S)
BORINS, S. F., Social Sciences (S)
BORODIN, A. B., Computer Science
BOSSONS, J. D., Economics
BOTHWELL, R., History
BOUISSAC, P., French (C)
BOURNE, L. S., Geography
BOURSIER, N. T., French
BRAUN, A., Political Science (E)
BRITTON, J., Geography
BROOK, T. J., History
BROOKS, D. R., Zoology
BROOKS, L. J., Management Studies (E)
BROWN, I. R., Zoology (S)
BROWN, J. R., Philosophy
BROWN, R. C., History
BROWN, R. M., Humanities (S)
BROWNLEE, J. S., East Asian Studies
BRUCKMANN, P., English (T)
BRUMER, P. W., Chemistry
BRYAN, R. B., Geography (S)
BRYM, R. J., Sociology
BURKE, J. F., Spanish and Portuguese
BURTON, F. D., Anthropology (S)
BUTLER, D. G., Zoology
CALLAHAN, W., History
CAMERON, D. R., Political Science
CAMERON, E., University College Programme
CANFIELD, J. V., Philosophy (E)
CAPOZZI, R., Italian Studies
CARENS, J. H., Political Science
CARLBERG, R. G., Physical Sciences (S)
CARR, J. L., Economics
CARSTENS, W. P., Anthropology
CASAS, F. R., Economics
CASE, F. I., French (N)
CHAMBERLIN, J. E., English
CHAMBERS, D. D., English (T)
CHAMBERS, J. K., Linguistics
CHING, J. C., Religious Studies
CHO, H. R., Physics
CHOI, M. D., Mathematics
CHOUDHRY, N. K., Economics
CHU, R., East Asian Studies
CIAVOLELLA, M., Italian Studies
CLARKSON, S. H. E., Political Science
CLEMENT, M. J. Y., Astronomy
CLIVIO, G. P., Italian Studies
CLOUTIER-WOJCIECHOWSKA, C., French
CODE, R. F., Physics (E)
COOK, E., English (C)
COOK, S. A., Computer Science
CORMAN, B., English Literature (E)
CORNEIL, D. G., Computer Science
CRAIK, F. I. M., Psychology
CRAWFORD, G., Anthropology
CSIZMADIA, I. G., Chemistry
CUMMINS, W. R., Botany (E)
CUNNINGHAM, F. A., Philosophy

CUPCHIK, G. C., Life Sciences (S)
DAINARD, J. A., French
DANESI, M., Italian Studies
DAY, R. B., Political Economy (E)
DEL JUNCO, A., Mathematics
DENGLER, N. G., Botany
DENNY, M. G. S., Economics
DENT, J., History
DE QUEHEN, A. H., English
DESAI, R. C., Physics
DE SOUSA, R., Philosophy
DESSER, S. S., Zoology
DEWEES, D. N., Political Economy
DION, K. K., Psychology (S)
DION, K. L., Psychology
DION, P.-E., Near Eastern Studies
DOLEZELOVA, M., East Asian Studies
DONNELLY, M. W., Political Science
DOUCETTE, L. E., French (S)
DRAKE, T. E., Physics
DREWITT, R. B., Anthropology
DRUMMOND, J. R., Physics
DUFFY, J. D., English
DUNHAM, D. W., Zoology
DUNLOP, D. J., Physics (E)
DUPRÉ, J. S., Political Science
DUTKA, J., English Literature (E)
DYCK, H. L., History
DYER, C. C., Physical Sciences (S)
EDDIE, S. M., Political Economy (E)
EDWARDS, R. N., Physics
EKSTEINS, M., Philosophy (S)
ELINSON, R. P., Zoology
ELLIOTT, G. A., Mathematics
ELLIS, K. A. A., Spanish and Portuguese
ENRIGHT, W. H., Computer Science (S)
EPSTEIN, L. G., Economics
ERICKSON, B. H., Sociology
ESTES, J. M., History (C)
EVANS, M. J., Statistics
EYLES, N., Physical Sciences (S)
FALCONER, A. G., French
FALKENHEIM, V. C., East Asian Studies
FAWCETT, J. J., Geology
FERNIE, J. D., Astronomy
FEUERVERGER, A., Statistics
FITCH, B. T., French (T)
FLEMING, A. S., Psychology (E)
FLOYD, J. E., Political Economy (E)
FOLEY, J. E., Life Sciences (S)
FOOT, D. K., Economics
FORBES, H. D., Political Science
FORGUSON, L. W., University College
FORRIN, B., Psychology (S)
FRANCESCHETTI, A., Italian Studies (S)
FRANK, R., English
FREEDMAN, J. L., Psychology
FRIEDLANDER, J. B., Mathematics (S)
FRIEDMANN, H. B., Sociology (E)
FUREDY, J. J., Psychology
FUSS, M. A., Economics
GALLINI, N. T., Economics
GALLOWAY, J. H., Geography
GARRISON, R. F., Astronomy
GARTNER, R. I., Sociology
GENNO, C., German (C)
GERTLER, M. S., Geography
GERVERS, M., History (S)
GILLIS, A. R., Sociology
GITTINS, J., Geology
GOFFART, W. A., History
GOERING, J., History
GOLDSTICK, D., Philosophy
GOMBAY, A. M., Philosophy (E)
GORDON, A. M., Spanish and Portuguese
GOVIND, C. K., Life Sciences (S)
GRACIE, G., Surveying Science (E)
GRAHAM, I. R., Mathematics (E)
GRAHAM, W. C., Humanities (S)
GRANT, J. N., Classics
GRAYSON, A. K., Near Eastern Studies
GRAZIANI, R. I. C., English
GREENWOOD, B., Geography (S)
GREER, A. R., History
GREINER, P. C., Mathematics
GRENDLER, P. F., History
GRIFFEN, P. A., Physics (S)
GRIFFITHS, F. J. C., Political Science
GROSS, M. R., Zoology
GUNDERSON, M. K., Economics
GURD, J. W., Biochemistry (S)
GWYNNE, D. T., Biology (E)
HAGAN, J. L., Sociology
HALEWOOD, W. H., English
HALLS, H. C., Geological Sciences (E)
HALPERIN, J. S., Mathematics
HAMEL, G. A., English
HANLY, C. M. T., Philosophy
HANSELL, R. I. C., Zoology
HAQUE, W., Mathematics, Political Economy
HARE, M. J., Economics (E)
HARVEY, E. R., English (C)
HARVEY, H. H., Zoology
HAYNE, B. S., English
HEATH, M. C., Botany
HEHNER, E. C. R., Computer Science
HEINEMANN, E. A., French
HELLEBUST, J. A., Botany
HELLEINER, G. K., Economics
HELMSTADTER, R. J., History
HERMAN, C. P., Psychology
HIGGINS, V. J., Botany
HIGGS, D. C., History
HINTON, G. E., Computer Science
HOFF, F. P., East Asian Studies
HOGAN, J. A., Psychology
HOLDOM, B., Physics
HOLLADAY, J. S., Near Eastern Studies
HOLLANDER, S., Economics
HOLT, R. C., Computer Science
HORGEN, P. A., Botany (E)
HOROWITZ, G., Political Science
HOSIOS, A. J., Economics (E)
HOUSTON, C. J., Geography (E)
HOWARD, W. J., English (S)
HOWELL, N., Sociology
HOWSON, S. K., Social Sciences (S)
HUTCHEON, L. A., English
HYNES, J. A., Economics (E)
IANNUCCI, A. A., Italian Studies
IMLAY, R. A., Philosophy
INGHAM, J. N., History
INWOOD, B. C., Classics
IRIBARNE, L., Slavic Languages and Literature
ISAJIW, W. W., Sociology (S)
ISRAEL, M., History
IVRII, V., Mathematics
JAAKSON, R., Geography
JACKSON, H., English
JACKSON, J. R., English (C)
JACKSON, K. R., Computer Science
JACOBS, A. E., Physics (S)
JAIN, S., Physical Sciences (S)
JAMES, E. F., French
JEFFERIES, R. L., Botany
JEPSON, A. D., Computer Science (E)
JOHN, S., Physics
JOHNSON, W. M. L. A., Fine Art
JOHNSTON, A., English (C)
JONES, C. L., Sociology
JONES, J. B., Chemistry
JUMP, G. V., Economics
JURDJEVIC, V., Mathematics
KAPRAL, R. E., Chemistry
KEITH, W. J., English
KENNEDY, J. M., Psychology (S)
KERVIN, J. B., Sociology (E)
KEY, A. W., Physics
KHOVANSKII, A., Mathematics
KING, J. D., Physics (S)
KIRKHAM, M. C., English
KLAUSNER, D. N., English
KLEIN, M. A., History
KLEINDIENST, M. R., Anthropology (E)
KLUGER, R. H., Chemistry
KOTOWITZ, Y., Economics
KOVRIG, B., Political Economy
KRAMES, L., Psychology (E)
KRASHINSKY, M., Social Sciences (S)
KROGER, R. O., Psychology
KRONBERG, P. P., Astronomy (S)
KUITUNEN, M. T., Italian Studies
KUKLA, A., Psychology (S)
KUPKA, I., Mathematics
LAMBEK, M. J., Social Sciences (S)
LANCASHIRE, A. C., English
LANCASHIRE, D. I., English (E)
LANTZ, K. A., Slavic Languages and Literature
LEDUC, L., Political Science
LEE, M. J., Physics (S)
LEE, R. B., Anthropology
LEGGATT, A. M., English
LEHMAN, A. B., Computer Science
LE HUENEN, R., French (C)
LEHOUCK, E., French
LEMON, J. T., Geography
LÉON, P. R., French (S)
LEPROHON, R. J., Near Eastern Studies
LESTER, J. B., Astronomy (E)
LEVENSON,, J. L., English (T)
LEVESQUE, H. J., Computer Science
LIMAN, A. V., East Asian Studies
LINDHEIM, N., English
LLOYD, T. O., History
LOCK, C. J., English (E)
LOCKHART, J. E., Psychology
LOCKHART, R. S., Psychology
LOMBARDI, C., Botany (S)
LORIMER, J. W., Mathematics
LUK, S. H., Geography (E)
LUSTE, G. J., Physics
LUONG, H. V., Anthropology
MCCLELLAND, J. A., French (C)
MCCLELLAND, R. A., Chemistry (S)
MCCOOL, J., Mathematics
MCDONOUGH, C., Classics (T)
MCDUNNOUGH, P. J., Statistics
MACKAY, R. J., Zoology
MCLEAN, S., Chemistry
MACLEOD, C. M., Life Sciences (S)
MCLEOD, W. E., Classics (C)
MACPHERSON, J., English (C)
MACHIN, J., Zoology
MAGILL, D. W., Sociology
MAGOCSI, P. R., Political Science
MALLOCH, D. W., Botany
MANZER, R. A., Political Economy (S)
MARKER, F. J., English
MARMURA, M. E., Mid East Islamic Studies
MARRUS, M. R., History
MARTIN, P. J., French
MASSON, D. R., Mathematics
MASUI, Y., Zoology
MATHEWSON, G. F., Political Economy
MAURY, N., French
MATHON, R. A., Computer Science
MATTHEWS, R. O., Politcial Science
MAURY, N., French
MAVALWALA, J. D., Anthropology
MAY, A. D., Physics
MAYER, H., German (C)
MELBYE, F. J., Anthropology (E)
MELINO, A., Economics
MELTZ, N. M., Political Economy (W)
MENDELSOHN, E., Mathematics (S)
MENDELZON, A. O., Computer Science
MENZINGER, M., Chemistry
MERRILEES, B., French (C)
METTRICK, D. F., Zoology
MIALL, A. D., Geology
MICHELSON, W., Sociology
MILGRAM, N. W., Life Sciences (S)
MILLGATE, J., English (C)
MILMAN, P., Mathematics
MIRON, J. R., Geography (S)
MOFFAT, J. W., Physics
MOGGRIDGE, D. E., Economics
MOLLE, M. L., Computer Science
MORGAN, K. P., Philosophy
MORGAN, P. F., English
MORRIS, G. K., Zoology (E)
MORRIS, R. H., Physical Sciences (S)
MORRISON, J. C., Philosophy
MORTON, D. P., History (E)
MROSOVSKY, N., Psychology, Zoology
MOSCOVITCH, M., Psychology (E)

Moskovits, M., Chemistry
Munro, D. S., Geography (E)
Munro, J. H. A., Economics
Murty, V., Mathematics
Mylopoulos, J., Computer Science
Nagata, S., Anthropology
Naldrett, A. J., Geology
Neglia, E. G., Spanish (E)
Nicholson, G. A., Philosophy
Normore, C. S., Philosophy (E)
Norris, G., Geology
Nowlan, D. M., Political Economy
O'Brien, M. J., Classics
O'Day, D., Zoology (E)
O'Donnell, P. J., Physics (S)
O'Toole, R., Sociology (S)
Oliver, W. A., French
Orchard, I., Zoology
Orr, R. S., Physics
Orwin, C. L., Political Science
Oxtoby, W. G., Religious Studies (T)
Ozin, G. A., Chemistry
Paloheimo, J. E., Zoology
Pangle, T. L., Political Science
Parker, R. B., English (T)
Paterson, J. M., French (E)
Paul, D. A. L., Physics
Peltier, W. R., Physics
Percy, J. R., Astronomy (E)
Perron, P., French (C)
Perz, J. M., Physics (S)
Peters, M. H., Economics
Petit, T. L., Life Sciences (S)
Philpott, S. B., Anthropology
Pietersma, A., Near Eastern Studies
Pietersma, H., Philosophy (C)
Pliner, P. L., Psychology (E)
Poirier, D. J., Economics
Polanyi, J. C., Chemistry
Polivy, J., Psychology (E)
Pomeranz, B. H., Zoology
Ponomareff, C. V., Russian (S)
Powell, J., Chemistry
Priestley, L. C., East Asian Studies
Pruessen, R. W., History (E)
Prugovecki, E., Mathematics
Raby, D. L., History (E)
Rackoff, C. W., Computer Science
Ranger, K. B., Mathematics
Rayside, D. M., Political Science
Rea, K. J., Economics
Rea, S. A., Economics (E)
Redford, D. B., Near Eastern Studies
Regier, H. A., Zoology
Reibetanz, J. H., English (C)
Reich, P. A., Linguistics
Reid, F. J., Economics (E)
Reid, N., Statistics
Reisz, R. R., Zoology (E)
Reiter, R., Computer Science
Reitz, J. G., Sociology
Relph, E. C., Social Sciences (S)
Repka, J. S., Mathematics
Revell, E. J., Near Eastern Studies (C)
Reynolds, W. F., Chemistry
Rice, K. D., Linguistics
Richardson, D. S., Fine Art
Richardson, G. P., Religious Studies
Rifat, D., Fine Art
Rising, J. D., Zoology
Rist, J. M., Classics
Robin, P. Y., Geological Science (E)
Robinson, T. M., Philosophy
Rosenthal, P., Mathematics
Rossos, A., History
Rowe, D. J., Physics
Rucklidge, J. C., Geology
Russell, P. H., Political Science
Rutherford, P., History
Saddlemyer, A., English (C)
Salaff, J. W., Sociology
Samuel, A. E., Classics
Sandbrook, K. R. J., Political Science
Schiff, B. B., Psychology
Schlepp, W. A., East Asian Studies
Schneider, B. A., Psychology (E)
Schwartz, D. V., Political Science
Schwerdtner, W. M., Geology
Scott, S. D., Geology
Seager, W. E., Philosophy (S)
Seaquist, E. R., Astronomy
Seary, P. D., English
Selick, P., Mathematics (S)
Sen, D. K., Mathematics
Sevcik, K. C., Computer Science
Sharpe, R. W., Mathematics (S)
Shatzmiller, J., History
Shaw, J. W., Fine Art
Shaw, W. D., English (C)
Shettleworth, S. J., Psychology
Shirley, R. W., Anthropology (S)
Sidnell, M., English (T)
Sigal, I. M., Mathematics
Sigmon, B. A., Anthropology (E)
Silcox, P., Political Science (E)
Simeon, R., Political Science
Simmons, J. W., Geography
Silva, E. T., Sociology (E)
Silver, J. C., Life Sciences (S)
Simpson, J. H., Sociology (E)
Sipe, J. E., Physics
Skogstad, G. D., Political Science (S)
Skyrme, R., Humanities (S)
Slater, J. G., Philosophy
Smith, D. W., French (C)
Smith, J. E., Political Science
Smith, J. J. B., Zoology
Smith, L. B., Political Economy
Smith, M. C., Psychology (S)
Smith, S. H., Mathematics
Smyth, D., History
Sobel, J. H., Philosophy (S)
Sohm, P. L., Fine Art
Solomon, P. H., Political Science
Solomon, S., Political Science (S)
Spence, I., Psychology
Spivakovsky, M., Mathematics (E)
Spooner, E. T., Geology
Sprules, W. G., Zoology (E)
Srivastava, M. S., Statistics
Stager, D. A., Economics
Stein, J., Political Science
Stevensen, J. T., Philosophy
Still, I. W. J., Chemistry (E)
Stren, R. E., Political Science
Straus, N. A., Botany
Struk, D. S., Slavic Languages and Literature
Sulem, C., Mathematics
Sullivan, R., English (E)
Sumner, L. W., Philosophy
Sweet, R. F., Near Eastern Studies
Tall, F. D., Mathematics
Taylor, R., French (C)
Telford, G. M., Zoology
Tepperman, L. J., Sociology
Thompson, J. C., Chemistry
Thompson, M., Chemistry
Thompson, R. P., Humanities (S)
Thomson, R. D. B., Slavic Languages and Literature
Thornton, M., Philosophy (C)
Tidwell, T. T., Chemistry (S)
Tobe, S. S., Zoology
Tolton, C., French (C)
Traill, J., Classics (C)
Trehub, S. E., Psychology (E)
Tsotsos, J. K., Computer Science
Tsukimura, R., East Asian Studies
Turner, D. H., Anthropology
Urquhart, A. I. F., Philosophy
Valdes, M. J., Spanish and Portuguese
Valleau, J. P., Chemistry
Van Driel , H. M., Physics (E)
Van Loon, J. C., Geology
Vanstone, J. R., Mathematics
Visser, C. W., English
Von zur Gathen, J., Physical Sciences (S)
Wagle, N. K., History
Walker, A., Physical Sciences (S)
Walker, M. B., Physics
Wall, A., M., Psychology
Wallace, S., Chemistry
Walters, G. C., Psychology
Warden, J. R., Classics (S)
Wardhaugh, R., Linguistics
Warkentin, G., English (C)
Waterhouse, A., Geography
Waterhouse, D. B., East Asian Studies
Watkins, M. H., Political Economy
Watson, A. M., Economics
Waverman, L., Economics
Webster, J. R., Spanish and Portuguese
Weiss, W. A., Mathematics (E)
Wellman, B. S., Sociology
Welsh, B. M., Fine Art (E)
Welsh, R. P., Fine Art
West, G. F., Physics
Westgate, J. A., Geology
Wetzel, H. E. M., German
Wheaton, B., Sociology (E)
White, R. R., Geography (E)
Whittington, S. G., Chemistry
Wilker, J. B., Physical Sciences (S)
Williams, D. D., Life Sciences (S)
Williams, J. P., Botany (T)
Wilson, F. F., Philosophy
Wilson, T. A., Political Economy
Winter, R. A., Economics
Winnick, M. A., Chemistry (E)
Wittmann, H., Humanities (S)
Wong, S. S. M., Physics (E)
Wooders, M. H., Economics (E)
Wooldridge, T. R., French
Wortman, D. B., Computer Science
Yeomans, J. S., Psychology
York, D., Physics
Youson, J. H., Zoology (S)
Zimmerman, A. M., Zoology
Zworski, M., Mathematics

Faculty of Medicine:

Aberman, A., Medicine
Ackermann, U., Physiology
Alberti, P. W. R. M., Otolaryngology
Amankwah, S., Obstetrics and Gynaecology
Anderson, G. H., Nutrition and Food Sciences
Anwar, R. A., Biochemistry
Archer, M. C., Nutritional Studies
Ashby, P., Medicine
Ashley, M. J., Preventive Medicine and Biostatistics
Atwood, H. L., Physiology
Badgley, R. F., Behavioural Science and Paediatrics
Baines, A. D., Clinical Biochemistry
Baker, M. A., Medicine
Baker, R. R., Medicine
Barber, B. H., Immunology
Balfe, J. W., Paediatrics
Baumal, R., Pathology
Bayliss, C. E., Surgery
Bear, R. A., Medicine
Becker, A. J., Medical Genetics
Biggar, W. D., Paediatrics
Birt, B. D., Otolaryngology
Blendis, L. M., Medicine
Bombardier, C., Medicine
Bouzina, A., Immunology
Britt, B. A., Anaesthesia
Broder, I., Medicine
Burnham, W. M., Pharmacology
Camerman, N., Biochemistry
Campbell, J. B., Microbiology
Cardella, C. J., Medicine
Carlen, P. L., Medicine
Carver, J. P., Medical Genetics
Casper, R. F., Obstetrics and Gynaecology
Cattran, D. C., Medicine
Chan, V. L., Microbiology
Charlton, M. P., Physiology
Cheng, H. P. L., Anatomy
Chipman, M. L., Preventive Medicine and Biostatistics
Coburn, D., Behavioural Science
Cohen, H., Medicine
Connon, J. J., Medicine

COREY, P. N., Preventive Medicine and Biostatistics
CORMACK, D. H., Anatomy
COWAN, D. H., Medicine
COWELL, C. A., Obstetrics and Gynaecology
CRYSDALE, W. S., Otolaryngology
DANEMAN, D., Paediatrics
DEBER, R., Health Administration
DEBONI, U., Physiology
DE PETRILLO, A. D., Obstetrics and Gynaecology
DETSKY, A., Health Administration
DIAMANT, N. E., Medicine
DIRKS, F., Medicine
DIRKS, J. H., Medicine
DITTAKAVI, S. R., Pathology
DORRINGTON, J. H., Banting and Best Medical Research
DOSTROVSKY, J. O., Physiology
DOWNAR, E., Medicine
DUFFIN, J., Anaesthesia
DUNN, E. V., Family and Community Medicine
EDELIST, G. E., Anaesthesia
EDMEADS, J. G., Medicine
EHRLICH, R. M. E., Paediatrics
ENDRENYI, L., Pharmacology
FAM, A. G., Medicine
FERNIE, G. R., Surgery
FISHER, R. H. G., Family and Community Medicine
FRANCOMBE, W. H., Medicine
FROM, L., Medicine
FRECKER, R., Biomedical Engineering
GANOZA, M. C., Banting and Best Medical Research
GARFINKEL, P. E., Psychiatry
GARVEY, M. B., Medicine
GILBERT, J. R., Family and Community Medicine
GLADMAN, D. D., Medicine
GOLD, M., Medical Genetics
GOLD, R., Paediatrics
GOLDBERG, D., Medicine
GOLDENBERG, G. J., Medicine
GOLDMAN, B. S., Surgery
GOLDSTEIN, M. B., Medicine
GORCZYNSKI, R. M., Surgery
GORDON, D. A., Medicine
GOTLIEB, A. I., Pathology
GREENBERG, G. R., Medicine
GREENBERG, M. L., Paediatrics
GREENBLATT, J. F., Banting and Best Medical Research
GULLANE, P. J., Otolaryngology
HALLETT, P. E., Physiology
HALPERIN, M. L., Medicine
HASTINGS, D. E., Surgery
HATTORI, T., Anatomy and Cell Biology
HAY, J. B., Immunology
HO PING KONG, Medicine
HOFFSTEIN, V., Medicine
HOLLENBERG, C. H., Medicine
HORNER, A. A., Physiology
HSIEH, J. J., Preventive Medicine and Biostatistics
HUANG, S.-N., Pathology
HUNTER, G. A., Surgery
HYLAND, R. H., Medicine
INABA, T., Pharmacology
INGLES, C. J., Banting and Best Medical Research
INMAN, R. D., Medicine
ISENMAN, D. E., Biochemistry
ISSEKUTZ, T., Medicine
JEEJEEBHOY, K. N., Medicine
JENKINS, D. J. A., Nutritional Science
JOHNSON, D. H., Family and Community Medicine
JORGENSEN, A. O., Anatomy and Cell Biology
KADAR, D., Pharmacology
KALNINS, V. I., Histology
KELNER, M., Behavioural Science
KENNEDY, S. H., Psychiatry
KENSHOLE, A. B., Medicine
KEYSTONE, J. S., Medicine
KHANNA, J. M., Pharmacology
KREPINSKY, J. J., Medical Genetics
KUCHARCZYK, W., Radiology
KUKSIS, A., Banting and Best Medical Research
LANE, B. G., Biochemistry
LANGER, B., Surgery
LANGILLE, B. L., Pathology
LANSDOWN, E. L., Radiology
LAWEE, D. H., Family and Community Medicine
LAWFORD, H. G., Biochemistry
LEATT, P., Health Administration
LEVY, G. A., Medicine
LEWIS, P. N., Biochemistry
LIEBGOTT, B., Anatomy
LIEW, C. C., Clinical Biochemistry
LIVINGSTONE, R. A., Obstetrics and Gynaecology
LOGAN, A. G., Medicine
LOGAN, W. J., Paediatrics
LUMSDEN, C. J., Medicine
MACDONALD, J. F., Physiology
MCLAUGHLIN, P. R., Medicine
MACLENNAN, D. H., Banting and Best Medical Research
MACLUSKY, N. J., Obstetrics and Gynaecology
MACMILLAN, V. H., Medicine
MAHON, W. A., Microbiology
MARKS, A., Medical Research
MARSHALL, V. W., Behavioural Science
MILLER, A. B., Preventive Medicine
MILLER, R. G., Immunology
MOLDOFSKY, H., Psychiatry
MORGAN, J. E., Obstetrics and Gynaecology
MORTIMER, C. B., Ophthalmology
MURIALDO, H., Medical Genetics
MURRAY, D., Pathology
MURRAY, R. K., Biochemistry
MURRAY, T. M., Medicine
MYERS, M. G., Medicine
NARANJO, C. A., Pharmacology
NEDZELSKI, J. M., Otolaryngology
NOBLE, W. H., Anaesthesia
NORRIS, J. W., Medicine
NORWICH, K. H., Physiology
NOYEK, A. M., Otolaryngology
OGILVIE, R. I., Medicine
OKEY, A. B., Pharmacology
OREOPOULOS, D. G., Preventive Medicine and Biostatistics
OSMOND, D. H., Physiology
PAI, E., Biochemistry
PAINTER, R. H., Biochemistry
PAPSIN, F. R., Obstetrics and Gynaecology
PAUL, P., Medicine
PENNER, J. L., Microbiology
PHILLIPS, M. J., Pathology
PHILLIPSON, E. A., Medicine
PINKERTON, P. H., Pathology
PULLEYBLANK, D. E., Biochemistry
RAKOWSKI, H., Medicine
READ, S. E., Paediatrics
REITHMEIER, R., Medicine
RITCHIE, J. W. K., Obstetrics and Gynaecology
ROBERTSON, D., Medicine
ROBINSON, G., Psychiatry
RODIN, G. M., Psychiatry
ROOTMAN, I., Health Promotion
ROSSER, W., Medicine
ROTHMAN, A. I., Medical Education
ROTSTEIN, O. D., Surgery
SADOWSKI, P. D., Medical Genetics
SAKINOFSKY, I., Psychiatry
SAUDER, D. N., Medicine
SCHATZKER, J., Surgery
SCHIMMER, B. P., Medical Research
SEIDELMAN, W. E., Family and Community Medicine
SEEMAN, M., Psychiatry
SEEMAN, P., Pharmacology
SELLERS, E. M., Pharmacology
SEYFRIED, P. L., Microbiology
SHAH, C. P., Preventive Medicine and Biostatistics
SHAPIRO, C., Psychiatry
SHARPE, J. A., Medicine
SHEPHERD, F. A., Medicine
SHIER, R. M., Obstetrics and Gynaecology
SHIME, J., Obstetrics and Gynaecology
SHORTER, E. L., History of Medicine
SHULMAN, H. S., Radiology
SHULMAN, K. I., Psychiatry
SHULMAN, M. J., Immunology
SHUMAK, K. H., Medicine
SILVER, M. D., Pathology
SILVERMAN, M., Medicine
SIU, C. H., Banting and Best Medical Research
SKINNER, H. A., Preventive Medicine and Biostatistics
SKORECKI, K. L., Medicine
SLUTSKY, A. S., Medicine
SMALLHORN, J. F., Paediatrics
SMITH, B. T. S., Paediatrics
SOLE, M. J., Medicine
SONNENBERG, H., Physiology
SPERO, L., Pharmacology
STEINER, G., Medicine
STEINHAUER, P. D., Psychiatry
STEWART, D. E., Psychiatry
STEWART, P. A., Anatomy and Cell Biology
STURGESS, J. M., Medicine
SUN, A., Physiology
TANSWELL, A., Paediatrics
TATOR, C. H., Surgery
TAYLOR, I. M., Anatomy
THOMPSON, L., Nutrition
THOMPSON, W., Biochemistry
TILE, M., Surgery
TINKER, D. O., Biochemistry
UROWITZ, M. B., Medicine
VAN DER KOOY, D. J., Anatomy and Cell Biology
VELLEND, H., Medicine
VRANIC, M., Physiology
WADDELL, J. P., Surgery
WALFISH, P. G., Medicine
WALKER, P. M., Surgery
WAXMAN, M. B., Medicine
WEBB, G. D., Medicine
WEISEL, R. D., Surgery
WHERRETT, J. R., Medicine
WONG, J. T. F., Biochemistry
WU, T. W., Clinical Biochemistry
YIP, C. C., Banting and Best Medical Research
ZINMAN, B., Medicine

Faculty of Applied Science and Engineering:

ABDELMESSIH, A. H. A., Mechanical Engineering
ADAMS, B. J., Civil Engineering
BALKE, S. T., Chemical Engineering
BALMAIN, K. G., Electrical Engineering
BARHAM, D., Chemical Engineering
BASMADJIAN, D., Chemical Engineering
BIRKEMOE, P. C., Civil Engineering
BOOCOCK, D. G. B., Chemical Engineering
BOULTON, P. I. P., Electrical Engineering
BYER, P. H., Civil Engineering
CHAFFEY, C. E., Chemical Engineering
CHARLES, M. E., Chemical Engineering
COBBOLD, R. S. C., Institute of Biomedical Engineering
COLLINS, M. P., Civil Engineering
COLLINS, R. A., Civil Engineering
CORMACK, D. E., Chemical Engineering
COX, B., Metallurgy
CURRAN, J. H., Civil Engineering
CURRIE, I. G., Mechanical Engineering
DAVISON, E. J. A., Electrical Engineering
DELAURIER, J. D., Aerospace Studies
DEWAN, S. B., Electrical Engineering
DIOSADY, L. L., Chemical Engineering
DODSON, C. T., Chemical Engineering
FENTON, R. G., Mechanical Engineering
FOULKES, F. R., Chemical Engineering
FOX, M. S., Industrial Engineering

FRANCIS, B. A., Electrical Engineering
GOLDENBERG, A. A., Mechanical Engineering
GOTTLIEB, J. J., Aerospace Studies
HAASZ, A. A., Aerospace Studies
HANSEN, J. S., Aerospace Studies
HAUER, E., Civil Engineering
HEINKE, W., Civil Engineering
HUGHES, P. C., Aerospace Studies
HURDLE, V. F., Civil Engineering
IIZUKA, K., Electrical Engineering
IRAVANI, M. R., Electrical and Computer Engineering
JAMES, D. F., Mechanical Engineering
JARDINE, A. K. S., Industrial Engineering
JOY, M., Electrical and Computer Engineering
KAWAJI, M., Chemical Engineering
KEFFER, J. F., Mechanical Engineering
KENNEY, T. C., Civil Engineering
KIRK, D. W., Chemical Engineering
KUNOV, H., Biomedical Engineering
KWONG, R. H., Electrical Engineering
LAVERS, J. D., Electrical Engineering
LEE, E. S., Electrical Engineering
LEON-GARCIA, A., Electrical Engineering
LUUS, R., Chemical Engineering
MCCAMMOND, D., Mechanical Engineering
MACKAY, D., Chemical Engineering
MCLEAN, A., Metallurgy and Materials Science
MANDELIS, A., Mechanical Engineering
MARTIN, K., Electrical Engineering
MEASURES, R. M., Aerospace Studies
MEGUID, S. A., Mechanical Engineering
MILLER, E. J., Civil Engineering
MILLER, W. A., Metallurgy and Materials Science
MIMS, C. A., Chemical Engineering
NEUMANN, A. W., Mechanical Engineering
NORTH, T. H., Metallurgy and Materials Science
PACKER, J. A., Civil Engineering
PASUPATHY, S. P., Electrical Engineering
PHILLIPS, M. J., Chemical Engineering
PIGGOTT, M. R., Chemical Engineering
POSNER, M. J., Industrial Engineering
REEVE, D. W., Chemical Engineering
REID, L. D., Aerospace Studies
RISTIC, V. M., Electrical Engineering
SADLEIR, C. D., Industrial Engineering
SALAMA, C. A. T., Electrical Engineering
SEFTON, M. V., Chemical Engineering
SELBY, K. A., Civil Engineering
SHADWICK, W., Fields Institute for Research in Mathematics
SHEIKH, S. A., Civil Engineering
SMITH, J. W., Chemical Engineering
SMITH, K. C., Electrical Engineering
SMITH, P. W., Electrical Engineering
SOBERMAN, R. M., Civil Engineering
SOMMERVILLE, I. D., Metallurgy and Materials Science
STANGEBY, P. C., Aerospace Studies
STEUART, G. N., Civil Engineering
SULLIVAN, P. A., Aerospace Studies
TENNYSON, R. C., Aerospace Studies
TIMUSK, J., Civil Engineering
TOGURI, J. M., Metallurgy and Materials Science
TRAN, H. N., Chemical Engineering
TRASS, O., Chemical Engineering
TURKSEN, I. B., Industrial Engineering
VECCHIO, F. J., Civil Engineering
VENETSANOPOULOS, A. N., Electrical Engineering
VENTER, R. D., Mechanical Engineering
VRANESIC, Z. G., Electrical Engineering
WALLACE, J. S., Mechanical Engineering
WARD, C. A., Mechanical Engineering
WILL, G. T., Civil Engineering
WONHAM, W. M., Electrical Engineering
WRIGHT, P. M., Civil Engineering
XU, J., Electrical and Computer Engineering
ZAKY, S. G., Electrical Engineering
ZUKOTYNSKI, S., Electrical Engineering

Faculty of Education:
AITKEN, J. L.
BIEMILLER, A. J.
BOOTH, D. W.
BOWERS, A. A.
CASE, T. R.
CORTER, C. M.
DIAMOND, P.
FRASER, D. L.
FULLAN, M.
GALBRAITH, D. I.
GARTH, D. W.
KELLY, B. G.
KUZMICH, N.
MCLEOD, K. A.
RIDGE, H. L.
SELBY, D. E.
SHACKEL, D. S. J.
TAN WILLIAM, C. A.
THIESSEN, D.
VOLPE, R. J.
WOLFE, T. J. E.

Faculty of Library and Information Sciences:
AUSTER, E. W.
FASICK, A. M.
FLEMING, E. P.

Faculty of Forestry:
AIRD, P. L.
BALATINECZ, J. J.
BLAKE, T. J.
CARROW, J. R.
HUBBES, M.
NAUTIYAL, J. C.
ROY, D. N.
TIMMER, V. R.

Faculty of Music:
AIDE, W.
BUCZYNSKI, W. J.
CHANDLER, R. E.
CHENETTE, S.
ELLIOTT, D. J.
FALCK, R. A.
HAWKINS, J.
HOLMAN, D.
HUGHES, A.
KLEIN, L. K.
LAUFER, E. C.
MCGEE, T. J.
MANIATES, M. R., History and Literature of Music
MOREY, C. R.
PEDERSEN, M. R.
SHAND, P. M.
ZAFER, D.

Faculty of Dentistry:
BENNICK, A.
DAVIES, J.
DEPORTER, D. A.
ELLEN, R. P.
FERRIER, J. M.
FREEMAN, E.
HEERSCHE, J. N. M.
LEAKE, J. L.
LEVINE, N.
LEWIS, D. W., Community Dentistry
LOCKER, D.
MCCOMB, D.
MCCULLOCH, C. A.
MAIN, J. H. P., Oral Pathology
MAYHALL, J. T.
MELCHER, A. H.
MOCK, D.
PILLIAR, R. M.
SANDHAM, H. J.
SESSLE, B. J.
SODEK, J.
SYMINGTON, J. M.
TEN CATE, A. R.
TENENBAUM, H. C.
WATSON, P. A.
ZARB, G. A., Prosthodontics

Faculty of Pharmacy:
O'BRIEN, P. J.
PANG, K. S.
PERRIER, D. G.
ROBINSON, J. B.
SEGAL, H.
STIEB, E. W., History of Pharmacy
THIESSEN, J. J.
UETRECHT, J. P.

Faculty of Law:
BEATTY, D. M.
DICKENS, B. M.
DUNLOP, J. B.
FRIEDLAND, M. L.
JANISCH, H. N.
LANGILLE, B. A.
MEWETT, A. W.
RISK, R. C. B.
SCANE, R. E.
SCHIFF, S. A.
SWINTON, K. E.
TREBILCOCK, M. J.
WADDAMS, S. M.
WEINRIB, E. J.

Faculty of Architecture and Landscape Architecture:
CORNEIL, C. S.
EARDLEY, A.

School of Physical and Health Education:
GOODE, R. C.

Faculty of Social Work:
BOGO, M. C.
BRETON, M. M.
HULCHANSKI, J. D.
IRVING, H. H.
LIGHTMAN, E. S.
MARZIALI, E. A.
NEYSMITH, S. M.
SHAPIRO, B. Z.
WELLS, L.

Faculty of Nursing:
CHAPMAN, J. S.
HODNETT, E.
PRINGLE, D. M. P.
YOSHIDA, M. A.

Faculty of Management Studies:
AMERNIC, J. H.
ARNOLD, H. J.
BOOTH, L. D.
CRISPO, J. H. G., Industrial Relations
EVANS, M. G.
HALPERN, P. J.
HULL, J. C.
KALYMON, B. A.
KOLODNY, H. F.
LATHAM, G.
MENZEFRICKE, U.
MINTZ, J. H.
MITCHELL, A. A.
ONDRACK, D. A.
PAULY, P.
RUGMAN, A. M.
SETHI, S. P.
SIEGEL, J. P.
SMIELIAUSKAS, W. J.

School of Graduate Studies:
ANGENOT, M., Comparative Literature
BEATTIE, J. M., Criminology
BOND, R. J., Theoretical Astronomy
BRYDEN, R., Drama
COHEN, J. S., Graduate Studies
DOOB, A. N., Criminology
HACKING, I. M., History and Philosophy of Science and Technology
HARIANTO, F., International Studies
HEALEY, A. D., Medieval Studies
HERNANDEZ, C., International Studies
KAISER, N., Theoretical Astronomy
LEVERE, T. H., History and Philosophy of Science and Technology
MARKER, L. L., Drama
MARTIN, P. G., Theoretical Astronomy
NESSELROTH, P. W., Comparative Literature
PESANDO, J. E., Policy Analysis

RIGG, A. G., Medieval Studies
SHEARING, C. D., Criminology
STENNING, P. C., Criminology
STOCK, B. C., Comparative Literature
TREMAINE, S. D., Theoretical Astronomy
VALVERDE, M. V., Criminology
WINSOR, M. P., History and Philosophy of Science and Technology

UNIVERSITY COLLEGES

Erindale College: 3359 Mississauga Rd North, Mississauga, Ont. L5L 1C6; tel. 828-5211; f. 1964; Principal D. MORTON.

Innis College: 2 Sussex Ave, Toronto, Ont. M5S 1A1; tel. 978-7023; f. 1964; Principal W. ROLPH (acting).

New College: 300 Huron St, Toronto, Ont. M5S 1A1; tel. 978-2460; f. 1962; Principal Prof. F. I. CASE.

Scarborough College: 1265 Military Trail, Scarborough, Ont. M1C 1A4; tel. 284-3300; f. 1964; Principal Dr PAUL THOMPSON.

University College: 15 King's College Circle, Toronto, Ont. M5S 1A1; tel. 978-3170; f. 1853; Principal PAUL J. PERRON.

Woodsworth College: 117–119 St George St, Toronto, Ont. M5S 1A1; tel. 978-4444; f. 1974; Principal N. M. MELTZ.

FEDERATED UNIVERSITIES

University of St Michael's College: 81 St Mary St, Toronto, Ont. M5S 1J4; tel. (416) 926-1300; f. 1958; conducted by the Basilian Fathers; Pres. Dr RICHARD ALWAY.

University of Trinity College: 6 Hoskin Ave, Toronto, Ont. M5S 1H8; tel. (416) 978-2522; f. 1851; Vice-Chancellor and Provost R. PAINTER.

Victoria University, Toronto: 73 Queen's Park Cres., Toronto, Ont. M5S 1K7; tel. (416) 585-4524; f. 1836; Pres. E. KUSHNER.

FEDERATED COLLEGES

Emmanuel College: 75 Queen's Park Cres., Toronto, Ont. M5S 1K7; tel. (416) 585-4540; f. 1928; United Church of Canada theological college; Principal JOHN HOFFMAN.

Knox College: 59 St George St, Toronto, Ont. M5S 2E5; tel. (416) 978-4500; Presbyterian theological college; Principal Rev. Dr RAYMOND HUMPHRYES (acting).

Regis College: 15 St Mary St, Toronto, Ont. M4Y 2R5; tel. (416) 922-5474; f. 1930; Roman Catholic theological college (Society of Jesus); Pres. Rev. JOHN E. COSTELLO.

Wycliffe College: 5 Hoskin Ave, Toronto, Ont. M5S 1H7; tel. (416) 979-2870; Anglican theological college; Principal Rev. H. S. HILCHEY (acting).

AFFILIATED INSTITUTES

Massey College: University of Toronto, Toronto, Ont. M5S 2E1; tel. (416) 978-2895; f. 1963; residential college for graduates and senior scholars engaged in research; Master J. S. DUPRE.

Ontario Institute for Studies in Education: 252 Bloor St West, Toronto, Ont. M5S 1V6; f. 1965; an independent college, affiliated for degree-granting purposes only; courses lead to certificate of standing and graduate degrees in education; extensive library; Dir WALTER PITMAN; publs *Interchange, Curriculum Theory Network*, (quarterly), *Orbit* (5 a year).

Pontifical Institute of Medieval Studies: 59 Queen's Park Cres. East, Toronto, Ont. M5S 2C4; affiliated to Univ. of St Michael's College; grants degrees in its own right, offering pontifical Licentiate in Mediaeval Studies (MSL) and Doctorate in Mediaeval Studies (MSD); Pres. Prof. M. DIMNIK.

TRENT UNIVERSITY

POB 4800, Peterborough, Ont. K9J 7B8
Telephone: (705) 748-1011
Fax: (705) 748-1246

Founded 1963
Language of instruction: English
Academic year: September to May (two semesters with reading periods intervening)

Chancellor: MARY MAY SIMON
President and Vice-Chancellor: BONNIE M. PATTERSON
Vice-President (Administration): SALLY YOUNG
Vice-President (Academic and Provost): GRAHAM TAYLOR
Vice-President (Advancement): SUSAN MACKLE
Registrar: PAUL THOMSON
University Librarian: TOM EADIE
Director of Communications: KATHLEEN BAIN

Number of teachers: 345
Number of students: 5,401

Publication: *Journal of Canadian Studies.*

DEAN AND PROVOST

Faculty of Arts and Science: ROBERT CAMPBELL

PROFESSORS

ADAMS, W. P., Geography
BANDYOPADHYAY, P., Comparative Development Studies
BARKER, J. C., History
BARRETT, P. F., Chemistry
BERRILL, M., Biology
BEWS, J. P., Ancient History and Classics
BOUNDAS, C. V., Philosophy
BRUNGER, A. G., Geography
BUTTLE, J., Geography
CARTER, R. E., Philosophy
CHAKRAVARTTY, I. C., Mathematics
COGLEY, J. G., Geography
CURTIS, D. C. A., Economics
DAWSON, P. C., Physics
DELLAMORA, R. J., English Literature and Cultural Studies
ERNEST, C. H., Psychology
EVANS, D., Environmental Studies
EVANS, W., Environmental Studies, Physics
FEKETE, J. A., English Literature, Cultural Studies
HAGMAN, R. S., Anthropology
HEITLINGER, A., Sociology
HELMUTH, H. S., Anthropology
HILLMAN, J., Comparative Development, Sociology
HUTCHINSON, T., Environmental Studies, Biology
HUXLEY, C. V., Sociology and Comparative Development Studies
JOHNSON, R. G., Physics
JOHNSTON, G. A., English Literature
JONES, E. H., History
JONES, R., Biology
JURY, J. W., Physics and Computer Studies
KANE, S., English Literature, Cultural Studies
KINZL, K. H., Classical Studies
KITCHEN, H. M., Economics
LASENBY, D. C., Biology
LEWARS, E. G., Chemistry
MACKAY, D., Environmental Studies and Chemistry
MARCH, R. E., Chemistry
MARSH, J. S., Geography
MAXWELL, E. A., Mathematics
MCCALLA, D., History
MCCASKILL, D. N., Native Studies
MCLACHLAN, I., Cultural Studies
METCALFE, C., Environmental Studies
MILLOY, J., Native Studies and History
MITCHELL, O. S., English Literature
MORRISON, D. R., Political Studies and Comparative Development Studies
MORTON, P. M., History
MURPHY, T. N., Mathematics
NADER, G. A., Geography
NORIEGA, T. A., Spanish
PAEHLKE, R. C., Political Studies, Environmental Studies
PETERMAN, M., English Literature
POLLOCK, Z., English Literature
REKER, G. T., Psychology
ROBSON, S. T., History
SANGSTER, J., History and Women's Studies
SLAVIN, A. J., Physics
SMITH, C. T., Psychology
SO, J. K.-F., Anthropology
STANDEN, S. D., History
STOREY, I. C., Ancient History and Classics
STRUTHERS, J. E., Canadian Studies, History
SUTCLIFFE, J., Biology
TODD, E. M., Anthropology
TOPIC, J. R., Anthropology
TREADWELL, J. M., English Literature
TROMLY, F. B., English Literature
VERDUYN, C., Canadian Studies, Women's Studies
WADLAND, J. H., Canadian Studies
WALDEN, K., History
WERNICK, A. L., Cultural Studies
WINOCUR, G., Psychology

TRINITY WESTERN UNIVERSITY

7600 Glover Rd, Langley, BC V2Y 1Y1
Telephone: (604) 888-7511
Fax: (604) 513-2061

Founded 1962, university status 1979
Private control
Language of instruction: English
Academic year: September to April (two terms)

President: Dr R. NEIL SNIDER
Vice-President (Academic Affairs): Dr DONALD PAGE
Executive Vice-President: Dr GUY SAFFOLD
Vice-President (Student Life): THOMAS F. BULICK
Vice-President (University Enterprises): Dr LOU SAWCHENKO
Vice-President (Advancement): RONALD KUEHL
Registrar: Dr LAWRENCE H. VANBEEK
Librarian: DAVID TWIEST

Library of 387,777 vols
Number of teachers: 84 full-time, 68 part-time
Number of students: 2,319

Publications: *Calendar* (annually), *TWU Tip-off, Mars'Hill, Roots.*

DEANS

Arts and Religious Studies: Dr PHILLIP WIEBE
Business and Economics: JOHN SUTHERLAND
Natural and Applied Sciences: Dr JOHN VAN DYKE
Social Sciences and Education: Dr ROBERT BURKINSHAW

DEPARTMENT HEADS

Art: Dr PHILLIP WIEBE
Biology: Dr RICHARD PAULTON
Business: JOHN SUTHERLAND
Drama: Dr LLOYD ARNETT
Chemistry: Dr CHRISTINE CROSS
Communications: Dr WILLIAM STROM
English and Modern Languages: Dr JOHN ANONBY
Geography, History and Political Science: Dr ROBERT BURKINSHAW
Linguistics: Dr MICHAEL WALROD
Music: Dr DAVID RUSHTON
Mathematical Sciences: Dr JOHN BYL
Nursing: Dr JULIA EMBLEN
Philosophy: Dr PHILLIP WIEBE
Physical Education and Recreation: MURRAY HALL
Psychology, Sociology and Anthropology: Dr RONALD PHILIPCHALK
Religious Studies: Dr CRAIG BROYLES
Teacher Education: Dr JOY MCCULLOUGH
Graduate Biblical Studies: Dr CRAIG EVANS
Graduate Psychology: Dr PAUL WONG

ATTACHED INSTITUTES

Dead Sea Scrolls Institute: Dir Dr CRAIG EVANS.

Ethics Institute: Dir Dr PHILLIP WIEBE.

Family Research Institute: Dir Dr PAUL WONG.

AFFILIATED COLLEGES

Canadian Baptist Seminary: Pres. Dr HOWARD ANDERSON.

Northwest Baptist College and Seminary: Pres. Dr LARRY MCCULLOUGH.

Trinity Western Seminary: Pres. Dr R. NEIL SNIDER

UNIVERSITY OF VICTORIA

POB 1700, Victoria, BC V8W 2Y2
Telephone: (604) 721-7211
Fax: (604) 721-7212

Founded 1963
Language of instruction: English
Provincial control
Academic year: September to April; Summer Studies: May to August, including Summer Session, July and August

Chancellor: NORMA I. MICKELSON
President and Vice-Chancellor: D. F. STRONG
Vice-President (Academic) and Provost: PENNY CODDING
Vice-President (Finance and Operations): J. DONALD ROWLATT
Vice-President (Research): Dr S. MARTIN TAYLOR
University Secretary: SHEILA SHELDON COLLYER
Administrative Registrar: D. C. THOMAS
University Librarian: MARGARET C. SWANSON

Number of teachers: 661 (full-time)
Number of students: 17,519

Publications: *Calendar* (annually), *Malahat Review*.

DEANS

Faculty of Business: ROGER N. WOLFF
Faculty of Education: BRUCE HOWE
Faculty of Engineering: MICHAEL MILLER
Faculty of Fine Arts: S. ANTHONY WELCH
Faculty of Graduate Studies: GORDANA LAZAREVICH
Faculty of Human and Social Development: ANITA MOLZAHN
Faculty of Humanities: G. R. IAN MACPHERSON
Faculty of Law: DAVID S. COHEN
Faculty of Science: JOHN T. WEAVER
Faculty of Social Sciences: JOHN A. SCHOFIELD

PROFESSORS

AGATHOKLIS, P., Electrical and Computer Engineering
ALKIRE, W. H., Anthropology
ANDRACHUK, G. P., Hispanic and Italian Studies
ANTONIOU, A., Electrical and Computer Engineering
ARMITAGE, A., Social Work
ASTBURY, A., Physics and Astronomy
AUSIO, J., Biochemistry and Microbiology
AVIO, K. L., Economics
BACHOR, D. G., Psychological Foundations
BALFOUR, W. J., Chemistry
BARCLAY, J. A., Mechanical Engineering
BARNES, C., Earth and Ocean Sciences
BARNES, G. E., Child and Youth Care
BASKERVILLE, P. A., History
BAVELAS, J. B., Psychology
BECKMAN, D., School of Business
BEDESKI, R. E., Political Science
BEER, G. A., Physics and Astronomy
BERRY, E. I., English
BEST, M. R., English
BHARGAVA, V. K., Electrical and Computer Engineering
BHAT, A. K. S., Electrical and Computer Engineering
BISH, R. L., Public Administration
BISHOP, J., Earth and Ocean Sciences
BLANK, K., English
BOAG, D. A., School of Business
BRADLEY, C. H., Mechanical Engineering
BRADLEY, K. R., Classics
BRENER, R., Visual Arts
BROWNING-MOORE, A., Music
BRUNT, H., Nursing
BRYANT, D., Pacific and Asian Studies
BUCKLEY, A. G., Computer Science
BUCKLEY, J. T., Biochemistry and Microbiology
BURBANK, I. K., Education
BURKE, R. D., Biology
CALLAHAN, M., Social Work
CAMPBELL, M., Human and Social Development
CARR, G. A., Physical Education
CARROLL, W. K., Sociology
CASSELS, J. L., Law
CASSWELL, D. G., Law
CELONA, J., Music
CHAPPELL, N. L., Sociology
CHEFFINS, R. I., Public Administration
COBLEY, E., English
COCKAYNE, E. J., Mathematics and Statistics
COLLIS, M. L., Physical Education
COOPERSTOCK, F. I., Physics and Astronomy
COWARD, H. G., History
CROIZIER, L., Writing
CROIZIER, R. C., History
CRUMRINE, N. R., Anthropology
CUNNINGHAM, J. B., Public Administration
CUTT, J., Public Administration
DANIELS, C. B., Philosophy
DASTMALCHIAN, A., School of Business
DAVIDSON, R. R., Mathematics and Statistics
DEARDEN, P., Geography
DEVOR, H., Sociology
DEWEY, J. M., Physics and Astronomy
DIMOPOULOS, N., Electrical and Computer Engineering
DIPPIE, B. W., History
DIXON, K. R., Chemistry
DIXON, R. A., Psychology
DOBELL, A. R., Public Administration
DOCHERTY, D., Physical Education
DONALD, L. H., Anthropology
DOST, S., Mechanical Engineering
EDWARDS, A. S., English
EL GUIBALY, F. H., Electrical and Computer Engineering
ELLIS, D. V., Biology
ENGLAND, A. B., English
EVANS, P. O., Education
FARQUHARSON, A., Social Work
FELLOWS, M., Computer Science
FERGUSON, G. A., Law
FITCH, J. G., Classics
FLEMING, T., Education
FOSTER, H., Law
FOSTER, H. D., Geography
FOWLER, R., Social and Natural Sciences
FRANCE, H., Psychological Foundations
FUNG, I., Earth and Ocean Studies
FYLES, T. M., Chemistry
GALAMBOS, N., Psychology
GALLAGHER, Nursing
GARRETT, C., Physics
GIFFORD, R. D., Psychology
GILES, D. E., Economics
GLICKMAN, B., Biology
GODFREY, W. D., Creative Writing
GOOCH, B. N. S., English
GOUGH, T. E., Chemistry
GRANT, P. J., English
GREGORY, P. T., Biology
HADLEY, M. L., Germanic Studies
HARKER, W. J., Education
HARTWICK, F. D. A., Physics and Astronomy
HAWRYSHYN, C., Biology
HEDLEY, R. A., Sociology
HESS, T., Linguistics
HOBSON, L., Biology
HOCKING, M., Chemistry
HODGINS, J., Creative Writing
HOEFER, W. J. R., Electrical and Computer Engineering
HOFFMAN, P. F., Earth and Ocean Sciences
HOGYA, G., Theatre
HOPPE, R. A., Psychology
HORITA, R. E., Physics and Astronomy
HORSPOOL, R. N., Computer Science
HOWE, B. L., Physical Education
HOWELL, R. G., Law
HUENEMANN, R. W., Economic Relations with China
HULTSCH, D. F., Psychology
ILLNER, R., Mathematics and Statistics
ISHIGURO, E. E., Biochemistry and Microbiology
JACKSON, J. J., Public Administration
JENKINS, A., English
JOHNSON, T. D., Education
JOHNSTON, D. M., Law
JONES, J. C. H., Economics
JURICIC, Z. B., Slavonic Studies
KAY, W. W., Biochemistry and Microbiology
KEELER, R., Physics and Astronomy
KELLER, P., Geography
KERBY-FULTON, K., English
KESS, J. F., Linguistics
KINDERMAN, W., Music
KIRK, A. D., Chemistry
KIRLIN, R. L., Electrical and Computer Engineering
KLUGE, E.-H., Philosophy
KNOWLES, D. W., Education
KOENIG, D., Sociology
KOSTER, P., English
KREBS, H., Music
KWOK, H. H. L., Electrical and Computer Engineering
LAI, D. C.-Y., Geography
LANGFORD, J. W., Public Administration
LAZAREVICH, G., Music
LEEMING, D. J., Mathematics and Statistics
LIDDELL, P., Germanic Studies
LIEDTKE, W. W., Education
LIMBRICK, E., French Language and Literature
LINDSAY, S., Psychology
LOBB, D. E., Physics and Astronomy
LONERGAN, S. C., Geography
LU, W.-S., Electrical and Computer Engineering
MACGREGOR, J. N., Public Administration
MACKIE, G. O., Biology
MACLEOD, R. A., Mathematics and Statistics
MACPHERSON, G. R. I., History
MAGNUSSON, W., Political Science
MALONEY, M. A., Law
MANNING, E. G., Computer Science
MANTLE, J. H., Nursing
MARTIN-NEWCOMBE, Y., Communication and Social Foundations
MASON, G. R., Physics and Astronomy
MASSON, M. E. J., Psychology
MATHESON, A. T., Biochemistry and Microbiology
MAY, R. B., Psychology
MAYFIELD, M., Education
MCAULEY, A., Chemistry
MCDAVID, J. C., Public Administration
MCDOUGALL, I., Music
MCLAREN, A. G., History
MCLAREN, J. P. S., Law
MCRAE, J. J., Public Administration
MIERS, C. R., Mathematics and Statistics
MITCHELL, D. H., Anthropology
MITCHELL, R. H., Chemistry
MOEHR, J. R., Health Information Service
MOLZAHN, A., Nursing
MORE, B. E., Music
MORGAN, C. G., Philosophy
MOSK, C. A., Economic Relations with Japan
MUIR, W., Education
MULCAHEY, M., History
MURPHY, P., Communication and Social Foundations
MURPHY, P. E., Geography
MUZIO, J. C., Computer Science
NEILSON, W. A. W., Law

NEUFELDT, V. A., English
NG, I., Business
NICHOLS, D., Physical Education
ODEH, R. E., Mathematics and Statistics
OGMUNDSON, R., Sociology
OLAFSON, R. W., Biochemistry and Microbiology
OLESKY, D., Computer Science
OLESON, J. P., Classics
OLLILA, L. O., Education
OSBORNE, J., History in Art
OWENS, J. N., Biology
PARTRIDGE, C. J., English
PEARSON, T. W., Biochemistry and Microbiology
PENCE, A. R., Child and Youth Care
PFAFFENBERGER, W. E., Mathematics and Statistics
PHILLIPS, J., Mathematics and Statistics
PICCIOTTO, C. E., Physics and Astronomy
PODHORODESKI, R. P., Mechanical Engineering
PORAC, C. K., Psychology
PORTEOUS, J. D., Geography
PREECE, A., Education
PRINCE, M. J., Social Policy
PRITCHET, C. J., Physics
PROTTI, D. J., Health Information Science
PROVAN, J. W., Mechanical Engineering
PUTNAM, I., Mathematics and Statistics
RANGER, L., Music
REED, W. J., Mathematics and Statistics
REID, R. G. B., Biology
RICKS, F. A. S., Child and Youth Care
RIEDEL, W. E., Germanic Studies
RING, R. A., Biology
ROBINSON, L. R., Law
ROLLAND, N., Anthropology
ROMANIUK, P., Biochemistry and Microbiology
ROTH, E., Anthropology
ROTH, E. A., Anthropology
ROTH, W.-M., Social and Natural Sciences
ROY, P., History
RUNTZ, M. G., Psychology
RUSKEY, F., Computer Science
RUSSELL, L. W., Creative Writing
RUTHERFORD, M., Economics
SAGER, E. W., History
SCARFE, C. D., Physics and Astronomy
SCHAAFSMA, J., Economics
SCHAARSCHMIDT, G. H., Slavonic Studies
SCHOFIELD, J. A., Economics
SCHULER, R., English
SCHWANDT, E., Music
SCOBIE, S. A. C., English
SCOTT, D. S., Mechanical Engineering
SCULLY, S, Classics
SERRA, M., Computer Science
SHERWOOD, N., Biology
SHERWOOD, T. G., English
SHRIMPTON, G., Greek and Roman Studies
SMITH, H. F., English
SMITH, P. L., Classics
SOUROUR, A. R., Mathematics and Statistics
SRIVASTAVA, H. M., Mathematics and Statistics
STEPANENKO, Y., Mechanical Engineering
STEPHENSON, P. H., Anthropology
STOBART, S. R., Chemistry
STRAUSS, E., Psychology
STRONG, D. F., Earth and Ocean Sciences
SUMMERFIELD, H. E., English
SYMINGTON, R. T. K., Germanic Studies
TABARROK, B., Mechanical Engineering
TATUM, J. B., Physics and Astronomy
THALER, D., French Language and Literature
THATCHER, D. S., English
THOMAS, P., Social and Natural Sciences
TOLMAN, C. W., Psychology
TRUST, T. J., Biochemistry and Microbiology
TUCKER, J., English
TULLER, S., Geography
TUNNICLIFFE, V. J., Earth and Ocean Sciences
TURKINGTON, D., Education
TURNER, N., Environmental Studies
UHLEMANN, M. R., Education
VAHLDIECK, R., Electrical and Computer Engineering
VALGARDSON, W. D., Creative Writing
VAN DEN DRIESSCHE, P., Mathematics and Statistics
VAN DEN DRIESSCHE, R., Biology
VAN EMDEN, M., Computer Science
VANCE, J. H., Education
VANDENBERG, D. A., Physics
VEEVERS, J. E., Sociology
VICKERS, G. W., Mechanical Engineering
WADGE, W. W., Computer Science
WALDRON, M. A., Law
WALKER, R. B. J., Political Science
WALTER, G. R., Economics
WAN, P. C., Chemistry
WATTON, A., Physics and Astronomy
WEAVER, A., Earth and Ocean Sciences
WEAVER, J. T., Physics
WELCH, S. A., History in Art
WENGER, H. A., Physical Education
WHARF, B., Social Welfare
WILL, H. J., Public Administration
WILLIAMS, T., English
WOON, YUEN-FONG, Pacific Asian Studies
WOOTTON, D., History
WUESTER, T. J., Law
WYNAND, D., Creative Writing
YORE, L. D., Education
ZIELINSKI, A., Electrical and Computer Engineering
ZIETLOW, E., English
ZIMMERMAN, D., History
ZUK, W., Arts in Education

UNIVERSITY OF WATERLOO

Waterloo, Ont. N2L 3G1

Telephone: (519) 888-4567
Telex: 069-55259
Fax: (519) 746-8088
E-mail: watquest@nh1adm.uwaterloo.ca

Founded 1957
Provincially supported
Language of instruction: English
Academic year: September to April (Co-operative programmes September to August, Summer Session July to August)

Chancellor: M. V. O'DONOVAN
President and Vice-Chancellor: Dr J. DOWNEY
Vice-President (Academic and Provost): J. G. KALBFLEISCH
Vice-President (University Research): C. M. HANSSON
Vice-President (University Relations): I. H. LITHGOW
Associate Provost (Academic and Student Affairs): T. G. WALLER
Associate Provost (General Services and Finance): D. E. HUBER
Associate Provost (Human Resources and Student Services): C. SCOTT
Associate Provost (Information Systems and Technology): J. P. BLACK
Registrar: K. A. LAVIGNE
Librarian: M. C. SHEPHERD

Number of teachers: 706 (full-time)
Number of students: 21,213

Publications: *Admissions Handbook, Calendars, Gazette, Imprint, New Quarterly.*

DEANS

Faculty of Arts: B. P. HENDLEY
Faculty of Engineering: D. J. BURNS
Faculty of Environmental Studies: G. R. MCBOYLE
Faculty of Applied Health Sciences: M. T. SHARRATT
Faculty of Mathematics: J. D. KALBFLEISCH
Faculty of Science: J. E. THOMPSON
Graduate Studies: P. M. ROWE

DEPARTMENT CHAIRMEN AND DIRECTORS OF PROGRAMMES AND SCHOOLS

Accounting: H. ARMITAGE
Anthropology and Classical Studies: P. Y. FORSYTH
Applied Mathematics: F. O. GOODMAN
Architecture: E. R. HALDENBY
Biology: W. D. TAYLOR
Canadian Studies: R. NEEDHAM
Chemical Engineering: I. CHATZIS
Chemistry: T. MCMAHON
Civil Engineering: J. F. SYKES
Combinatorics and Optimization: I. P. GOULDEN
Computer Science: N. J. CERCONE
Drama and Speech Communication: J. GREENBERG
Earth Sciences: E. A. STUDICKY
East Asian Studies: G. CUTHBERT BRANDT
Economics: J. A. BROX
Electrical and Computer Engineering: S. CHAUDHURI
English: M. G. MCARTHUR
Environmental Engineering: W. C. LENNOX
Environment and Resource Studies: J. E. ROBINSON
Fine Arts: D. I. MACKAY
French Studies: P. SOCKEN
Geography: P. J. HOWARTH
Geological Engineering: M. DUSSEAULT
Germanic and Slavic Languages and Literatures: D. G. JOHN
Health Studies and Gerontology: P. WAINWRIGHT
History: D. WRIGHT
Independent Studies: G. A. GRIFFIN
International Studies: G. HAYES
Kinesiology: J. FRANK
Legal Studies and Criminology: C. G. BRUNK
Management Sciences: J. D. FULLER
Management Studies: S. W. KARDASZ
Mechanical Engineering: R. J. PICK
Middle East Studies: L. CURCHIN
Music: L. ENNS
Optometry: J. G. SIVAK
Peace and Conflict Studies: L. EWERT
Human Resources Management: S. W. KARDASZ
Philosophy: R. H. HOLMES
Physics: J. LEPOCK
Political Science: S. D. BURT
Print Journalism: A. V. MORGAN
Psychology: M. P. ZANNA
Pure Mathematics: W. J. GILBERT
Recreation and Leisure Studies: R. JOHNSON
Religious Studies: T. YODER NEUFELD
Social Development Studies: M. SMYTH
Society, Technology and Values: N. R. BALL
Sociology: R. D. LAMBERT
Russian and East European Studies: R. KARPIAK
Spanish: A. FAMA
Statistics and Actuarial Science: M. E. THOMPSON
Studies in Personality and Religion: J. GOLLNICK
Studies in Sexuality, Marriage and the Family: J. REMPEL
Systems Design Engineering: K. HIPEL
Planning: R. NEWKIRK
Women's Studies: V. GOLINI

FEDERATED UNIVERSITY

St Jerome's University: Waterloo, Ont. N2L 3G3; f. 1864; federated 1960; Roman Catholic, conducted by the Congregation of the Resurrection; Pres. D. R. LETSON.

AFFILIATED COLLEGES

Conrad Grebel College: Waterloo, Ont. N2L 3G6; Mennonite; Pres. J. E. TOEWS.

Renison College: Waterloo, Ont. N2L 3G4; f. 1959, affiliated 1960; Anglican; Principal G. CUTHBERT BRANDT.

St Paul's United College: Waterloo, Ont. N2L 3G5; United Church; Principal H. MILLS.

UNIVERSITY OF WESTERN ONTARIO

London, Ont. N6A 3K7

Telephone: (519) 679-2111

Telex: 0647134

Fax: (519) 661-3388

Founded 1878

Charter last revised 1974

Academic year: September to April

Chancellor: P. GODSOE

President and Vice-Chancellor: P. DAVENPORT

Vice-President (Administration): P. MERCER

Vice-President (Academic) and Provost: G. MORAN

Vice-President (Research): W. BRIDGER

Vice-President (External): Dr E. GARRARD

Director of Libraries: CATHERINE A. QUINLAN

Number of teachers: 1,434 full-time, 496 part-time

Number of students: 19,619 full-time, 5,358 part-time

Publications: *Medical Journal, Dental Journal, Gazette* (student daily), *Alumni Gazette, The Business Quarterly, The Science Terrapin, Reflections, The President's Report, Western News* (weekly newsletter), Calendars for all Faculties and Schools.

DEANS

Faculty of Arts: J. GOOD

Faculty of Music: J. L. STOKES

Faculty of Science: C. Y. KANG

Faculty of Social Science: P. NEARY

Faculty of Education: A. T. PEARSON

Faculty of Engineering: R. M. MATHUR

Faculty of Medicine and Dentistry: R. Y. MCMURTRY

Faculty of Law: E. E. GILLESE

Faculty of Graduate Studies: A. C. WEEDON

Richard Ivey School of Business: L. TAPP

Faculty of Communications and Open Learning: G. MORAN (acting)

Faculty of Health Sciences: A. BELCASTRO

PROFESSORS

Faculty of Arts:

BELL, J. L., Philosophy
BENTLEY, D. M. R., English
BRADY, K., English
BRONAUGH, R. N., Philosophy
CHEETHAM, M. A., Visual Arts
COLLINS, T. J., English
DAVEY, F. W., English
DEMOPOULOS, W. G., Philosophy
DRAGLAND, S. L., English
GERBER, D. E., Classical Studies
GOLDSCHLAGER, A. J., French
GREEN, R. F., English
GRODEN, M. L., English
HAIR, D. S., English
HARPER, W. L., Philosophy
HILLMAN, R. W., English
HOFFMASTER, C. B., Philosophy
KREISWIRTH, M., English
LENNON, T. M., Philosophy
LEONARD, J., English
LITTLEWOOD, A. R., Classical Studies
MARRAS, A., Philosophy
MURISON, C. L., Classical Studies
POTTER, P. M. J., History of Science and Medicine
PURDY, A., French
RAJAN, T., English
SOMERSET, J. A. B., English
SURETTE, L., English
TAUSKY, T. E., English
WATSON, N., English
WYLIE, M. A., Philosophy

Faculty of Music:

BAILEY, T.
BEHRENS, J.
FENYVES, L.
FISKE, H.
KOPROWSKI, P. P.
PARKS, R. S.
SKELTON, R. A.
TOFT, R.

Faculty of Science:

ALLNATT, A. R., Chemistry
ANKNEY, C. O., Zoology
ATKINSON, B. G., Zoology
BAIRD, N. C., Chemistry
BANCROFT, G. M., Chemistry
BELLHOUSE, D. R., Statistical and Actuarial Sciences
BRUEN, A. A., Mathematics
CALDWELL, W. G. E., Earth Sciences
CASS, F. P. A., Mathematics
CAVENEY, S., Zoology
CAVERS, P. B., Plant Sciences
CHURCH, W. R., Earth Sciences
COTTAM, M. G., Physics
DAY, A. W., Plant Sciences
DEAN, P. A. W., Chemistry
DONNER, A., Epidemiology and Biostatistics
EDGAR, A. D., Earth Sciences
ELIAS, V. W., Applied Mathematics
FAHSELT, D., Plant Sciences
FLEET, M. E. L., Earth Sciences
GARGANTINI, I., Computer Science
GOLDMAN, P. S., Physics
GRAY, D. F., Astronomy
GREEN, R. H., Zoology
GUTHRIE, J. P., Chemistry and Biochemistry
HAQ, M. S., Statistical and Actuarial Sciences
HEINICKE, A. G., Mathematics
HOCKING, W. K., Physics and Astronomy
HOLT, R. A., Physics
HUNER, N. P. A., Plant Sciences
HUNTER, D. H., Chemistry
JARDINE, J. F., Mathematics
JEFFREY, D. J., Mathematics
JONES, J., Physics
JÜRGENSEN, H., Computer Science
KANE, R. M., Mathematics
KANG, C. Y., Zoology
KING, J. F., Chemistry
LACHANCE, M. A., Plant Sciences, Microbiology and Immunology
LANDSTREET, J. D., Astronomy
LEAIST, D. G., Chemistry
LIPSON, R. H., Chemistry
LONGSTAFFE, F. J., Earth Sciences
LOOKMAN, T., Applied Mathematics
LOWE, R. P., Physics
LUKE, T. M., Applied Mathematics Physics
MACRAE, N. D., Earth Sciences
MANSINHA, L., Earth Sciences
MARLBOROUGH, J. M., Astronomy
MAUN, A., Plant Sciences
MCINTYRE, N. S., Chemistry
MCKEON, D. G. C., Applied Mathematics
MCLEOD, A. I., Statistical and Actuarial Sciences
MEATH, W. J., Chemistry
MIGNERON, J. H. R., Applied Mathematics, Physics
MILLAR, J. S., Zoology
MILNES, P., Mathematics
MITCHELL, I. V., Physics
MITCHELL, J. B. A., Physics
MOORCROFT, D. R., Physics
NESBITT, H. W., Earth Sciences
NORTON, P. R., Chemistry
ORLOCI, L., Plant Sciences
PALMER, H. C., Earth Sciences
PAYNE, N. C., Chemistry
PETERSEN, N. O., Chemistry
PHIPPS, J. B., Plant Sciences
PODESTA, R. B., Zoology
PUDDEPHATT, R. J., Chemistry
RASMUSSEN, H., Applied Mathematics
RENNER, L. E., Mathematics
ROSNER, S. D., Physics
ST MAURICE, J.-P., Physics
SHAM, T. K., Chemistry
SHIVERS, R. R., Zoology
SINGH, M. R., Physics and Astronomy
SINGH, S. M., Zoology
STARKEY, J., Earth Sciences
STILLMAN, M. J., Chemistry
SULLIVAN, P. J., Applied Mathematics
TONG, B. Y., Physics
WEEDON, A. C., Chemistry
WIEBE, J. P., Zoology
WILLIS, C. J., Chemistry
YOUNG, G. M., Earth Sciences
ZAMIR, M., Applied Mathematics, Medical, Biophysics
ZINKE-ALLMANG, M., Physics and Astronomy

Faculty of Social Science:

ALLAHAR, A., Sociology
AVERY, D. H., History
AVISON, W. R., Sociology
BALAKRISHNAN, T. R., Sociology
BEAUJOT, R. P., Sociology
BHATIA, K. B., Economics
BLOMQVIST, A. G., Economics
BOYER, R. S, Economics
BURCH, T. K., Sociology
BURGESS, D. F., Economics
CAIN, D. P., Psychology
CARROLL, M. P., Sociology
CARTWRIGHT, D. G., Geography
CARTWRIGHT, J. R., Political Science
CLARK, S., Sociology
CONNIDIS, I. A., Sociology
CREIDER, C. A., Anthropology
DARNELL, R., Anthropology
DAVENPORT, P., Economics
DAVIES, J. B., Economics
DAWSON, W. F., Political Science
DREYER, F. A., History
EBANKS, G. E., Sociology
EMERSON, R. L., History
EVANS, D.R., Psychology
FISHER, W. A., Psychology
FLAHERTY, D. H., History
FLEMING, M., Political Science
FREEDMAN, J. M., Anthropology
GARDNER, R. C., Psychology
GOODALE, M., Psychology
GRABB, E. G., Sociology
GREEN, M. B., Geography
GRINDSTAFF, C. F., Sociology
GUINSBURG, T. N., History
HARLEY, L. K., Economics
HUMPHREY, K. G., Psychology
HYATT, A. M. J., History
KATZ, A. N., Psychology
KEATING, M., Political Science
KIMURA, D., Psychology, Neurology
KING, R. H., Geography
KNIGHT, J., Economics
KUIPER, N. A., Psychology
KUNKEL, J. H., Sociology
KYMLICKA, B. B., Political Science
LAIDLER, D. E. W., Economics
LEITH, J. C., Economics
LIPMAN, B., Economics
LUCKMAN, B. H., Geography
LUPKER, S. J., Psychology
MCDOUGALL, J. N., Political Science
MEYER, J. P., Psychology
MORAN, G., Psychology
MURRAY, H. G., Psychology
NEARY, P. F., History
NEUFELD, R. W. J., Psychology
NOEL, S. J. R., Political Science
OLSON, J. M., Psychology
OSSENKOPP, K.-P., Psychology
PARKIN, J. M., Economics
RINEHART, J. W., Sociology
ROBERTS, W. A., Psychology
ROBINSON, C. M. G. F., Economics
ROBSON, A. J., Economics
ROLLMAN, G. B., Psychology
RUSHTON, J. P., Psychology
RUUD, C. A., History

SANCTON, A. B., Political Science
SANTOSUOSSO, A., History
SEGAL, U., Economics
SELIGMAN, C., Psychology
SHATZMILLER, M., History
SHERRY, D., Psychology
SORRENTINO, R. M., Psychology
SPENCE, M. W., Anthropology
STEELE, I. K., History
TEEVAN, J. J., Sociology
THOMPSON, J. N., History
TIMNEY, B. N., Psychology
TROUGHTON, M. J., Geography
VANDERWOLF, C. H., Psychology
VERNON, P. A., Psychology
VERNON, R. A., Political Science
WHALLEY, J., Economics
WHITEHEAD, P. C., Sociology
WINTROBE, R. S., Economics
WOLFE, D., Psychology
YOUNG, R. A., Political Science

Faculty of Medicine and Dentistry:

AHMAD, D., Medicine
ARNOLD, J. M. O., Medicine
BAILEY, W. H., Surgery
BAIN, J. A., Anaesthesia
BALL, J. K., Biochemistry, Oncology
BANTING, D. W., Community Dentistry, Epidemiology and Biostatistics
BARR, R. M., Medicine, Oncology
BATTISTA, J. J., Oncology, Medical Biophysics
BELL, D. A., Medicine
BELLAMY, N., Medicine, Epidemiology and Biostatistics
BELLHOUSE, D. R., Epidemiology
BEND, J. R., Pharmacology and Toxicology
BIEHN, J. T., Family Medicine
BLUME, W. T., Clinical Neurological Sciences, Paediatrics
BOLTON, C. F., Clinical Neurological Sciences, Medicine
BONDY, D. C., Medicine
BOUGHNER, D. R., Medicine, Medical Biophysics
BOURNE, R. B., Orthopaedic Surgery, Medical Biophysics
BRAMWELL, V. H. C., Oncology, Medicine
BRIDGER, W. A., Biochemistry
BROOKE, R. I., Oral Medicine, Oral Biology
BROWN, J. D., Clinical Neurological Sciences
CAIRNCROSS, J. G., Oncology, Medicine, Clinical Neurological Sciences
CANHAM, P. B., Medical Biophysics
CARROLL, S. E., Surgery
CARRUTHERS, S. G., Pharmacology and Toxicology
CHACONAS, G., Biochemistry
CHAMBERS, A. F., Physiology, Anatomy
CHANCE, G. W., Paediatrics, Obstetrics and Gynaecology
CHERIAN, G. M., Pathology, Pharmacology and Toxicology
CHODIRKER, W. B., Medicine
CIRIELLO, J., Physiology, Anatomy
CLARK, W. F., Medicine
COLCLEUGH, R. G., Surgery
COOK, M. A., Pharmacology and Toxicology, Physiology
COOK, R. A., Biochemistry
COOKE, J. D., Physiology
COOPER, A. J., Psychiatry
CORDY, P. E., Medicine
CRADDUCK, T. D., Diagnostic Radiology and Nuclear Medicine, Medical Biophysics, Oncology
CUNNINGHAM, D. A., Physiology
DEL MAESTRO, R., Clinical Neurology Sciences, Oncology
DELOVITCH, T. L., Microbiology
DONNER, A. P., Epidemiology and Biostatistics, Family Medicine
DRIEDGER, A. A., Diagnostic Radiology and Nuclear Medicine, Medicine, Oncology
DUFF, J. H., Surgery
DUNN, S. D., Biochemistry
EBERS, G. C., Clinical Neurological Sciences, Medicine
EDMONDS, M. W., Medicine
ELLIS, C. G., Medical Biophysics
FEIGHTNER, J. W., Family Medicine
FELDMAN, R. D., Pharmacology and Toxicology
FENSTER, A., Diagnostic Radiology and Nuclear Medicine, Oncology
FERGUSON, G. G., Clinical Neurological Sciences, Medical Biophysics
FINNIE, K. J. C., Medicine
FISHER, W. A., Obstetrics and Gynaecology
FLINTOFF, W., Microbiology and Immunology
FLUMERFELT, B. A., Anatomy
FOWLER, P. J., Surgery
FOX, A. J., Diagnostic Radiology, Clinical Neurological Sciences
FREWEN, T. C., Paediatrics
GELB, A. W., Anaesthesia, Clinical Neurological Sciences
GERACE, R. V., Medicine
GIBSON, G. A., Family Medicine
GILBERT, J. J., Pathology, Clinical Neurological Sciences
GIROTTI, M. J., Surgery
GIRVAN, D., Surgery, Paediatrics
GIRVIN, J. P., Clinical Neurological Sciences, Physiology, Surgery
GORDON, B. A., Biochemistry
GRACE, D. M., Surgery
GRANT, C. W. M., Biochemistry
GRANT, D. R., Surgery, Microbiology and Immunology, Pathology
GUIRAUDON, C. M., Pathology
GUIRAUDON, G. M., Surgery
HAASE, P., Anatomy
HACHINSKI, V., Clinical Neurological Sciences, Medicine, Physiology, Epidemiology and Biostatistics
HAHN, A. F. G., Clinical Neurological Sciences, Medicine
HAINES, D. S. M., Biochemistry
HAMILTON, J. T., Pharmacology and Toxicology
HAMMOND, G. L., Obstetrics and Gynaecology, Oncology
HAN, V. K. M., Paediatrics, Anatomy, Biochemistry
HARDING, P. G. R., Obstetrics and Gynaecology
HARTH, M., Medicine
HAYES, K. C., Physical Medicine and Rehabilitation, Physiology
HELEWA, A., Epidemiology
HENDERSON, A. R., Biochemistry
HENNEN, B. K. E., Family Medicine
HERSEY, L. W., Anaesthesia
HILL, D. J., Medicine
HIRST, M. M., Pharmacology
HOBBS, B. B., Diagnostic Radiology and Nuclear Medicine
HODSMAN, A. B., Medicine
HOFFMASTER, C. B., Family Medicine
HOLLIDAY, R., Surgery
HOLLOMBY, D., Medicine
HORE, J., Physiology
HUFF, M. W., Medicine, Biochemistry
HURLEY, R. M., Paediatrics
HURST, L. N., Surgery
INWOOD, M. J., Medicine, Oncology
JAIN, S. C., Psychiatry
JAMIESON, W. G., Surgery
JONES, D. L., Physiology, Medicine
JUNG, J. H., Paediatrics, Obstetrics and Gynaecology
KANG, C. Y., Microbiology and Immunology
KARLIK, S. J., Diagnostic Radiology and Nuclear Medicine, Physiology, Clinical Neurological Sciences
KARMAZYN, M., Pharmacology and Toxicology
KAVALIERS, M. I., Oral Biology
KAZARIAN, S. S., Psychiatry
KENNEDY, T. G., Obstetrics and Gynaecology, Physiology
KERTESZ, A., Clinical Neurological Sciences, Medicine
KIDDER, G. M., Physiology, Obstetrics and Gynaecology
KIERNAN, J. A., Anatomy
KILLINGER, D. W., Medicine
KIRK, M. E., Pathology
KLEIN, G. J., Medicine
KLINE, R. L., Physiology
KOGON, S. L., Oral Medicine, Radiology
KOSTUK, W. J., Medicine
KVIETYS, P. R., Physiology
LALA, P. K., Anatomy
LAMPE, H. B., Otolaryngology
LAZAROVITS, A. I., Medicine, Microbiology and Immunology
LEEPER, H. A., Otolaryngology
LEFCOE, M. S., Diagnostic Radiology and Nuclear Medicine
LELLA, J. W., History of Medicine
LEUNG, F. Y., Biochemistry
LEUNG, L. W. S., Physiology
LEVIN, L., Oncology, Medicine, Obstetrics and Gynaecology
LINDSAY, R. M., Medicine
LLOYD, D., Medicine
LO, T. C., Biochemistry
MCDONALD, J. W. D., Medicine
MCDONALD, T. J., Medicine
MCGRATH, P. A., Paediatrics
MCKENZIE, F. N., Surgery
MCLACHLAN, R. S., Clinical Neurological Sciences, Physiology
MCMURTRY, R. Y., Surgery
MCSHERRY, J. A., Family Medicine
MALLA, A. K., Psychiatry, Family Medicine
MARTIN, A. H., Anatomy
MELENDEZ, L. J., Medicine
MILNE, J. K., Obstetrics and Gynaecology
MOOTE, D. W., Medicine
MORGAN, W. K. C., Medicine
MORRISSY, J. R., Family Medicine
MUIR, J. M., Anaesthesia
MUIRHEAD, N., Medicine
MURKIN, J. M., Anaesthesia
NARAYANAN, N., Physiology
NATALE, R., Obstetrics and Gynaecology
NEUFELD, R. W. J., Psychiatry
NISKER, J. A., Obstetrics and Gynaecology
PASSI, R. B., Surgery
PATERSON, N. A. M., Medicine, Pharmacology and Toxicology
PAYTON, K. B., Medicine
PERSAD, E., Psychiatry
PHILP, R. B., Pharmacology
POMERANTZ, P. K., Physiology, Obstetrics and Gynaecology
POSSMAYER, F., Biochemistry, Obstetrics and Gynaecology
POTTER, P. M. J., History of Medicine and Science
POZNANSKY, M. J., Biochemistry
PRATO, F. S., Diagnostic Radiology and Nuclear Medicine, Medical Biophysics, Anaesthesia
RALPH, E., Medicine
RANKIN, R. N., Diagnostic Radiology and Nuclear Medicine
REID, G., Microbiology and Immunology, Surgery
RICE, G. P. A., Clinical Neurological Sciences; Microbiology and Immunology
RICHARDSON, B. S., Obstetrics and Gynaecology, Physiology
ROACH, M. R., Medical Biophysics, Medicine
RODGER, N. W., Medicine
RORABECK, C. H., Surgery
ROTH, J. H., Surgery
RUTLEDGE, F. S., Medicine, Anaesthesia
RUTT, B. K., Diagnostic Radiology and Nuclear Medicine
RYLETT, R. J., Physiology
SANGSTER, J. F., Family Medicine
SELLERY, G. R., Anaesthesia
SIBBALD, W. J., Medicine
SILCOX, J. A., Obstetrics and Gynaecology

SINCLAIR, N. R., Microbiology and Immunology
SINGH, B., Microbiology and Immunology
SINGHAL, S. K., Microbiology and Immunology
SMITH, D. R., Medicine
SOLTAN, H. C., Paediatrics, Anatomy
SOUTHERN, R. F., Medicine
SPENCE, J. D., Medicine, Pharmacology and Toxicology, Clinical Neurological Sciences
STEWART, M. A., Family Medicine, Epidemiology and Biostatistics
STILLER, C. R., Medicine
TEPPERMAN, B. L., Physiology
TEVAARWERK, G. J. M., Medicine, Diagnostic Radiology and Nuclear Medicine
THOMPSON, J. M., Medicine
TOOGOOD, J. H., Medicine
TRENHOLM, H. L., Pharmacology
TREVITHICK, J. R., Biochemistry
TYML, K., Pharmacology and Toxicology
VILIS, T., Physiology, Ophthalmology
VINGILIS, E. R., Family Medicine
WALL, W. J., Surgery
WANG, J. H. C., Biochemistry
WEAVER, L. C., Physiology
WESTON, W. W., Family Medicine
WEXLER, D., Medicine
WILLIS, N. R., Ophthalmology
WISENBERG, G., Medicine, Diagnostic Radiology and Nuclear Medicine
WOLFE, B. M., Medicine
WOLFE, D. A., Psychiatry
WONG, P. T., Pharmacology
WRIGHT, G. Z., Orthodontics, Paediatric Dentistry
WRIGHT, V. C., Obstetrics and Gynaecology
WYATT, J. K., Surgery
WYSOCKI, G. P., Pathology
YOUNG, G. B., Clinical Neurological Sciences, Medicine
ZAMIR, M., Microbiology

Faculty of Law:
BACKHOUSE, C. B.
BARTON, P. G.
BROWN, C.
BRYANT, A. W.
FELDTHUSEN, B. P.
GILLESE, E. E.
HOLLAND, W. H.
HOVIUS, B.
MCLAREN, R. H.
MCLEOD, J.
MARTIN, R. I.
MERCER, P.
OOSTERHOFF, A. H.
SOLOMON, R.
USPRICH, S. J.
WELLING, B.

Faculty of Engineering Science:
BADDOUR, R. E., Civil
BASE, T. E., Mechanical
BEECKMANS, J. M., Chemical and Biochemical
BRIENS, C. L., Chemical and Biochemical
CASTLE, G. S. P., Electrical
DAVENPORT, A. G., Civil
DE LASA, H., Chemical and Biochemical
DICKINSON, S. M., Mechanical
FLORYAN, J. M., Mechanical
GREASON, W. D., Electrical
INCULET, I. I., Electrical
KUCEROVSKY, Z., Electrical
LAU, I. W. M., Materials
MARGARITIS, A., Chemical and Biochemical
MATHUR, R. M., Electrical
MOORE, I. D., Civil
MORCHED, A. S., Electrical and Computer
MURTHY, K. M. S., Electrical and Computer
NOWAK, E. S., Mechanical
ROSATI, P. A., Civil
ROWE, R. K., Civil
SHEASBY, J. S., Materials
SHINOZAKI, D. M., Materials
SURRY, D., Civil
TARASUK, J. D., Mechanical
TO, C. W. S., Mechanical
VICKERY, B. J., Civil
WEBSTER, A. R., Electrical

Richard Ivey School of Business:
ARCHIBALD, T. R.
BEAMISH, P. W.
BELL, P. C.
DEUTSCHER, T. H.
DI STEFANO, J. J.
FRY, J. N.
GANDZ, J.
HARDY, K. G.
HATCH, J. E.
HOWARD, J. H.
HUFF, S.
JONES, N. R.
LECRAW, D. J.
LEENDERS, M. R.
MCLEOD, J.
MIKALACHKI, A.
MORE, R.
RYANS, A. B.
SHAW, D. C.

Faculty of Education:
AYIM, M., Educational Policy Studies
BARAK, A., Educational Psychology
CREALOCK, C., Educational Psychology
DICKINSON, G. M., Educational Policy Studies
GOODSON, I., Curriculum Studies
LEE, D. Y., Educational Psychology
MCPECK, J., Educational Policy Studies
MAJHANOVICH, S. E. W., Curriculum Studies
PEARSON, A. T., Educational Policy Studies
RAY, D., Educational Policy Studies
SITKO, M. C., Educational Psychology

Faculty of Information and Media Studies:
CRAVEN, T. C.
DESBARATS, P.
HARRIS, R. M.
MARTIN, R. I.
ROSS, C. L.

Faculty of Health Sciences:
BARNEY, R. K., Kinesiology
BUCKOLZ, E., Kinesiology
CARRON, A. V., Kinesiology
COOKE, J. D., Physical Therapy
COX, B., Nursing
CUNNINGHAM, D. A., Kinesiology
FOWLER, P. J., Kinesiology
HALL, C. R., Kinesiology
HELEWA, A., Physical Therapy
JAMIESON, D., Communicative Disorders
LEEPER, H. A., Communicative Disorders
LEYSHON, G. A., Kinesiology
MEIER, K. V., Kinesiology
MILLER, D. I., Kinesiology
MORROW, L. D., Kinesiology
PATERSON, D. H., Kinesiology
POLATAJKO, H., Occupational Therapy
SEEWALD, R. C., Communicative Disorders
SEMOTIUK, D. M., Kinesiology
TAYLOR, A. W., Kinesiology

AFFILIATED INSTITUTIONS

Huron College: 1349 Western Rd, London, Ont. N6G 1H3; f. 1863; arts and theological college; Principal D. BEVAN.

PROFESSORS

BLOCKER, J. S., History
GELLATELY, R., History
HYLAND, P., English
KEYPOUR, D., French
READ, C., History
SCHACHTER, J. P., Philosophy

Brescia College: 1285 Western Rd, London, Ont. N6G 1H2; f. 1919; arts subjects; Principal Sr DOLORES KUNTZ.

PROFESSORS

KUNTZ, Sr. DOLORES, Psychology
MCKENZIE, Sr MARY LOUISE, English
SHARP, Sr CORONA, English
TOPIC, T., Anthropology

King's College: 266 Epworth Ave, London, Ont. N6A 2M3; f. 1912 (Seminary), 1955 (College); seminary and college of arts; Principal G. KILLAN.

PROFESSORS

BAHCHELI, T., Political Science
BLOM, D., Social Work
KILLAN, G., History
KOPINAK, K., Sociology
LELLA, J. W., Sociology
MACGREGOR, D., Sociology
MORGAN, J. D., Philosophy
PATERSON, G. H., English
PRIEUR, M. R., Religious Studies
SCHMEISER, J. A., Religious Studies
SKINNER, N. F., Psychology
SNYDER, J. J., Philosophy
WERSTINE, P., English

WILFRID LAURIER UNIVERSITY

Waterloo, Ont. N2L 3C5
Telephone: (519) 884-1970
Telex: 06955476
Fax: (519) 886-9351

Founded 1911; formerly Waterloo Lutheran University; name changed 1973
Language of instruction: English
State control
Academic year: September to May (two terms)
Chancellor: JOHN CLEGHORN
President and Vice-Chancellor: Dr ROBERT ROSEHART
Vice-President (Academic): Dr ROWLAND SMITH
Vice-President (Finance and Administration): Dr ROBIN L. ARMSTRONG (acting)
Registrar: Dr JOHN METCALFE
Librarian and Archivist: VIRGINIA GILLHAM

Number of teachers: 289 full-time, 215 part-time
Number of students: 5,625 full-time, 2,177 part-time

Publications: *Calendars, Laurier Campus* (quarterly), *Laurier News* (weekly), *The Cord Weekly.*

DEANS

Faculty of Arts and Science: Dr ARTHUR READ
Waterloo Lutheran Seminary: Dr RICHARD CROSSMAN
Faculty of Social Work: Dr JANNAH MATHER
Faculty of Graduate Studies: Dr BARRY MCPHERSON
Faculty of Music: Dr ANNE HALL
School of Business and Economics: Dr SCOTT CARSON

DEPARTMENT CHAIRS

Biology: Dr DAVID R. PEIRSON
Business Administration: Dr R. ELLIS
Chemistry: Dr R. RODRIGO
Classics: Dr G. SCHAUS
Economics: Dr T. LEVESQUE
English: Dr M. MOORE
Geography: Dr R. SHARPE
History: D. LORIMER
Mathematics: Dr S. STACK
Modern Languages and Literatures: Dr J. SKIDMORE
Philosophy: Dr R. JACOBSEN
Physics and Computing: Dr J. LIT
Political Science: Dr B. TANGUAY
Psychology: Dr K. HORTON
Religion and Culture: Dr KAY KOPPEDRAYER
Sociology and Anthropology: Dr L. CHRISTIE

UNIVERSITY OF WINDSOR

Windsor, Ont. N9B 3P4
Telephone: (519) 253-4232
Founded 1857

Provincially assisted
Language of instruction: English
Academic year: September to May (2 semesters)

Chancellor: (vacant)
Vice-Chancellor and President: (vacant)
Senior Vice-President for Development and Alumni Affairs: P. CASSANO
Vice-President (Finance and Services): ERIC HARBOTTLE
Vice-President (Academic): W. E. JONES
Registrar: F. L. SMITH
Librarian: GWENDOLYN EBBETT

Number of teachers: 470 (full-time)
Number of students: 14,775 (full- and part-time)

Publications: *The Lance* (weekly), *The Ambassador*, *Windsor University Magazine* (quarterly), *Review*, *Undergraduate Calendar*, *Graduate Calendar* (both every 2 years).

DEANS

Faculty of Arts: S. G. MARTIN
Faculty of Social Science: K. E. MCCRONE
Faculty of Science: B. J. FRYER
Faculty of Engineering: H. EL MARAGHY
Faculty of Business Administration: N. SOLOMON
Faculty of Education: M. A. AWENDER
Faculty of Graduate Studies and Research: S. CAMERON
Faculty of Law: J. WESTMORELAND-TRAORÉ
Faculty of Human Kinetics: M. SALTER
Student Affairs: R. G. PRICE

PROFESSORS

Faculty of Arts:

AMORE, R. C., Religious Studies
BAXTER, I., Visual Arts
BERTMAN, S., Classical Studies
BIRD, H. W., Classical Studies
BLAIR, J. A., Philosophy
BROWN, J. V., Philosophy
BUTLER, E. G., Music
CASSANO, P., French
DEVILLERS, J. P., French
DILWORTH, T. R., English
DITSKY, J. M., English
GOLD/SMITH, S. B., Visual Arts
HERENDEEN, W. H., English
HOUSEHOLDER, R., Music
JANZEN, H. D., English
JOHNSON, R. H., Philosophy
KING, J. N., Religious Studies
KINGSTONE, B. D., French
LEWIS, J. U., Philosophy
MCINTYRE, P. P., Music
MACKENDRICK, L. K., English
MACLEOD, A., English
MARTIN, S. G., Dramatic Art
MEHTA, M., Religious Studies
PALMER, D., Music
SARKAR, K. K., Classical Studies
SMEDICK, L., English
SPELLMAN, J. W., Classical Studies
STARETS, M., French
VAN DEN HOVEN, A., French
WARREN, B., Dramatic Art
WENDT-HILDEBRANDT, S., Classical Studies
WHITNEY, B., Religious Studies
WRIGHT, J., Philosophy

Faculty of Social Science:

ADAM, B. D., Sociology
BALANCE, W. D., Psychology
BRIGGS, E. D., Political Science
BROOKS, S., Political Science
BROWN-JOHN, C. L., Political Science
CHACKO, J., Social Work
COHEN, J. S., Psychology
CUNNINGHAM, S. B., Communication Studies
CUTHBERT, M. Communication Studies
FORTUNE, J. N., Economics
GILLEN, W. J., Economics
GOLD, M., Communication Studies
GUCCIONE, A., Economics
HOLOSKO, M. J., Social Work
INNES, F. C., Geography
KOBASIGAWA, A., Psychology
KROEKER, B. J., Social Work
LINTON, J. M., Communication Studies
MCCABE, A. E., Psychology
MCCRONE, K. E., History
MENG, R., Economics
MINTON, H. L., Psychology
ORR, R. R., Psychology
PAGE, J. S., Psychology
PHIPPS, A. G., Geography
PRICE, R. G., Political Science
PRYKE, K. G., History
RAMACHARAN, S., Sociology
REYNOLDS, D. V., Psychology
ROMSA, G. H., Geography
ROURKE, B. P., Psychology
SCHNEIDER, F. W., Psychology
SELBY, S. A., Communication Studies
SODERLUND, W. C., Political Science
STEBELSKY, I., Geography
STRICK, J. C., Economics
TRENHAILE, A. S., Geography
WAGENBERG, R. H., Political Science

Faculty of Science:
(Some professors are also attached to the Faculty of Engineering)

AROCA, R., Chemistry and Biochemistry
ATKINSON, J. B., Physics
BANDYOPADHYAY, S., Computer Science
BARRON, R. M., Mathematics and Statistics
BAYLIS, W. E., Physics
BLACKBURN, W. H., Earth Sciences
BRITTEN, D. J., Mathematics and Statistics
CAMERON, W. S., Nursing
CARON, R. J., Mathematics and Statistics
CARTY, L., Nursing
CHANDNA, O. P., Mathematics and Statistics
COTTER, D. A., Biological Sciences
DRAKE, G. W., Physics
DRAKE, J. E., Chemistry and Biochemistry
FACKRELL, H. B., Biological Sciences
FROST, R. A., Computer Science
FRYER, B. J., Earth Sciences
FUNG, K. Y., Mathematics and Statistics
GLASS, E. N., Physics
HAFFNER, G. D., Biological Sciences
HELBING, R. K. B., Physics
HUDEC, P. P., Earth Sciences
JONES, W. E., Chemistry and Biochemistry
KALONI, P. N., Mathematics and Statistics
KENT, R. D., Computer Science
LEMIRE, F. W., Mathematics and Statistics
LOEB, S. J., Chemistry and Biochemistry
LOVETT DOUST, J. N., Biological Sciences
LOVETT DOUST, L., Biological Sciences
MCCONKEY, J. W., Physics
MCDONALD, J. F., Mathematics and Statistics
MCINTOSH, J. M., Chemistry and Biochemistry
MCKENNEY, D. J., Chemistry and Biochemistry
MAEU, R. G., Physics
MUTUS, B., Chemistry and Biochemistry
PAUL, S. R., Mathematics and Statistics
ROSENBAUM, J. N., Nursing
SALE, P. F., Biological Sciences
SIMPSON, F., Earth Sciences
SMITH, T. E., Earth Sciences
SYMONS, D. T. A., Earth Sciences
SZABO, A. G., Chemistry and Biology
TAYLOR, N. F., Chemistry and Biochemistry
THOMAS, B. C., Nursing
THOMAS, D., Biological Sciences
TRACY, D. S., Mathematics and Statistics
TUREK, A., Earth Sciences
VAN WIJNGAARDEN, A., Physics
WARNER, A., Biological Sciences
WONG, C. S., Mathematics and Statistics
ZAMANI, N. G., Mathematics and Statistics

Faculty of Business Administration:

ANDIAPPAN, P.
ANEJA, Y. P.
BART, J.
BRILL, P. H.
CHANDRA, R.
CROCKER, O.
DICKINSON, J. R.
FARIA, A. J.
FIELDS, M.
KANTOR, J.
LAM, W. P.
MORGAN, A.
OKECHUKU, C.
ROSENBAUM, E.
SOLOMON, N. A.
TEMPLER, A.
THACKER, J. W.
WEST, E. N.
WITHANE, S.

Faculty of Education:

AWENDER, M. A.
CRAWFORD, W. J. I.
LAING, D. A.

Faculty of Engineering:

ABDEL-SAYED, G., Civil and Environmental Engineering
AHMADI, M., Electrical Engineering
ALPAS, A. T., Mechanical and Materials Engineering
ASFOUR, A. A., Civil and Environmental Engineering
BEWTRA, J. K., Civil and Environmental Engineering
BISWAS, N., Civil and Environmental Engineering
BUDKOWSKA, B. B., Cultural and Environmental Engineering
DUTTA, S. P., Industrial Engineering and Manufacturing Systems Engineering
EL MARAGHY, H., Industrial Engineering and Manufacturing Systems Engineering
EL MARAGHY, W., Industrial Engineering and Manufacturing Systems Engineering
HACKAM, R., Electrical Engineering
JULLIEN, G. A., Electrical Engineering
KENNEDY, J. B., Civil and Environmental Engineering
KWAN, H. K., Electrical Engineering
LASHKARI, R. S., Industrial Engineering and Manufacturing Systems Engineering
MADUGULA, M. K. S., Civil and Environmental Engineering
MILLER, W. C., Electrical Engineering
NORTH, W., Mechanical and Materials Engineering
RAJU, G. R. G., Electrical Engineering
RANKIN, G. W., Mechanical and Materials Engineering
SID-AHMED, M., Electrical Engineering
SOLTIS, J., Electrical Engineering
TEMPLE, M. C., Civil and Environmental Engineering
WATSON, A., Electrical Engineering
WATT, D. F., Mechanical and Materials Engineering
WILSON, N. W., Mechanical and Materials Engineering

Faculty of Human Kinetics:

BOUCHER, R. L., Athletics and Recreational Studies
MARINO, W., Kinesiology
METCALFE, A., Kinesiology
MORIARTY, R. J., Kinesiology
OLAFSON, G. A., Kinesiology
SALTER, M. A., Kinesiology

Faculty of Law:

BOGART, W. A.
BROWN, R. E.
BUSHNELL, I. S.
CONKLIN, W.
GOLD, N.
IANNI, R. W.
IRISH, M.
MANZIG, J. G.
MARASINGHE, M. L.

MAZER, B. M.
MENEZES, J. R.
MURPHY, P. T.
STEWART, G. R.
WESTMORELAND-TRAORÉ, J.
WILSON, L. C.
WYDRZYNSKI, C. J.

FEDERATED UNIVERSITY

Assumption University: 400 Huron Church Rd, Windsor, Ont.; Pres. Rev. U. E. PARÉ.

AFFILIATED COLLEGES

Canterbury College: 172 Patricia Rd, Windsor, Ont.; Principal D. T. A. SYMONS.

Holy Redeemer College: Cousineau Rd, Windsor, Ont.; Principal Rev. R. CORRIVEAU.

Iona College: Sunset Ave, Windsor, Ont.; Principal Rev. D. G. GALSTON.

ATTACHED INSTITUTES

Fluid Dynamics Research Institute: Dir R. M. BARRON

Great Lakes Institute: Dir G. D. HAFFNER.

UNIVERSITY OF WINNIPEG

515 Portage Ave, Winnipeg, Man. R3B 2E9
Telephone: (204) 786-7811
Fax: 786-8656

Founded 1871; University status 1967
Controlled jointly by the Government of Manitoba and the United Church of Canada
Language of instruction: English
Academic year: September to April

Chancellor: C. SHIELDS
President and Vice-Chancellor: M. P. HANEN
Vice-Presidents: G. LANE (Administration), G. TOMLINSON (Academic)
University Secretary: R. A. KINGSLEY
Director of Registrarial Services: N. LATOCKI
Librarian: W. R. CONVERSE

Number of teachers: 232
Number of students: 6,152

DEANS

Arts and Science: M. N. ZAWOROTKO
Collegiate: M. FOX
Theology: R. L. WHITHEAD
Continuing Education: C. NORDMAN

DEPARTMENT CHAIRMEN

Faculty of Arts and Science:
Anthropology: P. CLARKSON
Biology: R. BOLLMAN
Business Computing/Administrative Studies: S. RAMANNA
Chemistry: A. ABD-EL-AZIZ
Classics: I. MCDOUGALL
Economics: H. GRANT
Education: A. MAYS
English: N. BESNER
French Studies and German Studies: S. VISELLI
Geography: W. F. RANNIE
History: S. MCKINNON
Mathematics: H. HOWLADER
Philosophy: B. KEENAN
Physics: E. TOMCHUK
Political Science: C. WRIGHT
Psychology: H. BRADBURY
Physical Activity and Sport Studies: E. BROWN
Religious Studies: P. DAY
Sociology: S. KIRBY
Statistics: H. HOWLADER
Theatre and Drama: D. ARRELL

PROFESSORS

ABD-EL-AZIZ, Chemistry
ABIZADEH, S., Economics
BAILEY, D. A., History
BASILEVSKY, A., Statistics
BECKER, G., Psychology
BESNER, N., English
BLACKBURN, B. J., Chemistry
BOLLMAN, R., Biology
BRADBURY, H., Psychology
BRASK, P., Theatre and Drama
BROWN, J., History
BROWN, W., Economics
BURBANK, G., History
BURLEY, D., History
BYARD, E., Biology
CARLYLE, W. J., Geography
CARTER, T., Geography
CHAN, F. Y., Business Computing
CHEAL, D. J., Sociology
CHEKKI, D. A., Sociology
CLARK, J., Psychology
CONROY, J. C., Biology
DANIELS, B. C., History
DANNEFAER, S., Physics
DAY, P., Religious Studies
DHRUVARAJAN, V., Sociology
ERBACH, D., Administrative Studies, Business Computing
EVANS, M., English
FEHR, B., Psychology
FRIESEN, K., Chemistry
GHORAYSHI, P., Sociology
GINSBERG, J., Mathematics
GOLDEN, M., Classics
GRANZBERG, G., Anthropology
GREENHILL, P., Women's Studies
HARVEY, C. J., French Studies
HATHOUT, S., Geography
HEWLETT, D., Theatre and Drama
HOFLEY, J. R., Sociology
HOWLADER, H., Statistics
IZYDORCZYK, Z., English
JEWISON, D., English
KERR, D. P., Physics
KHAN, R. A., Political Science
KUNSTATTER, G., Physics
KUZ, T., Geography
KYDON, D. W., Physics
LEHR, J., Geography
LEO, C., Political Science
LOCKERY, A. R., Geography
MCCORMACK, A. R., History
MCCORMACK, R., History
MCDERMOTT, W. J., History
MCDOUGALL, I., Classics
MCINTYRE, M., Psychology
MCKINNON, S., History
MEADWELL, K., French Studies
MEIKLEJOHN, C., Anthropology
MILLS, A., Political Science
MOODIE, G. E. E., Biology
NNADI, J., French Studies
NODELMAN, P. M., English
NORTON, R., Psychology
NOVAK, M., Biology
NOVEK, J., Sociology
PARAMESWARAN, U., English
PEELING, J., Chemistry
PIP, E., Biology
RANNIE, W., Geography
ROCKMAN, G., Psychology
RODRIGUEZ, L., French
SCHAEFER, E., Psychology
SCHULTZ, K., Psychology
SCOTT, G., Geography
SELWOOD, J., Geography
SILVER, J., Political Science
SKENE, R. R., Theatre and Drama
SPIGELMAN, M., Psychology
STANIFORTH, R., Biology
STONE, D. Z., History
STONE, K., English
STRUB, H., Psychology
TOMCHUK, E., Physics
TOMLINSON, G., Chemistry
TOPPER, D. R., History
VISELLI, S., French Studies
WALTON, D. N., Philosophy
WIEGAND, M., Biology
WOODS, R. A., Biology
WRIGHT, C., Political Science
YOUNG, R. J., History

ATTACHED INSTITUTES

Institute of Urban Studies: 515 Portage Ave, Winnipeg; Dir T. CARTER.

Menno Simons College: 515 Portage Ave, Winnipeg; Pres. G. RICHERT.

YORK UNIVERSITY

4700 Keele St, Toronto, Ont. M3J 1P3
Telephone: (416) 736-2100
Telex: 065-24736
Fax: (416) 736-5700

Founded 1959, independent 1965
Public control
Language of instruction: English (Glendon College: English and French)
Academic year: September to December, January to April

Chancellor: A. J. BENNETT
President and Vice-Chancellor: L. R. MARSDEN
Vice-President (University Advancement): G. J. SMITH
Vice-President (Academic Affairs): H. M. STEVENSON
Vice-President (Administration): P. CLARK
Vice-President (Enrolment and Student Services): D. HOBSON
Librarian: ELLEN HOFFMANN

Number of teachers: 1,132 (full-time)
Number of students: 28,856

Publications: *Profiles* (quarterly), *York Gazette* (36 a year), *Student Handbook* (annually), Calendars, College newspapers, faculty newsletters.

DEANS

Schulich School of Business: D. HORVATH
Arts: G. B. FALLIS
Environmental Studies: P. A. VICTOR
Fine Arts: S. FELDMAN
Graduate Studies: D. R. LEYTON-BROWN
Law: P. W. HOGG
Pure and Applied Science: R. H. PRINCE
Education: S. M. SHAPSON
Joseph E. Atkinson College: L. VISANO
Glendon College: D. ADAM (Principal)

PROFESSORS

Schulich School of Business:
BEECHY, T. H., Accounting
BURKE, R. J., Organizational Behaviour/Industrial Relations
BUZACOTT, J., Management Science
COOK, W. D., Management Science
CRAGG, A. W., Business Ethics
CUFF, R., Policy
DERMER, J. D., Policy/Accounting
FENWICK, I. D., Marketing
HEELER, R. M., Marketing
HORVATH, D., Policy
LITVAK, I. A., Policy
MCKELLAR, J., Real Property Development
MCMILLAN, C. J., Policy
MORGAN, G. H., Organizational Behaviour/Industrial Relations
OLIVER, C. E., Organizational Behaviour/Industrial Relations
PETERSON, R., Policy
PRISMAN, E., Finance
ROBERTS, G. S., Finance
ROSEN, L. S., Accounting
SMITHIN, J. N., Economics
THOMPSON, D. N., Marketing
TRYFOS, P., Management Science
WILSON, H. T., Policy
WOLF, B. M., Economics
ZOHAR, U., Economics

Faculty of Arts:
ABRAMSON, M., Mathematics and Statistics
ANISEF, P., Sociology
APPELBAUM, E., Economics
ARMSTRONG, C., History
ARMSTRONG, P., Sociology

AXELROD, P., Social Science
BAYEFSKY, A. F., Political Science
BIALYSTOK, E., Psychology
BIRBALSINGH, F. M., English
BLUM, A. F., Sociology
BOURAOUI, H. A., French Studies
BROWN, M. G., Humanities
BURNS, R. G., Mathematics and Statistics
CARLEY, J., English
CHAMBERS, D., Physical Education
CODE, L. B., Philosophy
COHEN, D., English
COTNAM, J., French Studies
CUFF, R. D., History
DANZIGER, L., Economics
DARROCH, A. G. L., Sociology
DAVIES, D. I., Social Science and Sociology
DAVIS, J. T., Geography
DEWITT, D. B., Political Science
DONNENFELD, S., Economics
DOSMAN, E. J., Political Science
DOW, A. S., Mathematics and Statistics
ELLIS, D., Sociology
EMBLETON, S. M., Languages, Literatures and Linguistics
ENDLER, N. S., Psychology
EVANS, P. M., Political Science
FAAS, E., Humanities
FANCHER, R. E., Psychology
FLAKIERSKI, H., Social Science and Economics
FLETCHER, F. J., Political Science
FLETT, G. L., Psychology
FOWLER, B. H., Physical Education
FREEMAN, D. B., Geography
FROLIC, M. B., Political Science
GEWURTZ, M. P., Humanities
GILL, S., Political Science
GLEDHILL, N., Physical Education
GREEN, B. S., Sociology
GREENBERG, L., Psychology
GREENGLASS, E. R., Psychology
GREER-WOOTTEN, B., Geography
GUIASU, S., Mathematics and Statistics
GUY, G. R., Languages, Literatures and Linguistics
HABERMAN, A., Humanities
HARRIES-JONES, P., Anthropology
HARRIS, L. R., Psychology
HATTIANGADI, J. N., Philosophy
HEIDENREICH, C., Geography
HELLMAN, J., Political Science and Social Science
HELLMAN, S., Political Science
HILL, A. R., Geography
HOBSON, D. W., Humanities
HOFFMAN, R. C., History
HRUSKA, K. C., Mathematics and Statistics
INNES, C., English
IRVINE, W. D., History
JARVIE, I. C., Philosophy
KANYA-FORSTNER, A. S., History
KAPLAN, H., Political Science and Social Science
KATZ, E., Economics
KELLMAN, M. C., Geography
KING, R. E., Languages, Literatures and Linguistics
KLEINER, I., Mathematics and Statistics
KOCHMAN, S. O., Mathematics and Statistics
KOHN, P. M., Psychology
LAFRAMBOISE, J., Mathematics and Statistics
LANDA, J. T., Economics
LANPHIER, C. M., Sociology
LENNOX, J. W., English
LEYTON-BROWN, D., Political Science
LIGHTMAN, B. V., Humanities
LIPSIG-MUMMÉ, C., Social Science
LOVEJOY, P. E., History
MCROBERTS, K. H., Political Science
MADRAS, N. N., Mathematics and Statistics
MAIDMAN, M. P., History
MANN, S. N., History
MARSHALL, J. U., Geography
MASSAM, B. H., Geography
MASSAM, H., Mathematics and Statistics
MOUGEON, R., French Studies
MULDOON, M. E., Mathematics and Statistics
MURDIE, R. A., Geography
MURRAY, A. L., Social Science
NAGATA, J., Anthropology
NELLES, H. V., History
NOBLE, D., Social Science
NORCLIFFE, G. B., Geography
NORTH, L., Political Science
O'BRIEN, G. L., Mathematics and Statistics
OLIN, P., Mathematics and Statistics
OLIVER, P. N., History
ONO, H., Psychology
PANITCH, L., Political Science
PASCUAL-LEONE, J., Psychology
PELLETIER, J. M., Mathematics and Statistics
PEPLER, D. J., Psychology
PLOURDE, C., Economics
POLKA, B., Humanities
POPE, R. W. F., Languages, Literatures and Linguistics
PROMISLOW, S. D., Mathematics and Statistics
PYKE, S., Psychology
REGAN, D. M., Psychology
RENNIE, D. L., Psychology
ROBBINS, S. G., Physical Education
RODMAN, M. C., Anthropology
ROGERS, N. C. T., History
ROGERS, P. K., Mathematics and Statistics
SALISBURY, T., Mathematics and Statistics
SAYWELL, J. T., History
SHUBERT, A., History
SIEGEL, A., Social Science
SILVERMAN, I., Psychology
SILVERMAN, M., Anthropology
SIMMONS, H., Political Science
SIMPSON-HOUSLEY, P., Geography
SMITHIN, J. N., Economics
SOLITAR, D., Mathematics and Statistics
STAGER, P., Psychology
STEPRANS, J., Mathematics and Statistics
STEVENSON, H. M., Political Science
SUBTELNY, O., History and Political Science
TAYLOR, P. A., Mathematics and Statistics
THOLEN, W., Mathematics and Statistics
VAN ESTERIK, P., Anthropology
WAKABAYASHI, B. T., History
WATSON, W. S., Mathematics and Statistics
WHITAKER, R., Political Science
WHITELEY, W. J., Mathematics and Statistics
WONG, M., Mathematics and Statistics
WU, J., Mathematics and Statistics

Faculty of Education:

BUNCH, G.
DUDLEY-MARLING, C.
EWOLDT, C.
HESHUSIUS, L.
ROBBINS, S.
ROGERS, P. K.
SHAPSON, S.

Faculty of Environmental Studies:

BELL, D. V. J.
DALY, G. P.
FENTON, M. B.
FOUND, W. C.
GREER-WOOTTEN, B.
HOMENUCK, H. P. M.
LANG, R. S.
MCQUEEN, D. J.
MURRAY, A. L.
SALTER, L.
SPENCE, E. S.
VICTOR, P. A.
WEKERLE, G. R.
WILKINSON, P. F.

Faculty of Fine Arts:

BIELER, T., Visual Arts
MÉTRAUX, G. P. R., Visual Arts
MORRIS, P., Film and Video
RUBIN, D., Theatre
TENNEY, J., Music
THURLBY, M., Visual Arts
TOMCIK, A., Visual Arts
WHITEN, T., Visual Arts

Osgoode Hall Law School:

ARTHURS, H. W.
BROOKS, W. N.
CASTEL, J.-G.
EVANS, J. M.
GEVA, B.
GRANT, A.
GRAY, R. J. S.
HALÉVY, B. J.
HASSON, R. A.
HATHAWAY, J. C.
HOGG, P. W.
HUTCHINSON, A. C.
MCCAMUS, J. D.
MANDEL, M. G.
MONAHAN, P. J.
MOSSMAN, M. J.
PARKER, G. E.
RAMSAY, I. D.
SALTER, R. L.
VAVER, D.
WATSON, G. D.
WILLIAMS, S. A.
ZEMANS, F. H.

Faculty of Pure and Applied Science:

ALDRIDGE, K. D., Earth and Atmospheric Science
ARJOMANDI, E., Computer Science
BARTEL, N. H., Physics and Astronomy
BOHME, D. K., Chemistry
CAFARELLI, E. D., Physical Education
CALDWELL, J. J., Natural Science, Physics and Astronomy
CANNON, W. H., Physics and Astronomy
CARSWELL, A. I., Natural Science, Physics and Astronomy
COLMAN, B., Biology
COUKELL, M. B., Biology
DAREWYCH, J. W., Physics and Astronomy
DAVEY, K. G., Biology
DE ROBERTIS, M. M., Physics and Astronomy
DYMOND, P. W., Computer Science
FENTON, M. B., Biology and Environmental Science
FILSETH, S. V., Chemistry
FORER, A., Biology
FREEDHOFF, H. S., Physics and Astronomy
GLEDHILL, N., Physical Education
GOODINGS, J. M., Chemistry
HARRIS, G. W., Chemistry
HASTIE, D. R., Chemistry
HEATH, I. B., Biology
HEDDLE, J. A. M., Biology
HOLLOWAY, C. E., Chemistry
HOPKINSON, A. C., Chemistry
HORBATSCH, M., Physics and Astronomy
INNANEN, K. A., Physics and Astronomy
KONIUK, R., Physics and Astronomy
LAFRAMBOISE, J. G., Physics and Astronomy
LEE-RUFF, E., Chemistry
LEVER, A. B. P., Chemistry
LEZNOFF, C. C., Chemistry
LICHT, L. E., Biology and Environmental Science
LIU, J. W. H., Computer Science
LOGAN, D. M., Biology and Natural Science
LOUGHTON, B. G., Biology
MCCALL, M., Physics and Astronomy
MCCONNELL, J. C., Earth and Atmospheric Science
MCQUEEN, D. J., Biology and Environmental Science
MILLER, J. R., Physics and Astronomy
MOENS, P. B., Biology
PEARLMAN, R. E., Biology
PRINCE, R. H., Physics and Astronomy
REGAN, D., Biology
RUDOLPH, J., Chemistry
SALEUDDIN, A. S. M., Biology
SAPP, J. A., Biology
SHEPHERD, G. G., Earth and Atmospheric Science

SIU, K. W. M., Chemistry
SMYLIE, D. E., Earth and Atmospheric Science
SOKOLOWSKI, M. B., Biology
STAUFFER, A. D., Mathematics and Statistics, Physics and Astronomy
STEEL, C. G., Biology
TAYLOR, P. A., Earth and Atmospheric Science
WEBB, R. A., Biology

Atkinson College:

ADELMAN, H., Philosophy
ARTHUR, R. G., Humanities
BARTEL, H., Administrative Studies
BEER, F. F., English
BORDESSA, R., Geography
CALLAGHAN, B., English
COWLES, M. P., Psychology
DRACHE, D., Political Science
DROST, H., Economics
ELLENWOOD, W. R., English
FLEMING, S. J., Psychology
GRAY, P. T., Humanities
GRAYSON, J. P., Sociology
HERREN, M., Classics and Humanities
HOPKINSON, A. C., Science Studies
JARRELL, R. A., Science Studies
KATER, M. H., History
LEVY, J., Nursing
LUXTON, M., Social Science
MAHANEY, W. C., Geography
MALLIN, S. B., Philosophy
OKADA, R., Psychology
PARASKEVOPOULOS, C. C., Economics
SAUL, J. S., Social Science
SHANKER, S. G., Philosophy
STEINBACH, M. J., Psychology
TOURLAKIS, G., Computer Science and Mathematics
UNRAU, J. P., English
WEISS, A. I., Computer Science and Mathematics
WILSON, B. A., Humanities
WOOD, J. D., Geography

Glendon College:

ABELLA, I. M., History
ALCOCK, J., Psychology
BAUDOT, A., French Studies
COHEN, R. L., Psychology
CUMMINGS, M. J., English
DOOB, P. B., English
ESCOBAR, J., Hispanic Studies
FICHMAN, M., Multidisciplinary Studies
GENTLES, I. J., History
HORN, M. S. D., History
KIRSCHBAUM, S. J., Political Science
KLEIN-LATAUD, C., Translation
MAHANT, E., Political Science
MORRIS, R. N., Sociology
OLSHEN, B. N., English and Multidisciplinary Studies
ONDAATJE, P. M., English
SHAND, G. B., English
TATILON, C., French Studies
TWEYMAN, S., Philosophy
WALLACE, R. S., English
WHITFIELD, A., Translation

ATTACHED INSTITUTES

Centre for Atmospheric Chemistry: 006 Steacie Science, York University, 4700 Keele St, Toronto, Ont. M3J 1P3; Dir G. W. HARRIS.

Centre for International and Security Studies: 375 York Lanes, York University, 4700 Keele St, Toronto, Ont. M3J 1P3; Dir D. B. DEWITT.

Centre for Feminist Research: 228 York Lanes, York University, 4700 Keele St, Toronto, Ont. M3J 1P3; Dir N. MANDELL.

Canadian Centre for German and European Studies: 230 York Lanes, York University, 4700 Keele St, Toronto, Ont. M3J 1P3; Dir M. WEBBER.

Centre for Jewish Studies: 250 Vanier College, York University, 4700 Keele St, Toronto, Ont. M3J 1P3; Dir M. G. BROWN.

Centre for Health Studies: 214 York Lanes, York University, Toronto, Ont. M3J 1P3; Dir G. FELDBERG.

Centre for Refugee Studies: 322 York Lanes, York University, 4700 Keele St, Toronto, Ont. M3J 1P3; Dir A. F. BAYEFSKY.

Centre for Research in Earth and Space Science: 249 Petrie Science Building, York University, 4700 Keele St, Toronto, Ont. M3J 1P3; Dir G. SHEPHERD.

Centre for Research in Earth and Space Technology: 4850 Keele St, Toronto, Ont. M3J 3K1; Pres. and CEO I. H. ROWE.

Centre for Research on Latin America and the Caribbean: 240 York Lanes, York University, Toronto, Ont. M3J 1P3; Dir R. GRINSPUN.

Centre for Public Law and Public Policy: 435 Osgoode, York University, 4700 Keele St, Toronto, Ont. M3J 1P3; Dir P. J. MONAHAN.

Centre for Research on Work and Society: 276 York Lanes, York University, Toronto, Ont. M3J 1P3; Dir C. LIPSIG-MUMMÉ.

Centre for the Study of Computers in Education: S817 Ross, York University, 4700 Keele St, Toronto, Ont. M3J 1P3; Dir R. D. OWSTON.

LaMarsh Centre for Research on Violence and Conflict Resolution: 217 York Lanes, York University, 4700 Keele St, Toronto, Ont. M3J 1P3; Dir D. J. PEPLER.

Robarts Centre for Canadian Studies: 227 York Lanes, York University, 4700 Keele St, Toronto, Ont. M3J 1P3; Dir D. DRACHE.

York Institute for Social Research: 242A Schulich School of Business, York University, 4700 Keele St, Toronto, Ont. M3J 1P3; Dir J. P. GRAYSON.

Innovation York: 124 Farquarson, York University, 4700 Keele St, Toronto, Ont. M3J 1P3; Dir M. B. FENTON.

Joint Centre for Asia Pacific Studies: 270K York Lanes, York University, 4700 Keele St, Toronto, Ont. M3J 1P3; Dir B. FROLIC.

Centre for Practical Ethics: 102 McLaughlin, York University, 4700 Keele St, Toronto, Ont. M3J 1P3; Dir C. D. MACNIVEN.

Centre for Vision Research: 103 Farquharson, York University, 4700 Keele St, Toronto, Ont. M3J 1P3; Dir. I. HOWARD.

Centre for Applied Sustainability: 355 Lumbers, York University, 4700 Keele St, Toronto, Ont. M3J 1P3; Dir. D. BELL.

Nathanson Centre for the Study of Organized Crime and Corruption: 321A Osgoode, York University, 4700 Keele St, Toronto, Ont. M3J 1P3; Dir M. BEARE.

Schools of Art and Music

Alberta College of Art and Design: 1407 14th Ave NW, Calgary, Alta T2N 4R3; tel. (403) 284-7600; fax (403) 289-6682; e-mail arthur.greenblatt@acad.ab.ca; f. 1926; 100 teachers, 750 students; library of 22,000 vols and collection of 97,331 slides, 83 periodical titles; 4-year Degree and Diploma programmes in Visual Arts and Design; Pres. ARTHUR E. GREENBLATT.

Banff Centre: POB 1020, Banff, Alta T0L 0C0; tel. (403) 762-6100; fax (403) 762-6444; f. 1933; comprises the Centre for the Arts (programmes at advanced and professional levels in music, theatre arts, aboriginal arts, theatre crafts and design, writing and publishing, media and visual arts), the Centre for Management (intensive courses for leaders in business, government, aboriginal, environment, arts management and non-profit communities, the Centre for Mountain Culture, and the Centre for Conferences; Pres. and CEO Dr GRAEME D. MCDONALD.

Conservatoire de Musique de Montréal: 100 est rue Notre-Dame, Montréal, Qué. H2Y 1C1; f. 1942; tel. (514) 873-4031; fax (514) 873-4601; a government-controlled institution, largest of a network of seven in Quebec Province; 76 teachers, 340 students; library of 58,000 books and scores, 125 rare books, 20 MSS., 10,000 recordings and 80 periodicals; Dir ALBERT GRENIER.

Conservatoire de Musique de Québec: 270 rue St-Amable, Québec, Qué. G1R 5G1; tel. (418) 643-2190; fax (418) 644-9658; e-mail cmq@mcc.gouv.qc.ca; f. 1944; 50 teachers, 250 students; library of 68,000 vols, recordings, scores and periodicals; Dir GUY CARMICHAEL (acting).

Maritime Conservatory of Music: 6199 Chebucto Rd, Halifax, NS B3L 1K7; f. 1887; Dir Dr JACK BROWNELL.

Ontario College of Art: 100 McCaul St, Toronto, Ont. M5T 1W1; tel. (416) 977-6000; fax (416) 977-6006; f. 1876; library of 24,000 print vols, 225 periodical subscriptions, 44,000 pictures, 70,000 slides, etc.; post-secondary education in fine art and design; 250 teachers; 1,500 full-time students, 3,000 part-time; Pres. CATHERINE HENDERSON.

Royal Canadian College of Organists: 112 St Clair Ave W, Suite 302, Toronto, Ont. M4V 2Y3; tel. (416) 929-6400; fax (416) 929-0415; e-mail rcco@the-wire.com; f. 1909; Exec. Dir PETER NIKIFORUK; publ. *The American Organist* (in asscn with American Guild of Organists).

Royal Conservatory of Music: 273 Bloor St West, Toronto Ont. M5S 1W2; tel. (416) 408-2824; fax (416) 408-3096; f. 1886; 350 teachers, 10,000 students; Pres. PETER C. SIMON.

CENTRAL AFRICAN REPUBLIC

Research Institutes

GENERAL

Institut Français de Recherche Scientifique pour le Développement en Coopération (ORSTOM): BP 893, Bangui; tel. (236) 61-20-89; telex 5217; fax (236) 61-68-29; f. 1949; soil science, geophysics, geology, medical entomology; library of 9,000 vols; Dir C. CENSIER. (See main entry under France.)

AGRICULTURE, FISHERIES AND VETERINARY SCIENCE

Centre d'Etudes sur la Trypanosomiase Animale: BP 39, Bouar; stations at Bewiti, Sarki; annexe at Bambari.

Institut de Recherches Agronomiques de Boukoko (Agricultural Research Institute): BP 44, M'Baiki, Boukoko; f. 1948; research into tropical agriculture and plant diseases, fertilization and entomology; library of 2,740 vols; Dir M. GONDJIA.

Institut d'Etudes Agronomiques d'Afrique Centrale: Ecole Nationale des Adjoints Techniques d'Agriculture de Wakombo, BP 78, M'Baiki; Dir R. ELIARD.

ECONOMICS, LAW AND POLITICS

Département des études de population à l'Union Douanière et Economique de l'Afrique Centrale: BP 1418, Bangui; tel. 61-45-77; telex 5254; f. 1964; Dir JEAN NKOUNKOU.

MEDICINE

Institut Pasteur: BP 923, Bangui; tel. 61-45-76; fax 61-01-09; e-mail morvan@intnet.cf; f. 1961; research on viral haemorrhagic fevers, polio virus, tuberculosis, AIDS and simian retroviruses; WHO Regional Centre for poliomyelitis in Africa; Dir Dr J. M. MORVAN; publ. *Rapport Annuel*.

RELIGION, SOCIOLOGY AND ANTHROPOLOGY

Mission sociologique du Haut-Oubangui: BP 68, Bangassou; f. 1954; sociological and archaeological study of societies and cultures from the CAR, especially from the Gbaya, Nzakara and Zandé countries; historical maps and sociological documents; Head Prof. E. DE DAMPIERRE; publ. *Recherches oubanguiennes*.

TECHNOLOGY

Institut National de Recherches Textiles et Cultures Vivrières: BP 17, Bambari; Dir GABRIEL RAMADHANE-SAÏD.

Station Expérimentale de la Maboké: par M'Baiki; f. 1963 under the direction of the Muséum National d'Histoire Naturelle, Paris; studies in the protection of materials in tropical regions, mycology, entomology, virology, zoology, botany, anthropology, parasitology, protection of natural resources; Dir ROGER HEIM.

Libraries and Archives

Bangui

Bibliothèque Universitaire de Bangui: BP 1450, Bangui; tel. 61-20-00; telex 5283; f. 1980; 26,000 vols, 600 periodicals (Central Library); 9,144 vols (École Normale Supérieure); 5,240 vols, 168 periodicals (Faculty of Health Sciences); Dir JOSEPH GOMA-BOUANGA.

University

UNIVERSITÉ DE BANGUI

Avenue des Martyrs, BP 1450, Bangui
Telephone: 61-20-00
Telex: 5283
Fax: 61-78-90
Founded 1969
Language of instruction: French
Academic year: October to June
Rector: MAMADOU-NESTOR NALI
Vice-Rector: GASTON-MANDATA NGUEREKATA
Secretary-General: GABRIEL NGOUAMENE
Librarian: JOSEPH NGOMA-BOUANGA
Library: See Libraries
Number of teachers: 154
Number of students: 4,492

Publications: *Annales de l'Université de Bangui Wambesso, Revue d'Histoire et d'Archéologie Centrafricaine, Espace francophone.*

DEANS

Faculty of Letters and Humanities: GABRIEL NGOUANDJI-TANGA
Faculty of Law and Economics: DAMIENNE NANARE
Faculty of Science and Technology: Lic. MABOUA BARA
Faculty of Health Science: Prof. MAMADOU NESTOR NALI

DIRECTORS

Dept of Mathematics and Computer Studies: DANIEL SEGALEN
University Institute of Business Administration: MICHEL CREPON
Polytechnic Institute: JEAN BIANDJA
University Institute of Rural Development: GEORGES NGONDJO
Institute of Applied Language Studies: FRANÇOIS LIM
University Institute for Research in Mathematics Teaching: JOSEPH DENAMGANAI

Colleges

Ecole Centrale d'Agriculture: Boukoko.

Ecole Nationale des Arts: BP 349, Bangui; f. 1966; music, dance, dramatic art and plastic arts.

Ecole Territoriale d'Agriculture: Grimari.

CHAD

Research Institutes

AGRICULTURE, FISHERIES AND VETERINARY SCIENCE

Institut de Recherches du Coton et des Textiles Exotiques (IRCT): BP 764, N'Djamena; f. 1939; cotton research (entomology, agronomy and genetics); Head of station at Bebedja M. RENOU; Regional Dir M. YEHOUESSI. (See main entry under France.)

Laboratoire de Recherches Vétérinaires et Zootechniques de Farcha: BP 433, N'Djamena; tel. 52-74-75; telex 5248; fax 52-83-02; f. 1952; veterinary and stockbreeding research and production of vaccines; library of 3,500 vols; Dir Dr IDRISS ALFAROUKH; publ. *Rapport annuel.*

EDUCATION

Centre de Recherche, des Archives et de Documentation, Commission nationale pour l'UNESCO: BP 731, N'Djamena; Sec.-Gen. Dr KHALIL ALIO; publ. *COMNAT: Bulletin d' Information.*

RELIGION, SOCIOLOGY AND ANTHROPOLOGY

Institut National des Sciences Humaines: BP 1117, N'Djamena; tel. 51-62-68; f. 1961; palaeontology, prehistory, proto-history, linguistics, sociolinguistics, history, ethno-sociology, sociology, anthropology, geography, social sciences, oral traditions; 6 researchers; library of 1,000 vols and 400 archive documents; Dir MOUKTHAR DJIBRINE MAHAMAT; Gen. Sec. DJONG-YANG OÜANLARBO; publ. *Revue de Tchad.*

Museums and Art Galleries

N'Djamena

Musée National: BP 503, N'Djamena; tel. 36-86; f. 1963; attached to Institut National des Sciences Humaines (see above); *c.* 100 collections; in process of re-formation after the war; depts of palaeontology, prehistory and archaeology, ethnography, scientific archives; Dir DJAMIL MOUSSA NENE.

University

UNIVERSITÉ DE N'DJAMENA

BP 1117, N'Djamena
Telephone: 51-44-44
Fax: 51-40-33

Founded 1971

State control

Languages of instruction: French, Arabic

Academic year: October to June

Rector: ISSAYA ZOZABE
Vice-Rector: ALIO KHALIL
Secretary-General: ADOUM DOUTOUM MAHAMAT
Librarian: DOUMTANGAR KOULASSIM

Library of 12,000 vols
Number of teachers: 131
Number of students: 3,198

Publication: *Annuaire.*

DEANS

Faculty of Letters and Human Sciences: ALI MOUSTAPHA MAHAMAT
Faculty of Exact and Applied Sciences: YAYA MAHMOUT
Faculty of Law and Economics: MANDIGUI YOKABDJIM
Faculty of Health Sciences: Dean DOUPHANG-PHANG IVOULSOU

Colleges

Ecole Nationale d'Administration: BP 768, N'Djamena; f. 1963; set up by the Government and controlled by an Administrative Council to train students as public servants; Dir N. GUELINA.

Ecole Nationale des Télécommunications: Sarh.

CHILE

Learned Societies

GENERAL

Instituto de Chile: Almirante Montt 453, Clasificador 1349, Correo Central, 6500445 Santiago; tel. (2) 6382847; f. 1964; promotes cultural, humanistic and scientific studies; Pres. CARLOS RIESCO GREZ; Gen. Sec. ANTONIO DOUGNAC; publ. *Anales*.

Constituent academies:

Academia Chilena de la Lengua (Chilean Academy of Language): Clasificador 1349, Correo Central, Santiago; tel. (2) 382847; f. 1885; fmrly Academia Chilena; corresp. mem. of the Real Academia Española, Madrid; 36 mems; Dir ALFREDO MATUS OLIVIER; Sec. JOSÉ LUIS SAMANIEGO ALDAZÁBAL; publ. *Boletín de la Academia Chilena*.

Academia Chilena de la Historia (Chilean Academy of History): Almirante Montt 454, Santiago; tel. and fax (2) 6399323; f. 1933; 36 mems; library of 2,500 vols; Pres. JAVIER GONZÁLEZ ECHENIQUE; publs *Boletín de la Academia, Archivo de D. Bernardo O'Higgins*.

Academia Chilena de Ciencias (Chilean Academy of Sciences): Clasificador 1349, Correo Central, Santiago; tel. 6382847; fax 6332129; f. 1964; 36 Academicians, 21 corresp., 5 hon. Academicians; promotes research in pure and applied sciences; Pres. Dr JORGE E. ALLENDE; Sec. Dr JOSE CORVALÁN DÍAZ; publs *Boletín* (irregular), *Figuras señeras de la Ciencia en Chile* (irregular).

Academia Chilena de Ciencias Sociales, Políticas y Morales (Chilean Academy of Social, Political and Moral Sciences): Clasificador 1349, Correo Central, Santiago; tel. 382847; f. 1964; 36 mems; library of 7,000 vols; Pres. JUAN DE DIOS VIAL LARRAIN; Sec. HERNÁN GODOY URZÚA; publs *Boletín* (3 a year), *Anales* (annually), *Folletos*.

Academia Chilena de Medicina (Chilean Academy of Medicine): Almirante Montt 453, 6500445 Santiago; tel. (2) 6331902; fax (2) 6640775; f. 1964; 75 Academicians, 45 hon. foreign mems; library of 900 vols; Pres. Dr JAIME PÉREZ-OLEA; Sec. Dra SYLVIA SEGOVIA POLLA; publs *Boletín, Proceedings on the Chilean History of Medicine*, monographs, annuals.

Academia Chilena de Bellas Artes (Chilean Academy of Fine Arts): Clasificador 1349, Correo Central, 6500445 Santiago; tel. (2) 6331902; fax (2) 6337460; f. 1964; 31 Academicians, 10 corresp. mems, 3 hon. mems; Pres. CARLOS RIESCO GREZ; Sec. ALEJANDRO SIEVEKING; publ. *Boletín*.

AGRICULTURE, FISHERIES AND VETERINARY SCIENCE

Colegio de Ingenieros Forestales: San Isidro 22, Of. No. 503 Casilla 9686, Santiago; tel. 393289; f. 1972; 350 mems; Pres. JORGE I. CORREA DRUBI; Sec. LEONARDO ARAYA VALDEBENITO; publs *Actas de las Jornadas Forestales* (2 a year), *Renarres* (every 2 months).

Sociedad Agronómica de Chile (Agronomical Society of Chile): Casilla 4109, Calle Mac-Iver 120, Of. 36, Santiago; tel. 384881; f. 1910; 1,900 mems; library of 1,600 vols; Pres. Dr L. ANTONIO LIZANA M.; Sec. HECTOR E. NÚÑEZ; publ. *Simiente* (3 a year).

Sociedad Chilena de Producción Animal: Santa Rosa No. 11735, Casilla 2, Correo 15, La Granja, Santiago; tel. 5587042, ext. 307; f. 1979; 115 mems; Pres. Dr ALEJANDRO LÓPEZ V.; Sec./Treas. Dra MARÍA SOL MORALES S.

Sociedad de Medicina Veterinaria de Chile (Chilean Veterinary Society): Avda Italia 1045, Casilla 13384, Correo 21, Santiago; tel. (2) 2093471; fax (2) 3415408; f. 1926; 152 mems; Pres. Dr LAUTARO GOMEZ RAMOS; Sec.-Gen. Dr RODERIGO PALACIOS MORAGA; publ. *Boletín*.

Sociedad Nacional de Agricultura (National Society of Agriculture): Casilla 40-D, Tenderini 187, Santiago; tel. (2) 6396710; fax (2) 6337771; e-mail gusrojas@eutelchile.net; f. 1838; library of 3,500 vols; research in agricultural, social and economic problems; controls a plant genetics experimental station and a broadcasting chain with stations in several cities; register of pedigree cattle kept; technical assistance to farmers; annual international and agricultural show since 1869, and home show since 1980; Pres. RICARDO ARIZTÍA; Sec. LUIS QUIROGA; publs *Revista El Campesino, Boletín Económico y de Mercado, Vocero Agrícola, Informatoivo Frutícola, SNAFAX News*.

ARCHITECTURE AND TOWN PLANNING

Colegio de Arquitectos de Chile (Chilean College of Architects): Avda Libertador Bernardo O'Higgins 115, Casilla 13377, Santiago; tel. (2) 6398744; fax (2) 6398769; e-mail colegio@colegio-arquitectos.cl; f. 1942 for all Chilean and foreign architects working in Chile; 5,500 mems; library of 2,000 vols, 2,500 journals; Pres. RENÉ MORALES MORALES; Gen. Man. ERICO LUEBERT CID; publs *Revista CA* (quarterly), *Boletín* (monthly), *Bienal de Arquitectura* (every 2 years), *Congreso Nacional de Arquitectos* (every 2 years).

BIBLIOGRAPHY, LIBRARY SCIENCE AND MUSEOLOGY

Colegio de Bibliotecarios de Chile, AG: Diagonal Paraguay 383, Depto 122, Torre 11, Santiago; tel. 2225652; f. 1969; 1,439 mems; Pres. ESMERELDA RAMOS RAMOS; Sec. MÓNICA NÚÑEZ N.; publs *Micronoticias* (every 2 months), *Indice de Publicaciones Periódicas en Bibliotecología* (quarterly), *Documento de Trabajo* (annually).

Sociedad de Bibliófilos Chilenos (Society of Chilean Bibliophiles): Casilla 895, Santiago; f. 1945; Pres. ALAMIRO DE AVILA; Sec. RAMÓN EYZAGUIRRE; 100 mems; publ. *El Bibliófilo Chileno* (annual).

ECONOMICS, LAW AND POLITICS

Servicio Médico Legal (Forensic Medicine Service): Avda La Paz 1012, Santiago; tel. 7371268; fax 7371323; f. 1915; advises tribunals on forensic medicine; 305 mems; library of 800 vols; Dir Dr MARCO ANTONIO MEDINA MOLINA; publs *Monografías Servicio Médico Legal* (3 a year), *Revista de Medicina Legal* (3 a year).

EDUCATION

Asociación de Psicólogos Infanto-Juveniles: Bustamante 30, Dpto 21, Santiago; Pres. SOFIA LECAROS; Sec. GABRIELA SEPÚLVEDA.

Consejo de Rectores de Universidades Chilenas (Council of Rectors of Chilean Universities): Moneda 673, 8° piso, Casilla 14798, Santiago; tel. 39-7415; f. 1954; study of higher education problems, university information and co-ordination; Pres. AGUSTÍN TORO DÁVILLA; Gen. Sec. HUGO ARANEDA DORR; publs *Documentos, Cuadernos, Boletines Informativos*.

Oficina Regional de Educación de la Unesco para América Latina y el Caribe/ Santiago Unesco Regional Office for Education in Latin America and the Caribbean: POB 3187, Enrique Delpiano 2058, Providencia, Casilla 3187, Santiago; tel. 204-9032; telex 340258; fax 2091875; f. 1963; library and documentation centre; provides technical assistance to regional member states in preparation and implementation of educational plans; trains teachers and specialists in education and administration; organizes a conference of Ministers of Education of the region; 40 mems; library of 30,000 vols; Dir ANA LUIZA MADRADO PINHEIRO; publs *Boletín del Proyecto Principal, Contacto, Inovación* (all quarterly).

FINE AND PERFORMING ARTS

Asociación Plástica Latina Internacional de Chile (APLICH) (Chilean International Plastic Arts Association): Av. P. de Valdivia 1781, Casilla 177, Correo 29, Santiago; tel. and fax 2233444; f. 1990; Pres. ALICIA ARGANDOÑA R.; Sec.-Gen. SERGIO FUZAM NUMAN.; publ. *APLICH al Día*.

HISTORY, GEOGRAPHY AND ARCHAEOLOGY

Instituto Geográfico Militar (Military Geographical Institute): Nueva Santa Isabel 1640, Santiago; tel. (2) 6968221; fax (2) 6988278; e-mail igm@reuna.cl; f. 1922; 400 mems; library of 3,500 vols, 25,000 maps; Dir Bgr SERGIO MATEU MARTÍNEZ-CONDE; publ. *Revista Terra Australis* (annually).

Sociedad Chilena de Historia y Geografía (Chilean Society of History and Geography): Casilla 1386, Santiago; tel. 6382489; f. 1911; 304 mems, 13 hon., 70 corresponding; library of 12,600 vols; Pres. SERGIO MARTÍNEZ BAEZA; Sec.-Gen. RENE ARTIGAS MOREIRA; publs *Revista Chilena de Historia y Geografía*, related works.

LANGUAGE AND LITERATURE

Sociedad Chilena de Lingüística (Chilean Linguistics Society): La Verbena 3882, (Providencia) Santiago; f. 1971; over 100 mems; Pres. AMBROSIO RABANALES; Sec. MARIO BERNALES; publ. *Actas*.

MEDICINE

Colegio de Químico-Farmacéuticos de Chile (College of Pharmacists): Casilla 1136, Santiago; tel. 392505; f. 1942; 2,500 regional councils in 12 main towns; Pres. ANTONIO MORRIS; publ. *Revista*.

Sociedad Chilena de Cancerología: Fundación Arturo López Pérez, Rancagua 878, Santiago; tel. (2) 2047919 ext. 304; fax (2) 2280705;

f. 1964; 142 mems; Pres. José Manuel Ojeda; Sec. Jorge Gallardo; publ. *Revista Chilena de Cancerología* (3 a year).

Sociedad Chilena de Cardiología y Cirugía Cardiovascular: Esmeralda 678, 3° piso, Casilla 23-D, Santiago; tel. 30705; f. 1949; Pres. Dr Carlos Akel A.; Sec. Dr Jorge Carabantes C.; publ. *Revista*.

Sociedad Chilena de Citología: Casilla 10-D, Correo 13, San Miguel, Santiago; tel. 492247; f. 1970; 103 mems; Pres. Dr Ramón Gonzalez Munizaga; Sec.-Gen. Dr Eduardo Morales Barria; publ. *Cito-Notícias* (quarterly).

Sociedad Chilena de Dermatología y Venereología: Depto Dermatología, Hosp. J. J. Aguirre, Santos Dumont 999, Santiago; tel. 779484; f. 1938; Pres. Dra Julia Quiroz M.; Exec. Sec. Dra María Maira P.

Sociedad Chilena de Endocrinología y Metabolismo: Casilla 166, Correo 55, Santiago; tel. and fax (2) 3412909; f. 1961; Pres. Dr Juan Donoso; Sec.-Gen. Dr Nestor Soto.

Sociedad Chilena de Enfermedades Respiratorias: Bernarda Morín 488, Providencia, Santiago; tel. 2691742; fax 2238946; e-mail ser@ctcreuna.cl; f. 1930; 410 mems; Pres. Dr Juan Carlos Rodriguez D.; Sec. Dra Carmen Velasco P.; publs *Revista Chilena de Enfermedades Respiratorias* (4 a year), *Boletín Informativo* (monthly).

Sociedad Chilena de Gastroenterología: Casilla 166, Correo 55, Santiago; tel. (2) 3413106; fax (2) 3413836; f. 1938; Pres. Dr Roque Saenz F.; publ. *Normas de Diagnóstico en Enfermedades Digestivas* (every 2 years).

Sociedad Chilena de Gerontología (Chilean Gerontological Society): Avda Bulnes 377, Dpto 605, Santiago; tel. 6967176; f. 1961; 60 mems; library of 300 vols; Pres. Dr José Fromovich S.; Sec. Dr Víctor Acle.

Sociedad Chilena de Hematología: Clasificador 1, Correo 27, Santiago; tel. 2243175; f. 1943; 90 mems; Pres. Dr Diego Mezzano A.; Dr Jaime Pereira G.

Sociedad Chilena de Inmunología: Casilla 70061, Santiago 7; tel. 370081; f. 1972; 55 active mems; Pres. Dra Alicia Ramos; Sec. Dra Cecilia Sepúlveda.

Sociedad Chilena de Neurocirugía: Casilla 3717, Santiago; tel. 2237109; Pres. Dr Jorge Méndez S.; Sec.-Gen./Treas. Dr Enrique Colin B.

Sociedad Chilena de Obstetricia y Ginecología: Román Díaz 205, Oficina 205, Providencia, Santiago; tel. (2) 2350133; fax (2) 2351294; f. 1935; Pres. Dr Alfredo Saumann B.; Sec. Dra Mercedes Ruiz F.; publ. *Revista Chilena de Obstetricia y Ginecología*.

Sociedad Chilena de Oftalmología: Casilla 16197, Correo 9, Providencia, Santiago; tel. (2) 3410765; fax (2) 2096146; f. 1931; 390 mems; library of 1,300 vols; special collection of cassettes and video tapes; Pres. Dr Ricardo Colvin T.; Sec. Dr Juan Stoppel O.; publ. *Archivos Chilenos de Oftalmología* (2 a year).

Sociedad Chilena de Ortopedia y Traumatología: Jofré 039, Dpto 41, Casilla 117, Correo 22, Santiago; tel. (2) 2227233; fax (2) 2227233; e-mail schot@mail.bellsouth.cl; f. 1949; 508 mems; library of 500 vols; Pres. Dr Eduardo Zamudio; Sec.-Gen. Dr Ignacio Dockendorff B.; publ. *Revista Chilena de Ortopedia y Traumatología* (quarterly).

Sociedad Chilena de Parasitología: Condell 303, Casilla 50470, Santiago 1; tel. (2) 6785532; fax (2) 5416840; f. 1964; 150 mems; Pres. Dra Texia Gorman; Sec. Miryam Lorca; publ. *Parasitologia al Dia*.

Sociedad Chilena de Pediatría: Avda Eliodoro Yáñez 1984, Dpto 405, Casilla 16257, Correo 9, Santiago; tel. (2) 2254393; fax (2) 2232351; e-mail sochipe@reuna.cl; f. 1922; 1,230 mems; Pres. Dr Juan José Latorre; Sec.-Gen. Dra Carmen Larrañaga; publ. *Revista Chilena de Pediatría* (every 2 months).

Sociedad Chilena de Reumatología: Casilla 23-D, Santiago; f. 1950; Pres. Dr Gonzalo Astorga P.; Sec. Dr Alberto Valdés S.; publ. *Boletín* (quarterly).

Sociedad de Cirujanos de Chile (Chilean Society of Surgeons): Román Díaz 205, Of. 401, Casilla 2843, Santiago; tel. 2362831; fax 2351741; f. 1949; 640 mems; Pres. Dr Attila Csendes J.; Sec.-Gen. Dr Carlos Azolas S.; publ. *Revista Chilena de Cirugía* (every 2 months).

Sociedad de Farmacología de Chile: Casilla 70.000, Santiago 7; tel. (2) 6786050; fax (2) 7774216; f. 1979; 88 mems; Pres. Dra Lutske Tampier; Sec. Dra Teresa Pelissier

Sociedad de Neurología, Psiquiatría y Neurocirugía de Chile: Calle Carlos Silva V 1292, Plaza Las Lilas, Providencia, Casilla 3757, Correo 21, Santiago; tel. (2) 2329347; fax (2) 2319287; f. 1932; Pres. Dr César Ojeda F.; Dir Fredy Holzer M.; publ. *Revista Chilena de Neuropsiquiatría* (quarterly).

Sociedad de Ortodoncia de Chile (Society of Dentistry): Casilla 9895, Santiago; f. 1942; 200 mems; Pres. Dr Jorge Pavic M.; Sec.-Gen. Dr Alejandro Illanes V.; publ. *Revista Chilena de Ortodoncia* (2 a year).

Sociedad Médica de Concepción (Medical Society): Casilla 60-C, Concepción; f. 1886; Pres. Dr Enrique Bellolioz; publ. *Anales Médicos de Concepción*.

Sociedad Médica de Santiago (Santiago Medical Society): Casilla 168, Correo 55, Santiago; tel. 2748985; fax 3413068; f. 1869; library of 100 periodical titles; 1,500 mems; Pres. Dr Hernán Iturriaga; Sec. Dr Jaime Valenzuela; publ. *Revista Médica de Chile* (monthly).

Sociedad Médica de Valparaíso (Medical Society of Valparaíso): Hontaneda 2653, Valparaíso; f. 1913; 271 mems; library of 3,500 vols; Pres. Dr Arturo Villagran Valdes; Sec. Dr Manuel Barros; publ. *Revista Médica de Valparaíso* (quarterly).

Sociedad Odontológica de Concepción: Casilla 2107, Concepción; f. 1924; 300 mems; Pres. Dr Eduardo Navarete; Sec. Dr Sergio Esquerré S.; publ. *Anuario*.

NATURAL SCIENCES

General

Academia Chilena de Ciencias Naturales (Chilean Academy of Natural Sciences): Medinacelli 1233, Santiago; f. 1926; Pres. Dr Hugo Gunckel L.; Sec. Hans Niemeyer F.; publ. *Anales*.

Asociación Científica y Técnica de Chile (Scientific and Technical Association of Chile): Carlos Antúnez 1885, Dpto 205, Casilla 10332, Santiago; f. 1965; Pres. Héctor Cathalifaud Argandoña; Sec.-Gen. Elena Torres Seguel.

Corporación para el Desarrollo de la Ciencia: Marcoleta 250, Casilla 10332, Santiago; f. 1978; Pres. Fernando Díaz A.; Sec. Gen. Héctor Cathalifaud A.; publ. *Revista CODECI*.

Sociedad Científica Chilena 'Claudio Gay' (Chilean Scientific Society): Casilla 2974, Santiago; tel. (2) 7455066; fax (2) 7455176; f. 1955; 45 mems; library of 5,000 vols; Dir Alfredo Ugarte.

Biological Sciences

Asociación Chilena de Microbiología: Casilla 59, Correo 22, Santiago; tel. (2) 2093503; fax (2) 2258427; f. 1964; 194 mems; Pres. Dr Eugenio Spencer; Sec. Dr Matilde Jashes; publ. *Acta Microbiológica* (2 a year).

Sociedad Chilena de Entomología (Entomological Society): POB 21132, Santiago 21; f. 1922; 150 mems; library of *c.* 4,000 periodicals; Pres. Dr Ernesto Prado C.; Sec. Lic. Eduardo Fuentes C.; publ. *Revista Chilena de Entomología* (annually).

Sociedad de Biología de Chile: Casilla 16164, Santiago 9; f. 1928; 565 mems; Pres. A. Cecilia Hidalgo T.; Sec. Dr Miguel Bronfman A.; publs *Biological Research*, *Revista Chilena de Historia Natural*.

Sociedad de Genética de Chile: Casilla 70061, Correo 7, Santiago; tel. (2) 6786454; f. 1964; 100 mems; Pres. Dra Patricia Iturra; Sec.-Gen. Dr Raúl Godoy-Herrera; publs *Biological Research*, *Revista Chilena de Historia Natural*.

Sociedad de Vida Silvestre de Chile (Chilean Wildlife Society): Casilla 1705, Temuco; tel. 210773, ext. 310; f. 1975; 300 mems; Pres. Darcy Rios Leal; Sec.-Gen. Enrique Hauenstein Barra; publs *Boletín de Vida Silvestre* (annually), *Enlace* (quarterly).

Mathematical Sciences

Sociedad de Matemática de Chile: Casilla 653, Santiago; tel. and fax 2713882; f. 1976; 250 mems; Pres. Patricio Felmer; Sec. Oscar Barriga; publs *Gaceta*, *Notas*, *Revista del Profesor de Matemáticas*.

Physical Sciences

Asociación Chilena de Astronomía y Astronáutica: Casilla 3904, Santiago 1; tel. 6327556; f. 1957; union of amateur astronomers; arranges courses and lectures; astronomy, astrophotography, telescope making; owns the observatory of Mt Pochoco, near Santiago; 350 mems; library of 1,000 vols; Pres. Gabriel Rodriguez Jaque; Sec. Elías Ruiz; publ. *Boletín ACHAYA* (monthly).

Asociación Chilena de Sismología e Ingeniería Antisísmica (Chilean Association of Seismology and Earthquake Engineering): Casilla 2796, Santiago; f. 1963; Pres. Dr Patricio Ruiz.

Comisión Chilena de Energía Nuclear: Amunátegui 95, Casilla 188-D, Santiago; tel. 6990070; fax 6991618; e-mail gtorres@gopher.cchen.cl; f. 1965; library of 9,000 vols, 200,000 reports; Pres. Eduardo Bobadilla; Exec. Dir Gonzalo Torres Oviedo; publs *Nucleotécnica* (2 a year), *Memoria Anual*.

Comité Oceanográfico Nacional: Casilla 324, Valparaíso; tel. (32) 266520; fax (32) 266522; e-mail cona@shoa.cl; f. 1971; coordinates oceanographic activities in the country; Pres. Capt. Rafael Mac-kay; Exec. Sec. Alejandro Cabezas; publ. *Ciencia y Tecnología del Mar* (annually).

Liga Marítima de Chile (Chilean Maritime League): Avda Errázuriz 471, 2° piso, Casilla 117-V, Valparaíso; f. 1914; runs course in nautical education; Pres. Rear Admiral Eri Solis Oyarzún; Vice-Pres. Rubén Luzzi Villanueva; Sec. Julio Allard Aguirre; 1,350 mems; brs in Iquique, Tocopilla, Santiago, Concepción, Tomé, Valdivia, Puerto Montt and Punta Arenas; publ. *Mar* (annually).

Sociedad Chilena de Física: Casilla 73, Correo 5, Santiago; tel. 3412723; fax 2258427; f. 1965; 278 mems; Pres. Sergio Hojman.

Sociedad Chilena de Fotogrametría y Percepción Remota: Nueva Santa Isabel 1640, Santiago; tel. (2) 6968221; fax (2) 6988278; e-mail igm@reuna.cl; library of 3,500 vols, 25,000 maps; Pres. Bgr Sergio Mateu Martínez-Conde; Sec. Tcl. Héctor Gajardo Sepúlveda.

Sociedad Chilena de Química: Casilla de Correo 2613, Concepción; tel. (41) 227815; fax (41) 235819; f. 1945; 1,000 mems; library of 1,500 vols and 400 periodicals; Pres. Guil-

LERMO CONTRERAS; Sec. EDUARDO DELGADO; publ. *Boletín* (quarterly).

Sociedad de Bioquímica y Biología Molecular de Chile: Casilla 16164, Santiago 9; tel. 209-3503; fax 225-8427; f. 1971; 130 mems; Pres. Dr RAFAEL VICUÑA; Sec. Dr OMAR ORELLANA.

Sociedad de Bioquímica de Concepción: Casilla 237, Escuela de Química y Farmacia y Bioquímica, Concepción; f. 1957; Pres. MARIO POZO LÓPEZ; Sec. FROILÁN HERNÁNDEZ CARTES.

Sociedad Geológica de Chile: Valentin Letelier 20, dpto 401, Casilla 13667, Correo 21, Santiago; tel. 6980481; f. 1962; 434 mems; Pres. ESTANISLAO GODOY; Sec.-Gen. WALDO VIVALLO; publs *Revista Geológica de Chile* (2 a year), *Comunicaciones* (annually).

TECHNOLOGY

Asociación Interamericana de Ingeniería Sanitaria y Ambiental: San Martín 352, Santiago; tel. 6984028; f. 1979; Pres. GUILLERMO RUIZ TRONCOSO; Sec. JULIO HEVIA MEDEL; publ. *Revista* (quarterly).

Colegio de Ingenieros de Chile, AG: Avda Santa María 0508, Casilla 13745, Santiago; tel. (2) 7779530; fax (2) 7778681; e-mail colinge@intercom.bellsouth.cl; f. 1958; professional engineering asscn; 22,000 mems; Pres. CARLOS ANDREANI LUCO; Gen. Man. PEDRO TORRES OJEDA; publs *Ingenieros* (every 2 months), *C.I. Informa* (monthly).

Instituto de Ingenieros de Chile (Institute of Chilean Engineers): San Martín 352, Casilla 487, Santiago; tel. 6984028; fax 6971136; f. 1888; 800 mems; library of 2,100 vols; publs *Revista Chilena de Ingeniería, Anales*.

Instituto de Ingenieros de Minas de Chile: Avda Bulnes 197, 6° piso, Casilla 14668, Correo 21, Santiago; tel. (2) 6953849; fax (2) 6972351; f. 1930; 1,100 mems; Pres. CARLOS VEGA; Sec. RICARDO SIMIAN; publ. *Minerales* (quarterly).

Sociedad Chilena de Tecnología de Alimentos: Clasificador 814, Santiago; tel. and fax (2) 6821752; f. 1962; Pres. Dr JORGE P. SILVA.; Sec. LAURA ALMENDARES; publ. *Revista Alimentos* (4 a year).

Sociedad Nacional de Minería (National Society of Mining): Avda Apoquindo 3000 (5° piso), Santiago; f. 1883; library of 1,500 vols, 15,000 documents on microfilm, 20,000 maps; Pres. HERNÁN HOCHSCHILD ALESSANDRI; Sec. Gen. JULIO ASCUÍ LATORRE; publ. *Boletín Minero*.

Research Institutes

AGRICULTURE, FISHERIES AND VETERINARY SCIENCE

Estación Experimental 'Las Vegas' de la Sociedad Nacional de Agricultura (National Agricultural Society Experimental Station): Huelquen-Paine, Santiago; f. 1924; library of 1,000 vols; Dir RAÚL MATTE VIAL; publ. *El Campesino* (monthly).

Instituto de Fomento Pesquero (Fishery Research Institute): Hulto 374, Casilla 8-V, Valparaíso; tel. (32) 2047858; telex 343664; fax (32) 2254362; f. 1964 for research into fisheries and development in the fields of Biology, Oceanography, Economy, Technology; library of 8,500 vols; Dir PABLO ALVAREZ-TUZA; publs *Investigación Pesquera* (annually), *Boletín Bibliográfico* (monthly), *Boletín Informativo: Mercado del Sector Pesquero* (quarterly), *Boletín de Estadísticas: Sistema de Información Pesquera* (monthly), *Boletín Estadístico Mensual: Exportaciones* (monthly).

Instituto de Investigaciones Agropecuarias: Casilla 439, Correo 3, Santiago; tel. 5417223; fax 5417667; f. 1964; conducts research on plant and livestock production, horticulture, viticulture, oenology, field crops; 170 research workers; library: see Libraries; Pres. FERNANDO MUJICA CASTILLO; 'Intihuasi' Agricultural Experiment Station, Dir CARLOS QUIROZ; 'Tamel-aike' Agricultural Experiment Station, Dir CHRISTIAN HEPP; 'La Platina' Agricultural Experiment Station, Dir JORGE VALENZUELA BARNECH; 'Carillanca' Agricultural Experiment Station, Dir ANGEL GABRIEL VIVALLO P.; 'Quilamapu' Agricultural Experiment Station, Dir ISAAC MALDONADO I.; 'Remehue' Agricultural Experiment Station, Dir RENÉ BERNIER V.; Kampenaike Agricultural Experiment Station, Dir NILO COVACEVICH; publs *Agricultura Técnica* (quarterly), *Memoria Anual, Bibliografía Agrícola Chilena* (annually), *Boletín Técnico* (irregular), *Tierra Adentro* (6 a year).

Instituto Forestal (Forestry Institute): Huérfanos 554, Casilla 3085, Santiago; tel. (2) 6930700; fax (2) 6381286; f. 1961; research and advice in all aspects of forestry; library of 4,500 vols; Dir GONZALO PAREDES VELOSO; publs *Informe Técnico, Boletín Estadístico, Ciencia e Investigación Forestal*.

ECONOMICS, LAW AND POLITICS

Instituto Latinoamericano y del Caribe de Planificación Económica y Social (ILPES) (Latin American and Caribbean Institute for Economic and Social Planning): Edif. Naciones Unidas, Avda Dag Hammarskjöld s/n, Casilla 1567, Santiago; tel. (2) 2102507; telex 240077; fax (2) 2066104; f. 1962; ILPES is a permanent ind. body that forms part of the system of the UN Economic Commission for Latin America and the Caribbean (ECLAC); supports Latin American and Caribbean governments in public policy planning and co-ordination; provides training, advisory services and research; organizes and administers intergovernmental forums, the Regional Council for Planning (40 member governments) and the System of Co-operation and Co-ordination among Planning Bodies of Latin America and the Caribbean; library of 60,000 vols, documents and periodicals; Dir ARTURO NÚÑEZ DEL PRADO; publs *Cuadernos del ILPES, ILPES Bulletin*.

Instituto Nacional de Estadísticas (Statistical Office): Casilla 498, Correo 3, Santiago; tel. (2) 3667777; fax (2) 6712169; e-mail inesdadm@reuna.cl; f. 1843; library of 13,100 vols; Dir Ing. MAXIMO AGUILERA REYES; publs *Compendio Estadístico* (annually), *Anuarios, Revista Estadística y Economía* (2 a year), *Indicadores Coyunturales* (monthly), *Metodologías*.

EDUCATION

Centro de Investigación y Desarrollo de la Educación (CIDE): Erasmo Escala 1825, Casilla 13608, Santiago; tel. (2) 6987153; fax (2) 6718051; e-mail cide@reuna.cl; f. 1965; independent research centre; aims to provide education relevant to the basic needs of the people; research into education and the family, education and work, education and social values; library of 50,000 vols, 7,000 documents; Dir JOHN SWOPE.

Latin American Information and Documentation Network for Education (REDUC): Casilla 13608, Santiago; tel. 698-7153; fax 671-8051; f. 1977; network of different educational research institutions; aims to disseminate information on education for research and policy making; mems: 27 institutions; documentation centre of 16,000 research summaries; Dir ORLANDO MELLA VALENZUELA; publs *Analytic Abstracts in Education (RAE)* (2 a year), *Index* (annually), microfiches.

HISTORY, GEOGRAPHY AND ARCHAEOLOGY

Instituto de Investigaciones Arqueológicas y Museo 'R.P. Gustavo Le Paige, S.J.': San Pedro de Atacama; tel. 851002; f. 1985; affiliated to the Universidad Católica del Norte, Antofagasta; research in archaeology and anthropology; library of 1,900 books, 5,000 periodicals; Dir Dr LAUTARO NUÑEZ A.; publ. *Estudios Atacameños* (irregular).

MEDICINE

Fundación Gildemeister: Augustinas esq. Amunátegui 178, 5° piso, Casilla 99-D, Santiago; f. 1947 to co-operate with public or private institutions, universities, etc., in medical research and particularly in the diffusion of the technique of thoracic surgery, cardiology, neurology and neurosurgery; Pres. WOLF VON HARPE; Hon. Sec. Dra ADRIANA CARRETERO.

Instituto de Medicina Experimental del Servicio Nacional de Salud (Institute of Experimental Medicine of the National Health Service): Avda Irarrázaval 849, Casilla 3401, Santiago; tel. 49 79 30; f. 1937; affiliated to WHO; physiology, neuroendocrinology and cancer research; maintains tumour bank, available for use by other research centres; 15 mems; library of 6,800 vols; Dir Dr SERGIO YRARRÁZAVAL; Chief Sec Mrs BERTA IRIBIRRA.

Instituto de Salud Pública de Chile (Chilean Public Health Institute): Avda Marathon 1000, Nuñoa, Casilla 48, Santiago; tel. 2391105; fax 2396960; f. 1980; centre for vaccine production, national control of pharmaceutical, food and cosmetic products, and for co-ordination of national network of health laboratories; 600 mems; central scientific library of 3,600 vols, Centre of Occupational Health and Air Pollution Library of 5,542 vols; Dir JORGE SÁNCHEZ VEGA; publs *Laboratorio al día, Boletín informativo de medicamentos, Manuales de Procedimiento de Laboratorio Clínico, Manual de Bioseguridad*.

NATURAL SCIENCES

General

Centro de Información de Recursos Naturales (CIREN) (Centre for Information on Natural Resources): Avda Manuel Montt 1164, Casilla 14995, Correo Central, Santiago; tel. 2236641; fax 2096407; e-mail ciren@reuna.cl; f. 1964; a privately run corporation; gathers data and provides a central information service in the areas of climate, soil, water, fruit production, afforestation, mining, agricultural resources; holds a land-owners register; library of 11,000 vols, 150 journals; Exec. Dir JOSÉ ANTONIO BUSTAMANTE GARRIDO.

Physical Sciences

Comité Nacional de Geografía, Geodesía y Geofísica (National Geographical, Geodetic and Geophysical Committee): Nueva Santa Isabel 1640, Santiago; tel. (2) 6968221; fax (2) 6988278; e-mail igm@reuna.cl; f. 1935 to encourage and co-ordinate research in the fields mentioned; 119 mems; Dir Bgr SERGIO MATEU MARTÍNEZ-CONDE; Sec. Tcl. HÉCTOR GAJARDO SEPÚLVEDA; publ. *Terra Australis* (1 a year).

Dirección Meteorológica de Chile (Meteorological Bureau): Casilla 63, Correo Aeropuerto Internacional, Santiago; tel. (2) 6763437; fax (2) 6019590; e-mail dirección@meteochile.cl; f. 1884; library of 3,000 vols; Dir Col NATHAN MAKUC; publs *Boletín Climatológico* (monthly), *Boletín Agrometeorológico* (monthly), *Boletín de Radiación Ultravioleta, Anuario Meteorológico, Anuario Agrometeoro-*

lógico, Informe Solarimetrico Semestral de Radiación e Insolación.

European Southern Observatory: Casilla 19001, Correo 19, Avda Alonso de Córdova 3107, Vitacura, Santiago; tel. (2) 2285006; fax (2) 2285132; f. 1962; astronomical observatory of the European Organization for Astronomical Research in the Southern Hemisphere (mem. countries: Belgium, Denmark, France, Germany, Italy, Netherlands, Sweden, Switzerland, and Portugal as assoc.); situated on top of Cerro La Silla at an altitude of 2,400 m in Province of Elqui, 600 km north of Santiago; geographical co-ordinates: Lat. 29°15′ south, Long. 70°44′ west; main field of research is photometry and spectrography of southern hemisphere astronomical objects; facilities for member-country astronomers and for non-mems; main equipment: 360-cm telescope operating in prime focus (f/3), Cassegrain (f/8) optical and (f/35) infrared foci; 358-cm NTT (New Technology Telescope) incorporating active optics, with Nasmyth (f/11) foci; 220-cm telescope with Cassegrain (f/8) optical and (f/35) infrared foci; 152-cm spectrographic telescope with f/15 spectrograph and f/30 coudé spectrograph; 140-cm coudé auxiliary telescope feeding the 360-cm coudé echelle spectrograph; 1,500-cm SEST (Swedish/ESO Submillimetre Telescope) with 1.3 and 3.0-mm receivers; publ. *The Messenger* (quarterly). (See also International–Science.)

Instituto Antártico Chileno: Luis Thayer Ojeda 814, Casilla 16521, Correo 9, Santiago; tel. 2310105; telex 346261; fax 2320440; f. 1963; a centre for technological and scientific development on matters relating to the Antarctic and adjacent ecosystems; 43 mems; library of 4,100 vols and 400 periodicals; Dir OSCAR PINOCHET DE LA BARRA; publs *Serie Científica* (annually), *Boletín Antártico Chileno* (2 a year).

Instituto de Oceanología: Universidad de Valparaíso, Casilla 13-D, Montemar, Viña del Mar; tel. (32) 831668; fax (32) 833214; f. 1941; research in marine biology, physical and chemical oceanography, pollution; 18 laboratories, aquarium, workshops (photography and drawings, carpentry, mechanics), auditorium; library of 5,000 books, 250 periodical titles; museum (see under Museums); Dir ROBERTO PRADO-FIEDLER; publ. *Revista de Biología Marina y Oceanografía.*

Instituto para la Investigación Astronómica Isaac Newton (Isaac Newton Institute for Astronomy): Casilla 8–9, Correo 9, Santiago; tel. 217-2013; fax 217-2352; e-mail inewton@reuna.cl; f. 1978; research in globular clusters, stellar and extragalactic astrophysics; Dir GONZALO ALCAINO.

Observatorio Astrofísico 'Manuel Foster' (Observatory of the Catholic University of Chile): Casilla 104, Santiago 22; tel. (2) 6864940; fax (2) 6864948; e-mail hquintana@astro.puc.cl; f. 1904; research in stellar and extragalactic astrophysics; 4 mems; 7,000 vols in library; Dir Dr HERNÁN QUINTANA.

Observatorio Astronómico Nacional (National Astronomical Observatory): Universidad de Chile, Departamento de Astronomía, Biblioteca, Casilla 36-D, Santiago 1; tel. (2) 2294002; fax (2) 2294101; email biblio@das .uchile.cl; f. 1852; attached to the Universidad de Chile; Repsold Meridian circle, Transit instrument, Gauthier refractor astrograph, Heyde visual refractor, Danjon astrolabe and Zeiss transit instruments; astronomical station at Cerro El Roble and radio-astronomical observatory at Maipu; library of 7,247 vols; Dir JOSÉ MAZA SANCHO; publ. *Preprints.*

Observatorio Interamericano de Cerro Tololo (Cerro Tololo Inter-American Observatory): Casilla 603, La Serena; tel. (51) 225415; fax (51) 205342; f. 1963; astronomical observation of stars only observable in the southern hemisphere; library of 20,000 vols; Dir Dr MALCOLM G. SMITH.

Servicio Hidrográfico y Oceanográfico de la Armada de Chile (Hydrographic and Oceanographic Service of the Chilean Navy): Errázuriz 232, Playa Ancha, Valparaíso; tel. 266666; telex 230362; fax 266542; e-mail shoa@shoa.cl; f. 1874; hydrographic surveys, nautical charts and publications, oceanography, maritime safety, national oceanographic data centre; library of 12,000 vols; Dir RAFAEL MAC-KAY B.; publs *Manual de Navegación, Anuario Hidrográfico, Tablas de Mareas* (annually), *Noticias a los Navegantes* (monthly), *Derroteros de la Costa de Chile,* etc.

Servicio Nacional de Geología y Minería: Avda Santa María 0104, Casilla 10465, Correo 21, Santiago; tel. (2) 7375050; fax (2) 7372026; e-mail mcortes@sernageomin.cl; f. 1981; geoscience and mining; library of 30,000 vols, 15,000 aerial photographs, 200 satellite photographs, 700 periodical titles, 6,000 maps; Dir RICARDO TRONCOSO SAN MARTÍN; publs *Revista Geológica de Chile, Boletín.*

RELIGION, SOCIOLOGY AND ANTHROPOLOGY

Instituto Latinoamericano de Doctrina y Estudios Sociales: Almirante Barroso 6, Santiago, Casilla 14446, Correo 21; tel. 6714072; fax 6986873; f. 1965 for the study, dissemination and renewal of social thought within the Church; teaching and research in economics and social sciences; in-service courses for teachers and professionals; 54 mems; Exec. Vice-Dir R. P. GONZALO ARROYO; publs *DOCLA, Revista de Análisis Económico, Persona y Sociedad.*

TECHNOLOGY

Comisión Nacional de Investigación Científica y Tecnológica (CONICYT) (National Commission for Scientific and Technological Research): Casilla 297-V, Santiago; tel. (2) 2744537; fax (2) 2096729; e-mail info@conicyt.cl; f. 1969; government agency in charge of studying, planning and proposing national scientific and technological policy to the govt and developing, promoting and improving science and technology; mem. of ICSU; mem. of FID; library of 4,500 vols; Pres. Prof. MAURICIO SARRAZIN; Information Dir ANA MARIA PRAT; publs *Series Información y Documentación, Series Bibliografías, Series Directorios,* irregular study reports, documentation reports and annual reports.

Instituto de Investigaciones y Ensayes de Materiales (IDIEM) Universidad de Chile (Institute for Materials Research and Testing): Plaza Ercilla 883, Casilla 1420, Santiago; fax (2) 6718979; f. 1898; library of 8,000 vols; Dir LUIS AYAYA R.

Instituto Nacional de Normalización (National Institute of Standardization): Casilla 995, Correo 1, Santiago; f. 1944; library of 160,000 technical standards; Dir LEE WARD.

Libraries and Archives

Concepción

Universidad de Concepción, Dirección de Bibliotecas: Barrio Universitario, Casilla 1807, Concepción; tel. 234985; fax 244796; f. 1919; 420,000 vols, 6,046 periodicals; special collections: chemistry, history; Dir MARÍA NIEVES ALONSO MARTÍNEZ.

Santiago

Archivos Nacionales (National Archives): Clasificador 1400, Miraflores No. 50, Santiago; tel. (2) 6325735; fax (2) 6325735; e-mail archinac@oris.renib.cl; f. 1927; incl. historic and public administration collns; Dir MARÍA EUGENIA BARRIENTOS.

Biblioteca Central de la Universidad de Chile: Calle Arturo Prat 23, Casilla 10-D, Santiago; f. 1843, reorganized 1936; contains more than 200,000 vols, comprising donations from Canada, Great Britain, the United States and Spain, and from private collections, including those of Pedro Montt and Pablo Neruda; collection of periodicals comprising 14,500 titles, with over 500,000 issues; there are 40 other libraries in the University with an aggregate of 1,000,000 vols; Dir of Central Library Prof. HUMBERTO GIANNINI IÑIGUEZ.

Biblioteca Central del Instituto de Investigaciones Agropecuarias: Casilla 439 Correo 3, Santiago; tel. 5417223; fax 5417223, ext. 225; e-mail selso@platina.inia.cl; f. 1947; 16,500 vols, 77,000 documents and pamphlets, 747 current periodicals; Librarian SONIA ELSO; publ. *Bibliografía Agrícola Chilena.*

Biblioteca del Congreso Nacional (Congress Library): Huérfanos 1117, 2° piso, Clasificador Postal 1199, Santiago; tel. (2) 6715331; fax (2) 6715331 ext. 3127; e-mail xfeliu@biblioteca.congreso.cl; f. 1883; 1,000,000 vols and 5,600 periodicals on law, social sciences, politics and economics, human sciences and literature; 13,500 leaflets, 12,000 rare books, 1,353 maps and topographical charts, 4,000,000 Chilean press cuttings; official depository for international organizations, legal depository for national publs; open to the public; Dir XIMENA FELIÚ SILVA; Asst Dir ALICIA ROJAS ESTIBIL; publs *Serie Estudios, Serie Bibliografía, Boletín Informativo, Boletín de Resumenes de Artículos de Publicaciones Periódicas, Alerta Ambicntal, Visión Semanal.*

Biblioteca Nacional de Chile (National Library): Avda B. O'Higgins 651, Clasificador 1105, Santiago; tel. (2) 3605200; fax (2) 6380461; f. 1813; 3,500,000 vols, 75,000 MSS., 83 incunabula; Dir MARTA CRUZ-COKE M.; publs *Bibliografía Chilena* (annually), *Mapocho* (2 a year), *Referencias Críticas sobre autores Chilenos,* bibliographies, catalogues.

Centro Latinoamericano de Documentación Económica y Social (CLADES) (Latin American Centre for Economic and Social Documentation): Casilla 179-D, Avda Dag Hammarskjöld, Santiago; tel. 210-2427; telex 240077; fax 210-2422; f. 1971; part of UN Economic Comm. for Latin America and the Caribbean (ECLAC); collaborates with Latin American and Caribbean states in the development of their documentation centres; aims to establish the means for easy access to economic and social information for planners, researchers, public and private institutions and international bodies; undertakes research, technical assistance, training, information processing; 10 staff (documentalists); library of 1,500 vols, 98 periodicals, 500 micro-films; Dir CLAUDIONOR EVANGELISTA; publs *PLANINDEX, Informativo Terminológico: Hoja informativa latino-americana sobre terminología del desarrollo económico y social.*

Dirección de Bibliotecas de la Universidad de Santiago de Chile: Casilla 4637, Correo 2, Santiago; tel. 776-1220; telex 441674; fax 681-1422; f. 1979; 150,000 vols; Dir JORGE EDUARDO DEMANGEL RUÍZ.

Pontificia Universidad Católica de Chile, Sistema de Bibliotecas: Campus San Joaquín, Vicuña Mackenna 4860, Casilla 306, Correo 22, Santiago; tel. (2) 6864615; fax (2) 6865852; f. 1901; 10 university libraries;

1,560,000 vols; Dir MARÍA LUISA ARENAS FRANCO.

Valdivia

Sistema de Bibliotecas, Universidad Austral de Chile: Correo 2, Valdivia; tel. (63) 221290; fax (63) 221360; f. 1962; 114,000 vols, 1,600 periodicals; specializes in science; Dir SONIA SEGUEL INOSTROZA.

Valparaíso

Biblioteca Central de la Universidad Técnica 'Federico Santa María': Avda España 1680, CP 110-V, Valparaíso; tel. (32) 654147; fax (32) 797483; f. 1926; 110,000 vols, 2,400 periodicals; audiovisual material: cassettes, video cassettes, maps, microfilms, slides; specializes in science and technology; Dir MARÍA EUGENIA LAULIÉ; publs *Scientia: Serie A Mathematical Sciences, Gestión tecnológica* (quarterly), *USM Noticias* (monthly), acquisitions list (weekly).

Biblioteca de la Universidad Católica de Valparaíso: Avda Brasil 2950, Casilla 4059, Valparaíso; tel. (32) 273261; fax (32) 273183; f. 1928; 204,000 vols; Librarian ATILIO BUSTOS GONZALEZ.

Biblioteca Publica No. 1 'Santiago Severin' de Valparaíso: Plaza Simón Bolívar, Valparaíso; tel. and fax 213375; f. 1873; includes a collection of historical books on Chile and America and a collection of 17th- to 19th-century books; 94,149 vols, 166,814 periodicals; Dir YOLANDA SOTO VERGARA.

Museums and Art Galleries

Angol

Museo Dillman S. Bullock: Casilla 8-D, Angol; tel. and fax 712395; f. 1946; general local flora and fauna; extensive local archaeological collection; library of 5,000 vols; undertakes research, scientific expeditions; Dir ALBERTO E. MONTERO.

Antofagasta

Museo Regional de Antofagasta: Bolívar No 188, Casilla 746, Antofagasta; tel. 227016; f. 1984; archaeology, history, ethnography, geology; small library; Curator IVO KUZMANIĆ PIEROTIĆ.

Arica

Museo Arqueológico San Miguel de Azapa, Universidad de Tarapacá: Facultad de Ciencias Sociales, Administrativas y Económicas, Depto de Arqueología y Museología, Casilla 6-D, Arica; tel. (58) 205551; fax (58) 224248; e-mail csantoro@vitor.faci.uta.cl; f. 1959; exhibits related to research on pre-Columbian, colonial and modern Andean people; anthropological library of 15,000 vols; history library; Dean CALOGERO M. SANTORO; publs *Chungara* (2 a year), *Cuadernos de Trabajo* (irregular).

Cañete

Museo Folklórico Araucano de Cañete 'Juan A. Ríos M.': Casilla 28, Cañete; f. 1968; to conserve, exhibit and research the Mapuche culture from its origins to contact with Spanish culture; to recreate the environment which Valdivia saw in 1552 when he built the Tucapel Fort (near the museum); anthropological research of the native Mapuche settlements which still exist; archaeological excavations in the surrounding area; library of 2,000 vols; Curator GLORIA CARDENAS TRONCOSO.

Concepción

Museo de Historia Natural de Concepción (Concepción Natural History Museum): Plaza Luis Acevedo, Concepción; tel. and fax (41) 310932; e-mail musconce@ctcreuna.cl; f. 1902; 6,732 vols; Curator MARCO SÁNCHEZ AGUILERA; publ. *Comunicaciones del Museo de Concepción*.

Museo de Hualpen (Hualpen Museum): Parque Pedro del Rio Zañartu, Casilla 2656, Concepción; tel. 227305; f. 1882; collections of Greek, Roman and Egyptian archaeology; Chilean arms and numismatic collections; Oriental art; Chilean and American folk arts; Chilean archaeology; eighteenth- and nineteenth-century furniture; Pres. VICTOR LOBOS LÁPERA.

Copiapó

Museo Regional de Atacama: Atacama 98, Casilla 134, Copiapó; tel. 212313; fax (52) 212313; f. 1973; archaeology, mineralogy, ecology and history; library of 15,000 vols; Dir MIGUEL CERVELLINO.

Iquique

Museo Antropológico de Iquique: Universidad Arturo Prat de Iquique, Casilla 121, Campus Pedro Lagos, Pedro Lagos y Grumete Bolados Sts, Iquique; f. 1987; attached to the Centro de Estudios del Desierto of the University; permanent exhibition showing the cultural development of the people of the region from 10,000 BC to 1900; research in archaeology, rural development of farming communities, history and ethnography; specialized library; Dir Arq. ÁLVARO CAREVIC RIVERA; publ. research findings.

Museo Regional de Iquique: Baquedano 951, Iquique; tel. (57) 411034; fax (57) 413278; attached to the Dept of Social Development of the Municipality of Iquique; f. 1960; permanent exhibition of regional archaeology, ethnography and history; Dir CORA ROMY MORAGAS.

La Serena

Museo Arqueológico de La Serena (La Serena Archaeological Museum): Calle Cordovez esq. Cienfuegos, Casilla 617, La Serena; tel. 224492; fax 225398; f. 1943; sections on archaeology, pre-history, physical anthropology, colonial history, ethnology and palaeontology; library of 23,000 vols, 18,043 slides, 28,150 photographs; Dir GONZALO AMPUERO B.; specialized library; publ. *Boletín* (annually).

Linares

Museo de Arte y Artesanía de Linares: Casilla 272, Linares; f. 1966; arts and crafts from the Inca period to the present; valuable collections including unique clay miniatures; collection of Huaso implements; ceramics; exhibition of history and people of Linares; exhibition on the sugar industry; conferences, lectures, films, etc.; Dir PEDRO OLMOS MUÑOZ.

Ovalle

Museo del Limari: Calle Independencia 329, Casilla 59, Ovalle; tel. (53) 620029; f. 1963; archaeology; Curator MARCOS BISKUPOVIC MAZZEI.

Puerto Williams

Museo 'Martín Gusinde': Puerto Williams, Magallanes; f. 1975; situated at the naval base on Navarino Island; history and geography of the southern most archipelagos of America; aboriginal culture, flora, fauna and minerals of the area; library of 500 vols; Curator MAURICE VAN DE MAELE S.

Punta Arenas

Museo Histórico Regional de Magallanes: Centro Cultural Braun-Menéndez, Hernando de Magallanes 949, Casilla 97, Punta Arenas; tel. (61) 244216; fax (61) 221387; f. 1983, fmrly Museo de la Patagonia, f. 1967; Patagonian history; specialized library of 3,500 vols; Curator Sra DESANKA URSIĆ V.

Museo Regional Salesiano 'Maggiorino Borgatello' (Salesian Regional Museum 'Maggiorino Borgatello'): Avda Bulnes 374, Casilla 347, Punta Arenas; f. 1893; scientific and ethnographical (notable relics of extreme South American and Tierra del Fuegan tribes), petroleum industry; Scientific Dir Prof. SERGIO LAUSIĆ GLASINOVIĆ.

Santiago

Museo Chileno de Arte Precolombino: Casilla 3687, Bandera 361, Santiago; tel. 6953851; fax 6972779; f. 1981 by the council of Santiago City and the Fundación Familia Larraín Echenique; 2,000 items of precolumbian art and 1,000 items in ethnographic collections from Mapuche and Aymara cultures; textiles, ceramics, metal work, stone sculptures; large collection of photographs, slides, video and audio cassettes; laboratory for textile and pottery conservation; laboratory for archaeological research; research on precolumbian music, rock art, Tiahuanaco, Aymara, Atacama and Araucanian cultures, prehistoric architecture, Andean textiles and symbolism; educational programmes; music archive; library of 3,300 vols, 300 periodicals; special collection of precolumbian art, conservation and archaeology; Dir CARLOS ALDUNATE DEL SOLAR; publ. *Boletín* (annually), *Mundo Precolombino,* catalogue of exhibitions (occasionally).

Museo de Arte Colonial de San Francisco: Alameda Bernardo O'Higgins 834, Santiago; tel. (2) 6398737; fax (2) 6398737; f. 1968 by the Franciscan Order; 16th–19th-century art; includes the most important collection of 17th-century paintings in Chile; the life of St Francis depicted in 53 pictures; the life of San Diego de Alcalá depicted in 35 pictures; also other religious works of art, furniture, icons, etc.; valuable library; Dir ROSA PUGA D.

Museo de Arte Contemporáneo (Contemporary Art Museum): Universidad de Chile, Parque Forestal frente a Mosqueto, Santiago; tel. (2) 6395486; fax (2) 6394945; f. 1947; contemporary and fine arts; Dir ROSARIO LETELIER VIAL.

Museo de Arte Popular Americano (Museum of American Folk Art): Parque Forestal s/n, Casilla 2100, Universidad de Chile, Santiago; tel. (2) 6821480; fax (2) 6821481; e-mail museopop@abello.dic.uchile.cl; f. 1943; objects of American folk art in pottery, basketware, wood and metal, Araucanian silverware; Dir SYLVIA RIOS MONTERO.

Museo de Historia Natural de San Pedro Nolasco (Natural History Museum): MacIver 341, Santiago; tel. 30691; f. 1922; library of 58,000 vols; special collections: Claudio Gay, G. Cuvier, A. E. Brehrm, Ch. Darwin.

Museo Histórico Nacional (National Historical Museum): Palacio de la Real Audiencia, Plaza de Armas, Casilla 9764, Santiago; tel. 6381411; fax 6331815; f. 1911; sections: Prehispanic, Conquest, Colonial, Independence, Republican periods; library of 12,000 vols; costume, iconographic, arms, arts and crafts, and numismatic collections; dept of education; research in textile, paper and photographic restoration; Dir SOFÍA CORREA SUTIL.

Museo Nacional de Bellas Artes (National Museum of Fine Arts): Parque Forestal, Casilla 3209, Santiago; tel. 6330655; f. 1880; paintings, engravings, etchings and sculpture, Chilean and European paintings of 15th–20th centuries; library of 15,000 vols; Dir MILAN IVELIC; publs exhibitions catalogues.

Museo Nacional de Historia Natural (National Museum of Natural History): Casilla 787, Santiago; tel. (2) 6814095; fax (2) 6817182; e-mail webmaster@mnhn.cl; f. 1830; Departments: Zoology, Entomology, Hydrobiology, Botany, Mineralogy, Palaeontology, Anthropology, Museology, Education; Curator Dr ALBERTO CARVACHO; publs *Boletín*, *Noticiario mensual*.

Museo Pedagógico Carlos Stuardo Ortiz: Compañía 3150, 2° piso, Santiago; tel. 91938; f. 1941; records cultural and educational heritage of the country; educational research; translations; bibliographies; library of 25,000 vols; Dir DAVID VERGARA TORRES; publ. *Boletín* (quarterly)

Talca

Museo O'Higginiano y de Bellas Artes de Talca: 1 Norte No. 875, Casilla 189, Talca; tel. 227330; f. 1964; paintings, sculpture, Chilean history, archaeology, religious artefacts, antique furniture, arms; library of 430 vols; video tapes; Curator SERGIO ULLOA ROJOS; publ. *La Casona durante la Colonia*.

Temuco

Museo Regional de la Araucania (Araucania Museum): Avda Alemania 084, Casilla 481, Temuco; tel. (45) 211108; fax (45) 234881; f. 1940; opened to the public 1943; archaeological, artistic and ethnographic exhibits of the Araucanian, or Mapuche, Indians of South Chile, and others relating to the Conquest, Pacification and Colonization of Araucania as well as the history of Temuco city itself; maintains research section; specialized library of 886 vols about Mapuche culture and regional history; 1,400 reprints and maps of Mapuche reservations and foreign colonization; Dir HÉCTOR ZUMAETA ZÚÑIGA; publ. *Bulletin*.

Valdivia

Museo Histórico y Antropológico de la Universidad Austral de Chile: Casilla 586, Valdivia; tel. and fax (63) 212872; e-mail museo@entelchile.net; f. 1967; Centre for Conservation of Historical Monuments, Archaeology, Museums and Historical Archives; undertakes teaching, research, training of museum staff, conservation, museology; library of 3,000 vols, 4,000 photographs; Dir JORGE E. INOSTROZA SAAVEDRA.

Valparaíso

Museo de Historia Natural de Valparaíso (Natural History Museum): Calle Condell 1546, Casilla 3208, Correo 3, Valparaíso; tel. (32) 257441; fax (32) 220846; f. 1876; natural sciences and anthropology; library of *c*. 3,000 vols; Curator ANA AVALOS VALENZUELA; publ. *Anales*.

Vicuña

Museo Gabriela Mistral de Vicuña: Casilla 50, Vicuña; tel. 411223; f. 1971 to preserve the cultural legacy of the poetess, Gabriela Mistral (Nobel prize for Literature 1945); documents, photographs and personal effects; replica of birthplace of poetess, talks, films, music, etc.; library of 6,000 vols; Dir RODRIGO IRIBARREN AVILÉS; publs *Boletín del Museo*, etc.

Viña del Mar

Museo Comparativo de Biología Marina: Instituto de Oceanología, Universidad de Valparaíso, Casilla 13-D, Viña del Mar; tel. (32) 832702; fax (32) 833214; f. 1955; echinoderms, molluscs and other invertebrates; algae and marine lichens from the coastal regions of the SE Pacific; Curator ISABEL SOLIS; publ. *Revista de Biología Marina y Oceanografía*.

Universities and Technical Universities

PONTIFICIA UNIVERSIDAD CATÓLICA DE CHILE
(Catholic University of Chile)

Casilla 114-D, Santiago

Telephone: 2224516

Fax: 2225515

E-mail: soporte@puc.cl

Founded 1888

Private control

Academic year: March to July, August to December

Grand Chancellor: Arz. FRANCISCO JAVIER ERRÁZURIZ OSSA

Vice-Grand Chancellor: Mgr ELISEO ESCUDERO HERRERO

Rector: JUAN DE DIOS VIAL CORREA

Pro-Rector: JUAN IGNACIO VARAS CASTELLÓN

Vice-Rectors: RICARDO RIESCO JARAMILLO (Academic Affairs), ARTURO DEL RÍO LEYTON (Economics and Administration)

General Secretary: PEDRO BANNEN LANATA

Director of Distance Education: CARLOS ISAAC PALYI

Librarian: MARÍA LUISA ARENAS

Library: see Libraries

Number of teachers: 2,413

Number of students: 17,103

Publications: *Revista Universitaria* (2 a year), *Catálogo General* (every 2 years), *Revista Humanitas* (3 a year), various faculty publs.

ACADEMIC UNITS AND DEANS

Faculty of Agronomy: GUILLERMO DONOSO HARRIS

Faculty of Architecture and Fine Arts: FERNANDO PÉREZ OYARZÚN

Faculty of Biological Sciences: RENATO ALBERTINI BORTOLAMEOLLI

Faculty of Economics and Management Sciences: FRANCISCO ROSENDE RAMÍREZ

Faculty of Social Sciences: PEDRO MORANDÉ COURT

Faculty of Law: RAÚL LECAROS ZEGERS

Faculty of Education: OSVALDO ASTUDILLO CASTRO

Faculty of Philosophy: JUAN DE DIOS VIAL LARRAÍN

Faculty of Physics: RICARDO RAMÍREZ LEIVA

Faculty of History, Geography and Political Sciences: JOSÉ IGNACIO GONZÁLEZ LEIVA

Faculty of Engineering: ALDO CIPRIANO ZAMORANO

Faculty of Communication: SILVIA PELLEGRINI RIPAMONTI

Faculty of Mathematics: CLAUDIO FERNÁNDEZ JAÑA

Faculty of Medicine: PEDRO ROSSO ROSSO

Faculty of Chemistry: LUIS HERNÁN TAGLE DOMÍNGUEZ

Faculty of Theology: R. P. SERGIO SILVA GATICA

BRANCH CAMPUS

Sede Regional de Villarrica: Casilla 111; Dir Mons. PAUL WEVERING WEIDEMANN

UNIVERSIDAD ADOLFO IBAÑEZ

Balmaceda 1625, Casilla 17, Recreo, Viña del Mar

Telephone: (32) 503500

Fax: (32) 664006

Founded 1989 (previously faculty of economics of Univ. Técnica 'Federico Santa María')

Private control

Language of instruction: Spanish

Academic year: March to December

Chancellor: JUAN IGNACIO DOMÍNGUEZ COVARRUBIAS

Academic Vice-Chancellor: VICTOR KÜLLMER KIEKEBUSCH

Executive Director: PABLO JAVIER CANEPA BALDASSARE

Director of Administration and Finance: JORGE CAMPODONICO COSTA

Librarian: MARÍA ZINA JIMÉNEZ

Number of teachers: 37 (full-time)

Number of students: 1,498

DEANS

Faculty of Business and Economic Sciences: VÍCTOR KULLMER, K.

Faculty of Law: FERNANDO FARREN CORNEJO

Faculty of Science and Technology: ARTURO PARTARRIEU IBÁÑEZ

UNIVERSIDAD DE ANTOFAGASTA

Avda Angamos 601, Casilla 170, Antofagasta

Telephone: (56) 083-247804

Telex: 325054

Fax (56) 083-247786

Founded 1981

State control

Language of instruction: Spanish

Academic year: March to January

Rector: JAIME GODOY

Vice-Rector: RAUL HENRIQUEZ

Vice-Rector (Finance): MARCOS CRUTCHIK

Director-General of Administration: MANUEL RIVERA

Director of Research: OSCAR ZUÑIGA

Director-General for Student Affairs: ALBERTO JAMETT

Director of Extension and Co-operation: EILEEN STOCKINS

Director of Teaching: VANESSA CHIANG

Director of Planning and Research: RAUL IBARRA

Secretary-General: MARIO BAEZA

Head of Rectorial Cabinet: SILVIA OLIVOS

Director of Admission: LUIS WITTWER

Librarian: NORMA MONTERREY

Number of teachers: 190

Number of students: 4,657

Publications: *Estudios Oceanológicos, Hombre y Desierto, Innovación.*

DEANS

Faculty of Education and Human Sciences: DANIEL CARRIZO

Faculty of Basic Sciences: GUILLERMO MONDACA

Faculty of Health Sciences: MARCOS CIKUTOVIC

Faculty of Engineering: PEDRO CÓRDOVA

Faculty of Marine Resources: HERNAN BAEZA

Faculty of Law: DOMINGO CLAPS

HEADS OF DEPARTMENTS

Physics: MANUEL SANTANDER

Chemistry: AMBROSIO RESTOVIC

Mathematics: PEDRO HUERTA

Electrical Engineering: RICARDO MARQUEZ

Mechanical Engineering: RENE YUNG

Mining Engineering: OSVALDO HERREROS

Chemical Engineering: SARA PAREDES

Systems Engineering: GONZALO FLORES

Medical Technology: ALEJANDRO FUENTES

Biomedical: ELVIRA MORENO

Kinesiology: MITZI CATALAN

Nursing: VERONICA ITURRA

Obstetrics and Child Health: DIANA RUIZ

Nutrition and Food Technology: NELSON IRIBARREN

Aquaculture: LUIS TAPIA

Geomensural Engineering: HERNÁN TITICHOCA

ATTACHED INSTITUTES

Instituto de Investigaciones Oceanológicas: research in marine life of northern coast of Chile; Dir LUIS RODRIGUEZ.

Instituto de Investigaciones Antropológicas: research in archaeology, anthropology, linguistics and literature of North Chile; Dir PATRICIO NÚÑEZ.

Instituto del Desierto: research in energy and water resources of Atacama desert; agriculture and solar energy in the desert; Dir RENÉ CONTRERAS.

UNIVERSIDAD ARTURO PRAT

Avda 11 de Septiembre 2120, Iquique
Telephone: (57) 441208
Fax: (57) 441009

Founded 1984
State control
Language of instruction: Spanish
Academic year: March to July, August to December

Rector: CARLOS MERINO PINOCHET
Vice-Rector (Academic): CÉSAR ARANCIBIA CÓRDOVA
Administrative Director: CARLOS LADRIX OSES
Librarian: MARÍA CABRERA JIMÉNEZ

Number of teachers: 297
Number of students: 3,060

HEADS OF DEPARTMENTS

Marine Sciences: ROSALINO FUENZALIDA FUENZALIDA
Chemistry: VENECIA HERRERA APABLAZA
Education and Humanities: MATILDE NIÑO VALENZUELA
Economics and Administration; DANIEL GREENHILL MARTÍNEZ
Engineering: JORGE IPINZA ABARCA
Desert Farming: JOSÉ DELATORRE HERRERA
Auditing and Information Systems: SERGIO ETCHEVERRY GUTIÉRREZ
Physics and Mathematics: ROBERTO ARAVIRE FLORES
Law and Social Sciences: SERGIO GONZALEZ MIRANDA.

UNIVERSIDAD DE ATACAMA

Casilla 240, Copiapó
Telephone: (52) 212005
Fax: (52) 212662

Founded 1981
State control
Language of instruction: Spanish
Academic year: March to December

Rector: MARIO MATURANA CLARO
Vice-Rector: ENRIQUE LILLO ANTÚNEZ
Director of Administration and Finance: NEYLÁN VALDIVIA ROJO
Librarian: MARIANELA VIVANCO CORTÉS

Number of teachers: 95
Number of students: 2,950

Publications: *Revista de Ingeniería* (annually), *Revista de Derecho de Aguas* (annually), *Revista de Derecho de Minas* (annually).

DEANS

Faculty of Engineering: MARIO MEZA MALDONADO
Faculty of Humanities and Education: JUAN IGLESIAS DÍAZ

DIRECTORS

Department of Mines: HUGO OLMOS NARANJO
Department of Metallurgy: OSVALDO PAVEZ MIQUELES
Department of Mathematics and Computer Science: ELISEO MARTÍNEZ HERRERA
Department of Natural Sciences: JUAN DÍAZ VARAS
Department of Education: ORLANDO ZULETA GONZÁLEZ
Department of Humanities: OSCAR PAINEAN BUSTAMANTE
Department of Physical Education, Sport and Recreation: ARMANDO OLIVA GONZÁLEZ
Language Institute: RICARDO VERA MARTÍNEZ

ATTACHED INSTITUTES

Instituto de Investigaciones Científicas y Tecnológicas: Casilla 240, Copiapó; tel. and fax (52) 218770; Dir GERMÁN CÁCERES ARENAS.

Instituto Tecnológico: Casilla 240, Copiapó; tel. and fax (52) 218018; Dir TIMUR PADILLA BOCIC.

Instituto Derecho de Minas y Aguas: Moneda 673, 8° piso, Santiago; tel. (2) 6328290; fax (2) 6383452; Dir ALEJANDRO VERGARA BLANCO.

Instituto Asistencia a la Minería: Casilla 240, Copiapó; tel. (52) 212006; fax (52) 212662; Dir JUAN NAVEA DANTAGNAN.

UNIVERSIDAD AUSTRAL DE CHILE
(Southern University of Chile)

Casilla 567, Valdivia
Telephone: (63) 221960
Fax: (63) 221765

Founded 1954
Private control
Language of instruction: Spanish
Academic year: March to July, August to December

Rector: MANFRED MAX NEEF
Vice-Rector for Academic Affairs: GERMÁN CAMPOS P.
Vice-Rector for Economic and Administrative Affairs: GUILLERMO URRUTIA S.
Secretary-General: JUAN ANDRÉS VARAS B.
Director of Undergraduate Studies: ANGEL ENZO CROVETTO E.
Director of Student Affairs: JUAN MARTÍNEZ C.
Director of Postgraduate Studies: ALEJANDRO ROMERO M.
Director of Research: CARLOS HUMBERTO DEL CAMPO R.
Director of Extension: IVÁN CARRASCO M.
Director of Public Relations: VIELLA SHIPLEY
Registrar: MARIA C. BARRIGA RAMÍREZ

Library: see Libraries
Number of teachers: 832
Number of students: 8,785

Publications: *Estudios Filológicos, Medio Ambiente, English Notes, Estudios Pedagógicos* (annually), *Agro Sur, Bosque, Archivos de Medicina Veterinaria.*

DEANS

Faculty of Philosophy and Humanities: CARLOS AMTMANN M.
Faculty of Economic and Administrative Sciences: HERIBERTO FIGUEROA S.
Faculty of Medicine: CLAUS GROB B.
Faculty of Agriculture: RENÉ ANRIQUE G.
Faculty of Forestry Sciences: ANDRES IROUMÉ A.
Faculty of Veterinary Science: VÍCTOR CUBILLOS G.
Faculty of Sciences: EDUARDO QUIROZ REYES
Faculty of Engineering Sciences: FREDY RÍOS MARTÍNEZ
Faculty of Juridical and Social Sciences: KARIN EXSS KRUGMANN
Faculty of Fishery and Oceanography: IKER URIARTE

DIRECTORS

Faculty of Philosophy and Humanities:
- Institute of Social Sciences: FREDDY FORTOUL V.
- Institute of Philosophy and Education: GLADYS JADUE J.
- Institute of Social Communication: GUSTAVO RODRÍGUEZ B.
- Institute of Linguistics and Literature: MAURICIO PILLEUX D.

Faculty of Economic and Administrative Sciences:
- Institute of Administration: MÓNICA RADDATZ T.
- Institute of Economics: ANGELA SÁIZ
- Institute of Statistics: OSVALDO ROJAS QUINTANILLA
- Institute of Tourism: SILVIA COSTABEL G.

Faculty of Medicine:
- Institute of Physiology: RICARDO CASTILLO D.
- Institute of Human Anatomy: HUGO HERNÁNDEZ PARADA
- Institute of Clinical Microbiology: LUIS ZAROR CORNEJO
- Institute of Histology and Pathology: SILVIA HEIN GALLI
- Institute of Surgery: JUAN PÉREZ PÉREZ
- Institute of Medicine: HUMBERTO IBARRA VARGAS
- Institute of Paediatrics: MARIO CALVO GIL
- Institute of Obstetrics and Gynaecology: RAÚL PUENTES P.
- Institute of Psychiatry: FERNANDO OYARZÚN PEÑA
- Institute of Specializations: EDGARDO ROBLES FERNANDEZ
- Institute of Locomotive Apparatus and Rehabilitation: PEDRO VALDIVIA CARVAJAL
- Institute of Neurology and Neurosurgery: BORIS FLÁNDEZ ZBINDEN
- Institute of Haematology: ALVARO LEÓN RIVERA
- Institute of Nursing: ZOILA MUÑOZ JARAMILLO
- Institute of Maternal Nursing: LILIANA MARTÍNEZ G.
- Institute of Public Health: FRANCISCO MARÍN H.
- Institute of Immunology: PATRICIO ESQUIVEL S.
- Institute of Parasitology: PATRICIO TORRES H.

Faculty of Agriculture:
- Institute of Animal Production: OSCAR BALOCCHI L.
- Institute of Agricultural Economy: JUAN LERDÓN S.
- Institute of Plant Production and Health: ROBERTO CARRILLO LL.
- Institute of Agricultural Engineering and Soils: ROBERTO MACDONALD H.
- Institute of Food Science and Technology: BERNANDO FRASER R.

Faculty of Forestry Sciences:
- Institute of Silviculture: ANTONIO LARA A.
- Institute of Forestry Management: VÍCTOR SANDOVAL
- Institute of Technology of Forestry Products: JUAN E. DÍAZ-VAZ O.

Faculty of Veterinary Sciences:
- Institute of Veterinary Anatomy: EDMUNDO BUTENDIECK B.
- Institute of Animal Reproduction: JORGE CORREA SOTO
- Institute of Stockbreeding: ROBERTO IHL B.
- Institute of Veterinary Preventive Medicine: ERIKA GESCHE R.
- Institute of Clinical Veterinary Sciences: NÉSTOR TADICH B.
- Institute of Animal Pathology: GEROLD SIEVERS P.
- Institute of Pharmacology: FREDERICK AHUMADA M.
- Institute of Meat Sciences and Technology: JOSE A. DE LA VEGA MALINCONI
- Centre of Artificial Insemination: JORGE EHRENFELD VAN HASSELT

Faculty of Sciences:
- Institute of Mathematics: MANUEL BUSTOS V.
- Institute of Physics: DINER MORAGA O.
- Institute of Chemistry: CARLOS CABEZAS CUEVAS
- Institute of Geosciences: MARIO PINO QUIVIRA
- Institute of Biochemistry: JUAN CARLOS SLEBE T.
- Institute of Zoology: GERMÁN PEQUEÑO R.
- Institute of Botany: MIREN ALBERDI L.
- Institute of Microbiology: GERMÁN REINHARDT VATER
- Institute of Ecology and Evolution: CARLOS MORENO M.

Institute of Embryology: OSCAR GOICOECHEA BELLO
Institute of Marine Biology: JORGE NAVARRO A.

Faculty of Engineering Sciences:
Institute of Electricity and Electronics: PEDRO REY CLERICUS
Institute of Industrial Design and Method: ROBERTO CÁRDENAS PARRA
Institute of Civil Engineering: HERIBERTO VIVANCO BILBAO
Institute of Nautical and Maritime Sciences: RAÚL NAVARRO ARROYO
Institute of Acoustics: JORGE SOMMERHOFF HYDE
Institute of Thermomechanics Materials and Methods: ERNESTO ZUMELZU DELGADO
Institute of Information Science and Quantitative Methods: WLADIMIR RÍOS M.

Faculty of Juridical and Social Sciences:
Institute of Juridical Sciences: JUAN ANDRÉS VARAS B.
Institute of Juridical Specialisms: TEODORO CROQUEVIELLE B.

Faculty of Fishery and Oceanography:
Institute of Fishery and Oceanography: FERNANDO JARA S.
Institute of Natural and Exact Sciences: DORIS SOTO B.

UNIVERSIDAD DEL BÍOBÍO

Avda Collao 1202, Casilla 5-C, Concepción
Telephone: (41) 314364
Telex: 260010 (Concepción)
Fax: (41) 313897 (Concepción)

Founded 1988
State control
Language of instruction: Spanish
Academic year: March to July, August to December
Campus also at Avda Andrés Bello s/n, Chillán

Rector: ROBERTO GOYCOOLEA INFANTE
Pro-Rector (Chillán): FELIX MARTINEZ RODRÍGUEZ
Vice-Rector (Academic): HILARIO HERNÁNDEZ GURRUCHAGA
Vice-Rector (Financial): HÉCTOR GAETE FERES
Secretary-General: RODOLFO WALTER DIAZ
Librarian: ROBERTO PAREDES DURÁN

Number of teachers: 540
Number of students: 8,500

Publications: *Noticias UBB* (weekly), *Proyección UBB* (monthly), *Mercado de suelo de Concepción* (3 a year), *Arquitecturas del Sur* (3 a year), *Cuadernos de Edificación en Madera* (3 a year), *Theoría* (annually), *Tiempo y Espacio* (annually), *Memoria Anual Institucional* (annually).

DEANS

Faculty of Architecture, Construction and Design: RICARDO HEMPEL HOLZAPFEL
Faculty of Business Management: OSCAR GERICKE BRANDAU
Faculty of Education and Humanities (Chillán): MARCO AURELIO REYES COCA
Faculty of Engineering: PETER BACKHOUSE ERAZO
Faculty of Health and Food Sciences: NORA PLAZA CEBALLOS
Faculty of Sciences: JORGE PLAZA DE LOS REYES ZAPATA

DIRECTORS

Faculty of Architecture, Construction and Design:
School of Architecture: FLAVIO VALASSINA SIMONETTA
School of Civil Engineering: RAMIRO GARCÍA PEÑA
School of Industrial Design: PATRICIO MORGADO URIBE
School of Graphic Design: HUGO CÁCERES JARA
Department of Design and Theory of Architecture: ROBERTO BURDILES ALLENDE
Department of Planning and Urban Design: ROBERTO LIRA OLMOS
Department of Building: CECILIA POBLETE ARREDONDO
Department of Visual Communication: NINÓN JEGÓ ARAYA

Faculty of Health and Food Sciences:
School of Food Engineering: RICARDO VILLALOBOS CARVAJAL
School of Nursing: GLADYS VÁSQUEZ ZAVALA
School of Nutrition and Dietetics: TERESA PINCHEIRA RODRÍGUEZ
Department of Agroindustry: JOSÉ MIGUEL BASTÍAS MONTES
Department of Nutrition and Public Health: MARÍA ANGÉLICA GONZÁLEZ STAGER
Department of Nursing: SILVIA ALARCÓN SANHUEZA

Faculty of Engineering:
School of Civil Engineering: JUAN MARCUS SCHWENK
Department of Mechanical Engineering: LUIS SAN JUAN SEPÚLVEDA
Department of Electrical Engineering: JORGE SALGADO SAGREDO
Department of Wood Engineering: GUSTAVO CHIANG ACOSTA
Department of Civil Industrial Engineering: LUIS CEBALLOS ARANEDA

Faculty of Sciences:
Department of Physics: MAURICIO CATALDO MONSALVE
Department of Chemistry: ALEJANDRO LLANOS CONCHA
Department of Mathematics: HUMBERTO VALENZUELA MOLINÉ
Department of Basic Sciences (Chillán): FERNANDO TOLEDO MONTIEL

Faculty of Business Management:
Department of Auditing and Management: MAURICIO GUTIÉRREZ URZÚA
Department of Information Systems: LUIS CONTRERAS VILLAR
Department of Auditing and Computer Science: ALEX MEDINA GIACOMOZZI

Faculty of Education and Humanities:
Department of General Studies: MARÍA TERESA ULLOA ENRÍQUEZ
Department of Educational Sciences: MARIO CASTILLO PEÑAILILLO
Department of Arts and Literature: VIVIANA PRADO MEIJER
Department of History, Geography and Social Sciences: JAIME REBOLLEDO VILLAGRA

UNIVERSIDAD CENTRAL

Toesca 1783, Casilla 285-V, Correo 21, Santiago
Telephone: 699-51-51
Fax: 672-29-28

Founded 1982
Private control
Language of instruction: Spanish
Academic year: March to January

Rector: HUGO GÁLVEZ GAJARDO
Vice-Rectors: GONZALO HERNANDEZ URIBE (Academic), VICENTE KOVACEVIC POCKLEPOVIC (Planning and Finance), ENRIQUE MARTIN DAVIS (Administration), PEDRO CRUZAT FUSCHLOCHER (Development)
Secretary General: CARMEN HERMOSILLA VALENCIA
Librarian: NELLY CORNEJO MENESES

Number of teachers: 662
Number of students: 6,177

Publications: *Revista de Derecho*, *Revista de Psicología*, *Revista de Arquitectura*, *Perspectiva*, *Parthenon* (2 a year), *Universidad y Sociedad*, *Boletín Informativo*.

DEANS

Faculty of Architecture and Fine Arts: RENÉ MARTÍNEZ LEMOINE
Faculty of Law: RUBEN OYARZUN GALLEGOS
Faculty of Economics and Administration: FERNANDO ESCOBAR CERDA
Faculty of Physical Sciences and Mathematics: LUIS LUCERO ALDAY
Faculty of Social Sciences: ARISTIDES GIAVELLI ITURRIAGA

DIRECTORS

School of Architecture and Fine Arts: ELIANA ISRAEL JACARD
School of Environmental Studies, Ecology and Landscape Architecture: PABLO VODANOVIC VENEGAS
School of Psychology: LEONARDO VILLARROEL ILICH
School of Primary Education: SELMA SIMONSTEIN FUENTES
School of Law: VICTOR SERGIO MENA VERGARA
School of Economics and Administration: EUGENIO ARRATIA DUQUE
School of Civil Construction: ROBERTO PERALTA CARRASCO
School of Civil Engineering (Public Construction): FERNANDO BONHOME CERDA
School of Engineering in Administration and Agrarian Business: BENJAMIN LABBE VERGARA
School of Accounting: MARTÍN GARRIDO ARAYA
School of Political and Administrative Sciences: HECTOR AGUILERA SEGURA
School of Data Processing and Computer Sciences: SERGIO QUEZADA GONZÁLEZ
School of Business Administration: ROBERTO SZEDERKENYI DICKINSON

ATTACHED RESEARCH CENTRES

Centre of Economic and Administrative Research: San Ignacio 414, Santiago; tel. 6954010; fax 6727377; Dir CARLOS RETAMAL UMPIERREZ.

Centre of Housing Research: José Joaquin Prieto 10001, Casilla 6D, San Bernardo; tel. 5585311; fax 5270323; Dir ALFONSO RAPOSO MOYANO.

Centre of Juridical Research: Lord Cochrane 417, Santiago; tel. 6957533; fax 6727377; Dir RUBEN CELIS RODRIGUEZ.

UNIVERSIDAD DE CHILE

Avda Bernardo O'Higgins 1058, Casilla 10-D, Santiago
Telephone: (2) 6781003
Fax: (2) 6781012

Founded 1738 as Universidad Real de San Felipe; inaugurated 1843 as Universidad de Chile
State control
Academic year: March to December

Rector: Dr JAIME LAVADOS MONTES
Pro-Rector: ALFREDO LAHSEN AZAR
Academic Vice-Rector: Dr FERNANDO LOLAS STEPKE

Library: see Libraries
Number of teachers: 4,369 (including all branch institutions)
Number of students: 19,605

Publications: *Anales de la Universidad de Chile, Actualidad Universitaria,* several journals of the different faculties.

DEANS

Faculty of Architecture and Town Planning: MANUEL FERNÁNDEZ HECHENLEITNER
Faculty of Fine Arts: LUIS MERINO MONTERO

Faculty of Sciences: CAMILO QUEZADA BOUEY
Faculty of Chemical and Pharmaceutical Sciences: HUGO ZUNINO VENEGAS
Faculty of Dentistry: JOSÉ MATAS COLOM
Faculty of Economic and Administrative Sciences: LUIS RIVEROS CORNEJO
Faculty of Law: ROBERTO NAHUM ANUCH
Faculty of Medicine: EDUARDO ROSSELOT JARAMILLO
Faculty of Philosophy and Humanities: LUCIA INVERNIZZI SANTA CRUZ
Faculty of Physical and Mathematical Sciences: VÍCTOR PÉREZ VERA
Faculty of Veterinary Sciences and Cattle Breeding: IÑIGO DÍAZ CUEVAS
Faculty of Agrarian and Forestry Sciences: EDMUNDO ACEVEDO HINOJOSA
Faculty of Social Sciences: MARIO ORELLANA RODRÍGUEZ

DIRECTORS

Institute of International Studies: Condell 249, Santiago; JOAQUÍN FERMANDOIS HUERTA
Institute of Nutrition and Food Technology: Avda José Pedro Alessandri 5540, Santiago; RICARDO UAUY DAGACH-I
Institute of Political Science: María Guerrero 940, Santiago; RICARDO ISRAEL ZIPPER
Clinical Hospital of the University of Chile: Avda Santos Dumont 999, Santiago; Dr LUIS BAHAMONDE BRAVO

UNIVERSIDAD DE CONCEPCIÓN

Casilla 20-C, Concepción

Telephone: (41) 234985
Telex: 260004
Fax: 227455

Founded 1919
Private control
Language of instruction: Spanish
Academic year: March to January

Rector: AUGUSTO PARRA MUÑOZ
Academic Vice-Rector: GONZALO MONTOYA RIVERA
Vice-Rector for Financial Affairs and Personnel: CARLOS CÁCERES SANDOVAL
General Secretary: CARLOS ALVAREZ NUÑEZ
Library Director: MARÍA NIEVES ALONSO MARTÍNEZ

Number of teachers: 1,304
Number of students: 14,000

Publications: *Atenea* (monthly; science, art and literature); *Revista de Derecho* (quarterly); *Gayana, Acta Literaria, RLA—Revista de Lingüística Aplicada, Agro-Ciencia* (2 a year), *Informativo de Rectoría—PANORAMA* (Public Relations).

DEANS

Faculty of Forestry Sciences: JAIME GARCÍA SANDOVAL
Faculty of Biological Sciences: SERGIO MANCINELLI HUIDOBRO
Faculty of Chemical Sciences: SERGIO QUADRI CLEONARES
Faculty of Physical Sciences and Mathematics: ERNESTO FIGUEROA
Faculty of Natural Sciences and Oceanography: ALBERTO LARRAIN PRAT
Faculty of Economic and Administrative Sciences: JUAN SAAVEDRA GONZÁLEZ
Faculty of Education: JORGE ALEGRÍA ALEGRÍA
Faculty of Pharmacy: CARLOS CALVO
Faculty of Engineering: SERGIO LAVANCHY MERINO
Faculty of Law and Social Sciences: SERGIO CARRASCO.
Faculty of Medicine: ELSO SHIAPPACASSE FERRETTI
Faculty of Dentistry: ALVARO CELIS SAN FÉLIX
Faculty of Agriculture: RICARDO MERINO HINRICHSEN
Faculty of Veterinary Medicine: ALEJANDRO SANTA MARIA SANZANA
Faculty of Agricultural Engineering: LUIS SALGADO SEGUEL

HEADS OF DEPARTMENTS

Faculty of Forestry Sciences:
- Silviculture: MIGUEL ESPINOZA BANCALARI
- Forestry Management and Environment: FERNANDO DRAKE ARANDA

Faculty of Biological Sciences:
- Molecular Biology: MARIO ALARCÓN ALVAREZ
- Physiological Science: HERNÁN CÁRDENAS ALVAREZ
- Microbiology: RAÚL ZEMELMAN ZAMBRANO
- Histology and Embryology: RODOLFO PAZ OSORIO
- Pharmacology: MARCELO MEDINA VARGAS
- Physiopathology: ELIAS APUD SIMÓN

Faculty of Chemical Sciences:
- Analytical and Inorganic Chemistry: HERNÁN MATURANA
- Physical Chemistry: JUAN GODOY ALMIRALL
- Organic Chemistry: SARA GNECCO
- Earth Sciences: SANTIAGO COLLAO ITURRA
- Polymers: BERNABÉ RIVAS QUIROZ

Faculty of Physical Sciences and Mathematics:
- Physics: JUAN MORALES TORO
- Atmospheric and Oceanographic Physics: DANTE FIGUEROA
- Mathematical Engineering: GABRIEL GATICA PÉREZ
- Statistics: LUIS CID SERRANO
- Mathematical Methods: GUSTAVO AVELLO JOFRÉ

Faculty of Natural Sciences and Oceanography:
- Botany: MARIO SILVA
- Zoology: JORGE ARTIGAS COCH
- Oceanography: MARÍA IRENE LÉPEZ

Faculty of Economics and Administrative Sciences:
- Administration: LUIS MORENO PARRA
- Economics: ARCADIO CERDA URRUTIA

Faculty of Education:
- Curricula and Instruction: CARMEN DOMÍNGUEZ
- Physical Education: VICENTE GARCÍA GUAJARDO
- Educational Sciences: OSVALDO ARANEDA PERALTA

Faculty of Pharmacy:
- Instrumental Analysis: DIETRICH VON BAER LOCHOW
- Applied Biochemistry: CARLOS CALVO MONFÍL
- Bromatology, Nutrition and Dietetics: NÉSTOR MENDOZA CAMPOS
- Pharmacy: VÍCTOR JARAMILLO MENA

Faculty of Engineering:
- Civil Engineering: VÍCTOR AROS ARAYA
- Electrical Engineering: RICARDO SÁNCHEZ SCHULZ
- System Engineering: YUSSEF FARRAN LEIVA
- Mechanical Engineering: JOEL ZAMBRANO VALENCIA
- Metallurgical Engineering: RAÚL BENAVENTE GARCÍA
- Chemical Engineering: ALFREDO GORDON STRASSER
- Industrial Engineering: LORENA PRADENAS

Faculty of Law and Social Sciences:
- Economic Law: ABUNDIO PÉREZ RODRIGO
- Procedural Law: HÉCTOR OBERG YÁÑEZ
- Private Law: HERNÁN TRONCOSO LARRONDE
- Public Law: TARCICIO OVIEDO SOTO
- Labour Law: MARIO ROMERO GUGGINSBERG
- History and Philosophy of Law: JESÚS ESCANDÓN ÁLOMAR
- Social Service: OLGA MORA MARDONES
- Penal Law: MARCELO TORRES DUFFAU
- Political and Administrative Sciences: MARCELO SAN MARTIN CERUTTI

Faculty of Medicine:
- Surgery: ALBERTO GYHRA SOTO
- Nursing: VERÓNICA BEHM
- Specialities: RAÚL GONZÁLEZ RAMOS
- Obstetrics and Gynaecology: MILTON NIEDBALSKI MIRANDA
- Obstetrics and Paediatrics: TERESA URIARTE AVILÉS
- Internal Medicine: RUBÉN BERMÚDEZ OYARCE
- Normal and Pathological Anatomy and Legal Medicine: LUIS VIELMA BUSTAMANTE
- Psychiatry and Mental Health: BENJAMIN VICENTE PARADA
- Paediatrics: VERA WILHELM PERELMAN
- Public Health: GUSTAVO MOLINA MARTINEZ

Faculty of Dentistry:
- Surgical Stomatology: JORGE ESPEJO ARGANDOÑA
- Restorative Dentistry: ALFONSO CATALÁN SEPÚLVEDA
- Pathology and Diagnosis: ALBERTO RIVERA ARAYA
- Oral Paediatrics: ALFREDO SAAVEDRA CRUZ
- Public Health: LUIS VARGAS SANHUEZA

Faculty of Agriculture:
- Animal Production: FERNANDO BÓRQUEZ LAGOS
- Vegetable Production: ALFREDO VERA MANRÍQUEZ
- Soils: IVÁN PARRA VIDAL

Faculty of Veterinary Medicine:
- Clinical Sciences: ARMANDO ISLAS LETELIER
- Pathology and Preventive Medicine: HERNÁN GONZÁLEZ HENRÍQUEZ
- Animal Production and Reproduction: JOSÉ COX URETA

Faculty of Agricultural Engineering:
- Energy and Mechanization: MARIO IBÁÑEZ CIFUENTES
- Products and Structural Processes: PEDRO MELÍN MARÍN
- Irrigation and Drainage: LUIS SALGADO SEGUEL

ATTACHED CENTRES

Centro EULA Chile: Dir OSCAR PARRA BARRIENTOS; environmental sciences.
Centro GEA: Dir JOSÉ FRUTOS JARA; applied and geological sciences.

UNIVERSIDAD DIEGO PORTALES

Avda Ejército 412, Santiago

Telephone (2) 6762000
Fax: (2) 6762112

Founded 1982

Rector: MANUEL MONTT BALMACEDA
Vice-Rector: FRANCISCO VALDÉS NAGEL
Vice-Director (Academic): SERGIO TUTELEERS RAMÍREZ
General Director (Economic and Administrative): NELSON BRAVO CORREA
Director for Development: JAIME TORREALBA CUBILLOS
General Director for Student Affairs: ROBERTO VEGA MASSÓ
Librarian: PATRICIA GONZÁLEZ MARTÍNEZ

Number of teachers: 796
Number of students: 7,337

Publications: *El Portaliano, Noticias Académicas.*

DEANS

Faculty of Law: CARLOS PEÑA GONZÁLEZ
Faculty of Business Administration: TOMISLAV MANDAKOVIC FANTA
Faculty of Human Sciences: JUAN PABLO TORO CIFUENTES
Faculty of Communication and Information Science: LUCÍA CASTELLON AGUAYO

Faculty of Industrial Engineering and Data Processing: LUIS COURT MOOCK
School of Design: HERNÁN GARFIAS ARTE

UNIVERSIDAD GABRIELA MISTRAL

Avda Ricardo Lyon 1177, Santiago
Telephone: 2734545

Founded 1981

Academic year: March to January

Rector: ALICIA ROMO ROMÁN
Administrative Director: ESTANISLAO GALOFRÉ
Librarian: CARMEN BUSQUETS

Number of teachers: 450
Number of students: 3,500

DIRECTORS

Department of Law: LISANDRO SERRANO
Department of Economics and Business Administration: FRANCISCO JAVIER LABBÉ
Department of Education: SYLVIA SAILER
Department of Engineering: RODOLFO MARTÍNEZ
Department of Psychology: HERNÁN BERWART
Department of Social Sciences: RICARDO RIESCO
Department of Journalism: LURETO CAVIEDES

ATTACHED INSTITUTES

Instituto de Economía.

Instituto de Estudios del Pacífico.

Instituto de Lenguas.

Centro de Estudios de la Mujer.

Centro de Estudios Económicos, Jurídicos, Administrativos y Sociales de la Empresa.

UNIVERSIDAD DE LA FRONTERA

Avda Francisco Salazar 01145, Casilla 54-D, Temuco

Telephone: (45) 325000
Fax: (45) 325950

Founded 1981
State control
Academic year: March to July, August to December

Rector: Dr HEINRICH VON BAER VON LOCHOW
Vice-Rector (Academic): CÉSAR BURGUEÑO MORENO
Vice-Rector (Administration and Finance): JOSÉ MIGUEL LÓPEZ SANTA MARÍA
Secretary-General: FERNANDO MARCHANT TAIBA
Library Director: HERNÁN BURGOS VEGA

Number of teachers: 830
Number of students: 7,061

Publications: *Cubo* (annually), *Pekuntun* (2 a year), *ENLACES* (quarterly), *Chilean Review of Biological Medical Sciences* (2 a year), *Chilean Review of Anatomy* (2 a year), *Frontera* (annually), *Vertientes UFRO* (monthly), *Uni-Letter* (quarterly).

DEANS

Faculty of Engineering and Administration: SANTIAGO RAMÍREZ MORALES
Faculty of Education and Humanities: OMAR GARRIDO PRADENAS
Faculty of Medicine: RAÚL SALVATICI SALAZAR
Faculty of Agricultural and Forestry Sciences: ALFONSO AGUILERA PUENTE

HEADS OF DEPARTMENT

Faculty of Medicine:

- Basic Sciences: MARIANO DEL SOL CALDERÓN
- Surgery and Traumatology: PLÁCIDO FLORES ORTIZ
- Medicine (specialized): EDUARDO ILLANES VERDUGO
- Internal Medicine: EDUARDO LANAS ZANETTI
- Obstetrics and Gynaecology: WILFRED DIENER OJEDA
- Pre-clinical Sciences: CARLOS SCHULZ RIQUELME
- Paediatrics and Infant Surgery: EDUARDO HEBEL WEISS
- Public Health: JAIME SERRA CANALES
- Integral Odontology: GILDA CORSINI MUÑOZ

Faculty of Engineering and Administration:

- Physical Sciences: MARIO VILLOUTA SANHUEZA
- Chemical Sciences: EDDIE PERICH TOLEDO
- Electrical Engineering: MANUEL VILLARROEL MORENO
- Mechanical Engineering: MARIO INOSTROZA DELGADO
- Chemical Engineering: XIMENA INOSTROZA HOFFMANN
- Systems Engineering: EDUARDO NAVARRETE SUÁREZ
- Mathematics and Statistics: PEDRO VALENZUELA TAPIA
- Civil Engineering: JAIME RIQUELME CARRERA
- Administration and Economy: FERNANDO URRA JARA

Faculty of Education and Humanities:

- Education: IRAMA LABRAÑA MÉNDEZ
- Social Sciences: ARACELY CARO PUENTES
- Language, Literature and Communication: HUGO CARRASCO MUÑOZ
- Psychology: BEATRIZ VIZCARRA LARRAÑAGA
- Social Work: ANA MARÍA SALAMÉ COULON
- Physical Education, Sports and Recrea-tion: HERNÁN MERCADO AMPUERO

Faculty of Agricultural and Forestry Sciences:

- Agricultural Sciences and Natural Resources: RAMÓN REBOLLEDO RANZ
- Agricultural Production: JAIME GUERRERO CONTRERAS

ATTACHED INSTITUTES

Institute of Agroindustry: Dir RODOLFO PIHÁN SORIANO.

Institute of Environment: Dir JAIME GOMÁ MARTÍNEZ.

Institute of Indigenous Studies: JULIO TEREUCÁN ANGULO.

Institute of Information Science in Education: PEDRO HEPP KUSCHEL.

UNIVERSIDAD DE LA SERENA

Avda Raúl Bitrán N. s/n, La Serena
Telephone: (51) 204000
Fax: (51) 204310

Founded 1981
State control
Academic year: March to December

Rector: JAIME POZO CISTERNAS
Vice-Rector (Academic): MARÍA LINA BERRIOS SALAS
Vice-Rector (Administrative): JOSÉ AGUILERA MUÑOZ
Secretary-General: LUIS NÚÑEZ OLIVARES
Librarian: MARIA A. CALABACERO JIMENEZ

Number of teachers: 268
Number of students: 6,200

Publications: *Revista de Educación* (annually), *Revista de Investigación y Desarrollo* (annually), *Notas Científicas* (annually).

DEANS

Faculty of Engineering: MARIO CÁCERES VALENZUELA
Faculty of Humanities: BERTA SAN MARTÍN ALVAREZ
Faculty of Sciences: SERGIO MARTÍNEZ SILVA

HEADS OF DEPARTMENTS

Faculty of Engineering:

- Civil Engineering: MARIO DURAN LILLO
- Mining Engineering: JORGE OYARZÚN MUÑOZ
- Civil Industrial Engineering: FEDERICO CAROZZI SALVATIERRA
- Mechanical Engineering: RICARDO CASTILLO BOZZO
- Food Engineering: LUIS DIAZ NEIRA

Faculty of Humanities:

- Education: JORGE SALGADO SANHUEZA
- Music: LINA BARRIENTOS PACHECO
- Social Sciences: GUIDO VÉLIZ CANTUARIAS
- Arts and Letters: CRISTIÁN NOEMI PADILLA
- Psychology: MARÍA LOURDES CAMPOS
- Economic and Administrative Sciences: EDUARDO MONREAL MONREAL

Faculty of Sciences:

- Biology: SERGIO ZEPEDA MALUENDA
- Chemistry: IVAN FERNÁNDEZ ROJAS
- Mathematics: MICHAEL NEUBURG GRUND
- Physics: PEDRO VEGA JORQUERA
- Agronomy: LILIAM RUBIO MUÑOZ
- Nursing: ANA MARÍA VÁSQUEZ AQUEVEQUE

HEADS OF SCHOOLS

Faculty of Engineering:

- School of Civil Engineering; ALBERTO CORTES ALVAREZ
- School of Architecture: PAZ WALKER FERNANDEZ
- School of Civil Construction: GLORIA LLAMBIAS ABATTE
- School of Technical Engineering: JUAN CAMPOS FERREIRA
- School of Food Engineering: MARIO PEREZ WON

Faculty of Humanities:

- School of Teaching Humanities: ANA MARIA CORTES ALCAYAGA
- School of Psychology: PEDRO BOLGERI ESCORZA
- School of Teaching Music: OLIVIA CONCHA MOLINARI
- School of Journalism: VIRGINIA AGUIRRE JORQUERA
- School of Design: RAFAEL PAREDES ROJAS
- School of Commercial Engineering: LUPERFINA ROJAS ESCOBAR
- School of Tourism Administration: EDUARDO MONREAL MONREAL
- School of Auditing: CALIXTO VEAS GAZ

Faculty of Sciences:

- School of Agronomy: CARMEN JORQUERA JARAMILLO
- School of Teaching Sciences: GUSTAVO LABBÉ MORALES
- School of Nursing: ANA MARIA VASQUEZ AQUEVEQUE
- School of Chemical Laboratories: JULIO PONCE TRENGOVE
- School of Computation Engineering: ERIC JELSTCH FIGUEROA

UNIVERSIDAD DE LOS LAGOS

Casilla 933, Osorno
Telephone: 235377
Fax: 239517

Founded 1993; fmrly Instituto Profesional de Osorno

State control
Academic year: March to December

Rector: DANIEL LÓPEZ STEFONI
Vice-Rector: FRANCISCO VERGARA CUBILLOS
Academic Director: GLAUCO TORRES ROJAS
Administrative Director: GABRIEL HIDALGO AEDO
Librarian: EDUARDO BARROS BARROS

Number of teachers: 121 full-time, 97 part-time
Number of students: 2,500

Publications: *Biota* (aquatic sciences), *Alpha* (humanities), *Leader* (social sciences).

DIRECTORS

Department of Aquaculture and Aquatic Resources: CARLOS VARELA SANTIBAÑEZ
Department of Administration: JUAN ABELLO ROMERO

Department of Food and Forest Resources: Lucía de la Fuente Jiménez
Department of Physical Education: Ramón Arcay Montoya
Department of Basic Sciences: Gonzalo Gajardo Galvez
Department of Exact Sciences: Hernán Muñoz Hernández
Department of Social Sciences: Juan Sánchez Alvarez
Department of Education: Drago Vrsalovic Mihoevic
Department of Humanities and Art: Nelson Vergara Muñoz
Department of Fisheries (in Puerto Montt): Luis Ferreira Osses
Coyhaique Campus: Margarita Oyarco Igor

UNIVERSIDAD DE MAGALLANES

Casilla 113-D, Punta Arenas

Telephone: 212945
Fax: 219276

Founded 1964 (previously branch of Universidad Técnica del Estado)
State control
Language of instruction: Spanish
Academic year: begins in March

Rector: Dr Víctor Fajardo Morales
Vice-Rector (Academic): Luis Oval González
Secretary-General: Magdalena Aguero Caro
Librarian: Iluminanda Rojas Palacios

Number of teachers: 131
Number of students: 2,700

Publications: *Austrouniversitaria*, *Anales del Instituto de la Patagonia*.

DEANS

Faculty of Engineering: Juan Oyarzo Pérez
Faculty of Humanities and Social Sciences: Luis Poblete Davanzo
Faculty of Sciences: Octavio Lecaros Palma

HEADS OF DEPARTMENTS

Electrical Engineering: Luis González Veloso
Mechanical Engineering: Humberto Oyarzo Pérez
Mathematics and Physics: Víctor Valderrana Vergara
Chemical Engineering: José Retamales Espinoza
Administration and Economics: Ricardo Méndez Romero
Education and Humanities: Elia Mella Garay
Health Sciences: Susana Loaiza Miranda
Science and Natural Resources: Orlando Dollenz Alvarez
Computer Science: Serafin Ruiz Rebolledo
Agricultural and Aquacultural Resources Science and Technology: Sergio Kusanovic Mimica

ATTACHED INSTITUTE

Instituto de la Patagonia: Avda Bulnes 01890, Casilla 113-D, Punta Arenas; tel. 217173; fax 212973; f. 1969; scientific, cultural and social development of the South American region; Dir Mateo Martinic Beros.

UNIVERSIDAD METROPOLITANA DE CIENCIAS DE LA EDUCACIÓN

Casilla 147, Correo Central, Santiago

Telephone: 2257731

Founded 1889

Rector: Ariel Leporati Parra
Vice-Rector: Maximino Fernandez Fraile
Director of Administration: Rosana Sprovera Manriquez
Librarian: María Isabel Bruce

Number of teachers: 440
Number of students: 4,400

Publications: *Academia, Dimensión histórica de Chile, Educación Física, Acta Entomológica chilena*.

DEANS

Faculty of History, Geography and Literature: Silvia Vyhmeister Tzschabran
Faculty of Arts and Physical Education: Milton Cofre Iluffi
Faculty of Philosophy and Education: Jaime Araos San Martin
Faculty of Basic Sciences: Mafalda Schiappacasse Costa

UNIVERSIDAD CATÓLICA DEL NORTE

Avda Angamos 0610, Casilla 1280, Antofagasta

Telephone: 241148
Telex: 225097
Fax: 241724

Founded 1956
Language of instruction: Spanish
Private control
Academic year: March to July, August to December

Chancellor: Most Rev. Patricio Infante Alfonso
Rector: Juan A. Music Tomicic
Vice-Rectors: Raúl Apaz Vargas (Academic Affairs), Miriam Atienzo Soto (Economic Affairs), Renzo Follegatti Ghio (Coquimbo campus)
General Secretary: Victoria González Stuardo
Head of Admissions Office: Carlos Sainz López
Librarian: Drahomíra Srýtrová Tomásová

Library of 99,000 vols
Number of teachers: 398
Number of students: 8,033

Publications: *Boletín de Educación, Revista Reflejos, Revista Proyecciones, Revista Vertiente, Estudios Atacameños, Revista de Derecho, Cuadernos de Arquitectura*, etc.

DEANS

Antofagasta Campus:

Faculty of Architecture, Civil Engineering and Construction: Pablo Reyes Franzani
Faculty of Economics: Patricio Aroca González
Faculty of Engineering and Geological Sciences: Teodoro Politis Jaramis
Faculty of Sciences: Ramón Correa Soto
Faculty of Humanities: Mario Cortés Flores

Coquimbo Campus:

Faculty of Marine Sciences: Wolfgang Stotz Uslar

ATTACHED INSTITUTES

Archaeological Research Institute and Museum 'R. P. Gustavo Le Paige': Dir Lautaro Núñez Atencio.

Institute of Astronomy: Dir Luis Barrera Salas.

Institute of Applied Regional Economics: Dir (vacant).

Coastal Centre of Aquaculture and Marine Research.

UNIVERSIDAD DE PLAYA ANCHA DE CIENCIAS DE LA EDUCACIÓN

Avda Playa Ancha 850, Casilla 34-V, Valparaíso

Telephone: (32) 281758
Fax: (32) 285041

Founded 1948
Languages of instruction: Spanish, English, French, German
State control
Academic year: March to December

Rector: Norman Cortes Larrieu
Pro-Rector: German Campos Pardo
Head of Administration and Finance: Sergio Infante Barra
Librarian: Maria Eugenia Olguin Steenbecker

Number of teachers: 328
Number of students: 3,700

Publications: *Diccionario Ejemplificado de Chilenismos, Revista de Orientación, Diálogos Educacionales, Nueva Revista del Pacífico, Notas Históricas y Geográficas, Visiones Científicas, Proyección Universitaria*.

DEANS

Faculty of Educational Sciences: Rene Flores Castillo
Faculty of Physical Education: Antonio Maurer Furst
Faculty of Natural and Exact Sciences: Guillermo Riveros Gomez
Faculty of Arts: Belfort Ruz Escudero
Faculty of Humanities: Daniel Lagos Altamirano

HEADS OF DEPARTMENTS

Faculty of Educational Sciences:

Systematic Teaching: Maria Isabel Muñoz Rojo
Educational Sciences: Gaston Aguilar Pulido

Faculty of Natural and Exact Sciences:

Mathematics and Physics: Jose Rubio Valenzuela
Biology and Chemistry: Sergio Zamorano Pozo

Faculty of Humanities:

Languages and Information Sciences: Lidia Contardo Hogtert
Philosophy of Social Sciences: Enrique Muñoz Mickle

Faculty of Arts:

Music: Maria Teresa Devia Lubet
Visual Arts: Alberto Madrid Letelier

Faculty of Physical Education:

Physical Education: Elias Marin Valenzuela
Sports and Recreation: Pamela Galleguillos Guerrero

UNIVERSIDAD SAN SEBASTIÁN

Casilla 3427, Correo Concepción

Telephone: (41) 230116
Fax: (41) 244563
E-mail: uss@mater.uss.cl

Founded 1989
Private control
Academic year: March to December

Rector: Guido Alfredo Meller Mayr
Vice-Rector: Soledad Ramírez Gatica
Registrar: Fernando Canitrot Martínez
Librarian: Margarita Valderrama Cáceres

Library of 6,000 vols
Number of teachers: 174
Number of students: 1,714

DEANS

School of Law: Marcelo Contreras Hauser
School of Information Sciences: Cristián Antoine Faúndez
School of Social Services: Marta Montory Torres
School of Medicine: Dr Alexis Lama Toro
School of Business Studies and Administration: José Luis Parra Arias
School of Psychology: Carmen Bonnefoy Dibarrart
School of Child Education: Magdalena Burmeister Campos

UNIVERSIDAD DE SANTIAGO DE CHILE

Alameda Libertador Bernardo O'Higgins 3363, Casilla 442, Correo 2, Santiago
Telephone: (2) 6811100
Telex: 441674
Fax: (2) 6812663

Founded 1947 as Universidad Técnica del Estado, renamed 1981
State control
Language of instruction: Spanish
Academic year: March to December

Rector: EDUARDO MORALES SANTOS
Pro-Rector: MANUEL VEGA PEREZ
Teaching and Extension Vice-Rector: GERARDO GALINDO GRIFFITH
Vice-Rector for Student Affairs: RENE SCHIFFERLI DELARZE
Vice-Rector for Research and Development: MAURICIO ESCUDEY CASTRO
Vice-Rector for Administrative and Financial Affairs: PEDRO NARVARTE ARREGUI
Secretary-General: ANIBAL REYES TRONCOSO
Academic Registrar: JAIME CAZENAVE PONTANILLA
Librarian: JORGE DEMANGEL RUIZ

Number of teachers: 2,025
Number of students: 18,431

Publications: *Contribuciones Científicas y Tecnológicas, Boletín APYME* (every 2 months), *Avances en Investigación y Desarrollo* (quarterly), *Educación en Ingeniería, Manutención e Industria* (quarterly), *Cuadernos de Humanidades, Comunicación Universitaria, Comunicaciones en Desarrollo de Creatividad, Educación para el Desarrollo, Presencia.*

DEANS

Faculty of Engineering: JORGE GAVILAN LEON
Faculty of Administration and Economics: CARLOS ARAYA VILLALOBOS
Faculty of Sciences: NORMA GREZ VIELA
Faculty of Humanities: VICTOR AGUILERA VASQUEZ
Faculty of Medicine: FRANCISCO MARDONES RESTAT
Faculty of Technology: MIGUEL PORTUGAL CAMPILLAY
School of Journalism: JUAN JORGE FAUNDES
School of Psychology: ORLANDO SALAMANCA OSORIO
School of Architecture: HANS FOX TIMMLING

ATTACHED INSTITUTE

Instituto de Estudios Avanzados: Román Díaz 89, Santiago; Dir CARMEN NORAMBUENA CARRASCO.

UNIVERSIDAD DE TALCA

2 Norte 685, Talca
Telephone: 200101
Fax: 228054

Founded 1981
State control
Language of instruction: Spanish
Academic year: March to December

Rector: Dr ÁLVARO ROJAS MARÍN
Vice-Rector for Student Affairs: CARLOS HOJAS ALONSO
Vice-Rector for Finance and Administration: PATRICIO ORTÚZAR RUIZ
Vice-Rector for Academic Affairs: JUAN ANTONIO ROCK TARUD
Secretary-General: JUAN FRANCO DE LA JARA
Librarian: MARIA ANGÉLICA TEJOS MUÑOZ

Number of teachers: 186 full-time, 161 part-time
Number of students: 4,300

Publications: *Universum* (annually), *Panorama Socio Económico* (annually), *Acontecer* (monthly), *Ius et Praxis* (2 a year).

DEANS

Faculty of Business Administration: ARCADIO CERDA URRUTIA
Faculty of Juridical and Social Sciences: HUMBERTO NOGUEIRA ALCALÁ
Faculty of Engineering: JORGE OSSANDÓN GAETE
Faculty of Forestry Sciences: IVAN CHACON CONTRERAS
Faculty of Agricultural Sciences: JAVIER LUIS TRONCOSO CORREA
Faculty of Health Sciences: CARLOS GIGOUX CASTELLÓN

DIRECTORS

Faculty of Business Administration:
- School of Commercial Engineering: LUIS REY VERDUGO
- School of Auditing: VICTOR HUGO RUIZ ROJAS
- School of Postgraduate Studies: JOSÉ ROJAS MÉNDEZ

Faculty of Juridical and Social Sciences:
- School of Law: RUPERTO PINOCHET OLAVE

Faculty of Engineering:
- School of Mechanical Engineering: FELIPE TIRADO DÍAZ
- School of Civil and Industrial Engineering: CARLOS TOLEDO ABARCA

Faculty of Forestry Sciences:
- School of Forestry Engineering: OSCAR VALLEJOS BARRA

Faculty of Agronomy:
- School of Agronomy: RAMON RODRIGUEZ HERRERA

Faculty of Health Sciences:
- School of Odontology: (vacant)
- School of Medical Technology: SILVIA VIDAL FLORES

ATTACHED INSTITUTES

Instituto de Estudios Humanísticos Abate Juan Ignacio Molina: Dir JAVIER PINEDO CASTRO.

Instituto de Investigación y Desarrollo Educacional: Dir GUSTAVO HAWES BARRIOS.

Instituto de Matemática y Física: Dir JUAN PABLO PRIETO COX.

Instituto de Química de Recursos Naturales: Dir JOSE SAN MARTIN ACEVEDO.

Instituto de Biología Vegetal y Biotecnología: Dir JOSE SAN MARTIN ACEVEDO.

UNIVERSIDAD DE TARAPACÁ

Gral Velásquez 1775, Casilla 7-D, Arica
Telephone: (58) 222800
Fax: (58) 232135

Founded 1981
State control
Language of instruction: Spanish
Academic year: March to July, August to December

Rector: Ing. LUIS TAPIA ITURRIETA
Vice-Rector for Academic Affairs: CLAUDIO DÍAZ MELENDEZ
Vice-Rector for Finance and Administration: MAURICIO NESPOLO COVA
Librarian: INÉS RODRÍGUEZ RIQUELME

Library of 73,300 vols, 622 periodicals
Number of teachers: 215 full-time, 67 part-time
Number of students: 4,728

Publications: *Idesia, Chungará, Diálogo Andino, Administración y Economía, Graa, Aportes Matemáticos, Revista Facultad de Ingeniería y Temas Regionales.*

DEANS

Faculty of Social Sciences, Business Administration and Economics: PABLO JIMENEZ QUIÑONES
Faculty of Engineering: JORGE BENAVIDES SILVA
Faculty of Sciences: ARTURO FLORES FRANULIC
Faculty of Education and Humanities: CARLOS HERRERA SAAVEDRA
Research Institute for Agricultural Sciences: EUGENIO DOUSSOULIN ESCOBAR

UNIVERSIDAD TÉCNICA 'FEDERICO SANTA MARÍA'

Avda España 1680, Casilla 110V, Valparaíso
Telephone: 626364
Fax: 660504

Founded 1926
Private control
Language of instruction: Spanish
Academic year: March to December

Rector: ADOLFO ARATA ANDREANI
Vice-Rectors: DANIEL ALKALAY LOWITT (Academic), GIOVANNI PESCE SANTANA (Economic and Administrative Affairs)
Secretary-General: FRANCISCO GHISOLFO ARAYA
Library Director: MARÍA EUGENIA LAULIÉ

Library: see Libraries
Number of teachers: 486
Number of students: 6,800

Publications: *Scientia* (annually), *Gestión Tecnológica* (2 a year).

BRANCH CAMPUSES

Sede José Miguel Carrera: Casilla 920, Viña del Mar; Dir ROSENDO ESTAY MARTÍNEZ.

Sede Rey Balduino de Bélgica: Casilla 457, Talcahuano; Dir ALEX ERIZ SOTO.

Campus Santiago: El Golf 243, Las Condes, Santiago; Dir SERGIO OLAVARRÍA SIMONSEN.

Campus Rancagua: Gamero 212, Rancagua; Dir SERGIO ESTAY VILLALÓN.

UNIVERSIDAD DE VALPARAÍSO

Casilla 123-V, Valparaíso
Telephone: (32) 213071
Fax: (32) 220071

Founded 1981; previously branch of University of Chile
State control
Academic year: two terms, beginning March and August

Rector: AGUSTÍN SQUELLA NARDUCCI
Pro-Rector: JULIO CASTRO SEPÚLVEDA
Academic Director-General: OSVALDO BADENIER BUSTAMENTE
Secretary-General: ALDO VALLE ACEVEDO

Number of teachers: 200 full-time, 560 part-time
Number of students: 5,407

Publications: *Revista de Ciencias Sociales, Revista de Biología Marina, Boletín Micológico.*

DEANS

Faculty of Law and Social Sciences: ITALO PAOLINELLI MONTI
Faculty of Medicine: Dr DAVID SABAH JAIME
Faculty of Architecture: JAIME FARÍAS CÓRDOVA
Faculty of Dentistry: Dr LUIS OLIVARES MELÉNDEZ
Faculty of Economics and Administration: JUAN RIQUELME ZUCCHET
Faculty of Science: ANTONIO GLARÍA BENCOECHEA

UNIVERSIDAD CATÓLICA DE VALPARAÍSO

Avda Brasil 2950, Casilla 4059, Valparaíso
Telephone: (32) 27-30-00
Telex: 230389
Fax: (32) 21-27-46

Founded 1928
Private control

Academic year: March to July, August to December

Chancellor: Mgr Francisco Javier Errazuriz Ossa

Rector: Prof. Bernardo Donoso Riveros

Vice-Rectors: Alfonso Muga Naredo (Academic Affairs); Claudio Elortegui Raffo (Administrative and Financial Affairs), David Cademartori Rosso (Development Affairs)

Secretary-General: Gabriel Yany Gonzalez

Registrar: Victor Diaz Flores

Librarian: Atilio Bustos Gonzalez

Library: see Libraries

Number of teachers: 545

Number of students: 8,200

Publications: *Revista Geográfica de Valparaíso, Revista Investigaciones Marinas, Revista de Derecho, Revista de Estudios Históricos Jurídicos, Revista Philosophica, Revista Signos, Revista Perspectiva Educacional.*

DEANS

Faculty of Agronomy: Fundo La Palma, Quillota; Eduardo Salgado Varas

Faculty of Architecture: Avda Matta 12, Recreo, Viña del Mar; Salvador Zahr Maluk

Faculty of Basic Sciences and Mathematics: Avda Brasil 2950; Enrique Montenegro Arcila

Faculty of Economics and Administration: Avda Brasil 2950; Fernando Alvarado Quiroga

Faculty of Law and Social Sciences: Avda Brasil 2950; Enrique Aimone Gibson

Faculty of Philosophy and Education: Avda Brasil 2950; Renato Ochoa Disselkoen

Faculty of Engineering: Avda Brasil 2147; Feliciano Tomarelli Zapico

Faculty of Natural Resources: Avda Altamirano 1480; Esteban Morales Gamboa

Institute of Religious Studies: Avda Errázuriz 2734; Kamel Harire Seda

INSTITUTO PROFESIONAL DE SANTIAGO

Calle Dieciocho 161, Casilla 9845, Santiago

Telephone: 6981950

Founded 1981

Rector: Luis Pinto Faverio

Pro-Rector: Manuel Hevia Soto

Academic Vice-Rector: Sergio Gallardo E.

Vice-Rector for Administration: Félix Durán Fierro

Vice-Rector for Finance: Víctor Rocher Ferrada

Secretary: Miguel Avendaño Berríos

Librarian: Ximena Sánchez Staforelli

Number of teachers: 458

Number of students: 5,600

Publications: *Trilogía, Anuario Investigación del Departamento de Humanidades, Boletín Investigación del Departamento de Humanidades* (quarterly).

DIRECTORS

Department of Basic Sciences and Mathematics: Claudio Vila Ceppi (acting)

Department of Humanities: Juan Berrueta Castro (acting)

School of Administration: Luis Valenzuela Silva

School of Librarianship: Bruna Benzi Bistolfi

School of Computer Studies: Nina Valdivía Arenas (acting)

School of Social Work: Marta Jala Rubilar

School of Accountancy: Guillermo Zárate Gibert

School of Technology: Tomás Massardo Pérez

School of Civil Engineering: René Zorrilla Fuenzálida

School of Design: Waldo González Herve

Colleges

Escuela Militar 'General Bernardo O'Higgins': Los Militares 4500, Las Condes, Santiago; fax 2082946; f. 1817 (by General O'Higgins); 90 military instructors and officials, 80 civilian instructors, 700 students; library of 25,000 vols; Dir Col Oscar Izurieta Ferrer; Librarians Oscar Cornejo C., Juan Carlos Medina V.; publ. *Revista 'Cien Aguilas'* (annually), *Memorial del Ejército, Armas y Servicio.*

Facultad Latinoamericana de Ciencias Sociales (FLACSO)—Programa Santiago: Facultad Latinoamericana de Ciencias Sociales (FLACSO)—Programa Santiago:Casilla 3213, Correo Central, Santiago; tel. (2) 2256955; fax (2) 2741004; f. 1957; postgraduate training and research centre for Latin America; 35 staff; library of 17,000 vols, 700 periodicals; Dir Francisco Rojas Aravena; Librarian María Inés Bravo; publs *Documentos de Trabajo, Serie Libros FLACSO.*

Instituto Agrícola Metodista 'El Vergel' (Methodist Agricultural Institute): Casilla 2-D, Angol; tel. (45) 712103; fax (45) 711202; f. 1919; ornamental plant nursery, fruit nursery, fruit-garden, dairy, cattle ranch, apiculture, tourism, workshops, packing; museum; Administrator Rev. Mario Mayer.

PEOPLE'S REPUBLIC OF CHINA

Learned Societies

GENERAL

Chinese Academy of Sciences: 52 San Li He Rd, Beijing 100864; tel. (10) 68597219; fax (10) 68511095; f. 1949; academic divisions of Mathematics and Physics (Dir Prof. WANG SHOUGUAN), Biological Science (Dir Prof. ZOU CHENGLU), Chemistry (Dir Prof. ZHANG CUNHAO), Earth Sciences (Dir Prof. TU GUANGZHI), Technological Sciences (Dir Prof. SHI CHANGXU); 584 mems, 13 foreign mems; attached research institutes: see Research Institutes; libraries: see Libraries and Archives; Pres. Prof. LU YONGXIANG; Sec.-Gen. Prof. ZHU XUAN.

Chinese Academy of Social Sciences: 5 Jianguomen Nei Da Jie, Beijing 100732; tel. 65137744; f. c. 1977; attached research institutes: see Research Institutes; Pres. HU QIAOMU; Sec.-Gen. MEI YI.

AGRICULTURE, FISHERIES AND VETERINARY SCIENCE

China Society of Fisheries: 31 Minfeng Lane, Beijing 100032; tel. 66020794; fax 66062346; 15,000 mems; library of 12,000 vols; Pres. ZHANG YANXI; publs *Journal of Fisheries of China, Marine Fisheries, Freshwater Fisheries, Deep-sea Fisheries, Scientific Fish Farming*.

Chinese Academy of Agricultural Sciences: 30 Bai Shi Qiao Rd, Beijing 100081; tel. 62174433; fax 62174142; f. 1957; 40 attached research institutes; library of 650,000 vols, 7,000 periodicals; Pres. LU FEIJIE; publs *Acta Agronomica Sinica, Acta Horticulturae Sinica, Acta Phyliphulacica Sinica* etc.

Chinese Academy of Forestry: Wan Shou Shan, 100091 Beijing; tel. (10) 62582211; fax (10) 62584229; f. 1958; 4,700 mems; attached research institutes: see Research Institutes; library of 400,000 vols; Pres. JIANG ZEHUI; publs *Scientia Silvae Sinicae, Forestry Science and Technology, Chemistry and Industry of Forest Products, Forestry Research, Wood Industry, China Forestry Abstracts, Foreign Forestry Abstracts, Foreign Forest Product Industry Abstracts, World Forestry Research*.

Chinese Agricultural Economics Society: Agro-Exhibition, Beijing; Pres. CAI ZIWEI.

Chinese Association of Agricultural Science Societies: Ministry of Agriculture and Fisheries, 11 Nongzhanguan Nanli, Beijing 100026; telex 22233; f. 1917; Pres. HONG FUZENG; Sec.-Gen. LI HUAIZHI.

Chinese Sericulture Society: Sibaidu, Zhenjiang, Jiangsu 212018; tel. 626721 ext. 317; fax 622507; f. 1963; library of 50,000 vols; Pres. ZHU ZHUWEN; Sec.-Gen. HUANG JUNTING; publ. *Sericultural Science* (quarterly).

Chinese Society for Horticultural Science: 30 Baishiqiao Rd, Beijing 100081; tel. (10) 62174433 ext. 2629; f. 1930; Pres. XIANG CHONGYANG.

Chinese Society of Agricultural Machinery: 1 Beishatan, Deshengmen Wai, Beijing 100083; tel. (10) 64882231; fax (10) 64883508; e-mail bhmetecj@public3.bta.net.cn; f. 1963; 26,245 mems; library of 1,500,000 vols; Pres. LI SHOUREN; Sec.-Gen. GAO YUANEN; publs *Transactions of the Chinese Society of Agricultural Machinery* (quarterly), *Farm Machinery* (monthly), *Rural Mechanization* (6 a year), *China Agricultural Mechanization* (6 a year), *Tractor and Automobile Drivers* (6 a year).

Chinese Society of Forestry: Wanshoushan, Beijing 100091; tel. (10) 62889817; fax (10) 62888312; e-mail csf@csf.forestry.ac.cn; f. 1917; 75,000 mems; Pres. LIU YUHE; publ. *Scientia Silvae Sinicae* (6 a year).

Chinese Society of Tropical Crops: Baodao Xincun, Danzhou, Hainan; tel. and fax (890) 3300157; e-mail qbchen@scuta.edu.cn; f. 1978; 4,088 mems; library of 250,000 vols; Chair. ZHENG YIZHUANG, YU RANGSHUI; Sec.-Gen. ZHENG WENRONG; publ. *Chinese Journal of Tropical Crops* (4 a year).

Crop Science Society of China: Institute of Crop Breeding and Cultivation, 30 Bai Shi Qiao Rd, Beijing 100081; tel. (10) 62176667 ext. 2116; telex 222720; fax (10) 62174865; f. 1961; 22,000 mems; Pres. WANG LIANZHENG; Sec.-Gen. LI CHUNHUA; publs *Crops* (6 a year), *Acta Agronomica Sinica* (6 a year).

Soil Science Society of China: POB 821, Nanjing 210008; tel. 7713360; fax 3353590; f. 1945; 15,000 mems; Dir Prof. CAO ZHIHONG; publs *Acta Pedologica Sinica* (4 a year), *Journal of Soil Science* (6 a year).

ARCHITECTURE AND TOWN PLANNING

Architectural Society of China: Bai Wanzhuang, West District, Beijing; tel. (10) 68393659; fax (10) 68393428; e-mail asc@mail.cin.gov.cn; f. 1953; 14,000 mems; library of 20,000 vols; Pres. YE RUTANG; publs *Architectural Journal* (monthly), *Journal of Building Structure* (every 2 months), *Architectural Knowledge* (monthly).

Chinese Society for Urban Studies: Bai Wanzhuang, Beijing 100835; tel. 68992424; telex 222302; f. 1984; part of Min. of Construction; 30,000 mems; Pres. LIAN ZHONG; Standing Deputy Sec.-Gen. LI MENGBAI ; publ. *China Cities and Towns* (monthly).

BIBLIOGRAPHY, LIBRARY SCIENCE AND MUSEOLOGY

Chinese Archives Society: 21 Fengshen Hutong, Beijing; tel. 665797; telex 222919; f. 1981; 52 institutional mems, 3,783 individual mems; Chair. FENG ZIZHI; publ. *Archival Information* (every 2 months).

Chinese Association of Natural Science Museums: 126 Tian Qiao South St, Beijing 100050; tel. (10) 67024431; fax (10) 67021254; f. 1979; 1,200 individual mems, 320 group mems; Sec.-Gen. XIE YENGHUAN; publs *Newsletter* (quarterly), *China Nature* (6 a year, jointly with Beijing Natural History Museum and China Wildlife Conservation Association).

Chinese Society of Library Science: 39 Bai Shi Qiao Rd, Beijing 100081; tel. 68415566 ext. 5563; telex 222211; fax 68419271; f. 1979; 10,150 mems; Pres. LIU DEYOU; publ. *Journal of Library Science in China* (in Chinese, every 2 months).

ECONOMICS, LAW AND POLITICS

China Law Society: 6 Xizhi Men Nan Da Jie, Beijing 100035; tel. 66150114; telex 22505; fax 66182128; f. 1982; ind. academic instn for study of the Chinese socialist legal system; 523 corporate mems, 100,000 individual mems; library of 40,000 vols, incl. China Catalogue of Law Books; Pres. REN JIANXIN; Sec.-Gen. SONG SHUTAO; publs *Democracy and Law Journal, China Law Yearbook, Law of China*.

Chinese Association for European Studies: 5 Jiannei, Beijing 100732; tel. 65138428; f. 1981; 1,000 mems; Chair. Prof. QIU YUANLUN; publ. *European Studies* (every 2 months, coedited with Inst. of West European Studies).

Chinese Association of Political Science: C/o Chinese Academy of Social Sciences, 5 Jianguomennei Ave, Beijing; tel. 65125048; f. 1980; asscn of workers in the field of political science; 1,025 mems; Pres. JIANG LIU; Sec.-Gen. ZHANG ZHIRONG; publs *Studies in Political Science* (every 2 months), *Political Science Abroad* (every 2 months).

Chinese Legal History Society: Law Dept, Beijing University, Haidian District, Beijing 100871; tel. 62561166; telex 22239; f. 1979; studies history of Chinese and foreign legal systems; 300 mems; Pres. Prof. ZHANG GUOHUA; Chief Sec. RAO XINXIAN; publs *Review of Legal History, Communications of Legal History*.

Chinese Research Society for the Modernization of Management: C/o China Association for Science and Technology, Sanlihe, Xijiao, Beijing; tel. 68318877 ext. 524; f. 1978; Pres. XIE SHAOMING; publ. *Modernization of Management*.

Chinese Society of the History of International Relations: 12 Poshangcun, Haidian District, Beijing; Pres. WANG SHENGZU.

EDUCATION

Chinese Education Society: 35 Damucang Lane, Beijing 100816; telex 22014; Pres. ZHANG CHENGXIAN.

HISTORY, GEOGRAPHY AND ARCHAEOLOGY

Chinese Historical Society: 5 Jianguomennei St, Beijing 100732.

Chinese Society for Future Studies: 32 Baishiqiao Rd, Haidian District, Beijing 100081; f. 1979; 1,000 mems; CEO DU DAGONG; publ. *Future and Development* (quarterly).

Chinese Society of Geodesy, Photogrammetry and Cartography: Baiwanzhuang, Beijing; tel. 68992229; telex 222302; f. 1959; 3,000 mems; Pres. Prof. WANG ZHIZHUO; Sec.-Gen. Prof. YANG KAI; publ. *Acta Geodetica et Cartographica Sinica*.

Chinese Society of Oceanography: 10 Fuxingmenwai, Beijing; telex 22536; Pres. PENG DEQING.

Geographical Society of China: 917 Bldg, Datun Rd, Beijing 100101; tel. and fax (10) 64911104; f. 1909; 15,000 mems; Pres. WU CHUANJUN; Sec.-Gen. ZHANG JIAZHEN; publs *Acta Geographica Sinica* (6 a year), *Economic Geography* (4 a year), *Geographical Knowledge* (monthly), *Journal of Glaciology and Geocryology* (4 a year), *Remote Sensing Journal* (4 a year), *Human Geography* (4 a year), *Mountain Research* (4 a year), *World Regional Studies* (2 a year), *The Journal of Chinese Geography* (English Edition, 4 a year), Historical Geography (1 a year).

LANGUAGE AND LITERATURE

Chinese Writers' Association: 2 Shatanbeijie, Beijing 100720; 20,000 mems; Chair. BA JIN; publs include *People's Literature* (monthly), *Chinese Writers* (every 2 months), *Poetry* (monthly), *Minority Literature* (monthly), *Literature and Arts* (weekly newspaper).

MEDICINE

China Academy of Traditional Chinese Medicine: 18 Beixincang, Dongzhimennei, Beijing 100700; tel. (10) 64014411 ext. 2435; fax (10) 64016387; f. 1955; 12 attached research institutes; library of 300,000 vols; Pres. FU SHIYUAN; publs *Journal of Traditional Chinese Medicine, Chinese Acupuncuture and Moxibustion, Chinese Journal of Integrated Traditional and Western Medicine.*

China Association of Traditional Chinese Medicine: A4 Yinghualu, Hepingli Dongjie, Beijing 100029; tel. 64212828; fax 64220867; f. 1979; 80,000 mems; Chair. CUI YULI; Gen. Sec. (vacant); publ. *China Journal of Traditional Chinese Medicine* (every 2 months).

China Association of Zhenjiu (Acupuncture and Moxibustion): 18 Beixincang Dongcheng Qu, Beijing 100700; tel. 64030611; telex 210340; f. 1979; 13,000 mems; Pres. HU XIMING; Sec.-Gen. LI WEIHENG; publ. *Chinese Acupuncture and Moxibustion.*

Chinese Academy of Medical Sciences and Peking Union Medical College: 9 Dongdan Santiao, Beijing 100730; tel. 553447; fax 5124876; f. 1917 (College), 1956 (Academy); the two instns have a single governing body; attached research institutes: see Research Institutes; Pres. Dr BA DENIAN; publ. *Chinese Medical Sciences Journal.*

Chinese Anti-Cancer Association: Huanhuxi Rd, Tiyuanbei, Tianjin 300060; tel. 23359958; fax 23526512; e-mail caca@mail.zlnet.com.cn; 3359984; f. 1985; 18,000 mems; Pres. Dr XU GUANGWEI; publs *Chinese Journal of Clinical Oncology* (monthly), *Prevention and Research of Cancer* (quarterly), *Chinese Journal of Cancer Research* (English, quarterly), *Chinese Anti-Cancer Gazette* (every 2 weeks).

Chinese Anti-Tuberculosis Society: 42 Dung-si-xi-da St, Beijing; tel. 553685; Pres. HUANG DINGCHEN; publ. *Bulletin* (quarterly).

Chinese Association for Mental Health: 5 An Kang Hutong, De Wai, Beijing 100088; tel. (10) 62013330; f. 1985; 5,000 mems; Pres. CHEN XUE SHI; Sec. CAI CHAO JI; publ. *Chinese Mental Health Journal* (every 2 months).

Chinese Association of Integrated Traditional and Western Medicine: 18 Beixincang, Dongzhimennei, Beijing; tel. (10) 64010688; fax (10) 64010688; e-mail kjchen@mimi.cnc.ac.cn; f. 1981; 20,000 mems; Pres. CHEN KEJI; Sec.-Gen. CHEN SHIGUI; publ. *Chinese Journal of Integrated Traditional and Western Medicine* (monthly in Chinese, 4 a year in English).

Chinese Medical Association: 42 Dongsi Xidajie, Beijing; tel. 551943; tel. and fax (10) 65265331; f. 1915; library of 80,000 vols; Pres. BAI XIQING; publs *Chinese Medical Journal* (English edition, monthly), *National Medical Journal of China* (monthly), *Chinese Journal of Internal Medicine* (monthly), *Chinese Journal of Surgery* (monthly).

Chinese Nursing Association: 42 Dongsi Xidajie, Beijing 100710; tel. and fax (10) 65265331; f. 1909; Pres. ZENG XIYUAN; publ. *Chinese Journal of Nursing* (monthly).

Chinese Nutrition Society: 29 Nanwei Rd, Beijing 100050; tel. 63043472; telex 8761; fax 63011875; f. 1981; 5,120 mems; Pres. CHEN XIAOSHU; publ. *Acta Nutrimenta* (Chinese and English, quarterly).

Chinese Pharmaceutical Association: A38 Lishi Rd N., Beijing 100810; tel. 68316576; f. 1907; Pres. QI MAIJIA.

Chinese Pharmacological Society: 1 Xian Nong Tan St, Beijing 100050; tel. 63013366 ext. 404; telex 8602; fax 63017757; f. 1979; Pres. Prof. ZHANG JUNTIAN; Sec.-Gen. Prof. LIN ZHIBIN; publs *Acta Pharmacologica Sinica, Chinese Journal of Pharmacology and Toxicology, Chinese Pharmacological Bulletin, Pharmacology and Clinics of Chinese Materia Medica.*

NATURAL SCIENCES

General

China Association for Science and Technology (CAST): 54 Sanlihe Rd, Beijing 100863; tel. and fax 68321914; telex 20035; f. 1958; organizes academic exchanges, int. conferences and in-service training for scientists, engineers and technicians; almost all socs in China are affiliated mems; library of 50,000 vols; Pres. ZHU GUANGYA.

Chinese Society for Oceanology and Limnology: 7 Nanhai Rd, Qingdao 266071; tel. (532) 2879062 ext. 3402; fax (532) 2870882; f. 1950; 7,000 mems; Pres. QIN YUNSHAN; Sec.-Gen. ZHOU MINGJIANG; publs *Oceanologia et Limnologia Sinica* (in Chinese, every 2 months), *Chinese Journal of Oceanology and Limnology* (quarterly, in English).

Chinese Society of the History of Science and Technology: 137 Chao Nei St, Beijing 100010; tel. (10) 64043989; fax (10) 64017637; f. 1980; 1,500 mems; Pres X. ZEZONG, LU YONGXIANG; publs *Studies in the History of Natural Sciences* (quarterly), *China Historical Materials of Science and Technology* (quarterly).

Biological Sciences

Biophysical Society of China: 15 Datun Rd, Chaoyang District, 100101 Beijing; tel. (10) 62022025; fax (10) 62027837; f. 1980; 2,000 mems; Pres. Prof. LIANG DONGCAI; Sec.-Gen. Prof. SHEN XUN; publ. *Acta Biophysica Sinica* (quarterly).

Botanical Society of China: 141 Xizhimenwai Tajie, Beijing; Pres. WANG FUXIANG.

China Zoological Society: 19 Zhong Guan Cun Lu, Beijing; tel. 62561873; fax 62565689; e-mail fauna@panda.ioz.ac.cn; f. 1934; Pres. SONG DAXIANG; publs *Acta Zoologica Sinica* (quarterly), *Acta Zootaxonomica Sinica* (quarterly), *Acta Theriologica Sinica* (quarterly), *Acta Arachnologica Sinica* (2 a year), *Acta Parasitologica et Medica Entomologica Sinica* (quarterly).

Chinese Association for Physiological Sciences: 42 Dongsixidajie, Beijing 100710; Pres. CHEN MENGQIN.

Chinese Association of Animal Science and Veterinary Medicine: 33 Nongfengli, Dongdaqiao, Chao Yang District, Beijing 100020; tel. (10) 65005934; fax 65005670; f. 1936; 50,000 mems; Pres. CHEN YAOCHUN; Sec.-Gen. JIN JIAZHEN; publs *Chinese Journal of Animal and Veterinary Sciences, Chinese Journal of Animal Science, Chinese Journal of Veterinary Medicine.*

Chinese Society for Anatomical Sciences: 42 Dongsi Xidajie, Beijing 100710; tel. 65133311 ext. 247; fax 65123754; f. 1920; 3,000 mems; Pres. XU QUNYUAN; Sec.-Gen. LIU BIN; publs *Acta Anatomica Sinica, Chinese Journal of Anatomy, Chinese Journal of Clinical Anatomy, Journal of Neuroanatomy, Chinese Journal of Histochemistry and Cytochemistry, Progress of Anatomical Sciences* (all quarterly).

Chinese Society for Microbiology: Zhong-Guan Cun, Beijing 100080; tel. 62554677; f. 1952; Pres. LI JI-LUN; publs *Acta Microbiologica Sinica, Acta Mycologica Sinica, Chinese Journal of Biotechnology, Chinese Journal of Virology, Microbiology, Chinese Journal of Zoonoses.*

Chinese Society of Biochemistry and Molecular Biology: 15 Datun Rd, Chao Yang District, Beijing 100101; tel. (10) 62022027; fax (10) 62022026; f. 1979; 1,000 mems; Pres. C. L. TSOU; Sec.-Gen. J. M. ZHOU; publs *Chemistry of Life* (every 2 months), *Chinese Journal of Biochemistry and Molecular Biology* (every 2 months).

Chinese Society of Environmental Sciences: 115 Xizhimennei Nanxiaojie, Beijing; tel. 661006; telex 222359; f. 1979; 22,000 individual mems, 20 industrial/corporate mems; Pres. LI JINGZHAO; Sec.-Gen. QU GEPING; publs *China Environmental Science, China Environmental Management, Environmental Chemistry, Environmental Engineering, Environment.*

Chinese Society of Plant Physiology: 300 Fongling Rd, Shanghai; tel. 64042090; telex 33275; fax 64042385; f. 1963; 4,000 mems; Chair. Prof. TANG ZHANGCHENG; publs *Acta Phytophysiologica Sinica* (quarterly), *Plant Physiology Communications* (every 2 months).

Ecological Society of China: 19 Zhongguancun Lu, Beijing 100080; tel. (10) 62565694; fax (10) 62562775; f. 1979; 5,500 mems; Pres. Prof. WANG ZUWANG; Sec.-Gen. Prof. WANG RUSONG; publs *Journal of Ecology* (6 a year), *Acta Ecologica Sinica* (6 a year), *Journal of Applied Ecology* (4 a year).

Entomological Society of China: 19 Zhonguancun, Beijing 100080; tel. (10) 62552266; fax (10) 62565689; e-mail zss@panda.ioz.ac.cn; f. 1944; 11,000 mems; Pres. ZHANG GUANGXUE; publs *Acta Entomologica Sinica, Acta Zootaxonomia Sinica, Entomological Knowledge, Entomologia Sinica* (in English).

Genetics Society of China: Bldg 917, Datun Rd, Andingmenwai, Beijing 100101; tel. 64919944; fax 64914896; f. 1978; 400 nat. mems, 6,600 mems of local socs; Pres. LI ZHENSHENG; Sec.-Gen. CHEN SHOUYI; publs *Acta Genetica Sinica, Hereditas* (every 2 months).

Palaeontological Society of China: 39 E. Beijing Rd, Nanjing 210008; tel. (25) 3612664; telex 342301; fax (25) 3357026; e-mail muxinan@public.1.ptt.js.cn; f. 1929; 1,230 mems; Pres. MU XINAN; Sec.-Gen. SUN GE; publ. *Acta Palaeontologica Sinica* (4 a year).

Mathematical Sciences

Chinese Mathematical Society: C/o Institute of Mathematics, Chinese Academy of Sciences, Beijing 100080; tel. (10) 62551022; fax (10) 62568356; e-mail cms@math08.math.ac.cn; f. 1935; Pres. K. C. CHANG; Sec.-Gen. LI WENLIN.

Physical Sciences

Acoustical Society of China: 17 Zhongguancun St, Beijing 100080; tel. (10) 62553765; telex 222525; fax (10) 62553898; f. 1985; 3,030 mems; Pres. CHEN TONG; Sec.-Gen. HOU CHADHUAN; publs *Acta Acustica* (every 2 months), *Applied Acoustics* (quarterly), *Chinese Journal of Acoustics* (quarterly, English version of *Acta Acustica*).

Chinese Academy of Geological Sciences: 26 Baiwanzhuang Rd, Beijing 100037; tel. 68310893; fax 68310894; f. 1959; attached research institutes: see Research Institutes; Pres. CHEN YUCHUAN; publs *Bulletin, Acta Geologic Sinica, Geological Review.*

Chinese Academy of Meteorological Sciences: 7 Block 11, Hepingli, Beijing; tel.

64211631; fax 64218703; attached research institutes: see Research Institutes.

Chinese Aerodynamics Research Society: POB 2425, Beijing; Pres. ZHUANG GENGGAN.

Chinese Astronomical Society: Purple Mountain Observatory, Nanjing, Jiangsu 210008; Pres. LI QIBIN.

Chinese Chemical Society: POB 2709, Beijing 100080; tel. (10) 62564020; fax (10) 62568157; e-mail quixb@infoc3.icas.ac.cn; f. 1932; Pres. XI FU; publs *Chinese Journal of Chemistry* (6 a year), *Acta Chimica Sinica* (monthly).

Chinese Geological Society: 26 Baiwanzhuang, Beijing 100037; telex 222721; fax 68310894; f. 1922; 71,000 mems; Pres. ZHANG HONGREN; Sec.-Gen. ZHAO XUN; publs *Acta Geologica Sinica*, *Geological Review*.

Chinese Geophysical Society: Institute of Geophysics, POB 941, Beijing; f. 1948; 4,000 mems; Pres. GU GONGXU; Sec.-Gen. FU CHENGYI; publ. *Acta Geophisica Sinica* (every 2 months).

Chinese High-Energy Physics Society: POB 918, Beijing; tel. 68213344; telex 22082; fax 68213374; f. 1981; 820 mems; Chair. ZHENG LINSHENG; Sec. WANG XUEYING; publs *High Energy Physics and Nuclear Physics*, *Modern Physics*.

Chinese Meteorological Society: 46 Baishiqiao Rd, Beijing 100081; f. 1924; 21,000 mems; Pres. ZHOU JINGMENG; Sec.-Gen. PENG GUANGYI; publs *Acta Meteorologica Sinica*, *Meteorological Knowledge*.

Chinese Nuclear Physics Society: POB 275, Beijing; tel. 69357487; telex 222373; fax 69357008; f. 1979; 1,300 mems; Pres. SUN ZUXUN; Sec.-Gen. XU JINCHENG; publ. *Chinese Journal of Nuclear Physics*.

Chinese Nuclear Society: POB 2125, Beijing 100822; f. 1980; Pres. JIANG SHENGJIE; publ. *Chinese Journal of Nuclear Science and Technology*.

Chinese Physics Society: C/o Institute of Physics, Academia Sinica, Zhongguancun, Beijing 100080; tel. 62562425; Pres. HUANG KUN; Sec.-Gen. YANG GUOZHEN.

Chinese Society for Mineralogy, Petrology and Geochemistry: 73, Guanshui Rd, Guiyang 550002, Guizhou Province; tel. (851) 5860823; fax (851) 5822982; f. 1978; 6,500 mems; library of 10,000 vols and periodicals; Pres. OUYANG ZIYUAN; publs *Acta Mineralogica Sinica*, *Acta Petrologica Sinica*, *Chinese Journal of Geochemistry* (in English), *Acta Sedimentologica Sinica*, *Bulletin of Mineralogy, Petrology and Geochemistry*, (all quarterly), *Geochemistry* (6 a year).

Chinese Society for Rock Mechanics: POB 9701, Jia No 11, Anwai Datun Lu, Beijing; tel. (10) 62011118; telex 7594; fax (10) 62031995; e-mail csrme@c-geos15.c-geos.ac.cn; f. 1985; 72 group mems, 12,250 individual mems; Pres. Prof. SUN JUN; Sec.-Gen. FU BINGJUN; publs *Chinese Journal of Rock Mechanics and Engineering* (6 a year in Chinese), *News of Rock Mechanics and Engineering* (4 a year in Chinese).

Chinese Society of Space Research: 1 Second Southern Ave, Zhongguancun, Beijing 100080; tel. (10) 62559882; f. 1980; Pres. Prof. WANG XIJI; publ. *Chinese Journal of Space Science* (quarterly).

Seismological Society of China: 5 Minzu Xueyuan Nanlu, Beijing 100081; tel. (10) 68417858; f. 1979; 4,771 mems; Pres. Prof. CHEN YUNTAI; publs *Acta Seismologica Sinica* (quarterly, in Chinese and English editions).

PHILOSOPHY AND PSYCHOLOGY

Chinese Psychological Society: Institute of Psychology, Chinese Academy of Sciences, Beijing 100012; tel. (10) 62022071; fax (10) 62022070; e-mail zhangk@psych.ac.cn; f. 1921; 1,500 mems; Pres. Prof. YONGMING CHEN; Sec.-Gen. Prof. KAN ZHANG; publs *Acta Psychologica Sinica* (4 a year), *Psychological Science* (6 a year).

RELIGION, SOCIOLOGY AND ANTHROPOLOGY

Chinese Sociological Research Society: C/o Chinese Academy of Social Sciences, 5 Jianguomen Nei Da Jie, Beijing; f. 1979; Pres. FEI XIAOTONG; Exec. Sec. WANG KANG.

Chinese Study of Religion Society: Xi'anmen Ave, Beijing; Pres. REN JIYU.

TECHNOLOGY

Chemical Industry and Engineering Society of China: POB 911, Beijing; tel. 466025; telex 22492; f. 1922; 40,000 mems; Pres. YANG GUANGQI; Sec.-Gen. YIN DELIN; publs *Huagong Xuebao* (Journal of Chemical Engineering, quarterly), *Huagong Jinzhan* (Chemical Engineering Progress, every 2 months).

China Coal Society: Hepingli, Beijing 100013; tel. (10) 64214931; fax (10) 64219234; f. 1962; 53,000 mems; Pres. FAN WEITANG; Sec.-Gen. PAN HUIZHENG; publs *Journal*, *Modern Miners*.

China Computer Federation: POB 2704, Beijing 100080; tel. (10) 62562503; fax (10) 62567724; e-mail ccf@ns.ict.ac.cn; f. 1962; 40,000 individual mems; Chair. ZHANG XIAOXIANG; Sec.-Gen. CHEN SHUKAI; publs *Chinese Journal of Computers*, *Journal of Computer Science and Technology* (in English), *Journal of Computer-aided Design and Computer Graphics*, *Journal of Software*, *Chinese Journal of Advanced Software Research*.

China Electrotechnical Society: 46 Sanlihe Rd, POB 2133, Beijing 100823; tel. (10) 68595355; fax (10) 68511242; e-mail cesintl@public.bta.net.cn; f. 1981; 50,000 mems; Pres. ZHAO MINGSHENG; Sec.-Gen. ZHOU HELIANG; publs *Transactions* (quarterly), *Electrotechnical Journal* (every 2 months), *Electricity Age* (monthly), *Early Youth Electrical World* (monthly).

China Energy Research Society: 54 San Li He Rd, Beijing 100863; tel. and fax (10) 68511816; f. 1981; 18,000 mems; Pres. HUANG YICHENG; Sec.-Gen. BAO YUNQIAO; publs *Energy Policy Research Newsletter* (monthly), *Guide to World Energy* (every 2 weeks).

China Engineering Graphics Society: POB 85, Beijing 100083; tel. 62015346; Pres. TANG RONGXI; publ. *Computer Aided Drafting, Design and Manufacturing* (2 a year).

China Fire Protection Association: 14 Dong Chang An St, Beijing 100741; tel. (10) 65283122; fax (10) 65282846; f. 1984; 30,000 mems; Pres. HU ZHIGUANG; Sec.-Gen. LIU SHIPU; publs *Fire Science and Technology*, *Fire Technique and Products Information*, *Fire Protection in China*.

Chinese Abacus Association: Sidaokou, Xizhimenwai, Shidaokou, Beijing; tel. 896275; f. 1979; 500,000 mems; Pres. ZHU XI-AN; Sec.-Gen. HU JING; publs *Chinese Abacus* (monthly), *Chinese Abacus News* (monthly).

Chinese Academy of Space Technology: 31 Baishiqiao, POB 2417, Beijing 100081; tel. 68379439; fax 68378237; 4 mems; attached research institutes: see Research Institutes; Pres. QI FAREN.

Chinese Association of Automation: POB 2728, 100080 Beijing; tel. 62544415; fax 62620908; e-mail wangh@sunserver.ia.ac.cn; f. 1961; 20,000 mems; Pres Prof. CHEN HANFU, Prof. YANG JIACHI; publs *Acta Automatica Sinica* (every 2 months), *Information and Control* (every 2 months), *Robot and Automation* (every 2 months).

Chinese Ceramic Society: Bai Wan Zhuang, Beijing 100831; tel. 68313364; telex 22076; fax 68311497; Pres. YAN DONGSHENG.

Chinese Civil Engineering Society: Bai Wan Zhuang, POB 2500, 100835 Beijing; tel. 68311313; fax 68313669; f. 1953; Pres. MAO YISHENG; Sec.-Gen. ZHAO XICHUN; publ. *Civil Engineering Journal*.

Chinese Hydraulic Engineering Society: 2-2 Bai Guang Rd, Beijing 100053; tel. (10) 63202171; fax (10) 63202154; f. 1931; 80,000 mems; Pres. YAN KEQIANG; Sec.-Gen. ZHENG LIANDI; publ. *Journal of Hydraulic Engineering*.

Chinese Information Processing Society: POB 2704, Beijing; Pres. QIAN WEICHANG.

Chinese Light Industry Society: B22 Fuchengmenwai Ave, Beijing 100037; tel. 894147; f. 1979; Pres. JI LONG.

Chinese Mechanical Engineering Society: 46 Sanlihe Rd, Beijing 100823; tel. (10) 68595319; fax (10) 68533613; f. 1936; 180,000 mems; Pres. HE GUANGYUAN; publs *Journal of Mechanical Engineering* (quarterly), *Mechanical Engineering of China* (every 2 months).

Chinese Petroleum Society: POB 766, Liu Pu Kang, Beijing 100724; tel. (10) 62095615; fax (10) 62014787; 1979; academic asscn of petroleum engineers; 60,000 mems; library of 20,000 books, 560 periodicals; Pres. JIN ZHONGCHAO; Sec.-Gen. LU JIMENG; publ. *Acta Petrolei Sinica* (Exploration and Development, and Refining and the Petrochemical Industry, each edition quarterly).

Chinese Railway Society: 10 Fuxing Rd, POB 2499, Beijing; f. 1978; railway transport, construction and rolling stock manufacture; Pres. LIU JIANZHANG; Sec.-Gen. ZHAO XICHUN; publs *Railway Journal*, *Railway Knowledge*.

Chinese Society for Metals: 46 Dongsi Xidajie, Beijing 100711; tel. 65133322 ext. 3390; telex 222753; fax 65124122; f. 1956; 90,000 mems; library of 50,000 vols, 20,000 serials, 1,270 periodicals; Pres. LI MING; Sec.-Gen. ZHONG ZENGYONG; publs *Iron and Steel* (monthly), *Acta Metallurgica* (monthly), *Journal of Materials Science & Technology* (every 2 months).

Chinese Society for Scientific and Technical Information: 15 Fuxinglu, Beijing; tel. 68014024; telex 20079; fax 68014025; f. 1964; organizes academic activities about information science and technology; 13,000 mems; Pres. WU HENG; publ. *Journal of the China Society for Scientific and Technical Information* (every 2 months).

Chinese Society of Aeronautics and Astronautics: 5 Liangguochang Rd, Dongcheng District, Beijing 100010; tel. (10) 64021416; telex 22318; fax (10) 64021413; f. 1964; 30,000 mems; Pres. ZHU YULI; Sec.-Gen. ZHOU JIAQI; publs *Aerospace Knowledge* (monthly), *Acta Aeronautica et Astronautica Sinica* (monthly), *Chinese Journal of Aeronautics* (quarterly), *Model Aeroplane* (every 2 months).

Chinese Society of Astronautics: POB 838, Beijing 100830; tel. 68354602; telex 20026; fax 68372081; f. 1979; 8,000 mems; Pres. LIU JIYUAN; First Sec.-Gen. LIU JINGSHENG; publs *Space Flight*, *Journal*.

Chinese Society of Electrical Engineering: 1 Lane 2, Baiguang Rd, Beijing 10076; Pres. ZHANG FENGXIANG.

Chinese Society of Engineering Thermophysics: POB 2706, Zhong Guan Cun, Beijing; f. 1978; 5,000 mems; Sec.-Gen. Prof.

XU JIANZHONG; publ. *Journal of Engineering Thermophysics* (quarterly).

Chinese Society of Naval Architects and Marine Engineers: POB 817, Beijing; tel. 68340527; telex 22335; fax 68313380; f. 1943; Pres. WANG RONGSHENG; Sec.-Gen. WANG SHOUDAO; publs *Shipbuilding of China* (quarterly, contents and abstracts), *Ship Engineering* (every 2 months), *Naval and Merchant Ships* (monthly).

Chinese Society of Theoretical and Applied Mechanics (CSTAM): 15 Zhong-Guan-Cun, Beijing 100080; tel. (10) 62559588; fax (10) 62561284; e-mail cstam@sun.ihep.ac.cn; f. 1957; 21,000 mems; Dir Prof. ZHUANG FENGGAN; publs *Acta Mechanica Sinica* (6 a year, in English 4 a year), *Mechanics and Practice* (6 a year), *Journal of Experimental Mechanics* (4 a year), *Acta Mechanica Solida Sinica* (6 a year, in English 4 a year), *Journal of Computational Mechanics* (4 a year), *Explosion and Shock Waves* (4 a year), *Engineering Mechanics* (4 a year).

Chinese Textile Engineering Society: 3 Middle St, Yanjing Li, East Suburb, Beijing 100025; tel. (10) 65016537; fax (10) 65016538; f. 1930; 60,000 mems; Pres. JI GUOBIAO.

Nonferrous Metals Society of China: B12, Fuxing Rd, Beijing 100814; tel. and fax (10) 63965399; f. 1984; 36,638 mems; Pres. WU JIANCHANG; Sec.-Gen. MA FUKANG; publs *Journal of Rare Metals* (quarterly, with English version), *Journal of Nonferrous Metals* (quarterly, with English Abstracts), *Transactions of Nonferrous Metals Society of China* (quarterly, with English version).

Society of Automotive Engineers of China: 46 Fucheng Rd, Beijing 100036; tel. (10) 68121894; fax (10) 68125556; f. 1963; 1,520 mems; Pres. ZHANG XINGYE; publs *Automotive Engineering* (6 a year), *Auto Fan* (monthly).

Systems Engineering Society of China: Institute of Systems Science, Zhongguancun, Beijing 100080; tel. 62541827; fax 62568364; f. 1980; 3,000 individual mems, 150 collective mems; Pres. GU JIFA; Sec.-Gen. CHEN GUANGYA; publs *Systems Engineering* (quarterly), *Systems Engineering – Theory and Practice* (monthly), *Journal of Systems Science and Systems Engineering* (quarterly, in English).

Research Institutes

AGRICULTURE, FISHERIES AND VETERINARY SCIENCE

Chinese Research Institute of the Wood Industry: Wan Shou Shan, Beijing 100091; attached to Chinese Acad. of Forestry.

Forest Economics Research Institute: He Ping Li, Beijing; tel. 64210476; attached to Chinese Acad. of Forestry.

Forest Resource and Insect Research Institute: Kunming, Yunnan Province; attached to Chinese Acad. of Forestry.

Forestry Research Institute: Wan Shou Shan, Beijing 100091; attached to Chinese Acad. of Forestry.

Institute of Agricultural Meteorology: 7 Block 11, Hepingli, Beijing; attached to Chinese Acad. of Meteorological Sciences.

Institute of Soil Science: POB 821, Nanjing 210008; tel. 7712572; fax 3353590; f. 1953; attached to Chinese Acad. of Sciences; library of 110,000 vols; Dir Prof. ZHAO QIGUO; publs *Soils, Advance of Soil Science, Acta Pedologica Sinica, Soil Science Research Report, Pedosphere*.

Sub-Tropical Forestry Research Institute: Fuyang, Zhejiang Province 311400; attached to Chinese Acad. of Forestry; Dir YANG PEISHOU.

Tropical Forestry Research Institute: Longdong, Guangzhou, Guandong Province 510520; attached to Chinese Acad. of Forestry.

BIBLIOGRAPHY, LIBRARY SCIENCE AND MUSEOLOGY

State Archives Bureau of China: 21 Feng Sheng Hutong, Beijing; tel. 665797; Dir FENG ZIZHI; publ. *Archival Work* (monthly).

ECONOMICS, LAW AND POLITICS

American Studies Institute: 5 Jianguomennei Ave, Beijing 100732; tel. 65137559; f. 1981; attached to Chinese Acad. of Social Sciences; Dir LI SHENZHI.

Economics Institute: 2 Yuetanxiaojie N., Fuchengmenurai, Beijing 100836; tel. 895323; attached to Chinese Acad. of Social Sciences; Dir ZHAO RENWEI.

Industrial Economics Institute: 2 Yuetanbeixiao Street, Fuchengmenwai, Beijing 100836; f. 1978; attached to Chinese Acad. of Social Sciences; Dir ZHOU SHULIAN.

Institute of European Studies: 5 Jianguomennei Ave, Beijing 100732; f. 1980; attached to Chinese Acad. of Social Sciences; Dir Prof. QIU YUANLUN.

Japanese Studies Institute: Dong Yuan, 3 Zhangzhizhong Rd, Beijing 100007; f. 1980; attached to Chinese Acad. of Social Sciences; Dir HE FANG.

Latin American Studies Institute: POB 1113, Beijing; tel. 444375; f. 1961; attached to Chinese Acad. of Social Sciences; Dir SU ZHENXING (acting).

Law Institute: 15 Shatan St N., Beijing 100720; tel. 64014045; f. 1958; attached to Chinese Acad. of Social Sciences; Dir WANG JIAFU.

Marxism-Leninism and Mao Zedong Thought Institute: Cegongzhuang, Beijing; f. 1980; attached to Chinese Acad. of Social Sciences; Dir SU SHAOZHI.

Political Science Institute: Shatan Bei Jie, Beijing 100720; f. 1981; attached to Chinese Acad. of Social Sciences; Dir YAN JIAQI.

Quantitative and Technical Economics Institute: 5 Jianguomennei Ave, Beijing 100732; attached to Chinese Acad. of Social Sciences; Dir LI JINGWEN.

Rural Development Institute: Ritan Rd, Beijing; attached to Chinese Acad. of Social Sciences; Dir CHEN JIYUAN.

Soviet and East European Studies Institute: 3 Zhangzhizhong Rd, Beijing 100007; tel. 64014020; f. 1976; attached to Chinese Acad. of Social Sciences; Dir XU KUI.

Taiwan Studies Institute: 5 Jianguomennei Ave, Beijing 100732; attached to Chinese Acad. of Social Sciences; Dir KAN NIANYI.

Trade, Finance and Material Supply Institute: 2 Yuetanbeixiao St, Beijing 100836; attached to Chinese Acad. of Social Sciences; Dir ZHANG ZHUOYUAN.

West Asian and African Studies Institute: 3 Zhangzhizhong Rd, Beijing 100007; f. 1980; attached to Chinese Acad. of Social Sciences; Dir GE JIE.

World Economy and Politics Institute: 5 Jianguomennei Ave, Beijing 100732; telex 22061; attached to Chinese Acad. of Social Sciences; Dir PU SHAN.

HISTORY, GEOGRAPHY AND ARCHAEOLOGY

Archaeology Institute: 27 Wangfujing Ave, Beijing 100710; f. 1950; attached to Chinese Acad. of Social Sciences; Dir WANG ZHONGSHU.

Changchun Institute of Geography: 16 Gongnong Rd, Changchun 130021, Jilin Province; tel. and fax (431) 5652931; f. 1958; attached to Chinese Acad. of Sciences; Dir Prof. HE YAN.

Chinese Academy of Surveying and Mapping, National Bureau of Surveying and Mapping: 16 Bei Tai Ping Lu, Beijing 100039; tel. (10) 68212277; telex 221081; fax (10) 68218654; f. 1959; library of 50,000 vols; Dir LIU XIANLIN; publs *Remote Sensing Information, Trends in Science and Technology of Surveying and Mapping*.

History (Chinese) Institute: 5 Jianguomennei Ave, Beijing 100732; attached to Chinese Acad. of Social Sciences; Dir LI XUEQIN.

History (Modern Chinese) Institute: 1 Dongcheng Lane, Wangfu Ave, Beijing 100006; tel. 555400; attached to Chinese Acad. of Social Sciences; Dir WANG QINGCHENG.

History (World) Institute: 1 Dongcheng Lane, Wangfu Ave, Beijing 100006; f. 1964; attached to Chinese Acad. of Social Sciences; Dir ZHANG CHUNNIAN.

Institute of Geography: Bldg 917, Datun Rd, Anwai, Beijing 100101; tel. (10) 64914841; fax (10) 64911844; f. 1940; attached to Chinese Acad. of Sciences; library of 90,000 vols; Dir Prof. ZHENG DU; publ. *Geographical Research* (quarterly).

LANGUAGE AND LITERATURE

Applied Linguistics Institute: 51 Nanxiao Street, Chaoyangmennei, Beijing 100010; tel. 557146; f. 1984; attached to Chinese Acad. of Social Sciences; Dir CHEN YUAN.

Chinese Literature Institute: 5 Jianguomennei Ave, Beijing 100732; attached to Chinese Acad. of Social Sciences; Dir LIU ZAIFU.

Foreign Literature Institute: 5 Jianguomennei Ave, Beijing 100732; attached to Chinese Acad. of Social Sciences; Dir ZHANG YU.

Institute of Linguistics: 5 Jianguomenmei Dajie, Beijing 100732; tel. and fax (10) 65737403; f. 1950; attached to Chinese Acad. of Social Sciences; Dir JIANG LANSHENG; publs *The Chinese Language and Writing, Dialects, Linguistics Abroad*.

Journalism Institute: 2 Jintai Rd W., Chaoyang District, Beijing 100026; attached to Chinese Acad. of Social Sciences; Dir SUN XUPEI.

Literature of Minority Nationalities Institute: 5 Jianguomennei Ave, Beijing 100732; f. 1981; attached to Chinese Acad. of Social Sciences; Dir LIU KUILI.

MEDICINE

Basic Medicine Institute: 5 Dongdan Santiao, Beijing 100005; tel. 65134466; fax 65124876; attached to Chinese Acad. of Medical Sciences; Dir DENG XIXIAN.

Biomedical Engineering Institute: POB (25) 204, Tianjing 300192; fax (22) 361095; attached to Chinese Acad. of Medical Sciences; Deputy Dir WANG PENGYAN.

Blood Transfusion Institute: Renmin Rd N., Chengdu, Sichuan 61008; tel. and fax (28) 332125; attached to Chinese Acad. of Medical Sciences; Dir YANG CHENGMIN.

Cancer Institute and Hospital: Faculty of Oncology, Peking Union Medical College, Panjiayuan, Chaoyang District, Beijing 100021; tel. (10) 67781331; fax (10) 67713359; attached to Chinese Acad. of Medical Sciences; Dir DONG ZHIWEI.

Cardiovascular Diseases Institute: A167 Beilishi Rd, Beijing 100037; tel. 68314466; fax 68313012; e-mail fuwaih@public.bta.net.cn; attached to Chinese Acad. of Medical Sciences; Dir GAO RUNLIN.

Clinical Medicine Institute: 1 Shuaifuyuan Lane, Beijing 100730; tel. 65127733; fax 65124875; attached to Chinese Acad. of Medical Sciences; Dir LU ZHADLIN.

Dermatology Institute: 12 Jiangwangmiao St, Nanjing, Jiangsu 210042; tel. (25) 5411040; fax (25) 5414477; attached to Chinese Acad. of Medical Sciences; Dir YE SHUNZHANG.

Haematology Institute: 228 Nanjing Rd, Tianjing 300020; tel. (22) 707939; fax (22) 706542; attached to Chinese Acad. of Medical Sciences; Dir HAO YUSHU.

Health School: Badachu, Xishan, Beijing 100041; tel. 68862233; fax 68864137; attached to Chinese Acad. of Medical Sciences; Dir CHI XINGQIU.

Institute of Laboratory Animal Science: 5 Pan Jia Yuan Nan Li, Chao Yang District, Beijing 100021; fax 67780683; attached to Chinese Acad. of Medical Sciences; Dir LIU YINONG.

Institute of Microcirculation: 5 Dongdan Santiao, Beijing 100005; tel. (10) 65126407; fax (10) 62015012; f. 1984; attached to Chinese Acad. of Medical Sciences; Dir Prof. XIU RUIJUAN.

Institute of Plastic Surgery: Ba-Da-Chu, Beijing 100041; tel. (10) 68874826; fax (10) 68864137; e-mail yeguang@cdm.imicams.ac.cn; f. 1957; attached to Chinese Acad. of Medical Sciences; library of 20,000 vols; Dir Prof. SONG YEGUANG; publ. *Chinese Journal of Plastic Surgery and Burns*.

Materia Medica Institute: 1 Xiannongtan St, Beijing 100050; tel. 63013366; fax 63017757; attached to Chinese Acad. of Medical Sciences; Dir ZHANG JUNTIAN.

Medical Biology Institute: Huahongdong, Kunming, Yunnan 650160; f. 1959; attached to Chinese Acad. of Medical Sciences.

Medical Biotechnology Institute: 1 Tiantanxili, Beijing 100050; tel. 757315; fax 63017302; attached to Chinese Acad. of Medical Sciences; Dir ZHANG ZHIPING.

Medicinal Plant Development Institute: Xibeiwang, Haidian District, Beijing 100094; tel. 62581114; fax 62581330; attached to Chinese Acad. of Medical Sciences; Dir XIAO PEIGENG.

Radiation Medicine Institute: POB 71, Tianjin 300192; attached to Chinese Acad. of Medical Sciences.

Shanghai Institute of Materia Medica: 294 Tai-Yuan Rd, Shanghai 200031; tel. (21) 64311833; fax (21) 64370269; f. 1932; attached to Chinese Acad. of Sciences; development of new drugs; library of 80,000 vols, 600 current periodicals; Dir CHEN KAIXIAN; publ. *Acta Pharmocologica Sinica*.

NATURAL SCIENCES

General

Fujian Institute of Research on the Structure of Matter: Xihe, Fuzhou, Fujian 350002; tel. (591) 3714517; fax (591) 3714946; e-mail fjirsm@ms.fjirsm.ac.cn; f. 1960; attached to Chinese Acad. of Sciences; library of 75,000 vols; Dir Prof. HUANG JINSHUN; publ. *Journal on Structural Chemistry* (6 a year).

Institute of Oceanology: 7 Nanhai Rd, Qingdao 266071; tel. (532) 2879062; fax (532) 2870882; e-mail iocas@ms.qdio.ac.cn; f. 1950; attached to Chinese Acad. of Sciences; library of 180,000 vols; Dir ZHOU MINGJIANG; publs *Studia Marina Sinica* (Chinese with English abstracts, 1 a year), *Marine Sciences* (Chinese, 6 a year), *Chinese Journal of Oceanology and Limnology* (in English, 4 a year), *Oceanologia et Limnologia Sinica* (Chinese, 6 a year).

Institute of the History of Natural Sciences: 137 Chao Nei St, Beijing 100010; tel. (10) 64043989; fax (10) 64017637; f. 1957; attached to Chinese Acad. of Sciences; library of 150,000 vols; publs *Studies in the History of Natural Sciences* (quarterly), *China Historical Materials of Science and Technology* (quarterly).

Qinghai Institute of Salt Lakes: 7 Xinning Rd, Xinning, Qinghai Province 810008; tel. 44306; fax 46002; f. 1965; attached to Chinese Acad. of Sciences; library of 85,000 vols; Dir LIU DEJIANG; publ. *Journal of Salt Lake Science*.

South China Sea Institute of Oceanology: 164 West Xingang Rd, Guangzhou 510301; tel. (20) 84451335; fax (20) 84451672; e-mail scsio@ms.gzb.ac.cn; f. 1959; attached to Chinese Acad. of Sciences; library of 67,209 vols; Dir PAN JINPEI; publs *Tropic Oceanology* (quarterly), *Nanhai Studia Marina Sinica* (irregular, Chinese with English abstracts).

Biological Sciences

Institute of Applied Ecology: POB 417, Shenyang 110015; tel. (24) 3902096; fax (24) 3843313; f. 1954; attached to Chinese Acad. of Sciences; library of 95,000 vols; Dir SUN TIEHANG; publs *Chinese Journal of Ecology*, *Chinese Journal of Applied Ecology*.

Institute of Biophysics: 15 Datun Road, Chaoyang District, Beijing 100101; tel. (10) 62022029; fax (10) 62027837; attached to Chinese Acad. of Sciences; Dir WANG SHURONG.

Institute of Botany: 141 Xizhimen Wai St, Beijing 100044; attached to Chinese Acad. of Sciences; Dir ZHANG XINSHI.

Institute of Developmental Biology: POB 2707, Beijing; fax 62561269; f. 1980; attached to Chinese Acad. of Sciences; specializes in biotechnology of fish and mammals; Dir YAN SHAOYI.

Institute of Genetics: Bldg 917, Datun Rd, Andingmenwai, Beijing 100101; tel. and fax (10) 64914896; attached to Chinese Acad. of Sciences; Dir Prof. SHOUYI CHEN.

Institute of Hydrobiology: Luojiashan, Wuhan 430072, Hubei Province; tel. (27) 87883482; fax 7825132; e-mail plan@lily.whihb.ac.cn; f. 1930; attached to Chinese Acad. of Sciences; freshwater ecology and biotechnology; library of 60,000 vols; fish museum; Dir ZHU ZUOYAN; publ. *Acta Hydrobiologica Sinica* (quarterly).

Institute of Microbiology: Zhongguancun, Haidian District, Beijing 100080; tel. 62552178; fax 25160912; f. 1958; attached to Chinese Acad. of Sciences; Dir ZHOU PEIJIN; publs *Acta Mycologica Sinica*, *Acta Microbiologica Sinica*, *Chinese Journal of Microbiology*, *Microbiology*.

Institute of Vertebrate Palaeontology and Palaeo-Anthropology: Academia Sinica, Beijing; f. 1929; attached to Chinese Acad. of Sciences; Dir QIU ZHANXIANG.

Institute of Zoology: Chinese Academy of Sciences, 19 Zhongguancun Rd, Haidian, Beijing 100080; tel. 62552219; fax 62565689; attached to Chinese Acad. of Sciences; Dir Prof. WANG ZU-WANG.

Kunming Institute of Zoology: Kunming 650223, Yunnan Province; tel. (871) 5140390; fax (871) 5151823; f. 1959; attached to Chinese Acad. of Sciences; library of 180,000 vols; Dir SHI LIMING; publ. *Zoological Research* (quarterly).

Nanjing Institute of Geology and Palaeontology: 39 East Beijing Rd, Chi-Ming-Ssu, Nanjing 210008, Jiangsu Province; tel. (25) 7714437; telex 342301; fax (25) 3357026; f. 1951; attached to Chinese Acad. of Sciences; library of 26,000 vols; Dir MU XINAN; publs *Palaeontologia Sinica* (irregular), *Memoirs* (irregular), *Bulletin* (irregular), *Journal of Stratigraphy* (quarterly), *Acta Palaeontologica Sinica* (quarterly), *Palaeontologia Cathayana*, *Acta Micropalaeontologica Sinica* (quarterly), *Palaeontological Abstracts* (quarterly), *Palaeoworld* (irregular), *Acta Palaeobotanica et Palynologica Sinica* (irregular).

Research Center for the Eco-Environmental Sciences: POB 2871, Beijing 100085; tel. 62555019; fax 62555381; f. 1975; attached to Chinese Acad. of Sciences; library of 30,000 vols; publs *Acta Scientiae Circumstantiae* (quarterly, with English abstracts), *Huanjing Kexue* (Environmental Sciences, every 2 months), *Huanjing Huaxue* (Environmental Chemistry, every 2 months), *Annual Report*.

Shanghai Institute of Biochemistry: Chinese Academy of Sciences, 320 Yue-Yang Rd, Shanghai 200031; tel. (21) 64374430; fax (21) 64338357; attached to Chinese Acad. of Sciences; Dir Prof. LI BOLIANG.

Shanghai Institute of Cell Biology: 320 Yue-Yang Rd, Shanghai; tel. (21) 64315030; fax (21) 64331090; e-mail jhc@sunm.shcnc.ac.cn; f. 1950; attached to Chinese Acad. of Sciences; Dir Dr GUO LI-HE; publs *Acta Biologiae Experimentalis Sinica*, *Chinese Journal of Cell Biology*, *Cell Research*.

Shanghai Institute of Entomology: 225 Chongqing S. Rd, Shanghai 200025; tel. 3282039; f. 1959; attached to Chinese Acad. of Sciences; Dir CHEN YUANGUANG.

Shanghai Institute of Physiology: 320 Yue-Yang Rd, Shanghai; tel. (21) 64370080; fax (21) 64332445; e-mail sls@fudan.ac.cn; f. 1944; attached to Chinese Acad. of Sciences; library of 150,000 vols; Dir XIONG-LI YANG; publ. *Acta Physiologica Sinica* (in Chinese with English abstract, every 2 months).

Shanghai Institute of Plant Physiology: 300 Fongling Rd, Shanghai 200032; tel. (21) 64042090; fax (21) 64042385; e-mail sipp@iris.sipp.ac.cn; f. 1944; attached to Chinese Acad. of Sciences; library of 150,000 vols; Dir Prof. Z. C. TANG.

South China Institute of Botany: Wushan, Guangzhou, 510650 Guangdong Province; tel. 87705626; f. 1929; attached to Chinese Acad. of Sciences; library of 59,000 vols; botanic garden, herbarium and arboretum; Dir LIANG CHENGYE; publs *Acta Botanica Austro Sinica*, *Journal of Tropical and Sub-tropical Botany* (4 a year).

Xishuangbanna Tropical Botanical Garden: Menglun, Mengla County, Yunnan 666303; tel. (Jinghong) 905; telex (Mengla) 0954; f. 1959; attached to Chinese Acad. of Sciences; library of 50,000 vols; Dir Prof. XU ZAIFU; publs *Tropical Plants Research* (quarterly), *Collected Research Papers on Tropical Botany* (annually).

Mathematical Sciences

Institute of Applied Mathematics: Academia Sinica, Box 2734, Beijing 100080; tel. 62562939; fax 62541689 f. 1979; attached to Chinese Acad. of Sciences; Dir ZHANG XIANGSUN.

Institute of Mathematics: Zhongguancun, Beijing 100080; attached to Chinese Acad. of Sciences; Dir YANG LE.

Physical Sciences

562 Comprehensive Geological Brigade: Yanqiaozhen 101601, Sanhe County, Hebei; attached to Chinese Acad. of Geological Sciences.

Beijing Observatory: Zhongguancun, Beijing 100080; telex 22040; attached to Chinese Acad. of Sciences; Dir WANG SHOUGUAN.

Changchun Institute of Applied Chemistry: 109 Stalin St, Changchun, Jilin Province; tel. 5682801; fax 5685653; f. 1948; attached to Chinese Acad. of Sciences; library of 120,000 vols; Dir Prof. WANG ERKANG; publs

Analysis Chemistry (monthly), *Applied Chemistry* (every 2 months).

Changchun Institute of Physics: 1 Yan An Rd, Changchun 130021, Jilin Province; tel. (431) 5952215; fax (431) 5955378; f. 1958; attached to Chinese Acad. of Sciences; luminescence and its application, integrated optics; library of 69,800 vols; Dir JIN YIXIN; publs *Chinese Journal of Luminescence* (quarterly), *Chinese Journal of Liquid Crystal and Displays* (quarterly).

Chengdu Institute of Geology and Mineral Resources: 101 Renmin N. Rd, Chengdu 610082, Sichuan; attached to Chinese Acad. of Geological Sciences.

Chinese Institute of Atomic Energy: POB 275, Beijing; tel. 69357487; telex 222373; fax 69357008; f. 1958; attached to Chinese Acad. of Sciences; Dir Prof. SUN ZUXUN; publs *Annual Report, Chinese Journal of Nuclear Physics* (quarterly), *Journal of Nuclear and Radiochemistry* (quarterly), *Atomic Energy Science and Technology* (every 2 months), *Isotopes* (quarterly).

Commission for the Integrated Survey of Natural Resources: POB 9717, Beijing 100101; tel. (10) 64913580; fax (10) 64914230; e-mail zhaosd@cern.ac.cn; f. 1956; attached to Chinese Acad. of Sciences and State Planning Comm.; co-ordinates the integrated survey teams for the exploitation, utilization, conservation and evaluation of natural resources; multi-disciplinary research; library of 40,096 vols; Dir Prof. ZHAO SHIDONG; publ. *Journal of Natural Resources* (quarterly, with English abstracts).

Dalian Institute of Chemical Physics: 161 Zhongshan Rd, Dalian; tel. 3631841; telex 86436; fax 363426; f. 1949; attached to Chinese Acad. of Sciences; library of 70,000 vols; Dir YUAN QUAN; publs *Journal of Catalysis* (quarterly), *Chinese Journal of Chromatography* (every 2 months).

Guangzhou Institute of Chemistry: Academia Sinica, Guangzhou 510650; tel. 7708817; fax 7705319; f. 1958; attached to Chinese Acad. of Sciences; library of 80,000 vols; Dir CONG GUANGMIN; publs *Guangzhou Chemistry* (quarterly), *Journal of Cellulose Science and Technology* (quarterly).

Institute for the Application of Remote Sensing Information: Changsha 410114, Hunan; attached to Chinese Acad. of Geological Sciences.

Institute of Acoustics: 17 Zhongguancun St, Beijing 100080; tel. (10) 62553765; telex 222525; fax (10) 62553898; f. 1964; attached to Chinese Acad. of Sciences; Dir LI QIHU.

Institute of Atmospheric Physics: Qijiahezi, Beijing 100029; tel. 64919693; fax 62028604; f. 1928; attached to Chinese Acad. of Sciences; library of 55,000 vols and periodicals; Dir Prof. ZENG QINGCUN; publs *Scientia Atmospherica Sinica* (in Chinese), *Chinese Journal of Atmospheric Sciences, Advances in Atmospheric Sciences* (all quarterly), *Collected Papers of the Institute of Atmospheric Physics* (in Chinese).

Institute of Atmospheric Sounding: 7 Block 11, Hepingli, Beijing; attached to Chinese Acad. of Meteorological Sciences.

Institute of Chemical Metallurgy: 1 Beiertiao, Zhongguancun, Beijing; tel. (10) 62554241; fax (10) 62561822; e-mail office@home.icm.ac.cn; f. 1958; attached to Chinese Acad. of Sciences; library of 171,500 vols; Dir Prof. XIE YUSHENG; publs *Engineering Chemistry and Metallurgy* (quarterly), *Computer and Applied Chemistry* (quarterly).

Institute of Chemistry: Zhongguancun, Haidian District, Beijing; tel. 282281; fax 62569564; f. 1956; attached to Chinese Acad. of Sciences; library of 100,000 vols; Dir Prof. HU YADONG.

Institute of Climatology: 7 Block 11, Hepingli, Beijing; attached to Chinese Acad. of Meteorological Sciences.

Institute of Geochemistry: Chinese Academy of Sciences, 73 Guanshui Rd, Guiyang, Guizhou 550002; tel. (851) 5814495; fax (851) 5822982; f. 1966; attached to Chinese Acad. of Sciences; library of 150,000 vols; Dir LIU CONGQIANG; publs *Bulletin of Mineralogy, Petrology and Geochemistry* (quarterly), *Chinese Journal of Geochemistry* (quarterly), *Acta Mineralogica Sinica* (quarterly), *Geology-Geochemistry* (4 a year).

Institute of Geology: 26 Baiwanzhuang Rd, Beijing 100037; attached to Chinese Acad. of Geological Sciences.

Institute of Geomechanics: Fahuasi, Beijing 100081; tel. (10) 68412303; fax (10) 68422326; f. 1956; attached to Chinese Acad. of Geological Sciences; Pres. Prof. WU GANGUO; publ. *Journal of Geomechanics* (quarterly).

Institute of Geophysics: A-11 Datun Rd, Chao Yang District, Beijing 100101; tel. (10) 64871497; attached to Chinese Acad. of Sciences; Dir ZHENG TIANYU.

Institute of Geotectonics: Academia Sinica, Changsha, Hunan Province 410013; tel. (731) 8859150; telex 5106; fax (731) 8859137; f. 1961; attached to Chinese Acad. of Sciences; library of 35,000 vols; Dir CHEN GUODA; publ. *Geotectonica et Metallogenia* (quarterly).

Institute of High Energy Physics: POB 918, Beijing; attached to Chinese Acad. of Sciences; Dir Prof. ZHENG LINSHENG; publ. *Modern Physics*.

Institute of Karst Geology: 40 Seven Stars Rd, Guilin 541104, Guangxi; attached to Chinese Acad. of Geological Sciences.

Institute of Mesoscale Meteorology: 7 Block 11, Hepingli, Beijing; attached to Chinese Acad. of Meteorological Sciences.

Institute of Metal Research: Academia Sinica, 72 Wenhua Rd, Shenyang 110015; tel. (24) 3843531; telex 80095; fax (24) 3891320; f. 1953; attached to Chinese Acad. of Sciences; library of 85,000 vols, 2,300 periodicals; publs *Journal of Materials Science and Technology* (every 2 months), *Acta Metallurgica Sinica* (monthly), *Materials Science Progress* (every 2 months).

Institute of Mineral Deposits: 26 Baiwanzhuang Rd, Beijing 100037; attached to Chinese Acad. of Geological Sciences.

Institute of Photographic Chemistry: Academia Sinica, Bei Sha Tan, Beijing 100101; tel. (10) 62017061; fax (10) 62029375; f. 1975; attached to Chinese Acad. of Sciences; library of 32,000 vols; Dir CHEN-HO TUNG; publ. *Photographic Science and Photochemistry*.

Institute of Physics: Zhongguancun, Haidian District, Beijing 100080; telex 210208; fax 282271; attached to Chinese Acad. of Sciences; Dir YANG GUOZHEN.

Institute of Rock and Mineral Analysis: 26 Baiwanzhuang Rd, Beijing 100037; tel. (10) 68311550; fax (10) 68320365; f. 1978; attached to Chinese Acad. of Geological Sciences.

Institute of Space Physics: Zhongguancun, Beijing 100080; tel. 288052; attached to Chinese Acad. of Sciences.

Institute of Synoptic and Dynamic Meteorology: 7 Block 11, Hepingli, Beijing; attached to Chinese Acad. of Meteorological Sciences.

Institute of the Corrosion and Protection of Metals: Academia Sinica, 62 Wencui Rd, Shenyang 110015; tel. 3894313; telex 80095; fax 3894149; f. 1982; attached to Chinese Acad. of Sciences; library of 7,000 vols, 500 journals; Dir Prof. WU WEITAO; publs *Annual Report, Corrosion Science and Protection Technology* (quarterly).

Institute of Theoretical Physics: Academia Sinica, POB 2735, Beijing 100080; tel. (10) 62555058; fax (10) 62562587; f. 1978; attached to Chinese Acad. of Sciences; library of 10,000 vols; Dir SU ZHAOBIN; publ. *Communications in Theoretical Physics* (in English, every 2 months).

Institute of Weather Modification: 7 Block 11, Hepingli, Beijing; attached to Chinese Acad. of Meteorological Sciences.

Lanzhou Institute of Glaciology and Geocryology: 260 Donggang Rd W., Lanzhou; tel. (931) 8818203;; fax (931) 8885241; e-mail liggplan@ns.lzb.ac.cn; f. 1965; attached to Chinese Acad. of Sciences; library of 34,000 vols, 1,000 periodicals; Dir Prof. CHENG GUODONG; publs *Journal of Glaciology and Geocryology* (in Chinese, 4 a year), *Cryosphere* (in English, 1 a year).

Lanzhou Institute of Physics: POB Lanzhou 94; attached to Chinese Acad. of Space Technology.

Nanjing Institute of Geology and Mineral Resources: 534 Zhongshan E. Rd, Nanjing 210016, Jiangsu; attached to Chinese Acad. of Geological Sciences.

Purple Mountain Observatory: 2 West Beijing Rd, Nanjing 210008, Jiangsu; tel. (25) 3300818; telex 34144; fax (25) 3300818; f. 1934; attached to Chinese Acad. of Sciences; library of 36,000 vols; Dir LIU BENQUI; publs *Acta Astronomica Sinica* (quarterly), *Publications of Purple Mountain Observatory*.

Shaanxi Astronomical Observatory: POB 18, Lintong, Xian; tel. (29) 3890326; fax (29) 3890196; e-mail pub2@ms.sxso.ac.cn; f. 1966; attached to Chinese Acad. of Sciences; library of 3,500 vols; Dir Prof. LI ZHIGANG; publ. *Time and Frequency* (monthly).

Shanghai Astronomical Observatory: 80 Nandan Rd, Shanghai 200030; tel. (21) 64384522; fax (21) 64384618; e-mail office@center.shao.ac.cn; f. 1872; attached to Chinese Acad. of Sciences; library of 80,000 vols; Dir Prof. ZHAO JUNLIANG; publs *Progress in Astronomy* (quarterly), *Annals of Shanghai Observatory*.

Shanghai Institute of Metallurgy: Chinese Academy of Sciences, 865 Changning Rd, Shanghai 200050; tel. 2511070; fax 2513510; f. 1928; attached to Chinese Acad. of Sciences; Dir ZOU SHICHANG.

Shanghai Institute of Nuclear Research: POB 800-204, Shanghai 201800; tel. (21) 59553998; fax (21) 59553021; f. 1959; attached to Chinese Acad. of Sciences; Dir Prof. YANG FUJIA; publs *Nuclear Science and Techniques* (quarterly), *Journal of Radiation Research and Radiation Processing* (quarterly), *Nuclear Technology* (in Chinese, monthly).

Shanghai Institute of Organic Chemistry: 345 Fenglin Lu, Shanghai; tel. (21) 64163300; fax (21) 64166128; f. 1950; attached to Chinese Acad. of Sciences; library of 300,000 vols; Dir Prof. LIN GUOQIANG; publs *Acta Chimica Sinica* (monthly in Chinese), *Chinese Journal of Chemistry* (every 2 months in English), *Organic Chemistry* (every 2 months in English).

Shenyang Institute of Geology and Mineral Resources: Beiling Ave, Shenyang 110032, Liaoning; attached to Chinese Acad. of Geological Sciences.

Southwestern Institute of Physics: POB 15, Leshan, 614007 Sichuan; POB 432, Chengdu 610041, Sichuan; tel. (833) 2130701 (Leshan), (28) 5581122 (Chengdu); fax (833) 2132721 (Leshan), (28) 5581053 (Chengdu); e-mail yegaoy@public2.dta.net.cn; f. 1965;

attached to China National Nuclear Corporation; controlled nuclear fusion and application of intermediate technology; library of 150,000 vols, 630 periodicals; Dir Prof. SHANG ZHENKUI; publ. *Nuclear Fusion and Plasma Physics* (quarterly).

Tianjin Institute of Geology and Mineral Resources: 4 8th Rd, Dazhigu, Tianjin, 300170; tel. (22) 24314386; fax (22) 24314292; e-mail tjigmr@public.tpt.tj.cn; f. 1962; attached to Chinese Acad. of Geological Sciences; Dir LU SONGNIAN; publ. *Progress in Precambrian Research* (4 a year).

Xi'an Institute of Geology and Mineral Resources: 160 Eastern to Youyi Rd, Xian 710054, Shaanxi; attached to Chinese Acad. of Geological Sciences.

Yichang Institute of Geology and Mineral Resources: PO Box 502, Yichang 443003, Hubei; attached to Chinese Acad. of Geological Sciences.

Yunnan Observatory: POB 110, Kunming 650011; fax (871) 3911845; e-mail ynao@public.km.yn.cn; f. 1972; attached to Chinese Acad. of Sciences; library of 35,000 vols; Dir Prof. TAN HUISONG; publ. *Publications of Yunnan Observatory* (quarterly).

PHILOSOPHY AND PSYCHOLOGY

Institute of Psychology: POB 1603, Beijing 100012; tel. 64919520; fax 64872070; e-mail yangyf@psych.ac.cn; f. 1951; attached to Chinese Acad. of Sciences; library of 145,000 vols, 1,500 periodicals; Dir Dr YANG YUFANG; publs *Acta Psychologica Sinica* (quarterly), *Journal of Developments in Psychology* (quarterly).

Philosophy Institute: 5 Jianguomennei Ave, Beijing 100732; f. 1977; attached to Chinese Acad. of Social Sciences; Dir XING FONSI.

RELIGION, SOCIOLOGY AND ANTHROPOLOGY

Centre for Population Studies: 5 Jianguomennei Ave, Beijing 100732; attached to Chinese Acad. of Social Sciences; Dir TIAN XUEYUAN.

Institute of World Religions: 5 Jianguo Mennei St, Beijing 100732; tel. (10) 65138523; f. 1964; attached to Chinese Acad. of Social Sciences; Dir Prof. WU YUNGUI; publs *Studies on World Religions* (quarterly), *World Religious Culture* quarterly).

Nationalities Studies Institute: Baishiqiao, Beijing; attached to Chinese Acad. of Social Sciences; Dir ZHAONA SITU.

Sociology Institute: 5 Jianguomennei Ave, Beijing 100732; f. 1979; attached to Chinese Acad. of Social Sciences; Dir HE JIANZHANG.

TECHNOLOGY

Beijing Institute of Control Engineering: POB 729, Beijing 100080; attached to Chinese Acad. of Space Technology.

Beijing Institute of Spacecraft Systems Engineering: POB 9628, Beijing 100086; attached to Chinese Acad. of Space Technology.

Changchun Institute of Optics and Fine Mechanics: 112 Stalin St, Changchun, Jilin Province; tel. 684692; fax 682346; f. 1950; attached to Chinese Acad. of Sciences; Dir WANG JIAQI; publ. *Optics and Precision Engineering* (every 2 months).

Chemical Processing and Forest Products Utilization Research Institute: Longpan Rd, Nanjing, Jiangsu Province; attached to Chinese Acad. of Forestry.

China Coal Research Institute: Qingniangou, Hepingli, Beijing 100013; tel. (10) 64214931; fax (10) 64219234; e-mail office@ccri.ac.cn; f. 1957; attached research institutes: see Research Institutes; Dir Prof. Dr ZHU DEREN.

China State Bureau of Technical Supervision (CSBTS): POB 8010, Beijing; tel. 62025835; telex 210209; fax 62031010; f. 1988; research and development for national standards and quality control; colln of nat. standards from 56 countries; Dir-Gen. ZHU YULI; publs *Standards Journal*, *Technical Supervision Journal*.

Institute of Automation: Zhong Guan Cun, Haidian District, Beijing; tel. (10) 62551397; fax (10) 62545229; f. 1956; attached to Chinese Acad. of Sciences; Dir HU FENGFENG; publs *Acta Automatica Sinica* (in Chinese, 6 a year), *Chinese Journal of Automation* (in English, quarterly).

Institute of Coal Chemistry: POB 165, Taiyuan 030001, Shanxi Province; tel. (351) 4041267; fax (351) 4041153; f. 1954; attached to Chinese Acad. of Sciences; Dir Prof. ZHONG BING; publ. *Journal of Fuel Chemistry and Technology* (quarterly).

Institute of Computer Technology: 6 Kexueyuan S. Rd, Haidian District, Beijing; tel. 62565533; telex 22638; fax 62562946; attached to Chinese Acad. of Sciences; Dir YAN PEILIN.

Institute of Computer Technology: 24 Section 2, Sanhao St, Shenyang 110001, Liaoning; tel. 7705360; fax 7705319; attached to Chinese Acad. of Sciences; Dir CONG GUANGMIN.

Institute of Electronics: 17 Zhong Guan Cun Rd, POB 2702, Beijing 100080; tel. 62554424; telex 222582; fax 62567363; f. 1956; attached to Chinese Acad. of Sciences; library of 35,000 vols; Dir Prof. ZHU MINHUI; publs *Journal of Electronics* (every 2 months, in Chinese), *Journal of Electronics (China)* (quarterly, in English).

Institute of Engineering Mechanics: 9 Xuefu Rd, Harbin 150080; tel. 6662901; telex 87051; fax 6664755; f. 1954; attached to Chinese Acad. of Sciences; earthquake and safety engineering; library of 100,000 vols; Dir XIE LILI; publs *Earthquake Engineering and Engineering Vibration* (quarterly), *World Information on Earthquake Engineering* (quarterly), *Journal of Natural Disasters* (quarterly).

Institute of Engineering Thermophysics: 12B Zhongguancun Rd, Beijing; tel. 62554126; telex 2575913; f. 1980; attached to Chinese Acad. of Sciences; Dir CAI RUIXIAN; publ. *Journal of Engineering Thermodynamics* (quarterly).

Institute of Hydrogeology and Engineering Geology: Zhengding County 050303, Hebei; attached to Chinese Acad. of Geological Sciences.

Institute of Mechanics: 15 Zhongguancun Rd, Beijing 100080; attached to Chinese Acad. of Sciences; Dir ZHENG ZHEMIN.

Institute of Meteorological Instrument Calibration: 7 Block 11, Hepingli, Beijing; attached to Chinese Acad. of Meteorological Sciences.

Institute of Optics and Electronics: POB 350, Shuangliu, Chengdu, Sichuan Province; tel. (28) 5180032; telex 600069; fax (28) 5180070; f. 1970; attached to Chinese Acad. of Sciences; library of 90,000 vols; Dir MA JIAGUANG; publ. *Opto-Electronics Engineering* (6 a year).

Institute of Semiconductors: POB 912, Beijing 100083; tel. (10) 288131; telex 22474; fax (10) 62562389; f. 1960; attached to Chinese Acad. of Sciences; Dir WANG QIMING.

Institute of Systems Science: 1A Nansi St, Zhongguancun, Beijing 100080; tel. (10) 62553005; fax (10) 62568364; e-mail issb@bamboo.iss.ac.cn; f. 1979; attached to Chinese Acad. of Sciences; Dir Prof. CHEN HANFU; publs *Journal of Systems Science and Mathematics* (4 a year), *Journal of Systems Science and Systems Engineering* (6 a year).

Science and Technology Development Corporation: 26 Baiwanghuang Rd, Beijing 100037; attached to Chinese Acad. of Geological Sciences.

Shanghai Institute of Ceramics: 1295 Ding Xi Rd, Shanghai 200050; tel. (21) 62512990; telex 33309; fax (21) 62513903; f. 1959; attached to Chinese Acad. of Sciences; library of 80,000 vols; Dir SHI ERWEI; publs *Journal of Inorganic Materials* (quarterly), *Shanghai Silicate* (quarterly).

Shanghai Institute of Optics and Fine Mechanics: POB 800-211, Shanghai; tel. 9534890; fax 9528812; attached to Chinese Acad. of Sciences; laser science and technology; Dir Prof. XU ZHIZHAN; publs *Acta Optica Sinica* (monthly), *Chinese Journal of Lasers* (monthly).

Shanghai Institute of Technical Physics: 420 Zhong Shan Bei Yi Rd, Shanghai; tel. 5420850; fax 3248028; f. 1958; attached to Chinese Acad. of Sciences; infrared technology and physics, optoelectronics and remote sensing; library of 35,000 vols; Dir KUANG DINGBO; publs *Chinese Journal of Infrared Research* (every 2 months), *Chinese Journal of Infrared and Millimetre Waves*.

Xian Institute of Optics and Precision Mechanics: Xian, Shaanxi; tel. (29) 5261376; fax (29) 5261473; f. 1962; attached to Chinese Acad. of Sciences; library of 120,000 vols; Dir Prof. ZHAO BAOCHANG; publ. *Acta Photinica Sinica* (6 a year).

Xian Institute of Space Radio Technology: POB 165, Xian 710000; tel. (29) 5290500; fax (29) 5290588; f. 1965; attached to Chinese Acad. of Space Technology.

Zhengzhou Institute of the Multi-Purpose Utilization of Mineral Resources: 26 Funu Rd, Zhengzhou 450006, Henan Province; tel. (371) 8984974; fax (371) 8984942; f. 1956; attached to Chinese Acad. of Geological Sciences; library of 200,000 vols; Dir Prof. Dr ZHANG KEREN; publ. *Conservation and Utilization of Mineral Resources* (6 a year).

Libraries and Archives

Baoding

Hebei University Library: 2 Hezuo Rd, Baoding, Hebei Province; tel. (312) 5022922 ext. 417; telex 26294; fax (312) 5022648; f. 1921; 1,960,000 vols, 3,923 current periodicals, 3,000 back copies; special collection: 4,397 vols of Chinese ancient books, incl. local chronicles and family trees; Dir LOU CHENGZHAO; publ. *Journal of Hebei University*.

Beijing

Beijing Normal University Library: Xinjiekouwai Dajie St, Beijing 100875; tel. (10) 62208163; fax (10) 62200567; e-mail libli@bnu.cn; f. 1902; 2,700,000 vols, 14,436 periodicals; rich collection of thread-bound Chinese ancient books, incl. 1,500 titles of remarkable editions, 2,800 titles of local chronicles, 1,300 series; Dir YIU TIANCHI.

Beijing University Library: Haidian District, Beijing; tel. (10) 62751051; f. 1902; 4,610,000 books, 650,000 vols of bound periodicals; rich collection on philosophy, politics, economics, language, literature and history, and systematic collection of major reference books on the histories of philosophy and literature, complete collection of major abstract journals; special collection: 1,600,000 vols of thread-bound Chinese ancient books, incl. 160,000 vols of rare books, copy of *Complete*

Works of Shakespeare (publ. 1623), Dante's *Divine Comedy* (publ. 1896), and plays by Schiller, etc.; Dir Prof. LIN BEIDIAN; publs *Catalogue of Remarkable Edition Books Held by Beijing University Library, Union Catalogue of Books in Western Languages held by State Education Commission.*

Capital Library: 15 Guozijian St, Dongcheng District, Beijing; tel. and fax (10) 64040905; f. 1913; municipal library; 2,574,000 vols, 142,000 current periodicals; spec. collns incl. traditional opera, folk customs; Dir JIN PEILIN.

Central Archives of China: Wenquan, Haidian District, Beijing; tel. 62556611; f. 1959; revolutionary historical archives from the May 4th Movement of 1919 to the founding of the People's Republic in 1949, and archives of CPC and central government offices; 8,000,000 files; Curator WANG GANG; publs *CPC Documents, Central Archives of China Series, Collection of PCC Documents*, etc.

Centre for Social Science Information and Documentation: 5 Jianguomennei Ave, Beijing 100732; attached to Chinese Acad. of Social Sciences; Dir (vacant).

Documentation and Information Centre of the Chinese Academy of Sciences (DICCAS), and Library of Academia Sinica (LAS): 8 Kexueyuan, Nanlu, Zhongguancun, Beijing 100080; tel. 62566847; telex 83020; fax 62566846; f. 1950; 5,620,000 vols, 6,000 current periodicals, 24,000 back copies, conference proceedings, research reports; spec. collns incl. local chronicles, collected works of the Ming and Qing Dynasties, 30,000 rubbings from stone tablets; Dir XU YINCHI; publs *Foreign Sci-Tech Policy and Management* (monthly), *Progress in Biological Engineering* (every 2 months), *Mathematical Abstracts of China* (every 2 months), *Physical Abstracts of China* (every 2 months), *Library and Information Service* (every 2 months), *R&D Information* (monthly), *New Technology of Library and Information Service* (6 a year).

First Historical Archives of China: Palace Museum inside Xihuamen, 100031 Beijing; tel. (10) 63096489; f. 1925; 10,000,000 files; historical archives of Ming and Qing Dynasties and all other historical periods; Curator XU YIPU; publ. *Historical Archives* (quarterly).

Institute of Meteorological, Scientific and Technical Information: 7 Block 11, Hepingli, Beijing; attached to Chinese Acad. of Meteorological Sciences.

Institute of Scientific and Technical Information of China (ISTIC): 15 Fu Xing Lu, POB 3827, Beijing 100038; tel. (10) 68514020; fax (10) 68514025; f. 1956; 18,000,000 items from China and abroad, incl. research reports, conference proceedings, periodicals, patents, standards, catalogues and samples and audiovisual material; Dir-Gen. ZHU WEI; publs *Scientific and Technical Trends Abroad, Review of World Inventions, Journal of Scientific and Technical Information*, etc.

Institute of Scientific and Technological Information on Forestry: Wan Shou Shan, Beijing 100091; tel. (10) 62582211; fax (10) 62582317; attached to Chinese Acad. of Forestry.

Medical Information Institute: 3 Yabaolu, Chaoyang District, Beijing 100020; tel. and fax 65128176; attached to Chinese Acad. of Medical Sciences; Dir LU RUSHAN.

Medical Library: 9 Dongdan Santiao, Beijing 100730; tel. 65127733; attached to Chinese Acad. of Medical Sciences; Dir LU RUSHAN.

National Library of China: 39 Baishiqiao Rd, Haidian District, Beijing 100081; tel. (10) 68415566; fax (10) 68419271; e-mail cjsun@sun.ihep.ac.cn; f. 1909; 20,000,000 vols, 19,000 current periodicals, 9,000,000 back copies, 956,000 microforms and audiovisual items; collects all kinds of Chinese publs incl. those in minority languages; foreign books, periodicals and newspapers, UN publs and govt publs of certain countries; blockprinted editions, books of rubbings, and other antique items; spec. collns incl. 291,696 vols of rare books of imperial libraries in the Southern Song, Ming and Qing dynasties; Dir Prof. REN JIYU; publs *Documents* (quarterly), *Journal of the National Library of China* (quarterly), *National Bibliography.*

Qinghua University Library (Tsinghua University Library): Qinghuayuan, West Suburb, Beijing; tel. 62594591; telex 22617; fax 62562768; f. 1911; 2,500,000 vols, 15,495 periodicals (foreign 5,902); special collections: Chinese ancient books 30,000 titles (300,000 vols), including rare editions, only existing copies and handcopies, 3,000 titles (30,000 vols); rich collections of academic books and periodicals, conference literature, engineering historical data, local chronicles, collected papers on special subjects, major abstract journals, complete set of nearly 200 foreign periodicals; Dir Prof. ZHU WENHAO; publs *Tsinghua Journal* (Natural Sciences and Social Sciences edns), *Tsinghua University Selections of Scientific Theses, Science Report.*

Renmin University of China Library: 175 Haidian Rd, Beijing; tel. 62511371; fax 62566374; f. 1937; 2,500,000 vols, 2,400 current periodical titles, 400,000 back copies; publs on philosophy, politics, law, economics, etc.; rich collection of philosophy of Marxism, law, economics, modern and contemporary history of China; special collection: Chinese revolutionary documents in liberated and base areas, ancient rare books of Song, Yuan, Ming and Qing Dynasties (2,400 titles); 154 staff; Dir Prof. YANG DONGLIANG; publs *Index to the Complete Works of Marx and Engels, Classification of the Renmin University of China Library, Index to the ancient rare books of RUC Library.*

Changchun

Jilin Provincial Library: 10 Xinmin Ave, Changchun, Jilin Province; tel. 5643796; f. 1958; 2,700,000 vols; Dir JIN ENHUI; publ. *Research in Library Science* (every 2 months).

Jilin University Library: 117 Jiefang Rd, Changchun 130023, Jilin Province; tel. 8923189; f. 1946; 2,154,000 vols, 3,078 current periodicals, 299,808 back copies; special collection: local chronicles, clan trees, Asian Series, documents of Manchurian railways; Dir Prof. WANG TONGCHE.

Northeast Normal University Library: 138 Renmin St, Changchun, Jilin Province; tel. 5684174; f. 1946; 2,300,000 vols, 4,000 current periodicals, 11,600 back copies; publs from time of the War of Resistance Against Japan, rare Chinese ancient books; Dir SUN ZHONGTIAN; publ. *Jilin Libraries of Colleges and Universities* (quarterly).

Changsha

Hunan Provincial Library: 38 Shaoshan Rd, Changsha, Hunan Province; tel. 25653; f. 1904; 3,090,000 vols, 130,000 bound vols of periodicals, 900,000 ancient books.

Chengdu

Sichuan Provincial Library: 6 Lu Zongfu, Chengdu 610016, Sichuan Province; tel. (28) 6659219; f. 1940; 3,760,000 vols, 13,485 periodicals, historical material; Dir WANG ENLAI (acting); publ. *Librarian* (every 2 months).

Chongqing

Chongqing Library: 1 Changjiang Rd A, Chongqing, Sichuan Province; tel. 54832; f. 1947; 3,137,198 vols, 690,183 bound periodicals, 65,514 technical reports, 35,000 antique books, historical documents, UN publs; Dir LI PUJIE.

Dalian

Dalian City Library: 7 Changbai, Xigang District, Dalian, Liaoning Province; tel. (411) 3630033; fax (411) 3623796; f. 1907; 2,000,000 vols, 5,502 periodicals; 700 ancient books; Dir LIU ZHENWEI.

Fuzhou

Fujian Provincial Library: 37 Dongfanghong Dajie St, Fuzhou, Fujian Province; tel. 31604; f. 1913; 2,200,000 vols, 4,350 current periodicals, historical material; spec. collns incl. data on Taiwan and Southeast Asia.

Guangzhou

South China Teachers' University Library: Shipai, Tianhe District, Guangzhou, Guangdong Province; tel. 774911; 1,600,000 vols, over 3,000 current periodicals, 7,145 back copies; special collection: 180,000 vols of Chinese ancient books, incl. 1,025 titles of local chronicles; 106 staff; Deputy Dir YANG WEIPING.

Zhongshan Library of Guangdong Province: 211 Wenming Rd, Guangzhou, Guangdong Province; tel. 330676; f. 1912; 3,300,000 vols, 6,000 current periodicals, historical documents; spec. collns incl. research materials on Dr Sun Yat-sen; Dir HUANG JUNGUI; publs *Journal of Guangdong Libraries* (quarterly), *Library Tribune* (quarterly).

Guilin

Guilin Library of Guangxi Zhuang Autonomous Region: 15 North Ronghu Rd, Guilin, Guangxi Zhuang Autonomous Region; tel. 223494; f. 1909; 1,380,000 vols, 15,275 current periodicals, historical material; Deputy Dir YANG JIANHONG; publs *Catalogue of Guangxi Local Documents, Catalogue of Materials on Guangxi Minority Study* (vols 1–2).

Guiyang

Guizhou Provincial Library: 31 Beijing Rd, Guiyang, Guizhou Province; tel. 25562; f. 1937; 1,270,000 vols, 5,000 periodicals, historical material; publs *Journal* (quarterly), *Chronological Table of the Historical Calamities of Guizhou Province, Collected Papers on the Mineral Products of Guizhou Province.*

Hangzhou

Zhejiang Provincial Library: 3 Baishaqiuan Shuguang Rd, Hangzhou 310007, Zhejiang Province; tel. (571) 7046414; fax (571) 7046263; e-mail zjlib@public.hz.zj.cn; f. 1900; 3,800,000 vols, 7,564 current periodicals; Chief Officer WANG XIAOLIANG; publ. *Library Science Research and Work* (quarterly).

Hankou

Wuhan Library: 86 Nanjing Rd, Hankou, Hubei Province; tel. 24334; f. 1953; 1,400,000 vols, 2,018 periodicals, 200,000 ancient books, historial material.

Harbin

Heilongjiang Provincial Library: 22 Wen Chang St, Harbin, Heilongjiang Province; tel. 224581; f. 1958; 2,185,000 vols, 5,000 ancient books, historical material; spec. collns incl. Russian publs, 1920s–1940s Japanese publs; Dir WANG SHENGMAO; publ. *Heilongjiang Libraries* (every 2 months).

Hefei

Anhui Provincial Library: 38 Wuhu Rd, Hefei, Anhui Province; tel. 257602; f. 1913; 2,108,608 vols, 5,400 current periodicals, 30,000 antique books, historical documents; Dir WANG BAO SHENG; publs. *Library Work* (quarterly), *Bulletin of Anhui Libraries* (quarterly).

Huhhot

Nei Monggol Autonomous Region Library (Inner Mongolia Autonomous Region Library): People's Park, Huhhot 010020, Nei Monggol Autonomous Region; tel. 27948; f. 1950; 1,260,000 vols, 2,131 current periodicals; spec. collns incl. Mongolia; Dir ZHANG XIANGTANG; publ. *Nei Monggol Library Work* (quarterly, in Mongolian and Chinese).

Jinan

Shandong Provincial Library: 275 Daminhu Rd, Jinan, Shandong Province; tel. 612338; f. 1908; 3,500,000 vols, 3,500 periodicals, ancient books, historical documents.

Shandong University Library: Jinan, Shandong Province; tel. 803861; f. 1901; 2,000,000 vols, 3,000 current periodicals, 260,000 back copies; 77% of holdings are on liberal arts; special collection: rare books, rubbings from stone inscriptions, calligraphy and paintings, revolutionary documents; 118 staff; Dir Prof. XU WEN-TIAN.

Kunming

Yunnan Provincial Library: 2 South Cuihu Rd, Kunming, Yunnan Province; tel. 5298; f. 1950; 2,150,000 vols, 7,172 periodicals, historical material.

Lanzhou

Gansu Provincial Library: 250 Binghedong Rd, Lanzhou, Gansu Province; tel. 28982; f. 1916; 2,400,000 vols, historical material; spec. collns incl. Imperial Library of Qianlong; Dir PAN YINSHENG; publ. *Library and Information* (quarterly).

Nanchang

Jiangxi Provincial Library: 160 North Hongdu Rd, Nanchang, Jiangxi Province; tel. (791) 8517065; f. 1920; 2,200,000 vols, 6,600 periodicals, historical material; publ. *Journal of the Jiangxi Society of Library Science* (quarterly).

Nanjing

Nanjing Library: 66 Chengxian St, Nanjing, Jiangsu Province; tel. 7717619; f. 1907; 6,600,000 vols, 7,000 current periodicals, 1,700,000 ancient books; publ. *Journal of Jiangsu Libraries* (every 2 months).

Nanjing University Library: 22 Hankou Rd, Nanjing 210093, Jiangsu Province; tel. and fax (25) 3592943; f. 1902; 3,560,000 vols, 32,330 current periodicals, 566,400 bound vols of periodicals; systematic collection of literature, history, philosophy, economics, law, mathematics, physics, chemistry, astronomy, geology, geography, meteorology, environmental science, computer science, biology and medicine, in Chinese and foreign languages; fairly complete collection of reference books from most countries, rich collection of major retrieval serials; special collection: 1,452 titles of rare books (Song, Yuan, Ming and Qing Dynasties), 10,000 sheets of rubbings from stone inscriptions, many paintings, MSS and handcopies, 4,600 titles (40,000 vols) of local chronicles, mainly of Jiangsu and Sichuan Provinces, also books on orientalism, bibliography and archaeology; Dir Prof. ZHANG YIBING; publs *Catalogue of Remarkable Editions of Chinese Ancient Books Held by Nanjing University Library, Catalogue of Local Chronicles Held by Nanjing University Library, Catalogue of Local Chronicles Held by Nanjing University Library, Catalogue of Foreign Serials and Chinese Serials Held by Nanjing University Library, Journal of Serials Management and Research.*

Second Historical Archives of China: 309 East Zhongshan Rd, Nanjing, Jiangsu Province; tel. 4409996; f. 1951; archive material of the Republic of China (1912–1949); 1,740,000 files, 246,000 periodicals; Curator XU HAO; publs *Republican Archives* (quarterly), *Collected Archives Series of the History of the Republic of China.*

Nanning

Guangxi Zhuang Autonomous Region Library: 61 Minzu Dadao St, Nanning, Guangxi Zhuang Autonomous Region; tel. 5860297; f. 1931; 2,050,000 vols, 4,575 current periodicals, historical material; Dir WANG XUEGUANG; publ. *Library World* (quarterly).

Shanghai

East China Normal University Library: 3663 North Zhongshan Rd, Shanghai; tel. (21) 62579196; f. 1951; 2,640,000 vols, 5,187 current periodicals, 237,000 back copies; notable collection on pedagogy, psychology, geography, classical philosophy, local histories and bibliography; the earliest editions of thread-bound Chinese ancient books are those of the Song Dynasty and of foreign books (publ. 1630); rubbings from stone inscriptions; Dir WANG XIJING; publ. *Library Information* (monthly).

Fudan University Library: 220 Handan Rd, Shanghai 200433; tel. 65643162; fax 65649814; e-mail zfqin@fudan.edu.cn; f. 1918; 3,500,000 vols, incl. remarkable editions of Chinese ancient books; special collections: 709 different editions of *The Books of Songs* and 3,000 titles of collected works of famous writers of Qing Dynasty; Dir Prof. QIN ZENG-FU.

Shanghai Library: Huaihai Rd, Shanghai; tel. (21) 3273176; fax (21) 3278493; f. 1952; 8,200,000 vols, 14,449 periodicals, 152,270 technical reports, early MSS, historical material, microforms, audio-visual material; Dir ZHU QING ZHO; publs *Catalog of Chinese Series* (1959), *Contents of Modern Chinese Journals, Catalog of Shanghai Library Collections of Local Histories, Catalog of Works and Translations by Guo Moruo, National Index of Newspapers and Periodicals.*

Shenyang

Liaoning Provincial Library: Shenyang, Liaoning Province; f. 1948; 1,923,366 vols, 13,307 periodicals.

Taiyuan

Shanxi Provincial Library: 1 Wenguan Lane, South Jiefang Rd, Taiyuan, Shanxi Province; f. 1918; 1,700,000 vols, 9,900 periodicals.

Tianjin

Nankai University Library: 94 Weijin Rd, Tianjin 300071; tel. 3502410; fax 3505633; f. 1919; 2,300,000 vols, 6,000 current periodicals, 4,000 back copies; special collections: 2,000 titles of rare books, 4,000 titles of local chronicles, 10,000 titles of different reference books, complete set of 100 periodicals with back issues of more than 50 years; Dir Prof. FENG CHENGBO; publs *Catalog of Rare Books Held by Nankai University Library, Catalog of Thread-Bound Ancient Books Held by Nankai University Library.*

Tianjin Library: 12 Chengdedao Rd, Heping District, Tianjin; tel. 315171; f. 1907; 2,800,000 vols, 3,900 current periodicals, 500,000 ancient books; Dir DONG CHANGXU; publ. *Library Work and Research* (quarterly).

Urumqi

Xinjiang Library: 11 South Xinhua Rd, Urumqi, Xinjiang Uygur Autonomous Region; f. 1946; 546,800 vols, 3,723 periodicals, historical documents; spec. collns incl. books in Xinjiang nationality languages.

Wuhan

Central China Teachers' University Library: Mt Guizishan, Wuhan, Hubei Province; tel. 72631; f. 1951; 1,255,000 vols, 6,486 periodicals.

Hubei Provincial Library: 45 Wuluo Rd, Wuchang District, Wuhan 430060, Hubei Province; tel. 871284; f. 1904; 2,605,000 vols, 930,000 vols of periodicals, 50,000 antique books; Dir XIONG JINSHAN; publ. *Library & Information Science Tribune* (quarterly).

Wuhan University Library: Mt Luojiashan, Wuhan, Hubei Province; tel. and fax 7872290; e-mail jwshen@lib.whu.edu.cn; f. 1913; 2,900,000 vols, 6,000 current periodicals, 300,000 back copies; rich collection of works on basic theories, and newspapers and periodicals published before 1949; special collection: 180,000 vols of thread-bound local chronicles, over 500 titles of rare books of Yuan, Ming and Qing Dynasties; 141 staff; Dir SHEN JIWU.

Xiamen

Xiamen University Library: Daxue Rd, Xiamen, Fujian Province; tel. 227127; f. 1921; 1,700,000 vols, 6,000 current periodicals, 90,000 back copies; publs on natural and social sciences, especially economics, biology, chemistry, and data on Southeast Asia and Taiwan; 130 staff; Dir SUN JINHUA.

Xian

Shaanxi Provincial Library: 146 Xi Ave, Xian, Shaanxi Province; f. 1909; 2,300,000 vols.

Shaanxi Teachers' University Library: Wujiafen, South Suburb, Xian 710062, Shaanxi Province; tel. 711946, ext. 248; f. 1953; 1,884,487 vols, 2,628 current periodicals, 6,116 back copies; as one of the largest university libraries of Northwest China, it has a fairly rich collection of publications on philosophy, social sciences, literature, linguistics and philology, natural sciences, and thread-bound remarkable editions of Chinese ancient books, local chronicles, 7,000 sheets of rubbings from bronze and stone tablets of the Zhou, Qing, Han and Tang Dynasties, elhi textbooks and materials on pedagogy; 119 staff; Exec. Dir WANG KEJUN.

Xian Jiaotong University Library: Xianning Rd, Xian, Shaanxi Province 710049; tel. (29) 3268102; fax (29) 3237910; e-mail lib@xjtu.edu.cn; f. 1896; 1,840,000 vols, 4,373 current periodicals, 9,000 back copies; systematic collection of scientific and technical publs, complete sets of 15 world-famous sci-tech periodicals having a history of over 100 years; 143 staff; Dir Prof. LI RENHOU.

Xining

Qinghai Provincial Library: 44 Jiefang Rd, Xining, Qinghai Province; f. 1935; 1,354,000 vols, 2,819 periodicals; publ. *Libraries in Qinghai* (quarterly).

Yinchuan

Ningxia Library: Tongxin Rd N, Yinchuan, Ningxia Hui Autonomous Region; f. 1958; 1,300,000 vols.

Zhengzhou

Henan Provincial Library: 150 Song Shan Nan Rd, Zhengzhou, Henan Province; tel. (371) 7972396; f. 1909; 2,360,000 vols, 4,419 current periodicals, 700,000 antique books, historical material; Dir TONG JIYONG; publ. *Journal of Henan Libraries* (quarterly).

Museums and Art Galleries

Beijing

Arthur M. Sackler Museum of Art and Archaeology: Peking University, Dept of Archaeology, Beijing 100871; tel. and fax 62751667; f. 1993; attached to Peking University; Dir Prof. LI BOQIAN.

Beijing Lu Xun Museum: Ritiao, Gongmenkou, Beijing; Curator LI HELIN.

Beijing Natural History Museum: 126 Tianqiao South St, Beijing; tel. (10) 67024431; fax (10) 67021254; e-mail bnhm@public3bta.net.cn; f. 1951; library of 50,000 vols; Dir AI CHUNCHU; publs *Memoirs* (with English abstract), *China Nature* (with English contents, jointly with the China Wildlife Conservation Assn, the Chinese Assn of Natural Science Museums and Beijing Natural History Museum).

China Art Gallery: 1 Wu Si St, East City District, Beijing; tel. 442152; f. 1958; traditional Chinese painting and sculpture; library of 13,700 vols; Dir LIU KAIQU.

Military Museum of the Chinese People's Revolution: 9 Fuxing Rd, Beijing 100038; tel. 68014441; f. 1958; Curator QIN XINGHAN; publ. *Military History* (every 2 months).

Museum of Chinese History: Tiananmen Square, Beijing 100006; tel. 65128986; f. 1912; Curator YU WEICHAO.

Museum of the Chinese Revolution: Eastern side of Tiananmen Square, Beijing 100006; tel. 65129347; f. 1950; affiliated to State Admin. of Cultural Relics; library of 259,000 vols; Dir ZHUZHU; publ. *Study on the Modern History of China*.

National Geological Museum: 15 Yangru Hutong, Xisi, Beijing 100034; tel. (10) 66168135; fax (10) 66168870; f. 1916; attached to Chinese Acad. of Geological Sciences; Dir Prof. Dr JI QIANG.

Palace Museum: 4 Jingshan Qianjie, Beijing 100009; tel. 65132255; fax 65123119; f. 1925; paintings, ceramics; library of 600,000 vols; Dir (vacant); publs *Palace Museum Journal*, *Forbidden City* (4 a year).

Quanzhou

Quanzhou Museum for Overseas Communications History: Quanzhou City, Fujian Province; tel. (595) 226655; f. 1959; Chinese foreign trade and China's int. relations in the fields of culture, science and religion; Curator WANG LIANMAO; publ. *Research into Overseas Communications History* (published jointly with the China Society of Research on Overseas Communications History, 2 a year).

Shanghai

Shanghai Museum: 201 Ren Min Da Dao, Shanghai 200003; tel. (21) 63723500; fax (21) 63728522; cultural history of China; library of 200,000 vols; Dir MA CHENGYUAN.

Universities and Colleges

BEIJING COAL MINING MANAGEMENT INSTITUTE

Dingfuzhuang 2, Chaoyang District, Beijing 100024

Telephone: 65761031
Fax: 65763474

Founded 1982

President: GUO FUSHAN
Vice-Presidents: WANG RUIXIANG, WANG JIADI, FAN HUONGNAN, DING ZHENGYUAN
Library Director: LU CHUNYUAN

Library of 280,000 vols
Number of teachers: 422
Number of students: 3,500

Publication: *Enterprise Management of Coal Mining*.

HEADS OF DEPARTMENTS

Enterprise Management: Prof. CHENG YULING
Mining Engineering Management: Prof. YU DEMIAN
Administrative and Political Management: Prof. TIAN WEIYI
Foreign Languages: Prof. CHEN BIAN ZHI
Mining Safety: Prof. HAO YUSHEN
Economics: Prof. WU DAWEI
Finance Management: Prof. DING ZHENYUAN
Economics: Prof. WU DAWEI
Elementary: DUAN JIWANG

BEIJING FILM ACADEMY

Xi Tu Cheng Lu 4, Hai Dian District, Beijing 100088

Telephone: 62012132
Telex: 22084
Founded 1950

President: SHEN SONGSHENG
Vice-Presidents: XIE FEI, MENG HAIFENG
Deputy Librarians: CHEN WENJING, LU SHIPING

Library of 150,000 vols
Number of teachers: 273
Number of students: 286 (29 postgraduate)

Publication: *Journal*.

HEADS OF DEPARTMENTS

Film Direction: ZHENG DONGTIEN
Acting: CHIAN XIEGE
Cinematography: ZHENG GAOEN
Screen Script: WANG DI
Sound Recording: WANG JUNZHI
Design: LU ZHICHONG

BEIJING FOREIGN STUDIES UNIVERSITY

2 North Xisanhuan Ave, Haidian District, Beijing 100081

Telephone: 68420276
Telex: 222378
Fax: 68423144

Founded 1941

Chancellor: Prof WANG FUXIANG
Vice-Chancellors: Prof. MU DAYING, SHEN CHUNSENG, Prof. ZHUANG YICHUAN, Prof. HE QIXIN

Library of 600,000 vols
Number of teaching staff: 700
Number of students: 3,500

Publications: *Foreign Language Teaching and Research*, *Foreign Literatures*, *Soviet Art and Literature*, etc.

HEADS OF DEPARTMENTS

English: GUO QIQING
Russian: ZHANG JIANJUA
French: CHEN ZHENYAO
German: YIN TONGSHENG
Spanish: LIU JIAHAI
Afro-Asian Languages: CEN RONGLIN
Eastern European Languages: ZHANG ZHIPENG
English Language Communication: GU YUEGUO
Arabic: GUI YUNCHANG
Japanese: ZHU CHUNYUE
Chinese: YANG TIANGE
UN Interpreter-training: ZHUANG MINGLIANG

BEIJING FORESTRY UNIVERSITY

Xiaozhuang, Haidan District, Beijing 100083

Telephone: 62338279
Fax: 62325071

Founded: 1952

Rector: Prof. HE QINGTANG
Registrar: Prof. ZHOU XINCHEN
Librarian: Prof. GAO RONGFU

Library of 560,000 vols
Number of teachers: 700
Number of students: 3,500

HEADS OF DEPARTMENTS

School of Adult Education: Assoc. Prof. YAN JINMING
School of Forest Engineering and Products: Prof. LU ZHENYOU
School of Forest Resources and Environment: Prof. XIU JURU
School of Forestry Economics and Management: Prof. REN HENGQI
School of Landscape Architecture: Prof. ZHANG QIXIAN
School of Plant Sciences: Prof. LI FENGLAN
School of Soil and Water Conservation: Prof. SUN BAOPING
Department of Foreign Languages: Prof. SHI BAOHUI
Department of Postgraduate Studies: Prof. XIE MINGSHU
Department of Social Science: Prof. BAN DAOMING

BEIJING INSTITUTE OF BUSINESS

33 Fu-cheng Rd, Beijing 100037

Telephone: (10) 68904774
Fax: (10) 68417834

Founded 1950

President: Prof. WANG XIANGUIN
Vice-Presidents: LI ZHONG, LIU XIUSHENG, LI DIANFU, ZHANG ZEZHOU, MIAO LEI, XIE ZHIHUA, PAN BOZHOU
Librarian: GAO YUNZHI

Number of teachers: 300
Number of students: 6,000 (200 graduate)

Publications: *Journal* (every 2 months), *Commercial Economy Research* (monthly), *Correspondence Department Report* (quarterly).

HEADS OF DEPARTMENTS

Graduate Study: LI CHUN
Economics and Trade: LIANG KIAOMIN
Management: LAN LING
Accounting: TANG GULIANG
Finance: SU ZANGFU
Law: LI RENYU
Technical Economics: HE MINGKE
Tourism: LIU FEI
Journalism: SHEN YI

BEIJING INSTITUTE OF TECHNOLOGY

7 Beishiqiao Rd, Haidian District, Beijing 100081

Telephone: 68416688
Telex: 22011
Fax: 68412889

Founded 1940

President: Prof. WANG YUE
Vice-Presidents: LI ZHIXIANG, ZHAO XUREN, NING RUXIN, YU XIN, FAN BUOYAN, KUANG JINGMIN, ZHANG JINXIU

Dean of Graduate School: Prof. WANG YUE
Librarian: JIANG XIANJIN

Library of 800,000 vols
Number of teachers: 1,604
Number of students: 10,986 (incl. 1,418 postgraduates and 5,452 correspondence students)

Publication: *BIT Bulletin* (English).

DEANS

College of Vehicular Engineering: Prof. SUN YEBAO
College of Chemical Engineering and Material Science: Prof. LI QIANSU

CHAIRMEN OF DEPARTMENT

Flight Vehicles: Assoc. Prof. LIU ZHAOZHEN
Automatic Control: Assoc. Prof. GONG ZHIHAO
Optical Engineering: Prof. NI GUOQIANG
Electronic Engineering: Prof. LIU TIANQIN
Mechanical Engineering: Assoc. Prof. WANG HONGFU
Mechanics and Engineering: Prof FENG SUNSHANG
Computer Science and Engineering: Assoc. Prof. LIN GUOZHANG
Industrial Management: Assoc. Prof. HAN BUOTAN
Applied Mathematics: Assoc. Prof. SHI RONGCHANG
Applied Physics: Prof. BAO CHONGGUANG
Applied Mechanics: Prof. MEI FENGXIANG
Industrial Design: Prof. YUAN BAOXIANG
Foreign Languages: Prof. ZHANG SHULIANG
Humanities and Social Science: Assoc. Prof. ZHANG HONGJUN

BEIJING MEDICAL UNIVERSITY

38 Xue Yuan Lu, Northern Suburb, Beijing 100083

Telephone: 62092000
Fax: 62015681

Founded 1912
Languages of instruction: Chinese and English
Academic year: August to July (2 terms)

President: WANG DEBING
Vice-Presidents: CHENG BOJI, HAN QIDE
Dean for Education: ZHU XUEGUANG
Director of Libraries: LIAN ZHIJIAN

Library of 730,000 vols, 66,500 periodicals
Number of teachers: 3,721
Number of students: 6,274

Publications: *Journal* (every 2 months), various departmental journals.

DEANS

School of Basic Medicine: FAN SHAOGUANG
First School of Medicine: XU WENHUAI
Second School of Medicine: DU RUYU
Third School of Medicine: HOU KUANYONG
School of Public Health: Prof. LI LIMING
School of Oral Medicine: Prof. YU GUANGYAN
School of Pharmacy: Prof. ZHANG LIHE
School of Nursing: Dr YAO JINGPENG
School of Mental Health: SHEN YUCUN

There are 19 research institutes, 11 research centres and six affiliated hospitals.

BEIJING METALLURGICAL MANAGEMENT INSTITUTE

Guan Zhuang Chao Yang District, Beijing

Telephone: 65762934
Fax: 65762807

Founded 1984

President: MA DEQING
Vice-Presidents: HUANG ZHENGYU, LI YAN
Librarian: ZHAO ZONGDE

Library of 70,000 vols
Number of teachers: 126
Number of students: 1,700

HEADS OF DEPARTMENTS

Management Engineering: YAO GUANGYE
Economics: MA YIMIN
Foreign Languages: LIU YAMING
Information Engineering: LIU ZHENWU
Research Institute of Economic Management and Adult Education: SUN YU

BEIJING NORMAL UNIVERSITY

Xinjiekouwai St 19, Beijing 100875

Telephone: (10) 62207960
Fax: (10) 62200074

Founded 1902
State control

President: LU SHANZHEN
Vice-Presidents: YUAN GUIREN, WANG YINGJIE, ZHENG JUNLI, XIE WEIHE, YANG ZHANRU, ZHENG SHIQU
Librarian: Prof. CAO CAIHAN

Library: see Libraries
Number of teachers: 3,200
Number of students: 7,148 full-time, 6,670 part-time

Publication: *Journal* (Natural Science edition, 4 a year; Social Science edition, 6 a year).

There are 18 research institutes.

BEIJING UNIVERSITY OF AERONAUTICS AND ASTRONAUTICS

37 Xueyuan Rd, Beijing 100083

Telephone: 62017251
Fax: 62028356

Founded 1952
Controlled by the aviation industries of China
Languages of instruction: Chinese, English
Academic year: September to August

President: Prof. SHEN SHITUAN
Vice-Presidents: Prof. DENG XUEYING, XU CONGWEI, FEI BINJUN, WU ZHE
Director, International Academic Exchange: CUI DEYU
Librarian: Prof. JIN MAOZHONG

Library of 1,100,000 vols, 98,000 periodicals
Number of teaching and research staff: 2,300
Number of students: 12,600 (2,000 postgraduate)

Publications: *Journal* (quarterly), *Journal of Aerospace Power* (quarterly), *Acta Aeronautica et Astronautica Sinica* (monthly), *Journal of Engineering Graphics* (2 a year), *Acta Materiae Compositae Sinica* (quarterly), *Model World* (quarterly), *Aerospace Knowledge* (monthly), *College English* (every 2 months), *DADDM* (2 a year), *China Aeronautical Education* (quarterly).

DEPARTMENTAL DEANS

Materials Science and Engineering: Prof. XU HUIBIN
Electronic Engineering: Prof. ZHANG XIAOLIN
Automatic Control: Prof. LI XINGSHAN
Propulsion: Prof. LI QIHAN
Flying Vehicle Design and Applied Mechanics: Prof. WANG JINJUN
Computer Sciences and Engineering: Prof. JIN MAOZHONG
Manufacturing Engineering: Prof. TANG XIAOQING
Mechanical and Electrical Engineering: Prof. YANG ZONGXU
Foreign Languages: Prof. LI BAOKUN
Systems Engineering: Prof. YANG WEIMIN

PRINCIPALS

School of Continuing Education: Prof. WANG BAORAI.
School of Management: Prof. JIANG XIESHENG
Graduate School: Prof. DENG XUEYING
School of Astronautics: Prof. ZHANG ZHENPENG
Flying College: Exec. Dir Prof. WANG XIAOWAN
School of Haidian Applied Technology: Prof. LIU TIANSHEN
School of Science: Prof. GUAN KEYING (Dean)
School of Humanities and Social Sciences: Prof. SHENG SHUREN (Dean)

ATTACHED RESEARCH INSTITUTES

Chinese Aeronautical Establishment BUAA Branch: Dir Prof. SHEN SHITUAN
Research Institute of Higher Education: Dir Assoc. Prof. LEI QING
Research Institute of Thermal Power Engineering: Dir Prof. ZHOU SHENG
Research Institute of Fluid Mechanics: Dir Prof. LU ZHIYONG
Research Institute of Solid Mechanics: Dir Prof. GAO ZHENTONG
Research Institute of Unmanned Flight Vehicle Design: Prof. LI CHUNJIN
Research Institute of Computer Software Engineering: Dir Prof. JIN MAOZHONG
Research Institute of Manufacturing Engineering: Dir Prof. TANG XIAOQING
Research Institute of Robotics: Dir Prof. WANG YINMIAO
Research Institute of Reliability Engineering: Dir Prof. YANG WEIMIN

BEIJING UNIVERSITY OF POSTS AND TELECOMMUNICATIONS

10 Xi Tu Cheng Rd, Haidian District, Beijing 100088

Telephone: (10) 62282628
Fax: (10) 62281774
E-mail: faoffice@bupt.edu.cn

Founded 1954
Under control of Ministry of Posts and Telecommunications
Academic year: September to July

President: ZHU XIANGHUA
Vice-Presidents: LIN JINTONG, ZHONG YIXIN, ANG XIUFEN, ZHANG YINGHAI, RENG XIAOMIN, MI JIANHU
Chief Administrative Officer: WANG CHENGCHU
Librarian: MA ZIWEI

Library of 700,000 vols
Number of teachers: 800
Number of students: 8,000

Publications: *Academic Journal of BUPT* (quarterly), *Journal of China University of Posts and Telecommunications.*

DEANS

Correspondence College: ANG XIUFEN
Graduate School: SONG JUNDE
Telecommunications College: LIN JINTONG
Fuzhou Extension: ANG XIUFEN
Management Humanities College: TANG SHOULIAN

HEADS OF DEPARTMENT

Mechanical Engineering: Prof. SHI LIANGPING
Computer Engineering: Prof. AI BO
Applied Science and Technology: Prof. LIU JIE
Information Engineering: Prof. ZHANG HUIMIN
Foreign Language: Prof. YING YASHU

ATTACHED RESEARCH INSTITUTES

BUPT-BNR (Nortel China) Advanced Telecommunications R&D Centre: 10 Xi Tu Cheng Rd, Beijing 100088; Dir (China) ZHU QILIANG.

Research Institute: 10 Xi Tu Cheng Rd, Beijing 100088; communications systems and networks, information theory and processing, signal processing, artificial intelligence, neural networks and applications; Dir WU WEILING.

Institute of Communications and Optoelectronic Information Processing: 10 Xi Tu Cheng Rd, Beijing 100088; optical fibres, optical wave guides, holography and optical information processing; Dir XU DAXIONG.

CENTRAL ACADEMY OF ARTS AND DESIGN

34 North Dong Huan Rd, Beijing 100020
Telephone: 65026391
Founded 1956
President: CHANG SHANA
Vice-Presidents: WANG MING ZHI, YANG YONG SHAN, WANG ZHONG XIN
Library Director: QIU CHENGDE
Library of 170,000 vols
Number of teachers: 240
Number of students: 900 (36 postgraduates)
Publications: *Decoration* (quarterly), *College Journal* (monthly), *Reference on Arts and Crafts* (monthly).

HEADS OF DEPARTMENTS

Textile Dyeing and Fashion Design: LIU YUAN FENG
Ceramics: CHENG JIN HAI
Commercial Fine Arts Design: WANG GUO LUN
Interior Design: ZHANG YIMAN
Industrial Design: LIU GUANZHONG
Special Arts and Crafts: ZHANG CHANG
History of Arts and Crafts: XI JING ZHI

CENTRAL INSTITUTE OF FINE ARTS

5 Xiaowei hutong, East District, Beijing 100730
Telephone: 65254731
Founded 1950 by merger of Nat. Beijing College of Art and Fine Arts Dept of North China United University
President: JIN SHANGYI
Deputy Presidents: DU JIAN, YE YUZHONG
Librarian: TANG CHI
Library of over 170,000 vols (25,000 in foreign languages), 8,500 vols periodicals
Number of teachers: 164
Number of students: 519, including 28 postgraduates

HEADS OF DEPARTMENTS

Chinese traditional painting: YAO YOUDUO
Oil painting: SUN WEIMIN
Graphic arts: TAN QUANSHU
Sculpture: CAO CHUNSHENG
History of Fine Art: XUE YONGNIAN
Mural paintings: LING YUNGING
Sculpture Research Studio: WANG KEQING

CHANGCHUN UNIVERSITY OF EARTH SCIENCES

6 Ximinzhu St, Changchun, Jilin Province 130026
Telephone: (431) 822391
Telex: 83150
Founded 1952
Languages of instruction: Chinese, English, Russian, Japanese
Academic year: September to January, March to July
Chancellor: Prof. ZHANG YIXIA
Vice-Chancellors: MA ZHIHONG, LIU BAOREN, Prof. SHUN YUNSHENG
Librarian: XIANG TIANYUAN
Number of teachers: 830
Number of students: 3,890
Library of 800,000 vols
Publications: *Journal, Geology of the World.*

HEADS OF DEPARTMENTS

Geology: SUN DEYU
Hydrogeology and Engineering Geology: YU GUOGUANG
Applied Geophysics: HE QIAODENG
Geological Instrumentation: CAO MUYI
Rock and Mineral Testing and Analysis and Geochemistry: DUAN GUOZHENG
Drilling Engineering: ZHANG ZUPEI
Energy Geology: YANG BINGZHONG
Industry Administration: YAN FENGZENG
Social Sciences: MAO JIAN
Basic Sciences: YANG TIANXING
Foreign Language: LI YINGDA

CHANGCHUN INSTITUTE OF POSTS AND TELECOMMUNICATIONS

20 Nanhu St, Changchun, Jilin Province 130012
Telephone: 5171220
Fax: 5176342
Founded 1947
Controlled by the Ministry of the Information Industry
Language of instruction: Chinese
Academic year: September to July
President: SUN MUQIAN
Registrar: LIU YAN
Librarian: YU JIE
Library of 380,000 vols
Number of teachers: 407
Number of students: 2,125 (and 2,005 corresponding students)
Publication: *Journal of Changchun Institute of Posts and Telecommunications.*

HEADS OF DEPARTMENTS

Telecommunications Engineering: SHENG DESHEN
Computer Science: TANG JIQUN
Management: WANG ZHIXUE

CHENGDU UNIVERSITY OF TRADITIONAL CHINESE MEDICINE

37 Shierqiao Rd, Chengdu, Sichuan 610075
Telephone: (28) 7784542
Fax: (28) 7763471
Founded 1956
State Control
Language of Instruction: Chinese
Academic Year: September to August
President: Prof. LI MINGFU
Vice-Presidents: WAN DEGUANG, XIE KEQING, SUN LINGGEN
Chief Administrative Officer: ZHENG QIJIANG
Librarian: JIANG YONGGUANG
Library of 403,200 vols
Number of teachers: 260
Number of students: 4,311
Publications: *Journal, Information on Chinese Medicine and Herbs*.

HEADS OF DEPARTMENTS

Chinese Medicine: LUO CAIGUI
Acupuncture: LIANG FANRONG
Chinese Pharmacology: ZHOU GUANGCHUN
Basic Chinese Medicine: DENG ZHONGJIA
Adult Education: FU CHUNHUA

CHINA CENTRAL RADIO AND TELEVISION UNIVERSITY

160 Fuxing Men Nei St, Beijing 100031
Telephone: (10) 66039048
Fax: (10) 66039025
Founded 1979 on the 'open university' principle
State control
Forty-four provincial campuses, 690 branch schools
President: Dr WEI YU
Vice-Presidents: SONG CHENDONG, CHEN ZHILONG, SUN LUYI, SUN TIANZHEN
Library Director: SUN LUYI
Library of 97,000 vols (CRTVU), 17,000,000 vols (provinces)
Number of teachers: 180 full-time, 205 part-time (CRTVU), 18,130 full-time, 11,761 part-time (provinces)
Number of students: 547,925
Publication: *China TV University Education* (every 2 months).

HEADS OF DEPARTMENTS

Core Courses: CAI SHU
Economics: HUANG CHANGMING
Engineering: WANG SHUXIA
Humanities: YAN BIN
Teacher Training: XU NAIYIN
China Liaoyuan Radio and TV School: SUN TIAN ZHEN
Electrical Engineering: LI LIQUN
Chemical Engineering: WANG SHUXIA

CHINA TEXTILE UNIVERSITY

1882 West Yan-An Rd, Shanghai 200051
Telephone: 62199898
Fax: 62194722
Founded 1951
Academic year: September to July.
President: Prof. SHAO SHI-HUANG
Vice-Presidents: Prof. JIN JIA-YOU, Prof. HU XUE-CHAO, Prof. XUE YOU-YI, Prof. DAN DE-ZHONG
Registrar: Prof. ZHANG JIA-YU
Librarian: Prof. ZHU SHU-KANG
Library of 810,000 vols and periodicals
Number of teachers: 1,165
Number of students: 8,000
Publications: *Journal* (every 2 months, English edn 2 a year), *Textile Technology Overseas* (every 2 months).

HEADS OF SCHOOL

School of Fashion: Prof. ZHANG WEI-YUAN
School of Business Administration: Prof. SUN JUN-KANG, Prof. GU QING-LIANG

HEADS OF DEPARTMENTS

Textile Engineering: Prof. DIN XIN
Textile Chemical Engineering: Prof. DAI JIN-JIN
Mechanical Engineering: Prof. WANG SHEN-ZE
Electrical and Computer Engineering: Prof. SHAO YUE-XIANG
Basic Sciences: Prof. XIE HAN-KUN
Social Science: Prof. HE SHAN-KAN
Computer Science: Prof. WANG YI-GANG
Environmental Science Engineering: Prof. XI DAN-LI
Polymer Science and Engineering: Prof. CHEN YAN-MO
Foreign Languages: Prof. SHENG BAI-YAO
Physical Education: Prof. LIN SHENG-GEN

CHINA UNIVERSITY OF GEOSCIENCES (WUHAN)

Yujiashan, Wuhan, Hubei 430074
Telephone: (27) 7801330
Fax: (27) 7801736
Founded 1952
President: YIN HONGFU
Vice-Presidents: YANG CHANGMING, YAO SHUZHEN, ZHANG HANKAI
Library of 670,000 vols, over 3,852 periodicals
Number of teachers: 900
Number of students: 10,000
Publications: *Earth Science*, *Journal of China University of Geosciences* (in English and Chinese), *Geological Science and Technology Information, Journal of Geoscience Translations.*
The university has 30 specialities in 7 colleges and 6 departments.

CHINA UNIVERSITY OF MINING AND TECHNOLOGY

Xuzhou City, Jiangsu Province 221008
Telephone: (516) 3885745

Fax: (516) 3888682

Founded 1909
State control
Academic year: September to July

President: Prof. GUO YUGUANG
Vice-Presidents: Prof. CHEN SHILIN, Prof. WANG YUEHAN, Prof. GE SHIRONG, Prof. YANG GENGYU, Prof. KE WENJIN, Prof. WANG FENGYU
Registrar: Prof. XING YONGCHANG
Director of International Division: Prof. SU XINLIAN
Librarian: Prof. XING YONGCHANG

Library of 1,242,747 vols
Number of teachers: 1,500
Number of students: 11,000

Publication: *Journal* (quarterly in Chinese, annually in English).

HEADS OF DEPARTMENTS

Mining Engineering: Prof. CAI QINGXIANG
College of Architecture and Civil Engineering: Assoc. Prof. WANG JIANPING
College of Resource and Environmental Science: Prof. ZENG YONG
College of Information and Electrical Engineering: Prof. TAN DEJIAN
College of Mechatronic Engineering: Prof. ZHANG YONGZHONG
Energy Resources and Chemical Engineering: Prof. ZHAO YUEMIN
Social Sciences: Prof. WU ZHONGHAI
Applied Mathematics and Mechanics: Prof. PAN ZHI
Foreign Languages: Prof. WU FENG
College of Business Administration: Prof. TAO XUEYU
Computer Science: Prof. WU MIAO
College of Adult Education: Prof. ZHAO SENNAN
Beijing Campus: Prof. KE WENJIN

CHINESE TRADITIONAL OPERA COLLEGE

3 Li Ren St, Xuan Wu District, Beijing 100054

Telephone: 33-5156

Founded 1978

President: YU LIN
Vice-Presidents: ZHU WENXIANG, GE SHILIANG
Librarian: LIU SHIYUAN

Library of 150,000 vols
Number of teachers: 246
Number of students: 329

Publication: *Traditional Opera Art* (quarterly).

HEADS OF DEPARTMENTS

Stage Art: ZHAO YINGMIAN
Traditional Opera Literature: ZHOU CHUANJIA
Performance: SU YI
Directing: JING TONG
Music: GUAN YANONG

CHONGQING UNIVERSITY

Chongqing, Sichuan Province 630044

Telephone: (23) 65102449
Fax: (23) 65316656
E-mail: fao@cqu.edu.cn

Founded 1929
State control
Languages of instruction: Chinese, English
Academic year: February to July, September to January

President: LIN FEI
Vice-President: WU ZHONGFU
Chief Administrative Officer: CHEN DEWEN
Librarian: TANG YIKE

Number of teachers: 2,000
Number of students: 14,000

Publication: *Journal* (every 2 months).

HEADS OF DEPARTMENT

First Department of Mechanical Engineering: YOU LIHUA
Second Department of Mechanical Engineering: LI HUAJI
Department of Optical Electronic Precision Machinery: PAN YINGJUN
Department of Engineering Mechanics: ZHANG PEIYUAN
Department of Thermal Engineering: HE ZHUWEI
Department of Electrical Engineering: SUN CAIXIN
College of Resources and Environmental Engineering: LI XIAOHONG
Department of Metallurgical Engineering and Materials: GAO JIACHENG
College of Electronic Information Engineering: CAO ZEHAN (Dean)
Department of Radio Engineering: SHU XIANSHU
Department of Computer Science: ZHU QINGSHENG
Department of Automation: HUANG XIYUE
College of Business Administration: YANG XIUTAI
Department of Applied Mathematics: YANG DADI
Department of Applied Physics: YUN ZHIQIANG
College of Chemical Engineering: GAN GUNANGZHONG (Dean)
College of Foreign Languages: JIANG ZHIWEN (Dean)
College of Trade and Law: HE RONGWEI (Dean)
Institute of Bio-engineering: CAI SHAOXI

DALIAN MARITIME UNIVERSITY

1 Linhai Rd, Dalian 116026, Liaoning Province

Telephone: 4671611
Telex: 86175
Fax: 4671395

Founded 1953
State control
Academic year: September to July

President: Prof. SI YUZHUO
Vice-Presidents: WU ZHAOLIN, CONG XUANBIN, GUO YU, LU DENGYOU, WANG JIUCHANG
Registrar: GUO YU
Librarian: WU ZHAOLIN

Number of teachers: 798
Number of students: 5,326

Publications: *World Maritime Shipping* (quarterly), *Liaoning Navigation* (quarterly), *Higher Education Research in Areas of Communications* (6 a year).

DEANS

Navigation College: REN MAODONG
Marine Engineering College: YIN PEIHAI
Shipping Management College: XING YUEHUA
Market Economics and Law College: WANG SONGSHAN
International Business College: QIAN YAOPENG
Adult Education: SHUN LICHENG

ATTACHED INSTITUTES

Institute of Marine Machine Repair and Manufacture Engineering and Metal Technology: Deputy Dir YAN LI

Automation Institute: Deputy Dir NIU BAOLAI

Nautical Technology Institute: Dir XIA GUOZHONG

Marine Engineering Institute: Dir WU HENG

Systems Engineering Institute: Dir SUN ZHANSHAN

Port and Shipping Management Institute: Dir WANG JIAHUA

Iron-Plating Technology Institute: Dir DONG YUHUA

Higher Education Institute: Dir LI CAYING

DALIAN UNIVERSITY OF TECHNOLOGY (DUT)

2 Linggong Rd, Ganjingzi District, Dalian 116023, Liaoning Province

Telephone: (411) 4671929
Telex: 86231
Fax: (411) 4671009

Founded 1949 as Dalian Institute of Technology
State control
Academic year: September to January, March to July

President: Prof. CHENG GENGDONG
Vice-Presidents: Prof. JI ZHUOSHANG, Prof. SHEN HONGSHU, Prof. WANG LIANSHENG, Prof. WANG LIANSHENG
Librarian: XIE MAOZHAO

Library of 1,760,000 vols, 6,700 periodicals
Number of teachers: 2,800 (including 330 profs, 720 assoc. profs)
Number of students: 15,006 (including 2,400 postgraduates)

Publications: *DUT Journal* (every 2 months), *Mathematical Research and Exposition*, *Computational and Structural Mechanics and Application Journal*, *Library and Information Science*, *Studies of Higher Education*, *Educational Technology in Foreign Countries*, *Northeast China Water Power Journal* (all quarterly).

Nine schools, 24 depts, 42 research institutes.

DONGBEI UNIVERSITY OF FINANCE AND ECONOMICS

217 Jianshan St, Shahekou District, Dalian 116025

Telephone: (411) 4691503
Fax: (411) 4691862
E-mail: dufe1952@pub.dl.inpta.net.cn

Founded 1952
State control
Languages of instruction: Chinese, English
Academic year: September to July

President: Prof. YU YANG
Vice-Presidents: Prof. GUO CHANGLU, Assoc. Prof. LIU JIANMIN, Prof. QIU DONG
President's Assistant: Assoc. Prof. ZHOU LIANSHENG
Librarian: ZHANG LI

Library of 900,000 vols
Number of teachers: 561
Number of students: 11,815 (incl. 5,678 correspondence)

Publication: *Research on Finance and Economics Issues*.

HEADS OF SCHOOL

School of Accountancy: Prof. LIU YONGZE
School of Finance and Taxation: Prof. MA GOUQIANG
School of Business Management: Prof. LIU QINGYUAN
School of Hotel Management: Assoc. Prof. LI LI
School of Adult Education: Prof. CONG JIZENG
School of International Chinese: Assoc. Prof. ZHANG WENFENG

HEADS OF DEPARTMENTS

Postgraduate: Prof. HE JIAN
MBA Centre: Prof. Dr YU LI
Banking: Prof. ZHANG GUILE
Planning and Statistics: Assoc. Prof. YU HONGPING
Foreign Trade Economics: Prof. LI ZIZHI
Investment: Prof. MA XIUYAN
Law: Prof. GUI LIYI
Economic Information Management: Prof. ZHANG BUTONG
International Foreign Languages for Business: Assoc. Prof. HU YINGKUN
Economics: Prof. Dr WANG XUN

ATTACHED RESEARCH INSTITUTES

Research Institute of Economics: Dir Prof. JIN FENGDE.

Research Institute of Quantitative Economics: Dir Prof. LIU XINGQUAN.

Research Institute of Industrial Economics: Dir Prof. WANG XIANGCHUN.

Research Institute of Population: Dir Prof. JIANG PING.

Institute for Artificial Intelligence: Dir Prof. CHEN YOUGANG.

Research Institute of Stocks: Dir Prof. DAI YULIN.

Research Institute of Finance and Taxation: Dir Prof. MA GUOQIANG.

Research Institute of Investment: Dir Prof. MA XIUYAN.

Research Institute of Historical Maps: Dir Prof. LI KE.

Research Institute of Law: Dir Prof. GUI LIYI.

Research Institute of Banking: Dir Prof. LIN JIKEN.

Research Institute of Financial Management: Dir Prof. DONG WENQUAN.

Research Institute of Insurance: Dir Prof. ZHANG GUILE.

Research Centre for Japan: Dir Prof. JIN FENGDE.

Research Institute of Chinese Economics: Dir Prof. GAO LIANGMOU.

Research Institute of Commercial Economics: Dir Prof. LIU QINGYUAN.

Research Centre for Hong Kong, Macau and Taiwan: Dir Prof. WANG TIEJUN.

Research Institute of Statistics: Dir Prof. WANG QINGSHI.

Sanyou Research Institute of Accountancy: Dir Prof. LIU YONGZE.

Research Institute of Tourism: Dir Prof. LI LI.

EAST CHINA NORMAL UNIVERSITY

3663 Zhongshan Rd North, Shanghai 200062
Telephone: (21) 62577257
Telex: 33328
Fax: (21) 62576217

Founded 1951
Controlled by the State Education Commission of China
Academic year: September to July (two semesters)

President: ZHANG RUIKUN
Vice-Presidents: WANG JIANPAN, TAO ZENGLE, WANG TIEXIAN, ZHANG ZHIJING, XUE PEIJIAN
Registrar: XUE BOXING
Librarian: WANG XIJING

Library of 2,612,776 vols
Number of teachers: 1,532
Number of students: 14,788

DEANS

College of Educational Science and Technology: JIN LINXIANG
College of Educational Administration: MA QINRONG
College of Adult Education: HUA YUEXIAN
Graduate School: WANG JIANPAN
College of Humanities: FENG SHAOLEI
College of Literature and Art: QI SENHUA
College of Foreign Languages: ZHANG MINLUN
College of International Business: GUI SHIXUN
College of Science and Engineering: WANG ZUGENG
College of Chemistry and Life Science: JIN LITONG
College of Resources and Environmental Science: XU SHIYUAN
International College of Chinese Culture: WANG TIEXIAN

EAST CHINA UNIVERSITY OF SCIENCE AND TECHNOLOGY

130 Meilong Rd, Shanghai 200237
Telephone: 4775678
Fax: 4777138

Founded 1952 (until 1993, East China University of Chemical Technology)

President: Prof. WANG XINGYU
Vice-Presidents: Prof. DAI GANCE, LIN ZHUYUAN, Prof. ZHU ZIBIN, Prof. ZHANG DONGSHAN.

Library of 1,240,000 vols, 4,500 periodicals in 11 languages
Number of teachers: 1,841
Number of students: 8,322

Publication: *Journal* (every 2 months).

Departments of applied mathematics, applied physics, automatic control and electronic engineering, biochemical engineering, business management, chemical engineering, chemistry, computer science, environmental engineering, English for business, fine chemicals technology, foreign languages, industrial design, inorganic materials, management engineering, mechanical engineering, petroleum processing, polymer materials, social science.

Research institutes of agrochemical bioregulators, applied chemistry, applied mathematics, biomedical engineering, bioreactors (national lab.) chemical engineering, chemical environmental engineering, chemical physics, chemical reaction engineering (joint lab.), culture, economic development, fine chemicals technology, heterogeneous reaction engineering (national lab.), higher education, industrial automation, industrial design, inorganic chemical technology, inorganic materials, Marxism and ideological education, materials science, petroleum processing, process equipment and pressure vessels, speciality chemicals, technical chemical physics.

FUDAN UNIVERSITY

220 Handan Rd, Shanghai 200433
Telephone: 5492222
Telex: 33317
Fax: (86-21) 5491875

Founded 1905
State control
Languages of instruction: Chinese and English
Academic year: September to July (two semesters)

President: Prof. YANG FUJIA
Vice-Presidents: Prof. YAN SHAOZONG, Assoc. Prof. SHI YUEQUN, Assoc. Prof. ZONG YOUHENG, XU MINZHI
Librarian: Prof. QIN ZENGFU

Library of 3,400,000 vols
Number of teachers: 2,430
Number of students: 6,578 (and 1,620 postgraduates

Publications: *Fudan Social Sciences Journal*, *Fudan Natural Sciences Journal*, *Mathematics Annals*.

DEANS

School of Technological Science: Prof. YUAN QU
School of Management: Prof. ZHENG SHAOLIAN
School of Economics: Prof. HONG YUANPENG
School of Life Science: Prof. LI YUYANG
School of Journalism: Prof. DING GANLIN
School of Cultural Relics and Museum Science: Prof. ZHUANG XICHANG

CHAIRMEN OF DEPARTMENTS

Chinese Language and Literature: Prof. CHEN YUNJI
Foreign Languages and Literature: Prof. LU GUOQIANG
Journalism: Prof. DING GANLIN
Sociology: Prof. PENG XIZHE
History: Prof. YANG LIQIANG
Economics: Prof. SHU YUAN
World Economy: Prof. HUA MIN
International Finance: Prof. HU QINGKANG
International Politics: Prof. WANG HUNING
Philosophy: Prof. HUANG SONGJIE
Law: Prof. LI CHANGDAO
Mathematics: Prof. JIANG ERXIONG
Statistics and Operational Research: Prof. GUAN MEIGU
Physics: Prof. WANG WENCHENG
Nuclear Science: Prof. ZHENG CHENGFA
Chemistry: Prof. XIANG YIFEI
Biochemistry: Prof. HUANG WEIDA
Microbiology and Microbiological Engineering: Prof. ZHOU DEQING
Physiology and Biophysics: Prof. XU SUJUAN
Environmental and Resources Biology: Prof. ZHENG SHIZHANG
Genetics and Genetic Engineering: Prof. MAO YUMIN
Electronic Engineering: Prof. SHAO XIANGYI
Computer Science: Prof. SHI BOLE
Materials Science: Prof. ZONG XIANGFU
Polymer Science: Prof. YANG YULIANG
Applied Mechanics: Prof. LIU ZHAORONG
Light Sources and Illumination Engineering: Prof. HE MINGGAO
Management Science: Prof. XUE HUACHENG
Enterprise Management: Prof. WANG FANGHUA
Finance: Prof. OUYANG GUANGZHONG
Accounting: Prof. QIANG SHIZHENG
International Business Management: Prof. XUE QIUHE
Cultural Relics and Museum Science: Prof. WU HAOKUN
Technology of Cultural Relics Protection: Prof. XU ZHIZHENG

There are research institutes attached to almost all departments.

FUJIAN AGRICULTURAL COLLEGE

Jinshan, Fujian Province, 350002
Telephone: (591) 3741721
Fax: (591) 3741251

Founded 1936
State control
Language of instruction: Chinese

President: Prof. LU LIUXIN
Vice-Presidents: Prof. YE SHANGQING, PAN TINGGUO, YOU MINSHENG
Librarian: HU FANPING

Library of 560,000 vols
Number of teachers: 843
Number of students: 3,880

Publications: *Journal of Fujian Agricultural University*, *Overseas Agricultural Science: Sugarcane*, *Current Communications on Overseas Agricultural Science and Technology*, *Wuyi Science*, *Journal of Entomology in Eastern China*.

HEADS OF COLLEGE

College of Crop Science: LIN YANQUAN

College of Animal Science: HUANG YIFAN

College of Economics and Trade: HUANG JIANCHENG

College of Adult Education: YE YICHUN

ATTACHED RESEARCH INSTITUTES:

Biological Control Institute: Dir ZHAO JINGWEI.

Institute of Plant Virology: Dir XIE LIANHUI.

Synthetic Research Institute of Sugarcane: Dir CHEN RUKAI.

Research Institute of Genetics and Crop Breeding: Dir YANG RENCUI.

Institute of Subtropical Fruits: Dir LIN SHUNQUAN.

Biotechnology Centre: Dir GUAN XIONG.

Research Laboratory of Fungus-Grass: Dr LIN ZHANXI.

FUJIAN MEDICAL COLLEGE

Jinshan, Fuzhou, Fujian

Telephone: 557861

Founded 1937

President: Prof. WU ZHONGFU
Vice-Presidents: LUO GUEILIN, LIN KEHUA
Head of Postgraduate Department: KANG YUANYUAN
Librarian: HUANG HUISHANG

Library of 258,448 vols
Number of teachers: 398
Number of students: 2,306

Publications: *Journal, Medical Education Study.*

HEADS OF DEPARTMENTS

Medicine: LAN YUFU
Public Health: FU MINGSHENG
Stomatology: FAN RUXIONG
Medical Laboratory Science: DAI GENGSHUEN

GANSU AGRICULTURAL UNIVERSITY

Yingmentan, Anning District, Lanzhou, Gansu Province 730070

Telephone: (931) 7668011
Fax: (931) 7668010
E-mail: wujp@gsau.edu.cn

Founded 1958

President: Prof. HUANG SHENZHAO
Vice-Presidents: Prof. ZHAO YOUZHANG, Prof. LI ZHENGXIAO, LU JIANHUA, Prof. WANG DI
Librarian: LIU XI

Library of 500,000 vols
Number of teachers: 600
Number of students: 5,000 (125 postgraduates)

Publication: *Journal.*

DEANS

Animal Science: CUI XIAN
Veterinary Science: LIU YING
Grassland Science: CAO ZHIZHONG
Agronomy: LI WEI
Plant Protection: ZHANG XINGHU
Soil Chemistry: SHI YINGFU
Forest Science: JIANG ZHIRONG
Horticulture: ZHANG FUQUAN
Agricultural Machinery and Engineering: WU JIANMING
Water Conservation: CHENG ZIYONG
Agricultural Business and Trade: WANG CENGLIN
Food Science: YU QUNLI
Basic Courses: YUAN TONGSHENG
Social Science: SHANG ZHENHAI

ATTACHED INSTITUTES

Foodstuffs and Feeding Institute.

Wool Institute.

Melon Institute.

Turf Institute.

GUANGDONG COLLEGE OF MEDICINE AND PHARMACY

40 Guang Han Zhi, Haizhu District, Guangzhou, Guangdong Province 510224

Telephone: 4429040

Founded 1978

President: Prof. DU QI ZHANG (acting)
Vice-Presidents: LI TINGJIE, CHENG SHENGHAO
Librarian: LIAO MING QING

Library of 160,000 vols
Number of teachers: 300
Number of students: 1,800

Publication: *Journal.*

HEADS OF DEPARTMENTS

Preventive Medicine: Prof. WU ZHEN QIANG
Pharmacy: Prof. CHEN JIAN YU
Clinical Medicine: Prof. HE YIEXIONG
Basic Medical Sciences: Prof. LAI MUXIAN

PROFESSORS

FENGHE, H., Pharmacology
FENGMING, Z., Epidemiology
JINCHENG, H., Pharmaceutical Chemistry
JINGXIAN, J., Internal Medicine
JINGZHI, H., Human Parasitology
JIPENG, L., Pharmacognosy
MUXIAN, L., Biochemistry
PUSHENG, W., Traditional Chinese Medicine
QIHUA, W., Human Anatomy
QIYUN, Y., Phytochemistry
QIZHANG, D., Pharmacology
SHIDE, S., Statistics
YIYUAN, Z., Dermatology
ZHICHENG, C., Hygiene
ZHUHUA, L., Microbiology

GUANGXI UNIVERSITY

10 Xixiangtang Rd, Nanning, Guangxi Zhuang Autonomous Region 530004

Telephone: (771) 3832391
Fax: (771) 3823743
E-mail: gxugjc@public.nn.gx.cn

Founded 1928
State control
Academic year: September to June

President: Prof. TANG JILIANG
Registrar: Prof. FU ZHENFANG
Librarian: Prof. CHEN DAGUANG

Library of 2,020,000 vols
Number of teachers: 1,735
Number of students: 17,290

Publication: *Guangxi University Journal.*

DEANS

College of Forestry: Prof. JIN DAGANG (Exec. Vice-Dean)
College of Animal Science and Technology: Prof. YANG NIANSHENG
College of Agronomy: Prof. MO TIANYAN
College of Mechanical Engineering: Prof. LI SHANGPING
College of Electrical Engineering: Prof. LU ZUPEI
College of Chemistry and Chemical Engineering: Prof. TONG ZHANGFA
College of Computer Science and Information Technology: Prof. LI TAOSHEN
College of Civil Engineering: Prof. YAN LIUBIN
College of Biological Technology and Sugar Industrial Engineering: Prof. LU JIAJIONG
College of Natural Resources and the Environment: Prof. MA SHAOJIAN
College of Sciences: Prof. XI HONGJIAN
College of Business: Prof. LIU CHAOMING
College of Culture and Mass Communication: Prof. LIANG YANG
College of Foreign Languages: Prof. ZHOU YI
College of Social Sciences and Management: Prof. XIE SHUN
College of Law: Prof. MENG QINGUO
College of Adult Education: Prof. HE BAOCHONG
Department of Physical Education: Prof. XU MINGRONG
Department of Teacher-Training: Prof. WANG HAIYIN (Vice-Dean)

GUANGXI COLLEGE OF TRADITIONAL CHINESE MEDICINE

21 Mingxiudong Rd, Nanning, Guangxi Zhuang Autonomous Region 530001

Telephone: (771) 3137401
Fax: (771) 3135812

Founded 1956

President: Prof. WEI GUIKANG
Vice-Presidents: Prof. LI WEITAI, Assoc. Prof. ZHU HUA, Assoc. Prof. DEN JIAGANG
Librarian: LI JIANGUANG

Library of 300,000 vols
Number of teachers: 296
Number of students: 1,849

Publications: *Guangxi Journal of Traditional Chinese Medicine, Study in Higher Education of Traditional Chinese Medicine.*

HEADS OF DEPARTMENTS

Traditional Chinese Medical Science: Assoc. Prof. JIANG YINGSHI
Pharmaceutical and Chinese Materia Medica: Assoc. Prof. LIU HUAGANG
No. 1 Clinical Medicine: Assoc. Prof. LAN QINGQIANG
No. 2 Clinical Medicine: Prof. XU FUYE

ATTACHED RESEARCH INSTITUTES

Institute of Traditional Chinese Medical Treatment and Medicine: Prof. WONG TAILAI.
Institute of TCM Orthopaedics and Traumatology: Prof. WEI GUIKANG.
Zhuang Institute of Medical Science: Prof. HUANG JINGMING.
Institute of Acupuncture and Moxibustion: Assoc. Prof. XIE GANGONG.
Institute of Traditional Chinese Medicine: Assoc. Prof. LUO WEISHENG.
Institute of the Combination of Traditional Chinese Medicine and Western Medicine: Assoc. Prof. XIAO TINGGANG.

GUANGZHOU UNIVERSITY

Xiao Bei Xia Tang, Guangzhou 510091

Telephone: (20) 83597348
Fax: (20) 83502750

Founded 1983

President: Prof. ZHANG SHIXUN
Vice-Presidents: Prof. LI PEIHAO, Assoc. Prof. FENG GUOGUANG, Assoc. Prof. ZHANG XIAOKUA
Director of General and Foreign Affairs Office: Assoc. Prof. SUNYUN
Education Administration Office: Prof. WU JONGPING
Library Director: YU QINGRONG

Library of 300,000 vols
Number of teachers: 550
Number of students: 4,000

HEADS OF DEPARTMENTS

Chinese Language: Assoc. Prof. WANG SHOUCHEN
Foreign Languages: Assoc. Prof. WU KEXIAN
Economics: Assoc. Prof. ZHANG DUANMING
Law: Assoc. Prof. LEE LI
Management Science: Assoc. Prof. ZHANG XIAOHUA
Arts Design: Assoc. Prof. TANG ZHONGXI
Architectural Engineering: Assoc. Prof. LI RUNGENG
Electronic Engineering: LUO JUMING
Industrial Chemistry: Prof. ZHENG CHEN
Laboratory Centre: MA GUOXI
Physical Education: Assoc. Prof. CAO DONG
Social Science: Prof. HUANG JUNPING
Natural Science: Assoc. Prof. TAN YONGZHANG

ATTACHED RESEARCH INSTITUTES

Institute of Architectural Design: Dir RONG RUQIN.

Institute of Knowledge Engineering: Prof. WANG PEIZHUANG.

Economic Research Institute: Assoc. Prof. FENG GUOGUANG.

Nanfang Law Research Centre (Foreign Affairs): Prof. WANG MINGCAN.

Food Technology Research and Development Centre: Dir CHEN ZHAOJIN.

GUIZHOU RENMIN UNIVERSITY (Guizhou People's University)

180 Xiangsi Rd, Guiyang, Guizhou

Telephone: 42234

Founded 1983

President: Assoc. Prof. ZHANG GENGGUANG
Librarians: ZHAO TIANXIONG, ZHEN YANGYIN

Library of 27,000 vols
Number of teachers: 55
Number of students: 801

Depts of engineering science (environmental protection, industrial enterprise, village and town construction, engineer and operational safety, standardized management), liberal arts (English, secretarial/archives, administration management, industrial accounting).

GUIZHOU UNIVERSITY OF TECHNOLOGY

Caijiaguan, Guiyang, Guizhou Province 550003

Telephone: 4842486

Founded 1958

President: HU GUOGEN
Registrar: WANG YI
Secretary-General: YUAN HUAJUN
Librarian: HE LIQUAN

Library of 520,000 vols, 1,500 periodicals
Number of teachers: 780
Number of students: 8,000

Publication: *Journal* (6 a year).

HEADS OF DEPARTMENTS

Resource Engineering: ZHU LIJUN
Mining Engineering: YANG HOUHUA
Metallurgical Engineering: WU XIANXI
Mechanical Engineering: NIU MINGQI
Electrical Engineering: WU RUSHAN
Chemical Engineering: ZENG XIANGQIN
Civil Engineering: ZHANG HUI
Light Industry: ZHANG YIMING
Architecture: BAI NAIPENG
Computer Science: FU JIAXIANG
Foreign Languages: ZHANG CAIFENG
Engineering Management: YE ZHUGUANG
Adult Education No. 1: LIU ZHAOJIAN
Adult Education No. 2: LU KUN
Basic Science Courses: ZHOU GUOLI
Liberal Arts and Social Sciences: WU JIALING
Science Research: XIE QINSHENG
Physical Culture: LIU WEI

HANGZHOU UNIVERSITY

34 Tian Mu Shan Rd, Hangzhou, Zhejiang Province 310028

Telephone: 81224
Telex: 351082
Fax: 570159

Founded 1952, university status 1958

President: SHEN SHANHONG
Vice-Presidents: XIA YUEJIONG, DONG RUBIN, XIE TINGFAN, JIANG XINMO
Dean of Studies: LU JIAN
Librarian: HUANG SHIJIAN

Number of teachers: 2,673
Number of students: 7,330 (430 postgraduate)

Publications: *Journal* (quarterly), *Hangzhou University Post* (fortnightly), *Guide to Chinese Language and Literature* (monthly), *Applied Psychology* (quarterly).

HEADS OF DEPARTMENTS

Political Science: WANG XUEQI
Chinese Language and Literature: WU XIONGHE
Philosophy: MA ZHIZHENG
Law: YU TIANLONG
Economics: SHI JINCHUAN
Tourism: CHEN GANG
Finance: ZHANG MINGLIANG
Journalism: ZHANG DAZHI
Foreign Languages: REN SHAOZENG
History: JIN PUSEN
Education: SHAO ZUDE
Psychology: ZU ZUXIANG
Mathematics: LI ZHENGYAN
Physics: WANG SHAOMING
Chemistry: ZHANG YONGMIN
Biology: DING RENRUI
Geography: WANG DEHAN
Physical Culture: WANG MINGHAI
Computer Science: ZHANG SEN
Regional Planning and Urban Sciences: SONG XIAODI
Electronic Engineering: ZUO SHUSHENG
Foreign Languages of Non-Majors: WAN CHANGSHENG
Physical Culture of Non-Majors: GUO DONGSHENG

ATTACHED RESEARCH INSTITUTES

Research Institute of Biology: Dir MAO SHUJIAN.

Research Institute of Chinese Archaic Works: Dir JIANG LIANGFU.

Research Institute of Population: Dir WANG SIJUN.

Research Institute of Higher Education: Dir WANG CHENGXU.

Research Office of Catalysis: Dir JIN SONGSHOU.

Research Office of Estuaries and Ports: Dir ZHANG ZHIZONG.

Research Office of Land Planning: Dir MA YUXIANG.

Research Office of Information Display: Dir YE SICHAO.

Research Office of Historical Geography: Dir CHEN QIAOYI.

Research Office of Engineering Psychology: Dir ZHU ZUXIANG.

Research Office of Chinese Language and Literature: Dir ZHANG SONGNAN.

Research Office of the History of Song Dynasty: Dir XU GUI.

Research Office of French History: Dir SHEN LIANZHI.

Research Office of Ancient Greek Philosophy: Dir CHEN CUNFU.

Research Office of the History of Chinese Education: Dir CHEN XUEXUE.

Research Office of Foreign Education: Dir WANG CHENGXU.

Research Office of the History of the Chinese Communist Party: Dir WANG XUEQI.

Research Office of International Issues: Dir BIAN PENGFEI.

HANGZHOU UNIVERSITY OF COMMERCE

29 Jiao Gong Rd, Hangzhou, Zhejiang 310035

Telephone: (571) 8071024
Fax: (571) 8053079
E-mail: huc1@zjpta.net.cn

Founded 1911
Under control of Ministry of Internal Trade
Academic year: February to July, September to January

President: Prof. HU ZUGUANG
Vice-Presidents: Prof. WANG GUANGMING, DING ZHENGZHONG, HU WEIMIN, ZHANG JIANPING, ZHOU DAJUN
Chief Administrative Officer: KE LI
Librarian: ZHU SHANGWU

Library of 620,000 vols
Number of teachers: 326
Number of students: 5,100 full-time, 3,600 part-time

Publications: *Economics and Business Administration, Academic Periodical.*

HEADS OF DEPARTMENTS

Accounting: LIU JIANCHANG
Applied Fine Arts: ZHANG JIANCHUN
Business Administration: ZHU MINGWEI
Computer and Information Engineering: JU CHUNHUA
Electronic Engineering: REN ZHIGUO
Food Science and Technology: ZHONG LIREN
Foreign Languages: HUANG ZHIHONG
International Economics: YANG SENLIN
Investment Economics: HAN DEZHONG
Law: RUAN ZANLIN
Social Sciences: CHEN RONGFU
Statistics: LI JINCHANG
Tourism Management: XU ZHIWEI
Trade Economics: WANG CHUANWEI

HARBIN ENGINEERING UNIVERSITY

Wen Miao Jie, 11, Nangangqu, Harbin, Heilongjiang 150001

Telephone: (451) 2530010
Fax: (451) 2530010

Founded 1953

President: Prof. WU DEMING
Vice-Presidents: QIU CHANGHUA, YANG YAOGEN, LI GUOBIN, XU YURU, HUANG SHENG, ZHANG SHU, ZHOU RUITIAN

Library of 900,000 vols (special collections 150,000 vols)
Number of teachers: 1,800
Number of students: 8,000

Publications: *Journal of HEU, Marine Science and Technology, Transactions of Science and Technology, Marine Education.*

HEADS OF DEPARTMENT

Naval Architecture and Ocean Engineering: NIE WU
Civil Architecture Engineering: LIU DIANKUI
Marine Power Engineering: LIU ZHIGANG
Automation Engineering: SUN YAO
Electronic Engineering: HE YINGMIN
Underwater Acoustic Engineering: SAN ENFANG
Mechanical and Electrical Engineering: MENG QINGXIN
Computer and Information Science: GU GUOCHANG
Management Engineering: HUANG LUCHENG
Chemistry Engineering: ZHANG BAOHONG
Social Science: LUO JINLIAN
Physics: SU JINGHUI
Mathematics and Mechanics: SANG DAZHONG
Foreign Languages: ZHU ZICHAO
Computer Centre: WU CHANGLING
Adult Education Institute: ZHOU ZHENRONG

HARBIN INSTITUTE OF ELECTRICAL TECHNOLOGY

53 Daqing Rd, Harbin, Heilongjiang Province 150040

Telephone: 6221000
Fax: 51623

Founded 1950
Academic year: September to July

President: HE LIAN
Vice-Presidents: ZHOU SHICHANG, BAO SHAOXUAN, LIANG YUANHUA

Registrar: LU MINGJUAN
Librarian: BAO SHAOXUAN

Library of 270,000 vols
Number of teachers: 537
Number of students: 2,015 (incl. 95 postgraduates)

Publication: *Journal* (quarterly).

HEADS OF DEPARTMENTS

Electrical Machinery Engineering: LI ZHESHENG
Electromagnetic Measurement and Instrumentation: MA HUAIJIAN
Computer Engineering: SUN XINGRU
Electrical Material Engineering: YANG JIAXIANG
Mechanical Engineering: JIANG CHEN
Basic Courses: LU CIQING
Social Sciences: SONG DIANQING
Administration: GUAN ZHIYAO
Foreign Languages: XU XIANG

ATTACHED INSTITUTE:

Adult Education Institute: Dir YANG QI.

HARBIN INSTITUTE OF TECHNOLOGY

92 West Dazhi St, Harbin, Heilongjiang Province 150001

Telephone: 6412114
Telex: 87217
Fax: 6221048

Founded 1920

President: Prof. YANG SHIQIN
Vice-Presidents: LIU JIAQU, WANG SHUGUO, WANG ZUWEN, SHI GUANGJI, ZHANG DACHENG
Librarian: SHI HUILAI

Library of 1,000,000 vols
Number of teachers: 2,300
Number of students: 14,843 (incl. 2,652 postgraduates)

Publications: *Journal, Technology of Energy Conservation, Metal Science and Technology, Higher Engineering Education, Studying Computers*.

DEANS

School of Astronautics: Prof. JIA SHILOU
School of Management: LI YIJUN
School of Energy Science and Engineering: Prof. WANG ZUWEN
School of Computer and Electrical Engineering: Prof. HONG WENXUE
School of Electric Mechanical Engineering: Prof. WANG SHUGUO
School of Materials Science and Engineering: Prof. ZHAO LIANCHENG
School of Science: Prof. GENG WANZHEN
School of Humanities and Social Sciences: Prof. JIANG ZHENHUA

HEBEI MEDICAL COLLEGE

5 Changan West Rd, Shijiazhuang City, Hebei Province 050017

Telephone and fax: 6048177

Founded 1915

President: WEI BAOLIN
Vice-Presidents: WU XING, XU JINGFENG, YANG YUEFENG
Head of Graduate School: ZHOU DAQUAN
Librarian: Prof. JIA MINYI

Library of 300,000 vols
Number of teachers: 563
Number of students: 4,149

Publications: *Acta Academiae Medicinae Hebei, Chinese Journal of Physical Medicine, Foreign Medicine: Respiratory System section*.

HEADS OF DEPARTMENTS

Medical Sciences: WANG KECHENG, SUN SUFANG, Prof. MA ZHIXUE
Pharmacy: Prof. ZHANG LIDE
Stomatology: Prof. DU JIEJUN
Public Health: Prof. LIANG SIQUAN

HEBEI UNIVERSITY OF ECONOMICS AND TRADE

Wu Qi Rd, Shijiazhuang, Hebei Province 050061

Telephone: (311) 6039189
Fax: (311) 6039123

Founded 1982

President: YU RENGANG
Vice-Presidents: CUI YUANMIN, HU DONGYANG, YAO JINGGUAN, MAZHI ZHONG, WU SHENGCHEN, HU BAOZHONG
Librarian: MA KE

Library of 250,000 vols
Number of teachers: 900
Number of students: 10,000

Publication: *Economics and Management*.

HEADS OF DEPARTMENTS

Industrial Economic Management: LU CHANGFU
Agricultural Economic Management: QIN WENBO
Planning and Statistical Economic Management: LIU YAOHUA
Financial and Accounting Management: FAN CHANGYING
Labour Economics and Management: HAO BING
Political Work in Business: LI SHUZENG
Economics and Trade: YIE JIANFENG

HEFEI UNIVERSITY OF TECHNOLOGY

59 Tunxi Rd, Hefei, Anhui Province 230009

Telephone: (551) 4655210
Telex: 90040
Fax: (551) 4651517

Founded 1945

President: CHEN XINZHAO
Vice-Presidents: XU HUIPENG, WANG DEZE, TANG JIAN, LIU GUANGFU, ZHENG ZHIXIANG
Registrar: ZHOU XU
Librarian: SUN XUANYIN

Number of teachers: 4,513
Number of students: 18,216

Publications: *Journal, Teaching and Study of Industrial Automation, Engineering Mathematics, Forecasting, Techniques Abroad, Tribology Abroad*.

Fifteen departments.

HENAN COLLEGE OF TRADITIONAL CHINESE MEDICINE

1 Jin-Shui Rd, Zhengzhou, Henan Province 450003

Telephone: 556348
Fax: 555650

Founded 1958
State Control

President: SHANG CHICHANG
Vice-Presidents: FENG MINGAQING, WANG CHUNCHANG
Registrar: BO PENG
Librarian: LI XIAOWEN

Library of 300,000 vols
Number of teachers: 2,000, including 700 teachers and 600 doctors
Number of students: 2,000

Publications: *Henan Traditional Chinese Medicine* (every 2 months), *Journal of Henan Traditional Chinese Medicine* (seasonally).

HEADS OF DEPARTMENTS

Traditional Chinese Medicine (TCM): Prof. TANG SONG
Traditional Materia Medica (TMM): Prof. ZHANG GUANGQIANG
Acupuncture and Moxibustion: Prof. LIU MAOLIN

PROFESSORS

CAI, F. Y., TCM
CHEN, G. Z., Philosophy
CHEN, R. F., Internal Medicine
DONG, Y. S., Acupuncture
FENG, M. Q., TCM
GAO, T. S., TCM
HOU, S. L., TMM
JI, C. R., TMM
LI, X. W., TCM
LI, Y. L., Paediatrics
LI, Z. H., TCM
LI, Z. S., Internal Medicine
LOU, D. F., TCM Traumatology
LU, S. C., Qigong
MA, Z. H., TCM
SHANG, C. C., TCM
SHAO, J. M., Acupuncture
SHI, G. Q., TCM
SHUN, L. H., Acupuncture
SUN, C. Q., Physiology
SUN, H. B., Parasitology
SUN, J. Z., Internal Medicine
TANG, S., TCM
WANG, A. B., TCM History
WANG, R. K., Diagnostics
WANG, Y. M., Pharmaco-Chemistry
YANG, L. Y., Anatomy
YANG, Y. S., TMM
ZHANG, G. Q., TMM
ZHENG, J. M., TCM Paediatrics
ZHAO, M. Q., TCM
ZHOU, W. C., TCM

HOHAI UNIVERSITY

1 Xikang Rd, Nanjing 210098

Telephone: (25) 3323777
Telex: 34101
Fax: (25) 3315375

Founded 1915 (fmrly East China Technical Univ. of Water Resources), name changed 1985
State control
Languages of instruction: Chinese, English
Academic year: September to July

President: Prof. JIANG HONGDAO
Vice-Presidents: Prof. LIU XINREN, Prof. JIN ZHONGQING, Prof. ZHANG CHANG
Librarian: DONG TINGSONG

Number of teachers: 1,343
Number of students: 8,000

Publications: *Journal*†, *Advances in the Science and Technology of Water Resources*†, *Economics of Water Resources*†, *Water Resources Protection*†, *Journal of Higher Education*.

DEANS

College of Civil Engineering: Prof. ZHUO JIASHOU
College of Water Resources and Environment: Prof. WANG HUIMIN
College of Harbour, Waterway and Coastal Engineering: Prof. ZHANG CHANGKUAN
College of Water Conservancy and Hydropower Engineering: Prof. SUO LISHENG
College of Electrical Engineering: Prof. YANG JINTANG
College of Mechanical and Electrical Engineering: Prof. JIN YAHE
College of Computer and Information Engineering: Assoc. Prof. ZHU YAOLONG
College of International Industry and Commerce: Assoc. Prof. ZHANG YANG
College of Technical Economics: Prof. ZHENG CHUIYONG

HUAQIAO UNIVERSITY

Quanzhou 362011, Fujian
Telephone: (595) 2693630
Fax: (595) 2681940
E-mail: wsc@hqu.edu.cn

Founded 1960
State control
Academic year starts September

President: Prof. ZHUANG SHANYU
Vice-Presidents: Prof. WU CHENGYE, Prof. GUO HENGQUN, Assoc. Prof. HUANG YANCHENG, Assoc. Prof. DU CHENGJIN
Registrar: Assoc. Prof. WANG JIANCHENG
Librarian: Assoc. Prof. WENG CHANGWU

Library of 812,000 vols, 6,885 periodicals
Number of teachers: 514 (full-time)
Number of students: 8,765

Publications: *Journal of Huaqiao University* (Natural Science and Social Science editions, 4 a year, in Chinese), *Research in Higher Education by Overseas Chinese* (2 a year, in Chinese).

DEANS

College of Teaching Chinese as a Foreign Language: Assoc. Prof. LI JIJIE
Training College: Assoc. Prof. CHEN QINGJUN
Institute of Application Technology: Assoc. Prof. LIN YIXIONG

HEADS OF DEPARTMENTS

Management Information Science: Prof. ZHENG YONGSHU
Electrical Technology: Assoc. Prof. WANG JIAXIAN
Applied Chemistry: Prof. XU JINRUI
Computer Science: Assoc. Prof. WU QINGJIANG
Civil Engineering: Prof. WANG QUANFENG
Architecture: Assoc. Prof. HONG JIEXU
Precision Mechanical Engineering: Prof. HONG SHANGREN
Chemical and Biochemical Engineering: Assoc. Prof. FANG BAISHAN
Electronic Engineering: Assoc. Prof. ZHANG YINMING
Chinese Culture: Prof. GU SHENGHAO
Foreign Languages: Assoc. Prof. WANG GE
Fine Arts: Assoc. Prof. JIANG SONG
Law: Assoc. Prof. ZHU SUIBIN
Industrial and Commercial Management: Assoc. Prof. YE MINQIANG
General Social Science: Assoc. Prof. ZHANG YUDONG
Tourism: Prof. ZHENG XIANMIN

ATTACHED INSTITUTES

Institute of Material Physical Chemistry: Dir Assoc. Prof. WU JIHUAI.

Institute of Overseas Chinese Studies: Dir Assoc. Prof. XIAO BEIYING.

Institute of Environmental Protection: Assoc. Prof. LIN YIXIONG.

Institute of Taiwanese Economy: Prof. WU CHENGYE.

Institute of Stone-machining: Dir Assoc. Prof. XU XIPENG.

HUAZHONG AGRICULTURAL UNIVERSITY

Shizhishan, Wuhan 430070, Hubei
Telephone: (27) 7393766
Fax: (27) 7396057
E-mail: hau@maple.edu.cn

Founded 1952, present name 1985
State control

Languages of instruction: Chinese, English
Academic year: September to July

President: ZHANG DUANPIN
Vice-Presidents: DENG XIUXIN, RUAN GUIMEN, WANG XINGWANG
Registrar: LI ZHONGYUN
Librarian: WAN JIQIN

Library of 620,000 vols
Number of teachers: 2,281
Number of students: 5,385

Publication: journal.

DEANS

College of Animal Husbandry and Veterinary Science: CHEN HUANCHUN
College of the Fishing Industry: WANG MINGXUE
College of Life Sciences and Technology: ZHANG QIFA
College of Arts and Humanities: WANG XULANG
College of Land Management: LEI HAIZHANG
College of Economics and Trade: (vacant)
College of Adult Education: ZHANG DUANPIN

HEADS OF DEPARTMENTS

Agronomy: WANG WEIJIN
Plant Protection: XU GUANJUN
Resources, Environment and Agrochemistry: WANG YUNHUA
Horticulture: LUO ZHENGRONG
Forestry: BAO MANZHU
Food Science and Technology: ZHANG JIANIAN
Agricultural Engineering: XU QICHUAN
Foreign Languages: LIU YANXIU (Vice-Dean)
Basic Sciences: XIE JIJIAN

HUAZHONG UNIVERSITY OF SCIENCE AND TECHNOLOGY

Wuhan 430074, Hubei
Telephone: (27) 87542102
Fax: (27) 87545438

Founded 1953

President: Prof. ZHOU JI
Vice-Presidents: Prof. ZHOU SHOUBING, Prof. ZHOU ZUDE, Prof. QIN YI, Assoc. Prof. YU QINGSHUANG, Assoc. Prof. WANG YANJUE
Librarian: Assoc. Prof. WANG JINWEI

Library of 2,250,000 vols, 8,000 periodicals in Chinese and foreign languages
Number of teachers: 2,580
Number of students: 15,381

Publications include: *Journal* (every 2 months), *Applied Mathematics, Journal of Solid State Mechanics, New Architecture, Linguistics Research, Studies in Higher Education, Higher Engineering Education in China, Journal of Social Science.*

DEANS

Graduate School: Prof. YANG SHUZI
School of Adult Education: Prof. ZUO WUXIN
School of Economics: Prof. WU XIEHE
College of Architecture: Prof. YUAN PEIHUANG
College of Science: Prof. HUANG ZHIYUAN
College of Mechanical Science and Engineering: Prof. LI PEIGEN
School of Materials Science and Engineering: Prof. XIE JUCHEN
School of Energy Resource Science and Engineering: Prof. ZHANG YONGCHUAN
School of Computer Science and Technology: Prof. LU ZHENGDING
School of Navigation and Maritime Engineering: Prof. SHI ZHONGKUN
School of Laser Technology and Engineering: Prof. LI ZHENGJIA
College of Biological Science and Engineering: Prof. LIN JIARUI
School of Liberal Arts: Prof. WEICHI ZHIPING
College of Business Administration: Prof. CHEN RONGQIOU
School of Journalism and Information Circulation: Prof. WU TINGJUN

HEADS OF DEPARTMENTS

Mathematics: Prof. HU SHIGENG
Chemistry: Prof. HUANG KAIXUN
Solid State Electronics: Prof. XU CHONGYANG
Physics: Prof. XIAO YI
Mechanical Engineering: Prof. CHEN CHUANYAO
Bioengineering: Prof. MEI XINGGUO
Foreign Languages: Prof. QIN AOSONG
Structural Engineering: Prof. TANG JIAXIANG
Optoelectronic Engineering: Prof. HUANG DEXIU
Automobile Engineering: Prof. JIN GUODUNG
Electric Power Engineering: Prof. YING XIANGGEN
Power Engineering: Prof. LIU WEI
Computer Electronics Engineering: Prof. ZHU GUANGXI
Electronics Science and Technology: Prof. XU CHONGYANG
Radio Engineering: Prof. YAO TIANREN
Automatic Control Engineering: Prof. SUN DEBAO
Sociology: Prof. FENG XIAOTIAN
Arts; Prof. LI CHUNFU
Philosophy: Prof. YIN ZHENGKUN
Chinese Language and Literature: Prof. HUANG GUOYING
Finance: Prof. WU XIEHE
Physical Education: Prof. XIE YANGFENG

HUNAN MEDICAL UNIVERSITY

88 Xiang Ya Rd, Changsha, 410078 Hunan
Telephone: (731) 4471347
Fax: (731) 4471339

Founded 1914
Academic year: September to July

President: Prof. HU DONGXU
Vice-Presidents: Prof. SUN ZHENGQIU, Prof. WU ZHONGQI, Prof. ZHOU HONGHAO, Prof. HU TIEHUI, Prof. TIAN YONGQUAN, Prof. CHEN ZHUCHU
Librarian: Assoc. Prof. LIU XIACHUN

Library of 560,000 vols
Number of teachers: 652 (full-time)
Number of students: 3,846 (incl. 585 postgraduates)

Publications: *Bulletin* (6 a year), *Journal of Foreign Medicine—Psychiatry, Neurology and Neurosurgery, Physiology and Pathology Sections, Journal of Modern Medicine* (monthly), *Chinese Journal of General Surgery* (fortnightly), *Journal of Medical Degree and Postgraduate Education* (4 a year), *Higher Medical Education Management* (4 a year), *Journal of Applied Uro-Surgery* (4 a year), *Chinese Journal of Otolaryngological and Craniosacral Surgery, Chinese Journal of Endoscopy* (4 a year), *Chinese Journal of Psychology* (4 a year).

DIRECTORS

Faculty of Basic Medical Sciences: WEN JIFANG
1st Affiliated Hospital (Clinical Medicine): TIAN YONGQUAN
2nd Affiliated Hospital (Clinical Medicine): LIAO ERYUAN
3rd Affiliated Hospital (Clinical Medicine): LIU XUNYANG
Faculty of Laboratroy Research: CHEN ZHENGYAN
Faculty of Stomatology: JIAN XINCHUN
Faculty of Mental Health: CHEN YUANGUANG
Faculty of Library and Information Sciences: LIU XIAOCHUN
Faculty of Nursing: ZHOU CHANGJU
Faculty of Pharmacology: TANG GUISHAN (Deputy Dir)
Faculty of Preventive Medicine: TANG HONGZHUAN (Deputy Dir)

PROFESSORS

LU GUANGXIU, Biology and Genetics
WEN JIFANG, Pathology
FAN JUNYUAN, Organic Chemistry
HUANG GANCHU, Physics and Chemistry
ZHANG YANXIAN, Pathology
CHENG RUIXUE, Pathology
YOU JIALU, Pathophysiology

ZENG XIANFANG, Parasitology
YI XINYUAN, Parasitology
DENG HANWU, Pharmacology
LI YUANJIAN, Pharmacology
GUO ZHAOGUI, Clinical Pharmacology
GUO SHISHI, Immunology
LIU LIHOU, Anatomy
LUO XUEGANG, Anatomy
SUN XIUHONG, Physiology
LI JUNCHENG, Physiology
MA CHUANTAO, Cardiovascular Physiology
SONG HUIPING, Biochemistry
HAN FENGXIA, Biology
CHEN SHUZHEN, Microbiology
ZHU JIMING, Histology and Embryology
XU YOUHENG, Haemophysiology
WANG QIRU, Haemophysiology
JIANG DEZHAO, Haemophysiology
YAO KAITAI, Experimental Oncology
LI GUIYUAN, Molecular Biology
HU WEIXIN, Tumour Molecular Biology
CAO YA, Tumour Molecular Biology
CHEN ZHUCHU, Tumour Cellular Biology
XIA JIAHUI, Biology and Medical Genetics
LI LUYUN, Medical Genetics
DENG HANXIANG, Biology and Medical Genetics
ZHAO SHUYING, Children's Health
TANG MINGDE, Environmental Health
HU MANLING, Health Chemistry
HUANG ZHENNAN, Health Statistics
SUN ZHENGQIU, Health Statistics
HUANG YIMING, Nutritious Food and Health
CHEN ZHENGYAN, Clinical Biochemistry
CHA GUOZHANG, Clinical Microbiology and Immunology
LIU XIAOCHUN, Library and Information Sciences
FANG PING, Library and Information Sciences
ZHOU HONGHAO, Pharmacology
HU DONGXU, Cardiac Surgery
HU TIEHUI, Cardiac Surgery
HU JIANGUO, Cardiac Surgery
YIN BANGLIAN, Cardiac Surgery
GONG GUANGFU, Cardiac Surgery
CHEN SHENGXI, Cardiac Surgery
LI XUERONG, Medical Psychology
CHEN YUANGUANG, Psychiatry
YANG DESEN, Psychiatry
LUO JIAN, Internal Medicine (Kidney Diseases)
CAO ZHIHAN, Internal Medicine (Kidney Diseases)
JI LONGZHEN, Internal Medicine (Kidney Diseases)
ZHAO SHUIPING, Internal Medicine (Cardiology)
WANG ZHONGLIN, Internal Medicine (Cardiology)
CHEN GANREN, Internal Medicine (Cardiology)
QI SHUSHAN, Internal Medicine (Cardiology)
ZHANG GUANGSEN, Internal Medicine (Haematology)
LU HANBO, Internal Medicine (Haematology)
LU YINZHU, Internal Medicine (Cardiovascular Diseases)
SUN MING, Internal Medicine (Cardiovascular Diseases)
YIN BENYI, Internal Medicine (Cardiology)
WU ESHENG, Internal Medicine (Respiratory Diseases)
ZHANG XICHUN, Internal Medicine (Digestive Diseases)
HAN XIUYUN, Internal Medicine (Endocrinology)
LIAO ERYUAN, Internal Medicine (Endocrinology)
CAO PING, Internal Medicine (Haematology)
CHEN FANGPING, Internal Medicine (Haematology)
QI ZHENHUA, Internal Medicine (Haematology)
XIE ZHAOXIA, Internal Medicine (Haematology)
LI HEJUN, Orthopaedic Surgery
ZHOU JIANGNAN, Orthopaedic Surgery
FU YINYU, Orthopaedic Surgery
LIU REN, Uro-Surgery
HUANG XUN, Uro-Surgery
JIANG XIANZHEN, Uro-Surgery
QI FAN, Uro-Surgery
SHEN PENGFEI, Uro-Surgery
HU FUZEN, General Surgery
LIU XUNYANG, General Surgery
CHEN DAOJING, General Surgery
ZHANG YANGDE, General Surgery
LU XINSHENG, General Surgery
LU WENNENG, General Surgery
OU YANG ZHITING, General Surgery
XU LILI, Gynaecology and Obstetrics
LIN QIUHUA, Gynaecology and Obstetrics
ZHOU CHANGJU, Gynaecology and Obstetrics
YI ZHUWEN, Paediatrics
YANG YUJIA, Paediatrics
YE YIYAN, Paediatrics
YU XIAOLIANG, Paediatrics
SU XIANSHI, Infectious Diseases
TANG DEMING, Infectious Diseases
OU YANG KE, Infectious Diseases
HU GUOLING, Infectious Diseases
JIANG YOUQIN, Ophthalmology
HUANG PEIGANG, Ophthalmology
LU YONGDE, Otorhinolaryngology
XIE DINGHUA, Otorhinolaryngology
TAO ZHENGDE, Otorhinolaryngology
XIAO JIANYUN, Otorhinolaryngology
TIAN YONGQUAN, Otorhinolaryngology
CHEN QIZHI, Anaesthesiology
LI DETAI, Radiology
BAI XIANXIN, Radiology
SU JIANZHI, Isotopes in Medicine
PAN AIYIN, Isotopes in Medicine
ZHU WEIGUANG, Chinese Traditional Medicine
LI XINGQUN, Chinese Traditional Medicine
LI JIABANG, Chinese Traditional Medicine
JIN YIQIANG, Chinese Traditional Medicine
HUANG ZHAOMIN, Rebabilitation
WANG LIZHUANG, Emergency Medicine
LUO XUEHONG, Emergency Medicine
GAO JIESHENG, Internal Medicine (Rheumatology)
LI RUIZHEN, Ultrasound Diagnosis
CHEN FUWEN, Dermatology
LIU ZHIRAN, Dermatology
MA ENQING, Burns Medicine
LU BINGQING, Neurology
YANG QIDONG, Neurology
LIU YUNSHENG, Neurosurgery
YUAN XIANRUI, Neurosurgery
SHEN ZIHUA, Stomatology
JIAN XINCHUN, Stomatology
XU XIUHUA, Infection
WU ZHONGQI, Medical Hyperbaric Oxygen

JIANGXI AGRICULTURAL UNIVERSITY

Meiling, Nanchang, Jianxi Province 330045

Founded 1980

President: Prof. LUO MING

Library of over 400,000 vols
Number of teachers: 530
Number of students: 2,900

Publication: *Journal*.

Departments of agronomy, forestry, plant protection, horticulture, animal husbandry and veterinary science, farm engineering, agricultural economics.

ATTACHED INSTITUTES

Jiangxi Feed Science Research Institute.

Farm Animal Disease Prevention Research Institute.

Farm Crop Research Institute.

Insect Research Institute.

JILIN UNIVERSITY

123 Jiefang Dalu, Changchun, Jilin Province 130023

Telephone: 8922331
Telex: 83040
Fax: 8923907

Founded 1946

Academic year: September to July (two semesters).

President: LIU ZHONGSHU
Vice-Presidents: LI SHUJIA, ZHANG WENXIAN, QIU SHILUN, JIN SHUO, QI XIANG, GONG ZHIZHONG, YU CHANGYUN
Head of Graduate School: QIU SHILUN
Librarian: BAO CHENGGUAN

Library of 2,510,000 vols
Number of teachers: 1,593
Number of students: 9,301

Publications: *Chemical Research in Chinese Universities* (Chinese and English edns), *Journal of Natural Science, Mathematics of Northeastern China, Northeast Asian Forum, Journal of Historical Studies, Higher Education Research and Practice, Legal Systems and Social Development, Modern Japanese Economy, Journal of Demography.*

HEADS OF COLLEGES

College of Administration: Prof. ZHOU GUANGHUI
College of Law: Prof. WANG MU
College of Economics and Management: Prof. ZHENG GUITING
College of Business: Prof. DONG WENQUAN
College of Foreign Languages: Prof. YU CHANGMING
College of Philosophy and Sociology: Prof. MENG XIANZHONG

HEADS OF DEPARTMENTS

Mathematics: Prof. GAO WENJIE
Physics: Prof. HUI RUIFA
Chemistry: Prof. WU TONGHAO
Electronics Science: Prof. XU BAOKUN
Computer Science: Prof. LIU DAYOU
Molecular Biology: Prof. LI QINGSHAN
Materials Science: Prof. CHEN GANG
Environmental Science: Prof. DONG DEMING
Packaging Engineering: LIU XISHENG
Chinese Language and Literature: Prof. HAO CHANGHAI
History: LIU DEBIN
Economics: Prof. WU YUHUI
Economic Management: Prof. CAI XINGYANG
Management Science: Prof. WANG JINGONG
International Economics: Prof. LI JUNJIANG
Jurisprudence: Prof. LIU XINFU
Philosophy: Prof. AI FUCHENG
Political Science: Prof. SHUN XIAOHUI
Foreign Languages: Prof. YU CHANGMING
Archaeology: Prof. WEI CUNCHENG

College of Administration:

Political Science: Prof. HAN DONGXUE
Adminstration and Management: Prof. LI DEZHI
Office Automation: FANG ZHIWEN
Moral Education: Prof. WANG CAIBO
Small Town Development and Management: Prof. LIU QINGCAI

College of Law:

Jurisprudence: Prof. LIU XINFU
Economic Law: Prof. ZHAO XINHUA
International Law: Prof. CHE PEIZHAO

College of Economics and Management:

Economics: Prof. WU YUHUI
Economic Management: Prof. XU CUANCHEN
International Economy: Prof. LI JUNJIANG

College of Business:

Business: Prof. LIU YOUCHEN
Management Science: Prof. WANG JINGONG
Accounting: Prof. ZHAO CHENQUAN

College of Foreign Languages:

English Language and Literature: Prof. WU JINGHUI
Japanese: Prof. CUI QIN
Russian: Prof. XIAO LIANHE
Korean: Prof. CUI CHENGDE

College of Philosophy and Sociology:
Philosophy: Prof. AI FUNCHENG
Sociology: Prof. LIU SHAOJIE

JINAN UNIVERSITY

Shipai, 510632 Guangzhou, Guangdong Province

Telephone: 5516511
Telex: 44645
Fax: 5516941

Founded 1906, university status 1927
State control
Language of instruction: Chinese
Academic year: September to July

President: Prof. LIU RENHUAI
Vice-Presidents: Assoc. Prof. WU GUOJI, Prof. ZHANG YONGAN, Assoc. Prof. HUANG XUHUI, Assoc. Prof. LAI JIANGJI
Director of the Library: HE RENJIN
Vice-Directors of the Library: Prof. JIANG SHUZHUO, Assoc. Prof. LUO WEIQI, Assoc. Prof. LI WEISHU

Library of 1,347,000 vols
Number of teachers: 1,100
Number of students: 13,012 (incl. 615 postgraduates)

Publications: *Journal I* (Literature, History, Economics), *Journal II* (Science, Technology, Medicine), *Jinan Education, World Literature and Arts, University Newspaper, Jinan Bulletin.*

HEADS OF COLLEGES

Liberal Arts: Prof. WEI ZHONGLIN
Science and Technology: Prof. WU GONGSHUN
Economics: Prof. WANG FUCHU
Medicine: Prof. WANG MINGCHUN
Chinese Language and Culture: Assoc. Prof. LAI JIANGJI
Travel: Prof. REN KELEI
Adult and Lifelong Education: Prof. PENG DAHUO

HEADS OF DEPARTMENTS AND RESEARCH ORGANIZATIONS

Chinese Language and Literature: WEI ZHONGLIN
History: ZHANG XIAOHUI
Foreign Languages and Literatures: DAI WEIHUA
Journalism: WU WENHU
Foreign Languages Centre: LIANG DONGHUA
Chinese Languages and Culture Centre: LIAN WENGUANG
Basic Social Science: CHEN YOUWEN
Economics: LIN LIQIONG
Business Management: LUO LONGCHANG
Commerce: CHEN JIHUAN
Finance: DENG RUILIN
Accounting: YE CHANG
Statistics and Planning: CHEN GUANGCHAO
Economic Law: ZHANG ZENGQIANG
Mathematics: BO YUANHUAI
Chemistry: HUANG NINGXING
Physics: HUANG GUOCHUN
Biology: LIU JIESHENG
Computer Science: YE JIANYUAN
Electronic Engineering: LIU TAO
Stomatology: TANG LIANG
Medicine: ZHANG RENHUA
Physical Education Department: WEN SHISHENG
Preparatory School: CHEN WEIXIANG

ATTACHED INSTITUTES

Institute for Southeast Asian Studies: Dir CHEN QIAOZHI.

Institute for Overseas Chinese Studies: Dir Prof. HUANG KUNZHANG.

Institute for Studies in the Economy of the Special Economic Zones of Hong Kong and Macau: Dir FENG XIAOYUN.

Institute of Chinese History and Culture: Dir MAO QINGQI.

Institute of Biomedical Engineering: Dir ZOU HAN.

Research Centre of Reproductive Immunology: Dir PAN SHANPEI.

Institute of Hydrobiology: Dir QU YUZAO.

Institute for Biological Engineering: Dir LIN JIAN.

KUNMING MEDICAL COLLEGE

84 Renmin Xilu, Kunming, Yunnan Province 650031

Telephone: 81933

Founded 1956
Academic year: September to January, March to August

President: Prof. LIANG LIQUAN
Vice-Presidents: Prof. CHEN DECHANG, Prof. WANG ZICANG, ZHANG CHAO
Chief Administrative Officer: JIANG RUNSHENG

Library of *c.* 170,000 vols, 1,659 periodicals
Number of teachers: over 1,200
Number of students: 2,789 (including 118 postgraduates)

HEADS OF DEPARTMENTS

Medicine (1): Prof. TANG JINQING
Medicine (2): Assoc. Prof. GUO YONGZHANG
Stomatology: Prof. LI JIE
Public Health: Prof. WANG TONGYING
Forensic Medicine: YAO FANGSHENG

KUNMING UNIVERSITY OF SCIENCE AND TECHNOLOGY

1 Wenchangxiang, 12.1 Ave, Kunming, Yunnan 650093

Telephone: (871) 5144212
Fax: (871) 5158622

Founded 1954
Academic year: September to July

President: Prof. ZHANG WENBIN
Vice-Presidents: Prof. TAO HENGCHANG, Prof. XIANG NAIMING, Prof. HE TIANCHUN
Assistant President: Prof. SUN JIALIN
Registrar: Prof. ZHOU RONG
Librarian: Prof. LIU ZHONGHUA

Library of 1,100,000 vols
Number of teachers: 800
Number of students: 8,000

Publications: *Journal, Science and Technology in KUST, Research in Higher Education in KUST.*

HEADS OF COLLEGE

College of Adult Education: Prof. XU BAOZHONG
College of Management and Economy: Prof. YANG BAOJIAN
College of Social Science ad Art: LI XUEYOU

HEADS OF DEPARTMENTS

Geology and Survey Engineering: Prof. LIANG YONGNING
Mineral Processing and Mining: Prof. YANG SHIYONG
Metallurgy: Prof. WANG HUA
Mechanical Engineering: Prof. CHENG CHANGHUA
Automation: Prof. ZHANG YUNSHENG
Environmental Engineering and Chemistry: Prof. NING PING
Architectural Engineering and Mechanics: Prof. CHENG HEMING
Foreign Languages: Prof. HE YI
Basic Science: Prof. LI JIBIN
Computer Science: Prof. ZHANG HUAINING
Materials Engineering: Prof. SUN YONG
Physical Education: Assoc. Prof. WANG YUEZHOU
Graduate Study: Prof. XIE GANG

LANZHOU UNIVERSITY

298 Tianshui Rd, 730000 Lanzhou, Gansu Province

Telephone: 8828111
Fax: 8885076

Founded 1909
Academic year: September to July (2 semesters)

President: LI FASHEN
Vice-Presidents: YANG JUN, ZHAN XIU, ZHANG JIQING, LI LIAN, SHEN WEIGUO
Administrative Director: FENG YUYE
Librarian: ZHU ZISHENG

Number of teachers: 1,400
Number of students: 8,000

Publications: *Journal, Historical and Geographical Review of Northwest China, Collections of Articles on Dunhuang Studies,* etc.

HEADS OF DEPARTMENTS

Chinese: ZHANG WENXUAN
History: YANG JIANXIN
Journalism: WANG ZUOREN
Philosophy: LIN LI
Economics: LI ZONGZHI
Law: LI GONGGUO
Library Science: WANG GUIZHONG
Foreign Languages and Literature: FENG JIANWEN
Mathematics: WANG MINLIANG
Marxist Studies: LIU JIASHENG
Physics: CHEN GUANGHUA
Modern Physics: LIU ZHENMING
Electronics and Information Science: LU ZHENSU
Mechanics: YU HUANRAN
Computer Science: XU DEQI
Material Science: WANG TIANMING
Chemistry: PAN XINFU
Geography: ZHOU SHANGHE
Geology: HAN WENFENG
Administration: HE HENGXIN
Atmospheric Science: CHOU JIFAN

NANJING FORESTRY UNIVERSITY

Longpan Rd, Nanjing 210037, Jiangsu Province

Telephone: (25) 5427206
Fax: (25) 5412500

Founded 1952

President: Prof. YU SHIYUAN
Vice-Presidents: Prof. HONG QIQING, Prof. CHEN JINGHUAN, Prof. SHI JISEN, Prof. WU DIRONG
Librarian: LIU XIUHUA

Library of 600,000 vols
Number of teachers: 731
Number of students: 4,000 (incl. 274 postgraduates)

Publications: *Journal of Nanjing Forestry University, Bamboo Research, Development of Forestry Science and Technology, Interiors.*

HEADS OF COLLEGES AND DEPARTMENTS

Forest Resources and Environment: Prof. CAO FULIANG
Wood Science and Technology: Prof. TAN SHOUXIA
Chemical Engineering: Prof. AN XINNAN
Mechanical and Electronic Engineering: Prof. ZHOU YONGZHAO
Forest Economics and Management: Prof. CHEN GUOLIANG
Civil Engineering: Prof. ZHAO CHEN
Adult Education: Prof. GUAN SUQI
Graduate Studies: Prof. YE JIANREN
Basic Courses Division: Assoc. Prof. WEI SHUGUANG
Social Sciences Division: Assoc. Prof. WANG GUOPIN

PROFESSORS

XIONG WENYUE, Forest Ecology
ZHU ZHENGDE, Forest Botany
LI ZHONGZHENG, Chemical Processing of Forest Products
CHEN ZHI, Chemical Processing of Forest Products
HUA YUKUN, Wood Processing
SU JINYUN, Forest Engineering
CHEN GUOLIANG, Forest Economics
SHEN GUANFU, Forest Mechanics

NANJING INSTITUTE OF METEOROLOGY

Pancheng, Nanjing, Jiangsu Province 210044
Telephone: 7792648

Founded 1960
State control
Language of instruction: Chinese
Academic year: September to July

President: TU QIPU
Vice-President: SUN ZHAOBO
Dean: RUAN JUNSHI
Chief Administrative Officer: LU JICHENG
Librarian: ZHU FUCHENG

Library of 350,000 vols
Number of teachers: 350
Number of students: 2,800

Publications: *Journal* (quarterly), *Meteorological Education and Science and Technology.*

CHAIRMEN OF DEPARTMENTS

Meteorology: HE JINHAI
Atmospheric Physics: TANG DAZHANG
Agrometeorology: CHU CHANGSHU
Basic Sciences: GAO XUEHAO
Social Science: ZHANG YONGKUN
Computer and Information Engineering: CHENG JIELUN
Adult Education: SUN DONGYUAN

NANJING MEDICAL UNIVERSITY

140 Hanzhong Rd, Nanjing, Jiangsu 210029
Telephone: (25) 6612696
Fax: (25) 6508960

Founded 1934

President: ZHANG ZHENSHENG
Vice-Presidents: CHEN RONGHUA, WU GUANLING, XU XINDONG, XU YAOCHU
Registrar: PANG KANGLI
Librarian: ZHANG ZHENGHUI

Library of over 400,000 vols
Number of teachers: 1,160
Number of students: 4,000

HEADS OF DEPARTMENTS

Clinical Medicine: HUANG JUN
Nursing Science: DONG WEICI
Paediatrics: CHEN RONGHUA
Stomatology: YU WEIYI
Preventive Medicine: WANG XINRU

NANJING NORMAL UNIVERSITY

122 Ninghai Rd, Nanjing 210097, Jiangsu
Telephone: (25) 3720999
Fax: (25) 3706565

Founded 1902

Provincial govt control
Academic year: September to August
President: Prof. GONG PIXIANG
Vice-Presidents: Prof. LU BINGSHOU, Prof. CHEN GUOJUN, Prof. TU GUOHUA, Prof. CHEN LINGFU, Prof. WANG XIAOPENG, Prof. ZHU XIAOMAN, Prof. HUANG TAO
Dean of Postgraduate Studies: PAN BAIQI
Librarian: WU JIN

Library of 1,650,000 vols
Number of teachers: 1,100
Number of students: 7,000 (incl. 430 postgraduates)

Publications: *Periodicals of Nanjing Normal University* (social sciences, natural sciences), *References for Educational Research, Fine Arts Education in China,* text books.

HEADS OF DEPARTMENTS AND COLLEGES

College of Economics and Law: GONG TINGTAI
College of Journalism and Communication: YUE BINGLONG
Jinling Women's College: HUANG TAO
Adult Education College: ZHANG QIYUAN
Educational Science College: YANG QILIANG
International Culture and Education College: LU TONGQUN
Chinese Language and Literature: HE YONGKANG
History and Sociology: YU KUNQI
Foreign Languages and Literature: CHEN AIMIN
Mathematics: SONG YONGZHONG
Physics: HUANG KELIANG
Chemistry: ZHOU ZHIHUA
Biology: SHI GUOXIN
Geography Science College: SHA RUN
Music: YU ZIZHENG
Fine Arts: FAN YANG
Physical Education: FAN WENBIN
Computer Science: CAI SHAOJI
Physics and Chemistry Laboratory: LIU GUOJIN
Classical Books and Documents Institute: YU XIANHAO
Education Research Institute: YANG QILIANG
Chinese Literature Institute: ZHONG ZHENZHEN
Jiangsu Teachers' Training Centre for Institutions of Higher Learning: ZHU XIAOMAN
Jiangsu Journalists' Training Centre: CHEN GUOJUN
Jiangsu Teachers' Training Centre for Pre-School Education: YANG JIUJUN
Jiangsu International Economic and Cultural Exchange Centre: SHEN ZHENGCHAI
Jiangsu Personnel Training Centre for Intellectual Property Rights Protection: CHEN LINGFU
Audiovisual Education Centre: ZHEN KEN

NANJING UNIVERSITY

22 Hankou Rd, Nanjing, Jiangsu 210093
Telephone: 6637651
Fax: 3302728

Founded 1902
State control
Language of instruction: Chinese
Academic year starts September

President: QU QINYUE
Vice-Presidents: CHEN YI, XIE LI, YUAN CHUANRONG, ZHANG YONGTAO, LI CUN
Librarian: BAO ZHONGWEN

Number of teachers: 2,200
Number of students: 14,000

Publications: *Journal (Humanities and Social Sciences), Journal (Natural Sciences), Journal of Computer Science, Journal of Inorganic Chemistry, Progress in Physics, Contemporary Foreign Literature, Approximation Theory and its Application, Mathematics in Higher Education, Geology in Higher Education, Research in Higher Education, Mathematics Review* (2 a year).

DEANS

Graduate School: SUN YISUI
Medical School: ZHANG ZHUXUAN
International Business School: ZHOU SANDUO
Adult Education School: YAN YONGQUAN
School of Humanities: DONG JIAN
School of Law: FAN JIAN (acting)
School of Foreign Studies: LIU HAIPING
School of Natural Sciences: GONG CHANGDE
School of Chemistry and Chemical Engineering: YAO TIANYANG
School of Technology: SUN ZHONGXIU
School of Geoscience: WANG DEZI
School of Life Science: ZHU DEXI

HEADS OF DEPARTMENTS

Astronomy: FANG CHENG
Atmospheric Science: NI YUNQI
Basic Medicine: ZHENG YISHOU
Biochemistry: ZHU DEXI
Biological Science and Technology: WANG WEIZHONG
Business Communications: (vacant)
Chemical Engineering: (vacant)
Chemistry: XIN XINGQUAN
Chinese Language and Literature: HU RUODING
Clinical Medicine: ZHENG YISHOU
Computer Science and Technology: CHEN SHIFU
Earth Science: CHEN JUN
Economics: LIU ZHIBIAO
Economic Law: ZHANG CUN
Electronic Science and Technology: SUN GUANGRONG
English: WANG SHOUREN
Environmental Science and Technology: JIN HONGJUN
Foreign Languages and Literatures: LIU HAIPING
Geoscience: CHEN KERONG
History: ZHANG XIEWEN
Information Management: ZHOU ZHIREN
International Accounting: LU ZHENFEI
International Economic Law: SUN NANSHENG
International Economy and Trade: LIU HEJUN
International Enterprise Management: (vacant)
International Finance: PEI PING
Land and Ocean Science: ZHANG HESHENG
Law: XIN HONGFEI
Library Science: ZOU ZHIREN
Macromolecular Materials Science and Engineering: XUE QI
Mass Communication: DING BOQUAN
Materials Science and Technology: MIN NAIBEN
Mathematics: SU WEIYI
Philosophy: LIN DEHONG
Physics: JIANG SHUSHENG
Political Science: ZHANG YONGTAO
Russian and Japanese Languages and Literature: SHI GUOXIONG
Sociology: SONG LINFEI
Western Studies: XU JUAN
Audio-Visual Centre: DAI WENLIN
Centre for Chinese and American Studies: CHEN YONGXIANG (Chinese Co-Dir)
Computer Centre: CHEN HUASHENG

NANJING UNIVERSITY OF ECONOMICS

128 Tielubeijie, Nanjing 210003
Telephone and Fax: (25) 3418207

Founded 1956, present status 1981
State control
Academic year: September to July

President: Dr XU CONGCAI
Vice-Presidents: LI SHIHUA, WANG SUITING, GAO YADONG, ZHANG ZHENGGANG, WANG JIAXIN
Librarian: DING DAKE

Library of over 500,000 vols
Number of teachers: 565
Number of students: 5,600 (incl. correspondence courses 3,000)

Publication: *Journal of Nanjing University of Economics.*

HEADS OF DEPARTMENTS

Trade and Economics: QIAO JUN
Accounting: WANG KAITIAN
Business Management: LI YAFEI
Finance: LING YINGBING
Tourism: LI YAFEI

Economics: LI QUANGEN
Law (incl. Political Science and Philosophy): CAO KE
Basic Courses: ZHU LINGMEI
Adult Education School: CUI XINYOU
China Training Centre for Grain Distribution Management: Dir XU CONGCAI

NANJING UNIVERSITY OF POSTS AND TELECOMMUNICATIONS

66 Xin Mofan Ma Lu, Nanjing, Jiangsu

Telephone: (25) 3492038
Fax: (25) 3492349
E-mail: nupt@njupt.edu.cn

Founded 1942

President: XIE LING
Vice-Presidents: ZHANG XIAOQIANG, YIE ZHANGZHAO, ZHANG SHUNYI, TANG JINTU
Librarian: YANG ZHUYING

Library of over 600,000 vols
Number of teachers: 768
Number of students: 4,300 undergraduates, 270 postgraduates

Publications: *NIPT Periodical, Reports on Science and Technology.*

HEADS OF DEPARTMENTS

Management Engineering: WANG LIANGYUAN
Communications Engineering: FENG GUANGZENG
Information Engineering: YU ZHAOMIN
Computer Science and Technology: WANG SHAOLI
Electrical Engineering; WANG SHUOPING
Basic Courses: CHEN HEMING
Social Science: XU RURONG
Physical Education: WANG KUANZHENG
Foreign Languages: HUAN SHUXIAN
Optical Fibre Communication Research Institute: SHEN JIANHUA
Information Network Technology Institute: ZHANG SHUNYI
Image Processing and Image Communications Institute: BI HOUJIE

PROFESSORS

BI HOUJIE, Image Communications
CAO WEI, Microwave Communications
CHEN TINGBIAO, Information Engineering
CHEN XI SHENG, Telecommunications Engineering
FENG GUANGZENG, Satellite Communications
HU JIANZHANG, Information Engineering
JU TI, Computer Engineering Science
KAN JIAHAI, Mathematics
LI BIAOQING, Telecommunications Engineering
LUO CHANGLONG, Computer Science
MI ZHENGKUN, Communications Engineering
QI YUSHENG, Mobile Communication
QIN TINGKAI, Electrical Engineering
SHEN JINLONG, Computer Communication
SHEN YUANLONG, Electrical Engineering
SUN JINLUN, Communications Engineering
TANG JIAYI, Computer Science
WANG SHAOLI, Computer Communication
WANG SHUOPING, Electrical Engineering
WU XINYU, Electrical Engineering
WU ZHIZHONG, Electrical Engineering
XU CHENGQI, Telecommunications Engineering
YANG ZHUYIING, Electrical Engineering
YIE ZHANGZHAO, Mathematics
YU ZHAOMIN, Information Engineering
ZHANG LIJUN, Telecommunications Engineering
ZHANG SHUNYI, Computer Communications
ZHANG XIAOQIANG, Communication Systems
ZHANG ZHIYONG, Electrical Engineering
ZHENG BAOYU, Telecommunications Engineering
ZHU XIUCHANG, Information Engineering

NANKAI UNIVERSITY

94 Weijin Rd, Tianjin 300071
Telephone: (22) 23508229
Fax: (22) 23502990
Founded 1919
President: Prof. HOU ZIXIN
Vice-Presidents: WANG WENJUN, CHENG JINPEI, PANG JINJU, LIU ZHENXIANG
Provost: Prof. CHE MINGZHOU
Librarian: Prof. FENG CHENGBO
Library of 2,500,000 vols
Number of teachers: 1,650
Number of students: 17,000
Publications: *Nankai Journal* (philosophy and social science edn, every 2 months), *Nankai History* (2 a year), *Nankai Economic Journal* (every 2 months).

DEANS OF COLLEGES

Economics: Prof. HAO SHOUYI
Life Sciences: Prof. GENG YUNQI
Medicine: Prof. ZHU TIANHUI
Chinese Language and Culture: Prof. WANG ZHENKUN
Adult Education: Prof. LIU XINTING
Humanities: Prof. CHEN YANQING
Law and Political Science: Prof. CHE MINGZHOU
International Business: Prof. XUE JINGXIAO
Chemistry: Prof. HE XIWEN
Mathematics: Prof. SHEN SHIYI
Information Science and Technology: Prof. QIN SHICAI

CHAIRMEN OF DEPARTMENTS

Chinese Language and Literature: Prof. CHEN HONG
History: Prof. ZHU FENGHAN
Economics: Prof. HE ZILI
Law: Prof. CHENG KAIYUAN
Risk Management and Insurance: Prof. LIU MAOSHAN
Finance: Prof. MA JUNLU
Foreign Languages and Literature: Prof. JIANG HUASHANG
Chemistry: Prof. ZHU ZHIANG
Physics: Prof. PANG SHIHONG
Electronics: Prof. WANG CHAOYING
Mathematics: Prof. SHEN SHIYI
Biology: Prof. GAO YUBAO
Microbiology: Prof. XING LAIJUN
Biochemistry and Molecular Biology: Prof. HUANG XICHUNG
Computer and Systems Science: Prof. LU GUIZHANG
Environmental Science: Prof. DAI SHUGUI
Sociology: Prof. HOU JUNSHENG
Political Science: Prof. CHE MINGZHOU
Philosophy: Prof. CHEN YANQING
Tourism: Prof. DU JIANG
International Economics and Trade: Prof. TONG JIADONG
Oriental Culture and Art: Prof. DU ZILING
Information Resources Management: Prof. ZHONG SHOUZHEN
Accounting: Prof. LIU ZHIYUAN
General Foreign Languages: Prof. ZHANG SHUDONG
Physical Education: Prof. XING CHUNGUI
Education in Marxist-Leninist Theory: Prof. LI JIANSONG
International Business: Prof. LI GUOJIN
Foreign Languages for Foreign Trade: Prof. WANG WENHAN

PROFESSORS

Department of Mathematics:

CHEN JIXIANG, Basic Mathematics
DING GUANGGUI, Basic Mathematics
FU FANGWEI, Probability and Mathematical Statistics
GUO JINGMEI, Basic Mathematics
HOU ZIXIN, Basic Mathematics
HU CHUANGAN, Basic Mathematics
HU JIANWEI, Computing Mathematics
HUANG YUMIN, Basic Mathematics
LI CHENGZHANG, Basic Mathematics
LIN JINKUN, Basic Mathematics
LIU GUANGXU, Basic Mathematics
LUO JIASHUN, Basic Mathematics
MENG DAOYI, Basic Mathematics
SHEN SHIYI, Probability and Mathematical Statistics
SUN CHE, Partial Computing Mathematics
TANG HUAIMIN, Computing Mathematics
WANG GONGSHU, Probability and Mathematical Statistics
WU RONG, Probability and Mathematical Statistics
WU XIZHI, Probability and Mathematical Statistics
ZHANG RUNCHU, Probability and Mathematical Statistics
ZHOU XINGWEI, Computing Mathematics
ZHOU XUEGUANG, Basic Mathematics

Department of Chemistry:

CAI ZUNSHENG, Physical Chemistry
CHEN RONGTI, Physical Chemistry
CHEN YOUQI, Computer Software
CHENG JINPEI, Organic Chemistry
CHENG PENG, Inorganic Chemistry
DENG GUOCAI, Physical Chemistry
GAN WEITANG, Analytical Chemistry
GU ZHUOYING, Physical Chemistry
GUAN NAIJIA, Physical Chemistry
HAN WEIHUAN, Computer Software
HE XIWEN, Analytical Chemistry
HU QINGMEI, Organic Chemistry
HU SHUNJU, Operational Research and Control Theory
HUANG JIAXIAN, Polymer Chemistry
HUANG SHUJI, Computer Software
HUANG YALOU, Pattern Recognition and Intelligence Control
JIANG ZONGHUI, Inorganic Chemistry
LAI CHENGMING, Structural Chemistry
LI HEXUAN, Physical Chemistry
LIANG ZHENYUAN, Computer Application
LIAO DAIZHENG, Inorganic Chemistry
LIN HUAKUAN, Physical Chemistry
LIN YIJIA, Computer Application
LIU JING, Computer Software
LIU JINGJIANG, Physical Chemistry
LIU RUITING, Computer Application
LIU YU, Physical Chemistry
LU GUIZHANG, Pattern Recognition and Intelligence Control
MENG JIBEN, Organic Chemistry
NU WENCHENG, Physics of Semiconductors and Semiconductor Devices
PAN FURANG, Physical Chemistry
PAN YINMING, Physical Chemistry
PIAO XIANHE, Physical Chemistry
QIN SHICAI, Physics of Semiconductors and Semiconductor Devices
SHAO SHUMIN, Electron, Ion and Electrovacuum Physics
SHEN HANXI, Analytical Chemistry
SHEN PANWEN, Inorganic Chemistry
SONG LICHENG, Organic Chemistry
TANG SHIXIONG, Organic Chemistry
TAO KEYI, Physical Chemistry
TU FENGSHENG, Theory and Application of Automatic Control
WANG CHAOYING, Physics of Semiconductors and Semiconductor Devices
WANG GENGLIN, Inorganic Chemistry
WANG JITAO, Inorganic Chemistry
WANG XIUFENG, Theory of and Application of Automatic Control
WANG YI, Theory and Application of Automatic Control
WANG ZHIBAO, Theory and Application of Automatic Control
WU GONGYI, Computer Application
XIANG SHOUHE, Physical Chemistry
XIE TAO, Chemical Engineering
YAN SHAOLIN, Radioelectronics
YUAN WANQING, Analytical Chemistry

YUAN ZHUZHI, Theory and Application of Automatic Control
YUN XIQIN, Physical Chemistry
ZHANG CHUNXU, Analytical Chemistry
ZHAO WEIJUN, Physical Chemistry
ZHAO XUEZHUANG, Physical Chemistry
ZHOU DAMING, Radioelectronics
ZHOU QING, Electron, Ion and Electro-vacuum Physics
ZHOU XIUZHONG, Organic Chemistry
ZHOU YONGQIA, Inorganic Chemistry
ZHU DUANHUI, Polymer Chemistry
ZHU RUIXIANG, Computer Software
ZHU SHENJIE, Organic Chemistry
ZHU SHOURONG, Physical Chemistry
ZHU SIYOU, Teaching of Computer Theory
ZHU ZHIANG, Physical Chemistry
ZUO JU, Polymer Chemistry
ZUO YUMIN, Organic Chemistry

Department of Physics:

CAI CHONGHAI, Theoretical Physics
CHANG SHUREN, Basic Physics
CHEN TIANLUN, Theoretical Physics
CHEN XIAOBO, Condensed Matter Physics
CHENG LU, Optics
DING DATONG, Condensed Matter Physics
HAN SHAOXIAN, Basic Physics
HE JINGGANG, Theoretical Physics
KANG HUI, Optics
LAN GUOXIANG, Condensed Matter Physics
LI XUEQIAN, Theoretical Physics
LI ZENGFA, Condensed Matter Physics
LI ZIYUAN, Basic Physics
LIU SIMIN, Condensed Matter Physics
LU JINGFA, Theoretical Physics
LU ZHENQIU, Theoretical Physics
LUO MA, Theoretical Physics
MEN ZHENYU, Experimental Physics
NING PINGZHI, Theoretical Physics
PAN SHIHONG, Condensed Matter Physics
TIAN JIANGUO, Condensed Matter Physics
WANG LEIGUANG, Biological Physics
WANG YUGUI, Condensed Matter Physics
WEN JINGSONG, Theoretical Physics
WENG XINGUANG
WU FANGXIANG, Optics
XU JINGJUN, Condensed Matter Physics
XUE ZHAONAN, Theoretical Physics
YANG WENXIU, Biophysics
ZHAN YUANLING, Optics
ZHANG CHUNPING, Condensed Matter Physics
ZHANG CUNZHOU, Condensed Matter Physics
ZHANG GUANGYIN, Condensed Matter Physics

Department of Electronics:

DING SHOUQIAN, Electron Optics
LIU YOUYING, Physics of the Electron, Ion and Vacuum
NIU WENCHENG, Electronic Material and Sensors
QIN SHICAI, Micro-Physics and Physics of Semi-Conductor and Semi-Conductor Devices
TAN GUANRONG, Radio Electronics
WANG CHAOYING, Physics of Semi-Conductor and Semi-Conductor Devices
YAN SHAOLIN, Superconductivity Electronics
ZHOU QING, Physics of the Electron, Ion and Vacuum

Department of Computer and Systems Science:

CHEN RUYU, Organic Chemistry
CHEN ZONGTING, Organic Chemistry
GAO RUYU, Organic Chemistry
HUANG RUNQIU, Pesticide Science and Agricultural Chemistry
JIN GUIYU, Pesticide Science
LI GUANGREN, Organic Chemistry
LI JING, Organic Chemistry
LI YUCHANG, Organic Chemistry
LI ZHENGMING, Pesticide Science and Agricultural Chemistry
LIAO RENAN, Organic Chemistry
LIN CHUI, Applied Chemistry
LIN SHAOFAN, Applied Computer Science
LIU LUNZU, Organic Chemistry
LIU TIANLIN, Pesticide Science and Agricultural Chemistry
LIU ZHUN, Organic Chemistry
SHANG ZHIZHEN, Agricultural Biology
SHAO RUILIAN, Organic Chemistry
SUN JIABIN, Organic Chemistry
TANG CHUCHI, Organic Chemistry
WANG DERUN, Physical Chemistry
WANG LIKUN, Pesticide Science and Agricultural Chemistry
WANG QINSUN, Organic Chemistry
XIE QINGLAN, Organic Chemistry
YUANG HUAZHENG, Pesticide Science and Agricultural Chemistry
YAO XINKAN, Applied Chemistry
ZHANG JINPEI, Applied Computer Science
ZHANG ZHENGZHI, Organic Chemistry
ZHAO ZHONGREN, Agricultural Biology

Departments of Biology, Microbiology and Biochemistry:

CHEN RUIYANG, Genetics
DU RONGQIAN, Molecular Biology
GAO YUBAO, Botany
GENG YUNQI, Molecular Biology
HUANG XITAI, Biochemistry
LI JIANMIN, Biochemistry
LI YUHE, Zoology
LING QILANG, Biochemistry
LIU ANXI, Cell Biology
LIU XIUYE, Zoology
MA ZULI, Animal Physiology
QIU ZHAOZHI, Zoology
REN GAIXIN, Entomology
TANG TINGGUI, Botany
WANG YUEWU, Microbiology
XING LAIJUN, Microbiology
ZHANG JINZHONG, Cell Biology
ZHANG ZILI, Genetics
ZHAO JIAN, Genetics
ZHAO XIAOJUN, Plant Biology
ZHENG LEYI, Entomology
ZHONG YICHENG, Zoology
ZHOU YULIANG, Microbiology
ZHU LIANGJI, Biochemistry

Department of Environmental Science:

CHEN PUHUA, Environmental Chemistry
CHEN TIANYI, Environmental Biology
CHEN XIULONG, Environmental Biology
DAI SHUGUI, Environmental Chemistry
FENG JIANXING, Environmental Chemistry
FU XUEQI, Environmental Chemistry
HUANG GUOLAN, Environmental Chemistry
ZHU TAN, Environmental Chemistry
ZHUANG YUANYI, Environmental Chemistry

Department of Chinese Language and Literature:

CHEN HONG, Ancient Chinese Literature
CUI BAOHENG, World Literature
FENG ZHIBAI, History of the Chinese Language
JIAO SHANGZHI, Modern and Contemporary Chinese Literature
LANG BAODONG, Literature and Art
LI JIANGUO, Ancient Chinese Literature
LIU HUIZHEN, Modern and Contemporary Chinese Literature
LIU SHUXIN, Modern Chinese
LUO ZONGQIANG, History of Chinese Literary Criticism
MA QINGZHU, Modern Chinese
REN ZIFENG, World Literature
SHI FENG, Languages and Literatures of Minority Nationalities
SUN CHANGWU, Ancient Chinese Literature
XIE HUIQUAN, History of Chinese Language
ZHANG YI, Editing

Department of Foreign Languages and Literature:

CAI LIWEN, English Literature
CHANG YAOXIN, English Literature
GU HENGDONG, English
GU QINAN, English Literature
LIU SHICONG, English Translation
XU QIPING, English Literature
ZHANG MAIZENG, English Linguistics
ZHENG RONGXUAN, English Linguistics

Department of History:

CAO ZHONGPING, Modern and Contemporary Chinese History
CHEN ZHENJIANG, Modern and Contemporary Chinese History
CHEN ZHIQIANG, Ancient and Medieval World History
FENG CHENGBO, Museology
FENG ERKANG, Ancient Chinese History
FU MEI, Museology
LI XISUO, Modern and Contemporary Chinese History
LI ZHIAN, Ancient Chinese History
LIU ZEHUA, Ancient Chinese History
LOU XIANGSHE, Modern and Contemporary World History
WANG DUNSHENG, Ancient and Medieval World History
WANG LIANSHENG, Ancient Chinese History
WANG YONGXIANG, Modern and Contemporary Chinese History
WEI HONGYUN, Modern and Contemporary Chinese History
ZHANG GUOGANG, Ancient Chinese History
ZHANG HONGXIANG, Ancient and Medieval World History
ZHANG XIYING, Museology
ZHU FENGHAN, Ancient Chinese History

Department of Sociology:

HOU JUNSHENG, Applied Sociology
LIU JUNJUN, Applied Sociology
WANG CHUHUI, Applied Sociology
YUE GUOAN, Applied Sociology
ZHANG XIANGDONG, Applied Sociology

Department of Political Science:

CAI TUO, Political Science
CHE MINGZHOU, Western Philosophy
LIU TINGYA, Political Science
WANG QINTIAN, Political Science
ZHU GUANGLEI, Political Science

Department of Philosophy:

CHEN YANQING, Marxist Philosophy
CUI QINGTIAN, Logic
FENG LICHANG, Natural Dialectics
LI LANZHI, Chinese Philosophy
LIU WENYING, Chinese Philosophy
LU SHENGFA, Chinese Philosophy
TANG GUIXIAN, Marxist Philosophy
TONG TAN, Aesthetics
WANG NANSHI, Marxist Philosophy

Department of Information Sources Management:

WANG ZHIJIN, Information Science
ZHONG SHOUZHEN, Library Science

Department of Law:

CHENG KAIYUAN, Civil Law
WANG WENTONG, Theory of Law
ZHOU CHANGLING, Theory of Law

Department of Oriental Culture and Art:

DU ZILING, Traditional Chinese Painting
FAN ZENG, Painting
PENG XIUYIN, Aesthetics
XUE BAOKUN, Literature and Art
ZHENG QINGHENG, Painting

Department of Economics:

GAO FENG, Political Economy
GUO HONGMAO, Urban Economy
HAO SHOUYI, Urban Economy
LI HONGSHUO, Marxist Economic Theory
LI WEIAN, Political Economy
LU XUEMING, Marxist Economic Theory
WAN CHENGLIN, Political Economy
WANG SHUYING, Political Economy
YANG YUCHUAN, Political Economy
ZHANG RENDE, Political Economy
ZHANG SHIQING, Political Economy
ZHU GUANGHUA, Political Economy

Department of International Economics and Trade:

CHEN YUE, World Economy
TONG JIADONG, World Economy
XUE JINGXIAO, World Economy
YU ZHIDA, World Economy
ZHANG QIANG, World Economy
ZHANG ZHICHAO, World Economy

Department of Management:

HAN JINGLUN, Business Management
JIN MINGLU, Business Management
QI YINFENG, Business Management
ZHANG JINCHENG, Business Management

Department of Finance:

LIU YUCAO, International Finance
MA JUNLU, International Finance
QIAN RONGKUN, International Finance

Department of Accounting:

BAO GUOMING, Auditing
CUI TONG, Auditing
ZHOU GAIRONG, Auditing

Department of Risk Management and Insurance:

LIU MAOSHAN, Money and Banking

Department of Tourism:

LI TIANYUAN, Tourism
LI WEISHU, English

Department of General Foreign Languages:

CHEN ZONGXIAN, German Language
HOU MEIXUE, English Language
MENG XIANMING, English Language
WANG SHIBIN, English Language
ZHANG CHENGYI, English Language
ZHANG SHUDONG, English Language

Department of Physical Education:

MENG QINGSHAN, Boxing
XING CHUNGUI, Volleyball
XUE DEHUI, Track and Field

Department of Education in Marxist-Leninist Theory:

LI JIANSONG, Political Economy
LI ZHENYA, History of the Chinese Communist Party
LIU JINGQUAN, History of the Chinese Communist Party
SHAO YUNRUI, History of the Chinese Communist Party
WANG YUANMING, Marxist Philosophy
YANG GUIHUA, Marxist Philosophy
YU FUQIAN, Ideological and Political Education
ZHANG HONGWEN, Socialist Construction

Institute of Mathematics:

CHEN YONGCHUAN, Basic Mathematics
GE MOLIN, Theoretical Physics
LONG YIMING, Basic Mathematics
SHU SHUZHONG, Basic Mathematics
XU SHURUN, Theoretical Physics
YAN ZHIDA, Basic Mathematics
ZHANG WEIPING, Basic Mathematics

Institute of Modern Optics:

CHEN WENJU, Optics and Optical Instruments
DONG XIAOYI, Optics and Optical Instruments
GUO ZHUANYUN, Optics and Optical Instruments
LIN MEIRONG, Optics and Optical Instruments
MU GUOGUANG, Optics and Optical Instruments
TANG GUOQING, Optics and Optical Instruments
WANG ZHAOQI, Optics and Optical Instruments
ZHAI HONGCHEN, Optics and Optical Instruments
ZHANG YANXIN, Optics and Optical Instruments

Institute of Thin Film Devices and Technology:

GENG JIANHUA, Physics of Semiconductors and Semiconductor Devices
LI CHANGJIAN, Physics of Semiconductors and Semiconductor Devices
SUN ZHONGLIN, Physics of Semiconductors and Semiconductor Devices
XIONG SHAOZHEN, Physics of Semiconductors and Semiconductor Devices

Institute of Machine Intelligence:

WANG QINGREN, Pattern Recognition and Intelligence Control

Institute of Polymer Chemistry:

GUO XIANQUAN, Polymer Chemistry and Physical Chemistry
HE BINGLIN, Polymer Chemistry and Physical Chemistry
HUANG WENQIANG, Polymer Chemistry and Physical Chemistry
LI CHAOXING, Polymer Chemistry and Physical Chemistry
LI HONG, Polymer Chemistry and Physical Chemistry
LIN XUE, Polymer Chemistry and Physical Chemistry
MA JIANBIAO, Polymer Chemistry and Physical Chemistry
SHI ZUOQING, Polymer Chemistry and Physical Chemistry
SONG MOUDAO, Polymer Chemistry and Physical Chemistry
YAN HUSHENG, Polymer Chemistry and Physical Chemistry
ZHANG BANGHUA, Polymer Chemistry and Physical Chemistry

Institute of New Energy Material Chemistry:

DONG WEIYI, Physical Chemistry
SONG DEYING, Inorganic Chemistry
YAN JIE, Inorganic Chemistry
ZHANG YUNSHI, Inorganic Chemistry
ZHI YUAN, Polymer Chemistry and Physical Chemistry

Institute of Molecular Biology:

CHEN CHANGZHI, Biomedical Materials and Enzyme Engineering
CHEN DEFENG, Molecular Genetics
GAO CAICHANG, Genetic Engineering
YU YAOTING, Biomaterials and Enzyme Engineering

Institute of History:

CAI JIMING, Political Economy
CAO ZHENLIANG, Political Economy
CHEN ZONGSHENG, Political Economy
DING CHANGQING, History of the Chinese Economy
JI RENJUN, Economic Geography
LIU FODING, History of the Chinese Economy
LIU XIN, Political Economy
PANG JINJU, Political Economy
PENG ZHENYUAN, Political Economy
WANG GUANGWEI, Political Economy
ZHOU LIQUN, Political Economy

Institute of Economics:

BAO JUEMIN, Economic Geography
CAI JIMING, Basic Theory and Methodology of Economics
CAO ZHENLIANG, Real Estate Economics and Management
CHANG XIUZE, Micro-economic Operation of Socialist Economics
CHEN ZONGSHENG, Development Economics
DING CHANGQING, History of Contemporary Chinese Economy
GU SHUTANG, Theory of the Socialist Economy
JI RENJUN, Economic Geography
LIU FODING, History of Contemporary Chinese Economy
PANG JINJU, Macro-economic Operation of Socialist Economics
ZHU XIUQIN, History of Chinese Economy

Institute of International Economics:

CHEN LIGAO, World Economy
GAO ERSEN, International Economic Law
GONG ZHANKUI, World Economy
TENG WEIZAO, World Economy
XIAN GUOMING, World Economy
XIONG XINGMEI, World Economy
ZHANG YANGUI, World Economy

Institute of Population and Development:

LI JINGNENG, Population Economics
TAN LIN, Population Economics
WU GUOCUN, Population Economics

College of Chinese Language and Culture:

WANG ZHENKUN, Modern Chinese Language
XIE WENQING, Modern Chinese Language

College of Medical Science:

ZHU TIANHUI, Medical Science

ATTACHED RESEARCH INSTITUTES

Institute of History: Dir Prof. NAN BINGWEN.
institute of Ancient Chinese Books and Culture: Dir Prof. ZHAO BOXIONG.
Institute of Comparative Literature: Dir Prof. YE JIAYING.
Institute of Economics: Dir Prof. CHEN ZONGSHENG.
Institute of International Economics: Dir Prof. XIAN GUOMING.
Institute of Transportation Economics: Dir Prof. SANG HENGKANG.
Institute of International Insurance: Dir Prof. DUAN KAILING.
Institute of Population and Development: Dir Prof. TAN LIN.
Institute of the Taiwanese Economy: Dir Prof. LI HONGSHUO.
Institute of International Economic Law: Dir Prof. GAO ERSEN.
Institute of Mathematics: Dir Prof. ZHOU XINGWEI.
Institute of Molecular Biology: Dir Prof. GENG YUNQI.
Institute of Modern Physics: Dir Prof. ZHANG GUANGYIN.
Institute of Modern Optics: Dir Prof. MU GUOGUANG.
Institute of Thin Film Devices and Technology: Dir Prof. SUN ZHONGLIN.
Institute of Machine Intelligence: Dir Prof. HAN WEIHUAN.
Institute of Polymer Chemistry: Dir Prof. ZHANG ZHENGPU.
Institute of Elemento-Organic Chemistry: Dir Prof. LI JING.
Institute of New Energy Material Chemistry: Dir Prof. ZHANG YUNSHI.
Centre for APEC Studies: Dir Prof. XUE JINGXIAO.
Centre for International Studies: Dir Prof. FENG CHENGBO.
Centre for Sino-Canadian Studies: Dir Prof. CHEN BINGFU.
Centre for Japanese Studies: Dir Prof. YANG DONGLIANG.
Centre for American Studies: Dir Prof. FENG CHENGBO.
Centre for Latin-American Studies: Dir Prof. HONG GUOQI.
Centre for Northeast Asian Studies: Dir Prof. CHENG YUE.
Centre for Transnational Corporation Studies: Dir Prof. XIONG XINGMEI.
Centre for Pesticide Engineering: Dir Prof. LI ZHENGMING.

NORMAN BETHUNE UNIVERSITY OF MEDICAL SCIENCES

8 Xinmin St, Changchun 130021, Jilin
Telephone: (431) 5645911
Telex: 83016
Fax: (431) 5644739

Founded 1939
State control
President: Prof. WU JIAXIANG
Vice-Presidents: Prof. ZHU XUN, Prof. FAN HONGXUE, Prof. LI YULIN, Prof. YAN YONGFU, Assoc. Prof. CHANG ZHONGXIAN, Assoc. Prof. YOU HONG
Dean of Education Department: Assoc. Prof. NIE SUBIN
Chief Librarian: Assoc. Prof. CHEN QIAN
Library of 485,000 vols, 3,570 periodicals
Number of teachers: 2,099
Number of students: 4,400
Publications: *Journal* (every 2 months), *Foreign Medicine—Gerontology* (every 2 months), *Journal of Stroke and Neurological Diseases* (quarterly), *Clinical Journal of Liver and Biliary Diseases* (quarterly).

DEANS

Basic Medical Sciences: YU YONGLI
First Clinical College: YU DESHUN
Second Clinical College: MU DELIN
Third Clinical College: GAO FENGTONG
Preventive Medicine: SHU SHIJIE
Endemic Diseases: LI CAI
Stomatology: XU YONGZHONG

PROFESSORS

School of Basic Medical Sciences:
CHENG, Y. Y., Pathological Anatomy
DU, K. Q., Physiopathology
FU, N., Immunology
HONG, M., Biochemistry
JIN, B., Anatomy
LI, F., Anatomy
LI, Y. L., Pathological Anatomy
LI, Z. B., Electron Microscope
LIU, M., Physiology
LU, Z., Pharmacology
NIE, Y. X., Histology and Embryology
WANG, S., Physiology
WANG, S. L., Histology and Embryology
WEI, J. J., Organic Chemistry
WEI, Y. D., Organic Chemistry
WEN, Z. G., Biology
WU, D. C., Anatomy
WU, G. X., Inorganic Chemistry
WU, J. X., Pathological Anatomy
YANG, G. Z., Immunology
YANG, H. Y., Biochemistry
YANG, S. J., Pharmacology
YU, Y. L., Immunology
ZHAO, X. J., Physiopathology
ZHONG, G. G., Physiology
ZHONG, R. Y., Pharmacology
ZHOU, Z. Z., Histology and Embryology
ZHU, S., Physiopathology
ZHU, X, Immunology

School of Preventive Medicine:
FAN, H. X., Radiation Toxicology
GUO, S. P., Epidemiology
JIN, Y. K., Radiation Injuries
JU, G. Z., Radiation Biology
LI, X., Radiation Biology
LIU, J., Radiation Toxicology
LIU, S. Z., Radiation Biology
SHU, Q., Epidemiology
SU, S. J., Radiation Protection
SUI, Z. R., Nutriology
WAN, X. Z., Radiation Injuries
WEI, J., Radiation Biology
YU, H., Radiation Toxicology
ZHANG, M., Radiation Biology
ZHANG, Y. M., Labour Health
ZHAO, H., Biostatistics
ZHAO, Q., Nutriology

First Clinical College:
BU, G. X., Oto-rhino-laryngology
CAI, S., Oto-rhino-laryngology
CAO, L. N., General Surgery
DU, B. D., Oto-rhino-laryngology
FENG, W., Paediatrics
FU, W. Y., Paediatrics
GUO, X. F., Oto-rhino-laryngology
GUO, X. W., Cardiovascular Diseases
HAN, G. X., Laboratory Tests
HUO, S. F., Paediatrics
HU, K. H., Paediatrics
JI, Z. D., Chest Surgery
LE, J., Gynaecology and Obstetrics
LI, S., Haematology
LI, T. Y., Paediatrics
LI, X., Traditional Chinese Medicine
LIANG, B. Y., Psychology
LIANG, Z. X., Paediatrics
LIN, S. H., Neurology
LIU, D. M., Cardiovascular Diseases
LIU, F. C., Neurosurgery
LIU, G. J., Oncology
LU, J., Paediatrics
LU, M. D., Infectious Diseases
QIAO, R. J., Ophthalmology
RAO, M., Neurology
SONG, G. P., Diseases of Digestive System
SUO, J. X., Neurosurgery
TAN, K. A., Respiratory Diseases
TAN, Y., Laboratory Tests
TAN, Y. Q., General Surgery
WANG, C. K., Neurosurgery
WANG, F., Anaesthesia
WANG, G. C., Internal Medicine
WANG, J., Diseases of Digestive System
WANG, M., Neurology
WANG, Y., CAT Scanners
WANG, Y. D., General Surgery
XU, G. B., Electrodiagnosis
XU, J., Ophthalmology
XU, X., Infectious Diseases
XU, X., Internal Medicine
XU, X. X., Orthopaedics
YANG, J. W., Cardiovascular Diseases
YANG, J. Y., Paediatrics
YANG, Z. Q., Oto-rhino-laryngology
YI, Y. L., Haematology
YIN, G., Internal Medicine
YU, G. D., Electrodiagnosis
ZHAN, Q. Q., Infectious Diseases
ZHANG, J. B.
ZHANG, L., Dermatology
ZHANG, S. D., Internal Medicine
ZHANG, S. Q., Neurology
ZHANG, X., Orthopaedics
ZHANG, Y., Neurology
ZHAO, D. C., Cardiovascular Diseases
ZHAO, J., Neurology
ZHAO, W., General Surgery
ZHAO, Z., General Surgery
ZHENG, P. R., Internal Medicine
ZHOU, B., Oncology
ZHU, D., Radiotherapy

Second Clinical College:
AN, Q. Z., Gynaecology and Obstetrics
GAO, F., General Surgery
GUAN, W., General Surgery
HAN, G., Paediatrics
HE, G. Z., Respiratory Diseases
HUANG, D. H., General Surgery
JIN, X. Z., Dermatology
LI, H., Ophthalmology
LI, S. R., Gynaecology and Obstetrics
LI, Z., Traditional Chinese Medicine
LIN, S. Q., Internal Medicine
LIU, W. C., Internal Medicine
LIU, Y. R., Paediatrics
MA, Y. D., Oto-rhino-laryngology
QI, B., Orthopaedics
QIU, T. S., General Surgery
SONG, Y. F., Internal Medicine
TIAN, R. G., Chest Surgery
WANG, N., General Surgery
WANG, Z. D., Gynaecology and Obstetrics
WEI, S. L., General Surgery
WU, S. D., Traditional Chinese Medicine
XU, Y. H., Oto-rhino-laryngology
YANG, X. Q., Gynaecology and Obstetrics
ZHANG, M. F., Dermatology
ZHANG, W., Internal Medicine
ZHANG, W. Y., Gynaecology and Obstetrics
ZHANG, Y., Neurology
ZHANG, Z. D., General Surgery
ZHAO, Z. G., Child Health
ZHOU, J., Neurosurgery
ZHU, F. Q., Gynaecology and Obstetrics

Third Clinical College:
CHEN, Y., Internal Medicine
CHENG, L., Radiotherapy
CIU, Z. M., Cardiovascular Diseases
DUAN, D. S., Orthopaedics
FENG, J., Diseases of Digestive System
GAO, F., Nuclear Medicine
HE, E. S. T., General Surgery
HE, S. L., General Surgery
JANG, H. Z., Orthopaedics
KAN, X. X., Laboratory Tests
LI, Z., Orthopaedics
LIU, B. Y., General Surgery
LIU, Y., Orthopaedics
LIU, Y. H., Orthopaedics
LU, X., Urological Surgery
MENG, X. M., General Surgery
SONG, X. L., Chest Surgery
SUN, D., Orthopaedics
SUN, R. W., Laboratory Tests
SUN, X. D., Stomatology
WAN, L. Z., Radiotherapy
WAN, M., Electrodiagnosis
WANG, M. C., Neurosurgery
WANG, M. X., Internal Medicine
WANG, S. Q., Traditional Chinese Medicine
WANG, S. X., Paediatrics
WANG, W., General Surgery
WANG, W. Z., Laboratory Tests
XIAO, Y. L., Nuclear Medicine
YANG, H. S., Radiotherapy
YU, C., Paediatrics
YU, S. F., Physiotherapy
YU, W., Gynaecology and Obstetrics
ZHAN, X. M., Haematology
ZHANG, D., General Surgery
ZHANG, M., Internal Medicine
ZHAO, E. C., Paediatrics
ZHAO, F., Radiotherapy
ZHAO, H. X., Chest Surgery
ZHAO, L., Internal Medicine
ZHAO, S. H., Traditional Chinese Medicine
ZHEN, X., Oto-rhino-laryngology
ZHENG, Z. L., General Surgery
ZHOU, F., Internal Medicine

School of Dentistry:
CAI, J. J., Oral Paediatrics
LIANG, T., Orthodontics
LIU, J., Oral Surgery
LIU, Z., Oral X-Ray
OUYANG, J., Oral Pathology
WANG, G. Y., Oral Internal Medicine
XU, Y. Z., Oral Surgery

Research Institute of Endemic Diseases:
AN, R. G., Analytical Chemistry
HOU, L. Z., Biochemistry
JIANG, X. L., Analytical Chemistry
LI, G. S., Pathology
WANG, F., Pathology
YAN, W., Biochemistry
YANG, T. S., Biochemistry

NORTH CHINA ELECTRIC POWER UNIVERSITY

204 Qingnian Rd, Baoding, Hebei Province 071003
Campuses in Baoding and Beijing
Telephone: (312) 5024951 (Baoding), (10) 69795666 (Beijing)
Fax: (312) 5016156 (Baoding), (10) 69795105 (Beijing)
E-mail: dicncepu@public.bdptt.he.cn
Founded 1958
Controlled by State Power Corporation
Academic year: September to July
President: XU DAPING

Vice-Presidents: LIU JIZHEN, YANG ZHIYUAN, CHEN ZHIYE, WANG WANJIN
Chief Administrative Officer: AN LIANSUO
Librarians: KONG QINGPIN (Assistant Librarian, Baoding), LI XIAOYUN (Beijing)

Number of teachers: 864
Number of students: 9,801

Publications: *Journal* (4 a year), *Information on Electric Power* (4 a year), *Modern Electricity* (4 a year).

HEADS OF DEPARTMENT

Electric Power Engineering (Baoding): LI HEMING
Thermal Power Engineering (Baoding): HAN PU
Mechanical Engineering (Baoding): TANG YUNXI
Environmental Engineering (Baoding): ZHAO YI
Electronic Engineering (Baoding): GAO QIANG
Economics (Baoding): QI JIANXUN
Fundamental Science (Baoding): GUAN BAOGUO
Management (Beijing): XIAO GUOQUAN
Power Engineering (Beijing): WANG QINGZHAO
Information (Beijing): LIU KEQIN
Social Science (Beijing): ZHANG WENHUA
Electric Power (Beijing): QU HENAN

NORTHEAST FORESTRY UNIVERSITY

26 Hexing Rd, Harbin 150040, Heilongjiang Province

Telephone: (451) 2190015
Fax: (451) 2110146

Founded 1952

President: Prof. LI JIAN
Vice-Presidents: Prof. HUO JIANYU, Prof. YANG CHUANPING, Prof. CHAO JUN, Assoc. Prof. CHEN WENBIN, Assoc. Prof. HU WANYI
Dean of Graduate School: FAN DELIN
Librarian: WU QIJUN

Library of 570,000 vols
Number of teachers: 846
Number of students: 5,482 (307 postgraduates)

Publications: *Bulletin of Botany Research, Chinese Wildlife, Forest Fire Protection, Science of Logging Engineering, Forestry Finance and Accounting, Journal of Northeast Forestry University* (in English), *Forestry Research in Northern China* (in English).

HEADS OF COLLEGES AND DEPARTMENTS

College of Forest Resources and Environment: Prof. WANG FENGYOU
College of Wildlife Resources: Prof. MA JIANZHANG
College of Forest Products: Prof. WANG FENGHU
College of Economics and Management: Prof. LIU GUOCHENG
College of Humanities: Prof. WANG YAOXIAN
College of Civil Engineering: Prof. ZHANG YINGE
College of Electromechanical Engineering: Prof. LI DONGSHENG
College of Landscape Architecture: Prof. ZHUO LIHUAN
Normal College: Prof. SONG YE
Department of Forestry Engineering: Prof. WANG LIHAI
Department of Foreign Languages: Prof. PAN ZHENDUO
Department of Physical Education: Prof. MO SHONGSHAN
Correspondence College: CAO XIAOGUANG

PROFESSORS

DING, B., Silviculture
GE, M., Wood Science, Wood Chemistry
HU, Y., Forest Entomology
HUANG, Q., Plan Statistics
JIANG, M., Forestry Economics
LI, G., Forest Resources
LI JIAN, Wood Science and Technology, Wood Surface Chemistry
LI JINGWEN, Ecosystems, Community Ecology
LIU, G., Financial Accounting
LU, R., Wood and Composites Technology and Manufacturing
MA, J., Wildlife Management, Natural Reserves
MA, L., Forest Machinery
NIE, S., Phytocommunity Ecology, Phytotaxonomy
SHAO, L., Forest Disease Epidemiology, Taxonomy of Pathogenic Fungi
SHI, J., Forest Engineering
WANG, F., Ecosystems, Community Ecology
WANG, Y., Ecosystems, Physical and Chemical Ecology
WANG, Z., High Yield Forests
XIAN, K., Forest Protection, Water and Soil Conservation
XIANG, C., Taxonomy of Pathogenic Fungi, Management of Forest Diseases
YUE, S., Pest Control
ZHOU, X., Ecosystems, Economic Ecology
ZHOU, Y., Phytocommunity Ecology, Phytotaxonomy
ZHU, G., Forestry Vehicles, Sawing Equipment
ZU, Y., Unlinear Phytoecology

NORTHEASTERN UNIVERSITY

No. 11, Lane 3, Wenhua Lu, Heping District, Shenyang, Liaoning 110006

Telephone: (24) 3893000
Fax: (24) 3892454
E-mail: neu@ramm.neu.edu.cn

Founded 1923 as Northeastern University; became Northeast University of Technology in 1950; reverted to former name in 1993
Controlled by Ministry of Metallurgical Industry
Academic year: September to July (two semesters)

President: HE JICHENG
Prof. JIANG ZHONGLE
Vice-Presidents: YANG PEIZHEN, WANG ZHI, WANG QIYI, ZHOU GUANGYOU, LIU JIREN, WANG WANSHAN
Provost: Prof. DUAN YUEHU
Dean of General Affairs: Assoc. Prof. MENG QINGXIAN
Librarian: Prof. YANG HUAI

Library of 1,650,000 vols
Number of teachers: 1,950
Number of students: 18,814 undergraduates, 1,807 postgraduates

Publications: *Journal, Economics and Management of Metallurgical Enterprise, China Engineer, Control and Decision, Basic Automation.*

DEANS

Graduate School: Prof. HE JICHENG
Liaoning Branch: Prof. MAO TIANYU
Qinhuangdao Branch: Prof. WANG ZHENFAN
Adult Education School: Prof. ZHAO LIANGZHEN
College of Business Administration: Prof. BI MENGLIN
College of Humanities and Law: Prof. PENG DINGAN
College of Mechanical Engineering: Prof. WANG DEJUN
College of Resources and Civil Engineering: Prof. CHEN BAOZHI
College of Materials and Metallurgical Engineering: Prof. HAO SHIMING
College of Information Science and Engineering: Prof. GU SHUSHENG
College of Gold Metallurgy: Prof. YANG LI

ATTACHED RESEARCH INSTITUTES

Computer Software Research Centre: Dir Prof. LIU JIREN.

Automation Research Centre: Dir Prof. CAI TIANYOU.

National Laboratory of Automated Tandem Rolling: Dir Prof. WANG GUODONG.

NORTHERN JIAOTONG UNIVERSITY

Shangyuancun, Xizhimenwai, Beijing 100044
Telephone: 63240500
Fax: 62255671

Founded 1909
State control
Languages of instruction: Chinese and English
Academic year: September to January, February to July

President: WANG JINHUA
Vice-Presidents: ZHOU QIMING, TAN ZHENHUI, YAN WUER, NING BIN
Chief Administrative Officer: ZHEN JICHUN
Librarian: SHI JUNCHEN

Number of teachers: 2,044
Number of students: 7,662

Publication: *Journal* (quarterly).

HEADS OF INSTITUTE

Telecommunications and Control Engineering: RUAN QIUQI
Civil Engineering: XIA HE
Mechanical Engineering and Electrification: YANG CHAO
Economic, Industrial and Commercial Management: JU SONGDONG
Liberal Arts and Science: ZHAO XUEYI
Transport Management: WU YUJIAN
Adult Education: ZHANG PINGZHI

ATTACHED RESEARCH INSTITUTES

Information Science Research Institute: Dir YUAN BAOZONG.

Management Science Research Institute: Dir YE QINGYU.

Applied Systems Analysis Research Institute: Dir YIN XIANGYONG.

Engineering Mechanics Research Institute: Dir GUO ZHANQI.

Lightwave Technology Research Institute: Dir JIAN SHUISHENG.

Automation Research Institute: Dir ZHANG ZHONGYI.

NORTHWEST UNIVERSITY

Tai Bai Bei Lu, Xian 710069, Shaanxi Province

Telephone: 7215036
Telex: 70005
Fax: 7212323

Founded 1912
Academic year: September to August.

President: Prof. HAO KEGANG
Vice-Presidents: LIU SHUNKANG, WANG JIAN, WANG SHUANCAI, CHEN ZONGXING
Librarian: Prof. ZHOU TIANYOU

Library of 1.6 million vols
Number of teachers: 1,135
Number of students: 10,466 (incl. 571 postgraduates)

Publications: *Journal* (Arts and Social Science, Natural Sciences, quarterly), *Annual Report of Lu Xun Studies, Literature of the Tang Dynasty, Middle East, Studies in the History of North Western China, Studies in Higher Education.*

HEADS OF DEPARTMENTS

Chinese Language and Literature: Prof. YANG CHANGLONG

History: Prof. ZHOU WEIZHOU
Philosophy: Prof. SHEN ZHONGYING
Foreign Languages and Literature: Prof. ZHOU SHIZHONG
Mathematics: Prof. GAO ZHIMIN
Physics: Prof. LIU JUCHENG
Chemistry: Prof. WANG JIANHUA
Chemical Engineering: Prof. LI BAOZHANG
Biology: Prof. SUN LIANKUI
Geology: Prof. MEI ZHICHAO
Geography: Prof. YE SHUHUA
Computer Science: Prof. LIU DEAN
Law: Prof. ZHANG TIANJIE
Library and Information Science: Prof. ZHOU TIANYOU
Tourism: Prof. ZHANG HUI
Economic Management: Prof. HE LIANCHENG
Electronics: Prof. WANG DAKAI

NORTHWESTERN POLYTECHNICAL UNIVERSITY

Xi'an, Shaanxi 710072
Telephone: (29) 8493119
Telex: 70185
Fax: (29) 8491000
E-mail: office@nwpu.edu.cn

Founded 1957 by merger of Northwestern Engineering College and Xi'an Institute of Aeronautics
State control
Languages of instruction: Chinese and English
Academic year: September to July (2 semesters).

Honorary President: Prof. JI WENMEI
President: Prof. DAI GUANZHONG
Vice-Presidents: Prof. HUA JUN, Prof. HI BAOSHENG, Prof. XU DEMIN, Prof. WU BIN, Prof. GAO DEYUAN, Prof. YANG HAICHENG
Dean of Studies: Prof. REN GUANGHUA
Director of Foreign Affairs: Prof. JIANG JIESHENG
Librarian: Prof. ZHANG HONGCAI

Number of teachers: 1,000, incl. 234 professors
Number of students: 8,373, incl. 1,700 postgraduates

Publications: *University Journal* (quarterly), *Mechanical Science and Engineering* (quarterly), *Journal of Theoretical and Applied Mechanics* (quarterly).

DEANS

Graduate School: Prof. XU DEMIN
College of Management: Prof. XU DEMIN
College of Continuing Education: Prof. NA ZHENCHUN
College of Marine Engineering: Prof. MA YUANLIANG
College of Astronautics: Prof. YUAN JIANPING
College of Civil Aviation Engineering: Prof. LIU YUANYONG (acting)
College of Test Pilot Training: Prof. DING YUANJIE (acting)
College of Materials Science: (vacant)
College of Electronics: (vacant)

HEADS OF DEPARTMENTS

Applied Mathematics: Prof. NIE TIEJUN
Mechanical Engineering: Prof. LIU GENG
Aircraft Engineering: Prof. LÜ GUOZHI
Aero-Engines: Prof. CAI YUANHU
Aeronautical Manufacturing Engineering: Prof. YANG HAICHENG
Social Sciences: Prof. BAI BAOLI
Foreign Languages: Prof. FENG JIANLI
Architectural and Civil Engineering: Prof. ZHANG DESI
Engineering Mechanics: Prof. JIAO GUIQIONG
Applied Physics: Prof. LU FUYI

PROFESSORS

AI, S., Welding
AN, J. W., Automatic Control
BAI, B. L., Political Economy
CAI, Q., CAD/CAM Technology
CAI, T. M., Computational Thermophysics
CAI, Y. H., Aeroengines
CHEN, B. X., Flight Mechanics
CHEN, G. D., Drafting
CHEN, M., Gyroscope and Inertial Navigation
CHEN, Z., Metallic Materials and Heat Treatment
CHENG, L. F., Physical Metallurgy
DAI, G. Z., Theory and Application of Automatic Control
DANG, J. B., Solid Mechanics
DENG, J. H., Aircraft Engineering
DENG, X. J., Engine Machinery Manufacturing
DONG, D. Q., Sensing Technology and Signal Processing
DONG, G. M., Electronic Engineering
DONG, G. Z., Linguistics (English)
DONG, M. A., Aeroengines Technology
DONG, Z. X., Computer Information and Control
DUAN, L. Y., Welding
DUAN, Z. M., Signal Circuit and Systems Engineering
FAN, S. Q., Aeroengines
FAN, X. Y., Computer Applications
FANG, Z. D., Mechanical Engineering
FENG, J. L., Linguistics (Japanese)
FU, H. Z., Physical Metallurgy
FU, L. Z., Mathematics
GAO, D. Y., Computer Science and Engineering
GAO, H., Flight Mechanics
GAO, M. T., Drafting
GAO, X. G., Command Systems Engineering
GAO, Y. X., Physical Metallurgy
GAO, Z. H., Aerodynamics
GU, J. L., Vibration Engineering
GUI, Y. Y., Aircraft Manufacturing Engineering
GUO, L., Electronics and Communication
GUO, X. Z., Library Science
GUO, Y. Q., Electrical Technology
HAN, Z. G., Linguistics (German)
HAO, C. Y., Space Vehicle Design
HE, C. A., Automatic Control
HE, G. Y., Metallic Materials and Heat Treatment
HE, H. C., Computer and Artificial Intelligence
HE, H. Q., Rocket Engines
HE, K. M., Aircraft Aerodynamics
HE, M. Y., Signal Circuit and Systems Engineering
HE, X. S., General Mechanics
HONG, Y. L., Radio Technology
HOU, Y., Applied Mathematics
HU, Z. G., Computer Software
HUA, J., Aerodynamics
HUANG, J. G., Applied Electronic Technology
HUANG, W. D., Physical Metallurgy
HUANG, Z. X., Radio Technology
JI, W. M., Theoretical Mechanics
JIANG, G. L., Automatic Control of Flight Vehicles
JIANG, J. S., Vibration Engineering
JIANG, Y., Automatic Control
JIAO, G. Q., Solid Mechanics
JIE, W. Q., Physical Metallurgy
JING, Z. L., Theory and Application of Control
KANG, F. J., Physical Metallurgy
LAI, X. X., Casting Engineering
LAN, L. W., Applied Polymer Science
LEI, W. Y., Applied Polymer Science
LI, B. X., Rocket Engines
LI, B. Y., Acoustic Engineering
LI, B. Y., Acoustic Engineering
LI, F. W., Aerodynamics
LI, H. J., Metallic Materials and Heat Treatment
LI, J. G., Physical Metallurgy
LI, N., Aeroengines
LI, T. Y., Detection Technology
LI, W. J., Structural Mechanics and Optimization
LI, W. L., Physics
LI, W. Y., Ball Games
LI, X. L., Applied Mathematics
LI, X. P., Satellite Communication and Navigation
LI, Y. J., Automatic Control
LI, Y. L., Fracture Mechanics
LI, Y. Z., Applied Polymer Science
LI, Y. Z., Mathematics
LI, Z. M., Electrical Engineering
LI, Z. S., Underwater Technology
LIAN, X. C., Aeroengines
LIAO, M. F., Aeroengines
LIN, Q. A., Automatic Control
LIU, B., Aero-engines
LIU, D., Structural Mechanics
LIU, G., Mechanical Design
LIU, H. L., Underwater Technology
LIU, L., Casting
LIU, R. G., Mechanical Drawing
LIU, S. L., Thermal Engineering
LIU, S. P., Mechanics
LIU, X. H., Structural Mechanics
LIU, X. Q., Underwater Technology
LIU, Y. Y., Engineering Fracture
LIU, Z. W., Aeroengines
LU, C. D., Engines Technology
LU, F. Y., Physics
LU, G. Z., Structural Mechanics
LUO, J., Theory and Application of Automatic Control
LUO, X. B., Mathematics
LUO, Z. J., Metal Forming
MA, H. J., Radio Technology
MA, R., Aeroengine Design
MA, Y. L., Underwater Acoustics Engineering
MA, Y. Q., Aeroengines
MENG, Q. L., Computer Science
NA, Z. C., Radio Technology
NIE, T. J., Computational Mathematics
QIAO, S. R., Metallic Materials and Heat Treatment
QIAO, Z. D., Computational Aerodynamics
REN, G. H., Fluid Transmission and Control
REN, Z., Automatic Control
REN, Z. G., Mechanical Manufacturing
SHEN, Y. W., Mechanical Design
SHI, H. S., Radio Communication
SHI, J. M., Structural Mechanics
SHI, Y. K., Electrical Equipment
SHI, Z. K., Theory and Application of Automatic Control
SONG, J. S., Radio Technology
SONG, S. X., Physics
SU, C. W., Applied Mathematics
SUN, J. C., Applied Acoustics and Noise Control Engineering
TANG, C. R., Metal Forming
TANG, D. Y., Aeroengines
TANG, S., Flight Mechanics
TIAN, C. S., Metallic Materials and Heat Treatment
TIAN, Y. T., Physics
TIAN, Y. Y., Applied Electronic Technology
TIAN, Z., Applied Mathematics
TIAN, Z. R., Solid Mechanics
WANG, B. H., Space Vehicle Design
WANG, G. W., Electronic Technology
WANG, J. P., Aerodynamics
WANG, J. X., Aircraft Design
WANG, L., Fuzzy Control
WANG, L., Rocket Engines
WANG, R. X., Numerically Controlled Machine Tools
WANG, W., Automatic Control
WANG, W. L., Electronic Engineering
WANG, Y. G., Control Engineering in Aeroengines
WANG, Y. S., Radio Technology
WEI, B. B., Materials Science
WEI, S. M., CAD/CAM Technology
WENG, Z. Q., Navigation Systems
WU, B., Radio
WU, L., Welding
WU, S. C., Metal Forming
XI, Z. X., Aerodynamics
XIANG, J. L., Detection Technology

XIAO, S. T., Structural Mechanics of Flight Vehicles
XIE, C. J., Underwater Acoustics
XIE, Y. Q., Applied Electronic Technology
XIN, K., Linguistics (English)
XU, D. M., Analysis and Design of Control Systems
XU, J. D., Microwave and Antenna Technology
XU, J. N., Aircraft Design
XU, N. P., Information Systems Engineering
YAN, C. J., Aeroengines
YAN, X. M., Machine Tool Automation
YAN, X. Y., Aeroengines
YAN, Y. S., Underwater Acoustics Engineering
YANG, G. C., Physical Metallurgy
YANG, G. Y., Linguistics (English)
YANG, H., Metal Forming
YANG, H. C., CAD/CAM Technology
YANG, J. J., Underwater Acoustics Engineering
YANG, N. C., Aircraft Design
YANG, Y. F., Linguistics (English)
YANG, Y. N., Aerodynamics
YANG, Y. Q., Metallic Materials and Heat Treatment
YANG, Z. S., Computer Science
YE, F., Radio Transmission
YE, T. Q., Computational Mechanics
YE, Z. Y., Machinery Manufacturing
YU, B. Z., Electronic Engineering
YU, H. Q., Metal Forming
YU, Q. H., Rocket Engines
YU, R. L., Machinery Manufacturing
YU, X. R., Applied Polymer Science
YUAN, J. P., Flight Mechanics
YUAN, P. Y., Aeroengines
ZENG, Q. F., Aeroengines
ZHANG, D., Space Vehicle Design
ZHANG, D. H., CAD/CAM Technology
ZHANG, G. C., Physical Metallurgy
ZHANG, H. C., Theory and Application of Automatic Control
ZHANG, H. F., Thermal and Solar Energy Engineering
ZHANG, H. G., Linguistics (German)
ZHANG, K. D., Structural Strength
ZHANG, K. H., Applied Polymer Science
ZHANG, K. S., Solid Mechanics
ZHANG, L. T., Physical Metallurgy
ZHANG, Q., Automatic Control
ZHANG, T. C., CAD/CAM Technology
ZHANG, W., Applied Polymer Science
ZHANG, X. K., Machinery Design and Manufacturing
ZHANG, Y. Z., Automatic Control
ZHAO, J. W., Underwater Acoustics and Electronic Engineering
ZHAO, R. C., Signal and Graph Processing
ZHAO, X. P., Solid Mechanics
ZHENG, S. T., Solid Mechanics
ZHENG, X. L., Metal Fatigue and Fracture
ZHONG, X. D., Aircraft Design
ZHOU, F. Q., Aircraft Technology
ZHOU, W. C., Physical Metallurgy
ZHOU, X. H., Aeroengines
ZHOU, X. S., Computer Applications
ZHU, D. P., Structural Mechanics
ZHU, M. Q., Measurement Technology in Mechanical Engineering
ZHU, Y. A., Computer Applications
ZUO, P. C., Aerodynamics

ATTACHED RESEARCH INSTITUTES AND CENTRES

Institute of Aircraft Structures: Dir Prof. YANG ZHICHUN.

Institute of Pilotless Mini-Aircraft: Dir Prof. DANG JINBAO.

Institute of Computer Science and Information Engineering: Dir Prof. KANG JICHANG.

Centre for Automatic Control Research: Dir Prof. LOU JIAN.

Centre for Composite Material Research: Dir Prof. ZHANG LITONG.

Institute of Vibration Engineering: Dir Prof. JIANG JIESHENG.

Centre for Aerofoil Research: Dir Prof. QIAO ZHIDE.

Institute of Artificial Intelligence: Dir Prof. HE HUACAN.

Institute of Electronic Science: Dir Prof. XU JIADONG.

Institute of Monitoring and Control for Rotating Machinery and Wind Turbines (NPU and TU-Berlin): Dirs ROBERT GASCH, LIAO MINGFU.

Institute of Material and Thermal Technology: Dir Prof. FU HENGZHI.

Institute of Natural Dialectics: Dir Prof. SHIU YUNHUA.

Institute of Underwater Technology: Dir Prof. MA YUANLIANG.

Institute of Higher Learning: Dir Prof. BAO GUOHUA.

Institute of Computer-Integrated Circuit Manufacturing Systems (CIMS): Dir Prof. GAO DEYUAN.

Institute of Architectural Design: Dir Prof. YUAN MINGZHAO.

Institute of Rare Earth Permanent Magnetism Motor (REPM): Dir Prof. LI ZHONGMING.

Institute of High Technology Applications: Dir Prof. LIN QIAO.

Institute of Applied Mathematics: Dir Prof. NIE TIEJUN.

Institute of Aeronautical Equipment Systems: Dir Prof. ZHANG ZILIE.

Institute of Mechanical Electronic Engineering: Dir Prof. WANG RUNXIAO.

Institute of Public Security Technology: Dir Prof. LIU YUANYONG.

Shaanxi Provincial Friction Welding Engineering and Technology Centre: Dr DUAN LIYU.

Institute of Friction Welding: Dir Prof. DUAN LIYU.

Shaanxi Provincial CAD Engineering and Technology Centre: Dr YANG HAICHENG.

CAD/CAM Centre: Dir Prof. ZHANG DINGHUA.

Centre for Industrial Robots: Dir Prof. SUN SHUDONG.

Shaanxi Provincial Fan and Pump Engineering Research Centre (F & P SERC): Dir Dr XI DEKE.

Computer Centre: Dir Prof. WANG FUBAO.

Software Development Centre, NPU: Dir Dr ZHANG YANYUAN.

Centre for Moulding: Dir Prof. MA ZE'EN.

Centre for Computational Thermophysics Research: Dir Prof. SHEN HUILI.

Centre for Electromagnetism Studies: Dir Prof. WAN WEI.

Centre for Astronautical Technology: Dir Prof. ZHOU JUN.

Centre for Active Control Technology (ACT): Dir Prof. JIN XIYUE.

Centre for Target Prediction: Dir Prof. ZHANG HONGCAI.

Centre for Research and Development into High Technology Forging and Casting: Dir Prof. LUO ZIJIAN.

Centre for Microcesmic Detection: Dir Assoc. Prof. SONG SHIXIAN.

Centre for Data Processing: Dir Prof. LI ZHONGWEI.

Centre for Global Positioning Systems: Dir Prof. YUAN JIANPING.

PEKING UNIVERSITY

1 Loudouqiao, Hai Dian, Beijing 100871
Telephone: 62752114
Fax: 62751207

Founded 1898
Languages of instruction: Chinese and English
Academic year: September to January, February to June.

President: CHEN JIAER
Vice-Presidents: WANG YIQIU, MIN WEIFANG, CHI HUISHENG, MA SHUFU, HE FANGCHUAN, CHEN ZHANGLIANG, LIN JUNJING
Registrar: LI KE'AN
Librarian: LIN BEIDIAN

Library of 4,610,000 vols
Number of teachers: 2,513
Number of students: 24,000

Publication: *Peking University Academic Journal.*

HEADS OF DEPARTMENTS

School of Mathematical Science: JIANG BOJU
Department of Mechanics: FANG JING
Department of Physics: GAN ZIZHAO
Department of Geophysics: HUANG JIAYOU
Department of Technical Physics: YE YANLIN
Department of Electronics: XIANG HAIGE
Department of Computer Science and Technology: YANG FUQING
College of Molecular and Chemical Engineering: ZHAO XINSHENG
College of Life Sciences: ZHOU ZENGQUAN
Department of Geology: LI MAOSONG
Department of Urban and Environmental Sciences: YANG KAIZHONG
Department of Psychology: WANG LEI
Department of Chinese Language and Literature: FEI ZHENGGANG
Department of History: WANG TIANYOU
Department of Archaeology: LI BOQIAN
Department of Philosophy: YE LANG
School of International Studies: LIANG SHOUDE
School of Economics: YAN ZHIJIE
Guanhua School of Management: LI YINING
Department of Law: WU ZHIPAN
Department of Information Management: WU WEICI
Department of Political Science and Public Administration: WANG PUJU
Department of Sociology: WANG SHIBIN
Department of Oriental Studies: WANG BANGWEI
Department of Western Languages and Literature: LIN CHENGQIN
Department of Russian Language and Literature: REN GUANXUAN
Department of English Language and Literature: HU JIALUAN
Department of Arts: YE LANG
School of Marxism: CHENG ZHANAN

There are also 82 research institutes.

PEOPLE'S UNIVERSITY OF CHINA

39 Haidian Rd, Haidian District, Beijing 100872
Telephone: 62563399
Telex: 222653
Fax: 62566374

Founded 1937
State control
Academic year starts September.

President: LI WENHAI
Vice-Presidents: LI SHAOGONG, LI KANGTAI, DU HOUWEN, LUO GUOJIE, YANG DEFU, ZHENG HANGSHENG, MA SHAOMENG
Librarian: DAI YI

Number of teachers: 1,595
Number of students: 14,289 (incl. 1,284 postgraduates)

Publications: *Teaching and Research*, *Economic Theory and Business Management*, *Information Service News*, *Population Research*, *Archival News* (every 2 months), *The History of Qing Dynasty Research News-*

letter, *International Journalism World* (quarterly), *Learned Journal of the People's University of China* (every 2 months).

HEADS OF DEPARTMENTS

Philosophy: CHEN XIANDA
International Politics: YIE ZONGKUI
Economics: YU XUEBEN
Economic Planning: LIU CHENGRUI
Statistics: YUAN WEI
Industrial Economics: DENG RONGLING
Agricultural Economics: ZHOU ZHIXIANG
Commercial Economics: LI JINXUAN
College of Labour and Personnel Administration: ZHAO LUKUAN
Finance and Banking: HAN YINGJIE
Economic Information Management: CHEN YU
Law: ZENG XIANYI
Journalism: HE ZIHUA
Population Studies: GUO ZHIGANG
Chinese Language and Literature: CHEN CHUANCAI
History: GU XUESHUN
Land Management: ZHOU ZHIXIANG
Accounting: ZHU XIAOPING
Investment Economics: LANG RONGSHEN
Commodity Studies: ZHANG DALI
International Economics: (vacant)
College of Archives: CAO XICHEN
Sociology: ZHENG HANGSHENG
Foreign Languages: JIANG CHUNYU
Centre of Physical Education: LI DEYIN
College of Correspondence Education: FANG JIA
Centre of Teaching Chinese as a Foreign Language: LIU JIN

ATTACHED INSTITUTES

Institute of Economic Studies: Dir HU NAIWU

Institute of Foreign Economy and Management: Dir HUANG MENGFAN

Institute of East European Studies: Dir ZHOU XINCHENG

Institute of Sociology: Dir SHA LIANXIANG

Institute of Population Theory: Dir GUO ZHIGANG

Institute of Chinese Language and Writing: Dir HU RUICHANG

Institute of the History of the Qing Dynasty: Dir LI WENHAI

Institute of Legal Research: Dir WANG YIYING

Institute of Public Administration: Dir QI MINGSHAN

Institute of Soft Sciences: Dir LI ZHONGSHANG

QINGHAI NATIONALITIES COLLEGE

25 Ba Yi Rd, Xining, Qinghai 810007

Telephone: 76803

Founded 1949

President: DUO JIE JIAN ZAN
Vice-Presidents: ZHUO MA CAI DAN, Assoc. Prof. YU DEYUAN, SHAO DESHAN
Librarian: YAO KERANG

Library of 550,000 vols
Number of teachers: 330
Number of students: 1,572

Publication: *Journal of Qinghai Nationalities Institute, Qinghai Nationalities Research.*

HEADS OF DEPARTMENTS

Chinese: HU ANLIANG
Politics: MEI JINCAI
Law: SUN XIANZHEN
Minority Nationalities Languages and Literature: GE MING DUO JIE
Physics and Chemistry: WU QIXUN
Mathematics: NIAN KUN
Preparatory Courses: QU TAI
Basic Courses: ZHANG WENKUI

PROFESSORS

FENG, Y., Theory of Arts
HU, A., Ancient Chinese
MI, Y., History of Chinese
ZHU, K., Modern Literature

QINGHUA UNIVERSITY

1 Qinghuayuan, Beijing 100084
Telephone: 62561144
Telex: 226172
Fax: 62562768

Founded 1911

President: Prof. WANG DAZHONG
Vice-Presidents: Prof. LIANG YOUNENG, Prof. YU SHOUWEN, Prof. SUN JIMING, Prof. GUAN ZHICHENG, Prof. HE JIANKUM
Provost: Prof. YU SHOUWEN
Librarian: Prof. LIU GUILIN

Number of teachers: 3,311
Number of students: 14,125 (incl. 3,694 graduate)

Publication: *Journal* (every 2 months).

DEANS

Graduate School: Prof. YU SHOUWEN
School of Sciences: Prof. ZHOU GUANGZHAO
School of Economic Management: Prof. ZHU RONGJI
School of Continuing Education: Prof. MA ZUYAO
School of Architecture: Prof. HU SHAOXUE
School of Humanities and Social Sciences: Prof. TENG TENG (acting)

HEADS OF DEPARTMENTS

Architecture: Prof. LI DEXIANG
Urban Planning: Prof. ZENG GUANGZHONG
Civil Engineering: Prof. LIU XILA
Hydraulic Engineering: Prof. LEI ZHIDONG
Environmental Engineering: Prof. HAO JIEMING
Mechanical Engineering: Prof. LU ANLI
Automobile Engineering: Prof. CHENG QUANSHI
Thermal Engineering: Prof. WU ZANSONG
Precision Instruments and Mechanology: Prof. ZHOU ZHAOYING
Electrical Engineering: Prof. HAN YINGDUO
Information Electronics: Prof. DONG ZAIWANG
Computer Science and Technology: Prof. WANG DINGXIN
Automation: Prof. HU DONGCHENG
Engineering Physics: Prof. JING ZHAOXIONG
Engineering Mechanics: Prof. QIAN ZHANGZHI
Chemical Engineering: Prof. DAI YOUYUAN
Applied Mathematics: Prof. XIAO SHUTIE
Modern Applied Physics: Prof. GU BINGLIN
Chemistry: Prof. LIAO MUZHENG
Biological Science and Technology: Prof. SUI SENFANG
Economics: Prof. LI ZINAI
Management Engineering: Prof. XU GUOHUA
Management Information Systems: Prof. ZHAO CHUNJUN
International Trade and Finance: Prof. ZHAO JIAHE
Social Sciences: Prof. LI RENHAI
Foreign Languages: Prof. CHENG MUSHENG
Chinese Language and Literature: Prof. XU BAOGEN

SHANDONG INSTITUTE OF ECONOMICS

4 East Yanzishan Rd, Jinan 250014, Shandong

Telephone: (531) 8934161

Founded 1958

President: Prof. HU JIJIAN
Vice-Presidents: Prof. LIU SHIFAN, Prof. REN HUI, LI RENQUAN
Librarian: LI ZIRUI

Number of teachers: 322
Number of students: 2,118

Publications: *Shandong Economy, Accountant, Statistics and Management.*

HEADS OF DEPARTMENTS

Industrial and Commercial Economics: LONG ZENGRUI
Planning and Statistics: ZHANG XIAOFEI
Financial Accounting: LIU XUEYAN
Finance and Banking: TANG RUOYAN International Trade: XIE HONGZHONG
Computer Science and Management: ZHAO XIQING

SHANDONG UNIVERSITY

25 Shanda Rd S, Jinan 250100, Shandong Province

Telephone: 643861
Telex: 39196
Fax: 642167

Founded 1901

Languages of instruction: Chinese and English
Semesters starting September and February
President: Prof. PAN CHANGDONG
Vice-Presidents: Prof. ZENG FANREN, Prof. MA CHANGYI, Prof. JIANG MINHUA, Prof. QIAO YOUMEI
Librarian: AN JINYU

Library of 2,100,000 vols
Number of teachers: 1,831
Number of students: 9,000

Publications: *Wen Shi Zhe* (Literary, History and Philosophy Journal), *Shandong Da Xue Xue Bao* (University Journal). *Folklore Studies, ICHING Studies, American Literature Studies, Russian Literature.*

DEANS

Weihai College: Prof. XU YUQI
Economics and Business: Prof. ZHUANG DEJUN
Chemistry: Prof. GU YUEZHU

HEADS OF DEPARTMENTS

Chinese Language and Literature: KONG FANJIN
History: LI DEZHENG
Foreign Languages and Literature: LI NAIKUN
Scientific Socialism: ZHAO MINGYI
Philosophy: TAN XINTIAN
Economics: CHEN NAISHENG
Law: FENG DIANMEI
Mathematics: YUAN YIRANG
Computer Science: WANG JIAYE
Physics: HE MAO
Optics: CHEN WENYI
Chemistry: GAO ZILI
Biology: LU HAOQUAN
Microbiology: QIAN XINMIN
Sociology: XU JINGZE
Scientific Management: MO WENCHUAN

ATTACHED INSTITUTES

Institute of Literature, History and Philosophy: Dir Prof. LU HUIJUAN
Institute of Modern American Literature: Dir Prof. WANG YUGONG
Institute of Research in Ancient Texts: Dir Prof. DONG ZHIAN
Institute of Crystal Materials: Dir Prof. JIANG MINHUA
Institute of Mathematics: Dir Prof. PAN CHANGDONG
Institute of Microbiology: Dir Prof. QIAN XINMIN
Institute of Infra-red Remote Sensing: Dir Prof. HU XIERONG
Institute of Theorectical Chemistry: Dir Prof. JU GUANZHI
Institute of ECIWO Biology: Dir Prof. ZHANG YINGQING
Institute of ICHING Studies: Dir Prof. LIU DAJUN

Institute of New Materials: Dir Prof. CHEN JIANHUA
Institute of High-Energy Physics: Dir Prof. WANG CHENGRUI
Institute of Photo-Electronic Devices: Dir Prof. MA HONGLEI
Institute of Colloid Chemistry: Dir Prof. WANG GUOTING
Institute of Computing and Information: Dir Prof. WANG JIAYE
Institute of Conservation and the Environment: Dir Prof. WANG HUIREN
Institute of Electronic Technology: Dir Prof. CHENG GANGWU

SHANGHAI INTERNATIONAL STUDIES UNIVERSITY

550 Dalian Rd (W), Shanghai 200083
Telephone: 65311900
Telex: 33505
Fax: 65420225

Founded 1949 as Foreign Language College

President: DAI WEIDONG
Vice-Presidents: TAN JINGHUA, WU YOUFU, SHENG YULIANG, ZHU JIANGUO

Library of 1,100,000 vols
Number of students: 4,000

Publications: *Foreign Languages* (every 2 months), *Comparative Literature* (2 a year), *Arabian World* (quarterly), *Media in Foreign Language Instructions* (quarterly), *Foreign Language World* (quarterly), *International Survey* (quarterly), *English Self-study* (monthly)

Departments of English, Russian, French, German, Japanese, Spanish, Arabic language and literature, international journalism, international economics and trade, Chinese as a foreign language, communications.

SHANGHAI JIAO TONG UNIVERSITY

1954 Hua Shan Rd, Shanghai 200030
Telephone: 62812444
Fax: 62821369

Founded 1896
Academic year: September to July.

President: XIE SHENGWU
Vice-Presidents: SHENG HUANYE, BAI TONGSHUO, YE QUYUAN, SHEN WEIPING, ZHANG SHENGKUN, XU XIAOMING
Director of President's Office: ZHANG WEI
Librarian: CHEN ZHAONEN

Library of 1,826,000 vols
Number of teachers: 2,889
Number of students: 13,882 (incl. 2,831 post-graduates)

Publication: *Journal* (also in English, every 2 months).

HEADS OF SCHOOL

School of Naval Architecture and Ocean Engineering: LI RUNPEI
School of Power and Energy Resources Engineering: XU JIJUN
School of Electronics and Information Technology: XI YUGENG
School of Electric Power Engineering: HOU ZHIJIAN
School of Materials Science and Engineering: WU JIANSHENG
School of Machinery Engineering: YAN JUNQI
School of Science: SHI ZHONGCI
School of Life Sciences and Technology: TANG ZHANGCHENG
School of Humanities and Social Sciences: YE DUNPING
School of Civil Engineering and Mechanics: LIU ZHENGXING
School of Chemistry and Chemical Engineering: TANG XIAOZHENG
School of Management: ZHANG XIANG
School of Foreign Languages: ZHENG SHUTANG
Department of Physical Education: SUN QILING
Department of Plasticity Technology: RUAN XUEYU

RESEARCH INSTITUTES

Structural Mechanics Institute of Naval Architecture and Ocean Engineering: Dir JIN XIANDING.

Hydromechanics Institute of Naval Architecture and Ocean Engineering: Dir WANG GUOQIANG.

Institute of Underwater Engineering: Dir ZHU JIMAO.

Institute of Harbour Engineering and Hydraulic Engineering: Dir SHI ZHONG.

National Key Ocean Engineering Laboratory: Dir LI RUNPEI.

Research Centre for Vibration, Shock and Noise (National Key Laboratory): Dir HAN ZHUSHUN.

Institute of Engineering Thermophysics and Energy Resources: Dir CHENG HUIER.

HDTV Institute: Dir HUANG BAOLIN.

Institute of Image Processing and Pattern Recognition: Dir SHI PENGFEI.

Institute of Optical Fibre Technology: Dir YE AILUN.

Institute of Large-Scale Integrated Circuits: Dir LIN ZHENGHUI.

Institute of Computer Networks: Dir YANG CHUANHOU.

Institute of Composite Materials: Dir SHUN KANG.

National Key Laboratory of Base Metals: Dir GU MINGZHI.

Institute of Manufacturing Technology and Automation: Dir HU DEJIN.

Institute of Production Systems and Control: Dir CHAI JIANGUO.

Institute of Computer Integrated Systems: Dir MA DENGZHE.

Institute of Motor Design and Manufacturing: Dir ZHANG JIANWU.

Institute of Electromechanical Control: Dir FENG ZHENGJIN.

Institute of Robotics: Dir LU TIANSHENG.

Institute of Mechanical Engineering Design and Automation: Dir YE QINGTAI.

Institute of Graphic Technology and Computer-Aided Design: Dir JIANG SHOUWEI.

Institute of Mechanics and Automated Design: Dir HUANG WENZHEN.

Institute of Mathematics, Science and Technology: Dir FANG AINONG.

Institute of Optics and Photonics: Dir CHEN YINGLI.

Institute of Condensed Material Physics: Dir ZHENG HANG.

Institute of Solar Energy: Dir GUO LIHUI.

Institute of Space and Astrophysics: Dir YOU JUNHAN.

Institute of Biomedical Instruments: Dir CHEN YAZHU.

Institute of Health Science and Technology: Dir ZHU ZHANGYU.

Institute of Ecology and the Environment: Dir XU DAQUAN.

Institute of Social Science and Engineering: Dir ZHANG YUYU.

Institute of Science, Technology and Social Development: Dir QIAN XUECHENG.

Institute of Ideological and Political Education and Ethics: Dir YU YAPING.

Institute of Philosophy and Public Policy: Dir LIU FENG.

Institute of Architectural Design: Dir LIU SHUOTAN.

Institute of Polymeric Materials: Dir XU XI.

Institute of Pure Chemical Industry: Dir HUANG DEYIN.

Institute of Environmental Chemical Industry: Dir JIA JINPING.

Institute of Systems Engineering: Dir WANG HUANCHEN.

Institute of Human Resources Management: Dir LI DE.

SHANGHAI MEDICAL UNIVERSITY

138 Yixueyuan Lu, Shanghai 200032
Telephone: (21) 64041900
Fax: (21) 64037268

Founded 1927
State control

President: YAO TAI
Vice-Presidents: PENG YUWEN, CAO SHILONG, CHEN JIE, XIE RONGGUO, WANG WEIPING
Chief Administrative Officer: HU TIANNE
Librarian: CHEN GUIZHANG

Library of 490,000 vols
Number of teachers: 8,778
Number of students: 5,074

Publication: *Acta* (6 a year).

SHANGHAI SECOND MEDICAL UNIVERSITY

280 South Chongqing Rd, Shanghai 200025
Telephone: 3286590
Telex: 30314
Fax: 3202916

Founded 1952
Languages of instruction: Chinese, English, French
Academic year: September to July

Chancellor: WANG YIFEI
Vice-Chancellors: Prof. XUE CHUNLIANG, Assoc. Prof. FAN GUANRONG, Assoc. Prof. CHEN ZHIXING
Registrar: Prof. ZHU MINGDE
Librarian: YU XICHEN

Library of 420,000 vols
Number of teachers: 3,379
Number of students: 5,000

Publications: *Journal of Shanghai Second Medical University* (in Chinese and English), *Journal of Clinical Paediatrics* (in Chinese), *Chinese Journal of Endocrinology and Metabolism* (in Chinese), *Shanghai Journal of Immunology* (in Chinese).

DEANS

College of Basic Medical Sciences: Prof. TANG XUEMING
Faculty of Clinical Medicine in Rui Jin Hospital: Prof. LI HONGWEI
Faculty of Clinical Medicine in Ren Ji Hospital: Prof LI XUEMING
Faculty of Paediatrics and Clinical Medicine in Xin Hua Hospital: Prof. ZHANG YICHU
School of Stomatology: Prof. QUI WEILIU
Faculty of Clinical Medicine in No. 6 People's Hospital: Prof. LIN FAXIONG
Department of Social Sciences: DING YINKUI
Junior Medical College in Bao Gang Hospital: SHEN ZEMING
Health School: WANG TONGMIN

ATTACHED INSTITUTES

Basic Medical Research Centre of SSMU

Research and Training Centre for Reproductive Medicine of Shanghai

Research Centre for Clinical Pharmacology of SSMU

Research Centre for Traditional Chinese Medicine of SSMU

Shanghai Biomaterial Research and Test Centre
Shanghai Institute of Biomedical Engineering
Shanghai Institute of Burns
Shanghai Institute of Digestive Diseases
Shanghai Institute of Endocrinology
Shanghai Institute of Haematology
Shanghai Institute of Hypertension
Shanghai Institute of Immunology
Shanghai Institute of Orthopaedics and Traumatology
Shanghai Institute of Paediatrics
Shanghai Institute of Plastic and Reconstructive Surgery
Shanghai Institute of Stomatology
Shanghai Municipal Key Laboratory of Medical Technology

There are five affiliated hospitals.

SHANGHAI TIEDAO UNIVERSITY

450 Zhennan Lu, Shanghai 200333
Telephone and fax: (21) 2506812

Founded 1995 by merger of Shanghai Institute of Railway Technology and Shanghai Railway Medical College
State control
Academic year: September to July (two terms)

President: Prof. CHEN GUANMAO
Vice-Presidents: Prof. ZHU GUANGJIE, Prof. LI MENG, Prof. MA WENZENG, Prof. MAO YONGJIANG, Prof. XU LONG, Assoc. Prof. SUN ZHANG
Registrar: Prof. MIAO RUNSHEN
Librarian: Prof. WU WENQI

Library of 850,000 vols, 2,900 periodicals
Number of teachers: 1,164
Number of students: 6,354

Publication: *Journal*.

HEADS OF DEPARTMENTS

Mechanical and Electrical Engineering: Prof. QI WENXING
International Economics and Management: Prof. PEN YUNO
Medicine: Prof. XU LONG
Information Science and Technology: Prof. ZHANG SHUJING
Civil Engineering: Prof. CHAO XUQIN
Foreign Languages: Prof. HUA WEI

PROFESSORS

AI, Y., Hygienics
CAI, N., Physiology
CAI, T., Surgery
CHAO, X., Bridge, Tunnel and Structural Engineering
CHEN, D. L., Dermatology
CHEN, D. Y., Fluid Drive
CHEN, H., Mechanical Engineering
CHEN, J., Railway Locomotives and Rolling Stock
CHEN, S., Railway Locomotives and Rolling Stock
CHENG, S., Pathology
DENG, N., Internal Medicine
DU, Q., Electrification and Automation
FAN, P., Mechanical Engineering
FENG, Z. Q., Histology and Embryology
FENG, Z. Z., Railway Vehicles
GONG, J., Railway Locomotives and Rolling Stock
GUO, D. F., Railway Location and Construction
GUO, D. P., Orthopaedics
HOU, H., Neuropathology
HU, B., Anatomy
HU, K., Bridge, Tunnel and Structural Engineering
HU, M., Computer Communication
HUA, W., English
HUANG, S., Transport Management
JI, L., Transport Management
JIANG, E., Internal Combustion Engines
LE, S., Stomatology
LI, D., Surgery
LI, H., Mathematics
LI, J., Ophthalmology
LI, M., Applied Computer Technology
LI, S., Internal Medicine
LI, Y., Mechanics
LIN, Z., Ultrasonic Diagnosis
LIU, C., Internal Medicine
LIU, Q., Hydraulic Pressure Technology
LIU, X., Railway Automation
LIU, Y., Electrical Appliances
LIU, Z., Paediatrics
LU, G., Civil Engineering
LU, Y., Civil Engineering
NIE, C., Fluid Drive and Control
PAN, K., Stomatological Surgery
PENG, Y. O., Economics
QI, W., Internal Combustion Engines
QIU, W., Medical Genetics
REN, J., Transport Management
RUAN, Y., Computer Engineering
SHAO, B., Power Electronics Technology
SHEN, P., Railway Locomotives and Rolling Stock
SHEN, Z., Infectious Diseases
SHI, S., Stomatology
SONG, J., Anaesthesia
SUN, P., Surgery
SUN, Q., Railway Location and Construction
SUN, S., Parasitology
SUN, Y., Laborary Testing
TAN, B., Mechanical Engineering
TAO, S., Computer Engineering
TAO, Z., Fluid Drive
TONG, D., Wheel-rail System
WANG, B., Applied Computer Technology
WANG, B., Surgery
WANG, D., Telecommunications
WANG, F., Railway Vehicles
WANG, Q., Railway Electrification and Automation
WANG, R., Mathematics
WANG, W., Railway Engineering
WANG, Y., Biochemistry
WU, F., Telecommunications
WU, J., Railway Location and Construction
WU, W. Q., Transport Signals and Control
WU, W. Y., Psychiatry
WU, X., Railway Location and Construction
WU, Z. K., Electrical Appliances
WU, Z. R., Civil Engineering
XIA, Y., Mechanics
XIONG, W., Mechanics
XU, T., Mechanics
YANG, G., Mechanics
YANG, H. C., Histology and Embryology
YANG, H. Y., Transport Management
YANG, X., Civil Engineering
YE, E., Hygienics
YIN, L., Mechanics
YU, W., Pharmacology
YUAN, S., Stomatology
ZHANG, D. X., Railway Locomotives and Rolling Stock
ZHANG, D. Z., Railway Locomotives and Rolling Stock
ZHANG, J., Gynaecology and Obstetrics
ZHANG, S. C., Stomatology
ZHANG, S. J., Telecommunications and Information Processing
ZHANG, W. C., Civil Engineering
ZHANG, X., Mechanics
ZHANG, Y. J., Electrical Technology
ZHANG, Y. Z., Internal Medicine
ZHANG, Z., Railway Locomotives and Rolling Stock
ZHAO, S., Politics
ZHENG, G., Stomatology
ZHENG, T., Power Electronics Technology
ZHOU, Z., Stomatological Surgery
ZHU, J., Railway Location and Construction
ZHU, M., Mechanics
ZHU, P., Theoretical Physics
ZHU, X., Mathematics
ZONG, G., Structural Engineering

SHANGHAI UNIVERSITY

1220 Xin Zha Rd, Shanghai 200041
Telephone: (21) 2553062
Fax: (21) 2154780

Founded 1983

Chancellor: Prof. WANG SHENGHONG
Deputy Chancellor: Prof. LIN JIONGRU
Vice-Chancellors: Prof. CAO ZHONGXIAN, Prof. LI MINGZHONG
University Dean: Prof. WENG SHIRONG
University Co-ordinator for Foreign Affairs and International Programmes: ZHONG GUOXIANG

Number of teachers: 1,200, incl. 296 profs
Number of students: 7,500

Publications: *Journal, Sociology, Secretariat.*

PRESIDENTS

College of Engineering: Prof. MA GUOLIN
College of Liberal Arts: Prof. WANG XIMEI
College of Business: Prof. JIANG JIAJUN
College of Fine Arts: Prof. LI TIANXIANG
College of International Business: Prof. LU GUANQUAN
College of Political Science: Prof. WANG XIMEI

HEADS OF DEPARTMENTS

College of Engineering:
- Machinery: Prof. SHEN JIMIN
- Computer Science and Microwave: Prof. YU SHIQUAN
- Radio Technology: Prof. FU XUANYING
- Electrical Technology: Prof. XIE SHEN
- Engineering Technology: Prof. ZHANG SONGSHAN

College of Liberal Arts:
- Chinese Language and Literature: Prof. WU HUANZHANG
- History: Prof. YUAN JUNQING
- Law: Prof. XU YIREN
- Sociology: Prof. SHEN GUANBAO
- Secretarial Science: Prof. WANG LIXIN
- Archive Science: Prof. ZHANG JUNYAN
- Information Science: Prof. LI QI

College of Business:
- Business Administration and Technology: Prof. WANG NAILIANG
- Trade and Economics: Prof. CHEN XINJIAN
- Accounting and Statistics: Prof. HONG JIAMIN
- Food: Prof. YANG ZHONGYI
- Applied Computer Science: Prof. WANG XILIN

College of International Business:
- English: Prof. ZHANG GUANPEI
- International Business and Economics: Prof. WANG GUOMING
- Japanese: Prof. SHEN SHOUZHEN

College of Fine Arts:
- Art Design: Prof. WANG YIXIAN
- Traditional Chinese Painting: Prof. GU BINGXIN
- Oil Painting: Prof. JIONG JIUNMO
- Sculpture: Prof. ZHANG YONGHAO

College of Political Science:
- Political Science: Prof. ZHANG ZHIFU

SHENZHEN UNIVERSITY

Nantou, Shenzhen, Guangdong 518060
Telephone: (755) 6660166
Fax: (755) 6660462

Founded 1983
State control
Academic year: September to July

President: XIE WIEXIN
Vice-Presidents: Prof. ZHANG BIGONG, Prof. ZHANG BAOQUAN, Prof. LIANG GUILIN
Registrar: LI GUANGYIA

Librarian: MAO ZHUOMING

Library of 580,000 vols

Number of teachers: 614

Number of students: 9,138

Publications: *Shenzhen University Journal* (Social Sciences and Humanities), *Shenzhen University Journal* (Natural Sciences), *World Architecture Review*.

HEADS OF FACULTIES

Faculty of Arts: Prof. YU LONGYU
Faculty of Economics: Prof. CAO LONGQI
Faculty of Science: Prof. SHU QIQING
Faculty of Information Engineering: Prof. XIE WEIXIN
Faculty of Architecture and Civil Engineering: Prof. XU ANZHI
Faculty of Engineering Technology: Prof. ZHU QIN
Faculty of Art: Prof. LIAO XINGQIAO
Faculty of Golf Sport and Management: Prof. LIN ZUJI
Faculty of Adult Education: Prof. YANG ZHONGXIN
Teachers' College: Prof. ZHANG BIGONG
Department of English: Prof. CAO YIAJUN
Sports Department: Prof. CHEN XIAORONG

ATTACHED INSTITUTES

Joint Institute of Applied Nuclear Technology: Dir GUO CHENGZHAN.

SEZ Economic Studies Institute: Dir SU DONGBIN.

New Energy Research Institute: Dir WANG ENTANG.

Telecommunications Technology Research Institute: Dir JIN BINGRONG.

Advanced Technology Research Centre: Dir YANG SHUWEN.

Holographic Material Research Institute: Dir YE JINGDE.

SICHUAN UNION UNIVERSITY

Jiuyanqiao, Chengdu 610064
Telephone: (28) 5412233
Fax: (28) 5410187
E-mail: scuu@sun.scuu.cdnet.edu.cn

Founded 1994 by merger of Sichuan University and Chengdu University of Science and Technology
State control
Language of instruction: Chinese
Academic year: September to July

President: LU TIECHENG
Vice-Presidents: CHEN JUNKAI, LIU YINGMING, LONG WEI, LI ZHIQIANG, ZHANG YIZHENG, YANG JIRUI
Registrar: XIAO DINGQUAN
Librarians: LIU YINGMING, CAI SHUXIAN, FENG ZESI

Library of 3,650,000 vols
Number of teachers: 3,660
Number of students: 19,150

Publications: *South Asian Studies Quarterly, Religion Studies, Oil-field Chemistry, Journal of Atomic and Molecular Physics, Polymeric Material Science and Technology, Sichuan Union University Journal of Natural Science, Sichuan Union University Journal of Social Science, Sichuan Union University Journal of Engineering Science.*

DEANS

College of Humanities: CAO SHUNQING
College of Law: TANG LEI
College of Foreign Languages: (vacant)
College of Journalism: QIU PEIHUANG
College of Economics and Management: CHEN GAOLIN
College of Sciences: (vacant)
College of Life Sciences and Engineering: CHEN FANG
College of Information Science and Engineering: TAO FUZHOU
College of Materials Science and Engineering: GU YI
College of Manufacturing Science and Engineering: (vacant)
College of Energy Resources Science and Engineering: (vacant)
College of Urban and Rural Construction and Environmental Protection: LUO TEJUN
College of Chemical Science and Engineering: ZHU JIAHUA
College of Light Science and Engineering: WU DACHENG
College of Fine Art: DENG SHENGQING
School of Adult Education and Vocational Education: WANG ZHONGMING

HEADS OF DEPARTMENT

College of Humanities:
- Chinese Languages and Literature: GONG HANXIONG
- History: WANG TINGZHI

College of Law:
- Philosophy: DENG SHENGQING
- Law: TANG LEI

College of Foreign Languages:
- Foreign Languages and Literature: SHI JIAN

College of Economics and Management:
- Economics: ZHAO HUAISHUN
- Economic Management: LIAO JUNPEI
- Foreign Economics and Trade: ZHAO CHANGWEN
- Commercial and Industrial Administration: YANG JIANG
- Finance, Tax and Investment: ZHAO YUHUA
- Management Engineering: LI SHIYAN

College of Science:
- Mathematics: XIONG HUAXIN
- Applied Mathematics: LIU GUANGZHONG
- Physics: XIE MAONONG
- Applied Physics: WANG ZHAOQING
- Chemistry: FU HEJIAN

College of Life Sciences and Engineering:
- Biology: JIA YONGJIONG
- Bioengineering: HU YONGSONG

College of Information Science and Engineering:
- Information Management: ZHANG XIAOLIN
- Secretaryship and Archiving: LIU CHENGZHI
- Radioelectronics: HUANG KAMA
- Optical Electronics: CHEN JIANGUO
- Automation: ZHAO YAO
- Applied Electronics: DONG BAOWEN
- Computer Science: LI ZHISHU

College of Materials Science and Engineering:
- Inorganic Materials: RAN JUNGUO
- Polymer Materials: (vacant)
- Plastics Engineering: FAN WUYI
- Materials Science: FEN LIANGHUAN

College of Manufacturing Science and Engineering:
- Mechanical Engineering: YIN GUOFU
- Metallic Materials: LI NING
- Testing Technology and Control Engineering: ZHAO SHIPING

College of Energy Resources Science and Engineering:
- Electric Power Engineering: LI XINGYUANG
- Hydraulic Engineering: LIANG CHUAN

College of Urban and Rural Construction and Environmental Protection:
- Architectural Engineering: LUO TEJUN
- Environmental Science and Engineering: SHI JIANFU
- Civil Engineering and Applied Mechanics: TIAN YONGQIAN

College of Chemical Science and Engineering:
- Chemical Mechanics: HUANG WEIXING
- Chemical Engineering: LIANG BIN
- Applied Chemistry: XIE CHUAN

College of Light Industry and Textile Engineering:
- Leather Technology and Engineering: CHEN WUYONG
- Food Science and Engineering: LU LIANTONG
- Textile Engineering: GU DAZHI

ATTACHED INSTITUTES

Institute of Humanities and Social Sciences: (vacant).

Institute of Materials Science: Dir ZHANG XINGDONG.

Polymer Institute: Dir XU XI.

Institute of Classical Texts: Dir SHU DAGANG.

Institute of South Asian Studies: (vacant).

Institute of Population Studies: Dir HE JINGXI.

Institute of Nuclear Physics: Dir SUN GUANQING.

Institute of High-temperature and High-pressure Atomic and Molecular Physics: Dir HONG SHIMING.

Institute of Religion: Dir LI GANG.

National Laboratory of Polymer Materials: Dir LI HUILIN.

National Laboratory of High-speed Hydraulics: Dir YANG YONGQUAN.

Analytical and Testing Centre: Dirs ZHANG XINGDONG, TU MINDUAN.

Open Laboratory of Radiation Physics and Application: Dir LIN LIBIN.

SOUTH CHINA AGRICULTURAL UNIVERSITY

Wushan, Guangzhou 510642
Telephone: (20) 85511299
Fax: (20) 85511393

Founded 1952
State control
Academic year: September to July

President: Prof. LUO SHIMING
Vice-Presidents: Prof. LUO XIWEN, Prof. LUO FUHE, Prof. ZHANG YUEHENG, Assoc. Prof. CHEN CHANGSHENG
Librarian: Assoc. Prof. LIN PAI

Library of 526,000 vols
Number of teachers: 777
Number of students: 5,487

Publications: *Journal* (quarterly), *Journal of the Research Library of Ancient Chinese Agricultural Literature* (quarterly), *Poultry Husbandry and Disease Control* (monthly), *Guangdong Agricultural Sciences* (jointly published with Guangdong Acad. of Agricultural Science) (monthly).

DEANS

College of Forestry: Assoc. Prof. CHEN BEIGUANG
College of Adult Education: Assoc. Prof. KE KAILI
Polytechnic College: Prof. LUO XIWEN
College of Economics and Trade: Prof. WEN SIMEI
College of Biotechnology: Assoc. Prof. WANG XIAOFENG
College of Science: Prof. LI WEICHANG
College of Liberal Arts: Assoc. Prof. LIANG SHENHONG
College of Resources and Environment: Prof. WANG ZHENZHONG
Department of Agronomy: Prof. TAN ZHONGWEN
Department of Horticulture: Assoc. Prof. OUYANG RUO
Department of Sericulture: Assoc. Prof. TAN BINGAN
Department of Animal Science: Prof. BI YINGZUO
Department of Animal Medicine: Prof. HUANG QINGYUN

Department of Food Science: Assoc. Prof. CHEN YONGQUAN
Department of Physical Education: Prof. HUANG MAOWU

PROFESSORS

BI, Y. Z., Animal Nutrition and Immunology
CHEN, B. X., Veterinary Diagnosis
CHEN, D. C., Pomology
CHEN, W. K., Insect Toxicology
CHEN, Z. D., Forest Product Processing
CHEN, Z. L., Veterinary Medicine
FAN, H. Z., Plant Pathology
FENG, Q. H., Veterinary Medicine
FENG, Z. X., Plant Pathology
FU, W. L., Animal Physiology
GU, Y. K., Forest Ecology
HE, Y. K., Plant Genetics and Breeding
HU, L. Z., Agricultural Architecture
HU, S. X., Education Management
HUANG, H. B., Fruit Tree Physiology
HUANG, M. W., Physical Education
HUANG, Z. R., Silkworm Diseases and Insect Pest Control
HUANG, Z. X., Insecticide Toxicology
JI, Z. L., Agricultural Product Storage and Processing
JIAN, Y. Y. Plant Biotechnology
KUANG, Y. H., Biophysics
LAI, Y. G., Philosophy
LI, B. T., Plant Taxonomy
LI, F. H., Statistics
LI, H. Z., Soil Science
LI, J. P., Soil Chemistry
LI, M. Q., Plant Physiology
LI, S. M., Plant Pathology
LI, Y. Q., Crop Cultivation
LIANG, G. W., Insect Ecology
LIAO, Z. W., Soil Science and the Environment
LIN, C. C., Physical Education
LIN, J., Scientific Management
LIN, L. Y., History of Chinese Revolution
LIN, M. Z., Silviculture
LIN, W. Q., Poultry Disease
LIU, D. B., Agricultural Engineering
LIU, F. A., Veterinary Medicine
LIU, Q. Y., Biophysics
LIU, Y. M., Forest Soil
LIU, Z. H., Agricultural Systems Engineering and Management Engineering
LU, C. C., Forest Protection
LU, K. M., Silkworm Pathology
LU, Y. G., Plant Genetics
LUO, B. L., Agricultural Economics and Management
LUO, F. H., Forest Management
LUO, S. M., Agroecology
LUO, X. W., Agricultural Mechanization
MEI, M. T., Plant Biotechnology
OU, Y. G., Agricultural Engineering
PANG, X. F., Insect Ecology and Taxonomy
PENG, S. J., Ancient Agricultural History
QI, P. K., Plant Pathology
SHAO, Y. J., Agricultural Engineering
TAN, S. M., Silviculture
TAN, Z. W., Plant Genetics and Breeding
TANG, W. W., Plant Virology
WAN, B. H., Plant Genetics and Breeding
WANG, Z. Z., Plant Pathology
WEN, S. M., Agricultural Economics and Management
WU, D. H., Vegetable Breeding
WU, Q. T., Agricultural Environment Protection
WU, S. Z., Plant Breeding
XIAO, J. C., Agricultural Economics
XIE, W. H., Mathematical Statistics
XIN, C. A., Poultry Disease
XU, F. C., Plant Physiology
XU, H. T., Philosophy
XU, X. Z., Mathematics
YAN, X. C., Botany
YOU, Z. L., Soil Science
ZENG, X. M., Plant Pathology
ZHANG, J. N., Forest Pathology
ZHANG, L. Q., Plant Genetics and Breeding
ZHANG, T. L., Agricultural Mechanization
ZHANG, Y. H., Agricultural Economics and Management
ZHAO, S. H., Insect Toxicology
ZHENG, C., Animal Nutrition
ZHONG, S. Q., Silkworm Genetics and Breeding
ZHOU, Z. J., History of Agricultural Science

SOUTH CHINA UNIVERSITY OF TECHNOLOGY

Wushan, Guangzhou, Guangdong Province 510641

Telephone: (20) 87110000
Fax: (20) 85516386

Founded 1952
State control
Academic year: September to July

President: LIU HUANBIN
Vice-Presidents: HAN DAJIAN, HUANG SHISHENG, JIA XINZHEN, LIU SHUDAO, CHEN NIANQIANG
Registrar: LIN YANGSU
Librarian: LI JIANBIN

Library of 1,350,000 vols
Number of teachers: 2,200
Number of students: 14,000

Publications: *Journal*, *Control Theory and Applications*.

DEANS

School of Electric Power: WU JIE
School of Chemical Engineering: CHEN HUANQIN
School of Light Chemical Engineering and Food Engineering: GAO DAWEI
School of Business Administration: SUN DONGCHUAN
School of Materials Science and Engineering: JIA DEMIN
School of Electrical Communication: ZHU XUEFENG
School of Adult Education: WU MAN

HEADS OF DEPARTMENT

School of Electric Power:
- Department of Power Engineering: YANG ZELIANG
- Department of Electrical Power Engineering: WU JIE

School of Chemical Engineering:
- Department of Chemical Engineering: LI ZAIZI
- Department of Applied Chemistry: ZHANG HANWEI

School of Light Chemical Engineering and Food Engineering:
- Department of Light Chemical Engineering: ZHANG HUAIYU
- Department of Food Engineering: LI TIANYI
- Department of Biological Engineering: GUO YONG

School of Business Administration:
- Department of International Business Administration: CAI GUOQIANG
- Department of International Trade: KUANG GUOLIANG
- Department of International Finance and Investment Economics: LAN HAILIN

School of Materials Science and Engineering:
- Department of Inorganic Materials Science and Technology: DENG ZAIDE
- Department of Polymer Materials Science and Technology: ZHAO YAOMING
- Department of Electrical Materials Science and Engineering: CHEN XUMING

School of Electrical Communication:
- Department of Radio Engineering: ZHANG LING
- Department of Automation: ZHU XUEFENG
- Department of Computer Science and Engineering: WANG ZUOXIN

Departments not attached to a School:
- Electric Machinery and Engineering: XIE CUNXI
- Architecture: WU QINGZOU
- Civil Engineering: CAI JIAN
- Automatic Control and Industrial Equipment Engineering: QU JINPING
- Applied Mathematics: WANG GUOQIANG
- Applied Physics: LI GUANQI
- Social Sciences: CHEN JIANXIN
- Foreign Languages: QIN XIUBAI

ATTACHED INSTITUTES

Institute of Architectural Design: Dir HE JINGTANG.

Institute of Chemical Engineering: Dir YANG XIAOXI.

Institute of Environmental Science: Dir WAN YINHUA.

Institute of Light Chemical Engineering: Dir YANG LIANSHENG.

National Key Laboratory of Pulp and Paper Engineering: Dir LU XIANHE.

SOUTHEAST UNIVERSITY

Si Pai Lou 2, Nanjing 210096

Telephone: 6631700
Fax: 7712719

Founded: 1902

President: Prof. CHEN DUXIN
Vice-Presidents: Prof. MAO HENGCAI, Prof. HE LIQUAN, HU LINGYUN, QIAN MINGQUAN, LI YANBAO, ZHONG BINGLIN, SHENG ZHAOHAN
Librarian: KONG QINGXI

Library of *c.* 1.5 million vols
Number of teachers: 2,100
Number of students: 13,000 (incl. 1,500 postgraduates)

Publication: *Journal*.

DEANS

Graduate: Prof. YU WEI
Sciences: Prof. WANG YUANMIN
Arts: Prof. LIU DAOYONG
Management: Prof. QIU XIANGYANG
Continuing Education: Prof. WU JIEYI
Communication and Transport Engineering: Prof. CHEN RONGSHEN

HEADS OF DEPARTMENTS

Architecture: Prof. WANG GUOLIANG
Mechanical Engineering: Prof. ZHONG BINGLIN
Power Engineering: Prof. QIAN RUINIAN
Radio Engineering: Prof. LU JIREN
Civil Engineering: Prof. JIANG YONGSHENG
Electronic Engineering: Prof. GAO ZHONGLIN
Mathematics and Mechanics: Prof. WANG YUANMIN
Automatic Control Engineering: Prof. CHEN WEINAN
Computer Science and Engineering: Prof. XING HANCHENG
Physics: Prof. HU MEIWEN
Chemistry and Chemical Engineering: Prof. LIU JUZHENG
Biomedical Engineering: Prof. GAN QIANG
Social Science: Prof. LIU DAOYONG
Material Science and Engineering: Prof. SUN WEI
Philosophy and Science: Prof. FAN HEPING
Electrical Engineering: Prof. GONG LENIAN
Instrument Science and Engineering: Prof. CHEN MINGFA
Foreign Languages: Prof. ZOU CHANGZHENG
Physical Education and Research: Prof. WANG ZHISU
Art: Prof. ZHANG DAOYI
Law: Prof. LIU DAOYONG
Chinese Culture: Prof. YU XUECAI

ATTACHED INSTITUTES

Research Institute of Automatic Control: Dir Prof. CHEN WEINAN
Architecture Design Institute: Dir Prof. SUN GUANGCHU
Research Institute of Architecture: Dir Prof. QI KANG
Centre of Material Analysis and Testing: Dir Prof. SHEN KECHENG
Centre for Vibration Testing: Dir Prof. GAO WEI
Research Institute of Higher Engineering Education: Dir Prof. CHEN MINGXI
Audio and Visual Centre: Dir Prof. XU ZHIRUI
Research Institute of Thermal Engineering: Dir Prof. ZHANG MINYAO
State Key Laboratory for Millimetre Wave Research: Dir Prof. SUN ZHONGLIANG
Mobile Radio and Point-to-Multipoint Communication Systems Research Laboratory (State Key Laboratory): Dir Prof. CHEN SHIXIN
State Professional Laboratory for Computer-Aided Architectural Design: Dir Prof. QI KANG
Laboratory of Molecular and Biomolecular Electronics: Dirs Prof. YU WEI, Prof. LU ZHUHONG
CIMS Research Centre: Dir Prof. GU GUANQUN
New and High Definition Display Tube Laboratory: Dir Prof. TONG LINSHU
National Engineering Technology Centre: Dir SUN DAYOU
Centre for Integrated Engineering: Dir Prof. CHEN DUXIN
Oriental Culture Research Institute: Dir Dr TAO SIYAN
Electric Light Research Centre: Dir Prof. LI GUANGAN

Computer Network for Chinese Education and Research:

East China (Northern Region) Network Centre: Dir Prof. HE LIQUAN
Jiangsu Education and Research Computer Network Centre: Dir Prof. HE LIQUAN

SUN YAT-SEN UNIVERSITY OF MEDICAL SCIENCES

74 Zhongshan Rd II, Guangzhou 510089, Guangdong Province

Telephone: 778223
Fax: (20) 765679

Founded 1866

State control
Languages of instruction: Chinese and English

President: LU GUANGQI
Vice-Presidents: ZHUO DAHONG, ZHU JIAKAI, TAN XUCHANG, GU JIANHUI
Librarian: HUANG RUXUEN

Library of 545,900 vols
Number of teachers: 1,101
Number of students: 3,825 (incl. 489 postgraduates)

Publications: *Academic Journal, Chinese Journal of Neurology and Psychiatry, Chinese Journal of Nephrology, Chinese Journal of Microsurgery, New Chinese Medicine, Ophthalmic Science, Cancer, Family Doctor.*

DEANS

School of Basic Sciences: LI GUIYUN
First School of Clinical Medicine: XIAO GUANHUI
Second School of Clinical Medicine: ZHANG XUMING
Third School of Clinical Medicine: GU CAIRAN
School of Public Health: CHENG CHENZHANG
Faculty of Stomatology: REN CAI-NIAN

There are eight research institutes, 30 research laboratories, an attached ophthalmic centre, four hospitals, and an affiliated school of nursing.

TIANJIN CONSERVATORY OF MUSIC

57 Eleventh Meridian Rd, Hedong District, Tianjin 300171

Telephone: 412882

Founded 1958

President: Prof. YANG JINHAO (acting)
Vice-Presidents: Prof. CHEN JIXU, Assoc. Prof. XU YONGKUN, Assoc. Prof. SHI WEIZHENG
Librarian: Assoc. Prof. WANG ZHIJIAN

Library of 99,106 vols, 20,000 records
Number of teachers: 178
Number of students: 344 (incl. 9 postgraduates)

Publication: *Music Study and Research* (quarterly).

DEANS

Composition: Prof. CHEN ENGUANG
Vocal: Assoc. Prof. XIA ZHONGHENG
Chinese Traditional Music: Assoc. Prof. SONG GUOSHENG
Orchestra: Prof. YAN ZHENGPING
Education: Assoc. Prof. YANG LIZHONG

TIANJIN INSTITUTE OF TEXTILE SCIENCE AND TECHNOLOGY

63 Cheng lin Zhuang Rd, Hedong District, Tianjin

Telephone: (22) 4344477
Fax: (22) 4515672

Founded 1958

President: Prof. QIU GUANXIONG
Vice-Presidents: Prof. CUI YONGFANG, Assoc. Prof. LEI KEJIAN
Registrar: Prof. JING TAO
Librarian: Assoc. Prof. WANG CUN

Library of 600,000 vols, 960 periodicals
Number of teachers: 700
Number of students: 5,000 undergraduates, 150 postgraduates

Publication: *Journal.*

HEADS OF DEPARTMENTS

Textile Engineering: Prof. HUANG GU
Textiles: Prof. GU ZHENYA
Materials Science: Prof. XIAO CHANGFA
Mechanical Engineering: Prof. CUI RUNZENG
Automation: Prof. LI LANYOU
Management Engineering: Prof. WANG SHOUMAO
Garments: Assoc. Prof. LIU RUIPU
Basic Courses: Prof. SUN MINGZHU
Membrane Separation Institute: Assoc. Prof. LI XINMIN
Textile Composites Research Institute: Prof. LI JIALU

There are 73 research institutes and laboratories.

TIANJIN MEDICAL COLLEGE

22 Qi Xiang Tai Rd, Heping District, Tianjin 300070

Telephone: 341234
Fax: 319429

Founded 1951

President: WU XIANZHONG
Vice-Presidents: CUI YITAI, FANG PEIHUA, XING KEHAO, LI JINGFU
Chief Librarian: BAI JINGWEN

Library of *c.* 284,000 vols
Number of teachers: 761
Number of students: 1,883

Publications: *Journal of Tianjin Medical College* (quarterly), *Foreign Medicine* (quarterly), *Medical Inquiry* (every 2 months), *Medical Translation* (quarterly), *Medical Education Research* (2 a year).

CHAIRMEN

Medicine: ZHANG NAIXIN
Stomatology: SHI SHUJUN
Public Health: LAI ZEMIN
Nursing: ZOU DAOHUI
Biomedical Engineering: LI YUANMING

HEADS OF DEPARTMENTS

Basic Courses of Internal Medicine: YU XIANWU
Microbiology: REN ZHONGYUAN
Pathology: ZHANG NAIXIN
Pathophysiology: TANG TE
Histology and Embryology: ZHANG YANCHENG
Parasitology: YANG SHUSEN
Physiology: ZHANG JI GUO
Biochemistry: TANG XINZHI
Pharmacology: ZHANG CAILI
Electron Microscopy: BAI JINGWEN
Immunology: PAN JUFEN
Anatomy: CHEN ZHONGXIN
Chemistry: YE QINGXIAN
Physics: SU GUANGJUN
Foreign Languages: YANG GUANGWU
Nutrition and Hygiene: WANG DUSHENG
Labour Hygiene: CHENG WEINAN
Epidemiology: GENG GUANYI

PROFESSORS

Internal Medicine

SHI YUSHU
HUANG XIANGQIAN
DU WENBIN
ZHOU JINTAI
YIN WEI
HUANG TIGANG
WANG PEIXIAN
CHENG YUQIAN
HUANG NAIXIA

Surgery

YU SONGTING
GUO SHIFU
LIU ZIKUAN
WU XIANZHONG
LI QINGRUI
WANG PENGZHI
DAI ZHIHUA
DONG KEQUAN
SHENG XIKUN

Obstetrics and Gynaecology

ZHAI ZHANCAN
JIAO SHUZHU

Paediatrics

LIU YUJI
HUANG HONGHAI

Ophthalmology

YUAN JIAQING
WANG YANHUA
SONG GUOXIANG
ZHANG LIANJING
YING SHIHAO

Oto-rhino-laryngology

YAN CHENGXIAN
GUO QIXIN
WANG YANYOU

Dermatology

FU ZHIYI
SHEN JIANMING

Radiology

WU ENHUI
YANG TIANEN
LIAN ZHONGCHENG
LI JINGXUE
ZHAO CHANGJIANG
HE NENGSHU

Neurology

XUE QINGCHENG
CHEN SHIJUN
JIANG DEHUA
YANG LUCHUN
PU PEIYU

Isotope

LU TIZHANG
FANG PEIHUA
ZHENG MIAORONG

Endocrinology

PANG ZHILING
MA LIYUN
LI LIANGE

Stomatology

SUN XUEMIN
HOU ZHIYAN

ATTACHED INSTITUTE

Institute of Endocrinology: Dir GAO YUQI.

TIANJIN UNIVERSITY

92 Weijin Rd, Tianjin 300072
Telephone: (22) 27406148
Fax: (22) 23358706

Founded 1895
State control
Academic year: August/September to July (two semesters)

President: Prof. SHAN PING
Vice-Presidents: Prof. WANG YULIN, Prof. GAO WENXIN, Prof. YU DAOYIN, Prof. KOU JISONG, Prof. HU XIAOTANG
Secretary-General: Prof. SU QUANZHONG (Deputy)
Dean of Studies: Prof. CHEN RONGJIN
Chief for General Affairs: Prof. LI JINPU
Librarian: Prof. YANG JIACHENG

Library of 1,740,000 vols, 148,854 periodicals
Number of teachers: 2,438
Number of students: 18,000

Publications: *Journal* (quarterly), *Collection of Research Achievements,* various departmental publs.

DEANS

School of Management: Prof. ZHANG SHIYING
School of Precision Instruments and Opto-Electronics Engineering: Prof. JIN SHIJIU
School of Electronic Information Engineering: RING RUNTAO
School of Architecture: Prof. ZHANG QI
School of Electrical Automation and Energy Resources Engineering: Prof. SUNG YUGENG
School of Sciences: JIANG ENYONG
School of Chemical Engineering: Prof. ZHAO XUEMING
School of Mechanical Engineering: Prof. ZHANG CE
School of Constructional Engineering: Prof. GU XIAOLU
School of Materials Science and Engineering: Prof. LI JIAJUN
School of Letters: Assoc. Prof. LIU YUSHAN
Graduate School: Prof. YU DAOYIN
School of Adult Education: Prof. CHEN RONGJIN
School of Petrochemical Engineering: Prof. CHEN HONGFANG (Dir)

DIRECTORS OF DEPARTMENTS

School of Management:

Management Engineering: Assoc. Prof. WANG XUEQING
Industrial Engineering: Assoc. Prof. SONG GUOFANG
International Project Management: Assoc. Prof. LI CHANGYAN
Engineering Economics: Assoc. Prof. FAN YICHANG
International Enterprises Management: Prof. HE JINSHENG
Management Information Systems: Assoc. Prof. LI MINQIANG

School of Precision Instruments and Opto-Electronics Engineering:

Precision Instruments Engineering: Assoc. Prof. LIN YUCHI
Opto-Electronics Information Engineering: Prof. CHEN CAIHE
Biomedical Engineering and Scientific Instrumentation: Prof. FAN SHIFU

School of Electronic Information Engineering:

Electronic Information Technology: ZHAO YAXING
Computer Science and Technology: HE PILIAN
Microelectronics: WU XIAWAN

School of Architecture:

Architecture: Assoc Prof. ZHANG YUKUN
Urban Planning: Assoc. Prof. YUN YINGXIA

School of Electrical Automation and Energy Resources Engineering:

Electrical Power Engineering: Prof. CHEN CHAOYING
Automation: Prof. XU ZHENLIN
Thermoenergy and Refrigeration Engineering: Assoc. Prof. LI WEIYI

School of Sciences:

Applied Mathematics: CAI GAOTING
Applied Physics: LIN JIADI
Applied Chemistry: TIAN YILING

School of Chemical Engineering:

Chemical Engineering: Assoc. Prof. ZHANG FENGBAO
Applied Chemistry and Pure Chemical Engineering: Assoc. Prof. LIU DONGZHI
Biochemical Engineering: Prof. SUN YAN
Chemical Engineering Equipment and Machinery: Prof. CHEN XU
Organic Synthesis and Polymer Chemical Engineering: Assoc. Prof. HAN JINYU
Catalysis Science and Engineering: Assoc. Prof. WANG RIJIE

School of Mechanical Engineering:

Mechanics: Prof. KANG YILAN
Mechanical and Electronics Engineering I: Prof. HUANG TIAN
Mechanical and Electronics Engineering II: Prof. LI WUSHEN
Automobile Engineering: Prof. SHU GEQUN
Mechanical Design: DONG GANG

School of Constructional Engineering:

Civil Engineering: Prof. JIANG XINLIANG
Environmental Engineering: Assoc. Prof. JI MIN
Construction Equipment Engineering: Assoc. Prof. ZHANG YUFENG
Hydraulic and Hydroelectric Construction Engineering: Assoc. Prof. LIAN JIJIAN
Naval Engineering: Assoc. Prof. HUANG YANSHUN
Port Engineering: Prof. LI YANBAO
Ocean Engineering: Prof. SHI QINGZENG
Communications and Transport Engineering: Assoc. Prof. ZHANG ZHIQIANG

School of Materials Science and Engineering:

Inorganic Non-Metallic Materials Science and Engineering: Prof. XU TINGXIAN
Polymer Science and Engineering: Assoc. Prof. CHENG GUOXIANG
Metal Materials Science and Engineering: Assoc. Prof. QU YUANFANG

School of Letters:

English: Assoc. Prof. ZHOU KERONG
Law: Assoc. Prof. SUN ZAIYOU
Social Sciences: Prof. ZONG WENJU
Chinese: Assoc. Prof. MENG XIANTANG
Foreign Languages Teaching Section for Postgraduate Students: Prof. XIA YIHU
Japanese Teaching Section: Assoc. Prof. ZHENG YUHE
College English Teaching Section: Assoc. Prof. JI WEIWU

ATTACHED RESEARCH INSTITUTES

Institute of Systems Engineering: Dir Prof. ZHANG WEI.

Institute of Management Science: Dir Prof. WU YUHUA.

Institute of Information and Control: Dir Assoc. Prof. WANG YIZHI.

Institute of Opto-Electronics and Precision Engineering: Dir Prof. ZHANG YIMO.

Institute of Sensor Technology: Dir Prof. WANG MINGSHI.

Institute of Illumination Technology: Dir Prof. FA SHIFU.

Institute of Opto-Electronic Measuring and Control Technology: Dir Prof. HU XIAOTANG.

Institute of Lasers and Opto-Electronics: Dir Prof. YAO JIANQUAN.

Institute of Biomedical Engineering: Dir Prof. WANG MINGSHI.

Research Centre for Opto-Electronic Information: Dir Prof. ZHANG YIMO.

Centre for Precision Instruments: Dir Senior Eng. HAN RUCONG.

State Key Laboratory for Precision Measuring Technology and Instruments: Dir Prof. YE SHENGHUA.

Laboratory for Photoelectronics and Information Engineering (National Ministry of Education): Dir Prof. YU DAOYIN.

Institute of Television and Image Formation Processing: Dir YU SILE.

Electronics Practice and Experiment Centre: Dir LI TAN.

IBM New Technology Centre: Dir SUN JIZHOU.

Institute of Architectural Design and Theory: Dir Prof. ZOU DENONG.

Institute of Architectural Science and Technology: Dir Assoc. Prof. MA JIAN.

Institute of Architectural Environmental Art: Dir Assoc. Prof. DONG YA.

Wang Xuezhong Art Research Institute: Dir Prof. WANG XUEZHONG.

Institute of Electric Power and Automation Engineering: Dir Prof. HE JIALI.

Institute of Thermoenergy Engineering: Dir Prof. MA YITAI.

Institute of Electric Power and Electronics Application Technology: Dir Prof. SUN YUGENG.

Geothermal Research and Training Centre: Dir Prof. ZHANG QI.

Centre for Modern Electrical Engineering and Electronics: Dir Assoc. Prof. ZHOU SHUTANG.

Centre for Building Automation: Dir Assoc. Prof. WU AIGUO.

Electric Power Research and Training Centre: Dir Prof. HE JIALI.

Electrical Automation Engineering Technology Centre: Dir Assoc. Prof. QIAO JIANSHENG.

Institute of Chemical Engineering: Dir Prof. ZHOU MING.

Centre for Chemical Engineering Experimentation: Dir Assoc. Prof. GUO HONGYU.

ECL Chemical Engineering Laboratory: Dir Prof. XU XI'EN.

Key Laboratory for Distillation Technology: Dir Prof. YUAN XIGANG.

Institute of Engineering Mechanics and Measuring Techniques: Dir Prof. KANG YILAN.

Institute of Advanced Manufacturing Technology: Dir Prof. HUANG TIAN.

Institute of Mechanical and Electronics Engineering: Dir Assoc. Prof. ZHANG HAIGEN.

Institute of Vehicles and Motors: Dir Prof. SHU GEQUN.

Institute of Welding Engineering Technology: Dir Prof. LI WUSHEN.

Institute of New Materials for Welding: Dir Prof. CHEN BANGGU.

Experimental Centre for Mechanical Design: Dir Prof. DONG GANG.

National Key Laboratory for Combustion Engines: Dir Prof. SU WANHUA.

Institute of Structural Engineering: Dir Prof. JIANG XINLIANG.

Institute of Environmental Engineering: Dir Assoc. Prof. JI MIN.

Institute of Hydraulic Engineering: Dir Prof. CAO ZHIXIAN.

Institute of Ocean and Naval Engineering: Dir Prof. YU JIANXING.

Institute of Geotechnical Engineering: Dir Prof. YAN SHUWANG.

Testing Centre for Structural Engineering: Dir Prof. JIANG XINLIANG.

Centre for Hydraulic Engineering Experimentation: Dir Senior Eng. GENG JIUYUE.

Institute of Materials Science and Engineering: Dir Prof. SHENG JING.

Institute of Advanced Ceramics: Dir Prof. YUAN QIMING.

Institute of Polymer Materials Science and Engineering: Dir Prof. YAO KANGDE.

Institute and Experimental Base for a Military Project on Ceramic Materials and Appliances: Dir Prof. XU TINGXIAN.

Analysis Centre of Tianjin University: Dir Assoc. Prof. FAN GUOLIANG.

Research Centre for Form Memorization Alloy Engineering (State Education Commission): Dir Prof. LIU WENXI.

Institute of Traditional Culture and Humanities: Dir Prof. ZONG WENJU.

Institute of Taiwan: Dir Prof. CAI JIARUI.

Centre for Science and Technology and the Study of Society: Dir Prof. WANG SHUEN.

Institute of Architectural Design: Dir Prof. YANG CHANGMING.

Tianjin Internal Combustion Engine Research Institute: Dir Prof. LI DEKUAN.

TIANJIN UNIVERSITY OF COMMERCE

Jinba Highway E, Tianjin 300400

Telephone: 26-4345
Telex: 23174
Fax: 268222

Founded 1981

President: Prof. LI BINGWEI

Library of 400,000 vols, 2,000 periodicals
Number of teachers: 400
Number of students: 5,000 (incl. 40 postgraduate and 1,000 adult education)

Publications: *University Periodical, University Journal.*

HEADS OF DEPARTMENT

Food Engineering: JIN TIESHENG
Refrigeration Engineering: GAO ZUKUN, XUE TIANPENG
Commercial Enterprise Management: ZHOU TIE
Packing Engineering: WANG SHIZHAO
Management Engineering: SHAO YONGQI
Basic Courses: QI ZHIGUANG
Politics and Laws: CHEN JINGSHENG

TIANJIN UNIVERSITY OF LIGHT INDUSTRY

1038 Dagu Nanlu, Tianjin 300222

Telephone: (22) 8340538
Fax: (22) 8341536
E-mail: tjili@tju.edu.cn

Founded 1958
State control
Languages of instruction: Chinese, English

President: TAN GUOMIN
Vice-Presidents: YANG SHUHUI, CHANG RUXIANG, XU MINLIANG, LI JUN
Chief Administrative Officer: LI ZHENG

Library of 450,000 vols
Number of teachers: 552
Number of students: 5,109

Publication: *Journal.*

Divisions of mechanical and electrical engineering, chemistry and chemical engineering, biotechnology and food technology, industrial art engineering, management and systems engineering, applied liberal arts and sciences.

TONGJI MEDICAL UNIVERSITY

13 Hang Kong Lu, Wuhan, Hubei 430030

Telephone: (27) 3622284
Fax (027) 5858920

Founded 1907
State control
Languages of instruction: Chinese, English, German
Academic year: September to July

Chancellor: Prof. LIU SHUMAO
President: Prof. XUE DELIN
Vice-Presidents: Prof. LIU SHENGYUAN, Prof. WANG CAIYUAN, Prof. WANG XIMING, Prof. WEN LIYANG, Prof. LI GUOCHENG, Prof. WANG ZUQIN
Registrar: Prof. LUO WUJIN
Librarian: Prof. XU FENGYING (Deputy Librarian)

Library of 400,000 vols
Number of teachers: 2,692
Number of students: 7,962

Publications: *Acta Universitatis Medicinae Tongji* (Chinese and English, every 2 months), *Journal* (Chinese, quarterly), *China Higher Medical Education* (Chinese, every 2 months), various departmental publs.

DIRECTORS

College of Basic Medicine: Prof. SHI YOU'EN
College of Public Health: Prof. CHEN XUEMIN
College of Pharmacy: Prof. TIAN SHIXIONG
First College of Clinical Medicine: (vacant)
Second College of Clinical Medicine: Prof. HONG GUANG XIANG
College for Continuing Medical Education: Prof. XIANG CHUNTING
Faculty of Forensic Medicine: Prof. QIN QISHENG
Faculty of Medical Library and Information Sciences: Prof. LI DAOPING (Deputy Dir)
Faculty of Foreign Languages: Prof. ZHANG HONGQING
Faculty of Social Sciences: Prof. HU JICHUN
Faculty of Maternal and Child Health: Prof. LIU XIAOXIAN
Faculty of Paediatrics: Prof. HONG GUANGXIANG

AFFILIATED HOSPITALS

Xiehe Hospital: Dir (vacant)

Tongji Hospital: Dir Prof. HONG GUANGXIANG

ATTACHED INSTITUTES

Institute of Reproductive Medicine: Dir Prof. XIA WENJIA.

Institute of Organ Transplantation: Dir Prof. XUE DELIN.

Institute of Cardiovascular Diseases: Dir Prof. YANG CHENYUAN.

Institute of Basic Medicine: Dir Prof. SHI YUO'EN.

Institute of Integration of Traditional Chinese Medicine and Western Medicine: Dir Prof. HUANG GUANG YING.

Institute of Environmental Medicine: Dir Prof. CHEN XUEMIN.

Institute of Social Medicine: Dir Prof. CHEN SHIRONG.

Institute of Occupational Medicine: Dir Prof. HE HANZHEN.

Institute of Haematology: Dir Prof. SONG SHANJUN.

Institute of Hepatopathy: Dir Prof. WANG JIALONG.

Institute of Medical Education: Dir Prof. ZHOU DAIYAN.

Institute of Medical Information Science: Dir Prof. QIN HUIJI (Deputy Dir).

TONGJI UNIVERSITY

1239 Siping Rd, Shanghai 200092

Telephone: 65982200
Fax: 65028965

Founded 1907

President: WU QIDI
Vice-Presidents: GU GUOWEI, ZHENG SHILING, ZHOU ZHEN, YU XINHUI, XU ZUOZHANG, DONG CONGQI
Librarian: MA ZAITIAN

Number of teachers: 2,300 (incl. 293 professors)

Number of students: 15,500 (incl. 2,100 postgraduates)

Publications: *Tongji Journal* and several technical publications.

DEANS

Graduate School: WU QIDI
Professional Education and Correspondence School: WU QIDI
College of Economics and Management: HUANG YUXIANG
College of Architecture and Urban Planning: CHEN BINZHAO
College of Structural Engineering: FAN LICHU
College of Mechanical Engineering: MAO QINGXI
College of Environmental Engineering: LIU SUIQING
College of Computer Science: XUAN GUORONG
College of Humanities and Law: DENG WEIZHI
Sino-German School: WU QIDI

HEADS OF DEPARTMENTS

Management Engineering: LIN ZHIYAN
Business Administration: WU DONGMING
Architectural Engineering: ZHAO XIUHENG
Urban Planning: CHEN BINZHAO
Road and Traffic Engineering: SUN LIJUN
Industrial Design: YIN ZHENGSHENG
Landscape and Tourism: LIU BINYI
Art and Culture: SHI JIANWEI
Building Engineering: SHI MINHUA
Bridge Engineering: YUAN WANCHENG
Automobile Engineering: CHEN LIFAN
Heat Engineering: CHEN YI
Underground Building and Engineering: YANG LINDE
Real Estate and Surveying: ZHAO CAIFU
Mechanical Engineering: XU BAOFU
Environmental Engineering: YANG HAIZHEN
Computer Science and Engineering: ZHAO YIGUN
Marine Geology and Geophysics: WANG JIALIN
Applied Mathematics: SHAO JIAYU
Materials Science and Engineering: WANG XINYOU
Physics: CHEN HONG
Chemistry: SHI XIANFA
Engineering Mechanics and Technology: ZHANG RUOJING
Foreign Languages: WANG JIASHU
German: ZHU JIANHUA
Japanese: TAN JIANHAO
Social Science: SUN QIMING
Law: WANG WEIDA
Economics and Trade: DONG JINGHUAN
Electrical Engineering: XIAO YUNSHI
Preparatory School for German Language: HANG GUOSHENG

UNIVERSITY OF ELECTRONIC SCIENCE AND TECHNOLOGY OF CHINA

4 North Jian She Rd, Chengdu, Sichuan 610054

Telephone: (28) 3202353
Telex: 60202
Fax: (28) 3202365
E-mail: whfu@uestc.edu.cn

Founded 1956

Academic year: March to July, September to January

President: Prof. LIU SHENGGANG
Librarian: Prof. WU WEIGONG

Library of *c.* 1 million vols
Number of teachers: 1,380
Number of students: 13,000 (820 postgraduate)

Publication: *Journal* (every 2 months).

Sixteen departments, ten research institutes, and six centres.

UNIVERSITY OF INTERNATIONAL BUSINESS AND ECONOMICS

Hui Xin Dong Jie, He Ping Jie N., Beijing 100029

Telephone: 64965522
Fax: 64968036
E-mail: uibe@chinaonline.com.cn.net

Founded 1954 as Beijing Institute of Foreign Trade

Control: Ministry of Foreign Trade and Economic Co-operation

Academic year: September to July

President: Prof. SUN WEIYAN
Vice-Presidents: Prof. YE CAIWEN, Prof. HUANG ZHENHUA, Prof. FANG MAOTIAN, Prof. XU BINGREN
Chief Administrative Officer: LIU YUAN
Librarian: SHI SHIYU

Number of teachers: 813
Number of students: 17,000

Publications: *University Journal* (every 2 months), *International Business* (monthly), *Japanese Language Studies* (monthly).

DEANS

School of International Trade and Economics: Prof. LIN GUIJUN
Faculty of Customs Administration: Assoc. Prof. ZHENG JUNTIAN
School of International Business Management: Prof. MA CHUNGUANG
School of International Studies: Prof. WANG XUEWEN
School of Law: Prof. SHEN SIBAO
Faculty of Humanities: Assoc. Prof. ZHENG BAOYIN
School of Continuing Education: Prof. YANG FENGHUA
Faculty of Economic Information Management: Assoc. Prof. DANG JIAN
Department of Graduate Studies: Assoc. Prof. LIU YUAN

PROFESSORS

School of International Trade and Economics:

YE CAIWEN
WANG SHAOXI, International Trade
WANG SHOUCHUN, International Trade
XUE RONGJIU, International Business
CHEN TONGCHOU, International Trade
LI XIAOXIAN, International Trade
QIU NIANZHU, International Trade
SHI YUCHUAN
QIAO RONGZHEN, International Trade
LI KANG
XIA SHEN
WANG YUQING, Technology Trade
YU JUNNIAN
ZHAO XIUCHEN
LIU SHUNIAN
XIA XIURUI, History of China's Foreign Trade
FEI XIUMEI, International Finance
SHI YUXING, International Finance
LEI RONGDI, International Insurance
YAN QIMING, International Transport
WANG LINSHENG
LI KANGHUA
ZHANG XIGU
MENG JICHENG
LI SHI
CHU XIANGYIN
XIA YOUFU
LIN GUIJUN

School of International Business Management:

PENG YUSHU, Accountancy
HU HENIAN, Financial Management
GAO GUOPEI, International Marketing
MA CHUNGUANG, International Management
LIU YAOWEI
JIA HUAIQIN, Statistics
XU ZIJIAN
YU SHULIAN

School of International Studies:

SUN WEIYAN
HUANG ZHENHUA
FANG MAOTIAN
WANG XUEWEI, Business English
HE ZENGMEI, English
WU SHUNCHANG, English
WU FENG, Linguistics (English)
ZHANG BINGZI, Business English
YANG CHAOGUANG, Linguistics
SHI TIANLU, Business English
LU YONG, Business Russian
YANG NAIJUN, Linguistics (Russian)
DAI MINGPEI, Business French
XIAO TIANYOU, Linguistics (Italian)
ZIANG XINDAO, Linguistics (Korean)
ZHAO RUN, German Economics
YANG YANHONG
WANG ZHENGFU, Business German
ZHANG SUWO
SUN JIANQIU
YAN SHANMING
CHEN ZHUNMIN
LI WEIZHONG
LI WENTIAN
WANG TIANQING
ZHENG YUMIAO
HUANG MEIBO
CHENG HAIBO
DING HENGQI
ZHANG CAILIANG, Linguistics (German)
LIAO YAZHANG
CHEN JIANPING
LI BOJIE
CHANG LI
LI ZHENGZHONG
ZHU KAI

School of Law:

SHEN DAMING
SHEN SIBAO
GAO XIQING
WANG JUN

School of Continuing Education:

YANG FENGHUA

Faculty of Humanities:

GE GUANGQIAN, Political Economy
CHEN YUJIE, Political Economy
JIANG YONGHE
GUAN XIGUO
ZHANG YINGJU
LI ZUOSHU
ZHANG FANJIA
CHEN YANLIN
WANG XUEMIN
HUANG WEIZHI
LUO HANXIN

Faculty of Economic Information Management:

CAO ZELAN
YU JINKANG
LI XIAO

UNIVERSITY OF SCIENCE AND TECHNOLOGY BEIJING

30 Xueyuan Lu, Beijing 100083

Telephone: (10) 62332312
Fax: (10) 62327283

Founded 1952, present name 1988

President: Prof. YANG TIANJUN
Vice-President: Prof. XU JINWU
Head of Foreign Relations: LIU YONGCAI

Library of 837,000 vols
Number of teachers: 2,849
Number of students: 5,122 undergraduates, 1,424 graduates

Publications: *Journal of UST Beijing, Higher Education Research.*

UNIVERSITY OF SCIENCE AND TECHNOLOGY OF CHINA

96 Jinzhai Rd, Hefei, Anhui

Telephone: (551) 3601000
Fax: (551) 3631760
E-mail: iao@ustc.ac.cn

Founded 1958 by Chinese Academy of Sciences

Academic year: September to January, March to July

President: TANG HONGGAO
Vice-Presidents: FAN WEICHENG, FENG KEQIN, JIN DASHEN, LI GUODONG, ZHU QINSHI
Dean of Studies: ZHU BIN
Secretary-General: XI FUYUN
Director of Foreign Affairs: SHI WENFANG
Library Director: LI NANQIU

Library of 1,740,000 vols, 230,000 periodicals
Number of teachers: 1,650
Number of students: 7,500

Publications: *Education and Modernization, Experimental Mechanics.*

HEADS OF DEPARTMENTS

Mathematics: CHENG YI
Physics: LIU WENHAN
Modern Chemistry: HE TIANJING
Modern Physics: YUN CHANGXUAN
Modern Mechanics: HE SHIPING
Radio Electronics: XU SHANJIA
Earth and Space Sciences: ZHENG YONGFEI
Biology: LIU JING
Precision Machinery and Instrumentation: XIA YUANMING
Automatic Control: SUN DEMIN
Computer Science and Technology: WANG XIFA
Applied Chemistry: PAN ZHONGXIAO
Engineering Thermophysics: CHEN YILIANG
Material Science and Engineering: FAN HONGYI
Information Management and Decision Science: LIANG LIANG
Management Science: CHENG XIAOJIAN
Statistics and Finance: MIAO BOQI
Foreign Languages: GONG LI
Chemistry: LIN XIANGQIN
Polymer Science: PAN CAIYUAN
Centre for Electronic Engineering: ZHUANG ZHENGQUAN
Centre for Basic Physics: XIANG SHOUPING
Centre for Philosophical and Social Science: SUN XIANYUAN
Special Class for the Gifted Young: CHEN JIAFU

ATTACHED RESEARCH INSTITUTES

Centre for Astrophysics: ZHOU YOUYUAN
Centre for Children's Amblyopia and Strabismus: SHOU TIANDE
Centre for Nonlinear Science: WANG KELIN
Centre for Petroleum Research: XU GUOMING
Fast Electronics Laboratory: WANG YANFANG
Information Processing Centre: LIU ZHENKAI
Institute of Applied Mechanics: WU XIAOPING

Institute of Biomedical Engineering: ZHANG ZUOSHENG
Institute of High Precision Technology: LI MING
Institute of Industrial Automation: SUN DEMIN
Institute of Information and Decision Science: LUO KUANG
Institute of Intelligence and Information Technology: ZHUANG ZHENQUAN
Institute of Management Science: ZHANG YUNGANG
Institute of Microstructure: XIN HOUWEN
Institute of Molecular Biophysics: SHI YUNYU
Institute of Natural Science History: HE ZUOXIU
Institute of Quantum Chemistry: XIN HOUWEN
Institute of Science and Technology Strategy and World Development: SUN XIANYUAN
Institute of Signal Statistical Processing: WANG YUE
Institute of Solid State Chemistry and Inorganic Membranes: MENG GUANGYAO
Institute of SUN-USTC: CHEN YIYUAN
Institute of Superconductivity: WU HANGSHEN
Institute of Theoretical Physics: ZHU DONGPEI
Joint Institute for High Energy Physics of ETHZ and USTC: BIAN ZUHE
Laboratory for Atomic and Molecular Physics: LI JIANMING
Laboratory for Nuclear Technology Applications: HONG PINGSHUN
Laboratory for Plasma Physics: YU CHANGXUAN
Research Centre for Green Science and Technology: ZHU QINSHI
Research Centre for Thermal Safety Engineering and Technology: FAN WEICHENG

WEST CHINA UNIVERSITY OF MEDICAL SCIENCES

17 Renminnanlu 3 Duan, Chengdu, Sichuan 610044

Telephone: (28) 5501000
Fax: (28) 5583252

Founded 1910
State control
Languages of instruction: Chinese, English
Academic year: September to January, February to July

President: ZHANG ZHAODA
Vice-Presidents: LU CHONGJIU, ZHAO XIAOWEN, BAO LANG, ZHOU TONGFU
Chief Administrative Officer: TANG HONGGUANG
Librarian: CHEN HUAIQING

Library of 650,000 vols
Number of teachers: 1,057
Number of students: 4,998

Publications: *West China Journal of Stomatology, Journal of West China University of Medical Sciences, West China Journal of Pharmaceutical Sciences, Chinese Journal of Medical Genetics, West China Medical Journal, Chinese Journal of Ocular Fundus Diseases, Chinese Journal of Reparative and Reconstructive Surgery, Modern Preventive Medicine.*

DEANS

School of Medicine: Dr SHI YINGKANG
School of Stomatology: Dr ZHOU XUEDONG
School of Public Health: Dr ZHANG CHAOWU
School of Pharmacy: WANG FENGPENG
School of Basic Medical Sciences: Dr BAO LANG
School of Continued Education: Dr ZHANG YUFANG

DISTINGUISHED PROFESSORS

School of Basic Medical Sciences:

BAO LANG, Pathophysiology
CAI MEIYING, Immunology
CHEN HUAIQING, Biomedical Engineering
CHEN JUNJIE, Biochemistry
CHEN MANLING, Biochemistry
DAI BAOMIN, Pathophysiology
FU MINGDE, Biochemistry
HU XIAOSHU, Parasitology
LI RUIXIANG, Anatomy
LIU BINGWEN, Biochemistry
LU ZHENSHAN, Histology and Embryology
OU KEQUN, Histology and Embryology
WANG BOYAO, Pathophysiology
WU LIANGFANG, Histology and Embryology
ZHU BIDE, Histology and Embryology

School of Medicine:

CAO ZEYI, Obstetrics and Gynaecology
CAO ZHONGLIANG, Infectious Diseases
CHEN WENBIN, Internal Medicine
DENG XIANZHAO, Genito-Urinary Surgery
FANG QIANXUN, Ophthalmology
GAO LIDA, Neural Surgery
HU TINGZE, Paediatric Surgery
HUANG DEJIA, Diagnostic Imaging
HUANG MINGSHENG, Psychiatry and Mental Health
LEI BINGJUN, Infectious Diseases
LI GANDI, Pathology
LI XIUJUN, Internal Medicine
LIAO QINGKUI, Paediatrics
LIN DAICHENG, Otolaryngology
LIU XIEHE, Psychiatry and Mental Health
LUO CHENGREN, Ophthalmology
LUO CHUNHUA, Paediatrics
MIN PENGQIU, Diagnostic Imaging
OUYANG QIN, Gastroenterology
PENG ZHILAN, Obstetrics and Gynaecology
SHEN WENLU, General Surgery
SHI YINGKANG, Cardiological Surgery
TANG TIANZHI, Nuclear Medicine
TANG XIAODA, Genito-Urinary Surgery
TANG ZEYUAN, Paediatrics
WANG SHILANG, Obstetrics and Gynaecology
WANG ZENGLI, Internal Medicine
WEI FUKANG, Paediatric Surgery
XIAO LUJIA, General Surgery
YAN LUNAN, General Surgery
YAN MI, Ophthalmology
YANG GUANGHUA, Pathology
YANG YURU, Genito-urinary Surgery
YANG ZHIMING, Orthopaedics
ZHANG ZIZHONG, Medical Genetics
ZHANG ZHAODA, General Surgery
ZHAO LIANSAN, Infectious Diseases

School of Pharmacy:

LI TUN, Pharmaceutics
LIAO GONGTIE, Pharmaceutics
LU BIN, Pharmaceutics
WANG FENGPENG, Chemistry of Natural Medicinal Products
WANG XIANKAI, Pharmaceutical Chemistry
WENG LINGLING, Pharmaceutical Chemistry
XU MINGXIA, Pharmaceutical Chemistry
ZHENG HU, Pharmaceutical Chemistry
ZHONG YUGONG, Pharmaceutical Chemistry

School of Public Health:

LI CHANGJI
NI ZONGZAN
PENG SHUSHENG, Nutrition and Food Hygiene
SUN MIANLING, Environmental Health
WANG RUISHU, Nutrition and Hygiene
WANG ZHIMING, Occupational Health and Occupational Diseases
WU DESHENG, Environmental Health
YANG SHUQIN, Health Statistics
ZHANG CHAOWU
ZHANG CHENLIE, Occupational Health and Occupational Diseases

School of Stomatology:

CAO YONGLIE, Orthodontics
DU CHUANSHI, Prosthodontics
LI BINGQU, Oral Medicine
LI SHENWEI, Maxillofacial Surgery
LIU TIJIA, Oral Medicine
LUO SONGJIAO, Orthodontics
MAO ZHUYI, Maxillo-facial Surgery
WANG DAZHANG, Maxillo-facial Surgery
WANG HANZHANG, Maxillo-facial Surgery
WEI ZHITONG, Orthodontics
WEN YUMING, Maxillo-facial Surgery
XIAO ZHUERAN, Oral Medicine
YUE SONGLING, Oral Medicine
ZHANG YUNHUI, Oral Medicine
ZHAO YUNFENG, Orthodontics
ZHOU XIUKUN, Orthodontics

Faculty of Forensic Medicine:

WU MEIYUN, Forensic Medicine

WUHAN UNIVERSITY

Wuhan 430072, Hubei

Telephone: (27) 812712
Fax: 712661

Founded 1913

President: Prof. QI MINYOU
Vice-Presidents: Assoc. Prof. REN XINLIAN, Prof. TAO DELIN, Prof. WANG RENHUI, Assoc. Prof. DAI LIBIN, Assoc. Prof. LI JINCAI
Secretary-General: Assoc. Prof. ZHANG QINGMING
Director of Foreign Affairs Office: Prof. YANG RONGHAO
Librarian: Assoc. Prof. SHEN JIWU

Number of teachers: 2,262
Number of students: 9,700

Publications: *Journal* (Natural Sciences edn, Social Sciences edn), *Writing, French Studies, Russian-Soviet Literature, Journal of Mathematics, Law Review, Knowledge of Library Information.*

HEADS OF SCHOOLS

Postgraduate: Prof. TAO DELIN
Law: Prof. MA JUNJU
Economics: Prof. LI YUYI
Business Management: Prof. ZHANG YAOTING
Library Science: Prof. PENG PEIZHANG
Adult Education: Assoc. Prof. LIANG DAQUAN
Foreign Languages: Prof. ZHU ZAOAN

ATTACHED INSTITUTES

Institute of Chinese Studies (3rd to 9th centuries): Dir Prof. TANG CHANG-RU.
Institute of North American Economics: Dir Prof. GUO WUXIN.
Institute of World History: Dir Prof. WU YU-JIN.
Institute of French Studies: Dir Prof. JIANG HUOSHENG.
Institute of International Law: Dir Prof. HAN DEPEI.
Institute of Library Information: Dir Prof. ZONG FUBANG.
Institute of Virology: Prof. ZHANG CHUYU.
Institute of Applied Chemistry: Dir Prof. ZHA QUANXING.
Institute of Electromagnetic Wave Propagation and Space Physics: Dir Prof. LU JIANKE.
Institute of Higher Education: Dir Prof. WU YIGU.
Institute of Resources and Applicable Techniques: Dir Prof. DU YUMIN.
Institute of Software Engineering: Dir Prof. KANG DINGSHAN.
Institute of Demography: Dir Prof. GU SHENGZU.
Institute of Aesthetics: Dir Prof. LUI GANGJI.
Institute of Writing: Dir Assoc. Prof. ZHANG GUANGMING.

XIAMEN UNIVERSITY

422 Siming Rd S, Xiamen, Fujian 361005

Telephone: (592) 2182229
Fax: (592) 2086526

Founded 1921
Academic year: September to July

President: LIN ZUGENG
Vice-Presidents: ZHU CONGSHI, ZHENG XUEMENG, ZHU ZHIWEN, PAN SHIMO
Foreign Affairs Office: SU ZIXING
Registrar: YANG BING

Librarian: CHEN MINGGUANG

Library of 1,800,000 vols
Number of teachers: 1,397
Number of students: 12,000

Publications: *Xiamen University Journal* (philosophy and social sciences edn and natural sciences edn, both quarterly), *China's Social Economics* (quarterly).

DEANS

College of Economics: Prof. QIU HUABING
College of Politics and Law: Prof. LIAO YIXING
College of Art Education: Prof. LIU YIGUANG
College of Engineering: Prof. XU KEPING
College of Overseas Education: Prof. ZHOU SHIXIONG
Graduate School: Prof. LIN ZUGENG
College of Chemical Engineering: WAN HUILING
School of Business Administration: WU SHILONG
College of Marine and Environmental Science: HONG HUASHEN
Medical College: LIM YEAN LENG
School of Southeast Asian Studies: LIAO SHAOLIANG (acting)

HEADS OF DEPARTMENTS AND INSTITUTES

Liberal Arts:

Chinese Language and Literature: HUANG MINGFEN
History: CHEN ZHIPING
Journalism and Communication: CHEN PEIAI
Foreign Languages and Literature: LIAN SHUNEN
Institute of Taiwan Studies: FAN XIZHOU
Institute of Higher Education: LIU HAIFENG
Institute of Chinese Language and Literature: HE GENGFENG
Institute of Anthropology: GUO ZHICHAO

Science and Engineering:

Mathematics: LIANG YIXING
Computer Science: LI TANGQIU
Physics: CHEN JINCAN
Chemistry: SUN SHIGANG
Biology: ZHENG WENZHU
Oceanography: SU YONGQUAN
Scientific Instrumentation: HAN LEI
Architecture: LING SHIDE
Electrical Engineering: CHENG CAISHENG
Institute of Environmental Science: ZHENG TIANLING
Physics and Chemistry Institute: LIAO DAIWEI
Cancer Research Centre: YANG DONG
Subtropical Oceanology Institute: LI WENGUAN

College of Economics:

Planning and Statistics: ZENG WUYI
Accounting: WANG GUANGYUAN
Business Management: LIN ZHIYANG
Finance and Banking: ZHANG XIN
Foreign Trade: DENG LIPING
Economics: ZHUANG ZONGMING

College of Politics and Law:

Philosophy: XU MENGJIU
Law: LIAO YIXING
Political Science: HUANG QIANG

College of Art Education:

Music: WU PEIWEN
Fine Arts: CHENG RENGUANG

XIAN JIAOTONG UNIVERSITY

28 West Xianning Rd, Xian 710049
Telephone: (29) 3268234
Fax: (29) 3234781
E-mail: mailxjtu@xjtu.edu.cn

Founded 1896
State control
Academic year: September to July (two semesters)

President: JIANG DEMING
Registrar: LI NENGGUI
Administrative Officer: CHEN QINGLIANG
Librarian: LI RENHOU

Number of teachers: 1,800
Number of students: 16,000 (including 3,000 postgraduates)

Publications: *Journal*, *Applied Mechanics*, *Engineering Mathematics*.

DEANS

Graduate School: ZHANG WENXIU
Academy of Science and Engineering: SUN GUOJI
School of Management: XI YOUMIN
School of Mechanical Engineering: XING JIANDONG
School of Energy and Power Engineering: TAO WENQUAN
School of Electrical Engineering: WANG ZHAOAN
School of Electronics and Communications Engineering: WU HONGCAI
School of Architectural Engineering and Mechanics: CHEN YIHENG
School of Chemistry and Chemical Engineering: YU YONGZHANG
School of Materials Science and Engineering: JIN ZHIHAO
School of Science: XU ZONGBEN
School of Humanities and Social Science: PAN JI
School of Adult Education: LI NENGGUI

There are 79 research institutes and 78 research laboratories.

XIAN MEDICAL UNIVERSITY

205 Zhuquedajie, Nanjiao, Xian, Shaanxi Province 710061
Telephone: (29) 526-1609
Fax: (29) 526-7364
E-mail: mail1@irix.xamu.edu.cn

Founded 1937
Controlled by Ministry of Health
Language of instruction: Chinese
Academic year: September to January, March to July (3-year, 4-year, 5-year and 7-year courses)

President: Prof. REN HUIMIN
Vice-Presidents: Prof. FAN XIAOLI, Prof. CHEN HENGYUAN
Library Director: MA XINGFU

Number of teachers: 4,972
Number of students: 4,000

Publications: *Journal*, *Abstracts of Medicine, P.R. China (Dermatology)*, *Journal of Audio-Visual Medical Education*, *Journal of Chinese Medical Ethics*, *Journal of Medical Geography Overseas*, *Journal of Medical Education in Northwest China*, *Journal of Modern TCM (Traditional Chinese Medicine)*, *Journal of Maternity and Child Health Overseas*, *Journal of Pharmacy in Northwest China*, *Journal of Children's Health*, *Academic Journal of Xian Medical University* (Chinese and English editions).

DEANS

First Clinical Medical School: PAN CHENGEN
Second Clinical Medical School: CHEN JUNCHANG
Pre-clinical Medical School: GAO HONGDE
Secondary Health School: NI KAI
School of Stomatology: HU YONGSHENG
School of Pharmacy: YANG SHIMI
School of Forensic Medicine: LI SHENGBIN
School of Public Health: YAN HONG
School of Social Medicine: LI JINSUO
School of Adult Training: FENG XINZHOU
Faculty of Biomedical Engineering: JIN JIE
Faculty of Health Administration: GAO JIANMIN
Faculty of Foreign Languages: BAI YONGQUAN
Faculty of Maternal and Child Care: ZHANG MINGHUI
Faculty of Nursing: SHAO WEIWEI

PROFESSORS

BAI YONGQUAN, English
CHEN JUNCHANG, Surgery
CUI CHANGZONG, Internal Medicine
DENG YUNSHAN, Dermatology
DIAO GUIXIANG, Pathology
DING DONGNING, Chemistry
DING HUIWEN, Cardiology
DONG LEI, Digestive Medicine
FANG XIAOLI, Physiology
FENG XUELIANG, Internal Medicine
FENG YINQUN, Orthopaedics
GU JIANZHANG, Paediatrics
GUO YINGCHUN, Cardiology
HE LANGCHONG, Pharmaceutical Analysis
HU GUOYING, Isotopes
HU HAOBO, Health Administration
HU YONGSHENG, Stomatology
JI ZONGZHENG, Surgery
JIN JIE, Physics
KONG XIANGZHEN, Pathophysiology
LEI LIQUAN, Pathophysiology
LEI XIAOYING, Ultrasonic
LI GUOWEI, Surgery
LI RONG, Oncology
LI SHUXI, Digestive Medicine
LI YIMING, Surgery
LI YINGLI,, Pharmacognosy
LI ZHE, Parasitology
LI ZHONGMIN, Internal Medicine
LIU HONGTAO, English
LIU HUIXI, Gynaecology and Obstetrics
LIU JINYAN, Internal Medicine
LIU SHANXI, Internal Medicine
LIU XIAOGONG, Surgery
LIU ZHIQUAN, Internal Medicine
LU GUILIN, Gynaecology and Obstetrics
LU ZHUOREN, Cardiology
MA AIQUN, Internal Medicine
MA XIUPING, Endocrine Medicine
MEI JUN, Physiology
MEN BOYUAN, Epidemics
NAN XUNYI, Urology
PAN CHENGEN, Surgery
PANG ZHIGONG, Analytical Chemistry
PIAN JANPING, Health Care of Children
QIN ZHAOYIN, Surgery
QIU SHUDONG, Histology and Embryology
QU XINZHONG, Gynaecology and Obstetrics
REN HUIMIN, Anatomy
RUAN MEISHENG, Stomatology
SHI JINGSEN, Surgery
SHI WEI, Neurology
SONG TIANBAO, Histology and Embryology
SU MIN, Pathological Anatomy
SUN NAIXUE, Ophthalmology
TAN SHENGSHUN, Dermatology
TAN TINGHUA, Physical Chemistry
WANG BAOQI, Inorganic Chemistry
WANG BINGWEN, Pharmacology
WANG HUI, History of the Communist Party
WANG JINGUI, Physical Education
WANG KUNZHENG, Orthopaedics
WANG QIANG, Stomatology
WANG SHICHEN, Internal Medicine
WANG SHIYING, Stomatology
WANG XUELIANG, Epidemics
WANG ZEZHONG, Radiology
WANG ZIMING, Urology
WU YINGYUN, Respiratory Medicine
XU WENYOU, Pharmacology
YANG DINGYI, Internal Medicine
YANG GUANGFU, Radiological Diagnosis
YE PINGAN, Anaesthesiology
YU BOLANG, Medical Image Diagnosis
YUAN BINGXIANG, Pharmacology
YUE JINSHENG, Infectious Diseases
ZHANG AHUI, Chemistry
ZHANG HUAAN, Pharmacology
ZHANG MINGHUI, Gynaecology and Obstetrics
ZHANG QUANFA, Cardiology
ZHANG SHULIN, Infectious Diseases
ZHANG YONGHAO, Parasitology
ZHANG ZHEFANG, Radiology
ZHAO GENRAN, Anatomy

ZHAO JUNYONG, Biochemistry
ZHAO ZHONGRONG, Radiology
ZHU HONGLIANG, Otorhinolaryngology
ZHU JIAQING, Cardiology

XIAN MINING INSTITUTE

14 Yanta Road, Xian, Shaanxi Province 710054

Telephone: (29) 5262056
Fax: (29) 5262034

Founded 1958
Academic year: September to July

President: Prof. XU ZISHAN
Vice-Presidents: Prof. YANG HENGQING, Prof. CHANG XINTAN, Prof. NING ZHONGLIANG, Prof. ZHANG MIAOFENG
Librarian: Prof. WANG TINGMAN

Library of 420,000 vols
Number of teachers: 472
Number of students: 3,634

Publication: *Journal* (monthly).

HEADS OF DEPARTMENTS

Development of Resources and Management Engineering: Prof. XU JINGCAI
Civil Engineering: Prof. ZHANG FULING
Mechanical Engineering: Prof. GUO WEI
Communications: Prof. LU JIANJUN
Computer Engineering: Prof. GONG SHANGFU
Automation Engineering: YANG SHIXING
Geology: Prof. XIA YUCHENG
Basic Courses: Prof. LI YONG
Social Sciences: WANG ZHIYING
New Materials: Prof. CHOU ANNING

XIAN PETROLEUM INSTITUTE

18 Dian Zi Er Lu, Xian, Shaanxi Province 710061

Telephone: 5253253
Fax: 5263449

Founded 1958
Controlled by National Petroleum Corporation
Language of instruction: English

President: LIN RENZI
Vice-Presidents: XIN XIXIAN, XUE ZHONGTIAN, YANG ZHENGYI
Registrar: WANG XIAOQUAN
Librarian: XIE KUN

Library of 280,000 vols, 2,000 periodicals
Number of teachers: 558
Number of students: 4,000

Publications: *Journal* (natural science and social science editions), *Petroleum Library and Information, Supervision of Petroleum Industry Technology.*

HEADS OF DEPARTMENTS

Petroleum Engineering: ZHONG ZONGMING
Mechanical Engineering: CHEN CHAODA
Chemical Engineering: CHEN MAOTAO
Petroleum Exploration Instruments and Automation: ZHANG LIWEI
Business Management: HU JIAN
Computer Science: WANG JIAHUA

PROFESSORS

CHEN XIAOZHENG, Petroleum Economics
FU XINGSHENG, Earth Strata Slope Angles, Well-logging Methods and Instruments
GAO CHENGTAI, Well-testing
GAO JINIAN, Applied Electric-Hydraulic Control Technology
HU QI, Petroleum Instruments
LI DANG, Mechanism of High-Energy Gas Fracturing
LU JIAO, Petroleum Instruments
PANG JUFENG, Physics and Nuclear Well Logging
SHENG DICHENG, Walking Beam Pumping Units
WANG JIAHUA, Computers
WANG SHIQING, Mechanical Engineering
WANG YIGONG, Management Systems of Petroleum Machinery
WU KUN
WU YIJIONG, Pumping Wells
ZHANG SHAOHUAI, Drilling
ZHANG ZONGMING, Petroleum Tectonics of China
ZHAO GUANGCHANG, Economics and Management

XIAN UNIVERSITY OF ARCHITECTURE AND TECHNOLOGY

13 Yanta Rd, Xian, Shaanxi Province 710055

Telephone: (29) 2202169
Fax: (29) 2224571
E-mail: xudelong@xuat.edu.cn

Founded 1956
Academic year: September to July

President: Prof. XU DELONG
Vice-Presidents: Prof. GUI ZHONGYUE, Prof. GAO MINGZHANG, Prof. DUAN ZHISHAN, Prof. GU QIANG
Graduate School Head: Assoc. Prof. YUAN SHOUQIAN
Librarian: Prof. LIU LIN

Library of 710,000 vols
Number of teachers: 1,002
Number of students: 6,000 (400 postgraduates)

Publications: *Journal* (quarterly), *Study of Higher Education, Science and Technology of Xian University of Architecture and Technology* (quarterly).

HEADS OF COLLEGES AND DEPARTMENTS

College of Architecture: Prof. ZHOU RUOQI
College of Mechanical Engineering: Prof. LIU XINEN
College of Metallurgical Engineering: Prof. WANG HAIBO
Department of Construction Engineering: Assoc. Prof. SU SANQING
Department of Environmental Engineering: Prof. WANG ZHIYING
Department of Engineering Management: Prof. JIN WEIXING
Department of Mining Engineering: Prof. LI RONGFU
Department of Industrial Automation Engineering: Prof. WU WEISHAN
Department of Basic Courses: Prof. HUANG ZEMIN
Department of Humanities and Sociology: Assoc. Prof. ZHANG TONGLE
Department of Materials Science and Engineering: Assoc. Prof. JIANG MINGXUE
Department of Foreign Studies: Assoc. Prof. NIU DEHUA

XIAN UNIVERSITY OF TECHNOLOGY

5 Jinhua Rd (South), Xian, Shaanxi Province 710048

Telephone: (29) 3239700
Fax: (29) 3230026
E-mail: chenzm@xaut.edu.cn

Founded 1949; until 1993, Shaanxi Institute of Mechanical Engineering
Controlled by Ministry of Machine-Building Industry
Academic year: September to July

President: Prof. CHEN ZHIMING
Vice-Presidents: Prof. HUANG YUMEI, Prof. CUI DUWU, Assoc. Prof. WANG XIANYUN, Assoc. Prof. LIAN YONGJIE
Librarian: Prof. LIU FAGUAN

Library of 550,000 vols
Number of teachers: 700
Number of students: 8,000

Publications: *Journal of Xi'an University of Technology, Hydraulic Engineering Asphalt and Impervious Technology.*

DEANS

Faculty of Mechanical Engineering: Prof. GUO JUNJIE
Faculty of Printing and Packaging Engineering: Prof. XU WENCAI
Faculty of Automation Engineering and Information Science: Prof. LIU DING
Faculty of Water Conservancy and Hydroelectric Power: Prof. ZHOU XIAODE
Faculty of Science: Prof. HE QINXIANG
Graduate School: Prof. JING XIAOTIAN
Faculty of Humanities and Social Sciences: Prof. ZHAO YANXIN
Continuing Education College: CHENG LINGHAN
Faculty of Management: Prof. DANG XINHUA
Faculty of Materials Science and Engineering: Prof. YUAN SENG

ATTACHED INSTITUTES

Institute of Growth Equipment for Crystals: Dir LU YANGBIN.
Institute of Cast Iron: Dir Prof. GAN YU.

XIANGTAN UNIVERSITY

Yanggutang, Xiangtan, Hunan Province 411100

Telephone: 24812

Founded 1975
State control
Language of instruction: Chinese

President: Prof. YANG XIANGQUN

Number of teachers: 950
Number of students: 7,600

Publication: *Journal* (social science and natural science editions).

XIDIAN UNIVERSITY

2 Tai Bai Rd, Xian, Shaanxi

Telephone: (29) 8228200
Telex: 70034
Fax: (29) 5262281

Founded 1931

President: Prof. LIANG CHANGHONG
Vice-Presidents: CAO TIANSHUN, XIE WEIXIN, CHEN BISEN, HAO YUE, LI LI
Head of Graduate Department: XIE WEIXIN
Librarian: YANG QIDONG

Library of 917,000 vols
Number of teachers: 1,571
Number of students: 12,462 (incl. 705 postgraduates)

Publication: *Journal.*

HEADS OF DEPARTMENTS

Communication Engineering: LIU ZENGJI
Electronic Engineering: YANG WANHAI
Computers: WANG BAOSHU
Electronic Mechanics: DUAN BAOYAN
Technical Physics: AN YUYING
Microwave Telecommunications Engineering: GUAN GUOHUA
Economics and Management: XU GUOHUA
Applied Mathematics: LIU SANYANG
Foreign Languages: QIN DIHUI
Social Sciences: ZHAO BOFEI
Physics: GE DEBIAO
Detection and Instruments: ZHANG PING

ATTACHED RESEARCH INSTITUTES

Institute of Information Science: Dir LI JIANDONG.

Institute of Electronic Engineering: Dir WU SHUNJUN.

Institute of Antenna Research: Dir LIU QIZHONG.

Institute of Circuit-Aided Design: Dir LI YUSHAN.

Institute of Software Engineering: Dir JIN YIMIN.
Institute of Microelectronics: Dir ZHANG YIMEN.
Centre for Antenna Development: Dir XIAO LIANGYONG.
Centre for Computer Telemechanics: Dir YE MING.

XINJIANG ENGINEERING INSTITUTE

21 Youhao Rd, Urumqi, Xinjiang Uygur Autonomous Region 830008
Telephone: 41911
Founded 1953
Rector: SUN DESHUI
Vice-Rectors: JIN MINGSHAN, HUJIHAN HAKAMOFU, ZHANG XIAN
Librarian: DING ZHAOMING
Library of 215,000 vols
Number of teachers: 566
Number of students: 2,826 (incl. 27 postgraduates)
Publications: *Journal* (Science and Engineering edn, Literary Art edn).

DEANS

Geology: (vacant)
Electrical Engineering: LOU GUOZHONG
Mechanical Engineering: WANG YU
Construction Engineering: (vacant)
Chemical Engineering: LIOU CHUNMING
Textile Engineering: CHEN HONGKUN
Preparatory Courses: KAXIMOFU
Basic Courses: LIANG CHENGCHAO
Basic Technical Courses: WANG WEIGUO
Marxist Theory Teaching and Research Section: WAHAPU HEIBIR
Physical Culture Teaching and Research Section: (vacant)

YANTAI UNIVERSITY

Yantai, Shandong Province 264005
Telephone: (535) 6888995
Fax: (535) 6888801
Founded 1984
State control
Languages of instruction: Chinese and English
President: ZHANG JIANYI
Registrar: LU XUEMING
Librarian: SUN JILIANG
Library of 40,000 vols
Number of teachers: 450
Number of students: 3,839
Publication: *Journal.*

Degree programmes in Chinese language and literature, foreign languages and literature, law, electronics and computing, biochemical engineering, chemical engineering, machine design and manufacture, architecture, industrial and civil engineering, applied mathematics, applied physics, finance and economics and management, international business, fisheries industry, physical education.

YUNNAN FINANCE AND TRADE INSTITUTE

Shangmacun, North Suburb, Kunming, Yunnan 650221
Telephone: 51723
Founded 1981
President: Prof. WU JIANAN
Vice-Presidents: Assoc. Prof. MA GUANGBI, WU TANXUE, YANG LIZHI
Registrar: ZHOU ANFAN
Librarian: LIU SHUNDE
Library of 280,000 vols
Number of teachers: 289
Number of students: 2,620
Publications: *Journal*, *Foreign Economic Theory and Administration.*

HEADS OF DEPARTMENTS

Banking: Assoc. Prof. ZHOU HAOWEN
Finance: Assoc. Prof. DING ZHI
Planning and Statistics: Assoc. Prof. XU SHULONG
Accounting: Assoc. Prof. MO GUOJIANG
Business Administrative Economics: Assoc. Prof. ZHAO GAN
Industrial Economics: WANG JIANG

YUNNAN INSTITUTE FOR THE NATIONALITIES

420 Huanchengbei Rd, Kunming, Yunnan 650031
Telephone: (871) 5154308
Fax (871) 5154304
Founded 1951
State control
Languages of instruction: Chinese, English, Thai, Burmese and some minority languages
Academic year: September to July
President: ZHAO JIAWEN
Vice-Presidents: HUANG HUIKUN, PU TONGJIN, ZHAO JUNSHAN
Chief Administrative Officer: DI HUAYI
Librarian: DUAN SHENG'OU
Library of 430,000 vols, 28 special collections
Number of teachers: 385
Number of students: 4,969
Publication: *Journal* (Social Sciences edition and Science edition, quarterly).

HEADS OF DEPARTMENTS

Chinese Language and Literature: LI SHUREN
Minority Languages and Literature: LU YI
Foreign Languages and Literature: LI DANHE
History: XIE BINGKUN
Social Science: ZHANG JIANGUO
Economics and Management: SUN GUOCHANG
Mathematics: CHEN NAIXIN
Physics: TAO ZHIWEI
Chemistry: DONG XUECHANG
Ethnic Studies Centre: HUANG HUIKUN
In-Service Training: ZHANG YOUJING
Preparatory: MA QINGLIN
Minority Arts: YANG JUN

YUNNAN UNIVERSITY

52 N. Cuihu Rd, Kunming, Yunnan 650091
Telephone: (871) 5148533
Telex 3164124
Fax (871) 5153832
Founded 1923
State control
Academic year: September to July
President: Prof. ZHU WEIHUA
Vice-Presidents: Prof. XU KEMIN, Prof. WU SONG, Prof. HONG PINJIE, Prof. LIN CHAOMIN, Assoc. Prof. FANG YINGXIANG
Registrar: Prof. WU SONG
Librarian: Prof. LI ZIXIAN
Library of 1,170,000 vols
Number of teachers: 888
Number of students: 7,160

PROFESSORS

Department of Chinese Language and Literature:
- JIN DANYUAN, Aesthetics
- LI CONGZONG, Modern Literature
- QIAO CHUANZAO, Writing
- SUN QINHUA, Literature Survey
- WANG KAILIAN, Classical Chinese Language
- YANG ZHENKUN, Modern Literature
- ZHANG FUSAN, Ethnic and Folk Literature
- ZHANG GUOQING, Classical Chinese Writings
- ZHAO HAORU, Classical Literature

Department of History:
- LI JIABIN, Ancient World History
- LI YAN, History of the Chinese Feudal Economy
- LIN CHAOMIN, Ethnic History
- TANG MIN, Modern World History
- XU KANGMING, Modern World History
- ZHU HUIRONG, Historical Geography

Department of Archives:
- YOU ZHONG, History of Chinese Minorities
- ZHANG XINCHANG, History and Archives of Chinese Minorities

Department of Politics and Administration:
- DONG JIMEI, Philosophy
- SHI SHILONG, Chinese Revolutionary History
- WANG YONGKANG, History of Western Philosophy
- WU SONG, Philosophy

Department of Law:
- CHEN ZIGUO, Civil Law
- XU ZHISHAN, Constitution

Department of Economics:
- HONG HUAXI, Economics

Department of International Trade:
- LIU XUEYU, History of Foreign Economies
- ZHU YINGGENG, Ideological History of Western Economics

Department of Mathematical Statistics:
- SUN WENSHUANG, Mathematical Statistics
- WANG ZHONGHUA, Mathematical Statistics

Department of Foreign Languages and Literature:
- GONG NINGZHU, Lao, Vietnamese
- LI JIGANG, English
- ZHANG XINHE, English

Department of Mathematics:
- DAI ZHENGDE, Basic Mathematics
- GUO YUQI, Algebra
- HE XIANGFAN, Mathematical Model
- LIAO HONGZHI, Calculating Mathematics
- LUI ZHENGRONG, Differential Equations
- QU CHAOCHUN, Basic Mathematics
- WANG GUODONG, Matrix, Generalized Inverses
- YANG GUANGJUN, Basic Mathematics
- ZHANG SHENG, Applied Mathematics
- ZHAO XIAOHUA, Differential Equations

Department of Computer Science:
- LIU WEIYI, Fuzzy Database Theory
- TIAN ZHILIANG, Management Operating Systems

Department of Physics:
- BAO DEXIU, Applied Physics
- CHENG ERGANG, Electronic and Ionic Physics
- CHENG XUEQUAN, Semiconductors
- CHENG ZHONGXIAN, Theory of Nonlinear Dynamic Systems
- HU WENGUO, Electronic and Ionic Physics
- JIANG SHIJI, Thin Film Physics
- LIN LIZHONG, Optics
- MU CHONGJUN, Electronic and Ionic Physics
- PENG KUANGDING, Statistics of Physics
- PENG SHOULI, Theoretical Physics
- TIAN ZIHUA, Surface Physics
- WU XINGHUI, Semiconductors
- ZHANG SHIJIE, Theoretical Physics
- ZHAO SHUSONG, High-Energy Physics
- ZHOU WENDE, Cosmic Physics

Department of Telecommunications:
- LI TAILING, Electrocircuits and Communication
- LI TIANMU, Electronics and Information Systems
- ZHENG WENXING, Correspondence

Department of Earth Sciences:
- BU YUKANG, Synoptic Dynamics
- XIE YINGQI, Atmospheric Science, Mathematics

Department of Chemistry:

DAI SHUSHAN, Physics and Chemistry
HE SENQUAN, Organic Chemistry
HONG PINJIE, Microwave Plasma
LI LIANG, Organic Chemistry
LIU FUCHU, Organic Chemistry
LIU SONGYU, Analytical Chemistry
TAO YUANQI, Quantum Organic Chemistry
WANG CHANGYI, Organic Chemistry
XU QIHENG, Analytical Chemistry
YANG CHUNJIN, Inorganic Chemistry
YANG PIPENG, Organic Chemistry
YIN JIANGUO, Inorganic Chemistry

Department of Biology:

HU ZHIHAO, Botany
HUANG SUHUA, Botany
LI QIREN, Plant Cell Engineering
LIU XINHUA, Soil Ecology
ZAN RUIGUANG, Cell Biology
ZHANG ZHUO, Microbiology
ZUO YANGXIAN, Invertebrates

International Modern Design Art College:

HUANG GUOQIANG, Chinese Painting and Design

AFFILIATED RESEARCH INSTITUTES

Institute of Ecology and Botany
Yunnan Institute of Microbiology
Institute of Cosmogony
Institute of Southeast Asian Studies
Institute of Demography
Institute of Electronic Information and Technology
Institute of Applied Chemistry
Institute of Bioresource Development
Yunnan Institute of Applied Mathematics
Institute of Applied Statistics
Transducer and Technology Research Centre
Institute of Applied Physics
Institute of Physics
Institute of New Materials
Institute of Synthesis Chemistry
Institute of Economic Reform and Development
Institute of Tourism
Institute of Ethnic Law
Institute of the History of Southwest Frontier Ethnic Groups
Institute of Ancient Books of the Southwest
East Asia Institute of Visual Anthropology

ZHEJIANG AGRICULTURAL UNIVERSITY

268 Kaixuan Road, Hangzhou, Zhejiang 310029

Telephone: 6041733
Fax: 6049815

Founded 1910
State control
Languages of instruction: Chinese and English
Academic year: September to August

President: Prof. CHENG JIAAN
Vice-Presidents: TONG SHAOSU, ZHU JUN, CAI LISAN, HUANG ZUHUI, ZHAO YUN
Registrar: LOU CHENGFU
Librarian: XU TONG

Library of 78,000 vols
Number of teachers: 800
Number of students: 5,000 (incl. graduate and overseas students)

Publication: *Acta* (quarterly).

DEANS

College of Economics and Trade: HUANG ZUHUI
College of Animal Science: LIU JIANXIN
College of Agricultural Engineering: YING YIBIN
College of Environment and Resources: HUANG CHANGYONG
College of China Town and Village Enterprise: CHENG WENXIANG
College of Adult Education: HE YONGSHENG
College of Southeast Land Management: WU CIFANG

HEADS OF DEPARTMENTS

Agronomy: ZHANG GUOPING
Plant Protection: ZHENG ZHONG
Horticulture: CHEN LIGENG
Sericulture: LU XINGMENG
Tea Science: LIANG YUERONG
Food Science and Technology: HE GUOQING

ATTACHED INSTITUTES

Institute of Nuclear Agricultural Sciences: Dir SUN JINHE
Institute of Biotechnology: Dir LI DEBAO
Institute of Pesticide Environmental Toxicology: Dir FAN DEFANG
Institute of Applied Fungi: Dir JIANG JIAYU
Institute of Feed Science: Dir XU ZIRONG
Institute of Tea Science: Dir LIANG YUERONG
Institute of Vegetable Science: Dir ZENG GUANGWEN
Institute of Applied Insects: Dir CHEN JIAAN
Institute of Genetics and Plant Breeding: XUE QINGZHONG
Institute of Agro-chemistry: Dir TAO QUINNAN
Institute of Soil and Soil Fertility Science: Dir HUANG CHANGYONG
Institute of Environmental Science: Dir YE ZHAOJIE
Institute of Agroecology: Dir WANG ZHAOQIAN
Institute of Agricultural Remote Sensing and Information Systems Application: Dir WANG RENCHAO
Institute of Agricultural Bio-environmental Control Engineering: Dir CUI SHAORONG
Institute of Biochemistry: Dir ZHANG YAOZHOU
Institute of Rural Economy: Dir YUAN FEI

ZHEJIANG UNIVERSITY

20 Yugu Road, Hangzhou 310027, Zhejiang Province

Telephone: (571) 7951583
Fax: (571) 7951358
E-mail: ipo@sun.zju.edu.cn

Founded 1897
State control
Language of instruction: Chinese and (for foreign students) English
Academic year: September to June

President: Prof. PAN YUNHE
Vice-Presidents: Prof. HU JIANXIONG, Prof. GU WEIKANG, Prof. WU SHIMING, Prof. HUANG DAREN, Prof. FENG PEIEN, Prof. NI MINGJIANG, Prof. BU FANXIAO
Director of International Programmes Office: Prof. QIU JIZHEN
Librarian: Prof. CAO CHUNAN

Number of teachers: 1,792
Number of students: 18,712 (including 5,329 part-time)

Publications: *University Journal of Natural Science* (every 2 months), *University Journal of Social Science* (quarterly), *Industrial Engineering and Engineering Management* (quarterly), *Chemical Reaction Engineering and Technology* (quarterly), *Applied Mathematics, Chinese Universities Journal* (quarterly), *Chemical Engineering in Chinese Universities* (quarterly), *Materials Science and Engineering* (quarterly), *The World of Light* (quarterly).

HEADS OF DEPARTMENTS

Mathematics: Prof. CHEN SHUPING
Physics: Prof. BAO SHINING
Chemistry: Prof. XU ZHUDE
Polymer Science and Engineering: Prof. FENG LINXIAN
Mechanics: Prof. XU JINQUAN
Electrical Engineering: Prof. XU DEHONG
Chemical Engineering and Technology: Prof. LI BOGENG
Chemical Machinery: Prof. TONG SHUIGUANG
Biochemical Engineering: Prof. YAO SHANJING
Environmental Science and Engineering: Prof. WANG DAHUI
Control Science and Engineering: Prof. LI PING
Optoelectronic Information Engineering: Prof. LU ZHUKANG
Instrumentation Science and Engineering: Prof. ZHENG XIAOXIANG
Management Engineering: Prof. XIANG BAOHUA
Civil Engineering: Prof. GONG XIAONAN
Information and Electronic Engineering: Prof. QIU PEILIANG
Mechanical Engineering: Prof. TAN JIANRONG
Computer Science and Engineering: Prof. CHEN CHUN
Energy Engineering: Prof. YAN JIANHUA
Materials Science and Engineering: Prof. SHEN JINLIN
Earth Science: Prof. ZHU GUOQIANG
Architecture: Prof. SHEN JIHUANG
Life Science and Biomedical Engineering: Prof. ZHENG XIAOXIANG
Biological Science and Technology: Prof. SHEN GONGYU
Business Management and Marketing: Prof. XU JINFA
Finance and Accounting: Prof. ZHENG MINGCHUAN
Political Science: Assoc. Prof. YU XIAOFENG
Philosophy and Sociology: Assoc. Prof. SHENG XIAOMING
Economics and Finance: Prof. JIN XUEJUN
Foreign Languages: Prof. SHAO YONGZHEN
Chinese Language and Literature: Prof. XU DAI
International Trade: Prof. ZHANG XIAODI
International Economic Law: Prof. LU JIANPING

ZHEJIANG UNIVERSITY OF TECHNOLOGY

District 6, Zhaohui Xincun, Hangzhou, Zhejiang 310032

Telephone: (571) 8320114
Fax: (571) 5237605
E-mail: zgd@pub.zjpta.net.cn

Founded 1953
Academic year: September to January, March to July

President: Prof. WU TIANZU
Vice-Presidents: GE ZHONGHUA, ZHANG LIBIN, HAN YIXIANG
Librarian: Prof. CHANG JIAQIANG

Library of 760,000 vols
Number of teachers: 1,243
Number of students: 10,000

Publication: *Journal* (quarterly).

HEADS OF DEPARTMENTS

Mechanical Engineering: Prof. JIA GAOSHUN
Chemical Engineering: Prof. HU WEIXIAO
Electrical and Computer Engineering: Prof. YANG YANG
Architecture and Civil Engineering: Prof. FAN LIANGBEN
Light Industrial Engineering: Prof. BOYANG NAN
Business Administration: Prof. WU TIANZU
Vocational and Technical Education: Prof. SHEN ZHONGWEI

ZHONGSHAN (SUN YATSEN) UNIVERSITY

135 Xingang Rd, Guangzhou, Guangdong 510275

Telephone: (20) 84186300
Fax: (20) 84189173
E-mail: adpo@zsu.edu.cn

Founded 1924
State control
Academic year: September to July

President: WANG XUNSHANG
Vice-Presidents: LI CHONG, GUO SIGAN, WU ZENGSHENG, XU YUANTONG, LIU MEINAN
Librarian: ZHAO YANQUN

Library of 2,758,000 vols
Number of teachers: 1,685
Number of students: 16,113

Publications: *Journal* (Social Science, Natural Science edns, quarterly), *Journal of the Graduates*, *South China Population*, *Pearl River Delta Economy*.

HEADS OF SCHOOL

Graduate School: Prof. WANG XUNZHANG
College of Continuing Education: Prof. LUO WEIYIN
School of Humanities: Prof. ZENG XIANTONG
School of Chemistry and Chemical Engineering: Prof. JI LIANGNAN
School of Earth and Environmental Sciences: Prof. LUO HUIBANG
School of Foreign Languages: Prof. WU ZHITONG
School of Law and Political Science: Prof. WANG LEFU
School of Life Sciences: Prof. ZHOU CHANGQING
School of Management: Prof. GU BAOYAN
School of Information Science and Technology: Prof. LI ZHIXIAN
School of Physical Science and Engineering: Prof. ZHOU JIANYING
School of Mathematics and Computational Science: Prof. DENG DONGGAO
Lingnan (University) College: Prof. SU YUAN

HEADS OF DEPARTMENT

School of Humanities:
- Chinese Language and Literature: Prof. ZENG XIANTONG
- History: Prof. QIU JIE
- Anthropology: Assoc. Prof. SU JIANLING
- Philosophy: Prof. ZHANG HAISHAN

School of Chemistry and Chemical Engineering:
- Chemistry: Prof. ZHU XIHAI
- Applied Chemistry: Prof. DENG QINYING
- Polymer and Material Science: Prof. MAI KANCHENG

School of Earth and Environmental Sciences:
- Urban Planning: Assoc. Prof. CHEN JUNHE
- Earth Science: Prof. CHEN GUONENG
- Atmospheric Science: Prof. FAN SHAOJIA
- Environmental Science: Prof. WANG JINSAN

School of Foreign Languages:
- English: Prof. HUANG JIAYOU
- Foreign Languages: Prof. LIANG QIYAN
- College English: Prof. GUO SHE

School of Law and Political Science:
- Law: Prof. WANG ZHONGXING
- Political Science and Public Administration: Prof. WANG LEFU
- Sociology: Prof. CAI HE

School of Life Sciences:
- Biology and Biotechnology: Prof. HE JIANGUO
- Biochemistry: Prof. XU ANLONG
- Pharmacy: Prof. XU SHIBO

School of Management:
- Management: Prof. LI XINCHUN
- Accounting and Auditing: Prof. TAN JINSONG
- Tourism and Hotel Management: Prof. ZHAN JUNCHUAN

School of Information Science and Technology:
- Computer Science: Prof. LI SHIXIAN
- Radio-electronics: Prof. YU SHUNZHENG
- Information Management: Prof. CHENG HUANWEN

School of Physical Science and Engineering Technology:
- Physics: Prof. WU SHENSHANG
- Applied Mechanics and Engineering: Prof. SUN MINGGUANG

School of Mathematics and Computational Science:
- Mathematics: Prof. ZHAO YI
- Scientific Computation and Computer Application: Prof. LUO XIAONAN

Lingnan (University) College:
- Economics: Prof. DONG XIAOLIN
- International Business: Assoc. Prof. YU SHIYOU
- Public Finance and Taxation: Assoc. Prof. YANG WEIHUA
- Finance: Assoc. Prof. LU JUN
- Economic Management: Assoc. Prof. WANG JUN

HONG KONG

Learned Societies

GENERAL

Royal Asiatic Society, Hong Kong Branch: GPO Box 3864, Hong Kong; f. 1847, re-established 1959; for the encouragement of history, the arts, science and literature in relation to Asia, particularly Hong Kong; lectures and social activities; 500 mems, 150 overseas mems; library of 2,200 vols; Pres. Dr DAN WATERS; Hon. Sec. Dr PETER BARKER; publ. *Journal* (1 a year).

BIBLIOGRAPHY, LIBRARY SCIENCE AND MUSEOLOGY

Hong Kong Library Association: GPO Box 10095, Hong Kong; f. 1958; 520 mems; Pres. ALIMA TUET; Hon. Sec. LOUISA LAM; publs *Journal* (irregular), *Newsletter* (4 a year).

ECONOMICS, LAW AND POLITICS

Hong Kong Management Association: 14/F, Fairmont House, 8 Cotton Tree Drive, Central, Hong Kong; tel. 25266516; fax 28684387; f. 1960; management training courses, management consultancy services, library information, seminars, forums, awards and competitions; Chair. Hon. DAVID K. P. LI; Dir-Gen. ELIZABETH SHING; publ. *The Hong Kong Manager* (4 a year).

Hong Kong Society of Accountants: Belgian Bank Tower (17th Floor), 77 – 79 Gloucester Road, Wanchai, Hong Kong; tel. 2529-9271; fax 2865-6603; f. 1973; Pres. T. BRIAN STEVENSON; Exec. Dir and Registrar LOUIS L. W. WONG; publ. *The Hong Kong Accountant*.

Law Society of Hong Kong: 1403–1413 Swire House, 11 Chater Rd, Hong Kong; tel. 28460500; fax 28450387; f. 1907; 4,200 mems; Pres. ANTHONY CHOW; publ. *Hong Kong Lawyer*.

LANGUAGE AND LITERATURE

Hong Kong Chinese PEN Centre: POB 78521, Mongkok Post Office, Kowloon, Hong Kong; f. 1955; 92 mems; library of 1,600 vols; Pres. CHU CHIH-TAI; Sec. WILLIAM HSU; publ. *PEN News* (weekly in Chinese).

MEDICINE

Hong Kong Medical Association: 5/f, 15 Hennessy Rd, Hong Kong; tel. 28650943; fax 25278285; e-mail hkma@hkma.org; f. 1920 to promote the welfare and protect the lawful interests of the medical profession, to promote co-operation with national and international medical societies, and to work for the advancement of medical science; 4,800 mems; Pres. Dr LEE KIN HUNG; Hon. Sec. Dr KO WING MAN; publs *HKMA News* (monthly), *Journal* (quarterly).

Research Institutes

NATURAL SCIENCES

Physical Sciences

Hong Kong Observatory: 134A Nathan Rd, Kowloon, Hong Kong; tel. 29268200; fax 23119448; e-mail mailbox@hko.gcn.gov.hk; f. 1883; govt dept which operates weather forecasting, cyclone warning and other meteorological and geophysical services; library of 40,000 vols; Dir Dr H. K. LAM; publs *Hong Kong Observatory Almanac*, *Hong Kong Observatory Calendar*, *Hong Kong Tide Tables* (annually), *Daily Weather Chart*, *Marine Climatological Summaries* (annually), *Summary of Meteorological Observations in Hong Kong* (annually), *Tropical Cyclones* (annually), *Summary Charts for the South China Seas* (annually), *Monthly Weather Summary*, *Occasional Papers* (irregular), *Technical Memoirs* (irregular), *Technical Notes* (irregular), *Technical Notes (Local)* (irregular).

Libraries and Archives

Hong Kong

Chinese University of Hong Kong University Library System: Shatin, New Territories, Hong Kong; f. 1963; 6 branch libraries: Chung Chi College Library, f. 1951; New Asia College Library, f. 1949; United College Library, f. 1956; Li Ping Medical Library, f. 1980; American Studies Library, f. 1993; Architecture Library, f. 1994; 1,359,000 vols in Oriental and Western languages, 9,197 current periodicals; special collections: rare Chinese books, Korean 13th-century *Tripitaka* printed from wood blocks, modern Chinese drama comprising *c.* 1,850 titles; collection of 56 oracle bones; University Librarian MICHAEL M. LEE.

Hong Kong Polytechnic University Pao Yue-Kong Library: Kowloon, Hong Kong; tel. 2766-6857; fax 2765-8274; f. 1972; 900,000 vols; over 10,000 current periodicals, a comprehensive collection of standards, a collection of audio-visual materials, a newspaper clippings collection and a slide collection; CD-ROM Centre; Librarian BARRY L. BURTON; publ. *Directory of Professional Associations and Learned Societies in Hong Kong*.

Provisional Regional Council Public Libraries: 38 Sai Lau Kok Rd, 6/F, Tsuen Wan Central Library, Tsuen Wan, Hong Kong; tel. 2920-3068; fax 2415-8211; three central libraries, 22 brs and 4 mobile libraries; joint bookstock of 754,139 vols in English, 1,694,857 vols in Chinese, 1,752 titles of current newspapers and periodicals, 177,420 items of audiovisual material; reference, adult and junior libraries, newspapers and periodicals reading rooms, study rooms, audio-visual services, extension activities; Asia Development Bank depository colln; Chief Librarian ALIMA TUET.

Public Records Office of Hong Kong: 2 Murray Rd, Central, Hong Kong; tel. 2526-0031; fax 2845-4107; f. 1972; 22,000 Hong Kong Government publs; newspapers collection; photographs collection; map collection; Archivist SIMON F. K. CHU.

Sun Yat-Sen Library: 172 – 174 Boundary St, Kowloon, Hong Kong; f. 1953; public library; 140,190 vols; Dir K. FUNG; Librarian Mrs MEGIE M. L. TONG.

University of Hong Kong Libraries: Pokfulam Rd, Hong Kong; tel. 28597000; fax 28589420; e-mail libadmin@hkucc.hku.hk; f. 1911; 980,000 vols in Western languages, including the Hong Kong and Morrison collections, 20,000 current periodicals, 29,000 audiovisual items, 26,000 reels of microfilm, 305,000 microfiches, 350 CD-ROM bibliographies; Librarian Dr LAI-BING KAN.

Urban Council Public Libraries: City Hall High Block, Sixth Floor, Central, Hong Kong; tel. (852) 2921-2688; fax (852) 2877-2641; e-mail ucpl@ucplft.uc.gov.hk; f. 1962; 38 static libraries, 4 mobile libraries; joint bookstock of 2,209,000 vols in Chinese, 973,000 vols in English, 8,665 titles of current newspapers and periodicals, 219,000 items of audiovisual material; reference, adult and junior libraries; local collection, Hok Hoi and Kotewall Collections of Chinese materials; depository library for ADB, ILO, UN, UNESCO, WB, WFP and WTO publications; Chief Librarian MICHAEL MAK.

Museums and Art Galleries

Hong Kong

Hong Kong Museum of Art: 10 Salisbury Rd, Tsim Sha Tsui, Kowloon, Hong Kong; tel. 2734-2167; fax 2723-7666; f. 1962; Chinese antiquities, incl. the Henry Yeung collection; historical paintings, prints and drawings of Hong Kong, Macao and China, incl. Chater, Sayer, Law and Ho Tung collections; contemporary works by local artists; Chinese paintings and calligraphy, incl. the Xubaizhai Collection; Chief Curator GERARD C. C. TSANG.

Hong Kong Museum of History: Kowloon Park, Haiphong Rd, Tsimshatsui, Hong Kong; tel. 2367-1124; fax 2312-0962; f. 1975; archaeology, ethnography, natural history and local history of Hong Kong, including central repository of archaeological finds from Hong Kong; Chinese fishing junk models; historical photographs and documents; postal history and numismatics collection; active excavations, education services and field work; branches at Lei Cheng Uk Han Tomb and Law Uk Folk Museum; Chief Curator JOSEPH S. P. TING; publ. *Newsletter* (quarterly), exhibition handbooks.

Hong Kong Science Museum: 2 Science Museum Rd, Tsim Sha Tsui East, Kowloon, Hong Kong; tel. 2732-3201; fax 2311-2248; e-mail hkscm1@usd.gov.hk; f. 1991; Chief Curator LINCOLN W. L. TSUI; publ. *Newsletter* (quarterly).

Hong Kong Space Museum: 10 Salisbury Rd, Tsim Sha Tsui, Kowloon, Hong Kong; tel. 2734-2722; fax 23115804; f. 1980 to promote interest in astronomy and related sciences by exhibitions, lectures, film shows, etc; *c.* 100 staff; library of 1,700 vols, also films and videos; Curator CHEE-KUEN YIP; publs *Newsletter* (quarterly), *Astrocalendar* (annually).

Universities

CHINESE UNIVERSITY OF HONG KONG

Shatin, New Territories, Hong Kong

Telephone: 2609-7000
Fax: 2603-5544

Founded 1963
Chung Chi College, New Asia College, United College and Shaw College are constituent colleges of the University (see below)
Languages of instruction: Chinese and English
Academic year: August to July
The University is controlled by a self-governing corporation

Chancellor: Chief Executive of the Hong Kong Special Administrative Region
Chairman of Council: H. C. LEE
Vice-Chancellor: ARTHUR K. C. LI
Pro-Vice-Chancellors: A. Y. C. KING, PAK-WAI LIU, KENNETH YOUNG
Treasurer: RAYMOND P. L. KWOK
Secretary: JACOB S. K. LEUNG
Registrar: RICHARD M. W. HO
Librarian: MICHAEL M. LEE

Library: see Libraries
Number of teachers: 1,016
Number of students: 10,282 full-time, 2,061 part-time

Publications: *University Calendar* (annually), *University Student Handbooks* (annually), *University Bulletin* (2 a year), *CUHK Newsletter* (fortnightly), *Annual Report, Research Projects and Publications* (annually).

DEANS

Graduate School: KENNETH YOUNG
Faculty of Arts: H. H. HO
Faculty of Business Administration: K. H. LEE
Faculty of Education: STEPHEN Y. P. CHUNG
Faculty of Engineering: P. C. CHING
Faculty of Medicine: JOSEPH C. K. LEE
Faculty of Science: O. W. LAU
Faculty of Social Science: KENNETH K. L. CHAU

PROFESSORS

BOND, M. H., Psychology
CHAN, H. L., History
CHAN, K. H., Accountancy
CHAN, K. M., Orthopaedics and Traumatology
CHANG, A. M. Z., Obstetrics and Gynaecology
CHAU, K. K. L., Social Work
CHOW, M. S. S., Pharmacy
CHUNG, S. S. C., Surgery
COCKRAM, C. S., Medicine and Therapeutics (Medicine)
CRITCHLEY, J. A. J. H., Medicine and Therapeutics (Clinical Pharmacology)
DICKINSON, J. A., Community and Family Medicine (Family Medicine)
GOSLING, J. A., Anatomy
HAW, G. I. M., Accountancy
HJELM, N. M., Chemical Pathology
HSU, C. Y., History
INGENE, C. A., Marketing
JIN, S. S. H., Translation
JOHNSON, P. J., Clinical Oncology
JONES, R. L., Pharmacology
KAO, M. C., Fine Arts
KING, A. Y. C., Sociology
KING, W. W. K., Surgery (Head, Neck and Reconstructive)
KONG, Y. C., Biochemistry
KUAN, H. C., Government and Public Administration
LAM, J. Y. L., Educational Administration and Policy
LANG, L. H. P., Finance
LAU, J. W. Y., Surgery
LAU, K. S., Mathematics
LAU, L. W. M., Physics (Materials Science)
LAU, S. K., Sociology
LEE, C. Y., Biochemistry
LEE, J. C. K., Anatomical and Cellular Pathology (Morbid Anatomy)
LEE, K. H., Marketing
LEE, R. P. L., Sociology
LEE, S. H., Community and Family Medicine (Community Medicine)
LEE, S. Y., Statistics
LEE, T. T., Information Engineering
LEONG, A. S. Y., Anatomical and Cellular Pathology
LEUNG, P. C., Orthopaedics and Traumatology
LEUNG, Y., Geography
LI, A. K. C., Surgery
LI, R. S. Y., Information Engineering
LIU, P. W., Economics
LIU, S. H., Philosophy
MACKENZIE, A. E., Nursing (Clinical Nursing)
MAK, T. C. W., Chemistry
METREWELI, C., Diagnostic Radiology and Organ Imaging
MUN, K. C., International Business Marketing (Marketing)
PARKIN, A. T. L., English
RAYMOND, K., Pharmacy
SUN, S. S. M., Biology
TO, C. Y., Community and Family Medicine (Education)
TSO, M. O. M., Ophthalmology and Visual Science
VAN HASSELT, C. A., Surgery (Otorhinolaryngology)
WAH, B. W. S., Computer Science and Engineering
WENG, B. S. J., Government and Public Administration
WILSON, I. H., Electronic Engineering
WING, O., Information Engineering
WONG, C. K., Computer Science and Engineering
WONG, H. N. C., Chemistry
WONG, P. Y. D., Physiology
WONG, W. S., Information Engineering
WOO, J., Medicine and Therapeutics (Medicine)
WU, H. I., Chinese Language and Literature
YANG, C. N., Distinguished Professor at Large
YAO, D. D., Systems Engineering and Engineering Management
YAU, S. T., Mathematics
YEUNG, Y. M., Geography
YOUNG, K., Physics
YOUNG, L., Finance

YU, E. S. H., Decision Sciences and Managerial Economics
YUM, P. T. S., Information Engineering

CONSTITUENT COLLEGES

Chung Chi College: Shatin, Hong Kong; f. 1951; 285 teachers (full-time); 2,256 students (full-time); College Head RANCE P. L. LEE.

New Asia College: Shatin, Hong Kong; f. 1949; 258 teachers (full-time); 2,258 students (full-time); College Head P. C. LEUNG.

United College: Shatin, Hong Kong; f. 1956; 240 teachers (full-time); 2,255 students (full-time); College Head C. Y. LEE.

Shaw College: Shatin, Hong Kong; f. 1988; 230 teachers (full-time); 2,233 students (full-time); College Head Y. M. YEUNG.

ATTACHED INSTITUTES

Graduate School: f. 1966; 2,873 students; Dean KENNETH YOUNG.

School of Continuing Studies: f. 1965; Dir C. C. WAN.

Institute of Chinese Studies: f. 1967; Dir F. C. CHEN.

Research Institute for the Humanities: f. 1991; Dir Y. S. LEUNG.

Asia-Pacific Institute of Business: f. 1990; Exec Dir L. YOUNG.

Hong Kong Institute of Educational Research: f. 1993; Dir LESLIE N. K. LO.

Hong Kong Cancer Institute: f. 1990; Dir P. J. JOHNSON.

Institute of Science and Technology: f. 1965; Dir T. C. W. MAK.

Institute of Mathematical Sciences: f. 1993; Dirs C. N. YANG, S. T. YAU.

Hong Kong Institute of Asia-Pacific Studies: f. 1990; Dir Y. M. YEUNG.

Hong Kong Institute of Biotechnology: f. 1988; Dir A. Y. CHANG.

CITY UNIVERSITY OF HONG KONG

83 Tat Chee Ave, Kowloon, Hong Kong
Telephone: 2788-7654
Fax: 2788-1167

Founded 1984 as City Polytechnic of Hong Kong; present name 1995
Autonomous control, financed by the University Grants Cttee
Language of instruction: English
Academic year: September to August

President: Prof. H. K. CHANG
Vice-Presidents: Prof. P. S. CHUNG, JOHN DOCKERILL, Prof. EDMOND KO, Prof. Y. S. WONG, JAMES NG
Registrar: Dr J. T. YU
Librarian: Dr P. W. T. POON

Library of 439,000 vols
Number of teachers: 790 full-time, 237 part-time
Number of students: 11,381 full-time, 6,473 part-time

Publications: *Annual Report, Research Report, Annual Report on Liaison with Institutions in China, Linkage* (monthly), *Bulletin* (3 a year).

DEANS AND PRINCIPAL

Faculty of Business: Prof. RICHARD Y. K. HO
Faculty of Humanities and Social Sciences: Dr JULIA P. W. TAO
Faculty of Science and Technology: Prof. RODERICK WONG
College of Higher Vocational Studies: Prof. H. K. WONG
School of Graduate Studies: Prof. P. S. CHUNG
School of Creative Media: (vacant)
School of Law: (vacant)

HEADS OF DEPARTMENTS/DIVISIONS

Faculty of Business:
- Accountancy: J. S. L. TSUI
- Management Sciences: Dr S. K. TSE
- Management: Dr KWAKU ATUAHENE-GIMA
- Marketing: Dr J. ZHOU
- Economics and Finance: Prof. STEPHEN CHEUNG
- Information Systems: Dr M. K. O. LEE

Faculty of Humanities and Social Sciences:
- Applied Social Studies: W. T. CHAN
- Chinese, Translation and Linguistics: Prof. L. J. XU
- English: Dr A. TAYLOR
- Public and Social Administration: Dr ANTHONY CHEUNG

Faculty of Science and Technology:
- Biology and Chemistry: Prof. R. S. S. WU
- Building and Construction: Prof. A. P. JEARY
- Computer Science: Prof. H. IP
- Electronic Engineering: Prof. EDWARD K. N. YUNG
- Manufacturing Engineering and Engineering Management: Prof. K. V. PATRI
- Mathematics: Dr J. ZHANG
- Physics and Material Science: Dr MICHAEL STOKES

College of Higher Vocational Studies:
- Commerce: T. K. GHOSE
- Social Studies: Dr A. K. C. YEUNG
- Computer Studies: L. O. CLUBB
- Building Science and Technology: J. K. M. MO
- Language Studies: CHAN CHE-SING

ATTACHED INSTITUTES

Asia Pacific Financial and Markets Research Centre: Dir Prof. R. Y. K. HO.

School of Continuing and Professional Education: Dir C. K. H. WONG.

Contemporary China Research Centre: Dir Prof. J. Y. S. CHENG.

Language Information Sciences Research Centre: Dir Prof. B. K. Y. T'SOU.

English Language Centre: JEAN YOUNG.

Materials Research Centre: Dir Prof. J. K. L. LAI.

Telecommunications Research Centre: Head Prof. E. K. N. YUNG.

Centre for Chinese and Comparative Law: Dir Prof. G. G. WANG.

Centre for Environmental Science and Technology: Dir Prof. RUDOLF S. S. WU.

HONG KONG BAPTIST UNIVERSITY

Kowloon Tong, Kowloon
Telephone: 23397400
Fax: 23389987

Founded 1956

President and Vice-Chancellor: Dr DANIEL C. W. TSE
Vice-President (Academic): Prof. JERRY W. BARRETT
Vice-President (Research and Support Services): Prof. HERBERT H. TSANG
Vice-President (Administration) and Secretary: Dr MOK MANHUNG
Librarian: SHIRLEY LEUNG

Library of 566,000 vols, 6,670 current periodicals
Number of teachers: 314 f.t.e.
Number of students: 4,239 full-time, 2,445 part-time

Publications: *Annual Report, Research Report, Calendar / Bulletin* (1 a year), New Horizons (3 a year), *The Baptist Fax* (5 a year), *The Young Reporter* (5 a year).

DEANS

Faculty of Arts: Prof. JANE LAI
School of Business: Prof. FAN YIUKWAN
Faculty of Science: Prof. NG CHINGFAI
Faculty of Social Sciences: Prof. PAUL WONG
School of Communication: Prof. LEONARD L. CHU
School of Continuing Education: Dr BETTY C. CHANG

HONG KONG POLYTECHNIC UNIVERSITY

Yuk Choi Rd, Hung Hom, Kowloon
Telephone: 2766-5111
Telex: 38964
Fax: 2764-3374

Founded 1972 (formerly Hong Kong Polytechnic); present name *c.* 1995
Autonomous control, financed by the University Grants Committee. Awards its own degrees
Language of instruction: English
Academic year: September to July

Chancellor: Chief Executive of the Hong Kong Special Administrative Region
President: Prof. POON CHUNG-KWONG
Deputy President: (vacant)
Vice-Presidents: Prof. J. S. L. WONG (Multimedia Development), ALEXANDER TZANG (Institutional Advancement and Secretary to Council), Prof. E. J. HEARN (Planning), Prof. T. P. LEUNG (Quality Assurance), Prof. EDWIN CHENG (Research and Postgraduate Studies)
Librarian: B. L. BURTON

Library: see Libraries
Number of teachers: 1,034 full-time
Number of students: 10,799 full-time, 2,432 sandwich, 557 part-time day release, 3,039 part-time evening, 9,083 part-time, 886 distance learning

Publications: *Prospectus, Annual Report, Student Handbook, Continuing Education Programme, Library Handbook, Newsletters,* etc.

DEANS

Faculty of Applied Science and Textiles: Prof. K. W. YEUNG
Faculty of Business and Information Systems: Prof. PETER WALTERS
Faculty of Communication: Prof. J. S. L. WONG
Faculty of Construction and Land Use: Prof. M. ANSON
Faculty of Engineering: Prof. M. S. DEMOKAN
Faculty of Health and Social Studies: Prof. GEORGE WOO

HEADS OF DEPARTMENTS

Faculty of Applied Science and Textiles:
- Applied Biology and Chemical Technology: Prof. ALBERT S. C. CHAN
- Applied Mathematics: Dr S. H. HOU
- Applied Physics: Prof. C. L. CHOY
- Institute of Textiles and Clothing: Dr PATRICK CHONG

Faculty of Business and Information Systems:
- Accountancy: Prof. JOSEPH CHEUNG
- Business Studies: VANESSA STOTT
- Computing: Prof. DANIEL YEUNG
- Hotel and Tourism Management: Dr RAY PINE
- Management: Dr C. K. WAN (acting)

Faculty of Communication:
- Chinese and Bilingual Studies: Dr K. H. CHEUNG
- English: Prof. LIZ HEMP-LYONS
- School of Design: Prof. J. H. FRAZER
- Chinese Language Centre: (vacant)
- English Language Centre: PAMELA SMITH
- General Education Centre: Dr STEPHEN LAU (acting)

Faculty of Construction and Land Use:
- Building and Real Estate: Prof. DAVID SCOTT
- Building Services Engineering: Prof. J. BURNETT
- Civil and Structural Engineering: Prof. J. M. KO
- Land Surveying and Geo-Informatics: Prof. Y. Q. CHEN

Faculty of Engineering:
- Electrical Engineering: Prof. A. K. DAVID
- Electronic Engineering: Prof. W. C. SIU
- Manufacturing Engineering: Prof. W. B. LEE
- Mechanical Engineering: Prof. RONALD M. C. SO
- Maritime Studies: C. K. NG

Faculty of Health and Social Studies:
- Applied Social Studies: Prof. DIANA P. S. MAK
- Health Sciences: Prof. IDA MARTINSON
- Optometry and Radiography: Dr MAY WU (acting)
- Rehabilitation Engineering Centre: Prof. ARTHUR MAK
- Rehabilitation Sciences: Prof. CHRISTINA W. Y. HUI-CHAN

HONG KONG UNIVERSITY OF SCIENCE AND TECHNOLOGY

Clear Water Bay, Kowloon, Hong Kong

Telephone: 23586000
Fax: 23580545

Founded 1988; first student intake 1991
State control
Language of instruction: English
Academic year: September to June
Chancellor: Chief Executive of the Hong Kong Special Administrative Region
President: Prof. CHIA-WEI WOO
Vice-President for Academic Affairs: Prof. SHAIN-DOW KUNG
Vice-President for Administration and Business: PAUL BOLTON
Vice-President for Research and Development: Dr OTTO C. C. LIN
Director of Research Centre: Prof. J. C. CHEN
Director of Language Centre: Dr G. C. A. JAMES
Director of Library: MIN-MIN CHANG

Number of teachers: 458
Number of students: 6,290

Publications: *HKUST Newsletter*, *Annual Report, Academic Calendar.*

DEANS

Science: Prof. LEROY L. CHANG
Engineering: Prof. PING K. KO
Business and Management: Prof. YUK-SHEE CHAN
Humanities and Social Science: Prof. PANG-HSIN TING

PROFESSORS

BIDDLE, G. C., Accounting
CAO, X., Electrical and Electronic Engineering
CH'I, H. S., Social Science
CHAN, K. K. C., Finance
CHAN, Y. S., Finance
CHANG, D. C., Biology
CHANG, L. L., Physics
CHANG, P. T. Y., Civil and Structural Engineering
CHANSON, S., Computer Science
CHEN, J. C., Mechanical Engineering
CHEN, N. F., Finance
CHENG, L., Economics
CHENG, P., Mechanical Engineering
CHENG, S. Y., Mathematics
CHEUNG, P. W., Electrical and Electronic Engineering
CHIN, R. T., Computer Science
CUE, N., Physics
DOBSON, P. N. Jr., Physics
GORN, G., Marketing
HEINKE, G. W., Civil and Structural Engineering
HIRAOKA, H., Chemistry
HSIEH, D. H. T., Biology
HSIEH, D. Y., Mathematics
HUANG, H. J. C., Civil and Structural Engineering
HUI, G. W. H., Mathematics
HUNG, C. T., Humanities
KO, P. K., Electrical and Electronic Engineering
KUNG, S. D., Biology
KWOK, H. S., Electrical and Electronic Engineering
LEE, J. C. W., Accounting
LEE, L. F., Economics
LI, L., Information and Systems Management and Accounting
LIOU, M., Electrical and Electronic Engineering
LO, A. Y., Information and Systems Management
LOCHOVSKY, F. H., Computer Science
LOY, M. M., Physics
NOREEN, E., Accounting
SHEN, C. K., Civil and Structural Engineering
SHEN, V. Y. S., Computer Science
SHENG, P., Physics
TANG, W. H., Civil and Structural Engineering
TING, P. H., Humanities
TONG, P., Mechanical Engineering
TSENG, M. M., Industrial Engineering and Engineering Management
TSONG, T. Y., Biochemistry
TSUI, A., Management of Organizations
TUNG, Y. K., Civil and Structural Engineering
VANHONACKER, W. R., Marketing
WALDER, A., Social Science
WANG, J. C. Y., Humanities
WANG, J. H. C., Biochemistry
WONG, G. K., Physics
WONG, J. T. F., Biochemistry
WONG, S. S., Electrical and Electronic Engineering
WOOD, D., Computer Science
WU, M. C. S., Biology
YANG, C. C., Mathematics
YU, K., Mathematics
YU, M. L., Physics
YU, N. T., Chemistry
YU, T., Mechanical Engineering
YUE, P. L., Chemical Engineering

ATTACHED INSTITUTES

Advanced Manufacturing Institute: Dir Prof. P. KO.

Advanced Materials Research Institute: Dir Prof. N. CUE.

Biotechnology Research Institute: Dir Dr N. IP.

Centre for Asian Financial Markets: Dir Dr J. WEI.

Centre for Display Research: Dir Prof. H. S. KWOK.

Centre for Economic Development: Dir Dr F. T. LUI.

Co-operative Research Centre in Wireless Communication: Dir R. MURCH.

Cyberspace Centre for the Software Industry: Dir Prof. S. CHANSON.

Drug Delivery Technology Centre: Dir Prof. J. WONG.

Hainan Institute: Dir Prof. C. W. WOO.

Hong Kong Telecom Institute of Information Technology: Dir Prof. M. LIOU.

HKUST Multimedia Centre: Dir Dr GERALD PATCHELL.

Institute for the Environment and Sustainable Development: Dir Prof. G. HEINKE.

Institute for Infrastructure Development: Dir (vacant).

Institute for Microsystems: Dir Prof. P. K. KO.

Institute for Scientific Computation: Dir Prof. G. W. H. HUI (acting).

Materials Characterization and Preparation Centre: Dir Prof. M. L. YU.

Microelectronics Fabrication Centre: Dir (vacant).

Sino Software Research Institute: Dir Dr T. C. PONG.

Technology Transfer Centre: Dir Dr K. WHITE-HUNT.

Traditional Chinese Medicine Safety Information Centre: Dir Dr C. T. CHE.

OPEN UNIVERSITY OF HONG KONG

30 Good Shepherd St, Homantin, Kowloon, Hong Kong

Telephone: 2789-6600
Fax: 2789-0323

Founded 1989 as Open Learning Institute of Hong Kong; university status 1997.

President: Prof. S. W. TAM
Vice-President (Academic): Prof. DANNY WONG
Registrar: R. T. ARMOUR
Librarian: WAI-MAN MOK
Number of teachers: 870
Number of students: 23,000

DEANS

Business and Administration: Dr DANNY Y. K. IP (acting)
Arts and Social Sciences: Prof. P. K. IP
Science and Technology: Prof. T. M. WONG
Education and Languages: Prof. RONNIE CARR

UNIVERSITY OF HONG KONG

Pokfulam Rd, Hong Kong

Telephone: 2859-2111
Fax: 2559-9459

Founded 1911

Chancellor: Chief Executive of the Hong Kong Special Administrative Region
Pro-Chancellor: Hon. T. L. YANG
Vice-Chancellor: Prof. Y. C. CHENG
Deputy Vice-Chancellor: Prof. Y. K. CHEUNG (acting)
Pro-Vice-Chancellors: Prof. W. I. R. DAVIES, Prof. K. M. CHENG, Prof. F. F. WU, Prof. S. L. WONG
Treasurer: The Hon. D. K. P. LI
Registrar: Prof. Y. K. CHEUNG (acting)
Librarian: Dr L. B. KAN
Number of teaching staff: 863 full-time
Number of students: 14,685

Publications: *Calendar, Review, Research and Scholarship, Univ. Gazette, Interflow, Undergrad* (students).

DEANS

Faculty of Architecture: B. F. WILL
Faculty of Arts: Dr M. R. MARTIN
Faculty of Dentistry: Prof. F. C. SMALES
Faculty of Education: Dr F. K. S. LEUNG
Faculty of Engineering: Dr P. Y. S. CHEUNG
Faculty of Law: Prof. A. H. Y. CHEN
Faculty of Medicine: Prof. G. W. K. TANG
Faculty of Science: Prof. K. F. CHENG
Faculty of Social Sciences: Dr S. M. SHEN

PROFESSORS

BRANICKI, F. J., Surgery
BRAY, M., Education
BURNS, J. P., Politics and Public Administration
CHAN, C., Computer Science
CHAN, C. C., Electrical and Electronic Engineering
CHAN, C. L. W., Social Work and Social Administration
CHAN, D. K. O., Zoology

CHAN, F. H. Y., Electrical and Electronic Engineering
CHAN, H. C., Civil and Structural Engineering
CHAN, L. C., Pathology
CHAN, L. K. C., History
CHAN, S. T. H., Zoology
CHAN, V. N. Y., Medicine
CHAN, Y. S., Physiology
CHANG, E. C., School of Business
CHE, C. M., Chemistry
CHEAH, K. S. E., Biochemistry
CHEN, A. H. Y., Law
CHENG, K. F., Chemistry
CHENG, K. M., Education
CHENG, K. S., Physics
CHEUNG, S. N. S., School of Economics and Finance
CHEUNG, Y. K., Civil and Structural Engineering
CHILD, J., School of Business
CHIN, F. Y. L., Computer Science
CHIU, L. Y., Chinese
CHO, C. H., Pharmacology
CHOW, N. W. S., Social Work and Social Administration
CHOW, S. P., Orthopaedic Surgery
CHWANG, A. T., Mechanical Engineering
COOKE, M. S., Faculty of Dentistry
DAVIES, W. I. R., Faculty of Dentistry
DICKMAN, M. D., Ecology and Biodiversity
DIXON, A. S., Medicine
DUDGEON, A. D. M., Ecology and Biodiversity
DUGGAN, B. J., Mechanical Engineering
FAN, S. T., Surgery
FANG, H. H. P., Civil and Structural Engineering
FLETCHER, P., Speech and Hearing Sciences
FUNG, P. C. W., Physics
GANESAN, S., Architecture
GHAI, Y. P., Law
GOLDSTEIN, L., Philosophy
HAGG, E. U. O., Faculty of Dentistry
HANSEN, C., Philosophy
HE, G. W., Surgery
HEDLEY, A. J., Community Medicine
HILLS, P. R., Centre of Urban Planning and Environmental Management
HO, D. Y. F., Psychology
HO, K. P. H., Chinese
HO, P. C., Obstetrics and Gynaecology
HODGKISS, I. J., Ecology and Biodiversity
HOOSAIN, R., Psychology
HUI, S. S. C., School of Professional and Continuing Education
HWANG, K., Computer Science, Electrical and Electronic Engineering
IP, M. S. M., Medicine
JIM, C. Y., Geography and Geology
KAO, H. S. R., Psychology
KARLBERG, J. P. E., Paediatrics
KING, N. M., Faculty of Dentistry
KO, N. W. M., Mechanical Engineering
KO, R. C. C., Zoology
KUMANNA, C. R., Medicine
KUNG, A. W. C., Medicine
KWONG, Y. L., Medicine
LAI, C. L., Medicine
LAI, K. N., Medicine
LAM, K. S. L., Medicine
LAM, S. K., Medicine
LAM, T. H., Community Medicine
LAM, W. K., Medicine
LAU, C. P., Medicine
LAU, P. S. S., Architecture
LAU, Y. L., Paediatrics
LAWTON, J. W. M., Pathology
LEE, C. F., Civil and Structural Engineering
LEE, J. H. W., Civil and Structural Engineering
LEE, K. S., Chinese
LEONG, J. C. Y., Orthopaedic Surgery
LEUNG, M. P., Paediatrics
LI, V. O. K., Electrical and Electronic Engineering
LI, W. K., Statistics
LIANG, R. H. S., Medicine
LIE KEN JIE, M. S. F., Chemistry
LIU, M. C., Mathematics
LIU, M. W., Chinese
LOH, T. T., Physiology
LOW, L. C. K., Paediatrics
LUCAS, P. W., Anatomy
LUI, A. Y. C., History
LUK, K. D. K., Orthopaedic Surgery
LUNG, D. P. Y., Architecture
LYE, K. C., Architecture
MA, C. Y., Botany
MACKEOWN, P. K., Physics
MAK, K. L., Industrial and Manufacturing Systems Engineering
MAK-LIEH, F., Psychiatry
MALPAS, J. G., Earth Science
MAN, R. Y. K., Pharmacology
MOK, N. M., Mathematics
MOORE, F. C. T., Philosophy
MORRIS, P. J. T. F., Curriculum Studies
MORTON, B. S., Ecology and Biodiversity
MUSHKAT, R., Law
NG, M. H., Microbiology
NG, M. L., Psychiatry
NG, T. S., Electrical and Electronic Engineering
NGAN, H. Y. S., Obstetrics and Gynaecology
NUNAN, D. C., English Centre
OWEN, N. G., History
PANG, S. F., Physiology
PEARSON, V. J., Social Work and Social Administration
PEH, W. C. G., Diagnostic Radiology
PORTER, B., Industrial and Manufacturing Systems Engineering
REFSING, R., Japanese Studies
SAING, H., Surgery
SAMARANAYAKE, L. P., Faculty of Dentistry
SHAM, J. S. T., Radiation Oncology
SHERRIN, C. H., Professional Legal Education
SHORTRIDGE, K. F., Microbiology
SIN, C. Y., Chinese
SIT, V. F. S., Geography and Geology
SIU, M. K., Mathematics
SMALES, F. C., Faculty of Dentistry
SMALES, R. J., Faculty of Dentistry
SO, K. F., Anatomy
SPINKS, J. A., Psychology
SULLIVAN, P. L., Nursing Studies
TAM, P. K. H., Surgery
TAMBLING, J. C. R., Comparative Literature
TAN, S. T., Mechanical Engineering
TANG, F., Physiology
TANG, G. W. K., Obstetrics and Gynaecology
TIDEMAN, H., Faculty of Dentistry
TONG, D. S. Y., Physics
TONG, H., Statistics
TSE, D. K. C., School of Business
TSUI, A. B. M., Curriculum Studies
TUNG, S. S. L., School of Business
WACKS, R. I., Law
WALKER, A., Real Estate and Construction
WATKINS, D. A., Education
WEI, W. I., Surgery
WESLEY-SMITH, P., Law
WILKINSON, R. M., Professional Legal Education
WONG, J., Surgery
WONG, R. L. C., Obstetrics and Gynaecology
WONG, R. Y. C., School of Economics and Finance
WONG, S. K., Chinese
WONG, S. L., Sociology
WONG, T. M., Physiology
WONG, V. C. N., Paediatrics
WONG, Y. C., Anatomy
WU, F. F., Electrical and Electronic Engineering
YAM, V. W. W., Chemistry
YANG, E. S., Electrical and Electronic Engineering
YANG, J. C. S., Anaesthesiology
YEH, A. G. O., Centre of Urban Planning and Environmental Management
YEUNG, C. Y., Paediatrics
YOUNG, E. C. M., School of Professional and Continuing Education.
YUEN, K. Y., Microbiology
YUNG, B., Music
ZEE, S. S. Y., Botany

Colleges

Hong Kong Academy for Performing Arts: 1 Gloucester Rd, Hong Kong; tel. 25848500; fax 28024372; f. 1984; 3-year B.F.A. and B.Mus. programmes, 2-year diploma, 2-year advanced diploma, 1-year professional diploma programmes, 2-year advanced certificate, 2-year certificate, 1-year professional certificate programmes; 75 full-time, 250 part-time teachers; 700 students; library of 60,000 vols; Dir LO KING-MAN; Assoc. Dir (Administration) and Registrar ANNIE P. LAU; Assoc. Dir (Resources) WILLIAM JOHN TUSTIN; Assoc. Dir (Operations) PHILIP SODEN; Librarian LING WAI-KING; publs *Prospectus, Library Handbook, Annual Report*, monographs, *Dramatic Arts* (1 a year).

DEANS

Dance: MARGARET CARLSON
Drama: CHUNG KING-FAI
Film and Television: RICHARD WOOLLEY
Music: ANTHONY CAMDEN
Technical Arts: AUBREY WILSON

Lingnan College: Tuen Mun, Hong Kong; tel. 26168888; fax 24638363; f. 1967; 143 teachers, 2,121 students; library of 217,000 vols; Pres. Prof. EDWARD K. Y. CHEN; Vice-Pres. Prof. MEE-KAU NYAW; Sec. Dr KATHERINE Y. B. YAO; Registrar LOK-WOOD MUI.

DEANS

Arts: Prof. JOSEPH S. M. LAU
Business: Prof. TSANG-SING CHAN
Social Sciences: Prof. YAK-YEOW KUEH

RESEARCH CENTRES

Centre for Asian Pacific Studies: Dir Prof. YAK-YEOW KUEH

Centre for Literature and Translation: Dir Prof. CHING-CHIH LIU.

Centre for Public Policy Studies: Dir Prof. LOK-SANG HO.

Hong Kong Institute of Business Studies: Dir Prof. MEE-KAU NYAW.

Asia-Pacific Institute for Ageing Studies: Dir Prof. DAVID PHILLIPS.

Morrison Hill Technical Institute: 6 Oi Kwan Rd, Wanchai, Hong Kong; tel. 5745321; f. 1969; courses in commercial studies, construction, electronic engineering, mechanical engineering, general studies, computing; 100 full-time and 350 part-time teachers; 9,906 full-time and part-time students; library of 32,532 vols; Principal CHAN FU-KA; Vice-Principal WAN WING-TAI.

CHINA (TAIWAN)

Learned Societies

GENERAL

Academia Sinica (Chinese Academy of Sciences): Nankang, Taipei 11529; tel. (2) 27822120; fax (2) 27853847; f. 1928; 120 mems; attached research institutes: see Research Institutes; library of 780,000 vols; Pres. Dr LEE YUAN-TSEH; Dir-Gen. Dr LIU HSI-CHIANG; Chief of Secretariat TSENG CHIU-YU.

China Academy: Hwa Kang, Yang Ming Shan; f. 1966; private instn for sinological studies, consisting of 20 academic asscns and research institutions and Chinese and foreign mems; 591 acads, 312 hon. acads, 1,815 fellows; library of 450,000 vols; Pres. CHANG CHI-YUN; Sec.-Gen PAN WEI-HO; publs *Sino-American Relations* (quarterly in English), *Beautiful China Pictorial Monthly* (bilingual Chinese and English), *Sinological Monthly* (Chinese), *Sinological Quarterly* (Chinese), *Renaissance Monthly* (Chinese), *Chinese Culture* (quarterly in English).

China National Association of Literature and the Arts: 4 Lane 22, Nuigpo St W, Taipei.

China Society: 7 Lane 52, Wenchow St, Taipei; f. 1960; centre for Chinese studies; 100 mems; Pres. Dr CHEN CHI-LU; publ. *Journal* (annually).

AGRICULTURE, FISHERIES AND VETERINARY SCIENCE

Agricultural Association of China: 14 Wenchow St, Taipei; tel. (2) 23636681; f. 1917; mems: 159 instns, 2,554 individuals; Pres. TSONG-SHIEN WU; publ. *Journal* (quarterly).

Chinese Forestry Association: 2 Sec. 1, Hang-chaw South Rd, Taipei; f. 1948; 1,545 mems; Pres. CHI-YOU HSU; publs *Taiwan's Forestry Monthly, Quarterly Journal of Chinese Forestry.*

BIBLIOGRAPHY, LIBRARY SCIENCE AND MUSEOLOGY

Library Association of China: C/o National Central Library, 20 Chungshan S. Rd, Taipei; tel. (2) 23312475; fax (2) 23700899; e-mail lac@msg.nel.edu.tw; f. 1953; Pres. Dr MARGARET C. FUNG; Sec.-Gen. TERESA WANG CHANG; publs *Bulletin, Newsletter.*

ECONOMICS, LAW AND POLITICS

Chinese National Foreign Relations Association: 3rd Floor, 94 Nanchang St, Sec. 1, Taipei; Pres. HUANG KUO-SHU.

National Bar Association: 124 Chungking South Rd, Sec. 1, Taipei.

HISTORY, GEOGRAPHY AND ARCHAEOLOGY

Academia Historica (Academy of History): 406 Sec. 2, Pei Yi Rd, Hsintien, Taipei; tel. (2) 22171535; fax (2) 22171640; f. 1947; responsible for matters relevant to editing the nat. history; 158 mems; library of 5,294,000 items (nat. archives, books, documents); Pres. CHU SHAO-HWA; Sec.-Gen. Prof. CHU CHUNG-SHENG; publ. *Journal.*

LANGUAGE AND LITERATURE

Chinese Language Society: C/o Taiwan Normal University, Hoping East Rd, Taipei; f. 1953; Dir MAO TZU-SHUI; publ. *Chinese Language Monthly.*

MEDICINE

Chinese Medical Association: 201 Shih-Pai Rd, Sec. II, Taipei; f. 1915; 1,672 mems; Pres. Dr KWANG-JUEI LO; Sec.-Gen. Dr YANG-TE TSAI; publ. *Chinese Medical Journal* (monthly).

NATURAL SCIENCES

General

Chinese Association for the Advancement of Science: 5 Chungshan South Rd, Taipei; f. 1917; Pres. CHENG TIEN-FONG; publ. *Science Education.*

Mathematical Sciences

Chinese Statistical Association: 1 Nan Chung Rd, Sec. 1, Taipei; f. 1941; 1,082 mems; Pres. C. C. LEE; publ. *Chinese Statistical Journal.*

Mathematical Society of the Republic of China: Dept of Mathematics, National Cheng Kung University, Tainan 70101; fax (6) 2743191; Pres. LEE YUH-JIA; Sec. HUANG YOUNG-YE.

Physical Sciences

Astronomical Society of the Republic of China: C/o Taipei Observatory, Yuan Shan, Taipei 104; f. 1958; 200 mems; Pres. Dr M. H. WU; Gen. Sec. CHANG-HSIEN TSAI.

Chemical Society: POB 609, Taipei; fax (2) 23118464; f. 1932; 8,195 mems; Pres. JOHNSEE LEE; publs *Journal* (6 a year in English), *Hua Hsueh* (4 a year in Chinese).

Committee on the Promotion of the Peaceful Uses of Atomic Energy: 110 Yenping South Rd, Taipei; Pres. MILTON J. T. SHIEH.

Physical Society of China: POB 23-30, Taipei.

PHILOSOPHY AND PSYCHOLOGY

Confucius-Mencius Society of the Republic of China: 45 Nanhai Rd, Taipei; f. 1960; spreads knowledge about Confucius and Mencius, seeks the improvement of public morals and the creation of a better society; 3,900 mems; Chair. Dr CHEN LI-FU; Sec. HUA CHUNG-LIN; publs include *Confucius-Mencius Monthly, Journal of Confucius-Mencius Society.*

RELIGION, SOCIOLOGY AND ANTHROPOLOGY

Chinese Association for Folklore: 422 Fulin Rd, POB 68-1292, Shihlin, Taipei; f. 1932; Chinese and Asian folklore; 47 mems; library of 1,000 vols and MSS; Chair. Prof. LOU TSU-KUANG; Sec. AMY LOU.

TECHNOLOGY

Chinese Institute of Civil and Hydraulic Engineering: POB 499, Taipei; f. 1973; 7,500 mems; Pres. YU CHENG; publ. *Journal of Civil and Hydraulic Engineering* (quarterly), *Journal of the Chinese Institute of Civil and Hydraulic Engineering* (quarterly).

Chinese Institute of Engineers: 3rd and 4th Floors, 1 Jen-Ai Rd, Sec. 3, Taipei; tel. (2) 23925128; fax (2) 23973003; f. 1912; 11,501 mems; library of 7,334 vols, 60 periodicals; Pres. HAN M. HSIA; publs *Engineering Journal* (monthly), *Newsletter* (quarterly), *Transactions (Series A–D).*

Research Institutes

GENERAL

National Institute for Compilation and Translation: 247 Choushan Rd, Taipei; fax (2) 23629256; f. 1932; translates foreign books, examines and approves textbooks, standardizes scientific and technical terms; library of 60,000 vols; Dir NANCY CHAO LI-YUN; publs *The Journal*, periodicals (2 a year).

AGRICULTURE, FISHERIES AND VETERINARY SCIENCE

Council of Agriculture (COA): 37 Nanhai Rd, Taipei; tel. (2) 23812991; fax (2) 23310341; f. 1984; govt agency under the Exec. Yuan, with ministerial status; administers nat. agriculture, forestry, fisheries, livestock farming and food; library of 18,000 vols; Chair. Dr TJIU MAUYING; Sec.-Gen. Dr LEE JENCHYUAN; publs *General Reports* (annually), technical papers, news releases (irregular).

Taiwan Agricultural Research Institute: 189 Chung-Cheng Rd, Wan-Feng, Wu-Feng, Taichung; tel. (4) 3302301; fax (4) 3338162; f. 1895; insect collection; Dir LIN CHIEN-YIH; publs *Journal of Agricultural Research of China* (quarterly), *Annual Report, Special Publication.*

Taiwan Fisheries Research Institute: 199 Hou-Ih Rd, Keelung 220; tel. (2) 24622101; fax (2) 24629388; f. 1933; library of 16,000 vols; Dir-Gen I-CHIU LIAO; publs *Journal*, research reports.

Taiwan Forestry Research Institute: 53 Nan-Hai Rd, Taipei; tel. (2) 23817107; fax (2) 23142234; f. 1895; library of 33,000 vols; Dir YANG JENG-CHUAN; Sec. CHI SHENG-CHUNG; publ. *Journal of Forest Science* (quarterly).

Taiwan Sugar Research Institute: 54 Sheng Chan Rd, Tainan; tel. (6) 2671911; fax (6) 2685425; f. 1902; supported by Taiwan Sugar Corpn; library of 46,800 vols; Dir CHWAN-CHAU WANG; publs *Report* (quarterly in Chinese, English summary), *Annual Report* (in English), *Technical Bulletin, Extension Bulletin,* monographs.

ECONOMICS, LAW AND POLITICS

Co-operative League of the Republic of China: 11-2 Fu Chow St, Taipei; tel. (2) 23219343; telex 2995; fax (2) 23517918; f. 1940; co-operative business research and education; Chair. YANG CHIA-LIN; Exec. Dir/Sec.-Gen. HSU WEN-FU; publs *CLC Co-operative News* (annually), *Co-operative Economics* (quarterly).

Institute of Economics: C/o Academia Sinica, Nankang, Taipei 11529; attached to Academia Sinica; Dir Dr YUNG-SAN LEE.

FINE AND PERFORMING ARTS

National Taiwan Art Education Institute: 47 Nan Hai Rd, Taipei; tel. (2) 23714256; fax (2) 23122555; f. 1957; in charge of the research, extension and guidance of art education in Taiwan; Dir CHUN-CHIEH CHANG; publs *Art Education* (monthly), *Brief Information of Art Education* (monthly), *Catalogue of NTAEI Collection*.

HISTORY, GEOGRAPHY AND ARCHAEOLOGY

Institute of History and Philology: C/o Academia Sinica, Nankang, Taipei 11529; attached to Academia Sinica; Dir Dr TUNG-KUEI KUAN.

Institute of Modern History: C/o Academia Sinica, Nankang, Taipei 11529; attached to Academia Sinica; Dir Prof. YU-FA CHANG.

MEDICINE

Institute of Biomedical Sciences, Preparatory Office: C/o Academia Sinica, Taipei 115; attached to Academia Sinica; Dir Dr CHENG-WEN WU.

NATURAL SCIENCES

General

National Science Council: 106 Ho-ping East Rd, Section 2, Taipei; tel. (2) 27377501; fax (2) 27377668; e-mail tlyang@nsc.gov.tw; f. 1959; supports scientific and technological research and development; library of 24,000 vols; Chair. (vacant); publs *NSC Review* (annually, in English and Chinese), *Proceedings of NSC, Part A: Physical Science and Engineering* (6 a year in English), *Part B: Life Sciences* (4 a year in English), *Part C: Humanities and Social Sciences* (4 a year in Chinese and English), *Part D: Mathematics, Science and Technology Education* (3 a year in English), *Journal of Biomedical Science* (6 a year in English), *Science Bulletin* (monthly in English), *NSC Monthly* (in Chinese), *Indicators of Science and Technology* (annually in Chinese and English), *Yearbook of Science and Technology* (annually in Chinese, 2 a year in English).

Biological Sciences

Central Laboratory of Molecular Biology, Preparatory Office: C/o Academia Sinica, Nankang, Taipei 11529; attached to Academia Sinica; Dir Dr CHIEN HO.

Institute of Biological Chemistry: C/o Academia Sinica, Nankang, Taipei 11529; attached to Academia Sinica; Dir Dr WEN-CHANG CHANG (acting).

Institute of Botany: C/o Academia Sinica, Nankang, Taipei 11529; attached to Academia Sinica; Dir Dr JEI-FU SHAW.

Institute of Zoology: C/o Academia Sinica, Nankang, Taipei 11529; attached to Academia Sinica; Dir Dr JEN-LEIH WU

Mathematical Sciences

Institute of Mathematics: C/o Academia Sinica, Nankang, Taipei 11529; attached to Academia Sinica; Dir Dr KO-WEI LIH.

Institute of Statistical Science: C/o Academia Sinica, Nankang, Taipei 11529; attached to Academia Sinica; Dir Dr MIN-TE CHAO.

Physical Sciences

Atomic Energy Council: 67 Lane 144, Keelung Rd, Sec. 4, Taipei 106; tel. (2) 23634180; telex 26554; fax (2) 23635377; f. 1955; govt agency for the peaceful application of atomic energy; library of 11,000 vols, deposit library at the National Tsing Hua Univ. of 36,000 vols and 424,000 microcards; Chair. Dr YIH-YUN HSU; Sec.-Gen. KUANG-CHI LIU; publs *Nuclear Science Journal* (every 2 months), *Nuclear Climate* (monthly).

Central Geological Survey: POB 968, Taipei 100; tel. (2) 29462793; fax (2) 29429291; f. 1946; library of 12,000 vols; Dir CHAO-HSIA CHEN; publs *Bulletin, Special Publication* (irregular); maps and annual reports.

Institute of Atomic and Molecular Sciences, Preparatory Office: C/o Academia Sinica, Nankang, Taipei 11529; attached to Academia Sinica; Dir Dr CHAO-TIN CHANG.

Institute of Chemistry: C/o Academia Sinica, Nankang, Taipei 11529; attached to Academia Sinica; Dir Dr SUNNEY I. CHAN.

Institute of Earth Sciences: C/o Academia Sinica, Nankang, Taipei 11529; tel. (2) 27839910; fax (2) 27839871; attached to Academia Sinica; Dir Dr YEH YIH-HSIUNG.

Institute of Information Science: C/o Academia Sinica, Nankang, Taipei 11529; attached to Academia Sinica; Dir Dr YUE-SUN KUO (acting).

Institute of Nuclear Energy Research: POB 3, Lung-Tan 32500; tel. (2) 3651717; fax (3) 4711064; f. 1968; research in peaceful uses of atomic energy; Dir Dr HSIA DER-YU; publs *INER report series*.

Institute of Physics: C/o Academia Sinica, Nankang, Taipei 11529; attached to Academia Sinica; Dir Dr TUNG-MIN HO (acting).

PHILOSOPHY AND PSYCHOLOGY

Sun Yat-sen Institute for Social Sciences and Philosophy: C/o Academia Sinica, Nankang, Taipei 11529; attached to Academia Sinica; Dir Dr CHAO-CHENG MAI.

RELIGION, SOCIOLOGY AND ANTHROPOLOGY

Institute of American Culture: C/o Academia Sinica, Nankang, Taipei 11529; attached to Academia Sinica; Dir Dr LIANG-TSAI WEI.

Institute of Ethnology: C/o Academia Sinica, Nankang, Taipei 11529; attached to Academia Sinica; Dir Dr HSU CHENG-KUANG.

TECHNOLOGY

Industrial Technology Research Institute: 195 Chung Hsing Rd, Sec. 4, Chu-Tung, Hsinchu; tel. (35) 820100; fax (35) 820045; f. 1973; library of 130,000 vols; Pres. Dr OTTO C. C. LIN; publs *Chemical Industry Notes, CFC Newsletter, Mechatronics Journal, Electro-optics Development Journal, UCL Chemical Information Digest, Materials and Society, Reports of Center for Measurement Standards* (all monthly, in Chinese), *Superconductor Applications News, Metrology Information* (both every 2 months, in Chinese), *Opto-Electronics and Systems, Mining Technology, Energy-Resources and Environment* (quarterly, in Chinese), *MRL Bulletin of Research and Development* (2 a year, in English).

Research laboratories:

Energy and Resources Laboratories: Hsinchu; Dir Dr ROBERT J. YANG.

Mechanical Industry Research Laboratories: Hsinchu; Dir Dr C. RICHARD LIU.

Electronics Research and Service Organization: Hsinchu; Dir Dr DAVID C. T. HSING.

Materials Research Laboratories: Hsinchu and Kaohsiung; Dir Dr LI-CHUNG LEE.

Union Chemical Laboratories: Hsinchu; Dir Dr JOHN-SEE LEE.

Opto-Electronics and Systems Laboratories: Hsinchu; Dir Dr MIN-SHYONG LIN.

Centre for Measurement Standards: Hsinchu; Dir Dr CHANG HSU.

Centre for Pollution Control Technology: Hsinchu; Dir Dr LING-YUAN CHEN.

Computer and Communication Research Laboratories: Hsinchu; Dir Dr STEVEN CHENG.

Centre for Industrial Safety and Health Technology: Hsinchu; Dir Dr ADA W. S. MA.

Centre for Aviation and Aerospace: Hsinchu; Dir Dr RICHARD Y. H. LIN.

National Bureau of Standards: Ministry of Economic Affairs, 3rd Floor, 185 Hsinhai Rd, Sec. 2, Taipei 106; tel. (2) 27380007; fax (2) 27352656; f. 1947; nat. standards, weights and measures, patents, trademarks; library of 20,000 vols, 500 periodicals; Dir-Gen. MING-BANG CHEN; publs *Official Gazette for Standards* (monthly), *Official Gazette for Patents* (3 a month), *Official Gazette for Trademarks* (2 a month), *Chinese National Standards* (irregular), *Catalogue of Chinese National Standards* (annually), *Standards and Metrology Yearbook* (annually), *Patents and Trademarks Yearbook* (annually).

Libraries and Archives

Tainan

National Cheng Kung University Library: 1 Ta Hsueh Rd, Tainan 70101; tel. (6) 2757575 ext. 81000; fax (6) 2378232; f. 1927; 760,000 vols, 11,000 periodicals; Dir Dr WEN-TA TSAI; publs *Bulletin* (quarterly), *Newsletter* (monthly).

Taipei

Agricultural Science Information Center: POB 7-636, Taipei 106; tel. (2) 23626222; f. 1977; 11,000 vols, 638 periodicals, databases; Dir WAN-JIUN WU.

Dr Sun Yat-sen Library: 2F, 505 Jen Ai Rd, Sec. 4, Taipei; tel. (2) 27297030; fax (2) 27582460; f. 1929; 299,345 vols on Dr Sun Yat-sen's writings and studies on San Min Chu Yih and modern Chinese history; Curator SHAW MING-HUANG; publ. *Modern China* (every 2 months).

Fu Ssu-Nien Library, Institute of History and Philology: 130 Yen Chiu Yuan Rd, Sec. 2, Nankang, Taipei 11521; tel. (2) 27829555 ext. 136; fax (2) 27868834; f. 1928; 420,000 vols, 3,000 periodicals; spec. collns incl. 33,889 stone and bronze rubbings, 13,100 folk plays, 310,000 cabinet records of Ming and Ch'ing dynasties; Dir JUEI-HSIU WU.

Library and Information Service, Legislative Yuan: 1 Chung San S Rd, Taipei 10040; tel. (2) 23211531 ext. 384; fax (2) 23223557; f. 1947; general reference, govt publs, legal documents; 113,000 vols; Dir PAUL FAN; publs *Newsletter of books and documentation* (quarterly), *Chinese legislative news review index* (monthly), *Code resource pathfinder* (every two months), *Code and reference book catalogue* (irregular), *Gazette, proceedings and serials catalogue* (irregular), *LEGISIS thesaurus* (irregular), *Chinese legislative news reviews series* (irregular), *Selective abstracts of US Congressional Records* (irregular), *Index to Legal Periodicals* (irregular), *Legislative Decision Support Service* (monthly), *Subject Guide to Chinese Code* (irregular), *Code Amendment Cyclopedia* (irregular), *Index to Chinese Legislative Literature* (every 2 months), *Selected Dissemination of Information Series* (every 2 months), *The Legislative Yuan Library Catalogue* (irregular), *Collection of Interpellation Records* (irregular), *Legislative Microform Catalog* (irregular), *Index of Legislative Records* (every 3 years).

National Central Library: 20 Chung Shan South Rd, Taipei 10040; tel. (2) 23619132; fax (2) 23110155; f. 1933; 1,615,414 items incl. 190,000 rare books, stone rubbings; historical material; maintains centre for Chinese studies; Dir Dr CHUANG FANG-JUNG; publs *Chinese*

National Bibliography (monthly), *Bulletin* (2 a year), *Index to Chinese Periodicals* (quarterly), *NCL Newsletter* (quarterly, English), *NCL News Bulletin*, various catalogues and indexes, etc.

Branch library:

Taiwan Branch Library, National Central Library: 1 Hsinshen South Rd, Sec. 1, Taipei; f. 1915; 592,023 vols; spec. collns incl. Taiwan and Southern Asia; Dir LIN WEI-JEI; publs *The Annotative Catalogue of Taiwan Documents; Index to Taiwan-Related Periodical Literature collected in NCL Taiwan Branch, Union Catalogue of Taiwan-Related Bibliographies, Catalogue on China in Western Languages, Catalogue on China in Japanese Languages, Catalogue of Materials for the Blind, Catalogue of NCL Taiwan Branch Collection on Southeast Asia, List of Non-Chinese Serials in NCL Taiwan Branch*.

National War College Library: Yangmingshan, Taipei; 156,639 vols on political subjects; Librarian LO MOU-PIN.

Taipei City Library: 46 Chinan Rd, Sec. 2, Taipei; f. 1952; 125,000 vols; 4 brs; Dir CHIH-SHIH YANG; publ. *Taipei Municipal Library Annals*.

Museums and Art Galleries

Taichung

Taiwan Museum of Art: 2 Wu-Chuan West Rd, Taichung; tel. (4) 3723552; fax (4) 3721195; f. 1986; mostly works of Taiwan and of Chinese artists working abroad; library of 27,000 vols; Dir DANG-HO LIU; publs *Taiwan Museum of Art Newsletter*, *Journal of Taiwan Museum of Art*.

Taipei

Chinese Postal Museum: 45 Chungking South Rd, Sec. 2, Taipei 100; tel. (2) 23945185; f. 1966; library of 45,000 vols; Curator WEI MING.

Hwa Kang Museum: Ta Yi Bldg, Chinese Culture University, Yang Ming Shan, Taipei; tel. (2) 28610511 ext. 409; f. 1961; Chinese folk arts, pottery, porcelain, calligraphy and paintings; Dir CH'EN KUO-NING.

National Museum of History: 49 Nan Hai Rd, Taipei 10728; tel. (2) 23610270; fax (2) 23610171; f. 1955; Chinese historical and archaeological artifacts; library of 12,000 vols; Dir HUANG KUANG-NAN; publ. *Bulletin*.

National Palace Museum: Wai-shuang-hsi, Shih-lin, Taipei; tel. (2) 28821230; fax (2) 28821440; e-mail service@ss20.npm.gov.tw; f. 1925; colln consists chiefly of historic and archaeological treasures brought from the mainland; library of 120,000 vols, 1,000 periodical titles, 184,000 rare books, 387,000 documents; Dir CHIN HSIAO-YI; publs incl. *Newsletter* (4 a year in English and Chinese), *Bulletin* (6 a year in English), *Research Quarterly* (in Chinese), *National Palace Museum Monthly of Chinese Art* (in Chinese), illustrated catalogues, handbooks, research monographs.

National Taiwan Science Education Center: 41 Nan Hai Rd, Taipei; tel. (2) 23116734; f. 1958; planetarium, science exhibitions, lectures and films; Dir SHIH-BEY CHEN; publ. *Science Study Monthly*.

Taiwan Museum: 2 Siangyang Rd, Taipei; fax (2) 23822684; f. 1908; natural history, geology, ethnography; spectroscopic dating laboratory for fossils; Dir MINGFA SHIH; publ. *Journal of Taiwan Museum* (in English).

Universities

CHINESE CULTURE UNIVERSITY

55 Hwa Kang Rd, Yang Ming Shan, Taipei
Telephone: 28610511
Fax: 28615031

Founded 1962
Private control

President: LIN TSAI-MEI

Library of 630,000 vols, 3,500 periodicals
Number of teachers: 531
Number of students: 20,013

Colleges of arts, journalism and mass communication, science, engineering, business, agriculture, liberal arts, law, foreign languages and literature; graduate and evening schools.

CHUNG YUAN CHRISTIAN UNIVERSITY

Chung Li
Telephone: (3) 456-3171
Fax: (3) 456-3160

Founded 1955
Private control
Academic year: August to July

President: Dr SAMUEL K. C. CHANG

Library of 250,000 vols
Number of teachers: 12,491
Number of students: 11,798

Publications: *CYCU News*, *Chung Yuan Journal*.

Colleges of science, engineering, business, design; evening department.

FENG CHIA UNIVERSITY

100 Wenhwa Rd, Seatwen, Taichung 40724
Telephone: (4) 451-7250
Fax: (4) 451-4907
E-mail: adm_iac@fcu.edu.tw

Founded 1961
Private control
Languages of instruction: Chinese and English
Academic year: mid-September to end of June

President: AN-CHI LIU
Vice-President: YUAN-TONG LEE
Secretary-General: SHAW-JYH SHIN
Chief Librarian: SHU-LING LIN

Library of 469,000 vols
Number of teachers: 881
Number of students: 17,728 undergraduates, 756 graduates

Publications: *Civil Engineering Journal, Architecture Quarterly, Textile Science, Mechanical Engineering, Industrial Engineering, Computer Science, Banking and Insurance, Co-operative Research, Statistics Journal, Accounting Journal, Finance Research, International Trade, Feng Chia Hsueh Pao, Feng Chia Monthly.*

DEANS

Dean of Academic Affairs: HAN-CHU LIU
Dean of Student Affairs: LUNG-SHIH YANG
Dean of General Affairs: YUAN-TUNG LEE
College of Engineering: CHIU-YUE LIN
College of Business: CHING-CHONG LAI
College of Management: I-CHANG CHOW
College of Arts and Sciences: TAI-LI HU
Centre for Humanities and Social Studies: RUN-KEN TAI
Evening Division: TSONG-JEN YANG (Dir)

HEADS OF DEPARTMENTS

College of Engineering
- Aeronautical Engineering: TE LIANG
- Architecture: TSUNG-JUNG CHENG
- Automatic Control Engineering: SHYAN-LUNG LIN
- Chemical Engineering: CHIH-CHIEH CHANG
- Civil Engineering: JUN-PING PU
- Electrical Engineering: CHIH-CHIEH CHANG
- Electronic Engineering: MAN-LONG HER
- Hydraulic Engineering: CHAO-FU LIN
- Industrial Engineering: CHING-JU FENG
- Computer Engineering: YI-WEN WANG
- Mechanical Engineering: WEN-JINN LIOU
- Textile Engineering: MING-FEN LIN
- Urban Planning: DA-LIH WANG

College of Business
- Accounting: YU-CHIH LIN
- Co-operative Economics: YAO-MEN YU
- Economics: SHIH-WEN HU
- Finance: ALPHA LOWE
- Insurance: YUE-MIN KANG
- International Trade: JWU-RONG LIN
- Public Finance and Taxation: KUNG-CHENG LIN
- Statistics: SHEN-MING LEE

College of Arts and Sciences
- Applied Mathematics: SHIN-FENG HWANG
- Chinese Literature: TSUNG-MING LIN
- Environmental Engineering and Science: DONG-CHIR HUANG
- Materials Science: KEN-CHANG CHENG

College of Management
- Business Administration: YUAN-HSI HSU
- Land Management: MEI-YING CHANG
- Traffic and Transportation Engineering and Management: YAO T. HSU

DIRECTORS OF GRADUATE INSTITUTES

Applied Mathematics: SHING-FENG HWANG
Architecture and Urban Planning: DAH-LIH WANG
Automatic Control Engineering: SHYAN-LUNG LIN
Chemical Engineering: CHIH-CHIEH CHAN
Chinese Literature: TSUNG-MING LIN
Civil and Hydraulic Engineering: JUN-PING PU
Economics: SHIH-WEN HU
Electrical Engineering: SHEAU-SHONG BOR
Computer Engineering: YI-WEN WANG
Insurance: YUE-MIN KANG
Land Management: MEI-CHING CHANG
Materials Science: KEN-CHANG CHEN
Mechanical Engineering: WEN-JINN LIOU
Statistics and Actuarial Science: SHEN-MING LEE
Textiles Engineering: MING-FENG LIN

FU-JEN CATHOLIC UNIVERSITY

Hsin-Chuang 510 Chungcheng Rd, Taipei
Telephone: (2) 2903-1111-20
Fax. (02) 2901-7391
E-mail: soci1002@mails.fju.edu.tw

Founded in Beijing 1929, reopened in Taiwan 1961
Academic year: August to July

President: Dr PETER TUEN-HO YANG
Vice-Presidents: V. Rev. ANTHONY LAU, Rev. MICHAEL KWO, Rev. LOUIS GENDRON
Secretary-General: Rev. JOSEPH WONG
Dean of Academic Affairs: Dr BERNARD C. C. LI
Dean of Student Affairs: Dr SIH-MING KO
Dean of General Affairs: Dr SHANG-SHING CHOU
Registrar: LIANG-CHIUNG CHEN
Librarian: Dr CHWEN-CHWEN CHANG

Library of 699,000 vols
Number of teachers: 1,448
Number of students: 20,242

Publications: *Fu Jen Studies* (quarterly), *Fu Jen Philosophical Studies, Catholic Observer, China News Analysis.*

DEANS

College of Liberal Arts: Prof. SHIANG-YANG HWANG

College of Foreign Languages: Dr SHEI-FU LIN
College of Science and Engineering: Dr KANG C. JEA
College of Human Ecology: Dr NING-YUEAN LEE
College of Fine Arts: Rev. ANTHONY LAU
College of Law: Dr TAI-HSING DAISY DAY
College of Management: Dr DENG-YUAN HUANG
Evening School: Rev. JOSEPH TENG
College of Medicine: Rev. MARK CHU

There are 41 departments and 31 graduate programmes, an education programme, extension programmes, a faculty of theology and a Chinese (Mandarin) language centre.

NATIONAL CENTRAL UNIVERSITY

Chung-Li

Telephone: (3) 4227151

Founded 1968 as re-establishment of National Central University (Nanking)

Academic year: February to July, September to January

President: Prof. CHAO-HAN LIU
Vice-President: Prof. KUANG-FU CHENG
Dean of Studies: Prof. KUAN-CHING LEE
Dean of Student Affairs: Prof. GIEN-MING GUE
Dean of General Affairs: Prof. YAU-TARNG JUANG
Dean of Research and Development: Prof. GUEY-KUEN YU
Director of Secretariat: Prof. WEI-LING CHIANG
Librarian: Prof. EDMOND LIH-WU HOURNG

Number of teachers: 438
Number of students: 7,025

Publications: *Bulletin of Geophysics* (2 a year), *Journal of Humanities East/West* (2 a year).

DEANS

College of Liberal Arts: Prof. LAI-JEH HANG
College of Science: Prof. TUNG-JUNG CHUANG
College of Engineering: Prof. KUO-SHONG WANG
College of Management: Prof. PI-CHEN WANG

HEADS OF GRADUATE INSTITUTES

Institute of Mathematics: Prof. CHIANG LIN
Institute of Statistics: Prof. MING-CHENG YANG
Institute of Physics and Astronomy: Prof. WEN-HSIEN LI
Institute of Geophysics: Prof. CHIEN-YING WANG
Institute of Atmospheric Physics: Prof. JOUGH-TAI WANG
Institute of Chemical Engineering: Prof. CHENG-TUNG CHOU
Institute of Civil Engineering: Prof. HUEI-WEN CHANG
Institute of Information Engineering: Prof. JANG-PIN SHEU
Institute of Mechanical Engineering: Prof. JYH-CHENG CHEN
Institute of Electro-Optical Science: Prof. YIH-SHYANG CHENG
Institute of Industrial Economics: Prof. DACH-RAHN WU
Institute of Chinese: Prof. PING-HO LIN
Institute of Philosophy: Prof. SHUI-CHUEN LEE
Institute of Finance Management: Prof. MIN-TEN YU
Institute of Environmental Engineering: Prof. SHU-LIANG LIAW
Institute of Space Science: Prof. YEN-HSYANG
Institute of Applied Geology: Prof. CHIEH-HOU YANG
Institute of Astronomy: Prof. WEI-HSIN SUNG
Institute of Life Sciences: Prof. SHIR-LY HUANG
Institute of Human Resource Management: JOSEPH S. LEE
Institute of Industrial Management: JEN-MING CHEN
Institute of History: SUN-YEN CHANG
Institute of Art Studies: MING-MING LEE

DEPARTMENT HEADS

Mathematics: Prof. CHIANG LIN
Physics: Prof. WEN-HSIEN LI
Geophysics: Prof. CHIEN-YING WANG
Atmospheric Physics: Prof. JOUGH-TAI WANG
Chemical Engineering: Prof. CHENG-TUNG CHOU
Civil Engineering: Prof. HUEI-WEN CHANG
Mechanical Engineering: Prof. JYH-CHENG CHEN
Electrical Engineering: Prof. JYH-WONG HONG
Chinese: Prof. PING-HO LIN
English: Prof. YUH-JYH LIN
French: Prof. SHIU-I LIU
Information Management: Prof. TONG-AN HSU
Business Administration: Prof. LIN-CHIEN HUANG
Economics: Prof. DACHRAHN WU
General Courses: Prof. FEI-LONG CHEN
Finance: Prof. MIN-TEN YU
Chemistry: Prof. TUNG-JUNG CHUANG
Computer Science and Information Technology: JANG-PING SHEU

NATIONAL CHENGCHI UNIVERSITY

Wenshan 116, Taipei

Telephone: (2) 2939-3091
Fax: (2) 2939-8043

Founded 1927, university status 1946; Government financed

Languages of instruction: Chinese

Academic year: September to July (two semesters)

President: TING-WONG CHENG
Dean of Academic Affairs: ZONG-DE LIU
Dean of Student Affairs: JEAW-MEI CHEN
Dean of General Affairs: BAU-CHENG DUNG
Librarian: OU-LAN HU

Library of 2,289,000 vols
Number of teachers: 948 (full- and part-time)
Number of students: 11,554

DIRECTORS OF GRADUATE SCHOOLS

East Asia Studies: KUEN-HSUEN CHIU
Dr Sun Yat-Sen Graduate Institute for Interdisciplinary Studies: CHUEN-YUEN WANG
Technology and Innovation Management: SE-HUA WU
Library and Information Sciences: MEI-HUA YANG
Labour Research: HUI-LING WANG
Russian Studies: CHUEN-SHAN CHAO
Linguistics: YI-LI YANG

DEANS

College of Liberal Arts: CHE-LANG CHANG
College of Science: SE-CHIA CHUNG
College of Social Sciences: HSIAO-HONG CHEN
College of Law: CHUNG-MIN DUAN
College of Commerce: YI-YU WANG
College of Communication: JUI-CHENG CHENG
College of Foreign Languages: CHANG-KENG HSU

HEADS OF DEPARTMENTS

Chinese Literature: CHIN-YU DUNG
Oriental Languages and Cultures: CHI-HUI HUANG
English Language and Literature: CHI-KUEI LO
Education: MENG-CHUIN CHIN
Journalism: WEN-HUI LO
History: NENG-SHIH LIN
Philosophy: HSIN-CHUEN HO
Mathematical Sciences: CHUAN-CHIN SUNG
Psychology: MEI-CHEN LIN
Arabic Language and Literature: CHUAN-TIEN LI
Advertising: TSU-LONG CHENG
Political Science: FU-SHENG HSIEH
Law: CHUNG-MIN DUAN
Diplomacy: DENG-KE LI
Sociology: KAO-CHIAO HSIEH
Radio and Television: TSUEI-CHEN WU
Public Finance: CHU-WEI TSENG
Public Administration: CHUNG-EN WU
Land Economics: SEN-TIEN LIN
Economics: WEI-LING MAO
International Trade: LIEN-KUO HU
Statistics: TIEN-TSO CHENG
Accountancy: LING-TAI CHO
Money and Banking: HAO-MIN CHU
Business Administration: CHUO-MIN YU
Management Information Systems: WO-TSUNG LIN
Finance: CHI-HUANG LIN
Risk Management and Insurance: CHENG-TSUNG HUANG
Computer Science: YAO-NAN LIEN
Russian: HUNG-MEI CHUNG
Ethnology: HSIU-CHE LIN

NATIONAL CHENG KUNG UNIVERSITY

1 Ta-Hsueh Rd, Tainan 70101

Telephone: (6) 275-7575
Fax: (6) 236-8660
E-mail: em50000@mail.ncku.edu.tw

Founded 1931 as Tainan Technical College, renamed Taiwan Provincial College of Engineering 1946, present name 1971

State control

Languages of instruction: Chinese and some English

Academic year: September to January, February to June

President: Dr CHENG-I WENG
Dean of Academic Affairs: Dr CHIEN-ER LEE
Registrar: TZU-TSAN KUNG
Librarian: Dr WEN-TA TSAI

Number of teachers: 1,208
Number of students: 15,333

Publications: *Journal of National Cheng Kung University* (annually), *Faculty Publication List* (annually), *Newsletter* (quarterly), *Bulletin of National Cheng Kung University* (annually).

DEANS

College of Liberal Arts: Dr SAN-CHING WANG
College of Sciences: Dr LOU-CHUANG LEE
College of Engineering: Dr SHAN-HWEI OU
College of Management Science: Dr CHIANG KUO
College of Medicine: Dr NAI-SAN WANG

Graduate institutes are attached to the College of Liberal Arts, the College of Engineering, the College of Sciences, the College of Management Science, the College of Medicine and the College of Social Sciences.

NATIONAL CHIAO TUNG UNIVERSITY

1001 Ta Hsueh Rd, Hsinchu

Telephone: (35) 712121
Fax: (35) 721500

Founded 1896, re-established in Hsinchu 1958

Languages of instruction: Chinese and English

Academic year: August to July (two semesters)

President: Dr CHI-FU DEN
Dean of Academic Affairs: Dr LONG-ING CHEN
Dean of Student Affairs: Dr FU-WHA HAN
Dean of General Affairs: Dr CHUNG-BIAU TSAY
Dean of the Research and Development Council: Dr CHUNG-YU WU
Chief Secretary: Prof. HSIN-SEN CHU
Registrar: Assoc. Prof. CHIN-SHYONG CHEN
Chief Librarian: Dr RUEI-CHUAN CHANG

Library of 170,329 vols, 2,373 periodicals
Number of teachers: 415 (full-time)
Number of students: 4,896

Publications: *Chiao Ta Management Review*, *List of Publications of Faculty Members*, abstracts of papers and research reports.

DEANS AND HEADS OF DEPARTMENTS

College of Electrical Engineering and Computer Science: Dr CHE-HO WEI
Electronics Engineering: Dr WEN-ZEN SHEN

Control Engineering: Dr CHING-CHENG TENG
Communication Engineering: Dr SONG-TSUEN PENG
Computer Science and Information Engineering: Dr HSI-JIAN LEE
Computer and Information Science: Dr CHIA-HOANG LEE
College of Engineering: Dr TAI-YAN KAM
Mechanical Engineering: Dr HSIN-SEN CHU
Civil Engineering: Dr CHUN-SUNG CHEN
College of Science: Dr DER-SAN CHUU
Electrophysics: Dr RU-PIN CHAO PAN
Applied Mathematics: Dr GERARD J. CHANG
Applied Chemistry: Dr CHAIN-SHU HSU
College of Management: Dr PAO-LONG CHANG
Management Science: Dr HER-JIUN SHEU
Transportation Engineering and Management: Dr HSIN-LI CHANG
Industrial Engineering and Management: Dr FUH-HWA LIU

DIRECTORS OF GRADUATE INSTITUTES

Electronics: Dr TAN-FU LEI
Management Science: Dr SOUSHAN WU
Computer Science and Information Engineering: Dr SHU-YUEN HWANG
Communication Engineering: Dr CHUNG-JU CHANG
Traffic and Transportation: Dr YUAN-CHING HSU
Control Engineering: Dr DER-CHERNG LIAW
Applied Mathematics: Dr GERARD J. CHANG
Mechanical Engineering: Dr HSIN-SEN CHU
Electro-Optical Engineering: Dr CI-LING PAN
Applied Chemistry: Dr CHAIN-SHU HSU
Civil Engineering: Dr YUNG-SHOW FANG
Information Management: Dr CHI-CHUN LO
Materials Science and Engineering: Dr TZENG-FENG LIU
Electrophysics: Dr MING-CHIH LEE
Computer and Information Science: Dr RONG-HONG JAN
Industrial Engineering: Dr CHAO-TON SU
Environmental Engineering: Dr JEHNG-JUNG KAO
Statistics: Dr CHAO-SHENG LEE
Physics: Dr JSIN-FU JIANG
Biological Science and Technology: Dr CHENG ALLEN CHANG
Management Technology: Dr SHANG-JYH LIU
Communication Studies: Dr SHIN-MIN CHEN
Applied Arts (Design and Music): Dr MING-CHUEN CHUANG

DIRECTORS OF RESEARCH CENTRES

Computer Center: Dr RUEI-CHUAN CHANG
Semiconductor Research Center: (vacant)
Microelectronics and Information Science and Technology Research Center: Dr MING SZE
Center for Telecommunications Research: Dr SIN-HORNG CHEN
National Nano Device Center: Dr CHUN-YEN CHANG

NATIONAL CHUNG HSING UNIVERSITY

250 Kuokuang Rd, Taichung

Telephone: (4) 2872991
Fax: (4) 2853813

Founded 1961

President: Dr CHENG-CHANG LI
Secretary-General: MU-CHIOU HUANG
Librarian: ELLEN F. LIU

Number of teachers: 866
Number of students: 17,258

DEANS

College of Agriculture: MING-TSAO CHEN
College of Law and Commerce: SEN-TIAN WU
College of Science: TENG-KUEI YANG
College of Liberal Arts: CHU SENG HU
College of Engineering: J. SHIH-SHYN WU

HEADS OF DEPARTMENTS AND INSTITUTES

Chinese Literature: JAW-HWA SHYU
English Literature and Language: HSIN-FA WU
History: MING-SUN WANG
Law: CHENG-HERO LIN
Public Administration: CHUNG-YI LIN
Economics: TEIN-CHEW CHOU
Sociology and Social Work: LIN-LIN CHERING
Public Finance: JYH-LUH SUN
Accounting: SHIOU-CHIH WANG
Statistics: RUEY-TAY PAN
Business Administration: ING-SAN HWANG
Co-operative Economics: HSIANG-HSI LIU
Land Economics and Administration: SUNG-SAN WANG
Institute of Statistics: JIN-YUH CHANG
Institute of Urban Planning: HSUEH-TAO CHIEN
Institute of Public Policy: SENG-LEE WONG
Institute of Public Finance: SHIH-HSIN HUANG
Institute of Natural Resource Management: CHIU-YANG CHEW
Agronomy: CHI-FUU YEIN
Horticulture: YAN-SHIANG YANG
Forestry: CHERN-HSING OU
Agricultural Economics: SHIANG-TYAN SHYU
Agricultural Marketing: MING-MING WU
Plant Pathology: DER-SHY TZENG
Entomology: YU-CHANG LIU
Animal Science: JENN-CHUNG HSU
Veterinary Medicine: CHENG-I LIU
Soil Science: CHEN FANG LIN
Soil and Water Conservation: JIE-DAR CHEN
Food Science: SHIN LU
Agricultural Machinery Engineering: CHUNG-TEH SHENG
Institute of Agricultural Extension Education: JIH MIN SUNG
Chemistry: JEN-FON JEN
Botany: PEI-CHUNG CHEN
Applied Mathematics: CHANG-TAI PING
Physics: MING-KEH CHEN
Institute of Molecular Biology: WEN-HWEI HSU
Institute of Computer Science: WOEI LIN
Mechanical Engineering: REIYU R. CHEIN
Civil Engineering: CHIEN-HUNG LIN
Environmental Engineering: CHIH-JEN LU
Electrical Engineering: CHUNG-YUAN KUNG
Chemical Engineering: JIANG-JEN LIN
Institute of Materials Engineering: SHIOW-KANG YEN
Computer Centre: JINN-KE JAN
Agricultural Biotechnology Laboratory: ROGER FENG-NAN HOU

NATIONAL OPEN UNIVERSITY

172 Chung Cheng Rd, Lu Chow, Taipei 24702

Telephone: (2) 2282-9355
Fax: (2) 2288-6061

Founded 1986
Language of instruction: Chinese
Academic year: September to January, February to June

President: Dr YIH-YOUNG CHEN
Registrar: LI-CHI HSIEH
Dean of Academic Affairs: Dr LI-SHEN LIN

Number of teachers: 84 full-time, 1,614 part-time
Number of students: 39,007

CHAIRMEN OF DEPARTMENTS

Domestic Science: Dr JENG-RONG DUH
Public Administration: Dr WILLIAM FU-HSIN WU
General Study: Dr CHENG-CHIH HSU
Business: Dr SHENG-SHIUANG HWANG
Humanities: Dr HSIANG-HUEI TSAI
Social Science: Dr DWO-YAN CHANG
Management and Information: Dr YUNG-MENG WU
Production and Programming: Dr JESSE CHOU
Student Affairs: Assoc. Dr TE-CHUNG CHANG
Research and Development: Dr JU-SHAN CHEN
General Affairs: Dr SHIH-TSAI LEE

NATIONAL TAIWAN INSTITUTE OF TECHNOLOGY

43 Keelung Rd, Sec. 4, Taipei

Telephone: (2) 27333141
Fax: (2) 27376107

Founded 1974
Academic year: August to July (two semesters)

President: CHING-TIEN LIOU
Dean of Studies: SHI-SHUENN CHEN

Library of 230,000 vols
Number of teachers: 306
Number of students: 5,881

HEADS OF DEPARTMENTS

Graduate School of Engineering and Technology: SHI-SHUENN CHEN
Industrial Management: KUN-JEN CHUNG
Electronic Engineering: CHING-WEN HSUE
Mechanical Engineering: ZONE-CHING LIN
Textile Engineering: ING-JING WANG
Construction Engineering: CHANG-YU OU
Chemical Engineering: HO-MU LIN
Electrical Engineering: HONG-CHAN CHANG
Business Administration: DAY-LANG LIU
Information Management: YUE-LI WANG
Humanities: MAO-SUNG LIN
Architectural Design: YUNG-HORNG PERNG
Industrial and Commercial Design: WEN-CHIH CHANG

NATIONAL TAIWAN NORMAL UNIVERSITY

162 East Ho Ping Rd, Sec. 1, Taipei 10610

Telephone: (2) 23625101
Fax: (2) 23922673

Founded 1946
Language of instruction: Chinese
State control
Academic year: August to July (two semesters).

President: HSI-MUH LEU
Vice-President: MAW-FA CHIEN
Secretary-General: HSI-PING WANG
Registrar: CHIN-CHAO LIN
Library Director: SHENG-YEE LIN

Number of teachers: 819
Number of students: 6,667

Publications: *Bulletin*, *General Information*, *Public Lecture Series*, *NTNU Alumni* (monthly), *A-V Education* (every 2 months), *Secondary Education* (every 2 months), graduate institutional and departmental journals.

DEANS

College of Education: CHEN-SHAN LIN
College of Liberal Arts: MING-TEH LAI
College of Fine and Applied Arts: YU-CHIOU CHEN
College of Sciences: JAN-D CHEN
Extension Division: HENG-CHENG LIANG
Dean of Studies: TAI-WEI LEE
Dean of Students: CIN-HSIUNG YOU
Dean of General Affairs: HSU-HSIUNG LI

NATIONAL TAIWAN OCEAN UNIVERSITY

2 Pei-Ning Rd, Keelung

Telephone: (2) 24622192
Fax: (2) 24620724

Founded 1953 (formerly National Taiwan College of Marine Science and Technology)
Academic year: August to July

President: JIANN-KUO WU
Vice-President: HSING-CHEN CHEN
Dean of Academic Affairs: KUO-TIEN LEE
Dean of Student Affairs: CHING-MING MAO
Dean of General Affairs: RAN HUANG
Librarian: WEN-PING YANG

Library of 140,000 vols, 2,000 periodicals
Number of teachers: 474

Number of students: 5,106

DEANS OF COLLEGES

Maritime Science: HO-PING CHOU
Fisheries Science: TUU-JYI CHAI
Science and Engineering: HSIEW-WEN LI
Technology: TAI-SHENG LEE

HEADS OF DEPARTMENTS

Merchant Marine: YUAN-ERH TSAI
Marine Engineering: YIH-HWANG LIN
Shipping and Transportation Management: YIE-SHENG CHEN
Nautical Technology: PI-KUEI KUO
Marine Engineering and Technology: RONG-HUA YEH
Maritime Technology: JUNG-JAE CHAO
Maritime Law: CHANG-HUA YIN
Fisheries Science: YAU-SHOU CHOW
Marine Food Science: SHANN-JZONG JIANG
Marine Biology: SHIU-MEI LIU
Aquaculture: YEW-HU CHIEN
Fisheries Economics: DAVID S. LIAO
Marine Biotechnology: YIN-SI HWANG
Naval Architecture: JEUN-LEN WU
Harbour and River Engineering: SU-CHIH CHEN
Electrical Engineering: JIUNN-JYE CHANG
Oceanography: MING-KUANG HSU
Materials Engineering: PEE-YEW LEE
Applied Geophysics: CHENG-SUNG WANG
Computer and Information Sciences: IN-JEN LIN

NATIONAL TAIWAN UNIVERSITY

1 Roosevelt Rd, Section 4, Taipei 106
Telephone: (2) 2363-0231

Founded in 1928 during the Japanese occupation as the Taihoku Imperial University; taken over and renamed by Chinese Government in 1945
Language of instruction: Chinese
Academic year: August to June (two semesters)

President: WEI-JAO CHEN
Vice-President: CHENG-HONG CHEN
Dean of Academic Affairs: SI-CHEN LEE
Dean of Student Affairs: CHI-PENG HO
Dean of Business Affairs: YIH-MING CHEN
Library Director: MING-DER WU

Library of 1,851,000 vols
Number of teachers: 3,189
Number of students: 23,474

Publications: *Acta Geologica Taiwanica, Acta Botanica Taiwanica, Acta Oceanographica Taiwanica, History and Chinese Literature Series, List of Publications of the Faculty and Staff Members of the NTU,* various department publs, etc.

DEANS

College of Liberal Arts: YAO-FU LIN
College of Science: MING-CHANG KANG
College of Law: CHIEH-LIN HSU
College of Medicine: BOR-SHEN HSIEH
College of Engineering: YIH-NAN CHEN
College of Agriculture: TIAN-FUH SHEN
College of Management: HONG-CHANG CHANG
College of Public Health: CHIU-SEN WANG

DIRECTORS OF GRADUATE INSTITUTES

Chinese Literature: WEI-TAI LEE
History: TONG-HWA LEE
Philosophy: HSIN-AN TSAI
Anthropology: JIH-CHANG HSIEH
Library Science: HSUEH-HUA CHEN SUN
Foreign Languages and Literature: TIEN-EN KAO
Art History: PAO-CHEN CHEN
Linguistics: SHUAN-FAN HUANG
Theatre and Drama: JOHN Y. H. HU
Japanese Language and Literature: YIH-LANG HSIEH
Musicology: YING-FEN WANG
Mathematics: HUNG CHEN
Physics: WOEI-YANN HWANG
Chemistry: YING-CHIN LIN
Geography: TZU-HOW CHU
Geology: HUANN-JIH LO
Zoology: TAI-SHENG CHIU
Botany: YUNG-REUI CHEN
Psychology: CHIA-HUNG HSU
Atmospheric Sciences: CHENG-SHANG LEE
Oceanography: NAI-KUANG LIANG
Biochemical Science: MU-CHIN TZENG
Fisheries Science: HUAI-JEN TSAI
Political Science: TZONG-HO BAU
Law: TZU-YI LIN
Economics: CHING-HSI CHANG
Journalism: LIN-LIN KU
Sociology: WAN-I LIN
San-Min-Chu-I (Philosophy of the Father of the Republic): YEONG-KUANG GER
Business Administration: NENG-PAI LIN
Finance: TSUN-SIOU LEE
Accounting: YANG-TZONG TSAY
International Business: CHING-SUNG WU
Information Management: WEN-HSIEN CHEN
Dentistry: CHI-CHUAN HSIEH
Medical Technology: JAU-TSUEN KAO
Nursing: SHU-JEN SHIAU
Anatomy: SEU-MEI WANG
Physiology: YUAN-FEEN TSAI
Biochemistry: TA-HSIU LIAO
Pharmacology: MING-JAI SU
Pharmaceutical Sciences: SHOEI-SHENG LEE
Toxicology: TZUU-HUEI UENG
Molecular Medicine: SHENG-CHUNG LEE
Immunology: RONG-HWA LIN
Clinical Medicine: MING-YANG LAI
Microbiology: TSUEY-YING HSU
  Bacteriology Division: TSUEY-YING HSU
  Parasitology Division: SEN-CHI LU
Pathology: SU-MING HSU
Public Health: TUNG-LIANG CHIANG
Occupational Medicine and Industrial Hygiene: JUNG-DER WANG
Organization Administration: CHIH-LIANG YAUNG
Environmental Health: FUNG-CHANG SUNG
Agronomy: CHING-HUEI KAO
Agricultural Chemistry: YEI-SHUNG WANG
Plant Pathology and Entomology: WEN-SHI WU
Horticulture: PUNG-LING HUANG
Industrial Engineering: MAW-HUEI LEE
Electro-optical Engineering: HUNG-CHUN CHANG
Civil Engineering: JEONG-BIN YANG
Mechanical Engineering: HON SO
Electrical Engineering: SOO-CHANG PEI
Chemical Engineering: SHI-CHERN YEN
Naval Architecture Engineering: FORNG-CHER CHIU
Information Engineering: CHING-CHI HSU
Environmental Engineering: SHANG-LIEN LO
Materials Engineering: WEN-HSIUNG WANG
Applied Mechanics: TSUNG-TSONG WU
Building and Planning: HERNG-DAR BIH
Agricultural Engineering: FI-JOHN CHANG
Forestry: YA-NAN WANG
Animal Science: JEN-HSOU LIN
Agricultural Economics: MING C. CHEN
Agricultural Extension: WEN-RUEY LEE
Agricultural Machinery Engineering: FU-MING LU
Veterinary Medicine: CHAW-KING LIU
Food Science and Technology: WEN-CHANG CHIANG
Evening Division: RONG-RUEY DUH

NATIONAL TSING HUA UNIVERSITY

101, Sec. 2, Kuang Fu Rd, Hsinchu
Telephone: 886-35-715131

Re-founded 1956
Language of instruction: Chinese
Academic year: August to July

President: CHUN-SHAN SHEN
Librarian: JAMES T. LIN

Number of teachers: 459
Number of students: 6,001

Publications: *Tsing Hua Hsiao Yu T'ung Hsun* (Alumni News, quarterly), *Tsing Hua Shuang Chou K'an* (Review, fortnightly), *Tsing Hua Hsiao K'an* (Newsletter, irregular), *Tsing Hua Journal of Chinese Studies.*

DEANS

College of Science: CHUN-CHEN LIAO
College of Engineering: WEN-HWA CHEN
College of Nuclear Science: CHUEN-HORNG TSAI
College of Humanities and Social Sciences: BIH-ER CHOU
College of Life Science: TSE-WEN CHANG

HEADS OF DEPARTMENTS

College of Science:
  Chemistry: Prof KUEI-JUNG CHAO
  Mathematics: Prof. JER-SHYONG LIN
  Physics: Prof. JUH-TZENG LUE
  Computer Science: Prof. YOUN-LONG LIN
  Graduate Institute of Statistics: ANNE CHAO

College of Engineering:
  Chemical Engineering: Prof. KAN-SEN CHOU
  Electrical Engineering: CHING-TSAI PAN
  Industrial Engineering: HSIAO-FAN WANG
  Materials Science and Engineering: TSONG-PYNG PERNG
  Power Mechanical Engineering: Prof. JING-TANG YANG

College of Nuclear Science:
  Nuclear Science: Prof. MO-HSIUNG YANG
  Engineering and Systems Science: TIEN-KO WANG
  Graduate Institute of Radiation Biology: WEI-YUAN CHOW

College of Humanities and Social Sciences:
  Chinese Literature: Prof. YING-CHUN TSAI
  Foreign Languages and Literature: Prof. SAMUEL WANG
  Economics: Prof. KUO-PING CHANG
  Graduate Institute of History: Prof. CHANG YUAN
  Graduate Institute of Linguistics: Prof. CHINFA LIEN
  Graduate Institute of Sociology and Anthropology: WEI-AN CHANG
  Graduate Institute of Philosophy: FENG-FU TSAO

College of Life Science:
  Life Science: YIU-KAY LAI

SOOCHOW UNIVERSITY

Wai Shuang Hsi, Shihlin, Taipei
Telephone: (2) 28819184
Fax: (2) 28829310

Founded 1900
Private control
Languages of instruction: Chinese and English
Academic year: September to June (two semesters)

President: YUAN-TSUN LIU
Vice-President for Academic Affairs: MING-CHE TSAI
Registrar: CHENG-TSUN -LIN
Librarian: JOSEPH C. I. WANG

Library of 502,000 vols
Number of teachers: 1,093
Number of students: 13,004

DIRECTORS

School of Arts and Social Sciences: MING-CHE TSAI
School of Science: MAO-TING CHIEN
School of Foreign Languages and Cultures: CHIH-WEI HSIEH
School of Law: CHIA-JUI CHENG
School of Business: CHAO-CHUAN YU
Extension School: CHAO-HUNG WANG

TAMKANG UNIVERSITY

151 Ying-Chuan Rd, Tamsui, Taipei 25137

Telephone: (2) 2621-5656
Fax: (2) 2622-3204

Founded 1950 (formerly Tamkang College of Arts and Sciences)
Private control
Language of instruction: Chinese and English
Academic year: August to June

President: Dr Yun-shan Lin
Vice-Presidents: Dr Horng-jinh Chang (Academic), Dr Flora Chia-i Chang (Administrative)
Secretary-General: Prof. Ching-jen Hung
Dean of Academic Affairs: Dr Ting-chi Hsu
Dean of Student Affairs: Dr Huan-chao Keh
Dean of General Affairs: Prof. Edward F. Niu
Librarian: Prof. Hong-chu Huang

Library of 680,000 vols, 3,900 periodicals
Number of teachers: 1,220
Number of students: 24,672

Publications: *Tamkang Journal, Tamkang Review, Tamkang Chair Lecture Series, Tamkang Mathematics, Educational Media and Library Science, Journal of Future Studies, International Journal of Information and Management Science*, etc.

DEANS OF COLLEGES

Liberal Arts: Dr Hsi-jen Fu
Science: Dr Wen-fa Sye
Engineering: Dr Chao-kang Feng
Business: Dr Joug-rong Chiou
Management: Dr Miao-sheng Chen
Foreign Languages and Literature: Dr Sen-ling Lin
International Studies: Dr Yang Chi
Technocracy: Prof. Hsin-fu Tsai
Extension Education Centre: Prof. Ching-tang Lu

DIRECTORS OF GRADUATE INSTITUTES

Western Languages and Literature: Dr Lily Hwei-mei Chen
European Studies: Dr Wei-penn Chang
American Studies: Dr Thomas B. Lee
Mathematics: Dr Shou-jen Hu
Chemistry: Prof. Bo-cheng Wang
Physics: Dr Jenn-an Lin
Information Engineering: Dr Ding-an Chiang
Mechanical Engineering: Dr Chien-jong Shih
Management Science: Dr Hai-ming Chen
Architecture: Dr Sheng-fong Lin
Civil Engineering: Dr Shi-chi Chu
International Affairs and Strategic Studies: Dr Ming-hsien Wong
Japanese Studies: Dr Rueih-shyurng Jang
Water Resources and Environmental Engineering: Dr Po-chien Lu
Money, Banking and Finance: Dr Gin-chung Lin
Chinese Literature: Dr Po-yuan Kao
Slavic Studies: Dr Alexander Pisarev
China Studies: Dr Andy W. Y. Chang
Information Management: Dr Hung-chang Lee
Chemical Engineering: Dr Kuo-chen Huang
Educational Media Library Science: Dr Jeong-yeou Chiu
Aerospace Engineering: Dr Tjeng-yuan Chen
International Business: Dr Chao-nan Chia
Industrial Economics: Dr Ping-chen Li
Accounting: Prof. Mei-lan Wang
Electrical Engineering: Dr Po-jen Chuang
Latin-American Studies: Dr Kwo-wei Kung
Southeast Asian Studies: Dr Juo-yu Lin

TUNGHAI UNIVERSITY

181 Taichung Harbour Rd, Sec. 3, Taichung
Telephone: (4) 3590121
Fax: (4) 3590361

Founded 1955 under the auspices of the United Board for Christian Higher Education in Asia
Languages of instruction: Chinese and English
Academic year: September to July (two semesters)

President: Kang-pei Wang
Dean of Studies: Fang-bo Yeh
Dean of Students: Sheng-hsiung Liao
Dean of General Affairs: Morgan C. Y. Wang
Librarian: Cheng-tung Lin

Number of teachers: 826
Number of students: 13,000

Publications: *Tunghai Journal, Tunghai Bulletin, Tunghai News, The Vineyard.*

DEANS

College of Arts: Ming-shui Hung
College of Science: I-chao Hsiao
College of Engineering: Chung-hsing Li
College of Management: Tsai-ding Lin
College of Social Sciences: Tseng-lu Li
College of Agriculture: Chun-chin Kuo

Colleges and Institutes

China Medical College: 91 Hseuh Shih Rd, Taichung 404; tel. (4) 2057153; f. 1958; private control; two campuses (in Taichung and Peikang), six graduate institutes, 12 undergraduate schools, Chiang Kai-shek Medical Center, two teaching hospitals; 625 staff, 4,666 students; Pres. Mason Chen.

Kaohsiung Medical College: 100 Shih Chuan 1st Rd, Kaohsiung; tel. (7) 311-7820; fax (7) 321-2062; f. 1954; private control; 562 teachers, 4,485 students; library of 134,000 vols, 2,408 periodicals; schools of medicine, dentistry, pharmacy, nursing (including evening school of nursing), technology for medical sciences, public health, psychology, rehabilitation medicine, medical sociology, biology and chemistry; graduate institutes of medicine, pharmaceutical sciences, dental sciences, public health, nursing, oral health science, natural products, behavioural sciences, biochemistry, occupational safety and health; research centres: health and social services policy, industrial hygiene; college hospital; Pres. Juei-Hsiung Tsai; publ. *Kaohsiung Journal of Medical Sciences* (monthly).

National Institute of the Arts: 1 Hsueh Yuan Rd, Kuan-Tu, Taipei 112; tel. (2) 28961000; f. 1982; depts of music, fine arts, theatre, dance, traditional music, theatrical design, and graduate programmes of music, art history, theatre, dance, traditional arts; grants BFA and MFA degrees; 301 teachers; 950 students; library of 130,000 vols; Pres. Dr Kun-liang Chiu; publ. *Arts Review.*

National Kaohsiung Institute of Technology: 415 Chien-Kung Rd, Kaohsiung 807; tel. (7) 3814526; fax (7) 3838435; f. 1963; depts of chemical, civil, mechanical, electrical, electronic, industrial and mould- and die-making engineering, accounting and statistics, business management, banking and insurance; 9,951 students; library of 53,000 vols; Pres. Dr Kuang-chih Huang; publ. *Journal* (annually).

National Pingtung Polytechnic Institute: 1 Hseuh-Fu Rd, Nei Pu Hsiang, Pingtung Hsien; tel. (8) 7703660; fax (8) 7702226; f. 1954; depts of Plant Industry, Forest Resources Management and Technology, Aquaculture, Animal Production, Plant Protection, Veterinary Medicine, Environmental Protection, Civil Engineering, Mechanical Engineering, Natural Resources Conservation Technology, Forest Products Technology, Food Science and Technology, Agribusiness Management, Applied Life Science, Rural Planning and Landscaping, Management Information Systems, Industrial Management, Business Management, Child Care Technology; 150 professors, 4,500 students; library of 96,470 vols; Pres. Shanda Liu; publs *Bulletin* (annually), etc.

Taipei Institute of Technology: 3, Sec. 1, Shin-sheng South Rd, Taipei; f. 1912; 8,973 students; library of 112,000 vols; Pres. Dr Chih Tang.

Taipei Medical College: 250 Wu Hsing St, Taipei; tel. (2) 27361661; fax (2) 27362824; f. 1960; private control; undergraduate and graduate programmes; 570 teachers; 3,970 students; library of 82,000 vols; Pres. Chung-hong Hu; Vice-Pres. Meei-shiow Lu; Dean of Studies Chau-yang Chen; publ. *Journal* (2 a year).

Tatung Institute of Technology: 40 Chungshan N Rd, Sec. 3, Taipei; tel. 25925252; telex 11348; fax 25921813; f. 1956; private control; graduate programmes in business management, electrical engineering, mechanical engineering, chemical engineering, information engineering and materials engineering; depts of mechanical, electrical, chemical, information and materials engineering, business management, industrial design, applied mathematics and bioengineering (research centres attached); 265 teachers; library of 128,949 vols; Pres. T. S. Lin; Dean of Studies Cheng C. Huang.

School of Art and Music

National Taiwan Academy of Arts: Panchiao Park, Taipei; f. 1955; cinema, drama, radio, TV, fine arts, painting, graphic arts, industrial arts, Chinese music, dance, sculpture; 381 teachers, 2,128 students; library of 74,500 vols; Pres. S. L. Ling.

COLOMBIA

Learned Societies

GENERAL

Academia Colombiana de la Lengua (Colombian Academy): Apdo Aereo 13922, Bogotá; f. 1871; corresp. of the Real Academia Española (Madrid); 29 mems, 50 corresp. and hon. mems; library of 40,000 vols; Dir (vacant); Permanent Sec. IGNACIO CHAVES CUEVAS; Exec. Sec. HORACIO BEJARANO DÍAZ; publ. *Boletín*.

Casa de la Cultura de la Costa (House of Caribbean Coast Culture): Carrera 3, No. 19–60, Of. 401, Bogotá; tel. 243-3898; f. 1981; study centre for development of the Colombian coastal regions and int. Caribbean studies; mems: 36 companies and individuals, 86 congressmen from the coast; library of 2,000 vols; Pres. MARCO ANTONIO CONTRERAS; Sec. GERARDO MORA MEDINA; publ. *Revista Caribe Internacional* (monthly).

Instituto Colombiano de Cultura: Calle 8, No. 6–97, Bogotá; tel. 2828596; fax 2820854; f. 1968; conservation of the national heritage, organization of the development of arts and letters, promotion of national folklore; administers all cultural activity through 3 main depts: Cultural Heritage, Cultural Communications, Fine Arts; 1,000 staff; Dir LILIANA BONILLA OTOYA; Sec.-Gen. LINA MARÍA PÉREZ G.; publs *Colección Popular* (monthly), *Autores Nacionales* (monthly), *Revista Gaceta* (monthly), *Biblioteca Básica Colombiana* (2 a year), *Historia Viva*, special publications, children's literature.

AGRICULTURE, FISHERIES AND VETERINARY SCIENCE

Sociedad de Agricultores de Colombia (Colombian Farmers' Society): Carrera 7 No 24–89, 44° piso, Apdo Aéreo 3638, Bogotá; tel. 2821989; fax 2844572; f. 1871; consultative body for the Government; 400 mems; library of 5,500 vols, 435 periodical titles; Pres. JUAN MANUEL OSPINA RESTREPO; Sec. GABRIEL MARTINEZ PELAEZ; publs *Revista Nacional de Agricultura* (quarterly), *El Editorial Agrario* (irregular), *Documentos Independientes*.

BIBLIOGRAPHY, LIBRARY SCIENCE AND MUSEOLOGY

Asociación Colombiana de Bibliotecarios (ASCOLBI) (Colombian Association of Librarians): Calle 10, No. 3–16, Apdo Aéreo 30883, Bogotá; tel. 269-4219; f. 1942; 1,200 mems; Pres. SAUL SANCHEZ TORO; Gen. Sec. B. N. CARDONA DE GIL; publ. *Boletín* (quarterly).

Centro Regional para el Fomento del Libro en América Latina y el Caribe (CERLALC) (Regional Centre for the Promotion of Books in Latin America and the Caribbean): Calle 70 No. 9–52, Apdo Aéreo 57348, Bogotá; tel. (1) 3217501; fax (1) 3217503; e-mail cerlalc@impsat.net.co; f. 1972 by UNESCO and Colombian govt, later joined by most states in the area; promotes production and circulation of books, and development of libraries; provides training; promotes protection of copyright; library of 5,600 documents, 100 periodicals; Dir CARMEN BARVO BARCENAS; publs *El Libro en América Latina y el Caribe* (quarterly), *Boletín Informativo CERLALC* (4 a year).

Fundación para el Fomento de la Lectura—(FUNDALECTURA): Avenida calle 40 No. 16-46, Apdo 048902, Santafé de Bogotá; tel. 3201511; fax 2877071; e-mail fundalec@impsat.net.co; f. 1984; promotion of reading, and children's and juvenile literature; library of 4,500 vols; Dir SILVIA CASTRILLÓN; publs *Hojas de Lectura* (4 a year), *Revista Latinoamericana de Literatura Infantil y Juvenil* (2 a year), *Cincuenta Libros Sin-Cuenta* (2 a year).

ECONOMICS, LAW AND POLITICS

Academia Colombiana de Jurisprudencia (Colombian Academy of Jurisprudence): Calle 17 No. 4–95, Oficina 210, Bogotá; tel. 2414716; f. 1894; 50 mems; Pres. HERNANDO MORALES M.; publs *Revista* (2 a year), *Anuario*.

Sociedad Colombiana de Economistas: Carrera 20, No. 36–41, Apdo Aéreo 8429, Bogotá; tel. 2459637; f. 1957; to promote the improvement of the teaching of economic sciences and economics as a profession, for the economic and social development of the country; 5,500 mems; library of 25,000 vols; Pres. JORGE VALENCIA JARAMILLO; Dir. LUIS ALBERTO AVILA; publ. *Revista* (every 2 months).

EDUCATION

Asociación Colombiana de Universidades (Colombian Universities Association): Apdo Aéreo 252367, Calle 93, No. 16–43, Bogotá; tel. 2185145; fax 2185098; f. 1957; 68 mem. univs; Pres. Dr ALFONSO OCAMPO L.; Exec. Dir Dr JAIME TOBÓN V.; Sec.-Gen. Dr JORGE RIVADENEIRA; publs *ASCUN, Mundo Universitario* (annually).

Instituto Colombiano de Crédito Educativo y Estudios Técnicos en el Exterior (ICETEX) (Colombian Institute for Educational Loans and Advanced Studies Abroad): Carrera 3A, No. 18–24, Apdo Aéreo 5735, Bogotá; tel. (1) 2867780; fax (1) 2843510; e-mail icetex3@gaitana.interred.net.co; f. 1950; provides undergraduate and postgraduate grants; selects Colombian students for foreign scholarships, and finances foreign postgraduate students in Colombia; information and documentation centres; library of 15,000 vols; Dir Dr CARLOS A. BURITICÁ GIRALDO; publ. *Boletín Interno*.

HISTORY, GEOGRAPHY AND ARCHAEOLOGY

Academia Antioqueña de Historia (Antioquia Academy of History): Carrera 43, Nos 53–37, Apdo Aéreo 7175, Medellín; tel. (942) 395576; f. 1903; 60 mems; Pres. JAIME SIERRA GARCIA; Sec. ALICIA GIRALDO GÓMEZ; publs *Repertorio Histórico* (3 a year), *Bolsilibros*.

Academia Boyacense de Historia (Boyaca Academy of History): Casa del Fundador, Tunja; tel. (9792) 3441; f. 1905; publication and encouragement of historical, literary and anthropological studies in Boyaca; 30 mems; library of 1,000 vols, 600 MSS from the period 1539–1860; Pres. JAVIER OCAMPO LOPEZ; Sec. RAMÓN CORREA; publ. *Repertorio Boyacense* (2 a year).

Academia Colombiana de Historia (Colombian Academy of History): Calle 10 No. 8–95, Apdo Aéreo 14428, Bogotá; f. 1902; 40 mems excluding Colombian and foreign corresp. mems; library of 45,000 vols; Pres. Dr GERMÁN ARCINIEGAS; Sec. ROBERTO VELANDIA; Library Dir Dr RAFAEL SERRANO CAMARGO; publ. *Boletín de Historia y Antigüedades*.

Academia de la Historia de Cartagena de Indias (Cartagena Academy of History): Casa de la Inquisición, Plaza Bolívar, Cartagena; tel. 645432; f. 1918; 24 mems, and 48 Colombian, and 48 foreign corresponding mems; library of 10,000 vols; special collections on the history of Cartagena and Colombia; Pres. DONALDO BOSSA HERAZO; Sec.-Gen. CELEDONIO PIÑERES DE LA ESPRIELLA; publ. *Boletín Historial* (quarterly).

Sociedad Bolivariana de Colombia: Calle 19A No 4–40E, Apdo 11812, Bogotá; tel. 2431166; f. 1924; 20 hon. mems; library of 1,000 vols, specialized bibliography on Simón Bolívar; Pres. Col ALBERTO LOZANO; publ. *Revista Bolivariana* (3 a year).

Sociedad Geográfica de Colombia (Colombian Geographical Society): Observatorio Astronómico Nacional, Apdo 2584, Bogotá; tel. 2348893; f. 1903; 40 mems; Pres. CLEMENTE GARAVITO; Sec. RAFAEL CONVERS PINZON; publs *Boletín* (3 a year), *Cuadernos de Geografía Colombiana*; branch socs in Barranquilla, Pasto, Medellín, Tunja, Sibundoy.

LANGUAGE AND LITERATURE

Instituto Caro y Cuervo: Carrera 11 No. 64–37, Apdo Aéreo 51502, Bogotá; tel. 2557753; e-mail carocuer@openway.com.co; f. 1942; Hispanic philology and literature; 20 mems; library of 66,000 vols, 25,000 periodicals; Dir IGNACIO CHAVES CUEVAS; Sec-Gen. Dr GUILLERMO RUIZ LARA; publs *Thesaurus* (3 a year), *Biblioteca de Publicaciones del Instituto, Series Minor, Clásicos Colombianos, Filólogos Colombianos, Anuario Bibliográfico Colombiano, Serie Bibliográfica, Diccionario de Construcción y Régimen de la Lengua Castellana* vols I–VIII, *Archivo Epistolar Colombiano, Biblioteca Colombiana, La Granada Entreabierta, Biblioteca 'Ezequiel Uricoechea', Atlas Lingüístico-Etnográfico de Colombia*, vols I–VI, *Noticias Culturales* (every 2 months), *Cuadernos del Seminario Andrés Bello, Litterae*.

PEN Internacional, Colombia: Apdo Aéreo 101830 Zona 10, Bogotá; tel. (1) 2846761; fax (1) 2184236; f. 1983; 50 mems; library of 1,000 vols; Pres. Dr CECILIA BALCÁZAR; Sec. GLORIA GUARDIA; publ. *Noticias del Pen* (monthly).

Unión Nacional de Escritores (National Writers' Union): Carrera 6 No. 10–42, Of. 402, Apdo 28846, Bogotá; tel. 2439814; f. 1980; Pres. JAIME MEJIA DIQUE; Sec. ARTURO ALAPE.

MEDICINE

Academia Nacional de Medicina (National Academy of Medicine): Carrera 7A No. 69–05, Bogotá; tel. 2493122; f. 1890; 228 mems; library of 10,000 vols; Pres. Dr JOSÉ FELIX PATIÑO RESTREPO; Perm. Sec. CÉSAR AUGUSTO PANTOJA; publs *Medicina* (quarterly), *Temas Médicos* (annually).

Asociación Colombiana de Facultades de Medicina (Colombian Association of Medical Faculties): Apdo 53751, Calle 39A No. 28–63, Bogotá; tel. 3686711; e-mail sascome@col1.telecom.com.co; f. 1959 to further higher education and research in medicine; divisions of Education, Evaluation, Health and Social

Security, Information; membership: 24 medical faculties (institutional mems), 4,500 individuals, 7 affiliated mems; library of 3,500 vols, 100 periodicals and audiovisual materials; Pres. JOSE MARIA MAYA; Exec. Dir. JULIO ENRIQUE OSPINA; publs *Boletín de Medicamentos y Terapéutica* (quarterly), *Gaceta Médica, Revista de ASCOFAME, Cuadernos de Actualización Médica Permanente, Boletín del Centro de Etica Médica y Bioética.*

Asociación Colombiana de Fisioterapía: Carrera 23 No. 47–51, Of. 3N-06-A, Bogotá; tel. 2876106; f. 1953; 950 mems; library of 300 vols; Pres. ELISA JARAMILLO DE LOPEZ; Exec. Sec. CLARA INES DE AMAYA; publ. *Revista* (annually).

Asociación Colombiana de Sociedades Científicas: Hospital Militar Central, Transversal 5a No. 49–00, Entrepiso 1, Apdo Aéreo 6658, Bogotá; tel. 245-44-81; f. 1957, present name 1970; health sciences; 3,692 mems; Exec. Dir Dr RAFAEL SARMIENTO MONTERO; Sec. Dr MAURICIO BERNAL; publ. *Boletín* (quarterly).

Capitolo Colombiano de las Federaciones Latinoamericanas de Asociaciones de Cancer (Colombian Chapter of Latin American Cancer Asscns): Clínica del Country, Carrera 15 No. 84–13, Bogotá; tel. 2361168; f. 1983; Pres. CALIXTO NOGUERA.

Federación Médica Colombiana: Calle 72 No. 6–44, 11° piso, Bogotá; tel. 2110208; f. 1935; Pres. ISMAEL ROLDAN VALENCIA; Sec. SERGIO ROBLEDA RIAGA; publ. *Directorio Médico Asistencial* (annually).

Instituto Nacional de Medicina Legal y Ciencias Forenses (National Institute of Legal Medicine and Forensic Sciences): Calle 7A, A 12–61, Santafé de Bogotá; tel. (1) 233854; f. 1914; staff of 800; library of 30,000 vols; Dir RICARDO MORA IZQUIERDO; publ. *Revista.*

Sociedad Colombiana de Cardiología (Colombian Cardiological Society): Avda 19 No. 97-31 Of. 401, Apdo Aéreo 1875, Bogotá; tel. and fax 6234603; f. 1950; 245 mems; Pres. ALBERTO SUAREZ; Sec. RICARDO ROZO; publ. *Revista SCC* (4 a year).

Sociedad Colombiana de Cirugía Ortopédica y Traumatología: Transv. 14 No. 126-10 Of. 210, Bogotá; tel. (1) 6260077; fax (1) 6155563; f. 1959; 640 mems; Pres. Dr RODRIGO PESANTEZ; Gen. Sec. Dr MIGUEL ANGEL MURCIA R.; publ. *Revista Colombiana de Ortopedia* (quarterly).

Sociedad Colombiana de Obstetricia y Ginecología: Carrera 23, No. 39–82, Apdo Aéreo 34188, Bogotá; tel. 2681485; f. 1943; 300 mems; library of 1,000 vols; Pres. Dr JAIME FERRO CAMARGO; Vice-Pres. Dra MARIA TERESA PERALTA ABELLO; Sec.-Gen. Dr PIO IVÁN GÓMEZ SÁNCHEZ; publ. *Revista Colombiana de Obstetricia y Ginecología* (quarterly).

Sociedad Colombiana de Patología: Dpto de Patología, Universidad del Valle, Cali; f. 1955; to improve all aspects of pathology studies; 155 mems; Pres. Dr EDGAR DUQUE; Sec. and Treas. Dr JOSÉ A. DORADO.

Sociedad Colombiana de Pediatría (Colombian Paediatrics Society): Avdo 4 Norte, No. 16–23, Apdo 3124, Cali; tel. 611407; fax 673614; f. 1917; 150 mems; library of 2,300 vols; Pres. CESAR A. VILLAMIZAR LUNA; Sec. ALBERTO LEVY F.; publs *Pediatría* (quarterly), *Acta Pedriatrica Colombiana.*

Sociedad Colombiana de Psiquiatría: POB 52053, Bogotá; tel. 561148; fax 6162706; f. 1961; 350 mems; Pres. Dr ROBERTO CHASKEL; Sec. Dr ALVARO FRANCO; publ. *Revista Colombiana de Psiquiatría* (quarterly).

Sociedad Colombiana de Radiología (Radiological Society): Carrera 13A No. 90–18, Of. 208, Bogotá; tel. (1) 6183895; fax (1) 6183775; f. 1945; 400 mems; library of 3,000 vols, collections of journals; Pres. CAYO DUARTE; Sec. PATRICIA CASTRO S.

NATURAL SCIENCES

General

Academia Colombiana de Ciencias Exactas, Físicas y Naturales (Colombian Academy of Exact, Physical and Natural Sciences): Carrera 3A, No. 17–34, 3° piso, Apdo Aéreo 44763, Santafé de Bogotá 1, DC; tel. (1) 341-48-05; fax (1) 283-85-52; f. 1929; 9 hon. mems, 40 mems; Pres. LUIS EDUARDO MORA-OSEJO; Sec. JOSÉ A. LOZANO; publs *Revista, Collección Jorge Alvarez, Collección Julio Carrizosa, Collección Enrique Pérez, Collección Memorias.*

Sociedad de Ciencias Naturales Caldas: Apdo Aéreo 1180, Medellín; f. 1938; Dir MARCO A. SERNA D.; publs occasional articles.

Biological Sciences

Sociedad Colombiana de Biología: Calle 73 No. 10–10, Apartamento 301, Bogotá; Pres Dr GONZALO MONTES; Sec. MARGARET ORDÓÑEZ SMITH.

Mathematical Sciences

Sociedad Colombiana de Matemáticas: Apdo Aéreo 2521, Bogotá 1; tel. 2216829; f. 1955; 800 mems; library of 7,000 vols; Pres VICTOR SAMUEL ALBIS GONZALEZ; publs *Revista Colombiana de Matemáticas, Monografías Matemáticas, Lecturas Matemáticas, Monografías Elementales.*

Physical Sciences

Sociedad Colombiana de Ciencias Químicas: Apdo Aéreo 10968, Bogotá; tel. 2216920; fax 3150751; f. 1941 to promote chemical research in Colombia, to uphold professional ethical standards, to serve as an advisory body for public and private organizations, to maintain relations with similar institutions at home and abroad; 350 mems; Pres. FABIO H. VELANDIA CASALLAS; Sec. GILMA DAZA CASILIMAS; publ. *Química e Industria* (2 a year).

RELIGION, SOCIOLOGY AND ANTHROPOLOGY

Instituto Colombiano de Cultura Hispánica: Calle 12, No. 2–41, Apdo 5454, Bogotá; tel. 3-413857; fax 2811051; f. 1951; study and conservation of the traditions of Hispanic peoples; contains important editions of 'Flora of the Botanic Expedition' of the New Kingdom of Granada in conjunction with the Instituto de Cooperación Iberoamericana, Madrid; library of 50,000 vols (open to public); Dir WILLIAM JARAMILLO MEJÍA; Gen. Sec. CLEMENCIA VALLEJO DE MEJÍA; publ. *Revista Ximénez de Quesada.*

TECHNOLOGY

Asociación Colombiana de Industrias Gráficas—ANDIGRAF (Graphic Industry National Asscn): Carrera 4A No. 25B–46, Apdo Aéreo 45243, Bogotá; tel. 2819611; f. 1975; 200 company mems; Pres. JOSE GRANADA RODRIGUEZ; publs *Colombia Gráfica* (annually), *Boletín Informativo* (monthly).

Asociación Colombiana de Usuarios de Computadores (Colombian Asscn of Computer Users): Calle 39A No. 14–58, Apdo 4542, Bogotá; tel. 2455932; f. 1970; 400 company mems; library of 1,500 documents; Pres. JOSE GUILLERMO JARAMILLO G.; Exec. Dir CESAR AUGUSTO SALAZAR U.; publs *ACUC Noticias* (every 2 months), *Boletín El Usuario* (monthly), *Catálogo Nacional de Software—Guía de Servicios Informáticos* (annually).

Sociedad Antioqueña de Ingenieros y Arquitectos (Society of Engineers and Architects): Calle 71 No. 65–100, Apdo 4754, Medellín; tel. (942) 573900; f. 1913; 950 mems; Pres. JOEL MORENO SANTOS; Exec. Dir MERY ROCIO PALACIOS SALDARRIAGA; publs *Noti SAI* (irregular), *Revista Técnica SAI* (quarterly).

Sociedad Colombiana de Ingenieros (Colombian Society of Engineers): Carrera 4, No. 10–41, Apdo 340, Bogotá; tel. 2862200; fax 2816229; f. 1887; 2,000 mems; library of 5,000 vols; Pres. HERNANDO MONROY VALENCIA; Exec. Dir SANTIAGO HENAO PÉREZ; publ. *Anales de Ingeniería* (quarterly).

Research Institutes

GENERAL

Institut Français de Recherche Scientifique pour le Développement en Coopération (ORSTOM): Apto Aéreo 32417, Cali; tel. (2) 6675560; fax (2) 6602247; biotechnology, agriculture, geography, demography, social sciences, biology, microbiology, mineralogy, geology; Rep. DIDIER ALAZARD. (See main entry under France.)

Instituto Colombiano para el Desarrollo de la Ciencia y la Tecnología 'Francisco José de Caldas' (Colciencias): Transversal 9A No. 133–28, Apdo Aéreo 051580, Santafé de Bogotá; tel. 2169800; fax 6251788; f. 1968; to promote scientific and technical development; co-ordinates and finances projects; library of 15,000 vols, 225 periodicals, 10,000 databases; Dir LUIS FERNANDO CHAPARRO OSORIO; Sec.-Gen. JUAN RICARDO MORALES ESPINEL; publs serials: *Carta de Colciencias* (monthly), *Colombia Ciencia y Tecnología* (quarterly).

AGRICULTURE, FISHERIES AND VETERINARY SCIENCE

Instituto Colombiano Agropecuario (Colombian Agricultural and Livestock Institute): Apdo Aéreo 7984, Calle 37 No. 8–43, 4°, 5° pisos, Bogotá; tel. 2855520; telex 44309; fax 2854351; f. 1962 to promote, co-ordinate and carry out research, teaching and development in agriculture and animal husbandry; specialized library (see under Libraries); Dir-Gen. JUAN MANUEL RAMIREZ; publs *Revista ICA* (quarterly), *ICA-Informa* (quarterly), *Informe Anual,* bulletins.

ECONOMICS, LAW AND POLITICS

Centro de Estudios sobre Desarrollo Económico (Centre for Economic Development Studies): Universidad de los Andes, Carrera 1E No. 18A–10, Apdo Aéreo 4976, Bogotá; tel. 3412240; fax 2815771; f. 1958; library of 35,000 vols; Dir JOSÉ LEIBOVICH; publ. *Desarrollo y Sociedad* (2 a year).

Departamento Administrativo Nacional de Estadística (Statistics Office): Centro Administrativo Nacional, Avda El Dorado-CAN, Apdo Aéreo 80043, Bogotá; tel. 2221750; fax 2222305; e-mail dane@impsat.net.co; f. 1953; library of 12,000 vols, 850 periodicals received; Dir ELGARDO ALBERTO SANTIAGO MOLINA; publs *Boletín Mensual de Estadística, Anuario de Industria Manufacturera, Anuario de Comercio Exterior, Informe al Congreso Nacional, Cuentas Nacionales de Colombia, Colombia Estadística,* and others.

EDUCATION

Centro de Investigación y Educación Popular: Carrera 5 No 33A-08, Apdo 25916, Bogotá; tel. 2858977; fax 2879089; f. 1962; private, non-profit org. specializing in social sciences education, and analysis of the Colombian system; library of 23,000 vols; Dir FERNAN

GONZALEZ G.; publ. *Cien Días* (quarterly), *Controversia* (irregular).

Instituto Colombiano para el Fomento de la Educación Superior: Apdo Aéreo 6319, Calle 17, No. 3–40, Bogotá; tel. 2819311; fax 286-80-45; e-mail snies@icfes.gov.co; f. 1968; branch of the Ministry of Education; govt body supervizing the running of higher education; co-ordinates the country's distance education system; documentation centre specializing in higher, distance and 'open' education, and national film collection: 9,200 vols, 2,500 documents, 2,527 periodicals, 1,015 films, a/v items and videocassettes; Dir LUIS CARLOS MUÑOZ URIBE; publs *Revista ICFES* (irregular), *Memorias de Eventos Científicos, Estadísticas de la Educación Superior.*

HISTORY, GEOGRAPHY AND ARCHAEOLOGY

Instituto Geográfico 'Agustín Codazzi': Apdo 6721, Carrera 30 No. 48–51, Santafé de Bogotá; tel. 2682055; fax 2694146; f. 1935; prepares topographical, cadastral, sectional, national, and agricultural maps of the country, and geophysical, cadastral and geodetic surveys; prepares geographical studies of Colombia; library of 10,000 vols; Dir GLORIA CECILIA BARNEY DURÁN.

MEDICINE

Instituto Nacional de Cancerología: Calle 1, No. 9–85, Bogotá; tel. 3336216; fax 2802246; f. 1934; diagnosis, therapy, control, teaching and research in cancer; runs a national cancer programme with 13 regional units throughout the country; library of 26,000 vols; Dir Dr JUAN MANUEL ZEA; publs *Boletín del INC* (quarterly), *Revista del INC, Informe del INC* (annually).

Instituto Nacional de Salud INPES (National Institute of Health): Avda el Dorado Carrera 50, Apdo Aéreo 80334, Bogotá; tel. 2221059; fax 2220194; f. 1968; library of 10,000 vols, 500 periodicals; Dir Dr MOISES WASSERMAN; publs *Biomédica, Informe Quincenal de Casos y Brotes de Enfermedades* (fortnightly), *Boletín Epidemiológico.*

NATURAL SCIENCES

Biological Sciences

Instituto de Ciencias Naturales—Museo de Historia Natural (Institute of Natural Sciences—Natural History Museum): Universidad Nacional de Colombia, Bogotá, Apdo 7495, Santafé de Bogotá; tel. 3681380; fax 3681345; f. 1936 to conduct scientific research; four main sections: botany, zoology, geology and anthropology; 35 mems; library of 8,000 vols; Dir PEDRO M. RUIZ C.; publs *Caldasia, Lozania* (Zoology), *Mutisia* (Botany), *Catálogo Ilustrado de las Plantas de Cundinamarca, Notas Divulgativas, Flora de Colombia, Biblioteca José Jerónimo Triana.*

Instituto de Investigaciones Marinas de Punta de Betín 'José Benito Vives de Andreis' (INVEMAR): Apdo Aéreo 1016, Santa Marta; tel. 211380; fax 211377; f. 1963; institute of COLCIENCIAS; aims to study and preserve the marine wildlife of the Colombian Caribbean; library of 10,000 vols; Dir Dra LEONOR BOTERO; publ. *Anales.*

Physical Sciences

Observatorio Astronómico Nacional (National Astronomical Observatory): Carrera 8, Calle 8, Apdo Aéreo 2584, Bogotá; tel. 2423786; f. 1803; library of 3,000 vols; Dir JORGE ARRAS DE GREIFF; publs *Anuario del Observatorio,* occasional publications.

RELIGION, SOCIOLOGY AND ANTHROPOLOGY

Instituto Colombiano de Antropología (Colombian Institute of Anthropology): Calle 8A, No. 8–87, Apdo Aéreo 407, Bogotá; tel. (1) 2461040; fax (1) 2330960; f. 1941; Dir MARÍA VICTORIA URIBE ALARCÓN; publs *Revista Colombiana de Antropología, Informes Antropológicos.* This Institute also administers the National Parks of San Agustín, Tierradentro and Ciudad Perdida.

TECHNOLOGY

Instituto Colombiano de Normas Técnicas y Certificación (ICONTEC): Carrera 37, No. 52–95, Bogotá; tel. 3150377; telex 42500; fax 2221435; f. 1963; 1,200 mems; library of 500,000 vols; Exec. Dir Ing. FABIO TOBON; Admin. Dir ALVARO PERDOMO B.; publs *Boletín Informativo* (monthly), *Standards* (monthly), *Normas y Calidad* (4 a year).

Instituto de Ciencias Nucleares y Energías Alternativas (Institute for Nuclear Sciences and Alternative Energy): Avda Eldorado, Carrera 50, Apdo Aéreo 8595, Santafé de Bogotá, DC; tel. 2220071; telex 42416; fax 2220173; f. 1959 to study the application of atomic and nuclear energy for peaceful uses, the development of alternative energy sources and the efficient use of energy; library of 18,000 vols, 60 periodicals, 70,000 reprints, 120,000 microforms; Dir Dr CESAR HUMBERTO ARIAS PABON; publs scientific reports, annual report.

Instituto de Investigaciones en Geociencias, Minería y Química (INGEOMINAS): Diagonal 53, No. 34–53, Apdo Aéreo 4865, Bogotá; tel. 2221811; fax 2223597; f. 1940 as National Geological Survey, name changed 1969; basic geological research, environmental geology, mineral exploration and pre-feasibility studies; library of 4,300 books, periodicals, 1,896 newspaper titles; 3,500 reports and magazines; Dir Dr ADOLFO ALARCÓN GUZMÁN; publs *Boletín Geológico* (annually 3 vols), *Revista Ingeominas, Informe de Actividades Anuales.*

Libraries and Archives

Barranquilla

Biblioteca Pública Departamental: Carrera 38–B, No. 38–21, Barranquilla; tel. (95) 312015; f. 1923; 32,000 vols; Dir OLGA CHAMS.

Bello

Biblioteca del Marco Fidel Suárez: Avda Suárez, Bello, Antioquia; tel. (942) 750774; f. 1957; public library and regional centre; 2,615 vols; Dir WALTER GIL.

Bogotá

Archivo Nacional de Colombia: Archivo General de la Nación, Calle 24 No. 5–60, 4° piso, Bogotá; tel. 416015; f. 1868; *c.* 40,600 vols and 3,135 metres of documents; Dir JORGE PALACIOS PRECIADO; publs *Revista, Catálogos,* and series of historic documents.

Biblioteca Agropecuaria de Colombia: Inst. Colombiano Agropecuario, Apdo Aéreo 240142, Bogotá; e-mail fsalazar@caldas.colciencias.gov.co; f. 1954; 45,000 vols devoted to agriculture and livestock, 45,000 pamphlets, 1,900 journals, 27,000 documents, 170 maps, 150 audiovisual titles, 497 tapes; Dir FRANCISCO SALAZAR ALONSO.

Biblioteca Central de la Pontificia Universidad Javeriana: Carrera 7A, No. 41–00, Bogotá; tel. 285-8177; fax 2850973; e-mail lmcabarc@javercol.javeriana.edu.co; f. 1931; 285,000 vols; Dir LUZ MARIA CABARCAS SANTOYA.

Biblioteca 'Luis-Angel Arango' del Banco de la República (Bank of the Republic Library): Calle 11 No. 4–14, Apdo Aéreo 3531, Santafé de Bogotá DC; tel. 2827840; fax 2863881; e-mail wbiblio@banrep.gov.co; f. 1932; 450,000 vols, 4,000 maps, 60,000 slides; 8 reading-rooms, conference hall, exhibition hall, research rooms, concert-hall; also *Hemeroteca 'Luis López de Mesa':* 8,000 serials, 1,200 newspapers; Dir JORGE ORLANDO MELO; publ. *Boletín Cultural y Bibliográfico* (quarterly).

Biblioteca Nacional de Colombia (National Library): Calle 24, No. 5–60, Apdo 27600, Bogotá; tel. 3414029; fax 3414030; f. 1777; 800,000 vols, 22,000 periodicals; rare book section (*c.* 28,000 vols); Dir CARLOS JOSÉ REYES POSADA; publ. *Revista Senderos.*

Biblioteca Seminario Conciliar de San José de Bogotá (Library of the San José Seminary): Avda 7 No. 94–80, Bogotá 8; tel. (1) 2367144; fax (1) 2181096; f. 1581; 40,000 vols specializing in philosophy and theology; Dir Rev. JAIME ALBERTO MANCERA CASAS.

Departamento de Bibliotecas, Universidad Nacional de Colombia: Ciudad Universitaria, Apdo Aéreo 14490, Santafé de Bogotá; tel. 2691743; f. 1867; 230,000 vols; Dir VÍCTOR ALBIS.

División de Documentación e Información Educativa, Ministerio de Educación Nacional (Educational Documentation and Information Division, Ministry of Education): Avda El Dorado, CAN, Bogotá; tel. 222800; co-ordinates the Educational Documentation and Information Sub-system, the School Libraries National Programme and runs the National Educational Documentation Centre; 10,000 vols, 300 pamphlets, 6,000 documents, 300 periodicals; Dir MARY LUZ ISAZA; publs *Memorias del Ministro de Educación al Congreso Nacional* (annually), *Correo Educativo.*

Cali

Biblioteca Departamental de Cali: Calle 14 Norte No 9-45, Cali; tel. (923) 613018; 54,000 vols; Dir MARIA VICTORIA DE GOMEZ; publ. *Boletín Bibliovalle* (every 2 months).

Biblioteca Municipal del Centenario: Carrera 5a, No. 7–10, Cali; f. 1910; 22,000 vols; Dir ALFONSO ZAWADKY.

Cartagena

Sección de Bibliotecas y Recursos Educativos, Universidad de Cartagena: Calle de la Universidad, Apdo Aéreo 1382, Cartagena; tel. (95) 6646182; fax (95) 6697778; f. 1828; 49,800 vols; Librarian PERLA ECHEVERRI LEMA.

Manizales

Biblioteca Central, Universidad de Caldas: Apdo Aéreo 275, Manizales; tel. (968) 861250 ext. 115; fax (968) 862520; f. 1958; 53,000 vols, 5,500 documents, 1,300 periodicals; Librarian SAUL SANCHEZ TORO; publs *Revista de la Universidad de Caldas, Revista de Agronomia, Revista de Medicina Veterinaria y Zootecnia.*

Biblioteca Pública Municipal: Calle 23 No. 20–30, Manizales; tel. (9688) 31697; f. 1931; 8,100 vols; Librarian NELLY AGUIRRE DE FIGUEROA.

Medellín

Biblioteca de la Universidad Pontificia Bolivariana: Apdo Aéreo 1178, Medellín; tel. 2162222; fax 2396683; f. 1936; 41,191 vols, 1,332 periodicals, 1,726 pamphlets, 3,179 audioivisual records; Librarian Lic. OLGA BEATRIZ BERNAL LONDOÑO; *Revista Universidad Pontificia Bolivariana, Revista de la Facultad de Filosofia, Cvestiones Teológicas, Revista de la Facultad de Derecho y Ciencias Políticas.*

Biblioteca Pública Piloto de Medellín (Pilot Public Library of Medellín): Carrera 64 con Calle 50 No. 50–32, Apdo Aéreo 1797, Medellín; tel. 230-24-22; fax 230-53-89; f. 1954 under the auspices of UNESCO; 85,000 vols; special collections: Antioquia and Antioquian authors, UNESCO depository; Dir GLORIA INES PALOMINO L.

Departamento de Bibliotecas, Universidad de Antioquia: Apdo Aéreo 1226, Medellín; tel. (4) 2105140; fax (4) 2116939; f. 1935; 180,000 vols, 8,715 periodicals; Dir CARLOS A. CADAVID A.; publs *Leer y Releer, Revista*.

Popayán

Departamento de Bibliotecas, Universidad del Cauca: Apdo Nacional 113, Calle 5 No 4–70, Popayán; tel. 233032; f. 1827; 70,000 vols; Dir JOSÉ MARÍA SERRANO PRADA; publs *Catálogo del Archivo Central del Cauca, Boletín Bibliográfico, Boletín Informativo, Cuadernos de Medicina, Boletín del Comité de Investigaciones Científicas, Revista Cátedra*.

Tunja

Universidad Pedagógica y Tecnológica de Colombia, Biblioteca Central, Tunja: Apdo Aéreo 1234, Tunja; tel. 400668; f. 1932; 68,000 vols; 1,800 periodical titles; special collections: theses, Fondo E. Posada, rare books, learned works; Dir BARBARA MARTIN MARTIN; publs *Lista de Canje, Apuntes del CENES, Educación y Ciencia, Cuadernos de Linguística hispánica-UPTC, Agricultura y Ciencia, Perspectiva Proceso Salud-Enfermedad, Inquietud Empresarial, Revista Facultad de Ingeniería, Revista de Ciencias Sociales*.

Museums and Art Galleries

Bogotá

Casa-Museo 'Jorge Eliécer Gaitán': Calle 42, No. 15–23, Bogotá; tel. (1) 2450368; fax (1) 2879093; f. 1948; collection relating to the history of Bogotá; run by the Centro Jorge Eliécer Gaitán; Dir GLORIA GAITÁN.

Jardín Botánico de Bogotá 'José Celestino Mutis': Avda 57 No. 61–13, Bogotá; tel. 2313965; fax 2506798; e-mail jardin@gaitana.interred.net.co; f. 1955; conservation, research and education; library of 3,000 vols; Dir HILARIO PEDRAZA TORRES; publs *Pérez-Arbelaezia* (2 a year), *Guía*, etc.

Museo Bolivariano (Bolivar Museum): Calle 20, No. 3–23 Este, Bogotá; tel. 2846819; f. 1922 in the country house occupied by Simón Bolívar in 1820, where relics of the Liberator and his epoch are exhibited; is administered by the Sociedad de Mejoras y Ornato de la Ciudad de Bogotá and maintained by the Ministry of Public Works; library and collection of paintings; Dir MARÍA SUSANO DE OJEDA.

Museo Colonial (Museum of the Colonial Period): Carrera 6, No. 9–77, Bogotá; tel. (1) 3362350; fax (1) 2841373; f. 1942; paintings, sculpture, furniture, gold and silver work, drawings, etc., of the Spanish colonial period (16th, 17th and 18th centuries); education dept: library of 1,000 vols; it is installed in a building erected by the Jesuits in 1622 to house the first Javeriana University; Dir TERESA MORALES DE GÓMEZ.

Museo del Oro (Gold Museum): Calle 16 No. 5–41, Parque de Santander, Bogotá; tel. (1) 3348748; fax (1) 2847450; f. 1939; 36,000 pre-Columbian gold objects representing the gods, myths, and customs of the Quimbaya, Muisca, Tairona and other native Indian cultures; Dir CLEMENCIA PLAZAS; publ. *Boletín* (2 a year).

Museo Nacional (National Museum): Carrera 7, No. 28–66, Bogotá; tel. 3342129; fax 3347447; f. 1823; archaeology, ethnology, history since Spanish conquest; collections of portraits, arms, banners, medals, coins, ceramics, fine arts; theatre; exhibition gallery; Dir ELVIRA CUERVO DE JARAMILLO.

Museo Nacional de Antropología (National Museum of Anthropology): Calle 8, No. 8-87, Bogotá; tel. 2462481; fax 2330960; f. 1941; ceramics, stone carvings, gold objects, textiles, etc., from all districts of Colombia; is a department of the Instituto Colombiano de Antropología; Dir MYRIAM JIMENO SANTOYO; publs *Revista Colombiana de Antropología, Informes Antropológicos*.

Medellín

Museo de Ciencias Naturales del Colegio de San José (Natural Science Museum): Apdo Aéreo 1180, Medellín; f. 1913; natural history in general, zoology, botany, mineralogy, anthropology; library of 500 vols and 1,000 magazines; Dir H. MARCO A. SERNA D.; publs *Avancemos* (monthly), *El Colombiano* (daily), *Boletín Cultural* (quarterly), catalogues.

Museo Filatélico del Banco de la República: Edif. Banco de la República, Parque de Berrió, Medellín; tel. 515579; f. 1977; collections of Colombian postage stamps, and stamps from other countries; Dir HERNÁN GIL PANTOJA; publ. *Revista*.

Museo Universitario: Universidad de Antioquia, Apdo Aéreo 1226, Medellín; fax 2638282; f. 1942; sections of anthropology, history, natural sciences, visual arts; Dir ROBERTO L. OJALVO PRIETO.

Roldanillo

Museo Omar Rayo: Calle 8a, 8–53, Roldanillo, Valle del Cauca; tel. 2229-8623; f. 1976, opened 1981; run by Fundación Museo Rayo; specializes in modern works on or with paper, fundamentally graphic art and design, by Latin American artists or those working in Latin America; a large collection has been donated by the artist Omar Rayo; library of 2,003 vols; Pres. of Foundation and Dir-Gen. OMAR RAYO REYES; publ. *Ediciones Embalaje*.

National Universities

UNIVERSIDAD DE ANTIOQUIA

Apdo Aéreo 1226, Ciudad Universitaria, Medellín, Antioquia

Telephone: (4) 2105020
Fax: (4) 2638282

Founded 1822
State control
Academic year: January to June, August to November

Rector: JAIME RESTREPO CUARTAS
Vice-Rector (General): LUIS FERNANDO JARAMILLO SALAZAR
Academic Vice-Rector: Dra GLORIA ISABEL OCAMPO ARANGO
Administrative Vice-Rector: FRANCISCO OSORIO GIRALDO
Research Vice-Rector: Dr GUSTAVO VALENCIA RESTREPO
Extension Vice-Rector: CLARA INÉS GIRALDO MOLINA
Secretary-General: LUIS FERNANDO MEJÍA VÉLEZ
Librarian: Dr CARLOS CADAVID ARANGO

Library: see Libraries
Number of teachers: 1,002 (f.t.e.)
Number of students: 19,257

Publications: *Revista Universidad de Antioquia* and various faculty publications.

DEANS

Faculty of Social and Human Sciences: JAIME OCHOA ANGEL
Faculty of Exact and Natural Sciences: GUSTAVO QUINTERO BARRERA
Faculty of Arts: DIEGO LEÓN ARANGO GÓMEZ
Faculty of Education: RAFAEL FLÓREZ OCHOA
Faculty of Economics: JORGE LOTERO CONTRESAS
Faculty of Law and Political Science: TERSITA ARIAS DE OJALVO
Faculty of Media Communication: LUIS IVÁN BEDOYA MONTOYA
Faculty of Engineering: ASDRÚBAL VALENCIA GIRALDO
Faculty of Medicine: ALBERTO URIBE CORREA
Faculty of Veterinary Medicine and Animal Husbandry: LUIS JAVIER ARROYAVE MORALES
Faculty of Dentistry: GILBERTO NARANJO PIZANO
Faculty of Pharmaceutical Chemistry: PIEDAD RESTREPO DE ROJAS
National Faculty of Public Health: ALVARO FRANCO GIRALDO
Faculty of Nursing: MARÍA CONSUELA CASTRILLÓN AGUDELO

DIRECTORS

School of Bacteriology and Clinical Laboratory: LUZ MARIELA OCHOA SÁNCHEZ
School of Nutrition and Dietetics: LIGIA MARTINEZ MALVENDAS
Institute of Physical Education and Sports: RODRIGO ARBOLEDA SIERRA
Institute of Philosophy: JOSÉ OLIMPO SUÁREZ MOLANO
School of Languages: EDGAR LEÓN VÉLEZ ARENAS
Institute of Political Sciences: WILLIAM RESTREPO RIAZA
Institute of Regional Studies: HERNÁN HENAO DELAGADO
Interamerican School of Librarianship: BEATRIZ CÉSPEDES DE BAYONA

ATTACHED INSTITUTE

Escuela Interamericana de Bibliotecología de la Universidad de Antioquia (Interamerican School of Librarianship): Apdo Aéreo 1307, Medellín; f. 1956; training in librarianship to postgraduate level; technical assistance on administration and organization of information centres and libraries; 10 full-time, 5 part-time staff; 300 students; library of 16,000 vols; Dir Prof. BERTHA NELLY CARDONA DE GIL; publ. *Revista Interamericana de Bibliotecología*.

UNIVERSIDAD DEL ATLÁNTICO

Carrera 43, No. 50–53, Apdo Aéreo 1890, Barranquilla, Atlántico

Telephone: 313-513

Founded 1941
Undergraduate courses

Rector: CRISTIAN UJUETA TOSCANO
Secretary-General: PABLO ARTETA MANRIQUE
Librarian: CARMEN VASQUEZ ARRIETA

Number of teachers: 592
Number of students: 8,798

Publication: *Economía*.

DEANS

Faculty of Fine Arts: Dr HUGO VASQUEZ
Faculty of Economics: ROBERTO PERSAND BARNES
Faculty of Pharmacy and Chemistry: JOSE LLANOS AMARIS
Faculty of Law and Political Science: GUSTAVO DE SILVESTRI
Faculty of Chemical Engineering: AGUSTIN QUINTERO
Faculty of Architecture: RAFAEL RUIZ ZAPATA
Faculty of Education: ESTEBAN RODRIGUEZ
Faculty of Nutrition and Dietetics: LORIS JABBA DE TRUJILLO

UNIVERSIDAD DE CALDAS

Apdo Aéreo 275, Manizales, Caldas
Telephone: (968) 861250
Fax: 862520

Founded 1943
State control
Language of instruction: Spanish
Academic year: February to December (two semesters)

Rector: JORGE RAAD ALJURE
Academic Vice-Rector: DARIO MEJIA GUTIERREZ
Registrar: LUCY AMPARO GIL ZULUAGA
Librarian: SAUL SANCHEZ TORO

Library: see Libraries
Number of teachers: 488
Number of students: 3,620

Publications: *Revista*, faculty publs.

DEANS

Faculty of Agriculture: Dr ELMER CASTAÑO RAMIREZ
Faculty of Law: Dr IVAN GUILLERMO ASMAR RESTREPO
Faculty of Family Development: LUISA FERNANDA GIRALDO
Faculty of Education: MARIA LEONOR VILLADA SALAZAR
Faculty of Philosophy and Letters: ROBERTO VELEZ RAMIREZ
Faculty of Medicine: TULIO MARULANDA MEJIA
Faculty of Nursing: ALBA LUCIA VELEZ ARANGO
Faculty of Social Work: LUZ STELLA VALENCIA GIRALDO
Faculty of Veterinary Medicine and Zootechnics: URIEL GIRALDO GALLON
Faculty of Fine Arts: OLIVA MANCHOLA LASTRA
Faculty of Geology: BERNARDO CALLE ZAPATA

UNIVERSIDAD DE CARTAGENA

Apdo Aéreo 1382, Cartagena, Bolívar
Telephone: 65-44-80
Fax: 65-04-26

Founded 1827
State control
Academic year: February to December

President of the Council: Dr GUILLERMO PANIZA RICARDO
Rector: Dra BEATRIZ BECHARA DE BORGE
Academic Vice-Rector: Dr JAIME BARRIOS AMAYA
Administrative Director: Dr CLARET BERMUDEZ CORONEL
Chief Administrative Officer: Dr EDGAR REY SINNING
Librarian: PERLA ECHEVERRI LEMA

Library: see Libraries
Number of teachers: 560
Number of students: 4,310

Publications: *Prospecto Universidad, Revista Facultad de Economía, Revista Facultad de Medicina, Boletín Informativo, Revista Ciencia, Tecnología y Educación.*

DEANS

Faculty of Law: Dr ALCIDES ANGULO PASSOS
Faculty of Medicine: Dr ROBERTO GUERRERO FIGUEROA
Faculty of Dentistry: Dr LUIS ALVAREZ GARCIA
Faculty of Pharmaceutical Chemistry: Dra THELMA DEL CASTILLO DE SALAZAR
Faculty of Engineering: Dr ALVARO CUBAS MONTES
Faculty of Economics: Dr GUILLERMO QUINTANA SOSSA
Faculty of Nursing: Lic. YADIRA FERREIRA DE SIERRA
Faculty of Social Work: Lic. NATACHA MORILLO DE RODRIGUEZ

UNIVERSIDAD DEL CAUCA

Apdo Nacional 113, Calle 5 No. 4–70, Popayán, Cauca
Telephone: 21893

Founded 1827
State control
Language of instruction: Spanish
Academic year: January to June, July to December

Rector: Ing. HAROLD ALBERTO MUÑOZ MUÑOZ
Academic Vice-Rector: Ing. JUAN MARTÍN VELASCO MOSQUERA
President of Supreme Council: Dr HAROLD CASAS VALENCIA
General Secretary: Lic. LUZ HELENA CAJIAO DE COHEN
Administrative Director: Dr ALVARO HURTADO TEJADA
Planning Head: Ing. PABLO GRECH MAYOR
Library Director: Lic. JOSÉ MARÍA SERRANO PRADA

Library: see Libraries
Number of teachers: 473
Number of students: 3,729

Publication: *Crónica Universitaria.*

DEANS

Faculty of Law, Political and Social Sciences: Dra MARÍA TERESA OTOYA DE MUÑOZ
Faculty of Civil Engineering: Ing. GALO ALBERTO COSME VARGAS
Faculty of Electrical Engineering: Ing. HENRY CEBALLOS AGUIRRE
Faculty of Health Sciences: Dr PEDRO NIEVES OVIEDO
Faculty of Accountancy: C. P. T. ALVARO MEDRANO CARDOZO
Faculty of Education Sciences: Lic. ELIO FABIO GUTIÉRREZ RUIZ
Faculty of Humanities: Lic. LUCIA ARCINIEGAS DE GUERRERO
Conservatory of Music: Dr JOSÉ TOMÁS ILLERA
School of Nursing: Lic. LOLA MOGOLLÓN DE RUEDA (Dir)
School of Geotechnics: Ing. MARGARITA POLANCO DE HURTADO (Dir)

DIRECTORS OF POSTGRADUATE INSTITUTES

Transport: Ing. HERNÁN OTONIEL FERNÁNDEZ ORDÓÑEZ
Development and Research into Electronics and Telecommunications: Ing. HERNANDO PULIDO MOSQUERA
Co-operativism: Lic. SIGIFREDO TURGA A.

UNIVERSIDAD DE CÓRDOBA

Apdo Aéreo 354, Carretera a Cereté, Km. 5, Montería, Córdoba
Telephone: 33-81

Founded 1964
Academic year: April to March

Rector: Dr LAUREANO MESTRA DÍAZ (acting)
Academic Vice-Rector: Dr EFRAIN PASTOR NIEVES
Administrative Director: Dr ALVARO VIDAL OROZCO
Library Director: CARLOS HENAO TORO

Number of teachers: 270
Number of students: 2,493

Publications: *Revista, Trabajos de Grado presentados en la Universidad.*

DEANS

Faculty of Veterinary Medicine and Animal Husbandry: Dr FRANCISCO AGUILAR MADERA
Faculty of Agricultural Engineering: Dr MAXIMILIANO ESPINOSA PERALTA
Faculty of Education: Dr JOSÉ MORALES MANCHEGO
Faculty of Nursing: Dra GISELLE FERRER FERRER
Faculty of Science: Dr AQUILES GONZÁLEZ SALAZAR

UNIVERSIDAD DE LA GUAJIRA

Apdo Aéreo 172, Riohacha
Telephone: 273856
Fax: 273856

Founded 1976
State control
Language of instruction: Spanish
Academic year: February to July, August to November

Rector: FRANCISCO JUSTO PÉREZ VAN-LEENDEN
Vice-Rector: ROSALBA CUESTA LÓPEZ
Chief Administrative Officer: CRISTÓBAL VEGA GUTIÉRREZ
Librarian: MARINELA MENGUAL MEZA

Number of teachers: 107
Number of students: 1,258

Publications: *WOUMMAINPA, Revista Universidad de La Guajira, Anuario Estadístico.*

DEANS

Faculty of Business Administration: ISIDORO OSPINO MERIÑO
Faculty of Industrial Engineering: JAIRO SALCEDO DAVILA
Faculty of Education: JOSÉ CLEMENTE MARTÍNEZ

HEADS OF DEPARTMENTS

Faculty of Business Administration:

- Introduction to Law: HERNAN REINA
- Industrial Psychology, Professional Ethics: EFRAIN DELUQUE
- Principles of Administration: ERUNDINA ILLIDGE
- Development and Management Control: ALBERTO BRITTO
- Sport: SEGISMUNDO BERMUDEZ
- Tax Legislation: OSCAR PACHECO
- Administration III: WILLIAM GOMEZ
- Humanities II: ALVARO CUELLO
- Administration I: CRISTOBAL VEGA G.
- Macroeconomics: ABIMAEL SANCHEZ R.
- Principles of Administration: HERNANDO BEDOYA
- Introduction to Economics: WILMER ZUBIRIA
- Introduction to Law: NIDIA RESTREPO
- Mathematics I: CARLOS GUTIERREZ
- Spanish: RAFAEL CUENTAS FIGUEROA

Faculty of Industrial Engineering:

- Marketing: HERNANDO BEDOYA
- Industrial Psychology: EFRAIN DELUQUE
- Production: MIGUEL MURGAS
- Labour Legislation: ALAN PEREZ
- General Mechanics, Resistance of Materials: MIGUEL PITRE
- Electrical Engineering: JOSE F. PIRAQUIVE
- Engineering Materials: GONZALO CASTRO
- Electrical Engineering Laboratory: JONNYS ORTEGA
- Process Laboratory: MIGUEL PEÑA
- Plant Distribution, Mathematics I: ROLLAND PINEDO
- Humanities II: CESAR ARISMENDY
- English II: LUZ MARINA BOHADA DE P.

UNIVERSIDAD DISTRITAL 'FRANCISCO JOSÉ DE CALDAS'

Carrera 8, No. 40–78, Bogotá
Telephone: 2451420

Founded 1950

Rector: ABILIO LOZANO CABALLERO

Undergraduate courses in sciences, social sciences, engineering, languages and literature, forestry.

UNIVERSIDAD FRANCISCO DE PAULA SANTANDER

Avda Gran Colombia 12E–96, Barrio Colsag, Apdo Aéreo 1055, Cúcuta, Norte de Santander
Telephone: (75) 753172

Founded 1962
State control
Affiliated to the Universidad Nacional
Undergraduate courses

Chancellor: PATROCINIO ARARAT DÍAZ
Secretary-General: ALVARO ORLANDO PEDROZA ROAJS
Administrative Director: HÉCTOR MIGUEL PARRA LÓPEZ
Academic Vice-Chancellor: JOSÉ LUIS TOLOSA CHACÓN
Librarian: GLORIA MATILDE MELO SALCEDO

Library of 5,000 vols
Number of teachers: 350
Number of students: 6,500

DEANS

Faculty of Engineering: HUGO ALBERTO PORTILLA DUARTE
Faculty of Basic Sciences: JOSÉ LUIS MALDONADO
Faculty of Business Studies: JOSÉ RAMÓN VARGAS TOLOSA
Faculty of Education, Arts, Humanities and Sciences: RICARDO GARCIA
Faculty of Health Sciences: FANNY MARTINEZ
Faculty of Environmental Sciences: CIRO ESPINOSA

UNIVERSIDAD NACIONAL DE COLOMBIA

Ciudad Universitaria, Apdo Aéreo 14490, Bogotá

Telephone: 2699111

Founded 1867
Academic year: January to July, August to December
Campuses in Manizales, Medellín, Palmira

Rector: ANTANAS MOCKUS CIVICKAS
Academic Vice-Rector: GUILLERMO PÁRAMO
Vice-Rector for Medellín Campus: ALONSO HOYOS

Library: see Libraries
Number of teachers: 9,137
Number of students: 28,000 (20,000 at Bogotá)

Publications: *Revista,* various faculty reviews.

DEANS

Faculty of Arts: GONZALO VIDAL PERDOMO
Faculty of Science: JOSÉ GRANÉS SELLARES
Faculty of Agriculture: JORGE TORRES OTAVO
Faculty of Humanities: JORGE BOSSA SEGRERA
Faculty of Medicine: AUGUSTO CORREDOR ARJONA
Faculty of Law: RICARDO SÁNCHEZ ANGEL
Faculty of Economics: SALOMÓN KALMANOVITZ KRAUTER
Faculty of Engineering: VICTORIA BEATRIZ DURÁN
Faculty of Nursing: LUCY MUÑOZ DE RODRÍGUEZ
Faculty of Dentistry: JORGE HERNANDO ESPITIA
Faculty of Veterinary Science: JOSÉ YESID CAMPOS OVIEDO

Medellín Campus: Apdo Aéreo 568, Medellín
Faculty of Architecture: EDGAR MEJÍA ESCOBAR
Faculty of Stockbreeding: FERNANDO ALVAREZ MEJÍA
Faculty of Sciences: LUIS ALFONSO VÉLEZ MORENO
Faculty of Humanities: MARIO FRANCO HERNANDEZ
Faculty of Mining: HORACIO SIERRA RESTREPO

Manizales Campus: Carrera 27, No. 64-60
Faculty of Architecture and Engineering: FERNANDO MEJÍA
Faculty of Science and Administration: GERMÁN BUITRAGO ALFONSO

Palmira Campus: Apdo Aéreo 237, Palmira
Faculty of Stockbreeding: FRANCO ALIRIO VALLEJO

UNIVERSIDAD DE NARIÑO

Carrera 22, No. 18–109, Pasto, Nariño

Telephone: 35654

Founded in 1827 as Colegio Provincial by General Francisco de Paula Santander; later named Colegio Académico; university status 1964
First degree courses

Rector: HERNAN BURBANO ORJUELA
Vice-Rector: EFREN CORAL QUINTERO
Secretary: HECTOR RODRIGUEZ GUERRON
Librarian: LAURA VELASQUEZ

Central library of 10,000 vols; agronomy library of 15,000 vols
Number of teachers: *c.* 700
Number of students: *c.* 4,500

Publications: *Anales, Foro Universitario, Revista de Ciencias Agrícolas Meridiano, Awasca, Revista de Zootecnia.*

DEANS

Faculty of Law: JOSÉ L. RODRIGUEZ CABRERA
Faculty of Education: PEDRO V. OBANDO ORDONEZ
Faculty of Agronomy: LUCIO LEGARDA BURBANO
Faculty of Arts: MIREYA USCATEGUI DE JIMENEZ
Faculty of Economics: ROSENDO MARTINEZ PONCE
Faculty of Civil Engineering: CARLOS H. OCAÑA JURADO
Faculty of Stockbreeding: JORGE N. LOPEZ MACIAS

UNIVERSIDAD DE PAMPLONA

Apdo Aéreo 1046, Carrera 4 No. 4–38, Pamplona, Santander del Norte

Telephone: 682960
Fax: 680581

Founded 1960, university status 1970
State control
Language of instruction: Spanish
Academic year: January to June, July to December

Rector: CIRO ALFONSO CAKEDO CAMARGO
Academic Vice-Rector: GABRIEL SANTAFÉ SANTAFÉ
Administrative Vice-Rector: YOLANDA GALLARDO DE PARADA
Secretary-General: JOSÉ ALCIDES ACERO JAÚREGUI

Number of teachers: 122
Number of students: 3,714

Publications: *Bistua, Boletín Estadístico.*

DEANS

Humanities and Languages: NUBIA FERNÁNDEZ DE FUENTES
Sciences: HÉCTOR SÁNCHEZ ROSERO
Education: BELISARIO LAGUADO BUENO
Distance Learning: Dr ALBERTO JAIMES GÓMEZ
Postgraduate School: Dra FLOR DELIA PULIDO CASTELLANOS

DEPARTMENTAL CHAIRPERSONS

Microbiology: CLAUDIA CLAVISO OLMOS
Food Technology: ORLANDO MARTÍNEZ CÁCERES
Biology and Chemistry: FREDDY SOLANO
Mathematics and Computer Sciences: JAMES VELASCO MOSQUERA
Physical Education: GUSTAVO ROA ACEVEDO
Educational Administration: JUAN MANUEL VILLAMIZAR RAMÍREZ
Education and Psychology: VICTOR MANUEL BASTOS FERNÁNDEZ
English and French: ROGERIO VILLAMIZAR FLÓREZ
Spanish and English: ROGERIO VILLAMIZAR FLÓREZ
Social Sciences, Regional Development and Education: ALBERTO JAIMES GÓMEZ
Methodology of Teaching Spanish and Literature: ANGEL DELGADO TORRES
Leisure: CARLOS JOSÉ GIL JURADO
Gerontology: SELMA MANASSE ACEVEDU

UNIVERSIDAD PEDAGÓGICA NACIONAL

Apdo Aéreo 75144, Calle 73, No. 11–73, Santafé de Bogotá

Telephone: 3473562
Fax: 3473535

Founded 1955
State control
Languages of instruction: Spanish and English
Academic year: January to December (two semesters)

Rector: Dr ADOLFO RODRÍGUEZ BERNAL
Administrative Vice-Rector: Dr HERNÁN VÁSQUEZ ROCHA
Academic Vice-Rector: Dr MANUEL ERAZO PARGA
Librarian: Dr CAMILO ROJAS LEÓN

Number of teachers: 660
Number of students: 4,190

Publications: *Revista Colombiana de Educación, Pedagogia y Saberes.*

DEANS

Faculty of Humanities: Dra GLORIA RINCÓN CUBIDES
Faculty of Science and Technology: Dr RAFAEL HUMBERTO RAMÍREZ GIL
Faculty of Education: Dra MYRIAM PARDO TORRES

HEADS OF DEPARTMENTS

Fine Arts: FRANÇOIS KHOURY
Biology: JUDITH ARTETA DE MOLINA
Chemistry: FIDEL ANTONIO CÁRDENAS
Physics: JULIAN URREA BELTRÁN (acting)
Mathematics: MARGARITA ROJAS DE ROA
Social Sciences: LUIS ENRIQUE SUÁREZ QUEVEDO
Physical Education: LUIS ALFONSO GARZÓN
Languages: NOHORA PATRICIA MORENO GARCÍA
Technology: CARLOS JULIO ROMERO CASTRO
Educational Psychology: BLANCA AZUCENA S. DE OSORIO
Postgraduate School: LIBIA STELLA NIÑO ZAFRA

ATTACHED INSTITUTE

Instituto Pedagógico Nacional: Calle 127 No. 12A-20, Santafé de Bogotá; 2,178 students; Dir LUIS ERNESTO OJEDA SUÁREZ.

UNIVERSIDAD PEDAGÓGICA Y TECNOLÓGICA DE COLOMBIA

Apdo Aéreo 1094 y 1234, Carretera Central del Norte, Tunja, Boyacá

Telephone: 422175
Fax: 424311

Founded 1953
State control
Language of instruction: Spanish
Academic year: February to June, August to December

Rector: CARLOS ALBERTO SANDOVAL FONSECA
Vice-Rector for Administration: ALBERTO LEMOS VALENCIA
Vice-Rector for Academic Affairs: CARLOS AUGUSTO SALAMANCA ROA
Secretary-General: BETTINA MESA DISHINGTÓN
Librarian: BARBARÁ MARTÍN MARTÍN

Number of teachers: 540
Number of students: 13,500

Publications: *Gaceta Universitaria,* reviews.

DEANS AND DIRECTORS

Faculty of Education: JAIME BELTRÁN JIMÉNEZ
Faculty of Sciences: GUILLERMO BUITRAGO ROJAS
Faculty of Engineering: GONZALO PÉREZ BUITRAGO

Faculty of Health Sciences: ABEL MARTÍNEZ MARTÍN
Faculty of Agricultural Sciences: PABLO EMILIO CONTRERAS SERRANO
Faculty of Law and Social Sciences: Dr FRANCISCO GUILLERMO VEGA SUPELANO
Faculty of Economics and Business Administration: SIGIFREDO RODRÍGUEZ NIETO
Sectional Faculty, Duitama: OTTO CARO NIÑO
Sectional Faculty, Sogamoso: FRANCISCO MANOSALVA CERÓN
Sectional Faculty, Chiquinquirá: CARLOS HERNANDO PALACIOS AGUILAR (acting)
Institute of Open Learning and Correspondence Courses: Dir ROSENDO CASTRO JIMÉNEZ
Centre of Educational Research: Dir JOSEFINA RONDÓN NUCETTE

UNIVERSIDAD DEL QUINDÍO

Cra. 15, Cl. 12 N, Avda Bolívar, Apdo Aéreo 460, Armenia, Quindío

Telephone: (67) 450099
Fax: (67) 462563

Founded 1960
State control
Language of instruction: Spanish
Academic year: January to June, July to December

Rector: HECTOR POLANIA RIVERA
Vice-Rector (Academic): MARCO AURELIO ARISTIZABAL OSORIO
Vice-Rector (Administrative): MARTHA MARIA MARIN MEJIA
Secretary-General: BERNARDO VELASQUEZ MAHECHA
Dean of Research Committee: AMPARO AGUDELO DE ARANGO
Registrar: NELLY RESTREPO SÁNCHEZ
Librarian: Lic. LUZ MARINA PATIÑO ZULUAGA

Library of 26,250 vols
Number of teachers: 697
Number of students: 16,626

Publications: *Revista Facultad de Formación Avanzada e Investigaciones*, *Revista de la Universidad del Quindío*.

DEANS

Faculty of Open and Distance Learning: ROBERTO GIRALDO VIGOYA
Faculty of Health Sciences: DIEGO GUTIÉRREZ MEJÍA
Faculty of Civil Engineering: DIEGO GUERRERO CASTRO
Faculty of Public Accounting: CONSTANZA LORETH FAJARDO
Faculty of Basic and Technological Sciences: MARCO AURELIO CERON MUÑOZ
Faculty of Human Sciences: NELSON JOSÉ MURILLO VENEZ

UNIVERSIDAD INDUSTRIAL DE SANTANDER

Apdo Aéreo 678, Bucaramanga, Santander

Telephone: 343656
Fax: 976-451136

Founded 1947
Academic year: February to June, August to December

Rector: JORGE GÓMEZ DUARTE
Administrative Vice-Rector: HUMBERTO PRADILLA ARDILA
Academic Vice-Rector: GERMÁN OLIVEROS VILLAMIZAR
Secretary-General: Dra LILIA AMANDA PATIÑO DE CRUZ
Research Director: LUIS ALFONSO MALDONADO CERÓN
Librarian: ESPERANZA MÉNDEZ BRAVO

Number of teachers: 455
Number of students: 9,684

DEANS

Sciences: AUGUSTO LÓPEZ ZAGARRA
Physical/Mechanical Sciences: ROBERTO MARTÍNEZ ANGEL
Physical/Chemical Sciences: CARLOS JULIO MONSALVE MORENO
Health: GERMAN GAMARRA HERNÁNDEZ
Human Sciences: EMILIA ACEVEDO DE ROMERO
Distance Education: GLORIA INÉS MARÍN MUÑOZ

HEADS OF DEPARTMENTS

Sciences:
- Biology: ROSA AURA GAVILÁN DÍAZ
- Physics: MILTON FLÓREZ SERRANO
- Mathematics: ROSALBA OSORIO AGUILLÓN
- Chemistry: VICTOR GABRIEL OTERO GIL

Physical/Mechanical Sciences:
- Electrical Engineering: FRANCISCO A. RUEDA PATIÑO
- Civil Engineering: EDUARDO A. CASTAÑEDA PINZÓN
- Mechanical Engineering: ALFONSO GARCÍA CASTRO
- Industrial Engineering: FRANCISCO JAVIER MOSQUERA ROBBIN
- Systems Engineering: ELBERTO CARRILLO RINCÓN
- Design and Graphic Analysis: HÉCTOR JULIO PARRA MORENO

Physical/Chemical Sciences:
- Geology: JORGE ENRIQUE ZAMBRANO ARENAS
- Metallurgy: ORLANDO JOSÉ GÓMEZ MORENO
- Chemical Engineering: LEONARDO ACEVEDO DUARTE
- Petroleum Engineering: JOSÉ GREGORIO OCANDO RODRÍGUEZ

Human Sciences:
- Literature: MARIELA GÓMEZ DE OSSMA
- Arts: JESÚS ALBERTO REY MARIÑO
- Economics and Administration: SUSANA VALDIVIESO CANAL
- Social Sciences: BLANCA INÉS PRADA MÁRQUEZ
- Physical Education: JUAN JOSÉ MAYORGA CABALLERO
- Education: CONSTANZA VILLAMIZAR DE SUÁREZ
- History: AMADO ANTONIO GUERRERO RINCÓN

Health:
- Morphology and Pathology: ALFREDO ACEVEDO SARMIENTO
- Physiological Sciences: ÁLVARO GÓMEZ TORRADO
- Microbiological Sciences: GLADYS ORTEGA VANEGAS
- Nursing: MARÍA ANTONIETA FORERO DE LEÓN
- Internal Medicine: MARÍA EUGENIA RAMÍREZ QUINTERO
- Paediatrics: JAIRO RODRÍGUEZ HERNÁNDEZ
- Gynaecology and Obstetrics: MARTHA AGUDELO GARCÍA
- Surgery: HERNANDO CALA RUEDA
- Nutrition and Physical Rehabilitation: ESPERANZA CRUZ SOLANO
- Preventive Medicine and Public Health: ALBERTO ZÁRATE MARTÍNEZ
- Psychiatry: RODOLFO REY NUNCIRA

Distance Education:
- Professional Courses: LUZ EMILIA REYES ENCISO
- Advanced Training: GILBERTO GÓMEZ MANCILLA
- Continuing Education: LUCILA GUALDRÓN DE ACEROS

UNIVERSIDAD DE SUCRE

Apdo Aéreo 406, Cra. 28 No. 5-267, Sincelejo, Sucre

Telephone: 821240
Fax: 821240

Founded 1977
State control
Academic year: February to December

Rector: GUSTAVO VERGARA ARRÁZOLA
Chief Administrative Officer: VICTOR RAÚL CASTILLO JIMÉNEZ
Secretary-General: AMIRA VALDÉS ALTAMAR
Librarian: IRMA OCHOA DE FONSECA

Library of 12,000 vols
Number of teachers: 65
Number of students: 910

DEANS

Faculty of Engineering: PABLO ALFONSO CARO RETTIZ
Faculty of Sciences and Humanities: CARMEN PAYARES PAYARES
Faculty of Stockbreeding: JULIO ALEJANDRO HERNÁNDEZ
Faculty of Health Sciences: CARMEN CECILIA ALVIS DE PUENTES

UNIVERSIDAD SURCOLOMBIANA

Avda Pastrana Borrero con Carrera 1A, Neiva, Huila

Telephone: 745444

Founded 1970
State control
Language of instruction: Spanish
Academic year: February to December

Rector: ALVARO LOZANO OSORIO
Academic Vice-Rector: CARLOS BOLIVAR BONILLA
Administrative Vice-Rector: MARIA BEATRIZ PAVA MARÍN
Chief Administrative Officer: EFRAÍN POLANÍA VIVAS
Secretary: JOSÉ PIAR IRIARTE VELILLA
Librarian: LUIS ALFREDO PINTO

Number of teachers: 450
Number of students: 4,500

DEANS

Accountancy and Administration: ALFONSO MANRIQUE MEDINA
Educational Science: FABIO LOSADA PÉREZ
Engineering: ALFONSO ORTÍZ
Medicine and Health: ANTONIO ACEVEDO A.

HEADS OF DEPARTMENTS

Accountancy: HUMBERTO RUEDA
Business Administration: ORLANDO RODRIGUEZ
Mathematics and Physics: HERNANDO GONZALEZ S.
Pre-school Education: BEATRIZ PERDOMO DE G.
Educational Administration: GRACE ALVAREZ
Linguistics and Literature: MAGDALENA ARIAS B.
Agricultural Engineering: EDUARDO PASTRANA
Petroleum Engineering: ROBERTO VARGAS C.
Physical Education: ALVARO MOTTA MILLÁN
Nursing: MARIA ESNEDA BARRERA
Open University: NOHORA ELENA ROJAS
Post-Degrees Centre: AURA ELENA BERNAL

UNIVERSIDAD DEL TOLIMA

Apdo Aéreo No. 546, Santa Elena, Ibagué, Tolima

Telephone: (82) 649219
Fax: (82) 644869
E-mail: ut@utolima.ut.edu.co

Founded 1945
State control
Academic year: January to June, June to December

Rector: ISRAEL LOZANO MARTÍNEZ
Academic Vice-Rector: ARMANDO GARRIDO PÉREZ
Administrative Vice-Rector: RAMÓN ANTONIO CASTILLO CASTILLO
Vice-Rector for Development and Educational Resources: ANTONIO OSORIO JARAMILLO
Registrar: HUGO ERNESTO VARGAS ACOSTA
Librarian: CIELO URUEÑA LOZANO

Number of teachers: 500
Number of students: 12,000

Publications: *Revista Panorama Universitario, Revista de la Universidad del Tolima Serie Ciencia y Tecnología, Revista de la Universidad del Tolima Serie Humanidades y Ciencias.*

DEANS

Faculty of Agricultural Engineering: RAMÓN ASCENCIO MURILLO
Faculty of Agroindustrial Engineering: RAMÓN ASCENCIO MURILLO
Faculty of Veterinary Medicine and Zootechnics: FRANCISCO SEGURA CANIZALES
Faculty of Forestry Engineering: RAFAEL VARGAS RÍOS
Faculty of Business Administration: HERNANDO SÁNCHEZ CASTAÑEDA
Faculty of Educational Science: SANDRA CECILIA AMAYA DE PUJANA
Faculty of Technology: ALBERTO GONZÁLEZ DÍAZ
Faculty of Health Sciences: JESÚS RAMÓN RIVERA BULLA
Institute of Science: NEFTALÍ MESA LÓPEZ
Institute of Distance Education: LUIS ALBERTO MALAGÓN PLATA

HEADS OF DEPARTMENT

Faculty of Health Science:

Clinical Nursing: BETTY SÁNCHEZ DE PARADA

Faculty of Veterinary Medicine and Zootechnics:

Cattle Breeding: CARLOS ALFONSO POVEDA H.
Animal Health: GUILLERMO TORRES MORENO

Faculty of Technology:

Topography: YESID SALAZAR BEDOYA
Drawing: SAMUEL APARICIO ALBARÁN

Faculty of Forestry Engineering:

Forest Science: OMAR AURELIO MELO CRUZ
Engineering: HENRY GARZÓN SÁNCHEZ

Faculty of Education:

Spanish and English: LUIS ALFONSO CRUZ LONDOÑO
Social Studies: ELSA BONILLA PIRATOVA
Educational Psychology: HERNANDO VARGAS PEREA
Physical Education, Sport and Recreation: HUMBERTO ARBONA LORENZO

Faculty of Business Administration:

Administration, Marketing and Law: JUAN FERNANDO REINOSO LASTRA
Economics and Finance: JUAN DE J. RAMÍREZ SEDANO

Faculty of Agricultural Engineering:

Soils and Water: ALVARO ARTURO RODRÍGUEZ ALDANA
Agricultural Expansion: FABIO JARAMILLO PALMA
Vegetable Health and Production: ARMANDO EMILIO REY TORRES

Institute of Basic Science:

Biology: FRANCISCO ANTONIO VILLA N.
Physics: HECTOR HUGO CHACÓN MOLINA
Chemistry: YOLANDA FLÓREZ ORJUELA
Mathematics and Statistics: CARLOS A. TOVAR CASTAÑEDA.

UNIVERSIDAD DEL VALLE

Ciudad Universitaria, Meléndez, Apdo Aéreo 25360, Apdo Nacional 439, Cali, Valle del Cauca
Telephone: 392310
Fax: 398484

Founded 1945
State control
Language of instruction: Spanish
Academic year: January to June, August to December

Rector: JAIME E. GALARZA SANCLEMENTE
Vice-Rectors: CARLOS E. DULCEY BONILLA (Academic Affairs), Dr ALBERTO LOPEZ SANCHEZ (Administration), Dr HUMBERTO REY VARGAS (Research), Dr CECILIA MADRIÑAN POLO (University Welfare)
Library Director: Lic. ISABEL ROMERO DE DULCEY

Library of 267,656 vols
Number of teachers: 962
Number of students: 9,640 full-time, 5,000 part-time

Publications: *Revista Universidad del Valle, Poligramas, Boletín Socioeconómico, Humboltia, Heurística, Colombia Médica, Revista de Ciencias, Fin de Siglo, Praxis Filosófica, Historia y Espacio, Cuadernos de Administración, Pliegos Administrativos, La Palabra, Planta Libre, Revista Estomatología, Lenguaje.*

DEANS

Faculty of Architecture: Dr CARLOS ENRIQUE DULCEY BONILLA E.
Faculty of Engineering: Dr SILVIO DELVASTO
Faculty of Health: Dr HECTOR RAUL ECHAVARRIA ABAD
Faculty of Economics and Social Sciences: Dr LUGARDO ALVAREZ AGUDELO
Faculty of Humanities: Dr HUMBERTO VÉLEZ RAMÍREZ
Faculty of Education: Dr MARIO DIAZ
Faculty of Science: Dr LUIS FERNANDO CASTRO
Faculty of Administrative Science: Dr BERNARDO BARONA

HEADS OF DEPARTMENTS

Faculty of Engineering:

Department of Mechanical Engineering: Dr RICARDO RAMÍREZ
Department of Electrical Engineering: Dr HÉCTOR CADAVID
Department of Information and Systems: Dra MARTHA CECILIA GÓMEZ
Department of Fluid and Heat Sciences: Dr DIEGO MONTAÑA PALACIOS
Department of Chemical and Biological Processes: Dr CARLOS VELEZ

Faculty of Health:

Department of Morphology: Dr CAROLINA ISAZA DE LOURIDO E.
Department of Physiology: Dr FELIX EDUARDO MELO GONZALEZ
Department of Pathology: Dr EDWIN CARRASCAL
Department of Anaesthesiology: Dr MARIO VELÁSQUEZ
Department of Internal Medicine: Dr ALVARO MERCADO
Department of Surgery: Dr JAIME ROBERTO ARIAS
Department of Paediatrics: Dr FABIO PEREIRA
Department of Obstetrics and Gynaecology: Dr EDGAR IVAN ORTIZ
Department of Psychiatry: Dr CARLOS CLIMENT
Department of Social and Preventive Medicine: Dr ALFREDO AGUIRRE
Department of Microbiology: Dr SILVIO ARANGO
Department of Stomatology: Dr JOSÉ DOMINGO GARCÍA
Department of Nursing: Dr BLANCA AGUIRRE DE CABAL
Department of Physical Medicine and Rehabilitation: Dr ORLANDO QUINTERO FLOREZ E.
Department of Internal Medicine: (Resident Staff): Dr JOSÉ FRANCISCO DIAZ

Faculty of Architecture:

Department of Environmental Technology and Construction: Dr OTTO VALDERRUTEN
Department of Environmental Planning: Dr CARLOS ENRIQUE BOTERO
Department of Design: Dr RICARDO AGUILERA

Faculty of Science:

Department of Mathematics: Dr CARLOS RODRIGUEZ
Department of Physics: Dr CARLOS JULIO URIBE
Department of Chemistry: Dr ALONSO JARAMILLO
Department of Biology: Dr HÉCTOR ARMANDO VÁRGAS

Faculty of Social and Economic Sciences:

Department of Economics: Dr MAX ENRIQUE NIETO
Department of Social Sciences: Dr RENAN JOSÉ SILVA

Faculty of Humanities:

Department of Languages: Dra BLANCA DE ESCOCIA
Department of History: Dr JORGE ELIECER SALCEDO SAAVEDRA
Department of Music: Dra MARTHA LUCIA CALDERON
Department of Philosophy: Dr JEAN PAUL MARGOT
Department of Communications: Dr ALEJANDRO ULLO SANMIGUEL
Department of Social Work: Dr VICTOR MARIO ESTRADA
Department of Letters: Dr CARLOS ENRIQUE RESTREPO ACUÑA

Faculty of Education:

Department of Teacher Training: Dra MARIELA DE BRAND
Department of Psychology: Dr MIRALBA CORREA DE ROBLEDO
Department of Curriculum: Dr HUMBERTO QUICENO
Department of Educational Administration and Planning: Dr GUILLERMO SALAZAR
Department of Physical Education and Sports: Dr GILDARDO PEREZ

Faculty of Administrative Science:

Department of Business Administration: Dr MARÍA PAOLA CROCE DI PETTA
Department of Information, Accounting and Finance: Dr LUIS ENRIQUE POLANCO

UNIVERSIDAD TECNOLÓGICA DEL CHOCÓ 'DIEGO LUIS CÓRDOBA'

Carrera 2A, Nro., 25–22, Quibdó, Chocó
Telephone: 94096-616

Founded 1972
State control
Language of instruction: Spanish
Academic year: February to June, July to November

Rector: HECTOR D. MOSQUERA BENITEZ
Academic Vice-Rector: ALVARO GIRALDO GOMEZ
Administrative Vice-Rector: VICTOR RAUL MOSQUERA BENITEZ
Registrar: LEONILA BLANDÓN ASPRILLA
Librarian: ZAHILY SARRAZOLA MARTINEZ

Number of teachers: 125
Number of students: 1,500

Publications: *Obras Literarias,, Libros Tecnicos en diferentes areas del Conocimieto.*

DEANS

Faculty of Education: EFRAIN MORENO RODRIGUEZ
Faculty of Health and Social Security: MELIDA MORENO MURILLO
Faculty of Technology: LORENZO PORTOCARRERO SIERRA

HEADS OF DEPARTMENTS

Faculty of Education:

Mathematics and Physics: FRANCIA A. BEJARANO
Languages: CÉSAR E. RIVAS LARA
Social Science: JORGE E. PEREA PEÑA

Chemistry and Biology: JUAN MORENO TEHERAN
Psycho-pedagogy and Educational Administration: MANUEL GREGORIO RAMIREZ
Social Work: BERTHA CONTO GARCIA

Faculty of Technology:

Civil Works: ROSA OROZCO ABADIA
Mining: ALBERTO ERIK MARTINEZ HERRERA
Fishing: ALBEIRO VELEZ GOMEZ
Farming: FREDDY PINO MOSQUERA
Industrial Administration: JESUS LOZANO ASPRILLA

UNIVERSIDAD TECNOLÓGICA DE LOS LLANOS ORIENTALES

Apdo Aéreo 2621, Villavicencio, Meta

Telephone: 3-4892
Fax: 23325

Founded 1974
State control
First degree courses
Academic year: January to December

Rector: MAURICIO GONZALEZ MEDINA
Academic Vice-Rector: HECTOR ANTONIO TORRES RONCANCIO
Administrative Officer: ARISTOBULO SALCEDO MURILLO
Librarian: NANCY STELLA COLLAZOS DE PINEDA

Number of teachers: 120
Number of students: 1,345

Publications: *Catálogo, Boletín, Boletín Estadístico.*

DEANS

Faculty of Education: ANA MARIA HORRILLO DE PARDO
Faculty of Nursing: SARA MARIA PEREZ SAENZ
Faculty of Agricultural Engineering: LAZARO HUGO LEMUS ALARCON
Faculty of Veterinary Medicine and Animal Husbandry: PABLO EMILIO CRUZ CASALLAS

UNIVERSIDAD TECNOLÓGICA DEL MAGDALENA

Apdo Aéreo 731, Santa Marta

Telephone: 36150

Founded 1962

Rector: OSVALDO SAAVEDRA BALLESTEROS
Academic Vice-Rector: JAIME SILVA BERNIER
Chief Administrative Officer: ALFONSO GONZALEZ VIVES
Library Director: CARLOS COTES DIAZGRANADOS

Number of teachers: 156
Number of students: 2,009

Publications: *Revista Agronómica, Revista Económica, Revista Facultad Ingeniería Pesquera.*

UNIVERSIDAD TECNOLÓGICA DE PEREIRA

Apdo Aéreo 97, Pereira, Risaralda

Telephone: (6) 3213884
Fax: (6) 3215839
E-mail: buzon@utp.edu.co

Founded 1958
State control
Academic year: February to July, August to December

Rector: CARLOS ALBERTO OSSA OSSA
Academic Vice-Rector: CARLOS ALBERTO OROZCO HINCAPIE
Administrative Vice-Rector: FERNANDO NOREÑA JARAMILLO
Librarian: PAMELA SLINGSBY

Library of 30,000 vols, 1,400 periodicals
Number of teachers: 378
Number of students: 4,220

Publications: *Scientia et Technica, Revista de Ciencias Humanas, Revista Médica de Risaralda.*

DEANS

Faculty of Electrical Engineering: Ing. JORGE JUAN GUTIERREZ GRANADA
Faculty of Mechanical Engineering: Ing. CAMILO ANTONIO ECHEVERRY ZULUAGA
Faculty of Industrial Engineering: Ing. FERNANDO OROZCO JOHN
Faculty of Basic Sciences: Fis. CARLOS ARTURO HOLGUIN TABARES
Faculty of Environmental Sciences: Dr SAMUEL OSPINA MARIN
Faculty of Medicine: Dr JESUS HERNEY MORENO ROJAS
Faculty of Fine Arts and Humanities: Maestro MANUEL GUILLERMO CANTOR SANCHEZ
Faculty of Education: Lic. ROSA ELENA AMAYA ATEHORTUA
Faculty of Technology: Ing. LUIS JOSE RUEDA PLATA

ESCUELA SUPERIOR DE ADMINISTRACIÓN PÚBLICA

Apdo Aéreo 29745, Diagonal 40 No. 46A–37, Santafé de Bogotá

Telephone: 2224700
Fax: 2224356

Founded 1958
State control
Language of instruction: Spanish
Academic year: February to November

Director-General: SAMUEL OSPINA MARÍN
Administrative Deputy Director: GUILLERMO LEÓN REY
Academic Deputy Director: TITO ANTONIO HUERTAS PORRAS
Secretary-General: GERMÁN PUENTES GONZÁLEZ
Librarian: MARÍA CRISTINA ESCOBAR DE ARANGO

Library of 27,000 vols
Number of teachers: 91
Number of students: 905

Publications: *Administración y Desarrollo* (2 a year), *Documentos ESAP.*

DEANS

Faculty of Advanced Studies: OCTAVIO BARBOSA CARDONA
Faculty of Political and Administrative Sciences: TITO ANTONIO HUERTAS PORRAS

ATTACHED INSTITUTES

Institute of Human Rights 'Guillermo Cano': Dir GUILLERMO GONZÁLEZ RAMÍREZ.
Institute of International Studies: Dir HERNANDO ROA SUÁREZ.

Private Universities

UNIVERSIDAD CATÓLICA DE MANIZALES

Apdo 357, Carrera 23 No. 60–63, Manizales

Telephone: (68) 860019
Fax: (68) 860575
E-mail: sucatomz@col2.telecom.co

Founded 1954
Private control
Language of instruction: Spanish
Academic year: February to June, July to November

Rector: JUDITH LEON GUEVARA
Vice-Rectors: GORIA ARRIETA DE PLATA (Professional Teaching), Sr CECILIA GOMEZ JARAMILLO (Administrative), Sr BEATRIZ PATINO GARCIA (University Environment), MARCO FIDEL CHICA LASSO (Research), SILVIO CARDONA GONZALEZ (Higher Teaching), JORGE OSWALDO SANCHEZ BUITRAGO (Planning and Development)
Registrar: FANNY CASTELLANOS TORO
Librarian: GABRIEL DEL ROSARIO

Number of teachers: 248
Number of students: 2,567

Publications: *Boletín Informativo, Revista de Investigaciones, Protocolo.*

HEADS OF STUDIES

Undergraduate Course in Bacteriology: Mag. LUZ ESTELLA RAMIREZ ARISTIZÁBAL
Undergraduate Course in Audiology: Esp. MARIA CONSTANZA MONTOYA NARANJO
Undergraduate Course in Nutrition and Diet: Nut. PIEDAD ROLDÁN JARAMILLO
Undergraduate Course in Respiratory Therapy: Mag. MARTHA LUCÍA CUJIÑO QUINTERO
Undergraduate Course in Advertising: Esp. ARMANDO SÁNCHEZ SUÁREZ
Undergraduate Course in Tourism Administration: Esp. MIRIAM ASTRID VELÁSQUEZ HENAO
Undergraduate Course in Education: Esp. MARIA LUCIEL MONTOYA GÓMEZ
Undergraduate Course in Architecture, Town Planning and Construction: Arq. ORLANDO CASTRO M.
Undergraduate Course in Telematic Engineering: Ing. MARCELO LOPEZ TRUJILLO
Undergraduate Course in Technology and Computer Science: Ing. CARLOS CUESTA IGLESIAS
Postgraduate Studies in University Teaching: Esp. ALEYDA HENAO DE NARANJO
Postgraduate Studies in Educational Planning; Esp. ALDEMAR GIRALDO DE DIAZ
Postgraduate Studies in Human Rights: Esp. FRANCISCO JAVIER JARAMILLO O.
Postgraduate Studies in Speech Therapy: Esp. OLGA LUCIA OCAMPO GÓMEZ
Postgraduate Studies in Curriculum Management: Esp. GLADYS ESTELLA GÍRALDO DE DÍAZ
Postgraduate Studies in Audioprosthesis: Mag. CARMEN CECILIA GALLEGO GÓMEZ
Masters Course in Microbiology: Mag. MARTHA EVA BURITICÁ DE MONSALVE

ATTACHED INSTITUTES

Centro de Estudios de la Comunicacíon Humana (CECH): Dir L. T. SULAY ROCÍO ECHEVERRY DE F.
Institute of Food-farming quality Management (INGECAL): Dir PIEDAD CIRO BASTO.

UNIVERSIDAD AUTÓNOMA DE BUCARAMANGA

Calle 48, 39-234, Apdo Aéreo 1642, Bucaramanga

Telephone: 436261
Fax: 433958

Founded 1952
Private control
Language of instruction: Spanish
Academic year: January to May, July to November

Rector: Dr GABRIEL BURGOS MANTILLA
Administrative Vice-Rector: Dr JORGE HUMBERTO GALVIS COTE
Academic Vice-Rector: Dra GRACIELA MORENO URIBE
Librarian: ELENA UVAROVA

Number of teachers: 491
Number of students: 7,601

Publications: *Revista Reflexiones, Revista Prospectiva, Revista Cuestiones, Revista Temas Socio-Jurídicos, Revista Facultad de Contaduría, Periódico Zeta, Revista Medunab.*

DEANS

Faculty of Business Administration: MARTHA YOLANDA DIETTES LUNA

Faculty of Accountancy: Cont. SAMUEL ALBERTO MANTILLA BLANCO
Faculty of Law: JUAN CARLOS ACUÑA GUTIÉRREZ
Faculty of Education: AMPARO GALVIS DE ORDUZ
Faculty of Communication: MARÍA ISABEL LEÓN CARREÑO
Faculty of Systems Engineering: GUILLERMO RUEDA RUEDA
Faculty of Marketing Engineering: FELIPE DORADO ILLERA
Faculty of Finance Engineering: ARNALDO HELÍ SOLANO RUIZ
Faculty of Business Psychology: VICTORIA EUGENIA ARIAS NAVARRO
Faculty of Music: SERGIO ACEVEDO GÓMEZ
Faculty of Medicine: VIRGILIO GALVIS RAMÍREZ
Faculty of Hospitality and Tourism Administration: LUIS GUSTAVO ALVAREZ RUEDA

FUNDACIÓN UNIVERSIDAD DE BOGOTÁ 'JORGE TADEO LOZANO'

Apdo Aéreo 34185, Carrera 4, No. 22–61, Bogotá

Telephone: (1) 3341777
Fax: (1) 2826197
E-mail: btadeo12@andinet.lat.net

Founded 1954
Private control
Academic year: February to December (two semesters)

President: GUILLERMO RUEDA MONTAÑA
Rector: EVARISTO OBREGON GARCES
Vice-Rector (Academic): JUAN MANUEL CABALLERO PRIETO
Vice-Rector (Postgraduate Studies): MIGUEL BERMUDEZ PORTOCARRERO
Vice-Rector (Administrative): FANNY MESTRE DE GUTIERREZ
Secretary-General: OSCAR AZUERO RUIZ
Librarian: MARIA CONSUELO MONCADA CAMACHO

Number of teachers: 1,020
Number of students: 11,500

Publications: *Ecotropica, La Tadeo, Agenda cultural, Tadeísta.*

DEANS

Faculty of Business Administration: Dra CONSUELO VIDAL DE BRUGGEMAN
Faculty of Agriculture and Stockbreeding Administration: INES ELVIRA TAMARA
Faculty of Agrology: Dr TOMAS LEON SICARD
Faculty of Fine Arts: NATALIA GUTIERREZ E.
Faculty of Marine Biology: IVAN REY CARRASCO
Faculty of International Commerce: HUGO VILLAMIL P.
Faculty of Social Communication: Dr MARGOTH RICCI DE GOSSAIN
Faculty of Public Accountancy: Dr GENOVEVA CAMACHO DE CONSTAIN
Faculty of Interior Design: Dr DICKEN CASTRO DUQUE
Faculty of Graphic Design: Dra PASTORA CORREA DE AMAYA
Faculty of Industrial Design: Dr FERNANDO CORREA MUÑOZ
Faculty of International Relations: ESTHER LOZANO DE REY
Faculty of Economic Sciences: JOAQUIN FLOREZ TRUJILLO
Faculty of Food Technology: JANETH LUNA
Faculty of Geographic Engineering: Dr JAIME VILLAREAL MORALES
Faculty of Marketing: JESUS ANTONIO POVEDA
Faculty of Publicity: Dr CHRISTIAN SCHRADER
Faculty of Computer Science: JUAN ORLANDO LIZCANO
Faculty of Law: CAMILO NOGUERA
Health Services Management: ALFONSO LEON CANCINO
Workers' Health: LEONARDO CAÑON ORTEGON
International Business Management: CIRO AREVALO Y.
Food Business Management: PEDRO LUIS JIMENEZ

DIRECTORS

Agroindustrial Marketing: ISMAEL PEÑA DIAZ
Marketing Management: ALEJANDRO SCHNARCH KIRBERG
Regional Development Planning: CARLOS A. GONZALEZ PARRA
International Relations: DIEGO URIBE VARGAS
Commercial Logistics: JORGE URIBE ROLDAN
History and Fine-Art Criticism: FRANCISCO GIL TOVAR

FUNDACIÓN UNIVERSIDAD CENTRAL

Carrera 5A No. 21–38, Bogotá

Telephone: 2341966

Founded 1966

Rector: Dr JORGE ENRIQUE MOLINA M.
Secretary-General: Dr JESÚS ALBERTO PLATA MARTINEZ

Number of students: *c.* 4,500

Faculties of economics, administration, accountancy. School of journalism and advertising. Graduate courses.

FUNDACIÓN UNIVERSIDAD EXTERNADO DE COLOMBIA

Calle 12, No. 1–17 Este, Apdo Aéreo 034141, Bogotá

Telephone: 2826-066
Fax: 2843-769
E-mail: uextpub3@impsat.net.co

Founded 1886
Private control
Language of instruction: Spanish
Academic year: February to December

Rector: Dr FERNANDO HINESTROSA
Secretary-General: Dr HERNANDO PARRA NIETO
Administrative Director: (vacant)
Librarian: Dra LINA ESPITALETA DE VILLEGAS

Number of teachers: 639
Number of students: 7,000

Publications: *Catálogo General, Informativo, Informe Estadístico, Externadista, Boletín Bibliográfico, Paradigma, Revista Derecho Penal y Criminología, Externado Revista Jurídica.*

DEANS

Faculty of Law: Dr FERNANDO HINESTROSA
Faculty of Economics: Dr MAURICIO PÉREZ
Faculty of Business Administration: Dra DIANA CABRERA
Faculty of Hotel Management and Tourism: Dr LUIS CARLOS CRUZ
Faculty of Finance and International Relations: Dr ROBERTO HINESTROSA
Faculty of Social Work: Dra LUCERO ZAMUDIO
Faculty of Education: Dra MIRYAM OCHOA
Faculty of Social Communication and Journalism: Dr MIGUEL MENDEZ
Faculty of Furniture Restoration: Dra HELENA WIESNER

HEADS OF DEPARTMENTS

Public Law: Dra SANDRA MORELLI
Civil Law: Dr WILLIAM NAMEN
Commercial Law: Dr SAÚL SOTOMONTE
Criminal Law: Dr JAIME BERNAL
Labour Law: Dr HERNANDO FRANCO
Procedural Law: Dr HERNÁN FABIO LÓPEZ
Mathematics and Computer Science: (vacant)
Economic and Business Law: Dr EMILIO JOSÉ ARCHILA
Juridical Computer Science: Dra TERESA VARGAS
Municipal Government: Dr LUIS VILLAR BORDA

AFFILIATED INSTITUTES

Instituto de Estudios Interdisciplinarios: Dir Dr LUIS FERNANDO GÓMEZ.

Instituto de Estudios Internacionales: Dir Dr ROBERTO HINESTROSA.

Instituto Iberoamericano de Derecho Constitucional: Dir Dr CARLOS RESTREPO.

Instituto de Especialización en Derecho Laboral y Relaciones Industriales: Dir Dr HERNANDO FRANCO.

Instituto de Estudios Constitucionales 'Carlos Restrepo Piedrahita': Dir Dra SANDRA MORELLI.

INSTITUTO COLOMBIANO DE ESTUDIOS SUPERIORES

Apdo Aéreo 25608 (Unicentro), Santiago de Cali, Valle del Cauca

Telephone: 5552334
Fax 5552345
E-mail: frapie@cesi.edu.co

Founded 1979
Private control
Academic year: January to June, August to December

Rector: FRANCISCO PIEDRAHITA
Vice-Rector: HIPOLITO GONZALEZ
Secretary-General: MARIA CRISTINA NAVIA
Library Director: MARTA C. LORA GARCÉS

Number of teachers: 170
Number of students: 2,400

Publication: *Publicaciones ICESI* (quarterly).

PONTIFICIA UNIVERSIDAD JAVERIANA

Carrera 7, No. 40–76, Apdo Aéreo 56710, Bogotá

Telephone: 287-57-91
Fax: 571-288-23-35

Founded 1622 by the Jesuit Fathers; re-established 1931, present status 1937
Academic year: January to November (two semesters)

Grand Chancellor: R. P. P.-H. KOLVENBACH
Vice-Grand Chancellor: P. HORACIO ARANGO
Rector: P. GERARDO ARANGO
Vice-Rectors: P. JORGE HUMBERTO PELÁEZ (Academic), P. EDUARDO URIBE (University Affairs), P. JAVIER GONZÁLEZ (Cali section)
Financial Director: Dr PEDRO PABLO MARTÍNEZ
Administrative Director: Ing. LUZ MARINA ALZATE
Secretary-General: P. JAIME BERNAL

Library: see Libraries
Number of teachers: 2,940
Number of students: 27,353

Publications: *Theologica Xaveriana, Universitas Médica* (quarterly), *Universitas Jurídica, Universitas Humanistica, Universitas Economica, Universitas Canonica, Universitas Odontologica, Universitas Philosophica, Signo y Pensamiento* (2 a year), *Cuadernos de Agroindustria y Economía Rural, Ingeniería y Universidad.*

DEANS

Faculty of Theology: P. CARLOS NOVOA
Faculty of Canon Law: Dr RAFAEL GOMEZ
Faculty of Arts: M. GUILLERMO GAVIRIA
Faculty of Social Communication: P. GABRIEL JAIME PÉREZ
Faculty of Medicine: Dr JAIME ALVARADO
Faculty of Law: Dr GUSTAVO ZAFRA
Faculty of Economic and Administrative Sciences: Dr LUIS GARCÍA
Faculty of Social Sciences and Education: P. GERARDO REMOLINA
Faculty of Engineering: Dr JORGE IGNACIO VÉLEZ
Faculty of Education: Dr RAFAEL CAMPO

Faculty of Political Sciences and International Relations: P. JAVIER SANÍN
Faculty of Sciences: Dr CARLOS CORREDOR
Faculty of Architecture: Arq. RAFAEL URIBE
Faculty of Philosophy: Dr MANUEL DOMÍNGUEZ
Faculty of Psychology: Dr ARNOLDO ARISTIZABAL
Faculty of Dentistry: Dr NELSON CONTRERAS
Faculty of Nursing: Dra MARTA LOPEZ
Department of Languages: ANGELA DE TORO
Faculty of Engineering (in Cali): Ing. PABLO GRECH
Faculty of Economic and Administrative Sciences (in Cali): Dra ANA MILENA YOSHIOKA
Faculty of Humanities and Social Sciences (in Cali): P. MARCO TULIO GONZÁLEZ

AFFILIATED INSTITUTES

Instituto Geofísico—Universidad Javeriana (Geophysical Institute): Bogotá; f. 1941; Dir Dr PEDRO PABLO MARTÍNEZ.

San Ignacio University Hospital: Dir Dr JAIME ALVARADO.

Institute of Aesthetic Research: Dir Arq. ANDRÉS GAVIRIA

Institute for Human Genetics: Dir Dr JAIME BERNAL VILLEGAS

Institute for Rural Development: Dir Dr RICARDO DÁVILA.

Institute of Environmental Studies for Development: Dir Dr FRANCISCO GONZÁLEZ.

Institute for Energy Studies: Dir Ing. DIEGO OTERO.

Javeriana Institute for Housing and Urban Planning: Dir Arq. DORIS TARCHOPULOS.

UNIVERSIDAD AUTÓNOMA LATINOAMERICANA

Carrera 55 (Tenerife), No. 49–51, Apdo 3455, Medellín

Telephone: 5112199
Fax: 5123418

Founded 1966
Private control with state supervision
Language of instruction: Spanish
Academic year: February to November

President: Dra ROSITA TURIZO CALLEJAS
Rector: Dr JAIRO URIBE ARANGO
Vice-Rector: Dr JOSÉ RAUL JARAMILLO R.
Registrar: Dr VICENTE JOSÉ IGLESIAS ESCORCE
Librarian: Dr ALONSO GUILLERMO MERINO G.

Number of teachers: 265
Number of students: 2,300

Publications: *Boletín Informativo* (monthly), *Revista Unaula* (annually), *Sociología* (annually), *Visión Autónoma* (2 a year), *Actividad Contable* (annually), *Apuntes de Economía* (annually), *Cículo de Humanidades* (2 a year).

DEANS

Faculty of Law: Dr ALBERTO VILLEGAS MUÑOZ
Faculty of Education: Dr FERNANDO CORTÉS GUTIÉRREZ
Faculty of Sociology: Dr NÉSTOR RAUL PÉREZ JARAMILLO
Faculty of Accountancy: Dr JAIME ALBERTO LARA JIMÉNEZ
Faculty of Economics: Dr HERIBERTO ESCOBAR GALLO
Faculty of Industrial Engineering: Dr ANÍBAL VÉLEZ MUÑOZ
Faculty of Postgraduate Studies: Dr HÉCTOR ORTIZ CAÑAS

UNIVERSIDAD CATÓLICA POPULAR DEL RISARALDA

Avenida Sur, Frente al Parque Metropolitano del Café, Apdo Aéreo 2435, Pereira

Telephone: (963) 375940
Fax: (963) 375635
E-mail: ucpr@avan.net

Founded 1975
Private control
Academic year: January to June, July to November

Grand Chancellor: Mons. FABIO SUESCÚN MUTIS
Rector: Fr ALVARO EDUARDO BETANCUR JIMÉNEZ
Vice-Rector: Dr DUFFAY ALBERTO GÓMEZ RAMÍREZ
Administrative Director: Dr HÉCTOR FABIO LONDOÑO PARRA
Librarian: Dra JUDITH GÓMEZ GÓMEZ

Number of teachers: 117
Number of students: 1,299

Publication: *Páginas de la UCPR* (5 a year).

DEANS

Faculty of Industrial Economics: Dr MARIO ALBERTO GAVIRIA RÍOS
Faculty of Business Administration: Dr JAIME MONTOYA FERRER
Faculty of Religious Studies: Dr HÉCTOR CÓRDOBA VARGAS
Faculty of Industrial Design: Dra PATRICIA MORALES LEDESMA
Faculty of Architecture: Dr EDGAR SALOMÓN CRUZ MORENO
Faculty of Social Communication and Journalism: Dra CRISTINA BOTERO SALAZAR

UNIVERSIDAD ESCUELA DE ADMINISTRACIÓN Y FINANZAS Y TECNOLOGÍAS

Apdo Aéreo 3300, Avda Las Vegas, Carrera 49 No. 7–50, Medellín, Antioquia

Telephone: 2660-500

Founded 1960
Private control
Language of instruction: Spanish
Academic year: February to June, August to December

Rector: GUILLERMO SANÍN ARANGO
Registrar: LUIS EDUARDO GÓMEZ
Librarian: ANGELA RESTREPO MORENO

Library of 13,000 vols
Number of teachers: 286
Number of students: 3,166

Publications: *Temas Administrativos* (quarterly), *Boletín Informativo* (monthly), annual booklet.

DEANS

School of Engineering: JUAN FERNANDO MOLINA
Postgraduate School: Dr RAÚL VÉLEZ V.
School of Administration and Accountancy: Dr ALFONSO VÉLEZ R.

UNIVERSIDAD INCCA DE COLOMBIA

Apdo Aéreo 14817, Bogotá

Telephone: (2) 86-5200
Telex: 42531
Fax: (2) 82-4932

Founded 1955
Private control
Academic year: January to December

Rector: Dra LEONOR GARCIA DE ANDRADE
Vice-Rector: Dra MARUJA GARCIA DE CORDOBA
Administrative Vice-Rector: Dr JORGE ROJAS ALARCON
Academic Registrar: Dr MOISES NAJAR SANABRIA
General Secretary: Dr JOSE LUIS ROBAYO LEON
Librarian: MARTHA ISABEL ANGEL GIRALDO

Number of teachers: 520
Number of students: 6,700

DEANS

Faculty of Postgraduate Studies: Mg. CC. Biol. GERMAN PACHON OVALLE
Faculty of Basic and Natural Sciences: Bio. Mg. OVER QUINTERO CASTILLO
Faculty of Technical and Engineering Sciences: Ing. Sis. MARIO MARTINEZ ROJAS
Faculty of Human and Social Sciences: Mg. Mat. MESTOR BRAVO SALINAS
Faculty of Economic and Management Sciences: Sc. Oec. JULIO SILVA COLMENARES
Faculty of Judicial and State Sciences: Ab. Doc. OSCAR DUEÑAS RUIZ

UNIVERSIDAD LA GRAN COLOMBIA

Carrera 6A, No. 13–40, Apdo Aéreo 7909, Bogotá

Telephone: 2868200

Founded 1953
Private control
Academic year: January to November (two semesters)

Chancellor: JESUS ALBERTO HERNANDEZ RAMIREZ
Rector: JOSÉ GALAT NOUMER
Vice-Rector: CARLOS CORSI OTALORA
Head of Administration: JESUS ALBERTO HERNANDEZ RAMIREZ
Librarian: CONSTANZA GOMEZ DE NOVOA

Number of teachers: 649
Number of students: 9,256

DEANS

Faculty of Law: JESUS MARIA HERMIDA MOLINA
Faculty of Architecture: LUIS ALFREDO QUIÑONES SARMIENTO
Faculty of Educational Sciences: AURA FELISA PEÑA GALVIS
Faculty of Accountancy: JOSE DONADO UCROS
Faculty of Economics: RAFAEL LEON PARDO
Faculty of Civil Engineering: JOHN ELKIN GEITHNER CASTRILLON

UNIVERSIDAD DE LA SABANA

Sede Puente del Común Chía, Apdo Aéreo 140013, Bogotá

Telephone: 6760377
Fax: 6761864
E-mail: susabana@coll.telecom.com.co

Founded 1979
Private control
Languages of instruction: Spanish, English

Chancellor: JAVIER ECHEVARRÍA RODRÍGUEZ
Rector: Dr ALVARO MENDOZA RAMIREZ
Vice-Rectors: Dr PABLO ARANGO RESTREPO (Academic), Dra MERCEDES SINISTERRA POMBO (University Welfare), Dr RAFAEL GONZALEZ CACIGAS (Institutional Development)
Secretary-General: Dr JAIME PUERTA VASQUEZ
Head of Administration: Dr JAVIER MOJICA SANCHEZ
Academic Secretary: Dr JAIME MARTINEZ BALLESTEROS
Librarian: Dra ALIX RINCON DE DUQUE

Number of teachers: 464
Number of students: 7,976

DEANS

Faculty of Economic and Business Sciences: Dr HERNAN DARIO SIERRA ARANGO
Faculty of Social Communication and Journalism: Dra DIANA SOFIA GIRALDO DE MELO
Faculty of Law: Dr EDUARDO DEVIS MORALES
Faculty of Education: Dra TERESA GARZON DE COTRINO
Faculty of Nursing: Dra LEONOR PARDO NOVOA
Faculty of Medicine: Dr EDUARDO BORDA CAMACHO
Faculty of Psychology: Dra MARÍA EUGENIA DE BERMÚDEZ
Faculty of Engineering: Dr EVARISTO AYUSO MARTINEZ

UNIVERSIDAD LIBRE DE COLOMBIA (Colombia Free University)

Carrera 6, No. 8–06, Bogotá

Telephone: 2630851

Founded 1923
Rector: JORGE ENRIQUE CÓRDOBA P.
Number of teachers: *c.* 250
Number of students: *c.* 5,000
Faculties of accountancy, law and politics, metallurgy, education. Campuses in Calí, Pereira, Socorro, Cúcuta, Barranquilla.

UNIVERSIDAD LIBRE, SECCIONAL DE PEREIRA

Apdo Aéreo 1330, Calle 40 No. 7–30, Pereira
Telephone: 366025
Founded 1971
Academic year: February to December
Rector: JAIME ARIAS LOPEZ
Librarian: LUZ MARIA HINCAPIE
Number of teachers: 121
Number of students: 1,311
Publication: *Boletín del Centro de Investigaciones* (quarterly).

DEANS
Faculty of Law: RODRIGO RIVERA CORREA
Faculty of Economics: BERNARDO VÁSQUEZ CORREA

UNIVERSIDAD DE LOS ANDES

Carrera 1, No. 18 A-70, Santafé de Bogotá
Telephone: 3520466
Telex: 42343
Fax: 2841890
E-mail: secgral@uniandes.edu.co
Founded 1948
Private control
Languages of instruction: Spanish and English
Academic year: January to December (two semesters)
President: PABLO NAVAS
Rector: CARLOS ANGULO
Vice-Rectors: ALFONSO MEJÍA, CONSUELO DE SANTAMARÍA
Secretary-General: MARGARITA GÓMEZ
Registrar: ALEJANDRO RICO RESTREPO
Librarian: ANGELA MARÍA MEJÍA DE RESTREPO
Library of 136,000 vols
Number of teachers: 1,009 (full and part-time)
Number of students: 9,500
Publications: *Texto y Contexto, Historia Crítica, Colombia Internacional, Coleccion Somosur, Revista de Ingeniería, Memos de Investigación de Facultad de Ingeniería.*

DEANS
Faculty of Administration: JORGE HERNÁN CÁRDENAS
Faculty of Economics: SANTIAGO MONTENEGRO
Faculty of Engineering: JOSÉ TIBERIO HERNÁNDEZ
Faculty of Architecture: KAREN ROGERS
Faculty of Arts and Humanities: CLAUDIA MONTILLA
Faculty of Social Sciences: FRANCISCO LEAL
Faculty of Sciences: JOSÉ RAFAEL TORO
Faculty of Law: MANUEL JOSÉ CEPEDA

UNIVERSIDAD DE MEDELLÍN

Apdo Aéreo 1983, Carrera 87 No. 30–65, Belén Los Alpes, Medellín, Antioquia
Telephone: 341-44-55
Fax: 341-49-13
Founded 1950
Academic year: February to December
Rector: CESAR AUGUSTO FERNANDEZ POSADA
Secretary-General: ESPERANZA RESTREPO DE ISAZA
Administrative Director: MARIA TRINIDAD PINEDA CUERVO
Academic Director: ALVARO JARAMILLO GUZMAN
Director of Postgraduate Studies: CARLOS TULIO MONTOYA HERRERA
Librarian: MARTA LUZ TAMAYO PALACIO
Number of teachers: 600
Number of students: 7,515
Publications: *Revista Universidad de Medellín* (2 a year), *Revista Con-Textos* (2 a year).

DEANS
Faculty of Law: JUAN CARLOS VASQUEZ RIVERA
Faculty of Industrial Economy: NESTOR GAMBOA ARDILA
Faculty of Administrative Sciences: NORBERTO OSPINA MONTOYA
Faculty of Statistics and Informatics: ALBERTO QUIJANO MANCHERI
Faculty of Civil Engineering: ARTURO ALBERTO ARISMENDY JARAMILLO
Faculty of Educational Sciences: MARIA EVA QUINTERO BERNAL
Faculty of Public Accountancy: ESTELLA SABA LOPEZ
Faculty of Communication and Corporate Relations: LUIS MARIANO GONZALEZ AGUDELO
Faculty of Environmental Engineering: JUAN CARLOS BUITRAGO BOTERO
Faculty of Systems Engineering: MARTA CECILIA MESA

AFFILIATED INSTITUTE
Instituto de Derecho Penal y Criminología: Apdo Aéreo 1983, Medellín; Dir (vacant).

UNIVERSIDAD DEL NORTE

Apdo Aéreo 1569, 51820 Barranquilla, Atlántico
Telephone: (53) 598700
Fax (53) 598805
Founded 1966
Academic year: January to May, July to December
Rector: JESÚS FERRO BAYONA
Academic Director: ALBERTO ROA VARELO
Dean of Students: GINA PEZZANO
Academic Secretary: CARMEN H. DE PEÑA
Librarian: HILDA DE VENGOECHEA
Library of 36,000 vols
Number of teachers: 771
Number of students: 7,372

DEANS
Faculty of Business Administration: MIGUEL PACHECO SILVA
Faculty of Humanities and Social Sciences: JOSE AMA AMAR
Faculty of Engineering: PEDRO GUTIÉRREZ VISBAL
Faculty of Health Sciences: CARLOS MALABET SANTORO
Faculty of Law: LUIS ALBERTO GOMEZ ARAUJO

UNIVERSIDAD PONTIFICIA BOLIVARIANA

Apdo Aéreo, Circular 1A No. 70–01, Medellín, Antioquia
Telephone: (4) 4159015
Fax (4) 2502080
Founded 1936
Private Control
Academic year: January to December (two semesters)
Chancellor: Mgr ALBERTO GIRALDO
Rector: Pbro GONZALO RESTREPO RESTREPO
Academic Vice-Rector: Pbro JULIO JARAMILLO MARTÍNEZ
Financial Vice-Rector: Dr GABRIEL NARANJO PIZANO
Administrative Vice-Rector: Dra JULIETA MONTOYA DE LÓPEZ
Secretary-General: Dra BEATRIZ MARÍA ARANGO
Library Director: OLGA BEATRIZ BERNAL LONDOÑO
Library: see under Libraries
Number of teachers: 1,746
Number of students: 9,048
Publications: *Revista Universidad Pontificia Bolivariana* (2 a year), *Boletín de Programación de Radio Bolivariana* (every 2 months), *Revista Contaminación Ambiental* (annually), *Escritos*, *Administracion UPB* (annually), *Comunicacion Social UPB* (annually), *Cuestiones Teologicas y Filosoficas* (2 a year), *Revista de Medicina UPB* (2 a year), *Integral Industrial* (annually).

DEANS
School of Business Administration: TULIO VÉLEZ MAYA
School of Architecture: JORGE ALBERTO PEREZ JARAMILLO
School of Communications: ELVIA LUCÍA RUIZ
School of Law: MARIO VELASQUEZ SIERRA
School of Design: CLEMENCIA RESTREPO POSADA
School of Divinity: Mgr CARLOS LUQUE AGUILERA
School of Education: MARIA ISABEL MONSALVE TABORDA
School of Humanities: LUCILA GARCÍA VÉLEZ
School of Electrical Engineering: FRANCISCO LUIS MEJÍA DUQUE
School of Electronic Engineering: FRANCISCO LUIS MEJÍA DUQUE
School of Mechanical Engineering: CARLOS ALBERTO BUILES RESTREPO
School of Chemical Engineering: FRANCISCO JOSE PALACIO RAMIREZ
School of Medicine: ALVARO LEON ECHEVERRI BUSTAMANTE
School of Social Work: OLGA CECILIA OSPINA DE GIRALDO
School of Basic Science: JAIRO AUGUSTO LOPERA PEREZ
School of Economics: AUGUSTO URIBE MONTOYA
School of Psychology: OFELIA ACOSTA DE PEREZ
School of Agro-Industrial Engineering: JUAN ARTURO TOBON RESTREPO
School of Nursing: GLORIA ANGEL JIMENEZ
School of Textile Engineering: ALVARO GOMEZ BERNAL
School of Advertising: ANGELA MARIA RESTREPO RESTREPO
School of Philosophy: Pbro SERGIO DUQUE HERNÁNDEZ
Graduate School: Pbro JORGE IVÁN RAMÍREZ

UNIVERSIDAD SANTIAGO DE CALI

Apdo Aéreo 4102, Calle 5 No. 62-00 (Pampalinda), Cali, Valle del Cauca
Telephone: (2) 5134600
Fax: (2) 5528531
Founded 1958
Languages of instruction: Spanish, English
Academic year: January to June, July to December
Rector: RICARDO MAYA CORREA
Academic Vice-Rector: UBERNEY MARULANDA GIRALDO
Administrative Vice-Rector: ULISES ARTEAGA SIERRA
Vice-Rector for University Welfare: ALVARO URIBE RESTREPO
General Secretary: JORGE ELIECER TAMAYO M.
Academic Registrar: LUZ MARIA CANO ARIAS
Librarian: HIMILICE ORALIA SERNA
Number of teachers: 1,300
Number of students: 17,000
Faculties of social communication, economics, industrial engineering, dentistry, coastal and marine resource administration, business administration, business and foreign affairs, modern languages, mathematics, social sciences, biology, chemistry, pre-school and primary education, law and political science, accountancy, adult and community education.

UNIVERSIDAD DE SAN BUENAVENTURA

Calle 73, No. 10–45, Apdo Aéreo 50679, Santafé de Bogotá

Telephone: 2354942
Fax: 2115890

Founded 1708, University status 1961
Private control
Language of instruction: Spanish
Academic year: February to November
Campuses in Santafé de Bogotá, Cali, Cartagena and Medellín

Rector General: Fr Luis Javier Uribe Muñoz
Secretary-General: Fr Luis Armando Romero Gaona

Santafé de Bogotá Campus

Transversal 26, No. 172–08, Apdo Aéreo 75010, Santafé de Bogotá

Telephone: (1) 6776077
Fax: (1) 6773003

Rector: Fr Ruben Dario Vanegas Montoya
Academic Director: Dr Emilio González Pardo
Administrative Director: Dra Beatriz Carvajal Gómez
Librarian: Lic. Edelmira Vargas

Number of teachers: 235
Number of students: 2,880

Publications: *Itinerario Educativo* (3 a year), *Franciscanum* (3 a year), *Management*.

DEANS

Faculty of Education: Dr Jorge Abel Trujillo Niño
Faculty of Philosophy: Fr Publio Restrepo González
Faculty of Theology: Fr Luis Fernando Benítez Arias
Faculty of Business Administration: Dr Hernán Romero (acting)
Faculty of Engineering: Dr Augusto Guarín Rodríguez
Faculty of Gerontology: Dr Ismael Morales

Cali Campus

La Umbría, Carretera a Pance, Apdo Aérero 25162, Cali

Telephone: (23) 552007
Fax: (23) 552006

Rector: Fr Luis Javier Uribe Muñoz
Academic Director: Dr Delio Merino Escobar
Administrative Director: Dr Francisco Velasco Velez
Librarian: Cicilia Libreros

Number of teachers: 360
Number of students: 5,041

Publications: *Economia* (2 a year), *Contaduria* (2 a year), *Ingeniería de Sistemas* (2 a year), *Educacion* (2 a year), *Derecho* (2 a year), *Boletín Institucional* (fortnightly), *Architectura*.

DEANS

Faculty of Architecture: Dr Carlos Angel
Faculty of Accountancy: Dr Lubier Chavarriaga
Faculty of Law: Dr Humberto Aragón Salazar
Faculty of Economics: Dr Francisco José Rizo
Faculty of Education: Dr Jorge Guerrero
Faculty of Systems Engineering: Dr Ricardo Llano
Faculty of Business Administration: Dr Didier Navarro

Cartagena Campus

Calle Real de Ternera, Apdo Aéreo 7833, Cartagena

Telephone: (53) 610465
Fax: (53) 630943

Rector: Fr Alberto Montealegre González
Secretary-General: Fr Pablo Castillo Nova

Number of teachers: 68
Number of students: 961

DEANS

Faculty of Engineering: Nicanor Espinosa Ballestas
Faculty of Law: Aníbal Pérez Chaín
Faculty of Business Administration: Ignacio Burgos Corrales
Faculty of Psychology: Liliana Castillo Herrera
Distance Learning: Nora Medina Alarcón de Pineda

Medellín Campus

Carrera 56c No. 51–90, Apdo Aéreo 5222-7370, Medellín

Telephone: (4) 5113600
Fax: (4) 2316191

Rector: Fr Germán Alfonso Bautista Romero
Administrative Director: Fr Alfredo Pérez Alvárez
Secretary-General: Fr Hernando Arias Rodríguez
Librarian: Lic. Angela María Restrepo Vásquez

Number of teachers: 249
Number of students: 2,640

DEANS

Faculty of Education: Lic. María Elena Restrepo Vélez
Faculty of Sociology: Carmen Sofia Pabón de Rodas
Faculty of Systems Engineering: Mag. León Jairo Madrid Salazar
Faculty of Psychology: Fr Hector Jaime Ramírez Avila

UNIVERSIDAD SANTO TOMÁS

Carrera 9a, No. 51–23, Apdo Aéreo 75032, Bogotá 2, DE

Telephone: 2357312
Fax: 591-2116368

Founded 1580; restored 1965
Academic year: February to June, August to December

Rector: P. Dr Alvaro Galvis Ramírez
Vice-Rector (Academic): Dr Jorge Vergel Villamizar
Secretary-General: Dr Jorge Enrique Prieto Monroy
Librarian: P. Luis Francisco Sastoque Poveda

Library of 50,186 vols
Number of teachers: 642
Number of students: 15,142

Publications: *Análisis*, *Cuadernos de Filosofía Latinoamericana*.

DEANS

Faculty of Law and Political Science: Dr Rafael Piñeros Jiménez
Faculty of Public Accounting: Fernando Arturo Rodríguez Martínez
Faculty of Civil Engineering: Ing. Pedro Alfonso Acosta Vélez
Faculty of Electronic Engineering: Ing. Luis Alfonso Infante Peña
Faculty of Philosophy: P. Joaquín Zabalza Iriarte
Faculty of Economics: Conrado Pérez Rubiano
Faculty of Sociology: Dra Ana Medina de Ruiz
Faculty of Psychology: Jorge Vergel Villamizar
Department of Administrative Law: Dr Reynaldo Chavarro Buriticá

POSTGRADUATE INSTITUTES

Clinical and Family Psychology: Dir Jairo Estupiñan Mojica.
Economics: Dir Conrado Pérez Rubiano.
Education: Dir Dr Cayento Paéz Castro.
Planning and Socio-Economic Development: Dir Dra Ana Medina de Ruiz.
Latin-American Philosophy: Dir P. Joaquín Zabalza Iriarte.
Computer Systems Auditing: Dir Dr Fernández Arturo Rodríguez Martínez.

Bucaramanga Campus:

Carrera 18, No. 9–27, Apdo Aéreo 75010

Telephone: 32342
Telex: 1076

Sectional Rector: Dr José Antonio Balaguera Cepeda
Academic and Administrative Vice-Rector: Generoso Gutíerrez Morán
General Secretary: Dr Manuel Eduardo Serrano Baquero

Library of 50,000 vols
Number of teachers: 355
Number of students: 4,234

UNIVERSIDAD DE LA SALLE

Apdo Aéreo 28638, Bogotá

Telephone: 2842606
Fax: 2815064

Founded 1964
Academic year: February to May, July to October

Rector: Bro. Jose Vicente Henry Valbuena
Academic Vice-Rector: Bro. Luis Humberto Bolívar Rodríguez
Administrative Vice-Rector: Dr Orlando Ortiz Peña
Vice-Rector for Promotion and Human Development: Bro. Jose Antonio Rodríguez Otero
Secretary-General: Dr Juan Guillermo Durán Mantilla
Librarian: Dr Napoleón Muñoz Neda

Number of teachers: 1,000
Number of students: 11,300

Publications: *Revista de la Universidad*, *Ensayo en Administración, Reflejos*.

DEANS

Faculty of Architecture: Dr Tomás Fernando Uribe
Faculty of Civil Engineering: Dr Miguel Ortega Restrepo
Faculty of Economics: Dr Sebastián Arango Fonnegra
Faculty of Education: Dra Luz Amparo Martínez R.
Faculty of Philosophy and Letters: Dr Luis Enrique Ruíz López
Faculty of Optometry: Dr Carlos Hernando Mendoza
Faculty of Library Science and Archives: Dr Hugo Noel Parra Flórez
Faculty of Agricultural Administration: Dr Carlos Arturo González
Faculty of Accountancy: Dr Jesús María Peña Bermúdez
Faculty of Sanitary Engineering: Dr Camilo H. Guáqueta R.
Faculty of Veterinary Medicine: Dr Gonzalo Luque Forero
Faculty of Social Work: Dra Rosa Margarita Vargas
Faculty of Stockbreeding: Dr Germán Serrano Quintero
Faculty of Food Engineering: Luis Felipe Mazuera
Faculty of Business Administration: Dr Jesús Santos Amaya
Division of Advanced Training: Dr Felipe Reyes de la Vega

COLEGIO MAYOR DE NUESTRA SEÑORA DEL ROSARIO

Calle 14, No. 6-25, Santafé de Bogotá

Telephone: 282-00-88

Fax: 281-85-83

Founded 1653
Private control
Language of instruction: Spanish
Academic year: February to June, July to November

Rector: MARIO SUÁREZ MELO
Vice-Rector: Dr SERGIO CALLE ACOSTA
Secretary-General: Dra ANGÉLICA URIBE GAVIRIA
Librarian: MARYVONNE MOLINA DE ATEHORTUA

Number of teachers: *c.* 540
Number of students: *c.* 2,300

Publication: *Revista*.

DEANS

Faculty of Law: ADELAIDA ANGEL ZEA
Faculty of Economics: MIGUEL GÓMEZ MARTÍNEZ
Faculty of Philosophy: MAGDALENA HOLGUIN
Faculty of Medicine: ALFONSO TRIBÍN FERRO
Faculty of Business Administration: SONIA ARCINIEGAS B.

Schools of Art and Music

Conservatorio Nacional de Música (National Conservatory of Music): Dpto de Música, Facultad de Artes, Universidad Nacional, Bogotá; fax (1) 3681551; f. 1882 as Academia Nacional de Música, present name 1910; basic and university-level courses; 60 teachers; 900 students; library of 11,000 vols, scores and records; Dir LUIS E. AGUDELO.

Conservatorio de Música de la Universidad del Atlántico: Calle 68, No. 53–45, Apdo Aéreo 1890, Barranquilla; f. 1939; 21 teachers, 400 students; Dir Prof. GUNTER RENZ.

Conservatorio del Tolima: Calle 9, No. 1–18, Apdo Aéreo 615, Ibagué; tel. 639139; f. 1906; 121 teachers; library of 3,216 vols; Rector AMINA MELENDRO DE PULECIO.

Escuela de Música: Universidad de Nariño, Calle 21 No. 23-90, Pasto, Nariño; Dir FAUSTO MARTINEZ.

Escuela de Pintura y Artes Plásticas: Universidad del Atlántico, Calle 68, No. 53–54, Barranquilla; f. 1961; teaching of plastic arts; staff of 11; library of 1,900 vols; Dir Dr EDUARDO VIDES CELIS.

Instituto Musical de Cartagena: Apdo Aéreo No. 17–67, Cartagena, Bolívar; f. 1890; 12 teachers, 340 students; library of 1,500 vols; Dir Prof. JIRI PITRO M.

DEMOCRATIC REPUBLIC OF THE CONGO

Learned Societies

BIBLIOGRAPHY, LIBRARY SCIENCE AND MUSEOLOGY

Association des Archivistes, Bibliothécaires et Documentalistes: BP 805, Kinshasa XI; f. 1973, to assist the Government in the planning and organization of archives, libraries and documentation centres; professional training and seminars.

HISTORY, GEOGRAPHY AND ARCHAEOLOGY

Société des Historiens: BP 7246, Lubumbashi; f. 1974; dependent on the Min. of Higher Education and Scientific Research; aims to bring about a better understanding of the nation's past; to organize meetings, etc. for historians; to preserve the national archives, works of art, and archaeological remains; Pres. Prof. NDAYWEL È NZIEM; Sec.-Gen. Prof. Dr TSHIBANGU MUSAS KABET; publs *Likundoli*, (2 a year), *Etudes d'Histoire Africaine* (annually).

Research Institutes

GENERAL

Centre de Recherche en Sciences Humaines (CRSH): BP 3474, Kinshasa/Gombe; f. 1985 by fusion of IRS and ONRD; economics, law, administration, philosophy, linguistics, literature, sociology, social sciences, education, psychology, history; 94 research mems; library of 4,000 vols and 12,000 periodicals; Dir-Gen. MAKWALA MA MAVAMBU YE BEDA; publs *Cahier Zaïrois de Recherche en Sciences Humaines* (quarterly), *IRS—Information*.

AGRICULTURE, FISHERIES AND VETERINARY SCIENCE

Institut National pour l'Etude et la Recherche Agronomique (INERA): BP 2037, Kinshasa 1; tel. 32332; telex 21419; f. 1933; agronomical study and research; 2,250 staff; library of 38,428 vols; Pres. Dr Ir. MASIMANGO NDYANABO; publs *Rapport Annuel*, *Programme d'Activités* (annually), *Bulletin Agroclimatologique* (annually), *Bulletin Agricole du Zaïre* (2 a year), *Info-INERA* (monthly).

HISTORY, GEOGRAPHY AND ARCHAEOLOGY

Institut Géographique: 106 blvd du 30 Juin, BP 3086, Kinshasa-Gombe; f. 1949; geodetic, topographical, photogrammetric and cartographic studies; small library; Dir-Gen. Major LUBIKU LUSIENSE BELANI.

MEDICINE

Institut de Médecine Tropicale: BP 1697, Kinshasa; f. 1899; clinical laboratory serving Hôpital Mama Yemo with reference laboratory functions for other medical services in Kinshasa; Dir Dr DARLY JEANTY.

NATURAL SCIENCES

Biological Sciences

Institut pour la Conservation de la Nature: BP 868, Kinshasa I; tel. 31401; f. 1925, name changed 1975 from *Institut de la Conservation de la Nature;* 2,295 staff; library of 2,500 vols; Pres. MANKOTO MA MBAELELE; Dir/Admin. MOKWA VANKANG IZMTSHO; publ. *Revue Leopard*.

TECHNOLOGY

Bureau de Recherches Géologiques et Minières (BRGM): BP 1974, Kinshasa I; copper mining; Dir G. VINCENT. (See main entry under France.)

Centre de Recherches Géologiques et Minières: BP 898, 44 ave des Huileries, Kinshasa I; f. 1939; staff of 180 undertake mineral exploration and geological mapping; library of 7,305 vols; Dir Prof. Dr MONAMA ODONGO; publ. *Annales Géologiques*.

Commissariat Général à l'Energie Atomique: BP 868-184, Kinshasa XI; f. 1959; scientific research in peaceful applications of atomic energy; 140 staff; library of 3,000 vols; Commissary Gen. Prof. MALU WA KALENGA; publs *Revue Zaïroise des Sciences Nucléaires*, *Rapport de Recherche* (annually), *Bulletin d'Information Scientifique et Technique* (quarterly).

Libraries and Archives

Kinshasa

Archives Nationales: BP 3428, 42A ave de la Justice, Kinshasa-Gombe; tel. 31-083; f. 1947; *c.* 3,000 vols; Curator KIOBE LUMENGA-NESO.

Bibliothèque Centrale de l'Université de Kinshasa: BP 125, Kinshasa XI; f. 1954; 300,000 vols; Chief Librarian (vacant); publs *Liste des Acquisitions, Nouvelles du Mont Amba* (weekly).

Bibliothèque Publique: BP 410, Kinshasa; f. 1932; 24,000 vols; Librarian B. MONGU.

Kisangani

Bibliothèque Centrale de l'Université de Kisangani: BP 2012, Kisangani; tel. 2948; telex 19; f. 1963; 90,000 vols; Chief Librarian MUZILA LABEL KAKES.

Lubumbashi

Bibliothèque Centrale de l'Université de Lubumbashi: POB 2896, Lubumbashi; f. 1955; 300,000 vols, 1,000 periodicals, 500,000 microfiches and microfilms; Librarian MUBADI SULE MWANANSUKA; publs *Séries A, Lettres, Cahiers Philosophiques Africains* (every 2 months), *Likundoli* (irregular).

Museums and Art Galleries

Kananga

Musée National de Kananga: BP 612, Kananga.

Kinshasa

Musée National de Kinshasa: BP 4249, Kinshasa.

Lubumbashi

Musée National de Lubumbashi: BP 2375, Lubumbashi.

Universities

UNIVERSITÉ AMBAKART

BP 151, Kinshasa-Limete

Telephone: 25-732

Founded 1991

President: KAYIJI MUTOMBO ADSIR
Rector: Prof. KATALA SOK-MAYAZ

Library of 1,800 vols
Number of teachers: 18
Number of students: 250

Publication: *L'Ambakart*.

Faculties of agronomy and economics, faculty institute of rural development; other faculties are planned.

UNIVERSITÉ DE KINSHASA

BP 127, Kinshasa XI

Telephone: 30-123
Telex: 98223068

Founded 1954
Founded as the Université Lovanium by the Université Catholique de Louvain in collaboration with the Government; reorganized 1971 and 1981
Language of instruction: French
Academic year: October to July

Rector: BOGUO MAKELI
Secretary-General: KAPETA NZOVU

Library: see Libraries
Number of teachers: 536
Number of students: 5,800

Publications: *Cahiers Economiques et Sociaux* (quarterly), *Annales* (faculty publs, 2 a year).

DEANS

Faculty of Law: KISAKA KIA KOY
Faculty of Economics: KINTAMBO MAFUKU
Faculty of Sciences: MUKANA WA MURANA
Polytechnic Faculty: ANDRE DE BOECK
Faculty of Medicine: Dr NGALA KENDA
Faculty of Pharmacy: MULUMBA BIPI

ATTACHED RESEARCH INSTITUTES

Institut de recherches économiques et sociales (IRES): BP 257, Kinshasa XI; Dir ILUNGA ILUKAMBA.

Centre Interdisciplinaire d'Etudes et de Documentation Politiques (CIE-DOP).

Centre de Recherche pour l'Exploitation de l'Energie Renouvelable (CREER).

Centre de Recherches pour le Développement.

Laboratoire d'Analyses des Médicaments et des Aliments.

Centre de Cardiologie.

Institut d'Etudes et de Recherche Historique du Temps Présent.

Centre de Recherche Interdisciplinaire pour le Droit de l'Homme.

UNIVERSITÉ DE KISANGANI

BP 2012, Kisangani, Haut-Zaire

Telephone: 2152
Telex: 19

Founded 1963; present name 1981
State control
Language of instruction: French
Academic year: October to July (three terms)

Rector: MWABILA MADELA
Administrative Secretary: GUDIJIGA A GIKAPA
Academic Secretary: BOKULA MOISO
Budget Administrator: LINDONGA TEMELE-ZEMAKA

Library: see Libraries
Number of teachers: 216
Number of students: 2,439

Publications: *Revue Zaïroise de Psychologie et de Pédagogie* (2 a year), *Le Cahier du CRIDE*.

Faculties of science, medicine, social sciences, political science, administration.

ATTACHED RESEARCH INSTITUTES

Bureau Africain des Sciences de l'Education (BASE): BP 14, Kisangani; Dir A. S. MUNGALA.

Centre de Recherche Interdisciplinaire pour le Développement de l'Education (CRIDE): BP 1386, Kisangani; Dir KALALA NKUDI.

UNIVERSITÉ DE LUBUMBASHI

BP 1825, Lubumbashi

Telephone: 22-5285
Telex: 41079

Founded 1955; reorganized 1971 and 1981
Language of instruction: French
State control
Academic year: October to July (October–February, March–July)

Rector: Prof. MUSINDE KILANGA
Secretary-General (Academic): Prof. OKENGE OSOKONDA
Secretary-General (Administrative): ZEMAKA LINDONGA-TEMELE
Chief Librarian: SUKA MUBADI

Number of teachers: 442
Number of students: 13,158

Publications: *Recherches Linguistiques et Littéraires* (2 a year), *Likundoli* (2 a year), *Cahiers Philosophiques Africains*, various faculty publs, *Cahiers d'Études Politiques et Sociales* (2 a year), *Études d'Histoire Africaine* (2 a year), *Prospective et Perspective* (2 a year),*Mitunda* (African cultures, 2 a year).

DEANS

Faculty of Letters: Prof. ADNAN HADDAD
Faculty of Social Sciences: Prof. KINYAMBA SHOMBA
Faculty of Economics: Prof. KASANGANA MWALABA
Faculty of Law: Prof. KAZADI TSHITAMBWE
Faculty of Sciences: Prof. LUGALI MADI
Polytechnic Faculty: Prof. NGOY KALENGA
Faculty of Veterinary Medicine: Prof. NTINUNU KINDELE
Faculty of Medicine: Prof. KAMBALE K. MUNABE

AFFILIATED RESEARCH INSTITUTES

Centre d'Etudes Socio-Politiques en Afrique Centrale (CEPAC); Dir Prof. TSHIMPAKA.

Centre de Recherche et de Diffusion des Langues et Littératures Africaines: Dir Prof. WAMENKA N'SANDA.

Centre d'Etudes et de Recherches Documentaires sur l'Afrique Centrale (CERDAC); Dir Prof. BILONDA LWAMBA.

Centre d'Etudes et de Recherches en Philosophie Africaine: Dir Prof. KUBELA MOMBO.

University Institutes

Centre interdisciplinaire pour le développement et l'éducation permanente (CIDEP): BP 2.307, Kinshasa I; training courses in management; branches at Kisangani, Lubumbashi and Karanga; politics and administration, commerce, social sciences, applied education, applied technology; 1,785 students; Sec.-Gen. MBULAMOKO ZENGE MOVOAMBE.

Institut des sciences et techniques de l'information (ISTI): BP 14.998, Kinshasa I; first degrees and doctorates; 15 staff, 103 students; Dir-Gen. MALEMBE TAMANDIAK.

Institut facultaire des sciences agronomiques (IFA): BP 1232, Kisangani (Haut-Zaïre); f. 1973; first degrees and doctorates in agriculture; 38 teachers, 683 students; library of 7,141 vols, 14,574 periodicals; Rector Dr Ir Prof. MAMBANI BANDA; publ. *Annales*.

Institut supérieur d'arts et métiers (ISAM): BP 15.198, Kinshasa I; f. 1968; management training for the clothing industry; 18 staff, 101 students; Dir OMONGA OKAKO DENEWADE.

Institut supérieur d'études agronomiques de Bengamisa: BP 202, Kisangani (Haut-Zaïre); 31 staff, 328 students; Dir-Gen. LUMPUNGU KABAMBA.

Institut supérieur d'études agronomiques de Mondongo: BP 60, Lisala (Région de l'Equateur); f. 1973; 73 mems; library of 1,353 vols; Dir NGUBA WA ELEMBA; publ. *Les Annales des ISEA*.

Institut supérieur d'études sociales de Lubumbashi: BP 825, Lubumbashi 1; tel. 4315; f. 1956; 18 full-time staff, 785 students; Dir KITENGE YA.

Institut supérieur de commerce, Kinshasa: BP 16.596, Kinshasa I; 37 staff, 600 students; Dir-Gen. PANUKA D'ZENTEMA.

Institut supérieur de commerce, Kisangani: BP 2.012, Kisangani (Haut-Zaïre); Dir KABAMBI MULAMBA.

Institut supérieur de développement rural de Bukavu: BP 2849, Bukavu (Kivu); f. 1972; 19 staff, 350 students; library of 4,000 vols; Dir DIUR KATOND; publs *Amuka* (quarterly), *Cahiers du CERPRU*.

Institut supérieur de statistique (ISS): BP 2471, Lubumbashi (Shaba); tel. 3905; f. 1967; 72 staff, 700 students; library of 3,000 vols, 10 periodicals; Dir-Gen. Prof. Dr MBAYA KAZADI; Academic Sec.-Gen. Prof. Dr ANYENYOLA WELO; Administrative Sec.-Gen. Lic. BIHINI YANKA; publ. *Annales*.

Institut supérieur de techniques appliquées (ISTA): BP 6593, Kinshasa 31; tel. 20727; f. 1971; technical training; 513 staff; 5,814 students; library of 3,443 vols, 2,486 periodicals, 2,789 dissertations; Dir-Gen. Prof. MUKANA WA MUANDA (acting); publ. *Revue Zaïroise des Techniques Appliquées* (2 a year).

Institut supérieur des bâtiments et travaux publics (IBTP): BP 4.731, Kinshasa II; 83 staff, 916 students; Dir-Gen. BUTASNA BU NIANGA.

Institut supérieur des techniques médicales (ISTM): BP 774, Kinshasa XI; tel. 22-113; f. 1981; 80 staff, 1,005 students; Dir-Gen. Dr PHAKA MBUMBA.

Colleges

Académie des beaux-arts (ABA): BP 8.349, Kinshasa I; 44 staff, 248 students; Dir BEMBIKA NKUNKU.

Institut national des arts (INA): BP 8332, Kinshasa I; 72 staff, 147 students; Dir Prof. BAKOMBA KATIK DIONG.

REPUBLIC OF CONGO

Learned Societies

GENERAL

Union Panafricaine de la Science et de la Technologie (UPST): BP 2339, Brazzaville; tel. 83-65-35; fax 83-21-85; f.1987; coordinates research into development; mems: *c.* 409 associations, academies, societies and research institutes; Pres. Prof. EDWARD S. AYENSU; publ. *Nouvelles de l'UPST* (quarterly).

LANGUAGE AND LITERATURE

PEN Centre of Congo: BP 2181, Brazzaville; tel. and fax 81-36-01; Pres. E.B. DONGALA.

Research Institutes

GENERAL

Direction Générale de la Recherche Scientifique et Technique: BP 2499, Brazzaville; tel. 81-06-07; telex 5210; f. 1966; special commissions for medical science, natural sciences, industrial and technological sciences, social sciences and agricultural sciences; library of 4,500 vols; Dir-Gen. Prof. MAURICE ONANGA; publ. *Sciences et Technologies*.

Institut Français de Recherche Scientifique pour le Développement en Coopération (ORSTOM): BP 1286, Pointe-Noire; fax 94-39-81; f. 1950; biological and physical oceanography, ethnolinguistics, pedology, nematology, botany, plant ecology, plant physiology; library; Dir A. JOSEPH. (See main entry under France.)

Institut Français de Recherche Scientifique pour le Développement en Coopération (ORSTOM–DGRST): BP 181, Brazzaville; tel. 83-26-80; fax 83-29-77; f. 1947; bioclimatology, hydrology, soil science, botany, entomology, medical epidemiology, phytopathology, nutrition, microbiology, demography and sociology; library of 16,000 vols; Dir C. REICHENFELD; publ. *ORSTOM Congo Actualités*. (See main entry under France.)

AGRICULTURE, FISHERIES AND VETERINARY SCIENCE

Centre d'Etudes sur les Ressources Végétales (CERVE): BP 1249, Brazzaville; tel. 81-21-83; f. 1985; attached to Min. of Scientific Research; catalogues plant species of the Congo; promotes traditional phytotherapy; develops indigenous and exotic fodder plants; library of 100 vols; Dir Prof. LAURENT TCHISSAMBOU.

Centre de Recherche Forestière du Littoral: BP 764, Pointe-Noire; tel. and fax 94-39-12; f. 1992; forestry research; Dir Dr MAURICE DIABANGOUAYA.

Station Fruitière du Congo: BP 27, Loudima; f. 1963; Dir C. MAKAY.

HISTORY, GEOGRAPHY AND ARCHAEOLOGY

Centre de Recherche Géographique et de Production Cartographique: Ave de l'OUA, BP 125, Brazzaville; tel. 81-07-80; f. 1945; attached to Min. of Scientific Research; library of 2,786 vols; Dir F. ELONGO.

LANGUAGE AND LITERATURE

Institut Africain: Mouyondzi; living African languages.

MEDICINE

Direction de la Médecine Préventive: BP 236, Brazzaville; tel. (242) 81-43-51; f. 1978; attached to Ministry of Health and Social Affairs; responsible for carrying out policy on endemo-epidemic illnesses; 98 staff; Dir Dr RÉNÉ CODDY-ZITSAMELE: publs various reports and research papers.

TECHNOLOGY

Centre de Recherche et d'Initiation des Projets de Technologie (CRIPT): BP 97, Brazzaville; tel. 81-17-74; telex 5325; f. 1986; under the Ministry of Scientific Research and the Environment; aims to develop farming and forestry, to promote the creation of heavy industry, to set up projects concerned with industrial science and technology, and to adapt imported technology for local requirements; Dir GASTON GABRIEL ELLALY.

Libraries and Archives

Brazzaville

Bibliothèque des Sciences de la Santé et Centre de Documentation/AFRO Health Sciences Library and Documentation Centre: BP 6, Brazzaville; tel. 83-38-60-65; telex 5217; fax 83-18-79; f. 1952; 7,000 vols; Librarian A. IKAMA-OBAMBI.

Bibliothèque Nationale Populaire: BP 1489, Brazzaville; tel. 83-34-85; f. 1971; 15,000 vols (7,000 in branches); Dir PIERRE MAYOLA.

Bibliothèque Universitaire, Université Marien Ngouabi: BP 2025, Brazzaville; tel. 83-14-30; f. 1992; 78,000 vols; Chief Librarian INNOCENT MABIALA; publs *Cahiers congolais d'anthropologie et d'histoire, Cahiers de la Jurisprudence, Conglaise de Droit, Revue*.

Centre d'Information des Nations Unies: BP 1018, Brazzaville; tel. 83-50-90; telex 5399; f. 1983; affiliated to UN Dept of Information in New York; 4,378 vols (mostly NGO publs); Dir ISMAEL A. DIALLO: publs *Notes d'Information*, monthly list of acquisitions.

Museums and Art Galleries

Brazzaville

Musée National: BP 459, Brazzaville; f. 1965; ethnographic collection and national history; library of 285 vols; Dir JOSEPH NGOUBELI.

Kinkala

Musée Régional André Grenard Matsoua: BP 85, Kinkala; tel. 85-20-14; f. 1978; under the Min. of Culture and the Arts; ethnography; 5 staff; library; Curator BIVINGOU-NZEINGUI.

Pointe Noire

Musée Régional Ma-Loango Diosso: BP 1225, Pointe-Noire; tel. 94-15-79; f. 1982; attached to Min. of Culture and Arts; collects historical, ethnographical, scientific, artistic materials as a source of information on Congolese culture; Curator JOSEPH KIMFOKO-MADOUNGOU; publ. guide.

University

UNIVERSITÉ MARIEN-NGOUABI

BP 69, Brazzaville

Telephone: 81-24-36
Telex: 5331 KG

Founded 1961 as Centre d'Enseignement Supérieur; University status 1971
State control
Language of instruction: French

Rector: CHRISTOPHE BOURAMOUÉ
Vice-Rector: ALPHONSE EKOUYA
Secretary-General: MARIE ALPHONSE
Librarian: INNOCENT MABIALA

Number of teachers: 674
Number of students: 10,310

Publications: *Annales, Annuaire, Statistique, DIMI, Cahiers d'anthropologie et d'histoire, Revue médicale du Congo, Mélanges.*

DEANS

Faculty of Letters and Human Sciences: ABRAHAM NDINGA-MBO
Faculty of Sciences: JEAN MOALI
Faculty of Economics: LOUIS BAKABADIO
Faculty of Law: JEAN CLAUDE MAVILA

ATTACHED INSTITUTES

Ecole Normale Supérieure: BP 237, Brazzaville; f. 1962 under UN Special Fund; Dir CASPARD MBEMBA.

Institut Supérieur des Sciences de la Santé (INSSSA): BP 69, Brazzaville; f. 1976; Dir ASSORI ITOUA-NGAPORO.

Institut Supérieur de Gestion: BP 2469, Brazzaville; f. 1976; Dir MWAZIBI-OLINGOBA.

Institut de Développement Rural (IDR): BP 69, Brazzaville; f. 1976; Dir DANIEL AMBOULOU.

Institut Supérieur d'Education Physique et Sportive (ISEPS): BP 1100, Brazzaville; f. 1976; Dir JOACHIM BONGBELE.

Ecole Nationale d'Administration et de Magistrature (ENAM): BP 69, Brazzaville; f. 1980; Dir ZACHARIE SAMBA.

Ecole Normale Supérieure de l'Enseignement Technique (ENSET): BP 69, Brazzaville; f. 1981; Dir URBAIN MAKOUMBOU.

Institut Supérieur Pédagogique de Dolisie: BP 83, Dolisie; f. 1982; Dir MARIUS BANTSIMBA.

Colleges

Centre d'Etudes Administratives et Techniques Supérieures: Brazzaville; administrative and judicial centre, school of arts.

Collège d'Enseignement Technique Agricole: BP 30, Sibiti; f. 1943; Dir JEAN BOUNGOU.

Collège Technique, Commercial et Industriel de Brazzaville (et Centre d'Apprentissage): Brazzaville; f. 1959; Dir HUBERT CUOPPEY.

Ecole Supérieure Africaine des Cadres des Chemins de Fer (Higher School for Railway Engineers); Brazzaville; f. 1977; management and technical courses.

COSTA RICA

Learned Societies

BIBLIOGRAPHY, LIBRARY SCIENCE AND MUSEOLOGY

Asociación Costarricense de Bibliotecarios (Costa Rican Association of Librarians): Apdo 3308, San José; f. 1949; responsible for national bibliography; Pres. EFRAIM ROJAS R.; Sec.-Gen. NELLY KOPPER; publs *Boletín* (irregular), *Anuario Bibliográfico Costarricense* (annually).

HISTORY, GEOGRAPHY AND ARCHAEOLOGY

Academia de Geografía e Historia de Costa Rica (Costa Rican Academy of Geography and History): Apdo 4499, San José; 31 mems; Pres. Lic. CARLOS MELÉNDEZ; Sec. Dr OSCAR AGUILAR B.; publ. *Anales*.

LANGUAGE AND LITERATURE

Academia Costarricense de la Lengua (Costa Rican Academy of Language): Apdo 157-1002, Paseo de los Estudiantes, San José; f. 1923; corresp. of the Real Academia Española (Madrid); 18 mems; Dir ARTURO AGÜERO CHAVES; Sec. VIRGINIA SANDOVAL DE FONSECA; publ. *Boletín*.

MEDICINE

Asociación Costarricense de Cirugía (Surgery Association): POB 548, 1000 San José; f. 1954; 150 mems; Pres. Dr EDUARDO FLORES MONTERO; Sec. Dr LUIS MORALES ALFARO.

Asociación Costarricense de Pediatría (Costa Rican Paediatrics Association): Apdo 1654, 1000 San José; tel. and fax 221-68-21; f. 1951; organizes national conference every October; 250 mems; Pres. Dr MANUEL SOTO; Sec. Dra MARÍA UMAÑA; publ. *Acta Pediátrica Costarricense*.

Asociación de Cardiología (Cardiology Association): Apdo 527, Pavas, San José; tel. 222-01-22; f. 1978; 36 mems; library of 50 vols; Pres. Dr ABDÓN CASTRO BERMÚDEZ.

Asociación de Medicina Interna (Association of Internal Medicine): Hospital San Juan de Díos, San José.

Asociación de Obstetricia y Ginecología (Obstetrics and Gynaecology Association): Hospital San Juan de Díos, San José.

Research Institutes

GENERAL

Consejo Nacional de Investigaciones Científicas y Tecnológicas (CONICIT): Apdo postal 10318, 1000 San José; tel. 224-41-72; fax 225-26-73; e-mail conicit@www.conicit.go.cr; f. 1973; promotes development of science and technology for peaceful purposes; makes available funds for research; works in co-operation with the Min. of National Planning and Min. of Science and Technology; maintains an inventory of human, material and institutional resources which constitute the nation's scientific and technological potential; library of 3,500 vols; special collection: UNISIST program; publs *Prociencia, Boletín de Biotecnología*.

AGRICULTURE, FISHERIES AND VETERINARY SCIENCE

Centro Agronómico Tropical de Investigación y Enseñanza (CATIE): 7170 Turrialba; tel. 556-64-31; fax 556-15-33; f. 1973 by the IICA and the Costa Rican Government as a non-profit-making scientific and educational asscn for research and graduate education in farming, forestry, natural resources and environment in Belize, Brazil, Bolivia, Costa Rica, El Salvador, Panama, Nicaragua, Honduras, Guatemala, Dominican Republic, Mexico and Venezuela; library of 90,000 vols, 11,300 periodicals; Dir RUBÉN GUEVARA MONCADA; publs *Informe Anual, Boletín Informativo – Manejo Integrado de Plagas, Revista MIP, Chasquis* (3 a year), *Agroforestría en las Américas, Revista Forestal Centro Americana, Boletín Mejoramiento de Semillas Forestales*.

ECONOMICS, LAW AND POLITICS

Dirección General de Estadística y Censos: Apdo 10163, 1000 San José; tel. 233-36-71; fax 233-08-13; f. 1883; 250 mems; library of 10,867 vols; Dir Lic. MARITA BEGUERÍ P.; publs *Indice de Precios al Consumidor de Ingresos Medios y Bajos del Area Metropolitana de San José* (monthly), *Costa Rica Cálculo de Población por Provincia, Canton y Distrito* (2 a year), *Encuesta Hogares de Propósitos Multiples Módulo de Empleo* (annually), *Indice de Precios de los Insumos Básicos de la Industria de la Construcción* (monthly).

Instituto Centroamericano de Administración Pública (ICAP) (Central American Institute of Public Administration): Apdo 10025, 1000 San José; tel. 234-10-11; fax 225-20-49; e-mail icapcr@sol.racsa.co.cr; f. 1954; technical assistance from UNDP; public administration, economic and social development and integration; library of 30,800 vols; Dir HUGO ZELAYA CÁLIX; publ. *Revista*.

Instituto Latinoamericano de las Naciones Unidas para la Prevención del Delito y Tratamiento del Delincuente (UN Latin American Institute for Crime Prevention and Treatment of Offenders): Apdo 10071, 1000 San José; tel. 221-38-86; telex 2849; fax 233-71-75; f. 1975 as a UN regional agency; training, advice and research in the fields of law and criminology, crime prevention and treatment of offenders; specialized library and data bank for international use; arranges symposia, ministerial meetings; projects include standardization of criminal statistics, human rights in the administration of justice, female and juvenile crime, 'white-collar' crime; Dir Dr RODRIGO PARÍS STEFFENS; publs *ILANUD* (2 a year), *Research Reports, Bulletin* (quarterly).

EDUCATION

Centro Multinacional de Investigación Educativa (CEMIE): Ministerio de Educación Pública, Edif. Raventós, 6° piso, Apdo 10087, San José; tel. 223-16-66 ext. 285; f. 1971; project financed by the OAS; library of 1,000 vols; Dir MA EUGENIA PANIAGUA PADILLA; publ. *Boletín Informativo*.

HISTORY, GEOGRAPHY AND ARCHAEOLOGY

Instituto Geográfico Nacional: Apdo 2272, San José; tel. 226-11-25; f. 1944; library of 3,000 vols; Dir Ing. FERNANDO MAURO RUDÍN RODRÍGUEZ.

MEDICINE

Centro de Estudios Médicos Ricardo Moreno Cañas: Apdo 314, Escazú; f. 1942; 400 mems; Pres. Dr E. GARCÍA CARRILLO; Sec. Dr R. CÉSPEDES FONSECA.

Centro Internacional de Investigación y Adiestramiento Médico de la Universidad del Estado de Louisiana (Louisiana State University Int. Center for Medical Research and Training): Apdo 10155, San José; f. 1962; research on infectious and parasitic diseases; library of *c.* 4,000 vols; Dir Dr RONALD B. LUFTIG.

Instituto Costarricense de Investigación y Enseñanza en Nutrición y Salud (INCIENSA) (Institute of Research and Teaching in Nutrition and Health): Apdo 4, Tres Ríos; tel. 279-99-11; fax (506) 279-55-46; f. 1977; attached to Min. of Health and affiliated to the University of Costa Rica; 150 staff; library of 4,500 vols; Dir Dr JORGE ELIZONDO.

NATURAL SCIENCES

General

Instituto de Alajuela (Alajuela Institute): Calle 5 y 7, Avda 7, Alajuela; scientific research station; Dir JULIO C. SOLERA.

Biological Sciences

Organization for Tropical Studies: Apdo 676-2050, San Pedro; tel. 240-66-96; fax 240-67-83; e-mail oet@ns.ots.ac.cr; f. 1963; education, research, better usage, understanding of tropical ecology; field stations include Las Cruces (humid lowlands) Biological Station, Wilson Botanical Garden, Palo Verde (dry forest) station; consortium of 50 American and Costa Rican universities; library of 10,000 vols; Dir JORGE JIMÉNEZ; publs *OTS al DIA, Liana & Amigos Newsletter*.

Tropical Science Centre: Apdo 8-3870-1000, San José; tel. 253-32-67; e-mail cecitrop@sol.racsa.co.cr; fax (506) 253-49-63; f. 1962; private non-profit asscn; research and training in tropical science; consultation on tropical ecology, land use capability and planning, environmental assessments; biological reserve and field station at Monteverde Cloud Forest; 45 staff; library of 7,000 vols; Exec. Dir JULIO CALVO ALVARADO; publ. *Occasional Paper Series* (irregular).

Physical Sciences

Instituto Meteorológico Nacional: Apdo 7-3350, 1000 San José; tel. 222-56-16; fax 223-18-37; f. 1888; climatology, hydrometeorology, agrometeorology, synoptic and aeronautical meteorology; 100 mems; Dir-Gen. PATRICIA RAMÍREZ O.

TECHNOLOGY

Comisión de Energía Atómica de Costa Rica (National Atomic Energy Commission): Calle 5, No 555, Apdo 6681, San José; tel. 224-15-91; fax 224-12-93; f. 1969; Pres. ENRIQUE GÓNGORA TREJOS; Dir LILLIANA SOLÍS DÍAZ.

Libraries and Archives

San José

Archivo Nacional de Costa Rica: Apdo 41, 2020 Zapote; tel. 234-72-23; fax 234-73-12; e-mail ancost@sol.racsa.co.cr; f. 1881; 5,000 vols, 8.5 shelf-km of documents; Dir-Gen. Lic. VIRGINIA CHACÓN ARIAS; publs *Revista del Archivo Nacional* (annually), *Cuadernillos del Archivo Nacional* (4 a year).

Biblioteca 'Alvaro Castro J.': Calle 2, Avda 4–6, Apdo 10058, San José; tel. 233-42-33; telex BANCEN 2163; f. 1950; attached to the Central Bank; specializes in economics; 43,028 vols; Librarian DEYANIRA VARGAS DE BONILLA.

Biblioteca del Ministerio de Relaciones Exteriores: Apdo 10.056, Calle 11 a 7, San José; f. 1960; 12,500 vols; Librarian MARITZA RODRÍGUEZ QUESADA.

Biblioteca 'Mark Twain' – Centro Cultural Costarricense-Norteamericano: Apdo 1489, San José; tel. 225-94-33; fax 224-14-80; e-mail bncsjcr@sol.racsa.co.cr; f. 1945; 9,000 vols; Librarian GUISELLA RUIZ.

Biblioteca Nacional: Apdo 10008, 1000 San José; tel. 233-17-06; fax 223-55-10; f. 1888; 270,000 vols; Dir GUADALUPE RODRIGUEZ MÉNDEN; publ. *Bibliografía Nacional*.

Departamento de Servicios Bibliotecarios, Documentación e Información de la Asamblea Legislativa: Apdo 75-1013, San José; tel. 243-23-94; fax 243-24-00; f. 1953; social sciences; 40,000 vols, 500 periodicals; Dir Lic. JULIETA VOLIO G.; publs *C. R. Leyes, decretos: índice mensual de la legislación costarricense*, *Colección de Leyes, decretos y reglamentos* (2 a year).

Sistema de Bibliotecas, Documentación e Información: Ciudad Universitaria Rodrigo Facio, 2060 San Pedro; tel. 253-61-52; fax 207-41-63; e-mail mazamora@sibdi.bldt.ucr.ac.cr; f. 1946; 437,251 vols, 11,827 periodicals; Dir Licda AURORA ZAMORA G. (acting).

Museums and Art Galleries

Alajuela

Museo Histórico Cultural Juan Santamaría: Apdo 785-4050, Alajuela; tel. 441-47-75; fax 441-69-26; e-mail mhcjscr@sol.racsa.co.cr; f. 1974; attached to Ministry of Culture, Youth and Sports; 19th-century collection; library of *c.* 2,000 vols; Dir Prof. RAÚL AGUILAR PIEDRA; publ. *11 de Abril: Cuadernos de Cultura*.

San José

Fundación Museos Banco Central: Avda Central y 2, Calle 5, Plaza de la Cultura, Apdo 12388, 1000 San José; tel. 223-05-28; fax 257-06-51; e-mail museoro@sol.racsa.co.cr; f. 1950; permanent exhibitions of precolumbian gold and colonial coins, temporary exhibitions of fine arts; Dir DORA SEQUEIRA.

Galerías Teatro Nacional Enrique Echandi y Joaquín García Monge: Apdo 5015, San José 1000; tel. 221-13-29; fax 223-49-90; plastic arts; Dir GRACIELA MORENO ULLOA.

Museo de Arte Costarricense: Apdo 378, Fecosa 1009, San José; tel. 222-71-55; fax 222-72-47; attached to Ministry of Culture, Youth and Sport; f. 1977; collects and exhibits representative works of Costa Rican art; promotes artistic work through workshops and grants; supervision and preservation of state art collections; library of *c.* 2,000 vols; Dir ROCÍO FERNÁNDEZ DE ULIBARRI; publs catalogues.

Museo Indígeno (Native Museum): Seminario Central, San José; f. 1890; library of 40,000 vols; Dir Rev. WALTER E. JOVEL CASTRO.

Attached museum:

Museo de Historia Eclesiástica 'Anselmo Liorente y Lafuente': f. 1972; collection of sacred objects, articles owned by the bishops, and important documents on the history of the church in Costa Rica.

Museo Nacional de Costa Rica: Calle 17, Avda Central y 2, Apdo 749, San José 1000; tel. 221-44-29; fax 233-74-27; e-mail museonac@sol.racsa.co.cr; f. 1887; general museum: precolumbian art, colonial and republican history, national herbarium, natural history, culture; library of 70,000 vols; Dir MELANIA ORTIZ VOLIO; publs *Brenesia* (natural sciences), *Trees and Seeds from the Neotropics*, *Vínculos* (anthropology) (2 a year), occasional papers.

Has affiliated:

Museo de Zoología: Dpto de Biología, Univ. de Costa Rica, San José; mammals, herpetology, fish; small library.

Museo de Entomología: Faculty of Agronomy, Univ. de Costa Rica, San José.

Universities

UNIVERSIDAD AUTÓNOMA DE CENTRO AMERICA

Apdo 7637, San José 1000

Telephone: 234-07-01
Fax: 224-03-91

Founded 1976
Private control
Language of instruction: Spanish
Academic year: January to December (3 terms)

Rector: Lic. GUILLERMO MALAVASSI VARGAS
Chancellor: MARIO GRANADOS MORENO
Vice-Chancellor: PABLO ARCE
Registrar: PABLO ARCE
Librarian: VIRGINIA ALVARADO

Number of teachers: 2,500
Number of students: 5,000

Publications: *Ordenanzas y Anuario Universitario, Acta Académica* (2 a year).

CONSTITUENT COLLEGES

Studium Generale Costarricense: Apdo 7651-1000 San José; tel. 223-67-66; fax 222-65-28; Dean Lic. MARIO GRANADOS.

Collegium Academicum: Apdo 1703-1002, San José; tel. 221-89-19; Dean GASTÓN CERTAD.

Colegio de Artes Plásticas: Apdo 6177-1000 San Jóse; tel. and fax 221-00-53; Dean Lic. WILBERTH VILLEGAS.

Escuela Autónoma de Ciencias Médicas: Apdo 638-1007 San José; tel. 231-21-94; fax 221-45-38; Dean ALVARO FERNÁNDEZ SALAS.

Colegio Leonardo da Vinci: Apdo 44-1009, San José; tel. 233-70-35; Dean TERESITA BONILLA.

Colegio Andrés Bello: Apdo 455-2010, San José; tel. 223-92-82; fax 233-05-98; Dean Lic. HERBERTH SASSO.

Collegium Santa Paula: Apdo 3595-1000, San José; tel. 221-68-10; fax 221-53-31; Dean MARÍA EUGENIA VARGAS.

Colegio Iñigo de Loyola: Apdo 12345-1000, San José; tel. 224-72-20; fax 225-07-63; Dean ELIO BURGOS.

UNIVERSIDAD DE COSTA RICA

Ciudad Universitaria 'Rodrigo Facio', San Pedro de Montes de Oca, San José

Telephone: 253-53-23
Telex: 2544
Fax 234-04-52
E-mail: hernanr@sibdi.bldt.ucr.ac.cr

Founded 1843, re-founded 1940
Autonomous control
Language of instruction: Spanish
Academic year: March to November

Rector: Dr GABRIEL MACAYA TREJOS
Registrar: Sr JORGE RECOBA VARGAS (acting)
Librarian: Lic. AURORA ZAMORA GONZÁLEZ (acting)

Library: see Libraries.
Number of teachers: 3,800
Number of students: 28,986

Publications: school reviews.

DEANS

Faculty of Agronomy: Ing. ADOLFO SOTO AGUILAR
Faculty of Fine Arts: Dr LUIS DIEGO HERRA RODRÍGUEZ
Faculty of Economics: Dr JUSTO AGUILAR FONG
Faculty of Science: Dr RAMIRO BARRANTES MESÉN
Faculty of Letters: M.L. ENRIQUE MARGERY PEÑA
Faculty of Law: Dra MARÍA ANTONIETA SAÉNZ ELIZONDO
Faculty of Education: ALEJANDRINA MATA SEGREDA
Faculty of Pharmacy: Dra LIDIETTE FONSECA GONZÁLEZ
Faculty of Engineering: Ing. JOSÉ JOAQUÍN CHACÓN LEANDRO
Faculty of Medicine: Dr CARLOS DE CÉSPEDES MONTEALEGRE
Faculty of Microbiology: Dr EDUARDO BRILLA SALAZAR
Faculty of Dentistry: Dr FERNANDO SAÉNZ FORERO
Faculty of Social Sciences: Dr ROBERTO SALOM ECHEVERRIA (acting)
Graduate Studies: Dra MAIA PÉREZ YGLESIAS

There are 21 research institutes attached to the various faculties.

REGIONAL CENTRES

Centro Regional del Occidente: Dir Dr ELIAM CAMPOS BARRANTES.

Centro Regional del Atlántico: Dir Ing. CARLOS CALVO PINEDA.

Centro Regional de Guanacaste: Dir Ing. RAFAEL MONTERO ROJAS.

Centro Regional de Limón: Dir Dr ENRIQUE ZAPATA DUARTE.

Centro Regional del Pacífico: Dir MARIANA CHAVES ARAYA (acting).

UNIVERSIDAD ESTATAL A DISTANCIA (Open University)

Apdo 474, 2050 San Pedro de Montes de Oca, San José

Telephone: 253-21-21
Telex: 3003
Fax: 253-49-90

Founded 1977
State control
Language of instruction: Spanish
Academic year: March to November

Rector: Dr CELEDONIO RAMÍREZ RAMÍREZ
Vice-Rector for Planning: ANABELLE CASTILLO LÓPEZ
Executive Vice-Rector: RODRIGO ARIAS CAMACHO
Academic Vice-Rector: Lic. JOSÉ JOAQUIN VILLEGAS GRIJALBA
Administrative Director: Lica LIGIA MENESES SANABRÍA
Librarian: Lica ROSARIO SOLANO MURILLO

Number of teachers: 235
Number of students: 12,000

DIRECTORS

Academic Centre: RODRIGO BARRANTES ECHAVARRÍA
Academic Programmes: Lic. RODRIGO BARRANTES ECHAVARRÍA
Education: Dr CARLOS LÉPIZ JIMÉNEZ
Health Services Administration: Lica ROSA MARINA LÓPEZ-CALLEJA
Humanities: Lic. JOSÉ LUIS TORRES RODRÍGUEZ
Business Administration: Lica ROXANA ESCOTO LEIVA
Co-operative Business Administration: Lica ROXANA ESCOTO LEIVA
Social Service for Children: Lica ELISA DELGADO MOREIRA
Farming Administration: WALTER ARAYA NARANJO
Educational Administration: Dr CARLOS LÉPIZ

There are 28 regional centres where students can register, receive instruction, sit examinations and use library facilities.

UNIVERSIDAD LATINOAMERICANA DE CIENCIA Y TECNOLOGIA (ULACIT)

Apdo 10235, 1000 San José

Telephone: 257-57-67
Fax: 233-16-03

Founded 1987
Private control
Campuses in San José, San Ramón and Limón, and in Panama City (Panama)

Rector: ALVARO CASTRO-HARRIGAN
Registrar: CARLOS QUESADA CARMONA
Librarian: ELORY CORDERO

Library of 19,000 vols
Number of teachers: 262
Number of students: 3,150

DEANS

Faculty of Managerial Sciences: JAVIER SÁNCHEZ CORRALES
Faculty of Odontology: Dr RAYMOND PAULY S.
Faculty of Tourism: Dr EDUARDO LEITÓN R.
Faculty of Law: JAVIER SÁNCHEZ CORRALES

UNIVERSIDAD NACIONAL

Apdo 86-3000, Heredia

Telephone: 237-63-63
Telex: 7550
Fax: 237-75-93

Founded 1973
State control
Language of instruction: Spanish
Academic year: March to November

Chancellor and Rector: Lic. ROSE MARIE RUÍZ BRAVO
Vice-Rectors: Lic. VIRGINIA SÁNCHEZ (Teaching), LORENA SAN ROMÁN (Research), HERNÁN MORA (University Extension), Lic. CARLOS CARRANZA (Administration), GABRIEL CORONADO (Student Affairs), RONALD DORMOND (Regional Centres)
Secretary-General: JORGE MORA ALFARO
Librarian: Lic. MARCO TULIO GARCÍA

Number of teachers: 1,200
Number of students: 12,000

Publications: *Gaceta Universitaria, Repertorio Americano, UNICENCIA,* various faculty publications.

DEANS

Faculty of Exact and Natural Sciences: Lic. SANDRA LEÓN
Faculty of Earth and Sea Sciences: Dr JORGE CAMACHO
Faculty of Philosophy and Letters: Lic. ALBÁN BONILLA
Faculty of Health Sciences: Dr LUIS VARGAS ARÁUZ
Faculty of Social Sciences: OLGA MARTA SÁNCHEZ

ATTACHED CENTRES

Centre of General Studies: Lic. HAZEL VARGAS
Centre for Research and Teaching in Education: EDDIE VARGAS
Centre for Research, Teaching and Extension in Fine Arts: Lic. JUAN FERNANDO CERDAS
Liberia Regional Centre: Lic. JOSÉ ROSALES
Pérez Zeledón Regional Centre: Lic. LOVELIA MESÉN

INSTITUTO TECNOLÓGICO DE COSTA RICA

POB 159, 7050 Cartago

Telephone: 552-53-33
Fax: 551-53-48

Founded 1971
State control
Language of instruction: Spanish
Academic year: February to December

Rector: ALEJANDRO CRUZ MOLINA
Vice-Rector for Research and Extension: RICARDO AGUILAR DÍAZ
Vice-Rector for Management: ISABEL SOLANO BRENES
Vice-Rector for Academic Services and Students: ANA TERESA HIDALGO MURILLO
Vice-Rector (Academic): RONALD ELIZONDO CAMPOS
Registrar: WILLIAM VIVES BRENES
Librarian: ANA CECILIA CHAVES SEGURA

Library of 54,000 vols
Number of teachers: 455
Number of students: 6,000

Publications: *Tecnología en Marcha* (3 a year), *Comunicación* (2 a year), *Serie Informativa Tecnología Apropiada* (2 a year), *Módulo* (2 a year).

Departments of Agricultural Management Engineering, Agricultural Engineering, Agronomy, Forestry Engineering, Construction Engineering, Metallurgy, Industrial Maintenance, Industrial Production, Industrial Design, Electronics, Computer Science, Business Administration, Biology, Mathematics, Social Sciences, Communication, Sciences, Physics, and Chemistry.

ATTACHED RESEARCH CENTRES

Research Centre for Housing and Building: Dir Ing. R. VEGA GUZMÁN R.
Research Centre in Computer Science: Dir L. SANCHO CH.
Research Centre for Forestry-Industry Integration: Dir Ing. A. MEZA MONTOYA
Research Centre in Biotechnology: Dir D. FLORES MORA
Research Centre in Environmental Protection: Dir H. QUESADA CARVAJAL
Research Centre in Evaluation and Modern Technology Transfer in Manufacture: Dir R. BOLAÑOS MAROTO

Colleges

Escuela de Agricultura de la Region Tropical Húmeda (EARTH) (Agricultural College of the Humid Tropical Region): Apdo Postal 4442-1000, San José; tel. 255-20-00; fax 255-27-26; e-mail admision@ns.earth.ac.cr; f. 1990; BSc courses in agriculture for the humid tropics; 40 teachers, 400 students; library of 25,000 vols; Dir-Gen. Dr JOSÉ A. ZAGLUL SLON.

Instituto Centroamericano de Administración de Empresas (INCAE): Apdo 960, 4050 Alajuela; tel. 433-05-06; telex 7040; fax 433-91-01; f. 1964 in Nicaragua with technical assistance from Harvard Univ.; Costa Rica campus opened 1983; 2-year master's courses in business administration, managerial economics, natural resources, industrial administration and technological administration; executive training programmes; management research and consultation; library of 40,000 vols in fields of business administration, economic development, natural resources and Latin American economic and social conditions; Rector Dr BRIZIO BIONDI-MORRA; Librarian Lic. THOMAS BLOCH. (See also under Nicaragua.)

CÔTE D'IVOIRE

Research Institutes

GENERAL

Institut Français de Recherche Scientifique pour le Développement en Coopération (ORSTOM): 08 BP 2002, Abidjan 08; tel. 32-65-54; telex 22563; f. 1946; Dir J. LAUNAY. (See main entry under France.)

AGRICULTURE, FISHERIES AND VETERINARY SCIENCE

Centre Technique Forestier Tropical de Côte d'Ivoire: 08 BP 33, Abidjan 08; tel. 442858; f. 1962; research in forestry and wood technology; library of 2,500 vols; Dir KAMONON DIABATE.

Institut de Recherches sur le Caoutchouc (IRCA) (Institute of Rubber Research): 01 BP 1536, Abidjan 01; f. 1956; agronomy, physiology and technology; 15 staff; library of 1,100 vols; Dir Y. BANCHI; publ. *Revue Générale des Caoutchoucs et Plastiques*.

Institut de Recherches sur les Fruits et Agrumes (IRFA): 01 BP 1740, Abidjan 01; tel. (225) 32-13-09; Dir J. P. MEYER. (See main entry under France.)

Institut des Forêts (IDEFOR) (Forestry Institute): 01 BP 1001, Abidjan 01; tel. 21-95-10; fax: 22-69-85; Dir MARTIN KOUAME BROU.

Institut des Savanes: BP 633, Bouaké 01; tel. 63-35-26; fax 63-31-26; f. 1982; agriculture, livestock farming; library of 6,000 vols; stations at Bouaké, Ferkessedougou, Gagnoa, Man; Dir Dr KOFFI GOLI.

ECONOMICS, LAW AND POLITICS

Institut Africain pour le Développement Economique et Social (INADES): 08 BP 2088, Abidjan 08; tel. 44-15-94; fax 44-84-38; e-mail inades@africaonline.co.ci; f. 1962 by the Society of Jesus to promote the development of newly-independent countries; research in development planning, economics, sociology, ethnology; library of 48,000 vols, 230 periodicals; 18 staff; Dir MICHEL GUÉRY; publ. *Fichier-Afrique* (fortnightly).

Institut de Formation et de Recherches Appliquées de Côte d'Ivoire: Cidex 02C24, Abidjan; tel. 21-69-52; f. 1979; research and studies in marketing; advice to local or foreign businesses; Dir ALBERT TAIEB.

MEDICINE

Institut d'Hygiène: Abidjan.

Institut Pasteur de Côte d'Ivoire: 01 BP 490, Abidjan 01; tel. 45-33-30; fax 45-76-23; f. 1972; research laboratories for the study of viral diseases, such as yellow fever, poliomyelitis, rabies, influenza, hepatitis, AIDS, etc.; clinical analysis laboratories used by the Centre Hospitalier Universitaire, Cocody; small library in process of formation; Dir Pr A. EHOUMAN.

Institut Pierre Richet: BP1500, Bouaké; tel. 63-37-46; fax 63-27-38; e-mail carnevale@bouake2.ozstom.ci; f. 1973; research into tropical endemic diseases: Malaria, Onchocerciasis, Trypanosomiasis; part of *Organisation de Coordination et de Coopération pour la lutte contre les Grandes Endémies (OCCGE)*; training on 2 levels: technician in medical entomology, and medical entomologist; missions and field studies carried out as required by member countries of OCCGE; library containing special collection and all the field data of the OCP; Dir P. CARNEVALE.

NATURAL SCIENCES

General

Centre de Recherches Océanographiques: BP V18, Abidjan; tel. 35-50-14; telex 214235; fax 35-11-55; f. 1958; 40 staff; biological oceanography, physics and chemistry, hydrobiology; library of 30,000 vols; publs *Journal Ivoirien d'Océanologie et de Limnologie, Archives Scientifiques*.

Physical Sciences

Station Géophysique de Lamto: BP 31, N'Douci; tel. 62-90-95; fax 62-92-20; f. 1965; seismological, atmospherical and climatological studies; Dir Dr P. ROUDIL.

RELIGION, SOCIOLOGY AND ANTHROPOLOGY

Centre des Sciences Humaines: BP 1600, Abidjan; f. 1960; ethnological and sociological research, especially in the cultural and religious field; museology, conservation, exhibitions; Dir Dr B. HOLAS; see also Musée de la Côte d'Ivoire.

TECHNOLOGY

Bureau de Recherches Géologiques et Minières (BRGM): 01 BP 1335, Abidjan 01; gold-mining stations at Ity, Bondoukou, Fetekio, Yaouré, Toulepleu.

Société pour le Développement Minier de la Côte d'Ivoire (SODEMI): 01 BP 2816, Abidjan 01; tel. 44-29-95; telex 26162; fax 44-08-21; f. 1962; carries out a programme of geological and geophysical minerals prospecting; mineral mining; library of 5,435 vols, 28 current periodicals, 2,556 geological or prospecting reports, 3,500 topographic and geological maps; Dir-Gen. J. N'ZI; publ. *Rapport annuel*.

Libraries and Archives

Abidjan

African Development Bank Library: 01 BP 1387, Abidjan 01; tel. 20-44-44; telex 23717; f. 1970; 40,000 vols, 10,000 pamphlets, 350 periodicals; Dir A. ALAIN N'DIAYE: publs *Quarterly Bulletin of Statistics, Selected Statistics on Regional Member Countries, Compendium of Statistics, Annual Report of ADB and ADF, Economic Report on Africa, ADB Basic Information, African Development Review.*

Archives de Côte d'Ivoire: BP V126, Abidjan; tel. 32-41-58; telex 22296; f. 1913; Dir DOMINIQUE TCHRIFFO.

Bibliothèque Centrale de la Côte d'Ivoire: BP 6243, Abidjan-Treichville; f. 1963; a service of the Ministry of National Education; public lecture service; 14,000 vols; founded with help of UNESCO; Librarian P. ZELLI ANY-GRAH.

Bibliothèque Centrale de l'Université Nationale de Côte d'Ivoire: 22 BP 384, Abidjan; tel. 44-08-47; f. 1963; 95,000 vols, 1,650 periodicals; Librarian Mme F. N'GORAN.

Bibliothèque du Centre Culturel Français: 01 BP 3995, 01 Abidjan; tel. 22-56-28; fax 22-71-32; 32,014 vols (adult library), 6,352 vols (children's library), and 5,000 vols in African Documentation section; 197 periodicals and reviews; Dir MICHEL JANNIN; Librarian GÉRARD AUDOUIN.

Bibliothèque du Service d'Information: BP 1879, Abidjan.

Bibliothèque Municipale: Platena, Abidjan; 50,000 vols.

Bibliothèque Nationale: BPV 180, Abidjan; f. 1968; scientific library of 75,000 vols and 135 current periodicals; part of the former centre of the Institut Français d'Afrique Noire; Dir AMBROISE AGNERO; publ. *Bibliographie de la Côte d'Ivoire* (annually).

Museums and Art Galleries

Abidjan

Musée de la Côte d'Ivoire: BP 1600, Abidjan; exhibits of ethnographical, sociological, artistic and scientific nature; attached to the Centre des Sciences Humaines; Dir Dr B. HOLAS.

Universities

UNIVERSITÉ DE COCODY

BP V34, Abidjan 01

Telephone: 44–90–00
Telex: 26138
Fax: 44-14-07

Founded as the Centre d'Enseignement Supérieur d'Abidjan 1958; became Université Nationale de Côte d'Ivoire 1964; present name *c.* 1996

State control
Language of instruction: French
Academic year: September to July

President: ASSEYPO HAUHOUOT
General Secretary: JULIENNE BADIA
Librarian: FRANÇOISE N'GORAN

Number of teachers: 990
Number of students: 31,233

Publications: *Annales de l'Université,* bulletins of research institutes.

DEANS

Faculty of Law: YOLANDE TANO
Faculty of Letters, Arts and Humanities: SIMON PIERRE EKANZA M'BRA
Faculty of Medicine: AUGUSTE AKA KADIO
Faculty of Sciences and Technology: BIALLI SERI
Faculty of Economics and Management: ALLECHI M'BET
Faculty of Pharmacy: ETIENNE YAPO ABE
Institute of Odontostomatology: JOHANNES KOUAMÉ EGANKOU

PROFESSORS

Faculty of Law:

BLEOU, D. M., Public Law
DEGNI-SEGUI, R., Public Law
ISSA, S., Private Law

Oble, L., Private Law
Sarassoro, H., Private Law
Wodie, V. F., Public Law
Yao-N'Dre, P., Public Law

Faculty of Letters:

Ano, N.
Boka, M.
Dibi, K.
Hauhouot, A.
Kodjo, N.
Komenan, A. L.
Konate, Y.
Kone Boni, T.
M'Bra, E.
Niamket, K.
Niangoran, B.
Semi-Bi, Z.
Tano, J.

Faculty of Medicine:

Andoh, J.
Attia Y. R.
Bamba, M.
Beda, Y. B.
Bouhoussou, K. M.
Coulibaly, O. A.
Dago, A. B. A.
Djedje, M.
Dosso, B. M.
Ehouman, A.
Gadegbeku, A. S.
Kadio, A.
Kanga, J. M.
Kanga, M.
Keita, A. K.
Kone, N.
Kouakou, N. M.
Kouame, K. J.
Lambin, Y.
Mobiot, M. L.
N'Dori, R.
N'Dri, K. D.
N'Guessan, K. G.
Niamket, E. K.
Odehouri, K. P.
Odi, A. M.
Roux, C.
Sangare, A.
Sangare, I. S.
Sombo, M. F.
Timite Adjoua, M.
Waota, C.
Welffens-Ekra, C.

Faculty of Sciences and Technology:

Achy Seka, A., Atmospheric Physics
Aidara, D.
Assa, A.
Bokra, Y.
Degny, E.
Djakoure, A. L.
Ebby, N.
Ehile, E. E.
Honenou, P.
Kamenan, A.
Kopoh, K.
Kouakou, G.
Kouassi, N., Zoology
Kra, G.
Lorougnon, G.
N'Diaye, A. S., Cell Biology
Nezit, P., Mathematics
N'Guessan, Y. T., Organic Chemistry
Offoumou, A. M.
Seri, B.
Toure, S., Mathematics
Toure, S.
Toure, V., Organic Chemistry

Faculty of Economic Sciences:

Atsain, A.
Allechi, M.
Koulibaly, M.

Faculty of Pharmacy:

Bamba, M.
Kone, M.
Marcy, R.
Ouattara, L.
Yapo, A.E.

Faculty of Odontostomatology:

Angoa, Y.
Brou, K. E.
Bakayoko, L. R.
Egnankou, K.
Roux, H.
Toure, S.

DIRECTORS

Institute of Ethnosociology: Lancina Sylla
Institute of Applied Linguistics: Assy Adopo
Institute of Criminology: Alain Cissoko
Institute of African History of Art and Archaeology: Zan Semi-bi
Institute of African Literature and Aesthetics: Theophile Koui
University Centre for French Studies: N'Guessan Kouassi
Centre for Communication Teaching and Research: Regina Serie Traore
Institute of Teacher-Training and Teaching Research: Adou Aka
Centre for Architectural and Urban Research: N'Guessan Aloko

UNIVERSITÉ D'ABOBO-ADJAMÉ

BP 801, Abidjan 02

Telephone: 37-81-22
Fax: 37-81-18

President: Daouda Aïdara

UNIVERSITÉ DE BOUAKÉ

BP V 18, Bouaké 01

Telephone: 63-48-57
Fax: 63-59-84

President: François Kouakou N'Guessan

Colleges

Académie Régionale des Sciences et Techniques de la Mer: BP V 158, Abidjan; tel. 37-18-23; telex 3399; f. 1975 by 17 African countries; in process of organization; courses will include merchant shipping, training for radio officers, marine management; library in process of formation; Dir-Gen. Souleimane Sogodogo.

Ecole Nationale d'Administration: BP V 20, Abidjan; fax 41-49-63; f. 1960; 954 students; library of 11,600 vols; Dir Djah Kouacou.

Ecole Nationale des Postes et Télécommunications: Abidjan 18.

Ecole Normale Supérieure d'Agronomie: BP 1313, Yamoussoukro; tel. 64-07-70; fax 64-17-49; f. 1996; 58 teachers, 600 students; library of 6,000 vols; Dir Dr Kama Berte.

Ecole Nationale Supérieure de Statistique et d'Economie Appliquée: 08 BP3, Abidjan 08, Cocody; tel. 44-08-40; f. 1961; 120 students; library of 5,200 vols; Dir François Yattien-Amiguet.

Ecole Nationale Supérieure des Travaux Publics: BP 1083, Yamoussoukro; tel. 64-01-00; telex 72112; fax 64-03-06; f. 1963; comprises l'Ecole Préparatoire, l'Ecole Nationale Supérieure des Ingénieurs, le Centre de Formation Continue, Ecole Nationale des Techniciens Supérieurs; library of 60,000 vols; 97 teachers, 567 students; Dir S. Kacou.

Ecole Supérieure Interafricaine de l'Electricité/Interafrican Electrical Engineering College: BP 311, Bingerville; tel. 40-33-12; fax 40-35-07; f. 1979; bilingual (English/French) training to graduate level in electrical engineering for students sponsored by power supply authorities or private companies from all Africa; Dir-Gen. Mamadou Alioune Ndiaye.

Institut National Supérieur de l'Enseignement Technique: BP 1093, Yamoussoukro; tel. 64-05-41; telex 72110; fax 64-04-06; f. 1975; technical and vocational training; comprises Ecole Supérieure d'Ingénieurs, Ecole Supérieure de Commerce, Ecole de Technologie Tertiaire, Ecole de Technologie Industrielle; library of 10,000 vols; 237 teachers, 1,400 students; Dir-Gen. Nahounou Bobouo; publs *Akounda* (annually), *Leader* (quarterly).

CROATIA

Learned Societies

GENERAL

Društvo za Proučavanje i Unapredenje Pomorstva (Society for Research and Promotion of Maritime Sciences): Rijeka, Rade Končara 44/V, POB 391; f. 1962; research divided into 9 sections: economics, history, law, technology, natural sciences, nautical sciences, literature, ethnology, medicine; 323 elected mems; Pres. Adm. BOGDAN PECOTIĆ; Sec. Dr DRAGO CRNKOVIĆ; publ. *Pomorski Zbornik* (Maritime Annals, annually).

Hrvatska Akademija Znanosti i Umjetnosti (Croatian Academy of Sciences and Arts): 10000 Zagreb, Zrinski trg 11; tel. (1) 433-661; fax (1) 433-383; f. 1866; sections of Social Sciences, of Mathematical Sciences and Physics, of Natural Sciences, of Medical Sciences, of Philology, of Modern Literature, of Art, of Music; 146 mems; 18 attached research institutes; library: see Libraries and Archives; Pres. Dr IVAN SUPEK; Gen. Sec. Dr MILAN MOGUŠ; publs *Rad* (Memoirs), *Ljetopis* (annually) etc.

BIBLIOGRAPHY, LIBRARY SCIENCE AND MUSEOLOGY

Hrvatsko Knjižničarsko Društvo (Croatian Library Association): 10000 Zagreb Hrvatske bratske zajednice b.b.; tel. (1) 616-4111; fax (1) 616-4186; e-mail hbd@nsk.hr; f. 1948; 1,100 mems; Pres. Mag. DUBRAVKA KUNŠTEK; Sec. DUNJA GABRIEL; publs *Vjesnik bibliotekara Hrvatske* (quarterly), *Novosti* (2 a year).

Hrvatsko Muzejsko Drustvo (Croatian Museums Association): 10000 Zagreb, Habdelićeva 2; tel. and fax (1) 431-404; f. 1945; 500 mems; Pres. NADA VRKLJAN-KRIŽIĆ; publ. *News of Museum Custodians and Conservators of Croatia* (quarterly).

ECONOMICS, LAW AND POLITICS

Economists' Society of Croatia: Zagreb, Berislavićeva 6.

EDUCATION

Pedagoško-književni zbor, savez pedagoških društava Hrvatske (Pedagogical and Literary Union of Croatia): Zagreb, Trg Maršala Tita 4; tel. 420-601; f. 1871; 3,000 mems in 17 socs; Pres. HRVOJE VRGOČ; Sec. ANTE BIKIĆ; publ. *Pedagoški rad* (quarterly).

HISTORY, GEOGRAPHY AND ARCHAEOLOGY

Croatian Geographic Society: 10000 Zagreb, Marulićev trg 19; tel. (1) 446-728; f. 1897; 600 mems; library of 6,550 vols, 9,570 in special collections; Pres. Dr ZLATKO PEPEONIK; publs *Geografski glasnik* (annually), *Geografski horizont* (quarterly).

Hrvatsko numizmatičko društvo (Croatian Numismatic Society): 10000 Zagreb, Habdelićeva 2, POB 181; tel. (1) 431-426; f. 1928; *c.* 500 mems; library of 1,600 vols; Pres. EDGAR FABRY; Secs Prof. BORIS PRISTER, BERISLAV KOPAC; publs *Numizmatičke vijesti* (annually), *Numizmatika*, *Obol* (annually).

MEDICINE

Croatian Medical Association: 10000 Zagreb, Šubićeva ul. 9; tel. (1) 416-820; fax (41) 416-820; f. 1874; 29 regional brs, 88 mem. socs, 8,500 individual mems; Pres. Prof. Dr ANTE DRAŽANČIĆ; Gen. Sec. Prof. Dr IVAN BAKRAN; publs *Liječnički Vjesnik* (Medical Journal), *Liječničke novine* (Medical News), *Acta Stomatologica Croatica*.

Croatian Pharmaceutical Society: 10000 Zagreb, Masarykova 2; tel. (1) 427-944; fax (1) 431-301; f. 1945; 1,040 mems; library of 2,000 vols; Chair. KREŠIMIR RUKAVINA; publs *Farmaceutski glasnik* (monthly), *Acta Pharmaceutica* (quarterly).

NATURAL SCIENCES

General

Hrvatsko Prirodoslovno Društvo (Croatian Society of Natural Sciences): Zagreb, Ilica 16/III; tel. and fax (1) 425-288; e-mail periodicumbiologorum@public.srce.hr; f. 1885; Pres. Prof. Dr VELIMI PRAVDIĆ; Sec. Doc. Dr DAMIR KRALJ; publs *Priroda* (Nature, monthly), *Periodicum Biologorum* (scientific journal with papers on biomedicine and biochemistry, 4 a year).

TECHNOLOGY

Union of the Societies of Engineers and Technicians of Croatia: 10000 Zagreb, Berislavićeva 6; f. 1970; 3,017 mems; library of 5,000 vols; Chief Officer Prof. Dr Ing. ERVIN NONVEILLER; publ *Gradevinar.*

Research Institutes

GENERAL

Zavod za povijest i filozofiju znanosti Hrvatske akademije znanosti i umjetnosti (Institute for the History and Philosophy of Sciences of Croatian Academy of Sciences and Arts): Medical Sciences: 10000 Zagreb, Demetrova 18; Natural and Mathematical Sciences: 10000 Zagreb, Ante Kovačicá 5; Philosophy: 10000 Zagreb, Ante Kovačicá 5; f. 1960; incorporates Institute of the History of Pharmacy of the Croatian Pharmaceutical Society, Institute for the History of Medicine, Medical Faculty, University of Zagreb, Cabinet for the History of Veterinary Medicine, Museum of the Society of Physicians of Croatia and Institute for the Philosophy of Sciences; scientific institution to foster research into the history of science, especially that of the Croats; plans to study problems of methodology, to organize at Zagreb higher education for the study of the history of science, to collaborate with analogous institutes at home and abroad; library of 8,000 vols; Dir Prof. Dr ŽARKO DADIĆ; publ. *Rasprave i Gradja za Povijest Nauka* (annually).

Zavod za Znanstveni i Umjetnički rad Hrvatske Akademije Znanosti i Umjetnosti (Institute for Science and Art of the Croatian Academy of Sciences and Arts): 21000 Split, Trg Braće Radića 7, POB 100; f. 1925 as Maritime Museum, re-constituted 1985 as Institute for Science and Art; library of 6,000 vols; Dir Prof. Dr VLADIMIR IBLER; publ. *Adrias*.

AGRICULTURE, FISHERIES AND VETERINARY SCIENCE

Institut za oceanografiju i ribarstvo (Institute of Oceanography and Fisheries): Split, Šetalište Ivana Meštrovića 63; tel. (21) 358-688; fax (21) 358-650; f. 1930; research in oceanography, hydrography, geology, marine biology, marine fisheries, ichthyology, mariculture and fishery technology; postgraduate study in fisheries; has a hatchery, a research vessel and a staff of 55 naturalists; library of 15,000 vols; Dir Dr IVONA MARASOVIĆ; publs *Acta Adriatica*, *Notes*.

Poljoprivredni Institut Osijek (Osijek Agricultural Institute): 31000 Osijek, Južno Predgrade 17, POB 149; tel. (31) 122-458; fax (31) 551-414; e-mail zjurkov@ratar.poljinos.hr; f. 1916; agricultural and scientific research; 160 mems; library of 5,380 vols; Dir JOSIP KOVAČEVIĆ; publ. *Poljoprivreda* (2 a year).

ARCHITECTURE AND TOWN PLANNING

Zavod za Arhitekturu i Urbanizam (Institute of Architecture and Town Planning): 10000 Zagreb, Ulica braće Kavurića 1; tel. (1) 449-897; f. 1952 for the scientific study of the history of architecture and town planning and of methods of protection, conservation and presentation of monuments; 5 mems; library of 2,000 vols, 30 periodicals; Dir ANA DEANOVIĆ; publs *Rad JAZU* (irregular), *Bulletin Razreda za likovne umjetnosti* (2 a year), *Monographs* (irregular).

BIBLIOGRAPHY, LIBRARY SCIENCE AND MUSEOLOGY

Directorate for the Protection of the Cultural Heritage: Zagreb, Ilica 44; tel. (1) 427-200; fax (1) 426-386; f. 1910; library of 10,200 vols; photo collection of *c.* 54,000 negatives, 10,000 charts; Dir MARIO KEZIĆ; publs *Spomenici u Hrvatskoj njihova rasprostranjenost i opća valorizacija*, *Gradja za proučavanje starih kamenih mostova*, *Godišnjak zaštite spomenika kulture Hrvatske* (Yearbook of Protection of Croatian Cultural Monuments).

Regionalni zavod za zaštitu spomenika kulture (Regional Institute for the Protection of Historic Monuments): 21000 Split, Poljudsko šetalište 15, p.p. 191; tel. (21) 342-327; fax (21) 48993; f. 1854; library of 12,000 vols and periodicals, 130,000 photographs and negatives; Dir Dr JOŠKO BELAMARIĆ; Sec. NEIRA STOJANAC; publ. *Prilozi povijesti umjetnosti u Dalmaciji*.

Zavod za Restauriranje Umjetnina (Institute for the Restoration of Works of Art): 10000 Zagreb, Zmajevac br. 8; tel. (1) 433-967; fax (1) 420-157; f. 1948; restoration and research into the conservation of paintings, historic architecture, and wooden sculpture and other wooden objects; Dir MARIO BRAUN.

ECONOMICS, LAW AND POLITICS

Institute for International Relations – IMO: 10000 Zagreb, POB 303, Ul. Lj. Farkaša Vukotinovića 2/II; tel. 454-522; fax 444-059; f. 1963; attached to Univ. of Zagreb; interdisciplinary study of development processes and international relations, and cooperation in the field of economics, culture, science, environmental protection and politics; organizes international conferences, and is a focal point for international network (Culturelink); library of 9,000 vols, 400 periodicals; Dir Prof. Dr MLADEN STANIČIĆ; publs *Razvoj International* (2 a year, in English), *Culturelink* (3 a year and special issue in English), *Croatian International Relations Review* (quarterly, in English), *Euroscope* (6 a year, in Croatian), *Euroscope Reports* (2 a year, in English).

Jadranski zavod Hrvatske akademije znanosti i umjetnosti (Adriatic Institute of the Croatian Academy of Sciences and Arts): 10000 Zagreb, Frane Petrića 4; tel. and fax (1) 425-123; f. 1945; research in maritime law; library of 25,000 vols; Dir Prof. Dr VLADIMIR-DJURO DEGAN; publs *Zbornik za pomorsko pravo* (irregular), *Uporedno pomorsko pravo* (Comparative Maritime Law, quarterly).

LANGUAGE AND LITERATURE

Leksikografski Zavod 'Miroslav Krleža' ('Miroslav Krleža' Lexicographic Institute): 10000 Zagreb, Frankopanska 26; tel. (1) 4556-244; fax (1) 434-948; f. 1951; collects and processes MSS for encyclopaedic, lexicographic, bibliographic, monographic and other scientific editions; publishes results of research and co-operates with similar institutions abroad; 10,000 contributors, specialists in all fields; specialized library of 35,000 vols; Dir DALIBOR BROZOVIĆ.

Staroslavenski institut (Old Church Slavonic Institute): 10000 Zagreb, Demetrova 11; tel. (1) 272-957; fax (1) 278-684; e-mail staslav@filolog.hfi.hr; f. 1952; research in palaeo-Slav language, literature and culture; library of 20,000 vols; Dir. Dr ANICA NAZOR; Sec. MARINA ŠANTIĆ; publs *Slovo*, *Radovi Staroslavenskog zavoda*.

MEDICINE

Institute for Medical Research and Occupational Health: 10000 Zagreb, Ksaverska cesta 2, POB 291; tel. (1) 420-412; fax (1) 420-398; f. 1949 to study the influence of ecological factors upon health; 160 mems; library of 7,300 vols; Dir Dr SANJA MILKOVIĆ-KRAUS; publ. *Archives of Industrial Hygiene and Toxicology* (quarterly).

NATURAL SCIENCES

General

Institut 'Rudjer Bošković' (Rudjer Bošković Institute): 10001 Zagreb, Bijenička cesta 54, POB 1016; tel. (1) 4561-111; telex 21383; fax (1) 425-497; f. 1950; part of Univ. of Zagreb, Univ. of Rijeka and Univ. of Osijek; research in physics (theoretical, nuclear and atomic, medical, biophysics), chemistry (physical, organic, and biochemistry), biology (molecular biology, biomedicine), electronics; marine research centres in Zagreb and Rovinj; library of 35,000 books and 400 current periodicals; Dir Gen. Dr NIKOLA ZOVKO.

Biological Sciences

Bureau for Nature Conservation: 10000 Zagreb, Ilica 44/II; tel. (1) 432-022; fax (1) 431-515; f. 1961; 16 mems; library of 5,400 vols; photo collection of 12,200 negatives, 12,000 photos and 1,240 colour slides; Dir Prof. Dr MIHO MILJANIĆ.

Physical Sciences

Hidrometeorološki Zavod Hrvatske (Hydro-Meteorological Institute of Croatia): Zagreb, Grič 3; tel. (1) 421-222; telex 21356; f. 1947; meteorology, climatology, ecological studies, etc.; library of 7,000 vols, 45 periodicals; Dir Dipl. Eng. TOMISLAV VUČETIĆ; publs *Rasprave* (papers, annually), *Annual Report of the Meteorological Observatory Split-Marjan, Puntijarka*, *Annual Report of the Meteorological-aerological Observatory Zagreb-Maksimir*.

PHILOSOPHY AND PSYCHOLOGY

Institute for the Philosophy of Science and Peace: Zagreb, A. Kovačića 5; f. 1965; concerns itself with the synthesis and social ethics of sciences and arts; 5 mems; Pres. IVAN SUPEK.

RELIGION, SOCIOLOGY AND ANTHROPOLOGY

Institute for Social Research: 10000 Zagreb, POB 280, Amruševa 8/3; f. 1964; attached to Univ. of Zagreb; research in all fields of sociology, social anthropology, psychology; library of 16,400 vols and periodicals; Dir. RUŽA FIRST-DILIĆ; publs *Sociologija Sela* (Rural Sociology, quarterly), *Revija za Sociologiju* (Sociology Review).

Institute of Ethnology and Folklore Research: Zagreb, Zvonimirova 17; f. 1948; library of 25,500 vols; 165,000 items of archives and documentation; Dir ZORCA VITEZ; publ. *Narodna Umjetnost*.

TECHNOLOGY

Končar – Institut za elektrotehniku d.d.: 10001 Zagreb, Baštijanova ul. b.b.; tel. (1) 315-202; telex 21-104; fax (1) 334-170; f. 1991; R & D division within Končar Group of companies; research and development in all fields of electrical engineering; library of 30,000 vols, 350 periodicals, etc.; Dir Dr ANTE MILIŠA.

Libraries and Archives

Dubrovnik

Znanstvena knjižnica Dubrovnik (Scientific Library, Dubrovnik): Dubrovnik, Gjiva Natali 11; tel. and fax (20) 432-986; f. 1936; 263,000 vols, 77 incunabula, 1,400 MSS, 849 letters, 13,490 books belonging to the Republic of Dubrovnik up to 1808 (Old Ragusina), collection of 13,000 vols from New Ragusina, 6,000 vols of periodicals; Chief Officer MIRJANA URBAN.

Pula

Sveučilišna knjiznica u Puli (University Library of Pula): 52000 Pula, Herkulov prolaz 1; tel. (52) 213-888; fax (52) 214-603; e-mail skpu@knjiga.skpu.hr; f. 1861; 2,730 mems; copyright and lending library attached to Rijeka University; 300,000 vols; special collections: the Istrian area, Austro-Hungarian Naval Library (20,000 vols); Dir BRUNO DOBRIĆ; publ. *Nova Istra* (literary review, 4 a year).

Rijeka

Sveučilišna knjižnica Rijeka (Rijeka University Library): 51000 Rijeka, Dolac 1, POB 132; tel. (51) 336-911; fax (51) 332-006; e-mail ravnatel@knjiga.svkri.hr; f. 1627; special collection of material on the Istria, Rijeka and Gorski kotar regions, Glagolitica; 305,000 vols, 23 incunabula; Chief Officer JURAJ LOKMER; publs *Informacije o novim knjigama* (every 6 months), *Dometi*, *La Batana*, *Fluminensia*, *Riječ*, *Književna Rijeka*, *Rival*.

Split

Sveučilišna knjižnica u Splitu (Split University Library): 21000 Split, Zagrebačka 3; tel. (21) 361-231; fax (21) 361-474; e-mail office@svkst.hr; f. 1903; central university library of Dalmatia; 3,000 mems; 400,000 vols, 20,000 periodicals, 700 manuscripts, 5,000 rare books; Dir PETAR KROLO.

Varaždin

Gradska knjižnica i čitaonica 'Metel Ožegović' (Public Library): 42000 Varaždin, Trg Slobode 8A; tel. and fax (42) 212-767; e-mail grknjizmo@vz.tel.hr; f. 1838; library of 125,000 vols; Dir MARIJAN KRAŠ.

Zadar

Znanstvena Knjižnica (Research Library): Zadar, Ante Kuzmanića b.b.; tel. (23) 211-365; fax (23) 312-129; f. 1855; 700,000 vols.

Zagreb

Gradska knjižnica (Municipal Library): Zagreb, Starčevićev trg 6; tel. (1) 445-8560; fax (1) 421-486; e-mail kgz@zg.tel.hr; f. 1907; 279,000 vols; 1,400 periodicals; Dir LILIAN SABLJAK.

Hrvatski državni arhiv (Croatian State Archives): 10000 Zagreb, Marulićev trg 21; tel. (1) 424-144; fax (1) 482-9000; e-mail hda@arhiv.hr; f. 1643; 20,000 linear metres of records dating from 10th century, concerning the history of Croatia; 18,000,000 metres of film; library of 150,000 vols, 600,000 photographs; Dir JOSIP KOLANOVIĆ; publs *Arhivski vjesnik* (Archives Bulletin), *Bulletin – Hrvatski drzavni arhiv* (Bulletin – Croatian State Archives), *Fontes – HDS* (Sources – CSA).

Knjižnica Hrvatske akademije znanosti i umjetnosti (Library of the Croatian Academy of Sciences and Arts): 10000 Zagreb, Trg Nikole Šubića Zrinskog 11; tel. (1) 481-3344; fax (1) 481-9979; e-mail library@hazu.hr; f. 1867; 288,000 vols, 1,290 current periodicals, 1,500 current serials; Dir Dr D. SEČIĆ.

Nacionalna i sveučilišna knjižnica (National and University Library): 10000 Zagreb, Ul. Hrvatske bratske zajednice b.b., POB 550; tel. (1) 616-4009; fax (1) 616-4186; f. 17th century; 1,840,000 vols, 187 incunabula, 67,000 rare and precious books, 165,595 vols of newspapers, 328,992 vols of periodicals, 16,300 prints and drawings, 27,906 maps, 18,737 scores, 29,793 records, 8,500 microfilms, 125,000 posters and leaflets; copyright and deposit library; Chief Librarian Dr JOSIP STIPANOV; publ. *Hrvatska bibliografija* (monthly and annually).

Radnička biblioteka 'Božidar Adžija' Zagreb (Workers' Library): Zagreb, Trg Kralja Petra Krešimira IV, 2; tel. (1) 412-508; f. 1927; 149,016 vols; Dir MARIJA PICHLER.

Museums and Art Galleries

Dubrovnik

Muzej Dubrovačkog Pomorstva (Maritime Museum): 20000 Dubrovnik, St John's Fortress; tel. (20) 26465; f. 1872; collecting and exhibiting items illustrating Dubrovnik's maritime past; library of 9,000 vols; publ. *Materials Concerning the Maritime History of Dubrovnik*.

Muzej Srpske Pravoslavne Crkve (Museum of the Serbian Orthodox Church): 20000 Dubrovnik, Od Puća 2; f. 1953; collection of portraits, and over 170 icons from Serbia, Crete, Corfu, Venice, Russia, Greece, Dubrovnik, Boka-Kotorska; the palace which houses the collection is also of historical interest and there is a library of 25,000 vols.

Umjetnička Galerija Dubrovnik: 20000 Dubrovnik, Frana Supila 45; f. 1945; modern paintings and sculptures; library of 2,418 vols; Dir Prof. ANTUN KARAMAN; publs catalogues.

Rijeka

Moderna Galerija (Museum of Modern Art): 51000 Rijeka, Dolac 1; tel. (51) 334-280; fax (51) 330-982; e-mail modgalri@ri.tel.hr; f. 1948; paintings, sculpture and graphics from Croatia and other countries; library of 2,100 vols; Dir Prof. BERISLAV VALUSEK; publs catalogues.

Prirodoslovni muzej (Natural History Museum): 51000 Rijeka, Lorenzov Prolaz 1; tel. and fax (51) 334-988; e-mail primuzri@ri.tel.hr; f. 1946; library of 4,024 vols; Dir MILVANA ARKO-PIJEVAC.

Slavonski Brod

Brlić House (Ivana Brlić-Mažuranić Memorial): 55000 Slavonski Brod, Titov trg 8; f. 1933; private family house containing archives, furniture, library (8,000 vols) showing the evolution over 300 years of a Croatian middle-class family; Ivana Brlić (1874–1938) was a writer and first woman mem. of the Yugoslav Acad. of Sciences and Arts; Curator VIKTOR RUŽIĆ.

Split

Arheološki muzej u Splitu (Archaeological Museum): 21000 Split, Zrinjsko-Frankopanska 25; tel. (21) 44-574; fax (21) 44-685; f. 1820; prehistoric collections, relics from the Greek colonies on the east shore of the Adriatic Sea, Roman and Christian relics from Salonae and Dalmatia; Croatian medieval monuments from 9th to 13th century; numismatic collection; library of 30,000 vols, special collection: Dalmatica; Dir Prof. EMILIO MARIN; publ. *Vjesnik zu arheologiju i historiju dalmatinsku* (Bulletin of Dalmatian Archaeology and History, annually).

Etnografski muzej Split (Ethnographical Museum): 21000 Split, Iza Lože 1; tel. and fax (21) 344-164; e-mail etnografski-muzej-st@st.tel.hr; f. 1910; 19,500 items; national costumes, jewels, weapons, and traditional technological objects from Dalmatia, Dinaric Alps area and other neighbouring regions; illustrations section and textbook library (3,000 vols); Dir SILVIO BRAICA.

Galerija umjetnina (Art Gallery): 21000 Split, Lovretska 11; f. 1931; 2,300 paintings and sculptures (ancient and modern); library of 10,000 vols; Dir Prof. MILAN IVANIŠEVIĆ.

Ivan Meštrović Foundation: 21000 Split, Šetalište Ivana Meštrovića 46; f. 1952; permanent exhibition of sculptures of Ivan Meštrović (1883–1962); Dir Prof. MARINA BARIČEVIĆ.

Muzej grada Splita (City Museum of Split): 21000 Split, Papalićeva 1; tel. and fax (21) 341-240; e-mail muzej-grada-st@st.tel.hr; f. 1946; political and cultural history of Split; library of 10,000 vols; Dir Prof. GORAN BORČIĆ; publ. *Editions*.

Prirodoslovni muzej (Museum of Natural Sciences): 21000 Split; f. 1924; contains more than 100,000 exhibits of mineralogical, palaeontological and zoological specimens from Dalmatia and the Adriatic Sea; collections of coleoptera, shells and birds (mostly Dalmatian); library of 3,500 vols; zoological garden (Vrh Marjana 1); Dir Prof. ANTUN CVITANIĆ.

Zagreb

Arheološki muzej u Zagrebu (Archaeological Museum): 10000 Zagreb, Zrinski trg 19; tel. (1) 421-420; fax (1) 427-724; e-mail amz@zg.tel.hr; f. 1846; museum of archaeological finds from neolithic times to the 13th century, chiefly from Croatia; library of 45,000 vols; Dir Prof. ANTE RENDIĆ-MIOČEVIĆ; publ. *Vjesnik Arheološkog Muzeja u Zagrebu* (annually).

Etnografski muzej (Ethnographical Museum): 10000 Zagreb, Mažuranićev trg 14; tel. (1) 455-8544; fax (1) 455-0711; f. 1919; cultural traditions of the three ethnographic regions of Croatia: Pannonic, Dinaric, Adriatic; department of non-European collections; library of 13,000 vols; Dir DAMODAR FRLAN; publ. *Ethnographical Researches* (2 a year).

Glyptothèque: 10000 Zagreb, Medvedgradska 2; f. 1937; collection of medieval frescos and plaster casts of ancient, medieval and recent sculptures and architecture; originals of sculptures of the 19th and 20th centuries in Croatia; Dir MONTANI MIRO.

Hrvatski muzej naivne umjetnosti (Croatian Museum of Naive Art): 10000 Zagreb, Cirilometodska 3; tel. and fax (1) 423-669; f. 1952; Dir Prof. FRANJO MRZLJAK.

Hrvatski povijesni muzej (Croatian Historical Museum): 10000 Zagreb, Matoševa 9; tel. (1) 277-991; fax (1) 425-515; f. 1846; history of Croatia with collections of different historical objects, arms, paintings, prints, stone monuments, etc.; library of 43,000 vols; Dir Prof. ANKICA PANDŽIĆ; Librarian Prof. ZORA GAJSKY.

Hrvatski prirodoslovni muzej (Croatian Natural History Museum): 10000 Zagreb, Demetrova 1; tel. (1) 428-615; fax (1) 424-998; e-mail hpm@hpm.hr; f. 1846; departments of zoology, mineralogy and petrography, geology and palaeontology, botany; library of 30,000 vols; Dir Dr NIKOLA TVRTKOVIĆ; publ. *Natura croatica* (quarterly).

Hrvatski školski muzej (Croatian School Museum): 10000 Zagreb, Trg m. Tita 4; tel. (1) 420-604; fax (1) 420-627; e-mail hrskmuz@zg.tel.hr; f. 1901; history of the school system and education in Croatia; library of 37,000 vols on the history of schools and education in general; Dir IVAN VAVRA; publ. *Anali za povijest odgoja* (Annals of the History of Education, annually).

Kabinet Grafike (Print Room): 10000 Zagreb, A. Hebranga 1; tel. and fax (1) 420-431; f. 1951; 12,000 prints, drawings, and 4,000 posters; Dir Prof. SLAVICA MARKOVIĆ.

Moderna Galerija (Gallery of Modern Art): 10000 Zagreb, Andrije Hebranga 1; tel. and fax (1) 433-802; f. 1905; 19th- and 20th-century Croatian arts; collections of painting, sculpture and graphic arts; 1,945 medals; library of 2,423 vols; Dir IGOR ZIDIĆ.

Muzej grada Zagreba (City Museum of Zagreb): 10000 Zagreb, Opatička 20–22; tel. and fax (1) 428-294; f. 1907; arranged so as to depict Zagreb from prehistoric times to 20th century; library of 14,000 vols; Dir Prof. VINKO IVIĆ; publ. *Iz starog i novog Zagreba* (from Old and New Zagreb, irregular).

Muzej Suvremene Umjetnosti: 10000 Zagreb, Habdelićeva 2; tel. (1) 431-343; fax (1) 431-404; f. 1961 (fmrly Galerije Grada Zagreba); library; Dir SNJEŽANDA PINTARIĆ; publ. *Dokumenti* (Documents).

Controls:

Centar za Fotografiju, Film i Televiziju (Centre for Photography, Film and Television): 10000 Zagreb, Katarinin trg 2; tel. (1) 425-227; f. 1973; Chief Curator MLADEN LUČIĆ.

Galerija 'Benko Horvat': 10000 Zagreb, Habdelićeva 2; f. 1946; private collection of antique and renaissance art; Chief Curator ŽELIMIR KOŠČEVIĆ.

Galerija Suvremene Umjetnosti (Gallery of Contemporary Art): 10000 Zagreb, Katarinin trg 2; tel. (1) 425-227; fax (1) 273-469; f. 1954; Chief Curator MARIJAN SUSOVSKI.

Muzej za umjetnost i obrt (Museum of Arts and Crafts): 10000 Zagreb, Trg maršala Tita 10; tel. (1) 4554-122; fax (1) 482-8088; e-mail muo@muo.hr; f. 1880; applied arts from the 14th to the 20th century: furniture, textiles, ceramics, glass, metalwork, sculpture, paintings, photography, costumes, clocks and watches, ivory, architecture, design and posters; art library of 35,000 vols; Dir Prof. VLADIMIR MALEKOVIĆ.

Strossmayerova galerija starih majstora (Strossmayers' Gallery of Old Masters): 10000 Zagreb, Trg Nikole Šubića Zrinskog 11; tel. (1) 481-3344; fax (1) 481-9979; f. 1884; 14th to 19th centuries; library of 4,000 vols; Dir Prof. ĐURO VANDURA; publs *Bulletin, Razreda za likovne umjetnosti, HAZU*.

Tehnički muzej (Technical Museum): 10000 Zagreb, Savska cesta 18; tel. (1) 435-446; fax (1) 428-431; e-mail tehnicki-muzej@zg.tel.hr; f. 1954; library of 4,000 vols; Dir BOŽICA ŠKUW.

Universities

SVEUČILIŠTE JOSIPA JURJA STROSSMAYERA U OSIJEKU (Josip Juraj Strossmayer University of Osijek)

31000 Osijek, Trg sv. Trojstva 3
Telephone: (31) 132-100
Fax: (31) 124-767

Founded 1975
State control
Academic year: October to September

Rector: GORDANA KRALIK
Vice-Rectors: RADOSLAV GALIĆ, DRAŽENKA JURKOVIĆ, MARIJAN ŠERUGA
Chief Administrative Officer: ZDENKA BARIŠIĆ
Librarian: DRAGUTIN KATELENAC

Number of teachers: 441
Number of students: 9,272

Publications: *Pravni vjesnik* (Law Courier), *Ekonomski vjesnik* (Economic Courier), *Medicinski vjesnik* (Medical Courier), *Tehnički vjesnik* (Technical Courier), *Poljoprivreda* (Agriculture), *Glasnik Osječkog Sveučilišta* (Osijek University News).

DEANS

Faculty of Agriculture: ŽELJKO BUKVIĆ
Faculty of Food Technology: VLASTA PILIŽOTA
Faculty of Economics: MARCEL MELER
Faculty of Law: VLADIMIR LJUBANOVIĆ
Faculty of Education: ZDRAVKO FAJ
Faculty of Mechanical Engineering: DRAGOMIR KRUMES
Faculty of Civil Engineering: BARBARA MEDANIĆ
Faculty of Electrical Engineering: RUDOLF SCITOVSKI

PROFESSORS

Faculty of Agriculture:

- BERTIĆ, B., Agrochemistry
- IVEZIĆ, M., Entomology with Phytopharmacy and Plant Protection
- JURIĆ, I., Fundaments of Agriculture
- JURKOVIĆ, D., Plant Protection, Phytopharmacy
- KALINOVIĆ, I., Storage and Technology of Agricultural Products
- KNEŽEVIĆ, I., Cattle Breeding
- KNEŽEVIĆ, M., Botany
- KOVAČEVIĆ, V., Cereal Crop Production
- KRALIK, G., Husbandry of Swine, Poultry and Fur-bearing Animals
- MADAR, S., Agricultural Improvement
- MARTINČIĆ, J., Seeds and Seed Production, Plant Breeding
- PETRIČEVIĆ, A., Animal Products and Meat and Milk Technology
- RASTIJA, T., General Cattle Raising
- SKENDER, A., Agricultural Phytocentology
- STEINER, Z., Nutrition of Domestic Animals
- VUKADINOVIĆ, V., Plant Physiology
- ŽUGEC, I., General Crop Production

Faculty of Food Technology:

- MANDIĆ, M., Quality Control, Sensor Analyses, Fundamentals of Food Technology

NOVAKOVIĆ, P., Milk and Dairy Products Technology, Meat and Fish Technology
PILIŽOTA, V., Raw Materials in Food Industry, Technology of Fruit and Vegetable Preserving and Processing
PURKAT, L., Sociology, Political Systems

Faculty of Economics:

BABAN, L. J., Theory of Marketing, International Economics
BARKOVIĆ, D., Operational Research
JELINIĆ, S., Business Law
LAUC, A., Sociology
MANDIĆ, I., Regional Economics
MATIĆ, B., Statistics
MELER, M., Introduction to Marketing, Marketing Management
PRDIĆ, J., Economic Operation Analysis
SINGER, V., Business Policy, Cybernetics

Faculty of Law:

BABAC, B., Administrative Law, Administrative Science
JELINIĆ, S., Commercial Law
LAUC, Z., Constitutional Law
MECANOVIĆ, I., Constitutional Law
MILUŠIĆ, A., History of Law
NOVOSELEC, P., Criminal Law, Criminology
ROMŠTAJN, I., Transport Law
SRB, V., Financial Law and Sciences

Faculty of Education:

BABIĆ, A., Teaching of Drawing and Art
BABIĆ, N., Pre-School Education, Teaching Methods in Pre-School Education, Educational Communication
BABIĆ, T., General Botany
BRLENIĆ-VUJIĆ, B., Comparative Literature
JERKOVIĆ, J., Conducting, Choir
MARIANOVIĆ, S., Old Croatian Literature
MIKUSKA, J., Animal Ecology and Zoogeography, Special Zoology
NIKČEVIĆ, M., Methodology of Scientific Work, Methodics of Literature Teaching
PETROVIC, V., Linguistics and Syntax of the German Language
PLANINIĆ, J., Introduction to Physics

Faculty of Mechanical Engineering:

HNATKO, E., Heat Engines and Devices
KATALINIĆ, B., Automation
KRUMES, D., Materials, Heat Processing
LUKAČEVIĆ, Z., Technology, Quality Control, Welding, New Technologies and Materials
MAJDANDŽIĆ, N., Computers and Information Systems, Production Process, Artificial Intelligence, Planning Methods

Faculty of Civil Engineering:

MEDANIĆ, B., Construction Management
ŠEPER, K., Mathematics

Faculty of Electrical Engineering:

JOVIĆ, F., Information and Communications, Computers and Processes, Computer and Terminal Networks
PERIĆ, N., Automatic Processing, Electric Machine Processing
SCITOVSKI, R., Mathematics, Mathematical Analysis, Statistical and Numerical Analysis
STEFANKO, S., Fundamentals of Electrical Engineering, Theoretical Electrical Engineering
STIPANCIC, M., Physics
VALTER, Z., Fundamentals of Electromechanical Engineering

SVEUČILIŠTE U RIJECI (University of Rijeka)

51000 Rijeka, Trg braće Mažuranića 10
Telephone: (51) 218-288
Fax: (51) 216-671
E-mail: ured@uniri.hr

Founded 1973
State control
Language of instruction: Croatian (and some courses in Italian)
Academic year: October to July

Rector: Prof. Dr DANILO PAVEŠIĆ (acting)
Vice-Rectors: Prof. Dr JOSIP BRNIĆ, Prof. Dr MLADEN KRIŽ, Prof. Dr MILENA PERŠIĆ
Secretary-General: MIROLJUB SABALIĆ
Librarian: JURAJ LOKMER (Rijeka), BRUNO DOBRIĆ (Pula)

Number of teachers: 792
Number of students: 12,482

Publications: *Gaudeamus* (several times a year), *Sveučilišni vodič* (Guide to Curriculums, annually).

DEANS

Faculty of Medicine in Rijeka: Prof. Dr LJILJANA RANDIĆ (Deputy Dean)
Faculty of Engineering in Rijeka: Assoc. Prof. Dr JURAJ LJUBETIĆ (Deputy Dean)
Faculty of Civil Engineering in Rijeka: Assoc. Prof. Dr SERDJO BLAŽIĆ
Maritime Faculty in Rijeka: Assoc. Prof. Dr PAVAO KOMADINA
Faculty of Economics in Rijeka: Prof. Dr VINKO KANDŽIJA
Faculty of Hotel Management in Opatija: Prof. Dr IVANKA AVELINI HOLJEVAC
Faculty of Economics and Tourism 'Dr Mijo Mirković' in Pula: Assoc. Prof. Dr LOVRE BOŽINA
Faculty of Philosophy: Prof. Dr GORAN KALOGJERA
Faculty of Education in Pula: Assoc. Prof. Dr IVAN ZORIČIĆ (acting)
Faculty of Law in Rijeka: Assoc. Prof. Dr BERISLAV PAVIŠIĆ

SVEUČILIŠTE U SPLITU (University of Split)

21000 Split, Livanjska 5/I
Telephone: (21) 355-966
Fax: (21) 355-163

Founded 1974
State control
Language of instruction: Croatian
Academic year: October to September

Rector: Prof. Dr PETAR SLAPNIČAR
Vice-Rectors: Prof. Dr IVAN BILIČ, Prof. Dr PAVAO MAROVIĆ
Secretary-General: JOSIP ALAJBEG

Library of 369,000 vols
Number of teachers: 575
Number of students: 11,571

Publication: *Sveučilišni godišnjak.*

DEANS

Faculty of Law: Dr IVO GRABOVAC
Faculty of Electrical, Mechanical and Naval Engineering: Dr IGOR ZANCHI
Faculty of Arts (Zadar): Dr NIKICA KOLUMBIĆ
Faculty of Economics: Dr DAVOR POJATINA
Faculty of Technology: Dr NJEGOMIR RADIĆ
Faculty of Civil Engineering: Dr ANTE MIHANOVIĆ
Faculty of Tourism and Foreign Trade (Dubrovnik): Dr DJURO BENIĆ
Maritime Faculty (Dubrovnik): Dr JOSIP LOVRIĆ
Faculty of Natural Sciences and Arts: Dr KOSTA UGRINOVIĆ

PROFESSORS

Faculty of Law:

BILIĆ, I., Political Economy
BORKOVIĆ, I., Administrative Law
BOSNIĆ, P., International Private Law
CARIĆ, A., Criminal Law
CVITAN, O., Administrative Sciences
DUJIĆ, A., Modern Political Systems
GRABOVAC, I., Maritime and Transport Law
PETRIĆ, I., Economic Politics
PETRINOVIĆ, I., History of Political Theories
RUDOLF, D., International Public Law
ŠMID, V., Civil Law
VISKOVIĆ, N., Theory of State and Law

Faculty of Electrical, Mechanical and Naval Engineering:

DEŽELIĆ, R., Materials Technology
GRISOGONO, P., Industrial Furnaces and Fuels, Industrial Transportation
JADRIĆ, M., Electromagnetic Theory and Electrical Machinery
KURTOVIĆ, M., Asynchronous Machines, Electric Motor Plants, General Theory of Electric Machines
PILIĆ, L., Fluid Mechanics
SLAPNIČAR, P., Circuits

Faculty of Arts (Zadar):

BATOVIĆ, Š., Prehistoric Archaeology
BELOŠEVIĆ, J., Medieval Archaeology
CAMBJ, N., Classical and Old Christian Archaeology
ĆOSIĆ, V., French Language
DUKAT, Z., Greek Language and Literature
FRANIĆ, A., Modern Croatian Literature
GERERSDORFER, V., French Language and Medieval Literature
GRGIN, T., General and Systematic Psychology
JURIĆ, B., Political Economy and National Economic History
KALENIĆ, A. S., Latin Language and Literature
KOLUMBIĆ, N., Old Croatian Literature
MANENICA, I., Systematic Psychology
MIKIĆ, P., German Language
OBAD, S., Modern History
PEDERIN, S., German Literature
PETRICIOLI, I., Art History
SKLEDAR, N., Sociology
ZELIĆ, I., Visual Arts, Teaching Methods
ŽIVKOVIĆ, P., Croatian History up to 1918

Faculty of Economics:

ANDRIJIĆ, S., Macroeconomics, Econometrics
BUBLE, M., Organization Design, Job Evaluation
DOMANČIĆ, P., International Finance
DULČIĆ, A., Economics of Trade and Tourism
JELAVIĆ, A., Business Economics
LUKŠIĆ, B., Business Economics
ŠTAMBUK, D., Regional Economics

Faculty of Technology:

KOVAČIĆ, T., Polymers
KRSTULOVIĆ, R., Chemistry and Technology of Non-Metals
MEKJAVIĆ, I., Physical Chemistry
PETRIĆ, N., Thermodynamics
ROJE, U., Organic Industry – Technological Processes; Catalysis; Polymerization
RADOŠEVIĆ, J., Electrochemistry
VOJNOVIĆ, I., Materials and Energy Balance
ŽANETIĆ, R., Measuring and Process Operation

Faculty of Civil Engineering:

BONACCI, O., Hydrology
DAMJANIĆ, F., Technical Mechanics
JOVIĆ, V., Hydromechanics
MARGETA, J., Water Supply
MAROVIĆ, P., Strength of Materials, Testing of Structures
MIHANOVIĆ, A., Mechanics, Stablity and Dynamics of Structures
MILIČIĆ, J., Construction and Construction Machines
STOJIĆ, P., Hydrotechnical Systems
ŠESTANOVIĆ, S., Geology and Petrology
ŠKOMRLJ, J., Technology and Organization of Construction
VOJNOVIĆ, J., Building Construction
VRDOLJAK, B., Mathematics

Faculty of Tourism and Foreign Trade (Dubrovnik):

KONJHODŽIĆ, H., International Finance

MARKOVIĆ, M., Economics and Business Organization
REŠETAR, M., Travel Agency Management; Business Analysis
PAPARELA, I., International Finance and Business Finance
ŽABICA, T., Economic and Tourist Geography

Maritime Faculty:

FABRIS, O., Thermodynamics; Ships' Refrigerating Plants
LOVRIĆ, J., Ship Maintenance
SJEKAVICA, I., Terrestrial Navigation

Faculty of Natural Sciences and Arts:

JAKELIĆ, P., Graphic Design
KALOGJERA, A., Methods of Education
KRSTULOVIĆ, I., Painting
MARASOVIĆ, T., Croatian and European Medieval Art
MIDŽOR, A., Sculpture
MILAT, J., General Pedagogy
OMAŠIĆ, V., History

SVEUČILIŠTE U ZAGREBU
(University of Zagreb)

10000 Zagreb, Trg maršala Tita 14, POB 815

Telephone: (1) 456-4233

Founded 1669

Academic year: October to September

Language of instruction: Croatian

Rector: Dr BRANKO JEREN

University Vice-Rectors: Dr HELENA JASNA MENCER, Dr DRAGAN MILANOVIĆ, Dr ZDENKO KOVAČ, Dr VLADO LEKO

Chief Administrative Officer: ANA RUŽIČKA

Number of teaching staff: 4,800

Number of students: 53,000

Publication: *Sveučilišni vjesnik* (University Herald).

DEANS OF FACULTIES

Catholic Theology: Dr F. ŠANJEK
Philosophy: Dr S. BOTICA
Law: Dr U. DUJŠIN
Economic Sciences: Dr B. VUKONIĆ
Natural Sciences and Mathematics: Dr I. GUŠIĆ
Medicine: Dr N. ZURAK
Stomatology: Dr V. JEROLIMOV
Veterinary Medicine: Dr Z. BIDJIN
Pharmacy and Biochemistry: Dr N. KUJUNDŽIĆ
Architecture: Dr H. AUF-FRANIĆ
Civil Engineering: Dr A. SZAVITS-NOSSAN
Geodesy: Dr T. FIEDLER
Mechanical Engineering and Shipbuilding: Dr S. KRALJ
Electrical Engineering: Dr S. TONKOVIĆ
Chemical Engineering and Technology: Dr S. ZRNČEVIĆ
Food Technology and Biotechnology: Dr D. KARLOVIĆ
Mining Engineering, Geology and Petroleum: Dr D. MAYER
Agriculture: Dr Z. MUSTAPIĆ
Forestry: Dr S. M. FIGURIĆ
Political Sciences: Dr Z. POSAVEC
Defectology: Dr LJ. IGRIĆ
Physical Education: Dr B. MATKOVIĆ
Organization and Informatics (in Varaždin): Dr B. AURER
Metallurgy (in Sisak): Dr A. MARKOTIĆ
Academy of Fine Arts: D. BABIĆ
Academy of Dramatic Arts: M. RODICA-VIRAG
Academy of Music: I. GJADROV
Graphics: Dr S. BOLANČA
Textiles Technology: Dr I. SOLJAČIĆ
Geotechnics (in Varaždin): Dr I. GOTIĆ
Traffic and Transport: Dr J. BOŽIĆEVIĆ
Pedagogical Sciences: Dr I. SOVIĆ

College

Inter-University Centre Dubrovnik: 20000 Dubrovnik, Frana Bulića 4, POB 104; tel. (20) 413-626; fax (20) 413-628; f. 1972; an independent institution for international co-operation in teaching and research; Dir-Gen. Prof. HYLKE TROMP.

CUBA

Learned Societies

GENERAL

Academia de Ciencias de Cuba (Cuban Academy of Sciences): Capitolio Nacional, Havana 10200; tel. 626606; fax 338054; f. 1962; attached research institutes: see Research Institutes; National Archive: see Libraries and Archives; Pres. Dr ROSA ELENA SIMEÓN; publs *Boletín del Archivo Nacional* (annually), *Estudios de Historia de la Ciencia y la Tecnología* (annually), *Estudios de Politica Científica y Tecnología* (annually), *Boletín Señal* (weekly), *Boletín de Síntesis, Cablegráfica* (monthly), *Revista Ciencias Técnicas, Físicas y Matemáticas* (2 a year), *Revista Ciencias Biológicas* (2 a year), *Revista Ciencias de la Tierra y del Espacio* (2 a year), *Actas Botánicas Cubanas* (annually), *Poeyana* (annually), *Revista Cubana de Ciencias Sociales* (2 a year), *Datos Astronómicos para Cuba* (annually), *Datos Astronómicos para el Caribe* (2 a year), *Boletín Climática* (annually), *Boletín Meteorológico Marino* (3 a year), *Revista Cubana de Meteorología* (2 a year), *Resumen Climático de Cuba* (annually), *Boletín Oficial de la ONIITEM* (annually), *Revista Ciencia de la Información* (quarterly), *Directorio Biotec* (annually), *Anuario L.L. sobre estudios Lingüísticos*, *Anuario L.L. sobre estudios Literarios*, *Tablas de Mareas* (annually).

Ateneo de La Habana (Havana Athenaeum): Avda 5 No. 608, Vedado, Havana; f. 1902; Pres. Dr JOSÉ M. CHACÓN Y CALVO; Sec. Dr JOSÉ ENRIQUE HEYMANN Y DE LA GÁNDARA.

Casa de las Américas (House of the Americas): Calle 3ra esquina a G, El Vedado, Havana 10400; tel. 552706; telex 511019; fax 334554; f. 1959; cultural instn supporting Latin American literature, art and science; organizes festivals, exhibitions, conferences; maintains the 'José A. Echeverría' public library; documentary centre; Pres. ROBERTO FERNÁNDEZ RETAMAR; publs *Casa de las Américas* (3 a year), *Conjunto* (quarterly), *Boletín de Música* (2 a year), *Anales del Caribe* (annually), *Criterios* (annually).

EDUCATION

Consejo Nacional de Universidades (National University Council): Ministerio de Educación Superior, Ciudad Libertad, Havana 1; f. 1960; co-ordinating body for educational and scientific activities and for the administration of the four nat. univs; Pres. JOSÉ RAMÓN FERNÁNDEZ; Sec. Ing. MIGUEL MARRERO VALLET.

Oficina Regional de Cultura de la Unesco para América Latina y el Caribe/Unesco Regional Office for Culture in Latin America and the Caribbean: Apdo 4158, Havana 4; tel. 327741; fax 333144; f. 1950; library of 14,000 vols; Dir Dra GLORIA LÓPEZ MORALES; publs *Informaciones Trimestrales, Oralidad*.

LANGUAGE AND LITERATURE

Academia Cubana de la Lengua (Cuban Academy of Language): Avda 19 No. 502, Esq. a E, Vedado, Havana 4; f. 1926; corresp. of the Real Academia Española (Madrid); Dir Dra DULCE M. LOYNAZ; Sec. Dr DELIO CARRERAS.

Unión de Escritores y Artistas de Cuba (Writers' and Artists' Union of Cuba): Calle 17 No. 351, Vedado, Havana; tel. 324551; f. 1961; 4,589 mems; Pres. CARLOS MARTÍ BRENES; Exec. Sec. MARTIZA HERNANDEZ; publs. *Ediciones Unión, La Gaceta de Cuba* (monthly), *Unión* (quarterly), *Literatura Cubana* (2 a year).

MEDICINE

Sociedad Cubana de Hipnosis (Cuban Hypnosis Society): Gaveta postal 6773, Havana 10600; tel. 791410; fax 8686150; f. 1986; 300 mems; Pres. Dr BRAULIO MARTÍNEZ PERIGOD; Exec. Sec. Dr MOISÉS ASÍS.

Sociedad Cubana de Historia de la Medicina (Cuban Society for the History of Medicine): Calle L No. 406 esq. 23 y 25, Vedado, Havana 4; e-mail amaro@abril.sld.cu; Pres. Dr RUBÉN RODRÍGUEZ GAVALDÁ; Sec. Dra MARÍA DEL CARMEN AMARO CANO; publ. *Cuadernos*.

Sociedad Cubana de Radiología (Cuban Radiology Society): Calle L 406 esq. 23 y 25, Vedado, Havana 10400; f. 1968; Pres. Prof. Dr CARLUS UGARTE; Sec. Prof. Dr JORGE BANASCO.

TECHNOLOGY

Sociedad Cubana de Ingenieros (Cuban Engineers' Association): Avda de Bélgica 258, Havana; f. 1908; 500 mems; library of 9,000 vols; Pres. Ing. GUSTAVO STERLING; Sec. Ing. HONORATO COLETE; publ. *Revista* (every 2 months).

Research Institutes

AGRICULTURE, FISHERIES AND VETERINARY SCIENCE

Centro de Investigación para el Mejoramiento Animal (Research Centre for the Improvement of Livestock): Carretera Central Km 21½, Loma de Tierra, Cotorro, Havana; tel. (7) 338909; f. 1970; library of 4,000 vols; Dir JOSÉ R. MORALES; publ. *Revista Cubana de Reproducción Animal* (2 a year).

Centro de Investigaciones Pesqueras (Fisheries Research Centre): Barlovento, Santa Fé, Playa, Havana; f. 1959; library of 4,230 vols, 1,500 periodicals; Dir Lic. ADELA PRIETO T.; publ. *Ciencia y Tecnología Pesquera* (quarterly).

Estación Experimental Apícola (Experimental Station for Beekeeping): Arroyo Arenas, El Cano, La Lisa, Havana 19190; tel. (7) 220027; fax (7) 662318; f. 1982; library of 1,800 vols; Dir ADOLFO M. PÉREZ PIÑEIRO.

Instituto Cubano de Investigaciones de los Derivados de la Caña de Azúcar (ICIDCA) (Cuban Institute for Research on Sugar Cane By-Products): Vía Blanca y Carretera Central 804, Apdo 4026, San Miguel del Padrón, Havana; fax 338236; e-mail icidca@ceniai.inf.cu; f. 1963; library of 7,000 vols; Dir LUIS O. GÁLVEZ TAUPIER; publ. *Sobre los derivados de la Caña de Azúcar* (quarterly).

Instituto de Investigaciones Agropecuarias 'Jorge Dimitrov' (Jorge Dimitrov Livestock Research Institute): Carretera de Bayamo a Manzanillo, Km 17, Paralejo a Bayamo, Granma; tel. 5239; attached to Cuban Acad. of Sciences; Dir Dr ISMAEL LEONARD ACOSTA.

Instituto de Investigaciones Avícolas (Poultry Research Institute): Calle 15, No. 853 e/4 y 6, Vedado, Ciudad Havana.

Instituto de Investigaciones de Sanidad Vegetal (Research Institute for the Food Quality of Vegetables): Calle 110 No. 514 entre 5ta B y 5ta F, Miramar, Playa, Havana 11300; tel. (7) 229366; fax (7) 240535; e-mail inisav@ceniai.inf.cu.

Instituto de Investigaciones en Riego y Drenaje (Research Institute for Irrigation and Drainage): Avda Camilo Cienfuegos y calle 27, A. Naranjo, Havana.

Instituto de Investigaciones en Viandas Tropicales (Research Institute for Tropical Vegetables): Apdo 6, Santo Domingo 53000, Villa Clara; tel. (42) 42344; fax (42) 42201; e-mail inivit@quantum.inf.cu; f. 1967; library of 9,000 vols, Dir Dr SERGIO RODRIGUEZ MORALES; publ. *Agrotecnia de Cuba*.

Instituto de Investigaciones Forestales (Institute of Forestry Research): Calle 174 No 1723 e/ 17B y 17C, Siboney, Municipio Playa, Havana 16; f. 1969; library of 10,000 vols; Dir JUAN A. HERRERO ECHEVARRÍA; publ. *Revista Forestal Baracoa* (2 a year).

Instituto de Investigaciones Fundamentales en Agricultura Tropical 'Alejandro de Humboldt' (Alejandro de Humboldt Institute of Basic Research in Tropical Agriculture): Calle 2, Esq. a 1, Santiago de las Vegas; tel. (7) 579010; fax (7) 579014; e-mail inifat@ceniai.inf.cu; f. 1904; library of 2,600 vols; Dir Dr ADOLFO RODRÍGUEZ NODALS.

Instituto de Investigaciones para la Mecanización Agropecuaria (Research Institute for Mechanization in Livestock Farming): Avda de las 3 Palmas No. 13926, Capdevila, Havana.

Instituto de Investigaciones Porcinas (Pig Research Institute): Carretera del Guatao Km 1, Punta Brava, Bauta, Havana.

Instituto de Suelos y Agroquímica (Research Institute for Soils and Agrochemicals): Calle 150 y 21A, Siboney, Havana.

Instituto Tecnológico de la Caña de Azúcar 'Carlos M. de Cespedes' (Carlos M. de Cespedes Sugar-Cane Technology Institute): La Inagua, Apdo 164, Guantánamo, Oriente; Dir MIGDONIO CAUSSE.

ECONOMICS, LAW AND POLITICS

Instituto de Administración (Institute for Administration): Miguel E. Capote 351, Bayamo, Oriente; Dir AIDA RAMÍREZ.

EDUCATION

Instituto de Superación Educacional (ISE) (Institute of Educational Advancement): Ciudad Libertad, Marianao, Havana; Dir Dra MARÍA LUISA RODRÍGUEZ CÓLOMBIÉ.

HISTORY, GEOGRAPHY AND ARCHAEOLOGY

Instituto de Geografía Tropical (Institute of Tropical Geography): 13 No. 409 esquina F. Vedado, Plaza de la Revolución, Havana 10400; tel. (7) 324293; fax (7) 334616; f. 1962;

attached to Min. of Science, Technology and Environment; Dir Dr JOSÉ RAMÓN HERNÁNDEZ SANTANA.

LANGUAGE AND LITERATURE

Instituto de Literatura y Lingüística (Institute of Literature and Linguistics): Salvador Allende No. 710 esquina Soledad y Castillejo, Havana 10300; tel. 786486; f. 1793; attached to Min. of Science, Technology and the Environment; Dir Dra NURIA GREGORI TORADA; publs *Anuario Lingüístico, Anuario Literario*.

MEDICINE

Centro Nacional de Información de Ciencias Médicas (National Centre for Information on Medical Science): E No. 454, Entre 19 y 21 Vedado, Havana; tel. (7) 322004; fax (7) 333063; e-mail ojito@infomed.sld.cu; Dir Dr JEREMÍAS HERNÁNDEZ OJITO; publs *Revista Cubana de Medicina*, and other specialized medical journals.

Instituto Nacional de Higiene, Epidemiología y Microbiología (National Institute of Hygiene, Epidemiology and Microbiology): Infanta No. 1158/Llinás y Clavel, Havana 3; tel. 71479; telex 0511017; f. 1943; library of 3,000 vols; Dir Dr PEDRO MÁS BERMEJO.

Instituto Nacional de Oncología y Radiobiología de La Habana (National Institute of Oncology and Radiobiology in Havana): 29 y F, Vedado, Havana; tel 327297; telex 512662; fax 328480; f. 1961; library of 2,700 vols; Dir Prof. ROLANDO CAMACHO RODRÍGUEZ; publ. *Revista Cubana de Oncología*.

NATURAL SCIENCES

General

Centro de Estudios de Historia y Organización de la Ciencia 'Carlos J. Finlay' (Carlos J. Finlay Study Centre for the History and Organization of Science): POB 70, Cuba No. 460, Esquina Amargura y Fte. Rey, Havana; tel. 634823; f. 1977; attached to Cuban Acad. of Sciences; Dir Dr FRANCISCO GARCÍA VALLS; publs *Estudios de Historia de la Ciencia y la Tecnología* (annually), *Estudio de Politica Científica y Tecnológica* (annually).

Centro Nacional de Investigaciones Científicas (National Centre for Scientific Research): Avda 25 No. 15202 esq. 158, Reparto Cubanacán, Havana; tel. (7) 219446; fax (7) 330497; e-mail cnic@reduniv.edu.cu; f. 1965; 6 service laboratories; library of 100,000 vols; Dir Dr CARLOS GUTIERREZ CALZADO; publs *Revista CNIC Ciencias Biológicas*, (3 a year), *Revista CNIC Ciencias Químicas* (3 a year).

Centro Nacional para la Divulgación de la Ciencia y la Técnica (CNDCT) (National Centre for the Popularization of Science and Technology): Calle B, 352 esquina a 15 Vedado, Plaza de la Revolución, Havana 10400; tel. 301451; attached to Cuban Acad. of Sciences; Dir Lic. ROBERTO CARRASCO VILCHES; publs *Boletin Señal* (weekly), *Boletín de Síntesis Cablegráfica* (monthly).

Instituto de Oceanología (Institute of Oceanology): Calle 1ra. No. 18406 esquina 184 y 186, Rpto. Flores, Playa, Havana 12100; tel. 210342; f. 1965; attached to Cuban Acad. of Sciences; Dir Ing. JORGE FOYO HERRERA; publ. *Tablas de Mareas* (annually).

Biological Sciences

Centro Nacional de Producción de Animales de Laboratorio (CENPALAB) (National Centre for the Breeding of Laboratory Animals): Finca Tinabeque, Carretera de Bejucal, Cacahual, Santiago de las Vegas, Bejucal, Havana; tel. 3566; attached to Cuban Acad. of Sciences; Dir Dr FERNANDO GONZÁLEZ BERMÚDEZ.

Instituto de Ecología y Sistemática (Institute of Ecology and Systemization): Carretera Varona Km 3½, Capdevila Boyeros, Havana 14200; tel. 448819; f. 1959; attached to Cuban Acad. of Sciences; terrestrial ecology; Dir Dr PEDRO PÉREZ ALVAREZ; publs *Actas Botánicas* (annually), *Poeyana* (20 a year).

Mathematical Sciences

Instituto de Investigaciones Estadísticas (Institute for Statistical Research): Calle 28 No. 504 esq. 5a y 7a, Miramar, Municipio Playa, Havana; tel. 23815; f. 1982; library of 5,000 vols; Dir Dr RAMÓN SABADÍ RODRÍGUEZ; publs *Temas Estadísticos, Revista Estadística*.

Physical Sciences

Centro de Sismología (Centre for Seismology): Calle 17, No. 61 esquina 4 y 6, Rpto. Vista Alegre, Santiago de Cuba; tel. 41623; attached to Cuban Acad. of Sciences; Dir Ing. LUIS SIERRA QUESADA.

Instituto Cubano de Investigaciones Mineras y Metalúrgicas (Cuban Institute of Mineral and Metallurgical Research): Aguiar 207 e/Empedrado y Tejadillo, Havana; Dir CARLOS COCA OLIVER.

Instituto de Cibernética, Matemática y Física (ICIMAF) (Institute of Cybernetics, Mathematics and Physics): 15 esquina C. Vedado, Plaza de la Revolución, Havana 10400; attached to Cuban Acad. of Sciences; Dir Ing. RAIMUNDO FRANCO PARELLADA.

Instituto de Geofísica y Astronomía (Institute of Geophysics and Astronomy): Calle 212 No. 2906 entre 29 y 31, La Coronela, La Lisa, Havana 11600; tel. (7) 214331; fax (7) 339497; e-mail iga@cidet.icmf.inf.cu; f. 1964; attached to Min. of Science, Technology and the Environment; library of 1,000 vols; Dir Dra LOURDES PALACIO SUÁREZ; publ. *Datos Astronómicos para Cuba* (annually).

Instituto de Meteorología (Institute of Meteorology): Loma de Casablanca, Apdo 17032, Havana 11700; tel. (7) 617500; fax (7) 338010; attached to Min. of Science, Technology and Environment; Dir Dr TOMÁS GUTIERREZ PÉREZ ; publs *Revista Cubana de Meteorología* (2 a year), *Boletín Meteorológico Marino* (2 a year).

PHILOSOPHY AND PSYCHOLOGY

Instituto de Filosofía (Institute of Philosophy): Calzada No. 251 esq. J., Vedado, Havana 10400; tel. 321887; f. 1968; attached to Cuban Acad. of Sciences; library of 3,000 vols; Dir Dra OLGA FERNÁNDEZ RÍOS; publ. *Revista Cubana de Ciencias Sociales* (2 a year).

RELIGION, SOCIOLOGY AND ANTHROPOLOGY

Centro de Antropología (Centre for Anthropology): Buenos Aires No. 111 esquina Agua Dulce y Diana, Cerro, Havana 13000; tel. 708220; attached to Min. of Science, Technology and Environment; Dir Dra LOURDES SERRANO PERALTA.

Centro de Investigaciones Psicológicas y Sociológicas (CIPS) (Centre for Research in Psychology and Sociology): Calle 0 esquina 17 y 19 Vedado, Plaza de la Revolución, Havana 10400; tel. 328945; attached to Cuban Acad. of Sciences; undertakes socio-psychological surveys which relate to social politics in Cuba and the means of ensuring the participation of workers in the different levels of social planning; Dir Lic. ANGELA CASAÑAS MATA.

TECHNOLOGY

Centro de Desarrollo Científico de Montañas (Centre for the Scientific Development of Mountainous Regions): Matazón, Sabaneta, El Salvador, Guantanamo; tel. 99230; attached to Cuban Acad. of Sciences; Dir Ing. FRANCISCO VELÁZQUEZ RODRÍGUEZ.

Centro de Desarrollo de Equipos e Instrumentos Científicos (CEDIC) (Centre for the Development of Scientific Equipment and Instruments): Luz No. 375 esquina Compostela y Picota, Havana; tel. 612846; attached to Cuban Acad. of Sciences; laser technology and its application in medicine, nutrition and electronics; Dir Ing. LUIS EMILIO GARCÍA MAGARINO.

Centro de Diseño de Sistemas Automatizados de Computación (CEDISAC) (Centre for the Design of Automated Computer Systems): Industria esquina Dragones y San Jose, Havana 12400; tel. 626531; attached to Cuban Acad. of Sciences; Dir Lic. BEATRIZ ALONSO BECERRA.

Centro de Investigaciones de Energía Solar (Centre for Research into Solar Energy): Carretera Siboney, Km 5½ Abel Santa María, Santiago de Cuba; tel. 47186; attached to Cuban Acad. of Sciences; Dir Lic. JOSÉ S. CABRERA GARCÍA.

Centro de Investigaciones para la Industria Minero Metalúrgica (Research Centre of the Metal-Mining Industry): Finca 'La Luisa' Km. 1½, Carretera Varona No. 12028, Apdo 8067, Boyeros, Havana; tel. 442643; fax 802617; f. 1967; library of 4,000 vols; Dir EDUARDO ACEVEDO DEL MONTE; publs *Revista Tecnológica* (every 4 months), *Boletín de Información Factográficat* (2 a year), *Boletín de Información Señal* (monthly), *Resenas*, *Bibliografías temáticas*.

Instituto Tecnológico de Electrónica 'Fernando Aguado Rico' (Fernando Aguado Rico Technological Institute of Electronics): Belascoaín y Maloja, Havana; Dir Ing. GONZALO IGLESIAS Y RODRÍGUEZ-MENA.

Libraries and Archives

Havana

Archivo Nacional (National Archive): Compostela 906, Esq. a San Isidro, Havana; tel. 629436; fax 338089; e-mail arnac@ceniai.cu; f. 1840; 25,000 linear metres of archive material; library of 8,000 vols; Dir Dra BERARDA SALABARRÍA ABRAHAM; publ. *Boletín*.

Biblioteca Central 'Rubén Martínez Villena' de la Universidad de la Habana (Rubén Martínez Villena Central Library of the University of Havana): Vedado, Havana 4; tel. (7) 333768; fax (7) 335774; f. 1728; 945,000 vols; Dir Dr MARÍA CRISTINA SANTOS LABOURDETTE; publs *Biología* (1 a year), *Investigación Operacional* (3 a year), *Revista de Ciencias Matemáticast* (3 a year), *Revista de Investigaciones Marinas* (3 a year), *Revista del Jardín Botánico Nacional* (3 a year), *Revista Cubana de Educación Superior* (3 a year), *Revista Cubana de Física* (3 a year), *Revista Cubana de Psicología* (3 a year), *Universidad de la Habana* (1 a year), *Economía y Desarrollo* (3 a year), *Debates Americanos* (3 a year).

Biblioteca del Instituto Pre-universitario de La Habana (Library of the Havana Pre-University Institute of Education): Zuleta y San José, Havana; f. 1894; 32,000 books, newspaper library; Dir José Manuel Castellanos Rodiles.

Biblioteca 'Fernando Ortiz' del Instituto de Literatura y Lingüística (Fernando Ortiz Library of the Institute of Literature and Linguistics): Salvador Allende 710 entre Soledad y Castillejo, Havana 10300; tel. (7) 785405; f. 1793; 1,000,000 items; Librarian Lic. Pedro Luis Suárez Sosa.

Biblioteca Histórica Cubana y Americana (Cuban and American History Library): Municipio de La Habana, Oficina del Historiador de la Ciudad, Havana; f. 1938.

Biblioteca 'José Antonio Echeverría' (José Antonio Echeverría Library): Calle 3ra esquina a G, El Vedado, Havana 10400; tel. 552705; fax 334554; f. 1959; Caribbean and Latin American books; 150,000 vols, 8,500 journals; Dir Ernesto Sierra; publ. *Boletín* (monthly).

Biblioteca 'Manuel Sanguily' (Manuel Sanguily Library): Ministerio de Relaciones Exteriores, Calzada y G., Vedado, Havana; f. 1960; 29,512 vols; Dir Dra Madeleine Terán.

Biblioteca Nacional 'José Martí' (José Martí National Library): Apdo 6881, Avda de Independencia e/20 de Mayo y Aranguren, Plaza de la Revolución José Martí, Havana; tel. 708277; f. 1901; 2,628,800 items; Dir Marta Terry González; publs *Revista de la Biblioteca Nacional José Martí, Revista Bibliotecas, Indice General de Publicaciones Periódicas Cubanas, Bibliografía Cubana* (annually), *Catálogo Cuba en Publicaciones Extranjeras*.

Biblioteca Provincial 'Rubén Martínez Villena' (Rubén Martínez Villena Provincial Library): Obispo 160, Entre Mercaderes y San Ignacio, Edif. MINED, Havana; tel. 614895; f. 1960; 94,328 vols; spec. braille colln; Dir Lic. Ela Ramos Rodríguez.

Centro de Información Científica y Económica, Banco Nacional de Cuba (Scientific and Economic Information Center, National Bank of Cuba): Amargura 158, Havana 10100; tel. 628001; fax 48878269 (via Paris) ext. 35; f. 1950; periodicals and 29,000 books on economics, finance and banking; Man. Nuadis Planas García; Library Dept Chief Jorge Fernández Pérez; publs *Cuba: Half Yearly Economic Report, Economic Report* (annually).

Centro de Información y Documentación Agropecuario (Livestock Information and Documentation Centre): Gaveta postal 4149, Havana 4; tel. 818808; telex 1219; fax 335086; f. 1971; library of 20,000 vols, 1,400 journals; Dir Dr David Williams Cantero; publs numerous journals.

Instituto de Información Científica Tecnológica (IDICT) (Institute of Scientific and Technical Information): Capitolio Nacional, Apdo 2213, Havana 2; tel. 626501; fax 338237; f. 1963; attached to Min. of Science, Technology and Environment; library of 150,000 vols, 8,000 journals; Dir-Gen. Nicolas Garriga; publs. incl. *Ciencias de la Información* (quarterly), *Ciencia, Innovación y Desarrollo* (quarterly), *Boletín FID/CLA* (quarterly), *Newsletter* (quarterly).

Santiago

Biblioteca Central de la Universidad de Oriente (Central Library of the University of Oriente): Avda Patricio Lumumba s/n, Santiago de Cuba; tel. 31973; f. 1947; 42,000 vols; Librarian Lic. Maura González Pérez; publs *Revista Santiago, Revista Cubana de Química*.

Biblioteca Provincial 'Elvira Cape' (Elvira Cape Provincial Library): Calle Heredia 259, Santiago de Cuba 90100, Oriente; tel. 54836; f. 1899; 169,000 vols, 1,760 periodicals; Dir Rosa Digna Gutiérrez Calzado.

Museums and Art Galleries

Camagüey

Museo Ignacio Agramonte (Ignacio Agramonte Museum): Camagüey; paintings, furniture, relics from the colonial period.

Cárdenas

Museo Municipal Oscar M. de Rojas (Oscar M. de Rojas Muncipal Museum): Avda de José Martí, Cárdenas; f. 1903; exhibits relating to Martí; library; Curator Oscar M. de Rojas y Cruzat.

Havana

Acuario Nacional (National Aquarium): Ave. 1ra y Calle 60, Miramar, Playa, Havana 11300; tel. (7) 236401; fax (7) 241442; e-mail acuario@cidea.unepnet.inf.cu; f. 1960; attached to Cuban Acad. of Sciences; Dir Lic. Guillermo García Montero.

Jardín Botánico Nacional de Cuba (National Botanical Garden of Cuba): Carretera del Rocío Km 3½, CP 19230, Calabazar, Boyeros, Havana; tel. (7) 445525; fax (7) 335350; f. 1968; administered by Universidad de la Habana; library of 3,800 vols, 1,225 periodicals; herbarium; Dir-Gen. Dra. Angela Leiva; publs *Revista* (annually), *Index Seminum* (every 2 years), *Reporte Annual*.

Museo Agrícola (Agricultural Museum): Ministerio de Agricultura, Havana; Curator Archibald Durland y Nieto.

Museo Antropológico Montané (Montané Anthropological Museum): Facultad de Biología, Universidad de La Habana, Havana 4; tel. 329000; f. 1903; library of 5,000 vols; Dir Dr Antonio J. Martínez Fuentes.

Museo Casa Natal José Martí (House Museum of José Martí): Leonor Pérez 314, Havana; relics of José Martí and his works; Curator Maria de la Luz Ramirez Estrada.

Museo de Arte Colonial de la Habana (Havana Museum of Colonial Art): Plaza de la Catedral, Havana; housed in mansion built 1720; Dir Margarita Suárez.

Museo de Historia Natural 'Felipe Poey' (Felipe Poey Museum of Natural History): Departamento de Biología Animal y Humana, Facultad de Biología, Universidad de la Habana, Calle 25 e/J e I, Vedado, Havana 4; tel. 329000; fax 321321; f. 1842; zoology; library of 80,520 vols; Dir Lic. Martín Acosta Cruz.

Museo Ernest Hemingway (Ernest Hemingway Museum): Finca Vigía, San Francisco de Paula, Havana 19180; tel. 910809; f. 1962; house, library and personal items of Ernest Hemingway who lived here 1939–60; Dir Danilo M. Arrate Hernández.

Museo Municipal de Guanabacoa (Guanabacoa Muncipal Museum): Martí 108, Esquina a Versalles, Guanabacoa 11, Havana; tel. (7) 979117; f. 1964; popular Cuban religions of African origin; Dir Maria Cristina Peña Reigosa.

Museo Nacional y Palacio de Bellas Artes (National Museum and Palace of Fine Arts): Animas entre Zulueta y Monserrate, Havana Vieja 10200; tel. (7) 639042; fax (7) 613857; f. 1913; ancient Egyptian, Greek and Roman art, 16th- to 19th-century European art, Cuban art from the Colonial period to the present; Dir Pilar Fernández Prieto.

Attached museums:

Museo de Artes Decorativas (Museum of Decorative Arts): Calle 17, No. 502 entre D y E, Vedado, Havana 10100; tel. 320924; fax 613857; f. 1964; 17th- to 20th-century European and oriental decorative art; Dir Katia Varela.

Castillo de la Real Fuerza de la Havana (Castle of the Royal Garrison of Havana): O'Reilly entre Avda del Puerto y Tacón, Plaza de Armas, Havana Vieja 10100; tel. 616130; fax 613857; f. 1977; 20th-century ceramic exhibits, 16th-century fortification; Dir Alejandro G. Alonso.

Museo Napoleónico (Napoleonic Museum): San Miguel y Ronda, Havana; f. 1961; historical objects and works of art of Revolutionary and Imperial France; specialized library.

Museo Numismático (Numismatic Museum): Banco Central de Cuba, Oficios 8, Havana 1; tel. 615857; telex 1124; f. 1975; coins, banknotes, medals and decorations; library; Dir Inés Morales García.

Museo y Archivo Histórico Municipal de la Ciudad de La Habana (Havana Muncipal Historical Museum and Archive): Oficina del Historiador, Palacio de los Capitanes Generales, Plaza Carlos Manuel Céspedes, Havana; f. 1947; historical items from 1550 to the present.

Parque Zoológico Nacional (National Zoological Garden): Carretera de Varona Km 3½, Capdevila, Boyeros, Apdo 8010, Havana 10800; tel. (7) 441870; fax (7) 330802; f. 1975; attached to Cuban Acad. of Sciences; library of 1,300 vols; Dir Lic. Gilda del Cueto Jiménez.

Mariel

Museo de Pesca de la Escuela Naval del Mariel (Museum of Marine Fauna of the Mariel Naval Academy): Naval Academy, Mariel, Pinar del Río; f. 1943; specimens of deep-sea fish; Dir Luis Howell Rivero.

Matanzas

Museo Provincial de Matanzas (Matanzas Provincial Museum): Palacio de Junco, Calle de Milanés y Magdalena, Plaza de la Vigía, Matanzas; tel. 3195; f. 1959; history, natural history, decorative arts; library of 1,000 vols; Dir Lic. Gonzalo Domínguez Cabrera; publ. *Museo* (2 a year).

Remedios

Museo de Remedios 'José Maria Espinosa' (José Maria Espinosa Museum in Remedios): Maceo 32, Remedios; f. 1933; history, science, art; Dir. Alberto Vigil y Coloma.

Santiago

Museo 'Emilio Bacardi Moreau' (Emilio Bacardi Moreau Museum): Aguilera y Pio Rosado, Apdo 759, Santiago; tel. 8402; f. 1899; history, art; Curators José A. Arocha Rovira, Fidelia Pérez González.

Universities

UNIVERSIDAD DE LA HABANA

Calle San Lázaro esq. L, Vedado, Havana 4

Telephone: 7-3231, 70-5896

Founded 1728, reorganized 1976

Rector: Dr Fernando Rojas Avalos
Secretary-General: Lic. Isaura S. Sarmiento

Library: see Libraries
Number of teachers: 1,635
Number of students: 15,980

Publications: *Universidad de la Habana, Boletín Universitario,* and various scientific and technical publs.

DEANS

Faculty of Philosophy and History: Dr OSCAR GUZMÁN BETANCOURT
Faculty of Political Economy: Dra DELIA L. LÓPEZ GARCÍA
Faculty of Planning for the National Economy: Lic. ALFONSO FARNÓS MOREJÓN
Faculty of Accounting and Finance: Lic. JORGE MÁRQUEZ BUENO
Faculty of Psychology: FERNANDO GONZALEZ
Faculty of Arts and Letters: Dra ELENA SERRANO PARDIÑAS
Faculty of Journalism: Dra LÁZARA PEÑONES
Faculty of Foreign Languages: Lic. NURIA GARCÍA MENÉNDEZ
Faculty of Law: Dr LUIS SOLÁ VILA
Faculty of Physics: Dr CARLOS RODRÍGUEZ CASTELLANOS
Faculty of Mathematics: Dr FRANCISCO GUERRA VÁZQUEZ
Faculty of Chemistry: Dr JACQUES RIEUMONT BRIONES
Faculty of Geography: Lic. ARTURO RÚA DE CABO
Faculty of Pharmacology and Food: Dra RUTH DAYSI HENRÍQUEZ HERNÁNDEZ
Faculty of Biology: Lic. MARIO L. RODRÍGUEZ SUÁREZ
Faculty of Nuclear Sciences and Technology: Dr EVELIO BELLO VARELA

ATTACHED RESEARCH INSTITUTES

Departamento de Investigaciones Económicas en la Educación Superior: Dir Dra GRETA CRESPO GÓMEZ.

Departamento de Estudios para el Perfeccionamiento de la Educación Superior: Dir Ing. JESÚS GARCÍA DEL PORTAL.

Centro de Informática Aplicada a la Gestión: Dir Dra OLGA LODOS HERNÁNDEZ.

Centro de Investigaciones Marinas: Dir Dra MARÍA ELENA IBARRA MARTÍN.

Laboratorio de Investigaciones en Electrónica del Estado Sólido: Dir Dr PEDRO DÍAZ ARENCIBIA.

Centro de Estudios Demográficos: Dir Dr ERAMIS BUENO SÁNCHEZ.

Departamento de Investigaciones sobre los Estados Unidos: Dir Lic. ESTEBAN MORALES DOMÍNGUEZ.

Jardín Botánico Nacional: Dir Dra ANGELA LEYVA SANCHEZ.

UNIVERSIDAD DE ORIENTE

Avda Patricio Lumumba s/n, 90500 Santiago de Cuba

Telephone: (226) 31860
Fax: (226) 32689
E-mail: marcosc@rect.uo.edu.cu

Founded 1947
Academic year: September to July

Rector: Dr ENRIQUE J. MARAÑON REYES
Vice-Rectors: Dr PEDRO A. BEATÓN SOLER, Dr PEDRO HORRUITINER SILVA, ELIO CASTELLANOS, Dr PEDRO ARAFET PADILLA
Secretary-General: JOAQUÍN RODRÍGUEZ PEÑA
Librarian: Profa MYRIAM SANG SARABIA
Library: see Libraries and Archives

Number of teachers: 853
Number of students: 5,500 (undergraduate), 19,000 (postgraduate and continuing education)

Publications: *Revista Santiago* (every 6 months), *Revista Cubana de Química* (3 a year).

DEANS

Faculty of Natural and Exact Sciences: Dr ALEJANDRO GARCÉS CALVELO
Faculty of Economics: ULISES PACHECO
Faculty of Law: ZAIDA VALDÉS
Faculty of Social Sciences: Dra CARIDAD FRUTOS ESPINOSA
Faculty of Chemical Engineering: Dr WILLIAM SUÁREZ SANTOS
Faculty of Mechanical Engineering: Dr ROBERTO ZAGARÓ ZAMORA
Faculty of Electrical Engineering: Dr SERGIO CANO ORTIZ
Faculty of Building Construction: Arq. SONIA QUESADA MILIÁN

UNIVERSIDAD CENTRAL MARTA ABREU DE LAS VILLAS

Carretera a Camajuaní Km. 5½, CP 54830, Santa Clara, Villa Clara

Telephone: (422) 81178
Fax: (422) 81608
E-mail: uclvdri@ucentral.quantum.inf.cu

Founded: 1952
Academic year: September to July

Rector: Dr ANDRÉS OLIVERA RANERO
Vice-Rector: Dr FRANCISCO LEE TENORIO
Secretary-General: Lic. FERNANDO ECHERRI FERRANDIZ
Librarian: Ing. JOSÉ RIVERO DÍAZ

Library of 386,000 vols
Number of teachers: 962
Number of students: 5,436

Publications: *Centro Agrícola, Centro Azúcar, Construcción de Maquinaria, Islas* (quarterly).

DEANS

Faculty of Economics and Industrial Engineering: FELIPE GONZALEZ
Faculty of Mechanical Engineering: Dr CARLOS RENÉ GÓMEZ
Faculty of Electrical Engineering: Dr FRANCISCO HERRERA FERNÁNDEZ
Faculty of Chemistry and Pharmacy: SERAFÍN MACHADO
Faculty of Building: Dr MIGUEL PINO RODRÍGUEZ
Faculty of Social Sciences and Humanities: Dr EDGARDO ROMERO FERNÁNDEZ
Faculty of Mathematics, Computing and Physics: Dr RAFAEL BELLO PÉREZ
Faculty of Agricultural Sciences: Ing. PEDRO QUESADA

UNIVERSIDAD DE CAMAGÜEY

Carretera de Circunvalación Norte, Km 5½, Camagüey 74650

Telephone: 61019
Fax: 61126
E-mail: root@reduc.cmw.edu.cu

Founded as a branch of University of Havana 1967, present name 1974
State control
Academic year: September to July

Rector: Dr ANGEL VEGA GARCÍA
Vice-Rectors: Dr RAFAEL LARRUA, CARLOS BASULTO, JOSÉ LEÓN
Registrar: Lic. RAÚL GARRIGA CORZO
Librarian: Lic. SARA ARTILES VISBAL

Number of teachers: 450
Number of students: 3,200

Publication: *Revista de Producción Animal.*

DEANS

Faculty of Chemistry and Pharmacology: Ing. LUIS RAMOS
Faculty of Electromechanics: Dr LUIS CORRALES BARRIOS
Faculty of Construction: ANA ISABEL CARDOSO
Faculty of Economics: Lic. PEDRO LINO DEL POZO
Faculty of Law: Lic. NATALIA CARO
Faculty of Animal Sciences: Dr NELSON IZQUIERDO

HEADS OF DEPARTMENTS

Chemistry and Pharmacology:
- Chemical Engineering: Lic. NOELIA VARGAS
- Pharmacy: Lic. GILBERTO PARDO ANDREU
- Chemistry: MARLEN VILLALONGA
- English: Lic. ADDYS PALOMINO

Electromechanics:
- Electrical Engineering: Ing. DAVEL BORGES VASCONCELLOS
- Mechanical Engineering: Ing. DORIS VASCONCELLOS VILATÓ
- Physics: Lic. ELOY ORTIZ
- Computer Studies: Lic. BÁRBARA VALDEZ

Construction:
- Architecture: Arq. MARÍA ELENA GUTIÉRREZ
- Civil Engineering: Dr WILFREDO MARTÍNEZ LÓPEZ DEL CASTILLO
- Mathematics: Lic. JOSÉ MANUEL RUIZ SOCARRÁS

Economics:
- Economics: Dr JOSÉ PANTOJA GUERRA
- Accountancy: Dr ROLANDO LA TORRE GUIRCE
- Business and Public Administration: Lic. ANGELA PALACIOS
- Regional Development: Dr RAMÓN GONZÁLEZ FUENTES

Animal Sciences:
- Morphophysiology: NIRIAM NIETO MARTÍNEZ
- Veterinary Science: Dr MAGALY COLLANTES CÁNOVAS
- Agriculture: Dr MANUEL HERNÁNDEZ VICTORIA

ATTACHED INSTITUTES

Centre for Research in Education: Dir Dra MARÍA TERESA MORENO.

Centre for Research on Animal Production: Dir Ing. REDIMIO PEDRAZA OLIVERA.

Centre for Research on the Conservation of Historic Monuments: Dir Dra LOURDES GÓMEZ.

Centre for Research into the Repair of Equipment: Dir Ing. PABLO OÑOZ GUTIÉRREZ.

CENTRO UNIVERSITARIO DE PINAR DEL RÍO

Martí 270 esq. a 27 de Noviembre, Pinar del Río 20100

Telephone and fax: 5813
Telex: 053103

Founded 1972
State control
Academic year: September to August

Rector: Prof. Dr YNOCENTE BETANCOURT FIGUERAS
Vice-Rectors: Prof. Dr JOSÉ A. DÍAZ DUQUE, Prof. Dr ANGEL NOTARIO DE LA TORRE, Ing. ALFREDO GARCÍA RODRÍGUEZ
Secretary-General: Lic. MILAGROS DIAZ JEREZ
Librarian: Prof. Dr JORGE MARIN CLEMENTE

Number of teachers: 311
Number of students: 4,000

Publications: *Anuario Científico, Boletín de Geociencias, Cuadernos Científicos.*

DEANS

Faculty of Agronomy and Forestry: Dr FRANCISCO VALDES VALDES
Faculty of Economics: Lic. MAYRA CARMONA GONZÁLEZ
Faculty of Technical Sciences: Prof. Dr ANTONIO DE LA FLOR SANTALLA
Faculty of Mining: Dr ESTEBAN GARCÍA QUIÑONES

HEADS OF DEPARTMENTS

Physical Culture: Lic. GELASIO LÓPEZ GONZÁLEZ
Post-Graduate Studies: Lic. MARTA BERMÚDEZ CASTRO
Social Sciences: Dr ALBERTO RIVERA HERNÁNDEZ
Accounting: Dra MARÍA E. FERNÁNDEZ HERNÁNDEZ
Universal and Sectorial Economy: Lic. MARICELA GONZÁLEZ DÍAZ
Languages: Lic. PEDRO R. GOMÉZ MARRERO
Forestry Production: Dr FERNANDO HERNÁNDEZ MARTÍNEZ
Vegetable Production: Dr ALEIDO DÍAZ GUERRA
Botany: Lic. ANGELES DE LA TORRE TABARES
Chemistry: Lic. JUAN PASTOR BUSTAMANTE
Mathematics: Ing. MARÍA A. LEÓN SÁNCHEZ
Physics: Lic. JORGE SÁNCHEZ CABRERA
Computer Studies: Dr OSCAR GONZÁLEZ CHONG
Geology: Ing. CARLOS ALBERTO GARCÍA PÉREZ
Mechanics: Ing. JUAN C. HORTA GUTIERREZ
Electronics: Ing. CARLOS CANDANEDO CASTRO

AFFILIATED INSTITUTE

Orquideario Soroa: Apdo postal 5, Candelaria, Pinar del Río; f. 1952; study and conservation of orchids from Cuba and other countries; includes herbarium, laboratories and specialized library; Dir Ing. ROLANDO PEREZ MARQUEZ.

Colleges

Instituto Superior Agrícola: Carretera a Morón Km. 9, Ciego de Avila 69450; tel. 2-5702; fax (7) 335040; e-mail isaca@reduniv.edu.cu; f. 1978; agronomy, economics, irrigation, agricultural mechanization; 270 teachers, 1,500 students; library of 34,000 vols; Rector Dr HIPÓLITO PERALTA BENÍTEZ.

Instituto Superior de Ciencas Médicas de Camagüey: Carretera Central Oestey Madam Curie, Camagüey; tel 92100; telex 31104; f. 1981 from medical faculty of Univ. of Camagüey 70100; schools of dentistry, medicine, nursing; biomedical, clinical and sociomedical research; 587 teachers; 3,500 students; Rector Dr ALBERTO CLAVIJO CORTIELES; pubs. *Revista de Cienicias Médicas de Camagüey* (every 6 months).

Instituto Superior de Relaciones Internacionales 'Raul Roa García': Calle 22 111 e/1ra y 3ra, Miramar, Playa, Havana; tel. 22-2571; f. 1971; library of 14,000 vols; special collection containing the personal library of Dr Raúl Roa García; 61 teachers; Rector Dr OSCAR GARCÍA FERNÁNDEZ; Sec.-Gen. Dr RAFAEL MORENO.

Instituto Superior Politecnico 'José Antonio Echeverría': Calle 127, s/n, CUJAE, Marianao, CP 19390, Havana; tel. (7) 200641; telex 512217; fax (7) 277129; e-mail julio@tesla.ispjae.edu.cu; f. 1976, fmrly Faculty of Technology of University of Havana; library of 165,000 vols; 1,000 teachers; 5,000 students; Rector Dr ANTONIO ROMILLO TARKE; Sec. Ing. RAÚL CAPETILLO ALVAREZ; publs *Ingeniería Estructural y Vial, Ingeniería Electrónica, Automática y Comunicaciones, Ingeniería Industrial, Ingeniería en Transporte, Ingeniería Hidráulica, Ingeniería Energética, Arquitectura y Urbanismo* (all 3 a year).

DEANS

Architecture: RUBÉN BANCROFFT HERNÁNDEZ
Civil Engineering: NORBERTO MARRERO DE LEÓN
Electrical Engineering: ANGEL FERRAT ZALDO
Mechanical Engineering: DIMAS HERNÁNDEZ GUTIÉRREZ
Chemical Engineering: LOURDES ZUMALACÁRREGUI DE CÁRDENAS
Industrial Engineering: JOSÉ A. DÍAZ BATISTA

RESEARCH CENTRES

Hydraulic Research Centre.
Electroenergetic Test Research Centre.
Microelectronic Research Centre.

Universidad 'Camilo Cienfuegos' de Matanzas: Km 3½ Carretera Vía Blanca, Matanzas; tel. (52) 61013; telex 52248; fax (52) 53101; f. 1972.

Rector: Ing. JORGE RODRÍGUEZ PÉREZ
Vice-Rectors: Ing. MIGUEL SARRAF GONZÁLEZ, (Teaching), Dr ARTURO BOFFIL PLACERES (Research), Ing. FERNANDO ENRIQUE MATÍAS (Economics)
Library of 81,000 vols
Number of teachers: 470
Number of students: 4,060

Publications: *Revista Pastos y Forrajes, El Universitario.*

DEANS

Faculty of Mechanical Engineering: Dr ROBERTO RAMÍREZ MESA
Faculty of Chemistry: Dra JUANA ZOILA JUNCO
Faculty of Agronomy: Ing. REYNOLD VALENZUELA GALINDO
Faculty of Economics: Lic. ANGEL MENDOZA TORRIENTE
Faculty of Languages: Lic. ZOE DOMÍNGUEZ GÓMEZ

Universidad de Holguín 'Oscar Lucero Moya': Avda 20 Aniversario, Nuevo Holguín, Gaveta Postal 57, 80100 Holguín; tel. 481302; e-mail isth@reduniv.edu.cu; f. 1973; library of 90,000 vols; 290 teachers; 2,893 students; Rector Dr SEGUNDO PACHECO TOLEDO; Librarian Dr RAMÓN MARTÍNEZ BATISTA; publs *Diéresis, Ambito.*

DEANS

Faculty of Engineering: Ing. MANUEL VEGA ALMAGUER
Faculty of Economics: Lic. SIGFREDO CARBALLOSA PARRA

Schools of Art and Music

Conservatorio Alejandro García Caturla: Avda 31 y Calle 82, Marianao, Havana.

Conservatorio de Música Amadeo Roldán: Rastro y Lealtad, Havana.

Escuela Nacional de Bellas Artes 'San Alejandro' (National School of Fine Arts): Dragones 308, Havana; f. 1818 as Academia de San Alejandro; formerly Escuela de Pintura, organized by the French painter, Jean Baptiste Vermay; 800 students; Dir DOMINGO RAMOS ENRÍQUEZ.

CYPRUS

Learned Societies

GENERAL

Etaireia Kypriakon Spoudon (Society of Cypriot Studies): POB 1436, Nicosia; tel. (2) 463205; f. 1936; aims: the collection, preservation and study of material concerning all periods of the history, dialect and folklore of Cyprus; the Society maintains a Museum of Cypriot Folk Art; 250 mems; library of Kypria 4,000 vols; Pres. KYPROS CHRYSANTHIS; Sec. A. SPYRIDAKIS; publs *Demosievmata, Kypriakai Spoudai* (Cypriot Studies, annually).

BIBLIOGRAPHY, LIBRARY SCIENCE AND MUSEOLOGY

Library Association of Cyprus: POB 1039, Nicosia; f. 1962; promotes library science and professional activities; 45 mems; Pres. COSTAS D. STEPHANOU; Sec. PARIS G. ROSSOS.

HISTORY, GEOGRAPHY AND ARCHAEOLOGY

Cyprus Geographical Association: POB 3656, Nicosia; tel. (2) 463205; f. 1968; research and study of the geography of Cyprus; aims to improve the teaching of geography, and safeguard professional interests of geographers; 200 mems; library of 500 vols; Pres. ANDREAS SOPHOCLEOUS; Gen. Sec. ANDREAS CHRISTODOULOU; publ. *The Geographical Chronicles* (annually).

Research Institutes

GENERAL

Cyprus Research Centre (Kentron Epistemonikōn Erevnōn): POB 1952, Nicosia; under the jurisdiction of the Ministry of Education and Culture; f. 1967; aims: the promotion of scientific research in Cyprus with special reference to the historico-philological disciplines and the social sciences; research library; sections: (a) Historical Section: editing and publication of the sources of the history of Cyprus; (b) Ethnographic Section: collection, preservation, and publication of materials relating to the local culture of the island; (c) Philological and Linguistic Section: collection of lexicographic materials, the preparation of a historical dictionary of the Cypriot dialect, and the editing of literary and dialect texts; (d) Oriental Section: promotion of oriental studies in Cyprus, with special reference to Ottoman studies; (e) Archives Section: collection and preservation of MSS. and documents relating to all aspects of the society of Cyprus; Dir Dr COSTAS YIANGOULLIS; publs *Texts and Studies of the History of Cyprus, Publications, Epeteris* (annually).

HISTORY, GEOGRAPHY AND ARCHAEOLOGY

Cyprus American Archaeological Research Institute: 11 A. Demetriou St, Nicosia 1066; tel. (2) 451832; fax (2) 461147; e-mail caaridir@spidernet.com.cy; f. 1978; one of the American Schools of Oriental Research; promotes the study of archaeology and related disciplines in Cyprus; encourages communication among scholars interested in Cyprus and provides residence facilities; library of 6,000 books, 100 periodicals; representative ceramic, geological, lithic, archaeometallurgical and faunal reference collections, slide archive; Dir Dr NANCY SERWINT.

Libraries and Archives

Famagusta

Municipal Library: POB 41, Famagusta; f. 1954; reference and lending sections, including many books on Cyprus and in several languages; the Famagusta Municipal Art Gallery, with a historical maps section, is attached; 18,000 vols; Librarian and Curator CH. CHRISTOFIDES.

Limassol

Municipal Library: Limassol; f. 1945; 12,000 vols; Librarian Miss A. KYRIAKIDES.

Nicosia

Cyprus Library: Eleftheria Square Post Office, Nicosia; tel. 30-3180; f. 1987; 60,000 vols; special collection: Cypriot studies; Librarian ANDREAS G. THOMAS.

Cyprus Museum Library: POB 2024, Nicosia; tel. (2) 304167; fax (2) 303148; f. 1883; incorporated in Dept of Antiquities 1934; 15,000 vols (excluding bound periodicals), Pierides collection of 1,400 vols; Librarian MARIA D. ECONOMIDOU; publs *Annual Report of the Department of Antiquities Cyprus*, *Report of the Department of Antiquities Cyprus*.

Cyprus Turkish National Library: Kızılay Ave, Nicosia; tel. (2) 283257; f. 1961; 56,000 vols; Chief Librarian FATMA ÖNEN.

Library of the Archbishop Makarios III Foundation: POB 1269, Nicosia; tel. (2) 430008; fax (2) 430667; f. 1983; research library; incorporates the library of Phaneromeni, the library of the Holy Archbishopric of Cyprus, the library of the Society of Cypriot Studies, and the Foundation library; 55,000 vols relating mostly to Greek, Byzantine and post-Byzantine studies, Christian theology and recent political history of Cyprus; Dir Dr A.P. VITTI.

Library of the Pedagogical Institute: C/o Ministry of Education, Nicosia; tel. (2) 305933; f. 1972; 35,000 vols, mainly on education; Librarians MARIA DEMETRIOU, SOULA AGAPIOU.

State Archives of the Republic of Cyprus: Ministry of Justice and Public Order, Nicosia; tel. (2) 302664; fax (2) 667680; f. 1978; 9,000 vols; 159,000 Secretariat Archives files, 2.82 km of linear shelving of archival holdings; State Archivist EFFY PARPARINOU.

Sultan's Library: Evcaf, Nicosia; f. by Sultan Mahmud II; collection of Turkish, Persian and Arabic books.

Museums and Art Galleries

Limassol

Cyprus Medieval Museum: Limassol Castle; tel. (5) 330419; f. 1987; rich collection of local and imported pottery from the Early Christian, Byzantine and medieval periods; unique collections of medieval tombstones, coats of arms and architectural exhibits from palaces, castles and churches; coins, arms, cannons, etc.

Nicosia

Cyprus Folk Art Museum: POB 1436, Nicosia; tel. (2) 463205; f. 1950; Cyprus arts and crafts from early to recent times; mainly Cypriot Greek items; Dir Dr ELENI PAPADEMETRIOU.

Cyprus Historical Museum and Archives: Pentelis 50, Strovolos, Nicosia; f. 1975; a private enterprise to create a cultural centre; aims to tape-record accounts of historical events in Cyprus, to photocopy all existing historical material about Cyprus, to liaise with the Ministry of Culture and Greek historians, to find and publicize historical treasures in private collections; library of 3,000 vols; Pres. PETROS STYLIANOU; Gen. Sec. CLEITOS SYMEONIDES.

Cyprus Museum: POB 2024, Nicosia; tel. (2) 302189; f. 1882; inc. in Dept of Antiquities 1934; collection of (1) pottery from the Neolithic and Chalcolithic periods to the Graeco-Roman Age; (2) terracotta figures of the Neolithic Age to Graeco-Roman times, including the Ayia Irini group; (3) limestone and marble sculpture from the Archaic to the Graeco-Roman Age; (4) jewellery from the Neolithic period, especially Mycenaean (1400–1200 BC), to early Byzantine times, and coins from the 6th century BC to Roman times; (5) miscellaneous collections, including inscriptions (Cypro-Minoan, Phoenician, Cypro-syllabic, Latin, Greek), bronzes, glass, alabaster, bone, etc.; exhibitions of jewellery, seals, coins; reconstructed tombs; extensive reserve collections are available for students; an archaeological library (see above) is housed in the Cyprus Museum building and is open to students; Curator Dr PAVLOS FLOURENTZOS; publs *Report of the Department of Antiquities*, *Annual Report of the Director of Antiquities*, monographs.

Universities

EASTERN MEDITERRANEAN UNIVERSITY

POB 95, Gazi Mağusa, Turkish Republic of Northern Cyprus (via Mersin 10, Turkey)

Telephone: (Turkey 392) 366 6588

Telex: 57101

Fax (Turkey 392) 366 4479

E-mail: registrar@management.cc.emu.edu.tr

Founded 1979 as Higher Technological Institute; university status 1986

Language of instruction: English

State control

Academic year: September to June (two semesters)

Rector: Prof. Dr ÖZAY ORAL

Vice-Rectors: Assoc. Prof. Dr ERBİL AKBIL, Prof. Dr ABDULLAH ÖZTOPRAK, Assoc. Prof. Dr TAHİR ÇELİK, Assoc. Prof. Dr MEHMET ALTINAY

Secretary-General: CANER BARIN

Registrar: GÜROL ÖZKAYA

Librarian: FİLİZ ÇERMEN

Library of 110,000 vols, 900 periodicals
Number of teachers: 606 full-time, 124 part-time
Number of students: 10,300

Publications: *Journal of Cypriot Studies* (in Turkish and English, 4 a year), *EMU Bulletin* (in English, 1 a year), *AGENDA* (newsletter, in English, monthly).

DEANS

Faculty of Business and Economics: Assoc. Prof. Dr MEHMET TAHİROĞLU
Faculty of Engineering: Prof. Dr ERDİL RIZA TUNCER
Faculty of Architecture: Prof. Dr IBRAHIM NUMAN
Faculty of Law: Assoc. Prof. Dr TURGUT TURHAN
Faculty of Arts and Sciences: Assoc. Prof. Dr AYHAN BILSEL
Faculty of Communication and Media Studies: Prof. Dr AYSEL AZIZ
Faculty of Medicine: (vacant)

DIRECTORS

Institute for Research and Graduate Studies: Assoc. Prof. Dr ZEKA MAZHAR.
School of Computers and Technology: Assoc. Prof. Dr OSMAN YILMAZ
School of Tourism and Hospitality Management: Asst Prof. Dr TURGAY AVCI
English Preparatory School: Assoc. Prof. Dr GULSHEN MUSAYEVA

ATTACHED INSTITUTES

EMU European Research and Information Centre: Dir Assoc. Prof. Dr HASAN ALİ BIÇAK.

Centre for Ataturk Studies and Applied Research: Dir Assoc. Prof. Dr HASAN CICIOĞLU.

EMU Centre of Cyprus Studies: Dir ISMAİL BOZKURT.

Centre for Environmental Research and Policy: Dir METIN BAYTEKİN.

Centre for Cultural Heritage Studies and Archaeological Research: Dir Prof. Dr COŞKUN ÖZGÜNEL.

Information Technologies Research and Development Centre: Dir Asst Prof. Dr DERVIŞ DENİZ.

UNIVERSITY OF CYPRUS

Kallipoleos 75, POB 537, 1678 Nicosia

Telephone: (2) 756186
Fax (2) 756198

Founded 1989
State control
Languages of instruction: Greek and Turkish
Academic year: September to June

President: MICHALAKIS A. TRIANTAFYLLIDES
Vice-President: ANDREAS PATSALIDES
Rector: Prof. MILTIADES CHACHOLIADES
Vice-Rector: Prof. NICOLAS PAPAMICHAEL
Director of Administration and Finance: Dr NICOS VAKIS
Librarian: (vacant)

Number of teachers: 139
Number of students: 2,234

DEANS

Faculty of Economics and Management: Prof. CHRISTAKIS CHARALAMBOUS
Faculty of Humanities and Social Sciences: Assoc. Prof. YIANNIS E. IOANNOU
Faculty of Letters: Prof. MICHAEL PIERIS
Faculty of Pure and Applied Sciences: Assoc. Prof. CHARIS R. THEOCHARIS

PROFESSORS

Faculty of Humanities and Social Sciences:
- DAVY, J., Foreign Languages and Literature
- DEMETRIOU, A., Education
- HAZAI, GY., Turkish Studies
- NATSOPOULOS, D., Education

Faculty of Economics and Management:
- CHACHOLIADES, M., Economics
- CHARALAMBOUS, C., Public and business Administration
- PASHIARDES, P., Economics
- SPANOS, A., Economics
- TRIGEORGIS, L., Public and Business Administration
- ZENIOS, ST., Public and Business Administration

Faculty of Pure and Applied Sciences:
- KERAVNOU-PAPAILIOU, E., Computer Science
- PAPAMICHAEL, N., Mathematics

Faculty of Letters:
- CHRYSOS, E., History and Archaelogy
- PIERIS, M., Byzantine and Modern Greek Studies

EUROPEAN UNIVERSITY OF LEFKE

Gemıkonağı, Lefke, Mersin 10, Turkey
Telephone: (Turkey 392) 727-7362
Fax (Turkey 392) 727-7528

Founded 1990
Language of instruction: English
Controlled by Cyprus Science Foundation
Academic year: October to July

Rector: Dr HALÜK KABAALIO ĞLU
Vice-Rector: Dr MALCOLM MARSH
Chief Administrative Officer: AHMET ATANER
Registrar: ESAT HILMI IŞCAN
Librarian: HELEN GIERFELD

Library of 10,000 vols
Number of teachers: 61
Number of students: 820

DEANS

Faculty of Economics and Administrative Sciences: Assoc. Prof. Dr OSMAN KÜCÜKAHMETOĞLU
Faculty of Architecture and Engineering: Dr KARIM HADJRI (acting)
Faculty of Arts and Sciences: Dr MALCOLM WALSH (acting)

HEADS OF DEPARTMENT

Faculty of Economics and Administrative Sciences:
- Business and Economics: Assoc. Prof. Dr OSMAN KÜCÜKAHMETOĞLU
- International Relations: Dr LEONARD STONE

Faculty of Architecture and Engineering:
- Architecture and Interior Architecture: Dr KARIM HADJRI
- Civil Engineering: Dr MALEK BATEYNAH

Faculty of Arts and Sciences
- Computer Science: Dr LAMI KAYA
- English: Dr NEIL BRATTON
- Journalism and Broadcasting: Dr BEKIR AZGIN

ATTACHED INSTITUTE

Institute of Languages and Communication Sciences: Dir ESTAT TÜLEK.

Colleges

Cyprus College: POB 2006, Nicosia; tel. (2) 462062; telex 4646; f. 1961; 2-year associate degree courses, 3- and 4-year bachelor degree courses in business administration and computer science, MBA programme; 51 teachers, 1,020 students; library of 21,000 vols; Dir ANDREAS ELEFTHERIADES; Dean of Admissions MARINA ALEXANDROU; publs *The Observer, Journal of Business & Society.*

Cyprus College of Art: Lemba Paphos; tel. 245-557; f. 1969; one-year post-graduate course in painting/sculpture; three year diploma course in fine arts; also part-time courses and summer school; Dir STASS PARASKOS.

Cyprus Forestry College: Prodromos, Limassol; tel. (5) 462048; fax (5) 462646; f. 1951; technical-level and advanced training in forestry; 7 teachers, 42 students; library of 1,800 vols, 7 periodicals; Principal CHR. ALEXANDROU.

Cyprus International Institute of Management: 21 Akademias Ave, Aglandjia, POB 378, Nicosia; tel. (2) 330052; fax 331121; f. 1990; 1-year full-time and 2-year part-time courses leading to MBA and MPSM degrees and Advanced Diploma; library of 3,000 vols; Dir Dr JIM LEONTIADES.

Higher Technical Institute: POB 423, Nicosia; tel. 305030; telex 4070; fax 494953; f. 1968; 3-year courses in civil, electrical, mechanical and marine engineering, computer studies; 90 teachers; 655 students; library of 11,000 vols; Dir DEMETRIOS LAZARIDES; publ. *HTI Review* (annually).

Intercollege (International College): 6 Makedonitissa Ave, POB 4005, Nicosia; tel. (2) 357735; telex 4969; fax (2) 357481; f. 1980; private control; instruction in English; undergraduate and postgraduate courses lead to qualifying examinations for local, British and US degrees; also centres at Limassol and Larnaca; 70 teachers; 1,700 students (350 at Limassol and 340 at Larnaca); library of 20,000 vols; Dean of Academic Affairs ANDREAS POLEMITIS; Executive Dean NICOS PERISTIANIS; publ. *Cyprus Review* (2 a year).

Mediterranean Institute of Management: POB 536, 1679 Nicosia; tel. (2) 377992; fax (2) 376872; f. 1976; postgraduate management diploma course; library of 7,000 vols; 19 teachers, 30 students; Dir THEODOROS IOANNOU.

University College of Arts and Science: 10 Pikionis St, NAAFI Area, POB 1243, Limassol; tel. 66336; (br. at Nicosia: 59 Archbishop Makarios Ave, POB 2140, Nicosia; tel. 41876); f. 1967; library of 6,500 vols; 19 teachers, 125 students; first degree and diploma courses; Vice-Chancellor and Principal N. M. MICHAELIDES; Librarian Mrs A. NICOLAOU; publ. *Annual Journal.*

CZECH REPUBLIC

Learned Societies

GENERAL

Česká Akademie Věd (Czech Academy of Sciences): 111 42 Prague 1, Národní tř. 3; tel. (2) 24-22-03-84; fax (2) 24-24-05-31; divisions of Life and Chemical Sciences (Dir Dr HELENA ILLNEROVÁ), Humanities and Social Sciences (Dir Dr VILÉM HEROLD), Mathematics and Physical and Earth Sciences (Dir Ing. KAREL JUNGWIRTH; 112 academicians, 202 corresp. mems, 88 foreign mems; attached research institutes: see Research Institutes; library and archive; see Libraries and Archives; Pres. Prof. RUDOLF ZAHRADNÍK; Chair. of Scientific Ccl Dr BEDŘICH VELICKÝ; Admin. Dir Ing. LUDĚK KOPŘIVA; publs incl. *Acta entomologica bohemica, Acta technica, Acta virologica, Aplikace matematiky, Archeologické rozhledy, Archív orientální, Biologia Plantarum, Biologické listy, Bulletin of the Astronomical Institutes of the Czech Republic, Byzantinoslavica, Collection of Czech Chemical Communications, Czech Journal of Physics, Czech Mathematical Journal, Časopis pro mineralogii a geologii, Časopis pro pěstováni matematiky, Česká literatura, Česká mykologie, Česká fysiologie, Česká psychologie, Česká rusistika, Český časopis historický, Český časopis pro fysiku, Český lid, Dějiny věd a techniky, Ekonomicko-matematický obzor, Estetika, Filozofický časopis, Folia biologica, Folia geobotanica et phytotaxonomica, Folia microbiologica, Folia morphologica, Folia parasitologica, Folia zoologica, Hudební věda, Chemické listy, Kybernetika, Lidé a země, Listy filologické, Naše řeč, Nový Orient, Památky archeologické, Pedagogika, Philologica Pragensia, Photosynthetica, Phyziologia bohemica, Pokroky matematiky, fyziky a astronomie, Politická ekonomie, Právník, Preslia, Přírodovědné práce ústavů ČAV v Brně, Rozpravy České akademie věd, Sborník České geografické společnosti, Silikáty, Slavia, Slezský sborník, Slovo a slovesnost, Sociologický časopis, Studia geophysica et geodaetica, Umění, Vesmír, Věstník České akademie věd, Věstnik České společnosti zoologické, Věstník Ústředního ústavu geologického, Zdravotní technika a vzduchotechnika, Živa.*

AGRICULTURE, FISHERIES AND VETERINARY SCIENCE

Česká Akademie Zemědělských Věd (Czech Academy of Agricultural Sciences): 117 05 Prague 1, Těšnov 65; tel. 232-05-82; fax 232-88-98; f. 1924; sections of Crop Production (Chair. (vacant)), Livestock Production (Chair. (vacant)), Veterinary Medicine (Chair. Doc. MVDr KAREL HRUŠKA), Farm Technology, Construction and Energy (Chair. (vacant)), Foodstuffs Equipment and Technology (Chair. Prof. Ing. PAVEL KADLEC), Human Nutrition and Food Quality (Chair. Prof. Ing. JAN POKORNÝ), Economics, Management, Sociology and Information (Chair. Doc. Ing. ZDENĚK PODĚBRADSKÝ), Forestry (Chair. Ing. JOSEF KONOPKA), Soil Science and Land Improvement (Chair. BOHDAN JURÁNI); 179 mems; Pres. (vacant); publs *Rostlinná výroba* (Plant Production), *Živočišná výroba* (Animal Production), *Veterinární medicína* (Veterinary Medicine), *Zemědělská technika* (Agricultural Technology), *Zemědělská ekonomika* (Agricultural Economy), *Lesnictví* (Forestry), *Ochrana rostlin* (Plant Protection), *Genetika a šlechtění* (Genetics and Breeding), *Zahradnictví* (Gardening), *Potravinářské vědy* (Food Sciences).

Česká společnost pro vědy zemědělské, lesnické, veterinární a potravinářské (Czech Society for Agriculture, Forestry, Veterinary Sciences and Food Technology): 160 21 Prague 6, Suchdol VŠZ; tel. 32-36-40; f. 1968; 750 mems; Pres. Prof. Ing. F. HRON; Sec. Doc. Dr M. VALLA.

ARCHITECTURE AND TOWN PLANNING

Obec architektů (Society of Architects): 118 45 Prague 1, Letenská 5; tel. (2) 57-32-10-68; fax (2) 57-32-10-51; f. 1989; 1,300 mems; Pres. JIŘÍ MOJŽÍŠ; publ. *Architekt* (fortnightly).

ECONOMICS, LAW AND POLITICS

Česká společnost ekonomická (Czech Economic Association): 110 00 Prague 1, Tř. Politických vězňů 11; tel. 24-21-05-71; f. 1962; 600 mems; Pres. Dr P. KYSILKA; Sec. Dr L. KLAUSOVÁ; publ. *Bulletin* (3 a year).

Česká společnost pro mezinárodní právo (Czech Society for International Law): 116 91 Prague 1, Národní tř. 18; tel. (2) 24-91-22-58; fax: (2) 24-91-04-95; f. 1969; 96 mems; Pres. JUDr V. MIKULKA; Sec. JUDr Ing. J. ZEMÁNEK; publ. *Studie z mezinárodního práva* (Studies in International Law).

Česká společnost pro politické vědy (Czech Society for Political Sciences): 137 60 Prague 3, Nam. W. Churchilla 4; tel. 24-09-52-04; fax 24-22-06-57; e-mail skaloud@vse.cz; f. 1964; 200 mems; Pres. Prof. JAN ŠKALOUD; Sec. VLADIMÍR PROROK; publ. *Politologická Revue* (2 a year).

EDUCATION

Česká komise pro UNESCO (Czech Commission for Co-operation with UNESCO): 118 00 Prague 1, Toskán, Hradčanské nám. 5; tel. 24-31-05-42; fax 24-31-05-43.

Česká pedagogická společnost (Czech Society for Education): 660 88 Brno, Arne Nováka 1; tel. (5) 41-12-11-36; fax (5) 41-12-14-06; e-mail rybicka@dahlia.vszbr.cz; f. 1964; 350 mems; Pres. Doc. Dr Z. VESELÁ; Sec. Dr M. RYBIČKOVÁ; publ. *Pedagogická orientace* (quarterly).

FINE AND PERFORMING ARTS

Asociace hudebních umělců a vědců (Association of Music Artists and Musicologists): 118 01 Prague 1, Maltézské nám. 1; tel. 53-36-61; f. 1990; 1,200 mems; Pres. Mgr LUBOŠ SLUKA; Exec. Sec. MARCELA POSEJPALOVÁ; publ. *Hudební rozhledy* (monthly).

Česká hudební společnost (Czech Music Society): 150 00 Prague 5, Janáčkovo nábř. 59; tel. (2) 53-08-68; fax (2) 53-15-82; f. 1973; 5,000 mems; Pres. MÍLA SMETÁČKOVÁ; Sec.-Gen. EVA ŠTRAUSOVÁ; publ. *Information* (monthly).

Český filmový a televizní svaz (FITES) (Czech Film and Television Association): 120 00 Prague 2, Pod Nuselskými schody 3; tel. and fax (2) 691-03-10; f. 1966; 760 mems; Pres. MARTIN SKYBA.

Český spolek pro komorní hudbu (Czech Society for Chamber Music): C/o Česká filharmonie Rudolfinum, 110 00 Prague 1, Alšovo nábřeží 12; f. 1894; 3,500 mems.

Divadelní ústav (Theatre Institute): 110 00 Prague 1, Celetná 17; tel. 24-81-27-54; fax 232-61-00; f. 1956; research and documentation on Czech theatre; Czech centre of the International Theatre Institute (ITI); library of 100,000 vols; Dir ONDŘEJ ČERNÝ; publs *Theatre Czech* (2 a year), *Ročenka českých divadel* (annually), *Informační servis Divadelního ústavu* (monthly), *Divadelní noviny* (2 a month), *Loutkář* (10 a year), *Divadelní revue* (quarterly).

Společnost pro estetiku (Society for Aesthetics): 110 00 Prague 1, Celetná 20; tel. 24-49-13-84; f. 1969; Pres. PhDr H. JAROŠOVÁ; Sec. K. NOVOTNÁ.

Unie výtvarných umělců (Union of Creative Artists): 110 00 Prague 1, Masarykovo nábr. 250; tel. 29-22-15; fax 29-24-42; e-mail uvucr@brn.pvnet.cz; f. 1990; 3,000 mems; Pres. VÁCLAV KUBÁT; Sec.-Gen. VÍT WEBER; publs *Výtvarné umění* (quarterly), *Atelier* (fortnightly), *Technologia Artis* (annually), *Art Folia* (annually).

HISTORY, GEOGRAPHY AND ARCHAEOLOGY

Česká archeologická společnost (Czech Archaeological Society): 118 01 Prague 1, Letenská 4; tel. (2) 24-51-12-29; f. 1919; 580 mems; Pres. Dr K. SKLENÁŘ; Sec. Dr P. VAŘEKA.

Česká demografická společnost (Czech Demographic Society): 130 67 Prague 3, Nám. W. Churchilla 4; f. 1964; 450 mems; Pres. ZDENĚK PAVLÍK; Sec. FELIX KOSCHIN.

Česká geografická společnost (Czech Geographical Society): 128 00 Prague 2, Oldřichova 19; f. 1894; 805 mems; Pres. Assoc. Prof. I. BIČÍK; Sec. Dr D. DRBOHLAV; publ. *Sborník* (journal, quarterly).

Matice moravská (Moravian Society of History and Literature): 602 00 Brno, Gorkého 14; tel. (5) 75-00-50; fax (5) 75-30-50; f. 1849; 560 mems; Pres. Prof. Dr JAN JANÁK; Sec. Dr JIŘÍ MALÍŘ; publ. *Časopis Matice moravské* (2 a year).

LANGUAGE AND LITERATURE

Český esperantský svaz (Czech Union of Esperantists): 111 21 Prague 1, PS 1069; tel. and fax (2) 80-36-08; f. 1969; 1,300 mems; Pres. Ing. V. KOČVARA; publ. *Starto* (6 a year).

Czech Centre of International PEN: 118 00 Prague 1, POB 23; tel. (2) 57-07-27-83; fax (2) 57-07-25-09; f. 1924; 207 mems; Pres. J. STRÁNSKÝ; Sec. Ing. L. LUDVIKOVÁ.

Literárněvědná společnost (Literary Society): 110 00 Prague 1, Valentinská 1; tel. 232-01-67; f. 1934; 285 mems; Pres. Dr SLAVOMÍR WOLLMAN; Sec. JOSEF VLÁŠEK.

Obec spisovatelů (Society of Writers): 111 47 Prague 1, Národní 11; tel. 235-83-88; Pres. PhDr MILAN JUNGMANN.

MEDICINE

Česká imunologická společnost (Czech Society for Immunology): 142 20 Prague 4, Vídeňská 1083; tel. (2) 475-25-19; fax (2) 44-47-22-78; e-mail tlaskalo@biomed.cas.cz; f. 1986; 600 mems; Pres. Dr HELENA TLASKALOVÁ; Sec. Dr MARTIN BILEJ; publ. *Imunologický zpravodaj* (3 a year).

Česká lékařská společnost J. E. Purkyně (J. E. Purkyně Czech Medical Society): 120 26 Prague 2, Sokolská 31; tel. 24-91-51-95; fax 24-21-68-36; f. 1947; Pres. Prof. MUDr JAROSLAV BLAHOŠ; publs 27 medical journals.

NATURAL SCIENCES

General

Český svaz vědeckotechnických společností (Czech Association of Scientific and Technical Societies): 116 68 Prague 1, Novotného lávka 5; tel. (2) 21-08-22-95; fax (2) 24-23-74-03; e-mail dah@csvts.cz; f. 1990; Pres. Ing. DANIEL HANUS; Sec. Ing. ZDENKA DAHINTEROVÁ.

Společnost pro dějiny věd a techniky (Society of the History of Science and Technology); 170 78 Prague 7, Kostelní 42; tel. (2) 90-02-89-32; fax (2) 37-91-51; e-mail iso@ntm.anet.cz; f. 1965; 350 mems; library of 20,000 vols; Pres. Dr PAVEL DRÁBEK; Sec. (vacant); publ. *Dějiny věd a techniky* (quarterly).

Biological Sciences

Česká biologická společnost (Czech Biological Society): 662 43 Brno, Joštova 10; tel. (5) 42-12-62-68; fax (5) 42-12-62-00; f. 1922; 1,550 mems; Pres. Prof. Dr O. NEČAS; Sec. Dr R. JANISCH.

Česká botanická společnost (Czech Botanical Society): 128 01 Prague 2, Benátská 2; tel. 29-79-41; f. 1912; 1,040 mems; library of 33,700 vols; Chair. Dr J. HOLUB; Sec. Dr L. HROUDA; publs *Preslia* (quarterly), *Zprávy ČBS* (irregular).

Česká parazitologická společnost (Czech Society for Parasitology): 128 44 Prague 2, Viničná 7; tel. (2) 21-95-32-06; fax (2) 29-97-13; f. 1993; 167 mems; Pres. Prof. J. KULDA; Sec. Dr P. HORÁK; publ. *Zprávy České parazitologické společnosti* (quarterly).

Česká společnost bioklimatologická (Czech Society for Bioclimatology): 141 31 Prague 4, Boční II 1401; tel. (2) 67-10-33-21; fax (2) 76-15-49; f. 1965; 140 mems; Pres. Dr V. KREČMER; Sec. Dr V. PASÁK; publ. *Digests of Science Reports* (annually).

Česká společnost entomologická (Czech Entomological Society): 128 00 Prague 2, Viničná 7; tel. (2) 29-87-26; f. 1904; 1,050 mems; library of 19,000 vols; Pres. Dr SVATOPLUK BÍLÝ; Sec. Dr DAVID KRÁL; publ. *Klapalekiana* (2 a year).

Česká společnost histo- a cytochemická (Czech Society for Histochemistry and Cytochemistry): 128 00 Prague 2, Studničkova 2; tel. 29-17-51; f. 1962; 210 mems; Pres. Prof. MUDr Z. LOJDA; Sec. MUDr I. JULIŠ.

Česká společnost pro biomechaniku (Czech Society for Biomechanics): 160 00 Prague 6, J. Martiho 31; tel. and fax (2) 20-61-02-19; e-mail otahal@ftvs.cuni.cz; f. 1990; 168 mems; Pres. S. OTAHAL; Sec. M. SOCHOR; publ. *Bulletin* (2 a year).

Česká společnost zoologická (Czech Zoological Society): 128 44 Prague 2, Viničná 7; tel. 29-46-06; f. 1927; 350 mems; library of 16,000 vols; Pres. Prof. Dr J. BUCHAR; Sec. Dr K. ABSOLON; publ. *Acta Soc. Zool. Bohemicae* (quarterly).

Česká vědecká společnost pro mykologii (Czech Scientific Society for Mycology): 111 21 Prague 1, POB 106; tel. 24-49-72-59; f. 1946; 220 mems; Pres. Dr ZDENĚK POUZAR; Sec. Dr ALENA KUBÁTOVÁ; publs *Czech Mycology*, *Mykologické Listy* (quarterly).

Československá společnost mikrobiologická (Czechoslovak Society for Microbiology): 142 20 Prague 4, Vídeňská 1083; tel. (2) 475-24-94; fax (2) 471-32-21; f. 1928; 1,000 mems; Pres. L. EBRINGER; Sec. J. HÄUSLER; publs *Bulletin* (Czech, Slovak, quarterly), *Folia microbiologica* (English, every 2 months).

Mathematical Sciences

Jednota českých matematiků a fyziků (Union of Czech Mathematicians and Physicists): 117 10 Prague 1, Žitná 25; tel. (2) 24-23-08-77; fax (2) 24-22-76-33; f. 1862; 2,700 mems; Pres. Š. ZAJAC; Sec. M. KOČANDRLOVÁ; publs *Pokroky matematiky, fyziky a astronomie*, *Rozhledy matematicko-fyzikální*, *Matematika-Fyzika-Informatika*, *Učitel matematiky*.

Physical Sciences

Česká astronomická společnost (Czech Astronomical Society): 170 00 Prague 7, Královská obora 233; tel. 37-08-40; f. 1917; 700 mems; Pres. Dr JIŘÍ GRYGAR; Sec. Ing. JAN VONDRÁK.

Česká geologická společnost (Czech Geological Society): 182 09 Prague 8, V. Holešovičkách 41; tel. 66-00-93-23; fax 66-41-06-49; f. 1923; 700 mems; Pres. Dr V. KACHLÍK; Sec. Dr J. OTAVA; publ. *Journal* (quarterly).

Česká meteorologická společnost (Czech Meteorological Society): 143 06 Prague, Na Šabatce 17; tel. (2) 21-91-25-48; f. 1958; 230 mems; Pres. Prof. RNDr JAN BEDNÁŘ; Sec. RNDr EVA ŽIŽKOVÁ.

Česká společnost chemická (Czech Chemical Society): 116 68 Prague 1, Novotneho lavka 5; tel. (2) 21-08-23-83; fax (2) 792-45-64; e-mail drasar@uochb.cas.cz; f. 1866; 2,950 mems; Pres. Prof. RNDr MUDr VILIM SIMANEK; publs *Chemické Listy* (monthly), *Bulletin* (quarterly).

Spektroskopická společnost J. Marca Marci (J. Marcus Marci Spectroscopic Society): 166 29 Prague, Thákurova 7; tel. 311-23-43; f. 1949; 970 mems; Pres. Dr K. VOLKA; Sec. Dr M. RYSKA.

Vědecká společnost pro nauku o kovech (Metals Society): 616 62 Brno, Žižkova 22; tel. 726-84-17; fax 41-21-23-01; e-mail vrestal@chemi.muni.cz; f. 1966; 170 mems; Pres. Prof. VLADIMÍR ČÍHAL; Sec. Ing. BOŘIVOJ MILLION.

PHILOSOPHY AND PSYCHOLOGY

Jednota filosofická (Philosophical Association): 110 00 Prague 1, Jilská 1; tel. (2) 231-18-20; fax (2) 231-45-24; f. 1990; 250 mems; Chair. Dr L. HEJDÁNEK: Sec. Dr J. MOURAL; publ. *Česká Mysl* (occasionally).

RELIGION, SOCIOLOGY AND ANTHROPOLOGY

Česká společnost antropologická (Czech Anthropological Association): 120 00 Prague 2, Salmovská 5; tel. 29-83-23; f. 1964; 180 mems; Pres. RNDr J. JELÍNEK; Sec. Doc. Dr V. NOVOTNÝ; publ. *Zprávy* (quarterly).

Masarykova česká sociologická společnost (Masaryk Czech Sociological Society): 110 00 Prague 1, Husova 4; tel. 24-22-09-97; f. 1964; 414 mems; Pres. Dr ELIŠKA RENDLOVÁ; Sec. Doc. Ing. Dr VĚRA MAJEROVÁ.

Národopisná společnost (Ethnographical Society): 117 20 Prague 1, Národní třída 3; tel. (2) 53-54-95; f. 1893; 280 mems; Pres. Mgr JIŘINA VESELSKÁ; Sec. Dr HELENA MEVALDOVÁ; publ. *Národopisný věstník* (annually).

TECHNOLOGY

Česká společnost pro kybernetiku a informatiku (Czech Society for Cybernetics and Informatics): 182 07 Prague 8, Pod vodárenskou věží 2; tel. (2) 66-05-39-01; fax (2) 858-57-89; e-mail cski@utia.cas.cz; f. 1966; 500 mems; Pres. IVAN KRAMOSIL; Sec. DAGMAR HARMANCOVÁ; publs *Kybernetika* (in English, every 2 months), *Zpravodaj* (monthly).

Česká společnost pro mechaniku (Czech Society for Mechanics); 182 00 Prague 8, Dolejškova 5; tel. and fax (2) 858-77-84; e-mail csm@bivoj.it.cas.cz; f. 1966; 634 mems, 15 organizational mems; Pres. L. FRÝBA; Sec. M. OKROUHLÍK; publ. *Bulletin* (3 a year).

Česká společnost pro vědeckou kinematografii (Czech Society for Scientific Cinematography): 613 00 Brno, Zemědělská 1; tel. (5) 45-13-50-21; f. 1923; 150 mems; Pres. Ing. V. BOUČEK; Sec. Ing. L. RYGL; publ. *Bulletin* (annually).

Research Institutes

ARCHITECTURE AND TOWN PLANNING

Architecture and Building Foundation: 111 21 Prague 1, Václavské nám. 31; tel. 24-22-50-00; fax 24-21-60-04; e-mail fibiger@abf.cz; f. 1991; library of 10,000 vols; Dir Dr JAN FIBIGER; publs *ABF Forum* (quarterly), *Building Products Review* (annually), *Forum of Architecture and Building* (monthly).

ECONOMICS, LAW AND POLITICS

Národohospodářský ústav AV ČR (Economics Institute AS CR): 111 21 Prague 1, POB 882, Politických vězňů 7; tel. (2) 24-00-51-11; fax (2) 24-22-71-43; f. 1992; attached to Czech Acad. of Sciences; library of 25,000 vols; Dir Prof. JAN ŠVEJNAR.

Ústav pro výzkum mezinárodní politiky (Institute for International Political Studies): 110 00 Prague 1, Národní 18; tel. (2) 24-91-22-75; fax (2) 24-81-09-87; attached to Czech Acad. of Sciences; Dir Dr PETR MAREŠ.

Ústav státu práva AV ČR (Institute of State and Law AS CR): 116 91 Prague 1, Národní 18; tel. (2) 24-91-20-02; fax (2) 24-91-04-95; e-mail ilaw@ilaw.cas.cz; attached to Czech Acad. of Sciences; library of 40,000 vols, 100 periodicals; Dir Dr VLADIMÍR BALAŠ; publ. *Právník* (monthly).

EDUCATION

Institut základů vzdělanosti Univerzity Karlovy (Charles University Institute of Fundamental Learning): 120 00 Prague 2, Legerova 63; tel. (2) 90-00-26-17; attached to Czech Acad. of Sciences and Charles University; Dir Doc. PhDr ZDENĚK PINC.

FINE AND PERFORMING ARTS

Ústav dějin umění AV ČR (Institute of the History of Art AS CR): 110 00 Prague 1, Husova 4; tel. (2) 231-93-52; fax (2) 24-22-94-36; e-mail lahoda@kav.cas.cz; attached to Czech Acad. of Sciences; Dir Dr VOJTĚCH LAHODA.

Ústav pro hudební vědu AV ČR (Institute of Musicology AS CR): 160 00 Prague 6, Puškinovo nám. 9; tel. and fax (2) 24-31-12-12; e-mail uhv@site.cas.cz; attached to Czech Acad. of Sciences; library of 25,000 vols; Dir Prof. Dr IVAN POLEDŇÁK; publ. *Hudební věda* (musicology, 4 a year).

HISTORY, GEOGRAPHY AND ARCHAEOLOGY

Archeologický ústav AV ČR, Brno (Archaeological Institute AS CR, Brno): 612 64 Brno, Královopolská 147; tel. (5) 41-21-21-40; fax (5) 41-21-11-68; attached to Czech Acad. of Sciences; Dir Dr JAROSLAV TEJRAL.

Archeologický ústav AV ČR, Praha (Archaeological Institute AS CR, Prague): 118 01 Prague 1, Letenská 4; tel. (2) 57-32-09-42; fax (2) 53-93-61; e-mail sommer@site

.cas.cz; f. 1919; attached to Czech Acad. of Sciences; Dir Dr PETR SOMMER.

Historický ústav AV ČR (Institute of History AS CR): 190 00 Prague 9, Prosecká 76; tel. (2) 88-75-13; e-mail rakova@hiu.cas.cz; attached to Czech Acad. of Sciences; Dir Prof. JAROSLAV PÁNEK.

Orientální ústav AV ČR (Oriental Institute AS CR): 182 08 Prague 8, Pod vodárenskou věží 4; tel. (2) 66-05-24-84; fax (2) 858-56-27; e-mail kolmas@orient.cas.cz; f. 1922; attached to Czech Acad. of Sciences; Dir Prof. JOSEF KOLMAŠ; publs *Archív orientální* (quarterly), *Nový Orient* (monthly).

Slovanský ústav (Slavonic Institute): 110 00 Prague 1, Valentinská 1; tel. (2) 231-20-94; fax (2) 232-30-96; attached to Czech Acad. of Sciences; Dir Prof. ANTONÍN MĚŠTAN.

Ústav pro klasická studia AV ČR (Institute for Classical Studies AS CR): 120 00 Prague 2, Máchova 7; tel. and fax (2) 25-40-94; attached to Czech Acad. of Sciences; Dir Doc. Dr JAN BAŽANT; publs *Listy filologické* (2 a year), *Eirene* (on classical studies, annually).

Ústav pro soudobé dějiny AV ČR (Institute of Contemporary History AS CR): 118 40 Prague 1, Vlašská 9; tel. (2) 57-32-04-66; fax (2) 53-90-72; e-mail tuma@usd.cas.cz; attached to Czech Acad. of Sciences; Dir Dr OLDŘICH TŮMA; publ. *Soudobé dějiny* (4 a year).

Výzkumný ústav geodetický, topografický a kartografický (Research Institute of Geodesy, Topography and Cartography): 250 66 Zdiby 98; tel. (2) 685-73-75; fax (2) 685-70-56; e-mail odis@vugtk.anet.cz; f. 1954; library of 70,000 vols; Dir Dr Ing. VÁCLAV SLABOCH; publ. *Proceedings of Research Works* (every 2 years).

LANGUAGE AND LITERATURE

Ústav pro českou literaturu AV ČR (Institute of Czech Literature AS CR): 110 15 Prague 1, Nám. Republiky 1; tel. (2) 24-81-09-82; fax (2) 231-51-28; e-mail uclavcr@mail602.cz; f. 1947; attached to Czech Acad. of Sciences; library of 150,000 vols; Dir Dr VLADIMÍR MACURA; publ. *Česká literatura* (6 a year).

Ústav pro jazyk český AV ČR (Czech Language Institute AS CR): 118 51 Prague 1, Letenská 4; tel. (2) 57-32-09-42; fax (2) 53-62-12; attached to Czech Acad. of Sciences; Dir Prof. JIŘÍ KRAUS.

MEDICINE

Farmakologický ústav AV ČR (Institute of Pharmacology AS CR): 142 20 Prague 4 – Krč, Vídeňská 1083; tel. (2) 61-71-00-24; fax (2) 475-21-09; attached to Czech Acad. of Sciences; Dir Dr JAROSLAV SEIFERT.

Ústav experimentální medicíny AV ČR (Institute of Experimental Medicine AS CR): 142 20 Prague 4, Vídeňská 1083; tel. (2) 475-22-30; fax (2) 475-27-82; e-mail uemavcr@biomed.cas.cz; attached to Czech Acad. of Sciences; Dir Prof. JOSEF SYKA.

NATURAL SCIENCES

General

Ústav geoniky AV ČR (Institute of Geonics AS CR): 708 00 Ostrava – Poruba, Studentská 1768; tel. (69) 691-86-51; fax (69) 691-94-52; attached to Czech Acad. of Sciences; Dir Prof. PETR KONEČNÝ.

Biological Sciences

Biofyzikální ústav AV ČR (Institute of Biophysics AS CR): 612 65 Brno, Královopolská 135; tel. (5) 41-51-71-11; fax (5) 41-21-12-93; e-mail slotova@ibp.cz; attached to Czech Acad. of Sciences; Dir Dr JANA ŠLOTOVA.

Botanický ústav AV ČR (Institute of Botany AS CR): 252 43 Průhonice; tel. (2) 643-65-73; fax (2) 643-65-29; attached to Czech Acad. of Sciences; Dir Dr JAN ŠTĚPÁNEK.

Entomologický ústav AV ČR (Institute of Entomology AS CR): 370 05 Česke Budějovice, Branišovská 31; tel. (38) 408-22; fax (38) 436-25; attached to Czech Acad. of Sciences; Dir Prof. Dr FRANTIŠEK SEHNAL.

Fyziologický ústav AV ČR (Institute of Physiology AS CR): 142 20 Prague 4, Videňská 1083; tel. (2) 475-11-11; attached to Czech Acad. of Sciences; Dir Prof. PAVEL MAREŠ.

Hydrobiologický ústav AV ČR (Hydrobiological Institute AS CR): 370 05 České Budějovice, Na sádkách 7; tel. (38) 454-84; fax (38) 457-18; attached to Czech Acad. of Sciences; Dir Dr VĚRA STRAŠKRABOVÁ.

Mikrobiologický ústav AV ČR (Institute of Microbiology AS CR): 142 20 Prague 4, Vídeňská 1083; tel. (2) 44-47-22-72; fax (2) 44-47-12-86; e-mail spizek@biomed.cas.cz; attached to Czech Acad. of Sciences; Dir Dr JAROSLAV SPÍŽEK.

Parazitologický ústav AV ČR (Institute of Parasitology AS CR): 370 05 České Budějovice, Branišovská 31; tel. (38) 411-58; fax (38) 477-43; attached to Czech Acad. of Sciences; Dir Dr LIBOR GRUBHOFFER.

Ústav ekologie krajiny AV ČR (Institute of Vertebrate Biology AS CR): 603 65 Brno, Květná 8; tel. (5) 43-32-13-06; fax (5) 43-21-13-46; f. 1954; attached to Czech Acad. of Sciences; Dir Ing. MILAN PEŇÁZ; publ. *Folia Zoologica* (quarterly).

Ústav experimentální botaniky AV ČR (Institute of Experimental Botany AS CR): 165 02 Prague 6, Rozvojová 135; tel. (2) 20-39-04-53; fax (2) 20-39-04-56; e-mail machackova@ueb.cas.cz; attached to Czech Acad. of Sciences; Dir Prof. IVANA MACHÁČKOVÁ.

Ústav fyziky plazmatu AV ČR (Institute of Plasma Physics AS CR): 182 21 Prague 8, POB 17, Za Slovankou 3; tel. (2) 66-05-20-52; fax (2) 858-63-89; e-mail ipp@ipp.cas.cz; attached to Czech Acad. of Sciences; Dir Prof. PAVEL CHRÁSKA.

Ústav molekulární biologie rostlin AV ČR (Institute of Plant Molecular Biology AS CR): 370 05 České Budějovice, Branišovská 31; tel. (38) 817; fax (38) 414-75; attached to Czech Acad. of Sciences; Dir Dr VÍT NAŠINEC.

Ústav molekulární genetiky AV ČR (Institute of Molecular Genetics AS CR): 166 37 Prague 6, Flemingovo nám. 2; tel. (2) 20-18-31-11; fax (2) 24-31-09-55; e-mail office@img.cas.cz; attached to Czech Acad. of Sciences; Dir Prof. JAN SVOBODA; publs *Folia Biologica (Praha)* (6 a year), *Biologické listy* (4 a year).

Ústav organické chemie a biochemie AV ČR (Institute of Organic Chemistry and Biochemistry AS CR): 166 10 Prague 6, Flemingovo nám. 2; tel. (2) 20-18-31-11; fax (2) 24-31-00-90; attached to Czech Acad. of Sciences; Dir Dr ANTONÍN HOLÝ.

Ústav půdní biologie AV ČR (Institute of Soil Biology AS CR): České Budějovice, Na sádkách 7; tel. (38) 402-49; fax (38) 410-01; f. 1979; attached to Czech Acad. of Sciences; Dir Dr JOSEF RUSEK.

Ústav živočišné fyziologie a genetiky AV ČR (Institute of Animal Physiology and Genetics AS CR): 277 21 Liběchov, Rumburská 89; tel. (206) 69-70-24; fax (206) 69-71-86; attached to Czech Acad. of Sciences; Dir Dr PETR RÁB.

Mathematical Sciences

Český statistický úřad (Czech Statistical Office): 186 04 Prague 8, Sokolovská 142; tel. 82-73-19; fax 66-31-12-43; f. 1993; library of 175,000 vols; Pres. EDVARD OUTRATA; publs *Statistical Yearbook of the Czech Republic*, *Monthly Statistics of the Czech Republic*, *Quarterly Statistical Bulletin*, *Selected Economic and Social Indicators of the Czech Republic* (quarterly), *Bulletin Poland – Hungary – Czech Republic – Slovak Republic* (quarterly).

Matematický ústav AV ČR (Mathematical Institute AS CR): 115 67 Prague 1, Žitná 25; tel. (2) 22-21-16-31; fax (2) 22-21-16-38; e-mail mathinst@math.cas.cz; attached to Czech Acad. of Sciences; Dir Prof. KAREL SEGETH.

Physical Sciences

Astronomický ústav AV ČR (Astronomical Institute AS CR): 251 65 Ondřejov; tel. (204) 64-92-01; fax (204) 62-01-10; attached to Czech Acad. of Sciences; Dir Dr JAN PALOUŠ.

Český geologický ústav (Czech Geological Survey): 118 21 Prague 1, Klárov 3; tel. 24-00-22-06; fax 57-32-04-38; f. 1919; library: see Libraries; Dir Dr MILOŠ RŮŽIČKA; publs *Bulletin* (quarterly), *Journal of Geological Sciences* (annually), *Czech Mineralogical and Geological Bibliography* (annually), *Special Papers* (quarterly).

Fyzikální ústav AV ČR (Institute of Physics AS CR): 180 40 Prague 8, Na Slovance 2; tel. (2) 66-05-21-21; fax (2) 82-35-09; attached to Czech Acad. of Sciences; Dir Dr VLADIMÍR DVOŘÁK.

Geofyzikální ústav AV ČR (Geophysical Institute AS CR): 141 31 Prague 4, Boční II/1401; tel. (2) 67-10-33-27; fax (2) 71-76-15-49; e-mail gfu@ig.cas.cz; f. 1953; attached to Czech Acad. of Sciences; Dir Dr ALEŠ ŠPIČÁK; publs *Studia Geophysica et Geologica*, *Travaux Géophysiques*.

Geologický ústav AV ČR (Geological Institute AS CR): 165 02 Prague 6 – Lysolaje, Rozvojová 165; tel. (2) 24-31-14-21; fax (2) 24-31-15-78; e-mail inst@gli.cas.cz; f. 1957; attached to Czech Acad. of Sciences; library of 10,000 vols; Dir Dr PAVEL BOSÁK; publ. *Geolines* (2 a year).

Společná laboratoř chemie pevných látek AV ČR a Univerzity Pardubice (Joint Laboratory of Solid State Chemistry of the AS CR and Pardubice University): 530 09 Pardubice, Studentská 84; tel. (40) 603-61-50; fax (40) 603-60-11; attached to Czech Acad. of Sciences; Head Dr LADISLAV TICHÝ.

Státní úřad pro jadernou bezpečnost (State Office for Nuclear Safety): 110 00 Prague 1, Senovážné nám. 9; tel. (2) 21-62-41-11; fax (2) 21-62-47-04.

Ústav analytické chemie AV ČR (Institute of Analytical Chemistry AS CR): 611 42 Brno, Veveří 97; tel. (5) 726-81-11; fax (5) 41-21-21-13; attached to Czech Acad. of Sciences; Dir Dr PETR BOČEK.

Ústav anorganické chemie AV ČR (Institute of Inorganic Chemistry AS CR): 250 68 Řež u Prahy; tel. (2) 687-58-62; fax (2) 687-58-63; attached to Czech Acad. of Sciences; Dir Prof. LUBOMÍR NĚMEC.

Ústav chemických procesů AV ČR (Institute of Chemical Processes AS CR): 165 02 Prague 6, Rozvojová 135; tel. (2) 20-39-01-11; fax (2) 20-92-06-61; e-mail postmaster@icpt.cas.cz; attached to Czech Acad. of Sciences; Dir Prof. JIŘÍ DRAHOŠ.

Ústav fyzikální chemie Jaroslava Heyrovského AV ČR (Jaroslav Heyrovský Institute of Physical Chemistry AS CR): 182 23 Prague 8, Dolejškova 3; tel. (2) 858-30-14; fax (2) 858-23-07; attached to Czech Acad. of Sciences; Dir Prof. VLADIMÍR MAREČEK.

Ústav fyziky atmosféry AV ČR (Institute of Atmospheric Physics AS CR): 141 31 Prague 4, Boční II/1401; tel. (2) 76-97-00; fax (2) 76-37-45; e-mail ufa@ufa.cas.cz; f. 1964; attached to Czech Acad. of Sciences; library of 7,000 books, 20 periodicals; Dir Dr JAN LAŠTOVIČKA.

Ústav fyziky materiálů AV ČR (Institute of Physics of Materials AS CR): 616 62 Brno, Žižkova 22; tel. (5) 726-81-11; fax (5) 41-21-86-57; e-mail secretar@ipm.cz; f. 1956; attached to Czech Acad. of Sciences; Dir Prof. VÁCLAV SKLENIČKA; publ. *Metallic Materials* (6 a year).

Ústav jaderné fyziky AV ČR (Nuclear Physics Institute AS CR): 250 68 Řež; tel. (2) 66-17-11-11; fax (2) 685-70-03; e-mail ujf@ujf.cas.cz; attached to Czech Acad. of Sciences; Dir JAN DOBEŠ.

Ústav jaderného výzkumu Řež a.s. (Řež Nuclear Research Institute Řež plc): 250 68 Řež; tel. 66-17-11-11; telex 122626; fax 685-75-67; f. 1955; nuclear power and safety; library of 101,200 vols, 21,000 reports; Dir FRANTIŠEK PAZDERA; publs *Nucleon* (quarterly), *Annual Report*.

Ústav makromolekulární chemie AV ČR (Institute of Macromolecular Chemistry AS CR): 162 06 Prague 6; Heyrovského nám. 2; tel. (2) 36-03-41; fax (2) 36-79-81; e-mail office@imc.cas.cz; attached to Czech Acad. of Sciences; Dir Dr KAREL ULBRICH.

Ústav pro hydrodynamiku AV ČR (Institute of Hydrodynamics AS CR): 166 12 Prague 6, Pod Patankou 5; tel. (2) 24-31-06-71; fax (2) 32-21-81; attached to Czech Acad. of Sciences; Dir Dr PAVEL VLASÁK.

Ústav struktury a mechaniky hornin AV ČR (Institute of Rock Structure and Mechanics AS CR): 182 09 Prague 8, V Holešovičkách 41; tel. (2) 66-00-91-11; fax (2) 688-06-49; f. 1958; attached to Czech Acad. of Sciences; library of 28,000 vols; Dir VLADIMÍR RUDAJEV; publ. *Acta Montana* (in English, irregular).

Ústav termomechaniky AV ČR (Institute of Thermomechanics AS CR): 182 00 Prague 8, Dolejškova 5; tel. (2) 688-51-58; fax (2) 858-46-95; e-mail secr@it.cas.cz; f. 1954; attached to Czech Acad. of Sciences; library of 12,000 vols; Dir Dr IVAN DOBIÁŠ; publ. *Engineering Mechanics* (6 a year).

PHILOSOPHY AND PSYCHOLOGY

Centrum pro teoretická studia Univerzity Karlovy (Centre for Theoretical Study at Charles University): 110 00 Prague 1, Jilská 1; tel. (2) 231-18-20; fax (2) 231-45-24; e-mail ctsadm@mbox.cesnet.cz; attached to Czech Acad. of Sciences; Dir Dr IVAN M. HAVEL.

Filozofický ústav AV ČR (Institute of Philosophy AS CR): 110 00 Prague 1, Jilská 1; tel. (2) 24-22-09-79; fax (2) 24-22-02-57; attached to Czech Acad. of Sciences; Dir Dr MILAN MRÁZ.

Psychologický ústav AV ČR (Institute of Psychology AS CR): 602 00 Brno, Veveří 97; tel. (5) 726-81-11; fax (5) 74-46-67; attached to Czech Acad. of Sciences; Dir Dr LIDUŠKA OSECKÁ.

RELIGION, SOCIOLOGY AND ANTHROPOLOGY

Sociologický ústav AV ČR (Institute of Sociology AS CR): 110 00 Prague 1, Jilská 1; tel. (2) 24-22-02-56; fax (2) 24-22-02-78; e-mail socmail@soc.cas.cz; f. 1990; attached to Czech Acad. of Sciences; Dir Dr MICHAL ILLNER; publs *Czech Sociological Review* (in English, 2 a year), *Sociologický časopis* (4 a year).

Ústav pro etnografii a folkloristiku AV ČR (Institute of Ethnology AS CR): 120 00 Prague 2, Máchova 7; tel. (2) 25-46-40; fax (2) 25-04-30; attached to Czech Acad. of Sciences; Dir Dr STANISLAV BROUČEK.

TECHNOLOGY

Laboratoř anorganických materiálů (Laboratory of Inorganic Materials): 166 28 Prague 6, Technická 5; tel. (2) 24-31-03-71; fax (2) 24-31-10-82; attached to Czech Acad. of Sciences and Institute of Chemical Technology; Dir Prof. LUBOMÍR NĚMEC.

Státní výzkumný ústav textilní (State Textile Research Institute): 460 97 Liberec, U jezu 2; tel. 321; telex 186231; fax 244-42.

SVÚSS a.s. – Státní výzkumný ústav pro stavbu strojů (State Research Institute for Machine Design): 190 11 Prague–Běchovice; tel. (2) 74-32-33; telex 121333; fax (2) 74-20-78; f. 1946; library of 10,000 vols; Man. Dir Ing. PETR ŠTULC.

TESLA-Výzkumný ústav pro sdělovací techniku (TESLA Research Institute for Telecommunications): 142 21 Prague 4, Novodvorská 994; tel. 476-11-11; telex 121444; fax 472-35-51; f. 1952; library of 25,000 vols.

Ústav informatiky a výpočetní techniky AV ČR (Institute of Computer Science AS CR): 182 07 Prague 8, Pod vodárenskou věží 2; tel. (2) 688-42-44; fax (2) 858-57-89; attached to Czech Acad. of Sciences; Dir Prof. PETR HÁJEK.

Ústav přístrojové techniky AV ČR (Institute of Scientific Instruments AS CR): 612 64 Brno, Královopolská 147; tel. (5) 41-51-41-11; fax (5) 41-51-44-02; attached to Czech Acad. of Sciences; Dir Prof. RUDOLF AUTRATA.

Ústav pro elektrotechniku AV ČR (Institute of Electrical Engineering AS CR): 182 00 Prague 8, Dolejškova 5; tel. (2) 66-05-11-11; fax (2) 66-41-34-22; attached to Czech Acad. of Sciences; Dir Ing. IVO DOLEŽEL.

Ústav radiotechniky a elektroniky AV ČR (Institute of Radio Engineering and Electronics AS CR): 182 51 Prague 8, Chaberská 57; tel. (2) 688-18-04; fax (2) 688-02-22; e-mail ure@ure.cas.cz; f. 1955; attached to Czech Acad. of Sciences; library of 16,000 vols, 150 periodicals; Dir Ing. JAN ŠIMŠA.

Ústav teoretické a aplikované mechaniky AV ČR (Institute of Theoretical and Applied Mechanics AS CR): 190 00 Prague 9, Prosecká 76; tel. (2) 88-53-82; fax (2) 88-46-34; e-mail pirner@itam.cas.cz; attached to Czech Acad. of Sciences; Dir Prof. MIROŠ PIRNER.

Ústav teorie informace a automatizace AV ČR (Institute of Information Theory and Automation AS CR): 182 08 Prague 8, Pod vodárenskou věží 4; tel. (2) 688-46-69; fax (2) 688-49-03; attached to Czech Acad. of Sciences; Dir Prof. VLADIMÍR KUČERA.

VÚTS Liberec (Research Institute for Textile Machinery, Liberec): 461 19 Liberec, U jezu 4; tel. (48) 530-11-11; fax (48) 530-24-02; e-mail inf-vuts@falco.vslib.cz; f. 1951; library of 10,000 vols; Chief Man. MIROSLAV VÁCLAVÍK.

Libraries and Archives

Brno

Knihovna Moravské galerie v Brně (Library of the Moravian Gallery in Brno): 662 26 Brno, Husova 18; tel. (5) 42-21-57-53; fax (5) 42-21-57-58; f. 1873; 110,000 vols; Dir Dr HANA KARKANOVÁ; publs art catalogues, *Bulletin MG*.

Moravská zemská knihovna (Moravian Provincial Library): Brno, Kounicova 1; tel. (5) 42-16-21-50; fax (5) 74-77-58; f. 1808; humanities, social and natural sciences; 3,727,000 vols, 4,300 periodicals; spec. collns incl. technology, education; Dir Dr J. KUBÍČEK; publs various catalogues and bibliographies.

Ústřední knihovna a informační středisko Veterinární a farmaceutické univerzity (Central Library and Information Centre of the University of Veterinary and Pharmaceutical Sciences): 612 42 Brno, Palackého 1–3; tel. (5) 41-56-20-06; fax (5) 41-21-11-51; f. 1919; 197,000 vols; Librarian VÁCLAV SVOBODA; publ. *Acta veterinaria Brno* (quarterly).

České Budějovice

Státní vědecká knihovna (State Research Library): 370 59 České Budějovice, Riegrova ul. 3; tel. 278-34; f. 1885; 1,500,000 vols; Dir K. CEMPÍRKOVÁ.

Hradec Králové

Státní vědecká knihovna (State Research Library): 500 49 Hradec Králové, Pospíšilova 395; tel. (49) 551-48-71; fax (49) 551-17-81; e-mail knihovna@svkhk.cz; 273-81; f. 1949; 1,023,000 vols; Dir PhDr JOSEF VLČEK.

Liberec

Státní vědecká knihovna (State Research Scientific Library): 460 53 Liberec, Nám. Dr. E. Beneše 23; tel. 48-42-29-37; fax 48-42-11-04; e-mail library@svkli.cz; f. 1945; 663,000 books, 1,600 periodicals, 25,530 vols of printed music, 8,300 sound recordings, 3,100 vols of maps; Dir VĚRA VOHLÍDALOVÁ; publ. *Výroční zpráva* (annual report).

Olomouc

Státní vědecká knihovna (State Research Library): 771 77 Olomouc, Bezručova 2; tel. (68) 522-34-41; fax (68) 522-57-74; f. 1566; 1,660,000 vols, 1,448 MSS, 1,800 incunabula, 70,000 old prints; Dir Dr M. NÁDVORNÍKOVÁ; publ. *Knihovní obzor* (quarterly).

Ostrava

Státní vědecká knihovna v Ostravě (State Research Library in Ostrava): 728 00 Ostrava, Prokešovo nám. 9; tel. (69) 22-13-57; fax (69) 22-44-47; e-mail prchalova@svkos.cz; f. 1951; 863,000 vols; Dir LEA PRCHALOVÁ.

Ústřední knihovna Vysoké školy báňské v Ostravě (Central Library of the Technical University of Mining and Metallurgy of Ostrava): 708 33 Ostrava-Poruba, Tř. 17 listopadu 15; tel. 699-27-81; f. 1849; 450,000 vols; Dir DANIELA TKAČÍKOVÁ; publ. *Sborník vědeckých prací Vysoké školy báňské v Ostravě* (Transactions) (irregular).

Plzeň

Státní vědecká knihovna (State Research Library): 305 48 Plzeň, Smetanovy sady 2; tel. 722-40-80; fax 22-54-78; e-mail svk@svkpl.cz; f. 1950; 791,000 books, 1,700 current periodicals, 793,000 documents; Dir Dr JAROSLAV VYČICHLO; publs *Západni Čechy v tisku* (West Bohemia in Print), *Přírůstky zahraniční literatury* (foreign accessions, quarterly).

Prague

Archiv AV ČR (Archives of the Czech Academy of Sciences): 181 00 Prague 8 – Bohnice, V zámcích 56/76; tel. (2) 854-17-65; fax (2) 854-15-60; e-mail kostlan@cesnet.cz; f. 1953; attached to Czech Acad. of Sciences; 80,000 vols; Dir Dr ANTONÍN KOSTLÁN; publs *Studie o rukopisech* (Codicological Studies), *Studia historiae academiae scientiarum – Práce z dějin akademie věd* (Studies on the history of the Academy of Sciences).

Knihovna Akademie věd České republiky (Library of the Academy of Sciences of the Czech Republic): 115 22 Prague 1, Národní tř. 3; tel. 24-24-05-24; fax 24-24-06-11; f. 1952; 1,000,000 vols, 2,102 periodicals; HQ of the network of information centres and special libraries of academic institutes; Dir IVANA KADLECOVÁ.

Knihovna Archeologického ústavu AV ČR (Library of the Archaeological Institute of the Czech Academy of Sciences): 118 01

Prague, Letenská 4; tel. 57-32-09-42; fax 53-93-61; f. 1919; 63,000 vols; Chief Librarian EVA ŠOUFKOVÁ; publs *Památky archeologické* (2 a year), *Archeologické rozhledy* (quarterly), *Výzkumy v Čechách* (irregular), *Castrum Pragense* (irregular), *Castellologica bohemica*(irregular).

Knihovna Bedřicha Smetany (Bedřich Smetana Library): 115 72 Prague 1, Mariánské nám. 1; tel. 24-48-21-95; fax 232-82-30; f. 1893; music dept of City Public Library; 210,000 vols, 51 periodicals; Dir Mgr JANA NAVRÁTILOVÁ.

Knihovna Českého geologického ústavu (Library of the Czech Geological Survey): 118 21 Prague 1, Klárov 3; tel. (2) 24-00-21-11; fax (2) 24-51-04-80; e-mail jarch@ns.cgu.cz; f. 1919; 200,000 vols; Dir Dr MIROSLAV REJCHRT; publs *Geological Bibliography of the Czech Republic* (annually), *Library of the Geological Survey* (irregular).

Knihovna Evangelické teologické fakulty Univerzity Karlovy (Library of the Protestant Theological Faculty of the Charles University): 115 55 Prague 1, Černá 9; tel. (2) 21-98-86-01; fax (2) 21-98-82-15; f. 1919; 190,000 vols, 185 current periodicals; Librarian M. ŠÍROVÁ; publs *Communio Viatorum* (3 a year), *Teologická reflexe* (2 a year).

Knihovna Národní galerie (Library of the National Gallery): 119 04 Prague 1, Hradčanské nám. 15; tel. 20-51-45-99; e-mail library@ngprague.cz; f. 1887; 80,000 vols; Dir VÍT VLNAS.

Knihovna Národního muzea (Library of the National Museum): 115 79 Prague 1, Václavské nám. 68; tel. (2) 24-49-71-11; fax (2) 24-22-64-88; f. 1818; 3,600,000 vols; Dir Dr HELGA TURKOVÁ; publ. *Acta Musei Nationalis Pragae*, Series C (quarterly).

Knihovna Národního technického muzea (Library of the National Museum of Technology): 170 78 Prague 7, Kostelní 42; tel. (2) 20-39-91-11; fax 37-91-51; e-mail med@ntm.anet.cz; f. 1833; 200,000 vols; Chief Librarian RICHARDA SVOBODOVÁ.

Knihovna Orientálního ústavu Akademie věd České republiky (Library of the Oriental Institute of the Czech Academy of Sciences): 182 08 Prague 8, Pod vodárenskou věží 4; tel. (2) 66-05-24-01; fax (2) 689-72-60; e-mail prosecky@orient.cas.cz; f. 1922; Chinese library of 66,000 vols, general library of 200,000 vols; Librarian PhDr JIŘÍ PROSECKÝ; publs *Archív orientální* (quarterly), *Nový Orient* (monthly).

Knihovna Uměleckoprůmyslového muzea (Museum of Decorative Arts Library): 110 01 Prague 1, 17 listopadu 2; tel. (2) 232-84-72; fax (2) 24-81-16-66; e-mail upminfo@ms.anet.cz; f. 1885; 150,000 vols; Dir PhDr JARMILA OKROUHLÍKOVÁ; publs *Acta UPM* (irregular), catalogue.

Městská knihovna v Praze (Prague City Library): 115 72 Prague 1, Mariánské nám. 1; tel. (2) 22-11-33-00; fax (2) 22-11-33-05; e-mail bimkovaa@mlp.cz; f. 1891; 2,230,000 vols; 57 brs; Dir ANNA BIMKOVÁ.

Národní knihovna České republiky (National Library of the Czech Republic): 110 01 Prague 1, Klementinum 190; tel. (2) 24-21-32-76; fax (2) 24-22-77-96; e-mail sekret.ur@nkp.cz; f. 1366; 5,500,000 vols, 9,000 MSS, 3,900 incunabula, 500,000 prints; Dir Dr VOJTĚCH BALÍK: publs *Česká národní bibliografie ČR* (Czech National Bibliography, monthly), *Národní knihovna* (every 2 months), *Miscellanea oddělení rukopisů a starých tisků* (annually), etc.

Branch libraries:

Slovanská knihovna (Slavonic Library): 110 01 Prague 1, Klementinum 190; tel. (2) 24-22-60-02; e-mail milena.klimova@nkp.cz; 800,000 vols; Dir MILENA KLÍMOVÁ.

Národní lékařská knihovna (National Medical Library): 121 32 Prague 2, Nové Město, Sokolská 31; tel. (2) 24-26-60-48; fax (2) 24-26-60-51; e-mail nml@nlkdec.nlk.anet.cz; f. 1949; 85,000 vols, 1,000 current periodicals, 6,000 doctoral theses, 70,000 microfiches; WHO documentation centre; Dir OTAKAR PINKAS; Chief Librarian MICHAL GLYKNER; publs *Bibliographia medica čechoslovaca* (monthly), *Novinky literatury* (4 a year), *Referátový výběr* (series of 14 abstracts journals, quarterly or every 2 months).

Státní pedagogická knihovna Komenského: (Comenius State Library of Education): 116 74 Prague 1, Mikulandská 5; tel. 29-10-84; f. 1919; 400,000 vols; youth br. (Suk Library) of 50,000 vols; Dir LUDMILA ČUMPLOVÁ; publ. *Přehled pedagogické literatury* (survey of Czech pedagogic literature, every 2 months).

Státní technická knihovna (State Technical Library); 110 01 Prague 1, Mariánské nám. 5, POB 206; tel. (2) 21-66-31-11; fax (2) 24-22-92-24; e-mail techlib@stk.cz; f. 1718; 1,102,000 vols, 1,400 periodicals, 181,000 items of trade literature; Dir MARTIN SVOBODA.

Ústav dějin Univerzity Karlovy a Archiv Univerzity Karlovy (History Institute and Archives of Charles University): 116 36 Prague 1, Ovocný trh 5; history of education and of universities; 33,000 vols, 70 periodicals; Librarian Dr JIŘINA URBANOVÁ; publs *Acta Universitatis Carolinae, Historia Universitatis Carolinae Pragensis* (1 a year).

Ústav vědeckých informací 1. lékařské fakulty, Univerzita Karlova (Institute of Scientific Information, First Medical Faculty, Charles University): 121 08 Prague 2, Kateřinská 32; tel. (2) 29-77-15; fax (2) 24-91-54-13; f. 1949; 450,512 vols, 712 current periodicals; Dir PhDr FRANTIŠEK CHOC; publs *Acta Universitatis Carolinae Medica, Monografia, Proceedings of the Scientific Conferences, Sborník lékařský, Bulletin*.

Ústav zemědělských a potravinářských informací (Institute of Agricultural and Food Information): 120 21 Prague 2, Londýnská 55; tel. (2) 25-00-51; fax (2) 66-31-28-12; e-mail perlin@uzpi.cz; f. 1993; library of 1,000,000 vols (agriculture), 30,000 vols (food); Dir Ing. C. PERLÍN; publs *Rostlinná výroba* (Plant Production), *Živočišná výroba* (Livestock Production), *Veterinární medicina* (Veterinary Medicine), *Zemědělská ekonomika* (Agricultural Economics), *Lesnictví* (Forestry), (all monthly, with English summaries), *Potravinářské vědy* (Food Sciences) (6 a year), *Genetika a šlechtění* (Genetics and Plant Breeding), *Ochrana rostlin* (Plant Protection), *Zemědělská technika* (Agricultural Engineering), *Zahradnictvi* (Horticulture), (all quarterly, with English summaries).

Ustředí patentových informací (Centre for Information on Patents): 160 68 Prague 6, Antonína Čermáka 2A; tel. (2) 24-31-15-55; fax (2) 32-00-13; 24,000,000 documents; Dir Ing. JAROSLAV PAULÍK.

Ústřední knihovna pedagogické fakulty Univerzity Karlovy, Středisko vědeckých informací (Central Library of the Faculty of Pedagogy, Charles University, Scientific Information Centre): 116 39 Prague 1, M. D. Rettigové 4; tel. and fax (2) 96-24-24-20; f. 1948; 180,000 vols, 370 periodicals; Dir PhDr PAVLA LIPERTOVÁ.

Ústřední tělovýchovná knihovna (Central Library of Physical Training): 162 52 Prague 6, José Martiho 31; tel. (2) 20-17-21-58; fax (2) 20-17-20-18; e-mail utk@ftvs.cuni.cz; f. 1927; 300,000 vols; Dir JANA BĚLÍKOVÁ; publ. *Acta Universitatis Carolinae Kinanthropologica*.

Ústřední zemědělská a lesnická knihovna (Central Agricultural and Forestry Library): 120 56 Prague 2, Slezská 7; tel. (2) 24-25-50-74; fax (2) 24-25-39-38; e-mail ihoch@uzpi.cz; f. 1926; a section of the Institute of Agricultural and Food Information; 1,100,000 vols; Dir PhDr IVO HOCH; publs *Přehled novinek ve fondu ÚZLK* (New Accessions, every 2 months), *Přehled rešerší a tematických bibliografií* (quarterly review of retrievals and bibliographies), *Seznam časopisů* (List of Periodicals, annually).

Ústí nad Labem

Státní vědecká knihovna (State Research Library): 401 34 Ústí nad Labem, POB 134, Velká hradební 49; tel. (47) 522-08-11; fax (47) 520-00-45; e-mail library@svkul.cz; f. 1945; 690,000 vols; Dir ALEŠ BROŽEK; publs *Výběr kulturních výročí* (every 6 months), *Ústí nad Labem v tisku* (monthly).

Museums and Art Galleries

Brno

Moravská galerie v Brně (Moravian Gallery in Brno): 662 26 Brno, Husova 18; tel. (5) 42-21-57-59; fax (5) 42-21-57-58; e-mail m-gal@brno.ics.muni.cz; f. 1873; mostly European art of all periods; library of 110,000 vols; Dir PhDr KALIOPI CHAMONIKOLA; publs *Bulletin*, art catalogues.

Moravské zemské muzeum (Moravian Provincial Museum): 659 37 Brno, Zelný trh 6; tel. (5) 42-32-12-05; fax (5) 42-21-27-92; e-mail mzm@mzm.anet.cz; f. 1817; history, natural history, geology, arts; library of 230,000 vols; Dir Dr PETR ŠULEŘ; publs *Acta Musei Moraviae, Anthropologie, Folia Mendeliana, Folia Numismatica, Folia Ethnografica, Krystalinikum*.

Muzeum města Brna (Brno Municipal Museum): 662 24 Brno, Špilberk Castle; tel. 42-21-15-84; f. 1904; history of Brno and Špilberk as a state prison; Dir Dr JIŘÍ VANĚK; publ. *Forum Brunense* (annually).

Technické muzeum v Brně (Brno Museum of Technology): 612 00 Brno, Purkyňova 99; tel. (5) 41-21-44-19; fax (5) 41-21-44-18; f. 1961; library of 40,000 vols; Dir VLASTIMIL VYKYDAL; publs *Sborník technického muzea v Brně, Muzejní noviny*.

České Budějovice

Jihočeské muzeum České Budějovice (České Budějovice Museum of South Bohemia): 370 51 České Budějovice, Dukelská 1; tel. 731-15-28; fax 564-47; history, natural history, arts; Dir P. ŠAFR; publs *Archeologické výzkumy v jižních Čechách* (Archaeology, annually), *Sborník přírodní vědy* (Nature, annually), *Jihočeský sborník historický* (History, annually).

Cheb

Chebské muzeum (Cheb Museum): 350 01 Cheb, Františkánské nam. 12; tel. (166) 42-23-86; f. 1874; history, local ceramics; library of 15,000 vols; spec. colln: library of Franciscan order; Dir PhDr EVA DITTERTOVÁ; publ. *Sborník chebského muzea* (annually).

Chrudim

Muzeum loutkářských kultur (Museum of Puppetry): 537 60 Chrudim, Břetislavova 74; tel. (455) 62-03-10; fax (455) 62-06-50; e-mail puppets@cps.cz; f. 1972; Dir ALENA EXNAROVÁ.

Harrachov

Muzeum skla (Glass Museum): 51246 Harrachov, Novosad a Syn, Sklárna; tel. (432) 52-81-41; f. 1972; Dir K. PIPEK.

Hluboká nad Vltavou

Alšova jihočeská galerie (Aleš South Bohemian Gallery): 373 41 Hluboká nad Vltavou; tel. (38) 96-50-41; fax (38) 96-54-36; e-mail ajg@jcu.cz; f. 1953; 13th- to 20th-century Czech art, 16th- to 18th-century European art, 20th-century Czech and world ceramics; library of 11,000 vols; Dir PhDr HYNEK RULÍŠEK.

Hradec Králové

Muzeum východních Čech, Hradec Králové (Museum of East Bohemia, Hradec Králové): 500 01 Hradec Králové, Eliščino nábř. 465; tel. (49) 551-46-24; fax (49) 551-28-99; e-mail mvc@mvc.anet.cz; f. 1879; natural sciences, history; library of 70,000 vols; Dir PhDr ZDENĚK ZAHRADNÍK; publs *Acta* (irregular), *Fontes* (irregular).

Hukvaldy

Památník Leoše Janáčka (Leoš Janáček Memorial Museum): 739 46 Hukvaldy; tel. (97) 252; f. 1933; life and work of the composer; Dir B. VOLNÝ.

Jablonec nad Nisou

Muzeum skla a bižuterie (Museum of Glass and Jewellery): 466 00 Jablonec nad Nisou, Jiráskova 4; tel. (428) 31-16-81; fax (428) 31-17-04; f. 1961; Bohemian glass, Jablonec jewellery; library of 15,000 vols; Dir Ing. JAROSLAVA SLABÁ.

Karlovy Vary

Galerie umění Karlovy Vary (Karlovy Vary Art Gallery): 360 01 Karlovy Vary, Goethova stezka 6; tel. (17) 243-87; fax (17) 243-88; f. 1953; 20th-century Czech art; Dir MIROSLAV LEPŠÍ.

Karlovarské muzeum (Karlovy Vary Museum): 360 01 Karlovy Vary, Nová louka 23; tel. 262-52; f. 1870; history, natural history, arts; Dir K. KROČA.

Zlatý klíč muzeum (Golden Key Museum): 360 01 Karlovy Vary, Lázeňská 3; tel. 238-88; f. 1960; art nouveau paintings; Dir K. KROČA.

Kolín

Regionální muzeum v Kolíně (Kolín Regional Museum): 280 02 Kolín, I. Karlovo nám. 8; tel. and fax 229-88; f. 1895; local history; open-air museum at Kouřim; library of 49,500 vols; Dir JARMILA VALENTOVÁ.

Kopřivnice

Technické muzeum Tatra Kopřivnice (Tatra Kopřivnice Museum of Technology): 742 21 Kopřivnice, Janáčkovy sady 226; tel. (656) 89-28-25; f. 1947; Tatra cars and lorries; Dir ALOIS HAVEL.

Kutná Hora

Okresní muzeum v Kutné Hoře (Kutná Hora Regional Museum): 284 80 Kutná Hora-Hrádek, Barborská 28; tel. 51-21-59; f. 1877; medieval castle, medieval mining; Dir S. KRŠÁKOVÁ.

Lešany u Týnce nad Sázavou

Vojenské technické muzeum (Military Technology Museum): Lešany u Týnce nad Sázavou; tel. (2) 20-20-49-26; hardware for ground warfare 1890–1990.

Liberec

Oblastní galerie v Liberci (Liberec Regional Art Gallery): 460 01 Liberec, U tiskárny 1; tel. (48) 510-63-25; fax (48) 510-63-21; e-mail oblgal@ogl.cz; f. 1873; 16th- to 18th-century Dutch and Flemish painting, 19th-century French landscapes, 20th-century Czech art; Dir VĚRA LAŠTOVKOVÁ.

Severočeské muzeum v Liberci (North Bohemian Museum in Liberec): 460 01 Liberec 1, Masarykova tř. 11; tel. (48) 510-82-52; fax (48) 510-83-19; f. 1873; European and Bohemian glass and industrial arts, regional history, natural history; library of 35,000 vols; Dir ALOIS ČVANČARA; publ. *Sborník Severočeského musea* (one issue each on history and natural history, every 2 years).

Lidice

Památník Lidice (Lidice Memorial Museum): 273 54 Lidice, Kladno district; tel. (312) 92-34-42; f. 1948; history of the destruction of the village of Lidice in the Second World War; Dir M. ČERMÁK.

Litoměřice

Galerie výtvarného umění Litoměřice (Litoměřice Gallery of Fine Arts): 412 01 Litoměřice, Michalská 7; tel. (416) 73-23-82; fax (416) 73-23-83; f. 1956; 12th- to 20th-century European art, spec. colln of naive art; library of 13,000 vols; Dir PhDr JAN ŠTÍBR.

Mariánské Lázně

Městské muzeum v Mariánských Lázních (Mariánské Lázně Municipal Museum): 353 01 Mariánské Lázně, Goethovo nám. 11; tel. (165) 27-40; f. 1887; history, geology; open-air geological park; Dir PETR BOUŠE.

Mladá Boleslav

Auto Museum Škoda (Škoda Motor Vehicle Museum): 293 60 Mladá Boleslav, Tř. Václava Klementa 294; tel. (326) 83-11-34; fax (326) 83-20-28; e-mail museum@skoda-auto.cz; f. 1974; Dir (vacant).

Opava

Slezské zemské muzeum (Silesian Provincial Museum): 746 46 Opava, Tyršova 1; tel. 21-13-06; f. 1814; history, natural history, arts; arboretum at Nový Dvůr; library of 200,000 vols; Dir Dr JAROMÍR KALUS; publs. *Index Seminum* (annually), *Vlastivědné listy Slezska a severní Moravy* (2 a year), *Časopis Slezského zemského muzea* (natural sciences and historical sciences series, each 3 a year).

Pardubice

Vychodočeské muzeum (Museum of Eastern Bohemia): 531 02 Pardubice, Zámek č. 1; tel. (40) 51-81-21; fax (40) 51-60-61; f. 1880; history, natural history, arts; library of 40,000 vols; Dir Dr F. ŠEBEK; publs *Vychodočeský sborník přírodovědný, Vychodočeský sborník historický.*

Plzeň

Západočeská galerie v Plzni (West Bohemian Gallery in Plzeň): 301 14 Plzeň, Pražská 16; f. 1954; tel. and fax 22-29-70; Czech art from 14th century to the present; Dir PhDr JANA POTUŽÁKOVÁ.

Západočeské muzeum v Plzni (West Bohemian Museum in Plzeň): 301 50 Plzeň, Kopeckého sady 2; tel. (19) 22-41-05; fax (19) 723-65-41; e-mail zpcm@pm.cesnet.cz; f. 1878; history, natural history, arts; Dir Dr F. FRÝDA; publs *Folia Musei Rerum Naturalium Bohemiae Occidentalis* (series *Zoologica, Geologica, Botanica*) (2 a year), *Sborník* (*Příroda:* 5 a year; *Historie:* annually).

Prace u Brna

Mohyla míru (Peace Monument): 664 58 Prace u Brna; tel. and fax (5) 917-24; f. 1910; battle of Slavkov (Austerlitz); Dir Mgr ANTONÍN REČEK.

Prague

Armádní muzeum Žižkov (Army Museum, Žižkov): 130 05 Prague 3, U. Památníku 2; tel. (2) 20-20-49-26; fax (2) 627-96-57; Czech military history 1914–1945.

České muzeum výtvarných umění (Czech Museum of Fine Arts): 110 01 Prague 1, Husova 19/21; tel. (2) 24-22-20-68; fax (2) 90-00-38-28; f. 1963; temporary exhibitions of modern and contemporary art, and permanent exhibition of Czech Cubist art and design (Celetná 34); Dir Dr JAN SEKERA.

Galerie hlavního města Prahy (Prague City Gallery): 160 00 Prague 6, Mickiewiczova 3; tel. (2) 32-04-24; fax (2) 32-94-23; f. 1963; Pragensia, works by 19th- and 20th-century Czech artists; library of 1,400 vols; Dir JAROSLAV FATKA.

Letecké muzeum Kbely (Aviation Museum, Kbely): Prague 9, Kbely, Letiště Praha; tel. (2) 20-20-75-04.

Muzeum Aloise Jiráska a Mikoláše Alše (Alois Jirásek and Mikoláš Aleš Museum): Prague 6, Letohradek Hvězda; tel. 36-79-38; f. 1951; life and work of writer A. Jirásek and painter M. Aleš; Prague massacre of 1620; library of 14,000 vols; Dir JANA WEISEROVÁ.

Muzeum hl. města Prahy (Museum of the City of Prague): 110 00 Prague 1, Na Poříčí 52; tel. (2) 24-22-36-96; fax (2) 24-21-43-06; e-mail museum@monet.cz; f. 1883; history of Prague, archaeology, fine art; library of 17,000 vols; Dir Z. MÍKA; publ. *Archeologica pragensia* (annually).

Národní galerie v Praze (National Gallery in Prague): 119 04 Prague 1, Hradčanské nám. 15; tel. (2) 232-93-31; fax (2) 232-46-41; f. 1796; art of all periods; library of 71,000 vols; Dir Mgr MARTIN ZLATOHLÁVEK; publ. *Bulletin* (irregular).

Národní muzeum (National Museum): 115 79 Prague 1, Central Bldg, Václavské nám. 68; tel. 24-49-71-11; fax 24-22-64-88; f. 1818; library: see Libraries; Dir Dr MILAN STLOUKAL; publs *Sborník Národního muzea v Praze (Acta Musei Nationalis Pragae), Časopis Národního muzea, Muzejní a vlastivědná práce, Numismatické listy* (and see below).

Constituent museums:

Historické muzeum (Historical Museum): 115 79 Prague 1, Václavské nám. 68; tel. 24-49-71-11; history of Czechoslovakia, history of money, ethnography of the Czech Republic, sport, Czech theatre; Dir Dr EDUARD ŠIMEK; publs *Fontes archaeologici Pragenses* (irregular), etc.

Přírodovědecké muzeum (Natural History Museum): 115 79 Prague 1, Václavské nám. 68; tel. 24-49-71-11; Dir Ing. JIŘÍ ČEJKA; publs *Lynx, Sylvia, Acta Faunistica, Acta Entomologica* (all irregular), etc.

Muzeum české hudby (Museum of Czech Music): 110 00 Prague 1, Novotného lávka 1; tel. 24-22-90-75; f. 1936; incl. Dvořák (Prague 2, Ke Karlovu 20), Smetana (Prague 1, Novotného lávka 1), Mozart (Prague 5, Mozartova 169, Bertramka); library, sound archives; Dir Dr MARKÉTA HALLOVÁ.

Náprstkovo muzeum asijských, afrických a amerických kultur (Náprstek Museum of Asian, African and American Cultures): 110 01 Prague 1, Betlémské nám. 1; tel. 24-22-08-99; f. 1862; Dir Dr J. SOUČKOVÁ; publ. *Annals.*

Národní technické muzeum (National Museum of Technology): 170 78 Prague 7, Kostelní 42; tel. 20-39-91-11; fax 37-91-51; e-mail med@ntm.anet.cz; f. 1908; library: see Libraries; Dir Dr Ing. IVO JANOUŠEK; publs *Sborník Národního technichéko muzea v Praze, Rozpravy Národního technického muzea, Bibliografie a prameny Národního technického muzea.*

Národní zemědělské muzeum (National Museum of Agriculture): 170 00 Prague 7, Kostelní 44; tel. 37-39-42; fax 37-92-59; e-mail med@ntm.anet.cz; f. 1891; exhibition of agriculture and food industry located in Kačina Castle near Kutná Hora, of agricultural machinery located in Zdechovice, of forestry, hunting, fishery in Ohrada Castle near České Budějovice, and of horticulture in Lednice Castle near Břeclav; library of 120,000 vols, photographic archive; Dir A. HÁJEK; publs *Vědecké práce ZM.* (Scientific Studies), *Acta Museorum agriculturae*, *Prameny a studie* (Sources and Studies).

Památník národního písemnictví (Museum of Czech Literature): 118 38 Prague 1, Strahovské nádv. 1; tel. (2) 20-51-66-95; fax (2) 20-51-72-77; f. 1953; literary archives containing six million objects; library of 600,000 vols; Dir EVA WOLFOVÁ; publs *Literární archív*.

Pedagogické muzeum J. A. Komenského (J. A. Comenius Pedagogical Museum); 118 00 Prague 1, Valdštejnská ul. 20; tel. (2) 57-32-00-39; fax (2) 53-09-97; f. 1891; documents illustrating the development of national education and the life and work of Comenius; library of 25,000 vols; Dir Ing. LUDOVÍT EMANUEL.

Poštovní muzeum (Postal Museum): 110 00 Prague 1, Nové mlýny 2; tel. 231-20-06; Dir Dr PAVEL ČTVRTNÍK.

Uměleckoprůmyslové muzeum (Museum of Decorative Arts): 110 00 Prague 1, Ulice 17 listopadu 2; tel. 24-81-12-41; fax 24-81-16-66; e-mail directory@upm-praha.anet.cz; f. 1885; general (but spec. colln of glass); library of 150,000 vols; Dir Dr HELENA KOENIGSMARKOVÁ.

Vojenské historické muzeum (Military Historical Museum): 110 00 Prague 1, Hradčanské nám. 2; tel. (2) 53-64-88; Czech military history up to 1914.

Židovské muzeum v Praze (Jewish Museum in Prague): 110 01 Prague 1, Jáchymova 3; tel. 24-81-00-89; fax 231-06-81; e-mail zmp@ort.ecn.cz; f. 1906; liturgical objects, textiles, medieval synagogue and cemetery; library of ancient books and Hebrew MSS, archives of Bohemian and Moravian Jewish communities; Dir PhDr LEO PAVLÁT; publ. *Judaica Bohemiae* (annually).

Rožnov pod Radhoštěm

Valašské muzeum v přírodě (Wallachian Open-Air Museum): 756 61 Rožnov pod Radhoštěm, Palackého 147; tel. (651) 523-31; fax (651) 552-12; f. 1925; open-air museum in the form of a wooden town, a Wallachian village and a mill valley; methodological centre for open-air museums; library of 14,000 vols; Dir PhDr JAROSLAV ŠTIKA.

Slavkov u Brna

Historické muzeum ve Slavkově (Slavkov Historical Museum): 684 01 Slavkov u Brna, Zámek; tel. and fax (5) 44-22-16-35; f. 1949; Napoleonic wars (particularly the battle of Slavkov (Austerlitz)), 17th- and 18th-century paintings, chapel of the Holy Cross; library colln on Napoleon; Dir JAN SPATNÝ.

Tábor

Husitské Muzeum (Hussite Museum): 390 01 Tábor, Nám. Mikoláše z Husi 44; tel. (361) 25-22-42; fax (361) 25-22-45; f. 1878; Hussite movement; library of 40,000 vols; Dir MILOŠ DRDA; publ. *Husitský Tábor* (annually).

Teplice

Regionální muzeum v Teplicích (Teplice Regional Museum): 415 01 Teplice, Zámecké nám. 14; tel. (417) 288-76; fax (417) 414-61; f. 1896; history, natural history, arts; library of 60,000 vols; Dir Dr D. ŠPIČKA; publs *Zprávy a studie*, *Monografické studie*, *Archeologický výzkum*.

Terezín

Památník Terezín (Terezín Memorial): 411 55 Terezín, Alej Principova 304; tel. (416) 78-22-25; fax (416) 78-22-45; f. 1947; museums of the Small Fortress (resistance and political persecution 1940–45) and the wartime Jewish ghetto of Terezín; art gallery; library of 11,000 vols; Dir Dr JAN MUNK; publ. *Terezínské listy* (annually).

Uherské Hradiště

Slovácké muzeum (Slovácko Museum): 686 11 Uherské Hradiště, Smetanovy sady 179; tel. and fax 55-10-59; f. 1914; history, art; library of 30,000 vols; Dir Dr IVO FROLEC; publ. *Slovácko* (annually).

Uherský Brod

Muzeum J. A. Komenského v Uherském Brodě (Uherský Brod J. A. Comenius Museum): 688 12 Uherský Brod, Ul. Přemysla Otakara II 37; tel. (63363) 22-88; fax (63363) 40-78; e-mail muzeum@uhbrod.anet.cz; f. 1898; life, work and heritage of Comenius; library of 40,000 vols; Dir Dr PAVEL POPELKA; publ. *Studia Comeniana et historica* (2 a year).

Zlín

Muzeum jihovýchodní Moravy (Museum of South-Eastern Moravia): 762 57 Zlín, Soudní 1; tel. and fax (67) 305-03; e-mail muzeum@mbox.vol.cz; history, natural history; library of 21,800 vols; Dir PETR STAROSTA; publ. *Acta Musealia*.

Obuvnické muzeum (Footwear Museum): 762 57 Zlín, Tř. Tomáše Bati 1970, POB 175; tel. (67) 852-22-03; fax (67) 305-03; e-mail muzeum@mbox.vol.cz; f. 1959; library of 3,000 vols; Dir MIROSLAVA ŠTÝBROVÁ.

Universities

JIHOČESKÁ UNIVERZITA
(University of South Bohemia)

370 05 České Budějovice, Branišovská 31

Telephone and fax: (38) 402-20

Founded 1991
State control
Academic year: September to June

Rector: Prof. Ing. FRANTIŠEK STŘELEČEK
Vice-Rectors: Doc. PhDr JIŘÍ DIVÍŠEK (Study Programmes), Prof. Ing. VÁCLAV ŘEHOUT (University Development), Doc. RNDr MILAN STRAŠKRABA (Public Relations), Doc. Ing. MARTIN KŘÍŽEK (Science)

Number of teachers: 418
Number of students: 5,000

DEANS

Faculty of Agriculture: Prof. Ing. JAN FRELICH
Faculty of Biological Sciences: Doc. RNDr PAVEL BLAŽKA
Faculty of Health and Social Welfare: Doc. MUDr VLADIMÍR VURM
Faculty of Education: Doc. RNDr FRANTIŠEK MRÁZ
Faculty of Theology: Prof. ThDr KAREL SKALICKÝ
Faculty of Management: Doc. Ing. ZDENĚK ŽEMLIČKA

ATTACHED INSTITUTES

Institute of Entomology: Dir Prof. RNDr FRANTIŠEK SEHNAL.
Institute of Hydrobiology: Dir RNDr VĚRA STRAŠKRABOVÁ.
Institute of Landscape Ecology: Dir Ing. MILAN PEŇÁZ.
Institute of Parasitology: Dir RNDr LIBOR GRUBHOFFER.
Institute of Plant Molecular Biology: Dir RNDr VÍT NAŠINEC.
Institute of Soil Biology: Dir RNDr JOSEF RUSEK.
Institute of Botany, Section of Plant Ecology at Třeboň: Dir of Section RNDr JAN POKORNÝ.
Institute of Microbiology, Division of Autotrophic Micro-organisms at Třeboň: Head of Division Ing. JIŘÍ DOUCHA.

UNIVERZITA KARLOVA
(Charles University)

116 36 Prague 1, Ovocný trh 5

Telephone: (2) 24-49-11-11

Founded 1348
State control
Language of instruction: Czech
Academic year: September to June

Rector: Prof. Dr KAREL MALÝ
Vice-Rectors: Prof. Dr P. ČEPEK, Prof. Dr P. KLENER, Prof. Dr J. PÁNEK, Doc. Ing. I. WILHELM, Prof. Dr J. KOUTECKÝ, Dr M. PETRUSEK
Questor: Ing. JOSEF KUBÍČEK

Library: see Libraries
Number of teachers: 3,062
Number of students: 29,520

Publications: *Acta Universitatis Carolinae*—series: *Mathematica et Physica, Biologica, Geologica, Geographica, Oeconomica, Medica, Gymnica, Philosophica et Historica, Iuridica, Philologica, Historia Universitatis Carolinae Pragensis, Prague Bulletin of Mathematical Linguistics, Psychologie v ekonomické praxi* (quarterly).

DEANS

Faculty of Mathematics and Physics: Prof. Dr B. SEDLÁK
Faculty of Sciences: Prof. Ing. K. ŠTULÍK
1st Faculty of Medicine: Doc. Dr P. HACH
2nd Faculty of Medicine: Doc. Dr M. BOJAR
3rd Faculty of Medicine: Prof. Dr M. ANDĚL
Faculty of Medicine in Plzeň: Doc. Dr B. KREUZBERG
Faculty of Medicine in Hradec Králové: Doc. Dr K. BARTÁK
Faculty of Pharmacy in Hradec Králové: Doc. Dr E. KVASNIČKOVÁ
Faculty of Philosophy: Doc. Dr F. VRHEL
Faculty of Law: Prof. Dr D. HENDRYCH
Faculty of Social Sciences: Prof. Ing. L. MLČOCH
Faculty of Catholic Theology: Prof. Dr J. VÁCLAV
Faculty of Hussite Theology: Prof. Dr Z. KUČERA
Faculty of Gospel Theology: Prof. Dr. P. POKORNÝ
Faculty of Physical Training and Sport: Doc. Dr J. KARGER
Faculty of Education: Prof. Dr Z. HELUS

PROFESSORS

Faculty of Law:

BAKEŠ, M., Financial Law
BALÍK, S., History of State and Law
BOGUSZAK, J., Theory of State and Law
CÍSAŘOVÁ, D., Criminal Law
HENDRYCH, D., Administrative Law
KALENSKÁ, M., Labour Law
KNAPPOVÁ, M., Civil Law
KUČERA, Z., International Law
MALÝ, K., History of State and Law
NOVOTNÝ, O., Criminal Law
PAVLÍČEK, V., Constitutional Law and Civic Sciences
PELIKÁNOVÁ, I., Commercial Law
POTOČNÝ, M., International Law
RŮŽEK, A., Criminal Law
ŠVESTKA, J., Civil Law
URFUS, V., History of State and Law
WINTEROVÁ, A., Civil Law

1st Faculty of Medicine:

Bednář, B., Pathological Anatomy
Bencko, V., Hygiene
Betka, J., Oto-rhino-laryngology
Boguszaková, J., Ophthalmology
Brodanová, M., Internal Medicine
Broulík, P., Internal Medicine
Čech, E., Gynaecology
Doležal, A., Gynaecology and Obstetrics
Dvořáček, J., Urology
Eliška, O., Anatomy
Faber, J., Neurology
Fučíková, T., Immunology and Allergology
Horký, K., Internal Medicine
Hynie, S., Pharmacology
Jirsa, M., Biochemistry
Klener, P., Oncology
Kraml, J., Biochemistry
Křen, V., Medical Genetics
Laštovka, M., Oto-rhino-laryngology
Lojda, Z., Pathological Anatomy
Mára, M., Medical Microbiology and Immunology
Mareček, Z., Internal Medicine
Marek, J., Internal Medicine
Martínek, J., Histology and Embryology
Mazánek, J., Stomatology
Mířejovský, P., Pathological Anatomy
Nečas, E., Normal and Pathological Physiology
Pafko, P., Surgery
Pešková, M., Surgery
Petrášek, J., Internal Medicine
Petrovický, P., Anatomy
Povýšil, C., Pathological Anatomy
Raboch, J., Medical
Raboch, J., Psychiatry
Racek, J., Stomatology
Rakovič, M., Nuclear Medicine
Řehák, R., Surgery
Rozkovcová, E., Dental Medicine
Rybka, V., Orthopaedic Surgery
Schreiber, V., Internal Medicine
Seichert, V., Anatomy
Škach, M., Orthodontics
Šobra, J., Internal Medicine
Sonka, J., Internal Medicine
Sosna, A., Surgery
Štejskal, L., Neurosurgery, Neurology
Štěpán, J., Biochemistry
Štípek, S., Biochemistry
Strejc, P., Forensic Medicine
Strouhal, E., Anthropology
Teršíp, K., Surgery
Těšík, I., Histology and Embryology
Tichý, J., Neurology
Trojan, S., Medical Physiology
Vítek, F., Biophysics
Vosmík, F., Dermatovenerology
Záruba, F., Dermatovenerology
Zeman, M., Surgery
Živný, J., Gynaecology and Obstetrics
Zvolský, P., Psychiatry

2nd Faculty of Medicine:

Bouška, I., Forensic Medicine
Brožek, G., Physiology
Brůnová, B., Ophthalmology
Druga, R., Anatomy
Dvořák, J., Surgery
Dylevský, I., Anatomy
Goetz, P., Biology
Herget, J., Pathological Physiology
Hořejší, J., Gynaecology and Obstetrics
Kölbel, F., Internal Medicine
Konrádová, V., Histology and Embryology
Koutecky, J., Oncology
Kučera, M., Physiotherapy
Lisá, L., Paediatrics
Němec, J., Nuclear Medicine
Seemanová, E., Genetics
Šnajdauf, J., Surgery
Švihovec, J., Pharmacology
Tomášová, H., Medical Chemistry and Biochemistry
Tůma, S., X-ray Imaging Methods
Vízek, M., Pathological Physiology
Zapletal, A., Paediatrics

3rd Faculty of Medicine:

Anděl, M., Internal Medicine
Gregor, P., Internal Medicine
Horák, J., Internal Medicine
Höschl, C., Psychiatry
Jelínek, R., Histology and Embryology, Anatomy
Kršiak, M., Pharmacology
Kuchynka, P., Ophthalmology
Malina, L., Dermatology
Rokyta, R., Pathological Physiology
Stingl, J., Anatomy

Faculty of Medicine in Plzeň:

Ambler, Z., Neurology
Bouda, J., Gynaecology
Fakan, F., Pathological Anatomy
Kilian, J., Stomatology
Šolc, J., Paediatrics
Těšínský, P., Ophthalmology
Topolčan, O., Internal Medicine
Valenta, J., Surgery

Faculty of Medicine in Hradec Králové:

Fixa, B., Internal Medicine
Hejzlar, M., Microbiology
Hrnčíř, Z., Internal Medicine
Hybášek, I., Oto-rhino-laryngology
Král, B., Internal Medicine
Kvasnička, J., Internal Medicine
Malý, J., Internal Medicine
Martínková, J., Pharmacology
Němeček, S., Histology and Embryology
Nožička, Z., Pathological Anatomy
Pidrman, V., Internal Medicine
Rozsíval, P., Ophthalmology
Špaček, J., Pathological Anatomy
Šrb, V., Hygiene
Šteiner, I., Pathological Anatomy
Stransky, P., Biophysics
Vobořil, Z., Surgery
Vodička, I., Biophysics
Zadák, Z., Internal Medicine

Faculty of Sciences:

Boublík, T., Physical and Macromolecular Chemistry
Bouška, V., Geological Mineralogy
Buchar, J., Zoology
Čepek, P., Geology
Černý, M., Organic Chemistry
Chlupáč, I., Geology
Drobník, J., Biotechnology
Feltl, L., Analytical Chemistry
Gardavský, V., Regional Geography
Hampl, M., Regional Geography
Hůrka, K., Zoology
Kalvoda, J., Physical Geography
Klinot, J., Organic Chemistry
Kořínek, V., Biology
Marek, F., Geology
Mareš, S., Geophysics
Matolín, M., Geophysics
Mejsnar, J., Biology
Nátr, M., Plant Physiology
Neubauer, Z., Philosophy of Natural Sciences
Novotný, I., Biology and Physiology of Animals
Pavlík, Z., Demography
Pertold, Z., Geology
Pešek, J., Geology
Podlaha, J., Inorganic Chemistry
Rieder, M., Geology
Smolíková, L., Physical and Macromolecular Chemistry
Stehlík, E., Mathematics
Stemprok, M., Geology
Štrunecká, A., Biology
Štulik, A., Analytical Chemistry
Štys, P., Entomology
Tichá, M., Biochemistry
Váňa, J., Botany
Vávra, J., Parasitology
Zadražil, S., Genetics and Microbiology

Faculty of Philosophy:

Adamec, P., Russian Language
Bouzek, J., Classical Archaeology
Buchvaldek, M., Archaeology
Cejpek, J., Scientific and Technical Information
Čermák, F., Czech Language
Červenka, M., Theory of Literature
Dohalská, M., Phonetics
Doleželova, M., Sinology
Dušková, L., English Language
Hilsky, M., English Literature
Hledíková, Z., Auxiliary Historical Sciences
Homolka, J., Theory and History of Graphic Art
Hoskovec, J., Psychology
Hrala, M., Russian Literature
Hroch, M., History
Janáčková, J., Czech Literature
Janoušek, J., Psychology
Jindra, Z., Economic History
Kárník, Z., Czech and Czechoslovak History
Kohák, E., Philosophy
Kolař, Z., Pedagogy
Königová, M., Information and Librarianship
Král, O., Sinology
Kvaček, R., Czech and Czechoslovak History
Kvapil, M., Slavistics
Lukeš, M., Theatre and Film Science
Machovec, M., Philosophy
Macurová, A., Czech Language
Maur, E., Czech History
Mikšík, O., Psychology
Mouchova, B., Classical Philosophy
Nakonečný, M., Psychology
Oliverius, J., History of Arab Literature
Opatrný, J., General History
Palek, B., General Linguistics
Palková, Z., Phonetics and Phonology
Pánek, J., Czech and Slovak History
Sadek, V., Philosophy
Šimečková, A., German Language
Skřivan, A., General History
Sobotka, M., History of Philosophy
Sousedík, S., History of Philosophy
Stich, A., Czech Language
Syllaba, T., Politology
Tomeš, I., Labour Law
Tretera, I., History of Philosophy
Uličný, O., Czech Language
Vacek, J., Sanskrit and Tamil Philosophy
Veselý, J., History of German Literature
Veselý, R., Oriental Studies and Culture of the Near East
Verner, M., Egyptology
Vojtěch, I., Music Studies
Wittlich, P., Theory of History of Graphic Art

Faculty of Mathematics and Physics:

Anděl, J., Mathematics and Statistics
Bednář, J., Physics
Bičák, J., Theoretical Physics
Bican, L., Mathematics
Čápek, V., Theoretical Physics
Červený, V., Geophysics
Dupač, V, Mathematics and Statistics
Dupačová, J., Mathematics and Statistics
Feistauer, M., Mathematics
Finger, M., Physics
Formánek, J., Theoretical Physics
Hajčová, E., Information Science
Haslinger, J., Physics
Höschl, P., Physics
Hrach, R., Electronic Physics
Hušek, M., Mathematics
Jurečková, J., Probability and Statistics
Kowalski, O., Mathematics
Král, J., Mathematical Informatics
Kratochvíl, P., Physics
Kvasil, J., Experimental Physics
Lukáč, P., Experimental Physics
Lukeš, J., Mathematical Analysis
Mandl, P., Mathematics and Statistics
Marek, I., Mathematics

NEČAS, J., Mathematics
NEŠETŘIL, J., Mathematics
NETUKA, I., Mathematics
NOVÁK, B., Mathematics
PANEVOVÁ, J., Information Science
PROCHÁZKA, L., Mathematics
PULTR, A., Mathematics
ROB, L., Nuclear and Sub-nuclear Physics
SECHOVSKÝ, V., Physics
ŠEDLÁK, B., Physics
SÍCHA, M., Physics
SKÁLA, L., Physics
SOKOLOVSKÝ, P., Information Science
ŠPRUŠIL, B., Physics
ŠTĚPÁN, J., Mathematics
SUK, M., Nuclear Physics
SVOBODA, E., Theoretical Physics
TICHÝ, M., Physics
TRNKOVÁ, V., Mathematics
VALVODA, V., Physics
VLACH, M., Cybernetics
VOPENKA, P., Mathematics
ZIMMERMANN, K., Information Science

Faculty of Education:

BRABCOVÁ, R., Czech Language
HEJNÝ, M., Mathematics
HELUS, Z., Pedagogical Psychology
JELÍNEK, S., Russian Language
KOMAN, M., Mathematics
KOTÁSEK, J., Education
PARIZEK, V., Education
PEŠKOVÁ, J., Philosophy
PIŤHA, P., Philosophy
VULTERIN, J., Analytical Chemistry

Faculty of Social Sciences:

HLAVÁČEK, Economics
KOUBA, K., Political Economy
KŘEN, J., Czechoslovak History
MLČOCH, L., Economics
PETRUSEK, M., Sociology
SOJKA, M., Economic Theory
URBAN, L., Political Economy

Faculty of Physical Education and Sport:

BLAHUŠ, P., Sports Education
DOBRÝ, L., Theory of Physical Education and Sport
DYLEVSKÝ, I., Anatomy
HOŠEK, V., Psychology of Sport
KOVÁŘ, R., Kinanthropology
PFEIFFER, J., Neurology
SLEPIČKA, P., Teaching of Physical Education
SVOBODA, B., Sports Education
TEPLÝ, Z., Human Movement

Faculty of Pharmacy in Hradec Králové:

DRŠATA, J., Biochemistry
FENDRICH, Z., Pharmacology
JAHODÁŘ, L., Pharmacognosy
KARLÍČEK, R., Analytical Chemistry
LÁZNÍČEK, M., Radiopharmacy
SIKYTA, B., Microbiology and Immunology
VIŠŇOVSKÝ, P., Pharmacology
WAISSER, K., Organic Chemistry

Faculty of Catholic Theology:

KADLEC, J., History
MATĚJKA, J., Practical Theology
POLC, J., Church History
WOLF, V., Systematic Theology
ZEDNÍČEK, M., Canon Law

Faculty of Evangelical Theology:

FILIPI, P., Practical Theology
HEJDÁNEK, L., Philosophy
HELLER, J., Old Testament
POKORNÝ, P., New Testament
REJCHRTOVÁ, N., Church History
TROJAN, J., Social Ethics

Faculty of Hussite Theology:

KUČERA, Z., Systematic Theology
SALAJKA, M., Pastoral Theology
SÁZAVA, Z., Biblical Theology

UNIVERZITA MASARYKOVA
(Masaryk University)

601 77 Brno, Žerotínovo nám. 9

Telephone: (5) 41-12-81-11
Fax: (5) 41-12-83-00

Founded 1919
State control
Language of instruction: Czech
Academic year: September to August

Rector: Prof. Dr JIŘÍ ZLATUŠKA
Vice-Rectors: Prof. Dr JIŘÍ FUKAČ, Prof. Dr EDUARD SCHMIDT, Assoc. Prof. Dr ZUZANA BRÁZDOVÁ, Assoc. Prof. Dr ZDEŇKA GREGOROVÁ
Bursar: Ing. FRANTIŠEK GALE

Library of *c.* 1,291,000 vols
Number of teachers: 1,403
Number of students: 15,197

Publications: *Universitas* (4 a year), *Scripta Medica* (8 a year), *Archivum mathematicum*, and various faculty publs.

DEANS

Faculty of Medicine: Prof. Dr JIŘÍ VORLÍČEK
Faculty of Natural Sciences: Prof. Dr ROSTISLAV BRZOBOHATÝ
Faculty of Arts: Prof. Dr JANA NECHUTOVÁ
Faculty of Law: Dr JOSEF BEJČEK
Faculty of Education: Dr OTA ŘÍHA
Faculty of Economics and Administration: Ing. LADISLAV BLAŽEK
Faculty of Informatics: Prof. JIŘÍ ZLATUŠKA

PROFESSORS

Faculty of Medicine:

BENDA, K., Radiology
BILDER, J., Stomatology
BRAVENÝ, P., Physiology
ČECH, S., Histology
ČERBÁK, R., Surgery
ČERNÝ, J., Surgery
DAPECI, A., Stomatology
DÍTĚ, P., Internal Medicine
DVOŘÁK, I., Internal Medicine
DVOŘÁK, K., Pathology
FIŠER, B., Pathology and Physiology
GERYLOVOVÁ, A., Social Medicine
HABANEC, B., Pathology
HOLČÍK, J., Social Medicine
HORKÝ, D., Histology
HORN, V., Dermatology
HRAZDIRA, I., Biophysics
KAMARÝT, P., Internal Medicine
KORBIČKA, J., Forensic Medicine
KOTULÁN, J., Preventive Medicine
KOVANDA, M., , Orthopaedics
LOKAJ, J., Immunology
NEČAS, O., Biology
OLEJNÍČEK, M., Internal Medicine
PÁČ, L., Anatomy
PEŇÁZ, J., Physiology
PILKA, L., Gynaecology and Obstetrics
PLACHETA, Z., Internal Medicine
POTRUSIL, B., Surgery
REKTOR, I., Neurology
ŠEMRÁD, B., Internal Medicine
ŠMARDA, J., Biology
ŠTEJFA, M., Internal Medicine
ŠULCOVÁ, A., Pharmacology
ŠVESTKA, J., Psychiatry
SVOBODA, A., Biology
TÁBORSKÁ, D., Anaesthetics and Resuscitation
VÁCHA, J., Pathological Physiology
VLACH, O., Orthopaedics
VLAŠÍN, Z., Dermatology
VLKOVÁ, E., Ophthalmology
VORLÍČEK, J., Internal Medicine
ŽÁČEK, A., Social Medicine
ZÁHEJSKÝ, J., Dermatology
ZELNÍČEK, E., Biochemistry
ZEMAN, K., Internal Medicine
ZOUHAR, A., Neurology

Faculty of Law:

HAJN, P., Economic Law
KLOKOCKA, V., Constitutional Law and Political Science
VLČEK, E., History of State and Law

Faculty of Arts:

BARTONĚK, A., Classics
BARTOŠ, L., French Language
ČERMÁK, V., Social Philosophy
DOROVSKÝ, I., Slavic Literatures
ERHART, A., Indo-European Linguistics
FIRBAS, J., English Language
FLODR, M., Archive Studies
FRYČER, J., French Literature
FUKAČ, J., Musicology
HLADKÝ, J., English Language
HOLÝ, D., Ethnology
HORÁK, P., Philosophy
JANÁK, J., History
JELÍNEK, M., Czech Language
JEŘÁBEK, D., Czech and Slovak Literature
JEŘÁBEK, R., Ethnology
KOPECKÝ, M., Czech and Slovak Literature
KOŽMÍN, Z., Czech Literature
KŠICOVÁ, D., History of Russian Literature
LIBROVÁ, H., Sociology
MASAŘÍK, Z., German Language
MATERNA, P., Philosophy
MEZNÍK, J., History
MÍČEK, L., Psychology
MOŽNÝ, I., Sociology
NEČAS, C., History
NECHUTOVÁ, J., Classics
PEČMAN, R., History of Music
PODBORSKÝ, V., Archaeology
POSPÍŠIL, J., History of the Russian Literature
SMÉKAL, V., Psychology
SRBA, B., Theatre Studies
STŘÍTECKÝ, J., Philosophy
ŠVOBODA, M., Psychology
ŠLOSAR, D., Czech Language
ŠRÁMEK, J., History of Romance Literature
ŠTĚDROŇ, M., Musicology
ŠVANCARA, J., Psychology
VÁLKA, J., History
VEČERKA, R., Old Church Slavonic
ŽAŽA, S., Russian Language

Faculty of Natural Sciences:

BARTUŠEK, M., Analytical Chemistry
BENEŠ, J., Anthropology
BRÁZDIL, R., Physical Geography
BRZOBOHATÝ, R., Palaeontology
CETL, J., Genetics
FOJT, B., Mineralogy and Petrography
GAISLER, J., Zoology
GLOSER, J., Plant Physiology
HÁLA, J., Inorganic Chemistry
HAVEL, J., Analytical Chemistry
HORSKÝ, J., Theoretical Physics
HUMLÍČEK, J., Physics
JANČA, J., Physics
JONAS, J., Organic Chemistry
KAPIČKA, V., Physics
KNOZ, J., Biology
KOČA, J., Organic Chemistry
KOLÁŘ, I., Algebra and Geometry
KRATOCHVÍL, M., Organic Chemistry
LUKEŠ, F., Physics
MACHOLÁN, L., Biochemistry
MALINA, J., Archaeology
MUSIL, R., Geology and Palaeontology
NOVÁK, V., Mathematics
NOVOTNÝ, J., Physics
RÁB, M., Mathematics
RELICHOVÁ, J., Genetics
ROSICKÝ, J., Mathematics
ROSYPAL, S., Biology
ROZKOŠNÝ, R., Entomology
ŠCHMIDT, E., Physics
ŠIK, F., Algebra and Geometry
ŠIMEK, M., Animal Physiology
SKULA, L., Mathematics
SOMMER, L., Analytical Chemistry

Staněk, J., Mineralogy and Petrography
Suk, M., Mineralogy
Vetešník, M., Theoretical Physics and Astrophysics
Vetterl, V., Biophysics
Vicherek, J., Botany
Vřešťál, J., Physical Chemistry
Žák, Z., Inorganic Chemistry

Faculty of Education:
Buček, M., Musical Arts
Chalupa, P., Geography
Chvalina, J., Mathematics
Demek, J., Geography
Hauser, P., Czech Studies and Linguistics
Havlíček, P., Physical Education
Hladký, J.
Horník, S., Geography
Kosmák, L., Mathematics
Maňák, J., Pedagogy
Marečková, M., History
Motyčka, J., Physical Education
Novák, V., Mathematics
Přadka, M., Pedagogy
Šrámek, R., Czech Studies and Linguistics

Faculty of Economics and Administration:
Ivánek, L., Economics
Jakš, J., Trade
Máša, M., Management
Novák, V., Economics
Ondrčka, P., Finance
Sejbal, J., Finance
Vojtíšek, J., Economics

Faculty of Informatics:
Dokulil, M., Philosophy
Gruska, J., Informatics
Král, J., Informatics
Materna, P., Philosophy
Novotný, M., Mathematics and Informatics
Zlatuška, J., Informatics

ATTACHED INSTITUTE

Institute of Computer Science: 602 00 Brno, Botanická 69A; Dir Dr Václav Račanský.

UNIVERZITA PALACKÉHO V OLOMOUCI
(Palacký University)

771 47 Olomouc, Křížkovského 8
Telephone: (68) 522-14-55
Fax: (68) 522-27-31
E-mail: dvor@risc.upol.cz

Founded 1573, re-opened 1946
State control
Languages of instruction: Czech, English, German
Academic year: September to June

Rector: Prof. RNDr Lubomír Dvořák
Pro-Rectors: Prof. RNDr Karel Lenhart, RNDr Josef Tillich, Doc. PhDr Libuše Hornová, Doc. PhDr Jindřich Schulz
Registrar: Ing. Jiří Jirka
Librarian: PhDr Rostislav Hladký

Number of teachers: 980
Number of students: 12,000

Publication: *Acta Universitatis Palackianae* (quarterly).

DEANS

Faculty of Philosophy: Doc. PhDr Vladimír Řehan
Faculty of Science: Doc. RNDr Jan Lasovský
Faculty of Medicine: Prof. MUDr et PhDr Jana Mačáková
Faculty of Education: Doc. RNDr Jan Šteigl
Sts Cyril and Methodius Faculty of Theology: Doc. ThDr Pavel Ambros
Faculty of Physical Culture: Prof. PhDr František Vaverka
Faculty of Law: Doc. Ing. Jiří Blažek

PROFESSORS

Faculty of Medicine:
Duda, M., Surgery
Dušek, J., Pathology
Eber, M., Stomatology
Gladkij, J., Social Medicine
Holibka, V., General Anatomy
Houdek, M., Neurosurgery
Hřebíček, J., Pathological Physiology
Hubáček, J., Oto-Rhino-Laryngology
Hušák, V., Applied Physics
Indrák, K., Internal Diseases
Janout, V., Epidemiology
Jezdinský, J., Pharmacology
Jírava, E., Stomatology
Jirka, Z., Sports Medicine
Kamínek, M., Stomatology
Klačansky, J., Oto-Rhino-Laryngology
Kod'ousek, R., Pathological Anatomy
Kolář, Z., Pathology
Kolek, V., Internal Diseases
Komenda, S., Education
Kosatík, A., Forensic Medicine
Král, V., Surgery
Krč, I., Internal Medicine
Kudela, M., Gynaecology
Lenhart, K., General Biology
Lichnovský, V., Histology and Embryology
Lukl, J., Internal Diseases
Mačák, J., Pathology
Mačákova, J., Pathological Physiology
Malínský, J., Histology and Embryology
Mrňa, B., Psychiatry
Nekula, J., Radiology
Neoral, L., Forensic Medicine
Ošťádal, O., Internal Diseases
Pazdera, J., Stomatology
Petřek, J., Physiology
Scheinar, J., Urology
Ščudla, V., Internal Diseases
Šimánek, V., Medical Chemistry
Urbánek, K., Neurology

Faculty of Philosophy:
Andreš, J., Slavonic Studies
Bartoněk, L., Classical Philology
Černý, J., General Linguistics
Damborský, J., Slavonic Studies and Polish Language
Floss, P., History of Philosophy
Horejsek, J., World History
Hrabová, L., General History
Hudec, V., Music
Jařab, J., American Studies and American Literature
Komárek, M., Slavonic Studies and Czech Language
Kořenský, J., Slavonic Studies and Czech Language
Kostřica, V., Russian Literature
Kratochvíl, S., Clinical Psychology
Látal, J., History of French Literature
Lotko, E., Czech Language
Macháček, J., English Studies and English Language
Možný, I., Sociology
Nechutová, J., Classical Philology
Petrů, E., Theory and History of Czech Literature
Poledňák, I., Theory and History of Music
Tárnyiková, J., English Studies and English Language
Trapl, M., Czech and Slovak History
Václavek, L., History of German Literature
Vičar, J., Theory and History of Music
Zahrádka, M., Russian Literature

Faculty of Science:
Andres, J., Mathematical Analysis
Bičík, V., Zoology
Cabák, I., Experimental Physics
Chajda, I., Algebra and Geometry
Demek, J., Geography
Dvořák, L., Biophysics
Hlůza, B., Botany
Kubáček, L., Mathematical Statistics
Machala, F., Geometry and Topology
Majerník, V., Physics
Peřina, J., Optoelectronics
Peřinová, V., General Physics and Mathematical Physics
Pospíšil, J., Experimental Physics
Rachůnek, J., Algebra
Rachůnková, I., Mathematical Analysis
Rychnovská, M., Ecology
Slouka, J., Organic Chemistry
Sodomka, L., Applied Physics
Stránský, Z., Analytical Chemistry
Stužka, V., Analytical Chemistry
Štěrba, O., Ecology
Vyšín, V., Theoretical Physics
Zapletal, J., Geology

Faculty of Education:
Kovaříček, V., Theory of Education
Kučera, Z., Visual Arts
Mezihorák, F., Czechoslovak History
Stoffa, J., Electrical Engineering

Faculty of Physical Culture:
Frömel, K., Kinanthropology
Hodaň, B., Theory of Physical Culture
Měkota, K., Anthropomotory
Vaverka, F., Kinanthropology

Faculty of Law:
Císařová, D., Criminal Law
Haderka, J., Civil Law
Holländer, P., Constitutional Law
Kubů, L., Theory of State and Law
Vlček, E., History of State and Law

Sts Cyril and Methodius Faculty of Theology:
Tkadlčík, V., Greek

VETERINÁRNÍ A FARMACEUTICKÁ UNIVERZITA BRNO
(University of Veterinary and Pharmaceutical Sciences, Brno)

612 42 Brno, Palackého 1–3
Telephone: (5) 41-56-20-02
Fax: (5) 75-04-78
E-mail: zima@dior.ics.muni.cz

Founded 1918
State control
Languages of instruction: Czech, English
Academic year: September to August

Rector: Prof. RNDr Stanislav Zima
Vice-Rectors: Prof. RNDr Emanuel Sucman, Doc. Ing. MVDr Pavel Suchý
Registrar: Ing. Jaroslav Černy
Librarian: Vaclav Svoboda

Library: see Libraries
Number of teachers: 186
Number of students: 1,499

Publication: *Acta Veterinaria Brno* (quarterly).

DEANS

Faculty of Veterinary Medicine: Doc. MVDr et RNDr Petr Hořín
Faculty of Veterinary Hygiene and Ecology: Prof. MVDr Augustin Buš
Faculty of Pharmacy: Prof. RNDr Václav Suchý

PROFESSORS

Faculty of Veterinary Medicine:
Bouda, J., Internal Medicine
Celer, V., Microbiology
Černý, H., Anatomy
Červený, Č., Anatomy
Hanák, J., Equine Diseases
Hofírek, B., Internal Medicine
Chroust, K., Parasitology
Jurajda, V., Avian Diseases
Kříž, H., Avian Medicine
Kudláč, E., Gynaecology
Němeček, L., Veterinary Surgery
Pospíšil, Z., Epizootiology
Svoboda, M., Diseases of Small Animals

Faculty of Veterinary Hygiene and Ecology:
Buš, A., Veterinary Pharmacology
Fišer, A., Veterinary Hygiene
Hrabák, R., Biology

LUKÁŠOVÁ, J., Food Microbiology
MINKS, J., Tropical Veterinary Medicine
SMUTNÁ, M., Veterinary Chemistry and Biochemistry
ŠTĚRBA, O., Veterinary Morphology
SUCMAN, E., Veterinary Chemistry and Biochemistry
ZIMA, S., Veterinary Chemistry

Faculty of Pharmacy
BENEŠ, L., Pharmaceutical Chemistry
SUCHÝ, V., Pharmacognosy

ATTACHED INSTITUTE

Centre for Special Cultivation Sera: Dir Doc. Dr J. DERKA

ČESKÉ VYSOKÉ UČENÍ TECHNICKÉ V PRAZE
(Czech Technical University in Prague)

166 36 Prague 6, Zikova 4
Telephone: (2) 2435-1111
Fax: (2) 2431-0783

Founded 1707; reorganized 1806, 1863, 1920, 1960
State control
Languages of instruction: Czech, English
Academic year: October to June

Rector: Prof. Ing. P. ZUNA
Vice-Rectors: Doc. Ing. A. POKORNÝ, Prof. Ing. V. HAVLÍČEK, Doc. Ing. P. FIALA, Prof. Ing. arch. V. ŠLAPETA, Prof. Ing. J. ŠEJNOHA
Chief Administrative Officer: Doc. Ing Z. VOSPĚL

Number of teachers: 1,350
Number of students: 17,800

Publications: *Acta Polytechnica, Informační Bulletin Rektorátu.*

DEANS

Faculty of Civil Engineering: Doc. Ing. LADISLAV LAMBOJ
Faculty of Mechanical Engineering: Prof. Ing. JAN MACEK
Faculty of Electrical Engineering: Prof. Ing. JAN UHLÍŘ
Faculty of Nuclear Science and Physical Engineering: Prof. Ing. JAROSLAV MUSÍLEK
Faculty of Architecture: Doc. Ing. Arch. BOHUMIL FANTA
Faculty of Transportation Sciences: Prof. Ing. P. MOOS

HEADS OF DEPARTMENT

Faculty of Civil Engineering:
Mathematics: ČERNÝ, J.
Physics: VODÁK, F.
Physical Education: DRNEK, J.
Languages: JOHNOVÁ, J.
Social Sciences: VANÍČEK, V.
Construction Technology: LADRA, J.
Building Materials: NOVÁK, J.
Building Structures: WITZANY, J.
Construction Engineering Equipment: PAPEŽ, K.
Construction Management and Economics: ANTON, P.
Town and Regional Planning: MANSFELDOVÁ, A.
Applied Informatics: KLVAŇA, J.
Architecture: VODĚRA, S.
Structural Mechanics: ŠEJNOHA, J.
Concrete Structures and Bridges: KŘÍSTEK, V.
Steel Structures: STUDNIČKA, J.
Geotechnics: LAMBOJ, J.
Road Engineering: LEHOVEC, F.
Railway Engineering: KUBÁT, B.
Hydraulics and Hydrology: MAREŠ, K.
Hydrotechnics: BROŽA, V.
Irrigation, Drainage and Landscape Engineering: VRÁNA, K.
Sanitary Engineering: GRÜNWALD, A.
Geodesy and Land Adjustments: BLAŽEK, R.
Advanced Geodesy: ZEMAN, A.
Cartography: VEVERKA, B.
Special Geodesy: PROCHÁZKA, J.
Experimental Centre: HOŠEK, J.
Centre of Experimental Geotechnics: PACOVSKÝ, J.
Laboratory of Ecological Risks in Urban Drainage: POLLERT, J.
Computing Centre: HORA, V.

Faculty of Mechanical Engineering:
Technical Mathematics: KOZEL, K.
Applied Physics: SOPKO, B.
Physical Education: SCHMID, J.
Languages: KYBICOVÁ, H.
Mechanics: KONVIČKOVÁ, S.
Fluid Dynamics and Power Engineering: PETR, V.
Environmental Engineering: NOVÝ, R.
Social Sciences: KLIMEŠ, F.
Process Engineering: RIEGER, F.
Automotive and Aerospace Engineering: BAUMRUK, P.
Manufacturing Technology: MÁDL, J.
Materials Engineering: STEIDL, J.
Production Machines and Mechanisms: TALÁCKO, J.
Instrumentation and Control Engineering: ZÍTEK, P.
Management and Economics: MACÍK, K.

Faculty of Electrical Engineering:
Mathematics: DEMLOVÁ, M.
Physics: KUBEŠ, P.
Sports and Physical Education: FILANDR, J.
Languages: VLAČIHOVÁ, Z.
Mechanics and Materials Science: BOUDA, V.
Electrotechnology: MACH, P.
Electric Drives and Traction: PAVELKA, J.
Electroenergetics: DOLEŽAL, J.
Economics, Management and Humanities: TOMEK, G.
Electromagnetic Field: MAZÁNEK, M.
Circuit Theory: DAVIDEK, V.
Telecommunications Engineering: ŠIMÁK, B.
Microelectronics: HUSÁK, M.
Control Engineering: MAŘÍK, V.
Computer Science: KOLÁŘ, J.
Radioelectronics: VEJRAŽKA, F.
Measurements: HAASZ, V.

Faculty of Nuclear Science and Physical Engineering:
Mathematics: HAVLÍČEK, M.
Physics: TOLAR, J.
Languages: DVOŘÁKOVÁ, I.
Solid State Engineering: VRATISLAV, S.
Physical Electronics: FIALA, P.
Materials: NEDBAL, I.
Nuclear Chemistry: BENEŠ, P.
Nuclear Reactors: MATĚJKA, K.
Dosimetry and Application of Ionizing Radiation: ČECHÁK, T.
Microtron Laboratory: VOGNAR, M.

Faculty of Architecture:
Fine Arts: MOJŽÍŠ, F.
Theory of Architecture and Social Sciences: ŠLAPETA, V.
History of Architecture and Fine Arts: PAVLÍK, M.
Architectural Conservation: PAVLÍK, M.
Interior and Exhibition Design: BEDNÁŘ, P.
Architectural Modelling: POSPÍŠIL, J.
Industrial and Agricultural Buildings: ŠTĚDRÝ, F.
Design of Buildings: ŠTÍPEK, J.
Urban Design and Planning: MUŽÍK, J.
Mathematical Sciences: MUK, J.
Load-bearing Structures: KALOUSEK, J.
Construction Engineering I: PŠENIČKA, F.
Construction Engineering II: POKORNÝ, A.
Construction Management: POKORNÝ, A.
Languages: CARAVANASOVÁ, L.
Design I: ŠAFER, J.
Design II: NAVRÁTIL, A.
Design III: LÁBUS, L.

Faculty of Transportation Sciences:
Automation in Transport and Telecommunications: MOOS, P.
Economics and Management in Transport and Telecommunications: DUCHOŇ, B.
Transport Systems: JIRAVA, P.
Applied Mathematics: VLČEK, M.
Humanities: KUBIŠOVÁ, V.
Transport Technology: DUNOVSKÝ, J.
Logistics and Transport Processes: SVOBODA, V.
Mechanics and Materials Science: JÍRA, J.

ATTACHED INSTITUTES

Klokner Institute: Dir Ing. T. KLEČKA
Masaryk Institute of Advanced Studies: Dir Doc. Ing. J. PETR
Centre for Biomedical Engineering: Dir MUDr Ing. L. POUŠEK

VYSOKÉ UČENÍ TECHNICKÉ V BRNĚ
(Technical University of Brno)

601 90 Brno, Kounicova 67A
Telephone: (5) 4112-5111
Fax: (5) 4121-1309
E-mail: vavrin@ro.vutbr.cz

Founded 1899
State control
Language of instruction: Czech
Academic year: September to July

Rector: Prof. Ing. PETR VAVŘÍN
Pro-Rectors: Prof. Ing. JAROSLAV KADRNOŽKA, Asst Prof. PETR DUB, Prof. Ing. arch. HELENA ZEMÁNKOVÁ, Asst Prof. Ing. LEONARD HOBST, Asst Prof. Ing. PETR SÁHA
Registrar: Dr ALEXANDER ČERNÝ
Librarian: NATAŠA JURSOVÁ

Number of teachers: 946
Number of students: 13,378

Publication: *Události na VUT v Brně.*

DEANS

Faculty of Civil Engineering: Asst Prof. Ing. LADISLAV ŠTĚPÁNEK
Faculty of Mechanical Engineering: Prof. Ing. JAN VRBKA
Faculty of Electrical Engineering and Computer Science: Asst Prof. Ing. JAN HONZÍK
Faculty of Technology: Asst Prof. RNDr JIŘÍ DOSTÁL
Faculty of Architecture: Asst Prof. Ing. arch. ALOIS NOVÝ
Faculty of Chemistry: Prof. Ing. LUBOMÍR LAPČÍK
Faculty of Fine Arts: Prof. VLADIMÍR PRECLÍK
Faculty of Business and Management: Asst Prof. Ing. KAREL RAIS
Faculty of Management and Economics: Asst Prof. PhDr ALOIS GLOGAR

PROFESSORS

Faculty of Civil Engineering:
FIXEL, J., Geodesy
HORÁK, M., Metal and Timber Structures
KADLČÁK, J., Structural Mechanics
KOČÍ, J., Building Construction
KOKTAVÝ, B., Physics
KRATOCHVÍL, J., Hydraulics and Hydrotechnics
MALÝ, J., Chemistry
MARŠÍK, Z., Geodesy and Cartography
MELCHER, J., Metal and Timber Structures
MUSIL, F., Technology of Structures
MYSLÍN, J., Building Construction
NOVOSAD, Z., Geodesy
PYTLÍK, P., Precast Building Technology
ŠÁLEK, J., Water Resources Management
ŠAMALÍKOVÁ, M., Geotechnics
ŠIKULA, J., Physics
STRÁSKÝ, J., Concrete and Masonry Structures
TEPLÝ, B., Structural Mechanics
TRÁVNÍČEK, I., Geotechnics

VORÁČEK, J., Mathematics

Faculty of Mechanical Engineering:

BOHÁČEK, F., Machine Design
BUMBÁLEK, B., Technology
DUBŠEK, F., Thermomechanics and Nuclear Energy
ERENBERGER, Z., Production Machines and Industrial Robots
FILAKOVSKÝ, K., Aircraft Design
FLEISCHNER, P., Hydraulic Machines and Industrial Robots
JANÍČEK, P., Mechanics of Solids
KAČUR, J., Mathematics
KADRNOŽKA, J., Heat and Nuclear Power
KAVIČKA, F., Heat and Nuclear Power
KOCMAN, K., Production Engineering
KOHOUTEK, J., Process Engineering
KOMRSKÁ, J., Physics
KRATOCHVÍL, O., Mechanics of Solids
KULČÁK, L., Aerospace Engineering
LIŠKA, M., Physics
MEDEK, J., Process Engineering
NOVÁK, V., Mathematics
PÍŠTĚK, V., Combustion Engines and Motor Vehicles
POCHYLÝ, F., Heat and Nuclear Power
POKLUDA, J., Physics
RUSÍN, K., Foundry Engineering
SCHNEIDER, P., Process Engineering
SLAVÍK, J., Mechanics of Solids
ŠTĚPÁNEK, M., Automation and Computer Science
STRÁNSKÝ, K., Materials Engineering
ŠVEJCAR, J., Materials Engineering
VLK, F., Combustion Engines and Motor Vehicles
VRBKA, J., Mechanics of Solids
ŽENÍŠEK, A., Mathematics

Faculty of Electrical Engineering and Computer Science:

AUTRATA, R., Electrical and Electronic Technology
BIOLEK, D., Telecommunications
BRZOBOHATÝ, J., Microelectronics
DIBLÍK, J., Mathematics
DOSTÁL, T., Radioelectronics
DVOŘÁK, V., Computer Science and Engineering
HAVEL, V., Mathematics
HRUŠKA, K., Physics
JAN, J., Biomedical Engineering
MELKES, F., Mathematics
MIKULA, V., Radioelectronics
POSPÍŠIL, J., Radioelectronics
PROCHÁZKA, P., Electrical Engineering
ŘÍČNÝ, V., Radioelectronics
ŠEBESTA, V., Radioelectronics
SERBA, I., Computer Science and Engineering
SVAČINA, J., Radioelectronics
VALSA, J., Electrical Engineering
VAVŘÍN, P., Automation and Measurement Engineering
VRBA, K., Telecommunications

Faculty of Technology

KLÁSEK, A., Environmental Technology and Chemistry
LANGMEIER, F., Leather and Shoe Technology
MLÁDEK, M., Leather and Shoe Technology
RYBNIKÁŘ, F., Rubber and Plastics Technology

Faculty of Architecture

GŘEGORČÍK, J., Urban Studies
KYSELKA, M., Rural Architecture
MARTÍNEK, M., Rural Architecture
RULLER, I., Public Constructions
VAVERKA, J., Building Construction
ZEMANKOVA, H., Industrial Architecture

Faculty of Chemistry

KUČERA, M., Chemistry of Materials
LAPČÍK, L., Chemistry
MATOUŠEK, J., Environmental Chemistry and Technology
NEŠPŮREK, S., Chemistry
PELIKÁN, P., Chemistry
RYCHTERA, M., Food Science and Biotechnology
SCHAUER, F., Environmental Chemistry and Technology
SOMMER, L., Chemistry and Technology of Environmental Protection

Faculty of Fine Arts

NAČERADSKÝ, J., Painting
PRECLÍK, V., Sculpture

Faculty of Business and Management

DVOŘÁK, J., Economy and Management
KONEČNÝ, M., Economy and Management
MEZNÍK, I., Mathematics
NĚMEČEK, P., Economy and Management

VYSOKÁ ŠKOLA BÁŇSKÁ – TECHNICKÁ UNIVERZITA OSTRAVA (Technical University of Ostrava)

708 33 Ostrava-Poruba, třída 17 listopadu 15
Telephone: (69) 699-1111
Fax: (69) 691-8647

Founded 1716
State control
Academic year: September to August

Rector: Prof. Ing. VACLAV ROUBÍČEK
Vice-Rectors: Prof. Ing. JAROMÍR POLÁK, Prof. Ing. TOMÁŠ ČERMÁK, Prof. Ing. PETR WYSLYCH
Registrar: Ing. STANISLAV DZIOB
Librarian: Mgr DANIELA TKAČÍKOVÁ

Number of teachers: 731
Number of students: 12,734

Publications: *Sborník vědeckých prací VŠB-TU Ostrava* (irregular), *Akdemické Fórum* (6 a year).

DEANS

Faculty of Mining and Geology: Prof. Ing. CTIRAD SCHEJBAL
Faculty of Metallurgy and Material Engineering: Prof. Ing. LUDOVIT DOBROVSKÝ
Faculty of Mechanical Engineering: Prof. Ing. ANTONÍN VÍTIČEK
Faculty of Electrical Engineering and Informatics: Doc. Ing. KAREL CHMELÍK
Faculty of Economics: Prof. Ing. MIROSLAV NEJEZCHLEBA
Faculty of Civil Engineering: Prof. Ing. JINDŘICH CIGÁNEK

PROFESSORS

Faculty of Mining and Geology:

FOLDYNA, J., Geology
GRYGÁREK, J., Underground Mining
HAVELKA, J., Economic Geology
LÁNÍČEK, J., Mathematics
MÁDR, V., Physics
OTÁHAL, A., Mine Ventilation
PALAS, M., Economic Geology
PIŠTORA, J., Applied Physics
PROKOP, P., Mine Ventilation
SCHEJBAL, C., Economic Geology
STRAKOŠ, V., Automation in Mining
VAŠÍČEK, Z., Geology
VIDLÁŘ, J., Mineral Processing
WYSLYCH, P., Applied Physics
ZAMARSKÝ, V., Geology and Mineralogy

Faculty of Metallurgy and Material Engineering:

ADOLF, Z., Steel-making
BAZAN, J., Steel-making
DEMBOVSKÝ, V., Materials Science
DOBROVSKÝ, L., Physical Metallurgy
HYSPECKÁ, L., Physical Metallurgy
JELÍNEK,, P., Casting
KALOČ, M., Technology of Fuels
OBROUČKA, K., Thermal Engineering
PŘÍHODA, M., Thermal Engineering
ROUBÍČEK, V., Technology of Fuels
SOMMER, B., Metal Forming
VROŽINA, M., Automation of Metallurgical Processes
WEISS, Z., Mineralogy
WICHTERLE, K., Chemical Engineering

Faculty of Mechanical Engineering:

ANTONICKÝ, S., Transportation and Technology
BAILOTTI, K., Transportation and Preparation Equipment
DANĚK, J., Transportation and Technology
DEJL, Z., Machine Parts and Mechanisms
GONDEK, H., Mining Machinery
JANALÍK, J., Hydraulic Machines and Mechanisms
KOLAT, P., Thermal and Nuclear Power Engineering
KOUKAL, J., Engineering Technology
KUČERA, J., Technical Mechanics
LENERT, J., Mechanics
NOSKIEVIČ, P., Power Engineering
ONDROUCH, J., Technical Mechanics
POKORNÝ, A., Metallurgy
POLAK, J., Transportation and Manipulation Technology
PURMENSKÝ, J., Mechanical Technology
VÍTEČEK, A., Automation of Machines and Technological Processes
VNUK, V., Machine Parts and Mechanisms

Faculty of Electrical Engineering and Informatics:

BLUNÁR, K., Communications Technology
ČERMÁK, T., Electrical Drives
DOSTÁL, Z., Applied Mathematics
HASLINGER, J., Applied Mathematics
HRADÍLEK, Z., Electrical Power Engineering
LITSCHMANN, J., Engineering Cybernetics
NEVŘIVA, P., Technical Cybernetics
SANTARIUS, Electric Power Engineering

Faculty of Economics:

BALHAR, V., Foreign Trade Economics
HADERKA, J., Civil Law
JUREČKA, V., General Economics
KALUŽA, J., Informatics in Economics
KOLIČ, P., Enterprise and Management
MOČKOŘ, J., Algebra and Theory of Numbers
NEJEZCHLEBA, M., Finance
SMOLÍK, D., Environmental Protection and Reclamation
SNAPKA, P., Mining Economics and Management
STAVKOVÁ, J., Statistics
VLČEK, D., Systems Engineering

Faculty of Civil Engineering:

ALDORF, J.
BRADAC, J.
CIGANEK J.
MAREK, P.
TOMICA, V.

VYSOKÁ ŠKOLA CHEMICKO-TECHNOLOGICKÁ V PRAZE (Institute of Chemical Technology, Prague)

166 28 Prague 6, Technická 1905
Telephone: 24-35-11-11
Fax: 24-31-10-82

Founded 1807
State control
Languages of instruction: Czech
Academic year: September to June

Rector: Dr JOSEF KOUBEK
Vice-Rectors: Prof. OSKAR SCHMIDT (Science and Research), Dr JIŘÍ HAVRDA (Education), Dr JAN STANĚK (Development), Dr VLASTIMIL RŮŽIČKA (Foreign)
Registrar: Dr TOMÁŠ BARTOVSKÝ
Librarian: Dr ANNA SOUČKOVÁ

Library of 225,000 vols
Number of teachers: 360
Number of students: 2,700

Publication: *Sborník VŠCHT v Praze*.

DEANS

Faculty of Chemical Technology: Prof. LIBOR ČERVENÝ
Faculty of Environmental Engineering: Assoc. Prof. GUSTAV ŠEBOR
Faculty of Food and Biochemical Technology: Prof. PAVEL KADLEC
Faculty of Chemical Engineering: Prof. KAREL KADLEC

PROFESSORS

BASAŘOVÁ, G., Fermentation Chemistry and Biotechnology
BURYAN, P., Gas, Coke and Air Protection
ČERNÝ, C., Physical Chemistry
ČERVENÝ, L., Organic Technology
ČURDA, D., Food Preservation
DAVÍDEK, J., Food Chemistry and Technology
DEMNEROVÁ, K., Biochemistry and Microbiology
DOHÁNYOS, M., Water Technology and Environmental
DUCHÁČEK, V., Polymers
HAJŠLOVÁ, J., Food Chemistry and Analysis
HANIKA, J., Organic Technology
HLAVÁČ, J., Silicate Technology
HORÁK, J., Organic Technology
HUDEC, L., Technology of Materials for Electronics
JURSÍK, F., Inorganic Chemistry
KADLEC, P., Sugar Technology
KÁŠ, J., Biochemistry
KRÁLOVÁ, B., Biochemistry and Microbiology
KSANDR, Z., Analytical Chemistry
KUBÍČEK, M., Mathematics
KURAŠ, M., Environmental Engineering
KUTHAN, J., Organic Chemistry
LIŠKA, F., Organic Chemistry
MALIJEVSKÝ, A., Physical Chemistry
MAREK, M., Chemical Engineering
MATOUŠEK, J., Silicate Technology
NOVÁK, J., Physical Chemistry
PÁCA, J., Fermentation Chemistry and Biotechnology
PALAČEK, J., Organic Chemistry
PALETA, O., Organic Chemistry
PAŠEK, J., Organic Technology
PECKA, K., Petroleum Technology and Petrochemistry
PELIKÁN, J., Power Engineering
PITTER, P., Water Technology and Environmental Engineering
POKORNÝ, J., Food Chemistry and Technology
RAUCH, P., Biochemistry
RYCHTERA, M., Fermentation Chemistry and Biotechnology
SCHMIDT, O., Automated Control Systems
SLÁDEČKOVÁ, A., Water Technology and Environmental Engineering
STANĚK, J., Glass and Ceramics
ŠTIBOR, I., Organic Chemistry
ŠAŠEK, L., Silicate Technology
ŠEBOR, G., Petroleum Technology and Petrochemistry
ŠILHÁNKOVÁ, L., Biochemistry
VELÍŠEK, J., Food Chemistry and Technology
VOLKA, K., Analytical Chemistry
WANNER, J., Water Technology and Environmental Engineering

UNIVERZITA PARDUBICE (University of Pardubice)

532 10 Pardubice, Studentská 95

Telephone: (40) 603-61-11
Fax: (40) 603-63-61
E-mail: promotion@upce.cz

Founded 1950 as Vysoká Škola Chemicko-Technologická v Pardubicích; present name and status 1994
State control
Languages of instruction: Czech and English
Academic year: September to August

Rector: Prof. Ing. OLDŘICH PYTELA
Vice-Rectors: Doc. Ing. MIROSLAV LUDWIG, Doc. Ing. JAROSLAV JANDA, Doc. Ing. JAN ČAPEK
Bursar: Ing. MILAN BUKAČ
Librarian: IVA PROCHÁSKOVÁ

Library of 180,000 vols
Number of teachers: 310
Number of students: 3,660

Publications: *Scientific Papers* (annually), *Zapravodaj Univerzity Pardubice* (quarterly).

DEANS

Faculty of Chemical Technology: Doc. Ing. JOSEF KOTYK
Faculty of Economics and Administration: Doc. Ing. RADIM ROUDNÝ
Jan Perner Faculty of Transport: Prof. Ing. MILAN LÁNSKÝ
Institute of Languages and Humanities: Doc. PhDr VĚRA POLÁČKOVÁ

TECHNICKÁ UNIVERZITA V LIBERCI (Technical University of Liberec)

461 17 Liberec, Hálkova 6

Telephone: (48) 254 41-9
Fax: (48) 510-58-82

Founded 1953
State control
Languages of instruction: Czech and English
Academic year: September to June

Rector: Assoc. Prof. DAVID LUKÁŠ
Pro-Rectors: Prof. ZDENĚK KOVÁŘ, Assoc. Prof. PETR GOLKA
Registrar: PETR STRÁDAL
Librarian: VLADIMÍR STUDENÝ

Number of teachers: 426
Number of students: 5,055

Publication: *Sborník vědeckých prací Technické univerzity* (Annals of Scientific Research).

DEANS

Faculty of Mechanical Engineering: Prof. JAROSLAV EXNER
Faculty of Textile Engineering: Prof. JIŘÍ MILITKÝ
Faculty of Education: Assoc. Prof. JAROSLAV VILD
Faculty of Economics and Business Administration: Prof. JAN EHLEMANN
Faculty of Architecture: Assoc. Prof. JIŘÍ SUCHOMEL
Faculty of Mechatronics: Assoc. Prof. VOJTĚCH KONOPA

PROFESSORS

BAKULE, V., Finance and Credit
BENEŠ, S., Construction of Machines and Appliances
ČERNÝ, I., Mathematical Analysis
CIHELSKÝ, L., Statistics
EHLEMAN, J., Information Management
EXNER, J., Mechanical Engineering Technology
FOUSEK, J., Electromechanical Properties of Dielectrics
HONCŮ, J., Machine Design
JANOVEC, V., Electromechanical Properties of Dielectrics
KAŇOKOVÁ, J., Statistics
KOPKA, J., Teaching of Mathematics
KOVÁŘ, Z., Combustion Engines
KRATOCHVÍL, J., Thermomechanics and Fluid Mechanics
KRYŠTŮFEK, J., Textile Technology
LANDOROVÁ, A., Financing
MIKEŠ, V., Mechanical Engineering Technology
MILITKÝ, J., Textile Technology
NECKÁŘ, B., Structure of Textiles
NOSEK, S., Textile Machines
NOŽIČKA, F., Mathematics
ŠKALOUD, M., Mechanics
ŠPINAR, J., Political Economics
STŘEDA, I., Thermomechanics
STŘÍŽ, B., Elasticity and Strength
SVOBODA, S., Accountancy
VĚCHET, V., Technical Cybernetics
VODÁČEK, L., Information Management
VOKURKA, K., Applied Physics
VOSTATEK, J., Finance
ZELENKA, J., Radioelectronics
ZELINKA, B., Mathematical Informatics and Theoretical Cybernetics

ZÁPADOČESKÁ UNIVERZITA (University of West Bohemia)

306 14 Plzeň, Univerzitní 8

Telephone: (19) 27-93-63
Fax: (19) 27-93-61

Founded 1949 as college, present name 1991
State control
Language of instruction: Czech
Academic year: September to June

Rector: Prof. Ing. ZDENĚK VOSTRACKÝ
Pro-Rectors: Prof. Ing. JOSEF ROSENBERG, Doc. Ing. JAROMÍR HORÁK, Doc. Ing. ŠTĚPÁN RUSŇÁK
Registrar: Doc. Ing. JOSEF PRŮŠA
Librarians: Mgr ALENA SCHOŘOVSKÁ, PhDr MILOSLAVA FAITOVÁ

Library of 424,000 vols
Number of teachers: 688
Number of students: 9,645

Publication: *Sborník vědeckých prací.*

DEANS

Faculty of Mechanical Engineering: Doc. Ing. PETR HOFMANN
Faculty of Electrical Engineering: Doc. Ing. VLASTIMIL SKOČIL
Faculty of Applied Sciences: Prof. RNDr STANISLAV MÍKA
Faculty of Economics: Doc. Ing. JIŘÍ BECK
Faculty of Education: Doc. RNDr JAROSLAV DRÁBEK
Faculty of Law: Dr VLADIMÍR BALÁŠ

PROFESSORS

Faculty of Mechanical Engineering:

KOTT, J., Nuclear Power Equipment and Alternative Energetics
KOUTSKÝ, J., Physical Metallurgy and Physics of Strength and Plasticity
ŠKOPEK, J., Thermal Power Equipment
ŽENÍŠEK, J., Theory and Design of Machine Tools and Accessories

Faculty of Electrical Engineering:

BERAN, M., Electric Power Generation and Distribution
JERHOT, J., Electronics
KULE, L., Electrical Drives
MAYER, D., Electrical Machines and Apparatus
RYBÁŘ, J., Electrical Machines
ŠVAJCR, L., Electrical Machines and Apparatus
VONDRÁŠEK, F., Electrical Drives
VOSTRACKÝ, Z., Electrical Apparatus

Faculty of Applied Sciences:

DRÁBEK, P., Mathematical Analysis
KLÁTIL, J., Mathematical Analysis
KUFNER, A., Mathematical Analysis
MÍKA, S., Mathematical Analysis
PLÁNIČKA, F., Physical Metallurgy and Physics of Strength and Plasticity
ROSENBERG, J., Mechanics of Rigid and Deformable Bodies and Systems
ZEMAN, V., Mechanics of Rigid and Deformable Bodies and Systems

Faculty of Education:

JÍLEK, T., History
KLIMEŠ, L., Czech Language
KRAITR, M., Analytical Chemistry, Chemical Technology
MACEK, Z., General History
MIŠTERA, L., Economic and Regional Geography

ATTACHED RESEARCH INSTITUTES

Institute of Physical Engineering: Dir Prof. MIROSLAV BALDA.

VYSOKÁ ŠKOLA EKONOMICKÁ (Prague University of Economics)

130 67 Prague 3, Nám. W. Churchilla 4

Telephone: (2) 24-09-51-11
Fax: (2) 24-22-06-57

Founded 1953
State control
Language of instruction: Czech
Academic year: September to June

Rector: Prof. JAN SEGER
Vice-Rectors: Prof. JAROSLAVA DURČÁKOVÁ, Prof. MIROSLAV MAŇAS; Prof. ALEXEJ ŠVAGR

Number of students: 10,600

Faculties of Finance and Accounting, International Relations, Business Administration, Informatics and Statistics, Public Administration, Management.

ČESKÁ ZEMĚDĚLSKÁ UNIVERZITA V PRAZE (Czech University of Agriculture, Prague)

165 21 Prague 6, Suchdol, Kamýcká 129

Telephone: 338-11-11
Fax: 34-19-69

Founded 1906
State control
Language of instruction: Czech
Academic year: September to August

Rector: Prof. Dr JAN HRON
Pro-Rectors: Prof. Dr JOSEF KOZÁK, Prof. Dr IVAN VRANA, Prof. Dr PAVEL KOVÁŘ, Prof. Dr JOSEF PECEN
Registrar: Dr MILOŠ FRÝBORT
Librarian: Dr IVAN HAUZNER

Library of 225,000 vols
Number of teachers: 429
Number of students: 3,700

Publications: *Scientific Papers*, *Agricultura tropica et subtropica* (1 or 2 a year), *Scientia Agriculturae Bohemica* (quarterly).

DEANS

Faculty of Agricultural Economics and Management: Prof. Dr MIROSLAV SVATOŠ
Faculty of Agronomy: Prof. Dr VÁCLAV VANĚK
Faculty of Forestry: Prof. Dr IVAN ROČEK
Technical Faculty: Prof. Dr SLAVOMÍR PROCHÁZKA
Institute of Applied Ecology: RNDr ZDENĚK LIPSKÝ (Vice-Dean)
Institute of Tropical and Subtropical Agriculture: Prof. Dr JAN BLÁHA

HEADS OF DEPARTMENTS

Faculty of Agricultural Economics and Management:

Agricultural Economics: M. SVATOŠ
General Economics: J. KEILL
Computer Science: I. VRANA
Languages: M. DVOŘÁKOVÁ
Law: J. HOMOLKOVÁ
Management: J. HRON
Operational Research: J. ZÍSKAL
Philosophy and Sociology: K. HAUZER
Psychology: Z. PECHAČOVÁ
Statistics: B. KÁBA
Trade and Finance: A. VALDER

Faculty of Agronomy:

Agrochemistry and Plant Nutrition: J. VOSTAL
Animal Nutrition: Z. MUDŘÍK
Botany and Plant Physiology: K. DOLEJŠ
Cattle Breeding: F. LOUDA
Chemistry and Quality of Products: J. KOVÁŘ
Forage Crops: J. ŠANTRŮČEK
General Animal Husbandry: I. MAJZLÍK
General Plant Production and Agrometeorology: V. ŠKODA
Genetics and Breeding: J. ČERNÝ
Horticulture: J. DUFFEK
Microbiology and Biotechnology: L. VOŘÍŠEK
Zoology and Fishery: M. BARTÁK
Pig and Poultry Breeding: E. TŮMOVÁ
Plant Protection: V. TÁBORSKÝ
Soil Science and Geology: J. KOZÁK
Special Plant Production: J. VAŠÁK
Veterinary Medicine: F. JÍLEK

Faculty of Forestry:

Dendrology: V. CHALUPA
Ecology: J. FIGALA
Forest Economics and Management: K. PULKRAB
Forest Protection: V. KALINA
Forest Surveys and Management: V. KOUBA
Landscape Management: M. JANEČEK
Logging Technology and Timber Processing: I. ROČEK
Silviculture: V. GLOMB
Water Management: F. HRÁDEK

Technical Faculty:

Agricultural Machines: A. RYBKA
Electrical Engineering and Automation: K. POKORNÝ
Exploitation of Tractors and Machines: M. KAVKA
Farmyard Mechanization: M. PŘIKRYL
Materials and Technologies: M. BROŽEK
Mathematics: V. SLAVIK
Mechanics and Engineering: J. SCHELLER
Operational Reliability of Machines: J. POŠTA
Physics: J. PECEN
Tractors and Automobiles: V. KŘEPELKA

MENDELOVA ZEMĚDĚLSKÁ A LESNICKÁ UNIVERZITA V BRNĚ (Mendel University of Agriculture and Forestry, Brno)

613 00 Brno, Zemědělská 1

Telephone: 451-311-11
Fax: 452-111-28

Founded by State Law in 1919
State control
Language of instruction: Czech
Academic year: September to January, February to June

Rector: P. JELÍNEK
Pro-Rectors: K. VINOHRADSKÝ, J. ZELENKA, V. ŽIDEK, Z. POŠVÁŘ
Chief Administrative Officer: V. SEDLÁŘOVÁ
Chief Librarian: V. KELLEROVÁ

Library of 400,000 vols
Number of teachers: 350
Number of students: 4,587 full-time, 423 part-time

Publications: *Acta Universitatis Agriculturae et Silviculturae Mendelianae Brunensis*, *Folia Universitatis Agriculturae.*

DEANS

Faculty of Agronomy: I. INGR
Faculty of Horticulture: M. RAJNOCH
Faculty of Economics: J. STÁVKOVÁ
Faculty of Forestry and Wood Technology: L. SLONEK

HEADS OF DEPARTMENTS

Faculty of Agronomy:

Agricultural Mechanization: J. ČERVINKA
Agricultural Plant Protection: K. VEVERKA
Agrochemistry and Plant Nutrition: R. RICHTER
Anatomy and Physiology of Farm Animals: P. JELÍNEK
Basis of Mechanization and Machinery Repairs: M. HAVLÍČEK
Botany and Plant Physiology: S. PROCHÁZKA
Chemistry and Biochemistry: V. KUBÁŇ
Farm Animal Breeding: J. ŽIŽLAVSKÝ
Fisheries and Hydrobiology: P. SPURNÝ
Forage Crops and Feed Production: F. HRABĚ
General Plant Production: J. KŘEN
Genetics: J. DVOŘÁK
Landscape Ecology: J. PALL
Molecular Embryology: P. DVOŘÁK
Nuclear Methods: M. PÖSCHL
Nutrition and Feeding of Farm Animals: J. ZELENKA
Physical Education: L. ŠTEFL
Plant Production and Breeding: O. CHLOUPEK
Processing of Agricultural Products: J. MAREČEK
Soil Science and Microbiology: M. TESAŘOVÁ
Technology of Agricultural Products: S. GAJDŮŠEK
Zoology and Apiculture: Z. LAŠTŮVKA

Faculty of Economics:

Accounting: V. VYBÍHAL
Business Economics: L. GREGA
Finance: O. REJNUŠ
Humanities: S. HUBÍK
Informatics: A. MOTYČKA
Law: M. JANKŮ
Management: J. ERBES
Marketing and Trade Business: J. STÁVKOVÁ
Statistics and Operational Analysis: M. RAŠOVSKÝ

Faculty of Forestry and Wood Technology:

Basic Wood Processing: L. SLONEK
Economics and Management: F. KALOUSEK
Forest Botany, Dendrology and Typology: J. KOBLÍŽEK
Forest Ecology: E. KLIMO
Forest Engineering and Reclamation: J. HERYNEK
Forest Establishment: E. PALÁTOVÁ
Forest Management: J. SIMON
Wood Science: P. HORÁČEK
Forest Protection: R. MRKVA
Forestry and Wood Technology: A. SKOUPÝ
Furniture and Special Wood Products: F. ŠVANCARA
Game Management: J. HROMAS
Geomatics: V. ŽIDEK
Languages: A. ŘEHÁKOVÁ
Mathematics: G. VOSMANSKÁ
Silviculture: P. KANTOR
Soil Science and Geology: B. HRUŠKA

Faculty of Horticulture:

Biotechnology of Landscape Vegetation: M. RAJNOCH
Breeding and Propagation of Horticultural Plants: V. ŘEZNÍČEK
Fruit Growing and Viticulture: B. KRŠKA
Horticultural Technology: J. ŽUFÁNEK
Landscape Gardening and Architecture: J. DAMEC
Post-harvest Technology of Horticultural Plants: J. GOLIÁŠ
Vegetable Growing and Floriculture: K. PETŘÍKOVÁ
Mendeleum Experimental Station: M. KADLEC

All-University Departments:

Botanical Garden and Arboretum: A. NOHEL
Computer Centre: V. FIŠER
Institute of Scientific Information: J. POTÁČEK

Faculties of Theology

EVANGELIKÁ TEOLOGICKÁ FAKULTA UNIVERSITY KARLOVY

(Protestant Theological Faculty of the Charles University in Prague)

115 55 Prague 1, Černá 9

Telephone: (2) 21-98-82-00
Fax: (2) 21-98-82-15

Founded 1919

Dean: PETR POKORNÝ
Pro-Deans: PAVEL FILIPI, JINŘICH HALAMA, PETR MACEK, JAKUB TROJAN
Library of 190,000 vols

Number of teachers: 24
Number of students: 300

Publication: *Communio viatorum* (3 a year).

HUSITSKÁ TEOLOGICKÁ FAKULTA UNIVERSITY KARLOVY V PRAZE

(Hussite Faculty of Theology of the Charles University in Prague)

160 00 Prague 6, Wuchterlova 5

Telephone: 24-32-34-20
Fax: 24-32-34-19

Founded 1919

Dean: Prof. Dr ZDENĚK KUČERA
Vice-Dean: Dr VLADIMIR ŠTVERÁK

Number of teachers: 25
Number of students: 350

KATOLICKÁ TEOLOGICKÁ FAKULTA UNIVERSITY KARLOVY V PRAZE

(Roman Catholic Faculty of Theology of Charles University in Prague)

160 00 Prague 6, Thákurova 3

Telephone: 33-15-600
Fax: 33-15-215

Founded 1348

Dean: Prof. Dr VÁCLAV WOLF

Number of teachers: 30
Number of students: 180/350

Schools of Art and Music

AKADEMIE MÚZICKÝCH UMĚNÍ

(Academy of Performing Arts)

118 00 Prague 1, Malostranské nám. 12

Telephone: 53-09-43
Fax: 53-05-01
E-mail: tamara.curikova@amu.cz

Founded 1945

Rector: JAROSLAV MALINA
Vice-Rectors: ZDENĚK KIRSCHNER, PETER TOPERCZER, VÁCLAV SYROVÝ
Registrar: TAMARA ČUŘÍKOVÁ
Library of 97,000 vols

Number of teachers: 254
Number of students: 1,101

DEANS

Faculty of Film and Television: JAN BERNARD
Faculty of Music: IVAN KURZ
Faculty of Theatre: VLADIMÍR MIKEŠ

Publications: *Acta Academica Informatorium* (10 a year), *Acta Academica* (1 a year).

AKADEMIE VÝTVARNÝCH UMĚNÍ

(Academy of Fine Arts)

170 22 Prague 7, U akademie 4

Telephone: (2) 37-36-41
Fax: (2) 37-57-81

Founded 1799

Courses in painting, drawing, sculpture, architecture, graphic art, intermedia, video art and restoration

Rector: Doc. Dr JIŘÍ T. KOTALÍK
Pro-Rectors: Prof. ZDENĚK BERAN, Dr JIŘÍ ŠEVČÍK
Registrar: Ing. VLADIMÍR KALUGIN
Library of 50,000 vols

Number of teachers: 53
Number of students: 237

Publications: *Almanach*, *Catalogues*.

JANÁČKOVA AKADEMIE MÚZICKÝCH UMĚNÍ

(Janáček Academy of Music and Dramatic Art)

662 15 Brno, Komenského nám. 6

Telephone: (5) 42-32-13-07
Fax: (5) 42-21-32-86
E-mail: hajda@jamu.cz

Founded 1947

Rector: Prof. ALOIS HAJDA
Vice-Rectors: Prof. B. HAULIK, Prof. P. SCHERHAUFER
Registrar: E. GONDEK

Library of 100,000 vols; special collections of printed music and records

Number of teachers: 112
Number of students: 519

Publications: *Sborníky a spisy JAMU*, etc.

VYSOKÁ ŠKOLA UMĚLECKOPRŮMYSLOVÁ

(Academy of Applied Arts)

116 93 Prague 2, nám. Jana Palacha 80

Telephone: 21-70-81-11
Fax: 21-70-82-40

Founded 1885

Rector: Dr JOSEF HLAVÁČEK
Vice-Rector: Dr J. VYBÍRAL
Registrar: Ing. LUBOŠ KVAPIL

Number of teachers: 55
Number of students: 360

Janáčkova konzervatoř v Ostravě: 729 62 Moravská Ostrava, Českobratrská 40; tel. (69) 611-20-07; fax (69) 611-14-43; f. 1953; 145 teachers, 376 students; library of 23,000 vols, 7,000 records; Dir MILAN BÁCHOREK.

Konzervatoř, Brno (Conservatoire in Brno): 662 54 Brno, třída kpt. Jaroše 45; tel. and fax (5) 45-21-55-68; f. 1919; music and drama departments; 124 professors, 360 students; library of 7,000 vols, 29,900 scores, 1,600 records; Dir Mgr E. ZÁMEČNÍK.

Konzervatoř P. J. Vejvanovského, Kroměříž: 767 64 Kroměříž, Pilařova 7; tel. 225-01; e-mail mus.cons-km@snt.cz; f. 1949; 55 teachers, 190 students; library of 16,000 vols, 4,600 records; Dir M. ŠIŠKA.

Konzervatoř, Pardubice: 530 02 Pardubice, Sukova tř 1260; tel. and fax (40) 513-503; f. 1978; 79 teachers, 172 students; library of 2,200 books, 7,500 vols of music, 1,100 records; Dir Mgr MILOSLAV STŘÍTESKÝ.

Konzervatoř, Plzeň: 301 35 Plzeň, Kopeckého sady 10; tel. (19) 722-63-25; fax (19) 722-63-87; f. 1961; 78 teachers, 158 students; library of 1,500 books, 1,400 records and CDs, 7,000 scores; Dir KAREL FRIESL.

Konzervatoř, Praha: 110 00 Prague 1, Na Rejdišti 1; tel. 231-91-02; fax 232-64-06; e-mail conserv@prgeons.cz; f. 1808; 254 professors, 600 students; library of 85,000 vols, 19,000 records; Dir Prof. VĚROSLAV NEUMANN; Chief of Library (Archives) PhDr JITŘENKA PEŠKOVÁ.

Konzervatoř, Teplice: 415 01 Teplice, Českobratrská 15; tel. 264-01; fax 427-89; f. 1971; 80 teachers, 200 students; library of 10,000 vols, 800 records; Dir MILAN KUBÍK.

Taneční Konzervatoř (Prague Conservatory of Dance): 110 00 Prague 1, Křižovnická 7; tel. 231-91-45; fax 232-49-77; f. 1945; 60 teachers, 175 students; small library; Dir J. PACLÍK; publ. *Taneční listy* (Dance Review).

DENMARK

Learned Societies

GENERAL

Kongelige Danske Videnskabernes Selskab (Royal Danish Academy of Science and Letters): H. C. Andersens Blvd 35, 1553 Copenhagen V; tel. 33-11-32-40; fax 33-91-07-36; e-mail pg@royalacademy.dk; f. 1742; sections of History and Philosophy (Chair. DAVID FAVRHOLDT), Mathematics and Natural Sciences (Chair. TOM FENCHEL); 234 Danish mems, 265 foreign mems; Pres. BIRGER MUNK OLSEN; Sec. THOR A. BAK; Chief of Secretariat PIA GRÜNER; publs *Oversigt* (annually), *Meddelelser*, (Mathematics and Physics, History and Philosophy), *Skrifter* (History and Philosophy, Biology).

AGRICULTURE, FISHERIES AND VETERINARY SCIENCE

Dansk Skovforening (Danish Forestry Society): Amalievej 20, 1875 Frederiksberg C; tel. 33-24-42-66; fax 33-24-02-42; f. 1888; attends to the commercial and professional interests of Danish forestry; Chair. GUSTAV BERNER; Gen. Man. JAN SØNDERGAARD; publ. *Skoven* (monthly).

Dansk Veterinærhistorisk Samfund (Danish Veterinary History Society): Svalgårdsvej 20, Sjørring, 7700 Thisted; tel. and fax 97-97-10-01; f. 1934; 300 mems; Pres. ANTON ROSENBOM; publ. *Dansk Veterinærhistorisk Årbog* (every 2 years).

Foreningen af Mejeriledere og Funktionærer (Association of Dairy Managers): Det gamle Mejeri, Landbrugsvej 65, 5260 Odense S; f. 1887; tel. 66-12-40-25; 900 mems; Dir K. MARK CHRISTENSEN; publ. *Maelkeritidende* (fortnightly).

Jordbrugsakademikernes Forbund (Danish Federation of Graduates in Agriculture, Horticulture, Forestry and Landscape Architecture): Strandvejen 863, 2930 Klampenborg; tel. 39-97-01-00; fax 39-97-01-19; e-mail post@jordbrugsakademikerne.dk; f. 1976; 5,300 mems; Chair. LISBETH ARBOE JAKOBSEN; publ. *Jord og Viden*.

Kongelige Danske Landhusholdningsselskab, Det (Royal Danish Agricultural Society): Mariendalsvej 27, 2., 2000 Frederiksberg; f. 1769; Pres JON KRABBE, IVER TESDORPF, KIRSTEN JAKOBSEN, NIELS KÆRGÅRD, BRITTA SCHALL HOLBERG; Dir GRETHE ERSKOV.

ARCHITECTURE AND TOWN PLANNING

Dansk Byplanlaboratorium (Danish Town Planning Institute): Peder Skramsgade 2B, 1054 Copenhagen K; tel. 33-13-72-81; fax 33-14-34-35; e-mail db@byplanlab.dk; f. 1921; educational services and seminars; library of 17,000 vols; complete collection of public documents and reports concerning urban and regional planning in Denmark; Chair. PEDER BALTZER NIELSEN; Sec. OLE DAMSGAARD.

Danske Arkitekters Landsforbund/ Akademisk Arkitektforening (Federation of Danish Architects): Bredgade 66, Postbox 1163, 1260 Copenhagen K; f. 1951; 5,900 mems; Pres. VIGGO GRUNNET; Dir BENTE BEEDHOLM; publs *Arkitekten, Arkitektur*.

BIBLIOGRAPHY, LIBRARY SCIENCE AND MUSEOLOGY

Danmarks Biblioteksforening (Danish Library Association): Telegrafvej 5, 2750 Ballerup; tel. 44-68-14-66; fax 44-68-11-03; f. 1905; Dir WINNIE VITZANSKY; publs *Bogens Verden* (World of Books, 6 a year), *Danmarks Biblioteker* (Newsletter, 10 a year), *Biblioteksvejviser* (Directory, annually).

Danmarks Forskningsbiblioteksforening (Danish Research Library Association): Odense Universitetsbibliotek, Campusvej 55, 5230 Odense M; tel. 66-15-67-68; fax 66-15-81-62; f. 1978; 700 personal, 140 institutional mems; Pres. ERLAND KOLDING NIELSEN; publ. *DF-Revy*.

Dansk Biblioteks Center a.s.: Tempovej 7-11, 2750 Ballerup; tel. 44-86-77-77; fax 44-86-78-91; f. 1991; provides bibliographical services for Danish libraries, including centralized cataloguing, national bibliographies, book lists and special bibliographies for Danish libraries; Man. Dir MOGENS BRABAND JENSEN; Dir KIRSTEN WANECK; publs the Danish National Bibliography of books, audiovisual materials, articles and reviews on database (DanBib) and CD-ROM, etc.

Dansk Kulturhistorisk Museumsforening: Nr. Madsbadvej 6, 7884 Fur; tel. 97-59-35-66; fax 97-59-31-63; f. 1929; annual assemblies and study meetings; 167 institutional mems; Curator LARS HOLST; Sec. KIRSTEN REX ANDERSEN.

Foreningen af Danske Kunstmuseer (Union of Danish Art Museums): Nr. Madsbadvej 6, 7884 Fur; tel. 97-59-35-66; fax 97-59-31-63; f. 1978; 50 institutional mems; Chair. LARS KÆRULF MOELLER; Sec. KIRSTEN REX ANDERSEN.

Foreningen af Danske Museumsmaend (Association of Danish Museum Curators): Zoologisk Museum, 15 Universitetsparken, 2100 Copenhagen Ø; f. 1928; 250 mems; Pres. TOVE HATTING; Sec. BI SKAARUP.

ECONOMICS, LAW AND POLITICS

Danmarks Jurist- og Økonomforbund (Danish Lawyers and Economists Association): Gothersgade 133, 1123 Copenhagen K; tel. 33-95-97-00; fax 33-95-99-99; f. 1972; 35,000 mems; Dir ROLF TVEDT; publ. *DJØF Efteruddannelse* (2 a year).

Dansk Selskab for Europaforskning (Danish Society for European Studies): Studiestrade 6, 1455 Copenhagen K; tel. 35-32-31-29; fax 35-32-40-00; f. 1975; aims to promote Danish academic study and teaching of the legal, economic, political and social aspects of European integration by means of seminars, publishing a newsletter, etc.; 130 mems; Chair. Prof. H. RASMUSSEN.

International Law Association – Danish Branch: c/o Hon. Sec. A. KAUFMANN, Skoubogade 1, 1000 Copenhagen K; f. 1925; Pres. Prof. ALLAN PHILIP.

Nationalekonomisk Forening (Danish Economic Association): Danmarks Nationalbank, Havnegade 5, 1093 Copenhagen K; tel. 33-14-14-11; fax 33-91-30-41; f. 1873; 1,500 mems; Chair. Prof. NIELS CHRISTIAN NIELSEN; Sec. LISBETH BORUP; publ. *Nationaloekonomisk Tidsskrift* (3 a year).

Udenrigspolitiske Selskab (Foreign Policy Society): Amaliegade 40A, 1256 Copenhagen K; tel. 33-14-88-86; fax 33-14-85-20; e-mail udenrigs@udenrigs.dk; f. 1946; studies, debates, courses and conferences on international affairs; library of 100 periodicals; Dir K. CARSTEN PEDERSEN; Chair. UFFE ELLEMANN-JENSEN; publs *Udenrigs, Udenrigspolitiske Skrifter, Lande i Lommeformat*.

EDUCATION

Folkeuniversitetsudvalget (Committee for University Extension Services in Denmark): University of Odense, 5230 Odense M; f. 1898; Chair. Prof. CARL F. WANDEL; Man. Dir Dr JENS E. OLESEN.

Mellemfolkeligt Samvirke (Danish Association for International Co-operation): Borgergade 14, 1300 Copenhagen K; tel. 33-32-62-44; fax 33-15-62-43; e-mail ms@ms-dan.dk; f. 1944; administration of Danish development workers and International Work Camps; public information service on the problems of the developing countries and international co-operation; 5,200 mems; specialized library of 30,000 vols on third world issues, immigrants and refugees in Denmark, 400 periodicals; Gen. Sec. BJOERN FOERDE; publs *Kontakt* (8 a year), *Zapp* (6 a year), *MS-revy* (8 a year).

Rektorkollegiet (Danish Rectors' Conference): Vester Voldgade 121A (4. sal), 1552 Copenhagen V; f. 1967; tel. 33-92-54-05; fax 33-92-50-75; e-mail hr@rks.dk; consulting authority for co-operation and communication between institutions of higher education and the Ministry of Education; mems: the rectors of the 17 institutions of higher education in Denmark; Chair. Prof. HANS PETER JENSEN; Sec. ELLEN HANSEN.

FINE AND PERFORMING ARTS

Billedkunstnernes Forbund (Artists' Association): Vingårdstræde 21, 1070 Copenhagen K.; tel. 33-12-81-70; 1,250 mems; Pres. JANE BALSGÅRD; Sec. ANNE MARIE NEHAMMER.

Dansk Billedhuggersamfund (Danish Sculptors' Society): Høgstedgård, Hyrup 7140 Stouby; tel. 75-89-75-15; f. 1905; 120 mems; Chair. MARKAN CHRISTENSEN.

Dansk Komponistforening (Danish Composers' Society): Gråbrødretorv 16, 1, 1154 Copenhagen K; tel. 33-13-54-05; fax 33-14-32-19; f. 1913; 166 mems; Chair. MOGENS WINKEL HOLM; Sec. KIRSTEN WREM.

Dansk Korforening (Danish Choral Society): Absalonsgade 3, 4180 Sorø; f. 1911; mems: 27 choirs; Pres. ASGER LARSEN.

Danske Kunsthåndværkeres Landssammenslutning (DKL) (Danish Arts and Crafts Association): Linnésgade 20, 1361 Copenhagen K; tel. 33-15-29-40; fax 33-15-26-76; f. 1976; arranges exhibitions; professional advice for schools, museums, etc.; 380 mems; 8 regional groups of artist-craftsmen; Exec. Sec. NINA LINDE; publ. *Dansk Kunsthåndværk* (quarterly).

Kunstforeningen i København (Copenhagen Art Association): Gl. Strand 48, 1202 Copenhagen K; tel. 33-36-02-60; fax 33-36-02-66; e-mail admin@kunstforeningen.dk; f. 1825; exhibitions of modern and contemporary art; Dir HELLE BEHRNDT.

Kunstnerforeningen af 18. November (Artists' Association of the 18th November): Frederiksgade 8, 1265 Copenhagen K; tel. 33-15-96-14; f. 1842; workshop, lectures, concerts, exhibitions, art collection and library of *c.* 300 vols; 150 mems; Pres. NIELS WAMBERG; Vice-Pres. MOGENS HØVER.

Ny Carlsbergfondet (New Carlsberg Foundation): Brolæggerstræde 5, 1211 Copenhagen K; f. 1902; supports art and history of art in Denmark; Pres. H. E. NØRREGÅRD-NIELSEN.

Samfundet til Udgivelse af Dansk Musik (Society for Publication of Danish Music): Gråbrødrestræde 18, 1156 Copenhagen K; tel. 33-13-54-45; fax 33-93-30-44; e-mail sales@samfundet.dk; f. 1871; Chair. KLAUS IB JØRGENSEN; Sec. NIELS PRINS.

Sammenslutningen af Danske Kunstforeninger (National Committee of Danish Art Societies): Skt. Annæ Plads 10C, 1250 Copenhagen K; f. 1942; arranges touring art exhibitions with government support; 15,000 mems; Pres. AGNETE SØRENSEN; Sec. RUTH KOBBELTVEDT.

HISTORY, GEOGRAPHY AND ARCHAEOLOGY

Arktisk Institut (Arctic Institute): Strandgade 100 H, 1401 Copenhagen K; tel. 32-88-01-50; fax 32-88-01-51; f. 1954; information, scientific and historic activities; library of 8,000 vols, archives of Arctic expeditions, diaries, and over 50,000 photographs, mainly of Greenland; Man. JENS FABRICIUS.

Dansk Selskab for Oldtids- og Middelalderforskning (Danish Society for Research of Ancient and Medieval Times): Nationalmuseet, 1220 Copenhagen K; f. 1934; 120 mems; Pres. RIKKE AGNETE OLSEN; Sec. KELD GRUNDE HANSEN; publ. *Classica et Mediaevalia*, Vols 1–35.

Danske Historiske Forening (Danish Historical Society): Njalsgade 102, 2300 Copenhagen S; tel. 35-32-82-45; fax 35-32-82-41; f. 1839; Chair. Prof. Dr E. LADEWIG PETERSEN; Secs Dr A. MONRAD MØLLER, Dr C. DUE-NIELSEN; publ. *Historisk Tidsskrift* (historical review, 2 a year).

Jysk Arkaeologisk Selskab (Jutland Archaeological Society): Moesgård, 8270 Højbjerg; tel. 89-42-45-04; fax 86-27-23-78; f. 1951; lectures and publication of primary archaeological and ethnological investigations; 1,500 mems; Pres. STEEN HVASS; Sec.-Gen. H. J. MADSEN; publs *KUML* (annually), *Jysk Arkaeologisk Selskabs Skrifter* (monographs, irregular), *Handbooks* (irregular).

Jysk Selskab for Historie (Jutland Historical Society): Historisk Institut, Århus Universitet, 8000 Århus C; f. 1866; 1,100 mems; Pres. Dr Phil. HENNING POULSEN; Sec. HENRIK FODE; publs *Historie*, *Nyt fra Historien* (2 a year).

Kongelige Danske Geografiske Selskab (Royal Danish Geographical Society): Øster Voldgade 10, 1350 Copenhagen K; f. 1876; 450 mems; the library contains *c.* 100,000 vols; Protector HM QUEEN MARGRETHE; Pres. HRH PRINCE HENRIK; Vice-Pres. Gen. Maj. S. HASLUND-CHRISTENSEN, Prof. Dr N. KINGO JACOBSEN; Sec. Prof. S. CHRISTIANSEN; publs *Geografisk Tidsskrift*, *Folia Geographica Danica*, *Kulturgeografiske Skrifter* and *Atlas of Denmark*.

Kongelige Danske Selskab for Fædrelandets Historie (Royal Danish Society for National History): C/o Kgl. Mønt- og Medaillesamling, Nationalmuseet, Frederiksholms Kanal 12, 1220 Copenhagen K; tel. 33-47-31-40; f. 1745; 60 mems; 20 foreign correspondents; Pres. VAGN SKOVGAARD-PETERSEN; Sec. JØRGEN STEEN JENSEN; publ. *Danske Magazin*.

Kongelige Nordiske Oldskriftselskab (Royal Society of Northern Antiquaries): Prinsens Palais, Frederiksholms Kanal 12, 1220 Copenhagen K; f. 1825; *c.* 1,300 mems; library in the National Museum; Vice-Pres. NIELS-KNUD LIEBGOTT; Sec. PETER VANG PETERSEN; publs *Aarbøger for Nordisk Oldkyndighed og Historie*, *Nordiske Fortidsminder*.

Samfundet for Dansk Genealogi og Personalhistorie (Danish Genealogical and Biographical Society): Groennevej 23, 2830 Virum; f. 1879; 1,100 mems; Chair. FINN ANDERSEN; Sec. POUL STEEN; publ. *Personalhistorisk Tidsskrift* (2 a year), *Hvem forsker Hvad* (yearly).

Selskabet for Dansk Kulturhistorie (Society for the History of Danish Culture): Rosenborg Palace, Øster Voldgade 4A, 1350 Copenhagen K; tel. 33-15-32-86; fax 33-15-20-46; f. 1936; 30 mems; Pres. STEFFEN HEIBERG; Sec. PETER WAGNER; publ. *Kulturminder*.

LANGUAGE AND LITERATURE

Dansk Forfatterforening (Danish Writers' Association): Tordenskjolds Gård, Strandgade 6, st., 1401 Copenhagen K; tel. 32-95-51-00; fax 32-54-01-15; e-mail danskff@postb.tele.dk; f. 1894; 1,382 mems; Chair. KNUD VILBY; publ. *Forfatteren* (8 a year).

Danske Sprog- og Litteraturselskab (Society for Danish Language and Literature): Christians Brygge 1 (1.), 1219 Copenhagen; tel. 33-13-06-60; fax 33-14-06-08; f. 1911; 75 mems; Dir Dr IVER KJAER.

Filologisk-Historiske Samfund (Philological-Historical Society): Inst. of Classical Studies, Univ. of Copenhagen, Nialsgade 92, 2300 Copenhagen S; f. 1854; 300 mems; Pres. Prof. M. SKAFTE JENSEN; publ. *Studier fra Sprog- og Oldtidsforskning*.

Íslenzka fræðafélag (Icelandic Literary Society): Helsevej 21, 3400 Hillerød; f. 1912; Sec. P. JÓNASSON.

MEDICINE

Almindelige Danske Lægeforening, Den (Danish Medical Association): Trondhjemsgade 9, 2100 Copenhagen Ø; tel. 35-44-85-00; fax 35-44-85-05; f. 1857; professional and educational activities; 18,000 mems; Dir JØRGEN REEDTZ FUNDER; publs *Ugeskrift for Laeger* (weekly), *Danish Medical Bulletin* (English, 6 a year).

Danmarks Farmaceutiske Selskab (Danish Pharmaceutical Society): c/o Danmarks farmaceutiske Højskole, 2 Universitetsparken, 2100 Copenhagen Ø; f. 1912; to encourage the scientific and practical development of Danish pharmacy; 765 mems; Pres. Prof. EBBA HOLME HANSEN.

Dansk Farmaceutforening (Asscn of Danish Pharmacists): Toldbodgade 36A, 1253 Copenhagen K; f. 1873; library of 16,000 vols; 3,205 mems; Pres. GERD ASKAA; publ. *Farmaceuten* (every 2 weeks).

Dansk Medicinsk Selskab (Danish Medical Society): Kristianiagade 14 (4 tv), 2100 Copenhagen Ø; tel. 35-44-84-07; f. 1919; an asscn of 82 socs covering all aspects of medical science; 18,081 mems; Pres. JOERN NERUP; Sec. KARSTEN BECH.

Dansk Tandlægeforening (Danish Dental Association): Amaliegade 17, Postboks 143, 1004 Copenhagen K; tel. 33-15-77-11; fax 33-15-16-37; e-mail dtf-dk@inet.uni-c.dk; f. 1873; 5,633 mems; publ. *Tandlaegebladet* (18 a year).

Medicinske Selskab i København (Medical Society of Copenhagen): Trondhjemsgade 9, 2100 Copenhagen Ø; f. 1772; 2,616 mems; Pres. Dr GRETE KRAG JACOBSEN; Sec. MARIANNE PONTOPPIDAN.

NATURAL SCIENCES

General

Selskabet for Naturlærens Udbredelse (Society for the Promotion of Natural Science): UNI-C, Vermundsgade 5, 2100 Copenhagen Ø; f. 1824 by H. C. ØRSTED; 200 mems; Pres. Prof. DORTE OLESEN; Sec. Dr JØRN JOHS. CHRISTIANSEN; publ. *KVANT/Fysisk Tidsskrift* (quarterly).

Biological Sciences

Biologisk Selskab (Danish Biological Society): Department of Cell Biology and Anatomy, Institute of Zoology, Universitetsparken 15, 2100 Copenhagen; tel. 35-32-12-27; fax 35-32-12-00; f. 1896; 750 mems; Pres. Dr MICHAEL G. PALMGREN; Sec. Prof. CORNELIS GRIMMELIKHUIJZEN.

Danmarks Naturfredningsforening (Danish Society for the Conservation of Nature): Noerregade 2, 1165 Copenhagen K; f. 1911; 265,000 mems; Pres. Prof. SVEND BICHEL; Dir LONE JOHNSEN; publ. *Tidsskriftet natur og miljø* (quarterly).

Dansk Botanisk Forening (Danish Botanical Society): Sølvgade 83, 1307 Copenhagen K; f. 1840; 1,350 mems; Pres. POUL MØLLER PEDERSON; publ. *Urt* (popular botanical journal).

Dansk Naturhistorisk Forening (Danish Natural History Society): Universitetsparken 15, 2100 Copenhagen Ø; tel. 35-32-11-20; fax 35-32-10-10; f. 1833; 525 mems; Pres. REINHARDT MØBJERG KRISTENSEN; publs *Årsskrift for Dansk Naturhistorisk Forening* (annually), *Danmarks Fauna*.

Dansk Ornithologisk Forening (Danish Ornithological Society): Vesterbrogade 138–140, 1620 Copenhagen V; tel. 33-31-44-04; fax 33-31-24-35; e-mail dof@dof.dk; f. 1906; 12,000 mems; Pres. CHR. HJORTH; publs *Tidsskrift* (quarterly), *Fugle og Natur* (quarterly), *DOF-Nyt*† (quarterly).

Entomologisk Forening (Entomological Society): Zoological Museum, Universitetsparken 15, 2100 Copenhagen Ø; f. 1868; 360 mems; Pres. NIELS PEDER KRISTENSEN; Sec. OLE GUDIK-SØRENSEN; publ. *Entomologiske Meddelelser* (quarterly).

Physical Sciences

Astronomisk Selskab (Astronomical Society); Observatoriet, Juliane Maries Vej 30, 2100 Copenhagen Ø; tel. 35-32-59-99; fax 35-32-59-89; e-mail palbre@post11tele.dk; f. 1916; 700 mems; Dir PALLE BREDEGAARD: publs *Astronomisk Tidsskrift*† (jointly with asscns in Norway and Sweden, quarterly), *Knudepunktet* (quarterly).

Dansk Fysisk Selskab (Danish Physical Society): c/o Prof. Preben Alstrøm, Niels Bohr Institute, Blegdamsvej 17, 2100 Copenhagen Ø; f. 1972; arranges conferences; 500 mems; Pres. PREBEN ALSTRØM; Sec. PETER BODIN; publ. *Kvant* (jointly with Danish Association for the Advancement of Science, quarterly).

Dansk Geologisk Forening (Geological Society of Denmark): Øster Voldgade 5-7, DK-1350 Copenhagen K; tel. 35-32-23-54; fax 35-32-23-25; f. 1893; 800 mems; Sec. LARS CLEMMENSEN; publs *Bulletin*, *Arsskrift*.

Kemisk Forening (Danish Chemical Society); H. C. Ørsted Institutet, Universitetsparken 5, 2100 Copenhagen Ø; tel. 35-32-02-87; fax 35-32-02-99; f. 1879; 900 mems; Chair. POUL ERIK HANSEN: Sec. I. TRABJERG.

PHILOSOPHY AND PSYCHOLOGY

Dansk Psykolog Forening (Danish Psychologists' Association): Bjerregårds Sidevei 4, 2500 Valby; tel. 31-16-33-55; f. 1947; 3,400 mems; Chair. JOHANNE BRATBO; Sec.-Gen. OLE MÜNSTER; publ. *Psykolog Nyt* (every 2 weeks).

RELIGION, SOCIOLOGY AND ANTHROPOLOGY

Danske Bibelselskab (Danish Bible Society): Frederiksborggade 50, 1360 Copenhagen K; tel. 33-12-78-35; f. 1814; editing and distributing Bibles and other biblical scriptures; Chair. GAI FRIMODT-MØLLER; Gen. Sec. Rev. MORTEN AAGAARD; publ. *News* (quarterly), *Annual Report*.

Grønlandske Selskab, Det (The Greenland Society): Kraemer Hus, L. E. Bruunsvej 10, 2920 Charlottenlund; tel. 39-63-57-33; fax 39-63-55-43; f. 1905; 1,500 mems with interest in Greenland and its people; Chair. H. SCHULTZ-LORENTZEN; publ. *Grønland* (8 a year).

Orientalsk Samfund (Institute of Asia Studies): University of Copenhagen, 17–19 Snorresgade, 2300 Copenhagen S; f. 1915; 50 mems; Pres. Dr LEIF LITTRUP; Sec. Prof. JES P. ASMUSSEN; publ. *Acta Orientalia*.

TECHNOLOGY

Akademiet for de Tekniske Videnskaber (Danish Academy of Technical Sciences): 266 Lundtoftevej, 2800 Lyngby; tel. 45-88-13-11; fax 45-93-13-77; e-mail atvmail@atv.dk; f. 1937; divisions of fundamental and ancillary sciences, chemical science and engineering, mechanical engineering, civil engineering, electrical engineering, agricultural and food engineering, industrial organization and economics, biology and hygiene; 630 mems; Chair. Prof. Dr JENS R. ROSTRUP-NIELSEN; CEO Dr VIBEKE Q. ZEUTHEN.

Byggecentrum (Building Centre): Dr Neergaards Veg 15, 2970, Hoersholm; tel. 45-76-73-73; fax 45-76-76-69; e-mail byggec@byggecentrum.dk; f. 1956; acts as centre for construction information; bookshop, database services, postgraduate training, exhibitions, training centre; Man. Dir JOERN VIBE ANDREASEN.

Dansk Husflidsselskab (Danish Society of Domestic Crafts): Tyrebakken 11, 5300 Kerteminde; tel. 65-32-20-96; fax 65-32-56-11; f. 1873; promotes domestic crafts on an artistic and craftsmanship basis; 6,602 mems; publ. *Husflid* (every 2 months).

Dansk Ingeniørforening (Danish Society of University Engineers): Ingeniørhuset, Vester Farimagsgade 31, 1780 Copenhagen V; tel. 33-15-65-65; fax 33-93-71-71; f. 1892; to promote professional matters and advance scientific technical education and research; 20,500 mems; Chair. HANS-OLE SKOUGAARD; Dir. HELGE STRANGE HENRIKSEN; publ. *Ingeniøren* (weekly).

Elektroteknisk Forening (Society of Danish Electrotechnicians): Sct. Annagade 43, 3000 Helsingør; tel. 49-20-18-19; fax 49-20-18-39; f. 1903; arranges lectures; 3,000 mems; Sec.-Gen. AAGE HANSEN; publ. *Elteknik* (11 a year).

Ingeniør-Sammenslutningen (Society of Engineers of Denmark); Domus Technica, 18 Ved Stranden, 1061 Copenhagen K; tel. 31-12-13-11; fax 33-93-46-22; f. 1937; 23,000 mems (graduates of the Danish engineering colleges); Man. JESPER GINNERUP; publ. *Ingeniøren* (weekly).

Research Institutes

GENERAL

Carlsberg Laboratoriet: Gl. Carlsbergvej 8–10, 2500 Copenhagen Valby; attached to Carlsberg Foundation; scientific work in chemistry and physiology; Dirs Prof. K. BOCK (Chemistry), Prof. R. OLIVER (Physiology), M. C. KIELLAND-BRANDT (Yeast Genetics).

Forskningsministeriet (Ministry of Research): H. C. Andersens Blvd 40, 1553 Copenhagen V.; tel. 33-11-43-00; central administrative unit for research policy; co-operates with the international research policy organizations of EEC, OECD, Council of Europe, UNESCO and UN; provides comprehensive R & D statistics, planning and forecasts; Permanent Sec. KNUD LARSEN; publs Annual Reports.

Attached bodies:

Forskningspolitisk Råd (Danish Council for Research Policy): Copenhagen; f. 1989: 9 mems appointed by the Minister of Research and Technology; advisory body to government in research policy matters; makes proposals on resources, structures, etc. required for the development and exploitation of Danish research; Dir Dr EVA STEINESS.

Statens Naturvidenskabelige Forskningsråd (Danish Natural Science Research Council): Copenhagen; f. 1968; 15 mems appointed by the Minister of Research and Technology; advisory body to public authorities and institutions in the natural sciences; initiates, supports and co-ordinates research, national and international; awards grants and fellowships for scientific research; Chair. Prof. Dr BENT CHRISTENSEN.

Statens Sundhedsvidenskabelige Forskningsråd (Danish Medical Research Council): Copenhagen; f. 1968; 15 mems appointed by the Minister of Research and Technology; advisory body to public authorities and institutions in medical sciences, including odontology and pharmacy; initiates and supports research, co-ordinates research, national and international; awards grants and fellowships to scientific research; Chair. Dr MIKAEL RØRTH.

Statens Jordbrugs- og Veterinærvidenskabelige Forskningsråd (Danish Agricultural and Veterinary Research Council): Copenhagen; f. 1968; 15 mems appointed by the Minister of Research and Technology; advisory body to public authorities and institutions in the agricultural and veterinary sciences; initiates and supports national and international research; awards grants and fellowships for scientific research; Chair. Dr KIRSTEN JAKOBSEN.

Statens Samfundsvidenskabelige Forskningsråd (Danish Social Science Research Council): Copenhagen; f. 1968; 15 mems appointed by the Minister of Research and Technology; advisory body to public authorities and institutions in the social sciences; initiates and supports national and international research; awards grants and fellowships for scientific research; Chair. Prof. Dr JOHN MARTINUSSEN.

Statens Humanistiske Forskningsråd (Danish Research Council for the Humanities): Copenhagen; f. 1968; 15 mems appointed by the Minister of Research and Technology; advisory body to public authorities and institutions in the humanities; initiates and supports national and international research; awards grants and fellowships for scientific research; Chair. Prof. Dr PER BOJE.

Statens Teknisk-Videnskabelige Forskningsråd (Danish Technical Research Council): Copenhagen; f. 1973, to replace *Danmarks teknisk-videnskabelige Forskningsrad* and *Statens teknisk-videnskabelige Fond.*; 15 mems appointed by the Minister of Education; advisory body to public authorities in the technical sciences; initiates and supports national and international research; awards grants and fellowships for scientific research; Chair. Prof. KNUD OESTERGAARD.

DANDOK (Danish Committee for Scientific and Technical Information and Documentation): Copenhagen; f. 1970; 8 mems; advisory body to public and private authorities and institutions in scientific and technical information and documentation; prepares and evaluates Danish participation in international co-operation in the field; Chair. NIELS CHRISTIAN NIELSEN.

AGRICULTURE, FISHERIES AND VETERINARY SCIENCE

Danish Institute of Agricultural Sciences: POB 50, 8830 Tjele; tel. 89-99-19-00; fax 89-99-19-19; f. 1882; research in agriculture and connected subjects; Pres. NIELS W. HOLM; Dir ARENT B. JOSEFSEN.

Hedeselskabet (Danish Land Development Service): POB 110, 8800 Viborg; tel. 86-67-61-11; f. 1866; forestry, forest nurseries, shelter belts, soil improvement, environmental protection, environmental engineering, land reclamation, drainage, irrigation, hydrology and research; specialists carry out practical assignments and research; technical projects designed and administered for farmers, foresters, industry, government authorities in Denmark and abroad; publ. *Vakst* (every 2 months).

ECONOMICS, LAW AND POLITICS

Center for Udviklingsforskning (Centre for Development Research): Center for Udviklingsforskning, Gammel Kongevej 5, 1610 Copenhagen V; tel. 33-85-46-00; fax 33-25-81-10; e-mail cdr@cdr.dk; f. 1969; library of 45,000 vols; undertakes research in the economic and social development of developing countries and in relations between industrialized and developing countries; Dir POUL ENGBERG-PEDERSEN; publs *Den Ny Verden* (4 a year), *CDR Research Reports*, *CDR Working Papers*, *Annual Report* (in English), *Researching Development* (in English, 4 a year).

Danmarks Statistik: Sejrøgade 11, 2100 Copenhagen Ø; tel. 39-17-39-17; fax 39-17-39-99; e-mail dst@dst.dk; f. 1849; central institution for all Danish statistics; library: see Libraries; Dir JAN PLOVSING; publs *Statistisk Årbog* (annually), *Statistisk Månedsoversigt* (monthly), *Nyt fra Danmarks Statistik* (300 a year), *Statistisk Tiårsoversigt* (statistical ten-year survey, annually), and other statistical publications.

EDUCATION

Danmarks Paedagogiske Institut (Danish National Institute for Educational Research): Hermodsgade 28, 2200 Copenhagen N.

HISTORY, GEOGRAPHY AND ARCHAEOLOGY

Danske Komité for Historikernes Internationale Samarbejde (Danish Cttee for Int. Historical Co-operation): Copenhagen University, 2300 Copenhagen S; f. 1926; 43 mems; Chair. Prof. NIELS STEENSGAARD.

MEDICINE

Finsen Center–Rigshospitalet: Blegdamsvej 9, 2100 Copenhagen; tel. 35-45-40-90; fax 31-35-69-06; f. 1896; cancer research; Pres. Prof. HEINE H. HANSEN.

Institute of Cancer Biology: Strandboulevarden 49, 2100 Copenhagen; tel. 35-25-75-00; fax 35-25-77-21; f. 1949; experimental cancer research; Chair. Dr JES FORCHHAMMER; publ. *Report* (every 2 years, in English).

NATURAL SCIENCES

Biological Sciences

Arctic Station, University of Copenhagen: Box 504, 3953 Godhavn, Greenland; tel. 47384; fax 47385; e-mail mrarksta@greennet.gl; f. 1906 for study of Arctic nature; laboratory; library; research cutter 'Porsild'; Governors: Dr NIELS NIELSEN, Prof. REINHARDT MØBJERG KRISTENSEN, Dr HELGE A. THOMSEN, Dr GUNUER KRARUP PEDERSEN; Scientific Dir Dr PETER FUNCH; correspondence to Botanisk Institut, Øster Farimagsgade 2D, 1123 Copenhagen K; tel. 35-32-21-60; e-mail anetteh@bot.ku.dk.

Danmarks Fiskeriundersøgelser (Danish Institute for Fisheries Research): Jægersborgvej 64–66, 2800 Lyngby; tel. 33-96-33-00; fax 33-96-33-49; e-mail dir@dfu.min.dk; f. 1952; fisheries, aquaculture, marine and freshwater research; large specialist library of fisheries and biology texts; Dir NIELS AXEL NIELSEN; publ. *Fisk og Hav.*

Statens Seruminstitut: Artillerivej 5, 2300 Copenhagen; tel. 32-68-32-68; telex 31316; fax 32-68-38-68; f. 1902; microbiological and immunological research institute and centre for the prevention and control of infectious diseases and congenital disorders; 110 scientists; the library contains *c.* 19,000 vols; Dir LARS PALLESEN.

Zoologisk Have (Copenhagen Zoo): Sdr Fasanvej 79, 2000 Frederiksberg; tel. 36-30-25-55; fax 36-44-24-55; f. 1859; Dir LARS LUNDING ANDERSEN.

Physical Sciences

Danmarks Meteorologiske Institut (Danish Meteorological Institute): Lyngbyvej 100, 2100 Copenhagen; tel. 39-15-75-00; fax 39-27-10-80; f. 1872; meteorology and geophysics; library contains 40,000 vols; 400 mems; Dir L. P. PRAHM; publs include *Magnetic Results* (Godhavn and Thule, Greenland), *Danmarks Klima* (annually).

Danmarks og Grønlands Geologiske Undersøgelse (Geological Survey of Denmark and Greenland): 8 Thoravej, 2400 Copenhagen NV; tel. 38-14-20-00; telex 19999; fax 38-14-20-50; f. 1995; library of 30,000 vols; Man. Dir OLE WINTHER CHRISTENSEN; publs *Geology of Denmark* (survey bulletin), *Geology of Greenland* (survey bulletin).

Kort & Matrikelstyrelsen: (National Survey and Cadastre): Rentemestervej 8, 2400 Copenhagen NV; tel. 35-87-50-50; telex 15184; fax 35-87-50-51; f. 1989, by amalgamation of former Geodetic Inst., Danish Cadastral Dept and Hydrographic Div.; responsible for geodetic survey of Denmark, Faroe Islands and Greenland; topographic survey and mapping of those areas, also nautical charting and issue of nautical publs; cadastral survey, registration, and mapping of Denmark; seismographic service in Denmark, Faroe Islands and Greenland; research and development within geodesy and seismology; development of digital maps and charts; library of 30,000 vols; Dir PETER JAKOBSEN.

Niels Bohr Institutet for Astronomi, Fysik og Geofysik (Niels Bohr Institute for Astronomy, Physics and Geophysics): Astronomisk Observatorium, Københavns Universitet, Juliane Maries Vej 30, 2100 Copenhagen Ø; tel. 35-32-59-99; fax 35-32-59-89; e-mail library@astro.ku.dk; f. 1642; library of *c.* 12,000 vols, 100 periodicals; Dir O. HANSEN.

NORDITA (Nordisk Institut for Teoretisk Fysik) (Nordic Institute for Theoretical Physics): Blegdamsvej 17, 2100 Copenhagen Ø; tel. 35-32-55-00; telex 15216; fax 31-38-91-57; f. 1957; member countries: Denmark, Finland, Iceland, Norway and Sweden; Chair. of Board KAARE OLAUSSEN; Dir PAUL HOYER.

RELIGION, SOCIOLOGY AND ANTHROPOLOGY

Instytut Polsko-Skandynawski/Polsk-Skandinavisk Forskningsinstitut: POB 2532, 2100 Copenhagen Ø; fax 39-29-98-26; f. 1985; independent research institute for Polish-Scandinavian studies; organizes research in the field of history and political sciences; organizes symposia, lectures, and workshops; 30 mems; archive and library of 3,000 vols; Dir Prof. Dr hab. E. S. KRUSZEWSKI; publs *Rocznik* (Annals), monographs.

Socialforskningsinstituttet (Danish National Institute of Social Research): Herluf Trolles Gade 11, 1052 Copenhagen K; tel. 33-48-08-00; fax 38-48-08-33; f. 1958; independent research body under Ministry of Social Affairs; library of 32,500 vols; Dir-in-Chief JØRGEN SØNDERGAARD; publ. *Social Forskning* (quarterly).

TECHNOLOGY

Forskningscenter Risø (Risø National Laboratory): POB 49, DK-4000 Roskilde; tel. 46-77-46-77; fax 42-36-06-09; f. 1958; technological research and development; library of 500,000 vols, 1,500 current periodicals; Dir JØRGEN KJEMS; publs *RisØ Reports*, *Annual Reports*.

Libraries and Archives

Ålborg

Aalborg Universitetsbibliotek (Aalborg University Library): Langagervej 2, POB 8200, 9220 Aalborg Øst; tel. 96-35-94-00; fax 98-15-68-59; e-mail aub@aub.auc.dk; f. 1973; open to the public; 650,000 vols; Chief Librarian KIRSTEN RØNBØL.

Nordjyske Landsbibliotek (Central Library for the County of North Jutland): Nytorv 26, Postboks 839, 9100 Ålborg; tel. 99-31-44-00; fax 99-31-44-33; f. 1895; 1,000,000 vols, 1,300 current periodicals; 14 brs and 3 mobile libraries; also a medical library; Chief Librarian KIRSTEN BOEL.

Århus

Århus Kommunes Biblioteker (Århus Public Library): Møllegade 1, 8000 Århus C; tel. 87-30-45-00; fax 87-30-46-39; f. 1934; 1,415,000 vols (including audiovisual materials); Chief Librarian ROLF HAPEL.

Erhvervsarkivet. Statens Erhvervshistoriske Arkiv (Danish National Business History Archives): Vester Allé 12, 8000 Århus C; f. 1948; also a research institute for economic and social history; Chief Archivist HENRIK FODE; publ. *Erhvervshistorisk Årbog* (Business History Yearbook).

Handelshøjskolens Bibliotek (Library of the Århus School of Business): Fuglesangs Allé 4, 8210 Århus V; tel. 89-48-66-88; fax 86-15-93-39; e-mail merkur@bib.hha.dk; f. 1939; 170,000 vols, 3,000 periodicals; special collection: European documentation centre for EEC; Chief Librarian: TOVE BANG.

Statsbiblioteket (State and University Library): Universitetsparken, 8000 Århus C; tel. 89-46-20-22; telex 64515; fax 89-46-22-20; f. 1902; legal deposit library; 3,297,289 vols, including special collections of books on foreign missions, music and books on Schleswig-Holstein, also collection of Friesland and Friesian literature from all Friesian areas; State newspaper collection and National Sound Archive; Dir NIELS MARK.

Copenhagen

Administrative Bibliotek, Det: Slotsholmsgade 12, 1216 Copenhagen K; tel. 33-92-46-91; fax 33-91-06-29; e-mail dab@dab.dk; f. 1924; attached to Min. of Research; library and documentation centre for the central administration; 125,000 vols; special collection: Danish governmental publs; Chief Librarian ULLA JEPPESEN; publ. *Prima Vista* (6 a year).

Danmarks Biblioteksskoles Bibliotek (Library of the Royal School of Librarianship): Birketinget 6, 2300 Copenhagen S; tel. 31-58-60-66; fax 32-84-02-01; f. 1956; 180,000 vols; Librarian IVAR A. L. HOEL.

Danmarks Farmaceutiske Bibliotek (Danish Pharmaceutical Library): Universitets-parken 2, 2100 Copenhagen Ø; tel. 35-37-08-50; fax 35-37-08-52; e-mail dfhlib@mail.dfh.dk; f. 1892; 55,000 vols; Head of Library Service ALICE NØRHEDE.

Danmarks Natur- og Lægevidenskabelige Bibliotek, Universitetsbiblioteket: (Danish National Library of Science and Medicine, University Library): Nørre Allé 49, 2200 Copenhagen N; tel. 35-39-65-23; fax 35-39-85-33; e-mail dnlb@dnlb.dk; f. 1482; 1,500,000 vols; Dir METTE STOCKMARR; publs *Acta historica scientiarum, naturalium et medicinalium* (irregular), *Skrifter udg. af Danmarks Natur- og Lægevidenskabelig Bibliotek* (irregular).

Danmarks Paedagogiske Bibliotek (National Library of Education): Danmarks Laererhøjskole, Emdrupvej 101, Postbox 840, 2400 Copenhagen NV; tel. 39-69-66-33; fax 39-55-10-00; e-mail dpbasen@bib.dlh.dk; f. 1887; 960,000 vols, 4,154 current periodicals, 543,000 microcards; Dir LEIF LØRRING.

Danmarks Statistiks Bibliotek (Danish Statistical Library): Sejrøgade 11, DK-2100 Copenhagen Ø; tel. 39-17-30-30; fax 39-17-30-03; e-mail bib@dst.dk; f. 1849; attached to Danmarks Statistik (Danish National Central Statistical Bureau); 231,000 vols; Librarian SØREN CARLSEN.

Danmarks Veterinaer- og Jordbrugsbibliotek (Danish Veterinary and Agricultural Library): Bülowsvej 13, 1870 Frederiksberg C; tel. 35-28-21-80; fax 35-28-21-38; f. 1783; 500,000 vols; Chief Librarian INGER MATHIESEN.

Frederiksberg Bibliotek (Public Library): Solbjergvej 21–25, 2000 Frederiksberg; tel. 38-34-48-77; fax 38-33-36-77; e-mail hl3@fkb.dk; f. 1887; 610,000 vols; 3 brs; also a music library and a special genealogy section; Chief Librarian ANNE MØLLER-RASMUSSEN.

Handelshøjskolens Bibliotek (Copenhagen Business School Library): Rosenørns Allé 31, 1970 Frederiksberg C, Copenhagen; tel. 38-15-36-66; fax 38-15-36-63; e-mail hbk.lib@cbs.dk; f. 1922; 241,000 vols, 3,200 current periodicals; Dir MICHAEL COTTA-SCHØNBERG.

Københavns Kommunes Biblioteker (Copenhagen Public Libraries): Administrationen, Islands Brygge 37 (4. sal), 2300 Copenhagen S; tel. 33-66-46-50; fax 33-66-70-61; e-mail ibertelsen@kultfrit.kk.dk; f. 1885; 2,113,000 vols; Librarian JAN ØSTERGAARD BERTELSEN; publs *Årsberetning* (annually).

Københavns Stadsarkiv (Copenhagen City Archives): Rådhuset, DK-1599 Copenhagen V; tel. 33-66-23-74; fax 33-66-70-39; first mentioned 1563; 30 linear km. of archive material, 50,000 maps and drawings; Dir HENRIK GAUTIER; publ. *Historiske Meddelelser om København 1907* ff. (annually).

Kongelige Bibliotek (Royal Library): POB 2149, 1016 Copenhagen K; tel. 33-47-47-47; telex 15009; fax 33-93-22-18; f. 1482 as university library, 1653 as the King's Library, merged 1989; acts as the Danish National Library, principal research library and university library for Theology, the Humanities, Law and the Social Sciences; nat. deposit library for int. orgs; nat. archive for MSS and archives of prominent Danes; 4,700,000 vols, 4,500 incunabula, 6,100 metres of manuscripts and archives, 10,624,000 graphic documents, 268,000 maps and prints, 271,000 musical items; incl. Danish Museum of Books and Printing, National Museum of Photography; open to the public; Dir-Gen. ERLAND KOLDING NIELSEN; publs include *Fund og Forskning i Det Kongelige Biblioteks Samlinger* (annually), *Magasin fra Det Kongelige Bibliotek* (quarterly).

Kongelige Garnisonsbibliotek (Royal Army Library): Kastellet 46, 2100 Copenhagen Ø; tel. 33-47-95-25; fax 33-47-95-36; f. 1785; Army central research library; 200,000 vols, 200 periodicals; Librarian Lt-Col S. HOEGENHAUG.

Kunstakademiets Bibliotek (Royal Danish Academy of Fine Arts Library): Kgs Nytorv 1, Postbox 3053, 1021 Copenhagen K; tel. 33-74-48-00; fax 33-74-48-88; e-mail kab@kb.dk; f. 1754; 150,000 vols on history of art and architecture, 205,000 architectural drawings, 364,000 photographs, 164,000 slides; Dir (vacant).

Marinens Bibliotek (Danish Naval Library): Overgaden oven Vandet 62B, 1415 Copenhagen K; tel. 31-54-73-82; f. 1765; naval affairs and Greenland literature; 33,000 vols; Librarian Commdr A. HOLM.

Patentdirektoratet Bibliotek (Library of the Danish Patent Office): Helgeshoj Allé 81, 2630 Taastrup; tel. 43-50-80-00; telex 16046; fax 43-50-80-01; f. 1894; 28,860 vols; 28,000,000 patent specifications; Heads of Library JON FINSEN, LIZZI VESTER; publs *Dansk Patenttidende* (Danish Patent Gazette, weekly), *Dansk Varemarketidende* (Danish Trademark Gazette, weekly), *Dansk Mønstertidende* (Danish Design Gazette, every 2 weeks), *Dansk Brugsmodeltidende* (Danish Utility Models Gazette, every 2 weeks).

Rigsarkivet (Danish State Archives): Rigsdagsgården 9, 1218 Copenhagen K; tel. 33-92-33-10; fax 33-15-32-39; e-mail mailbox@ra.sa.dk; f. 1582; consists of a central record office in Copenhagen, four Provincial Archives (*Landsarkiver*), situated in Copenhagen, Odense, Viborg and Aabenraa, the National Business Archives in Aarhus and the Danish Data Archives in Odense. The central record office contains most of the medieval documents (1200–1559), the archives of the Central Administration, and the armed forces, and the papers of the Royal family and of famous statesmen; Dir JOHAN PETER NOACK; publs historical series; *Arkiv*.

Statens Bibliotekstjeneste: (National Library Authority): Nyhavn 31 E, 1051 Copenhagen K; tel. 33-73-33-73; fax 33-73-33-72; e-mail sbt@sbt.dk; f. 1990 by merging of Rigsbibliotekarembedet and Bibliotekstilsynet; adviser to Govt on matters concerning academic and special libraries, public libraries, and information and documentation problems; National Librarian MORTEN LAURSEN VIG; publ. *Nyt fra Nyhavn* (quarterly).

Esbjerg

Centralbiblioteket for Ribe Amt (Ribe County Central Library): Nørregade 19, 6700 Esbjerg; tel. 75-12-13-77; fax 75-12-16-68; f. 1897; 725,000 vols; Chief Librarian JOHANNES BALSLEV.

Hellerup

Gentofte Bibliotekerne (Public Library): Ahlmanns Allé 6, 2900 Hellerup; tel. 39-62-75-00; fax 39-62-75-07; f. 1918; 671,388 vols; 5 brs; Chief Librarian LONE GLADBO.

Lyngby

DTV – Technical Knowledge Centre and Library of Denmark: POB 777, Anker Engelunds Vej 1, 2800 Lyngby; tel. 45-88-30-88; fax 45-88-30-40; e-mail dtv@dtv.dk; f. 1942; a nat. centre for scientific information and library for the Technical University of Denmark; 700,000 vols, 4,000 current periodicals; Dir LARS BJØRNSHAUGE.

Odense

Landsarkivet for Fyn (Provincial Archives of Funen): Jernbanegade 36A, 5000 Odense C; tel. 66-12-58-85; e-mail mailbox@lao.sa.dk; f. 1893; the archives include records of local administration of Funen and neighbouring islands and collections of private papers. The Karen Brahe Library, the only nearly complete private Danish library from the 17th century, with about 3,400 printed books and 1,153 MSS, is deposited in the Archives; Dir DORRIT ANDERSEN.

Odense Centralbibliotek (County Library, Odense): 5000 Odense C.; f. 1924; 945,000 vols, 118,000 records, compact discs and cassettes; Chief Librarian SØREN EGELUND.

Odense Universitetsbibliotek (Odense University Library): Campusvej 55, 5230 Odense M; tel. 66-15-86-00; fax 66-15-81-62; e-mail oub@freja.ou.dk; f. 1965; languages, literature, philosophy, history, music, economics, social sciences, natural sciences, medicine; 1,018,000 vols, 7,600 periodicals; Dir AASE LINDAHL.

Roskilde

Roskilde Universitetsbibliotek (Roskilde University Library): POB 258, Marbjergvej 35, DK-4000 Roskilde; tel. 46-75-77-11; fax 46-75-61-02; e-mail rub@bib.ruc.dk; f. 1971; open to general public; humanities, social sciences and natural sciences; 500,000 vols, 190,000 units of non-book material; Dir NIELS SENIUS CLAUSEN.

Silkeborg

Silkeborg Bibliotek (Public Library): 8600 Silkeborg; tel. 86-82-02-33; fax 86-80-26-79; f. 1900; 216,000 vols, plus 128,000 in the Children's Dept, 50,000 records and cassettes; Chief Librarian PETER BIRK.

Vejle

Biblioteket for Vejle By og Amt (Vejle County and Central Library): Willy Sørensens Plads 1, 7100 Vejle; tel. 75-82-32-00; fax 75-82-32-13; e-mail vejlebib@bvba.bibnet.dk; f. 1895; 410,000 vols; Chief Librarian JØRN GODRUM BECH.

Viborg

Landsarkivet for Nørrejylland (Provincial Archives of Northern Jutland): 8800 Viborg; tel. 86-62-17-88; fax 86-60-10-06; e-mail mailbox@lav.sa.dk; f. 1889, opened 1891; Dir C. R. JANSEN.

Museums and Art Galleries

Ålborg

Aalborg Historiske Museum: Algade 48, 9000 Aalborg; tel. 98-12-45-22; fax 98-16-11-31; f. 1863; archaeology, history, ethnology, glass; Dir TORBEN WITT.

Nordjyllands Kunstmuseum (Museum of Contemporary Art): Kong Christians Allé 50, 9000 Aalborg; tel. 98-13-80-88; fax 98-16-28-20; f. 1877, building inaugurated 1972; 20th-century Danish and international art: painting, sculpture, graphics, sculpture park; Dir NINA HOBOLTH.

Århus

Aarhus Kunstmuseum (Aarhus Art Museum): Vennelystparken, 8000 Aarhus C; tel. 86-13-52-55; fax 86-13-33-51; f. 1859; 19th- and 20th-century art; Dir JENS ERIK SØRENSEN.

Naturhistorisk Museum (Natural History Museum): Universitetsparken, Bygning 210, 8000 Århus C; tel. 86-12-97-77; fax 86-13-08-82; e-mail nm@nathist.aau.dk; f. 1921; permanent field laboratory: 'Molslaboratoriet', Femmöller, 8400 Ebeltoft; the museum laboratories are open to scientists, and specialize in terrestrial ecology, limnology, entomology, acarology, mammalogy, ornithology and bioacoustics; the library contains 15,000 vols; Pres. SVEND KAABER; Dir A. HOLM JOENSEN; publs *Natura Jutlandica* (in English), *Natur og Museum* (in Danish).

Auning

Dansk Landbrugsmuseum (Danish Agricultural Museum): Gl. Estrup, 8963 Auning, Jutland; tel. 86-48-30-01; fax 86-48-41-82; f. 1889; Dir HENRIK VENSILD.

Charlottenlund

Ordrupgaard: Vilvordevej 110, 2920 Charlottenlund; tel. 39-64-11-83; fax 39-64-10-05; f. 1918; museum for French and Danish 19th and early 20th century works; Dir ANNE-BIRGITTE FONSMARK.

Copenhagen

Botanisk Have (Botanical Gardens): Øster Farimagsgade 2B, 1353 Copenhagen K; tel. 35-32-22-22; fax 35-32-22-21; f. 1874; 25 acres of landscape garden, palm-house and greenhouses; rare trees, plants (15,000 species), etc.; Dir OLE HAMANN.

Filmmuseet: Vognmagergade 10, 1120 Copenhagen K; tel. 33-74-34-00; fax 33-74-35-99; f. 1941; a film archive with collections of films, books, posters, documentation and film shows; library of 48,000 vols, 13,500 scripts, 370 periodicals; Dir DAN NISSEN; publ. *Kosmorama* (2 a year).

Geologisk Museum: Øster Voldgade 5–7, 1350 Copenhagen K; tel. 35-32-23-45; fax 35-32-23-25; f. 1772; minerals, rocks, meteorites and fossils; geology of Denmark and Greenland; Origin of Man; plate tectonics; volcanoes; salt in the subsoil; Chairs NIELS HALD, Prof. DAVID BRIDGWATER, Prof. DAVID HARPER.

Københavns Bymuseum (Copenhagen City Museum): Vesterbrogade 59, 1620 Copenhagen V; tel. 33-21-07-72; fax 33-25-07-72; history of Copenhagen including pictures, architecture, models; houses the collection of Kierkegaard relics; includes an outdoor museum street; Dir JØRGEN SELMER.

Kunstindustrimuseet (Danish Museum of Decorative Art): Bredgade 68, 1260 Copenhagen K; tel. 33-14-94-52; fax 33-11-30-72; f. 1890; European applied art from the Middle Ages to modern times, Chinese and Japanese art, and a library of 63,000 vols on applied art; Pres. OLAV GRUE; Dir BODIL BUSK LAURSEN.

Musikhistorisk Museum og Carl Claudius' Samling (Musical History Museum and Carl Claudius Collection): Åbenrå 30, 1124 Copenhagen K; tel. 33-11-27-26; fax 33-11-60-44; f. 1898; collection of musical instruments; concerts, library, archives; Dir Dr LISBET TORP.

Nationalmuseet (National Museum): Frederiksholms Kanal 12, 1220 Copenhagen; tel. 33-13-44-11; fax 33-47-33-30; f. 1807 on basis of the older Royal Collections; consists of 6 divisions; Dir STEEN HVASS; Keepers of divisions: Danish Prehistory, Middle Ages, Coins and Medals, Classical Antiquities, Inst. of Maritime Archaeology at Roskilde and Natural Science Research Unit NIELS-KNUD LIEBGOTT; Denmark 1660 – Today (including

Bredemuseet at Brede, Frilandsmuseet (open-air museum) at Sorgenfri, and Museum of Danish Resistance 1940–1945) (vacant); Ethnographic Collection TORBEN LUNDBÆK; Department of Public Services JETTE SANDDAHL, Department of Conservation JØRGEN NORDQVIST; Department of Administration and Technical Services EBBE HOLMBOE; publs *Nationalmuseets Arbejdsmark* (annually), *Skrifter* (in 3 series), *Nyt fra Nationalmuseet* (quarterly), catalogues.

Ny Carlsberg Glyptotek: Dantes Plads 7, 1556 Copenhagen V; tel. 33-41-81-41; fax 33-91-20-58; f. 1888; 19th- and 20th-century Danish and French sculpture and painting, Egyptian, Greek, Roman and Etruscan art, mainly sculpture; Pres. HANS EDVARD NØRREGÅRD-NIELSEN; Dir SØREN DIETZ; publ. *Meddelelser* (annually).

Orlogsmuseet (Royal Danish Naval Museum): Overgaden oven Vandet 58, 1415 Copenhagen K; tel. 32-54-63-63; fax 32-54-29-80; ship-models, weapons, ships' decorations, maritime art; Dir OLE LISBERG JENSEN.

Rosenborg Slot (Rosenborg Palace): Øster Voldgade 4A, 1350 Copenhagen K; tel. 33-15-76-19; fax 33-15-20-46; contains 'The Chronological Collections of the Danish Kings'; the collection was founded by Frederik III about 1660, and consists of arms, apparel, jewellery, and furniture from 1470 to 1863; the Royal Regalia and the Crown Jewels are also here; Dir Chamberlain NIELS EILSCHOU HOLM; Museum Dir MOGENS BENCARD.

Statens Museum for Kunst (National Gallery): Sølvgade 48-50, 1307 Copenhagen K; tel 33-74-84-94; fax 33-74-84-04; contains the main collection of Danish paintings and sculpture; a number of works by other 19th- and 20th-century Scandinavian artists; J. Rump collection of modern French art; about 1,000 paintings by old masters of the Italian, Flemish, Dutch and German Schools (chiefly derived from the old royal collection, which was est. as an art gallery in the 1760s). The Print Room includes about 300,000 Danish and foreign prints and drawings. Library of about 130,000 vols. Dir ALLIS HELLELAND; publ. *Statens Museum for Kunst Journal*.

Teatermuseet: Christiansborg, Ridebane 10 and 18, 1218 Copenhagen K; tel. 33-11-51-76; f. 1922; situated in the old Court theatre, dating from 1767; illustrates the development of the Danish theatre from the 18th century to the present day; Dir LISBET GRANDJEAN.

Thorvaldsens Museum: Porthusgade 2, 1213 Copenhagen K; tel. 33-32-15-32; fax 33-32-17-71; e-mail thm@thorwaldsensmuseum.dk; f. 1839–48; sculptures and drawings by the Danish sculptor Bertel Thorvaldsen (1770–1844), his collections of contemporary European paintings, drawings and prints, classical antiquities and his library of 876 vols; museum library of 8,000 vols; Dir STIG MISS; publs catalogues and books in Danish, English, French and German, *Meddelelser* (Bulletin, irregular).

Tøjhusmuseet (Royal Danish Arsenal Museum): Administration: Frederiksholms Kanal 29, 1220 Copenhagen K; main entrance: Tøjhusgade 3, Copenhagen; f. 1838; central state museum for the history of the Danish defence forces and for arms and armour; history of arms in Europe, from the introduction of gunpowder till the present time; history and development of international military materials; Dir OLE LOUIS FRANTZEN.

Zoologisk Museum (University of Copenhagen Zoological Museum): Universitetsparken 15, 2100 Copenhagen Ø; tel. 35-32-10-00; fax 35-32-10-10; e-mail henghoff@zmuc.ku.dk; f. 1770; Danish and foreign colln (incl. Arctic and deep-sea animals, Danish and South American quaternary fossils); Dir HENRIK ENGHOFF; publs *Steenstrupia*, *Atlantide Report*, *Galathea Report*.

Dronningmølle

Rudolph Tegners Museum og Statuepark: Villingerød pr. Dronningmølle, 3120 Dronningmølle; tel. 49-71-91-77; f. 1938; open April to October.

Elsinore

Danmarks Tekniske Museum (Danish Museum of Science and Industry): Office: Ole Roemers Vej, 3000 Elsinore; tel. 49-22-26-11; fax 49-22-62-11; Exhibition Halls: Ndr. Strandvej 23, 3000 Elsinore, Ole Roemers Vej 15, 3000 Elsinore; f. 1911; more than 12,000 items, particularly relating to Danish inventions; library of 18,000 vols; Dir JENS BREINEGAARD; publ. *Arbog* (Yearbook).

Handels- og Søfartsmuseet (Danish Maritime Museum): Kronborg Castle, 3000 Elsinore; tel. 49-21-06-85; fax 49-21-34-40; f. 1914; maritime library of 28,000 vols; special collection of logbooks; Dir HANS JEPPESEN.

Kronborg: 3000 Elsinore; tel. 49-21-30-78; fax 49-21-30-52; fortified royal castle dating from the end of the 16th century; contains the Royal Apartments (furniture, tapestry, etc.), banqueting hall, chapel; known as Hamlet's castle.

Hillerød

Nationalhistoriske Museum paa Frederiksborg Slot, Det (Museum of National History at Frederiksborg Castle): Frederiksborg Slot, 3400 Hillerød; tel. 48-26-04-39; fax 48-24-09-66; castle built in 1560s and 1600–20 and endowed as museum in 1878; contains a chronological collection of portraits and paintings illustrating the history of Denmark, all arranged in rooms, the furniture and appointments in keeping with the period of the paintings; *c.* 10,000 exhibits; library contains 15,000 vols; Pres. NIELS EILSCHOU HOLM, Chamberlain; Dir JESPER KNUDSEN; publs various catalogues and illustrated guides.

Højbjerg

Moesgård Museum: Moesgård, 8270 Højbjerg; tel. 89-42-11-00; fax 86-27-23-78; f. 1861; collections of Danish prehistoric antiquities; research organization in environmental, Danish and Oriental archaeology and ethnology; Dir JAN SKAMBY MADSEN.

Hørsholm

Jagt- og Skovbrugsmuseet (Danish Museum of Hunting and Forestry): 2970 Hørsholm; tel. 42-86-05-72; fax 45-76-20-02; f. 1942; Curator J. BAAGØE; publ. *Yearbook*.

Humlebæk

Louisiana Museum of Modern Art: Gl. Strandvej 13, 3050 Humlebæk; tel. 49-19-07-19; fax 49-19-35-05; e-mail press@louisiana.dk; f. 1958; neo-classic villa and estate transformed into a modern museum of art; collection of Danish and international art; exhibitions of modern art; cinema, concerts, theatre; Dirs CRISTINA LAGE HANSEN, STEINGRIM LAURSEN; publ. *Louisiana Revy*.

Odense

Odense Bys Museer (Odense City Museums): Bangs Boder 5, 5000 Odense C; tel. 66-14-88-14; fax 65-90-86-00; e-mail museum@post.odkomm.dk; f. 1860; Dir TORBEN GRØNGAARD JEPPESEN; publ. *Fynske Minder* (Bygone Funen, annually).

Selected museums:

Hollufgård-Arkæologi og Landskab: Hestehaven 201, 5220 Odense SØ; archaeology.

Møntergården – Odense Bymuseum: Overgade 48–50, 5000 Odense C; local history, coins and medals.

Fynske Landsby (Funen Village): Sejerskovvej 20, 5260 Odense S; open-air museum.

Fyns Kunstmuseum: Jernbanegade 13, 5000 Odense C; art gallery.

Hans Christian Andersens Hus: Hans Jensens Stræde 37–45, 5000 Odense C; poet's life and work.

Carl Nielsen Museet: Claus Bergs Gade, 5000 Odense C; composer's life and work.

Roskilde

Vikingeskibshallen i Roskilde (Viking Ship Museum): Strandengen, POB 298, 4000 Roskilde; tel. 46-30-02-00; fax 46-32-21-15; f. 1969; exhibits the five Viking ships found at Skuldelev in 1962, and aims to promote research in ship-building history in general; research on maritime subjects is carried out in co-operation with the Institute of Maritime Archaeology of the National Museum (Havnevej 7, 4000 Roskilde; tel. 46-35-64-29); Dir TINNA DAMGÅRD-SØRENSEN.

Universities and Technical Universities

AALBORG UNIVERSITET

POB 159, Fredrik Bajers Vej 5, 9100 Aalborg
Telephone: 96-35-80-80
Fax: 98-15-22-01

Founded 1974
State control
Academic year: September to July

Rector: SVEN CASPERSEN
Vice-Rector: JØRGEN ØSTERGAARD
Administrative Officer: PETER PLENGE
Librarian: KIRSTEN RØNBØL

Number of teachers: 700
Number of students: 10,000

Publications: *Uglen* (10 a year), *Videnskabet* (2 a year), *Biannual Report*.

DEANS

Faculty of Humanities: OLE PREHN
Faculty of Social Sciences: MARGRETHE NØRGAARD
Faculty of Technology and Science: FINN KJAERSDAM

ATTACHED RESEARCH DEPARTMENTS

Department of Social Studies and Organization
Department of Economics, Politics and Public Administration
Department of Business Studies
Department of Development and Planning
Department of Chemistry and Applied Engineering
Department of Civil Engineering
Department of Building Technology and Structural Engineering
Department of Physics
Department of Mechanical Engineering
Department of Energy Technology
Department of Production
Department of Music and Music Therapy
Department of Communication
Department of Languages and Intercultural Studies
Institute of Electronic Systems

AARHUS UNIVERSITET

Nordre Ringgade, 8000 Aarhus C
Telephone: 89-42-11-66

Fax: 86-19-70-29

Founded 1928
State controlled
Academic year: September to June

Rector: H. LEHMANN
Pro-Rector: PALLE BO MADSEN
Director: STIG MØLLER
Library: see Libraries

Number of professors: 185
Number of students: 19,500

Publication: *Årsberetning* (yearbook).

DEANS

Faculty of Arts: ANDRÉ WANG HANSEN
Faculty of Health Services: ARVID MAUNSBACH
Faculty of Social Sciences: NIELS CHR. SIDENIUS
Faculty of Theology: PETER WIDMANN
Faculty of Science: KARL PEDERSEN

PROFESSORS

Faculty of Arts:

ALBERTSEN, L. L., Germanic Philology
ANDERSEN, P. B., Information Service
BACH, S., Latin Languages
BOHN, O.-S., English
DUE, O. S., Classical Languages
ENGBERG, J., History
FOGSGÅRD, L., Roman Languages
HANNESTAD, N., Classical Archaeology
JUUL JENSEN, U., Philosophy
KYNDRUP, M., Aesthetics and Culture
LANGSTED, J., Drama
MARSCHNER, B., Music
MORTENSEN, F., Media Science
OTTO, T., Ethnography
POULSEN, H., Modern History
ROESDAHL, E., Medieval Archaeology
SCHANZ, H.-J., History of Ideas
SØRENSEN, P. E., Scandinavian Studies
THRANE, H., Prehistoric Archaeology
TOGEBY, O., Scandinavian Studies
WEDELL-WEDELLSBORG, A., Chinese

Faculty of Health Sciences:

AALKJAER, C., General Physiology
ANDERSEN, J. P., Molecular Physiology
ANDREASEN, F., Clinical Pharmacology
ASTRUP, J., Neurosurgery
AUTRUP, H. N., Environment and Occupational Medicine
BJERRING, P., Laser-based Measuring Methods
BLACK, F. T., Medicine
BOLUND, L., Clinical Genetics
BÜNGER, C., Experimental Orthopaedic Surgery
CELIS, J., Biochemistry
CHRISTENSEN, E. I., Structural Cell Biology
CHRISTIANSEN, G., Medical Molecular Biology
CHRISTIANSEN, J. S., Clinical Growth Hormone Research
CLAUSEN, T., Physiology
DAHL, R., Lung Diseases and Allergology
DAM, M., Epileptology
DANSCHER, G., Neurobiology
DJURHUUS, J. C., Surgery
EHLERS, N., Ophthalmology
ELLEGAARD, J., Medicine
ELSASS, P., Medical Physiology
ENGBERG, B. I., Physiology
FALK, E., Ischaemic Heart Disease
FEJERSKOV, O. B., Dental Pathology, Dentistry and Endodontics
FOLDSPANG, A., Health Service Research
FUGGER, L., Clinical Immunology
FÆRGEMAN, O., Preventive Cardiology
GJEDDE, A., Positron Tomography
GLIEMANN, J., Biochemistry
GREEN, A., Epidemiology
GREGERSEN, M., Forensic Medicine
GUNDERSEN, H. J., Stereology
GYLDENSTED, G., X-ray Diagnostics
HAMILTON-DUTOIT, S., Pathological Anatomy
HVID, I., Experimental Orthopaedics
JAKOBSEN, J. K., Neurology
JENSEN, O. M., Pathology
JENSEN, S. L., Surgery
JENSEN, T. S., Pain Research
JENSENIUS, J. C. T., Immunology
KARRING, T., Periodontology
KILIAN, M., Microbiology and Immunology
KRAGBALLE, K., Psoriasis Research
KØLVRAA, S., Clinical Genetics
KÖNÖNEN, M., Prosthetics
LAMBERT, J., Neurophysiology
LAURBERG, S., Surgery
LAURITZEN, T., General Practice
MAASE, H. VON DER, Oncology
MAUNSBACH, A., Anatomy
MELSEN, B., Orthodontics
MELSEN, F., Pathology
MOGENSEN, C. E. S., Medicine
MOGENSEN, S. C., Microbiology and Immunology
MOSEKILDE, L., Bone Diseases
MULVANY, M., Cardiovascular Pharmacology
MØLLER, J. V., Biophysics
NERSTRØM, B., Urology
NEXOE, E., Clinical Biochemistry
NIELSEN, S., Structural Cell Biology and Pathophysiology
NIELSEN, T. T., Cardiology
NIELSEN-KUDSK, F., Pharmacology
OLESEN, F., General Practice
OLSEN, J., Social Medicine
OVERGAARD, J., Experimental Cancer Research
PAASKE, W., Cardiovascular Surgery
PARNVIG, H.-H., Diabetic Microangiopathy
PAULSEN, P. K., Surgery
PEDERSEN, C. B., Oto-rhino-laryngology
PEDERSEN, F. S., Molecular Oncology
POULSEN, S., Paediatric Dentistry
REISBY, N., Psychiatry
RIZZA, R., Medicine and Metabolism
ROSENBERG, R., Psychiatry
SARACCI, R., Basic Epidemiology Research
SCHIØTZ, P. O., Paediatrics
SECHER, N. J., Gynaecology
SINDET-PEDERSEN, S., Oral and Maxillofacial Surgery
SNEPPEN, O., Orthopaedic Surgery
THESTRUP-PEDERSEN, K., Dermato-venereology
THOMSEN, P. H., Psychiatry for Children and Adolescents
TOENNESEN, E., Anaesthesiology
VESTERGAARD, P., Psychiatry
VÆTH, M., Biostatistics
VIIDIK, A., Anatomy
VILSTRUP, H., Hepatology
WEEKE, J., Medical Endocrinology
WENZEL, A., Oral Radiology
WOLF, H., Surgery
ØRSKOV, H., Experimental Clinical Research

Faculty of Social Sciences:

AGERVOLD, M., Psychology
ANDERSEN, T. M., Economic Planning
BASSE, E. M., Jurisprudence
BORRE, O., Political Science
CARSTENSEN, V. U., Jurisprudence
CHRISTENSEN, B. J., Economic Planning
CHRISTENSEN, J. G., Political Science
CHRISTENSEN, J. P., Jurisprudence
DALBERG-LARSEN, J. V., Jurisprudence
DAMGAARD, E., Political Science
DIDERICHSEN, B., Psychology
DÜBECK, I., Jurisprudence
FENGER, O., Jurisprudence
GENEFKE, J., Economic Planning
GERMER, P., Jurisprudence
HYLLEBERG, S. A. F., National Economy
JEPSEN, G. T., National Economy
JESPERSEN, H. K., Jurisprudence
KATZENELSON, B., Psychology
KVALE, S., Psychology
LARSEN, S. F., Psychology
MADSEN, O. Ø., Economic Planning
MADSEN, P. B., Jurisprudence
MATHIASSEN, J., Jurisprudence
NANNESTAD, P., Political Science
NIELSEN, G. T., Jurisprudence
NYBORG, H., Psychology
PALDAM, N. M., Economic Planning
PEDERSEN, P. J., Economics
PEDERSEN, J., Jurisprudence
PETERSEN, N., Political Science
ROERSTED, B., Economic Planning
REVSBECH, K., Jurisprudence
SOERENSEN, C., Political Science
SOERENSEN, G., Political Science
THOMSEN, S. R., Political Science
TOGEBY, L., Political Science
VASTRUP, C., Economics
YNDGAARD, E., National Economy

Faculty of Theology:

ANDERSEN, S., Ethics and Philosophy of Religion
GEERTZ, A., History of Religions
HVIDBERG-HANSEN, F. O., Semitic Philology
NIELSEN, K., Old Testament Exegesis
THODBERG, C., Practical Theology
WILDMANN, P., Dogmatics

Faculty of Science:

ANDERSEN, H. H., Mathematics
ANDERSEN, J. U., Experimental Physics
ANDERSEN, T., Physics
BALSLEV, E., Mathematics
BALSLEV, H., Biology
BARNDORFF-NIELSEN, O., Mathematics
BESENBACHER, F., Experimental Solid State Physics
BØTTIGER, J., Materials Science
CHRISTENSEN, K. R., Biological Oceanography
CHRISTENSEN, N. T. E., Theoretical Solid State Physics
CHRISTENSEN-DALSGAARD, J., Astronomy
CHRISTIANSEN, F. V. B., Population Biology
CLARK, B., Chemistry
JACOBSEN, H. J., Chemistry
JANTZEN, J. C., Mathematics
JENSEN, J. L., Mathematical Statistics
JØRGENSEN, K. A., Organic Chemistry
KORSTGÅRD, J. A., Structural Geology and Basin Tectonics
KRAGH, H., History of Science
KRISTENSEN, L., Mathematics
LANGANKE, K., Physics
LINDERBERG, J., Chemistry
LOESCHKE, V., Biology
MADSEN, I. H., Mathematics
MADSEN, O. L., Computer Science
MARCKER, K., Biological Biochemistry
MAYOH, B. H., Computer Science
MICHELSEN, O. J., Marine Geology
NIELSEN, J. A., Mathematical Finance
OGILBY, P. R., Chemistry
POULSEN, E. T., Mathematics
REVSBECH, N. P., Microbial Ecology
UGGERHØJ, E., Physics
VOLLRATH, F., Zoology
WANDEL, C. F., Physics
WEBER, R. E., Zoophysiology
WINSKEL, G., Computer Science

ATTACHED INSTITUTES

School of Post-Basic Nursing: f. 1938.

Institute of Occupational Therapy and Physiotherapy: f. 1959.

Institute of Home Economics: f. 1945.

JYSK AABENT UNIVERSITET
(Jutland Open University)

Nordre Ringgade 1, 8000 Aarhus C
Telephone: 89-42-11-66
Telex: 64767
Fax: 89-42-11-10

Founded 1982 as a joint venture between the Universities of Aalborg, Aarhus and Esbjerg; co-ordinates all the Open University teaching from these universities, mainly in the humanities

Courses are organized as distance learning and part-time study, with residential weekend seminars 4 or 5 times a year. One-year courses and BA degrees are offered

Chairman of Steering Committee: Prof. JOERGEN BANG

Head of Administration: KIRSTEN ANDERSEN

Library of 150 vols; access to the libraries of Aalborg, Aarhus and Esbjerg Universities

Number of teachers: 59 part-time

Number of students: 864

Publications: *Report* (annually), newsletters.

KØBENHAVNS UNIVERSITET
(University of Copenhagen)

Frue Plads/Noerregade 10, POB 2177, 1017 Copenhagen K

Telephone: 35-32-26-26

Fax: 35-32-26-28

Founded 1479

State control

Language of instruction: Danish

Academic year: September to August (2 terms)

Rector: Prof. Med. Dr KJELD MØLLGÅRD

Pro-Rector: Assoc. Prof. JENS BRINCKER

Number of teachers: 2,000

Number of students: 28,000

DEANS

Faculty of Theology: JENS GLEBE-MØLLER

Faculty of Law: STEEN RØNSHOLDT

Faculty of Social Sciences: CHRISTIAN HJORTH-ANDERSEN

Faculty of Medicine: HANS HULTBORN

Faculty of Arts: JOHN KUHLMANN MADSEN

Faculty of Science: HENRIK JEPPESEN

PROFESSORS

Faculty of Theology:

GLEBE-MØLLER, J., Dogmatics
GRANE, L., Church History
GRØN, A., Ethics and Philosophy of Religion
HANSEN, H. B., Church History
HYLDAHL, N. C., New Testament Exegesis
JØRGENSEN, T., Dogmatics
KJELDGAARD-PEDERSEN, S., Church History, History of Dogma
LAUSTEN, M. S., Theology, Danish Church History
LEMCHE, N. P., Old Testament Exegesis
MÜLLER, M., New Testament Exegesis
THOMPSON, T. L., Old Testament Exegesis

Faculty of Law:

BALVIG, F., Legal Sociology and Sociology of Law
BLUME, P., Legal Informatics
BONDESON, U., Criminology
BRYDE ANDERSEN, M., Private Law, Computer Law
DUE, O., European Union Law
FOIGEL, I., Law of Taxation
GREVE, V., Criminal Law
KETSCHER, K., Social Law
KOKTVEDGAARD, M., Law of Competition, Intellectual Property Law
KRARUP, O., Public Law
LOOKOFSKY, J., Law of Contracts and Torts, Private International Law
NIELSEN, L., Family Law
RASMUSSEN, H., International Law and European Union Law
RØNSHOLDT, S., Administrative Law
SMITH, E., Legal Procedure
TAKSØE-JENSEN, F., Family Law, Law of Wills and Succession
TAMM, D., History of Law
VON EYBEN, B., Law of Property
ZAHLE, H., Jurisprudence

Faculty of Social Sciences:

ANDERSEN, E., Economics
ANDERSEN, E. B., Theoretical Statistics
BERTILSSON, M., Sociology
ESTRUP, H., Economics
GRODAL, B. K., Economics
GUNDELACH, P., Sociology
GØRTZ, E., Social Description
HASTRUP, K., Anthropology
HEURLIN, B., Political Science
HJORTH-ANDERSEN, C., Economics
JUSELIUS, K., Economics
JØRGENSEN, T. B., Political Science
KEIDING, H., Economics
KNUDSEN, T., Political Science
PEDERSEN, O. K., International Politics
PEDERSEN, O. K., Political Science
SCHULTZ, C., Economics
SJØBLOM, B. G., Political Science
SØRENSEN, P. B., Economics
THYGESEN, N. C., Economics
VIND, K., Economic

Faculty of Medicine:

ASMUSSEN, E., Dental Materials
BENDIXEN, G., Internal Medicine
BOCK, E. M., Cellular Biology
BOCK, J. E., Obstetrics and Gynaecology
BOLWIG, T. G., Psychiatry
BOYSEN, G., Neurology
BRETLAU, P., Oto-rhino-laryngology
BUUS, S., Basic Immunology
CHRISTENSEN, N. J., Internal Medicine
CHRISTOFFERSEN, P., Pathological Anatomy
DABELSTEEN, S. E., Oral Diagnosis
DEURS, B. G., Structural Cell Biology
DIRKSEN, A., Internal Medicine
GALBO, H., Physiopathology
GJERRIS, F. O., Neurosurgery
GYNTELBERG, F., Occupational Medicine
HALD, T., Surgery
HAUNSØ, S., Internal Medicine
HEMMINGSEN, R. P., Psychiatry
HENRIKSEN, J. H., Clinical Physiology
HJØRTING-HANSEN, E., Oral and Maxillofacial Surgery
HOLLNAGEL, H., General Practice
HOLMSTRUP, P., Periodontology
HOLST, J. J., Medical Physiology
HORNSLET, A., Virology
HULTBORN, H., Neurophysiology
HØIBY, N., Microbiology
KEHLET, N., Surgery
KEIDING, N., Statistics
KRASILNIKOFF, P. A., Paediatrics
KRASNIK, A., Social Medicine
KREIBORG, S., Paedodontics
LARSEN, J. F., Obstetrics and Gynaecology
LARSEN, S., Pathological Anatomy
LORENZEN, I., Internal Medicine
LUND, B., Surgery
LUND-ANDERSEN, H., Eye Diseases
MELLERGÅRD, M. J., Psychiatry
MENNÉ, T., Dermatology
MICHELSEN, N., Clinical Social Medicine
MOGENSEN, J. V., Anaesthesiology
MORLING, N., Forensic Genetics
NIELSEN, J. O., Epidemic Diseases
NORÉN, O., Biochemistry
OLESEN, J., Neurology
OTTESEN, B., Obstetrics and Gynaecology
PAULSON, O. B., Neurology
PETERSEN, P. E., Community Dentistry and Postgraduate Education
PETTERSON, G., Thoraxsurgery
PHILIP, J., Obstetrics and Gynaecology
POULSEN, H. E., Clinical Pharmacology
PRAUSE, J. U., Eye Diseases
QUISTOR, F. F., Biochemistry
REHFELD, J. F., Clinical Chemistry
REIBEL, J., Oral Pathology and Oral Medicine
ROSTGAARD, J., Normal Anatomy
ROVSING, H. C., Radiology
RØRTH, M., Clinical Oncology
SCHOU, J., Pharmacology
SCHROEDER, T. V., Surgery
SCHROLL, M., Geriatrics
SCHWARTZ, T. W., Molecular Pharmacology
SIGGAARD-ANDERSEN, O., Clinical Chemistry and Laboratory Technique
SIMONSEN, J., Forensic Pathology
SJÖSTRÖM, H., Biochemistry
SKAKKEBÆK, N., Paediatrics
SKINHØJ, P., Epidemic Diseases
SKOUBY, F., Paediatrics
SOLOW, B., Orthodontics
SØRENSEN, T. I. A., Clinical Epidemiology
STADIL, F. W., Surgery
SVEJGAARD, A., Clinical Immunology
THYLSTRUP, A., Cardiology
TOMMERUP, N., Medical Genetics
TOS, M., Oto-rhino-laryngology
VEJLSGAARD, G., Dermato-venereology
WULF, H. C., Dermato-venereology
WULFF, H. R., Clinical Decisiontheory and Ethics
ØLGAARD, K., Internal Medicine
ÖWALL, B., Prosthodontics

Faculty of Arts:

ASMUSSEN, J., Iranian Philology
BERGSAGEL, J. D., Music
BREDSDORFF, H. T., Danish Literature
BUNDENSEN, C., Cognitive Psychology
CALLEWAERT, S., Pedagogics
ELSASS, P., Clinical Psychology
FELDBAEK, O., History
GEMZELL, C.-A., Modern History
GREGERSEN, F., Danish Language
GRODAL, T. K., Film and Media Studies
HANSEN, E., Danish Language
HERTEL, H. C., Nordic Literature
HJORT, Ø., History of Art
JOHANSEN, K. F., Ancient and Medieval Philosophy
JØRGENSEN, S. AA., German Philology
KOCK, C., Rhetoric
KUSCHEL, R., Social Psychology
KVAM, K., Theatre Studies
LEVINE, P., American Languages and Literature
LOCK, C., English Literature
LOUIS-JENSEN, J., Icelandic Language and Literature
MADSEN, P., Literary History
OLSEN, B. M., Romance Languages and Literature
PEDERSEN, J., Romance Languages and Literature
RISCHEL, J., Phonetics
SCHØSLER, L., Romance Languages
SKYDSGAARD, J. E., Ancient History
STEENSGAARD, N. P., History
THOMSEN, N. J., History
TOLL, C. C., Semitic Philology
ZETTERSTEN, A., English Language and Literature
ØHRGAARD, P. C., German Philology

Faculty of Science:

ALS-NIELSEN, J., Experimental Condensed-Matter Physics
ANDERSEN, H. H., Physics
ANDERSEN, S. O., Biochemistry
BAK, P., Theoretical Physics
BATES, J. R., Meteorology
BERCHTOLD, M., Molecular Cell Biology
BERG, C., Mathematics
BILLING, G. D., Chemistry
BJÖRCK, S., Geology
BREUNING-MADSEN, H., Geography
BRIDGWATER, D., Geology
BRØNS, H., Mathematical Statistics
CHRISTENSEN, B., Zoology
CHRISTIANSEN, C., Geography, Geomorphology
CHRISTIANSEN, S. E., Geography
CVITANOVIC, P., Theoretical Physics
EGEL, R., Genetics
ENGHOFF, H., Zoological Systematics and Zoological Geography
FENCHEL, T. M., Marine Biology
FJELDSÅ, J., Biodiversity

FRIIS, I., Systematic Botany and Plant Geography
GARRET, R., Biology
GISLASON, H., Fisheries Biology
GRIMMELIKHUIJZEN CORNELIS, J. P., Zoology
GRUBB, G., Mathematics
HAMANN, O., Botany
HAMMER, C. U., Geophysics
HANSEN, J., Physics
HANSEN, O., Physics
JACKSON, A. O., Theoretical Nuclear Physics
JENSEN, C. U., Mathematics
JOHANSEN, P., Computer Science
JOHANSEN, S., Mathematical Statistics
JONASSON, S. E., Ecological Botany
JONES, N. D., Computer Science
JØRGENSEN, H. E., Astronomy
JØRGENSEN, P., Physiology
KRARUP, J. F., Computer Science
KRISTENSEN, N. P., Systematic Entomology
KRISTENSEN, R. M., Invertebrate Zoology
LARSEN, E. H., Zoophysiological Laboratory
MAKOVICKY, E., Geology
MATTHIESSEN, C. W., Geography
MOESTRUP, Ø., Spore Plants
MUNDY, J., Plant Physiology
NAUR, P., Computer Science
NIELSEN, H. B., Theoretical Physics
NIELSEN, M. S., Freshwater Biology
NORBERG, R., Insurance Mathematics
NOVIKOV, I., Astronomy
PEDERSEN, G. K., Mathematics
RICHTER, E. A., Exercise Physiology, Human Physiology
SALTIN, B., Theory of Gymnastics
SCHÄFFER, C. E., Inorganic Chemistry
SHAFFER, G., Geophysics
SKELBOE, S., Computer Science
SMITH, H., Physics
SOLOVEJ, J. P., Mathematics
STRID, A., Botany
SURLYK, F., Geology
TIND, J., Mathematical Economics
TSCHERNING, C., Geophysics
WENGEL, J., Organic Chemistry

KONGELIGE VETERINÆR- OG LANDBOHØJSKOLE (Royal Veterinary and Agricultural University)

Bülowsvej 13, 1870 Frederiksberg C
Telephone: 35-28-28-28
Fax: 35-28-23-26
E-mail: kvl@kvl.dk

Founded 1856

Rector: B. SCHMIDT-NIELSEN
Pro-Vice-Chancellor of Education: Prof. FLEMMING FRANDSEN
Pro-Vice-Chancellor of Research: Prof. TORBEN GREVE
Head of Administration: E. GRAVESEN
Head of the College Arboretum in Hørsholm: SØREN ØDUM

Library: see under Libraries
Number of teachers: 341, including 61 professors
Number of students: 2,902, including 352 postgraduates

PROFESSORS

ANDERSEN, A. S., Agricultural Sciences
ASTRUP, A., Human Nutrition
BAUER, R., Mathematics and Physics
BISGAARD, M., Veterinary Microbiology
BLIXENKRONE-MØLLER, M., Veterinary Microbiology
BOGETOFT, P., Economics and Natural Resources
BORGGÅRD, O., Chemistry
CHRISTENSEN, L. P. G., Animal Sciences and Animal Health
CHWALIBOG, A., Animal Science and Animal Health
ESBJERG, P., Ecology and Molecular Biology
FLAGSTAD, A., Clinical Sciences
FLENSTED-JENSEN, M., Mathematics and Physics
FRANDSEN, F., Ecology and Molecular Biology
FREDHOLM, M., Animal Sciences and Animal Health
FRIIS, C., Pharmacology and Pathobiology
GREVE, T., Clinical Sciences
HANSEN, A. K., Pharmacology and Pathobiology
HAVE, H., Agricultural Sciences
HELLES, F., Economics and Natural Resources
HENNINGSEN, K. W., Clinical Sciences
HESSELHOLT, M., Clinical Sciences
HOLM, A. V., Chemistry
HYLDGAARD-JENSEN, J., Anatomy and Physiology
HYTTEL, P., Anatomy and Physiology
JACOBSEN, N., Botany and Forest Genetics
JAKOBSEN, M., Agricultural Sciences
JENSEN, A. L., Clinical Sciences
JENSEN, H. E., Agricultural Sciences
KJELDSEN-KRAGH, S., Economics and Natural Sciences
KÆRGAARD, N., Economics and Natural Resources
LADEWIG, J., Animal Sciences and Animal Health
LARSEN, J. B., Economics and Natural Resources
LARSEN, J. L., Veterinary Microbiology
LARSEN, L. E., General and Inorganic Chemistry
MUNCK, L., Dairy and Food Sciences
MØLLER, B. LINDBERG, Plant Biology
NANSEN, P., Veterinary Microbiology
NIELSEN, J. P., Clinical Sciences
NIELSEN, N. E., Agricultural Sciences
OLESEN, P. O., Agricultural Sciences
OLSEN, I. A., Economics and Natural Resources
OLSEN, J. E., Veterinary Microbiology
PALMGREN, M., Plant Biology
POULSEN, K., Anatomy and Physiology
PRIMDAHL, J., Economics and Natural Resources
PURSLOW, P., Agricultural Sciences
QVIST, K. B., Dairy and Food Sciences
RAJAGOPAL, R., Plant Biology
RUDEMO, M., Mathematics and Physics
SANDSTRÖM, B., Human Nutrition
SKADHAUGE, E., Anatomy and Physiology
SKIBSTED, L. H., Dairy and Food Sciences
SKOVGAARD, I. M., Mathematics and Physics
SMEDEGAARD, V., Plant Biology
STAUN, H., Animal Sciences and Animal Health
STREIBIG, J. C., Agricultural Sciences
SVALASTOGA, E., Clinical Sciences
SVENDSEN, O., Pharmacology and Pathobiology
SØRENSEN, J., Ecology and Molecular Biology
WILLEBERG, P., Animal Sciences and Animal Health
WULFF, H., Economics and Natural Resources
AASTED, B., Veterinary Microbiology

ODENSE UNIVERSITET

Campusvej 55, 5230 Odense M
Telephone: 66-15-86-00
Fax: 66-15-84-28
E-mail: ou@ou.dk

Founded 1964
State control
Languages of instruction: Danish and English
Academic year: September to June (two semesters)

Rector: HENRIK TVARNØ
Pro-Rector: KIM BRØSEN
Chief Administrative Officer: H. MUHLE LARSEN

Library: see under Libraries
Number of teachers: 640
Number of students: 11,000

Publication: *Nyt fra Odense Universitet* (20 a year).

DEANS

Faculty of Arts: FLEMMING G. ANDERSEN
Faculty of Social Sciences and Business Studies: TAGE KOED MADSEN
Faculty of Natural Sciences: JENS ODDERSHEDE
Faculty of Medicine: MOGENS HØRDER

PROFESSORS:

Faculty of Arts:

BACHE, C., English Language and Literature
BASBØLL, H., Scandinavian Language
BOYSEN, G., French Language
FAVRHOLDT, D., Philosophy
JENSEN, B., Slavic Studies
JENSEN, M. S., Classical Language and Culture
JESPERSEN, K. J. V., History
JOHANSEN, H. C., History
JOHANSEN, J. D., Comparative Literature
MOESTRUP, J., Romance Philology
MORTENSEN, F. H., Scandinavian Language and Literature
NYE, D., American Studies
NØJGAARD, M., Romance Philology
SAUERBERG, L. O., English Language and Literature
SCHMIDT, P., Danish Textual and Cultural History
SØRENSEN, B. A., German Language and Literature

Faculty of Social Sciences and Business Studies:

AMIR, R., Business Studies
BOUCHET, D., Business Studies
CHRISTENSEN, J. A., Business Studies
CHRISTENSEN, P. O., Business Studies
CLAUSEN, N. J., Law
HANSEN, J. D., Business Studies
IVERSEN, B., Law
JØRGENSEN, S., Business Studies
KLAUSEN, K. K., Public Organization Theory
MADSEN, T. K., Business Studies
MATTHIESSEN, L., National Economics
MOURITZEN, P. E., Political Sciences
OBEL, B., Business Studies
PEDERSEN, M. N., Political Sciences
PETERSEN, J. H., Social Science
SØGAARD, J., Health Economics
SØRENSEN, C. J., National Economics

Faculty of Natural and Engineering Sciences:

BERNSEN, N. O., Information Technology
BJERREGAARD, P., Biology
CANFIELD, D., Biology
HAAGERUP, U., Mathematics
ISSINGER, O., Biochemistry
JOOSEN, W., Information Technology
JØRGENSEN, B., Statistics
KNUDSEN, J. K., Biochemistry
KORNERUP, P., Computer Science
KRISTENSEN, B. B., Information Technology
LUNTZ, A. C., Physics
MICHELSEN, A., Biology
NIELSEN, H. T., Chemistry
ODDERSHEDE, J., Chemistry
PEDERSEN, E. K., Mathematics
PERRAM, J. W., Information Technology
PETERSEN, H., Mathematics
RANKIN, J. C., Biology
ROEPSTORFF, P., Molecular Biology
SIGMUND, H. P., Physics
VALENTIN-HANSEN, P., Molecular Biology

Faculty of Health Sciences:

ANDERSEN, K. E., Dermato-venerology
BECK-NIELSEN, H., Medical Endocrinology
BENDIX, T., Biomechanics
BENTZEN, N., General Practice
BJERRE, P., Neurosurgery
BRØSEN, K., Clinical Pharmacology
CORDER, E., Genetic Epidemiology
GRAM, L. F., Pharmacology

GRANDJEAN, P. A., Environmental Medicine
HAGHFELT, T., Cardiology
HØILUND-CARLSEN, P., Clinical Physiology
HØRDER, M, Clinical Chemistry
JØRGENSEN, K. E., Oto-rhino-laryngology
JUNKER, P., Rheumatology
KILDEBERG, P. A., Paediatrics
KRAG-SØRENSEN, P., Psychiatry
KRONBORG, P., Surgery
MANNICHE, C., Biomechanics
NEDERGAARD, O. A., Pharmacology
PEDERSEN, C., Infectious Medicine
PETERSEN, S., Asthma and Allergy in Childhood
RASMUSSEN, J. Z., Anatomy
RITSKES-HOITINGA, M., Comparative Medicine and Laboratory Animal Science
SCHAFFALITZKY DE MUCKADELL, O. B., Internal Medicine
SIBONI, K., Microbiology
SJØGAARD, G., Physical Education and Health
SKØTT, O., Physiology
SVEHAG, S. E., Microbiology
SØRENSEN, T., Psychiatry
THOMSEN, J., Forensic Medicine
VACH, W., Medical Statistics
VAUPEL, J. W., Demographic Studies
WALTER, S., Surgery
WESTERGAARD, J. G., Obstetrics

ROSKILDE UNIVERSITETSCENTER

POB 260, Universitetsvej 1, 4000 Roskilde
Telephone: 46-74-20-00
Telex: 43158
Fax: 46-74-30-00
Founded 1970
State control
Academic year: September to June (two semesters)
Rector: HENRIK TOFT JENSEN
Pro-Rector: KAREN SJÖRUP
Administrative Officer: ERIK EBBE
Librarian: NIELS SENIUS CLAUSEN
Library of 450,000 vols
Number of teachers: 390 full-time, 75 part-time
Number of students: 6,300
Publications: *Ruc-Nyt* (fortnightly), *Fructus* (occasionally), *Annual Calendar*.

PROFESSORS

Humanities:

BAGGESEN, S., Science of Texts, Scandinavian and American Literature
BJERG, J., Educational Psychology
BRASK, P., Science of Texts, Theory and Methodology of Literary Analysis
BRYLD, C., History
HELTOFT, L., Danish
KJØRUP, S., Philosophy and Communication
MCGUIRE, B. P., History
MORTENSEN, A. T., Philosophy and Communication
NISSEN, G., History
OLESEN, H. S., Educational Psychology
OLSEN, M., French
PEDERSEN, S., Philosophy
PREISLER, B., English
WUCHERPHENNIG, W. P., German

Natural Sciences:

AGGER, P., Environmental Planning
ANDERSEN, O., Environmental Science
BONDESEN, E., Geology
BRANDT, J., Geography
CLAUSEN, J., Biochemistry
HANSEN, P. E., Chemistry
ILLERIS, S., Geography
NISS, M., Mathematics
PRÆSTGAARD, E., Chemistry
SIMONSEN, K. F., Geography
SVEINSDOTTIR, E., Computer Science
SØRENSEN, B. E., Physics
THULSTRUP, E., Chemistry

Social Sciences:

AAGE, H., Political Economy
BOGASON, P., Public Administration
DAVIS, J. D., Economics, Public Sector
JESPERSEN, J., Welfare State Studies
MARTINUSSEN, J., Economics, Political and Social Sciences
MATTSON, J., Business Administration
NIELSEN, K., Industrial Theory
OLSEN, O. J., Planning
SUNDBO, J., Business Administration

POLYTEKNISKE LAEREANSTALT DANMARKS TEKNISKE UNIVERSITET (Technical University of Denmark)

Bygning 101, 2800 Lyngby
Telephone: 45-25-25-25
Fax: 45-88-17-99
Founded 1829
President: Dr HANS PETER JENSEN
Vice-President: Prof. KNUT CONRADSEN
University Director: ANNE GRETE HOLMSGAARD
Number of professors: 67
Number of students: 6,100

DEANS OF FACULTY COMMITTEES

Mechanical Engineering, Energy and Production: Prof. P. TERNDRUP PEDERSEN
Civil and Environmental Engineering: Assoc. Prof. KNUD CHRISTENSEN
Chemistry, Chemical Engineering and Biotechnology: Prof. JOHN VILLADSEN
Information Technology, Electronics and Mathematics: Prof. ERIK BRUUN
Electrical Engineering and Physics: Prof. STEEN MØRUP

PROFESSORS

ADLER-NISSEN, J. L., Biotechnology
ALTING, L., Mechanical Engineering
BENDSØE, M., Applied Functional Analysis
BJØRNER, D., Computer Science
BOE, C., Engineering Design
BOHR, J., Physics of Structure Formation
BOHR, J., Physics
BRO-RASMUSSEN, F., Environmental Science and Ecology
BRUUN, K. E., Analog Electronics
BUCHHAVE, P., Optics
CHRISTENSEN, TH. H., Environmental Engineering
CONRADSEN, K., Statistical Image Analysis
COTTERILL, R. M. J., Materials Science
DAHL, J. P., Chemical Physics
DAM JOHANSEN, K., Combustion and Chemical Reaction Engineering
DITLEVSEN, O. D., Actions on Structures and Structural Reliability
FANGER, P. O., Heating and Air Conditioning
FOGED, N., Geotechnical Engineering
FREDSØE, J., Marine Hydraulics
GIMSING, N. J., Structural Engineering
GRAM, C., Computer Science
GAARSLEV, A., Construction Management
HAMMER, K., Microbiology
HANSEN, B., Soil Mechanics
HANSEN, C. P., Scientific Computing
HANSEN, E., Hydrology
HANSEN, E. B., Applied Mathematics
HANSEN, E. H., Analytical Chemistry
HANSEN, J. R., Electric Power Supply
HANSEN, V. L., Mathematics
HARREMOES, P., Sanitary Engineering
HOAM, J. M., Microelectronics
HØLMER, G., Industrial Human Nutrition
JACOBI, O., Surveying and Photogrammetry
JENSEN, J. A., Biomedical Signal Processing
JENSEN, L. B., Acoustics
JEPPESEN, P., Optical Communication
JUSTESEN, J., Telecommunication
JØRGENSEN, N. O., Traffic
JØRGENSEN, S. B., Technical Chemistry
KOPS, J., Polymer Chemistry and Engineering
KRENK, S., Structural Mechanics
LARSEN, P. S., Fluid Mechanics
LEISTIKO, O., Semiconductor Physics
LIND, M., Control Systems
LYNGAAE-JOERGENSEN, J., Polymer Technology
MAAHN, E., Corrosion Science
MADSEN. K., Numerical Analysis
MEYER, N., Physics
MOLIN, S., Applied Microbiogenetics
MOURITZEN, O. G., Physical Chemistry
NIELSEN, M. P., Structural Analysis
NILSSON, J. F., Artificial Intelligence
NØRSKOV, J. K., Theoretical Physics
OTT, S., Town Planning
PEDERSEN, F. B., Hydrodynamics
PEDERSEN, P. T., Strength of Materials
QVALE, B., Mechanical Engineering
ROENNE-HANSEN, J., Electric Power Engineering
STAUNSTRUP, J., Digital System Construction
STENBY, H. E., Applied Thermodynamics and Separation Processes
SVENDSEN, SV. AA. HØJGAARD, Energy Technology in Buildings
TANNER, D., Organic Chemistry
THAGESEN, B. M., Road Building
THOMASSEN, C., Mathematics
TRUMPY, G., Physics
TVERGAARD, V., Mechanics of Materials
TØNNESEN, O., Experimental High Voltage Technique
ULSTRUP, J., Inorganic Chemistry
VILLADSEN, J., Biotechnology
VILLUMSEN, A., Geology
WANHEIM, T., Machine Engineering
ØLGAARD, P. L., Reactor Physics and Nuclear Engineering
ØSTERGAARD, K., Chemical Engineering

Other Institutions of Higher Education

Århus Tandlægehøjskole (Royal Dental College, Århus): Vennelyst Boulevard, 8000 Århus C; f. 1958; 124 teachers, including 10 professors; 483 students; Dean Prof. SVEN POULSEN; Administrator RIGMOR ASTRUP ANDERSEN; Librarian P. JUNKER JACOBSEN.

Arkitektskolen i Aarhus (Aarhus School of Architecture): Nørreport 20, 8000 Aarhus C; tel. 89-36-00-00; fax 86-13-06-45; f. 1965; architectural design, planning, furniture and industrial design; 106 teachers, including 6 professors; library of 44,000 vols; Rector PETER KJÆR; Administrator OLE GRAAH; publs *Årsberetning*, *Skolehåndbogen* (annually).

Danmarks Biblioteksskole (Royal School of Library and Information Science): Birketinget 6, 2300 Copenhagen S; tel. 32-58-60-66; fax 32-84-02-01; e-mail db@db.dk; f. 1956; 75 teachers; 1,000 students; library of 186,000 vols; Rector OLE HARBO.

Danmarks Biblioteksskole Aalborgafdeling (Royal School of Library and Information Science, Aalborg Branch); Langagervej 4, 9220 Aalborg Øst.

Danmarks Farmaceutiske Højskole (Royal Danish School of Pharmacy): Universitetsparken 2, 2100 Copenhagen Ø; tel. 35-37-08-50; fax 35-37-57-44; f. 1892; Library: see under Libraries; 150 teachers; 1,300 students; Rector Prof. BIRTHE JENSEN; Administrator BJØRN ANDERSEN; publ. *Lægemiddelforskning* (1 a year).

Danmarks Journalisthøjskole (Danish School of Journalism): Olof Palmes Allé 11, 8200 Århus N.; tel. 89-44-04-40; fax 86-16-89-10; f. 1971; 46 teachers; 800 students; Dean

KIM MINKE; Head of Administration KIRSTEN JENSEN.

Danmarks Laererhøjskole (Royal Danish School of Educational Studies): Emdrupvej 101, 2400 Copenhagen NV; 9 local brs; tel. 39-69-66-33; fax 39-66-00-81; f. 1856; library: see Libraries; 115 teachers (*c*. 1,800 part-time), including 15 professors; 18,600 full-time, 16,000 part-time students; Rector TOM PLOUG OLSEN; Pro-Rector NILS HOLDGAARD SOERENSEN; Administrator JAKOB KLINGERT; Pedagogic Inspector CHRESTEN KRUCHOV; Chief Librarian LEIF LOERRING.

CHAIRMEN OF INSTITUTES

Educational Studies and Research: MOGENS NIELSEN
Early Childhood Education: HANS VEJLESKOV
Psychology and Special Education: NIELS EGELUND
Department of Humanities: FINN LOEKKEGAARD
Arts, Crafts, Media and Music: JOHN HOEBYE
Biology, Geography and Domestic Sciences: HANS LEVIN HANSEN
Mathematics, Physics, Chemistry and Informatics: MOGENS LYSTER

Dansk Teknologisk Institut (Danish Technological Institute): Gregersensvej, 2630 Tåstrup; tel. 43-50-43-50; fax 43-50-72-50; *and at* Teknologiparken, 8000 Århus C; tel. 89-43-89-43; fax 89-43-89-89; f. 1906; building technology, energy, environment, industry, industrial and business development; 15,000 course participants; Pres. LARS OLE KORNUM.

Fynske Musikkonservatorium (Carl Nielsen Academy of Music): Islandsgade 2, 5000 Odense C; tel. 66-11-06-63; fax 66-17-77-63; f. 1929; 75 teachers; 140 students; library of 33,000 books and scores; Pres. BERTEL KRARUP.

Handelshøjskolen i Århus (The Århus School of Business): Fuglesangs Allé 4, 8210 Århus V; tel. 89-48-66-88; fax 86-15-01-88; f. 1939; 183 full-time teachers including professors, 315 part-time; 5,448 students; Rector MORTEN BALLING; Sec. JAN HALLE; Librarian TOVE BANG.

PROFESSORS

ANDERSEN, P. K., Company Law
BALLING, M., Finance
BERGENHOLTZ, H., Lexicography
DAHLGAARD, J. J., Quality Management
ERIKSSON, T., Economics
GRUNERT, K. G., Marketing
HASSELBALCH, O., Business Law
HILDEBRANDT, S., Organization Theory and Management
KOCH, W., German
KRISTENSEN, K., Applied Statistics
MICHELSEN, Å., Tax Law
MØLLER, P. F., Financial Accounting
NØLKE, H., French Language
PRINTZ, L., Organization Theory and Management
PROVSTGAARD, B., Accountancy
SMITH, N., Economics
STRANDSKOV, J., International Business
THOMSEN, S., International Business
THRANE, T., English
WESTERGAARD-NIELSEN, N., Economics (Labour Economics)
ÖLANDER, F., Economic Psychology

Handelshøjskolen i København (Copenhagen Business School): Struenseegade 7–9, 2200 Copenhagen N; tel. 38-15-38-15; fax 38-15-20-15; f. 1917; State control; Academic year: September to July; teaching and research in business economics and modern languages; Library: see under Libraries; 325 full-time, 1,000 part-time teachers; 15,000 students; Pres. FINN JUNGE-JENSEN; Sec. JAKOB VOLTELEN; publ. *CEBAL, ARK, SPRINT, Yearbook*.

Handelshøjskole Syd – Ingeniørhøjskole Syd: (Southern Denmark School of Business and Engineering): Grundtvigs Allé 150, 6400 Sønderborg; tel. 79-32-11-11; fax 79-32-12-87; e-mail hhs@hhs.dk; f. 1984; library of 72,000 vols; 87 full-time teachers, 204 part-time; 3,000 students; Pres. JENS HOHWÜ; Administrator NIELS HENRIK ASSING.

DEANS

Faculty of Business Administration: AXEL SCHULTZ-NIELSEN
Faculty of Engineering: ERIK URTH
Faculty of Modern Languages: ANNELISE GRINSTED

Ingeniørhøjskolen i Aarhus: Dalgas Ave 2, 8000 Aarhus C; tel. 86-13-62-11; fax 86-13-64-88; e-mail rektorat@aarhus.ih.dk; f. 1903; 110 teachers; 1,100 students; library of 18,000 vols; Rector HARRY SVANHEDE PEDERSEN

HEADS OF DEPARTMENTS

Civil Engineering: JØRGEN KORSGÅRD
Mechanical Engineering: LAURIDS ØSTERGAARD
Electrical Power Engineering: ERLING JOHANSEN
Electronic Engineering: LEIF MUNKØE
Computer Engineering: LEIF MUNKØE

Ingeniørhøjskolen i Horsens: Chr. M. Østergaards Vej 4, 8700 Horsens; tel. 75-62-88-11; fax 75-62-64-56; f. 1915; library of 27,000 vols; 50 teachers; 452 students; Rector HANS JØRN HANSEN; Pro-Rector HANS EMBORG; Sec. POVL THOMSEN.

DEANS

Faculty of Civil Engineering: WERNER BAI
Faculty of Mechanical Engineering: AAGE PEDERSEN
Faculty of Export Engineering: ANKER STÆHR-JØRGENSEN

Ingeniørhøjskolen, Københavns Teknikum: Lautrupvang 15, 2750 Ballerup; tel. 42-97-80-88; fax 42-97-81-72; e-mail ig@cph.ih.dk; f. 1963; applied sciences; 186 teachers; 2,100 students; library of 32,900 vols; Rector VERNER DAUGAARD.

Ingeniørhøjskolen Odense Teknikum: Niels Bohrs Alle 1, 5230 Odense M; tel. 66-13-08-27; fax 66-13-48-27; f. 1905; library of 30,000 vols; 130 teachers; 1,200 students; Rector BENT POULSEN; Sec. F. JOHANSEN.

DEANS

Faculty of Civil and Construction Engineering: A. HANSEN
Faculty of Electrical Engineering: HENNING ANDERSEN
Faculty of Chemical Engineering: THORKILD SCHRØDER
Faculty of Mechanical Engineering: STEEN ANDERSEN
Faculty of Production Engineering: H. C. JUHL

Ingeniørhøjskolen Sønderborg Teknikum: Voldgade 5, 6400 Sønderborg; tel. 74-42-55-50; fax 74-43-17-35; f. 1962; 24 teachers; 290 students; library of 10,000 vols; Rector K. CLEMEN JORGENSEN.

HEADS OF DEPARTMENTS

Electronics: ERIK URTH
Mechanics: EGON VILLUMSEN
Production: SVEND HANSEN

Jyske Musikkonservatorium, Det (Royal Academy of Music Århus): Fuglesangs Allé 26, 8210 Århus V; tel. 89-48-33-88; fax 89-48-33-22; f. 1927; 100 teachers; 200 students; Pres. ERIK BACH; Administrator SANDER ANGELSØ.

Københavns tekniske Skole (Copenhagen Polytechnic): Rebslagervej 11, POB 899, 2400 Copenhagen NV; tel. 31-81-22-90; fax 31-81-35-90; 500 staff, *c*. 6,000 students; Dir MOGENS NIELSEN.

Kongelige Danske Kunstakademi (Royal Danish Academy of Fine Arts); Charlottenborg, Kgs. Nytorv 1, 1050 Copenhagen K; tel. 33-74-45-00; fax 33-74-45-55; f. 1754; 20 professors; 1,350 students; library: see under Libraries; Rectors THORKEL DAHL (School of Architecture), ELSE MARIE BUKDAHL (School of Fine Arts), RENÉ LARSEN (School of Conservation).

Kongelige Danske Musikkonservatorium (Royal Danish Academy of Music): Niels Brocksgade 1, 1574 Copenhagen V; tel. 33-69-22-69; fax 33-14-09-11; f. 1867; library of 50,000 vols; 170 teachers; *c*. 400 students; Principal STEEN PADE; Administrator BJARNE BACH ØSTERGAARD; Librarian TOVE KRAG.

Nordjysk Musikkonservatorium (Academy of Music, Aalborg): Ryesgade 52, 9000 Aalborg; tel. 98-12-77-44; fax 98-11-37-63; f. 1930; 100 students; Rector JENS-OLE BLAK.

Sociale Højskole Esbjerg, Den (School of Social Work, Esbjerg): Storegade 182, 6705 Esbjerg Ø, tel. 75-13-35-00; fax 75-12-09-04; f. 1971; library of 14,500 vols; 22 teachers; 400 students; Dir GRETHE ERICHSEN; Registrar LILLIAN SØEBORG.

Sydjysk Universitetscenter (South Jutland University Centre): Niels Bohrs Vej 9, 6700 Esbjerg; tel. 79-14-11-11; fax 79-14-11-99; f.1972; private research institution; postgraduate courses and seminars in social sciences and humanities; library of 111,332 vols; Rector JAN MAGNUSSEN; Librarian EDITH CLAUSEN; publs *Vindue mod Ost* (East Window, quarterly), *Folk og forskning* (People and Research, quarterly).

ATTACHED INSTITUTES

Institute of Industrial and Social Development: Dir TORBEN BAGER.
Institute of Fisheries Economics: Dir HANS FROST.
Institute of Maritime Medicine: Dir OLAF JENSEN (acting).
Institute of Thrombosis Research: Dir JØRGEN JESPERSEN.
Institute of Biomass Utilization and Biorefinery: Dir PAULI KIEL.
Centre of East-West Research: Dir FINN LAURSEN.
Danish Centre of Ethnicity and Migration Research: Dirs TORBEN BAGER, JAN HJARNOE.
GRID-Denmark (Global Resource Database – UN/UNEP): Dir HENNING SMIDT-HANSEN.

Vestjysk Musikkonservatorium (Academy of Music, Esbjerg): Kirkegade 61–63, 6700 Esbjerg; tel. 76-10-43-00; fax 76-10-43-10; f. 1946; 120 students; Dir AXEL MOMME.

FAROE ISLANDS

Learned Societies

GENERAL

Føroya Fróðskaparfelag/Societas Scientiarum Faeroensis (Faroese Society of Science and Letters): POB 209, 100 Tórshavn; tel. 31-53-02; fax 31-89-29; f. 1952; aims to procure scientific and scholarly literature and to promote research work; 150 mems; Pres. EYÐUN ANDREASSEN; publs *Fróðskaparrit* (Annals), *Supplementa*.

AGRICULTURE, FISHERIES AND VETERINARY SCIENCE

Føroya Búnadarfelag (Faroese Agricultural Society): Yviri við Strond 8, Tórshavn; f. 1924; to promote the agricultural industry; advisory service; 1,500 mems; Chair MORTAN WINTHER POULSEN.

HISTORY, GEOGRAPHY AND ARCHAEOLOGY

Føroya Forngripafelag (Faroese Archaeological Society): POB 1173, 110 Tórshavn; f. 1898; works in conjunction with the National Museum of Antiquities; 325 mems; Pres. MORTAN WINTHER POULSEN.

LANGUAGE AND LITERATURE

Felagid 'Varðin' ('Varðin' Literary Society): 100 Tórshavn; f. 1919; Pres. JOHAN HENDRIK W. POULSEN; publ. *Varðin* (The Cairn) (quarterly).

Rithøvundafelag Føroya (Faroese Writers Union): POB 1124, 110 Tórshavn; fax (298) 10133; f. 1957; to promote the growth of Faroese literature and to protect authors' rights; 73 mems; Pres. HEDIN KLEIN.

NATURAL SCIENCES

Biological Sciences

Føroya Náttúra—Føroya Skúli (Natural History Society): Hoydalar, 3800 Tórshavn; f. 1951; 150 mems; Pres. ÁSMUNDUR JOHANNESEN.

TECHNOLOGY

Føroya Verkfrøðingafelag (Chartered Engineers Assen): Tvørgøta 3, POB 2133, 165 Argir; tel. 298-14826; f. 1967; 140 mems; Pres. SÍMUN HAMMER; publ. *Verkfrøði* (3 a year).

Research Institutes

AGRICULTURE, FISHERIES AND VETERINARY SCIENCE

Fiskirannsóknarstovan (Marine Research Institute): Nóatún, Postboks 3051, 110 Tórshavn; tel. 298-15092; fax 298-18264; f. 1951; fishery biology and oceanography; Dir HJALTI Í JÁKUPSSTOVU; publ. *Fiskirannsóknir* (1 or 2 a year).

Heilsufrøðiliga Starvsstovan (Food and Environmental Institute): Debesartrøð, 100 Tórshavn; tel. (298) 15300; fax (298) 10508; f. 1975; research, services, quality control and inspection in the fish and food industry and in the environment; government dept; Dir BARÐUR ENNI; publ. *Ársfrágreiðing* (annual report).

Libraries and Archives

Tórshavn

Býarbókasavnid (Public Library): Niels Finsensgøta 7, POB 358, 110 Tórshavn; f. 1969; 60,000 vols; Dir ANNA BRIMNES.

Føroya Landsbókasavn (National Library): POB 61, Tórshavn; tel. (298) 11626; fax (298) 18895; e-mail fonalib@flb.fo; f. 1828; 130,000 vols (20,000 scientific); open to the public; Dir MARTIN NÆS; publ. *Føroyskur Bókalisti* (annual list of Faeroese publs).

Føroya Landsskjalasavn (National Archives of the Faroe Islands): W.U. Hammershaimbsgøta 24, 100 Tórshavn; tel. 316677; fax 318677; e-mail fararch@lss.fo; f. 1932; medieval documents (1298-1599), archives of parliament and central and local administration (1615-1980); Dir JÓANNES DALSGAARD.

Museums and Art Galleries

Tórshavn

Føroya Fornminnissavn (National Museum): Hoyvík, POB 1155, 110 Tórshavn; tel. 31-07-00; fax 31-22-59; e-mail apnethor@fms.fo; f. 1898, taken over by State 1952; archaeology, ethnology, inspection of ancient monuments; Antiquary ARNE THORSTEINSSON.

Føroya Náttúrugripasavn (Natural History Museum): Debesartrød, 100 Tórshavn; f. 1955; depts of geology, botany, zoology; Dir DORETE BLOCH.

Savnid 1940-45 (Faroe-British Museum): Brekkuni 7, 100 Tórshavn; tel. 13813; f. 1983; military and civilian artefacts from Second World War British occupation.

University

FRÓDSKAPARSETUR FØROYA/ UNIVERSITAS FÆROENSIS (University of the Faroe Islands)

Debesartrød, 100 Tórshavn

Telephone: 31-53-02
Fax: 31-89-29

Founded 1965

Rector: ARNE NØRREVANG
Secretary-General: INGIBJØRG BERG

Number of teachers: 14
Number of students: 70 full-time

Departments of Faeroese, natural sciences, computer science, history and sociology; evening classes and public lectures.

GREENLAND

Learned Societies

GENERAL

Grønlandske Selskab, Det (The Greenland Society): see under Denmark.

Nunani Avannarlerni piorsarsimassutsikkut Attaveqaat (NAPA) (The Nordic Institute in Greenland): POB 770, DK-3900 Nuuk; tel. 24733; fax 25733; f. 1986; financed by the 5 nordic countries and 3 home rule areas within them; purpose is to advance and sponsor all sorts of inter-nordic cultural relations; Dir OLE OXHOLM; Sec. MARGRETHE GUNDEL.

FINE AND PERFORMING ARTS

'Simerneq' (Artists' Society): POB 1009, DK-3900 Nuuk; f. 1978; arranges exhibitions of works of members and others; Sec. INGER HAUGE.

LANGUAGE AND LITERATURE

Kalaallit Atuakkiortut (Greenlandic Authors' Society): POB 43, DK-3900 Nuuk; tel. 28485; fax 28585; f. 1975; copyrights for authors and translators; 83 mems; Chair. AQQALUK K. LYNGE.

Research Institutes

AGRICULTURE, FISHERIES AND VETERINARY SCIENCE

Forsøgsstationen 'Upernaviarsuk' (Experimental Station 'Uper'): POB 152, 3920 Qaqortoq; tel. 38006; fax 38003; governmental institution carrying out experiments in sheep rearing, fodder crops, tree planting and gardening in a polar environment.

NATURAL SCIENCES

General

Commission for Scientific Research in Greenland: Strandgade 100H, 1401 Copenhagen; tel. 32-88-01-00; fax 32-88-01-01; an independent board that decides public sponsoring of public and private research projects in Greenland; Chair. J. P. HART HANSEN.

Danish Polar Center: Strandgade 100H, 1401 Copenhagen; tel. 32-88-01-00; fax 32-88-01-01; e-mail dpc@dpc.dk; f. 1989; supports and co-ordinates arctic and antarctic research in Denmark and Greenland and provides information on polar issues; Dir MORTEN MELDGAARD; publ. *Polarfronten* (4 a year).

Biological Sciences

Arctic Station, University of Copenhagen: see under Denmark.

Danmarks Miljøundersøgelser, Afdeling for Arktisk Miljø (Danish Environmental Research Institute, Department of Arctic Environment): Tagensvej 135, 4th floor, 2200 Copenhagen N; tel. 35-82-14-15; fax 35-82-14-20; monitors esp. effects of mineral exploitation; Dir HANNE K. PETERSEN.

Grønlands Naturinstitut (Greenland Institute of Natural Resources): Postboks 570, 3900 Nuuk; tel. 32-10-95; fax 32-59-57; applied research in natural resources, environmental protection and biodiversity; Dir KLAUS HOYER NYGAARD.

Physical Sciences

Dansk Meteorologisk Institut (Danish Meteorological Institute): see under Denmark.

Libraries and Archives

Nuuk

Nunatta Atuagaateqarfia/Grønlandske Landsbibliotek (National Library of Greenland): POB 1011, DK-3900 Nuuk; tel. 21156; fax 23943; Dir ELISA JEREMIASSEN.

Museums and Art Galleries

Nuuk

Nunatta Katersugaasivia Allagaateqarfialu/Grønlands Nationalmuseum og Arkiv (Greenland National Museum and Archive): POB 145, 3900 Nuuk; tel. 22611; fax 22622; f. 1966; research into archaeology, ethnology, art, history, public archival matters; Dir EMIL ROSING.

Colleges

Eqqumiitsuliornermik Ilinniarfik/Kunstskolen (School of Arts): POB 286, DK-3900 Nuuk; tel. 22644; f. 1973; Dir ARNANNGUAQ HØEGH.

Ilisimatusarfik (University of Greenland): POB 279, 3900 Nuuk; tel. 32-45-66; fax 32-47-11; e-mail university@greennet.gl; f. 1984; Greenlandic language and literature, cultural and historical sciences, administration, theology; library of 17,000 vols; Rector CLAUS ANDREASEN; Dir Prof. ROBERT PETERSEN; publ. *Grønlandsk Kultur- og Samfunds-Forskning* (annually).

Ilinniarfissuaq: POB 1026, 3900 Nuuk; tel. 21191; teacher training college, social pedagogical and social administrative education and in-service training; Dir Rektor HENDRIK LENNERT.

Niuernermik Ilinniarfik/Grønlands Handelsskole: POB 1038, 3900 Nuuk; tel. 32-30-99; fax 32-32-55; f. 1980; courses and in-service training in journalism, interpreting and mercantile matters, also technical mercantile training; Dir BO NÓRRESLET.

DOMINICAN REPUBLIC

Learned Societies

GENERAL

Instituto de Cultura Dominicana: Biblioteca Nacional, César Nicolás Penson, Santo Domingo; f. 1971; to promote the cultural tradition of the country, encourage artistic creation in general, and the expression of the spirit of the Dominican people; Pres. ENRIQUE APOLINAR HENRÍQUEZ; Sec. PEDRO GIL ITURBIDES.

BIBLIOGRAPHY, LIBRARY SCIENCE AND MUSEOLOGY

Asociación Dominicana de Bibliotecarios, Inc. (ASODOBI) (Librarians' Association): c/o Biblioteca Nacional, Plaza de la Cultura, César Nicolás Penson 91, Santo Domingo; tel. 688-4086; f. 1974 to develop library services in the Republic, increase the standing of the profession and encourage the training of its members; 90 mems; Pres. PRÓSPERO J. MELLA CHAVIER; Sec.-Gen. V. REGÚS; publ. *El Papiro* (quarterly).

Sociedad Dominicana de Bibliófilos Inc.: Las Damas 106, Santo Domingo; Pres. Lic. FRANK MOYA PONS.

EDUCATION

Asociación Dominicana de Rectores de Universidades (Dominican Assn of University Presidents): Apdo 2465, Calle Luperón esq. Hostos (altos), Edif. Comisión de Monumentos, Zona Colonial, Santo Domingo; tel. 689-4931; telex 3460898; fax 687-7401; f. 1981; 9 full mems, 8 regular mems; Exec. Dir Dra. GERTRUDYS MIESES.

HISTORY, GEOGRAPHY AND ARCHAEOLOGY

Academia Dominicana de la Historia (Dominican Academy of History): Calle Mercedes 204, Casa de las Academias, Santo Domingo; tel. 689-3446; fax 535-7891; f. 1931; 18 mems, 24 nat. corresp. mems, 60 foreign corresp. mems; Pres. Dr JULIO G. CAMPILLO PEREZ; Sec. Dr CARLOS DOBAL; publ. *Clio* (quarterly).

LANGUAGE AND LITERATURE

Academia Dominicana de la Lengua (Dominican Academy): Avda Tiradentes 66, Ensanche La Fe, Santo Domingo; Corresp. of the Real Academia Española (Madrid); 13 mems; library of 50,000 vols; Pres. MARIANO LEBRÓN SAVIÑÓN; Sec. MANUEL GOICO CASTRO.

MEDICINE

Asociación Médica de Santiago (Santiago Medical Association): Apdo 445, Santiago de los Caballeros; f. 1941; library of 1,500 vols; 65 mems; Pres. Dr RAFAEL FERNÁNDEZ LAZALA; Sec. Dr JOSÉ COROMINAS P.; publ. *Boletín Médico* (quarterly).

Asociación Médica Dominicana (Dominican Medical Association): Apdo 1237, Santo Domingo; f. 1941; 1,551 mems; Pres. Dr ANGEL S. CHAN AQUINO; Sec. Dr CARLOS LAMARCHE REY; publ. *Revista Médica Dominicana*.

Research Institutes

AGRICULTURE, FISHERIES AND VETERINARY SCIENCE

Instituto Azucarero Dominicano (Dominican Sugar Institute): Avda Jiménez Moya, Apdo 667, Santo Domingo; tel. 532-5571; Dir JIMMY GARCÍA SAVIÑÓN.

HISTORY, GEOGRAPHY AND ARCHAEOLOGY

Instituto Cartográfico Militar de las Fuerzas Armadas (Military Cartographic Institute): Base Naval 27 de Febrero, Santo Domingo; tel. 686-2954; f. 1950; photogrammetry, cartography, geodesy, hydrography, photographic laboratory; Dir Capt. DOMINGO GÓMEZ.

Libraries and Archives

Baní

Biblioteca 'Padre Billini': Calle Duarte No. 6, Baní; f. 1926; *c.* 38,000 vols; Dir Lic. FERNANDO HERRERA.

Moca

Biblioteca Municipal 'Gabriel Morillo': Calle Antonio de la Maza esq. Independencia, Moca; f. 1942; 6,422 vols; Dir Lic. ADRIANO MIGUEL TEJADA E.

San Pedro de Macorís

Biblioteca del Ateneo de Macorís (Library of the Athenaeum of Macorís): San Pedro de Macorís; f. 1890; 6,274 vols; Pres. Lic. JOSÉ A. CHEVALIER.

Santiago de los Caballeros

Biblioteca de la Sociedad Amantes de la Luz: España esq. Avda Central, Santiago de los Caballeros; f. 1874; public library of cultural society; 18,000 vols; Dir Lic. BERENI ESTRELLA DE INOA.

Santo Domingo

Archivo General de la Nación: Calle M. E. Diaz, Santo Domingo; f. 1935; 3,000 vols; Dir MARISOL FLORÉN; publ. *Boletín* (quarterly).

Biblioteca de la Cámara de Comercio y Producción del Distrito Nacional (Library of the Chamber of Commerce and Production): Arzobispo Nouel No. 206, Apdo 815, Santo Domingo; tel. 682-2688; fax 685-2228; f. 1848; 6,000 vols.

Biblioteca de la Secretaría de Estado de Relaciones Exteriores (Library of the Secretariat of Foreign Affairs): Estancia Ramfis, Santo Domingo; special collections relating to international law; Dir Dr PRÓSPERO J. MELLA CHAVIER.

Biblioteca de la Universidad Autónoma de Santo Domingo (Library of Santo Domingo University): Ciudad Universitaria, Apdo 1355, Santo Domingo; 104,441 vols (Dominicana, historical archives, prints, maps, microfilms, etc.), 782,795 reviews (chiefly foreign, relating to the different faculties), microfilms, gramophone records; Dir Dra MARTHA MARÍA DE CASTRO COTES; publ. *Boletín de Adquisiciones*.

Biblioteca Dominicana: Santo Domingo; housed in a chapel of the Dominican Order dating from 1729; f. 1914; over 6,000 vols, of which Dominican authors comprise 700; collections of periodicals; also contains a students' reading-room, text-books, maps; Dir JOSÉ RIJO.

Biblioteca Municipal de Santo Domingo (Municipal Library of Santo Domingo): Padre Billini No. 18, Santo Domingo; Librarian LUZ DEL CARMEN RAPOZO.

Biblioteca Nacional: César Nicolás Penson, Santo Domingo; f. 1971; collects government publs; houses National Bibliography; exhibitions, conferences, research and documentation; 153,955 vols; Dir Lic. ROBERTO DE SOTO.

Departamento de Documentación y Bibliotecas, Secretaría de Estado de Educación y Cultura (Library and Documentation Section): Santo Domingo; Dir Lic. ELIDA JIMÉNEZ V.

Museums and Art Galleries

Santo Domingo

Galería Nacional de Bellas Artes (National Fine Arts Gallery): Santo Domingo; f. 1943; contains the later paintings and sculptures previously exhibited in the Museo Nacional; controlled by the Dirección General de Bellas Artes (Fine Arts Council); Dir Dr JOSÉ DE J. ALVAREZ VALVERDE.

Museo de Arte Moderno: Avda Pedro Henríquez Ureña, Plaza de la Cultura 'Juan Pablo Duarte', Santo Domingo; f. 1976; state controlled; modern art of national and foreign artists; permanent and exchange exhibitions; organizes lectures, conferences, films and children's workshops; art library of 2,047 vols, children's library of 2,050 vols; Dir Lic. PORFIRIO HERRERA; publs catalogue, guide, *Revista especializada, Boletín mensual de actividades*, monographs.

Museo de las Casas Reales (Museum of the Royal Houses): esq. Mercedes Las Damas, Apdo 2664, Santo Domingo; f. 1976; buildings used to be the headquarters of the colonial government; exhibition of items from that period (1492–1821); arms and armour, ceramics and items from shipwrecks; library of 17,700 vols; Dir Arq. EUGENIO PÉREZ MONTÁS; publ. *Casas Reales* (3 a year).

Museo del Hombre Dominicano (Museum of Dominican Man) (fmrly Museo Nacional): Calle Pedro Henríquez Ureña, Plaza de la Cultura, Santo Domingo; tel. 687-3622; f. 1973; 19,000 exhibits: *Pre-Columbian* (Indian archaeological; anthropological and ethnographical exhibits; ceramics, wooden objects, idols, amulets, charms, weapons and tools, pots, osseous remains); *Colonial* (weapons and armour, parts of ships, Spanish religious objects, ceramics, bells, etc.); library of 4,000 vols; Dir Dr FERNANDO MORBÁN LAUCER; publs *Boletín, Serie Investigaciones Antropológicas*, etc.

Museo Nacional de Historia Natural: Plaza de la Cultura, Santo Domingo; tel. 685-1580; fax 689-0100; e-mail jaragua@tricom.net; f. 1974; zoology, geology, palaeontology;

library of 3,000 vols, 10 periodicals; Dr CARLOS ML. RODRÍGUEZ; publs *Hispaniolana* (journal, occasionally), *Boletín Informativo* (4 a year).

Museo Nacional de Historia y Geografía: Calle Pedro Henríquez Ureña, Plaza de la Cultura, Santo Domingo; tel. 686-6677; fax 686-4943; f. 1982; history, geographical features and phenomena of the island of Santo Domingo; Dir Lic. VILMA BENZO DE FERRER; publ. *Revista de Historia y Geografía*.

Oficina de Patrimonio Cultural: Las Atarazanas 2, Santo Domingo; tel. 682-4750; f. 1967; Dir Arq. MANUEL E. DEL MONTE URRACA.

Controls:

Alcázar de Diego Colón (Columbus Palace): museum f. 1957; the castle, built in 1510, was the residence of Don Diego Columbus, son of Christopher Columbus, and Viceroy of the island; period furniture and objects, paintings, musical instruments, ceramics, and the most important collection of tapestries in the Caribbean.

Museo de la Familia Dominicana Siglo XIX (Museum of the Dominican Family): f. 1973; a 16th-century house displaying household items for a noble family of the 19th century.

Casa-Fuerte de Ponce de León (Ponce de León's Fort): San Rafael del Yuma, Higüey; museum f. 1972; the residence of Ponce de León who discovered Florida and Puerto Rico; authentic furniture and household items from a 16th-century house.

Fortaleza de San Felipe (St Philip's Fortress): Puerto Plata; museum f. 1972; 16th-century fort; archaeological objects found during restoration.

Sala de Arte Prehispánico: Apdo 723, Santo Domingo; f. 1973; run by the García Arévalo Foundation; studies and exhibits culture of pre-Hispanic times; library of 6,000 vols on anthropology and the history of Santo Domingo and the Caribbean; Dir MANUEL ANTONIO GARCÍA ARÉVALO; publs *Salida Semestral, Caney*.

Universities

PONTIFICIA UNIVERSIDAD CATÓLICA MADRE Y MAESTRA

Autopista Duarte, Santiago de los Caballeros

Telephone: (809) 580-1962
Telex: 346-1032
Fax: (809) 581-7750
E-mail: anunez@pucmmsti.edu.do

Founded 1962
Private control
Academic year: August to May (two semesters) and a summer session May to July

Rector: Mgr AGRIPINO NÚÑEZ COLLADO
Academic Vice-Rector: Ing. NELSON GIL
Executive Vice-Rector: Lic. SONIA GUZMÁN DE HERNÁNDEZ
Registrar: Lic. DULCE RODRÍGUEZ DE GRULLÓN
Librarian: Lic. ALTAGRACIA PEÑA

Number of teachers: 755
Number of students: 9,918

Publications: *Boletín de Noticias*, *Revista de Ciencias Jurídicas*.

DEANS

Faculty of Engineering: Ing. VICTOR COLLADO
Faculty of Humanities and Social Sciences: Lic. SARAH GONZÁLEZ
Faculty of Health Sciences: Dr RAFAEL FERNANDEZ LAZALA

Campuses in Santo Domingo, Puerto Plata, Bonao

UNIVERSIDAD APEC

Avda Máximo Gómez 72, esq. México, Santo Domingo

Telephone: 686-0021
Fax: 685-5581
E-mail: univ.apec@.codetel.net.do

Founded 1965

President: Lic. OPINIO ALVAREZ BETANCOURT
Rector: Dr FRANKLYN HOLGUÍN HACHÉ
Vice-Rector (academic): Lic. BALTASAR GONZÁLEZ CAMILO
Vice-Rector (development): Lic. GISELA VARGAS ORTEGA
Librarian: Lic. BIENVENIDA MIRABAL

Library of 19,000 vols
Number of teachers: 345
Number of students: 9,400

Publications: *Investigación y Ciencia*, *Coloquios Jurídicos*, *Boletín Trimestral*, *Cuadernos de Estudio*.

UNIVERSIDAD AUTÓNOMA DE SANTO DOMINGO

Ciudad Universitaria, Apdo 1355, Santo Domingo

Telephone: 533-1104
Telex: 5460182
Fax: 533-1106

Founded 1538 by Papal Bull of Paul III, closed 1801–15; reopened as a lay institution in 1815, reorganized in 1914. It is the oldest university in the Americas

Rector: Dr JULIO RAVELO ASTACIO
Vice-Rectors: Lic. RAMÓN CAMACHO JIMÉNEZ (Academic), Lic. JULIO URBÁEZ (Administrative)
Secretary-General: MARIO SURIEL
Personnel Director: Lic. JULIO CÉSAR RODRÍGUEZ

Number of teachers: 1,665
Number of students: 26,040

Publications: *Ciencia, Derecho y Política*.

DEANS

Faculty of Humanities: Lic. ANA DOLORES GUZMÁN DE CAMACHO
Faculty of Law and Politics: Lic. ROBERTO SANTANA
Faculty of Medicine: Dr CÉSAR MELLA MEJÍAS
Faculty of Sciences: Lic. PLÁCIDO CABRERA
Faculty of Engineering and Architecture: Ing. MIGUEL ROSADO MONTES DE OCA
Faculty of Agronomy and Veterinary Science: Ing. Agr. FRANK M. VALDÉZ L.
Faculty of Economic and Social Sciences: Dr EDILBERTO CABRAL

UNIVERSIDAD CENTRAL DEL ESTE

Avda de Circunvalación, San Pedro de Macorís

Telephone: 529-3562
Fax: (809) 529-5146

Founded 1970
Private control
Academic year: January to December (3 terms)

President and Rector: Dr JOSÉ E. HAZIM FRAPPIER
Vice-President: Dr JOSÉ A. HAZIM AZAR
Vice-Rector (Academic): Lic. RICHARD F. PEGUERO
Vice-Rector (Administration): Ing. MARILYN DÍAZ PÉREZ
Secretary General: Lic. PIEDAD L. NOBOA MEJÍA
Registrar: Lic. OLGA CHALAS
Librarian: Lic. ROSA DORIVAL

Library of 150,000 vols
Number of teachers: 677
Number of students: 6,700

Publications: *Anuario Científico*, *UCE*, *Publicaciones Periódicas*.

DEANS

Faculty of Medicine: Dr JUAN A. SILVA SANTOS
Faculty of Engineering and Natural Resources: Ing. OLGA BASORA
Faculty of Sciences and Humanities: Dr JOSÉ A. HAZIM AZAR
Faculty of Administration and Systems: Lic. SENCIÓN IVELISSE ZOROB
Faculty of Law: Dr ANTONIO LEÓN SASSO

UNIVERSIDAD EUGENIO MARÍA DE HOSTOS

Apdo Postal 2694, Santo Domingo

Telephone: 532-2495

Founded 1981
Private control

Rector: Lic. CARMEN MARÍA CASTILLO SILVA
Academic Vice-Rector: Lic. CARMEN ROSA MARTÍNEZ V.
Administrative Vice-Rector: Rev. RAFAEL MARCIAL SILVA
General Administrator: Dr JORGE DÍAZ VARGAS

DIRECTORS

Faculty of Health Sciences: Dr JOSÉ RODRÍGUEZ SOLDEVILLA
School of Medicine: Dr RAÚL ALVAREZ STURLA
School of Oral Medicine: Dr CÉSAR LINARES IMBERT
School of Veterinary Medicine: Dr TULIO S. CASTAÑOS VÉLEZ
School of Nursing: Lic. AMANDA PEÑA DE SANTANA
School of Public Health: Dr MANUEL TEJADA BEATO
School of Law: Lic. CECILIO GÓMEZ PÉREZ
School of Computer Studies: Lic. SANDY SANTOS
School of Marketing Studies: Lic. PEDRO MELO
Campus in Ozama: Lic. GUILLERMO DÍAZ
Campus in San Cristóbal: Lic. EMILIANO DE LA ROSA

UNIVERSIDAD NACIONAL 'PEDRO HENRÍQUEZ UREÑA'

Apdo 1423, Santo Domingo

Telephone: 562-6601
Fax: 566-2206

Founded 1966
Private control
Academic year: August to July

Rector: Arq. ROBERTO BERGÉS FEBLES
Vice-Rector for Administrative Affairs: Lic. BIENVENIDO DE LA CRUZ
Vice-Rector for Academic Affairs: Lic. DANIELA FRANCO DE GUZMÁN
Vice-Rector for Development Affairs: Ing. EZEQUIEL GARCÍA TATIS
Registrar: Dra SARI DUVERGÉ MEJÍA
Librarian: Dra CARMEN IRIS OLIVO

Library of 80,000 vols
Number of teachers: 759
Number of students: 8,000

Publications: *Biblionotas*, *Aula*, *Cuadernos Jurídicos*, *Cuadernos de Filosofía*, *Nuestra UNPHU*, *Campus*.

DEANS

Faculty of Agronomy and Veterinary Science: Dr HECTOR LUIS RODRÍGUEZ
Faculty of Humanities: Dr CARLOS ESTEBAN DEIVE
Faculty of Law and Politics: Dr MANUEL BERGÉS CHUPANI
Faculty of Engineering and Technology: Ing. JOSE DEL CARMEN BAUTISTA
Faculty of Health Science: Dr MARIANO DEFILLÓ RICART
Faculty of Architecture and Arts: Arq. ATILIO LEÓN LEBRÓN
Faculty of Science: Lic. MAYRA SÁNCHEZ DE PÉREZ

Faculty of Economics and Social Sciences: Lic. GENARO SORIANO
Faculty of Postgraduate Studies: Dr EURIBÍADES CONCEPCIÓN

AFFILIATED INSTITUTES

Centro de Información de Drogas: Santo Domingo; Dir Dra ROSA RICOURT.

Centro de Investigación: Santo Domingo; Dir Dr LUCIANO SBRIZ.

Instituto de Estudios Biomédicos: Santo Domingo; Dir Dr SANTIAGO COLLADO CHASTEL.

UNIVERSIDAD NORDESTANA

Apdo 239, San Francisco de Macorís

Telephone: (809) 588-3239

Founded 1978

Rector: Mons. JESÚS MARÍA DE JESÚS MOYA
Vice-Rectors: Lic. JULIO CÉSAR PINEDA, Lic. PEDRO MANUEL LORA
Librarian: Lic. EMELDA RAMOS

Number of teachers: 179
Number of students: 1,850

Faculties of medicine, economic and social sciences, agriculture, law, engineering, humanities

UNIVERSIDAD TECNOLÓGICA DE SANTIAGO (UTESA)

Avda Estrella Sadhala (esq. Mirador del Yaque), Apdo 685, Santiago

Telephone: 582-7156
Fax: 582-7644

Founded 1974
Private control
Academic year: January to April, May to August, September to December

Rector: Dr PRIAMO RODRÍGUEZ CASTILLO
Vice-Rector (Academic): Licda JOSEFINA CRUZ DE SANTOS
Vice-Rector (Administration): Lic. MANUEL RODRÍGUEZ CASTILLO
Vice-Rector (Campus Premises): Lic. ARNALDO PEÑA VENTURA
Secretary-General: Lic. RAMÓN ANÍBAL CASTRO R.
Registrar: Lic. ANDRÉS VIVAS
Librarian: Ing. ILUMINADA DE LA HOZ

Library of 15,000 vols
Number of teachers: 758
Number of students: 22,000

Publications: *Ciencias y Tecnología, Revista Universitas.*

Faculties of social and economic sciences, architecture and engineering, health sciences, science and humanities, secretarial studies

Colleges

Centros APEC de Educación a Distancia (CENAPEC): POB A-38, Santo Domingo; tel. 688-4403 ext. 235; fax 686-2277; f. 1972; offer low-cost educational programmes by means of the distance education system; 22,000 students; Pres. CARLOS A. ELMÚDESI; Exec. Dir MARIANO MELLA; publ. *Boletín CENAPEC* (6 a year).

Instituto Superior de Agricultura (ISA) (Higher Institute of Agriculture): Apdo 166, Santiago; tel. (809) 247-2000; fax (809) 247-2626; f. 1962; independent institution but operates joint programme in agriculture with the Universidad Católica Madre y Maestra; training in agricultural sciences at high school and undergraduate level; subjects for degree course: horticulture, food technology, animal production, irrigation, agrarian reform, agricultural economics, administration; library of 14,000 vols; Pres. Dr FRANK JOSEPH THOMEN; Dir Ing. BENITO A. FERREIRAS; publs occasional research papers.

Instituto Tecnológico de Santo Domingo: Avda de los Próceres, Galá, Apdo 342-9, Santo Domingo; tel. 567-9271; telex 4184; fax 566-3200; e-mail desarrollo@mail.intec.edu.do; f. 1972; undergraduate and postgraduate teaching and research.
Rector: Lic. RAFAEL TORIBIO
Academic Vice-Rector: Lic. ALTAGRACIA LÓPEZ
Librarian: Lic. LUCERO ARBOLEDA DE ROA

Library of 44,000 books, 1,400 periodicals
Number of students: 2,300

Publications: *Documentos Intec* (annually), *Ciencia y Sociedad* (quarterly), *Indice de Publicaciones de Universidades* (annually).

DIRECTORS

Basic and Environmental Sciences: Dr JOSÉ CONTRERAS
Health Sciences: Dr RAYMUNDO JIMENEZ
Social Sciences: Lic. REINA ROSARIO
Humanities: Dr MANUEL MATOS MOQUETE
Civil Engineering: Ing. DANIEL COMARAZAMY
Industrial and Electromechanical Engineering: Ing. CARLOS CONDERO
Business: Lic. AMARILIS GARCÍA

Schools of Art and Music

Dirección General de Bellas Artes (Fine Arts Council): Santo Domingo; Dir JOSÉ DELMONTE PEGUERO.

Controls the following:

Academias de Música (Academies of Music): Villa Consuelo and Villa Francisca, Santo Domingo; also 19 provincial towns.

Conservatorio Nacional de Música (National Conservatoire of Music and Elocution): Santo Domingo.

Escuela de Arte Escénico (School of Scenic Art): Santo Domingo.

Escuela Nacional de Bellas Artes (Fine Arts School): Santo Domingo.

Escuela de Artes Plásticas (School of Plastic Arts): Santiago.

Escuela de Bellas Artes (School of Fine Arts): San Francisco de Macorís.

Escuela de Bellas Artes: San Juan de la Maguana.

ECUADOR

Learned Societies

GENERAL

Casa de la Cultura Ecuatoriana 'Benjamín Carrión': Apdo 67, Avda 6 de Diciembre 794, Quito; f. 1944; covers all aspects of Ecuadorian culture; Pres. Lcdo CAMILO RESTREPO; Sec.-Gen. Lcdo SERGIO VÉLEZ; publs regular journals in sciences, culture, art, etc.

EDUCATION

Consejo Nacional de Universidades y Escuelas Politécnicas: Avda 9 de Octubre 624 y Carrión, Quito; tel. 569-898; telex 21442; fax 563685; f. 1982; mems: 24 universities, 5 polytechnics; library in process of formation; Pres. Dr MEDARDO MORA; Sec.-Gen. Lic. DARIO MOREIRA; publs *Boletín Bimensual* (6 a year), *Planinformativo*, *Investigación Universitaria* (2 a year).

LANGUAGE AND LITERATURE

Academia Ecuatoriana de la Lengua (Academy of Ecuador): Apdo 3460, Quito; f. 1875; Corresp. of the Real Academia Española (Madrid); library of 3,000 vols; Dir GALO RENÉ PÉREZ; Sec. PIEDAD LARREA BORJA; publs *Memorias* (quarterly), *Obras de la Literatura Ecuatoriana* (quarterly).

MEDICINE

Academia Ecuatoriana de Medicina (Ecuadorian Academy of Medicine): Apdo postal 17-11-6202, Quito; f. 1958.

Federación Médica Ecuatoriana (Medical Federation of Ecuador): Avda N. Unidas e Iñaquito, Quito; tel. 452-660; fax 456-812; f. 1942; 1,435 mems; Pres. Dr EDGAR MONTALVO MENDOZA; Sec. Dr ALBERTO CORDERO AROCA.

Sociedad Ecuatoriana de Pediatría (Paediatrics Society of Ecuador): Casilla 5865, Guayaquil; f. 1945; scientific extension courses and lectures; Pres. Dr ISIDORO MARTÍNEZ MCKLIFF; Sec. Dr ARTURO VALERO ROJAS; publ. *Revista Ecuatoriana de Pediatría*.

Research Institutes

GENERAL

Institut Français de Recherche Scientifique pour le Développement en Coopération (ORSTOM): Apdo 17.11.06596, Quito; tel. (2) 504-856; fax (2) 569-396; f. 1974; geology, pedology, hydrology, botany and vegetal biology, agronomy, geography, human sciences, economics; library of 550 vols, 400 periodicals, 80 extracts; Dir Dr F. KAHN. (See main entry under France.)

AGRICULTURE, FISHERIES AND VETERINARY SCIENCE

Instituto Interamericano Agricultural Experimental (Inter-American Experimental Agricultural Institute): Conocoto, Línea 63, Quito; part of OAS Interamerican Agricultural Institute.

Instituto Nacional Autónomo de Investigaciones Agropecuarios (Autonomous National Institute of Agricultural Research): Av. Amazonas y Eloy Alfaro, Edif. MAG (4° piso), Quito; f. 1959; Dir-Gen. Dr JAIME TOLA CEVALLOS; publs scientific articles, annual report, bulletins.

Instituto Nacional de Pesca (National Fishery Institute): Letamendi 102 y La Ría, Casilla 5918, Guayaquil; f. 1960; fishing research and development; library of 20,000 vols; Dir Dr ROBERTO JIMÉNEZ S.; publs *Boletín Científico y Técnico*, *Revista Científica de Ciencias Marinas y Limnología*, *Boletín Informativo*.

ECONOMICS, LAW AND POLITICS

Instituto Latinoamericano de Investigaciones Sociales (ILDIS) (Latin American Social Sciences Research Institute): Casilla 17-03-367, Quito; tel. 562-103; telex 2539; fax 504337; f. 1974; affiliated to the Friedrich-Ebert Foundation (*q.v.*); research in economics, sociology, political science and education; library of 15,000 vols; Dir Dr REINHART WETTMANN; publs various.

Instituto Nacional de Estadística y Censos (National Statistics and Census Institute): Juan Larrea 543 y Riofrío, Quito; tel. (2) 231602; fax (2) 509836; e-mail inec1@ecnet.ec; f. 1944; library of 6,000 vols; Dir Ing. JOHNY CEVALLOS MUÑOZ.

HISTORY, GEOGRAPHY AND ARCHAEOLOGY

Centro de Investigaciones Históricas (Centre of Historical Research): Apdo 7,110, Guayaquil; f. 1930; library of 6,000 vols; Pres. Dr ABEL ROMEO CASTILLO; Sec.-Gen. JULIO ESTRADA YCAZA; publ. *Revista*.

Instituto Geográfico Militar (Military Geographical Institute): Casilla 17-01-2435, Quito; tel. (2) 522-148; fax (2) 522-495; f. 1928; part of Ministry of Defence; main activity is preparation of national map series; undertakes projects for public and private organizations; provides cartographic and geographic documentation for national development and security; library of 10,500 vols; Dir Col Eng. JULIO AROSTEGUÍ CÁCERES; publs *Revista Geográfica* (2 a year), *Indices Toponímicos*, *Atlas Universal y del Ecuador*.

MEDICINE

Instituto de Investigaciones para el Desarrollo de la Salud (Research Institute for Health Development): Calle Buenos Aires 340, 3 piso, Quito; tel. and fax (2) 544-597; e-mail lopezjar@pi.pro.ec; f. 1988, by merger of Instituto Nacional de Investigaciones Nutricionales y Médico-Sociales and Instituto de Recursos Odontológicos del Area Andina; research on main aspects of public health; Dir PATRICIO LÓPEZ-JARAMILLO; publs *La Situación de la Salud en el Ecuador*, *La Situación de Salud en Areas Urbano Marginales*, *Control contra Bocio Endémico*, etc.

Instituto Nacional de Higiene y Medicina Tropical 'Leopoldo Izquieta Pérez' (National Institute of Hygiene): Julian Coronel 905 y Esmeraldas, Guayaquil; tel. (4) 281-540; telex 3334; fax (4) 394-189; f. 1941; 120 departments and sections; library of 5,600 vols; Dir Dra ARACELY ALAVA A.; Gen. Sec. Ab. PEDRO MENDOZA; publ. *Revista Ecuatoriana de Higiene y Medicina Tropical*.

NATURAL SCIENCES

General

Instituto Oceanográfico de la Armada (Naval Oceanographic Institute): Avda 25 de Julio, Apdo 5940, Guayaquil; f. 1972 to study oceanography and hydrography; 250 staff; library of 2,500 vols; Dir Commdr HERNAN MOREANO ANDRADE; publ. *Acta Oceanográfica del Pacífico* (2 a year).

Biological Sciences

Charles Darwin Research Station: Pto Ayora, Santa Cruz, Galapagos Islands; fax (593-2) 443-935; f. 1964 under the auspices of the Ecuadorian Government, UNESCO and the Charles Darwin Foundation to study and preserve the flora and fauna of the Archipelago; maintains meteorological stations, a herbarium, a zoological museum and a marine laboratory; breeding programme for endangered reptiles; library of 4,000 vols, 10,000 separates; Dir Dr ROBERT BENSTED-SMITH; publs *Noticias de Galápagos* (2 a year), *Annual Report*, *Newsletter*.

Instituto Ecuatoriano de Ciencias Naturales (Ecuadorian Institute of Natural History): Apdo 408, Quito; tel. 215-497; f. 1940; research into natural resources and conservation; 46 mems, 24 foreign mems; library of 48,450 vols; Dir Prof. Dr MISAEL ACOSTA-SOLÍS; publs *Flora* (official organ), contributions and monographs.

Physical Sciences

Instituto Nacional de Meteorología e Hidrología (Hydrometeorological Office): Iñaquito 700 y Corea, Quito; tel. (2) 265330; fax (2) 433934; f. 1961; library of 6,500 vols; Dir Ing. NELSON SALAZAR D.; publs. *Anuario Meteorológico*, *Anuario Hidrológico*, *Boletín Climatológico* (monthly).

Observatorio Astronómico de Quito (Astronomical Observatory): Apdo 17-01-165, Parque Alameda, Quito; tel. (2) 570765; telex 22650; fax (2) 567848; f. 1869; astronomy, astrophysics, seismology, meteorology and archaeoastronomy; library of 3,160 vols; Dir Dr ERICSON LÓPEZ IZURIETA; publs *Boletín Astronómico* Series A, B., *Boletín Meteorológico; Boletín del Observatorio Astronómico de Quito* (every 6 months)

RELIGION, SOCIOLOGY AND ANTHROPOLOGY

Instituto Ecuatoriano de Antropología y Geografía (Ecuadorian Institute of Anthropology and Geography): POB 17-01-2258, Quito; premises at: Avda Orellana 557 y Coruña, Quito; tel. (2) 506-324; fax (2) 509-436; f. 1950; research in anthropology, folklore, history, social psychology and national questions; library of 5,000 vols; Dir Lcdo RODRIGO GRANIZO R.; publ. review *Llacta* (2 a year).

TECHNOLOGY

Comisión Ecuatoriana de Energía Atómica (Atomic Energy Commission of Ecuador): Avda González Suárez 2351 y Bosmediano, Casilla 17-01-2517, Quito; tel. (2) 458-013; fax (2) 253-097; f. 1958; 40 mems; research in nuclear physics, radioisotopes, radiobiology, chemistry, medicine; library of 5,000 vols; Exec. Dir Ing. CELIANO ALMEIDA; publ. *Noticias Trimestrales*.

Corporación de Desarrollo e Investigación Geológico-Minero-Metalúrgica (CODIGEM): Casilla 17-03-23, Av. 10 de Agosto 5844 y Pereira, Quito; tel. (2) 254-673; fax (2) 254-674; f. 1991 to replace Instituto Ecuatoriano de Minería; responsible for mineralogical research and prospecting in Ecuador, and for providing information to the public; produces national geological map; library of 1,205 vols, 22 periodicals; Exec. Pres. Ing. EFRÉN GALÁRRAGA SOTO; publs *Minería Ecuatoriana, Folleto Potencial Minero Ecuatoriano*.

Dirección General de Hidrocarburos (General Directorate of Hydrocarbons): Avda 10 de Agosto 321, Quito; f. 1969; supervises enforcement of laws relating to petroleum exploration and development, and sets standards for mining-petroleum industry; 210 mems; Dir Gen. Ing. GUILLERMO BIXBY; Sec. ERNESTO CORRAL; publs *Estadística Petrolera, Reporte Geológico de la Costa Ecuatoriana, Indice de Leyes y Decretos de la Industria Petrolera*.

Instituto de Ciencias Nucleares (Institute of Nuclear Science); Escuela Politécnica Nacional, Apdo 2759, Quito; f. 1957; library with department of microcards and microfilms; equipment for application of radioisotopes to chemistry, agriculture, medicine and radiation control; cobalt source-60 2,400 curies; 4 departments: Department of Application to Chemistry and Agriculture, Dir RICARDO A. MUÑOZ; Department of Biomedical Applications, Dir RODRIGO FIERRO B.; Department of Natural Resources, Dir Dr ERNESTO GROSSMAN; Department of Radiation Control, Dir Ing. FREDDIE ORBE M.

Libraries and Archives

Cuenca

Biblioteca de Autores Nacionales 'Fray Vicente Solano': Apdo 01-01-222, Cuenca; f. 1929; 43,000 vols; Dir JUAN CARLOS GONZALEZ V.

Biblioteca Hispano-Americana (Hispanic-American Library): Mariscal Sucre 338, Apdo 133, Cuenca; f. 1934; 54,700 vols; Dir CELIANO A. VINTIMILLA V.

Biblioteca 'Juan Bautista Vázquez' de la Universidad de Cuenca (Cuenca University Library): Apdo 168, Cuenca; f. 1882; 62,185 vols; Dir CELIANO A. VINTIMILLA V.

Biblioteca Panamericana (Pan-American Library): Apdo 57, Cuenca; tel. (593-7) 826130; f. 1912; 64,000 vols; Dir CLAUDIO ALBORNOZ V.

Biblioteca Pública Municipal (Public Municipal Library): Apdo 202, Cuenca; f. 1927; 50,000 vols; Dir JUAN TAMA MÁRQUEZ.

Guayaquil

Biblioteca 'Angel Andrés Garcia' de la Universidad 'Vicente Rocafuerte': Vélez 2203, Apdo 330, Guayaquil; f. 1847; 13,000 vols; Dir HERNÁN CABEZAS CANDEL; publs *Revista de la Universidad 'Vicente Rocafuerte'* and students' periodicals.

Biblioteca de Autores Nacionales 'Carlos A. Rolando' (Library of Ecuadorian Writers): Palacio Municipal, Guayaquil; f. 1913; 12,000 vols, 15,000 pamphlets, 17,000 leaflets, 3,000 MSS relating to Ecuadorian authors and foreign works about Ecuador; Dir Dr CARLOS A. ROLANDO.

Biblioteca de la Casa de la Cultura Ecuatoriana: Núcleo de Guayas, 9 de Octubre y Pedro Moncayo, Apdo 3542, Guayaquil; f. 1945; 16,748 vols; Dir Lic. RUTH GARAICOA SORIA.

Biblioteca General, Universidad de Guayaquil: Casilla 3834, 09-01 Guayaquil; tel. 28-24-40; f. 1901; 50,000 vols; Dir Lic. LEONOR VILLAO DE SANTANDER; publs. *Revista, El Universitario*.

Biblioteca Histórica y Archivo Colonial (Historical Library and Colonial Archives): Palacio de la Municipalidad, Apdo 75, Guayaquil; f. 1930; Dir Dr CARLOS A. ROLANDO; Sec. Prof. GUSTAVO MONROY GARAICOA.

Biblioteca Municipal 'Pedro Carbo' (Public Library): Avda 10 de Agosto, Calle Pedro Carbo, Guayaquil; f. 1862; 120,000 vols; Dir PATRICIA DE QUEVEDO (see also under Museums).

Quito

Archivo-Biblioteca de la Función Legislativa: Palacio Legislativo, Quito; f. 1886; scientific and cultural; 27,000 vols; Dir Lic. RAFAEL A. PIEDRA SOLÍS; publs *Clave de la Legislación Ecuatoriana, Diario de Debates de la Legislatura*.

Archivo Nacional de Historia (National Historical Archives): Avda 6 de Diciembre 332, Apdo 67, Quito; f. 1938; 2,500 vols; colonial documents of the 16th to 19th centuries; Dir JORGE A. GARCÉS Y GARCÉS; Sec. JUAN R. FREKE-GRANIZO; publ. *Arnahis*.

Biblioteca de la Universidad Central del Ecuador (Central University Library): Quito; f. 1826; 170,000 vols; Dir ALONSO ALTAMIRANO; publs *Anales, Bibliografía Ecuatoriana, Anuario Bibliográfico*.

Biblioteca del Banco Central del Ecuador: Reina Victoria y Jorge Washington, Apdo 17-21-366 Eloy Alfaro, Quito; tel. 568957; fax 568973; f. 1938; 100,000 vols, 2,000 periodicals; specializes in economics, administration, banking and finance, social sciences; open to the public; Dir CARLOS LANDAZURI; publ. *Boletín Bibliográfico* (irregular).

Has attached:

Hemeroteca : Calle Arenas y 10 de Agosto Apdo 17-15-0029-C, Quito; tel 561521; 5,000 periodicals; Dir JULIO OLEAS.

Musicoteca: Calles García Moreno y Sucre, Apdo 339, Quito; tel. 572784; music and video library; Dir ADRIANA ORTIZ.

Biblioteca Ecuatoriana 'Aurelio Espinosa Pólit': Apdo 17-01-160, Quito; f. 1928; Ecuadorian library, archive, Ecuadorian art and history museum; 300,000 vols; Librarian JULIAN G. BRAVO.

Biblioteca Municipal (Municipal Library): Casa de Montalvo, Apdo 75, Quito; f. 1886; 12,500 vols, 300 MSS, 4 incunabula.

Biblioteca Nacional del Ecuador (National Library): 12 de Octubre 555, Apdo 67, Quito; f. 1792; 70,000 vols of which 7,000 date from the 16th to 18th centuries; shares legal deposit with municipal libraries; Dir Dr EUGENIO ESPEJO.

Attached library:

Biblioteca de la Casa de la Cultura Ecuatoriana (Library of Ecuadorian Culture): Apdo 67, Avda Colombia, Quito; f. 1944; 12,000 vols and over 20,000 periodicals; includes the 'Laura de Crespo' Room of National Authors.

Museums and Art Galleries

Guayaquil

Museo Antropológico del Banco Central: Guayaquil; tel. (4) 327707; telex 043257; fax (4) 322792; f. 1974; archaeology of the Ecuadorian coast; gallery of contemporary Latin American art; research; library of 7,500 vols; Dir Arq. FREDDY OLMEDO R.; publ. *Miscelánea Antropológica Ecuatoriana*, occasional papers on art and archaeology.

Museo Municipal (Municipal Museum): Avda 10 de Agosto, Calle Pedro Carbo, Guayaquil; f. 1862; historical, ethnographical, palaeontological, geological exhibits; colonial period and modern paintings and numismatics (see also Libraries).

Quito

Casa de la Cultura Ecuatoriana 794, Avenue 6 de Diciembre, Quito; tel. 566-070; fax 521-451; f. 1944; Pres Milton Barragán Dumet.

Has attached:

Museo de Arte Moderno: Quito; 19th-century and contemporary art from Ecuador and Latin America.

Museo de Arte Colonial: Cuenca St and Mejía St, Quito; tel. 212-297; f. 1914; many examples of art from the Escuela Quiteña of the colonial epoch (17th and 18th centuries).

National Library and Museo del Libro: Quito; 500,000 vols; concerts, theatre, cinema, dance and music performances; publ. *Letras del Ecuador* (every 3 months).

Museo Antropológico 'António Santiana': Universidad Central del Ecuador, Quito; f. 1925; sections of anthropology, archaeology, ethnography; library of 2,000 vols; Dir Dr HOLGUER JARA; publs *Humanitas, Boletín Ecuatoriano de Antropología* (irregular).

Museo de Arqueología y Etnología del Instituto Ecuatoriano de Antropología y Geografía (Museum of Archaeology and Ethnology): Casilla 2258, Quito; f. 1950; precious stones, ceramics, prehistoric sculptures.

Museo de Ciencias Naturales de la Escuela Militar 'Eloy Alfaro': Avda Orellana, La Pradera 400, Quito; f. 1937; geological specimens and fauna from the Galapagos Islands; taxidermy and anatomy illustrated, especially of mammals and birds; Taxidermist LUIS ALFREDO PÉREZ VACA; publ. *Revista Anual del Plantel*.

Museo Jacinto Jijón Caamaño (Jacinto Jijón y Caamaño Museum): Pontifícia Universidad Católica, Avda 12 de Octubre y Carrión, Apdo 17-01-2184, Quito; tel. (2) 565-627; fax (2) 544-995; e-mail museo-jjc@puceuio.puce.edu.ec; f. 1969; archaeology, art; library of 2,000 vols; Dir ERNESTO SALAZAR.

Museo Municipal de Arte e Historia 'Alberto Mena Caamaño' (Civic Museum of Arts and History): Espejo 1147 y Benalcázar, Apdo 17-01-3346, Quito; tel. 214018; f. 1930; archaeology, colonial art, 19th-century art, items of historical interest; history archive (1583–1980), information library; Dir ALFONSO ORTIZ CRESPO; publ. *Revista Caspicara*.

Museo Nacional de la Dirección Regional del Banco Central del Ecuador: Reina Victoria y Jorge Washington (esquina), Apdo 339, Quito; tel. 220547; fax 568972; f. 1969; prehistorical archaeological exhibits; colonial and modern art (sculpture, paintings, etc.); library of 6,000 vols; Dir Arq. JUAN FERNANDO PÉREZ ARTETA; publs material on Pre-Columbian cultures of Ecuador.

Universities and Technical Universities

UNIVERSIDAD CENTRAL DEL ECUADOR

Avda América y A. Pérez Guerrero, Apdo 3291, Quito

Telephone: 226-080
Fax: 501-207

Founded 1586 as Universidad de San Fulgencio; became Real y Pontificia Universidad de San Gregorio in 1622, Universidad de Santo Tomás de Aquino in 1688, then Universidad Central del Sur de la Gran Colombia; present name 1826.
State control
Language of instruction: Spanish
Academic year: September to July

Rector: Dr TIBERIO JURADO CEVALLOS
Vice-Rector: Ing. VICTOR HUGO OLALLA
Registrar: Lic. MARCELO REYES CALDERÓN
Librarian: ALFONSO ARMAS

Number of teachers: 4,000
Number of students: 55,000

Publication: *Casona*.

DEANS

Faculty of Jurisprudence and of Political and Social Sciences: Dr GUILLERMO BOSANO
Faculty of Economics: Econ. JOSÉ DÁVALOS HERRERA
Faculty of Medicine: Dr ENRIQUE CHIRIBOGA
Faculty of Chemistry and Pharmacy: Dr BYRON CAICEDO
Faculty of Odontology: Dr SALOMÓN CABEZAS
Faculty of Architecture: Arq. ANTONIO NARVAEZ
Faculty of Philosophy and Education: Lic. FRANKLIN CABASCANGO
Faculty of Engineering, Physics and Mathematics: Ing. HUGO BRAVO
Faculty of Agriculture: Ing. ALBERTO ORTEGA
Faculty of Administration: Dra MERCEDES BRAVO
Faculty of Arts: Lic. MANUEL MEJÍA
Faculty of Psychology: Dr FAUSTO GAVILANEZ
Faculty of Veterinary Medicine and Zootechnology: Dr NELSON JARAMILLO
Faculty of Geology, Mining and Petroleum Technology: Dr AGUSTIN PALADINES
Faculty of Social Communication: Lic. MARCELO PÉREZ

Campus at Riobamba offers courses in philosophy, literature, education.

PONTIFICIA UNIVERSIDAD CATÓLICA DEL ECUADOR

Avda 12 de Octubre 1076 y Carrión, Apdo 17-012184, Quito

Telephone: 529-240
Fax: 567-117

Founded 1946
Private control
Language of instruction: Spanish
Academic year: September to July

GOVERNING COUNCIL

Grand Chancellor: Dr ANTONIO GONZÁLEZ ZUMÁRRAGA
Vice-Chancellor: Rev. JORGE CARRIÓN
Rector: Dr JULIO TERÁN DUTARI
Vice-Rector: Dr CARLOS JIMENEZ SALAZAR
Librarian: Lic. OSWALDO ORBE

Number of teachers: 610
Number of students: 4,664

Publications: *Revista PUCE* (2 a year), *Boletín Informativo* (monthly), *Sumario de Revistas* (quarterly).

DEANS

Faculty of Jurisprudence: Dr GONZALO ZAMBRANO
Faculty of Engineering: Ing. PATRICIO TORRES
Faculty of Economics: Econ. GUILLERMO LANDÁZURI
Faculty of Education: Dr NOHEMY OLEAS
Faculty of Humanities: Lic. MILTON BENÍTEZ
Faculty of Nursing: Lic. CARMEN FALCONÍ
Faculty of Administrative Sciences: Ing. BASEN BADER
Faculty of Linguistics and Languages: Dr JULIO PAZOS
Faculty of Exact and Natural Sciences: Dr LAURA ARCOS
Faculty of Psychology: Lic. MERCEDES CORDERO

DIRECTORS

School of Medical Technology: Lic. MARY ECHEVERRÍA
School of Social Work: Dr JOSÉ GONZÁLEZ POYATOS
School of Philosophy: Dr EFRAIN SANTACRUZ

Ambato Campus: Parroquia Isamba, Apdo 124, Ambato; tel. 822050; courses in computer technology and English; Pro-Rector Dr ANGEL JADÁN PERALTA.

Esmeraldas Campus: Casilla 65, Esmeraldas; tel. 710-545; 391 students; courses in education, accountancy, nursing, English; Pro-Rector Dr JOAQUÍN ZURUTUZA.

Ibarra Campus: Casilla 734, Ibarra; tel. 952-352; 741 students; courses in administration and accountancy, tourism and hotel management, design, civil engineering; Pro-Rector Dr JOSÉ MARÍA SANCHO.

UNIVERSIDAD ESTATAL DE BOLÍVAR

Casilla 92, Guaranda

Telephone: 980121
Fax: 980123

Founded 1989
State control

Rector: Ing. GABRIEL AQUILES GALARZA LOPEZ
Vice-Rector: Lcdo PEDRO PABLO LUCIO GAIBOR
Registrar: Ing. GONZALO LOPEZ RIVADENEIRA
Librarian: Ing. RODRIGO SALTOS CHAVES

Number of teachers: 182
Number of students: 2,091

Publication: *Enlace Universitario*

DEANS

Faculty of Health Sciences: Dr MANUEL ALBÁN LUCIO
Faculty of Agriculture: Ing. MANUEL RODRIGO GAIBOR
Faculty of Administrative Sciences: Ing. DIÓMEDEZ NÚÑEZ MINAYA
Faculty of Education: Lcdo. MANUEL ALAVA MAGALLANES

UNIVERSIDAD CATÓLICA DE CUENCA

POB 01-01-1937, Cuenca

Telephone: 7-84-26-06
Telex: 04-8567
Fax: 7-83-10-40

Founded 1970
Private control
Academic year: October to July (3 terms)

Rector: Dr CÉSAR CORDERO MOSCOSO
Associate Rector: Dr HUGO DARQUEA LÓPEZ
Academic Vice-Rector: Dr TITO DOMÍNGUEZ IZQUIERDO
Administrative Vice-Rector: Dr NELSON CORDOVA ALVAREZ
Extension Vice-Rector: Dr MARCO VICUÑA DOMÍNGUEZ
Academic Director: Dr HUGO ORTIZ SEGARRA
Finance Director: Eco. RODRIGO SARMIENTO SEGARRA
Chief Administrative Officer: Eco. ESTUARDO RUBIO AUQUILLA
Secretary-General: Dr RODRIGO CISNEROS AGUIRRE
Librarian: Ing. JORGE GÓMEZ JUCA

Library of 5,000 vols
Number of teachers: 500
Number of students: 5,000

Publications: *Panoramas*, *Estudios*, *Retama*, *Presencia*, *Diálogo*, manuals.

DEANS

Faculty of Law and Social Sciences: Dr HUGO DARQUEA
Faculty of Education and Psychology: Dr JOSÉ ESCANDÓN MEJÍA
Faculty of Medicine and Health Sciences: Dr CARLOS DARQUEA LOPEZ
Faculty of Informatics Systems: Dr EDUARDO CORONEL DIAZ
Faculty of Civil Engineering and Architecture: Ing. MARCELO DARQUEA LÓPEZ
Faculty of Economics: Dr JORGE VIVAR IDROVO
Faculty of Commercial Engineering: Eco. LUIS CISNEROS GONZALEZ
Faculty of Enterprise Engineering: Ing. FRANCISCO ZEA ZAMORA
Faculty of Chemical and Industrial Engineering: Dr ALEJANDRO VÁSQUEZ CHICA.
Faculty of Agricultural Engineering, Mines and Veterinary Science: Dr EDUARDO CORONEL DIAZ
Faculty of Distance Learning: Dr HUGO ORTIZ SEGARRA
School of Social Service: Dr CLAUDIO PEÑAHERRERA M.
Bilingual Secretarial School: Eco. JULIO HERNANDEZ VINTIMILLA B.
Delegation in Europe: Prof. Dr FRANZ KANEHL (Germany)
Extension University at Macas: Lic. JOSÉ MERINO V.
Extension University at Méndez: Dr EDUARDO CORONEL DIAZ
Extension University at Azogues: Dr MARCO VICUÑA DOMÍNGUEZ
Extension University at Cañar: Dr JUSTINIANO CRESPO VERDUGO
Extension University at San Pablo, Troncal: Lawyer MARCELO ROMO LOYOLA
School of Drama and Aerobics: Lcdo FERNANDO ESPINOZA HERMIDA
School of Physical Education: Dr FRANCISCO PIEDRA LOJA
Communications, Radio and Television Channel 2: Dr HUGO ORTIZ SEGARRA
School of Journalism and Communications: Dra PRISCILA TAMAYO DE PALACIOS
University Hospital: Dr CARLOS DARQUEA LÓPEZ
Institute of Nursing: Dr OSWALDO VINTIMILLA MARCHÁN
Institute of Languages: Dr JOSÉ ESCANDÓN MEJÍA
Distance Learning and Open University: Dr MARCO VICUÑA DOMÍNGUEZ

UNIVERSIDAD DE CUENCA

Avda 12 de Abril, Sector 16, Apdo 168, Cuenca

Telephone: 831-556
Fax: 835197

Founded 1868
Academic year: October to July

Rector: Dr GUSTAVO VEGA-DELGADO
Vice-Rector: Dr JAIME ASTUDILLO R.
Secretary-General: Dr WILSON ANDRADE R.
Administrative Director: MARGARITA GUTIERREZ
Librarian: MARGARITA GUTIERREZ

Number of teachers: 613
Number of students: 8,500

Publications: *Anales de la Universidad de Cuenca*, *IURIS—Revista de la Facultad de Jurisprudencia*, *Revista de la Facultad de Ciencias Médicas*, *Revista de la Facultad de Ciencias Agropecuarias*, *Revista del IDIS*, *Revista del IICT*, *Revista del IDICSA*, *Informe de Coyuntura-Facultad de Ciencias Económicas*, etc.

DEANS

Faculty of Jurisprudence: PABLO ESTRELLA V.
Faculty of Medical Sciences: Dr RUBÉN DARÍO SOLÍS C.
Faculty of Engineering: Ing. FABIÁN CARRASCO C.

Faculty of Philosophy and Letters: Dr JORGE VILLAVICENCIO V.
Faculty of Chemistry: Dr LUÍS TONÓN P.
Faculty of Dentistry: Dr RAÚL CORDERO R.
Faculty of Architecture: Arq. LEOPOLDO CORDERO O.
Faculty of Economics: Econ. LEONARDO ESPINOZA
Faculty of Agriculture: Ing GERMÁN ARCOS

DIRECTORS

Planning Unit: Ing. RAFAEL ESTRELLA A.
Institute of Physical Education: Lcdo. JULIO ABAD
Research Institute: Dr ALBERTO QUEZADA R.
Institute of Computing and Information Science (ICEI): Ing. SALVADOR MONSALVE R.

UNIVERSIDAD DE GUAYAQUIL

Casilla 09-001-471, Guayaquil
Telephone: (4) 329905
Telex: 3179
Fax: (4) 329905

Founded 1867
Private control
Language of instruction: Spanish
Academic year: April to February (2 semesters)

Rector: Arq. JAIME POLIT ALCIVAR
Vice-Rectors: Ab. GUSTAVO ITURRALDE NÚÑEZ, Dr JOSÉ APOLO PINEDA (Academic) (acting), Ing. OSWALDO AYALA NÚÑEZ (Administrative)
Secretary-General: Dr ALBERTO SÁNCHEZ BALDA
Librarian: Lic. LEONOR V. DE SANTANDER

Number of teachers: 2,848
Number of students: 60,000

Publication: *Revista*.

DEANS

Faculty of Law, Social Sciences and Politics: Dr PUBLIO DAVILA ALAVA
Faculty of Philosophy, Literature and Education: Dr FRANCISCO MORÁN MÁRQUEZ
Faculty of Medicine: Dr SALOMON QUINTERO ESTRADA
Faculty of Mathematics and Physics: Ing. NESTOR LAYANA ROMERO (acting)
Faculty of Industrial Engineering: Ing. ALFREDO ARÉVALO MOSCOSO
Faculty of Odontology: Dr JOSÉ APOLO PINEDA
Faculty of Architecture: Arq. ALFONSO CORREA RODAS
Faculty of Chemistry: Dr JULIO ALVAREZ CASTRO
Faculty of Chemical Engineering: Ing. LUIS PACTONG ASSAN
Faculty of Administrative Sciences: Ing. Com. EDWARD FAGGIONI CAMACHO
Faculty of Economics: Eco. LEONARDO VICUÑA IZQUIERDO
Faculty of Psychology: Dra LIDIA ANDRADE BORRERO
Faculty of Social Communication: Ab. ALBA CHÁVEZ DE ALVARADO
Faculty of Agricultural Engineering: Ing. Agr. VICTOR VILLAO ROSALES (acting)
Faculty of Veterinary Medicine: Dr OMAR LOOR RISCO (acting)
Faculty of Natural Sciences: Bio. RAFAEL BECERRA SILVA
Faculty of Physical Education, Sport and Recreation: Dr CÉSAR HERMIDA BAQUERIZO

ATTACHED INSTITUTE

Institute of Diplomacy and International Studies: Dir Ab. REYNALDO HUERTA ORTEGA.

Campuses in Milagro, Vinces and Guaranda.

UNIVERSIDAD NACIONAL DE LOJA

Casilla Letra 'S', Ciudadela Universitaria, Loja
Telephone: 561-841
Telex: 4535

Founded 1869 as the Junta Universitaria; university status 1943
State control
Language of instruction: Spanish
Academic year: October to July

Rector: Ing. GUILLERMO FALCONÍ ESPINOSA
Vice-Rectors: Dr CÉSAR JARAMILLO CARRIÓN (Administrative), Dr REINALDO VALAREZO GARCÍA (Academic)
Secretary-General: Dr JAIME GUZMÁN REGALADO
Librarian: Dr ENITH COSTA MUÑOZ

Library of 3,500 volumes
Number of teachers: 720
Number of students: 13,280

Publications: *Estudios Universitarios, Revista Científica*, and various faculty bulletins.

DEANS

Faculty of Agriculture: Ing. ALFREDO SAMANIEGO VÉLEZ
Faculty of Law, Political, Social and Economic Sciences: Dr CÉSAR MONTAÑO ORTEGA
Faculty of Medicine: Dr ALONSO ARMIJOS LUNA
Faculty of Philosophy, Literature and Education: Lic. HÉCTOR SILVA VILEMA
Faculty of Veterinary Science: Dr EDUARDO VÉLEZ RUIZ
Faculty of Administrative Sciences: Dr FULVIO FERNANDEZ MACAS
Faculty of Science and Technology: Ing. ERMEL LOAIZA
Faculty of Arts: Lic. OSWALDO MORA RIVAS

ATTACHED INSTITUTES

Instituto de Lenguas: Lic. NUMA REINOSO LARREA.

Instituto de Ciencias Básicas: Ing. WILMER MARINO A.

Instituto Tecnológico: Yanzatza; Ing. JOSÉ RAMÍREZ.

Instituto Tecnológico: Alamor; Dir Econ. GLADYS GARCÍA.

Instituto Tecnológico: Cariamanga; Lic. LUIS TORRES.

Instituto Tecnológico: Catacocha; Dir Ing. ALFREDO SILVA.

Instituto Tecnológico: Macará; Lic. CARMEN CEVALLOS.

UNIVERSIDAD CATÓLICA DE SANTIAGO DE GUAYAQUIL

Casilla 09-01-4671, Guayaquil
Telephone: 200-801
Fax: 200-071

Founded 1962
Private control
Academic year: May to April

Rector: Dr GUSTAVO NOBOA BEJARANO
Vice-Rector: Dra NILA VELÁSQUEZ COELLO
Secretary-General and Registrar: Ab. GUILLERMO VILLACRES SMITH
Librarian: Lcda CLEMENCIA MITE DE SANTILLÁN

Library of 32,974 vols
Number of teachers: 612
Number of students: 6,249

Publications: *Revista Universidad, Revista Cuadernos*.

DEANS

Faculty of Law, Social and Political Sciences: Ab. VLADIMIRO ALVAREZ
Faculty of Economics: Econ. LUIS FERNANDO HIDALGO
Faculty of Engineering: Ing. ANTONIO BELTRÁN
Faculty of Architecture: Arq. RAÚL CHIRIBOGA
Faculty of Philosophy, Literature and Education: Dra OLGA AGUILAR
Faculty of Medicine: Dr MICHAEL DOUMET
Faculty of Technical Education for Development: Ing. GONZALO-ARGUDO

Department of Theology: Fr JOSÉ CIFUENTES ROMERO

UNIVERSIDAD TÉCNICA DE AMBATO

Casilla 18-01-334, Ambato
Telephone: 82-90-30
Fax: 84-91-64

Founded 1969

Rector: Ing. VÍCTOR HUGO JARAMILLO
Vice-Rector: Lic. ANÍBAL JARA ANDINO
Secretary-General: Dr JOSÉ ERNESTO JARAMILLO
Librarian: Lic. ELSA NARANJO

Number of teachers: 332
Number of students: 5,332

DEANS

Faculty of Accountancy: Lic. MARCELLO MEZA
Faculty of Administration:Ing. JAIME VIERA
Faculty of Civil Engineering: Ing. LUIS AMOROSO
Faculty of Education: Dr JAIME PROAÑO
Faculty of Food Technology: Ing. MARIO MANJARREZ
Faculty of Agricultural Engineering: Ing. OCTAVIO BELTRÁN
Faculty of Systems Engineering: Ing. WASHINGTON MEDINA

UNIVERSIDAD TÉCNICA DE BABAHOYO

Apdo 66, Via Flores, Babahoyo, Los Ríos
Telephone: 730208

Founded 1971

Rector: Dr BOLÍVAR LUPERA ICAZA
Vice-Rector: Ab. HUGOLINO ORELLANA VILLACRÉS
Secretary-General: ALBERTO BRAVO MEDINA
Librarian: Lic. MIGUEL BASTIDAS

Number of teachers: 450
Number of students: 5,000

DEANS

Faculty of Agriculture: Ing. Agr. WÁSHINGTON URQUIZA B.
Faculty of Education: Ab. AUSBERTO COLINO GONZALVO
Research (Director): Ing. Agr. CARLOS MIÑAN FIALLOS
Quevedo Campus (Director): Lic. ANGEL GUANOPATÍN

UNIVERSIDAD TÉCNICA DE ESMERALDAS

Avda Nuevo Horizonte, Apdo 179, Esmeraldas
Telephone: 711-851

Founded 1970

Rector: Lic. ANTONIO PRECIADO
Vice-Rector: Ing. ALFREDO ARÉVALO
Secretary-General: Ab. MARCO REINOSO CAÑOTE
Librarian: SOLANDA GOBEA

Number of teachers: *c.* 180
Number of students: *c.* 800

DEANS

Faculty of Stockbreeding: Ing. RAÚL TELLO
Faculty of Administration: Dr CARLOS RIOFRÍO
Faculty of Education: Lic. MIGUEL LARA
Faculty of Sociology and Social Work: Lic. JOSÉ LUNA CH.
Faculty of Mechanical Engineering: Ing. LEONARDO MERA.

UNIVERSIDAD TÉCNICA PARTICULAR DE LOJA

Casilla 11-01-608, Loja
Telephone: (7) 570204
Fax: (7) 584893
E-mail: utpl@accessinter.net

Founded 1971
Private control

Language of instruction: Spanish
Academic year: October to March, April to August

Chancellor: Pe Dr LUIS MIGUEL ROMERO FERNÁNDEZ
Rector: Ing. JAIME GERMÁN GUAMÁN
Vice-Rector: Lic. FANNY AGUIRRE DE MOREIRA
Secretary-General: Dr CARLOS RAMÍREZ ROMERO
Director of Distance Education: Dra MARÍA JOSÉ RUBIO GÓMEZ
Librarian: Lic. AMADA JARAMILLO LOJÁN

Library of 25,000 vols
Number of teachers: 190 full-time, 121 distance education
Number of students: 2,200 full-time, 7,218 distance education

Publications: *Universidad Técnica Particular de Loja* (annually), *Universidad* (monthly), *El Reloj* (monthly).

DEANS

Faculty of Civil Engineering: Ing. JORGE HIDALGO TORRES
Faculty of Economics: Econ. FERNANDO MORA JIMÉNEZ
Faculty of Agricultural Engineering: Ing. HÉCTOR RAMÍREZ
Faculty of Architecture: Arq. JORGE AUQUILLA
Faculty of Languages: Lic. GEOVANNY CASTILLO
Distance Education Faculty of Education: Lic. GERMÁN GONZÁLEZ

DIRECTORS

School of Fine Arts: Lic. FABIÁN FIGUEROA
School of Mines: Ing. RUDY VALDIVIESO L.
Institute of Computer Science: Ing. LILIANA ENCISO
School of Accountancy and Auditing: Lic. ELSA CÁRDENAS S.School of Industrial Mechanics: (vacant)
School of Hotel Management and Tourism: Dr JAIME BUSTAMENTE
Executive Secretarial School: Lic. ENITH BRAVO L.
Graduate School: Dr LUIS VARELA E.
Institute of Basic Sciences: Dr CONSTANTE RAMÍREZ
Institute of Human Sciences and Religious Studies: Lic. ALONSO GUAMÁN
Zamora Campus: Ing. ALFONSO OCHOA
Cariamanga Campus: Lic. ANGEL J. CABRERA M.

UNIVERSIDAD TÉCNICA DE MACHALA

Casilla 466, Machala
Telephone: 939-631

Founded 1969
State control
Language of instruction: Spanish
Academic year: March to January

Rector: Ing. VÍCTOR HERNÁN CABRERA JARAMILLO
Vice-Rector: Ing. EDDIE PLAZA CRIOLLO
Secretary-General: Ab. JOSÉ ANTONIO ROMERO TANDAZO
Librarian: MARÍA UNDA SERRANA DE BARREZUETA

Library of 5,000 vols
Number of teachers: 300
Number of students: 5,000

Publication: *Revista de la Facultad de Agronomía y Veterinaria*.

DEANS

Faculty of Agronomy and Veterinary Science: Ing. OSCAR SÁNCHEZ GUILLÉN
Faculty of Chemical Sciences: Dr RODRIGO VINTIMILLA CALDREÓN
Faculty of Sociology: Soc. FÉLIX CADENA ALVARADO
Faculty of Civil Engineering: Ing. LUIS ORDÓÑEZ JARAMILLO
Faculty of Business Administration and Accountancy: Ing. CÉSAR GARCÍA PAZMIÑO
Institute of Languages: LAURA LEÓN DE ASTUDILLO
School of Nursing: Lic. DAYSI ESPINOZA DE RAMÍREZ

UNIVERSIDAD TÉCNICA DE MANABÍ

Casilla 82, Portoviejo, Manabí
Telephone: 636-867

Founded 1954
State control
Academic year: May to January (two semesters)

Rector: Dr GUIDO ALAVA PÁRRAGA
Secretary: Dr PLUTARCO GARCÍA SALTOS
Librarian: MARÍA ANGELA DE CORONEL

Number of teachers: 489
Number of students: 8,000

Publication: *Revista*.

DEANS

Faculty of Administration and Economics: Econ. SEGUNDO ZAMBRANO
Faculty of Agricultural Engineering: Ing. RÉGULOS CEBALLOS
Faculty of Chemistry, Mathematics and Physics: Ing. ELIÉCER RODRÍGUEZ INDARTE
Faculty of Agronomy: Ing. MARCOS MEDINA NARANJO
Faculty of Health Sciences: Dr FÉLIX MOGRO
Faculty of Social Sciences and Education: Dr NILO PALMA PALMA
Faculty of Veterinary Sciences: Dr IGNACIO PALACIOS MACÍAS
Faculty of Zootechnology: Dr MARIO MATA MOREIRA

UNIVERSIDAD TÉCNICA ESTATAL DE QUEVEDO

Casilla 73, Quevedo, Los Ríos
Telephone: (5) 751430
Fax: (5) 753300

Founded 1984
State control

Rector: Ing. Forest. MANUEL HAZ ALVAREZ
Vice-Rector: Dr. MARCO ARGUDO SEMPÉRTEGUI
Librarian: CARMEN VELASCO LÓPEZ

Number of teachers: 122
Number of students: 1,569

DEANS

Faculty of Agricultural Sciences: Ing. TITO CABRERA VICUÑA
Faculty of Zoology: Dr MARCELO HAÓN JAMA

UNIVERSIDAD LAICA 'VICENTE ROCAFUERTE' DE GUAYAQUIL

Avda de las Américas, Apdo 11-33, Guayaquil
Telephone: (4) 287200
Fax: (4) 287431
E-mail: u.laica@impsat.net.ec

Founded 1847; university status 1966
Private control
Language of instruction: Spanish
Academic year: April to January

Rector: Dra ELSA ALARCÓN SOTO
Vice-Rectors: Ing. ALFREDO AGUILAR ALAVA (General), Econ. ALFONSO SÁNCHEZ GUERRERO (Academic)
General Secretary: Ab. ALFONSO AGUILAR ALAVA
Librarian: Ab. CECILIA RODRÍGUEZ GRANDA

Library of 8,000 vols
Number of teachers: 307
Number of students: 9,317

Publications: *Boletín de Información Académica* (annually), *Boletín el Contador Laico*.

Faculties of Administrative Sciences, Jurisprudence, Agricultural Engineering, Journalism, Education, Civil Engineering, Economics, Architecture. Schools of Secretarial Administration, Social Work, English, Accountancy, Publicity and Marketing, Design.

ESCUELA POLITÉCNICA NACIONAL (National Polytechnic School)

Ladrón de Guevara s/n, Apdo 17-01-2759, Quito
Telephone: 562400
Fax: 567848

Founded 1869
Autonomous control
Language of instruction: Spanish
Academic year: October to February, March to July

Rector: Ing. RODRIGO ARROBO RODAS
Vice-Rector: Dr GERMÁN ROJAS IDROVO
Secretary: Attorney Dr HERNÁN LARREÁTEGUI YÉPES
Librarian: MARÍA KUONQUÍ

Number of teachers: 800
Number of students: 7,000

Publication: *Politécnica*.

DEANS

Faculty of Civil Engineering: Ing. CIRO MENÉNDEZ
Faculty of Electrical Engineering: Ing. LUIS TACO
Faculty of Geology, Mines and Petroleum: Ing. JOSÉ CARRIÓN
Faculty of Mechanical Engineering: Ing. JORGE ESCOBAR
Faculty of Chemical Engineering: Ing. MARIO SÁNCHEZ
Faculty of Sciences: Dr LUIS HORNA
Faculty of Systems Engineering: Ing. VINICIO BAQUERO

DIRECTORS

Postgraduate Studies: Dr GERMÁN ROJAS
School of Technology: Ing. PABLO LÓPEZ
Institute of Basic Sciences: Ing. ABRAHAM ULLOA
Institute of Social Science: Dr FRANCISCO RHON
Institute of Technology Research: Ing. MARGOTH AVILA
Institute of Nuclear Science: Ing. RICARDO MUÑOZ
Institute of Geophysics: Dr MINARD HALL
Department of Biological Sciences: Dr RAMIRO BARRIGA
Centre of Continuing Education: Ing. OTHON ZOVALLOS

ESCUELA SUPERIOR POLITÉCNICA DE CHIMBORAZO

Casilla 4703, Riobamba
Telephone: 96-1099
Telex: 25046

Founded 1972
Autonomous control
Language of instruction: Spanish
Academic year starts October

Rector: Ing. RODRIGO JARAMILLO G.
Vice-Rector: Dr. FERNANDO RODRÍGUEZ P.
Secretary-General: Dr PATRICIO PAZMIÑO F.
Librarian: Sr. CARLOS RODRÍGUEZ C.

Library of 35,000 vols, 80,000 periodicals
Number of teachers: 264
Number of students: 4,500 (excluding students from the Dept of Languages

Publication: *GACETA* (every 3 months).

DEANS

Faculty of Nutrition and Dietetics: Lcda. CARMEN PLAZA N.
Faculty of Mechanical Engineering: Ing. PACÍFICO RIOFRÍO
Faculty of Agronomy: Ing. BAYARDO ULLOA E.

Department of Chemistry: Dr JOSÉ MONTESINOS J.
Faculty of Business Administration: Econ. JORGE RÍOS CH.
Faculty of Sciences: Dr CARLOS DONOSO F.
Faculty of Mathematics and Physics: Ing. GUSTAVO MANCHENO T.
Department of Physical Education: Lcdo. RAÚL RODRÍGUEZ
Faculty of Animal Husbandry: WILFRIDO CAPELO B.

ESCUELA SUPERIOR POLITÉCNICA DEL LITORAL

La Prosperina, Km 30½ Vía Perimetral, Guayaquil

Telephone: (4) 269269
Fax: (4) 854629
E-mail: cee@ecua.net.ec

Founded 1958
State control
Language of instruction: Spanish
Academic year: May to February

Rector: VICTOR BASTIDAS JIMÉNEZ
Provost and Vice-President (Academic Affairs): MARCOS VELARDE T.
Vice-President (Business Affairs and Finances): DANIEL TAPIA FALCONÍ
Vice-President (Student Affairs): ROBERT TOLEDO ECHEVERRÍA
Secretary-General: Lic. JAIME VÉLIZ LITARDO
Librarian: ELOÍSA PATIÑO LARA

Library of 47,000 vols
Number of teachers: 550
Number of students: 12,005

Publications: *Boletín Informativo Polipesca, Tecnológica, Informes de Actividades*.

DIRECTORS

Department of Electrical Engineering and Computer Science: CARLOS VILLAFUERTE
Department of Geology, Mines and Petroleum Engineering: MIGUEL A. CHÁVEZ
Department of Maritime Engineering: EDUARDO CERVANTES
Department of Mechanical Engineering: EDUARDO RIVADENEIRA
Institute of Physics: JAIME VÁSQUEZ
Institute of Chemistry: JUSTO HUAYAMAVE
Institute of Mathematics: JORGE MEDINA
Institute of Humanities: OMAR MALUK
Graduate School of Business: MOISÉS TACLE
Computer Science School: ALEXANDRA PALADINES
Food Science School: MA. FERNANDA MORALES
Fisheries School: FRANCISCO PACHECO
Furniture and Cabinet School: VÍCTOR FERNÁNDEZ
Mechanics School: MIGUEL PISCO
Electrical and Electronics School: CAMILO ARELLANO
Agriculture School: HAYDÉE TORRES
Center for the Study of Foreign Languages: Lic. DENNIS MALONEY S.

Colleges

Colegio Nacional de Agricultura 'Luis A. Martínez': Casilla 286, Ambato; f. 1913; Dir Dr CÉSAR VÁSCONEZ S.; Sec. CÉSAR EDUARDO COBO N.; 500 students; publ. *Germinación*.

Colegio Nacional '24 de Mayo', Quito: Quito; f. 1934; an experimental institution for women's higher education; assisted by UNESCO; departments of modern humanities for students preparing for universities and commerce, administration and professional training; Rector Dra MARÍA A. CARRILLO DE MATA M.; number of teachers 122; number of students 3,388.

Centro Internacional de Estudios Superiores de Comunicación para América Latina (International Centre for Advanced Studies in communications for Latin America): Diego de Almagro 2155 y Andrade Marín, Apdo 584, Quito; tel. 548011; telex 22474; fax 524177; f. 1959 with UNESCO aid; training, documentation and research; 67 staff; library of 16,500 documents, 2,000 vols; Dir-Gen. Dr ASDRÚBAL DE LA TORRE; publ. *Chasqui* (quarterly).

Escuela de Agricultura: Daule.

Escuela de Agricultura: Ibarra.

Schools of Art and Music

Conservatorio Nacional de Música (National Academy of Music): Madrid 1159 y Andalucía, Quito; tel. 544883; fax 564792; f. 1900; library of 5,000 vols; Rector LUCIANO CARRERA; publ. *Conservatorio*.

Conservatorio de Música 'José María Rodríguez': Cuenca; teaching staff 11; Dir Prof. RAFAEL SOJOS JARAMILLO.

EGYPT

Learned Societies

GENERAL

Academy of the Arabic Language: 15 Aziz Abaza St, Zamalek, Cairo; tel. 3405931; fax 3412002; e-mail aal@idsc-gov.eg; f. 1932; 40 Egyptian active mems, also corresp. mems, hon. mems and foreign active mems; library of 60,000 vols; Pres. Prof. Dr AHMED SHAWKY DHEIF; Sec.-Gen. IBRAHIM ABDEL MEGEED; publ. *Review* (2 a year).

African Society: 5 Ahmed Hishmat St, Zamalik, Cairo; tel. 3407658; f. 1972 to promote knowledge about Africa and national liberation movements in the Afro-Arab world and encourage research on Africa; organizes lectures, debates, seminars, symposia and conferences; participates in celebration of African national occasions; arranges cultural and scientific exchange with similar African societies; publishes bulletins and books in Arabic and English; 500 mems; library of 1,500 vols in Arabic, 2,000 vols in other languages; Sec.-Gen. M. FOUAD EL BIDEWY; publs *African Studies* (irregular), *Africa Newsletter* (in Arabic).

Institut d'Égypte (Egyptian Institute): 13 Sharia Sheikh Rihane, Cairo; f. 1798 by Napoleon Bonaparte; literature, arts and science relating to Egypt and neighbouring countries; 60 mems, 50 assoc. mems, 50 corresp. mems; library of 160,000 vols; Pres. Dr SILEMAN HAZIEN; Sec.-Gen. P. GHALIOUNGUI; publs *Bulletin* (annually), *Mémoires*.

AGRICULTURE, FISHERIES AND VETERINARY SCIENCE

Egyptian Society of Dairy Science: 1 Ouziris St, Garden City, Cairo; f. 1972; Pres. Dr ISMAEL YOUSRY; publ. *Egyptian Journal of Dairy Science*.

BIBLIOGRAPHY, LIBRARY SCIENCE AND MUSEOLOGY

Egyptian Association for Library and Information Science: c/o Dept of Archives, Librarianship and Information Science, Faculty of Arts, Univ. of Cairo, Cairo; tel. 5676365; fax 5729659; f. 1956; 4,000 mems; Pres. Dr S. KHALIFA; Sec. M. HOSAM EL-DIN.

National Information and Documentation Centre: Al-Tahrir St, Dokki, Cairo; tel. 701696; f.1955; accumulates and disseminates information in all languages and in all branches of science and technology; comprises five depts: Libraries, Scientific and Technological Information, Reprography, Editing and Publishing, Training; 33,600 vols, 2,000 periodicals; special collections: UNESCO and WHO; 210 staff; Dir Dr MOSTAGA ESMAT EL-SARHA; publs 18 scientific journals.

ECONOMICS, LAW AND POLITICS

Egyptian Society of International Law: 16 Sharia Ramses, Cairo; tel. 743162; f. 1945; objects: to promote the study of international law and to work for the establishment of international relations based on law and justice; Pres. Dr FOUAD ABDEL MONCIM RIAD; Sec.-Gen. Dr MOUFEED CHEHAB; Admin. Dir GEORGE HARFOUSH; 650 mems; library contains 4,100 books and 120 periodicals; publ. *Revue Egyptienne de Droit International* (annually).

Egyptian Society of Political Economy, Statistics and Legislation: 16 Sharia Ramses, Cairo, POB 732; tel. 750797; f. 1909; 3,018 mems; library contains 18,259 vols; Pres. Dr ATIF SIDKY; Gen.-Sec. MAHMOUD HAFEZ GHANEM; publs *L'Egypte Contemporaine* (quarterly, in Arabic, English and French), and numerous other publications on economics and law.

EDUCATION

Supreme Council of Universities: Cairo University Buildings, Giza; tel. (2) 5738583; fax (2) 5728722; f. 1950; delineates general policy of university education and scientific research in order to attain national objectives in social, economic, cultural and scientific development plans; determines admission numbers, fields of specialization, equivalences, etc.; the Egyptian Universities network (EUN) links university computer centres and research institutes throughout Egypt, and is the Egyptian gateway to the INTERNET and TERENA; library of 3,300 vols (English and Arabic); Pres. The Minister of Higher Education; Sec.-Gen. Prof. Dr MOFID SHEHAB.

FINE AND PERFORMING ARTS

Armenian Artistic Union: 3 Sharia Soliman, El-Halaby, POB 1060, Cairo; f. 1920; aims: promotion of Armenian and Arabic culture; 300 mems; Pres. VAHAG DEPOYAN.

'Atelier, L': 6 Victor Bassili St, 6 Pharaana St, Azarita, Alexandria; tel. 4820526; fax 4837662; f.1934; society of artists and writers; 350 mems; library of 5,500 vols; Hon. Pres. Prof. NAIMA EL-SHISHINY; Hon. Sec. D. FAROUK WAHBA; publ. *Bulletin*.

High Council of Arts and Literature: 9 Sharia Hassan Sabri, Zamalek, Cairo; f. 1956; publs books on literature, arts and social sciences.

Institute of Arab Music: 2 Sharia Tewfik, Alexandria; Pres. AHMED BEY HASSAN; Hon. Sec. ALY SAAD.

Institute of Arab Music: 22 Sharia Ramses, Cairo; tel. 750702; f. 1924; promotion and teaching of Arab music; libraries of records, tapes and scores of Arab music; Chair. of Board HASSAN TAKER MOK; Sec.-Gen. FARZY RASHAD.

HISTORY, GEOGRAPHY AND ARCHAEOLOGY

Egyptian Geographical Society: Sharia Kasr El-Aini (Jardin du Ministère d'Irrigation), PO Garden City, Cairo; tel. 3545450; f. 1875, reorganized 1917; library of 29,000 vols; Pres. SOLIMAN A. HUZZAYN; Sec.-Gen. YUSEF ABULHAGGAG; publ. *Bulletin*.

Hellenic Society of Ptolemaic Egypt: 20 Sharia Fouad I, Alexandria; f. 1908; Pres. Dr G. PARTHENIADIS; Sec. COSTA A. SANDI.

Société Archéologique d'Alexandrie: 6 Mahmoud, Moukhtar St, POB 815, Alexandria 21111; tel. (203) 48-20-650; f. 1893; 248 mems; Pres. Dr A. SADEK; Sec.-Gen. M. EL ABADI; publ. *Bulletin*.

Society for Coptic Archaeology: 222 Sharia Ramses, Cairo; f. 1934, for the study of Coptic archaeology, linguistics, papyrology, church history, liturgy and art; 360 mems; library of 15,000 vols; Pres. WASSIF BOUTROS GHALI; Sec.-Gen. Dr A. KHATER; Librarian Dr MARGIT TÓTH; publs *Bulletin* (annually), monographs: *Fouilles, Textes et documents*, MSS, etc.

MEDICINE

Alexandria Medical Association, The: 4 G. Carducci St, Alexandria; f. 1921; 1,200 mems; Pres. Prof. H. S. EL-BADAWI; Sec.-Gen. Prof. Dr TOUSSOUN ABOUL-AZI; publ. *The Alexandria Medical Journal* (English, French and Arabic, quarterly).

Cairo Odontological Society: 39 Kasr El-Nil, Cairo; Pres. Dr ABULNAGA M. ABDEL-AZIM; Sec. Dr J. ALCÉE.

Egyptian Medical Association: 42 Sharia Kasr El-Aini, Cairo; f. 1919; 2,142 mems; Pres. Prof. Dr A. EL-KATEB; Sec.-Gen. Prof. Dr A. H. SHAABAN; Vice-Pres. Prof. Dr M. IBRAHIM; publ. *Journal* (monthly, in Arabic and English).

Egyptian Orthopaedic Association: 16 Sharia Houda Shaarawi, Cairo 11111; tel. (2) 3930013; f. 1948; scientific and social activities in the field of orthopaedic surgery and traumatology; holds bi-annual scientific meetings, monthly clinical meetings; 1,700 mems; Pres. HASAN ELZAHER HASAN; Sec.-Gen. NABIL KHALIFA; publ. *Egyptian Orthopaedic Journal* (4 a year).

Ophthalmological Society of Egypt: Dar El Hekma, 42 Sharia Kasr El-Aini, Cairo; f. 1902; Pres. Prof. Dr EL-SAID KHALIL ABOU SHOUSA; Hon. Sec. Dr AHMAD EZ EL-DIN NAIM; 480 mems; publ. *Annual Bulletin*.

NATURAL SCIENCES

Biological Sciences

Egyptian Botanical Society: 1 Ozoris St, Tager Bldg, Garden City, Cairo; f. 1956 to encourage students of botany and links between workers in botany; organizes conferences, seminars, lectures, and field trips for collecting, preserving and identifying plants; 230 mems; Pres. Prof. Dr A. M. SALAMA; Sec. Dr MOHAMED FAWZY; publ. *Egyptian Journal of Botany* (3 a year).

Egyptian Society of Parasitology: 1 Ozoris St, Tager Bldg, Garden City, Cairo; f. 1967; holds scientific meetings, annual conference; covers subjects in the fields of helminthology, medical entomology, protozoology, molluscs, insect control, immuno-diagnosis of parasitic diseases, treatment, etc.; 350 mems; Pres. Prof. MAHMOUD HAFEZ; Sec.-Gen. Prof. TOSSON A. MORSY; publ. *Journal* (2 a year).

Société Entomologique d'Egypte: 14 Sharia Ramses, POB 430, Cairo; f. 1907; 502 mems; publs bulletins and economic series, library of 28,000 vols; Pres. MAHMOUD HAFEZ; Vice-Pres. Dr ABDEL AZIZ HAFEZ SOLIMAN, Dr ABDEL AZIZ KAMEL; Sec.-Gen. Dr ABDEL HAKIM M. KAMEL.

Zoological Society of Egypt: Giza Zoo, Giza; f. 1927; aims to promote zoological studies and to foster good relations between zoologists in Egypt and abroad; field courses, lectures, etc; library of 2,500 vols; 260 mems; Pres. Dr HASSAN A. HAFEZ; Sec. MOHAMED H. AMER; publ. *Bulletin*.

PHILOSOPHY AND PSYCHOLOGY

Egyptian Association for Mental Health: 1 Sharia 'Ilhami, Qasr al-Doubara, Cairo; f. 1948; 630 mems.

Egyptian Association for Psychological Studies: 1 Osiris St, Tager Bldg, Garden City, Cairo; tel. 3541857; f. 1948; 1,200 mems; Pres. Dr FOUAD A-L. H. ABOU-HATAB; publ. *Yearbook of Psychology*.

RELIGION, SOCIOLOGY AND ANTHROPOLOGY

Institut Dominicain d'Etudes Orientales: Priory of the Dominican Fathers, 1 Sharia Masna al-Tarabish, BP 18, Abbassiah 11381, Cairo; tel. (2) 4825509; fax (2) 2820682; e-mail ideo@link.com.eg; f. 1952; library of 60,000 vols; Dir Père R. MORELON; publ. *Mélanges* (annually).

Social Sciences Association of Egypt: Cairo; f. 1957; 1,234 mems.

TECHNOLOGY

Egyptian Society of Engineers: 28 Sharia Ramses, Cairo; f. 1920; Pres. Prof. Dr IBRAHIM ADHAM EL-DEMIRDASH; Sec. Dr MOHAMED M. EL-HASHIMY.

Research Institutes

GENERAL

Academy of Scientific Research and Technology: 101 Kasr El-Eini St, Cairo; tel. 3542714; telex 93069; fax 356280; f. 1971; the national body responsible for science and technology, with many instns affiliated to it; library of 34,000 vols, 50,000 periodicals; Pres. Prof. Dr ALI A. HEBEISH.

Affiliated institutions (see also below): National Network for Technology and Development (UNTD), Egyptian National Scientific and Technological Information Network, General Directorate of Satistics on Science and Technology, Scientific Instruments Centre, Science Museum, National Research Centre, Central Metallurgical Research and Development Institute, Institute of Oceanography and Fisheries, Institute of Astronomy and Geophysics, National Institute for Standards, Petroleum Research Institute, Remote Sensing Centre, Scientific Instrument Centre, National Information and Documentation Centre.

National Research Centre: Al-Tahrir St, Dokki, Cairo; tel. 701010; telex 94022; fax 700931; f. 1956; began functioning in 1947 and laboratory work started in 1956; fosters and carries out research in both pure and applied sciences; the 54 laboratories are divided into 13 sections: textile industries, food industries and nutrition, pharmaceutical industries, chemical industries, engineering, agriculture and biology, medical, applied organic and inorganic chemistry, physics, basic sciences, environment, genetic engineering and biotechnology; library of 12,000 vols; Pres. Prof. A. EL-SHERBEINY; publ. *Bulletin, NRC News*.

AGRICULTURE, FISHERIES AND VETERINARY SCIENCE

Agricultural Research Centre, Ministry of Agriculture: Giza; Chair. H. E. Prof. Dr YOUSSEF WALLY.

Attached research institutes:

Agricultural Economy Research Institute: Nadi El Said St, Dokki, Cairo; tel. 702318; f. 1973; Dir Dr OSMAN EL KHOLY.

Agricultural Extension and Rural Development: Nadi El Said St, Dokki, Cairo; tel. 706133; f. 1977; Dir Dr SHAFIE SALLAM.

Agricultural Machinery Research Institute: Nadi El Said St, Dokki, Giza; tel. 707247; Dir Dr AHMED EL SAHRIGI.

Animal Health Research Institute: Nadi El Said St, Dokki; tel. 703520; f. 1928; Dir Dr SAMIR AFRAM.

Animal Production Research Institute: Nadi El Said St, Dokki, Cairo; tel. 702934; f. 1938; Dir Dr MAMDOUH SHRAF ELDEEN.

Animal Reproduction Research Institute: Pyramids Rd, Giza; tel. 8954325; Dir Dr MAHMOUD SABRI.

Central Laboratory for Agricultural Industries: Cairo University St, Giza; tel. 722042; Dir Dr AHMED KHORSHID.

Central Laboratory for Agricultural Pesticides: Cairo University St, Giza; tel. 703860; Dir Dr ZAKARIA EL ATTAL.

Central Laboratory for Food and Feed: Cairo University St, Giza; tel. 732280; Dir Dr AKILA SALEH.

Central Laboratory for Statistical Design and Analysis: Cairo University St, Giza; tel. 723000; Dir Dr AHMED ABDEL HALIM.

Cotton Research Institute: Cairo University St, Giza; tel. 725135; f. 1919; Dir Dr AHMED EL GOHARY.

Field Crops Research Institute: Cairo University St, Giza; tel. 736515; f. 1971; Dir RASHAD ABOU EL-ENIN.

General Department of Agricultural Research Stations and Experiments: Cairo University St, Giza; tel. 721027; f. 1961; Dir Dr ISMAIL DARRAG.

Horticultural Research Institute: Cairo University St, Giza; tel. 720617; f. 1948; Dir. Dr KAMLA MANSOUR.

Plant Pathology Research Institute: Cairo University St, Giza; tel. 724893; f. 1919; research in various aspects of disease survey: ecology, biology, epidemiology and control measures; *c.* 170 research staff; library of 1,098 vols; Dir Dr MOKHTAR SATOUR; publs *Agricultural Research Review, Egyptian Phytopathology, Journal of Applied Microbiology*.

Plant Production Research Institute: Nadi El Said St, Dokki, Cairo; tel. 702193; Dir Dr AHMED ABDEL SALAM KHATTAB.

Plant Protection Research Institute: Nadi El Said St, Dokki, Giza; tel. 702193; Dir Dr AHMAD KHATTAB.

Soil and Water Research Institute: Cairo University St, Giza; tel. 720608; f. 1969; Dir Dr NABIL EL MOWILHI.

Sugar Crops Research Institute: Cairo University St, Giza; tel. 731465; Dir AHMED HASAN NOUR.

Vaccine and Serum Research Institute: Abbasiya, Cairo; tel. 821866; Dir Dr SAIED SALAMA.

Alexandria Institute of Oceanography and Fisheries: Kayed Bey, Alexandria; f. 1931; library: see Libraries; Dir Prof. Dr SAAD K. EL-WAKEEL; Sec. Sheik EL-ARAB SADEEK; publ. *Bulletin* (annually).

Institute of Freshwater Fishery Biology: 10 Hassan Sabry St (Fish Garden), PO Zamalik, Cairo; f. 1954; undertakes research in fish biology and culture; 7 scientists; Dir Prof. A. R. EL BOLOCK.

Institute of Oceanography and Fisheries: 101 Sharia Kasr El-Aini, Cairo; tel. (202) 3551381; telex 93069; f. 1931 in connection with the Faculty of Science, Cairo; undertakes oceanographical, environmental and fisheries research at Alexandria, the Red Sea, inland waters and fish farms; attached to the Academy of Scientific Research; contains a library and a museum; regular correspondence is kept up with more than 350 scientific institutions; 280 researchers; Dir Prof. Dr A. AL-RIFAI BAYOUMI; publ. *Bulletin*.

ARCHITECTURE AND TOWN PLANNING

General Organization for Housing, Building and Planning Research: POB 1770, Cairo; tel. 711564; telex 94025; attached to the Ministry of Development, New Communities, Housing and Public Utilities; carries out basic and applied research work on building materials and means of construction; also provides technical information and acts as consultant to the different authorities concerned with building and construction materials; eight specialized laboratories; Chair. Prof. Dr H. F. EL-SAYED FAHMY; publs bulletins, reports.

ECONOMICS, LAW AND POLITICS

Centre d'Etudes et de Documentation Economique, Juridique et Sociale: 14 Gameyet el-Nisr St, Mohandessin, Dokki, Cairo; tel. (2) 3611932; fax (2) 3493518; e-mail cedej@idsc.gov.eg; f. 1968; attached to Sous-direction des Sciences sociales et humaines (MAE) and Centre National de la Recherche Scientifique (CNRS), Paris; co-operation, documentation and research on an exchange basis between Egypt and France; research on Egypt (19th and 20th century) and the Arab world; university exchanges in co-operation with Egyptian Govt; library of 30,000 vols; 8 documentalists scan and classify *c.* 40 Egyptian periodicals; Dir PHILIPPE FARGUES.

Institute of Arab Research and Studies: POB 229, 1 Tolombat St, Garden City, Cairo; tel. 3551648; telex 92642; fax 3562543; f. 1953; affiliated to the Arab League Educational, Cultural and Scientific Organization (ALECSO); library of *c.* 71,000 vols, 1,040 periodicals; studies in contemporary Arab affairs, economics, sociology, history, geography, law, literature, linguistics; Dir Prof. AHMED YOUSSEF AHMED; publ. *Bulletin of Arab Research and Studies* (annually).

Institute of National Planning: Salah Salem St, Nasr City, Cairo; tel. 2627840; telex 93261; fax 2631747; f. 1960; research, training, documentation and information; organized in 11 scientific and technical centres; library of 70,000 vols; Chief Board of Dirs Dr KAMAL EL GANZOURY; publs *Egyptian Review of Development and Planning, Issues in Planning and Development* (irregular).

EDUCATION

National Centre for Educational Research: Central Ministry of Education, 33 Sharia Falaky, Cairo; f. 1972; co-ordinates current educational policy with that of the National Specialized Councils; exchanges information with like institutions throughout the world; provides local and foreign documents on education; Dir Dr YOUSSEF KHALIL YOUSSEF; publs. *Contemporary Trends in Education* (2 a year), *Educational Information Bulletin* (monthly), and various works on education in Egypt and the Arab world.

HISTORY, GEOGRAPHY AND ARCHAEOLOGY

Deutsches Archäologisches Institut (German Institute of Archaeology): 22 Sharia Gezira al Wusta, Cairo-Zamalek; Dir Prof. Dr RAINER STADELMANN.

Institut Français d'Archéologie Orientale (French Institute of Oriental Archaeology): 37 rue Sheikh Ali Youssef, BP 11562, Cairo; tel. 3548248; fax 3544635; e-mail cvelud@ifao.eg-net.net; f. 1880; excavations, research and publications intended to widen knowledge of Egyptian history from the Pharaohs to the Islamic period; 6 scientific mems; library of 60,000 vols; Dir Prof. NICOLAS GRIMAL; Dir of Studies CHRISTIAN VELUD; publs *Bulletin* (annually), *Annales Islamologiques* (annually), *Bulletin Critique des Annales Islamologiques, Cahiers des Annales Islamologiques, Cahiers de la Céramique Égyptienne, Bulletin de la Céramique Égyptienne, Bulletin d'Information Archéologique.*

MEDICINE

Bilharz, Theodor, Research Institute: Warak El Hadar, Embaba, POB 30, Giza; tel. 3405633; f. 1979; field work dealing with national health problems; 928 staff; Dir Prof. Dr AHMED ALI EL GAREM; publ. *Egyptian Journal of Bilharziasis.*

Central Health Laboratories: Ministry of Health, 19 Sheikh Rehan, Cairo; f. 1885; Dir-Gen. Dr ABDEL MONEIM EL BEHAIRY; Bacteriology: Dr GUERGUIS EL MALEEH; Clinical Pathology: Dr NADIR MOHARRAM; Sanitary Chemistry: MOUNIR AYAD; Toxicology: DALAL ABDEL REHIM; Food Microbiology: Dr MAGDA RAKHA; Library of 2,000 vols; publs *Bacteriology, Virology, Sera and Vaccines Production.*

Egyptian Organization for Biological Products and Vaccines: 51 Sharia Wezarat El Zeraa, Agouza, Giza.

Memorial Institute for Ophthalmic Research: Sharia Al-Ahram, Giza, Cairo; f. 1925; library of 2,800 vols; Dir Dr ABDEL MEGID ABDEL RAHMAN; publ. *Report.*

National Organization for Drug Control and Research: 6 Abou Hazem St, Giza; f. 1976; 300 staff; Chair. Dr ALI HIGAZI.

Nutrition Research Institute: 16 Kasr El-Aini St, Cairo; tel. 847476; telex 22895; f. 1955; 250 staff; Dir MOHAMED AMR HUSSEIN; publ. *Bulletin.*

Research Institute for Tropical Medicine: 10 Sharia Kasr El-Aini, Cairo; f. 1932; sections: clinical parasitology, helminthology, entomology, biochemistry, physiology and pharmacology, radiology, radiotherapy and radioisotopes, bacteriology, pathology, haematology, endoscopy, serology, immunology, malacology, animal house and field research units; library of 4,000 vols; Dir-Gen. M. HATHOUT.

NATURAL SCIENCES

Physical Sciences

Geological Survey and Mining Authority: Post Bag Ataba No. 11511, Cairo; fax (2) 4820128; f. 1896; regional geological mapping, mineral prospecting, evaluation of mineral deposits, and granting mineral exploration and exploitation rights; cartography laboratory; 763 research workers; library of 82,000 vols; Chair. Board GABER NAIM; publs occasional papers, maps.

Institute of Astronomy and Geophysics: Helwan, Cairo; tel. 780645; telex 93070; f. 1903; carries out research studies in geophysics and astronomy; comprises the Helwan Observatory, the Kottamyia Observatory, the Misallat geomagnetic observatory, the seismic stations at Helwan, Aswan, Matrouh, and the satellite tracking stations at Helwan and Abu Simbel; attached to the Academy of Scientific Research and Technology; library of 10,594 vols; Dir Prof. R. MOHAMED KEBESY; publs bulletins.

Remote Sensing Center: 101 Sharia Kasr El-Aini, Cairo; tel. 3557110; telex 93069; f. 1972 by Academy of Scientific Research in co-operation with the USA; covers geology, mineral and energy resources, hydrogeology, agriculture, soils, geophysics, photogrammetry, engineering, physics and data processing; one of the few centres which applied LANDSAT imagery interpretations from an early stage; operates advanced digital data processing facility for satellite and aircraft data, also Beechcraft King-Air aeroplane with most advanced remote sensing equipment; 65 specialist scientists, as well as technical staff; Dir Dr MOHAMED ABDEL HADY; publs *Proceedings* of various conferences and symposiums, technical reports.

TECHNOLOGY

Central Metallurgical Research and Development Institute: POB 87, Helwan, Cairo; tel. (2) 5010642; telex 23116; fax (2) 5010639; e-mail rucmrdi@rusys.eg.net; f. 1972; attached to the Ministry of Scientific Research; extractive metallurgy, ore dressing, technical services, metal-forming and working, welding research; library of 4,000 vols; Chair. Prof. Dr ADEL NOFAL.

Egyptian Atomic Energy Organization: 101 Sharia Kasr El-Aini, Cairo; f. 1957; Pres. Prof. Dr HISHAM FOUD ALY.

Attached research centres:

Nuclear Research Centre (NRC): Inshas; main facilities include a 2 MW research reactor, a 2.5 Van de Graaff accelerator, a radio-isotope production laboratory, nuclear fuel research and development laboratory, laboratories for application of radio-isotopes, electronic instrumentation laboratory and radiation protection laboratory; Chair. Prof. Dr NASF CAMSAN.

National Centre for Radiation Research and Technology (NCRRT): Nasr City, Cairo; main facilities include a 400,000 Ci, Co-60 unit and an electron accelerator; Chair. Prof. Dr AMIN EL-BAHY.

Egyptian Petroleum Research Institute: 7th Region, Nasr City, Cairo; tel. 2747847; telex 21300; fax 2747433; f. 1976; organ of the Ministry for Scientific Research; joint Board with Egyptian General Petroleum Corporation; seven research sections, dealing with all aspects of petroleum and energy-related problems; contract research and commercial services to local oil companies; library of over 5,000 books and periodicals; 850 staff; Dir Dr FAROUK EZZAT; publ. *Egyptian Journal of Petroleum.*

Hydraulics Research Institute: Delta Barrage 13621; f. 1949; tel. (2) 2188268; fax (2) 2189539; e-mail draulics@intouch.com; Dir Prof. Dr M. B. A. SAAD.

Middle Eastern Regional Radioisotope Centre for the Arab Countries: Sharia Malaeb El Gamaa, Dokki, 11321 Cairo; tel. 3370569; fax 3371082; f. 1963; trains specialists in the applications of radioisotopes, particularly in the medical, agricultural and industrial fields; conducts research in hydrology, tropical and sub-tropical diseases, fertilizers, and entomology; promotes the use of radioisotopes in the Arab countries; Dir Prof. Dr Y. M. MEGAHED; publs *Annual Report, Bulletin* (2 a year).

National Institute for Standards: El-Tahrir St, Dokki, Cairo; tel. 701944; attached to the Minister of Scientific Research and Technology; 350 staff; responsible for maintenance of national standards for physical units and their use for purposes of calibration; research on scientific metrology, to develop new techniques for measurements, calibrations, and development of new standards; consists of the following laboratories: electricity, photometry, frequency, thermometry, radiation, acoustics, mass, length metrology, engineering metrology, testing of materials, safety tests and textile testing, ultrasonics, rubber; Dir Dr M. M. AMMAR.

Textile Consolidation Fund: El-Syouf, Alexandria; incl. textiles quality control centre and textiles development centre; library of 5,000 vols; Gen. Man. MAGDI EL-AREF.

Unesco Regional Office for Science and Technology in the Arab States (ROSTAS): 11511 Cairo; telex 93772; fax 3545296; f. 1947; advisory services, trains personnel, undertakes studies and research; co-ordination at regional level for Unesco activities; depository library for Unesco publs; Dir Dr ADMAN SHIHAB EL-DIN; publ. *ROSTAS Bulletin* (quarterly).

Libraries and Archives

Alexandria

Alexandria Municipal Library: 18 Sharia Menasha Moharrem Bey, Alexandria; f. 1892; 22,390 Arabic vols, 35,399 European vols, 4,086 MSS; Chief Librarian Sheikh BESHIR BESHIR EL-SHINDI.

Alexandria University Library: 22 Sharia Al-Gueish, Shatby, Alexandria; f. 1942; consists of the Central Library (122,225 vols), 7 faculty libraries, and the Library of the Institute of Chemical Technology; over 1,000,000 vols; Dir ESSMAT EL-ASHRY.

Library of the Greek Orthodox Patriarchate of Alexandria: POB 2006, Alexandria; f. 10th century; 41,000 vols, 542 MSS, contains 2,241 rare editions; Librarian DIMITRIOUS TH. MOSCONAS.

Assiut

Assiut University Library: Assiut; 250,000 vols; Dir S. M. SAYED.

Cairo

Al-Azhar University Library: Nasr City, Cairo; 80,000 vols, including 20,000 MSS; Librarian M. E. A. HADY.

American University in Cairo Library: 11 Youssef El Guindi St, POB 2511, Bab El Louk, Cairo; tel. 3576904; telex 92224; fax: 3557565; e-mail selsawy@aucegypt.edu; f. 1919; 275,000 vols; Librarian SHAHIRA EL-SAWY.

Arab League Information Centre (Library): Midan Al-Tahir, Cairo; f. 1945; 30,000 vols, 250 periodicals.

Cairo University Library: Orman, Giza; f. 1932; 1,407,000 vols, 10,000 periodicals; Gen. Dir FATMA IBRAHIM MAHMOUD.

Central Library of the Agricultural Research Centre: Gamaa St, Giza; tel. 723000, ext. 331; f. 1920; 25,000 vols; Dir ISMAIL ABDEL SAMIE; publ. *Agricultural Review.*

Centre of Documentation and Studies on Ancient Egypt: 3 Sharia El-Adel Abou Bakr, Zamalek, Cairo; f. 1956; scientific and documentary reference centre for all Egyptian Pharaonic monuments; 4,500 vols, 33,000 photographs; Dir-Gen. Dr MAHMOUD MAHER-TAHA; publs a wide range of specialist material on ancient Egypt.

Egyptian Library: Abdin Palace, Cairo; over 20,000 vols; Dir ABDEL HAMID HOSNI.

Egyptian National Library (Dar-ul-Kutub): Sharia Corniche El-Nil, Bulaq, Cairo; f. 1870; 1,500,000 vols (400,000 European); 11 brs with 250,000 vols, including fine arts library; deposit library; Dir Gen. ALI ABDUL-MOHSEN.

Library of the Central Bank of Egypt: 153 Mohamed Farid St, Cairo; tel. 3905427; telex 22386; fax 3904232; f. 1961; 15,430 vols; publs *Economic Review* (quarterly), *Annual Report.*

Library of the Ministry of Education: 16 Sharia El-Falaki, Cairo; tel. (2) 8544805; f. 1927; 55,966 vols (European and Arabic); Dir of Libraries HASSAN ABDEL SHAFI.

Library of the Ministry of Health: Sharia Magles esh-Shaab, Cairo; over 27,000 vols.

Library of the Ministry of Justice: Midan Lazoghli, Cairo; f. 1929; over 90,000 vols and periodicals in Arabic, French and English (law and social science); private library for the use of judges and members of the Parquet (public prosecution and criminal investigation authority); a centre attached to the library contains the latest texts of local and comparative legislature on Personal Status; Dir F. ABOU-EL-KHEIR.

Library of the Ministry of Supply and Internal Trade: 99 Sharia Kasr el-Aini, Cairo; over 20,000 vols.

Library of the Ministry of Waqfs: Sharia Sabri Alu Alam, Ean el-Luk, Cairo; f. 1942; 20,219 vols.

Library of the Monastery of St Catherine: 18 Midan El Daher, Cairo; f. 6th century; over 4,000 Greek, Oriental and Slavonic MSS; contains the Codex Sinaiticus Syriacus; Librarians Monks DANIEL and SYMEON.

Library of the National Research Institute of Astronomy and Geophysics: Helwan, Cairo; f. 1903; 11,000 vols; Dir Prof. R. M. KEBEASY; publ. *Bulletin*.

National Archives Central Administration: Corniche El Nil, Boulac, Cairo; tel. 752883; f. 1954; Dir IBRAHIM FATALLAH AHMAD.

National Assembly Library: Palace of the National Assembly, Cairo; f. 1924; over 50,000 vols; Dir ANTOUN MATTA.

Damanhour

Damanhour Municipal Library: Damanhour; 13,431 vols.

Mansoura

Mansoura Municipal Library: Mansoura; contains 17,984 vols (Arabic 13,036, European 4,948).

Zagazig

Sharkia Provincial Council Library: Zagazig; contains 12,238 vols (Arabic 7,861, European 4,377).

Museums and Art Galleries

Alexandria

Greco-Roman Museum: Museum St, Alexandria; f. 1892; exhibits from the Greek, Roman and Byzantine eras; library of 15,500 vols, Omar Tousson collection of 4,000 vols; Dir DOREYA SAID; publs *Annuaire du Musée Gréco-Romain, Guide to the Alexandrian Monuments*.

National Maritime Museum: Alexandria; Dir Dr MEHREZ EL HUSSEINI.

Cairo

Agricultural Museum: Dokki, Cairo; tel.700063; f. 1938; exhibits of ancient and modern Egyptian agriculture and rural life, horticulture, irrigation; botanical and zoological sections; library of 8,885 vols; Dir SAMIR M. SULTAN.

Al-Gawhara Palace Museum: The Citadel, Cairo; f. 1954, refurnished 1956; built in 1811 in the Ottoman style, the Palace retains much of its original interior, contains Oriental and French furniture, including gilded throne, Turkish paintings, exhibitions of clocks, glass, 19th-century costumes.

Anderson Museum: Beit el-Kretlia, Cairo; f. 1936; private collections of Oriental art objects bequeathed to Egypt by R. G. Gayer Anderson Pasha in 1936; Curator YOUNES MAHRAN.

Cairo Geological Museum: POB Dawawin 11521, Cairo; premises at: Cornish El-Nil, Maadi Rd, Cairo; tel. 3187056; telex 22695; fax 820128; a general dept of the Egyptian Geological Survey; f. 1904; 50,000 specimens, mostly Egyptian; depts: vertebrates, invertebrates, rocks and minerals; library of 4,200 vols and 6,000 periodicals; Dir-Gen. MOHAMMED AHMED EL-BEDAWI.

Cairo Museum of Hygiene: Midan-el-Sakakini, Daher, Cairo; Dir Dr FAWZI SWEHA.

Coptic Museum: Old Cairo, Cairo; f. 1910; sculpture and frescoes, MSS, textiles, icons, ivory and bone, carved wood, metalwork, pottery and glass; library of 6,587 vols; Dir Dr MAHAR SALIB.

Cotton Museum: Gezira, Cairo; f. 1923; established by the Egyptian Agricultural Society; all aspects of cotton growing, diseases, pests, and methods of spinning and weaving are shown; Dir M. EL-BAHTIMI.

Egyptian (National) Museum: Midan-el-Tahrir, Cairo; f. 1902; exhibits from prehistoric times until the 3rd century AD; excludes Coptic and Islamic periods; established by decree in 1835 to conserve antiquities; the Antiquities Department administers the archaeological museums and controls excavations; library of 40,000 vols; Dir Dr MOHAMED SALEH; publs *Annals of the Antiquities Service of Egypt*, etc.

Egyptian National Railways Museum: Cairo Station Buildings, Ramses Square, 11669 Cairo; tel. 763793; telex 92616; fax 5740000; f. 1933; contains models of foreign and Egyptian railways, and technical information and statistics of the evolution and development of the Egyptian railway services; library of 5,595 vols (Arabic 2,694, European 2,901); Curator IBRAHIM SALEH ALY.

Museum of Islamic Art: Ahmed Maher Sq, Bab al-Khalq, Cairo 11638; f. 1881; collection of 86,000 items representing the evolution of Islamic art from the first quarter of 7th century up to 1900; Dir-Gen. Dr NIMAT M. ABU-BAKR; library of 15,000 vols; publs *Islamic Archaeological Studies* (annually), catalogues on Islamic decorative arts.

Museum of Modern Art: 4 Sharia Kasr El-Nil, Cairo; f. 1920; Curator SALAH E. TAHER.

War Museum: The Citadel, Cairo; library of 6,000 vols.

Universities

AIN SHAMS UNIVERSITY

Kasr El-Zaafaran, Abbasiya, Cairo

Telephone: 2847827

Fax: 2847824

Founded 1950

President: Prof. Dr ABDEL WAHAB ABDEL HAFEZ

Vice-President for Undergraduate Studies: Prof. Dr HASSAN GHALLAB

Vice-President for Graduate Studies and Research: Prof. Dr ALI RAMZI

Secretary-General: AL-SAID M. ALY

Librarian: NASR EL-DIN ABDEL RAHMAN

Number of teachers: 6,452

Number of students: 126,835

Publications: Faculty reviews.

DEANS

Faculty of Medicine: Prof. Dr HAMED SHATLA

Faculty of Arts: Prof. Dr MAHMOUD OUDA

Faculty of Science: Prof. Dr ABDUL-GAWAD RABIE

Faculty of Engineering: Prof. Dr IBRAHIM AL-NOMEIRY

Faculty of Agriculture: Prof. Dr ABDU S. SHEHATA

Faculty of Commerce: Prof. Dr MOHAMED REDA AL-EDEL

Faculty of Law: Prof. Dr IBRAHIM AL-ANANY

Faculty of Women: Prof. Dr ALIA A. SHOKRY

Faculty of Education: Prof. Dr MOHAMED AL-MOFTY

Faculty of Languages: Prof. Dr SALMAN SELEIM SALMAN

Faculty of Dentistry: Prof. Dr HASSAN A. BADRAN

Faculty of Pharmacy: Prof. Dr AHMED SHAWKY GENEIDY

Faculty of Computer Science and Information: Prof. Dr MOHAMED F. TOLBA

DIRECTORS

Institute of Childhood Studies: (vacant)

Institute of Environmental Studies and Research: Prof. Dr ADEL YASSIN MOHARRAM

Middle East Research Centre: Prof. Dr MOHAMED REDA AL-EDEL

Computer Centre: Prof. Dr MOHAMED F. TOLBA

Centre for Childhood Studies: Prof. Dr GAILAN ABDEL HAMID OSMAN

Centre for the Development of Science: Prof. Dr YOSSEF SALAH EL-DIN KOTB

Centre for Papyrus Studies: Prof. Dr ALIA H. HASSANEIN

ALEXANDRIA UNIVERSITY

22 El-Geish Ave, El-Shatby, Alexandria

Telephone: 5971675

Telex: 54467

Fax: 5960720

Founded 1942

State control

Academic year: September to May

Languages of instruction: Arabic and English

President: Prof. Dr ESSAM AHMED SALEM

Vice-President for Community Development and Environment: Prof. Dr MOHAMED AHMED ABDELLAH

Vice-President for Graduate Studies: Prof. Dr FATHI MOHAMED ABOU AYANAH

Vice-President for Postgraduate Studies: Prof. Dr MOSTAFA HASSAN MOSTAFA

Secretary-General: MOHAMED IBRAHIM AYOUB

Chief Librarian: KHALID EL-RAMADY

Library: see Libraries

Number of teachers: 5,550

Number of students: 130,500

Publications: Faculty Bulletins, *University Monthly Gazette* (for staff and personnel), *Collection of Public Affairs Lectures*.

DEANS

Faculty of Arts: Prof. Dr MOHAMED ABDOU MAHGOUB

Faculty of Law: Prof. Dr MOHAMED AL-SAID AL-DAKKAK

Faculty of Commerce: Prof. Dr AHMED MOHAMMED NOUR

Faculty of Science: Prof. Dr SALEM MOHAMED SALEM

Faculty of Medicine: Prof. Dr MOHAMED AHAB AL-MANSI

Faculty of Engineering: Prof. Dr MOHAMED ABDEL FATTAH SHAMA

Faculty of Agriculture: Prof. Dr AHMED MAHMOUD YOUSSEF

Faculty of Pharmacy: Prof. Dr ADEL MOHAMED METAWE

Faculty of Dentistry: Prof. Dr ABDEL RAHMAN WASFI

Faculty of Education: Prof. Dr SAMIR AHMED ABOU ALY

Faculty of Veterinary Medicine: Prof. Dr HELMY AHMED AL-SAYED TORKY

Higher Institute of Public Health: Prof. Dr MOHAMED AL-AMIN ABDEL FATTAH (see also under Colleges)
Institute of Medical Research: Dir Prof. Dr SHEHATA MAHMOUD AL-SEWEIDY
Higher Institute of Nursing: Dir Prof. Dr FERIAL ABDEL AZIZ
Faculty of Tourism and Hotels: Prof. Dr MONA OMAR BARAKAT
Institute of Higher Studies and Research: Prof. Dr MOHAMED EZ AL-DIN AL-RAEL
Faculty of Agriculture (in Saba Basha): Prof. Dr IBRAHIM ABDEL SALAM EL SAMRAH
Faculty of Fine Arts: Prof. Dr ATTIA MOHAMED HUSSEIN
Faculty of Physical Education (Males): Prof. Dr ESSAM AL-DIN ABDEL KHALEK
Faculty of Physical Education (Females): Prof. Dr NABILA ABDEL RAHMAN

ATTACHED INSTITUTES

Centre for Advancement of Postgraduate Science Studies: Alexandria; f. 1972 with Unesco and UNDP aid; Dir Prof. Dr ABDEL-RAHMAN EL-SADR.

Computer Science Centre: Alexandria; Dir Prof. Dr MOHAMED ABDEL HAMID ISMAIL.

AL-AZHAR UNIVERSITY

Cairo
Telephone: 2623278
Fax: 2623284
Founded 970, modernized and expanded 1961
Rector: Prof. AHMAD OMAR HASHEM
Library: see Libraries
Number of teachers: 6,000
Number of students: 155,000 (on several campuses)
Publications: *Annual Report,* University and Faculty Calendars.

DEANS

Faculty of Islamic Theology: Prof. ABDEL-MOUTI MOHAMMAD BAYOMI
Faculty of Islamic Jurisprudence and Law: Prof. ALI AHMAD MAREE
Faculty of Arabic Studies: Prof. SAAD ABDEL-MAQSOOD ZALLAM
Faculty of Engineering: Prof. HUSSEIN ABBAS
Faculty of Medicine: Prof. ISMAEEL KHALAF
Faculty of Commerce: Prof. BAKRY TAHA ATIA
Faculty of Agriculture: Prof. AMIN YOUSSEF
Islamic Women's College: Prof. SAIED ABDEL-TAWAB ABDEL-HADY
Faculty of Arabic and Islamic Studies: Prof. MAHMOUD EL-SAIED SHAIKHOON
Faculty of Language and Translation: Prof. AHMAD BASEM ABDEL-GHAFFAR
Faculty of Science: Prof. ABDEL-WAHAB AL-SHARKAWI

AMERICAN UNIVERSITY IN CAIRO

POB 2511, 113 Sharia Kasr El-Aini, Cairo
Telephone: 3542969
Telex: 92224
Fax: 3557596
American Address: 866 United Nations Plaza, New York, NY 10017
Founded 1919
Private control
Language of instruction: English
Academic year: September to June
President: Dr DONALD MACDONALD
Vice-Presidents: Dr MOHAMMED ABDEL KHALEK ALLAM, ANDREW SNAITH, ROBERT HOLLBACK
Provost and Dean of the Faculty: Dr ANDREW KEREK
Registrar: HODA HAMED
Librarian: SHAHIRA EL-SAWY
Library: see Libraries
Number of teachers: 361
Number of students: 4,477
Publications: *Cairo Papers in Social Science, Journal of Comparative Poetics*.

HEADS OF DEPARTMENTS

Center for Arabic Studies: Dr G. SCANLON
Arabic Language Institute: Dr S. EL-BADAWI
Economics: Dr A. BISHAI
Political Science: Dr E. SULLIVAN
Mass Communication: J. NAPOLI
Engineering: Dr E. FAHMY
Computer Science: Dr A. GONEID
English and Comparative Literature: Dr D. SHOUKRI
Performing and Visual Arts: Dr T. HARING-SMITH
Management: Dr S. YOUSSEF
Science: Dr M. H. OMAR
Sociology, Anthropology and Psychology: Dr A. BAYAT
English Language Institute: Dr PAUL STEVENS

ATTACHED UNITS

Center for Adult and Continuing Education: non-credit study programme for 11,265 students per semester; offers courses and post-secondary and post-graduate career programmes in Arabic/English, Arabic/French translation, English language, business and secretarial skills, and computing; Dean Dr HARRY MILLER.
Social Research Center: current research projects on demography and human resettlement; Dir Dr HUDA RASHAD.
Desert Development Center: Dir Dr M. SABAH (acting).

ASSIUT UNIVERSITY

Assiut
Telephone: (88) 324040
Fax: (88) 312564
Founded 1957
Languages of instruction: Arabic and English
President: Prof. MOHAMED RAAFAT MAHMOUD
Vice-President for Community Services and Environmental Affairs: Prof. ABD. EL-MOEZ AHMED ISMAIL
Vice-President for Postgraduate Studies and Research: Prof. MOHAMED AHMED MOHAMED SHALABY
Vice-President for Undergraduate Affairs: Prof. HUSSAIN AHMED EL-GALIL AHMED
Secretary-General: MOHAMED MOHAMED EL-GREATLY
Number of teachers: 2,405
Number of students: 56,960

DEANS

Faculty of Science: Prof. YASEEN MOHAMED HUSSAIN TEMEREK
Faculty of Engineering: Prof. MAHMOUD GABER MOUESY
Faculty of Agriculture: Prof. ABD. EL-RAZIK ABD. EL-ALEEM AHMED EL-RAZIK
Faculty of Medicine: Prof. MAHMOUD RAAFI ABD. EL-FATTAH HASSAN
Faculty of Pharmacy: Prof. AHMED ABD. EL-RAHMAAN ALI IBRAHIM
Faculty of Veterinary Medicine: Prof. NABIL AHMED ALY MESK
Faculty of Commerce: Prof. ISMAAIL SUBRY MAKLAD
Faculty of Education: Prof. WAGEEB AHMED MOHAMED GOBEEL (acting)
Faculty of Law: Prof. AHMED MOHAMED MELEEGI MOUSA
Faculty of Physical Education: Prof. Dr WADIA M. DAWOUD (acting)
Faculty of Social Work: Prof. BADRIN SHAWKY ABD. EL-WAHNAB
Faculty of Arts: Prof. FERDOUS ABD. EL-HAMEED EL-BAHNASSAWI
Higher Institute of Nursing: Prof. SAFEYA ALI TOHAMI (acting)
Institute of Sugar Studies and Technology: Prof. HASSANEIN GOMAA HASSANEIN
Faculty of Education (New Valley Branch): Prof. ABD. EL-TAWAB ABD. ELLAH ABD. EL-TAWAH

CAIRO UNIVERSITY

POB 12611, Orman, Giza, Cairo
Telephone: (2) 5729584
Fax: (2) 628884
Founded 1908
State control
Language of instruction: Arabic (English in practical faculties)
Academic year: October to June
President: Prof. Dr MOUFID SHEHAB
Vice-President for Education and Student Affairs: Prof. Dr HASSAN MAHMOUD EMAM
Vice-President for Graduate Studies and Research: Prof. Dr FAROUK ISMAIL
Vice-President for Society Service and Environment Development: Prof. Dr HASSANAIN RABIA
Vice-President for Khartoum Branch: Prof. Dr ALI EL-NAASSAN
Vice-President for Fayoum Branch: Prof. Dr MOHAMED SAEED SOLIMAN
Vice-President for Beni-Suef Branch: Prof. Dr HASSANAIN OBAID
Secretary-General: MOHAMED FAREED
Director-General of the Central University Library: FATMA IBRAHIM
Library: see Libraries
Number of teachers: 4,970
Number of students: 101,427

DEANS

Faculty of Arts: Prof. Dr MOHAMED HAMDI IBRAHIM
Faculty of Law: Prof. Dr MOHMOUD SAMIR EL-SHARKAWI
Faculty of Medicine: Prof. Dr MOHAMED MOTAZ EL-SHERBINI
Faculty of Economics and Political Science: Prof. Dr ALI EL-DEEN HELAL
Faculty of Science: Prof. Dr MOHAMED EL-SHARKAWI
Faculty of Commerce: Prof. Dr MAHMOUD BAZARAA
Faculty of Engineering: (vacant)
Faculty of Oral and Dental Medicine: Prof. Dr MAGEED AMIN MOHAMED
Faculty of Pharmacy: Prof. Dr AHMED ABD-EL BARI ABD-EL-RAHMAN
Faculty of Agriculture: Prof. Dr AHMED MOSTAGEER
Faculty of Dar El-Oloum: Prof. Dr MOHAMED BELTAGI HASSEN
Faculty of Veterinary Medicine: Prof. Dr ABD-EL KARIM MAHMOUD ABD EL-KARIM
Faculty of Mass Communication: Prof. Dr FAROUK ABU ZAID
Faculty of Archaeology: Prof. Dr SALAH EL-DEEN AL-BEHERI
Faculty of Physiotherapy: Prof. Dr AZZA ABD-EL-AZIZ
Faculty of Regional and Urban Planning: Prof. Dr ABD-EL-MOHSEN BARADA
Higher Institute of Nursing: Prof. Dr EMAN MOSTAFA MOURAD
National Cancer Institute: Prof. Dr MOHAMED NABIL EL-BOLKENI
Institute of Statistical Studies and Research: Prof. Dr IBRAHIM FARAG ABD-EL RAHMAN
Institute of African Studies and Research: Prof. Dr EL-SAEED IBRAHIM EL-BADAWI
Faculty of Agriculture (in Fayoum): Prof. Dr SAAD ZAKI NASSAR
Faculty of Science (in Fayoum): Prof. Dr ABD-EL-FATAH EL-SHERSHABI
Faculty of Education (in Fayoum): Prof. Dr MOHAMED ABD EL-RAHMAN EL-SHARNOBY

Faculty of Engineering (in Fayoum): Prof. Dr Galal Mostafa M. Saeed
Faculty of Social Service (in Fayoum): Prof. Dr Abd-El-Aziz Abd-Alla Moukhtar
Faculty of Arabic and Islamic Studies (in Fayoum): Prof. Dr Mohamed Salah El-Deen Mostafa
Faculty of Tourism and Hotels (in Fayoum): Prof. Dr Mahmoud Atwa Howadi
Faculty of Archaeology (in Fayoum): Prof. Dr Salah El-Behari
Faculty of Commerce (in Beni-Suef): Prof. Dr Mohamed Mahmoud El Kashef
Faculty of Arts (in Beni-Suef): Prof. Dr Said Hanafi Hassanain
Faculty of Science (in Beni-Suef): Prof. Dr Abd-El-Hamid El-Said Harhash
Faculty of Law (in Beni-Suef): Prof. Dr Mohamed Anas Kassem
Faculty of Veterinary Medicine (in Beni-Suef): Prof. Dr Salah Deeb
Faculty of Education (in Beni-Suef): Prof. Dr Ali-Hussain Hassan.
Faculty of Pharmacy (in Beni-Suef): Prof. Dr Ahmed Abd-El-Bary
Faculty of Arts (in Khartoum): Prof. Dr Mohamed Hamdi Ibrahim
Faculty of Law (in Khartoum): Prof. Dr Ahmed Shawki Mahmoud
Faculty of Commerce (in Khartoum): Prof. Dr Mona Abd-El-Fatah

HELWAN UNIVERSITY

96 Ahmed Ouraby St, Mohandissen, Giza

Telephone: 3446441

Founded 1975, incorporating existing institutes of higher education
State control
Languages of instruction: Arabic and English
Academic year: September to June

President: Prof. Dr Mohamed Mahmoud El-Gawhary
Vice-Presidents: Prof. Dr Abd El-Hay El-Refai Ebeid (Undergraduate Studies and Student Affairs); Prof. Dr Hassan Mohamed Hosny (Postgraduate Studies and Research), Prof. Dr Amal Ahmed Moukhtar Sadek (Community Service and Environmental Development)
Secretary-General: Ibrahiem El-Dosoky
Librarian: Khayrya El-Rafey

Library of 299,283 vols
Number of teachers: 2,525
Number of students: 36,833

Publication: *Science and Arts* (quarterly).

DEANS

Faculty of Engineering and Technology (Helwan): Prof. Dr Sayed Mostafa El-Sherbiny
Faculty of Engineering and Technology (Mataria): Prof. Dr Amr M. Radwan
Faculty of Commerce and Business Administration: Prof. Dr Mohamed Rehan Hussein
Faculty of Art Education: Prof. Dr Soliman M. Hassan
Faculty of Musical Education: Prof. Dr Safinaz H. Kamal
Faculty of Fine Arts: Prof. Dr Asem E. El-Embaby
Faculty of Applied Arts: Prof. Dr Emad El-Deen Abd El-Latif
Faculty of Social Work: Prof. Dr Ryad Amin Hamzawy
Faculty of Physical Education for Boys (Cairo): Prof. Dr Kamal El-Deen Darwish.
Faculty of Physical Education for Girls (Cairo): Prof. Dr Adela Teleb
Faculty of Home Economics: Prof. Dr Seham Zaki A. Mosa
Faculty of Tourism and Hotel Management: Prof. Dr Hazem Ahmed Atiatalla
Faculty of Education: Prof. Dr Ahmed Esmaiel Heggy
Faculty of Science: Prof. Dr Abdalla Barakat M. Kamal
Faculty of Law: Prof. Dr Hosny Ahmed El-Gendy
Faculty of Art: Prof. Dr Asem Ahmed El-Desoky
Faculty of Pharmacy: Prof. Dr Sobhy M. Ali Said

MANSOURA UNIVERSITY

Univ. Post Office 35516, Mansoura

Telephone: (50) 347054
Telex: 23768

Founded 1973 from the Mansoura branch of Cairo University
State control
Languages of instruction: Arabic and English
Academic year: October to June

President: Prof. Dr Mohamed H. M. Emarah
Vice-President for Graduate Studies and Research: Prof. Dr Sayed Mohamed Khair Allah
Vice-President for Undergraduate Studies: Prof. Dr Farouk Amin Ezzat
Secretary-General: Saafa El-Din Sayed Arafat
Librarian: Madiha Mahmoud Elemam

Number of teachers: 3,144
Number of students: 30,588 undergraduates, 2,029 postgraduates

Publications: faculty bulletins (annually).

DEANS

Faculty of Dentistry: Prof. Dr Omar Hassan Khashaba
Faculty of Medicine: Prof. Dr Mohamed Refat El-Nahass
Faculty of Science: Prof. Dr Abd El-Galeel Mohamed Khalil
Faculty of Education: Prof. Dr Roshdy Ahmed Tiema
Faculty of Commerce: Prof. Dr Ibrahim Mohamed Badawy Mahdy
Faculty of Engineering: Prof. Dr Saeed Abd El-Ghany Ashour
Faculty of Agriculture: Prof. Dr Ibrahim Mahmoud Tantawy
Faculty of Law: Prof. Dr Fathy Abdul Rihim Abd Allah
Faculty of Pharmacy: Prof. Dr Mohamed Mahmoud El-Kerdawy
Faculty of Arts: Prof. Dr Hussin Abdul Rihim Eliwa
Faculty of Education (in Domiatt): Dr Zaki Mohamed Abdullah
Faculty of Science (in Domiatt): Dr Shawky Mohamed Hassan

MENIA UNIVERSITY

Menia

Telephone: 2498

Founded 1976, incorporating existing faculties of Assiut University

President: Prof. Dr Yehia Aly Shaheen
Vice-President for Graduate Studies and Research: Prof. Dr Yousry Abd El-Razek El-Gohary
Vice-President for Undergraduate Studies: Prof. Dr Mohamed Abd El-Wahab El-Naghy
Secretary-General: Ahmed Fathy Mohamed Kayed

Number of teachers: 770
Number of students: 16,120

DEANS

Faculty of Agriculture: Prof. Dr Gamal Abu El-Makarem Rezk
Faculty of Arts: Prof. Dr Abd El-Hady El-Gohary
Faculty of Medicine: Prof. Dr Hafez Mahmoud Khafagy
Faculty of Science: Prof. Dr Kamal Abd El-Hady Mohamed
Faculty of Education: Prof. Dr Mohamed El-Naghy
Faculty of Engineering and Technology: Prof. Dr Maher Abd El-Wahab Mohamed
Faculty of Physical Education for Boys: Prof. Dr Hanafy Mahmoud Mokhtar
Faculty of Fine Arts: Prof. Dr Ahmed Anwar Ismail
Faculty of Arabic Studies: Prof. Dr Abd El-Khalek Mohamed Abd El-Khalek

MENOUFIA UNIVERSITY

Shebeen El-Kome

Telephone: (48) 224155
Telex: 23832
Fax: (2) 777620

Founded 1976

State control
Languages of instruction: Arabic and English
Academic year: September to July

President: Prof. Sakr A. Sakr
Vice-President for Community and Environmental Development: Prof. Ali Z. Al-Fayomy
Vice-President for Graduate Studies and Research: (vacant)
Vice-President for Undergraduate Education: Prof. Taher Sabry
Secretary-General: Farok Al-Ngar
Librarian: Hamid Arafa

Number of teachers: 1,787
Number of students: 46,965

DEANS

Faculty of Agriculture: Prof. Zaki El-Shennawi
Faculty of Engineering and Technology: Prof. Ibrahim Zakariya
Faculty of Electrical Engineering (in Menouf): Prof. Farhg El-Halfawi
Faculty of Education: Prof. Sami Abo Bih
Faculty of Science: Prof. Mohamed M. Al-Zaydeya
Faculty of Medicine: Prof. Mohamed A. Shoeib
Faculty of Commerce: Rafat H. El-Hennawi
Faculty of Arts: Prof. Fathi El-Moslhi
Faculty of Law: Prof. Abdel Ghfar Saleh
Liver Institute: Prof. Ahmed A. M. Raouf
Higher Institute of Nursing: Prof. Dalal M. Khalil
Faculty of Home Economics: Prof. Mohamed S. Al-Dashlouti
Faculty of Sports: Gamal Hamadh
Genetic Engineering and Biotechnology Research Institute: Prof. Mahmoud Nasr

SUEZ CANAL UNIVERSITY

El-Shikh Zayed, Ismailia

Telephone: 229976
Telex: 225176
Fax: 325208

Founded 1976
State control
Languages of instruction: Arabic and English
Academic Year: September to June

President: Prof. Dr Ahmed Ismail Khodair
Vice-Presidents: Prof. Dr Ahmed Dwedar El-Bassiouny (Postgraduate and Research Affairs), Dr Abdel-Hamid Shafek Shalaby (Undergraduate Affairs), Prof. Dr Abdel-Fattah Mohamed Abdel-Wahab (Environmental and Community Affairs)
Registrar: Mohammed Abd El-Rahman El-Kady
Librarian: Hayat Anwar Hamid

Number of teachers: 683
Number of students: 12,312 undergraduate, 1,588 postgraduate

DEANS

Faculty of Science (Ismailia): Prof. Dr Salah El Deen K. Aly

Faculty of Agriculture (Ismailia): Prof. Dr AHMED S. ABDEL-AZIZ
Faculty of Environmental and Agricultural Sciences (El Arish): Prof. Dr SAMIR IBRAHIM GHONEEM
Faculty of Education (Ismailia): Prof. Dr NABIL AID RAGAB EL ZAHAR
Faculty of Education (El Arish): Prof. Dr DARWEESH AHMED EL-SAYED
Faculty of Education (Suez): Prof. Dr SAED ABDALLAH MOHAMED
Faculty of Medicine (Ismailia): Prof. Dr FATHY ABDEL HAMID MAKLDY
Faculty of Veterinary Medicine (Ismailia): Prof. Dr MOHAMED ALY SHELEH
Faculty of Engineering (Port Said): Prof. Dr FAROUK MAHMOUD ABDEL KADER
Faculty of Petroleum and Mining Engineering (Suez): Prof. Dr MOHAMED A. T. ELGENDY
Faculty of Commerce (Port Said): Prof. Dr ZAIN EL-ABEDIN FARIS
Faculty of Commerce (Ismailia): Prof. Dr FAROUK MOHAMED SHALABI
Faculty of Physical Education (Port Said): Prof. Dr ADEL ABD EL-BASEER ALY
Faculty of Education (Port Said): Prof. Dr MAHMOUD MOHAMED MITWALLY
Higher Institute of Nursing (Port Said): Prof. Dr MOUSA ABDEL HAMID MOVSA

TANTA UNIVERSITY

Tanta Elgeish St, Tanta
Telephone: 327929
Telex: 23605
Fax: 331800

Founded 1972
State control
Language of instruction: English
President: Prof. Dr RAAFAT MOSTAFA ISSA
Vice-President for Undergraduate Studies: Prof. Dr MOUSA RAAD ELDIN EL-SHERBINY
Vice-President for Graduate Studies and Research: Prof. Dr EL ASHRY HUSSEN DARWISH
Vice-President for Kafr El Sheikh Branch: Prof. Dr ABD EL-TAWAB ABDEL AZIZ EL-YAMANY
Chief Administrative Officer: IBRAHEM MOHAMED MAREE
General Secretary: ABDEL RAHMAN M. HASSAN
Librarian: MOHAMED MOHAMED EL SETEHA

Number of teachers: 1,037
Number of students: 35,507

DEANS

Faculty of Medicine: Prof. Dr MOSTAFA FAHMY SHAMLULA
Faculty of Science: Prof. Dr MOHAMED ELMETWALI GHONIEM
Faculty of Education: Prof. Dr MOHAMED AHMED SALAMA
Faculty of Commerce: Prof. Dr SHAWKY EL SAIED KHATER
Faculty of Arts: Prof. Dr ABDEL RAHEEM M. ZALAT
Faculty of Pharmacy: Prof. Dr MOSTAFA KAMAL YOUSEF
Faculty of Law: Prof. Dr YOUSR ANWAR ALI
Faculty of Dentistry: Prof. Dr YAHIA MAHMOUD BAGDADY
Higher Institute of Nursing: Prof. Dr FOUAD K. HARRAS
Faculty of Agriculture (at Kafr El Sheikh): Prof. Dr RUSHDY A. OMAR
Faculty of Education (at Kafr El Sheikh): Prof. Dr HOSNEY Y. EL-BARADEY
Faculty of Engineering (at Kafr El Sheikh): Prof. Dr MOHAMED A. KASEEM
Faculty of Veterinary Science (at Kafr El Sheikh): Prof. Dr MOSTAFA A. MOHAMED

ZAGAZIG UNIVERSITY

Zagazig
Telephone: (55) 322926
Fax: (55) 345452

Founded 1974, incorporating existing faculties of Ain-Shams University
State control
Languages of instruction: Arabic, French, English
President: Prof. Dr MOHAMED RAMZY EL-SHAER
Vice-President for Student Affairs (Undergraduate Studies): Prof. Dr AHMED SAMIR AWAD
Vice-President for Community Service and Environment: Prof. Dr MOHAMED AMIN AMER
Vice-President for Graduate Studies and Research: Prof. Dr MAHMOUD SAMIR TOUBAR
Vice-President for Banha Branch: Prof. Dr AHMED FOUAD MANSOUR EL-SHEIKH
General Secretary: AHMED AMIN FARAC
Librarian: MOHAMED ABD EL-MONSEF

Number of teachers: 5,634
Number of students: 110,952

DEANS

Faculty of Arts: Prof. Dr ISMAIEL ABD EL-BARY
Faculty of Law: Prof. Dr KAMAL MOHAMED ABOU SERIE
Faculty of Commerce: Prof. Dr MOHMED AHMED SHAWKI
Faculty of Science: Prof. Dr AHMED HASHEM BASIONY
Faculty of Medicine: Prof. Dr ABDEL ZAHER TANTAWY
Faculty of Pharmacy: Prof. MAHER EL-DOMIATY
Faculty of Engineering: Prof. Dr AL-ADWI METWALY SHABAAN
Faculty of Agriculture: Prof. Dr ADEL EL-BADAWY
Faculty of Veterinary Medicine: Prof. Dr AHMED M. MOHAMED EL-TAHER
Faculty of Education: Prof. Dr MOHAMED A. DESOUKI
Faculty of Commerce (in Banha): Prof. Dr TARIK ABDEL AZIEM
Faculty of Medicine (in Banha): Prof. Dr HOSNY A. ABD EL-RAHMAN
Faculty of Engineering (in Banha): Prof. Dr MOSTAFA ZAKI ZAHRAN
Faculty of Science (in Banha): Prof. Dr MAHMOUD A. MOSA
Faculty of Arts (in Banha): Prof. Dr MOHAMED IBRAHEEM EBADA
Faculty of Law (in Banha): Prof. Dr MOHAMED EL-SHAFEE ABO-RAAS
Faculty of Veterinary Medicine (in Banha): Prof. Dr HOUSSAM EL-DEEN MOHAMED ABD. EL-AZIZ EL-ATTAR
Faculty of Education (in Banha): Prof. Dr HASSAN EL-BILAWY
Faculty of Agriculture (in Moshtoher): Prof. Dr FOUAD M. A. ASHOUR
Faculty of Physical Education (Boys): Prof. Dr MAHMOUD YEHIA SAAD
Faculty of Physical Education (Girls): Prof. Dr KARIMAN SROUR
Higher Institute of Nursing: Prof. Dr LAILA ABD EL-MOHSEN ZAKY
Institute of Efficient Productivity: Prof. Dr ABDEL HAMIED BAHGAT FAIED
Institute of Near Eastern Studies: Prof. Dr MOHMED AMER (Supervisor)
Institute of Asian Research and Studies: Prof. Dr RAFAT EL-SHIFKHI (Supervisor)

Colleges

Cairo Polytechnic Institute: 108 Shoubra St, Shoubra, Cairo; f. 1961; engineering, agriculture, commerce; Dir H. H. MOHAMED.

Higher Industrial Institute: Aswan; f. 1962; state control; courses in mechanical, electrical and chemical engineering, mining and natural sciences.

Higher Institute of Public Health: 165 Sharia Gamal Abd El Nasser, El-Hadra PO, Alexandria; an autonomous unit of the Univ. of Alexandria; f. 1955; undertakes fundamental teaching and applied public health research; 81 staff mems and 50 instructors; departments of public health administration, biostatistics, nutrition, epidemiology, tropical health, microbiology, occupational and environmental health, family health; library of 10,000 vols; Dean Prof. YASSIN M. EL-SADEK; publ. *Bulletin*.

Mansoura Polytechnic Institute: Mit-Khamis St, Mansoura; f. 1957; 147 teachers, 2,290 students; library of 21,400 vols; Dir Dr ESAYED SELIM ELMOLLA.

Regional Centre for Adult Education (ASFEC): Sirs-el-Layyan, Menoufia; tel. (48) 351596; f. 1952 by UNESCO; training of specialists in fields of literacy, adult education and education for rural development; production of prototype educational material, research in community development problems; advisory service; Chair. F. A. GHONEIM; Dir SALAH SHARAKAM.

Sadat Academy for Management Sciences: Kernish el Nile el Maadi, PO Box 2222, Cairo; tel. 3501033; fax 3502901; f. 1981; principal governmental organization for management development in Egypt; activities carried out through ten academic depts: business administration, public administration, economics, production, administration law, personnel and organizational behaviour, accountancy, insurance and quantitative analysis, computer and information systems, languages; also consists of four professional centres: Training, Consultation, Research and Local Administration; and Faculty of Management (undergraduate) and National Institute of Management Development (postgraduate); library of 32,000 vols, 250 periodicals; 124 teachers, 4,948 students; Pres. Prof. Dr MOUSTAFA REDA ABD AL-RAHMAN; Sec.-Gen. MOHAMMED BAKRI; publ. *Magalet Al-Behouth Al Edaria* (Administrative Research Review, quarterly, in Arabic and English).

Garden City Branch: 5 El Bergas St, Garden City, Cairo; tel. 3551793.
Ramsis Branch (Faculty of Management): 14 Ramsis St, Cairo; tel. 753350; fax 777175.
Alexandria Branch: 59 Mohandis Mahmoud Ismail St, Moharram Bey, POB 1176, Alexandria; tel. 4227125; fax 220485.
Tanta Branch: 5 Quateni St, Tanta; tel. 32083.
Assyot Branch: 19 El-Nour St, Assyot; tel. 322429.
Port Said Branch: Abdel-Salam Arif St, Port Said; tel. 235926.

Université internationale de langue française au service du développement africain/Université Senghor: BP 21111-415, 1 Midan Ahmed Orabi, El Mancheya, Alexandria; tel. (3) 4843371; fax (3) 4843374; e-mail secretariat-general@refer.org.eg; f. 1989; two-year courses (mainly post-graduate) in African development, nutrition and health, project management, financial institutions, managing the environment, managing cultural heritage; students are from francophone countries and intend to work in Africa; Rector Prof. SOULEYMANE SECK; Sec.-Gen. Prof. NAHWAT ABDALLA.

Schools of Art and Music

Academy of Arts: El-Afghany St, off Alharam Ave, Giza; tel. 854985; telex 20272; fax 850034; f. 1959; comprises eight institutes of university status; Pres. Prof. Dr FAWZY FAHMY AHMED; publ. *Alfann Almuasir* (quarterly).

Higher Institute of Ballet: Cairo; tel. 853999; f. 1958; 2 branches in Alexandria and Ismailia; depts of classical ballet, choreography, post-graduate studies; library of 3,500 vols; 21 teachers, 21 students; Dean Dr MAGDA EZZ.

Higher Institute of Cinema: Cairo; tel. 850291; f. 1959; depts of scriptwriting, directing, editing, photography and camerawork, scenery design, sound production, animation and cartoons; post-graduate studies; library of 5,000 vols; 90 teachers, 450 students; Dean Dr SHAWKY ALY MOHAMED.

Higher Institute of Theatre Arts: Cairo; tel. 853233; f. 1944; depts of acting and directing, drama and criticism, scenic and stage design; postgraduate studies; library of 15,500 vols; 90 teachers, 330 students; Dean Dr SANAA SHAFIE.

Higher Institute of Arab Music: Cairo; tel. 851561; f. 1967; depts of instrumentation, singing, theory of composition; postgraduate studies; library of 11,000 vols; 125 teachers, 280 students; Dean Dr SAID HAIKUL.

Higher Institute of Music (Conservatoire): Cairo; tel. 853451; f. 1959; depts of composition and theory, piano, string instruments, wind instruments, percussion, singing, solfa and music education, musicology; postgraduate studies; library of 24,000 vols, 3,000 records; 90 teachers, 78 students; Dean Prof. Dr NIBAL MOUNIB.

Higher Institute of Folklore: Cairo; tel. 851230; f. 1981; dept of postgraduate studies; library of 6,000 vols; 25 teachers, 60 students; Dean Dr ALYAA SHOUKRY.

Higher Institute of Art Criticism: Cairo; library of 2,500 vols; 8 teachers; 90 students; Dean Dr NAHIL RACHAB.

Higher Institute of Child Arts: Cairo; tel. 850727; f. 1990; postgraduate studies.

EL SALVADOR

Learned Societies

GENERAL

Academia Salvadoreña (El Salvador Academy): 13 Calle Poniente, San Salvador; Corresp. of the Real Academia Española (Madrid); 22 mems; Dir ALFREDO MARTÍNEZ MORENO; Sec. Prof. ALFREDO BETANCOURT.

Ateneo de El Salvador: 13A Calle Poniente, Centro de Gobierno, San Salvador; tel. 222-9686; f. 1912; library of 2,800 vols; 50 mems, 100 corresponding mems; Pres. Lic. LUIS ALONSO APARICIO; Sec.-Gen. Lic. JOSÉ OSCAR RAMÍREZ PÉREZ; publ. *Revista Ateneo* (2 a year).

HISTORY, GEOGRAPHY AND ARCHAEOLOGY

Academia Salvadoreña de la Historia (El Salvador Academy of History): Km. 10 Planes de Renderoz, Col. Los Angeles, Villa Lilia 13, San Salvador; f. 1925; Corresp. of the Real Academia de la Historia (Madrid); 18 mems; library of 9,000 vols; Dir JORGE LARDÉ Y LARÍN; Sec. PEDRO ESCALANTE MENA; publ. Boletín (irregular).

MEDICINE

Colegio Médico de El Salvador: Final Pasaje 10, Col Miramonte, San Salvador; f. 1943; tel. 267403; 1,710 mems; promotes medical research and cooperation; Pres. Dr MIGUEL OQUELÍ COLINDRES; publs. *Archivos*. (3 a year), *Revista Lealo* (every 2 months).

Sociedad de Ginecología y Obstetricia de El Salvador: Colegio Médico de El Salvador, Final Pasaje 10, Col. Miramonte, San Salvador; tel. and fax 235-3432; f. 1947; 150 mems; library of 2,000 vols; Pres. Dr JORGE CRUZ GONZALEZ; Sec. Dr HENRY AGREDA RODRIGUEZ.

Sociedad Médica de Salud Pública: Colegio Médico, Final Pasaje 10, Col. Miramonte, San Salvador; f. 1960; 85 mems.

Research Institutes

AGRICULTURE, FISHERIES AND VETERINARY SCIENCE

Centro Nacional de Tecnología Agropecuaria (CENTA): Final la Avda Norte, San Salvador; f. 1942; research and development of seeds; 400 staff; library of 6,500 vols, incl. periodicals; publs *Agricultura en El Salvador* (irregular), *Boletín Técnico* (occasional), *Circular* (occasional).

Instituto Salvadoreño de Investigaciones del Café: Ministerio de Agricultura, 23 Avda Norte No. 114, San Salvador; f. 1956; administered by the Ministry of Agriculture; publs monographs, *Boletín Informativo* (every 2 months).

ECONOMICS, LAW AND POLITICS

Dirección General de Estadística y Censos (Statistical Office): c/o Ministerio de Economía, 1A Calle Poniente y 43 Avda Norte, San Salvador; f. 1881; Dir-Gen. Lic. LUZ ELENA RENDEROS DE HERNÁNDEZ; publs *Anuario Estadístico, IPC* (monthly), *Avance Estadístico* (every 2 months).

NATURAL SCIENCES

Physical Sciences

Centro de Investigaciones Geotécnicas: Apdo 109, San Salvador; tel. 22-98-00; reorganized 1964; departments of seismology, soil mechanics, building materials, geological surveys; 250 mems; library of 1,000 vols; Dir Eng. JULIO BRAN VALENCIA; publs *Investigaciones Geológicas, reports*.

Servicio de Meteorología e Hidrología, El Salvador: Cantón El Matasano, Soyapango; tel. and fax 294-4750; f. 1889; formerly Servicio Meteorológico; library of 2,000 vols; Dir Lic. LEONARDO MERLOS; publs *Almanaque Salvadoreño, Anuario Hidrológico, Boletín CLICOM Centroamericano, Boletines Agrometeorológicos*.

TECHNOLOGY

Comisión Salvadoreña de Energía Nuclear (COSEN): c/o Ministerio de Economía, 1A Calle Poniente y 73 Avda Norte, San Salvador; f. 1961; to consider the applications in medicine, agriculture and industry of radioisotopes and nuclear energy.

Libraries and Archives

San Salvador

Archivo General de la Nación: Palacio Nacional, San Salvador; tel. 222-9418; f. 1948; 2,000 vols; Dir ALBERTO ATILIO SALAZAR; publ. *Repositorio*.

Biblioteca Ambulantes, Ministerio de Educación: 8A Avda Sur No. 15, San Salvador; f. 1951; 25,000 vols; Librarian VALENTÍN AMAYA.

Biblioteca Central de la Universidad de El Salvador: Final 25 Avda Norte, Ciudad Universitaria, Apdo postal 2923, San Salvador; tel. and fax 225-0278; e-mail sb@biblio.ues.edu.sv; f. 1847; 30,000 vols; Dir Lic. ANA AURORA DE KAPSALIS.

Biblioteca del Ministerio de Economía: Apdo (01) 19, Paseo General Escalón #4122, San Salvador; tel. 98-1963; fax 23-2586; f. 1950; 14,000 vols; Librarian ROBERTO GALEANO Y SOMOZA.

Biblioteca del Ministerio de Relaciones Exteriores (Library of the Ministry of Foreign Affairs): Carretera a Santa Tecla, San Salvador; 10,000 vols; Librarian MANUEL ANTONIO LÓPEZ.

Biblioteca Nacional (National Library): 8A Avda Norte y Calle Delgado, San Salvador; tel. 21-6312; f. 1870; 150,000 vols; special collections: old books, titles on int. organizations, Braille room; Dir JOSÉ ASTUL YANES.

Museums and Art Galleries

San Salvador

Museo de Historia Natural de El Salvador: Col. Nicaragua, Final Calle Los Viveros, San Salvador; tel. 70-9228; f. 1976; Dir JOSÉ ENRIQUE BARRAZA.

Museo Nacional 'David J. Guzmán' (National Museum): Avda la Revolución, Colonia San Benito, San Salvador; f. 1883; specializes in history, archaeology, ethnology, library science and restoration; travelling exhibits programme; Dir MANUEL R. LÓPEZ; publs *Anales, Colección Antropología e Historia, La Cofradía, El Xipe*.

Also administers:

Museo Tazumal: Chalchuapa, Dpto de Santa Ana; f. 1951; archaeological site museum.

Museo San Andrés: Sitio San Andrés, Km. 32 carretera Panamericana, Dpto de La Libertad; f. 1987; archaeological site museum.

Parque Zoológico Nacional: Final Calle Modelo, San Salvador; tel. 270-0828; fax 270-1387; f. 1953; recreation, environmental education and research, conservation; library of 1,800 vols; Dir Lic. ELIZABETH DE QUANT.

Universities

UNIVERSIDAD CATÓLICA DE OCCIDENTE

1A Calle Pte No. 32, Santa Ana
Telephone: 41-3217
Fax: 41-2655

Founded 1982
Private control
Language of instruction: Spanish
Academic year: February to December

Rector: Mons. Lic. MARCO RENÉ REVELO Y CONTRERAS
Vice-Rector: Mons. Dr FERNANDO SÁENZ LACALLE
Secretary-General: Lic. MARGARITO CALDERÓN
Librarian: ENRIQUE LEONEL ASENCIO ALEMÁN

Number of teachers: 87
Number of students: 1,019

DEANS

Faculty of Science and Humanities: Dra. DINA DEL CARMEN GAMERO FLORES
Faculty of Agricultural Engineering: Lic. JOSÉ ANTONIO PUIG
Faculty of Engineering: Ing. MARIO ANTONIO SÁNCHEZ GUTIÉRREZ
Faculty of Economic Sciences: Lcda. PATRICIA ORELLANA DE RAMÍREZ
Faculty of Law: Lic. ROBERTO ANTONIO SAYES

ATTACHED INSTITUTES

Instituto de Promoción Humana: promotes courses in administration, administration for rural cooperatives, nutrition, administration for small businesses.

Instituto de Desarrollo Rural: promotes extra-curricular activities in the rural sphere, projects on agricultural development, training courses for the rural population, technical analysis for agricultural cooperatives and environmental health and hygiene projects.

Departamento de Educación a Distancia: promotes teacher training courses.

UNIVERSIDAD DE EL SALVADOR

Apdo 1703, San Salvador
Telephone: 25-9427

Telex: 20794
Fax: 25-9427

Founded 1841
State control
Academic year: May to September, November to March
Branches at Santa Ana and San Miguel

Rector: Lic. José Luis Argueta Antillón
Vice-Rector: Dr Herberth W. Barillas
Secretary-General: Lic. Raul Madriz
Librarian: Lic. Luis Melgar Brizuela

Number of teachers: 1,500
Number of students: *c.* 32,000

Publications: *El Universitario, Boletin International, La Universidad, Coyuntura Economica.*

DEANS

Faculty of Chemical Sciences: Lic. Salvador Castillo Arevalo
Faculty of Dentistry: Dr José Benjamin Lopez Guillen
Faculty of Sciences and Humanities: Lic. Catalina Machuca de Merino
Faculty of Engineering and Architecture: Ing. Roberto Bran Giralt
Faculty of Economics: Lic. Hortensia Dueñas de Garcia
Faculty of Agriculture: Ing. Agr. Hector Armando Marroquin Arevalo
Faculty of Medicine: Dr Rafael Antonio Monterrosa Rogel
Faculty of Jurisprudence and Social Sciences: Dr Hector Armando Hernandez Turcios

UNIVERSIDAD CENTROAMERICANA 'JOSÉ SIMEÓN CAÑAS'

Apdo (01) 168, San Salvador

Telephone: 273-4400
Fax: 273-1010

Founded 1965
Private control (Society of Jesus)
Language of instruction: Spanish
Academic year: March to December

Rector: Lic. José María Tojeira
Secretary-General: Lic. René Alberto Zelaya
Librarian: Lic. Dra Katherine Miller

Number of teachers: 310
Number of students: 8,393

Publications: *Estudios Centroamericanos (ECA), Revista de Administración de Empresa, Revista Realidad Económica Social, Revista Proceso, Revista Carta a las Iglesias, Revista de Teología.*

DEANS

Faculty of Economics: Lic. Francisco Javier Ibisate
Faculty of Engineering: Ing. Celina Pérez
Faculty of Human and Natural Sciences: Lic. Héctor Samour

HEADS OF DEPARTMENTS

Faculty of Engineering:
- Natural Sciences and Agriculture: Ing. Herman Feussier Binder
- Systems and Processing Technology: Dr Francisco Armando Chávez
- Electronics and Information: Ing. William Ernesto Marroquin
- Structural Mechanics: Ing. Patricia Méndez de Hasbun
- Energy and Power Sciences: Ing. Ismael Antonio Sánchez Figueroa
- Spacial Planning: Arq. Bernardo Pohl

Faculty of Economics:
- Business Administration: Lic. Fidel Ernesto Zablah
- Law: Licda. Emma Dinora de Avelar
- Economics: Licda. Sonia Ivette Sánchez

Faculty of Human and Natural Sciences:
- Sociology: Lic. Sergio René Bran Molina
- Philosophy: Dr Antonio González
- Psychology: Lic. Erick Cabrera
- Literature: Lic. Ferran Caum
- Mathematics: Lic. David Navarro
- Education: Maestro Joaquín Samayoa

Institute of Human Rights: Dr Benjamín Cuéllar
Centre of Information, Documentation and Investigation Support (CIDAI): Lic. Luis Armando González
Master of Business Administration: Maestro Rafael Parada
Master of Theology: Dr Rafael de Sivatte

UNIVERSIDAD 'DR JOSÉ MATÍAS DELGADO'

Apdo 1849, Carretera a la Libertad, San Salvador 01158

Telephone: 289-0926
Fax: 289-0927

Founded 1977
Private control
Language of instruction: Spanish
Academic year: January to June, July to December

Rector: Dr David Escobar Galindo
Vice-Rector: Lic. Carlos Quintanilla Schmidt
Academic Vice-Rector: Dr Fernando Basilio Castellanos

Number of teachers: 380
Number of students: 4,000

DEANS AND DIRECTORS

School of Architecture: Arq. Luis Salazar Retana
School of Medicine: Dr Juán José Fernández
School of Industrial Engineering: Ing. Silvia Barrios de Ferreiro
School of Law: Dr Humberto Guillermo Cuestas
School of Liberal and Fine Arts: Dr David Escobar Galindo
School of Business Administration and Marketing: Lic. Patricia Linares de Hernández
School of Public Administration: Lic. José Hernández y Hernández
School of Agro-Industrial Research: Lic. María Georgía Gómez de Reyes
School of Economics: Ing. Roberto Sorto Fletes
School of Graphic Design: Lic. Rosemarie Vázquez L.
School of Psychology: Lic. Roxana Vides
School of Communications and Journalism: Arq. Luis Salazar Retana

UNIVERSIDAD SALVADOREÑA ALBERTO MASFERRER

19 Avda Norte, Entre Alameda Juan Pablo II y 3a Calle Poniente No 1040, Apdo postal 2053, San Salvador

Telephone: 221-1136
Fax: 222-8006
E-mail: usames@sal.gbm.net

Founded 1979
State control
Language of instruction: Spanish
Academic Year: January to June, June to December

Rector: Dr Amilcar Avendano y Ortiz
Vice Rector: Dr Miguel Antonio Barrios
Secretary-General: Lic. Daysi C. M. de Gomez
Registrar: Lic. Leonel Ayala
Librarian: Lic. Ximena Tiznado

Number of teachers: 264
Number of students: 3,122

DEANS

Faculty of Medicine: Dr y Lic. Carlos Uriarte González
Faculty of Dentistry: Dr Joaquín Parr Sánchez
Faculty of Pharmacy: Lic. Socorro Valdez
Faculty of Veterinary Medicine: Dr Francisco Antonio Parker
Faculty of Law and Social Sciences:: Dr Julio E. Acosta

UNIVERSIDAD TECNOLÓGICA DE EL SALVADOR

Calle Arce 1006, Apdo postal 1770, San Salvador

Telephone: 271-5990
Fax: 271-4764
E-mail: infoutec@utec.edu.sv

Founded 1981
Private control
Academic year: January to December

President and Rector: Lic. José Mauricio Loucel
Vice-President: Lic. Carlos Reynaldo López Nuila
Vice-Rector: Ing. Nelson Zárate Sánchez
Secretary General: Dr José Enrique Burgos
Prefect: Lic. Mario Antonio Juárez
Librarian: Lic. María Elsa Lémus Flores

Library of 16,000 vols
Number of teachers: 349
Number of students: 14,618

Publications: *Catálogo, Revista de Aniversario, Manual de Bienvenida, Manual de Ingreso, Revista Entorno, Revista Redes, Boletín Comunica.*

DEANS

Faculty of Economics: Lic Benjamin Cañas
Faculty of Engineering and Architecture: Ing. Francisco Armando Zepeda
Faculty of Humanities and Natural Sciences: Lic. Arely de Parada
Faculty of Law and Social Sciences: Dr José Enrique Burgos Martinez

Colleges

Central American Technical Institute: Apdo 133, Santa Tecla, La Libertad; tel. 228-0845; fax 228-1277; f. 1969; courses in agricultural engineering, civil and construction engineering, architecture, electronics, mechanical engineering; library of 6,000 vols; Dir Ing. Rolando Marín Coto.

Departamento de Música del Centro Nacional de Artes: 6a Avda Norte 319, San Salvador; tel. 21-31-84; f. 1970; trains teachers and performers; library of 2,675 vols; Dirs Prof. Luis Mario Flamenco Sevilla, José Atilio Martínez Cáceres.

Escuela Nacional de Agricultura 'Roberto Quiñónez': Km 33½ Carr. a Sta Ana, Apdo 2139, San Salvador; tel. 28-2735; f. 1956; 350 students, 60 teachers; library of 7,000 vols; Dir Ing. Mauricio Arévalo.

ERITREA

Libraries and Archives

Asmara

Asmara Public Library: 82 Ras Alula St, POB 259, Asmara; tel. 127044; f. 1955; 28,345 vols; branch library with 11,000 vols in north Asmara; Dir KEFELA KOKUBU.

British Council Library: POB 997, Asmara; f. 1971; 20,000 vols, 30 periodicals; Librarian MICHAEL TEKIE.

Massawa

Massawa Municipal Library: POB 17, Massawa; f. 1997; 10,000 vols; Chief Librarian MUHAMMED NUR SAID.

University

UNIVERSITY OF ASMARA

POB 1220, Asmara

Telephone: (1) 161926

Telex: 42091

Fax: (1) 162236

Italian section founded 1958; English section received charter 1968

State control

Language of instruction: English

Academic year: September to June (two semesters)

Chancellor: ISAYAS AFEWERKI

President: Dr WOLDE-AB YISAK

Vice-President for Business Affairs: Dr TESFAYESUS MEHARY (acting)

Director of Administration: TEKIE ASEHUN

Librarian: ASSEFAW ABRAHA

Library of 60,000 vols

Number of teachers: 206 full-time, 39 part-time

Number of students: 3,180

Publication: *Seismic Bulletin* (2 a year).

DEANS AND DIRECTORS

Science: Dr GHEBREBERHAN OGBAZGHI

Arts and Language Studies: Dr SETH I. NYAGAVA

Agriculture and Aquatic Sciences: Dr MOHAMMED KHEIR OMER

Business and Economics: MEHARI TEWOLDE

Health Sciences: Dr ASEFAW TEKESTE

Education: Dr BELAYNESH ARAYA

Eritrean Institute of Management: Dr GAFER ABUBAKER

Freshman Programme: Dr ABDULKADER SALEH

HEADS OF DEPARTMENT

Biology: Prof. AFEWERKI MAASHO

Chemistry: Dr MOBAE AFEWERKI

Mathematics: Dr GHIDEY ZEDINGLE

Physics: MEHRETEAB TSEGAI

Engineering: BERAKI GHEBREYEESUS

Language Studies: FESSEHAYE TECLE

Liberal Arts: Dr ALEXANDER NATY

Agricultural Science: Dr BISSIRAT GHEBRU

Marine Biology: ZEKARIA ABDULKERIM

Plant Sciences: Dr ANWAR UL HAG

Accounting: ESTIFANOS HAILEMARIAM

Economics and Finance: MELAKE TEWELDE

Business Management and Public Administration: GHEBREMEDHIN HAILE

Law: MENGISTEAB NEGASH

Consultancy, Training and Testing Institute: OGBAI ZERU

ESTONIA

Learned Societies

GENERAL

Estonian Academy of Sciences: 0001 Tallinn, Kohtu 6; tel. 44-21-29; fax 45-18-05; f. 1938; divisions of Astronomy and Physics (Head R. Villems, Learned Sec. J. Jaaniste), Informatics and Technical Sciences (Head B. Tamm, Learned Sec. I. Timmerman), Biology, Geology and Chemistry (Head D. Kaljo, Learned Sec. J. Lasn), Humanities and Social Sciences (Head P. Tulviste, Learned Sec. Ü. Sirk); 60 mems, 10 foreign mems; Pres. J. Engelbrecht; Sec.-Gen. Ü. Margna; publs *Toimetised* (Proceedings: Physics and Mathematics, Engineering, Chemistry, Geology, Biology/Ecology), *Trames, Acta Historica Tallinnensia, Oil Shale, Linguistica Uralica*.

HISTORY, GEOGRAPHY AND ARCHAEOLOGY

Estonian Geographical Society: 0001 Tallinn, Kohtu 6; Pres. Jaan-Mati Punning; Scientific Sec. Laine Merikalju.

LANGUAGE AND LITERATURE

Estonian Mother Tongue Society: 0001 Tallinn, Roosikrantsi 6; Chair. Tiit-Rein Viitso; Scientific Sec. Mart Meri.

NATURAL SCIENCES

General

Estonian Union of the History and Philosophy of Science: 0001 Tallinn, Estonia puiestee 7; Chair. Karl Siilivask; Scientific Sec. Karl Martinson.

Biological Sciences

Estonian Naturalists' Society: 2400 Tartu, POB 43; Pres. Tõnu Möls; Scientific Sec. Linda Kongo.

Research Institutes

GENERAL

Institute for Islands Development: 3300 Kuressaare, Rootsi 7; tel. and fax (45) 574-40; e-mail marins@si.edu.ee; Dir Maret Pank.

AGRICULTURE, FISHERIES AND VETERINARY SCIENCE

Estonian Agrobiocentre: 2400 Tartu, Rõõmu 10; tel. and fax (7) 33-97-17; e-mail eabc@pb.uninet.ee; attached to Min. of Agriculture; veterinary research; Dir Jüri Kumar.

Estonian Institute of Agrarian Economics: Harjumaa, 3400 Saku, Teaduse 1; tel. (2) 72-13-83; fax (2) 72-14-08; e-mail msepp@online.ee; attached to Min. of Agriculture; Dir Mati Sepp.

Estonian Institute of Agricultural Engineering: Harjumaa, 3400 Saku, Teaduse 13; tel. (2) 72-18-54; fax (2) 72-19-61; e-mail ergo@peak.edu.ee; attached to Min. of Agriculture; Dir Arvi Kallas.

Estonian Plant Biotechnical Research Centre: Harjumaa, 3400 Saku, Teaduse 6A; tel. (2) 72-14-84; fax (2) 72-16-52; attached to Min. of Agriculture; Dir Viive Rosenberg.

Estonian Research Institute of Agriculture: 3400 Saku, Teaduse 4/6; tel. (2) 72-11-68; fax (2) 72-25-99; e-mail annet@netekspress.ee; Dir Hindrek Older.

Jõgeva Plant Breeding Institute: 2350 Jõgeva; tel. (77) 225-65; fax (77) 601-26; e-mail vahur@sort.sai.ee; attached to Min. of Agriculture; Dir Hans Küüts.

ARCHITECTURE AND TOWN PLANNING

Estonian Building Research Institute: 0001 Tallinn, Estonia blvd 7; tel. 645-49-58; fax (2) 44-23-25; e-mail etui@online.ee; f. 1947; Dir Viljar Hämalane.

ECONOMICS, LAW AND POLITICS

Estonian Institute for Futures Studies: 0001 Tallinn, Lai 34; tel. 641-11-65; fax 641-17-59; e-mail eti@eti.online.ee; future scenarios for the development of Estonia and its neighbouring areas; Dir Erik Terk.

Estonian Institute for Market Research: 0001 Tallinn, Rävala puiestee 6; tel. (2) 45-44-50; fax 646-64-37; e-mail eki@online.ee; Dir Marje Josing.

Estonian Institute of Economics: 0100 Tallinn, Estonia puiestee 7; tel. 44-45-70; fax 630-88-51; Dir Olev Lugus.

HISTORY, GEOGRAPHY AND ARCHAEOLOGY

Institute of History: 0001 Tallinn, Rüütli 6; tel. 644-65-94; fax 644-37-14; Dir Priit Raudkivi.

LANGUAGE AND LITERATURE

Institute of the Estonian Language: 0001 Tallinn, Roosikrantsi 6; tel. and fax 641-14-43; Dir Asta Õim.

Under and Tuglas Literature Centre: 0001 Tallinn, Roosikrantsi 6; tel. 44-31-47; fax 44-01-77; Dir Dr T. Liiv.

MEDICINE

Estonian Institute of Cardiology: 0007 Tallinn, Ravi 18; tel. 620-72-50; fax 620-72-51; attached to Min. of Social Affairs; Dir Jüri Kaik.

Estonian Institute of Experimental and Clinical Medicine: 0016 Tallinn, Hiiu 42; tel. (2) 51-43-00; fax 670-68-14; e-mail toomas@ekmi.online.ee; attached to Min. of Social Affairs; Dir Toomas Veidebaum.

Pärnu Institute of Health Resort Treatment and Medical Rehabilitation: 3600 Pärnu, Kuuse 4; tel. and fax (44) 417-79; Dir Endel Veinpalu.

NATURAL SCIENCES

General

Estonian Marine Institute: 0001 Tallinn, Lai 32, tel. 631-30-05; fax 631-30-04; Dir T. Saat.

Biological Sciences

Estonian Biocentre: 2400 Tartu, Riia 23; tel. 42-04-43; fax 42-01-94; e-mail rvillems@ebc.ee; Dir Richard Villems.

Institute of Ecology: 0001 Tallinn, Kevade 2; tel. (2) 45-16-34; fax (2) 45-37-48; e-mail eco@eco.edu.ee; f. 1992; Dir J. M. Punning.

Institute of Experimental Biology: 3051 Harju rajoon, Harku, Instituudi tee 11; tel. (2) 51-24-56; fax (6) 50-60-91; e-mail ebi@ebi.ee; Dir A. Aaviksaar.

Institute of Zoology and Botany: 2400 Tartu, Riia 181; tel. (7) 47-19-88; fax (7) 38-30-13; e-mail zbi@zbi.ee; Dir Urmas Tartes.

International Centre for Environmental Biology: 0019 Tallinn, Klostrimetsa tee 44/52; tel. 23-90-01; fax 23-84-68; Dir J. Martin.

Physical Sciences

Estonian Meteorological and Hydrological Institute: 0001 Tallinn, Rävala puiestee 8; tel. 646-15-63; fax (2) 45-42-77; e-mail emhi.karing@torn.ee; attached to Min. of the Environment; Dir Peeter Karing.

Geological Survey of Estonia: 0026 Tallinn, Kadaka tee 80/82; tel. 672-00-94; fax 672-00-91; e-mail egk@estpak.ee; attached to Min. of the Environment; Dir. Vello Klein.

Institute of Chemical Physics and Biophysics: 0001 Tallinn, Rävala puiestee 10; tel. (2) 44-13-04; fax (2) 44-06-40; Dir Endel Lippmaa.

Institute of Chemistry: 0026 Tallinn, Akadeemia tee 15; tel. (2) 53-64-50; fax 654-75-24; e-mail kann@argus.chemnet.ee; Dir J. Kann.

Institute of Geology: 0001 Tallinn, Estonia puiestee 7; tel. 641-00-91; fax 631-20-74; e-mail inst@gi.ee; f. 1947; Dir Rein Vaikmäe; publ. *Proceedings* (4 a year).

Institute of Physics: 2400 Tartu, Riia 142; tel. (7) 42-81-02; fax (7) 38-30-33; e-mail dir@fi.tartu.ee; f. 1973; library of 27,000 vols, 50 periodicals; Dir K. Haller.

Oil Shale Research Institute: 2020 Kohtla-Järve, Järveküla tee 12; tel. (33) 445-50; fax (33) 447-82; f. 1958; library of 100,000 vols; Dir Richard Joonas.

Tartu Observatory: 2444 Tartu Maakond, Tõravere; tel. (7) 41-02-65; fax (7) 41-02-05; e-mail aai@aai.ee; f. 1946; library of 57,000 vols; Dir T. Viik.

RELIGION, SOCIOLOGY AND ANTHROPOLOGY

Estonian Interuniversity Population Research Centre: 0090 Tallinn, POB 3012; tel. 640-94-51; fax 640-94-53; e-mail asta@ekdk.estnet.ee; Dir Kalev Katus.

Institute of International and Social Studies: 0100 Tallinn, Estonia puiestee 7; tel. (2) 45-49-27; fax (2) 44-66-08; Dir Klara Hallik (acting).

TECHNOLOGY

Computer Research and Design Division 'Ekta': 0026 Tallinn, Akadeemia tee 21/G; tel. 639-79-00; fax 639-79-01; Dir H. Tani.

Estonian Energy Research Institute: 0001 Tallinn, Paldiski maantee 1; tel. (2) 45-29-73; fax 646-02-06; Dir (vacant).

Institute of Cybernetics: 0026 Tallinn, Akadeemia tee 21; tel. (2) 52-54-35; fax 639-70-39; e-mail dir@ioc.ee; Dir Jaan Penjam.

Libraries and Archives

Tallinn

Estonian Academic Library: 0100 Tallinn, Rävala Ave 10; tel. 645-47-04; fax 645-40-49; e-mail tar@maxi.tatr.ee; f. 1946; 2,600,000 vols, incunabula; Dir Anne Valmas; publs *Eesti retrospektiivne rahvusbibliograafia, Estonica: Humanitaar- ja Sotsiaalteadused* (annually), *Soome-ugri etnograafia & folkloor* (annually).

National Library of Estonia: 0100 Tallinn, Tõnismägi 2; tel. (6) 30-75-00; fax 631-14-10; f. 1918; nat. and parliamentary library with public access; 3,000,000 vols; Gen. Dir Dr Ivi Eenmaa; publ. *Raamatukogu* (The Library, 6 a year).

Tartu

Tartu University Library: 2400 Tartu, Struve 1; tel. (7) 37-57-02; fax (7) 37-57-01; e-mail library@utlib.ee; f. 1802; 3,751,000 vols, 504,000 theses, 28,000 MSS; Dir P. Olesk.

Museums and Art Galleries

Tallinn

Art Museum of Estonia: 0001 Tallinn, Kiriki Plats 1; tel. (2) 44-93-40; fax (2) 44-20-94; e-mail muuseum@ekm.estnet.ee; f. 1919; fine and applied art; library of 135,975 vols; Dir Marika Valk.

Estonian History Museum: 0001 Tallinn, Pikk 17; tel. 641-16-30; fax 244-34-46; e-mail post.eam@tallinn.astronet.ee; f. 1842; library of 11,000 vols; Dir T. Tamla.

Estonian Open Air Museum: 0035 Tallinn, Vabaöhumuuseumi tee 12; tel. 656-02-30; fax 656-02-27; e-mail e.v.m.@online.ee; f. 1957; 18th- to 20th-century architectural and ethnographical objects; Dir M. Lang.

Estonian Theatre and Music Museum: 0001 Tallinn, Müürivahe 12; tel. 44-21-32; f. 1924; library of 50,000 vols; Dir A. Saar; publ. *Eesti NSV Teatribibliograafia* (annually).

Tallinn City Museum: 0001 Tallinn, Vene 17; tel. (6) 44-18-29; f. 1937; library of 6,000 vols; Dir Maruta Varrak.

Tartu

Estonian Literary Museum: 2400 Tartu, Vanemuise 42, POB 368; tel. (7) 43-00-35; fax (7) 42-04-26; e-mail krista@kirmus.ee; f. 1909; Dir Krista Aru.

Estonian National Museum: 2400 Tartu, Veski 32; tel. (7) 42-12-79; fax (7) 42-22-54; e-mail enm@erm.tartu.ee; f. 1909; ethnology and culture of the Estonian and Finno-Ugric people; library of 24,000 vols; Dir Jaanus Plaat; publs *Eesti Rahva Muuseumi Aastaraamat* (Yearbook of the Estonian National Museum), *Pro Ethnologia*.

Museum of Classical Antiquities of Tartu University: 2400 Tartu, Ülikooli 18; tel. (7) 46-53-84; fax (7) 46-54-40; f. 1803; mainly plaster reproductions of ancient sculpture, gems and coins, 15th- to 19th-century Western European graphic works; library of 6,600 vols; Dir A. Laansalu.

Tartu Art Museum: 2400 Tartu, Vallikraavi 14; tel. and fax (7) 44-11-43; f. 1940; 19th- and 20th-century Estonian and European art; library of 20,000 vols; Dir E. Talvistu.

Universities

TALLINN TECHNICAL UNIVERSITY

0026 Tallinn, Ehitajate tee 5

Telephone: 620-20-02
Fax: 620-20-20

Founded 1918
Languages of instruction: Estonian and Russian
Academic year: September to June

Rector: Prof. O. Aarna
Vice-Rectors: Prof. T. Kaps, Prof. R. Küttner
Executive Vice-Rector: Dr J. Tanner
Librarian: M. Ideon

Number of teachers: 518
Number of students: 6,150

Publications: *Tehnikaülikool* (newsletter, weekly).

DEANS

Faculty of Chemistry: Prof. A. Öpik
Faculty of Civil Engineering: Prof. Karl-Peeter Õiger
Faculty of Economics and Business Administration: Prof. Alari Purju
Faculty of Mechanical Engineering: Prof. Jakob Kübarsepp
Faculty of Power Engineering: Prof. Enno Reinsalu
Faculty of Mathematics and Physics: Prof. Rein-Karl Loide
Faculty of Humanities: Prof. Väino Rajangu
Faculty of Systems Engineering: Prof. Leo Mõtus
Faculty of Information Processing: Prof. Rein Jürgenson

PROFESSORS

Faculty of Chemistry:

Kallas, J., Chemical Engineering
Kaps, T., Woodworking
Lopp, M., Organic Chemistry
Metsis, M., Molecular Biology
Mölder, L., Fuel Chemistry and Technology
Munter, R., Environmental Technology
Öpik, A., Physical Chemistry
Paalme, T., Food Science and Technology
Pehk, T., Chemical Physics
Saarma, M., Molecular Diagnostics
Truve, E., Gene Technology
Viikna, A., Textile Technology
Vilu, R., Biochemistry
Vokk, R., Food Chemistry

Faculty of Civil Engineering:

Engelbrecht, J., Applied Mechanics
Hääl, K., Heating and Ventilation
Koppel, T., Hydrodynamics
Laving, J., Traffic and Transportation Engineering
Loigu, E., Environmental Protection
Loorits, K., Steel Structures
Metsaveer, J., Solid Mechanics
Mölder, H., Water Engineering
Oiger, K., Timber and Plastic Structures
Sürje, P., Road Engineering
Sutt, J., Construction Economics and Management

Faculty of Information Processing:

Arro, I., Signal Processing
Jürgenson, R., Software Engineering
Kalja, A., Systems Programming
Keevallik, A., Digital Systems Design
Schults, E., Telecommunications
Taklaja, A., Microwave Engineering
Tepandi, J., Applied Artificial Intelligence
Ubar, R.-J., Computer Engineering and Diagnostics

Faculty of Systems Engineering:

Aarna, O., Process Control Engineering
Hinrikus, H., Radio and Laser Engineering
Kukk, V., Circuit and Systems Theory
Männamaa, V., Applied Electronics
Min, M., Electronic Measurement
Mõtus, L., Real Time Systems
Penjam, J., Theoretical Computer Science
Rang, T., Electronics Design
Rüstern, E., Automatic Control and Systems Analysis
Velmre, E., Applied Electronics

Faculty of Economics and Business Administration:

Kallas, K., Financial Accounting
Kalle, E., Labour Science
Kerem, K., Economic Theory
Kilvits, K, Economic Policy
Kolbre, E., Management Economics
Kukrus, A., Economic Law and Regulation
Kumm, K., Economic Theory
Leimann, J., Organization and Management
Lepp, R., Economic Mathematics
Pavelson, M., Economic Sociology
Purju, A., Public Economics
Saat, M., Business Administration
Teder, J., Small Businesses
Vensel, V., Theory of Statistics and Econometrics

Faculty of Mathematics and Physics:

Kallavus, U., Materials Research
Kukk, P.-E., Semiconductor Physics
Loide, R.-K., Theoretical Particle Physics
Puusemp, P., Algebra and Geometry
Tammeraid, L., Mathematical Analysis
Vaarmann, O., Applied Mathematics

Faculty of Mechanical Engineering:

Ajaots, M., Fine Mechanics
Kiitam, A., Quality Engineering
Kübarsepp, J., Metal Processing
Kulu, P., Materials Science
Küttner, R., Computer-aided Design and Manufacturing
Laaneots, R., Metrology and Measurement Techniques
Mellikov, E., Semiconductor Materials Technology
Pappel, T., Machine Mechanics
Papstel, J., Production Engineering
Põdra, P., Machine Elements
Reedik, V., Product Development
Tamre, M., Mechatronics

Faculty of Power Engineering:

Adamson, A., Rock Engineering
Jarvik, J., Electrical Machines
Laugis, J., Electrical Drives and Electricity Supply
Lehtla, T., Robotics
Meldorf, M., Transfer in Power Systems
Ots, A., Thermal Power Engineering
Pirrus, E., Applied Geology
Reinsalu, E., Mining
Tiikma, T., Heat Engineering
Valdma, M., Power Systems

Faculty of Humanities:

Mäeltsemees, S., Regional Policy
Rajangu, V., Educational Policy
Teichmann, M., Psychology

UNIVERSITY OF TARTU

2400 Tartu, Ülikooli 18

Telephone: (7) 37-51-00
Fax: (7) 37-54-40

Founded 1632
State control
Language of instruction: Estonian
Academic year: September to June

Rector: Prof. Jaak Aaviksoo
Pro-Rectors: Prof. Hele Everaus, Prof. Teet Seene, Prof. Volli Kalm
Academic Secretary: Ivar-Igor Saarniit

Library Director: PEETER OLESK

Library: see Libraries
Number of teachers: 791
Number of students: 8,870

Publications: *Acta et Commentationes Universitatis Tartuensis* (44 series), collections of research papers in 14 disciplines.

DEANS

Faculty of Biology and Geography: (vacant)
Faculty of Economics and Business Administration: Prof. J. SEPP
Faculty of Law: Dr P. PRUKS
Faculty of Mathematics: Prof. T. LEIGER
Faculty of Medicine: Prof. A. PEETSALU
Faculty of Philosophy: Prof. J. ROSS
Faculty of Physics and Chemistry: Prof. J. TAMM
Faculty of Physical Education and Sports Sciences: Asst Prof. M. PÄÄSUKE
Faculty of Theology: Asst Prof. T. KULMAR
Faculty of Social Sciences: Prof. J. ALLIK

Other Higher Educational Institutes

Estonian Academy of Arts: 0001 Tallinn, Tartu maantee 1; tel. 626-73-09; fax 626-73-50; e-mail public@artun.ee; f. 1914; faculties of fine arts (painting, stage design, sculpture, graphics), applied art (textiles, fashion design, leather work, ceramics, glass and metal work), architecture (interior design, architecture), design (product design, graphic design), art history; 160 teachers, 523 students; library of 54,427 vols; Rector Prof. ANDO KESKKÜLA.

Estonian Agricultural University: 2400 Tartu, Kreutzwaldi 64; tel. (7) 42-20-66; telex 173839; fax (7) 42-28-60; f. 1951; specialized areas: agronomy, horticulture, animal husbandry, veterinary medicine, meat and dairy technology, forestry, household economics, food production and marketing, agricultural engineering and energetics, agricultural economics and entrepreneurship, finance, land surveying, landscape architecture and management, water management, agricultural buildings; 268 teachers, 2,038 students; library of 500,000 vols; Rector MAIT KLAASSEN; publ. *Eesti Põllumajandusülikooli Teaduslike Tööde Kogumik*.

Tallinn Conservatoire: 0009 Tallinn, Vabaduse pst. 130; tel. 51-45-98; f. 1919; departments: singing, orchestral instruments, choral conducting, piano, organ, composition, music teaching, musicology, theatre; 134 teachers; 500 students; library of 200,000 vols; Rector V. LAUL; publ. *Scripta Musicalia* (quarterly).

ETHIOPIA

Learned Societies

AGRICULTURE, FISHERIES AND VETERINARY SCIENCE

Association for the Advancement of Agricultural Sciences in Africa: POB 30087, Addis Ababa; tel. 44-35-36; f. 1968; aims to promote the development and application of agricultural sciences and the exchange of ideas, to encourage Africans to enter training and to hold seminars annually in different African countries; crop production and protection, animal health and production, soil and water management, agricultural mechanization, agricultural economics, agricultural education, extension and rural sociology, food science and technology; *c.* 1,200 mems (individual and institutional); library of 5,000 items; Admin. Sec.-Gen. Prof. M. El-Fouly (acting); publs *African Journal of Agricultural Sciences, AAASA Newsletter*, Proceedings of workshops, conferences.

BIBLIOGRAPHY, LIBRARY SCIENCE AND MUSEOLOGY

Ethiopian Library and Information Association: POB 30530, Addis Ababa; tel. 110844; f. 1961; to promote the interests of libraries, archives, documentation centres, etc., and to serve those working in them; 150 mems; Pres. Mulugeta Hunde; Sec. Girma Makonnen; publs *Bulletin* (2 a year), *Directory of Ethiopian Libraries*.

MEDICINE

Ethiopian Medical Association: POB 2179, Addis Ababa; f. 1961; Pres. Dr Abebe Haregewoin; publ. *Ethiopian Medical Journal* (quarterly).

NATURAL SCIENCES

Physical Sciences

Geophysical Observatory: Addis Ababa University, POB 1176, Addis Ababa; tel. 117253; telex 21205; fax 551863; f. 1958; research in seismology, gravity, tectonics, crustal deformation and geodesy; library of 100 vols and 10 periodicals; Dir Laike M. Asfaw.

Research Institutes

AGRICULTURE, FISHERIES AND VETERINARY SCIENCE

Institute of Agricultural Research: POB 2003, Addis Ababa; tel. 612633; telex 21749; fax 611222; f. 1966; agronomy and crop physiology, crop protection, research extension, animal production, animal feeds and nutrition, animal health, agricultural mechanization, horticulture, soil science economics, field crop; aid from UNDP/FAO and other sources; 23 research centres and stations; library of 32,000 vols and 150 journals; Gen. Man. Dr Tadesse G. Medhin; publs *Proceedings* (annually), *Newsletter* (quarterly), *Annual Report, Research Report, Working Paper, Extension Bulletins, Ethiopian Journal of Agricultural Sciences*.

Institute of Agricultural Research: Awasa Centre, POB 6, Awasa, Sidamo; tel. (06) 200224; f. 1967; soil and water management, crop protection, horticulture, field crops, agronomy and crop physiology, agricultural economics and farming systems; library of 2,300 vols, 28 journals; Man Terefe Belehu; publs *ILEIA Newsletter* (quarterly), *Tropical Agriculture* (quarterly), *Agroforestry* (quarterly), *CERES* (monthly), *Journal of the American Society of Horticultural Science* (monthly), *Review of Plant Pathology* (monthly).

HISTORY, GEOGRAPHY AND ARCHAEOLOGY

Ethiopian Mapping Authority: POB 597, Addis Ababa; tel. (1) 518445; fax (1) 515189; e-mail ema@telecom.net.et; f. 1955; under Min. of Economic Development and Co-operation; conducts land surveying, mapping, remote sensing and geographical research; 400 mems; library of 3,000 vols; Gen. Man. Hadgu G. Medhin; publ. *Geo-Information Bulletin Ethiopia* (2 a year).

Institut d'Archéologie: POB 1907, Addis Ababa; conducts archaeological excavations in the Soddo region and at Axum, Yeha and Matara; undertakes preservation work at Axum, Gondar and Tana; Dir Dr Berhanou Abbébé; publ. *Annales d'Ethiopie*.

NATURAL SCIENCES

Biological Sciences

Desert Locust Control Organization for Eastern Africa (DLCO-EA): POB 4255, Addis Ababa; f. 1962; mems: Djibouti, Eritrea, Ethiopia, Kenya, Somalia, Sudan, Tanzania, Uganda; research into and control of desert locust and other pests, including armyworm, quelea and tsetse fly; library of 2,000 vols; Dir Dr A. M. H. Karrar; publs *Annual Report, Technical Reports*.

National Herbarium: University of Addis Ababa, POB 3434, Addis Ababa; tel. 114323; fax 552350; e-mail nat.heb@telecom.net.et; f. 1959; Dir Dr Sebsebe Demissew; publ. *Flora of Ethiopia*.

Physical Sciences

Ethiopian Institute of Geological Surveys: POB 2302, Addis Ababa; tel. 159926; telex 21042; fax 517874; f. 1968; library of 2,000 vols; Man. Shiferaw Demessie; Chief Geologist Ketema Tadesse.

RELIGION, SOCIOLOGY AND ANTHROPOLOGY

Institute of Ethiopian Studies: Addis Ababa University, POB 1176, Addis Ababa; telex 21205; f. 1963; advanced study and documentation centre; library: see Libraries; 50 mems; ethnological-historical museum; Dir Dr Abdussamad H. Ahmad; Librarian Ato Degfe G. Tsadik; Curator Ahmad Zekaria (acting); publs include *Journal of Ethiopian Studies* (2 a year), *IES Bulletin* (quarterly), various minor bibliographies and indexes compiled by Library staff.

Libraries and Archives

Addis Ababa

Addis Ababa University Libraries: POB 1176, Addis Ababa; tel. 115673; telex 21205; fax 550655; e-mail kennedy.aau@telecom.net.et; f. 1950; 500,000 vols; collection includes 90,000 vols on Ethiopia; central library, seven branch libraries and campus library in Debrezeit; Librarian Dr Taye Tadesse.

British Council Library: POB 1043, Artistic Bldg, Adwa Ave, Addis Ababa; tel. 55-00-22; telex 21561; fax 55-25-44; f. 1959; 51,000 vols, 137 periodicals; Librarian Ato Mulugeta Hunde.

Institute of Ethiopian Studies Library: Addis Ababa University, POB 1176, Addis Ababa; tel. 55-08-44; telex 21205; fax 55-26-88; f. 1963; collection of printed and non-printed materials on Ethiopia, Somalia, Djibouti, Red Sea, Indian Ocean, Sudan; also materials on Middle East; 110,000 vols, 9,000 MSS: Librarian Degife Gabre Tsadik; publ. *Journal of Ethiopian Studies*.

National Library and Archives: POB 717, Addis Ababa; tel. 512241; f. 1944; 125,000 vols; legal repository; includes Public Library section; Head Feleke Wolde; publ. *Ethiopian Publications Bibliography*.

Museums and Art Galleries

Addis Ababa

Musée Archéologique: c/o Institut Ethiopien d'Archéologie, POB 1907, Addis Ababa.

Museum of the Institute of Ethiopian Studies: University of Addis Ababa, POB 1176, Addis Ababa; tel. 550844; telex 21205; fax 552688; f. 1963; sections: exhibit of Haile Sellasie's bedroom, material culture (household artefacts, clothing, handicrafts, etc.); ethno-musicology (all types of Ethiopian musical instruments, religious music and poetry, record archive of oral tradition and folklore); traditional art (church paintings and furnishings, icons, etc., Islamic calligraphy); stamps, coins and banknotes of Ethiopia; Curator Ahmed Zekaria (acting).

Universities

ADDIS ABABA UNIVERSITY

POB 1176, Addis Ababa

Telephone: 550844

Telex: 21205

University College founded 1950, University 1961; extension centres in Addis Ababa, Awassa and Bahir Dar

State control

Language of instruction: English

Academic year: September to July

President: Prof Alemayehu Teferra

Academic Vice-President: Dr Mekonnen Dilgassa

Vice-President for Business and Development: Dr Ayele Tirfe

Librarian: Ato Adhane Mengisteab

Number of teachers: 871

Number of students: 19,149 (incl. 7,702 in continuing education)

Publications: *Journal of Ethiopian Studies, SINET: An Ethiopian Journal of Science,*

Ethiopian Journal of Development Research, Ethiopian Journal of Education, Register of Current Research on Ethiopia and the Horn of Africa, Ethiopian Publications.

DEANS

College of Social Sciences: Dr TADDESSE TAMRAT
Faculty of Business and Economics: Dr JOHANNIS KINFU
Faculty of Science: Dr THEODROS SOLOMON
Faculty of Technology: Dr HAILU AYELE
Faculty of Education: Dr SEYOUM TEFERRA
Faculty of Law: Ato DANIEL HAILE
Faculty of Medicine: Prof. EDEMARIAM TSEGA
Gondar College of Medical Sciences: Dr DESSALEGNE MERSHA
School of Pharmacy: Dr KALEAB ASRES
Awassa College of Agriculture: Dr ASSEFA G. AMLAK
Bahir Dar Teachers' College: Dr YALEW INGIDAYEHU
School of Graduate Studies: Dr DEMISSU GEMEDU
Faculty of Veterinary Medicine: Dr GERESSU BIRRU
Institute of Language Studies: Dr DEJENIE LETA
School of Information Studies: Ato GETACHEW BIRRU

DIRECTORS

Institute of Ethiopian Studies: Dr TADDESE BEYENE
Institute of Pathobiology: Prof. SHIBRU TEDLA
Institute of Development Research: Dr ANDARGACHEW TESFAYE
Institute of Educational Research: Dr DARGE WOLE

ALEMAYA UNIVERSITY OF AGRICULTURE

POB 138, Dire Dawa

Telephone: (5) 11-13-99
Fax: (5) 11-40-08

Founded 1952; university status 1985
State control
Language of instruction: English
Academic year: September to January, February to June

President: Dr DESTA HAMITO
Vice-President (Academic): Dr BELAY KASSA
Vice-President (Research and Development): Dr EFREM BECHERE
Vice-President (Administrative): (vacant)
Registrar: Dr BROOK LEMMA
Librarian: TESFAYE SALILEW

Number of teachers: 182
Number of students: 1,730 (and 1,008 evening students)

Publications: *The Alemayan, Alemaya Annual Research Report, Debre Zeit Annual Research Report, AUA News Letter.*

DEANS

School of Graduate Studies: Dr TEMAM HUSSEIN
Faculty of Agriculture: Dr HELUF GEBRE-KIDAN
Faculty of Education: MOLLA JEMERE
Faculty of Health Sciences: MELAKE DAMENA
Continuing Education Programme: Dr LISANEWORK NIGATU

RESEARCH CENTRES

Alemaya Agricultural Research Centre: POB 138, Dire Dawa; Dir Dr BELAY SIMANE.

Debre Zeit Agricultural Research Centre: POB 32, Debre Zeit; Dir TEKALIGN MAMO.

Colleges

Jimma College of Agriculture: POB 307, Jimma; tel. (7) 11-01-02; f. 1952; library of 14,000 vols; 65 teachers, 500 students; Dean Dr SOLOMON MOGES; Registrar Ato DAGNACHEW GIRMA; Librarian Ato GOITOM GHEBRU.

Polytechnic Institute: POB 26, Bahir-Dar; tel. (08) 200277; f. 1963; electrical, mechanical, civil and chemical engineering, agromechanics technology, industrial chemistry, electrical technology, wood technology, textile technology and metal technology; 350 students; 57 teachers; library of 500 vols; Dean MESFIN TEREFE WOLDU; Dean of Students GIRMA KEBEDE.

Yared National School of Music: POB 30097, Addis Ababa; tel. 55-01-66; f. 1967; 120 students; Head EZRA ABATE.

FIJI

Learned Societies

GENERAL

Fiji Society, The: Box 1205, Suva; f. 1936; is concerned with subjects of historic and scientific interest to Fiji and other islands of the Pacific; Pres. IVAN WILLIAMS; publ. *Transactions* (irregular).

ECONOMICS, LAW AND POLITICS

Fiji Law Society, The: POB 144, Ba; Pres. K. N. GOVIND; Sec. G. P. SHANKAR.

MEDICINE

Fiji Medical Association: 2 Brown St, Box 1116, Suva; tel. 315388; fax 315869; f. 1960; 215 mems; Pres. Dr SACHIDA MUDALIAR; publ. *Fiji Medical Journal* (4 a year).

Libraries and Archives

Nadi

Sri Ramakrishna Mission Library: Nadi; tel. 702786; fax 702193; f. 1927; books, periodicals, a/v cassette tapes, video cassette tapes; Librarian Rev. SWAMI DAMODARANANDA.

Suva

Library Service of Fiji: Ministry of Education, POB 2526, Govt Bldgs, Suva; tel. 315344; fax 314994; f. 1964; public special and school library service; 3 mobile libraries, 28 school media centres, 37 govt dept libraries; 960,000 vols; Principal Librarian HUMESH PRASAD; publ. *Fiji National Bibliography* (annually).

National Archives of Fiji: POB 2125, Government Bldgs, Suva; tel. 304144; f. 1954 as the Central Archives of Fiji and the Western Pacific High Commission; Government records from 1871, Anglican and Methodist church records from 1860s; 10,000 vols of monographs on the South Pacific, files on local newspapers from 1869, Fiji official publs from 1874, 2,800 reels of microfilm; Archivist SETAREKI TUINACEVA.

Suva City Library: POB 176, Suva; tel. 313433; fax 302158; f. 1909, known as Carnegie Library, until 1953; public lending library; 77,000 vols (48,000 in children's library, 29,000 in adults' library), 25 periodicals; special collection: Fiji and the Pacific; mobile library service for schools; Chief Librarian HUMESH PRASAD.

Museums and Art Galleries

Suva

Fiji Museum: POB 2023, Suva; tel. 315944; fax 305143; e-mail fijimuseum@is.com.fj; f. 1904; contains archaeological, ethnological and historical collections relating to Fiji; archives of Fijian oral traditions; photographic archives; Dir KATE VUSONIWAILALA; publs *Bulletin* (irregular), *Domodomo* (quarterly), Historic Reprint Series, special publications (irregular).

University

UNIVERSITY OF THE SOUTH PACIFIC

Suva

Telephone: 313900
Telex: 2276
Fax: 301305

Founded 1968

State control; regional university with 12 island State mems

Language of instruction: English

Academic year: February to November (two semesters)

Extension centres in the Cook Islands, Fiji, Kiribati, Marshall Islands, Nauru, Niue, Samoa, Solomon Islands, Tonga, Tuvalu, Vanuatu; link arrangements with Tokelau; the university's second campus is in Alafua, Samoa; third campus is in Vanuatu

Chancellor: Sir TULANGA MANUELLA
Pro-Chancellor: SAVENACA SIWATIBAU
Vice-Chancellor: E. SOLOFA
Deputy Vice-Chancellor: Prof. RAJESH CHANDRA
Pro-Vice-Chancellors: PIO MANOA, Prof. JOHN LYNCH
Registrar: SAROJINI D. PILLAY
Librarian: ESTHER WININAMAORI WILLIAMS

Library of 600,000 vols
Number of teaching staff: 355
Number of students: 4,000 on campus, 6,000 extension students

Publications: *Calendar*, *School/Institute Reports, School Handbooks* (annually), *Bulletin* (weekly), *Journal of Pacific Studies, Pacific Perspective, Directions* (Inst. of Education), *Pacific Islands Communications Journal, Alafua Agricultural Bulletin, SSED Review* (quarterly), *South Pacific Agricultural News* (fortnightly).

HEADS OF SCHOOLS

School of Humanities: Prof. KONAI THAMAN
School of Pure and Applied Sciences: Dr SURENDRA PRASAD
School of Social and Economic Development: Dr VIJAY NAIDU
School of Agriculture (Alafua Campus): Dr MAREKO TOFINGA (acting). (See also under Samoa).
School of Law: Prof. ROBERT HUGHES

PROFESSORS

AALBERSBERG, W., Natural Products Chemistry
AGGARWAL, S., Management and Public Administration
BABA, T., Education
FIRTH, S., Politics
FORSYTH, D. J. C., Economics
FULLERTON, R., Business Administration
GASKEL, I., Literature and Language
HAVOTA, E., Oceania Centre for Arts and Culture
HUGHES, R., Law
LYNCH, J., Pacific Languages
MCARTHUR, A., Physics
NEWELL, P., Biology
NUNN, P., Geography
PATTERSON, D., Pacific Law
PATTIE, W., Agriculture
PLANGE, N., Sociology
RAVUVU, A., Pacific Studies
SHARMA, M. D., Banking
SOTHEESWARAN, S., Chemistry
SOUTH, R., Marine Studies
SUBRAMANI, Literature and Language
SZILVASSY, C., Technology
THAMAN, R., Geography
WALSH, A. C., Development Studies
WHITE, M., Accounting and Financial Management

ATTACHED INSTITUTES

Institute of Education: Dir CLIFF BENSON.

Institute of Marine Resources: Dir GUNNU PILLAI.

Institute of Applied Sciences: Dir R. BEYER.

Institute of Pacific Studies: Dir A. RAVUVU.

Institute for Research, Extension and Training in Agriculture: Dir MOHAMMED UMAR.

Institute of Social and Administrative Studies: Dir HARI RAM.

Institute of Justice and Applied Legal Studies: Dir MERE PULEA.

Colleges

Fiji College of Agriculture: Koronivia, Nausori; f. 1954, reorganized 1962; three-year diploma course in tropical agriculture; library of 9,000 monographs, 450 periodicals; 130 students; Principal RUSSELL DUNHAM; publs *Fiji Farmer, Annual Report, Fiji Agricultural Journal* (2 a year), *Annual Research Report*.

Fiji Institute of Technology: POB 3722, Samabula, Suva; tel. 381044; fax 370375; f. 1964; courses in building and civil engineering, business studies, electrical and electronic engineering, mechanical engineering, aeronautical engineering, maritime studies, printing, graphic design, hospitality and tourism, automobile engineering, applied computing, applied science, secretarial studies, agricultural engineering; 210 full-time teachers, 5,000 students; library of 10,000 vols; Dir Dr JOHN HARRÉ.

Fiji School of Medicine: Private Mail Bag, Hoodless House, CWM Hospital Campus, Suva; tel. 311700; f. 1885, reorganized as Central Medical School 1928; external MBBS course of Univ. of the South Pacific and Allied Health Sciences Diploma courses; postgraduate courses; 522 students; library of 16,000 vols; Head Dr JIMIONE SAMISONI; Librarian Mr CHANDRAIYA.

FINLAND

Learned Societies

GENERAL

Finska Vetenskaps-Societeten/Suomen Tiedeseura (Finnish Society of Sciences and Letters): Mariankatu 5A, 00170 Helsinki; tel. (9) 633005; fax (9) 661065; f. 1838; 323 mems; Pres. Prof. DAN-OLOF RISKA; Permanent Sec. Prof. CARL G. GAHMBERG; publs *Årsbok-Vuosikirja A,B* (Yearbook), *Commentationes Humanarum litterarum, Scientiarum socialium, Bidrag till kännedom av Finlands natur och folk.*

Suomalainen Tiedeakatemia (Finnish Academy of Science and Letters): Mariankatu 5, 00170 Helsinki; tel. (9) 636800; fax (9) 660117; f. 1908; 615 mems; Pres. JARMO VISAKORPI; Sec.-Gen. PENTTI KAURANEN; publs *Annales Academiae Scientiarum Fennicae, Folklore Fellows' Communications, Yearbook.*

Suomen Akatemia (Academy of Finland): Vilhonvuorenkatu 6, POB 99, 00501 Helsinki; tel. (9) 774881; fax (9) 77488299; e-mail keskus@aka.fi; f. 1969; central governmental organ for research admin. and the development of nat. science policy, reporting directly to Min. of Education; 25 acad. professorships; library of 21,000 vols; Pres. REIJO VIHKO; Dir of Admin. HEIKKI KALLIO; Dir of Research JORMA HATTULA.

Tieteellisten seurain valtuuskunta/ eration of Finnish Learned Societies): Mariankatu 5, 00170 Helsinki; tel. 22869222; fax 22869291; f. 1899 to promote scholarly publishing, scientific information, scientific co-operation and science policy; 213 mem. socs; houses exchange centre for scientific literature; Pres. Prof. PÄIVIÖ TOMMILA; Dir HANNU HEIKKILÄ; publ. *Catalogue* (every 2 years).

AGRICULTURE, FISHERIES AND VETERINARY SCIENCE

Meijeritieteellinen Seura r.y. (Finnish Society for Dairy Science): Dept of Food Technology, Dairy Science, POB 27 (Viikki B), 00014 University of Helsinki; f. 1938 to promote research work and co-operation in the field of dairy science; 300 mems; Chair. Prof. Dr ESKO UUSI-RAUVA; Sec. EEVA-LIISA RYHÄNEN; publ. *Meijeritieteellinen Aikakauskirja* (Finnish Journal of Dairy Science).

Suomen Eläinlääkäriliitto (Finnish Veterinary Asscn): Makelankatu 2C, 00500 Helsinki; tel. 701-1388; fax 701-8397; f. 1892 to promote veterinary science and the practice of veterinary medicine; 1,355 mems; Chief Officers TIMO ESTOLA, KALEVI JUNTUNEN; publ. *Suomen Eläinlääkärilehti* (Finnish Veterinary Journal).

Suomen Maataloustieteellinen Seura (Scientific Agricultural Society of Finland): Institute of Resource Management, Agricultural Research Centre of Finland, 31600 Jokioinen; tel. (3) 41881; fax (3) 4188396; f. 1909; 581 mems; Pres. Prof. ASKO MÄKI-TANILA; Sec. Dr MARKKU YLI-HALLA; publ. *Journal* (4–6 a year).

Suomen Metsätieteellinen Seura (Finnish Society of Forestry Science): Unioninkatu 40A, 00170 Helsinki; tel. (9) 85705235; fax (9) 85705677; e-mail sms@helsinki.fi; f. 1909 to encourage forest research work in Finland; composed of persons devoting themselves to the study of forestry and its underlying theory; 550 mems; Pres. CARL JOHAN WESTMAN; Sec. JARI LISKI; publs *Acta Forestalia Fennica, Silva Fennica* (quarterly).

BIBLIOGRAPHY, LIBRARY SCIENCE AND MUSEOLOGY

Suomen Kirjastoseura (Finnish Library Association): Vuorikatu 22 A 18, 00100 Helsinki; tel. (9) 6221399; fax (9) 6221466; e-mail fla@fla.fi; f. 1910; 2,100 mems; Pres. KAARINA DROMBERG; Sec.-Gen. SINIKKA SIPILÄ (acting); publ. *Kirjastolehti* (Bulletin, monthly).

Suomen Museoliitto/Finlands Museiförbund (Finnish Museums Association): Annankatu 16 B 50, 00120 Helsinki; tel. (9) 649001; fax (9) 608330; e-mail museoliitto@museoliitto.fi; f. 1923; 170 museums; library of 2,000 vols; Sec.-Gen. ANJA-TUULIKKI HUOVINEN; publ. *Museo* (quarterly).

Suomen Tieteellinen Kirjastoseura (Finnish Research Library Association): POB 217, 00171 Helsinki; tel. (3) 3653148; fax (3) 3652907; e-mail meri.kuula@arcada.fi; f. 1929; 696 mems; Pres. ARJA-RIITTA HAARALA; Sec. MERI KUULA; publ. *Signum* (Bulletin) (8 a year).

ECONOMICS, LAW AND POLITICS

Ekonomiska Samfundet i Finland (Economic Society of Finland): Swedish School of Economics, POB 479, 00101 Helsinki; f. 1894; 900 mems; Pres. BO HARALD; Sec. JAN-ERIK KRUSBERG; publ. *Tidskrift* (Journal, 3 a year).

Hallinnon Tutkimuksen Seura r.y./ Sällskapet för Förvaltningsforskning (Finnish Association for Administrative Studies): Dept of Administrative Sciences, University of Tampere, POB 607, 33101 Tampere; tel. (3) 632119; f. 1981; aims: to function as a common link for depts and researchers studying administrative questions, to co-ordinate the planning and surveillance of training in administrative sciences, to hold lectures and discussions, to take part in international scientific co-operation; a mem. of the European Group of Public Administration; 598 individual mems, 8 organizational mems; Pres. Assoc. Prof. IIRIS AALTIO-MARJOROLA; Sec. JYRI LEHTINEN; publs *Hallinnon Tutkimus* (quarterly), *Hallinnon Tutkimuksen Seura Tiedottaa* (Newsletter, 3–6 a year).

International Institute of Administrative Sciences, Finnish Branch: f. 1956; 80 mems; Pres. Prof. MARKKU TEMMES; Sec. PETRI UUSIKYLA, Dept of Political Science, POB 54, 00014 University of Helsinki; tel. (9) 1918825.

International Law Association, Finnish Branch: c/o Advocate Klaus Lagus, Tehtaankatu 4 B 11, 00140 Helsinki; tel. 666726; fax: 631054; f. 1946; 105 mems; Pres. Prof. BENGT BROMS; Hon. Sec. MATTI TUPAMÄKI.

Ius Gentium Association (Law of the Nations Association): PL 208, 00171 Helsinki; tel. 191-2468; telex 124690; fax 191-3076; f. 1983; research on international law and legal theory; Pres. JUHANI KORTTEINEN; publs *Kansainoikeus/Ius Gentium, Finnish Yearbook on International Law, Acta Societatis Fennicae Iuris Gentium,* A, B and C Series.

Juridiska Föreningen i Finland (Law Society of Finland): Advokatbyrå Hannes Snellman Ab, Södra Kajen 8, 00130 Helsinki; tel. (9) 228841; fax (9) 636992; f. 1862; 794 mems; Pres. PER LINDHOLM; Sec. ULRIKA FORSBERG; publs *Tidskrift utgiven av Juridiska Föreningen i Finland,* various legal publications.

Kansantaloudellinen Yhdistys (Finnish Economic Association): c/o Sinimaaria Ranki, Bank of Finland, POB 160, 00101 Helsinki; f. 1884; 1,012 mems; Pres. SINIKKA SALO; Sec. SINIMAARIA RANKI; publs *Kansantaloudellinen Aikakauskirja* (Finnish Economic Journal) and *Kansantaloudellisia Tutkimuksia* (Economic Studies).

Suomalainen Lakimiesyhdistys (Finnish Lawyers' Association): Kasarmikatu 23 A 17, 00130 Helsinki; tel. (9) 603567; fax (9) 604668; e-mail sly@suomalainenlakimesyhdistys.fi; f. 1898; 4,000 mems; Pres. PEKKA HALLBERG; Sec. RITVA ERMA; publs *Lakimies, Suomalaisen Lakimiesyhdistyksen Julkaisuja,* series A-D, *Lakimies-aikakauskirja.*

Suomen Tilastoseura/Statistiska Samfundet i Finland (Finnish Statistical Society): c/o Statistics Finland, POB 4A, 00022 Statistics Finland; tel. 17341; fax 1734 3251; f. 1920; aims to promote the development of theoretical and applied statistics, to unite statisticians working in various fields, to promote statistical education and research; 500 mems; Pres. ANTTI KANTO; Sec. LEENA HIETANIEMI; publs *Publications, Statistical Research Reports, Yearbook.*

Suomen Väestötieteen Yhdistys (Finnish Demographic Society): c/o University of Helsinki, Dept of Sociology (Pia Mäkelä), POB 18, 00014 University of Helsinki; tel. (9) 19123897; fax (9) 19123967; f. 1973; population studies; 145 mems; Chair. Dr TAPANI VALKONEN; Sec. PIA MÄKELÄ.

Suomen Ympäristöoikeustieteen Seura/ Miljörättsliga Sällskapet i Finland (Finnish Society of Environmental Law): POB 1225, 00101 Helsinki; tel. (9) 27091890; fax (9) 4775004; e-mail erkki.hollo@helsinki.fi; f. 1980 to support and promote legal and administrative research of environmental problems, and to promote co-operation between researchers and authorities; 400 mems; Chair. E. J. HOLLO; Sec. M. KUOPPALA; publs *Ympäristöjuridiikka-Miljöjuridik* (Environmental Law), *Publications* (series, foreign summaries).

Taloushistoriallinen Yhdistys (Economic History Society): Dept of Economic and Social History, University of Helsinki; f. 1952; studies economic and social history; 55 mems; Chair. Dr RIITTA HJERPPE; Hon. Sec. MATTI LAKIO; publ. *Scandinavian Economic History Review* (in co-operation with other Scandinavian societies for the advancement of the study of economic history).

EDUCATION

Suomen Yliopistojen Rehtorien Neuvosto (Finnish Council of University Rectors): POB 3 (Fabianinkatu 33), 00014 University of Helsinki; tel. 191-22335; fax 191-22194; Chair. Dr PAAVO URONEN; Sec.-Gen. Dr T. MARKKANEN.

FINE AND PERFORMING ARTS

Suomen Musiikkitieteellinen Seura r.y./ Musikvetenskapliga Sällskapet i Finland r.f. (Finnish Musicological Society): PL 35 (Vironkatu 1), 00014 Helsingin Yliopisto; fax

(9) 1917955; e-mail taurula@cc.helsinki.fi; aims to encourage musicological research, develop international exchanges, and to function for the good of Finnish musical life by broadening knowledge of music and musical culture; *c.* 250 mems; Chair. Prof. EERO TARASTI; Sec.-Gen. TARJA TAURULA; publs *Musiikki, Acta Musicologica Fennica, Musiikkitieteen Kirjasto.*

Suomen Näytelmäkirjailjalitto (Finnish Dramatists' Society): Vironkatu 12B, 00170 Helsinki 17; f. 1921; Pres. ESKO SALERVO; Sec. PIRJO WESTMAN.

Suomen Säveltäjät r.y. (Society of Finnish Composers): Runeberginkatu 15A 11, 00100 Helsinki 10; tel. (9) 445589; fax (9) 440181; e-mail saveltajat@compose.pp.fi; f. 1945; 116 mems; Pres. MIKKO HEINIÖ; Sec. ANNU MIKKONEN.

Suomen Taideyhdistys (Fine Arts Society of Finland): Helsingin Taidehalli, Nervanderinkatu 3, 00100 Helsinki; tel. 45420611; fax 45420610; f. 1846; arranges exhibitions, presents awards and scholarships; 3,000 mems; Pres. JAAKKO ILONIEMI; Sec. TIMO VALJAKKA.

Suomen Taiteilijaseura/Konstnärsgillet i Finland (Artists' Association of Finland): Yrjönkatu 11, 00120 Helsinki; tel. (9) 607171; fax (9) 607561; f. 1864; mem. socs consist of the Painters' Union of Finland, the Sculptors' Union of Finland, the Association of Graphic Artists in Finland, the Finnish Association of Artists in Photography and the Federation of the Fine Arts Associations in Finland; promotes professional interests of artists and holds an annual exhibition; Chair. KARI JYLHÄ; Sec.-Gen. ESKO VESIKANSA; publs *Taide* (Art), *Taiteilijamatrikkeli* (Dictionary of Finnish Artists), *Taiteilija* (newsletter for mems).

Taidehistorian seura/Föreningen för konsthistoria r.y. (Society for Art History in Finland): Unioninkatu 34, 00014 University of Helsinki; f. 1974 to promote research in art history in Finland; 425 mems; Chair. PEKKA KORVENMAA; Sec. ELINA RÄSÄNEN; publ. *Taidehistoriallisia tutkimuksia/Konsthistoriska studier* (Studies in Art History).

Turun Soitannollinen Seura (Turku Music Society): Sibelius Museum, Piispankatu 17, Turku; f. 1790; 625 mems; Pres. ALARIK REPO; Sec. ILPO TOLVAS.

HISTORY, GEOGRAPHY AND ARCHAEOLOGY

Historian Ystäväin Liitto (Society of the Friends of History): Kaupinkatu 22 A 5, 33500 Tampere; f. 1926; 1,500 mems; Sec. M. LINNA; publ. *Historiallinen Aikakauskirja* (Finnish Historical Review, quarterly), *Historian Aitta, Historiallinen Kirjasto* (both irregular).

Suomen Historiallinen Seura (Finnish Historical Society): Arkadiankatu 16B 28, 00100 Helsinki 10; tel. (9) 440369; fax (9) 441468; e-mail shs@histseura.fi; f. 1875; 850 mems; Chair. Dr Prof. TOIVO NYGÅRD; Sec. RAUNO ENDÉN; publs *Historiallinen Arkisto* (Historical Archives), *Historiallisia Tutkimuksia* (Historical Researches), *Suomen historian lähteitä* (Sources of the History of Finland), *Käsikirjoja* (Handbooks), *Studia Historica* (Historical studies in German, French and English).

Suomen Kirkkohistoriallinen Seura (Finnish Society of Ecclesiastical History): Dept of Church History, POB 33 (Aleksanterinkatu 7), 00014 University of Helsinki; tel. (9) 19123040; fax (9) 19123033; e-mail hannu.mustakallio@helsinki.fi; f. 1891; 900 mems; Pres. Prof. S. HEININEN; Sec. Dr HANNU MUSTAKALLIO; publs *Vuosikirja-Årsskrift* (Yearbook), *Toimituksia-Handlingar* (research papers, 3 to 6 a year).

Suomen Maantieteellinen Seura/Geografiska Sällskapet i Finland (Geographical Society of Finland): C/o Dept of Geography, POB 4 (Hallituskatu 11), 00014 University of Helsinki; tel. 19122627; fax 19122641; f. 1888; 1,300 mems; library of *c.* 56,000 vols; Pres. H. VESAJOKI; Sec. L. HOUTSONEN; publs *Fennia* (2 a year), *Terra* (quarterly).

Suomen Muinaismuistoyhdistys/Finska Fornminnesföreningen (Finnish Antiquarian Society): POB 913, 00101 Helsinki 10; tel. 40501; f. 1870; 600 mems; Pres. TEPPO KORHONEN; Sec. MARIANNE SCHAUMAN-LÖNNQVIST; publs *Suomen Museo, Finskt Museum, Suomen Muinaismuistoyhdistyksen Aikakauskirja—Finska Fornminnesföreningens Tidskrift, Kansatieteellinen Arkisto, Iskos.*

Suomen Sukututkimusseura/Genealogiska Samfundet i Finland (Genealogical Society of Finland): Liisankatu 16A, 00170 Helsinki 1; tel. (9) 2781188; fax (9) 2781199; e-mail sukututkimusseura@genealogia.fi; f. 1917; 2,600 mems; library of 34,000 vols; Pres. JYRKI PAASKOSKI; Sec. PERTTI VUORINEN; publs *Vuosikirja—Årsskrift* (Yearbook), *Genos* (quarterly), *Julkaisuja—Skrifter* (monographs).

LANGUAGE AND LITERATURE

Finlands Svenska Författareförening (Society of Swedish Authors in Finland): Runebergsgatan 32 C 27, 00100 Helsinki; f. 1919; 190 mems; Pres. THOMAS WULFF (author); Vice-Pres MONIKA FAGERHOLM, NALLE VALTIALA (authors); Sec.-Gen. MERETE JENSEN.

Klassillis-filologinen yhdistys (Society for Classical Philology): Helsingin yliopisto, Klass. fil. laitos, PL 4 (Vuorikatu 3A), 00014 Helsinki; fax 191-22161; f. 1882; promotes the study of classical philology and classical antiquity in general; 134 mems; Pres. Prof. H. SOLIN; Sec. N. NYKOPP; publs *Arctos, Acta Philologica Fennica, Nova Series I* (1954–), *Supplementum I* (1968), *II* (1985).

Kotikielen Seura (Mother-Tongue Society): Castrenianum, PL 3, 00014 University of Helsinki; e-mail hanna.lappalainen@helsinki.fi; f. 1876; Finnish linguistics, especially dialectology, sociolinguistics, language planning; 680 mems; Pres. PIRKKO NUOLIJÄRVI; Sec. HANNA LAPPALAINEN; publ. *Virittäjä* (quarterly).

Suomalaisen Kirjallisuuden Seura (Finnish Literature Society): Hallituskatu 1, POB 259, 00171 Helsinki 17; tel. 131231; fax 13123220; f. 1831 to promote study of folklore, ethnology, literature and Finnish language; 3,400 mems; Pres. of Council Prof. ANNA-LEENA SIIKALA; Chair. Exec. Cttee Prof. PENTTI LEINO; Gen. Sec. URPO VENTO; see also under Libraries; publs *Studia Fennica: Ethnologica, Folkloristica, Linguistica* (yearly), *Suomi, Tietolipas, Toimituksia* (irregular).

Suomalais-Ugrilainen Seura (Finno-Ugrian Society): Mariankatu 7, POB 320, 00171 Helsinki; tel. 662149; fax 632501; e-mail riho.grunthal@helsinki.fi; f. 1883; Northern Eurasian linguistics and ethnography; 800 mems; Pres. Prof. Dr SEPPO SUHONEN; Sec. RIHO GRÜNTHAL; publs *Journal* (annually), *Mémoires* (2–5 a year), *Lexica Societatis F.U.* (irregular), *Travaux ethnographiques, Hilfsmittel* (irregular), *Finnisch-Ugrische Forschungen* (annually).

Suomen englanninopettajat r.y. (Association of Teachers of English in Finland): Rautatieläisenkatu 6A, 00520 Helsinki; tel. 145414; f. 1948; 2,900 mems; Pres. TUULA PENTTILÄ; Sec. AULI TALVI; publ. *Tempus* (8 a year).

Suomen Kirjailijaliitto (The Union of Finnish Writers): Runeberginkatu 32C, Helsinki; tel. (9) 445392; fax (9) 492278; e-mail suomen.kirjailijaliitto@cultnet.fi; f. 1897; allied to the Scandinavian Authors' Council and European Writers' Congress; 520 mems; Pres. JARKKO LAINE; Gen. Sec. PÄIVI LIEDES; publs *Suomen Runotar, Suomalaiset kertojat.*

Svenska litteratursällskapet i Finland (Swedish Literary Society in Finland): Riddareg. 5, 00170 Helsinki; tel. (9) 618777; fax (9) 632820; f. 1885; 1,100 mems; Pres. Prof. JOHAN WREDE; Sec. Prof. ANN-MARIE IVARS; see also under Libraries; publ. *Skrifter.*

Uusfilologinen Yhdistys (Modern Language Society): POB 4, 00014 University of Helsinki; f. 1887; 300 mems; Pres. Prof. OLLI VÄLIKANGAS; Hon. Sec. PEKKA KUUSISTO; Editorial Sec. PÄIVI PAHTA; publs *Mémoires* (irregular), *Neuphilologische Mitteilungen* (Bulletin, quarterly).

MEDICINE

Cancer Society of Finland: Liisankatu 21 B 9, 00170 Helsinki; Pres. RISTO JOHANSSON; Sec.-Gen. LIISA ELOVAINIO.

Finska Läkaresällskapet (Medical Society of Finland): POB 316, 00171 Helsinki; tel. 665576; fax 1356463; f. 1835; 1,000 mems; library of 35,000 vols; Pres. Prof. LEIF ANDERSON; Sec. Dr MARIANNE GRIPENBERG; publ. *Finska Läkaresällskapets Handlingar.*

Suomalainen Lääkäriseura Duodecim (Finnish Medical Society Duodecim): Kalevankatu 11A, 00100 Helsinki; tel. (9) 618851; fax (9) 61885200; e-mail seura@duodecim.fi; library Haartmaninkatu 4, 00290 Helsinki; f. 1881; 14,000 mems; library of 17,000 vols; Pres. JUSSI HUTTUNEN; Sec. JAN LINDGREN; publs *Duodecim* (24 a year), *Annals of Medicine*. (every 2 months)

Suomen Farmaseuttinen Yhdistys/Farmaceutiska Föreningen i Finland (Finnish Pharmaceutical Society): POB 56, 00014 University of Helsinki; tel. (9) 70859136; fax (9) 70859138; f. 1887; 290 mems; Pres. PIA VUORELA; Sec. SIRKKU SAARELA.

Suomen Hammaslääkäriseura (Finnish Dental Society): Bulevardi 30 B 5, 00120 Helsinki; tel. (9) 6803120; fax (9) 646263; f. 1892; 5,800 mems; Pres. Prof. MARIA MALMSTRÖM; Sec. Dr ULLA PAJARI; publ. *Finnish Dental Journal* (with Finnish Dental Association).

NATURAL SCIENCES

Biological Sciences

Kasvinsuojeluseura r.y. (Plant Protection Society): Agricultural Research Centre, 31600 Jokioinen; tel. (3) 41881; e-mail minna-maria.linna@mtt.fi; f. 1931; research on, and protection from, diseases, pests and weeds; arranges meetings and excursions, awards grants to researchers; 1,500 mems; Chair. RISTO TAHVONEN; Sec. MINNA-MARIA LINNA; publ. *Kasvinsuojelulehti.*

Societas Amicorum Naturae Ouluensis/Oulun Luonnonystäväin Yhdistys r.y.: Dept of Biology (Botany), University of Oulu, 90570 Oulu; tel. (8) 5531546; telex 32375; fax (8) 5531500; f. 1925; 436 mems; Pres. Prof. P. LAHDESMAKI; Sec. S. KONTUNEN-SOPPELA; publs *Aquilo, Ser. Botanica, Aquilo, Ser. Zoologica.*

Societas Biochemica, Biophysica et Microbiologica Fenniae (Biochemical, Biophysical and Microbiological Society of Finland): c/o Jarmo Juuti, Dept of Biosciences, Division of Plant Physiology, POB 56 (Viikinkaari 9), 00014 University of Helsinki; tel. (9) 70859440; fax (9) 70859552; f. 1945; 1,200 mems; Pres. Dr TUULA TEERI; Sec. Dr JARMO JUUTI.

Societas Biologica Fennica Vanamo/Suomen Biologian Seura Vanamo: POB 56, 00014 University of Helsinki; f. 1896; Pres. PERTTI UOTILA; Sec. KURT FAGERSTEDT; Exchange Librarian ILKKA TERÄS; publs *Atlas Florae Europaeae, Luonnon Tutkija* (The Naturalist, 5 a year).

Societas Entomologica Fennica/ Suomen Hyönteistieteellinen Seura (Entomological Society of Finland): P. Rautatiekatu 13, 00100 Helsinki 10; tel. 1917392; fax 19174443; f. 1935; library; Pres. Dr ANTTI PEKKARINEN; Sec. ILPO MANNERKOSKI; publ. *Entomologica Fennica* (quarterly).

Societas pro Fauna et Flora Fennica: Botanical Museum (R. Skytén), POB 47, 00014 University of Helsinki; tel. (9) 7084787; fax (9) 7084830; e-mail roland.skyten@helsinki.fi; f. 1821; discussion and research on all aspects of animals and plants in Finland; 940 mems; library of 44,000 vols; Pres. Prof. C.-A. HÆGGSTRÖM; Sec. R. SKYTEN; publ. *Memoranda Societatis pro Fauna et Flora Fennica* (quarterly).

Suomen Lintutieteellinen Yhdistys: (Finnish Ornithological Society); Helsingin yliopisto, PL 17 (P. Rautatiekatu 13), 00014 University of Helsinki; tel. 1917453; fax 1917443; f. 1924; Pres. Dr JARI KOUKI; Sec. JAAKKO JÄRVINEN; publ. *Ornis Fennica* (quarterly).

Physical Sciences

Geofysiikan Seura/Geofysiska Sällskapet (Geophysical Society of Finland): C/o Finnish Meteorological Institute, POB 503, 00101 Helsinki; tel. (9) 19293148; fax (9) 19293146; e-mail kirstijylha@fmi.fi; f. 1926; aims to promote geophysical research and provide links between researchers; 250 mems; Pres. RAINO HEINO; Sec. KIRSTI JYLHÄ; publ. *Geophysica* (2 a year).

Maanmittaustieteiden seura r.y. (Finnish Society of Surveying Sciences): POB 84, 00521 Helsinki; tel. (9) 1481900; fax (9) 1483580; f. 1926; 760 mems; Pres. MATTI VAHALA; Sec. JAANA JÄRVINEN; publ. *Surveying Science in Finland*.

Suomen Geologinen Seura (Geological Society of Finland): POB 96, 02151 Espoo; tel. 2055011; fax 2055012; f. 1886; 925 mems; Pres. KALEVI KORSMAN; Sec. I. MÄNTTÄRI; publs *Bulletin* (1 or 2 a year), *Geologi* (10 a year).

Suomen Kemian Seura/Kemiska Sällskapet i Finland (Asscn of Finnish Chemical Societies): Hietaniemenkatu 2, 00100 Helsinki; tel. (9) 4542040; fax (9) 408780; e-mail skks@kemia.pp.fi; f. 1970 to promote research in chemistry, chemical education, chemical industry; to organize the annual Finnish Chemical Congress; to act as a link between the three mem. societies, and to support and co-ordinate their activities; represents the mem. societies in common matters; 14 sections: wood and polymer chemistry, biotechnology, mass spectrometry, NMR spectroscopy, metal analysis, chromatography, chemometrics, explosives, optical spectroscopy, computational chemistry, catalysis, EURACHEM—Finland, synthetic chemistry, and NBC protection, rescue and safety; library of c. 800 vols; Pres. Dr SIRPA HERVE; publs *Kemia-Kemi, Acta Chemica Scandinavica*.

Constituent societies:

Suomalaisten Kemistien Seura (Finnish Chemical Society): Hietaniemenkatu 2, 00100 Helsinki; f. 1919; 3,480 mems; Pres. Dr TIMO HIRVI; Sec. HELEENA KARRUS.

Finska Kemistsamfundet/Suomen Kemistiseura: (Chemical Society of Finland): Hietaniemenkatu 2, 00100 Helsinki; f. 1891; 564 mems; Pres. OLLE TELEMAN; Sec. URBAN WIIK.

Kemiallisteknillinen Yhdistys (The Finnish Society of Chemical Engineers): Hietaniemenkatu 2, 00100 Helsinki; f. 1970; 816 mems; Pres. JAAKKO E. LAINE; Sec. JUHA VIRTANEN.

PHILOSOPHY AND PSYCHOLOGY

Suomen Filosofinen Yhdistys (Philosophical Society of Finland): Dept of Philosophy, POB 24 (Unioninkatu 40), 00014 University of Helsinki; tel. (9) 1917631; fax (9) 1917627; e-mail risto.vilkko@helsinki.fi; f. 1873; promotes the study of philosophy and related disciplines in Finland; 700 mems; Pres. Prof. ILKKA NIINILUOTO; Sec. RISTO VILKKO; publs *Acta Philosophica Fennica, Ajatus*.

Suomen Psykologinen Seura r.y. (Finnish Psychological Society): Liisankatu 16A, 00170 Helsinki; tel. (9) 2782122; f. 1952; 1,800 mems; small library; Pres. KLUUO ALHO; Sec. TAINA SCHAKIR; publs *Psykologia* (every 2 months), *Acta Psychologica Fennica* series A (irregular) and series B (annually).

RELIGION, SOCIOLOGY AND ANTHROPOLOGY

Suomalainen Teologinen Kirjallisuusseura (Finnish Theological Literature Society): PL 33 (Aleksanterinkatu 7), 00014 University of Helsinki; tel. 19122076; fax 19123033; 1,160 mems; Chair. Prof. EEVA MARTIKAINEN.

Suomen Antropologinen Seura/Antropologiska Sällskapet i Finland (Finnish Anthropological Society): Pl 322, 00171 Helsinki; tel. 19123094; fax 19123006; f. 1975 to promote co-operation between scholars from different fields of anthropology; organizes meetings, conferences etc; 500 mems; Pres. ANNA MARIA VILJANEN; Sec. KATJA UUSIHAKALA; publ. *Suomen Antropologi / Antropologi i Finland*.

Suomen Itämainen Seura (Finnish Oriental Society): c/o Dept of Asian and African Studies, POB 13 (Meritullink. 1B), 00014 University of Helsinki; fax (9) 19122094; f. 1917; 160 mems; Pres. Prof. ASKO PARPOLA; Sec. Prof. TAPANI HARVIAINEN; publ. *Studia Orientalia*.

TECHNOLOGY

Rakenteiden Mekaniikan Seura (Finnish Society for Structural Mechanics): Dept of Mechanical Engineering, Helsinki University of Technology, Otakaari 4, 02150 Espoo; tel. 4513498; fax 4513419; f. 1970 for promoting research and exchange of knowledge on engineering materials, structural mechanics and design; 222 individual mems, 10 collective mems; Chair. KAJ RISKA; Sec. MIKA REIVINEN; publ. *Rakenteiden Mekaniikka* (Journal of Structural Mechanics, quarterly).

Suomen Atomiteknillinen Seura/Atomtekniska Sällskapet i Finland r.y. (Finnish Nuclear Society): C/o VTT Energy, Nuclear Energy, POB 1604, 02044 VTT; tel. (9) 4561; fax (9) 4565000; f. 1966 to promote knowledge and development of nuclear technology in Finland, and exchange information on international level; 650 individual mems, 20 institutional mems; Chair. Dr SEPPO VUORI; Sec. VESA TANNER; publ. *ATS Ydintekniikka* (4 a year).

Svenska Tekniska Vetenskapsakademien i Finland (Swedish Academy of Engineering Sciences in Finland): Teknikvägen 12, 02150 Esbo; tel. (9) 455-4565; fax (9) 455-4626; f. 1921; to promote research in engineering sciences; 154 mems; Pres. Prof. JOHAN GULLICHSEN; Sec. PhD NIKLAS MEINANDER; publs *Forhandlingar* (Proceedings), *Meddelanden* (Reports).

Tekniikan Akateemisten Liitto TEK r.y. (The Finnish Association of Graduate Engineers TEK): Ratavartijankatu 2, 00520 Helsinki; tel. 229121; fax 22912944; f. 1896; serves as a link between engineers and architects, promotes technical sciences and industry, fosters Finnish economic life, coordinates a European education and training network UETP-EEE; 38,000 mems; Chair. MARKKU MARKKULA; publs *Tekniikan Akateemiset* (monthly), *Tekniikka ja Talous* (44 a year), *Talouselämä* (41 a year), *EEE Bulletin* (quarterly).

Tekniikan edistämissäätiö (Technological Foundation): Aleksanterinkatu 4, 00170 Helsinki 17; f. 1949 to provide yearly fellowships for the advancement of technology; Pres. HARRI HINTIKKA; Sec.-Gen. ONNI JUVA; Sec. TAPANI KOIVUMÄKI.

Teknillisten Tieteiden Akatemia/Akademin för Tekniska Vetenskaper r.y. (Finnish Academy of Technology): Tekniikantie 12, 02150 Espoo; tel. 455-4565; fax 455-4626; f. 1957 to promote technical-scientific research; 390 mems; Pres. JUHANI AHAVA; Sec. Gen. Prof. MARTTI M. KAILA; publs *Acta Polytechnica Scandinavica* (monographs), *High Technology from Finland* (every 2 years).

Tekniska Föreningen i Finland (The Engineering Society in Finland—TFiF): Banvaktsg. 2, 00520 Helsinki; tel. (9) 4767718; fax (9) 4767333; f. 1880; 2,650 mems; Pres. HENRIK JANSON; Man. Dir FREJ GUSTAFSSON; publ. *Forum för ekonomi och teknik*.

Research Institutes

AGRICULTURE, FISHERIES AND VETERINARY SCIENCE

Maatalouden tutkimuskeskus (Agricultural Research Centre): 31600 Jokioinen; tel. (3) 4188-1; fax (3) 4188-222; f. 1898; Dir-Gen. Prof. ESKO POUTIAINEN: consists of 5 research units, 7 regional research stations, 4 service units; publs *Agricultural and Food Science in Finland* (Journal), *Koetoiminta ja Käytäntö* (Experimental Work and Practice).

Research units:

Kasvintuotannon tutkimus (Plant Production Research): 31600 Jokioinen; Dir Prof. AARNE KURPPA.

Kotieläintuotannon tutkimus (Animal Production Research): 31600 Jokioinen; Dir Prof. ASKO MÄKI-TANILA.

Elintarvikkeiden tutkimus (Food Research): 31600 Jokioinen; Dir Prof. HANNU KORHONEN.

Luonnonvarojen tutkimus (Resource Management Research): 31600 Jokioinen; Dir Prof. SIRPA KURPPA.

Maatalousteknologian tutkimus (Agricultural Engineering Research): Vakolantie 55, 03400 Vihti; tel. (9) 2246211; fax (9) 2246210; Dir Dr MARKUS PYYKKÖNEN.

Metsäntutkimuslaitos (Finnish Forest Research Institute): Unioninkatu 40A, 00170 Helsinki; tel. (9) 857-051; fax (9) 625308; f. 1917; maintains 2 research centres and 10 stations; library of 43,000 vols; Dir-Gen. ELJAS POHTILA; publs *Acta Forestalia Fennica, Folia Forestalia, Silva Fennica*,

BIBLIOGRAPHY, LIBRARY SCIENCE AND MUSEOLOGY

Museovirasto (National Board of Antiquities): POB 913, 00101 Helsinki; tel. 40501; fax 4050300; f. 1884; directs and supervises Finland's administration of antiquities, researches its cultural heritage, preserves artefacts, buildings and sites of cultural and historical value; maintains the National Museum and other museums; with the Finnish Antiquarian Society, a library of 156,000 vols; Dir-Gen. HENRIK LILIUS.

ECONOMICS, LAW AND POLITICS

Elinkeinoelämän Tutkimuslaitos, ETLA (Research Institute of the Finnish Economy): Lönnrotinkatu 4B, 00120 Helsinki; tel. (9) 609900; fax (9) 601753; f. 1946; research in economics, business economics and social policy; library of 20,000 vols; Man. Dir Dr PENTTI VARTIA; publ. *The Finnish Economy*.

Liiketaloustieteellinen Tutkimuslaitos (Helsinki Research Institute for Business Administration): Meritullinkatu 3 D, 00170 Helsinki; tel. 171-600; fax 170-950.

Tilastokeskus (Statistics Finland): Työpajakatu 13, 00022 Statistics Finland; tel. (9) 17341; fax (9) 1734 2279; f. 1865; library: see Libraries; Dir TIMO RELANDER; chief publs *Suomen tilastollinen vuosikirja* (Statistical Yearbook of Finland), *Tietoaika* (Statistical Magazine, monthly), *Official Statistics of Finland* (28 series and indexes), *Tutkimuksia* (Studies, irregular).

EDUCATION

Suomen Kasvatustieteellinen Seura r.y./Samfundet för Pedagogisk Forskning (Finnish Society for Educational Research): Jyväskylän yliopisto/OKL, Seminaarinkatu 15, 40100 Jyväskylä; f. 1967; 245 mems; publ. *Kasvatus*.

MEDICINE

Minerva Foundation Institute for Medical Research: Tukholmankatu 2, 00250 Helsinki; tel. 4771001; fax 4771025; f. 1959; non-profit organization owned by Minerva Foundation; basic and experimental biomedical, genetic and nutritional research; library of 4,000 vols; Pres. Prof. JIM SCHRÖDER; Chief of Inst. Prof. FREJ FYHRQUIST.

NATURAL SCIENCES

Physical Sciences

Geodeettinen Laitos (Geodetic Institute): POB 15, 02431 Masala; tel. (9) 29550; fax (9) 29555208; e-mail fgi@fgi.fi; f. 1918; 45 mems; library of 40,000 vols; Dir Prof. Dr JUHANI KAKKURI; publs *Suomen Geodeettisen laitoksen julkaisuja* (Publications of the Finnish Geodetic Institute), *Suomen Geodeettisen laitoksen tiedonantoja* (Reports of the Finnish Geodetic Institute).

Geologian Tutkimuskeskus (Geological Survey of Finland): POB 96, 02151 Espoo; tel. 2055011; fax 2055012; f. 1885; library of 147,000 vols; Dir-Gen. Prof. RAIMO MATIKAINEN; Dir Prof. MARKKU MÄKELÄ; publs *Vuosikertomus* (Annual Report), *Geological Survey of Finland, Bulletin, Geological Maps, Tutkimusraportti* (Report of Investigation), *Special Paper*.

Ilmatieteen laitos (Finnish Meteorological Institute): POB 503, Vuorikatu 24, 00101 Helsinki; tel. (9) 19291; fax (9) 179581; f. 1838; library of 37,000 vols; 10,000 offprints; Dir-Gen. Dr ERKKI JATILA; publ. *Suomen meteorologinen vuosikirja* (Meteorological Yearbook of Finland, in Finnish and English).

Merentutkimuslaitos (Finnish Institute of Marine Research): POB 33, Lyypekinkuja 3A, 00931 Helsinki; tel. (9) 613941; fax (9) 61394494; f. 1918; physical, chemical and biological oceanography; library of 47,000 vols; Dir Prof. PENTTI MÄLKKI; publs *Boreal Environment Research, Meri* (The Sea), *Vuosikertomus* (Annual Report).

Säteilyturvakeskus (Radiation and Nuclear Safety Authority): POB 14, 00881 Helsinki; tel. (9) 759-881; fax (9) 7598-8500; f. 1958; government institute for radiation protection and nuclear safety, including inspection and research in the field; library of 30,000 vols; Dir-Gen. Prof. JUKKA LAAKSONEN; publs *STUK-A Reports* (irregular), *Alara* (quarterly).

RELIGION, SOCIOLOGY AND ANTHROPOLOGY

Donnerska institutet för religionshistorisk- och kulturhistoriskforskning – Steinerbiblioteket (Donner Institute for Research in Religious and Cultural History–The Steiner Memorial Library): POB 70, Gezeliusg. 2, 20501 Åbo; tel. (2) 2654315; fax (2) 2311290; e-mail donner. institute@abo.fi; f. 1959 to promote research in comparative religion; library of 65,000 vols; Dir Dr TORE AHLBÄCK; publs *Scripta Instituti Donneriani Aboensis*, *Contenta Religionum* (5 a year).

TECHNOLOGY

Oy Keskuslaboratorio - Centrallaboratorium Ab KCL (Finnish Pulp and Paper Research Institute): POB 70, 02151 Espoo; tel. (9) 43711; fax (9) 464305; f. 1916; technical and scientific research in the pulp, paper and board industry; library of 50,000 vols; Man. Dir ANTTI ARJAS; publ. *Annual Report*.

Valtion teknillinen tutkimuskeskus (Technical Research Centre of Finland): POB 1000, 02044 VTT; premises at: Vuorimihentie 5, Espoo; tel. (9) 4561; fax (9) 4567000; f. 1942; incl. 9 research institutes; applied research for industry and society, contract research and testing services for industry, research into electronics, information technology, automation, chemical technology, biotechnology and food research, energy, manufacturing technology, building technology, and communities and infrastructure; Dir-Gen. Prof. Dr MARKKU MANNERKOSKI; publs *Annual Report*, *VTT Symposium*.

Libraries and Archives

Espoo

Espoon kaupunginkirjasto – maakuntakirjasto (Espoo City Library–Regional Central Library): Vanha maantie 11, 02600 Espoo; tel. 517022; telex 124574; fax 513036; f. 1869; 1,000,000 vols; special collections: Uusimaa-Nylandica (provincial collection), Norwegian collection; Chief Librarian ULLA PACKALÉN.

Teknillisen Korkeakoulun Kirjasto (Library of Helsinki University of Technology): POB 7000, 02015 Helsinki University of Technology; located at: Otaniementie 9, 02150 Espoo; tel. 4514112; fax 4514132; e-mail infolib@hut.fi; f. 1849; the national resource library for technology; 1,000,000 vols, 2,000 periodicals on engineering and allied sciences, mathematics, environmental sciences, architecture, urban planning and industrial economy; publs *Study Programme of the University, Annual Bibliography, Research in Progress*; online databases: index to Finnish technical periodical articles, Masters' theses in engineering and architecture.

Helsinki

Eduskunnan Kirjasto (Library of Parliament): 00102 Helsinki; tel. 4321; fax 432-3495; e-mail library@eduskunta.fi; f. 1872; 590,000 vols on administration, law, political and social sciences; the library is open to the public; Chief Librarian TUULA H. LAAKSOVIRTA; publs *Eduskunnan kirjaston julkaisuja* (Library of Parliament Publications 1–5), *Valtion virallisjulkaisut* (Government publications in Finland 1961–), *Bibliographia iuridica fennica 1982–*.

Helsingin Kauppakorkeakoulun Kirjasto (Library of the Helsinki School of Economics and Business Administration): Runeberginkatu 22–24, 00100 Helsinki; tel. (9) 43131; fax (9) 43138539; e-mail library@hkkk.fi; f. 1911; 280,000 vols; several on-line and CD-ROM data bases; Librarian EEVA-LIISA LEHTONEN; publs HELECON International on CD-ROM, HELECON Nordic on CD-ROM (every 6 months).

Helsingin Kaupunginkirjasto (Helsinki City Library): Rautatieläisenkatu 8, 00520 Helsinki; tel. (9) 3108511; fax (9) 31085517; f. 1860; national central public library; 34 br. libraries; total 1,980,000 vols (1,384,000 Finnish, 200,000 Swedish, 175,000 foreign), 134,000 sound recordings, 1,200 newspapers; Dir MAIJA BERNDTSON; publ. *Helsingin kaupungin toimintakertomus* (Annual Report of Helsinki City Library).

Helsingin Yliopisto, Luonnontieteiden Kirjasto (University of Helsinki, Science Library): POB 26, 00014 University of Helsinki; tel. (9) 7084-4114; fax (9) 7084-4498; e-mail natura@helsinki.fi; f. 1899 as Library of the Scientific Societies; natural sciences, especially biosciences; 8,000 shelf metres; Librarian SISKO HYVÄMÄKI.

Helsingin Yliopiston Historiallis-Kielitieteellinen Kirjasto (Helsinki University History and Philology Library): POB 4 (University Street 3), 00014 University of Helsinki; e-mail hhkk_kir@helsinki.fi; f. 1904; *c.* 180,000 vols; Chief Librarian MARJA-LEENA STRANDSTRÖM.

Helsingin Yliopiston Kirjasto (Helsinki University Library): POB 15 (Unioninkatu 36), 00014 University of Helsinki; tel. (9) 19122709; fax (9) 19122719; e-mail hyk_palvelu@helsinki.fi; f. 1640 in Turku (Åbo), moved to Helsinki 1828; general library of the University of Helsinki, national library of Finland and central library of arts and humanities; comprehensive collection of books printed in Finland, large foreign collection; Nordenskiöld collection (cartography); approx. 3,000,000 vols, *c.* 1,700 shelf metres MSS, and 400 incunabula; Librarian Prof. ESKO HÄKLI; publs *Suomen kirjallisuus* (The Finnish National Bibliography), *Helsingin yliopiston kirjaston julkaisuja* (Publications of the Helsinki University Library), *Books from Finland* (quarterly).

Helsingin Yliopiston Kirjasto, Slaavilainen Kirjasto (Helsinki University Library, Slavonic Library): POB 37 (Neitsytpolku 1B), 00014 University of Helsinki; tel. 1913902; fax 1913975; the library held a legal deposit right to all publications printed in Russia from 1828 to 1917; now acquires available literature in arts and humanities in Slavonic languages; 400,000 vols; Librarian JARMO SUONSYRJÄ.

Helsingin Yliopiston Maatalouskirjasto (Helsinki University Agricultural Library): POB 27, 00014 University of Helsinki; tel. (9) 70851; fax (9) 7085011; e-mail maatalouskirjasto@helsinki.fi; f. 1930; national central library for agricultural, food and household sciences, depository library for FAO publications; 324,000 vols, 2,620 periodicals; Chief Librarian HELI MYLLYS; publ. *Helsingin yliopiston maatalouskirjaston julkaisuja* (Publications of Helsinki University Library of Agriculture).

Helsingin Yliopiston Metsäkirjasto (Helsinki University Library of Forestry): POB 24 (Unioninkatu 40B), 00014 University of Helsinki; tel. (9) 1917610; fax (9) 1917619; e-mail forest-lib@helsinki.fi; f. 1862 in Evo, Helsinki 1908; national forestry library; 222,500 vols, 1,200 periodicals; Chief Librarian ANNIKKI KARJALAINEN.

Helsingin Yliopiston Oikeustieteellisen Tiedekunnan Kirjasto (The Law Library of the University of Helsinki): POB 4 (Fabianinkatu 24A), 00014 University of Helsinki; tel.

(9) 19122033; fax (9) 19122174; e-mail hotki@otdk.helsinki.fi; f. 1910; 90,000 vols; Librarian MARJATTA SULEVO; the library is open to University teachers and students.

Helsingin Yliopiston Teologisen Tiedekunnan Kirjasto (Theology Library, University of Helsinki): POB 33 (Aleksanterinkatu 7), 00014 University of Helsinki; tel. (9) 1911; fax (9) 19123879; e-mail teol-kirjasto@helsinki.fi; f. 1902; 68,000 vols, 6,500 theses; Librarian LIISA RAJAMÄKI.

Helsingin Yliopiston Valtiotieteellisen Tiedekunnan Kirjasto (The Social Science Library, University of Helsinki): POB 18 (Unioninkatu 35), 00014 University of Helsinki; fax (9) 19122048; f. 1950; 90,000 vols; Chief Librarian MARJA-LIISA HARJU-KHADR.

Kansallisarkisto (National Archives): POB 258, 00171 Helsinki 17; f. 1869; library of 76,800 vols, 39,800 metres of documents, 174,000 cartographic items, 23,500 reels of reading copies, 109,600 microfiches; central office for public archives; controls seven Provincial Archives at Turku, Hämeenlinna, Mikkeli, Vaasa, Oulu, Jyväskylä and Joensuu; holds historical documents and archives of the Government, Supreme Court and other court records, and private papers of statesmen and politicians; the Provincial Archives contain documents relating to regional and local administration; Dir-Gen. PhDr KARI TARKIAINEN; publs series of historical documents and guides.

Has attached:

Helsingin Kaupunginarkisto (Helsinki City Archives): 00530 Helsinki 53, 2 linja 4 F; f. 1945; central archive repository for City Administration; Dir M. A. JUHANI LOMU.

Sota-arkisto (Military Archives): POB 223, 00171 Helsinki 17; f. 1918; central archive repository of the Defence Forces; Dir M. A. VELI-MATTI SYRJÖ.

Sibelius-Akatemian Kirjasto (Sibelius Academy Library): Töölönk 28, Helsinki; tel. (9) 4054539; fax (9) 4054542; e-mail ikoskimie@siba.fi; f. 1882; 65,000 scores, 23,000 records, 11,000 books; Librarian IRMELI KOSKIMIES.

Suomalaisen Kirjallisuuden Seuran Kirjasto (Library of the Finnish Literature Society): Hallituskatu 1, POB 259, 00171 Helsinki; tel. (9) 131231; fax (9) 13123220; e-mail sks-kirjasto@helsinki.fi; f. 1831; 230,000 vols on folklore, ethnology, cultural anthropology, Finnish literature, history and language; Librarian HENNI ILOMÄKI.

Has attached:

Suomalaisen Kirjallisuuden Seuran Kansanrunousarkisto (Folklore Archives of the Finnish Literature Society): Hallituskatu 1, POB 259, 00171 Helsinki; 3,500,000 documents, 15,000 hours of audiovisual material, 107,000 photographs; Archivist PEKKA LAAKSONEN.

Suomalaisen Kirjallisuuden Seuran Kirjallisuusarkisto (Literary Archives of the Finnish Literature Society): Hallituskatu 1, POB 259, 00171 Helsinki; fax 131 23268; 30,000 MSS, correspondence, recordings and photographs on Finnish literature, history and language; Archivist KAARINA LAMPENIUS SALA.

Svenska Handelshögskolans Bibliotek (Library of the Swedish School of Economics and Business Administration): Arkadiagatan 22, POB 479, 00101 Helsinki; tel. (9) 431331; fax (9) 43133425; e-mail biblioteket@shh.fi; f. 1909; 95,000 vols; Librarian MARIA SCHRÖDER.

Svenska litteratursällskapet i Finland Folkkultursarkivet (Folk Culture Archives): Sörnäs strandv. 25, 00500 Helsinki; tel. 7731077; fax 7731527; f. 1937; 1,800 collections, 300,000 photographs; publs *Meddelanden från Folkkultursarkivet, Folklivsstudier.*

Terveystieteiden keskuskirjasto (National Library of Health Sciences): Haartmaninkatu 4, 00290 Helsinki; tel. (9) 2410385; fax (9) 19126644; e-mail terkkoinfo@helsinki.fi; f. 1965; the national medical library; 100,000 vols, 1,300 periodicals; Dir (vacant); publs *Finmed* (bibliography of Finnish medical literature not included in international data bases), MEDIC data base (on Finnish publications), and access to int. data bases.

Tilastokirjasto (Library of Statistics): Statistics Finland, 00022 Tilastokeskus; premises at: Työpajakatu 13 (2nd Floor), Helsinki; tel. (9) 1734-2220; fax (9) 1734-2279; f. 1865; 265,000 vols, 6,400 periodicals, 26,000 microfiches, 500 electronic publications; Chief Librarian HELLEVI YRJÖLÄ.

Joensuu

Joensuun kaupunginkirjasto – Pohjois-Karjalan maakuntakirjasto (Joensuu City Library–Central Library of North Carelia): Box 114, Koskikatu 25, 80101 Joensuu; tel. (13) 2677111; fax (13) 2676210; e-mail maire.nuutinen@jns.fi; f. 1862; 450,000 vols; special collection of N. Carelia; Chief Librarian MAIRE NUUTINEN.

Jokioinen

Maatalouden Tutkimuskeskuksen Kirjasto (Agricultural Research Centre Library): 31600 Jokioinen; tel. (3) 41881; fax (3) 4188339; f. 1935; 80,000 vols, 600 periodicals; Information Specialist MAJ-LIS AALTONEN.

Jyväskylä

Jyväskylän Yliopiston Kirjasto (Jyväskylä University Library): POB 35 (Seminaarinkatu 15), 40351 Jyväskylä; tel. (14) 601211; fax (14) 603371; e-mail jyk@bibelot.jyu.fi; f. 1912; deposit library for Finnish prints and a/v material; national resource library for education, physical education and psychology; 1,350,000 vols; Dir KAI EKHOLM; publs *Jyväskylän yliopiston kirjaston julkaisuja* (Publications), *Jyväskylän yliopiston kirjaston katsauksia ja oppaita* (Guides and reviews), *Jyväskylän yliopiston kirjaston bibliografioita* (Bibliographies), *Suomalaisten äänitteiden luettelo* (Catalogue of Finnish recordings), *Kulttuuritutkimus* (cultural studies, quarterly).

Kuopio

Kuopion kaupunginkirjasto — Pohjois-Savon maakuntakirjasto (Kuopio City Library — Central Library of North Savo): Maaherrankatu 12, Box 157, 70101 Kuopio; tel. (17) 182111; fax (17) 182340; f. 1872; 700,000 vols; collections: letters of the author Minna Canth, Kuopio Lyceum collection, Iceland collection, North Saivo region collection; Chief Librarian HILKKA KOTILAINEN; publ. *Kuopion Kaupunginkirjaston toimintakertomus* (Annual Report).

Oulu

Oulun yliopiston kirjasto (Oulu University Library): POB 450, 90571 Oulu; tel. (8) 5531011; fax (8) 5569135; e-mail kirjasto@oulu.fi; f. 1959; 1,600,000 vols; depository library; European Documentation Centre; spec. collns incl. material concerning Northern and Arctic research; Chief Librarian PÄIVI KYTÖMÄKI; publs *Publications of Oulu University Library, Guide to the Library, Acta Universitatis Ouluensis*.

Pori

Porin kaupunginkirjasto – Satakunnan maakuntakirjasto (Pori City Library, Satakunta County Library): Gallen-Kallelankatu 12, POB 200, 28101 Pori; tel. (2) 895800; fax (2) 6332582; f. 1858; 623,000 vols; centre of Hungarian literature; Librarian MARJAANA KARJALAINEN.

Tampere

Tampereen kaupunginkirjasto – Pirkanmaan maakuntakirjasto (Tampere City Library–Pirkanmaa Regional Library): Pirkankatu 2, PL 152, 33101 Tampere; tel. (3) 2584111; fax (3) 2584100; e-mail tampereen.kaupunginkirjasto@tt.tampere.fi; f. 1861; 1,100,000 vols, 160 newspapers, 1,100 periodicals, 120,000 items of audiovisual material, 11,000 microfilms; special collections: Poland, Pirkanmaa region; Chief Librarian TUULA MARTIKAINEN.

Tampereen teknillisen korkeakoulun kirjasto (Tampere University of Technology Library): POB 537, 33101 Tampere; tel. (3) 3652111; fax (3) 3652907; f. 1956; 180,000 vols, 1,300 periodicals; Librarian ARJA-RIITTA HAARALA.

Tampereen yliopistollisen sairaalan lääketieteellinen kirjasto (Medical Library of Tampere University Hospital): Box 2000, 33521 Tampere; fax (3) 2474364; e-mail mervi.ahola@tays.fi; f. 1962; 50,000 vols, 900 periodicals; Librarian MERVI AHOLA.

Tampereen yliopiston kirjasto (Tampere University Library): POB 617, 33101 Tampere; tel. (3) 2156111; fax (3) 2157493; f. 1925 in Helsinki; 1,000,000 vols, 3,100 periodicals; deposit library for UN and EDC publs; Chief Librarian HANNELE SOINI; publ. *Annual Report*.

Turku

Åbo Akademis Bibliotek (Åbo Akademi University Library): 20500 Åbo, Domkyrkogatan 2–4; tel. (2) 21531; telex 62301; fax (2) 2154795; f. 1918; general library; 1,600,000 vols (excluding pamphlets and MSS); Chief Librarian SIV STORÅ; publ. *Skrifter utgivna av Åbo Akademis bibliotek*.

Turun Kauppakorkeakoulun Kirjasto (Library of the Turku School of Economics): 20500 Turku, Rehtorinpellonkatu 3; tel. (2) 338311; fax (2) 2503131; f. 1950; 100,000 vols; Librarian PENTTI RAUTIAINEN; various publications.

Turun Yliopiston Kirjasto (Turku University Library): 20500 Turku; tel. (2) 3336177; telex 62123; fax (2) 3335050; f. 1922; 1,842,000 vols; large collection of old Finnish literature; Librarian MARJA ENGMAN; publ. *Annales Universitatis Turkuensis*.

Museums and Art Galleries

Helsinki

Finnish National Gallery: Kaivokatu 2, 00100 Helsinki; tel (9) 173361; f. 1887 as the Ateneum, re-organized in 1990; comprises Museum of Finnish Art (Ateneum), Museum of Contemporary Art, Museum of Foreign Art, Central Art Archives; library of 15,000 vols, 80 periodicals, 20,000 catalogues; Dir-Gen. MARJA-LIISA RÖNKKÖ; Dir, Museum of Finnish Art SOILI SINISALO; Dir, Museum of Contemporary Art TUULA ARKIO; Dir, Central Art Archives ULLA VIHANTA; publ. *The Art Museum of the Ateneum Bulletin*.

Helsinki City Museum: Sofiankatu 4, 00170 Helsinki; tel. 1691; fax 667665; f. 1911; cultural history museum; main exhibition on the history of Helsinki; special exhibitions to highlight various features of the city's past; collection of 200,000 objects; documentation and inventory pertaining to different eras; Helsinki landscape paintings and graphics; library of 15,000 vols; photo archive of 650,000 photos from 1860s to the present; Dir LEENA ARKIO-LAINE; publs *Narinkka, Memoria*, Guide books.

Luonnontieteellinen Keskusmuseo/Naturhistoriska Centralmuseet (Finnish Museum of Natural History): P. Rautatiekatu 13, POB 17, 00014 University of Helsinki; tel. (9) 17484; fax (9) 17488; Dir. J. LOKKI.

Constituent museums:

Eläinmuseo/Zoologiska Museet (Zoological Museum): P. Rautatiekatu 13, POB 17, 00014 University of Helsinki; tel. (9) 17430; fax (9) 17443; Dir O. BISTRÖM.

Geologian Museo/Geologiska Museet (Geological Museum): Snellmaninkatu 3, POB 11, 00014 University of Helsinki; tel. (9) 123424; fax (9) 123466; Dir M. LEHTINEN.

Kasvimuseo/Botaniska Museet (Botanical Museum): Unioninkatu 44, POB 7, 00014 University of Helsinki; tel. (9) 18620; fax (9) 18656; Dir P. UOTILA.

Mannerheim-museum: Kalliolinnantie 14, 00140 Helsinki; tel. (9) 635443; fax (9) 636736; e-mail mannerheim@museo.pp.fi; f. 1951; Marshal Mannerheim's home as it was in the 1930s; Curator VERA VON FERSEN.

Suomen kansallismuseo (National Museum of Finland): Mannerheimintie 34, 00100 Helsinki; tel. 40501; fax 4050400; f. 1893; history, ethnography, numismatics; open-air museum at Seurasaari; Cygnaeus Gallery at Kaivopuisto, and several historical buildings throughout Finland; Dir RITVA WÄRE.

Taideteollisuusmuseo Konstindustrimuseet (Museum of Applied Arts): Laivurinkatu 3, 00150 Helsinki; tel. 6220540; fax 626733; f. 1873; exhibits of industrial design and handicrafts; library of 10,000 vols; Dir JARNO PELTONEN.

Oulu

Pohjois-Pohjanmaan Museo: PL 17, 90101 Oulu; f. 1896; tel. (8) 55847160; fax (8) 3110375; specializes in historical-ethnological research on Ostrobothnia; Dir ILSE JUNTIKKA.

Pori

Satakunnan Museo: Pori; f. 1888; 72,000 archaeological and historical exhibits and 200,000 photographs relating to the history of the province of Satakunta; 13,000 vols in reference library and 8,500 old books; Dir LEENA SAMMALLAHTI.

Tampere

Sara Hildénin Taidemuseo (Sara Hildén Art Museum): Särkänniemi, 33230 Tampere; tel. (3) 2143134; fax (3) 2229971; e-mail sara .hilden@tampere.fi; f. 1979; exhibition centre for the works of the Sara Hildén Foundation collection (Foundation f. 1962 when Sara Hildén donated all her art works to it); modern art, with emphasis on Finnish and foreign art of the 1960s and 1970s; library of 9,000 vols; Dir TIMO VUORIKOSKI.

Tampereen museot (Tampere Museums): POB 87, 33211 Tampere.

Include:

Tampereen Teknillinen Museo (Tampere Technical Museum): Lapintie 1, POB 87, 33211 Tampere; f. 1958; technical history of Finland; reference library of 2,000 vols, notably works on early aviation and watch-making; Dir TOIMI JAATINEN.

Tampereen Kaupunginmuseo (Tampere City Museum): Lapintie 1, POB 87, 33211 Tampere; f. 1970; history of Tampere; reference library of 10,000 vols; Dir TOIMI JAATINEN.

Tampereen Luonnontieteellinen Museo (Tampere Natural History Museum): Hämeenpuisto 20, 33210 Tampere; f. 1961; flora and fauna of northern Satakunta and northern Häme provinces; nature conservation service; Dir TOIMI JAATINEN.

Hämeen Museo (Häme Museum): Näsilinna, 33210 Tampere; f. 1904; prehistory and folk art of the cultural district of Tampere and the old Häme province; Dir TOIMI JAATINEN.

Amurin Työläismuseokortteli (Amuri Museum of Workers' Housing): Makasiininkatu 12, 33210 Tampere; f. 1974; the development of workers' housing 1880–1970, with authentic buildings; Dir TOIMI JAATINEN.

Turku

Sibeliusmuseum (Musikvetenskapliga Institutionen vid Åbo Akademi) (Sibelius Museum at Åbo Akademi): Biskopsgatan 17, Turku; f. 1926; contains archives and library relating to Sibelius and to Finnish music, and possesses a collection of musical instruments; Curator M. A. ILPO TOLVAS; publs *Acta Musica, Källskrifter och studier utg. av Musikvetenskapliga institutionen vid Åbo Akademi.*

Turun maakuntamuseo (Turku Provincial Museum): POB 286, 20101 Turku; tel. (2) 2620111; fax (2) 2620444; f. 1881; consists of the Castle of Turku with the collections of Turku Historical Museum, Luostarinmäki Handicrafts Museum, Pharmacy Museum and the Qwensel House, Kylämäki Village of living history, Turku Biological Museum, Turku Maritime Museum and Astronomical Collection; furniture, paintings, costumes, textiles, porcelain, glass, silver, copper, fire-arms, uniforms, weapons, coins and medals, etc.; Dir JUHANI KOSTET; publs *Aboa* (yearbook), research reports, museum guides.

Turun Taidemuseo (Turku Art Museum): Puolalanpuisto, 20100 Turku 10; tel. (2) 2747570; fax (2) 2747599; e-mail turuntaidemuseo@pp.weppi.fi; f. 1891; paintings, sculpture, prints and drawings, mainly of Finnish and Scandinavian art from early 19th century to present; Pres. ROGER BROO; Dir BERNDT ARELL.

Vasikka-aho

Väinö Tuomaalan Museosäätiö: Väinöntalo-Evijärvi, 62540 Vasikka-aho; f. 1960; exhibits illustrate the rural life of the Järviseutu district; library of 2,500 vols; Pres. JUHANI TUOMAALA; Sec. JUOKO TUOMAALA; publs *Järviseudun Joulu, Evijärven Väinöntalo, Runo Soinin kirkosta, Pietersaaren ylämaalaisten käräjäjutut vuosilta 1543–1600, Erkki Lahti, pohjalainen kuvanveistäjä 1816–58, Kotiseututyön opas.*

Universities

ÅBO AKADEMI
(Finland-Swedish University of Åbo)

Domkyrkotorget 3, 20500 Åbo

Telephone: (2) 21531
Fax: (2) 2517553

Founded 1918
Language of instruction: Swedish
State control
Academic year: September to May

Chancellor: BERTIL ROSLIN
Rector: GUSTAV BJÖRKSTRAND
Vice-Rectors: OLLE ANCKAR, SVEN-ERIK HANSÉN
Administrative Director: ROGER BROO
Chief Librarian: SIV STORÅ

Number of teachers: 345, including 71 professors

Number of students: 6,534

Publications: *Årsberättelse* (Annual Review), *Acta Academiae Aboensis*, *Åbo Academy Press*.

DEANS

Faculty of Arts: Prof. E. ANDERSSON
Faculty of Mathematics and Natural Sciences: Prof. J. MATTINEN
Faculty of Economics and Social Sciences: Prof. P. WETTERSTEIN
Faculty of Chemical Engineering: Prof. H. SAXÉN
Faculty of Theology: Prof. I. DAHLBACKA
Faculty of Education: Prof. H. ANDERSSON
Faculty of Social and Caring Sciences: Prof. KAJ BJÖRKQVIST

PROFESSORS

Faculty of Arts:

ANDERSSON, E., Swedish Language
ENGMAN, M., History
GENRUP, K., Scandinavian Ethnology and Folklore
HÄKKINEN, K., Finnish Language and Literature
HERTZBERG, L. H., Philosophy
HOLM, N. G., Comparative Religion
JUNGAR, S. H., Scandinavian History
KORKMAN, M., Psychology
LINDBERG, B., Art History
LINDMAN, R., Psychology
LÖNNQVIST, B., Russian Language and Literature
MOISALA, P., Musicology
NEUENDORFF, D., German Language
SELL, R., English Language and Literature
SVANE, B., French Language
ZILLIACUS, C. R., Literature

Faculty of Mathematical and Natural Sciences:

BACK, R.-J., Computer Science
EHLERS, C. W., Geology and Mineralogy
HÖGNÄS, N. G., Mathematics
JOHNSON, M., Biochemistry and Pharmaceutical Chemistry
KURKIJÄRVI, J., Theoretical Physics
LEPPÄKOSKI, E., Ecotoxicology and Environmental Toxicology
MATTINEN, J. T., Organic Chemistry
PANULA, P., Biology
ROSENHOLM, J. B., Physical Chemistry
SLOTTE, J. P., Biochemistry
STAFFANS, O., Mathematics
STUBB, H., Experimental Physics
TÖRN, A., Computer Science

Faculty of Economics and Social Sciences:

ANCKAR, D. B. B., Political Science
ANCKAR, O., Economics
BÄCKMAN, G. M., Social Policy
CARLSSON, C., Management Science
GINMAN, M., Library and Information Science
HELANDER, V., Public Administration
HONKA, H., Commercial Law
KARVONEN, L., Political Science
KOVALAINEN, A. K., Sociology
NORDBERG, L. B., Statistics and Econometrics
ÖSTERMARK, R., Accounting
SCHEININ, M., Constitutional and International Law
SILIUS, H., Women's Studies
WETTERSTEIN, L. P. L., Civil Law and Jurisprudence
WILLNER, J., Economics

Faculty of Chemical Engineering:

EKLUND, D., Paper Chemistry and Technology
HOLMBOM, B., Forest Products Chemistry
HUPA, M., Inorganic Chemistry
IVASKA, A., Analytical Chemistry
LEWENSTAM, A., Sensor Technology
LINDFORS, L.-E., Chemical Technology
LÖNNBERG, K. B., Pulping Technology
SALMI, T., Chemical Technology
STENLUND, B., Polymer Technology
WALLER, K. V. T., Automatic Control
WESTERLUND, K. T., Chemical Engineering

WILÉN, C.-E., Polymer Technology

Faculty of Theology:

DAHLBACKA, I., Church History
HANSSON, K.-J., Practical Theology
ILLMAN, K.-J., Old Testament Exegesis and Jewish Studies
KURTÉN, T., Systematic Theology
KVIST, H.-O., Systematic Theology
SANDELIN, K.-G., New Testament Exegesis

Faculty of Education:

ANDERSSON, L. P. H., Education
HANSÉN, S.-E., Education, Teacher-Training
LAHTINEN U., Special Education
WENESTAM, C.-G., Education

Faculty of Social and Caring Sciences:

BJÖRKQVIST, K., Psychology

ATTACHED INSTITUTES

Computing Centre: Dir S.-G. LINDQVIST.

National PET Centre: Dir S.-E. HESELIUS.

Language Centre: Dir H. NORDSTRÖM.

Centres for Continuing Education: Dirs M. VAINIO, C. ROSENGREN.

Institute of Parasitology: Dir G. BYLUND.

Institute for Advanced Management Systems Research: Dir C. CARLSSON.

Institute for Social Research concerning Swedish Finland (Vasa): Dir F. FINNÄS.

Institute for Human Rights: Dir M. SUKSI.

Institute of Local Life Studies: Dir C.-E. KNIIVILÄ.

Institute of Women's Studies: Dir H. SILIUS.

Centre for Biotechnology: Dir M. SKURNIK.

Combustion Chemistry Research Group: Dir M. HUPA.

Institute of Medieval Studies: Dir Å. RINGBOM.

British Studies Centre: Dir R. SELL.

Institute of Comparative Nordic Politics and Administration: Dir K. STÅHLBERG.

Institute of Maritime and Commercial Law: Dir H. HONKA.

Institute of Ecumenics and Social Ethics: Dir H.-O. KVIST.

Institutum Judaicum Aboense: Dir K.-J. ILLMAN.

Donner Institute for Research in Religious and Cultural History: Dir T. AHLBÄCK.

South-East Asian Studies Centre: Dir K. WIKSTRÖM.

Turku Centre for Computer Science: Dir R. BACK.

HELSINGIN YLIOPISTO/ HELSINGFORS UNIVERSITET

(University of Helsinki)

POB 33 (Yliopistonkatu 4), 00014 Helsingin Yliopisto
Telephone: (9) 1911
Telex: 124690
Fax: (9) 19123008
E-mail: tiedotus@helsinki.fi

Founded 1640 Turku (Åbo), 1828 Helsinki
Languages of instruction: Finnish and Swedish
State control
Academic year: September to May (two terms)

Chancellor: Prof. R. V. A. IHAMUOTILA
Rector: Prof. K. O. RAIVIO
Vice-Rectors: Prof. T. K. J. WILHELMSSON, Prof. I. M. O. NIINILUOTO, Assoc. Prof. R. T. SOLLAMO
Director of Administration: S. S. MERTANO
Librarian: Prof. E. A. HÄKLI

Number of teachers: 1,712
Number of students: 33,419

DEANS

Faculty of Theology: Prof. M. K. J. HEIKKILÄ
Faculty of Law: Prof. O. I. MÄENPÄÄ
Faculty of Medicine: Assoc. Prof. M. J. TIKKANEN
Faculty of Arts: Prof. F. G. KARLSSON
Faculty of Science: Prof. M. E. KOSONEN
Faculty of Education: Prof. J. J. HAUTAMÄKI
Faculty of Social Sciences: Prof. H. O. NIEMI
Faculty of Agriculture and Forestry: Prof. K. J. A. VON WEISSENBERG
Faculty of Veterinary Medicine: Prof. H. SALONIEMI

PROFESSORS

Faculty of Theology:

HEIKKILÄ, M. K. J., Practical Theology
HEININEN, S. K. M., General Church History
HELANDER, E. M., Church Sociology
KNUUTTILA, S. J. I., Theological Ethics and Philosophy of Religion
MANNERMAA, T. S., Ecumenics
MARTIKAINEN, E., Modern Theology
PENTIKÄINEN, J. Y., Study of Religions
RUOKANEN, M. M., Doctrinal Theology
RÄISÄNEN, H. M., New Testament Exegetics
SEPPO, J. V., Finnish and Scandinavian Church History
VEIJOLA, T. K., Old Testament Exegetics

Faculty of Law:

ANDERSSON, E. W., Public Law
AUREJÄRVI, E. I., Civil Law
FRÄNDE, D. G., Criminal Law and Judicial Procedure
HAVANSI, E. E. T., Judicial Procedure
HIDÉN, M. J. V., Constitutional and International Law
HOLLO, E. J., Environmental Law
JOUTSAMO, K. J., European Law
KEKKONEN, J. T., Judicial History and Roman Law
KLAMI, H. T., General Law and Private International Law
KOSKENNIEMI, M. A., International Law
KOSKINEN, P. T., Criminal Law
KOULU, R., Insolvency Law
LAHTI, R. O. K., Criminal Law
LAPPALAINEN, J. A., Judicial Procedure
MAJAMAA, V. V., Environmental Law
MÄENPÄÄ, O. I., Administrative Law
NOUSIAINEN, K. I., Women's Law
RISSANEN, K. K., Commercial Law
TEPORA, J. K., Civil Law
TIITINEN, K.-P., Labour Law
TIKKA, K. S., Financial Law
TUORI, K. H., Administrative Law
UUSITALO, P. A., Legal Sociology
WILHELMSSON, T. K. J., Private and Commercial Law

Faculty of Medicine:

AHONEN, P. J., Surgery
ALITALO, K. K., Cancer Biology
ALMQVIST, S. F., Child Psychiatry
ANDERSSON, L. C. L., Pathological Anatomy
BROMMELS, M. H., Health Care Administration
ERIKSSON, M. K. E. M., Nursing
FYHRQVIST, F. Y., Internal Medicine
HALTIA, M. J. J., Neuropathology
HERNESNIEMI, J. A., Neurosurgery
HÄYRY, P. J., Transplantation Surgery and Immunology
IIVANAINEN, M. V., Child Neurology
JALKANEN, S. T., Immunology
JOENSUU, H. T., Radiotherapy and Oncology
JÄNNE, O. A., Physiology
KARMA, P. H., Otorhinolaryngology
KEKKI, P. V., General Practice and Primary Health Care
KESKI-OJA, J. K., Cell Biology
KIVILAAKSO, E. O., Surgery
KLOCKARS, L. G. M., General Practice
KLOCKARS, M. L. G., General Practice
KONTULA, K. K., Molecular Medicine
KÖNÖNEN, M. H. O., Stomatognatic Physiology and Prosthetic Dentistry
LAATIKAINEN, L. T., Ophthalmology
LAITINEN, L. A. I., Tuberculosis and Pulmonary Medicine
MATTILA, S. P., Surgery
MEURMAN, J. H., Dentistry
MURTOMAA, H. T., Oral Public Health
NEUVONEN, P. J., Clinical Pharmacology
NIEMINEN, M. S., Cardiology
PALO, J. H. I., Neurology
PALOTIE, L. P. M., Medical Genetics
PENTTILÄ, M. A., Forensic Medicine
PERHEENTUPA, J. P., Paediatrics
RAIVIO, K. O., Perinatal Medicine
RANKI, P. A., Dermatology and Venereology
RANNIKKO, S. A. S., Urology
RIMÓN, H. R., Psychiatry
ROSENBERG, P. H., Anaesthesiology
SAKSELA, E. J., Pathological Anatomy
SALASPURO, M. P. J., Alcohol Diseases
SANTAVIRTA, S. S., Orthopaedics and Traumatology
SEPPÄLÄ, M. T., Obstetrics and Gynaecology
SOVIJÄRVI, A. R. A., Clinical Physiology
STANDERTSKJÖLD-NORDENSTAM, C. G. M., Diagnostic Radiology
TASKINEN, M.-R., Internal Medicine
THESLEFF, I. P. N., Pedodontics and Orthodontics
TILVIS, R. S., Geriatrics
VAARA, M. S., Bacteriology
VAHERI, A. I., Virology
VAPAATALO, H. I., Pharmacology and Toxicology
VIRKKUNEN, M. E., Forensic Psychiatry
VIRTANEN, I. T., Anatomy
WIKSTRÖM, M. K. F., Medical Chemistry
YKI-JÄRVINEN, H., Internal Medicine
YLIKORKALA, R. O., Obstetrics and Gynaecology
ÅKERBLOM, H. K., Paediatrics

Faculty of Arts:

CARLSON, L., Language Theory and Translation
HAAPALA, A. K., Aesthetics
HAKULINEN, A. T., Finnish Language
HARVIAINEN, J. M. T., Semitic Languages
HURSKAINEN, A. J., African Languages and Cultures
IIVONEN, A. K., Phonetics
IVARS, A.-N., Scandinavian Languages
JANHUNEN, J.-A., East Asian Languages and Culture
KAIMIO, M., Greek Language and Literature
KARLSSON, F. G., General Linguistics
KAUKIAINEN, Y. M. A., History
KELTIKANGAS-JÄRVINEN, A. L., Applied Psychology
KIVINIEMI, E. O., Finnish Language
KLINGE, M., History
KORHONEN, J. A., German Philology
KOSKENNIEMI, K. M., Computer Linguistics
KOURI, E. I., General History
LEHTONEN, J. U. E., Finno-Ugrian Ethnology
LEINO, P. A., Finnish Language
LINDSTEDT, J. S., Slavonic Philology
MAZZARELLA, S. M., Scandinavian Literature
MUSTAJOKI, A. S., Russian Language and Literature
NENOLA, A. A., Women's Studies
NEVALAINEN, T. T. A., English Philology
NIINILUOTO, I. M. O., Theoretical Philosophy
NIKULA, R. K., Art History
NÄÄTÄNEN, R. K., General Psychology
PALVA, H. V. K., Arabic Language
PARPOLA, A. H. S., Indology
PARPOLA, S. K. A., Assyriology
PÖRN, I. G., Philosophy
RAUD, R., Japanese Languages and Culture
RIIHO, T. T., Iberian Languages and Romanian
RIIKONEN, H. K., General Literature
RISSANEN, M. J., English Philology
SAARI, M. H., Scandinavian Languages

SAARILUOMA, P., Cognate Science
SALOMIES, O. I., Latin Language and Roman Literature
SARMELA, M. E., Cultural Anthropology
SIIKALA, A. A.-L., Folklore
SIIRIÄINEN, A. P., Archaeology
SOLIN, H. L. A., Latin Philology
SUHONEN, S. T., Baltic-Finnic Languages
SUMMALA, K. H. I., Psychology
TARASTI, E. A. P., Musicology
VIIKARI, A. I., Finnish Literature
VIRSU, V. V. E., Neuropsychology
YLIKANGAS, H. E., Finnish and Scandinavian History

Faculty of Science:

AHTEE, L. M., Pharmacology
ANTTILA, A. J., Physics
ARJAS, E., Biometry
CHAICHIAN, M., High Energy Physics
ERONEN, M. J., Geology and Palaeontology
FORTELIUS, H. L. M., Ecological Palaeontology
GAHMBERG, C.-G., Biochemistry
HAAPALA, I. J., Geology and Mineralogy
HAEGSTRÖM, C.-A., Botany
HALONEN, L. O., Physical Chemistry
HANSKI, I. A., Morphology and Ecology
HASE, T. A., Organic Chemistry
HILTUNEN, R. V. K., Pharmacognosy
HOYER, P. G., Elementary Particle Physics
ILLMAN, S. A., Mathematics
JAAKKOLA, T. V. A., Radiochemistry
KAILA, K. K., Physiological Zoology
KAIRESALO, T. A., Freshwater Ecology
KAJANTIE, K. O., Theoretical Physics
KEINONEN, J., Applied Physics
KOPONEN, T. J., Botany
KORHONEN, T. K., General Microbiology
KOSKINEN, H. E. J., Space Physics
KOSONEN, M. E., Planning Geography
KULMALA, M. T., Environmental Physics and Chemistry
KUPIAINEN, A. J., Mathematics
LESKELÄ, M. A., Inorganic Chemistry
LUMME, K. A., Astronomy
LUUKKALA, M. V., Physics
MANNILA, H. O., Computer Science
MARTIO, O. T., Mathematics
MARVOLA, M. L. A., Biopharmacy
MATTILA, V. A. K., Astronomy
MÄKELÄINEN, T. O. T., Applied Mathematics
NIEMI, A. A., Ecology
PALVA, E. T., Genetics
PYYKKÖ, V. P., Chemistry
RAUVALA, H. M. E., Molecular and Cell Biology
REUTER, T. E., Zoology
RICKMAN, S. U., Mathematics
RIEKKOLA, M.-L., Analytical Chemistry
RIKKINEN, K. V., Geography
RISKA, D.-O. W., Physics
SIIVOLA, A. T., Physics
SIMOLA, L. K., Botany
SUNDHOLM, F., Polymer Chemistry
TASKINEN, J. A. A., Pharmaceutical Chemistry
TIENARI, M. J., Computer Science
TUKIA, P. P., Mathematics
UKKONEN, E. J., Computer Science
VÄISÄLÄ, J. I., Mathematics
VÄLIAHO, H. S., Applied Mathematics
YLIRUUSI, J. K., Pharmaceutical Technology

Faculty of Education:

HAUTAMÄKI, J. J., Special Pedagogics
KANSANEN, P. J., Pedagogics
KONTIAINEN, S. A., Adult Education
LEINO, A.-L., Pedagogics
NIEMI, H. M., Pedagogics
RAUSTE-VON WRIGHT, M.-L., Pedagogical Psychology
SUOJANEN, U. T., Textile, Clothing and Craft Design
UUSIKYLÄ, K. T., Pedagogics

Faculty of Social Sciences:

AIRAKSINEN, T., Practical Philosophy
ALAPURO, R. S., Sociology
COWEN, M. P., Development Studies
ERÄSAARI, R. O., Social Policy
HEISKANEN, I. J., Political Science
HELKAMA, K. E., Social Psychology
HENTILÄ, S. J., Political History
HONKAPOHJA, S. M. S., Economics
JUSSILA, O. T., Political History
KANNIAINEN, V. L., Economics
KARISTO, A. O., Social Policy
KIVIKURU, U., Journalism
KOSKELA, E. A., Economics
MARTIKAINEN, T. T., Political Science
MUSTONEN, S. J., Statistics
NIEMI, H. O., Statistics
ROOS, J. P., Social Policy
SUNDBERG, J. H., Political Science
TUOMELA, R. H., Practical Philosophy
VALKONEN, Y. T., Sociology
VARTIA, Y. O., Economics
VÄYRYNEN, R. V. A., Political Science
ÅBERG, L. E. G., Communication

Faculty of Agriculture and Forestry:

AHLSTRÖM, A. G., Nutrition
ELORANTA, P V., Limnology
FRIED, J. S., Geoinformatics
HAARLAA, R. H. T., Forest Technology
HARI, P. K. J., Forest Ecology
HARTIKAINEN, H. H., Soil and Environment Chemistry
HATAKKA, A., Environmental Biotechnology
HELENIUS, J. P., Agroecology
HELIÖVAARA, K. T., Forest Zoology
HOKKANEN, H. M. T., Agricultural Zoology
HYVÖNEN, L. E. T., Food Technology
HYVÖNEN, S. M., Marketing
JAAKKOLA, A. O., Agricultural Chemistry and Physics
JUSLIN, H. J., Forest Products Marketing
KAUPPI, P. E., Environmental Protection
KELTIKANGAS, M., Business Economics of Forestry
KOSKELA, M. O., Food Economics
KOSKINEN, E., Animal Physiology
KUULUVAINEN, J. T. M., Social Economics of Forestry
LEHTONEN, H. V. T., Fish Biology and Science
LUUKKANEN, M. O., Silviculture in Developing Countries
MIKKONEN, E. U. A., Logging and Utilization of Forest Products
OJALA, M. J., Animal Breeding
PEHKONEN, A. I., Agricultural Engineering
PEHU, E. P., Plant Breeding
PIIRONEN, V. I., Food Chemistry
POSO, S. J., Forest Mensuration and Management
PUOLANNE, T. E. J., Meat Technology
PUTTONEN, P. K., Silviculture
PÄIVÄNEN, E. J., Peatland Forestry
SALKINOSA-SALONEN, M. S., Microbiology
SALOVAARA, H. O., Cereal Technology
SYRJÄLÄ-QVIST, L., Animal Husbandry
TIGERSTEDT, P. M. A., Plant Breeding
WEISSENBERG, K. J. A. VON, Forest Pathology
YLATALO, E. M. O., Agricultural Economics

Faculty of Veterinary Medicine:

KATILA, M. T. H., Animal Breeding
LINDBERG, L.-A., Anatomy
PALVA, A., Veterinary Microbiology
SALONIEMI, H., Animal Hygiene
SANDHOLM, M., Pharmacology and Toxicology
TULAMO, R.-M., Veterinary Surgery
WESTERMARCK, E., Medicine

ATTACHED INSTITUTES

Institute of Seismology: Dir (vacant).

Helsinki Institute of Physics: Dir E. A. BYCKLING.

Helsinki University Centre for Continuing Education: Dir S. KOIVULA.

Institute of Biotechnology: Dir Acad. M. SAARMA.

Finnish Institute for the Verification of the Chemical Weapons Convention: Dir M. M. RAUTIO.

Alexander Institute: Dir M. J. KIVINEN.

JOENSUUN YLIOPISTO
(University of Joensuu)

POB 111, 80101 Joensuu
Telephone: (13) 251-111
Telex: 46223
Fax: (13) 251-2050
E-mail: intl@joyl.joensuu.fi

Founded 1969
Language of instruction: Finnish and English
State control
Academic year: August to July (two terms)

Rector: PAAVO PELKONEN
Vice-Rectors: HANNES SIHVO, KARI TUUNAINEN
Director of Administration: MATTI HALONEN
Librarian: TUULIKKI NURMINEN

Number of teachers: 500
Number of students: 6,000

Publications: *Julkaisuja* (Publications), *Sanansaattaja Joensuusta* (News), *Silva Carelica*.

DEANS

Faculty of Education: ANNA RAIJA NUMMENMAA
Faculty of Humanities: ILKKA SAVIJÄRVI
Faculty of Science: ILPO LAINE
Faculty of Social Sciences: KYÖSTI PULLIAINEN
Faculty of Forestry: TANELI KOLSTRÖM

PROFESSORS

AHMED, M., Business Economics
AHO, L., Education
ALHO, J., Statistics
ANTIKAINEN, A., Sociology of Education
FRIBERG, A., Physics
HARSTELA, P., Forest Technology
HEIKKINEN, A., History of Finland
HEINONEN, R., Common Theology
HIRVONEN, P., English Language
HYVÄRINEN, H., Biology
HÄLLSTRÖM, G. AF, Systematic Theology
HÄYRYNEN, Y.-P., Psychology
JÄÄSKELÄINEN, T., Physics
KÄRKKÄINEN, M., Wood Science
KAUKINEN, L., Textiles
KELLOMÄKI, S., Forestry
KNUUTTILA, S., Folklore
LAINE, I., Mathematics
MAKKONEN, H., Practical Theology
MANNERKOSKI, H., Forest Soil Science
NIEMELÄ, P., Forest Ecology
PAKKANEN, T., Chemistry
PELKONEN, P., Production of Wood and Peat for Energy
PENTTONEN, M., Computer Science
POHJOLAINEN, T., Public Law
PUKKALA, T., Forest Management Planning
PULLIAINEN, K., Economics
RÄISÄNEN, A., Finnish Language
SALO, M., Social Policy
SAVIJÄRVI, M., Russian Language
SEPPO, S., Education
SIHVO, H., Literature
SOPANEN, T., Botany
SORVALI, T., Mathematics
TIRKKONEN-CONDIT, S., Linguistic Theory and Translation
TURUNEN, J., Electronics
TUUNAINEN, K., Special Education
VARTIAINEN, P., Geography and Regional Planning
WIKSTRÖM, K., Swedish Language

ATTACHED INSTITUTES

Karelian Research Institute: Dir Dr ANTTI LAINE.

Mekrijärvi Research Station: Dir Dr JORMA AHO.

JYVÄSKYLÄN YLIOPISTO
(University of Jyväskylä)

POB 35, 40351 Jyväskylä
Telephone: (14) 601211
Fax: (14) 601021

Founded as Teacher Training School 1863, became College of Education 1934, and University 1966
Language of instruction: Finnish
State control
Academic year: September to July (three terms)

Rector: Prof. AINO SALLINEN
Vice-Rectors: Prof. PEKKA NEITTAANMÄKI, HEIKKI LYYTINEN
Administrative Director: JUHO HUKKINEN
Chief Librarian: KAI EKHOLM

Number of teachers: 575
Number of students: 12,383

Publications: *Studia Historica Jyväskyläensia, Studia Philologica Jyväskyläensia, Jyväskylä Studies in Education, Psychology and Social Research, Jyväskylä Studies in the Arts, Jyväskylä Studies in Computer Science, Economics and Statistics, Jyväskylä Studies in Sport, Physical Education and Health, Kasvatus* (Finnish Journal of Education), *Biological Research Reports, Jyväskylän Studies in Communication.*

DEANS

Faculty of Education (including Dept of Teacher Training): Assoc. Prof. JORMA EKOLA
Faculty of Social Sciences: Prof. ISTO RUOPPILA
Faculty of Humanities: Prof. KARI SAJAVAARA
Faculty of Mathematics and Natural Sciences: Prof. MATTI MANNINEN
Faculty of Sport and Health Sciences: Prof. PAULI VUOLLE

PROFESSORS

Faculty of Education:

HIRSJÄRVI, S., Education
KARI, J., Education
KUUSINEN, J., Education
MOBERG, S., Special Education
VAHERVA, T., Adult Education

Faculty of Social Sciences:

AALTONEN, J., Psychology (Family Therapy)
ILMONEN, K., Sociology
KANGAS, A., Cultural Management
LAGERSPETZ, E., Philosophy
LYYTINEN, H., Developmental Neuropsychology
LYYTINEN, K., Data Processing
MARIN, M., Social Gerontology
OJA, H., Statistics
PALONEN, K., Political Science
PULKKINEN, L., Psychology
RUOPPILA, I., Developmental Psychology

Faculty of Humanities:

HJERPPE, R., Economic History
JÄNTTI, A., German Philology
KUNNAS, T., Literature
LEHTONEN, J., Organizational Communication
LEIWO, M., Finnish Language
LÖNNQVIST, B., Ethnology
MERISALO, O., Romance Philology
NYGÅRD, T., History
PEKKANEN, T., Latin
PEURANEN, E., Russian Language and Literature
RAHKONEN, M., Scandinavian Philology
ROUTILA, L., Art Education
SAJAVAARA, K., Applied Language Studies
SALLINEN, A., Speech Communication
SALOKANGAS, R., Journalism
VAINIO, M., Musicology
ZETTERBERG, S., History

Faculty of Mathematics and Natural Sciences:

ALATALO, R., Ecology
ALEN, R., Applied Chemistry
ASTALA, K., Mathematics
BAGGE, P., Hydrobiology
HEINO, J., Biology
JULIN, R., Physics
KORPPI-TOMMOLA, J., Chemistry
MANNINEN, M., Physics
MATTILA, P., Mathematics
NEITTAANMÄKI, P., Applied Natural Sciences
OIKARI, A., Environmental Sciences
ORPONEN, P., Applied Mathematics
PEKOLA, J., Physics
RISSANEN, K., Chemistry
RUUSKANEN, V., Theoretical Physics
TIMONEN, J., Applied Physics
VALKONEN, J., Chemistry
ÄYSTÖ, J., Physics

Faculty of Sport and Health Sciences:

HEIKKINEN, E., Gerontology
KANNAS, L., Health Education
KIRJONEN, J., Sport Psychology
KOMI, P., Biomechanics
MÄLKIÄ, E., Physiotherapy
TAKALA, T., Physiology of Exercise
TELAMA, R., Physical Education
VIDEMAN, T., Sport Medicine
VUOLLE, P., Sociology of Sport

School of Business and Economics:

KOIRANEN, M, Entrepreneurship
NÄSI, J., Business Management
PENTO, T., Marketing
VEHMANEN, P., Management Accountancy

ATTACHED INSTITUTES

Koulutuksen tutkimuslaitos (Institute for Educational Research): Dir JOUNI VÄLIJÄRVI.

Laskentakeskus (Computer Centre): Dir EERO BLÅFIELD.

Täydennyskoulutuskeskus (Continuing Education Centre): Dir JUKKA ALAVA.

Yliopiston kielikeskus (Language Centre): Dir MAIJA KALIN.

Yliopiston museo (University Museum): Dir JANNE VILKUNA.

Ympäristöntutkimuskeskus (Centre for Environmental Research): Dir JARMO MERILÄINEN.

KUOPION YLIOPISTO
(University of Kuopio)

Box 1627, 70211 Kuopio
Telephone: (17) 162-211
Fax: (17) 162131

Founded 1966
State control
Language of instruction: Finnish
Academic year: August to June

Rector: P. PARONEN
Vice-Rectors: S. SAARIKOSKI, K. M. VEHVILÄINEN-JULKUNEN
Administrative Director: T. T. TEITTINEN
Librarian: R. L. HUUHTANEN

Number of teachers: 400, including 90 professors and associate professors
Number of students: 3,000, plus 1,000 postgraduate students

Publications in the fields of pharmaceutical sciences, natural and environmental sciences, medical sciences, social sciences, university affairs.

DEANS

Pharmacy: J. GYNTHER
Medicine: P. KIRKINEN
Social Sciences: P. NIEMELÄ
Natural and Environmental Sciences: Prof. P. J. KALLIOKOSKI
A. I. Virtanen Institute: J. JÄNNE

PROFESSORS

Faculty of Medicine:

ALHAVA, E., Surgery
HELMINEN, H., Anatomy
HORSMANHEIMO, M. T., Dermatology
HUSMAN, K. R. H., Occupational Medicine
HÄNNINEN, O. O. P., Physiology
JOHANSSON, R. T., Radiotherapy and Oncology
LAAKSO, M. H. S., Internal Medicine
LEHTONEN, P. O. J. B., Psychiatry
LOUHEVAARA, V. A., Ergonomics
MAKAROW, M. T., Medical Biochemistry
MÄNTYJÄRVI, M. I., Ophthalmology
MÄNTYJÄRVI, R. A., Clinical Microbiology
NISSINEN, A., Community Health
PENTTILÄ, I. M., Clinical Chemistry
RIEKKINEN, P. J. Sr, Neurology
RÄSÄNEN, E., Child Psychiatry
SAARIKOSKI, S. V., Gynaecology and Obstetrics
SALONEN, J. T., Community Health (Epidemiology)
SIVENIUS, J., Neurology (Epilepsy and Rehabilitation)
SOIMAKALLIO, S., Diagnostic Radiology
SULKAVA, R., Geriatrics
SYRJÄNEN, K., Pathology
TAKALA, J., Anaesthesiology
TAKALA, J., General Practice
TIIHONEN, J., Forensic Medicine
TUKIAINEN, H. O., Pulmonary Diseases
UUSITUPA, M. I. J., Clinical Nutrition
VAPALAHTI, M., Neurosurgery

Faculty of Natural and Environmental Sciences:

HYNYNEN, K. H., Medical Physics
JUHOLA, K. M. I., Computer Science
JÄNNE, J. E., Biotechnology
KALLIOKOSKI, P. J., Environmental Sciences (Industrial Hygiene)
KÄRENLAMPI, L. V., Environmental Sciences (Ecology)
LAATIKAINEN, R., Chemistry
LINDQVIST, O. V., Applied Zoology
MÄENPÄÄ, P. H., Biochemistry
RAUNEMAA, T., Environmental Sciences
RUUSKANEN, J., Environmental Health (Air Protection)
VALTONEN, M., Veterinary Medicine

Faculty of Pharmacy:

ENLUND, K. H., Social Pharmacy
MÄNNISTÖ, P., Pharmacology
PARONEN, T. P., Pharmaceutical Technology
SAVOLAINEN, K. M., Toxicology
URTTI, A. O., Biopharmacy

Faculty of Social Sciences:

GRÖNFORS, M., Sociology
LAUKKANEN, M., Entrepreneurship and Management
LAURINKARI, J., Social Policy
NIEMELÄ, P., Social Policy
SINKKONEN, S. E., Nursing and Health Care Administration
SINTONEN, H. P., Health Economics
VEHVILÄINEN-JULKUNEN, K. M., Nursing Science

A. I. Virtanen Institute:

KAUPPINEN, R., Biochemical NMR
YLÄ-HERTTUALA, S., Molecular Medicine

ATTACHED INSTITUTES

Centre for Training and Development: Dir PÄIVI NERG.

Computing Centre: Dir Y. JOKINEN.

Language Centre: Dir A. HILDÉN.

National Laboratory Animal Centre: Dir T. NEVALAINEN.

Research Institute of Public Health: Dir J. T. SALONEN.

LAPIN YLIOPISTO
(University of Lapland)

POB 122, 96101 Rovaniemi
Telephone: (16) 3241
Fax: (16) 324-207
Founded 1979
Languages of instruction: Finnish and English
State funded
Academic year: August to July
Rector: Prof. ESKO RIEPULA
Vice-Rector: Prof. KYÖSTI URPONEN
Dir of Administration: JUHANI LILLBERG
Librarian: LEA KARHUMAA
Library of 180,000 vols
Number of teachers: 195
Number of students: 3,070
Publication: *KIDE* (monthly).

DEANS

Faculty of Education: Prof. RAIMO RAJALA
Faculty of Law: Prof. TERTTU UTRIAINEN
Faculty of Social Sciences: Prof. MARTTI SIISIÄINEN
Faculty of Arts and Design: Assoc. Prof. VEIKKO KAMUNEN

DIRECTORS

Centre for Continuing Education: Dr HELKA URPONEN
Northern Institute for Environmental and Minority Law: Dr FRANK HORN
Language Centre: RÜTTA SALLINEN
Arctic Centre: Dr JANNE HUKKINEN
Meri-Lappi Institute: AARO TIILIKAINEN
Teacher-Training School: HELVI HEISKANEN

PROFESSORS

Faculty of Education:

JUSSILA, J., Pedagogics
KURTAKKO, K., Adult Education
RAJALA, R., Pedagogics

Faculty of Law:

HAKAPÄÄ, K., International Law
HARLE, V., International Relations
HOLMA, K., Environmental Law
KOSKINEN, S., Labour Law
KUNLA, J., Marketing
LINNAKANGAS, E., Public Economy
MINCKE, W., Legal Informatics
PANULA, J., Marketing
PÖYHÖNEN, J., Civil Law
RUDANKO, M., Business Law
SAARENPÄÄ, A., Family and Inheritance Law
SARAVIITA, I., Public Law
UTRIAINEN, T., Criminal Law
VIROLAINEN, J., Juridical Procedure

Faculty of Social Sciences:

AHO, S., Tourism
HAVERI, A., Public Administration
KÄHKÖNEN, I., Business Economics
PAASO, I., Public Law
RIEPULA, E., Public Law
SIISIÄINEN, M., Sociology
URPONEN, K., Social Policy
VIMONEN, T., Economics

Faculty of Art and Design:

KAMUNEN, V., Industrial Design
RAJAKANGAS, L., Clothing and Textile Design
SEITAMAA-ORAVALA, P., Art Education
VOTILA, M., Clothing and Textile Design
YLÄ-KOTOLA, M., Media Studies

LAPPEENRANNAN TEKNILLINEN KORKEAKOULU
(Lappeenranta University of Technology)

Box 20, 53851 Lappeenranta 85
Telephone: (5) 62111
Fax: (5) 6212350
Founded 1969
Languages of instruction: Finnish and English
State control
Academic year: August to July (two terms)
Rector: Prof. MARKKU LUKKA
Vice-Rectors: Prof. JARMO PARTANEN, Prof. RAIMO IMMONEN
Administrative Officer: ARTO OIKKONEN
Librarian: ANJA UKKOLA
Library of 127,000 vols
Number of teachers: 200
Number of students: 3,300
Publications: *Tieteellisiä julkaisuja* (research papers).

PROFESSORS

AALTIO-MARJOSOLA, I., Management and Organization
ESKELINEN, P., Electronics
HANDROOS, H., Machine Automation
IMMONEN, R., Business Law
JORMAKKA, J., Telecommunications
KALLI, H., Nuclear Engineering
KERTTULA, E., Telematics
LUKKA, A., Logistics (esp. transport), Inventories, Purchasing
LUKKA, M., Applied Mathematics
LUUKKO, A., Physics
MANNER, H., Paper Technology
MARTIKAINEN, J., Welding Technology
NAOUMOV, V., Telecommunications
NEILIMO, K., Accounting and Business Accounting
NYSTRÖM, L., Process Technology
NYSTRÖM, M., Membrane Technology
PAATERO, E., Chemical Technology
PALOSAARI, S., Chemical Engineering
PARKKINEN, J., Information Processing
PARTANEN, J., Electrical Systems
PÖYHÖNEN, I., Wood Technology
PYRHÖNEN, J., Electrical Machines and Drives
SARKOMAA, P., Technical Thermodynamics
TALONEN, P., Industrial Economics
TARJANNE, R., Energy Management and Economics
TIUSANEN, T., International Operations of Industrial Firms
TUOMINEN, M., Industrial Engineering and Management
VERHO, A., Structural Design of Machinery

OULUN YLIOPISTO
(University of Oulu)

Kirkkokatu 11A, PL 191, 90101 Oulu
Telephone: (8) 5534011
Fax: (8) 371158
Founded 1958
Language of instruction: Finnish
State control
Academic year: September to May (two terms)
Rector: Prof. L. LAJUNEN
Vice-Rectors: Prof. J. KOISO-KANTTILA, Prof. I. SORVALI
Administrative Director: P. HEIKKINEN
Librarian: P. KYTÖMÄKI
Number of teachers: 850
Number of students: 12,650

DEANS

Faculty of Humanities: Prof. L. HUHTALA
Faculty of Education: Assoc. Prof. J. LUUKKONEN
Faculty of Science: Prof. E. RAHKAMAA
Faculty of Technology: Prof. U. KORTELA
Faculty of Medicine: Prof. V. MYLLYLÄ

PROFESSORS

Faculty of Humanities:

FÄLT, O. K., History
HUHTALA, L., Literature
KEINÄSTÖ, K., German
LEHTIHALMES, M., Logopedics
MANNINEN, J., History of Science and Ideas
NUÑEZ, M., Archaeology
NYYSSÖNEN, H., English
PENNANEN, J., Cultural Anthropology
SAMMALLAHTI, P., Saami (Lapp) Language and Culture
SORVALI, I., Scandinavian Languages
SULKALA, H., Finnish

Faculty of Education:

HUJALA, E., Early Childhood Education
RUISMÄKI, H., Music Education
SILJANDER, P., Education
SUORTTI, J., Education
SYRJÄLÄ, L., Education

Faculty of Science:

AARIO, R., Soil Geology
ANTTILA, R., Physics
HILTUNEN, K., Biochemistry
HJELT, S.-E., Geophysics
IIVARI, J., Information Processing Science
JÄRVILEHTO, M., Animal Physiology
KALLIO, A., Theoretical Physics
KEMMINK, J., Structural Elucidation of Macromolecules by NMR Spectroscopy
KOSKINEN, A., Organic Chemistry
LAAJOKI, K., Geology and Mineralogy
LAASONEN, K., Physical Chemistry
LAJUNEN, L., Inorganic Chemistry
LAKOVAARA, S., Genetics
LÄHDESMÄKI, P., Plant Physiology
NAUKKARINEN, A., Human Geography and Regional Planning
PAASI, A., Geography
PÄIVÄRINTA, L., Mathematics
PULLIAINEN, E., Zoology
RAHKAMAA, E., Structural Chemistry
SARANEN, J., Applied Mathematics
SIMILÄ, J., Information Processing Science
TANSKANEN, P., Physics
TUOMINEN, I., Astronomy
TURAKAINEN, P., Mathematics
TURMI, J., Botany

Faculty of Technology:

BRONER-BAUER, K., Architecture
EHROLA, E., Road Construction
GLISIC, S., Telecommunication
HOOLI, J., Hydraulic Engineering
HYTTINEN, E., Statics and Bridge Engineering
HÄRKKI, J., Metallurgy
KALLIOMÄKI, K., Measurement Technology
KARJALAINEN, P., Physical Metallurgy
KILPELÄINEN, M., Structural Engineering
KOISO-KANTTILA, J., Architecture
KORTELA, U., Control and Systems Engineering
KOSTAMOVAARA, J., Electronics
LAPPALAINEN, P., Electrical Instrumentation
LEINONEN, T., Machine Design
LEIVISKÄ, K., Process Engineering
LEPPÄVUORI, S., Microelectronics
METSÄ-KETELÄ, H., Industrial Design
MYLLYLÄ, R., Optoelectronics and Electronic Measurement Technology
NEVALA, K., Mechatronics
NIEMINEN, J., Mathematics
NISKANEN, J., Machine Construction
NYMAN, K.-E., Planning and Urban Design
PERTTUNEN, J., Business Administration
PIETIKÄINEN, M., Computer Technics
POHJOLA, V., Chemical Process Engineering
PRAMILA, A., Technical Mechanics
SALONEN, E., Radio Technology
SILVÉN, O., Signal Processing
SOHLO, J., Heat and Mass Transfer Processes
TASA, J., Architecture
TUOMAALA, J., Machine Construction
VÄYRYNEN, S., Work Science
YLINEN, R., Automation Technology

Faculty of Medicine:

AIRAKINNEN, I. J., Ophthalmology
ALVESALO, L., Dentistry
HALLMAN, H., Paediatrics
HAUSEN, H., Dentistry

HENTINEN, M., Nursing Science
HILLBOM, M., Neurology
HIRVONEN, J., Forensic Medicine
ISOHANNI, M., Psychiatry
KAIRALUOMA, M., Surgery
KAPRIO, J., Public Health Science
KESÄNIEMI, A., Internal Medicine
KIVELÄ, S.-L., General Practice
KIVIRIKKO, K., Medical Biochemistry
KNUUTTILA, M., Parodontology
KOIVUKANGAS, J., Neurosurgery
LARMAS, M., Dentistry
LEHTO, V.-P., Pathology
LEPPÄLUOTO, J., Physiology
MOILANEN, I., Child Psychiatry
NUUTINEN, J., Oto-rhino-laryngology
NUUTINEN, L., Anaesthesiology
OIKARINEN, H., Dentistry
PELKONEN, O., Pharmacology
PIHLAJANIEMI, T., Medical Biochemistry
RAJANIEMI, H., Anatomy
RAUSTIA, A., Dentistry
RUSKOSKO, H., Molecular Pharmacology
SURAMO, I., Diagnostic Radiology
VANHARANTA, H., Physical Medicine and Rehabilitation
VIHKO, R., Clinical Chemistry
VILKMAN, E., Phoniatrics

ATTACHED INSTITUTES

Thule Institute: 90570 Oulu; Dir B. SEGERSTÄHL.

Continuing Education Centre: 90570 Oulu; Dir P. KESS.

Computer Services Centre: 90570 Oulu; Dir P. KORHONEN.

Language Centre: 90570 Oulu; Dir P. LEHTINEN.

Institute of Electron Optics: 90570 Oulu; Dir S. SIVONEN.

Research and Development Centre of Kajaani: 87100 Kajaani; Dir A. MIKKONEN.

Sodankylä Geophysical Observatory: 99600 Sodankylä; Dir J. KANGAS.

TAMPEREEN TEKNILLINEN KORKEAKOULU (Tampere University of Technology)

Box 527, 33101 Tampere
Telephone: (3) 3652111
Telex: 22-313
Fax: (3) 3652170

Founded 1965
Language of instruction: Finnish
State control
Academic year: September to May

Rector: Prof. TIMO LEPISTÖ
Vice-Rector: Prof. MARKKU MATTILA
Director of Administration: SEPPO LOIMIO
Librarian: ARJA-RIITTA HAARALA

Number of teachers: 440
Number of students: 7,000

DEANS

Department of Architecture: Prof. JUHANI KATAINEN
Department of Automation: Assoc. Prof. PENTTI LAUTALA
Department of Civil Engineering: Prof. RALF LINDBERG
Department of Electrical Engineering: Prof. GUNNAR GRAEFFE
Department of Environment: Assoc. Prof. HELGE LEMMETYINEN
Department of Industrial Engineering and Management: Prof. ERKKI UUSI-RAUVA
Department of Mechanical Engineering: Prof. ASKO RIITAHUHTA
Department of Information Technology: Prof. JAAKKO ASTOLA
Department of Materials Science: Prof. TUOMO TIAINEN

PROFESSORS

AITTOMÄKI, A., Refrigeration Technology
ASTOLA, J., Digital Signals Processing
AUMALA, O., Metrology
ERIKSSON, J.-T., Electrodynamics and Magnetism
GRAEFFE, G., Physics
HAAVISTO, P., Signal Processing
HAIKALA, I., Computer Science
HARJU, J., Telecommunications
HARTIKAINEN, J., Soil Mechanics and Foundation Engineering
JAAKKOLA, H., Information Technology
JALLINOJA, R., Architectural Theory
JARSKE, P., Telecommunications
KARVINEN, R., Fluid Dynamics and Heat Transfer
KASKI, K., Microelectronics
KATAINEN, J., Architectural Design
KIVIKOSKI, M., Industrial Electronics
KOIVO, H., Industrial Automation
KOSKI, J., Structural Mechanics
KURKI-SUONIO, R., Computer Science and Engineering
KÄRNÄ, J., Electrical Power Engineering
LAKERVI, E., Electrical Power Engineering
LAPINLEIMU, I., Production Engineering
LEPISTÖ, T., Mathematics
LEPISTÖ, TOIVO, Electron Microscopy
LINDBERG, R., Structural Engineering
MALMIVUO, J., Bioelectronics
MATTILA, M., Occupational Safety Engineering
MAULA, J., Urban Planning
NOUSIAINEN, P., Textile Technology
NYBERG, T., Paper Machine Automation
OTALA, M., Industrial Management
PESSA, M., Semiconductor Technology
REIJONEN, A., Textile Technology
RENFORS, M., Telecommunications Engineering
RIITAHUHTA, A., Machine Design
RISSANEN, J., Scientific Computing
SAARINEN, J., Signal Processing Laboratory
SALOKANGAS, R., Construction Economics
SAVOLAINEN, A., Process Engineering
SIEKKINEN, V., Maintenance Technology
SIIKANEN, U., Architectural Construction
TALLQVIST, T., History of Architecture
TUOKKO, R., Automation Technology
TUOMALA, M., Structural Mechanics
TÖRMÄLÄ, P., Plastics Technology
UUSI-RAUVA, E., Industrial Management and Engineering
VIITASAARI, M., Water and Environmental Engineering
VILENIUS, M., Hydraulic Machines

ATTACHED INSTITUTES

Institute of Digital Media: Box 553, 33101 Tampere; f. 1994; Dir J. ASTOLA.

Research Institute of Materials Science: Box 589, 33101 Tampere; f. 1988; Dir TOIVO LEPISTÖ.

TAMPEREEN YLIOPISTO (University of Tampere)

PL 607, Kalevantie 4, 33101 Tampere
Telephone: (3) 2156111
Fax: (3) 2134473

Founded 1925
Language of instruction: Finnish
State control
Academic year: September to May

Chancellor: Dr H. KOSKI
Rector: Prof. J. SIPILÄ
Vice-Rectors: Prof. M. JYLHÄ, Assoc. Prof. K. VARANTOLA
Administrative Director: T. LAHTI
Librarian: H. SOINI

Number of teachers: 605, including 94 professors
Number of students: 19,000
Publication: *Acta Universitatis Tamperensis*.

DEANS

Faculty of Social Sciences: Prof. M. ALESTALO
Faculty of Humanities: Prof. M.-L. PIITULAINEN
Faculty of Economics and Administration: Prof. S. LAAKSO
Faculty of Medicine: Prof. A. PASTERNACK
Faculty of Education: Prof. P. RUOHOTIE

PROFESSORS

Faculty of Social Sciences:

ALASUUTARI, P., Sociology
ALESTALO, M., Sociology
APUNEN, O., International Politics
BORG, O., Political Science
GORDON, T., Women's Studies
JÄRVELIN, K., Information Studies
KOSKIAHO-CRONSTRÖM, B., Social Policy (General)
NORDENSTRENG, K., Journalism and Mass Communication
PERÄKYLÄ, A., Social Psychology
PIETILÄ, V., Journalism and Mass Communication
SCHIENSTOCK, G., Work Research
SIPILÄ, J., Social Work
VAKKARI, P., Information Studies
VARIS, T., Media Culture and Communication Education

Faculty of Humanities:

HIETALA, M., General History
LEINONEN, M., Slavonic Languages, Russian
LEISIÖ, T., Ethnomusicology
MANNINEN, O., Finnish History
NORRMAN, R., English Philology
PAUNONEN, H., Finnish Language
PIITULAINEN, M-L., German Philology
PITKÄNEN, A. J., Nordic Languages, Swedish
RENVALL, Y. J., Actor Training
TAMMI, P., Comparative Literature
VARPIO, Y., Finnish Literature

Faculty of Economics and Administration:

AHONEN, P., Financial Administration and Public Sector Accounting
AHTIALA, P., Economics
HAAHTI, A., Service Entrepreneurship
HAILA, Y., Environmental Policy
HAUTAMÄKI, L., Regional Studies
HOIKKA, P., Local Government
HYYRÖ, S., Mathematics
JÄRVINEN, P., Computer Science
JUHOLA, M., Computer Science
KOSKIMIES, K., Computer Science
LAAKSO, S., Public Law
LEHTINEN, U., Marketing
LISKI, E., Statistics
MEKLIN, P., Local Public Economics
MIETTINEN, A., Management and Organization
MYLLMÄKI, A., Public Law
NISKANEN, J., Accounting and Finance
NUOLIMAA, R., Commercial Law
PENTTILÄ, S., Tax Law
RÄIHÄ, K., Computer Science
RANTALA, V., Philosophy
SIIRILÄ, S., Regional Studies
TUOMALA, M., Economics
VAINIOMÄKI, J., Economics
VARTOLA, J., Public Administration
YLÄ-LIEDENPOHJA, J., Economics

Faculty of Medicine:

FREY, H., Neurology
HURME, M., Microbiology and Immunology
JÄRVINEN, M., Surgery
KARHUNEN, P., Forensic Medicine
KELLOKUMPU-LEHTINEN, P., Radiotherapy and Oncology
KNIP, M., Paediatrics
LAASONEN, E. M., Radiology
MATTILA, K., General Practice
NIEMINEN, M., Pulmonary Medicine
NISKANEN, P., Psychiatry
OJA, S., Physiology
PASTERNACK, A., Internal Medicine
PAUNONEN, M., Nursing

PUHAKKA, H., Otorhinolaryngology
PUNNONEN, R., Obstetrics and Gynaecology
REUNALA, T., Dermatology and Venereology
SALMINEN, L., Ophthalmology
TAMMINEN, T., Child Psychiatry
TUOHIMAA, P., Anatomy
UUSITALO, A., Clinical Physiology
VESIKARI, T., Virology
YLITALO, P., Clinical Pharmacology and Toxicology

Faculty of Education:
JÄRVINEN, A., Adult Education
RAIVOLA, R., Education
RUOHOTIE, P., Education (Vocational Policy)

AFFILIATED INSTITUTES

Yhteiskuntatieteiden tutkimuslaitos (Research Institute for Social Sciences): Tampere; f. 1945; Dir A. AARNIO.

Tietokonekeskus (Computer Centre): Tampere; f. 1966; Dir T. KANKAANPÄÄ.

Täydennyskoulutuskeskus (Institute for Extension Studies): Tampere; f. 1970; Dir M. LEPPÄALHO.

Puheopin laitos (Institute of Speech Communication and Voice Research): Tampere; f. 1973; Dir T. LEINO.

Kielikeskus (Language Centre): Tampere; f. 1975; Dir U.-K. TUOMI.

International School of Social Sciences (ISSS): Language of instruction: English; Dir O. APUNEN.

Lääketieteellisen teknologian instituutti (Institute of Medical Technology): Tampere; f. 1995; Dir K. KROHN.

Terveystieteen laitos (Tampere School of Public Health): Tampere; f. 1995; Dir A. RIMPELÄ.

TEKNILLINEN KORKEAKOULU
(Helsinki University of Technology)

POB 1000, 02015 Helsinki University of Technology

Telephone: (9) 4511
Fax: (9) 4512017

Founded 1908
Language of instruction: Finnish, with some lectures in Swedish and English
State control
Academic year: September to May

Rector: Prof. PAAVO URONEN
Vice-Rectors: Assoc. Prof. M. PURSULA, Prof. A. RÄISÄNEN
Administrative Director: E. LUOMALA
Library Director: S. KOSKIALA

Number of teachers: 475 (full-time)
Number of students: 12,000

DEANS

Department of Engineering, Physics and Mathematics: Prof. RAINER SALOMAA
Department of Computer Science and Engineering: Prof. OLLI SIMULA
Department of Industrial Management: Prof. PAUL LILLRANK
Department of Electrical and Communications Engineering: PEKKA WALLIN
Department of Mechanical Engineering: Prof. SEPPO LAINE
Department of Automation and Systems Technology: Prof. AARNE HALME
Department of Chemical Technology: Prof. JUKKA SEPPÄLÄ
Department of Materials Science and Rock Engineering: KARI HEISKANEN
Department of Forest Products Technology: TERO PAAJANEN
Department of Architecture: Prof. TOM SIMONS
Department of Surveying: Prof. TEUVO PARM
Department of Civil and Environmental Engineering: Prof. VESA PENTTALA

PROFESSORS

AIRILA, M., Machine Design
BYCKLING, E., Technical Physics
ELORANTA, E., Industrial Management
FOGELHOLM, C-J., Energy Engineering
GULLICHSEN, J., Pulping Technology
HAGGREN, H., Photogrammetry
HALLIKAINEN, M., Space Technology
HALME, A., Automation Engineering
HALME, S., Communication Engineering
HALONEN, K., Integrated Circuit Design, Microelectronics Design
HALONEN, L., Power Systems and Illumination Engineering
HARTIKAINEN, O.-P., Road and Railway Engineering
HARTIMO, I., Computer Technology
HAUTOJÄRVI, P., Physics
HEISKANEN, K., Mechanical Process Engineering and Recycling
HELANDER, V., History of Architecture
HOLAPPA, L., Metallurgy, Theoretical Process Metallurgy
HÄMÄLÄINEN, R., Applied Mathematics
HÄNNINEN, H., Engineering Materials
IKONEN, E., Quantitative Science and Technology
JOKINEN, T., Electromechanics
JUTILA, A., Bridge Engineering
KANERVA, P., Structural Engineering and Building Physics
KARILA, A., Data Communication Software
KARJALAINEN, M., Acoustics, Audio and Speech Processing
KASKI, K., Computational Engineering
KATILA, T., Biomedical Engineering
KAUPPINEN, V., Production Technology
KIIRAS, J., Construction Economy and Management
KIVILAHTI, J., Materials and Manufacturing Technology for Electronics
KLEIMOLA, M., Combustion Engines
KOIVO, H., Control Engineering
KOMONEN, M., Architecture
KORHONEN, A., Processing and Heat Treatment of Materials
KOSKINEN, K., Information Technology in Automation
KRAUSE, O., Industrial Chemistry
KUIVALAINEN, P., Microelectronics
LAAKSO, S., Biochemistry
LAAKSO, T., Telecommunications
LAINE, S., Aeronautical Engineering
LAKERVI, E., Power Systems
LAMPINEN, M., Applied Thermodynamics
LAUKKANEN, R., Water Supply
LEISOLA, M., Bioprocess Engineering
LEPPIHALME, M., Photonics
LILLRANK, P., Quality Management
LINDELL, I., Electromagnetics
LINDROOS, V., Physical Metallurgy
LOUNASMAA, M., Organic Chemistry
MARTIKAINEN, O., Data Communication Software
MIKKOLA, M., Mechanics
MÄKELÄINEN, P., Steel Structures
MÄNTYLÄ, M., Information Technology
MÄÄTTANEN, M., Strength of Materials
NEVANLINNA, O., Mathematics
NIEMINEN, R., Physics
NIINI, H., Economic Geology
NIINISTÖ, L., Inorganic Chemistry
NORDÉN, H. V., Chemical Engineering
OITTINEN, P., Graphic Arts
OJA, E., Computer and Information Sciences
OJALA, L., Digital Systems
OVASKA, S., Industrial Electronics
PAAJANEN, T., Wood Technology
PAAVILAINEN, S., Architecture
PALOHEIMO, E., Wood Building
PARM, T., Geodesy
PAULAPURO, H., Paper Technology
PENTTALA, V., Building Materials Technology
PITKÄRANTA, J., Mathematics
PORRA, V., Electronic Circuit Engineering
RAUTAMÄKI, M., Landscape Architecture
RISKA, K., Arctic Technology
RÄISÄNEN, A., Radio Engineering
SAARELMA, H., Graphic Arts
SALOMAA, R., Technical Physics
SÄRKKÄ, P., Rock Engineering
SEPPÄLÄ, J., Polymer Technology
SEPPÄNEN, O., Heating, Ventilation and Air Conditioning Technology
SHARMA, A., Communications Systems
SIHVOLA, A., Electromagnetics
SIITONEN, T., Housing Design
SIMONS, T., Landscape Architecture
SIMULA, O., Computer and Information Sciences
SINKKONEN, J., Electron Physics
SÖDERLUND, J.-H., Building Technology
SOISALON-SOININEN, E., Information Processing Science
STENIUS, P., Physical Chemistry of Forest Products Technology
SULONEN, R., Information Processing
SUNDHOLM, G., Physical Chemistry
SYRJANEN, M., Knowledge Engineering
TAKALA, T., Data Communication Software
TEIKARI, V., Industrial Psychology
TUOMI, T., Physics
URONEN, P., Process Control
VAKKILAINEN, P., Hydrology and Water Resources Management
VALTONEN, M., Circuit Theory
VARSTA, P., Naval Architecture and Marine Engineering
VIRTAMO, J., Telecommunications Technology
VUORINEN, J., Foundry Technology
YLÄSAARI, S., Corrosion Science and Technology

ATTACHED INSTITUTES

Lifelong Learning Institute: Dir J. RAUTIAINEN.
Centre for Urban and Regional Planning: Dir H. LEHTONEN.
Low Temperature Laboratory: Dir Prof. M. PAALANEN.
Metsähovi Radio Research Station: Dir S. URPO.
Language and Communication Centre: Dir KRISTIINA VOLMARI-MÄKINEN.
IIA Research Centre: Dir J. KANERVA.
Computing Centre: Dir JUHANI MARKULA.

TURUN YLIOPISTO
(University of Turku)

20014 Turku

Telephone: (2) 33351
Fax: (2) 3336363

Founded 1920
Language of instruction: Finnish
State control
Academic year: August to July (two semesters)

Chancellor: K. PAUNIO
Rector: K. VIRTANEN
Vice-Rectors: P. KOSONEN, A. SALMI
Director of Administration: K. HYPPÖNEN
Librarian: M. ENGMAN

Number of teachers: 819, including 120 professors

Number of students: 14,947

Publication: *Annales Universitatis Turkuensis*.

DEANS

Faculty of Humanities: Assoc. Prof. R. KERO
Faculty of Mathematics and Natural Sciences: Prof. V.-P. SALONEN
Faculty of Medicine: Prof. E. VIROLAINEN
Faculty of Law: Prof. A. SAARNILEHTO
Faculty of Social Sciences: Prof. K. SALAVUO
Faculty of Education: Prof. E. OLKINUORA

PROFESSORS

Faculty of Humanities:
ANTTONEN, V., Comparative Religion

HAKANEN, A. K., Finnish Language
HEINIÖ, M. K., Musicology
HILTUNEN, R., English Philology
HOVI, A. K., General History
KARKAMA, P. J., Finnish Literature
LAPPALAINEN, J., Finnish History
LEIMU, P., Finnish and Comparative Ethnology
LUUKKAINEN, M., German Language and Culture
SAARILUOMA, L., Comparative Literature and Drama
TAAVITSAINEN, J.-P., Finnish and Comparative Archaeology
VILJAMAA, T., Classical Philology
VIRTANEN, K., Cultural History

Faculty of Mathematics and Natural Sciences:

GYLLENBERG, M., Applied Mathematics
HAUKIOJA, E., Animal Ecology and Systematics
HIRVONEN, J.-P., Materials Science
HYVÖNEN, J., Plant Systematics and Ecology
HÖLSÄ, J., Inorganic Chemistry
JÄRVI, T. H. J., Computer Science
KALLIO, H., Food Chemistry
KANKARE, J., Analytical Chemistry
KARHUMÄKI, G., Mathematics
KAUPPINEN, J. K., Physics
LÖNNBERG, H., Organic Chemistry
LÖVGREN, T., Biotechnology
MÄNTSÄLÄ, P. I., Biochemistry
NIKINMAA, M., Animal Physiology
PAPUNEN, H., Geology and Mineralogy
PIHLAJA, K., Physical Chemistry
PORTIN, P., Genetics
PUNKKINEN, M., Physics
PURSIHEIMO, U. J., Applied Mathematics
SALO, J., Biodiversity Research
SALOMAA, A. K., Mathematics
SALONEN, V.-P., Quaternary Geology
SEWÓN, P. I., Plant Physiology
TIETÄVÄINEN, A. A., Mathematics
TUHKANEN, S., Physical Geography
VALTONEN, M., Astronomy
YLI-JOKIPII, P., Human Geography

Faculty of Medicine:

AULA, P., Medical Genetics
ERKKOLA, R., Obstetrics and Gynaecology
FINNE, J., Medical Biochemistry
HAVU, V. K., Dermatology and Venereal Diseases
HUHTANIEMI, I., Physiology
JUVA, K., Clinical Chemistry
KANTO, J., Anaesthesiology
KORMANO, M. J., Diagnostic Radiology
KORPI, E., Pharmacology
KOSKENVUO, M., Public Health
LAURI, S., Nursing Science
LEHTONEN, A., Geriatrics
NEVALAINEN, T. J., Pathology
NIINIKOSKI, J. H. A., Surgery
PIHA, J., Child Psychiatry
RINNE, U. K., Neurology
SAARI, K. M., Ophthalmology
SALMI, A., Virology
SALOKANGAS, R., Psychiatry
SAUKKO, P., Forensic Medicine
SCHEININ, M., Clinical Pharmacology
SILLANPÄÄ, M., Paediatric Neurology
SIMELL, O. G., Paediatrics
SOINI, E., Medical Physics and Engineering
SYRVÄNEN, S., Oral Pathology
TENOVUO, J. O., Cariology
TERHO, E. O., Pulmonary Diseases and Clinical Allergology
TOIVANEN, A., Internal Medicine
TOIVANEN, P. U., Bacteriology and Serology
VÄÄNÄNEN, K., Anatomy
VIROLAINEN, E., Otorhinolaryngology
VUORIO, E., Molecular Biology
WICKSTRÖM, G., Occupational Health
YLI-URPO, A., Dental Prosthetics

Faculty of Law:

BACKMAN, E. V., Criminal Law
BJÖRNE, L., Roman Law and Legal History
JOKELA, A. T., Procedural Law
JYRÄNKI, A., Constitutional and International Law
KARTIO, L., Civil Law
KULLA, H., Administrative Law
KUUSINIEMI, K., Environmental Law
LARYAVA, H., Periodontology
NÄRHI, M., Stomatognatic Physiology
PYRHÖNEN, S., Oncology and Radiotherapy
SAARNILEHTO, A., Civil Law
TOLONEN, H., Jurisprudence
VIKSTRÖM, K. T., Financial Law

Faculty of Social Sciences:

ANTOLA, E., European Institutions and Civilizations
HAKOVIRTA, H., Political Science, International Politics
HILPINEN, R., Theoretical Philosophy
KALELA, J., Political History
KANGAS, O., Social Policy
KIVINEN, O., Sociology of Education
NIEMI, P., Psychology
NURMI, H., Political Science
PIETARINEN, V. J., Practical Philosophy
SALAVUO, K., Social Policy
SULKUNEN, P., Sociology
VIRÉN, M., Economics
VUORELA, E., Economics

Faculty of Education:

LEHTINEN, E., Learning Environment and Educational Technology
NIINISTÖ, K. P., Education (Teacher Training)
OLKINUORA, E. T., Education
PELTONEN, J., Education (Teaching of Handicrafts)
RINNE, R., Adult Education

ATTACHED INSTITUTES

Archipelago Research Institute: Head Dr I. VUORINEN.

Cardiorespiratory Research Unit: Head Assoc. Dr P. KÄÄPÄ.

Centre for Extension Studies: Head Dr M. JULKUNEN.

Centre for Maritime Studies: Head Dr J. VAINIO.

Language Centre: Head V. VÄÄTÄJÄ.

Kevo Subarctic Research Institute: Head Dr S. NEUVONEN.

Satakunta Environmental Research Centre: Head Dr M. OJANEN.

Tuorla Observatory: Head Prof. M. VALTONEN.

Turku Centre for Biotechnology: Head Dr M. SKURNIK.

Turku Centre for Computer Science: Head Prof. R.-J. BACK.

Turku PET Centre: Head Dr J. KNUUTI.

VAASAN YLIOPISTO
(University of Vaasa)

POB 700 (Yliopistonranta), 65101 Vaasa
Telephone: (6) 3248111
Fax: (6) 3248179
E-mail: international.affairs@uwasa.fi

Founded 1966
Languages of instruction: Finnish, Swedish, English
State control
Academic year: September to May

Rector: MATTI JAKOBSSON
Vice-Rector: KAUKO MIKKONEN
Administrative Director: EILA REKILÄ
Librarian: VUOKKO PALONEN

Library of 120,000 vols
Number of teachers: 160
Number of students: 3,500
Publication: *Acta Wasaensia.*

DEANS

Faculty of Accounting and Industrial Management: Prof. ILKKA VIRTANEN
Faculty of Business Administration: Prof. VESA ROUTAMAA
Faculty of Humanities: Prof. ANTERO NIEMIKORPI
Faculty of Social Sciences: Prof. ISMO LUMIJÄRVI

PROFESSORS

Faculty of Business Administration:

GAHMBERG, H., Management and Organization
LAAKSONEN, M., Marketing
LAAKSONEN, P., Marketing
LARIMO, J., International Marketing
LEHTONEN, A., Law
MIKKONEN, K., Regional Studies
OKKO, P., Economics
ROUTAMAA, V., Management and Organization
SUUTARI, V., Management and Organization
TOLONEN, J., Business Law
VESALAINEN, J., Management and Organization

Faculty of Accounting and Industrial Management:

ALANDER, J., Production Automation
JAKOBSSON, M., Information Technology
LAITINEN, E. K., Accounting and Business Finance
NIEMI, V., Mathematics
PYNNÖNEN, S., Statistics
SALMI, T., Accounting and Business Finance
TAKALA, J., Production Economics
VEKARA, T., Electrical Engineering
VIRTANEN, I., Operations Research and Management Science
YLI-OLLI, P., Accounting and Business Finance

Faculty of Social Sciences:

HOVI, J., Public Law
KOSKINEN, T., Economic Sociology
LUMIJÄRVI, I., Public Administration
SALMELA, R., Social and Health Administration
SALMINEN, A., Public Administration

Faculty of Humanities:

INGO, R., Modern Finnish
LAURÉN, CH., Swedish
MALMBERG, T., Informatics
NIEMIKORPI, A., Modern Finnish
NIKULA, H., Modern German
NORDMAN, M., Swedish
NUOPPONEN, A., Applied Linguistics
PARRY, CH, German Literature
POUSSA, P., English Language, Literature and Culture

ATTACHED INSTITUTES

Centre for Continuing Education: Dir J. PELTONIEMI.
Computer Centre: Dir M. TAANONEN.
Technology Research Centre Technobothnia: Dir I. RAATIKAINEN.
University of Vaasa Research Centre: Dir H. KATAJAMÄKI.

University Institutions

HELSINGIN KAUPPAKORKEAKOULU
(Helsinki School of Economics and Business Administration)

Runeberginkatu 14–16, 00100 Helsinki
Telephone: (9) 43131
Fax: (9) 43138707

Founded 1911
Language of instruction: Finnish
State control
Academic year: September to May

Chancellor: AATTO PRIHTI
Rector: EERO KASANEN
Vice-Rectors: RISTO TAINIO, OLLI AHTOLA
Head of Administration: ESA AHONEN
Librarian: EEVA-LIISA LEHTONEN

Number of teachers: 142, including 37 professors
Number of students: 4,362

Publications: *Acta Academiae Oeconomicae Helsingiensis*, Series B, C, D, F, M.

PROFESSORS

AHTOLA, O., Marketing
ANTTILA, M., Marketing
HAAPARANTA, P., International Economics
HAKKARAINEN, H., German Language
ILMAKUNNAS, P., Industrial and Labour Economics
KALLIO, M., Management Systems
KANTO, A., Statistics
KASANEN, E., Finance
KINNUNEN, J., Financial Accounting
KIVIJÄRVI, H., Information Systems
KORHONEN, P., Management Science
KYLÄKOSKI, K., Management Accounting
LAHTI, A., Entrepreneurship
LEPPINIEMI, J., Finance and Capital Markets
LILJA, K., Business Administration
LUOSTARINEN, R., International Marketing
MARTIKAINEN, T., Finance
MÖLLER, K., Business Economics
NISKAKANGAS, H., Law
NUOLIJÄRVI, P., Finnish Language
PIHKALA, E., Economic History
POHJOLA, M., Economics
RÄSÄNEN, K., Organization and Management
SÄÄKSJÄRVI, M., Business Information Systems
SAARINEN, T., Information Systems
SALO, S., Applied Mathematics
TAINIO, R., Business Administration
TOMBAK, M., Technology Management
UUSITALO, L., Marketing Communications and Consumer Theory
VEPSÄLÄINEN, A., Logistics
VIRTANEN, K., Management Accounting
WALLENIUS, J., Decision Making and Planning

ATTACHED INSTITUTES

International Centre: Dir JYRKI WALLENIUS.

Programme for Development Cooperation: Dir LIISA TERVO.

Centre for Management Development: Dir LEENA MASALIN.

Information Technology: Dir MARKKU KUULA.

SVENSKA HANDELSHÖGSKOLAN (Swedish School of Economics and Business Administration)

POB 479, 00101 Helsinki

Telephone: (9) 431331
Fax: (9) 431333
E-mail: postmaster@shh.fi

Founded 1909
Languages of instruction: Swedish, English
State control
Academic year: September to May

Rector: M. STENIUS
Vice-Rectors: M. LINDELL, J. KNIF
Administrative Director: M. LINDROOS
Librarian: M. SCHRÖDER

Number of teachers: 95, including 31 professors
Number of students: 2,097

Publications: *Ekonomi och Samhälle* (main series), Reports, Working Papers (Swedish or English).

PROFESSORS

BERGLUND, T., Economics
BJÖRK, P., Marketing and Corporate Geography
BJÖRKMAN, I., Management and Organization
BLOMQVIST, H. C., Economics
BRUUN, N., Commercial Law
EKHOLM, B.-G., Accounting
ERIKSSON, I., Statistics and Computer Science
GRÖNROOS, C., Marketing and Corporate Geography
HANSSON, M., Finance
HELENIUS, R., Political Science
HOLMLUND, M., Marketing and Corporate Geography
KNIF, J., Finance
KOCK, S., Entrepreneurship and Management (at Vasa)
LERVIKS, A.-E., Marketing and Corporate Geography
LILJEBLOM, E., Finance
LINDELL, M., Management and Organization
LINDQVIST, L.-J., Marketing and Corporate Geography
LÖFLUND, A., Finance
MÄNTYSAARI, P., Commercial Law
RINGBOM, S., Economics
ROSENQVIST, G., Statistics and Computer Science
RYYNÄNEN, O., Commercial Law
SEVÓN, G., Management and Organization
STENBACKA, R., Economics
STENIUS, M., Finance
STRANDVIK, T., Marketing and Corporate Geography
SUNDGREN, S., Accounting
TANDEFELT, M., Languages and Communication
TÖRNROOS, J.-Å., Marketing and Corporate Geography
TROBERG, P., Auditing
WALLIN, J., Accounting

Vasa Branch: Biblioteksgatan 16, 65100 Vasa; tel. (6) 3247511; fax. (6) 3128020.

SVENSKA SOCIAL- OCH KOMMUNALHÖGSKOLAN VID HELSINGFORS UNIVERSITET (Swedish School of Social Science)

PB16 (Topeliusgatan 16), 00014 Helsingfors Universitet, Helsinki

Telephone: (9) 405001
Fax: (9) 40500295

Founded 1943

Rector: HENRIK HÄGGLUND

Library of 36,000 vols
Number of teachers: 50
Number of students: 500

TAIDETEOLLINEN KORKEAKOULU (University of Art and Design)

Hämeentie 135C, 00560 Helsinki

Telephone: (9) 75631
Fax: (9) 75630223

Founded 1871
State control
Languages of instruction: Finnish, English, Swedish
Academic year: September to May

Rector: YRJÖ SOTAMAA
Vice-Rectors: MERJA SALO, YRJÄNÄ LEVANTO
Director of Administration: ILKKA HUOVIO
Librarian: LIISA KEMPPI

Library of 39,700 vols
Number of teachers: 73 (full-time), 500 (part-time)
Number of students: 1,482

Publications: *Vuosikertomus* (annual report), *Opinto-opas* (Study guide), *Arttu* (bulletin, every 2 months), *UIAH* series A, B and C.

HEADS OF DEPARTMENT

Department of Art Education: LIISA PIIRONEN
Department of Graphic Design: JUHO HÄMÄLÄINEN
Department of Theatre, Film and Television Design: EEVA IJÄS
Department of Photography: MERJA SALO
Department of Film and Television: Prof. LAURI TÖRHÖNEN
Department of Ceramic and Glass Design: TAPIO YLI-VIIKARI
Department of Interior Architecture and Furniture Design: JAN VERWIJNEN
Department of Textile Art and Clothing Design: ELISA ANVO-PORKOLA
Department of Industrial Design: RAIMO NIKKANEN
Department of General Studies: Prof. SAKARI MARILA

ATTACHED INSTITUTES

Institute for Research in Art and Design: Dir PEKKA KORVENMAA.
West Finland Design Centre (MUOVA): Dir Prof. ARI SALONEN.
Finnish Design Management Institute: Dir Prof. Y. SOTAMAA.
Medialab: Head PHILIP DEAN.
Centre for Advanced Studies: Dir PEKKA SAARELA.

TURUN KAUPPAKORKEAKOULU (Turku School of Economics and Business Administration)

Rehtorinpellonkatu 3, 20500 Turku

Telephone: (2) 338311
Fax: (2) 3383299

Founded 1950
Language of instruction: Finnish
State control
Academic year: August to July

Rector: T. REPONEN
Vice-Rector: R. MAJALA
Chief Administrative Officer: A. LEINO
Librarian: P. RAUTIAINEN

Number of teachers: 89
Number of students: 1,900

PROFESSORS

HAKKARAINEN, P., Economic Sociology (acting)
HANSÉN, S.-O., International Marketing
IKÄHEIMO, S., Accounting and Finance (acting)
KIVIKARI, U., International Economics
LÄHTEENMÄKI, S., Management and Organization (acting)
LUKKA, K., Accounting and Finance
MAJALA, R., Accounting and Finance
MÄKINEN, E. H., Marketing
NURMI, R. W., Management and Organization
OJALA, L., Logistics
PAASIO, A., Business Administration (entrepreneurship)
PIHLANTO, P. H., Accounting and Finance
REINIKAINEN, V., Economics
SAVIRANTA, J., Economic Geography
SEPPÄLÄ, T., Economic Mathematics and Statistics (acting)
SILLANPÄÄ, M., Commercial Law
SUOMI, R. V., Information Systems Science
TAINA, J., Shipping Economics
VAPAA VUORI, A., Commercial Law
VIHANTO, M., Economics (acting)
VUOKKO, P., Marketing (acting)

ATTACHED CENTRES

Business Research and Development Centre: Head Prof. ANTTI PAASIO.

Institute for East-West Trade: Head Prof. URPO KIVIKARI.

Institute for European Studies: Head Prof. ESA STENBERG.

Finland Futures Research Centre: Head TARJA MERISTÖ.

Other Colleges and Institutes

Arcada (Polytechnic): Metsäpojankuja 3, 02130 Espoo; tel. (9) 525-321; fax (9) 525-32207; f. 1996; healthcare and social work, business and services, technology; library of 12,500 vols; Rector HENRIK WOLFF.

Helsingin Teknillinen Oppilaitos (Technical Institute of Helsinki): Bulevardi 31, 00180 Helsinki; tel. 680481; fax 68048200; f. 1881; 250 teachers; 2,300 students; library of 32,000 vols; Rector JUHA KAUNISMAA.

Turun Ammattikonkeakoulu (Turku Polytechnic): Sepänkatu 1, 20700 Turku; tel. (10) 55000; fax (10) 5500791; f. 1849; 2,000 students; Rector Dr KAJ MALM.

Työterveyslaitos (Finnish Institute of Occupational Health): Topeliuksenkatu 41a A, 00250 Helsinki; tel. (9) 47471; fax (9) 2414634; f. 1945; 240 researchers; regional institutes in Kuopio, Lappeenranta, Oulu, Tampere, Turku and Uusimaa; information service centre of 40,000 vols and 500 journals; Dir-Gen. JORMA RANTANEN; publs *Scandinavian Journal of Work, Environment and Health* (every 2 months), *Työ-Terveys-Turvallisuus* (15 a year).

Schools of Art and Music

SIBELIUS-AKATEMIA

POB 86, 00251 Helsinki

Telephone: (9) 4054-41
Fax: (9) 4054-600

Founded 1882
Languages of instruction: Finnish and Swedish
State control
Academic year: September to May
University status

Rector: LASSI RAJAMAA
Vice-Rector: TUULA KOTILAINEN
Administrative Director: SEPPO SUIHKO

Library: see Libraries
Number of teachers: 189 full-time, 350 part-time
Number of students: 1,760
Publication: *Sibis* (newsletter).

DEANS

Composition and Music Theory: MATTI SAARINEN
Solo Performance: MARGIT RAHKONEN
Music Education: MARJUT LAITINEN
Church Music: OLLI PORTHAN
Folk Music: KRISTIINA ILMONEN
Jazz: JARNO KUKKONEN
Church Music in Kuopio: OLAVI HAUTSALO
Opera: RIITTA -LIISA KYYKKÄ

PROFESSORS

GOTHONI, R., Chamber Music
HEININEN, P., Composition
HELASVUO, M., Wind Music
HYNNINEN, J., Singing
KARMA, K., Music Education
KURKELA, K., Research into Musical Performance
NORAS, A., Cello
ORAMO, I., Theory of Music
PELTO, P., Church Music
POHJOLA, L., Piano
PORTHAN, O., Organ
ROUSI, M., Cello
SAARIKETTU, K., Violin
SEGERSTAM, L., Conducting
TAWASTSTJERNA, E. T., Piano
TUKIAINEN, S., Violin

Kuvataideakatemia (Academy of Fine Arts): Yrjönkatu 18, 00120 Helsinki; tel. 680-3320; fax 680-33260; f. 1848; degree courses in painting, sculpture, graphics and media arts; 11 teachers; 200 students; Rector ERKKI SOININEN.

ÅLAND ISLANDS

Learned Societies

GENERAL

Ålands kulturstiftelse (Åland Cultural Foundation): POB 172, 22101 Mariehamn; f. 1951; promotes research of Åland history, promotes cultural life in the islands; Pres. BÖRJE KARLSSON; Sec. ANITA PENSAR.

Libraries and Archives

Mariehamn

Mariehamns stadsbibliotek–Centralbibliotek för Åland (Mariehamn City Library–Central Library of Åland): Strandgatan 29, 22100 Mariehamn; fax 531419; e-mail biblioteket@mariehamn.aland.fi; 120,000 vols; special collection: Alandica collection; Chief Librarian TOM ECKERMAN.

Museums and Art Galleries

Lappo

Skärgårdsmuseet (Museum of the Archipelago): 22840 Lappo; tel. 56621; specializes in fishermen's tools and other ethnographica from 19th century.

Mariehamn

Ålands konstmuseum (Art Museum): POB 60, 22101 Mariehamn; tel. (18) 25426; emphasis on local artists from 19th century onwards; Curator ANNA-LENA DREIJER.

Ålands Museum: 22100 Mariehamn; tel. 25000; e-mail info@aland-museum.aland.fi; f. 1934; prehistoric, historic and ethnological material; library of 27,000 vols; Dir KJELL EKSTRÖM; publs *Åländsk Odling* (annually), *Ålands Folkminnesförbund, Bygdeserien.*

Ålands Sjöfartsmuseum (Maritime Museum): PB 98, 22101 Mariehamn; tel. (18) 19930; fax (18) 19936; e-mail staff@maritime-museum.aland.fi; f. 1935; ships' documents, model ships, etc; Pres. BO LINDHOLM; Dir Capt. HENRIK KARLSSON.

Colleges

Ålands Högskola (Åland University College): POB 160, 22101 Mariehamn; tel. (18) 25000; fax (18) 22160; e-mail hogskolan@ah.aland.fi; f. 1981; Dir BRITTMARI WIKSTRÖM.

FRANCE

Learned Societies

GENERAL

Académie des Jeux Floraux: Hotel d'Assézat, 31000 Toulouse; f. 1323; all human sciences; composed of 40 'mainteneurs' and 25 'Maîtres ès Jeux Floraux'; Permanent Sec. JEAN SERMET; publ. *Recueil* (annually)

Académie des Sciences, Agriculture, Arts et Belles-Lettres d'Aix: 2A rue du 4-Septembre, 13100 Aix-en-Provence; tel. 4-42-38-38-95; f. 1829; library of 100,000 vols; collections of ceramics, paintings, sculptures; Pres. PAUL JOURDAN; Perm. Sec. GEORGES SOUVILLE; publ. *Bulletin*.

Académie des Sciences, Arts et Belles-Lettres de Dijon: 5 rue de l'Ecole de Droit, 21000 Dijon; f. 1740; 550 mems; library; Pres. MICHEL PAUTY; Sec. MARTINE CHAUNEY-BOUILLOT; publs *Mémoires de l'Académie* (every 2 years), *Mémoires de la Commission des Antiquités de la Côte d'Or* (every 2 years).

Académie des Sciences, Belles-Lettres et Arts de Lyon: Palais Saint-Jean, 4 ave Adolphe Max, 69005 Lyon; tel. 4-78-38-26-54; f. 1700; 52 elected mems; library of 60,000 vols; Pres. J. BOIDIN; Chancellor P. MALAPERT; publ. *Mémoires* (annually).

Académie des Sciences d'Outre-mer: 15 rue Lapérouse, 75116 Paris; tel. 1-47-20-87-93; fax 1-47-20-89-72; f. 1922; library of 50,000 vols and 2,000 periodicals; 275 mems (incl. 100 corresponding, 50 assoc., 25 free mems) attached to sections on Geography, Politics and Administration, Law, Economics and Sociology, Science and Medicine, Education; Perm. Sec. GILBERT MANGIN; publs *Mondes et Cultures*, *Hommes et Destins* (Biographical Dictionary).

Académie Goncourt: Société de Gens de Lettres, c/o Drouant, Place Gaillon, 75002 Paris; f. 1896 by Edmond de Goncourt; composed of 10 members. The prize awarded at the end of each year by the Academy is regarded as a very high literary distinction; Pres. FRANÇOIS NOURISSIER; Sec.-Gen. DIDIER DECOIN.

Académie Mallarmé: Hôtel de Massa, 38 rue du Faubourg Saint-Jacques, 75014 Paris; 30 mems, 30 corresp.; awards an annual prize; Pres. JEAN ORIZET; Sec.-Gen. CHARLES DOBZYNSKI.

Agence de Coopération Culturelle et Technique: 13 quai André Citroën, 75015 Paris; tel. 1-44-37-33-00; telex 201916; fax 1-45-79-14-98; f. 1970; an intergovernmental organization of French-speaking countries for co-operation in the fields of education, culture, science, technology, and in any other ways to bring the peoples of those countries closer together; 47 mems; Sec.-Gen. JEAN-LOUIS ROY.

Alliance Française: 101 blvd Raspail, 75270 Paris Cedex 06; tel. 1-45-44-38-28; fax 1-45-44-89-42; e-mail afparis_ecole@compuserve.fr; f. 1883; the oldest-established French language school for foreigners; independent institution; 20,000 students; Pres. JACQUES VIOT; Sec.-Gen. JEAN HARZIC; Dir of the School JOSEPH COMMETS.

Comité des Travaux Historiques et Scientifiques: 1 rue Descartes, 75005 Paris; tel. 1-46-34-47-57; fax 1-46-34-47-60; f. 1834, reorg. 1991 as part of Min. of Ed.; research and publs in the fields of history, archaeology, geography, human sciences, natural sciences, life sciences; organizes annual national congress of learned societies; 300 mems; Admin. Sec. MARTINE FRANÇOIS; publs *Actes du Congrès national des Sociétés savantes*, etc.

Euskaltzaindia/Académie de la Langue Basque: 37 rue Pannecau, 64100 Bayonne; tel. 5-59-25-64-26; fax 5-59-59-45-59. See also under Spain, Academies.

Institut de France: 23 quai de Conti, 75006 Paris; tel. 1-44-41-44-41; fax 1-44-41-43-41; e-mail com@institut-de-france-fr; f. 1795; Chancellor MARCEL LANDOWSKI; Dir of Services ERIC PEUCHOT.

Constituent academies:

Académie Française: 23 quai de Conti, 75006 Paris; f. 1635; 40 mems; Permanent Sec. MAURICE DRUON; Dir JEAN-DENIS BREDIN.

Academie des Inscriptions et Belles-Lettres: 23 quai de Conti, 75006 Paris; f. 1663; 45 mems, 10 free mems, 20 foreign assocs, 30 French and 40 foreign corresp. mems; Pres. CLAUDE NICOLET; Permanent Sec. JEAN LECLANT; publs *Comptes Rendus*, *Journal des Savants*, *Mémoires*, and various on orientalism, classical antiquity and the Middle Ages.

Académie des Sciences: 23 quai de Conti, 75006 Paris; f. 1666; sections of Mathematics, of Physics, of Mechanics, of Science of the Universe, of Chemistry, of Cellular and Molecular Biology, of Animal and Plant Biology, of Human Biology and Medical Sciences; 140 mems, at most 120 foreign assocs and 180 corresp. mems; Pres. JACQUES-LOUIS LIONS; Permanent Secs JEAN DERCOURT (Mathematical and Physical Sciences and their Applications), FRANÇOIS GROS (Chemical, Natural, Biological and Medical Sciences and their Applications); publs *Comptes Rendus*, *La Vie des Sciences*, newsletter.

Académie des Beaux-Arts: 23 quai de Conti, 75006 Paris; f. 1648; sections of Painting, Sculpture, Architecture, Engraving, Musical Composition, Free Members, Artistic Creation (Cinema and Audiovisual Arts); 50 mems, 15 foreign assocs, 50 corresp. mems; Pres. JEAN CARDOT; Permanent Sec. ARNAUD D'HAUTERIVES.

Académie des Sciences Morales et Politiques: 23 quai de Conti, 75006 Paris; f. 1795; sections of Philosophy, of Moral and Sociological Sciences, of Legislation, Public Law and Jurisprudence, of Political Economy, Statistics and Finance, of History and Geography, of General Interest; 50 mems, 12 foreign assocs, 60 corresp. mems; Pres. ROGER ARNALDEZ; Permanent Sec. PIERRE MESSMER; publs *Revue des Sciences morales et politiques*, *Ordonnances des Rois de France*, *Notices biographiques et bibliographiques*.

AGRICULTURE, FISHERIES AND VETERINARY SCIENCE

Académie d'Agriculture de France: 18 rue de Bellechasse, 75007 Paris; tel. 1-47-05-10-37; fax 1-45-55-09-78; f. 1761; 120 mems, 60 foreign mems, 180 corresp. mems, 60 foreign corresp. mems; Pres. RAYMOND MÉRILLON; Perm. Sec. GEORGES PÉDRO; library of 80,000 vols, 500 periodicals; publ. *Comptes rendus*.

Académie Vétérinaire de France: 60 blvd Latour-Maubourg, 75007 Paris; f. 1844; 44 mems; Sec.-Gen. Prof. M. CATSARAS; publ. *Bulletin* (quarterly).

Association Centrale des Vétérinaires: 10 place Léon Blum, 75011 Paris; f. 1889; 3,000 mems; Pres. Dr J. P. MARTY.

Association Française pour l'Etude du Sol: INRA, Domaine de Limère, ave de la Pomme de Pin, 45160 Ardon; f. 1934; e-mail afes@orleans.inra.fr; pedology, agronomy; 950 mems; Pres. M. JAMAGNE; publ. *Etude et Gestion des Sols*.

Société Française d'Economie Rurale: INA-PG, 16 rue Claude Bernard, 75231 Paris Cedex 05; tel. 1-47-07-47-86; f. 1949; two study sessions a year; 400 mems; Pres. PHILIPPE LACOMBE; Sec.-Gen. LUCIEN BOURGEOIS; publ. *Economie Rurale* (every 2 months).

Société Nationale d'Horticulture de France (SNHF): 84 rue de Grenelle, 75007 Paris; tel. 1-44-39-78-78; fax 1-45-44-96-57; f. 1827; 13,000 mems, 800,000 affiliated mems; library of 15,000 vols; Pres. MICHEL COINTAT; Gen. Sec. GEORGES SOUBEYRAND; publ. *Jardins de France* (10 a year).

Société Vétérinaire Pratique de France: 10 place Léon Blum, 75011 Paris; f. 1879; 750 mems; Pres. JEAN-PIERRE BORNET; Sec.-Gen. JACQUES DOUCET; publ. *Bulletin* (monthly).

ARCHITECTURE AND TOWN PLANNING

Académie d'Architecture: 9 place des Vosges, 75004 Paris; f. 1840 as Société Centrale des Architectes, name changed 1953; 100 elected mems; Pres. WLADIMIR MITROFANOFF; Gen. Sec. GUY AUTRAN.

Association Nationale pour la Protection des Villes d'Art: 39 ave de La Motte-Picquet, 75007 Paris; tel. 1-47-05-37-71; f. 1963; an association of local societies in 85 cities for the protection and restoration of historic and artistic buildings; Pres. J. DE SACY.

Compagnie des Experts-Architectes près la Cour d'Appel de Paris: 24 rue Bezout, 75014 Paris; tel. 1-43-27-59-69; fax 1-43-20-47-96; f. 1928; 125 mems; Pres. MICHEL AUSTRY; Gen. Sec. ROBERT LEGRAS.

Conseil National de l'Ordre des Architectes: 25 rue du Petit Musc, 75004 Paris; tel. 1-53-01-95-55; fax 1-53-01-95-69; e-mail info@cnoa.com; f. 1977 as the official regulating body for the architectural profession; Pres. of Conseil YVES MAGNAN; Sec. ALAIN FABREGA; publ. *d'Architectures* (monthly).

Institut Français d'Architecture: 6 rue de Tournon, 75006 Paris; tel. 1-46-33-90-36; fax 1-46-33-02-11; f. 1980; funded by Min. of Culture; contemporary French architecture; library of 10,000 vols, 70 periodicals; Pres. FRANÇOIS BARRÉ; Dir. LUCIANA RAVANEL; publ. *Bulletin d'informations architecturales* (monthly).

Office Général du Bâtiment et des Travaux Publics: 55 ave Kléber, 75784 Paris Cedex 16; tel. 1-40-69-51-00; f. 1918; combines the majority of societies, unions and federations of architects and contractors; Pres. M. MICHEL MARCONNET.

Société Française des Architectes: 55 rue du Cherche-Midi, 75006 Paris; tel. 1-45-48-53-10; fax 1-42-84-01-99; f. 1877; cultural association; 1,000 mems; Pres. LAURENT SALOMON; publ. *Tribune d'Histoire et d'Actualité de l'Architecture* (2 a year).

Société pour la Protection des Paysages, et de l'Esthétique de la France: 39 ave de la Motte-Picquet, 75007 Paris; f. 1901; 5,000 mems; Pres. P. ALBRECHT; publ. *Sites et Monuments* (quarterly).

BIBLIOGRAPHY, LIBRARY SCIENCE AND MUSEOLOGY

Association des Archivistes Français: 60 rue des Francs-Bourgeois, 75141 Paris Cedex 03; tel. 1-40-27-60-00; f. 1904; 700 mems; Pres. JEAN-LUC EICHENLAUB; Sec. JEAN LE POTTIER; publ. *La Gazette des Archives* (quarterly).

Association des Bibliothécaires Français: 31 rue de Chabrol, 75010 Paris; tel. 1-55-33-10-30; fax 1-55-33-10-31; e-mail abf@wanadoo.fr; f. 1906; 2,500 mems; Pres. CLAUDINE BELAYCHE; Gen. Sec. MARIE-MARTINE TOMITCH; publ. *ABF Bulletin d'Informations* (quarterly).

Association des Conservateurs de Bibliothèques: INA-PG, 16 rue Claude Bernard, 75005 Paris; tel. and fax 1-44-08-18-62; f. 1967; organizes conferences, study groups, study tours, etc. and collaborates with other similar bodies to further research and training in all aspects of librarianship; 600 mems; Pres. NOËL TANAZACQ; Sec. BERNADETTE JOSEPH; publs *Annuaire* (every 2 years), *ACB Infos* (quarterly).

Association des Professionnels de l'Information et de la Documentation (ADBS): 25 rue Claude Tillier, 75012 Paris; tel. 1-43-72-25-25; fax 1-43-72-30-41; e-mail adbs@adbs.fr; f. 1963; 5,000 mems; organizes bi-annual congress with Asscn Nationale de la Recherche Technique; Pres. FLORENCE WILHELM; Gen. Man. OLIVIER THIEBAULD; publs *Documentaliste, Sciences de l'Information* (every 2 months), *ADBS/Informations* (monthly).

Association Générale des Conservateurs des Collections Publiques de France: 6 rue des Pyramides, 75041 Paris Cedex 01; tel. 1-40-15-36-49; fax 1-47-03-44-82; f. 1922 to promote and improve museums and museums' curatorship; 1,000 mems; Pres. JACQUES MAIGRET; publ. *Musées et Collections Publiques de France* (quarterly).

Centre d'Archives et de Documentation Politiques et Sociales: 86 blvd Haussmann, 75008 Paris; f. 1949; Dir Dr G. ALBERTINI; publs *Informations Politiques et Sociales* (weekly in France, Africa and Asia), *Est et Ouest* (monthly), *Le Monde des Conflits* (monthly).

ECONOMICS, LAW AND POLITICS

Association d'Etudes et d'Informations Politiques Internationales: 86 blvd Haussmann, 75008 Paris; f. 1949; Dir G. ALBERTINI; publs *Est & Ouest* (Paris, twice monthly), *Documenti sul Comunismo* (Rome), *Este y Oeste* (Caracas).

Fondation Nationale des Sciences Politiques: 27 rue Saint Guillaume, 75337 Paris Cedex 07; tel. 1-45-49-50-50; fax 1-42-22-31-26; f. 1945; administers the Institut d'Etudes Politiques de Paris (*q.v.*), promotes research centres and social science studies, documentation service; library of 700,000 vols; Pres. RENÉ RÉMOND; Admin. R. DESCOINGS; Scientif. Dir J. L. DOMENACH; publs *Revue Française de Science Politique* (every 2 months), *Bulletin Analytique de Documentation* (monthly), *Mots* (4 a year), *Revue Economique* (every 2 months), *Revue de l'OFCE* (quarterly), *Vingtième Siècle, Revue d'Histoire* (quarterly).

Institut des Actuaires Français: 59 rue de la Boétie, 75008 Paris; tel. 1-45-63-61-35; f. 1890; 600 mems; library of 5,000 vols; Pres. JEAN BERTHON; publ. *Bulletin* (quarterly).

Institut d'Histoire Sociale: 4 ave Benoît-Frachon, 92023 Nanterre Cedex; tel. 1-46-14-09-29; fax 1-46-14-09-25; e-mail bibihs@aol.com; f. 1935; study of Communist and Soviet activities; library of 40,000 vols specializing in political sciences and history of workers' movements since beginning of 19th century, trade union periodicals and political reviews; Dir MORVAN DUHAMEL; publs *Cahiers d'Histoire Sociale* (2 a year), *Chronique Economique Syndicale et Sociale* (monthly).

Institut Français des Relations Internationales: 27 rue de la Procession, 75740 Paris Cedex 15; tel. 1-40-61-60-00; fax 1-40-61-60-60; f. 1979; studies foreign policy, economy, defence and strategy; 900 mems; library of 30,000 vols; Dir THIERRY DE MONTBRIAL; publs *Politique Etrangère* (quarterly), *Lettre d'Information* (every 3 months), *Enjeux internationaux—Travaux et Recherches, Notes de l'IFRI, RAMSES (Rapport Annuel sur le Système Economique et les Stratégies)* (annually).

Société d'Economie et de Science Sociales: 80 rue Vaneau, 75007 Paris; f. 1856; concerned with social reforms and sociology; 300 mems; library of 3,000 vols, including collection 'La Réforme Sociale'; Pres. EDOUARD SECRETAN; publ. *Les Etudes Sociales* (2 a year).

Société d'Etudes Jaurésiennes: 21 blvd Lefebvre, 75015 Paris; tel. 1-48-28-25-89; f. 1959 to promote all aspects of the life and works of Jean Jaurès; promotes the publication or re-edition of his speeches and writings; 300 mems; Pres. MADELEINE REBERIOUX; Sec.-Gen. VINCENT DUCLERT; publ. *Bulletin* (quarterly), *Cahiers trimestriels* (quarterly).

Société d'Histoire du Droit: 158 rue Saint Jacques, 75005 Paris; f. 1913; 550 mems; Pres. Prof. OLIVIER GUILLOT; Sec. A. LEFEBVRE.

Société de Législation Comparée: 28 rue St Guillaume, 75007 Paris; tel. 1-44-39-86-23; fax 1-44-39-86-28; e-mail slc@sky.fr; f. 1869; comparative law; library of 100,000 vols; 1,700 mems; Pres. XAVIER BLANC-JOUVAN; Gen. Sec. MARIE-ANNE GALLOT LE LORIER; publ. *Revue Internationale de Droit Comparé* (quarterly).

Société Statistique de Paris: C/o Institut Henri Poincaré, 11 rue Pierre et Marie Curie, 75231 Paris Cedex 05; f. 1860; 1,040 mems; library of 60,000 vols; Gen. Sec. ANNIE MORIN; Librarian Mme DEVILLERS; publs *Journal de la Société de Statistique de Paris*, *Revue trimestrielle internationale des statisticiens d'expression française*.

EDUCATION

Association Francophone d'Education Comparée: 1 ave Léon Journault, 92310 Sèvres; tel. 1-45-07-60-00; f. 1973 to promote comparative education among francophone teachers and educationalists; organizes one seminar a year and participates in meetings of the Comparative Education Society in Europe and the World Council of Comparative Educational Societies; 100 mems; Pres. JEAN-MICHEL LECLERCQ; Sec.-Gen. ANTOINE BEVORT; publs *Bulletin de liaison et d'information* (3 a year), *Education comparée* (annually).

Centre Culturel Calouste Gulbenkian: 51 ave d'Iéna, 75116 Paris; tel. 1-53-23-93-93; fax 1-53-23-93-99; f. 1955; non-profit-making; exhibitions, lectures, seminars; awards grants in the fields of education, art, science and charity; attached to Calouste Gulbenkian Foundation in Lisbon (*q.v.*); library of 60,000 vols; Dir ANTONIO COIMBRA MARTINS.

Conférence des Présidents d'Université: 103 blvd Saint-Michel, 75005 Paris; tel. 1-44-32-90-00; fax 1-44-32-91-58; f. 1971; consultative body at the disposition of the Minister of Education; also studies questions of interest to all universities and co-ordinates the activities of various commissions on all aspects of education; mems: 96 presidents of universities and state institutions; Pres. The Minister for Education; First Vice-Pres. JEAN-MARC MONTEIL.

Conférence des Recteurs Français: La Houssinière, BP 972, 44076 Nantes Cedex 03; f. 1967 to establish personal and permanent links between mems, to encourage the discussion of professional problems, and to establish relations with national and international bodies concerned with education, science and culture; 28 mems; the Rectors are Chancellors of the State univs in their administrative area; Pres. JEAN-CLAUDE MAESTRE (Acad. de Nantes); Sec. Gen./Treas. CLAUDE LAMBERT (Acad. de Creteil).

Fédération interuniversitaire de l'enseignement à distance français (FIED): Bureau E 217, Université de Paris X, 200 ave de la République, 92001 Nanterre Cedex; tel. 1-40-97-75-51; fax 1-47-29-18-21; e-mail fied@telesup.univ-mrs.fr; f. 1987; promotes distance learning by encouraging co-operation between French and international universities and institutions; 26 mems; Pres. Mme CH. GUILLARD; Secretary M. J. VAUTHIER.

Fondation Biermans-Lapôtre: 9A blvd Jourdan, 75690 Paris Cedex 14; tel. 1-40-78-72-00; fax 1-45-89-00-03; f. 1924; promotes academic and scientific exchanges between France and Belgium; offers grants, etc.; affiliated to Fondation Universitaire (see Belgium chapter); Pres. ALFRED CAHEN; Dir FERNAND MORAY.

Office National d'Information sur les Enseignements et les Professions: 12 mail B. Thimonnier, BP 86 Lognes, 77423 Marne la Vallée, Cedex 02; tel. 1-64-80-35-00; fax 1-64-80-35-01; f. 1970; Dir MICHEL VALDIGUIÉ; publs *Avenirs, ONISEP Communiqué* (every 2 months), *Bulletin d'Information* (monthly), *Réadaptation* (monthly), *Les Cahiers de l'ONISEP.*

Société Française de Pédagogie: 6 rue du Champ de l'Alouette, 75013 Paris; f. 1902; 10,000 mems; studies educational theories and teaching methods; Pres. M. BONISSEL; Gen. Sec. M. GEVREY; publ. *Bulletin Trimestriel*.

Union des Professeurs de Spéciales (Mathématiques et Sciences Physiques): 3 rue de l'École Polytechnique, 75005 Paris; tel. and fax 1-43-26-97-92; f. 1928; 2,500 mems; Pres. M. ROOY; Sec. M. DI VALENTIN.

FINE AND PERFORMING ARTS

Association du Salon d'Automne: Grand Palais, Porte H, 75008 Paris; f. 1903; sections: painting, engraving, mural and decorative art, sculpture, photography; Pres. JEAN-FRANÇOIS LARRIEU.

Jeunesses Musicales de France: 20 rue Geoffroy l'Asnier, 75004 Paris; tel. 1-44-61-86-86; telex 215901; fax 1-44-61-86-88; f. 1944; encourages young audiences, promotes concerts, dance, etc.; 5,000 delegates in 3,200 towns; Pres. J. L. TOURNIER; Dir ROBERT BERTHIER.

Société d'Histoire du Théâtre: 98 blvd Kellermann, 75013 Paris; tel. 1-45-88-46-55; fax 1-45-89-87-63; f. 1948; *c.* 1,000 mems; library of 45,000 vols; Pres. FRANÇOIS PÉRIER; Sec.-Gen. ROSE MARIE MOUDOUES; publ. *Revue d'Histoire du Théâtre* (quarterly).

Société de l'Histoire de l'Art Français: 1 rue Berbier du Mets, 75013 Paris; f. 1873; 1,000 mems; Pres. JEAN COURAL; Gen. Sec.

Bruno Foucart; publs *Bulletin, Archives de l'Art Français, Annuels.*

Société des Amis du Louvre: 34 quai du Louvre, 75001 Paris; tel. 1-40-20-53-34; f. 1897; 72,000 members; Pres. Marc Fumaroli; Sec.-Gen. Serge-Antoine Tchekhoff; publs. *Chronique, Bulletin Trimestriel* (quarterly).

Société des Artistes Décorateurs (SAD): Grand Palais, Porte H, Ave Winston Churchill, 75008 Paris; tel. 1-43-59-66-10; f. 1901 to promote modern art; 400 mems; Pres. Jean-Pierre Khalifa.

Société des Artistes Français: Grand Palais, Porte H., ave Winston-Churchill, 75008 Paris; tel. 1-43-59-52-49; fax 1-45-62-85-97; f. 1882; 5,000 members; its exhibition is held annually; Pres. Jean Campistron; publ. *Bulletin.*

Société des Artistes Indépendants: Grand Palais des Champs-Elysées, Ave Winston Churchill, Porte H, 75008 Paris; f. 1884; 2,500 members; unites the majority of artists of modern tendency; annual exhibition of paintings, sculpture, engravings and decorative art; Pres. Jean Monneret; Sec.-Gen. Suzanne Vincent.

Société des Auteurs, Compositeurs et Editeurs de Musique: 225 ave Charles-de-Gaulle, 92521 Neuilly sur Seine Cedex; tel. 1-47-15-47-15; fax 1-47-45-12-94; f. 1851; 80,000 mems; deals with collection and distribution of performing rights; Pres. Jacques Demarny; Pres. of the Directory Jean-Loup Tournier.

Société Française de Musicologie: 2 rue Louvois, 75002 Paris; tel. 1-47-03-75-49; f. 1917; 550 mems; Pres. Jean Gribenski; Sec.-Gen. Anik Devries-Lesure; publs *Revue* (2 a year), *Publications* (40 vols).

Société Française de Photographie: 4 rue Vivienne, 75002 Paris; tel. 1-42-60-05-98; fax 1-47-03-75-39; e-mail sfp@wanadoo.fr; f. 1854; 430 mems; library of 10,000 vols, and 25,000 old photographs; Pres. Michel Poivert; publs *Bulletin* (quarterly), *Etudes photographiques* (2 a year).

Société Nationale des Beaux-Arts: 11 rue Berryer, 75008 Paris; f. 1890; organizes art exhibitions; Pres. François Baboulet; Gen. Sec. Etienne Audfray.

HISTORY, GEOGRAPHY AND ARCHAEOLOGY

Association de Géographes Français: 191 rue Saint-Jacques, 75005 Paris; tel. 1-44-32-14-00; fax 1-45-29-13-40; f. 1920; 470 mems; Pres. A. Metton; Sec. J.-P. Charvet; publs *Bulletin* (every 2 months), *Bibliographie géographique annuelle.*

Association des Amis de la Revue de Géographie de Lyon: 18 rue Chevreul, 69362 Lyon Cedex 07; f. 1923; Pres. Nicole Commerçon; publ. *Revue de Géographie de Lyon* (quarterly).

Centre International d'Etudes Romanes: 13 Cour du Cloître, 71700 Tournus; tel. 3-85-32-54-45; fax 3-85-32-18-98; f. 1952; 400 mems; Pres. Geoffroy de Gislain de Bontin; Sec.-Gen. Marguerité Thibert; publ. *Bulletin* (annually, with Société des Amis des Arts et des Sciences de Tournus).

Comité National Français de Géographie: 191 rue Saint-Jacques, 75005 Paris; coordinates French geographical activity and participates in the work of the International Geographical Union; 400 mems; Pres. J. R. Pitte; Sec.-Gen. P. J. Thumerelle; publ. *Bibliographie Géographique Internationale* (published jointly with the International Geographical Union).

Comité Scientifique du Club Alpin Français: 24 ave de Laumière, 75019 Paris; tel. 1-53-72-87-13; fax 1-53-72-87-16; f. 1874; 20 mems; Dir J. Malbos.

Demeure Historique: Hôtel de Nesmond, 57 quai de la Tournelle, 75005 Paris; tel. 1-43-29-02-86; fax 1-43-29-36-44; f. 1924; 3,000 members; study, research and conservation of historic buildings, châteaux, etc.; Pres. Marquis de Breteuil; publ. *La Demeure Historique* (quarterly).

Fédération Française de Spéléologie: 130 rue Saint-Maur, 75011 Paris; tel. 1-43-57-56-54; fax 1-49-23-00-95; e-mail adherents@ffspeleo.fr; f. 1963; speleology; 12,000 mems; library of 2,000 vols, 600 periodicals; Pres. C. Viala; publs *Spelunca* (quarterly), *Karstologia* (2 a year), *Spelunca Mémoires, Karstologia Mémoires, Bulletin Bibliographique Spéléologique.*

Institut des Sciences Historiques: Société Archéologique de France, 45 rue Rémy Dumoncel, 75014 Paris; tel. 1-43-27-50-45; fax 1-40-47-04-09; f. 1816; historical research in Europe; 150 mems; Dir-Gen. Philippe Montillet; Sec.-Gen. Fabien Gandrille; publ. *La Science Historique* (quarterly).

Institut Français d'Etudes Byzantines: 21 rue d'Assas, 75006 Paris; tel. 1-44-39-52-24; fax 1-44-39-52-36; f. 1897; Byzantine research, particularly on sources of ecclesiastical history; 4 mems; library of 50,000 vols; publ. *Revue des Etudes Byzantines* (annually).

Institut Français d'Histoire Sociale: Centre de documentation et de recherche, Archives Nationales, 60 rue des Francs-Bourgeois, 75141 Paris Cedex 03; tel. 1-40-27-64-49; f. 1948; 200 mems; library of 12,000 vols, 50,000 pamphlets, large collection of periodicals, manuscripts and illustrated documents; Pres. Jean-Pierre Chaline; Vice-Pres. Henri Bartoli.

Société d'Emulation du Bourbonnais: 4 place de l'Ancien Palais, 03000 Moulins; tel. 4-70-44-39-03; f. 1846; 600 mems; activities in the fields of history, science, arts and literature; library of 30,000 vols; folklore museum; Pres. Jacques Lougnon; publ. *Bulletin* (quarterly).

Société d'Ethnographie de Paris: 6 rue Champfleury, 75007 Paris; f. 1859; 400 mems; Dirs A.-M. d'Ans, R. Lacombe; publ. *L'Ethnographie* (2 a year).

Société d'Ethnologie Française: 6 ave du Mahatma Gandhi, 75116 Paris; tel. 1-44-17-60-00; 500 mems; holds annual national conference and study sessions; Pres. F. Lautman; Sec.-Gen. F. Maguet; publ. *Ethnologie Française* (quarterly).

Société d'Etude du XVIIe Siècle: Collège de France, 11 place Marcelin-Berthelot, 75231 Paris Cedex 05; f. 1948; 1,250 mems; Pres. J. Berenger; publ. *XVIIe Siècle* (quarterly).

Société d'Histoire Générale et d'Histoire Diplomatique: 13 rue Soufflot, 75005 Paris; tel. 1-43-54-05-97; fax 1-46-34-07-60; f. 1887; history and diplomatic relations; 400 mems; publ. *Revue d'Histoire Diplomatique.*

Société d'Histoire Moderne et Contemporaine: C/o CHEVS, 44 rue du Four, 75006 Paris; tel. 1-45-43-42-40; fax 1-42-22-59-62; f. 1901; 1,100 mems; 16th–20th century French and foreign history; Pres. Daniel Roche; Sec.-Gen. Guy Boquet; publ. *Bulletin-Revue d'Histoire Moderne et Contemporaine* (4 parts a year).

Société de Biogéographie: 57 rue Cuvier, 75231 Paris Cedex 05; f. 1924; 350 mems; Pres. C. Sastre; Sec.-Gen. M. Salomon; publs *Biogeographica, Mémoires hors série.*

Société de Géographie: 184 blvd St-Germain, 75006 Paris; tel. 1-45-48-54-62; f. 1821; library of 400,000 vols at 8 rue des Petits-Champs, 75002 Paris (Librarian Mlle Pelletier); 700 mems; Pres. Prof. Bastié; Sec.-Gen. M. Florin; publ. *Acta Geographica* (quarterly).

Société de Géographie Humaine de Paris: 8 rue Roquépine, 75008 Paris; f. 1873; Pres. Jacques Augarde; library of 2,000 vols; publ. *Revue Economique Française* (quarterly).

Société de l'Histoire de France: Ecole des Chartes, 19 rue de la Sorbonne, 75005 Paris; f. 1834; Pres. Henri Dubois; Sec. Philippe Contamine; publs *Annuaires-Bulletins, Mémoires, Textes inédits de l'Histoire de France.*

Société des Etudes Historiques: 44 rue de Rennes, 75006 Paris; f. 1833; Pres. Christian Schaffer; Sec.-Gen. M. Deborde de Montgorin; Dir Emm. Rodocanachi; publ. *Revue des Études Historiques.*

Société des Océanistes: Musée de l'Homme, Palais de Chaillot, 75116 Paris; tel. 1-47-04-63-40; f. 1945; 560 mems; Pres. Michel Panoff; Sec.-Gen. Philippe Missotte; publs *Journal* (2 a year), *Publications.*

Société Française d'Archéologie: Musée National des Monuments Français, 1 place du Trocadéro, 75116 Paris; tel. 1-47-04-78-96; fax 1-44-05-94-25; f. 1834; mem. of CSSF; 2,800 mems; Pres. Jean Mesqui; publs *Bulletin Monumental* (quarterly), *Congrès Archéologiques de France* (annually).

Société Française d'Egyptologie: Collège de France, Place Marcelin-Berthelot, 75231 Paris Cedex 05; f. 1923, 1,010 mems; Pres. D. Valbelle; Sec. V. Laurent; publs *Bulletin, Revue d'Egyptologie.*

Société Française d'Histoire d'Outre-Mer: 15 rue Catulienne, 93200 Saint Denis; tel. and fax 1-48-13-09-09; f. 1913; 500 mems; Pres. Marc Michel; Sec.-Gen. Daniel Lefeuvre; publ. *Revue Française d'Histoire d'Outre-Mer* (quarterly).

Société Française de Numismatique: Bibliothèque Nationale, Cabinet des Médailles, 58 rue de Richelieu, 75084 Paris Cedex 02; tel. 1-47-03-83-44; f. 1865; 700 mems; Pres. Jean Hiernard; Gen. Sec. Jacqueline Pilet-Lemiere; publs *Revue Numismatique, Bulletin de la S.F.N.* (monthly).

Société Historique, Archéologique et Littéraire de Lyon: Archives municipales de Lyon, 4 ave Adolphe Max, 69005 Lyon; f. 1807; Pres. J. P. Gutton; Sec. Paul Feuga; publ. *Bulletin.*

Société Nationale des Antiquaires de France: Palais du Louvre, Pavillon Mollien, 75001 Paris; f. 1803; mems: 55 full, 380 corresponding; history, philology and archaeology of Antiquity and the Middle Ages; publs *Bulletin de la Société nationale des Antiquaires de France* (annually), *Mémoires de la Société nationale des Antiquaires de France* (irregular).

Vieilles Maisons Françaises: 93 rue de l'Université, 75007 Paris; tel. 1-40-62-61-71; fax 1-45-51-12-26; f. 1958; the society seeks to bring together all those who own buildings of historical interest and those who help to preserve them; 16,000 mems; Pres. Baron de Grandmaison; publ. *Vieilles Maisons Françaises.*

LANGUAGE AND LITERATURE

Académie Montaigne: Le Doyenné, 72140 Sillé-le-Guillaume; f. 1924; for the study of literature; awards an annual prize for research; 20 mems; Sec. Constant Hubert.

Association des Ecrivains de Langue Française (ADELF) (French Language Writers Asscn): 14 rue Broussais, 75014 Paris; tel. 1-43-21-95-99; fax 1-43-20-12-22; f. 1926 as 'Société des romanciers et auteurs coloniaux français' to bring together writers of all nationalities whose works are published in

French; awards 13 literary prizes; 2,000 mems in 79 countries; library of 2,000 vols; Pres. EDMOND JOUVE; Sec.-Gen. SIMONE DREYFUS; publs *Annuaire, Lettres et Cultures de langue française* (annually), *Le Point au...* (quarterly), *Actes* of annual colloquium.

Association Française des Professeurs de Langues Vivantes: 19 rue de la Glacière, 75013 Paris; f. 1902; 3,000 mems; Pres. CHRISTIAN PUREN; Gen. Sec. SYLVESTRE VANUXEM; publ. *Les Langues Modernes* (quarterly), *Le Polyglotte* (quarterly).

Association Guillaume Budé: 95 blvd Raspail, 75006 Paris; f. 1917; 3,000 mems; edits ancient Greek, Latin and Byzantine, classical texts with French translations and studies on history, philology and archaeology, which are published by the Société d'éditions 'Les Belles Lettres' at the same address; Pres. P. POUTHIER; Vice-Pres. A. MICHEL, J. JOUANNA; periodical publs *Bulletin* and *Lettres d'Humanité*.

Centre National du Livre: 53 rue de Verneuil, 75007 Paris; tel. 1-49-54-68-68; fax 1-45-49-10-21; f. 1946, present name 1993, to uphold and encourage the work of French writers; to give financial help to writers, editors and public libraries; to promote translation into French; Pres. JEAN-SEBASTIEN DUPUIT; Sec.-Gen. ANDRÉ-MARC DELOCQUE-FOURCAUD; publ. *Lettres*.

Fondation Saint-John Perse: Espace Méjanes, 10 rue des Allumettes, 13098 Aix-en-Provence Cedex 2; tel. 4-42-25-98-85; fax 4-42-27-11-86; f. 1975; contains all MSS, books, correspondence, private library and personal belongings of Saint-John Perse (Nobel Prize for literature 1960); organizes annual exhibition and symposium; 500 mems; Dir JOËLLE GARDES-TAMINE; publs *Cahiers Saint-John Perse* (irregular), *Souffle de Perse* (annually).

France Latine, La: 16 rue de la Sorbonne, 75005 Paris; tel. 1-40-46-27-44; fax 1-40-46-25-11; f. 1957 to preserve Latin culture and civilization in all its forms, maintains regional traditions and the 'Langue d'Oc'; Literary Dir S. THIOLIER-MÉJEAN; publ. *Revue* (2 a year).

Maison de Poésie (Fondation Emile Blémont): 11 bis rue Ballu, 75009 Paris; tel. 1-40-23-45-99; f. 1928; library of over 16,000 vols; annual prizes: Grand Prix de la Maison de Poésie, Prix Paul Verlaine, Prix Edgar Poe, Prix Gabriel Vicaire, Prix Léon Riotor, Prix Van Lerberghe, Prix Fernand Dauphin; Pres. JACQUES CHARPENTREAU; Sec. ROBERT HOUDELOT.

Organisation de la Jeunesse Esperantiste Française (JEFO): 4 bis rue de la Cerisaie, 75004 Paris; tel. 1-42-78-68-86; f. 1969; promotes Esperanto among young people; 300 mems; Pres. BRUNO FLOCHON; publs *Koncize, JEFO informas* (every 2 months).

PEN International (Centre français): 6 rue François-Miron, 75004 Paris; tel. 1-42-77-37-87; fax 1-42-78-64-87; f. 1921; 550 mems; Pres. JEAN ORIZET; Sec.-Gen. BERTRAND GALIMARD FLAVIGNY; publ. *Bulletin* (every 2 months).

Société d'Etudes Dantesques: Centre Universitaire Méditerranéen, 65 Promenade-des-Anglais, 06000 Nice; f. 1935; Sec.-Gen. SIMON LORENZI; publ. *Bulletin*.

Société d'Histoire Littéraire de la France: 112 rue Monge, 75005 Paris; tel. and fax 1-45-87-23-30; f. 1894; 300 mems; Pres. R. POMEAU; Dir S. MENANT; publ. *Revue d'Histoire Littéraire de la France* (every 2 months).

Société de Linguistique de Paris: Ecole Pratique des Hautes Etudes, 4e section, Sorbonne, 47 rue des Ecoles, 75005 Paris; f. 1864; 800 mems; Sec. Prof. J. PERROT; Admin. Prof. B. CARON; publs *Collection Linguistique, Bulletin, Mémoires* (annually).

Société des Anciens Textes Français: 19 rue de la Sorbonne, 75005 Paris; f. 1875; 125 mems; Pres. Prof. A. VERNET; Dir Prof. F. LECOY; Gen. Sec. Prof. J. MONFRIN.

Société des Auteurs et Compositeurs Dramatiques: 11 bis rue Ballu, 75442 Paris Cedex 09; tel. 1-40-23-44-44; fax 1-45-26-74-28; e-mail infosacd@sacd.fr; f. 1777; to protect the rights of authors of theatre, radio, cinema, television and multimedia; Pres. MARCEL BLUWAL; publ. *La Revue de la SACD*.

Société des Etudes Latines: 1 rue Victor-Cousin, 75230 Paris Cedex 05; f. 1923; Sec.-Gen. Prof. MICHÈLE DUCOS; Administrator Prof. ALAIN MICHEL; publs *Revue des Etudes Latines* (1 a year), *Collection d'études latines*.

Société des Gens de Lettres: Hôtel de Massa, 38 rue du Faubourg St Jacques, 75014 Paris; tel. 1-53-10-12-00; fax 1-53-10-12-12; f. 1838; Pres. FRANÇOIS COUPRY; Gen. Sec. MARIE-FRANCE BRISELANCE.

Société des Poètes Français: 38 rue du Faubourg St Jacques, 75014 Paris; f. 1902; 1,600 mems; presents prizes annually; Pres. VITAL HEURTEBIZE; Sec.-Gen. JEAN-MARC EULBRY; publ. *Bulletin trimestriel*.

MEDICINE

Académie Nationale de Chirurgie: 'Les Cordeliers', 15 rue de l'École de Médecine, 75006 Paris; tel. 1-43-54-02-32; fax 1-43-29-34-44; e-mail academie@chirurgie.org; f. 1731; 500 mems; library of 5,000 vols; Sec.-Gen. MARCEL GUIVARC'H; publ. *Chirurgie* (6 a year).

Académie Nationale de Médecine: 16 rue Bonaparte, 75272 Paris Cedex 06; tel. 1-42-34-57-70; fax 1-40-46-87-55; f. 1820 by Louis XVIII; library of 300,000 vols; 130 mems attached to sections on Medicine, Surgery, Hygiene, Biological Sciences, Social Sciences, Veterinary Medicine, and Pharmacy; Pres. CLAUDE LAROCHE; Perm. Sec. RAYMOND BASTIN; publ. *Bulletin de l'Académie nationale de médecine* (9 a year).

Académie Nationale de Pharmacie: 4 ave de l'Observatoire, 75006 Paris; tel. 1-43-25-54-49; fax 1-43-29-45-85; f. 1803; 325 mems; Pres. Prof. C. DREUX; Gen. Sec. Dr F. BOURILLET; publ. *Annales Pharmaceutiques Françaises*.

Association des Anatomistes: BP 184, 54505 Vandoeuvre-lès-Nancy; e-mail grignon@facmed.u-nancy.fr; f. 1899; 1,005 mems; Gen. Sec. Prof. G. GRIGNON; publ. *Bulletin* (quarterly).

Association Française d'Urologie: C/o Convergences, 120 ave Gambetta, 75020 Paris; tel. 1-43-64-77-77; fax 1-40-31-01-65; f. 1896; 750 mems; Pres. J. M. BUZELIN; Vice-Pres. F. RICHARD; Sec.-Gen. P. TEILLAC; publs *Mémoires* (annually), *Progrès en Urologie*.

Association Générale des Médecins de France: 60 blvd de Latour-Maubourg, 75327 Paris Cedex 07; Pres. P. BAUDOUIN; Sec. Dr TOUCHARD; publ. *Bulletin*.

Association Scientifique des Médecins Acupuncteurs de France (ASMAF): 2 rue du Général de Larminat, 75015 Paris; tel. 1-42-73-37-26; f. 1945 as Société d'Acupuncture; 1,500 mems; Pres. Dr GEORGES CANTONI; Sec.-Gen. Dr H. OLIVO; publ. *Méridiens* (quarterly).

Centre d'Etude de l'Expression: Centre hospitalier Sainte-Anne, 100 rue de la Santé, 75014 Paris; f. 1973 to develop psychopathological and psychological studies of various forms of expression: plastic, verbal, mimic, body-language, musical, theatrical; Pres. Prof. B. SAMUEL-LAJEUNESSE; Sec.-Gen. Dr. A. M. DUBOIS.

Comité National contre les Maladies Respiratoires et la Tuberculose: 66 blvd Saint-Michel, 75006 Paris; tel. 1-46-34-58-80; fax 1-43-29-06-58; e-mail cnmrt@magic.fr; f. 1916; research, information, health education, assistance for the handicapped; Pres. FRANÇOIS BONNAUD; publ. *La Lettre du Souffle* (4 a year).

Confédération des Syndicats Médicaux Français: 60 blvd de Latour-Maubourg, 75340 Paris Cedex 07; tel. 1-40-62-68-00; fax 1-45-51-97-58; f. 1930; 16,000 mems; Pres. Dr MAFFIOLI; Sec.-Gen. Dr WANNEPAIN; publs *Bulletin, Le Médecin de France*.

Fédération des Gynécologues et Obstétriciens de Langue Française: Clinique Baudelocque, 123 blvd de Port Royal, 75014 Paris; tel. 1-42-34-11-37; e-mail jean-rene.zorn@cch.ap.hop-paris.fr; f. 1950; 2,000 mems; Pres. Prof. H. BOSSART; Sec.-Gen. Prof. J.-R. ZORN (Paris); publ. *Journal de Gynécologie Obstétrique et Biologie de la Reproduction* (8 a year).

Fédération Nationale des Médecins Radiologues et Spécialistes en Imagerie Diagnostique et Thérapeutique: 60 blvd la Tour-Maubourg, 75327 Paris Cedex 07; f. 1907; 3,000 mems; Pres. Dr A. TAÏEB; publ. *Bulletin*.

Société d'Histoire de la Pharmacie: 4 ave de l'Observatoire, 75270 Paris Cedex 06; f. 1913; 1,300 mems; Pres. Doyen JEAN FLAHAUT; Sec. M. WAROLIN; publ. *Revue d'Histoire de la Pharmacie* (quarterly).

Société d'Ophtalmologie de Paris: 108 rue du Bac, 75007 Paris; f. 1888; Sec. Gen. Dr JEAN-PAUL BOISSIN; publ. *Bulletin* (monthly).

Société de Chirurgie Thoracique et Cardio-vasculaire de Langue Française: 1 rue Cabanis, 75014 Paris; tel. 1-53-62-91-19; fax 1-53-62-91-20; f. 1948; 643 mems; studies problems linked with thoracic and cardiovascular surgery; Pres. Prof. YVES LOGEAIS; Sec.-Gen. Dr R. NOTTIN; publ. *Journal de chirurgie thoracique et cardiovasculaire* (4 a year).

Société de Médecine de Strasbourg: Faculté de Médecine, 4 rue Kirschleger, 67085 Strasbourg Cedex; f. 1919; 450 mems; organizes medical conferences; Pres. Prof. J. MCWARTER; Sec.-Gen. Dr MOISE; publ. *Journal de Médecine de Strasbourg* (monthly).

Société de Médecine Légale et de Criminologie de France: 2 place Mazas, 75012 Paris; tel. 1-43-43-42-54; f. 1868; Pres. Prof. L ARBUS; Sec. M. PENNEAU; publs *Médecine légale, Droit médical*.

Société de Neurochirurgie de Langue Française: 60 blvd Latour-Maubourg, 75327 Paris Cedex 7; f. 1948; 700 mems; Pres. J. BROTCHI; Sec. J. P. HOUTTEVILLE; publ. *Neurochirurgie* (every 2 months).

Société de Neurophysiologie Clinique de Langue Française: Hôpital Sainte Anne, 1 rue Cabanis, 75674 Paris Cedex 14; tel. 1-40-48-82-03; f. 1948; 520 mems; Pres. Dr P. PLOUIN; Sec.-Gen. Dr B. GUEGUEN; publ. *Neurophysiologie Clinique* (every 2 months).

Société de Pathologie Exotique: 25 rue du Docteur-Roux, 75015 Paris; tel. 1-45-66-88-69; fax 1-45-66-44-85; e-mail socpatex@club-internet.fr; f. 1908; 750 mems; library of 2,000 vols, 125 periodicals; Pres. Prof. MARC GENTILINI; Sec.-Gen. Dr A. CHIPPAUX; publ. *Bulletin* (5 a year).

Société de Pneumologie de Langue Française: 66 blvd Saint-Michel, 75006 Paris; tel. 1-46-34-03-87; fax 1-46-34-58-27; e-mail 100731.3566@compuserve.com; Pres. M. FOURNIER; Secs-Gen. J. F. CORDIER, J. P. GRIGNET, B. HOUSSET, E. LEMARIÉ; publ. *Revue des Maladies Respiratoires*.

Société Française d'Allergologie et d'Immuno-Allergie Clinique: Institut Pasteur, 25 rue du Dr Roux, 75015 Paris; tel. 1-45-68-82-41; fax 1-40-61-31-60; f. 1947; 860 mems; Pres. Prof. D. VERVLOET; publ. *Revue Française d'Allergologie et d'Immunologie clinique* (5 a year).

Société Française d'Anesthésie et de Réanimation: 74 rue Raynouard, 75016 Paris; tel. 1-45-25-82-25; fax 1-40-50-35-22; f. 1960; 4,298 mems; Pres. Dr GÉZY BOULARD; Sec.-Gen. Prof. JEAN-LOUIS POURRIAT; publ. *Annales françaises d'Anesthésie et de Réanimation* (11 a year).

Société Française d'Angéiologie: 153 ave Berthelot, 69007 Lyon; tel. 4-78-72-38-98; f. 1947; 350 mems; Sec.-Gen. Dr H. BUREAU DU COLOMBIER.

Société Française d'Endocrinologie: c/o Masson Edit., 120 blvd Saint-Germain, 75280 Paris Cedex 06; f. 1939; 1,000 mems; Sec.-Gen. Prof. BERNARD CONTE-DEVOLX; publ. *Annales d'Endocrinologie* (every 2 months).

Société Française d'Histoire de la Médecine: 38 bis rue de Courlancy, 51100 Reims; tel. 3-26-48-32-60; fax 3-26-48-32-71; f. 1902; 700 mems; library; Pres. Prof. GUY PALLARDY; Gen. Sec. Dr ALAIN SEGAL; publ. *Histoire des Sciences médicales* (quarterly).

Société Française d'Hydrologie et de Climatologie Médicales: DGS Laboratoire National d'Hydrologie, 1 rue Lacietelle, 75015 Paris; tel. 1-55-76-17-37; f. 1853; 413 mems; Pres. Dr HENRI FOUNAU; Sec.-Gen. Dr ANDRÉ AUTHIER; publ. *La Presse Thermale et Climatique* (quarterly).

Société Française d'Ophtalmologie: 9 rue Mathurin-Régnier, 75015 Paris; tel. 1-47-34-20-21; f. 1883; annual conference; 7,200 mems; Pres. Dr J. FLAMENT; Sec.-Gen. Dr J. L. DUFIER; publs *Rapport* (annually), *Ophtalmologie* (6 a year).

Société Française d'Oto-Rhino-Laryngologie et de Pathologie Cervico-Faciale: 9 rue Villebois-Mareuil, 75017 Paris; f. 1880; 1,500 mems; Pres. Dr R. BATISSE; Sec. Prof. CHARLES FRECHE; publs *Comptes Rendus* and *Rapports Discutés au Congrès*.

Société Française d'Urologie: 6 ave Constant Coquelin, 75007 Paris; f. 1919; 50 mems; Pres. Dr BOISSONNAT; publ. *Journal d'Urologie*.

Société Française de Biologie Clinique: Laboratoire de Chimie Clinique et Biologie Moléculaire, 15 rue de l'Ecole de Médecine, 75270 Paris Cedex 06; Sec. Prof. L. HARTMANN.

Société Française de Chirurgie Orthopédique et Traumatologique: Secrétariat: 56 rue Boissonade, 75014 Paris; 1,950 mems; Pres. J. M. THOMINE; publ. *Revue de Chirurgie Orthopédique*.

Société Française de Chirurgie Pédiatrique: Chirurgie Infantile, Hôpital Hautepierre, 67098 Strasbourg Cedex; tel. 3-88-12-73-02; fax 3-88-12-73-03; f. 1959; 350 mems; Pres. Prof. PAUL MITROFANOFF; Sec.-Gen. Prof. J. L. CLAVERT; publ. *European Journal of Paediatric Surgery* (every 2 months).

Société Française de Chirurgie Plastique, Reconstructive et Esthétique: 26 rue de Belfort, 92400 Courbevoie; tel. 1-46-67-74-85; fax 1-46-67-74-89; f. 1953; Pres. Prof. J. BAUDET; Sec.-Gen. Prof. J. P. CHAVOIN.

Société Française de Gynécologie: 20 rue Clément Marot, 75008 Paris; 582 mems; Pres. J. P. WOLFF; Sec.-Gen. ANDRÉ GORINS; publ. *Gynécologie* (every 2 months).

Société Française de Médecine Aérospatiale: Laboratoire de Médecine Aérospatiale du Centre d'Essais en Vol, 91228 Brétigny sur Orge Cedex; tel. 1-69-88-23-80; fax 1-69-88-27-25; f. 1960; publishes papers on experimental and clinical studies; 1,100 mems; Sec.-Gen. Prof. MAROTTE; publ. *Médecine Aéronautique et Spatiale* (quarterly).

Société Française de Mycologie Médicale: 25 rue du Docteur-Roux, 75724 Paris Cedex 15; tel. 1-40-61-32-54; fax 1-45-68-84-20; f. 1956; 500 mems; Sec.-Gen. Prof. B. DUPONT; publ. *Journal de Mycologie Médicale* (quarterly).

Société Française de Neurologie: Service de Neurologie 1, Clinique Paul Castaigne, Hôpital de la Salpêtrière, 47 blvd de l'Hôpital, 75651 Paris Cedex 13; tel. 1-42-16-18-28; fax 1-44-24-52-47; f. 1899; 550 mems; library of 22,000 vols; Sec.-Gen. Prof. C. PIERROT-DESEILLIGNY; publ. *Revue Neurologique* (monthly).

Société Française de Pédiatrie: Hôpital Robert Debré, 48 blvd Sérurier, 75935 Paris Cedex 19; tel. and fax 1-42-06-69-17; f. 1929; Pres. Prof. G. LASFARGUES; Sec.-Gen. Prof. FRANÇOIS BEAUFILS.

Société Française de Phlébologie: 46 rue Saint-Lambert, 75015 Paris; tel. 1-45-33-02-71; fax 1-42-50-75-18; f. 1947; 2,000 mems; Pres. M. PERRIN; Sec.-Gen. F. VIN; publ. *Phlébologie—Annales Vasculaires* (quarterly).

Société Française de Phytiatrie et de Phytopharmacie: CNRA, Route de Saint Cyr, 78000 Versailles; tel. 1-49-50-75-22; f. 1951; 1,000 mems.

Société Française de Radiologie et d'Imagerie Médicale: Hôpital Laënnec, 42 rue de Sèvres, 75007 Paris; tel. 1-45-44-48-04; fax 1-45-44-47-66; e-mail sfrmail@sfr./francenet.fr; f. 1909; 3,900 mems; Sec. G. FRIJA.

Société Française de Santé Publique: BP 7, 54501 Vandoeuvre lès Nancy Cedex; tel. 3-83-44-87-47; fax 3-83-44-37-76; e-mail sante.publique@sfsp-publichealth.org; f. 1877; 750 mems; Pres. Prof. M. BRODIN; publ. *Santé publique* (quarterly).

Société Française du Cancer: 34 rue d'Ulm, 75231 Paris Cedex 05; f. 1920; 440 mems; quarterly meetings, annual symposium; offers grants to doctors from abroad or French doctors for work abroad; publ. *Bulletin du Cancer.*

Société Internationale de Recherches pour l'Environnement et la Santé: 4 rue Pérignon, 75007 Paris; tel. 1-47-34-21-68; f. 1979; aims to study health in its widest sense, involving research in food, environment, psychosociology; to make known the results of effective research on health and environment; 135 personal mems, 9 asscns; Pres. Prof. JEAN KEILLING; publ. *Cahiers* (quarterly).

Société Médicale des Hôpitaux de Paris: 45 quai de la Tournelle, 75005 Paris; tel. 1-43-25-71-95; fax 1-43-25-40-92; Sec. LOÏC GUILLEVIN; publ. *Annales de Médecine Interne*.

Société Médico-Psychologique: 14/16 ave Robert Schuman, 92100 Boulogne; f. 1852; 675 mems; Pres. Prof. MICHEL LAXENAIRE; Sec.-Gen. Dr PIERRE MARCHAIS; publ. *Annales médico-psychologiques* (monthly).

Société Nationale Française de Gastro-Entérologie: Pavillon Pointeau du Ronceray, Hôpital Pontchaillou, 35033 Rennes Cedex; tel. 2-99-28-24-15; fax 2-99-28-24-14; e-mail snfge@snfge.asso.fr; Sec.-Gen. Prof. JEAN-FRANÇOIS BRETAGNE; publ. *Gastroentérologie clinique et biologique*.

Société Odontologique de Paris (SOP): 239 rue du Faubourg Saint-Martin, 75010 Paris; tel. 1-42-09-29-13; 2,500 mems; Pres. Dr M. FITOUSSI; Sec.-Gen. Dr Y. BISMUTH; publs *Revue d'Odonto-Stomatologie* (4 a year), *Journal de la Société Odontologique de Paris*.

Société Scientifique d'Hygiène Alimentaire: 16 rue de l'Estrapade, 75005 Paris; f. 1904; 1,182 mems; Pres. Dr GUY EBRARD.

NATURAL SCIENCES

General

Comité National Français des Recherches Arctiques et Antarctiques: C/o Expéditions Polaires Françaises, 47 ave du Maréchal Fayolle, 75016 Paris; Pres. J.-C. HUREAU.

Fédération Française des Sociétés de Sciences Naturelles: 57 rue Cuvier, 75231 Paris Cedex 05; tel. 1-43-36-20-84; f. 1919; groups 175 societies; natural sciences and nature conservation; Pres. J. LESCURE; Gen. Sec. J.-F. VOISIN; publs *Revue de la FFSSN* (annually), *Faune de France* (irregular).

Fondation 'Pour la Science', Centre International de Synthèse (Foundation for International Scientific Co-ordination): see under International.

Biological Sciences

Naturalistes Parisiens, Les: 45 rue de Buffon, 75005 Paris; f. 1904 to undertake research in natural history and deepen the scientific knowledge of its members; 600 mems; Sec. C. DUPUIS; publs *Cahiers des Naturalistes*, *Bulletin* (quarterly).

Société Botanique de France: rue J. B. Clément, 92296 Châtenay-Malabry Cedex; tel. 1-46-83-55-20; fax 1-46-83-13-03; f. 1854; 800 mems; Gen. Sec. M. BOTINEAU; publs *Acta Botanica Gallica* (6 or 7 a year), *Le Journal de Botanique* (4 a year).

Société d'Etudes Ornithologiques de France: Muséum National d'Histoire Naturelle, Laboratoire d'Ecologie Générale, 4 ave du Petit Château, 91800 Brunoy; tel. 1-47-30-24-48; fax 1-60-46-57-19; f. 1993; scientific study of wild birds; 1,000 mems; library of 4,000 vols; Sec. B. FROCHOT; publs *Alauda, Revue Internationale d'Ornithologie* (quarterly).

Société de Biologie: Collège de France, 75231 Paris Cedex 05; tel. 1-44-27-13-40; f. 1848; 140 hon. mems, 50 elected mems, 25 associates, 190 corresp.; Pres. Prof. JACQUES PICARD; Sec. Prof. JACQUES POLONOVSKI; publ. *Comptes Rendus* (every 2 months).

Société Entomologique de France: 45 rue Buffon, 75005 Paris; tel. 1-40-79-33-84; f. 1832; 650 mems; specialized entomological library; 80 entomological periodicals, 12,000 vols; Gen. Sec. H. PIGUET; publs *Annales* (quarterly), *Bulletin* (5 a year), *L'Entomologiste* (6 a year).

Société Française d'Ichtyologie: 43 rue Cuvier, 75231 Paris Cedex 05; tel. 1-40-79-37-49; fax 1-40-79-37-71; f. 1976; fish culture, biology and systematics of fish, sea and freshwater fisheries; 280 mems; library of 5,000 vols, 800 periodicals; Pres. J. ALLARDI; Sec. G. DUHAMEL; publ. *Cybium* (quarterly).

Société Française de Physiologie Végétale: 4 place Jussieu, 75230 Paris Cedex 05; f. 1955; 600 mems; Pres. P. GADAL; Sec.-Gen. A.-L. ETIENNE; publ. *Plant Physiology and Biochemistry* (monthly).

Société Mycologique de France: 20 rue Rottembourg, 75012 Paris; tel. 1-44-67-96-90; f. 1884; 1,800 mems; Pres. GUY REDEUILH; Sec.-Gen. PATRICK VANHECKE; publ. *Bulletin Trimestriel*.

Société Nationale de Protection de la Nature: 9 rue Cels, 75014 Paris; tel. 1-43-20-15-39; fax 1-43-20-15-71; f. 1854; 4,000 mems; Pres. FRANÇOIS RAMADE; Gen. Sec. MICHEL ECHAUBARD; publs *La Terre et la Vie* (quarterly), *Le Courrier de la Nature* (every 2 months).

Société Zoologique de France: 195 rue St Jacques, 75005 Paris; tel. 1-40-79-31-10; f. 1876; zoology, evolution; 600 mems; Pres. Prof. J. CHAUDONNERET; Gen. Sec. Dr J. L. D'HONDT; publs *Bulletin* (quarterly), *Mémoires* (irregular).

Mathematical Sciences

Comité National Français de Mathématiciens: C/o P. Arnoux, Institut de Mathématiques de Luminy, 163 ave de

Luminy, Case 907, 13288 Marseille Cedex 9; tel. 4-91-26-96-72; fax 4-91-26-96-55; e-mail arnoux@iml.univ-mrs.fr; f. 1951; Pres. P. Arnoux; Sec. Y. Brenier.

Société Mathématique de France: Institut Henri Poincaré, 11 rue Pierre et Marie Curie, 75231 Paris Cedex 05; tel. 1-44-27-67-96; f. 1872; 1,800 mems; Pres. J.-J. Risler; publs *Bulletin, Mémoires* (both quarterly), *Officiel des Mathématiques* (9 a year), *Astérisque* (monthly), *Gazette des Mathématiciens* (quarterly), *Revue d'Histoire des Mathématiques* (2 a year).

Physical Sciences

Association Française d'Observateurs d'Etoiles Variables: Observatoire Astronomique, 11 rue de l'Université, 67000 Strasbourg; tel. 3-88-84-37-11; e-mail afoev@astro.u-strasbg.fr; f. 1921; 110 mems; Pres. E. Schweitzer; Secs-Gen. D. Proust, M. Verdenet; publ. *Bulletin de l'AFOEV* (quarterly).

Association Française pour l'Etude du Quaternaire: Maison de la géologie, 79 rue Claude Bernard, 75005 Paris; f. 1962 to prepare scientific publications and exchange information on the Quaternary; 600 mems; Pres. Dr M. T. Morzadec; Sec. Dr D. Lefèvre; publ. *Quaternaire* (quarterly).

Association Scientifique et Technique pour l'Exploitation des Océans: Immeuble Ile de France, La Défense 9, 4 place de la Pyramide, 92070 Paris La Défense Cedex 33; tel. 1-47-67-25-32; telex 620430; f. 1967; oil technology and allied activities, pollution control, polymetallic nodules, sand and gravel workings, fishing technology and fish farming; 80 mem. industries; Chair. Pierre Jacquard; Man. Dir B. E. Dimont; publ. *Annuaire Technique et Industriel*.

Société Astronomique de France: 3 rue Beethoven, 75016 Paris; tel. 1-42-24-13-74; fax 1-42-30-75-47; e-mail saf@calvanet.calvacom.fr; f. 1887; 2,700 mems; Pres. Roger Ferlet; Sec.-Gen. Nicole Née; publs *L'Astronomie* (monthly), *Observations et Travaux* (4 a year).

Société de Chimie Industrielle: 28 rue Saint-Dominique, 75007 Paris; tel. 1-53-59-02-10; fax 1-45-55-40-33; f. 1917; 4,000 mems; Pres. P. Trifarol; Del.-Gen. G. Mattioda; publs *l'Actualité chimique, Informations Chimie, Analusis*.

Société des Experts-Chimistes de France: 23 rue du Commandant Jean Duhail, 94120 Fontenay-sous-Bois; tel. 1-48-76-17-24; fax 1-48-76-60-15; f. 1912; 1,200 mems; Pres. Michel Derbesy; Sec.-Gen. Jacques Botrel; publ. *Annales des Falsifications de l'Expertise Chimique et Toxicologique*.

Société Française de Biochimie et Biologie Moléculaire: 4 ave de l'Observatoire, 75270 Paris Cedex 06; f. 1914; 1,320 mems; Pres. J. C. Patte; Gen. Secs J. Agneray, J. P. Ebel; publs *Biochimie, Regard sur la Biochimie*.

Société Française de Chimie: 250 rue St Jacques, 75005 Paris; tel. 1-40-46-71-60; fax 1-40-46-71-61; f. 1857; 4,600 mems; Pres. Marc Julia; Sec.-Gen. Jean-Claude Brunie; publs *L'Actualité chimique* (monthly), *Analusis* (10 a year), *Journal de Chimie physique* (10 a year).

Société Française de Minéralogie et de Cristallographie: 4 place Jussieu, Tour 16, casier 115, 75252 Paris Cedex 05; tel. and fax 1-44-27-60-24; f. 1878; 600 mems; Sec. Hélène Suquet; publ. *Bulletin de Liaison, European Journal of Mineralogy*.

Société Française de Physique: 33 rue Croulebarbe, 75013 Paris; tel. 1-47-07-32-98; fax 1-43-31-74-26; f. 1873; 2,500 mems; Pres. Marianne Lambert; Gen. Sec. Claude Sebenne; publs *Bulletin, Catalogue de l'Exposition de Physique, Journal de Physique, Annales de Physique, Colloques*.

Société Géologique de France: 77 rue Claude-Bernard, 75005 Paris; tel. 1-43-31-77-35; fax 1-45-35-79-10; e-mail sgfr@worldnet.fr; f. 1830; 2,000 mems; library of 50,000 vols, 500 periodicals; Pres. Jacques Kornprobst; publs *Bulletin* (6 a year), *Mémoires* (irregular), *Géochronique* (4 a year).

Union des Physiciens: 44 blvd Saint-Michel, 75270 Paris Cedex 06; tel. 1-43-25-61-53; fax 1-43-25-07-48; f. 1906; 9,500 mems; Pres. J. Tinnes; publ. *Bulletin* (monthly).

PHILOSOPHY AND PSYCHOLOGY

Société Française d'Etudes des Phénomènes Psychiques: 1 rue des Gâtines, 75020 Paris; tel. 1-43-49-30-80; f. 1893; conducts experiments in psychic clairvoyance and undertakes research to prove the immortality of the soul; Pres. A. Croonenberghs: publ. *La Tribune Psychique* (quarterly).

Société Française de Philosophie: 12 rue Colbert, 75002 Paris; f. 1901; 180 mems; Pres. Bernard Bourgeois; Vice-Pres. Jacques Havet, Jean-Marie Beyssade; Sec.-Gen. Christiane Menasseyre; publs *Bulletin de la Société Française de Philosophie, Revue de Métaphysique et de Morale* (quarterly).

Société Française de Psychologie: 28 rue Serpente, 75006 Paris; tel. 1-40-51-99-36; fax 1-40-46-96-51; e-mail sfp@psycho.univ-paris5.fr; f. 1922; 1,000 mems; Pres. Michèle Carlier; Sec.-Gen. Dana Castro; publs *Psychologie Française* (3 a year), *Pratiques Psychologiques* (3 a year).

RELIGION, SOCIOLOGY AND ANTHROPOLOGY

Association Française des Arabisants: Collège de France, 52 rue du Cardinal Lemoine, 75005 Paris; f. 1973 to promote Arabic studies, to study questions of doctrine and practice relative to teaching and research in Arabic; to keep its members informed of ideas and activities of interest to teachers, researchers and students of Arabic; 450 mems; Pres. Floréal Sanagustin; publs *L'Arabisant, Annuaire des Arabisants* (every 2 years), *Lettre d'Information* (2 a year), *Actes des journées d'etudes arabes* (irregular).

Société Asiatique: 3 rue Mazarine, 75006 Paris; tel. 1-44-41-43-14; fax 1-44-41-43-16; f. 1822; library of 100,000 vols; 725 mems; Pres. Danile Gimaret; publs *Journal Asiatique* (2 a year), *Cahiers*.

Société d'Anthropologie de Paris: Musée de l'Homme, place du Trocadéro, 75116 Paris; tel. 1-44-05-72-65; fax 1-44-05-72-41; f. 1859; biological anthropology; 310 mems; Pres. Olivier Dutour; Sec.-Gen. Alain Froment; publ. *Bulletins et Mémoires* (quarterly).

Société d'Histoire religieuse de la France: 26 rue d'Assas, 75006 Paris; f. 1910; 750 mems; Pres. Marc Venard; Sec.-Gen. Bernard Barbiche; publ. *Revue d'Histoire de l'Eglise de France*.

Société de l'Histoire du Protestantisme Français: 54 rue des Saints-Pères, 75007 Paris; tel. 1-45-48-62-07; fax 1-45-44-94-87; f. 1852; 150,000 vols, 12,000 MSS in library, 2,000 periodical titles; Pres. Laurent Theis; Sec.-Gen. Jean-Hugues Carbonnier; publs *Bulletin, Cahiers de Généalogie Protestante* (quarterly).

Société de Mythologie Française: 3 rue St-Laurent, 75010 Paris; tel. 1-42-05-30-57; f. 1950; 300 mems; Pres. H. Fromage; publ. *Bulletin* (quarterly).

Société des Africanistes: Musée de l'Homme, Place du Trocadéro, 75116 Paris; tel. 1-47-27-72-55; f. 1931; 400 mems; Sec. Françoise le Guennec-Coppens; publ. *Journal des Africanistes*.

Société des Américanistes: Musée de l'Homme, 17 place du Trocadéro, 75116 Paris; tel. 1-47-04-63-11; f. 1895; 500 mems; Pres. Claude Baudez; Gen. Sec. Dominique Michelet; publ. *Journal* (annually).

Société Française de Sociologie: 59/61 rue Pouchet, 75849 Paris Cedex 17; tel. 1-40-25-10-99; fax 1-42-28-95-44; f. 1962; Pres. Dominique Schnapper; Sec.-Gen. Gérard Mauger.

TECHNOLOGY

Académie de Marine: BP 11, 00300 Armées; premises at: 21 place Joffre, 75007 Paris; tel. 1-44-38-40-33; fax 1-44-38-40-65; f. 1752; 66 mems and 24 corresp. mems, attached to sections on History, Law, Naval Equipment, Navigation, Military Affairs, Economics, Yachting, Mercantile Marine; Pres. I. G. A. (GM) René Bloch; Permanent Sec. V. A. Henri Cochet.

Association Aéronautique et Astronautique de France (AAAF): 66 route de Verneuil, BP 3002, 78133 Les Mureaux Cedex; tel. 1-39-06-33-01; fax 1-39-06-36-15; f. 1972; 1,800 mems; formed by merger of Association Française des Ingénieurs de l'Aéronautique et de l'Espace and Société Française d'Astronautique; Pres. J. C. Poggi; publ. *La Nouvelle Revue d'Aéronautique et d'Astronautique* (every 3 months).

Association des Anciens Elèves de l'Ecole Nationale Supérieure des Industries Agricoles et Alimentaires: 9–11 ave Franklin D. Roosevelt, 75008 Paris; tel. 1-42-25-92-48; 1,500 mems; Pres. Jean-Louis Tixier; Sec.-Gen. Michel Mery; publ. *Industries Alimentaires et Agricoles* (monthly).

Association des Chimistes, Ingénieurs et Cadres des Industries Agricoles et Alimentaires: 51 rue Jean-Jacques Rousseau, 75001 Paris; tel. and fax 1-40-13-91-74; f. 1883; publ. *Revue IAA* (10 a year).

Association Française du Froid: 17 rue Guillaume Apollinaire, 75006 Paris; tel. 1-45-44-52-52; fax 1-42-22-00-42; f. 1908; 1,200 mems; Pres. Michel Barth; Sec.-Gen. Louis Millot; publ. *Revue Générale du Froid* (10 a year).

Association Française pour la Cybernetique Economique et Technique: 156 blvd Péreire, 75017 Paris; tel. 1-47-66-24-19; fax 1-42-67-93-12; f. 1968; aims to consolidate the six fields of automatic control, office automation, management / computerization / decision aiding, data processing, applied mathematics, systems applications; study sessions, symposia, conferences, working groups, etc.; 4,500 individuals and institutional mems; Pres. Eric Jacquet-Lagreze; publs *AFCET INterflash, Ingénierie des Systèmes d'Information, Technique et Sciences informatiques, Automatique, Productique et Informatique industrielles, Recherche opérationnelle, Informatique théorique et applications*.

Association Nationale de la Recherche Technique: 101 ave Raymond Poincaré, 75116 Paris; tel. 1-44-17-36-36; fax 1-45-01-85-29; f. 1953 to promote technical research and organizations, and to foster contact with technical research institutions abroad; Pres. Francis Mer; publ. *La lettre Européenne du Progrès Technique* (10 a year).

Conseil National des Ingénieurs et des Scientifiques de France: 7 rue Lamennais, 75008 Paris; tel. 1-44-13-66-88; fax 1-42-89-82-50; f. 1848; publ. *I.D.*

Institut Français de l'Energie: 3 rue Henri-Heine, 75016 Paris; tel. 1-45-24-46-14; telex 615867; fax 1-40-50-07-54; f. 1952; organizes training courses (Ecole de Thermique, Ecole de Chauffe de la Région Parisienne, Centre de Travaux Pratiques de Taverny), documentation, and studies and information centre; library of 35,000 vols; Pres. ALBERT ROBIN; Gen. Dir YVES CHAINET; publs *Revue Générale de Thermique* (monthly), and others.

Société d'Encouragement pour l'Industrie Nationale: 4 place Saint-Germain-des-Prés, 75006 Paris; f. 1801; publ. *L'Industrie Nationale*.

Société des Electriciens et des Electroniciens (SEE): 48 rue de la Procession, 75724 Paris Cedex 15; tel. 1-44-49-60-00; fax 1-44-49-60-49; f. 1883; 6,000 mems; Pres. MICHEL FENEYROL; Gen. Sec. GERARD MARSOT; publ. *Revue de l'Electricité et de l'Electronique* (monthly).

Société Française de Métallurgie et de Matériaux (SF2M): 1 rue de Craïova, 92024 Nanterre Cedex; tel. 1-41-02-03-90; fax 1-41-02-03-88; e-mail sfmm@wanadoo.fr; f. 1945; 1,400 mems; Pres. YVES FARGE; Sec.-Gen. YVES FRANCHOT.

Société Française de Photogrammétrie et de Télédétection: 2 ave Pasteur, 94160 St Mandé; tel. 1-43-98-80-73; f. 1959; photogrammetry and remote sensing; 615 mems; Pres. G. BEGNI; Sec.-Gen. I. VEILLET; publ. *Bulletin* (quarterly).

Société Française des Microscopies: 9 quai Saint Bernard, 75005 Paris; tel. 1-44-27-26-21; fax 1-44-27-26-22; f. 1959; to further all types of microscopy, electronic optics and electronic diffraction, spectroscopy, microprobe, cellular biology; 1,600 mems; Pres. Dr DANIÈLE HERNANDEZ-VERDUN; publs *Biology of the Cell* (9 a year), *Microscopy, Microanalysis, Microstructures* (every 2 months).

Société Hydrotechnique de France: 199 rue de Grenelle, 75007 Paris; tel. 1-47-05-13-37; fax 1-45-56-97-46; f. 1912; fluid mechanics, applied hydraulics, geophysical hydraulics and water conservation; 600 mems; Pres. M. MAURIN; Gen. Dir MAX PERRIN; publs *La Houille Blanche Revue Internationale de l'Eau* (8 a year), *Proceedings, Journées de l'Hydraulique* (every 2 years), guides on hydroelectricity and flood forecasts, research documents.

Research Institutes

GENERAL

Centre National de la Recherche Scientifique (CNRS) 3–5 rue Michel-Ange, 75794 Paris Cedex 16; tel. 1-44-96-40-00; fax. 1-44-96-50-00; f. 1939; co-ordinates and promotes scientific research, and proposes to the Govt means of doing research and how to allocate funds; makes grants-in-aid to scientific bodies and to individuals to enable them to carry out research work; subsidizes or sets up laboratories for scientific research; controls 1,370 laboratories and research centres, covering all scientific fields; funds 19,391 researchers and engineers and 7,263 technicians and admin. staff; sectors of Nuclear and Particle Physics (Scientific Dir CLAUDE DÉTRAZ), Mathematics and Physics (Scientific Dir DANIEL THOULOUZE), Physical Sciences for Engineers (Scientific Dir JEAN-JACQUES GAGNEPAIN), Chemistry (Scientific Dir PAUL RIGNY), Earth and Space Sciences (Scientific Dir MICHEL AUBRY), Life Sciences (Scientific Dir PIERRE TAMBOURIN), Humanities and Social Sciences (Scientific Dir ALAIN D'IRIBARNE); Pres. EDOUARD BREZIN; Dir-Gen. CATHERINE BRÉCHIGNAC; Sec.-Gen. SIMONE TOUCHON.

I. Nuclear and Particle Physics:

Laboratoire souterrain de Modane (LSM): 90 rue Polset, 73500 Modane; tel. 4-79-05-22-57; fax 4-79-05-24-74; Dir SERGE JULLIAN.

Centre de spectrométrie nucléaire et de spectrométrie de masse (CSNSM): Bâtiment 104–108, 91405 Orsay Campus; tel. 1-69-41-52-13; fax 1-69-41-52-68; f. 1946; Dir PHILIPPE QUENTIN.

Centre de recherches nucléaires (CRN): BP 20 CR, 67037 Strasbourg Cedex; tel. 3-88-28-63-01; fax 3-88-28-09-90; f.1960; Dir FRANCIS BECK.

Grand accélérateur national d'ions lourds (GANIL): BP 5027, 14021 Caen Cedex; tel. 2-31-45-46-47; fax 2-31-45-46-65; Dir SAMUEL HARAR.

Laboratoire national Saturne (SATURNE): Commissariat à l'Energie Atomique, 91191 Gif-sur-Yvette Cedex; tel. 1-69-08-22-03; fax 1-69-08-29-70; Dir JACQUES ARVIEUX.

Laboratoire d'Annecy-le-Vieux de physique des particules (LAPP): BP 110, 74941 Annecy-le-Vieux Cedex; tel. 4-50-09-16-00; fax 4-50-27-94-95; f. 1975; Dir DENIS LINGLIN.

Institut des sciences nucléaires (ISN): Université de Grenoble 1, 53 ave des Martyrs, 38026 Grenoble Cedex; tel. 4-76-28-40-00; fax 4-76-28-40-04; Dir BERNARD VIGNON.

Institut de physique nucléaire de Lyon (IPNL): Université de Lyon 1, 43 blvd du 11 Novembre 1918, 69622 Villeurbanne Cedex; tel. 4-72-44-80-00; fax 4-78-89-19-02; Dir JEAN-PIERRE BURQ.

Laboratoire de l'accélérateur linéaire (LAL): Université de Paris 11, Centre d'Orsay, Bâtiment 200, 91405 Orsay Cedex; tel. 1-64-46-83-00; fax 1-69-07-94-04; Dir MICHEL DAVIER.

Institut de physique nucléaire (IPN): Université de Paris 11, BP 1, 91406 Orsay Cedex; tel. 1-69-41-67-50; fax 1-69-41-64-70; Dir HENRI SERGOLLE.

Laboratoire de physique nucléaire des hautes énergies (LPNHE): Université de Paris 6 (Pierre et Marie Curie), 4 place Jussieu, 75230 Paris Cedex 05; tel. 1-44-27-44-27; fax 1-46-33-41-42; Dir BERNARD GROSSETÊTE.

Centre d'études nucléaires de Bordeaux-Gradignan (CENBG): Université de Bordeaux 1, Le Haut-Vigneau, 33170 Gradignan; tel. 5-56-89-18-00; fax 5-56-75-11-80; Pres. ALAIN FLEURY.

Laboratoire de physique corpusculaire de Clermont (LPC Clermont): Université de Clermont-Ferrand 2, Complexe scientifique des Cézeaux, BP 45, 63177 Aubière Cedex; tel. 4-73-26-41-10; fax 4-73-26-45-98; Dir JEAN-CLAUDE MONTRET.

Laboratoire de physique corpusculaire de Caen (LPC Caen): Université de Caen, blvd du Maréchal-Juin, 14032 Caen Cedex; tel. 2-31-45-25-16; Dir CHRISTIAN LE BRUN.

Laboratoire de physique corpusculaire du Collège de France (LPC): Collège de France, 11 place Marcelin-Berthelot, 75231 Paris Cedex 05; tel. 1-44-27-12-11; fax 1-43-54-69-89; Dir MARCEL FROISSART.

Centre de physique des particules de Marseille (CPPM): Université d'Aix-Marseille 2, Centre universitaire de Luminy, Case 907, 70 route Léon Lachamp, 13288 Marseille Cedex 09; tel. 4-91-26-90-00; fax 4-91-41-91-26; Dir JEAN-JACQUES AUBERT.

Laboratoire de physique nucléaire des hautes énergies (LPNHE X): École Polytechnique, plateau de Palaiseau, 91128 Palaiseau Cedex; tel. 1-69-33-47-36; fax 1-69-41-88-46; Dir FRANÇOIS JACQUET.

Laboratoire de physique nucléaire (LPN Nantes): Université de Nantes, 2 rue de la Houssinière, 44072 Nantes Cedex 03; tel. 2-40-37-30-66; Dir DANIEL ARDOUIN.

II. Mathematics and Physics:

Théorie des collisions atomiques: Université de Bordeaux 1, 351 cours de la Libération, 33405 Talence; tel. 5-56-84-61-81; fax 5-56-84-61-87; Dir ROBERT GAYET.

Laboratoire de physique théorique de l'ENS: École normale supérieure, 24 rue Lhomond, 75231 Paris Cedex 05; tel. 1-44-32-37-79; fax 1-45-87-34-89; f. 1974; Dir JEAN ILIOPOULOS.

Laboratoire de photophysique moléculaire: Université de Paris XI, Bâtiment 213, 91405 Orsay Cedex; tel. 1-69-41-61-30; fax 1-69-41-67-77; f. 1972; Dir MICHEL GAILLARD.

Centre de physique théorique: Centre de Luminy, Case 907, 13288 Marseille Cedex 9; tel. 4-91-26-95-00; fax 4-91-26-95-53; f. 1967; Dir JACQUES SOFFER.

Laboratoire Aimé Cotton: Campus d'Orsay Bâtiment 505, 91405 Orsay Cedex; tel. 1-69-82-40-50; fax 1-69-07-68-91; f. 1947; Dir CATHERINE BRECHIGNAC.

Service national des champs intenses (SNCI): 25 avenue des Martyrs, BP 166X, 38042 Grenoble Cedex; tel. 4-76-88-10-00; fax 4-76-87-21-97; f. 1971; Dir PETER WYDER.

Laboratoire d'optique quantique: École polytechnique, route de Saclay, 91128 Palaiseau Cedex; tel. 1-69-33-41-27; fax 1-69-33-30-17; f. 1971; Dir FRANÇOIS PRADÈRE.

Laboratoire de physique des solides: 1 place Aristide-Briand, 92190 Meudon; tel. 1-45-07-51-53; fax 1-45-07-58-99; f. 1970; Dir JACQUES CHEVALLIER.

Laboratoire de physique du solide et énergie solaire: Parc de Valbonne Sophia-Antipolis, Rue Bernard Grégory, 06034 Valbonne; tel. 4-93-95-42-00; fax 4-93-95-83-61; Dir PIERRE GIBART.

Laboratoire de magnétisme et matériaux magnétiques: 1 place Aristide-Briand, 92195 Meudon; tel. 1-45-07-53-18; fax 1-45-07-58-22; f. 1970; Dir VLADIMIR CAGAN.

Laboratoire de physique des matériaux: 1 place Aristide-Briand, 92195 Meudon; tel. 1-45-07-51-65; fax 1-45-07-58-99; f. 1948; Dir JACQUES CASTAING.

Centre de recherches sur les très basses températures: 25 avenue des Martyrs, BP 166X, 38042 Grenoble Cedex; tel. 4-76-88-10-00; fax 4-76-87-50-60; f. 1962; Dir PIERRE MONCEAU.

Laboratoire de magnétisme Louis Néel: 25 avenue des Martyrs, BP 166X, 38042 Grenoble Cedex; tel. 4-76-88-10-89; fax 4-76-88-11-91; f. 1971; Dir DOMINIQUE GIVORD.

Laboratoire des propriétés mécaniques et thermodynamiques des matériaux: Université de Paris 13, Ave Jean-Baptiste Clément, 93430 Villetaneuse; tel. 1-49-40-35-00; f. 1973; Dir ANDRÉ ZAOUI.

Centre de recherches sur les solides à organisation cristalline imparfaite (CRSOCI): 1B rue de la Férollerie, 45071 Orléans Cedex; tel. 2-38-63-39-37; f. 1969; Dir HENRI VAN DAMME.

Laboratoire de cristallographie: 25 avenue des Martyrs, BP 166X, 38042 Grenoble Cedex; tel. 4-76-88-10-00; fax 4-76-88-10-38; f. 1971; Dir DENIS RAOUX.

Centre d'élaboration de matériaux et d'études structurales/Laboratoire d'optique électronique: 29 rue Jeanne-Marvig, BP 4347, 31055 Toulouse Cedex;

tel. 5-62-25-78-00; fax 5-62-25-79-99; f. 1949; Dir JEAN GALY.

Centre de recherche sur les mécanismes de la croissance cristalline (CRMC2): Campus de Luminy, Case 913, 13288 Marseille Cedex 9; tel. 4-91-17-28-00; fax 4-91-41-89-16; f. 1975; Dir MICHEL BIENFAIT.

Laboratoire Léon Brillouin (LLB): Centre d'Etudes Nucléaires de Saclay, 91191 Gif-sur-Yvette Cedex; tel. 1-69-08-52-41; fax 1-69-08-82-61; f. 1974; Dir MARIANNE LAMBERT.

Laboratoire de l'utilisation du rayonnement électromagnétique (LURE): Université de Paris 11, Bâtiment 209C, 91405 Orsay Cedex; tel. 1-64-46-80-00; f. 1977; Dir YVES PETROFF.

Centre interdisciplinaire de recherches avec les ions lourds (CIRIL): BP 5133, 14040 Caen Cedex; tel. 2-31-45-46-01; fax 2-31-45-46-65; f. 1982; Dir JEAN-CLAUDE JOUSSET.

Laboratoire d'études des propriétés électroniques des solides: 25 ave des Martyrs, BP 166, 38042 Grenoble Cedex; tel. 4-76-88-10-39; f. 1983; Dir FRANÇOISE CYROT.

Centre de physique théorique: Ecole polytechnique, Route de Saclay, 91128 Palaiseau Cedex; tel. 1-69-33-40-87; fax 1-69-33-30-08; Dir GUY LAVAL.

Service des champs magnétiques intenses: 156 ave de Rangueil, 31077 Toulouse Cedex; tel. 5-61-55-95-15; fax 5-61-55-96-24; f. 1967; Dir SALOMON ASKENAZY.

Recherches mathématiques et documentation en vue de la recherche à l'IHP: Université de Paris 6, Institut Henri Poincaré, 11 rue Pierre-et-Marie-Curie, 75231 Paris Cedex 05; tel. 1-43-54-42-10; f. 1985; Dir NICOLE EL KAROUI.

Spectrométrie nucléaire et spectrométrie de masse: Campus d'Orsay, Bâtiment 104–108, BP 1, 91406 Orsay Campus; tel. 1-69-41-52-22; Dir HARRY BERNAS.

Microscopie électronique, analytique et quantitative: Université de Paris 11, Laboratoire de physique des solides, Bâtiment 510, 91405 Orsay Cedex; tel. 1-69-41-53-70; f. 1984; Dir CHRISTIAN COLLIEX.

Laboratoire de microstructures et microélectroniques (L2M): Centre national d'étude des télécommunications, Centre Paris B, 196 ave Henri Ravera, 92220 Bagneux; tel. 1-42-31-76-93; fax 1-45-31-73-78; f. 1984; Dir HUGUETTE LAUNOIS.

Laboratoire commun CNRS/Saint-Gobain: CRPAM, BP 109, 54704 Pont-à-Mousson Cedex; tel. 1-83-83-24-24; fax 1-83-82-89-62; f. 1986; Dir ANDRÉ THOMY.

Laboratoire grenoblois de recherche sur les ions, les plasmas et la physique atomique (LAGRIPPA): CENG, BP 85X, 38041 Grenoble Cedex; tel. 4-76-88-40-01; fax 4-76-88-51-60; f. 1983; Dir JURGEN ANDRA.

Institut de physique et chimie des matériaux de Strasbourg (IPCM): Université de Strasbourg 1, 4 rue Blaise-Pascal, 67070 Strasbourg Cedex; tel. 3-88-41-60-00; fax 3-88-28-09-90; f. 1988; Dir FRANÇOIS GAUTIER.

Laboratoire d'étude des microstructures: ONERA, 20 ave de la Division-Leclerc, 92320 Châtillon-sous-Bagneux; tel. 1-46-57-11-60; fax 1-46-56-25-23; f. 1988; Dir PATRICK VEYSSIÈRE.

Spectroscopie en lumière polarisée: ESPCI, 10 rue Vauquelin, 75231 Paris Cedex 05; tel. 1-40-79-46-03; fax 1-43-31-42-22; f. 1967; Dir CLAUDE BOCCARA.

Magnétisme et optique des solides: 1 place Aristide-Briand, 92190 Meudon; tel. 1-45-34-75-50; fax 1-45-34-46-96; f. 1975; Dir HENRI LE GALL.

Structures organiques dissymétriques: Université de Paris 11, Centre Pharmaceutique, Laboratoire de Physique, Tour B, Avenue J.-B.-Clément, 92290 Châtenay-Malabry; tel. 1-46-83-56-23; fax 1-46-83-13-03; f. 1975; Dir COLETTE DE RANGO.

Problèmes d'interactions non-linéaires: Université Paris 7, Tour 33-43, 2 place Jussieu, 75251 Paris Cedex 05; tel. 1-43-36-25-25; f. 1975; Dir RAYMOND JANCEL.

Théorie des processus atomiques et moléculaires à basse énergie: Observatoire de Meudon, 5 place Jules Janssen, 92195 Meudon Cedex; tel. 1-45-07-75-30; fax 1-45-07-74-69; f. 1983; Dir MARYVONNE LE DOURNEUF.

Département d'astrophysique relativiste et de cosmologie (DARC): Observatoire de Meudon, 5 place Jules-Janssen, 92195 Meudon Principal Cedex; tel. 1-45-07-74-16; fax 1-45-07-74-69; f. 1975; Dir JEAN-PIERRE LASOTA.

Physique moléculaire et applications: Université Paris 6, Tour 13, 4 place Jussieu, 75252 Paris Cedex 05; tel. 1-44-27-44-83; fax 1-44-27-70-33; f. 1973; Dir JEAN-MARIE FLAUD.

Laboratoire de rhéologie: Université de Grenoble 1, 38041 Grenoble; tel. 4-76-82-51-70; Dir JEAN-MICHEL PIAU.

III. Physical Sciences for Engineers:

Laboratoire d'aérothermique: 4 ter route des Gardes, 92190 Meudon; tel. 1-45-07-54-38; fax 1-45-07-58-20; f. 1938; Dir JEAN-CLAUDE LENGRAND.

Laboratoire d'automatique et d'analyse des systèmes (LAAS): 7 ave du Colonel Roche, 31077 Toulouse; tel. 5-61-33-62-00; fax 5-61-55-35-77; f. 1967; Dir ALAIN COSTES.

Institut de science et de génie des matériaux et des procédés: BP 5, Odeillo-Via, 66120 Font-Romeu; tel. 4-68-30-77-00; fax 4-68-30-29-40; f. 1950; Dir CLAUDE DUPUY.

Laboratoire de mécanique et d'acoustique (LMA): 31 chemin Joseph-Aiguier, 13402 Marseille Cedex 9; tel. 4-91-22-40-00; fax 4-91-22-08-75; f. 1941; Dir CLAUDE GAZANHES.

Laboratoire de physique et de métrologie des oscillateurs: 32 ave de l'Observatoire, 25000 Besançon; tel. 3-81-66-69-99; fax 3-81-66-69-98; f. 1973; Dir DANIEL HAUDEN.

Laboratoire des signaux et systèmes (L2S): Ecole supérieure d'électricité, Plateau du Moulon, 91192 Gif-sur-Yvette; tel. 1-69-41-80-40; fax 1-69-41-30-60; f. 1974; Dir PIERRE BERTRAND.

Laboratoire d'électrostatique et de matériaux diélectriques: BP 166, 25 ave des Martyrs, 38042 Grenoble Cedex; tel. 4-76-88-10-76; fax 4-76-88-79-45; f. 1971; Dir JEAN-PIERRE GOSSE.

Laboratoire d'informatique pour la mécanique et les sciences pour l'ingénieur (LIMSI): Université de Paris XI, Bâtiment 508, BP 133, 91406 Orsay Cedex; tel. 1-69-85-80-85; fax 1-69-85-80-88; f. 1945; Dir JOSEPH MARIANI.

Laboratoire des sciences du génie chimique: BP 451, 1 rue Grandville, 54001 Nancy Cedex; tel. 3-83-35-21-21; fax 3-83-35-29-75; f. 1975; Dir DANIEL TONDEUR.

Laboratoire de combustion et systèmes réactifs: 1C ave de la Recherche-Scientifique, 45071 Orléans Cedex 2; tel. 2-38-63-06-17; fax 2-38-64-26-70; f. 1969; Dir HENRY MELLOTTÉE.

Laboratoire d'ingéniérie, des matériaux et des hautes pressions: Centre universitaire Paris XII, Ave Jean-Baptiste-Clément, 93430 Villetaneuse; tel. 1-49-40-34-37; fax 1-49-40-34-14; Dir Prof. BERNARD DECOMPS.

Laboratoire d'énergétique moléculaire et macroscopique, combustion: Ecole centrale de Paris, gde-Voie des Vignes, 92295 Châtenay-Malabry; tel. 1-47-02-70-56; fax 1-47-02-80-35; f. 1970; Dir EMILE ESPOSITO.

Thermique de l'habitat (RAMSES): Université de Paris XI, bâtiment 508, 91405 Orsay Cedex; tel. 1-69-41-82-50; f. 1985; Dir LOUIS-MARIE CHOUNET.

Equipe de combinatoire: Université de Paris VI, 4 place Jussieu, 75252 Paris Cedex 05; tel. 1-44-27-38-08; fax 1-44-27-40-01; f. 1975; Dir M. LAS VERGNES.

Groupe de représentation et traitement des connaissances (GRTC): 31 chemin Joseph-Aiguier, 13402 Marseille Cedex 09; tel. 4-91-22-40-00; fax 4-91-71-08-08; f. 1984; Dir EUGÈNE CHOURAQUI.

Ingénierie électronique assistée par ordinateur: Institut méditerranéen de technologie, Technopile Château Combert, 13451 Marseille Cedex 13; fax 4-91-05-43-43; f. 1988; Dir JEAN MERMET.

Techniques de l'informatique, des mathématiques, de la microélectronique et de la microscopie quantitative: IMAG, 46 rue Félix-Viallet, 38031 Grenoble Cedex; tel. 4-76-57-46-22; fax 4-76-47-38-14; f. 1986; Dir BERNARD COURTOIS.

Laboratoire de physique des décharges: École supérieure d'électricité, plateau du Moulon, 91192 Gif-sur-Yvette; tel. 1-69-41-80-40; fax 1-69-41-30-60; f. 1972; Dir EMMANUEL MARODE.

Laboratoire de l'horloge atomique: Université de Paris XI, Bâtiment 221, 91405 Orsay Cedex; tel. 1-69-41-78-61; fax 1-69-41-08-80; f. 1973; Dir MICHEL DÉSAINTFUSCIEN.

Optique physiologique et fonctions visuelles: Muséum national d'histoire naturelle, 43 rue Cuvier, 75231 Paris Cedex 05; tel. 1-40-79-37-24; fax 1-40-79-37-16; f. 1983; Dir HANS BRETTEL.

Laboratoire de physique des interfaces et des couches minces: École polytechnique, plateau de Palaiseau, 91128 Palaiseau Cedex; tel. 1-69-33-40-09; fax 1-69-33-30-06; f. 1983; Dir BERNARD EQUER.

Laboratoire de physique des milieux ionisés: École polytechnique, plateau de Palaiseau, 91128 Palaiseau Cedex; tel. 1-65-33-41-15; fax 1-69-33-20-23; f. 1975; Dir JEAN VIRMONT.

Laboratoire de physique et applications des semi-conducteurs: Centre de recherches nucléaires, Université de Strasbourg II, 23 rue de Loess, BP 20, 67037 Strasbourg Cedex; tel. 3-88-28-65-43; fax 3-88-28-09-90; f. 1985; Dir PAUL SIFFERT.

Laboratoire pour l'utilisation des lasers intenses: École polytechnique, plateau de Palaiseau, 91128 Palaiseau Cedex; tel. 1-60-33-41-12; fax 1-69-33-30-09; f. 1988; Dir EDOUARD FABRE.

Institut de mécanique statistique de la turbulence: Université d'Aix-Marseille II, 12 ave Général-Leclerc, 13003 Marseille; tel. 4-91-50-54-39; fax 4-91-08-16-37; f. 1969; Dir MICHEL COANTIC.

Institut de mécanique des fluides de Marseille: Université d'Aix-Marseille II, 1 rue Honnorat, 13003 Marseille; tel. 4-91-08-16-90; f. 1966; Dir BERNARD FORESTIER.

Laboratoire réacteurs catalytiques en milieu triphasique: Rhône-Poulenc Industrialisation, 24 ave Jean-Jaurès, BP 166, 69151 Décines-Charpieu Cedex; tel. 4-72-05-25-52; fax 4-72-05-20-45; f. 1987; Dir JEAN JENCK.

Laboratoire des matériaux et structures du génie civil: CNRS Laboratoire central des ponts et chaussées, 58 blvd Lefebvre, 75732 Paris Cedex 15; tel. 1-40-43-50-96; fax 1-40-43-54-98; Dir MICHEL FREMOND.

Laboratoire d'application des lasers de puissance: 16 bis ave du Prieur de la Côte d'Or, 94114 Arcueil; tel. 1-42-31-91-94; fax 1-42-31-97-46; Dir RÉMY FABBRO.

Action recherche et applications MATRA-IRIT en interface homme-système: Zone industrielle du Palays, 31 rue des Cosmonautes, 31077 Toulouse; tel. 5-61-39-66-25; fax 5-61-39-69-65; Dir JEAN-PAUL DENIER.

IV. Chemistry:

Physique des liquides et électrochimie: Université de Paris 6, 4 place Jussieu, Tour 22, 75230 Paris Cedex 05; tel. 1-43-36-25-25; fax 1-43-54-40-97; Dir MICHEL FROMENT.

Laboratoire de chimie quantique: Université de Strasbourg 1, Institut Le Bel, 4 rue Blaise Pascal, 67000 Strasbourg; tel. 3-88-41-61-28; fax 3-88-60-75-50; Dir ALAIN DEDIEU.

Chimie métallurgique des terres rares: 1 place Aristide Briand, 92195 Meudon Bellevue; tel. 1-45-34-75-50; fax 1-45-34-46-96; Dir JEAN CLAUDE ACHARD.

Eléments de transition dans les solides: 1 place Aristide Briand, 92190 Meudon; tel. 1-45-34-75-50; fax 1-45-34-46-96; Dir GÉRARD SCHIFFMACHER.

Physicochimie des matériaux par techniques avancées: 1 place Aristide Briand, 92190 Meudon; tel. 1-45-34-75-50; fax 1-45-34-46-96; Dir BERNARD BLANZAT.

Laboratoire des matériaux moléculaires: 2–8 rue Henri-Dunant, BP 28, 94320 Thiais; tel. 1-46-87-33-55; Dir FRANCIS GARNIER.

Dynamique des interactions moléculaires: Université de Paris 6, Tour 22, 4 place Jussieu, 75252 Paris Cedex 05; tel. 1-43-26-09-82; Dir MARCEL ALLAVENA.

Chimie des interactions moléculaires: Collège de France, bâtiment C, 11 place Marcelin-Berthelot, 75231 Paris Cedex 05; tel. 1-44-27-12-11; Dir JEAN-MARIE LEHN.

Nouveaux procédés de synthèse organique: École normale supérieure, Laboratoire de chimie, 24 rue Lhomond, 75231 Paris Cedex 05; tel. 1-43-29-12-25; Dir GERARD LINSTRUMELLE.

Centre de biophysique moléculaire: 1A ave de la Recherche Scientifique, 45045 Orléans Cedex; tel. 2-38-51-55-88; fax 2-38-63-15-17; f. 1967; Dir MICHEL DAUNE.

Institut de recherches sur la catalyse: 2 ave Einstein, 69609 Villeurbanne Cedex; tel. 4-72-44-53-00; fax 4-78-89-47-69; f. 1958; Dir DANIÈLE OLIVIER.

Centre d'études de chimie métallurgique: 15 rue Georges-Urbain, 94400 Vitry-sur-Seine; tel. 1-46-87-35-93; fax 1-46-75-04-33; f. 1936; Dir JEAN-PIERRE CHEVALIER.

Centre d'études et de recherches de chimie organique appliquée (CERCOA): 2–8 rue Henry-Dunant, BP 28, 94320 Thiais; tel. 1-46-87-33-55; fax 1-46-87-17-27; f. 1946; Dir MICHEL LANGLOIS.

Laboratoire de chimie du solide: Université de Bordeaux I, 351 cours de la Libération, 33405 Talence Cedex; tel. 5-56-84-60-00; f. 1974; Dir JEAN ETOURNEAU.

Centre de recherches 'Paul Pascal': CNRS, Château Brivazac, ave A. Schweitzer, 33600 Pessac Cedex; tel. 5-56-84-56-56; f. 1963; Dir PIERRE BOTHOREL.

Institut de chimie des substances naturelles: Avenue de la Terrasse, BP 1, 91198 Gif-sur-Yvette; tel. 1-69-82-30-30; fax 1-60-67-72-47; f. 1959; Dir PIERRE POTIER.

Laboratoire Maurice Letort: Route de Vandoeuvre, BP 104, 54600 Villers-lès-Nancy; tel. 3-83-27-60-10; f. 1963; Dir BOYAN MUTAFTSCHIEV.

Centre d'études et de recherches par irradiation: 3A rue de la Ferollerie, 45071 Orléans Cedex; tel. 2-38-51-54-26; fax 2-38-64-26-70; f. 1974; Dir DIDIER ISABELLE.

Laboratoire d'électrochimie interfaciale: 1 place Aristide-Briand, 92195 Meudon; tel. 1-45-34-75-50; fax 1-45-34-46-96; f. 1946; Dir MAX COSTA.

Centre de recherches sur les macromolécules végétales: BP 53X, 38402 Saint-Martin-d'Hères Cedex; tel. 4-76-54-11-45; fax 4-76-54-72-03; f. 1967; Dir MARGUERITE RINAUDO.

Service central d'analyse: BP 22, Autoroute Lyon-Vienne, Echangeur de Solaize, 69390 Vernaison; tel. 4-78-02-22-22; fax 4-78-02-71-87; f. 1958; Dir ALAIN LAMOTTE.

Centre de thermodynamique et de microcalorimétrie: 26 rue du 141e R.I.A., 13003 Marseille; tel. 4-91-95-62-17; fax 4-91-50-38-29; f. 1959; Dir JEAN ROUQUEROL.

Centre de recherches sur la physicochimie des surfaces solides: 24 ave du Président-Kennedy, 68200 Mulhouse; tel. 3-89-42-01-55; fax 3-89-32-09-96; f. 1967; Dir JACQUES SCHULTZ.

Laboratoire 'Pierre Sue': CEN-Saclay, Bâtiment 637, 91191 Gif-sur-Yvette Cedex; tel. 1-69-08-46-17; fax 1-69-08-69-23; f. 1969; Dir GILLES REVEL.

Laboratoire de spectrochimie infrarouge et Raman (LASIR): 2 rue Henry Dunant, BP 28, 94320 Thiais; tel. 1-46-87-33-55; fax 1-20-43-49-95; f. 1965; Dir JACQUES CORSET.

Laboratoire de chimie de coordination: CNRS, 205 route de Narbonne, 31077 Toulouse Cedex; tel. 5-61-33-31-00; fax 5-61-55-30-03; f. 1974; Dir IGOR TKATCHENKO.

Laboratoire des matériaux organiques: BP 24, Autoroute Lyon-Vienne, Echangeur de Solaize, 69390 Vernaison; tel. 4-78-02-22-22; fax 4-78-02-71-87; f. 1977; Dir ALAIN GUYOT.

Chimie du phosphore et des métaux de transition: DCPH-École Polytechnique, 91128 Palaiseau; tel. 1-69-41-82-00; fax 1-69-41-33-92; f. 1987; Dir FRANÇOIS MATHEY.

Centre de recherches sur la physique des hautes températures: 1D ave de la Recherche-Scientifique, 45071 Orléans Cedex; tel. 2-38-51-55-14; fax 2-38-64-26-70; f. 1968; Dir JEAN-PIERRE COUTURES.

Institut Charles Sadron: 6 rue Boussingault, 67083 Strasbourg Cedex; tel. 3-88-41-40-00; fax 3-88-41-40-99; f. 1947; Dir GILBERT WEILL.

Laboratoire CNRS Roussel-Uclaf: Roussel-Uclaf, BP 9, 102 route de Noisy, 93230 Romainville; tel. 1-48-91-52-80; f. 1984; Dir ROBERT LETT.

Physicochimie des biopolymères: BP 28, 94320 Thiais; tel. 1-46-87-33-55; fax 1-46-87-17-27; f. 1985; Dir BERNARD SEBILLE.

Electrochimie, catalyse et synthèse organique: 2 rue Henri-Dunant, 94320 Thiais; tel. 1-46-87-33-55; f. 1985; Dir JACQUES PÉRICHON.

Génie catalytique des réacteurs de raffinage: BP 22, 69360 St-Symphorien-d'Ozon; tel. 4-72-51-82-34; f. 1986; Dir JEAN-RENÉ BERNARD.

Génie de la fabrication des catalyseurs hétérogènes: Institut Français du Pétrole, BP 3, 69390 Vernaison; tel. 4-78-02-20-20; fax 4-78-02-10-51; f. 1986; Dir PIERRE TRAMBOUZE.

Précurseurs organométalliques de matériaux: Université de Montpellier II, 2 place E.-Bataillon, 34060 Montpellier Cedex; tel. 4-67-41-39-80; fax 4-67-54-30-79; f. 1986; Dir ROBERT CORRIU.

Laboratoire des composites thermostructuraux: Europarc, 3 ave Léonard-de-Vinci, 33600 Pessac; tel. 5-56-07-06-80; f. 1988; Dir ROGER NASLAIN.

Laboratoire de RMN et de modélisation moléculaire: Institut de Chimie, BP 296 R/8, 67008 Strasbourg; tel. 3-88-41-61-85; f. 1988; Dir PIERRE GRANGER.

Chimie et biochimie macromoléculaire: ENS, 46 allée d'Italie, 69364 Lyon Cedex 07; tel. 4-72-72-83-59; f. 1988; Dir BERNARD MANDRAND.

Polymères thermostables et leurs applications: IFP, BP 3, 69390 Vernaison; tel. 4-78-02-20-77; fax 4-78-02-10-51; f. 1988; Dir BERNARD SILLION.

Institut de physique et chimie des matériaux: Université de Nantes, UFR de Chimie, 2 rue de la Houssinière, 44072 Nantes Cedex; tel. 2-40-37-39-39; fax 2-40-37-39-91; f. 1988; Dir (vacant).

Conception d'analogues de biomolécules: application aux antiviraux: Université de Montpellier 2, UFR de Chimie, Place Eugène Bataillon, 34060 Montpellier Cedex; tel. 4-67-54-58-73; Dir JEAN-LOUIS IMBACH.

Stéreochimie et interactions moléculaires: ENS de Lyon, 46 allée d'Italie, 69364 Lyon Cedex 07; tel. 4-72-72-80-00; fax 4-72-72-80-80; Dir ANDRÉ COLLET.

V. Earth and Space Sciences:

Astrophysique nucléaire et nucléosynthèse: CEN-Saclay, DPHG, SAP Bât. 28, 91191 Gif-sur-Yvette Cedex; tel. 1-69-41-80-00; Dir HUBERT REEVES.

Magnétisme des roches et ses applications géologiques et géophysiques: Université de Paris 6, Laboratoire de géomagnétisme du parc St-Maur, 4 ave de Neptune, 94107 Saint-Maur-des-Fosses Cedex; tel. 1-48-86-32-72; fax 1-48-89-44-33; Dir LUCIEN DALY.

Ecologie et biochimie microbienne du milieu marin: Université d'Aix-Marseille 1, Laboratoire de microbiologie marine, Campus de Luminy, Case 907, 70 route Léon Lachamp, 13288 Marseille Cedex 9; tel. 4-91-26-90-51; Dir ARMAND BIANCHI.

Dynamique terrestre et planétaire: Centre national d'études spatiales, 18 ave Edouard Belin, 31055 Toulouse Cedex; tel. 5-61-27-40-11; Dir MARC SOURIAU.

Physique mathématique, modélisation et simulation: 3A ave de la Recherche Scientifique, 45071 Orléans Cedex 2; tel. 2-38-63-00-86; fax 2-38-63-01-48; Dir MARC FEIX.

Service d'aéronomie (SA): BP 3, 91371 Verrières-le-Buisson; tel. 1-69-20-01-83; fax 1-69-20-29-99; f. 1958; Dir PIERRE BAUER.

Laboratoire d'astronomie spatiale (LAS): Traverse du Siphon, les Trois Lucs,

13012 Marseille; tel. 4-91-05-59-00; fax 4-91-05-59-66; f. 1965; Dir PAUL CRUVELLIER.

Institut d'astrophysique de Paris (IAP): 98 bis blvd Arago, 75014 Paris; tel. 1-43-20-14-25; f. 1936; Dir ALAIN OMONT.

Centre géologique et géophysique de Montpellier (CGGM): Université de Montpellier II, 2 Place Eugène Bataillon, 34060 Montpellier Cedex; tel. 4-67-14-30-30; fax 4-67-54-36-48; f. 1974; Dir MICHEL PRÉVOT.

Laboratoire de géologie du quaternaire (LGQ): Université d'Aix-Marseille 2, UER de Luminy, case 907, 13288 Marseille Cedex 9; tel. 4-91-26-96-50; f. 1958; Dir YVES LANCELOT.

Laboratoire de glaciologie et de géophysique de l'environnement (LGGE): rue Molière, BP 96, 38402 St Martin d'Hères Cedex; tel. 4-76-42-58-72; f. 1947; Dir ROBERT DELMAS.

Centre de recherches en physique de l'environnement (CRPE): 38–40 rue du Général Leclerc, 92231 Issy-les-Moulineaux; tel. 1-45-29-44-44; fax 1-45-29-60-52; telex 200570; f. 1975; Dir GILLES SOMMERIA.

Laboratoire de météorologie dynamique: Ecole Polytechnique, Route départementale 36, 91128 Palaiseau Cedex; tel. 1-60-19-41-43; f. 1939; Dir ROBERT SADOURNY.

Observatoire de Haute-Provence (OHP): 04870 Saint-Michel-l'Observatoire; tel. 4-92-70-64-00; fax 4-92-76-62-95; f. 1937; Dir PHILIPPE VÉRON.

Centre de pédologie biologique (CPB): 17 rue Notre-Dame-des-Pauvres, BP 5, 54500 Vandoeuvre-lès-Nancy; tel. 3-83-51-08-60; f. 1961; Dir ADRIEN HERBILLON.

Centre de recherches pétrographiques et géochimiques (CRPG): 15 rue Notre-Dame-des-Pauvres, BP 20, 54501 Vandoeuvre-lès-Nancy Cedex; tel. 3-83-51-22-13; f. 1953; Dir SIMON SHEPPARD.

Centre des faibles radioactivités (CFR): Ave de la Terrasse, 91190 Gif-sur-Yvette; tel. 1-69-82-30-30; f. 1961; Dir JEAN-CLAUDE DUPLESSY.

Centre de géochimie de la surface (CGS): 1 rue Blessig, 67084 Strasbourg Cedex; tel. 3-88-35-85-00; f. 1963; Dir BERTRAND FRITZ.

Centre armoricain d'études structurales des socles (CAESS): Institut de géologie, ave du Général-Leclerc, 35042 Rennes Cedex; tel. 2-99-28-61-10; f. 1974; Dir PIERRE CHOUKROUNE.

Centre de recherches sur la synthèse et la chimie des minéraux (CRSCM): 1A rue de la Férollerie, 45071 Orléans Cedex; tel. 2-38-51-53-96; fax 2-38-64-26-70; f. 1969; Dir MICHEL PICHAVANT.

Institut d'astrophysique spatiale: BP 10, 91370 Verrières-le-Buisson; tel. 1-64-47-43-15; fax 1-69-20-39-07; f. 1979; Dir ALAN GABRIEL.

Centre d'étude spatiale des rayonnements (CESR): Université de Toulouse III, 9 ave du Colonel Roche, BP 4346, 31029 Toulouse Cedex; tel. 5-61-55-66-66; f. 1979; Dir GILBERT VEDRENNE.

Laboratoire de physique et chimie de l'environnement (LPCE): 3A ave de la Recherche Scientifique, 45071 Orléans Cedex 2; tel. 2-38-51-52-00; fax 2-38-63-01-48; f. 1982; Dir CHRISTIAN BEGHIN.

Laboratoire des écoulements géophysiques et industriels: Université de Grenoble, 38041 Grenoble; tel. 4-76-82-50-50; Dir GILBERT BINDER.

Laboratoire des sols, solides, structures et leurs interactions: Université de Grenoble 1, 38041 Grenoble; tel. 4-76-82-51-26; Dir PHILIPPE TROMPETTE.

Laboratoire d'etude des transferts en hydrologie et environnement: Université de Grenoble 1, 38041 Grenoble; tel. 4-76-82-50-56; Dir MICHEL VAUCLIN.

VI. Life Sciences:

Laboratoire de neurobiologie cellulaire et moléculaire: Avenue de la Terrasse, 91198 Gif-sur-Yvette Cedex; tel. 1-69-82-36-61; fax 1-69-07-05-38; Dir LADISLAV TAUC.

Institut de biologie et chimie des protéines: 43 blvd du 11 Novembre 1918, 69622 Villeurbanne; tel. 4-72-44-81-86; fax 4-72-44-08-03; Dir ALAIN COZZONE.

Centre de biochimie: Université de Nice, Parc Valrose, 06034 Nice Cedex; tel. 4-93-52-99-23; fax 4-93-52-99-17; Dir GÉRARD AILHAUD.

Centre de recherches de biochimie macromoléculaire: Route de Mende, BP 5051, 34033 Montpellier Cedex; tel. 4-67-61-33-21; fax 4-67-52-15-59; f. 1973; Dir JACQUES DEMAILLE.

Centre de service des animaux de laboratoire (SAL): 3 bis rue de la Férollerie, 45071 Orléans Cedex 02; tel. 2-38-63-29-48; f. 1953; Dir CLAUDE AUZANNEAU.

Centre d'études biologiques des animaux sauvages (CEBAS): Villiers-en-Bois, BP 14, 79360 Beauvoir-sur-Niort; tel. 5-49-09-61-11; f. 1967; Dir PIERRE JOUVENTIN.

Laboratoire de recherche génétique sur les modèles animaux: CNRS, BP 8, 7 rue Guy Mocquet, 94801 Villejuif Cedex; tel. 1-47-26-46-58.

Laboratoire de biologie moléculaire eucaryote: 118 route de Narbonne, 31062 Toulouse Cedex; tel. 5-61-33-58-86; Dir FRANÇOIS AMALRIC.

Laboratoire de microbiologie et génétique moléculaire: 118 route de Narbonne, 31062 Toulouse Cedex; tel. 5-61-33-58-86; Dir MICHAEL CHANDLER.

Institut Jacques Monod: Université de Paris VII, 2 place Jussieu, tour 43, 75251 Paris Cedex 05; tel. 1-43-36-25-25; fax 1-46-33-23-05; f. 1966; molecular biology research institute; Dir JACQUES RICARD.

Institut de biologie moléculaire et cellulaire (IBMC): 15 rue René Descartes, 67084 Strasbourg Cedex; tel. 3-88-41-70-00; fax 3-88-61-06-80; f. 1973; Dir GUY DIRHEIMER.

Centre technique pour le soutien de la recherche sur le cancer: 16 ave Vaillant-Couturier, BP 3, 94801 Villejuif Cedex; tel. 1-46-78-57-57; fax 1-47-26-04-75; f. 1981; Dir JACQUES CROZEMARIE.

Laboratoire de chimie bactérienne: 31 chemin Joseph Aiguier, case 901 Luminy, BP 71, 13277 Marseille Cedex 9; tel. 4-91-22-40-75; fax 4-91-22-08-75; f. 1962; Dir JEAN-CLAUDE PATTE.

Institut d'embryologie cellulaire et moléculaire: 49 bis ave de la Belle-Gabrielle, 94736 Nogent-sur-Marne Cedex; tel. 1-48-73-60-90; fax 1-48-73-43-77; f. 1947; Dir NICOLE LE DOUARIN.

Laboratoire d'enzymologie: Avenue de la Terrasse, 91198 Gif-sur-Yvette Cedex; tel. 1-69-82-34-88; fax 1-69-82-31-29; f. 1959; Dir DOMINIQUE PANTALONI.

Laboratoire de génétique des virus: Bât. 14, Avenue de la Terrase, 91198 Gif-sur-Yvette Cedex; tel. 1-69-82-30-30; f. 1946; Dir ANNE FLAMAND.

Laboratoire de neurobiologie moléculaire des interactions cellulaires: 5 rue Blaise Pascal, 67084 Strasbourg Cedex; tel. 3-88-61-48-48; f. 1965; Dir GUY VINCENDON.

Centre de recherches sur la nutrition: 9 rue Jules Hetzel, 92190 Meudon; tel. 1-45-07-52-18; f. 1946; Dir JEAN GIRARD.

Centre national de coordination des études et recherches sur la nutrition et l'alimentation (CNERNA): 11 rue Jean Nicot, 75007 Paris; tel. 1-42-75-93-24; f. 1945; Dir JACQUES FLANZY.

Laboratoire de pharmacologie et de toxicologie fondamentale: 205 route de Narbonne, 31077 Toulouse Cedex; tel. 5-61-17-59-00; f. 1960; Dir JEAN CROS.

Laboratoire de physiologie des organes végétaux après récolte: 4 ter route des Gardes, 92190 Meudon; tel. 1-45-34-75-50; f. 1942; Dir JEAN DAUSSANT.

Centre d'écologie et physiologie énergétiques: CNRS, 23 rue du Loess, 67087 Strasbourg; tel. 3-88-28-69-00; Dir YVON LE MAHO.

Institut Alfred Fessard: Avenue de la Terrasse, 91198 Gif-sur-Yvette Cedex; tel. 1-69-82-34-23; fax 1-69-07-05-38; f. 1972; Dir JEAN-DIDIER VINCENT.

Centre d'écologie des ressources renouvelables: 29 rue Jeanne-Marvig, BP 4009, 31055 Toulouse Cedex; tel. 5-61-25-40-87; f. 1947; Dir HENRI DECAMPS.

Laboratoire de biologie et de génétique évolutives: Bât. 13, Avenue de la Terrasse, 91198 Gif-sur-Yvette Cedex; tel. 1-69-82-37-23; f. 1947; Dir JEAN DAVID.

Laboratoire de biologie et technologie des membranes et des systèmes intégrés: 43 blvd du 11 Novembre 1918, 69622 Villeurbanne Cedex; tel. 4-72-44-80-00; fax 4-78-89-47-69; f. 1976; Dir DANIÈLE GAUTHERON.

Centre d'immunologie de Marseille-Luminy: Case 906, Luminy, 13288 Marseille Cedex 09; tel. 4-91-26-94-00; fax 4-91-26-94-30; f. 1976; Dir MICHEL PIERRES.

Laboratoire de génétique moléculaire des eucaryotes: 11 rue Humann, 67085 Strasbourg Cedex; tel. 3-88-37-12-55; f. 1977; Dir PIERRE CHAMBON.

Laboratoire de génétique et biologie cellulaires (LGBC): Centre Universitaire de Luminy, case 907, 13288 Marseille Cedex 9; tel. 4-91-26-96-00; f. 1981; Dir ROLAND ROSSET.

Laboratoire de physiologie neurosensorielle: 15 rue de l'Ecole de Médecine, 75006 Paris; tel. 1-43-29-61-54; f. 1981; Dir ALAIN BERTHOZ.

Centre de neurologie cellulaire et moléculaire: 67 rue Maurice-Günsbourg, 94205 Ivry-sur-Seine; tel. 1-46-72-18-00; f. 1969; Dir BERNARD PESSAC.

Centre d'études d'océanographie et de biologie marine: Station biologique, place Georges Teissier, 29211 Roscoff; tel. 2-98-69-72-30; fax 2-98-61-26-55; f. 1946; Dir PIERRE LASSERRE.

Laboratoire de physiologie et psychologie environnementales: 21 rue Becquerel, 67087 Strasbourg Cedex; tel. 3-88-28-67-83; fax 3-88-28-09-90; f. 1986; Dir ALAIN MUZET.

Laboratoire de neurobiologie: 31 chem. Joseph Aiguier, BP 71, 13402 Marseille Cedex 9; tel. 4-91-22-40-00; fax 4-91-22-08-75; f. 1986; Dir JEAN-LUC CLÉMENT.

Laboratoire des neurosciences fonctionnelles: 31 chem. Joseph Aiguier, BP 71, 13402 Marseille Cedex 09; tel. 4-91-22-40-00; fax 4-91-22-08-75; f. 1986; Dir JEAN MASSION.

Centre de recherches souterraines: 09200 Saint-Girons; tel. 5-61-66-31-26; f. 1948; Dir CHRISTIAN JUBERTHIE.

Institut de biochimie cellulaire: 1 rue Camille-Saint-Saëns, 33077 Bordeaux Cedex; tel. 5-56-98-24-22; f. 1980; Dir BERNARD GUÉRIN.

Centre CNRS-INSERM de pharmacologie, endocrinologie: rue de la Cardonille, 34094 Montpellier Cedex; tel. 4-67-54-37-18; fax 4-67-54-24-32; f. 1982; Dir JOËL BOCKAËRT.

Laboratoire de biologie moléculaire des relations plantes-microorganismes: BP 27, 31326 Castanet-Tolosan; tel. 5-61-28-50-28; f. 1981; Dir PIERRE BOISTARD.

Institut de pharmacologie moléculaire et cellulaire: Sophia-Antipolis, 06560 Valbonne; tel. 4-93-95-77-77; fax 4-93-95-77-01; Dir MICHEL LAZDUNSKI.

Institut des sciences végétales: BP 1, 91198 Gif-sur-Yvette Cedex; tel. 1-69-82-36-36; fax 1-69-82-36-95; Dir ADAM KONDOROSI.

Relations structure-fonction des constituants membranaires: Université de Lille I, 59655 Villeneuve-d' Ascq Cedex; tel. 3-20-43-48-83; fax 3-20-43-49-95; Dir ANDRÉ VERBERT.

Biologie et génétique moléculaires: 7 rue Guy Môquet, BP 8, 94802 Villejuif; tel. 1-47-26-46-58; fax 1-47-26-88-36; Dirs DANIEL BLANGY, ANNE-MARIE DE RECONDO.

Oncologie virale: 7 rue Guy Môquet, BP 8, 94802 Villejuif; tel. 1-47-26-46-58; fax 1-47-26-76-02; Dir ION GRESSER.

Oncologie moléculaire: 7 rue Guy Môquet, BP 8, 94802 Villejuif; tel. 1-47-26-46-58; Dir PIERRE MAY.

Centres réactionnels photosynthétiques: BP 1, 91198 Gif-sur-Yvette; tel. 1-69-82-38-11; fax 1-69-82-35-62; Dir ANNE-LISE ETIENNE.

Centre d'écologie fonctionelle et évolutive Louis Emberger (CEFE): BP 5051, route de Mende, 34033 Montpellier Cedex; tel. 4-67-61-32-00; fax 4-67-41-21-38; Dir FERNAND WAREMBOURG.

Centre de génétique moléculaire: Bât. 26, Avenue de la Terrasse, 91198 Gif-sur-Yvette; tel. 1-69-82-30-30; fax 1-69-07-53-22; Dir JEAN-CLAUDE MOUNOLOU.

Centre de recherches sur le polymorphisme génétique des populations humaines: Hôpital Purpan, Ave de la Grande-Bretagne, 31300 Toulouse; tel. 5-61-49-60-80; Dir ANNE CAMBON-THOMSEN.

Recombinaisons génétiques: Université de Paris VII, Hôpital St-Louis, Centre Georges-Hayem, 1 avenue Claude Vellefeaux, 75475 Paris Cedex 10; tel. 1-42-02-16-05; fax 1-42-41-14-70; Dir FRANCIS GALIBERT.

Rétrovirus et rétrotransposons des vertébrés: Université de Paris VII, Hôpital St-Louis, 12 bis rue Grange-aux-Belles, 75475 Paris Cedex 10; tel. 1-42-40-13-82; Dir GEORGES PERIES.

Laboratoire de génétique moléculaire: 7 rue Guy Môquet, 94802 Villejuif; tel. 1-47-26-46-58; fax 1-47-26-88-36; Dir ALAIN SARASIN.

Ontogénèse du comportement et vie sociale: 31 chemin Joseph-Aiguier, 13402 Marseille Cedex 09; tel. 4-91-22-40-00; Dir JACQUES GERVET.

Institut de biologie moléculaire des plantes (IBMP): 12 rue du Gén. Zimmer, 67000 Strasbourg; tel. 3-88-41-72-00; Dirs JACQUES-HENRI WEIL, CLAUDE GIGOT.

Régulation de l'expression des gènes eucaryotes: 7 rue Guy Môquet, BP 8, 94802 Villejuif; tel. 1-47-26-46-58; Dir JANINE DOLY.

Biochimie fonctionnelle des membranes végétales: Bât. 9, BP 1, 91190 Gif-sur-Yvette; tel. 1-69-82-38-57; fax 1-69-07-83-10; Dir ANTOINE TREMOLIÈRES.

Génétique moléculaire et cellulaire: Université de Lyon I, 43 blvd du 11 Novembre-1918, 69622 Villeurbanne Cedex; tel. 4-72-44-80-00; fax 4-72-44-05-55; Dir JACQUELINE GODET.

Immunovirologie moléculaire et cellulaire, virologie moléculaire: Université de Lyon I, rue Guillaume-Paradin, 69372 Lyon Cedex 08; tel. 4-78-77-86-00; fax 4-78-01-43-22; Dir LOUIS GAZZOLO.

Laboratoire des interactions plastescytoplasmes mitochondries: Centre d'Etudes nucléaires, BP 85X, 38041 Grenoble Cedex; tel. 4-76-88-37-85; fax 4-76-88-51-55; Dir JACQUES JOYARD.

Neuropharmacologie moléculaire: Université de Lyon I, rue Guillaume-Paradin, 69372 Lyon; tel. 4-78-77-86-32; fax 4-78-01-35-47; Dir JEAN-FRANÇOIS PUJOL.

Laboratoire de biologie moléculaire et cellulaire: ENS de Lyon, 46 all. d'Italie, 69364 Lyon Cedex 07; tel. 4-72-72-81-72; fax. 4-72-72-80-80; Dir JACQUES SAMAROT.

Phytotron: Bât. 23, Avenue de la Terrasse, 91198 Gif-sur-Yvette; tel. 1-69-82-37-82; Dirs ROGER GUILLET, JACQUES TEMPE.

VII. Humanities and Social Sciences:

Centre de recherches archéologiques (CRA): Sophia-Antipolis, 06565 Valbonne Cedex; tel. 4-93-95-42-99; f. 1970; includes 14 research units; Dir FRANÇOISE AUDOUZE.

Institut de recherche et d'histoire des textes (IRHT): 40 ave d'Iéna, 75116 Paris; tel. 1-47-23-61-04; f. 1937; Dir LOUIS HOLTZ.

Laboratoire d'économie et de sociologie du travail (LEST): 35 ave Jules Ferry, 13626 Aix-en-Provence Cedex; tel. 4-42-37-85-00; f. 1969; Dir JEAN-JACQUES SILVESTRE.

Institut national de la langue française (INALF): 52 blvd Magenta, 75010 Paris; tel. 1-42-45-00-77; f. 1960; includes nine units of linguistic research; Dir BERNARD QUEMADA.

Mission permanente à Karnak: Centre franco-égyptien des temples de Karnak, Service de la valise, Ministère des Relations extérieures, 37 quai d'Orsay, 75007 Paris; f. 1974; Dir FRANÇOIS LARCHÉ.

Institut de recherche en architecture antique: 28 place des Martyrs-de-la-Résistance, 13100 Aix-en-Provence; tel. 4-42-21-03-80; Dir PIERRE GROS.

Centre d'études de géographie tropicale (CEGET): Domaine Universitaire, 33405 Talence Cedex; tel. 5-56-84-68-30; f. 1968; Dir M. SINGARAVELOU.

Centre de géomorphologie: Rue des Tilleuls, 14000 Caen; tel. 2-31-86-48-00; f. 1963; Dir JEAN-PIERRE LAUTRIDOU.

Centre de recherche en droit comparé: 27 rue Paul-Bert, 94204 Ivry-sur-Seine Cedex; tel. 1-46-70-02-43; f. 1952; Dir JEAN HILAIRE.

Langues et civilisations à tradition orale (LACITO): 44 rue de l'Amiral-Mouchez, 75014 Paris; tel. 1-45-80-96-73; f. 1976; Dir JACQUELINE THOMAS.

IMAGEO: Centre de géographie, 191 rue St Jacques, 75005 Paris; tel. 1-43-29-31-39; f. 1976; Dir FERNAND VERGER.

Centre d'études et de recherches écogéographiques (CEREG): Université de Strasbourg 1, 3 rue de l'Argonne, 67083 Strasbourg Cedex; tel. 3-88-35-43-00; f. 1976; Dir JEAN-LUC MERCIER.

Institut de recherche en pédagogie de l'économie et en audiovisuel pour la communication dans les sciences sociales (IRPEACS): 93 chemin des Mouilles, 69131 Ecully Cedex; tel. 4-72-29-30-30; f. 1975; Dir ANDRÉE TIBERGHIEN.

Centre de sociologie des organisations (CSO): 19 rue Amélie, 75007 Paris; tel. 1-45-55-04-14; f. 1975; Dir CATHERINE GREMION.

Institut d'histoire moderne et contemporaine (IHMC): Ecole normale supérieure, 45 rue d'Ulm, 75005 Paris; tel. 1-43-29-12-25; f. 1979; Dir DANIEL ROCHE.

Institut d'histoire du temps présent (IHTP): 44 rue de l'Amiral-Mouchez, 75014 Paris; tel. 1-45-80-90-46; f. 1978; Dir ROBERT FRANK.

Centre d'ethnologie française: 6 ave du Mahatma Gandhi, 75116 Paris; tel. 1-40-67-90-00; f. 1966; Dir MARTINE SEGALEN.

Institut des textes et manuscrits modernes (ITEM): 61 rue Richelieu, 75084 Paris Cedex 02; tel. 1-42-96-30-94; f. 1978; Dir ALMUTH GRÉSILLON.

Inventaire général des monuments et des richesses artistiques de la France: 10 rue du Parc-Royal, 75003 Paris; tel. 1-42-71-22-02; f. 1986; Dir PAUL-ALBERT FÉVRIER.

Centre de recherches sur la conservation des documents graphiques (CRCDG): 36 rue Geoffroy St Hilaire, 75005 Paris; tel. 1-45-87-06-12; f. 1964; Dir FRANÇOISE FLIEDER.

Centre de recherches historiques (CRH): 54 blvd Raspail, 75006 Paris; tel. 1-49-54-25-25; f. 1979; Dir LOUIS BERGERON.

Centre d'analyse et de mathématique sociale (CAMS): 54 blvd Raspail, 75270 Paris Cedex 06; tel. 1-49-54-20-00; f. 1967; Dir MARC BARBUT.

Laboratoire d'anthropologie sociale: 52 rue du Cardinal Lemoine, 75005 Paris; tel. 1-44-27-12-11; f. 1980; Dir FRANÇOISE HÉRITIER-AUGÉ.

Laboratoire de recherche économie appliquée (LAREA): Université de Paris X, 200 avenue de la République, 92001 Nanterre; tel. 1-40-97-72-00; f. 1985; Dir PHILIPPE HUGON.

Transformations de l'appareil productif et structuration de l'espace sociale (LATAPSES): Université de Nice, 34 avenue Robert Schuman, 06000 Nice; tel. 4-93-97-70-00; f. 1986; Dir RICHARD ARENA.

Centre de recherche médecine, maladie et sciences sociales (CERMES): 201 rue de Vaugirard, 75015 Paris; tel. 1-45-67-90-34; f. 1986; Dir CLAUDINE HERZLICH.

Institut de recherches et d'études sur le monde arabe et musulman (IREMAM): 3 et 5 ave Pasteur, 13100 Aix-en-Provence; tel. 4-42-21-59-88; f. 1988; Dir MICHEL CAMAU.

Laboratoire d'économie des transports (LET): 14 avenue Berthelot, 69363 Lyon Cedex 07; tel. 4-72-72-64-03; f. 1988; Dir ALAIN BONNAFOUS.

Département et laboratoire d'économie théorique et appliquée (DELTA): ENS, 48 blvd Jourdan, 75014 Paris; tel. 1-45-89-08-33; Dir FRANÇOIS BOURGUIGNON.

Laboratoire de recherche sur les arts du spectacle: CNRS, 27 rue Paul-Bert, 94200 Ivry-sur-Seine; tel. 1-49-60-40-40; f. 1983; Dir ELIE KONIGSON.

Groupe de sociologie du travail: Université de Paris VII, Tour centrale, 2 place

Jussieu, 75251 Paris Cedex 05; tel. 1-43-36-25-25; f. 1980; Dir CLAUDE DURAND.

Groupe de sociologie des religions: 59–61 rue Pouchet, 75849 Paris Cedex 17; tel. 1-40-25-10-25; fax 1-42-28-95-44; f. 1970; Dir FRANÇOISE LAUTMAN.

Groupe de recherches sociologiques: Université de Paris X, Bâtiment G, 2 rue de Rouen, 92001 Nanterre Cedex; tel. 1-40-97-77-96; f. 1970; Dir MARCEL JOLLIVET.

Institut d'économie et de politique de l'énergie (IEPE): Université de Grenoble II, BP 47X, 38040 Grenoble Cedex; tel. 4-76-42-45-84; f. 1970; Dir DOMINIQUE FINON.

Laboratoire d'histoire des sciences et des techniques: 49 rue Mirabeau, 75016 Paris; tel. 1-45-27-66-30; f. 1968; Dir JEAN DHOMBRES.

Institut de recherche sur l'économie de l'education (IREDU): BP 138, 21004 Dijon Cedex; tel. 3-80-39-54-50; f. 1986; Dir FRANÇOIS ORIVEL.

Laboratoire de sociologie du changement des institutions (LSCI): 59–61 rue Pouchet, 75849 Paris Cedex 17; tel. 1-40-25-10-25; fax 1-42-28-95-44; f. 1986; Dir RENAUD SAINSAULIEU.

Laboratoire d'anthropologie urbaine: CNRS, 27 rue Paul-Bert, 94200 Ivry-sur-Seine; tel. 1-49-60-40-83; f. 1988; Dir JACQUES GUTWIRTH.

Geste et Image: anthropologie de la gestuelle et didactique de la communication (GIAGEDIC): c/o AGI, BP 233, 75227 Paris Cedex 05; tel. 1-45-44-21-22; f. 1988; Dir BERNARD KOECHLIN.

Communication et politique: 27 rue Damesme, 75013 Paris; tel. 1-45-89-96-66; f. 1988; Dir DOMINIQUE WOLTON.

La préhistoire du Midi de la France et de la vallée du Rhône: Faculté St-Jérôme, 13397 Marseille Cedex 13; tel. 4-91-98-90-10; f. 1968; Dirs JEAN COMBIER, JEAN-LOUIS ROUDIL.

Culture écrite du Moyen Age tardif: Centre d'histoire des sciences et des doctrines, 156 ave Parmentier, 75010 Paris; tel. 1-42-03-06-35; f. 1968; Dir EZIO ORNATO.

Recherches philosophiques de la Renaissance aux Lumières: 156 ave Parmentier, 75010 Paris; tel. 1-42-03-06-35; f. 1969; Dir HENRY MECHOULAN.

Histoire des doctrines de la fin de l'Antiquité et du haut Moyen Age: Centre d'histoire des sciences et des doctrines, 156 ave Parmentier, 75010 Paris; tel. 1-42-03-06-35: f. 1969; Dir MARIE-ODILE GOULET-CAZE.

Histoire et structure des orthographes et systèmes d'écritures (HESO): CNRS, 27 rue Paul-Bert, 94204 Ivry-sur-Seine Cedex; tel. 1-46-60-40-40; f. 1971; Dir CLAUDE GRUAZ.

Centre de recherche sur le droit des marchés et des investissements internationaux (CREDIMI): Université de Dijon, 4 blvd Gabriel, 2100 Dijon; tel. 3-80-66-81-34; f. 1972; Dir PHILIPPE KAHN.

Études d'ethnomusicologie: Musée de l'Homme, Département d'ethnomusicologie, 17 place du Trocadéro, 75116 Paris; tel. 1-47-04-58-63; Dir BERNARD LORTAT-JACOB.

Droits de propriété industrielle et intellectuelle: CUERPI, Université de Grenoble II, BP 47, 3840 Grenoble Cedex; tel. 4-76-82-56-58; f. 1974; Dir CHRISTIAN LE STANC.

Techniques et culture: CNRS, 27 rue Paul-Bert, 94204 Ivry-sur-Seine; tel. 1-46-60-40-40; f. 1975; Dir GENEVIÈVE BEDOUCHA.

Mouvements internationaux de capitaux: Service d'étude de l'activité économique, 4 rue Michelet, 75006 Paris; tel. 1-43-54-50-66; f. 1975; Dir PATRICK MESSERLIN.

Mari et le Proche-Orient ancien, travaux épigraphiques et archéologiques: 9 rue de la Perle, 75003 Paris; tel. 1-48-87-22-24; f. 1975; Dir JEAN-MARIE DURAND.

Centre de recherche sur le bien-être (CEREBE): 140 rue du Chevaleret, 75013 Paris; tel. 1-45-86-87-83; f. 1977; Dir PHILIPPE D'IRIBARNE.

Laboratoire d'économétrie de l'École polytechnique: École polytechnique, 1 rue Descartes, 75230 Paris Cedex 05; tel. 1-46-34-35-35; f. 1977; Dir MICHEL BALINSKI.

Nouvelle Gallia Judaica: École pratique des hautes études V[e] section, 45 rue des Écoles, 75005 Paris; tel. 1-47-35-55-89; f. 1977; Dir GÉRARD NAHON.

Dynamique bioculturelle: Pavillon Lenfant, 346 route des Alpes, 13100 Aix-en-Provence; tel. 4-42-23-57-94; f. 1978; Dir EMILE CROGNIER.

Géographie sociale et gérontologie: Université de Paris VII, Centre de géographie, 191 rue St-Jacques, 75005 Paris; tel. 1-46-34-51-96; f. 1982; Dir FRANÇOISE CRIBIER.

Sciences sociales du monde iranien contemporain: CNRS, 27 rue Paul-Bert, 94204 Ivry-sur -Seine Cedex; tel. 1-49-60-40-40; f. 1982; Dir JEAN PIERRE DIGARD.

Équipe de recherche d'anthropologie sociale: morphologie, échanges (ERASME): EHESS, 44 rue de la Tour, 75116 Paris; tel. 1-45-03-21-20; f. 1983; Dir DANIEL DE COPPET.

Anthropologie alimentaire différentielle: Muséum national d'histoire naturelle, Laboratoire d'ethnobotanique, 57 rue Cuvier, 75231 Paris Cedex 05; tel. 1-47-07-36-25; f. 1983; Dir IGOR DE GARINE.

Fondements des sciences: Université de Strasbourg I, Institut de physique, 3 rue de l'Université, 67084 Strasbourg; tel. 3-88-36-35-32; f. 1983; Dir HERVÉ BARREAU.

Groupe d'étude sur la division sociale et sexuelle du travail (GEDISST): 59–61 rue Pouchet, 75849 Paris Cedex 17; tel. 1-40-25-12-06; fax 1-42-28-95-44; f. 1984; Dirs DANIÈLE CHABAUD-RYCHTER, GHISLAINE DONIOL-SHAW.

Centre de sociologie urbaine (CSU): 59–61 rue Pouchet, 75849 Paris Cedex 17; tel. 1-40-25-10-25; f. 1984; Dir CHRISTIAN TOPALOV.

Groupe d'analyse des politiques publiques (GAPP): Université de Paris I, 13 rue du Four, 75006 Paris; tel. 1-43-54-11-09; f. 1984; Dir JEAN-CLAUDE THOENIG.

Centre d'anthropologie des sociétés rurales Europe méditerranéenne: EHESS, 56 rue du Taur, 31000 Toulouse; tel. 5-61-23-29-53; f. 1979; Dir JEAN GUILAINE.

Civilisations protohistoriques de la France méditerranéenne: Centre archéologique, Mas Saint-Saveur, route de Perols, 34970 Lattes; tel. 4-67-65-31-67; f. 1983; Dir GUY BARRUOL.

Groupe de recherches sur l'Amérique Latine (GRAL): Université de Toulouse II, 5 allée Antonio-Machado, 31058 Toulouse Cedex; tel. 5-61-41-11-05; f. 1987; Dir CLAUDE BATAILLON.

Dynamique - espace et variation en Insulinde (DEVI): 22 rue d'Athènes, 75009 Paris; tel. 1-45-26-15-12; f. 1985; Dir CHRISTIAN PELRAS.

Ethnologie comparative de l'Asie du Sud-Est: 22 rue d'Athènes, 75009 Paris; tel. 1-45-26-15-12; f. 1985; Dir CHARLES MACDONALD.

Milieux, société et culture en Himalaya: 1 place Aristide-Briand, 92190 Meudon; tel. 1-45-34-75-50; f. 1985; Dir GÉRARD TOFFIN.

Chypre et le Levant: Maison de l'Orient méditerranéen, 7 rue Raulin, 69007 Lyon; tel. 4-78-72-02-53; f. 1986; Dir MARGUERITE YON.

Les pays grecs de la Méditerranée orientale: épigraphie, géographie, historique et sociétés: Maison de l'Orient, 7 rue Raulin, 69007 Lyon; tel. 4-78-72-02-53; f. 1986; Dir BRUNO HELLY.

Laboratoire de recherches sur l'Afrique orientale: CNRS, Place Aristide-Briand, 92190 Meudon; tel. 1-45-34-75-50; f. 1986; Dirs GINETTE AUMASSIP, JEAN POLET.

Archéologie du Mexique et de l'Amérique centrale: Musée de l'homme, Palais de Chaillot, place du Trocadéro, 75116 Paris; tel. 1-47-04-63-11; f. 1986; Dir PIERRE BECQUELIN.

Préhistoire des régions andines: 27 rue Paul-Bert, 94204 Ivry-sur-Seine; tel. 1-49-60-40-40; f. 1986; Dir DANIÈLE LAVALLÉE.

Centre Fustel de Coulanges: École normale supérieure, Laboratoire d'archéologie, 45 rue d'Ulm, 75230 Paris Cedex 05; tel. 1-43-29-12-25; f. 1986; Dir CHRISTIAN PEYRE.

Archéologie de l'Asie centrale, peuplement, milieux et techniques: 23 rue du Maroc, 75940 Paris Cedex 19; tel. 1-40-38-74-74; f. 1986; HENRI-PAUL FRANCFORT.

Centre de recherches archéologiques Indus-Baluchistan: Musée Guimet, 6 place d'Iéna, 75116 Paris; tel. 1-47-23-76-70; f. 1986; Dir JEAN-FRANÇOIS JARRIGE.

Recherches épistémologiques et historiques sur les sciences exactes et les institutions scientifiques (REHSEIS): 49 rue Mirabeau, 75016 Paris; tel. 1-46-47-47-16; f. 1986; Dir ROSHDI RASHED.

Laboratoire d'analyse secondaire et de méthodes appliquées en sociologie (LASMAS): IRESCO, 59–61 rue Pouchet, 75849 Paris Cedex 17; tel. 1-40-25-10-25; fax 1-42-28-95-44; f. 1986; Dir ALAIN DEGENNE.

Champ des activités surréalistes (CAS): 27 rue Paul-Bert, 94200 Ivry-sur-Seine; tel. 1-49-60-40-40; f. 1986; Dirs JACQUELINE CHENIEUX-GENDRON, MARIE-CLAIRE DUMAS.

Équipe de recherche en ethnologie amérindienne (EREA): IRESCO 59–61 rue Pouchet, 75017 Paris; tel. 1-40-25-11-73; fax 1-42-28-95-44; f. 1986; Dir FRANCE-MARIE CASEVITZ.

Anthropologie et paléoenvironnement des civilisations armoricaines et atlantiques: Université de Rennes I, Laboratoire d'anthropologie, 35042 Rennes Cedex; tel. 2-99-36-48-15; f. 1967; Dirs JACQUES BRIARD, JEAN-LAURENT MONNIER.

Environnement climatique: statistique, modélisation, cartographie: Université de Grenoble 1, Laboratoire de biologie végétale, BP 53, 38041 Grenoble; tel. 4-76-51-46-00; f. 1967; Dir ANNICK DOUGUEDROIT.

Alimentation, cultures, espaces, sociétés: Faculté de médecine, BP 184, 54505 Vandoeuvre-lès-Nancy; tel. 3-83-56-56-56; f. 1988; Dir CLAUDE THOUVENOT.

Gallia et Gallia préhistoire: CNRS, 6 rue Jean-Calvin, 75005 Paris; tel. 1-43-37-50-72; f. 1982; Dir CHRISTIAN GOUDINEAU.

Antiquités africaines: Université d'Aix-Marseille I, 29 ave Robert-Schuman, 13621 Aix-en-Provence; tel. 4-42-59-26-83; f. 1982; Dir GEORGES SOUVILLE.

Centre d'anthropologie de la Chine du sud et de la péninsule indochinoise (CACSPI): 27 rue Damesme, 75013 Paris; tel. 1-45-80-27-90; fax 1-45-88-01-84; Dir JACQUES LEMOINE.

Littérature orale, dialectologie et ethnologie du domaine arabo-berbère: Ecole des hautes études en sciences sociales, 44 rue de la Tour, 75016 Paris; tel. 1-45-03-21-20; Dir CAMILLE LACOSTE-DUJARDIN.

Institut de recherche sur l'architecture antique (IRAA): 28 place des Martyrs de la Résistance, 13100 Aix-en-Provence; tel. 4-42-21-03-80; Dir PIERRE GROS.

Computer Centres:

Centre inter-régional de calcul électronique: Bâtiment 506, BP 167, 91403 Orsay Cedex; tel. 1-69-82-41-41; fax 1-69-28-52-73; f. 1969; Dir PHILIPPE SALZEDO.

Centre de calcul de Strasbourg: 23 rue de Loess, BP 20 CR, 67037 Strasbourg Cedex; tel. 3-88-28-68-66; f. 1968; Dir CLAUDE GAILLARD.

Centre de calcul, Antenne de Paris de l'IN2P3: 11 quai St Bernard, 75230 Paris Cedex 05; tel. 1-43-26-77-68; fax 1-43-26-82-76; f. 1966; Dir JACQUES COHEN-GANOUNA.

Centre de calcul de physique nucléaire de l'IN2P3: 27–29 blvd du 11 Novembre 1918, 69622 Villeurbanne Cedex; tel. 4-78-93-08-80; fax 78-94-30-54; Dir JACQUES COHEN-GANOUNA.

AGRICULTURE, FISHERIES AND VETERINARY SCIENCE

Centre de Coopération Internationale en Recherche Agronomique pour le Développement (CIRAD): 42 rue Scheffer, 75116 Paris; tel. 1-53-70-20-00; fax 1-53-70-20-34; (laboratories: BP 5035, 34032 Montpellier Cedex 1; tel. 4-67-61-58-00); f. 1970, present name 1986; state-owned; research and development within the framework of French scientific and technical co-operation with developing countries; stations in over 50 countries; library of 134,000 vols; Dir-Gen. BERNARD BACHELIER; Sec.-Gen. MICHEL EDDI; publs *Annual Report,* scientific periodicals.

Research departments:

Département d'élevage et de médecine vétérinaire (CIRAD-EMVT): Campus international de Baillarguet, BP 5035, 34032 Montpellier Cedex 1; tel. 4-67-59-37-10; fax 4-67-59-37-95; f. 1948; research and missions to countries of Africa, Asia and South America; Dir JOSEPH DOMENECH; publ. *Revue d'Elevage et de Médecine Vétérinaire des Pays Tropicaux* (quarterly).

Département des cultures annuelles (CIRAD-CA): 2477 ave Agropolis, BP 5035, 34032 Montpellier Cedex 1; tel. 4-67-61-58-00; fax 4-67-61-59-88; f. 1992; experts stationed in Benin, Brazil, Burkina Faso, Burundi, Cameroon, Chad, Colombia, Costa Rica, Côte d'Ivoire, Dominica, Gabon, Ghana, Guinea, Honduras, Laos, Madagascar, Mali, Niger, Paraguay, Philippines, Central African Republic, Senegal, Thailand, Togo, Turkey, Viet Nam; Dir: HUBERT MANICHON; publ. *Agriculture et développement* (quarterly, abstracts in French, English and Spanish).

Département des cultures pérennes (CIRAD-CP): 2477 ave Agropolis, BP 5035, 34032 Montpellier Cedex 1; tel. 4-67-61-58-00; fax 4-67-61-56-59; f. 1992; research and technical assistance relating to cocoa, coconuts, coffee, oil palm and rubber; Dir PATRICE DE VERNOU; publ. *Plantations, recherche, développement* (in French and English or Spanish).

Département des productions fruitières et horticoles (CIRAD-FLHOR): 2477 ave Agropolis, BP 5035, 34032 Montpellier Cedex 1; tel. 4-67-61-58-00; fax 4-67-61-58-71; f. 1945; activities in the technical, scientific and economic aspects of horticulture (from product research to distribution) in tropical and Mediterranean zones and with respect to related agro-industries; many overseas brs; Dir JEAN-PIERRE GAILLARD; publs *Fruits, FruiTrop.*

Département forestier (CIRAD-Forêt): Campus international de Baillarguet, BP 5035, 34032 Montpellier Cedex 1; tel. 4-67-59-37-10; fax 4-67-59-37-55; forestry; Dir JACQUES VALEIX; publ. *Bois et forêts des tropiques.*

Département des systèmes agroalimentaires et ruraux (CIRAD-SAR): 73 ave Jean-François Breton, BP 5053, 34032 Montpellier Cedex 1; tel. 4-67-61-58-00; fax 4-67-61-12-23; rural and food-crop systems; Dir JEAN PICHOT; publ. *Les cahiers de la recherche et du développement.*

Département de gestion, recherche, documentation et appui technique (CIRAD-GERDAT): 2477 ave Agropolis, BP 5053, 34032 Montpellier Cedex 1; tel. 4-67-61-58-00; fax 4-67-61-56-59; management, research, documentation, technical support; Dir JACQUES MEUNIER; publ. *Sésame bulletin.*

Centre de Recherches de Jouy: Domaine de Vilvert, 78352 Jouy-en-Josas Cedex; tel. 1-34-65-21-21; telex 695431; fax 1-34-65-20-51; f. 1950; linked to Institut National de la Recherche Agronomique (*q.v.*); scientific research on animal production, food technology, human nutrition, food safety and biotechnology; library of 6,000 vols, 2,200 periodicals.

Institut d'Immunologie Animale et Comparée (Institute of Animal and Comparative Immunology): Ecole Nationale Vétérinaire d'Alfort, 7 ave du Général de Gaulle, 94704 Maisons-Alfort Cedex; tel. 1-43-68-98-82; f. 1981; organizes courses; research in immunostimulation, clinical immunology, immunopathology; Dir Prof. CH. PILET.

Institut National de la Recherche Agronomique (INRA): 147 rue de l'Université, 75338 Paris Cedex 07; tel. 1-42-75-90-00; f. 1946; agricultural research, including agricultural and food industries, rural economics and sociology, plant and animal production and forestry; administers and subsidizes a large number of centres, laboratories and experimental farms in France; Pres. GUY PAILLOTIN; Dir-Gen. PAUL VIALLE; publs *Annales de Zootechnie* (5 a year), *Reproduction Nutrition Development* (every 2 months), *Productions Animales* (5 a year), *Genetics Selection Evolution* (every 2 months), *Agronomie* (10 a year), *Annales des Sciences Forestières* (every 2 months), *Apidologie* (every 2 months), *Le Lait* (every 2 months), *Veterinary Research* (every 2 months), *Annales de Zootechnie* (5 a year), *Cahiers d'Economie et Sociologie rurales* (every 3 months), *INRA Sciences Sociales* (every 2 months).

Laboratoire Central de Recherches Vétérinaires: BP 67, 22 rue Pierre Curie, 94703 Maisons-Alfort Cedex; tel. 1-49-77-13-00; fax 1-43-68-97-62; f. 1901; 140 mems; study of contagious diseases in domestic and wild animals; supervises sanitary regulations for import and export of livestock; Dir Dr ERIC PLATEAU.

ECONOMICS, LAW AND POLITICS

Centre d'Etudes Prospectives et d'Informations Internationales (Centre for International Prospective Studies and Information): 9 rue Georges Pitard, 75015 Paris; tel. 1-53-68-55-00; fax 1-53-68-55-03; e-mail postmaster@cepii.fr; f. 1978 by the Government, under the aegis of Commissariat Général du Plan; aims to aid public and private decision-makers in the international economic field by conducting synthetic studies of the global economic environment in the mid-term (5–10 years), constructing economic models and data bases, and by providing a coherent statistical information system of the world economy and its major participants; 50 mems; library of 20,000 vols, 500 periodicals; Dir JEAN-CLAUDE BERTHÉLEMY; publs incl. *Economie Internationale* (quarterly), *La Lettre du CEPII* (11 a year), *CEPII Newsletter* (2 a year).

Institut de Sciences Mathématiques et Economiques Appliquées: 14 rue Corvisart, 75013 Paris; tel. 1-44-08-51-42; e-mail denoel@univ-mlv.fr; f. 1944; study of economic problems and exchange of ideas with other countries; library of 14,500 vols; Chair. G. DESTANNE DE BERNIS; publs *Economies et Sociétés* (monthly), *Economie Appliquée* (quarterly), *Mondes en Développement* (quarterly).

Institut National d'Etudes Démographiques: 27 rue du Commandeur, 75675 Paris Cedex 14; tel. 1-42-18-20-00; fax 1-42-18-21-99; f. 1945; library of 40,000 vols; Dir PATRICK FESTY; publs *Population* (every 2 months), *Population et Sociétés* (monthly), *Cahiers de Travaux et Documents de l'INED* (4–6 a year), *Congrès et Colloques* (2–4 a year).

Institut National de la Statistique et des Etudes Economiques: 18 blvd Adolphe Pinard, 75675 Paris Cedex 14; tel. 1-41-17-66-11; fax 1-41-17-66-66; f. 1946; statistical research: population census, economic indices and forecasts; library: see Libraries; Dir-Gen. PAUL CHAMPSAUR; publs *Annuaire Statistique, Bulletin Mensuel de Statistique, Tableaux de l'économie française* (yearbook), La France et ses régions (every 2 years), *Insee Première* (60 a year), Economie et Statistique (monthly), *Données Sociales* (every 3 years), *Annales d'Economie et de Statistique* (quarterly), *Note de Conjoncture* (quarterly), *Tableau de bord hebdomadaire* (50 a year), *Courrier des Statistiques* (quarterly), *Insee Méthodes, Insee Résultats, Insee News, Insee Actualités.*

EDUCATION

Centre International d'Etudes Pédagogiques de Sèvres: 1 ave Léon Journault, BP 75, 92318 Sèvres Cedex; tel. 1-45-07-60-00; fax 1-45-07-60-01; f. 1945; research and studies in comparative education; training overseas teachers in French as a foreign language; 170 mems; Dir M. LÉOUTRE; publ. *Revue Internationale d'Education.*

Institut National de Recherche Pédagogique: 29 rue d'Ulm, 75230 Paris Cedex 05; f. 1879; 500 mems; library: see Libraries; Dir ANDRÉ HUSSENET; publs *Revue Française de Pédagogie* (quarterly), *Repères, Histoire de l'Education, Etapes de la Recherche, Recherche et Formation, Perspectives Documentaires, Aster.*

FINE AND PERFORMING ARTS

Institut de Recherche et Coordination Acoustique et de la Musique: Centre National d'Art et de Culture Georges-Pompidou, 75191 Paris Cedex 04; tel. 1-44-78-12-33; attached to Centre National d'Art et de Culture Georges-Pompidou; interdisciplinary research centre for musicians and scientists; data processing, electroacoustics, instrumental and vocal research; Dir LAURENT BAYLE.

HISTORY, GEOGRAPHY AND ARCHAEOLOGY

Centre d'Études Supérieures de la Renaissance: 59 rue Néricault-Destouches, BP 1328, 37013 Tours Cedex; tel. 2-47-70-17-00; fax 2-47-70-17-01; f. 1956; also a specialized library of 45,000 vols; Dir Prof. G. CHAIX; Sec. M. ANCELIN.

Centre de Recherches Historiques: Ecole des Hautes Etudes en Sciences Sociales et CNRS, UMR C0019, 54 blvd Raspail, 75006 Paris; tel. 1-49-54-24-42; fax 1-49-54-23-99; e-mail crh@msh-paris.fr; f. 1950; joint research in economic, social, cultural and political history; 126 mems; Dirs ALAIN BOUREAU, PAUL-ANDRÉ ROSENTAL, GÉRARD BÉAUR.

Centre de Recherches sur les Monuments Historiques: Palais de Chaillot, Aile Paris, 1 place du Trocadéro, 75116 Paris; tel. 1-47-27-84-64; fax 1-47-04-55-83; f. 1942; Dir JEAN-DANIEL PARISET.

Institut Géographique National: 136 bis rue de Grenelle, 75700 Paris; tel. 1-43-98-80-00; fax 1-43-98-84-00; f. 1940; satellite-image, aerial and ground surveys, map printing; national map and aerial photograph library, scientific library; administers *Ecole Nat. des Sciences Géographiques;* Pres. (vacant); Dir-Gen. JEAN POULIT; publ. *Bulletin d'Information* (quarterly).

Sous-Direction de l'Archéologie: 4 rue d'Aboukir, 75002 Paris; tel. 1-40-15-77-81; fax 1-40-15-77-00; e-mail patrick.monod@culturc.fr; f. 1964; library of 2,000 vols, 47 periodicals; Dir PATRICK MONOD.

MEDICINE

Institut Alfred-Fournier: 25 blvd Saint-Jacques, 75014 Paris; research into sexually transmitted diseases; Dir Dr P. BARBIER.

Institut Arthur-Vernes: 36 rue d'Assas, 75006 Paris; tel. 1-44-39-53-00; fax 1-42-84-26-09; f. 1981; Pres. J. C. SERVAN-SCHREIBER.

Institut Gustave-Roussy: 39 rue Camille Desmoulins, 94805 Villejuif Cedex; tel. 1-42-11-42-11; fax 1-42-11-53-00; f. 1921; diagnosis and treatment of cancer, research, and training in oncology (affiliated with Univ. Paris-Sud for teaching purposes); library of 11,000 vols, with special collections on cancerology; Dir Prof. THOMAS TURSZ.

Institut National de la Santé et de la Recherche Médicale (INSERM): 101 rue de Tolbiac, 75654 Paris Cedex 13; tel. 1-44-23-60-00; fax 1-44-23-60-99; f. 1941 as Institut National d'Hygiène, renamed 1964; assisted by scientific commissions and the Scientific Council; 270 research units throughout France; Gen. Dir CLAUDE GRISCELLI; publs *Annuaire des laboratoires, rapport d'activité, INSERM Actualités*, Collections, etc.

Institut Pasteur: 25–28 rue du Dr Roux, 75015 Paris; tel. 1-45-68-80-00; f. 1887; Pres. PHILIPPE ROUVILLOIS; Dir-Gen. MAXIME SCHWARTZ; Gen. Sec. MARIE-HÉLÈNE MARCHAND; publs *Annales Research in Virology, Immunology and Microbiology* (16 a year), *Bulletin* (quarterly), *Annales: Actualités.*

NATURAL SCIENCES

General

Institut Français de Recherche Scientifique pour le Développement en Coopération (ORSTOM): 211 rue La Fayette, 75480 Paris Cedex 10; tel. 1-48-03-77-77; telex 214627; f. 1943; a public corporation charged to aid developing countries by means of research, both fundamental and applied, in the non-temperate regions, with special application to human environment problems and food production; 50 centres in 30 countries; 2,600 staff; library and documentation centre; Pres. PHILIPPE LAZAR; Dir-Gen. JEAN NEMO.

Maintains the following services:

Centre ORSTOM de Bondy: 72 route d'Aulnay, 93143 Bondy Cedex; tel. 1-48-47-31-95; geophysics, geodynamics, social sciences, entomology, applied computer science, scientific information (cartography, documentation, audiovisual); Dir JEAN-FRANÇOIS TURENNE.

Centre ORSTOM de Montpellier: 2501 ave du Val de Montferrand, 34032 Montpellier Cedex: tel. 4-67-52-11-71; hydrology, hydrobiology and oceanography, soil biology, agrarian research, phytopathology, phytovirology, applied zoology, medical entomology, nutrition, geology, Dir JEAN-PIERRE TROUCHAUD.

Laboratoire de Géochronologie commun ORSTOM/Université de Nice: Parc Valrose, 06000 Nice; geology.

Laboratoire de Tropicalisation: 2 place de la Gare de Ceinture, 78210 St-Cyr l'Ecole.

Centre ORSTOM de Brest: c/o IFREMER, BP 70, 29263 Plouzane; oceanography.

Antenne ORSTOM auprès de l'INRA: Station d'Hydrobiologie Lacustre, Ave de Corzent, 74203 Thonon les Bains; hydrobiology.

Antenne ORSTOM auprès du Laboratoire de Phanérogamie: Muséum National d'Histoire Naturelle, 16 rue de Buffon, 75231 Paris Cedex 05; botany.

Antenne ORSTOM auprès du CEN: Centre d'Etudes Nucléaires de Cadarache, c/o DB. SRA, BP1, 13115 St Paul lez Durance; nuclear agronomy.

Antenne ORSTOM, Station Météorologique: Nouveau Sémaphore, Quai des Abeilles, 76600 Le Havre; oceanography.

Biological Sciences

Institut de Biologie Physico-chimique: 13 rue Pierre et Marie Curie, 75005 Paris; f. 1927; Dir Prof. B. PULLMAN; Dirs of Laboratories: Dr D. HAYES (Cellular Chemistry), Dr R. BANERJEE (Biophysics), Mrs M. GRUNBERG MANAGO (Biochemistry), Prof. P. DOUZOU (Biospectroscopy), Dr P. JOLIOT (Photosynthesis), Dr A. M. MICHELSON (Physical Biochemistry), B. PULLMAN (Theoretical Chemistry).

Institut de Biologie Structurale (IBS): 41 ave des Martyrs, 38027 Grenoble Cedex 1; tel. 4-76-88-95-50; fax 4-76-88-54-94; jointly financed by the Commissariat à l'Énergie Atomique (CEA) and the Centre National de la Recherche Scientifique (CNRS); Dir Prof. MICHEL VAN DER REST.

Station Biologique de Roscoff: Place Georges-Teissier, BP 74, 29682 Roscoff Cedex; tel. 2-98-29-23-23; fax 2-98-29-23-24; e-mail postmaster@sb-roscoff.fr; f. 1872; attached to Univ. Paris VI and CNRS; chemical and biological oceanography, plankton research, microbiology, biology of hydrothermal vent fauna, cell cycle and developmental biology, cell and molecular biology on macroalgae; library of 5,000 vols, 1,000 periodicals; Dir Prof. ANDRÉ TOULMOND; publs *CBM-Cahiers de Biologie marine* (quarterly), *Travaux* (annually).

Physical Sciences

Association Nationale pour l'Etude de la Neige et des Avalanches (ANENA): 15 rue Ernest Calvat, 38000 Grenoble; tel. 4-76-51-39-39; fax 4-76-42-81-66; f. 1971; to aid research and study by public or private organizations, to facilitate co-operation with other countries and to advise on safety; 820 mems; library of 2,000 vols; Pres. HERVÉ GAYMARD; Dir FRANÇOIS SIVARDIÈRE; Sec. SERGE RIVEILL; publ. *Neige et Avalanches* (quarterly).

Bureau de Recherches Géologiques et Minières (BRGM): 3 ave Claude Guillemin, BP 6009, 45060 Orléans Cedex 2; tel. 2-38-64-34-34; telex 780 258; fax 2-38-64-35-18; f. 1959; publicly-owned industrial and trading organization; study and development of underground resources in France and abroad; library of 22,000 vols, 4,000 scientific journals, 55,000 maps; Dir-Gen. Y. LE BARS; publs *Géologie de la France* (quarterly), *Hydrogéologie* (quarterly), *Chronique de la Recherche minière* (quarterly), *Géochronique* (publ. with Société géologique de France, quarterly), geological maps, bibliographies, SDI and retrospective searches.

Bureau des Longitudes: Palais de l'Institut, 3 rue Mazarine, 75006 Paris; f. 1795 by Convention Nationale; 50 mems and corresp.; Pres. R. CAYREL; Vice-Pres. J.-L. LE MOUËL; Sec. N. CAPITAINE; publs *Ephémérides Astronomiques, Connaissance des Temps, Ephémérides Nautiques, Cahier des Sciences de l'Univers,* and supplements to *Connaissance des Temps* (annually).

Centre d'Etudes Marines Avancées: c/o Équipe Cousteau, 7 rue Amiral d'Estaing, 75116 Paris; tel. 1-53-67-77-77; fax 1-53-67-77-71; f. 1953; underwater exploration, study and research; Pres. (vacant); Sec.-Gen. HENRI JACQUIER; publ. *Calypso Log* (monthly).

Centre de Recherches Atmosphériques: 8 route de Lannemezan, 65300 Campistrous; tel. 5-62-40-61-00; fax 5-62-40-61-01; e-mail pvdinh@aero.obs-mip.fr; f. 1960; cloud physics, atmospheric chemistry, planetary boundary layer; library of 2,000 vols; Dirs B. BENECH, B. CAMPISTRON, J. DESSENS; publ. *Atmospheric Research* (quarterly).

Centre International pour la Formation et les Echanges Géologiques (CIFEG): 3 ave Claude Guillemin, BP 6517, 45065 Orléans Cedex 2; tel. 2-38-64-33-67; fax 2-38-64-34-72; e-mail jc.napias@brgm.fr; f. 1981; geological training and documentation centre; exchanges between developed and developing countries; library of 2,800 vols, 250 periodicals, 4,000 maps; Pres. J. GIRI; Dir J. C. NAPIAS; publs *PANGEA* (2 a year), *African Geology* (quarterly).

Centre National de Recherches Météorologiques: 42 ave G. Coriolis, 31057 Toulouse Cedex; tel. 5-61-07-93-70; fax 5-61-07-96-00; f. 1946; meteorological research; 250 staff; Dir D. CARIOLLE.

Commissariat à l'Energie Atomique (CEA): 31–33 rue de la Fédération, 75752 Paris Cedex 15; tel. 1-40-56-10-00; f. 1945; basic and applied nuclear research, energy generator studies; library; five affiliated civil research centres; Pres. of Atomic Energy Cttee The Prime Minister; Man. Dir YANNICK D'ESCATHA; publs *Les Défis du CEA, Rapport Annuel, Clefs CEA.*

Attached research centres:

Centre CEA de Cadarache: 13108 St-Paul-lez-Durance Cedex; tel. 4-42-25-70-00; fax 4-42-25-45-45; f. 1960; reactor development, nuclear safety and environmental protection, fundamental research; industrial innovation; Dir MARCEL DE LA GRAVIÈRE.

Centre CEA de Fontenay-aux-Roses: BP 6, 92265 Fontenay-aux-Roses Cedex; tel. 1-46-54-70-80; fax 1-46-54-90-27; f. 1945; first French reactor; Zoé natural uranium, heavy water moderated; nuclear safety and environmental protection, radiobiology; research and development in remote handling and robotics for nuclear, military and medical needs, corrosion studies, high activity chemistry; Dir ALAIN DEBIAR.

Centre CEA de Grenoble: 17 rue des Martyrs, 38054 Grenoble Cedex 9; tel. 4-76-88-44-00; fax 4-76-88-34-32; f. 1957; applied nuclear research on heat transfer studies and on behaviour of nuclear fuels; fundamental research on physics, chemistry, biology, materials science; advanced technologies: microelectronics, optronics, instrumentation, materials, heat exchangers, life sciences and tracer studies; library of 31,000 vols; Dir GEORGES CAROLA.

Centre CEA de Saclay: 91191 Gif-sur-Yvette Cedex; tel. 1-69-08-60-00; f. 1949; equipped with two high-flux experimental reactors, six particle accelerators and special laboratories: spent fuel study facility, isotope and labelled molecule production laboratories, activation analysis centre, ionizing radiations applications centre; laboratories specializing in research on reactors, nuclear metallurgy and chemistry, elementary particle physics, nuclear physics, astrophysics, condensed-matter physics, earth sciences, biology, radioactivity measurement and electronics; library of 48,000 vols, 400,000 reports; Dir ELIANE LOQUET.

Centre CEA de la Vallée du Rhône: BP 171, 30207 Bagnols-sur-Cèze Cedex; tel. 4-66-79-60-00; fax 4-66-90-14-35; f. 1982; fuel cycle research and development: uranium isotopic enrichment, spent fuel processing, waste conditioning, dismantling; fast reactors; Dir JEAN-YVES GUILLAMOT.

Institut Curie: 26 rue d'Ulm, 75231 Paris Cedex 05; tel. 1-44-32-40-00; telex 270479; fax 1-43-29-02-03; f. 1978 (fmrly Fondation Curie–Inst. du Radium); treatment, research and teaching in cancer; library of 7,000 vols; two sections: Research (Dir D. LOUVARD), Medicine (Dir J. P. CAMILLERI); Pres. C. BURG.

Institut Français de Recherche pour l'Exploitation de la Mer (IFREMER): 155 rue J. Jacques Rousseau, 92138 Issy-les-Moulineaux Cedex; tel. 1-46-48-21-00; fax 1-46-48-22-96; f. 1967; research in all fields of oceanography and ocean technology; Pres./Dir-Gen. PIERRE DAVID; publs *Rapport Annuel*, series of scientific and technical publs.

Attached institutes:

Centre IFREMER de Brest: BP 337, 29273 Brest Cedex; f. 1968; Dir J. QUERELLOU.

Centre IFREMER de Toulon: BP 330, 83507 La Seyne sur Mer; Dir JEAN JARRY.

Centre IFREMER Océanologique du Pacifique: BP 7004, Taravao, Tahiti; tel. 7-12-74; f. 1972; development of ocean resources: minerals, fishing and aquaculture in French South Pacific territories; 70 staff; library of 200 vols; Dir J.-L. MARTIN.

Centre IFREMER de Nantes: BP 1049, 44037 Nantes Cedex; Dir J.-P. DRENO.

Laboratoire d'Astronomie de l'Université des Sciences et Techniques de Lille-Flandres-Artois: 1 impasse de l'Observatoire, 59000 Lille; tel. 3-20-52-44-24; f. 1934; astronomy, celestial mechanics; Dir L. DURIEZ.

Météo-France: 1 quai Branly, 75340 Paris Cedex 07; tel. 1-45-56-71-71; telex 202876; fax 1-45-56-70-05; f. 1945; Dir JEAN-PIERRE BEYSSON; publs *METEO-HEBDO, Monographies, Bulletin Climatique, Données et Statistiques, Notes techniques, Bibliographies, La météorologie, Met/Mar.*

Observatoire de Bordeaux: Université de Bordeaux I, CNRS, 2 ave P. Sémirot, BP 89, 33270 Floirac; tel. 5-57-77-61-00; fax 5-57-77-61-10; f. 1879; astrometry, astrodynamics, solar physics, radioastronomy, helioseismology, planetary atmosphere, radio aeronomy; library of 3,300 vols; Dir J. COLIN; publs *Rapport*, *Publications*.

Observatoire de la Côte d'Azur: BP 229, 06304 Nice Cedex 4; tel. 4-92-00-30-11; fax 4-92-00-30-33; f. 1881; astronomy and astrophysics; library of 12,000 vols, 250 periodicals; Dir J. A. DE FREITAS PACHECO.

Observatoire de Lyon: 9 ave Charles-André, 69561 Saint-Genis-Laval Cedex; tel. 4-78-86-83-83; fax 4-78-86-83-86; e-mail amtumes@obs.univ-lyon1.fr; f. 1880; specializes in two-dimensional photometry and infrared imagery; library of 20,000 vols; Dir ROLAND BACON.

Observatoire de Marseille: 2 place Le Verrier, 13248 Marseille Cedex 4; tel. 4-95-04-41-00; fax 4-91-62-11-90; e-mail postmaster@observatoire.cnrs-mrs.fr; library of 5,000 vols; Dir Dr G. COMTE.

Observatoire de Paris: 61 ave de l'Observatoire, 75014 Paris; f. 1667; library of 60,000 vols; Dir M. COMBES.

Attached stations:

Observatoire de Paris, Site de Meudon: 5 place Jules Janssen, 92195 Meudon Principal Cedex; administered by the Observatoire de Paris; f. 1875; astrophysics; Dir M. COMBES.

Station de Radioastronomie de Nançay: administered by the Observatoire de Paris; f. 1953; study of the sun, comets, planets and radio sources; radio telescopes; Dir M. COMBES.

Observatoire de Physique du Globe de Clermont-Ferrand: 12 ave des Landais, 63000 Clermont-Ferrand; tel. 4-73-40-73-80; f. 1871; specializes in atmospheric physics and earth sciences: radar and satellite meteorology, microphysics, seismology, geochemistry, geochronology, volcanology; Dir JACQUES KORNPROBST.

Observatoire de Strasbourg: 11 rue de l'Université, 67000 Strasbourg; tel. 3-88-15-07-10; fax 88-15-07-60; f. 1882; specializes in astronomical data and information, galactic evolution, cosmology, high-energy astrophysics; houses the Strasbourg Astronomical Data Centre (CDS); library of 16,000 vols; Dir DANIEL EGRET; publs *Bulletin du Centre de Données Stellaires* (2 a year), *Publications de l'Observatoire* (irregular).

Observatoire des Sciences de l'Univers de Besançon: BP 1615, 41 bis ave de l'Observatoire, 25010 Besançon Cedex; tel. 3-81-66-69-00; fax 3-81-66-69-44; f. 1882; theoretical, observational and instrumental research (galactic structure, stellar binaries, comets, celestial mechanics, metrology of time); 30 staff; library of *c.* 15,000 vols; Dir SONIA CLAIREMIDI.

Observatoires du Pic du Midi et de Toulouse: *Headquarters:* 65200 Bagnères-de-Bigorre; library of 50,000 vols; solar, planetary, stellar, galactic and extragalactic astrophysics, atmospheric physics; Dir Dr J.-P. ZAHN; publ. *Travaux*.

Service des Equipements et des Techniques Instrumentales de la Météorologie: 7 rue Teisserenc de Bort, 78195 Trappes Cedex; tel. 1-30-13-60-00; telex 699727; fax 1-30-13-60-60; f. 1896; Dir M. ROCHAS; publs *Notes techniques*, *Recueil de fiches instrumentales.*

RELIGION, SOCIOLOGY AND ANTHROPOLOGY

Centre Européen de Recherches sur les Congrégations et Ordres Religieux (CERCOR): Maison Rhône-Alpes des Sciences de l'Homme, 35 rue du 11 Novembre, 42023 Saint-Etienne Cedex 2; tel. 4-77-38-96-67; f. 1981; a research group of CNRS (*q.v.*); studies the influence of monastic and religious orders on European life, from their origins to the 20th century; 1,400 researchers in 35 countries; co-ordinates and promotes research (conferences, etc.), runs a specialized documentation service, publishes texts, etc.; Dir Prof. PIERRETTE PARAVY; publ. *Bulletin* (2 a year).

Collège des Etudes Juives (Beit Hamidrach): 45 rue La Bruyère, 75009 Paris; tel. 1-53-32-88-55; fax 1-48-74-51-33; e-mail aiu@imaginet.fr; f. 1986 to unite researchers, organize seminars, study days and colloquia based on the library of the Alliance Israélite Universelle (the most important private Judaic-Hebrew library in Europe); 400 students annually; library of over 120,000 items; Dir Dr SHMUEL TRIGANO; publs *Les Cahiers du Judaïsme* (quarterly), *Bulletin des Etudes Juives, Cahiers de l'Alliance.*

Institut d'Ethnologie du Muséum National d'Histoire Naturelle: Musée de l'Homme, Palais de Chaillot, Place du Trocadéro, 75116 Paris; tel. 1-44-05-73-45; fax 1-44-05-73-44; f. 1925; social anthropology, archaeology, linguistics; Dir Prof. J. GUIART; publs *Collections Travaux et Mémoires, Mémoires, microform archives and documents.*

Institut d'Etudes Augustiniennes: 3 rue de l'Abbaye, 75006 Paris; tel. 1-43-54-80-25; fax 1-43-54-39-55; f. 1943; research into life, thought and times of St Augustine; specialized public library of 35,000 vols; Dir J.-C. FREDOUILLE; publs *Revue des Etudes Augustiniennes* (quarterly), *Recherches Augustiniennes.*

Institut du Monde Arabe: 1 rue des Fossés Saint Bernard, 75005 Paris; tel. 1-40-51-38-38; fax 1-43-54-76-45; f. 1980 by France and 21 Arab countries to promote knowledge of Arab culture and civilization; aims to encourage cultural exchanges, communication and co-operation between France and the Arab world, particularly in the fields of science and technology; international library and documentation centre of 60,000 vols, 1,200 periodicals; museum of Arab-Islamic civilization covering 7th–19th century; exhibitions of Arab contemporary art; audio-visual centre; Pres. CAMILLE CABANA; Dir MOHAMED BENNOUNA; publs *Qantara* (4 a year), *Al-Moukhtarak, MARS.*

Institut International d'Anthropologie: 1 place d'Iéna, 75116 Paris; tel. 1-47-93-09-73; f. 1920; 400 mems; affiliated to Ecole d'Anthropologie (*q.v.*); special collection: intercultural documentation centre; Pres. Prof. L. BRUMPT; Sec.-Gen. Dr. B. HUET; publ. *Nouvelle Revue Anthropologique* (monthly).

Institut Kurde de Paris (Kurdish Institute): 106 rue La Fayette, 75010 Paris; tel. 1-48-24-64-64; fax 1-47-70-99-04; f. 1983; research into Kurdish language, culture and history; Kurdish language teaching and publication of textbooks, maps, music cassettes, video films in Kurdish; library of 6,500 vols (open to the public); Pres. KENDAL NEZAN; publs *Information Bulletin* (monthly), *Kurmancî* (2 a year).

Maison des Sciences de l'Homme: 54 blvd Raspail, 75270 Paris Cedex 06; tel. 1-49-54-20-00; telex 203-104; fax 1-45-48-83-53; f. 1963 to support research and int. co-operation in the social sciences; library of 90,000 vols, 1,800 current periodicals; Administrator M. AYMARD; publ. *MSH Informations* (quarterly).

Maison Rhône-Alpes de Sciences de l'Homme (MRASH): 14 ave Berthelot, 69363 Lyon Cedex 07; tel. 4-72-72-64-64; fax 4-72-80-00-08; f. 1988 to support research in the social sciences; Dir ALAIN BONNAFOUS.

TECHNOLOGY

Association Française pour la Protection des Eaux: Secrétariat Administratif, 4 rue Ménard, 78000 Versailles; f. 1960; brings to public notice the necessity of protecting and preserving the quality and quantity of water-supplies, studies problems of water pollution and its prevention; 800 mems; Pres. P. L. TENAILLON; publ. *L'Eau Pure* (quarterly).

Centre National d'Etudes des Télécommunications (CNET): 38–40 rue du Général Leclerc, 92131 Issy les Moulineaux; tel. 1-45-29-44-44; telex 250317; f. 1944; as the France Telecom research centre, is engaged in the development of future communications systems; as a technical centre, is responsible for according official approval for telecommunications equipment; 4,200 staff; library of 2,500 vols, 1,000 periodicals; Dir MICHEL FENEYROL; publs. *L'Echo des Recherches* (quarterly), *Annales des Télécommunications* (every 2 months), *Bulletin Signalétique des Télécommunications* (monthly), *Annual Report, Innovation Telecom* (monthly).

Centre National d'Etudes Spatiales (CNES): 2 place Maurice Quentin, 75001 Paris; f. 1961; prepares national programmes of space research, provides information, promotes international co-operation; Pres. ALAIN BENSOUSSAN; Dir-Gen. (vacant).

Institut d'Hydrologie et de Climatologie: Faculté de Médecine, Pitié-Salpétrière, 91 blvd de l'Hôpital, 75013 Paris; tel. 1-45-83-69-92; 5 main laboratories in Paris, and further laboratories at the principal spas; Gen. Sec. Prof. G. OLIVE.

Institut Français du Pétrole: 1 et 4 ave de Bois-Préau, BP 311, 92506 Rueil-Malmaison Cedex; tel. 1-47-52-60-00; telex 634202; fax 1-47-52-70-00; f. 1945; scientific and technical organization for the purpose of research, development and industrialization, training specialists at the Ecole Nationale Supérieure du Pétrole et des Moteurs, information and documentation, international technical assistance in the different fields of the oil, gas and automotive engineering industries; library of 275,000 vols; Chair. and CEO P. JACQUARD; publs *Revue*, scientific treatises and monographs, practical handbooks, etc.

Institut Max von Laue-Paul Langevin (ILL): BP 156, 38042 Grenoble Cedex 9; tel. 4-76-20-71-11; fax 4-76-48-39-06; f. 1967 by France and Fed. Repub. of Germany, UK became third equal partner in 1973; associated scientific members are Spain (1987), Switzerland (1988), Austria (1990) and Italy (1997); research on fundamental and nuclear physics, solid state physics, metallurgy, chemistry and biology by using reactor neutrons; receives 1,500 guest scientists a year and carries out experiments on 25 ILL-funded instruments and several instruments funded by collaborating research groups; central facility is high flux beam reactor producing maximum flux of $1.5 \times 10^{15} n/cm^2/s$; library of 11,000 vols, 250 periodicals; Dirs D. DUBBERS (Germany), A. LEADBETTER (UK), P. LECONTE (France); publs *Annual Report*, *Neutron Research Facilities*, scientific and technical reports, etc.

Institut National de l'Audiovisuel: 4 ave de l'Europe, 94366 Bry-sur-Marne Cedex; tel. 1-49-83-32-06; fax 1-49-83-26-83; f. 1975; two research depts: *Recherche Prospective* (research combining telecommunications, computer science and audiovisual science); *Groupe de Recherches Musicales* (numerical development of synthesis and treatment of sound; psychoacoustics and musical perception, technology of electroacoustical instruments); library of 3,000 vols; Pres. JEAN-PIERRE TEYSSIER; publ. *Dossiers Audiovisuels* (every 2 months).

Institut National de l'Environnement Industriel et des Risques (INERIS) (National Institute for Environmental Technology and Hazards): Parc Technologique ALATA, BP 2, 60550 Verneuil-en-Halatte; tel. 3-44-55-66-77; fax 3-44-55-66-99; e-mail ineris@ineris.fr; f. 1990; library of 28,000 vols; Dir-Gen. GEORGES LABROYE; publs *Lettre de l'INERIS* (6 a year), *Références INERIS* (quarterly).

Institut National de Recherche en Informatique et en Automatique (INRIA): Domaine de Voluceau, Rocquencourt, BP 105, 78153 Le Chesnay Cedex; tel. 1-39-63-55-11; fax 1-39-63-59-60; e-mail communication@inria.fr; f. 1967; five research units; library of 45,000 vols; Pres./Dir-Gen. BERNARD LARROUTUROU; publs *INédit* (newsletter), *Thésauria* (bulletin), *Rapports de Recherche, Rapports Techniques, Séminaires, Inriathèque.*

Institut National des Sciences et Techniques Nucléaires (INSTN) (National Institute of Nuclear Science and Technology): CEA-Saclay, 91191 Gif-sur-Yvette Cedex; f. 1956; provides courses in nuclear engineering, robotics and computer integrated manufacturing (CIM) and, in co-operation with the Universities, postgraduate courses in reactor physics, dynamics of structures, analytical chemistry, radiochemistry, metallurgy, data processing, robotics, radiobiology, energy management, the use of radioisotopes in medicine and pharmacy; Dir JEAN-PIERRE LE ROUX; Pres. Council of Instruction R. PELLAT.

Institut Technique du Bâtiment et des Travaux Publics: 6-14 rue La Pérouse, 75784 Paris Cedex 16; tel. 1-40-69-53-09; fax 1-45-53-58-77; f. 1933; Lecture Centre for engineers, building contractors, architects, and students, for architecture, building construction and public works.

Laboratoire de Biotechnologie de l'Environnement: Ave des Etangs, 11100 Narbonne; tel. 4-68-42-51-51; fax 4-68-42-51-60; f. 1895; attached to INRA; research in microbiological wastewater treatment; library of 5,000 vols; Dir RENÉ MOLETTA; publ. *Water Research*.

Office International de l'Eau: 15 rue Edouard Chamberland, 87065 Limoges Cedex; tel. 5-55-11-47-80; fax 5-55-77-72-24; f. 1991; documentation centre on water problems; library of 35,000 vols and 170,000 articles; Pres. M. RENARD; Dir M. NEVEU; publ. *Information Eaux* (monthly).

Office National d'Etudes et de Recherches Aérospatiales (ONERA): 29 ave de la Division-Leclerc, 92320 Châtillon; tel. 1-46-73-40-40; fax 1-46-73-41-41; f. 1946 to develop, direct, and co-ordinate scientific and technical research in the field of aeronautics and space; library of 40,000 vols, 150,000 reports, 11,000 microfiches, 850 periodicals; Pres. MICHEL SCHELLER; publ. *Aerospace Science and Technology* (English edn, 8 a year).

Libraries and Archives

Abbeville

Bibliothèque Municipale: Jardin d'Emonville, place Clemenceau, BP 10, 80101 Abbeville Cedex; tel. 3-22-24-95-16; fax 3-22-19-03-97; f. 1643; 120,000 vols; Librarian Mme HAZEBROUCK.

Aix-en-Provence

Bibliothèque de l'Université d'Aix-Marseille III: 3 ave Robert-Schuman, 13626 Aix-en-Provence Cedex 1; tel. 4-42-59-22-91; fax 4-42-52-38-92; 156,000 vols, 273,000 periodicals, 86,000 theses; Librarian J. C. RODA

Bibliothèque Mejanes: 8–10 rue des Allumettes, 13098 Aix-en-Provence Cedex 2; tel. 4-42-25-98-88; telex 441502; fax 4-42-25-98-64; f. 1810; 450,000 vols; Chief Librarian DANIÈLE OPPETIT.

Albi

Bibliothèque Municipale: 28 rue Rochegude, 81000 Albi; tel. 5-63-54-22-40; fax 5-63-49-99-02; f. during the French Revolution; 300,000 vols; Librarian MARIELLE MOURANCHE.

Amiens

Bibliothèque de l'Université de Picardie Jules Verne: Chemin du Thil, 80025 Amiens Cedex 01; tel. 3-22-82-72-72; f. 1966; 250,000 vols, 3,000 periodicals; Co-Dir B. LOCHER.

Bibliothèque Municipale: 50 rue de la République, BP 542, 80005 Amiens Cedex 1; tel. 3-22-97-10-10; fax 3-22-97-10-70; f. 1826; 500,000 vols, 2,500 MSS, 300 incunabula; Chief Librarian CHRISTINE CARRIER.

Angers

Bibliothèque Municipale: 49 rue Toussaint, 49100 Angers; tel. 2-41-24-25-50; fax 2-41-81-05-72; e-mail cl.belayche@wanadoo.fr; f. during the French Revolution; 400,000 vols, 2,120 MSS, 111 incunabula; Librarian CLAUDINE BELAYCHE.

Bibliothèque Universitaire d'Angers: 5 rue Le Nôtre, 49045 Angers Cedex: tel. 2-41-35-21-00; fax 2-41-35-21-05; e-mail bib@univangers.fr; Dir J.-C. BROUILLARD.

Avignon

Bibliothèque Municipale: 2 bis rue Laboureur, BP 349, 84025 Avignon Cedex 1; tel. 4-90-85-15-59; fax 4-90-14-65-61; f. 1810; 300,000 vols, 7,000 MSS, 700 incunabula, 2,700 musical scores, 40,000 engravings and maps, 30,000 coins; Chief Librarian PIERRE GAILLARD.

Bibliothèque Universitaire: 74 rue Louis Pasteur, 84018 Avignon Cedex 1; tel. 4-90-16-27-60; fax 4-90-16-27-70; f. 1968; 68,000 vols, 900 periodicals; Librarian Mlle FRANÇOISE FEBVRE.

Besançon

Bibliothèque de l'Université de Franche-Comté: 32 rue Mégevand, BP 1057, 25001 Besançon Cedex; tel. 3-81-66-51-26; f. 1880; Dir ALAIN BONNEFOY.

Bibliothèques Municipales: 1 rue de la Bibliothèque, BP 09, 25012 Besançon Cedex; tel. 3-81-81-20-89; fax 3-81-61-98-77; e-mail helene.richard@besancon.com; f. 1694; 350,000 vols, 3,800 MSS, 1,000 incunabula, etc.; Chief Librarian HÉLÈNE RICHARD.

Bordeaux

Bibliothèque Municipale: 85 cours du Maréchal Juin, 33075 Bordeaux Cedex; tel. 5-56-24-32-51; fax 5-56-24-94-08; f. 1736; 900,000 vols, 4,200 MSS, 333 incunbula, 1,000 current periodicals; Chief Librarian PIERRE BOTINEAU.

Service Interétablissements de Coopération Documentaire: Ave des Arts, BP 120, 33402 Talence Cedex; tel. 5-56-84-86-86; fax 5-56-84-86-96; 1,270,000 vols; Dir GÉRARD BRIAND.

Brest

Service Commun de Documentation: 10 ave Victor-Le-Gorgeu, 29287 Brest Cedex; tel. 2-98-01-64-04; fax 2-98-47-75-25; Dir ALAIN SAINSOT.

Caen

Bibliothèque de l'Université de Caen: Esplanade de la Paix, BP 5186, 14032 Caen Cédex; tel. 2-31-56-58-70; fax 2-31-56-56-13; Dir FRANÇOISE BERMANN.

Bibliothèque Municipale: Place Louis-Guillouard, 14027 Caen Cedex; tel. 2-31-86-22-01; fax 2-31-86-20-05; f. 1809; 550,000 vols, 608 periodicals, 12,000 pre-1800 printed items, 50,000 slides, 2,000 video-cassettes, 12,000 compact discs, 7,000 talking books for the visually impaired, 1,345 software disks for micro-computer, 300 CD-ROMs; special Normandy collection; Librarian PHILIPPE DUPONT.

Cambrai

Bibliothèque Municipale Classée: 37 rue St Georges, BP 179, 59403 Cambrai Cedex; tel. 3-27-82-93-93; fax 3-27-82-93-94; f. 1791; 130,000 vols, 1,400 MSS, 600 incunabula; Librarian BÉNÉDICTE TEROUANNE.

Carpentras

Bibliothèque Inguimbertine: 234 blvd Albin-Durand, 84200 Carpentras; f. 1745; 265,000 vols, 3,126 MSS; Librarian ISABELLE BATTEZ.

Châlons-sur-Marne

Bibliothèque Municipale: 1 passage Henri Vendel, 51038 Châlons-sur-Marne Cedex; tel. 3-26-69-38-50; fax 3-26-69-38-54; f. 1803; 335,000 vols, 1,660 MSS, 120 incunabula; Librarian FRANÇOISE BÉRARD.

Chambéry

Bibliothèque de l'Université de Savoie: route de l'Eglise, Jacob-Bellecombette BP 1104, 73011 Chambéry Cedex; tel. 4-79-75-85-64; f. 1962; 119,000 vols, 568 periodicals; Chief Librarian COLETTE COMMANAY.

Clermont-Ferrand

Bibliothèque Municipale et Interuniversitaire: 1 blvd Lafayette, BP 27, 63001 Clermont-Ferrand Cedex 01; tel. 4-73-40-62-40; fax 4-73-40-62-19; e-mail berard@cicsun .univ-bpclermont.fr; f. 1902; 600,000 vols, 1,700 current periodicals; Dir RAYMOND BÉRARD.

Colmar

Bibliothèque de la Ville de Colmar: 1 place des Martyrs de la Résistance, 68000 Colmar; tel. 3-89-24-48-18; fax 3-89-23-33-80; f. 1803; 400,000 vols, 1,300 MSS, 2,500 incunabula; Chief Librarian FRANCIS GUETH.

Dijon

Bibliothèque de l'Université de Bourgogne: 6 rue Sully, 21000 Dijon; tel. 3-80-39-51-20; Dir Mme F. HAGENE.

Bibliothèque Municipale: 3–7 rue de l'Ecole-de-Droit, 21000 Dijon; tel. 3-80-44-94-14; fax 3-80-44-94-34; f. 1701; 460,000 vols; Chief Librarian ANDRÉ-PIERRE SYREN.

Douai

Bibliothèque Municipale: rue de la Fonderie, 59500 Douai; tel. 3-27-97-88-51; fax 3-27-99-71-80; f. 1770; 250,000 vols, 2,000 MSS, 300 incunabula, 200 periodicals; Librarian MICHELE DEMARCY.

Grenoble

Bibliothèque Municipale: 12 blvd Maréchal Lyautey, BP 1095, 38000 Grenoble; tel. 4-76-86-21-00; fax 4-76-86-21-19; e-mail bmei-@upmf.grenoble.fr; f. 1772; 600,000 vols, 654 incunabula, 20,980 MSS, 81,000 prints, 2,575 maps; special collection: local history; Dir CATHERINE POUYET.

Service de Coopération Documentaire Sciences-Médecine: BP 66, 38402 St Martin d'Hères; linked with university science and medical libraries.

Service Interétablissements de Coopération Documentaire: Domaine universitaire BP 85, 38402 St Martin d'Hères Cedex; tel. 4-76-82-61-61.

Haguenau

Bibliothèque et Archives de la Ville: 9 rue du Maréchal Foch, BP 261, 67504 Haguenau Cedex; tel. 3-88-93-79-22; fax 3-88-93-48-12; f. 1899; 120,000 vols; Dir PIA WENDLING; publ. *Etudes Haguenoviennes* (annually).

La Rochelle

Bibliothèque Municipale: 28 rue Gargoulleau, 17025 La Rochelle Cedex; f. 1750; 360,000 vols; Librarian BRUNO CARBONE.

Le Havre

Bibliothèque Municipale: 17 rue Jules Lecesne, 76600 Le Havre; tel. 2-35-42-04-53; f. 1803; public borrowing, reference, record library; 450,000 vols, 1,000 periodicals, 700 MSS; Librarian MATHILDE LEPAPE.

Le Mans

Bibliothèque de l'Université du Maine: Avenue Olivier Messiaen, 72017 Le Mans Cedex; 68,000 vols, 827 periodicals; Dir C. MENIL.

Lille

Bibliothèque de l'Université des Sciences et Technologies de Lille: Service commun de la documentation de Lille I: Ave Henri Poincaré, BP 155, 59653 Villeneuve d'Ascq Cedex; tel. 3-20-43-44-10; fax 3-20-33-71-04; 115,000 books, 60,000 theses; economics, humanities, technology, science; Chief Librarian JEAN-BERNARD MARINO.

Bibliothèque Municipale: 34 rue Edouard Delesalle, 59043 Lille Cedex; tel. 3-20-15-97-20; fax 3-20-63-94-54; f. 1726; 595,000 vols; Librarian MIle GENEVIÈVE TOURNOUËR.

Service commun de la documentation de Lille II (Secteur Médecine/Pharmacie and Secteur Droit/Gestion): 1 place Déliot, BP 179, 59017 Lille Cedex; tel. 3-20-90-76-50; fax 3-20-90-76-54; Chief Librarian BRIGITTE MULETTE.

Service commun de la documentation de l'Université de Lille III – Charles de Gaulle: Domaine universitaire du Pont-de-bois, BP 99, 59652 Villeneuve d'Ascq Cedex; tel. 3-20-41-70-00; fax 3-20-91-46-50; Dir JEAN-PAUL CHADOURNE.

Limoges

Bibliothèque de l'Université de Limoges: 39C rue Camille-Guérin, 87031 Limoges Cedex; tel. 5-55-43-57-00; fax 5-55-43-57-01; e-mail rohou@unilim.fr; f. 1965; 100,000 vols; Dir ODILE ROHOU.

Bibliothèque Francophone Multimédia: 2 rue Louis Longequeue, 87032 Limoges Cedex; tel. 5-55-45-96-00; fax 5-55-45-96-96; f. 1804; 530,000 vols, 900 periodicals, 14,000 videos, 32,000 records; spec. collns incl. enamels, ceramics, porcelain; Librarian: ALAIN DUPERRIER.

Lyons

Bibliothèque Municipale: 30 blvd Vivier-Merle, 69431 Lyon Cedex 03; tel. 4-78-62-18-00; fax 4-78-62-19-49; e-mail bm@bm-lyon.fr; f. 1693; 1,700,000 vols, *c.* 11,000 MSS, 1,000 incunabula, 30,000 prints, 7,900 periodicals, 137,000 records; special collections: Lyons and Rhône-Alpes area, Chinese, medical anthropology; Dir PATRICK BAZIN.

Service Interétablissements de Coopération Documentaire: 5 ave Mendès France, Case 11, 69676 Bron Cedex; tel. 4-78-77-23-54; fax 4-78-77-69-21; Dir M. THOUMIEUX.

Marseilles

Bibliothèque de l'Université de la Méditerranée (Aix-Marseille II): 27 blvd Jean Moulin, 13385 Marseille Cedex 05; tel. 4-91-32-45-37; fax 4-91-25-60-22; e-mail m-h .bournat@bu2.univ-mrs.fr; Dir Mme BOURNAT.

Bibliothèque et Centre de Documentation, Chambre de Commerce et d'Industrie Marseille-Provence: Palais de la Bourse, La Canebière, BP 1856, 13222 Marseille Cedex 1; tel. 4-91-39-33-99; fax 4-91-91-42-25; f. 1872; economics, law, business, industry, commerce, agriculture, marine, Provence, overseas, history, geography; on-line information service; 60,000 vols, 60,000 brochures, 3,000 periodicals; Librarian FRANÇOIS NICOULAUD.

Bibliothèque Municipale: 38 rue du 141e RIA, 13331 Marseille Cedex 3; tel. 4-91-55-36-44; f. 1800; 750,000 vols; Chief Librarian CLAUDINE IRLES.

Metz

Bibliothèque Municipale: 1 cour Elie Fleur, 57000 Metz; tel. 3-87-55-53-33; fax 3-87-30-42-88; f. 1811; 400,000 vols, 1,195 MSS, 5,000 engravings, 463 incunabula; video cassettes, slides; Chief Librarian PIERRE LOUIS.

Service Commun de Documentation de l'Université de Metz: Ile du Saulcy, 57045 Metz Cedex 1; tel. 3-87-31-50-80; fax 3-87-33-22-90; e-mail lamarche@scd.univ-metz.fr; f. 1972; 250,000 vols, 1,100 periodicals; Dir SIMONE LAMARCHE.

Montpellier

Bibliothèque Interuniversitaire: Administration: 4 rue Ecole Mage, 34965 Montpellier ; tel. 4-67-84-77-70; fax 4-67-60-63-97; e-mail biu.secretariat@sc.univ-montp1.fr; Chief Librarian PIERRE GAILLARD.

Bibliothèque Municipale: 37 blvd Bonne Nouvelle, 34000 Montpellier; tel. 4-67-60-16-16; fax 4-67-66-03-09; f. during the French Revolution; 720,000 vols; Librarian M. G. GUDIN DE VALLERIN.

Mulhouse

Bibliothèque de l'Université de Haute Alsace: 8 rue des Frères Lumière, 68093 Mulhouse; tel. 3-89-59-63-60; fax 3-89-59-63-79; Dir. JACQUES REIBEL.

Bibliothèque de l'Université et de la Société Industrielle de Mulhouse (Section Histoire des Sciences): 12 rue de la Bourse, 68100 Mulhouse; tel. 3-89-56-12-74; f. 1826; 29,000 vols, 700 (and 150 current) periodicals; Dir PHILIPPE RUSSELL.

Nancy

Bibliothèque Municipale: 43 rue Stanislas, 54042 Nancy Cedex; tel. 3-83-37-38-83; fax 3-83-37-63-29; f. 1750; 500,000 vols; Chief Librarian ANDRÉ MARKIEWICZ.

Service Commun de Documentation: 46 ave de la Libération, BP 3408, 54015 Nancy Cedex; tel. 3-83-96-80-50; fax 3-83-96-43-41; e-mail heddeshf@bu.u-nancy.fr; 356,000 vols, 4,100 periodicals; Chief Librarian FRANCINE HEDDESHEIMER.

Nantes

Bibliothèque Municipale: 15 rue de l'Heronnière, BP 44113, 44041 Nantes Cedex 01; tel. 2-40-41-95-95; f. 1753; 900,000 vols; Chief Librarian AGNÈS MARCETTEAU.

Bibliothèque Universitaire de Nantes: Chemin de la Censive du Tertre, BP 32211, 44322 Nantes Cedex 03; tel. 2-40-14-12-30; Chief Librarian MICHELLE GUIOT.

Nice

Bibliothèque de l'Université de Nice–Sophia Antipolis: Parc Valrose, BP 2053, 06101 Nice Cedex 02; tel. 4-92-07-60-00; f. 1963; 260,000 vols, 4,400 periodicals; Dir LOUIS KLEE.

Bibliothèque Municipale de Nice: Direction du service, 33 ave Jean Médecin, 06000 Nice; tel. 4-93-82-42-73; fax 4-93-87-77-49; f. 1802; 663,000 vols, 1,500 periodicals, 139,000 compact discs, records and cassettes, 5,000 video cassettes; Michel Butor special collection; Chief Librarian JOËL MARTRES.

Nîmes

Carré d'Art Bibliothèque: place de la Maison-Carrée, 30033 Nîmes Cedex; tel. 4-66-76-35-03; fax 4-66-76-35-10; e-mail bibiotheque.carre.art.de.nimes@wanadoo.fr; f. 1803; 323,000 vols, 590 periodicals, 800 MSS, 40,000 ancient books, 19,000 CDs; Chief Librarian J.-M. MASSADAU; publ. *Journal Carré d'Art* (3 a year).

Orléans

Médiathèque d'Orléans: 1 place Gambetta, 45043 Orléans Cedex 1; tel. 2-38-65-45-45; fax 2-38-65-45-40; e-mail orleans-medi@wanadoo-fr; f. 1714; 420,000 vols; 2,550 MSS; Librarian AGNÈS CHEVALIER.

Service Commun de la Documentation de l'Université d'Orléans: Domaine de la Source, rue de Tours, 45072 Orléans Cedex 02; tel. 2-38-41-71-84; f. 1965; 180,000 vols and theses, 800 periodicals; Dir Mme DESBORDES.

Paris

American Library in Paris: 10 rue du Général Camou, 75007 Paris; tel. 1-53-59-12-60; fax 1-45-50-25-83; e-mail 100142.1066@compuserve.com; branches in Angers, Montpellier, Nancy and Toulouse; f. 1920; private English-language lending and reference library open to all nationalities; 90,000 vols, 450 periodicals; access to library of American University of Paris (50,000 vols); Chair. JOHN H. RIGGS, Jr; Dir KAY RADER.

Archives de France: 56 rue des Francs-Bourgeois, 75141 Paris Cedex 03; tel. 1-40-27-60-00; f. 1790; *c.* 480 km. documents; Dir ALAIN ERLANDE-BRANDENBURG.

Has attached:

Centre des Archives contemporaines: 2 rue des Archives, 77300 Fontainebleau; Chief Curator CHRISTINE PETILLAT.

Centre des Archives d'Outre-Mer: 29 chemin du Moulin-Detesta, 13090 Aix-en-Provence; f. 1962; Chief Curator FRANÇOISE DURAND-EVRARD.

Centre des Archives du Monde du Travail: Carrefour de l'Europe, 59100 Roubaix; f. 1993; Chief Curator GEORGES MOURADIAN.

Centre historique des Archives nationales: 60 rue des Francs-Bourgeois, 75141 Paris Cedex 03; Chief Curator MARIE-PAULE ARNAULD.

Dépôt central de Microfilms: Domaine d'Espeyran, 30800 St-Gilles-du-Gard; Chief Curator ANNE DEBANT.

Bibliothèque Administrative de la Ville de Paris: Hôtel de Ville, 75196 Paris RP; tel. 1-42-76-48-87; fax 1-42-76-63-78; f. 1872; 500,000 vols (reports, studies, statistics, official texts, budgets, etc.); 3,200 periodicals, 8,000 photographs, 1,800 MSS, 12,000 architectural designs, 40,000 microfiches, 2,000 microfilms; French and foreign local administration; French legislation; economic, political and social history; legislation of ex-French colonies; general biography; Chief Librarian PIERRE CASSELLE.

Bibliothèque Centrale de l'Ecole Polytechnique: 91128 Palaiseau Cedex; tel. 1-69-33-40-42; telex 601596; fax 1-69-33-30-01; f. 1794; 300,000 vols, 760 periodicals; Chief Librarian MADELEINE DE FUENTES.

Bibliothèque Centrale du Muséum National d'Histoire Naturelle: 38 rue Geoffroy-Saint-Hilaire, 75005 Paris; tel. 1-40-79-36-27; fax 1-40-79-36-56; f. 1635; 800,000 vols, 7,050 MSS, 10,135 periodicals; Chief Librarian MONIQUE DUCREUX.

Bibliothèque d'Art et d'Archéologie Jacques Doucet: 2–4 rue Vivienne, 75083 Paris Cedex 02; tel. 1-47-03-76-20; fax 1-47-03-89-25; e-mail baa@bnf.fr; f. 1918; 483,000 vols, 6,200 periodicals; Chief Librarian FRANÇOISE LEMELLE.

Bibliothèque de Documentation Internationale Contemporaine: Centre Universitaire, 6 allée de l'Université, 92001 Nanterre Cedex; tel. 1-40-97-79-00; fax 1-40-97-79-40; f. 1914; over 1,000,000 vols, 90,000 series of periodicals, history of the two World Wars and international relations in 20th century, social and revolutionary movements, political emigrations; Dir GENEVIÈVE DREYFUS-ARMAND; Sec.-Gen. MARC PETIT.

Bibliothèque de Géographie: 191 rue Saint-Jacques, 75005 Paris; tel. 1-44-32-14-63; fax 1-44-32-14-67; e-mail bibgeo@univ-paris1.fr; 78,000 vols, 4,000 periodicals, 25,000 maps, 40,000 photographs; Librarian Mme JOSEPH.

Bibliothèque de l'Académie Nationale de Médecine: 16 rue Bonaparte, 75006 Paris; tel. 1-46-34-60-70; fax 1-43-25-84-14; f. 1840; over 350,000 vols, 113 incunabula, 500 periodicals; 8,000 portraits, 1,100 medals, 135 sculptures, 75 paintings; Archives of the Société Royale de Médecine and Académie Royale de Chirurgie; Librarian Mme FRANÇOISE DE SAINTE MARIE; publ. *Bulletin de l'Académie nationale de Médecine*.

Bibliothèque de l'Arsenal: 1 rue de Sully, 75004 Paris; tel. 1-53-01-25-25; fax 1-42-77-01-63; f. 1756 by the Marquess of Paulmy, public library in 1797; inc. with Bibliothèque Nationale 1934; specializes in literature; open to scholars; contains 1,000,000 vols; 15,000 MSS, many autographs; includes archives of the Bastille; 100,000 prints, 18th-century maps; houses the performing arts collection of the Bibliothèque Nationale (2,500,000 vols and other items); Dir (vacant).

Bibliothèque de l'Assemblée Nationale: Palais Bourbon, 75007 Paris; tel. 1-40-63-64-74; telex 260420; f. 1796; 690,000 vols, 1,870 MSS, and 80 incunabula, 2,800 periodicals, 50,000 microfiches, 2,500 microfilms, mainly on history, political science, law, economy; Dir FRANÇOISE MONET; publs *Sélection d'articles de périodiques*; *Sélection d'ouvrages récemment acquis* (8 a year).

Bibliothèque de l'Ecole Nationale Supérieure des Mines: 60 blvd Saint-Michel, 75272 Paris Cedex 06; tel. 1-40-51-90-56; fax 1-43-25-53-58; e-mail bib@bib.ensmp.fr; f. 1783; 300,000 vols, 3,820 periodicals, 30,000 maps; Chief Librarian Mme F. MASSON.

Bibliothèque de l'Ecole Normale Supérieure: 45 rue d'Ulm, 75230 Paris Cedex 05; f. 1810; 500,000 vols; Chief Librarian PIERRE PETITMENGIN.

Bibliothèque de l'Institut de France: 23 quai de Conti, 75006 Paris; tel. 1-44-41-44-10; fax 1-44-41-44-11; f. 1795; 1,500,000 vols, 11,000 periodicals, 8,000 MSS; Chief Curator MIREILLE PASTOUREAU.

Bibliothèque de l'Institut National de Recherche Pédagogique: 29 rue d'Ulm, 75230 Paris Cedex 05; tel. 1-46-34-90-62; fax 1-43-54-32-01; f. 1879; 550,000 vols, 5,000 periodicals, 100,000 textbooks; educational research; Chief Librarian MARIE-LOUISE SOULA; publs *Histoire de l'Education* (quarterly), *Revue Française de Pédagogie* (quarterly), *Repères pour l'enseignement du Français* (3 a year).

Bibliothèque de la Cour des Comptes: 13 rue Cambon, 75100 Paris RP; tel. 1-42-98-97-12; fax 1-42-60-01-59; e-mail scda@courrier.cour-des-comptes-crc.fr; f. 1807 by Napoleon I; 50,000 vols on finance, law and economy; Librarian (vacant).

Bibliothèque de la Direction Générale de l'Institut National de la Statistique et des Etudes Economiques: 18 blvd Adolphe Pinard, 75675 Paris Cedex 14; tel. 1-41-17-53-43; fax 1-41-17-50-69; f. 1946; 150,000 vols, 9,600 periodicals; Head of Documentation Division YVES ANTHEAUME; Curator MARGUERITE WEIL; publ. *Scribeco* (every 2 months).

Bibliothèque de la Sorbonne: 47 rue des Ecoles, 75257 Paris Cedex 05; tel. 1-40-46-30-27; fax 1-40-46-30-44; e-mail adminst@biu.sorbonne.fr; f. 1762; over 3 million vols, 13,000 periodicals; Chief Librarian MARIE-BERNADETTE JULLIEN; publ. *Mélanges de la Bibliothèque de la Sorbonne*.

Bibliothèque des Avocats à la Cour d'Appel: Palais de Justice, 75001 Paris; f. 1708; confiscated during the Revolution, but refounded in 1810; 160,000 vols; not open to the public; Librarian MICHEL BRICHARD.

Bibliothèque du Conservatoire National des Arts et Métiers: 292 rue St-Martin, 75141 Paris Cedex 03; tel. 1-40-27-27-03; telex 240-247; fax 1-40-27-29-87; f. 1794; 150,000 vols, 3,600 periodicals on science, technology, political economy; special collections: exhibition catalogues, Bartholdi, Organum; Librarian Mme BRIGITTE ROZET.

Bibliothèque du Ministère des Affaires Etrangères: 37 quai d'Orsay, 75351 Paris; tel. 1-43-17-42-71; fax 1-47-53-45-85; f. in 18th century; over 500,000 vols; admin. by Asst Curator of the Archives Dept; Librarian MARIE-THÉRÈSE DENIS.

Bibliothèque du Sénat: Palais du Luxembourg, 75291 Paris Cedex 06; tel. 1-42-34-35-39; telex 260-430; fax 1-42-34-27-05; f. 1818; 450,000 vols, chiefly on history and law, 1,343 MSS and 45,000 prints; open to members of Parliament; Dir PHILIPPE MARTIAL.

Bibliothèque du Service Historique de l'Armée de Terre: Château de Vincennes, BP 107, 00481 Armées; over 600,000 vols; f. *c.* 1800 science and military history; Librarian Lieut-Col DE GISLAIN DE BONTIN.

Bibliothèque du Service Historique de la Marine: Château de Vincennes, BP2, 00300 Armées; tel. 1-43-28-81-50; fax 1-43-28-31-60; f. 1919; 100,000 vols on naval history; Chief Curator PHILIPPE HENWOOD.

Bibliothèque et Archives des Musées Nationaux: 6 rue des Pyramides, 75041 Paris Cedex 01; tel. 1-40-20-52-66; fax 1-40-20-51-69; f. 1871; 150,000 vols; books and MSS connected with the Louvre and the National Museums (Egyptology collection, Oriental antiquities, Greco-Roman antiquities, drawings, paintings and sculptures); open only to curators and authorized persons; Archivist and Librarian ISABELLE LE MASNE DE CHERMONT.

Bibliothèque et Archives du Conseil d'Etat: Place du Palais-Royal, 75100 Paris 01 SP; tel. 1-40-20-81-31; fax 1-42-61-69-95; e-mail biblio.ce@wanadoo.fr; f. 1871; 100,000 vols on jurisprudence, administrative science, political science and legislation; Librarian SERGE BOUFFANGE.

Bibliothèque Forney: 1 rue du Figuier, 75004 Paris; tel. 1-42-78-14-60; fax 1-42-78-22-59; f. 1886; 135,000 vols, 20,000 periodicals, *c.* 250,000 other items, chiefly on arts and crafts; Librarian A.-C. LELIEUR.

Bibliothèque Georges Duhamel: Square Brieussel Bourgeois, 78200 Mantes-la-Jolie; tel. 1-34-78-80-73; f. 1797; encyclopaedic library; 88,882 vols; record library: 6,400 records, 1,500 compact discs; permanent exhibitions in Georges Duhamel picture gallery; Dir PAUL JOLAS; publ. *Rencontres Artistiques et Littéraires*.

Bibliothèque Historique de la Ville de Paris: 24 rue Pavée, 75004 Paris; tel. 1-44-59-29-40; fax 1-42-74-03-16; f. 1871; 650,000 vols, 15,000 MSS on history of Paris; Curator JEAN DERENS.

Bibliothèque Interuniversitaire Cujas de Droit et Sciences Economiques: 2 rue Cujas, 75005 Paris; tel. 1-46-34-99-87; fax 1-46-34-98-32; f. 1876; 1,000,000 vols; Chief Librarian DOMINIQUE ROCHE.

Bibliothèque Interuniversitaire de Médecine: 12 rue de l'Ecole-de-Médecine, 75270 Paris Cedex 06; tel. 1-40-46-16-16; fax 1-44-41-10-20; f. 1733; 1,000,000 vols; Chief Librarian PIERRETTE CASSEYRE.

Bibliothèque Interuniversitaire de Pharmacie: 4 ave de l'Observatoire, 75270 Paris Cedex 06; tel. 1-53-73-95-23; fax 1-53-73-95-20; e-mail piketky@pharmacie.univ-paris5.fr; f. 1570; centre for the acquisition and dispersion of scientific and technical information (CADIST) on beauty care; 280,000 vols, 945 periodicals, archives of Parisian apothecaries; Dir Mme FRANÇOISE MALET.

Bibliothèque Interuniversitaire des Langues Orientales: 4 rue de Lille, 75007 Paris; tel. 1-44-77-87-20; fax 1-44-77-87-30; f. 1868; languages and cultures of countries in Asia, Africa and Europe, and Oceanian and Amerindian languages; 560,000 vols, 9,600 periodicals; Dir NELLY GUILLAUME.

Bibliothèque Mazarine: 23 quai de Conti, 75006 Paris; tel. 1-44-41-44-06; fax 1-44-41-44-07; f. 1643 by Cardinal Mazarin, since 1945 attached to Institut de France; 500,000 vols, 4,600 MSS, 2,500 incunabula; Dir CHRISTIAN PÉLIGRY.

Bibliothèque-Musée de l'Opéra: 8 rue Scribe, 75009 Paris; tel. 1-47-42-07-02; fax 1-42-65-10-16; f. 1875; a service of Bibliothèque Nationale, music dept; 200,000 vols, 30,000 scores, 80,000 libretti, 100,000 drawings, 40,000 lithographs, 100,000 photographs, 2,000 periodicals; Librarians PIERRE VIDAL, ROMAIN FEIST, MARIE-JOSÉ KERHOAS.

Bibliothèque Gustav Mahler: 11 bis rue Vézelay, 75008 Paris; tel. 1-53-89-09-10; fax 1-43-59-70-22; f. 1985; reference collection for musicians, students, researchers; 20,000 vols, 8,000 musical scores, 6,000 reviews, 40,000 records; archives: MSS, letters, photos, etc. on Mahler's life and works; also 2,000 dossiers on contemporary composers, autographs and MSS of 19th- and 20th-century musicians; Pres. HENRY-LOUIS DE LA GRANGE; Librarian (vacant); publ. *Bulletin d'information de la BMGM* (quarterly).

Bibliothèque Nationale de France: quai François Mauriac, 75013 Paris; tel. 1-53-79-53-79; f. 14th century; specialized depts: printed books (11m. vols), periodicals (350,000 titles), maps and plans (890,000), prints and photographs (11m.), MSS (350,000 bound vols), coins, medals and antiques (580,000 items), music (incl. Bibliothèque-Musée de l'Opéra (q.v.), sound archive and audiovisual aids (1m. discs and tape recordings, 20,000 films, 40,000 video materials), performing arts (3m. items), Bibliothèque de l'Arsenal (q.v.); Pres. JEAN-PIERRE ANGREMY; Dir-Gen. PHILIPPE BELAVAL; publs *Chronique de la Bibliothèque Nationale de France* (6 a year), *Bibliographie nationale Française* (fortnightly).

Bibliothèque Polonaise: 6 quai d'Orléans, 75004 Paris; tel. 1-43-54-35-61; f. 1854; 200,000 vols, 25,000 drawings and engravings, sculptures, paintings, 8,000 maps (16th to 20th centuries), 5,000 photographs, archives of 19th- and 20th-century Polish emigration to France; Chopin memorabilia; also posters, medals and periodicals; Mickiewicz museum; specializes in 19th- and 20th-century history, literature and art; admin. by Société Historique et Littéraire Polonaise; Dir L. TALKO.

Bibliothèque Publique d'Information: Centre Georges-Pompidou, 75197 Paris Cedex 04; tel. 1-44-78-12-33; fax 1-44-78-12-15; f. 1977; reference library, closed to the public until January 2000, pending refurbishment (BPI Brantôme offers a smaller colln in the interim); 400,000 books, 2,610 periodicals, 2,333 newspapers, 2,425 films, 10,000 music records; also language laboratory, current events hall (4,500 documents), picture collection on 3 interactive video-discs (150,000 views) and exhibitions.

Bibliothèque Sainte-Geneviève: 10 place du Panthéon, 75005 Paris; tel. 1-44-41-97-97; fax 1-44-41-97-96; e-mail bsgmail@univ-paris1.fr.; f. 1624 by Cardinal F. de La Rochefoucauld; 1,200,000 vols, 13,000 periodicals, 120,000 early printed books, 1,500 incunabula and 4,200 MSS, 50,000 prints; encyclopaedic library; special collection: Bibliothèque Nordique (160,000 vols, 3,500 periodicals), Estonian collection (1,000 vols); Dir NATHALIE JULLIAN.

Bibliothèque Thiers: 27 place Saint-Georges, 75009 Paris; tel. 1-48-78-14-33; fax 1-42-80-26-10; f. 1905; attached to Institut de France; 130,000 vols, 3,000 MSS and 30,000 engravings on 19th-century history; Dir DANUTA MONACHON.

Bibliothèques de l'Institut Catholique de Paris: C/o Bibliothèque de Fels, 21 rue d'Assas, 75270 Paris Cedex 06; tel. 1-44-39-52-30; fax 1-44-39-52-98; e-mail bibliotheque.dc.fels@icp.fr; f. 1875; philosophy, theology, history, literature, psychology; 700,000 vols; Chief Librarian MADELEINE COLOMB.

CÉDIAS Musée Social: 5 rue Las-Cases, 75007 Paris; tel. 1-45-51-66-10; fax 1-44-18-01-81; f. 1894; social information and documentation; public library containing 100,000 vols; Dir BRIGITTE BOUQUET; publs *Vie Sociale* (every 2 months), *Répertoires des établissements sanitaires et sociaux de France.*

Centre de Documentation Contemporaine et Historique de l'Ecole Nationale des Ponts et Chaussées: 6 et 8 ave Blaise Pascal, Cité Descartes, Champs sur Marne, 77455 Marne-la-Vallée Cedex 2; tel. 1-64-15-34-60; fax 1-64-15-34-79; e-mail coronio@enpc.fr; f. 1747; over 200,000 vols on building, civil engineering, urban and regional planning, and transport, 3,200 MSS, 3,000 maps, 10,000 photographs 1850–1900; Dir G. CORONIO.

Centre de Documentation Economique de la Chambre de Commerce et d'Industrie de Paris: 16 rue de Châteaubriand, 75008 Paris; tel. 1-55-65-72-72; fax 1-55-65-72-86; f. 1821; economics, business information, management, market surveys, companies; 300,000 vols, 1,000 periodicals; economic data bank (DELPHES); Dir GÉRARD FALCO.

Centre de Documentation et d'Information Scientifique pour le Développement (CEDID): 209 rue La Fayette, 75010 Paris; tel. 1-48-03-75-95; telex 214627; fax 1-48-03-08-29; f. 1985 by ORSTOM (*q.v.*); 70,000 documents on development and North-South cooperation, world environment, tropical agriculture, health, evolving societies, and women in third-world countries; 200 general and scientific reviews, press cuttings, database, etc.; open to the public.

Direction des Services d'Archives de Paris: 18 blvd Sérurier, 75019 Paris; tel. 1-53-72-41-23; fax 1-53-72-41-34; f. 1791; collections of various kinds of documents relating to the history of Paris; library of 30,000 vols specializing in history of Paris and administrative publications; Dir FRANÇOIS GASNAULT.

Unesco Library: Unesco, 7 Place de Fontenoy, 75352 Paris; tel. 1-45-68-03-56; telex 204461; fax 1-45-67-16-90; f. 1947; reference and general collection 200,000 vols, 2,000 periodicals; incl. Unesco publs and documents (on microfiche); on-line bibliographic searches and listings; reference and referral services; co-ordination of the documentation network of Unesco; Chief, Information, Library and Archives Division (vacant); publs *Unesco List of Documents and Publications* (quarterly, annual and triennial cumulations), *Unesco Library Acquisitions* (quarterly), *Unesco Library Periodical Checklist* (annually).

Pau

Bibliothèque de l'Université de Pau et des Pays de l'Adour: Campus universitaire, 64000 Pau; tel. 5-59-92-33-60; fax 5-59-92-33-62; f. 1962; 142,000 vols, 2,067 periodicals; Dir SYLVAINE FREULON.

Bibliothèque Municipale: Square Paul-Lafond, BP 1621, 64016 Pau Cedex; tel. 5-59-27-15-72; fax 5-59-83-94-47; 350,000 vols; includes municipal archives; special collections on Henri IV and Béarn; Librarian OLIVIER CAUDRON.

Périgueux

Bibliothèque Municipale: 12 ave Georges Pompidou, 24000 Périgueux; tel. 5-53-53-32-51; fax 5-53-53-17-85; f. 1809; 170,000 vols; Librarian J. L. GLÉNISSON.

Perpignan

Bibliothèque Universitaire: BP 1062, Moulin à Vent, 52 ave de Villeneuve, 66870 Perpignan Cedex; tel. 4-68-50-07-63; fax 4-68-50-37-72; e-mail bu-perp@univ-perp.fr; f. 1962; 123,000 vols and 90,000 theses; 1,600 periodicals; special collections: Catalan, Mexican studies, history of Languedoc-Roussillon, renewable energy, materials science, geology of north Africa; Dir F.-G. BELLEDENT.

Poitiers

Bibliothèque Municipale: 43 place Charles-de-Gaulle, BP 619, 86022 Poitiers Cedex; tel. 5-49-41-16-86; fax 5-49-37-86-72; f. during the French Revolution; 400,000 vols, 1,800 MSS, 286 incunabula; Librarian JEAN-MARIE COMPTE.

Bibliothèque Universitaire de Poitiers: BP 605, 86022 Poitiers Cedex; tel. 5-49-45-33-11; fax 5-49-45-33-56; f. 1879; Dir GENEVIÈVE FIROUZ-ABADIE.

Reims

Bibliothèque de l'Université de Reims: Ave François Mauriac, 51095 Reims Cedex; tel. 3-26-05-39-28; fax 3-26-05-39-30; e-mail mj.poisson@univ-reims.fr; f. 1970; 260,000 vols, 1,700 periodicals; Dir MARIE-JEANNE POISSON.

Bibliothèque Municipale: 2 place Carnegie, 51095 Reims; tel. 3-26-84-39-60; fax 3-26-84-39-68; f. 1809; 348,000 vols, 2,800 MSS; Librarian NICOLAS GALAUD.

Rennes

Bibliothèque de l'Université de Rennes I: 4 rue Lesage, BP 1123, 35014 Rennes Cedex; tel. 2-99-38-25-83; fax 2-99-36-73-87; e-mail jean-yves.roux@univ-rennes1.fr.; f. 1855; 550,000 vols; Chief Librarian J.-Y. ROUX.

Bibliothèque de l'Université de Rennes II: 19 ave de la Bataille Flandres-Dunkerque, 35043 Rennes Cedex; tel. 2-99-14-12-55; fax 2-99-14-12-85; Librarian E. LEMAU.

Bibliothèque Municipale: 1 rue de La Borderie, 35042 Rennes Cedex; tel. 2-99-87-98-98; fax 2-99-87-98-99; e-mail bm-rennes@univ-rennes1.fr; f. 1794; 650,000 vols; Chief Librarian MARIE-THÉRÈSE POUILLIAS.

Rouen

Bibliothèque de l'Université de Rouen–Haute-Normandie: Anneau central, rue Lavoisier, 76821 Mont-Saint-Aignan Cedex; tel. 2-35-14-60-00; Dir YANNICK VALIN.

Bibliothèque Municipale: 3 rue Jacques-Villon, 76043 Rouen Cedex; f. 1791; 500,000 vols incl. 600 incunabula; Chief Librarian M. F. ROSE.

St-Etienne

Bibliothèque de l'Université Jean-Monnet: 1 rue Tréfilerie, 42023 St-Etienne Cedex 2; tel. 4-77-42-16-99; Dir MARIE-CLAUDE ACHARD.

Strasbourg

Bibliothèque Nationale et Universitaire: 6 place de la République, BP 1029/F, 67070 Strasbourg Cedex; tel. 3-88-25-28-00; fax 3-88-25-28-03; e-mail bnus@bnus.u-strasbg.fr; f. 1871; 3,000,000 vols; Chief Librarian G. LITTLER.

Toulon

Bibliothèque de l'Université de Toulon et du Var: BP 122, 83957 La Garde Cedex; e-mail scd@univ-tln.fr; f. 1971; general library; Dir J. KERIGUY.

Toulouse

Bibliothèque de l'Université de Toulouse 1: 11 rue des Puits-Creusés, 31070 Toulouse Cedex; tel. 5-62-15-01-40; fax 5-62-15-01-50; f. 1879; 900,000 vols; special collections: Fonds Pifteau (books printed in Toulouse, books on regional history and geography), Fonds Chabaneau (18th-century books), Fonds Liguge (Spanish history), Fonds Claude Perroud (French Revolution), Fonds Montauban (History of Protestantism); Chief Librarian M. D. HEUSSE.

Bibliothèque Municipale: 1 rue de Périgord, BP 7092, 31070 Toulouse Cedex 7; tel. 5-61-22-21-78; fax 5-61-22-34-30; f. 1782; 20 brs; 914,000 vols, 3,700 periodicals; Chief Librarian PIERRE JULLIEN (acting).

Tours

Bibliothèque Municipale Classée de Tours: 2 bis, ave André Malraux, 37042 Tours Cedex; tel. 2-47-05-47-33; fax 2-47-61-93-26; e-mail ville.tours.biblio@wanadoo.fr; f. 1791; original library destroyed in 1940; 501,000 vols, 3,000 periodicals; Librarian (vacant).

Service Commun de la Documentation de l'Université de Tours: 5 rue des Tanneurs, 37041 Tours Cedex (Letters and Law); Parc de Grandmont, 37200 Tours (Sciences and Pharmacy); 2 *bis* blvd Tonnellé, 37032 Tours Cedex (Medicine).

Troyes

Bibliothèque Municipale: 1 rue Chrestien-de-Troyes, BP 2014, 10010 Troyes Cedex; tel. 3-25-70-40-10; fax 3-25-81-05-45; f. 1651; 400,000 vols; Librarian THIERRY DELCOURT.

Valence

Médiathèque Publique et Universitaire: Place Charles Huguenel, 26000 Valence; tel. 4-75-79-23-70; fax 4-75-79-23-82; f. 1775; 330,000 vols; Librarian ESTHER HERANZ.

Valenciennes

Bibliothèque Municipale: 2–6 rue Ferrand, 59300 Valenciennes; tel. 3-27-22-57-00; fax 3-27-22-57-01; f. 1598; 200,000 vols; Librarian MARIE-PIERRE DION.

Vandoeuvre-lès-Nancy

Institut de l'Information Scientifique et Technique (INIST): 2 allée du Parc de Brabois, 54514 Vandoeuvre-lès-Nancy Cedex; tel. 3-83-50-46-00; fax 3-83-50-46-50; f. 1988; collects, processes and distributes international research findings; produces two databases: PASCAL (Sciences, Technology, Medicine) and FRANCIS (Humanities, Social Sciences, Economics); 23,000 serial titles, 60,000 conference proceedings, 100,000 French doctoral theses, 56,000 French research reports; Dir-Gen. ALAIN CHANUDET.

Versailles

Bibliothèque Municipale: 5 rue de l'Indépendance-Américaine, 78000 Versailles; tel. 2-39-07-13-20; fax 2-39-07-13-22; f. 1803; 642,000 vols; Chief Librarian CLAIRE CAUCHETEUX.

Museums and Art Galleries

Agen

Musée des Beaux-Arts: Place du Docteur Esquirol, 47916 Agen Cedex 9; tel. 5-53-69-47-23; f. 1876; local, Roman and medieval archaeology; paintings of Corneille de Lyon, Goya, the Impressionists, Roger Bissière and François-Xavier Lalanne; ceramics; Chinese art; Curator Mlle YANNICK LINTZ.

Aix-en-Provence

Musée Granet: Place St Jean de Malte, 13100 Aix-en-Provence; tel. 4-42-38-14-70; fax 4-42-26-84-55; f. 1765; Egyptian, Greek, Celto-Ligurian, Roman and Gallo-Roman archaeology; pictures of Cézanne and the French Schools, with special emphasis on Provence; Italian, Spanish, Flemish, Dutch and German Schools; modern painting; sculpture; furniture of 16th, 17th and 18th centuries; Curator DENIS COUTAGNE.

Alençon

Musée des Beaux-Arts et de la Dentelle: Rue Charles Aveline, 61000 Alençon; tel. 2-33-32-40-07; fax 2-33-26-51-66; 17th–19th-century French, Dutch and Flemish paintings, 16th–19th-century French, Italian and Dutch drawings, 16th–20th-century French, Flemish, Italian and Eastern European lace; 16th–19th-century French and British prints; ethnology from Kampuchea.

Amboise

Musée de l'Hôtel de Ville: 37400 Amboise; tel. 2-47-23-47-23; fax 2-47-23-19-80; history of Amboise; collection includes tapestries, and autographs of the kings of France; Curator MARIE-HELLENE LE GAL-BRUCKERT.

Musée de la Poste: 6 rue Joyeuse, 37400 Amboise; tel. 2-47-57-00-11; fax 2-47-23-19-80; f. 1971; collection includes material on historic postal services and transport; Curator MARIE-HELLENE LE GAL-BRUCKERT.

Amiens

Musée de Picardie: 48 rue de la République, 80000 Amiens; tel. 3-22-91-36-44; f. 1854; fine collection of paintings of Northern and French Schools; murals by Puvis de Chavannes and Sol Le Witt; Egyptian, Greek and Roman antiquities; prehistoric, Iron and Bronze age collections; objets d'art of Middle Ages and Renaissance; 19th-century sculpture; 20th-century paintings; Chief Curator MATTHIEU PINETTE.

Angers

Musée des Beaux-Arts: 10 rue du Musée, 49100 Angers; tel. 2-41-88-64-65; fax 2-41-86-06-38; f. 1797; housed in 15th-century 'logis Barrault'; paintings of 18th-century French School and 17th-century Dutch and Flemish Schools; sculpture, including busts by Houdon; Dir PATRICK LE NOUËNE.

Affiliated museums:

Galerie David d'Angers: 33 bis rue Toussaint, 49100 Angers; tel. 2-41-87-21-03; fax 2-41-86-06-38; f. 1984; sited in restored gothic church; almost all the sculptor's work.

Musée Jean Lurçat et de la Tapisserie Contemporaine: 4 blvd Arago, 49100 Angers; tel. 2-41-24-18-45; (Musée Jean Lurçat), 2-41-24-18-48 (Musée de la Tapisserie Contemporaine); fax 2-41-86-06-38; occupies 12th-century Hôpital Saint-Jean; paintings of Jean Lurçat and tapestry.

Musée Pincé: 32 bis rue Lenepveu, 49100 Angers; tel. 2-41-88-94-27; fax 2-41-86-06-38; f. 1889; Greek, Roman, Etruscan and Egyptian antiquities; Chinese and Japanese art.

Antibes

Musée Picasso: Château Grimaldi, 06600 Antibes; tel. 4-92-90-54-20; fax 4-92-90-54-21; f. 1948; 230 works by Picasso; collection of modern and contemporary art: Atlan, Miró, Calder, Richier, Ernst, Hartung and others; Nicolas de Staël room with works from Antibes period; sculpture garden; Dir MAURICE FRÉCHURET; publs catalogues.

Arras

Musée d'Arras: Ancienne Abbaye Saint-Vaast, 22 rue Paul Doumer, 62000 Arras; tel. 3-21-71-26-43; fax 3-21-23-19-26; f. 1825; medieval sculpture, 17th- and 19th-century paintings, porcelain, also temporary exhibitions each year; Curator Mme ANNICK NOTTER; publ. *Les nouvelles des Musées* (every 2 months), catalogues.

Arromanches

Exposition Permanente du Débarquement (Permanent Exhibition of the Landings): 14117 Arromanches; tel. 2-31-22-34-31; f. 1954; exhibition of the Normandy landings of D-Day, 6th June 1944; comprises artificial port and museum of relief maps, working models, photographs, diorama and films.

Avignon

Musée Calvet: 65 rue Joseph Vernet, 84000 Avignon; tel. 4-90-86-33-84; f. 1810; fine art of 16th century to present; Curator PIERRE PROVOYEUR.

Musée du Petit Palais: Place du Palais des papes, 84000 Avignon; tel. 4-90-86-44-58; fax 4-90-82-18-72; f. 1976; in the old archbishop's palace (14th–15th-century); medieval paintings of the Avignon and Italian Schools, medieval sculpture from Avignon; Curator ESTHER MOENCH.

Musée Lapidaire: 27 rue de la République, 84000 Avignon; tel. 4-90-85-75-38; f. 1933; ancient Egyptian, Greek and Gallo-Roman sculpture; Curator ODILE CAVALIER.

Bayonne

Musée Basque de Bayonne: Château-Neuf/Maison Dagourette, 64100 Bayonne; tel. 5-59-59-08-98; fax 5-59-59-03-71; f. 1922; four sections covering the history and folklore of the town of Bayonne, the French Basque country, the Spanish Basque country, and the Basques in the New World; library of 30,000 vols; Dir O. RIBETON; publ. *Bulletin* (quarterly).

Besançon

Musée des Beaux-Arts et d'Archéologie: 1 place de la Révolution–place du Marché, 25000 Besançon; tel. 3-81-81-44-47; f. 1694, moved to present buildings 1843; Danish (pre- and protohistoric), Egyptian, Greek, Etruscan and Roman antiquities; regional (pre- and protohistoric, Gallo-Roman, early medieval) antiquities; medieval objets d'art; 15th–20th-century European paintings (especially French 18th–19th-century), sculpture, ceramics and objets d'art; 15th–20th century drawings in temporary exhibitions; Curators F. SOULIER-FRANÇOIS, P. LAGRANGE, F. THOMAS-MAURIN.

Biot

Musée National Fernand Léger: 06410 Biot; tel. 4-92-91-50-30; fax 4-92-91-50-31; permanent exhibition of paintings, drawings, ceramics.

Blérancourt

Musée National de la Coopération Franco-Américaine: Château de Blérancourt, 02300 Blérancourt; tel. 3-23-39-60-16; f. 1924 to contain collections presented to the State by Mrs Anna Murray Dike, Miss Anne Morgan, and other French and American benefactors, relating to the history of Franco-American relations; the castle, formerly the ancestral home of the Ducs de Gesvres, is classed as an historical monument; library of 3,500 vols; Curator PHILIPPE GRUNCHEC.

Bordeaux

Musée d'Aquitaine: 20 cours Pasteur, 33000 Bordeaux; tel. 5-56-01-51-00; fax 5-56-44-24-36; f. 1987; regional prehistory, history and ethnology; library of 18,000 vols; Curator CHANTAL ORGOGOZO.

Musée d'art contemporain de Bordeaux: Entrepôt Lainé, 7 rue Ferrère, 33000 Bordeaux; tel. 5-56-00-81-50; fax 5-56-44-12-07; f. 1984 by 'capc' asscn (f. 1974), financed by Direction des Musées de France and Bordeaux town; temporary exhibitions; permanent collection; library of 25,000 vols, mostly catalogues; photos, slides, videos; education service for schools; publs *Catalogue* (quarterly), *Calendrier* (5 a year).

Musée des Beaux-Arts: 20 cours d'Albret, 33000 Bordeaux; tel. 5-56-10-17-49; fax 5-56-44-98-16; e-mail beaux-arts@atlantel.fr; f. 1801; 2,300 paintings, 504 sculptures, 2,370 drawings; Curator FRANCIS RIBEMONT.

Caen

Musée de Normandie: Château de Caen, 14000 Caen; tel. 2-31-86-06-24; fax 2-31-85-27-94; e-mail mdn@mairie-caen.fr; f. 1946; history, archaeology and ethnology of Normandy; Dir J.-Y. MARIN; publs *Annales de Normandie* (quarterly), *Publications* (irregular).

Carnac

Musée de Préhistoire: 10 place de la Chapelle, BP 80, 56340 Carnac; tel. 2-97-52-22-04; municipal museum; f. 1881, new site 1984; local prehistory and archaeology; most important museum in the world for collections from megalithic period; research library; photographic archive (3,000 items); Dir ANNE-ELISABETH RISKINE.

Chantilly

Musée et Château de Chantilly (Musée Condé): BP 70243, 60631 Chantilly Cedex; tel. 3-44-62-62-62; fax 3-44-62-62-61; f. 1886; paintings, miniatures, furniture, drawings, 70,000 books, 3,000 MSS, etc.; Curator NICOLE GARNIER; publ. *Le Musée Condé* (2 a year).

Compiègne

Musée National du Château de Compiègne: BP 204, 60200 Compiègne; tel. 3-44-38-47-00; royal palace of the first kings of France, reconstructed under Louis XV and Louis XVI and partly redecorated under the First Empire; furniture of 18th and 19th centuries, mostly First Empire period; tapestries of 18th century; collections from the Second Empire period; souvenirs of the Empress Eugénie; Chief Curator JEAN-MARIE MOULIN.

Affiliated museum:

Musée National de la Voiture et du Tourisme: 60200 Château de Compiègne; f. 1927 with the co-operation of the Touring Club de France; old carriages, sedan chairs, survey of development of the bicycle and the automobile; 180 vehicles; Chief Curator JEAN-MARIE MOULIN.

Dijon

Musée des Beaux-Arts: Palais des Etats, Cour de Bar, 21000 Dijon; tel. 3-80-74-52-70; f. 1787 and housed in the Palace of the Dukes of Burgundy and the Palace of the States of Burgundy; Swiss primitives; paintings of Franco-Flemish School of 15th century and of other French and foreign schools; prints and drawings; sculptures from tombs of the Dukes of Burgundy; marble, ivory, armour; modern art; Granville collection; Chief Curator EMMANUEL STARCKY.

Musée Magnin: 4 rue des Bons-Enfants, 21000 Dijon; tel. 3-80-67-11-10; fax 3-80-66-43-75; Curator EMMANUEL STARCKY.

Fontainebleau

Musée National du Château de Fontainebleau: 77300 Château de Fontainebleau; tel. 1-60-71-50-70; fax 1-60-71-50-71; buildings 12th–19th centuries; paintings, interior decoration and furniture of the Renaissance, 17th and 18th centuries, 1st and 2nd Empires and 19th century; Curators AMAURY LEFÉBURE, DANIELE DENISE, YVES CARLIER, VINCENT DROGUET, NICOLE BARBIER.

Giverny

Claude Monet Foundation: 27620 Giverny; tel. 2-32-51-28-21; f. 1980 after restoration; consists of Monet's house and garden where he lived from 1883 to 1926; it was left by his son in 1966 to the Académie des Beaux-Arts; the house contains Monet's collection of Japanese engravings; Curator GERALD VANDER KEMP; Sec.-Gen. Mme C. LINDSEY.

Grenoble

Musée de Grenoble: 6 place Lavalette, 38000 Grenoble; tel. 4-76-63-44-44; fax 4-76-63-44-10; f. 1796; art and antiquities; library of 40,000 vols; Dir SERGE LEMOINE.

Musée Stendhal: Ancienne Mairie, Jardin de Ville, 38000 Grenoble; tel. 4-76-54-44-14; f. 1933; documents relating to Stendhal's life; 18th-century setting; Dir Y. JOCTEUR-MONTROZIER.

Langeais

Château de Langeais: 37130 Langeais; tel. 2-47-96-72-60; fax 2-47-96-54-44; built in 15th century and given to the Institut de France in 1904; furniture and tapestries of the 13th–15th centuries and 15th-century architecture.

Le Havre

Musée des Beaux-Arts 'André Malraux': Blvd J. F. Kennedy, 76600 Le Havre; tel. 2-35-42-33-97; f. 1845; rebuilt 1961; permanent collection from 14th to 20th centuries (Boudin, Impressionists, Dufy); exhibitions; Dir F. COHEN.

Affiliated museums:

Musée du Prieuré de Graville: Rue Elisée Reclus, 76600 Le Havre; f. 1926; sculpture from the 12th to 18th centuries; models of old houses; exhibitions; Dir CH. MAUBANT.

Musée de l'Ancien Havre: Rue Jérôme Bellarmato, 76600 Le Havre; tel. 2-35-42-27-90; f. 1955; drawings and documents on the history of Le Havre from 1517 to the 20th century; naval models; Dir CH. MAUBANT.

Espace Maritime et Portuaire du Havre: Quai Frissard, 76600 Le Havre; tel. 2-35-24-51-00; fax 2-35-26-76-69; Le Havre maritime and port history since 1830; Dir CH. MAUBANT.

Le Mans

Musée Automobile de la Sarthe: Circuit des 24 Heures du Mans, BP 424, 72009 Le Mans Cedex; tel. 2-43-72-72-24; fax 2-43-85-38-96; cars, cycles and motorcycles; Man. FRANCIS PIQUERA.

Musée de la Reine Bérengère: 9–13 rue de la Reine Bérengère,72000 Le Mans; tel. 2-43-47-38-51; 16th-century architecture, folklore, ceramics, etc.; Curator FRANÇOISE CHASERANT.

Musée de Tessé: 2 ave de Paderborn, 72000 Le Mans; tel. 2-43-47-38-51; fax 2-43-47-49-93; fine arts, paintings and sculpture, archaeology, Egyptology; Curator FRANÇOISE CHASERANT.

Lille

Musée des Beaux-Arts: 18 *bis* rue de Valmy, 59800 Lille; tel. 3-20-06-78-00; fax 3-20-06-78-15; f. 1801; paintings of Flemish, Italian, Spanish, German, French and Dutch Schools; exceptional collection of drawings; sculpture, ceramics and archaeological exhibits; Chief Curator ARNAULD BREJON DE LAVERGNÉE.

Limoges

Musée Municipal de l'Evêché: Place de la Cathédrale, 87000 Limoges; tel. 5-55-34-44-09; fax 5-55-34-44-14; f. 1912; paintings, drawings, engravings; Limoges enamels; Egyptian collection; archaeological and lapidary collection; library of 5,000 vols; Curator VÉRONIQUE NOTIN.

Musée National Adrien Dubouché: Place Winston Churchill, 87000 Limoges; tel. 5-55-33-08-50; fax 5-55-33-08-55; f. 1900; ceramics and glass; Curator CHANTAL MESLIN-PERRIER.

Lyons

Musée des Beaux-Arts: 20 place des Terreaux, 69001 Lyon; tel. 4-72-10-17-40; fax 4-78-28-12-45; f. 1801 and housed in the former Benedictine Abbey of the Dames de Saint-Pierre, built in 1659; the important collection contains paintings of French, Flemish, Dutch, Italian and Spanish Schools, and sections devoted to local painters, modern art, and murals by Puvis de Chavannes; ancient, medieval and modern sculpture; French, Italian, Oriental and Hispano-Moorish ceramics; drawings, prints, furniture, numismatic collection; Egyptian, Greek, Roman and Near and Middle Eastern antiquities; library of 30,000 vols; Chief Curator PHILIPPE DUREY; publs *Bulletin des Musées et Monuments Lyonnais* (quarterly), illustrated guides.

Magny-les-Hameaux

Musée National des Granges de Port-Royal: 78114 Magny-les-Hameaux; tel. 1-30-43-73-05; f. 1952; history of Port-Royal and Jansenism; presented in the house of 'Petites Ecoles' where Racine studied; Curator VÉRONIQUE ALEMANY.

Maisons-Laffitte

Musée du Château: 78600 Maisons-Laffitte; tel. 1-39-62-01-49; fax 1-39-12-34-37; château dates from 1642; contains paintings, sculptures, tapestries; Curator FLORENCE DE LA RONCIÈRE.

Marseilles

Musée Cantini: 19 rue Grignan, 13006 Marseille; tel. 4-91-54-77-75; fax 4-91-55-03-61; f. 1936; modern and contemporary art; library of 20,000 vols on 20th-century art; Curators NICOLAS CENDO, OLIVIER COUSINOU.

Musée d'Archéologie Méditerranéenne: 2 rue de la Charité, 13002 Marseille; tel. 4-91-14-58-80; fax 4-91-14-58-81; f. 1863; Egyptian, Greek, Cypriot, Etruscan, Roman and Gallo-Roman antiquities; library of 4,500 vols; Curators AGNÈS DURAND, BRIGITTE LESCURE.

Affiliated museum:

Musée des Docks Romains: 28 place Vivaux, 13002 Marseille; tel. 4-91-91-24-62; f. 1963; ancient commerce; exhibits include amphorae, ingots and marine archaeology; Curator AGNÈS DURAND.

Musée de la Marine et de l'Economie de Marseille: Chambre de Commerce et d'Industrie Marseille-Provence, Palais de la Bourse, La Canebière, BP 1856, 13221 Marseille Cedex 1; tel. 4-91-39-33-33; fax 4-91-39-56-15; e-mail patrick.boulanger@marseille-provence.ccr.fr; f. 1932; history of Marseilles and Mediterranean shipping; models of ships, paintings, drawings, plans, etc.; 25,000 tape recordings; Nossof, Cantelar and Grimard collections (history of steam ships); Archivist, Chief of Cultural Heritage Dept PATRICK BOULANGER.

Musée des Beaux-Arts: Palais de Longchamp, 13004 Marseille; tel. 4-91-14-59-30; fax 4-91-14-59-31; f. 1802; paintings (French, Italian, Flemish and Dutch); murals by Puvis de Chavannes; collection of paintings and sculptures by Puget; sculptures by Daumier and Rodin; Curators M.-P. VIAL, L. GEORGET.

Metz

La Cour d'Or, Musées de Metz: 2 rue du Haut Poirier, 57000 Metz; tel. 3-87-75-10-18; fax 3-87-36-51-14; f. 1839; prehistory, protohistory, arts and popular traditions of northern Lorraine, and natural history collections (not open to public); architecture; fine arts (15th to 20th centuries); archaeology and history; military collections; audiovisual programmes; library of 5,000 vols, 100 periodicals; Dir MONIQUE SARY; publs catalogues, guides.

Montpellier

Musée Atger: Faculté de Médecine, 2 rue de l'Ecole de Médecine, 34000 Montpellier; tel. 4-67-66-27-77; f. 1823; drawings and paintings of French, Italian and Flemish schools, 16th to 18th centuries (Fragonard, Natoire, Tiepolo); Curator Mme C. NICQ.

Musée Fabre: Blvd Bonne Nouvelle, 34000 Montpellier; tel. 4-67-14-83-00; fax 4-67-66-09-20; f. 1825 by the painter Fabre; paintings of French (Greuze, Delacroix, Courbet, Bazille, Géricault), Italian, Spanish, Dutch and Flemish Schools; drawings, sculpture (Houdon), furniture, tapestries, porcelain, silver; Dir MICHEL HILAIRE.

Mulhouse

Musée de l'Impression sur Etoffes: 14 rue Jean-Jacques Henner, 68100 Mulhouse; tel. 3-89-46-83-00; fax 3-89-46-83-10; f. 1955; 18th- to 20th-century printed textiles; Curator JAQUELINE JACQUÉ; publ. *L'Imprimé* (2 a year).

Musée National de l'Automobile, Collection Schlumpf: 192 ave de Colmar, 68100 Mulhouse; tel. 3-89-42-29-17; fax 3-89-32-08-09; f. 1982; privately owned; 500 vehicles from early models to modern times; notable collection of 125 Bugattis; includes the Espace Découvert, opened in 1989, which enables visitors to discover how a car works; library of 4,500 vols; Dir PATRICK GARNIER.

Nancray

Musée de Plein Air des Maisons Comtoises: 25360 Nancray; tel. 3-81-55-29-77; fax 3-81-55-23-97; f. 1984; folklore of Franche-Comté; 60,000 illustrations of rural architecture; Curator PIERRE BOURGIN; publs *Barbizier, Revue Régionale d'Ethnologie Comtoise* (annually).

Nancy

Musée des Beaux-Arts: Place Stanislas, 54000 Nancy; tel. 3-83-85-30-72; fax 3-83-85-30-76; f. 1793; paintings, sculpture, drawings, prints and glass from 15th to 20th century; temporary exhibitions; Curator BÉATRICE SALMON.

Nantes

Musée des Beaux-Arts: 10 rue Georges-Clemenceau, 44000 Nantes; tel. 2-40-41-65-65; fax 2-40-41-67-90; e-mail musees@mairie-nantes.fr; f. 1800; 2,200 paintings; library of 10,000 vols; Curator JEAN AUBERT.

Nice

Direction des Musées de Nice: Palais Masséna, 65 rue de France, 06050 Nice Cedex 1; tel. 4-93-88-11-34; fax 4-93-82-39-79; f. 1921; Dir C. FOURNET.

Comprises:

Musée d'Art et d'Histoire: Palais Masséna, 65 rue de France, 06050 Nice Cedex 1; tel. 4-93-88-11-34; fax 4-93-82-39-79; art and history; Dir C. FOURNET; Curator LUC THEVENON.

Musée des Beaux-Arts: 33 ave des Baumettes, 06000 Nice; tel. 4-93-44-50-72; fax 4-93-97-67-07; painting and sculpture 18th and 19th centuries, (Impressionists, Van Dongen); works of Jules Chéret; Dir C. FOURNET; Curators BÉATRICE DEBRABANDERE, JEAN FORNERIS.

Musée d'Archéologie: 160 Ave des Arènes de Cimiez, 06000 Nice; tel. 4-93-81-59-57; fax 4-93-81-08-00; Curator Mlle D. MOUCHOT.

Musée Matisse: 164 ave des Arènes de Cimiez, 06000 Nice; tel. 4-93-81-08-08; fax 4-93-53-00-22; collections of paintings and sculptures by Henri Matisse; Curator MARIE-THÉRÈSE PULVÉNIS DE SELIGNY.

Musée du Vieux-Logis: 59 ave Saint Barthélémy, 06100 Nice; tel. 4-93-84-44-74; medieval furniture; Curator C. FOURNET.

Muséum d'Histoire Naturelle: 60 *bis* blvd Risso, 06300 Nice; tel. 4-93-55-15-24; f. 1823; Curator G. THOMEL.

Palais Lascaris: 15 rue Droite, 06300 Nice; tel. 4-93-62-05-54; 17th- and 18th-century frescoes and furniture; Curator CH. ASTRO.

Galerie des Ponchettes–Musée Dufy: 77 quai des Etats-Unis, 06300 Nice; tel. 4-93-62-31-24; Curator C. FOURNET.

Musée Alexis et Gustav-Adolf Mossa: 59 quai des Etats-Unis, 06300 Nice; tel. 4-93-62-37-11; Curator C. FOURNET.

Musée d'Art Moderne et d'Art Contemporain: Promenade des Arts, 06300 Nice; tel. 4-93-62-61-62; fax 4-93-13-09-01; f. 1990; collection 'Nice à partir des années 60'; nouveaux réalistes, pop art, fluxus, color field painting. Dir C. FOURNET; Curators P. CHAIGNEAU, G. PERLEIN.

Musée de Paléontologie—Terra Amata: 25 blvd Carnot, 06300 Nice; tel. 4-93-55-59-93; fax 4-93-89-91-31; Curator Mme M. GOUDET.

Musée Naval: Tour Bellanda, Colline du Château, 06300 Nice; tel. 4-93-80-47-61; Curator JEAN WURSTHORN.

Musée International d'Art Naïf Anatole Jakovsky: Château Ste Hélène-ave Val-Marie, 06200 Nice; tel. 4-93-71-78-33; fax 4-93-72-34-10; Dir CLAUDE FOURNET; Curator Mme ANNE DEVROYE-STILZ.

Musée National Message Biblique Marc Chagall: Ave du Dr Ménard, 06000 Nice; tel. 4-93-53-87-20; fax 4-93-53-87-39; f. 1973; permanent collection of the artist's biblical works; temporary exhibitions; library of 3,000 vols; Curator JEAN LACAMBRE.

Nîmes

Musée archéologique: 13 blvd Amiral-Courbet, 30000 Nîmes; tel. 4-66-67-25-57; fax 4-66-21-33-23; f. 1823; protohistoric and Gallic and Roman archaeology; library of 6,000 vols; Curator DOMINIQUE DARDE.

Musée d'Art Contemporain: Carré d'Art, place de la Maison Carrée, 30000 Nîmes, tel. 4-66-76-35-70; fax 4-66-76-35-85; Dir GUY TOSATTO.

Musée d'Histoire Naturelle et de Préhistoire: 13 blvd Amiral-Courbet, 30000 Nîmes; tel. 4-66-67-25-57; library of 3,000 vols; Curator RENÉ JEANTET.

Musée du Vieux Nîmes: Mairie de Nîmes, Place de l'Hôtel de Ville, 30033 Nîmes Cedex; located at: Place aux Herbes, 30000 Nîmes; tel. 4-66-36-00-64; fax 4-66-21-29-97; f. 1921; local history, folklore and traditional employments; Curator MARTINE NOUGARÈDE.

Orléans

Musée des Beaux-Arts: 1 rue Fernand Rabier, 45000 Orléans; tel. 2-38-79-21-55; fax 2-38-79-20-08; f. 1823; sculpture; French, Flemish, Italian, Dutch, German and Spanish paintings and pastels (especially of 17th and 18th centuries); Max Jacob Room, Malfray and Gaudier-Brzeska rooms; Curator E. MOINET.

Attached museum:

Musée Historique et Archéologique de l'Orléanais: Hôtel Cabu, Place Abbé Desnoyers, Orléans; f. 1855; Roman bronzes, Gallo-Roman collection from Neuvy-en-Sullias, 18th- and 19th-century silverware; popular prints and ceramics from Orléans; Curator E. MOINET.

Paris

Cité des Sciences et de l'Industrie: 30 ave Corentin Cariou, 75930 Paris Cedex 19; tel. 1-40-05-70-00; telex 213785; fax 1-40-05-73-44; f. 1986; located in La Villette complex; permanent exhibitions: the universe, the earth, the environment, space, life, communication, etc; multimedia public library (300,000 vols, 2,700 periodicals, 4,000 films, 1,300 educational software discs), history of science multimedia library, the Louis Braille room for the visually handicapped, Science Newsroom; Pres. GÉRARD THÉRY.

Galerie nationale du Jeu de Paume: 1 Place de la Concorde, 75008 Paris; tel. 1-47-03-12-50; fax 1-47-03-12-51; re-f. 1991; devoted to temporary exhibitions of contemporary art; Dir DANIEL ABADIE.

Galeries nationales du panthéon bouddhique: 19 ave d'Iéna, 75116 Paris; tel. 1-40-73-88-11; Chinese and Japanese art; Curator JEAN-FRANÇOIS JARRIGE.

Maison de Balzac: 47 rue Raynouard, 75016 Paris; tel. 1-42-24-56-38; f. 1971; museum and library of 13,000 books and periodicals; documents relating to life and work of Honoré de Balzac; first editions and autographed letters; comprehensive range of work from the romantic period; Curator JUDITH MEYER-PETIT; publs catalogues and documents.

Maison de Victor Hugo: 6 place des Vosges, 75004 Paris; tel. 1-42-72-10-16; fax 1-42-72-06-64; f. 1903; personal belongings, correspondence, first editions; library of 8,000 vols, 3,000 pamphlets; drawings by Victor Hugo, etc.; Chief Curator DANIELLE MOLINARI.

Musée Astronomique de l'Observatoire de Paris: 61 ave de l'Observatoire, 75014

Paris; f. 1667; astronomical instruments of the 16th, 17th, 18th and 19th centuries; statues and pictures of celebrated astronomers.

Musée Carnavalet: 23 rue de Sévigné, 75003 Paris; tel. 1-42-72-21-13; fax 1-42-72-01-61; f. 1880; archaeology and history of Paris and of the Revolution, dept of prints and drawings; Chief Curator JEAN-MARC LÉRI; publ. *Bulletin* (annually).

Musée Cernuschi: 7 ave Vélasquez, 75008 Paris; tel. 1-45-63-50-75; fax 1-45-63-78-16; f. 1896; Chinese art; Dir GILLES BEGUIN; publs catalogues.

Musée Cognacq-Jay: 8 rue Elzévir, 75003 Paris; tel. 1-40-27-07-21; fax 1-40-27-89-44; f. 1929; 18th-century works of art, French and English paintings, pastels, sculptures, porcelain, furniture, etc; Curator JACQUELINE LAFARGUE.

Musée d'Art Moderne de la Ville de Paris: 9 rue Gaston de Saint-Paul, 75116 Paris; located at: 11 ave du Président Wilson, 75116 Paris; tel. 1-53-67-40-00; fax 1-47-23-35-98; f. 1961; modern and contemporary art; Curator SUZANNE PAGE.

Musée d'Ennery: 59 ave Foch, 75116 Paris; tel. 1-45-53-57-96; fax 1-45-05-02-66; f. 1903; 17th- to 19th-century Far East decorative arts; Curator JEAN-FRANÇOIS JARRIGE.

Musée d'Histoire Contemporaine: Hôtel National des Invalides, 75007 Paris; tel. 1-45-51-93-02; f. 1914; attached to Bibliothèque de Documentation Internationale Contemporaine (see under University Libraries); 400,000 documents (paintings, engravings, posters, cartoons, etc.); 800,000 photographs and postcards; tel. 44-42-54-91; Curator LAURENT GERVEREAU.

Musée d'Orsay: 1 rue de Bellechasse, 75007 Paris; tel. 1-40-49-48-14; telex 201717; fax 1-45-44-63-82; f. 1986; works from the second half of the 19th century and early 20th century; paintings and pastels, sculptures, art objects, photographs, also plans, sketches, etc.; audiovisual information, database, cultural service, exhibitions and dossier-exhibitions, cinema, lectures, concerts; Dir HENRI LOYRETTE.

Musée de l'Air et de l'Espace: BP 173, Aéroport du Bourget, 4-93352 Le Bourget Cedex; tel. 1-49-92-71-99; fax 1-49-92-70-95; f. 1919; aeronautics, representative collection of aircraft; library of 30,000 vols; Dir Gen. JEAN-PAUL SIFFRE; publ. *Pégase* (quarterly).

Musée de l'Armée: Hôtel des Invalides, 75007 Paris; tel. 1-44-42-37-67; f. 1905; collections of artillery, arms, armour, uniforms, flags; history of French Army from its origin to present day; library of 50,000 vols, 60,000 prints, 74,400 photographs; Dir B. DEVAUX; publ. *Revue de la Société des Amis du Musée de l'Armée* (annually).

Musée de l'Histoire de France: Centre historique des Archives nationales, 60 rue des Francs-Bourgeois, 75141 Paris Cedex 03; tel. 1-40-27-62-18; fax 1-40-27-66-45; f. 1867; frequent exhibitions showing original documents from the National Archives tracing the principal events in the history of France; also historical objects and iconography; Dir MARIE-PAULE ARNAULD; Curator LUC FORLIVESI.

Musée de l'Homme: Palais de Chaillot, place du Trocadéro, 75116 Paris; tel. 1-44-05-72-72; f. 1878; library of 250,000 vols, 5,000 periodicals, 1,000 microfiches; ethnography, anthropology, prehistory; attached to the Muséum National d'Histoire Naturelle (*q.v.*); also a research and education centre; Profs BERNARD DUPAIGNE, ANDRÉ LANGANEY, HENRY DE LUMLEY.

Musée de l'Orangerie: Jardin des Tuileries, 75001 Paris; tel. 1-42-97-48-16; permanent exhibition of the 'Nymphéas' (Water Lilies) murals by Claude Monet, and Walter-Guillaume collection; Dir PIERRE GEORGEL.

Musée de la Marine: Palais de Chaillot, Place du Trocadéro et du 11 novembre, 75116 Paris; tel. 1-53-65-69-69 ext. 130; fax 1-53-65-69-46; f. 1827; collection of models and paintings of the navy; oceanographic research; library of 50,000 documents, 176,000 photographs; Dir Rear-Adm. GEORGES PRUD'HOMME; publs *Neptunia* (quarterly), catalogues.

Musée de la Monnaie: Monnaie de Paris, 11 quai de Conti, 75270 Paris Cedex 06; tel. 1-40-46-55-33; fax 1-40-46-57-09; f. 1771; collections of coins, medals, drawings, paintings, old machines, engravings and stained glass windows; Dir EVELYNE COHEN.

Musée des Monuments Français (fmrly Musée de Sculpture Comparée): Palais de Chaillot, Place du Trocadéro, 75116 Paris; tel. 1-44-05-39-10; fax 1-47-55-40-13; f. 1882; library: 10,000 works on history of art, 200,000 photographs, collection of scale reproductions of murals of the Middle Ages and materials connected with building and decoration; casts of portions of monuments and sculptures from beginning of Christianity to 20th century; architectural models; Dir GUY COGEVAL; publ. *Guides*. (In 1998 the museum was reported to be closed for refurbishment.)

Musée des Plans en Reliefs: Hôtel National des Invalides, 75007 Paris; tel. 1-45-51-95-05; fax 1-47-05-11-07; f. 1668; models of fortified towns of the French border. (Part of the museum was reported in 1998 to be closed for restoration, but a provisional exhibition explained the history of the collection and siege warfare.)

Musée du Louvre: 75058 Paris Cedex 01; tel. 1-40-20-50-50; fax 1-40-20-54-42; f. 1793; Dir PIERRE ROSENBERG; depts and curators: Oriental Antiquities (ANNIE CAUBET), Egyptian Antiquities (CHRISTIANE ZIEGLER), Greek, Etruscan and Roman Antiquities (ALAIN PASQUIER), Sculpture (JEAN-RENÉ GABORIT), *Objets d'art* (DANIEL ALCOUFFE), Paintings (JEAN-PIERRE CUZIN), Drawings and Prints (FRANÇOISE VIATTE).

Musée du Petit Palais: Ave Winston Churchill, 75008 Paris; tel. 1-42-65-12-73; fax 1-42-65-24-60; municipal museum, f. 1900; paintings, sculptures and works of art from antiquity to 1925; Dir Mlle THÉRÈSE BUROLLET.

Musée Galliera: 10 ave Pierre Ier de Serbie, 75116 Paris; tel. 1-47-20-85-23; fax 1-47-23-38-37; f. 1977; temporary exhibitions of French costumes and accessories from 1725 to the present day; library; Curator CATHERINE JOIN-DIETERLE; publs catalogues.

Musée Gustave Moreau: 14 rue de la Rochefoucauld, 75009 Paris; tel. 1-48-74-38-50; fax 1-48-74-18-71; f. 1902 from a bequest by the painter Gustave Moreau of his house and contents, including paintings, watercolours, sketches, wax sculptures and designs; Curator GENEVIÈVE LACAMBRE.

Musée Jacquemart-André: 158 blvd Haussmann, 75008 Paris; tel. 1-42-89-04-91; f. 1912; painting, tapestry and furniture from Renaissance to 18th century.

Musée Marmottan: 2 rue Louis Boilly, 75016 Paris; tel. 1-42-24-07-02; fax 1-40-50-65-84; f. 1932; Primitives, Renaissance, Empire and Impressionists; Wildenstein Collection of medieval miniatures; permanent exhibition 'Monet et ses Amis'; affiliated to the *Académie des Beaux-Arts – Fondation Rouart*; Dir ARNAUD D'HAUTERIVES.

Musée National d'Art Moderne: 75191 Paris Cedex 04; tel. 1-44-78-12-33; attached to Centre National d'Art et de Culture Georges-Pompidou; 20th-century painting, sculpture, prints, drawings, photographs, art films; Dir WERNER SPIES.

Musée National de la Légion d'Honneur et des Ordres de Chevalerie: 2 rue de Bellechasse, 75007 Paris; tel. 1-40-62-84-25; fax 1-47-53-79-50; f. 1925; contains histories of National Orders from the Middle Ages until the present and Awards of all countries: unique collection of decorations, costumes, arms, documents, etc.; Centre de Documentation International de l'Histoire des Ordres et des Décorations; also collection and documents relating to Napoleon I; Dir-Curator ELIZABETH PAULY.

Musée National des Arts Asiatiques Guimet: 6 place d'Iéna, 75116 Paris; tel. 1-47-23-61-65; fax 1-47-20-57-50; f. 1889; Asiatic Dept of National Museums; library of 100,000 vols; art, archaeology, religions, history, literature and music of India, Central Asia, Tibet, Afghanistan, China, Korea and Japan, Khmer, Thailand and Indonesia; Chief Curator JEAN-FRANÇOIS JARRIGE; Librarian F. MACOUIN; publs *Annales, Arts Asiatiques*. (Much of the museum, though not the library, was expected to be closed until 1999.)

Musée National des Arts d'Afrique et d'Océanie: 293 ave Daumesnil, 75012 Paris; tel. 1-44-74-84-80; f. 1931 as Musée des Colonies, 1935 Musée de la France d'Outre-Mer, present name 1960; exhibits from Maghreb, Africa and the Pacific Islands; tropical aquarium; temporary exhibitions; library of *c.* 5,000 vols, 160 periodicals; Dir JEAN-HUBERT MARTIN.

Musée National des Arts et Traditions Populaires: 6 ave du Mahatma Gandhi, 75116 Paris; tel. 1-44-17-60-00; fax 1-44-17-60-60; f. 1937; 142,000 objects; library of 90,000 books, 2,000 periodicals; 281,000 photographic documents, 70,000 tape records; Curator MICHEL COLARDELLE; publs *Architecture rurale française, Mobilier traditionnel français, Récits et contes populaires, Archives d'Ethnologie Française, Guides Ethnologiques, Catalogues des Expositions, Ethnologie française* (4 a year).

Musée National des Techniques: 292 rue St Martin, 75003 Paris; tel. 1-40-27-23-71; fax 1-40-27-26-62; f. 1794; evolution of industrial technology from 16th century to present day; Dir DOMINIQUE FERRIOT.

Musée National du Moyen Âge: Thermes et Hôtel de Cluny, 6 place Paul Painlevé, 75005 Paris; tel. 1-53-73-78-00; fax 1-43-25-85-27; e-mail mnma@cluny.culture.fr; f. 1843; everyday life and fine and decorative arts of the Middle Ages; Dir VIVIANE HUCHARD.

Musée Picasso: 5 rue de Thorigny, 75003 Paris; tel. 1-42-71-25-21; fax 1-48-04-75-46; f. 1985 from a collection begun in 1979; traces the evolution of Picasso's art; 251 paintings, 160 sculptures, 107 ceramics, 1,500 drawings and engravings; library of *c.* 2,000 vols on Picasso and his world; Chief Curator GÉRARD RÉGNIER; publs catalogues and guides.

Musée Rodin: Hôtel Biron, 77 rue de Varenne, 75007 Paris; tel. 1-44-18-61-10; fax 1-45-51-17-52; e-mail penseur@musee-rodin.fr; f. 1919; sculpture and drawings by Rodin and objects from his collections; annexe in Meudon; Dir JACQUES VILAIN.

Muséum National d'Histoire Naturelle: see under State Colleges.

Palais de la Découverte: Ave Franklin D. Roosevelt, 75008 Paris; tel. 1-40-74-80-00; fax 1-40-74-81-81; f. 1937 as a scientific centre for the popularization of science; experiments explained to the public; departments of mathematics, astronomy, physics, chemistry, biology, medicine, earth sciences; also includes a Planetarium and cinema; library of 7,000 vols; Dir MICHEL DEMAZURE; publs *Revue*, *Monographies*.

Palais du Cinéma: Palais de Tokyo, 24 rue Hamelin, 75116 Paris; tel. 1-45-53-74-74; fax 1-45-53-74-76; exhibitions concerning motion pictures; motion picture theatres; library and film archive; Dir XAVIER NORTH. (The Palais is closed for refurbishment until 1999.)

Pavillon de l'Arsenal: 21 blvd Morland, 75004 Paris; tel. 1-42-76-33-97; fax 1-42-76-26-32; f. 1988; information and documentation centre on urban planning and architecture; permanent exhibition on Paris; temporary exhibitions, photo library, educational facilities, etc.; Dir Mme ANN-JOSÉ ARLOT; publs catalogues.

Pavillon des Arts: 101 rue Rambuteau, 75001 Paris; tel. 1-42-33-82-50; fax 1-40-28-93-22; f. 1983; municipal art gallery for temporary exhibitions; Dir BÉATRICE RIOTTOT EL-HABIB.

Union Centrale des Arts Décoratifs: Palais du Louvre, 107 rue de Rivoli, 75001 Paris; tel. 1-44-55-57-50; f. 1864; Gen. Man. GUY AMSELLEM; Gen. Curator MARIE-CLAUDE BEAUD

Includes:

Musée des Arts Décoratifs: Palais du Louvre, 107 rue de Rivoli, 75001 Paris; f. 1883; collection from middle ages to the present: woodwork, sculpture, tapestries, textiles, jewels, ceramics, furniture, painting, gold and silver work, glass; library of 100,000 vols, 1,500 periodicals.

Musée Nissim de Camondo: 63 rue de Monceau, 75008 Paris; tel. 1-53-89-06-40; bequeathed by Count Moïse de Camondo who collected unique 18th-century objects in his Hôtel Parc Monceau.

Musée de la Publicité: Palais du Louvre, 107 rue de Rivoli, 75001 Paris; tel. 1-44-55-57-50; permanent exhibitions (from June 1998), an advertising film library, a library open to the public, a documentation centre for publicity.

Musée de la Mode et du Textile: Palais du Louvre, 111 rue de Rivoli, 75001 Paris; tel. 1-44-55-57-50; f. 1985; fashion and textiles from 17th century to present.

Pau

Musée Bernadotte: 8 rue Tran, 64000 Pau; tel. 5-59-27-48-42; f. 1935; pictures and documents tracing the career of Jean Baptiste Bernadotte, Marshal under Napoleon, later King of Sweden; Swedish pictures; Curator PH. COMTE; publ. *Bulletin* (annually).

Musée des Beaux-Arts: 64000 Pau; tel. 5-59-27-33-02; f. 1864; pictures from French, Flemish, Dutch, English, Italian and Spanish schools; contemporary artists; sculptures, engravings and drawings; numismatic collections; Curator PH. COMTE.

Musée National du Château de Pau: 64000 Pau; tel. 5-59-82-38-00; f. 1927; 16th- and 17th-century collection of tapestries; state apartments of King Louis-Philippe I and Napoleon III; decorative arts and paintings on the legend of King Henry IV; engravings, drawings and 16th- and 17th-century library; Curator PAUL MIRONNEAU; publ. *Bulletin* (quarterly).

Musée Régional Béarnais: 64000 Pau; tel. 5-59-27-07-36; a collection relating to the Bearnese country.

Perpignan

Casa Pairal, Musée Catalan des Arts et Traditions Populaires: Mairie de Perpignan, BP 931, 66931 Perpignan Cedex; located at: Le Castillet, Place de Verdun, 66000 Perpignan; tel. 4-68-35-42-05; f. 1963; ethnography, folklore and anthropology of the Catalan region; Curator JACQUES-GASPARD DELONCLE; publ. brochure.

Poitiers

Conservation des Musées de Poitiers: 3 bis rue Jean-Jaurès, 86000 Poitiers; tel. 5-49-41-07-53; fax 5-49-88-61-63; f. 1794; library of 10,000 vols, 50 periodicals; Curators MICHEL REROLLE, MARIE-CHRISTINE PLANCHARD, MARYSE REDIEN, PHILIPPE BATA.

Comprises:

Baptistère Saint-Jean: Rue Jean-Jaurès, 86000 Poitiers; f. 1836; Merovingian archaeology.

Hypogée des Dunes: 101 rue du Père de la Croix, 86000 Poitiers; f. 1909; 7th- to 8th-century Merovingian archaeology.

Musée Sainte-Croix: 3 bis rue Jean-Jaurès, 86000 Poitiers; tel. 5-49-41-07-53; f. 1974; fine arts, history of Poitou (archaeological, ethnographical collections, sculpture and paintings post 1800).

Musée Rupert de Chièvres: 9 rue Victor Hugo, 86000 Poitiers; f. 1887; reconstruction of a 19th-century collector's private house; pre-1800 paintings, furniture, objets d'art.

Reims

Musée des Beaux-Arts: 8 rue Chanzy, 51100 Reims; tel. 3-26-47-28-44; fax 3-26-86-87-75; f. 1795; paintings (especially French School, 17th-century Le Nain, and 19th-century Corot–Delacroix), and Cranach drawings; 15th- and 16th-century 'Toiles Peintes'; collection of ceramics; Curator CATHERINE DELOT.

Musée Saint-Remi: 53 rue Simon, 51100 Reims; tel. 3-26-85-23-36; fax 3-26-82-07-99; the old Abbey of St Remi (12th to 18th centuries); Prehistoric, Celtic, Gallo-Roman, Romanesque and Gothic antiquities and sculptures; tapestries of St-Remi life (1530); old weapons; Chief Curator MARC BOUXIN.

Rennes

Musée de Bretagne: 20 quai Emile Zola, 35000 Rennes; tel. 2-99-28-55-84; fax 2-99-28-40-17; f. 1960; geology, prehistory, Armorica at the Roman period, medieval art, historical documents, popular art, furniture, 19th-century costumes, contemporary regional art and history; Curators J. Y. VEILLARD, FRANÇOIS HUBERT, LAURENCE PROD'HOMME, ERIC MORIN.

Musée des Beaux-Arts: 20 quai Emile Zola, 35000 Rennes; tel. 2-99-28-55-85; fax 2-99-28-55-99; f. 1799; paintings, drawings, engravings, sculpture of French and foreign Schools from the 15th century; archaeology; library of 35,000 vols; Curator LAURENT SALOMÉ.

Rouen

Musée des Beaux-Arts: Square Verdrel, 76000 Rouen; tel. 2-35-71-28-40; fax 2-35-15-43-23; f. 1801; paintings, drawings, sculpture, decorative art; Dir CLAUDE PÉTRY.

Rueil-Malmaison

Musée National des Châteaux de Malmaison et de Bois-Préau: 92500 Rueil-Malmaison; tel. 1-41-29-05-55; fax 1-41-29-05-56; f. 1906; historical collection of Napoleon I and Josephine; Curator BERNARD CHEVALLIER.

St-Denis

Musée d'Art et d'Histoire: 22 bis rue Gabriel Péri, 93200 St-Denis; tel. 1-42-43-05-10; f. 1901, moved 1981 to buildings of a disused 17th-century Carmelite monastery; collections: medieval archaeology and ceramics; history and memorabilia from the monastery and Madame Louise; the Paris Commune; paintings by Albert André; Paul Eluard and Francis Jourdain collections; remains of the old hospital; documentation room for researchers and students; Curator SYLVIE GONZALEZ.

St-Etienne

Musée d'Art et d'Industrie: Place Louis Comte, 42000 St-Etienne; tel. 4-77-33-04-85; f. 1833, at Palais des Arts since 1850; armaments, fabrics, bicycles; Curator NADINE BESSE. (Closed until 1998).

Attached museums:

Musée d'Art Moderne: La Terrasse, 42000 St-Etienne; tel. 4-77-79-52-52; fax 4-77-79-52-50; f. 1987; collection of modern and contemporary art; library; Curator BERNARD CEYSSON.

Musée de la Mine: 3 blvd Franchet d'Esperey, 42000 St-Etienne; tel. 4-77-43-83-23; fax 4-77-43-83-29; mining and industrial museum on the site of a former working mine.

St-Germain-en-Laye

Musée des Antiquités Nationales: 78103 St-Germain-en-Laye; tel. 1-39-10-13-00; f. 1862; Prehistoric, Bronze Age, Celtic, Gallo-Roman and Merovingian antiquities, comparative archaeology; library of 20,000 vols; Chief Curator PATRICK PÉRIN; publ. *Antiquités nationales* (annually).

St-Malo

Musée de St-Malo: Château de St-Malo, 35400 St-Malo; tel. 2-99-40-71-57; f. 1950; history of Saint-Malo and temporary exhibitions; Curator PH. PETOUT.

Attached museum:

Musée International du Long Cours: Tour Solidor, St-Servan, 35400 St-Malo; tel. 2-99-40-71-58; f. 1969; international history of sailing around the world, 16th to 20th centuries; Curator PH. PETOUT.

St-Paul-de-Vence

Fondation Maeght: 06570 St-Paul-de-Vence; f. 1964; tel. 4-93-32-81-63; fax 4-93-32-53-22; modern paintings and sculpture; library of 23,000 vols on modern arts and daily films on art and artists; Curator JEAN-LOUIS PRAT.

St-Tropez

L'Annonciade, Musée de St-Tropez: Place Georges Grammont, 83990 St-Tropez; tel. 4-94-97-04-01; fax 4-94-97-87-24; f. 1955; French paintings from 1890 to 1950; Curator JEAN-PAUL MONERY.

Saumur

Château Musée: Le Château, 49400 Saumur; tel. 2-41-51-30-46; fax 2-41-67-78-35; f. 1829 and reorganized 1960; local archaeology, the collection of Comte Charles Lair of decorative arts, including tapestries, furniture, wood carvings, liturgical ornaments; fine porcelain of 16th to 18th centuries; Curator Mlle JACQUELINE MONGELLAZ.

Sceaux

Musée de l'Ile de France: Château de Sceaux, 92330 Sceaux; tel. 1-46-61-06-71; fax 1-46-61-00-88; f. 1935; old and modern paintings, sculpture, engravings, furniture, decorative art, tapestries, history and drawings of the environs of Paris; documentation centre on the Paris region; educational services; documentation centre; annexes: Orangerie and Pavillon de l'Aurore (Parc de Sceaux); Dir CECILE DUPONT-LOGIÉ.

Sèvres

Musée National de Céramique: Place de la Manufacture, 92310 Sèvres; tel. 1-41-14-04-20; fax 1-45-34-67-88; f. 1824; ancient and modern ceramic art; Curator ANTOINETTE

HALLÉ; publ. *Revue de la Société des Amis du Musée National de Céramique* (annually).

Soissons

Musée Municipal: 2 rue de la Congrégation, 02200 Soissons; tel. 3-23-59-15-90; f. 1857; antiquities, medieval sculpture, paintings of 17th to 20th centuries, local history and prehistory; Curators DENIS DEFENTE, DOMINIQUE ROUSSEL.

Strasbourg

Palais Rohan: 2 place du Château, 67000 Strasbourg; tel. 3-88-52-50-00; fax 3-88-52-50-09.

Attached museums:

Musée Archéologique: C/o Palais Rohan, 2 place du Château, 67000 Strasbourg; f. 1856; prehistoric, Celtic, Gallo-Roman and Merovingian collections; results of excavations in Alsace; Curator B. SCHNITZLER.

Musée des Arts Décoratifs et Appartements Historiques: C/o Palais Rohan, 2 place du Château, 67000 Strasbourg; f. 1883; 18th- and 19th-century furniture; French paintings; ceramics; silver objects; musical instruments; wrought-iron and tin; Curator E. MARTIN.

Musée des Beaux-Arts: C/o Palais Rohan, 2 place du Château, 67000 Strasbourg; f. 1801; French and foreign paintings: Old Masters, 14th–19th-century, Italian, Spanish, Flemish, Dutch and French schools; Curator J. L. FAURE.

Toulouse

Musée des Augustins: 21 rue de Metz, 31000 Toulouse; tel. 5-61-22-21-82; fax 5-61-22-34-69; e-mail courrier@augustins.org; f. 1793 and housed in the former Augustine Convent, of which parts date from the 14th and 15th centuries; Roman and Gothic sculptures, local and foreign paintings; Curator ALAIN DAGUERRE DE HUREAUX.

Tours

Musée de la Société Archéologique de Touraine: Hôtel Gouin, 25 rue du Commerce, 37000 Tours; tel. 2-47-66-22-32; Gallic and Roman archaeology, medieval and 16th-century sculptures; iconography of Tours, 18th- and 19th-century pottery.

Musée des Beaux-Arts: 18 place François-Sicard, 37000 Tours; tel. 2-47-05-68-73; fax 2-47-05-38-91; f. 1793 and moved in 1910 to the former Archbishop's palace dating from the 17th and 18th centuries; paintings by Mantegna, Rubens, Vignon, Lancret, Boucher, Delacroix, Degas, Debré; sculpture by Le Moyne, Houdon, Bourdelle, Davidson, Calder; furniture, tapestries and objets d'art; Curator PHILIPPE LE LEYZOUR.

Affiliated museums:

Château d'Azay-le-Ferron: 36290 Azay-le-Ferron; tel. 2-54-39-20-06; buildings, objets d'art and furniture of the 16th to early 19th century. (In 1998 the Château was reported to be closed to the public.)

Musée Saint-Martin: 3 rue Rapin, 37000 Tours; tel. 2-47-64-48-87; fax 2-47-05-38-91; contains collection of souvenirs of St Martin.

Musée des Vins de Touraine: 16 rue Nationale (parvis Saint-Julien), 37000 Tours; tel. 2-47-61-07-93; f. 1975; Curator LAURENT BASTARD.

Musée du Compagnonnage: 8 rue Nationale, 37000 Tours; tel. 2-47-61-07-93; f. 1968; archives and historical masterpieces; Curator LAURENT BASTARD.

Ungersheim

Ecomusée d'Alsace: BP 71, 68190 Ungersheim; tel. 3-89-74-44-74; fax 3-89-48-15-30; f. 1984 by the Asscn Maisons Paysannes d'Alsace to safeguard the rural architecture of Alsace; an open-air museum comprising a reconstituted village of 70 cottages, showing life in olden days with a baker, an oil-mill, a blacksmith, a clog-maker, a sawmill working on site; nature walks, seminars, etc.; library of 950 vols, 4,000 drawings and reliefs, 25,000 photographs, videos; Pres. MARC GRODWOHL.

Vaison-la-Romaine

Musée Archéologique Théo Desplans: Colline de Puymin, 84110 Vaison-la-Romaine; tel. 4-90-36-50-00; fax 4-90-36-50-29; f. 1920, present site 1975; archaeological collection from excavations at Vaison; Curator CHRISTINE BEZIN.

Valenciennes

Musée des Beaux-Arts: blvd Watteau, 59300 Valenciennes; tel. 3-27-22-57-20; fax 3-27-22-57-22; painting, sculpture, archaeology, etc; Dir P. RAMADE.

Vallauris

Musée National Picasso 'La Guerre et la Paix': Place de la Libération, 06220 Vallauris; tel. 4-93-64-16-05; fax 4-93-64-50-32; f. 1959; works by Picasso including *La Guerre et la Paix* in 12th-century chapel; Curator JEAN LACAMBRE.

Verdun

Musée des Trois Guerres: Verdun; f. 1920; museum of the wars of 1870, 1914, 1939, Indochina, Suez, Algeria; Curator Comte R. DE LA ROCHEFOUCAULD.

Versailles

Musée National du Château de Versailles: 78000 Versailles; tel. 1-30-84-74-00; fax 1-30-84-76-48; f. 1837 by Louis-Philippe; historical painting and sculpture, furniture of the 17th to 19th centuries; Grand Trianon, Petit Trianon châteaux, Hameau de la Reine, park; Pres. HUBERT ASTIER.

Vizille

Musée de la Révolution Française: Château de Vizille, 38220 Vizille; tel. 4-76-68-07-35; fax 4-76-68-08-53; f. 1984; relics and art connected with the French Revolution of 1789; library of 16,000 vols, 25,000 microfiches; Dir ALAIN CHEVALIER.

State Universities

UNIVERSITÉ D'AIX-MARSEILLE I (UNIVERSITÉ DE PROVENCE)

3 place Victor Hugo, 13331 Marseille Cedex 3

Telephone: 4-91-10-60-00
Telex: 402014
Fax: 4-91-10-60-06

Founded 1970

President: GÉRARD DUFOUR
Vice-Presidents: YVES MATHIEU, JEAN-MARC FABRE, ROGER MARTIN
Secretary-General: LUCIEN DONNADIEU
Librarian: Mme GACHON

Library: see Libraries
Number of students: 26,000
Publication: *Guide de l'Etudiant.*

TEACHING AND RESEARCH UNITS

Aix-en Provence:

Psychology and Education Sciences: Dir CLAUDE BASTIEN
Anglo-Saxon and Germanic Languages: Dir DANIELLE BONNEAU
Civilization and Humanities: Dir GILLES DORIVAL
Literature, Art, Communication and Linguistics: Dir CLAUDE MAURON
Oriental, Slavonic, Romance Languages and Latin American Studies: Dir BARNARD MARTOCQ
Geography and Development: Dir MIREILLE PROVENSAL
Centre for the Training of Musicians at Nursery and Primary Schools: Dir YVES DARIE

Marseille:

Life Sciences, Earth Sciences and Environment: Dir JEAN PHILIP
Physical Sciences: Dir GILBERT ALBINET
Mathematics, Computer Science, Mechanics: Dir JIMMY ELHADAD
University Institute for Industrial Thermal Systems: Dir PATRICK GAUNE
Charles Fabry Institute for Training in Engineering: Dr JEAN-PIERRE SORBIER
Observatory: 2 place Leverrier, 13248 Marseille Cedex 04; Dir GEORGES COMTE

UNIVERSITÉ D'AIX-MARSEILLE II

Jardin du Pharo, 58 blvd Charles Livon, 13284 Marseille Cedex 07

Telephone: 4-91-39-65-00
Fax: 4-91-31-31-36

Founded 1973

Language of instruction: French
Academic year: October to June

President: DIDIER RAOULT
Vice-Presidents: ANDRÉ CARTAPANIS (Administrative Council), DANIEL DUFRESNE (Council of Studies and University Life), PIERRE MERY
Secretary-General: DOMINIQUE MARCHAND

Number of teachers: 1,166
Number of students: 19,160

TEACHING AND RESEARCH UNITS

Faculty of Economic Science: 14 ave Jules Ferry, 13621 Aix-en-Provence Cedex; tel. 4-42-33-48-00; fax 4-42-33-48-07; Dir ANDRÉ CARTAPANIS.
Institute of Labour: 12 traverse Saint-Pierre, 13100 Aix-en-Provence; tel. 4-42-21-40-37; fax 4-42-21-20-12; Dir JEAN RISACHER.
Institute of Technology: Ave Gaston Berger, 13625 Aix-en-Provence Cedex 1; tel. 4-42-93-90-00; fax 4-42-93-90-90; Dir R. KAZAN.
Faculty of Medicine: 27 blvd Jean Moulin, 13385 Marseille Cedex 5; tel. 4-91-32-43-00; fax 4-91-32-44-96; Dir GERARD GUERINEL.
Faculty of Pharmacy: 27 blvd Jean Moulin, 13385 Marseille Cedex 5; tel. 4-91-83-55-00; fax 4-91-80-26-12; Dir PIERRE TIMON-DAVID.
Faculty of Dental Surgery: 27 blvd Jean Moulin, 13385 Marseille; tel. 4-91-78-46-70; fax 4-91-78-23-43; Dir HENRY ZATTARA.
Faculty of Physical Education and Sport: 163 ave de Luminy, Case 910, 13288 Marseille Cedex 9; tel. 4-91-17-04-13; fax 4-91-17-04-19; Dir PIERRE THERME.
Faculty of Science: 163 ave de Luminy, 13288 Marseille Cedex 9; tel. 4-91-82-90-00; fax 4-91-82-92-00; Dir PIERRE MERY.
Institute of Mechanics: UNIMECA, Technopôle de Château Gombert, 60 rue Joliot Curie, 13453 Marseille Cedex 13; tel. 4-91-11-38-00; fax 4-91-11-38-38; Dir DANIEL DUFRESNE.
School of Mechanics: I.M.T., Technopôle de Château-Gombert, 13451 Marseille Cedex 20; tel. 4-91-05-44-34; fax 4-91-05-45-98; Dir ROBERT PELISSIER.
Oceanological Centre: Station Marine d'Endoume, 1 rue de la Batterie des Lions, 13007 Marseille; tel. 4-91-04-16-00; fax 4-91-04-16-35; Dir LUCIEN LAUBIEN.
School of Journalism and Communication: 21 rue Virgile Marron, 13392 Marseille Cedex 05; tel. 4-91-24-32-00; fax 4-91-48-73-59; Dir PATRICK BADILLO.
School of Engineering: 163 ave de Luminy, 13288 Marseille Cedex 9; tel. 4-91-82-85-00; fax 4-91-82-85-91; Dir JEAN-JACQUES AUBERT.

ATTACHED INSTITUTES

Centre de Recherche pour l'Enseignement des Mathématiques (IREM): Faculté des Sciences de Luminy, 163 ave de Luminy, 13288 Marseille Cedex 9; tel. 4-91-26-90-91; fax 4-91-26-93-43; research into the teaching of mathematics; Dir ROBERT ROLLAND.

Centre International de Formation et de Recherche en Didactique (CIFORD): Faculté des Sciences de Luminy, 163 ave de Luminy, 13288 Marseille Cedex 9; tel. 4-91-26-90-30; fax 4-91-26-93-55; Dir PAUL ALLARD.

Centre Universitaire Régional d'Etudes Municipales (CURET): 191 rue Breteuil, 13006 Marseille; tel. 4-91-37-61-62; fax 4-91-37-61-63; courses in local government administration; Dir M. FOUCHET.

Institut Universitaire Professionnalisé (IUP) Affaires et Finances: Faculté des Sciences Economiques, 14 ave Jules Ferry, 13621 Aix-en-Provence Cedex; tel. 4-42-33-48-70; fax 4-42-33-48-72; course on business and finance.

UNIVERSITÉ D'AIX-MARSEILLE III (UNIVERSITÉ DE DROIT, D'ECONOMIE ET DES SCIENCES)

3 ave Robert Schuman, 13628 Aix-en-Provence Cedex

Telephone: 4-42-17-27-18
Fax: 4-42-64-03-96

Founded 1973

President: C. LOUIT
Vice-Presidents: P. DJONDANG, G. PEIFFER, J. MESTRE, J. Y. NAUDET, D. NAHON
Secretary-General: W. BARKATE
Librarian: J. RODA

Number of teachers: 767
Number of students: 21,713

Publications: *L'Inter Cours* (monthly), *Spécial Etudiant* (every 2 months), *Livret de l'Etudiant* (annually), annual research reports.

DEANS

Faculty of Law and Political Science: J. M. LE BERRE
Faculty of Applied Economics: P. DJONDANG
Faculty of Science and Technology (St Jérôme): G. PEIFFER

TEACHING AND RESEARCH UNITS

Aix-en-Provence: Social Sciences:
Institute of Penal Sciences and Criminology: Dir J. BORRICAND
Institute of Business Law: Dir J. MESTRE
Legal Research Unit: Dir A. ROUX
Institute of Regional Development: Dir A. MOTTE
Institute of Business Management: Dir R. WEISZ
Institute of Political Studies: Dir J. .C. RICCI
Institute of French Studies for Foreign Students: Dir J.-J. BOUSQUET

Marseille: Sciences and Technology:
Propaedeutical Sciences Unit: Dir M. GILLET
Professional Training Unit: Dir G. LESGARDS
Scientific and Technical Research Unit: Dir A. M. SIOUFFI
Higher National School of Synthesis, Processes and Chemical Engineering at Aix-Marseille: Dir J. L. CHEVALIER
Higher National School of Physics: Domaine Universitaire de Saint Jérôme, ave Escadrille Normandie-Niémen, 13397 Marseille Cedex 20; tel. 91-28-86-00; Dir S. HUARD
University Institute of Technology: Dir R. OCCELLI
University Institute of Engineering Sciences: Dir J. C. BERTRAND

UNIVERSITÉ D'ANGERS

40 rue de Rennes, BP 3532, 49035 Angers Cedex

Telephone: 2-41-96-23-17
Fax: 2-41-96-23-00

Founded 1971; formerly Centre Universitaire d'Angers

President: PIERRE JALLET
Vice-President: JACQUES LOUAIL
Secretary-General: JEAN-CLAUDE CONNIN
Librarian: JEAN-CLAUDE BROUILLARD

Number of teachers: 772
Number of students: 16,925

Publication: *Plantes médicinales et phytothérapie, Journal of the Short Story in English, Publications du Centre de Recherche en Littérature et Linguistique de l'Anjou et des Bocages.*

DEANS

Faculty of Medicine: J. C. BIGORGNE
Faculty of Science: A. KERRIOU
Faculty of Law, Economic Sciences and Social Sciences: Y. DOLAIS
Faculty of Letters and Human Sciences: J. DEVOIZE
Faculty of Pharmacy: G. MAURAS

UNIVERSITÉ D'ARTOIS

9 rue du Temple, BP 665, 62030 Arras Cedex

Telephone: 3-21-60-37-00
Fax: 3-21-60-37-37

Founded 1991

Rector: ALAIN LOTTIN (acting)
Secretary-General: MARIE-PAULE DEJONGHE
Librarian: FRANÇOISE ROUBAUD

Number of teachers: 422 (incl. University Institutes of Technology)
Number of students: 11,185 (incl. University Institutes of Technology)

Publication: *Interpôles Artois* (8 a year).

TEACHING AND RESEARCH UNITS

Arras:
Arts: Dir CHRISTIAN MORZEWSKI
Languages: Dir JEAN-JACQUES POLLET
Economic and Social Administration: Dir GILLES FIEVET
History and Geography: Dir DENIS CLAUZEL
Professional University Institute of Heritage and Tourism: Dir CHARLES GIRY-DELOISON
Asian and Pacific Ocean Studies: Dir OLIVIER SEVIN

Béthune:
University School of Economics and Management: Dir AHMED HENNI
Applied Sciences: Dir FRANCIS NOTELET
University Institute of Technology: Dir PIERRE BOULET

Douai:
Law: Dir MANUEL GROS

Lens:
Science: Dir YOLANDE BARBAUX
Science and Technology of Sport and Physical Pursuits: Dir ANDRÉ GIUDICELLI
University Institute of Technology: Dir JOËL MULLER

UNIVERSITÉ D'AVIGNON ET DES PAYS DE VAUCLUSE

74 rue Louis Pasteur, 84029 Avignon Cedex 1

Telephone: 4-90-16-25-00
Fax: 4-90-16-25-10

Founded 1973; formerly UER Lettres et Sciences at the University of Provence

President: HENRI MÉLONI
Secretary-General: MICHEL PATIN
Librarian: Mlle FRANÇOISE FEBVRE

Number of teachers: 215
Number of students: 6,500

TEACHING AND RESEARCH UNITS

Sciences: Dir ANDRE PHILIPPE GALLO
Arts: Dir GUY CHEYMOL
Applied Sciences: Dir CHRISTIAN GROS
Faculty of Law: Dean JEAN VIRET

PROFESSORS

Sciences:
BENOIT, Computer Science
BLAVOUX, Geology
COULOMB, P., Cellular Biology
DE MORI BAJOLIN, Computer Science
DELORME, C., Physics
DUMOLIE, Communication
EL BEZE, M., Computer Science
ESPAGNAC, H., Plant Biology
GUIRAUD, R., Geology
LACOMBE, Chemistry
LAGANIER, Economics
LAMIZET, Communication
MAHÉ, J., Geology
MEDINA, Mathematics
MICHEL, R., Mathematics
PLANQUE, Economics
PUCCI, Chemistry
REIDENBACH, J.-M., Animal Biology
ROGGERO, J.-P., Chemistry
ROUX, B., Mathematics
SEEGER, Mathematics
VIVES, C., Physics
VOLLE, Mathematics
WILLIAMSON, Mathematics

Arts:
ABITEBOUL, English
AGOSTINI, English
AURIAC, F., Geography
BOUVIER-CAVORET, French
BRASSEUR, French
CHARRE, J., Geography
CHEYMOL, G., Literature
CHIFFOLEAU, Medieval History
FERRIÈRES, History
LUYAT, American
PROVOST, Roman History
REY-FLAUD, B., French
RISER, J., Geography
STRUBEL, French
ULPAT, A., English
VELASCO, Spanish

Law:
D'HAUTEVILLE, Law
PASQUALINI, Law
SCOFFONI, G., Law
VIRET, Public Law

ATTACHED INSTITUTES

Institut Universitaire Professionnalisé (IUP) en Génie Informatique et Mathématique: Rue Meinajaries, Agroparc, 84140 Mont Favet; Dir ALAIN SAMUEL.

Institut Universitaire de Technologie (IUT): 2 rue Meinajaries, Agroparc, 84140 Montfavet; Dir SYLVIE VIALA-TAVAKOLI.

UNIVERSITÉ DE BORDEAUX I

351 cours de la Libération, 33405 Talence Cedex

Telephone: 5-56-84-60-00
Fax: 5-56-80-08-37

President: MICHEL COMBARNOUS
Vice-Presidents: DIDIER DESJARDINS (Administration), FRANCIS HARDOUIN (Science), JEAN FRESNEL (Curriculum and University Life)
Secretary-General: MANUEL-ROBERT EDOUARD

Number of students: 14,000

TEACHING AND RESEARCH UNITS

Scientific Studies (First Cycle): Dir MARIE-FRANÇOISE BOURDEAU

Physics: Dir WILLY CLAEYS
Chemistry: Dir FRANÇOIS CARMONA
Mathematics and Computer Science: Dir PAUL MOREL
Biology: Dir JEAN-PAUL TRUCHOT
Earth and Marine Sciences: Dir MICHEL PUJOS

CONSTITUENT INSTITUTES AND SCHOOLS

Ecole d'Ingénieurs des Sciences et Techniques des Aliments (EISTAB): 351 cours de la Libération, 33405 Talence Cedex; tel. 5-56-84-87-60; Dir ANDRÉ DUCASTAING.

Observatoire: Av Pierre Sémirot, 33270 Floirac; tel. 5-56-86-43-30; Dir JACQUES COLIN.

Institut Universitaire de Technologie: Domaine Universitaire, 33405 Talence Cedex; tel. 5-56-84-57-02; Dir PIERRE LAFON.

UNIVERSITY PROFESSIONAL INSTITUTES

University Professional Institute of Electrical Engineering and Industrial Informatics: Dir YVES DANTO.

University Professional Institute of Mechanical Engineering: Dir MICHEL NOUILLANT

University Professional Institute of Computer-Assisted Management: Dir JEAN-GUY PENAUD.

University Professional Institute of Industrial Systems Engineering – Aircraft Maintenance: Dir ROGER LALANNE.

ATTACHED INSTITUTES:

(See under Colleges and Institutes)

École Nationale Supérieure d'Électronique et de Radioélectricité de Bordeaux (ENSERB)

École Nationale Supérieure de Chimie et de Physique de Bordeaux (ENSCPB)

UNIVERSITÉ VICTOR SEGALEN (BORDEAUX II)

146 rue Léo-Saignat, 33076 Bordeaux Cedex

Telephone: 5-57-57-10-10
Telex: 572237
Fax: 5-56-99-03-80

President: JOSY REIFFERS
Secretary-General: CORINNE DUFFAU
Number of teachers: 904
Number of students: 14,628

TEACHING AND RESEARCH UNITS

Medical Sciences I: Dir B. BEGAUD
Medical Sciences II: Dir G. GBIKPI-BENISSAN
Medical Sciences III: Dir P. HENRY
Pharmacy: Dir J. ROQUEBERT
Odontology: Dir G. DORIGNAC
Public Health and Epidemiology: Dir R. SALAMON
Biochemistry and Cellular Biology: Dir P. CANIONI
Social and Psychological Sciences: Dir M. FRESEL-LOZEY
Regional Institute of Physical Education: Dir A. MENAUT
Institute of Oenology: Dir Y. GLORIES
Mathematics, Information and Social Sciences: Dir M. NIKOULINE
Bordeaux Higher Technical School of Biomolecular Science: C. CASSAGNE

AFFILIATED RESEARCH INSTITUTES

Attached to INSERM (*q.v.*):

Unité de Recherche de Psychobiologie des Comportements Adaptifs: Rue Camille Saint-Saëns, 33000 Bordeaux; Dir Prof. LE MOAL.

Unité de Recherche de Structures et Fonctions des Rétrovirus: 229 cours de l'Argonne, 33000 Bordeaux; Dir B. GUILLEMAIN.

Unité de Recherche de Neurobiologie Intégrative: Rue Camille Saint-Saëns, 33000 Bordeaux; Dir R. DANTZER.

Unité de Recherche d'Athérosclérose, Déterminisme Cellulaire et Moléculaire: Dir Prof. J. BONNET.

Unité de Recherche sur la Neurogénétique et Stress: Dir P. MORMÈDE.

Unité de Recherche sur la Biologie Cellulaire et Moléculaire des Cellules Ciliées de l'Audition: Dir D. DULON.

Unité de Recherche sur la Physiologie Mitochondriale: Dir Prof. J. P. MAZAT.

Unité de Recherche sur les Biomatériaux et Réparation Tissulaire: 146 rue Léo-Saignat, 33076 Bordeaux Cedex; Dir C. BAQUEY.

Unité de Recherche d'Épidémiologie, Santé Publique et Développement: Dir R. SALAMON

Unité de Recherche sur la Neurobiologie Morphofonctionelle: 146 rue Léo-Saignat, 33076 Bordeaux Cedex; Dir D. POULAIN.

Unité de Recherche sur la Modulation Artificielle de Gènes Eucaryotes: 146 rue Léo-Saignat, 33076 Bordeaux Cedex; Dir J.-J. TOULME.

Attached to CNRS (*q.v.*):

Institut de Biochimie et Génétique Cellulaires, UPR 9026: Dir Prof. B. GUERIN.

UMR 5543 'Physiologie élémentaire et intégrée des systèmes nerveux et endocriniens': Dir B. DUFY.

UMR 5533 'Hémostase pathologie cellulaire': Dir A. NURDEN.

UMR 5536 'Résonance magnétique des systèmes biologiques': Dir Prof. P. CANIONI.

UPRES-A 5017 'Physiopathologie et pharmacologie vasculaire': Dir J. MIRONNEAU.

UMR 5540 'Immunomodulation par les médiateurs de l'inflammation': Dir Prof. N. GUALDE.

UMR 5541 'Interactions neuronales et comportement': Dir Prof. B. BLOCH.

UMR 5544 'Biogenèse membranaire': Dir Prof. C. CASSAGNE.

Réplication et expression des génomes eucaryotes et rétroviraux': Dir S. LITVAK.

UPRES-A 5016 'Biologie moléculaire et immunologie de protozoaires parasites': Dir Prof. T. BALTZ.

UPRES-A 5036 'Sociétés, santé, développement': Dir C. RAYNAUT.

'Mathématiques du vivant': Dirs Prof. M. LANGLAIS, CH.-H. BRUNEAU.

Attached to INRA (*q.v.*):

Laboratoire de Biologie Cellulaire et Moléculaire: La Grande Ferrade, 33140 Pont de la Maye; Dir M. GARNIER.

Laboratoire de Génétique Moléculaire et Amélioration des Champignons Cultivés: La Grande Ferrade, 33140 Pont de la Maye; Dir Prof. LABARÈRE.

Institut d'Oenologie: 351 cours de la Libération, 33405 Talence; Dir Prof. Y. GLORIES.

Laboratoire de Physiologie Végétale: Dirs PH. RAYMOND, J.-P. GAUDILLÈRE.

UNIVERSITÉ MICHEL DE MONTAIGNE (BORDEAUX III)

Espl. Michel-Montaigne, Domaine Universitaire, 33405 Talence Cedex

Telephone: 5-56-84-50-50
Fax: 5-56-84-50-90

President: Prof. ANNE-MARIE COCULA
Vice-Presidents: Prof. FRÉDÉRIC DUTHEIL, Prof. CHRISTIAN LERAT, Prof. JEAN MONDOT
Secretary-General: ANNE-MARIE DUDEZERT
Chief Librarian: M. GUERIN

Number of teachers: 671
Number of students: 15,886

Publications: *Revue des études anciennes, Cahier d'outre-mer, Bulletin hispanique, Annales du Midi, Revue Géographique des Pyrénées et du Sud-Ouest, Aquitania.*

TEACHING AND RESEARCH UNITS

Letters: JACK CORZANI
Philosophy: Dir CLAUDIE LAVAUD
History: Dir RAYMOND DESCAT
Geography: Dir JEAN-PAUL CHARRIÉ
Language, Literature and Civilization of Anglophone Countries: Dir CHRISTINE BOUVART
Foreign Languages: Dir ROGER BILLION
Germanic Studies: Dir JEAN MONDOT
Iberian and Latin American Studies: Dir JEAN-MICHEL DESVOIS
Institute of Information and Communication Sciences: Dir HUGUES HOTIER
Science, Information, Communication and Arts: Dir JEAN-PIERRE BERTIN-MAGHIT
University Institute of Technology: Dir DANIEL GARREC
Development and Natural Resources: Dir LOUIS HUMBERT
History of Art and Archaeology: Dir JACQUES DES COURTILS

PROFESSORS

ABECASSIS, A., Philosophy
AGOSTINO, M., Contemporary History
AGUILA, Y., Spanish
AUGUSTIN, J.-P., Geography
BARAT, J.-C., English
BART, F., Geography
BAUDRY, P., Sociology
BECHTEL, F., Physics applied to Archaeology
BERIAC, F., Medieval History
BERTIN-MAGHIT, J.-P., Cinema
BESSE, M. G., Portuguese Literature
BOHLER, D., Medieval Languages and Literature
BOST, J.-P., Ancient History
BOUCARUT, M., Petrography
BRAVO, F., Spanish
BRESSON, A., Medieval History
CABANES, J.-L., Contemporary French Literature
CAMBRONNE, P., Latin
CHAMPEAU, G., Spanish
CHARRIE, J.-P., Geography
COCULA, A.-M., Modern History
COCULA, B., French Language
CORZANI, J., Contemporary French Literature
COSTE, D., Comparative Literature
DEBORD, P., Ancient History
DE CARVALHO, P., Latin
DECOUDRAS, P. M., Land and Society in Tropical Environments
DEPRETTO, C., Russian
DESCAT, R., Greek History
DESCHAMPS, L., Latin
DES COURTILS, J., History of Art
DESVOIS, J.-M., Spanish
DI MÉO, G., Geography
DOTTIN ORSINI, M., Comparative Literature
DUBOIS, C., French
DUCASSE, R., Information Science
DURRUTY, S., English
DUTHEIL, F., Italian
DUVAL, G., English
FONDIN, H., Information and Communication Science
FOURTINA, H., English
FRANCHET D'ESPEREY, S., Latin
GARMENDIA, V., Spanish
GAUTHIER, M., American English
GILBERT, B., English
GORCEIX, P., German
GOZE, M., Urban Planning
GRANDJEAT, Y., North American Civilization
GUILLAUME, P., Modern History
GUILLAUME, S., Modern History
HOTIER, H., Information and Communications Science
HUMBERT, L., Geology
JARASSE, D., History of Modern Art
JOLY, M., Image Analysis
JOUVE, M., English

LACHAISE, B., Modern History
LACOSTE, J., History of Art
LAMORE, J., Spanish
LANGHADE, J., Arabic
LARRERE, C., Philosophy
LAVAUD, C., Philosophy
LAVEAU, P., German
LEBIGRE, J.-M., Physical Geography, Biogeography
LEPRUN-PIÉTON, S., Art, Plastic Arts
LERAT, C., English
LOPEZ, F., Spanish
LOUISE, G., Medieval History
LOUPES, P., History
LY, A., Spanish
MAILLARD, J.-C., Geography
MALEZIEUX, J.-M., Geology
MALLET, D., Arabic
MANTION, J.-R., 18th-century French Literature
MARIEU, J., Urban Planning and Projects
MARQUETTE, J.-B., History
MARTIN, D., French Language and Literature
MATHIEU, M., Contemporary Francophone Literature
MAZOUER, C., Contemporary French Literature
MONDOT, J., German
MORIN, S., Tropical Geography
MOULINE, L., Theatre
MULLER, C., General Linguistics
NAVARRI, R., French Language and Literature
NOTZ, M.-F., Medieval Language and Literature
OLLIER, N., English
ORPUSTAN, J.-B., Basque
PAILHE, J., Geography
PELLETIER, N., German
PERRIN-NAFFAKH, A.-M., Contemporary Language and Literature
PERROT, M., Information and Communications Science
PEYLET, G., Contemporary Language and Literature
PICCIONE, M.-L., Contemporary Language and Literature
PONCEAU, J.-P., Medieval Language and Literature
PONTET, J., Modern History
PORTINE, H., Teaching French as a Foreign Language
POUCHAN, P., Geology
RABATE, D., Contemporary French Literature
RAMOND, C., Philosophy
REYNIER-GIRARDIN, C., English
RIBEIRO, M., Portuguese
RICARD, M., Tropical Pacific Phytoplankton
RIGAL-CELLARD, B., English
RITZ, R., English
ROCHER, A., Japanese
RODDAZ, J.-M., Ancient History
ROSSI, G., Geography
ROUCH, M., Italian
ROUDIE, P., Geography
ROUYER, M.-C., English
ROUYER, P., Plastic Art
RUIZ, A, German
SALOMON, J.-N., Geography
SCHVOERER, M., Physics applied to Archaeology
SENTAURENS, J., Spanish
SEVESTRE, N., Music and History of Music
SHEN, J., Applied Mathematics
SHUSTERMAN, R., English
SINGARAVELOU, Geography
TAILLARD, C., History of Modern Art
TERREL, J., Philosophy
VADE, Y., Contemporary Language and Literature
VAGNE-LEBAS, M., Social Communication
VIGNE, M.-P., English
VITALIS, A., Information and Communication Science
VLES, V., Urban Planning
ZAVIALOFF, N., Russian

UNIVERSITÉ MONTESQUIEU (BORDEAUX IV)

Av. Léon-Duguit, 33608 Pessac

Telephone: 56-84-85-86
Fax: 56-37-00-25
E-mail: umb4@montesquieu.u-bordeaux.fr

Founded 1995 from units formerly within the University of Bordeaux I
State control

President: JEAN DU BOIS DE GAUDUSSON
Secretary-General: MARIE-FRANCE DUBERNET
Librarian: D. MONTBRUN-ISRAËL

Number of students: 13,500

TEACHING AND RESEARCH UNITS

Juridical Studies (First Cycle): Dir ANTOINE VIALARD
Private Law and History of Institutions: Dir BERNARD SAINTOURENS
Public Law and Political Science: Dir SLOBODAN MILACIC
Economics and Management Studies: Dir VELAYOUDOM MARIMOUTOU
Intensive Curricula in Economics and Business Studies: Dir SERGE EVRAERT
Management of Economic and Social Institutions: Dir GÉRARD BORDENAVE

CONSTITUENT INSTITUTE

Regional Institute of Management and Business Administration: Dir GÉRARD HIRIGOYEN

ATTACHED INSTITUTE

Institute of Political Studies: Dir PIERRE SADRAN

UNIVERSITÉ DE BOURGOGNE

Maison de l'Université, Esplanade Erasme, BP 138, 21004 Dijon Cedex

Telephone: 3-80-39-50-11
Fax: 3-80-39-50-69

Founded 1722 as Dijon Faculty of Law

President: JOCELYNE PERARD
Secretary-General: D. MARTINY
Librarian: F. HAGENE

Number of students: 29,098

Publications: *Annuaire*, *Journal d'Information*, *Publications de l'Université* (irregular series of monographs), *Limet de la recherche*.

TEACHING AND RESEARCH UNITS

Law, Political and Administrative Science: Dir O. BOUSCARY
Economics and Business Studies: Dir B. ROUGET
Literature and Philosophy: Dir J. FERRARI
Foreign Languages, Literature and Civilization: Dir T. MCCARTHY
Human Sciences: Dir J. CHIFFRE
Mathematics, Computer Science, Physics, Chemistry: Dir J.-C. MARCUARD
Life Sciences and Environment: Dir J.-L. CONNAT
Pharmacy and Biology: Dir J.-P. SCHREIBER
Institute of Earth Sciences: Dir M. CAMPY
Physical Education and Sport: Dir J. VANHOECKE
Medicine: Dir H. PORTIER
University Institute of Technology (Dijon): Dir J.-L. BAILLY
University Institute of Technology (Le Creusot): Dir J.-L. GISCLON
Higher National School of Applied Biology: Dir D. LORIENT
Viticulture and Oenology Experimental Centre: Dir M. FEUILLAT
Higher Institute of Transport and the Car: Dir S. AIVAZZADEH
University Professional Institute of Management in Education, Training and Culture: Dir T. CHEVAILLIER
Preparatory Institute for General Administration: Dir M. DRAN
University Professional Institute in Burgundy for Industrial Engineering: Dir B. BOBIN
Training of Research Engineers in Materials Science and Technology: Dir A. DORMOND

PROFESSORS

Arts Faculties:

ABDI, Psychology
ALI BOUACHA, French Linguistics
BASTIT, Philosophy
BAVOUX, Geography
BENONY, Psychology
BERCOT, Mme, Modern Literature
CHAPUIS, Geography
CHARRIER, Geography
CHARUE, German
CHARUE, Mme, German
CHEVIGNARD, American English
CHIFFRE, Geography
COMANZO, English
COURTOIS, Mme, Comparative Literature
DOBIAS, Mme, Classical Literature
DUCHENE, History
DUCOS, Mme, Classical Literature
DURIX, English
DURU, Mme, Education
FAYARD, Mme, Modern History
FAYOL, Psychology
FERRARI, Philosophy
FOYARD, French Philology
GARNOT, Modern History
HAAS, Mme, French Linguistics
IMBERTY, Italian
JACOBI, Information and Communication Science
JOLY, Mlle, Latin
LAMARRE, Geography
LARRAZ, Romance Languages
LAVAUD, Mme, Spanish
LAVAUD, Spanish
MCCARTHY, English
MORDANT, Protohistory
NOUHAUD, Spanish
PELLAN, Mlle, English
PERARD, Mme, Geography
PERROT, Mlle, Philosophy
PIROELLE, Mme, English
PITAVY, English
PITAVY, Mme, English
POURKIER, Mme, Greek
QUILLIOT, Philosophy
RATIE, English
REFFET, German
RONSIN, Modern History
SADRIN, Mme, English
SADRIN, French Literature
SAINT-DENIS, Medieval History
SAURON, Audiology
SOUILLER, Comparative Literature
SOUTET, Linguistics, Phonetics
TABBAGH, Medieval Archaeology
TAVERDET, French Philology
TUROWSLI, History of Art
VINTER, Mme, Psychology
WOLIKOW, History and Civilization
WUNENBURGER, Philosophy ZAGAR, Psychology
ZAGAR, Psychology

Science Faculties:

ANDREUX, Geochemistry
BELLEVILLE, J., Animal Physiology
BERGER, Physics
BERTRAND, Chemistry
BESANÇON, Chemistry
BOBIN, Physics
BONNARD, Mathematics
BOQUILLON, Physics
CAMPY, Geology
CEZILLY, Ecology
CHABRIER, Computer Sciences
CHAMPION, Physics
CLOUET, Animal Physiology
COLSON, Chemistry

CONNAT, Animal Biology
COQUET, Physics
CORTET, Mathematics
DEMARQUOY, Animal Physiology
DEREUX, Physics
DOLECKI, Mathematics
DORMOND, Chemistry
DULIEU, Animal Physiology
FANG, Mathematics
FLATO, Mathematics
FRANGE, Chemistry
FROCHOT, B., Ecology
GAUTHERON, B., Chemistry
GOUDONNET, Physics
GUILARD, R., Mathematics
GUIRAUD, Geology
JANNIN, Physics
JANNOT, Physics
JAUSLIN, Physics
JOUBERT, Mathematics
KUBICKI, Chemistry
LALLEMANT, Chemistry
LANG, J., Geology
LANGEVIN, Mathematics
LARPIN, Physical Chemistry
LASSALE, Mathematics
LATRUFFE, Biochemistry
LAURIN, Geology
LENOIR-ROUSSEAU, Zoology
LINES, Mathematics
LOETE, Physics
LOREAU, Geology
MARCUARD, Statistical Probability
MARNIER, Physics
MARTY, Plant Biology
MATVEEV, Mathematics
MAUME, B., Biochemistry
MEUNIER, Chemistry
MICHELOT, Mme, Physics
MICHON, Mathematics
MILAN, Electronics
MILLOT, Physics
MOÏSE, C., Chemistry
MOUSSU, Mathematics
MUGNIER, Chemistry
NIEPCE, J.-CL., Chemistry
PAINDAVOINE, Automatics
PALLO, Informatics
PAUL, Plant Biology
PAUTY, Physics
PERRON, Mathematics
PIERRE, Physics
PINCZON, Mathematics
PRIBETICH, Electronics
PUGIN, Biochemistry
RACLIN, Mechanics
REMOISSENET, Physics
ROUSSARIE, Mathematics
SCHMITT, Mathematics
SEMENOV, Mathematics
SIEROFF, Neurophysiology
SIMON, Mathematics
STEINBRUNN, Chemistry
THIERRY, Geology
TOURNEFIER, Mme, Biology
VALLADE, Plant Biology
WABNITZ, Physics
YETONGNON, Informatics

Faculties of Law and Economic Science:

BALESTRA, Economic Sciences
BART, Law, Roman Law
BAUMONT, Mme, Economics
BODINEAU, History of Law
BOLARD, Private Law
BROUSSOLLE, Public Law
CASIMIR, Management
CHADEFAUX, Management
CHAPPEZ, Public Law
CHARREAUX, Management
CLERE, History of Law
COURVOISIER, Political Sciences
DE MESNARD, Economics
DESBRIÈRES, Economics
DOCKES, Private Law
DUBOIS, Public Law
FILSER, Management Sciences
FORTUNET, Mme, History of Law
FRITZ, Political Sciences
GADREAU, Mme, Economics
HURIOT, Economic Sciences
JACQUEMONT, Management
JOBERT, History of Law
KORNPROBST, Public Law
LOQUIN, Private Law
MARTIN-SERF, Mme, Private Law
MATHIEU, Public Law
MICHELOT, Economics, Mathematics
PAUL, Economics of Education
PERREUR, Economic Sciences
PICHERY, M. C., Economics
PIERI, History of Law
PIERI, Mme, Private Law
PIZZIO, Private Law
ROUGET, Economics
SALMON, Political Economy
SIMON, Public Law

Faculties of Medicine and Pharmacy:

ARTUR, Physical Biochemistry
AUTISSIER, Anatomy
AUTISSIER, Mme, Physical Chemistry
BEDENNE, Gastroenterology
BELON, Pharmacology
BESANCENOT, Internal Medicine
BINNERT, Radiology
BLETTERY, Resuscitation
BONNIN, Parasitology
BRALET, Physiology
BRENOT, Vascular Surgery
BRON, Ophthalmology
BROSSIER, Physical Chemistry
BRUN, Endocrinology
BRUNOTTE, Biophysics
CAMUS, Pneumology
CARLI, Mme, Haematology
CASILLAS, Rehabilitation
CHAILLOT, Pharmacy
CHAVANET, Infectious Diseases
COUGARD, Surgery
CUISENIER, Surgery
DAVID, Thoracic and Cardiac Surgery
DELCOURT, Pharmacy
DIDIER, Rehabilitation
DUBOIS-LACAILLE, Mme, Pharmacognosy
DUMAS, Mme, Pharmacology
DUMAS, Neurology
DUSSERRE, Biostatistics
ESCOUSSE, Clinical Pharmacology
FANTINO, Physiology
FAIVRE, Gastroenterology
FAVRE, General Surgery
FELDMAN, Gynaecology and Obstetrics
FREYSZ, Anaesthesiology
GAMBERT, Biochemistry
GIRARD, Anaesthesiology
GIROUD, Neurology
GISSELMANN, Epidemiology
GOUYON, Paediatrics
GRAMMONT, Orthopaedic Surgery and Traumatology
GUERRIN, Cancerology
HILLON, Hepatology, Gastroenterology
HORIOT, Radiotheraphy
HUICHARD, Mme, Pharmaceutical Law
JEANNIN, Pneumology
JUSTRABO, Mlle, Pathological Anatomy
KAZMIERCZAK, Bacteriology, Virology
KRAUSE, Radiology
LAMBERT, Dermatology
LORCERIE, Internal Medicine
LOUIS, Cardiology
MABILLE, S. P., Radiology
MACK, Biochemistry
MALKA, Stomatology and Maxillo-facial Surgery
MARTIN, F., Immunology
MOURIER, Neurosurgery
NEEL, Biochemistry
NIVELON, Paediatrics
PADIEU, Biological Chemistry
PFITZEMEYER, Internal Medicine
PIARD, Mme, Pathological Anatomy
PORTIER, Infectious and Tropical Diseases
POTHIER, Bacteriology
POURCELOT, Mme, Pharmacy
RAT, General Surgery
RIFLE, Nephrology
ROCHAT, Mme, Pharmacy
ROCHETTE, Pharmacy
ROMANET, Oto-rhino-laryngology
ROUSSET, Bacteriology
SAGOT, Gynaecology
SAUTREAUX, Neurosurgery
SCHREIBER, Pharmacy
SMOLIK, Occupational Medicine
SOLARY, Haematology
TAVERNIER, Rheumatology
TEYSSIER, Cytogenetic Histology
THEVENIN, Pharmacy
THIERRY, Neurosurgery
TRAPET, Adult Psychiatry
TROUILLOUD, Orthopaedic Surgery and Anatomy
VERGES, Endocrinology of Metabolic Diseases
WEILLER, Radiology
WILKENING, Anaesthesiology
WOLF, Cardiology
ZAHND, Embryology

University Institute of Technology:

BELEY, Biology, Applied Biochemistry
BERLIÈRE, Contemporary History
BESSIS, Botany
BERNARD, Physiology and Nutrition
BIZOUARD, M., Thermodynamics
BUGAUT, Biochemistry
CHANUSSOT, Physics
DIOU, Industrial Computer Science
GORRIA, Computer Engineering
GREVEY, Materials
POISSON, Biochemistry
SACILOTTI, Physics
TRUCHETET, Computer Engineering

Higher National School of Applied Biology:

BELIN, Alimentary Biotermology
BESNARD, Physiology of Nutrition
DIVIES, Microbiology
GERVAIS, Process Engineering
LE MESTE, Physical Chemistry of Food
L'HUGUENOT, Biochemistry
MOLIN, Mathematics
TAINTURIER, Organic Chemistry
VOILLEY, Mme, Biology, Biochemistry

University Professional Institute of Management in Education, Training and Culture:

JAROUSSE, J.-P., Education
PATRIAT, C., Informatics and Communication
SOLAUX, A., Education

Physical Education and Sport:

MORLON, B., Biophysics
VANHOECKE, J., Physical Education and Sport

Viticulture and Oenology Experimental Centre:

CHARPENTIER, O., Oenology
FEUILLAT, M., Oenology

Higher Institute of Transport and the Car:

AIVAZZADEH, S., Mechanics
LESUEUR, Mechanics
VERCHERY, Mechanics

UNIVERSITÉ DE BRETAGNE OCCIDENTALE

Site 1–3, Rue des Archives, BP 808, 29285 Brest Cedex

Telephone: 2-98-01-60-20
Fax: 2-98-01-60-01

President: PIERRE APPRIOU
Secretary-General: RENÉ FIRMIN
Librarian: ALAIN SAINSOT

Number of teaching staff: 820
Number of students: 19,090

TEACHING AND RESEARCH UNITS

Letters and Social Sciences: Dean BERNARD SELLIN
Département Administration Economique et Sociale (AES): Dir PATRICK LE GUIRRIEC
Science and Technology: Dean CHRISTIAN MADEC
Institut Universitaire Professionnalisé (IUP): Dir MICHEL MOAN
Euro-Institut d'Actuariat (EURIA): Dir HERVÉ LE BORGNE
Ecole Supérieure de Microbiologie et Sécurité Alimentaire de Brest (ESMISAB): Dir DANIEL THOUVENOT
Medicine: Dean JEAN-MICHEL BOLES
Law and Economics: Dean HERVÉ THOUEMENT
Dentistry: Pres. HERVÉ FORAY
University Institute of Technology (Brest): Dir RENÉ PERRON
University Institute of Technology (Quimper): Dir ROGER PRAT

UNIVERSITÉ DE CAEN

Esplanade de la Paix, 14032 Caen Cedex
Telephone: 2-31-56-55-00
Fax: 2-31-56-56-00
Founded 1432; reorganized 1985
Rector: MARYSE QUÉRÉ
President: JOSETTE TRAVERT
Vice-President: EUGÈNE DUBOIS
Secretary-General: (vacant)
Librarian: FRANÇOISE BERMANN
Library: see Libraries
Number of teachers: 1,154
Number of students: 26,667

TEACHING AND RESEARCH UNITS

Law and Political Science: Dir J. HERON
Economics and Management Science: Dir M. DUPUIS
Medicine: Dir M. BAZIN
Pharmacy: Dir P. DALLEMAGNE
Science of Man: Dir P. LESAGE
Life Sciences and Behavioural Sciences: Dir J. LANGLOIS
Earth Sciences and Regional Planning: Dir L. DUPRET
Modern Languages: Dir S. FABRIZIO-COSTA
History: Dir P. GOUHIER
Sciences: Dir E. DUBOIS
Business Studies: Dir P. JOFFRE
Institute of Biochemistry and Applied Biology: Dir J. BOUCAUD
University Institute of Technology: Dir J. F. LE QUERLER
General Administration Studies: Dir P. SAUNIER
Regional Institute for Physical Education and Sport: Dir M. DESRUES
Institut universitaire professionnalisé Banque-Assurance: Dir R. FERRANDIER
Institut universitaire professionnalisé: Agroalimentaire: Dir M. LE BRETON
Institut universitaire de technologie de Cherbourg: Dir M. LEMIÈRE
Ecole d'Ingénieurs de Cherbourg: Dir (vacant)

ATTACHED INSTITUTES

Institut des sciences de la matière et du rayonnement: Dir R. DEBRIE.

Institut universitaire de formation des maîtres: Dir M. GUGLIELMI.

UNIVERSITÉ DE CERGY-PONTOISE

8 Le Campus, 95033 Cergy-Pontoise Cedex
Telephone: 1-34-25-49-49
Fax: 1-34-25-49-04

UNIVERSITÉ DE CLERMONT-FERRAND I

49 blvd Gergovia, BP 32, 63001 Clermont-Ferrand Cedex
Telephone: 4-73-35-55-20
Founded 1976; present status 1985
President: ANNIE ROUHETTE
Secretary-General: JEAN ORTOLI
Librarian: Mlle SART
Number of teachers: 500
Number of students: 9,638

TEACHING AND RESEARCH UNITS

Medicine: 28 place Henri Dunant, BP 38, 63001 Clermont-Ferrand Cedex; tel. 4-73-60-80-00; Dir M. CLUZEL
Pharmacy: 28 place Henri Dunant, BP 38, 63001 Clermont-Ferrand Cedex; tel. 4-73-60-80-00; Dir D. CHATONIER
Law and Politics: 41 blvd Gergovia, 63002 Clermont-Ferrand Cedex; tel. 4-73-43-42-00; Dir M. JARNEVIC
Economic and Social Sciences: 41 blvd Gergovia, 63002 Clermont-Ferrand Cedex; tel. 4-73-43-42-00; Dir J. AULAGNIER
University Institute of Technology (Clermont-Ferrand): Ensemble universitaire des Céseaux, BP 86, 63170 Aubière; tel. 4-73-40-63-00; Dir P. ANDANSON
Dentistry: 11 blvd Charles de Gaulle, 63035 Clermont-Ferrand Cedex; tel. 4-73-43-64-00; Dir J.-C. BOREL

UNIVERSITÉ DE CLERMONT-FERRAND II (UNIVERSITÉ BLAISE PASCAL)

34 ave Carnot, BP 185, 63006 Clermont-Ferrand Cedex 1
Telephone: 4-73-40-63-63
Fax: 4-73-40-64-31
Founded 1810, present status 1984
President: JACQUES FONTAINE
Secretary-General: A. ROUME
Librarian: R. BERARD
Number of teachers: 710
Number of students: 18,555

TEACHING AND RESEARCH UNITS

Exact and Natural Sciences (Teaching): 24 ave des Landais, 63177 Aubière Cedex; Dir G. PRENSIER
Scientific and Technical Research: 24 ave des Landais, 63177 Aubière Cedex; Dir Y. SUREAU
Literature and Human Sciences: 29 blvd Gergovia, 63037 Clermont-Ferrand Cedex; Dir R. NEBOIT-GUILHOT
Geophysics Institute and Observatory (Puy-de-Dôme): 12 ave des Landais, 63001 Clermont-Ferrand Cedex; Dir J. KORNPROBST
Physical Education and Sport: Complexe Scientifique des Cézeaux, BP 104, 63172 Aubière Cedex; Dir M. J. BIACHE
University Institute of Technology (Montluçon): Ave Aristide Briand, BP 408, 03107 Montluçon Cedex; Dir C. BASILICO
National Higher School of Chemistry: Ensemble scientifique des Cézeaux, BP 187, 63174 Aubière Cedex; Dir J. GELAS
Engineering Sciences: Rue des Meuniers, BP 206, 63174 Aubière Cedex; Dir M. TROQUET
Applied Language and Communication: 34 ave Carnot, 63037 Clermont-Ferrand Cedex; Dir P. FAUCHÈRE
Psychology, Social Sciences and Educational Science: 34 ave Carnot, 63037 Clermont-Ferrand Cedex; Dir M. CHAMBON
Computer Engineering (ISIMA): Complexe des Cézeaux, BP 125, 63173 Aubière Cedex; Head A. QUILLIOT

UNIVERSITÉ DE TECHNOLOGIE DE COMPIÈGNE

Centre B. Franklin, BP 649, Rue Roger Couttolenc, 60206 Compiègne Cedex
Telephone: 3-44-23-44-23
Fax: 3-44-23-43-00
Founded 1972
Academic year: September to August (2 semesters)
President: FRANÇOIS PECCOUD
Secretary-General: LUC ZIEGLER
Librarian: ANNIE BERTRAND
Number of teachers: 220
Number of students: 3,000
Publications: *Guide de l'Etudiant*, *Informations UTC* (weekly).

DIRECTORS

Department of Industrial Affairs: MICHEL CORDONNIER
Department of Mechanical Engineering: GÉRARD BERANGER
Department of Biological Engineering: JOEL CHOPINEAU
Department of Chemical Engineering: PIERRE GUIGON
Department of Computer Science: MENAD SIDAHMED
Department of Pedagogy: JEAN-FRANÇOIS CHRETIEN
Department of Technology and Human Sciences: JEAN-MICHEL BESNIER
Department of Mechanical Engineering Systems: PIERRE ORSERO.

UNIVERSITÉ DE CORSE (Università di Corsica)

BP 52, 7 ave Jean-Nicoli, 20250 Corti
Telephone: 4-95-46-10-45
Founded 1976; opened 1981
President: JACQUES-HENRI BALBI
Secretary-General: ROBERT ALBERTI

DEANS

Faculty of Law, Economics and Politics: JEAN-YVES COPPOLANI
Faculty of Literature, Languages and Human Sciences: FRANCIS BERETTI
Faculty of Sciences and Technology: ANTOINE-FRANÇOIS BERNARDINI
University Institute of Technology: ANTOINE FRANCIONI

ATTACHED RESEARCH INSTITUTES

Institut de Développement des Iles Mediterranéennes: Dir ANNE CODACCIONI.

Centre de Recherche Corse en Lettres et Sciences Humaines.

Centre de Recherche des Langues et de la Communication: Dir BERNARD DEXANT.

Centre de Recherche Médicale: Dir Dr VOVAN.

Centre de Valorisation des Ressources Naturelles: Dir ANTOINE BERNARDINI.

Centre d'Energétique: Dir Prof. GEORGES PERI.

UNIVERSITÉ D'ÉVRY-VAL D'ESSONNE

Boulevard des Coquibus, 91025 Évry Cedex
Telephone: 1-69-47-70-10
Fax: 1-64-97-27-34

UNIVERSITÉ DE FRANCHE-COMTÉ

1 rue Claude Goudimel, 25030 Besançon Cedex
Telephone: 3-81-66-50-34
Fax: 3-81-66-50-36
E-mail: patrick-andre.lehmann@univ-fcomte.fr
Founded 1423 at Dole, 1691 at Besançon

President: CLAUDE OYTANA
Vice-Presidents: F. BEVALOT, M. LE BERRE, J. C. CHEVAILLER, P. M. BADOT, B. LEGEARD, C. SCHMITT
Secretary-General: MICHEL ROIGNOT

Library: see Libraries
Number of teachers: 1,093
Number of students: 22,362

Publications: *Annales Littéraires de l'Université, Journal de Médecine de Besançon, Annales Scientifiques de l'Université, Revue Géographique de l'Est, Annales de l'Observatoire de Besançon, En Direct, Tout l'U.*

TEACHING AND RESEARCH UNITS

Literature and Human Sciences: Dir J. F. GIRARDOT
Science and Technology: Dir J. BERGER
Law, Economics and Politics: Dir B. LIME
Medicine and Pharmacy: Dir G. CAMELOT
University Institute of Technology (Besançon): Dir M. TACHEZ
University Institute of Technology (Belfort): Dir D. RONDOT
Besançon Observatory: Dir S. CLAIREMIDI
Physical Education and Sport: Dir. E. PREDINE
Industrial Science, Management and Technology: Dir R. PORCAR

UNIVERSITÉ DE GRENOBLE I (UNIVERSITÉ JOSEPH FOURIER)

BP 53, 38041 Grenoble Cedex 9

Telephone: 4-76-51-46-00
Fax: 4-76-51-48-48

President: (vacant)
Vice-Presidents: JACQUES FOURNET, ALAIN DENEUVILLE, CLAUDE MOSER, ROGER MAYNARD
Secretary-General: JEAN JACQUES PELLEGRIN

Number of students: 18,000

TEACHING AND RESEARCH UNITS

Medicine: Dir J. L. DEBRU
Pharmacy: Dir J. ROCHAT
Biology: Dir P. CUCHET
Chemistry: Dir C. DUPUY
Physical Education and Sport: Dir P. CHIFFLET
Geography: Dir G. BOCQUET
Geology: Dir CH. PICARD
Applied Mathematics and Computer Sciences: Dir M. ADIBA
Mathematics: Dir J. BERTIN
Mechanical Engineering: Dir J. M. TERRIEZ
Physics: Dir N. LONGUEQUEUE

ATTACHED INSTITUTES

Institut de la Formation des Maîtres (IFM): Dir B. DARLEY.

Département Scientifique Universitaire (DSU): Dir R. DARVES-BLANC.

Institut Universitaire de Technologie: Dir C. MONLLOR.

Observatoire des Sciences de l'Univers: Dir G. PERRIER.

Science and Technology: Dir D. CORDARY.

UNIVERSITÉ DE GRENOBLE II (UNIVERSITÉ PIERRE MENDÈS-FRANCE)

BP 47X, 38040 Grenoble Cedex

Telephone: 4-76-82-54-00
Telex: 980910
Fax: 4-76-82-56-54

Founded 1970
Academic year: September to June

Rector: MICHEL TREUIL
President: BERNARD POUYET
Vice-Presidents: GUY ROMIER (Educational Affairs), MICHEL CHATELUS (Research), JACQUELINE DOMENACH (European and International Relations), FRANÇOIS PETIT (Continuing Education), FRANÇOIS SERVOIN (New Technology in Education), JANINE CHENE (Student and University Counselling)
Chief Administrative Officer: NICOLE MALASSIGNE

Library: see Libraries
Number of teachers: 500
Number of students: 18,500

Publications: *Guide de l'Etudiant, Intercours,* various scientific publications.

TEACHING AND RESEARCH UNITS

Law: Dean P. MAISTRE DU CHAMBON
Institute of Political Studies: Dir F. D'ARCY
Economic Sciences: Dir J. FONTANEL
Development, Economic Management and Society: Dir B. BILLAUDOT
Human and Social Sciences: Dir G. POUSSIN
Humanities: Dir G. MARTINIÈRE
Higher Institute of Business: J. TRAHAND
Centre for Research with Data Processing in the field of Social Sciences: R. ARRUS, Mlle S. ROBERT
Institute of Energy Policy and Economics: J.-M. MARTIN
University Institute of Technology II: Dir A. SPALANZANI
University Institute of Technology at Valence: Dir A. DE LACHEISSERIE

PROFESSORS

ALBOUY, M., Management
ANTONIADIS, A., Mathematics
ARNAUD, P., Sociology
BAILLE, J., Education
BARREYRE, P.-Y., Management
BEAUVOIS, J.-L., Psychology
BELLISSANT, C., Computer Science
BERBAUM, J., Education
BERNADIE, S., French Literature
BERNARD, J.-P., Political Science
BERNARD-CHEYRE, C., Language Centre
BERR, C., Private Law
BIAYS, J. P., Political Science
BILLAUDOT, B., Economics
BIZIERE, J., History
BOITTIAUX, J., Computer Science
BONNIN, B., History
BORNECQUE, R., History
BORRELLY, R., Economics
BOUTOT, A., Philosophy
BRECHON, P., Political Science
BRODEAU, F., Applied Mathematics
CAILLOSSE, J., Public Law
CALABRE, S., Economics
CAYEZ, P., History
CHALARON, Y., Private Law
CHAPAL, P., Public Law
CHATELUS, M., Economics
CHEVALLIER, F., Public Law
CHIANEA, G., History of Law
COURTIN, J., Informatics
COVIAUX, C., Private Law
CROISAT, M., Political Science
D'ARCY, F., Political Science
DEJEAN DE LA BATIE, N., Private Law
DESTANNE DE BERNIS, G., Economics
DIDIER, P., History of Law
DROUET D'AUBIGNY, G., Mathematics
DUC-JACQUET, M., Mathematics
DUFRESNOY, C., French Language
EUZEBY, A., Economics and Management
EUZEBY, C., Economics
FOUCHARD, A., History
FRANCILLON, J., Private Law
GIROD, P., Management
GLEIZAL, J.-J., Public Law
GOUTAL, J.-L., Private Law
GRANGE, D., History
GRELLIERE, V., Law
GROC, B., Computer Science
GUILHAUDIS, M., Public Law
GUILLEN, P., Modern History
HATWELL, Y., Experimental Psychology
HEIDSIECK, F., Moral Philosophy
HOLLARD, M., Economics
JOLIBERT, A., Management
JUDET, P., Economics
LABROT, G., History
LARGUIER, J., Private Law
LEFEBVRE, D., Private Law
LEROY, P., Public Law
LESCA, H., Management
LE STANC, C., Law
MAISONNEUVE, B., Mathematics
MARIGNY, J., History
MARTIN, C., Management
MARTINIERE, G., History
MEYER, M., Economics
MOTTE, A., Planning
N'GUYEN XUAN DANG, M.
NIZARD, L., Public Law and Political Science
OHLMANN, T., Psychology
PAGE, A., Management
PARAVY, P., History
PASCAL, G., Philosophy
PATUREL, R., Management
PECCOUD, F., Computer Science
PEISER, G., Public Law
PETIT, B., Private Law
PHILIBERT, M., Philosophy
PIETRA, R., Philosophy
POUSSIN, G., Psychology
POUYET, B., Public Law
QUERMONNE, J.-L., Political Science
REBOUD, L., Economics
RENARD, D., Political Science
RICHARD, A., Economics
ROCHE, J.-J., Political Science
ROMIER, G., Applied Mathematics
ROUAULT, J., Applied Mathematics
ROUSSET, M., Public Law
RUFFIOT, A., Psychology
SALVAGE, PASCALE, Law
SALVAGE, PHILIPPE, Law
SAMUELSON, A., Economics
SCHNEIDER, C., Public Law
SEGRESTIN, D., Industrial Engineering
SIRONNEAU, J.-P., Sociology
SOLE, J., History
SOULAGE, B., Political Science
TERCINET, M., Public Law
TESTON, G.
TEULIÉ, J., Management
TIBERGHIEN, G., Psychology
TRAHAND, J., Management
USUNIER, J. C., Management
VALETTE-FLORENCE, P.
VERNANT, D., Philosophy

UNIVERSITÉ DE GRENOBLE III (UNIVERSITÉ STENDHAL)

BP 25, 38040 Grenoble Cedex 9

Telephone: 4-76-82-43-00
Fax: 4-76-82-43-84

Founded 1970

President: ANDRÉ SIGANOS
Vice-Presidents: PIERRE MORÈRE, PAUL MATTEI
Secretary-General: GERARD LANCIAN

Number of teachers: 320
Number of students: 7,400

Publications: *Livret de l'étudiant, La Gazette de l'Université.*

TEACHING AND RESEARCH UNITS

Languages: Dir VINCENT SERVERAT
English: Dir JEAN DERIOZ
Modern and Classical Literature: Dir NATHALIE FOURNIER
Communication Sciences: Dir ISABELLE PAILLIART
Linguistic Science: Dir MADELEINE BRIOT

DIRECTORS OF DEPARTMENTS

Languages, Literature and Foreign Civilizations:

German and Dutch Studies: JEAN-FRANÇOIS MARILLIER

Iberian and Spanish-American Studies: ANNE-MARIE GONZALEZ-RAYMOND
Italian and Romanian Studies: ALAIN GODARD
Russian and Slav Studies: GILBERT MERLE
Oriental Studies: (vacant)
Trilingual Law and Economics: ROBERT GRIFFITHS
Applied Foreign Languages: (vacant)

Modern and Classical Literature:
Languages, Literatures and French Civilization: BERTRAND VIBERT
Classical Studies: BERNARD COLOMBAT
Comparative Literature: FRÉDÉRIC MONNEYRON

Sciences of Language:
French as a Foreign Language: VIOLAINE DE NUCHÈZE, JEAN EMMANUEL LE BRAY

UNIVERSITÉ DE HAUTE-ALSACE

2 rue des Frères Lumière, 68093 Mulhouse Cedex
Telephone: 3-89-33-60-00
Fax: 3-89-33-63-19
Founded 1975
President: GERARD BINDER
Secretary-General: ALAIN COLLANGE
Librarian: PHILIPPE RUSSELL
Number of students: 7,700

TEACHING AND RESEARCH UNITS

Letters and Humanities: Dir M. FAURE
Sciences: Dir M. GOZE
Institute of Technology Colmar: Dir G. MICHEL
Institute of Technology Mulhouse: Dir J. M. MEYER
Higher National School of Chemistry: Dir J. P. FOUASSIER
Higher National School of the Textile Industries: Dir M. RENNER
Faculty of Economic and Social Sciences: Dir D. CHASSIGNET
Higher School of Applied Engineering Sciences: Dir F. M SCHMITT

UNIVERSITÉ DU HAVRE

25 rue Philippe Lebon, BP 1123, 76063 Le Havre Cedex
Telephone: 2-35-19-55-00
Fax: 2-35-21-49-59
Founded 1984
State control
Academic year: September to July
President: JACQUES LE BAS
Vice-Presidents: CHARLES-HENRI FREDOUET, ROGER HEITZ, PHILIPPE MOREL
Secretary-General: ALEXIS MAVROCORDATO
Librarian: PIERRETTE PORTRON
Number of teachers: 343
Number of students: 7,292

TEACHING AND RESEARCH UNITS

Faculty of Science and Technology: Dean FRANÇOISE FLEURY
Faculty of International Affairs: Dean GILLES LEBRETON
University Institute of Technology: Dir SERGE CARPENTIER
Higher Institute of Logistics and Engineering: Dir ALAIN PORTRON

UNIVERSITÉ DE LILLE I (UNIVERSITÉ DES SCIENCES ET TECHNOLOGIES DE LILLE)

59655 Villeneuve d'Ascq Cedex
Telephone: 3-20-43-43-43
Fax: 3-20-43-49-95
Founded 1855 as Faculty of Sciences; present status 1971
President: JACQUES DUVEAU
Vice-Presidents: YVONNE MOUNIER, HERVE BAUSSART, HENRI DUBOIS
Secretary-General: YVES CHAIMBAULT
Number of teachers: 1,200
Number of students: 23,000

TEACHING AND RESEARCH UNITS

Pure and Applied Mathematics: Dir Mme DUVAL
Computer Science, Electronics; Electrical Engineering and Automation: Dir M. STEEN
Physics: Dir Mme DUPREZ
Chemistry: Dir M. LECLERCQ
Biology: Dir M. ANDRIES
Earth Sciences: Dir M. THIEBAULY
Geography and Spatial Development: Dir M. DUBOIS
Economics and Social Sciences: Dir M. ROLLET
University Institute of Technology (Lille): Dir M. BOCQUET
Institute of Business Studies: Dir M. GUILBERT
Agricultural Institute: Dir M. BOUQUELET
Higher National School of Chemistry in Lille: Dir M. BONNELLE
University Centre for the Economics of Permanent Education: Dir M. POISSON
University School of Engineers in Lille: Dir M. LEGRAND

PROFESSORS

BOILLY, B., Biology
BONNELLE, J.-P., Chemistry
BREZINSKI, C., Computer Sciences
BRUYELLE, P., Geography
CHAMLEY, H., Geotechnics
COEURE, G., Pure and Applied Mathematics
CONSTANT, E., Electronics
CORDONNIER, V., Calculus and Information Science
DAUCHET, M., Theoretical Computing
DEBOURSE, J.-P., Management Science
DEBRABANT, P., Engineering
DEGAUQUE, P., Electronics
DHAINAUT, A., Biology
DORMARD, S., Economics
DOUKHAN, J.-C., Engineering
DUPOUY, J.-P., Biology
DYMENT, A., Mathematics
ESCAIG, B., Solid State Physics
FOCT, J., Chemistry
FOURET, R., Physics
FRONTIER, S., Biology
GABILLARD, R., Electronics
GLORIEUX, P., Physics
GOSSELIN, G., Sociology
GOUDMAND, P., Energy Generation
GRUSON, L., Pure and Applied Mathematics
GUILBAULT, Biology
LABLACHE-COMBIER, A., Organic Chemistry
LAVEINE, J.-P., Palaeobotany
LEHMANN, D., Geometry
LENOBLE, Mme, Atmospheric Optics
LOMBARD, J., Sociology
LOUCHEUX, C., Macromolecular Chemistry
MACKE, B., Physics
MAILLET, P., Economic and Social Sciences
MICHEAUX, P., Mechanical Engineering
PAQUET, J., Applied Geology
PORCHET, M., Biology
PROUVOST, J., Mineralogy
RACZY, L., Computer Sciences
SALMER, G., Electronics
SCHAMPS, J., Physics
SEGUIER, G., Electro-Technology
SIMON, M., Economic and Social Sciences
SLIWA, H., Chemistry
SPIK, G., Biology
STANKIEWICZ, F., Economic Sciences
TOULOTTE, J.-M., Computer Sciences
TURREL, G., Chemistry
VERNET, P., Biology of Populations and Ecosystems
VIDAL, P., Automation
ZEYTOUNIAN, R., Mechanics

UNIVERSITÉ DE LILLE II (DROIT ET SANTÉ)

42 rue Paul Duez, 59800 Lille
Telephone: 3-20-96-43-43
Fax: 3-20-88-24-32
E-mail: ri@hp-sc.univ lille2.fr
Founded 1969
State control
Language of instruction: French
Academic year: October to June
President: Prof. JEAN LÉONARDELLI
Vice Presidents: Prof. JEAN-CHARLES FRUCHART, Prof. DANIEL VION
Secretary-General: G. BAILLIEUL
Number of teachers: 710
Number of students: 17,481

DEANS

Faculty of Medical Sciences: Prof. BERNARD DEVULDER
Faculty of Pharmacy: Prof. JEAN CLAUDE CAZIN
Faculty of Dentistry: Prof. PIERRE LAFFORGUE
Faculty of Legal, Political and Social Sciences: Prof. JEAN-LOUS THIEBAULT
Physical Education and Sport: Dir IRENE LAUTIER

CONSTITUENT INSTITUTES

Institut Universitaire de Technology: Dir JEAN PIERRE KRAWIEC.

Institut de Médecine Légale et Sociale: Dir Prof. DIDIER GOSSET.

Institut de Chimie Pharmaceutique: Dir Prof. DANIEL LESIEUR.

Institut de Préparation à l'Administration Générale: Dir Prof. PIERRE LECOCQ.

Institut des Sciences du Travail: Dir PIERRE YVES VERKINDT.

UNIVERSITÉ DE LILLE III, CHARLES DE GAULLE (SCIENCES HUMAINES, LETTRES ET ARTS)

BP 149, 59653 Villeneuve d'Ascq Cedex
Telephone: 3-20-41-60-00
Fax: 3-20-91-91-71
Founded 1560, present status 1985
President: GÉRARD LOSFELD
First Vice-President: ALAIN DEREMETZ
Vice-Presidents: JACQUES SYS (Doctoral Research), JACQUES AUBRET (Studies), JACQUES BOULOGNE (International Relations and Research), THOMAS FRASER (International Relations and Training), DOMINIQUE-GUY BRASSART (Research into Scientific Publishing), DANIELLE DELMAIRE (Documentation), PIERRE LECONTE (Research), MARC PARMENTIER (Teacher Training), PHILIPPE DANTOING (Students)
Secretary-General: DANIÈLE SAVAGE
Librarian: JEAN-PAUL CHADOURNE
Number of teachers: 599
Number of students: 23,986

Publications: *Revue du Nord* (history, 5 a year), *Revue des Sciences Humaines* (quarterly), *Etudes Irlandaises* (every 6 months), *Cahiers de Recherches de l'institut de Papyrologie et d'Egyptologie, Bulletin du Centre de Recherche en Techniques d'Expression Information Communication, Germanica* (1 or 2 a year), *Lexique* (annually), *Roman 20–50* (every 6 months), *Bien dire et bien aprandre, Uranie, Graphè.*

TEACHING AND RESEARCH UNITS

History, Art and Politics: Dir ROBERT VANDENBUSSCHE
English Language, Literature and Civilization: RICHARD LILLY
German Studies: Dir ANDRÉ COMBES

Romance, Slav and Oriental Studies: Dir KAMAL TAYARA
Classical Languages and Culture: DOMINIQUE MULLIEZ
Letters, Film and Music: Dir FRÉDÉRIC BRIOT
Mathematics, Economics and Social Sciences: Dir FLORENT CORDELIER
Philosophy: Dir MARC PARMENTIER
Psychology: Dir RÉGIS VERQUERRE
Applied Foreign Languages: Dir CLAIRE LECOINTRE
Education: Dir DOMINIQUE-GUY BRASSART
Information, Documentation and Scientific and Technical Information: Dir VINCENT CARADEC
Arts and Culture: Dir REYNOLD HUMPHRIES
University Institute of Technology B: Dir MICHEL BUGHIN
Training Centre for Accompanying Musicians: Dir PASCAL HAMEAUX
IUP–Information Communication: Dir OLIVIER CHANTRAINE
IUP–Artistic and Cultural Professions: Dir GEORGES VANDALLE

PROFESSORS (1ST CLASS AND EXCEPTIONAL)

History, Art and Politics:
MENAGER, B., Contemporary History
STALTER, M., Contemporary Art
VALBELLE, D., Egyptology

English Studies:
BECQUEMONT, D., History of Ideas, Phoenetics and Phonology
DURAND, R., North American Literature and Civilization
GOURNAY, J.-F., 19th-century Literature and Civilization
SYS, J., British Civilization, History of Ideas

German Studies:
COLONGE, P., 19th- and 20th-century Literature and Civilization
ROUSSEAU, A., Dutch Linguistics
VAYDAT, P., Anglo-German Relations: 1870–1914

Romance, Slav, Semitic and Hungarian Studies:
ALLAIN, L., Russian
COVO, J., Spanish
PIEJUS, M. F., Italian

Classics:
DUMONT, J.-CHR., Social History of the Roman Republic

French Linguistics and Literature:
ALLUIN, B., Modern and Contemporary Language and Literature
BONNEFIS, PH., 19th-century Literature
GUILLERM, J.-P., 19th-century Literature
HORVILLE, R., 17th-century Literature
LESTRINGANT, FR., 16th-century Literature
MALANDAIN, P., Modern and Contemporary Language and Literature

Mathematics, Economics, Social Sciences:
CELEYRETTE, J., Mathematics

Philosophy:
QUILLIEN, J., Metaphysics and the Philosophy of Language

Psychology:
LECONTE, P., Experimental Psychology

University Institute of Technology: 9 rue Auguste Angellier, 59046 Lille Cedex.

UNIVERSITÉ DE LIMOGES

Hôtel Burgy, 13 rue de Genève, 87065 Limoges Cedex
Telephone: 5-55-45-76-01
Fax: 5-55-45-76-34
Founded 1808, closed 1840, reopened 1965
Academic year: October to June
President: BERNARD VAREILLE
Secretary-General: DANIEL POUMEROULY
Librarian: ODILE ROHOU
Library: see Libraries
Number of teachers: 742
Number of students: 14,186

TEACHING AND RESEARCH UNITS

Law and Economic Sciences: Dir PASCAL TEXIER
Medicine: Dir CLAUDE PIVA
Pharmacy: Dir AXEL GHESTEM
Sciences: Dir JEAN-PIERRE BOREL
Letters and Social Sciences: Dir JEAN-PAUL LECERTUA
University Institute of Technology: Dir ANTONIN NOUAILLES

PROFESSORS

Medicine
ADENIS, J.-P., Ophthalmology
ALAIN, L., Infantile Surgery
ALDIGIER, J.-C., Cardiology
ARCHAMBEAUD, F., Clinical Medicine
ARNAUD, J. P., Orthopaedics, Traumatology, Plastic Surgery
BARTHE, D., Histology, Embryology
BAUDET, J., Obstetrics and Gynaecology
BENSAID, J., Clinical Cardiology
BERTIN, P., Therapeutics
BESSEDE, J.-P., Oto-rhino-laryngology
BONNAUD, F., Pneumo-Phthisiology
BONNETBLANC, J.-M., Dermatology, Venereology
BOULESTEIX, J., Paediatrics and Medical Genetics
BOUQUIER, J.-J., Clinical Paediatrics
BOUTROS, T. F., Epidemiology
BRETON, J.-C., Biochemistry
CATANZANO, G., Pathological Anatomy
COLOMBEAU, P., Urology
CUBERTAFOND, P., Digestive Surgery
DARDE, M. L., Parasitology
DE LUMLEY-WOODYEAR, L., Paediatrics
DENIS, F., Bacteriology, Virology
DENIZOT, N., Anaesthesiology
DESCOTTES, B., Anatomy
DUDOGNON, P., Occupational Therapy
DUMAS, J. PH., Urology
DUMAS, M., Neurology
DUMONT, D., Occupational Medicines
DUPUY, J.-P., Radiology
FEISS, P., Anaesthesiology
GAINANT, A., Digestive Surgery
GAROUX, R., Child Psychiatry
GASTINNE, H., Resuscitation
HUGON, J., Histology, Embryology
LABROUSSE, C., Occupational Therapy
LASKAR, M., Thoracic and Cardiovascular Surgery
LAUBIE, B., Endocrinology, Metabolism, Nutrition
LEGER, J.-M., Adult Psychiatry
LEROUX-ROBERT, C., Nephrology
MENIER, R., Physiology
MERLE, L., Pharmacology
MOREAU, J.-J., Neurosurgery
MOULIES, D., Infantile Surgery
PECOUT, C., Orthopaedics, Traumatology, Plastic Surgery
PICHON BOURDESSOULE, D., Haematology
PILLEGAND, B., Hepato-gastro-enterology
PIVA, C., Forensic Medicine and Toxicology
PRA LORAN, V., Haematology
RAVON, R., Neurosurgery
RIGAUD, M., Biochemistry
ROUSSEAU, J., Radiology
SAUVAGE, J.-P., Oto-rhino-laryngology
TABASTE, J.-L., Gynaecology, Obstetrics
TREVES, R., Rheumatology
VALLAT, J.-M., Neurology
VALLEIX, D., Anatomy
VANDROUX, J.-C., Biophysics
WEINBRECK, P., Tropical Medicine

Faculty of Law and Economics:
ALAPHILIPPE, F., Private Law and Criminology
ARCHER, R., Economics
CAVAGNAC, M., Economics
DARREAU, P., Economics
FLANDIN-BLETY, P., Legal and Institutional History
KARAQUILLO, J.-P., Private Law and Criminology
LENCLOS, J.-L., Public Law
MARGUENAUD, J.-P., Private Law
MOULY, J., Private Law
PAULIAT, H., Public Law
PRIEUR, M., Public Law
SAUVIAT, A., Economics
TARAZI, A., Economics
TEXIER, P., Legal and Institutional History
VAREILLE, B., Private Law

Faculty of Pharmacy:
BERNARD, M., Physical Chemistry and Pharmaceutical Technology
BOSGIRAUD, C., Biology
BROSSARD, C., Physical Chemistry and Pharmaceutical Technology
BUXERAUD, J., Pharmacology
CARDOT, PH., Physical Chemistry and Pharmaceutical Technology
CHULIA, A., Pharmacology
CLEMENT-CHULIA, D., Physical Chemistry and Pharmaceutical Technology
DELAGE, C., Physical and Mineral Chemistry
GHESTEM, A., Botany
HABRIOUX, G., Biochemistry
OUDART, N., Pharmacology

Faculty of Sciences:
BARONNET, J.-M., Energetics
CATHERINOT, A., Energetics
COLOMBEAU, B., Optics
COUDERT, J. F., Methodology, Plasma and Automation
DECOSSAS, J. L., E.E.A.
DESCHAUX, P., Physiology
DESMAISON, J., Mineral Chemistry
DUVAL, D., Mathematics
FAUCHAIS, P., Energetics
FRIT, B., Mineral Chemistry
GAUDREAU, B., Mineral Chemistry
GOURSAT, P., Mineral Chemistry
GUILLON, P., Electronics, Electrotechnology and Automation
JULIEN, R., Biochemistry
KRAUSZ, P., Organic, Analytical and Industrial Chemistry
LAUBIE, F., Mathematics
MARCOU, J., Electronics, Electrotechnology and Automation
MARTIN, C., Energetics
MAZET, M., Organic, Analytical and Industrial Chemistry
MERCURIO, D., Mineral Chemistry
MERCURIO, J.-P., Mineral Chemistry
MOLITON, A., Optics
MOLITON, J. P., E.E.A.
MORVAN, H., Biology
OBREGON, J., Electronics, Electrotechnology and Automatics
SABOURDY, G., Geology
THERA, M., Mathematics

Faculty of Letters and Humanities:
BALABANIAN, O., Geography and Development
BARRIÈRE, B., Medieval Archaeological History
BEDON, R., Ancient Language and Literature
BEHAR, P., Germanic and Scandinavian Language and Literature
CAPDEBOSCQ, A. M., Romance Language and Literature
CARON, P., Modern and Contemporary French Language and Literature
CHANDES, G., Middle Age to Renaissance French Language and Literature
DUMONT, J., Ancient World Archaeological History

El Gammal, J. M., World Medieval Archaeological History
Filteau, C., Modern and Contemporary French Language and Literature
Fontanille, J., Language Sciences
Gendreau-Massaloux, Romance Language and Literature
Grassin, J.-M., Comparative Literature
Grassin, M., Anglo-Saxon English Language and Literature
Leclanche, J.-L., Middle Age to Renaissance French Language and Literature
Lemoine, B., Anglo-Saxon English Language and Literature
Levet, J.-P., Ancient Language and Literature
Moreau, J.-P., Anglo-Saxon English Language and Literature
Nouhaud, M., Ancient Language and Literature
Rambaux, C., Ancient Language and Literature
Valadas, B., Economic and Regional Geography
Verdon, J., World Medieval Archaeological History

University Institute of Technology:

Berland, R., Electronics, Electrotechnology and Automatics
Besson, J.-L., Dense Media and Materials
Caperaa, S., Civil Engineering
Caron, A., Information Processing
Fray, C., Electronics, Electrotechnology and Automatics
Glandus, J.-C., Mechanics, Mechanical Engineering and Civil Engineering
Jecko, B., Electronics, Electrotechnology and Automatics
Jecko, F., Electronics, Electrotechnology and Automatics
Labbe, J.-C., Chemistry of Materials
Malaise, M., Mechanics, Mechanical Engineering and Civil Engineering
Nardou, F., Physical Chemistry
Platon, F., Mechanics, Mechanical Engineering and Civil Engineering
Quere, R., Electronics, Electrotechnology and Automation
Quintard, P., Dense Media and Materials
Ratinaud, M. M., Biochemistry and Biology

AFFILIATED INSTITUTES

Centre Limousin associé au Conservatoire National des Arts et Métiers: Dir Michèle Mouricout.

Institut Médical de Biologie Cellulaire et Moléculaire: Dir Michel Rigaud.

Institut d'Epidémiologie Neurologique et de Neurologie Tropicale: Dir Michel Dumas.

Textes et Langages: Dir Philippe Caron.

Sciences Historiques et Géographiques: Dir Bernadette Barrière.

Chimie, Biologie, Santé: Dir Albert-José Chulia.

Sciences de l'Environnement: Dir Michel Mazet.

Biotechnologie: Dir Raymond Julien.

Céramiques et Matériaux: Dir Bernard Frit

Mathématiques, Informatique Productique: Dir Guy Robin.

UNIVERSITÉ DU LITTORAL

Pôle Universitaire Lamartine, 49–79 place du Général-De-Gaulle, 59385 Dunkerque Cedex

Telephone: 3-28-66-10-50
Fax: 3-28-21-00-57

President: Alain Dubrulle

UNIVERSITÉ LYON I (UNIVERSITÉ CLAUDE-BERNARD)

43 blvd du 11 Novembre 1918, 69622 Villeurbanne Cedex

Telephone: 4-72-44-80-00
Telex: 330208
Fax: 4-72-43-10-20

Founded 1970
State control
Language of instruction: French
Academic year: October to June

President: Gérard Fontaine
Vice-Presidents: Yves Lemoigne (Health Sciences), Paul Zech (Sciences)
Secretary-General: Jacques Flacher

Number of teachers: 1,500
Number of students: 23,000

Publications: *Lettre FLASH/INFO* (quarterly), *Livret de l'Etudiant* (annually), *Annuaire sur la Recherche* (annually).

DIRECTORS OF TEACHING AND RESEARCH UNITS

Medicine:

Medicine 'Grange-Blanche': Hélène Pellet
Medicine 'Alexis-Carrel': Marc Dechavanne
Medicine 'Lyon-Nord': Louis Patricot
Medicine 'Sud': Jean-Pierre Gérard
Pharmacy: Jean Villard
Rehabilitation: Michel Eyssette
Dentistry: Jacques Doury

Sciences:

Material Sciences: Edgar Elbaz
Engineering and Technological Development: Jean Dimnet
Chemistry, Molecular and Cellular Biology: Annick Varagnat
Systems Analysis (Biology and Socio-Economics): Domitien Debouzie
Earth, Ocean, Atmospheric, Space and Environmental Sciences: Serge Elmi
Physical Education and Sport: Jacques Pontier
University Institute of Technology: Jean Gielly
University Institute of Technology: Jacques Pivot
Institute of Engineering: (vacant)
Observatory: Jean-Claude Ribes

ATTACHED INSTITUTES

Institut Cardiovasculaire: 8 ave Rockefeller, 69373 Lyon Cedex 08; Dir Pr. Termet.

Institut de Pharmacie Industrielle: 8 ave Rockefeller, 69373 Lyon Cedex 08; Dir Prof. J. Cotte.

Institut d'Audiophonologie: Hôpital Edouard-Herriot, Pavillon U, 5 place d'Arsonval, 69003 Lyon; Dir A. Morgon.

Institut de Stomatologie: Centre hospitalier Lyon Sud, Hôpital Jules Courmont, 69310 Pierre Bénite; Dir P. Freydel.

Institut de Médecine du Travail: 8 ave Rockefeller, 69373 Lyon Cedex 08; Dir G. Prost.

Institut d'Hydrologie et Climatologie: 8 ave Rockefeller, 69373 Lyon Cedex 08; Dir Prof. G. Meunier.

Institut de Médecine et d'Hygiène Tropicales: 8 ave Rockefeller, 69373 Lyon Cedex 08; Dir Prof. Jean-Paul Garin.

Institut de Science Financière et d'Assurance: 43 blvd du 11 Novembre 1918, 69622 Villeurbanne; Dir Prof. Ph. Picard.

Institut Michel-Pacha: Laboratoire Maritime de Physiologie, 83500 Tamaris-sur-Mer; Dir Georges Brichon.

Institut de Météorologie et Sciences Climatiques: 43 blvd du 11 Novembre 1918, 68622 Villeurbanne; Dir Guy Blanchet.

Institut de Recherche sur l'Enseignement des Mathématiques (IREM): 43 blvd du 11 Novembre 1918, 69622 Villeurbanne; Dir Yvon Gerard.

Institut de Médecine Légale et Criminologie Clinique 'Alexandre Lacassagne': 12 ave Rockefeller, 69373 Lyon Cedex 08; Dir M. Colin.

Institut de Recherches Chirurgicales: 8 ave Rockefeller, 69373 Lyon Cedex 08; Dir Dr Peix.

Institut d'Evolution Moléculaire: UER des Sciences de la Nature, Bât. 741, 43 blvd du 11 Novembre 1918, Villeurbanne; Dir Prof. Grantham.

Institut d'Epidémiologie: 8 ave Rockefeller, 69373 Lyon Cedex 08; Dir J. Fabry.

Institut d'Histoire de la Médicine: Hôpital cardiologique, 69500 Brom; Dir J. Normand.

UNIVERSITÉ LUMIÈRE LYON 2

86 rue Pasteur, 69365 Lyon Cedex 07

Telephone: 4-78-69-70-00
Telex: 330637
Fax: 4-78-69-56-01

President: Bruno Gelas
First Vice-President (Research and Documentary Policy): Gilbert Puech
Vice-President (Training): Régis Bernard
Vice-President (International Relations): Henri Béjoint
Vice-President (University Life and Communication): Dominique Bertin
Vice-President (Personnel): Christian Mercier
Vice-President (Resources and Budget): Christian le Bas
Secretary-General: Bernard Fradin

Number of teachers: 793
Number of students: 24,000

Publication: *Le Rayon Vert* (10 a year).

DEANS

Faculty of Literature, Science of Language and Arts: Jean-Yves Debreville
Faculty of Modern Languages: Claudette Fillard
Faculty of Geography, History, History of Art and Tourism: Richard Sceau
Faculty of Law: Jean-Luc Albert
Faculty of Anthropology and Sociology: Jacques Bonniel
Faculty of Economics and Business Studies: Jean-François Goux

DIRECTORS

Institute of Politics: Alain-Serge Mescheriakoff
Institute of Psychology: Jacques Gaucher
Institute of Teacher Training: Michel Develay
Institute of Communication: Serge Miguet
Institute of Labour and Trade Union Training: Florence Debord
Institute of Work Study: Jean-Marc Béraud
Institut Universitaire de Technologie Lumière: Paul Rousset
Centre International d'Etudes Françaises (CIEF): Robert Bouchard

UNIVERSITÉ LYON 3 (UNIVERSITÉ JEAN MOULIN)

1 rue de l'Université, BP 0638, 69239 Lyon Cedex 02

Telephone: 4-72-72-20-20
Telex: 380311
Fax: 4-72-72-20-50

Founded 1973

President: Gilles Guyot
Vice-Presidents: François Piquet, Marie Cariou, Guy Daude, Alain Teston
Secretary-General: Jean-Claude Migraine-George

Number of teachers: 1,643
Number of students: 20,000

Publication: *Lyon 3 Infos* (monthly).

DEANS

Faculty of Law: ADRIEN-CHARLES DANA
Faculty of Languages: CHARLES C. HADLEY
Faculty of Letters and Civilizations: JACQUES BONNET
Faculty of Philosophy: JEAN-CLAUDE BEAUNE
Institute of Business Administration and Management: (vacant)

UNIVERSITÉ DU MAINE

Ave Olivier Messiaen, 72085 Le Mans Cedex 9
Telephone: 2-43-83-30-00
Fax: 2-43-83-30-77
Founded 1977
President: GILLES COTTEREAU
Secretary-General: PHILIPPE WISLER
Number of teachers: 395
Number of students: 10,308
Publication: *Livret de l'Etudiant* (annually).

DEANS

Faculty of Sciences: J. PIERRE BUSNEL
Faculty of Letters and Human Sciences: R. THOLONIOT
Faculty of Economic, Legal and Social Sciences: Y. GUILLOTIN
University Institute of Technology: M. HENRY

UNIVERSITÉ DE MARNE-LA-VALLÉE

2 rue de la Butte Verte, 93166 Noisy-le-Grand Cedex
Telephone: 1-49-32-60-00
Fax: 1-64-73-70-70
Founded 1991
President: DOMINIQUE PERRIN
Secretary-General: GEORGES ROQUEPLAN
Dir of University Institute of Technology: DOMINIQUE PERRIN
Librarian: CHRISTIAN LUPOVICI
Number of teachers: 382
Number of students: 6,000

UNIVERSITÉ DE METZ

Ile du Saulcy, BP 80794, 57012 Metz Cedex 1
Telephone: 3-87-31-50-50
Telex: 930 462
Fax: 3-87-31-50-55
Founded 1970
President: G. NAUROY
Vice-Presidents: G. RHIN, M. POTIER-FERRY, G. GINTER
Secretary-General: MICHEL CLEMENS
Librarian: SIMONE LAMARCHE
Number of teachers: 623
Number of students: 16,484

DEANS

Letters and Human Sciences: M. SARY
Mathematics, Computer Science, Mechanics: A. ZEGHLOUL
Fundamental and Applied Sciences: C. CROCHARD
University Institute of Technology: M. SCHAAL
Law, Economics and Environmental Studies: M. SCHAEFER

HEADS OF DEPARTMENTS

Letters and Human Sciences:
Psychology: M. L. COSTANTINI
Language Science: J. F. HALTE
English: R. SPRINGER
German: M. GRUNEWALD
Spanish: A. CANSECO-JEREZ
Classics: E. AUBRION
Modern Languages: A. CULLIÈRE
History: M. SEVE
Geography: E. GILLE
Philosophy: J. P. RESWEBER
Religious Education: Y. LEDURE
Communication Sciences: N. NEL
Applied Foreign Languages: K. BIRAT
International Exchange: P. SCHAEFFER
Music: P. PREVOST
Plastic Arts: P.-D. HUYGHE
Sociology: S. GUTH
Dramatic Arts: L. JULLIER

Law and Economics:
Law: P. SCHAEFER
Management and Business Administration: B. SIBAUD
Environmental Sciences: Mlle VASSEUR

Mathematics, Computing and Mechanics:
Mathematics and Computer Science: A. ZEGHLOUL
Mechanics, Materials, Technology: J.-C. VÉRONIE

Fundamental and Applied Sciences:
Natural Sciences: J. C. PIHAN
Chemistry: J. C. MORETEAU
Physics and Electronics: M. F. CHARLIER

There are 33 attached research centres and laboratories.

UNIVERSITÉ DE MONTPELLIER I

BP 1017, 34006 Montpellier Cedex
Telephone: 4-67-41-20-90
Telex: 499302
Fax: 4-67-41-02-46
Founded 1970
State control
Language of instruction: French
Academic year: September to June
President: YVES LOUBATIÈRES
General Secretary: SYLVAIN SALTIEL
Librarian: BENOÎT LECOQ
Number of teachers: 829
Number of students: 18,538
Publications: *L'Economie Méridionale, Revue de la Société d'Histoire du Droit, Journal de Médecine, Le Ligament, Cadran.*

TEACHING AND RESEARCH UNITS

Law : Dir O. DUGRIP
Science and Economics: Dir J. PERCEBOIS
Economic and Social Administration: Dir YVES CHIROUZE
Medicine: Dir C. SOLASSOL
Pharmacy: Dir J.-L. CHANAL
Industrial Pharmacy: Dir H. DELONCA
Odontology: Dir P. PARGUEL
Alimentary, Oenological and Environmental Studies: Dir J. C. CABANIS
Physical Education and Sport: Dir L. BELEN

ATTACHED INSTITUTES

Montpellier Higher Institute for Business: Dir D. GATUMEL.

Research Institute for the Study of Juridical Information: Dir J.-L. BILON.

Regional Institute for Economic Study: Dir J.-M. BOISSON.

Institute for Preparation for General Administration: Dir P. DI MALTA.

UNIVERSITÉ DE MONTPELLIER II (SCIENCES ET TECHNIQUES DU LANGUEDOC)

Place Eugène Bataillon, 34095 Montpellier Cedex 5
Telephone: 4-67-14-30-30
Fax: 4-67-14-30-31
E-mail: presidence@univ-montp2.fr
President: YVES ESCOUFIER
Vice-President (Council of Administration): ALAIN FOURNIER
Vice-President (Scientific Council): MICHEL AVEROUS
Vice-President (Council of Studies and University Life): JACQUES MARIGNAN
Secretary-General: BERNARD BIAU
Librarian: MIREILLE GALCERAN
Number of teachers: 970
Number of students: 13,736
Publications: *Naturalia Monspelianesia, Paléobiologie Continentale—Paléovertebrata, Cahiers de Mathématiques.*

TEACHING AND RESEARCH UNITS

Basic and Applied Sciences: Dir CHRISTIANE UHEL
Institute of Engineering Sciences: Dir SERGE PEYTAVIN
Institute of Business Management: Dir PIERRE LOUIS DUBOIS
Higher National School of Chemical Engineers: 8 rue de l'Ecole Normale, 34075 Montpellier Cedex; tel. 4-67-63-52-73; Dir JEAN SARRAZIN
University Institute of Technology of Montpellier: 99 ave d'Occitanie, 34296 Montpellier Cedex 5; tel. 4-67-14-40-40; Dir JEAN-CLAUDE MARTIN
University Institute of Technology of Nîmes: 8 Rue Jules Raimu, 30907 Nîmes Cedex; tel. 4-66-62-85-00; Dir JOSEPH CALAS

UNIVERSITÉ DE MONTPELLIER III (UNIVERSITÉ PAUL VALÉRY)

Place de la Voie Domitienne, BP 5043, 34032 Montpellier Cedex
Telephone: 4-67-14-20-00
Fax: 4-67-14-20-52
Founded 1970
State control
Language of instruction: French
Academic year: October to June
President: PIERRE BENEDETTO
Vice-Presidents: HENRI PICHERAL, MICHEL LAUNAY, ANNIE ESCURET
Secretary-General: STANISLAS KUBIAK
Librarian: PIERRE LECCIA
Number of teachers: 480
Number of students: 18,000
Publications: 68 research periodicals.

TEACHING AND RESEARCH UNITS

Letters, Arts, Philosophy and Linguistics: Dir MICHÈLE WEIL
Anglo-American, Germanic, Slav and Oriental Studies: Dir MICHEL BANDRY
Human and Environmental Sciences: Dir JEAN-PIERRE LUMARET
Economic, Mathematical and Social Sciences: Dir DANY SERRATO
Science of Society: Dir DENIS BROUILLET
Mediterranean Romance Languages: Dir FRANCIS UTEZA

UNIVERSITÉ DE NANCY I (HENRI POINCARÉ)

24 rue Lionnois, BP 3069, 54013 Nancy Cedex
Telephone: 3-83-85-48-00
Fax: 3-83-85-48-48
E-mail: francoise.scheid@uhp.u-nancy.fr
Founded 1970
President: JEAN PIERRE FINANCE
Vice-Presidents: (Administration) CLAUDE BURLET, (Scientific) ALAIN NICOLAS, (Studies and University Life) BERNARD DECARIS
Secretary-General: GEORGES POULL
Number of teachers: 1,210
Number of students: 16,932

TEACHING AND RESEARCH UNITS

Medical Sciences: Dir JACQUES ROLAND
Pharmaceutical and Biological Sciences: Dir CLAUDE VIGNERON

Dental Surgery: Dir JEAN-PAUL LOUIS
Sciences: MICHEL AUBRUN
Biological Sciences: Dir CHRISTIAN DOURNON
Mathematics, Computing and Automation: Dir JEAN-RENÉ CUSSENOT
Materials Science and Processes: Dir PIERRE GUILMIN
Sport and Physical Education: Dir ALAIN ROSSIGNOL
University Institute of Technology (Nancy-Brabois): Dir GÉRARI KRZAKALA
University Institute of Technology (Longwy): Dir BERNARD GAYRAL
Higher School of the Science and Technology of Engineering: Dir CLAUDE HUMBERT
Higher School of the Science and Technology of the Wood Industry: Dir XAVIER DEGLISE
Higher School of Computing and its Applications: Dir JACQUES GUYARD

UNIVERSITÉ DE NANCY II

25 rue Baron Louis, BP 454, 54001 Nancy Cedex
Telephone: 3-83-34-46-00
Fax: 3-83-30-05-65
Founded 1970
State control
Language of instruction: French
Academic year: October to May

President: PIERRE BARDELLI
Vice-President, Administration Council: P. BARDELLI
Vice-President, Scientific Council: H. C. GREGOIRE
Vice-President, Council for Study and University Life: S. M. CEMBALO
Secretary-General: P. AIME
Librarian: J. B. MARINO

Library: see Libraries
Number of teachers: 531
Number of students: 22,000

Publications: *Les Annales de l'Est, Verbum, Revue Géographique de l'Est, Autrement dire, Etudes d'archéologie classique, La Revue française d'études américaines.*

TEACHING AND RESEARCH UNITS

Law, Economic Sciences and Management: Dir ETIENNE CRIQUI
Regional Institute of Labour: Dir MARC MAYOT
Institute of Administrative and Political Studies: Dir JEAN CLAUDE BONNEFONT
Institute of Commerce (Nancy): Dir JACQUES THEVENOT
European University Centre: Dir JEAN DENIS MOUTON
Literature: Dir G. BORRELI
Foreign Languages and Literature: Dir BRUNO TOPPAN
Historical and Geographical Sciences: Dir ANDRÉ WEISROCK
Philosophy, Psychology, Sociology and Educational Sciences: Dir E. GEHIN
Science of Languages: Dir HENRI-CLAUDE GRÉGOIRE
Mathematics and Computer Sciences: Dir JEANINE SOUQUIERES
University Institute of Technology (at Nancy): Dir JEAN-CLAUDE PETIT
University Institute of Technology (at Épinal): Dir HERBERT NERY (acting)
Institute of Cinematographic Studies: Dir ERIC SCHMULEVITCH

UNIVERSITÉ DE NANTES

1 quai de Tourville, BP 13522, 44035 Nantes Cedex 01
Telephone: 2-40-99-83-83
Fax: 2-40-93-83-00
E-mail: president@president.univ-nantes.fr
Founded 1962
State control

President: YANN TANGUY
First Vice-President: FRANÇOIS RESCHE
Vice-Presidents: JEAN MICHEL VIENNE (International Relations), SERGE LEFRANT (Scientific Council), JACQUES MARCHAND (Teaching), JULIEN BEZILLE (Students)
Secretary-General: C. PALU-LABOUREU
Librarian: MICHÈLE GUIOT

Number of teachers: 1,354
Number of students: 33,278

Publication: *Prisme* (6 a year).

TEACHING AND RESEARCH UNITS

Law: M. HELIN
Economics: M. OUISSE
Business Studies: M. BRECHET
Medicine: M. GROLLEAU
Pharmacology: M. SPARFEL
Dentistry: M. MARION
Sciences: M. GINSBURGER-VOGEL
Institute of Technology (Nantes): G. COEURDEUIL
Institute of Technology (St-Nazaire): M. LEFEVRE
Human Sciences: Mme GANGLER
History and Sociology: M. DURAND
Languages: M. LEES
Geography: M. MIOSSEC
Higher Institute of Electronics: M. REMAUD
Institute of Thermodynamics and Materials: M. SCHLEICH
Institute of Preparatory Administrative Studies: M. VINCENT

UNIVERSITÉ DE NICE SOPHIA ANTIPOLIS

28 parc Valrose, 06108 Nice Cedex 2
Telephone: 4-92-07-60-60
Telex: 970281
Fax: 4-92-07-66-00
Founded 1965
State control
Language of instruction: French

President: J. P. LAHEURTE
Vice-Presidents: F. GAYMARD, A. CHIAVELLI, P. FERRAN, Y. HERVIER
Secretary-General: C. KUNTZEL
Librarian: LOUIS KLEE

Number of teachers: 1,200
Number of students: 27,500

Publications: *Annuaire, Guide des formations de Recherche.*

TEACHING AND RESEARCH UNITS

Law, Economics and Management: 7 Ave R. Schuman; Dir R. CRISTINI
Institute of Business Administration: Ave Emile Henriot; Dir M. MARTIN
Law of Peace and Development Law: 7 Ave R. Schuman; Dir L. BALMOND
Medicine: Ave de Vallombrose; Dir P. RAMPAL
Odontology: Ave Joseph Vallot; Dir J. P. ROCCA
Sciences: Parc Valrose; Dir M. ROUILLARD
Letters, Arts and Human Sciences: 98 blvd Edouard Herriot; Dir J. P. ZIROTTI
Physical Education and Sports Sciences: 65 Ave Valrose; Dir J. GAULARD
Culture and Space: 98 blvd Edouard Herriot; Dir L. ROGNANT
Higher School of Information Sciences: 650 route des Colles, 06903 Sophia Antipolis Cedex; Dir J. P. RIGAULT
University Institute of Technology: 41 blvd Napoléon III; Dir J. L. CAVARERO
Higher School of Engineering: 2229 route des Crêtes, 06560 Valbonne; Dir A. CHAVE

PROFESSORS

Law, Economics and Management:

Private Law:

BERNARDINI, R.
COLLOMB, P.
CULIOLI, M.
DE BOTTINI, R.
DEPOULPIQUET, J.
FARJAT, G.
GASTAUD, J.-P.
HONORAT, A.
JULIEN, P.
MARTIN, G.
PIROVANO, A.
VACHET, G.
VIDAL, D.

Public Law:

ASSO, B.
BALMOND, L.
CHARLES, H.
CHARVIN, R.
CRISTINI, R.
GUILLOT COLI, A.
ISOART, P.
LINOTTE, D.
PIQUEMAL, A.
RAINAUD, J.-M.
RIDEAU, J.
TORRELLI, M.
TOUSCOZ, J.
VALLAR, CH.
WAGNER, F.

History of Law:

BOTTIN, M.
CARLIN, M.-L.
MALAUSSENA, P.

Economics:

ARENA, R.
BERTHOMIEU, C.
BOMEL, P.
GAFFARD, J.-L.
GUICHARD, J.-P.
LONGHI, A.
MAROUANI, A.
MAUNOURY, J.-L.
MOCKERS, J.-P.
RAINELLI, M.
RAVIX, J.
SPINDLER, J.

Management:

ALLA, J.
BOYER, A.
CHIAVELLI, A.
DALOZ, J.-P.
GIORDANO, Y.
GUYON, C.
LEBRATY, J.
MARTIN, M.
MICALLEF, A.
SAIDE, J.
SOLLE, G.
TELLER, R.
TOURNOIS, N.

Politics:

BASSO, J.
BIDEGARAY, C.
DABENE, O.

Letters, Arts and Human Sciences:

Sociology and Ethnology:

AFFERGAN, F.
DE VOS, C.
GAIGNEBET, C.
PAUL LÉVY, F.

Psychology:

BEAUVOIS, J. L.
GEFFROY, Y.
JUAN DE MENDOZA, J.-L.
LÉONARD, F.
MIOLLAN, C.
ROUGEUL, F.

Philosophy:

CHARLES, D.
JANICAUD, D.
LARTHOMAS, J.-P.
MATTEÏ, J.-F.
ROSSET, C.

Comparative Literature:

GAEDE, E.

French Literature:
ACCARIE, M.
AMIOT, A.-M.
BONHOMME, B.
BRUNET, E.
COTONI, M.-H.
EMELINA, J.
MARTINEAU, C.

French Philosophy:
GUEDJ, C.

History:
ARNAUD, P.
DERLANGE, M.
PERVILLE, G.
POMPONI, FR.
REBUFFAT, F.
SCHOR, R.
ZERNER, M.

Geography:
DAUPHINE, A.
ESCALLIER, R.
JULIAN, M.
LABORDE, J.-P.
PAULET, J.-P.
ROGNANT, L.

Linguistics and Phonetics:
DALBERA, J.-PH.
JUNKOVIC, Z.
KOTLER, E.
NICOLAI, R.
ZINGLE, H.

Greek:
RICHER, R.
THIVEL, A.

English:
BARDOLPH, J.
BONIFAS, G.
COUTURIER, M.
JUILLARD, M.
LAPRAZ, F.
LEMOSSE, M.
MURAIRE, A.
OLLIER, J.
REMY, M.
SOUESME, J.-C.
TERREL, D.
VIOLA, A.

German:
DARMAUN, J.
FAURE, A.
STOLWITZER, G.
VUILLAUME, M.

Latin:
BENEJAM, M.-J.
KIRCHER, C.
MUSTAPHA, M.

Romance Languages:
BARUCCO, P., Italian
BRAU, J.-L., Spanish
CADUC, E., French
CASTELA, P., Occitan
JAUBERT, A., French
LAVERGNE, G., Spanish
MOLITERNO, R., Italian
MOROLDO, A., Italian
OTTAVI, A., Italian
SPIZZO, J., Italian

Music:
LELEU, J.-L.

Information Science:
SANOUILLET, A.

Physical Education:
CLAMENS, D.

Sciences:
PETIT, L.

Mathematics:
AUBERT, G.
BRIANCON, J.
CATHELINEAU, J.-L.
CHAZARAIN, J.
CHENAIS, D.
DIENER, F.
DIENER, M.
ELENCWAJG, G.
HIRSCHOWITZ, A.
KOSTOV, V.
LABROUSSE-CASTAING, J.-PH.
LE BARZ, P.
LEMAIRE, J.
LEMAIRE, J.-M.
LOBRY, C.
MAISONOBE, P.
MARLIN, R.
MERLE, M.
MONTALDI, J.
PHAM, F.
PIRIOU, A.
POUPAUD, F.
RASCLE, M.
RIX, H.
ROUSSELET, B.
ROUVIÈRE, F.
WALTER, C.
WOJTKOWIAK, Z.
XIOA, G.

Information Sciences:
BOND, I.
BOUSSARD, J.-C.
CAVARERO, J.-L.
LE CARME, O.
LE THANH, N.
LITOVSKY, I.
MIRANDA, S.
PEYRAT, CL.
RUEHER, M.
SANDER, P.
THOMAS, M.-C.
RIGAULT, J.-P.
WATT, S.

Physics:
AZEMA, A.
ELÉGANT, L.
GILABERT, A.
KOFMAN, R.
LAHEURTE, J.-P.
LAPRAZ, D.
LÉVY-LEBLOND, J.-M.
LEYCURAS, C.
MEUNIER, J.-L.
OSTROWSKY, D.
OSTROWSKY, N.
PROVOST, J.-P.
ROMAGNON, J.-P.
VASILESCU, D.

Electronics and Industrial Computer Science:
ALENGRIN, G.
ANDRÉ, C.
CAMBIAGGIO, E.
CHAVE, A.
MENEZ, J.
PAPIERNIK, A.
ROSTAING, P.
THIELTGEN, A.

Astrophysics:
AIME, C.
BORGNINO, J.
LANTERI, H.
MARTIN. F.
RICORT, G.

Geology:
CARUBA, R.
CASANOVA, R.
DELTEIL, J.
LEPAGE, M.-TH.
STEPHAN, J.-F.
VIRIEUX, J.

Mineralogy, Geochemistry, Petrography, Applied Geology:
BERNAT, M.

General Chemistry:
ARDISSON, G.
CABROL BASS, D.
GRENET, J.-C.
GUION, J.
HUBERT, L.
LEROUX, J.
MARIA, H.

Organic, Mineral and Analytical Chemistry:
AZZARO, M.
CAMBON, A.
FELLOUS, R.
GAL, F.
GAYMARD, F.
GUEDJ, R.
PASTOR, R.
RIESS, J.
ROUILLARD, M.

Biochemistry:
AILHAUD, G.
CLERTANT, P.
CUPPO, A.
CUZIN, F.
FEHLMANN, M.
GLAICHENHAUS, N.
LAZDUNSKI, M.
NEGREL, R,
VINCENT, J.-P.

Physiology and Biology:
BORNANCIN, M., Cellular and Comparative Physiology
BROCH, H., Biophysics
EHRENFELD, J., Cellular and Comparative Physiology
FARGES, J.-P., Biophysics
FREDJ, G., Biological Oceanography
GIRARD, J.-P., Cellular and Comparative Physiology
GOTTESMANN, C., Psychophysiology
GREUET, C., Cytophysiology
JAUBERT, J., Experimental Ecology
LAHLOU, B., Cellular and Comparative Physiology
LE RUDULIER, D., Plant Biology and Microbiology
MEINESZ, A., Marine Ecology and Biology
NICAISE, G., Applied Microscopy
NICAISE, M.-L., Applied Microscopy
PAYAN, P., Cellular and Comparative Physiology
PUPPO, A., Plant Biology and Microbiology
RIGAUD, J., Plant Biology and Microbiology
VIANI, R., Biophysics

Higher School of Information Sciences:
FRANCHI-ZANNETTACCI, P.
GALLIGO, A.
GIULIERI, A.
LAFON, J.-C.

Non-Linear Institute of Nice:
COULLET, P.
DEMAY, Y.
GUÉRIN, F.
IOOSS, G.
LE BELLAC, M.
ROCCA, F.

University Institute of Technology:
BARLAUD, M.
BOERI, F.
DEMARTINI, J.
GUIRAUD, J.-L.
POMPEI, D.
TREDDICE, J.
TSCHAEGLE, A.

Physical Education and Sports Sciences:
ERRAIS, B.
MARCONNET, P.

Medicine:
AMIEL, J., Urology
ARGENSON, C., Surgery
AYRAUD, N., Genetics
BALAS, D., Histology
BATT, M., Surgery
BAUDOUY, M., Cardiology
BERNARD, A., Immunology
BLAIVE, B., Pneumology
BOCQUET, J.-P., Hygiene
BOURGEON, A., Anatomy
BOUTTE, P., Paediatrics
BRUNETON, J.-N., Radiology
BUSSIÈRE, F., Biophysics

CAMOUS, J.-P., Therapeutics
CANIVET, B., Internal Medicine
CAREL, C., Histology
CASSUTO, J.-P., Haematology
CHATEL, M., Neurology
COUSSEMENT, A., Radiology
DARCOURT, G., Psychiatry
DELLAMONICA, P., Infectious Diseases
DELMONT, J., Hepatology
DEMARD, F., Oto-rhino-laryngology
DESNUELLE, C., Cellular Biology
DOLISI, C., Physiology
DUJARDIN, P., Internal Medicine
DURJEUX, E., Haematology
FREYCHET, P., Endocrinology
FUZIBET, J.-G., Internal Medicine
GASTAUD, P., Ophthalmology
GILLET, J.-Y., Gynaecology
GRELLIER, P., Neurosurgery
GRIMAUD, D., Anaesthesiology
GUGENHEIM, J., Digestive Surgery
HARTER, M., Endocrinology
JOURDAN, J., Thoracic Surgery
KERMANREC, J., Pathological Anatomy
LACOUR, J.-P., Dermatology
LAMBERT, J.-CL., Genetics
LAPALUS, P., Pharmacology
LE BAS, P., Vascular Surgery
LE FICHOUX, Y., Parasitology
LEBRETON, E., Surgery
LEFEBVRE, J.-C., Bacteriology
MARIANI, R., Paediatrics
MATTEI, M., Resuscitation
MICHIELS, J.-F., Pathological Anatomy
MORAND, P., Cardiology
MOUIEL, J., Digestive Surgery
MYQUEL, M., Child Psychiatry
OLLIER, A., Forensic Medicine
ORTONNE, J.-P., Dermatology
PRINGUEY, D., Psychiatry
RAMPAL, P., Hepatology
RICHELME, H., General Surgery
SANTINI, J., Oto-rhino-laryngology
SCHNEIDER, M., Cancerology
SERRES, J.-J., Radiology
SUDAKA, P., Biochemistry
THYSS, A., Cancerology
TOUBOL, J., Urology
TRAN, D. K., Gynaecology
ZIEGLER, G., Rehabilitation
ZIEGLER, L., Rheumatology

Odontology:

EXBRAYAT, J.
JASMIN, J.
MONTEIL, R.
PALLANCA, C.
ROCCA, J.-P.

UNIVERSITÉ d'ORLÉANS

Château de la Source, BP 6749, 45067 Orléans Cedex 2

Telephone: 2-38-41-71-71
Fax: 2-38-41-70-69

Founded 1961
Language of instruction: French
Academic year: September to June

President: MICHEL MUDRY
Vice-Presidents: MICHEL PERTUÉ, JACQUES CHARVET, JEAN-MARIE GINESTA
Secretary-General: ANNE CHAUVIRÉ
Librarian: Mme DESBORDES

Number of teachers: 400
Number of students: 17,500

Publications: *Bulletin d'informations de l'Université* (5 a year), *Plaquette en direction des entreprises* (annually), *1er contact* (annually), *Internships* (annually), research catalogue.

TEACHING AND RESEARCH UNITS

Law, Economics and Management: Dir JEAN-PAUL POLLIN
Letters, Languages and Human Sciences: Dir JOËL MIRLOUP
Sciences: Dir ANDRÉ BARASSIN
University Institute of Technology (Orléans): Dir JEAN-PIERRE COÏC
University Institute of Technology (Bourges): Dir PIERRE MARCHÉ
University Institute of Technology (Chartres): Dir JEAN-MICHEL THOMAS
Higher School of Energy and Material Resources: Dir VINCENT PERTHUSIOT
Higher School of Electronics for Optics: Dir JACQUES THIEL
University Institute of Technology (Châteauroux): Dir J.-P. COLSON
School of Sports: Dir CH. CATHELINEAU

UNIVERSITÉ DE PARIS I (PANTHÉON-SORBONNE)

12 place du Panthéon, 75231 Paris Cedex 05

Telephone: 1-46-34-97-00

Founded 1971
State control
Language of instruction: French
Academic year: September to June

President: YVES JEGOUZO
First Vice-President: LÉON PRESSOUYRE
Secretary-General: DIDIER SABINE
Librarian: GENEVIÈVE SIMONOT

Number of teachers: 1,024
Number of students: 43,256

TEACHING AND RESEARCH UNITS

General Economics, Business Administration: Dir Prof. ROJOT
Economic Analysis and Politics, Econometrics, Labour and Human Resources: Prof. E. ARCHAMBAULT
Public Administration and Public Law: Dir Prof. PICARD (acting)
Business Law: Dir Prof. CHAPUT (acting)
Development, International, European and Comparative Studies: Dir Prof. MANIN
Geography: Dir Prof. POURTIER (acting)
History: Prof. PARISSE (acting)
Philosophy: Dir Prof. MOSCONI
Economic and Social Administration, Labour and Social Studies: Dir C. MILLS
Political Science: Dir Prof. BRAUD (acting)
Plastic Arts and Science of Art: Dir Prof. COHEN (acting)
History of Art and Archaeology: Dir Prof. ALAIN SCHNAPP
Mathematics, Statistics and Informatics: Dir Prof. BONNISSEAU (acting)

INSTITUTES

Institute of Business Administration: Dir Prof. HELFER
Institute of Demography: Dir Prof. DITTGEN (acting)
Institute of Economic and Social Development: Dir Prof. HAUBERT (acting)
Institute of Social Sciences: Dir Prof. PAULRE

DEPARTMENTS

Applied Modern Languages, Economics and Law: Dir L. THOMPSON (acting)
Applied Modern Languages, Humanities: Dir A. BIANCHI (acting)
Co-ordination of Juridic and Political Sciences: Dir Prof. CHAPUT
Social Sciences: Dir M. GRAS

PROFESSORS

Public Administration and Public Internal Law:

CASTAGNEDE, B., Public Finance
CLAISSE, A., Administrative Management
DUHAMEL, O., Constitutional Law
DUPUIS, G., Administrative Law and Institutions
DURUPTY, M., Public Law
GEST, G., Finance
GICQUEL, J., Public Law
GILLI, J. P., Administrative Law
JEGOUZO, Y., Administrative Law
LEGENDRE, P., Administrative Law and History of Law
LE MIRE, P., Public Law
MODERNE, F., Administrative Law
MORAND-DEVILLER, J., Administrative Law
PICARD, E., Administrative Law
TIMSIT, G., Public Law

Economic Analysis and Politics, Econometrics, Labour and Human Resources:

ANDREFF, V., Economy of the Transition
ARCHAMBAULT, E., Accountancy and Social Economics
BERTHELEMY, J., International Economics
CAHUC, P., Macroeconomics
CHAUVEAU, TH., Money and Finance
COHEN, D., Mathematical Economics
DE BOISSIEU, C., Monetary Economics
DE MASSON D'AUTUME, A., Macroeconomics
ENCAOUA, D., Industrial Economics
FARDEAU, Mme M., Health Economics, Social Economics
FAU, Mme J., Economic Analysis
GARDES, F., Econometrics
GOUX, C., Applied Macro-economics
GREFFE, X., Political Economy
HENIN, P., Macroeconomics
LAFAY, J. D., Public Economy
LANTNER, R., Economics and Industrial Politics
LAPIDUS, A., History of Economic Thought
LASSUDRIE-DUCHENE, B., International Economics
LEVY GARBOUA, L., Microeconomics
MENARD, C., Theory of Organizations
PASSET, R., Environmental Economics
PERROT, A., Macroeconomics
PHAN DUC LOI, International Economics
SOLLOGOUB, M., Microeconomics
THISSE, J., Mathematical Economics
VERNIERES, M., Economic Analysis
ZAGAME, P., Macroeconomics

History of Art and Archaeology:

CROISSANT, F., Greek Archaeology
DEMOULE, J.-P., Protohistory
DENTZER, J. M., Archaeology and History of Roman Art
HUOT, J. L., Oriental Archaeology
LICHARDUS, M., Protohistory
MENIER, M., History of Contemporary Art
MONNIER, G., History of Contemporary Art
PRESSOUYRE, L., Medieval Art and Archaeology
RABREAU, D., History of Arts
SCHNAPP, A., Greek Archaeology
SODINI, J. P., Byzantine Archaeology
TABORIN, Y., Prehistory
TREUIL, R. A., Archaeology and Protohistory
VOVELLE, M.-J., History of 20th-century Art

Plastic Arts:

BAQUE, P., Plastic Arts
CHATEAU, D., Aesthetics
CHIRON, E., Plastic Arts
CLANCY, G., Aesthetics
FRENAULT-DERUELLE, P., Semiotics
JIMENEZ, M., Aesthetics
LANCRI, J., Plastic Arts
LEBENSZTEJN, J. C., History of Art
MIEREANU, C., Musicology
NOGUEZ, D., Cinema and Audiovisual Arts
PALMIER, J.-M., Aesthetics
SERCEAU, D., Cinema and Audiovisual Arts

Business Law:

AYNES, L., Private and Civil Law
BIGOT, J., Civil and Insurance Law
BOULOC, B., Private Law and Criminology
CHAPUT, Y., Commerical Law
COLOMBET, C., Civil Law
GAVALDA, C., Banking and Commercial Law
GHESTIN, J., Civil Law
GUYON, Y., Commercial Law

HONORAT, J., Commercial Law
LABRUSSE, C., Civil Law
LUCAS DE LEYSSAC, C., Commercial Law
SCHMIDT, J. L., Fiscal Law
VINEY, G., Civil Law

Managerial Economics and Business:

BAETCHE, A., Scientific Methods Applied to Marketing
DE LA BRUSLERIE, H., Finance
GOFFIN, R., Finance
GREGORY, P., Marketing
JOBARD, J. P., Finance
LAURENT, P., Business Law
MUCHIELLI, J.-L., Industrial Economics
OPSOMER, C., Marketing
PARENT, J., Industrial Politics
PEYRARD, M., International and European Business
PONCET, P., Finance
RAIMBOURG, P., Finance
RAY, J.-E., Business Law
ROJOT, J., Theory of Organizations
ROLLAND, C., Informatics
ROURE, F., Finance
WOLFF, J., Sociology and Social Psychology

Development, International, European and Comparative Studies:

ALLIOT, M., African Institutions
BURDEAU, G., International Public Law
CARREAU, D., Economic Public Law
DELMAS-MARTY, M., Penal Law
FROMONT, M., Constitutional Law
HUDAULT, J., History of Law
JUILLARD, P., International Economic Law
LAGARDE, P., International Private Law
LE ROY, E., Legal Anthropology
LUCCHINI, L., International Public Law
MANIN, P., European Community Law
MAYER, P., International Private Law
MORISSON, C., Development Economics
STERN, B., International Public Law

Geography:

CAZES, G., Geography of Tourism
FAUGERES, L., Physical Geography
FISCHER, A., Regional Geography
GODARD, A., Physical Geography
MALEZIEUX, J., Regional Geography, Land Use
MERLIN, P., Urban Geography
NOIN, D., Population Geography
POURTIER, R., Tropical Geography
PUMAIN, D., Urban Geography
RAFFY, J., Physical Geography
ROCHEFORT, M., Urban and Human Geography
SAINT-JULIEN, TH., Human Geography, Statistics
SOPPELSA, J., Geopolitics
TABEAUD, M., Climatology

History:

BALARD, M., Mediterranean Medieval History
BERTAUD, J. P., History of the French Revolution
BOULEGUE, J.-M., History of Black Africa
CHARPIN, D., Near Eastern History
CHRISTOL, M., Roman History
CORBIN, A., Contemporary History
GAUVARD, C., Medieval History
GUERRA, F., History of Latin America
KAPLAN, M., Byzantine Medieval History
KASPI, A., History of North America
LEMAITRE, N., Modern History
LE ROY, C., Greek History
MARSEILLE, J., Economic and Social History
MELEZE, J., Ancient History
MICHEL, B., History of Eastern Europe
PROST, A., Contemporary History
ROCHE, D., Culture and Society in 'Ancien Régime' France
SALOMON-BAYET, C., History of Science and Technology
SERMAN, S., Contemporary Military History
SERRES, M., History of Science and Technology
WORONOFF, D., Economic and Social History

Philosophy:

BLOCH, O., History of Philosophy
BLONDEL, E., Moral and Political Philosophy
BONARDEL, F., Philosophy of Religion
BOURGEOIS, B., History of Philosophy
BOUVERESSE, J., Philosophy of Logic
BRAGUE, R., History of Philosophy
CARRIVE, P., English Philosophy
CHEDIN, O., History of Philosophy
COLETTE, C., General Philosophy
GRAS, A., Social Philosophy
LASCAULT, G., Aesthetics
MICHAUD, Y., History of Philosophy
PINTO, E., Aesthetics

Political Science:

BIRNBAUM, P., Political Sociology
BRAUD, P., Political Sociology
COLLIARD, J. C., Comparative Government
CONAC, G., Comparative Political Institutions
COT, J. P., International Law
COTTERET, J.-M., Political Communication
EMERI, C., Comparative Government
GAXIE, D., Political Sociology
KLEIN, J., International Relations
LAGROYE, J., Political Sociology
LESAGE, M., Theory of Organizations
PISIER, E., Political Philosophy
QUENEUDEC, J.-P., International Public Law
SFEZ, L., Communication
ZORGBIBE, C., International Relations

Economic and Social Administration, Labour and Social Studies:

BLANC-JOUVAN, X., International Civil Law
COUTURIER, G., Labour Law
GAZIER, B., Labour Economy
GUILLEMARD, A. M., Sociology
LENOIR, R., Sociology
RODIERE, P., Labour Law

Mathematics, Statistics and Computer Science:

ABDOU, J., Game Theory
AUSLENDER, A., Optimization
BALASKO, Y., Mathematical Economics
BONNISSEAU, J.-M., Mathematics and Economics
CORNET, B., Mathematics and Economics
COTTRELL, M., Probability, Statistics and Neural Networks
GIRE, F., Computer Science
GUYON, X., Probability and Statistics
HADDAD, G., Differential Equations and Functional Analysis
JOUINI, E., Mathematics and Economics

Business Administration:

GIARD, V., Operations Management
HELFER, J.-P., Marketing and Accounting
MAILLET, P., Finance
TRIOLAIRE, G., Management
WEISS, D., Management

Demography:

GROSSAT, B., Socio-Demography
NORVEZ, A., Socio-Demography

Economic and Social Development:

GRELLET, G., Economic Development
HAUBERT, M., Social Development
LAUTIER, B., Economic and Social Development

Institute of Social Sciences:

DELEBECQUE, P., Private Law
FREYSSINET, J., Economics
OFFERLE, M., Political Science
PAULRE, B., Economics

Applied Modern Languages, Economics and Law:

BULLIER, A.-J., Legal English Studies

UNIVERSITÉ DE PARIS II (UNIVERSITÉ PANTHÉON-ASSAS)

12 place du Panthéon, 75231 Paris Cedex 05

Telephone: 1-44-41-57-00
Fax: 1-44-41-55-13

Founded 1970

President: BERNARD TEYSSIÉ
Secretary-General: PATRICK LE GUERER
Librarian: GENEVIÈVE SONNEVILLE

Number of teachers: 300
Number of students: 13,000

TEACHING AND RESEARCH UNITS

Law (First cycle): JEAN-BERNARD BLAISE
Law (Second cycle) and Political Science: JEAN COMBACAU
Law (Third cycle) and Political Science: J. CHEVALLIER
Economics: ANTOINE BILLOT
Economic and Social Administration (First and Second cycles): C. LABROUSSE
Information Sciences (French Press Institute): Dir Prof. REMY RIEFFEL
Institute of Judicial Studies: Dir Prof. S. GUINCHARD
Institute of Advanced International Studies: Dirs C. LEBEN, P.-MARIE DUPUY
Institute of Comparative Law: Dir Prof. LOUIS VOGEL
Institute for Administration Training: Dir MICHEL VERPEAUX
Image and Communication Institute: Dir Prof. C. TUAL
Institute of Business Law: Dir Prof. MICHEL GERMAIN
Institute of Criminology: Dir Prof. JACQUES-HENRI ROBERT
Higher Institute for Defence Studies: Dir Prof. YVES CARO
Centre for Studies and Research in Construction and Housing: Dir Prof. P. MALINVAUD
Centre for Human Resources Training: Dir Prof. A. M. FERICELLI
IUP–Management: Dir Prof. RAYMOND TRÉMOLIÈRES

PROFESSORS

ALLAND, D., Public Law
ALPHANDERY, E., Economic Sciences
AMSELEK, P., Public Law
ANCEL, D., Private Law
AUBY, J. B., Public Law
AUDIT, B., Private Law
AVRIL, P., Political Science
BALLE, F., Political Science
BALLOT, G., Economic Sciences
BARRAT, J., Information Sciences
BENZONI, L., Economic Sciences
BERNARD, M., Education Sciences
BETBEZE, J.-P., Economic Sciences
BETTATI, M., Public Law
BIENVENU, J. J., Public Law
BILLOT, A., Economic Sciences
BLAISE, J.-B., Private Law
BLUMANN, C., Public Law
BOISIVON, J.-P., Management Science
BONET, G., Private Law
BONNEAU, T., Private Law
BOURNOIS, F., Management Science
BRESSON, G., Economic Sciences
BURDEAU, F., History of Law
CARBASSE, J. M., History of Law
CARO, J.-Y., Economic Science
CARTIER, M.-E., Private Law
CASTALDO, A., History of Law
CATALA, Mme N., Private Law
CAZENAVE, P., Economic Sciences
CHAGNOLAUD, D., Political Science
CHAMPENOIS, G., Private Law
CHARPIN, F., Economic Sciences
CHEVALLIER, J., Public Law
CHRISTIN, Y., Economic Sciences
COCATRE-ZILGIEN, P., History of Law
COHEN-JONATHAN, G., Public Law

COMBACAU, J., Public Law
CROCQ, P., Private Law
DECOCQ, A., Private Law
DELVOLVE, P., Public Law
DERIEUX, E., Information Science
DESNEUF, P., Economic Science
DESPLAS, M., Economic Sciences
DIBOUT, P., Public Law
DIDIER, P., Private Law
DISCHAMPS, J. C., Management Science
DONIO, J., Computing
DUPUY, G., Public Law
DURRY, G., Private Law
DUTHEIL DE LA ROCHÈRE, J., Public Law
FACCARELLO, G., Economic Sciences
FERICELLI, Mme A.-M., Economic Sciences
FEYEL, G., History
FOUCHARD, P., Private Law
FOYER, J., Private Law
GAUDEMET, Y., Public Law
GAUDEMET-TALLON, H., Private Law
GAUTIER, P. Y., Private Law
GERMAIN, M., Private Law
GHOZI, A., Private Law
GJIDARA, M., Public Law
GOBERT, Mme M., Private Law
GOYARD, C., Public Law
GRIMALDI, M., Private Law
GUINCHARD, S., Private Law
HAROUEL, J.-L., History of Law
HUET, J., Private Law
HUMBERT, M., History of Law
JAHEL, S., Private Law
JARROSON, C., Private Law
JAUFFRET-SPINOSI, C., Private Law
JAVILLIER, J.-C., Private Law
JEANNEAU, B., Public Law
LABROUSSE, C., Economic Sciences
LAFAY, G., Economic Sciences
LAINGUI, A., History of Law
LAMARQUE, J., Public Law
LARROUMET, C., Private Law
LEBEN, C., Public Law
LEFEBVRE-TEILLARD, A., History of Law
LE GALL, J.-P., Private Law
LEMENNICIER-BUCQUET, B., Economic Sciences
LEMOYNE DE FORGES, J. M., Public Law
LEQUETTE, Y., Private Law
LEVENEUR, L., Private Law
LOMBARD, M., Public Law
LOMBOIS, C., Private Law
LUBOCHINSKY, C., Economic Sciences
MALINVAUD, P., Private Law
MARTINEZ, J. C., Public Law
MERLE, P., Private Law
MONCONDUIT, F., Political Science
MORANGE, J., Public Law
MOREAU, J., Public Law
MOURGUES, Mme M. DE, Economic Sciences
NEME, Mme C., Economic Sciences
OLIVIER, J. M., Private Law
PELE, M., Management Science
PONDAVEN, C., Economic Sciences
PORTELLI, H., Political Science
QUENET, M., History of Law
RAYNAUD, P., Political Science
REDSLOB, A., Economic Sciences
RIALS, S., Public Law
RIEFFEL, R., Information Sciences
RIGAUDIERE, A., History of Law
ROBERT, J.-H., Private Law
ROUGEMONT, M. DE, Computing
SCANNAVINO, A., Economic Sciences
SCHWARTZENBERG, R. G., Public Law
SUR, S., Public Law
SYNVET, H., Private Law
TERLON, C., Education Sciences
TERRE, F., Private Law
TEYSSIÉ, B., Private Law
THERY, P., Private Law
TOUSSAINT-DESMOULINS, N., Information Science
TREMOLIÈRES, R., Management Science
TRUCHET, D., Public Law
TUAL, C., English
VEDEL, C., Economic Sciences
VENEZIA, J.-CL., Public Law
VERPEAUX, M., Public Law
VITRY, D., Economic Sciences
VOGEL, L., Private Law
ZOLLER, E., Public Law

UNIVERSITÉ DE PARIS III (SORBONNE-NOUVELLE)

17 rue de la Sorbonne, 75230 Paris Cedex 05

Telephone: 1-40-46-28-97
Fax: 1-43-25-74-71

Founded 1970
State control
Language of instruction: French
Academic year: October to June

President: JEAN-LOUIS LEUTRAT
Vice-Presidents: P. HAMON, A. ROCCHETTI, J. REVEL-MOUROZ
Secretary-General: DIDIER RAMOND
Librarian: Mme N. LE BRENN

Number of teachers: 480
Number of students: 20,000

TEACHING AND RESEARCH UNITS

Theatre Studies: Dir J. P. RYNGAERT
General and Comparative Literature: Dir D. PAGEAUX
Language, Literatures and Civilizations of English-Speaking Countries: Dir J. C. SERGEANT
German Institute: Dir H. SCHULTE
General Phonetics and Linguistics: Dir E. PIETRI
Institute of Latin American Studies: Dir G. COUFFIGNAL
French as a Foreign Language: Dir Mlle E. WAGNER
Indian, Oriental and North African Languages and Civilizations: Dir B. DAGENS
Higher School of Interpreters and Translators: Dir Mme LEDERER
Finnish and Hungarian Studies: Dir (vacant)
French Language and Literature: Dir M. DAMBRE
Italian and Romanian: Dir G. DE VAN
Iberian Studies: Dir G. LUQUET
Cinematographic Studies: Dir M. MARIE
Department of Studies of Contemporary Society: Dir J.-C. ALLAIN
Department of Techniques of Expression and Communication: Dir G. LOCHARD
Department of Cultural Mediation: Dir C. AZIZA
Centre of Finno-Ugrian Studies: Dir B. BOIRON
Applied Foreign Languages Centre: Dir G. GUILLARD

UNIVERSITÉ DE PARIS IV (PARIS-SORBONNE)

1 rue Victor-Cousin, 75230 Paris Cedex 05

Telephone: 1-40-46-22-11
Fax: 1-40-46-25-88
E-mail: georges.molinie@paris4.sorbonne.fr

Founded 1970
State control
Language of instruction: French
Academic year: October to June

President: GEORGES MOLINIÉ
Secretary-General: A. RICHART-LEBRUN
Librarian: B. VAN DOOREN

Number of teachers: 750
Number of students: 30,898

TEACHING AND RESEARCH UNITS

French Literature: Dir Prof. M. MURAT
French Language: Dir Prof. M. HUCHON
Latin Language and Literature: Dir Prof. H. ZEHNACKER
Greek: Dir Prof. J. JOUANNA
Philosophy: Dir Prof. A. RENAUT
History: Dir Prof. J. P. MARTIN
History of Art and Archaeology: Dir Prof. B. FOUCART
Geography: Dir Prof. CH. HUETZ DE LEMPS
English and North American Studies: Dir Prof. J. R. ROUGÉ
Germanic Studies: Dir Prof. J.-M. VALENTIN
Iberian Studies: Dir Prof. A. MOLINIÉ
Italian and Romanian: Dir Prof. C. BEC
Slavonic Studies: Dir Prof. F. CONTE
Applied Foreign Languages: Dir Prof. G. SCHNEILIN
Music and Musicology: Dir Prof. L. JAMBOU
Modern Western Civilization: Dir J. BÉRENGER
Institute of Applied Humanities: Dir Prof. F. CHAZEL
Institute of Information and Communication: Dir Prof. J. B. CARPENTIER
Centre for Applied Iberian and Latin-American Studies: Dir C. LESELBAUM

GRADUATE SCHOOLS

Sciences of Language and Communication: Dir Prof. P. VALENTIN
French and Comparative Literatures: Prof. F. MOUREAU
Foreign Literatures and Cultures: Prof. J. M. VALENTIN
Philosophy and Social Sciences: Prof. R. BOUDON
Classical World and its Legacy: Prof. J. JOUANNA
Medieval Studies: Prof. PH. MÉNARD
History of Modern Civilizations: Prof. J. P. POUSSOU
Contemporary Societies: Prof. G. H. SOUTOU
History of Art and Archaeology: Prof. PH. BRUNEAU
Geography and Urban Studies: Prof. P. CLAVAL
Sciences of Religion and Religious Anthropology: Prof. J. C. FREDOUILLE
Music and Musicology: Prof. L. JAMBOU

UNIVERSITÉ RENÉ DESCARTES (Paris V)

12 rue de l'École de Médecine, 75270 Paris Cedex 06

Telephone: 1-40-46-16-16
Fax: 1-40-46-16-15
E-mail: secretaire.general@univ-paris5.fr

Founded 1970
Academic year: October to June

President: PIERRE VILLARD
Vice-Presidents: P. DAUMARD, J. C. DEPEZAY, A. CARTRON, G. LANGOUET, D. DURAND, D. SICARD, H. MEAU-LAUTOUR, K. FINI
Secretary-General: M. RONZEAU
Librarian: J. KALFON

Number of teachers: 1,752
Number of students: 30,564

TEACHING AND RESEARCH UNITS

Human and Social Sciences: Dir PH. LABURTHE-TOLRA
Institute of Psychology: Dir S. IONESCU
Mathematics and Data Processing: Dir M. SCHREIBER
Medicine: Cochin—Port-Royal: Dir J. P. LUTON
Medicine: Necker—Enfants Malades: Dir PH. EVEN
Medicine: Paris-Ouest: Dir J. P. GALLET
Biomedicine: Dir A. COBLENTZ
Dentistry: Dir G. ZEILIG
Forensic Medicine and Medical Law: Dir A. HAERTIG
Pharmaceutical and Biological Sciences: Dir D. DURAND
University Institute of Technology: Dir J.-P. MATHERON
Physical Education and Sports: Dir P. FILIPPI
Faculty of Law: Dir H. MEAU-LAUTOUR

UNIVERSITÉ DE PARIS VI (PIERRE ET MARIE CURIE)

4 place Jussieu, 75252 Paris Cedex 05
Telephone: 1-44-27-44-27
Telex: 200 145

President: JEAN LEMERLE
Secretary General: P. ENDRIVET

TEACHING AND RESEARCH UNITS

Pure and Applied Mathematics: Dir M. GAVEAU
Mathematical Sciences and Engineering: Dir M. BOUGEROL
Computer Sciences: Dir M. HORLAIT
Mechanical and Robotic Engineering and Energy: Dir M. THELLIEZ
Electrical, Electronic and Automation, Applied Physics: Dir M. ALQUIE
Fundamental and Applied Physics: Dir M. PETROFF
Chemistry: Dir M. MASSART
Life Sciences: Dir M. GUERDOUX
Earth Sciences and the Evolution of Natural Environments: Dir M. RENARD
Medicine, Saint-Antoine: Dir M. THIBAULT
Medicine, Pitié-Salpétrière: Dir M. BRUNET
Medicine, Broussais-Hotel-Dieu: Dir M. BARIETY
Stomatology and Maxillofacial Surgery: Dir M. VAILLANT
Institute of Science and Technology: Dir M. LANDAU
Oceanological Observatory, Roscoff: Dir M. TOULMOND
Oceanological Observatory, Banyuls: Dir M. GUILLE
Oceanological Observatory, Villefranche-sur-Mer: Dir M. SOYER

UNIVERSITÉ DE PARIS VII (DENIS DIDEROT)

2 place Jussieu, 75251 Paris Cedex 05
Telephone: 1-44-27-53-67
Fax: 1-44-27-69-12

Founded 1970

President: MICHEL DELAMAR
Secretary-General: PIERRE MAUSSION

Number of teachers: 2,000
Number of students: 30,000

Publication: *VUES*.

TEACHING AND RESEARCH UNITS

Anthropology, Ethnology and Religious Studies: Dir P. DESHAYES
Biochemistry: Dir A. KLIER
Biology and Natural Sciences: Dir C. BERGMAN
Chemistry: Dir J. PINSON
Didactics of Disciplines: Dir L. BOASSON
Management and Environmental Protection: Dir J. P. FRANGI
Dental Surgery: Dir P. GIRARD
Medicine (Lariboisière-Saint-Louis): Dir D. KUNTZ
Medicine (Xavier-Bichat): Dir J. M. DESMONTS
Geography and Social Sciences: Dir P. KAPLAN
Institute of Haematology: Dir L. DEGOS
Institute of English: Dir M. ORIANO
Eastern Asian Languages and Literature: Dir F. JULLIEN
Intercultural Studies in Applied Languages: Dir J. ATHERTON
Mathematics: Dir L. ELIE
Computer Studies: Dir C. CHOFFRUT
Physics: Dir L. VALENTIN
Linguistic Research: Dir B. CERQUINGLINI
Clinical Human Sciences: Dir M. TORT
Earth and Physical Sciences: Dir J. P. COGNE
Sciences of Texts and Documents: Dir G. ROSA
Social Sciences: Dir S. DAYAN
Film, Communication and Information Studies: Dir S. LIANDRAT-GIGUES
University Institute of Technology: Dir A. JUNGMANN

UNIVERSITÉ DE PARIS VIII—VINCENNES À ST-DENIS

2 rue de la Liberté, 93526 St Denis Cedex 02
Telephone: 1-49-40-67-89
Fax: 1-48-21-04-46

Founded 1969
State control
Language of instruction: French

President: RENAUD FABRE
Vice-Presidents: HARALD WERTZ (Administration), JACQUES NEEFS (Scientific), ALAIN BLANCHET (Academic Studies and University Life)
Secretary-General: FRANÇOIS VIGNAUX
Librarian: MADELEINE JULLIEN

Number of teachers: 739
Number of students: 24,825

Publications: *Médiévales, Histoire, Epistémologie, Langage, Recherches linguistiques de Vincennes, Théorie, Littérature, Enseignement, Humoresques, Extrême-Orient, Extrême-Occident, Pratiques de Formation.*

TEACHING AND RESEARCH UNITS

Arts, Philosophy and Aesthetics: Dir J. P. OLIVE
Power, Administration, Trade: Dir F. VICTOR
Territory, Economics and Society: Dir F. PLET
History, Literature, Society: Dir J. MAURIN
Languages, Societies, Foreign Cultures: Dir D. BUSSY-GENEVOIS
Linguistics, Computer Studies, Technology: Dir F. MELLET
Psychology, Clinical and Social Practices: Dir T. NATHAN
Communication, Animation, Teaching: Dir A. COULON

ATTACHED INSTITUTES

Institut Français d'Urbanisme: Dir M. F. GRIBET.

Institut d'Etudes Européennes: Dir M. AZZOUG.

Institut Universitaire de Technologie: Dir P. P. REY.

UNIVERSITÉ DE PARIS IX (PARIS-DAUPHINE)

Place du Maréchal de Lattre de Tassigny, 75775 Paris Cedex 16
Telephone: 1-44-05-44-05
Fax: 1-44-05-41-41

Founded 1968
State control
Language of instruction: French

President: Prof. ELIE COHEN
Secretary-General: LOUIS JOUVE
Librarian: I. SABATIER

Number of teachers: 880
Number of students: 7,700

TEACHING AND RESEARCH UNITS

Business Studies, Applied Economics: Dir Prof. F. ETNER
Business Studies: Dir J. DE LA BRUSLERIE
Applied Economics: Dir M. ARMATTE
Organization Sciences: Dir H. LENA
Business Computer Science: Dir Prof. P. TOLLA
Applied Mathematics: Dir M. BELLEC

PROFESSORS

ALTER, N., Sociology
ARNOLD, V., Mathematics
AUBIN, J.-P., Mathematics
BENSOUSSAN, A., Applied Mathematics
BERLIOZ-HOUIN, B., Business Law
BERTHET, CH., Computer Studies
BIENAYME, A., Industrial Economics
BLONDEL, D., Economics
BOUQUIN, H., Finance
BRUNET, A., Civil Law
CAREY-ABRIOUX, C.
CAZES, P., Statistics
CHAITIN-CHATELIN, F., Mathematics
CHAVENT, G., Mathematics
CHEDIN, G., English Languages
CHEVALIER, J.-M., Economics
CLAASSEN, E., Economics
COHEN, E., Finance
COLASSE, B., Finance
COTTA, A., Business Organization
COUSOT, P., Computer Studies
DANA, R.
DE MONTMORILLON, B., Finance
DESMET, P.
DIDAY, E., Computer Studies
DOSS, H., Mathematics
EKELAND, I., Mathematics
ETNER, F., Economics
FLORENS, D., Mathematics
FRISON-ROCHE, M. A., Civil Law
GAUVIN, C., English Language
GEMAN, H., Finance
GHOZI, A., Civil Law
GIOVANNANGELI, J.-L., English Language and Literature
GOURIEROUX, C., Mathematics
GRELON, B., Civil Law
GUILLAUME, M., Economics
GUILLOCHON, B., Economics
HADDAD, S., Computer Studies
HAMON, J., Finance
HESS, C., Mathematics
JOMIER, G., Computer Studies
LARNAC, P.-M., Economics
LENA, H., Public Law
LE PEN, C., Economics
LE TALLEC, P., Mathematics
LEVY, E., Economics
LEVY, G., Computer Studies
LIONS, P.-L., Mathematics
LIU, M., Sociology
LOMBARD, M., Public Law
LORENZI, J.-H., Economics
MAILLES, D., Computer Studies
MANIN, A., Public Law
MARIET, F., Education
MATHIS, J., Finance
METAIS J., Economics
MEYER, Y., Mathematics
MICHALET, C., Economics
MOREL, J.-M., Mathematics
NUSSENBAUM, M., Finance
PALMADE, J., Sociology
PARLY, J.-M., Economics
PASCHOS, V., Computer Studies
PIGANIOL, B., Management
PILISI, D., Economics
PINSON, S., Computer Studies
PIQUET, M., English Language and Literature
PRAS, B., Finance
RICHARD, J., Finance
RIGAL, J.-L., Computer Studies
RIVES-LANGE, J. L., Civil Law
ROMELAER, P., Finance
ROUX, D., Business Economics
ROY, B., Scientific Methods of Management
SALIN, P., Monetary Economics
SCHMIDT, C., Sociology
SIMON, Y., Finance
SIROEN, J.-M., Economics
SULZER, J.-R., Finance
TERNY, G., Public Economics
THIETART, R., Finance
TOLLA, P., Computer Studies
TRINH-HEBREARD, S., Sociology
VALLEE, C., Public Law

UNIVERSITÉ DE PARIS X (PARIS-NANTERRE)

200 ave de la République, 92001 Nanterre Cedex
Telephone: 1-40-97-72-00
Fax: 1-40-97-75-71

President: ANDRÉ LEGRAND

Secretary-General: GILLES GAI
Librarian: JEAN MALLET

Number of teachers: 1,500
Number of students: 34,000

TEACHING AND RESEARCH UNITS

Economic Sciences: Dir M. GIBERT
Juridical Sciences: Dir Mme TALLINEAU
Psychology and Education Sciences: Dir M. SIROTA
History, Geography and Sociology: Dir M. LEVILLAIN
Letters, Linguistics and Philosophy: Dir Mme DELAVEAU
Anglo-American Studies: Dir Mme FRISON
German, Romance Languages, Slav and Applied Foreign Languages: Dir M. PHILLIPENKO
Institute of Technology (Ville d'Avray): Dir M. PRIOU
Science and Techniques of Physical and Sporting Activities: Dir M. PINARD

UNIVERSITÉ DE PARIS XI (Paris-Sud)

15 rue G. Clémenceau, 91405 Orsay Cedex
Telephone: 1-69-41-67-50
Fax: 1-69-41-61-35
E-mail: secretariat@presidence.u-psud.fr

Founded 1970
State control
Language of instruction: French
Academic year: September to June

President: ALAIN GAUDEMER
Secretary-General: DANIEL PERAULT
Librarian: ANNE-MARIE MOTAIS DE NARBONNE

Number of teachers: 1,720
Number of students: 28,000

Publications: *Aspects de la recherche* (annually), *Plein-Sud* (every 2 months).

TEACHING AND RESEARCH UNITS

Pharmacy (Châtenay-Malabry): 5 rue Jean Baptiste Clément, 92290 Châtenay-Malabry; tel. 1-46-83-57-89; fax 1-46-83-57-35; Dean ANNE-MARIE QUERDO
Medicine (Kremlin-Bicêtre): 63 rue Gabriel Péri, 94276 Le Kremlin-Bicêtre Cedex; tel. 1-49-59-67-67; fax 1-49-59-67-00; Dean BERNARD CHARPENTIER
Sciences (Orsay): 15 rue Georges Clémenceau, 91405 Orsay Cedex; tel. 1-69-41-67-50; fax 1-69-15-63-64; Dean JEAN-CLAUDE ROYNETTE
Law and Economic Science (Sceaux): 54 blvd Desgranges, 92331 Sceaux Cedex; tel. 1-40-91-17-00; fax 1-46-60-92-62; Dean PIERRE SIRINELLI

UNIVERSITY INSTITUTES

University Institute of Technology at Cachan: 9 ave de la Division Leclerc, 94230 Cachan; tel. 1-41-24-11-00; fax 1-46-64-62-18; Dir PIERRE DAUMEZON
University Institute of Technology at Orsay: BP 127, 91403, Orsay Cedex; tel. 1-69-33-60-00; fax 1-60-19-33-18; Dir MICHEL PEDOUSSAUT
University Institute of Technology at Sceaux: 8 ave Cauchy, 92330 Sceaux; tel. 1-40-91-24-99; fax 1-46-60-64-79; Dir RICHARD MILKOFF

ATTACHED INSTITUTION

Ecole Supérieure d'Optique: see under Independent Institutes.

UNIVERSITÉ DE PARIS XII (PARIS-VAL-DE-MARNE)

61 ave du Général de Gaulle, 94010 Créteil Cedex

Telephone: 1-45-17-10-00
Telex: 264167
Fax: 1-42-07-70-12

Founded 1970

President: HÉLÈNE LAMICQ
Vice-Presidents: P. BRUSTON, V. DARMON, J. F. DUFEU, J. ZEGUERMAN
Secretary-General: C. BARREIX
Librarian: P. CARBONE

Number of teachers: 1,000
Number of students: 23,000

TEACHING AND RESEARCH UNITS

Institute of Town Planning: Dir L. DAVEZIES
Medicine: 8 rue du Gén. Sarrail, 94010 Créteil Cedex; Dir J. P. LE BOURGEOIS
Law and Politics: 58 ave Didier, 94210 La Varenne-St Hilaire; Dir M. CAILLET
Economic Sciences: Dir J. C. LEROY
Letters and Humanities: Dir M. DUMAS
Science: Dir E. GARNIER-ZARLI
Public and Social Administration: Dir M. J. C. ATTUEL
Education and Social Sciences: Dir M. PARIAT
Institute of Technology (Créteil-Vitry): Dir M. DUPEYRAT
Institute of General Administration: Dir M. J. C. ATTUEL
Institute of Technology Sénart/Fontainebleau: Dir M. F. VASSE

UNIVERSITÉ DE PARIS XIII (PARIS-NORD)

Ave J.-B. Clement, 93430 Villetaneuse

Telephone: 1-49-40-30-00
Telex: 610670
Fax: 1-49-40-33-33

Founded 1970

President: J. F. MELA
Vice-President: M. DAVID
Secretary-General: M. BARBIER
Librarian: A. TANE

Number of teachers: 830
Number of students: 22,200

Publications: *Psychologie clinique, Annales du CESER, Cahiers de Linguistique Hispanique Médiévale.*

TEACHING AND RESEARCH UNITS

Scientific and Polytechnic Centre: Dir N. LEBLANC
Law and Political Science: Dir P. SUEUR
Letters and Humanities: Dir J. BIARNES
University Institute of Technology (Saint-Denis): Dir J. P. BERTHIER
University Institute of Technology (Villetaneuse): Dir G. VICARD
Medicine and Human Biology Experimental Centre: Dir M. CUPA
Economic Sciences and Business Administration: Dir D. PLIHON
Expression and Communications Sciences: Dir R. BAUTIER
Institute of Town and Health: Dir P. CORNILLOT

UNIVERSITÉ DE PAU ET DES PAYS DE l'ADOUR

Domaine Universitaire, Ave de l'Université, BP 576, 64012 Pau Université Cedex

Telephone: 5-59-92-30-00
Fax: 5-59-80-83-80

Founded 1970
State control

President: JEAN-LOUIS GOUT
Vice-Presidents: J.-C. DOUENCE, J.-P. GACON, C. POUCHAN, J. P. MONTFORT, C. FIÉVET, M. UHALDEBORDE, E. POQUET, M. PARSONS
Secretary-General: JEAN RAVON
Librarian: SYLVAINE FREULON

Number of teachers: 600
Number of students: 14,100

TEACHING AND RESEARCH UNITS

Faculty of Law, Economics and Management: Dean GÉRARD DENIS
Faculty of Exact Sciences: Dean ALAIN GRACIA
Faculty of Literature, Languages and Human Sciences: Dean CHRISTIAN MANSO
University Institute of Scientific Research: Dir JEAN PEYRELASSE
Multidisciplinary Faculty (in Bayonne): Dean HENRI LABAYLE
Institute of Business Administration: Dir J.-J. RIGAL
Higher National School of Industrial Engineering: Dir M. ROQUES
University Institute of Technology (in Bayonne): Dir BERNARD CAUSSE
University Institute of Technology (in Pau): Dir ROBERT HOO-PARIS

UNIVERSITÉ DE PERPIGNAN

Ave de Villeneuve, 66025 Perpignan Cedex
Telephone: 4-68-66-20-00

Founded 1971

President: JEAN-MICHEL HOERNER
Secretary-General: JEAN-POL ISAMBERT
Librarian: FERNAND BELLEDENT

Number of teachers: 230
Number of students: 4,500

TEACHING AND RESEARCH UNITS

Humanities, Juridical, Economic and Social Sciences: Dir JACQUELINE AMIEL DONAT
Exact and Experimental Sciences: Dir NAGUI EL GHANDOUR
University Institute of Technology: Dir CATHERINE SABATE

PROFESSORS

Humanities, Juridical, Economic and Social Sciences:

Humanities:

ANDIOC, R., Romance Languages and Literature
AUBAILLY, J.-C., French
BELOT, A., Romance Languages and Literature
BROC, N., Geography
DAUGE, Y., Classics
DELEDALLE, G., Philosophy
DENJEAN, A., English Language and Anglo-Saxon Literature
HOLZ, J. M., Geography
HUGUET, L., Germanic and Scandinavian Languages and Literature
ISSOREL, J., Spanish
LEBLON, B., Romance Languages and Literature
MEYER, J., Contemporary History
RETHORE, J., Literature
SAGNES, J., History

Law and Economics:

BLANC, F. P., History of Law
BREJON DE LAVERGNEE, N., Economic Dynamics
CONSTANS, L., Public Law
DONAT, Mme J., Private Law and Criminology
DOUCHEZ, M.-H., Administrative Law
HUNTZINGER, J., International Law
PEROCHON, F., Law
RUDLOFF, M., Economics
SAINT-JOURS, Y., Private Law and Criminology
SERRA, Y., Private Law

Exact and Experimental Sciences:

AMOUROUX, M., Applied Physics and Computer Science
BAILLY, J. R., Biochemistry
BERÇOT, P., Applied Organic Synthesis
BLAISE, P., Chemistry
BODIOT, D., Mineral Chemistry and Thermochemistry

BOMBRE, F., Solid State Physics
BONNARD, M., Algebraic Topology
BOURGAT, R., General Biology
BRUNET, S., Applied Physics and Computer Science
BRUSLE, J., Marine Biology
CAUVET, A. M., Plant Biology and Physiology
CHOU, C. C., Functional Analysis
CODOMIER, L., Biology and Chemistry of Marine Plants (Research)
COMBES, C., Animal Biology
CROZAT, G., Physics
DAGUENET, M., Thermodynamics and Energetics
DUPOUY, J., General Biology
EL JAÏ, A., Computer Science
FABRE, B., Thermology
FOUGERES, A., Mathematics
GIRESSE, P., Marine Sedimentology Research Centre
GONZALEZ, E., Organic Chemistry
GOT, H., Sedimentology and Marine Geochemistry
HENRI-ROUSSEAU, O., Theoretical Chemistry
HILLEL, R., Chemistry
HORVATH, C., Mathematics
HUYNH, V. C., Atomic and Molecular Physics
JUPIN, H., Plant Biology
MARTY, R., Mathematics applied to Human Sciences
MEYNADIER, CHR., Thermodynamics and Energetics
PENON, P., Plant Physiology
SOULIER, J., Organic Chemistry
SOURNIA, A., Atomic and Molecular Physics
SPINNER, B., Mineral Chemistry and Thermochemistry
VIALLET, P., Physical Chemistry

University Institute of Technology:

AZE, D., Mathematics
BARRIOL, R., Mechanical Engineering
BARUSSEAU, J. P., Marine Sedimentology
COMBAUT, G., Marine Chemistry
FARINES, M., Organic Chemistry
COSTE, C., Industrial Chemistry
GRELLET, P., Biochemistry, Applied Biology
MASSE, J., Organic Chemistry
MASSON, PH., Animal Husbandry

UNIVERSITÉ DE PICARDIE (JULES VERNE)

Chemin du Thil, 80025 Amiens Cedex 01

Telephone: 3-22-82-72-72
Fax 3-22-82-75-00

Founded 1965

President: PAUL PERSONNE
Secretary-General: GILLES GAY
Librarian: FRANÇOISE MONTBRUN

Number of teachers: 800
Number of students: 23,000

TEACHING AND RESEARCH UNITS

Law: Dir Prof. N. DECOOPMAN
Economics: Dir Prof. P. MAURISSON
Modern Languages: Dir Prof. J. DARRAS
Literature: Dir Prof. P. DEMONT
Philosophy and Human Sciences: Dir Prof. A. LANCRY
History and Geography: Dir Prof. N. CHALINE
Medicine: 12 rue des Laurels, Amiens; Dir Prof. M. LAUDE
Pharmacy: 3 rue des Louvels, 80037 Amiens Cedex; Dir J. G. GACEL
Sciences: 33 rue Saint-Leu, Amiens; Dir Prof. D. BEAUPÈRE
Mathematics: 33 rue Saint Leu, 80039 Amiens Cedex; Dir L. THIMONIER
University Institute of Technology: Ave des Facultés, Le Bailly, Amiens; Administrator E. MERIAUX
UER (Saint-Quentin): 48 rue Raspail, 02109 Saint-Quentin Cedex; Dir A. LEBRUN

UNIVERSITÉ DE POITIERS

15 rue de l'Hôtel-Dieu, 86034 Poitiers Cedex

Telephone: 5-49-45-30-00
Fax: 5-49-45-30-50
E-mail: communication@univ-poitiers.fr

Founded 1431

President: ALAIN TRANOY
Secretary-General: HÉLÈNE BROCHET-TOUTIRI
Librarian: GENEVIÈVE FIROUZ-ABADIE

Number of teachers: 1,200
Number of students: 27,000

Publications: *Les Cahiers de Civilisation Médiévale, La Licorne, Revue Norois, Migrinter.*

TEACHING AND RESEARCH UNITS

Fundamental and Applied Sciences: Dir GUY RENAULT
Medicine and Pharmacy: Dir ROBERT BARRAINE
Languages and Literatures: Dir JOËL DALANÇON
Human Sciences: Dir JEAN-MICHEL PASSERAULT
Centre for Higher Studies of Medieval Civilization: Dir GABRIEL BIANCIOTTO
Law and Social Sciences: Dir CHRISTIAN CHÊNE
Economics: Dir JEAN-PIERRE BERDOT
Physical Education and Sport: Dir PATRICK LEGROS
University Institute of Technology in Poitiers: Dir CHRISTIAN BERRIER
University Institute of Technology in Angoulême: Dir MICHEL PINÇON
University Institute of Business Administration: Dir SERGE PERCHERON
National Higher School of Mechanical and Aero-engineering: Dir FRANÇOIS ARMANET
Centre for Aerodynamic and Thermic Studies: Dir MICHEL GUILBAUD
Poitiers Higher School for Engineering (ESIP): Dir JEAN-HUGUES THOMASSIN
Preparatory Institute of General Administration: JEAN-LOUIS GOUSSEAU
Establishment for Research in Human Sciences and Society: ERIC ESPERET
Institute of Communication and New Technologies: Dir JACQUES DEBORD

UNIVERSITÉ DE REIMS CHAMPAGNE-ARDENNE

Villa Douce, 9 boulevard de la Paix, 51097 Reims Cedex

Telephone: 3-26-05-30-00
Fax: 3-26-05-30-98

Founded 1548, 1969

President: JACQUES MEYER
Vice-Presidents: JEAN-JACQUES ABNET, JACQUES BUR, MARCEL BAZIN
Secretary-General: MARTINE BEURTON

Library: see Libraries
Number of teachers: 1,000
Number of students: 26,000

Publications: *Flash-Infos* (weekly), *Livret de l'Université, Imaginaires, Etudes Champenoises* (annually), *Revue de l'Institut de Géographie* (termly), *Jurisprudence Cour d'appel* (quarterly), *Cahiers de l'Institut du Territoire et de l'Environnement de l'Université de Reims* (annually), *Cahiers du Centre de Recherches sur la Décentralisation Territoriale* (annually).

TEACHING AND RESEARCH UNITS

Exact and Natural Sciences: Dir JACQUES PERRIN
Medicine: Dir FRANÇOIS-XAVIER MAQUART
Pharmacy: Dir JEAN LÉVY
Letters and Human Sciences: Dir GÉRARD DUFOUR
Law and Political Sciences: Dir GÉRARD CLÉMENT
Odontology: Dir MICHEL MAQUIN
University Institute of Technology in Reims: Dir GUY DELABRE
University Institute of Technology in Troyes: Dir JOËL HAZOUARD
Economic Sciences and Management: Dir GILLES RASSELET
University Institute of Technical Training in Charleville: Dir JACQUES MALICET
Higher School of Packaging: Dir JEAN-CLAUDE PRUDHOMME

UNIVERSITÉ DE RENNES I

2 rue du Thabor, 35065 Rennes Cedex

Telephone: 2-99-25-36-36
Fax: 2-99-25-36-00

President: Prof. JACQUES LENFANT
Secretary-General: ANNIE JULIEN

Number of teaching staff: 1,300
Number of students: 27,000

TEACHING AND RESEARCH UNITS

Sciences Pharmaceutiques et Biologiques: Ave du Professeur Léon Bernard, 35043 Rennes Cedex; tel. 2-99-33-69-69; fax 2-99-33-68-88; Dean Prof. MICHEL CORMIER.
Médecine: Ave du Professeur Léon Bernard, 35043 Rennes Cedex; tel. 2-99-33-69-69; fax 2-99-54-13-96; Dean Prof. CLAUDE RIOUX.
Odontologie: 2 place Pasteur, 35000 Rennes; tel. 2-99-33-19-55; fax 2-99-38-24-77; Dean Prof. JEAN-CLAUDE ROBERT.
Droit et Science Politique: 9 rue Jean-Macé, 35042 Rennes Cedex; tel. 2-99-84-76-76; fax 2-99-84-76-55; Dean GEORGES FOURNIER.
Sciences Economiques: 7 place Hoche, 35000 Rennes; tel. 2-99-25-35-45; fax 2-99-38-80-84; Dean Prof. JEAN-JACQUES DURAND.
Institut de Gestion de Rennes: 11 rue Jean-Mace, BP 1997, 35019 Rennes Cedex; tel. 2-99-84-77-77; fax 2-99-84-78-00; Dir Prof. ARMEL LIGER.
Institut de Mathématiques de Rennes: Ave du Général Leclerc, 35042 Rennes Cedex; tel. 2-99-28-60-01; fax 2-99-28-67-90; Dir Prof. JACQUES CAMUS.
Structure et Propriété de la Matière: Ave du Général Leclerc, 35042 Rennes Cedex; tel. 2-99-28-62-44; fax 2-99-28-69-85; Dir Prof. CHRISTIAN WILLAIME.
Sciences de la Vie et de l'Environnement: Ave du Général Leclerc, 35042 Rennes Cedex; tel. 2-99-28-61-62; fax 2-99-28-69-15; Prof. PATRICK JEGO.
Philosophie: Ave du Général Leclerc, 35042 Rennes Cedex; tel. 2-99-28-63-02; fax 2-99-28-14-11; Dir Prof. JACQUELINE DELIAU-LAGRÉE
Institut de Préparation à l'Administration Générale: 3A place Saint-Melaine, 35000 Rennes; tel. 2-99-25-36-10; fax 2-99-25-36-27; Dir MARIE-LIESSE HOUBÉ.
Institut Universitaire de Technologie de Rennes: Rue du Clos-Courtel, BP 1144, 35014 Rennes Cedex; tel. 2-99-84-40-00; fax 2-99-84-40-01; Dir Prof. BERTRAND FORTIN.
Institut Universitaire de Technologie de Lannion: Rue Edouard Branly, BP 150, 22302 Lannion Cedex; tel. 2-96-48-43-34; fax 2-96-48-13-20; Dir Prof. JEAN-YVES LE BIHAN.
Ecole Nationale Supérieure des Sciences Appliquées et de Technologie: 6 rue de Kérampont, BP 447, 22305 Lannion Cedex; tel. 2-96-46-50-30; fax 2-96-37-01-99; Dir Prof. JEAN SEGUIN.
Institut de Formation Supérieure en Informatique et Communication: Ave du Général Leclerc, 35042 Rennes Cedex; tel. 2-99-84-71-00; fax 2-99-84-71-71; Dir Prof. YVES BEKKERS.

UNIVERSITÉ DE RENNES II (UNIVERSITÉ DE HAUTE BRETAGNE)

6 ave Gaston Berger, 35043 Rennes Cedex

Telephone: 2-99-14-10-00
Fax: 2-99-14-10-15

President: Dr JEAN BRIHAULT
First Vice-President: Dr JACQUELINE SAINCLIVIER
Secretary-General: BERNARD CHAIGNAUD

Number of teaching staff: 501
Number of students: 20,000

Publications: *Rennes 2 Actualités* (fortnightly), *R2 Recherche* (2 a year), *Tétrologiques* (annually), *Interférences* (annually), *Mondes hispanophones* (annually), *Annales de Bretagne et des Pays de l'Ouest* (annually), *Norois: revue de Géographes* (annually), *Arts de l'Ouest* (annually), *Plurial* (annually), *Annales du Levant* (annually), *Dossiers de Télédétection* (2 a year).

TEACHING AND RESEARCH UNITS

Arts: Dir J. C. BERTHOME
Literature: Dir M. TOURET
Geography and Environment: Dir A. SARNI
History and Political Sciences: Dir M. CHAUVIN
English: Dir L. MARCHAND
Modern Languages: Dir D. TOUDIC
Psychology, Sociology and Education: Dir A. AIT ABDELMALEK
Language and Culture: Dir J. LAISIS
Physical Education and Sport: Dir Y. LEZIART
Economic and Social Administration: Dir A. EVEN
Institute of the Social Sciences of Employment: 6 ave Gaston Berger, 35043 Rennes Cedex; tel. 2-33-33-52-52; Dir ANNIE JUNTER-LOISEAU
Armorican Institute of Economic and Human Research: 4 place St-Melaine, 35000 Rennes; tel. 2-99-63-27-77; Dir FRANÇOIS LEBRUN

UNIVERSITÉ DE ROUEN

1 rue Thomas Becket, Secrétariat-Général, 76821 Mont-Saint-Aignan Cedex
Telephone: 2-35-14-60-00
Telex: 770127
Fax: 2-35-14-63-48

Founded 1966
Academic year: September to June

President: ERNEST GIBERT
Vice-Presidents: MOHAMED KETATA, BERNARD PROUST
Secretary-General: (vacant)
Librarian: YANNICK VALIN

Number of teachers: 778
Number of students: 30,000

TEACHING AND RESEARCH UNITS

Medicine and Pharmacy: BP 97, 76800 Saint-Etienne-du-Rouvray; Dir P. LAURET
Sciences and Technology: Place Emile Blondel, 76821 Mont-Saint-Aignan Cedex; Dir M. LEREST
Letters and Humanities: Rue Lavoisier, 76821 Mont-Saint-Aignan Cedex; Dir J. MAURICE
Law and Economics: Blvd Siegfried, 76821 Mont-Saint-Aignan Cedex; Dir Y. SASSIER
Behavioural and Educational Sciences: Rue Lavoisier, 76821 Mont-Saint-Aignan; Dir R. WEIL
University Institute of Technology: Place Emile Blondel, 76821 Mont-Saint-Aignan; Dir P. MICHE
Sport: Blvd Siegfried, 76821 Mont-Saint-Aignan Cedex; Dir J. P. LEFEVRE

PROFESSORS

Medicine and Pharmacy:

ANDRIEU-GUTTRANCOURT, J., Otorhinolaryngology
AUGUSTIN, P., Neurology
BACHY, B., Infantile Surgery
BENOZIO, E., Radiology
BERCOFF, E., Internal Medicine
BESANÇON, P., Chemistry
BESSOU, J. P., Surgery
BEURET, F., Rehabilitation
BIGA, N., Orthopaedics
BLANQUART, F., Rehabilitation
BONMARCHAND, G., Resuscitation
BONNET, J. J., Pharmacology
BRASSEUR, G., Ophthalmology
BRASSEUR, P. H., Bacteriology
CAILLARD, J.-F., Industrial Medicine
CAPRON, R., Biophysics
COLIN, R., Gastroenterology
COLONNA, L., Psychiatry
COMOY, D., Biochemistry
COSTENTIN, J., Pharmacology
COURTOIS, H., Internal Medicine
CRIBIER, A., Cardiology
CZERNICHOW, P., Epidemiology
DEHESDIN, D., Otorhinolaryngology
DENIS, P., Physiology
DUCROTTE, P., Hepatology
DUVAL, C., Clinical Obstetrics
FESSARD, C., Paediatrics
FILLASTRE, J. P., Nephrology
FREGER, P., Anatomy
GARNIER, J., Botany and Cryptogamy
GODIN, M., Nephrology
GRISE, PH., Urology
HECKETSWEILER, P., Hepatology
HEMET, J., Pathological Anatomy
HUMBERT, G., Tropical and Infectious Diseases
JANVRESSE, C., Hygiene
JOLY, P., Dermatology
JOUANY, M., Toxicology
KUHN, J. M., Endocrinology
LAFONT, O., Organic Chemistry
LAURET, P., Dermatology
LAVOINNE, D., Biochemistry
LECHEVALLIER, J., Infantile Surgery
LEDOSSEUR, P., Radiology
LEFUR, R., Cancerology
LELOET, X., Rheumatology
LEMELAND, J. F., Hygiene
LEMOINE, J. P., Gynaecology
LEREBOURS, E., Nutrition
LEROY, J., Therapeutics
LETAC, B., Cardiology
MACE, B., Histology
MAITROT, B., Biochemistry
MALLET, E., Biology
MARCHAND, J., Chemical Pharmacology
MATRAY, F., Medical Biochemistry
METAYER, J., Anatomy
MICHOT, F., Digestive Tract Surgery
MIHOUT, B., Neurology
MITROFANOFF, P., Infantile Surgery
MONCONDUIT, M., Haematology
MUIR, J. F., Pneumology
NOUVET, G., Pneumology
ORECCHIONI, A.-M., Pharmacology
PASQUIS, P., Physiology
PEILLON, C., Orthopaedic and Traumatological Surgery
PERON, J. M., Stomatology
PETIT, M., Psychiatry
PIGUET, H., Immuno-haematology
PROTAIS, P., Physiology
PROUST, B., Forensic Medicine
SAOUDI, N., Cardiology
SORIA, C., Pharmaceutical Biochemistry
SOYER, R., Thoracic Surgery
TADIE, M., Neurosurgery
TENIERE, P., General Surgery
TESTART, J., Clinical Surgery
THIEBOT, J., Radiology
THOMINE, M., Orthopaedic and Traumatological Surgery
TILLY, H., Haematology
THUILLIEZ, C., Therapeutics
TRON, F., Immunology
TRON, P., Paediatrics
VANNIER, J. P., Pediatrics
WATELET, J., General Surgery
WINCKLER, C., Anaesthesiology
WOLF, L., Therapeutic Internal Medicine

Sciences and Technology:

ANTHORE, R., Physics
ATTIAS, J., Biochemistry
AUGER, P., Physics
BALANGE, P., Biochemistry
BANEGE, A., Physics
BARBEY, G., Chemistry
BLANCHARD, D., Mechanics
BLAVETTE, D., Physics
BOISARD, J., Vegetal Biology
BORGHI, R., Mechanics
BOUAZIZ, R., Chemistry
BRISSET, J. L., Chemistry
CAGNON, M., Physics
CALBRIX, J., Mathematics
CARLES, D., Electronics
CARPENTIER, J. M., Chemistry
CASTON, J., Biology
CAZIN, L., Biology
CHAMPRANAUD, J. M., Computer Sciences
CHARPENTIER, J., Physiology
CHERON, B., Thermodynamics
COMBRET, C., Chemistry
COTTEREAU, M. J., Thermodynamics
DAVOUST, D., Chemistry
DEBRUCQ, D., Electronics
DERRIDJ, M., Mathematics
DE SAM LAZARO, J., Mathematics
DESBENE, A., Chemistry
DESBENE, P., Chemistry
DONATO, P., Mathematics
DOSS, H., Mathematics
DUHAMEL, P., Chemistry
DUVAL, J.-P., Computer Sciences
DUVAL, P., Physics
FOUCHER, B., Biochemistry
FRILEUX, P. N., Biology
GALLOT, J., Physics
GAYOSO, J., Chemistry
GORALCIK, P., Computer Sciences
GRENET, J., Physics
GUESPIN, J., Microbiology
HANNOYER, B., Physics
HANSEL, G., Mathematics
HUSSON, A., Biology
LAMBOY, M., Geology
LANERY, E., Mathematics
LANGE, C., Chemistry
LECOURTIER, Y., Electronics
LEDOUX, M., Thermodynamics
LENGLET, M., Chemistry
LOPITAUX, J., Chemistry
MAHEU, B., Thermodynamics
MENAND, A., Physics
METAYER, M., Chemistry
MEYER, R., Geology
MICHON, J. F., Computer Sciences
OZKUL, C., Physics
PAULMIER, C., Chemistry
PEREZ, G., Chemistry
PETIPAS, C., Physics
POIRIER, J. M., Chemistry
QUEGUINNER, G., Chemistry
RIPOLL, C., Biochemistry
SELEGNY, E., Chemistry
STRELCYN, J. M., Mathematics
SURIN, A., Mathematics
TEILLET, J., Physics
UNANUE, A., Chemistry
VAILLANT, R., Animal Physiology
VAUTIER, C., Physics
VERCHERE, J. F., Chemistry
VIGER, C., Electronics
VIGIER, P., Physics
WEILL, M., Thermodynamics

Letters and Humanities:

ARNAUD, J. C., Geography
BALAN, B., Epistemology
BENAY, J., German
BERGER, PH., Spanish
CAITUCOLI, C., Linguistics
CAPET, A., English
COIT, K., English
CORTES, J., Linguistics
CYMERMAN, C., Spanish

DELAMOTTE, R., Linguistics
GARDIN, B., Linguistics
GRANIER, J., Philosophy
GUERMOND, Y., Geography
HUSSON, G., Greek
LE BOHEC, S., Ancient History
LECLAIRE, J., English
LECLERC, Y., French
LEGUAY, J.-P., Medieval History
LEMARCHAND, G., Modern History
LESOURD, M., Geography
MAQUERLOT, J. P., English
MAURICE, J., French
MAZAURIC, C., Modern History
MERVAUD, C., French
MERVAUD, M., Russian
MILHOU, A., Spanish
MORTIER, D., Comparative Literature
NIDERST, A., French
NOISETTE DE CRAUZAT, CL., Musical History
PASTRE, J. M., German
PHILONENKO, A., Philosophy
PICHARDIE, J. P., English
PIERROT, J., Modern French Literature and Language
PIGENET, M., Contemporary History
POINSOTE, J. L., Classics
PUEL, M., English
RAVY, G., German
RETAILLE, B., Geography
ROUDAUT, F., French
SALAZAR, B., Spanish
SOHNA, R., Modern History
THELAMON, F., Ancient History
TREDE, M., Classics
VAN DER LYNDEN, A. M., Spanish
WALLE, M., German
WILLEMS, M., English
ZYLBERBER, G. M., Modern History

Law and Economics:

BADEVANT, B., Law
BRAS, J. P., Public Law
CAYLA, O., Public Law
CHRETIEN. P., Public Law
COURBE, P., Private Law
DAMMAME, D., Political Science
EPAULARD, A., Economics
GOY, R., Public Law
KULLMANN, J., Private Law
LEHMANN, P., Economics
MONNIER, L., Economics
PORTIER, F., Economics
RENOUX, M. F., Law
SASSIER, Y., Law
TAVERNIER, P., Public Law
TEBOUL, G., Public Law
TONNEL, M., Economics
VATTEVILLE, E., Administration and Management
VESPERINI, J.-P., Economics

Behavioural and Educational Sciences:

ABALLERA, F., Sociology
ASTOLFI, J. P., Educational Sciences
DURAND, J., Sociology
GATEAUX, J., Educational Sciences
HOUSSAYE, J., Educational Sciences
KOKOSOWSKI, A., Educational Sciences
LEMOINE, CL., Psychology
MALANDAIN, CL., Psychology
MARBEAUX-CLEIRENS, B., Psychology
MELLIER, D., Psychology

UNIVERSITÉ JEAN MONNET

34 rue Francis Baulier, 42023 Saint-Etienne Cedex
Telephone: 4-77-42-17-00
Telex: 300816
Fax: 4-77-42-17-99

Founded in 1969 as Université de Saint-Étienne; present name 1991
State control
Language of instruction: French
Academic year: October to June

President: MAURICE VINCENT
Vice-Presidents: YVES BOUVERET, JEAN-BAPTISTE ORSINI, ANDRÉ GEYSSANT
Secretary-General: P. BESSENAY
Librarian: Mme ACHARD

Number of teachers: 592
Number of students: 13,684

Publications: *L'Université communique* (weekly), and various institute bulletins.

TEACHING AND RESEARCH UNITS

Law and Economics: Dir P. ANCEL
Letters and Human Sciences: Dir G. ARGOUD
Sciences: Dir B. BUISSON
Medicine: Dir P. QUENEAU
University Institute of Technology: Dir J. MAZERAN
Arts, Communication, Pedagogy: Dir CHRISTIANE LAUVERGNAT (acting)
Institute of Advanced Science and Technology (ISTA): Dir ROBERT ROUGNY
Institute of Industrial Management: Dir GÉRARD LABAURE

HEADS OF DEPARTMENT

Law and Economics:

Law: P. ANCEL
Economics: M. VINCENT

Letters and Human Sciences:

Letters: M. SADOULET
English Studies: P. BADONNEL
German Studies: A. SAUTER
Spanish Studies: M. OTT
Italian Studies: J. ALEXANDRE
History: J. BAYON
Geography: RENÉ CONNERE
Plastic Arts: M. GILLES
Music: M. RANEAU

Sciences:

Biology: A. PERRIN
Chemistry: B. BOINON
Geology: A. GIRET
Mathematics: A. LARGILLIER
Physics: A. CACHARD

Medicine:

Anatomy: J.-G. BALIQUE
Pathological Anatomy: S. BOUCHERON
Anaesthesiology: C. AUBOYER, J.-C. BERTRAND
Bacteriology/Virology: O. GAUDIN
Biochemistry: A. CHAMSON
Biophysics and Medical Computer Science: J.-C. HEALY
Cancerology: T. SCHMITT
Cardiology: G. BARRAL
Child Psychiatry: D. SIBERTIN-BLANC
General Surgery: J.-G. BALIQUE
Paediatric Surgery: Y. CHAVRIER
Dermatology and Venerology: A. CAMBAZARD
Emergency Medicine: J.-C. BERTRAND
Endocrinology: H. ROUSSET
Medical Genetics, Paediatrics: F. FREYCON, B. LAURAS
Gynaecology and Obstetrics: P. SEFFERT
Haemobiology: C. BRIZARD, D. GUYOTAT
Hepatology, Gastroenterology: H. FRAISSE, J.-C. AUDIGIER
Histology and Embryology: J.-L. LAURENT
Immunology/Haematology: C. BRIZARD, D. GUYOTAT, M. LE PETIT
Forensic Medicine, Toxicology: M. DEBOUT
Preventive Medicine, Hygiene, Rheumatology: C. ALEXANDRE
Labour Medicine: C. CABAL
Nephrology: F. BERTHOUX
Neurology: D. MICHEL
Neurosurgery: J. BRUNON
Nutrition: H. ROUSSET
Ophthalmology: J. MAUGERY
Oto-Rhino-Laryngology: C. MARTIN
Orthopaedics and Traumatology: G. BOUSQUET, J.-L. RHENTER
Parasitology: R. TRAN MANH SUNG
Pathology of Infectious Diseases: O. GAUDIN, R. LUCHT
Pharmacology: M. OLLAGNIER
Pneumo-phthysiology: A. EMONOT
Physiology: A. GEYSSANT
Psychiatry: J. PELLET
Medical Psychology: J. PELLET
Radiology: G. BARRAL
Rehabilitation: P. MINAIRE
Rheumatology: G. RIFFAT, C. ALEXANDRE
Public Health: J.-M. RODRIGUES
Semeiology: H. ROUSSET
Stomatology: P. SEGUIN
Surgical Semeiology: J.-G. BALIQUE
Therapeutics: P. QUENEAU
Urology: A. GILLOZ

University Institute of Technology:

Electrical Engineering: B. FAURE
Mechanical Engineering: M. LAUVERNET
Business Administration: G. DISSARD
Commerce: D. MOREAU
Physics: C. GONNET
Industrial Maintenance: R. PHILIPPE

ATTACHED RESEARCH INSTITUTES

Faculty of Law and Economics:

Centre de recherches économiques de l'Université de Saint-Etienne (CREUSET): Dir JOËL RAVIX

Centre d'études et de recherches critiques sur le droit (CERCRID): Dir ANTOINE JEAMMAUD

Centre d'études sociologiques appliquées à la Loire (CRESAL): Dir JACQUES ION

Centre d'études et de recherches sur l'administration publique (CERAPSE): Dir STÉPHANE CAPORAL

Institut de préparation aux études comptables: Dir JACQUES CAMUS

Faculty of Letters and Human Sciences:

Institut de la Renaissance et de l'âge classique: Dir ANTONY MACKENNA

Centre Jean Palerme: Dir GILBERT ARGOUD

Centre Jules Romains: Dirs PIERRE CHARRETON, BERNARD YON

Centre d'études comparatistes: Dir STÉPHANE MICHAUD

Centre de recherches sur l'environnement et l'aménagement (CRENAM): Dir THIERRY JOLIVEAU

Centre Max Jacob: Dir LOUIS THEUBET

Centre d'études du XVIIIe siècle: Dir HENRI DURANTON

Centre interdisciplinaire et de recherches sur les structures régionales: Dir JEAN MERLEY

Centre de recherche sur les pays ibériques et ibéro-américains: Dir JACQUES SOUBEYROUX

Centre européen de recherches sur les congrégations et ordres religieux (CERCOR): Dir PIERRETTE PARAVY

Centre d'etudes foréziennes: Dir FRANÇOIS TOMAS

Institut du travail: Dir FRANÇOISE VENNIN

Faculty of Science:

Laboratoire de traitement et instrumentation: Dir JEAN-PIERRE GOURE

Centre commun de physique et chimie des matériaux: Dir JEAN-MARIE VERGNIAUD

Laboratoire de théorie des nombres: Dir FRANÇOIS GRAMAIN

Laboratoire de rhéologie des matières plastiques: Dir JACQUES GUILLOT

Equipe d'analyse numérique: Dir ALAIN BOURGEAT

Laboratoire de recherche sur les capteurs à colloïdes et instrumentation: Dir JEAN MONIN

Laboratoire de biologie végétale

Equipe de géologie: Dir RENÉ-PIERRE MONOT

Equipe de statistiques et modèles: Dir JACQUES BERRUYER

Centre de ressources informatiques télécommunications et réseaux (CRITeR): Dir JEAN-LOUIS SUBTIL

Centre international de langues et civilisation (CILEC): Dir YVES BOUVERET

Faculty of Medicine:

Groupe de recherches sur les gomérulonéphrites et transplantation rénales: Dir FRANÇOIS BERTHOUX

Laboratoire de biophysique et information médicale: Dir JEAN-CLAUDE HEALY

Laboratoire d'histologie-embryologie: Dir JEAN-LOUIS LAURENT

Laboratoire de biochimie du collagène: Dir JACQUES FREY

Laboratoire de physiologie: Dir ANDRÉ GEYSSANT

Institut universitaire de réadaptation fonctionnelle: Dir PIERRE MINAIRE

Laboratoire de biologie du tissu osseux: Dir CHRISTIAN ALEXANDRE

Laboratoire d'immuno-dermatologie: Dirs GENIN, CAMBAZARD

Groupe de recherches sur l'immunité des muqueuses: Dir ODETTE GAUDIN

Laboratoire de pharmacologie médicale: Dir MICHEL OLLAGNIER

Groupe de recherche en oncologie médicale: Dir JEAN-MICHEL VERGNON

Equipe de neurologie réanimatrice hypoxie: Dir BERNARD LAURENT

Laboratoire d'anatomie et de cytologie pathologique: Dir ALEXANDRE BAIL

Institut de médecine du travail: Dir CHRISTIAN CABAL

Laboratoire d'hématologie cellulaire et moléculaire: Dir DENIS GUYOTAT

Service de psychiatrie: Dir JACQUES PELLET

Laboratoire de parasitologie: Dir ROGER TRAN MANH SONG

Groupe de recherches sur la thrombose: Dir HERVÉ DECOUSUS

Laboratoire de neurologie: Dir DANIEL MICHEL

Institut de biologie du sport de la Région Rhône-Alpes: Dir JEAN-RENÉ LACOUR

Centre de microscopie électronique Médecine-Sciences: Dir CHRISTIAN ALEXANDRE

Faculty of Arts, Communication and Pedagogy:

Centre interdisciplinaire d'études et de recherches sur l'expression contemporaine (CIEREC): Dir LOUIS ROUX

Centre de recherche en éducation: Dir DOMINIQUE GLASMAN

University Institute of Technology:

Centre de recherche et études de management public: Dir JACQUES MAZERAN

Groupe de recherches en techniques de commercialisation: Dir ODETTE DOMENACH

UNIVERSITÉ DE SAVOIE (CHAMBÉRY)

BP 1104, 73011 Chambéry Cedex

Telephone: 4-79-75-85-85
Telex: 320410
Fax: 4-79-75-84-44

Founded 1970

President: Prof. PIERRE BARAS
Vice-Presidents: PIERRE FAIVRE (Administrative Council), DANIEL DECAMP (Scientific Council), CHRISTIAN GULLERÉ (Council of Studies and University Life)
Secretary-General: JEAN-LOUIS REFFET
Librarian: COLETTE COMMANAY

Number of teachers: 416
Number of students: 11,229

Publications: *Annales* (annually), *CIRCE* (annually), *Etudes maistriennes.*

TEACHING AND RESEARCH UNITS

Faculty of Commerce and Sales, and Economics and Management: Dir JEAN MOSCAROLA
Faculty of Transport, Hotel Management, Tourism and Applied Foreign Languages: Dir PAUL CONSTABLE
Faculty of Language, Literature and Social Science: JEAN-LUC ROULIN
Faculty of Law and Economics: Dir GILLES PAISANT
Interdisciplinary Centre for Mountain Sciences: Dir JEAN-PAUL RAMPNOUX
Faculty of Applied Sciences: Dir GILBERT ANGENIEUX

ATTACHED INSTITUTES

Annecy National College of Engineering: Dir JACQUES DUFOUR
Chambéry National College of Engineering: Dir JACQUES DUFAU
Institute of Technology: Dir DOMINIQUE PACCARD

UNIVERSITÉ DE STRASBOURG I (UNIVERSITÉ LOUIS PASTEUR)

Institut Le Bel, 4 rue Blaise Pascal, 67070 Strasbourg Cedex

Telephone: 3-88-41-60-00
Telex: 870260
Fax: 3-88-60-75-50

Founded 1971

Rector: JEAN-PAUL DE GAUDEMAR
President: Prof. JEAN-YVES MÉRINDOL
Secretary-General: JACQUES SOULAS
Vice-Presidents: Prof. MICHEL CARA (Research and Doctoral Education), Prof. DANIEL ZACHARY (Personnel and Recruitment), ANNIE CHEMINAT (Initial and Continuing Education), Prof. P. LLERENA (Development and Means), VALERIE MELLET (Student Welfare), GUY VINCENDON (External Relations)
Librarian: MICHEL BOISSET

Number of teachers and research scientists: 1,320
Number of students: 20,000

TEACHING AND RESEARCH UNITS

Medical Sciences: 4 rue Kirschleger, 67085 Strasbourg Cedex; Dir P. GERLINGER
Dentistry: 4 rue Kirschleger, 67085 Strasbourg Cedex; Dir M. LEIZE
Pharmacy: 74 route du Rhin, 67400 Strasbourg Cedex; Dir D. GERARD
Mathematics and Computer Science: 7 rue René Descartes, 67084 Strasbourg Cedex; Dir M. MIGNOTTE
Chemistry: 1 rue Blaise Pascal, 67008 Strasbourg Cedex; Dir P. GRANGER
Physics: 3 rue de l'Université, 67084 Strasbourg Cedex; Dir B. CARRIERE
Earth and Life Sciences: 28 rue Goethe, 67083 Strasbourg Cedex; Dir M. HOFFERT
Environmental and Behavioural Sciences: 7 rue de l'Université, 67000 Strasbourg; Dir B. WILL
Economics and Management: 4 rue Blaise Pascal, 67070 Strasbourg Cedex; Dir R. EGE
Geography: 3 rue de l'Argonne, 67083 Strasbourg Cedex; Dir J. L. PIERMAY
Polymer Engineering Graduate School: 4 rue Boussingault, 67000 Strasbourg; Dir J. C. BERNIER
Observatory: 11 rue de l'Université, 67000 Strasbourg; Dir D. EGRET
Institute of Geophysics: 5 rue René Descartes, 67084 Strasbourg Cedex; Dir R. SCHLICH
School for Advanced Studies in Physics (ENSPS): Parc d'Innovation, Blvd Sébastien Brant, 67400 Illkirch-Graffenstaden; tel. 3-88-65-50-00; fax 3-88-65-52-49; Dir F. BECKER
University Technology Institute: 3 rue Saint-Paul, 67300 Schiltigheim; Dir B. OBRECHT
University School of Biotechnology (ESBS): Parc d'Innovation, Blvd Sébastien Brant, 67400 Illkirch-Graffenstaden; tel. 3-88-65-50-00; fax 3-88-65-53-30.

UNIVERSITÉ DE STRASBOURG II (SCIENCES HUMAINES)

22 rue Descartes, 67084 Strasbourg Cedex

Telephone: 3-88-41-73-00
Fax: 3-88-41-73-54
E-mail: hamm@ushs.u-strasbg.fr

Founded 1538
State control

President: ALBERT HAMM
Vice-President: DANIEL PAYOT
Secretary-General: CLAUDE PANARD

Number of teachers: 421
Number of students: 16,291

Publications: *Recherches anglaises et nord-américaines, Recherches ibériques et ibéro-américaines, Recherches germaniques, Bulletin analytique d'histoire romaine, Revue des sciences sociales de la France de l'Est, Travaux de l'Institut de Phonétique, KTEMA (Civilisations de l'Orient, de la Grèce et de Rome antique), Revue de Droit Canonique* (annually), *Revue des Sciences Religieuses* (quarterly).

DIRECTORS OF TEACHING AND RESEARCH UNITS

Classics: FRANÇOIS-XAVIER CUCHE
Modern Languages, Literature and Civilization: CHRISTIAN CIVARDI
Social Sciences, Social Work and Development: JUAN MATAS
Philosophy and Communication: DANIEL PAYOT
Languages and Applied Human Sciences: JEAN-JACQUES ALCANDRE
History: JEAN-MICHEL MEHL
Arts: JEAN-LOUIS FLECNIAKOSKA
Sport Science: BERNARD MICHON
French and Comparative Linguistics and Literature: JEAN-PAUL SCHNEIDER
Catholic Theology (9 place de l'Université, 67084 Strasbourg Cedex): SIMON KNAEBEL
Protestant Theology (9 place de l'Université, 67084 Strasbourg Cedex): JEAN-FRANÇOIS COLLANGE
Music Teacher Training Centre (Ecole Normale 1, rue Froehlich, 67600 Selestat): JEAN-LOUIS FLECNIAKOSKA

HEADS OF DEPARTMENTS

Classics:

- Institute of South Asian Studies: BORIS OGUIBENINE
- Institute of Greek: BERNARD LAUROT
- Institute of Latin: FRANÇOIS HEIM
- Institute of Linguistics and French Language: MARTIN RIEGEL
- Institute of General and Comparative Literature: OLIVIER BONNEROT
- Institute of Phonetics: JEAN-PIERRE ZERLING
- Institute of Papyrology (9 place de l'Université): JEAN GASCOU

Modern Languages, Literature and Civilization:

- Department of English and North American Studies: BRIAN WALLIS
- Department of German Studies: YOLANDE SIEBERT
- Department of Alsatian and Mosellan Dialectology: ARLETTE BOTHOREL
- Department of Scandinavian Studies: SOPHIE GRIMAL
- Department of Dutch: CLAUDIA HUISMAN
- Department of Iberian and Ibero-American Studies: BRENDA LACA

Department of Italian Studies: LUCA BADINI CONFALONIERI
Department of Romanian Studies: Mme HÉLÈNE LENZ
Department of Slavic and Soviet Studies: BELKIS-SONJA PHILONENKO
Department of Modern Greek Studies: LAURENT PERNOT
Department of Arab and Islamic Studies: MICHEL BARBOT
Department of Hebrew and Jewish Studies: JOSEPH ELKOUBY
Department of Turkish Studies: PAUL DUMONT
Department of Persian Studies: HOSSEIN BEIKBAGHBAN
Department of Japanese Studies: CHRISTIANE SEGUY
Department of Hungarian Studies: ILDIKÓ SZTRAPKOVICS
Department of Applied Linguistics and the Teaching of Living Languages: JÜRGEN OTT
Department of Chinese Studies: CHRISTIAN CIVARDI

Sport:

Institute of Physical Education and Sports Science: BERNARD MICHON

Social Sciences:

Institute of Sociology: PASCAL HINTERMEYER
Institute of Demography: ANNE-MARIE SAHLI
Institute of Ethnology: ERIC NAVET
Institute of Polemics: PATRICK WATIER
Institute of Town Planning and Regional Administration: STEPHAN JONAS

Philosophy and Communication:

Department of Philosophy: MARTINE DE GAUDEMAR
Department of General Linguistics: GEORGES KLEIBER
Department of Computer Studies: MICHEL EYTAN
Department of Education: MAURICE SACHOT

Languages and Applied Human Sciences:

Department of Applied Modern Languages: JEAN-JACQUES ALCANDRE

History:

Institute of Art History: ROLAND RECHT
Institute of Greek History: EDMOND LEVY
Institute of Roman History: ALAIN CHAUVOT
Institute of Medieval History: JEAN-MICHEL MEHL, DENIS MENJOT
Institute of the History of Alsace: BERNARD VOGLER
Institute of Modern History: JEAN-CLAUDE WAQUET
Institute of Contemporary History: CHRISTIAN BAECHLER
Institute of the History of Religions: FRANÇOIS BLANCHETIÈRE
Institute of Byzantine Art and Archaeology: JEAN-MICHEL SPIESER
Institute of the History and Archaeology of the Ancient East: DOMINIQUE BEYER
Institute of Classical Archaeology: GÉRARD SIEBERT
Institute of Egyptology: CLAUDE TRAUNECKER
Institute of National Antiquities: ANNE-MARIE ADAM
Institute of Geography: CATHERINE SELIMANOVSKI

Arts:

Department of Fine Art: JEAN-LOUIS FLECNIAKOSKA
Department of Cinema and Audio-Visual: JEAN-FRANÇOIS MORIS
Department of Music: JEAN-LOUIS FLECNIAKOSKA
Department of Plastic Arts: JACQUELINE CUSTODERO

Catholic Theology:

Institute of Religious Education: GILBERT ADLER
Institute of Canon Law: MARCEL METZGER

Protestant Theology:

Centre of Pedagogical Study and Practice: BERNARD KELLER
Centre of Theological Training: JEAN-FRANÇOIS COLLANGE
Centre of Training in Church Music: ULRICH ASPER

UNIVERSITÉ DE STRASBOURG III (UNIVERSITÉ ROBERT SCHUMAN)

1 place d'Athènes, BP 66, 67045 Strasbourg Cedex

Telephone: 3-88-41-42-00
Fax: 3-88-61-30-37

President: PIERRE ORTSCHEIDT
Vice-Presidents: J. FLECK, C. MESTRE, D. ALEXANDRE
Secretary-General: ALAIN MÈGE
Librarian: DOMINIQUE BAUDIN

Number of students: 9,600

Publication: *News d'Ill* (every 2 months).

TEACHING AND RESEARCH UNITS

Law, Political Sciences and Management: Dir N. OLSZAK
Law, Political and Social Research: Dir C. MESTRE
Institute of Labour: Dir F. KESSLER
Institute of Political Studies: Dir R. DORANDEU
Institute of Business Economics: Dir P. IMBS
Centre for International Patent Rights: Dir Y. REBOUL
University Centre for Journalistic Studies: Dir A. CHANEL
European Institute for Advanced Commercial Studies: Dir H. TÜMMERS
University Institute of Technology: Dir J. FLECK
Institute of Advanced European Studies: Dir J.-F. FLAUSS
Institute of Preparation for General Administration: Dr G. SIAT
Language Centre: Dir A. MARAGE
Adult Education Service: Dir B. CUBAYNES

PROFESSORS

ALEXANDRE, D., Private Law
ALIPRANTIS, N., Private Law
ARROUS, J., General Economics and Statistics
BAUD, J. P., History of Law
BAUMERT, H., Management
BISCHOFF, J. M., Private Law
BITSCH, M.-TH., History of Europe
BLED, J.-P., Modern History and Political Science
BRILL, J. P., Private Law
BURST, J. J., Private Law
CONSTANT, F., History
CONSTANTINESCO, V., Public Law
DELCOURT, X., Journalism
DELOYE, Y., Political Science
DEVOLUY, M., General Economics and Statistics
DIETSCH, M., General Economics and Statistics
DORANDEU, R., Political Science
FABREGUET, M., History
FLAUSS, J.-F., Public Law
GANGHOFER, R., Legal History
GARTNER, F., Public Law
GEORGES, P., Journalism
GIRAUDEAU, A., Physical Chemistry
GOYET, C., Private Law
GRANET, F., Private Law
GREWE, C., Public Law
GROSCLAUDE, J., Public Law
HERTZOG, R., Public Law
HETZEL, P., Management
HINDERMANN, J.-P., Applied Chemistry
HOFNUNG, M., Public Law
HUET, A., Private Law
JEANCLOS, Y., History of Law
JOUANJAN, O., Public Law
KNAUB, G., Public Law
KOERING, R., Private Law
KOVAR, R., Public Law
LAVOINNE, Y., Journalism
LEMOINE, P., Chemistry
LITTMANN, M.-J., Private Law
LLORENS, F., Public Law
MARCHESSOU, PH., Public Law
MATHIEN, M., Journalism
MESTRE, CH., Public Law
MOUSSON-LESTAING, J.-P., Modern History and Political Science
MUGUET, M.-P., Chemistry
MULLER, M.-P., Mathematics
OBRECHT, J.-J., Management
OLSZAK, N., History of Law
ORSCHEIDT, P., Private Law
PIETRI, N., History
POUGHON, J.-M., Legal History
PUECH, M., Private Law
REBOUL, Y., Private Law
RIEG, A., Private Law
ROHMER, F., Public Law
ROMER, J.-C., History
SCHEVIN, P., Management
SCHMIDT, D., Private Law
SIMLER, P., Private Law
SIMON, D., Public Law
SOLER-COUTEAUX, P., Public Law
STORCK, J.-P., Private Law
STORCK, M., Private Law
URBAN, S., Management
VERNET, D., Journalism
WACHSMANN, P., Public Law
WALINE, J., Public Law
WIEDERKEHR, G., Private Law

UNIVERSITÉ DE TOULON ET DU VAR

Ave de l'Université, BP 132, 83957 La Garde Cedex

Telephone: 4-94-75-90-50
Fax: 4-94-08-14-32

Founded 1970

President: JEAN-LOUIS VERNET
Vice-President: DANIELLE HOUVET
Secretary-General: HENRI LAFAGE
Librarian: JACQUES KERIGUY

Number of teachers: 380
Number of students: 8,500

TEACHING AND RESEARCH UNITS

Sciences and Technology: Dir BERNARD BARBAGELATA
Law Sciences: Dir MICHEL PAILLET
Economic Sciences: Dir MICHEL WEILL
Arts: JAMES DAUPHINE
University Institute of Technology: Dir BRUNO ROSSETO

UNIVERSITÉ DE TOULOUSE I (SCIENCES SOCIALES)

Place Anatole France, 31042 Toulouse Cedex

Telephone: 5-61-63-35-00
Fax: 5-61-63-37-98

Founded 1229
State control

President: BERNARD SAINT-GIRONS
Vice-President: JACQUES IGALENS
Secretary-General: DANIELE ROULLAND
Librarians: GERMAINE ROGÉ, MONIQUE PUZZO

Number of teachers: 411
Number of students: 19,027

Publications: *Livret de l'Etudiant, Annales, Livre de la Recherche, UT1 Magazine.*

TEACHING AND RESEARCH UNITS

Law: Dir H. ROUSSILLON
Economics: Dir B. BELLOC

Economic and Social Administration: Dir S. REGOURD
Information Science: Dir C. ERNST

ATTACHED INSTITUTES

Ecole Supérieure Universitaire de Gestion: 2 rue Albert Lautmann, 31042 Toulouse Cedex; tel. 5-61-21-55-18; fax 5-61-23-84-33; Dir P. SPITERI.

Institut d'Etudes Politiques: 2 ter rue des Puits Creusés, 31042 Toulouse Cedex; tel. 5-61-11-02-60; fax 5-61-22-94-80; Dir C. HEN.

Institut Universitaire Technologique de Rodez: 33 ave du 8 mai 1945, 12000 Rodez; tel. 5-65-77-10-80; fax 5-65-77-10-81; Dir B. ALLAUX.

Centre Universitaire d'Albi: 2 ave Franchet d'Espérey, 81011 Albi Cedex 09, tel. 5-63-48-19-79; fax 5-63-48-19-71; Dir O. DEVAUX.

Centre Universitaire de Montauban: 116 blvd Montauriol, 82017 Montauban Cedex; tel. 5-63-63-32-71; fax 5-63-66-34-07; Dir B. MARIZ.

UNIVERSITÉ DE TOULOUSE II (Le Mirail)

5 allées Antonio Machado, 31058 Toulouse Cedex 1

Telephone: 5-61-50-42-50
Fax: 5-61-50-42-09

President: ROMAIN GAIGNARD
Secretary-General: JEAN-CLAUDE SELSIS

Number of teachers: 781
Number of students: 26,504

Publications: *Caravelle* (2 a year), *Criticón* (3 a year), *Homo* (annually), *Kairos* (2 a year), *Littératures* (2 a year), *Pallas* (2 a year), *Cinémas d'Amérique Latine* (1 a year), *Clio* (2 a year), *Science de la Société* (3 a year), *Anglophonia* (2 a year), *Sud / Ouest Européen.*

TEACHING AND RESEARCH UNITS

Philosophy and Politics: Dir L. SALA-MOLINS
Psychology: Dir J.-R. HAIT (acting)
Social Sciences: Dir M. PERVANCHON (acting)
Behavioural Sciences, Education: Dir S. ALAVA
Modern Languages, Foreign Literatures and Civilizations and General Linguistics: Dir H. HOMBOURG
Studies of the English-Speaking World: Dir J. L. BRETEAU
Ancient Literature and Languages: Dir J.-P. MAUREL
French Literature, Languages and Music: Dir F. GEVREY
History, Archaeology and History of Art: Dir P. VAYSSIÈRE
Geography: Dir D. WEISSBERG
Mathematics, Computer Science Statistics, Economics and Business Studies: Dir P. CARBONNE
Hispanic and Hispano-American Studies: Dir C. CHAUCHADIS
University Institute of Technology: Dir J. J. MERCIER
Continuing Education: M. FOURNET
Audio-visual Studies: Dir G. CHAPOUILLIE
Latin-American Studies (IPEALT): Dir J. GILARD
Institut Universitaire de Formation de Musiciens Intervenant à l'Ecole Elémentaire et Pré-Elémentaire (IFMI): Dir J. BROUSSAUDIER

UNIVERSITÉ PAUL SABATIER (TOULOUSE III)

118 route de Narbonne, 31062 Toulouse Cedex

Telephone: 5-61-55-66-11
Telex: 521880
Fax: 5-61-55-64-70

Founded 1969
State control
Academic year: September to June

President: RAYMOND BASTIDE
Vice-Presidents: R. CAUBET (Scientific Council), G. SOUM (Council of Studies and University Life)
Secretary-General: Mme A. VERDAGUER
Librarian: Mme HEUSSE

Number of teachers and researchers: 1,650
Number of students: 28,000

Publication: *Campus CONTACT Actualité* (monthly).

DEANS

Faculty of Medicine (Rangueil): G. LAZORTHES
Faculty of Medicine (Purpan): B. GUIRAUD CHAUMEIL
Faculty of Dental Surgery: J. PH. LODTER
Faculty of Pharmacy: P. COURRIÈRE

TEACHING AND RESEARCH UNITS

Mathematics, Information Science, Management: Dir Prof. H. SENATEUR
Physics, Chemistry and Automation: Dir Y. SALAMERO
Earth and Life Sciences: Dir Prof. J. DERAMOND
Scientific Study of Physical and Sporting Activities: G. AUNEAU
University Institute of Technology: Dir M. EYCHENE
Modern Languages: Dir R. FAURE

UNIVERSITÉ DE TOURS (UNIVERSITÉ FRANÇOIS RABELAIS)

3 rue des Tanneurs, BP 4103, 37041 Tours Cedex

Telephone: 2-47-36-66-00
Fax: 2-47-36-64-10
E-mail: scuio@balzac.univ-tours.fr

Founded 1970
State control
Academic year: September to June

President: JACQUES GAUTRON
Vice-Presidents: CHRISTINE POIRIER, ISABELLE HANNEQUART, MICHEL LUSSAULT, MICHEL LÉCUREUIL
Secretary-General: PIERRE RICHARD
Librarian: A. M. FERRIER

Number of teachers: 1,093
Number of students: 26,500

Publication: *François Rabelais Informations.*

DIRECTORS OF TEACHING AND RESEARCH UNITS

Law, Economics and Social Sciences: N. GAUTRAS
Medicine: J. C. ROLLAND
Pharmacy: M. LECUREUIL
University Institute of Technology: C. VERSAVEL
Exact and Natural Sciences: M. C. VIGUIER-MARTINEZ
Centre for Renaissance Studies: G. CHAIX
Centre for Higher Studies in Planning: G. VERGNEAU
Art and Science of Man: F. TESTU
Classical and Modern Languages, Literatures, Civilizations: E. GENOUVRIER
Language, Literature and Civilization of English-speaking Countries: G. DELECHELLE
School of Industry-Related Computer Studies and Engineering: C. PROUST
University Branch at Blois: J.-F. LUSSEAU (Coordinator)
University Institute of Technology at Blois: A. RONCIN
Val-de-Loire School of Engineering (Blois): J. LEMEUR (acting)
National Higher School of Landscaping (Blois): J. F. DE BOISCUILLÉ

UNIVERSITÉ DE VALENCIENNES ET DU HAINAUT-CAMBRESIS

Le Mont Houy, BP 311, 59304 Valenciennes Cedex

Telephone: 3-27-14-12-34
Fax: 3-27-14-11-00
E-mail: uvhc@univ-valenciennes.fr

Founded 1964
State control
Language of instruction: French
Academic year: September to June

President: JEAN-CLAUDE ANGUÉ
Secretary-General: JEAN-PIERRE DARRAS
Librarian: A. STEINER

Library of 73,000 vols
Number of teachers: 485
Number of students: 12,000

Publications: *16 Lez Valenciennes* (annually), *Guide d'étudiant* (annually), *Rapport d'activité des laboratoires de recherche* (annually), *Lettre de l'Université* (monthly).

TEACHING AND RESEARCH UNITS

Institute of Science and Technology: Dir P. LEVEL
Institute of Technology: Dir J. M. DESRUMAUX
Literature, Modern Languages and Art: Dir J. VAILLANT
Law, Economics and Management: Dir M. DEFOSSEZ
Department of Administrative Studies: Dir X. MOREAU
School of Mechanics and Energetics: Dir YVES RAVALARD
School of Mechanics: Dir J. P. BRICOUT
School of Data Processing and Production Technology: Dir D. WILLAEYS

UNIVERSITÉ VERSAILLES/SAINT QUENTIN-en-YVELINES

23 rue du Refuge, 78000 Versailles

Telephone: 1-39-25-41-03
Fax: 1-39-25-41-07

Founded 1991

President: DOMINIQUE GENTILE

Number of students: 9,300

TEACHING AND RESEARCH UNITS

Unité de Formation et de Recherche St-Quentin-en-Yvelines: 47 blvd Vauban, 78280 Guyancourt; tel. 1-39-25-50-00; fax 1-39-25-53-55; courses in law, economics, social sciences, humanities; Dir JEAN-FRANÇOIS LEMETTRE.

Unité de Formation et de Recherche Versailles: 45 ave des Etats-Unis, 78000 Versailles; tel. 1-39-25-40-00; fax 1-39-25-40-19; courses in science; Dir JACQUES LAVERGNAT.

Polytechnic Institutes

INSTITUT NATIONAL POLYTECHNIQUE DE GRENOBLE

46 ave Félix Viallet, 38031 Grenoble Cedex 1

Telephone: 4-76-57-45-00
Fax: 4-76-57-45-01

Founded 1907

President: YVES BRUNET
Vice-Presidents: ROGER MORET, BERNARD GUERIN, JEAN-MICHEL DION, JEAN-CLAUDE SABONNADIÈRE
Secretary-General: PIERRE BALME

Number of teachers: 350
Number of students: 4,300

Publications: *Ingénieurs INPG* (weekly, monthly and termly).

CONSTITUENT SCHOOLS

Ecole Nationale Supérieure d'Electricité et de Radioélectricité (ENSERG): 23 rue des Martyrs, BP 257, 38016 Grenoble Cedex; Dir MICHEL BARIBAUD.

Ecole Nationale Supérieure d'Electrochimie et d'Electrométallurgie de Grenoble (ENSEEG): 1130 rue de la Piscine, Domaine Universitaire, BP 75, 38402 Saint-Martin-d'Hères Cedex; Dir JEAN-CLAUDE POIGNET.

Ecole Nationale Supérieure de Génie Industriel (ENSGI): 46 ave Félix Viallet, 38031 Grenoble Cedex 1; Dir SERGE TICHKIEWITCH.

Ecole Nationale Supérieure d'Ingénieurs Electriciens de Grenoble (ENSIEG): Rue de la Houille Blanche, Domaine Universitaire, BP 46, 38402 Saint-Martin d'Hères; Dir ARLETTE CHERVY.

Ecole Nationale Supérieure d'Informatique et de Mathématiques Appliquées de Grenoble (ENSIMAG): Domaine Universitaire, BP 72, 38402 St Martin d'Hères; Dir GUY MAZARÉ.

Ecole Nationale Supérieure d'Hydraulique et de Mécanique de Grenoble (ENSHMG): 1025 rue de la Piscine, Domaine Universitaire, BP 95, 38402 Saint-Martin-d'Hères Cedex; Dir JEAN-MICHEL GRESILLON.

Ecole Nationale Supérieure de Physique de Grenoble (ENSPG): rue de la Houille Blanche, BP 46, 38402 Saint-Martin-d'Hères; Dir CLAIRE SCHLENKER.

Ecole Française de Papeterie et des Industries Graphiques (EFPG): 461 rue de la Papeterie, Domaine Universitaire, BP 65, 38402 Saint-Martin-d'Hères Cedex; Dir CHRISTIAN VOILLOT.

Ecole Supérieure d'Ingénieurs en Systèmes Industriels Avancés Rhône-Alpes (ESISAR): 50 rue Barthélémy de Laffemas, BP 54, 26902 Valence Cedex 9; Dir MICHEL DANG.

Collège Doctoral: 46 ave Félix Viallet, 38031 Grenoble Cedex 1; Dir PIERRE GENTIL.

AFFILIATED INSTITUTE

Centre Universitaire d'Education et de Formation des Adultes (CUEFA): 701 rue de la Piscine, Domaine Universitaire, 38402 Saint-Martin-d'Hères; Dir MAXIME VINCENT.

INSTITUT NATIONAL POLYTECHNIQUE DE LORRAINE

2 ave de la Forêt de Haye, BP 3, 54501 Vandoeuvre

Telephone: 3-83-59-59-59
Fax: 3-83-59-59-55

Founded 1971

Language of instruction: French

President: MICHEL LUCIUS
Vice-Presidents: JEAN-CHARLES CHEVRIER, ANDRÉ LAURENT (Scientific Council), JEAN-PAUL TISOT (Council of Studies and University Life)
Secretary-General: NOËL GAND

Number of teachers: 400
Number of students: 4,000

CONSTITUENT SCHOOLS

Ecole Nationale Supérieure d'Agronomie et des Industries Alimentaires: 2 ave de la Forêt de Haye, BP 172, 54505, Vandoeuvre Cedex; tel. 3-83-59-59-59; fax 3-83-59-59-55; f. 1970; 45 full-time staff, 417 students; library of 7,500 vols; Dir JOËL HARDY; publ. *Bulletin Scientifique* (annually).

Ecole Nationale Supérieure d'Electricité et de Mécanique: 2 ave de la Forêt de Haye, 54500 Vandoeuvre; tel. 3-83-59-59-59; fax 3-83-59-59-55; 381 students; Dir Prof. JEAN-CLAUDE BRAUN.

Ecole Nationale Supérieure de Géologie: 94 ave de Lattre de Tassigny, BP 452, 54001 Nancy Cedex; tel. 3-83-32-85-86; fax 3-83-30-21-37; 247 students; Dir BERNARD DURAND.

Ecole Nationale Supérieure des Mines de Nancy: Parc de Saurupt, 54042 Nancy Cedex; tel. 3-83-58-42-32; telex 850 661; fax 3-83-57-97-94; f. 1919; 361 students; library of 37,500 vols, 180 periodicals; Dir CLAUDE CREMET.

Ecole Nationale Supérieure des Industries Chimiques: 1 rue Grandville, 54042 Nancy Cedex; tel. 3-83-35-21-21; fax 3-83-35-08-11; 345 students; Dir Prof. A. STORCK.

Ecole Nationale Supérieure en Génie des Systèmes Industriels: 4 allée Pelletier Doisy, 54600 Villiers lès Nancy; tel. 3-83-44-38-38; fax 3-83-44-04-82; 45 students; Dir Prof. CLAUDINE GUIDAT.

Ecole Européenne d'Ingénieurs en Génie des Matériaux: 6 rue B. Lepage, 54010 Nancy Cedex; tel. 3-83-36-83-00; fax 3-83-36-83-36; 191 students; Dir Dr TORBJORN HEDBERG.

Ecole Supérieure d'Ingénieurs des Techniques de l'Industrie: 2 rue de la Citadelle, 54000 Nancy; tel. 3-83-35-82-82; 131 students; Dir FRANÇOIS MOLLEYRE (acting).

Ecole d'Architecture de Nancy: Rue Bastien Lepage, BP 435, 54000 Nancy; tel. 3-83-30-81-00; fax 3-83-30-81-30; 476 students; Dir DENIS GRANDJEAN.

INSTITUT NATIONAL POLYTECHNIQUE DE TOULOUSE

Place des Hauts-Murats, BP 354, 31006 Toulouse Cedex 6

Telephone: 5-62-25-54-00
Fax: 5-61-53-67-21
E-mail: inp@inp-toulouse.fr

Founded 1970

President: ALAIN COSTES
Vice-Presidents: MM. BABILE, BELLET, CANDAU, GOURDON, GRANDPIERRE, KALCK, METZ
Secretary-General: J. L. BOUZINAC

Number of teachers: 270
Number of students: 2,866

CONSTITUENT SCHOOLS

Ecole Nationale Supérieure Agronomique: Ave de l'Agrobiopole, BP 107, Auzeville-Tolosane, 31326 Castanet-Tolosan Cedex; Dir M. COQUART.

Ecole Nationale Supérieure d'Electrotechnique, d'Electronique, d'Informatique et d'Hydraulique: 2 rue Camichel, 31071 Toulouse Cedex 7; Dir M. RODRIGUEZ.

Ecole Nationale Supérieure de Chimie: 118 rue de Narbonne, 31077 Toulouse Cedex 4; Dir M. MORANCHO.

Ecole Nationale Supérieure d'Ingénieurs de Génie Chimique: Chemin de la Loge, 31078 Toulouse Cedex 4; Dir M. CASAMATTA.

State Colleges and Institutes

(Due to space limitations, we are restricted to giving a selection of colleges. Almost every one is a 'Grande Ecole' and awards a national degree.)

GENERAL

COLLÈGE DE FRANCE

11 place Marcelin-Berthelot, 75231 Paris Cedex 05

Telephone: 1-44-27-12-11
Fax: 1-44-27-11-09

Founded 1530 by François I

Administrator: GILBERT DAGRON

Library of 85,000 vols
Number of teaching staff: 53 professors

PROFESSORS

Science:

BAULIEU, Fundamental Principles of Human Reproduction
BERTHOZ, Physiology of Perception and Action
CHAMBON, Molecular Genetics
CHANGEUX, Cellular Communications
COHEN-TANNOUDJI, Atomic and Molecular Physics
CONNES, Analysis and Geometry
CORVOL, Experimental Medicine
FROISSART, Particle Physics
GENNES, DE, Solid State Physics
GLOWINSKI, Neuropharmacology
JOLIOT, Cellular Bioenergetics
KOURILSKY, Molecular Immunology
LABEYRIE, Observational astrophysics
LE DOUARIN, Cellular and Molecular Embryology
LE PICHON, Geodynamics
LEHN, Chemistry of Molecular Interaction
LIONS, Mathematical Analysis of Systems
NOZIÈRES, Statistical Physics
RICQLÈS, DE, Historical Biology and Evolutionism
SCHELL, Plant Molecular Biology
TITS, Theory of Groups
YOCCOZ, Differential Equations and Dynamic Systems

Letters:

BOURDIEU, Sociology
BOUVERESSE, Philosophy of Language and Knowledge
COPPENS, Palaeoanthropology and Prehistory
COQUIN, Contemporary History of Russia
DAGRON, Byzantine History
FUMAROLI, Rhetoric and Society in Europe (16th–17th Centuries)
FUSSMAN, History of Civilization (of India)
GOUDINEAU, National Antiquities
GROTOWSKI, Theatre Anthropology
GUILAINE, Neolithic and Bronze Age Civilizations in Europe
HAGÈGE, Linguistic Theory
KELLENS, Indo-Iranian Languages and Religions
LE RIDER, Economic History of the Hellenistic East
LE ROY LADURIE, History of Modern Civilization
TARDIEU, History of syncretisms from the end of antiquity
TEIXIDOR, Semitic Antiquities
THUILLIER, History of French Art
TOUBERT, History of the Western Mediterranean in the Middle Ages
VEYNE, History of Rome
WACHTEL, History and Anthropology of Meso-American and South American Societies
WEINRICH, Romance languages and literature
WILL, History of Modern China
ZEMB, German Grammar and Thought
ZINK, French Medieval Literature

Ecole Pratique des Hautes Etudes: 45–47 rue des Ecoles, 75005 Paris; tel. 1-40-46-33-97; fax 1-40-46-33-98; f. 1868; library of 50,000 vols; Pres. BRUNO NEVEU.

Three divisions:

Natural Sciences: 46 rue Saint-Jacques, 75005 Paris; f. 1868; Pres. M. BONS; publ. *Annuaire*.

Historical and Philological Sciences: 45–47 rue des Ecoles, 75005 Paris; f. 1868; Pres. M. MONNIER; publ. *Annuaire*.

Religious Sciences: Sorbonne, 45–47 rue des Ecoles, 75005 Paris; f. 1886; Pres. M. LANGLOIS; publ. *Annuaire*.

ADMINISTRATION

Ecole Nationale d'Administration: 13 rue de l'Université, 75007 Paris; tel. 1-49-26-45-45; telex 214859; fax 1-42-60-26-95; f. 1945 to provide training for the higher ranks of the Civil Service; 600 teachers; 400 students; library of 25,000 vols; Dir RAYMOND-FRANÇOIS LE BRIS; Gen. Sec. JEAN-BENOÎT ALBERTINI.

Groupe Ecole Supérieure de Commerce: 4 blvd Trudaine, 63037 Clermont-Ferrand; tel. 4-73-98-24-24; fax 4-73-98-24-49; f. 1919; dependent on the Direction de l'Enseignement Supérieur du Ministre de l'Education; 200 teachers, 600 students; library of 9,000 vols; and Chamber of Commerce library of 12,000 vols; Dir L. HUA; publs *Point Zéro* (every 2 months), *Développements* (3 a year).

Institut International d'Administration Publique: 2 ave de l'Observatoire, 75272 Paris Cedex 06; tel. 1-44-41-85-00; telex 270229; fax 1-44-41-86-19; f. 1966 to train high-ranking civil servants at the request of governments from Europe, Africa, America, Asia and the Middle East; full-length courses in public management, int. relations, economic policy; special and proficiency courses; research in comparative administration; research and documentation services; library of 40,000 vols; scholarships can be granted; Dir DIDIER MAUS; publ. *Revue française d'Administration publique* (quarterly).

AGRICULTURE, FORESTRY, VETERINARY SCIENCE

Centre National d'Etudes Agronomiques des Régions Chaudes: 1101 ave Agropolis, BP 5098, 34033 Montpellier Cedex 1; tel. 4-67-61-70-00; fax 4-67-41-02-32; e-mail sauboa@cnearc.fr; f. 1902; library of 22,000 vols, 350 periodicals; Dir M. LATHAM.

Sections:

Cycle d'Etudes Supérieures d'Agronomie Tropicale.
Cycle d'Etudes d'Ingénieurs des Techniques Agricoles des Régions Chaudes.
Département de la Formation Continue.
Master Professionnel Natura 'Vulgarisation et Organisations Professionnelles Agricoles'.
Master of Science 'Développement Agricole Tropical'.

Ecole Nationale d'Ingénieurs des Travaux Agricoles de Clermont-Ferrand: Marmilhat, 63370 Lempdes; tel. 4-73-98-13-15; fax 4-73-98-13-98; f. 1984; 45 teachers; 300 students; library of 10,000 vols; Dir ROBERT HÈNNAF.

Ecole Nationale du Génie Rural des Eaux et des Forêts: Centre de Nancy, 14 rue Girardet, 54042 Nancy Cedex; tel. 3-83-39-68-00; fax 3-83-30-22-54; e-mail nom@engref.fr; f. 1965 by the fusion of the Ecole Nationale du Génie Rural and the Ecole Nationale des Eaux et Forêts; library of 40,000 vols, 1,100 periodicals; Dir M. DANGUY DES DÉSERTS; publ. *Revue Forestière française* (every 2 months).

Ecole Nationale Supérieure Agronomique de Montpellier: Place Viala, 34060 Montpellier Cedex 1; tel. 4-99-61-22-00; fax 4-99-61-25-80; e-mail bye@ensam.inra.fr; f. 1872; 474 students; library of 100,000 vols, 1,400 periodicals; Dir P. RAYNAUD.

Ecole Nationale Supérieure Agronomique de Rennes: 65 rue de Saint-Brieuc, 35042 Rennes Cedex; tel. 2-99-28-50-00; fax 2-99-28-75-10; f. 1830; library of 50,000 vols; 70 teachers; 520 students; Dir P. THIVEND.

Ecole Nationale Supérieure des Industries Agricoles et Alimentaires (ENSIA): 1 ave des Olympiades, 91744 Massy Cedex; tel. 1-69-93-50-50; fax 1-69-20-02-30; e-mail ensia@ensia.inra.fr; f. 1893; library of 7,000 vols; Dir Y. DEMARNE; publs *Industries Alimentaires* (monthly), *Compte Rendu d'Activités* (annually), *Livret de l'Etudiant* (annually).

Ecole Nationale Supérieure du Paysage: 4 rue Hardy, RP 914, 78009 Versailles Cedex; tel. 1-39-24-62-00; fax 1-39-24-62-01; f. 1975; rural development, ecology, humanities, plastic arts, architecture, landscaping, town planning; library of 6,000 vols, 75 periodicals; Dir J. B. CUISINIER; publ. *Les Carnets du Paysage* (4 a year).

Ecole Nationale Vétérinaire d'Alfort: 7 ave Général de Gaulle, 94704 Maisons-Alfort Cedex; tel. 1-43-96-71-00; fax 1-43-96-71-25; f. 1765; 72 teachers; library of 150,000 vols; Dean Prof. ANDRÉ-LAURENT PARODI; publ. *Le Recueil de Médecine Vétérinaire*.

Ecole Nationale Vétérinaire de Lyon: 1 ave Bourgelat, BP 83, 69280 Marcy L'Etoile; tel. 4-78-87-25-25; fax 4-78-87-82-62; f. 1762; library of 10,000 vols; Dir M. LAPRAS; 65 teachers; publs *Revue de Médecine Vétérinaire* (monthly), *Bulletin de la Société des Sciences Vétérinaires et de médecine comparée de Lyon* (every 2 months).

Ecole Nationale Vétérinaire de Nantes: Atlanpole-La Chantrerie, BP 40706, 44307 Nantes Cedex 03; tel. 2-40-68-77-77; fax 2-40-68-77-78; f. 1979; 69 teachers, 530 students; Dir Prof. MARYSE HURTREL.

Ecole Nationale Vétérinaire de Toulouse: 23 chemin des Capelles, 31076 Toulouse Cedex; tel. 5-61-19-38-01; fax 5-61-19-39-93; f. 1828; library of 50,000 vols; 63 teachers; Dir G. VAN HAVERBEKE; Sec.-Gen. J. G. MCCOOK; Librarian Prof. J. EUZEBY; publ. *Revue de Médecine Vétérinaire* (monthly).

Institut National Agronomique Paris-Grignon: Département Agronomie-Environnement, 16 rue Claude Bernard, 75231 Paris Cedex 05; tel. 1-43-37-15-50; f. 1972 with present title; teaching personnel 129; library of 50,000 vols and 1,700 periodicals; Dir (vacant).

Département des Sols de l'INAP-G: 78850 Thiverval-Grignon; tel. 1-30-54-45-10; f. 1979; library of *c.* 1,000 vols; publ. *Sols* (3 or 4 a year).

Institut National d'Horticulture: 2 rue Le Notre, 49045 Angers Cedex 01; tel. 2-41-22-54-54; fax 2-41-73-15-57; e-mail nil@angers.inra.fr; f. 1874; library of 16,000 vols; Dir A. NIL.

Institut National Supérieur de Formation Agro-Alimentaire: 65 rue de Saint-Brieuc, 35042 Rennes Cedex; tel. 2-99-28-50-00; fax 2-99-28-75-10; f. 1990; quality management, production management, marketing; library of 50,000 vols; 70 teachers; 238 students; Dir P. THIVEND.

ARCHITECTURE

Ecole d'Architecture de Lille et des Régions Nord: 2 rue Verte, quartier de l'Hôtel de Ville, 59650 Villeneuve d'Ascq; tel. 3-20-61-95-50; fax 3-20-61-95-51; f. 1755 as Ecole d'Architecture, reorganized 1968; library of 13,000 vols; 90 teachers, 750 students; Dir BERNARD WELCOMME.

Ecole d'Architecture de Paris-La Villette: 144 rue de Flandre, 75019 Paris; tel. 1-44-65-23-00; fax 1-44-65-23-01; f. 1969, present name 1982; attached to Min. of Culture; 80 teachers; 2,300 students; library of 25,000 vols; Dir GERARD CATTALANO.

Ecole Spéciale d'Architecture: 254 blvd Raspail, 75014 Paris; tel. 1-40-47-40-47; fax 1-43-22-81-16; f. 1865; 450 students, 60 teachers; library of 7,000 vols; Dir FRANÇOIS WEHRLIN.

ECONOMICS, LAW AND POLITICS

Centre des Hautes Etudes sur l'Afrique et l'Asie Modernes: 13 rue du Four, 75006 Paris; tel. 1-44-41-38-80; fax 1-40-51-03-58; f. 1936; affiliated to the Fondation Nationale des Sciences Politiques (*q.v.*); library of 14,000 vols; Dir J. P. DOUMENGE; publs *Publications du CHEAM, Notes africaines, asiatiques et caraïbes, Notes sur l'Afrique, l'Asie et le Moyen-Orient.*

Centre Français de Droit Comparé: 28 rue Saint-Guillaume, 75007 Paris; tel. 1-44-39-86-23; fax 1-44-39-86-28; e-mail cfdc@sky.fr; f. 1951; library of 100,000 vols; Pres. JACQUES ROBERT; Sec.-Gen. DIDIER LAMÈTHE; publs *Revue Internationale de Droit Comparé, Revue de Science Criminelle et de Droit Pénal Comparé* (quarterly).

Ecole des Hautes Etudes en Sciences Sociales: 54 blvd Raspail, 75006 Paris; tel. 1-49-54-25-25; fax 1-45-44-93-11; f. 1947; 3,200 students; Pres. JACQUES REVEL.

Ecole Nationale de la Magistrature: 10 rue des Frères Bonic, 33080 Bordeaux; tel.5-56-00-10-10; e-mail initiale@enm_magistrature.fr; f. 1958; 450 students; library of 50,000 vols; Dir DOMINIQUE MAIN; publs *Mémento de l'Instruction* (2 a year), *Instruction actualité* (every 2 months), *Revue* (annually).

Ecole Nationale de la Statistique et de l'Administration Economique (ENSAE): 3 ave Pierre Larousse, 92245 Malakoff Cedex; tel. 1-41-17-51-55; fax 1-41-17-38-53; e-mail info@ensae.fr; f. 1942; attached to the Institut National de la Statistique et des Etudes Economiques (see Research Institutes); economics, statistics, finance; 350 students; Chair. A. TROGNON.

Ecole Nationale de la Statistique et de l'Analyse de l'Information (ENSAI): Campus de Ker Lann, rue Blaise Pascal, 35170 Bruz; tel. 2-99-05-32-32; fax 2-99-05-32-05; f. 1942; attached to the Institut National de la Statistique et des Etudes Economiques (see Research Institutes); statistics and information processing; 260 students; Dir A. BOUVY.

Institut d'Etudes Politiques: Ave Ausone, BP 101, 33405 Talence Cedex; tel. 5-56-84-42-52; fax 5-56-37-45-37; f. 1948; affiliated with Univ. Bordeaux IV; politics and administration, economics, management; 200 teachers and researchers; 1,200 students; library of 80,000 vols; Dir PIERRE SADRAN.

Institut d'Etudes Politiques de Paris: 27 rue Saint-Guillaume, 75337 Paris Cedex 07; tel. 1-45-49-50-50; fax 1-42-22-31-26; f. 1945 as successor to l'Ecole Libre des Sciences Politiques; linked to Fondation Nationale des Sciences Politiques (*q.v.*); library of 700,000 vols; 4,000 students; Dir R. DESCOINGS.

EDUCATION

Ecole Normale Supérieure: 45 rue d'Ulm, 75230 Paris Cedex 05; tel. 1-44-32-30-00; telex 202601; fax 1-43-29-73-69; f. 1794 by the National Convention; library: see Libraries; 800 students; graduate and postgraduate studies in humanities, social sciences and science; Dir ETIENNE GUYON; Sec.-Gen. JEAN PASCAL BONHOTOF; Librarian PIERRE PETITMENGIN; publs *Presses de l'Ecole Normale Supérieure, Annales Scientifiques de l'Ecole Normale Supérieure.*

Ecole Normale Supérieure: 31 ave Lombart, 92260 Fontenay aux Roses; tel. 1-41-13-24-00; fax 1-41-13-24-09; f. 1880; library of 200,000 vols, 700 periodicals; 120 teachers; 450 students; Dir SYLVAIN AUROUX; Sec.-Gen. A. COURDAVAULT; Dir of Studies F. MAZIÈRE; publ. *Collections des Presses de l'ENS.*

Ecole Normale Supérieure de Cachan: 61 ave du Président Wilson, 94235 Cachan Cedex; tel. 1-47-40-20-00; telex 250948; fax 1-47-40-20-74; f. 1912; library of 55,000 vols;

145 teachers, 1,150 students; Dir BERNARD DECOMPS.

HEADS OF DEPARTMENTS

Mathematics: M. CORON
Physics: M. FORTUNATO
Chemistry: M. DELAIRE
Biology and Biochemistry: M. BENICOURT
Civil Engineering: M. COUDROY
Mechanical Engineering: Mme LENE
Industrial Design: Mme BRUNET
Economics and Business: M. MUNIER
Social Sciences: Mme PARADEISE
Foreign Languages: Mme BARBIER

Ecole Normale Supérieure de Lyon: 46 allée d'Italie, 69364 Lyon Cedex 07; tel. 4-72-72-80-00; fax 4-72-72-80-80; f. 1985; library of 43,000 vols, 800 periodicals; 380 teachers and researchers; 898 students; Dir JEAN GIRAUD; Sec.-Gen. FRANÇOISE GRANGER; Librarian ARLETTE MAURIES-TAPPAZ.

DIRECTORS OF RESEARCH LABORATORIES

Chemistry: A. COLLET
Theoretical Chemistry: B. BIGOT
Geology: PH. GILLET
Computing: Y. ROBERT
Biology: P. JALINOT, J. L. DARLIX, C. DUMAS
Physics: P. OSWALD
Astrophysics: R. BACON
Mathematics: E. GHYS

GEOGRAPHY

Ecole Nationale des Sciences Géographiques: 6 et 8 ave Blaise Pascal, Cité Descartes, Champs-sur-Marne, 77455 Marne-la-Vallée Cedex 2; tel. 1-64-15-30-01; fax 1-64-15-31-07; e-mail info@ensg-ign.fr; f. 1941; administered by Institut Géographique National; 200 students (including part-time); specialized library of 36,000 books, 950,000 maps, 2,100,000 aerial photographs; Dir M. DENÈGRE.

PROFESSORS

BEAUVILLAIN, E., Remote Sensing
BORDIN, P., Geographical Information Systems
BOUILLE, F., Programming
CHAPPART, G., Cartography
CHEDHOMME, J., Geomorphology
DUQUENNE, F., Astronomy, Geodesy
EGELS, Y., Photogrammetry
FERRIF, B., Geometry, Mathematics
HOTTIER, P., Numerical Analysis
KASSER, M., Physics
LAMY, S., Applied Mathematics
LEAUTHAUD, J. M., Topography
MOISSET, D., Photogrammetry
PRIOU, J. Y., Programming

HISTORY

Ecole Nationale des Chartes: 19 rue de la Sorbonne, 75005 Paris; tel. 1-55-42-75-00; fax 1-55-42-75-09; f. 1821, reorganized 1846; library of 150,000 vols; 170 students; Dir Y.-M. BERCÉ; Sec. J. BELMON; Chief Librarian I. DIU; publs *Bibliothèque de l'Ecole des Chartes*, *Mémoires et Documents*, *Matériaux pour l'Histoire*, *Etudes et Rencontres*, *Positions des thèses* (annually).

PROFESSORS

BARBICHE, B., History of French Institutions
BOURGAIN, P., Literary Manuscripts
CHARON, A., Bibliography and history of the book
DELMAS, B., Modern Archival Sciences
ERLANDE-BRANDENBURG, A., Archaeology
GIORDANENGO, G., History of Law
GUYOTJEANNIN, O., Diplomatics
JESTAZ, B., History of Art (16th- to 18th-century)
LENIAUD, J. M., History of Art (19th- and 20th-century)
SMITH, M. H., Palaeography
VIELLIARD, F., Philology

Ecole Nationale du Patrimoine: 117 blvd St Germain, 75006 Paris; tel. 1-44-41-16-41; fax 1-44-41-16-76; f. 1990; trains curators of museums, archives and historical monuments; Dir JEAN-PIERRE BADY.

LANGUAGE AND LITERATURE

Institut National des Langues et Civilisations Orientales: 2 rue de Lille, 75343 Paris Cedex 07; tel. 1-49-26-42-00; fax 1-49-26-42-99; f. 1669; 245 teachers; 11,108 students; Pres. ANDRÉ BOURGEY; Sec.-Gen. C. DELAFOSSE.

TEACHING AND RESEARCH UNITS

Africa: Dir G. PHILIPPSON
South Asia: Dir E. MEYER
Southeast and Northern Asia and the Pacific: Dir M. AUFRAY
Korea and Japan: Dir F. MACÉ
Central and Eastern Europe: Dir O. DANIEL
China: Dir C. DESPEUX
Near and Middle East, North Africa: Dir M. BEN ABDESSELEM
Russia and Eurasia: Dir J. RADVANYI

RESEARCH CENTRES

Centre d'études sur la Russie et l'Eurasie: Dir F. CORNILLOT.

Centre de recherche en ingénierie multilingue: Dir M. SLODZIAN.

Équipe de recherche interdisciplinaire sur les sociétés méditerranéennes: Dir M. BOZDEMIR.

Centre de poétique comparée: Dir M. R. DOR.

Centre d'études japonaises: Dir F. MACÉ.

Centre de recherche sur l'oralité: Dir D. REY-HULMAN.

Centre d'études chinoises: Dir C. DESPEUX.

Centre d'études et de recherche sur l'Asie du Sud-Est: Dir M. FOURNIE.

Centre de recherche et d'études sur le sous-continent indien contemporain: Dir A. MONTAUT.

Centre d'études balkaniques: Dir H. TONNET.

Centre d'études et de recherche sur l'Afrique orientale et centrale: Dir J.-L. VILLE.

Centre de recherche en traitement automatique des langues: Dir P. POGNAN.

Centre de recherche sur l'Océan Indien occidental: Dir P. VERIN.

Centre Georges Dumézil d'études sur le Caucase: Dir G. CHARACHIDZE.

Centre de recherche berbère et arabe maghrébin: Dir DOMINIQUE CAUBET.

Institut d'etudes turques: Dir RÉMY DOR.

ATTACHED INSTITUTE

Ecole des Hautes Etudes du Judaïsme: Dir R. SIRAT.

LIBRARIANSHIP

Ecole Nationale Supérieure des Sciences de l'Information et des Bibliothèques: 17/21 blvd du 11 Novembre 1918, 69623 Villeurbanne Cedex; tel. 4-72-44-43-07; fax 4-72-44-27-88; e-mail dupuigre@enssib.fr; f. 1963; 26 teachers, 300 students; library of 17,000 vols and 585 periodicals, also audio-visual items; Dir FRANÇOIS DUPUIGRENET DESROUSSILLES; publ. *Bulletin des Bibliothèques de France* (every 2 months).

MEDICINE

Ecole d'Application du Service de Santé des Armées: 1 place Alphonse Laveran, 75230 Paris Cedex 05; tel. 1-40-51-42-31; fax 1-40-51-47-74; f. 1850; mainly two-year graduate courses; library of 40,000 vols and 2,067 periodicals; Dir MGI DE SAINT-JULIEN; publ. *Médecine et Armées*.

Ecole Nationale de la Santé Publique: Ave du Professeur Léon Bernard, 35043 Rennes Cedex; tel. 2-99-02-22-00; fax 2-99-02-28-28; f. 1945; post-university courses; 60 full-time teachers; 500 full-time, 4,000 part-time students; library of 15,000 vols; Dir PASCAL CHEVIT.

SCIENCES

Ecole Nationale de la Météorologie: 42 ave G. Coriolis, 31057 Toulouse Cedex; tel. 5-61-07-90-90; telex 521990; fax 5-61-07-96-30; f. 1982; library of 4,000 vols; Dir M. CHALON.

Institut National des Sciences Appliquées de Lyon: 20 ave Albert Einstein, 69621 Villeurbanne Cedex; tel. 4-72-43-83-83; fax 4-72-43-85-00; e-mail dir@insa-lyon.fr; f. 1957; library of 80,000 vols; 450 teachers, 4,500 students; biochemistry, computer science, civil, electrical, energetics, production and mechanical engineering, material science; Dir JOËL ROCHAT.

Institut National des Sciences Appliquées de Rennes: 20 ave des Buttes de Coësmes, 35043 Rennes Cedex; f. 1961; physical and materials science, electronic engineering, civil engineering and town planning, computer science, communications systems, mechanical engineering and control; 130 teachers, 1,200 students; Dir DÉSIRÉ AMOROS.

Institut National des Sciences Appliquées de Rouen (INSA Rouen): Place Emile Blondel, BP 08, 76131 Mont-Saint-Aignan Cedex; tel. 2-35-52-83-00; fax 2-35-52-83-20; f. 1985; chemistry, mathematics, energy, mechanical engineering, technology and applied sciences; 109 teachers; 985 students; library of 15,000 vols, 200 periodicals; Dir Prof. GILBERT TOUZOT.

Muséum National d'Histoire Naturelle: 57 rue Cuvier, 75281 Paris Cedex 05; tel. 1-40-79-30-00; fax 1-40-79-34-84; f. 1635; teaching and research in natural history; administers the Zoological Garden, the Musée de l'Homme and several other natural history depts and institutions; Dir Prof. HENRY DE LUMLEY; Librarian MONIQUE DUCREUX.

PROFESSORS

BILLARD, R., Ichthyology
BLANDIN, P., Ecology
BODO, B., Applied Organic Chemistry
CAUSSANEL, C., Entomology
COINEAU, Y., Arthropods
COUDERC, H., Botany
COUTÉ, A., Cryptogamy
DEMENEIX, B., General and Comparative Physiology
DOUMENC, D., Biology of Marine Invertebrates and Malacology
DUBOIS, A., Zoology (Reptiles and Amphibians)
DUBOST, G., Conservation of Animal Species
DUPAIGNE, Ethnology
ERARD, C., Zoology
FABRIES, J., Mineralogy
GARESTIER, T., Biophysics
LANGANEY, A., Physical Anthropology
LEFEUVRE, J. C., Evolution of Natural Systems
LUMLEY, H. DE, Prehistory
MONNIER, Y., Ethnology-Biogeography
MORAT, P., Phanerogamy
REPERANT, J., Comparative Anatomy
REVAULT D'ALLONNES, M., Physical Oceanography
SANTUS, R., Photobiology
SCHREVEL, J., Parasitology
TAQUET, PH., Palaeontology
WEVER, P. DE, Geology

TECHNOLOGY

Conservatoire National des Arts et Métiers: 292 rue St Martin, 75141 Paris Cedex 03; tel. 1-40-27-20-00; f. 1794; 55 regional centres;

diploma and doctorate courses; 470 teachers, 82,000 students (full- and part-time); library: see Libraries; Administrator LAURENCE PAYE-JEANNENEY.

PROFESSORS

Department of Chemistry and Nuclear Science:

BONFAND, E., Technology of Nuclear Reactors
CATONNE, J.-C., Industrial Electrochemistry
DELACROIX, A., Industrial Chemistry
DESCARSIN, M.-T., Industrial Electrochemistry
DESJEUX, J.-F., Applied Biology
FAUVARQUE, J.-F., Industrial Electrochemistry
FOOS, J., Isotopic Radiation and Applications
GENTY, C., Physical-Chemical Methods of Analysis
GUETTÉ, J.-P., Applied Organic Chemistry
GUY, A., Applied Organic Chemistry
LEFRANÇOIS, B., Industrial Chemistry
LEMAIRE, G., Radioprotection
MORIFN, R., Biotechnology
NICOLAS, J., Industrial and Foodcrop Biochemistry
OLIVEROS, L., General Chemistry applied to Industry
VALEUR, B., General Chemistry applied to Industry

Department of Economics and Business Administration:

AIMETTI, J.-P., Business Strategy and Business Studies
BLOCH, J., Commercial Forecasting
BURLAUD, A., Management Accounting and Control
CURIEN, N., Telecommunications Policy and Economics
DE MONTBRIAL, T., Applied Economic Analysis
DIDIER, M., Industrial Economics and Statistics
DREYFUS, B., Administration and Management of Local Collectives
GODET, M., Industrial Forecasting
GUILLERME, A., History of Technology
LEBAN, R., Business Economics and Management
LEBAU, A., Spatial Techniques and Programmes
LESOURNE, J., Industrial Economics and Statistics
MERCADAL, B., Commercial Law
PETAUTON, P., Mathematical Theory of Insurance
SALOMON, J. J., Technology and Society
SCHEID, J.C., Finance and Accountancy
WISZIAK, M., Mathematics of Business Dealing
ZIV, J.-C., Transport and Logistics

Department of Informatics:

ANCEAU, F., Principles of Informatics
ARNAUD, J.-P., Networks
CARREZ, C., Business Informatics
DEWEZ, L., Informatics, Programming
FLORIN, G., Informatics, Programming
KAISER, C., Informatics, Programming
LEMAIRE, B., Operational Research
MATHELOT, P., Business Informatics
MEINADIER, J.-P., Systems Integration
NATKIN, S., Informatics, Programming
PRINTZ, J., Software Engineering
SCHOLL, M., Informatics, Programming
VIGUIE-DONZEAU-GOUGE, V., Informatics, Programming

Department of Mathematics:

DESTUYNDER, P., Scientific Calculus
HOCQUENGHEM, S., Applied Mathematics in Arts and Crafts
REINHARD, H., Mathematics in Engineering
SAPORTA, G., Applied Statistics
VELU, J., Applied Mathematics in Arts and Crafts

Department of Mechanical Engineering, Materials and Energetics:

BATHIAS, C., Metallurgy
CHAMPION, P., Minerals
CHOMETON, F., Industrial Applications of Aerodynamics
COLOMBIE, P., Metallurgy
CORDEBOIS, J.-P., Mechanical Manufacturing
DEPREZ, D., Geological Engineering in Construction
KERN, F., Civil Engineering
LASSAU, G., Industrial Mechanics
LAVAUR, R., Civil Engineering
LEGER, D., Minerals
LUCAS, J., Heat Transfer in Industry
MEUNIER, F., Applied Physics in Cryogenics and Industrial Applications
OHAYON, R., Industrial Mechanics
PLUMELLE, C., Geological Engineering in Construction
PLUVIOSE, M., Turbomachinery
RENAUDAUX, J.-P., Mechanical Manufacturing
VILLOUTREIX, G., Physical Chemistry and Applications of Macromolecular Materials
WOLFF, C., Physical Chemistry and Applications of Macromolecular Materials

Department of Physics and Electronics:

BELLANGER, M., Electronics
BONNET, J.-J., Applied Physics in Industry
CANIT, J.-C., Optics
CANRY, B., Industrial Robotics
FERNANDES, C., Physics of Electrical Components
FINO, B., Radiocommunications
GARCIA, A., Applied Accoustics
HIMBERT, M., Metrology
HINCELIN, G., Physics of Electrical Components
JOUHANEAU, J., Applied Acoustics
JUNCAR, P., Metrology
LATTUATTI, V., Industrial Robotics
LEPOUTRE, F., Physics of Captors and Measures
MANESSE, G., Electrotechnology
MISEREY, F., Physics of Electrical Components
RHUMELARD, C., Physics of Electrical Components
RIALLAND, J.-F., Electrotechnology
SOL, C., Electrotechnology
VIALLE, M., Applied Physics in Industry
VU THIEN, H., Signals and Systems

Department of Labour and Business Studies:

ADAM, G., Professional Relations
BARBIER, J. M., Training of Adults
CASPAR, P., Training of Adults
CUNY, X., Hygiene and Security
DEJOURS, C., Psychology of Work
FALZON, P., Ergonomics and Neurophysiology of Work
FARDEAU, M., Social integration of the Disabled
GILLET, B., Psychology of Work
LE COADIC, Y., Scientific and Technological Information and Communication
LUSSATO, B., Theories and Systems of Organization
MARCHAND, D., Labour Law and Social Security Law
PIOTET, F., Sociology of Work, Employment and Organizations
REYNAUD, J.-D., Sociology of Work and Professional Relations
RIBETTE, R., Personnel Administration
ROUX-ROSSI, D., Labour Law and Social Security Law
SCHMITT, J.-P., Labour and Management Organization

ATTACHED INSTITUTES

Institut d'Etudes Supérieures des Techniques d'Organisation: f. 1956; Dir M. SCHMITT.

Institut d'Informatique d'Entreprise: f. 1968; Dir M. BLOCH.

Institut Français du Froid Industriel: Dir F. MEUNIER.

Institut National de Formation des Cadres Supérieurs de la Vente: f. 1956; Dir A. BLOCH.

Institut National des Techniques de la Documentation: f. 1950; Dir C. BERTHO-LAVENIR.

Institut National des Techniques de la Mer: f. 1981; Dir J. C. GUARY.

Institut Scientifique et Technique de la Nutrition et de l'Alimentation: Dir S. HERCBERG.

Institut des Transports Internationaux et des Ports: f. 1980; Dir J.-C. ZIV.

Institut de la Construction et de l'Habitation: Dir J. CHAPUISAT.

Institut National des Techniques Economiques et Comptables: Dir J.-C. SCHEID.

Institut National d'Etude du Travail et d'Orientation Professionnelle: Dir J. GUICHARD.

Institut de Topométrie et Ecole Supérieure des Géomètres et Topographes: M. KASSER.

Centre d'Actualisation des Connaissances et de l'Etude des Matériaux Industriels: Dir M. COLOMBIE.

Ecole Nationale d'Assurances: Dir J. F. DE VULPILLIERES.

Institut d'Ingénierie Internationale: Dir J. P. MEINADIER.

Centre de Préparation au Diplôme d'Etat d'Audioprothésiste: Dir A. GARCIA.

Centre de Préparation de l'Ingénieur au Management: Dir R. LEBAN.

Institut Technique de Banque: Dir J.-C. LOINTIER.

Centre de Recherche Science Technologie et Société: Dir J. J. SALOMON.

Institut National de Métrologie: Dir M. HIMBERT.

Institut Aérotechnique de St Cyr: Dir E. SZECHNYI.

Centre de Recherche sur les Marchés de Matières Premières: Dir J. KLEIN.

Centre de Documentation d'Histoire des Techniques: Dir A. GUILLERME.

Centre de Recherche et d'Expérimentation pour l'Enseignement des Mathématiques: Dir S. HOCQUENGHEM.

Centre de Sociologie du Travail et de l'Entreprise: Dir J.-M. BARBIER.

Centre de Formation de Formateurs de Branche: Dir L. VOLERY.

Institut de Technologie: Dir P. BOUCLY.

Ecole Supérieure de Conception et Production Industrielles: Dir C. SOL.

Institut d'Hygiène Industrielle et de l'Environnement: Dir X. CUNY.

Ecole Centrale de Lille: Cité Scientifique, BP 48, 59651 Villeneuve d'Ascq Cedex; tel. 3-20-33-53-53; fax 3-20-33-54-99; f. 1872; 7 research laboratories; library of 10,000 vols; 82 teachers, 1,040 students; Dir Prof. JEAN-CLAUDE GENTINA.

Ecole Centrale des Arts et Manufactures: Grande Voie des Vignes, 92295 Châtenay-Malabry Cedex; tel. 1-41-13-10-00; telex 250659; fax 1-41-13-10-10; f. 1829; higher degrees in engineering; library of 60,000 vols and 340 periodicals; 1,400 students; Dir D. GOURISSE; publs *Centraliens* (monthly), *Les Echos de Centrale*.

Ecole des Mines de Douai: 941 rue Charles Bourseul, BP 838, 59508 Douai Cedex; tel. 3-

27-71-22-22; fax 3-27-71-25-25; f. 1878; library of 15,000 vols; 250 teachers, 650 students; Dir M. COTTE.

Ecole Nationale de l'Aviation Civile: BP 4005, 31055 Toulouse Cedex 4; tel. 5-62-17-40-00; telex 530452; fax 5-62-17-40-23; f. 1948; training of civil aviation personnel; advanced studies in engineering; library of 30,000 vols; 408 teachers and researchers; Dir M. SOUCHELEAU.

Ecole Nationale d'Ingénieurs de Belfort: Espace Bartholdi, Belfort Technopôle, BP 525, 90016 Belfort Cedex; tel. 3-84-58-23-00; fax 3-84-54-00-62; e-mail direction@enibe.fr; f. 1962; library of 4,600 vols; Dir CLAUDE CHICOIX.

Ecole Nationale d'Ingénieurs de Metz (ENIM): Ile du Saulcy, 57045 Metz Cedex 1; tel. 3-87-34-69-00; fax 3-87-34-69-35; e-mail padilla@enim.unim.univ-metz.fr; f. 1962; 800 students; Dir PIERRE PADILLA.

Ecole Nationale d'Ingénieurs de Tarbes (ENIT): 47 ave d'Azereix, BP 1629, 65016 Tarbes Cedex; tel. 5-62-44-27-00; fax 5-62-44-27-27; e-mail mugniery@enit.fr; f. 1963; mechanical, industrial and production engineering; 60 teachers; 850 students; library of 4,000 vols; Dir BERNARD MUGNIERY.

Ecole Nationale de la Photographie: 16 rue des Arènes, BP 149, 13631 Arles Cedex; tel. 4-90-99-33-33; e-mail comm.enp@provnet.fr; f. 1982; under auspices of Ministry of Culture; 3-year course; 7 teachers, 75 students; library of 10,000 vols; Dir ALAIN LELOUP.

Ecole Nationale des Ponts et Chaussées: 6 et 8 ave Blaise Pascal, Cité Descartes, Champs-sur-Marne, 77455 Marne-la-Vallée Cedex 2; tel. 1-64-15-30-30; f. 1747; civil and mechanical engineering, town and country planning, transport; library of 170,000 vols, 3,212 18th-century MSS, 900 maps, 3,000 photographs; 700 students, 343 teachers; Dir J. LAGARDÈRE; Sec.-Gen. L. SAUTRON; publs *Annales des Ponts et Chaussées, Revue Française de Géotechnique* (quarterly).

Ecole Nationale des Travaux Publics de l'Etat: Rue Maurice Audin, 69518 Vaulx en Velin Cedex; tel. 4-72-04-70-70; fax 4-72-04-62-54; f. 1953 in Paris, moved 1975; 100 teachers (full-time), 600 teachers (part-time), 500 students; library of 14,000 vols; Dir FRANÇOIS PERDRIZET.

Ecole Nationale du Génie de l'Eau et de l'Environnement de Strasbourg: 1 quai Koch, BP 1039, 67070 Strasbourg Cedex; tel. 3-88-25-34-50; fax 3-88-37-04-97; e-mail engees@engees.u-strasbg.fr; f. 1960; Dir D. LOUDIÈRE.

Ecole Nationale Supérieure de l'Aéronautique et de l'Espace: BP 4032, 31055 Toulouse Cedex 4; tel. 5-62-17-80-30; fax 5-62-17-83-33; e-mail panier@supaero.fr; f. 1909; 700 students; library of 15,000 vols; Dir J. KERBRAT.

Ecole Nationale Supérieure d'Electronique et de Radioélectricité de Bordeaux (ENSERB): Rue du Dr Schweitzer, 33402 Talence Cedex; tel. 5-56-84-65-00; affiliated with Univ. Bordeaux I; Dir BERNARD LEROUX.

Ecole Nationale Supérieure de Chimie et de Physique de Bordeaux (ENSCPB): Ave Pey Berland, BP 108, 33402 Talence Cedex; tel. 5-56-84-65-65; affiliated with Univ. Bordeaux I; Dir HENRI GASPAROUX.

Ecole Nationale Supérieure des Arts et Industries Textiles (ENSAIT): 9 rue de l'Ermitage, BP 30329, 59056 Roubaix Cedex; tel. 3-20-25-64-64; fax 3-20-24-84-06; e-mail jean-marie.castelain@ensait.fr; f. 1883; library of 4,000 vols, 70 periodicals; Dir JEAN-MARIE CASTELAIN.

Ecole Nationale Supérieure des Arts et Industries de Strasbourg: 24 blvd de la Victoire, 67084 Strasbourg Cedex; tel. 3-88-14-47-00; f. 1875; 5-year diploma courses in mechanical, electrical, civil, building services and energetics, land surveying, polymer and composite materials, mecatronics and architecture; 948 students; Dir A. COLSON.

Ecole Nationale Supérieure d'Arts et Métiers: 8 blvd Louis XIV, 59046 Lille Cedex; tel. 3-20-62-22-10; fax 3-20-53-55-93; university-level courses with emphasis on mechanical engineering; f. 1881; 340 students; Dir Prof. J.-P. FRACHET; Librarian MICHÈLE DECORTE.

Ecole Nationale Supérieure d'Arts et Métiers (ENSAM): 151 blvd de l'Hôpital, 75013 Paris; tel. 1-44-24-62-99; fax 1-44-24-63-26; f. 1780; mechanical, computer, engineering and industrial sciences; 3,500 students; library of 20,000 vols; Dir-Gen. GUY GAUTHERIN; Librarian C. OLLENDORF.

Ecole Nationale Supérieure d'Ingénieurs de Constructions Aéronautiques: 1 place Emile Blouin, 31056 Toulouse Cedex 5; tel. 5-61-61-85-00; fax 5-61-61-85-85; e-mail mcastel@ensica.fr; f. 1946; aeronautics and space; library of 10,000 vols; 410 students; Dir JEAN-LOUIS FRESON.

Ecole Nationale Supérieure de Céramique Industrielle: 47–73 ave Albert Thomas, 87065 Limoges Cedex; tel. 5-55-45-22-22; fax 5-55-79-09-98; e-mail secretdir@ensci.fr; f. 1893; library of 4,000 vols; 25 teachers, 150 students; Dir P. ABELARD; publ. *Annuaire*.

Ecole Nationale Supérieure de l'Electronique et de ses Applications (ENSEA): 6 ave du Ponceau, 95014 Cergy Pontoise Cedex; tel. 1-30-73-66-66; fax 1-30-73-66-67; e-mail ceschi@ensea.fr; f. 1952; electronics, telecommunications, instrumentation, digital signal processing; library of 6,000 vols, 150 periodicals; 80 teachers and researchers, 490 students; Dir ROGER CESCHI.

Ecole Nationale Supérieure de Mécanique: see under University of Nantes.

Ecole Nationale Supérieure de Meunerie et des Industries Céréalières (ENSMIC): 16 rue Nicolas-Fortin, 75013 Paris; tel. 1-44-23-23-44; fax 1-45-85-50-27; f. 1924; courses in milling, baking, cereal food industry and feed technology; 260 students; affiliated with UPMC-Univ. Paris VI (training of engineers); Dir CHRISTIANE MAZEL; publs *Industries des Céréales* (every 2 months), *Les Journées de l'ENSMIC* (annually).

Ecole Nationale Supérieure des Mines de Paris: 60 blvd St Michel, 75272 Paris Cedex 06; tel. 1-40-51-90-00; f. 1783; library of 500,000 vols and 2,500 periodicals; 920 students; Pres. J. P. CAPRON; Dir J. LEVY; Sec.-Gen. N. IMBERT-BOUCHARD; Librarian Mme MASSON; publ. *Rapport* (annually).

Ecole Nationale Supérieure des Mines de Saint-Etienne: 158 cours Fauriel, 42023 Saint-Etienne Cedex 2; tel. 4-77-42-01-23; fax 4-77-42-00-00; f. 1816; chemical process engineering, computer science, materials science; library of 10,000 vols; 250 teachers and researchers, 600 students; Dir M. HIRTZMAN.

Ecole Nationale Supérieure du Pétrole et des Moteurs: BP 311, 92506 Rueil-Malmaison Cedex; tel. 1-47-52-60-00; telex 634202; fax 1-47-52-67-65; f. 1954; five centres: geological or geophysical exploration; petroleum, production and offshore engineering; refining, engineering and construction, gas; internal combustion engines/petroleum and energy-generating product applications; economics and corporate management; Dir J. MASSERON.

Ecole Nationale Supérieure de Techniques Avancées: 32 blvd Victor, 75015 Paris; tel. 1-45-52-44-08; e-mail hoffmann@ensta.fr; f. 1765, refounded 1970; systems engineering, naval architecture, oceanology, mechanics, nuclear techniques, chemical engineering, electronics, information technology; 3-year curriculum; 160 students a year; graduate and postgraduate studies; library of 10,000 vols; Dir P. SINTES.

Ecole Nationale Supérieure des Télécommunications: 46 rue Barrault, 75634 Paris Cedex 13; tel. 1-45-81-77-77; fax 1-45-89-79-06; f. 1878; attached to France Telecom; Dir JEAN HERR.

Ecole Nationale Supérieure des Télécommunications de Bretagne: BP 832, 29285 Brest Cedex; tel. 2-98-00-11-11; telex 940729; fax 2-98-45-51-33; f. 1977; attached to Ministry of Technology, Information and Posts; 108 full-time teachers; 764 students (207 postgraduate); Dir BERNARD AYRAULT.

Ecole Polytechnique: 91128 Palaiseau Cedex; tel. 1-69-33-47-36; f. 1794; 362 teachers, 859 students; library of 300,000 vols; Dir-Gen. JEAN NOVACQ; Librarian MADELEINE DE FUENTES.

Ecole Supérieure de Physique et de Chimie Industrielles de la Ville de Paris: 10 rue Vauquelin, 75005 Paris; tel. 1-40-79-44-00; fax 1-40-79-44-25; f. 1882; training of research engineers; 17 research laboratories; library of 5,000 vols; 220 teaching and research staff, 300 students; Dir P.-G. DE GENNES.

Institut des Hautes Études Scientifiques: 35 route de Chartres, 91440 Bures-sur-Yvette; tel. 1-60-92-66-00; f. 1958; advanced research in mathematics, theoretical physics; library of 4,000 vols, 125 periodicals; Dir J.-P. BOURGUIGNON; publ. *Publications Mathématiques* (2 a year).

Institut National des Télécommunications: 9 rue Charles Fourier, 91011 Evry Cedex; tel. 1-60-76-40-40; fax 1-60-76-43-25; f. 1979; attached to Ministry of Industry, Post and Telecommunications; mem. of Conférence des Grandes Ecoles; engineering and business schools; 150 full-time teachers, 1,000 students; Dir MICHEL TRELLUYER.

ISMCM-CESTI Paris: 3 rue Fernand Hainaut, 93407 St Ouen Cedex; tel. 1-49-45-29-00; fax 1-49-45-29-91; f. 1948; 400 students; library of 3,000 vols; Dir HENRI VEYSSEYRE; publ. *La Lettre de l'ISMCM-CESTI* (2 a year).

CESTI-Toulon: Maison des Technologies, Place Georges Pompidou, Quartier Mayol, 83000 Toulon; tel. 4-94-03-88-00; fax 4-94-03-88-04; e-mail information@toulon.ismcm-cesti.fr; f. 1994; training of engineers, applied research in automation and industrial engineering; 100 students; Dir JEAN-MARC FAURE.

Catholic Colleges and Institutes

INSTITUT CATHOLIQUE DE PARIS

21 rue d'Assas, 75270 Paris Cedex 06

Telephone: 1-44-39-52-00
Fax: 1-45-44-27-14

Founded 1875
Academic year: October to June

Chancellor: Mgr JEAN-MARIE LUSTIGER
Rector: PATRICK VALDRINI
Vice-Rector: JEAN JONCHERAY
General Secretary: MARIE-LISE RAOUL
Librarian: MADELEINE COLOMB

Library: see Libraries

Number of teaching staff: 847, including 96 professors
Number of students: 11,000 (excluding affiliated schools)

Publications: *Transversalités, Revue de l'Institut Catholique de Paris* (quarterly).

DEANS AND DIRECTORS

Faculty of Theology: Abbé JEAN-FRANÇOIS BAUDOZ
  Biblical and Systematic Theology: Abbé JESUS ASURMENDI
  Higher Institute of Liturgy: Abbé PAUL DE CLERCK
  Higher Institute of Ecumenical Studies: Pasteur LOUIS SCHWEITZER
  Higher Institute of Pastoral Catechetics and University Extension: DENIS VILLEPELET
  Institute of Science and Theology of Religions: Abbé JEAN JONCHERAY
  Doctoral Studies: P. HERVÉ LEGRAND
  School of Ancient Oriental Languages: RENÉ LEBRUN
  Institute of Music and Liturgical Music: E. BELLANGER
  Institute of Sacred Art: Sr R. DU CHARLAT
Faculty of Canon Law: Père JEAN-PAUL DURAND
Faculty of Philosophy: Abbé P. CAPELLE
Faculty of Letters: N. NABERT
Higher Institute of Pedagogy: C. PAISANT
Institute of Social Sciences and Economics: JOSEPH MAÏLA
Institute for French Language and Culture and University Summer School: Dir PIERRE LE FORT
University for Retired People: Dir J. MENU

AFFILIATED SCHOOLS AND INSTITUTES

Ecole Supérieure des Sciences Economiques et Commerciales: 95000 Cergy; Dir G. VALIN.

Ecole de Psychologues-Praticiens: Paris; Dir J. P. CHARTIER.

Ecole de Formation Psycho-Pédagogique: Paris; Dir R. RENOUT.

Ecole de Bibliothécaires-Documentalistes: Paris; Dir J. VÉZIN.

Institut Supérieur d'Interprétation et de Traduction: Paris; Dir Mme DE DAX.

Institut Supérieur d'Electronique de Paris: Dir J. FONTENEAU.

Centre de Formation Pédagogique Pierre Faure: 78A rue de Sèvres, 75341 Paris Cedex 07; Dir Frère P. CORNECC.

Institut Polytechnique Saint-Louis: 95000 Cergy; Sec.-Gen. F. GARDÈRE.

  Ecole de Biologie Industrielle: 95000 Cergy; Dir F. DUFOUR.

  Institut d'Agro-Développement International: 95000 Cergy; Dir G. TANDEAU DE MARSAC.

  Ecole d'Electricité, de Production et des Méthodes Industrielles: 95000 Cergy; Dir J. P. RIGAUD.

  Ecole Pratique de Service Social: 95000 Cergy; Dir F. LETELLIER.

Ecole Supérieure de Chimie Organique et Minérale: 95000 Cergy; Dir P. SANDRIN.

Institut Géologique Albert-de-Lapparent: 95000 Cergy; Dir C. MONTENAT.

Institut Supérieur Agricole de Beauvais: Rue Pierre Waguet, 60000 Beauvais and 95000 Cergy; f. 1855; Dir M. A. BLANCHARD.

Institut Libre d'Education Physique Supérieure: 95000 Cergy; Dir M. D. JOVIS.

UNIVERSITÉ CATHOLIQUE DE LILLE

60 blvd Vauban, BP 109, 59016 Lille Cedex
Telephone: 3-20-13-40-00
Fax: 3-20-13-40-01

Founded 1875 as Faculty of Law, became university institution in 1877
Private (Roman Catholic) control

Rector: M. VANDECANDELAERE
Vice-Rector: Abbé J. BOULANGE
Administrative Officer: CH. HENIN
Librarian: J.-CH. DESQUIENS

Library: nearly 500,000 volumes
Number of teachers: 1,300
Number of students: 15,000

Publications: *Monographies de la Faculté libre de Médecine de Lille, Mémoires et Travaux, Mélanges de Science Religieuse* (3 a year), *Ensemble, Encyclopédie Catholicisme, Repères, La Lettre de la Catho, Catho Actualités, Vie et Foi.*

DEANS

Faculty of Theology: M. HUBAUT
Faculty of Economic Sciences: P. N'GAHANE
Faculty of Medicine: J. COUSIN
Faculty of Letters and Human Sciences: J. HEUCLIN
Faculty of Science: B. MILHAU
Faculty of Law: H. LEFÈVRE

FEDERATED INSTITUTES

Ecole des Hautes Etudes Industrielles (HEI): 13 rue de Toul, 59046 Lille Cedex; tel. 3-20-30-83-14; f. 1885; civil engineering, chemistry and electrical engineering; 1,180 students; Dir M. VITTU.

Ecole Supérieure des Techniques Industrielles et des Textiles (ESTIT): GAFIT, 52 Allée Lakanal, BP 209, 59654 Villeneuve d'Ascq Cedex; tel. 3-20-79-90-10; f. 1895; textile, engineering; 260 students; Dir B. AVRIN.

Institut Supérieur d'Agriculture (ISA): 41 rue du Port, 59046 Lille Cedex; tel. 3-20-30-83-14; f. 1963; agricultural, agro-engineering; five-year course; 525 students; Dir P. CODRON.

Institut Supérieur d'Electronique du Nord (ISEN): 41 blvd Vauban, 59046 Lille Cedex; tel. 3-20-30-62-20; f. 1956; electronics engineering; 65 teachers, 554 students; Dir-Gen. PAUL ASTIER; Dir J. N. DECARPIGNY.

Institut Catholique d'Arts et Métiers (ICAM): 6 rue Auber, 59046 Lille Cedex; tel. 3-20-22-61-61; f. 1898; 490 students; Dir-Gen. G. CARPIER; Dir J. G. PRIEUR.

Institut Supérieur de Technologie du Nord (ISTN): 65 rue Roland, 59000 Lille; tel. 3-20-22-36-00; f. 1990; 177 students; Dir J. L. BIGOTTE.

IEFSI L'Ingénieur – Manager (Institut d'Economie, d'Entreprise et de Formation Sociale pour Ingénieurs): 41 rue du Port, 59000 Lille; tel. 3-20-30-83-14; f. 1962; 51 students; Dir P. RENSY.

Ecole de Hautes Etudes Commerciales du Nord (EDHEC): 58 rue du Port, 59046 Lille Cedex; tel. 3-20-15-45-00; f. 1920; 1,400 students; Dirs-Gén. O. OGER, J.-L. TURRIÈRE.

  EDHEC Nice: 393 Promenade des Anglais, BP 116, 06202 Nice Cedex; tel. 4-93-18-99-66; 400 students.

Institut d'Economie Scientifique et de Gestion (IESEG): 3 rue de la Digue, 59800 Lille; tel. 3-20-54-58-92; f. 1964; 510 students; Dir J. P. AMMEUX.

Centre de Recherches Economiques, Sociologiques et de Gestion (CRESGE): 1 rue Norbert Segard, 59000 Lille; tel. 3-20-13-40-60; f. 1964; Dir J.-CL. SAILLY.

Conseils et Recherches en Economie Agricole et Agro-alimentaire (CREA): 1 rue Norbert Segard, 59046 Lille; tel. 3-20-78-26-95; f. 1981; Dir (vacant).

Institut d'Expertise Comptable (IEC): 60 blvd Vauban, BP 109, 59016 Lille Cedex; tel. 3-20-54-86-44; 550 students; Dir P. POUJOL.

Ecole Supérieure des Assistants de Direction (ESAD-ESBT): 81 blvd Vauban, BP 109, 58016 Lille Cedex; tel. 3-20-54-90-90; f. 1964; 320 students; Dir H. AMIOT CHANAL.

Ecole Supérieure de Traducteurs, Interprètes, et de Cadres du Commerce Extérieur (ESTICE): 60 blvd Vauban, BP 109, 59016 Lille Cedex; tel. 3-20-54-90-90; f. 1961; 100 students; Dir H. AMIOT CHANAL

Ecole de Service Social de la Région Nord (ESSRN): 68 blvd Vauban, BP 12, 59004 Lille Cedex; tel. 3-20-21-93-93; f. 1932; 267 students; Dir E. PRIEUR.

Ecole de Formation d'Animateurs Sociaux (EFAS): 105 rue d'Artois, 59800 Lille; tel. 3-20-58-15-40; f. 1973; 193 students; Dir J. D. VERNIER.

Ecole de Professeurs (EDP): 60 blvd Vauban, BP 109, 59016 Lille Cedex; tel. 3-20-13-41-20; f. 1962; 500 students; Dir J. BOULANGÉ.

Institut des Stratégies et Techiques de Communication (ISTC): 67 blvd Vauban, 59800 Lille; tel. 3-20-54-32-32; f. 1991; 62 students; Dir CLAUDE DOGNIN.

Institut de Formation en Soins Infirmiers (IFSI) et Ecole de Puéricultrices: 70 rue du Port, 59000 Lille; tel. 3-20-57-89-54; f. 1927; 424 students; Dir BERNADETTE MIROUX.

Ecole de Sages-Femmes (ESF): 115 rue du Grand But, 59160 Lomme; tel. 3-20-93-74-00; f. 1882; 61 students; Dirs M. DELCROIX, CHRISTIANE ROUX.

Institut de Formation en Kinésithérapie, Pédicurie et Podologie: 10 rue J. B. de la Salle, 59000 Lille; tel. 3-20-92-06-99; f. 1964; 325 students; Dirs M. PAPAREMBORDE, D. VENNIN.

Lycée Technologique OZANAM: 50 rue Saint Gabriel, 59000 Lille; tel. 3-20-21-96-50; 375 students; Dir R. LEHAMIEU.

Ecole des Délégués Médicaux de la Faculté Libre de Médecine: 56 rue du Port, 59046 Lille Cedex; tel. 3-20-13-41-80; f. 1988; 59 students; Dir (vacant).

Lycée privé Notre-Dame de Grâce: Quai des Nerviens, BP 127, 59602 Maubeuge Cedex; tel. 3-27-53-00-66; 100 students; Dir JEAN-PIERRE LAMQUET.

Lycée privé commercial 'De la Salle': 2 rue Jean Le Vasseur, 59046 Lille Cedex; tel. 3-20-93-50-11; 251 students; Dir JEAN-LOUIS CARON.

Lycée privé Saint-Joseph: 26 route de Calais, 62200 Saint-Martin-lez-Boulogne; tel. 3-21-99-06-99; 307 students; Dir MICHEL DUFAY.

Ecole Supérieure de Management et l'Entreprise (ESPEME): 23 rue Delphin Petit, 59046 Lille Cedex; tel. 3-20-15-45-00; f. 1988; 420 students; Dir FRANÇOIS DEFOORT.

  ESPEME Nice: 393 Promenade des Anglais, BP 116, 06202 Nice Cedex; tel. 4-93-18-99-66; 173 students; Dir BERNARD BOTTERO.

Ecole Supérieure Privée d'Application des Sciences (ESPAS): 83 blvd Vauban, 59800 Lille; tel. 3-20-57-58-71; f. 1988; 120 students; Dir O. TRANCHANT.

Institut de Formation d'Animateurs de Catéchèse pour Adultes (IFAC): 60 blvd Vauban, 59016 Lille Cedex; tel. 3-20-57-69-33; f. 1980; 25 students; Dir JACQUES BERNARD.

Institut Pratique d'Etudes Religieuses (IPER): 60 blvd Vauban, 59016 Lille Cedex; tel. 3-20-78-26-78; f. 1951; 35 students; Dir MICHEL VEYS.

Institut de Musique Liturgique (IML): 60 blvd Vauban, 59016 Lille Cedex; tel. 3-20-13-41-06; f. 1948; 70 students; Dir JEAN LEBON.

INSTITUT CATHOLIQUE DE TOULOUSE

31 rue de la Fonderie, BP 7012, 31068 Toulouse Cedex 7

Telephone: 5-61-36-81-00
Fax: 5-61-36-81-33
E-mail: savic@savic.unisoft.fr

Founded 1877 and administered by a Council of Bishops of the region

Chancellor: H.E. Mgr EMILE MARCUS, Archbishop of Toulouse
Rector: P. ANDRÉ DUPLEIX
Registrar: J. LANGUILLON
Librarian: P. GEORGES PASSERAT

Library of over 250,000 vols
Number of teachers: 238
Number of students: 3,133 (full-time), 2,263 (part-time)

Publications: *Bulletin de Littérature ecclésiastique* (quarterly), *Chronique* (supplement), *Revue Purpan*.

DEANS

Faculty of Theology: P. MARCHADOUR
Faculty of Canon Law: P. DAVID
Faculty of Philosophy: M. MALDAMÉ
Faculty of Letters: M. DAZET-BRUN

INSTITUT UNIVERSITAIRE CATHOLIQUE SAINT-JEAN

11 Impasse Flammarion, 13001 Marseille

Telephone: 4-91-50-35-50
Fax: 4-91-50-35-55

Founded 1991

Rector: GERARD DE BELSUNCE
Registrar: (vacant)

Library of 500 vols
Number of teachers: 30
Number of students: 250

UNIVERSITÉ CATHOLIQUE DE L'OUEST

3 place André Leroy, BP 808, 49008 Angers Cedex 01

Telephone: 2-41-81-66-00
Fax: 2-41-81-67-88

Founded 1875, under the patronage of the Bishops of the western region of France

Rector: Rev. CL. CESBRON
Vice-Rectors: G. BERTIN, R. ROUSSEAU
Secretary-General: P. LERAYS
Librarian: Y. LE GALL

Library of 200,000 vols and periodicals
Number of students: 11,231

Publications: *Annuaire, Impacts* (quarterly).

DEANS

Faculty of Theology: Rev. P. HAUDEBERT
Teacher Training Institute: R. MARTIN
Modern Languages Institute: D. STAQUET
Institute of Applied Psychology and Sociology: M.-T. NEUILLY
Applied Mathematics Institute: J. M. MARION
Basic and Applied Research Institute: J. P. BOUTINET
Literature and History Institute: B. HAM
Education and Communication Institute: M. SOETARD
International Centre for French Studies (for Foreign Students): R. COCHIN
Applied Ecology Institute: P. GILLET

AFFILIATED SCHOOLS

Ecole Supérieure d'Electronique de l'Ouest: 4 rue Merlet de la Boulaye, 49000 Angers; f. 1956; Dir M. V. HAMON.

Ecole Supérieure des Sciences Commerciales d'Angers: 1 rue Lakanal, 49000 Angers; Dir M. POTE.

Ecole Technique Supérieure de Chimie de l'Ouest: 50 rue Michelet, 49000 Angers; Dir B. DAVID.

Institut Supérieur d'Action Internationale et de Production: 18 rue du 8 Mai 1945, 49124 St Barthélemy; Dir J. Y. BIGNONET.

Institut de Formation en Education Physique et Sportive: 3 place André-Leroy, 49008 Angers Cedex 01; Dir F. GRANDIÈRE.

Institut de Formation et de Recherche pour les Acteurs du Développement et de l'Entreprise: 1 place A. Luoy, 49008 Angers Cedex 01; Dir L. PASQUIER.

UNIVERSITÉ CATHOLIQUE DE LYON

25 rue du Plat, 69288 Lyon Cedex 02

Telephone: 4-72-32-50-12
Fax: 4-72-32-50-19

Founded 1875

Rector: Père CHRISTIAN PONSON
Vice-Rector: Père PIERRE GIRE
Secretaries-General: C. BLOND, M. B. GRANDJANNY
Librarian: Mlle BEHR

Library of 240,000 vols
Number of teachers: 300
Number of students: 7,422
Publications: *Bulletin*, Cahiers.

DEANS

Faculty of Theology: P. GIBERT
Faculty of Philosophy: M. E. BELY
Faculty of Science: CH. RUGET
Faculty of Letters: J. P. GERFAUD
Faculty of Law: R. VALETTE

AFFILIATED INSTITUTIONS

Ecole Supérieure de Techniciens Biochimie-Biologie: Lyon; f. 1952; 16 teachers, 123 students; Dir CH. RUGET.

Ecole Supérieure pour le Développement Economique et Social: Lyon; f. 1987; 208 students; Dir J. BOLON.

Ecole Supérieure de Langues et Traduction: Lyon; f. 1968; 15 teachers, 173 students; Dir P. CARLEN.

CPE Lyon: 31 place Bellecour, 69002 Lyon; f. 1919 as Institut de Chimie; 41 teachers, 769 students; Dir J. C. CHARPENTIER.

Institut Supérieur d'Agriculture Rhône-Alpes: 31 place Bellecour, 69002 Lyon; f. 1968; 21 teachers, 404 students; Dir J. TRAYNARD.

Institut des Sciences de la Famille: Lyon; f. 1974; 10 teachers, 61 students; Dir B. BARTHELET.

Independent Institutes

GENERAL

American University of Paris, The: 31 ave Bosquet, 75007 Paris; tel. 1-40-62-06-00; fax 1-47-05-34-32; f. 1962; language of instruction: English; mem. of Middle States Assn of Colleges and Schools; 4-year arts and sciences undergraduate courses; two summer sessions; adult education programmes; large computer science laboratory; technical writing programme; library of over 100,000 vols; 800 students; Pres. Dr MICHAEL K. SIMPSON.

Schiller International University — France: for general details, see entry in Germany chapter.

Paris Campus: 32 Boulevard de Vaugirard, 75015 Paris; tel. 1-45-38-56-01; fax 1-45-38-54-30; Dir C. BARODY.

AGRICULTURE

Ecole Supérieure d'Agriculture: 55 rue Rabelais, BP 748, 49007 Angers Cedex 1; tel. 2-41-23-55-55; fax 2-41-23-55-00; f. 1898; library of 45,000 vols, 520 periodicals; 600 students; Dir AYMARD HONORÉ; publs *Cahiers Agriscope* (3 a year), *Bibliographie Agricole et Rurale* (5 a year).

Ecole Supérieure d'Agriculture de Purpan: 75 voie du Toec, 31076 Toulouse Cedex 3; tel. 5-61-15-30-30; fax 5-61-15-30-00; f. 1919; 5-year diploma course; library of 12,000 vols, 600 periodicals; 100 teachers (37 full-time), 700 students; Dir PIERRE TAPIE; publ. *Purpan* (quarterly).

Ecole Supérieure d'Ingénieurs et de Techniciens pour l'Agriculture: BP 607, 27106 Val de Reuil Cedex; tel. 2-32-59-14-59; fax 2-32-59-87-32; f. 1919; 5-year diploma courses for agricultural engineers; Dir P. DENIEUL.

COMMERCE, BUSINESS ADMINISTRATION AND STATISTICS

Centre d'Enseignement et de Recherche de Statistique Appliquée (CERESTA): 10 rue Bertin Poirée, 75001 Paris; tel. 1-42-33-97-14; f. 1952; Dir J. P. THERME.

Centre Européen d'Education Permanente (CEDEP): Blvd de Constance, 77305 Fontainebleau Cedex; f. 1971; management development courses in business administration for member companies (6 French, 4 Danish, 3 British, 1 Swedish, 3 Belgian, 1 Italian, 1 Indian, 2 Dutch, 1 German, 3 European); associated with the Institut Européen d'Administration des Affaires; Gen. Dir CLAUDE MICHAUD.

Ecole du Chef d'Entreprise (ECE): 24–26 rue Hamelin, 75116 Paris; f. 1944; business administration; 50 teachers; Pres. M. Y. CHOTARD; Dir C. GOURDAIN; Sec.-Gen. Mlle M. JANNOR.

Ecole Européenne des Affaires: 6 avenue de la Porte de Champerret, 75838 Paris Cedex 17; tel. 1-44-09-33-00; fax 1-44-09-33-59; f. 1973; brs in Oxford, Berlin and Madrid; European degree programme in management; library of 50,000 vols; Dir MICHEL RAIMBAULT; publ. *European Management Journal* (6 a year).

Ecole Nouvelle d'Organisation Economique et Sociale (ENOES): 62 rue de Miromesnil, 75008 Paris; tel. 1-45-62-87-60; fax 1-45-63-55-44; f. 1937; courses in transport and logistics, business administration and accountancy; Pres. MICHEL FRYBOURG; Gen. Sec. MICHEL OHAYON.

Ecole Supérieure d'Economie, d'Art et de Communication – Groupe E.A.C.: 13 rue de la Grange Batelière, 75009 Paris; tel. 1-47-70-23-83; fax 1-47-70-17-83; f. 1987; library of 500 vols; 70 teachers; 350 students; Dir CLAUDE VIVIER.

Ecole Supérieure de Commerce de Lille: Ave Willy Brandt, 59777 Euralille; tel. 3-20-21-59-62; fax 3-20-21-59-59; f. 1892; library of 3,700 vols, 270 periodicals; 1,000 students; Dir JEAN-PIERRE DEBOURSE.

Ecole Supérieure de Commerce de Montpellier: 2300 ave des Moulins, 34185 Montpellier Cedex 4; tel. 4-67-10-25-00; fax 4-67-45-13-56; e-mail info@supco-montpellier.fr; f. 1897; 210 teachers, 966 students; three-year courses in business administration and management sciences; Dir Dr DIDIER JOURDAN.

Ecole Supérieure de Commerce de Pau: 3 rue Saint John Perse, Campus Universitaire, 64000 Pau; tel. 5-59-92-64-64; fax 5-59-92-64-55; f. 1970 by the Chamber of Commerce; library of *c.* 5,000 vols; 16 full-time, 120 part-time teachers; 500 students; Dir LAURENT HUA.

Ecole Supérieure de Commerce de Poitiers: 11 rue de l'Ancienne Comédie, BP 5, 86001 Poitiers Cedex; tel. 5-49-60-58-00; fax 5-49-60-58-30; f. 1961; graduate management degree programme, master's and International M.B.A. degree programmes, continuing education and distance learning in management; courses in economics, marketing, finance, accountancy, management information systems, international business; master's degrees in business administration and information systems; 20 full-time, 200 part-time teachers; library of 4,500 vols; Dir FRANÇOISE VILAIN; publ. *Les Cahiers de Recherche de l'ESC Poitiers* (2 a year).

Ecole Supérieure de Commerce de Tours: 1 rue Léo-Delibes, BP 0535, 37205 Tours Cedex 3; tel. 2-47-71-71-71; fax 2-47-71-72-10; e-mail com@esctours.lenet.fr; f. 1982; run by the Tours Chamber of Commerce and Industry; 3-year programme, also executive programmes: seminars in company training; library of 7,000 vols; 30 full-time, 350 part-time teachers; 1,000 students; Dir GUY LEBOUCHER; publs *A Propos* (monthly), *Ligne Directe* (4 a year), *Cahier de Recherche* (monthly).

Ecole Supérieure de Commerce Marseille-Provence: Domaine de Luminy, BP 911, 13288 Marseille Cedex 09; tel. 4-91-82-79-00; fax 4-91-82-79-01; e-mail daloz@escmp.u-3mrs.fr; f. 1872; library of 15,000 vols; 500 teachers (38 full-time); Dir JEAN-PIERRE DALOZ.

Ecole Supérieure des Sciences Economiques et Commerciales (ESSEC): Ave Bernard Hirsch, BP 105, 95021 Cergy-Pontoise Cedex; tel. 1-34-43-30-00; fax 1-34-43-30-01; e-mail info-essec@edu.essec.fr; f. 1907; 3-year and 2-year degree courses; master's degree in business administration and management; M.Sc. in marketing, finance, logistics, information and decision systems, international law and management, and agribusiness management; library of 45,000 vols, 1,500 periodicals; 70 full-time, 300 part-time teachers; 1,700 students; Dir MAURICE THEVENET.

EM Lyon: BP 174, 23 ave Guy de Collongue, 69132 Ecully Cedex; tel. 4-78-33-78-00; fax 4-78-33-61-69; f. 1872; library of 12,927 vols; 80 teachers; Dir PATRICK MOLLE.

Affiliated Institutes:

Ecole Supérieure de Commerce de Lyon (ESC Lyon): 2-year master's course in management; Dir CHANTAL POTY.

Cesma MBA: Dir JUDITH RYDER.

Continuing Education: Dir PAUL-ANDRÉ FAURE.

Groupe CERAM: BP 085, 06902 Sophia Antipolis Cedex; tel. 4-93-95-45-45; fax 4-93-65-45-24; f. 1978 by Nice Chamber of Commerce; library of 16,000 vols; 100 full-time, 120 part-time teachers; 750 students, plus 100 on MS course; Dir MAXIME CRENER.

Groupe CPA – Centre de Perfectionnement aux Affaires: 14 ave de la Porte de Champerret, 75017 Paris; tel. 1-44-09-34-00; fax 1-44-09-34-99; f. 1930 by the Paris Chamber of Commerce and Industry; general management courses for top executives; Dir JEAN-LOUIS SCARINGELLA.

CPA Paris: 14 ave de la Porte de Champerret, 75017 Paris; tel. 1-44-09-34-00; fax 1-44-09-34-99; Dirs JOEL PINKHAM, FRÉDÉRIC VALLAUD.

CPA Jouy en Josas: 1 rue de la Libération, 78350 Jouy en Josas; tel. 1-69-41-82-22; fax 1-69-41-81-92; Dir OLIVIER DE LAVENERE-LUSSAN.

CPA Lyon: 93 chemin des Mouilles, 69130 Ecully Cedex; tel. 4-78-33-52-12; fax 4-78-33-37-06; Dir CHARLES AB-DER-HALDEN.

CPA Nord: 551 rue Albert Bailly, 59700 Marcq-en-Baroeul; tel. 3-20-25-97-53; fax 3-20-27-12-94; Dir JEAN-CLAUDE VACHER.

CPA Grand Sud-Ouest: 20 blvd Lascrosses, 31000 Toulouse; tel. 5-61-29-49-91; fax 5-61-13-98-31; Dir ALAIN MAINGUY.

CPA Méditerranée: C/o CERAM II, 60 rue Dostoïevski, 06902 Sophia Antipolis; tel. 4-92-96-96-95; fax 4-93-95-44-21; Dir ADRIEN CORBIERE-MEDECIN.

CPA Madrid: Calle Serrano 208, 28012 Madrid, Spain; tel. (1) 53837-59; fax (1) 53837-58; Dir TEODORO AGUADO DE LOS RÍOS.

Groupe Ecole Supérieure de Commerce de Bordeaux: Domaine de Raba, 680 cours de la Libération, 33405 Talence Cedex; tel. 5-56-84-55-55; fax 5-56-84-55-00; e-mail groupe.esc@esc.bordeaux.fr; f. 1874 by Chamber of Commerce; library of 11,000 vols; 94 teachers; 1,700 students; Dir GEORGES VIALA.

Groupe Ecole Supérieure de Commerce de Paris: 79 ave de la République, 75543 Paris Cedex 11; tel. 1-49-23-20-00; fax 1-49-23-22-12; f. 1819; graduate programmes, research centre, executive education; Dean VÉRONIQUE DE CHANTÉRAC-LAMIELLE.

Groupe ESC Brest: 2 ave de Provence, BP 7214, 29272 Brest Cedex; tel. 2-98-34-44-44; fax 2-98-34-44-69; f. 1962; library of 5,000 vols, 150 periodicals; 110 teachers; 533 students; Dir C. MONIQUE.

Groupe ESC Nantes Atlantique: 8 route de la Jonelière, BP 31222, 44312 Nantes Cedex 3; tel. 2-40-37-34-34; fax 2-40-37-34-07; f. 1900; library of 10,000 vols, 300 periodicals; 43 full-time, 300 part-time teachers; 1,000 students; Pres. JEAN-FRANÇOIS MOULIN; Dir-Gen and Dean AÏSSA DERMOUCHE.

Groupe ESC Reims: 59 rue Pierre-Taittinger, BP 302, 51061 Reims Cedex; tel. 3-26-77-47-47; fax 3-26-04-69-63; e-mail groupe.esc@reims.cci.fr; f. 1928; various courses, at different levels, in business administration; *c.* 1,700 students (20 per cent non-French); library of 7,500 vols, 150 periodicals; Dir DIDIER DEVELEY.

Groupe ESIDEC: 3 place Edouard Branly, Technopôle Metz 2000, 57070 Metz; tel. 3-87-56-37-34; fax 3-87-56-37-99; e-mail vlebrun@gr.esidec.fr.edu; f. 1988; run by the Moselle Chamber of Commerce and Industry; courses in management, logistics, marketing, finance, law, trade, purchasing; 40 teachers; 210 students; Dir THIERRY JEAN.

Groupe HEC: 78351 Jouy-en-Josas Cedex; tel. 1-39-67-70-00; fax 1-39-67-74-40; e-mail hecinfo@hec.fr; f. 1881; sponsored by the Paris Chamber of Commerce and Industry; three degree courses in management and executive development programmes; library of 60,000 vols; 106 full-time, 450 part-time staff; Dean BERNARD RAMANANTSOA; Dean for Administration and Finance: JEAN-LUC GULIN.

DIRECTORS

Faculté: J. KLEIN (Dean of Faculty and Research)

Institutions d'Enseignement:

Ecole des Hautes Etudes Commerciales et des Mastères HEC: NICOLE FERRY-MACCARIO

Institut Supérieur des Affaires: JEAN-LOUP ARDOIN

Doctorat HEC: MARC CHESNEY (Associate Dean)

Executive Programmes: BERTRAND MOINGEON

INSEAD: Blvd de Constance, 77305 Fontainebleau Cedex; tel. 1-60-72-40-00; fax 1-60-74-55-00; f. 1958; post-graduate MBA programme; PhD programme; executive development programmes; 100 professors; library of 40,000 vols; Chair. Board of Govs CLAUDE JANSSEN; Dean ANTONIO BORGES.

Institut de Formation d'Animateurs Conseillers d'Entreprises: 79 ave de la République, 75543 Paris Cedex 11; tel. 1-49-23-22-25; training programmes for trainers and training consultants (at national and European levels); Dir M. THIBERGE.

LAW AND POLITICAL SCIENCE

Académie Internationale de Science Politique et d'Histoire Constitutionnelle en Sorbonne: see under International.

Ecole des Hautes Etudes Internationales: 4 place Saint-Germain des Prés, 77553 Paris Cedex II; tel. 1-42-22-68-06; f. 1904; Pres. M. SCHUMANN; Dir P. CHAIGNEAU.

Ecole de Notariat d'Amiens: 7 rue Anne-Franck, 80136 Rivery; tel. 3-22-92-61-26; f. 1942; Dir M. DESCHAMPS.

Ecole de Notariat de Clermont-Ferrand: 25 rue de la Rotonde, 63000 Clermont-Ferrand; f. 1913; diploma course; library of 1,641 vols; Dir PH. LAVILLAINE.

Ecole de Notariat de Paris: 9 rue Villaret-de-Joyeuse, 75017 Paris; f. 1896; Dir M. P. MATHIEU.

Ecole Supérieure de Journalisme: 107 rue Tolbiac, 75013 Paris; tel. 1-45-70-73-37; f. 1899; Pres. M. SCHUMANN; Dir P. CHAIGNEAU.

Institut International des Droits de l'Homme (International Institute of Human Rights): 2 Allée Zaepfel, 67000 Strasbourg; tel. 3-88-45-84-45; fax 3-88-45-84-50; e-mail iidhiihr@sdv.fr; f. 1969 by René Cassin; post-graduate teaching in international and comparative law of human rights; annual study session during July; Pres. JACQUES LATSCHA; Sec.-Gen. JEAN-BERNARD MARIE.

International Centre for University Human Rights Teaching: Strasbourg; f. 1973 at the request of UNESCO; four-week courses for university teachers.

MEDICINE

Ecole Dentaire Française: 3 rue de l'Est, 75020 Paris; tel. 1-47-97-77-81; Dir R. J. CACHIA.

Ecole Supérieure Internationale d'Optométrie: 134 route de Chartres, 91440 Bures-sur-Yvette; tel. 1-69-07-93-23; fax 1-69-28-78-06; f. 1989; Dir Mme DUQUESNES.

RELIGION

Faculté Libre de Théologie Protestante de Paris: 83 blvd Arago, 75014 Paris; tel.1-43-31-61-64; fax 1-47-07-67-87; e-mail iptparis@club-internet.fr; f. 1877; religious history, old and new testament, ecclesiastical history, systematic theology, philosophy, practical theology, Hebrew, Greek, German, English; library of 60,000 vols; 12 professors, 180 students; Dean JACQUES-NOËL PÉRÈS.

Institut de Théologie Orthodoxe: 93 rue de Crimée, 75019 Paris; tel. 1-42-08-12-93; fax 1-42-08-00-09; f. 1925; 15 professors and 50 students; library of 30,000 vols; Dean Rev. Fr BORIS BOBRINSKOY; publ. *Pensée Orthodoxe* (every 2 years).

Institut Européen des Sciences Humaines: Centre Boutloin, 58120 Saint-Léger-de-Fougeret; tel. 3-86-79-40-62; fax 3-86-85-01-19; f. 1990; Muslim theology; library of 5,000 vols; 8 teachers; capacity for 200 students; Dir ZUHAIR MAHMOOD.

Institut Orthodoxe Français de Paris (Saint-Denis): 96 blvd Auguste-Blanqui, 75013 Paris; tel. 1-45-41-48-75; f. 1944; 20 professors and 125 students; library of 5,000 vols; faculties of theology and philosophy; Rector BERTRAND-HARDY, Bishop GERMAIN of Saint Denis; publ. *Présence Orthodoxe*.

Séminaire Israélite de France (Ecole Rabbinique): 9 rue Vauquelin, 75005 Paris; tel. 1-47-07-21-22; fax 1-43-37-75-92; f. 1829; Talmud, Bible, Jewish history and philosophy, Hebrew language and literature studies, rabbinical law; 26 students; library of 60,000 vols; Dir Chief Rabbi MICHEL GUGENHEIM.

SCIENCES

Ecole d'Anthropologie: 1 place d'Iéna, 75116 Paris; tel. 1-47-93-09-73; f. 1876 by Prof. Broca; pre-history, physical anthropology, ethnology, biology, genetics, immunology, ethnography, demography, third world problems, psychology, criminology, anthropotechnics, biometeorology; Dir Prof. BERNARD J. HUET; publ. *Nouvelle revue anthropologique* (monthly).

Ecole Supérieure de Biochimie et de Biologie: 31 bis blvd de Rochechouart, 75009 Paris; f. 1945; Dir FRANÇOISE SOUWEINE.

Institut de Paléontologie Humaine: 1 rue René Panhard, 75013 Paris; tel. 1-43-31-62-91; fax 1-43-31-22-79; f. 1910 by Prince Albert I of Monaco; 60 staff; library of 25,000 vols; vertebrate palaeontology, palynology, palaeoanthropology, prehistory, quaternary geology, sedimentology, geochronology; Dir HENRY DE LUMLEY; publs *Archives*, *L'Anthropologie*, *Etudes Quaternaires*.

PROFESSORS

DE LUMLEY, H., Quaternary Geology
HEIM, J. L., Anthropology
SIMONE, S., Statistical Analysis of Prehistoric Industries

Institut Edouard Toulouse: 1 rue Cabanis, 75014 Paris; tel. 1-45-65-81-38; f. 1983; teaching, training and research in psychiatry, seminars on psychoanalysis; Pres. Dr JEAN AYME; Sec. Dr MARCEL CZERMAK; publ. *Cahiers de l'Hôpital Henri Rousselle.*

Institut Océanographique: 195 rue Saint Jacques, 75005 Paris; tel. 1-44-32-10-70; fax 1-40-51-73-16; e-mail bvg@oceano.org; education, scientific research, museology, publishing; f. 1906 by Prince Albert I of Monaco; library of 15,000 vols; Pres. A. SAUNIER-SEÏTÉ; Dir G. GRAU; Sec. C. BEAUVERGER; publs *Annales* (2 a year), *Oceanis* (4 a year).

Musée Océanographique: see under Monaco.

SOCIAL AND ECONOMIC SCIENCES

CNOF – Management et Formation: Tour Manhattan, 6 place de l'Iris, 92400 Courbevoie; tel. 1-47-67-13-13; fax 1-47-78-82-24; f. 1926; provides executive, managerial and administrative training.

Collège Libre des Sciences Sociales et Economiques: 184 blvd Saint-Germain, 75006 Paris; f. 1895; composed of six sections: social, economic, international and public relations; evening and correspondence courses; diplomas conferred after two or three years' study, and submission of theses on some aspect of applied economics; Pres. J. RUEFF; Dir L. DE SAINTE-LORETTE.

Ecole de Hautes Etudes Sociales: 107 rue Tolbiac, 75013 Paris; tel. 1-45-70-73-37; f. 1899; Pres. M. SCHUMANN; Dir P. CHAIGNEAU.

Faculté des Lettres et Sciences Sociales: BP 800, 29200 Brest; tel. 2-98-80-19-87; f. 1960; library of 18,000 vols; 105 teachers; 2,752 students; President and Dean Prof. MICHEL QUESNEL.

Institut Européen des Hautes Etudes Internationales (IEHEI): 10 ave des Fleurs, 06000 Nice; tel. 4-93-37-69-24; fax 4-93-37-79-39; f. 1964; 40 teachers, 70 students; library of *c.* 3,200 vols; Pres. VLAD CONSTANTINESCO; Dir CLAUDE NIGOUL.

TECHNOLOGY

Ecole Catholique d'Arts et Métiers: 40 montée Saint-Barthélemy, 69321 Lyon Cedex 05; tel. 4-72-77-06-00; fax 4-72-77-06-11; f. 1900; 525 students, 60 professors; courses in electrotechnics, mechanics, metallurgy, physics, computer science; library of 5,000 vols; Dir BERNARD PINATEL; publ. *Bulletin* (quarterly).

Ecole Centrale de Lyon: BP 163, 36 ave Guy de Collongue, 69131 Ecully Cedex; tel. 4-72-18-60-00; fax 4-78-43-39-62; f. 1857; cultural, scientific and technical training for engineers in all branches of industry; library of 15,000 vols; 900 students; Dir E. PASCAUD; Sec.-Gen. C. LACROIX.

Ecole de Thermique: 3 rue Henri Heine, 75016 Paris; teaching centre for the Institut Français de l'Energie (IFE); Dir (vacant).

Ecole Française d'Electronique et d'Informatique: 10 rue Amyot, 75005 Paris; f. 1936; courses in telecommunications, electronic engineering and computer science; Dir H. MEUNIER.

Ecole Spéciale de Mécanique et d'Electricité A.M. Ampère: 4 rue Blaise-Desgoffe, 75006 Paris; Dir P. DOCEUL.

Ecole Spéciale des Travaux Publics, du Bâtiment et de l'Industrie: 57 blvd Saint-Germain, 75005 Paris; tel. 1-44-41-11-18; fax 1-44-41-11-12; e-mail estp@eyrolles.com; f. 1891; civil engineering for private and public enterprise; 2,000 students; library of 10,000 vols; Dir S. EYROLLES.

Ecole Supérieure d'Electricité: Plateau de Moulon, 91192 Gif sur Yvette Cedex; tel. 1-69-85-12-12; fax 1-69-85-12-34; campuses at Gif, Metz and Rennes; f. 1894; two- or three-year courses in electrical engineering, radio engineering, information science, electronics and computer science; 1,100 students; attached to Univ. Paris XI; Dir. Gen. J. J. DUBY; Dir of Studies F. MESA; Gen.-Sec. J. RENOUARD.

Ecole Supérieure d'Informatique: 94-98 rue Carnot, 93100 Montreuil; tel. 1-48-59-69-69; f. 1965; *c.* 90 teachers; *c.* 1,000 students; Dir LEO ROZENTALIS; publ. *Dossiers de l'Association pour la Promotion de l'Ecole Supérieure d'Informatique.*

Ecole Supérieure d'Ingénieurs de Marseille (ESIM): Technopôle de Château-Gombert, 13451 Marseille Cedex 20; tel. 4-91-05-45-45; f. 1891; specialist courses in electronics and industrial computing, electrotechnology and power electronics, thermal engineering, mechanical and civil engineering, materials science, marine engineering, industrial product design and project management; library of 8,000 vols; 70 teachers, 660 students.

Ecole Supérieure d'Ingénieurs en Electrotechnique et Electronique: Cité Descartes, BP 99, 93162 Noisy-le-Grand; tel. 1-45-92-65-10; fax 1-45-92-66-99; f. 1962; computer science, automation, telecommunications, signal processing, microelectronics; 1,000 students, 100 teachers; library of 18,000 vols; Dir ALAIN CADIX.

Ecole Supérieure d'Optique: Centre Universitaire, Bât. 503, BP 147, 91403 Orsay Cedex; tel. 1-69-35-88-88; fax 1-69-35-88-00; e-mail francoise.metivier@iota.u-psud.fr; attached to Univ. Paris XI; f. 1920; optical engineering; 150 students; Dir Prof. CHRISTIAN IMBERT.

Ecole Supérieure de Fonderie: Pôle Universitaire, 92916 Paris La Défense Cedex; tel. 1-41-16-12-30; fax 1-41-16-72-46; f. 1923; library of 2,150 vols; Dir G. CHAPPUIS.

Ecole Supérieure des Industries du Caoutchouc: 60 rue Auber, 94408 Vitry-sur-Seine Cedex; f. 1941; Dir M. G. BERTRAND.

Ecole Supérieure des Industries du Vêtement: 73 blvd Saint Marcel, 75013 Paris; Dir M. BOUDRY.

Ecole Supérieure des Industries Textiles d'Epinal: 85 rue d'Alsace, 88025 Epinal Cedex; tel. 3-29-35-50-52; fax 3-29-35-39-21; e-mail esite@wanadoo.fr; f. 1905; training of industrial textile engineers; library of 1,500 vols; Dir J. TIERCET.

Ecole Supérieure des Techniques Aéronautiques et de Construction Automobile: 34 rue Victor Hugo, 92300 Levallois-Perret; tel. 1-41-27-37-00; f. 1925; private school offering 5-year courses; 850 students; Dir M. BOUTTES.

Ecole Supérieure des Techniques Aérospatiales (ESTA): S/c Pôle Universitaire Léonard de Vinci, 12 rue Berthelot, 92916 Paris La Défense Cedex; tel. 1-41-16-72-45; fax 1-41-16-72-46; f. 1930; specialist training in aerospace engineering; Dir A. DUROLLET.

Ecole Supérieure du Bois: rue Christian Pauc, BP 10605, 44306 Nantes Cedex 3; tel. 2-40-18-12-12; fax 2-40-18-12-00; f. 1935; training of engineers and management for wood industry; 150 students; Dir X. MARTIN.

Ecole Supérieure du Soudage et de ses Applications (Welding Engineering): BP 50362, 95942 Roissy CDG Cedex; tel. 1-49-90-36-27; fax 1-49-90-36-50; e-mail jlbreat@easynet.fr; f. 1930; 55 teachers; Dir J.-L. BRÉAT.

Ecole Technique Supérieure du Laboratoire: 93–95 rue du Dessous-des Berges, 75013 Paris; tel. 1-45-83-76-34; e-mail etsl.75@wanadoo.fr; f. 1934; Pres. J. CHOMIENNE; Dir. F. LAISSUS.

European Institute of Technology: 8 rue Saint Florentin, 75001 Paris; tel. 1-40-15-05-69; fax 1-49-27-98-11; f. 1988 to strengthen industrial research and development, and to increase the contribution of technological innovation to economic growth in Europe; Sec.-Gen. JOHN M. MARCUM.

Fondation EPF – Ecole d'Ingénieurs: 3 bis rue Lakanal, 92330 Sceaux; tel. 1-41-13-01-65; fax 1-46-60-39-94; e-mail jeneveau@epf.fr; f. 1925; engineering training; Pres. Dr ALAIN JENEVEAU.

Institut Textile de France: ave Guy de Collongue, BP 60, 69132 Ecully Cedex; tel. 4-78-33-34-55; telex 330316; fax 4-78-43-39-66; f. 1946; library of 15,000 vols and documents; Dir M. SOTTON.

Institut Textile et Chimique de Lyon (ITECH): 181 Avenue Jean Jaurès, 69007 Lyon; tel. 4-78-72-28-31; fax 4-78-61-03-33; e-mail itech@asi.fr; f. 1899; diploma courses in leather technology, painting and adhesives technology, plastics, textiles; Dir J.-P. GALLET.

Schools of Art and Music

Conservatoire National de Région de Musique, Danse et d'Art Dramatique de Lyon: 4 montée Cardinal Decourtray, 69005 Lyon; tel. 4-78-25-91-39; 3,850 students; library of 2,600 vols, 40,000 scores, 4,500 records, 2,000 orchestral scores; Dir RENÉ CLEMENT.

Conservatoire National de Région de Musique et de Danse de Boulogne-Billancourt: 22 rue de la Belle-Feuille, 92100 Boulogne-Billancourt; tel. 1-55-18-45-85; fax 1-55-18-45-86; f. 1953, present name 1978; *c.* 90 teachers; 1,650 students; library of 20,000 scores, 2,500 books, 3,500 records; Dir ALFRED HERZOG.

Conservatoire National Supérieur d'Art Dramatique: 2 bis rue du Conservatoire, 75009 Paris; f. 1786; *c.* 100 students; library of 10,100 vols; Dir MARCEL BOZONNET.

Conservatoire National Supérieur de Musique et de Danse: 209 ave Jean Jaurès, 75019 Paris; tel. 1-40-40-45-45; fax 1-40-40-45-00; e-mail cnsmdp@cnsmdp.fr; f. 1795; 386 teachers; 1,413 students; Dir MARC-OLIVIER DUPIN.

Conservatoire National Supérieur de Musique de Lyon: 3 quai Chauveau, CP 120, 69266 Lyon Cedex 09; tel. 4-72-19-26-26; fax 4-72-19-26-00; f. 1980; 170 teachers; 550 students; library of 40,000 vols; Dir GILBERT AMY; Sec.-Gen. CLAIRE ALBAN-LENOBLE.

Ecole d'Art de Marseille-Luminy: 184 ave de Luminy, 13288 Marseille Cedex 9; tel. 4-91-41-01-44; fax 4-91-26-75-72; f. 1710; 420 students; library of 15,000 vols; Dir NORBERT DUFFORT; publs *Verba Volant* (2 a year), *Recherche et Création Artistiques* (monographs, 5 a year).

Ecole du Louvre: 34 quai du Louvre, 75001 Paris; tel. 1-40-20-56-14/15; fax 1-42-60-40-36; f. 1882; library of 20,000 vols; 3,000 students; Principal D. PONNAU; Sec.-Gen. M. C. DEVEVEY.

PROFESSORS

AMANDRY, M., Numismatics
ANDRE-SALVINI, B., Oriental Archaeology
BENOIT, A., Oriental Archaeology
BERNUS-TAYLOR, M., Islamic Art
BINET, J. L., Contemporary Art
BLISTENE, B., Contemporary Art
BOVOT, J. L., Egyptian Archaeology
BRESC, G., History of Sculpture, Museology
CAMBON, P., Archaeology of Korea
CARLIER, A., 18th-century Art
CAUBET, A., Oriental Archaeology
CHAZAL, G., Iconography
CHEW, H, Prehistory and National Antiquities
CLIQUET, D., National Antiquities
COGEVAL, G., 19th- and 20th-century Art
CREPIN-LEBLOND, T., Renaissance Art
DENOYELLE, M., Antique Ceramics
DESROCHES, J. P., Art in the Far East
DIJOUD, F., Museology
DION, A., History of Furniture
DUPUIS-LABBÉ, D., 20th-century Art
DURAND, J., Medieval Art
DUVAL, A., Pre-history and National Antiquities
ELISSEEFF, Art in the Far East
ETIENNE, M, Egyptian Archaeology
FAUVET-BERTHELOT, M. F., Precolumbian Arts
FEAU, E., African Art
FONTAN, E., Oriental Archaeology
FRIZOT, M., History of Photography
GABORIT, J. R., History of Sculpture
GAULTIER, F., Etruscan Archaeology
GLÜCK, D., Ethnography
GOURARIER, Z., Ethnography
GUÉNÉ, H., History of Architecture
HORNBY, P., Roman Archaeology
JAOUL, Mme M., Ethnography
JEAMMET, V., Greek Archaeology
JOANNIS, Mme, Ethnography
LEGRAND, C., History of Drawing
LEROY-JAY-LEMAISTRE, I., History of Sculpture
LOIRE, S., 17th-century Art
LORRE, C., National Antiquities
LOTH, A. M., Archaeology of India
MAFFRE, J. J., Iconography
MARINO, M. H., National Antiquities
METZGER, C., Christian Archaeology
NOLDUS, J. W., History of Foreign Painting
OURSEL, H., History of French Painting
PASQUIER, A., Greek Archaeology
PATTYN, C., Museology
PELTIER, P., Oceanian Art
POMMIER, E., Museology
PRÉAUD, M., History of Engraving
REVERSEAU, J. P., Military Archaeology
ROQUEBERT, A., 19th-century Art
RUTSCHKOWSKY, M., Christian Archaeology
SAMOYAULT, J.-P., Architecture and Decoration
TRICAUD, A., Ethnography
VALLET, Mlle, National Antiquities
ZEPHYR, Indian Archaeology

Ecole Nationale Supérieure des Arts Décoratifs: 31 rue d'Ulm, 75005 Paris; tel. 1-42-34-97-00; fax 1-42-34-97-85; f. 1766; visual arts and design; 161 teachers; library of 22,000 vols and special collections; Dirs RICHARD PEDUZZI, ELISABETH FLEURY; publ. *Journal des Arts-Déco* (3 a year).

Ecole Nationale Supérieure des Beaux-Arts: 14 rue Bonaparte, 75272 Paris Cedex 06; tel. 1-47-03-50-00; fax 1-47-03-50-80; f. 1648 as Académie Royale de Peinture et de Sculpture, and in 1671 as Académie Royale d'Architecture; library of 120,000 vols; 75 teachers, 650 students; Dir ALFRED PACQUEMENT; publs *Ecrits d'Artistes*, *Beaux-Arts Histoire*, *Espaces de l'art*.

Ecole Supérieure Régionale des Beaux-Arts: 11 rue Ballainvilliers, 63000 Clermont-Ferrand; tel. 4-73-91-43-86; fax 4-73-90-27-80; f. 1882; library of 6,000 vols and special collections; Dir F. BESSON.

Schola Cantorum: 269 rue St Jacques, 75005 Paris; tel. 1-43-54-15-39; f. 1896 by Vincent d'Indy; music, dance and dramatic art; Dir MICHEL DENIS.

FRENCH GUIANA

Research Institutes

GENERAL

Institut Français de Recherche Scientifique pour le Développement en Coopération (ORSTOM) Centre de Cayenne: BP 165, 97323 Cayenne Cedex; tel. 30-27-85; fax 31-98-55; f. 1947; teledetection, pedology, hydrology, sedimentology, botany and vegetal biology; medical and agricultural entomology, ornithology, phytopharmacology, oceanography, sociology; 60 staff; library; Dir GUY ROCHETEAU; publ. *L'homme et la nature en Guyane*. (See main entry under France.)

MEDICINE

Institut Pasteur de la Guyane Française: 97306 Cayenne Cedex; tel. 29-26-00; fax 30-94-16; f. 1940; medical and biological research; Dir J. P. MOREAU.

Libraries and Archives

Cayenne

Archives Départementales de la Guyane: Place Léopold Héder, 97307 Cayenne Cedex; tel. 30-05-00; fax 29-55-25; f. 1983; history of French Guiana; Dir ANNE-MARIE BRULEAUX.

Bibliothèque A. Franconie: 1 ave du Général de Gaulle, BP 5011, 97305 Cayenne Cedex; tel. 29-59-16; fax 29-55-25; f. 1885; general lending library; 30,000 vols; Dir Mme MARIE-ANNICK ATTICOT.

Service Commun de la Documentation de l'Université des Antilles et de la Guyane (Section Guyane): Campus St-Denis, BP 1179, 97346 Cayenne Cedex; tel. 31-94-60; fax 30-96-68; 17,000 vols, 475 periodicals; Dir of French Guiana Branch NICOLE CLÉMENT-MARTIN.

Museums and Art Galleries

Cayenne

Musée Local: 2 ave Général de Gaulle, 97300 Cayenne; flora and fauna of Guiana; historical documents.

Universities and Colleges

Université des Antilles et de la Guyane: Ave d'Estrée, Campus Saint-Denis, BP 792, 97337 Cayenne Cedex; tel. 30-42-00; fax 30-79-53; 239 students; library: see Libraries and Archives; Pres. JEAN-CLAUDE WILLIAM. (See also under Guadeloupe and Martinique.)

TEACHING AND RESEARCH UNITS

Institute of Higher Education in Cayenne: Dir H. CLERGEOT.

University Institute of Technology in Kourou: Dir C. MAILLE.

FRENCH POLYNESIA

Learned Societies

GENERAL

Maison de la culture Te Fare Tauhiti Nui: 646 Blvd Pomaré, BP 1709, Papeete; tel. 54-45-44; fax 42-85-69; f. 1998; promotes culture locally and abroad; sponsors many public and private cultural events; library of 13,000 vols, children's library of 7,000 vols; Dir JEAN-MARIE PAMBRUN (acting).

NATURAL SCIENCES

General

Société des Etudes Océaniennes: BP 110, Papeete; tel. 41-96-03; f. 1917; 450 mems; library; Pres. ROBERT KOENIG; publ. *Bulletin* (quarterly).

Research Institutes

GENERAL

Institut Français de Recherche Scientifique pour le Développement en Coopération (ORSTOM) Centre de Tahiti: BP 529, Papeete; tel. 50-62-00; fax 42-95-55; f. 1963; medical entomology, anthropology, oceanography; library of 7,000 vols; Dir F. X. BARD. (See main entry under France.)

AGRICULTURE, FISHERIES AND VETERINARY SCIENCE

Centre Océanologique du Pacifique: BP 7004, Taravao, Tahiti; tel. 54-60-00; fax 54-60-99; f. 1972; part of IFREMER (*q.v.*); research in aquaculture (crustacea, fish, shellfish); specialized library; Dir D. DUSSERT.

MEDICINE

Institut Territorial de Recherches Médicales 'Louis Malardé': BP 30, Papeete; tel. 41-64-64; fax 43-15-90; e-mail irm@malarde .pf; f. 1949; parasitology (in particular lymphatic filariasis), virology (dengue), microbiology, immunology, serology, biochemistry, pharmacotoxicology, bio-ecology and marine biochemistry, medical entomology; library of 1,000 vols, 9,185 periodicals; Dir Dr ELIANE CHUNGUE.

RELIGION, SOCIOLOGY AND ANTHROPOLOGY

Département des Traditions Orales, du Centre Polynésien des Sciences Humaines 'Te Anavaharau': Pointe de Pêcheurs, Punaauia Pk 15, Tahiti; tel. 58-34-76; study of Polynesian oral tradition.

Museums and Art Galleries

Tamanu

Musée de Tahiti et des Iles: BP 380354 Tamanu, Tahiti; f. 1974; aims: the collection, conservation and appreciation of Polynesian cultural heritage; Dir MANOUCHE LEHARTEL.

Taravao

Musée Paul Gauguin: BP 7029, Taravao, Tahiti; tel. 57-10-58; fax 57-10-42; f. 1965; 1,000 documents on Gauguin's life and work; library of unpublished documents; collection of paintings by R. Delaunay, S. Delaunay, Buffet and others; 20 original works by Gauguin (paintings, sculptures, watercolours); Curator G. ARTUR.

Universities and Colleges

Université française du Pacifique, Centre Universitaire de Polynésie Française: BP 6570, Aéroport de Faaa, Tahiti; tel. 80-38-03; fax 80-38-04; e-mail gautier@ufp.pf; library of 20,000 vols, 200 periodicals; 54 teachers, 1,600 students; Dir Prof. YVES GAUTIER.

The university centres in French Polynesia and New Caledonia (*q.v.*) have a common presidency: BP 4635, Papeete, Tahiti; tel. 42-16-80; fax 41-01-31; e-mail szabo@ufp.pf.; Pres. Prof. PIERRE VERIN. (It was announced in May 1998 that the Université française du Pacifique was to devolve into two separate universities, based respectively in French Polynesia and New Caledonia.)

GUADELOUPE

Research Institutes

GENERAL

Institut Français de Recherche Scientifique pour le Développement en Coopération (ORSTOM) Centre en Guadeloupe: BP 1020, 97178 Pointe-à-Pitre Cedex; tel. 82-05-49; fax 91-73-94; f. 1960; hydrology and demography; library of 3,000 vols; Dir ALAIN LAFFORGUE. (See main entry under France.)

AGRICULTURE, FISHERIES AND VETERINARY SCIENCE

Département des Productions Fruitières et Horticoles – Centre de Coopération Internationale en Recherche Agronomique pour le Développement (CIRAD-FLHOR): Station de Neufchâteau, 97130 Capesterre Belle Eau; tel. 86-30-21; fax 86-80-77; Dir C. VUILLAUME. (See main entry under France.)

Institut National de la Recherche Agronomique (INRA), Centre Antilles-Guyane: BP 515, 97165 Pointe-à-Pitre Cedex; tel. (590) 25-59-00; telex 919867; fax (590) 25-59-24; f. 1948; soil science, animal science, forestry, plant science, rural economy and sociology, zoology and biological control, technology transfer; controls four research units, three experimental farms and a documentation service; Pres. ALAIN XANDE. (See main entry under France.)

MEDICINE

Institut Pasteur de la Guadeloupe: BP 484, 97165 Pointe-à-Pitre Cedex; f. 1948; medical and microbiological analysis laboratories; international vaccination centre; Public Health Department certified laboratories for water and food analysis (chemical and microbiological); mycobacteria research centre; small library; Dir Dr R. GOURSAUD; publ. *Archives* (annually).

Libraries and Archives

Basse-Terre

Archives départementales de la Guadeloupe: BP 74, 97102 Basse-Terre; tel. 81-13-02; fax 81-97-15; f. 1951; library of 10,000 vols; Dir GHISLAINE BOUCHET; publ. *Bulletin de la Société d'Histoire de la Guadeloupe* (quarterly).

Pointe-à-Pitre

Bibliothèque Universitaire Antilles-Guyane (Section Guadeloupe): Campus de Fouillole, 97159 Pointe-à-Pitre Cedex; tel. 93-86-56; fax 93-86-53; e-mail catherine .vassilieff@univ-ag.fr; f. 1972; 58,000 vols, 715 periodicals; Dir of Guadeloupe Branch CATHERINE VASSILIEFF.

Museums and Art Galleries

Pointe-à-Pitre

Musée Schoelcher: 24 rue Peynier, 97110 Pointe-à-Pitre; tel. 82-08-04; f. 1883; exhibitions on Victor Schoelcher and slavery; Dir H. PETITJEAN ROGET.

Affiliated museums:

Fort Fleur d'Epée: Bas du Fort, Gosier 97190; f. 1759; military history, art gallery.

Musée Edgar Clerc: Parc de la Rosette, 97160 Le Moule; tel. 23-57-57; f. 1984; archaeological museum; library of 800 vols.

Ecomusée de Marie Galante: Habitation Murat, 97112 Grand Bourg, Marie Galante; tel. 97-94-41; f. 1980; local arts, history and traditions, and history of sugar cane; library of 400 vols; Dir C. MOMBRUN.

Universities and Colleges

Université des Antilles et de la Guyane: BP 250, 97157 Pointe-à-Pitre Cedex; tel. 82-38-22; fax 91-06-57; f. 1982; 271 teachers; 12,144 students; library: see Libraries and Archives; Pres. JEAN-CLAUDE WILLIAM; Sec.-Gen. RAPHAËL BOURDY. (See also under French Guiana and Martinique.)

TEACHING AND RESEARCH UNITS

Law and Economics: Dir E. NABAJOTH.

Sciences: Dean A. RANDRIANASOLO.

Medicine: Dean G. JEAN-BAPTISTE.

Science and Technology of Physical Activities and Sport: Dir M. LÉVÊQUE.

MARTINIQUE

Research Institutes

AGRICULTURE, FISHERIES AND VETERINARY SCIENCE

Centre de Coopération Internationale en Recherche Agronomique pour le Développement (CIRAD): BP 427, 97204 Fort de France Cedex; tel. (596) 51-17-05; Dir J. M. SERVANT.

Institut Français de Recherche Scientifique pour le Développement en Coopération (ORSTOM) Centre de la Martinique: BP 8006, 97259 Fort de France; tel. 70-28-72; fax 71-73-16; e-mail lordinot@outremer.com; f. 1958; soil science, nematology; library of 1,700 vols; Dir G. H. SALA. (See main entry under France.)

MEDICINE

Laboratoire Départemental d'Hygiène de la Martinique: 35 blvd Pasteur, BP 628, 97261 Fort de France Cedex; tel. 71-34-52; fax 71-33-50; f. 1977; hygiene research and analysis of human blood, food and water, entomology, immunology of parasitic diseases; Dir Dr J. M. P. LAFAYE.

Libraries and Archives

Fort-de-France

Archives départementales de la Martinique: BP 649, 19 rue Saint-John-Perse, Tartenson, 97263 Fort-de-France Cedex; f. 1949; 12,000 vols; Dir Mlle LILIANE CHAULEAU.

Bibliothèque Schoelcher: BP 640, Rue de la Liberté, Fort-de-France; tel. 70-26-67; fax 72-45-55; f. 1883; 226,000 vols; Dir JACQUELINE LEGER.

Schoelcher

Service Commun de la Documentation de l'Université des Antilles et de la Guyane (Section Martinique): BP 7210, 97275 Schoelcher Cedex; tel. 72-75-30; fax 72-75-27; e-mail p.berato@martinique.univ-ag.fr; f. 1972; 89,000 vols, 830 periodicals, administrative headquarters for the 3 branches of the univ. library (see also French Guiana and Guadeloupe); Dir of SCDUAG MARIE-FRANÇOISE BERNABÉ; Dir of Martinique Branch PHILIPPE BERATO.

Museums and Art Galleries

Fort-de-France

Musée Départemental d'Archéologie Précolombienne et de Préhistoire de la Martinique: 9 rue de la Liberté, 97200 Fort-de-France; tel. 71-57-05; fax 73-03-80; f. 1971; prehistory of Martinique; archaeological collections; Dir CÉCILE CELMA.

Musée du Père Pinchon: Fort de France Seminary, 97207 Fort-de-France.

Universities and Colleges

Université des Antilles et de la Guyane: Campus de Schoelcher, BP 7209, 97275 Schoelcher Cedex; tel. 72-73-00; fax 72-73-02; e-mail j.laviolette@martinique.univ-ag.fr; library: see Libraries; Pres. JEAN-CLAUDE WILLIAM. (See also under French Guiana and Guadeloupe.)

TEACHING AND RESEARCH UNITS

Law and Economics: Dean PHILIPPE SAINT-CYR.

Letters and Human Sciences: Dean JEAN BERNABÉ.

NEW CALEDONIA

Learned Societies

GENERAL

Association pour la Diffusion des Thèses sur le Pacifique Francophone (THESE-PAC): BP 920, Nouméa; tel. 25-15-98; fax 27-88-01; f. 1986; lists all theses and dissertations on the South Pacific, and aims to obtain copies, providing microfiches for the Service Territorial des Archives, and photocopies for the CTRDP; makes nine annual awards; 60 mems; library of 460 theses; Pres. PHILIPPE PALOMBO; publ. *THESE-PAC* (1 a year).

HISTORY, GEOGRAPHY AND ARCHAEOLOGY

Société d'Etudes Historiques de la Nouvelle-Calédonie: BP 63, 98845 Nouméa; f. 1968; research and study of the past; heritage conservation; publs books and periodicals on history, pre-history, Melanesian society, etc.; close contact with the univs of the Pacific area; 127 mems; archives; Pres. BERNARD BROU; Sec. Gen. DANIEL MORIGNAT; publ. *Bulletin* (quarterly).

RELIGION, SOCIOLOGY AND ANTHROPOLOGY

Société des Etudes Mélanésiennes: Nouméa; tel 27-23-42; f. 1938; anthropology; publ. *Etudes Mélanésiennes* (annually).

Research Institutes

GENERAL

Institut Français de Recherche Scientifique pour le Développement en Coopération (ORSTOM) Centre de Nouméa: BP A5, 98848 Nouméa; tel. 26-10-00; fax 26-43-26; e-mail gasser@noumea.orstom.nc; f. 1946; geology, geophysics, agropedology, hydrology, botany and plant ecology, pharmacology, phytopathology and applied zoology, physical and biological oceanography, archaeology, geography, microbiology; library of 11,000 items; Dir CHRISTIAN COLIN; publs *Sea Sciences*, *Life Sciences*, *Earth Sciences*, *Social Sciences*. (See main entry under France.)

EDUCATION

Centre Territorial de Recherche et de Documentation Pédagogiques de Nouvelle-Calédonie (New Caledonia Territorial Centre for Research and Pedagogic Documentation): BP 215, Nouméa; tel. 27-52-93; fax 28-31-13; f. 1978; research in education; library of 12,000 vols, 800 video tapes, 2,200 slide serials; Dir PHILIPPE BOYER.

MEDICINE

Institut Pasteur de Nouvelle Calédonie: BP 61, Nouméa; tel. 27-26-66; fax 27-33-90; f. 1954; medical analysis laboratory; research laboratory: arbovirology, leptospirosis, virology; library of 1,080 vols; Dir B. GENTILE; publ. *Rapport technique* (annually).

RELIGION, SOCIOLOGY AND ANTHROPOLOGY

Coordination pour l'Océanie des Recherches sur les Arts, les Idées et les Littératures (C.O.R.A.I.L.): BP 2448, 98846 Nouméa Cedex; fax 25-95-27; f. 1987; for the study of francophone and anglophone literatures and civilizations of the South Pacific; annual conference; Pres. DOMINIQUE JOUVÉ; Sec. MICHEL PÉREZ; publ. *Actes du Colloque* (annually).

Libraries and Archives

Nouméa

Bibliothèque Bernheim: BP G1, Nouméa Cedex; tel. 27-23-43; fax 27-65-88; f. 1905; 141,000 vols, 28,500 vols of children's books, 85 periodicals; public library (adults and children), record library; historical, ethnological collections of 2,500 vols dealing with New Caledonia and the Pacific Islands; Librarian J. F. CARREZ-CORRAL.

Service Territorial des Archives de Nouvelle Calédonie: BP 525, Nouméa; tel. 28-59-42; fax 27-12-92; f. 1987; manages the historical and administrative archives of the territory; 4,000 linear metres of archives, library of 8,000 vols; Dir BRUNO CORRE.

South Pacific Commission Library: South Pacific Commission, BP D5, 98848 Nouméa Cedex; tel. (687) 26-20-00; telex 3139; fax (687) 26-38-18; e-mail deveni@spc.org.nc; f. 1947; reference library on health, fisheries, and economic and social development in S. Pacific; 35,000 documents, 10,000 monographs, 3,000 current periodicals and annual reports; Librarian DEVENI TEMU; publs *New Additions to the Library* (quarterly), *Select List of Publications* (annually).

Universities and Colleges

Université Française du Pacifique, Centre Universitaire de Nouvelle Calédonie: BP 4477, Nouméa; tel. 26-58-00; fax 25-48-29; e-mail dedeckke@ufp.nc; library of 18,000 vols, 150 periodicals; 46 teachers, 1,200 students; Dir Prof. PAUL DE DECKKER.

Conservatoire National des Arts et Métiers: BP 3562, Nouméa Cedex; tel. 28-37-07; f. 1971; attached to the Conservatoire National des Arts et Métiers in Paris; 12 staff, 500 students; Pres. JEAN BEGAUD; Dir BERNARD SCHALL.

RÉUNION

Learned Societies

GENERAL

Académie de l'Île de la Réunion: 142 rue Jean-Chatel, 97400 Saint-Denis; tel. 20-10-09; f. 1913; 25 mems; Pres. SERGE YCARD; Sec. YVES DROUHET; publ. *Bulletin*.

HISTORY, GEOGRAPHY AND ARCHAEOLOGY

Association Historique Internationale de l'Océan Indien: c/o Archives Départementales, Le Chaudron, 97490 Sainte-Clotilde; f. 1960; 86 mems; Pres. CL. WANQUET; Sec.-Gen. B. JULLIEN; publ. *Bulletin de liaison et d'information* (2 a year).

Research Institutes

AGRICULTURE, FISHERIES AND VETERINARY SCIENCE

CIRAD–Département des Cultures Annuelles (CIRAD–CA): Station de la Réunion, 97487 Saint-Denis Cedex; tel. 52-80-10; fax 52-80-11; f. 1962; library of 5,000 vols; agronomic research, mainly on sugar cane, maize and fodder crops; Head J.-C. GIRARD; publ. *Rapport Annuel*.

CIRAD–Département des Productions Fruitières et Horticoles (CIRAD-FLHOR): BP 180, 97455 Saint-Pierre Cedex; tel. 57-98-98; fax 38-81-13; stations in Cilaos and Saint-Pierre; Dir (vacant). (See main entry under France.)

ECONOMICS, LAW AND POLITICS

Institut National de la Statistique et des Etudes Economiques – Direction Régionale de la Réunion: 15 rue de l'Ecole, BP 13, 97408 Saint-Denis Messag Cedex 9; tel. 29-51-57; fax 29-76-85; f. 1966; attached to INSEE in Paris; produces statistical data, economic studies, etc.; data base with 10,000 bibliographical references on the region, data bank with 2,000 chronological series; Dir RENÉ JEAN; publs *L'Economie de la Réunion* (every 2 months), *Tableau économique de la Réunion* (annually).

Libraries and Archives

St-Denis

Bibliothèque Centrale de Prêt: 1 place Joffre, 97400 St-Denis; tel. 21-03-24; fax 21-41-30; f. 1956; 100,000 vols; Dir MARIE-COLETTE MAUJEAN.

Bibliothèque Départementale: 52 rue Roland Garros, 97400 St-Denis; tel. 21-13-96; f. 1855; 95,000 vols; Dir ALAIN VAUTHIER.

Service Commun de la Documentation: Université de la Réunion, 15 ave René Cassin, BP 7152, 97715 St-Denis Cedex 9; tel. 93-83-79; fax 93-83-64; e-mail amblanc@univ-reunion.fr; f. 1971; arts, human sciences, law, economics, politics, social sciences, management, science, medicine; 96,000 vols; 1,500 current periodicals; special collections on the Indian Ocean islands; Dir ANNE-MARIE BLANC.

St-Pierre

Médiathèque de Saint-Pierre: rue du Collège Arthur, BP 396, 97458 St-Pierre Cedex; tel. 35-13-24; fax 25-74-10; f. 1967; 70,000 vols, 70,000 CDs, 2,500 videotapes; Dir LINDA KOO SEEN LIN.

Ste-Clotilde

Archives Départementales: Le Chaudron, 97490 Ste-Clotilde; specializes in the history of the Indian Ocean; 5,000 vols; Dir B. JULLIEN.

Museums and Art Galleries

St-Denis

Musée Léon-Dierx: 28 rue de Paris, 97400 St-Denis; tel. 20-24-82; fax 21-82-87; f. 1911; fine arts; Curator JEAN-PAUL LE MAGUET.

Muséum d'Histoire Naturelle: Jardin de l'Etat, 97400 St-Denis; tel. 20-02-19; fax 21-33-93; f. 1854; library of 6,000 vols; zoology collection; Dir S. RIBES.

St-Gilles-les-Hauts

Musée Historique: Domaine Panon-Desbassayns, 97435 St-Gilles-les-Hauts; tel. 55-64-10; fax 55-51-91; f. 1976; 18th-century plantation house and adjoining properties; French East India Co. furniture and china, prints, models, weapons, documents, etc.; Curator JEAN BARBIER.

Universities and Colleges

UNIVERSITÉ DE LA RÉUNION (UNIVERSITÉ FRANÇAISE DE L'OCÉAN INDIEN)

15 ave René Cassin, 97715 Saint-Denis Messag Cedex 9

Telephone: 93-80-80

Fax: 93-80-06

Founded 1970, university status 1982

Rector: JEAN-PIERRE BENEJAM

President: PATRICK HERVÉ

Vice-Presidents: MICHEL BOYER (Administration), ALAIN GEOFFROY (Science), BERNARD VIDAL (Studies and University Life), CLAUDE FERAL (External Relations)

Librarian: ANNE-MARIE BLANC

Library: see Service Commun de la Documentation, Réunion

Number of teachers: 286

Number of students: 9,103

DEANS

Faculty of Law, Political and Economic Sciences: J.-P. BOUSSEMART

Faculty of Arts and Humanities: M. LATCHOUMANIN

Faculty of Science: F. CADET

ATTACHED INSTITUTES

Institut Universitaire de Technologie: Dir RENÉ SQUARZONI.

Institut d'Administration des Entreprises: Dir MICHEL BOYER.

Institut de Linguistique et d'Anthropologie: Dir CHRISTIAN BARAT.

GABON

Research Institutes

GENERAL

Centre National de la Recherche Scientifique et Technologique (CENAREST): BP 842, Libreville; tel. 73-25-78; f. 1976; human sciences, tropical ecology, agronomy, medicinal plants, plant biotechnology; Dir CHARLES MEFANE.

AGRICULTURE, FISHERIES AND VETERINARY SCIENCE

Centre Technique Forestier Tropical, Section Gabon: BP 149, Libreville; f. 1958; silviculture, technology, genetic improvement; library of 500 vols; Dir J. LEROY DEVAL.

Institut de Recherches Agronomiques et Forestières (IRAF): BP 2246, Libreville; tel. 73-23-75; fax 73-25-78; f. 1977; agronomy, forestry; Dir JEAN-JACQUES ENGO.

MEDICINE

Centre International de Recherches Médicales de Franceville: BP 769, Franceville; tel. 677096; telex 6708; fax 677295; f. 1979; undertakes basic and applied research in medical parasitology (e.g. malaria, filariosis, trypanosomiasis) and viral diseases (e.g. HIV, Ebola); library of 1,800 vols, 72 periodicals, 20,000 microfiches; Dir-Gen. Prof. ALAIN J. GEORGES.

NATURAL SCIENCES

Biological Sciences

Laboratoire de Primatologie et d'Ecologie des Forêts Equatoriales (CNRS): BP 18, Makokou; f. 1970; study of the 17 species of primate living in the wild state; research on the general ecology of the equatorial forest; Dir A. BROSSET; publ. *Biologia Gabonica* (3 a year).

TECHNOLOGY

Bureau de Recherches Géologiques et Minières (BRGM): BP 175, Libreville; f. 1960; Dir. M. BERTUCAT. (See main entry under France.)

Libraries and Archives

Libreville

Bibliothèque du Centre d'Information: BP 750, Libreville; f. 1960; 6,000 vols; 80 current periodicals.

Direction Générale des Archives Nationales, de la Bibliothèque Nationale et de la Documentation Gabonaise (DGABD): BP 1188, Libreville; tel. 736310 (Archives Nationales), 730972 (Bibliothèque Nationale), 737247 (Documentation Gabonaise); f. 1969 (Nat. Archives and Nat. Library), 1980 (Gabonese Documentation); 36 mems; 25,000 vols, 2,000 periodical titles; 2 linear km archives; 639 microfilms; Archives Dir RENÉ G. SONNET-AZIZE; Nat. Library Dir JÉRÔME ANGOUNE-NZOGHE; Documentation Dir JEAN PAUL MIFOUNA; Dir-Gen. F. IBOUILI-NZIGOU.

Universities

UNIVERSITÉ OMAR BONGO

BP 13 131, Blvd Léon M'Ba, Libreville

Telephone: 73-20-33
Telex: 5336

Founded 1970, renamed 1978
State control
Language of instruction: French
Academic year: October to July

Rector: BONAVENTURE MVE-ONDO
Vice-Rectors: VINCENT MINTSA-MI-EYA, PAUL BONGUE-BOMA, PATRICE OTHA
Secretary-General: EMMANUEL ANGO-MEYE
Librarian: M. ABOGHE-OBIANG

Library of 12,000 vols
Number of teachers: 295
Number of students: 2,400

DEANS

Faculty of Law and Economics: ALBERT ONDO-OSSA
Faculty of Letters: VINCENT MOULENGUI-BOUKOSSOU
Faculty of Sciences: JEAN-REMY M'PARIA
National Law School: JESN-PIERRE AKOUMBOU M'OLUNA
Higher Teacher Training School: LUCHÉRI GAHILA
Higher Technical Teacher Training School: A. ISSEMBÉ
National Higher School of Engineering: M. BONDON
Health Science Centre: NGUEMBI-MBINA
National School of Administration: MBOU-YEMBI
National School of Forestry and Hydraulics: SYLVESTRE MENDENE
National School of Management: FABIEN OKOUE METOGO

UNIVERSITÉ DES SCIENCES ET TECHNIQUES DE MASUKU

BP 901, Franceville

Telephone: 67-77-25
Telex: 6723
Fax: 67-75-20

Founded 1986
State control
Language of instruction: French

Rector: JACQUES LEBIBI
Vice-Rector: BERTRAND M'BATCHI
Secretary-General: ANSELME PONGA
Librarian: YVES NTOUTOUME NKOUME

Library of 11,000 vols
Number of teachers and researchers: 110
Number of students: 800

DEANS

Faculty of Sciences: NDOB MAMBUNDU
Polytechnic: FELICIEN MENDENE M'EKWA

Colleges

Ecole Interprovinciale de Santé: BP 530, Mouila; tel. 86-11-77; f. 1981; 18 teachers; 76 students; Dir PIERRE FRANKLIN NGUEMA ONDO.

Institut Africain d'Informatique: BP 2263, Libreville; tel. 72-00-05; f. 1971 by member states of OCAM to train computer programmers and analysts; small library; 7 permanent teachers; Dir EGBAO BIDAMON.

GAMBIA

Learned Societies

NATURAL SCIENCES

Biological Sciences

Gambia Ornithological Society: POB 757, Banjul; tel. 495170; f. 1974; birdwatching, study and records; 56 mems; library of *c.* 24 vols; Chair. CHRIS WHITE; Hon. Sec. M. DALE; publs *Reports*.

Research Institutes

MEDICINE

Medical Research Council Dunn Nutrition Unit, Keneba: Keneba, West Kiang; f. 1974; field station of the Dunn Nutrition Unit laboratory in Cambridge; research on maternal undernutrition: work on paediatric gastroenterology and nutrition, the physiological adaptation of mothers to pregnancy and lactation, also maternal vitamin and mineral requirements; research into long-term effects of ante-natal and early post-natal nutrition; research on growth faltering, and the role of small differences in economic status on malnutrition; calorimetry research on comparisons of energy expenditure between Gambians and Europeans; Supervisor Dr E. POSKITT.

Medical Research Council Laboratories: POB 273, Fajara, near Banjul; tel. 495442; fax 495919; e-mail mrc@gam.healthnet.org; f. 1947; research on tropical diseases found in West Africa; 600 staff; Dir Prof. K. MCADAM.

Libraries and Archives

Banjul

Gambia National Library: PMB, Reg Pye Lane, Banjul; tel. 228312; fax 223776; f. 1946 by British Ccl, taken over by Govt 1962, autonomous 1985; serves as a public and national library; national deposit library; 115,400 vols, 85 periodicals; special collection of Gambiana; Chief Librarian MARY E. FYE; publs *National Bibliography, Wax Taani Xalel Yi* (children's magazine), *Annual Report*.

Museums and Art Galleries

Banjul

Gambia National Museum: Museum and Monuments Division, National Council for Arts and Culture, Independence Drive, Banjul; tel. 226244; fax 227461; library of 645 vols; f. 1982; Principal Cultural Officer B. A. CEESAY.

College

Gambia College: Brikama, Western Division; tel. 84812; f. 1978; library of 23,000 vols; 57 teachers; 400 students; Pres. N.S.Z. NJIE; Registrar N. S. MANNEH.

HEADS OF SCHOOLS

Agriculture: J. MANNEH
Education: W. A. COLE
Nursing and Midwifery: F. SARR
Public Health: B. A. PHALL

GEORGIA

Learned Societies

GENERAL

Georgian Academy of Sciences: 380008 Tbilisi, Pr. Rustaveli 52; tel. 99-88-91; fax 99-88-23; e-mail lado@acad.acnet.ge; depts of Mathematics and Physics (Academician-Sec. D. G. LOMINADZE, Learned Sec. L. A. GOGOLAURI), Earth Sciences (Academician-Sec. E. P. GAMKRELIDZE, Learned Sec. E. D. KILASONIA), Applied Mechanics, Machine Building and Control Processes (Academician-Sec. M. E. SALUKVADZE, Learned Sec. I. A. GORDADZE), Chemistry and Chemical Technology (Academician-Sec. G. G. GVELESIANI, Learned Sec. Z. P. TSINTSKALADZE), Agricultural Science Problems (Academician-Sec. O. G. NATISHVILI, Learned Sec. N. I. GIORGBERIDZE), Biology (Academician-Sec. M. M. ZAALISHVILI, Learned Sec. M. K. GRIGOLAVA), Physiology and Experimental Medicine (Academician-Sec. T. N. ONIANI, Learned Sec. N. R. KIKNADZE), Social Sciences (Academician-Sec. G. B. TEVZADZE, Learned Sec. L. I. LAZARASHVILI), Linguistics and Literature (Academician-Sec. G. SH. TSITSISHVILI, Learned Sec. L. G. DUMBADZE); 66 mems, 76 corresp. mems; attached research institutes: see Research Institutes; library: see Libraries and Archives; Pres. A. N. TAVKHELIDZE; Academician-Sec. L. K. GABUNIA; publs *Bulletin* (in Georgian and English, monthly), *Matsne* (Herald, dept of Social Sciences, monthly), *Metsnierba da Technika* (monthly).

HISTORY, GEOGRAPHY AND ARCHAEOLOGY

Georgian Geographical Society: 380007 Tbilisi, Ketskhoveli 11; attached to Georgian Acad. of Sciences; Chair. V. SH. DZHAOSHVILI.

Georgian History Society: 380008 Tbilisi, Rustaveli 52; attached to Georgian Acad. of Sciences; Vice-Chair. A. M. APAKIDZE.

LANGUAGE AND LITERATURE

Amateur Society of Basque Language: 380008 Tbilisi, Rustaveli 52; attached to Georgian Acad. of Sciences; Chair. SH. V. DZIDZIGURI.

MEDICINE

Georgian Bio-Medico-Technical Society: 380003 Tbilisi, Telavi 51; attached to Georgian Acad. of Sciences; Chair. K. SH. NADAREISHVILI.

Georgian Neuroscience Association: C/o Beritashvili Institute of Physiology, 380060 Tbilisi, Gotua 14; tel. (32) 37-42-16; fax (32) 94-10-45; e-mail mgt@physiol.acnet.ge; f. 1996; 55 mems; Pres. S. N. KHECHINASHVILI; Sec.-Gen. M. G. TSAGARELI.

Georgian Society of Patho-Anatomists: 380077 Tbilisi, V. Pshavela 27B; attached to Georgian Acad. of Sciences; Chair. T. I. DEKANOSIDZE.

NATURAL SCIENCES

Biological Sciences

Georgian Botanical Society: 380007 Tbilisi, Kodzhorskoe shosse; attached to Georgian Acad. of Sciences; Chair. G. SH. NAKHUTSRISHVILI.

Georgian Society of Biochemists: 380043 Tbilisi, University 2; tel. (32) 30-39-97; fax (32) 22-11-03; f. 1958; attached to Georgian Acad. of Sciences; 850 mems; Pres. Prof. NOUGZAR ALEKSIDZE; Sec. NANA ABASHIDZE.

Georgian Society of Geneticists and Selectionists: 380060 Tbilisi, Gotua 3; tel. 37-42-27; attached to Georgian Acad. of Sciences; Chair. T. G. CHANISHVILI.

Georgian Society of Parasitologists: 380079 Tbilisi, Chavchavadze 31; tel. (32) 22-33-53; attached to Georgian Acad. of Sciences; Pres. Prof. B. E. KURASHVILI; Sec. K. G. NIKOLAISHVILI.

Physical Sciences

Georgian Geological Society: 380008 Tbilisi, Rustaveli 52; attached to Georgian Acad. of Sciences; Chair. SH. A. ADAMIA.

Georgian National Speleological Society: 380093 Tbilisi, Merab Aleksidze (Bl. 8); tel. 36-74-49; f. 1980; attached to Georgian Acad. of Sciences; 25 mems; Chair. Z. K. TATASHIDZE; publ. *Caves of Georgia* (irregular).

PHILOSOPHY AND PSYCHOLOGY

Georgian Philosophy Society: 380008 Tbilisi, Rustaveli 29; attached to Georgian Acad. of Sciences; Chair. N. Z. CHAVCHAVADZE.

Georgian Society of Psychologists: 380007 Tbilisi, Jashvili 22; attached to Georgian Acad. of Sciences; Chair. N. Z. NADIRASHVILI.

Research Institutes

AGRICULTURE, FISHERIES AND VETERINARY SCIENCE

Gulisashvili, V. Z., Institute of Mountain Forestry: 380086 Tbilisi, E. Mindeli 9; tel. 31-36-91; attached to Georgian Acad. of Sciences; Dir G. N. GIGAURI.

Institute of Water Management and Engineering Ecology: 380030 Tbilisi, J. Chavchavadze 60; tel. 22-40-94; attached to Georgian Acad. of Sciences; Dir T. E. MIRSKHOULAVA.

Research Institute of Tea and Sub-Tropical Crops: Makharadzevsky raion, Pos. Anaseuli.

Scientific Research Centre of the Biological Basis of Cattle-Breeding: 380030 Tbilisi, Z. Paliashvili 87; tel. 29-40-03; attached to Georgian Acad. of Sciences; Dir A. R. DOLMAZASHVILI.

ARCHITECTURE AND TOWN PLANNING

Zavriev, K. S., Institute of Constructional Mathematics and Seismic Resistance: 380093 Tbilisi, Ul. Z. Rukhadze 1; tel. 36-59-28; attached to Georgian Acad. of Sciences; Dir G. K. GABRICHIDZE.

BIBLIOGRAPHY, LIBRARY SCIENCE AND MUSEOLOGY

Kekelidze, K. S., Institute of Manuscripts: 380093 Tbilisi, Ul. Z. Rukhadze 1; tel. 36-39-14; attached to Georgian Acad. of Sciences; Dir Z. N. ALEKSIDZE.

ECONOMICS, LAW AND POLITICS

Gugushvili, P. V., Institute of Economics: 380007 Tbilisi, Ul. Kikodze 22; tel. 93-22-60; attached to Georgian Acad. of Sciences; Dir V. G. PAPAVA.

Institute of State and Law: 380007 Tbilisi, Kikodze 14; tel. 99-86-14; attached to Georgian Acad. of Sciences; Dir J. V. PUTKARADZE.

Research Centre of National Relations: 380007 Tbilisi, Leselidze 4; attached to Georgian Acad. of Sciences; Dir G. V. ZHORZHOLIANI.

FINE AND PERFORMING ARTS

Chubinashvili, G. N., Institute of History of Georgian Art: 380008 Tbilisi, Rustaveli 52; Dir N. SH. DZHANBERIDZE.

HISTORY, GEOGRAPHY AND ARCHAEOLOGY

Centre for Archaeological Studies: 380002 Tbilisi, Uznadze 14; tel. 95-97-65; attached to Georgian Acad. of Sciences; Dir O. D. LORDKIPANIDZE.

Dzhavakhishvili, I. A., Institute of History and Ethnography: 380009 Tbilisi, Ul. Melikishvili 10; tel. 99-06-82; attached to Georgian Acad. of Sciences; Dir G. A. MELIKISHVILI.

Vakhushti Bagrationi Institute of Geography: 380093 Tbilisi, Merab Aleksidze 1 (Bl. 8); tel. 36-74-49; e-mail root@geogr.acnet.ge; f. 1933; attached to Georgian Acad. of Sciences; library of 68,000 vols; Deputy Dir R. D. KHAZARADZE.

LANGUAGE AND LITERATURE

Abkhazian D. I. Gulia Institute of Linguistics, Literature and History: 384932 Sukhumi, Ul. Rustaveli 34; tel. 2-42-84; attached to Georgian Acad. of Sciences; Dir (vacant).

Chikobava, A. S., Institute of Linguistics: 380007 Tbilisi, Ul. Ingorokva 8; tel. 93-45-30; attached to Georgian Acad. of Sciences; Dir G. SH. KVARATSKHELIA.

Shota Rustaveli Institute of Georgian Literature: 380008 Tbilisi, Ul. Kostava 5; tel. 99-14-15; attached to Georgian Acad. of Sciences; Dir G. D. BARNOV.

Tsereteli, G. V., Institute of Oriental Studies: 380062 Tbilisi, Ul. Akad. G. Tsereteli 3; tel. 23-31-14; attached to Georgian Acad. of Sciences; Dir T. V. GAMKRELIDZE.

MEDICINE

Beritashvili Institute of Physiology: 380060 Tbilisi, Gotua 14; tel. 37-12-31; fax 94-10-45; e-mail mgt@physiol.acnet.ge; f. 1935; library of 48,000 vols, 25 periodicals; attached to Georgian Acad. of Sciences; Dir V. M. MOSIDZE.

Georgian Institute of Roentgenology and Medical Radiology: Tbilisi, Ul. Ordzhonikidze 101; Dir G. NAZARISHNILI.

Georgian Scientific Research Institute of Industrial Hygiene and Occupational Diseases: 380002 Tbilisi, David Agmashenebeli Ave 60; tel. 95-65-94; f. 1927; library of 24,000 vols; Dir RUSUDAN DJAVAKHADZE; publs periodicals on occupational hygiene and industrial diseases (annually).

Institute of Experimental Pathology and Therapy: 384900 Sukhumi, Gora Trapetsiya, POB 66; Dir B. A. Lapin.

Institute of Medical Biotechnology: 380059 Tbilisi, Chiaureli 2; tel. 51-98-76; attached to Georgian Acad. of Sciences; Dir V. I. Bakhutashvili.

Kutateladze, I. G., Institute of Pharmaceutical Chemistry: 380059 Tbilisi, POB 71; tel. 51-16-29; attached to Georgian Acad. of Sciences; Dir E. P. Kemertelidze.

National Scientific Research Institute of Tuberculosis: 380108 Tbilisi, Zacomoldina 50; f. 1930; library of 32,000 vols; Dir N. V. Gogebashvili.

Natishvili, A. N., Institute of Experimental Morphology: 380059 Tbilisi, Chiaureli 2; tel. 51-00-46; attached to Georgian Acad. of Sciences; Dir N. A. Dzhavakhishvili.

Research and Teaching Clinical and Experimental Centre of Traumatology and Orthopaedics: 380002 Tbilisi, Ul. Kalinina 51; tel. 95-53-81; Dir B. Tsereteli.

Research Institute of Psychiatry: 380077 Tbilisi, Ul. M. Asatiani 10; tel. (32) 39-47-65; fax (32) 94-36-73; e-mail georgia@gamh.kheta.ge; f. 1925; library of 8,000 vols, 7,000 periodicals.

Research Institute of Skin and Venereal Diseases: 380064 Tbilisi, Ul. Ninoshvili 55; tel. (32) 95-35-64; fax (32) 96-48-02; e-mail dermat@nile.org.ge; f. 1935; library of 23,800 vols; Dir Dr Badzi Chlaidze; publ. *Trudy* (Proceedings, annually).

Research Institute of Vaccines and Sera: 380060 Tbilisi 42, Ul. L. Gotua 3; tel. 37-42-27.

Research Institute 'Radian': 380086 Tbilisi, Pr. Mira 32; tel. 37-29-44.

Scientific Research Centre for Radiobiology and Radiation Ecology: 380003 Tbilisi, Telavi 51; tel. 94-20-17; fax 93-61-26; e-mail radiobio!kiazo@acnet.ge; f. 1990; attached to Georgian Acad. of Sciences; Dir K. Sh. Nadareishvili; publs *Radiation Studies* (2 a year), *Biomedical Techniques* (2 a year), *Problems of Ecology* (2 a year).

Virsaladze Institute of Medical Parasitology and Tropical Medicine: Tbilisi 64, Ul. Plekhanova 139.

Zhordania Research Institute of Human Reproduction: Tbilisi, Ul. Kostava; Dir Prof O. E. Viazov.

NATURAL SCIENCES

Biological Sciences

Davitashvili, L. Sh., Institute of Palaeobiology: 380004 Tbilisi, Ul. Niagavari 4A; tel. 93-12-82; attached to Georgian Acad. of Sciences; Dir G. A. Mchedlidze.

Durmishidze, S. V., Institute of Plant Biochemistry: 380059 Tbilisi, Al. David Agmashenebeli 10km; tel. 95-81-45; fax 98-94-79; f. 1971; attached to Georgian Acad. of Sciences; library of 72,000 vols; Dir G. I. Kvesitadze.

Institute of Molecular Biology and Biological Physics: 380060 Tbilisi, L. Gotua 14; tel. 37-42-11; attached to Georgian Acad. of Sciences; Dir M. M. Zaalishvili.

Institute of Zoology: 380030 Tbilisi, Pr. Chavchavadze 31; tel. 22-01-64; attached to Georgian Acad. of Sciences; Dir I. I. Eliava.

Ketskhoveli, N., Institute of Botany: 380087 Tbilisi, Kodzhorskoe shosse; tel. 99-77-46; attached to Georgian Acad. of Sciences; Dir G. Sh. Nakhutsrishvili.

Mathematical Sciences

Institute of Computational Mathematics: 93 Tbilisi, Akuri 8; tel. (32) 36-24-38; e-mail postmaster@acnet.ge; f. 1956; attached to Georgian Acad. of Sciences; Dir Prof. N. N. Vakhania.

A. Razmadze Mathematical Institute: 380093 Tbilisi, M. Aleksidze 1; tel. (32) 98-76-32; e-mail kig@gmj.acnet.ge; f. 1935; attached to Georgian Acad. of Sciences; Dir I. T. Kiguradze; publ. *Proceedings* (in English, 3 a year).

Physical Sciences

Abastumani Astrophysical Observatory: 383762 Abastumani, Kanobili Mountain; tel. 2-10; attached to Georgian Acad. of Sciences; Dir D. G. Lominadze.

Dzanelidze, A. I., Geological Institute: 380093 Tbilisi, Ul. Z. Rukhadze 1; tel. 36-51-09; attached to Georgian Acad. of Sciences; Dir Sh. Adamia.

Institute of Geophysics: 380093 Tbilisi, Ul. Z. Rukhadze 1; tel. 36-54-80; attached to Georgian Acad. of Sciences; Dir T. L. Chelidze.

Institute of Hydrometeorology: 380012 Tbilisi, David Agmashenebeli 150A; tel. (32) 95-10-47; fax (32) 95-11-60; e-mail gsvan@hydmet.acnet.ge; f. 1953; attached to Georgian Acad. of Sciences; Dir G. G. Svanidze.

Institute of Inorganic Chemistry and Electrical Chemistry: 380086 Tbilisi, Ul. Z. Rukhadze 1; tel. 31-54-96; attached to Georgian Acad. of Sciences; Dir L. N. Dzhaparidze.

Institute of Physics: 380077 Tbilisi, Ul. Tamarashvili 6; tel. 39-87-83; telex 212236; attached to Georgian Acad. of Sciences; Dir G. A. Kharadze.

Melikishvili, P. G., Institute of Physical and Organic Chemistry: 380086 Tbilisi, Dzhikia 5; tel. 31-90-65; attached to Georgian Acad. of Sciences; Dir T. O. Andronikashvili.

Tavadze, F. N., Institute of Metallurgy: 380060 Tbilisi, Ul. Pavlova 15; tel. 37-02-67; attached to Georgian Acad. of Sciences; Dir I. B. Baratashvili.

Transcaucasian Hydrometeorological Research Institute: 380012 Tbilisi, Pr. Agmashenebeli 150A; tel. 95-43-77.

PHILOSOPHY AND PSYCHOLOGY

Institute of Philosophy: 380008 Tbilisi, Pr. Rustaveli 29; tel. 93-74-92; attached to Georgian Acad. of Sciences; Dir N. Z. Chavchavadze.

Uznadze, D. N., Institute of Psychology: 380007 Tbilisi, Ul. Iashvili 22; tel. 93-24-54; attached to Georgian Acad. of Sciences; Dir Sh. A. Nadirashvili.

RELIGION, SOCIOLOGY AND ANTHROPOLOGY

Berdzenishvili, N. A., Batumi Scientific Research Institute: 384516 Batumi, Ul. Ninoshvili 23; tel. 3-29-01; attached to Georgian Acad. of Sciences; Dir D. A. Khakhutaishvili.

Institute of Demography and Sociological Research: 380007 Tbilisi, Kikodze 14; tel. 99-67-25; attached to Georgian Acad. of Sciences; Dir L. L. Chikava.

Tskhinvali Scientific Research Institute: 383570 Tskhinvali, Ul. Lenina 3A; tel. 2-49-70; attached to Georgian Acad. of Sciences; Dir (vacant).

TECHNOLOGY

Institute of Control Systems: 380060 Tbilisi, K. Gamsakhurdia Ave 34; tel. (32) 37-20-44; fax (32) 384753; f. 1956; attached to Georgian Acad. of Sciences; library of 10,000 vols; Dir M. E. Salukvadze; publs *Control Theory and Devices* (annually), *Speech Recognition and Language Modelling* (annually).

Institute of Cybernetics: 380086 Tbilisi, Ul. S. Euli 5; tel. 31-25-19; attached to Georgian Acad. of Sciences; Dir G. L. Kharatishvili.

Institute of Engineering Geology and Hydrogeology: 380008 Tbilisi, Rustaveli 31; tel. 51-71-23; attached to Georgian Acad. of Sciences; Dir K. I. Dzhandzhgava.

Institute of Mechanics of Machines: 380086 Tbilisi, Nutsubidze 112; tel. 31-30-62; attached to Georgian Acad. of Sciences; Dir I. I. Dzhebashvili.

Scientific-Industrial Institute: 380090 Tbilisi, D. Guzamishvili 36; tel. 74-08-29; attached to Georgian Acad. of Sciences; Dir Z. E. Kruashvili.

Sukhumi I. N. Vekua Physical-Technical Institute: Sukhumi; attached to Georgian Acad. of Sciences; Dir R. G. Salukvadze.

Tsulukidze, G. A., Institute of Mining Mechanics: 380086 Tbilisi, A. Mindelli 7; tel. 31-47-16; attached to Georgian Acad. of Sciences; Dir L. A. Dzhaparidze.

Libraries and Archives

Tbilisi

Central Library of the Georgian Academy of Sciences: 380093 Tbilisi, M. Aleksidze St, Korp. 4; tel. 36-00-19; f. 1941; 3,200,000 vols; Dir N. A. Gurgenidze.

Mikeladze, G. S., Scientific and Technical Library of Georgia: Tbilisi 4, Ul. Dzneladze 27; 10,100,000 vols (without patents); Dir R. D. Gorgiladze.

National Library of Georgia: 380007 Tbilisi, Gudiashvili 7; tel. 99-92-86; fax 99-80-95; f. 1846; 6,000,000 vols, 24,000 periodicals; Dir Alexander Kartozia.

Scientific Information Centre for Social Sciences: 380030 Tbilisi, Paliashvili 87; tel. 22-41-04; attached to Georgian Acad. of Sciences; Dir N. I. Kikvadze.

Tbilisi State University Library: 380028 Tbilisi, Ul. 1 Chavchavadze 1; tel. 22-10-32; 3,000,000 vols; Dir S. Apakidze.

Museums and Art Galleries

Kutaisi

Berdzenishvili, N. A., Kutaisi State Museum of History and Ethnography: Kutaisi, Ul. Tbilisi 1; tel. 5-56-76; f. 1912; attached to Georgian Academy of Sciences; library of 25,000 vols; Dir Dr M. V. Nikoleishvili.

Sukhumi

State Museum of Abkhasia: Sukhumi, Ul. Lenina 22; f. 1915; history of the Abkhasian people; Dir A. A. Argun.

Sukhumi Botanical Garden: 384933 Sukhumi, Ul. Chavchavadze 20; tel. 2-44-58; attached to Georgian Acad. of Sciences; Dir (vacant).

Tbilisi

State Museum of Georgia: Tbilisi, Pr. Rustaveli 3; tel. 99-80-22; f. 1852; history, natural history; attached to Georgian Academy of Sciences; library of 250,000 vols; Dir L. A. Chilashvili; publ. *Moambe* (Bulletin).

Georgian State Art Museum: Tbilisi, Ul. Ketskhoveli 1; Dir S. Y. Amiranishvili.

Georgian State Museum of Oriental Art: Tbilisi, Ul. Azizbekova 3; Georgian fine and applied art; Dir G. M. Gvishiani.

Georgian State Picture Gallery: Tbilisi, Pr. Rustaveli 11; Dir M. A. Kipiani.

State Literary Museum of Georgia: 380004 Tbilisi, Ul. Djiordjiashivili 8; tel. 99-

86-67; f. 1930; 19th- and 20th-century Georgian literature; library of 11,893 vols; Dir I. A. ORDZHONIKIDZE; publ. *Literary Chronicle*.

Tbilisi State Museum of Anthropology and Ethnography: Tbilisi, Komsomolskii pr. 11; history and ethnography of Georgia; library of 150,000 vols; Dir A. V. TKESHELASHVILI.

Universities

ABKHAZIAN A. M. GORKII STATE UNIVERSITY

384900 Sukhumi, Ul. Tsereteli 9

Telephone: 2-25-98

Founded 1985

Number of students: 3,800

Faculties of physics and mathematics, economics, history and law, philology, biology and geography, teacher training.

GEORGIAN TECHNICAL UNIVERSITY

380075 Tbilisi, Ul. M. Kostava 77

Telephone: (32) 29-48-56
Telex: 212100
Fax: (32) 94-20-33

Founded 1990 (1922 as Georgia Polytechnic Institute)
State Control
Languages of Instruction: Georgian, Russian, English
Academic Year: September to June

Chancellor: Prof. R. KHURODZE
Vice-Rectors: Prof. T. JAPARIDZE, Prof. P. TURMANIDZE, Prof. R. STURUA, Prof. V. DIDMANIDZE, Prof. T. BATSIKADZE
Head of Teaching and Methodology: O. ZUMBURIDZE

Librarian: V. PAPASKIRI
Number of teachers: 2,050
Number of students: 16,000

Publication: *Agmshenebeli* (newspaper).

DEANS

Faculty of Civil Engineering: R. IMEDADZE
Faculty of Mining and Geology: Z. MGELADZE
Faculty of Power Engineering: D. LAOSHVILI
Faculty of Chemical Engineering: N. KUTSLAVA
Faculty of Mechanics and Machine-Building: B. BOKHOLISHVILI
Faculty of Basic Sciences: R. CHIKOVANI
Faculty of Information Technology: N. LOMINADZE
Faculty of Transport: A. CHKHEIDZE
Faculty of Architecture: G. SALUKVADZE
Faculty of Aviation: S. TEPNADZE
Faculty of Humanities: A. TSINTSADZE
Faculty of Metallurgy: G. KASHAKASHVILI
Faculty of Communication: T. KUPATADZE
Faculty of Hydraulic Engineering: L. GOGELIANI

JAVAKHISHVILI STATE UNIVERSITY

380028 Tbilisi, Pr. Chavchavadze 1

Telephone: 31-47-92
Founded 1918
State control
Language of instruction: Georgian
Academic year: September to June

Rector: Prof. David I. CHKHIKVISHVILI
Pro-Rectors: Prof. S. M. DZHORBENADZE, Dr G. A. CHILASHUILI, Dr A. KINTSURASHVILI
Chief Administrative Officer: A. I. KHARSHILADZE
Librarian: S. A. APAKIDZE
Library: see Libraries
Number of professors and lecturers: 1,659
Number of students: 16,000

Publications: *Tbilisi University* (weekly), *Proceedings* (quarterly, in two series).

DEANS

Faculty of Mechanics and Mathematics: Prof. L. GIGIASHVILI
Faculty of Cybernetics and Applied Mathematics: Dr R. KORDZADZE
Faculty of Physics: Prof. T. SANADZE
Faculty of Chemistry: Dr. S. MIKADZE
Faculty of Geography and Geology: Dr N. NACHKEBIA
Faculty of Biology: Prof. B. LOMSADZE
Faculty of History: Prof. A. SURGULADZE
Faculty of Philosophy and Psychology: Prof. G. TEVZADZE
Faculty of Philology: Prof. O. BAKANIDZE
Faculty of Western European Languages and Literature: Dr I. BACHIASHVILI
Faculty of Oriental Studies: Dr G. PUTURIDZE
Faculty of Economics: Prof. G. CHANUKVADZE
Faculty of Engineering Economics: Dr V. GABIDZASHVILI
Faculty of Economic Planning: Dr N. MESKHI
Faculty of Commercial Economics: Dr I. MUDZHIRI
Faculty of Law: Dr V. LORIA
Faculty of Fine Arts: Prof. V. GVAKHARIA
University Teachers' Training Faculty: Dr A. ISHKHNELI
School Teachers' Training Faculty: Dr D. DZHIKIA

ATTACHED INSTITUTES

Institute of Applied Mathematics: Tbilisi, Universitetskaya ul. 2.
Institute of Nuclear Physics.
Institute of Cybernetics.
Institute of Cosmic Rays.
Institute of Low Temperatures.
Institute of the Ionosphere.
Sarajishvili Institute of Neurology: Dir Prof. ROMAN SHAKARISHVILI.

TBILISI STATE MEDICAL UNIVERSITY

380077 Tbilisi, V. Pshavela 33

Telephone: (32) 39-38-01
Fax: (32) 94-25-19
E-mail: medic@ridmu.khetha.ge

Founded 1918

Rector: R. G. KHETSURIONI
Vice-Rectors: N. LOMIDZE (Education), V. KIPIANI (Research), O. GERZMAVA (Foreign Affairs)

Library of 500,000 vols

Number of teachers: 780
Number of students: 4,000

Publications: *Georgian Medical News* (monthly), *Research* (1 a year).

Schools of General Medicine, Paediatrics, Stomatology, Health Administration and Management, Pharmacy, Medical Biology and Nursing.

Other Higher Educational Institutes

Georgian Agricultural Institute: 380031 Tbilisi, Digomi, 13-km. Voenno-Gruzinskoi Dorogi; tel. 51-47-63; depts: agronomy, fruit and vegetable growing, viticulture, mechanization, electrification, forestry, economics and management, accounting, silkworm breeding, plant protection, wine making, preserving industry; library of 700,000 vols; Rector I. F. SARISHVILI.

Georgian Institute of Subtropical Cultivation: 384904 Sukhumi, Kelasuri; tel. 3-38-69; depts: subtropical agronomy, subtropical cultivation, mechanization, preserving industry; library of 90,000 vols; Rector I. A. GEORGBERIDZE.

Georgian S. Rustaveli State Institute of Dramatic Art: 380004 Tbilisi, Pr. S. Rustaveli 17; tel. 99-94-11; f. 1939; drama and cinema, musical comedy, stage management, puppetry; 122 teachers; 566 students; library of 85,000 vols; Rector E. N. GUGUSHVILI.

Georgian Veterinary Training and Research Institute: 380107 Krtsanisi, Tbilisi; tel. 72-37-52; f. 1932; 105 teachers; 2,250 students; library of 200,000 vols; Rector V. G. MAMATELASHVILI.

Gori Economics Institute: 383500 Gori, Pr. Chavchavadze 57; tel. 24-13.

Kutaisi N. I. Muskhelishvili Technical University: 384014 Kutaisi, Pr. Molodezhi 98; tel. 3-40-27; telex 601558; f. 1974; faculties: mechanical and technological, automotive, technology, humanitarian sciences, light industry; 360 teachers; 6,427 students; library of 148,800 vols; Rector ARCHIL KOSTAVA.

Tbilisi Academy of Arts: 380008 Tbilisi, Ul. Griboedova 22; tel. 93-69-59, 93-78-93; f. 1922; depts: decorative arts, applied arts, textiles, architecture, sculpture; library of 42,000 vols; publ. *Works* (annually).

Tbilisi State Pedagogical Institute of Foreign Languages: 380062 Tbilisi, Pr. Chavchavadze 45; tel. 22-17-03, 22-03-57.

Tbilisi V. Saradzhishvili State Conservatoire: 380004 Tbilisi, Ul. Griboedova 8; tel. 99-91-44; fax 99-91-44; f. 1917; courses: piano, singing, choral conducting, composition, orchestral instruments, musicology; 205 teachers; 700 students; library of 100,000 vols; Rector N. K. GABUNIA.

GERMANY

Learned Societies

GENERAL

Akademie der Künste (Academy of Arts): 10557 Berlin, Hanseatenweg 10; tel. (30) 390007-0; fax (30) 390007-71; f. 1696; sections of Fine Art, Architecture, Music, Literature, Performing Arts, Film and Media Arts; 256 mems; Pres. WALTER JENS; publ. *Hanseatenweg 10* (2 a year).

Akademie der Wissenschaften in Göttingen (Göttingen Academy of Sciences and Humanities): 37073 Göttingen, Theaterstr. 7; tel. (551) 395362; fax (551) 395365; f. 1751; sections of Philology and History, Mathematics and Physics; 317 mems and corresp. mems; Pres. Prof. Dr GERHARD GOTTSCHALK; Sec. Prof. HEINZ GEORG WAGNER; publs *Nachrichten, Abhandlungen, Göttingische Gelehrte Anzeigen*.

Akademie der Wissenschaften und der Literatur Mainz (Mainz Academy of Sciences, Humanities and Literature): 55131 Mainz, Geschwister Schollstr. 2; tel. (6131) 577-0; fax (6131) 577-111; f. 1949; sections of Mathematics and Natural Sciences (Vice-Pres. Prof. Dr ELKE LÜTJEN-DRECOLL), Philosophy and Social Sciences (Vice-Pres. Prof. Dr WOLFGANG P. SCHMID), Literature (Vice-Pres. WALTER HELMUT FRITZ); 98 mems; Pres. Prof. Dr CLEMENS ZINTZEN; Sec.-Gen. Dr WULF THOMMEL; publs *Abhandlungen, Forschungsreihen*.

Bayerische Akademie der Wissenschaften (Bavarian Academy of Sciences and Humanities): 80539 Munich, Marstallplatz 8; tel. (89) 23031-0; fax 23031-100; e-mail aw002aa@lrz1.lrz-muenchen.de; f. 1759; sections of Philosophy and History (Secs Prof. Dr KLAUS STRUNK, Prof. Dr PETER LANDAU), Mathematics and Natural Sciences (Secs Prof. Dr HUBERT ZIEGLER, Prof. Dr ROLAND BULIRSCH); 129 mems; Pres. Prof. Dr HEINRICH NÖTH.

Berlin-Brandenburgische Akademie der Wissenschaften (Berlin Academy of Sciences and Humanities): 10106 Berlin, Postfach 238; tel. (30) 20370-0; fax (30) 20370-500; e-mail bbaw@bbaw.de; f. 1700; sections of Humanities, of Social Sciences, of Mathematics and Natural Sciences, of Biological and Medical Sciences, of Engineering Sciences; 113 ordinary mems, 33 extraordinary mems, 3 hon. mems; Pres. Prof. Dr DIETER SIMON; Sec.-Gen. DIEPOLD SALVINI-PLAWEN.

Deutsche Akademie der Naturforscher Leopoldina (Leopoldina German Academy of Researchers in Natural Sciences): 06108 Halle/Saale, August-Bebel-Str. 50A; tel. (345) 2025014; fax (345) 2021727; e-mail president@leopoldina.uni-halle.de; f. 1652; sections of Medicine (Vice-Pres. Prof. Dr GOTTFRIED GEILER), Natural Sciences (Vice-Pres. Prof. Dr ALFRED SCHELLENBERGER); 950 mems; archive: see Libraries and Archives; Pres. Prof. Dr BENNO PARTHIER; Sec.-Gen. Dr AXEL NELLES; publs *Nova acta Leopoldina* (Neue Folge), *Leopoldina Informationen, Acta historica Leopoldina*.

Goethe-Gesellschaft in Weimar eV: 99403 Weimar, Burgplatz 4, Postfach 2251; tel. (3643) 202050; fax (3643) 202050; f. 1885; literature, art and history of Goethe's time; 4,500 mems; Pres. Prof. Dr WERNER KELLER; Dir Dr GUNTER RENTZSCH; publs *Goethe-Jahrbuch, Schriften der G.G.* (irregular).

Goethe-Institut: 80604 Munich, PF 190419; premises at: 80637 Munich, Helene-Weber-Allee 1; tel. (89) 15921-0; fax (89) 15921-450; e-mail zv@goethe.de; f. 1951 to promote a wider knowledge abroad of the German language and to foster cultural co-operation with other countries; 141 brs abroad, 18 in Germany; Pres. Prof. HILMAR HOFFMANN; Sec.-Gen. Dr JOACHIM SARTORIUS; publs *Jahrbuch, Spracharbeit*.

Heidelberger Akademie der Wissenschaften (Heidelberg Academy of Sciences and Humanities): 69117 Heidelberg, Karlstr. 4, Postfach 102769; tel. (6221) 543265; fax (6221) 543355; f. 1909; sections of Mathematics and Natural Sciences (Sec. Prof. Dr FRIEDRICH VOGEL), Philosophy and History (Sec. Prof. Dr GÉZA ALFÖLDY); Pres. Prof. Dr GOTTFRIED SEEBASS; Man. Dir GUNTHER JOST.

Institut für Auslandsbeziehungen (Institute for Foreign Cultural Relations): 70020 Stuttgart, Pf. 102463; 70173 Stuttgart, Charlottenplatz 17; tel. (711) 2225-0; telex 723772; fax (711) 2264346; e-mail info@infa.de; f. 1917; library of 380,000 vols; Pres. ALOIS GRAF VON WALDBURG-ZEIT; Gen. Sec. DR KURT-JÜRGEN MAASS; publs *Zeitschrift für Kulturaustausch, Materialien zum Internationalen Kulturaustausch, Reihe Dokumentation*.

Inter Nationes: 53175 Bonn, Kennedyallee 91–103; tel. (228) 880-0; telex 17228308; fax (228) 880457; f. 1952; non-profit organization with the object of strengthening cultural relations between foreign countries and Germany; Chair. Dr DIETER W. BENECKE; publs *Kulturchronik* (every 2 months), *Humboldt* (3 a year), *Fikrun wa fann* (2 a year), *Education and Science* (quarterly).

Konferenz der Deutschen Akademien der Wissenschaften (Conference of the German Academies of Sciences and Humanities): 55131 Mainz, Geschwister-Scholl-Str. 2; tel. (6131) 573735; fax (6131) 51316; f. 1973; consists of academies of sciences and humanities in Berlin, Düsseldorf, Göttingen, Heidelberg, Leipzig, Mainz and Munich; deals with research projects common to the academies and co-ordinates the work of their mems; Sec. (vacant); publ. *Akademie-Journal* (2 a year).

Nordrhein-Westfälische Akademie der Wissenschaften (Northrhine-Westphalia Academy of Sciences and Humanities): 40217 Düsseldorf, Palmenstr. 16; tel. (211) 342051; fax (211) 341475; f. 1950; sections of Natural, Engineering and Economic Sciences, Philosophy; 166 mems; Pres. Prof. Dr PAUL MIKAT; publs *Sitzungsberichte, Abhandlungen*.

Sächsische Akademie der Wissenschaften zu Leipzig (Saxon Academy of Sciences and Humanities in Leipzig): 04107 Leipzig, Karl-Tauchnitz-Str. 1; tel. (341) 711530; f. 1846; sections of Mathematics and Natural Sciences (Sec. Prof. Dr KLAUS BEYER), Philology and History (Sec. Prof. Dr KURT NOWAK), Technical Sciences (Sec. Prof. Dr EUGEN-GEORG WOSCHNI); 100 mems, 70 corresp. mems; Pres. Prof. Dr GOTTHARD LERCHNER; publs *Abhandlungen, Sitzungsberichte*.

AGRICULTURE, FISHERIES AND VETERINARY SCIENCE

Agrarsoziale Gesellschaft eV (ASG): 37001 Göttingen, Postfach 1144; premises at 37073, Göttingen, Kurze Geismarstr. 33; tel. (551) 497090; fax (551) 49709-16; e-mail asggoe@girdg.de; f. 1947; 389 mems, plus 168 corporate mems; library of 6,000 vols; Pres. MANFRED MERFORTH; Sec. Dr DIETER CZECH; publs *Ländlicher Raum-Rundbrief der ASG, Schriftenreihe für ländliche Sozialfragen, Materialsammlung der ASG, Arbeitsbericht der ASG, Kleine Reihe der ASG*.

Dachverband Wissenschaftlicher Gesellschaften der Agrar-, Forst-, Ernährungs-, Veterinär- und Umweltforschung eV: 60489 Frankfurt, a. M., Eschbormer Landstr. 122; tel. (69) 24788104; fax (69) 24788110; f. 1973; advancement and co-ordination of research; information; contacts; representation; 29 mems; Pres. Prof. Dr W. WERNER; Man. Dir R. DÖRRE.

Deutsche Landwirtschafts-Gesellschaft (German Agricultural Society): 60489 Frankfurt a.M., Eschborner Landstr. 122; tel. (69) 24788-0; fax (69) 24788110; e-mail info@DLG-Frankfurt.de; f. originally 1885, refounded 1947; 16,000 mems; Pres. PHILIP VON DEM BUSSCHE; Dir Dr DIETRICH RIEGER; publs *Mitteilungen, Das wirtschaftseigene Futter, Zeitschrift für Agrargeschichte und Agrarsoziologie* (quarterly), *Journal of International Agriculture, Entwicklung und ländlicher Raum, Zeitschrift für Bewässerungswirtschaft, Übersichten zur Tierernährung*.

Deutsche Veterinärmedizinische Gesellschaft: 35392 Giessen, Frankfurter Str. 89; tel. (641) 24466; fax (641) 25375; f. 1952; 4,000 mems; Pres. Prof. Dr HOLGER MARTENS; Sec. Prof. Dr Dr h.c. E. WEISS; publ. *Kongressbericht* (every 2 years).

Deutscher Forstwirtschaftsrat eV: 53359 Rheinbach bei Bonn, Münstereifeler Str. 19; tel. (2226) 2350; fax (2226) 5792; f. 1950; promotion of forestry; 64 mems; Pres. Bürgermeister HERMANN ILAENDER; Man. Forstdirektor MARTIN STRITTMATTER.

Verband Deutscher Landwirtschaftlicher Untersuchungs- und Forschungsanstalten eV (VDLUFA) (Association of German Agricultural Research Institutes): 64293 Darmstadt, Bismarckstr. 41A; tel. (6151) 26485; fax (6151) 293370; f. 1888; Pres. Prof. Dr habil. GERHARD BREITSCHUH; Sec. Gen. Dr CHRISTOF BRAUN; publs *Agribiological Research* (annual vol.), *Handbuch der landwirtschaftlichen Versuchs- und Untersuchungsmethodik, Mitteilungen, Presseinformationen, VDLUFA-Schriftenreihe*.

ARCHITECTURE AND TOWN PLANNING

DAI – Verband Deutscher Architekten- und Ingenieurvereine eV: 53113 Bonn, Adenauerallee 58; tel. (228) 211453; fax (228) 213213; f. 1871; 5,500 mems; Chair. Prof. Dr-Ing. JÜRGEN FISSLER; publ. *DAI-Verbandszeitschrift BAUKULTUR*.

Deutscher Verband für Wohnungswesen, Städtebau und Raumordnung eV (German Federation for Housing and Planning): 53119 Bonn, Ellerstr. 58; tel. (228) 657013; fax (228) 692271; f. 1946; independent research in housing, town and country planning; 700 mems; Pres. Bundesminister a.D. KARL RAVENS; Sec.-Gen. Dr HANS-LUDWIG OBERBECKMANN.

Fraunhofer-Informationszentrum Raum und Bau (IRB) (Fraunhofer Information Centre for Regional Planning and Building Construction): 70569 Stuttgart, Nobelstr. 12; tel. (711) 970-2500; telex 7255168; fax (711) 970-2508; e-mail irb@irb.fhg.de; f. 1941; collects, processes and provides specialized information on building, structural engineering, architecture, regional and urban planning, and housing; library of 105,000 vols and 50,000 research reports, standards, test certificates and licences; Dir Dr-Ing. W. WISSMANN; publs *Schadenfreis Bauen, Bauschäden-Sammlung, Bauforschung für die Praxis, Sanierungsgrundlagen Plattenbau, IRB Literaturdokumentationen, ARCONIS Wissen zum Planen und Bauen und zum Baumarkt, Internationale Zeitschrift für Bauinstandsetzen, Markt- und Planungsdaten für die Bauwirtschaft, Kurzberichte aus der Bauforschung*.

BIBLIOGRAPHY, LIBRARY SCIENCE AND MUSEOLOGY

Arbeitsgemeinschaft der Spezialbibliotheken eV: C/o Universitätsbibliothek Karlsruhe (attn Frau Eckl), 76049 Karlsruhe, Postfach 6920; tel. (721) 608-3128; fax (721) 608-4886; e-mail ub@ubka.uni-karlsruhe.de; f. 1946; service to specialized libraries; 664 mems; Pres. Dipl.-Ing. C.-H. SCHÜTTE; publs *Information, Berichte der Arbeits- und Fortbildungstagung* (every 2 years).

Deutsche Gesellschaft für Dokumentation eV: 60314 Frankfurt a.M., Ostbahnhofstr. 13; tel. (69) 430313; fax (69) 4909096; f. 1948; promotion of information and documentation, information science and practice; 2,000 mems; Pres. Prof. Dr JOACHIM-FELIX LEONHARD; publs *Deutscher Dokumentartag* (annually), *DGD-Online-Conference* (annually), *Nachrichten für Dokumentation* (every 2 months), *Information–Wissenschaft und Praxis*.

Deutscher Museumsbund eV (German Museums Association): C/o Deutsches Hygiene-Museum, 01069 Dresden, Lingnerplatz 1; tel. (351) 4846324; fax (351) 4955162; e-mail dmb@dhmd.de; f. 1917; to promote museums, their development and museology; 1,200 mems; Pres. Dr MARTIN ROTH; Vice-Pres. Dr WERNER HILGERS; publs *Museumskunde* (2 a year), *Bulletin* (quarterly).

Deutsches Bibliotheksinstitut: 10559 Berlin, Alt-Moabit 101A; tel. (30) 39077-0; fax (30) 39077-100; f. 1978; provides services, research publs and advanced training for librarians; 150 mems; Dir Prof. GÜNTER BEYERSDORFF; publs *Bibliotheksdienst* (monthly), *dbi—materialien* (irregular).

Internationale Vereinigung der Musikbibliotheken, Musikarchive und Musikdokumentationszentren Gruppe BRD (International Asscn of Music Libraries, FRG Branch): C/o Dr Joachim Jaenecke, Staatsbibliothek zu Berlin – Musikabteilung, 10102 Berlin; tel. (30) 2661673; fax (30) 2661624; Pres. Prof. Dr WOLFGANG KRÜGER.

Verein der Bibliothekare und Assistenten eV (Asscn of Librarians in Public Libraries): 72703 Reutlingen, POB 13 24, Gartenstr. 18; tel. (7121) 34910; fax (7121) 300433; e-mail bub.vba@t-online.de; f. 1949; 4,350 mems; Pres. Prof. Dr KONRAD UMALUF; Sec. KATHARINA BOULANGER; publ. *Buch und Bibliothek* (10 a year).

Verein Deutscher Bibliothekare eV (Association of German Librarians): 48043 Münster, Postfach 8029; premises at: 48143 Münster, Universitäts- und Landesbibliothek, Krummer Timpen 3–5; tel. (251) 8324023; fax (251) 8328398; e-mail hilgema@uni-muenster.de; f. 1900, re-f. 1948; Pres. Dr KLAUS HILGEMANN; Sec. Dr LYDIA JUNGNICKEL; publs *Zeitschrift für Bibliothekswesen und Bibliographie* (every 2 months), *Rundschreiben* (quarterly), *Jahrbuch der Deutschen Bibliotheken* (every 2 years).

Württembergische Bibliotheksgesellschaft (Society of Friends of the Württemberg State Library): 70047 Stuttgart, Postfach 105441; tel. (711) 212-4428; fax (711) 212-4422; f. 1946 to support the reconstruction of the Württemberg State Library, to hold lectures, meetings, exhibitions, etc.; 500 mems; Pres. (vacant); Chair. Dr WULF D. VON LUCIUS; Sec. ELISABETH TOSTA.

ECONOMICS, LAW AND POLITICS

Akademie für Fernstudium und Weiterbildung Bad Harzburg (Academy for Distance Study): 38667 Bad Harzburg, An den Weiden 15; tel. (5322) 906130; Dir DIETMAR BORSCH.

Deutsche Gesellschaft für Auswärtige Politik eV (German Society for Foreign Affairs): 53113 Bonn, Adenauerallee 131; tel. (228) 2675-0; fax (228) 2675-173; e-mail dgap@compuserve.com; and 10787 Berlin, Rauchstr. 18; tel. (30) 25423100; fax (30) 25423116; e-mail dgap.berlin@t-online.de; f. 1955; 1,650 mems; discusses and promotes research on problems of international politics; research library of 52,000 vols; Pres. Dr WERNER LAMBY; Exec. Vice-Pres. REINHARD SCHLAGINTWERF; Dirs Research Institute, Prof. Dr KARL KAISER, Dr JOACHIM KRAUSE; publs *Die Internationale Politik* (yearbook), *Internationale Politik* (monthly).

Deutsche Gesellschaft für Osteuropakunde eV (German Society for Eastern European Studies): 10719 Berlin, Schaperstr. 30; tel. (30) 21478412; fax (30) 21478414; e-mail dgo@zedat.fu-berlin.de; f. 1913; 800 mems; Pres OTTO WOLFF VON AMERONGEN; Dir Dr THOMAS BREMER; publs *Osteuropa* (monthly), *Osteuropa-Recht, Osteuropa-Wirtschaft* (quarterly).

Deutsche Gesellschaft für Versicherungsmathematik (Deutscher Aktuarverein): 50667 Cologne, Komödienstr. 44; tel. (221) 912554-0; fax (221) 912554-44; f. 1948; society for promotion of actuarial theory in collaboration with the universities; 838 mems; Pres Dr MARTIN BALLEER; Sec. KLAUS ALLERDISSEN; publ. *Blätter* (2 a year).

Deutsche Gesellschaft für Völkerrecht (International Law): 24098 Kiel, Olshausenstr. 40; f. 1917, re-f. 1949; 230 mems; Pres. Prof. Dr JOST DELBRÜCK; publ. *Berichte* (every 2 years).

Deutsche Statistische Gesellschaft: 14195 Berlin, Garystr. 21; tel. (30) 8385791; fax (30) 8386629; e-mail dgst@wiwiss.fu-berlin.de; f. 1911; 850 mems; Pres. Prof. Dr P.-TH. WILRICH; Sec. C. TERTON; publs *Allgemeines Statistisches Archiv* (quarterly), *Sonderhefte zum Allgemeinen Statistischen Archiv* (irregular).

Deutsche Vereinigung für Politische Wissenschaft (German Political Science Association): 64283 Darmstadt, Residenzschloss; tel. (6151) 163197; fax (6151) 162397; e-mail dvpw@hrz1.hrz.tu-darmstadt.de; f. 1951; 1,200 mems; Pres. Prof. Dr CHRISTINE LANDFRIED; Dir FELIX W. WURM; publ. *Politische Vierteljahresschrift* (quarterly).

Deutscher Juristentag eV: 53111 Bonn, Oxfordstr. 21, Sterntorhaus; tel. (228) 9839135; fax (228) 9839140; f. 1860; furthers discussion among jurists; 8,200 mems; Sec. Dr A. NADLER.

Gesellschaft für öffentliche Wirtschaft (Society for Public Economy): 12159 Berlin, Sponholzstr. 11; tel. (30) 8521045; f. 1951; 90 mems; research and information on public enterprises; Pres. FELIX ZIMMERMAN; Dir WOLF LEETZ; publ. *Zeitschrift für öffentliche und gemeinwirtschaftliche Unternehmen* (quarterly).

Gesellschaft für Rechtsvergleichung (Society for Comparative Law): 79098 Freiburg, Belfortstr. 16; tel. (761) 2032126; fax (761) 2032127; f. 1894; 1,400 mems; Chair. Prof. Dr UWE BLAUROCK; Sec.-Gen. Prof. Dr GERHARD HOHLOCH; publs *Arbeiten zur Rechtsvergleichung, Ausländische Aktiengesetze, Mitteilungen*.

Gesellschaft für Sozial- und Wirtschaftsgeschichte (Society for Social and Economic History): c/o The Pres. Prof. Dr J. Schneider, Lehrstuhl für Wirtschafts- und Sozialgeschichte, Universität Bamberg, Postfach 1549, 96045 Bamberg; tel. (951) 863-2324; f. 1961; 220 mems; Pres. Prof. Dr J. SCHNEIDER; Sec. Prof. Dr R. WALTER.

Kommission für Geschichte des Parlamentarismus und der politischen Parteien (Commission for History of Parliamentarism and Political Parties): 53115 Bonn, Colmantstr. 39; f. 1951; Pres. Prof. Dr R. MORSEY; Gen. Sec. Dr M. SCHUMACHER; publs *Beiträge zur Geschichte des Parlamentarismus und der politischen Parteien, Quellen zur Geschichte des Parlamentarismus und der politischen Parteien, Bibliographien, Handbücher, Photodokumente*.

EDUCATION

Deutscher Akademischer Austauschdienst (DAAD) (German Academic Exchange Service): 53175 Bonn, Postfach 200404; tel. 8820; telex 885515; fax (228) 882-444; branch offices: Jägerstr. 23, 10117 Berlin, Germany; DFHK, Deutsches Sekretariat, Schönborner Hof, Schillerstr. 11, 55116 Mainz, Germany; 34 Belgrave Sq, London SW1X 8QB, England; 9 rue Maspéro, 75116 Paris, France; Maison Heinrich Heine, 27C, bd Jourdan, 75014 Paris, France; 11 Sharia Saleh Ayyoub, Cairo-Zamalek, Egypt; 176 Golf Links, New Delhi 110003, India; 950 Third Ave, 19th Floor, New York, NY 10022, USA; Rua Pres. Carlos de Campos 417, 22231-080 Rio de Janeiro, Brazil; POB 14050 Nairobi, Kenya; Akasaka 7-5-56, Minato-ku, Tokyo 107, Japan; c/o CONARE, Apdo 374, 2050 San Pedro Montes de Oca, Costa Rica; Jl. Jend. SUDIRMAN, Kav. 61–62, Summitmas I, It.19, Jakarta 12190, Indonesia; Leninski Prospekt, 95A, 117313 Moscow, Russia; C/o Beijing Waiguoyu Daxue, POB 8110-46, Xisanhuanbeilu Nr. 2, 100081 Beijing, People's Republic of China; f. 1925; exchange of professors, lecturers in German for foreign universities, IAESTE—student-trainees, scholarships for German and foreign students and graduates, etc.; Pres. Prof. Dr THEODOR BERCHEM; Gen. Sec. Dr CHRISTIAN BODE.

Deutscher Volkshochschul-Verband eV (German Adult Education Association): 53225 Bonn, Obere Wilhelmstr. 32; tel. (228) 97569-0; f. 1953; 16 regional associations of 1,100 Volkshochschulen with 4,000 brs; f. 1979; Pres. Prof. Dr RITA SÜSSMUTH, MP; Chair. DORIS ODENDAHL, MP; Dir Dr VOLKER OTTO; publs *DVV magazin Volkshochschule* (quarterly), *Adult Education and Development* (2 a year, English, French and Spanish).

Hochschulrektorenkonferenz (Rectors' and Presidents' Conference): 53175 Bonn, Ahrstr. 39; tel. (228) 887-0; fax (228) 887110; f. 1949; the central voluntary body representing the universities and higher education institutions; 257 mems; Pres. Prof. Dr KLAUS LANDFRIED; Sec.-Gen. Dr JOSEF LANGE.

Humboldt Gesellschaft für Wissenschaft, Kunst und Bildung eV (Humboldt Society for Science, Art and Education): 68307 Mannheim 31, Riedlach 12; f. 1962; 710 mems; Pres. Prof. Dr HERBERT KESSLER; Chair. Prof. Dr GUDRUN HÖHL.

Katholischer Akademischer Ausländer-Dienst: 53129 Bonn, Hausdorffstr. 151; tel. 917580; fax 9175858; e-mail kaad-de@t-online .de; f. 1956; co-ordinates activities of Catholic organizations concerned with foreign students in Germany and grants scholarships; Pres. Prof. Dr PETER HÜNERMANN; Dir Dr HERMANN WEBER; publs *Jahresbericht*, *Jahresakademie* (all annually).

FINE AND PERFORMING ARTS

Bayerische Akademie der Schönen Künste: 80539 Munich, Max-Joseph-Platz 3; tel. (89) 290077-0; Pres. Prof. Dr WIELAND SCHMIED; Gen. Sec. Dr OSWALD GEORG BAUER.

Deutsche Gesellschaft für Photographie eV (German Society for Photography): 50676 Cologne, Overstolzenhaus, Rheingasse 8–12; tel. (221) 9232069; fax 9232070; f. 1951; 1,000 mems; Pres. Prof. Dr KARL STEINORTH; Gen. Sec. GERT KOSHOFER.

Deutsche Mozart-Gesellschaft eV (German Mozart Society): 86152 Augsburg, Frauentorstr. 30; tel. (821) 518588; fax (821) 157228; f. 1951; 3,500 mems; Pres. Dr FRIEDHELM BRUSNIAK; publ. *Acta Mozartiana*.

Deutscher Komponisten-Interressenverband eV (German Composers' Association): 12205 Berlin, Kadettenweg 80B; tel. (30) 833-4121; fax (30) 833-0713; f. 1954; 1,500 mems; Pres. KARL HEINZ WAHREN; Dir MANUEL NEUENDORF.

Deutscher Verein für Kunstwissenschaft eV (Society for the Study of German Art): 10623 Berlin, Jebensstr. 2; tel. (30) 3139932; f. 1908; 1,000 mems; Chair. Prof. Dr RAINER KAHSNITZ; Sec. (vacant); publs *Denkmäler deutscher Kunst*, *Zeitschrift*, *Schrifttum zur Deutschen Kunst*, *Forschungen zur deutschen Kunstgeschichte*.

Institut für den Wissenschaftlichen Film (Scientific Film Institute): 37075 Göttingen, Nonnenstieg 72; tel. (551) 5024-0; fax (551) 5024-400; e-mail iwf-goe@iwf.gwdg.de; f. 1956; 117 mems; library of 7,000 films for higher education; Deputy Dir Dr-Ing. HARTMUT RUDOLPH (acting); Man. Dr H. U. Frhr VON SPIEGEL; publs *Gesamtverzeichnis der wissenschaftlichen Filme*, *Encyclopaedia Cinematographica*, *Publikationen zu wissenschaftlichen Filmen*, *IWF aktuell*.

Kestner-Gesellschaft: 30159 Hanover, Goseriede 11; tel. (511) 70120-0; fax (511) 70120-20; f. 1916; 3,000 mems; activities concerned with the promotion of modern art; Pres. WILHELM SANDMANN; Dir Dr CARL HAENLEIN.

Stiftung Preussischer Kulturbesitz (Prussian Cultural Foundation): 10785 Berlin, Von-der-Heydt-Str. 16–18; f. 1961 to preserve, augment and reunite the Prussian cultural heritage; comprises 17 State Museums, the State Library, the State Privy Archives, the Iberian-American Institute and the State Institute for Research in Music with the Museum for Musical Instruments; Pres. (vacant).

Verband Deutscher Kunsthistoriker eV (Asscn of German Art Historians): C/o Dr Andrew John Martin, Zentralinstitut für Kunstgeschichte, 80333 Munich, Meiserstr. 10; tel. (89) 553488; fax (89) 54505221; f. 1948; 1,300 mems; Pres. Dr SYBILLE EBERT-SCHIFFERER; Sec. Dr ANDREW JOHN MARTIN; publ. *Kunstchronik* (monthly).

HISTORY, GEOGRAPHY AND ARCHAEOLOGY

Arbeitsgemeinschaft Historischer Kommissionen und Landesgeschichtlicher Institute (Association of Historic Councils and Regional History Institutes): 35037 Marburg/Lahn, Gisonenweg 5–7; tel. (6421) 1840; f. 1898; controls 56 societies and institutes; Pres. Prof. Dr RODERICH SCHMIDT.

Deutsche Akademie für Landeskunde (German Academy for Geography of Germany): 69120 Heidelberg, Im Neuenheimer Feld 348; tel. (6221) 1544536; fax (6221) 545585; f. 1882, re-f. 1946; study of German regional geography; Pres. Prof. Dr HANS GEBHARDT; Sec. Dr FRANZ SCHYMIK; publs *Berichte zur deutschen Landeskunde*, *Forschungen zur deutschen Landeskunde* (2 a year), *Neues Schrifttum zur deutschen Landeskunde*.

Deutsche Gesellschaft für Geographie: C/o Geographical Institute, Gerhard-Mercator-Universität Duisburg, 47048 Duisburg, Lotharstr. 1; tel. (203) 3792250; fax (203) 3793516; e-mail blotevogel@uni-duisburg.de; Pres. Prof. Dr HANS H. BLOTEVOGEL; Sec.-Gen. Dr GERALD WOOD.

Deutsche Gesellschaft für Kartographie eV: 80333 Munich, Karlstr. 6; tel. (89) 54506820; fax (89) 54506820; f. 1950; promotes scientific and practical cartography; 2,530 mems; Pres. Prof. Dr THEODOR WINTGES; Sec. RONALD BOYÉ; publ. *Kartographische Nachrichten* (every 2 months).

Deutsche Gesellschaft für Ortung und Navigation eV (German Institute of Navigation): 40211 Düsseldorf, Pempelforter Str. 47; fax (211) 351645; f. 1951 as Ausschuss für Funkortung, 1961 under present title; to promote research and development of methods and systems used for navigation; Pres. Dr G. BOUCKE; publ. *Ortung und Navigation* (3 a year).

Deutsche Quartärvereinigung eV (Quaternary Union): 30631 Hannover, POB 510153; located at: 30655 Hannover, Stilleweg 2; tel. (511) 6432487; fax (511) 6432304; f. 1950; 650 mems; Pres. Prof. Dr H. HAGEDORN; publ. *Eiszeitalter und Gegenwart*.

Deutscher Nautischer Verein von 1868 eV (German Nautical Association of 1868): 21147 Hamburg, Striepenweg 31; tel. (40) 796-0105; fax (40) 796-0806; f. 1868; 4,196 mems in 21 local Nautical Associations, 40 corporate mems; Pres. FRANK LEONHARDT; Sec. Capt. GARRIT LEEMREIJZE.

Fränkische Geographische Gesellschaft: 91054 Erlangen, Kochstr. 4; tel. (9131) 852645; fax (9131) 852013; f. 1954; library of 9,500 vols; 900 mems; Dir Prof. Dr HORST KOPP; Gen. Secs Prof. Dr HILMAR SCHROEDER, Prof. Dr UWE TRETER; publs *Mitteilungen* (annually), *Erlanger Geographische Arbeiten*.

Gesamtverein der Deutschen Geschichts- und Altertumsvereine (Union of German Historical and Archaeological Societies): 30169 Hanover, Am Archiv 1; f. 1852; 238 affiliated asscns; Pres. Dr D. BROSIUS; Treas. Dr M. TREML; publ. *Blätter für deutsche Landesgeschichte*.

Gesellschaft für Erd- und Völkerkunde (Geographical and Anthropological Society): 53115 Bonn, Meckenheimer Allee 166; tel. (228) 737506; f. 1910; 300 mems; Pres. Prof. Dr EBERHARD MAYER; Sec. Dr GÜNTER MENZ.

Gesellschaft für Erdkunde zu Berlin (Berlin Geographical Society): 12165 Berlin, Arno-Holz-Str. 14; tel. (30) 791-90-01; fax (30) 793-32-49; f. 1828; 500 mems; library of *c.* 100,000 vols; Pres. Dr DIETER BIEWALD; Sec. Dr KIRSTEN GEHRENKEMPER; publ. *Die Erde (Zeitschrift der Gesellschaft für Erdkunde zu Berlin)* (quarterly).

Monumenta Germaniae Historica: 80099 Munich 34, Ludwigstr. 16, Pf. 34 02 23; tel. (89) 28638384; fax (89) 281419; e-mail verlag@mgh .de; f. 1819; library of 87,000 vols; Pres. Prof. Dr RUDOLF SCHIEFFER; Sec. Dr WOLFRAM SETZ; Librarian Dr ARNO MENTZEL-REUTERS; publ. *Deutsches Archiv für Erforschung des Mittelalters*.

Verband der Historiker Deutschlands (Union of German Historians): C/o Prof. Dr Heinz Duchhardt, 55116 Mainz, Alte Universitätstr. 19; f. 1893, re-f. 1949; 2,300 mems; Pres. Prof. Dr JOHANNES FRIED; Gen. Sec. Dr HEINZ DUCHHARDT.

LANGUAGE AND LITERATURE

Deutsche Gesellschaft für Sprachwissenschaft (German Society for Linguistics): C/o Bernd Kortmann, Albert-Ludwigs-Universität Freiburg (Engl. Seminar), 79098 Freiburg i. Br.; fax (761) 2033330; e-mail kortmann@ruf.uni-freiburg.de; f. 1978 for the advancement of the scientific investigation of language, and the support of linguists engaged in this; 1,000 mems; Pres. Prof. Dr EKKEHARD KÖNIG; Sec. Prof. Dr BERND KORTMANN; publs *Mitteilungen der DGfS* (2 a year), *Zeitschrift für Sprachwissenschaft* (2 a year).

Gesellschaft für deutsche Sprache eV (Society for the German Language): 65183 Wiesbaden, Spiegelgasse 11; tel. (611) 999550; fax (611) 9995530; f. 1947; 2,500 mems; library of 9,000 vols; Dir Prof. Dr GÜNTHER PFLUG; publs *Muttersprache* (quarterly), *Der Sprachdienst* (every 2 months).

Hölderlin-Gesellschaft eV: 72070 Tübingen, Hölderlinhaus; tel. (7071) 22040; fax (7071) 22948; f. 1943, reconstituted 1946; 1,500 mems; Pres. Prof. Dr GERHARD KURZ; publs *Hölderlin-Jahrbuch* (every 2 years), *Schriften der Hölderlin-Gesellschaft* (irregular), *Turm-Vorträge*, *Lyrik im Hölderlinturm*.

Mommsen-Gesellschaft: 37073 Göttingen, Humboldt-allee 19 (Seminar für Klassische Philologie); tel. (551) 394743; f. 1950; 570 mems; association of university teachers of classics, ancient history and archaeology; Pres. Prof. Dr S. DÖPP; Sec. Dr MARCUS DEUFERT.

PEN Zentrum Bundesrepublik Deutschland: 64283 Darmstadt, Sandstr. 10; tel. (6151) 23120; fax (6151) 293414; f. 1951; 488 mems; Pres. CARL AMERY; Sec.-Gen. HANNS WERNER SCHWARZE.

MEDICINE

Anatomische Gesellschaft (Anatomical Society): 23538 Lübeck, Institut für Anatomie, Medizinische Universität, Lübeck, Ratzeburger Allee 160; tel. (451) 500-4030; fax (451) 5004034; f. 1886; 1,112 mems; Sec. Prof. Dr Med. WOLFGANG KÜHNEL; publ. *Anatomischer Anzeiger* (Annals of Anatomy).

Deutsche Dermatologische Gesellschaft: 72076 Tübingen, Hautklinik; f. 1888; 2,500 mems; Pres. and Sec.-Gen. Prof. Dr G. RASSNER; publ. *Hautarzt* (monthly).

Deutsche Gesellschaft für Anästhesiologie und Intensivmedizin: 90419 Nürnberg, Roritzerstr. 27; tel. (911) 933780; fax (911) 3938195; e-mail dgai@dgai-ev.de; f. 1953; 8,750 mems; Pres. Prof. Dr DETLEV PATSCHKE; Sec. Prof. Dr K. VAN ACKERN; publ. *Anästhesiologie und Intensivmedizin* (monthly).

Deutsche Gesellschaft für Angewandte Optik (German Society for Applied Optics): C/o Carl-Zeiss Jena GmbH, 73446 Oberkochen; tel. (7364) 203428; fax (7364) 204601; f. 1923; 680 mems; Pres. Dr F. MERKLE; Sec. Dr CH. BUDZINSKI; publ. *Optik* (monthly).

Deutsche Gesellschaft für Chirurgie (German Surgical Society): 81925 Munich, Elektrastr. 5; f. 1872; 3,444 mems; Pres. Prof. Dr C. HERFARTH; Sec. Prof. Dr W. HARTEL; publ. *Langenbecks Archiv für Chirurgie*.

Deutsche Gesellschaft für Endokrinologie: C/o Schering AG, 13342 Berlin; tel. (30)

46815802; telex 182030; fax (30) 46818056; f. 1953; 1,300 mems; Pres. Prof. Dr R. ZIEGLER; Sec. Dr URSULA-F. HABENICHT; publ. *Endokrinologie-Informationen* (6 a year).

Deutsche Gesellschaft für Gynäkologie und Geburtshilfe: 92224 Amberg, Mariahilfbergweg 7, Klinikum St. Marien, Frauenklinik; Pres. Prof. Dr D. BERG.

Deutsche Gesellschaft für Hals-Nasen-Ohren-Heilkunde, Kopf- und Hals-Chirurgie (Oto-rhino-laryngology): 53129 Bonn, Hittorfstr. 7; tel. (228) 231770; fax (228) 239385; e-mail dghnokhc@t-online.de; 10 European archives of oto-rhino-laryngology; Pres. Prof. Dr H. HILDMANN; Sec. Prof. Dr U. KOCH.

Deutsche Gesellschaft für Hygiene und Mikrobiologie: Hygiene-Institut der Universität, 69120 Heidelberg, Im Neuenheimer Feld 324; f. 1906; 1,700 mems; Chair. Prof. Dr E. STRAUBE; Sec. Prof. Dr Dr h.c. H.-G. SONNTAG.

Deutsche Gesellschaft für Innere Medizin (Internal Medicine): 65189 Wiesbaden, Humboldtstr. 14; tel. (611) 30-79-46; fax (611) 378260; f. 1882; 5,000 mems; Sec. Prof. Dr Dr h.c. mult. H.G. LASCH; publ. *Supplementum of abstracts* (annually).

Deutsche Gesellschaft für Kinderheilkunde und Jugendmedizin (Paediatrics and Adolescent Medicine): C/o Prof. Dr Lothar Pelz, Universitäts-Kinderklinik, Rembrandtstr. 16–17, 18057 Rostock; tel. (381) 494-7000; fax (381) 494-7002; f. 1883; 8,500 mems; Pres. Prof. Dr LOTHAR PELZ.

Deutsche Gesellschaft für Neurochirurgie: 45147 Essen, Hufelandstr. 55; f. 1950; 244 mems; Pres. Prof. Dr med. W. GROTE; Gen. Sec. Prof. Dr med. H. DIETZ.

Deutsche Gesellschaft für Orthopädie und Traumatologie: c/o Pres. Prof. Dr J. Kramer, Dir Orthop, Univ.-Klinik im St Josef-Hospital, Gudrunstr. 56, 44791 Bochum; f. 1901; Pres. Prof. Dr J. KRAMER.

Deutsche Gesellschaft für Physikalische Medizin und Rehabilitation: Klinik für Physikalische Medizin der Ludwig-Maximilians-Universität, 81377 Munich, Marchioninstr. 15; tel. (89) 70954050; fax (89) 70958836; f. 1886; physical medicine and rehabilitation; 550 mems; Pres. Prof. Dr E. SENN; publs *Physikalische Medizin*, *Rehabilitationsmedezin*, *Kurortmedizin* (every 2 months).

Deutsche Gesellschaft für Plastische und Wiederherstellungschirurgie eV (German Society for Plastic and Reconstructive Surgery): II Chir. Klinik f. Unfall-, Wiederherstellungs, Gefäss- u. Plastische Chirurgie, 27356 Rotenburg/Wümme, Diakoniekrankenhaus, Elise-Averdieck-Str. 17; f. 1962; 680 mems; Pres. Prof. Dr H. K. WEITZEL; Gen. Sec. Dr H. RUDOLPH.

Deutsche Gesellschaft für Psychiatrie, Psychotherapie und Nervenheilkunde (Psychiatry, Psychotherapy and Neurosciences): 45147 Essen, Virchowstr. 174; tel. (201) 7227201; fax (201) 7227303; f. 1842; 2,000 mems; Pres. Prof. Dr M. GASTPAR; Sec. Prof. Dr P. FALKAI; publs *Spektrum*, *Nervenarzt*.

Deutsche Gesellschaft für Psychoanalyse, Psychotherapie, Psychosomatik und Tiefenpsychologie (DGPT) eV: 20459 Hamburg, Johannisbollwerk 20 III; tel. (40) 319-26-19; fax (40) 319-43-00; f. 1949 to train psychotherapists; 2,400 mems; Pres. Dipl.-Psych. ANNE MARIE SCHLÖSSER; Dir HOLGER SCHILDT.

Deutsche Gesellschaft für Rechtsmedizin: 50823 Cologne, Melatengürtel 60–62; tel. (221) 478-4280; Pres. Prof. Dr med. MICHAEL STAAK.

Deutsche Gesellschaft für Sozialmedizin und Prävention (German Society for Social Medicine and Prevention): 39120 Magdeburg, Leipziger Str. 44; tel. (391) 532803; fax (391) 541-4258; f. 1964; 500 mems; Pres. Prof. Dr med. J. GOSTOMZYK; publ. *Das Gesundheitswesen* (monthly).

Deutsche Gesellschaft für Tropenmedizin und internationale Gesundheit: 20359 Hamburg, Bernhard-Nocht-Str. 74; f. 1962 to bring together persons interested in medical questions related to the tropics; 720 mems; Pres. Prof. J. KNOBLOCH; Sec. PD Dr G. D. BURCHARD.

Deutsche Gesellschaft für Zahn-, Mund- und Kieferheilkunde (German Scientific Society for Dentistry): 40237 Düsseldorf, Lindemannstr. 96; tel. (211) 682296; fax (211) 679-8132; e-mail info@dgzmk.de; f. 1859; 9,500 mems; Pres. Prof. Dr Dr W. WAGNER; Sec. Dr A. MEURER.

Deutsche Ophthalmologische Gesellschaft Heidelberg: 69120 Heidelberg, Berliner Str. 14; tel. (6221) 411787; fax (6221) 484616; f. 1857; 3,500 mems; Pres. Dr H. BUSSE; Sec. Prof. Dr H. E. VÖLCKER; publ. *Der Ophthalmologe* (monthly).

Deutsche Physiologische Gesellschaft eV: Physiologisches Institut der Universität, Kiel, Olshausenstr. 40, 24098 Kiel; tel. (431) 8802032; fax (431) 8804580; f. 1904; 820 mems; Pres. Prof. Dr med. Dr rer. nat. BURKHARDT BROMM; Sec. Prof. Dr med. MICHAEL ILLERT.

Deutsche Psychoanalytische Gesellschaft: 14195 Berlin, Arnimallee 12; f. 1910; psychoanalytic training, education and research; 500 mems; Pres. Prof. Dr JÜRGEN KÖRNER; publs *Forum der Psychoanalyse*, *Zeitschrift für Psychosomatische Medizin und Psychoanalyse*, *Praxis der Kinderpsychologie und Kinderpsychiatrie*.

Deutsche Psychoanalytische Vereinigung eV: 14199 Berlin, Sulzaer-Str. 3; tel. (30) 826-45-47; br. of the International Psychoanalytical Association; Pres. Dr E. GATTIG; Sec. Dr E. KAISER.

Vereinigung Westdeutscher Hals-, Nasen- und Ohrenärzte (Association of West German Oto-Rhino-Laryngologists): 51067 Cologne, HNO-Klinik, Städt. Krankenanstalten, Neufelderstr. 32; f. *c.* 1897; 1,370 mems; Sec. Prof. Dr med. T. BRUSIS.

NATURAL SCIENCES

General

Georg-Agricola Gesellschaft zur Förderung der Geschichte der Naturwissenschaften und der Technik eV: 44791 Bochum, Am Bergbaumuseum 28; tel. (234) 5877-140; fax (234) 5877-111; f. 1926; promotes study of the history of science and technology; 280 mems; 25 mem. asscns; Pres. Dr-Ing. H. GASSERT; Sec. Dr W. KROKER.

Gesellschaft Deutscher Naturforscher und Ärzte eV (German Society for Scientists and Doctors): 53604 Bad Honnef, Hauptstr. 5; tel. (2224) 9232-37; fax (2224) 9232-40; f. 1822; 5,700 mems; Pres. Prof. Dr DETLEV GANTEN; Gen. Sec. Dr ERNST TRUSCHEIT.

Görres-Gesellschaft zur Pflege der Wissenschaft: 50456 Cologne, Postfach 101618; f. 1876; over 3,000 mems; Pres. Prof. Dr Dr h.c. mult. PAUL MIKAT; Gen. Sec. Prof. Dr RUDOLF SCHIEFFER.

Joachim Jungius-Gesellschaft der Wissenschaften eV: 20146 Hamburg, Edmund-Siemers-Allee 1; tel. (40) 41-74-44; f. 1947; 92 ordinary mems; Pres. Prof. Dr OTTO KRAUS; Vice-Pres. Prof. Dr ERHARD KANTZENBACH; publs *Tagungen*, *Vorträge*, *Veröffentlichungen*, *Berichte*, *Wiss. Sitzungen*, *Kolloquien*.

Wissenschaftsrat (Science Council): 50968 Cologne, Brohlerstr. 11; tel. (221) 3776-0; e-mail post@wrat.de; f. 1957 through co-operation of Länder and Federal Governments; advisory and co-ordinating body for science policy; makes recommendations on the structural and curricular development of the universities and on the organization and promotion of science and research; 54 nominated mems in two commissions (Scientific and Administrative); Chair. Prof. Dr WINFRIED SCHULZE; Sec.-Gen. Dr WINFRIED BENZ; publ. *Empfehlungen und Stellungnahmen* (annually).

Biological Sciences

Bayerische Botanische Gesellschaft (Bavarian Botanical Society): 80638 Munich, Menzinger Str. 67; tel. (89) 17861-264 (-257); fax (89) 17861-193; f. 1890; research into the flora of Bavaria and adjacent countries; preservation of species and plant communities; 900 mems; library of 10,000 vols; Pres. Dr W. LIPPERT; publ. *Berichte*.

Deutsche Botanische Gesellschaft: C/o Lehrstahl für Pflanzenphysiologie, Universität Bayreuth, 95440 Bayreuth, Universitätsstr. 30; tel. (921) 552627; fax (921) 552642; e-mail christian.schaefer@uni-bayreuth.de; f. 1882; 1,050 mems; Pres. Prof. Dr E. BECK; publ. *Botanica Acta* (6 a year).

Deutsche Gesellschaft für allgemeine und angewandte Entomologie eV (German Society for General and Applied Entomology): 69221 Dossenheim, Schwabenheimer Str. 101; tel. (6221) 866238; fax (6221) 861222; f. 1976; 870 mems; Pres. Prof. Dr E. DICKLER; Sec.-Gen. Dr H. VOGT; publ. *Mitteilungen der DG aa E.*

Deutsche Gesellschaft für Züchtungskunde eV: 53113 Bonn, Adenauerallee 174; f. 1905; livestock breeding, animal housing, reproduction, hygiene, nutrition; *c.* 1,000 mems; Man. Dr K. WEMKEN; publ. *Züchtungskunde* (every 2 months).

Deutsche Malakozoologische Gesellschaft: 60325 Frankfurt a.M., Senckenberganlage 25; f. 1868; study of Mollusca; 270 mems; library of 20,000 vols; Pres. Dr VOLLRATH WIESE; Sec. Dr RONALD JANSSEN; publs *Archiv für Molluskenkunde* (2 a year), *Mitteilungen* (1–2 a year).

Deutsche Ornithologen-Gesellschaft eV: 78315 Möggingen/Radolfzell (Bodensee); f. 1850; 2,500 mems; Pres. Prof. Dr W. WILTSCHKÓ; publs *Journal für Ornithologie*, *Die Vogelwarte*.

Deutsche Phytomedizinische Gesellschaft eV (German Phytomedical Society): 53115 Bonn, Nussallee 9; f. 1949; 1,800 mems; Pres. Prof. Dr H.-W. DEHNE.

Deutsche Zoologische Gesellschaft eV (German Zoological Society): Poppelsdorfer Schloss, 53115 Bonn; f. 1890; 1,600 mems; Chair. Prof. Dr W. RATHMAYER; Sec. Dr HELGA EICHELBERG; publ. *Verhandlungen*.

Gesellschaft für Biochemie und Molekularbiologie: 60596 Frankfurt, Kennedyallee 70; tel. (69) 6303395; fax (69) 6303397; e-mail rose@gbm.uni-frankfurt.de; f. 1947; 5,000 mems; Chair. Prof. Dr H. BETZ; Sec. Prof. Dr U. BRANDT; publ. *BIOspektrum* (6 a year).

Gesellschaft für Naturkunde in Württemberg: 70191 Stuttgart, Rosenstein 1; tel. (711) 8936-115; fax (711) 8936-100; f. 1844; 860 mems; Pres. Prof. Dr U. KULL; publ. *Jahreshefte* (Editor Prof. Dr S. SEYBOLD).

Münchner Entomologische Gesellschaft eV (Munich Entomological Society): 81247 Munich, Münchhausenstr. 21; tel. (89) 81070; fax (89) 8107300; e-mail kld1109@mail

.lrz-muenchen.de; f. 1904; 550 mems; library of 10,000 vols, 651 periodicals; attached to library of the State Zoological Collection; Pres. Dr ROLAND GERSTMEIER; publs *Mitteilungen* (annually), *Nachrichtenblatt der Bayerischen Entomologen* (quarterly), *Bayerischer Entomologentag*.

Naturhistorische Gesellschaft Hannover (Hanover Society of Natural History): 30631 Hanover, Postfach 510153; tel. (511) 643-2470; fax (511) 643-2304; f. 1797; 605 mems; Pres. Dr J. KNOLL; publs *Berichte*, *Beihefte*.

Naturwissenschaftlicher Verein in Hamburg (Natural History Society of Hamburg): c/o Zoologisches Museum, 20146 Hamburg, Martin-Luther-King-Platz 3; f. 1837; *c.* 460 mems; Chair. Dr HANS-GEORG PEUKERT; Gen. Man. Prof. Dr OTTO KRAUS; publs *Abhandlungen*, *Verhandlungen*.

Naturwissenschaftlicher Verein zu Bremen (Bremen Natural Science Association): 28195 Bremen, Bahnhofsplatz 13, Übersee-Museum; tel. (421) 17-13-47; f. 1864; Sec. HEINRICH KUHBIER; about 500 mems; publ. *Abhandlungen des Naturwissenschaftlichen Vereins*.

Verein Naturschutzpark eV (Nature Reserves Federation): 29646 Bispingen Niederhaverbeck 7; tel. (5198) 408; fax (5198) 668; f. 1909; 6,000 mems; Sec. Dr EBERHARD JÜTTNER; publ. *Naturschutz- und Naturparke*.

Vereinigung für Angewandte Botanik eV (Applied Botany): 37077 Göttingen, Grisebachstr. 6; tel. (551) 39-37-48; f. 1902; *c.* 300 mems; Pres. Prof. Dr R. LIEBEREI; Sec. Prof. Dr H.-J. JÄGER; publ. *Angewandte Botanik* (3 a year).

Mathematical Sciences

Berliner Mathematische Gesellschaft eV (Berlin Mathematical Society): 10623 Berlin, Str. des 17 Juni 136; f. 1899; Sec. Prof. Dr E. J. THIELE; publ. *Sitzungsberichte*.

Deutsche Gesellschaft für Operations Research (DGOR) (German Society for Operational Research): 44795 Bochum, Am Steinknapp 14B; tel. (234) 462246; fax (234) 462245; fusion of *Deutsche Gesellschaft für Unternehmensforschung* and *Gesellschaft für Operations Research* (earlier *AKOR*); f. 1972; 850 mems; promotes development of operational research and encourages co-ordination of theoretical and practical branches of the subject; library of 4,000 vols; Pres. Prof. Dr Dr ULRICH DERIGS; Sec. BÄRBEL NIEDZWETZKI; publ. *OR-S 'Operations Research Spectrum'* (quarterly).

Deutsche Mathematiker Vereinigung eV (German Mathematical Association): 10117 Berlin, Mohrenstr. 39; f. 1890; 3,000 mems; Pres. Prof. INA KERSTEN; Sec. Prof. Dr D. FERUS; publs *Jahresbericht der DMV* (quarterly), *Mitteilungen der DMV* (quarterly).

Gesellschaft für Angewandte Mathematik und Mechanik (Society for Applied Mathematics and Mechanics): 93040 Regensburg, Naturwissenschaftliche Fakultät I – Mathematik, Universität Regensburg, Universitätsstr. 31; tel. (941) 943-4918; fax (941) 943-4005; f. 1922; advancement of scientific work and international co-operation in applied mathematics, mechanics and physics; 2,300 mems; Pres. Prof. Dr F. ZIEGLER; Sec. Prof. Dr-Ing V. ULBRICHT.

GMD—Forschungszentrum Informationstechnik GmbH (German National Research Centre for Information Technology): 53754 St Augustin, Schloss Birlinghoven; tel. (49) 224114-0; fax (49) 224114-2618; e-mail info@gmd.de; f. 1968; research and development in the fields of computer science and information technology; library of 110,000 vols; Dirs Dr jur. HEINZ-GEORG SUNDERMANN, Prof. Dr DENNIS TSICHRITZIS; publs *Berichte der GMD*, *GMD-Studien*, *Arbeitspapiere der GMD*, *GMD-Spiegel*.

Physical Sciences

Astronomische Gesellschaft: C/o Dr Reinhard Schielicke, Astrophysikalisches Institut und Universitäts-Sternwarte Jena, 07745 Jena, Schillergässchen 2; e-mail schied@astro.uni-jena.de; f. 1863; Pres. Prof. Dr WERNER PFAU; Sec. Dr REINHARD SCHIELICKE.

Deutsche Bunsen-Gesellschaft für Physikalische Chemie eV: 60486 Frankfurt a.M., Varrentrappstr. 40–42; tel. (69) 7917201; f. 1894; 1,700 mems; Sec. Dr H. BEHRET; publ. *Berichte*.

Deutsche Geologische Gesellschaft: 30631 Hannover, Alfred-Bentz-Haus, Postfach 510153; tel. (511) 643-2507; telex 923730; fax (511) 6432304; f. 1848; 2,700 mems; Pres. Prof. Dr P. NEUMANN-MAHLKAU; publs *Zeitschrift*, *Nachrichten*.

Deutsche Geophysikalische Gesellschaft eV: C/o GFZ, 14473 Potsdam, Telegrafenberg; f. 1922; 950 mems; Chair. Prof. Dr F. JACOBS; Sec. Dr W. WEBERS; publs *Geophysical Journal International* (monthly), *Mitteilungen* (quarterly).

Deutsche Gesellschaft für Biophysik eV: Institut für Physik, Medizinische Universität zu Lübeck, 23538 Lübeck, Ralzeburger Allee 160; tel. (451) 500-4200; fax (451) 500-4214; f. 1943; 460 mems; Pres. Prof. Dr J. HÜTTERMANN; Sec. Prof. Dr A. X. TRAUTWEIN.

Deutsche Gesellschaft für experimentelle und klinische Pharmakologie und Toxikologie eV: 55216 Ingelheim; tel. (6132) 772973; fax (6132) 773016; 2,500 mems; Chair. Prof. Dr M. GÖTHERT; Gen. Sec. Prof. Dr A. WALLAND.

Deutsche Meteorologische Gesellschaft eV: 56841 Traben-Trarbach, Mont Royal; tel. (6541) 18203; f. 1883; 1,750 mems; Pres. Prof. Dr G. TETZLAFF; Sec. Dr J. STRÜNING; publs *Meteorologische Zeitschrift* (every 2 months), *Beiträge zur Physik der Atmosphäre* (quarterly), *Mitteilungen DMG* (quarterly).

Deutsche Mineralogische Gesellschaft (German Mineralogical Society): Mineralogisch-Petrologisches Institut, 53115 Bonn, Poppelsdorfer Schloss; tel. (228) 732733; fax (228) 732763; e-mail stephan-hoernes@uni-bonn.de; f. 1908; crystallography, petrology, geochemistry, ore minerals, applied mineralogy; 1,700 mems; Sec. Prof. Dr S. HOERNES; publs *European Journal of Mineralogy (EJM)* (6 times a year), *Beihefte* (annually).

Deutsche Physikalische Gesellschaft eV: 53604 Bad Honnef, Hauptstr. 5; tel. (2224) 9232-0; fax (2224) 9232-50; f. 1845; 31,000 mems; Pres. Prof. Dr A. M. BRADSHAW; Sec. Dr V. HÄSELBARTH; publs *Physikalische Blätter* (monthly), *Verhandlungen der DPG* (7 a year).

Deutscher Zentralausschuss für Chemie: 60444 Frankfurt a.M., Postfach 90 04 40; premises at: 60486 Frankfurt a.M., Carl Bosch-Haus, Varrentrappstr. 40–42; tel. (69) 7917323; fax (69) 7917307; Sec. Prof. Dr Dr h.c. HEINDIRK TOM DIECK.

Deutsches Atomforum eV: 53113 Bonn, Heussallee 10; tel. (228) 507-0; fax (228) 507-219; f. 1959; 620 mems; library of 1,100 vols; promotes the peaceful uses of atomic energy; Pres. Dr WILFRIED STEUER; Sec.-Gen. Dr PETER HAUG.

Geologische Vereinigung eV (Geological Association): 56743 Mendig, Vulkanstr. 23; tel. (2652) 989360; fax (2652) 989361; e-mail geol.ver@t-online.de; f. 1910; 2,200 mems; Chair. Prof. Dr W. FRANKE; publ. *Geologische Rundschau* (quarterly).

Gesellschaft Deutscher Chemiker: 60444 Frankfurt a.M., Postfach 900440; located at: 60486 Frankfurt a.M., Carl Bosch-Haus, Varrentrappstr. 40–42; tel. (69) 7917320; fax (69) 7917307; e-mail gdch@gdch.de; f. 1946; 28,000 mems; Pres. Dr E. MEYER-GALOW; Sec.-Gen. Prof. Dr Dr h.c. HEINDIRK TOM DIECK; publs *Angewandte Chemie* (fortnightly, International Edn in English, fortnightly), *Chemie-Ingenieur-Technik* (monthly), *Chemie in unserer Zeit* (every 2 months), *European Journal of Inorganic Chemistry* (monthly), *European Journal of Organic Chemistry* (monthly), *Chemischer Informationsdienst* (weekly), *Nachrichten aus Chemie*, *Technik und Laboratorium* (monthly), *Chemistry – A European Journal* (monthly).

Paläontologische Gesellschaft: c/o Forschungsinstitut Senckenberg, 60325 Frankfurt a.M., Senckenberganlage 25; tel. (69) 97075139; fax (69) 97075137; f. 1912; Pres. Prof. Dr A. v. HILLEBRANDT; publs *Paläontologische Zeitschrift*, *Paläontologie aktuell*.

PHILOSOPHY AND PSYCHOLOGY

Allgemeine Gesellschaft für Philosophie in Deutschland eV: c/o Prof. Dr Christoph Hubig, 70049 Stuttgart, Institut für Philosophie, Pädagogik und Psychologie, Universität Stuttgart, Seidenstr. 36, Pf. 106037; tel. (711) 121-2491; fax (711) 121-2492; f. 1948; 760 mems; Pres. Prof. Dr JÜRGEN MITTELSTRASS; Sec. Prof. Dr CHRISTOPH HUBIG.

Deutsche Gesellschaft für Psychologie eV (German Psychology Association): Institut für Psychologie der Universität Frankfurt, 60054 Frankfurt, Georg-Voigt-Str. 8; tel. (69) 79825024; fax (69) 79828595; e-mail knopf@psych.uni-frankfurt.de; f. 1904 for the advancement of experimental psychology; 1,600 mems; Pres. Prof. Dr MANFRED AMELANG; Sec. Prof. Dr MONIKA KNOPF; publs *Kongressberichte* (every 2 years), *Psychologische Rundschau* (quarterly).

Gesellschaft für Geistesgeschichte eV (Society for the History of Ideas): 91056 Erlangen, Drosselweg 8; tel. (9131) 41187; f. 1958; 150 mems; Pres. Prof. Dr JULIUS H. SCHOEPS; Sec. JOACHIM FRICKE; publ. *Zeitschrift für Religions- und Geistesgeschichte*.

Gottfried-Wilhelm-Leibniz-Gesellschaft eV: 30169 Hannover, Waterloostr. 8 (Niedersächsische Landesbibliothek); tel. (511) 1267331; fax (511) 1267202; f. 1966; organizes lectures, symposia, congresses; 385 mems; 12 mem. asscns; Pres. Prof. Dr ERNST GOTTFRIED MAHRENHOLZ; Gen. Sec. Prof. Dr WILHELM TOTOK; publs *Studia Leibnitiana*, *Studia Leibnitiana Supplementa / Sonderhefte*.

RELIGION, SOCIOLOGY AND ANTHROPOLOGY

Albertus-Magnus-Institut: 53111 Bonn, Adenauerallee 19; tel. (228) 20146-0; fax (228) 20146-30; e-mail ami@ami.bn.shuttle.de; f. 1931; critical publishing of the works of Albertus Magnus; 8 mems; Dirs Prof. Dr L. HONNEFELDER, PD Dr M. DREYER.

Berliner Gesellschaft für Anthropologie, Ethnologie und Urgeschichte (Berlin Society for Anthropology, Ethnology and Prehistory): 14059 Berlin, Schloss Charlottenburg, Langhansbau; tel. (30) 32091-233; fax (30) 3226422; f. 1869; 350 mems; Pres. Dr H. ULLRICH; Sec. Dr CLAUDIUS MILLER; publ. *Mitteilungen*.

Deutsche Gesellschaft für Asienkunde eV (German Association for Asian Studies): 20148 Hamburg, Rothenbaumchaussee 32; tel. (40) 445891; fax (40) 4107945; e-mail ifahh.dga@uni-hamburg.de; f. 1967; promotion and co-ordination of contemporary Asian research;

600 mems; Pres. Dr CHRISTIAN SCHWARZ-SCHILLING; publ. *Asien* (quarterly).

Deutsche Gesellschaft für Bevölkerungswissenschaft eV (German Society for the Scientific Study of Population): 44780 Bochum, University of Bochum; tel. (234) 7002971; fax (234) 7094247; f. 1952 to promote all fields of demographic research and co-ordinate research work undertaken by demographers, inc. non-Germans; working sessions and publs; 250 mems; Pres. Prof. Dr HERMANN KORTE.

Deutsche Gesellschaft für Soziologie: c/o Institut für Soziologie, Universität, 55099 Mainz; tel. (6131) 392692; fax (6131) 393726; f. 1909; 1,200 mems; Pres. Prof. STEFAN HRADIL; publ. *Soziologie*.

Deutsche Gesellschaft für Volkskunde eV (German Society for European Ethnology): 37085 Göttingen, Friedländer Weg 2; f. 1904; 1,100 mems; Pres. Prof. Dr ROLF WILHELM BREDNICH; publs *Zeitschrift für Volkskunde*, *Internationale Volkskundliche Bibliographie*, *Mitteilungen der Deutschen Gesellschaft für Volkskunde (dgv-Informationen)*.

Deutsche Morgenländische Gesellschaft (German Oriental Society): Südasien-Institut, 69120 Heidelberg, Im Neuenheimer Feld 330; f. 1845; 698 mems; library of 50,000 vols; Sec. MANFRED HAKE; publs *Zeitschrift*, *Abhandlungen für die Kunde des Morgenlandes*, *Bibliotheca Islamica*, *Wörterbuch der Klassischen Arabischen Sprache*, *Beiruter Texte und Studien*, *Verzeichnis der orientalischen Handschriften in Deutschland*, *Journal of the Nepal Research Centre*.

Deutsche Orient-Gesellschaft eV (German Oriental Society): 14195 Berlin, Bitterstr. 8–12, Geschäftsstelle Altorientalisches Seminar der FU Berlin; tel. (30) 838-3347; f. 1898; 801 mems; Pres. Prof. Dr GERNOT WILHELM; Sec. Dr HELMUT FREYDANK; publs *Mitteilungen der DOG* (annually), *Wissenschaftliche Veröffentlichungen*, *Abhandlungen*.

Deutsche Religionsgeschichtliche Studiengesellschaft (German Society for Study of the History of Religion): 48341 Altenberge, Droste-Hülshoff-Str. 9B; f. 1970; promotion and co-operation in all fields of research on religion, and interconnection with other areas; Pres. Prof. Dr M.L.G. DIETRICH.

Deutsches Orient-Institut: 20148 Hamburg, Mittelweg 150; tel. (40) 4132050; fax (40) 441484; f. 1960; to study modern Near and Middle East; library of *c.* 22,000 vols; Dir Prof. Dr UDO STEINBACH; Deputy Dir THOMAS KOSZINOWSKI; publs *Orient* (quarterly), *Mitteilungen* (irregular), *Nahost-Informationsdienst* (fortnightly), *Schriften des Deutschen Orient-Instituts* (irregular), *Jahrbuch Nahost* (annually).

Gesellschaft für Anthropologie und Humangenetik (Society for Anthropology and Human Genetics): 28334 Bremen, Dept. für Humanbiologie/Anthropologie der Universität, Fachbereich Biologie; Pres. Prof. Dr H. WALTER.

Gesellschaft für Evangelische Theologie: 37085 Göttingen, Merkelstr. 49; f. 1940; *c.* 800 mems; Pres. Prof. Dr F. VOGEL, Prof. Dr E. WOLF; publ. *Verkündigung und Forschung* (2 a year).

Institut für Asienkunde (Institute of Asian Affairs): 20148 Hamburg, Rothenbaumchaussee 32; tel. (40) 443001; fax (40) 4107945; e-mail ifahh@uni-hamburg.de; f. 1956; research and documentation into all aspects of contemporary South, South-East and East Asia; 60,000 books; Pres. Dr W. RÖHL; Dir Dr W. DRAGUHN; publs *China aktuell*, *Südostasien aktuell*, *China Monthly Data*, *Japan aktuell* (6 a year).

Rheinische Vereinigung für Volkskunde: 53113 Bonn, Am Hofgarten 22; tel. (228) 737618; fax (228) 737562; f. 1947; regional ethnology of the Rhineland; *c.* 200 mems; Pres. Prof. Dr H. L. COX; publs *Rheinisches Jahrbuch für Volkskunde*, *Bonner kleine Reihe zur Alltagskultur*.

Wissenschaftliche Gesellschaft für Theologie eV: 10117 Berlin, Auguststr. 80; tel. (30) 28395-218; f. 1973; 629 mems in Federal Germany, Switzerland, Scandinavia, UK, Netherlands, Romania, Czech Republic, Hungary and Austria; six sections: Old Testament, New Testament, Church History, Systematic Theology, Practical Theology, Missions and Religion; Pres. Prof. Dr EILERT HERMS.

TECHNOLOGY

DECHEMA (Deutsche Gesellschaft für Chemisches Apparatewesen, Chemische Technik und Biotechnologie eV): 60486 Frankfurt a.M., Theodor-Heuss-Allee 25; tel. (69) 7564-0; fax (69) 7564-201; f. 1926; 4,200 mems; library of 25,000 vols; Pres. Prof. Dr rer. nat. UTZ-HELLMUTH FELCHT; Gen. Man. Prof. Dr rer. nat. GERHARD KREYSA; publs *Materialwissenschaft und Werkstofftechnik* (monthly), *Chemie – Ingenieur – Technik* (monthly), *Materials and Corrosion* (monthly).

Deutsche Gemmologische Gesellschaft eV (Gemmological Association of Germany): 55714 Idar-Oberstein, Postfach 12 22 60; tel. (6781) 43011; fax (6781) 41616; f. 1932; administers the German Gemmological Training Centre; 2,000 mems; library of 2,500 vols; Dir Dr U. HENN; publ. *Zeitschrift* (quarterly).

Deutsche Gesellschaft für Bauingenieurwesen eV (Constructional Engineering): 76137 Karlsruhe, Barbarossaplatz 2; f. 1946; 490 mems; Pres. Prof. Dr WILHELM STRICKLER; Sec. Dipl. Ing. GERHART BOCHMANN.

Deutsche Gesellschaft für Luft- und Raumfahrt – Lilienthal – Oberth eV (DGLR) (German Society for Aeronautics and Astronautics): 53175 Bonn, Godesberger Allee 70; tel. (228) 30805-0; fax (228) 30805-24; f. 1994; 3,200 mems; support of aeronautics and astronautics for all scientific and technical purposes; Pres. Dr-Ing. HANS J. RATH; Vice-Pres Dr-Ing. ROLF STÜSSEL, Dipl.-Ing. B. OSSENBÜHL; Sec.-Gen. H. LÜTTGEN; publs *Aerospace Science and Technology* (8 a year), *Luft- und Raumfahrt* (quarterly).

Deutsche Gesellschaft für Materialkunde eV (Materials Science and Engineering): 60486 Frankfurt, Hamburger Allee 26; tel. (69) 7917-750; fax (69) 7917-733; f. 1919; 3,000 mems; Pres. Prof. Dr F. JEGLITSCH; Sec. Dr P. P. SCHEPP; publs *Zeitschrift für Metallkunde*, *DGM-Aktuell*.

Deutsche Gesellschaft für Photogrammetrie und Fernerkundung: C/o Photogrammetrie und Kartographie, Technische Universität Berlin, Str. d. 17. Juni 135, 10623 Berlin; fax (30) 31421104; e-mail albertz@fpk.tu-berlin.de; f. 1909; 850 mems; Pres. Prof. Dr Ing. JÖRG ALBERTZ; publ. *Photogrammetrie-Fernerkundung-Geoinformation* (every 2 months).

Deutsche Gesellschaft für Zerstörungsfreie Prüfung eV (DGZfP) (Non-Destructive Testing): 13629 Berlin, Motardstr. 54; tel. (30) 386-29-910; fax (30) 386-29-917; f. 1933; conferences, training courses and personnel certification; 1,450 mems; Pres. Prof. Dr-Ing. D. SCHNITGER; Sec. Dr rer. nat. RAINER LINK; publ. *Materialprüfung* (monthly).

Deutsche Glastechnische Gesellschaft eV (German Society of Glass Technology): D-60325 Frankfurt a.M., Mendelssohnstr. 75–77; tel. (69) 975861-0; fax (69) 975861-99; e-mail dgg@hvg-dgg-de; f. 1922; 1,460 mems; on-line retrieval service; library of 19,500 vols; Chair. Dipl.-Ing. Dipl.-Kfm. M. WERNER; Sec. Prof. Dr rer. nat. HELMUT A. SCHAEFFER; publ. *Glass Science and Technology – Glastechnische Berichte* (monthly, in English and German).

Deutsche Keramische Gesellschaft eV (German Ceramic Society): 51147 Cologne, Am Grott 7; tel. (2203) 96648; fax 69301; e-mail blum@dkg.de; f. 1919; 1,400 mems; Pres. Dr HANNES WALTER; Sec. Dr MARKUS BLUMENBERG; publ. *cfi-ceramic forum international / Berichte der Deutschen Keramischen Gesellschaft* (monthly).

Deutsche Lichttechnische Gesellschaft eV: 10787 Berlin, Burggrafenstr. 6; tel. (30) 2601-2439; telex 184 273; fax (30) 2601-1255; f. 1912; 2,700 mems; Sec. Dr-Ing. M. SEIDL; publ. *Licht* (monthly).

Deutscher Beton-Verein eV (German Concrete Association): 65185 Wiesbaden, Bahnhofstr. 61; tel. (611) 1403-0; fax (611) 1403-150; f. 1898; quality control, research, standardization and construction advice; 750 mems; Pres. Dr-Ing. HANS LUBER; Chief Sec. Dr-Ing. HANS-ULRICH LITZNER; publs *Vorträge Betontag*, *Beton-Handbuch*, *Bemessungsbeispiele*.

Deutscher Kälte- und Klimatechnischer Verein eV (Refrigerating Association): 70569 Stuttgart, Pfaffenwaldring 10; tel. (711) 685-3200; fax (711) 685-3242; e-mail dkv@itw.uni-stuttgart.de; f. 1909; 5 sections for production and industrial application of refrigeration, food science and technology, storage, transport and air conditioning; 1,300 mems; Pres. Dr Ing. RAINER JAKOBS; Sec. IRENE REICHERT; publs *DKV-Forschungsberichte* (irregular), *DKV-Tagungsbericht* (annually), *DKV-Statusberichte* (irregular), *DKV-Aktuell* (quarterly).

Deutscher Markscheider Verein eV (Mining Surveyors): 45897 Gelsenkirchen-Buer, Horster Str. 165; Pres. Dr-Ing. HERBERT SPICKERNAGEL.

Deutscher Verband für Material-forschung und -prüfung eV (DVM) (Materials Research and Testing): 12205 Berlin, Unter den Eichen 87; tel. (30) 811-30-66; fax (30) 811-93-59; f. 1896; 350 mems; Pres. Prof. Dr MANFRED WILHELM; Sec. Frau INGRID MASLINSKI; publ. *Materialprüfung* (monthly).

Deutscher Verband für Schweissen und verwandte Verfahren eV (German Welding Society): 40010 Düsseldorf, Postfach 101965, Aachener Str. 172; tel. (0211) 1591-0; fax (211) 1591-200; f. 1947; welding and allied processes; 20,000 mems; Pres. Dr-Ing. KLAUS NÜRNBERG; Dir Prof. Dr-Ing. DETLEF VON HOFE; publs *Schweissen und Schneiden* (also English language edition), *Der Praktiker*, *Aufbau und Verbindungstechnik in der Elektronic* (also English edition), *Fachbuchreihe Schweisstechnik*, *DVS-Berichte*, *Die Schweisstechnische Praxis*, *Referateorgan Schweissen und verwandte Verfahren*, *DVS-Merkblätter*, *DVS-Richtlinien*, *Forschungsberichte Humanisierung des Arbeitslebens der Schweisser*, *Fachbibliographie Schweisstechnik*, *Fachwörterbücher*, *DVS-Videos*, *Schweissjytechnische Forschungsberichte*, *Schweisstechnische Software*.

Deutscher Verband für Wasserwirtschaft und Kulturbau eV: 10563 Berlin, Postfach 10 03 20; premises at: 10623 Berlin, Landesgruppe Nordost, C/o Technische Universität Berlin, Institut für Wasserbau und Wasserwirtschaft Str. des 17 Juni 142–144; tel. (30) 314-23328; fax (30) 313-2803; f. 1891; hydraulic engineering and hydrology; 118 mems; Dir Prof. Dipl.-Ing. P. FRANKE.

Deutscher Verband technisch-wissenschaftlicher Vereine (Union of Technical and Scientific Asscns): 40239 Düsseldorf, Graf-Recke-Str. 84; tel. (211) 621-44-99; fax

(211) 621-41-72; e-mail dvt@vdi.de; f. 1916; comprises 95 technical and scientific associations; Chair. Dr-Ing. H. GASSERT; Sec. Dr J. DEBELIUS.

Deutscher Verein des Gas- und Wasserfaches eV (DVGW) (German Technical and Scientific Association on Gas and Water): 53058 Bonn, Postfach 140362; tel. (228) 9188-5; fax (228) 9188-990; e-mail dvgw@dvgw.de; f. 1859; specifications and standardization, testing and certification, research and development, training, providing consultancy services and information; 6,700 mems; Pres. Dipl.-Ing. ROLF GÜNNEWIG; Man. Dir Prof. Dr-Ing. WOLFGANG MERKEL; publs *DVGW—Regelwerk, DVGW—Schriftenreihen, DVGW—Nachrichten, DVGW—Informationen.*

DIN Deutsches Institut für Normung eV (German Institute for Standardization): 10787 Berlin, Burggrafenstr. 6; tel. (4930) 2601-0; fax (4930) 2601-1231; e-mail postmaster@din.de; f. 1917; Pres. Dipl.-Ing. GOTTFRIED KREMER; Dir Prof. Dr-Ing. Sc.D. H. REIHLEN; publs *DIN-Mitteilungen* (monthly), *DIN-Catalogue* (annually).

Gesellschaft für Informatik eV: Wissenschaftszentrum, Ahrstr. 45, 53175 Bonn; tel. (228) 302-145; fax (228) 302-167; e-mail gs@gi-ev.de; f. 1969; promotion of informatics in research, education, applications; 20,000 mems; Pres. Prof. Dr GERHARD BARTH; Dir Dr HERMANN RAMPACHER; publs *Informatik Spektrum, Künstliche Intelligenz, Wirtschaftsinformatik.*

Informationstechnische Gesellschaft im VDE (ITG) (Information Technology Society within VDE): 60596 Frankfurt a.M., Stresemannallee 15; tel. (69) 6308360; fax (69) 6312925; e-mail vde_itg@compuserve.com; f. 1954; 13,000 mems; Chair. Dr-Ing. H. SCHÜSSLER; Sec. Dr-Ing. V. SCHANZ; publs *Nachrichtentechnische Zeitschrift (NTZ)* (monthly), *ETT (European Transactions on Telecommunications and Related Technologies)* (6 a year).

Institut für gewerbliche Wasserwirtschaft und Luftreinhaltung GmbH (Institute for Commercial Water Supply and the Prevention of Air Pollution): 50996 Cologne, Wankelstr. 33; tel. (2236) 3909-35; fax (2236) 3909-23; f. 1956; 2,500 mems; publs *IWL-Umweltbrief* (monthly), *IWL Forum* (irregular).

Rationalisierungs-Kuratorium der Deutschen Wirtschaft eV (RKW) (German Productivity and Management Association): 65760 Eschborn, Düsseldorfer Str. 40; tel. (6196) 495-1; f. 1921; 8,000 mems; Pres. Dr OTMAR FRANZ; Dir Dr HERBERT MÜLLER; publ. *Economy and Productivity* (monthly).

VDE Verband Deutscher Elektrotechniker eV (German Association of Electrical Engineers): 60596 Frankfurt a.M., Stresemannallee 15; tel. (69) 6308-0; f. 1893; 36,000 mems; Chair. Dipl.-Ing. HERMANN WOLTERS; Sec. Dr-Ing. F. D. ALTHOFF; publs *dialog VDE-Mitglieder-Information, Elektrotechnische Zeitschrift, Nachrichtentechnische Zeitschrift, VDE-Vorschriften, VDE-Fachberichte, VDE-Buchreihe, VDE-Schriftenreihe.*

Verein der Zellstoff- und Papier-Chemiker und -Ingenieure eV (Association of Pulp and Paper Chemists and Engineers): 64295 Darmstadt, Berliner Allee 56; tel. (6151) 332-64; fax (6151) 311076; f. 1905; 2,050 mems; Pres. Dr Ing. W. HEINRICH; Sec. Dipl.-Ing. R. WEIDENMÜLLER; Librarian Prof. Dr L. GÖTTSCHING; publ. *Das Papier.*

Verein Deutscher Eisenhüttenleute (German Iron and Steel Institute): 40237 Düsseldorf, Sohnstr. 65; tel. (211) 6707-0; telex 8582512; f. 1860; promotion of research, literature, documentation and information, education and training; 10,000 mems; library of 90,000 vols; Pres. Dr-Ing. K. A. ZIMMERMANN; Exec. Dir Dr D. SPRINGORUM; publs *Stahl und Eisen* (monthly), *Steel Research (Archiv für das Eisenhüttenwesen)* (monthly), *Literaturschau Stahl und Eisen* (fortnightly), *MPT Metallurgical Plant and Technology International* (every 2 months).

Verein Deutscher Giessereifachleute (German Foundrymen's Asscn): 40042 Düsseldorf, Postfach 105144, Sohnstr. 70; tel. (211) 68710; fax (211) 6871333; e-mail sekretariat@vdg.de; f. 1909; 3,100 mems; library of 35,000 vols; Chair. WILHELM KUHLGATZ; Sec. Dr-Ing. NIELS KETSCHER; publs *Giesserei* (monthly), *Giessereiforschung* (quarterly), *Casting Plant Technology International* (quarterly), seminars and courses.

Verein Deutscher Ingenieure (VDI) (Asscn of German Engineers): 40002 Düsseldorf, Postfach 101139; premises at: 40239 Düsseldorf, Graf-Recke-Str. 84; tel. (211) 6214-0; fax (211) 6214-575; e-mail vdie@vdi.de; f. 1856; technical and scientific co-operation in 18 engineering sections concerning all fields of technology; training courses for professional engineers; 130,000 individual mems, 2,000 corporate mems; documentation in various branches of engineering and prevention of air pollution and noise; Dir Dr-Ing. PETER GERBER; publs *VDI-Verlag: Program: VDI-Nachrichten* (weekly newspaper), technical journals, books, etc.

Wissenschaftlicher Verein für Verkehrswesen eV (WVV) (Transport Asscn): 40511 Düsseldorf, ISS, PO Box 11 11 36; tel. (211) 52360; fax (211) 5236456; f. 1956; 140 mems; Pres. Prof. Dr-Ing. PAUL BARON.

Research Institutes

GENERAL

Max-Planck-Gesellschaft zur Förderung der Wissenschaften eV (Max Planck Society for the Advancement of Science): 80084 Munich, Postfach 101062; tel. (89) 2108-0; fax (89) 2108-1111; f. 1911; Pres. Prof. Dr HUBERT MARKE; Sec.-Gen. Dr BARBARA BLUDAU.

Attached research institutes:

Max-Planck-Institut für Aeronomie (Aeronomy): 37189 Katlenburg-Lindau, Postfach 20; tel. (5556) 979-0; fax (5556) 979-240; Man. Dir Prof. Sir IAN AXFORD.

Max-Planck-Institut für Astronomie (Astronomy): 69117 Heidelberg, Königstuhl 17; tel. (6221) 5280; fax (6221) 528246; Man. Dir Prof. Dr STEVEN V. W. BECKWITH.

Max-Planck-Institut für Astrophysik (Astrophysics): 85748 Garching, Karl-Schwarzschild-Str. 1; tel. (89) 329900; fax (89) 32993235; Man. Dir Prof. Dr SIMON D. M. WHITE.

Max-Planck-Institut für Bildungsforschung (Human Development and Education): 14195 Berlin, Lentzeallee 94; tel. (30) 82406-0; fax (30) 8249939; Man. Dir Prof. Dr PAUL B. BALTES.

Max-Planck-Institut für Biochemie (Biochemistry): Am Klopferspitz 18A, 82152 Martinsried bei München; tel. (89) 85781; fax (89) 85783777; Man. Dir Prof. Dr ROBERT HUBER.

Max-Planck-Institut für die Erforschung globaler biogeochemischer Kreisläufe (Study of Global Biogeochemical Cycles): Jena; (In the process of formation).

Max-Planck-Institut für Biologie (Biology): 72076 Tübingen, Spemannstr. 32; tel. (7071) 601750; fax (7071) 601759; Man. Dir Prof. Dr PETER OVERATH.

Max-Planck-Institut für Biophysik (Biophysics): 60596 Frankfurt a.M., Kennedyallee 70; tel. (69) 6303-1; fax (69) 6303-244; Man. Dir Prof. Dr ERNST BAMBERG.

Max-Planck-Institut für Chemie (Otto-Hahn-Institut) (Chemistry): 55128 Mainz, Joh.-Joachim-Becher-Weg 27; tel. (6131) 3050; telex 4187674; fax (6131) 305388; Man. Dir Prof. Dr MEINRAT O. ANDREAE.

Max-Planck-Institut für biophysikalische Chemie (Karl-Friedrich-Bonhoeffer-Institut) (Biophysical Chemistry): 37077 Göttingen, Am Fassberg; tel. (551) 2011; fax (551) 201-1222; Man Dir Prof. Dr PETER GRUSS.

Max-Planck-Institut für demografische Forschung (Demographic Research): 18057 Rostock, Doberaner Str. 114; tel. (381) 2081-0; fax (381) 2081-219; Man. Dir Prof. Dr JAMES W. VAUPEL.

Max-Planck-Institut für Dynamik komplexer technischer Systeme (Dynamics of Complex Technical Systems): Magdeburg; (In the process of formation).

Max-Planck-Institut für Eisenforschung GmbH (Iron): 40074 Düsseldorf, Postfach 140 444; premises at: 40237 Düsseldorf, Max-Planck-Str. 1; tel. (211) 67921; fax (211) 6792268; Head Manager and Dir Prof. Dr PETER NEUMANN.

Max-Planck-Institut für experimentelle Endokrinologie (Experimental Endocrinology): 30625 Hanover, Feodor-Lynen-Str. 7; tel. (511) 5359-0; fax (511) 5359-203; Dir Prof. Dr GREGOR EICHELE.

Forschungsstelle 'Enzymologie der Proteinfaltung' der Max-Planck-Gesellschaft (Enzymology of the Peptide Bond): 06120 Halle/Saale, Kurt-Mothes-Str. 3; tel. (345) 5522800; fax (345) 5511972; Head Prof. Dr GUNTER S. FISCHER.

Max-Planck-Institut für Entwicklungsbiologie (Developmental Biology): 72076 Tübingen, Spemannstr. 35; tel. (7071) 6011; fax (7071) 601300; Man. Dir Prof. Dr FRIEDRICH BONHOEFER.

Max-Planck-Institut für Festkörperforschung (Solid-State Physics): 70569 Stuttgart, Heisenbergstr. 1; tel. (711) 6890; fax (711) 689-1010; Man. Dir Prof. Dr OLE KROGH ANDERSEN.

Friedrich-Miescher-Laboratorium für biologische Arbeitsgruppen in der Max-Planck-Gesellschaft: 72011 Tübingen, Postfach 2109; premises at: 72076 Tübingen, Spemannstr. 37-39; tel. (7071) 601-460; fax (7071) 601-455; biological research groups; Mans Dr MARTIN BÄHLER, Dr ALEXANDER BORST, Dr ANDREAS MAYER, Dr RALPH RUPP, Dr CHRISTOPH M. SCHUSTER.

Fritz-Haber-Institut der Max-Planck-Gesellschaft (Physical Chemistry): 14195 Berlin, Faradayweg 4–6; tel. (30) 8413-30; fax (30) 8413-3155; Man. Dir Prof. Dr ROBERT SCHLÖGL.

Max-Planck-Institut für molekulare Genetik (Molecular Genetics): 14195 Berlin (Dahlem), Ihnestr. 73; tel. (30) 8413-0; fax (30) 8413-1380; Man. Dir Prof. Dr HANS LEHRACH.

Max-Planck-Institut für Geschichte (History): 37073 Göttingen, Hermann-Föge-Weg 11; tel. (551) 49560; fax (551) 495670; library of 27,300 vols; Man. Dir Prof. Dr OTTO GERHARD OEXLE.

Max-Planck-Institut für Gesellschaftsforschung (Social Research): 50677 Cologne, Lothringer Str. 78; tel. (221) 336050; fax (221) 33605-55; Man. Dir Prof. Dr WOLFGANG STREECK.

Gmelin-Institut für anorganische Chemie und Grenzgebiete der Max-Planck-Gesellschaft (Inorganic Chemistry): 60444 Frankfurt a.M., Postfach 900467; premises at: 60486 Frankfurt a.M., Varrentrappstr. 40–42, Carl-Bosch-Haus; tel. (69) 79171; fax (69) 7917-391; Dir Prof. Dr HANSJÖRG W. VOLLMANN (acting).

Max-Planck-Institut für Gravitationsphysik (Gravitational Physics): 14473 Potsdam, Schlaatzweg 1; Man. Dir Prof. Dr JÜRGEN EHLERS.

Max-Planck-Institut für Hirnforschung (Brain Research): 60496 Frankfurt a.M., Postfach 710 662; premises at: 60528 Frankfurt a.M., Deutschordenstr. 46; tel. (69) 96769-0; fax (69) 96769-433; Man. Dir Prof. Dr HEINZ WÄSSLE.

Max-Planck-Institut für Immunbiologie (Immunobiology): 79108 Freiburg, Stübeweg 51; tel. (761) 51080; fax (761) 5108-221; Man. Dir Prof. Dr DAVOR SOLTER.

Max-Planck-Institut für Infektionsbiologie (Biology of Infection): 10117 Berlin, Monbijoustr. 2; tel. (30) 2802-6612; fax (30) 2802-6406; Dirs Prof. Dr STEFAN H. E. KAUFMANN, Prof. Dr THOMAS F. MEYER.

Max-Planck-Institut für Informatik (Information Science): 66123 Saarbrücken, Im Stadtwald; tel. (681) 9325-0; fax (681) 9325-999; Man. Dir Prof. Dr HARALD GANZINGER.

Max-Planck-Institut für Kernphysik (Nuclear Physics): 69117 Heidelberg, Saupfercheckweg 1; tel. (6221) 5160; fax (6221) 516-601; Man. Dir Prof. Dr KONRAD MAUERSBERGER.

Max-Planck-Institut für Kohlenforschung (Coal): 45470 Mülheim/Ruhr, Kaiser-Wilhelm-Platz 1; tel. (208) 3061; fax (208) 3062980; Dir Prof. Dr MANFRED REETZ.

Max-Planck-Institut für Kolloid- und Grenzflächenforschung (Colloids and Interfaces): 14513 Teltow, Kantstr. 55; tel. (3328) 46-0; fax (3328) 46215; Man. Dir Prof. Dr HELMUTH MÖHWALD.

Max-Planck-Institut für biologische Kybernetik (Biological Cybernetics): 72076 Tübingen, Spenmannstr. 38; tel. (7071) 601501; fax (7071) 601616; Man. Dir Prof. Dr KUNO KIRSCHFELD.

Max-Planck-Institut für Limnologie (Limnology): 24306 Plön/Holstein, August-Thienemann-Str. 2; tel. (4522) 763-0; fax (4522) 763-310; Man. Dir Prof. Dr WINFRIED LAMPERT.

Max-Planck-Institut für Mathematik (Mathematics): 53225 Bonn, Gottfried-Claren-Str. 26; tel. (228) 4020; fax (228) 402-277; Man. Dir Prof. Dr DON B. ZAGIER.

Max-Planck-Institut für Mathematik in den Naturwissenschaften (Mathematics in Natural Sciences): 04103 Leipzig, Inselstr. 22–26; tel. (341) 9959-50; fax (341) 9959-658; Man. Dir Prof. Dr EBERHARD ZEIDLER.

Max-Delbrück-Laboratorium in der Max-Planck-Gesellschaft: 50829 Cologne, Carl-von-Linné-Weg 10; tel. (221) 5062-601; fax (221) 5062613.

Max-Planck-Institut für experimentelle Medizin (Experimental Medicine): 37075 Göttingen, Hermann-Rein-Str. 3; tel. (551) 3899-0; fax (551) 3899389; Man. Dir Prof. Dr NORBERT HILSCHMANN.

Max-Planck-Institut für medizinische Forschung (Medical Research): 69120 Heidelberg, Jahnstr. 29; tel. (6221) 4860; fax (6221) 486-351; Man. Dir Prof. Dr BERT SAKMANN.

Max-Planck-Institut für Metallforschung (Metals Research): 70569 Stuttgart, Heisenbergstr. 1; tel. (711) 689-0; fax (711) 6891010; Man. Dir Prof. Dr MANFRED RÜHLE.

Max-Planck-Institut für Meteorologie (Meteorology): 20146 Hamburg, Bundesstr. 55; tel. (40) 41173-0; fax (40) 41173-298; Man. Dir Prof. Dr LENNART BENGTSSON.

Max-Planck-Institut für marine Mikrobiologie (Marine Microbiology): 28359 Bremen Fahrenheitstr. 1; tel. (421) 2028-50; fax (421) 2028-590; Man. Dir Prof. Dr FRIEDRICH WIDDEL.

Max-Planck-Institut für terrestrische Mikrobiologie (Terrestrial Microbiology): Karl-von-Frisch-Str., 35043 Marburg; tel. (6421) 178-0; fax (6421) 178-999; Man. Dir Prof. Dr RUDOLF K. THAUER.

Max-Planck-Institut für Mikrostrukturphysik (Microstructure Physics): 06120 Halle/Saale, Weinberg 2; tel. (345) 558250; fax (345) 5511223; Man. Dir Prof. Dr JÜRGEN KIRSCHNER.

Max-Planck-Institut für neurologische Forschung (Neurological Research): 50931 Cologne, Gleueler Str. 50; tel. (221) 4726-0; fax (221) 4726298; Man. Dir Prof. Dr WOLF-DIETER HEISS.

Max-Planck-Institut fur neuropsychologische Forschung (Cognitive Neuroscience): 04103 Leipzig, Inselstr. 22–26; tel. (341) 9940-0; fax (341) 9940-104; Dirs Prof. Dr ANGELA D. FRIEDERICI, Prof. Dr DETLEV YVES VON CRAMON.

Max-Planck-Institut für chemische Ökologie (Ecology-oriented chemistry): 07745 Jena, Johann-Friedrich-Str. 1; tel. (161) 6308-600; Man. Dir Prof. Dr WILHELM BOLAND.

Max-Planck-Institut für ausländisches und internationales Patent-, Urheber- und Wettbewerbsrecht (Foreign and International Patent, Copyright and Competition Law): 81675 Munich, Siebertstr. 3; tel. (89) 92461; fax (89) 9246-247; library of 20,000 vols; Man. Dir Prof. Dr GERHARD SCHRICKER.

Max-Planck-Institut für molekulare Pflanzenphysiologie (Molecular Plant Physiology): 14476 Golm, Karl-Liebknecht-Str. 24–25, Haus 20; tel. (331) 977-2300; fax (331) 977-2301; Man. Dir Prof. Dr LOTHAR WILLMITZER.

Max-Planck-Institut für Physik (Werner-Heisenberg-Institut) (Physics): 80805 Munich, Föhringer Ring 6; tel. (89) 32354-0; fax (89) 3226704; Man. Dir Prof. Dr VOLKER SOERGEL.

Max-Planck-Institut für Physik komplexer Systeme (Physics of Complex Systems): 01187 Dresden, Nöthnitzer Str. 38; tel. (351) 871-0; Dir Prof. Dr PETER FULDE.

Max-Planck-Institut für chemische Physik fester Stoffe (Solid-State Chemical Physics): Dresden; Man. Dir Prof. Dr FRANK STEGLICH; (In the process of formation).

Max-Planck-Institut für extraterrestrische Physik (Extraterrestrial Physics): 85748 Garching, Giessenbachstr.; tel. (89) 3299-00; fax (89) 32993569; Man. Dir Prof. Dr GERHARD HAERENDEL.

Max-Planck-Institut für molekulare Physiologie (Molecular Physiology): 44139 Dortmund, Rheinlanddamm 201; tel. (231) 12060; fax (231) 1206464; Man. Dir Prof. Dr ALFRED WITTINGHOFER.

Max-Planck-Institut für physiologische und klinische Forschung (Physiological and Clinical Research): W. G. Kerckhoff-Institut, 61231 Bad Nauheim, Parkstr. 1; tel. (6032) 7051; fax (6032) 705211; Man. Dir Prof. Dr WERNER RISAU.

Max-Planck-Institut für Plasmaphysik (Plasma Physics): 85748 Garching, Boltzmannstr. 2; tel. (89) 3299-01; fax (89) 32992200; Scient. Dir Prof. Dr KLAUS PINKAU.

Max-Planck-Institut für Polymerforschung (Polymer Research): 55128 Mainz, Ackermannweg 10; tel. (6131) 379-0; fax (06131) 379-100; Man. Dir Prof. Dr GERHARD WEGNER.

Max-Planck-Institut für ausländisches und internationales Privatrecht (Foreign and International Private Law): 20148 Hamburg, Mittelweg 187; tel. (40) 41900-0; telex 212 893; fax (40) 41900-288; Man. Dir Prof. Dr Dr KLAUS J. HOPT.

Max-Planck-Institut für Psychiatrie (Deutsche Forschungsanstalt für Psychiatrie) (Psychiatry): 80804 Munich, Kraepelinstr. 2 and 10; tel. (89) 30622-1; fax (89) 30622483; Man. Dirs Prof. Dr Dr FLORIAN HOLSBOER, Prof. Dr HARTMUT WEKERLE.

Max-Planck-Institut für Psycholinguistik (Psycholinguistics): NL 6525 XD Nijmegen, Wundtlaan 1, Netherlands; tel. (Netherlands) (24) 3521911; fax (Netherlands) (24) 3521213; Man. Dir Prof. Dr WILLEM J. M. LEVELT.

Max-Planck-Institut für psychologische Forschung (Psychological Research): 80750 Munich, Postfach 440 109; premises at: 80802 Munich, Leopoldstr. 24; tel. (89) 386021; fax (89) 342473; Man. Dir Prof. Dr FRANZ EMANUEL WEINERT.

Max-Planck-Institut für Quantenoptik (Quantum Optics): 85748 Garching, Hans-Kopfermann-Str. 1; tel. (89) 32 905-0; fax (89) 32905-200; Man. Dir Prof. Dr HERBERT WALTHER.

Max-Planck-Institut für Radioastronomie (Radioastronomy): 53121 Bonn, Auf dem Hügel 69; tel. (228) 5250; fax (228) 525-229; Man. Dir Prof. Dr RICHARD WIELEBINSKI.

Projektgruppe 'Recht der Gemeinschaftsgüter, der Max-Planck-Gesellschaft (Law of Common Goods): Bonn; (In the process of formation).

Max-Planck-Institut für europäische Rechtsgeschichte (European Legal History): 60489 Frankfurt a.M., Hausener Weg 120; tel. (69) 78978-0; fax (69) 78978169; Man. Dir Prof. Dr MICHAEL STOLLEIS.

Max-Planck-Institut für ausländisches und internationales Sozialrecht (Foreign and International Social Law): 80802 Munich, Leopoldstr. 24; tel. (89) 386021; fax (89) 399795; Man. Dir Prof. Dr BERND BARON VON MAYDELL.

Max-Planck-Institut für ausländisches und internationales Strafrecht (Foreign and International Criminal Law): 79100 Freiburg i. Br., Günterstalstr. 73; tel. (761) 70811; fax (761) 7081-294; library of 64,000 vols; Dirs Prof. Dr ALBIN ESER, Prof. Dr HANS-JÖRG ALBRECHT.

Max-Planck-Institut für Strahlenchemie (Radiation Chemistry): 45470 Mülheim/Ruhr, Stiftstr. 34–36; tel. (208) 306-0; fax (208) 3063951; Man. Dir Prof. Dr KARL WIEGHARDT.

Max-Planck-Institut für Strömungsforschung (Flow Research): 37018 Göttingen, Postfach 2853; premises at: 37073 Göttingen, Bunsenstr. 10; tel. (551) 5176-0; fax (551) 5176-704; Man. Dir Prof. Dr THEO GEISEL.

Max-Planck-Institut für Verhaltensphysiologie (Behavioural Physiology): 82319 Seewiesen, Post Starnberg/Obb.; tel.

(8157) 9320; fax (8157) 932-209; Man. Dir Prof. Dr WOLFGANG WICKLER.

Max-Planck-Institut für ausländisches öffentliches Recht und Völkerrecht (Comparative Public and International Law): 69120 Heidelberg, Im Neuenheimer Feld 535; tel. (6221) 4821; telex 461 505; fax (6221) 482-288; Man. Dir Prof. Dr JOCHEN A. FROWEIN.

Max-Planck-Institut zur Erforschung von Wirtschaftssystemen (Economic Systems): 07745 Jena, Kahlaische Str. 10; tel. (3641) 686-5; fax (3641) 686-990; Dir Prof. Dr MANFRED E. STREIT.

Max-Planck-Institut für Wissenschaftsgeschichte (History of Science): 10117 Berlin, Wilhelmstr. 44; tel. (30) 22667-0; fax (30) 22667-299; Dir Prof. Dr JÜRGEN RENN.

Max-Planck-Institut für Zellbiologie (Cell Biology): 68526 Ladenburg bei Heidelberg, Rosenhof; tel. (6203) 106-0; fax (6203) 106-122; Man. Dir Prof. Dr PETER TRAUB.

Max-Planck-Institut für Züchtungsforschung (Plant Breeding Research): 50829 Cologne, Carl-von-Linné-Weg 10; tel. (221) 5062-0; fax (221) 5062513; Man. Dir Prof. Dr HEINZ SAEDLER.

AGRICULTURE, FISHERIES AND VETERINARY SCIENCE

Bundesforschungsanstalt für Fischerei (Federal Research Centre for Fisheries): 22767 Hamburg, Palmaille 9; tel. (40) 389050; fax (40) 38905-200; e-mail 100565.1223@compuserve.com; f. 1948; research into inland and sea fishing, aquaculture; library of 65,500 vols; Man. Dir Prof. Dr HANS-STEPHAN JENKE; publs *Archive of Fishery and Marine Research*, *Schriften der Bundesforschungsanstalt für Fischerei*, *Informationen für die Fischwirtschaft*.

Attached research institutes:

Institut für Seefischerei: 22767 Hamburg; Dir Prof. Dr GERD HUBOLD.

Institut für Ostseefischerei: 18069 Rostock, An der Jägerbäk 2; Dir Dr OTTO RECHLIN.

Institut für Fischereitechnik: 22767 Hamburg; Dir Prof. Dr OTTO GABRIEL.

Institut für Biochemie und Technologie: 22767 Hamburg; Dir Dr HARTMUT REHBEIN (acting).

Institut für Fischereiökologie: 22589 Hamburg, Wüstland 2; Dir Prof. Dr HANS-STEPHAN JENKE.

Bundesforschungsanstalt für Landwirtschaft Braunschweig-Völkenrode (FAL) (Federal Agricultural Research Centre Braunschweig-Völkenrode): 38116 Braunschweig, Bundesallee 50; tel. (531) 596-1; fax (531) 596-814; f. 1947; library of 115,000 vols; Pres. Prof. Dr sc. agr. FOLKHARD ISERMEYER; 13 institutes for specialized agricultural research; publs *Landbauforschung Völkenrode* (3 or 4 a year), *Annual Report*, *Information* (quarterly).

Deutsche Gesellschaft für Holzforschung eV (Wood Research): 80335 Munich, Bayerstr. 57–59, 5 Stock; tel. (89) 5389057; fax (89) 531657; f. 1942; Pres. Dipl.-Ing. K. MOSER; Man. Dipl. Ing. JOACHIM TEBBE; publs *DGfH aktuell* (quarterly), *Informationsdienst Holz der Entwicklungsgemeinschaft Holzbau*, and several annual reports, etc.

Deutsche Gesellschaft für Hopfenforschung (Hops Research): 85283 Wolnzach, Hüll 5; tel. (8442) 3597; fax (8442) 2871; Pres. Dipl.-Ing. GEORG BALK; Dir H. SCHLICKER.

Forschungsgesellschaft für Agrarpolitik und Agrarsoziologie: 53115 Bonn, Meckenheimer Allee 125; tel. (228) 634781; fax (228) 634788; f. 1952; study and scientific investigation of economic and social problems of agriculture and rural areas; 70 mems; Pres. Prof. Dr W. HENRICHSMEYER; Dir Dr R. STRUFF.

ARCHITECTURE AND TOWN PLANNING

Akademie für Raumforschung und Landesplanung (Academy for Regional Research and Regional Planning): 30161 Hannover, Hohenzollernstr. 11; tel. (511) 34842-0; fax (511) 3484241; e-mail arl@mbox.arl.uni-hannover.de; f. 1946; 118 mems, 370 corresp. mems; library of 20,000 vols; Pres. Prof. Dr KLAUS WOLF; Gen. Sec. Dr Ing. DIETMAR SCHOLICH; publs *Proceedings of the Academy*, *Raumforschung und Raumordnung* (every 2 months).

Deutsche Akademie für Städtebau und Landesplanung (Town and Country Planning): 80803 Munich, Kaiserplatz 4; tel. (89) 33-20-77; f. 1922; 450 mems; library of 5,000 vols; Pres. Prof. Dr-Ing. G. ALBERS; publ. *Mitteilungen* (once or twice annually).

BIBLIOGRAPHY, LIBRARY SCIENCE AND MUSEOLOGY

Gutenberg-Gesellschaft (Gutenberg Society): 55116 Mainz, Liebfrauenplatz 5; tel. (6131) 22-64-20; fax (6131) 12-34-88; f. 1901; for the publication of research work on the art of printing and books from Gutenberg until the present day; 1,700 mems; Pres. The Mayor of the City of Mainz; Sec.-Gen. GERTRAUDE BENÖHR; Editor Prof. Dr STEPHAN FÜSSEL; publs *Gutenberg-Jahrbuch*, *Kleine Drucke*, *Veröffentlichungen*, etc.

ECONOMICS, LAW AND POLITICS

Arbeitsgemeinschaft deutscher wirtschaftswissenschaftlicher Forschungsinstitut eV (Asscn of German Economic Science Research Institutes): 14195 Berlin, Königin-Luise-Str. 5; f. 1949; 31 mem. institutes; co-ordinates programmes of the institutes and provides a permanent base for research exchange and co-operation; Chair. Prof. Dr LUTZ HOFFMANN; publ. *Gemeinschaftsdiagnose* (2 a year).

Member institutes:

Deutsches Institut für Wirtschaftsforschung (German Institute for Economic Research): 14195 Berlin, Königin-Luise-Str. 5; tel. (30) 897890; fax (30) 89789200; f. 1925; Pres. Prof. Dr LUTZ HOFFMANN; publs *Wochenbericht* (weekly), *Vierteljahrshefte zur Wirtschaftsforschung* (quarterly), *Economic Bulletin* (monthly).

Abteilung Wirtschaftswissenschaft im Osteuropa Institut an der Freien Universität Berlin (Economics Department of the East European Institute at the Free University, Berlin): 14195 Berlin-Dahlem, Garystr. 55; f. 1950; economic research on East European countries; 10 mems; library of 85,000 vols and 95 periodicals; Dir Prof. Dr ERICH KLINKMÜLLER; publs *Wirtschaftswissenschaftliche Veröffentlichungen*, *Berichte des Osteuropa Instituts/Reihe Wirtschaft und Recht*.

Forschungsinstitut der Friedrich-Ebert-Stiftung (Research Institute of Friedrich-Ebert-Foundation): 53175 Bonn, Godesberger Allee 149; tel. (228) 883-0; telex 885 479; fax (228) 883625; Dir GERHARD STÜMPFIG.

Institut für Landwirtschaftliche Marktforschung der Bundesforschungsanstalt für Landwirtschaft Braunschweig-Völkenrode (FAL) (Institute for Agricultural Market Research of the Federal Research Centre for Agriculture): 38116 Braunschweig, Bundesallee 50; tel. (531) 596566; fax (531) 596367; e-mail bachmann@mf.fal.de; Dir Dr E. NEANDER (acting).

Bremer Ausschuss für Wirtschaftsforschung (Bremen State Economic Research Institute): 28195 Bremen, Schlachte 10/11; tel. (421) 361-8801; fax (421) 361-8810; f. 1947; library of 20,000 vols; Dir Dr PETER FRANKENFELD; publs *Wirtschaftsdaten* (annually), *BAW-Monatsbericht* (monthly), *Bremer Zeitschrift für Wirtschaftspolitik BZW* (quarterly), *Regionalwirtschaftliche Studien* (irregular).

Rheinisch-Westfälisches Institut für Wirtschaftsforschung (Rhine-Westphalia Institute for Economic Research): 45128 Essen, Hohenzollernstr. 1–3; tel. (201) 8149-0; fax (201) 8149-200; e-mail rwi@rwi-essen.de; f. 1943; study of the structure and development of the West German economy; special research facilities, advice on administration and economics for firms and students; 70 mems; library of 53,000 vols; Pres. Prof. Dr PAUL KLEMMER; Dir Prof. Dr ULLRICH HEILEMANN; publs *Konjunkturberichte* (2 a year), *Mitteilungen* (quarterly), *Handwerksberichte* (annually), *Konjunkturbriefe*, *Schriftenreihe*, *Untersuchungen*, *RWI-Papiere* (all irregular).

Schmalenbach-Gesellschaft — Deutsche Gesellschaft für Betriebswirtschaft eV: 13629 Berlin, Nonnendammallee 101; tel. (30) 382-70-24; f. 1978; economic research; 1,500 mems; Pres. Dr JOACHIM FUNK; Man. Dr GERTRUD FUCHS-WEGNER; publ. *Schmalenbachs Zeitschrift für betriebswirtschaftliche Forschung (ZfbF)* (monthly).

Institut für Allgemeine Überseeforschung der Stiftung 'Deutsches Übersee-Institut' (Institute of Comparative Overseas Studies): 20354 Hamburg, Neuer Jungfernstieg 21; tel. 35-62-593; fax 35-62-547; e-mail duei@uni-hamburg.de; f. 1964; 40 mems; library of 8,000 vols and periodicals; Dir Dr W. DRAGUHN; publ. *NORD-SÜD aktuell* (quarterly).

HWWA-Institut für Wirtschaftsforschung-Hamburg (Hamburg Institute of Economic Research): 20347 Hamburg, Neuer Jungfernstieg 21; tel. (40) 35-62-354; fax (40) 35-19-00; f. 1908; research depts: business cycles, money and public finance, world business cycles, economic structures and economic systems, regional economics and regional policy, economic and financial relations between industrial countries, economic systems and economic relations of East European countries, development economics; library of 1,000,000 vols, 9,000 reference books, 3,200 periodicals; depository library for UN, FAO, GATT, OECD, EEC; Pres. (vacant); publs *Wirtschaftsdienst*, *Bibliographie der Wirtschaftspresse* (monthly), *Intereconomics* (every 2 months, in English).

Institut für Weltwirtschaft an der Universität Kiel: see under Christian-Albrechts-Universität.

Energiewirtschaftliches Institut an der Universität zu Köln: 50931 Köln, Albertus Magnus Platz; tel. (221) 4702258; fax (221) 446537; e-mail m.schmid@wiso.uni-koeln.de; f. 1943; energy economics; 14 mems; library of 12,000 vols, 90 periodicals; Dir Prof. Dr C. CHRISTIAN VON WEIZSÄCKER;

publ. *Zeitschrift für Energiewirtschaft* (quarterly).

Institut für Handelsforschung an der Universität zu Köln: 50935 Köln, Säckinger Str. 5; tel. (221) 943607-0; fax (221) 943607-99; Dir Prof. Dr L. MÜLLER-HAGEDORN.

Institut für Wirtschaftspolitik an der Universität zu Köln: 50969 Köln, Pohligstr.1; tel. (221) 470-5347; fax (221) 470-5350; economic policy, foreign trade policy, European Community research; Dirs Prof. Dr JUERGEN B. DONGES, Prof. Dr JOHANN EEKHOFF; publs *Zeitschrift für Wirtschaftspolitik* (3 a year), *Untersuchungen zur Wirtschaftspolitik*.

Wirtschafts- und Sozialwissenschaftliches Institut in der Hans-Böckler-Stiftung (Economic Research Institute of the Hans Böckler Foundation): 40227 Dusseldorf, Bertha-von-Suttner-Platz 1; tel. (211) 7778-0; fax (211) 7778-190; Dir Prof. Dr HEIDE PFARR.

Forschunginstitut für Wirtschaftspolitik an der Universität Mainz: see under Johannes Gutenberg-Universität.

IFO-Institut für Wirtschaftsforschung (IFO-Institute for Economic Research): 81679 Munich, Poschingerstr. 5; tel. 9224-0; telex 5-22269; fax 985369; f. 1949; empirical economic research; 230 staff; library of 90,000 vols; Pres. Prof. K. H. OPPENLÄNDER; publs *IFO-Schnelldienst* (3 a month), *Wirtschaftskonjunktur* (monthly), *IFO Digest* (quarterly, in English), *IFO-Studien* (quarterly).

Deutsches Wirtschaftswissenschaftliches Institut für Fremdenverkehr an der Universität München (German Institute for Economic Research in Tourism and Travel, University of Munich): 80331 Munich, Herman-Sack-Str. 2; tel. (89) 267091; fax (89) 267613; e-mail dwif@lrz.uni-muenchen.de; f. 1950; 6 staff; library of c. 8,000 vols; Dir Dr J. MASCHKE; publ. *Jahrbuch für Fremdenverkehr*.

Forschungsstelle für allgemeine und textile Marktwirtschaft an der Universität Münster (Research Institute for General and Textile Economics): 48149 Münster, Fliednerstr. 21; f. 1941; 25 mems; library of 15,000 vols; Dirs Prof. Dr GUSTAV DIECKHEUER, Prof. Dr DIETER AHLERT.

GfK-Nürnberg, Gesellschaft für Konsum-, Markt- und Absatzforschung eV (Society for Consumer and Market Research): 90319 Nuremberg, Nordwestring 101; 850 mems; Dir Prof. Dr FRANK WIMMER; publ. *Yearbook of Marketing and Consumer Research*.

Institut für Angewandte Wirtschaftsforschung Tübingen (Institute for Applied Economic Research): 72074 Tübingen, Ob dem Himmelreich 1; tel. (7071) 9896-0; fax (7071) 9896-99; e-mail iaw@oe.uni-tuebingen.de; f. 1957; analysis of issues in economic policy; research in economic theory; econometric macromodels; library of 12,500 vols; Dirs Prof. Dr GERD RONNING, Prof. Dr MANFRED STADLER; publ. *IAW-Mitteilungen* (quarterly).

Statistisches Bundesamt (Federal Statistical Office): 65180 Wiesbaden, Gustav-Streseman-Ring 11; tel. (611) 751; fax (611) 724000; f. 1950; library of 433,000 vols; Pres. JOHANN HAHLEN; publs *Wirtschaft und Statistik*, etc.

Institut der deutschen Wirtschaft eV: 50968 Cologne, Gustav-Heinemann-Ufer 84–88; tel. (221) 4981-1; fax (221) 4981-592; f. 1951; education and social sciences; economic and social policy; library and archives include 200,000 monographs; Dir Prof. Dr GERHARD FELS.

Osteuropa-Institut München: 81679 Munich, Scheinerstr. 11; tel. (89) 998396-0; fax (89) 9810110; e-mail oein@lnz.uni-muenchen.de; f. 1952; research in history and economics of Eastern Europe and fmr Soviet Union; library of 158,000 vols; Dir Prof. Dr G. HEDTKAMP; publs *Jahrbücher für Geschichte Osteuropas* (quarterly), *Economic Systems*, *Jahrbuch der Wirtschaft Osteuropas* (quarterly), working papers (irregular).

Institut für Wirtschaft und Gesellschaft Bonn eV (IWG BONN) (Bonn Institute for Economic and Social Research): 53175 Bonn, Wissenschaftszentrum, Ahrstr. 45; tel. (228) 372044; fax 375869; f. 1977; Chair. Prof. Dr MEINHARD MIEGEL.

Institut für Arbeitsmarkt- und Berufsforschung der Bundesanstalt für Arbeit: 90327 Nürnberg, Regensburger Str. 104; tel. (911) 179-0; fax (911) 179-3258; e-mail iab.ba@t-online.de; f. 1967; employment and labour market research; library of 45,000 vols; Dir Prof. Dr GERHARD KLEINHENZ; publ. *Mitteilungen aus der Arbeitsmarkt- und Berufsforschung* (quarterly).

Institut für Seeverkehrswirtschaft und Logistik (Institute of Shipping Economics and Logistics): 28359 Bremen, Universitätsallee GW 1 Block A; tel. (421) 22096-0; fax (421) 22096-55; f. 1954; shipping, shipbuilding, sea-port economics, seaborne trade, traffic and transport logistics; library of about 110,000 bibliographical units; 1,000 periodicals and annuals; Dir Prof. Dr WERNER E. ECKSTEIN; Man. Dirs Prof. Dr M. ZACHCIAL, Prof. Dr V. SPEIDEL; publs *Lectures and Contributions to International Shipping Research*, *Shipping Statistics and Market Review* (monthly figures of shipping, shipbuilding, sea-ports and sea-borne trade), *Shipping Statistics Yearbook*, *Book Series*, on maritime economics, port management, etc.

Arbeitsstelle Friedensforschung Bonn (Peace Research Information Unit, Bonn): 53173 Bonn, Beethovenallee 4; tel. (228) 35-60-32; fax (228) 356050; e-mail afb@bonn.iz-soz.de; f. 1984; information and advice on research into Peace; Dir Dr REGINE MEHL.

Arnold Bergstraesser Institut für kulturwissenschaftliche Forschung (ABI): 79110 Freiburg im Breisgau, Windausstr. 16; tel. (761) 85091; fax (761) 892967; e-mail abifr@ruf.uni-freiburg.de; f. 1960; socio-political research particularly on education and administration in Africa, Asia, Near East and Latin America; depts of overseas education and overseas admin.; four regional depts: Africa, Asia, Latin America, Middle East/North Africa; 30 mems; library of c. 60,000 vols; Dirs Prof. Dr T. HANF, Prof. Dr D. OBERNDÖRFER.

Bundesinstitut für ostwissenschaftliche und internationale Studien (Federal Institute for Russian, East European and International Studies): 50823 Cologne, Lindenbornstr. 22; tel. (221) 57-47-0; fax (221) 574-71-10; e-mail biost.koeln@mail.rrz.uni-koeln.de; f. 1961; autonomous, academic government institute; research and editorial work on current political, social, economic and legal developments in Eastern Europe, especially the former USSR, and the implications for international relations; library of 250,000 vols; Dir Prof. Dr HEINRICH VOGEL.

Deutsches Übersee Institut – Übersee Dokumentation (German Overseas Institute – Overseas Documentation): 20354 Hamburg, Neuer Jungfernstieg 21; tel. (40) 3562-598; fax (40) 3562-512; f. 1966; sections on Africa, Asia and South Pacific, Latin America, Near and Middle East; database of 400,000 documentary units (references to research literature) available online from the database of the 'Fachinformationsverbund Internationale Beziehungen und Länderkunde'; Head Dr GOTTFRIED REINKNECHT; publs *Ausgewählte neuere Literatur* (selected bibliographies of recent literature, by regions, quarterly; Latin America 3 a year), *Kurzbibliographien* (working/introductory bibliographies, irregular), *Reihe A-Spezialbibliographien* (specialized bibliographies, irregular), *Reihe B-Verzeichnisse* (directories, etc, irregular).

Frobenius-Institut an der Johann Wolfgang Goethe-Universität: 60323 Frankfurt a.M., Liebigstr. 41; tel. (69) 719199-0; fax (69) 719199-11; f. 1898; African, Indonesian and Melanesian cultures and history; library of 96,000 vols; Dir Prof. Dr KARL-HEINZ KOHL; publs *Paideuma* (annually), *Studien zur Kulturkunde* (irregular), *Sonderschriften des Frobenius-Instituts* (irregular), *Afrika-Archiv* (irregular).

Gesellschaft für Deutschlandforschung eV (Society for Research on Germany): 12119 Berlin, Postfach 410965; tel. (30) 8512851; f. 1978; contemporary research on Germany; seminars and conferences; Pres. Prof. Dr KARL ECKART (Universität Duisburg); Vice-Pres. Prof. Dr MANFRED WILKE (Berlin).

Herder-Institut eV: 35037 Marburg/Lahn, Gisonenweg 5–7; tel. (6421) 1840; fax (6421) 184139; e-mail herder@mailer.uni-marburg.de; f. 1950; historical research on countries and peoples of Eastern Central Europe; library: see Libraries; Dir Dr EDUARD MÜHLE; publ. *Zeitschrift für Ostmitteleuropa-Forschung* (quarterly).

Institut Finanzen und Steuern eV (Finance and Taxation Institute): 53072 Bonn, Postf. 7269; located at: 53111 Bonn, Markt 10 und 14; tel. (228) 98-22-10; fax (228) 98-22-150; f. 1949; Dir Dr A. UELNER.

Institut für Afrika-Kunde (Institute of African Affairs): 20354 Hamburg, Neuer Jungfernstieg 21; tel. (40) 3562523; fax (40) 3562511; e-mail iak@uni.hamburg.de; f. 1963; contemporary social science research, documentation, discussion groups, international contact with organizations and individuals with specialized knowledge of African affairs; library of 45,000 vols and 480 periodicals; Dir Dr ROLF HOFMEIER; publs *Afrika Spectrum* (3 a year), *Aktueller Informationsdienst Afrika* (2 a month), *Arbeiten aus dem Institut für Afrika-Kunde*, *Hamburger Beiträge zur Afrika-Kunde*, *Focus Afrika*, *Hamburg African Studies*.

Institut für international vergleichende Wirtschafts- und Sozialstatistik an der Ruprecht-Karls-Universität Heidelberg: 69117 Heidelberg, Hauptstr. 126; tel. (6221) 542924; f. 1958; methods of international comparisons; 6 mems; library of c. 20,000 vols; Dir Prof. H. KOGELSCHATZ; publ. *Diskussionsschriften* (quarterly).

Stiftung Wissenschaft und Politik, Forschungsinstitut für Internationale Politik und Sicherheit (Foundation for Science and Politics, Research Institute for International Politics and Security): 82067 Ebenhausen, Zellerweg 27; tel. (8178) 700; fax (8178) 70312; f. 1962; interdisciplinary research in international affairs and national security; library of 92,000 vols, 570 periodicals; 380 yearbooks; computerized information system for the fields of international relations and area studies (440,000 references), publicly-available database 'World Affairs Online'; Pres. Prof. Dr h.c. H. L. MERKLE; Dir Dr C. BERTRAM.

Wissenschaftszentrum Berlin für Sozialforschung: 10785 Berlin, Reichpietschufer 50; tel. (30) 25491-0; fax (30) 25491684; e-mail presse@medea.wz-berlin.de; f. 1969; a non-profit organization; aims to conduct international and interdisciplinary, empirical social science research and to communicate the results to the scientific and decision-making community; 4 research areas, 4 research groups; library of 100,000 vols, 600 periodicals, special collections on the themes of the research units; Pres. Prof. FRIEDHELM NEIDHARDT; publs *WZB-Mitteilungen* (quarterly), *WZB-Forschung* (3 a year), *WZB Abstracts* (1 a year).

EDUCATION

Deutsches Institut für Internationale Pädagogische Forschung: 60486 Frankfurt am Main, Schloss-Str. 29; tel. (69) 24708-0; fax (69) 24708-444; e-mail dipf@dipf.de; f. 1950; educational research; libraries (in Berlin and Frankfurt) of 875,000 vols; Dir Prof. Dr HERMANN AVENARIUS; publ. *Zeitschrift für internationale erziehungs- und sozialwissenschaftliche Forschung* (2 a year).

Gesellschaft für Pädagogik und Information eV: 33052 Paderborn, Pädagogisches Büro, Rathenaustr. 16, Postfach 2228; tel. (5251) 34024; f. 1964; 400 mems; to promote research and development in the field of educational technology and information science; Chair. Prof. Dr Dr G. E. ORTNER, Prof. Dr U. LEHNERT; publs *Schul Praxis—Wirtschaft und Weiterbildung*, *Pädagogik und Information*.

Gesellschaft zur Förderung Pädagogischer Forschung eV (Society for the Promotion of Educational Research): 60442 Frankfurt am Main, Postfach 900280; premises at: 60486 Frankfurt am Main, Schloss-Str. 29; tel. (69) 247080; telex 4170331; fax (69) 24708444; f. 1950; dissemination of research results, organization of communication processes between educational research and school practice; 400 mems; Pres. HANS KROLLMANN; Sec. P. DOEBRICH; publ. *Zeitschrift für internationale erziehungs- und sozialwissenschaftliche Forschung* (Journal for International Educational and Social Research).

FINE AND PERFORMING ARTS

Gesellschaft für Musikforschung: 34131 Kassel-Wilhelmshöhe, Heinrich-Schütz-Allee 35; f. 1946; 1,800 mems; Pres. Prof. Dr CHRISTOPH H. MAHLING; Treas. Dr HANSPETER BENNWITZ; publ. *Die Musikforschung* (quarterly).

Staatliches Institut für Musikforschung Preussischer Kulturbesitz mit Musikinstrumenten-Museum: 10785 Berlin, Tiergartenstr. 1; tel. (30) 254-81-0; fax (30) 254-81-172; e-mail sim@sim.spk-berlin.de; f. 1935; collects musicological material, instruments, records, phonograms and tape recordings; conducts research into the development and history of musicology, inc. acoustics, musical instruments and the style and practice of executing music of the past; archival and documentary research and comparative musicological research; open to the public; library of over 62,000 vols; lectures, concerts and exhibitions; Dir Dr THOMAS ERTELT; Dir of Museum Dr KONSTANTIN RESTLE; publs *Veröffentlichungen*, *Bibliographie des Musikschrifttums*, *Jahrbuch*, *Geschichte der Musiktheorie*, *Briefwechsel der Wiener Schule*, etc.

Zentralinstitut für Kunstgeschichte (History of Art): 80333 Munich, Meiserstr. 10; tel. (89) 5591-547; fax (89) 5504352; f. 1946; library of 323,000 vols; 650,000 photographs; Dir Dr WOLF TEGETHOFF; publs *Kunstchronik* (monthly), *Reallexikon zur deutschen Kunstgeschichte*.

HISTORY, GEOGRAPHY AND ARCHAEOLOGY

Deutsches Archäologisches Institut (German Archaeological Institute): 14195 Berlin, Podbielskiallee 69–71; tel. (030) 83008-0; fax (30) 83008168; f. 1829; Pres. Prof. Dr HELMUT KYRIELEIS; Dir Prof. Dr WALTER TRILLMICH; brs in Rome (Prof. Dr PAUL ZANKER), Athens (Prof. Dr KLAUS FITTSCHEN), Cairo (Prof. Dr RAINER STADELMANN), Istanbul (Prof. Dr HARALD HAUPTMANN), Madrid (Prof. Dr TILO ULBERT), Middle East (Prof. Dr RICARDO EICHMANN), Sana'a (Dr BURKHARD VOGT), Damascus (Dr KLAUS STEFAN FREYBERGER), Eurasia (Prof. Dr HERMANN PARZINGER) and Teheran; also Römisch-Germanische Kommission, Frankfurt am Main (Prof. Dr SIEGMAR FREIHERR VON SCHNURBEIN), Kommission für Alte Geschichte und Epigraphik, München (Prof. Dr M. WÖRRLE) and Kommission für Allgemeine und Vergleichende Archäologie, Bonn (Prof. Dr-Ing. WOLFGANG WURSTER); publs *Jahrbuch*, *Archäologischer Anzeiger*, *Berichte der Römisch-Germanischen-Kommission*, *Germania*, *Chiron*, *Athenische Mitteilungen*, *Römische Mitteilungen*, *Istanbuler Mitteilungen*, *Mitteilungen des DAI Kairo*, *Madrider Mitteilungen*, *Baghdader Mitteilungen*, *Teheraner Mitteilungen*, *Archäologische Berichte aus dem Yemen*, *Damaszener Mitteilungen*, monographs (40–50 a year) and others.

Institut für Europäische Geschichte (Institute for European History): 55116 Mainz, Alte Universitätsstr. 19; tel. (6131) 399360; fax (6131) 237988; e-mail iegl@inst-euro-history.uni.mainz.de; f. 1950; modern European and church history, specializing in the Reformation; provides fellowship support; library of 190,000 vols; Dirs Prof. Dr G. MAY (Abt Religionsgeschichte), Prof. Dr H. DUCHHARDT (Abt Universalgeschichte); publ. *Veröffentlichungen*.

Institut für Zeitgeschichte (Institute of Contemporary History): 80636 Munich, Leonrodstr. 46b; tel. (89) 126880; fax 1231727; f. 1949; German and European history research since 1918, particularly Weimar Republic, National Socialism and post 1945 history; library of 160,000 vols; Dir Prof. Dr HORST MOELLER; publs *Vierteljahrshefte für Zeitgeschichte* (quarterly), *Schriftenreihe der Vierteljahrshefte für Zeitgeschichte* (2 a year), *Studien zur Zeitgeschichte*, *Quellen und Darstellungen zur Zeitgeschichte*, *Kolloquien des Instituts für Zeitgeschichte*, *Pressedienst*, *Biographische Quellen zur Zeitgeschichte*, *Texte und Materialien zur Zeitgeschichte*, *Akten der Auswärtigen Politik der Bundesrepublik Deutschland*.

Vereinigung zur Erforschung der Neueren Geschichte eV (Modern History Research Association): 53115 Bonn, Argelanderstr. 59; f. 1957; 17th century to present-day history; Dir Prof. Dr KONRAD REPGEN; Man. Dr A. OSCHMANN; publs *Acta Pacis Westphalicae* (Sources of the Westphalian Peace Conference), *Schriftenreihe*.

LANGUAGE AND LITERATURE

Arbeitsstelle für österreichische Literatur und Kultur Robert-Musil-Forschung: 66041 Saarbrücken, Universität des Saarlandes, Gebäude 35/4. OG, Postf. 151150; tel. (681) 302-3334; fax (681) 302-3394; e-mail fzoelk@rz.uni-sb.de; f. 1970; library of 5,000 vols; archives; study programmes, publications, symposia, bibliography; Dirs Prof. Dr PIERRE BÉHAR, Prof. Dr MARIE-LOUISE ROTH, Dr ANNETTE DAIGGE, PATRIK H. FELTES; publ. research reports; (See also International Robert Musil Society).

Institut für Deutsche Sprache: 68016 Mannheim, POB 101621; premises at: 68161 Mannheim, R5 6–13; tel. (621) 1581-0; fax (621) 1581-200; f. 1964; scientific study of present-day German; library of 70,000 vols, 300 journals; Dir Prof. Dr GERHARD STICKEL; publs *Jahrbücher*, *Studienbibliographien Sprachwissenschaft*, *Schriften des Instituts für deutsche Sprache*, *Studien zur deutschen Sprache*, *Deutsche Sprache* (quarterly), *Phonai*, *Sprachreport* (quarterly).

MEDICINE

Bernhard-Nocht-Institut für Tropenmedizin (Tropical Medicine): 20359 Hamburg, Bernhard-Nocht-Str. 74; tel. (40) 31182401; fax (40) 31182400; e-mail bni@bni.uni-hamburg.de; f. 1900; tropical medicine and parasitology; library of 41,000 vols and 47,500 reprints; Dir Prof. Dr BERNHARD FLEISCHER; publ. *Scientific Report* (annually).

C. & O. Vogt-Institut für Hirnforschung, Universität Düsseldorf (Brain Research): 40001 Düsseldorf, Postfach 101007; tel. (0211) 8112777; fax (211) 8112336; f. 1937; morphometry, neuroanatomy; immunohistochemistry, psychopharmacology; neurochemistry; Dir Prof. Dr KARL ZILLES.

Chemotherapeutisches Forschungsinstitut Georg-Speyer-Haus: 60596 Frankfurt a.M., Paul-Ehrlich-Str. 42/44; tel. (69) 63395-0; fax (69) 63395297; f. 1904; research on AIDS, tumours and allergies; library of 27,664 vols; Dir Prof. Dr H. D. BREDE.

Deutsche Gesellschaft für Kardiologie – Herz- und Kreislaufforschung (German Cardiac Society): Ständige Geschäftsstelle: Inst. f. Exp. Chirurgie, Heinrich-Heine-Univ. Düsseldorf, Postfach 101007, 40001 Düsseldorf; located at: 40225 Düsseldorf, Universitätsstr. 1; tel. (211) 8115255; fax (211) 8113550; f. 1927; 3,788 mems; Sec. Prof. Dr G. ARNOLD; publ. *Suppelmentum Zeitschrift für Kardiologie* (annually).

Deutsche Gesellschaft für Sexualforschung eV (German Association for Sex Research): Abt. für Sexualforschung der Universität Hamburg, 20246 Hamburg, Martinistr. 52; f. 1950; 220 mems; Pres. Prof. Dr VOLKMAR SIGUSCH; Sec. Prof. Dr HERTHA RICHTER-APPELT; publ. *Zeitschrift für Sexualforschung*.

Deutsche Krebsgesellschaft eV (German Cancer Society): 60596 Frankfurt/Main, Paul-Ehrlich-Str. 41; tel. (69) 630096-0; fax (69) 639130; f. 1970; promoting research, treatment and prevention of cancer; mems: 3,000 individuals; Pres. Prof. Dr Dr CH. HERFARTH (Heidelberg); Sec.-Gen. Prof. Dr P. DRINGS; publs *Journal of Cancer Research and Clinical Oncology* (6 a year), *Mitteilungen* (German Cancer Society news, quarterly).

Forschungsvereinigung Feinmechanik und Optik eV (Precision Mechanics and Optic Research Association): 50667 Cologne, Pipinstr. 16; f. 1963; Dir. Dr ERNST POHLEN.

Geomedizinische Forschungsstelle der Heidelberger Akademie der Wissenschaften: 69117 Heidelberg, Karlstr. 4; tel. (6221) 543272; f. 1952; epidemiology of atherosclerotic diseases in Europe and Asia; 50 mems; library of 3,000 vols; Dir Prof. Dr G. SCHETTLER; publs *World Atlas of Epidemic Diseases* (3 vols 1952–1961), *World Maps of Climatology*, *Geomedical Monographs Series* (6 vols), geomedical studies.

GSF — Forschungszentrum für Umwelt und Gesundheit GmbH (National Research Centre for Environment and Health): 85764 Neuherberg, Ingolstädter Landstr. 1; tel. (89) 31870; f. 1964; controls 17 institutes; research into 3 subject areas; 1,700 mems; central library of 120,000 vols and 650 journals; Scientific and Technical Dir Prof. Dr Dr E.-G.

AFTING; Administrative Dir Dr CARL-HEINZ DUISBERG.

Herz- und Diabeteszentrum NRW: 32545 Bad Oeynhausen, Georgstr. 11; tel. (5731) 970; f. 1985; cardiology, thoracic and cardiovascular surgery, paediatric cardiology, diabetology, gastroenterology, nuclear medicine, anaesthesiology, radiology, molecular biophysics, radiopharmacy, laboratory and transfusion medicine; library of 3,000 vols and 180 periodicals; Dirs Dr R. KÖRFER, Dr O. FOIT.

Institut für Wasser-, Boden- und Lufthygiene, Forschungsstelle Bad Elster: Berlin; b. in Bad Elster: 08645 Bad Elster, Heinrich-Heine-Str. 12; tel. (37437) 760; fax (37437) 76219; f. 1962; fed. govt instn; research in drinking water and bathing water, microbiology, toxicology, chemical analysis and ecology; library of 17,000 vols; Dir (Berlin) Prof. Dr H. LANGE-ASSCHENFELDT.

Institut für Wasserchemie und Chemische Balneologie der Technischen Universität München: 81377 Munich, Marchioninistr. 17; tel. (89) 70957980; fax (89) 70957999; f. 1951; water chemistry, hydrogeology, environmental analytical chemistry; Dir Prof. Dr R. NIESSNER.

Max von Pettenkofer-Institut für Hygiene und Medizinische Mikrobiologie (Institute of Hygiene and Medical Microbiology): 80336 Munich, Pettenkoferstr. 9A; tel. (089) 5160-5200; fax (89) 5380584.

Medizinisches Institut für Umwelthygiene an der Heinrich-Heine-Universität Düsseldorf (Medical Institute for Environmental Hygiene): 40225 Düsseldorf, Auf'm Hennekamp 50; tel. (211) 33890; fax (211) 3190910; f. 1962; 180 mems; library of 15,000 vols; Dir Dr M. HERBST; publs *Umwelthygiene*, *Jahresberichte*.

Paul-Ehrlich-Institut, Bundesamt für Sera und Impfstoffe: 63225 Langen, Paul-Ehrlich-Str. 51-59; tel. (6103) 77-0; fax (6103) 77123; e-mail presse-pei@em.uni-frankfurt.de; f. 1896; depts of bacteriology, virology, immunology, veterinary medicine, allergology, medicinal biotechnology, haematology and transfusion medicine; library of 32,000 vols; Pres Prof. Dr. R. KURTH; publ. *Arbeiten aus dem Paul-Ehrlich-Institut*.

NATURAL SCIENCES

General

Forschungsinstitut und Naturmuseum Senckenberg (Research Institute and Natural History Museum): 60325 Frankfurt am Main, Senckenberganlage 25; tel. (69) 7542-0; fax (69) 746238; f. 1817; systematics, anatomy, distribution, ecology, evolution in zoology, botany, palaeozoology, palaeobotany, marine biology and geology, palaeoanthropology; 50 scientists; Dir Prof. Dr F. STEININGER; publs *Abhandlungen der SNG*, *Senckenbergiana biologica*, *Senckenbergiana lethaea*, *Senckenbergiana maritima*, *Archiv für Molluskenkunde*, *Senckenberg-Bücher*, *Aufsätze und Reden der Senckenbergischen Naturforschenden Gesellschaft*, *Natur und Museum*, *Kleine Senckenberg-Reihe*, *Courier Forschungsinstitut Senckenberg*, *Mitteilungen der Deutschen Malakozoologischen Gesellschaft*.

Fraunhofer-Gesellschaft zur Förderung der angewandten Forschung eV: 80636 Munich, Leonrodstr. 54; tel. (89) 1205-01; fax (89) 1205-317; e-mail info@zv.fhg.de; f. 1949; research in microelectronics and microsystems technology, information and communications technology, sensor systems, testing and measurement technology, production technology, materials and components, process engineering, energy technology, construction engineering, environmental research and public health, technical and economic studies, information transfer; Pres. Prof. Dr Dr-Ing. H.-J. WARNECKE; publ. *Fraunhofer Magazin* (quarterly).

Biological Sciences

Alfred-Wegener-Institut für Polar- und Meeresforschung (Alfred Wegener Institute for Polar and Marine Research): 27568 Bremerhaven, Columbusstr.; tel. (471) 4831-0; telex 0238695; fax (471) 4831149; e-mail awi-pr@awi-bremerhaven.de; f. 1981; library of 60,000 vols; Dir Prof. Dr JÖRN THIEDE; publ. *Berichte zur Polarforschung*.

Biologische Anstalt Helgoland (Biological Institution Helgoland): Central Laboratory: 22607 Hamburg, Notkestr. 31; tel. (40) 896930; fax (40) 89693115; Marine Station: 27483 Helgoland; Wadden Marine Station: 25992 List/Sylt; f. 1892; research in marine biology; 136 mems; library of 115,000 books and journals; Dir Prof. Dr W. NULTSCH; publs *Helgoländer Meeresuntersuchungen* (quarterly), *Berichte der Biologischen Anstalt Helgoland* (irregular).

Deutsche Gesellschaft für Moor- und Torfkunde (German Society for Bog and Peat Research): 30655 Hannover, Stilleweg 2; tel. (511) 643-2241; fax (511) 643-3681; f. 1970; 310 mems; Pres. Dr J. D. BECKER-PLATEN; publ. *TELMA* (annually).

Forschungszentrum Borstel – Zentrum für Medizin und Biowissenschaften (Borstel Research Centre for Medicine and Biological Sciences): 23845 Borstel, Parkallee 1–40; tel. (4537) 188-0; fax (4537) 188-404; f. 1947; research in fields of immunology, pulmonology, microbiology, cell biology, allergy, chemistry and medicine; library of 50,000 vols.

Institut für Vogelforschung 'Vogelwarte Helgoland' (Ornithological Research): 26386 Wilhelmshaven, Rüstersiel; tel. (4421) 96890; fax (4421) 968955; e-mail bairlein@ifv-terramare.fh.wilhelmshaven.de; f. 1910; re-opened 1947; biology, migration studies, ringing centre, ecology, morphology, ethology of birds and biology of sea birds, avian nutrition, etc.; Dir Prof. Dr FRANZ BAIRLEIN.

Naturforschende Gesellschaft Bamberg eV: 96129 Strullendorf, Litzendorferstr. 17; tel. (9505) 8629; f. 1834; 250 mems; library of 18,000 vols; Dirs Dipl.-Biol. K. WEBER, Dr D. BÖSCHE; publ. *Berichte*.

Naturforschende Gesellschaft Freiburg i. Br.: 79104 Freiburg i. Br., Albertstr. 23B; tel. (761) 2036484; fax (761) 2036483; f. 1821; 300 mems; Pres. Prof. Dr A. BOGENRIEDER; publ. *Berichte* (annually).

Institut für Allgemeine Botanik und Botanischer Garten der Universität (Institute for General Botany and Botanic Garden of the University): 22609 Hamburg, Ohnhorststr. 18; tel. (40) 82282-0; fax (40) 82282-254; e-mail sekretariat@botanik.uni-hamburg.de; f. 1821; research in plant physiology, cell biology, plant systematics, genetics and microbiology, applied plant molecular biology; botanical garden and herbarium comprising *c.* 800,000 specimens; *c.* 250 mems; library of 45,000 vols and 49,000 reprints; Man. Dir Prof. Dr HORST LÖRZ; publs *Mitteilungen*, *Institut für Allgemeine Botanik Hamburg*.

Institut für Angewandte Botanik (Institute of Applied Botany at Hamburg University): 20309 Hamburg, Marseiller Str. 7; fax (40) 41236593; f. 1885; *c.* 140 mems; library of 130,000 vols; research on plant products, agriculture and horticulture; Dir Prof. Dr GÜNTER ADAM; publ. *Jahresberichte* (every 2 years).

Mathematical Sciences

Mathematisches Forschungsinstitut Oberwolfach (Mathematical Research Institute): 77709 Oberwolfach, Lorenzenhof; tel. (7834) 979-0; fax (7834) 979-38; e-mail admin@mfo.de; f. 1944; Dir Prof. Dr MATTHIAS KRECK.

Physical Sciences

Astronomisches Institut der Universität Münster: 48149 Münster (Westf.), Wilhelm-Klemm-Str. 10; tel. (251) 83-33561; telex 892529; fax (251) 83-33565; e-mail aim@cygnus.uni-muenster.de; f. 1912; observational cosmology, variable stars, stellar physics; library of *c.* 22,000 books; Man. A. BRUCH.

Astronomisches Institut der Universität Würzburg: 97074 Würzburg, Am Hubland; f. 1967; astronomy, theoretical astrophysics; library of 5,000 vols, 50 journals; Dir Prof. Dr FRANZ-L. DEUBNER.

Astronomisches Rechen-Institut (Astronomical Institute): 69120 Heidelberg, 12–14 Mönchhofstr.; tel. (6221) 4050; fax (6221) 405297; e-mail library@ari.uni-heidelberg.de; f. 1700; theoretical astronomy; 50 mems; library of 26,000 vols; Dir Prof. Dr ROLAND WIELEN; publs *Apparent Places of Fundamental Stars*, *Astronomy and Astrophysics Abstracts*, *Veröffentlichungen*, *Astronomische Grundlagen für den Kalender*.

Astrophysikalisches Institut und Universitäts-Sternwarte: 07745 Jena, Schillergässchen 2; tel. (3641) 630323; fax (3641) 630417; e-mail obs@astro.uni-jena.de; f. 1813; Dir Prof. Dr W. PFAU.

Bundesamt für Seeschiffahrt und Hydrographie (Federal Maritime and Hydrographic Agency): 20359 Hamburg, Bernhard-Nocht-Str. 78; tel. (40) 3190-0; telex 923730; f. 1945, renamed 1990 (1868); under the Federal Ministry of Transport; oceanography, tides and currents, geomagnetism, gravimetry, nautical technics, navigating methods, tonnage measurement, hydrographic surveying and nautical geodesy, bathymetry, sea-bed geology, pollution control, ice information service, nautical charts and publications; library of 136,000 vols; hydrographic information service; 1,000 mems; Pres. Prof. Dr PETER EHLERS; publs *Deutsche Hydrographische Zeitschrift* (quarterly), *Jahresbericht*, *Nachrichten für Seefahrer* (weekly), *Eisberichte*, etc.

Bundesanstalt für Geowissenschaften und Rohstoffe (Federal Institute for Geosciences and Natural Resources): 30631 Hanover, Postfach 51 0153; tel. (511) 643-0; fax (511) 6432304; e-mail public.relations.bgr-nlfb@bgr.de; f. 1958; geoscientific investigation, evaluation of mineral resources, environmental protection, geotechnology, seismology, marine and polar research; library of 296,000 vols; Pres. Prof. Dr Ing. F.-W. WELLMER; publs *Geologisches Jahrbuch*, *Zeitschrift fur angewandte Geologie*.

Deutsche Stiftung Edelsteinforschung (German Foundation for Gemstone Research): 55714 Idar-Oberstein, Postfach 122260; tel. (6781) 43013; fax (6781) 41616; f. 1972; depts for applied gemmological research, gemmological documentation and gemstone identification; Dir Dr C. C. MILISENDA.

Deutscher Wetterdienst (German Meteorological Service): 63004 Offenbach am Main, Postfach 100465; premises at: 63067 Offenbach am Main, Frankfurter Str. 135; f. 1952; central office for the Federal Republic; 3,000 mems; library of 155,000 vols; Pres. UDO GÄRTNER; publs *Europäischer Wetterbericht*, *Monatlicher Witterungsbericht*, *Die Grosswetterlagen Europas* (monthly), *Jahresbericht*, *Deutsches Meteorologisches Jahrbuch* (annually), *promet-Meteorologische Fortbildung* (quarterly), *Annalen der Meteorologie*, *Berichte des Deutschen Wetterdienstes*, *Bibliographien*, *Leitfäden für die Ausbildung*.

Forschungsgemeinschaft Angewandte Geophysik eV (Applied Geophysical Research Association): 30032 Hanover, POB 3266; tel. (511) 76867-0; fax (511) 76867-22; f. 1954; Dir OTTO LENZ.

Forschungszentrum Jülich GmbH (Jülich Research Centre): 52425 Jülich; tel. (2461) 61-0; fax (2461) 615327; f. 1956; operated jointly by German federal govt (90%) and state of North Rhine-Westphalia (10%); research in information technology and physical basic research, energy (materials and technology), environmental life sciences; library of 600,000 vols, 250,000 microforms, 2,000 journal titles; CEO Prof. Dr JOACHIM TREUSCH.

Forschungszentrum Karlsruhe GmbH (Karlsruhe Research Centre): 76021 Karlsruhe, Postfach 3640; tel. (7247) 82-0; fax (7247) 82-5802; f. 1956; environmental research, conversion of energy, climate modelling, nuclear fusion, nuclear safety, nuclear waste management, superconductivity, microsystems technology, medical technology; 4,000 mems; library of 253,000 vols, 1,600 periodical titles, 587,000 reports; Chair. Prof. Dr MANFRED POPP; publs *Hausmitteilungen*, *Nachrichten*, *FZKA-Berichte*.

Fraunhofer-Institut für Bauphysik: 70504 Stuttgart 80, POB 800469, Nobelstr. 12; tel. (711) 970-00; telex 7255168; fax (711) 970-3395; f. 1929; acoustics, noise control, thermal insulation, heating, ventilation, energy technology, low-energy houses, daylighting technology, indoor climate, indoor air quality; Dir Prof. Dr Dr hc Dr E.h Dr E.h K. A. GERTIS; publ. *IBP Mitteilung* (irregular).

Geologisch-Paläontologisches Institut und Museum, Universität Hamburg (Geological and Palaeontological Institute and Museum): 20146 Hamburg, Bundesstr. 55; tel. (40) 41234999; fax (40) 41235007; f. 1907; 12 scientific mems; library of 80,000 vols; Dirs Prof. C.-D. REUTHER, Prof. K. BANDEL; publ. *Mitteilungen aus dem Geologisch-Paläontologischen Institut der Universität Hamburg* (annually).

Hahn-Meitner-Institut Berlin GmbH: 14109 Berlin, Glienicker Str. 100; tel. (30) 80620; telex 01 85 763; fax (30) 80622181; e-mail postmaster@hmi.de; f. 1957; solid state physics, atomic and molecular structures, solar energy (photovoltaic); 655 mems; library of 50,000 vols and 400,000 reports; Dirs Prof. Dr MICHAEL STEINER, Dr BERND-UWE JAHN; Librarian Dr ECKART KUPFER.

Hamburger Sternwarte: 21029 Hamburg, Gojenbergsweg 112; tel. (40) 7252-4112; fax (40) 7252-4198; f. 1833; cosmology, quasars, stellar physics, interstellar medium, astronometry; library of 62,000 vols; Dirs Prof. D. REIMERS, Prof. S. REFSDAL.

Institut für Astronomie und Astrophysik der Universität Tübingen: 72076 Tübingen, Waldhäuserstr. 64; tel. (7071) 2972486; fax (7071) 293458; EUV- and X-ray astronomy, optical astronomy; library of 13,000 vols; Head Prof. K. WERNER; Sec. HEIDRUN OBERNDOERFFER.

Institut für Spektrochemie und angewandte Spektroskopie: 44139 Dortmund, Bunsen-Kirchhoff-Str. 11; tel. (231) 1392-0; fax (231) 1392120; f. 1952; various aspects of fundamental and applied analytical spectrochemistry; Dir Prof. Dr D. KLOCKOW.

Institut für Umwelt- und Zukunftsforschung an der Sternwarte Bochum: 44797 Bochum-Sundern, Blankensteiner Str. 200A; tel. (234) 47711; development and testing of electronic equipment for tracking and reception of satellite data, development of display and reproduction systems for satellite imagery, photo-interpretation of satellite imagery for geo-scientific and environmental studies; remote sensing; Dir Prof. H. KAMINSKI.

Attached institution:

Sternwarte Bochum-Grossplanetarium: 44791 Bochum, Castroper Str. 67; tel. (234) 9103691.

Kiepenheuer-Institut für Sonnenphysik: 79104 Freiburg i.Br., Schöneckstr. 6; tel. (761) 3198-0; fax (761) 3198-111; e-mail secr@kis.uni-freiburg.de; observatories at Freiburg/Schauinsland, and Tenerife (Canary Islands); f. 1942; optical investigation of the solar atmosphere; 48 mems.

Landessternwarte auf dem Königstuhl bei Heidelberg: 69117 Heidelberg, Königstuhl; f. 1897; astronomical scientific research; 50 mems; library of 17,000 vols; Dir Prof. Dr I. APPENZELLER.

Remeis-Sternwarte (Remeis Observatory): 96049 Bamberg, Sternwartstr. 7; tel. (951) 952220; fax (951) 952222; f. 1889; stellar astrophysics; attached to Erlangen—Nürnberg University; Chairs Prof. Dr IRMELA BUES, Prof. Dr ULRICH HEBER.

Universitäts-Sternwarte — Institut für Astronomie und Astrophysik und Observatorium Wendelstein: 81679 Munich, Scheinerstr. 1; tel. (89) 922094-0; telex 529815; fax (89) 922094-27; f. 1816; extragalactic astronomy, plasma astrophysics, stellar atmospheres, stellar evolution, cosmochemistry; library of 18,000; Dirs Prof. Dr R. P. KUDRITZKI, Prof. Dr R. BENDER.

Universitäts-Sternwarte Göttingen: 37083 Göttingen, Geismarlandstr. 11; tel. (551) 39-50-42; fax (551) 395043; f. 1748; galactic and extragalactic astrophysics, high-energy astrophysics, solar physics, stellar spectroscopy and theoretical astrophysics; Dirs K. BEUERMANN, W. DEINZER, K. J. FRICKE, F. J. KNEER.

UWG Gesellschaft für Umwelt- und Wirtschaftsgeologie mbH: 12681 Berlin, Wolfener 36 (Aufg. K); geoscientific and environmental library (books, data, photographs (remote sensing), maps); Dir Dr KLAUS ERLER.

PHILOSOPHY AND PSYCHOLOGY

Institut für Gerichtspsychologie (IfG) (Institute of Forensic Psychology): 44789 Bochum, Gilsingstr. 5; tel. (234) 34091; f. 1951; 41 mems; Dir Dr FRIEDRICH ARNTZEN.

RELIGION, SOCIOLOGY AND ANTHROPOLOGY

Arbeitsgemeinschaft Sozialwissenschaftlicher Institute eV (Association of Social Science Institutes): 53113 Bonn, Lennéstr. 30; tel. (228) 2281-0; fax (228) 2281-120; e-mail sl@bonn.iz-soz.de; f. 1949 to promote research in social sciences; 100 mems; Pres. Prof. Dr HEINZ SAHNER; Man. Dir MATTHIAS STAHL; publs *Soziale Welt* (quarterly), *ASI-News*.

Forschungsgruppe für Anthropologie und Religionsgeschichte eV (Research Group for Anthropology and History of Religion): 48341 Altenberge, Droste-Hülshoff-Str. 9B; f. 1970; research and documentation refer to all fields of religion including interconnections with anthropology, psychology, culture and environment; methodology of research; international co-operation and exchange; Pres. Prof. Dr M. L. G. DIETRICH; publs *Mitteilungen für Anthropologie und Religionsgeschichte*, *Forschungen zur Anthropologie und Religionsgeschichte*.

Gesellschaft Sozialwissenschaftlicher Infrastruktureinrichtungen eV (German Social Science Infrastructure Services): 68072 Mannheim, POB 122155; tel. (621) 12460; fax (621) 1246100; f. 1986; infrastructural services on numerical data, information bases and research methods for social scientists; Chair Prof. Dr WOLFGANG ZAPF; Mans Prof. Dr PETER PH. MOHLER, EKKEHARD MOCHMANN, Prof. Dr JÜRGEN KRAUSE.

Informationszentrum Sozialwissenschaften (Social Sciences Information Centre): 53113 Bonn, Lennéstr. 30; tel. (49 228) 22810; fax (49228) 2281120; e-mail iz@bonn.iz-soz.de; f. 1969; collection and dissemination of information in the social sciences; Chair. Prof. Dr WOLFGANG SODEUR; Sci. Dir Prof. Dr JÜRGEN KRAUSE; publs *Forschungsarbeiten in den Sozialwissenschaften*, *Sozialwissenschaftlicher Fachinformationsdienst* (2 a year), numerous reference books; produces two databases: Forschungsinformationssystem Sozialwissenschaften (FORIS) and Sozialwissenschaftl. Literaturinformationssystem (SOLIS).

TECHNOLOGY

Arbeitsgemeinschaft industrieller Forschungsvereinigungen 'Otto von Guericke' eV (AiF): 50968 Köln, Bayenthalgürtel 23; tel. (221) 376800; fax (221) 3768027; f. 1954; promotion of co-operative research for small and medium-sized industry; Pres. Dipl.-Ing. HANS WOHLFART; Dir-Gen. Dr-Ing. HANS KLEIN.

Battelle-Institut eV, Forschung, Entwicklung, Innovation: 60486 Frankfurt a.M., Am Römerhof 35; tel. (69) 7908-0; telex 411966; fax (69) 790880; f. 1952; electronic systems, engineering, vehicle technology, biological and environmental sciences, research and development, system development, planning studies, consulting, project management; 520 staff mems; library of 50,000 vols; Man. Dir Dr GERT H. HEWIG; publ. *Battelle Information*.

Bundesanstalt für Materialforschung und -prüfung (Federal Institute for Materials Research and Testing): 12205 Berlin, Unter den Eichen 87; tel. (30) 8104-0; telex 183261; fax (30) 8112029; e-mail info@bam.de; f. 1870; library of 50,000 vols; Pres. Prof. Dr-Ing. Dr hc H. CZICHOS; publs *Jahresbericht* (annually), *BAMBerichte* (research reports, irregular).

Bundesforschungsanstalt für Ernährung (Federal Research Centre for Nutrition): 76131 Karlsruhe, Engesserstr. 20; tel. (721) 6625-0; fax (721) 6625-111; e-mail walter.spiess@bfe.uni-karlsruhe.de; f. 1974; 176 mems; library of 30,000 vols; Dir Prof. Dr Ing. W. E. L. SPIESS; incorporates: Institute for Hygiene and Toxicology: Dir Prof. Dr W. HOLZAPFEL; Institute for Chemistry and Biology: Dir Prof. Dr B. TAUSCHER; Institute for Nutrition Physiology: Dir Prof. Dr. G. RECHKEMMER; Institute for Economics and Sociology of Nutrition: Dir Dr U. OLTERSDORF; Institute for Process Engineering: Dir Prof. Dr Ing. W. E. L. SPIESS; Centre for Molecular Biology: Dir Prof. Dr K.-D. JANY.

Clausthaler Umwelttechnik-Institut GmbH (Clausthal Institute of Environmental Technology): 38678 Clausthal-Zellerfeld, Leibnizstr. 21 u. 23; tel. (5323) 933-0; fax (5323) 933-100; f. 1990; wholly owned by state of Lower Saxony; research into waste avoidance, recycling and disposal; Man. Dir Prof. Dr-Ing. Dr-Ing E.h. KURT LESCHONSKI.

Deutsche Forschungsanstalt für Lebensmittelchemie (German Research Institute for Food Chemistry): 85748 Garching, Lichtenbergstr. 4; tel. (89) 28914170; telex 17898174; fax (89) 28914183; f. 1918; library of *c*. 3,000 vols; Dir (vacant); publ. *Annual Research Report*.

Deutsche Forschungsanstalt für Luft- und Raumfahrt eV (DLR) (German Aerospace Research Establishment): 51147 Cologne, Linder Höhe; tel. (2203) 601-0; fax (2203) 67310; f. 1969; flight mechanics, guidance and control, fluid mechanics, structures and materials, telecommunication technology and remote sensing, energetics; library of 400,000 vols; Chair. Prof. Dr rer. nat. WALTER KRÖLL; publs *DLR-Forschungsberichte*, *DLR-Mitteilungen* (both irregular), *DLR-Nachrichten* (quarterly), *Zeitschrift für Flugwissenschaften und Weltraumforschung* (every 2 months).

DeutscheMontanTechnologie für Rohstoff, Energie, Umwelt (DMT): 44787 Bochum, Herner Str. 45; tel. (234) 968-01/02; telex 825701; fax (234) 968-3606; f. 1990; specialists in mining.

Deutsches Textilforschungszentrum Nord-West eV: Institut an der Gerhard-Mercator-Universität Duisburg — Gesamthochschule, 47798 Krefeld, Frankenring 2; f. 1990; 100 mems; Dir Prof. Dr ECKHARD SCHOLLMEYER.

Forschungsinstitut für Edelmetalle und Metallchemie (Precious Metals and Metals Chemistry): 73525 Schwäbisch Gmünd, Katharinenstr. 17; tel. (7171) 10060; fax (7171) 100654; e-mail femmail@compuserve.com; f. 1922; basic and applied research into precious metals science and technology, electrochemical deposition, corrosion, aluminium surface technology, physical vapour deposition, metallography, environmental techniques/analyses; library; Dir Dr H. JEHN.

Forschungsinstitut für Internationale Technische und Wirtschaftliche Zusammenarbeit der RWTH Aachen (FIZ) (Research Institute for International Technical and Economic Co-operation of Aachen University of Technology): 52056 Aachen, Ahornstr. 55; tel. (241) 88947-0; fax (241) 8888284; f. 1957; 36 mems; library of 100,000 vols; Dir Prof. Dr W. GOCHT; publs *Internationale Kooperation*, *intertechnik*, *Aachener Beiträge zur Internationalen Zusammenarbeit*.

Forschungsinstitut für Wärmeschutz eV München (Thermal Insulation, Testing, Research): 82166 Gräfelfing Lochhamer Schlag; tel. (89) 85800-0; fax (89) 8580040; f. 1918; 140 mems; Scientific Dir Dr J. ACHTZIGER U. H. ZEHENDNER; publ. *Mitteilungen aus dem F / W München*.

Fraunhofer-Institut für Verfahrenstechnik und Verpackung (Process Engineering and Packaging): 85354 Freising, Giggenhauser Str. 35; tel. (8161) 491-0; f. 1942; food processing, environmental technology, preservation and packaging, general packaging; library of 6,000 vols; Dir Dr-Ing. W. HOLLEY.

Gesellschaft für Schwerionenforschung (GSI), mbH: 64291 Darmstadt, Planckstr. 1; tel. (6159) 71-0; telex 0419593; f. 1969; carries out basic research with heavy ions in nuclear physics and chemistry, solid state and atomic physics, radiation biology, etc; heavy ion linear accelerator, synchrotron, storage ring and laboratory; library of 3,000 vols; Dirs HANS. J. SPECHT, H. ZEITTRÄGER; publ. *GSI-Scientific Report*.

Institut für Bauforschung eV (Building Research): 30163 Hanover, An der Markuskirche 1; f. 1946; Dir Prof. Dr-Ing. JOACHIM ARLT.

Institut für Erdöl- und Erdgasforschung (German Petroleum Institute): 38678 Clausthal-Zellerfeld, Walther-Nernst-Str. 7; tel. (5323) 711100; fax (5323) 711200; e-mail postmaster@ife-clausthal.de; f. 1943; oil and gas recovery, reservoir engineering, refinery technology, research in petroleum products, hydrocarbons and environment; 85 mems; library of 5,000 vols; Dir Prof. Dr D. G. KESSEL; publ. research report (annually).

Institut für Textil- und Verfahrenstechnik: 73770 Denkendorf, Körschtalstr. 26; f. 1921; 165 staff; library of 2,500 vols; Dir Prof. Dr-Ing. G. EGBERS.

Institut für Werkstoffkunde der Technischen Universität Darmstadt (Materials Science Institute): 64283 Darmstadt, Grafenstr. 2; tel. (6151) 162351; fax (6151) 166118; e-mail berger@mpa-ifw.tu-darmstadt.de; Dir Prof. Dr C. BERGER.

Landesumweltamt Nordrhein Westfalen: 45023 Essen, Postfach 102363; premises at: 45133 Essen, Wallneyer Str. 6; tel. (201) 7995-0; telex 8579065; fax (201) 7995-446; research and advice in the fields of air pollution and noise control; prevention of accidental releases; water, waste-water and waste management; library of 79,000 vols, 450 current periodicals, 21,000 microfilms; Pres. Dr HARALD IRMER; publs *Berichte über die Luftqualität an Rhein und Ruhr* (monthly), *Berichte* (irregular), *Berichte über die Luftqualität in Nordrhein-Westfalen* (irregular), *Wassergüteberichte*, *Jahresberichte*, *Wasser und Abfall*.

Physikalisch-Technische Bundesanstalt (Federal Institute of Physics and Metrology): 38023 Braunschweig, Postfach 3345; tel. (531) 5920; fax (531) 592-9292; e-mail helmut.klages@ptb.de; f. 1887; divisions for mechanics and acoustics, electricity, thermodynamics and explosion protection, optics, precision engineering, ionising radiation, temperature and synchrotron radiation, and medical physics and information technology; library of 125,000 vols; Pres. Prof. Dr E. O. GÖBEL; publs *PTB-Mitteilungen* (every 2 months), *Jahresbericht* (annual report), *PTB-Berichte* (scientific reports, irregular), *PTB Prüfregeln* (irregular, available in English and Spanish).

Libraries and Archives

Aachen

Bibliothek der Technischen Hochschule: 52056 Aachen, Templergraben 61; tel. (241) 80-4445; fax (241) 8888273; f. 1870; 1,104,000 vols; Dir Dr ULRICH FELLMANN.

Oeffentliche Bibliothek: 52058 Aachen, Couvenstr. 15; tel. (241) 4791-0; telex 832654; fax (241) 408007; f. 1831; general information about the city and the region; regional history; 570,000 vols; special collections: folklore, ethnology, archaeology, organ literature; Dir M. FALTER.

Amberg

Staatsarchiv Amberg: 92224 Amberg, Archivstr. 3; f. 1437, became state archive in 1921; 2 million items in archives, library of 28,000 vols; Dirs Dr K. O. AMBRONN, R. FRITSCH.

Augsburg

Staats- und Stadtbibliothek: 86044 Augsburg, Postfach 111909; located at: 86152 Augsburg, Schaezlerstr. 25; tel. (821) 3242739; fax (821) 3242127; f. 1537; 450,000 vols, 3,636 MSS, 2,798 incunabula, 16,100 drawings and engravings; Dir Dr HELMUT GIER.

Staatsarchiv Augsburg: 86159 Augsburg, Salomon-Idler-Str. 2; tel. (821) 575025; f. 1830 in Neuburg; 2m. items; Dir Dr REINHARD H. SEITZ.

Universitätsbibliothek: 86135 Augsburg, Universitätsstr. 22; tel. (821) 5985300; fax (821) 5985354; e-mail dir@bibliothek.uni-augsburg.de; f. 1970; 1,879,000 vols, 98,400 theses, 57,000 maps, 368,000 items of AV material and microforms, 1,000 incunabula, 1,500 MSS, 1,787 music MSS; Dir (vacant).

Aurich

Niedersächsisches Staatsarchiv Aurich: 26603 Aurich, Oldersumer Str. 50; f. 1872; library of 20,000 vols; Dir Dr BERNHARD PARISIUS.

Bamberg

Staatsarchiv Bamberg: 96047 Bamberg, Hainstr. 39; tel. (951) 986220; f. in 13th century, became Bavarian state archive in 1803; special collections: Frankish history, maps, plans, MSS, documents; library of 27,500 vols; Dir Dr WAGENHÖFER.

Staatsbibliothek Bamberg: 96049 Bamberg, Domplatz 8, Neue Residenz; tel. (951) 54014; fax (951) 54615; e-mail staatsbibliothek@unibib.uni-bamberg.de; f. 1803; 400,000 vols, including a special collection of old manuscripts (5,800), incunabula (3,400), and prints and drawings (70,000); Chief Librarian Dr BERNHARD SCHEMMEL; publ. *Katalog der MSS*.

Universitätsbibliothek: 96018 Bamberg, Postfach 2705; premises at: 96052 Bamberg, Feldkirchenstr. 21; tel. (951) 8631503; fax (951) 8631565; e-mail unibibliothek@unibib.uni-bamberg.de; f. 1973; 1,394,000 vols on theology, humanities and social sciences; Dir Dr DIETER KARASEK; publ. *Schriften der Universitätsbibliothek Bamberg*.

Bayreuth

Universitätsbibliothek: 95440 Bayreuth, Universitätsgelände; tel. (921) 553420; fax (921) 553442; f. 1973 to serve the university and the public; 1,290,000 vols; Dir Dr KARL BABL.

Berlin

Akademiebibliothek der Berlin-Brandenburgischen Akademie der Wissenschaften: 10109 Berlin, Postfach 355; premises at: 10117 Berlin, Unter den Linden 8; tel. (30) 20370487; fax (30) 2082367; f. 1700; 667,000 vols, 940 periodicals, 3,258 dissertations; special collection of the publications of academies and learned societies; Dir Dr STEFFEN WAWRA.

Bibliothek für Bildungsgeschichtliche Forschung: 10203 Berlin, PF 171138; premises at: 10243 Berlin, Warschauer Str. 34–38; tel. (30) 293360-0; fax (30) 293360-25; e-mail ritzi@bbf-dipf.de; f. 1876; 685,000 vols; Dir CHRISTIAN RITZI; publs *Auswahlbestandsverzeichnisse*, *Neuerwerbungsverzeichnis*, *Katalog zum Hör- und Sprachgeschädigtenwesen*, *Tagungsbände*, *Ausstellungskataloge*, *Reihe Bestandsverzeichnisse zur Bildungsgeschichte*, *Bibliographie Bildungsgeschichte* (annually), *Quellentexte aus der Bibliothek für Bildungsgeschichtliche Forschung*.

Geh. Staatsarchiv Preuss. Kulturbesitz: 14195 Berlin-Dahlem, Archivstr. 12/14; tel. (30) 83901-00; fax (30) 83901-180; f. 1598; material and research on history of Prussia and Brandenburg from 12th to 20th century; library of *c.* 120,000 vols, 650,000 records and files, 120,000 maps; Dir Dr J. KLOOSTERHUIS; publ. *Veröffentlichungen* (2–3 a year).

Ibero-Amerikanisches Institut Preussischer Kulturbesitz: 10785 Berlin, Potsdamer Str. 37; tel. (30) 2662502; fax (30) 2662503; f. 1930; research institute and library dedicated to Latin America, Spain and Portugal; library of 770,000 vols; Dir Prof. Dr DIETRICH BRIESEMEISTER; publs *Quellenwerke zur alten Geschichte Amerikas*, *Monumenta Americana*, *Bibliotheca Ibero-Americana*, *Stimmen Indianischer Völker*, *Miscellanea*

Ibero-Americana, Indiana, Ibero-Amerikanisches Archiv, Iberoamericana, Biblioteca Luso-Brasileira.

Kunstbibliothek Staatliche Museen zu Berlin: 10785 Berlin, Matthäikirchplatz 6; tel. (30) 266-6; fax (30) 2662958; f. 1867; 400,000 vols, special collections: ornamental and architectural books, Lipperheidesche Kostumbibliothek, artists' books, posters, photographs, graphic design, drawings.

Landesarchiv Berlin: 10777 Berlin, Kalckreuthstr. 1–2; tel. (30) 212830; f. 1948; legal documents, etc. for the Berlin area, and important material of all kinds on the history of Berlin; library of 76,000 vols and 5,200 film rolls; Dir Dr JÜRGEN WETZEL.

Senatsbibliothek Berlin: 10623 Berlin, Str. des 17 Juni 112; tel. (30) 39987-324; fax (30) 39987-322; f. 1949; central government library of Berlin and special library for urban and land planning and regional research; 493,000 vols, 4,700 periodicals; Dir MARION HECKER; publ. *Berlin-Bibliographie.*

Staatsbibliothek zu Berlin – Preussischer Kulturbesitz: 10117 Berlin, Unter den Linden 8; tel. (30) 2015-0; fax (30) 2015-1721; and 10785 Berlin, Potsdamer Str. 33 (Tiergarten); tel. (30) 266-1; fax (30) 266-2814; f. 1661; 9 m. vols, 38,000 current periodicals and newspapers, 17,200 occidental MSS, 66,200 musical MSS, 438,000 music prints, 889,000 maps, 4,300 incunabula, 97,000 autographs, 12 m. pictures, 2 m. microforms; Mendelssohn archive; international ISBN agency; Gen. Dir Dr ANTONIUS JAMMERS; Deputy Dir Dr GÜNTER BARON; publs *Jahresbericht, Mitteilungen* (3 a year).

Universitätsbibliothek der Freien Universität Berlin: 14195 Berlin, Garystr. 39; tel. 8384224; fax 8383738; f. 1952; 2,100,000 vols, 6,000 periodicals, 498,000 theses; Dir Prof. Dr rer. pol. ULRICH NAUMANN.

Universitätsbibliothek der Humboldt-Universität: 10117 Berlin, Dorotheenstr. 27; tel. (30) 2093-3200; fax (30) 2093-3207; e-mail info@unibib.hu-berlin.de; f. 1831; 2,933,000 vols, 2,988,000 vols in dept libraries; Dir Dr MILAN BULATY; publ. *Schriftenreihe.*

Universitätsbibliothek der Technischen Universität Berlin: 10623 Berlin, Str. des 17. Juni 135; tel. (30) 31422956; fax (30) 31421726; e-mail katalog@ub.tu-berlin.de; 2,111,000 vols, 7,184 periodicals, 60,000 architectural drawings, complete German standards; Dir Dipl.-Soz. A. HABERMANN.

Zentral- und Landesbibliothek Berlin (Berlin Central and Provincial Library): 10178 Berlin, Breite Str. 32–36; tel. (30) 902260; fax (30) 90226494; e-mail zlb@kulturbox.de; central public library of Berlin; 2,200,000 vols, 1,800 periodicals; Dir Dr CLAUDIA LUX.

Bochum

Stadtbücherei Bochum: 44777 Bochum, Willy-Brandt-Platz 2–6; tel. (234) 910-2480; fax (234) 910-2437; e-mail stadtbue@bochum.de; f. 1905; 518,000 vols; Dir I. MÄMECKE.

Universitätsbibliothek: 44780 Bochum, Postfach 102148; tel. (234) 7002350; fax (234) 7094213; e-mail erda.lapp@ruhr-uni-bochum.de; f. 1963; 1,942,000 vols, 371,000 theses; Dir Dr E. LAPP.

Bonn

Archiv der sozialen Demokratie (Friedrich-Ebert-Stiftung) (Archive of Social Democracy—Friedrich Ebert Foundation): 53175 Bonn, Godesberger Allee 149; f. 1969; contains material formerly in archives of the Sozialdemokratische Partei Deutschlands (SPD) concerning the history of the party since its formation in 1882; history of German and international social movement, labour movement, labour problems, political movements in the Third World; library of 230,000 vols, 8,000 periodicals; Dirs Dr ULRICH CARTARIUS (Archive), WERNER KRAUSE (Library).

Auswärtiges Amt, Referat Bibliothek, Dokumentation, Geographischer Dienst: 53113 Bonn, Adenauerallee 99-103; tel. (228) 172202; fax (228) 174179; e-mail lib@aabonn2.bn.eunet.de; 278,000 vols, 2,900 periodicals, 90,000 maps; Dir Dr HANS-JOCHEN PRETSCH.

Beethoven-Archiv: 53111 Bonn, Bonngasse 24–26; tel. (228) 9817511; f. 1927; books, periodicals, documents on Beethoven and his times; Dir S. BRANDENBURG; publs *Gesamtausgabe der Musikalischen Werke Beethovens, Ausgabe der Skizzen Beethovens, Gesamtausgabe der Briefe Beethovens, Beethoven-Jahrbuch, Schriften zur Beethoven-Forschung.*

Bibliothek der Deutschen Telekom AG: 53105 Bonn, Postfach 2000; tel. (228) 1819463; fax (228) 1818928; f. 1945; telecommunications; 80,000 vols; Dir RAINER BRAUER; publ. *Zugangsliste* (monthly).

Bibliothek der Hochschulrektorenkonferenz: 53175 Bonn, Ahrstr. 39; tel. (228) 887-0; fax (228) 887-110; f. 1954 (Westdeutsche Rektorenkonferenz); 68,000 vols, 800 periodicals, 93,000 records and acts; Head Dr WERNER BECKER.

Bibliothek des Deutschen Bundestages: 53113 Bonn, Bundeshaus; tel. (228)163073; telex 886808; fax (228) 1626087; e-mail vorzimmer@wd2.bundestag.dbp.de; f. 1949; 1,100,000 vols, 11,000 periodicals; special collections of German and foreign official publications and parliamentary papers; depository library of 12 int. organizations; 30,000 maps; Dir MARGA COING; publs *Neuerwerbungen der Bibliothek, Auswahlverzeichnis, Neue Aufsätze in der Bibliothek, Auswahlverzeichnis* (every 2 months), *Schnellinformation der Bibliothek* (fortnightly).

Deutsche Zentralbibliothek für Landbauwissenschaften ZBL (National Agricultural Library of Germany): 53014 Bonn, Postfach 2460A; premises at: 53115 Bonn, Nussallee 15A; tel. (228) 733405; fax (228) 733281; e-mail zbl@ulb.uni-bonn.de; f. 1848; agriculture, horticulture, forestry, nutrition; 460,000 vols, 4,743 current periodicals; Dir CHRISTIAN JUNG.

Politisches Archiv des Auswärtigen Amts: 53113 Bonn, Adenauerallee 99–103; tel. (228) 172159; telex 88-65-91; fax (228) 173948; f. 1920; Foreign Office archives; documents dating from 1867; Dir H. J. PRETSCH; publs *Akten zur deutschen auswärtigen Politik 1918–1945* (series), *Akten zur auswärtigen Politik der Bundesrepublik Deutschland 1949 ff.* (series).

Attached archive:

Aussenstelle Berlin: 10922 Berlin, Postfach 610187; tel. (30) 20186-0; archives of former Foreign Ministry of the German Democratic Republic 1949–1990.

Stadtarchiv und Stadthistorische Bibliothek: 53103 Bonn, Stadtverwaltung; tel. (228) 773707; fax (228) 774301; f. 1899; library of 110,000 vols; Archivist and Librarians Dr MANFRED VAN REY, Dr NORBERT SCHLOSSMACHER; publs *Bonner Geschichtsblätter* (annually), *Veröffentlichungen des Stadtarchivs Bonn, Studien zur Heimatgeschichte des Stadtbezirkes Bonn-Beuel.*

Universitäts- und Landesbibliothek: 53014 Bonn, Postfach 2460; premises at: 53113 Bonn, Adenauerallee 39–41; tel. (228) 737350; fax (228) 737546; f. 1818; 2,200,000 vols, 9,100 current periodicals; Dir Dr PETER RAU.

Bremen

Bibliothek des Instituts für Seeverkehrswirtschaft und Logistik: 28359 Bremen, Universitätsallee GW1, Block A; tel. (421) 22096-0; fax (421) 22096-55; f. 1954; 110,000 bibliographical units; Head B. OGIOLDA.

Staats- und Universitätsbibliothek: 28331 Bremen, Postfach 330160; tel. (421) 2182601; fax (421) 2182614; e-mail suub@uni-bremen.de; f. 1660; 3,000,000 vols, 12,600 current periodicals; Dir ANNETTE RATH-BECKMANN; publs *Jahresbibliographie Massenkommunikation, Schriften der Staats- und Universitätsbibliothek Bremen*, facsimiles of MSS, exhibition catalogues.

Staatsarchiv: 28203 Bremen, Am Staatsarchiv 1; tel. (421) 361-6221; fax (421) 361-10247; Dir Dr H. MÜLLER; publs *Veröffentlichungen aus dem Staatsarchiv der Freien Hansestadt Bremen, Bremisches Jahrbuch.*

Brunswick

Bibliothek der Biologischen Bundesanstalt für Land- und Forstwirtschaft: 38104 Brunswick, Messeweg 11/12; tel. (531) 299-3390; fax (531) 299-3000; f. 1950; plant protection and related fields; 59,000 vols, 1,200 periodicals, 44,000 reprints, 2,200 microfilms; Head MICHAEL SCHOLZ; publs *Nachrichtenblatt des Deutschen Pflanzenschutzdienstes* (monthly), *Amtliche Pflanzenschutzbestimmungen* (irregular), *Berichte aus der Biologischen Bundesanstalt für Land- und Forstwirtschaft, Pflanzenschutzmittel-Verzeichnis* (annually), *Amtliche Pflanzenschutzbestimmungen* (irregular), *BBA – Bekanntmachungen* (irregular).

Stadtarchiv: 38100 Brunswick, Löwenwall 18B; f. 1861; 10,000 documents since 1031, municipal records, charters, maps and plans since 1228, special collections on the history of the town; Dir Dr MANFRED GARZMANN.

Universitätsbibliothek der Technischen Universität: 38106 Brunswick, Pockelsstr. 13; tel. (531) 391-5011; fax (531) 391-5836; e-mail ub@tu-bs.de; f. 1748; 1,100,000 vols; Dir Prof Dr DIETMAR BRANDES.

Wissenschaftliche Stadtbibliothek: 38100 Brunswick, Steintorwall 15; tel. (531) 470-4601; f. 1861; 370,000 vols, medieval MSS, 426 incunabula, *c.* 2,500 maps and plans up to 1850; special collection on the history of the town; Dir Dr ANETTE NASS; publs *Braunschweiger Werkstücke, Kleine Schriften* (irregular).

Bückeburg

Niedersächsisches Staatsarchiv: 31675 Bückeburg, Schloss; tel. (5722) 96773; fax (5722) 1289; f. 1961; archives of the old county, later principality, of Schaumburg-Lippe and the district of Schaumburg; central workshops for restoration and security filming for Lower Saxony; 4,000 documents, 35,000 vols, 20,000 maps; Dir Dr HUBERT HÖING; publ. *Schaumburger Studien.*

Chemnitz

Stadtbibliothek: 09030 Chemnitz, Str. d. Nationen 33, Postfach 471/479; tel. (371) 4884222; fax (371) 4884299; e-mail biblio.chem.@sb.c.shuttle.de; f. 1869; 500,000 vols; special collection of literature on local government; Dir ELKE BEER.

Universitätsbibliothek: 09107 Chemnitz, Str. der Nationen 62; tel. (371) 5311283; fax (371) 5311569; f. 1836; 945,000 vols, 93,000 theses, 4,000 periodicals, 6,816,000 patents; Dir Dr HANS-J. HERMES.

Clausthal-Zellerfeld

Universitätsbibliothek der Technischen Universität: 38678 Clausthal-Zellerfeld, Leibnizstr. 2; f. 1810; 433,000 vols, 1,400 periodicals, 5,000 geological maps; Dir Dr H. CYNTHA; publ. *Katalog der Calvörschen Bibliothek*.

Coburg

Landesbibliothek: 96450 Coburg, Schlossplatz 1; f. *c.* 1775; 363,000 vols; Dir Dr JÜRGEN ERDMANN.

Staatsarchiv Coburg: 96450 Coburg, Herrngasse 11; tel. (9561) 92833; fax (9561) 94017; f. 13th century, present title since 1939; archives of the duchy and republic of Saxe-Coburg, since 1920 the rural district of Coburg; 280,000 documents; library of 8,000 vols; Dir Dr RAINER HAMBRECHT.

Cologne

Deutsche Zentralbibliothek für Medizin (German National Medical Library): 50924 Cologne, Joseph-Stelzmann-Str. 9; tel. (221) 4785600; fax (221) 4785697; e-mail zbmed .zbmed@uni-koeln.de; f. 1908; 1,000,000 vols and microforms; 8,000 current periodicals; Dir U. KORWITZ.

Erzbischöfliche Diözesan- und Dombibliothek: 50451 Cologne, Postfach 10-11-45; premises at: 50668 Cologne, Kardinal-Frings-Str. 1–3; tel. (221) 16423721; fax (221) 16423783; f. 1738; 403,000 vols; Dirs Dr J. A. CERVELLÓ-MARGALEF, Dr F. J. BUSCH, K. GROSS, Dr LENZ.

Historisches Archiv: 50676 Cologne, Severinstr. 222–228; tel. (221) 221-4450; fax (221) 221-2480; f. 1322; records date back to AD 875; library of 43,000 vols; Dir Dr E. KLEINERTZ; publ. *Mitteilungen aus dem Stadtarchiv von Köln*.

Kunst- und Museumsbibliothek: 50667 Cologne, Kattenbug 18–24; tel. (221) 221-2388; fax (221) 221-2210; f. 1957; 340,000 vols; Curator Dr K. STAMM.

Rheinisch-Westfälisches Wirtschaftsarchiv zu Köln eV: 50667 Cologne, Unter Sachsenhausen 10–26; tel. (221) 1640-800; fax (221) 1640-829; f. 1906; economic records of the region; research and publication of research results; lending and reference library of business documents; library of *c.* 15,000 vols; Dir Prof. Dr KLARA VAN EYLL; publ. *Schriften zur rheinisch-westfälischen Wirtschaftsgeschichte*.

Rheinisches Archiv- und Museumsamt, Abtl. Archivberatung: 50259 Pulheim 2, Ehrenfriedstr. 19; tel. (2234) 9854221; fax (2234) 9854349; f. 1929; archive of the Landschaftsverband Rheinland with sources of the last 200 years; library of 16,500 vols; collections relating to local history; Dir Dr KURT SCHMITZ; publs *Landschaftsverband Rheinland, Archivberatungsstelle Rheinland: Inventare nichtstaatlicher Archive, Archivhefte, Rheinprovinz*.

Universitäts- und Stadtbibliothek: 50931 Cologne, Universitätsstr. 33; tel. (221) 4702260; fax (221) 4705166; e-mail usbsekr@ub.uni-koeln.de; f. 1920; library of *c.* 2,500,000 vols; Dir Dr H. LIMBURG.

Darmstadt

Hessische Landes- und Hochschulbibliothek Darmstadt: 64283 Darmstadt, Schloss; tel. (6151) 165800; fax (6151) 165897; e-mail auskunft@lhb.th-darmstadt.de; f. 16th century; 1,500,000 vols, 4,090 MSS, 2,200 incunabula, 13,000 musicalia, 37,000 maps, 4,600,000 German and European patent documents; Dir Dr YORCK HAASE.

Hessisches Staatsarchiv: 64289 Darmstadt, Karolinenplatz 3; tel. (6151) 165900; fax (6151) 165901; f. 1567; Dir Prof. Dr FRIEDRICH BATTENBERG; publs *Darmstädter Archivenschriften, Geschichte im Archiv, Darmstädter Archivdokumente für den Unterricht*.

Dessau

Anhaltische Landesbücherei Dessau: 06844 Dessau, Zerbster Str. 10/35; tel. (340) 213264; fax (340) 212501; f. 1898; 274,000 vols, 133 incunabula, 516 MSS, 403 current periodicals; Dir GABRIELE SCHNEIDER.

Detmold

Lippische Landesbibliothek Detmold: 32756 Detmold, Hornsche Str. 41; tel. (5231) 926600; fax (5231) 92660-55; f. 1614; 440,000 vols, 7,000 MSS; Dir DETLEV HELLFAIER.

Staatsarchiv (Personenstandsarchiv): 32756 Detmold, Willi-Hofmann-Str. 2; tel. (5231) 7660; fax (5231) 766114; f. 1957 (formerly Lippisches Landesarchiv, f. 16th century); archives of former regions of Lippe (12th century to 1947) and Minden (1815 to 1947), Dominion of Vianen (Netherlands), Detmold (since 1947); special collections: genealogy, French Citizens' Registers, Parish Registers, Jewish and Dissenters' Registers of Westphalia (1808 to 1874); copies of registers of births, deaths and marriages (1874–1938); library of 60,000 vols; Dr KLAUS SCHOLZ.

Dortmund

Stadt- und Landesbibliothek Dortmund: 44137 Dortmund, Königswall 14; tel. (231) 50-23225; fax (231) 50-23199; f. 1907; 1,200,000 vols; special collection of MSS and autographs and material on Westphalia; music dept; Dir ULRICH MOESKE; publs *Mitteilungen aus dem Literaturarchiv Kulturpreis der Stadt Dortmund* (every 2 years), *Mitteilungen* (irregular), *Autographenausstellungen* (irregular).

Stiftung Westfälisches Wirtschaftsarchiv: 44141 Dortmund, Märkische Str. 120; tel. (231) 5417296; telex 231409; fax (231) 5417117; e-mail wwado@dortmund.ihk.de; f. 1941; records of the economic, social and industrial history of Westphalia and the Ruhr; research; 4,000 shelf-metres of records; library of 50,000 vols; Dir Dr KARL-PETER ELLERBROCK.

Universitätsbibliothek Dortmund: 44227 Dortmund, Vogelpothsweg 76; tel. (231) 755-4030; fax (231) 755-4032; f. 1965; 1,674,000 vols, 6,500,000 patents; Dir MARLENE NAGELSMEIER-LINKE.

Dresden

Sächsische Landesbibliothek – Staats- und Universitätsbibliothek Dresden: 01054 Dresden; tel. (351) 463-4308; fax (351) 463-7173; e-mail direktion@slub-dresden.de; f. 1996; 3,844,000 vols, 154,000 theses, 120,000 maps, 158,000 tapes and records, 1,850,000 photographs, 131,000 standards, 15,000 current periodicals; Dir-Gen. JURGEN HERING; publ. *SLUB- Kurier* (4 a year).

Sächsisches Hauptstaatsarchiv: 01074 Dresden, Postfach 100450; premises at: 01097 Dresden, Archivstr. 14; tel. (351) 80060; f. 1834; library of 63,000 vols; Head Archivist Dr GUNTRAM MARTIN; publs *Schriftenreihe des Sächsischen Hauptstaatsarchivs* (13 vols), *Einzelveröffentlichungen*.

Städtische Bibliotheken Dresden: 01008 Dresden, Postfach 120737, Freibergerstr. 33; tel. (351) 8648101; fax 8648102; e-mail mail@bibo-dresden.de; f. 1910; 900,000 vols; Dir Dr AREND FLEMMING.

Duisburg

Stadtarchiv Duisburg: 47049 Duisburg, Karmelplatz 5 (Am Innenhafen); tel. (203) 283-2154; fax (203) 283-4330; f. 12th century; administration, research into local and city history; reference library on local history and customs of Duisburg and Lower Rhine; library of 35,000 vols; Dir Dr HANS GEORG KRAUME; publs *Duisburger Forschungen, Schriftenreihe für Geschichte und Heimatkunde Duisburgs, Duisburger Geschichtsquellen*.

Stadtbibliothek: 47049 Duisburg, Düsseldorfer Str. 5–7; tel. (203) 283-4213; fax (203) 283-4294; f. 1901; public library; 858,000 vols, 785 periodicals; Dir H. SONN.

Düsseldorf

Hauptstaatsarchiv Nordrhein-Westfälisches: 40476 Düsseldorf, Mauerstr. 55; tel. (211) 944902; fax (211) 944497002; f. 1832; Dir Prof. Dr OTTFRIED DASCHER, Zweigarchiv Kalkum: Schloss Kalkum über Düsseldorf-Kaiserswerth, tel. (211) 940750; publs *Der Archivar, Mitteilungsblatt für deutsches Archivwesen*.

Heinrich-Heine-Institut: 40213 Düsseldorf, Bilker Str. 12–14; tel. (211) 8992902; fax (211) 8929044; f. 1970; library of *c.* 30,000 vols, 300 manuscripts, 35,000 autographs of 18th, 19th and 20th centuries, 130 bequests of literature, music, art and science and a special collection relating to the poet Heine; Dir Prof. Dr J. A. KRUSE; publs *Heine-Jahrbuch, Heine-Studien, Veröffentlichungen*.

Universitäts- und Landesbibliothek Düsseldorf: 40225 Düsseldorf, Universitätsstr. 1; tel. (211) 81-12030; fax (211) 81-13054; e-mail ulb@ub.uni-duesseldorf.de; f. 1970; 2,400,000 vols, 8,281 periodicals; Dir Dr E. NIGGEMANN.

Eichstätt

Universitätsbibliothek (University Library): 85072 Eichstätt, Universitätsallee 1; tel. (8421) 93-1330; fax (8421) 93-1791; f. 16th century; developed from former Library of Diocesan Seminary and State Library; special collections: theology, archives of Assen of German Catholic Press and of Assen of Catholic publishers and booksellers, Schlecht music library and MSS, Glossner oriental and judaistic library, German Institute of Pedagogics library, archives and library of the Inklings Society; 1,580,000 vols, 27,000 units of non-book materials, 2,254 MSS, 3,147 musical MSS, 1,055 incunabula, 4,338 periodicals; Dir Dr H. HOLZBAUER; publs *Schriften der Universitätsbibliothek Eichstätt, Kataloge der Universitätsbibliothek Eichstätt, Aus den Beständen der Universitätsbibliothek Eichstätt, Bibliographien der Universitätsbibliothek Eichstätt*.

Erfurt

Stadt- und Regionalbibliothek Erfurt: 99005 Erfurt, Postfach 243; premises at: 99084 Erfurt, Domplatz 1; tel. (361) 6551590; fax (361) 6551599; f. 1392; 596,000 vols (260,000 vols in scientific special collections), 979 MSS of Middle Ages, 17th–19th century MSS, 615 incunabula, 16th–18th century imprints, 760 periodicals; Dir HEIDEMARIE TRENKMANN.

Erlangen

Universitätsbibliothek: 91051 Erlangen; premises at: 91054 Erlangen, Universitätsstr. 4; tel. (9131) 852151; fax (9131) 859309; f. 1743; 4,700,000 vols, 830,000 theses, 2,364 MSS, 140 papyri, 2,136 incunabula; special collections on education, science and philosophy; Dir Dr K. WICKERT.

Frankfurt am Main

Bibliothek des Freien Deutschen Hochstifts: 60311 Frankfurt am Main, Grosser Hirschgraben 23–25; tel. (69) 28-28-24; fax (69) 29-38-22; f. 1859; 130,000 vols, 30,000 MSS; Dirs Prof. Dr CHRISTOPH PERELS, DORIS HOPP.

Bundesarchiv Aussenstelle Frankfurt: 60311 Frankfurt a.M., Seckbächer Gasse 4; tel. (69) 212-35220; f. 1953; books containing judgments of the Supreme Court of Justice of the German Reich 1495–1806, the central paper records of the German Confederation

1815–66, materials of the German National Assembly 1848/49, ministry files of temporary central govt. 1848/49, written heritages and public sources dealing with the revolution of 1848/49; 850 metres of paper records, 1,336 pictures; library of 13,400 vols; Dir Dr WOLFGANG MICHALKA.

Deutsche Bibliothek, Die: 60322 Frankfurt a.M., Adickesallee 1; tel. (69) 15250; fax (69) 15251010; e-mail info@dbf.ddb.de; Deutsche Bibliothek (Frankfurt) and Deutsche Bücherei (Leipzig) unified 1990; acts as deposit library for Germany since 1913 and functions as national library and bibliographic information centre; special collections: Reichsbibliothek 1848, German exile literature 1933–1945, Anne-Frank-Shoah-Bibliothek; Dir-Gen. Prof. KLAUS-DIETER LEHMANN; publs *Deutsche Nationalbibliographie* (weekly, half-yearly and five-yearly issues), special lists of periodicals, theses, records and printed music.

Incorporates:

Deutsche Bibliothek: 60322 Frankfurt a.M., Adickesallee 1; tel. (69) 15250; fax (69) 15251010; e-mail info@dbf.ddb.de; f. 1947; 6,770,000 vols.

Deutsche Bücherei: 04103 Leipzig, Deutscher Platz; tel. (341) 22710; fax (341) 2271444; e-mail info@dbl.ddb.de; f. 1912; library of 8,650,000 vols.

Deutsches Musikarchiv: 12207 Berlin, Gärtnerstr. 25-32; tel. (30) 770020; fax (30) 77002-299; e-mail info@dma.ddb.de.

Institut für Stadtgeschichte (Stadtarchiv) Frankfurt am Main: 60311 Frankfurt a.M., Karmelitergasse 5; fax (69) 21230753; f. 1436; municipal records; documents from the 9th century, registers from the 13th century, deeds from the 14th century; records on Frankfurt from other archives; historical records in writings, pictures and sound; library of over 40,000 vols and 750 current periodicals; Dir Prof. Dr D. REBENTISCH; publs various.

Stadt- und Universitätsbibliothek/Senckenbergische Bibliothek: 60325 Frankfurt, Bockenheimer Landstr. 134–138; Dir BERNDT DUGALL.

Comprises:

Stadt- und Universitätsbibliothek: 60325 Frankfurt, Bockenheimer Landstr. 134–138; tel. (69) 21239230; fax (69) 21239062; e-mail direktion@uni-frankfurt.de; f. 1484; collection of vols on the humanities and medicine; 3,560,000 vols.

Senckenbergische Bibliothek: 60325 Frankfurt, Bockenheimer Landstr. 134–138; tel. (69) 798-2365; fax (69) 798-3147; f. 1763; natural sciences; 1,100,000 vols.

Freiberg im Sachsen

Technische Universität Bergakademie Freiberg Universitätsbibliothek 'Georgius Agricola': 09599 Freiberg, Agricolastr. 10; tel. (3731) 392959; fax (3731) 393289; f. 1765; 640,000 vols, 2,800 autographs, 22,000 standards, 2,400 cards, 66,300 university publications; special collections: mining and metallurgy, geosciences; Head KARIN MITTENZWEI; publ. *Veröffentlichungen der Bibliothek 'Georgius Agricola' der TU Bergakademie Freiberg*.

Freiburg im Breisgau

Deutsches Volksliedarchiv (German Folksong Archive): 79100 Freiburg, Silberbachstr. 13; tel. (761) 705030; fax (761) 7050328; f. 1914; library of 56,000 vols; Head Prof. Dr MAX MATTER; publs *Deutsche Volkslieder mit ihren Melodien, Jahrbuch für Volksliedforschung, Studien zur Volksliedforschung, Handbuch des Volksliedes, Gottscheer Volkslieder, Melodietypen des deutschen Volksgesanges*.

Stadtarchiv Freiburg i. Br.: 79098 Freiburg, Grünwälderstr. 15; f. 1840; library of 45,000 vols; Dir Dr HANS SCHADEK; publs *Veröffentlichungen, Schau-ins-Land, Neue Reihe*.

Universitätsbibliothek: 79016 Freiburg, Werthmannplatz 2, Postfach 1629; tel. 2033900; fax 203-3987; e-mail info@ub.uni-freiburg.de; f. 1457; 3,150,000 vols, incl. dissertations; Dir BÄRBEL SCHUBEL.

Fulda

Hessische Landesbibliothek Fulda: 36037 Fulda, Heinrich von Bibra-Platz 12; tel. (661) 97490; f. 1778; 300,000 vols, 840 MSS and 431 incunabula; Dir Prof. Dr HARTMUT BROSZINSKI.

Giessen

Universitätsbibliothek Giessen: 35394 Giessen, Otto-Behaghelstr. 8; tel. (641) 991400; fax (641) 9914009; f. 1612; 894,000 vols; 380,455 dissertations; 2,430 MSS; 873 incunabula; 2,841 papyri; Dir (vacant).

Görlitz

Oberlausitzische Bibliothek der Wissenschaften bei den Städtischen Sammlungen für Geschichte und Kultur Görlitz: 02826 Görlitz, Neiss Str. 30, Postfach 300131; tel. (3581) 671350; fax (3581) 671351; f. 1950 (original library 1779); scientific, historical and general library including rare book collection; 116,000 vols; Librarian MATTHIAS WENZEL.

Gotha

Forschungs- und Landesbibliothek Gotha: 99851 Gotha, Schloss Friedenstein, PF 100 130; tel. 30800; fax 308038; f. 1647; 553,000 vols, 10,000 MSS; Dir SUSANNE WERNER.

Göttingen

Niedersächsische Staats- und Universitätsbibliothek: 37070 Göttingen, Platz der Göttinger Sieben 1; tel. (551) 395231; fax (551) 395222; f. 1734; 3,972,439 vols, 12,031 MSS, 3,100 incunabula, 14,670 periodicals; Dir Prof. Dr E. MITTLER; publ. *Göttinger Bibliotheksschriften*.

Greifswald

Universitätsbibliothek: 17487 Greifswald, Rubenowstr. 4; tel. (3834) 861515; fax (3834) 861501; e-mail ub@rz.uni.greifswald.de; f. 1604; 2,790,700 vols, including 4,600 periodicals, 653,514 theses, 2,081 autographs, 330 incunabula; Dir Dr HANS-ARMIN KNÖPPEL.

Halle

Bibliothek der Deutschen Akademie der Naturforscher Leopoldina: 06019 Halle/Saale, Postfach 110543; premises at: 06108 Halle/Saale, August-Bebel-Str. 50A; tel. (345) 202423; fax (345) 2021727; e-mail biblio@leopoldinauni-halle.de; f. 1732; 250,000 vols, 20,000 theses; Dir JOCHEN THAMM.

Universitäts- und Landesbibliothek Sachsen-Anhalt: 06098 Halle/S., August-Bebel-Str. 13; tel. (345) 552201; fax (345) 5527140; f. 1696; 4,400,000 vols, 575,000 theses; Ponickau collection on Thuringian and Saxon history and folklore; Dir Dr HEINER SCHNELLING.

Hamburg

Bibliothek des Max-Planck-Institut für ausländisches und internationales Privatrecht: 20148 Hamburg, Mittelweg 187; tel. (40) 41900-0; telex 212893; fax (40) 41900-288; f. 1926; 362,500 vols, 4,000 periodicals, of which 2,044 current; Dir Dr JÜRGEN C. GÖDAN.

Commerzbibliothek der Handelskammer Hamburg: 20457 Hamburg, Adolphsplatz; tel. (40) 36138373; fax (40) 36138437; f. 1735; 170,000 vols on law, economics and social science; historical map series; Librarian ULRIKE VERDIECK.

Deutsches Bibel-Archiv: 20146 Hamburg, Von Melle Park 6; tel. (40) 4123-2564; f. 1931; biblical traditions in German literature and art; Bible translations; library of 8,000 vols; Dir Prof. Dr HEIMO REINITZER; publs *Bibel und deutsche Kultur, Abhandlungen und Vorträge, Vestigia bibliae, Naturalis historia bibliae*.

Staats- und Universitätsbibliothek Hamburg 'Carl von Ossietzky': 20146 Hamburg, Von-Melle-Park 3 (the former book holdings in Speersort were to a large extent destroyed); tel. (40) 41232213; fax (40) 41233352; e-mail auskunft@sub.uni-hamburg.de; f. 1479; deposit library for literature published in Hamburg; special collections: political science, administrative science, literature on American Indians and Eskimos, sea and coastal fishing, literature on Portugal and Spain; 2.8 million vols and 11,752 MSS; Dir Prof. Dr HORST GRONEMEYER; publs *Kataloge der Handschriften, F. G. Klopstock, Werke und Briefe*.

Staatsarchiv: 22041 Hamburg, Kattunbleiche 19; tel. (40) 3681-0; f. 13th century; history of Hamburg; library of over 1,000,000 vols; Dir Prof. Dr HANS-DIETER LOOSE; publs *Hamburgisches Urkundenbuch, Veröffentlichungen*.

Hanover

Niedersächsische Landesbibliothek: 30169 Hanover, Waterloostr. 8; tel. (511) 12670; fax (511) 1267-202; f. 1665; 2,058,244 vols, 13,000 periodicals, 4,313 MSS, *c.* 80,000 autographs, 375 incunabula, several thousand maps, etchings, woodcuts; collection of coats of arms and seals; Leibniz archive; Dir Dr WOLFGANG DITTRICH.

Niedersächsisches Hauptstaatsarchiv in Hannover: 30169 Hanover, Am Archiv 1; tel. (511) 106-2840; fax (511) 106-2910; f. 892; 32,000 metres shelf-space; Dir Dr DIETER BROSIUS.

Stadtbibliothek: 30169 Hanover, Hildesheimer Str. 12; tel. (511) 168-2169; fax (511) 1686410; f. 1440; general information about the city and region; 700,000 vols, 2,200 periodicals; Dir WIEBKE ANDRESEN.

Universitätsbibliothek Hannover und Technische Informationsbibliothek (TIB): 30060 Hanover, Welfengarten 1B, Postfach 6080; tel. (511) 762-2268; fax (511) 71-59-36; e-mail ubtib@tib.uni-hannover.de; f. 1831; 4,750,000 vols and microforms, 18,000 current periodicals; German research reports, patent specifications, standards; conference proceedings; doctoral dissertations and American reports (microforms); special emphasis on technical and scientific literature in Eastern and East Asian languages; acts as central technical library of Federal Republic; Dir Dr-Ing. G. SCHLITT.

Heidelberg

Bibliothek des Max-Planck-Instituts für Ausländisches Öffentliches Recht und Völkerrecht: 69120 Heidelberg, Im Neuenheimer Feld 535; tel. (6221) 4821; fax (6221) 482288; f. 1924; 460,000 vols; Dir J. SCHWIETZKE.

Universitätsbibliothek: 69117 Heidelberg, Plöck 107–109; tel. (6221) 542380; fax (6221) 542623; e-mail ub@ub.uni-heidelberg.de; f. 1386; 2,800,000 vols, 6,862 MSS, 1,702 incunabula, 4,500 documents; 4,000 photographs and pieces of graphic art; Dir Dr HERMANN JOSEF DÖRPINGHAUS; publs *Heidelberger Bibliotheksschriften, Facsimilia Heidelbergensia, Schriften der Universitätsbibliothek, Schriftenverzeichnis Heidelberger Dozenten, Neuerwerbungslisten, Theke*.

Jena

Thüringer Universitäts- und Landesbibliothek: 07740 Jena, Postfach; located at: 07743 Jena, Ernst-Abbe-Platz 2; tel. (3641) 638770; telex 331506; fax (3641) 638775; f. 1558; 160 mems; 2,445,000 vols, 762,800 pamphlets, 3,247 MSS, 8,677 current periodicals; Dir Doz. Dr KONRAD MARWINSKI; publs *Thüringen-Bibliographie* (annually), *Mitteilungen der Thüringer Universitäts- und Landesbibliothek Jena* (5 a year).

Karlsruhe

Badische Landesbibliothek: 76133 Karlsruhe, Erbprinzenstr. 15; tel. (721) 175-0; fax (721) 175-2333; f. 1500; 1,508,000 vols; 6,081 MSS; 1,356 incunabula; Dir Dr PETER MICHAEL EHRLE.

Bibliothek des Bundesgerichtshofes: 76133 Karlsruhe, Herrenstr. 45A; tel. (721) 159300; fax 159824; e-mail sc11@rz.uni-karlsruhe.de; f. 1950; law library; 470,000 vols; Dir D. PANNIER.

Generallandesarchiv Karlsruhe: 76133 Karlsruhe, Nördliche Hildapromenade 2; tel. (721) 9262200; fax (721) 9262231; f. 1803; 130,000 documents, 42,000 MSS, 3,500,000 report files; library of 65,000 vols on Baden history; Dir Dr VOLKER RÖDEL; publ. *Zeitschrift für die Geschichte des Oberrheins* (annually).

Universitätsbibliothek: 76049 Karlsruhe, Postfach 6920; tel. (721) 608-3101; telex 17721166; fax (721) 608-4886; e-mail ub@ubka.uni-karlsruhe.de; f. 1840; 860,000 vols; Dir Dipl.-Ing. C.-H. SCHÜTTE.

Kassel

Gesamthochschul-Bibliothek Kassel—Landesbibliothek und Murhardsche Bibliothek der Stadt Kassel: 34111 Kassel, Diagonale 10; tel. (561) 804-2166; fax (561) 804-7162; e-mail direktion@bibliothek.uni-kassel.de; f. 1976; 1,524,000 vols, 10,000 MSS, 7,400 music, 10,000 maps, 20,000 autographs, 6,000 periodicals; Dir Dr H.-J. KAHLFUSS.

Kiel

Deutsche Zentralbibliothek für Wirtschaftswissenschaften: 24105 Kiel, Düsternbrooker Weg 120; tel. (431) 8814-383; fax (431) 8814-520; e-mail info@zbw.ifw-kiel.de; f. 1914; 2,500,000 vols; Librarian HORST THOMSEN.

Schleswig-Holsteinische Landesbibliothek: 24103 Kiel, Schloss; tel. (431) 9067172; fax (431) 9067167; f. 1895; culture, civilization, literature of Schleswig-Holstein, musical scores, special collection on chess; 200,000 vols and literary bequests of *c.* 100 authors and scholars; Dir Prof. Dr DIETER LOHMEIER.

Universitätsbibliothek: 24118 Kiel, Westring 400; e-mail sekretariat@ub.uni-kiel.de; f. 1665; 1,999,000 vols incl. 609,000 theses; Dir Dr G. WIEGAND.

Koblenz

Bundesarchiv: 56003 Koblenz, Postfach 320; premises at: 56075 Koblenz (Karthause), Potsdamer Str. 1; tel. (261) 5050; fax (261) 505-226; f. 1952; central archives of the Federal Republic; 238,593 shelf-metres of records of Reich, Federal and GDR Govts, agencies, political parties, private asscns; collection of private papers; 29,200 feature films, 133,000 documentaries and newsreels, 12,005,800 photographs; 588,000 maps, 227,000 technical drawings, 38,800 political posters, 168,000 official prints, 1,524,000 vols; collns held at various sites throughout Germany; Pres. Prof. Dr FRIEDRICH P. KAHLENBERG.

Landeshauptarchiv: 56068 Koblenz, Karmeliterstr. 1/3; tel. (261) 9129-0; fax (261) 9129-112; e-mail lhakoblenz@t-online.de; f. 1832; history of Rhineland Palatinate and former territories; library of 82,000 vols, 35,000 linear metres of archives; Dir Dr HEINZ-GÜNTHER BORCK; publs *Jahrbuch für westdeutsche Landesgeschichte* (annually), *Blätter für deutsche Landesgeschichte* (annually), reports.

Konstanz

Bibliothek der Universität: 78457 Konstanz, Universitätsstr. 10; tel. (7531) 88-2800; fax (7531) 883082; f. 1965; 1,800,000 vols, 110,000 theses; Dir Dr K. FRANKEN.

Landshut

Staatsarchiv: 84036 Landshut, Burg Trausnitz; tel. (871) 92328-0; fax (871) 92328-8; f. 1753; library of 34,000 vols; Dir Dr G. SCHWERTL.

Leipzig

Institut für Länderkunde e.V. Geographische Zentralbibliothek und Archiv für Geographie: 04329 Leipzig, Schongauer Str. 9; tel. (341) 2556500; f. 1892; central geographical library containing 176,000 vols, special collection of maps and atlases from 16th–18th century, geography archives; Chief Librarian Dr INGRID HÖNSCH; publs *Beiträge zur Regionalen Geographie* (annually), *Werte der deutschen Heimat* (irregular), *Europa regional* (quarterly), *Sonderpublikationen*.

Leipziger Städtische Bibliotheken: 04009 Leipzig, Postfach 100927; premises at: 04107 Leipzig, Wilhelm-Leuschner-Platz 10–11; tel. (341) 1235342; fax (341) 1235305; e-mail stadtbib@leipzig.de; f. 1677/1914; 1.2 m. vols; Dir REINHARD STRIDDE.

Stadtarchiv: 04092 Leipzig; premises at: 04318 Leipzig, Torgauer Str. 74; tel. (341) 2429-0; fax (341) 2429-121; f. *c.* 1100.

Universitätsbibliothek der Universität Leipzig: 04107 Leipzig, Beethovenstr. 6; tel. (341) 9730500; fax (341) 9730599; f. 1543; 4,604,000 vols; Dir Dr phil. EKKEHARD HENSCHKE.

Lübeck

Archiv der Hansestadt Lübeck: 23552 Lübeck, Mühlendamm 1–3; f. 1298; municipal archives and documents of the churches, recognized public bodies, institutions and private persons; library of 40,000 vols; Dir Dr A. GRASSMANN.

Bibliothek der Hansestadt Lübeck: 23552 Lübeck, Hundestr. 5–17; tel. (451) 1224111; fax (451) 1224112; f. 1616; 1,176,000 vols, 3,200 maps, 41,000 vols of printed music, 1,395 MSS; Dir J. FLIGGE.

Ludwigsburg

Staatsarchiv: 71638 Ludwigsburg, Arsenalplatz 3; tel. (7141) 18-6310; fax (7141) 18-6311; e-mail staatsarchiv@lb.lad-bw.de; f. 1868; archives for the administrative district of Stuttgart (Nordwürttemberg); 31,000 metres of deeds and documents; library of 43,000 vols; Dir Dr GERHARD TADDEY.

Magdeburg

Landesarchiv Magdeburg—Landeshauptarchiv: 39104 Magdeburg, Hegelstr. 25; tel. (391) 56643; f. 1823; archives of public record offices in state of Saxony-Anhalt; 44,000 documents, 26,000 metres of records, 76,000 maps; library of 56,000 vols; Dir Dr J. HARTMANN.

Stadtbibliothek Magdeburg: 39015 Magdeburg, Postfach 4025; tel. (391) 5404800; f. 1525; 650,000 vols.

Mainz

Stadtbibliothek: 55116 Mainz, Rheinallee 3B; tel. (6131) 12-26-49; f. 1477 as University Library, taken over by the City of Mainz in 1805; 560,000 vols, 2,363 incunabula, 1,256 MSS; Dir G. WELLMER-BRENNECKE; publs *Mainzer Zeitschrift*, *Beiträge zur Geschichte der Stadt Mainz*.

Universitätsbibliothek Mainz: 55030 Mainz, Postfach 4020; premises at: 55122 Mainz, Saarstr. 21; tel. (6131) 392644; fax (6131) 393822; 1,815,143 vols, 814 MSS; Dir Dr A. ANDERHUB.

Mannheim

Universitätsbibliothek: 68131 Mannheim, Schloss-Ostflügel; tel. (621) 292-5101; fax (621) 292-5162; e-mail biblubma@bib.uni-mannheim.de; 1,800,000 vols; Dir CHRISTIAN BENZ.

Marbach am Neckar

Schiller-Nationalmuseum und Deutsches Literaturarchiv: 71672 Marbach, Schillerhöhe 8–10; tel. (7144) 8480; fax (7144) 848299; f. 1895; German literature since 1750; large collection of autographs and documents, 1,000 legacies, 450,000 vols; Dir Dr ULRICH OTT; publs *Jahrbuch*, *Veröffentlichungen der Deutschen Schillergesellschaft*, *Marbacher Magazin*, *Deutsches Literaturarchiv* (Verzeichnisse, Berichte, Informationen), *Marbacher Schriften*, *Marbacher Faksimiles*.

Marburg

Bibliothek des Herder-Instituts: 35037 Marburg, Gisonenweg 5–7; tel. (6421) 1840; fax (6421) 184139; e-mail bibliothek.hi@mailer.uni-marburg.de; f. 1950; East Central European library of 325,000 vols; Chief Librarian Dr HORST VON CHMIELEWSKI.

Deutsches Adelsarchiv: 35037 Marburg, Schwanallee 21; f. 1945; genealogy of German nobility; library of 15,000 vols; Dir Dr CHRISTOPH FRANKE; publ. *Genealogisches Handbuch des Adels*.

Hessisches Staatsarchiv Marburg: 35037 Marburg, Friedrichsplatz 15, Postfach 540; tel. (6421) 92500; fax (6421) 161125; f. 1870; 121,000 books, 115,000 charts; 220,000 maps and plans; 40 km of records of the Electorate of Hesse-Kassel, the abbeys of Fulda, Hersfeld, the principality of Waldeck, etc; Dir Dr FRITZ WOLFF; publs *Repertorien*, *Schriften*.

Universitätsbibliothek: 35008 Marburg, Postfach 1920; located at: 35039 Marburg, Wilhelm-Röpke-Str. 4; tel. (6421) 281319; fax (6421) 286506; e-mail verwub@mailer.uni-marburg.de; f. 1527; 1,807,000 vols, 726,981 theses, 2,916 MSS; Dir Dr D. BARTH.

Mönchengladbach

Bibliothek Wissenschaft und Weisheit (Library of Theology and Philosophy): 41063 Mönchengladbach, Franziskanerstr. 30; tel. (2161) 899135; fax (2161) 899171; f. 1929; 70,000 vols; Dir Father O. GIMMNICH.

Stadtbibliothek: 41050 Mönchengladbach, Blücherstr. 6; tel. (2161) 256341; fax (2161) 256369; e-mail stbmg@aol.com; f. 1904; 538,000 vols; special collection on social and political questions, library of the 'Volksverein fur das katholische Deutschland 1890–1933'; Dir GUIDO WEYER.

Munich

Bayerische Staatsbibliothek: 80328 Munich; premises at: 80539 Munich, Ludwigstr. 16; tel. (89) 28638-0; fax (89) 28638-293; e-mail info@bsb.badw-muenchen.de; f. 1558; academic and research library; 7,084,000 vols, 895,000 microforms, 76,000 MSS, 42,000 current periodicals, 353,000 maps, 313,000 scores, 5,400 videos and films,

35,000 slides, 60,000 sound tapes, 1,200,000 photographs; deposit library for Bavaria; Dir Dr HERMANN LESKIEN; publ. *Jahresbericht* (annually).

Bayerisches Hauptstaatsarchiv: 80539 Munich, Schönfeldstr. 5; tel. (89) 28638-596; fax (89) 28638-615; f. 13th century, reorganized 1978; comprises five departments: (1) Ältere Bestände: 278,000 charters, 553,000 documents and vols, 80,700 maps and plans; (2) Neuere Bestände (19th and 20th centuries): 4,200 charters, 923,000 documents, 28,300 maps and plans; (3) Geheimes Hausarchiv: 10,100 charters, 14,000 documents and vols, 6,100 pictures; (4) Kriegsarchiv: 465,000 documents and vols, 130,300 maps and plans, 96,000 pictures; (5) Nachlässe und Sammlungen: collections of private papers, publications, posters, pictures, etc.; Dir Dr JOACHIM WILD; publs *Archivalische Zeitschrift*, *Bayerische Archivinventare*, *Mitteilungen für die Archivpflege in Bayern*, *Nachrichten aus den Staatlichen Archiven Bayerns*, *Kurzführer*, *Austellungskataloge*.

Bibliothek des Deutschen Museums: 80306 Munich, Deutsches Museum; tel. (89) 2179-213; fax (89) 2179262; f. 1903; 860,000 vols; Dir Dr ERNST H. BERNINGER.

Deutsches Bucharchiv München (Institut für Buchwissenschaften): Bibliothek und Dokumentationsstelle, Literaturhaus München, 80333 Munich, Salvatorplatz 1; tel. (89) 291951-0; fax (89) 291951-95; f. 1948; documentation, scientific and technical information about books and periodicals; library of 26,800 vols, 160 periodicals; Dir Prof. Dr LUDWIG DELP.

Deutsches Patentamt: 80297 Munich, Abt. Informationsdienste (Bibliothek); tel. (89) 2195-2606; telex 0523534; fax (89) 2195-2221; f. 1877; industrial property; library of 1,116,000 vols, 37,000,000 patent specifications; Dir JOACHIM PRETZSCH.

Evangelischers Presseverband für Bayern eV: 80636 Munich, Birkerstr. 22; tel. (89) 12172-0; fax (89) 12172-138; e-mail redaktion@epv.de; f. 1963.

Münchner Stadtbibliothek: 81667 Munich, Rosenheimer Strasse 5; tel. (89) 48098-203; fax (89) 48098-248; f. 1843; 3 million vols; Dir Dr WERNER SCHNEIDER.

Staatsarchiv: 80539 Munich, Schönfeldstr. 3; f. 1814; 11,295,125 files (records), 9,157 documents (charts), 30,455 maps and plans, 25,000 vols (library); Dirs Dr ZORN, Dr TAUSENDPFUND.

Stadtarchiv: 80797 Munich, Winzererstr. 68; tel. 1234031-34; f. 1520; library of 65,000 vols, 78,000 documents, 16,000 million deeds, 22,000 maps and plans, 1,200,000 photos and postcards, 3,050 soundtracks, 1,500 films, 26,629 posters; Dir Dr R. BAUER.

Universitätsbibliothek: 80539 Munich, Geschw.-Scholl-Platz 1; tel. (89) 21802428; f. 1472; 2,440,000 vols, 3,123 MSS; Dir Dr FRITZ JUNGINGER.

Universitätsbibliothek der Technischen Universität: 80333 Munich, Arcisstr. 21; tel. (89) 28928601; fax (89) 28928622; e-mail bibdir@biblio.tu-muenchen.de; f. 1868; 1,700,000 vols, 500,000 reports; Dir Dr HORST WERNER.

Münster

Nordrhein-Westfälisches Staatsarchiv Münster: 48147 Münster, Bohlweg 2; tel. (251) 4885-0; fax (251) 4885-100; f. 1829 as Provinzialarchiv for Westphalia, present title since 1946; 28,000 metres of documents dating from 9th century AD; library of 150,000 vols; Dir Dr WILFRIED REININGHAUS; publ. *Das Staatsarchiv Münster und seine Bestände*.

Universitäts- und Landesbibliothek: 48043 Münster, Postfach 8029, Krummer Timpen 3–5; tel. (251) 8324021; fax (251) 8328398; f. 1588, refounded 1902; 2,197,377 vols incl. 393,424 theses, 820 incunabula, 1,213 MSS, 9,604 periodicals; Dir Dr ROSWITHA POLL.

Westfälisches Archivamt Münster im Landschaftsverband Westfalen-Lippe: 48133 Münster, Jahnstr. 26; tel. (251) 5913886; fax (251) 591269; f. 1927; non-state archives; training of archivists; library of 13,000 vols; Dir Dr NORBERT REIMANN; publs *Inventare der nichtstaatlichen Archive Westfalens*, *Westfälische Quellen und Archivverzeichnisse*, *Archivpflege in Westfalen und Lippe* (Mitteilungsblatt), *Veröffentlichungen aus dem Archiv des Landschaftsverbandes*, *Texte und Untersuchungen zur Archivpflege*.

Nuremberg

Bibliothek des Germanischen Nationalmuseums: 90105 Nuremberg, Postfach 119580; premises at: 90402 Nuremberg, Kornmarkt 1; tel. (911) 1331-0; f. 1852; arts, history of civilization, German-speaking regions; 539,000 vols; Dir Dr EBERHARD SLENCZKA; publs *Anzeiger des Germanischen Nationalmuseums* (annually), *Schrifttum zur Deutschen Kunst* (annually).

Landeskirchliches Archiv der Evangelisch-Lutherischen Kirche in Bayern: 90489 Nuremberg, Veilhofstr. 28; tel. (911) 588690; fax (911) 5886969; f. 1930; library of 160,000 vols; Dir Dr H. BAIER.

Staatsarchiv: 90408 Nuremberg, Archivstr. 17; tel. (911) 93519-0; fax (911) 93519-99; under general administration of Bavarian State Archives, Munich; f. 1806; archives of middle Franconia from middle ages to 20th century; includes Nuremberg trial documents; library of 45,000 vols; Dir Dr KLAAR.

Stadtarchiv Nürnberg: 90317 Nuremberg, Egidienplatz 23; tel. (911) 231-2770; fax (911) 231-4091; e-mail av.@av.stadt.nuernberg; f. 1865; reference library of 40,000 vols; Dir Dr MICHAEL DIEFENBACHER; publs *Quellen zur Geschichte und Kultur der Stadt Nürnberg*, *Nürnberger Werkstücke zur Stadt- und Landesgeschichte*, *Ausstellungskataloge*.

Stadtbibliothek Nürnberg: 90317 Nuremberg, Egidienplatz 23; tel. (911) 2312790; telex 622903; fax (911) 2315476; f. 1370; 960,000 vols, 3,132 MSS, 2,140 incunabula, 32,000 recordings; Dir EVA HOMRIGHAUSEN.

Universitätsbibliothek Erlangen-Nürnberg, Wirtschafts- und Sozialwissenschaftliche Zweigbibliothek: 90403 Nuremberg, Egidienplatz 23; tel. (911) 22095; fax (911) 2449157; e-mail wszb00@uerx2.bib.uni-erlangen.de; f. 1919; 243,000 vols; Dir Dr MONIKA GATTINGER.

Offenbach am Main

Bibliothek des Deutschen Wetterdienstes (Library of the German Meteorological Service): 63004 Offenbach am Main, Postfach 100465; premises at: 63067 Offenbach am Main, Frankfurter Str. 135; tel. (69) 8062-2272; fax (69) 8062-2486; f. 1847; 155,000 vols (14,000 pre-1900); the national library for meteorology, climatology; comprehensive records of data published by German and foreign instns; Dir H.-D. KIRCH; Documentation M. GOESCH.

Oldenburg

Landesbibliothek: 26024 Oldenburg, Pferdemarkt 15, Postfach 3480; tel. (441) 799-2800; fax (441) 799-2865; f. 1792; regional library; 530,000 vols, 70,000 microforms, 818 MSS; Dir Dr E. KOOLMAN; Librarians J. BEUTIN, Dr R. FIETZ, Dr K.-P. MÜLLER; publs *Schriften*, *Kataloge*.

Niedersächsisches Staatsarchiv in Oldenburg: 26135 Oldenburg, Damm 43; tel. (441) 9244100; fax (441) 26504; f. before 1615; public record office for the former district of Oldenburg; library of 63,000 vols; record repository with 13,800 metres of files; contributes to *Veröffentlichungen der Niedersächsischen Archivverwaltung*.

Osnabrück

Niedersächsisches Staatsarchiv: 49074 Osnabrück, Schloss Str. 29; tel. (541) 28577; fax (541) 21929; f. 1869; library of 74,000 vols; Dir Dr STEINWASCHER.

Passau

Staatliche Bibliothek: 94032 Passau, Michaeligasse 11; tel. (851) 2712; fax (851) 31704; e-mail kastner.spa@bvbnt1.bib-bvb.de; f. 1612 as Jesuit library, refounded 1803 as national library; special collections: philosophy, theology, regional history and literature, emblematic, Jesuitica; 270,000 vols, 149 MSS, 345 incunabula; Dir Dr JÖRG KASTNER.

Universitätsbibliothek: 94032 Passau, Innstr. 29; tel. (851) 509-1600; fax (851) 509-1602; e-mail heinrich.wimmer@uni-passau.de; f. 1976; 1,650,000 vols, 80,000 theses; Dir Dr HEINRICH WIMMER; publ. *Jahresbericht*.

Potsdam

Brandenburgisches Landeshauptarchiv Potsdam: 14404 Potsdam, Postfach 600449; tel. (331) 5674-0; fax (331) 5674-112; f. 1949; library of 85,000 vols, 40,000 linear feet of files; Dir Dr KLAUS NEITMANN.

Stadt- und Landesbibliothek Potsdam: 14467 Potsdam; Am Kanal 47; tel. (331) 2842-0; fax (331) 2842102; f. 1969; 700,000 vols; Brandenburg collection, Gottfried Benn collection.

Regensburg

Bischöfliche Zentralbibliothek: 93047 Regensburg, St Petersweg 11–13; tel. (941) 58813; f. 1972; 258,000 vols, 417 journals, with special collections on ascetics and sacred music; includes the library of St Jacob's Irish monastery and Proske's music library; Dir PAUL MAI.

Staatliche Bibliothek: 93047 Regensburg, Gesandtenstr. 13; tel. (941) 54501; fax (941) 54501; e-mail sbr@bvbnt1.bib-bvb.de; f. 1816; special collection of regional history; 257,000 vols; Dir Dr MICHAEL DRUCKER.

Universitätsbibliothek: 93042 Regensburg; premises at: 93053 Regensburg, Universitätsstr. 31; tel. (941) 943-3900; fax (941) 943-3285; f. 1964; 3,000,000 vols, incl. 322,600 theses; Dir Dr FRIEDRICH GEISSELMANN.

Rostock

Universitätsbibliothek: 18055 Rostock, Universitätsplatz 5; tel. (381) 4982283; fax (381) 4982270; e-mail ubsekretariat@ub.uni-rostock.de; f. 1569; 2,000,000 vols, 329,000 theses, 3,800 journals, 3,400 MSS, 3,985,000 patents, 33,000 standards; Dir Dr-Ing. PETER HOFFMANN.

Saarbrücken

Landesarchiv Saarbrücken: 66024 Saarbrücken, Postfach 102431; tel. (681) 980390; f. 1948; 9,500 metres of archives concerning the Saar, 25,000 vols; Dir Dr WOLFGANG LAUFER; 170 official publs.

Saarländische Universitäts- und Landesbibliothek: 66041 Saarbrücken, Postfach 151141 (medical library in Homburg, Saar); tel. (681) 302-2070; fax (681) 302-2796; f. 1950; 1,705,000 vols incl. 375,000 theses; Dir Dr BERND HAGENAU.

Schleswig

Landesarchiv Schleswig-Holstein: 24837 Schleswig, Prinzenpalais; tel. (4621) 86-1800; fax (4621) 86-1801; e-mail lash-sl@t-online.de; f. 1870; 30,000 metres of documents, 99,000 vols; Dir Dr REIMER WITT; publ. *Veröffentlichungen*.

Schwerin im Meckl

Landesbibliothek Mecklenburg-Vorpommern: 19055 Schwerin, Am Dom 2; tel. (385) 558440; fax (385) 5584424; e-mail lb@lbmv.de; f. 1779; 595,000 vols; Dir Dr R.-J. WEGENER; publ. *Mecklenburg-Vorpommersche Bibliographie* (annually).

Sigmaringen

Staatsarchiv Sigmaringen: 72488 Sigmaringen, Karlstr. 1 und 3; tel. (7571) 101551; fax (7571) 101552; f. 1865; archives of Regierungsbezirk Tübingen; family archives of the princes of Hohenzollern, barons of Stauffenberg, etc.; *c.* 16,000 metres of archives dating from 11th century; library of 52,000 vols; Dirs Dr V. TRUGENBERGER, Dr O. H. BECKER; Dr J. TREFFEISEN.

Speyer

Landesarchiv: 67346 Speyer, Otto-Mayer-Str. 9; tel. (6232) 91920; f. 1817; historical archives of the Palatinate (878–1798), of the French administration until 1815 and the Bavarian administration until 1945; current accessions of administrations in the Palatinate and Rheinhesse; collection of maps; Dir Dr K. H. DEBUS.

Pfälzische Landesbibliothek: 67343 Speyer, Otto-Mayer-Str. 9, Postfach 1709; tel. (6232) 9192-0; fax (6232) 9192-200; e-mail info@plb.de; f. 1921; 800,000 vols on all subjects, with special reference to the Palatinate and the Saar; includes library of the Historischer Verein der Pfalz; Dir Dr HARTMUT HARTHAUSEN.

Stuttgart

Bibliothek der Staatlichen Hochschule für Musik und Darstellende Kunst: 70182 Stuttgart, Urbanstr. 25; tel. (711) 212-4664; fax (711) 2124663; f. 1857; 15,165 vols, 74,835 musical scores, 3,624 records, 2,997 CDs, 125 videos; Librarians CLAUDIA NIEBEL, CATHERINA BECKER.

Bibliothek des Instituts für Auslandsbeziehungen: 70020 Stuttgart, Postfach 102463; premises at: 70173 Stuttgart, Charlottenplatz 17; tel. (711) 2225147; fax (711) 2225-131; f. 1917; 380,000 vols, 2,900 periodicals regularly, 8,700 microfilms; Dir UDO ROSSBACH; publ. *Reihe Dokumentation* (new acquisitions).

Bibliothek für Zeitgeschichte: 70173 Stuttgart, Konrad Adenauer Str. 8; tel. (0711) 2364641; fax (711) 2361347; f. 1915; contemporary history, political sciences, military sciences, especially concerning World Wars I and II, and other 20th century conflicts; 300,000 vols, 900 current periodicals, and special collections (photographs, maps, leaflets, posters, microfiches etc.); Dir Dr GERHARD HIRSCHFELD; publs *Jahresbibliographie*, *Library of Contemporary History*, *Schriften der Bibliothek für Zeitgeschichte–Neue Folge*, *Stuttgarter Vorträge zur Zeitgeschichte*.

Hauptstaatsarchiv Stuttgart: 70173 Stuttgart, Konrad-Adenauer-Str. 4; tel. (711) 212-4335; fax (711) 212-4360; history and regional studies of south-west Germany, with particular reference to Württemberg and Baden-Württemberg from 9th to 20th centuries; archives of *c.* 107,000 charters, *c.* 18,000 metres of files and vols, *c.* 40,000 maps and plans, 100,000 seals and arms; Dir (vacant).

Rathausbücherei der Landeshauptstadt Stuttgart: 70049 Stuttgart, Postfach 106034; tel. (711) 2163301; fax (711) 2163506; f. archives 1928; history of Stuttgart and Württemberg; library of 115,000 vols; spec. collns incl. 18th- and 19th-century first editions published in Stuttgart; Dir Dipl.-Bibliothekar GABY VOLLMER; publ. *Veröffentlichungen des Archives der Stadt Stuttgart*.

Universitätsbibliothek: 70043 Stuttgart, Holzgartenstr. 16, Postfach 104941; tel. (711) 121-2222; fax (711) 121-3502; e-mail ub@ub.uni-stuttgart.de; f. 1829; 1,150,000 vols, including 200,000 theses, and 4,100 German and foreign periodicals; Dir WERNER STEPHAN.

Universitätsbibliothek Hohenheim: 70599 Stuttgart, Garbenstr. 15; tel. (711) 4592097; fax (711) 4593262; e-mail ubmail@uni-hohenheim.de; f. 1818; 450,000 vols; agriculture, sciences, economics; Dir Dr JÖRG MARTIN.

Württembergische Landesbibliothek: 70047 Stuttgart, Konrad Adenauerstr. 8, Postfach 105441; tel. (711) 212-4424; fax (711) 212-4422; e-mail direktion@mailserver.wlb-stuttgart.de; f. 1765; 2.7 million vols, 6,965 incunabula; large collection of old Bibles; 15,212 MSS; Hölderlin archive and Stefan George archive; Dir B. SCHNEIDER.

Trier

Bibliothek des Priesterseminars Trier: 54203 Trier, Postfach 1330; located at: 54290 Trier, Jesuitenstr. 13; tel. (651) 9484-141; fax (651) 9484-181; f. 1805; 400,000 vols on philosophy and theology, 300 theological manuscripts, and 120 incunabula; Librarian Dr MICHAEL EMBACH.

Stadtbibliothek Trier: 54290 Trier, Weberbach 25; tel. 718-2430; fax 718-3432; f. 1804; developed from the former Jesuit Library (f. 1560) and University Library; contains 385,000 books, 2,500 MSS and about 2,500 incunabula; scientific library; Chief Librarian Dr GUNTHER FRANZ; publs *Kurtrierisches Jahrbuch*, *Rheinland-pfälzische Bibliographie*, *Ausstellungskataloge Trierer Bibliotheken*.

Universitätsbibliothek: 54296 Trier, Universitätsring 15; tel. (651) 201-2496; fax (651) 201-3977; f. 1970; open to the public; 1,200,000 vols; Dir Dr LAURENZ BÖSING.

Tübingen

Universitätsbibliothek: 72016 Tübingen, Wilhelmstr 32; tel. (7071) 2972577; fax (7071) 293123; e-mail sekretariat@b-u-tuebingen.de; f. in the last quarter of 15th century; 3,000,000 books, journals, microfilms and microfiches, 2,600,000 vols and journals in faculty libraries, 1,994 incunabula, 8,863 MSS; Dir Dr B. VON EGIDY; publs *Tübinger Bibliotheksinformationen*, *Neuerwerbungen Theologie*, *Allgemeine Religionswissenschaft* (monthly), *Alter Orient*, *Neuerwerbungen Südasien* (7 a year), *Neuerwerbungen Kriminologie* (every 6 months), *Zeitschrifteninhaltsdienst Theologie* (monthly).

Ulm

Stadtbibliothek Ulm: 89070 Ulm, Weinhof 12; tel. (731) 161-4100; fax (731) 161-1633; f. 1516; special collections: the arts, regional history; 445,000 vols; Dir J. LANGE.

Weimar

Herzogin Anna Amalia Bibliothek: 99423 Weimar, Platz der Demokratie 1; tel. (3643) 545200; fax (3643) 545220; f. 1691; history of literature, art and music; special collections: German literature of the Classical Period, Faust, Liszt, Nietzsche; 850,000 vols; Dir Dr MICHAEL KNOCHE; publ. *Internationale Bibliographie zur deutschen Klassik*.

Thüringisches Hauptstaatsarchiv Weimar: 99408 Weimar, Postfach 2726; premises at: 99423 Weimar, Marstallstr. 2; tel. (3643) 870-0; fax (3643) 870-100; f. 1547; Dir Dr habil. VOLKER WAHL.

Wiesbaden

Bibliothek-Dokumentation-Archiv Statistisches Bundesamt: 65189 Wiesbaden, Gustav-Stresemann-Ring 11; tel. (611) 751; fax (611) 724000; e-mail bibliothek.stba@t-online.de; f. 1948; collection and dissemination of statistical records, esp. on the economic and demographic development of all countries; 536,000 vols; Dir Dr KARL SCHOER.

Hessische Landesbibliothek Wiesbaden: 65185 Wiesbaden, Rheinstr. 55–57; tel. (611) 334-2670; fax (611) 334-2694; e-mail 43@hlw1.hlbwi.tu-darmstadt.de; f. 1813; 650,000 vols, manuscripts and incunabula; Dir Dr DIETER WOLF.

Hessisches Hauptstaatsarchiv Wiesbaden: 65187 Wiesbaden, Mosbacher Str. 55; tel. (611) 8810; fax (611) 881145; e-mail poststelle@hhstaw.hesseu.de; Dir Dr WINIFRED SCHÜLER; publ. *Nassauische Annalen* (annually).

Wolfenbüttel

Herzog August Bibliothek: 38299 Wolfenbüttel, Lessingplatz 1, Postfach 1364; tel. (5331) 8080; fax 808134; f. 1572; cultural history from the Middle Ages to the Enlightenment; 765,000 vols, 12,000 manuscripts, 3,500 incunabula; Dir Prof. Dr HELWIG SCHMIDT-GLINTZER; publs *Ausstellungskataloge*, *Kleine Schriften*, *Wolfenbütteler Beiträge*, *Wolfenbütteler Barocknachrichten*, *Wolfenbütteler Notizen zur Buchgeschichte*, *Wolfenbütteler Renaissance-Mitteilungen*, *Wolfenbütteler Forschungen*, *Wolfenbütteler Hefte*, *Wolfenbütteler Bibliotheks-Informationen*, *Repertorien zur Erforschung der frühen Neuzeit*, *Malerbuch-Kataloge*.

Niedersächsisches Staatsarchiv: 38302 Wolfenbüttel, Forstweg 2; tel. (5331) 9350; f. 16th century; contains documents and records of the province of Brunswick; library of *c.* 60,000 vols; Dir Dr HORST-RÜDIGER JARCK.

Worms

Stadtarchiv im Raschi Haus: 67547 Worms, Hintere Judengasse 6; tel. (6241) 853345; Judaic museum; large collection of records, documents and maps; Head Archivist Dr GEROLD BOENNEN.

Stadtbibliothek: 67547 Worms, Marktplatz 10; tel. (6241) 853504; fax (6241) 853505; e-mail stadtbibliothek@stbwo.worms.de; f. 1881; 350,000 vols, 162 incunabula; special collections on Luther and Kant; Dir Dr BUSSO DIEKAMP; publ. *Der Wormsgau*.

Wuppertal

Stadtbibliothek (Public Library): 42103 Wuppertal, Kolpingstr. 8; tel. (202) 563-6001; fax (202) 306594; e-mail stabi.wuppertal@t-online.de; f. 1852; special collections: theology, early Socialism; Else Lasker-Schüler-Archiv, Armin T. Wegner-Archiv; 749,000 vols; Dir UTE SCHARMANN.

Würzburg

Staatsarchiv Würzburg: 97070 Würzburg, Residenzplatz 2; tel. (931) 35529-0; f. in Middle Ages, situated in Residenzplatz since 1764; archives of Lower Franconia dating from Middle Ages; library of 34,200 vols, 6,500,000 documents; Man. Dir Dr KALLFELZ.

Universitätsbibliothek: 97074 Würzburg, Am Hubland; tel. (931) 888-5943; fax (931) 888-5970; f. 1619; 3,056,000 vols, 308,000 theses, 2,949 incunabula, 2,250 manuscripts, 73 papyri; special Franconian collection; Dir (vacant).

Museums and Art Galleries

Aachen

Internationales Zeitungsmuseum der Stadt Aachen (International Newspaper Museum): 52058 Aachen, Pontstr. 13; tel. (241) 4324508; fax (241) 4090656; e-mail zeitung@izm.org.de; f. 1886; 160,000 newspapers; Dir Dr CHRISTOF SPULER.

Suermondt-Ludwig-Museum: 52070 Aachen, Wilhelmstr. 18; tel. (241) 47980-0; fax (241) 37075; f. 1882; antiques, sculpture of Middle Ages, paintings, particularly 17th-century Dutch School and modern collection, prints and drawings; history of art library of 15,000 vols; Dir Dr ULRICH SCHNEIDER; publ. *Aachener Kunstblätter* (annually).

Baden-Baden

Staatliche Kunsthalle: 76530 Baden-Baden, Lichtentaler Allee 8A; tel. (7221) 23250; fax (7221) 38590; f. 1909; international exhibitions of classical and contemporary art; Dir Dr MARGRIT BREHM (acting); publs catalogues.

Bayreuth

Richard-Wagner-Museum mit Nationalarchiv und Forschungsstätte der Richard-Wagner-Stiftung: 95444 Bayreuth, Richard-Wagner-Str. 48; tel. (921) 757280; fax (921) 7572822; f. 1976; museum and archive of the life and works of Richard Wagner and of the history of the Bayreuth festival; Dir Dr SVEN FRIEDRICH.

Bensheim-Auerbach

Grossherzogliche Porzellansammlung: 64625 Bensheim-Auerbach, Damenbau, Im Staatsbau Fürstenlager; tel. (6251) 788547; f. 1907; European porcelain, paintings, furniture, faïence; Owner MORITZ Landgraf VON HESSEN; Dir GUDRUN ILLGEN.

Berlin

Botanischer Garten und Botanisches Museum Berlin-Dahlem: 14191 Berlin, Königin-Luise-Str. 6–8; tel. 83006-0; fax 83006-186; e-mail zebgbm@zedat.fu-berlin.de; f. 1679, Herbarium f. 1815, Schaumuseum f. 1879; attached to Freie Universität Berlin; plant taxonomy and phytogeography; library of 141,000 vols; Dir Prof. Dr W. GREUTER; publs *Willdenowia*, *Englera*.

Brücke-Museum: 14195 Berlin, Bussardsteig 9; tel. 831-20-29; f. 1967; German expressionism, paintings, sculptures and graphic art of the Brücke group; Dir Dr MAGDALENA MOELLER; publ. *Brücke Archiv* (annually).

Deutsches Historisches Museum (German Historical Museum): 10117 Berlin, Unter den Linden 2; tel. (30) 203040; fax (30) 20304543; f. 1987; Gen. Dir Prof. Dr CHRISTOPH STÖLZL.

Haus der Wannsee-Konferenz (Wannsee Conference Building): Am Grossen Wannsee 56–58, 14109 Berlin; tel. (30) 8050010; fax (30) 80500127; f. 1992; memorial and educational centre, with a permanent exhibition documenting the persecution of Jews in Europe 1933–1945; educational department; library of 14,000 vols; Dir Dr NORBERT KAMPE.

Käthe-Kollwitz-Museum: Fasanenstr. 24, 10719 Berlin; tel. (30) 882-52-10; f. 1986; private museum (collection of Prof. Hans Pels-Leusden); permanent exhibition of Käthe Kollwitz's work; temporary exhibitions of artists related to Käthe Kollwitz; Dir MARTIN FRITSCH.

Landesmuseum für Kultur und Geschichte Berlins: 10178 Berlin, Poststr. 13–14; tel. (30) 24002-0; fax (30) 24002-187; f. 1874; illustrates history of Berlin, its culture and its art; library of 50,000 vols; Dir Prof. REINER GÜNTZER; publ. *Jahrbuch*.

Museum für Naturkunde der Humboldt-Universität zu Berlin (Natural History Museum): 10115 Berlin, Invalidenstr. 43; tel. (30) 2093-8544; fax (30) 2093-8561; e-mail dieter.stoeffler@rz.hu-berlin.de; f. 1889; incl. research institutes of palaeontology, of mineralogy, of systematic zoology; Dir Prof. Dr D. STÖFFLER.

Staatliche Museen zu Berlin – Preussischer Kulturbesitz: 10785 Berlin, Stauffenbergstr. 41; tel. (30) 2662610; telex 183160; fax (30) 2662992; f. 1957; supervises museums and collections on several sites, incl. the following selection: Museum of Pre- and Proto-History (Dir Prof. Dr WILFRIED MENGHIN), Museum of Indian Art (Dir Prof. Dr. MARIANNE YALDIZ), Museum of Islamic Art (Dir VOLKMAR ENDERLEIN), Museum of Far Eastern Art (Dir Prof. Dr WILLIBALD VEIT), Ethnology Museum (Dir. Prof. Dr KLAUS HELFRICH), Museum of German Folkore (Dir Dr ERIKA KARASEK), National Gallery (Dir (vacant)), Collection of Prints and Drawings (Dir Prof. Dr ALEXANDER DÜCKERS), Pergamonmuseum (containing Museum of West Asian Antiquities, (Dir Prof. Dr BEATE SALJE), Department of Classical Antiquities (Dir Prof. Dr WOLF-DIETER HEILMEYER), Bodemuseum (containing Egyptian Museum and Papyrus Collection, Dir Prof. Dr DIETRICH WILDUNG), Picture Gallery (Dir Prof. Dr JAN KELCH), Collection of Coins and Medals (Dir Prof. Dr BERND KLUGE), Museum of Late Classical and Byzantine Art (Dir Prof. Dr ARNE EFFENBERGER), Department of Sculpture (Dir Prof. Dr ARNE EFFENBERGER), Museum of Applied Arts (Dir Prof. Dr BARBARA MUNDT); Gen. Dir Prof. Dr WOLF-DIETER DUBE.

Verwaltung der Staatlichen Schlösser und Gärten, West-Berlin (Administration of State Castles and Gardens): 10585 Berlin, Schloss Charlottenburg Luisenplatz; tel. (30) 32091-1; f. 1927; the administration controls Charlottenburg Castle, Grunewald Hunting Castle (with collection of paintings), Glienicke Castle and Peacock Island (Castle and Park); library of 5,000 vols; Chief Officers Prof Dr JÜRGEN JULIER, Prof. Dr HELMUT BÖRSCH-SUPAN; Prof. Dr WINFRIED BAER.

Bonn

Beethoven-Haus: 53111 Bonn, Bonngasse 20; f. 1889; Beethoven's birthplace; Beethoven archives; 1,000 mems; library of 40,000 vols; Pres. Dr F. WILHELM CHRISTIANS.

Kunstmuseum Bonn: 53113 Bonn, Friedrich-Ebert-Allee 2; tel. (228) 776260; f. 1882, restored 1948; collection of 20th-century art; German expressionist painting, with important August Macke collection; contemporary international graphic art, contemporary German art; library of *c.* 15,000 vols; Dir Prof. Dr DIETER RONTE; publs catalogues.

Rheinisches Landesmuseum Bonn (Rhineland Museum in Bonn): 53121 Bonn, Fraunhoferstr. 8; tel. (228) 9881-0; fax (228) 9881-299; f. 1820; prehistoric, Roman and Frankish antiquities of the Rhineland; Rhenish sculpture, painting and applied arts up to the 20th century; Dutch paintings; library of 135,000 vols; Dir Prof. Dr FRANK GÜNTER ZEHNDER; publs *Bonner Jahrbücher des Rheinischen Landesmuseums und des Vereins von Altertumsfreunden im Rheinlande* (since 1842), *Das Rheinische Landesmuseum Bonn* ((quarterly)); (The museum was expected to be closed for reconstruction until April 2001).

Zoologisches Forschungsinstitut und Museum Alexander Koenig (Alexander Koenig Zoological Research Institute and Museum): 53113 Bonn, Adenauerallee 160; tel. (228) 9122-0; fax (228) 216979; f. 1912; zoology—vertebrates and insects; library of 150,000 vols; Dir Prof. Dr C. M. NAUMANN; publs *Bonner Zoologische Beiträge* (quarterly), *Bonner Zoologische Monographien* (irregular), *Myotis*, *Mitteilungsblatt für Fledermauskundler* (annually).

Bremen

Focke-Museum (District Museum for Art and Culture): 28213 Bremen, Schwachhauser Heerstr. 240; tel. (421) 3613575; f. 1900; exhibits from Middle Ages to 1900, pre- and early history, history of navigation, etc.; library of 40,000 vols; publ. *Hefte des Focke-Museums* (2 or 3 a year); Dir Dr JÖRN CHRISTIANSEN.

Kunsthalle Bremen: 22195 Bremen, Am Wall 195; tel. (421) 329080; fax (421) 3290847; e-mail office@kunsthalle-bremen.de; f. 1823; 15th–20th-century European paintings, prints and drawings; 17th–20th-century sculpture; Japanese drawings and books; library of 100,000 vols; Dir Dr WULF HERZOGENRATH.

Übersee-Museum Bremen: 28195 Bremen, Bahnhofsplatz 13; tel. (421) 3619176; fax (421) 3619291; f. 1896; ethnology, history of commerce, natural history, Third World subjects; library of 70,000 vols; Dir Dr VIOLA KÖNIG; publ. *TenDenZen* (annually).

Brunswick

Herzog Anton Ulrich-Museum: 38100 Brunswick, Museumstr. 1; tel. (531) 4842400; fax (531) 4842408; f. 1754; collection includes old pictures, prints and drawings, medieval art, ceramics, 16th-century French enamels, carvings in ivory, bronzes, collection of lace, old clocks, etc; art library of 55,000 vols; Dir Dr J. LUCKHARDT.

Städtisches Museum: 38100 Brunswick, Am Löwenwall; tel. (531) 4704505; fax (531) 4704555; f. 1861; collections illustrate topography, history and culture of the town; 19th- and 20th-century paintings, cabinet of medals (all periods and territories, with about 80,000 pieces); ethnographical collection of Dukedom of Brunswick; library of 39,000 vols; Dir Dr G. SPIES; publs *Braunschweiger Werkstücke*, *Arbeitsberichte*, *Miszellen*, *catalogues*.

Cologne

Agfa Foto-Historama: 50667 Cologne, Bischofsgartenstr. 1; tel. (221) 221-2411; fax (221) 221-4114; history of photography; collection of cameras, photographs, caricatures and documents; Dir Dr BODO VON DEWITZ.

Josef-Haubrich-Kunsthalle: 50676 Cologne, Josef-Haubrich-Hof; tel. (221) 221-2335; fax (221) 221-4552; f. 1967; Dir (vacant).

Kölnisches Stadtmuseum: 50667 Cologne, Zeughausstr. 1–3; tel. (221) 221-5789; fax (221) 221-4154; f. 1888; Dir Dr WERNER SCHÄFKE.

Museum für Angewandte Kunst: 50667 Cologne, An der Rechtschule; tel. (221) 221-6729; fax (221) 221-3885; f. 1888; library: see Libraries; Dir Prof. Dr BRIGITTE TIETZEL.

Museum für Ostasiatische Kunst: 50674 Cologne, Universitätsstr. 100; tel. (221) 940-5180; fax (221) 407-290; f. 1911; library of 12,000 vols; Dir Dr ADELE SCHLOMBS.

Museum Ludwig: 50667 Cologne, Bischofsgartenstr. 1; tel. (221) 221-2626; fax (221) 221-4114; f. 1976; paintings, modern sculpture, prints; library; Dir MARC SCHEPS.

Rautenstrauch-Joest-Museum: 50678 Cologne, Ubierring 45; tel. (221) 33694-13; fax (221) 33694-10; f. 1901; ethnological museum; library of 30,000 vols; Dir Dr GISELA VÖLGER; publ. *Ethnologica*.

Römisch-Germanisches Museum: 50667 Cologne, Roncalliplatz 4; tel. (221) 2212304; fax (221) 2214030; f. 1946; library of 11,000 vols; Dir Prof. Dr HANSGERD HELLENKEMPER; publ. *Kölner Jahrbuch für Vor- und Frühgeschichte*.

Schnütgen-Museum: 50667 Cologne, Cäcilienstr. 29; tel. (221) 221-2311; fax (221) 221-8489; f. 1906; library of 12,000 vols; Dir Dr HILTRUD WESTERMANN-ANGERHAUSEN.

Wallraf-Richartz-Museum: 50667 Cologne, Bischofsgartenstr. 1; tel. (221) 221-2626; fax (221) 221-2315; f. 1824; paintings, sculpture, prints; library: see Libraries; Dir Dr RAINER BUDDE; publ. *Wallraf-Richartz-Jahrbuch*.

Darmstadt

Hessisches Landesmuseum Darmstadt: 64283 Darmstadt, Friedensplatz 1; tel. (6151) 165703; fax (6151) 28942; f. 1820; archaeology, prehistory, zoology, geology-palaeontology, mineralogy; art collections and cultural history from 9th to 20th centuries, inc. crafts, prints and drawings, stained glass, sculptures, painting, post-1945 European art; library of 55,000 vols; Dir Dr INA BUSCH; publs *Kunst in Hessen und am Mittelrhein* (annually), *Kaupia. Darmstädter Beiträge zur Naturgeschichte* (2 a year).

Jagdmuseum Schloss Kranichstein: 64289 Darmstadt, Schloss Kranichstein; tel. (6151) 718613; f. 1918; pictures, hunting trophies and weapons, furnished rooms; owned by Stiftung Hessischer Jägerhof; Dir Dr A. ROSENSTOCK.

Schlossmuseum: 64283 Darmstadt, Residenzschloss; tel. (6151) 24035; f. 1920; Holbein Madonna, furnished rooms, ceremonial carriages and harness; Dir Dr V. ILLGEN.

Dortmund

Museum für Kunst und Kulturgeschichte Dortmund (Dortmund Museum of Art and Cultural History): 44137 Dortmund, Hansastr. 3; tel. (231) 5025522; fax (231) 5025511; f. 1883; collections include medieval art and sculpture, furniture of 15th–20th centuries, design, *objets d'art*, paintings, archaeology; library of 18,000 vols; publ. catalogues.

Dresden

Landesamt für Archäologie mit Landesmuseum für Vorgeschichte: Dresden, Japanisches Palais; tel. (351) 814450; fax (351) 8144666; f. 1874; preservation of ancient monuments, archaeological research and exhibitions; library of 40,000 vols specializing in prehistory; Dir Dr J. OEXLE; publs *Arbeits- und Forschungsberichte* (annually), *Veröffentlichungen*, *Kleine Schriften*, *archäologie aktuell im Freistaat Sachsen*.

Militärhistorisches Museum der Bundeswehr: 01099 Dresden, Olbrichtplatz 2; tel. (351) 8232800; fax (351) 8232805; f. 1972; German military history from the Middle Ages; exhibits include weapons, equipment, documents, uniforms and combat vehicles; cannons and caissons; also a mid-19th-century submarine, models, dioramas, paintings and sculptures.

Museum Schloss Moritzburg: 01468 Moritzburg bei Dresden, Schloss Moritzburg; tel. (35207) 8730; fax (35207) 87311; f. 1947; leather hangings, furniture, paintings, statues, porcelain, glasswork, principally of the 18th century; Dir INGRID MÖBIUS.

Staatliche Kunstsammlungen Dresden: Head Office: 01067 Dresden, Georg-Treu-Platz 2, Albertinum; tel. (351) 49140; fax (351) 4914777; f. 1560; library of 80,000 vols; Gen. Dir Dr SYBILLE EBERT-SCHIFFERER; publs *Jahrbuch*, *Dresdener Kunstblätter* (every 2 months).

Comprise:

Gemäldegalerie Alte Meister: 01067 Dresden, Zwinger, Theaterpl. 1; tel. (351) 4914620; fax (351) 4914694; Dir Prof. Dr HARALD MARX.

Gemäldegalerie Neue Meister: 01067 Dresden, Albertinum, Georg-Treu-Platz 2; tel. (351) 4914730; fax (351) 4914732; Dir Dr ULRICH BISCHOFF.

Grünes Gewölbe: 01067 Dresden, Albertinum, Georg-Treu-Platz 2; tel. (351) 4914590; fax (351) 4914599; Dir Dr DIRK SYNDRAM.

Kunstgewerbemuseum: 01326 Dresden, Schloss Pillnitz; tel. (351) 26130; fax (351) 261322; Dir Dr GISELA HAASE.

Kupferstich-Kabinett: 01307 Dresden, Güntzstr. 34; tel. (351) 4593813; fax (351) 4593891; Dir Dr WOLFGANG HOLLER.

Münzkabinett: 01307 Dresden, Güntzstr. 34; tel. (351) 4593813; fax (351) 4593891; Dir Dr PAUL ARNOLD.

Museum für Sächsische Volkskunst: 01097 Dresden, Jägerhof, Köpckestr. 1; tel. (351) 8030817; fax (351) 8044963; also a puppet theatre collection: 01445 Radebeul, Barkengasse 6; tel. 74373; Dir Dr JOHANNES JUST.

Porzellansammlung: 01067 Dresden, Zwinger, Sophienstr.; tel. (351) 4914627; fax (351) 4914629; Dir Dr ULRICH PIETSCH.

Rüstkammer: 01067 Dresden, Zwinger, Sophienstr.; tel. (351) 4914626; fax (351) 4914690; Dir Dr HEINZ-WERNER LEWERKEN.

Skulpturensammlung: 01067 Dresden, Albertinum, Georg-Treu-Platz 2; tel. (351) 4914740; fax (351) 4914350; Dir Dr HEINER PROTZMANN.

Staatlicher Mathematisch-Physikalischer Salon (Natural Sciences): 01067 Dresden, Zwinger; tel. (351) 4951364; fax (351) 4960201; f. 1560; historical watches and clocks, scientific instruments, etc.; library of 7,000 vols; Dir Dr SCHILLINGER; publ. *Veröffentlichungen* (irregular).

Staatliches Museum für Mineralogie und Geologie: 01067 Dresden, Augustusstr. 2; tel. (351) 4952446; fax (351) 4952468; f. 1728; library of 35,000 vols; letter archive; Dir FRITZ JÜRGEN OBST; publs *Abhandlungen* (annually), *Schriften* (1–2 a year).

Staatliches Museum für Tierkunde (Zoology): 01067 Dresden, Augustusstr. 2; tel. (351) 4952503; fax (351) 4952525; f. 1728; library of 60,000 vols; Dir FRITZ JÜRGEN OBST; publs *Entomologische Abhandlungen*, *Zoologische Abhandlungen*, *Malakologische Abhandlungen*, *Faunistische Abhandlungen*, *Reichenbachia Zeitschrift für entomolog. Taxonomie* (annually).

Staatliches Museum für Völkerkunde: 01097 Dresden, Japanisches Palais, Palaisplatz; tel. (351) 814450; fax (351) 8144888; f. 1875; ethnography, physical anthropology; library of 60,000 vols; Dir Dr ANNEGRET NIPPA; publs *Abhandlungen und Berichte*, *Kleine Beiträge* (annually), *Dresdner Tagungsberichte* (irregular), *Bibliographien* (irregular).

Stadtmuseum Dresden: 01067 Dresden, Wilsdruffer Str. 2; tel. 498660; f. 1891; 19,000 items; library of 7,500 vols, 22,500 pictures, 55,000 photographs; Dir MATTHIAS GRIEBEL; The Museum zur Dresdener Frühromantik, J. I. Kraszewski-Museum, Schillerhäuschen and Carl-Maria-von-Weber-Museum are attached to this Museum.

Verkehrsmuseum Dresden (Museum of Transport): 01067 Dresden, Augustusstr. 1; tel. (351) 8644-0; fax (351) 8644-110; f. 1952; collection of automobiles, motorcycles, bicycles, streetcars, aircraft, model ships and railways; library of 35,000 vols (7,000 vols in special collection); Dir Dr-Ing. DIETRICH CONRAD.

Düsseldorf

Kunstmuseum Düsseldorf im Ehrenhof (incorporating Sammlung Kunstakademie and Glasmuseum Hentrich): 40479 Düsseldorf, Ehrenhof 5; tel. (211) 899-2460; fax (211) 892-9046; f. 1913; European art and applied art from the Middle Ages to 1800; collection of 19th-century German painting; early Iranian bronzes and ceramics; 6,500 textiles from late antiquity to the 19th century; glass collection, mainly Art Nouveau, Jugendstil and Art Déco; collection of prints and drawings, including extensive collection of Italian Baroque drawings; contemporary art; design; museum for young visitors; library of 75,000 vols; Dir Dr HELMUT RICKE.

Kunstsammlung Nordrhein-Westfalen: 40213 Düsseldorf, Grabbeplatz 5; tel. (211) 8381-0; f. 1961; 20th-century art; Dir Dr ARMIN ZWEITE; Curators Dr VOLKMAR ESSERS, Dr ANETTE KRUSZYNSKI, Dr MARIA MÜLLER, Dr PIA MÜLLER-TAMM.

Löbbecke-Museum und Aquazoo: 40200 Düsseldorf, Kaiserswertherstr. 380; tel. (211) 899-6150; fax (211) 899-4493; f. 1904; natural science museum and large vivarium; 6,000 books; Dir Dr W. W. GETTMANN; publs *Westdeutscher Entomologentag Düsseldorf*, *Verhandlungen* (annually), *Jahresberichte* (annually).

Städtische Kunsthalle Düsseldorf: 40213 Düsseldorf, Grabbeplatz 4; tel. (211) 899-6241; fax (211) 8929168; reopened 1967; exhibitions of contemporary art; Dir J. HARTEN; publs catalogues.

Essen

Museum Folkwang: 45128 Essen, Goethestr. 41; tel. (201) 88-45316; fax (201) 88-45001; f. 1902; 19th- and 20th-century art, including drawings, prints, posters and photographs; library of 100,000 vols; Dir Dr G. W. KÖLTZSCH.

Flensburg

Museumsberg Flensburg: 24937 Flensburg; f. 1876; contains about 26,000 exhibits, mainly arts and crafts, peasant art, and prehistory of Schleswig; library of *c.* 12,000 vols; Dir Dr ULRICH SCHULTE-WÜLWER; publs *Nordelbingen*, *Beiträge zur Kunst- und Kulturgeschichte*.

Frankfurt am Main

Deutsches Architektur-Museum: Schaumainkai 43, 60596 Frankfurt; tel. (69) 212-38844; fax (69) 212-37721; f. 1979, opened 1984; international collection of plans, sketches, paintings and models primarily of present-day and 20th-century architecture; changing exhibitions, lectures, symposia; library and archive; publs *Jahrbuch Architektur*, monographs, exhibition catalogues.

Freies Deutsches Hochstift, Frankfurter Goethe-Museum (Goethe-Haus): 60311 Frankfurt a.M., Gr. Hirschgraben 23–25; tel. (69) 13880-0; fax (69) 13880-222; f. 1859; Goethe's birthplace; German literature of the Romantic period and of Goethe's time; selected 19th- and 20th-century works; 30,000 MSS of German poetry principally of Goethe period; 400 paintings, 16,000 etchings; library: see Libraries; Dir Prof. Dr CHRISTOPH PERELS; publs *Jahrbuch*, *Reihe der Schriften*, guides, literary editions, catalogues, etc.

Historisches Museum Frankfurt: 60311 Frankfurt a.M., Saalgasse 19; tel. (69) 212-35599; telex 413064; fax (69) 212-30702; f. 1878; history of Frankfurt; library of 50,000 vols; special collection: documents relating to elections of emperors 1562–1792, to the Assembly of Paulskirche 1848/49, and to trade fairs in the 16th to 18th centuries; Dir Prof. Dr RAINER KOCH; publ. *Schriften des Historischen Museums*.

Museum für Kunsthandwerk: 60594 Frankfurt, Schaumainkai 17; tel. (69) 212-34037; f. 1877; European applied art, Gothic to art nouveau and 20th-century art; Islamic and Far Eastern art; prints, Russian icons; library of *c.* 13,000 vols; Dir Dr ARNULF HERBST.

Museum für Moderne Kunst: Domstr. 10, 60311 Frankfurt am Main; tel. (69) 21230477; fax (69) 212-37882; opened 1991; art since the 1960s; library of 35,000 vols (open by appointment); Dir Dr JEAN-CHRISTOPHE AMMANN; Chief Curator Dr ROLF LAUTER.

Museum für Post und Kommunikation: 60596 Frankfurt a.M., Schaumainkai 53; tel. 49696060-0; telex 413014; fax 49696060123; f. 1872; items on history of Post and Telecommunications; library of 13,000 vols; Dir Dr HELMUT GOLD.

Museum für Vor- und Frühgeschichte–Archäologisches Museum: 60311 Frankfurt, Karmelitergasse 1; tel. (69) 212-35896; fax (69) 212-30700; f. 1937; prehistoric, Roman and early medieval objects from the Frankfurt area; Mediterranean and oriental archaeology; Dir Prof. Dr MEIER-ARENDT.

Städelsches Kunstinstitut und Städtische Galerie: 60596 Frankfurt, Dürerstr. 2; tel. (69) 605098-0; fax (69) 610163; f. 1816; paintings, drawings, prints, sculpture; library of 50,000 vols; Dir Prof. Dr HERBERT BECK.

Städtisches Museum für Völkerkunde: 60594 Frankfurt, Schaumainkai 29; tel. (69) 212-353-91; fax (69) 212-307-04; f. 1904; ethnographic collections from Third World cultures; research into Third World cultures; library of 60,000 vols; Dir Prof. Dr J. F. THIEL.

Freiburg im Breisgau

Städtische Museen (Municipal Collections): 79098 Freiburg im Breisgau, Salzstr. 32; f. 1862.

Comprise:

Adelhausermuseum: 79098 Freiburg im Breisgau, Gerberau 32; tel. (761) 2012566; f. 1895; native and exotic fauna; herb collection, mineralogy, precious stones, wood types, beekeeping, traditional arts and crafts from Africa, America, Asia and Oceania; library of 3,000 vols; Dir Dr EVA GERHARDS.

Augustinermuseum: 79098 Freiburg im Breisgau, Augustinerplatz; tel. (761) 2012521; f. 1923; art and culture of Upper Rhine area from Middle Ages to present day; library of 40,000 vols; Dir Dr SASKIA DURIAN-RESS.

Museum für Neue Kunst: 79098 Freiburg im Breisgau, Marienstr. 10A; tel. (761) 2012581; f. 1985; German art from 1910 to the present day; Dir Dr JOCHEN LUDWIG.

Museum für Ur- und Frühgeschichte: 79098 Freiburg im Breisgau, Colombischlössle; tel. (761) 2012571; f. 1867; collections from pre- and early history; library of *c.* 5,000 vols; Dir Dr HILDE HILLER.

Giessen

Liebig Museum: 35390 Giessen, Liebigstr. 12; exhibition of the life and work of Liebig through documents and pictures; pharmaceutical laboratory and display of chemical analysis from the 19th century.

Oberhessisches Museum und Gailsche Sammlungen der Stadt Giessen: 35390 Giessen, Brandplatz 2; f. 1879; palaeolithic collection, first Middle European flint tools; archaeological collections and treasures of Roman-German and Hessian Franconian culture; oil paintings, water-colours and copperplate engravings of present century; Dir Dr FRIEDHELM HÄRING.

Comprises:

Altes Schloss: 35390 Giessen, Brandplatz 2; houses furniture and art in 14th-century building; collections of Gothic, Baroque, Renaissance, 19th- and 20th-century artefacts.

Leib'sches Haus: 35390 Giessen, Georg-Schlosser-Str. 2; f. 1978; originally the seat of the Junkers of Rodenhausen; now museum of local history and culture; exhibits of material culture of Giessen and surrounding area; portraits, pictures, maps, engravings, textile manufacture and handicraft; furniture, farm implements, costumes, pottery; special exhibitions on the political thinkers Georg Büchner and Wilhelm Liebknecht (founder of the German Social Democratic Party).

Wallenfels'sches Haus: 35390 Giessen, Kirchenplatz 6, Am Stadtkirchturm; ethnological museum with artefacts dating from prehistoric times; examples from India, China, Japan, Ceylon, Java, East and West Africa, Egypt, New Guinea and Australia.

Gotha

Galerie am Hauptmarkt: 99867 Gotha, Hauptmarkt; tel. 51611; Dir MARLIES MIKOLAJCZAK.

Münzkabinett: 99867 Gotha, Schloss Friedenstein; tel. 53036; Dir UTA WALLENSTEIN.

Museum der Natur: 99853 Gotha, Postfach 100319; located at: 99867 Gotha, Parkallee 15; tel. (3621) 823010; fax (3621) 823020; animal and fossil exhibitions, with exhibition of local natural history; Dir RAINER SAMIETZ; publ. *Abhandlungen und Berichte*.

Museum für Kartographie: 99867 Gotha, Schloss Friedenstein; tel. (3621) 854016; Curator JUTTA SIEGERT.

Museum für Regionalgeschichte und Volkskunde: 99867 Gotha, Schloss Friedenstein; tel. (3621) 82315; exhibition of local history, with *Ekhof-Theater* (baroque theatre); Dir ELISABETH DOBRITZSCH; publ. *Abhandlungen und Berichte zur Regionalgeschichte*.

Schlossmuseum: 99867 Gotha, Schloss Friedenstein; tel. (3621) 82340; fax (3621) 852669; art collections, historical rooms, coin collections, Egyptological exhibition; Dir BERND SCHÄFER.

Göttingen

Städtisches Museum (Municipal Museum): 37073 Göttingen, Ritterplan 7; tel. (551) 400-2843; fax (551) 400-2059; f. 1889; prehistory and early history, ecclesiastical art, history of Göttingen and the University, arts and crafts, etc; library of 20,000 vols.

Halle

Landesamt für Archäologie Sachsen-Anhalt (Landesmuseum für Vorgeschichte) (Archaeological and Prehistory Museum): 06114 Halle, Richard-Wagner-Str. 9–10; tel. (345) 5247-30; f. 1882; pre- and medieval history; library of 60,000 vols; Archaeologist Dr habil. SIEGFRIED FRÖHLICH; publs *Jahresschrift für mitteldeutsche Vorgeschichte* (annually), *Veröffentlichungen* (annually), *Archäologische Berichte aus Sachsen-Anhalt* (annually).

Hamburg

Altonaer Museum in Hamburg/Norddeutsches Landesmuseum: 22701 Hamburg, Postfach 500125; premises at: 22765 Hamburg (Altona), Museumstr. 23; tel. (40) 3807514; fax (40) 38072122; f. 1863; collections on art and cultural history, folk art, shipping and fishing; library of 60,000 vols; Dir Prof. Dr G. KAUFMANN; publs *Altonaer Museum in Hamburg, Jahrbuch* (Yearbook), catalogues of collections and exhibitions.

Hamburger Kunsthalle: 20095 Hamburg, Glockengiesserwall; tel. (40) 24862612; fax (40) 2486-2482; f. 1869; paintings from 14th to 20th centuries, sculpture of 19th and 20th, drawings and engravings from 14th to 20th, Greek and Roman coins, medals from 14th to 20th centuries; library of 110,000 vols; Dir Prof. Dr UWE M. SCHNEEDE.

Hamburgisches Museum für Völkerkunde: 20148 Hamburg, Rothenbaumchaussee 64; tel. (40) 441952524; fax (40) 441952242; f. 1879; ethnological collections from Africa, America, Asia, Australia, Europe and the Pacific; library of 120,000 vols; Dir Prof. Dr W. KÖPKE; publs *Mitteilungen*, *Monographien zur Völkerkunde*, *Wegweiser zur Völkerkunde*, *Beiträge zur Mittelamerikanischen Völkerkunde*.

Museum für Hamburgische Geschichte: 20355 Hamburg, Holstenwall 24; f. 1839; political history of Hamburg, library, coins, handicrafts, models, etc; Dir Prof. Dr JÖRGEN BRACKER; publs *Hamburger Beiträge zur Numismatik*, *Numismatische Studien*, *Beiträge zur deutschen Volks- und Altertumskunde*.

Museum für Kunst und Gewerbe Hamburg: 20099 Hamburg, Steintorplatz 1; tel. (40) 2486-2732; fax (40) 2486-2834; f. 1877; 150,000 books; European sculpture and art from the Middle Ages onward, ancient art, art of the Near and Far East, European popular art, graphic, photographic and textile collections; Dir Prof. Dr WILHELM HORNBOSTEL; publs *Jahrbuch*, catalogues.

Hanover

Historisches Museum am Hohen Ufer: 30159 Hanover, Pferdestr. 6; tel. (511) 16843052; f. 1903 as Vaterländisches Museum, 1937–50 Niedersächsisches Volkstumsmuseum, 1950–66 as Niedersächsisches Heimatmuseum; three sections: Lower Saxon Folklore, History of the City of Hanover, History of the Kingdom of Hanover up to 1866; library of 8,000 vols; Dir Dr T. SCHWARK.

Kestner-Museum: 30159 Hanover, Trammplatz 3; tel. (511) 16842120; opened 1889; Egyptian, Greek, Etruscan and Roman art; illuminated MSS, incunabula, arts and crafts of Middle Ages to 20th century; ancient, medieval and modern coins, medals; Dir (vacant); Curator Prof. Dr ROSEMARIE DRENKHAHN.

Niedersächsisches Landesmuseum Hannover: 30169 Hanover, Willy-Brandt-Allee 5; tel. (511) 9807-5; fax (511) 9807-640; f. 1852; art, natural history, prehistory and ethnology sections; libraries attached to each section; Dirs Dr HEIDE GRAPE-ALBERS (also Dir art section), Dr Dr GÜNTER WEGNER (pre-history), Dr MICHAEL SCHMITZ (natural history), Dr THOMAS MICHEL (ethnology).

Heidelberg

Kurpfälzisches Museum der Stadt Heidelberg: 69117 Heidelberg, Hauptstr. 97; tel. (6221) 583400; f. 1879; Dir (vacant).

Hildesheim

Pelizaeus-Museum: 31134 Hildesheim, Am Steine 1–2; tel. (5121) 93690; fax (5121) 35283; f. 1911; collection of Egyptian and Graeco-Roman antiquities; Egyptological library for scientific use; library of 25,000 vols; Dir Dr ARNE EGGEBRECHT; publ. *Hildesheimer Ägyptologische Beiträge* (monographs).

Roemer-Museum: 31134 Hildesheim, Am Steine 1–2; tel. (5121) 93690; fax (5121) 35283; f. 1845; natural history, applied art, prehistory, ethnography, etc; library of 35,000 vols; Dir MANFRED BOETZKES.

Jena

Ernst-Abbe-Stiftung, Optisches Museum: 07743 Jena, Carl-Zeiss-Platz 12; tel. (3641) 443165; fax (3641) 443224; f. 1922; history and development of optical instruments; Dir Prof. Dr L. WENKE.

Goethe-Gedenkstätte (im Inspektorhaus des Botanischen Gartens): 07743 Jena, Fürstengraben 26; f. 1921; Admin. Friedrich-Schiller-Universität.

Jenaer Kunstsammlung und Romantiker-Gedenkstätte: 07743 Jena, Unterm Markt 12A; tel. (3641) 443263; Dir MARIA SCHMID.

Schiller-Gedenkstätte (Schillerhäuschen und -garten): 07743 Jena, Schillergässchen 2; tel. (3641) 30304; f. 1924; biographical and literary museum; Admin. Friedrich-Schiller-Universität, Sachgebiet Kultur.

Stadtmuseum Göhre: 07743 Jena, Markt 7; tel. (3641) 443245; f. 1903; library of 15,000 vols; Dir HOLGER NOWAK.

Karlsruhe

Badisches Landesmuseum: 76131 Karlsruhe, Schlossplatz 1; f. 1919; collection includes prehistoric, Egyptian, Greek and Roman antiquities, medieval, renaissance and baroque sculpture, works of art from the middle ages to the 20th century, weapons, folklore and coins, collection of Turkish trophies; library of 60,000 vols; Dir Prof. Dr HARALD SIEBENMORGEN.

Museum für Literatur am Oberrhein: 76133 Karlsruhe, Röntgenstr. 6; tel. (721) 843818; fax (721) 853544; f. 1965; exhibition of the works, manuscripts and pictures of various authors; library of 8,000 vols; Pres. Dr HANS-GEORG SCHMIDT-BERGMANN; publs *Mitteilungen*, *Jahresgabe*.

Staatliche Kunsthalle: 76133 Karlsruhe, Hans-Thoma-Str. 2–6; f. 1803; German, Dutch, Flemish, French and Italian paintings and sculpture, 14th to 20th centuries; print room; 90,000 prints and drawings; library of 110,000 vols; Dir Prof. Dr KLAUS SCHRENK.

Staatliches Museum für Naturkunde Karlsruhe (State Museum of Natural History, Karlsruhe): 76133 Karlsruhe, Erbprinzenstr. 13; tel. (721) 1752161; f. 1751; research and exhibitions in botany, zoology, mineralogy, geology, entomology, palaeontology, vivarium; library of *c.* 50,000 vols; Dir Prof. Dr S. RIETSCHEL; publs *Carolinea*, *Andrias*, *Führer zu Ausstellungen* (irregular).

Kassel

Brüder Grimm-Museum: 34117 Kassel, Brüder Grimm-Platz 4A; tel. (561) 103235; fax (561) 713299; e-mail grimm-museum@t-online.de; f. 1960; preservation of works of Jacob, Wilhelm and Ludwig Emil Grimm; collection of works by the brothers; original paintings, autographs, letters, drawings, etchings; Dir Dr BERNHARD LAUER.

Staatliche Museen Kassel (State Art Museums): 34131 Kassel, Schloss Wilhelmshöhe; tel. (561) 93777; fax (561) 9377666; f. 18th century; Dir Dr HANS OTTOMEYER; publ. *Kunst in Hessen und am Mittelrhein* (annually).

Comprise:

Hessisches Landesmuseum: Kassel, Brüder-Grimm-Platz 5; pre- and early history; arts-handicraft; folklore; wall papers.

Neue Galerie: Kassel, Schöne Aussicht 1; paintings and sculpture from 1750 to present day; temporary exhibitions of modern art.

Orangerie: Kassel, Karlsaue; astronomy and physics collection with history of technology section; planetarium.

Schloss Friedrichstein: Bad Wildungen; 15th–19th-century military and hunting exhibits.

Schloss Wilhelmshöhe: 34131 Kassel; department of classical antiquities, gallery of 15th–18th-century old master paintings, collection of drawings and engravings; library of 70,000 vols.

Torwache: Kassel, Brüder-Grimm-Platz 6; arts, handicraft and design from 1840 to present day.

Konstanz

Bodensee-Naturmuseum: 78462 Konstanz, Katzgasse 5–7; f. 1967; geology, palaeontology, zoology and botany of Lake Constance; Curator Dr INGO SCHULZ-WEDDIGEN.

Hus-Museum: 78462 Konstanz, Hussenstr. 64; tel. (7531) 29042; f. 1965; house of Jan Hus (d. 1415); display by Czechoslovak artists depicting Hus' life, Council of Constance and the Hussite wars; Dir MICHAEL MÜLLER.

Rosgarten Museum: 78459 Konstanz, Rosgartenstr. 3–5; f. 1870; central museum for Lake Constance area; prehistoric, early historic collection; arts and crafts from the Middle Ages to 19th century, coins, etc; library of 6,000 vols; Curator ELISABETH VON GLEICHENSTEIN.

Leipzig

Deutsches Buch- und Schriftmuseum der Deutschen Bücherei Leipzig (German Book Museum): 04103 Leipzig, Deutscher Platz; tel. 2271324; fax 2271444; e-mail dbsm@dbl.ddl.de; f. 1884; exhibits relate to history of books, writing and paper; library of 128,000 vols, 758 incunabula, 29,000 items of graphic art; collection of 425,000 watermarks; Dir LOTHAR POETHE.

Museum der bildenden Künste: 04109 Leipzig, Grimmaischestr. 1–7; tel. (341) 21699-0; fax (341) 9609925; f. 1837; Dir Dr HERWIG GURATZSCH.

Museum für Kunsthandwerk Leipzig, Grassi-Museum (Museum of Decorative Arts): 04103 Leipzig, Johannisplatz; tel. (341) 2142175; fax (341) 2142113; f. 1874; textiles, ceramics, glass, wood, and metal objects; collection of prints and patterns relating to design; library of 36,000 vols; Dir Dr EVA M. HOYER.

Museum für Völkerkunde zu Leipzig — Staatliche Forschungsstelle (Ethnographical Museum and State Research Centre): 04103 Leipzig, Täubchenweg 2; tel. (341) 21420; fax (341) 2142262; f. 1869; ethnographical collections from Asia, Australia, Pacific Islands, Africa, America, Europe; library of 80,000 vols; Dir Dr LOTHAR STEIN; publs *Jahrbuch* (Year Book), *Veröffentlichungen* (Publications), *Mitteilungen*.

Stadtgeschichtliches Museum Leipzig: 04109 Leipzig, Altes Rathaus, Markt 1; tel. (341) 9651-30; fax (341) 9651-352; e-mail stadtmuseum.leipzig@t-online.de; f. 1909; library of 300,000 items in special collections; Dir Dr VOLKER RODEKAMP.

Lübeck

Museum für Kunst und Kulturgeschichte (Museum for Art and Cultural History): 23552 Lübeck, Düvekenstr. 21; tel. (451) 1224134; library of 30,000 vols; Dir Dr GERHARD GERKENS; publs *Kataloge des St Annen-Museums*, *Katalog des Behnhauses*.

Branch museums:

St Annen-Museum: Lübeck, St Annenstr. 15; Late Gothic convent, built 1502–1515; medieval ecclesiastical art from Lübeck; domestic art from Lübeck, from Middle Ages to *c.* 1800.

Museum Behnhaus: Lübeck, Königstr. 11; museum of 19th- and 20th-century art in a late 18th-century patrician house.

Museum Drägerhaus: Lübeck, Königstr. 9–11; art from Overbeck to Munch; 18th-century rooms.

Museum Holstentor: Lübeck; built 1464–1478; history of the city.

Katharinenkirche: Lübeck; 14th century; formerly Franciscan monasteries church.

Völkerkundesammlung (Ethnographic Collection): 23552 Lübeck, Grosser Bauhof 14; collection at: Parade 10; tel. (451) 12-24342; fax (451) 12-26690; Dir Dr GERHARD GERKENS.

Lübstorf

Landesamt für Bodendenkmalpflege Mecklenburg-Vorpommern und Archäologisches Landesmuseum: 19069 Lübstorf, Schloss Wiligrad; tel. (3867) 8805; fax (3867) 8806; f. 1953; library of 44,000 vols; Dir Dr FRIEDRICH LÜTH; publs *Bodendenkmalpflege in Mecklenburg-Vorpommern Jahrbuch*, *Beiträge zur Ur- und Frühgeschichte Mecklenburg-Vorpommerns*, *Museumskataloge*, *Materialhefte*.

Magdeburg

Magdeburger Museen: 39104 Magdeburg, Otto von Guerickestr. 68–73; tel. (391) 5432645; fax (391) 5432646; e-mail museen@magdeburg.de; f. 1906; local history collection, art gallery, sculptures, handicrafts, graphics, bibliophilia, costumes, sociology, natural history and prehistory collection; Kulturhistorisches Museum, Kunstmuseum Kloster Unser Lieben Frauen, Museum für Naturkunde, Technikmuseum, Otto-von-Guericke Museum Lukasklause and Schulmuseum are affiliated; library of 50,000 vols; Dir MATTHIAS PUHLE; publs *Abhandlungen und Berichte Naturkunde und Vorgeschichte*, *Magdeburger Museumsschriften*, *Magdeburger Museumshefte*, *Kataloge*.

Mainz

Gutenberg-Museum: 55116 Mainz, Liebfrauenplatz 5; tel. (6131) 122640; f. 1900; world museum of typography; library of 70,000 vols; Dir Dr EVA-MARIA HANEBUTT-BENZ.

Landesmuseum Mainz: 55116 Mainz, Grosse Bleiche 49–51; tel. (6131) 2857-0; fax (6131) 285757; f. 1803; cultural history and art; Dir Dr GISELA FIEDLER-BENDER; publ. *Ausstellungskataloge*.

Münzsammlung (Coin Collection): Stadtarchiv Mainz, 55116 Mainz, Rheinallee 3B; tel. (6131) 122178; f. 1784; Dir FRIEDRICH SCHÜTZ.

Naturhistorisches Museum Mainz (Natural History Museum): 55116 Mainz, Reichklararstr./Mitternachtsplatz; tel. (6131) 12-26-46; fax (6131) 122975; e-mail lsnhmmz@goofy.zdv.uni-mainz.de; collections; f. 1834, museum f. 1910; mineralogy, geology, palaeontology, zoology and botany of Rheinland-Pfalz and Rwanda; library of 40,000 vols and 15,000 pamphlets; Dir Dr rer. nat. FR.-O. NEUFFER; publs *Mainzer Naturwissenschaftliches Archiv*, *Beihefte*, *Museumsführer*.

Römisch-Germanisches Zentralmuseum-Forschungsinstitut für Vor- und Frühgeschichte: 55116 Mainz, Ernst-Ludwig-Platz 2; tel. (6131) 91240; fax (6131) 9124199; f. 1852; studies in Old-world archaeology and prehistory, conservation of prehistoric, Roman and early medieval antiquities; library of 80,000 vols; Gen. Dir Dr K. WEIDEMANN; publs *Kataloge, Ausstellungskataloge, Führer durch die Ausstellungen, Jahrbuch, Arbeitsblätter für Restauratoren, Archäologisches Korrespondenzblatt, Corpus Signorum Imperii Romani, Studien zu den Anfängen der Metallurgie*, and various monographs.

Mannheim

Reiss-Museum der Stadt Mannheim: 68030 Mannheim, POB 103051, C5; tel. (621) 293-3151; fax (621) 293-3099; f. 1763; museum of art, crafts and decorative arts, local theatre-history, archaeology and prehistory, ethnology, local history and natural history; 82,000 books; Dir Prof. Dr KARIN VON WELCK.

Städtische Kunsthalle: 68165 Mannheim, Moltkestr. 9; tel. (621) 293-6413; fax (621) 293-6412; f. 1907; Dirs Prof. Dr MANFRED FATH, Dr JOCHEN KRONJÄGER, Dr HANS-JÜRGEN BUDERER, Dr INGE HEROLD, Dr MONIKA SCHULTE.

Marburg

Universitätsmuseum für Bildende Kunst: 35032 Marburg/Lahn, Biegenstr. 11, im Ernst von Hülsen-Haus; f. 1927; Dir Dr JÜRGEN WITTSTOCK.

Universitätsmuseum für Kulturgeschichte: 35032 Marburg/Lahn, Landgrafenschloss, Wilhelmsbau; f. 1875; Dir Dr JÜRGEN WITTSTOCK.

Mettmann

Neanderthal-Museum: 40822 Mettmann, Talstr. 300; tel. (2104) 979797; fax (2104) 979796; e-mail neanderthal-museum@t-online.de; f. 1936; human evolution from earliest times to the present; library of 4,000 vols; Dir PD Dr GERD-C. WENIGER.

Munich

Bayerische Staatsgemäldesammlungen (Bavarian State Art Galleries): 80799 Munich, Barerstr. 29; tel. (89) 238050; fax (89) 23805-221; medieval to modern art; Gen. Dir Prof. Dr PETER-KLAUS SCHUSTER; Dir Doerner Institute BRUNO HEIMBERG.

Bayerisches Nationalmuseum: 80538 Munich, Prinzregentenstr. 3; tel. (89) 21124-1; fax (89) 21124-201; f. 1855; European fine arts, especially sculpture, decorative art and folk art; library of 75,000 vols; Gen. Dir Dr REINHOLD BAUMSTARK; publs *Kataloge, Bildführer, Forschungshefte, Bayerische Blätter für Volkskunde*.

Deutsches Museum von Meisterwerken der Naturwissenschaft und Technik: 80306 Munich; premises at: 80538 Munich, Museumsinsel 1; tel. (89) 21791; fax (89) 2179324; f. 1903; presents the history of science and technology from its origins to the present day, exemplified by historical originals and hands-on experiments; library of 815,000 vols; special collection of manuscripts and autographs, trade literature, plans, pictorial art, films, commemorative medals; research institute for the history of science and technology; 'Kerschensteiner Kolleg' for museum education; Dir-Gen. Prof. Dr WOLF PETER FEHLHAMMER; publs guides, catalogues and monographs, *Abhandlungen und Berichte* (quarterly), *Kultur und Technik* (quarterly).

Affiliated museums:

Deutsche Museum Bonn: 53175 Bonn, Ahrstr. 45; tel. (228) 302252; fax (228) 302270; f. 1995; science and technology in Germany since 1945; Dir-Gen. Prof. Dr WOLF PETER FEHLHAMMER.

Deutsches Museum Flugwerft Schleissheim: 85764 Oberschleissheim, Effnerstr. 18; tel. (89) 3157140; fax (89) 31571450; f. 1992; aeronautical collection; Dir-Gen. Prof. Dr WOLF PETER FEHLHAMMER.

Generaldirektion der Staatlichen Naturwissenschaftlichen Sammlungen Bayerns, München (State Scientific Collections, Munich): 80638 Munich, Menzingerstr. 71; tel. (89) 1782066; fax (89) 177825; Gen. Dir Prof. Dr HEINZ SCHULZ.

Controls:

Anthropologische Staatssammlung: 80333 Munich, Karolinenpl. 2A; tel. (89) 595251; fax (89) 5501924; f. 1886; Dir Prof. Dr GISELA GRUPE.

Bayerische Staatssammlung für Paläontologie und historische Geologie: 80333 Munich, Richard-Wagner-Str. 10; tel. (89) 5203361; fax (89) 5203276; e-mail pal.sammlungen@lrz.uni-muenchen.de; f. 1759; Dir Dr PETER WELLNHOFFER; publs *Mitteilungen, Zitteliana*.

Botanische Staatssammlung: 80638 Munich, Menzinger-Str. 67; tel. (89) 17861265; fax (89) 17861193; e-mail bsm@botanik.biologie.uni-muenchen.de; f. 1813; Dir Prof. Dr JÜRKE GRAU; publ. *Sendtnera*.

Botanischer Garten: 80638 Munich, Menzingerstr. 61–65; tel. (89) 17861310; fax (89) 17861340; e-mail botgart@botanik.biologie.uni-muenchen.de; f. 1914; Dir Prof. Dr JÜRKE GRAU.

Geologische Staatssammlung: 80333 Munich, Luisenstr. 37; tel. (89) 52031; fax (89) 5203293; e-mail geol.sammlung@iaag.geo.uni-muenchen.de; f. 1924; Dir Prof. Dr HUBERT MILLER.

Jura-Museum: 85072 Eichstätt, Willibaldsburg; tel. (8421) 2956, (8421) 89609; natural history; Man Dr GÜNTER VIOHL.

Mineralogische Staatssammlung: 80333 Munich, Theresienstr. 41; tel. (89) 23944312; fax (89) 23944334; e-mail mineralogische . staatssammlung @ lrz.uni-muenchen.de; f. 1823; Dir Prof. Dr HEINZ SCHULZ.

Museum Mensch und Natur: 80638 Munich, Maria-Ward-Str. 1B; tel. (89) 171382; fax (89) 1784380; natural history; Man. Dr HANS-ALBERT TREFF.

Naturkunde-Museum Bamberg: 96047 Bamberg, Fleischstr. 2; tel. (951) 8631248; fax (951) 8631250; e-mail matthiasmaeser@en.uni.bamberg.de; Man. Dr MATTHIAS MÄUSER.

Rieskrater-Museum Nördlingen: 86720 Nördlingen, Hintere Gerbergasse 3; tel. (9081) 84143; fax (9081) 84144; natural history; Man. Dr MICHAEL SCHIEBER.

Urwelt-Museum Oberfranken: 95447 Bayreuth, Ludwig-Thoma-Str. 7; tel. (921) 56548; fax (921) 56548; e-mail urwelt-museum-oberfranken@t-online.de; f. 1997; natural history; Man. Dr JOACHIM RABOLD.

Zoologische Staatssammlung: 81247 Munich, Münchhausenstr. 21; tel. (89) 81070; fax (89) 8107300; f. 1807; Dir Prof. Dr. GERHARD HASZPRUNAR; publ. *Spixiana*.

Neue Sammlung—Staatliches Museum für angewandte Kunst (State Museum for Applied Arts): 80538 Munich, Prinzregentenstr. 3; tel. (89) 227844; fax (89) 220282; f. 1925; modern industrial arts and crafts, architecture, urban planning; industrial and graphic design; Dir Prof. Dr FLORIAN HUFNAGL.

Prähistorische Staatssammlung: 80535 Munich, Postfach 220028; tel. (89) 293911; fax (89) 225238; f. 1885; prehistoric, Roman and early medieval antiquities from Southern Germany, prehistoric archaeology of Mediterranean and Near East; Dir Prof. Dr L. WAMSER; publ. *Kataloge* (irregular).

Staatliche Antikensammlungen und Glyptothek: 80333 Munich, Meiserstr. 10; fax (89) 28927516; collections at: Königsplatz 1 & 3; Greek and Etruscan vases and bronzes, Greek and Roman sculpture, terracottas and bronzes, glass, jewellery.

Staatliche Graphische Sammlung: 80333 Munich, Meiserstr. 10; tel. (89) 28927650; fax (89) 28927653; f. 1758; collection of 15th–20th century German, also Dutch, French and Italian prints and drawings; library of 40,000 vols; Dir Dr TILMAN FALK.

Staatliche Münzsammlung (State Coin Collection): 80333 Munich, Residenzstr. 1; tel. (89) 227221; fax (89) 299859; f. 16th Century; coins from different countries and centuries; special collections: Greek, Roman and Byzantine coins, German and Italian Renaissance medals, Bavarian coins, precious stones from antiquity, Middle Ages and Renaissance; library of 14,300 vols; Dir Prof. Dr OVERBECK.

Staatliche Sammlung Ägyptischer Kunst (State Collection of Egyptian Art): 80333 Munich, Meiserstr. 10; premises at Munich, Hofgartenstr.; tel. (89) 5591486; fax (89) 5503754; f. 1966; small specialized library; Dir Dr SYLVIA SCHOSKE.

Staatliches Museum für Völkerkunde (State Museum of Ethnology): 80538 Munich, Maximilianstr. 42; tel. (89) 210136-0; fax (89) 210136-47; f. 1868; collections on Asia, America, Africa and the Pacific Islands; library of 50,000 vols; Dir Prof. Dr WALTER RAUNIG.

Städtische Galerie im Lenbachhaus: 80333 Munich, Luisenstr. 33; tel. (89) 233-32000; fax (89) 233-32003; f. 1925; Munich artists including paintings by Kandinsky, Klee and the Blaue Reiter group; int. contemporary art; exhibitions, lectures, performances; Dir Dr HELMUT FRIEDEL.

Münster

Westfälisches Landesmuseum für Kunst und Kulturgeschichte (Westphalian Museum of Art and Cultural History): 48143 Münster, Domplatz 10; tel. (251) 590701; f. 1908; 9th– 20th-century sculpture, painting, graphic art, goldsmith work; engraved portraits, history, numismatics; library of 90,000 vols; Dir Prof. Dr KLAUS BUSSMANN.

Nuremberg

Albrecht-Dürer-Haus: 90317 Nuremberg, Albrecht-Dürer-Str. 39; tel. (911) 2315421; f. 1828; life and work of Albrecht Dürer presented in his home 1509–28, cultural history of Nuremberg; Dir Dr JUTTA TSCHOEKE.

Germanisches Nationalmuseum: 90402 Nuremberg, Kartäusergasse 1; tel. (911) 1331-0; fax (911) 1331-200; f. 1852; German art and culture from prehistoric times to the present, fine art galleries, folk art, public library, archives, print room, musical instruments, arms, toys, etc; library of 500,000 vols and 1,500 current periodicals; Chief Dir Dr ULRICH GROSSMANN; publs *Anzeiger des Germ. Nationalmuseums, Werke und Dokumente, Schrifttum zur deutschen Kunst*, catalogues and guides.

Kunsthalle Nürnberg: 90402 Nuremberg, Lorenzer Str. 32; tel. (911) 231-2853; fax (911) 231-3721; f. 1967; changing exhibitions of international contemporary art; Dir Dr EVA MEYER-HERMANN; publs catalogues of exhibitions.

Stadtmuseum Fembohaus: 90317 Nuremberg, Burgstr. 15; tel. 2312271; f. 1958; art and cultural history of Nuremberg; Dir (vacant).

Offenbach am Main

Klingspor-Museum der Stadt: 63012 Offenbach a.M., Herrnstr. 80; tel. (69) 80652954; f. 1953; collection and exhibition of calligraphy, typography, bookbinding and modern book art; library of 47,000 vols; special collection of 20th-century calligraphy; Dir CHRISTIAN SCHEFFLER.

Pforzheim

Reuchlinhaus: 75173 Pforzheim, Schmuckmuseum Pforzheim und mod. Schmuckschau; tel. (7231) 392126; fax (7231) 391441; e-mail holzacc@stadt-pforzheim.de; f. 1938; Dir Dr FRITZ FALK, Kunst- und Kunstgewerbeverein (Kunst-Wechselausstellungen), tel. (7231) 21525; f. 1877; Pres Dr MARGA ANSTETT-JANSEN.

Potsdam

Brandenburgisches Landesmuseum für Ur- und Frühgeschichte (Pre- and Early History): 14482 Potsdam, Schloss Babelsberg; tel. (331) 708073; fax (331) 708074; f. 1953; Dir Prof. Dr J. KUNOW; publs *Veröffentlichungen des Brandenburgischen Landesmuseums für Ur- und Frühgeschichte* (annually), *Forschungen zur Archäologie im Land Brandenburg* (annually).

Recklinghausen

Museen der Stadt Recklinghausen (Recklinghausen City Museums): 45657 Recklinghausen, Grosse-Perdekamp-Str. 25–27; Dir Dr FERDINAND ULLRICH.

Comprise:

Städtische Kunsthalle (City Art Gallery): Recklinghausen; tel. (2361) 501931; fax (2361) 501932; e-mail kunst.re@t.online.de; paintings, drawings, prints and sculptures by contemporary artists.

Ikonen-Museum (Icon Museum): 45657 Recklinghausen, Kirchplatz 2A; tel. (2361) 501941; fax (2361) 501942; Russian, Byzantine and Balkan icons, miniatures, metal work, Coptic sculpture and textiles.

Vestisches Museum: 45659 Recklinghausen, Hohenzollernstr. 12; tel. (2361) 501946; fax (2361) 501932; Westphalian arts and crafts.

Schleswig

Archäologisches Landesmuseum der Christian-Albrechts-Universität (Provincial Museum of Archaeology): 24837 Schleswig, Schloss Gottorf; tel. (4621) 813300; fax (4621) 813535; f. 1835; archaeology of Schleswig-Holstein; library of 20,000 vols; Dir Prof. Dr K. SCHIETZEL; publs *Offa* (annually), *Offa Bücher* (irregular), *Die Funde der älteren Bronzezeit des nordischen Kreises* (irregular), *Die Ausgrabungen in Haithabu* (irregular), *Berichte über die Ausgrabungen in Haithabu* (irregular), *Ausgrabungen in Schleswig* (irregular), *Untersuchungen und Materialien zur Steinzeit in Schleswig-Holstein* (irregular).

Affiliated museum:

Wikinger Museum Haithabu (Museum of the Viking age settlement Haithabu): Schloss Gottorf.

Schleswig-Holsteinisches Landesmuseum: 24837 Schleswig, Schloss Gottorf; tel. (4621) 8130; f. 1875; exhibits of art and culture of Schleswig-Holstein and surrounding area; library of 50,000 vols; Dir Prof. Dr HEINZ SPIELMANN; publs *Kunst in Schleswig-Holstein*, *Jahresberichte*, *Kataloge zu Sonderausstellungen*.

Speyer

Historisches Museum der Pfalz (Historical Museum of the Palatinate): 67324 Speyer, Domplatz; tel. (6232) 13250; fax (6232) 132540; f. 1869; art and cultural history of the Palatinate, includes wine museum; and diocesan museum; library of 20,000 vols; Dir Dr MEINRAD MARIA GREWENIG; publs *Mitteilungen des Historischen Vereins* (annually), *Pfälzer Heimat* (quarterly).

Stralsund

Kulturhistorisches Museum Stralsund: 18439 Stralsund, Mönchstr. 25–27; tel. (3831) 292180; fax (3831) 280060; f. 1858; prehistory, ecclesiastical art, folklore, local history, furniture, history of navigation and navy, modern art, handicrafts, 18th-century products; Dir Dr ANDREAS GRÜGER.

Stuttgart

Galerie der Stadt Stuttgart: 70173 Stuttgart, Schlossplatz 2, Kunstgebäude; tel. (711) 2162188; fax (711) 216-7820; f. 1925; paintings, drawings, graphics and sculptures of 19th- and 20th-century artists in Germany; Otto Dix collection; Dir JOHANN-KARL SCHMIDT.

Linden-Museum Stuttgart, Staatliches Museum für Völkerkunde: 70174 Stuttgart, Hegelplatz 1; tel. (711) 2022-400; f. 1884; ethnographical museum; library of *c.* 30,000 vols; Dir Prof. Dr PETER THIELE; publs *Tribus* (yearbook), catalogues, etc.

Staatliches Museum für Naturkunde Stuttgart: 70191 Stuttgart, Rosenstein 1; tel. (711) 89360; fax (711) 8936-100; f. 1791; zoology, botany, palaeontology, geology and mineralogy; library of 68,000 vols; Dir Prof. Dr C. KÖNIG; publ. *Stuttgarter Beiträge zur Naturkunde*.

Staatsgalerie Stuttgart: 70182 Stuttgart, Urbanstr. 35; premises at: Stuttgart, Konrad-Adenauerstr. 30–32; tel. (711) 212-4050; fax (711) 212-4068; f. 1843; art from the Middle Ages to the 20th century; collection of prints, drawings and photographs; Oskar Schlemmer Archive, Will Grohmann Archive, Sohm Archive; Dir Prof. Dr CHRISTIAN VON HOLST.

Württembergisches Landesmuseum: 70173 Stuttgart, Altes Schloss; tel. (711) 2793400; f. 1862; archaeology from prehistoric to medieval times, textiles and costumes, glass, furniture from the Middle Ages to the present, Swabian sculpture, clocks and watches, coins, musical instruments, Württemberg crown jewels; Roman lapidarium; Dir Prof. Dr V. HIMMELEIN; Chief Curator Dr H.-U. ROLLER; publ. *Jahrbuch*.

Trier

Rheinisches Landesmuseum: 54290 Trier, Weimarer Allee 1; tel. (651) 9774-0; fax (651) 9774-222; f. 1877; prehistoric, Roman and early medieval exhibits excavated in Trier and district; medieval art; library of 70,000 vols; Dir Dr HANS-PETER KUHNEN; publs *Trierer Zeitschrift* (annually), *Funde und Ausgrabungen im Bezirk Trier* (annually), *Trierer Grabungen und Forschungen*, catalogues.

Ulm

Ulmer Museum: 89070 Ulm, Marktplatz 9; tel. (731) 1614300; f. 1924; collections of Ulm and Swabian Arts from 14th to 19th century, 20th-century international art; Dir Dr BRIGITTE REINHARDT.

Weimar

Kunstsammlungen zu Weimar: 99423 Weimar, Burgplatz 4; tel. (3643) 546-0; fax (3643) 546-101; f. 1921-28 (former art collections of the grand-dukes of Saxe-Weimar-Eisenach); art gallery, coins, Rococo museum, historical carriages, Bauhaus museum; Dir Dr ROLF BOTHE.

Stiftung Weimarer Klassik: 99423 Weimar, Burgplatz 4; tel. (3643) 545-0; fax (3643) 202174; f. 1981; directs the Goethe-National-museum (museums and houses connected with Goethe and Schiller, and other buildings, incl. Liszt's house; also Nietzsche-Archiv; Dir Prof. Dr GERHARD SCHUSTER (acting)), the Goethe- und Schiller-Archiv (800,000 MSS of German writers, artists, composers and scientists; Dir Dr JOCHEN GOLZ) and Herzogin Anna Amalia Bibliothek (850,000 vols; Dir Dr MICHAEL KNOCHE); Pres. Dr JÜRGEN SEIFERT; Admin. Dir MANFRED-UDO SCHMIDT.

Thüringisches Landesamt für Archäologische Denkmalpflege: 99423 Weimar, Humboldtstr. 11; tel. 903324; fax 903328; f. 1888; library of 28,000 vols; publs *Jahresschrift 'Alt-Thüringen'*, *Weimarer Monographien zur Ur- und Frühgeschichte*, *Restaurierung und Museumstechnik*, *Ausgabungen und Funde im Freistaat Thüringen*.

Wittenberg

Lutherhalle, reformationsgeschichtliches Museum (History of the Reformation Museum): 06886 Lutherstadt Wittenberg, Collegienstr. 54; tel. (3491) 42030; fax (3491) 420327; e-mail lutherhalle@wittenberg.de; f. 1883; portraits, MSS, pictures, woodcuts, copperplates, medallions and original works on the history of the Reformation; library of *c.* 15,000 vols; Dir Dr STEFAN RHEIN.

Worms

Museum der Stadt Worms: 67547 Worms, Weckerlingplatz 7; tel. (6241) 9463914; fax (6241) 24068; f. 1881; archaeology, town history of Worms; Dir THOMAS SCHIWEK; publs *Der Wormsgau*, *Zeitschrift der Kulturinstitute der Stadt Worms und des Altertumsvereins Worms*.

Stiftung Kunsthaus Heylshof: 67547 Worms, Stephansgasse 9; tel. (6241) 22000; f. 1923; 15th–19th-century paintings, sculptures, pottery, porcelains, glass; Curator CORNELIUS ADALBERT, FRH. V. HEYL.

Universities

FERNUNIVERSITÄT (Distance-Learning University)

58084 Hagen
Telephone: (2331) 98701
Fax: (2331) 987316
E-mail: postmaster@fernuni-hagen.de

Founded 1974
68 Regional Study Centres
State control
Languages of instruction: mainly German
Academic year: October to September

Rector: Prof. Dr-Ing. HELMUT HOYER
Vice-Rectors: Prof. Dr Dr VORMBAUM, Prof. Dr ENDRES, Prof. Dr BEEKMANN, Prof. Dr SIMONIS
Chief Executive: RALF BARTZ
Librarian: DIETER SCHMAUSS (acting)

Number of teachers: 350
Number of students: 54,800 (full- and part-time and associate)

Publications: *Contacte*, *Informationen zum Studium*, *Anleitung zur Belegung*, *Forschungsbericht*, *Jahresberichte*, *Schriftenreihen*.

DEANS

Department of Economics: Prof. Dr ARNOLD
Department of Education, Social Sciences and Humanities: Prof. Dr CZADA
Department of Electrical Engineering: Prof. Dr WUPPER
Department of Law: Prof. Dr EISENHARDT
Department of Mathematics: Prof. Dr MOESCHLIN
Department of Computer Sciences: Prof. Dr WEIHRAUCH

RHEINISCH-WESTFÄLISCHE TECHNISCHE HOCHSCHULE AACHEN

52056 Aachen
Telephone: (241) 801
Telex: 832704
E-mail: international@aaa.rwth-aachen.de
Founded 1870 as Polytechnikum, attained university status 1880
Rector: Prof. Dr rer. nat. R. WALTER
Pro-Rectors: Prof. Dr rer. nat. B. RAUHUT, Prof. Dr-Ing. M. JANSEN, Prof. Dr rer. pol. T. HARTMAN-WENDELS
Director-General: JÜRGEN KESSLER
Librarian: Dr rer. nat. U. FELLMANN
Library: see Libraries
Number of teachers: 2,290, including 405 professors
Number of students: 31,094
Publications: *Vorlesungsverzeichnis*, *Alma Mater Aquensis* (annual report), *RWTH – Themen* (2 a year), *Newsletter*.

DEANS

Faculty of Science: Prof. Dr rer. nat. J. SCHNAKENBERG
Faculty of Architecture: Prof. Dr-Ing. J. PIEPER
Faculty of Civil Engineering and Surveying: Prof. Dr-Ing. J. KÖNIGETER
Faculty of Mechanical Engineering: Prof. Dr-Ing. U. DILTHEY
Faculty of Mining, Metallurgy and Geological Science: Prof. Dr G. GOTTSTEIN
Faculty of Electrical Engineering: Prof. Dr rer. nat. B. WALKE
Faculty of Arts: Prof. Dr U. A. NICHELSEN
Faculty of Economics: Prof. Dr K. G. ZINN
Faculty of Medicine: Prof. Dr med. H. SASS

PROFESSORS

Faculty of Science:

BAADER, F., Theoretical Computer Science
BALLMANN, J., Mechanics
BAUMANN, H., Chemistry
BEMELMANS, V., Mathematics
BERGER, C., High Energy Physics
BERNDT, R., Physics
BERNREUTHER, W., Theoretical Physics
BETHKE, S., Experimental Physics
BLUEMICH, B., Macromolecular Chemistry
BOCK, H. H., Applied Statistics
BOEHM, A., Experimental Physics
BOLM, C., Chemistry
BRUECKEL, T., Physics
CAPELLMANN, H., Physics
DAHMEN, W., Mathematics
DEDERICHS, P. H., Theoretical Solid State Physics
DOHM, V., Theoretical Physics
DRONSKOWSKI, R., Chemistry
ENDERS, D., Organic Chemistry
ENGELS, H., Applied Mathematics
ENSS, V., Mathematics
ESSER, K.-H., Applied Mathematics
FELDERHOF, B. U., Theoretical Physics
FESSNER, W.-D., Organic Chemistry
FLEISCHHAUER, J., Theoretical Chemistry
FLÜGGE, G., Experimental Physics
FRENTZEN, M., Botany
GAIS, H.-J., Organic Chemistry
GERLACH, E., Physics
GÖRLICH, E., Mathematics
GRAEDEL, E., Mathematical Bases of Computer Science
GRAMBOW, H.-J., Plant Physiology
GÜNTHERODT, G., Experimental Physics
HABETHA, K., Engineering Mathematics
HANUS, M., Computer Sciences
HARTMEIER, W., Biotechnology
HAUSMANN, H. A., Experimental Physics
HAVERKORT, B., Computer Sciences
HEISE, U., Applied Mechanics
HERBERICH, G., Inorganic Chemistry
HERMANN, P., Mathematics
HISS, G., Mathematics
HÖCKER, H., Textile Chemistry and Macromolecular Chemistry
HÖLDERICH, W., Fuel Chemistry
HROMKOVIC, J., Computer Sciences
IBACH, H., Experimental Physics
INDERMARK, K., Computer Science
JANK, G., Engineering Mathematics
JARKE, M., Computer Science
JONGEN, H. TH., Mathematics
KASTRUP, H. A., Theoretical Physics
KEIM, W., Technical Chemistry and Petrochemistry
KIRCHNER, W., Didactics of Biology
KLINNER, U., Microbiology
KRAFFT, O., Statistics
KREIBIG, U., Experimental Physics
KREUZALER, F., Botany
KRIEG, A., Mathematics
KULL, H.-J., Physics
LAKEMEYER, G., Computer Sciences
LAUR, P., Inorganic Chemistry
LENGELER, B., Experimental Physics
LÜBELSMEYER, K., Experimental Physics
LUEKEN, H., Inorganic Chemistry
LÜTH, H., Physics
MATHAR, R., Stochastics
MÜLLER-KRUMBHAAR, H., Theoretical Physics
NAGL, M., Computer Science
NESSEL, R. J., Mathematics
NEY, H., Computer Science
OTTER, G., Physics
PAHLINGS, H., Mathematics
PAETZOLD, P., Inorganic Chemistry
PLESKEN GEN. WIGGER, W., Mathematics
PRIEFER, U., Terrestrial Ecology
RAUHUT, B., Statistics and Mathematics of Economics
REINERMANN, J., Mathematics
REUSKEN, A., Mathematics
RICHTER, J., Physical Chemistry
ROEPSTORFF, G., Theoretical Physics
ROHDE, H.-W., Mathematics
SALZER, A., Inorganic Chemistry
SCHMIDT, P., Zoology
SCHMINCKE, U.-W., Mathematics
SCHMITZ, D., Experimental Physics
SCHNAKENBERG, J., Theoretical Physics
SCHONWAELDER, U., Mathematics
SCHUPHAN, I., Biology
SLUSARENKO, A., Botany
SPANIOL, O., Computer Science
STAHL, A., Physics
THOMAS, H. G., Organic Chemistry
TRIESCHE, E., Mathematics
URBAN, K., Experimental Physics
VERSMOLD, H., Physical Chemistry
WAGNER, H., Biology
WALKE, B., Communication Networks
WENZL, H., Experimental Physics
WOLF, K., Microbiology
WIEGNER, M., Mathematics
WUTTIG, M., Physics
ZEIDLER, M., Physical Chemistry

Faculty of Architecture:

BAUM, M., Architectural Drawings
BEYER, A., History of Art
COERSMEIER, U., Interior Architecture
CURDES, G., Town and Regional Planning
DÖRING, W., Building Construction
EICHENBERG, K., Drawing and Painting
FÜHRER, W. F., Experimental Wing Assembly
FUHRMANN, P., Construction Planning
GAUBE, E., Industrial Construction
HEUSER, H., Town Planning
HOFFMANN, H., Design
JANSEN, M., History of Town Planning
KRAUSE, C., Landscape Ecology and Landscape Architecture
LAUENSTEIN, H., Free Space Planning
MARG, V., Town and Regional Planning
NIKOLIC, V., Building Construction
PIEPER, J., History of Architecture, Preservation of Historic Monuments
SCHMIDT, H., Conservation
SCHÖFL, G., Domestic Architecture
SCHULZE, M., Plastics
SIEBER, H., Extensions and Architectural Drawings
SPEIDEL, M., Theory of Architecture

Faculty of Civil Engineering and Surveying:

BENNING, W., Geodesy
DOHMANN, M., Water Supply
DORNBUSCH, J., Building Machines and Building Section
GÜLDENPFENNIG, J., Building Construction
HEGGER, J., Large Constructions
KÖNGETER, J., Civil Engineering
MESKOURIS, K., Architectural Studies
REICHERT, J., Water Supply
ROHDE, F., Water Supply
RÜBBEN, A., Synthetics
SASSE, H. R., Building Materials
SCHIESSL, P., Building Materials
SCHWANHÄUSSER, W., Transport and Railway Engineering
SEDLACEK, G., Structural Engineering (Steel)
SEELING, R., Planning Methods
STEINAUER, B., Road Construction
WITTKE, W., Waterway Engineering, Foundation and Soil Mechanics
WOLF, P., Airport Engineering

Faculty of Mechanical Engineering:

ALLES, W.
BEISS, P., Materials Technology
BETTEN, J., Mathematical Models of Engineering Materials
BEYLICH, A. E., Space Flight Technology
BOHN, D., Steam and Gas Turbines
BONKA, H., Radiation Protection in Nuclear Technology
BÜCHS, Z., Bioprocess Engineering
DILTHEY, U., Welding Technology
DITTRICH, G., Machine Dynamics
DREWS, P., Welding Technology
EL-MAGD, E. A., Engineering Materials
EVERSHEIM, W., Production Engineering
FREDERICH, F., Rail Traction, Cranes and Conveyors
GOLD, P., Machine Elements and Machine Design
HABERSTROH, E., Synthetic Rubber Technology
HENNING, K., Methods of Cybernetics in Engineering Sciences
JACOB, D., Aeronautics and Space Engineering
KLOCKE, F., Manufacturing Technology
KNOCHE, K.-F., Technical Thermodynamics
KOLLER, R., Machine Design
KOSCHEL, W., Jet Propulsion
KRAUSE, E., Aerodynamics
KUGELER, K., Reactor Security and Reactor Technology
LUCZAK, H., Science of Working
LUGSCHEIDER, E., Engineering Materials
MAIER, H.-R., Ceramic Components in Mechanical Engineering
MARQUARDT, W., Process Engineering
MELIN, T., Process Engineering
MICHAELI, W., Plastics Technology
MODIGELL, M., Mechanical Engineering
NASTASE, A.-M., Aircraft Aerodynamics
OLIVIER, H., High-Temperature Gas Dynamics
OSTEN-SACKEN, E. VON DER, Machine Elements
PETERS, N., Mechanics
PFEIFER, T., Measuring Technology
PFENNIG, A., Process Engineering
PISCHINGER, S., Combustion Engineering
PLESSMANN, K., Control Engineering
POPRAWE, R., Laser Technology
RAKE, H., Automatic Control
REIMERDES, H.-G., Light Construction

RENZ, U., Heat Transfer and Air Conditioning
SINGHEISER, L., Materials for Energy Technology
STOJANOFF, C.-G., High Temperature Thermodynamics
WALLENTOWITZ, H., Automotive Engineering
WECK, M., Tool Machine Design
WEICHERT, D., Mechanics
WORTBERG, G., Mechanics
WULFHORST, B., Textile Engineering
ZELLER, M., Air Conditioning

Faculty of Mining, Metallurgy and Geological Science:

Section of Mining:

FRENZ, W., Mining and Environment
HEIL, J., Coking Practice, Briquetting and Refining Technology
MARTENS, P. N., Mining Technology
NIEHAUS, K., Equipment for the Extraction of Minerals
PRETZ, T., Mineral Processing
PREUSSE, A., Mining Subsidence Engineering and Geophysics in Mining
SEELIGER, A., Mechanical Engineering in Mining
STOLL, R. D., Mining Technology

Section of Geological Science:

ECHLE, W., Mineralogy and Sedimentary Petrography
FLAJS, G., Geology and Palaeontology
FÖRSTER, H., Mineralogy and Petrography
HEGER, G., Crystallography
KASIG, W., General, Regional and Historical Geology
KRAMM, U., Mineralogy and Geochemistry
LANGGUTH, H. R., Hydrogeology
LITTKE, R., Geology and Geochemistry
MEYER, M., Mineralogy and Deposits
MULLER, A., General and Historical Geology
ROETH, G., Applied Crystallography and Mineralogy
SCHETELIG, K., Engineering Geology and Hydrogeology
URAI, J., Geology
WALTER, R., Geology and Palaeontology
WELTE, D., Geology and Geochemistry of Fuels
WOHLENBERG, J., Applied Geophysics

Section of Metallurgy and Material Technology:

BLECK, W., Ferrous Metallurgy
CONRAD, T., Glass and Ceramic Composites
EPPLE, U., Process Control Engineering
GOTTSTEIN, G., Metal Science
GUDENAU, H. W., Iron Production
HEINZ, D., Bonding Agents
KAYSSER, W. A., Metallurgy
KÖHNE, H., Heat and Mass Transfer
KOPP, R., Metal Forming
KRÜGER, J., Non-Ferrous and Electrolytical Metallurgy
NEUSCHÜTZ, D., Metallurgy of Nuclear Fuels and Theoretical Metallurgy
SAHM, P. R., Foundry Technology
TELLE, R., Glass and Ceramics

Faculty of Electrical Engineering:

BEMMERL, T., Operating Systems
DE DOCKER, R., Power Electronic and Electrical Drives
HAUBRICH, H.-J., Electrical Power Engineering
HEIME, K., Semiconductor Technology
HENNEBERGER, G., Electrical Machines
HILL, B., Technical Electronics
HOSSFELD, F., Computer Science
INDERMARK, K., Computer Science
JANSEN, R., Electromagnetic Theory
KAISER, W., History of Engineering
KRAISS, K.-F., Computer Science
KURZ, H., Semiconductor Technology
LÜKE, H. D., Telecommunications Engineering
MEYER-EBRECHT, D., Technology Measuring
MEYR, H., Electrical Control Engineering
MOKWA, W., Materials in Electronics Technology
MÖLLER, K., General Electrical and High Voltage Engineering
NOLL, T. G., General Electrical Engineering and Data Processing
PIETSCH, G., Electrical and Gas Discharge Engineering
RAU, G., Biomedical Engineering
REMBOLD, B., High Frequency Technology
VARY, P., Data Processing
VORLÄNDER, M., Technical Acoustics
WALKE, B., Communication Systems
WASER, R., Electrical Materials

Faculty of Arts:

BAUDLER, G., Catholic Theology
BAUM, R., Romance Philology
BECK, G., German Language
BEIER, R., Applied Philology
BERNING, V., Philosophy
BÖTTCHER, W., Political Science
BREUER, D., German Literature
BREUER, H., Applied Geography
BUTZKAMM, W., English Language
CRAEMER, H., Philosophy
DEBUS, G., Psychology
FELTEN, H., Romance Philology
FLICK, M., German Literature
FLOSS, J., Biblical Theology
GATZEMEIER, M., Practical Philosophy
GELLHAUS, A., German Literature
GRÄF, P., Economic Geography
HAMMERICH, K., Sociology
HARGASSER, F., Pedagogics
HAVLIK, D., Physical Geography
HELLER, D., Psychology
HILDEBRANDT, R., History
HILL, P. B., Sociology
HORCH, H.-O., German and Jewish Literature
HÖRNING, K.-H., Sociology
HORNKE, L., Psychology
JÄGER, L., German Philology
JANSEN, M., History of Town Planning
KERNER, M., Medieval and Modern History
KÖNIG, H., Political Science
KUHLMANN, W., Philosophy
LOHRMANN, D., History
MARTIN, R., English Philology
MEY, H., Sociology
MICHELSEN, V. A., Pedagogics
MOESSNER, L, English Language and Literature
PIEPER, J., History of Town Planning
RÖHSER, G., Bible Science
SCHMITZ, S., German Language
SCHULTZ, J., Physical Geography
SIEPMANN, H., Romance Languages and Literature
SONNEMANNS, H., Systematical Theology
SPIJKERS, W., Psychology
STETTER, C., Germanic Linguistics
WANDSCHNEIDER, D., Philosophy
WENZEL, P., English Language and Literature

Faculty of Economics:

BASTIAN, M., Operational Research
BRÖSSE, U., Political Economy
DORNER, K., Economy
DYCKHOFF, H., Industrial Management
GOCHT, W., International Technical and Economical Co-operation
GRETSCHMANN, K., Economics
HARTMANN-WENDELS, T., Industrial Management
HUBER, C., Science of Law
HÖMBURG, R., Business Management
MENKHOFT, L., Economics
MÖLLER, H. P., Industrial Management
SCHRÖDER, H.-H., Industrial Management
SEBASTIAN, H.-J., Economics
STEFFENHAGEN, H., Industrial Management and Marketing
THOMES, P., Economic History
VON NITZSCH, R., Economics
ZIMMERMANN, H.-J., Operational Research
ZINN, K. G., Political Economy

Faculty of Medicine:

ALTHOFF, H., Forensic Medicine
AMMON, J., Radiology and Radiotherapy
BEIER, H., Anatomy
BERNUTH, G. VON, Paediatric Cardiology
BÖCKING, A., Pathology
BOSSE, A., Pathology
BÜLL, U., Nuclear Medicine
BUSE, G., Molecular Biology of Proteins
DEUTICKE, B., Physiology
DIEDRICH, P., Dental Surgery
DOTT, W., Hygienics and Environment
DREXLER, J., Industrial Medicine
FÜZESI, L., Pathology
GERZER, R., Flight Medicine
GILSBACH, J., Neurosurgery
GREVEN, J., Pharmacology and Toxicology
GÜNTHER, R., Radiological Diagnostics
HANRATH, P., Internal Medicine
HEIMANN, G., Paediatrics
HEINRICH, P., Physiological Chemistry
HERPERTZ-DAHLMANN, B., Child and Youth Psychiatry
HÖRNCHEN, H., Paediatrics
HUBER, W., Neurolinguistics
HUEGEL, W., Thorax and Cardiovascular Surgery
JAKSE, G., Urology
JOOST, H. G., Pharmacology and Toxicology
KAUFMANN, P., Anatomy
KEYSERLINGK, D. GRAF VON, Anatomy
KIRCHHOF, B., Ophthalmology
KORR, H., Anatomy
KÜPPER, W., Veterinary Laboratory
LAMPERT, F., Preventive Dentistry
LUCKHOFF, A., Physiology
LUETTICKEN, R., Medical Microbiology
MARX, R., Dental Materials
MATERN, S., Internal Medicine
MERK, H., Dermatology
MESSMER, B. J., Cardiovascular Surgery
MITTERMAYER, C., Pathology
MURKEN, A. H., History of Medicine
NEULEN, J., Gynaecology
NEUSER, J., Psychology
NIETHARD, F. U., Orthopaedics
NOTH, J., Neurology
OSIEKA, R., Internal Medicine
PAAR, O., Surgery
PALLUA, N., Burns Surgery
PETZOLD, E., Psychosomatics and Psychotherapy
RATH, W., Gynaecology
RAU, G., Biomedical Engineering
RIEDIGER, D., Dentistry
RITTER, K., Virology
ROSSAINT, R., Anaesthesia
SASS, H., Psychiatrics
SCHMID-SCHÖNBEIN, H., Physiology
SCHMUTZLER, W., Pharmacology and Toxicology
SCHRÖDER, J. M., Neuropathology
SCHUMPELICK, V., Surgery
SIEBERTH, H.-G., Internal Medicine
SPIEKERMANN, H., Prosthetic Dentistry
SPITZER, K., Medical Computer Science
THRON, A., Neuroradiology
WESTHOFEN, M., Otolaryngology
WIENERT, V., Dermatology
WILLMES-VON-HINCKELDEY, K., Neuropsychology
WOLLMER, A., Structure and Function of Proteins

AFFILIATED INSTITUTIONS

Haus der Technik eV, Essen: 45127 Essen, Hollestr. 1; Dir Prof. Dr-Ing. E. STEINMETZ.

Technische Akademie, Wuppertal eV: 42117 Wuppertal-Elberfeld, Hubertus-Allee 18; Dir Dip.-Oec. E. GIESE.

Institut für Kunststoffverarbeitung in Industrie und Handwerk (Institute of Plastics Technology): 52062 Aachen, Pontstr. 49; Dir Prof. Dr-Ing. W. MICHAELI.

Deutsches Wollforschungsinstitut (German Wool Research Institut): 52062 Aachen, Veltmanplatz 8; Dir Prof. Dr rer. nat. H. HÖCKER.

Forschungsinstitut für Rationalisierung eV (Institute for Research in Rationalization): 52062 Aachen, Pontdriesch 14–16; Dir Prof. Dr-Ing. Dip.-Wirt. Ing. H. LUCZAK.

Forschungsstelle Technischwirtschaftliche Unternehmensstrukturen der Stahlindustrien (Research Department Technical and Economic Corporate Structures in the Steel Industries): 52072 Aachen, Intzestr. 1; Dir Prof. em. Dr rer. nat. Dr-Ing. c.h. W. DAHL.

Helmholtz-Institut für Biomedizinische Technik (Helmholtz Institute for Biomedical Engineering): 52074 Aachen, Pauwelsstr. 20; Head Prof. Dr rer. nat. G. RAU.

Interdisziplinärer Sonderbereich Umweltschutz (Department of Hygiene: Occupational Medicine): 52062 Aachen, Kármánstr. 11; Dir Prof. Dr med. H. J. EINBRODT.

Forschungsinstitut für Wasser- und Abfallwirtschaft eV (Research Institute for Water and Waste Management): 52074 Aachen, Mies-van-der-Rohe-Str 17; Dir Prof. Dr-Ing. M. DOHMANN.

Fraunhofer-Institut für Produktionstechnologie (Fraunhofer Institute for Production Technology): 52074 Aachen, Herwart-Opitz-Haus, Steinbachstr. 17; Dir Prof. Dr-Ing. F. KLOCKE.

Fraunhofer-Institut für Lasertechnik (Fraunhofer Institute for Laser Technology): 52074 Aachen, Steinbachstr. 15; Dir Prof. Dr REINHART POPRAWE.

Institut für Prozess- und Anwendungstechnik Keramik (Institute for Process and Application Technology in Ceramics): Aachen, Bruggemannstr. 12; Dir Prof. Dr.-Ing. H. R. MAIER.

Studienkolleg für Auslandische Studierende (Department for Foreign Students): 52056 Aachen; Head F.-J. MOHREN.

Aachener Centrum für Erstarrung unter Schwerelosigkeite eV (Aachen Centre for Solidification under Weightlessness): 52062 Aachen, Intzestr. 5; Dir Prof. Dr-Ing. PETER R. SAHM.

UNIVERSITÄT AUGSBURG

86159 Augsburg, Universitätsstr. 2
Telephone: (821) 598-0
Fax: (821) 5985505
Founded 1970
State control
Language of instruction: German
Academic year: November to February, May to July
Rector: Prof. Dr REINHARD BLUM
Vice-Rectors: Prof. Dr WILHELM M. GESSEL, Prof. Dr WILFRIED BOTTKE
Chancellor: Dr DIETER KÖHLER
Registrar: H. GOHL
Librarian: Dr RUDOLF FRANKENBERGER

Library: see Libraries
Number of teachers: 458
Number of students: 13,196

DEANS

Faculty of Economics and Social Science: Prof. Dr H. GIERL
Faculty of Catholic Theology: Prof. Dr H. HEINZ
Faculty of Jurisprudence: Prof. Dr H. BUCHNER
Faculty of Philosophy I: Prof. Dr H. ALTENBERGER
Faculty of Philosophy II: Prof. Dr TH. M. SCHEERER
Faculty of Natural Sciences: Prof. Dr U. ECKERN

PROFESSORS

Faculty of Catholic Theology:

GESSEL, W., Ecclesiastical History and Patristics
HEINZ, H., Catholic Pastoral Theology
IMMENKÖTTER, H., Church History
KIENZLER, K., Basic Theology
KILIAN, R., Old Testament Exegesis
KÜPPERS, K., Liturgy Science
LEROY, H., Biblical Studies and Hermeneutics
LISTL, J., Church Law
MÜLLER, S., Philosophy
PIEGSA, J., Moral Theology
RADL, W., New Testament Exegesis
WEIDMANN, F., Didactics of Catholic Theology
ZIEGENAUS, A., Dogmatics

Faculty of Economics and Social Science:

ATTESLANDER, P., Sociology
BAMBERG, G., Statistics
BLUM, R., Economics
BUHL, H. U., Business Administration
COENENBERG, A., Business Administration
EBERS, M., Business Administration
FLEISCHMANN, B., Business Administration
GAHLEN, B., Economics
GIEGLER, H., Sociology
GIERL, H., Business Administration
HANUSCH, H., Economics
HARTMANN, H. A., Psychology
HEINHOLD, M., Business Administration
HOFFMANN, F., Business Administration
NEUBERGER, O., Psychology
OPITZ, O., Mathematical Methods of Economics
PFAFF, A., Economics
PFAFF, M., Economics
SCHITTKO, U., Econometrics
STEINER, M., Business Administration
STENGEL, M., Psychology

Faculty of Jurisprudence:

BEHR, V., Civil Law
BOTTKE, W., Penal Law
BUCHNER, H., Civil Law
DÜTZ, W., Civil Law
HEINTSCHEL VON HEINEGG, W., Public Law
HERRMANN, J., Penal Law
HUBER, CH., Civil Law
JAKOB, W., Public Law
KNÖPFLE, F., Public Law
KÖHLER, H., Civil Law
MÖLLERS, TH., Civil Law
SCHLOSSER, H., Civil Law
SCHMIDT, R., Public Law
SIMSHÄUSER, W., Civil Law with Roman Law
TENCKHOFF, G., Penal Law
VEDDER, CH., Civil Law
VESTING, TH., Civil Law

Faculty of Philosophy I:

ALTENBERGER, H., Sports Education
BARUZZI, A., Philosophy
BLUM, E., Protestant Theology with Biblical Studies
DANCKWARDT, M., Music
GRAF, F. W., Protestant Theology
JOHN-WINDE, H., Art Education
KRAEMER, R. D., Musical Training
LAEMMERMANN, G., Protestant Theology with Didactics of Religion
MACHA, H., Pedagogics
MÄRZ, F., Pedagogics
MAINZER, K., Philosophy
MAURER, F., Pedagogics
MICHAELIS, W., Psychology
MÜHLEISEN, H.-O., Political Science
REIMANN, H., Sociology
ROTH, R., Didactics of Social Science
SCHÄFER, G. E., Pedagogics
SCHULTZE, R.-O., Political Science
STAMMEN, TH., Political Studies
ULICH, D., Psychology
WALDMANN, P., Sociology
WIATER, W., Pedagogics

Faculty of Philosophy II:

ABEL, F., Didactics of French
BECKER, J., Modern and Contemporary History
BUBLITZ, W., English Linguistics
BURKHARDT, J., History of Early Modern Times
DOERING-MANTEUFFEL, S., Folklore
FILSER, K., Didactics of History
FINKENSTAEDT, TH., English Language
FÖRSTER, S., New History
FRIED, P., Bavarian and Swabian History
GEPPERT, H. V., German and Comparative Literature
GLASER, E., German Philology
GÖTZ, D., English Language
GOTTLIEB, G., Ancient History
HERINGER, H.-J., German as a Foreign Language
JANOTA, J., German Language and Medieval Literature
KIESSLING, R., Bavarian and Swabian Linguistics
KOCKEL, V., Classical Archaeology
KOOPMANN, H., German Literature
KRAUSS, H., Romance Literature
KRUFT, H.-W., History of Art
LAUSBERG, M., Classical Philology
OETTINGER, N., Linguistics, Indo-European Linguistics
PACHE, W., English Literature
SCHEERER, T. M., Hispanic Studies
SCHIMMELPFENNIG, B., Medieval History
SCHRÖDER, K., Didactics of English
SPINNER, K., Didactics of German
TOENNESMANN, A., History of Art
WELLMANN, H., German Language
WERNER, R., Romance Languages
WILLIAMS, W., German Language and Medieval Literature
WOLF, L., Romance Philology
ZAPF, H., American Studies

Faculty of Mathematics and Natural Sciences:

AULBACH, B., Pure Mathematics
BEHRINGER, K., Physics
BORGWARDT, K.-H., Optimization
COLONIUS, F., Applied Mathematics
DOSCH, W., Theoretical Computer Science
ECKERN, U., Theoretical Physics
ESCHENBURG, J., Differential Geometry
FISCHER, K., Physical Geography
HAIDER, F., Physics
HÄNGGI, P., Theoretical Physics
HEFENDEHL-HEBEKER, L., Didactics of Mathematics
HEINTZE, E., Pure Mathematics
HILLENBRAND, H., Didactics of Geography
HILSCHER, H., Didactics of Physics
HOPPE, R. H. W., Applied Mathematics
HORN, S., Physics
INGOLD, G.-L., Theoretical Physics
JUNGNICKEL, D., Applied Mathematics, Discrete Mathematics, Optimation, Operations Research
KAMPF, A., Physics
KIELHÖFER, H.-J., Applied Analysis
KIESSLING, W., Theoretical Computer Science
LOHKAMP, J., Analysis and Geometry
LOIDL, A., Physics
MANNHART, J., Physics
MÖLLER, B., Practical Computer Science
MÜLLER, V., Applied Physics
POTT, A., Applied Mathematics
PUKELSHEIM, F., Applied Mathematics
RAUSCHENBACH, B., Applied Physics
RITTER, J., Pure Mathematics
RÜDE, U., Applied Mathematics

SAMWER, K., Applied Physics
SCHÜTZ-GMEINEDER, G., Physics
SCHAFFER, F., Social and Economic Geography
SCHERTZ, R., Analysis
STEWART, G., Applied Physics
STRITZKER, B., Physics
TÖPFER, H.-J., Practical Computer Science
UNWIN, A., Computer-Oriented Statistics and Data Analysis
VOGELSANG, R., Regional Geography of Canada
VOGLER, W., Theoretical Computer Science
VOLLHARDT, D., Theoretical Physics
VORNDRAN, G., Geography
WIECZOREK, U., Didactics of Geography

ATTACHED INSTITUTES

Institute of Business Administration: Dir Prof. Dr MANFRED STEINER.

Institute of Economics: Dir Prof. Dr FRITZ RAHMEYER.

Institute of Social Economic Questions: Dir Prof. Dr MARTIN STENGEL.

Institute of Statistics and Mathematical Theory of Economics: Dir Prof. Dr OTTO OPITZ.

Institute of Civil Law: Dir Prof. Dr WILHELM DÜTZ.

Institute of Public Law: Dir Prof. Dr REINER SCHMIDT.

Institute of Penal Law: Dir Prof. Dr JÖRG TENCKHOFF.

Institute of European Law: Dir Prof. Dr VOLKER BEHR.

Institute of Environmental Law: Dir Prof. Dr REINER SCHMIDT.

Institute of Informatics: Dir Prof. Dr W. KIESSLING.

Institute of Mathematics: Dir Prof. Dr ANTONY UNWIN.

Institute of Physics: Dir Prof. Dr FERDINAND HAIDER.

Institute of Philosophy: Dir Prof. Dr KLAUS MAINZER.

Institute of Spanish and Latin American Studies: Dirs Prof. Dr PETER WALDMANN, Prof. Dr REINHOLD WERNER; Prof. Dr FRANCISCO LÓPEZ-CASERO.

Institute of Canadian Studies: Dir Prof. Dr RAINER-OLAF SCHULTZE.

Institute of European Cultural History: Dirs Prof. Dr JOHANNES BURKHARDT, Prof. Dr THEO STAMMEN.

OTTO-FRIEDRICH-UNIVERSITÄT BAMBERG

96047 Bamberg, Kapuzinerstr. 16
Telephone: (951) 863-0
Fax: (951) 863-1005
E-mail: rektorat@zuv.uni-bamberg.de

Founded 1647
State control
Academic year: October to September (two semesters)

Rector: Prof. Dr ALFRED HIEROLD
Vice-Rectors: Prof. Dr Dr GODEHARD RUPPERT, Prof. Dr HANS-PETER FREY
Chancellor: ALFRED HEMMERLEIN
Librarian: Dr DIETER KARASEK

Number of teachers: 300
Number of students: 8,500

Publications: *Bamberger Universitätszeitung "Dialog"* (5 a year), *Bamberger Geographische Schriften* (1–2 a year), *Bamberger Beiträge zur Englischen Sprachwissenschaft* (annually), *Gratia: Bamberger Schriften zur Renaissanceforschung* (2 a year), *Pressemitteilungen*, *Informationen* (irregular), *Personal- und Vorlesungsverzeichnis* (1 a term), *Bericht des Rektors*, *Forschungsforum* (annually), *Bamberger Editionen. Hg. v. H. Unger und H. Wentzlaff-Eggebert.*

DEANS

Faculty of Catholic Theology: Prof. Dr WOLFGANG KLAUSNITZER
Faculty of Education, Philosophy and Psychology: Prof. Dr HANS REINECKER
Faculty of Languages and Literature: Prof. Dr THOMAS ANZ
Faculty of History and Earth Sciences: Prof. Dr-Ing. MANFRED SCHULLER
Faculty of Social and Economic Sciences: Prof. Dr ELMAR J. SINZ
School of Social Work: Prof. Dr MANFRED HAIDL

PROFESSORS

Faculty of Catholic Theology:

EID, V., Moral Theology
FUCHS, O., Pastoral Theology
HEIMBACH-STEINS, M., Christian Social Theory
HOFFMANN, P., New Testament
KLAUSNITZER, W., Fundamental Theology and Theology of Ecumenical Movement
KOHLSCHEIN, F., Liturgy
KRAUS, G., Dogmatics
MÜLLER, L., Canon Law
RUPPERT, G., Catechetics and Didactics of Religious Education
STÖHR, J., Dogmatics

Faculty of Pedagogy, Philosophy and Psychology:

BAUMANN, M.-P., Folk Music
BAUMANN, S., Physical Education
BERG, D., School Psychology
BORN, J., Psycho-Physiology
DÖRNER, D., Psychology
ERLER, L., Pre-school Education
HÖRMANN, G., Pedagogics
LACHMANN, R., Protestant Theology and Religious Instruction
LAUX, L., Psychology
LIEBEL, H., Social Psychology
MÜHLFELD, C., Sociology of Social Work
ORTNER, R., Primary School Education
RAEHLMANN, I., Labour Economics
REINECKER, H., Clinical Psychology
REISCHMANN, J., Adult Education
RUPRECHT, H., Arts Education
SELG, H., Psychology
SIMON-SCHÄFER, R., Philosophy
WEIGELT, H., Protestant Theology
WEYER, R., Music Education
ZENCK, M., Historical Musicology

Faculty of Languages and Literature:

ANZ, TH., Diffusion Processes of Literature
BEISBART, O., German Language and Literary Instruction
BENNEWITZ, I., Medieval German Philology
BERGMANN, R., German Philology and Medieval Studies
BODE, C., English and American Literature
BOLLÉE, A., Romance Philology and Medieval Studies
BUS, H., American Studies
DÖRING, K., Classical Philology, Greek
FINSTER, B., Islamic Arts and Archaeology
FRAGNER, B., Iranian Studies
GIER, A., Romance Literature
GLÜCK, H., German Linguistics and German as a Foreign Language
GOCKEL, H., Modern German Literature
JOCHUM, K. P., English Literature
KEMPGEN, S., Slavic Linguistics
KREISER, K., Turkish Philology, History and Culture
LEISS, E., German Linguistics
PENZKOFER, G., Romance Philology
RIEKS, R., Classical Philology, Latin
RÜHL, M., Communication Science
SEGEBRECHT, W., Modern German Literature
THEILE, W., Romance Literature
THEIS-BERGLMAIR, A.-M., Communication Science and Journalism
THIERGEN, P., Slavic Philology
ULRICH, M., Romance Linguistics
VIERECK, W., English Language and Medieval Studies
WIELANDT, R., Islamic Studies

Faculty of History and Earth Sciences:

BECKER, H., Geography
BÜTTNER, F. O., Medieval Art History
DENZLER, G., Ecclesiastical History
ENZENSBERGER, H., History (Diplomatics and Paleography)
ERICSSON, J., Medieval and Modern History, Archaeology
GARLEFF, K., Physical Geography
GUTH, K., Folk Studies
HUBEL, A., Monument Preservation and Restoration
HUSS, W., Ancient History
KERKHOFF-HADER, B., Local History and Folklore
KRINGS, W., Historical Geography
MATSCHE, F., Modern Art History
MÖCKL, K., Modern History
PROTZNER, W., History Teaching
SCHIER, W., Prehistory and Early History
SCHMITT, E., Modern History
SCHNEIDER, J., Economic and Social History
SCHNEIDMÜLLER, B., Medieval History
SCHULLER, M., Historical Architecture
TREUDE, E., Economic Geography

Faculty of Social and Economic Sciences:

AUGSBURGER, W., Data Processing in Administration
BECKER, W., Business Administration
CREZELIUS, G., Tax Law
DAUSES, M. A., Public Law
DERLIEN, H.-U., Public Administration
DINKEL, R., Population Studies
DIRUF, G., Business Administration (Logistics)
ENGELHARD, J., European Management
FERSTL, O., Computer-Integrated Systems in Industry and Banking
HECKMANN, F., Sociology
HOFFMANN-LANGE, U., Political Science and Political Systems
KUPSCH, P., Business Administration (Auditing and Accounting)
MAUSSNER, A., Economics
MEINIG, W., Business Administration (Automobile Industry)
MEYER, U., Economics
MICKLITZ, H.-W., Private Law, European Business Law
MÜNCH, R., Sociology
OEHLER, A., Business Administration
PIEPER, R., Town and Social Planning
RATTINGER, H., Political Science
SCHMID, J., Population Studies
SCHMID, M., Economics
SCHULZE, G., Research Methods in Sociology
SINZ, E., Systems Development and Applications of Databases
TRENK-HINTERBERGER, P., Labour and Social Law
VASKOVICS, L., Sociology
VOGEL, F., Statistics
WENZEL, H., Economics (Finance)
WIMMER, F., Business Administration (Marketing)
ZINTL, R., Political Science

School of Social Work:

BIRK, U.-A., Law
BOTT, W., Political Science
CYPRIAN, G., Sociology
ESSING, H.-G., Social Medicine
FREY, H.-P., Sociology
GROSER, M., Political Science
HAIDL, M., Education

HASE, F., Law
HOSEMANN, W., Social Work
KLAPPROTT, J., Psychology
PLESSEN, H., Psychology
PLOIL, E., Social Work, Social Pedagogics
RIEBER, A., Philosophy, Social Ethics
RIEMANN, G., Social Work, Social Education
SPINDLER, W., Methodology
TRIPPMACHER, B., Pedagogics

UNIVERSITÄT BAYREUTH

95440 Bayreuth
Telephone: (921) 55-0
Telex: 921824
Fax: (921) 55-5214

Founded 1972

President: Prof. Dr Dr h.c. HELMUT RUPPERT
Vice-Presidents: Prof. Dr JOCHEN SIGLOCH, Prof. Dr HANS-WERNER SCHMIDT
Chancellor: WOLF-PETER HENTSCHEL
Librarian: Dr KARL BABL

Number of professors: 165
Number of students: 7,800

Publication: *Personen- und Vorlesungsverzeichnis* (2 a year).

DEANS

Department of Mathematics and Physics: Prof. Dr FRANK LEMPIO
Department of Biology, Chemistry and Geosciences: Prof. Dr KLAUS H. HOFFMANN
Department of Law and Economics: Prof. Dr ANDREAS REMER
Department of Language and Literature: Prof. Dr EWALD MENGEL
Department of Cultural Studies: Prof. Dr KLAUS ZIESCHANG
Department of Applied Natural Sciences: Prof. Dr-Ing. Dr Ing. E.h. FRANZ MAYINGER

PROFESSORS

Department of Mathematics and Physics:

BAPTIST, P., Mathematics
BRAND, H., Theoretical Physics
BRAUN, H.-F., Experimental Physics
BÜTTNER, H., Theoretical Physics
BUSSE, F., Theoretical Physics
DELLNITZ, M., Mathematics
DOSE, V., Experimental Physics
ESKA, G., Experimental Physics
HAARER, D., Experimental Physics
HUBER, P. J., Mathematical Statistics
KALUS, J., Experimental Physics
KERBER, A., Mathematics
KERNER, H., Pure Mathematics
KÖHLER, W., Experimental Physics
KRAMER, L., Theoretical Physics
KRÄMER, M., Mathematics
KÜPPERS, J., Experimental Physics
LAUE, R., Computer Science
LEMPIO, F., Mathematics
LEUGERING, G., Mathematics
MERTENS, F.-G., Theoretical Physics
MÜLLER, W., Pure Mathematics
PASCHER, H., Experimental Physics
PESCH, W., Theoretical Physics
PETERNELL, T., Mathematics
RAINER, D., Theoretical Physics
RIEDER, H., Mathematics
ROESSLER, E., Experimental Physics
SCHAMEL, H., Theoretical Physics
SCHITTKOWSKI, K., Mathematics
SCHREYER, F. O., Mathematics
SCHWOERER, M., Experimental Physics
SEILMEIER, A., Experimental Physics
SIMADER, C. G., Mathematics
VAN SMAALEN, S., Crystallography
WAHL, W. VON, Mathematics

Department of Biology, Chemistry and Geosciences:

BACH, L., Urban and Regional Planning
BECK, E., Plant Physiology
DETTNER, K., Animal Ecology
DRAKE, H. L., Soil Microbiology
ENGELS, C., Agrarian Ecology
FIEDLER, K., Animal Ecology
FOKEN, T., Micrometeorology
FRANK, H., Environmental Pollution
HAUHS, M., Ecological Modelling
HERBERHOLD, M., Inorganic Chemistry
HERRMANN, R., Hydrology
HOFFMANN, H., Physical Chemistry
HOFFMANN, K. H., Animal Ecology I
HOLST, D. VON, Animal Physiology
HÜSER, K., Geomorphology
HUWE, B. U., Soil Science
IBRAHIM, F., Social Geography
KLAUTKE, S., Biology
KLEINER, D., Microbiology
KOMOR, E., Plant Physiology
KRAUSCH, G., Physical Chemistry
KRAUSS, G., Biochemistry
LEHNER, C., Genetics
LIEDE, S., Plant Systematics
MACKWELL, ST., Experimental Geophysics of Solid Earth
MAIER, J., Economic Geography
MATZNER, E., Soil Sciences
MEYER, O., Microbiology
MONHEIM, R., Cultural Geography
MORYS, P., Inorganic Chemistry
MÜLLER-HOHENSTEIN, K., Biogeography
NICKEL, H., Cultural Geography
PLATZ, G., Physical Chemistry
RÖSCH, P., Structure and Chemistry of Biopolymers
RUBIE, D., Structure and Dynamics of Earth Materials
RUPPERT, H., Geography
SCHÄFER, K., Geology
SCHMID, F. X., Biochemistry
SCHMIDT, H.-W., Macromolecular Chemistry
SCHUMANN, W., Genetics
SEIFERT, F., Experimental Geosciences
SEIFERT, K., Organic Chemistry
SPITELLER, G., Organic Chemistry
SPRINZL, M., Biochemistry
STADLER, R., Macromolecular Chemistry
STEUDLE, E., Plant Ecology
STINGL, H., Geomorphology
TENHUNEN, J., Plant Ecology
WRACKMEYER, B., Inorganic Chemistry
ZECH, W., Soil Science and Soil Geography

Department of Law and Economics:

BERG, W., Public Law
BÖHLER, H., Economics
BREHM, W., Civil Law
DANNECKER, G., Criminal Law
EMMERICH, V., Civil Law
FRICKE, D., Economics
GITTER, W., Civil Law
GÖRGENS, E., Economics
HÄBERLE, P., Public Law
HEINZL, A., Economics
HERZ, B., Economics
KLIPPEL, D., Civil Law, History of Law
KÜHLMANN, T., Economics
LORITZ, K.-G., Civil Law
MICHALSKI, L., Civil Law
MÖSSLE, W., Public Law
OBERENDER, P., Economics
OTTO, H., Criminal Law
PFISTER, B., Civil Law
RANFT, O., Criminal Law
REMER, A., Economics
SCHLÜCHTERMANN, J., Economics
SCHMITT GLAESER, W., Public Law
SIGLOCH, J., Economics
SPELLENBERG, U., Civil Law
STREINZ, R., Public Law
WORATSCHEK, H., Economics
WOSSIDLO, P. R., Economics

Department of Language and Literature:

BERGER, G., Romance Linguistics
DÖHRING, S., Theatre Studies (Music Theatre)
GEBHARD, W., Modern German Literature, Teaching of German
HINDERLING, R., German Language Studies
KHAMIS, S., Literatures in African Languages
KLOTZ, P., German Language and Literature
LINK-HEER, U., General and Comparative Literary Studies
MENGEL, E., English Studies
MIEHE, G., African Linguistics
OSSWALD, R., Islamic Studies
OWENS, J., Arabistic Studies
RIESZ, J., Romance Studies
STEPPAT, M., English Literature
TAYLOR, R. D., Afro-English Studies
VILL, S., Theatre Studies
WIERLACHER, A., German as a Foreign Language
WOLF, G., Early German Philology

Department of Cultural Studies:

APEL, H.-J., Education
BARGATZKY, T., Ethnology
BERNER, U., Religious Studies
BOCHINGER, CH., Religious Socialization and Extramural Studies
BOSBACH, F., History
BREHM, W., Sport Science and Physical Education
EBNER, R., Catholic Religious Teaching
ENDRES, R., History (Bavaria)
FELDMEIER, R., Evangelical Theology
GÄHDE, U., Philosophy
GÜNZEL, W., Teaching of Physical Education
HEGSELMANN, R., Philosophy
HIERY, H., History
KOCH, L., Education
LANGE, D., History (Africa)
LINDGREN, U., History of Science
LÖW, K., Politics
PUTZ-OSTERLOH, W., Psychology
RITTER, W., Protestant Theology
SCHEIT, H., Social Philosophy
SCHLUMBERGER, J., History
SCHMIDT, W., Sports Medicine
SCHOBERTH, W., Evangelical Theology
SCHORCH, G., Education
SEGL, P., History
SPITTLER, G., Ethnology
WIESEND, R., Music Science
WINTER, J. C., Ethnology
ZIESCHANG, K., Sport Science and Physical Education
ZINGERLE, A., Sociology
ZÖLLER, M., Extramural Studies

Department of Applied Natural Sciences:

BERGMANN, H. W., Materials Science
RIEG, F., Design Theory
WILLERT-PORADA, M., Materials Processing
ZIEGLER, G., Materials Science

ATTACHED INSTITUTES

Forschungsinstitut für Musiktheater (Research Institute for Music Theatre): Dir Prof. Dr S. DÖHRING.

Bayerisches Forschungsinstitut für Experimentelle Geochemie und Geophysik (Bavarian Research Institute for Experimental Geochemistry and Geophysics): Dirs Prof. Dr D. RUBIE, Prof. Dr F. SEIFERT, Prof. Dr ST. MACKWELL.

Institut für Materialforschung (Institute for Materials Research): Dir Prof. Dr G. ZIEGLER (acting).

Bayreuther Institut für Makromolekülforschung (Bayreuth Institute for Macromolecular Research): Dir Prof. Dr M. SCHWOERER (acting).

Bayreuther Institut für Terrestrische Ökosystemforschung (Bavarian Institute for Terrestrial Ecology Research): Dir Prof. Dr E. MATZNER (acting).

Institut für Afrikastudien (Institute for African Studies): Dir Prof. Dr G. SPITTLER.

Afrikazentrum (Africa Centre): Dir Dr T. FÖRSTER.

FREIE UNIVERSITÄT BERLIN

14195 Berlin (Dahlem), Kaiserswerther Str. 16–18

Telephone: (30) 838-1

Telex: 018 40 19

Founded 1948

President: Prof. Dr iur. JOHANN WILHELM GERLACH

Chancellor: WOLF-DIETRICH VON FIRCKS

Librarian: Dr ULRICH NAUMANN

Library: see Libraries

Number of teachers: 2,800

Number of students: 43,000

Publications: *University Calendar*, *FU-Info*, annual reports, etc.

DIRECTORS OF DEPARTMENTS

Medicine: Prof. Dr M. PAUL
Veterinary Medicine: Prof. Dr K. HARTUNG
Law: Prof. Dr A. RANDELZHOFER
Economics and Business Administration: Prof. Dr H. TOMANN
Philosophy and Social Sciences I: Prof. Dr H. GANSSMANN
Philosophy and Social Sciences II: Prof. Dr G. GOBRECHT
Education: Prof. Dr H. KEMPER
History: Prof. Dr C. ULBRICH
Classics and Archaeology: Prof. Dr H. J. NISSEN
Political Science: Prof. Dr E. ALTVATER
German Literature and Philology: Prof. Dr G. MATTENKLOTT
Modern Languages and Literatures: Prof. Dr J. TRABANT
Mathematics: Prof. Dr E. FEHR
Physics: Prof. Dr H. GABRIEL
Chemistry: Prof. Dr F. HUCHO
Pharmacy: Prof. Dr R. H. MÜLLER
Biology: Prof. Dr E. HARTMANN
Geo-Sciences: Prof. Dr H. KEUPP

CENTRAL ATTACHED INSTITUTES

John F. Kennedy-Institut für Nordamerikastudien (J.F.K. Institute of North American Studies): Chair. Prof. Dr M. MAYER.

Lateinamerika-Institut (Central Institute of Latin American Studies): Chair. Prof. Dr U. THIEMER-SACHSE.

Osteuropa-Institut (East European Institute): Chair. Prof. Dr H. SUNDHAUSSEN.

Zentralinstitut für Fachdidaktiken (Central Institute of Didactics): Chair. Prof. B. WURL.

HUMBOLDT-UNIVERSITÄT ZU BERLIN

10099 Berlin, Unter den Linden 6

Telephone: (30) 2093-0

Telex: 305662

Fax: (30) 2093-2770

Founded 1809

State control

Academic year: October to March, April to September

President: Prof. Dr MARLIS DÜRKOP

Vice-Presidents: Prof. BERND BANK, Prof. DETLEF KRAUSS, Dr MONIKA ZIELINSKI, Prof. HANS-WOLFGANG PRESBER

Registrar and Chief Administrative Officer: RAINER NEUMANN

Librarian: Dr M. BULATY

Library: see Libraries

Number of teachers: 1,629

Number of students: 22,752

Publications: *Wissenschaftliche Zeitschrift*, *Humboldt-Spektrum*.

DEANS

Faculty of Law: Prof. B. SCHLINK
Faculty of Agriculture and Horticulture: Prof. ERNST LINDEMANN
Faculty of Mathematics and Natural Sciences I: Prof. MICHAEL VON ORTENBERG
Faculty of Mathematics and Natural Sciences II: Prof. KONRAD GRÖGER
University Hospital 'Charité'–Faculty of Medicine: Prof. Dr HARALD MAU
Faculty of Philosophy I: Prof. H. SCHILLING
Faculty of Philosophy II: Prof. W. RÖCKE
Faculty of Philosophy III: Prof. H. BREDEKAMP
Faculty Institute of Social Sciences: Prof. Dr HERFRIED MÜNKLER
Faculty Institute of Theory of Art and Culture: Prof. Dr HARTMUT BÖHME
Faculty Institute of Asian and African Studies: (vacant)
Faculty of Philosophy IV: Prof. D. BENNER
Faculty of Theology: Prof. Dr CILLIERS BREYTENBACH
Faculty of Economics: Prof. W. PLINKE

TECHNISCHE UNIVERSITÄT BERLIN

10623 Berlin, Str. des 17 Juni 135

Telephone: (30) 314-0

Telex: 182262

Fax: (30) 314-23222

The Bauakademie (Building Academy) of Berlin (f. 1799) and the Gewerbeakademie (f. 1821) were amalgamated in 1879 as the Technische Hochschule Berlin, which was opened under its present name in 1946.

President: Prof. Dr HANS-JÜRGEN EWERS

Chancellor: ULRICH PODEWILS

Librarian: Dipl.-Ing. KLAUS LAASCH

Library: see Libraries

Number of professors: 500

Number of students: 31,700

Publications: *Mitteilungsblatt der TUB* (fortnightly), *Vorlesungsverzeichnis* (2 a year), *Universitätsführer* (every two years), *TU International* (quarterly), *TU intern* (9 a year).

DIRECTORS

Communications and History: Prof. Dr W. BENZ
Education: Prof. Dr U. PREUSS-LAUSITZ
Mathematics: Prof. Dr K.-H. FÖRSTER
Physics: Prof. Dr A. HESE
Chemistry: Prof. Dr J. MÜLLER
Process Technology, Environmental Technology and Materials Sciences: Prof. Dr G. HINRICHSEN
Environment and Society: Prof. Dr G. SCHMIDT-EICHSTAEDT
Architecture: Prof. Dr R. SCHÄFER
Civil Engineering and Applied Geosciences: Prof. Dr ST. SAVIDIS
Transport and Applied Mechanics: Prof. Dr-Ing. G. CLAUSS
Mechanical Engineering and Production Technology: Prof. Dr W. BEITZ
Electrical Engineering: Prof. Dr H. HENKE
Computer Science: Prof. Dr-Ing. ST. JÄHNICHEN
Economics and Management: Prof. Dr K. SERFLING
Food Technology and Biotechnology: Prof. Dr-Ing. U. STAHL

UNIVERSITÄT BIELEFELD

33615 Bielefeld, Universitätsstr. 25

Telephone: (521) 106-00

Fax: (521) 1065844

Founded 1969

State control

Academic year: April to July, October to February

Rector: Prof. Dr GERT RICKHEIT

Pro-Rectors: Prof. Dr WIELAND, Prof. Dr P. BLANCHARD, Prof. Dr TIMMERMANN, Prof. Dr TROCKEL

Chancellor: K. H. HUVENDICK

Librarian: Dr WILHELM NEUBAUER

Number of teachers: 780

Number of students: 20,000

Publications: *Forschungsbericht* (every 2 years), *Forschungsmagazin* (quarterly), *Pressedienst Forschung* (irregular), *Bielefelder Universitätszeitung* (monthly), *Jahresbericht des Rektors* (annual), *Schriften zum Aufbau einer Universität* (irregular), *Personalverzeichnis / Lehrveranstaltungen* (2 a year).

DEANS

Faculty of Law: Prof. Dr JOST
Faculty of Mathematics: Prof. Dr RÖCKNER
Faculty of Sociology: Prof. Dr JAPP
Faculty of Education: Prof. Dr WITTWER
Faculty of History and Philosophy: Prof. Dr MERL
Faculty of Linguistics and Literature: Prof. Dr STROHNER
Faculty of Physics: Prof. Dr STEIDL
Faculty of Economics: Prof. Dr JAHNKE
Faculty of Biology: Prof. Dr EICHENLAUB
Faculty of Chemistry: Prof. Dr WENCK
Faculty of Psychology and Sport Science: Prof. Dr HARTJE
Faculty of Theology, Geography, Art and Music: Prof. Dr KAHRMANN
Faculty of Technology: Prof. Dr SAGERER
Faculty of Health Sciences: Prof. Dr HURRELMANN
Centre for Interdisciplinary Research: Prof. Dr GERTRUDE LÜBBE-WOLFF
School of Public Health: Prof. Dr BADURA

RUHR-UNIVERSITÄT BOCHUM

44721 Bochum, Postfach 102148

Premises at: 44801 Bochum, Universitätsstr. 150

Telephone: (234) 700-1

Fax: (234) 7094-201

Founded 1961

State control

Language of instruction: German

Academic year: April to September (summer semester), October to March (winter semester)

Rector: Prof. Dr MANFRED BORMANN

Pro-Rectors: Prof. Dr WERNER ENGELHARDT, Prof. Dr PETER SCHEID, Prof. Dr HARRO MÜLLER-MICHAELS

Chancellor: Dr B. WIEBEL

Librarian: Dr ERDMUTE LAPP

Number of teachers: 1,542

Number of students: 37,473

Publications: *RUBENS. Nachrichten, Berichte und Meinungen aus der Ruhr-Universität Bochum* (9 a year), *Rechenschaftsbericht des Rektorates* (annually), *Amtliche Bekanntmachungen* (irregular), *RUBIN Wissenschaftsmagazin der Ruhr-Universität Bochum* (every 6 months), *Bochumer Universitätsreden* (irregular).

DEANS

Faculty of Protestant Theology: Prof. Dr KLAUS WENGST
Faculty of Catholic Theology: Prof. Dr W. KNOCH
Faculty of Philosophy, Pedagogy and Journalism: Prof. Dr BERNHARD ROSEMANN
Faculty of History: Prof. Dr E. ISENMANN
Faculty of Philology: Prof. Dr K.-P. WEGERA
Faculty of Law: Prof. Dr H. SIEKMANN
Faculty of Economics: Prof. Dr V. NIENHAUS

Faculty of Social Sciences: Prof. Dr U. ANDERSEN
Faculty of East Asian Studies: Prof. Dr P. WEBER-SCHÄFER
Faculty of Sport Science: Prof. Dr med. HERMANN JOSEF HECK
Faculty of Psychology: Prof. Dr HEINRICH WOTTAWA
Faculty of Mechanical Engineering: Prof. Dr-Ing. G. SCHWEIGER
Faculty of Civil Engineering: Prof. Dr-Ing. H.-J. NIEMANN
Faculty of Electrical Engineering: Prof. Dr-Ing. J. MELBERT
Faculty of Mathematics: Prof. Dr E. BERTSCH
Faculty of Physics and Astronomy: Prof. Dr H. KOCH
Faculty of Geosciences: Prof. Dr h.c. LOTHAR DRESEN
Faculty of Chemistry: Prof. Dr MUHLER
Faculty of Biology: Prof. Dr ULRICH KÜCK
Faculty of Medicine: Prof. Dr med. U. EYSEL

DIRECTORS OF CENTRAL ACADEMIC INSTITUTIONS

Centre of Further Education: Man. Dip. Päd. K. HELLERMANN
Institute for Research in the European Labour Movement: Prof. Dr K. TENFELDE
Institute for Neuro-Computing: Prof. Dr CH. VON DER MALSBURG
Institute for Development Research and Development Policy: Prof. Dr H. DÜRR
Institute for Energy and Natural Resources Law: Prof. Dr P. J. TETTINGER
Institute for Industrial Science: (vacant)
Centre for Interdisciplinary Research in the Ruhr Area: Prof. Dr D. PETZINA
Institute for International Law of Peace and Human Rights: Prof. Dr K. IPSEN
Institute for Social Security Law: Prof. Dr F. E. SCHNAPP
Institute for German Cultural Studies: Prof. Dr P. G. KLUSSMANN

PROFESSORS

Faculty of Protestant Theology:
BALZ, H., Theology and New Testament History
BEYER, F.-H., Practical Theology
EBACH, J., Old Testament
FREY, C., Systematic Theology
GELDBACH, E., Ecumenical and Denominational Studies
GRÄB, W., Practical Theology
HASENFRATZ, H.-P., Theology of the History of Religion
LINK, C., Systematic Theology
RAISER, K., Systematic Theology
STROHM, C., Church History (Reformation and Modern)
THIEL, W., Old Testament
WENGST, K., New Testament Exegesis and Theology
WYRWA, D., Church History

Faculty of Catholic Theology:
BERG, W., Old Testament Exegesis and Theology
DSCHULNIGG, P., New Testament
GEERLINGS, W., Church History, Patrology
KNAPP, M., Dogmatics
KNOCH, W., Dogmatics
KOBUSCH, T., Philosophical and Theological Questions
KRAMER, H., Moral Theology
MEIER, J., Medieval and Modern Church History
POTTMEYER, H. J., Fundamental Theology
REINHARDT, H. J. F., Canon Law

Faculty of Philosophy, Education and Journalism:
ADICK, C., Comparative Education
BECKERS, E., Sports Education
DRIESCHNER, M., Natural Philosophy
FISCHER, H.-D., Journalism and Communication Studies
HAARDT, A., Philosophy
HERBIG, M., General Didactics and Methodology
KNOLL, J. H., Practical Education
KOBUSCH, T., Philosophy and Theology
KÖNIG, G., Philosophy
MEYER-DRAWE, K., History of Education
MOJSISCH, B., History of Philosophy
MÜLLER, D. K., Social History of Education
ROSEMANN, B., Educational Psychology
SASS, H.-M., Philosophy
SCHOLTZ, G., History and Theory of the Humanities
STRUBE, W., Philosophy
STUKE, F.-R., Media Studies
TERHART, E., Practical Education
WALDENFELS, B., Philosophy

Faculty of History:
ADANIR, F., Southeast European History
BLEEK, W., Sociology
BONWETSCH, B., East European History
BÜSING, H., Archaeology
EDER, W., Ancient History
FREI, N., Modern History
VON GRAEVE, V., Archaeology
HELBICH, W., North American History
HÖLSCHER, L., Theory of History
ISENMANN, E., Medieval History
PETZINA, D., Social and Economic History
PINGEL, V., Early History
SCHLEIER, R., History of Art
SCHMIDT, G., Political History
SCHMITZ, W., Ancient History
SCHULTE, R., Modern and Contemporary History, Racial History
STEINHAUSER, M., History of Art
SYKORA, K., History of Art
TENFELDE, K., Social History and the Socialist Movement
VOLLRATH, H., Medieval History
WALZ, R., Modern History
WEBER, W., Economic and Technical History
WYSS, B., History of Art

Faculty of Philology:
AHRENDS, G., English Philology
ALT, P.-A., Modern German Literature
BAUSCH, K.-R., Romance Philology
BEHRENS, R., Romance Philology
BEILENHOFF, W., Cinematography and Television Studies
BEYER, M., English Philology
BINDER, G., Classical Philology
BOETTCHER, W., Teaching of German Language and Literature
BOLLACHER, M., Modern German Literature
BORETZKY, N., Comparative Linguistics
DENIG, F., Psychology of Language
DILLER, H.-J., English Philology
EFFE, B., Classical Philology
EIKELMANN, M., German Philology
EIMERMACHER, K., Slavonic Studies
ENDRESS, G., Arabic and Islamic Studies
FECHNER, J.-U., Modern German Literature
FIGGE, U. L., Romance Philology
GALLOWAY, D., English Philology
GLEI, R., Classical Philology/Latin
HARTMANN, D., German Language
HARWEG, R., Linguistics
HISS, G., Theatre Studies
HOPKINS, E. A., Applied Linguistics
JACHNOW, H., Slavonic Studies
KETELSEN, U.-K., Modern German Literature
KNAUTH, K. A., Romance Philology
KOCH, G., Cinematography and Television Studies
KOCH, W. A., English Philology, Semiotics
KRAMARZ-BEIN, Scandinavian Studies
KRENN, H., Romance Philology
KRINGS, H., Applied Linguistics
LEBSANFT, F., Romance Philology
MAKRIS, G., Modern Greek and Byzantine Philology
MÜLLER-MICHAELS, H., Didactics of German Philology
NEU, E., Comparative Linguistics and Hittite Studies
REICHMUTH, S., Islamic Studies
SALJE, G., Cinematography and Television Studies
SAPPOK, C., Slavonic Studies
SCHIFFER, R., English Philology
SCHMITZ-EMAUS, M., General and Comparative Literature
SCHULZE, J., Romance Philology
SCHWERDTFEGER, I. C., Applied Linguistics
SPROCKHOFF, J. F., Indology and Religious Studies
STRATMANN, G., English Philology
TIETZ, M., Romance Philology
UHLENBRUCH, B., Russian and Soviet Culture
WAGNER-EGELHAAT, M., Modern German Literature
WEBER, I., English Philology
WEGERA, K.-P., History of German Language
WIEHL, P., Germanic Philology

Faculty of Law:
BERZ, U., Criminal Law, Criminal Procedural Law
VON DANWITZ, T., Public Law, European Law
GRAWERT, R., Public Law
HERZBERG, R. D., Criminal Law, Criminal Procedural Law, General Theory of Law
HÜFFER, U., Civil Law, Commercial Law
IPSEN, K., Public Law
KINDLER, P., Civil Law, Commercial Law, International Civil Law and Comparative Law
KRIECHBAUM, M., Civil Law, History of Law
MUSCHELER, K., History of German Law, Civil Law, Church Law
NAENDRUP, P.-H., Civil, Commercial, Labour and Civil Procedural Law
RÖHL, K. F., Civil Law, Insurance Law, Civil Procedural Law, Sociology of Law, Philosophy of Law
SCHILDT, B., History of Law, Civil Law
SCHLÜCHTER, E., Criminal Law, Criminal Procedural Law
SCHNAPP, F. E., Public Law
SCHREIBER, K., Civil Law, Procedural Law and Labour Law
SCHWIND, H.-D., Criminology
SEER, R., Tax Law and Administrative Law
SIEKMANN, H., Public Law
TETTINGER, P. J., Public Law
WANK, R., Civil Law, Commercial and Labour Law
WOLF, J., Public Law
ZEISS, W., Procedural Law, Civil Law and Labour Law
ZIMMER, D., Civil Law, German and European Commercial Law

Faculty of Economics:
BAYER, H.-W., Public Law
BENDER, D., International Business Relations
DIRRIGL, H., Controlling
FOLKERS, C., Finance
GABRIEL, R., Applied Information Science
HAMMANN, P., Applied Industrial Economics
HARTWIG, K.-H., Economic Policy
KERBER, W., National Economic Policy
KLEMMER, P., Economic Policy
KÖSTERS, W., Theoretical Political Economy
LÖSCH, M., Statistics and Econometrics
MAG, W., Theoretical Industrial Economics
NIENHAUS, V., Economic Policy
SCHNEIDER, D., Applied Industrial Economics
SEITZ, T., Theoretical Political Economy
STREIM, H., Theoretical Industrial Economics
SÜCHTING, J., Applied Industrial Economics
WERNERS, B., Business Research and Accountancy

Faculty of Social Sciences:

ANDERSEN, U., Political Science
BLEEK, W., Political Science
HEINZE, R. G., Sociology
LEHNER, F., Political Science
LENZ, I., Sociology
MINSSEN, H., Labour Organization
MÜLLER-JENTSCH, W., Participation and Organization
NEUMANN, L. F., Social Politics and Economy
NOLTE, H., Social Psychology
PETZINA, D., Social and Economic History
PÖHLER, W., Labour Organization
ROHWER, G., Methodology of Social Science and Social Statistics
SCHMIDT, G., Political Science
STROHMEIER, K. P., Sociology
TIEDE, M., Mathematical and Empirical Procedure in Social Sciences
VOIGT, D., Sociology of Sport
VOSS, W., Mathematical and Empirical Procedure in Social Sciences
WAGNER, G., Social Politics
WEBER-SCHÄFER, P., Political Science
WIDMAIER, Political Science
WOLFF, J., Sociology of Developing Countries

Faculty of East Asian Studies:

KLENNER, W., East Asian Economics
LENZ, I., Sociology
MARTIN, H., Chinese Language and Literature
MATHIAS, R., Japanese History
RICKMEYER, J., Japanese Language and Literature
WEBER-SCHÄFER, P., Political Science, East Asian Politics

Faculty of Sport Science:

BECKERS, E., Pedagogy of Sport
HECK, H. J., Medicine in Sport
NEUMAIER, A., Theory of Movement, Biomechanics
REULECKE, W., Sport Psychology
STEINHÖFER, D., Training
VOIGT, D., Sociology of Sport

Faculty of Psychology:

BIERHOFF, H.-W., Social Psychology
BOCK, M., Psychology of Language and Communication
DAUM, I., Clinical Neuropsychology
GÜNTÜRKÜN, O., Biopsychology
GUSKI, R., Cognitive and Environmental Psychology
REULECKE, W., Sport Psychology
ROSEMANN, B., Educational Psychology
SCHÖLMERICH, A., Development Psychology
SCHULTE, D., Clinical Psychology
WOTTAWA, H., Methodology, Diagnostic and Evaluation
ZIMOLONG, B., Industrial and Organizational Psychology

Faculty of Mechanical Engineering:

ABRAMOVICI, M., Informatics
BERNS, H., Materials Technology
EGGELER, G., Materials Science
HICKEN, E., Safety Research and Nuclear Engineering, Forschungszentrum Juelich GmbH
KREMER, H., Energy Conversion Engineering
PAPENFUSS, H.-D., Applied Fluid Mechanics
PFOST, H., Steam and Gas Turbines
POHL, M., Materials Testing
PREDKI, W., Mechanical Components
REINIG, G., Control Systems and Navigation Technology
ROGG, B., Fluid Mechanics
RÖHM, H.-J., Process and Environmental Engineering
SCHNAUBER, H., Production Planning
SCHWEIGER, G., Applied Laser Technology
STOFF, H., Hydraulic Machines
STÖVER, D. H. H., Materials
SVEJDA, P., Thermodynamics of Mixtures
UNGER, H., Nuclear and Renewable Energy Systems
WAGNER, G., Mechanical Components and Production Technology
WAGNER, W., Thermodynamics
WELP, E. G., Mechanical Components and Design
WEYER, H., Propulsion Engineering (DFVLR, Köln-Porz)

Faculty of Civil Engineering:

BRILON, W., Transport and Communications
BRUHNS, O. T., Engineering Mechanics
HARTMANN, D., Computational Engineering
JESSBERGER, H. L., Soil Mechanics and Civil Engineering
KALTHOFF, J. F., Experimental Mechanics
KINDMANN, R., Steel-Girder Construction
KRASS, K., Road and Railway Construction
KRÄTZIG, W. B., Structural Engineering and Dynamics
MAIDL, B., Process Engineering and Building Industry
NIEMANN, H.-J., Wind Engineering
ORTH, H., Environmental Engineering
REYER, E., Structural Design, Timber Construction and Building Physics
SCHERER, M., Geodesy
SCHMID, G., Structural Mechanics and Computer Simulation
SCHULTZ, G., Hydrology, Water Resources Management and Environmental Engineering
STANGENBERG, F., Reinforced and Prestressed Concrete Structures
STEIN, D., Pipe Construction and Maintenance
STOLPE, H., Environmental Engineering and Ecology
STUMPF, H., General Mechanics
WALLER, H., Computational Mechanics and Simulation

Faculty of Electrical Engineering:

BALZERT, H., Software Engineering
BLAUERT, J., Electrical Engineering and Acoustics
BLUME, S., Theoretical Electrical Engineering
BÖHME, J. F., Signal Theory
DULLENKOPF, P., Electronic Circuitry
EDENHOFER, P., Antennas and Wave Propagation
ERMERT, H., High-Frequency Engineering
FISCHER, H. D., Communications Engineering
GÖCKLER, H., Digital Signal Processing
HABEREY, F., Materials Science
HAHN, A., Materials Science
KUNZE, U., Materials Science
MELBERT, J., Electronic Switching and Metrology
MENTEL, J., Principles of Electrical Engineering
REIN, H.-M., Semiconductor Components
SCHIEK, B., High Frequency Measurement Techniques
SCHIFFNER, G., Electro-optics and Electrical Engineering
STEIMEL, A., Power Engineering
TÜCHELMANN, Y., Applied Computer Science
UNBEHAUEN, H., Control Engineering
WEBER, W., Data Processing

Faculty of Mathematics:

ABRESCH, U., Mathematics
ALBEVERIO, S., Mathematics
BARTENWERFER, W., Mathematics
BERTSCH, E., Computer Science
BÖGER, E., Mathematics
BÖHME, R., Mathematics
BRAESS, D., Mathematics
DETTE, H., Mathematics
ELLIGER, S., Mathematics
FLENNER, H., Mathematics
GERRITZEN, L., Mathematics
HUCKLEBERRY, A. T., Mathematics
KIRSCH, W., Mathematical Physics
SPALLEK, K., Mathematics
STORCH, U., Mathematics
VERFÜRTH, R., Mathematics
WASSERMANN, G., Differential Topology
YE, R.
ZIESCHANG, H., Mathematics

Faculty of Physics and Astronomy:

BORMANN, M., Teaching of Physics
CHINI, R., Astrophysics
DETTMAR, R.-J.
EFETOR, K., Theoretical Physics
ELSÄSSER, K., Theoretical Physics
FEUERBACHER, B., Experimental Physics
GARI, M., Theoretical Physics
GERWERT, K., Biophysics
GLÖCKLE, W., Theoretical Physics
GOEKE, K., Theoretical Physics
KOCH, H., Experimental Physics
KÖHLER, U., Experimental Physics
KUNZE, H.-J., Experimental Physics
MALSBURG, C. VON DER, Neuroinformatics
MEYER, W., Experimental Physics
PELZL, J., Experimental Physics
ROLFS, C., Experimental Physics
SOLTWISCH, H., Experimental Physics
WIECK, A., Experimental Physics
WIESEMANN, K., Experimental Physics
WINTER, J., Experimental Physics
WUNNER, G., Theoretical Physics
ZABEL, H., Experimental Physics

Faculty of Geosciences:

BRONGER, D., Geography
BUTZIN, B., Geography
CHATTERJEE, N. D., Mineralogy and Petrology
DODT, J., Geography, Remote Sensing
DRESEN, L., Seismics
DÜRR, H., Economic and Social Geography
FLEER, H., Climatology and Hydrogeology
GIES, H., Mineralogy and Crystallography
HARJES, H.-P., Geophysics
KLINK, H.-J., Geography
KROSS, E., Didactics of Geography
KUTTER, H., Rock Mechanics
LÖTSCHER, L., Geography and Cultural Geography
MARESCH, W. V., Mineralogy
MÜLLER, J.-C., Cartography
MUTTERLOSE, J., Palaeontology and Geology
NIGGEMANN, J., Geography
OBERMANN, P., Applied Geology
RUMMEL, F., Geophysics
SCHRÖDER, B., Geology
SCHWARZ, H.-U., Geology
STÖCKHERT, B., Geology
VEIZER, J., Sedimentology and Geochemistry
ZEPP, H., Physical Geography

Faculty of Chemistry:

BAERNS, M., Technical Chemistry
DRIESS, M., Inorganic Chemistry
FEIGEL, M., Organic Chemistry
GRÜNERT, W., Technical Chemistry
HASSELMANN, D., Organic Chemistry
HEMETSBERGER, H., Organic Chemistry
HEUMANN, R., Molecular Neurobiochemistry
HORN, H.-G., Inorganic Chemistry
HOVEMANN, B., Molecular Cell Biochemistry
VON KIEDROWSKI, G., Organic Chemistry
KUTZELNIGG, W., Theoretical Chemistry
MUHLER, M., Technical Chemistry
SABROWSKY, H., Inorganic Chemistry
SANDER, W., Organic Chemistry
SCHUHMANN, W., Analytical Chemistry
SHELDRICK, W. S., Analytical Chemistry
STAEMMLER, V., Theoretical Chemistry
STUHL, F., Physical Chemistry
WEINGÄRTNER, H., Physical Chemistry
WÖLL, C., Physical Chemistry

Faculty of Biology:

BERZBORN, R., Immunochemistry of Energy Transforming Membranes
BLÜM, V., Comparative Endocrinology
BOHEIM, G., Biophysical Chemistry
CURIO, E., Behavioural Research
GERWERT, K., Biophysics
GLITSCH, H., Muscle Physiology
HAEUPLER, H., Special Botany
HATT, H., Cell Physiology
HAUSER, M., Cell Biology and Zoology
HENGSTENBERG, W., Physiology of Micro-organisms
HOFFMANN, K.-P., General Zoology and Neurobiology
HOFMANN, D. K., Developmental Physiology of Animals
KLIPP, W., Biology of Micro-organisms
KÜCK, U., General Botany
LINK, G., Plant Cell Physiology and Molecular Biology
MACHEMER, H., Cell Physiology
RÖGNER, M., Plant Biochemistry
RÜGER, W., Molecular Genetics
SCHAUB, G., Special Zoology
STEFFAN, A. W., Zoology and Ecology
STÜTZEL, T., Special Botany
WÄGELE, J., Special Zoology
WAHLE, P., Zoology and Neurobiology
WEILER, E., Plant Physiology
WILDNER, G. F., Plant Biochemistry

Faculty of Medicine:

ALTMEYER, P., Dermatology and Venereology
ARCQ, M., Orthopaedics
BARMEYER, J.-P., Internal Medicine
BEYER, H.-K., Radiology
CUNITZ, G., Anaesthesiology
DUNTZE, W., Enzymology
DÜRING, M. VON, Anatomy
ENGERT, J., Paediatric Surgery
EPPLEN, J., Genetics
EYSEL, U., Physiology
FISCHER, H.-D., Medical Journalism
GEHLEN, W., Neurology and Psychiatry
GLEICHMANN, U., Cardiology
GRONEMEYER, U., Ophthalmology
GUZMAN Y ROTAECHE, J., Pathology
HANSTEIN, W., Physiological Chemistry
HARDERS, A. G., Neurosurgery
HECK, H. J., Sports Medicine
HEILMEYER, L., Physiological Chemistry
HEUSER, L., Radiology
HILDMANN, H., Otorhinolaryngology
HOHLBACH, G.-R., Surgery
JANSSEN, P. L., Psychosomatic Medicine and Psychotherapy
JENSEN, A. W. O., Gynaecology and Obstetrics
KALISCH, W.-E., Genetics
KIWULL, P., Physiology
KLEESIEK, K., Clinical Chemistry and Pathobiochemistry
KLEMPNAUER, J.
KLIESER, E., Psychiatry
KÖRFER, R., Thoracic and Cardiovascular Surgery
KÖSTER, O., Radiology
KRÄMER, J., Orthopaedics
KRIEG, M., Clinical Chemistry
KUNAU, W.-H., Physiological Chemistry
LACZKOVICS, A., Surgery, Thoracic and Cardiovascular Surgery
LAUBENTHAL, H., Anaesthesiology
LAUTERBACH, F., Pharmacology and Toxicology
LIERMANN, D., Radiology
MACHTENS, E., Maxillofacial Surgery
MALIN, J.-P., Neurology
MANNHERZ, H. G., Anatomy and Cell Biology
MAY, B., Internal Medicine
MELLER, K., Experimental Cytology
MEYER, H., Paediatric Cardiology
MORGENROTH, K., Pathology
MUHR, G., Surgery
MÜLLER, I., History of Medicine
MÜLLER, K.-M., Pathology
OPFERKUCH, W., Medical Microbiology and Immunology
PAYK, T., Neurology and Psychiatry
PESKAR, B., Clinical Experimental Medicine
PETZOLDT, R., Internal Medicine
PLATH, P., Otorhinolaryngology
POTT, L., Cellular Physiology
PRZUNTEK, H., Neurology
PUCHSTEIN, CH., Anaesthesiology
QUAKERNACK, K., Obstetrics and Gynaecology
RICKEN, D., Internal Medicine
RIEGER, CH., Paediatrics
SASS, H.-M., Philosophy
SCHATZ, H., Internal Medicine
SCHEID, P., Physiology
SCHLÄFKE, M., Physiology
SCHMIEGEL, W.-H., Internal Medicine
SCHULTZE-WERNINGHAUS, G., Internal Medicine
SENGE, T., Urology
STEINAU, H.-U., Surgery
TRAMPISCH, H. J., Medical Informatics and Biomathematics
TRAPPE, H.-J., Internal Medicine
WERCHAU, H., Medical Microbiology and Virology
WERNER, J., Biomedical Engineering
WILHELM, M., Hygiene
ZENZ, M., Anaesthesiology
ZIDEK, W., Internal Medicine
ZIERDEN, E., Internal Medicine
ZUMTOBEL, V., Surgery

Institute for Industrial Science:

KAILER, N., Personnel and Qualifications
MINSSEN, H., Organization of Work
PÖHLER, W., Organization of Work
SCHNAUBER, H., Working System Design
STAUDT, E., Economics of Work

Institute for Research in the European Labour Movement:

TENFELDE, K., Social History and Social Movements

Institute for Neuro-Computing:

VON DER MALSBURG, CH.
VORBRÜGGEN, J.

Institute for International Law of Peace and Human Rights:

IPSEN, K., Public Law

Institute for Energy and Natural Resources Law:

VON DANWITZ, T., Public Law, European Law
DRESEN, L., Seismology
HÜFFER, U., Civil Law, Commercial Law
IPSEN, K., Public Law
STEIN, D., Pipe Construction and Maintenance
TETTINGER, P. J., Public Law
UNGER, H., Nuclear and Modern Energy Systems

Institute for Development Research and Development Policy:

BENDER, D., International Business Relations
DURR, H., Geography
IPSEN, K., Public Law
NIENHAUS, V., Economic Policy
VOSS, W., Mathematical and Empirical Procedure in Social Sciences
WOLFF, J. H., Sociology of Developing Countries

Institute for German Cultural Studies:

ANDERSEN, U., Political Science
BLEEK, W., Political Science
IPSEN, K., Public Law
KROSS, E., Didactics of Geography
PETZINA, D., Social and Economic History
VOIGT, D., Sociology of Sport
VOSS, W., Mathematical and Empirical Procedure in Social Sciences

Institute for Social Security Law:

NAENDRUP, P.-H., Civil, Commercial, Labour and Civil Procedural Law
NEUMANN, L. F., Social Politics and Economics
RÖHL, K., Civil Law, Insurance Law, Civil Procedural Law, Sociology of Law, Philosophy of Law
SCHNAPP, F. E., Civil Law
TETTINGER, P. J., Public Law
WAGNER, G., Social Politics
WANK, R., Civil Law, Commercial and Labour Law

ATTACHED INSTITUTES

Institut für angewandte Innovationsforschung (Applied Research in Innovations): 44801 Bochum, Buscheyplatz 13; Chair. Prof. Dr E. STAUDT.

Forschungsinstitut für Arbeiterbildung (Research in Worker-Education): 45657 Recklinghausen, Kirchplatz 2; Dir Dr K. JOHANNSON.

Forschungsinstitut für Arbeitsmedizin (Research Centre for Industrial Medicine): 44789 Bochum, Bürkle-de-la-Camp-Platz 1; Dir Prof. Dr X. BAUR.

Institut für Umwelthygiene und Umweltmedizin des Hygiene-Instituts des Ruhrgebites in Gelsenkirchen (Environmental Hygiene and Medicine): 45879 Gelsenkirchen, Rotthauserstr. 19; Dir Dr rer. nat. E. SCHRAMMECK.

Institut für Kanalisationstechnik (Institute of Sewer Technology): 45886 Gelsenkirchen, Exterbruch 1; Dirs F. WEDDIGE, Prof. Dr-Ing. D. STEIN.

Institut für Wohnungswesen, Immobilienwirtschaft, Stadt- und Regionalentwicklung GmbH (Institute of Housing, Real Estate, Town and Regional Development Ltd): 44795 Bochum, Springorumallee 20; Dir Dr V. EICHENER.

RHEINISCHE FRIEDRICH-WILHELMS-UNIVERSITÄTBONN

53113 Bonn, Regina-Pacis-Weg 3
Telephone: (228) 731
Telex: 886657
Fax: (0228) 735579

Founded 1786, refounded 1818
State control
Academic year: October to March, April to September

Rector: Prof. Dr KLAUS BORCHARD
Chancellor: Dr REINHARDT LUTZ
Librarian: Dr P. RAU

Number of academic staff: 3,100
Number of students: 36,621

Publications: *Bonner Akademische Reden*, *Politeia*, *Alma Mater*, *Academica Bonnensia*, *Bonner Universitäts-Nachrichten*, *Studium Universale*.

DEANS

Faculty of Evangelical Theology: (vacant)
Faculty of Catholic Theology: Prof. Dr GERHARD HÖVER
Faculty of Law and Economics: (vacant)
Faculty of Medicine: Prof. Dr MANFRED GÖTHERT
Faculty of Philosophy: Prof. Dr H. ROTH
Faculty of Mathematics and Natural Sciences: Prof. Dr WIGHART VON KOENIGSWALD
Faculty of Agriculture: Prof. Dr ERNST BERG
Faculty of Education: HANS-JÜRGEN SCHALLER

PROFESSORS

Faculty of Evangelical Theology:

FAULENBACH, K. H., Church History
GÜTTGEMANNS, E., New Testament
HAUSCHILDT, E., Practical Theology

HONECKER, M., Systematic Theology, Social Ethics
KINZIG, W., Church History
MEYER-BLANCK, M., Theology Education
ZUR MÜHLEN, K. H., Church History
PRATSCHER, W., New Testament
SAUTER, G., Systematic Theology
SCHMIDT, W. H., Old Testament
SEEBASS, H., Old Testament
STOCK, K., Systematic Theology
WOLTER, M., New Testament

Faculty of Catholic Theology:
ADRIÁNYI, G., Church History
BITTER, G., Religious Education and Homilectics
FABRY, H. J., Old Testament
FINDEIS, H.-J., New Testament
FISCHER, I., Research into Women with regard to the Old Testament and Theology
FÜRST, W., Pastoral Theology
GERHARDS, A., Liturgy
HÖVER, G., Moral Theology
HOSSFELD, F.-L., Old Testament Science
MENKE, K.-H., Dogmatics, Theological Propaedeutics
MERKLEIN, H., New Testament
ROOS, L., Christian Sociology
SCHÖLLGEN, G., Ancient Church History and Patrology
SONNEMANS, H., Fundamental Theology
WOHLMUTH, J., Dogmatics

Faculty of Law and Economics:
BÖS, D., Political Economy
BREUER, R., Public Law
BREUER, W., Business Administration
DOLZER, R., German and International Public Law
FENN, H., Civil Law
GERHARDT, W., Civil Law
VON HAGEN, J., Economics
HEINZE, M., Civil Law
HERDEGEN, M., Public Law
HILDENBRAND, W., Economic Theory, Mathematical Theory of Economics
HUBER, U., Commercial Law
ISENSEE, J., Civil and Administrative Law
JAKOBS, G., Criminal Law, Philosophy of Law
JAKOBS, H. H., Civil and Roman Law
KINDHÄUSER, U., Criminal Law
KNÜTEL, R., Roman and Civil Law
KÖNDGEN, J., Civil Law
KORTE, B., Operational Research
KRÄKEL, M., Public Law
LÖWER, W., Public Law
MARQUARDT, H., Criminology
NEUMANN, M., Economic Policy
OSSENBÜHL, F., Civil and Administrative Law
PAEFFGEN, H.-U., Criminal Law
PIETZCKER, J., Public Law
ROTH, W.-H., Civil Law, International Private Law, and Comparative Law
RUDOLPHI, H.-J., Criminal Law and Philosophy of Law
SABEL, H., Business Administration
SCHILKEN, E., Civil Law
SCHMIDT, K., Civil Law
SCHÖN, W., Civil Law
SCHÖNFELD, P., Economics
SCHWEIZER, U., Economic Policy
SHAKED, A., Economic Policy
SONDERMANN, D., Statistics
ZIMMERMANN, K., Economic Policy

Faculty of Medicine:
BAUR, M. P., Medical Statistics
BIDLINGMAIER, F., Clinical Biochemistry
BIEBER, TH., Dermatology and Venereology
BIERSACK, H.-J., Nuclear Medicine
ELGER, C. E., Epileptology
EXNER, M., Hygiene
FRANZ, TH., Anatomy
GÖTHERT, M., Pharmacology, Toxicology
GROTE, J., Physiology
HANFLAND, P., Experimental Haematology
HANSIS, M. L., Emergency Surgery
HERBERHOLD, C., Oto-rhino-laryngology
HIRNER, A., Surgery
HOEFT, A., Anaesthesiology
JÄGER, A., Dentistry
KOECK, B., Dentistry
LENTZE, M. J., Paediatrics
LIEDTKE, R., Psychosomatic Medicine and Psychotherapy
LÜDERITZ, B., Internal Medicine, Cardiology
MADEA, B., Forensic Medicine
MAIER, W., Psychiatry
MÜLLER, ST., Urology
NOLDEN, R., Dentistry
PFEIFER, U., Pathology, Pathological Anatomy
PROPPING, P., Human Genetics
REICH, R., Oral and Maxillofacial Surgery
SAUERBRUCH, T., Internal Medicine
SCHAAL, K. P., Medical Microbiology
SCHILD, H. H., Radiology
SCHILLING, K., Anatomy
SCHMITT, O., Orthopaedics
SCHOTT, H., History of Medicine
SCHRAMM, J., Neurosurgery
SEITZ, H. M., Medical Parasitology
SPITZNAS, M., Ophthalmology
VETTER, H., Internal Medicine
WAHL, G., Oral Surgery
WIESTLER, O., Neuropathology

Faculty of Philosophy:
BONNET, A.-M., History of Art
BREDENKAMP, J., Psychology
BRÜGGEN, E., Germanic Studies
COX, H. L., Folklore
DAHLMANN, D., East European History
EHLERS, E., Social and Economic Geography
ESSER, J., English Philology
FEHN, K., Historical Geography
FISCHER, E., Musicology
FOHRMANN, J., Germanic Studies
GALSTERER, H., Ancient History
GROTZ, R., Geography
HESS, W., Communication and Phonetics
HILDEBRAND, K., Medieval and Modern History
HILGENHEGER, N., Education
HIRDT, W., Romance Philology
HOGREBE, W., Philosophy
HONNEFELDER, L., Philosophy
HÖNNIGHAUSEN, L., English Philology
KAISER, K., Political Science
KARSTEN, D., Political Science
KEIPERT, H., Slavonic Studies
KELZ, H., Phonetics
KLAUER, K. C., Psychology
KLEIN, TH., Germanic Studies
KLIMKEIT, H.-J., Comparative Religion
KOHRT, M., Germanic Studies
KÖLZER, T., Medieval and Modern History, Archival Science
KREINER, J., Japanology
KUBIN, W., Sinology
KÜHNHARDT, L., Political Science
LADENTHIN, V., Education
LANGE, W. D., Romance Philology
LAUREYS, M., Philology
MATZAT, WO., Romance Philology
MIELSCH, H., Archaeology
NEUBAUER, W., Psychology
OEHLER, D., Comparative Science of Literature
PANTZER, P., Japanology
POHL, H., Constitutional History, Economics, Social History
POTTHOFF, W., Slavonic Studies
PREM, H. J., Ethnology
PÜTZ, P., Modern German
REICHL, K., English Philology
ROECK, B., Medieval and Modern History
RÖSSLER, U., Egyptology
ROSEN, K., Ancient History
ROTH, H., Prehistory
SCHMITT, C., Roman Philology
SCHNEIDER, H., Germanic Studies
SCHOLZ, O. B., Psychology
SCHWARZ, H.-P., Political Science
SIMEK, R., Germanic Studies
STUHLMANN-LAEISZ, R., Logic and Foundations
WEEDE, E., Sociology
WILD, S., Semitic Philology
WINIGER, M., Geography
WOLF, H. J., Romance Philology
ZIMMER, ST., Linguistics
ZWIERLEIN, O., Classical Philology

Faculty of Mathematics and Natural Sciences:
ALBEVERIO, S., Mathematics
ALT, H. W., Mathematics
AUMANN, D., Chemistry
BALLMANN, W., Mathematics
BARGON, J., Physical Chemistry
BARTHLOTT, W., Botanics
BLECKMANN, H., Zoology
BÖHME, H., Botany
BRIESKORN, E., Mathematics
CREMERS, A. B., Computer Science
DE BOER, K., Astronomy
DIETZ, K., Theoretical Physics
DIKAU, R., Geography
DÖTZ, K. H., Organic Chemistry
ECKMILLER, R., Computer Science
EHLERS, E., Social and Economic Geography
FREHSE, J., Applied Mathematics
GLOMBITZA, K.-W., Pharmaceutical Biology
GRIEBEL, M., Scientific Computing
GROTZ, R., Geography
HAMENSTÄDT, U., Mathematics
HARDER, G., Mathematics
HERZOG, V., Cell Biology
HILDEBRANDT, S., Mathematics
HILGER, E., Experimental Physics
HUBER, M. G., Theoretical Atomic Physics
JANSEN, M., Inorganic Chemistry
KARPINSKI, M., Computer Science
KELLER, R., Zoology
KILIAN, K., Experimental Atomic Physics
KIRFEL, A., Mineralogy
KLEIN, F., Experimental Physics
KLEMPT, E., Experimental Physics
KOENIGSWALD, W. VON, Palaeontology
LEISTNER, E., Pharmaceutical Biology
LIEB, I., Mathematics
MADER, W., Inorganic Chemistry
MAIER, K., Experimental Physics
MASCHUW, R., Atomic Physics
MCKENNA, D., Chemistry
MEBOLD, U., Radio Astronomy
MENZ, G., Geography
MENZEL, D., Botany
MESCHEDE, D., Experimental Physics
MONIEN, H., Theoretical Physics
MÜLLER, W., Mathematics
NAHM, W., Mathematical Physics
NAUMANN ZU KÖNIGSBRÜCK, C., Zoology
NEUGEBAUER, H., Geophysics
NICKEL, P., Pharmaceutical Chemistry
NIECKE, E., Inorganic and Analytical Chemistry
NILLES, H. P., Theoretical Physics
PEYERIMHOFF, S., Theoretical Chemistry
RAITH, M., Geology and Petrology
SANDHAS, W., Theoretical Physics
SANDHOFF, K., Biochemistry
SAUER, K. P., Zoology and Ecological Studies
SCHOCH, B., Physics
SCHÖNHAGE, A., Informatics
SIMMER, C., Meteorology
SPETH, J., Theoretical Physics
STEFFENS, K. J., Pharmaceutical Technology
THEIN, J., Geology
TRÜPER, H. G., Microbiology
VÖGTLE, F., Chemistry
WANDELT, K., Physical Chemistry
WANDREY, CH., Biotechnology
WERMES, N., Experimental Physics
WILLECKE, K., Genetics
WINIGER, M., Geography

Faculty of Agriculture:

BERG, E., Agricultural Economics
BORCHARD, K., Housing and Town Planning
BRÜMMER, G., Soil Science
DEHNE, H., Phytopathology
FÖRSTNER, W., Photogrammetry
FÜHR, F., Agricultural Chemistry
GALENSA, R., Food Science and Food Chemistry
GOLDBACH, H., Plant Nutrition
HELFRICH, H.-P., Practical Mathematics
HENRICHSMEYER, W., Political Economy, Agricultural Politics and Information
ILK, K. H., Satellite-assisted Physical Geodesy
KOCH, K.-R., Theoretical Geodesy
KÖPKE, U., Ecological Agriculture
KROMER, K.-H., Agricultural Technology
KÜHBAUCH, W., Plant Breeding
KÜHL, R., Nutrition
KUNZ, B., Food Technology and Food Biotechnology
KUTSCH, TH., Agricultural and Domestic Sociology
LÉON, J., Plant Production and Breeding
MORGENSTERN, D., Cartography and Topography
NOGA, G., Fruit and Vegetable Production
PFEFFER, E., Animal Nutrition
SCHELLANDER, K., Animal Breeding
SCHIEFER, G., Agricultural Economy
SCHNABL, H., Botany
STEHLE, P., Nutrition
WEISS, E., House and Town Planning
WITTE, B., Geodesy
WITTMANN, D., Agricultural Zoology and Ecology
WOLFFRAM, R.-E., Market Research

Faculty of Education:

DUMKE, D., Educational Psychology
KARSTEN, D., Economics
KUHN, A., History
MECHLING, H., Sports
NEUBAUER, W., Psychology
SCHALLER, H.-J., Sports

ATTACHED INSTITUTES

Institute for Water Conservation Law and Waste Disposal Law: Dir Prof. Dr F. BREUER.

Franz Josef Dölger Institute: Dir Prof. Dr E. DASSMANN.

Max Planck-Institute for Radioastronomy: see under Research Institutes.

Old Catholic Theology: Dir Prof. Dr G. ESSER.

Max Planck Institute for Mathematics: see under Research Institutes.

Research Institute for Discrete Mathematics: Dir Prof. Dr B. KORTE.

Centre for European Integration Research: Dir Prof. Dr J. VON HAGEN.

North-South Centre for Development Research: Dir Prof. Dr J. VON BRAUN.

TECHNISCHE UNIVERSITÄT CAROLO WILHELMINA ZU BRAUNSCHWEIG

38106 Braunschweig, Pockelsstr. 14

Telephone: (531) 3910
Fax: 391-4577
E-mail: president@tu-bs.de

Founded in 1745 as the Collegium Carolinum, was established as a humanistic, mercantile and technical teaching centre in 1835, and was expanded in 1862 as the Herzogliche Polytechnische Schule. It was known as the Technische Hochschule from 1877 until 1968 when it acquired its present title as a technical university

State control

Academic year: October to September (two terms)

President: Prof. Dr iur. BERND REBE
Vice-Presidents: Prof. Dr phil. habil. ULRIKE VOGEL, Prof. Dr rer. nat. habil. FRED JOCHEN LITTERST
Chancellor: HARALD WAGNER
Librarian: Prof. Dr rer. nat. habil. DIETMAR BRANDES

Library: see Libraries
Number of teachers: 227 full-time professors
Number of students: 14,646

Publications: *Mitteilungen* (1 or 2 a year), *Personal- und Vorlesungsverzeichnis* (2 a year), *TU-aktuell* (every 2 months), *Forschungsberichtsband* (*c.* every 5 years), *Veröffentlichung der Technischen Universität* (annually).

DEANS AND HEADS OF DEPARTMENTS

Faculty of Natural Sciences: Prof. Dr phil. HEINER ERKE

Department 1 (Mathematics and Informatics): Prof. Dr rer. nat. HANS-DIETER EHRICH

Department 2 (Physics and Geosciences): Prof. Dr rer. nat. habil. OTTO RICHTER

Department 3 (Chemistry and Pharmacy): Prof. Dr rer. nat. WOLF-WALTHER DU MONT

Department 4 (Biosciences and Psychology): Prof. Dr rer. nat. RALF-RAINER MENDEL

Department 5 (Architecture): Prof. Dipl.-Ing. PER KRUSCHE

Faculty of Mechanical and Electrical Engineering: Prof. Dr-Ing. JÖRG SCHWEDES

Department 6 (Building Engineering): Prof. Dr rer. nat. HEINZ ANTES

Department 7 (Mechanical Engineering): Prof. JÜRGEN HESSELBACH

Department 8 (Electrical Engineering): Prof. Dr phil. nat. ROLAND SITTING

Department 9 (Philosophy, Economics and Social Sciences): Prof. Dr habil. HANS-JOACHIM BEHR

Department 10 (Education): Prof. Dr rer. pol. habil. GERHARD HIMMELMANN

There are 123 affiliated institutes

UNIVERSITÄT BREMEN

28334 Bremen, Postfach 330440
Located at: 28359 Bremen, Bibliothekstr.

Telephone: (421) 218-1
Fax: (421) 218-4259
E-mail: rektor@vwg.uni-bremen.de

Founded 1971
State control
Academic year: October to September (two terms)

Rector: Prof. Dr JÜRGEN TIMM
Chancellor: GERD-RÜDIGER KÜCK
Pro-Rectors: Prof. Dr H. DIEHL, Prof. Dr HAGEN LICHTENBERG, Prof. Dr W. MÜLLER
Librarian: ANNETTE RATH-BECKMANN

Number of teachers: 366
Number of students: 18,000

Publications: *Veranstaltungsverzeichnis* (5 a year), *Rechenschaftsbericht* (annually), *Impulse aus der Forschung* (2 a year), *Research Report* (every 2 years), *Bremer Uni Schlüssel* (5 a year).

DEANS

Department of Physics and Electrical Engineering: Prof. Dr STEFAN VON AUFSCHNAITER
Department of Biology and Chemistry: Prof. Dr G.-O. KIRST
Department of Mathematics and Computer Science: Prof. Dr H.-J. KREOWSKI
Department of Production Engineering: Prof. Dr F.-J. HEEG
Department of Geosciences: Prof. Dr O. BROCKAMR
Department of Law: Prof. Dr G. WINTER
Department of Economics: Prof. Dr A. LEMPER
Department of Social Sciences: Prof. Dr G. BAHRENBERG
Department of Cultural Sciences: Prof. Dr H. G. ARTUS
Department of Literature and Language Studies: Prof. Dr. G. PASTERNACK
Department of Health and Human Studies: Prof. Dr A. KEIL
Department of Social and Educational Sciences: Prof. Dr A. KRETSCHMANN

PROFESSORS

Department 1 (Physics; Electrical Engineering):

Physics:

AUFSCHNAITER, S. VON, Teaching of Physics
AUGSTEIN, E., Meteorology and Physics of the Oceans
BLECK-NEUHAUS, J., Experimental Physics
BONNING, K., Physics of the Oceans
BOSECK, S., Experimental Physics
BURROWS, P., Environmental Physics
CZYCHOLL, G., Theoretical Physics
DIEHL, H., Biophysics
DREYBRODT, W., Experimental Physics, Molecular Spectroscopy
EHRENSTEIN, D. VON, Experimental Physics
GUTOWSKI, J., Semiconductor Optics
HERZ, A., Theoretical Physics
HOMMEL, D., Epitaxy of Semiconductors
JÜPTNER, W., Laser Application
KRAUSE, G., Physical Oceanography
KÜNZI, K., Environmental Physics
LANGE, H., Sociology of Labour
MAYER-HENRICY, A., Biophysics
NIEDDERER, H., Teaching of Physics
NOACK, C. C., Theoretical Physics
OLBERS, D., Theoretical Physics
PAWELZIK, K., Theoretical Biology
RICHTER, P., Theoretical Physics
ROETHER, W., Physical Oceanography in the Polar Regions
RYDER, P., Physics of Metals
SCHMITZ-FEUERHAKE, I., Experimental Physics
SCHWEDES, H., Teaching of Science
SCHWEGLER, H., Theoretical Physics
SIMHAN, K., Fluid Physics
STAUDE, W., Experimental Physics

Electrical Engineering:

ANHEIER, W., Microelectronics
ARNDT, F., High Frequency Technology
BENECKE, W., Silicon-Micromechanics, Sensors and Actuators
BINDER, J., Micro- and Sensor-Systems, and Space Technology
GRÄSER, A., Automation Engineering
GRONWOLD, D., Electrical Technology
KAMMEYER, K.-D., Communications
LAUR, R., Electronics and Microelectronics
LOHMANN, B., Automatic Control
MARTE, G., Electronics
MEINERZHAGEN, B., Field Theory
MÜLLER, W., Analysis of the Engineering Professions
ORLIK, B., Electrical Drives and Power Electronics
RAUNER, F., Electrical Technology
ROY, S. C., Electronics
SILBER, D. H., Power Electronics and Devices

Department 2 (Biology; Chemistry):

Biology:

ARNTZ, W., Ocean Ecology
BLOHM, D., Biotechology
ENTRICH, H., Theory and Practice of Education in the Natural Sciences
FISCHER, H., Marine Microbiology
FLOHR, H., Biology

GRIMME, L. H., Biology, Biochemistry
HEYSER, W., Botany
HILDEBRANDT, A., Biology
KIRST, G.-O., Marine Botany
KOENIG, F., Botany
KREITER, A., Neurobiology
MOSSAKOWSKI, D., Evolutionary Biology
POERTNER, H.-O., Marine Biology
ROTH, G., Neurobiology
SAINT-PAUL, U., Marine Ecology
SCHLOOT, W., Genetics, Human Genetics
SMETACEK, V., Marine Biology
VALLBRACHT, A., Virology
WEIDEMANN, G., Ecology
WITTE, H., Zoology
WOLFF, M., Marine Ecology

Chemistry:

BALZER, W., Marine Chemistry
BEYERSMANN, D., Biochemistry
BREUNIG, H.-J., Inorganic Chemistry
GABEL, D., Organic Chemistry, Biochemistry
JAEGER, N., Physical Chemistry
JASTORFF, B., Organic Chemistry
JUST, E., Teaching of Chemistry
LEIBFRITZ, D., Organic Chemistry
MEWS, R., Inorganic Chemistry
MONTFORTS, F., Organic Chemistry
PLATH, P., Chemistry
RIEKENS, R., Teaching of Chemistry
RÖSCHENTHALER, G., Inorganic Chemistry
SCHREMS, O., Physical Chemistry
SCHROER, W., Physical Chemistry
SCHULZ-EKLOFF, G., Physical Chemistry
STOHRER, W.-D., Chemistry
THIEMANN, W., Physical Chemistry
WANCZEK, K., Inorganic Chemistry
WÖHRLE, D., Chemistry

Department 3 (Mathematics; Computer Science):

Mathematics:

ARNOLD, L., Probability and Statistics
BAENSCH, E., Technomathematics
BECKER, G., Teaching of Mathematics
BOEHM, M., Technomathematics
BUNSE-GERSTNER, A., Numerics
DENNEBERG, D., Mathematics
DEUTSCH, M., Teaching of Mathematics
DOMBROWSKI, H.-D., Mathematics
FISCHER, H. W., Teaching of Mathematics
GAMST, J., Theory of Dynamics
HENNING, J., Teaching of Mathematics
HERRLICH, H., Topology
HINRICHSEN, D., Theory of Dynamics
HOFFMANN, R.-E., Topology
HORNEFFER, K., Mathematics
HUPPERTZ, H., Teaching of Mathematics
KRAUSE, U., Mathematics
LINDENAU, V., Teaching of Mathematics
MAESS, P., Technomathematics
MÜNZNER, H.-F., Mathematics
OELJEKLAUS, E., Complex Analysis
OSIUS, G., Biometry
PEITGEN, H.-O., Applied Mathematics
PORST, H.-E., Algebra
SCHÄFER, R., Mathematics
SCHINDLER, M., Teaching of Mathematics
WISCHNEWSKY, M., Algebra

Computer Science:

BORMANN, U., Computer Networks
BRUNS, F.-W., Simulations
FRIEDRICH, J., Business Development
GOGOLLA, M., Database Systems
HAEFNER, K., Information Technology
HERZOG, O., Knowledge-Based Systems and Applications in Production Planning and Environmental Protection
KREOWSKI, H.-J., Computer Programming
KRIEG-BRÜCKNER, B., Computer Languages
KUBICEK, H., Applied Computer Science
MARTE, G., Information Systems
NAKE, F., Computer Programming and Computer Languages
PELESKA, J., Operations Systems, Distributed Systems
SZCZERBICKA, H., Computer Architecture and Modelling

Department 4 (Production Engineering):

BAUCKHAGE, K., Chemical Process Engineering
BRINKSMEIER, E., Manufacturing Engineering
GENTHNER, K., Technical Thermodynamics, Heat and Mass Transfer
GOCH, G., Measurement Control
GRATHWOHL, G., Ceramic Materials and Components
HARIG, H., Material Sciences
HEEG, F.-J., Ergonomics, Industrial and Human Engineering
HENNEMANN, O. D.
HIRSCH, B. E., Production Systems Design and Organization
KIENZLER, R., Applied Mechanics and Structural Mechanics
KUNZE, H.-D., Near-Net-Shape Manufacturing Technologies
MAYR, P., Material Sciences
MÜLLER, D. H., Engineering Design, CAE, CAD
RÄBIGER, N., Process Engineering, Environmental Technology
RATH, H. J., Technical Mechanics and Fluid Mechanics
SEPOLD, G., Laser and Plasma Technologies
VISSER, A., Production Facilities
WITTKOWSKY, A., Design and Development of Technology

Department 5 (Geosciences):

BLEIL, U., Marine Geophysics
BROCKAMP, O., Mineralogy, Petrography, Clay Mineralogy
FISCHER, R. X., Crystallography
FÜTTERER, D., Geology
HENRICH, R., Sedimentology, Palaeo-oceanography
HERTERICH, K., Palaeo-oceanographic Modelling
JÖRGENSEN, B. B., Biogeochemistry
KUSS, H. J., Geology, Stratigraphy, Sedimentology
MILLER, H., Geophysics
OLESCH, M., Geology of the Polar Regions, Petrology
SCHULZ, H., Geochemistry, Hydrogeology
SPIESS, V., Marine Technology, Marine Environmental Geophysics
VILLINGER, H., Marine Technology, Geophysical Sensor Development
WEFER, G., Geology
WILLEMS, H., Historical Geology and Palaeontology

Department 6 (Law):

BÖLLINGER, L., Criminal Law
BRÜGGEMEIER, G., Civil and Economic Law
DÄUBLER, B., Labour, Commercial and Economic Law
DAMM, R., Civil Law, Economic Law
DERLEDER, P., Civil and Banking Law
DUBISCHAR, R., Civil Law
FEEST, J., Criminal Law and Criminology
FRANCKE, R., Legal Didactics
GESSNER, V., Comparative Law and Legal Sociology
HART, D., Economic Law
HINZ, M., Public Law and Political and Legal Sociology
HOFFMANN, R., Public Law, Labour Law and Political Science
JOERGES, C., Civil and Comparative Law
KNIEPER, R., Civil and Economic Law
LICHTENBERG, H., Labour and European Law
REICH, N., Civil and European Law
RINKEN, A., Public Law
RUST, U., Gender Law
SCHEFOLD, D., Public Law
SCHMIDT, E., Civil Law and Procedure
SCHMINCK-GUSTAVUS, C., History of Law
SCHUMANN, K. F., Criminology
STUBY, G., Public Law and Political Science
THOSS, P., Criminal Law
WASHNER, R., Labour Law
WESSLAU, E., Criminal Law and Procedure
WINTER, G., Public and Environmental Law

Department 7 (Economics):

BAUER, E., Business Administration
BIESECKER, A., Economic Theory
BRITSCH, K., Economic Statistics
DWORATSCHEK, S., Project Management
ECKSTEIN, W., Economics of Logistic Systems
ELSNER, W., Economic, Industrial and Regional Policy, Institutional Economics
FRANCKE, R., Economic Theory
GERSTENBERGER, H., Theory of State and Society
GRENZDÖRFFER, K., Economic Statistics, Labour Economics
HAASIS, H.-D., Economics
HEIDE, H., Town and Country Planning
HICKEL, R., Public Finance
HUFFSCHMID, J., Political Economy of the Federal Republic
KALMBACH, P., Economics
KOPFER, H., Economics of Logistics Systems
LEITHÄUSER, G., Economic Policy and Development Policy
LEMPER, A., Foreign Trade Theory and Politics
LIONVILLE, J., International Economics
MARX, F. J., Financial Accounting and Business Taxation
PODDIG, TH., Finance
SCHAEFER, H., Theory, Forecasting and Control
SCHMÄHL, W., Economics and Social Policy
SCHWIERING, D., Economics
SELL, A., International Economics
STEIGER, O., General Economic Theory and Monetary Economics
STUCHTEY, R. W., Economics of Marine Transport
VRING, TH. VON DER, Political Economy
WOHLMUTH, K., Comparative Economic Systems
ZACHCIAL, M., Transport Science and Transport Planning

Department 8 (Sociology; Geography; History; Politics):

Sociology:

BILLERBECK, R., Political Sociology
BLOSSFELD, H.-P., Statistics and Empirical Social Research
FREYHOLD, M. VON, Social Science
KRÄMER-BADONI, T., Town and Regional Planning
KRAUSE, D., Educational Planning
KRÜGER, M., Social Analysis
LAUTMANN, R., General Sociology and Sociology of Law
PETER, L., Labour and Industrial Sociology
QUENSEL, S., Resocialization and Rehabilitation
REICHELT, H., Theory of Science and Society
SENGHAAS, D., Peace and Conflict Studies
WEYMANN, A., Social Theory, Educational Research

Geography:

BAHRENBERG, G., Social and Economic Geography
SCHRAMKE, W., Geography, Teaching of Geography
TAUBMANN, W., Cultural Geography
TIPPKÖTTER, R., Geography of Soils
VENZKE, J.-F., Physical Geography

History:

BARROW, L., Social and Political History of England
EICHWEDE, W., History and Politics of Socialist Countries
HÄGERMANN, D., Medieval History

HAHN, M., History of Business, Political Theories
HOEDER, D., Social History of the USA
KLOFT, H., Ancient History
KRAUSS, M., History of 19th- and 20th-century Social Economics
QUACK, S., Social and Gender History of the USA
RECH, M., Prehistoric and Medieval History
SCHMIDT, J., Curricula in Economic and Social Studies
STEINBERG, H.-J., Modern European History
WAGNER, W., Politics

Cultural History of Eastern Europe:
EICHWEDE, W., History and Politics of Socialist Countries
KRASNODEBSKY, Z., Polish Social and Cultural History
STÄDTKE, K., Cultural History of Eastern Europe

Politics:
ALBERS, D., Labour Relations
EICHWEDE, W., History and Politics of Socialist Countries
KOOPMANN, K., Didactics of Social Science Education
LOTHAR, R., Politics, and Federal and Constitutional Law
LUBERT, U., Comparative Politics, European Integration
PETERS, B., Political Theory and History of Ideas
SCHMIDT, M., Politics, Comparative Social Policies
WAGNER, W., Politics, History of Political Education
WIRTH, M., Parliamentary System of Federal Germany
ZOLL, R., History and Theory of Trade Unions
ZÜRN, M., Politics

Department 9 (Cultural Sciences):

Cultural Science:
DRÖGE, F., Mass Communication Research
DUERR, H. P., Ethnology and Cultural History
NADIG, M., European Ethnology and Cultural Anthropology
RICHARD, J., Teaching of Drama
RICHTER, D., German Literature

Art:
BUDDEMEIER, H., Communication, Mass Media
MÜLLER, M., Art History and Cultural Studies
PETERS, M., Art Education
SCHADE-THOLEN, S., Art History, Aesthetics

Music:
BRECKOFF, W., Teaching of Music
KLEINEN, G., Teaching of Music, Musicology
RIEGER, E., Musicology

Philosophy:
MOHR, G., Practical Philosophy
SANDKÜHLER, H. J., Theoretical Philosophy
STÖCKLER, M., Philosophy of Natural Sciences

Religious Science:
KIPPENBERG, H.-G., Theory and History of Religions
LOTT, J., Religious Education
SCHULZ, H., Comparative Religion

Sport:
ARTUS, H. G., Teaching of Physical Education
BRAUN, H., History of Sport
FIKUS, M., Psychomotor Behaviour
SCHEELE, K., Sports Medicine

Department 10 (Literature and Language Studies):

Communication:
BACH, G., Teaching of English
BARROW, L., Social and Political History of England
BÜRGER, P., French and Comparative Studies
DAHLE, W., German Language and Literature
EMMERICH, W., German Literature
FRANZBACH, M., Literature and Social History of Spain and Latin America
GALLAS, H., German Literature
JÄGER, H.-W., History of German Literature
KOCH, H. A., German and Comparative Literature
LIEBE-HARKORT, K., German as a Foreign Language
MENK, A.-K., Linguistics
METSCHER, T., English Literature
PASTERNACK, G., Theory of Literature
PAUL, L., Applied Linguistics
POURADIER DUTEIL, F., French Language
SAUTERMEISTER, G., History of German Literature
STEHL, T., Romance Philology and Italian Linguistics
STOLZ, TH., Linguistics
WAGNER, K.-H., Linguistics
WALTZ, M., French Literature
WILDGEN, W., Linguistics
ZIMMERMANN, K., Spanish and Portuguese Linguistics

Department 11 (Health and Human Studies):

Public Health:
FRENTZEL-BEYME, R., Occupational and Environmental Epidemiology
GREISER, E., Occupational Health and Social Medicine
MÜLLER, R., Health Policy, Occupational Health and Social Medicine

Work Study:
MÜLLER, R., Health Policy, Occupational Health and Social Medicine
SENGHASS-KNOBLOCH, E., Humanization of Work
SPITZLEY, H., Technology and Society

Teacher Training:
BOEHM, U., Structure and Development of Education
DRECHSEL, R., Education
GOERRES, ST., Social Gerontology
HOPPE, M., Mechanical Technology
HYAMS-PETER, H.-U., Social Education
KRÜGER-MÜLLER, H., Sociology
LITTEK, W., Theory and Practice of Vocational Education
MAANE, H. VAN, Nursing Sciences
ORTMANN, H., Educational Sciences
VOIGT, B., Teacher Training

Psychology:
BAUMGÄRTL, F., Psychological Diagnosis
BERNDT, J., Physiology
GNIECH, G., Psychology
HEINZ, W.-R., Sociology and Social Psychology
HENNING, H.-J., Psychology
LEITHÄUSER, T., Development Psychology
PETERMANN, F., Clinical Psychology
REINKE, E., Clinical Psychology
STADLER, M., Psychology
VETTER, G., Theory of Learning
VOGT, R., Psychology
VOLMERG, B., Psychology

Social Education:
AMENDT, G., Sub-Cultures
BAUER, R., Social Pedagogy
BLANDOW, J., Social Education
BROCKMANN, A.-D., Town and Regional Planning
HEINSON, G., Social Pedagogy
KEIL, A., General Education
LEIBFRIED, S., Social Planning
MERKEL, J., Pre-School Education

Department 12 (Social and Educational Sciences):

Work Experience:
FISCHER, W. C., Consumer Economics
FRÖLEKE, H., Nutrition
HUISKEN, F., Educational Science
SCHRÖDER, A., Textile Technology

Education Diploma:
DIETZE, L., Public Law
ROTH, L., Theory of Teaching
SCHÖNWÄLDER, H. G., Educational Planning and Economics
STRAKA, G., Extracurricular Education
ZIECHMANN, J., Psychology of Learning

Further Education:
GERL, H., Adult Education
GÖRS, D., Distance Education
HOLZAPPFEL, G., Curricular Planning
KUHLENKAMP, D., Educational Planning
MADER, W., Adult Education
SCHLUTZ, E., Adult Education
WOLLENBERG, J., Adult Education in Political Science

Teaching the Handicapped:
DÖHNER, O., Medicine of Mental Illness
FEUSER, G., Education of Mentally Disturbed Children
HOMBURG, G., Educating People with Speech Defects
JANTZEN, W., History of Educating the Handicapped
KRETSCHMANN, R., Training of Educationally Handicapped
PIXA-KETTNER, U., Educating People with Speech Defects
REINCKE, W., Education for the Mentally Disturbed

Primary Education:
MILHOFFER, P., Sociology and Political Education
SCHMITT, R., Developmental Psychology
SPITTA, G., Beginning of German Language

Educational Science:
BECK, J., Educational Social Sciences
DRECHSEL, W., Educational Social History
HUISKEN, F., Educational Political Economy
POLZIN, M., Aesthetic Education
PREUSS, O., Sociology of Education
UBBELOHDE, R., Educational Science
VINNAI, G., Analytical Social Psychology

ATTACHED INSTITUTES

Academy for Labour and Politics: Dir Prof. Dr TH. LEITHÄUSER.

Alfred Wegener Institute for Polar and Marine Research: Dir Prof. Dr M. TILZER.

ATB Institute for Applied Systems Technology Bremen GmbH: Dir Dr-Ing. U. KIRCHOFF.

Bremen Fibre Institute: Dir Prof. Dr-Ing. H. HARIG.

Bremen Institute for Applied Beam Technology: Dir Prof. Dr-Ing. G. SEPOLD.

Bremen Institute for Prevention Research and Social Medicine: Dir Prof. Dr E. GREISER.

Bremen Institute of Industrial Technology and Applied Work Science at the University of Bremen: Dir Prof. Dr F.-J. HEEG.

Centre for Applied Information Technologies: Dir Prof. Dr M. B. WISCHNEWSY.

Centre for Applied Space Technology and Microgravity: Dir Prof. Dr H. J. RATH.

Centre for Cognitive Sciences: Dir Prof. Dr G. ROTH.

Centre for Complex Systems and Visualization: Dir Prof. Dr H.-O. PEITGEN.

Centre for Continuing Education and Training: Dir Prof. Dr D. KUHLENKAMP.

Centre for European Law and Policy at the University of Bremen: Dirs Prof. Dr G. BRÜGGEMEIER, Prof. Dr U. K. PREUSS; Prof. Dr C. JOERGES.

Centre for Human Genetics and Genetic Counselling: Dir Prof. Dr rer. nat. med. habil. W. SCHLOOT.

Centre for Medical Diagnostic Systems and Visualization: Dir Prof. Dr H.-O. PEITGEN.

Centre for Environmental Research and Technology: Dir Prof. Dr B. JASTORFF.

Centre for Networking and Distributed Data Processing: Dir Dr W.-D. SCHWILL.

Centre for the Philosophical Foundations of the Sciences: Dir Prof. Dr H. J. SANDKÜHLER.

Centre for Social Policy Research: Dir Prof. Dr R. MÜLLER.

Centre for Tropical Marine Ecology: Dir Prof. Dr G. HEMPEL.

Foundation Institute of Materials Science and Engineering: Dir. Prof. Dr-Ing. habil. P. MAYR.

Fraunhofer Institute for Applied Materials Research: Dir Prof. Dr-Ing. H.-D. KUNZE.

Computing Science Technology Centre: Dir Prof. Dr O. HERZOG.

German Press Research Institute: Dir Prof. Dr H.-W. JÄGER.

Institute for Honey Analysis: Dir Dr C. LÜLLMAN.

Institute for Microsensors, Microactuators and Microsystems: Dir Prof. Dr. W. BENECEK.

Institute for Municipal Energy Management and Policy at the University of Bremen: Dir Prof. Dr-Ing. K. TRAUBE.

Institute for Science Transfer Through Further Education: Dir H.-J. ZAREMBA.

Institute for Shipping Economics and Logistics: Dir Prof. Dr W. ECKSTEIN.

Institute of Environmental Physics: Dirs Prof. Dr J. P. BURROWS, Prof. Dr K. KÜNZI.

Institute of Environmental Process Engineering: Dir Prof. Dr N. RÄBIGER.

Institute of Remote Sensing: Dirs Prof. Dr J. P. BURROWS, Prof. Dr K. KÜNZI.

Institute of Technology and Education: Dir Prof. Dr F. RAUNER.

Max Planck Institute for Marine Microbiology: Dir Prof. Dr F. WIDDEL.

Research Centre for Work and Technology: Dirs Prof. Dr H. LANGE, Prof. Dr W. MÜLLER.

Research Institute for Independent Literature and Social Movements in Eastern Europe: Dir Prof. Dr W. EICHWEDE.

Research Institute for Labour and the Region: Dir Prof. Dr TH. KRÄMER-BADONI.

TECHNISCHE UNIVERSITÄT CHEMNITZ

09107 Chemnitz

Telephone: (371) 531-0
Telex: 32483
Fax: (371) 531-1651

Founded 1836 as a royal trade school of Chemnitz; became Technische Universität Chemnitz-Zwickau 1986; present name *c*1997
State control
Academic year: October to September

Rector: Prof. Dr rer. nat. habil. CHRISTIAN VON BORCZYSKOWSKI
Vice-Rectors: Prof. Dr Ing. habil. KLAUS-JÜRGEN MATTHES, Prof. Dr rer. nat. habil. BERND STÖCKERT, Prof. Dr phil. habil. JOSEF SCHMIED
Chancellor: Dr-Ing. PETER REHLING
Librarian: Dr HANS-JOACHIM HERMES

Number of teachers: 173
Number of students: 5,430

Publication: *Spectrum*† (quarterly).

DEANS

Faculty of Computer Science: Prof. WOLFGANG BENN
Faculty of Economics: Prof. JOACHIM KÄSCHEL
Faculty of Electrical and Information Engineering: Prof. GUNTER EBEST
Faculty of Mathematics: Prof. EBERHARD LANCKAU
Faculty of Mechanical and Process Engineering: Prof. SIEGFRIED WIRTH
Faculty of Natural Science: Prof. MICHAEL SCHREIBER
Faculty of Philosophy: Prof. JOSEF KREMS

TECHNISCHE UNIVERSITÄT CLAUSTHAL

38678 Clausthal-Zellerfeld, Adolph-Roemer-Str. 2A

Telephone: (5323) 720
Telex: 953828
Fax: 723500

Founded 1775 as Bergakademie Clausthal, attained university status 1968
State control
Academic year: April to following March (two terms)

Rector: Prof. Dr-Ing. P. DIETZ
Chancellor: Dr Jur. PETER KICKARTZ
Vice-Chancellor: J. DRERUP
Librarian: Dr HELMUT CYNTHA

Number of teachers: 187, including 119 Ordinary Professors
Number of students: 2,900

Publications: *Mitteilungsblatt*, *Lösestunde*, *Vorlesungsverzeichnis* (annually).

DEANS

Faculty of Mathematics and Natural Sciences: Prof. Dr rer. nat. THOMAS HANSCHKE
Faculty of Mining, Metallurgy and Engineering: Prof. Dr-Ing. CLAUS MARX

HEADS OF DEPARTMENTS

Faculty of Mathematics and Natural Sciences:
- Mathematics and Computer Science: Prof. Dr G. MÜLLER
- Physics: Prof. Dr R. LABUSCH
- Chemistry: Prof. Dr G. SCHMIDT
- Earth Sciences: Prof. Dr REIK

Faculty of Mining, Metallurgy and Engineering:
- Mining and Raw Materials: Prof. Dr GOCK
- Metallurgy and Materials Science: Prof. Dr G. FRISCHAT
- Mechanical Engineering and Process Engineering: Prof. Dr HOFFMANN

BRANDENBURGISCHE TECHNISCHE UNIVERSITÄT COTTBUS

03013 Cottbus, Postfach 101344
Premises at 03044 Cottbus, Karl-Marx-Str. 17

Telephone: (355) 69-0
Fax: (355) 69-2721
E-mail: rektor@tu-cottbus.de

Founded 1991
State control

President: Prof. Dr rer. nat. habil. ERNST SIGMUND
Registrar: PETER LANGER

Library of 600,000 vols
Number of teachers: 620
Number of students: 3,000

DEANS

Faculty of Mathematics, Physics and Information Sciences: Prof. Dr rer. nat. habil. BERNHARD THALHEIM
Faculty of Architecture and Civil Engineering: Prof. Dipl.-Ing. WOLFGANG SCHUSTER
Faculty of Mechanical Engineering, Electrical Engineering and Industrial Engineering: Prof. Dr-Ing. GERHARD LAPPUS
Faculty of Environmental Sciences and Process Engineering: Prof. Dr-Ing. MICHAEL SCHMIDT
Centre of Technology and Society: Prof. Dr phil. habil. KLAUS KORNWACHS

TECHNISCHE UNIVERSITÄT DARMSTADT

64277 Darmstadt, Karolinenplatz 5

Telephone: (6151) 1601
Telex: 419579
Fax: (6151) 165489

Founded 1836 as Höhere Gewerbeschule, acquired university status in 1877

President: Prof. Dr-Ing. JOHANN-DIETRICH WÖRNER
Vice-President: Prof. Dr-Ing. PETER HAGEDORN
Chancellor: Dr jur. HANNS SEIDLER

Number of professors: 295
Number of students: 16,175

HEADS OF DEPARTMENTS

Department 1 (Law and Economics): Prof. Dr HEIKO KÖRNER
Department 2 (History and Social Sciences): Prof. Dr KLAUS DIETER WOLF
Department 3 (Education Science, Psychology and Sports Science): Prof. Dr KATRIN BORCHEDING
Department 4 (Mathematics): Prof. Dr PETER RENTROP
Department 5 (Physics): Prof. Dr HELMUT WIPF
Department 6 (Mechanics): Prof. Dr DIETMAR GROSS
Department 7 (Chemistry): Prof. Dr rer. nat. HANS GÜNTER
Department 10 (Biology): Prof. Dr rer. nat. WERNER HIMSTEDT
Department 11 (Geosciences and Geography): Prof. Dr rer. nat. WOLFGANG F. MÜLLER
Department 12 (Surveying): Prof. Dr-Ing. HARALD SCHLEMMER
Department 13 (Civil Engineering): Prof. Dr-Ing. ROLF KATZENBACH
Department 15 (Architecture): Prof. Dipl.-Ing. GÜNTER PFEIFER
Department 16 (Mechanical Engineering): Prof. Dr-Ing. JOHANNES JANICKA
Department 17 (Electrical Energy Technology): Prof. Dr-Ing. GERD BALZER
Department 18 (Electrical Engineering and Information Technology): Prof. Dr HANS STRACK
Department 20 (Computer Science): Prof. Dr ALEJANDRO BUCHMANN
Department 21 (Material Science): Prof. Dr-Ing. HORST HAHN

PROFESSORS

Law and Economic Sciences:
- AZZOLA, A., Public Law
- BECKS, R., Political Economy
- BETSCH, O., Industrial Economy
- CASPARI, V., Political Economy
- DOMSCHKE, W., Industrial Economy
- HEIKE, H.-D., Political Economy
- HOFMANN, P., Civil, Economic and Labour Law
- IPSEN, D., Political Economy
- KÖRNER, H., Political Economy
- NICKEL, E., Civil, Economic and Labour Law
- ORTNER, E., Business Computer Science

PETZOLD, H.-J., Industrial Economy
PFOHL, H.-CHR., Industrial Economy
POSER, G., Political Economy
REISS, W., Law of Taxation and Public Finance
RÜRUP, B., Political Economy
SCHNEIDER, U. H., Civil Economic and Labour Law
SPECHT, G., Industrial Economy
STADTLER, H., Industrial Economy
WURL, H.-J., Industrial Economy

History and Social Sciences:
ABROMEIT, H., Political Science
BÖHME, G., Philosophy
BÖHME, H., Modern History
BRUNLOP, E., Sociology
DAHMER, H., Sociology
DIPPER, CHR., Modern History
EGLOFF, G., Philology and Literature
FRYDE, N. FRIEFRAN STROMER VON REICHENBACH, Medieval History
GAMM, G., Philosophy
HEINELT, H., Political Science
HOBERG, R., Philology
JAEGER, C., Sociology
KRAIS, B., Sociology
MAYER, E., Sociology
NIXDORFF, P., Political Science
PROMIES, W., Philology and Literature
SCHMALZ-BRUNS, R., Political Science
SCHMIEDE, R., Sociology
SCHRÖDER, H.-C., Modern History
SIEGRIST, L., English Language
STAHL, M., Ancient History
WOLF, K. D., Political Science

Education Science, Psychology and Sport:
BORCHERDING, K., Psychology
DIGEL, H., Sport
FENGER, H., Vocational Education and Educational Planning
FERTIG, L., Education
HARTMANN, H., Sport
LEICHNER, R., Psychology
PAUL-KOHLHOFF, Vocational Education
PETERSEN, G., Didactics of Natural Sciences
PONGRATZ, L., Education
RÜTTINGER, B., Psychology
RÜTZEL, J., Vocational Education
SCHMIDT, R., Psychology
SCHMITZ, B., Psychology
SESINK, W., Education
SINGER, R., Sport
SORGATZ, H., Psychology
VOSS, H.-G., Psychology
WANDMACHER, J., Psychology
WIEMEYER, J., Sport

Mathematics:
ALBER, H.-D.
ARTMANN, B.
BOKOWSKI, J.
BRUHN, G.
BURMEISTER, P.
FARWIG, R.
FINCKENSTEIN, Graf K. VON
HEIL, E.
HOFMANN, K. H.
HOSCHEK, J.
KEIMEL, K.
KINDLER, J.
KRABS, W.
LAUGWITZ, D.
LEHN, J.
MÄURER, H.
MEISTER, E.
NOLTE, W.
RENTROP, P.
SCHEFFOLD, E.
SCHELLHAAS, H.
SPELLUCCI, P.
STEIN, G.
STREICHER, TH.
TREBELS, W.
WEGMANN, H.
WILLE, R.

Physics:
BRANN-MUNZINGER, P., Nuclear Physics
CLERC, H.-G., Nuclear Physics
ELSÄSSER, W., Applied Physics
FEILE, R., Solid State Physics
GREWE, N., Solid State Physics
HEBER, J., Solid State Physics
KAISER, F., Applied Physics
KÖRDING, A., Nuclear Physics
KÜBLER, J., Solid State Physics
MANAKOS, P., Nuclear Physics
MULSER, P., Applied Physics
NÖRENBERG, W., Nuclear Physics
RICHTER, A., Nuclear Physics
ROSE, H., Applied Physics
SAUERMANN, G., Solid State Physics
SAUERMANN, H., Solid State Physics
SEELIG, W., Applied Physics
STEGLICH, F., Solid State Physics
TSCHUDI, TH., Applied Physics
WAMBACH, J., Nuclear Physics
WIEN, K., Nuclear Physics
WIPF, H., Solid State Physics
ZILGES, A., Nuclear Physics

Mechanics:
GROSS, D., Mechanics
HAGEDORN, P., Mechanics
HAUGER, W., Mechanics
HUTTER, K., Mechanics
MARKERT, R., Mechanics
ROESNER, K., Mechanics
TSAKMAKIS, CH., Mechanics
WRIGGERS, P., Mechanics

Chemistry:
BÄCHMANN, K., Nuclear Chemistry
BRAUN, D., Organic and Macromolecular Chemistry
BRICKMANN, J., Physical Chemistry
BUCHLER, J. W., Inorganic Chemistry
DENCHER, N. A., Physical Biochemistry
DINSE, K., Physcial Chemistry
ELIAS, H., Inorganic Chemistry
FRIEDL, P., Biotechnology
GASSEN, H. G., Biochemistry
GAUBE, J., Chemical Technology
GRUBER, E., Macromolecular Chemistry
HAASE, W., Physical Chemistry
HOMANN, K.-H., Physical Chemistry
JOPPIEN, G., Inorganic Chemistry
KLEIN, H.-F., Inorganic Chemistry
KNIEP, R., Inorganic Chemistry
LICHTENTHALER, FR., Organic Chemistry
LINDNER, H. J., Organic Chemistry
LUFT, G., Chemical Technology
MARTIN, M., Physical Chemistry
NEUNHOEFFER, H., Organic Chemistry
SKERRA, A., Biochemistry
VOGEL, H., Inorganic Technology
WENDT, H., Inorganic Technology

Biology:
BUSCHINGER, A., Zoology
DANCKER, P., Zoology
GIERSCH, CH., Botany
HIMSTEDT, W., Zoology
KAISER, W., Zoology
KLUGE, M., Botany
LANGNER, G., Zoology
LAYER, P., Zoology
LÜTTGE, U., Botany
NIXDORFF, K., Microbiology
PFEIFER, F., Microbiology
SCHWABE-KRATOCHWIL, A., Geobotany
ULLRICH, W., Botany
WEIGL, J., Botany
ZIMMERMANN, F., Microbiology

Geosciences and Geography:
BLÜMEL, P., Mineralogy
EBHARDT, G., Geology and Palaeontology
GURSKY, H.-J., Regional Geology and Earth History
KEMPE, ST., Physical Geology
MAY, H.-D., Geography
MOLEK, H., Geology and Palaeontology
MÜLLER, W. F., Petrography and Stratigraphy
SCHUMANN, D., Geology and Palaeontology

Surveying:
GERSTENECKER, C.-E., Experimental Physical and Astronomical Geodesy
GÖPFERT, W., Cartography
GROTEN, E., Physical and Satellite Geodesy
SCHLEMMER, H., Geodesy
WOLFRUM, O., Surveying
WROBEL, B., Photogrammetry

Civil Engineering:
BÖHM, H. R., Environmental and Regional Planning
FRIEMANN, H., Steel Construction
GRAUBNER, C.-A., Solid Engineering
GRÜBL, P., Solid Engineering
JAGER, J., Solid Waste Technology
KATZENBACH, R., Geotechnics
MEISSNER, U., Construction Engineering, Data Processing
MOTZKO, CH., Construction Management
OSTROWSKI, M., Engineering Hydrology and Water Management
PÖPEL, H. J., Waste-Water Technology
SCHARDT, R., Statics
SCHRÖDER, W., Water Supplies and Economy
SCHUBERT, E., Construction Engineering
SEEGER, T., Steel Construction and Mechanics of Materials
TIEDT, W., Hydraulics and Hydrology
URBAN, W., Water Supply
WÖRNER, J.-D., Statics
ZANKE, U., Water Supplies and Economy

Architecture:
BODINI, F., Sculpture
BÖHM, H., Drawing, Painting and Graphic Art
BRANDT, A., Design of Buildings
BREDOW, J., Design, Housing Construction and Specialized Subjects
EBERLE, D., Architectural Design
EISELE, J., Architectural Design
FÜHRER, H., Design and Industrial Construction
GOERNER, S., Town Planning and Design
HAUSCHILD, M., Design of Surface Engineering
JAKUBEIT, B., Architectural Design
KNELL, H., Classical Archaeology
KÖRTE, A., Planning and Construction in Developing Countries
LIEBENWEIN, W., History of Art
MÜRB, R., Landscape Architecture
PETZINKA, K.-H., Design and Building Engineering
PFEIFER, G., Design of Surface Engineering
SEELINGER, F., Design and Visual Communication
SIEVERTS, TH., Town Planning and Design
STÖFFLER, J., Supporting Structures
WAECHTER, H.-G., Design, Structures and Country Planning
WEISCHEDE, D., Design and Building Engineering
WICK, R., Town Planning and Design
WILKES, W., Typography

Mechanical Engineering:
ANDERL, R., Computer Integrated Design
BEER, H., Technical Thermodynamics
BERGER, CH., Materials Technology
BIRKHOFER, H., Machine Elements and Construction Theory
BREUER, B., Vehicle Technology
ECKSTEIN, F., Machine Tools, Manufacturing Technology
EWALD, B., Aerodynamics and Measuring Techniques
GÖTTSCHING, L., Paper Technology
HAMPE, M. J., Chemical Process Engineering
HARS, CH., Printing Technology
HENNECKE, D., Flight Propulsion

HOHENBERG, G., Internal Combustion Engines
JANICKA, J., Energy and Powerplan Technology
KOLLMANN, F. G., Machine Dynamics
KUBBAT, W., Flight Mechanics
LANDAN, K., Work Studies
LOTH, R., Energy Technology and Reactors
NORDMANN, R., Mechatronic Systems
SCHMOECKEL, D., Transformer Technology
SCHULZ, H., Mechanical Technology and Manufacturing Technology
SCHÜRMANN, H., Lightweight Design and Construction
SPECKHARDT, H., Materials
SPURK, J. H., Fluid Dynamics
STOFFEL, B., Hydraulic Machines and Plant
WOELFEL, H., Machine Dynamics

Electrical Energy Technology:
BALZER, G., Electrical Energy Supply
HARTKOPF, TH., Renewable Energy
HASSE, K., Transformer-powered Propulsive Mechanisms
KÖNIG, D., High Voltage Technology
MUTSCHLER, P., Power Electronics and Drive Control
PFEIFFER, W., Electrical Measurement
SCHMIDT-CLAUSEN, J.-J., Illuminating Engineering
STENZEL, J., Automation and Control of Electrical Power Systems
ZÜRNECK, H., Foundations of Electrotechnology

Electrical Engineering and Information Technology:
CLAUSERT, H., Foundations of Electrical Engineering
DORSCH, B., Foundations of Electrical Engineering
EVEKING, H., Computer Systems
GLESNER, M., Microelectronic Systems
HÄNSLER, E., Theory of Signals
HARTNAGEL, H., High-Frequency Technology
HILBERG, W., Digital Circuits and Memories
HOFFMAN, K., Telecommunications
ISERMANN, R., Theory of Control Systems
JAKOBY, R., Microwave Technology
KOTKA, A., Semiconductor Electronics
LANGHEINRICH, W., Semiconductor Technology
MEISSNER, P., Optical Communications
STEINMETZ, R., Industrial Process and System Communications
STRACK, H., Semiconductor Technology
TOLLE, H., Theory of Control Systems
WEILAND, TH., Electromagnetic Theory
WEISSMANTEL, H., Electromechanical Apparatus
WERTHSCHÜTZY, R., Electromechanical Apparatus
ZSCHUNKE, W., Telecommunications

Computer Science:
BIBEL, W., Intellectics
BUCHMANN, A., Data Processing
BUCHMANN, J., Theoretical Computer Science
ENCARNAÇÃO, J., Data Processing
HENHAPL, W., Programming Languages and Compilers
HOFFMANN, H.-J., Programming Languages and Compilers
HOFFMANN, R., Micro Programming
HUSS, P., VLSI Systems
KAMMERER, P., Operating Systems
MATTERN, F., Distributed Systems
NEUHOLD, E., Publishing and Information Systems
WALDSCHMIDT, H., Operating Systems
WALTER, H., Automation Theory and Formal Languages
WALTHER, CHR., Computer Programming

Material Science:
EXNER, H., Physical Metallurgy
FUESS, H., Chemical and Physical Crystallography
HAHN, H., Thin Strata
ORTNER, H., Chemical Analysis in Material Science
RAUH, H., Theoretical Principles of Material Development
RIEDEL, R., Dispersed Solid Materials
RÖDEL, J., Non-metallic Inorganic Materials

UNIVERSITÄT DORTMUND

44221 Dortmund
Premises at: 44227 Dortmund-Eichlinghofen, August-Schmidtstrasse
Telephone: (231) 755-1
Telex: 822465
Fax: (231) 751532

Founded 1968
State control
Languages of instruction: German, English
Academic year: April to February

Rector: Prof. Dr ALBERT KLEIN
Vice-Rectors: Prof. Dr DIETER HOELTERSHINKEN, Prof. Dr URSULA GATHER, Prof. Dr KLAUS WEINERT
Chancellor: DOROTHEE DZWONNEK
Librarian: MARLENE NAGELSMEIER-LINKE

Library of 1,700,000 vols
Number of students: 25,389

Publications: *Unizet* (monthly), *UniReport* (2 a year), *International Newsletter* (2 a year).

DEANS

Department of Mathematics: Prof. Dr N. STEINMETZ
Department of Physics: Prof. Dr J. BAACKE
Department of Chemistry: Prof. Dr R. SCHMUTZLER
Department of Chemical Engineering: Prof. Dr S. ENGELL
Department of Urban and Regional Planning: Prof. Dr K. R. KUNZMANN
Department of Mechanical Engineering: Prof. Dr K. HEINZ
Department of Computer Sciences: Prof. Dr H. MÜLLER
Department of Statistics: Prof. Dr S. SCHACH
Department of Electrical Engineering: Prof. Dr U. SCHWIEGELSHOHN
Department of Building Construction and Architecture: Prof. Dr J. NEISECKE
Department of Economic and Social Sciences: Prof. Dr H. NEUENDORFF
Department of Education and Biology: Prof. Dr N. VORSMANN
Department of Special Education and Rehabilitation: Prof. Dr H. STADLER
Department of Sociology, Philosophy and Theology: Prof. Dr W. POST
Department of Language and Literature, Journalism and History: Prof. Dr H. HÖMIG
Department of Music, Arts, Sport and Geography: Prof. Dr H. HINKEL

PROFESSORS

Department of Mathematics:
BECKER, E., Algebra
BLUM, H.
ERLE, D., Topology
FLOER, J., Mathematics Teaching
FRANK, H., Differential Geometry and CAD
HAZOD, W., Analysis
KABALLO, W., Analysis
MÖLLER, H. M., Applied Mathematics
KILIAN, H., Mathematics Teaching
MAYER, K. H., Topology
MENKE, K., Analysis
MÖLLER, H. M., Applied Mathematics
MÜLLER, G., Mathematics Teaching
MÜLLER, M. W., Applied Mathematics
REIMER, M., Applied Mathematics
ROSENBERGER, G.
SCHARLAU, R., Geometry
SCHNEIDER, A., Analysis
SCHRAGE, G., Mathematics Teaching
STEINMETZ, N., Function Theory
THEDY, A., Algebra
WALTER, R., Differential Geometry
WINZEN, W., Mathematics Teaching
WITTMANN, E., Mathematics Teaching
ZAMFIRESCU, T., Geometry

Department of Physics:
BAACKE, J., Theoretical Physics
BRANDT, U., Theoretical Physics
FISCHER, H. E., Physics Teaching
FRÖHLICH, D., Experimental Physics
FUJARA, F., Experimental Physics
GERLACH, B., Theoretical Physics
GÖSSLING, K. F., Experimental Physics
KEITER, H., Theoretical Physics
PASCHOS, E. A., Theoretical Physics
PFLUG, A., Physics Teaching
REIHL, B., Experimental Physics
REYA, E., Theoretical Physics
SCHÜLKE, W., Experimental Physics
SUTER, D., Experimental Physics
WEBER, W., Theoretical Physics
WEGENER, D., Experimental Physics
WEIS, T., Experimental Physics
WILLE, K., Accelerator Physics

Department of Chemistry:
BLECKMANN, P., Organic Chemistry
BODDENBERG, B., Physical Chemistry
BROEKAERT, J., Inorganic Chemistry
EILBRACHT, P., Organic Chemistry
GEIGER, A., Physical Chemistry
JACOBS, H., Inorganic Chemistry
JURKSCHAT, K., Inorganic Chemistry
KELLER, H.-L., Inorganic Chemistry
KREHER, R. P., Organic Chemistry
KREISER, W., Organic Chemistry
LIPPERT, B., Inorganic Chemistry
MINKWITZ, R., Inorganic Chemistry
MITCHELL, T. N., Organic Chemistry
SCHMIDT, H.-J., Chemistry Teaching
SCHMUTZLER, R., Physical Chemistry
WINTER, R., Physical Chemistry

Department of Chemical Engineering:
BEHR, A., Technical Chemistry
ENGEL, S., Plant Technology
FRIEDRICH, C., Technical Microbiology
GÓRAK, A., Thermal Processes
KÖSTER, W., Materials and Corrosion
PETERMANN, J., Materials Science
SCHECKER, H.-G., Physical Chemistry, Processing Science
SCHMIDT-TRAUB, H., Plant Technology
SCHULZ, S., Thermodynamics
STRAUSS, K., Energy Processing
WEINSPRACH, P.-M., Thermal Process
WEISS, E., Chemical Plant Technology
WERNER, U., Mechanical Process
WICHMANN, R., Biological Process Engineering

Department of Urban and Regional Planning:
BADE, F.-J., Economics
BARON, P., Traffic
BECKER, R., Research into Women's Issues and Housing
DAVID, C.-H., Planning Law
FINKE, L., Landscape Ecology and Planning
HENNINGS, G., Industrial Planning
KRAUSE, K.-J., Town and Country Planning
KREIBICH, V., Geography
KROES, G., Political Economy
KUNZMANN, R., Regional Planning
RÖDDING, W., System Theory and Techniques
SCHMALS, K. M., Sociological Theory of Spatial Planning
SCHOOF, A., Town and Regional Planning
TUROWSKI, G., Development and Regional Planning
VELSINGER, P., Economics
ZLONICKY, P., Construction Supervision and Town Planning

Department of Mechanical Engineering:
CROSTACK, H.-A., Quality Control
DALL, O. F., Technical Didactics
FINCKENSTEIN, E. VON, Production Methods
HEINZ, K., Manufacturing Preparation
JANSEN, R., Logistics
JÜNEMANN, R., Mechanical Handling and Storage
KAUDER, K., Fluid Energy Machines
KESSEL, S., Mechanics
KREIS, W., Machinery
KUHN, A., Factory Organization
KÜNNE, B., Machine Elements in Transport Engineering
SCHÜLER, U., Technical Didactics
STEFFENS, H.-D., Physical Production Methods
THERMANN, K., Machine Dynamics
UHLE, M., Measurement
WEINERT, K., Cutting Production Methods

Department of Computer Science:
BANZHAF, W., Computer Science in Engineering
BEILNER, H., Quantitative Methods
BISKUP, U., Databases and Information Systems
DIETZFELBINGER, M., Parallel Algorithms
DITTRICH, G., Theory of Machines and Systems
DOBERKAT, E.-E., Software Technology
ECHTLE, K., Fault-tolerant Systems
FUHR, N., Data Structures and Information Systems
HERRMANN, T., Computer Science and Society
KRUMM, H., Distributed Systems
MARWEDEL, P., Computer-aided Design of Integrated Circuits
MORAGA, C., Theory of Machines
MORIK, K., Artificial Intelligence
MÜLLER, H., Computer Graphics
PADAWITZ, P., Keyboarding Theory
REUSCH, B., Machines and Switching Theory
SCHWEFEL, H. P., Systems Analysis
SIMON, U., Recursive Functions and Complexity Theory
WEDDE, H., Operating Systems and Computer Architecture
WEGENER, I., Efficient Algorithms and Complexity Theory

Department of Statistics:
GATHER, U., Statistics of Natural Sciences
HARTUNG, J., Statistics in relation to Engineering
HERING, F., Experimental Design
KRÄMER, W., Statistics of Economics and Sociology
KUNERT, J., Mathematical Statistics
SCHACH, S., Mathematical Statistics
TRENKLER, G., Econometry
URFER, W., Statistical Methods in Genetics
WEIHS, C., Computer-aided Statistics

Department of Economics and Sociology:
BERG, H., Political Economy
HOLLÄNDER, H., Economics
HUMMEL, S., Business Administration
JEHLE, E., Business Administration
KÄSEBORN, H.-G., Economics Teaching
KLANDT, H., Empirical Economics and Social Research
LACKES, R., Business Computing
LEININGER, W., Economic theory, Microeconomics
NEUENDORFF, H., Sociology
RECHT, P., Operations Research
REICHMANN, TH., Business Administration
RICHTER, W., Economics
SCHÜNEMANN, B., Private Law
SCHUMM-GARLING, U., Sociology
TEICHMANN, U., Manufacturing Preparation
WAHL, J., Investment and Finance
WELGE, M., Management

Department of Building Construction and Architecture:
ALBRECHT, P., Steel Structures
BLECKEN, U., Construction, Management, Machinery and Equipment
BOFINGER, H., Construction and Design
FISCHER, M., Steel Structures
HASSLER, U., Preservation of Historic Monuments, Building Research
HETTLER, A., Foundations
LEIMBÖCK, E., Construction
KLOPFER, H., Physics of Buildings
MÜLLER, H., Architecture in compliance with the Climate
NALBACH, G., Graphic Communication and Design
NEISECKE, J., Building Materials
NUSSBAUM, N., History of Building
OBRECHT, H., Structural Engineering
PFEIFFER, H., Planning
RANK, E., Numerical Calculation and Data Processing
SAWADE, J., Building Design, Industrial Buildings
SCHÄFER, H.-G., Concrete and Cement Building
SCHIFFERS, K.-H., Building Organization
SCHRAMEK, E.-R., Building Equipment Technology

Department of Electrical Engineering:
FREUND, E., Automation and Robotics Technology
GOSER, K., Electronic Components and Design
HANDSCHIN, E., Electrical Energy Maintenance
KIENDL, H., Electrical Application and Regulation
KULIG, T., Electric Machines, Drives and Power Engineering
PEIER, D., High Tension Technology
PONNER, J., Current Regulation
SCHEHRER, R., Electrical Systems and Applications
SCHRÖDER, H., Electronic Components
SCHUMACHER, K., Micro-Electronics
SCHWIEGELSHOHN, U., Data Processing Systems
VOGES, E., High Frequency
WENDLAND, B., Information Technology

Department of Education and Biology:

Institute of General, Comparative and Vocational Education:
PÄTZOLD, G.
RURIK, G.
SCHÄFER, K.-H.
VOGEL, P.

Institute of Teaching Science:
FLESSAU, K.-I.
GLUMPER, E.
KOCH, K.-H.
VORSMANN, N.
WIEDERHOLD, K.-A.

Institute of Social and Elementary Education:
HÖLTERSHINKEN, D.
RAUSCHENBACH, T.
THOLE, W.

Institute for Development Research:
ROLFF, H. G.
SCHÜLZ-ZANDER, R.

Biology:
SCHULTE, H.
STICHMANN, W.
VERBEEK, B.

Department of Special Education and Rehabilitation:

Theory of Special Education:
SOLAROVA, S.

Psychology:
FRANKE, A.
LAUTH, G. W.

Diagnosis for Special Education:
MOOG, W.

Sociology:
ADAM, C.
HORN, H.

Professional Training for Handicapped People:
BIERMANN, H.

Education of the Blind and Visually Handicapped:
WALTHES, R.

Education of Disturbed People:
PETERMANN, U.

Education of the Mentally Handicapped:
DÖNHOFF, K.

Education of the Physically Handicapped:
LEYENDECKER, CH.
STADLER, H.

Education of those with Speech Handicap:
DUPUIS, G.
KATZ-BERNSTEIN, N.

Education of those with Learning Difficulties:
SCHMETZ, D.
WEMBER, F. B.

Motor Theory:
HÖLTER, G.

Women's Research in Education of Handicapped People:
SCHILDMANN, U.

Art:
TÖNNE, R.

Music:
MERKT, I.

Department of Sociology, Philosophy and Theology:

Home Economics:
EISSING, G.
JOOSTEN, B.

Philosophy:
POST, W.
RAPP, F.
SCHMIDT, H. J.

Politics:
MEYER, T.
ROEMHELD, L.

Psychology:
GASCH, B.
HEUER, H.
KASTNER, M.
KLEINBECK, U.
LASOGGA, F.
ROEDER, B.
SCHADE, B.

Sociology:
BEER, U.
KALBITZ, R.
METZ-GÖCKEL, S.
NAEGELE, G.
STALLBERG, F. W.
VEELKEN, L.

Protestant Theology:
GREWEL, H.
JACOBS, F.
KONRAD, J.-F.
MAURER, E.
WIED, G.

Catholic Theology:
ESSER, W.
KOLLMANN, R.
MÖLLE, H.
RUSTER, T.

Department of Language and Literature, Journalism and History:

German:
BRÜNNER, G.
BUSCHA, J.
CONRADY, P.
ENGELEN, B.
KLEIN, A.

KÜHN, R.
LINK, J.
LYPP, M.
MOTTÉ, M.
QUASTHOFF, U. M.
RADEMACHER, G.
RIEMENSCHNEIDER, H.
ZABEL, H.

English:

BIMBERG, C.
GRUNZWEIG, W.
HEUER, H.
NOLD, G.
OPPERTSHÄUSER, O.
PETERS, H.

Journalism:

BOHRMANN, H.
BRANAHL, U.
EURICH, C.
HEINRICH, J.
KOPPER, G.
PÄTZOLD, U.
PÖTTKER, H.
RAGER, G.

History:

GOEBEL, K.
HÖMIG, H.
KEINEMANN, F.
LAMPE, K.

Department of Music, Arts, Sport and Geography:

Music:

ABEGG, W.
GECK, M.
HOUBEN, E. M.
RÖTTER, G.

Art:

BERTRAM, U.
GRÜNEWALD, D.
HINKEL, H.
SCHNEIDER, N.
SCHUBERT, P.
STUCKENHOFF, W.

Textile Design:

MENTGES, G.
NIXDORF, H.

Sport:

BRÄUTIGAM, M.
STARISCHKA, S.
STÖCKER, G.
VÖLKER, K.

Geography:

CORDES, G.
KAMINSKE, V.
THIEME, G.

ATTACHED INSTITUTES

Institut für Arbeitsphysiologie: 44139 Dortmund, Ardeystr. 67; Dir Prof. Dr H. M. BOLT.

Fraunhofer Institut für Materîalfluss und Logistik: Dir Prof. Dr R. JÜNEMANN.

Institut für Roboterforschung: Head Prof. Dr E. FREUND.

Institut für Spektrochemie und Angewandte Spektroskopie: Head Prof. Dr D. KLOCKOW.

Institut für Umweltschutz: Head Prof. Dr CH. ULLRICH.

Landesinstitut Sozialforschungsstelle Dortmund.

Institut für Landes- und Stadtenwicklungsforschung des Landes NW.

Institut für Gerontologie: Head Prof. Dr G. NAEGELE.

Technologie Zentrum Dortmund GmbH.

TECHNISCHE UNIVERSITÄT DRESDEN

01062 Dresden, Mommsenstr. 13
Telephone: (351) 4635358
Fax: (351) 4637738
E-mail: mader@pop3.tu-dresden.de

Founded 1828, University status 1961
State control
Academic year: October to September

Rector: Prof. Dr A. MEHLHORN
Pro-Rectors: Prof. Dr H.-J. HARDTKE, Prof. Dr H. WIESMETH, Prof. Dr W. SCHMITZ
Chief Administrative Officer: A. POST
Librarian (Saxony Regional Library and University Library): J. HERING

Number of teachers: 635
Number of students: 23,913

Publication: *Wissenschaftliche Zeitschrift* (six a year).

DEANS

Faculty of Natural Sciences and Mathematics: Prof. Dr H. FREIESLEBEN
Faculty of Computer Science: Prof. Dr H. VOGLER
Faculty of Electrical Engineering: Prof. Dr G. GERLACH
Faculty of Mechanical Engineering: Prof. Dr G. SÖRGEL
Faculty of Construction: Prof. Dr J. STRITZKE
Faculty of Economics and Business Management: Prof. Dr W. ESSWEIN
Faculty of Education: Prof. Dr U. SANDFUCHS
Faculty of Law: Prof. Dr P. HAY
Faculty of Medicine 'Carl Gustav Carus': Prof. Dr W. KIRCH
Faculty of Architecture: Prof. Dr H. KOKENGE
Faculty of Forestry, Hydrology and Geosciences: Prof. Dr W. KILLISCH
Faculty of Philosophy: Prof. Dr H. VORLÄNDER
Faculty of Literature and Linguistics: Prof. Dr P. STROHSCHNEIDER
Faculty of Transport and Traffic Engineering: Prof. Dr S. LIEBIG

GERHARD-MERCATOR-UNIVERSITÄT GESAMTHOCHSCHULE DUISBURG

47057 Duisburg, Lotharstr. 65
Telephone: (203) 3790
Fax: (203) 3793500

Founded 1972 by amalgamation and extension of the Pädagogische Hochschule and the Fachhochschule
Academic year: April to March (two semesters)

Rector: Prof. Dr rer. nat. WALTER EBERHARD
Co-Rectors: Prof. Dr phil. nat. EDGAR HEINEKEN, Prof. Dr-Ing. HEINZ LUCK, Prof. Dr rer nat PETER SARTORI
Chancellor: CARL-FRIEDRICH NEUHAUS
Librarian: SIGURD PRAETORIUS

Number of teachers: 620
Number of students: 15,013

Publications: *Amtliche Mitteilungen*†, *Universitäts-Report*†, *Vorlesungsverzeichnis*†.

DEANS

Department 1 (Philosophy, Evangelical Theology, Social Sciences): Prof. Dr JÜRGEN KRÜGER
Department 2 (Educational Science, Psychology): Prof. Dr ROLF DOBISCHAT
Department 3 (Linguistics): Prof. Dr HELMUT TERVOOREN
Department 5 (Economics): Prof. Dr jur. HANS LEUER
Department 6 (Chemistry and Geography): Prof. Dr GÜNTER GEISMAR
Department 7 (Construction Engineering): Prof. Dr-Ing. HANS-DIETER KOCHS
Department 8 (Metallurgy and Ceramics): Prof. Dr-Ing. HEINZ-JOSEF WOJTAS
Department 9 (Electrical and Control Engineering): Prof. Dr-Ing. ERICH KUBALEK
Department 10 (Physics and Technology): Prof. Dr RALF COURTHS
Department 11 (Mathematics): Prof. Dr GÜNTER TÖRNER

(There was no Department 4 as we went to press)

PROFESSORS

Department 1:

ALTER, P., History
AXT, H.-J., Political Science
BÄRSCH, C.-E., Political Science
BEHSCHNITT, W. D., History
BOSCH, G., Sociology
BROSE, H.-G., Sociology
BUSSMANN, C., History
CHRISTADLER, M., Political Science
DANCKWERTS, D., Sociology
EBERT, K., Protestant Theology
GEUENICH, D., History
GIRNDT, H., Philosophy
GRIPP-HAGELSTANGE, H., Sociology
GRUNOW, D., Political Science
HANTSCHE, I., History
HARTUNG, W., History
HEINZ, M., Philosophy
HENNING, H., Social History
HERWIG, H., Political Science
HOLLER, W., Sociology
HORN, F., Protestant Theology
HÜBNER, H., Social Work and Education
HUMMELL, H.-J., Sociology
KLIEMT, H., Philosophy
KRÜGER, J., Sociology
KULENKAMPFF, J., Philosophy
MEYNS, P., Political Science
NUSCHELER, F., Political Science
OELSCHLÄGEL, D., Social Work and Education
RICKERS, F., Protestant Theology
ROSENAU, H., Protestant Theology
RÜLCKER, C., Sociology
SCHATZ, H., Political Science
STEIN, G., Political Science
STÖVE, E., Protestant Theology
STRASSER, H., Sociology
ZIEGLER, R., History
ZIMMER, J., Social Work and Education

Department 2:

BAYER, M., Pedagogics
BRUNNER, R., Pedagogics
DOBISCHAT, R., Economic Pedagogics
FREY, S., Psychology
HEILAND, H., Pedagogics
HEINEKEN, E., Psychology
HELMER, K., Pedagogics
KUTSCHA, G., Pedagogics
LÖWISCH, D.-J., Pedagogics
MIETZEL, G., Psychology
RAATZ, U., Psychology

Department 3:

AMMON, U., German Philology
BECKERS, H., German in the Middle Ages
BIEHL, J., German Philology
BOGDAL, M., German Philology
BÖRNER, K., English Philology
BORNSCHEUER, L., German Philology
BRÖG, H., Art
GASSENMEIER, M., English Philology
GRIMM, G., German Philology
HAACK, D., English and American Philology
HARDT, M., Romance Philology
HOEPPNER, W., Computer Linguistics
JÄGER, S., German Philology/Linguistics
JÜTTNER, S., Romance Philology
KAISER, H., German Philology
KÖPF, G., German Philology
LINKE, N., Music
MATHIAS, R., Japanese Philology
MIHM, A., German Philology
PÜRSCHEL, H., Applied Linguistics
SIEPE, H. TH., Romance Philology

SPILLNER, B., Romance Philology
STAIB, B., Romance Linguistics
TERVOOREN, H., German Philology

Department 5 (Economics):
BARTH, K.
BODENSTEIN, G.
BREITHECKER, V.
BRETZKE, W.-R.
CASSEL, D.
CHAMONI, P.
COX, H.
GERPOTT, T.
HEIDUK, G.
HEILEMANN, U.
HERRMANN-PILLATH, C.
KALUZA, B.
KATH, D.
LANGE, W.
LEUER, H.
MEYER, B.
NIERHAUS, H.
PAFFENHOLZ, H.-J.
PASCHA, W.
PLACHETKA, M. G.
ROLFES, B.
SCHENK, H.-O.
SCHIRA, J.
TIEPELMANN, K.
TIETZEL, M.
WOHLGEMUTH, M.

Department 6:
BLOTEVOGEL, H.-H., Geography
BONNET, P.-H., Organic Chemistry
BORCHARD, W., Applied Physical Chemistry
BUSS, V., Theoretical Chemistry
DANNEEL, I., Biology
DÖPP, D., Organic Chemistry
DYKER, G., Metallorganic Chemistry
ECKART, K., Geography
FLEMMING, H.-C., Microbiology
FLÜCHTER, W., Geography
FROHN, H.-J., Inorganic Chemistry
GEISMAR, G., Inorganic Chemistry
GOLLOCH, A., Analytical Chemistry
HABRICH, W., Geography
HENKEL, G., Solid State Chemistry
HINZ, W., Zoology
KLEIN, W., Ecological Chemistry
MAYER, C., Physical Chemistry
MOLT, K., Analytical Chemistry
SARTORI, P., Inorganic Chemistry
SAUS, A., Applied Chemistry
SCHÖNBUCHER, A., Applied Chemistry
STRÄSSER, M., Geography
VEEMAN, W., Physical Chemistry
VOLLMER, G., Didactics of Chemistry

Department 7:
BENRA, F.-K., Turbomachinery
BESTER, H., Raw Materials
BRAUN, M., Technical Mechanics
ELBRACHT, D., Manufacturing
ELFERT, J., Foundry Machinery
FRIK, M., Technical Mechanics
GIMBEL, R., Chemical Engineering
HAGEN, P., Shipbuilding
HÄNEL, D., Numerical Fluid Dynamics
HERBELL, J.-D., Waste Treatment
HILLER, M., Applied Mechanics/Machine Dynamics
IVANTYSYNOVA, M., Surveying
KOCHS, H.-D., Information Technology and Communication
KÖHLER, P., Construction
KOSCHNITZKI, K., Technical Systems
LEDJEFF-HEY, K., Energy Technology
LUCAS, K., Thermodynamics
MÜLLER-SLANY, H.-H., Machine Dynamics
NOWACK, H., Raw Materials
ROTH, P., Dynamics
SCHLÜTER, H.-J., Shipbuilding
SCHMIDT, K. G., Chemical Engineering
SCHMIDT-OTT, A., Incineration and Gas Dynamics
SCHWARZ, H., Surveying
SHARMA, S. D., Shipbuilding
SIMON, H., Turbo-machinery
SPERLICH, V., Energy Technology
THIEL, J.-J., Shipbuilding
WIETASCH, K. W., Shipbuilding
WÜNSCH, D., Construction

Department 8:
BAUER, W., Energy Optimization
DETTE, M., Smelting Technology
DREXLER, W., Metallurgical Machines, and Mechanics
GOTTSCHLING, J., Mathematics for Engineers
HARTMANN, D. C., Science of Metals
KAESEMANN, K., Metallurgy
KAMPTZ, H. T. VON, Glass Technology
KRAUSS, S., Foundry Operation and Steel Production
STEINHÄUSER, T., Machines for Moulding
WOJTAS, H.-J., Moulding
ZEIHE, R., Glass Technology

Department 9:
BEYER, A., General and Theoretical Electrotechnics
BRAKELMANN, H., Electrical Energy Technology
DICKOPP, G., Communication Systems
FIEDLER, H.-L., Electronic Components and Circuits
FISSAN, H., Aerosol Measurement
FRANK, P. M., Electrical Surveying
FRITZ, W., Electrical Energy
GEISSELHARDT, W., Manufacturing
GERHARD, E., Electromechanical Construction
HERBERTZ, J., Electro-Acoustics
HOSTICKA, B., Electronic Components and Circuits
HUNGER, A., Manufacturing
JÄGER, D., Optoelectronics
KUBALEK, E., Electrotechnical Materials
LAWS, P., Communications
LUCK, H., Communications
MAIER, U., Measuring and Control-Engineering Technology
RASQUIN, W., Electrical Energy Technology
RIGOLL, G., Information Technology
RUMPEL, D., Electrical Engineering
TEGUDE, F.-J., Solid-state Electronics
WAGNER, H.-G., General and Theoretical Electrotechnics
WILLMS, I., Communications
WOLFF, I., General and Theoretical Electrotechnics
ZIERMANN, A., High Frequency Technology
ZIMMER, G., Electronic Components and Circuits

Department 10:
ACET, M., Experimental Physics
ARP, H., Technology
BORN, G., Physics
COURTHS, R., Experimental Physics
ENTEL, P., Theoretical Physics
FEDER, R., Theoretical Physics
FRANKE, H., Applied Physics
HARREIS, H., Physics
KEUNE, W., Applied Physics
KLEEMANN, W., Applied Physics
MÖNCH, W., Experimental Physics
PUTZER, D., Applied Physics
SANFLEBER, H., Technology
TREITZ, N., Physics Education
USADEL, K., Theoretical Physics
WASSERMANN, E., Experimental Physics
WENIG, W., Applied Physics
WERHEIT, H., Experimental Physics
WOLF, D., Theoretical Physics

Department 11 (Mathematics):
ARNOLD, H. J.
BAUER, J.
DONIG, J.
EBERHARD, W.
EBERSOLDT, F.
FREILING, G.
GONSKA, H. M.
HAUSSMANN, W.
HERKENRATH, U.
HOPPE, H. U.
JETTER, K.
KNOOP, H.-B.
LUTHER, W.
MOHN, K. H.
PITTNAUER, F.
PROFANT, M.
ROGGE, L.
SCHREIBER, W.
SIMM, G.
TÖRNER, G.
WEFELSCHEID, H.
WIEGMANN, K. W.

ATTACHED INSTITUTES

Deutsch-Französisches Institut für Automation und Robotik (IAR) Teilinstitut Duisburg: Speaker Prof. Dr-Ing. P. M. FRANK.

Rhein-Ruhr-Institut für Sozialforschung und Politikberatung e.V. (RISP): applied regional socio-economic research; promotes communication and co-operation between the academic world and public and private sector institutions in the Ruhrgebiet; Dir Prof. Dr HERIBERT SCHATZ.

Deutsches Textilforschungszentrum Nord-West e.V. Institut an der Universität-GH-Duisburg: Dir Prof. Dr ECKHARD SCHOLLMEYER.

Forschungsinstitut für wirtschaftlich-technische Entwicklungen in Japan und im Pazifikraum (FJP) an der Universität-GH-Duisburg: Dir Prof. Dr GÜNTER HEIDUK.

Institut für Umwelttechnologie und Umweltanalytik e.V. (IUTA): Dir KLAUS GERHARD SCHMIDT.

Rheinisch-Westfälisches Institut für Wasserchemie und Wassertechnologie GmbH: Dir GERD MÜLLER.

Salomon Ludwig Steinheim Institut für deutsche-jüdische Geschichte e.V. an der Universität-GH-Duisburg: research and adult education on German-Jewish relations from the Renaissance to the present; Dir Prof. Dr CLAUS-E. BÄRSCH.

Versuchsanstalt für Binnenschiffbau e.V. Duisburg (VBD) Forschungsinstitut für Flachwasserhydrodynamik: Dir Prof. Dr-Ing. E. MÜLLER.

Institut für Informatik: Dir Prof. Dr AXEL HUNGER.

Institut für Entwicklung und Frieden (INEF): Dir Prof. Dr FRANZ NUSCHELER.

Institut für Mechatronik (IMECH GmbH): Man. Prof. Dr-Ing. MANFRED HILLER.

Institut für Mobil- und Satellitenfunktechnik: Dir Prof. Dr-Ing. INGO WOLFF.

Institut für Ostasienwissenschaften: Dir Prof. Dr WINFRIED FLÜCHTER.

Institut für Schiffstechnik (ISD): Dir Prof. Dr-Ing. SOMDEO SHARMA.

Institut für Verbrennung und Gasdynamik (IVG): Dir Prof. Dr-Ing. PAUL ROTH.

HEINRICH-HEINE-UNIVERSITÄT DÜSSELDORF

40225 Düsseldorf, Universitätsstrasse 1
Telephone: (211) 81-00
Telex: 8587348
Fax: 342229

Founded 1965; formerly Medizinische Akademie, f. 1907
State control
Language of instruction: German
Academic year: Summer: April to September; Winter: October to March
Rector: Prof. Dr G. KAISER

Chancellor: ULF PALLME KÖNIG
Pro-Rectors: Prof. Dr J. SCHRADER, Prof. Dr D. RIESNER, Prof. Dr M. MAE
Head of Student Secretariat: K.-H. FEHR
Librarian: Dr E. NIGGEMANN

Library: see Libraries
Number of teachers: c.3,200
Number of students: 21,110

Publications: *Personen- und Vorlesungs verzeichnis* (2 a year), *Universitätszeitung* (6 a year), *Jahrbuch der Universität* (annually), *Amtliche Bekanntmachungen* (14 a year).

DEANS

Faculty of Economics: Prof. Dr W. HAMEL
Faculty of Mathematics and Natural Sciences: Prof. Dr H. M. JAHNS
Faculty of Philosophy: Prof. Dr R. KELLER
Faculty of Medicine: Prof. Dr H.-D. RÖHER
Faculty of Law: Prof. Dr H. DÖRNER

PROFESSORS

Faculty of Economics:

BERENS, Business Administration and Management
DEGEN, H., Statistics and Econometrics
GÜNTER, B., Business Administration and Marketing
HAMEL, W., Management and Business Administration
SCHIRMEISTER, Business Administration and Finance
SMEETS, H.-D., Economics
THIEME, H. J., Economics
WAGNER, G. R., Business Administration, Production Management and Environmental Economics

Faculty of Mathematics and Natural Sciences:

ALFERMANN, A.-W., Botany
AURICH, V., Mathematics
BAUMGARTEN, E., Physical Chemistry and Chemical Technology
BAUSCH, R., Theoretical Physics
BEHMENBURG, W., Experimental Physics
BESSENRODT, R., Theoretical Physics
BÖTTCHER, P., Inorganic and Structural Chemistry
BRAUN, M., Organic Chemistry
CIRIACY-WANTRUP, M., Microbiology
DECKER, G., Experimental Physics
DÖRING, B., Applied Mathematics
ECKMILLER, R., Physical Biology, Bio-cybernetics
ERNST, J. F., Microbiology
FISCHER, G., Mathematics
GLEBE, G., Geography
GRABITZ, H.-J., Psychology
GREVEN, H., Zoology
GRIESHABER, M., Zoology
HACKMANN, J., Experimental Physics
HÄGELE, G., Inorganic Chemistry
HARZHEIM, E., Mathematics
HEHL, F.-J., Psychology
HEIDE, G., Zoology
HESS, O., Genetics
HODAPP, V., Psychology
HOLLENBERG, C., Microbiology
HUSTON, J. P., Psychology
JAHNS, H. M., Botany
JANSSEN, A., Statistics and Documentation
JANSSEN, H.-K., Theoretical Physics
JANSSEN, K., Mathematics
KALVERAM, K., Psychology
KERNER, O., Mathematics
KISKER, E., Applied Physics
KLÄUI, W., Inorganic Chemistry
KLEINDIENST, H., Physical and Theoretical Chemistry
KLEINHANSS, H. E., Experimental Physics
KÖHNEN, W., Teaching of Mathematics
KOWALLIK, K. V., Botany
KRÄMER, R., Biotechnology
KRAUSE, G. H., Plant Physiology
KRAUTH, J., Psychology
KRÖNER-HERWIG, B., Psychology
KUCKLÄNDER, U., Pharmaceutical Chemistry
KULA, M.-R., Enzyme Technology
KUNZ, W., Genetics
LIPPOLD, B., Pharmaceutical Technology
LÖSCH, R., Botany
MARTIN, H. D., Organic Chemistry
MEINERS, D., Physics
MEISE, R., Mathematics
MICHALIS, G. F., Botany
MÖHRLE, H., Pharmacy
MOOTZ, D., Molecular Chemistry and Inorganic Chemistry
OTTO, A., Experimental Physics
PETERS, W., Zoology
PETRY, W., Instrumental Mathematics
POHST, M., Mathematics
RATSCHEK, H., Mathematics
REBHAN, E., Theoretical Physics
RIESNER, D., Physical Biology
SAHM, H., Biotechnology
SANTARIUS, K. A., Botany
SCHIRMER, W., Geology
SCHLUE, W.-R., Zoology
SCHMID, D., Solid Matter Spectroscopy
SCHMIDTKE, H.-H., Theoretical Chemistry
SCHULTZE, J., Physical Chemistry
SCHULZE, G. E., Raw Materials Science
SCHWOCHAU, M., Genetics
SCHWUGER, M., Physical Chemistry
SINGHOF, W., Mathematics
SPATSCHEK, K.-H., Theoretical Physics
SPECKENMEYER, E., Mathematics
SPINDLER, K. D., Zoology
STARK, D., Applied Physics
STEFFEN, K., Mathematics
STREHBLOW, H.-H., Physical Chemistry
STROTMANN, H., Botany
UHLENBUSCH, J., Experimental Physics
VOLLMER, G., Teaching of Chemistry
VORLAUFER, K., Geography
WAGNER, R., Physical Biology
WEBER, H., Pharmacy
WEIN, N., Teaching Geography
WEISS, H., Biochemistry
WENZENS, G., Geography
WESTHOFF, P., Botany
WILLUHN, G., Pharmaceutical Biology
WISBAUER, R., Mathematics
WIST, E. R., Psychology
WITSCH, K., Mathematics
WOLF, G. H., Plasma Physics
WULFF, G., Organic Chemistry
WUNDERLICH, F., Parasitology
ZACHARIAE, G., Soil Biology

Faculty of Philosophy:

ANTON, H., Modern German Literature
APTROOT, M., Yiddish Culture, Language and Literature
BAUMANN, U., English
BEEH, V., Germanic Philology
BERGER, D., English
BEUKER, F., Sports Medicine
BIRLEY, A. R., Ancient History
BIRNBACHER, D., Philosophy
BOLDT, H., Politics
BORSÒ, V., Romance Languages and Literature
BRANDES, D., Culture and History of Germans in the east of Europe
BÜHLER, A., Philosophy
BUSSE, W., English
CLAAS, D., English
DÜWELL, K., History
FLOHR, H., Politics
FRIEDL, H., English
FRIEDRICH, L., Education
GELDSETZER, L., Philosophy
GERUM, E., Theory of Organization
HARDACH, K., Economic History
HAUPT, B., German
HÄUSSLER, R., Classical Philology
HECKER, H., East European History
HEINZ, R., Philosophy
HELDMANN, W., General Education
HENRICHS, N., Philosophy and Information Science
HIESTAND, R., Medieval History
HOEBINK, H., East European History
HÖFLER, M., Romance Philology
HOGREBE, W., Philosophy
HUNING, A., Philosophy
KAISER, G., Ancient German Literature
KELLER, R., Germanic Philology
KILBURY, J., Computer Linguistics
KLESCZEWSKI, R., Romance Philology
KÖRNER, H., Art History
LABISCH, A., History of Medicine
LEGENHAUSEN, L., English
LÖNNE, K.-E., Modern History
LOUVEN, E., Institute of the east of Asia
LÜSCHEN, G., Sociology
MANUWALD, B., Classical Philology
MANZ, W., Psychology
MARGIES, D., Education
MEULEMANN, H., Social Science
MICHEL, G., Education
MOLITOR, H., Modern History
MOMMSEN, W. J., Modern History
MÜLLER, K., Modern History
MÜLLER, K., Modern Japan
MÜNCH, R., Social Science
NICKEL, H., Development and Educational Psychology
NIES, F., Romance Philology
POTT, H.-G., Modern German
RETTIG, W., Romantic Philology
RÖSCH, H. E., Sport
RUPP, G., German
SCHMIDT-BRASELMANN, P., Romance Languages and Literature
SCHORMANN, G., History
SCHRADER, L., Romance Philology
SCHWARZER, C., Education
SCHWEMMER, O., Philosophy
SEIDEL, T., English
SEMMLER, J., Medieval History
SIEGRIST, J., Medical Sociology
STEIN, D., English
STÖTZEL, G., German Philology and Linguistics
SÜSSMUTH, H., History
TEPE, P., German
TIEGEL, G., Sport
WEBER, CH., Modern History
WINDFUHR, M., Modern German Literature
WITTE, B., German
WUNDERLI, P., Romance Philology
WUNDERLICH, D., General Linguistics
YALDAI, S., Sport
ZIMMERMANN, B., Classical Philology

Faculty of Medicine:

ACKERMANN, R., Urology
ALBERTI, L., Psychosocial Disturbances
ARNDT, J. O., Experimental Anaesthesiology
ARNOLD, G., Anatomy
ARNOLD, G., Experimental Surgery
BARZ, J., Forensic Medicine
BAYER, R., Physiology
BECK, L., Obstetrics and Gynaeology
BECKER, H., Surgery
BENECKE, R., Neurology
BONTE, W., Forensic Medicine
BORCHARD, F., General Pathology and Pathological Anatomy
BOJAR, H., Physiological Chemistry
BOURGEOIS, M., Paediatrics
BRÜSTER, H. T., Paediatrics and Haematology
ESSER, G., Acoustic Medicine and Audiology
FEINENDEGEN, L. E., Nuclear Medicine
FREUND, H.-J., Neurology
FRITZEMEIER, C. U., Dentistry
GANZER, U., Oto-rhino-laryngology
GIANI, G., Medieval Statistics and Documentation
GÖBEL, U., Paediatrics
GOERZ, G., Dermatology and Venerology
GRABENSEE, B., Internal Medicine

GRIES, F. A., Internal Medicine
GRÜNEWALD, G.
HAAS, H., Neurophysiology
HADDING, U., Medical Microbiology and Virology
HAENSCH, R., Dermatology and Venerology
HARING, C., Psychiatry
HARTWIG, H.-G., Anatomy
HEINZ, H.-P., Medical Microbiology
HERFORTH, A., Dentistry
HERING, P., Clinical Physiology
HEUCK, C. C., Clinical Chemistry and Biochemistry
HOFMANN, N., Dermatology and Venerology
HÖLZLE, E., Dermatology and Venerology
HORSTER, F.-A., Internal and Nuclear Medicine
JANSEN, G., Industrial Medicine
JUNGBLUT, R. M., Medical Radiotherapy
KAUFMANN, R., Clinical Physiology
KRÖNER, H., Physiological Chemistry
KUPKE, I. R., Clinical Chemistry and Clinical Biochemistry
LABISCH, A., History of Medicine
LENARD, H.-G., Paediatrics
LENTRODT, J. E. CH., Maxillary and Facial
LINS, E. J. F., Neuroradiology
LOMBECK, I., Paediatrics
MAI, J. K., Neuroanatomy
MAJEWSKI, F., Human Genetics and Paediatrics
MANNHOLD, R., Investigation of Molecular active substances
MAU, J., Statistics and Biomathematics in Medicine
MÖDDER, U., Clinical Radiology
MOLINSKI, H., Psychosomatic Medicine and Psychotherapy
MORGENSTERN, J., Applied Biomedicine
MOSER, J., Clinical Psychology
NOACK, E. A., Pharma- and Toxicology
NOVOTNY, G. E. K., Anatomy
PFEUFFER, TH., Neurophysiology
PFITZER, P., General Pathology and Cytopathology
PIPER, H. M., Physiology
PODLESCH, I., Anaesthesiology
RECHENBERGER, I., Psychiatry of Gynaecology
REH, H., Forensic Medicine
REINAUER, H., Clinical Biochemistry
RICK, W., Clinical Chemistry
RÖHER, H. D., Surgery
RÖHRBORN, G., Human Genetics and Anthropology
ROSENBAUER, K., Anatomy
ROSS, H.-G., Physiology
ROTH, S.
RUTHER, W., Orthopaedics
SANDMANN, W., Surgery
SCHEIBNER, H., Neuropsychology
SCHEID, A., Medical Microbiology and Virology
SCHMIDT, E., Paediatrics
SCHMITT, G., Radio-oncology
SCHMITZ, R., Dentistry
SCHNEIDER, W., Internal Medicine
SCHRADER, J., Physiology
SCHRÖR, K., Pharmacology and Toxicology
SCHÜBEL, F., Dentistry
SCHULITZ, K.-P., Orthopaedics
SCHULTE, H.-D., Surgery
SCHULTHEISS, H.-P., Internal Medicine
SIES, H., Physiological Chemistry
STEINGRÜBER, H.-J., Medical Psychology
STRASSBURG, M., Dentistry
STRAUER, B.-E., Internal Medicine
STROHMEYER, G., Internal Medicine
STÜTTGEN, U., Dentistry
SUNDMACHER, R., Ophthalmology
TARNOW, J., Anaesthesiology
THÄMER, V., Physiology
THON, K., Surgery
TRESS, W., Psychiatry
VOSBERG, H., Internal and Nuclear Medicine
WAAG, K.-L., Surgery
WECHSLER, W., Neuropathology
WEISE, W., Dentistry
WIRTH, K., Pharmacology and Toxicology
WORTH, H., Internal Medicine
ZEPF, S., Out-patients Psychotherapy
ZILLES, K., Anatomy

Faculty of Law:

DÖRNER, H., Private International Law and Comparative Law
FRISTER, H., Criminal Law and Law of Criminal Procedure
HOEREN, TH., Civil Law and International Commercial Law
KOKOTT, J., German and Foreign Public Law, Public International Law and European Law
NOACK, U., Civil Law and Commercial Law
OEBBECKE, J., Public Law and Administration Science
OLZEN, D., Civil Law and Law of Civil Procedure
SACHS, M., Constitutional Law and Administrative Law
SCHLEHOFER, H., Criminal Law and Law of Criminal Procedure

ATTACHED INSTITUTES

Diabetes-Forschungsinstitut an der Heinrich-Heine-Universität Düsseldorf: 40225 Düsseldorf, Auf'm Hennekamp 65; Dirs Prof. Dr F. A. GRIES, Prof. Dr H. REINAUER.

Institut für Ernährungsberatung und Diätetik: 40225 Düsseldorf, Moorenstr. 5; Dir Prof. Dr F. A. GRIES.

Medizinisches Institut für Umwelthygiene (Environmental Health Research): see under Research Institutes.

Neurologisches Therapicentrum (NTC) an der Heinrich-Heine-Universität Düsseldorf: 40591 Düsseldorf, Hohensandweg 37; Dir Dr V. HÖMBERG.

Arbeitsgemeinschaft Elektrochemischer Forschungsinstitutionen AGEF e.V.: 40225 Düsseldorf, Universitatsstr. 1; Chair. Prof. Dr J. W. SCHULTZE.

Eichendorff-Institut – Literaturwissenschaftliches Institut der Stiftung Haus Oberschlesien: 40883 Ratingen 6-Hösel, Bahnhofstr. 71; Dir. Prof. ANTON.

Institut für Medizin, Forschungszentrum Jülich GmbH: 52428 Jülich; Dir Prof. Dr L. FEINENDEGEN.

Institut für Biotechnologie, Forschungszentrum Jülich GmbH: 52428 Jülich; Dir Prof. Dr H. SAHM.

Institut für Plasmaphysik, Forschungszentrum Jülich GmbH: 52428 Jülich; Dir Prof. Dr G. H. WOLF.

Institut für Angewandte Physikalische Chemie, Forschungszentrum Jülich GmbH: 52428 Jülich; Dir Prof. Dr-Ing. M. SCHWUGER.

Deutsches Krankenhausinstitut: 40474 Düsseldorf, Tersteegenstr. 9; Dir Prof. Dr EICHHORN.

Technische Akadamie Wuppertal e.V.: 42004 Wuppertal, Pf 100409; Man. Dir Dipl. oec. ERICH GIESE.

Institut für Internationale Kommunikation: 40215 Düsseldorf, Hildebrandtstr. 4; Man. Dir Priv.-Doz. Dr BELTEN.

KATHOLISCHE UNIVERSITÄT EICHSTÄTT

85072 Eichstätt, Ostenstrasse 26-28
Telephone: (8421) 93-0
Fax: (8421) 931796

Founded 1972, reviving a foundation of 1564
Academic year: May to July, November to February

President: Prof. Dr RUPRECHT WIMMER
Vice-President: Prof. Dr HEINZ OTTO LUTHE
Chief Administrative Officer: MANFRED HARTL
Librarian: Dr HERMANN HOLZBAUER

Library of 1,400,000 vols
Number of teachers: 460
Number of students: 3,800

Publications: *Eichstätter Hochschulreden* (6 a year), *Vorlesungsverzeichnis* (2 a year), *Agora* (3 a year), *Eichstätter Beiträge* (2 a year), *Eichstätter Studien* (3 a year), *Eichstätter Materialen* (2 a year).

DEANS

Faculty of Theology: Prof. Dr FRIEDRICH DIEDRICH
Faculty of Philosophy and Education: Prof. Dr GÜNTHER KÖPPEL
Faculty of Languages and Literature: Prof. Dr WALTER HÖMBERG
Faculty of History and Social Sciences: Prof. Dr SIEGFRIED LAMNEK
Faculty of Mathematics and Geography: Prof. Dr INGRID HEMMER
Faculty of Economic Sciences: Prof. Dr HELMUT FISCHER
Faculty of Religious Education: Prof. Dr MARKUS EHAM
Faculty of Social Studies: Prof. Dr HANS-JÜRGEN GÖPPNER

PROFESSORS

Faculty of Theology:

BUCHER, A., Practical Philosophy and History of Philosophy
DIEDRICH, F., Old Testament
ELSÄSSER, A., Moral Theology
FISCHER, N., Philosophy and Basic Questions of Theology
GLÄSSER, A., Fundamental Theology
GROSS, E., Religious Teaching and Catholic Theology
HOFMANN, J., Old Church History and Patrology
MAAS-EWERD, T., Liturgy
MAIER, K., Middle and New Church History
MAYER, B., New Testament
SEYBOLD, M., Dogmatics
SPÖLGEN, J., Catechetics and Religious Education
ZOTTL, A., Pastoral Theology

Faculty of Philosophy and Education:

FELL, M., Adult Education
FETZ, R., Philosophy
GEISER, G., Pedagogics of Work
HELLBRÜCK, J., Psychology
JENDROWIAK, H.-W., General Pedagogics
KNOPP, N., History of Art
KÖPPEL, G., Art
PAULIG, P., Pedagogics in Schools
PLAUM, E., Psychology
SCHLAGER, K. H., History of Music
SCHMIDT, H.-L., Social Pedagogics
SCHUMANN-HENGSTELER, R., Psychology
WAKENHUT, R., Psychology
WITTLING, W., Psychology

Faculty of Languages and Literature:

BAMMESBERGER, A., English Linguistics
BLAICHER, G., English Literature
GSELL, O., Romance Linguistics
HÖMBERG, W., Journalism
HUBER, W., German Linguistics
HUNFELD, H., Teaching of English Language and Literature
KLÖDEN, H., Romance Linguistics
KOHUT, K., Romance Literature
KRAFFT, P., Classical Philology
MUELLER, K., German as a Foreign Language
NEUMANN, M., Modern German Literature
NIGGL, G., German Literature
RENK, H. E., Teaching of German Language and Literature

RONNEBERGER-SIBOLD, E., Historic German Linguistics
STEER, G., Medieval German Literature
TONNEMACHER, J., Journalism
TSCHIEDEL, H.-J., Classical Philology
WEHLE, W., Romance Literature
WIMMER, R., Modern German Literature

Faculty of History and Social Sciences:

BALLESTREM, K., Political Science
DICKERHOF, H., Medieval History
GRECA, R., Sociology
KIESEWETTER, H., History of Economics and Social Development
KÖNIG, H. J., Latin American History
KRAMER, F., Regional History
LAMNEK, S., Sociology
LUKS, L., Eastern European History
LUTHE, H. O., Sociology
MALITZ, J., Ancient History
MÜLLER, R. A., Modern History
PÖTZL, W., Ethnology
RUPPERT, K., Modern and Contemporary History
SCHUBERT, K., Political Science
WITETSCHEK, H., Political Science

Faculty of Mathematics and Geography:

BLATT, H.-P., Mathematics
CORNEA, A., Mathematics
FALK, M., Mathematics
FELIX, R., Mathematics
GIESSNER, K., Physical Geography
HEMMER, I., Teaching of Geography
HOPFINGER, H., Geography
KUTSCH, H., Physical Geography
RESSEL, P., Mathematics
ROHLFS, J., Mathematics
SCHWERMER, J., Mathematics
SOMMER, M., Mathematics
STEINBACH, J., Geography

Faculty of Economic Sciences:

BURGER, A., General Business Management
DJANANI, C., General Business Management
FISCHER, H., Economics
FUCHS, M., Law for Economists
GENOSKO, J., Economic and Social Policy
HOMANN, K., Ethics of Economic Institutions and Business
KÜSTERS, U., Statistics
KUTSCHKER, M., General Business Management, International Management
REICHOLD, H., Law for Economists
RINGLSTETTER, M., General Business Management
SCHNEIDER, J., Economics
SCHUSTER, L., Business Administration, Banking and Finance
STAUSS, B., Business Administration and Marketing
WILDE, K., General Business Management and Economic Information Technology

Faculty of Religious Education (vocational courses):

EHAM, M., Music and Voice Training
HILBER, W., Pedagogics
KURTEN, P., Dogmatics
LOUIS, B., Psychology
MEIER, U., Religious Education
OBERRÖDER, W., Theory and Practice of Church Work
TAGLIACARNE, P., Old Testament
TRAUTMANN, M., New Testament
WILLERS, U., Fundamental Theology and Philosophy
ZIRKER, L., Moral Theology

Faculty of Social Studies (vocational courses):

BECHER, H., Sociology
ERATH, P., Pedagogics
GÖPPNER, H.-J., Psychology
KLUG, W., Social Work
MERKEL, C. M., Psychology
OXENKNECHT-WITZSCH, R., Law
SING, H., Political Science
ZIENER, A., Pedagogics

ATTACHED INSTITUTE

Zentralinstitut für Lateinamerika-Studien: Man. Dir Dr KARL-DIETER HOFFMANN; Dirs Prof. Dr HAN-JOACHIM KÖNIG, Prof. Dr KARL KOHUT.

Zentralinstitut für Mittel- und Osteuropastudien: Dir Prof. Dr NIKOLAUS LOBKOWICZ.

FRIEDRICH-ALEXANDER-UNIVERSITÄT ERLANGEN-NÜRNBERG

91054 Erlangen, Schlossplatz 4
Telephone: (9131) 85-0
Fax: (9131) 852131

Founded 1743; merged with Universität Altdorf 1809

Rector: Prof. Dr GOTTHARD JASPER
Pro-Rectors: Prof. Dr GÜNTHER KUHN, Prof. Dr BERND NAUMANN
Chancellor: THOMAS A. H. SCHÖCK
Librarian: (vacant)

Number of teachers: 1,775, including 253 Ordinary Professors
Number of students: 25,000

Publications: *Unikurier, Unikurier aktuell, Jahresbibliographie und Forschungsbericht, Jahresbericht, Personen- und Einrichtungsverzeichnis, Erlanger Bausteine zur fränkischen Heimatforschung, Erlanger Forschungen, Geologische Blätter für Nordost-Bayern und angrenzende Gebiete, Jahrbuch für fränkische Landesforschung, Sitzungsberichte der Physikalisch-Medizinischen Societät zu Erlangen, Erlanger Universitätsreden.*

DEANS

Faculty of Theology: Prof. Dr H. BRENNECKE
Faculty of Law: Prof. Dr F. STRENG
Faculty of Medicine: Prof. Dr B. FLECKENSTEIN
Faculty of Philosophy, History and Social Sciences: Prof. Dr K. MÖSENEDER
Faculty of Languages and Literatures: Prof. Dr F. J. HAUSMANN
Faculty of Mathematics and Physics: Prof. Dr P. KNABNER
Faculty of Biology and Chemistry: Prof. Dr W. HILLEN
Faculty of Geosciences: Prof. Dr R. KOCH
Faculty of Economic and Social Sciences: Prof. Dr H. DILLER
Faculty of Technology: Prof. Dr G. HEROLD
Faculty of Education: Prof. Dr H. SCHRETTENBRUNNER

PROFESSORS

Faculty of Theology:

BRANDT, H., Ecumenical Theology, Science of Missions and Religion
BRENNECKE, H.-C., Early Church History
FELMY, CH., Theology of the Christian East
HAMM, B., Historical Theology
HERON, A., Reformist Theology
MEIER-REUTTI, G., Christian Journalism
MERK, O., New Testament
NICOL, M., Pastoral Theology
POSCHARSKY, P., Christian Archaeology and History of Art
SCHMIDT, G., Teaching of Religion
SCHMIDT, L., Old Testament
SCHMITT, H.-C., Old Testament Theology
SPARN, W., Systematic Theology
ULRICH, J., Systematic Theology
WANKE, G., Old Testament
WISCHMEYER, O., New Testament

Faculty of Law:

BARTLSPERGER, R., Public Law
BLOMEYER, W., Civil Law, Commercial and Business Law, Labour Law, International Private Law and Comparative Law
GÖSSEL, K. H., Criminal Law and Criminal Procedure
GREGER, R., Civil Law, Civil Procedure and Non-Contentious Jurisdiction
HRUSCHKA, J., Criminal Law, Criminal Procedure and Legal Philosophy
LINK, CH., Ecclesiastical Law, Constitutional and Administrative Law
ROHE, M., Civil Law
SCHMIDT-PREUSS, M., Public Law
SIEMS, H., History of German and Bavarian Law and Civil Law
STRENG, F., Criminal Law and Criminology
VEELKEN, W., Civil Law, Commercial and Business Law, Copyright Law and Industrial Property Rights, International Private Law and Comparative Law
VIEWEG, K., Civil Law, Law and Data Processing, Personal Data Protection Law
VOLLKOMMER, M., Civil Law, Civil Procedure and Labour Law
ZIEMSKE, B., Public Law

Faculty of Medicine:

BAROCKA, A., Psychiatry
BAUTZ, W. A., Diagnostic Radiology
BECKER, C.-M., Biochemistry
BETZ, P., Forensic Medicine
BRAND, K., Biochemistry
BRUNE, K., Pharmacology and Toxicology
DANIEL, W. F., Internal Medicine
EMDE, J. VON DER, Heart Surgery
FAHLBUSCH, R., Neurosurgery
FLECKENSTEIN, B., Virology
HAHN, E. G., Internal Medicine
HANDWERKER, H. O., Physiology and Experimental Physiopathology
HIRSCHFELDER, U., Orthodontics
HOHENBERGER, W., Surgery
HOHMANN, D., Orthopaedics
KALDEN, J. R., Internal Medicine
KALENDER, W., Radiology
KESSLER, M., Physiology and Cardiology
KIRCHNER, T., Pathology and Anatomy
LANG, N., Gynaecology and Obstetrics
LEHNERT, G., Social and Environmental Medicine
LÜTJEN-DRECOLL, E., Anatomy
NAUMANN, G. O. H., Optics
MARK, K. VON DER, Experimental Medicine
NEUHUBER, W. L., Anatomy
NEUKAM, F. W., Maxillofacial Surgery
NEUNDÖRFER, B., Neurology
PETSCHELT, A., Restorative Dentistry and Periodontology
PFEIFFER, R. A., Human Genetics
PLATT, D., Gerontology
RASCHER, W., Paediatrics
RÖLLINGHOFF, M., Clinical Microbiology and Immunology
SAUER, R., Radiotherapy
SCHROTT, K.-M., Urology
SCHULER, G., Dermatology
SCHÜTTLER, J., Anaesthesiology
STERZEL, R. B., Internal Medicine
WIGAND, M. E., Oto-rhino-laryngology
WITTERN-STERZEL, R., History of Medicine

Faculty of Philosophy, History and Social Sciences:

ABELE-BREHM, A., Social Psychology
ALTRICHTER, H., East European History
BAHADIR, H., East European History
BECK-GERNSHEIM, E., Sociology
BENDA, H. VON, Psychology
BLESSING, W. K., Modern History and Regional History
BÖRKER, CHR., Classical Archaeology
EBERT, TH., Philosophy
ENGELHARDT, M. VON, Sociology
FORSCHNER, M., Philosophy
GEBHARDT, J., Political Science
GERLOFF, S., Prehistory and Early History
HANDL, J., Sociology

HÖGEMANN, P., Ancient History
HORN, W., Music
JASPER, W., Political Science
JENKS, S., Medieval History
KRANZ, P., Classical Archaeology
KROSIGK, F. VON, Political Science
KULENKAMPFF, J., Philosophy
KURER, O., Economics
LENGER, F., Modern and Contemporary History
LIEBAU, E., Education
LÖSEL, F., Psychology
MENNING, K., History of Modern and Contemporary Art
METZ, K.-H., Modern History
MÖSENEDER, K., History of Art
NEUHAUS, H., Modern History
OLBRICH, E., Psychology
PHILIPP, TH., Near and Middle Eastern History and Politics
RAUTENBERG, U., History
RECKOW, F., Music
REISCH, L., Prehistory and Early History
ROTHE, K., Political Science
SCHMID, A., Bavarian and Frankish History
SCHMIDT, G., Sociology
SCHÖLLGEN, G., Modern History
SRUBAR, I., Sociology
STURM, R., Political Science
STÜRMER, M., Medieval and Modern History
SÜNKEL, W., Education
THIEL, CHR., Philosophy
THOMPSON, M., Political Science
URBAN, R., Ancient History
WERBIK, H., Psychology

Faculty of Languages and Literatures:

ACKERMANN, P. D., Japanese
BOBZIN, H., Semitic Philology
BREINIG, H., American Studies
DAUSES, A., Romance Philology
ELM, TH., Modern German Literary History
ERDMANN-PANDZIC, E. VON, Slavic Philology
FELDMANN, D., English Philology
FLESSEL, K., Chinese Studies
FORSSMAN, B., Comparative Indo-European Linguistics
FREIBURG, R., English Philology
HAUSMANN, F. J., Romance Philology
HAUSSER, R., Linguistics
HERBST, TH., English Philology
HEYDENREICH, T., Romance Philology
HUDDE, H., Romance Philology
ICKLER, TH., German as a Foreign Language
JACOBSEN, P. CHR., Middle Latin Philology
JASTROW, O., Semitic Philology
KESSLER, K. H., Assyriology
KISSEL, W., Classical Philology
KOSTER, S., Classical Philology
KUGLER, H., German Philology
LANG, J., Romance Philology
LEHMANN, J., Modern German Literature
LÖFFLER, A., English Philology and Literature
LUTZ, A., English Philology and Language
MEINDL, D., North American Philology and Literature
MUNSKE, H. H., Germanic and German Linguistics
NAUMANN, B., Germanic and German Linguistics
NEUMANN, P. H., Modern German Literary History
PÖHLMANN, E., Classical Philology
SCHMITT, P., Theatre
SEELOW, H., Nordic Philology
STEINKE, K., Slavic Philology
VERWEYEN, TH., Modern German Literature
WITTING, G., Modern German Literature
WYSS, U., German Philology

Faculty of Mathematics and Physics:

ANTON, G., Experimental Physics
BARTH, W., Mathematics
BERENS, H., Applied Mathematics
BORCHERS, W., Applied Mathematics
BUES, I., Astrophysics
COFMAN, J., Mathematics Teaching Methods
DILLIG, M., Physics
DÖHLER, G., Semiconductor Physics
FAUSTER, TH., Solid State Physics
GERSTNER, O., Mathematics
GEYER, W.-D., Mathematics
GRABMÜLLER, H., Applied Mathematics
GREVEN, A., Mathematical Stochastics
HEBER, U., Astrophysics
HEINZ, K., Solid State Physics
HELBIG, R., Physics
HOFFMANN, D., Experimental Physics
HUELLER, A., Theoretical Physics
JAHN, J., Applied Mathematics
KELLER, G., Mathematics
KNABNER, P., Applied Mathematics
KÖHN, J., Mathematics
KÖLZOW, D., Mathematics
KURZWEIL, H., Mathematics
LANGE, H., Mathematics
LENZ, F., Theoretical Physics
LESCHKE, H., Theoretical Physics
LEUCHS, G., Optics
LEY, L., Experimental Physics
MAGERL, A., Crystallography
MÜLLER, P., Experimental Physics
PANKRATOV, O., Theoretical Solid State Physics
PLAUMANN, P., Mathematics
REINHARD, P.-G., Theoretical Physics
RITH, K., Physics
SCHMEISSER, G., Mathematics
SCHNEIDER, W., Physics Teaching Methods
SCHULZ, M., Applied Physics
STEFFENS, E., Experimental Physics
STRAMBACH, K., Mathematics
STRAUSS, H., Mathematics
THIES, M., Theoretical Physics
TOEPFFER, CH., Theoretical Physics
USTINOV, A., Experimental Physics
VOIT, H., Physics
WEIDNER, H.-G., Mathematics
WILSCH, H., Experimental Physics
ZIMMERMANN, H., Crystallography
ZOWE, J., Applied Mathematics

Faculty of Biology and Chemistry:

BREITINGER, D., Inorganic Chemistry
BÜNING, J., Zoology
DAHLENBURG, L., Inorganic Chemistry
ELDIK, R. VAN, Inorganic and Analytical Chemistry
ELLERMANN, J., Inorganic Chemistry
FEY, G., Genetics
FROITZHEIM, H., Physical Chemistry
GASTEIGER, J., Organic Chemistry
GLADYSZ, J. A., Organic Chemistry
GMEINER, P., Pharmaceutical Chemistry
HAAS, W., Zoology
HÄDER, D.-P., Botany
HARTMANN, K. M., Botany
HEINZE, J., Zoology
HELVERSEN, O. VON, Zoology
HILLEN, W., Microbiology
HIRSCH, A., Organic Chemistry
KISCH, H., Inorganic Chemistry
KNOBLOCH, K., Botany and Biology
KREIS, W., Pharmaceutical Biology
LADIK, J., Theoretical Chemistry
LEE, G., Pharmaceutical Technology
LÖHMANNSRÖBEN, H.-G., Physical Chemistry
LOTZ, W., Microbiology
OTTO, P., Theoretical Chemistry
SAALFRANK, R. W., Organic Chemistry
SAUER, N., Botany
SCHELOSKE, H.-W., Biology Teaching Methods
SCHNEIDER, S., Physical Chemistry
SCHWEIZER, E., Biochemistry
SEITZ, G., Zoology
SELLMANN, D., Inorganic and General Chemistry
STEINRÜCK, H.-P., Physical Chemistry
TROSCHÜTZ, R., Pharmaceutical Chemistry
WASSERTHAL, R., Zoology
WEISS, R., Organic Chemistry
WISSMANN, P., Physical Chemistry
ZENNECK, U., Inorganic Chemistry

Faculty of Geosciences:

BÄTZING, W., Geography
BAUSCH, W., Mineralogy
BUGGISCH, W., Geology
FLÜGEL, E., Palaeontology
HÖFLING, R., Palaeontology
HÜMMER, P., Geography Teaching Methods
KOCH, R., Palaeontology
KOPP, H., Geography
KREUTZMANN, H., Geography
KÜHNE, J., Geography
MOSER, M., Applied Geology
NOLLAU, G., Geology
RICHTER, M., Geography
SCHRÖDER, H., Geography
SCHWAB, R., Mineralogy
TOBSCHALL, H.-J., Applied Geology
TRETER, U., Geography

Faculty of Economic and Social Sciences:

BERNECKER, W. L., Modern and Contemporary History (Latin America, Southern Europe)
BODENDORF, F., Business Management
BUTTLER, G., Statistics
DILLER, H., Marketing
DOERRIES, R. R., English-Language Cultures
EULER, D., Education
FELDENKIRCHEN, W., Economic and Business History
GERKE, W., Banking, Finance and Stock Exchange
GRÜSKE, K.-D., Economics and Public Finance
HARBRECHT, W., International Economics
HERRMANN, H., Private Law
KLAUS, J., Political Economics
KLAUS, P., Logistics
KLEIN, I., Statistics and Econometrics
KREUTZ, H., Sociology and Social Anthropology
KUMAR, B., International Management
LACHMANN, W., Economic Policy and Development Economics
MÄNNEL, W., Business Management
MERTENS, P., Business Economics
MEYER, M., Business Economics
NEUMANN, M., Economics
PEEMÖLLER, V. H., Business Economics and Auditing
PFEIFFER, W., Industrial Management and Technology Management
RAUSCH, H., Communication Studies and Political Science
REISS, W., German and International Tax Law
RITTER, W., Economic and Social Geography
SCHACHTSCHNEIDER, K. A., Public Law
SCHEFFLER, W., Business Taxation
SCHERL, H., Social Policy
SCHULZ, W., Communication Studies and Political Science
STEINMANN, H., Business Administration

Faculty of Technology:

BLUM, W., Properties of Materials
BRAND, H., High Frequency Technology
BRUNK, M., Communications Technology
BRUNN, P. O., Fluid Mechanics
DAL CIN, M., Communication Networks
DURST, F., Fluid Mechanics
EHRENSTEIN, G., Raw Materials
EMIG, G., Technical Chemistry
ERTL, TH., Graphic Networks
FELDMANN, K., Production Engineering
GEIGER, M., Manufacturing Engineering
GIROD, B., Communication Technology
GLAUERT, W., Electrical Engineering
GÖRZ, G., Artificial Intelligence
GREIL, P., Raw Materials
GRETSCH, R., Electrical Engineering

HEROLD, G., Electrical Engineering
HERZOG, U., Communication Networks
HOFMANN, F., Operating Systems
HUBER, J., Communications Technology
HUBERT, A., Electrical Technology
JABLONSKI, ST., Database Systems
KÖNIG, A., Technical Chemistry
KUHN, G., Technical Engineering
LEEB, K., Automatic Theory and Formal Languages
LEIPERTZ, A., Technical Chemistry
MEERKAMM, H., Technical Construction
MOLERUS, O., Mechanical Engineering
MUGHRABI, H., Materials Science, General Material Properties
MÜLLER, G., Electrical Technology
MÜLLER, H., Hardware Architecture (Computer Science)
MÜNSTEDT, H., Raw Materials
NEESSE, TH., Recycling
NIEMANN, H., Pattern Recognition
PFAFF, G., Electrical Engineering
REPPICH, B., Materials Science
ROPPENECKER, G., Automatic Control
ROOSEN, A., Glass and Ceramics
RYSSEL, Technical Electronics
SCHNEIDER, H.-J., Programming Languages
SEIDEL, H.-P., Graphic Networks
SEITZER, D., Technical Electronics
SINGER, R. F., Materials Science, Metals Technology
STEINER, R., Technical Chemistry
STOYAN, H., Artificial Intelligence
STRATMANN, M., Corrosion
STRUNK, H., Materials Science
UNBEHAUEN, R., Electrical Engineering
VETTER, G., Mechanical Engineering
WECKENMANN, A., Manufacturing Engineering
WEDEKIND, H., Database Systems
WEISSMANN, R., Materials Science
WENDLER-KALSCH, E., Corrosion
WENZEL, H., Technical Chemistry
WINNACKER, A., Materials Science
WIRTH, K.-E., Mechanical Process Engineering

Faculty of Education:
BAUMANN, H., Sport
BECK, H., Work Theory
BRECHTKEN, J., Religious Education (Roman Catholic)
DANN, H.-D., Psychology
DIEGRITZ, TH., German Language
EINSIEDLER, W., Primary-School Teaching
ERDMANN, E., History
FISCHER, W. L., Mathematics
HELBIG, P., Primary-School Teaching
HELLER, H., Regional Studies and Ethnology
INEICHEN, H., Philosophy
KLINGER, W., Physical Education
KUGELMANN, C., Sports
LÄHNEMANN, J., Religious Education (Lutheran)
LIEDTKE, M., Education
OSWALD, W. D., Psychology
POMMERIN-GÖTZE, G., German Language
PFEIFER, P., Chemistry
SACHER, W., School Education
SCHABERT, T., Political Science
SCHMIDT, W., Art
SCHOBER, O., German
SCHRETTENBRUNNER, H., Geography
SCHROFNER, E., Theology
SPANHEL, D., Education
WALTER, G., English

UNIVERSITÄT-GESAMTHOCHSCHULE-ESSEN

45117 Essen
Telephone: (201) 183-1
Telex: 8579091 unie d
Fax: (201) 183-2151
E-mail: universitaet@uni-essen.de
Founded 1972
State control
Academic year: October to September (2 semesters)

Rector: Prof. Dr Dr h.c. KARL ROHE
Chancellor: Dr ELMAR LENGERS
Pro-Rectors: Prof. Dr KLAUS HÜBNER (Academic), Prof. Dr ELKE WINTERHAGER (Research), Prof. Dr ERNST SCHMACHENBERG (Personnel and Finance), Prof. Dr VOLKER BUCK (Structure and Planning)
Librarian: ALBERT BILO

Number of teachers: 1,350
Number of students: 23,000

Publication: *Vorlesungsverzeichnis* (2 a year).

DEPARTMENTS AND DEANS

Philosophy, Religious Studies and Sociology: Prof. Dr O. N. HABERL
Educational Sciences, Psychology and Physical Education: Prof. Dr K. KLEMM
Literature and Linguistics: Prof. Dr H. W. SCHMITZ
Design and Art Education: Prof. Dr INGO GRÜN
Economics: Prof. Dr INGOLF BAMBERGER
Mathematics and Computer Science: Prof. Dr N. KNOCHE
Physics: Prof. Dr DIETER MERGEL
Chemistry: Prof. Dr R. ZELLNER
Bioscience and Geosciences: Prof. Dr G. OBE
Civil Engineering: Prof. Dr-Ing. G. IVANYI
Surveying: Prof. Dr-Ing. W. ROCHOLL
Mechanical Engineering: Prof. Dr-Ing. J. WORTBERG
Medicine: Prof. Dr HANS GROSSE-WILDE

JOHANN WOLFGANG GOETHE-UNIVERSITÄT FRANKFURT

60054 Frankfurt am Main, Senckenberganlage 31, Postfach 111932
Telephone: (69) 798-1
Fax: (69) 798-28383
Founded 1914
Academic year: October to September (2 semesters)

President: Prof. Dr W. MEISSNER
Chancellor: Dr W. BUSCH
Librarian: B. DUGALL

Number of teachers: 2,000, including 596 professors
Number of students: 35,914

Publications: *Vorlesungs- und Personenverzeichnis*, *Studienführer*, *Rechenschaftsbericht* (annually), *Forschungsbericht*, *Uni-Report* (every three weeks in term-time), *Forschung Frankfurt* (quarterly).

DEANS

Department of Law: Prof. Dr P.-A. ALBRECHT
Department of Economics: Prof. Dr W. NEUBAUER
Department of Social Science: Prof. Dr W. GLATZER
Department of Education: Prof. Dr G. SCHOLZ
Department of Psychology: Prof. Dr W. BAUER
Department of Protestant Theology: Prof. Dr. W.-E. FAILING
Department of Catholic Theology: Prof. Dr H. WOLF
Department of Philosophy and History: Prof. Dr U. MUHLACK
Department of Classical Languages and Arts: Prof. Dr G. A. SEECK
Department of Modern Languages: Prof. Dr E. LOBSIEN
Department of East European and Non-European Languages and Cultures: Prof. Dr M. ERDAL
Department of Mathematics: Prof. Dr H. F. DE GROOTE
Department of Physics: Prof. Dr K. BETHGE
Department of Chemistry: Prof. Dr E. EGERT
Department of Biochemistry, Pharmacy and Food Chemistry: Prof. Dr C. R. NOE
Department of Biology: Prof. Dr R. WITTIG
Department of Geosciences: Prof. Dr C.-D. SCHÖNWIESE
Department of Geography: Prof. Dr V. ALBRECHT
Department of Human Medicine: Prof. Dr G. VON JAGOW
Department of Information Science: Prof. Dr O. DROBNIK
Department of Sport: Prof. Dr W. BANZER

PROFESSORS

Department of Law:
ALBRECHT, P., Criminology and Penal Law
BOTHE, M., Public Law
DENNINGER, E., Common Law
DILCHER, G., History of German Law, Canon and Civil Law
EBSEN, I., Public Law
FABRICIUS, D., Penal Law, Criminal Politics
FRANKENBERG, G., Public Law
GILLES, P., Legal Procedure, Civil and Comparative Law
HASSEMER, W., Theory of Law
KARGL, W., Theory of Law, Criminal Law
KOHL, H., Civil Law
KÜBLER, F., Economic and Civil Law
LOEWENHEIM, U., Civil, Commercial and Industrial Law
LÜDERSSEN, K., Criminal Law
MERTENS, H.-J., Civil Law, Commercial Law, Comparative Law and International Private Law
NAUCKE, W., Criminal Law
NEUMANN, U., Criminal Law
OGOREK, R., Roman Law, Civil Law
OSTERLOH, L., Public Law, Tax Law
PAUL, W., Legal Theory and Methodology
REHBINDER, E., Business, Environmental and Comparative Law
RUECKERT, J., History of Law
SCHMIDT, W., Public Law
SIMITIS, S., Labour and Civil Law and the Informatics of Law
STEINBERG, R., Public Law and Administration
STOLLEIS, M., Public Law, History of Law
TROJE, H. E., Roman Law, History of German Law
WANDT, M., German and International Civil Law
WEISS, M., Business and Civil Law
WEYERS, H.-L., Civil Law
WIETHÖLTER, R., Civil, Industrial and Economic Law
WOLF, M., Civil Law
ZULEEG, M., Civil, European and Common Law

Department of Economics:
ABB, F., Economic Theory and Policy
ANDEL, N., Public Finance
BARTELS, H. G., Business Administration, Operational Research
BAUER, T., Comparative Economics and Economic Systems
BIEHL, D., Political Economy
CZAYKA, L., Political Science
DUNN, M., International Development Economics
EISEN, R., Political Economy
EWERT, R.
FEESS, E., Economic Theory and Policy
FLEISCHMANN, G., Political Economics
GEBAUER, W., Political Economy
GEBHARDT, G., Economic Management
GEHRIG, G., Economics
GÜMBEL, R., Economic Management, especially Commerce
HAUSER, R., Social Legislation
HUJER, R., Statistics and Econometrics
ILLING, G., Economic Theory
ISERMANN, H., Economic Management
KAAS, K. P., Industrial Economics

KOENIG, W., Economic Management
KOSSBIEL, H. G., Business Management
KRAHNEN, J. P., Financial Management
KREIKEBAUM, H., Business Economics
LAUX, H., Theory of Organization
MATHES, H. D., Production Planning
MELLWIG, W., Industrial Economics
MITSCHKE, J., Political and Industrial Accountancy
MOXTER, A., Industrial Economy
MÜLLER, G., Programming
NEUBAUER, W., Statistics
OBERWEIS, A., Information Management
OHSE, D., Management Economics and Quantitative Methodology
ORDELHEIDE, D., Management Economics, Accounting and Auditing
RENDTEL, U., Statistics
RITTER, U., Political Science
ROMMELFANGER, H., Mathematics for Economists
SCHEFOLD, B., Political Economy
SCHMIDT, R., Economic Management
SPAHN, P. B., Public Finance

Department of Sociology:

ALLERBECK, K., Sociology
APITZSCH, U., Sociology
BOSSE, H., Theory of Socialization
BREDE, K., Social Psychology
BROCK, L., International Politics
CLEMENZ, M., Sociology of Education
ESSER, J., Study of Politics, Sociology
GERHARD-TEUSCHER, U., Sociology
GLATZER, W., Social Structures
GRESS, F., Political Science
HIRSCH, J., Political Science
HOFMANN, G., Methods of Social Research, Statistics
HONDRICH, K. O., Sociology
KELLNER, H.-F., Sociology
KÖNIG, H.-D., Sociology
KRELL, G., Political Science
MANS, D., Methods of Social Research
MAUS, I., History of Political Ideas
NEUMANN-BRAUN, K., Sociology
OEVERMANN, U., Sociology, Social Psychology
PROKOP, D., Mass Communications Research
PUHLE, H.-J., Political Science
RITSERT, J., Sociology
RODENSTEIN, M., Sociology
ROTTLEUTHNER-LUTTER, M., Methodology
SCHUMM, W., Sociology
SIEGEL, T., Sociology of Industrialized Societies
STEINERT, H., Sociology

Department of Education:

BECK-SCHLEGEL, G., Primary Education
BECKER, E., Pedagogics
BRAKEMEIER-LISOP, I., Economic Pedagogics
DEPPE-WOLFINGER, H., Special Education
DIAS, P., Pedagogics in the Third World
FAUST-SIEHL, G., Primary Education
HESS, H., Social Pedagogics
HOFMANN-MÜLLER, C. H., Pedagogics
IBEN, G., Health and Special Education
JACOBS, K., Special and Remedial Education
KADE, J., Theory and Practice of Adult Education
KALLERT, H., Social Pedagogics
MEIER, R., Primary Teacher Training
NYSSEN, F., Teacher Training
OVERBECK, A., Special Education
RADTKE, F.-O., Pedagogics
RANG, B., History and Pedagogics of Women's Studies
SCHLÖMERKEMPER, J., Pedagogics
SCHOLZ, G., Primary Education
ZANDER, H., Social Pedagogics
ZENZ, G., Social Pedagogics

Department of Psychology:

BAUER, W., General Psychology
DEGENHARDT, A., Diagnostic Psychology
DEUSINGER, I., Psychology
GIESEN, H., Educational Psychology
KNOPF, M., Psychology
LANGFELDT, H.-P., Pedagogical Psychology
LAUTERBACH, W., Clinical Psychology
MOOSBRUGGER, H., Psychological Methodology, Statistics
PREISER, S., Educational Psychology
ROHDE-DACHSER, CH., Psychoanalysis
SARRIS, V., Psychology
SCHWANENBERG, E., Social Psychology
WERTHMANN, H.-V., Psychoanalysis

Department of Protestant Theology:

FAILING, W.-E., Protestant Theology
HEIMBROCK, H. G., Protestant Theology
SPIEGEL, Y., Protestant Theology
WEBER, E., Protestant Theology

Department of Catholic Theology:

DENINGER-POLZER, G., Catholic Theology
HAINZ, J., Exegesis of the New Testament
HOFFMANN, J., Moral Theology, Social Ethics
KESSLER, H., Systematic Theology
RASKE, M., Practical Theology
SCHREIJÄCK, T., Catholic Theology
SCHRÖDTER, H., Philosophy of Religion
WIEDENHOFER, S., Systematic Theology
WOLF, H., Catholic Theology

Department of Philosophy and History:

BREUNIG, P., Archaeology
BRINGMANN, K., Ancient History
CLAUSS, M., Ancient History
DETEL, W., Philosophy
ESSLER, W. K., Philosophy, Logic and Educational Theory
FEEST, CHR., Ethnology
FRIED, J., Ancient History
GALL, L., Medieval and Modern History
GREFE, E.-H., History Teaching
HAMMERSTEIN, N., Medieval and Modern History
HENNING, J., Prehistory
KAMBARTEL, F., Philosophy
KAENEL, H. M. VON, Greek and Roman History
KOHL, K.-H., Ethnology
KULENKAMPFF, A., Philosophy
LENTZ, C., Ethnology
LÜNING, J., Prehistory
LUTZ-BACHMANN, M., Medieval Philosophy
MÜLLER, K., Folklore
MUHLACK, U., General History
PIERENKEMPER, T., Economic and Social History
RECKER, M.-L., Recent History
RÖTTGES, H., Philosophy
SCHEER, B., Philosophy
SCHMIDT, A., Philosophy and Sociology
WENDE, P., Medieval and Modern History

Department of Classical Philology and Arts:

BÜCHSEL, M., History of European Art
FISCHER, J., Art Teaching
GERMER, S., Art History
HERDING, K., Art History
MEYER, J.-W., Archaeology
NEU, T., Art Teaching
NEUMEISTER, C., Classical Philology
NOVA, A., Art History
NOWAK, A., Music
RAECK, W., Classical Archaeology
SCHÜTZ, O., Art Teaching
SEECK, G. A., Classical Philosophy
STAUDTE, A., Art Teaching

Department of Modern Languages:

BOHN, V., Modern German
BRACKERT, H., German Philology
BÜRGER, C., German Language and Literature
DEGENHARDT, I., German Language and Literature
EWERS, H., German Philology and Literature (Children's Literature)
FIEDLER, L. M., Modern German
FREY, W., German
GARSCHA, K., Romance Philology
GOEBEL, G., Romance Philology
GOMPF, G., Teaching of English Language
GREWENDORF, G., German Linguistics
HANSEN, O., American Studies
HERRMANN, W., Teaching of German Language and Literature
HOFMANN, K., English
JEZIORKOWSKI, K., Modern German
KELLER, U., English
KIMPEL, D., Modern German
KLEIN, H. G., Romance Philology
KÖNNEKER, B., German
KÜHNEL, W., English and American
LAUERBACH, G., English Studies
LEHMANN, H.-T., Theatre Studies
LEPPER, G., German
LEUNINGER, H., German Linguistics
LINDNER, B., German Language and Literature Teaching
LOBSIEN, E., English
MERKELBACH, V., German Language and Literature Teaching
METZNER, E., German
MITTENZWEI, I., Modern German
NEUBER, W., Modern German Literature
OPFERMANN, S., American Studies
QUETZ, J., English Teaching
RAITZ, W., History of German Literature
REICHERT, K., English/American Language
RIEMENSCHNEIDER, D., English
RÜTTEN, R., French Language and Literature
SCHARLAU, B., Romance Philology
SCHEIBLE, H., German Language and Literature
SCHLOSSER, H. D., German
SCHLÜPMANN, H., Film Science
SCHNEIDER, G., Romance Philology
SEITZ, D., German
SOLMECKE, G., Teaching of English Language
STEGMANN, T., Romance Languages and Literature
WEBER, G., Germanic and Scandinavian Philology
WEISE, W.-D., English Teaching
WIETHÖLTER, W., Modern German Literature
WOLFZETTEL, F., Romance Philology

Department of East European and Non-European Languages and Cultures:

CHANG, T.-T., Sinology
DAIBER, H., Oriental Studies
ERDAL, M., Turkish Studies
FREIDHOF, G., Slavic Languages
GIPPERT, J., Comparative Science of Languages
JUNGRAITHMAYR, H., African Languages
LANGER, G., Slavic Languages
MAY, E., Japanology
NOTHOFER, B., South-East Asian Studies
SCHLÜTER, M., Judaic Studies
VOSSEN, R., African Languages
WODARZ, H., Phonetics

Department of Mathematics:

BAUER, F.-W., Mathematics
BAUMEISTER, J. B., Optimum and Convex Functions
BEHR, H., Pure Mathematics
BIERI, R., Pure Mathematics
BLIEDTNER, J., Pure Mathematics
BORGES, R., Mathematics Teaching
BROSOWSKI, B., Information Science
CONSTANTINESCU, F., Mathematics
DINGES, H., Probability Theory and Statistics
FÜHRER, L., Mathematics Teaching
GROOTE, H. DE, Applied Mathematics
GÜTING, R. K., Mathematics Teaching
HOMAGK, F., Mathematics Teaching
KERSTING, G., Stochastics
KULZE, R., Mathematics
LUCKHARDT, H., Fundamental Mathematics

METZLER, W., Mathematics
MÜLLER, K. H., Applied Mathematics
REICHERT-HAHN, M., Mathematics
SCHNORR, C., Applied Mathematics
SCHWARZ, W., Mathematics
SIEVEKING, M., Applied Mathematics
WAKOLBINGER, A., Probability Theory
WEIDMANN, J., Mathematics
WOLFART, J., Mathematics

Department of Physics:

ASSMUS, W., Experimental Physics
BECKER, R., Applied Physics
BETHGE, K., Nuclear Physics
DREIZLER, R., Theoretical Physics
ELZE, T., Nuclear Physics
GERHARDT, U., Physics
GÖRNITZ, T., Physics Teaching
GREINER, W., Theoretical Physics
GROENEVELD, K.-O., Nuclear Physics
HAUG, H., Theoretical Physics
HIRST, L. L., Theoretical Physics
JELITTO, R., Theoretical Physics
KEGEL, W., Theoretical Physics
KING, D. A., History of Natural Sciences
KLEIN, H., Applied Physics
LACROIX, A., Applied Physics
LÜTHI, B., Experimental Physics
LYNEN, U., Nuclear Physics
MARUHN, J., Theoretical Physics
MESTER, R., Applied Physics
MOHLER, E., Experimental Physics
RAUCH, F., Physics
SALTZER, W., History of Science
SCHÄFER, A., Physics
SCHMIDT-BÖCKING, H., Experimental Atomic Physics
SCHUBERT, D., Physics for Doctors
SIEMSEN, F., Physics Teaching
STOCK, R., Experimental Nuclear Physics
STÖCKER, H., Theoretical Physics
STRÖBELE, H., Experimental Nuclear Physics
WOLF, D., Physics

Department of Chemistry:

BADER, H.-J., Chemistry Teaching
BRAUER, H.-D., Chemistry
BRUTSCHY, B., Physical Chemistry
EGERT, E., Organic Chemistry
ENGELS, F., Organic Chemistry
GRIESINGER, C., Organic Chemistry
HENSEN, K., Physical Chemistry
KARAS, M., Analytical Chemistry
KOHLMAIER, G., Theoretical and Physical Chemistry
KOLBESEN, B., Inorganic Chemistry
REHM, D., Physical and Organic Chemistry
SCHÜTH, F., Organic Chemistry
TRÖMEL, M., Inorganic Chemistry

Department of Biochemistry, Pharmacy and Food Chemistry:

BAMBERG, E., Biophysical Chemistry
DINGERMANN, T., Pharmaceutical Biology
DRESSMAN, J., Pharmaceutical Technology
FASOLD, H., Biochemistry
KREUTER, J., Pharmaceutical Technology
LAMBRECHT, G., Pharmacology
LUDWIG, B., Biochemistry
MOSANDL, A., Food Chemistry
NOE, CHR., Pharmaceutical Chemistry
RÜTERJANS, H., Physical Biochemistry
STEINHILBER, D., Pharmaceutical Chemistry

Department of Biology:

BEIER, W., Biology Teaching
BEREITER-HAHN, J., Cell Research
BRÄNDLE, K., Zoology
BRENDEL, M., Biology for Doctors
DÖHLER, G., Botany
ENTIAN, K.-D., Microbiology
FEIERABEND, F., Botany
FLEISSNER, G., Zoology
GIES, T., Biology Teaching
GNATZY, W., Zoology
HILGENBERG, W., Botany
HOLSTEIN, T., Zoology
KAHL, G., Botany
KOENIGER, N., Zoology
KROEGER, A., Microbiology
LANGE-BERTALOT, H., Botany
MASCHWITZ, U., Zoology
NOVER, L., Botany
OSIEWACZ, H., Botany
PONS, F., Microbiology
PRINZINGER, R., Zoology
PROTSCH VON ZIETEN, R., Anthropology
RHEINLAENDER, J., Zoology
SANDMANN, G., Botany
SCHAUB, H., Botany
STARZINSKI-POWITZ, A., Human Genetics
STEIGER, H., Microbiology
STREIT, B., Zoology
TROMMER, G., Biology Teaching
WILTSCHKO, W., Zoology
WINTER, C., Zoology
WITTIG, R., Botany
ZIMMERMANN, H., Zoology
ZIZKA, G., Botany

Department of Geosciences:

ANDRES, W., Physical Geography
BARTL, H., Crystallography and Mineralogy
BAUR, W., Crystallogaphy and Mineralogy
BREY, G., Mineralogy
BRINKMANN, W. L. F., Hydrology
HÄNEL, G., Meteorology
HERBERT, F., Theoretical Meteorology
HUSSNER, H., Geology and Palaeontology
JUNGE, A., Geophysics
KLEINSCHMIDT, G., Geology
KOWALCZYK, G., Geology
MÜLLER, G., Mathematical Geophysics
NAGEL, G., Geography
PLASS, W., Soil Science
PÜTTMANN, W., Environmental Analysis
SCHMELING, H., Solid Earth Physics
SCHMIDT, U., Atmospheric Physics
SCHÖNWIESE, C., Meteorological Environmental Research
SCHROEDER, R., Palaeontology
STEIN, N., Physical Geography
URBAN, H., Petrology and Stratigraphy
VOGEL, K.-P., Palaeontology
WINTER, J., Geology and Palaeontology

Department of Geography:

ALBRECHT, V., Geography Teaching
HASSE, J., Geography Teaching
LAMPING, H., Economic Geography
SCHAMP, E., Economic Geography
SCHICKHOFF, I., Human Geography
SULGER, E., Geography Teaching
THARUN, E., Cultural Geography
WOLF, K., Cultural Geography

Department of Medicine:

BITTER, K., Maxillo-facial Surgery
BÖHLES, H. J., Paediatrics
BÖTTCHER, H. D., Radiation Therapy
BRAAK, E., Anatomy
BRAAK, H., Anatomy
BRADE, V., Hygiene, Microbiology
BRANDT, U., Biochemistry
BRATZKE, H., Forensic Medicine
BRETTEL, H.-F., Forensic Medicine
BUSSE, R., Physiology
BROCK, R., Psychosocial Industrial Medicine
CASPARY, W., Internal Medicine and Gastroenterology
CHANDRA, P., Therapeutic Biochemistry
DEPPE, H.-U., Medical Sociology
DOERR, H. W., Medical Virology
DUDZIAK, R., Anaesthesiology
DUFEK, J., Forensic Medicine
EHRLY, A., Internal Medicine
ELSNER, G., Industrial Medicine
ENCKE, A., General and Abdominal Surgery
FÖRSTER, H., Applied Biochemistry
FRIAUF, E., Physiology
FRÖMTER, H., Applied Physiology
GALL, V., Child Audiology
GIERE, W., Documentation and Data Processing
GROSS, W., Physiological Chemistry
HANSMANN, M.-L., Pathology
HEIDEMANN, D., Dental and Maxillo-facial Medicine
HELLER, K., Surgery
HOELZER, D., Haematology
HÖR, G., Nuclear Medicine
HOFMANN, D., Child Health
HOFSTETTER, R., Child Cardiology
HOHMANN, W., Materials in Dentistry
HÜBNER, K., Pathology
ILBERG, C. VON, Oto-rhino-laryngology
JACOBI, G., Child Health
JAGOW, G. VON, Psychological Chemistry
JONAS, D., Urology
JORK, K., General Medicine
KAUERT, G., Forensic Toxicology
KAUFMANN, M., Gynaecology
KAUFMANN, R., Dermatology and Venerology
KERSCHBAUMER, F., Orthopaedics and Orthopaedic Surgery
KLINKE, R., Physiology
KOCH, F., Ophthalmology
KOLLATH, J., Radiation Medicine
KORF, H.-W., Anatomy
KORNHUBER, B., Child Health
KUHL, H., Experimental Endocrinology
LANGENBECK, U., Human Genetics
LAUER, H.-CHR., Dentistry
LEUSCHNER, U., Gastroenterology
LOEWENICH, V. VON, Child Health
LORENZ, R., General Neurosurgery
MAURER, K., Psychiatry
MELCHNER VON DYDIOWA, H., Clinical Molecular Biology
MILBRADT, R., Dermatology
MOELLER, M., Medical Psychology
MORITZ, A., Thoracic, Heart and Vessel Surgery
NENTWIG, G.-H., Dental and Maxillo-facial Medicine
NÜRNBERGER, F., Anatomy, Neurobiology
OFFENLOCH, K., Neurophysiology
OHRLOFF, CH., Ophthalmology and Experimental Ophthalmology
OVERBECK, G., Psychosomatics
PANNIKE, A., Surgery
PFEILSCHIFTER, J. M., Pharmacology and Toxicology
PFLUG, B., Psychiatry
PIESCHL, D., Psychiatry
POUSTKA, F., Child and Adolescent Psychiatry
RÄTZKE, P., Dental and Maxillo-facial Medicine
RIETBROCK, N., Pharmacology
SCHLOTE, W., Neuropathology
SCHMITT, E., Orthopaedics
SCHOPF, P., Maxillo-facial Surgery
SCHUBERT, R., Hygiene
SIEDENTOPF, H.-G., Gynaecology
SIEFERT, H., History of Medicine
SIGUSCH, V., Sexology
STÄRK, N., Ophthalmology
STILLE, W., Internal Medicine
STÜRZEBECHER, E., Medical Acoustics
STUTTE, H.-J., Pathology and Pathological Anatomy
TAUBERT, H.-D., Endocrinology
USADEL, K.-H., Internal Medicine
WINCKLER, J., Anatomy
ZANELLA, F., Neuroradiology
ZEIHER, A. M., Internal Medicine
ZICHNER, L., Orthopaedics

Department of Computer Science:

DROBNIK, O., Architecture and Business Systems
GEIHS, K., Practical Informatics
KEMP, R., Applied Informatics
SCHMIDT-SCHAUSS, M., Artificial Intelligence
SCHNITGER, G., Theoretical Informatics
WALDSCHMIDT, K., Applied Informatics
WOTSCHKE, D., Computer Languages
ZICARI, R., Databases

Department of Sport and Work Studies:
BALLREICH, R., Teacher Training
BANZER, W., Prevention and Rehabilitation
BÖS, K., Leisure Sport
HAASE, H., Psychology and Sociology of Sport
HORTLEDER, G., Sociology of Sport
KAHSNITZ, D., Polytechnic/Technical Instruction Course
ROPOHL, G., Polytechnic/Technical Instruction Course
SCHMID, A., Polytechnic/Technical Instruction Course
SCHMIDTBLEICHER, D., Scientific Training

EUROPA-UNIVERSITÄT VIADRINA (European University Viadrina)

Grosse Scharrnstr. 59, 15230 Frankfurt (Oder)
Telephone: (335) 5534-0
Fax: (335) 5534-305
Founded 1991
Language of instruction: German
President: Prof. Dr HANS N. WEILER
Registrar: BEATRIX ECKERT
Librarian: Dr ULRIKE EICH
Number of teachers: 173
Number of students: 2,800

DEANS

School of Law: Prof. Dr SIGURD LITTBARSKI
School of Economics: Prof. Dr EBERHARD STICKEL
School of Cultural Studies: Prof. Dr Dr ULRICH KNEFELKAMP

ATTACHED RESEARCH INSTITUTES

Heinrich von Kleist Institute for Literature and Politics.

Frankfurt Institute for Transformation Studies.

Interdisciplinary Ethics Centre.

ATTACHED COLLEGE

Collegium Polonicum: (situated in Slubice in Poland, and managed jointly by the Europa-Universität Viadrina and the Adam Mickiewicz University in Poznań).

TECHNISCHE UNIVERSITÄT BERGAKADEMIE FREIBERG

09596 Frieberg/Sachsen, Akademiestr. 6
Telephone: (3731) 39-0
Fax: (3731) 22195
E-mail: rektorat@zuv.tu-freiberg.de
Founded 1765
State control
Academic year: October to August
Rector: Prof. Dr ERNST SCHLEGEL
Pro-Rectors: Prof. Dr HORST BREZINSKI, Prof. Dr HEINRICH OETTEL
Chancellor: MARTIN KLEIN
Librarian: KARIN MITTENZWEI
Number of teachers: 430
Number of students: 2,300
Publication: *Freiberger Forschungshefte*†.

DEANS

Faculty of Mathematics and Computer Science: Prof. Dr WEGERT
Faculty of Chemistry and Physics: Prof. Dr ROEWER
Faculty of Geosciences, Geotechnology and Mining: Prof. Dr HERZIG
Faculty of Mechanical, Process and Energy Engineering: Prof. Dr OBERMEIER
Faculty of Materials Science and Technology: Prof. Dr TOMANDL
Faculty of Economics and Business Administration: Prof. Dr FRANCK

ALBERT-LUDWIGS-UNIVERSITÄT FREIBURG

79085 Freiburg i. Br., Werthmannplatz
Telephone: (761) 2031
Telex: 772740
Fax: (761) 203-4369
Founded 1457
Rector: Prof. Dr WOLFGANG JÄGER
Pro-Rectors: Prof. Dr SIEGFRIED HAUSER, Prof. Dr EDUARD FARTHMANN, Prof. Dr GREGOR HERTEN
Director of Administration: Dr JÜRGEN HESS
Librarian: BÄRBEL SCHUBEL
Number of teachers: 2,400
Number of students: 21,100

DEANS

Faculty of Theology: Prof. Dr EBERHARD SCHOCKENHOFF
Faculty of Law: Prof. Dr DIETRICH MURSWIEK
Faculty of Economics: Prof. Dr FRANZ SCHOBER
Faculty of Medicine: Prof. Dr ERWIN SCHÖPF
Faculty of Philosophy I: Prof. Dr KONRAD KÜSTER
Faculty of Philosophy II: Prof. Dr EVA TICHY
Faculty of Philosophy III: Prof. Dr ACHIM AURNHAMMER
Faculty of Philosophy IV: Prof. Dr DIETER MERTENS
Faculty of Mathematics: Prof. Dr DIETMAR KRÖNER
Faculty of Physics: Prof. Dr HERMANN GRABERT
Faculty of Chemistry and Pharmacology: Prof. Dr HEINO FINKELMANN
Faculty of Biology: Prof. Dr ALBRECHT SIPPEL
Faculty of Geosciences: Prof. Dr RÜDIGER MÄCKEL
Faculty of Forestry: Prof. Dr HEINRICH SPIEKER
Faculty of Applied Sciences: (vacant)

PROFESSORS

Faculty of Theology:
BÜSSE, H., Liturgy
CASPER, B., Christian Philosophy
FRANK, S., Old Church History
FÜRST, C. G., Canon Law
FUSS, M., Religious History
GLATZEL, N., Christian Society
GRESHAKE, W., Dogmatics and Ecumenical Theology
MÜLLER, J., Pastoral Theology
OBERLINNER, L., New Testament Literature
POMPEY, H., Caritas Science and Social Work
RUPPERT, L., Old Testament Literature
SCHOCKENHOFF, E., Moral Theology
SMOLINSKY, H., New Church History
VERWEYEN, H. J., Fundamental Theology
WALTER, P., Dogmatics

Faculty of Law:
BLOY, R., Penal Law
BÖCKENFÖRDE, E., Public Law
BULLINGER, M., State and Administrative Law
BUND, E., Greek Law
CRAUSHAAR, G. V., Civil Law
ESER, A., Penal Law
FRANK, R., Civil Law
FRISCH, W., Penal Law
HERREN, R., Criminal Law and Procedure
HOLLERBACH, A., History of Law, Church Law, Philosophy of Law
KÖBL, U., Social Insurance Law
KROESCHELL, K., German History of Law
LEIPOLD, D., Civil, Labour and Procedural Law
LIEBS, D., History of Modern Law
LÖWISCH, M., Civil, Labour, Social Insurance and Commercial Law
MURSWIEK, D., State Law
SCHLECHTRIEM, P., Civil, Trade Law, International Private Law
SCHOCH, F., Public Law
SCHWARZE, J., European and International Law
STOLL, H., Civil Law
STÜRNER, R., Civil Law
TIEDEMANN, K., Criminal Law and Procedure
WAHL, R., Administrative Law
WOLF, J. G., Roman Law
WÜRTENBERGER, T., State Law

Faculty of Economics:
BLÜMLE, G., Mathematical Economics
FRANCKE, H. H., Financial Economics
HILKE, W., Commercial Economics
KNIEPS, G., Political Economy
KÜLP, B., Social Politics
LANDMANN, O., Economic Theory
LÜDEKE, D., Statistics
MÜLLER, G., Computer Science
OBERHAUSER, A., Political Economy
REHKUGLER, H., Commercial Economics
SCHOBER, F., Computer Science
WITT, U., Regional Policy and Transport

Faculty of Medicine:
ANTONI, H., Physiology
BASSENGE, E., Physiology
BAUERLE, P., Biochemistry
BERGER, M., Psychiatry
BRANDIS, M., Paediatrics
BRECKWOLDT, M., Gynaecology
BREDT, W., Hygiene and Bacteriology
CHRIST, B., Anatomy
DASCHNER, F., Environmental Medicine
DECKER, K., Biochemistry
DEIMLING, O. VON, Chemical Pathology
FARTHMANN, E. H., Surgery
FROMMHOLD, H., Radiology
FROTSCHER, M., Anatomy
GEIGER, K., Anaesthesiology
GOEPPERT, S., Medical Psychology
GREGER, R., Physiology
HALLER, O., Virology
HASSE, J., Surgery
HELLWIG, E., Dentistry
JONAS, J., Dentistry
JUST, H., Internal Medicine
KEUL, J., Sport and Leisure Medicine
KLEIST, S. VON, Immunobiology
KREUTZ, W., Biophysics and Radiobiology
KUNER, E., Surgery
LANGER, M., Radiology
LASZIG, R., Otorhinolaryngology
LÜCKING, C., Neurology
MATTHYS, H., Pneumology
MERTELSMANN, R., Internal Medicine
MOSER, E., Radiology
OSTERTAG, C., Neurosurgery
PETER, H. H., Rheumatology
PFANNER, N., Biochemistry
PFLEIDERER, A., Gynaecology
POLLAK, S., Forensic Medicine
PRIEBE, H. J., Anaesthesiology
REICHELT, A., Surgery
SCHÄFER, H. E., Pathology
SCHILLI, W., Dentistry
SCHLOSSER, V., Surgery
SCHOLLMEYER, P., Internal Medicine
SCHÖPF, E., Dermatology
SCHUMACHER, M., Medical Statistics
SEEGER, W., Neurosurgery
SOMMERKAMP, H., Surgery
STARKE, K., Pharmacology and Toxicology
STRUB, J., Dentistry
STRUNK, P., Psychiatry
TRÖHLER, U., History of Medicine
TROSCHKE, J. VON, Medical Sociology
VOLK, B., Neuropathology
WIELAND, H., Clinical Chemistry
WIRSCHING, M., Psychiatry
WOLF, U., Human Genetics and Anthropology

Faculty of Philosophy I:
- BÜHRLE, M., Sports
- BUGGLE, F., Psychology
- CROTT, H., Psychology
- EIGLER, G., Philosophy and Pedagogics
- FAHRENBERG, J., Psychology
- JACOBI, K., Philosophy
- MISCHO, J., Psychology
- PRAUSS, G., Philosophy
- SCHLINK, W., History of Art
- SPADA, H., Psychology
- STROCKA, V., Classical Archaeology
- STRUBE, G., Cognitive Science
- TIPPELT, R., Pedagogics

Faculty of Philosophy II:
- ENDE, W., Islamic Studies
- GAUGER, H.-M., Romance Philology
- HAUSMANN, R., Romance Philology
- HESS, R., Romance Philology
- HINÜBER, O., Indology
- KULLMANN, W., Classical Philology
- LEFÈVRE, E., Classical Philology
- MESTAU, A., Slavonics
- RAIBLE, W., Romance Philology
- RIX, H., Indogermanic Languages
- SCHMIDT, G., Medieval Latin Philology
- STAUB, H., Romance Philology
- WEIHER, E., Slavonics

Faculty of Philosophy III:
- ARNHAMMER, A., German Philology
- FLUDERNIK, M., English Philology
- GOETSCH, P., English Philology
- KORTMANN, B., English Philology
- MAIR, C., English Philology
- MICHEL, W., German Philology
- PILCH, H., English Philology
- PÜTZ, M., English Philology
- SASSE, G., German Philology
- SCHMIDT, J., German Philology
- SCHUPP, V., German Philology
- STEGER, H., German Philology
- WERNER, O., German Philology

Faculty of Philosophy IV:
- DUX, G., Sociology
- ESSBACH, W., Sociology
- GEHRKE, H.-J., Ancient History
- JÄGER, W., Political Science
- KÜHNHARDT, L., Political Science
- MARTIN, J., Ancient History
- MERTENS, D., Medieval History
- MORDEK, H., Medieval History
- OBERNDÖRFER, D., Political Science
- OTT, H., Economic and Social History
- REINHARD, W., Modern History
- SCHRAMM, G., Modern and East European History
- SCHULIN, Modern History
- SCHWENGEL, H., Sociology
- SEIDLER, E., History of Medicine
- STEUER, H., Prehistory

Faculty of Mathematics:
- BANGERT, V., Mathematics
- DZIUK, G., Applied Mathematics
- EBBINGHAUS, H.-D., Mathematical Logic
- EBERLEIN, E., Stochastics
- FLUM, J., Mathematical Logic
- KEGEL, O., Mathematics
- KRÖNER, D., Applied Mathematics
- LAUSEN, G., Computer Science
- LERCHE, H. R., Stochastics
- MÜLLER, S., Mathematics
- OTTMANN, T., Computer Science
- RÜSCHENDORF, L., Stochastics
- SCHINZEL, B., Computer Science
- SCHNEIDER, R., Mathematics
- SOERGEE, W.
- SPILKER, J., Mathematics
- WALLISSER, R., Mathematics
- WOLKE, D., Mathematics
- ZIEGLER, M., Mathematical Logic

Faculty of Physics:
- BAMBERGER, A., Experimental Physics
- BLUMEN, A., Theoretical Physics
- BRENN, R., Experimental Physics
- BRIGGS, J. ST., Theoretical Physics
- GRABERT, H., Theoretical Physics
- HABERLAND, H., Experimental Physics
- HELM, H., Experimental Physics
- HERTEL, I. V., Experimental Physics
- HONERKAMP, J., Theoretical Physics
- MEHLHORN, W., Experimental Physics
- POHLMEYER, K., Theoretical Physics
- RÖMER, H., Theoretical Physics
- RÖPKE, H., Experimental Physics
- RÖSSLE, E., Experimental Physics
- RUNGE, K., Experimental Physics
- SCHLIER, C., Experimental Physics
- SCHMITT, H., Experimental Physics
- STROBL, G., Experimental Physics
- VAN DER BIJ, J., Theoretical Physics

Faculty of Chemistry and Pharmacy:
- BAUER, K., Pharmaceutical Technology
- BURCHARD, W., Molecular Chemistry
- EBERBACH, W., Organic Chemistry
- FINKELMANN, H., Molecular Chemistry
- FRAHM, A. W., Pharmaceutical Technology
- FRIEDRICH, K., Organic Chemistry
- KABUSS, S., Organic Chemistry
- KIEDROWSKI, G., Organic Chemistry
- KREUTZ, W., Biophysics
- LEHMANN, J., Biochemistry
- MÜLHAUPT, R., Molecular Chemistry
- MÜLLER, H., Inorganic Chemistry
- OTTO, H. H., Pharmaceutical Technology
- PRINZBACH, H., Organic Chemistry
- RIMPLER, H., Pharmaceutical Biology
- RÜCHARDT, C., Organic Chemistry
- SCHILL, G., Organic Chemistry
- SCHULZ, G. E., Biochemistry
- THIELE, G., Inorganic Chemistry
- VAHRENKAMP, H., Inorganic Chemistry

Faculty of Biology:
- BECK, C., Biology
- BOGENRIEDER, A., Geobotany
- FEIX, G., Biology
- FISCHBACH, K. F., Biology
- HAEHNEL, W., Biochemistry
- HAUSMANN, R., Biology
- HERTEL, R., Biology
- HILSE, K., Biology
- KÖSSEL, H., Biology
- MOHR, H., Botany
- PESCHKE, K., Zoology
- RAK, B., Biology
- SCHÄFER, E., Botany
- SCHINK, B., Limnology
- SCHWOERBEL, J., Limnology
- SIPPEL, A. E., Biophysics
- SITTE, P., Cell Biology
- SPATZ, H. C., Biophysics
- VOGT, K., Zoology
- WILMANNS, O., Geobotany

Faculty of Geosciences:
- BENZ, K. W., Crystallography
- BOHLE, H.-G., Geography
- BUCHER, K., Mineralogy
- GLAWION, R., Geography
- GOSSMANN, H., Geography
- KELLER, J., Mineralogy
- KÖHLER, U., Ethnology
- LEIBUNDGUT, CH., Hydrology
- MÄCKEL, R., Geography
- MAYER, H., Meteorology
- OTTO, J., Mineralogy
- PFLUG, R., Geology
- SEITZ, S., Ethnology
- STADELBAUER, J., Geography
- ZÖTTL, H., Geology

Faculty of Forestry:
- BECKER, M., Forest Policy
- BOPPRÉ, M., Forest Zoology
- FINK, S., Forest Botany
- GRAMMEL, R., Forest Management
- HUSS, J., Forest Production
- OESTEN, G., Forest Management
- PELZ, D. R., Biometrics
- RENNENBERG, H., Forest Botany
- SPIECKER, H., Forest Production
- VOLZ, K., Forest Policy
- ZÖTTL, H. W., Soil Science

Faculty of Applied Sciences:
- MENZ, W., Microsystems Technology
- OTTMANN, TH., Informatics

JUSTUS-LIEBIG-UNIVERSITÄT GIESSEN

35390 Giessen, Ludwigstr. 23

Telephone: (641) 990

Fax: (641) 9912289

Founded 1607

State control

Academic year: October to September (two terms)

President: Prof. Dr STEFAN HORMUTH

Vice-President: Prof. Dr BERND HOFFMANN

Chief Administrative Officer: Dr MICHAEL BREITBACH

Librarian: Dr HEINER SCHNELLING

Number of teachers: 399

Number of students: 20,169

Publication: *Spiegel der Forschung* (2 a year).

DEANS

- Faculty of Law: Prof. Dr WOLFRAM HOEFLING
- Faculty of Economics: Prof. Dr HELGA LUCKENBACH
- Faculty of Social Sciences: Prof. Dr HELMUT DUBIEL
- Faculty of Education: Prof. Dr WILFRIED LIPPITZ
- Faculty of Art, Music and Sport: Prof. Dr GUENTER KOEPPE
- Faculty of Psychology: Prof. Dr DIETER VAITL
- Faculty of Protestant Divinity and Catholic Divinity and its Teaching: Prof. Dr GERHARD DAUTZENBERG
- Faculty of History: Prof. Dr PETER MORAW
- Faculty of German: Prof. Dr DIETMAR ROESLER
- Faculty of English: Prof. Dr MICHAEL K. LEGUTKE
- Faculty of Mediterranean and East European Studies: Prof. Dr HELGA FINTER
- Faculty of Mathematics: Prof. Dr HANS-OTTO WALTHER
- Faculty of Physics: Prof. Dr CLAUS-DIETER KOHL
- Faculty of Chemistry: Prof. Dr WOLFGANG LAQUA
- Faculty of Biology: Prof. Dr CHRISTIAN KUNZE
- Faculty of Geology and Geography: Prof. Dr ECKHARD HINZE
- Faculty of Agriculture and Environmental Conservation: Prof. Dr PETER FELIX-HENNINGSEN
- Faculty of Veterinary Medicine: Prof. Dr ERNST-GUENTHER GRUENBAUM
- Faculty of Nutrition and Home Economics: Prof. Dr ELMAR SCHLICH
- Faculty of Medicine: Prof. Dr KLAUS KNORPP

PROFESSORS

Law:
- BRYDE, B.-O., Public Law
- EKKENGA, J., Civil Law, Commercial Law
- HAMMEN, H., Civil Law, Commercial Law
- HEINE, G., Criminal Law, Procedural Law
- HÖFLING, W., Public Law
- KREUZER, A., Criminology, Juvenile Criminal Law
- LANGE, K., Public Law, Administration Teaching
- LIPP, M., History of German Law and Civil Law
- SCHAPP, J., Civil Law and Philosophy of Law
- SÖLLNER, A., Roman Law and Civil Law, Labour and Social Law
- STEIGER, H., Public Law
- WALKER, W. D., Civil Law, Labour Law, Civil Procedural Law

WALTERMANN, R., Civil Law, Labour and Social Law
WEICK, G., Civil and Commercial Law
WIESER, E., Civil and Procedural Law
ZEZSCHWITZ, F. VON, Public and Tax Law

Economics:
ABERLE, G., Political Economy
ALEXANDER, V., Political Economy
BOHNET, A., Political Economy
ESCH, F.-R., Business Administration, Marketing
HAHN, D., Business Administration
HEMMER, H. R., Political Economy and Developing Countries
KRÜGER, W., Business Management
LUCKENBACH, H., Political Economy
MORLOCK, M., Business Management
MÜLLER, H., Political Economy
PAUSENBERGER, E., Industrial Economics
RINNE, H., Statistics
SCHERF, W., Economics and Public Finance
SELCHERT, F. W., Industrial Economics
WEINHARDT, C., Business Management and Computer Science

Social Sciences:
BERGMANN, J. R., Sociology
DÖRR, M., Politics
DUBIEL, H., Sociology
FRITZSCHE, K., Political Science
GIESEN, B., Sociology
GRONEMEYER, R., Sociology
HOLLAND-CUNZ, B., Political Science, Gender Studies
KREBS, D., Empirical Research in Social Sciences
KÜHNEL, S.-M., Empirical Research in Social Sciences
LEGGEWIE, C., Political Science
REIMANN, B., Sociology
SCHMIDT, P., Empirical Research in Social Sciences
SEIDELMANN, R., Political Science, International Relations and Foreign Policy

Education:
DUNCKER, L., Primary- and Secondary-Level Teaching
LIPPITZ, W., Systematic and Comparative Science of Education
MÜCKENHOFF, E., Comparative Education Studies
PRELL, S., Empirical Education Studies
SCHULZ, M., Education
SCHWANDER, M. W., Primary- and Secondary-Level Teaching
SEMBILL, D., Polytechnics and the Economy

Art, Music, Sport:
ANDRASCHKE, P., Music History
CRIEGERN, A. VON, Didactics of Art
JOST, E., Music
KÖPPE, G., Teaching of Sports
KÖTTER, E., Music Education
MEUSEL, H., Sports
MUNZERT, H.-J., Sports Psychology
NEUMANN, H., Sports
NITSCHE, P., Music Education
NOWACKI, P., Sports Medicine
PAPE, W., Music
RICHTER-REICHENBACH, K.-S., Teaching of Art
SPICKERNAGEL, E., Art History
THIELE, H., Practical Art

Psychology:
BORG, I., Methodology
FRESE, M., Work and Education Psychology
GLOWALLA, U., Educational Psychology
HAJOS, A., Psychology
HALDER-SINN, P., Psychological Diagnosis
HAUBENSAK, G., Psychology
KÖNIG, R., Psychology
MOSER, K., Labour, Business and Organization Psychology
NETTER, P., Differential Psychology
SPITZNAGEL, A., Pedagogic Psychology
SPORER, S., Social Psychology
TODT, E., Pedagogic Psychology
VAITL, D., Psychology
WENDELER, J., Pedagogic Psychology

Protestant Divinity and Catholic Divinity and its Teaching:
DAUTZENBERG, G., Bible Studies
DEUSER, H., Systematic Theology
FRITZ, V., Bible Studies, Old Testament and Biblical Archaeology
GRESCHAT, M., Ecclesiastical History
HAUSER, L., Systematic Theology
JENDORFF, B., Religious Education
KRIECHBAUM, F., Systematic Theology
KURZ, W., Religious Education
LEVIN, C., Bible Studies, Old Testament
SÄNGER, D., Bible Studies, New Testament

History:
BAUMGARTNER, M., Art History
BECKER, W., Philosophy
BERDING, H., Modern History
BERGMANN, K., Didactics of History
GESCHE, H., Ancient History
GRESCHAT, M., Ecclesiastical History
HELLER, K., East European History
KAMINSKY, H., Medieval History
LOTTES, G., Medieval and Modern History
MARTINI, W., Classical Archaeology
MEINHARDT, H., Philosophy
MENKE, M., Pre- and Early History
MORAW, P., Medieval History
QUANDT, S., History Teaching
RÖSENER, W., Medieval and Modern History
SCHRÖDER, H. J., Contemporary History
SPICKERNAGEL, E., History of Art
WERNER, N., Art History

German:
EHRISMANN, O., German Language
ERTZDORFF-KUPFFER, X. VON, Germanic Philology
FRITZ, G., German Language
GANSEL, R.-K., Teaching of German Language and Literature
GAST, W., German Language Teaching
INDERTHAL, K., German Literature
KARTHAUS, U., German Language and Literature Teaching
KLUGE, W., Didactics of German Language and Literature
KURZ, G., History of Modern German Literature
LEIBFRIED, E., General Literature
LUBKOLL, CHR., Comparative and Modern German Literature
OESTERLE, G., Modern Literature
RAMGE, H., Linguistics
RÖSLER, D., German as a Foreign Language
RÖTZER, H. G., Didactics of German Language and Literature
SEEL, M., Philosophy
VOLLHARDT, F., Modern German Literature

English:
BERGNER, H., English Language
BORGMEIER, R., Modern English and American Literature
BREDELLA, L., English Language and Literature Teaching
GRABES, H., Modern English and American Literature
HORSTMANN, U., Modern English and American Literature
JUCKER, A., English Language
LEGUTKE, M., English Language Teaching
NÜNNING, A., Modern English and American Literature

Mediterranean and East European Studies:
BERSCHIN, H., Romance Linguistics
FINTER, H., Applied Theatre Studies
FLOECK, W., Spanish Literature
GIESEMANN, G., Slavonic Philology
HARTMANN, A., Islamic Studies
JELITTE, H., Slavonic Philology
KÜPPERS, J., Classical Philology
LANDFESTER, M., Greek Philology
MEISSNER, F.-J., Teaching of French Language and Literature
PRINZ, M., Teaching of Romance Languages and Literatures
RIEGER, D., Romance Literature
STENZEL, H., Romance Literature
WINKELMANN, O., Romance Linguistics

Mathematics:
BARTSCH, T., Analysis
BAUMANN, B., Algebra
BEUTELSPACHER, A., Geometry and Discrete Mathematics
BRAUNSS, G.
EITER, T., Computer Science
FENSKE, C.
FILIPPI, S., Numeric and Instrumental Mathematics
FRANKE, M., Teaching of Mathematics
FRICKER, F.
HÄUSLER, E. K., Stochastics
HOISCHEN, L.
JAENISCH, S.
KRÖGER, H., Computer Science
METSCH, K., Geometry
PROFKE, L., Mathematics Teaching
STUTE, W., Stochastics
TIMMESFELD, F. G., Algebra
WALTHER, H.-O., Mathematical Analysis
WEIGAND, H. G., Teaching of Mathematics

Physics:
BOLTERAUER, H., Theoretical Physics
BUNDE, A., Theoretical Physics, Solid-state Physics
CASSING, W., Theoretical Physics
GRÜN, N., Theoretical Physics
HEIDEN, C., Applied Physics
HERMANN, G., Experimental Physics
KANITSCHEIDER, B., Philosophy of Science
KIEFER, J., Biophysics
KOHL, C. D., Applied Physics
KÜHN, W., Experimental Physics
LOHMANN, W., Biophysics
METAG, V., Experimental Physics
MEYER, B., Experimental Physics
MOSEL, U., Theoretical Physics
MÜLLER, A., Experimental Physics
SALZBORN, E., Nuclear Physics
SCHARTNER, K.-H., Experimental Physics
SCHEID, W., Theoretical Physics
SCHRAMM, H., Physics Teaching
SCHWARZ, G., Physics Teaching
SEIBT, W., Experimental Physics
WOLLNIK, H., Experimental Physics

Chemistry:
AHLBRECHT, H., Organic Chemistry
ASKANI, R., Organic Chemistry
BECK, J., Inorganic Chemistry
GEBELEIN, H., Chemistry Teaching
IPAKTSCHI, J., Organic Chemistry
LAQUA, W., Inorganic Chemistry
MAIER, G., Organic Chemistry
WINNEWISSER, M., Physical Chemistry

Biology:
BEL, A. J. E. VAN, General Botany
CLAUSS, W., Animal Physiology
EICHELBERG, D., Zoology
ESSER, G., Plant Ecology
GÖTTING, K.-J., Zoology
HOBOM, G., Microbiology
HOLL, A., Zoology
JÄGER, H. J., Experimental Plant Ecology
JOST, E., Genetics
KLEE, R., Biology Teaching
KLUG, G., Microbiology
KUNTER, M., Anthropology
KUNZE, C., Botany
PAHLICH, E., Botany
PINGOUD, A., Biochemistry
RENKAWITZ, R., Genetics
RINGE, F., Botany
SCHIPP, R., Zoology
SCHNETTER, R., Botany
SCHULTE, E., Zoology

SCHWARTZ, E., Zoology
TRENCZEK, M., Zoology
VOLAND, E., Philosophy of Life Sciences
WAGNER, G., Botany
WOLTERS, V., Animal Ecology
ZETSCHE, K., Botany

Geology and Geography:
EMMERMANN, R., Mineralogy
FRANKE, W., Geology
GIESE, E., Economic Geography
HAACK, U., Mineralogy
HAFFNER, W., Geography
HANDY, M., Geology
HAVERSATH, J.-B., Teaching of Geography
HINZE, E., Mineralogy
KING, L., Geography
KNOBLICH, K., Geology
MEYER, R., Geography
SCHOLZ, U., Geography
SEIFERT, V., Applied Geography
WERLE, O., Geography Teaching

Agriculture:
BAUER, S., Agricultural Regional and Project Planning
BODENSTEDT, A., Agrarian Sociology
BOLAND, H., Agricultural Extension and Communication
DZAPO, V., Animal Breeding and Genetics of Domestic Animals
ERHARDT, G., Animal Breeding and the Genetics of Domestic Animals
FELIX-HENNINGSEN, P., Soil Science, Land Conservation
FREDE, H.-G., Soil Science
FRIEDT, W., Plant Cultivation
GÄTH, S., Waste Management
HARRACH, T., Applied Soil Science
HERRMANN, R., Agricultural Policy
HERZOG, A., Comparative Genetic Pathology
HOY, S., Animal Husbandry and Biology of Animal Husbandry
HUMMEL, H., Plant Biology and Biotechnology
KÄMPFER, P., Microbiology of Recycling Processes
KOGEL, K.-H., Plant Diseases and Conservation
KÖHLER, W., Biometrics
KUHLMANN, F., Agricultural Management
NEUMANN, K.-H., Plant Nutrition
OPITZ VON BOBERFELD, W., Pastureland
OTTE, A., Landscape Ecology and Planning
OTTOW, J. C. G., General and Agricultural Microbiology
SAUERBORN, J., Plant Production in the Tropics and Subtropics
SCHINKE, E., Agricultural Economics of Socialist Countries
SCHLÖSSER, E., Plant Pathology
SCHMITZ, P. M., Agricultural and Development Policy
SEUFERT, H., Land Management
STEINBACH, J., Ecology of Domestic Animals
VIDAL, S., Applied Ecology
WEIGAND, E., Animal Nutrition
ZILAHI-SZABÓ, M. G., Computation and Data Processing

Veterinary Medicine:
BALJER, G., Hygiene and Infectious Diseases in Animals
BAUMGÄRTNER, W., Veterinary Pathology
BONATH, K., Experimental Surgery
BOSTEDT, H., Obstetrics
BÜLTE, M., Veterinary Nutrition
BÜRGER, H. J., Parasitology
DIENER, M., Veterinary Physiology
DOLL, K., Diseases of Ruminants
EIGENBRODT, E., Physiological Chemistry
FRESE, K., Pathological Anatomy
GRÜNBAUM, E.-G., Internal Medicine (Small Animals)
HOFFMANN, B., Physiology and Pathology
KALETA, E., Poultry Diseases
KRESSIN, M., Veterinary Anatomy, Histology and Embryology
LEISER, R., Veterinary Anatomy, Histology and Embryology
LITZKE, L.-F., Equine Surgery
LUTZ, F., Pharmacology
PETZINGER, E. D., Pharmacology and Toxicology
SASSE, H., Internal Medicine (Horses)
SCHIMKE, E., Surgery (Anaesthesiology)
SCHONER, W., Biochemistry
SERNETZ, M., Applied Biochemistry
THIEL, H.-J., Virology
WEISS, E., General Pathology, Pathological Anatomy and Histology of Animals
WENDT, M., Pig Diseases
WENGLER, G., Virology and Cellular Biology
ZAHNER, H., Parasitology

Nutrition and Home Economics:
BITSCH, I., Nutrition
BOTTLER, J., Home Economics
BRÜCKNER, H.-O., Food Science
DANIEL, H., Human Nutrition
EVERS, A., Comparative Health and Social Policy
LEONHÄUSER, J.-U., Nutrition and Consumption
MEIER, U., Home Economics
NEUHÄUSER-BERTHOLD, M., Human Nutrition
NEUMANN, K.-H., Plant Nutrition
PALLAUF, J., Animal Nutrition
SCHLICH, E., Budgeting
SCHNIEDER, B., Domestic Ecology
SCHUBERT, S., Plant Nutrition
WEIGAND, E., Animal Nutrition

Medicine:
ALTLAND, K., Human Genetics
ALZEN, G., Paediatric Radiology
BAUER, R., Nuclear Medicine
BAUMANN, C., Physiology
BECK, E., Molecular Biology
BECKMANN, D., Medical Psychology
BEIN, G., Clinical Immunology and Transfusion Medicine
BENEDUM, J., History of Medicine
BEUTEL, M., Psychotherapy
BLÄHSER, S., Anatomy
BÖKER, D.-K., Neurosurgery
CHAKRABORTY, T., Medical Microbiology
DREYER, F., Pharmacology
DUDECK, J., Medical Statistics and Documentation
DUNCKER, H. R., Anatomy
EIKMANN, T., Hygiene
FERGER, P., Dentistry
FLEISCHER, G., Anatomy
FRIEDRICH, R., Molecular Genetics and Virology
FRINGES, B., Pathology
GALLHOFER, B., Psychiatry
GERLICH, W., Medical Virology
GEYER, R., Biochemistry
GIELER, U., Psychosomatics and Psychotherapy
GLANZ, H., Oto-rhino-laryngology
HATTINGBERG, H. M. VON, Child Health
HEHRLEIN, F. W., Surgery
HEMPELMANN, G., Anaesthesiology
HOWALDT, H.-P., Surgery of the Mouth, Jaws and Face
IRNICH, W., Biomedical Electronics
JACOBI, K. W., Ophthalmology
JESSEN, C.-U., Physiology
KATZ, N., Biochemistry
KAUFMANN, H., Ophthalmology
KIESSLING, J., Audiology
KIRSCHNER, H., Dentistry
KLIMEK, J., Dental Health
KNORPP, K., Internal Medicine
KOCKAPAN, C., Oto-rhino-laryngology
KUMMER, W., Anatomy and Cytobiology
KÜNZEL, W., Gynaecology and Obstetrics
LAMPERT, F., Paediatrics
LAUBE, H., Internal Medicine
LIEVEN, H. VON, Radiology
LINDEMANN, H., Child Health
MATTHIAS, R., Internal Medicine
MEYLE, J., Parodontology
MÖLLER, W., Anatomy
MÜLLER, U., Human Genetics
NEUHÄUSER, G., Neuropaediatrics
NEUHOF, H., Clinical Pathophysiology
NÖSKE, H.-D., Urology
OEHMKE, H.-J., Anatomy
PANCHERZ, H. J., Orthopaedics
PIPER, H. M., Physiology
PRALLE, H., Internal Medicine
RASCHER, W., Paediatric Medicine
RAU, W., Radiological Diagnostics
REIMER, CHR., Clinical Psychosomatics
RITTER-HORN, R., Dentistry
SCHACHENMAYR, W., Neuropathology
SCHÄFFER, R., Cytopathology
SCHEER, J. W., Medical Psychology
SCHIEFER, H.-G., Cell Physiology and Medical Microbiology
SCHILL, W. B., Dermatology and Andrology
SCHMIDT, K.-L., Rheumatology, Physical Medicine and Balneology
SCHNETTLER, R., Accident Surgery
SCHRANZ, D., Paediatric Cardiology
SCHULZ, A., Pathology
SCHULZE, H.-U., Biochemistry
SCHWEMMLE, K., Surgery
SEEGER, W., Internal Medicine
SKRANDIES, W., Physiology
STÜRZ, H., Orthopaedics
SUTTORP, N., Internal Medicine and Physiopathology
TESCHEMACHER, H., Pharmacology
TILLMANNS, H., Internal Medicine, and Cardiology
TRAUPE, H., Neuroradiology
UECK, M., Anatomy
VAHRSON, H., Obstetrics and Gynaecology
VOGEL, W., Physiology
WEIDNER, W., Urology
WEILER, G., Forensic Medicine
WETZEL, W. E., Dentistry
WOITOWITZ, H.-J., Industrial Medicine
ZEISBERGER, E., Physiology

GEORG-AUGUST-UNIVERSITÄT GÖTTINGEN

37073 Göttingen
Telephone: (551) 390
Telex: 96703
Fax: (0551) 399612

Founded 1737
Academic year: April to March (two terms)
President: Prof. Dr HANS-LUDWIG SCHREIBER
Vice-Presidents: Prof. Dr LIPPE, Prof. Dr KUHN, Dr WÖHLER
Chancellor: Dr MARINA FROST
Number of teachers: 800
Number of students: 27,000
Publications: *Vorlesungsverzeichnis* (2 a year), *Jahresforschungsbericht* (every 2 years), *Georgia-Augusta*, *Nachrichten* (2 a year), *Hochschulzeitschrift Spektrum* (quarterly).

DEANS

Faculty of Theology: Prof. Dr EBERHARD BUSCH
Faculty of Law: Prof. Dr JÖRG-MARTIN JEHLE
Faculty of Medicine: Prof. Dr ROLF-HERMANN RINGERT
Faculty of History and Philology: Prof. Dr MARTIN STAEHLIN
Faculty of Philosophy: Prof. Dr GUSTAV-ADOLF LEHMANN
Faculty of Mathematics: Prof. Dr SAMUEL-JAMES PATTERSON
Faculty of Physics: Prof. Dr KLAUS BEUERMANN
Faculty of Chemistry: Prof. Dr ARMIN DE MEIJERE

Faculty of Earth Sciences: Prof. Dr KLAUS WEBER
Faculty of Biology: Prof. Dr DAVID R. ROBINSON
Faculty of Forestry: Prof. Dr FRIEDRICH BEESE
Faculty of Agriculture: Prof. Dr BERTRAM BRENIG
Faculty of Economics: Prof. Dr WILFRIED AHIBOM
Faculty of Social Sciences: Prof. Dr ERNST KUPER
Faculty of Education: Prof. Dr DIETRICH HOFFMANN

ERNST-MORITZ-ARNDT-UNIVERSITÄT GREIFSWALD

17487 Greifswald, Domstr. 11
Telephone: (3834) 86-0
Fax: (3834) 861105
E-mail: rektor@rz.uni-greifswald.de

Founded 1456
Academic year: October to September
Chancellor: KARL HEINZ JACOB
Rector: Prof. Dr JÜRGEN KOHLER
Pro-Rector: Prof. Dr rer. KLAUS FESSER
Librarian: Dr HANS-ARMIN KNÖPPEL

Number of teachers: 235
Number of students: 5,800

Publications: *Wissenschaftliche Beiträge* (irregular), *Greifswalder Universitätsreden* (irregular), *Universitätszeitung* (monthly).

DEANS

Faculty of Protestant Theology: Prof. Dr theol. habil. CHRISTOF HARDMEIER
Faculty of Law and Economics: Prof. Dr RAINER LEISTEN
Faculty of Medicine: Prof. Dr med. habil. EBERHARD WERNER
Faculty of Philosophy: Prof. Dr paed. habil. JÜRGEN ERICH SCHMIDT
Faculty of Mathematics and Natural Sciences: Prof. Dr rer. nat. habil. DETLEF HABERLAND

MARTIN LUTHER-UNIVERSITÄT HALLE-WITTENBERG

06099 Halle (Saale), Universitätsplatz 10
Telephone: 8320
Telex: 04353

Founded 1502 (Wittenberg), 1694 (Halle), 1817 (Halle-Wittenberg)
Rector: GUNNAR BERG

UNIVERSITÄT HAMBURG

20146 Hamburg, Edmund-Siemers-Allee 1
Telephone: 4123-1
Fax: (40) 4123-2449
E-mail: presse@rra.uni-hamburg.de

President: Dr JÜRGEN LUTHJE
Vice-President: Prof. Dr Dr L. C. WILFRIED HARTMANN
Chief Administrative Officer: HARTMUT HALFMEIER
State and University Librarian: Prof. Dr HORST GRONEMEYER

Number of teachers: 3,172
Number of students: 40,996

HEADS OF DEPARTMENTS

Protestant Theology: Prof. Dr GERHARD SELLIN
Law: Prof. Dr HANS-JOACHIM KOCH
Economic Sciences: Prof. Dr MANFRED HOLLER
Medicine: Prof. Dr HEINZ-PETER LEICHTWEISS
Philosophy and Social Sciences: Prof. Dr MARIE-ELISABETH HILGER
Education: Prof. Dr KARL-HEINZ SCHERLER
Philology: Prof. Dr KLAUS RÜHL
History: Prof. Dr FRANK GOLCZEWSKI
History of Culture: Prof. Dr ORTWIN SMAILUS
Oriental Studies: Prof. Dr SIEGBERT UHLIG
Mathematics: Prof. Dr REINER HASS
Physics: Prof. Dr BERNHARD KRAMER
Chemistry: Prof. Dr WITTKO FRANCKE
Biology: Prof. Dr REINHARD LIEBEREI
Geographical Sciences: Prof. Dr GÜNTER MIELICH
Psychology: Prof. Dr ERICH H. WITTE
Computer Science: Prof. Dr HORST OBERQUELLE
Physical Education: Prof. Dr K. MICHAEL BRAUMANN

PROFESSORS

Department of Protestant Theology:
AHRENS, T., Missions
CORNEHL, P., Practical Theology
DIERKEN, J., Systematic Theology
FISCHER, H., Systematic Theology
GRÜNBERG, W., Practical Theology
KOCH, T., Systematic Theology
KROEGER, M., Church History and Dogma
LINDNER, W. V., Practical Theology
MAGER, I., Church History and Dogma
RAU, E., New Testament
SCHRAMM, T., New Testament
SCHUMANN, O., Missions
SELLIN, G., New Testament
SPIECKERMANN, H., Old Testament
TIMM, S., Old Testament
WILLI-PLEIN, I., Old Testament

Department of Law:
BEHRENS, P., Civil, Commercial and International Private Law
BERGH, R. VAN DEN, Civil Law
BORK, R., Civil, Commercial, Economic and International Private Law
BRUHA, T., Public, European and International Law
BÜHNEMANN, B., Informatic Law
BULL, H., Constitutional and Administrative Law
FEZER, G., Criminal Law
GANTZEL, K.-J., International Affairs
GIEHRING, H., Criminal Law
HAAG, F., Sociology
HANSEN, U., Criminal Law
HILF, M., Public, European and International Law
HOFFMAN-RIEM, W., Public, Administrative, Revenue and Tax, and Economic Law
JOOST, D., Civil and Labour Law
KARPEN, U., Public Law
KELLER, R., Criminal Law
KOCH, H.-J., Public Law, Philosophy of Law
KÖHLER, M., Criminal Law, Philosophy of Law
KÖTZ, H., Civil, Comparative and International Law
KRIECHBAUM, M., Roman Law
LADEUR, K.-H., Public Law
LAGONI, R., Public, Maritime, International and Constitutional Law
LANDWEHR, G., History of German and Nordic Law, Civil and Commercial Law
LUCHTERHANDT, O., Public and Eastern Law
MAGNUS, U., Civil Law
MARTENS, K. P., Civil, Labour and Commercial Law
MORITZ, K., Civil and Labour Law, Sociology of Law
MÜNCH, I. VON, Constitutional Law, Administrative Law, International Law
OTT, C., Sociology of Law, Civil, Commercial and Company, and Economic Law
PASCHKE, M., Civil, Commercial and Economic Law
PFARR, H., Civil and Labour Law
RAMSAUER, U., Public Law
RANDZIO, R., Civil Law
RITTSTIEG, H., Public Law
SCHÄFER, H.-B., National Economy
SCHEERER, S., Criminology
SCHILLING, G., Criminal Law
SCHWABE, J., Public Law
SELMER, P., Public Law, Law of Finance, Law of Taxes
SESSAR, K., Criminology and Juvenile Criminal Law
SONNEN, B.-R., Criminal Law
STOBER, R., Economic Law
STRUCK, G., Civil Law
VILLMOW, B., Criminology
WALZ, R., Commercial, Economic, Civil and Tax Law
WERBER, M., Civil and Insurance Law
WINTER, G., Civil and Insurance Law, Comparative Law
ZIEGLER, K.-H., Roman Law, Civil Law

Department of Economic Sciences:
ADAMS, M., Economic Law
ALTROGGE, G., Business Administration
ARNOLD, B., National Economy
BÄNSCH, A., Business Administration
CZERANOWSKY, G., Business Administration
ENGELHARDT, G., National Economy
FELDMANN, H., Business Data Processing
FISCHER, L., General Business Administration
FREIDANK, C.-C., Business Administration, Auditing Taxation
FUNKE, M., National Economy
HANSEN, K., Business Administration
HANSMANN, K.-W., Business Administration
HASEBORG, F. L., Trade and Commerce
HASENKAMP, G., National Economy
HAUTAU, H., National Economy
HOFMANN, H., National Economy
HOLLER, M., National Economy
HUMMELTENBERG, W., Business Administration
KARTEN, W., Business Administration
KRAUSE-JUNG, G., International Finance
KÜPPER, W., Business Administration
LAYER, M., Business Administration
LORENZEN, G., National Economy
MAENNIG, W., National Economy
OEHSEN, J. H. VON, Finance
PFÄHLER, W., National Economy
PRESSMAR, D., Business Administration
RÄDLER, A., Business Administration, Taxation
REITSPERGER, W. D., Business Administration
RIETER, H., National Economy
RINGLE, G., Business Administration
SCHÄFER, H.-B., National Economy
SCHEER, C., Finance
SCHERF, H., National Economy, Statistics
SCHLITTGEN, R., National Economy, Statistics
SCHMIDT, H., Business Administration
SEELBACH, H., Business Administration
STAHLECKER, H.-P., National Economy, Statistics
STOBER, R., Economic Law
STREITFERDT, L., Business Administration
TIMMERMANN, V., National Economy
WEGSCHEIDER, K., National Economy, Statistics

Department of Medicine:
AGARWAL, D., Human Genetics
ALBERTI, W., Radiotherapy
BAHNSEN, J., Gynaecology
BAISCH, H., Biophysics
BAUMANN, K., Physiology
BECK, H., Anaesthesiology
BEIL, F. U., Internal Medicine
BEISIEGEL, U., Biochemistry
BENTELE, K., Paediatrics
BERGER, J., Mathematic and Computer Applications of Medicine
BERGER, M., Child Psychology
BERNER, W., Psychiatry
BRAENDLE, L.-W., Gynaecology and Obstetrics
BRAUMANN, K.-M., Internal-Physiological Sports Medicine
BROMM, B., Physiology

BSCHORER, R., Maxillary Surgery, Plastic Surgery
BÜCHELER, E., Roentgenology
BULLINGER, M., Medical Psychology
BURDELSKI, M., Paediatrics
BUSSCHE, H. VAN DEN, Didactics
CLAUSEN, M., Nuclear Medicine
DALLEK, M., Surgery, Accident Surgery
DAPPER, F., Surgery
DAVIDOFF, M., Anatomy
DELLING, G., General Pathology and Pathological Anatomy
DENEKE, F.-W., Psychosomatic Medicine
DONATH, K., Pathology, Pathological Anatomy
DÖRING, V., Surgery
EIERMANN, T., Transfusion Medicine
FLEISCHER, B., Immunology, Virology
FREITAG, H.-J., Neuroradiology
FRILLING, A., Surgery
GABBE, E., Physiological Chemistry
GAL, A., Medical Genetics
GÖTZE, P., Psychiatry
GRÄSSLIN, D., Experimental Endocrinology
GRETEN, H., Internal Medicine
GROSSNER, D., Surgery
GRUBEL, G., Neurosurgery
GÜLZOW, H. J., Dental Medicine
HAASE, W., Ophthalmology
HALATA, Z., Anatomy
HAMM, C., Internal Medicine
HAND, I., Psychiatry
HELLNER, K.-A., Applied Neurophysiology
HELLWEGE, H., Paediatrics
HELMCHEN, U., Pathology
HENKE, R.-P., Pathology
HERRMANN, H.-D., Neurosurgery
HÖHNE, K., Medical Data Processing
HÖLTJE, W.-J., Maxillary Surgery
HOLSTEIN, A.-F., Anatomy
HORN, H.-J., Forensic and Criminal Psychology
HORSTMANN, R., Internal Medicine
HOSSFELD, D., Internal Medicine
HÜBENER, K.-H., Radiology
HULAND, H., Urology
HUNEKE, A., Gynaecology and Obstetrics
IZBICKI, J., Surgery
JÄNICKE, F. K.-H., Gynaecology and Obstetrics
JANKE-SCHAUB, G., Paediatrics
JENTSCH, T., Cell Biology
JÜDE, H. D., Dental Medicine
JUNG, H., Biophysics and Radiobiology
KAHLKE, W., Internal Medicine
KAULFERS, P.-M., Medical Microbiology
KAUPEN-HAAS, H., Medical Sociology
KNABBE, C., Clinical Chemistry
KOCH, U., Oto-rhino-laryngology
KOCH-GROMUS, U., Medical Psychology
KOHLSCHÜTTER, A., Paediatrics
KOLLEK, R., Biotechnology
KORTH, M., Pharmacology
KRÄUSSLICH, H.-G., Cell Biology, Virology
KRAUSZ, M., Psychiatry
KREYMANN, K. G., Internal Medicine
KRUPPA, J., Physiological Chemistry
KRUSE, H.-P., Internal Medicine
KÜHNL, P., Transfusions, Immuno-Haematology
KUNZE, K., Neurology
LAMBRECHT, W., Surgery
LAUFS, R., Medical Microbiology and Immunology
LEICHTWEISS, H.-P., Physiology
LINDNER, C., Gynaecology and Obstetrics
LÖNING, T., General Pathology, Pathological Anatomy
MACK, D., Medical Microbiology, Infection Epidemiology and Hospital Hygiene
MANGOLD, U., Anatomy
MARQUARDT, H., General Toxicology
MAYR, G. W., Physiological Chemistry
MEINERTE, T., Cardiology
MILTNER, E., Law of Medicine
MOLL, I., Dermatology, Venereology
MÜHLHAUSER, I., Health
MÜLLER, D., Neurosurgery
MÜLLER-WIEFEL, D. E., Internal Medicine
NABER, D., Psychiatry
NEUMAIER, M., Clinical Chemistry
NICOLAS, V., Radiology
NIENHABER C., Internal Medicine
PFEIFFER, E., Hygiene
PFEIFFER, G., Neurology
PFORTE, A., Internal Medicine
PILLUNAT, L. C., Ophthalmology
PLATZER, U., Dentistry
PONGS, O., Neurology
PÜSCHEL, U., Forensic Medicine
RASSOW, B., Medical Optics
RICHARD, G., Ophthalmology
RICHTER, D., Physiological Chemistry
RICHTER, E., Paediatrics
RICHTER, R., Medical Psychology, Psychosomatics
RIEDESSER, P., Paediatric Psychology
ROTH, K., Dental Medicine
ROTHER, U., Radiological Diagnostics on Dental Medicine
RUEGER, J. M., Accident Surgery
RUMBERGER, E., Physiology
RUTHER, W., Orthopaedics
SCHACHNER, M., Neurobiology
SCHÄFER, H., General Pathology and Pathological Anatomy
SCHALLER, C., Neurobiology
SCHIFFNER, U., Dental Medicine
SCHLOSSER, G.-A., Surgery
SCHMALE, H., Biochemistry
SCHMELZLE, R., Dental Medicine
SCHMIDT, G., Sexology
SCHMOLDT, A., Forensic Medicine
SCHOLZ, H., Pharmacology and Toxicology
SCHOLZ, J., Anaesthesiology
SCHRÖDER, H. J., Physiology
SCHULTE AM ESCH, J., Anaesthesiology
SCHULTE-MARKWORT, M., Child and Youth Psychiatry
SCHULZE, C., Anatomy
SCHULZE, W., Anatomy
SCHUMACHER, U., Anatomy
SCHWARZ, J., Physiology
SEITZ, H.-J., Physiological Chemistry
SOEHENDRA, N., Surgery
STAHL, R., Internal Medicine
STARK, F.-M., Psychiatry
STAVROU, D., Neuropathology
STRÄTLING, W., Physiological Chemistry
SUPPRIAN, U., Psychiatry
SZADKOWSKI, D., Occupational Medicine
TROJAN, A., Social Medicine
ULLRICH, K. H. O., Paediatrics
VOGEL, C.-W., Biochemistry and Molecular Biology
VONDERLAGE, M., Physiology
WAGENER, C., Clinical Chemistry
WEIL, J., Paediatric Cardiology
WEISSER, U., History of Medicine
WESTENDORF, J., Toxicology, Pharmacology
WIEDEMANN, K. B., Biological Psychiatry
WIELAND, T., Pharmacology
WILL, R. P., Paediatrics
WILLIG, R.-H., Paediatrics
WINDLER, E., Internal Medicine
ZANDER, A., Bone Marrow Transplantation
ZEUMER, H., Neuroradiology
ZORNIG, C., Surgery
ZYWIETE, F., Biophysics, Radiobiology

Department of Philosophy and Social Sciences:

AHRENS, G., Social Sciences
BARTUSCHAT, W., Philosophy
BERMBACH, U., Political Science
DEICHSEL, A., Sociology
DIEDERICH, W., Philosophy
EICHNER, K., Sociology
FREDE, D., Philosophy
GANTZEL, K.-J., Political Science
GOERTZ, H.-J., Social and Economic History
GREVEN, M., Political Science
HEINEMANN, K., Sociology
HILGER, M.-E., Social and Economic History
KAUPEN-HAAS, H., Medical Sociology
KLEINSTEUBER, H. J., Political Science
KORTE, H., Sociology
KÜNNE, W., Philosophy
LANDFRIED, C., Political Science
LÜDE, R. VON, Sociology
MILLER, M., Sociology
NEVERLA, I., Journalism, Communications
PIEPER, M., Sociology
RASCHKE, J., Political Science
RASCHKE, P., Political Science
RECKI, B., Philosophy
RENN, H., Sociology
RUNDE, P., Sociology
SOMMERKORN, I., Didactics, Sociology of Education
STEINVORTH, U., Philosophy
TETZLAFF, R., Political Science
TRAUTMANN, G., Political Science
TROITZSCH, U., Social Sciences

Department of Education:

AUFENANGER, S.
BASTIAN, J.
BECK, I.
BOLLMANN, H.
BORRIES, B. VON
BRAND, W.
BRUHN, J.
BRUSCH, W.
BÜRGER, W.
BUTH, M.
CLAUSSEN, B.
COMBE, A.
DECKE-CORNILL, H.
DEGENHART, S.
DEHN, M.
DUSSMANN, G.
EHNI, H. W.
FAULSTICH, P.
FAULSTICH-WIELAND, H.
FIEDLER, U.
FILIPP, K.
GEGHARD, U.
GOGOLIN, I.
GRAMMES, T.
GRENZ, D.
GUDJONS, H.
GÜNTHER, K.-R.
HARTER-MEYER, R.
HARTMANN, W.
HEMMER, K.
JUNG, H. W.
KAISER, H.-J.
KALLENBACH, K.
KLEIN, P.
KOCH, F.
KOKEMOHR, R.
KRAUSE, H.-J.
KRAUTHAUSEN, G.
KRETSCHMER, J.
KÜNNE, W.
LAUFF, W.
LECKE, B.
LEGLER, W.
LOHMANN, I.
MARTENS, E.
MEYER, H.
MEYER, M.
MIELKE, R.
NEUMANN, U.
NEVERS, P.
NOLTE, M.
OPASCHOWSKI, H.
PAWLIK, W.
PAZZINI, K.-J.
PETERSEN, J.
PEUKERT, H.
RAUER, W.
REINHARDT, K.-H.
RICHTER, H.
SCARBATH, H.
SCHAACK, E.
SCHÄFER, H.-P.

SCHENK, B.
SCHERLER, K.
SCHIESS, G.
SCHLEICHER, K.
SCHREIER, H.
SCHUCK, K. D.
SEYD, W.
SIENKNECHT, H.
SPRETH, G.
STAEHR, G. VON
STEFFENSKY, F.
STRUCK, P.
STÜTZ, G.
TENFELDE, W.
TRAMM, T.
TYMISTER, H. J.
WAGNER, A.
WALLRABENSTEIN, W.
WARZECHA, B.
WEICHERT, W.
WEISSE, W.
WILLENBERG, H.
WITTNEBEN, K.
WOCKEN, H.
WUDTKE, H.
ZIMPEL, A.

Department of Philology:
AUER, P., German Linguistics
BERG, T., English Linguistics
BLESSIN, S., German Literature, German as a Foreign Language
BÖRNER, W., Linguistics
BRAUNMÜLLER, K., Germanic Philology
BRINKER, K., German Linguistics
BUNGARTEN, T., German Linguistics
CORTHALS, J., Comparative Language Studies
DAMMANN, G., German Literature
EDMONDSON, W., Language Instruction Research
FISCHER, L., German Literature
FISCHER, R., German Sign Language
FREYTAG, H., German Philology
FREYTAG, W., German Literature
FRIEDL, B., American Studies
GUTJAHR, O., Modern German Literature
GUTKNECHT, C., English Language
HABEL, C., Language Processing
HAHN, W. VON, Natural Language Systems
HARTENSTEIN, K., Russian
HELIMEKI, E., Finno-Ugrian Philology
HENKEL, N., German Philology
HENNIG, J., German Linguistics
HICKETHIER, K., German Literature
HILL, P., Slavonic Philology
HILLMANN, K., German Philology
HODEL, B., Slavonic Philology
HOTTENROTH, P.-M., French and Italian Linguistics
HOUSE, J., Language Instruction Research
HÜHN, P., English Philology
IBANEZ, R., Hispanic Linguistics
KÖSTER, U., German Literature
LATOUR, B., German as a Foreign Language
LEHMANN, V., Language Instruction Research
LLEO, C., Hispanic Linguistics
MARTENS, G., German Literature
MEIER, J., German Linguistics
MEISEL, J. M., Romance Philology
MEYER, W., Romance Philology
MEYER-ALTHOFF, M.
MEYER-MINNEMANN, K., Romance Philology
MÖHN, D., German Philology, esp. Low German
MÜLLER, H.-H., German Literature
PANTHER, K.-U., English Linguistics
PÉTURSSON, M., General Applied Phonetics
PRESCH, G., German Linguistics
PRILLWITZ, S., German Linguistics
RADDEN, G., English Philology and Linguistics
REDICKER, C. H., English Philology
REHBEIN, J., German Linguistics, German as a Foreign Language
REICHARDT, D., Romance Philology
REINITZER, H., German Literature
RODENBURG, H.-P., American Studies
ROSS, D., Applied Communications
RÜHL, K., Romance Philology
SAGER, S., German Linguistics
SCHLUMBOHM, D., Romance Philology
SCHMID, W., Slavonic Literature
SCHMIDT, J., English Philology
SCHMIDT-KNÄBEL, S., German Linguistics
SCHÖBERL, J., German Literature
SCHÖNERT, J., German Literature
SCHÖPP, J. K., American Studies
SCHULLER, M., German Literature
SCHULTZE, B., English Philology
SEGEBERG, H., German Literature
SETTEKORN, W., French
TERNES, E., Phonetics
TRAPP, F., Modern German Literature
VOIGT, B., Spanish
WERGIN, U., Modern German Literature
WINTER, H.-G., German Literature
WITTSCHIER, H. W., Romance Philology

Department of History:
ALPERS, K., Classical Philology
ANGERMANN, M., Medieval and Modern History
BOROWSKY, Modern History
DEININGER, J., Ancient History
DINGEL, J., Classical Philology
EIDENEIER, H., Byzantine and Modern Greek Philology
FINZSCH, N., Modern and North American History
GOETZ, H.-W., Medieval and Modern History
GOLCZEWSKI, F., Eastern European History
HALFMANN, H., Ancient History
HARDING, L., Modern History (Africa)
HARLFINGER, D., Classical Philology
HERGEMÖLLER, B.-U., Medieval History
HERZIG, A., Modern History
MEJCHER, H., Modern History
MOLTHAGEN, J., Ancient History
PIETSCHMANN, H., Modern History
SARNOWSKY, V., Medieval History
SCHMIDT, V., Classical Philology
SYWOTTEK, A., Modern History
VOGEL, B., Modern History
WENDT, B. J., Medieval and Modern History

Department of Cultural Studies:
DÖMLING, W., Music
FEHR, B., Classical Archaeology
GREEVE, B., Music
HENGAUTNER, T., Folklore
HIPP, H., History of Art
JENSEN, J., Folklore
KEMP, W., Art History
KOKOT, W., Ethnology
LEHMANN, A., German Archaeology and Folklore
MARX, H. J., Music
MISCHUNG, B., Ethnology
NIEMEYER, H. G., Archaeology
PETERSEN, P., Musicology
REUDENBACH, B., Art History
RÖSING, H., Systematic Music
ROLLE, R., Prehistory of Europe
SCHNEIDER, A., Systematic Music
SMAILUS, O., Ancient American Language and Culture
WAGNER, M., Art History
WARNKE, M., History of Art
ZIEGERT, H., Pre-history

Department of Oriental Studies:
ALTENMÜLLER, H., Egyptology
CARLE, R., Austronesian Languages and Cultures
EBERSTEIN, B., Sinology
EMMERICK, R., Iranian Studies
FRIEDRICH, M., Sinology
GENENZ, K., Japanese
GERHARDT, L., African Languages and Cultures
GRONEBERG, B., Ancient Oriental Languages and Cultures
JACKSON, D., Tibetology
KAPPERT, P., Turkish Studies
KURTH, D., Egyptology
NOTH, A., Islamic Studies
POHL, M., Japanese Politics
REH, M., African Languages and Cultures
ROTTER, G., Islamic Studies
SASSE, W., Chinese
SCHMITHAUSEN, L., Indology
SCHNEIDER, R., Japanese
STUMPFELDT, H., Sinology
TEEWIEL, B., Thai Language and Culture
UHLIG, S., African Languages and Cultures
VU, D.-T., Vietnamese Studies
WEZLER, A., Indology

Department of Mathematics:
ANDREAE, T.
BANDELT, H.-J.
BERNDT, R.
BREDENDIEK, E.
BRÜCKNER, H.
DADUNA, H.
ECKHARDT, V.
GEIGER, C.
GLASHOFF, K.
HASS, R.
HOFMANN, W. D.
HÜBNER, G.
HÜNEMÖRDER, C.
KERBY, W.
KRÄMER, H.
KREMER, E.
KREUZER, A.
MICHALICEK, J.
MÜLLER, H.
NEUHAUS, G.
OBERLE, H. J.
OPFER, G.
ORTLIEB, C.
PFEIFFER, D.
REICH, K.
RIEMENSCHNEIDER, O.
SCHRÖDER, E.
SEIER, W.
SLODOWY, P.
SONAR, T.
STRADE, H.
TAUBERT, K.
WERNER, B.
WEYER, J.
WOLFSCHMIDT, G.

Department of Physics:
BARTELS, J., Theoretical Physics
BLOBEL, V., Experimental Physics
BÜSSER, F.-W., Experimental Physics
FAY, D., Theoretical Physics
FREDENHAGEN, K., Theoretical Physics
GERAMB, H. V. VON, Theoretical Physics
GERDAU, E., Experimental Physics
HANSEN, W., Experimental Physics
HAZLEHURST, J., Astronomy
HEINZELMANN, G., Experimental Physics
HEITMANN, D., Applied Physics
HEMMERICH, A., Experimental Physics
HEYSZENAU, H., Theoretical Physics
HUBER, G., Experimental Physics
JOHNSON, R., Experimental Physics
KLANNER, R., Experimental Physics
KÖTZLER, J., Applied Physics
KRAMER, B., Theoretical Physics
KRAMER, G., Theoretical Physics
KUNZ, C., Experimental Physics
LINDNER, A., Theoretical Physics
MACK, G., Theoretical Physics
MERKT, U., Experimental Physics
NAROSKA, B., Experimental Physics
NEUHAUSER, W., Experimental Physics
REFSDAL, S., Astronomy
REIMERS, D., Astronomy
SCHARNBERG, K., Theoretical Physics
SCHMIDT-PARZEFALL, W., Experimental Physics
SCHMÜSER, P., Experimental Physics

SCOBEL, W., Experimental Physics
SONNTAG, B., Experimental Physics
SPITZER, H., Fundamental Physics
STROHBUSCH, U., Experimental Physics
TOSCHEK, P., Experimental Physics
VEGT, CH. DE, Astronomy
VOGT, D., Experimental Physics
WAGNER, A., Elementary Particle Physics
WENDKER, H., Astronomy
WICK, K., Experimental Physics
WIESENDANGER, R., Experimental Physics
WIIK, B., Experimental Physics
ZIMMERER, G., Experimental Physics

Department of Chemistry:

ALSEN, E., Nutrition
BEIER, U., Home Economics
BENNDORF, C., Physical Chemistry
BREDEHORST, R., Biochemistry
DANNECKER, W., Inorganic and Analytical Chemistry
DUCHSTEIN, H.-J., Pharmaceutical Chemistry
FISCHER, R. D., Inorganic Chemistry
FRANCKE, W., Organic Chemistry
GEFFKEN, D., Pharmaceutical Chemistry
HECK, J., Inorganic Chemistry
JENTSCH, J., Organic Chemistry
KAMINSKY, W., Inorganic Chemistry
KLAR, G., Inorganic Chemistry
KNÖCHEL, A., Inorganic Chemistry
KÖNIG, W., Organic Chemistry
KÖSTER, H., Organic Chemistry and Biochemistry
KRAMOLOWSKY, R., Inorganic Chemistry
KRICHELDORF, H., Applied Chemistry
KUBECZKA, K.-H., Pharmaceutical Biology
KULICKE, W., Technical Chemistry
LECHERT, H., Physical Chemistry
LÜHRS, K., Pharmaceutical Chemistry
MARGARETHA, P., Organic Chemistry
MESSINGER, P., Pharmaceutical Chemistry
MEYER, B., Organic Chemistry
MIELCK, J., Pharmaceutical Technology
MORITZ, H.-U., Technical and Macromolecular Chemistry
MÜHLHAUSER, I., Health
NAGORNY, K., Physical Chemistry
REHDER, D., Inorganic Chemistry
RELLER, A., Solid State Chemistry
STAHL-BISKUP, E., Pharmaceutical Biology
STEFFEN, M., Teaching of Chemistry
STEINBACH, F., Physical Chemistry
STEINHART, J., Food Chemistry
THIEME, F., Physical Chemistry
VOGEL, C.-W., Biochemistry and Molecular Biology
VOSS, J., Inorganic Chemistry
WELLER, H., Electrochemistry

Department of Biology:

ABRAHAM, R., Entomology
ADAM, G., Phytopathology
BAUCH, J., Timber Biology
BECKER, W., Zoology
BEUSMANN, V., Biotechnics, Society and Environment
BOCK, E., General Microbiology
BÖTTGER, M., General Botany
BRANDT, A., Zoology
BRETTING, H., Zoology
BUCHHELZ, F.
CHOPRA, V., Anthropology
DÖRFFLING, K., General Botany
DREYLING, G., Applied Botany
ECKSTEIN, D., Timber Biology
FLEISCHER, A., Work Science
FORTNAGEL, P., Botany
FRANCK, D., Zoology
FRÜHWALD, A., Mechanical Processing of Timber
GANZHORN, J., Zoology
GEWECKE, M., Zoology, Animal Physiology
GIERE, O., Zoology
GRIMM, R., Zoology
HAHN, H., Zoology, Ecology
HARTMANN, H., Systematic Botany
HEINZ, E., Botany
HEUVELDOP, J., International Forest Management
KAUSCH, H., Hydrobiology
KIES, L., General Botany
KNUSSMANN, R., Anthropology
KRISTEN, U., General Botany
KUBITZKI, K., Systematic Botany
LIEBEREI, R., Phytopathology
LÖRZ, H., Applied Plant Molecular Biology
MANTAU, U., Economics of Forestry
MERGENHAGEN, D., Cell Biology
MÜHLBACH, H.-P., Molecular Genetics
NELLEN, W., Hydrobiology
PARZEFALL, J., Zoology
PATT, R., Chemical Timber Technology
PETERS, N., Zoology
PRATJE, E., General Botany
REISE, K., Heligoland Biological Institute
RENWRANTZ, L., Zoology
RODEWALD, A., Anthropology and Human Genetics
SCHÄFER, W., Biology
SCHEMMEL, C., Zoology
SCHLIEMANN, H., Zoology
STRÜMPEL, H., Zoology
TEMMING, A., Fisheries Sciences
VOGEL, C.-W., General Botany
WEBER, A., General Botany
WIENAND, U., General Botany
WIESE, K., Neurophysiology
WILKENS, H., Zoology
ZANDER, C.-D., Zoology
ZEISKE, E., Zoology

Department of Earth Sciences:

ALPERS, W., Oceanography
BACKHAUS, J., Oceanography
BANDEL, K., Palaeontology and Historic Geology
BISMAYER, U., Mineralogy, Crystallography
BRÜMMER, B., Meteorology
DUDA, S. J., Geophysics
FIEDLER, K., Geology
FRAEDRICH, K, Meteorology
GAJEWSKI, D., Geophysics
GRASSL, H., Meteorology
GRIMMEL, E., Geography
GUSE, W., Mineralogy
HILLMER, G., Geology and Palaeontology
HOEBER, H., Meteorology
ITTEKKOT, V., Biogeochemistry
JASCHKE, D., Geography
LAFRENZ, J., Geography
LEUPOLT, B., Geography
MAKRIS, J., Geophysics
MEINCKE, J., Regional Oceanography
MIEHLICH, G., Soil Science
NAGEL, F. N., Geography
OSSENBRÜGGE, J., Geography
POHL, D., Mineralogy
RASCHKE, E., Meteorology
REUTHER, C.-D., Geology
ROSSMANITH, E., Mineralogy
SCHATZMANN, M., Meteorology
SCHLEICHER, H., Mineralogy, Petrography
SCHWARZ, R., Geography
SPAETH, CH., Geology and Palaeontology
SPIELMANN, H.-O., Geography
SÜNDERMANN, J., Oceanographpy
TARKIAN, M., Mineralogy
THANNHEISER, D., Geography
TIETZ, G. F., Sedimentary Petrography
VINX, R., Mineralogy
WIECHMANN, H., Soil Science
WONG, H. K., Geology
ZAHEL, W., Oceanography

Department of Psychology:

BAMBERG, E.
BERBALK, H.
BURISCH, M.
BUSE, L.
CROPLEY, A.
DAHME, B.
ECKERT, J.
HEINZE, B.
KREBS, G.
LANGER, I.
ORTH, B.
PAWLIK, K.
PROBST, P.
RHENIUS, D.
SCHMIDTCHEN, S.
SCHULZ VON THUN, F.
SCHWAB, R.
TONNIES, S.
UECKERT, H.
VAGT, G.
WITT, H.
WITTE, E.

Department of Computer Sciences:

BRUNNSTEIN, K., Computer Applications
DRESCHLER-FISCHER, L., Cognitive Systems
FLOYD, C., Software Technics
HABEL, C., Information and Documentation
HAHN, W. VON, Natural Language Systems
HEIDE, K. VON DER, Technical Basics of Computer Science
JANTZEN, M., Computer Theory
KAISER, K., Computer Applications
KUDLEK, M., Computer Theory
LAGEMANN, K., Computer Technology
LAMERSDORF, W., Technical Basics of Computer Science
MENZEL, W.
MERTSCHING, B.
NEUMANN, B., Cognitive Systems
OBERQUELLE, H., Computer Theory
PAGE, B., Computer Applications
ROLF, A., Computer Theory
SCHEFE, P., Computer Applications
STIEHL, H.-S., Cognitive Systems
VALK, R., Computer Theory
WOLFINGER, B., Computer Organization
ZÜLLIGHOVEN, H.

Department of Physical Education:

BRAUMANN, K.-M.
DIETRICH, K.
EICHLER, G.
FUNKE-WIENEKE, J.
KÖLBEL, R.
LANGE-AMELSBERG, J.
SCHRÖDER, W.
STRIPP, K.
TIEDEMANN, C.
TIWALD, H.
WEINBERG, P.

UNIVERSITY INSTITUTES

Office for Continuing Education.

Interdisciplinary Centre for University Didactics.

Computer Centre.

Institute for Theatre, Musical Theatre and Film.

International Tax Institute.

Biotechnology, Society, Environment.

Audio-Visual Centre.

Centre for Oceanography and Climate Research.

Museum of Geology and Palaeontology.

Museum of Zoology.

Museum of Mineralogy.

ASSOCIATED INSTITUTES

Mission Academy.

Institute for Integration Research.

Hans Bredow Institute for Radio and Television.

Institute for Peace Research and Security Policy.

Heinrich Pette Institute for Experimental Virology and Immunology.

Institute for Hormone and Reproduction Research.

UNIVERSITÄT DER BUNDESWEHR HAMBURG
(University of the Federal Armed Forces, Hamburg)

Holstenhofweg 85, 22043 Hamburg
Telephone: (40) 6541-0
Fax: (40) 6541-2869

Founded 1972
State control
Academic year: October to September

Chancellor: ECKHARD REDLICH
President: Prof. Dr GERHARD STRUNK
Vice-President: Prof. Dr HERMANN HARDE
Librarian: Dr MARTIN SKIBBE

Library of 500,000 vols
Number of teachers: 103
Number of students: 1,950

Publications: *Uniforum* (annually), *Uniforschung* (annually).

DEANS

Faculty of Economics and Management: Prof. Dr JÜRGEN HARTMANN
Faculty of Educational Science: Prof. Dr GISELA DAHME
Faculty of Electrical Engineering: Prof. Dr-Ing. HANS CHRISTOPH ZEIDLER
Faculty of Mechanical Engineering: Prof. Dr-Ing. HENDRIK ROTHE

TECHNISCHE UNIVERSITÄT HAMBURG-HARBURG

21071 Hamburg
Telephone: (40) 7718-0
Telex: 403696
Fax: (40) 7718-2040
E-mail: trinks@tu-harburg.de

Founded 1978

President: Prof. Dr HAUKE TRINKS
Vice-President: Prof. Dr MÜLLER
Head of Administration: Dr JUSTUS WOYDT
Librarian: INKEN FELDSIEN-SUDHAUS

Library of *c.* 2,500 vols
Number of teachers: 101
Number of students: 3,800

DEANS

Civil Engineering: Prof. Dr WIDMANN
Electrical Engineering: Prof. Dr SINGER
Mechanical Engineering: Prof. Dr ACKERMANN
Chemical and Process Engineering: Prof. Dr MÄRKL

MEDIZINISCHE HOCHSCHULE HANNOVER

30625 Hannover, Carl-Neuberg-Str. 1
Telephone: (511) 532-1
Fax: (511) 532-5550

Founded 1965

Rector: Prof. Dr KARL-MARTIN KOCH
Chancellor: Dr jur. WOLFGANG FRANKE-STEHMANN
Librarian: Dr FELSCH-KLOTZ

Library of 280,000 vols
Number of teachers: 614
Number of students: 3,197

UNIVERSITÄT HANNOVER

30167 Hannover, Welfengarten 1
Telephone: (511) 762-0
Fax: (511) 762-3456
E-mail: praesidialamt@uni-hannover.de

Founded 1831

President: Prof. LUDWIG SCHÄTZL
Vice-Presidents: Prof. R. POTT, Prof. L. GLAGE
Chancellor: J. GEHLSEN
Library Director: Dr-Ing. G. SCHLITT

Number of teachers: 1,272
Number of students: 31,880

DEANS

Department of Mathematics and Computer Science: Prof. LIPECK
Department of Physics: Prof. PFNÜR
Department of Chemistry: Prof. BINNEWIES
Department of Earth Sciences and Geography: Prof. FISCHER
Department of Biology: Prof. KOLB
Department of Architecture: Prof. ECKERLE
Department of Civil Engineering: Prof. ROTHERT
Department of Mechanical Engineering: Prof. REDEKER
Department of Electrical Engineering and Information Technology: Prof. HAASE
Department of Horticulture: Prof. STÜTZEL
Department of Landscape Development and Planning: Prof. LÖSKEN
Department of Literature and Linguistics: Prof. BEZZEL
Department of Education: Prof. SCHUCK
Department of History, Philosophy and Social Sciences: Prof. HIEBER
Department of Law: Prof. WAECHTER
Department of Economics: Prof. MEYER

PROFESSORS

Department of Mathematics and Computer Science:

DUSKE, J., Computer Science
EBELING, W., Mathematics
ERNÉ, M., Mathematics
FORSTER, P., Applied Mathematics
GRÜBEL, R., Probability Theory and Statistics
HEINE, J., Mathematics
HOTJE, H., Mathematics
HULEK, K., Mathematics
KOPFERMANN, K., Mathematics
LIPECK, U., Computer Science
MADER, W., Mathematics
MIELKE, A., Applied Mathematics and Partial Differential Equations
MUES, E., Mathematics
MÜHLBACH, G., Approximation Theory and Numerical Analysis
MÜLLER, D., Computer Science
PARCHMANN, R., Computer Science
PFEIFFER, H., Mathematical Logic
PODEWSKI, K.-P., Mathematics
PRALLE, H., Head of Regional Computer Centre, Lower Saxony
REINEKE, J., Mathematics
RIEGER, G. J., Number Theory
SCHMIDT-WESTPHAL, U., Mathematics
SCHNOEGE, K. J., Applied Mathematics
STEFFENS, K., Mathematics
STEPHAN, E., Applied Mathematics
WOLTER, F.-E., Computer Science

Department of Physics:

BREHM, B., Experimental Physics
DANZMANN, K., Experimental Physics
DEMMIG, F., Physics
DRAGON, N., Theoretical Physics
ERTMER, W., Experimental Physics
ETLING, D., Theoretical Meteorology
EVERTS, H.-U., Theoretical Physics
GROSS, G., Meteorology
GROSSER, J., Atomic Processes
HAUG, R., Experimental Physics
HENZLER, M., Experimental Physics
KOCK, M., Plasma Physics
LECHTENFELD, O., Theoretical Physics
LIU, M., Theoretical Physics
MICHEL, R., Head of Centre for Radiation Protection and Radioecology
MIKESKA, H. J., Theoretical Physics
PFNÜR, H., Experimental Physics
SAUER, P. U., Theoretical Physics
SCHULZ, H., Theoretical Physics
TIEMANN, E., Experimental Physics
WELLEGEHAUSEN, B., Applied Physics
ZAWISCHA, D., Theoretical Physics

Department of Chemistry:

ALVES, J., Graduate Centre for the Transformation of Natural Products
BEIL, W., Graduate Centre for the Transformation of Natural Products
BELLGARDT, K.-H., Technical Chemistry
BERGER, R. G., Applied Chemistry
BINNEWIES, M., Inorganic Chemistry
BUTENSCHÖN, H., Organic Chemistry
DUDDECK, H., Organic Chemistry
HALLENSLEBEN, M. L., Macromolecular Chemistry
HEITJANS, P., Physical Chemistry
HESSE, D., Technical Chemistry
HOFFMANN, H. M. R., Organic Chemistry
IMBIHL, R., Physical Chemistry
JUG, K., Theoretical Chemistry
NAUMANN, Domestic Technology
SCHEPER, T., Technical Chemistry
SCHMALZRIED, H., Physical and Electrical Chemistry
SCHMAUDERER, E., Food Science
SEWING, K.-F., Graduate Centre for the Transformation of Natural Products
URLAND, W., Inorganic Chemistry
WATKINSON, B. M., Food Science
WILLNER, H., Special Inorganic Chemistry
WINTERFELDT, E., Organic Chemistry
WÜNSCH, G., Inorganic Chemistry

Department of Earth Sciences:

ARNOLD, A., Human Geography
BÖTTCHER, J., Soil Science
BUCHHOLZ, H. J., Human Geography
BUHL, J.-CH., Mineralogy
FISCHER, R., Palaeontology
FISCHER, W. R., Soil Science
GÜNTHER, K., Geology
HENNINGSEN, D., Geology
HOLTZ, F., Mineralogy
JOHANNES, W., Petrology
MOSIMANN, T., Physical Geography
PLOEG, R. VAN DER, Soil Science
SCHÄTZL, L., Economic Geography
WINSEMANN, J., Palaeontology

Department of Biology:

ANDERS, A., Biophysics
AULING, G., Microbiology
DIEKMANN, H., Microbiology
FENDRIK, I., Biophysics
JACOBSEN, H.-J., Molecular Biology
KLENERT, M., Biophysics
KLOPPSTECH, K., Botany
KOLB, A., Biophysics
KUSTER, H., Palaeoecology
MÖLLER, H., Botany
NIEMEYER, R., Botany
POTT, R., Botany
SCHMIDT, A., Botany

Department of Architecture:

ECKERLE, E., Fine Arts
DWORSKY, A., Rural Design
EHRMANN, W., Work Methods and Processing of Wood and Artificial Materials
GABRIEL, I., Construction and Design
GENENGER, H.-G., Architecture
GERKEN, H., Planning Technology
HENCKEL, H., Rural Structural Research
KAPPELER, D., Painting and Graphic Arts
KAUP, P., Construction and Design
KENNEDY, M., Resource-saving in Building
LINDINGER, H., Industrial Design
MECKSEPER, C., History of Architecture
PARAVICINI, U., Theory of Architecture
POHL, W.-H., Building Materials Technology
SCHMID-KIRSCH, A., Drawing and Computer-Assisted Design
SCHOMERS, M., Design
SLAWIK, H., Construction and Design
TROJAN, K., Town Planning
TURKALI, Z., Construction and Design
ZIBELL, B., Theory of Architecture

Department of Civil Engineering:

BILLIB, M., Hydrology
BLÜMEL, W., Foundations, Dams
DAMRATH, R., Applied Informatics
DOEDENS, H., Water Supply
GRÜNBERG, J., Concrete Construction
GRÜNREICH, D., Cartography
HOFFMANN, B., Hydrology
HORST, H., Statics
IWAN, G., Construction Management
KONECNY, G., Photogrammetry and Engineering Surveying
KUNST, S., Water Supply
LECHER, K., Hydrology
LIERSE, J., Building Construction
MARKOFSKY, M., Flow Mechanics
MULL, R., Hydrology
MÜLLER, U., Graduate Centre for Environmentally Relevant Fluxes in Water and Soil
MÜLLER-KIRCHENBAUER, H., Foundations, Dams
NATKE, H. G., Theory of Vibrations and Metrology
PELZER, H., General Surveying
RIZKALLAH, V., Foundations, Dams
ROKAHR, R., Statics and Geomechanics
ROSEMEIER, G., Flow Mechanics
ROSENWINKEL, K.-H., Water Supply
ROTH, J., Building Construction
ROTHERT, H., Statics
SEEBER, G., Geodesy
SCHELLING, W., Building Technology
SCHNÜLL, R., Traffic Economics, Highway System, Town Planning
SIEFERT, T., Railways and Roads
SIEKER, F., Hydrology
STEIN, E., Building Mechanics
WELLNER, F., Traffic Economics, Highway System, Town Planning
ZIELKE, W., Flow Mechanics
ZIMMERMANN, C., Hydroengineering

Department of Mechanical Engineering:

BACH, F.-W., Materials
BESDO, D., Mechanics
BRAUNE, R., Mechanisms and Machine Elements
DOEGE, E., Metal Forming and Machines
GATZEN, H.-H., Microtechnology
GIETZELT, M., Steam and Fuel Engineering
HAFERKAMP, H. D., Materials
HAGER, M., Conveying Technology and Mining Machinery
HALLENSLEBEN, M. L., Macromolecular Chemistry
HEIMANN, B., Machine Dynamics
KABELAC, S., Thermodynamics
LOUIS, H., Material Testing
MEIER, G. E. A., Fluid Mechanics
MERKER, G. P., Internal Combustion Engine
MEWES, D., Chemical Engineering
POLL, G., Construction Science
POPP, K., Mechanics
RAUTENBERG, M., Radial Compressors
REDEKER, G., Factory Building
REHFELDT, D., Welding Technology
REITHMEIER, E., Measurement and Control Technology
RIESS, W., Turbo Machinery
ROSEMANN, H., Construction Science
SCHULZE, L., Department Planning, Control of Warehouse and Transport Systems
SCHWERES, M., Labour Science, Ergonomics
STEGEMANN, D., Nuclear Technology
TÖNSHOFF, H.-K., Production Engineering and Machine Tools
VOSS, G., Railway Machines
WIENDAHL, H.-P., Plant Engineering and Production Control

Department of Electrical Engineering:

BARKE, E., Microelectronic Systems
GARBE, H., Basic Electrical Engineering
GERTH, W., Control Technology
GOCKENBACH, E., High Voltage
GRAUL, J., Semi-Conductor Technology and Materials of Electrical Engineering
HAASE, H., Electrical Engineering
HOFMANN, K., Semi-Conductor Technology and Materials of Electrical Engineering
JOBMANN, K., General Communications Technology
KUCHENBECKER, H.-P., General Communications Technology
LIEDTKE, C.-E., Theoretical Communications Technology
MARQUARDT, J., High Frequency Technology
MUCHA, J., Theoretical Electrical Engineering
MÜLLER-SCHLOER, C., Computing Sciences
MUSMANN, H.-G., Theoretical Communications Technology
NEJDL, W., Knowledge-Based Systems
NESTLER, J., Power Electronics
OSWALD, B. R., Electricity Supply
PIRSCH, P., Microelectronical Engineering
SEINSCH, H. O., Electrical Machines and Drives
STÖLTING, H.-D., Electrical Machines and Drives
WAGNER, B., Electrical Systems and Teaching of Electrical Engineering

Department of Horticulture:

GIESECKE, M., Gardening Management
HAU, B., Phytopathology
HÖRMANN, D., Gardening Management
HORST, W., Plant Nutrition
HOTHORN, L., Biology Informatics
MAISS, E., Phytopathology
POEHLING, Phytopathology and Plant Protection
SCHENK, E.-W., Gardening Management and Accountancy
SCHENK, M., Plant Nutrition
SCHMIDT, E., Horticultural Economics
SCHMITZ, U. K., Applied Genetics
SCHERER, G., Crop Physiology
SCHÖNHERR, J., Fruit Science
SPETHMANN, W., Nursery Gardening
STÜTZEL, Vegetable Science
TANTAU, H.-J., Horticultural Engineering
TATLIOGLU, T., Applied Genetics
WAIBEL, H., Horticultural Economics
WIEBE, H.-J., Vegetable Science
ZIMMER, K., Ornamental Plants

Department of Landscape Development and Planning:

BARTH, H. G., Regional Planning
FÜRST, D., Regional Planning
HACKER, E., Conservation
HERLYN, U., Planning-related Sociology
KOWARIK, I., Plant Ecology
LÖSKEN, G., Open Space Planning and Garden Architecture
NAGEL, G., Open Space Planning and Garden Architecture
SCHRAMM, W., Development Planning and Structural Research
SEGGERN, H. VON, Open Space Planning
SELLE, K., Open Space Planning
TÖPFER, K., Landscape Planning
WÖBSE, H. H., Landscape Aesthetics and Design
WOLSCHKE-BULMAHN, J., Open Space Planning and Garden Architecture

Department of Literature and Linguistics:

BEZZEL, CH., German Language
BICKES, H., German Language
BIRKNER, G., English Philology
BRÜGGEMANN, H., Modern German Literature
DISCHNER-VOGEL, G., Modern German Literature
EGGS, E., Romance Philology and Language
FISCHER, H., German Literature
GLAGE, L., English Literature
HOEGES, D., Romance Philology and Literature
KREUTZER, L., Modern German Literature
KUPETZ, R., Teaching of English, Applied Linguistics
LENK, E., German Literature
LUDWIG, O., German Language
PETERS, J., Modern German Literature
RECTOR, M., Modern German Literature
ROHLOFF, H., English Philosophy
SANDERS, H., Romance Philology and Literature
SAUER, W., German Language
SCHLOBINSKI, P., German Language
SCHLÜTER, G., French Literature
SCHULZE, R., English Language and Linguistics
VASSEN, F., Modern German Literature
WEBER, H., English Philology
WENZEL, F., Scientific and Technical Russian

Department of History, Philosophy and Social Sciences:

History:

ASCHOFF, H.-G., Modern History and Ecclesiastical History
BARMEYER-HARTLIEB, H., Modern History
BERG, D., Medieval History
BLEY, H., Modern History
BRUEGGEMEIER, F. J., Modern and Environmental History
CALLIES, H., Ancient History
FÜLLBERG-STOLLBERG, O., Modern History
HAUPTMEYER, C.-H., Early Medieval History
NOLTE, H.-H., Medieval History
RIEDEL, M., Modern History
SALDERN, A. VON, Modern History
SCHMID, H.-D., History and History Teaching
SCHWARZ, B., Medieval History
WILHARM, I., History and History Teaching
WÜNDERICH, V., Latin American History

Philosophy:

BULTHAUP, P.
KORFF, F.-W.
MENSCHING, G.
RIES, W.

Political Science:

BLANKE, B.
BROKMEIER, P.
HAENSCH, D.
LEMKE, C.
MÜLLER, R.-W.
PERELS, J.
SCHÄFER, G.
VESTER, M.

Psychology:

BECKER-SCHMIDT, R.
KIESELBACH, T.
KNAPP, G.-A.
KROVOZA, A.
SCHMID, R.
WACKER, A.
WELLENDORF, F.
WELZER, H.

Sociology:

CLAUSSEN, D.
DUDEN, B.
GHOLAMASAD, D.
HIEBER, L.
MESCHKAT, K.
MICKLER, O.
NEGT, O.
WÜNDERICH, V.

Theology:

ANTES, P.

Department of Education:

ACHINGER, G., Sociology
BAYER, K., German
BEUTLER, K., Education
BILLMANN-MAHECHA, Psychology
BINDEL, W.-R., Special Education
BOLSCHO, D., Pedagogy
BÖNSCH, M., School Pedagogy
BRODTMANN, D., Sports

DITTRICH, J.-H., Technology of Clothing and Textiles
DORDEL, H. J., Sports
EBINGHAUS, H., Physics
EGGERT, D., Psychology
EHRHARDT, J., Education
EHRHARDT, M. L., German
FELDMANN, K., Sociology
FRACKMANN, M., Social Education
FRANZKE, R., Social Education
GIPSER, D., Special Education
GÖRTZ, H.-J., Roman Catholic Religious Education
HEINEMANN, M., Education
HERWIG, J., Music
HORSTER, D., Education
ILIEN, A., Education
JANSSEN, B., School Pedagogy
JETTER, K., Therapy
JOHANNSEN, F., Evangelical Religious Education
JUNGK, D., Vocational Education
KENTLER, H., Social Education
KLEINDIENST-CACHAY, Sports
KNOLL, J., Biology
KOETHEN, E., Art and Visual Media, Teaching of Art and Visual Media
KÖPCKE, K. M., German
KÜHNE, A., Psychology
KUNTZ, K. M., Education
LAGA, G., Sociology
LOHRER-PAPE, Arts
MANZ, W., Vocational Education
NARR, R., School Pedagogy
NAUMANN, German
NAUMANN, G., Home Technology
NOLL, A.-H., Social Studies
NOORMANN, Teaching of Evangelical Relations
OELSCHLÄGER, H., Educational Planning & Reform
PAEFGEN, E., German
PEIFFER, L., Sports
RADATZ, Mathematics
RAUFUSS, D., Education
REISER, H., Special Education
RUST, H., Sociology
RÜTTERS, K., Vocational Education
SCHAEFFNER, L., Adult Education
SCHMAUDERER, E., Food Science
SCHMIDT, M., Adult Education
SCHMIDT-WULFFEN, W.-D., Geography
SCHMITZ, K., Education
SCHÖNBERGER, F., Special Education
SCHREIBER, G., Technology of Clothing and Textile
SCHUCHARDT, E., Education
SIEBERT, H., Adult Education
TIEDEMANN, J., Psychology
TILCH, H., Social Education
TREBELS, A. H., Sports
TROCHOLEPCZY, B., Roman Catholic Religious Education
TSCHAMMER-OSTEN, B., Home Economics
URBAN, Psychology
WATKINSON, B. M., Food Science
WERNING, R., Education of the Mentally Handicapped
WILKEN, E., Special Education
WIPPERMANN, H., Mathematics
ZIEHE, T., Education

Department of Law:

ABELTSHAUSER, T., Civil Law
CALLIESS, R.-P., Criminal Law
DORNDORF, E., Civil Law
FABER, H., Public Law
FENGE, H., Civil Law
FOLZ, H.-E., Public Law
FRANK, J., Economics
HARTWIG, O., Civil Law
HESSE, H. A., Teaching of Law, Sociology of Law
KILIAN, W., Civil Law
KÜHNE, J.-D., Public Law
MAGOULAS, G., Economics
MASSING, O., Politics
MEDER, S., Civil Law, History of Law
MEIER, B.-D., Criminal Law
NAHAMOWITZ, P., Theory of Organization and Planning
OPPERMANN, B., Civil Law
PFEIFFER, C., Criminology
RÜPING, H., Criminal Law
SALJE, P., Civil Law
SCHNEIDER, H.-P., Public Law
SCHWERDTFEGER, G., Public Law
TREIBER, H., Theory of Organization and Planning
WAECHTER, K., Public Law
WALTHER, M., Teaching of Law and Philosophy
WENDELING-SCHRÖDER, U., Civil Law
WILMOWSKY, P. VON, Civil Law
ZIELINSKI, D., Criminal Law

Department of Economics and Business Administration:

GEIGANT, F., Money, Credit, Currency
GERLACH, K., Political Economy and Labour Economics
HANSEN, U., Marketing
HASLINGER, F., Economics
HEINEMANN, H.-J., International Economic Relations
HOMBURG, S., Public Economics
HÜBL, L., Economic Policy
HÜBLER, O., Econometrics
JÖHNK, M.-D., Econometrics and Statistics
MEYER, W., Economic Policy
MÜLLER, U., Economic Systems, Anti-Trust Policy and Stabilization
RIDDER, H.-G., Personnel Management
SCHREIBER, U., Business Taxation
SCHULENBURG, J.-M. GRAF VON DER, Insurance
SCHWARZE, J., Computer Science
STEFFEN, R., Production
STEINLE, C., Management Economics
TSCHAMMER-OSTEN, B., Domestic Science
WIEDMANN, K.-P., Marketing

TIERÄRZTLICHE HOCHSCHULE HANNOVER (Hanover School of Veterinary Medicine)

30545 Hannover, Buenteweg 2, Postfach 711180

Telephone: (511) 953-6
Fax: (511) 953-8050

Founded 1778 as Königliche Rossarzneischule, attained university status 1887
State control
Academic year: October to September

Rector: Prof. Dr V. MOENNIG
Pro-Rectors: Prof. Dr G. F. GERLACH, Prof. Dr EDDA TÖPFER-PETERSEN
Administrative Officer: HANS LINNEMANN
Librarian: Dr F. RUMP

Number of teachers: 122
Number of students: 2,160

Publication: *TiHo-Anzeiger* (8 a year).

HEADS

Institute of Anatomy: Prof. Dr H. WAIBL
Institute of Pathology: Prof. Dr S. UEBERSCHÄR
Institute of Physiology: Prof. Dr G. BREVES
Institute of Physiological Chemistry: Prof. Dr H. Y. NAIM
Institute of Microbiology and Epidemics: Prof. Dr K.-H. BOEHM
Department of Chemical Analysis and Endocrinology: Prof. Dr H.-O. HOPPEN
Department of Animal Ecology and Cell Biology: Prof. Dr H. LEHMANN
Institute of Animal Breeding and Genetics: Prof. Dr O. DISTEL
Institute of Parasitology: Prof. Dr A. LIEBISCH
Institute of Zoology: Prof. Dr E. ZIMMERMANN
Centre of Food Science: Prof. Dr G. HAMANN
Institute of Pharmacology, Toxicology and Pharmacy: Prof. Dr W. LÖSCHER
Poultry Clinic: Prof. Dr U. NEUMANN
Department of Virology: Prof. Dr V. MOENNIG
Institute of Animal Nutrition: Prof. Dr J. KAMPHUES
Department of Animal Hygiene and Animal Welfare: Prof. Dr J. HARTUNG
Department of Biometry and Epidemiology: Prof. Dr M. ROMMEL
Clinic for Pigs, Small Ruminants, Forensic Medicine and Ambulatory Service: Prof. Dr K.-H. WALDMANN
Horse Clinic: Prof. Dr E. DEEGEN
Clinic for Small Domestic Animals: Prof. Dr I. NOLTE
Clinic for Cattle Obstetrics and Gynaecology: Prof. Dr B. MEINECKE (acting)
Cattle Clinic: Prof. Dr H. SCHOLZ
Department of Reproductive Medicine: Prof. Dr B. MEINECKE

ATTACHED INSTITUTES

Unit for the History of Veterinary Medicine: Prof. Dr J. SCHÄFFER.

Unit for Medical Physics: Prof. Dr W. GIESE.

Unit for Fish Pathology and Fish Farming: Prof. Dr W. KÖRTING.

Unit for Immunology: Prof. Dr W. LEIBOLD.

Institute for Wildlife Research: Prof. Dr K. POHLMEYER.

RUPRECHT-KARLS-UNIVERSITÄT HEIDELBERG

69047 Heidelberg, Postfach 105760

Telephone: 06221-541
Telex: 461515
Fax: 06221-542618

Founded 1386

Rector: Prof. Dr JÜRGEN SIEBKE
Pro-Rectors: Prof. Dr HEINZ HORNER, Prof. Dr HARTMUT KIRCHHEIM, Prof. Dr HEINZ-DIETRICH LOEWE
Chancellor: ROMANA Gräfin VOM HAGEN
Librarian: Prof. Dr JOSEF DÖRPINGHAUS

Number of teachers: 2,020
Number of students: 27,400

Publications: *Unispiegel* (every 2 months), *Mitteilungsblatt des Rektors* (irregular), *Ruperto Carola* (quarterly), *Pressemitteilungen Personalia* (monthly), *Heidelberger Jahrbücher* (annually).

DEANS

Faculty of Theology: Prof. Dr HEIMO HOFMEISTER
Faculty of Law: Prof. Dr HERBERT ROTH
Faculty of Clinical Medicine (Heidelberg): Prof. Dr HANS-GÜNTER SONNTAG
Faculty of Clinical Medicine (Mannheim): Prof. Dr KLAUS VAN ACKERN
Faculty of Philosophy and History: Prof. Dr VOLKER SELLIN
Faculty of Oriental and Classical Studies: Prof. Dr HUBERT PETERSMANN
Faculty of Modern Philology: Prof. Dr WILHELM KÜHLMANN
Faculty of Economic Sciences: Prof. Dr EVA TERBERGER
Faculty of Social and Behavioural Sciences: Prof. Dr VOLKER LENHART
Faculty of Mathematics: Prof. Dr RAINER DAHLHAUS
Faculty of Chemistry: Prof. Dr PETER COMBA
Faculty of Pharmacy: Prof. Dr MICHAEL WINK
Faculty of Physics and Astronomy: Prof. Dr FRANZ EISELE
Faculty of Biology: Prof. Dr MARK SITT
Faculty of Geosciences: Prof. Dr RAINER ALTHERR

PROFESSORS (INSTITUTE DIRECTORS)

Faculty of Theology:

HOFMEISTER, H., Philosophy of Religion
RITSCHL, D., Systematic Theology
SCHMIDT, H., Practical Theology
STROHM, T., Practical Theology

Faculty of Law:

DÖLLING, D., Criminal Law
HOMMELHOFF, P., German and European Company and Business Law
JAYME, E., Foreign and International Private and Business Law
KIRCHHOF, P., Public Law, Finance and Tax Law
KÜPER, W., Criminal Law
MISERA, K., Historical Law
MUSSGNUG, R., Fiscal and Tax Law
NICKLISCH, F., German and European Technology and Environment Law

Faculty of Clinical Medicine (Heidelberg):

BARTRAM, C., Human Genetics
BASTERT, G., Gynaecology
BREMER, H.-J., Paediatrics
ECKART, W. U., History of Medicine
EWERBECK, V., Orthopaedics
FAHMI, D., Anatomy
HACKE, W., Neurology
HAUX, R., Medical Biometrics and Computer Science in Medicine
HERFARTH, CH., Surgery
HERWART, F. O., Pathology
KAUFFMANN, G., Radiology
KIRCHHEIM, H., Vivisection
KUNZE, S., Neurosurgery
LENZ, P., Dentistry
MARTIN, E., Anaesthesiology
MATTERN, R., Forensic Medicine
MEUER, S., Immunology
MUNDT, CH., Psychiatry
OTTO, H., Pathology
PETZOLDT, D., Dermatology
RUDOLF, G., Psychosomatic Medicine
SCHWABE, U., Pharmacology
SELLER, H., Physiology
SONNTAG, H.-G., Hygiene
TRIEBIG, G., Social and Industrial Medicine
VÖLCKER, H. E., Ophthalmology
WEIDAUER, H., Ear, Nose and Throat
WIELAND, F., Biochemistry (I)
ZIEGLER, R., Internal Medicine
ZIMMERMANN, M., Physiology (II)

Faculty of Clinical Medicine (Mannheim):

ACKERN, K. VAN, Anaesthesiology
ALKEN, P., Urology
BLEYL, U., General Pathology and Pathological Anatomy
ERTL, G., Internal Medicine (II)
GEORGI, M., Radiology
HEENE, D. L., Internal Medicine (I)
HEHLMANN, R., Internal Medicine (III)
HENN, F., Social Psychiatry
HENNERICI, M., Neurology
HOF, H., Medical Microbiology and Hygiene
HÖRMANN, K., Ear, Nose and Throat
JANI, L., Orthopaedics
JUNG, E., Dermatology and Venereal Diseases
LEMMER, B., Pharmacology and Toxicology
LIESENHOFF, H., Ophthalmology
MELCHERT, F., Obstetrics and Gynaecology
NIESSEN, K.-H., Paediatrics
SCHADENDORE, D., Clinical Co-operation Unit (Skin Cancer)
SCHMIEDEK, P., Neurological Surgery
SINGER, M. V., Internal Medicine (IV)
TREDE, M., Surgery
WAAG, K.-L., Children's Surgery
WEHLING, M., Clinical Pharmacology
WELLEK, S., Medical Statistics
WENTZENSEN, A., Casualty Surgery
WISSER, H., Clinical Chemistry
WOUDE, F. VAN DER, Internal Medicine (V)

Faculty of Philosophy and History:

BEYME, K. VON, Political Science
BUBNER, R., Philosophy
HERMANN, J., Palestine History
LEDDEROSE, L., History of the Arts
LEOPOLD, S., Musicology
LÖWE, H.-D., History of Eastern Europe
MIETHKE, J., Medieval and Modern History
SAURMA, L., History of Art

Faculty of Oriental and Classical Studies:

ALBRECHT, M., Classics (Greek and Latin)
ALFÖLDY, G., Ancient History
ASSMANN, J., Egyptology
HAGEDORN, D., Papyrology
HÖLSCHER, T., Classical Archaeology
MARAN, J., Prehistory and Early History
MAUL, S., Semitics
SCHAMONI, W., Japanese Studies
WAGNER, R., Sinology

Faculty of Modern Philology:

ALBRECHT, J., Translating and Interpreting
BERSCHIN, W., Latin Philology of the Middle Ages
HELLWIG, P., Computer Linguistics
HÖFELE, A., English Philology
KIESEL, H., German Philology
PANZER, B., Slavic Philology
POHL, E., Language Laboratory
ROTHE, A., Romance Philology
STRACK, F., German Studies

Faculty of Economics:

KOGELSCHATZ, H., Comparative Economic and Social Statistics
REQUATE, T., Interdisciplinary Institute for Environmental Economics
ROSE, M., Political Economics
SCHREMMER, E., History of Sociology and Economics

Faculty of Social and Behavioural Sciences:

FUNKE, J., Psychology
KOHL, J., Sociology
KRUSE, A., Gerontology
ROTH, K., Sport
SCHIERSMANN, CHR., Education
WASSERMANN, J., Ethnology

Faculty of Mathematics:

AMBOS-SPIES, K., Mathematics
RANNACHER, R., Mathematics

Faculty of Chemistry:

HELMCHEN, G., Organic Chemistry
SIEBERT, W., Inorganic Chemistry
WOLFRUM, J., Physical Chemistry

Faculty of Pharmacy:

NEIDLEIN, R., Pharmaceutical Chemistry
WINK, M., Pharmaceutical Biology

Faculty of Physics and Astronomy:

BILLE, J., Applied Physics
EISELE, F., Physics
HÜFNER, J., Theoretical Physics
PLATT, U., Atmospheric Physics
TITTEL, K., High Energy Physics
TSCHARNUTER, W., Theoretical Astrophysics

Faculty of Biology:

BAUTZ, E., Molecular Genetics
BEHNKE, H.-D., Cell Biology
HUTTNER, W., Neurobiology
LEINS, P., Botany
SCHALLER, H., Microbiology
STITT, M., Botany
STORCH, V., Zoology

Faculty of Geosciences:

ALTHERR, R., Mineralogy and Petrography
GEBHARDT, H., Geography
GREILING, R., Geology
LIPPOLT, H. J., Geochronology
SCHÖLER, H. F., Environmental Geochemistry

ATTACHED INSTITUTES

Südasien-Institut (South Asian Institute): 69120 Heidelberg, Im Neuenheimer Feld 330; Dir Prof. Dr M. BOEHM-TETTELBACH.

Zentrum für Molekulare Biologie Heidelberg: 69120 Heidelberg, Im Neuenheimer Feld 282; Dir Prof. Dr K. BEYREUTHER.

Interdisziplinäres Zentrum für Wissenschaftliches Rechnen: 69120 Heidelberg, Im Neuenheimer Feld 368; Dir Prof. Dr W. JÄGER.

UNIVERSITÄT HILDESHEIM

31141 Hildesheim, Marienburger Platz 22
Telephone: (5121) 8830
Fax: (5121) 867558

Founded 1978
State control
Academic year: October to September

President: Dr ULLA BOSSE
Vice-President: Prof. Dr Dr WERNER BRÄNDLE
Vice-Rector: Prof. Dr NORBERT WEGNER
Administrative Officer: Dr CHRISTIAN GRAHL
Librarian: PETER MARMEIN

Number of teachers: 156
Number of students: 3,900

Publications: *Vorlesungsverzeichnis* (2 a year), *Universitätszeitschrift* (2 a year).

DEANS

Faculty I (Education): Prof. Dr HUBERTUS KUNERT
Faculty II (Social Work and Cultural Education): Prof. Dr HANS-OTTO HÜGEL
Faculty III (Languages and Technology): Prof. Dr REINER ARNTZ
Faculty IV (Computer Science and Natural Sciences): Prof. Dr EBERHARD SCHWARZER

PROFESSORS

Faculty I:

BORSCHE, Philosophy
BRÄNDLE, Protestant Theology
CLOER, General Pedagogy
EBERLE, Social Pedagogy
FLINTROP, Philosophy
FRIEDRICH, Political Science
GÖLLNER, Catholic Theology
HEINEMEYER, Protestant Theology
HELFRICH-HÖLTER, Psychology
HOPF, Sociology
JÄGER, Sport
JAUMANN-GRAUMANN, Education
KECK, Education
KLAGES, Protestant Theology
KÖHNLEIN, General Natural Science
KUNERT, General Pedagogy
LEDER, Political Science
LÜTTGE, Psychology
MEIER-HILBERT, Geography
MOLTKE, Psychology
MÜLLER, Social Pedagogy
NICKEL, Sport
OVERESCH, History
PÖPPEL, Education
SCHAUB, General Natural Science
SCHREINER, Protestant Theology
STIENSMEIER-PELSTER, Psychology
STRANG, Social Pedagogy
WERNER, Catholic Theology
WOLFF, Social Pedagogy

Faculty II:

BERG, Media Education
DÜWEL, Cultural Administration
EGGEBRECHT, Fine Arts
GIFFHORN, Media Education
GORNIK, German Literature and Linguistics
GROMES, Theatre
GÜNZEL, Fine Arts and Visual Communication
HEINRICHS, Media Education
HÜGEL, Popular Culture

KUMHER, Fine Arts and Visual Communication
KURZENBERGER, Theatre
LÖFFLER, Music and Aural Communication
MENZEL, German Language and Linguistics
NOLTE, Fine Arts and Visual Communication
SCHAPER, Music and Aural Communication
TESKE, Fine Arts
VIETTA, Literature and Lingual Communication
WEBER, Music and Aural Communication

Faculty III:

ARNTZ, Romance Languages and Linguistics
BENEKE, English Linguistics and Intercultural Communication
BLIESENER, Language Didactics
FRANZBECKER, General Science
HAUENSCHILD, Computational Linguistics
KAISER, English Studies
KOLB, General Economics
SABBAN, Romance Languages and Linguistics
THEUERKAUF, Applied Electrical Engineering and Science Education
WEGNER, Technology
WERNER, English Studies

Faculty IV:

ALTEN, Mathematics
AMBROSI, Computer Science
BENTZ, Mathematics
DAHLMANN, Chemistry
FLECHSIG, Chemistry
KREUTZKAMP, Mathematics
SCHWARZER, Physics
STURM, Biology
WÜRDINGER, Biology

ATTACHED INSTITUTES

Institute for General Educational Theory: Dir Prof. Dr ERNST CLOER.

Institute for Applied Educational Science and General Teaching Methods: Dir Prof. Dr RUDOLF KECK.

Institute for Primary School Teacher Training: Dir Prof. Dr WALTER KÖHNLEIN.

Institute for Philosophy: Dir Dr TILMAN BORSCHE.

Institute for Psychology: Dir Prof. Dr DIETER LÜTTKE.

Institute for Social Sciences: Dir Prof. Dr CHRISTEL HOPF.

Institute for Evangelical Theology: Dir Prof. Dr WERNER BRÄNDLE.

Institute for Geography and History: Dir Prof. Dr MANFRED OVERESCH.

Institute for Catholic Theology: Dir Prof. Dr REINHARD GÖLLNER.

Institute for Social Education: Dir Prof. Dr BURKHARD MÜLLER.

Institute for Sport Science and Sport Education: Dir Prof. Dr ULRICH NICKEL.

Institute for Art and Aesthetics: Dir Prof. Dr ULRICH TESKE.

Institute for German Language and Literature: Dir Prof. Dr SILVIO VIETTA.

Institute for Media and Theatre: Dir Prof. Dr HARTWIN GROMES.

Institute for Audiovisual Media: Dir Prof. Dr WALTER THISSEN.

Institute for Music: Dir Prof. Dr RUDOLF WEBER.

Institute for Applied Linguistics: Dir Prof. Dr ANNETTE SABBAN.

Institute for Labour, Commerce and Engineering: Dir Dr WALTER FRANZBECKER.

Institute for Applied Electrical Engineering and Teaching of Engineering: Dir Prof. Dr WALTER THEUERKAUF.

Institute for Mathematics: Dir Prof. Dr THEO KREUTZKAMP.

Institute for the Theory of Business Management: Dir Prof. Dr KLAUS AMBROSI.

Institute for Physics and Computer Science in Technology: Dir Prof. Dr EBERHARD SCHNAUZER.

Institute for Biology and Chemistry: Dir Prof. Dr WOLFGANG DAHLMANN.

UNIVERSITÄT HOHENHEIM

70593 Stuttgart
Telephone: (711) 459-0
Fax: (711) 459-3960
E-mail: presse@uni-hohenheim.de

Founded 1818
Academic year: October to September

President: Prof. Dr K. MACHARZINA
Vice-Presidents: Prof. Dr Dr W. DROCHNER, Prof. Dr V. KOTTKE
Administrative Director: E. RÖDLER
University Librarian: Dr J. MARTIN

Number of teachers: 780
Number of students: 5,100

Publications: *Hohenheimer Arbeiten*, *Rechenschaftsbericht* (annually), *Universitätsführer* (annually), *Vorlesungsverzeichnis* (2 a year), *Amtliche Mitteilungen*.

DEANS

Faculty of General Natural Sciences: Prof. Dr K. BOSCH
Faculty of Biology: Prof. Dr A. PREISS
Faculty of Agricultural Sciences I (Plant Production and Ecology): Prof. Dr A. E. MELCHINGER
Faculty of Agricultural Sciences II (Agricultural Economics, Agricultural Technology and Animal Production): Prof. Dr JUNGBLUTH
Faculty of Economics and Social Sciences: Prof. Dr W. HABENICHT

PROFESSORS

Faculty of General Natural Sciences:

BECKER-BENDER, G., Physics
BIESALSKI, H. K., Biochemistry and Nutrition
BODE, C., Nutrition
BOSCH, K., Mathematics
CARLE, R., Food Technology
CLASSEN, H.-G., Toxicology and Pharmacology
DEHNHARDT, W., Informatics
DUFNER, J., Mathematics
EHRENSTEIN, W., Applied Physiology
FISCHER, A., Food Technology
FÜRST, P., Nutrition
HAGENMEYER, B., Mathematics
HAMMES, W., Food Technology
HAUBOLD, H., Inorganic Chemistry
ISENGARD, H.-D., Food Analysis
JETTER, K., Food Analysis
KOCH, J., Biochemistry
KOTTKE, V., Food Process Technology
KRAUS, W., Organic Chemistry
MENZEL, P., Chemistry and Ecology
PIEPER, H.-J., Food Technology
RAU, H., Physical Chemistry
RENZ, P., Biochemistry and Nutrition
SCHWACK, W., Food Chemistry
SPITZNER, D., Organic Chemistry
THÖNI, H., Biometry
WIESER, H.-P., Physics
WURSTER, R., Physics

Faculty of Biology:

BREER, H., Zoophysiology
EHRLEIN, H., Zoophysiology
FRANK, B., Zoology
HANKE, W., Zoophysiology
HESEMANN, C. U., Genetics
HESS, D., Plant Biotechnology
KUHN, A., Microbiology
KUHN, E., Plant Physiology
KÜPPERS, M., Botany
MACKENSTEDT, U., Zoology
PFITZNER, A., Virology
PREISS, A., Genetics
RAHMANN, H., Zoology
RÖSNER, H., Zoology
SALCHER, O., Microbiology
SPRING, O., Botany
SÜSSMUTH, R., Microbiology and Molecular Biology

Faculty of Agricultural Sciences I:

AUFHAMMER, W., Special Plant Production
BANGERTH, F., Applied Botany
BLAICH, R., Viticulture
BÖCKER, R., Landscape Ecology
BUCHENAUER, H., Plant Protection
CLAUPEIN, W., Plant Production
GEIGER, H. H., Genetics
HURLE, K., Plant Protection
JACOB, H., Crop and Plant Production
KANDELER, E., Soil Biology
KAUPENJOHANN, M., Soil Chemistry
KOHLER, A., Ecology
LEIHNER, D., Plant Production in Tropical and Subtropical Areas
LIEBIG, H.-P., Vegetable Cropping
MELCHINGER, A., Genetics and Plant Breeding
MÜLLER, W. A., Climatology
RÖMHELD, V., Plant Nutrition
ROTH, K., Soil Physics
SCHULTZE-KRAFT, R., Tropical Plant Production
STAHR, K., Soil Sciences
STEINER, A., Plant Physiology
STÖSSER, R., Applied Botany
UTZ, F., Plant Breeding
WEBER, G., Special Plant Breeding
ZEBITZ, C., Plant Protection

Faculty of Agricultural Sciences II:

AMSELGRUBER, W., Anatomy and Physiology of Domestic Animals
BECKER, K., Animal Nutrition in Tropical and Subtropical Areas
BECKER, T., Rural Markets and Rural Marketing
BESSEI, W., Animal Breeding
BÖHM, R., Veterinary Hygiene
CLAUS, R., Stockbreeding
DABBERT, S., Production Theory in Agriculture
DIEDRICHSEN, I., Applied Psychology
DOLUSCHITZ, R., Farm Management
DOPPLER, W., Farm Management in Tropical and Subtropical Areas
DROCHNER, W., Animal Nutrition
GELDERMANN, H., Stockbreeding
GROSSKOPF, W., Agricultural Politics
HAGMÜLLER, P., Agricultural Teaching
HAUSSMANN, A., Stockbreeding
HEIDHUES, F., Agricultural Economics in Tropical and Subtropical Areas
HENZE, A., Agricultural Politics
HOFFMANN, V., Agricultural Communication
JUNGBLUTH, T., Agricultural Technology
KLEISINGER, S., Agricultural Technology
KÖLLER, K., Agricultural Technology in Developing Countries
KROMKA, F., Agricultural Sociology
KUTZBACH, H.-D., Agricultural Technology
MOSENTHIN, R., Animal Nutrition
MÜHLBAUER, W., Energy Technology
OPPEN, M. VON, Agricultural Economics in Developing Countries
SCHENKEL, H., Animal Nutrition
WEBB, P., Nutrition and Politics
ZEDDIES, J., Agricultural Economics

Faculty of Economics and Social Sciences:

BAREIS, H.-P., Taxation and Management
BUSS, E., Sociology
CAESAR, R., Financing

DITTMAN, A., Law
EISELE, W., Micro-economics
GERYBADZE, A., International Management
HABENICHT, W., Industrial Economics
HAGEMANN, H., Economic Theory
HANF, E., Mathematical Economics and Operations Research
HERDZINA, K., Economics
HÖRSCHGEN, H., Economics and Marketing
JUNGKUNZ, D., Vocational Teaching
KAMMLER, H., Politics
KRCMAR, H., Informatics
KRUEDENER, Frhr J. VON, Social and Economic History
KUHNLE, H., Business Administration
MACHARZINA, K., Management and Organizational Research
MAST, C., Journalism
OHR, R., International Economics
SCHENK, M., Journalism
SCHMIDT, I., Competitive Politics
SCHULER, H., Psychology
SEEL, B., Household Management
SPAHN, P., Economics
STEIN, J. H. VON, Commercial Economy and Banking Management
TROSSMANN, E., Controlling
TURNER, G., Law
VOLLMER, L., Civil Law
WAGENHALS, G., Statistics and Econometry

TECHNISCHE UNIVERSITÄT ILMENAU

98684 Ilmenau, Pf. 100565
Premises at 98693 Ilmenau, Max-Planck-Ring 14
Telephone: (3677) 69-0
Fax: (3677) 69-1701
E-mail: webmaster@tu-ilmenau.de

Founded 1953 as Hochschule für Elektrotechnik; present name and status 1992
State control
Academic year: October to September

Rector: Prof. Dr-Ing. habil. WOLFGANG GENS
Vice-Rectors: Prof. Dr-Ing. habil. HEINRICH KERN (Teaching), Prof. Dr-Ing. habil. ILKA PHILIPPOW (Science)
Chancellor: Dr-Ing. habil. BERNHARD HAUPT
Librarian: Dr GOTTFRIED MÄLZER

Number of teachers: 400
Number of students: 3,500

Publications: *Tagungsberichte des Internationalen Kolloquiums* (annually), *"Information / Dokumentation"* (proceedings, every 2 years), *Wissenschaftliches Magazin*.

DEANS

Faculty of Mathematics and Natural Sciences: Prof. Dr rer. nat. habil. HANSJOACHIM WALTHER
Faculty of Electrical Engineering and Information Technology: Prof. Dr-Ing. habil. GERT WINKLER
Faculty of Computer Science and Automation: Prof. Dr-Ing. habil. ILKA PHILIPPOW
Faculty of Mechanical Engineering: Prof. Dr-Ing. habil. EBERHARD KALLENBACH
Faculty of Engineering and Business Economics: Prof. Dr-Ing. habil. PETER GMILKOWSKY

FRIEDRICH-SCHILLER-UNIVERSITÄT JENA

07743 Jena, Fürstengraben 1
Telephone: (3641) 9300
Fax: (3641) 931682

Founded 1558
Academic year: September to August

Chancellor: Dr KLAUS KÜBEL
Rector: Prof. Dr GEORG MACHNIK
Pro-Rectors: Prof. Dr WOLFGANG SCHWEICKARD, Prof. Dr KONRAD GOETZ
Librarian: Doz. Dr KONRAD MARWINSKI

Number of teachers: 320
Number of students: 12,600

Publications: *Jenaer Reden und Schriften, Mitteilungen der Thüringer Universitäts- und Landesbibliothek, Uni-Journal Jena, Forschungsmagazin.*

DEANS

Faculty of Theology: Prof. Dr MICHAEL TVOWITZSCH
Faculty of Law: Prof. Dr MONIKA SCHLACHTER
Faculty of Medicine: Prof. Dr GÜNTER STEIN
Faculty of Philosophy: Prof. Dr ANGELIKA GEYER
Faculty of Economics: Prof. Dr ROLF WALTER
Faculty of Mathematics and Computer Science: Prof. Dr BERND CARL
Faculty of Chemistry and Geosciences: Prof. Dr ROLAND MÄUSBACHER
Faculty of Biology and Pharmaceutics: Prof. Dr BERND LUCKAS
Faculty of Physics and Astronomy: Prof. Dr LUTZ WENKE
Faculty of Social and Behavioural Sciences: Prof. Dr RAINER K. SILBEREISEN

UNIVERSITÄT KAISERSLAUTERN

67663 Kaiserslautern, Erwin-Schrödinger-Str., Postfach 3049
Telephone: (631) 205-0
Telex: 04-5627
Fax: (631) 205-3200

Founded 1970 as Universität Trier Kaiserslautern, separated 1975
State control
Academic year: October to September

President: Prof. Dr phil. KLAUS LANDFRIED
Vice-Presidents: Prof. Dr phil. nat. WOLFGANG TROMMER, Prof. Dr-Ing. HARTMUT HOFRICHTER
Administrative Officer: STEFAN LORENZ
Librarian: Dipl.-Ing. DIETER JOHANNES

Number of teachers: 583
Number of students: 8,600

DEANS

Faculty of Mathematics: Prof. Dr GERT-MARTIN GREUEL
Faculty of Physics: Prof. Dr HANS-JÖRG JODL
Faculty of Chemistry: Prof. Dr WILFRIED MEYER
Faculty of Biology: Prof. Dr HELMUT SCHMIDT
Faculty of Mechanical Engineering: Prof. Dr-Ing. DETLEF ZÜHLKE
Faculty of Electrical Engineering: Prof. Dr-Ing. LOTHAR LITZ
Faculty of Architecture, Regional Planning and Civil Engineering: Prof. Dr-Ing. KLAUS WASSERMANN
Faculty of Computer Science: Prof. Dr MICHAEL RICHTER
Faculty of Social and Economic Sciences: Prof. Dr ROLF ARNOLD

PROFESSORS

Faculty of Mathematics:

BECKER, H., Mathematics
BRAKHAGE, H., Applied Mathematics
DEMPWOLFF, U., Mathematics
FRANKE, J., Stochastics
FREEDEN, W., Mathematics
GREUEL, G.-M., Topology
HAMACHER, H., Econometrics
LÜNEBURG, H., Mathematics
NEUNZERT, H., Mathematics
PFISTER, G., Computer Algebra
PRÄTZEL-WOLTERS, D., Mathematics
RADBRUCH, K., Mathematics, Teaching of Mathematics
SCHOCK, E., Applied Mathematics
SCHWEIGERT, D., Mathematics
TRAUTMANN, G., Pure Mathematics
v. WEIZÄCKER, H., Analysis

Faculty of Physics:

BERGMANN, K., Experimental Physics
DEMTRÖDER, W., Experimental Physics
EHRHARDT, H., Experimental and Applied Physics
FOUCKHARDT, H., Experimental Physics
HILLEBRANDS, B., Experimental Physics
HOTOP, H., Experimental Physics
JODL, H.-G., Teaching of Physics, Experimental Physics
KRÜGER, H., Theoretical Physics
KUPSCH, J., Theoretical Physics
LINDER, F., Experimental Physics
MÜLLER, V. F., Theoretical Physics
MÜLLER-KIRSTEN, H. J. W., Theoretical Physics
OECHSNER, H., Applied Physics
RÜHL, W., Theoretical Physics
SCHMORANZER, H., Experimental and Applied Physics
URBASSEK, H. M., Applied Physics
VANCURA, A., Theoretical Physics
WALLENSTEIN, R., Experimental and Applied Physics

Faculty of Chemistry:

BLUME, A., Physical Chemistry
EISENBRAND, G., Food Chemistry and Toxicology
ERNST, S., Technical Chemistry
FRANK, W., Inorganic Chemistry
HIMBERT, G., Organic Chemistry
KREITER, C., Inorganic Chemistry
KUBALL, H.-G., Physical Chemistry
METZLER, M., Food Chemistry and Toxicology
MEYER, W., Physical and Theoretical Chemistry
REGITZ, M., Organic Chemistry
SCHERER, O. J., Inorganic Chemistry
TROMMER, W., Organic Chemistry, Biochemistry
VILSMAIER, E., Organic Chemistry

Faculty of Biology:

ANKE, T., Biotechnology
BÄSSLER, U., Biology, Zoology
BÜDEL, D., Systematic Botany
CULLUM, J. A., Genetics
DEITMER, J. W., Zoology
FOCK, H., Botany
HAKENBECK, R., Microbiology
KAUSS, H., Botany
NAGL, W., Cell Biology
PFLUMM, W., Zoology
SCHMIDT, H., Physiological Ecology
ZANKL, H., Human Biology and Genetics

Faculty of Computer Science:

AVENHAUS, J., Algorithms
BRUNNETT, G., Computer-Aided Design, Computer Geometry
GOTZHEIN, R.
HÄRDER, T., Data Management Systems
HAGEN, H., Graphic Data Processing, Computer Geometry
HARTENSTEIN, R., Computers in Engineering
HEINRICH, S., Numeral Algorithms in Computer Science
MADLENER, K., Principles of Computer Science
MAYER, O., Principles of Programming and Computer Languages
MÜLLER, P., Integrated Communication Systems
NEHMER, J., Software Technology
v. PUTTKAMER, E., Process Computer Engineering
RICHTER, M., Artificial Intelligence
ROMBACH, D., Software Engineering
WIEHAGEN, R., Algorithmic Learning (Theory)
WIPPERMANN, H.-W., Programming Languages

ZIMMERMANN, G., VLSI — Design and Construction

Faculty of Mechanical Engineering:

BART, H.-J., Chemical Engineering
BROCKMANN, W., Materials and Surfaces Technology
DANKWORT, W., Computer-Aided Design
EBERT, F., Process Engineering
EIFLER, D., Materials Science
HABERLAND, R., Precision Engineering
HAHN, H. G., Mechanics
HELLMANN, D., Fluid Mechanics
MAURER, G., Thermodynamics
RENZ, R., Recyclability in Product Design and Disassembly
STEINHILPER, W., Machine Components
WARNECKE, G., Production Engineering, Labour Organization
WÜSTENBERG, D., Design and Manufacture of Machines and Apparatus
ZÜHLKE, D., Production Automation

Faculty of Electrical Engineering:

ACHILLES, D., Digital Signalling
BAIER, P. W., Principles of Electrical Engineering and High-frequency Transmission
BEISTER, J., Digital Technology
FREISE, W., High-voltage Engineering
HEINLEIN, W., Theoretical Electrical Engineering, Optical Telecommunications
KAHLEN, H., Electronic Performance, Electronics
LITZ, L., Automatic Control
NELLES, D., Electrical Energy Supply
PANDIT, M., Control Engineering, Signal Theory
RUPPRECHT, W., Public Telecommunications Engineering
TIELERT, R., Principles of Microelectronics
WEISS, P., High-voltage Engineering, Principles of Electrical Engineering
WENDT, S., Digital Systems
ZENGERLE, R., Theory of Electrical and Electronic Engineering, Optical Communications

Faculty of Architecture, Regional Planning and Civil Engineering:

BODE, H., Civil Engineering
BÖHM, W., Theory of Buildings and Design
DENNHARDT, H., Regional Planning
EISSLER, H., Architectural Design
ERMEL, H., Architectural Design
FRITZ, N., Structural Design and Planning
GÖPFERT, N., Statics of Rising Structures
HEINRICH, B., Building Physics and Equipment
HOFRICHTER, H., Architecture, History of Town Planning
KESPOHL, D., Building Materials and Testing of Materials
KISTENMACHER, H., Regional Planning
KOEHLER, G., Civil Engineering
MAHLER, K., Architectural Design
MEISSNER, H., Civil Engineering
MEYERSPEER, B., Industrial Construction I and Design
RAMM, W., Civil Engineering
RUMPF, G., Plastic Arts
SCHMITT, T. G., Water Management in Residential Areas
SEITZ, E., Room Design
SPANNOWSKY, W., Public Law
SPEER, A., Regional Planning
STICH, R., Public Law and Civil Engineering
STREICH, B., Computer-assisted Design and Construction
TOPP, H. H., Traffic Management
WASSERMANN, K., Civil Engineering
WITTEK, U., Civil Engineering
WÜST, H.-S., Landscaping

Faculty of Social and Economic Sciences:

ARNOLD, R., Education
BILLING, W., Politics
BLIEMEL, F., Business Management
CORSTEN, H., Business Administration, Production Economics
ENSTHALER, J., Business and Economic Law
FESER, H.-D., Economics and Economic Policy I
FRANZ, K.-P., Business Management, Accountancy
v. HAUFF, M., Economics and Economic Policy
HÖLSCHER, R., Finance and Investment
LANDFRIED, K., Politics
LAUX, J., Psychology
MÜLLER-MERBACH, H., Business Management
NEUSER, W., Philosophy
WEBER, H., Sociology
ZINK, K. J., Business Management

AFFILIATED INSTITUTES

Deutsches Forschungszentrum für Künstliche Intelligenz GmbH (DFKI) (Research Centre for Artificial Intelligence): Erwin-Schrödinger-Str. (Gebäude 57), Postfach 2080, 67663 Kaiserslautern; Dir (vacant).

Institut für Verbundwerkstoffe GmbH (IVW) (Institute for Composite Materials): Erwin-Schrödinger-Str., 67663 Kaiserslautern; Dir Prof. Dr-Ing. MANFRED NEITZEL.

Institut für Oberflächen- und Schichtanalytik GmbH (Institute for Surface and Coating Analysis): Erwin-Schrödinger-Str. (Gebäude 56), 67663 Kaiserslautern; Dir Prof. Dr rer. nat. HANS OECHSNER.

UNIVERSITÄT FRIDERICIANA KARLSRUHE

76128 Karlsruhe, Kaiserstr. 12
Telephone: 608-0
Telex: 721166
Fax: 0721-6084290

Founded 1825

The Universität Fridericiana (Technische Hochschule) was the first technical institute in Germany and the first to acquire university status

State control

Academic year: October to September

Rector: Prof. Dr SIGMAR WITTIG
Pro-Rectors: Prof. Dr MANFRED SCHNEIDER, Prof. Dr rer. nat. Dr rer. pol. WOLFGANG EICHHORN
Chancellor: Dr GERHARD SELMAYR
Librarian: Dipl.-Ing. CHRISTOPH-HUBERT SCHÜTTE

Number of teachers: 1,190
Number of students: 20,574

Publications: *Universitätsführer*, *Vorlesungsverzeichnis*, *Fridericiana*, *Uni-Information*, *Veröffentlichungsverzeichnis*, *Mitteilungsblatt*.

DEANS

Faculty of Mathematics: Prof. Dr rer. nat. C.-G. SCHMIDT
Faculty of Physics: Prof. Dr P. WÖLFLE
Faculty of Chemistry: Prof. Dr rer. nat. H.-J. KNÖLKER
Faculty of Biological and Geo-Sciences: Prof. Dr R. PAULSEN
Faculty of Art and Social Sciences: Prof. Dr phil. B. THUM
Faculty of Architecture: Prof. Dr M. KLINKOTL
Faculty of Construction Engineering: Prof. Dr-Ing. F. GEHHAUER
Faculty of Mechanical Engineering: Prof. Dr GÜNTER ERNST
Faculty of Chemical Engineering: Prof. Dr A. BRAUN
Faculty of Electrical Engineering: Prof. Dr H. SPÄTH
Faculty of Information Sciences: Prof. Dr rer. nat. H.-H. NAGEL
Faculty of Economics: Prof. Dr rer. nat. R. STUDER

PROFESSORS

Faculty of Mathematics:

ALEFELD, G., Applied Mathematics
BÜRGER, W., Theoretical Mechanics
FIEGER, W., Mathematical Stochastics
HENZE, N., Mathematical Stochastics
HERRLICH, F., Mathematis
HEUSER, H., Mathematics
KULISCH, U., Applied Mathematics
KUNLE, H., Mathematics, especially Geometry
MARTENSEN, E., Mathematics
NIETHAMMER, W., Practical Mathematics
SCHMIDT, C., Mathematics
SCHNEIDER, M., Mathematics
WALTER, W., Mathematics
WEIL, W., Mathematics

Faculty of Physics:

DORMANN, E., Experimental Physics
FIEDLER, F., Meteorology
FUCHS, K., Geophysics
HOLLIK, W., Theoretical Physics
HUBRAL, P., Applied Geophysics
HÜMMER, K., Crystallography
KLINGSHIRN, C., Applied Physics
KÜHN, J., Theoretical Physics
v. LÖHNEYSEN, H., Experimental Solid State Physics
SCHÖN, G., Theoretical Physics
SCHUBERT, K., Experimental Nuclear Physics
WEGENER, M., Applied Physics
WENZEL, F., Geophysics
WÖLFLE, P., Condensed Matter Physics
WÜHL, H., Experimental Nuclear Physics
ZEITNITZ, B., Experimental Nuclear Physics

Faculty of Chemistry:

ACHE, H. J., Instrumental, Analytic and Radio-Chemistry
AHLRICHS, R., Theoretical Chemistry
BALLAUF, M., Chemical Technology
BÄRNIGHAUSEN, H., Inorganic Chemistry II
BOCKHORN, H., Chemical Technology
EBERLE, Radiochemistry
FENSKE, D., Inorganic Chemistry
FREYLAND, W., Physical Chemistry I
HIPPLER, H., Physical Chemistry III
HIRSCH, A., Organic Chemistry
HÜTTINGER, K., Chemical Technology
KAPPES, M., Physical Chemistry II
KLÜFERS, Inorganic Chemistry
KNÖLKER, H.-W., Organic Chemistry I
RETEY, J., Biochemistry
SCHNÖCKEL, H., Analytical Chemistry
SCHRÖDER, G., Organic Chemistry II
WALDMANN, H., Organic Chemistry

Faculty of Biological and Geo-Sciences:

ALTHAUS, E., Mineralogy
BURGER, D., Mineralogy
CZURDA, K.-A., Geology
EISBACHER, G., Geology
HANKE, W., Zoology
HERRLICH, P., Genetics and Toxicology
HEUMANN, H.-G., Cytology
HÜTZL, H., Geology and Palaeontology
KILCHENMANN, A., Geography
KUHN, A., Applied Microbiology
LICHTENTALER, H., Botany
MEURER, M., Physical Geography
PAULSEN, R., Zoology
STUBEN, D., Geochemistry and Science of Deposits
WEISENSEEL, M., Botany and Pharmacology
WIRTHMANN, A., Geography
ZÖLLER, M., Applied Genetics
ZUMFT, W., Microbiology

Faculty of Arts and Social Sciences:

GLEITSMANN-TOPP, R.-J., History of Technology
GROSSKLAUS, G., Modern German Philology

GUTJAHR, O., Modern German Literary History
JAPP, U., Literature
KENNTNER, G., Sport
LENK, H., Philosophy
LILL, R., History
LIPSMEIER, A., Professional Education
PLEINES, J.-E., General Education and Philosophy
SCHÄFERS, B., Sociology
SCHULTE, H., Law

Faculty of Architecture:
EINSELE, M., Town Planning and Design
ERHARDT, H. M., Painting and Graphic Art
JANSON-WOLFRUM, A., Basic Architecture
KIENAST, D., Landscaping and Landscape Gardening
KOHLER, N., Industrial Building Construction
KRAMM, R., Building Construction and Design
LANGNER, J., History of Art
LEDERER, A., Building Construction and Design
NÄGELI, W., Building Planning and Design
SCHIRMER, W., History of Building
UHLIG, G., Housing
WENZEL, F., Building Construction

Faculty of Construction Engineering and Surveying:
BÄHR, H. P., Photogrammetry and Topography
BLASS, H. J., Timber Construction and Structural Theory
EIBL, J., Steel and Cement Construction
GEHBAUER, F., Machines in the Building Industry
GUDEHUS, G., Soil Mechanics and Foundation Construction
HAHN, H. H., Waterworks
HECK, B., Physical Satellite Geodesy
HEIDEMANN, C., Regional Sciences
HIERSCHE, E.-U., Road and Railway Construction
JIRKA, G., Fluid Mechanics
KÖHL, W., Town and Country Planning
LARSEN, P., Water Supply
MIERLO, J. VAN, Geodesy
NATAU, O., Rock Mechanics
NESTMANN, F., Waterworks
PLATE, E., Waterworks
SAAL, H., Steel and Light-metal Construction
SCHMITT, G., Mathematical and Data Processing
SCHWEIZERHOF, K., Mechanics
VIELSACK, P., Mechanics
WAGNER, W., Construction Statics
WINTER, J., Waste Management
ZUMKELLER, D., Transport

Faculty of Mechanical Engineering:
ARNOLD, D., Haulage
CACUCI, D., Nuclear Technology and Reactor Safety
ERNST, G., Technical Thermodynamics
GNADLER, R., Motor Vehicle Construction
GRABOWSKI, H., Use of Computers in Machine Construction
KUHN, P., General Machine Construction Technology
LÖHE, D., Raw Materials I
MENZ, W., Microstructure Technique
MESCH, F., Measurement and Regulation Techniques in Machine Construction and Operating Techniques
MUNZ, D., Reliability and Damage in Engineering
OERTEL, H., Hydrodynamics
SCHNACK, E., Technical Mechanics and Stability in Engineering
SPATH, D., Raw Materials II
SPATH, DIETER, Machine Tools and Factory Engineering
SPICHER, U., Combustion Engines
WEULE, H., Machine Tools and Factory Engineering
WITTENBURG, J., Technical Mechanics
WITTIG, S., Thermal Electric Machines
ZÜLCH, G., Industrial Science and Factory Organization
ZUM GAHR, K.-H., Raw Materials II

Faculty of Chemical Engineering:
BRAUN, A., Measurement Technology
BUGGISCH, N., Mechanical Engineering
FRIMMEL, F., Aquatic Chemistry
GRIESBAUM, K., Petrochemical and Organic Technology
LEUCKEL, W., Heating Technology
MARTIN, H., Thermal Process Engineering
OELLRICH, L., Refrigeration Technology
REIMERT, R., Petrochemical, Gas and Coal Technology
SCHABER, K., Technical Thermodynamics
SCHLÜNDER, E. U., Thermotechnics
SCHUBERT, H., Food Technology
STAHL, W., Mechanics

Faculty of Electrical Engineering:
BRAUN, M., Electric Drives and Power Electronics
GRAU, G. K., High Frequency Technique
HÄRDTL, K. H., Electrical Engineering
JONDRAL, F., Telecommunications Systems
JUTZI, W., Electronics in Computer Engineering
KIENCKE, U., Industrial Information Technology
KREBS, V., Regulation and Control Systems
MLYNSKI, D., Theoretical Electronic and Measuring Techniques
MÜLLER-GLASER, K., Information Processing Technology
POPP, H. P., Lighting
SCHWAB, A., Electrical Energy Systems, High-voltage Engineering
WIESBECK, W., High Frequency Technology

Faculty of Information Sciences:
BETH, TH., Algorithm Engineering and Data Systems
BRINKSCHULTE, U., Informatics
CALMET, Informatics
DEUSSEN, P., Deduction Systems
GOOS, G., Systems
GÖRKE, W., Fault-Tolerant Computer Systems
KRÜGER, G., Telematics
LOCKEMANN, P., Database and Information Systems
MENZEL, W., Logic, Program Verification and Complexity Theory
NAGEL, H. H., Pattern Recognition and Digital Image Evaluation
REMBOLD, U., Process Control and Autonomous Systems
SCHMID, D., Performance of Computer Systems and Design of VLSI Circuits
SCHMITT, A., Interactive Systems and Computer Graphics
SCHREINER, A., Organization of Datasystems
SCHWEIZER, G., Computerized Automation Systems
TICHY, W., Programming Systems
VOLLMAR, R., Computers in Engineering and Natural Sciences
WAIBEL, A., Knowledge- and Work-based Systems
WETTSTEIN, H., Operating Systems

Faculty of Economics:
BERNINGHAUS, S., Economics
BOL, Decision Theory
EGLE, Statistics
EICHHORN, W., Economics
FUNCK, R., Economics
GAUL, W., Industrial Management
GEMÜNDEN, G., Industrial Economics
GÖPPL, H., Industrial Management
HAMMER, G., Operations Research
HIPP, C., Insurance Science
KETTERER, K.-H., Finance and Currency Values
KNAUTH, P., Industrial Science
MORLOCK, M., Operations Research
NEUMANN, K., Operations Research
PALLASCHKE, D., Operations Research and Economic Theory
RENTZ, O., Industrial Economics
ROTHENGATTER, W., Economics
RUTSCH, M., Econometrics and Statistics
SCHMECK, H., Use of Computers in Economics
STUCKY, W., Applied Computer Sciences and Formal Description Methods
STUDER, R., Use of Computers in Economics
WALDMANN, K.-H., Information Economics

UNIVERSITÄT GESAMTHOCHSCHULE KASSEL

Präsidialverwaltung, 34109 Kassel, Mönchebergstr. 19

Telephone: (561) 8040
Fax: (561) 8042330
E-mail: aaa@hrz.uni-kassel.de

Founded 1971
State control
Language of instruction: German
Academic year: April to October, October to April (two terms)

President: Prof. Dr HANS BRINCKMANN
Vice-Presidents: Prof. Dr HERBERT HAF, Prof. HEIDE ANDRES-MÜLLER
Chancellor: Dr HANS GÄDEKE
Librarian: Dr HANS-JÜRGEN KAHLFUSS

Library of 1,300,000 books, 8,200 periodicals
Number of teachers: 380 professors
Number of students: 18,000

Publications: *Prisma* (2 a year), *GhK-Publik* (9 a year), *Preciosa Casselana und Studia Casselana*.

DEANS

Humanities and Education: Prof. Dr BEN BACHMAIR
Ergonomics, Vocational Education, Polytechnics: Prof. Dr KARLHEINZ FINGERLE
Psychology, Physical Education, Music: Prof. Dr KLAUS ZIMMERMANN
Social Sciences: Prof. Dr JENS FLEMMING
Social Work and Social Education: Prof. Dr FRIEDRICH ORTMANN
Philology, Romance, English and Anglo-American Studies: Prof. Dr INEZ DE FLORIO-HANSEN
Applied Social Sciences and Applied Law: Prof. Dr CLARITA MÜLLER-PLANTENBERG
Economics: Prof. Dr RAINER STÖTTNER
German Language and Literature: Prof. Dr HELMUT SCHEUER
Architecture: Prof. Dipl. Ing. ALEXANDER EICHENLAUB
Civil Engineering: Prof. Dr-Ing. HEINZ ZACKOR
Mechanical Engineering: Prof. Dr MARTIN LAWERENZ
Electrical Engineering: Prof. Dr-Ing. BERND WEIDEMANN
Mathematics: Prof. Dr KLAUS BARNER
Physics: Prof. Dr KLAUS RÖLL
Biology and Chemistry: Prof. Dr ULRICH KUTSCHERA
Agriculture, International Agricultural Development, Ecology and Environment: Prof. Dr ECKHARD BAUM
City and Landscape Planning: Prof. INGRID LÜBKE
Art: Univ.-Prof. FRIEDRICH SALZMANN
Visual Communication: Univ.-Prof. FLORIS M. NEUSÜSS
Product Design: Univ.-Prof. GERHARD FISCHER

ATTACHED INSTITUTES

Research Centre on Professional and University Education: Dir Prof. HANS-DIETER DANIEL.

Research Centre on Culture: Dir Prof. Dr JOHANNES WEISS.

Research Centre on Environmental Technology: Dir Prof. Dr JOSEPH ALCAMO.

CHRISTIAN-ALBRECHTS UNIVERSITÄT ZU KIEL

24098 Kiel
Telephone: (431) 88000
Telex: 29 26 56
Fax: (431) 880-2072

Founded 1665
State control
Academic year: October to July (two terms)

Rector: Prof. Dr RUPRECHT HAENSEL
Vice-Rectors: Prof. Dr REINHARD DEMUTH, Prof. Dr DIETER HARMS
Chancellor: HORST NEUMANN
Librarian: Dr GÜNTHER WIEGAND

Number of teachers: 600, incl. 430 full professors
Number of students: 23,000

Publications: *Personal- und Vorlesungsverzeichnis* (2 a year), *Christiana-Albertina* (2 a year), *Jahresbericht* (annually), *Universitätsreden* (irregular).

DEANS

Faculty of Theology: Prof. Dr theol. PETER LAMPE
Faculty of Law: Prof. Dr jur. HEIMO SCHACK
Faculty of Economics and Social Sciences: Prof. Dr jur. GÜNTER ENDRUWEIT
Faculty of Medicine: Prof. Dr med. HUBERTUS MAXIMILIAN MEHDORN
Faculty of Philosophy: Prof. Dr phil. BERNHARD SCHMALTZ
Faculty of Mathematics and Natural Sciences: Prof. Dr rer. nat. JÜRGEN BÄHR
Faculty of Agriculture: Prof. Dr sc. agr. Dr h.c. mult. ERNST KALM
Faculty of Engineering: Prof. Dr rer. nat. HELMUT FÖLL
Faculty of Education: Prof. Dr phil. WINFRIED ULRICH

PROFESSORS

Faculty of Theology:

BARTELMUS, R., Old Testament Studies, Biblical and Middle Eastern Languages
BECKER, J., New Testament
HÜBNER, U., Old Testament Studies and Biblical Archaeology
KRESS, R., Systematic Theology
LAMPE, P., New Testament
MECKENSTOCK, G., Systematic Theology
PREUL, R., Practical Theology
SCHILLING, J., Practical Theology
SCHMIDT-ROST, R., Practical Theology
SCHWÖBEL, C., Systematic Theology
STAATS, R., Church History and Dogma

Faculty of Law:

ALEXY, R., Public Law
DELBRÜCK, J., Public Law
ECKERT, J., History of German and European Law, Civil Law, Commercial Law
EINSELE, D., Civil Law, Commercial Law, Private International Law, Comparative Law
FROMMEL, M., Criminology, Criminal Law, Philosophy of Law and History of Law
HOFMANN, R., German and Foreign Public Law, International Law, European Law
HORN, E., Penal Law and Procedure, Philosophy of Law
IGL, G., Public Law, Social Law
JICKELI, J., Civil Law, Commercial Law
KREUTZ, P., Civil, Labour, Commercial and Economic Law
MUTIUS, A. VON, Public Law and Administration
REUTER, D., Civil, Commercial and Economic Law
ROTH, M., Civil Law, International Procedural and Business Law, Comparative Law
SAMSON, E., Penal Law and Procedure
SCHACK, H., International Civil Law, Private and Civil Trial Law, Copyright Law
SCHMIDT-JORTZIG, E., Public Law
SCHUBERT, W., Civil and Criminal Law
SONNENSCHEIN, J., Civil and Commercial Law
WAGNER, H., Penal Law and Procedure

Faculty of Economics and Social Sciences:

ALBERS, S., Industrial Economics
BROCKHOFF, K., Industrial Economics
CLAUSEN, L., Sociology
DREXL, A., Industrial Economics
ENDRUWEIT, G., Sociology
FRIEDL, B., Business Management
HANSEN, G., Econometrics
HAUSCHILDT, J., Industrial Economics
HERBERG, H., Political Economy
JECK, A., Theoretical Political Economics
KALTEFLEITER, W., History of Politics and Political Science
MITTNIK, S., Statistics
NIPPEL, P., Business Management
PROSI, G., Political Economy
RÖHRICH, W., Political Science
SEIDL, C., Political Economics
SIEBERT, H., Political Economics
VEIT, K.-R., Industrial Economics
WILLMS, M., Economic Structure
WOHLTMANN, H.-W., Political Economics

Faculty of Medicine:

ALBERS, H.-K., Dentistry
ALDENHOFF, J., Psychiatry, Psychotherapy
CHRISTOPHERS, E., Dermatology and Venereology
DECKER, W. DE, Ophthalmology
DEUSCHL, G., Neurology and Neurophysiology
FISCHER-BRANDIES, H., Tooth, Mouth and Jaw Medicine
FÖLSCH, U. R., Internal Medicine
GERBER, W.-D., Clinical Psychology
GIESELMANN, V., Biochemistry
GLÜER, C., Medicinal Physics
GROTE, W., Human Genetics
GUNDERMANN, K.-O., Hygiene and Health
HÄRLE, F., Dental Surgery
HARMS, D., General Pathology and Pathological Anatomy
HASSENPFLUG, J., Orthopaedics
HAVEMANN, D., Accident Surgery
HAVSTEEN, B., Physiological Chemistry
HELLER, M., Radiological Diagnosis
HENNE-BRUNS, D., Surgery
HENZE, E., Nuclear Medicine
HERDEGEN, T., Physiology, Molecular Pharmacology
ILLERT, U., Physiology
JONAT, W., Gynaecology and Obstetrics
KIMMIG, B. N., Clinical Radiology
KLÖPPEL, G., Pathology and Pathological Anatomy
KÖRBER, K., Dentistry
KOVÁCS, G., Radiotherapy
KRAMER, H.-H., Child Medicine, Child Cardiology
KREMER, B., Surgery
KRISCH, B., Anatomy
KRÖNKE, M., Immunology
LÖFFLER, H., Internal Medicine
MÁLYUSZ, M., Physiology
MEHDORN, H., Neurosurgery
METTLER, L., Obstetrics and Gynaecology
MÜLLER, M. J., Physiological Chemistry, Internal Medicine, Nutrition
NEPPERT, J., Clinical Immunology and Transfusion Medicine
NIEDERMAYER, W., Internal Medicine
NIELSEN, J. B., Physiology
PARWARESCH, R., Haematopathology
PLAGMANN, H.-CH., Dentistry
PROKSCH, E., Dermatology and Venereology
REGENSBURGER, D., Surgery
RIECKERT, H., Sports Medicine
ROCHELS, R., Eye Medicine
RUDERT, H., Oto-rhino-laryngology
SAUTER, K., Medical Informatics and Statistics
SCHAUB, J., Paediatrics
SCHAUER, R., Physiological Chemistry
SCHLEGELBERGER, B., Genetics
SCHMIDT, W. E., Internal Medicine
SCHMITT, H. J., Paediatrics
SCHRÖDER, J. M., Anatomy
SCHÜNKE, M., Anatomy
SCHÜTZE, G., Child and Adolescent Psychiatry
SEIFERT, J., Surgery
SIEVERS, J., Anatomy
SIMON, R., Cardiology
SPEIDEL, H., Psychotherapy and Psychosomatics
SPRENGER, E., General Pathology and Zytopathology
STEPHANI, U., Paediatrics, Neuropaediatrics
STÖCKLE, M., Urology
TILLMANN, B., Anatomy
ULLMANN, U., Medical Microbiology
UNGER, T., Pharmacology
WASSERMANN, O., Toxicology
WAWERSIK, J., Anaesthesiology
WOLF, J. H., History of Medicine
ZIEGLER, A., Molecular Pharmacology

Faculty of Philosophy:

BENZ, L., Classical Philology
BÖHM, R., English Philology
BRINKHAUS, H., Indology
BRINKMANN, W., Pedagogics
BUTTLAR, A. VON, Medieval and Modern Art History
DETERING, H., Modern German and Nordic Literature
DORMEIER, H., Medieval and Modern History
EICHINGER, L. M., German Philology
ENDRUWEIT, G., Sociology
ENGEL, A., Slavic Philology
FERSTL, R., Clinical Psychology
FLEISCHMANN, B., English Philology
FOUQUET, G., Economic and Social History
GÖTTSCH-ELTEN, S., Folklore
GROSS, K., English Philology
HAAG, H., Physical Education
HAARMANN, U., Oriental Philology
HAFFNER, A., Pre- and Early History
HAYE, T., Latin Philology
HELDMANN, K., Classical Philology
JANSSEN, J.-P., Sport Psychology
JAWORSKI, R., East European History
JONGEBLOED, H. C., Pedagogics
KAPP, V., Romance Philology
KERSTING, W., Philosophy
KÖHNKEN, G., Diagnostic and Differential Psychology
KOHLER, K., Phonetics
KONRADT, U., Industrial, Marketing and Organizational Psychology
KRUMMACHER, F., Music
KUDER, U., Art History
KULKE, H., Asiatic History
LARSSON, L. O., Art History
LINCK, G., Sinology
MAROLD, E., Old German, Nordic and Friesian Philology
MAUSFELD, R., Psychology
MEIER, A., Modern German Literature
MENKE, H., Low German and Dutch Philology
MOERKE, O., Early Modern and Modern History

Mosel, U., Linguistics
Müller-Oberhäuser, G., English Philology
Müller-Wille, M., Pre- and Early History
Nitsche, P., East European History
Petersen, J., Pedagogics
Rebas, H., Northern History
Riis, T., History of Schleswig-Holstein
Salewski, M., Medieval and Modern History
Schmaltz, B., Classical Archaeology
Schönfeldt, A., German Philology
Schwinge, E.-R., Classical Philology
Sommer, M., Philosophy
Sponheurer, B., Music
Teuber, B., Romance Philology
Thun, H., Romance Philology
Weiss, P., Ancient History
Wendt, D., Psychology
Wiesehöfer, J., Early History
Wode, H., English Philology
Wünsch, M., Modern German Literature

Faculty of Mathematics and Natural Sciences:

Achenbach, H., Geography
Adelung, D., Marine Zoology
Bähr, I., Geography
Bauer, T.
Bayrhuber, H., Teaching Methods of Biology
Bender, H., Mathematics
Bensch, W., Inorganic Chemistry
Bergweiler, W., Mathematics
Betten, D., Mathematics
Binding, H., Botany
Blaschek, W., Pharmaceutical Biology
Böger, H., Geology and Palaeontology
Böttger, K., Zoology
Brodowsky, H., Technical Chemistry
Carstensen, C., Mathematics
Cemič, L., Mineralogy and Petrology
Clement, B., Pharmaceutical Chemistry
Colijn, F., Coastal Ecology
Depmeier, W., Mineralogy and Crystallography
Dierssen, K., Botany
Dullo, W. C., Palaeo-Oceanography
Duphorn, K., Quaternary Geology
Flügel, H., Zoology
Fränzle, O., Geography
Götzky, M., Mathematics
Grootes, P., Experimental Physics, Isotope Research
Haensel, R., Experimental Physics
Hänsel, W., Pharmaceutical Chemistry
Hartl, G. B., Zoology
Hensler, G., Theoretical Physics
Hoernle, K., Vulcanology, Magmatic Petrology
Holweger, H., Astronomy and Theoretical Physics
Hormann, K., Geography
Imhoff, J., Marine Microbiology
Irle, A., Probability Theory and Mathematical Statistics
Jürgens, H. W., Anthropology
Kappen, L., Ecophysiology
Kern, H., Mineralogy and Petrography and Geochemistry
Klug, H., Geography
König, H., Mathematics
Koester, D., Astronomy and Astrophysics, Theoretical Physics
Kollmann, R., Botany
Koske, P., Practical Oceanography
Kruska, D., Zoology
Küppers, H., Crystallography
Kuhnt, W., Geology and Palaeontology
Lagaly, G., Inorganic Chemistry
Lemke, P., Meteorology
Lincke, R., Physics
Lüning, U., Organic Chemistry
Mattay, J. W., Organic Chemistry
Mayerle, R., Applied Coastal Geology
Milkereit, R., Geophysics
Müller, B., Pharmaceutical Technology
Müller, D., Mathematics
Piel, A., Experimental Physics
Pohl, P., Pharmaceutical Biology
Preetz, W., Inorganic Chemistry
Press, W., Experimental Physics
Rabbel, W., Geophysics
Ristow, D., Marine Geophysics
Rösler, U., Stochastics
Rohr, G. von, Geography
Rosenthal, H., Ichthyology
Rupprecht, E., Meteorology
Sarnthein-Lotichius, J. M., Geology and Palaeontology
Sauter, J., Botany
Schäfer, P., Geology
Schenk, V., Petrology and Mineralogy
Schiemenz, G. P., Organic Chemistry
Schlüter, D., Astrophysics
Schmidt, R., Mathematics
Schmincke, H.-U., Petrology of Ocean-Bed Rock Strata
Schnack, D., Ichthyology
Schönheit, P., Microbiology
Schott, F., Physical Oceanography
Schuster, H. G., Theoretical Physics
Siedler, G., Geophysics
Skibowski, M., Experimental Physics
Soll, J., Botany
Sommer, U., Sea-Floor Ecology
Spindler, M., Polar Ecology
Stattegger, K., Geology and Palaeontology
Stellmacher, B., Mathematics
Stoffers, P., Geology
Suess, E., Marine Environmental Geology
Temps, F., Physical Chemistry
Thiede, J., Geology
Thomm, M., Microbiology
Tochtermann, W., Organic Chemistry
Uhlarz, H., Botany
Ullerich, F.-H., General Zoology
Wagner, F., Theoretical Physics
Willebrandt, J., Oceanography
Wünnenberg, W., Zoology
Zeitzschel, B., Oceanography

Faculty of Agriculture:

Alvensleben, R. von, Agrarian Marketing
Blume, H.-P., Soil Science
Ebersdobler, H., Physiology, Physiological Chemistry, Nutrition Physiology
Hanf, C.-H., Agricultural Economics
Hanus, H., Agriculture
Hesse, K., Home Economics
Horn, R., Soil Science and Cultivation of Soil
Isensee, E., Plant Production
Jung, Ch., Plant Cultivation
Kalm, E., Animal Husbandry and Genetics
Koester, U., Agricultural Economics
Kollmann, R., Botany
Langbehn, C., Agricultural Economics
Müller, R., Agricultural Economics
Roweck, H., Landscape Ecology
Sattelmacher, B., Plant Feeding
Schallenberg, E., Animal Ownership
Scheper, W., Commercial Politics
Susenbeth, A., Animal Nutrition
Taube, F., Crop Cultivation
Verreet, J.-A., Phytopathology
Widmoser, P., Water Conservation
Wyss, U., Phytopathology

Faculty of Engineering:

Berghammer, R., Computer-aided Programme Development
Brocks, W., Materials Science
Brokate, M., Numerical Mathematics
Carstensen, C., Arithmetic
Dirks, H., General and Theoretical Electrical Engineering
Faupel, F., Composite Materials
Föll, H., Material Science
Fuchs, F. W., Electronics and Electrical Drives
Hackbusch, W., Practical Mathematics
Heuberger, A., Semiconductor Technology
Heute, U., Network and Systems Theory
Jäger, W., Microstructural Analysis
Jammel, A., Computer Science
Kandzia, P., Computer Science
Kluge, W., Computer Science
Knöchel, R., High-frequency Engineering
Langmaack, H., Computer Science
Röck, H., Control and Automation Engineering
Roever, W. P. de, Computer Science, Software Technology
Rosenkranz, W., Telecommunications and Transmission Engineering
Seegebrecht, P.
Sommer, G., Cognitive Systems Information
Thomas, W., Computer Science
Weppner, W., Solid-state Engineering

Faculty of Education:

Bauhoff, E. P., Teaching of Mathematics
Berge, O. E., Teaching of Physics
Biesterfeld, W., Teaching of German Literature
Biller, K., Education
Bodendiek, R., Teaching of Mathematics
Borchert, J., Remedial Education
Bruhn, H., Teaching of Music
Burgmer, M., Teaching of Engineering
Dahncke, H., Teaching of Physics
Dall'asta, E., Politics
Demuth, R., Teaching of Chemistry
Detering, K., Teaching of English
Etschenberg, K., Teaching of Biology
Gerling, M., Psychology
Haas, R., Teaching of English Language and Literature
Härtel, W., Teaching of Engineering
Hameyer, U., Education
Hanisch, M., Teaching of History
Hassenpflug, W., Teaching of Geography
Heidtmann, H., Special Education
Klemenz, D., Education
Klippstein, E., Psychology
Konersmann, R., Teaching of Philosophy
Korte, M., Teaching of Art
Krope, P., Education
Kruber, K.-P., Economics, Politics
Kürzdörfer, K., Teaching of Protestant Theology
Küttel, H., German
Müller, G., Teaching of German
Newig, J., Teaching of Geography
Niemann, F. J., Teaching of Catholic Theology
Pallasch, W., Education
Pohl, K. H., Teaching of History
Prahl, H.-W., Sociology
Schumacher, H., Teaching of Mathematics
Sielert, U., General Education
Spengler, U., Teaching of Mathematics
Spiess, W., Remedial Education
Steinhagen, K., Psychology
Strank, W., German
Tucholski-Däke, B.-C., Teaching of Art
Ulrich, W., German
Walburg, W.-R., Remedial Education
Walter, J., Special Education
Walther, G., Teaching of Mathematics
Wiechmann, J., Education

ATTACHED INSTITUTES

Institut für die Pädagogik der Naturwissenschaften an der Universität Kiel (Institute for Science Education): 24098 Kiel; Dir Prof. Dr H. Bayrhuber.

Institut für Meereskunde an der Universität Kiel (Institute of Marine Sciences): 24105 Kiel, Düsternbrooker Weg 20; Dir Prof. Dr F. Schott.

Institut für Weltwirtschaft (Institute for World Economics): 24105 Kiel, Düsternbrooker Weg 120; Pres. Prof. Dr H. Siebert.

Lorenz-von-Stein-Institut für Verwaltungswissenschaften (Lorenz von Stein Institute for Management Sciences): 24098 Kiel; Dir Prof. Dr von Mutius.

Max-Planck-Institut für Limnologie zu Plön (Max-Planck Institute of Limnology): see under Research Institutes.

Institut für Sicherheitspolitik an der Universität Kiel (Institute of Security Studies): 24098 Kiel; Dir Prof. Dr W. KALTEFLEITER.

Schleswig-Holsteinisches Institut für Friedenswissenschaften an der Christian-Albrechts-Universität Kiel (SCHIFF) (Schleswig Holstein Institute for Peace Studies): 24143 Kiel; Dir Prof. Dr K. POTTHOFF.

Forschungzentrum für Marine Geowissenschaften (GEOMAR) (Research Centre for Maritime Earth Sciences): 24148 Kiel; Dir Prof. Dr E. SUESS.

WISSENSCHAFTLICHE HOCHSCHULE FÜR UNTERNEHMENSFÜHRUNG, OTTO-BEISHEIM-HOCHSCHULE (Koblenz School of Corporate Management, Otto Beisheim Graduate School)

56179 Vallendar, Burgplatz 2

Telephone: (261) 6509-0
Fax: (261) 6509111
E-mail: info@whu-koblenz.de

Founded 1984
Private control
Languages of instruction: German, English
Academic year: September to May

Rector: Prof. Dr MICHAEL FRENKEL
Vice-Rector: Prof. Dr HORST G. CARUS
Librarian: HANNELORE STRAUB

Library of 26,000 vols
Number of teachers: 14 full-time, 20 part-time
Number of students: 260

PROFESSORS

ALBACH, H., International Management
CARUS, H., Corporate Policy
DUFEY, G., International Corporate Finance
FISCHER, T., Information Technology
FRENKEL, M., Economics II
HOMBURG, C., Marketing
HUCHZERMEIER, A., Energy, Materials, Production and Environment
JACOB, A.-F., Financial and Banking Management
JOST, P.-J., Organization and Management
ROSE, K., Economics I
WEBER, J., Control and Logistics

DEUTSCHE SPORTHOCHSCHULE KÖLN

50933 Köln, Carl-Diem-Weg 6

Telephone: (221) 4982-1
Fax: (221) 4971782

Founded 1920 in Berlin, reopened in Cologne 1947
State control
Academic year: October to March, April to September

Rector: Prof. Dr JOACHIM MESTER
Chancellor: Dr E. RESCHKE
Librarian: K.-H. LEMKE

Number of teachers: 230
Number of students: 6,672

DEANS

Faculty of Education, Humanities and Social Sciences: Prof. Dr WALTER TOKARSKI
Faculty of Medicine and Natural Sciences: Prof. HANS-JOACHIM APPELL
Faculty of Didactics and Methods in Sport: Prof. Dr RALF ERDMANN

UNIVERSITÄT ZU KÖLN

50931 Köln, Albertus-Magnus-Platz

Telephone: (221) 4701
Telex: 08 882 281
Fax: (221) 4705151

Founded 1388

Rector Magnificus: Prof. Dr Phil. BERNHARD KÖNIG
Pro-Rectors: Prof. Dr JENS PETER MEINCKE, Prof. Dr PETER MITTELSTAEDT, Prof. Dr CARL AUGUST LÜCKERATH
Chancellor: Dr jur. JOHANNES NEYSES
Librarian: Dr HANS LIMBURG

Number of teachers: 1,981
Number of students: 54,000

DEANS

Faculty of Economics and Social Sciences: Prof. Dr KARL-HEINZ HANSMEYER
Faculty of Law: Prof. Dr PETER WEIDES
Faculty of Medicine: Prof. Dr WALTER THÜSSMANN
Faculty of Philosophy: Prof. Dr WOLF-DIETRICH BALD
Faculty of Mathematics and Natural Sciences: Prof. Dr MICHAEL MELKONIAN
Faculty of Education: Prof. Dr HANS-RUDOLF BECHER
Faculty of Special Education and Therapy: Prof. Dr HANS-GÜNTHER RICHTER

PROFESSORS

Faculty of Economics and Social Sciences:

ANDEREGG, R. G., Political Economy
ANGER, H., Economic Psychology
BAUM, H., Political Economy
BEUERMANN, G., Economics
BIHN, W. R., Statistics and Economics
BÖSSMANN, E., Political Economy
BÜSCHGEN, H. E., Economics
DELFMANN, W., Economics
DERIGS, U., Economics
DÖRSCHEL, A., Economic Pedagogics
DONGES, J., Economics
ELLINGER, T., Economics
ENGELHARDT, W. W., Social Politics
FARNY, D., Insurance
FELDERER, B., Political Economy
FELDSIEPER, M., Political Economy
FRESE, E., Economics
FRIEDRICHS, J., Sociology
GLÄSSER, E., Economic Geography
GUTMANN, G., Political Economy
HANSMEYER, K.-H., Political Economy
HAX, H., Economics
HENNING, F.-W., Economic and Social History
HERDER-DORNEICH, PH., Social Politics
HERMENS, F. A., Political Science
KAISER, K., Political Science
KERN, W., Economics
KLEIN-BLENKERS, F., Economics
KLOOCK, J., Economics
KÖHLER, R., Economics
KÖNIG, R., Social Sciences
KOPPELMANN, U., Economics
LINK, W., Political Science
MACKSHEIDT, K., Political Economy
MANN, G., Economics
MATZ, U., Political Science
RETTIG, R., Economics
ROSE, G., Economics
SAVRAMIS, D., Sociology
SCHÄFFER, K.-A., Economic and Social Statistics
SCHEFFLER, W., Economics
SCHEUCH, E. K., Sociology
SCHIRMMEISTER, R., Economics
SCHMIEL, M., Business Studies
SCHMITT, K., Political Economy
SCHMITZ, P., Information Science
SCHMÖLDERS, G., State Economics
SCHNEIDER, H. K., Political Economics
SEIBT, D., Information Science and Economics
SIEBEN, G., Economics
SILBERMANN, A., Sociology
STRATENWERTH, W., Economic and Social Pedagogics
STÜDEMANN, K., Economics
SUNDHOFF, E., Economics
TWARDY, M., Economic and Social Pedagogics
VOPPEL, G., Economic Geography
WATRIN, CH., Political Economics
WEEDE, E., Sociology
WEIZSÄCKER, C. C. VON, State Science
WIED-NEBBELING, S., State Science
WIENDIECK, G., Economics and Social Psychology
WILLEKE, R., Political Economy
WILLGERODT, H., Political Economy
WISWEDE, G., Economic Psychology
ZERCHE, J., Social Politics
ZUNKEL, F., Economic and Social History

Faculty of Law:

BAUMGÄRTEL, G., German and International Civil Law
BAUR, J. F., Civil Law, Economic Law, European Law
BERNSMANN, K., Penal Law
BÖCKSTIEGEL, K.-H., International and Constitutional Law, German and International Economic Law
BÖRNER, B., Civil Law, Economic Law
BRINKMANN, K., Philosophy of Law
BRUNNER, G., Public Law, General State Law and East German Law
FASTENRATH, K., Public Law, Law of Nations
FRIAUF, H. H., State and Administration Law, Financial Law and Law of Taxation
FROST, H., Church Law, General State Law, Philosophy of Law
HANAU, P., Labour and Economic Law
HEPTING, R., Civil Law, International Private Law, International Civil Law and Comparative Law
HIRSCH, H.-J., Penal Law, Process Law, Philosophy of Law
HORN, N., Civil Law, German and International Commercial, Economic and Banking Law
HÜBNER, H., Civil Law, Commercial Law, Roman Law
HÜBNER, U., Civil Law
JAHRREISS, H., Public Law, Law of Nations
KEGLL, G., International Law
KLINGMÜLLER, E., Insurance Law, Civil Law, Commercial Law
KLUG, U., Penal Law, Penal Process Law, Philosophy of Law
KOHLMANN, G., Penal Law, Philosophy of Law
KRIELE, M., Philosophy of Law and Public Law
KRÜGER, H., Public Law
LANG, J., Taxation Law, Public Law
LANGE, R., Penal Law, Penal Process Law
LIEB, M., Civil and Labour Law
LÜDERITZ, A., Civil Law
LUIG, K., Civil Law, Roman Law
MEINCKE, J. P., Civil Law, Roman Law, Law of Taxation
MEISSNER, B., East European Law
OEHLER, D., Penal Law, Penal Process Law, Foreign and International Penal Law, Protestant Church Law
PLEYER, K., Civil, Commercial and Labour Law
PRÜTTING, H., Civil Law
RÜFNER, W., Public Law, Church Law
SCHIEDERMAIR, H., Public Law, Law of Nations, Philosophy of Law
SCHMITT-KAMMLER, A., State and Administrative Law
STERN, K., State and Administration Law
STRAUCH, D., Civil Law
TIPKE, K., Law of Taxation

WACKE, A., Roman Law, Civil Law
WAIDER, H., Penal Law, Philosophy of Law, Catholic Church Law
WALTER, M., Penal Law
WEIDES, P., Public Law
WEIGEND, T., Penal Law, Penal Process Law, Foreign and International Penal Law
WIEDEMANN, H., Labour Law, Commercial and Economic Law

Faculty of Medicine:

ABEL, M., Anaesthesiology
ACKERMANN, R., Neurology and Psychiatry
ADDICKS, K., Anatomy
BALDAMUS, C., Internal Medicine
BAUER, P., Medical Documentation and Statistics
BISTER, K., Biological Chemistry
BÖRNER, U., Anaesthesiology
BOLTE, A., Obstetrics and Gynaecology
BONHOEFFER, K., Anaesthesiology
DE BOOR, W., Neurology and Psychiatry
BRESSER, P. H., Neurology and Psychiatry
BRUNS, W., Pharmacology
BUZELLO, W., Anaesthesiology
DEBUCH, H., Physiological Chemistry
DIEHL, V., Internal Medicine
EGGERS, H. J., Virology
EIFINGER, F., Dentistry
ENGELKING, R., Urology
FISCHER, R., General Pathology and Pathological Anatomy
FRICKE, U., Pharmacology and Toxicology
FRIEDMANN, G., Clinical Radiology
FROWEIN, R., Neurosurgery
GIBBELS, E., Neurology and Psychiatry
GIELEN, W., Physiological Chemistry
GLADTKE, E., Paediatrics
HACKENBROCH, M. H., Orthopaedics
HADJIANGHELOU, O., Jaw and Facial Surgery
HAMACHER, J., Pharmacology and Toxicology
HAUSMANN, M. L., Pathology
HEIMANN, K., Ophthalmology
HEINEMANN, U., Normal and Pathological Physiology
HEINISCH, H.-M., Paediatrics
HEISS, W.-D., Neurology and Psychiatry
HENSSGE, C., Forensic Medicine
HILGER, H.-H., Internal Medicine
HIRCHE, H., Physiology
HÖPP, H.-W., Internal Medicine
HÜGEL, W., Thorax and Cardiovascular Surgery
ISENBERG, G., Normal and Pathological Physiology
ISSELHARD, W., Experimental Surgery
JETTER, D., History of Medicine
KAISER, R., Gynaecology
KARIMI-NEJAD, A., Neurosurgery
KAUFMANN, W., Internal Medicine
KERSCHBAUM, TH., Dentistry
KLAUS, W., Pharmacology and Toxicology
KLEIN, H. O., Internal Medicine
KLUG, N., Neurosurgery
KLUSSMANN, F., Physiology
KOEBKE, J., Anatomy
KÖHLE, K., Psychosomatic Medicine
KONEK, W., Ophthalmology
KRIEGLSTEIN, G., Ophthalmology
KRÜGER, G., General Pathology and Pathological Anatomy
KRÜGER, J., Immunology
KUMMER, B., Anatomy
LECHLER, E., Internal Medicine
LEHMANN, K., Anaesthesiology
LEHMKUHL, G., Child and Adolescent Psychiatry
LOESCHKE, G., Anaesthesiology
MACHLEIDT, W., Psychiatry
MAHRLE, G., Dermatology
MAUFF, G., Hygiene and Microbiology
MENNICKEN, U., Children's Cardiology
MERK, H., Dermatology and Venerology
MICHALK, D., Paediatrics
MÜLLER, R.-P., Radiology
NEISS, W. F., Anatomy
NITTNER, K., Neurosurgery
OETTE, K., Clinical Chemistry
PAPE, H.-D., Dental Surgery
PETERS, U.-H., Neurology and Psychiatry
PICHLMAIER, H., Surgery
PIEKARSKI, C., Industrial Medicine
PULVERER, G., Hygiene and Microbiology
PUTSCHER, M., History of Medicine
REHM, K. E., Surgery and Accident Surgery
ROTH, B., Paediatrics
RÜSSMANN, W., Ophthalmology
SCHICHA, H., Nuclear Medicine
SCHMIDT, J. G. H., Ophthalmology
SCHRÖDER, R., Neuropathology
SCHWARZE, C., Dentistry
SICKEL, W., Normal and Pathological Physiology
STAAK, M., Forensic Medicine
STAMMLER, A., Neurology and Psychiatry
STENNERT, E., Otolaryngology
STOFFEL, W., Physiological Chemistry
STURM, V., Neurosurgery
STURZ, J., Experimental Surgery
THIELE, J., Pathology
THUMFART, W. F., Otolaryngology
TROIDL, H., Surgery
UHLENBRUCK, G., Immunobiology
DE VIVIE, E. R., Thorax- and Cardio-Surger
VOSS, R., Dental Prosthetics
WEIDTMAN, V., Medical Documentation and Statistics
WINKELMANN, W., Internal Medicine

Faculty of Philosophy:

ALEXANDER, M., History
ANGERMANN, E., Anglo-American History
ANGERMEIER, W. F., Psychology
BALD, W.-D., Applied Linguistics
BIEG, L., Sinology
BINDING, G., Art History and Urban Conservation
BIRWÉ, R., Indian Philology
BONHEIM, H., Anglo-American Philology
BORK, H.-D., Romance Philology
BORMANN, K., Philosophy
BORSE, U., Catholic Theology
BOSINSKI, G., Prehistory and Early History
BRINCKEN, A. VON DER, History (Medieval)
BUCK, E., Theatre, Film and Television Studies
BUMKE, J., German Philology
BURIAN, P., History (Medieval and Modern)
CLAESGES, U., Philosophy
CONRADY, K. O., Modern German Literature
DÄMMER, H.-W., Prehistory and Early History
DANN, O., Modern History
DERCHAIN, PH., Egyptology
DIEM, W., Oriental Philology
DOMBRADY, G. S., Japanese Philology
DÜLFFER, F., Modern History
DÜSING, K., Philosophy
ECK, W., Ancient History
ELEY, L., Philosophy
ENGELS, O., Medieval and Modern History
ERICKSON, JON, Applied Linguistics
FALATURI, A., Islam Studies
FELDMANN, H., Romance Philology
FRICKE, J., Musicology
FRISCH, P., Classical Philology
FUNKE, F., Ethnology
GAUS, J., History of Art
GERMER, R., English Philology
GIMM, M., Sinology and Manchurian Philology
GOMPF, L., Middle Latin Philology
GÖRLACH, M., English Philology
GÖTZ, M., Islam Studies
GRAEVENITZ, A. VON, Art History
GREIVE, A., Romance Philology
GROENKE, U., Nordic and Finnish Philology
GRONEWALD, M., Classical Philology
GROOTHOFF, H.-H., Pedagogy
GRZESIK, J., Pedagogy
GÜNTHER, R., Musicology
HAUPTS, L., Modern History
HEIKE, G., Phonetics
HEINE, B., African Studies
HERRMANN, H.-V., Archaeology
HESBERG, H. VON, Classical Archaeology
HILGENHEGER, N., Pedagogy
HINCK, W., Modern German Language and Literature
HÜSCHEN, H., Musicology
HUSSY, W., Psychology
IRMSCHER, H. D., History of Modern German Literature
JANERT, K.-L., Indology
JANSSEN, P., Philosophy
JOHANSEN, U., Ethnology
KAEGBEIN, P., Library Science
KAHLE, G., Medieval and Modern History
KAPPELER, A., East European History
KASACK, W., Slavonic Literatures
KASSEL, R., Classical Philology
KELLER, W., Modern German Literature
KIRCHHOFF, R., Psychology
KLEIN, TH., German Philology
KNABE, P.-E., Romance Philology
KÖHLER, O., African Studies
KOLB, E., Medieval and Modern History
KÖNIG, B., Romance Philology
KRENTZER, G., Nordic Philology
KRÖNIG, W., Art History
KUNISCH, J., Medieval and Modern History
LADENDORF, H., Art History
LANDGREBE, L., Philosophy
LANGE, G., German Philology
LANGOSCH, K., Middle Latin Philology
LEBEK, W. D., Classical Philology
LEHMANN, G. A., Ancient History
LENERZ, J., German Philology
LINFERT, A., Classical Archaeology
LINKE, H., German Philology
MAIER, J., Hebraic Studies
MENZE, C., Pedagogy
MERKELBACH, R., Classical Philology
MEUTHEN, E., Medieval and Modern History
MÖHLIG, W., African Studies
MÖHRMANN, R., Theatre, Film and Television Studies
MÜLLER-BOCHAT, E., Romance Philology
NAGEL, W., Near East Studies
NEUHAUS, V., Modern German and Comparative Literature
NIEMÖLLER, K. W., Musicology
NIERMANN, J., Pedagogy
OBST, U., Slavonic Literatures
ÖNNERFORS, A., Middle Latin Philology
OST, H., Art History
PAPE, W., German Philology
PIEL, J., Romance Philology
RATHOFER, J., German Philology
ROELLENBLECK, G., Romance Philology
ROLSHOVEN, J., Philological and Linguistic Computing
RUBIN, B., Byzantine Studies
RÜPPELL, H., Pedagogy
SALBER, W., Psychology
SASSE, H.-J., Comparative Linguistics
SCHARPING, T., Sinology
SCHIEFFER, T., Medieval and Modern History
SCHMIDT, H., Musicology
SCHMIDT-DENTER, U., Psychology
SCHREINER, P., Byzantine Studies
SCHÜTZ, E., Pedagogy
SCHWARTE, K.-H., Ancient History
SCHWEIZER, G., Geography
SEILER, H., Comparative Linguistics
SORETH, M., Philosophy
SOWINSKI, B., German Philology
STEPHAN, E., Psychology
STRÖKER, E., Philosophy
TAUCHMANN, K., Common Ethnology
TAUTE, W., Pre-History
VAN THIEL, H., Classical Philologyy
TSCHOHL, P., Ethnology
UNDEUTSCH, U., Psychology
UNTERMANN, J., Comparative Linguistics

VATER, H., German Philology
VEKEMAN, H., Dutch Philology
VIVIAN, A., Hebraic Studies
VOLLRATH, E., Philosophy
VOSSKAMP, W., Modern German Literature
WEIHER, E. VON, Ancient Oriental Philology
WENTZLAFF-EGGEBERT, C., Romance Philology
WERNER, M., History
WIENBRUCH, U., Philosophy
WOLLMANN, A., Applied Linguistics and English Philology
WREDE, H., Classical Archaeology
WÜLFING, P., Classical Philology
WÜRZBACH, N., English Philology
ZAHRNT, M., Old History
ZICK, G., Art History
ZIMMERMANN, A., Philosophy
ZIMMERMANN, R. C., Modern German Literature
ZINTZEN, C., Classical Philology

Faculty of Mathematics and Natural Sciences:

ALEXANDER, H., Metallurgy
ANTON, H. J., Zoology
ARMBRUST, M., Mathematics
BACHEM, A., Applied Mathematics
BAUDLER, M., Inorganic and Analytical Chemistry
BAZLEY, N. W., Mathematics
BERGMANN, L., Botany
BESLER, H., Geography
BISCHOFF, G., Geology
BOTHE, H., Botany
BREMER, H., Geography
BRENTANO, P. VON, Experimental Physics
BRUNNACKER, K., Study of the Ice Ages
BRUNOTTE, E., Geography
BUDZIKIEWICZ, H., Organic Chemistry
BUNDSCHUH, P., Mathematics
CAMPOS-ORTEGA, J. A., Developmental Physiology
DAMBACH, M., Zoology
DIETZ, G., Physics
DOERFLER, W., Genetics
DOMBROWSKI, P., Mathematics
DOST, M., Physics
EBEL, A., Geophysics
EBERHARDT, W., Physics
EGELHAAF, A., Zoology
EHHALT, D. H., Geophysics
EHRING, R., Genetics
EILENBERGER, G., Theoretical Physics
ENGLÄNDER, H., Zoology
ERMER, O., Organic Chemistry
FAUTZ, B., Geography
FEHER, F., Inorganic Chemistry
FOLLMANN, G., Geobotany
GELBERG, A., Physics
GRIMME, W., Organic Chemistry
GRUHLE, W., Physics
HAJDU, J., Theoretical Physics
HAPP, H., Experimental Physics
HAUSEN, K., Zoology
HAUSER, U., Experimental Physics
HAUSSÜHL, S., Crystallography
HEHL, F., Theoretical Physics
HENKE, W., Mathematics
HERRMANN, M., Mathematics
HETZEL, W., Geography
HOHLNEICHER, G., Theoretical Chemistry
HUMMEL, D., Physical Chemistry
ILGENFRITZ, G., Physical Chemistry
JAENICKE, L., Biochemistry
JAHRREISS, H., Physics
JEHNE, W., Mathematics
JOHNEN, A. G., Zoology
JUX, U., Palaeontology
KAUPP, U., Biophysical Chemistry
KEMPER, B., Genetics and Genetic Technology
KEMPF, E. K., Geology
KLEINOW, W., Animal Physiology
KNESER, H., Genetics of Micro Organisms
KNUST, E., Developmental Physiology
KRUCK, TH., Inorganic Chemistry
KRUMSIEK, K., Geology
KÜPPER, T., Mathematics
LAMOTKE, K., Mathematics
LANDERS, D., Mathematics
LANGE, H., Mathematics
LEGLER, G., Biochemistry
LIEBERTZ, J., Crystallography
LIPOWSKY, R., Theoretical Physics
MEIS, TH., Mathematics
MELKONIAN, M., Botany
MITTELSTAEDT, P., Theoretical Physics
MÜHLSCHLEGEL, B., Theoretical Physics
MÜLLER, J., Developmental Physiology
MÜLLER-HARTMANN, E., Theoretical Physics
MÜLLER-HILL, B., Genetics
NAPP-ZINN, K., Botany
NAUMANN, D., Inorganic and Analytical Chemistry
NEUBAUER, F. M., Geophysics and Meteorology
NEUMANN, D., Zoology and Physiological Ecology
NEUWIRTH, W., Physics
NIMTZ, G., Physics
NIPPER, J., Geography
PAETZ GEN. SCHIECK, H., Physics
PFANZAGL, J., Mathematics
POHLEY, H.-J., Developmental Physiology
RADBRUCH, A., Genetics
RAJEWSKY, K., Molecular Genetics
RAMMENSEE, W., Mineralogy
RECKZIEGEL, H., Mathematics
REZNIK, H., Botany
RISTIG, M., Theoretical Physics
SCHLICHTER, D., Zoology
SCHMITZ, K., Botany
SCHNEIDER, C., Physical Chemistry
SCHNEIDER, P., Mathematics
SCHNEIDER-POETSCH, HJ., Botany
SCHRADER, R., Applied Mathematics
SCHRÖDER, J., Applied Mathematics
SCHULT, O., Nuclear Physics
SCHUSTER, H.-U., Inorganic Chemistry
SCHWEIZER, G., Geography
SECK, H. A., Mineralology
SEIDEL, E., Geochemistry
SPETH, P., Geophysics
STARLINGER, P., Genetics and Radiation Biology
STAUFFER, D., Theoretical Physics
STÖCKLIN, G., Nuclear Chemistry
STUTZKI, J., Physics
SWODENK, W., Technical Chemistry
TEBBE, K.-T., Inorganic Chemistry
TOPP, W., Zoology
TROTTENBERG, U., Applied Mathematics
VAHS, W., Zoology
VIELMETTER, W., Genetics and Microbiology
VOGEL, E., Organic Chemistry
VOLL, G., Mineralogy and Petrography
WALKOWIAK, W., Zoology
WASGESTIAN, F., Theoretical Inorganic Chemistry
WEISSENBÖCK, G., Botany
WENDLER, G., Zoology, Animal Physiology
WERNER, D., Geography
WILLE, W., Genetics
WILLENBRINK, J., Botany
WINNEWISSER, G., Experimental Physics
WOERMANN, D., Physical Chemistry
WOHLLEBEN, D., Applied Physics
WOPFNER, H., Geology
ZINN, W., Experimental Physics
ZIRNBAUER, M., Theoretical Physics
ZITTARTZ, J., Theoretical Physics

Faculty of Education:

ANACKER, U., General Pedagogy
ANGERMAIER, M., Psychology
ARNDT, H., English Linguistics
BAHRO, H., Political Science
BANNWARTH, H., Biology Teaching
BARTELS, G., Geography
BECHER, H.-R., General Education and Secondary Teaching
BERG, CH., General Education
BRAUN, E., Philosophy
BRICKENKAMP, R., Psychology
BRILLA, G., Human Biology
BROSSEDER, J., Catholic Theology
BURSCHEID, H. J., Mathematics
CHRIST, G., History of Rhineland
DIERS, L., Biology
DRÜE, H., Psychology
EFFERTZ, F. H., Physics
ESSER, H., Biology
FRESLE, F., Geography Teaching
FRIEDRICH, H., Economics
GIESELER, W., Music
GLÜCK, G., General Didactics and Teaching
GÜNTHER, H., General Didactics and Teaching
HAMMER, H. O., Chemistry
HEINEN, E., Modern History
HEINIG, P., Textile Design
HERFF, E., General Didactics and Teaching
HERING, H., Mathematics
HURRELMANN, B., German Language and Literature and its Teaching
KLEIN, K., Biology Teaching
KLEINSCHMIDT, G., German
KLINGMÜLLER, G., Textile Design
KÖRNER, K., Music Teaching
KRONEN, H., General Education and Secondary School Teaching
KÜNSTLINGER, R., Political Science
KUNZ, G., Sociology
LAMM, H., Psychology
LERMEN, B. J., German
LEWANDOWSKI, TH., German
LLARYORA, R., Sociology
LÖTTGEN, U., Mathematics
LÜCKERATH, C. A., History
MEFFERT, E., Geography and Didactics
MESSELKEN, H., German
MINSEL, W.-R., Psychology
MOCK, A., Psychology
MÜNCH, F., Textile Design
NOLL, G., Music Teaching
OFFERMANN, J., General Didactics and Teaching
PICKER, B., Mathematics
RADERMACHER, H., Philosophy
RAHN, W., English
RECH, P., Art
REICH, K., General Pedagogy
RIES, G., Psychology
RITTER, G., Geography
RÖHRIG, P., General Education
ROOSEN, H., Art
RUTT, TH., German Language and Method of Teaching
SAYLER, W., General Pedagogics
SCHEPPING, W., Chemistry Teaching
SCHLÖSSER, K., Chemistry
SCHMIDT, H., Physics
SCHMIDT, J. M., Lutheran Theology
SCHRÖDER, J., History
SEIBEL, H. D., Sociology
SPREY-WESSING, TH., General Education
STENGER, W., Roman Catholic Theology
STOCK, A., Roman Catholic Theology
THIEMANN, F., General Education
TIMM, U., Biology Teaching
TÖNNIS, G., Fine Arts Teaching
VOLKENBORN, A., Mathematics Teaching
WEISER, W., Mathematics Teaching
WICHELHAUS, M., Lutheran Theology
WICKERT, J., Psychology
WIEGERSHAUSEN, H., Fine Arts Teaching
WOLFF, G., German Language Teaching
WROBEL, R., Physics
ZEPF, H., Fine Arts Teaching
ZILLESSEN, D., Lutheran Theology

Faculty of Special Education and Therapy:

ADLER, M., Remedial Education
ALICH, G., Education of the Deaf and Hard of Hearing
ANTOR, G., General Therapy and Social Education
BUCHKREMER, H., General Therapy

DREHER, W., Education of the Mentally Handicapped
FEND-ENGELMANN, E., Psychology of the Educationally Subnormal
FENGLER, J., Remedial Education
GROHNFELD, M., Education of Children with Speech Defects
HARTMANN, K., Psychiatry
HOFMANN, TH., Education of the Mentally Retarded
JANSEN, G., Psychology of the Physically Handicapped
JUSSEN, H., Education of the Deaf and Hard of Hearing
KANTER, G., Education of the Mentally Subnormal
KIRFEL, B., Sociology of the Handicapped
KLINGHAMMER, H.-D., Psychology
KLUGE, K.-J., Education of Children with Behavioural Problems
KNURA, G., Education of Children with Speech Defects
KUCKARTZ, W., General Pedagogy
LENZEN, H., General Therapy and Social Education
LIST, G., Remedial Education
MASENDORF, F., Special Education and Rehabilitation of the Educationally Subnormal
MOOG, H., Music
NEISE, K., Psychology of the Mentally Handicapped
NELLES, M., Psychology of Children with Behavioural Problems
PEUSER, G., Applied Linguistics
RICHTER, H.-G., Arts and Crafts
SCHOLZ, H.-J., Education of Children with Speech Defects
SOMMER, M., Physical Education
TSCHERNER, K., Teaching of Educationally Subnormal
WEINWURM-KREUSE, E.-M., Special Education and Rehabilitation of the Physically Handicapped
WILLAND, H., Special Education and Rehabilitation of the Educationally Subnormal
WISOTZKI, K. H., Education of the Deaf and Hard of Hearing
WÖRNER, G., Remedial Education
WULFES, S., Teaching of Physically Handicapped

UNIVERSITÄT KONSTANZ

78457 Konstanz
Telephone: (7531) 800
Telex: 733359
Fax: (7531) 88-3688

Founded 1966
Academic year: October to September

Rector: Prof. Dr RUDOLF COHEN
Pro-Rectors: Prof. Dr MARC SCHOLL, Prof. Dr MAX EMANUEL GEIS, Prof. Dr GERHARD MÜLLER
Registrar: Dr ELKE LUISE BARNSTEDT
Librarian: Dr jur. K. FRANKEN

Number of teachers: 187
Number of students: 7,735

Publications: *Personal- und Veranstaltungsverzeichnis* (annually), *Uni-info*, *Studienführer*.

DEANS

Faculty of Mathematics and Computer Science: Prof. Dr R. RACHE
Faculty of Physics: Prof. Dr W. DIETERICH
Faculty of Chemistry: Prof. Dr W. WEYRICH
Faculty of Biology: Prof. Dr W. RATHMAYER
Faculty of Social Sciences: Prof. Dr B. ROCKSTROH
Faculty of Economics and Statistics: Prof. Dr F. BREYER
Faculty of Law: Prof. Dr A. STADLER
Faculty of Arts: Prof. Dr G. WOLTERS
Faculty of Administrative Sciences: Prof. Dr SCHNEIDER

PROFESSORS

Faculty of Mathematics and Computer Science:
BARTHEL, G.
BAUR, W.
BOHL, E.
HOFFMANN, D.
KAUP, L.
NEUBAUER, G.
PREZ, W.
PRESTEL, A.
PUPPE, V.
RACKE, R.
SCHOLL, M. H.
STOSS, H.-J.
STRASSEN, V.
WAGNER, D.
WATZLAWEK, W.
WOLFF, G.

Faculty of Physics:
AUDRETSCH, J.
BUCHER, E.
DEHNEN, H.
DIETERICH, W.
GANTEFÖR, G.
JÄCKLE, J.
KLEIN, R.
LEIDERER, P.
MARET, G.
MLYNEK, J.
REMPE, G.
SCHATZ, G.
WEBER, R.

Faculty of Chemistry:
BRINTZINGER, H.
DALTROZZO, E.
FELSCHE, J.
FISCHER, H.
GROTH, U.
JOCHIMS, J.
METZ, F.
MÜLLER, G.
PRZYBYLSKI, M.
SCHMIDT, R. R.
STEINER, U.
WEYRICH, W.

Faculty of Biology:
APELL, H.-J.
BADE, E.
BÖGER, P.
BOOS, W.
BRDICZKA, D.
COOK, A.
DIETRICH, D.
ECKMANN, R.
GHISLA, S.
HOFER, H.-W.
KIRCHNER, W.
KNIPPERS, R.
KRAWINKEL-BRENIG, U.
KRONECK, P.
KUTSCH, W.
MALCHOW, D.
MARKL, H.
MENDGEN, K.
MÜLLER, G.
NICOTERA, P.
PETTE, D.
PLATTNER, H.
RATHMAYER, W.
ROTHAUPT, K. O.
SCHINK, B.
STARK, G.
STÜRMER, C.
ULLRICH, V.
WELTE, W.
WENDEL, A.

Department of Psychology:
COHEN, R.
DELIUS, J. D.
ELBERT, TH.
GOLLWITZER, P.
ROCKSTROH, B.
STECK, P.
TROMMSDORF, G.
WALTER, H.

Faculty of Social Sciences:

Department of Sociology:
GEORG, W.
KANTOWSKY, D.
LÜSCHER, K.
SOEFFNER, H.-G.
WIEHN, E.

Department of Sports:
MIETHLING, W.-D.
RIEHLE, H.

Faculty of Economics and Statistics:

Department of Economics:
BREYER, F.
GENSER, B.
LÄUFER, N.
POHLMEIER, W.
RAMSER, H.-J.
SCHWEINBERGER, A.
URSPRUNG, H.
VOSGERAU, H.-J.
WULF, J.

Department of Statistics:
BERAN, J.
HEILER, S.
KEMPF-PALMBACH, W.
KOHLMANN, M.

Faculty of Law:
BROHM, W.
DAMRAU, J.
EBKE, W.
FEZER, K.-H.
GEIS, M.-E.
HAILBRONNER, K.
HAUSMANN, R.
HEINZ, W.
LORENZ, D.
MAURER, H.
RENGIER, R.
RÜTHERS, B.
STADLER, A.
STEIN, E.
STRÄTZ, H. W.
WILMS, H.

Faculty of Arts:

Department of Philosophy:
FUHRMANN, A.
MITTELSTRASS, J.
SCHLEICHERT, H.
SEEBASS, G.
SPOHN, W.
STEMMER, P.
WOLTERS, G.

Department of History:
AMBROSIUS, G.
BURCHARDT, L.
PATSCHOVSKY, A.
PIETROW-ENKER, B.
RICHTER, M.
SCHLÖGL, K.
SCHULLER, W.
SÜRENHAGEN, D.
WUNDER, B.

Department of Literature:
ASSMANN, A.
BAUDY, G.
FEICHTINGER, B.
GAIER, U.
GRAEVENITZ, G. VON
LACHMANN, R.
NISCHIK, R.
OETTINGER, K.
ORTMANN, CH.
PAECH, J.
SCHMIDT, P.-L.
SMIRNOV, I.
STIERLE, K.
STILLERS, R.

THÜRLEMANN, F.
TODOROV, A.

Department of Languages:

BREU, W.
CORRELL, CH.
COUPER-KUHLEN, E.
DI LUZIO, A.
EGLI, U.
HÖLKER, K.
LAHIRI, A.
PAUSE, E.
PLANK, F.
SCHWARZE, CH.

Faculty of Administrative Sciences:

ALBER, J.
GRABHER, G.
IMMERGUT, E.
KELLER, B.
KLIMECKI, R.
KUHLEN, R.
NEIDHART, L.
REITERER, H.
SCHNEIDER, V.
SCHNELL, R.
SIMON, K.
WEIBLER, J.

UNIVERSITÄT LEIPZIG

04009 Leipzig, Postfach 920
Premises at: 04109 Leipzig, Augustusplatz 10–11
Telephone: (341) 97108
Telex: 311432
Fax: (341) 9730099

Founded 1409
State control
Academic year: October to September (two semesters)

Rector: Prof. Dr CORNELIUS WEISS
Pro-Rectors: Prof. Dr Dr GÜNTHER WARTENBERG (Education), Prof. Dr MANFRED REINACHER (Research), Prof. Dr MICHAEL GEYER (Development)
Chancellor: PETER GUTJAHR-LÖSER
Librarian: Dr EKKEHARD HENSCHKE

Number of students: 21,137

Publication: *Universität Leipzig* (8 a year).

DEANS

Faculty of Theology: Prof. Dr MATTHIAS G. PETZOLDT
Faculty of Law: Prof. Dr ANDREAS BLASCHCZOK
Faculty of History, Art and Oriental Studies: Prof. Dr THOMAS TOPFSTEDT
Faculty of Philology: Prof. Dr LUDWIG STOCKINGER
Faculty of Education: Prof. Dr ROLAND LAUTERBACH
Faculty of Mathematics and Computer Science: Prof. Dr JÜRGEN STÜCKRAD
Faculty of Life Sciences, Pharmacy and Psychology: Prof. Dr KURT EGER
Faculty of Physics and Geosciences: Prof. Dr JÖRG KÄRGER
Faculty of Chemistry and Mineralogy: Prof. Dr HELMUT PAPP
Faculty of Social Sciences and Philosophy: Prof. Dr GEORG VOBRUBA
Faculty of Sports Science: Prof. Dr RICHARD RIECKEN
Faculty of Veterinary Medicine: Prof. Dr JÜRGEN GROPP
Faculty of Economic Sciences: Prof. Dr ADOLF WAGNER
Faculty of Medicine: Prof. Dr VOLKER BIGL

PROFESSORS

Faculty of Theology:

HANISCH, H., Religious Education
JUNGHANS, H., Church History
KÄHLER, C., New Testament
KÜHN, U., Systematic Theology
LUX, R., Old Testament
MAI, H., Christian Archaeology
NOWAK, K., Church History
PETZOLDT, M., Systematic Theology
PETZOLDT, M., Principles of Theology, Hermeneutics
RATZMANN, W., Practical Theology
RÜTERSWÖRDEN, U., Old Testament
VOGLER, W., New Testament
WARTENBERG, G., Church History
ZIEMER, J., Practical Theology

Faculty of Law:

BECKER-EBERHARD, E., Civil Law and Civil Action Law
BLASCHCZOK, A., Civil Law and Commercial Law
DEGENHART, C., Commercial, Environmental and Planning Law
DOLEZALEK, G., Civil Law
GEIGER, R., Public, International and European Law
GLASS, K., Public and Administrative Law
GOERLICH, H., Public, Constitutional and Administrative Law
GROPP, W., Criminal Law
HÄUSER, F., Civil, Industrial and Banking Law
KERN, B.-R., Civil and Medical Law, History of Law
OLDIGES, M., Public Law
RAUSCHER, TH., Private International Law, Comparative and Civil Law
SCHUMANN, H., Criminal and Commercial Law
SEEBODE, M., Criminal and Penal Law, Criminology
STADIE, M.-H., Tax Law and Public Law

Faculty of History, Art and Oriental Studies:

BAUMBACH, G., Drama
BELLMANN, D., Arabic and Oriental Philology
BLUMENTHAL, E., Egyptology
CAIN, H.-U., Classical Archaeology
ERKENS, F.-R., Medieval History
VON FRANZ, R., Modern Sinology
GIRSHAUSEN, TH., Drama
VON HEHL, U., Modern History
HELD, W., History of Saxony
HERBERGER, R., Teaching of Music
HEYDEMANN, G., Modern History
HÖPKEN, W., East and South-east European History
JONES, A., African History
KAPPEL, R., African Politics and Economy
KÖHLER, J., Teaching of Music
KÖLVER, B., Indology
MATSCHKE, K.-P., Medieval and Byzantine History
MEHNER, K., Systematic Musical Science
MORITZ, R., Classical Sinology
PREISSLER, H., History of Middle Eastern Religions
RICHTER, S., Japanology
RIECKHOFF-HESSE, S., Prehistory and Early History
RIEKENBERG, M., Comparative History and Ibero-American History
SCHÖNEMANN, B., Teaching of History
SCHRAMM, H., Drama
SCHUBERT, CH., Classical History
SCHULZ, E., Arabic Linguistic and Translation Science
SCHULZ, F., Teaching of Art
SEIDEL, W., History of Music
SEIWERT, H., General and Comparative Religion
SÖRENSEN, P. K., Central Asian Studies
STRECK, B., Ethnology
TOPFSTEDT, TH., History of Art
VOGTHERR, TH., Historical Complementary Sciences
WILCKE, C., Classical Oriental Studies
WOLFF, E., African Studies
ZÖLLNER, F., History of Art
ZWAHR, H., Social and Economic History

Faculty of Philology:

BARZ, I., Contemporary German Linguistics and Lexicology
BOCHMANN, K., Romance Linguistics
EILERT, H., Modern German Literature
FIX, U., Contemporary German Linguistics
GÄRTNER, E., Romance Linguistics
GOTTZMANN, C., Old German Literature
HENGST, K., Onomastics
HENRICH, G., Byzantine and Modern Greek Philology
HINRICHS, U., Southern Slavic Linguistics and Translation Science
HOFFMANN-MAXIS, A., General and Comparative Literature and Literary Theory
KEIL, H., North American Cultural History
KOENEN, A., American Literature
KÖNIGS, F., Teaching of Foreign Languages
KÖSSLING, R., Old German and Latin Literature
KRAMER, J., British Culture
LERCHNER, G., History of German Language
LÖRSCHER, W., English Linguistics
MASS, E., Romance Literature
MIETH, A., Teaching of German
NASSEN, U., Children's Literature and Juvenile Literature
ÖHLSCHLÄGER, G., German Linguistics
OLSEN, S., English Linguistics
PECHMANN, TH., Psycholinguistics
POLLNER, C., English Linguistics
PORSCH, P., Sociolinguistics and Dialectology
RICHTER, H., Modern German Literature
RITZER, M., Modern German Literature
SCHENKEL, E., English Literature
SCHMITT, A. P., Linguistics and Translation Studies (English)
SCHWARZ, W., Literature and Cultural History of the Western Slavs
SIER, K., Classical Philology and Greek Literature
STÄRK, C., Classical Philology
STEUBE, A., General Linguistics
STOCKINGER, L., Modern German Literature
DE TORO, A., Romance Literature
WIESE, I., Contemporary German Linguistics
WOTJAK, B., German as a Foreign Language, Lexicology of Contemporary German Linguistics
WOTJAK, G., Romance Linguistics and Translation Science (Spanish and French)
ZYBATOW, G., Slavic Linguistics

Faculty of Education:

ADAM, H., Teaching Mentally Handicapped People
EBNER, H., Vocational and Business Education
HEIMLICH, U., Teaching Children with Learning Disabilities
HOPPE-GRAFF, S., Educational Psychology
HÖRNER, W., Comparative Education
KNOLL, J., Adult Education
LAUTERBACH, R., Primary School Education
MELZER, M., School Education
MUTZECK, W., Behaviour Problems and Therapy
NEUMANN, K., Teaching Physically Handicapped People
SCHULZ, D., School Education
STACHOWIAK, F. J., Special Education, Language and Speech Pathology
STERN, E., Educational Psychology
TOEPELL, M., Teaching Primary School Mathematics
WOLFFERSDORFF, C., Social Education
WOLLERSHEIM, H. W., General Education

Faculty of Mathematics and Computer Science:

BEYER, K., Applied Mathematics
BORNELEIT, P., Teaching of Mathematics
EISENREICH, G., Theoretical Mathematics

FRITZSCHE, B., Probability Theory
GERBER, S., Computer Science
GIRLICH, H.-J., Stochastics
GÜNTHER, M., Partial and Differential Equations
HERZOG, B., Principles of Mathematics, Logic, Theory of Numbers
KIRSTEIN, B., Mathematical Statistics
KÜRSTEN, K.-D., Operator Algebra
MIERSEMANN, E., Calculus of Variations
RADEMACHER, H.-B., Differential Geometry
SCHMÜDGEN, K., Functional Analysis
SCHUMANN, R., Analysis
STÜCKRAD, J., Algebra
WOLLENBERG, M., Mathematical Physics

Faculty of Life Sciences, Pharmacy and Psychology:

BABEL, W., Microbial Physiology
COLLANI, G. VON, Cognitive Social Psychology
DRÖSSLER, K., Animal Physiology
EGER, K., Pharmaceutical Chemistry
ETTRICH, K. U., Developmental Psychology
GEHLHAAR, K.-H., Teaching of Biology
GEISSLER, H.-G., General Psychology
GUTHKE, J., Differential Psychology and Psychodiagnostics
HAHN, U., Biochemistry
HAUSCHILDT, S., Immunobiology
HOFMANN, H.-J., Biophysical Chemistry
JAKUBKE, H.-D., General Biochemistry
KLEBER, H.-P., Theoretical and Applied Enzymology
MOHR, G., Industrial and Organizational Psychology
MORAWETZ, W., Special Botany
NAUMANN, W., Developmental Neurobiology
NIEBER, K., Pharmacology
PETERMANN, H., Psychology of Personality and Psychological Intervention
PISCHEL, H., Pharmaceutical Chemistry
POEGGEL, G., Human Biology
RAUWALD, J.-W., Pharmaceutical Biology
REISSER, W., General and Applied Botany
RÜBSAMEN, R., Neurobiology
SASS, H., Genetics
SCHILDBERGER, K.-M., General Zoology
SCHLEGEL, M., Special Zoology
SCHRÖDER, H., Clinical Psychology
SÜSS, W., Pharmaceutical Technology
WILHELM, CHR., Plant Physiology
WITRUK, E., Educational Psychology

Faculty of Physics and Geosciences:

BEHN, U.
BIGL, F., Experimental Physics
BORGS, C., Theoretical Physics
BÖTTCHER, R.
BREUSTE, J., Geoecology
BUTZ, T., Experimental Physics
EISSMANN, L., Geology
ESQUINAZI, P. D., Experimental Physics
GESCHKE, D., Experimental Physics
GEYER, B., Theoretical Physics
GLÄSSER, W., Geology, Hydrogeology
GRILL, W., Experimental Physics
HEINTZENBERG, J., Atmospheric Physics
IHLE, D., Theoretical Physics
JACOBS, F., Geophysics
KÄRGER, J., Experimental Physics
KIRSTEIN, W.
KLOSE, G., Experimental Physics
KORN, M., Theoretical Geophysics
KREHER, K., Experimental Physics
KREMER, F., Experimental Physics
KÜHNEL, A., Theoretical Physics
LÖSCHE, M., Experimental Physics
MAYR, A., Regional Geography
METZ, W., Theoretical Meteorological
MEYER, H., Engineering and Environmental Geophysics
MICHEL, D., Experimental Physics
MÜLLER, A.
NEUMEISTER, H., Physical Geography
OEHME, W., Teaching of Physics
RENNER, E., Modelling of Atmospheric Processes
RUDOLPH, G., Theoretical Physics
SCHMIDT, H., Anthropogeography
SIBOLD, K., Theoretical Physics
TETZLAFF, G., Meteorology
WIESSNER, R.

Faculty of Chemistry and Mineralogy:

BENTE, K., Mineralogy, Crystallography
BEYER, L., Inorganic Chemistry
BORSDORF, R., Analytical Chemistry
BREDE, O., Physical Chemistry
BURGER, K., Organic Chemistry
ENGEWALD, W., Analytical Chemistry
HEY-HAWKINS, E., Inorganic Chemistry
KABISCH, K., Nature and Conservation
KIRMSE, R., Inorganic Chemistry
PAPP, H., Technological Chemistry
QUITZSCH, K., Physical Chemistry
REINHOLD, J., Theoretical Chemistry
SCHREITER, P., Technological Mineralogy
SIELER, J., Inorganic Chemistry
STOTTMEISTER, U., Technological Chemistry
SZARGAN, R., Physical Chemistry
WEISS, C., Theoretical Chemistry
WELZEL, P., Organic Chemistry
WENDT, G., Technological Chemistry
WERNER, G., Analytical Chemistry
WILDE, H., Organic Chemistry

Faculty of Social Sciences and Philosophy:

BARTELBORTH, TH., Theory of Science
BENTELE, G., Public Relations
ELSENHANS, H., Political Science and International Politics
ENGFER, H.-J., History of Philosophy
FACH, W., Politics
FENNER, C., Politics
FLAM, H., Sociology
FRÜH, W., Empirical Communications and Media Research
GERHARDS, J., Sociology
GIESEN, K.-G., International Politics
GOTTWALD, S., Logic
HALLER, M., Journalism
HUBER, M., Politics
HUININK, J., Sociology
KERLEN, D., Books, Economics of Book Publishing
KREISER, L., Logic, Classical Logic and Semantics
KUTSCH, A., Historical and Systematic Communication Studies
MEGGLE, G., Philosophy
MEUSCHEL, S., Politics
MÜHLER, K., Sociology
OPP, K.-D., Sociology
SCHORB, B., Teaching of Media Studies, Further Education
SIEGRIST, H., Theory and Philosophy of Culture
STEIMETZ, R., Media and Media Culture
STEKELER-WEITHOFER, P., Philosophy
STIEHLER, H.-J., Empirical Communications and Media Research
VOBRUBA, G., Sociology
VOSS, T., Sociology

Faculty of Sports Science:

ALFERMANN, D., Psychology of Sport
BUSSE, M., Sports Medicine
INNENMOSER, J., Sports Therapy, Sport for Handicapped People
KIRCHGÄSSNER, H., Movement and Training Science
RIECKEN, R., Sports Education
ZEUNER, A., Teaching of School Sports

Faculty of Veterinary Medicine:

ALBER, G., Immunology
BERGMANN, A., Epidemiology and Statistics
DITTRICH, A., Nutrition
ELZE, K., Herd Management and Reproduction
FEHLHABER, K., Food Hygiene and Consumer Protection
FERGUSON, J., Large-Animal Surgery
GÄBEL, G., Physiology
GROPP, J., Animal Nutrition, Diseases and Dietetics
GRÜN, E., Endocrinology
GÜRTLER, H., Physiological Chemistry
KIETZMANN, M., Toxicology
KRÜGER, M., Bacteriology and Mycology
MÜLLER, H., Virology
OECHTERING, G., Small-Animal Medicine
PRIETZ, G., Lameness in Large Animals
REINACHER, M., Veterinary Pathology
RIBBECK, R., Parasitology
SALOMON, F.-V., Anatomy
SCHARNER, E., Meat Hygiene
SCHNEIDER, J., Large-Animal Surgery
SCHNEIDER, J., Fish Diseases
SCHNURRBUSCH, U., Reproduction Biology and Andrology
SCHOON, H.-A., Histopathology and Clinical Pathology
SCHUSSER, G., Large-Animal Medicine
SEEGER, J., Histology and Embryology
SOBIRAJ, A., Obstetrics and Gynaecology
UNGEMACH, F.-R., Pharmacology and Pharmacy

Faculty of Economic Sciences:

BISKUP, R., Economics
EHRENBERG, D., Economics Computer Science
GOLDAMMER, G., Economics Computer Science
GRAW, K.-U., Foundations and Drainage
HIELSCHER, U., Business Management and Financing
KÖNIG, G., Large Structures, Materials Technology
LENK, T., Finance
LÖBLER, H., Business Management
MAY, A., Building and Construction Industry
PAHL, B., Planning and Design of Buildings
PARASKEWOPOULOS, S., Economics
PELZL, W., Real Estate
RAUTENBERG, H.-G., Business Accounting
SINGER, H. J., Banking
THIELE, R., Construction Engineering
VOLLMER, U., Economics
WAGNER, A., Economic Research
WIESE, H., Economics
VON ZELEWSKI, S., Production and Industrial Information

Faculty of Medicine:

ADAM, H., Anaesthesiology and Intensive Therapy
ALEXANDER, H., Obstetrics and Gynaecology
ANGERMEYER, M., Psychiatry
ARENDT, T., Neuroanatomy
ARNOLD, K., Medical Physics and Biophysics
BEHRENDT, W., Phoniatrics and Paediatric Audiology
BENNEK, J., Paediatric Surgery
BERR, F., Internal Medicine, Hepatology
BIGL, V., Neurochemistry
BOOTZ, F., Oto-rhino-laryngology
BRÄHLER, E., Medical Psychology
CRAMON, Y. VON, Cognitive Neurology
DANNHAUER, K.-H., Orthodontics
DETTMER, D., Biochemistry
DIETRICH, J., Diagnostic Radiology, Neuroradiology
DORSCHNER, W., Urology
EMMRICH, F., Clinical Immunology
ENGELMANN, L., Internal Medicine, Intensive Medicine
ESCHRICH, K., Biochemistry
ETTRICH, C., Child and Adolescent Psychiatry, Psychotherapy
FRIEDRICH, T., Pathology
FROSTER, U., Genetics
GEHRE, G., Dental Prosthetics and Materials
GERTZ, H.-J., Psychiatry
GEYER, M., Psychosomatic Medicine and Psychotherapy
GLANDER, H.-J., Andrology

GÖPFERT, E., Physiology
HANITZSCH, R., Physiology
HÄNTZSCHEL, H., Internal Medicine, Rheumatology
HAUSS, P., Abdominal, Transplantation and Vascular Surgery
HAUSTEIN, U.-F., Dermatology
HELBIG, W., Internal Medicine, Haematology, Oncology
HEMPRICH, A., Maxillofacial Surgery
HERBARTH, O., Environmental Medicine
HÖRMANN, D., Diagnostic Radiology
HORN, F., Molecular Immunology
HUTSCHENREITER, W., Cardiac Surgery
ILLES, P., Pharmacology and Toxicology
JOSTEN, CH., Traumatology
KAMPRAD, F.-W., Radiotherapy
KIEFEL, V., Transfusion Medicine
KÖHLER, U., Obstetrics and Gynaecology
KÖNIG, F., Anaesthesiology and Intensive Therapy
KOPPERSCHLÄGER, G., Biochemistry
LANGANKE, B., Maxillofacial Surgery
LIEBERT, U. G., Virology
LÖFFLER, M., Medical Informatics, Statistics and Epidemiology
MATZEN, P., Paediatric Orthopaedics
MERTE, K., Restorative Dentistry
METZNER, G., Clinical Immunology, Allergology
MOHR, F.-W., Cardiac Surgery
MÖSSNER, J., Internal Medicine, Gastroenterology
MÜLLER, K., Forensic Toxicology
OLTHOFF, D., Anaesthesiology and Intensive Therapy
PASCHKE, R., Internal Medicine, Endocrinology
PFEIFFER, D., Internal Medicine, Cardiology
PLIQUETT, F., Membrane and Cell Biophysics
PRAGER, W., Radiotherapy
PREISS, R., Clinical Pharmacology
RAUE, W., Paediatrics
REIBER, T., Dental Prosthetics and Materials
REICHENBACH, A., Neurophysiology
REUTER, W., Metabolic Disorders, Gerontology
RICHTER, V., Clinical Chemistry, Metabolic Disorders
RIHA, O., History of Medicine
RODLOFF, A., Medical Microbiology
ROTHER, P., Macroscopic Anatomy
SACK, G., Neurology
VON SALIS-SOGLIO, G., Orthopaedics
SANDNER, KH., Accident Surgery
SCHAUER, J., Internal Medicine, Pulmology
SCHMIDT, F., Diagnostic Radiology, Clinical Radiology
SCHMIDT, H., Periodontology
SCHMIDT, W., Anatomy
SCHNEIDER, P., Paediatric Cardiology
SCHOBER, R., Neuropathology
SCHÖNFELDER, M., Surgical Oncology
SCHREINICKE, G., Industrial Medicine
SCHULER, G., Cardiology
SCHULZ, H.-G., Radiological Diagnostics
SCHWOKOWSKI, CH., Surgical Oncology
SEIFERT, V., Neurosurgery
SPANEL-BOROWSKY, K., Anatomy
SPENKER, F.-B., Microbiology and Epidemiology
STIEHL, P., Pathology, Immunopathology
THOM, A., History of Medicine
TREIDE, A., Child Dentistry
VIEHWEG, B., Obstetrics
VITZTHUM, E., Neurosurgery
VOCK, R., Forensic Medicine
VOGTMANN, C., Neonatology and Paediatric Intensive Care
WAGNER, A., Neurology
WAGNER, D., Clinical Chemistry, Pathobiochemistry
WIEDEMANN, P., Ophthalmology
WILD, L., Anaesthesiology and Intensive Therapy
WILDFÜHR, W., Hygiene
WILLGERODT, H., Paediatric Endocrinology, Metabolic Disorders
WINTER, A., Medical Informatics
WITTEKIND, C., Pathology, Immunopathology
ZIMMER, H.-G., Physiology

Foreign Language Centre:

GLÄSER, R., Applied Linguistics

Institute of German Literature:

HASLINGER, J., Literary Aesthetics
JENTZSCH, B., Poetry
TREICHEL, H.-U., German Literature

Institute of Computer Science:

BREWKA, G., Intelligent Systems
GERBER, G., Automata and Formal Languages
HERRE, H., Formal Concepts of Computer Science
HEYER, G., Natural Language Processing
RAHM, E., Databases
SPRUTH, W., Computer Systems

MEDIZINISCHE UNIVERSITÄT ZU LÜBECK

23538 Lübeck, Ratzeburger Allee 160
Telephone: (451) 500-0
Telex: 26 492
Fax: (451) 500-3016

Founded 1963

Rector: Prof. Dr med. WOLFGANG KÜHNEL
Pro-Rectors: Prof. Dr med. HORST LORENZ FEHM, Prof. Dr rer. nat. ALFRED X. TRAUTWEIN
Chancellor: W.-D. VON DETMERING

Number of teachers: 220
Number of students: 1,800

Publications: *Forschungsbericht* , *Vorlesungsverzeichnis*, *Focus MUL* (4 a year).

DEANS

Faculty of Science and Technology: Prof. Dr PETER K. MÜLLER
Faculty of Medicine: Prof. Dr PETER SCHMUCKER

PROFESSORS

Faculty of Medicine:

ARNOLD, H., Neurosurgery
BRACH, M., Molecular Medicine
BRUCH, H.-P., Surgery
DIEDRICH, K., Gynaecology and Obstetrics
DILLING, H., Psychiatry
DOMARUS, H., Maxillary and Facial Surgery
DOMINIAK, P., Pharmacology, Toxicology and Clinical Pharmacology
FASSL, H., Medical Statistics and Documentation
FEHM, H. L., Internal Medicine
FENNER, A., Paediatrics
FLAD, H.-D., Immunology
GRADINGER, R., Orthopaedics
GROSS, W. L., Internal Medicine
HALSBAND, H., Surgery, Paediatrics
JELKMANN, W., Physiology
JOCHAM, Urology
KATUS, H. A., Internal Medicine
KESSEL, R., Industrial Medicine
KIRCHNER, H., Immunology and Transfusional Medicine
KNÖLKER, U., Child and Adolescent Psychiatry
KÖMPF, D., Neurology
KRUSE, K., Paediatrics
KÜHNEL, W., Anatomy
LAQUA, H., Ophthalmology
LORENTZ, K., Internal Medicine and Clinical Chemistry
OEHMICHEN, M., Forensic Medicine
RASPE, H.-H., Social Medicine
RICHTER, E., Radiotherapy and Nuclear Medicine
SCHLAAK, M., Internal Medicine
SCHMIELAU, F., Medical Psychology
SCHMUCKER, P., Anaesthesiology
SCHWINGER, E., Human Genetics
SIEVERS, H. H., Cardiac Surgery
SOLBACH, W., Medical Microbiology and Hygiene
STRUBELT, O., Pharmacology and Toxicology
WEERDA, H., Otolaryngology
WEISS, H.-D., Clinical Radiology
WOLFF, H. H., Dermatology and Venereology

Faculty of Science and Technology:

DOSCH, W., Software Technology
ENGELHARDT, D., History of Medicine and Science
HERCEG, M., Multimedia and Interactive Systems
HOGREFE, D., Telematics
LINNEMANN, V., Practical Informatics
MÜLLER, K.-P., Medical Molecular Biology
PETERS, TH., Physics
PÖPPL, S., Medical Informatics and Statistics
REISCHUK, K. R., Theoretical Informatics
RIETSCHEL, E.-TH., Immunochemistry and Biochemical Microbiology
SCHÄFER, G., Biochemistry
TRAUT, W., Biology
TRAUTWEIN, A., Physics

UNIVERSITÄT LÜNEBURG

21332 Lüneburg, Scharnhorststr. 1
Telephone: (4131) 78-0
Fax: (4131) 78-1097
E-mail: zuehlsdorff@uni-lueneburg.de

Founded 1946
State control
Academic year: April to September, October to March

Chancellor: Dr HANS-GEORG SCHULTZ-GERSTEIN
President: Prof. Dr HARTWIG DONNER
Vice-Presidents: Prof. Dr EDGAR KREILKAMP, Prof. Dr FERDINAND MÜLLER-ROMMEL
Registrar: DIETER GAWLIK
Librarian: Dr HILDEGARD MÜLLER

Library of 350,000 vols
Number of teachers: 389
Number of students: 6,768

Publications: *Berichte*, *Informationen*, *Meinungen* (every 6 months), *Forschungsberichte* (every 3 years), *Rechenschaftsbericht des Präsidenten* (every 2 years), *Vorlesungsverzeichnis* (every 6 months).

DEANS

Faculty of Educational Sciences: Prof. Dr HANS-JOACHIM PLEWIG
Faculty of Economics and Social Sciences: Prof. Dr EGBERT KAHLE
Faculty of Cultural Sciences: Prof. Dr THEODOR KLIMEK
Faculty of Environmental Sciences: Prof. Dr EDMUND BRANDT

PROFESSORS

Faculty of Educational Sciences:

CLASSEN-BAUER, I., Comparative Educational Sciences
COLLA-MÜLLER, H. E., Social Work and Therapy
CZERWENKA, K., Teacher Education
DE RUDDER, H., Sociology
ENGELHARDT, W., Social Studies and Science, Environmental Education
HÖFFKEN, P., Protestant Theology
KARSTEN, M.-E., Social Administration and Management
LENZ-JOHANNS, M., Aesthetic Education
PLEWIG, H.-J., Deviant Behaviour

RAMB, W., Psychiatric Social Work and Social Therapy
RINGSHAUSEN, G., Protestant Theology
ROSSBACH, H.-G., General Education
SIELAND, B., Psychology
STIMMER, F., Social Work and Therapy
STOLTENBERG, U., Social Studies and Science
STREHL, R., Mathematics and its Teaching
TITZE, H., General Education
UHLE, R., General Education
SALDERN, M. VON, Teacher Training
WOLFF, J., Judicature and Criminal Law relating to Juvenile Delinquency
ZIEGENSPECK, J., Psychology

Faculty of Economics and Social Sciences:

DÖRING, U., Business Administration
DONNER, H., Law
GRUNWALD, W., Psychology
GSCHWENDTER, H., Economics
HEILMANN, J., Law
KAHLE, E., Business Administration
KREILKAMP, E., Business Administration, Travel and Tourism
LINDE, R., Economics
MARTIN, A., Business Administration
MERZ, J., Research on Professions
REESE, J., Business Administration and Business-Related Computer Sciences
RUNKEL, G., Sociology
SIMON, J., Law
THAYSEN, U., Political Sciences
WAGNER, J., Economics
WEISENFELD-SCHENK, U., Business Administration
ZÜNDORF, L., Sociology

Faculty of Cultural Sciences:

AHNSEHL, P., Music
CLAUSBERG, K., Art History
FAMME, Philosophy
FAULSTICH, W., Media Studies and Public Relations
HAHN, B., Geography
HOPPE, O., German Language and Literature and their Teaching
JOST, E., Physical Education
KESSLER, H., Fine Arts
KLIMEK, T., English Language and its Teaching
KROHN, C.-D., Social and Cultural History
SCHLOTTHAUS, W., German Language and Literature and their Teaching
SCHWEPPENHÄUSER, H., Philosophy
STEGMANN, D., Social and Cultural History and its Teaching
WÖHLER, K., Travel, Tourism and Sociology

Faculty of Environmental Sciences:

AMELUNG, U., Physics
BRANDT, E., Environmental Law
COENEN-STASS, D., Ecology
HÄRDTLE, W., Ecology
KALLENRODE, M.-B., Physics
MICHELSEN, G., Ecology
MÜLLER-ROMMEL, F., Political Science
RUCK, W., Chemistry
STAMM, R. A., Biology

ATTACHED INSTITUTES

Institute of Business Administration: Dir Prof. Dr EGBERT KAHLE.

Institute of Ecology: Dir Prof. Dr WERNER HÄRDTLE.

Institute of Economics: Dir Prof. Dr JOACHIM WAGNER.

Institute of Educational Research: Dir Prof. Dr KURT CZERWENKA.

Institute of Environmental Communication: Dir Prof. Dr GERD MICHELSEN.

Institute of Environmental Strategy: Dir Prof. Dr EDMUND BRANDT.

Institute of Independent Professions: Dir Prof. Dr JOACHIM MERZ.

Institute of Jurisprudence: Dir Prof. Dr JOACHIM HEILMANN.

Institute of Media Studies: Dir Prof. Dr WERNER FAULSTICH.

Institute of Physical Education: Dir Prof. Dr EIKE JOST.

Institute of Small and Medium-Sized Businesses: Dir Prof. Dr ALBERT MARTIN.

Institute of Social Education: Dir Prof. Dr HERBERT E. COLLA-MÜLLER.

Institute of Social Sciences: Dir Prof. Dr LUTZ ZÜNDORF.

Institute of Systematic Pedagogics: Dir Prof. Dr REINHARDT UHLE.

OTTO-VON-GUERICKE-UNIVERSITÄT MAGDEBURG

39106 Magdeburg, Universitätsplatz 2

Telephone: (391) 6701
Fax: (391) 67-11156

Founded 1953, present status 1993
State control
Academic year: October to February, April to July (two semesters)

Chancellor: WOLFGANG LEHNECKE
Rector: Prof. Dr HARALD BÖTTGER
Vice-Rectors: Prof. Dr THOMAS STROTHOTTE (Planning and Development), Prof. Dr GÜNTHER GADEMANN (Research), Prof. Dr ECKHARD DITTRICH (Study)
Librarian: Dr-Ing. EKKEHARD OEHMIG

Library of 850,000 vols
Number of students: 5,600

Publications: *Personal- und Vorlesungsverzeichnis*, *Forschungsbericht*, *Wissenschaftsjournal*, *Preprint*.

DEANS

Faculty of Humanities and Social Sciences: Prof. Dr KLAUS ERICH POLLMANN
Faculty of Economics and Management: Prof. Dr JOACHIM WEIMANN
Faculty of Mathematics: Prof. Dr LUTZ TOBISKA
Faculty of Natural Sciences: Prof. Dr RAINER CLOS
Faculty of Medicine: Prof. Dr WOLFRAM NEUMANN
Faculty of Computer Science: Prof. Dr JÜRGEN DASSOW
Faculty of Mechanical Engineering: Prof. Dr WOLFGANG POPPY
Faculty of Electrical Engineering: Prof. Dr ULRICH KORN

PROFESSORS

Faculty of Humanities and Social Sciences:

BADER, R., Vocational Education
BAUDISCH, W., Special Education and Professional Rehabilitation
BELENTSCHIKOW, R., Slavic Linguistics
BERNARD, F., Metal Technology Teaching
BLASER, P., Administrative Sciences
BREIT, G., Political Education
BURKHARDT, A., German Linguistics
DIPPELHOFER-STIEM, B., Methodology in Social Research
DITTRICH, E., Macrosociology
DREHER, M., Ancient History
FORNDRAN, E., International Relations and Theory of Politics
FRITZSCHE, K.-P., Comparative Political Systems (esp. Study of Prejudice)
FUHRER, U., Developmental and Educational Psychology
GIRMES, R., General Didactics and School Theory
GOLZ, R., Historical and Comparative Educational Studies
HOHMANN, A., Physical Education and Training Science
HUISINGA, R., Vocational Teaching and Training (esp. in Economics and Management Studies)
IBLER, R., Slavic Literatures
KNOLLE, N., Music Education
KÖHLER, M., Voice
LAGING, R., Physical Education and Sports Education
LANGE, B.-P., English Literary and Cultural Studies
LINNEWEBER, V., Social Psychology
LOHMANN, G., Practical Philosophy
MÄKELÄ, T., Music Science
MAROTZKI, W., General Education
MEIER-SCHMID, M., Voice
MEYER, P. G., English Linguistics
PETERS, S., Industrial Educational Sciences
POLLMANN, K. E., Modern History and History of Science
RENZSCH, W., Political System and Political Sociology of the Federal Republic of Germany
ROS, A., Theoretical Philosophy
SCHILLING, M., Older German Literature
SCHÜTZE, F., Microsociology
SPRINGER, M., Medieval History
WELSCH, W., Philosophy of Culture and Technology
WITTPOTH, J., Media and Adult Education

Faculty of Economics and Management:

DEMOUGIN, D., Political Economy
ERICHSON, B., Business Management (Marketing)
FABEL, O., Business Management (Industrial and Labour Organization)
GISCHER, H., Political Economy (Money and Credit)
HOMMEL, M., Business Management (Auditing)
INDERFURTH, K., Business Management (Logistics)
LUHMER, A., Business Management (Controlling)
PAQUÉ, K.-H., Political Economy IV (International Economics)
SCHÜLER, W., Business Management (Organization)
SCHWÖDIAUER, G., Political Economy II
TIETBÖHL, G., Business Management (Operations Research and Statistics)
WEIMANN, J., Political Economy III
WIRL, F., Business Management (Public Enterprises)

Faculty of Mathematics:

BESSENRODT, C., Algebra
CHRISTOPH, G., Mathematical Stochastics
GAFFKE, N., Mathematical Stochastics
JUHNKE, F., Mathematical Optimization
POTTS, A., Discrete Mathematics
TOBISKA, L., Numerical Analysis
WARNECKE, G., Numerical Mathematics
WEISSBACH, B., Geometry

Faculty of Natural Sciences:

BÖTTGER, H., Theoretical Physics
CHRISTEN, J., Experimental Physics
CLOS, R., Experimental Physics
EDELMANN, C., Experimental Physics
EDELMANN, F. T., Inorganic Chemistry
ENGEL, A., Theoretical Physics
JÄNCKE, L., Psychology
KASSNER, K., Computational Physics
MÜLLER, S., Biophysics
REHBERG, I., Experimental Physics
RICHTER, J., Theoretical Physics
SCHINZER, D., Organic Chemistry

Faculty of Medicine:

ALLHOFF, E. P., Urology
ANSORGE, S., Experimental Internal Medicine and Immunology
AUGUSTIN, W., Patho-biochemistry
BEGALL, K.-G., Otorhinolaryngology
BEHRENS-BAUMANN, W., Ophthalmology
BOGERTS, B., Psychiatry
BOHNENSACK, R., General Biochemistry

BONNEKOH, B., Dermatology and Venereology, Allergology
DIETZMANN, K., Neuropathology
DÖHRING, W., Radiology
FELDER, S., Health Economics
FIRSCHING, R., Neurosurgery
FRANKE, A., Haematology and Oncology
FREIGANG, B., Otorhinolaryngology
FROMMER, J., Psychosomatic Medicine and Psychotherapy
GADEMANN, G., Radio-oncology
GERLACH, K.-L., Oral and Maxillofacial Surgery
GOLLNICK, H., Dermatology and Venereology
GRASSHOFF, H., Orthopaedic Surgery
GROTE, R., Interventional Radiology
HEIM, M., Transfusion Medicine and Immunohaematology
HEINZE, H.-J., Neurophysiology
HOFFMANN, W., Medical Chemistry and Molecular Biology
HÖLLT, V., Pharmacology and Toxicology
HUTH, C., Cardiothoracic Surgery
KEKOW, J., Rheumatology
KLEIN, H., Cardiology, Angiology and Pneumology
KLEINSTEIN, J., Reproductive Medicine and Gynaecological Endocrinology
KÖNIG, W., Medical Microbiology
KRAUSE, D., Forensic Medicine
KRUG, M., Neuropharmacology
LÄUTER, J., Medical Biometry
LEHNERT, H., Endocrinology
LIPPERT, H., General Surgery
LULEY, C., Clinical Chemistry
MALFERTHEINER, P., Gastroenterology and Hepatology
MITTLER, U., Paediatric Haematology and Oncology
MÜLLER, W., Parasitology
NEUMANN, K.-H., Nephrology
NEUMANN, W., Orthopaedic Surgery
NIEDER, J., Gynaecology and Obstetrics
OTTO, H. J., Nuclear Medicine
PAPE, H.-C., Physiology
REISER, G., Neurobiochemistry
ROBRA, B.-R., Public Health
ROESSNER, A., General Pathology
RÖSE, W., Anaesthesiology and Critical Care Medicine
SABEL, B., Medical Psychology
SCHNEIDER, W., Plastic, Reconstructive and Hand Surgery
SCHWARZBERG, H., Neurophysiology
SCHWEGLER, H., Neuroanatomy
VON SPECHT, H., Experimental Audiology and Medical Physics
THAL, W., Paediatric Pneumology
VOIGT, TH., Physiology
WALLESCH, C.-W., Neurology
WEISE, W., Gynaecology and Obstetrics
WENDLER, D., General Anatomy
WIEACKER, P., Human Genetics
WINCKLER, ST., Traumatology
WOLF, G., Neurobiological Medicine

Faculty of Computer Science:
DASSOW, J., Theoretical Computer Science
DUMKE, R., Software Engineering
HOFESTÄDT, R., Modelling and Animation in Biology and Medical Science
KRUSE, R., Neural and Fuzzy Systems
RAUTENSTRAUCH, C., Business Information Systems
RÖSNER, D., Knowledge-Based Systems and Document Processing
SAAKE, G., Databases and Information Systems
SCHRÖDER-PREIKSCHAT, W., Parallel Operating Systems
SMID, M., Computer Geometry
STROTHOTTE, T., Computer Graphics and Interactive Systems

Faculty of Mechanical Engineering:
AMBOS, E., Foundry Engineering
BERTRAM, A., Strength of Materials
BLUMENAUER, H., Materials Testing
DETERS, L., Machine Elements and Tribology
GABBERT, U., Numerical Mechanics
GROTE, K. H., Product Development and Engineering Design
HANSELKA, A.
HAUPTMANNS, U., Plant Design and Safety
HEROLD, H., Joining Engineering
KÄFERSTEIN, P., Heat Technology and Energy Industry
KASPER, R., Mechatronics
KECKE, H., Fluid Dynamics
KRAUSE, F., Conveying Engineering
KÜHNLE, H., Factory Operation and Manufacturing Systems
LIERATH, F., Cutting Procedures
MOLITOR, M., Manufacturing Measurement Technology and Quality Management
MÖRL, L., Chemical Apparatus Construction
POPPY, W., Construction Machinery
QUAAS, W., Ergonomics
REGENER, D., Materials Engineering
SCHMIDT, J., Technical Thermodynamics
SEIDEL-MORGENSTERN, A., Chemical Reaction Engineering
SPECHT, E., Technical Thermodynamics and Combustion
SPERLING, L., Vibration Engineering and Dynamics
TOMAS, J., Mechanical Process Engineering
TSCHÖKE, H., Piston Engines
TSOTSAS, E., Thermal Process Engineering
VAJNA, S., Computer Applications in Mechanical Engineering
ZIEMS, D., Logistics

Faculty of Electrical Engineering:
DÖSCHNER, C., Control Engineering
GÜTTLER, F., Telecommunication Engineering
HANISCH, H.-M., Control Engineering
HAUPTMANN, P., Measurement Technology and Microsystems
KLEINE, U., Electronic Circuits
KORN, U., Control Engineering
MATHIS, W., Electronics
MECKE, H., Power Electronics
MICHAELIS, B., Technical Computer Science
NITSCH, J., Electromagnetic Compatibility, Theory of Electrical Engineering
PALIS, F., Electrical Engineering
WOLLENBERG, G., Theoretical and General Electrical Engineering

JOHANNES GUTENBERG-UNIVERSITÄT MAINZ

55099 Mainz
Telephone: (6131) 39-0
Fax: (6131) 39-29-19

Founded 1477; closed 1816; re-opened 1946

President: Prof. Dr JOSEF REITER
Vice-Presidents: Prof. Dr MICHAEL LOOS, Prof. Dr ULRICH DRUWE
Administrative Director: GOETZ SCHOLZ
Librarian: Dr A. ANDERHUB

Library: see Libraries
Number of teachers: 2,357
Number of students: 30,000

Publications: *Bericht des Präsidenten*, *Personen- u. Studienverzeichnis*, *Universitätszeitung 'JOGU'*, *Forschungsmagazin*, *Forschungsbericht*.

DEANS

Faculty of Catholic Theology: Prof. Dr W. SIMON
Faculty of Evangelical Theology: Prof. Dr H. WISSMANN
Faculty of Law and Economics: H.-W. LAUBINGER
Faculty of Medicine: Prof. Dr S. O. HOFFMANN
Faculty of Philosophy and Pedagogics: Prof. Dr K. SPRENGARD
Faculty of Social Sciences: (vacant)
Faculty of Philology I: Prof. Dr T. KOEBNER
Faculty of Philology II: Prof. Dr W. HERGET
Faculty of Philology III: Prof. Dr W. GIRKE
Faculty of History: Prof. Dr P. C. HARTMANN
Faculty of Mathematics: Prof. Dr K.-J. SCHEIBA
Faculty of Physics: Prof. Dr D. DRECHSEL
Faculty of Chemistry and Pharmacy: Prof. Dr G. DANNHARDT
Faculty of Biology: Prof. Dr A. FISCHER
Faculty of Geosciences: Prof. Dr D. UTHOFF
Faculty of Applied Linguistics and Cultural Sciences: Prof. Dr A. F. KELLETAT
Faculty of Fine Arts: Prof. Dr W. REISS
Faculty of Music: L. DREYER
Faculty of Physical Education: Prof. Dr D. AUGUSTIN

PROFESSORS

Faculty of Catholic Theology:
ANZENBACHER, A., Christian Anthropology and Social Ethics
BAUMEISTER, TH., Ancient Church History and Patrology
BECKER, H., Liturgy and Homiletics
KNOBLOCH, ST., Pastoral Theology
KREINER, A., Fundamental Theology and Religious Studies
MEIER, J., Medieval and Modern Church History
MOSIS, R., Old Testament
REISER, M., New Testament
REITER, J., Moral Theology
RIEDEL-SPANGENBERGER, I., Canon Law, Law of State and Church
SCHENKE, L., New Testament
SCHNEIDER, TH., Dogmatics and Oecumenical Theology
SIMON, W., Religious Education Theory, Catechetics
WEISS, B., Dogmatics

Faculty of Evangelical Theology:
BEISSER, F., Systematic Theology
BÖCHER, O., New Testament
HORN, F., New Testament
MAY, G., Church Dogmatics and History
MAYER, G., Biblical History and Literature of Biblical and Postbiblical Judaism
MICHEL, D., Old Testament
VOLP, R., Practical Theology
WISSMANN, H., Studies for Religion and Mission

Faculty of Law and Economics:
BARTLING, H., Economics
BARTMANN, H., Economics
BECK, K., Vocational Education
BELLMANN, K., Business Administration and Production Theory
BOCK, M., Criminology, Criminal Law
BREUER, K., Vocational Education
BRONNER, R., Business Administration and Organization
DÖRR, D., Public Law, European Law, International Law
DREHER, M., European Law, Civil Law, Commercial Law, Comparative Law
ENDERS, C., Public Law
EULER, R., Business Administration and Taxes
GRUNEWALD, B., Civil Law, Commercial, Economic and Company Law
HADDING, W., Civil Law, Commercial, Economic and Civil Procedural Law
HARDER, M., Roman Law, Civil Law, History of Modern Private Law
HEIL, O., Marketing
HENTSCHEL, V., Economic History, Social History
HEPTING, R., Civil Law
HETTINGER, M., Criminal and Procedural Law

HUFEN, F., Public Law, Constitutional Law, Commercial Law
KARGL, H., Business Administration, Business Computing
KNOTH, J., Business Administration
KONZEN, H., Civil, Commercial, Industrial and Civil Procedural Law
KRÜMPELMANN, J., Criminal and Procedural Law
KUBIN, I., Theoretical Economics
LAUBINGER, H.-W., Public Law, Management
LÜCKE, J., Constitutional and Administrative Law, Foreign Public Law
MÜLLER, K., Civil Law, Commercial Law, Procedural Law, Foreign and International Private Law, Comparative Law
PECHER, H., Civil and Civil Procedural Law
PEFFEKOVEN, R., Economics and Public Finance
PERRON, W., Criminal Law and Procedure, Foreign Criminal Law and Procedure
PFLUG, H.-J., Civil Law, Commercial, Economic and Civil Procedural Law
PICK, E., Commercial Law, Civil Law, History of German Law, Constitutional Law
PRINZ, A., Economics
ROTH, A., Civil Law, History of Law
RUDOLF, W., Public Law
SANDMANN, K., Business Administration, Bank Management
SAUERNHEIMER, K., International Economics
SCHULZE, P., Statistics, Econometrics, Regional Economics
TEICHMANN, A., Jurisprudence, Civil Law, Commercial Law, German and European Economic Law
TILLMANN, G., Economics and Public Finance
TRAUTMANN, S., Business Administration and Public Finance
TRZASKALIK, CHR., Financial and Tax Law
ZOHLNHÖFER, W., Economics

Faculty of Medicine:

BENKERT, O., Psychiatry
BEYER, J., Internal Medicine (Endocrinology)
BHAKDI, S., Microbiology
BORK, K., Skin and Venereal Diseases
BRISENO, B., Dentistry
BROCKERHOFF, P., Gynaecology
BUHL, R., Pneumology
D'HOEDT, B., Dental Surgery
DICK, W., Anaesthesiology
DUSCHNER, H., Dentistry
ENK, A., Skin and Venereal Diseases
FÖRSTERMANN, U., Pharmacology
GLATZEL, J., Psychiatry
GOEBEL, H. H., Neuropathology
HALMÁGYI, M., Anaesthesiology
HEINRICHS, W., Anaesthesiology
HEINE, J., Orthopaedics
HEINEMANN, M., Communication Disorders
HIEMKE, CH., Psychiatry
HOFFMANN, S. O., Psychosomatic Medicine and Psychotherapy
HOFMANN VON KAP-HERR, K. S., Paediatrics
HOMMEL, G., Medical Statistics and Documentation
HOPF, H.-CH., Neurology
HUBER, C., Internal Medicine, Haematology
HUPPMANN, G., Psychology, Medical Sociology
JAGE, J., Anaesthesiology
JANSEN, B., Hygiene
JUNG, K., Internal Medicine, Sports Medicine
JUNGINGER, T., Surgery
KAINA, B., Toxicology
KEMPSKI, O., Neurosurgical Physiopathology
KILBINGER, H., Pharmacology and Toxicology
KIRKPATRICK, CH. J., Pathology
KNAPSTEIN, P.-G., Obstetrics and Gynaecology
KNOP, J., Dermatology
KONERDING, M., Anatomy
KONIETZKO, J., Industrial and Social Medicine
KRAFT, J., Dental Materials Technology
KÜMMEL, W., History of Medicine
KUTZNER, J., Radiology
LEUBE, R., Anatomy
LÖFFELHOLZ, K., Pharmacology
LOOS, M., Medical Microbiology
LÜDDENS, H., Psychiatry
MAELICKE, A., Physiological Chemistry and Pathobiochemistry
MANN, W., Otorhinolaryngology
MASCHEK, H., Pathology
MEYER, J., Internal Medicine
MICHAELIS, J., Medical Statistics and Documentation
MÜLLER, W. E. G., Physiological Chemistry
MÜLLER-ESTERL, W., Pathobiochemistry
MÜLLER-KLIESER, W., Physiology
MÜNTEFERING, H., General Pathology and Child Pathology
NIX, W., Neurology
OELERT, H., Heart, Thorax and Vascular Surgery
OESCH, F., Toxicology
OHLER, W., Internal Medicine
OLBERT, D., Ophthalmology
OTTO, G., Surgery and Transplants
PERNECZKY, A., Neurosurgery
PETUTSCHNIGK, D., Anatomy
PLACHTER, B., Virology
POHL, U., Psychology
POLLOW, K., Experimental Endocrinology
POMMERENING, K., Medical Statistics and Documentation
PRELLWITZ, W., Clinical Chemistry
REDDEHASE, M., Virology
REITTER, B., Paediatrics
RESKE-KUNZ, A., Allergology, Immunology
RITTNER, CH., Forensic Medicine
ROMER, F., Biology for Doctors
ROMMENS, P. M., Accident Surgery
ROSE-JOHN, S., Physiopathology
RÜDE, E., Immunology
SCHMIDT, B., Physiological Chemistry
SCHÖNBERGER, W., Paediatrics
SCHULTE, E., Anatomy
SCHUMACHER, R., Paediatrics
SERGL, H. G., Maxillary Surgery
STOETER, P., Neuroradiology
STOFFT, E., Anatomy
STOPFKUCHEN, H., Paediatrics
STREECK, R., Molecular Genetics (Medical Microbiology)
THELEN, M., Radiology
THÜROFF, J., Urology
TREEDE, R.-D., Physiology
URBAN, R., Forensic Medicine
VAUPEL, P., Physiology and Physiopathology
VOLLRATH, L., Histology and Embryology
VOTH, D., Neurosurgery
WAGNER, W., Oral and Maxillofacial Surgery
WALGENBACH, S., General and Abdominal Surgery
WANITSCHKE, R., Internal Medicine
WEILEMANN, L. S., Internal Medicine
WEINBLUM, D., Physiological Chemistry
WILLERSHAUSEN-ZÖNNCHEN, B., Dentistry
WOLF, H. K., Pathology
ZABEL, B., Paediatrics
ZANDER, R., Physiology

Faculty of Philosophy and Pedagogics:

BUCHHEIM, TH., Philosophy
BÜRMANN, J., Higher Education
CESANA, A., Philosophy
GERLACH, H.-M., Philosophy
HAMBURGER, F., Education
HEINEMANN, E., Special Education
HELSPER, W., Education
HUFNAGEL, E., Education
KRON, FR. W., Education
MEUELER, E., Adult Education
SEEBOHM, TH., Philosophy

Faculty of Social Sciences:

BIERSCHENK, T., Ethnology
DRUWE, U., Political Science
FALTER, J., Political Science
FRÖHLICH, W., Psychology
GERHARDT, R., Journalism
HEINTZ, B., Sociology
HOLTZ-BACHA, C., Journalism
HRADIL, ST., Sociology
KASTENHOLZ, R., African Philology
KEPPLINGER, H. M., Journalism
KNAPP, A., Psychology for Educationalists
KROHNE, H. W., Psychology
KUNCZIK, M., Journalism
LANDWEHRMANN, F., Sociology
MERKEL, W., Political Science
MOLS, M., Political Science
NEDELMANN, B., Sociology
OCHSMANN, R., Psychology
RENNER, K.-N., Journalism
RICKER, R., Journalism
SANDSCHNEIDER, E., Political Science
SCHNEIDER, N., Sociology
STRECKER, I., Ethnology
WERMUTH, N., Psychological Methods
WILKE, J., Journalism
WOLFF, V., Journalism

Faculty of Philology I:

BALME, C., Theatre Studies
DICK, M., Modern German Literature
DÜSING, W., Modern German Literature
FRITZ, H., General and Comparative Literature
HILLEBRAND, B., Modern German Literature
KAFITZ, D., Modern German Literature
KOEBNER, TH., Film Studies
KRUMMACHER, H.-H., Modern German Literature
KURZKE, H., Modern German Literature
LAMPING, D., General and Comparative Literature
RUBERG, U., Medieval German Literature
SCHWEDT, H., German Ethnology
VEITH, W. H., Descriptive Linguistics
VOSS, R., Medieval German Literature

Faculty of Philology II:

BISANG, W., General and Comparative Linguistics
ELIASSON, ST., Nordic and Baltic Languages
ERLEBACH, P., English Philology
FAISS, K., English Philology
HERGET, W., American Studies
HORNUNG, A., English and American Studies
LUBBERS, K., English and American Philology
REITZ, B., English Philology
RIEDEL, W., English Philology
SEELBACH, D., General Linguistics

Faculty of Philology III:

BLÄNSDORF, J., Classical Philology
BRAUN, E. A., Near East Archaeology
BRINGMANN, M., History of Art
FLEISCHER, R., Classical Archaeology
GEISLER, E., Romance Philology
GIRKE, W., Slavonic Philology
GÖBLER, F., Slavonic Literature
JANIK, D., Romance Philology
JOHANSON, L., Turcology
KROPP, M., Islamic Philology and Semitics
LEY, K., Romance Philology
MEISIG, K., Indology
PESCHLOW, U., Christian Archaeology and History of Byzantine Art
SALLMANN, K., Classical Philology
SCHRÖTER, E., History of Art
SCHULTZE, B., Slavonic Literature
SIEPE, H. T., Romance Philology
VENZLAFF, H., Islamic Culture and Philology
VERHOEVEN-VAN ELSBERGEN, U., Egyptology
WEHR, B., Romance Philology

WINTERFELD, D. VON, History of Art
WLOSOK, A., Classical Philology
ZELLER, D., Religion in the Hellenistic Period

Faculty of History:

ALTGELD, W., Modern and Contemporary History
AMENT, H., Pre- and Proto-history
BAUMGART, W., Modern and Contemporary History
BEER, A., Musicology
DOTZAUER, W., Modern History, Regional History
FELTEN, F. J., Medieval History
FISCHER, E., History of the Book Trade in the 19th and 20th Centuries
FÜSSEL, ST., History of the Book and other Media; Renaissance Studies
HARTMANN, P., General and Modern History
MAHLING, CH.-H., Musicology
MATHEUS, M., Medieval and Modern History, Comparative Regional History
MENZEL, J. J., Medieval History
OBERLÄNDER, E., East European History, Modern History
OLDENSTEIN, J., Pre- and Protohistory
PRINZING, G., Byzantine Studies
RÖDEL, W. G., Modern History, Comparative Regional History
SCHILSON, A., History of Western Religions
SCHUMACHER, L., Ancient History and Classical Culture

Faculty of Mathematics:

AMBERG, B., Mathematics
BÄUMER-SCHLEINKOFER, Ä., History of Natural Sciences
BÜHLER, W., Mathematical Statistics
DOERK, K., Mathematics
GÖTTLER, H., Computer Science
GOTTSCHLING, E., Mathematics
GRAMSCH, B., Mathematics
HEINZ, H.-P., Applied Mathematics
HELD, D., Mathematics
HOFMEISTER, G., Mathematics
KLÜPPELBERG, C., Mathematical Statistics
KRECK, M., Mathematics
LAUTEMANN, C., Computer Science
LEEB, B., Mathematics
LEINEN, F., Mathematics
MÜLTHEI, H., Applied Mathematics
PERL, J., Computer Science
PFISTER, A., Mathematics
ROWE, D., History of Mathematics and Natural Sciences
RÜSSMANN, H., Mathematics
SCHEIBA, K.-J., Mathematics
SCHLEINKOFER, G., Mathematics
SCHNEIDER, C., Mathematics
SCHUH, H.-J., Mathematics
STAUDE, U., Mathematics
VAN STRATEN, D., Mathematics

Faculty of Physics:

ADRIAN, H., Experimental Physics
ALT, E., Theoretical Physics
ARENDS, J., Physics
ARENHÖVEL, H., Physics
BACKE, H., Experimental Physics
BECKMANN, P., Theoretical Physics
BINDER, K., Theoretical Physics
BROCKMANN, R., Theoretical Nuclear Physics
DRECHSEL, D., Theoretical Physics
EHRFELD, W., Microtechnology
HARRACH, D. VON, Experimental Physics
HUBER, G., Experimental Physics
JAENICKE, R., Meteorology
JAKOBS, K., Experimental Physics
KLEINKNECHT, K., Experimental Physics
KÖPKE, L., Experimental Physics
KÖRNER, J., Theoretical Physics
MERLE, K., Experimental Physics, Data Processing
MÜNZENBERG, G., Experimental Physics
NEUHAUSEN, R., Physics
OTTEN, E. W., Experimental Physics
PALBERG, T., Experimental Physics
REUTER, M., Theoretical Physics
SANDER, H.-G., Experimental Physics
SCHECK, F., Experimental Theoretical Physics
SCHILCHER, K., Theoretical Physics
SCHILLING, R., Theoretical Physics
SCHÖNHENSE, G., Experimental Physics
STRÖHER, H., Experimental Physics
WALCHER, TH., Experimental Nuclear Physics
WERTH, G., Experimental Physics
ZIMMERMANN, G., Meteorology

Faculty of Chemistry and Pharmacy:

BASCUÉ, T., Physical Chemistry
BAUMANN, W., Physical Chemistry
BUTT, H.-J., Physical Chemistry
DANNHARDT, G., Pharmaceutical Chemistry
DENSCHLAG, J. O., Nuclear Chemistry
DRÄGER, M., Inorganic and Analytical Chemistry
EPE, B., Pharmacology and Toxicology for Pharmacists
FAHRENHOLZ, F., Biochemistry
GAUSS, J., Theoretical Chemistry
GEYER, E., Organic Chemistry
GÜTLICH, PH., Inorganic and Analytical Chemistry
HEUMANN, K., Analytical Chemistry
KIRSTE, R., Physical Chemistry
KOCH-BRANDT, C., Biochemistry
KRATZ, J.-V., Nuclear Chemistry
KRATZ, K.-L., Nuclear Chemistry
KUNZ, H., Organic Chemistry
MEIER, H., Organic Chemistry
MOLL, F., Pharmaceutical Technology
OKUDA, J., Inorganic Chemistry
PINDUR, U., Pharmaceutical Chemistry
RITTER, H., Organic Chemistry
RÖSCH, F., Nuclear Chemistry
SCHMIDT, M., Physical Chemistry
SILLESCU, H., Physical Chemistry
SINGER, H., Inorganic Chemistry
STÖCKIGT, J., Pharmaceutical Biology
TREMEL, W., Inorganic and Analytical Chemistry
UNGER, K., Inorganic Chemistry
VOGT, W., Organic and Macromolecular Chemistry
WOLF, B., Physical Chemistry

Faculty of Biology:

BERNHARD, W., Anthropology
CAMPENHAUSEN, C. VON, Zoology
CLASSEN-BOCKNOFF, R., Botany
DECKER, H., Molecular Biophysics
DORN, A., Zoology
DORRESTEIJN, A., Zoology
EISENBEIS, G., Zoology
FISCHER, A., Zoology
HENKE, W., Anthropology
HONOMICHL, K., Zoology
KADEREIT, J. W., Botany
KÖNIG, H., Microbiology
LÜPNITZ, D., Botany
MARKL, J., Zoology
MARTENS, J., Zoology
NEUMEYER, CH., Zoology
PAULSEN, H., Botany
RICHTER, M., Botany
ROMER, F., Zoology
ROTHE, G., Botany
RUPPRECHT, R., Zoology
SCHMIDT, E. R., Molecular Genetics
SEITZ, A., Zoology
SIEGERT, A., Botany
TECHNAU, G. M., Genetics
UNDEN, G., Microbiology
WEGENER, G., Zoology
WERNICKE, W., Botany

Faculty of Geosciences:

BAUMGARTNER, L. P., Mineralogy and Petrology
BERG, D. E., Palaeontology and Geology
BÖHM, H., Mineralogy and Crystallography
BOY, J., Palaeontology and Geology
DOMRÖS, M., Geography
DÜRR, S., Geology and Palaeontology
ESCHER, A., Geography
GRUNERT, J., Geography
HILDEBRANDT, H., Geography
JACOBY, W., Geophysics
KANDLER, O., Geography
KEESMANN, I., Mineralogy
KERSTEN, M., Geochemistry
KRÖNER, A., Geology
MEYER, G., Geography
PASSCHIER, C., Tectonic Physics
PREUSS, J., Geography
SCHENK, D., Applied Geology
SCHMIDT-KITTLER, N., Palaeontology and Geology
TRETTIN, R., Applied Mineralogy
UTHOFF, D., Geography
WILKEN, R.-D., Applied Hydrochemistry

Faculty of Applied Linguistic and Cultural Sciences:

BARDELEBEN, R. VON, American Studies
DRESCHER, H. W., English Philology
FORSTNER, M., Islamic Philology and Culture
HUBER, D., General and Applied Linguistics
KELLETAT, A., Comparative German Studies
PERL, M., Romance Studies
PÖCKL, W., Romance Philology
PÖRTL, K., Romance Philology
RUGE, H., Modern Greek Studies
STOLL, K.-H., English Philology
WORBS, E., Polish Philology

Faculty of Fine Arts:

BIEDERBICK, CH., Plastic Art
BREMBS, D., Drawing
ELLWANGER, V., Pottery (Ceramics)
GRIMM, A., Writing
HAHN, F., Painting
HELLMANN, U., Metal
KNOCHE-WENDEL, E., Textiles
LIESER, P. G., Environmental Design
LÖFFLER, A., Woodwork
LÖRINCZ, P., Graphic Arts
NIERHOFF, A., Plastic Art
REISS, W., Teaching of Art
SCHLEICHER, H., Film, Video
SPACEK, V., Photography
VIRNICH, W., Painting
VOGELGESANG, K., Drawing
ZIMMERMANN, J., Art Theory

Faculty of Music:

BERGER, J., Cello
BLUME, J., Theory of Music, Phrasing
CANTOR, E., Viola
DAUS, J., Conducting
DEWALD, TH., Singing
DOBNER, M., Double Bass
DREYER, L., Phrasing, Aural Training, Theory of Musical Form
EDER, C., Singing
FRANK, B., Jazz, Piano
GERMER, K., Piano
GUANN, G., Organ
KAISER, H.-J., Organ, Improvisation
MARX, K., Cello and Chamber Music
REICHERT, M., Contemporary Music
VETRE, O., Piano
VOLK, E., Conducting
WAHN, M., Flute
ZARBOCK, H., Piano

Faculty of Physical Education:

AUGUSTIN, D., Athletics and Theory of Training
JUNG, K., Sports Medicine
LETZELTER, H., Athletics and Theory of Training
LETZELTER, M., Theory of Training and Movement Theory
MESSING, M., Sociology of Sport
MÜLLER, N., History of Sport, Athletics

Petter, W., Teaching Practice and Psychology
Salomon, H., Teaching Practice and Athletics
Schöpe, H. G., Teaching Practice and Athletics
Ulmer, H.-V., Physiology

ATTACHED INSTITUTES

Forschungsinstitut für Wirtschaftspolitik (Institute for Economic Research): 55099 Mainz, Universität, Jakob-Welder-Weg 4; Dirs Prof. Dr Hartwig Bartling, Prof. Dr Werner Zohlnhöfer, Prof. Dr Helmut Diederich, Prof. Dr Walter Hamm.

Forschungsinstitut Lesen und Medien (Institute for Media Research): 55116 Mainz, Fischtorplatz 23; Dir Prof. Dr Stephan Füssel.

Institut für Europäische Geschichte (Institute for European History): see under Research Institutes.

Institut für Geschichtliche Landeskunde (Institute for Historical Regional Studies of Rhineland-Palatinate): 55099 Mainz, Universität, Johann-Friedrich-von-Pfeiffer-Weg 3; Dirs Prof. Dr M. Matheus, Prof. Dr W. Kleiber; Prof. Dr K. Düwell.

Institut für Internationales Recht des Spar-, Giro- und Kreditwesens (Institute for International Law of Banking): Universität, Saarstrasse 21, Haus Recht und Wirtschaft, 55122 Mainz; Dirs Prof. Dr W. Hadding, Prof. Dr U. H. Schneider.

Institut für Mikrotechnik GmbH (Institute for Microtechnology): 55071 Mainz, Postfach 421364; premises at: 55129 Mainz, Carl-Zeiss-Str. 18–20; Dir Prof. Dr W. Ehrfeld.

Tumorzentrum Rheinland-Pfalz e.V. (Tumour Centre Rhineland-Palatinate): Am Pulverturm 13, 55101 Mainz; Dir Prof. Dr C. Huber.

UNIVERSITÄT MANNHEIM

68131 Manheim, Schloss
Telephone: (621) 2920
Telex: 6211776
Fax: (621) 292-2587

Founded 1907 as Städtische Handelshochschule, attached to Heidelberg University 1933, re-opened as Wirtschaftshochschule 1946, University status 1967
Academic year: April to July, October to February

Rector: Prof. Dr Peter Frankenberg
Pro-Rectors: Prof. Dr Rainer Weissauer, Prof. Dr Hartmut Esser
Chancellor: Dr iur. Dietmar Ertmann
Librarian: Prof. Dr rer. nat. Manfred Kleiss
Press Officer: Martin Spieles

Number of teachers: *c.* 165
Number of students: *c.* 12,000

DEANS

Faculty of Law: Prof. Dr J. Taupitz
Faculty of Economics: Prof. Dr W. Bühler
Faculty of Political Economy and Statistics: Prof. Dr A. Börsch-Supan
Faculty of Social Sciences: Prof. Dr J. Handl
Faculty of Philosophy, Psychology and Pedagogy: Prof. Dr W. Wittmann
Faculty of Languages and Literature: Prof. Dr B. Henn-Memmesheimer
Faculty of History and Geography: Prof. Dr C. Jentsch
Faculty of Mathematics and Information Sciences: Prof. Dr M. Majster-Cederbaum

ATTACHED INSTITUTES

Institut für Aufbaustudien 'Internationale Wirtschaftsbeziehungen': Dir Prof. Dr Jürgen Schröder.

Institut für Empirische Wirtschaftsforschung: Dir Prof. Dr W. Bühler.

Otto-Selz-Institut für Psychologie und Erziehungswissenschaft: Dir Prof. Dr W. Bungard.

Rechenzentrum: Dir Prof. Dr Hans W. Meuer.

Mannheimer Zentrum für Europäische Sozialforschung: Dir Prof. Dr Urban Pappi.

Institut für Kommunikations- und Medienforschung/Sprachlabor: Dir Prof. Dr Rolf Klöpfer.

Institut für Versicherungswissenschaft: Dir Prof. Dr Egon Lorenz.

Institut für Volkswirtschaftslehre und Statistik: Dir Prof. Dr Heinz König.

Institut für Landeskunde und Regionalforschung: Dir Prof. Dr Pirmin Spiess.

Institut für Sport: Dir Dr Robin Kähler.

Institut für Mittelstandsforschung: Dir Prof. Dr E. Gaugler.

Dokumentations- und Datenbankszentrum: Dir Prof. Beate Kohler-Koch.

PHILIPPS-UNIVERSITÄT MARBURG

35032 Marburg, Biegenstrasse 10-12
Telephone: 280
Telex: 482372
Fax: 282500

Founded 1527
State control
Academic year: October to July (two terms)

President: Prof. Dr Werner Schaal
Vice-President: Prof. Dr Theodor Schiller
Chancellor: Bernd Höhmann
Librarian: Dr Dirk Barth

Library: see Libraries
Number of teachers: 650
Number of students: 17,900

Publication: *Marburger Universitätszeitung* (monthly).

PROFESSORS

Department of Law:
Beuthien, V., Civil Commercial, Economic and Labour Law
Buchholz, St., German Legal History and Civil Law
Detterbeck, S., Public Law
Freund, G., Criminal and Procedural Law, Philosophy of Law
Frotscher, W., Public Law
Gornig, G.-H., Public Law
Gounalakis, G., Civil and Comparative Law
Hippel, R. von, Criminal and Procedural Law
Koenig, C., Public Law
Langer, W., Criminal and Procedural Law
Lessmann, H., Civil, Commercial and Economic Law
Meurer, D., Criminal and Procedural Law, Philosophy of Law
Müller-Volbehr, J., Public Law
Mummenhoff, W., Civil and Labour Law
Rupprecht, H.-A., Papyrology
Schanze, E., Civil Law
Voit, W., Civil Law
Werkmüller, D., History of Law

Department of Economics:
Alpar, P., Economics, Computer Science
Fehl, U., Economic Theory
Gerum, E., Commerce
Göpfert, J., Commerce, Logistics
Hasenkamp, U., Business Management and Economic Information Studies
Krag, J.
Krüsselberg, H.-G., Political Economy
Lingenfelder, M., Marketing
Meyer, W., Political Economy—Methods and Hypothesis
Münkner, H.-H., Business Economics
Priewasser, E., Banking
Röpke, J., Economic Theory
Schimenz, B., Business Economics
Schüller, A., Economic Theory
Zimmermann, H., Political Economy

Department of Social Science and Philosophy:
Berg-Schlosser, D., Political Science
Boris, H.-D., Sociology
Brandt, R., Philosophy
Bredow, W. von, Political Science
Deppe, F., Political Science
Foltin, H.-F., European Ethnology
Fülberth-Sperling, G., Political Science
Janich, P., Philosophy
Käsler, D., Sociology
Kissler, L., Sociology
Köhle-Hezinger, C., European Ethnology
Kühnl, R., Political Science
Langer, I., Political Science
Lüdtke, H., Sociology
Münzel, M., Ethnology
Römer, P., Political Science
Rupp, H.-K., Political Science
Scharfe, M., European Ethnology
Schiller, Th., Political Science
Tuschling, B., Philosophy
Wyniger, W., Sociology
Zoll, R., Sociology

Department of Psychology:
Ehlers, T.
Florin, I.
Jacobs, A.
Lachnit, H.
Liebhart, E.
Röhrle, B.
Rösler, F.
Rost, D.
Scheiblechner, H.
Schulze, H.-H.
Sommer, G.
Stelzl, I.
Stemmler, G.
Wagner, U.

Department of Theology:
Barth, H.-M., Systematic Theology
Bienert, W., Church History
Conrad, D., Hebrew, Archaeology of Palestine
Elsas, C., Religious History
Gerstenberger, E., Old Testament
Hage, W., Church History
Harnisch, W., New Testament
Jeremias, J., Old Testament
Kaiser, J.-C., Church History
Keil, S., Social Ethics
Kessler, R., Old Testament
Koch, G., Christian Archaeology
Lührmann, D., New Testament
Martin, G. M., Practical Theology
Nethöfel, W., Social Ethnics
Schneider, H., Church History
Schunack, G., New Testament
Schwab, U., Practical Theology
Schwebel, H., Religious Communication
Stollberg, D., Practical Theology

Department of History:
Borscheid, P., Social and Economic History
Drexhage, H.-J., Ancient History
Errington, R. M., Ancient History
Hardach, G., Social and Economic History
Klein, T., Modern History
Krieger, W., Modern History
Krüger, P., Modern History
Lemberg, H., East European History
Malettke, K., Modern History
Petersohn, J., Medieval History
Rück, P., Historical Auxiliary Sciences
Schulze, H. K., Medieval History

Department of Antiquities:
Böhme, H. W., Prehistory
Froning, H., Classical Archaeology
Köngsen, E., Latin Philology

LAUTER, H., Classical Archaeology
SCHMITT, A., Classical Philology

Department of General and Germanic Linguistics and Philology:

ALBERT, R., German Language
BRANDT, W., German Linguistics and Medieval German Philology
HEINZLE, J., German Philology
HILDEBRANDT, R., German Linguistics and Philology
KETTNER, B.-U., German Linguistics
LOMNITZER, H., German Language and Old German Philology
PUTSCHKE, W., German Linguistics and Linguistic Informatics
RÖSSING-HAGER, M., German Linguistics and Philology
SCHANZE, H., German Language and Old German Philology
WIESE, R., German Linguistics

Department of Modern German Literature and Arts:

BAUER, B., Modern German Literature
BERNS, J. J., Modern German Literature
DEDNER, B., Modern German Literature
GIESENFELD, G., Modern German Literature
GLÜCK, A., Modern German Literature
HELLER, H.-B., Modern German Literature
HENZE-DÖHRING, S., Music
HEUSINGER, L., Informatics in History of Art
KRAUSE, K., History of Art
LICHTENSTERN, C., History of Art
OSINSKI, J., Modern German Literature
PICKERODT, G., Modern German Literature
PRÜMM, K., Media Teaching
SCHÄFER, G., Graphics and Painting
SCHÜTTE, W., History of Art
SOLMS-HOHENSOLMS-LICH, W., PRINZ ZU, Communication Sciences and Media Teaching
VOGT, G., German Language Teaching
WEYER, M., Theory and Practice of Music

Department of Modern Languages and Literature:

BISCHOFF, V., American Literature
GUTHMÜLLER, B., Romance Philology
HANDKE, J., English Linguistics
HOFER, H., Romance Philology
JÄNICKE, O., Romance Philology
LOPE, H. J., Romance Philology
SCHALLER, H., Slavic Philology
UHLIG, C., English and American Philology
WOLL, D., Romance Philology
ZIMMERMANN, R., English Linguistics

Department of Non-European Languages and Cultures:

HAHN, M., Indology
JOB, M., General and Comparative Language
MÜLLER, W. W., Semitic Studies
PAUER, E., Japanology
POPPER, E., General Language and Celtology
PYE, E. M., General and Comparative Religion
SOMMERFELD, W., Ancient Oriental Studies
STEINER, G., Ancient Oriental Studies
ÜBELHÖR, M., Sinology

Department of Mathematics:

BÖHMER, K.
DRESSLER, A.
GROMES, W.
GUMM, H.-P.
HANEKE, W.
HESSE, W.
KNÖLLER, F. W.
KÖRLE, H.-H.
LOOGEN, R.
MAMMITZSCH, V.
MIESNER, W.
PORTENIER, C.
REUFEL, M.
SEEGER, B.
SOMMER, M.
STEINEBACH, J.
ULTSCH, A.
UPMEIER, H.

Department of Physics:

ACKERMANN, H., Experimental Physics
ECKHORN, R., Applied Physics
FICK, D., Experimental Physics
FUHS, W., Experimental Physics
GANSSAUGE, E., Experimental Physics
GROSSMANN, S., Theoretical Physics
HÜHNERMANN, H., Experimental Physics
KERLER, W., Theoretical Physics
KOCH, S., Theoretical Physics
KRÖLL, W., Theoretical Physics
MAASS, W., Theoretical Physics
MELSHEIMER, O., Theoretical Physics
NEUMANN, H., Theoretical Physics
PÜHLHOFER, F., Experimental Physics
REITBÖCK, H., Applied Physics
RÜHLE, W., Experimental Physics
STÖCKMANN, H.-J., Experimental Physics
THOMAS, P., Theoretical Physics
WASSMUTH, H.-W., Experimental Physics
WEISER, G., Experimental Physics
WISSEL, C., Theoretical Physics

Department of Physical Chemistry:

BÄSSLER, H., Physical Chemistry
BRANDT, R., Nuclear Chemistry
FÖRSTERLING, H.-D., Physical Chemistry
HAMPP, N., Physical Chemistry
HEITZ, W., Polymer Chemistry
HENSEL, F., Physical Chemistry
PATZELT, P., Nuclear Chemistry
SCHWEIG, A., Physical Chemistry
WENDORFF, J., Physical Chemistry

Department of Chemistry:

AURICH, H. G., Organic Chemistry
BERNDT, A., Organic Chemistry
BOCHE, G., Organic Chemistry
DEHNICKE, K., Inorganic Chemistry
ELSCHENBROICH, CHR., Inorganic Chemistry
FRENKING, G., Chemistry-Related Computer Studies
HARBRECHT, B., Inorganic Chemistry
HOFFMANN, R. W., Organic Chemistry
KADENBACH, B., Biochemistry
KINDL, H., Biochemistry
KNOCHEL, T., Organic Chemistry
LORBERTH, J., Chemistry
MARAHIEL, M., Biochemistry
NEIDHART, B., Analytical Chemistry
PERST, H., Organic Chemistry
REICHARDT, C., Organic Chemistry
STORK, G., Inorganic and Analytical Chemistry
SUNDERMEYER, J., Metal-organic Chemistry

Department of Pharmacy and Nutrition:

DILG, P., History of Pharmacy
FAHR, A., Pharmaceutical Technology
HAAKE, M., Pharmaceutical Chemistry
HANEFELD, W., Pharmaceutical Chemistry
KISSEL, T., Pharmaceutical Technology and Biopharmacy
KLEBE, G., Pharmaceutical Chemistry
KLUMPP, S., Pharmaceutical Chemistry
KRAFFT, H. F., History of Pharmacy
KRIEGLSTEIN, J., Pharmacology and Toxicology
KUSCHINSKY, K., Pharmacology and Toxicology
MATERN, U., Pharmaceutical Biology
MATUSCH, R., Pharmaceutical Chemistry
SEITZ, G., Pharmaceutical Chemistry

Department of Biology:

BERTSH, A., Botany
BREMER, E., Microbiology
BUCKEL, W., Microbiology
GALLAND, P., Plant Physiology, Photobiology
HAGEN, H.-O. VON, Zoology, Evolution and Human Biology
HELDMAIER, G., Zoology
KIRCHNER, C., Zoology
KLEIN, A., Molecular Genetics
KOST, G., Botany, Mycology
LINGELBACH, U., Zoology, Parasitology
PLACHTER, H., Nature Conservancy Studies
POSCHLOD, P., Nature Conservancy
RENKAWITZ-POHL, R., Molecular Genetics
SCHÖNBOHM, E., Botany
SEITZ, K.-A., Comparative Anatomy
THAUER, R., Microbiology
THROM, G., Botany
WEBER, H. C., Botany
WEHRMEYER, W., Botany
WERNER, D., Botany and General Biology

Department of Geological Studies:

BUCK, P., Crystallography
HAFNER, S., Crystallography and Mineralogy
HAHN, G., Palaeontology
HOFFER, E., Petrology
PRINZ-GRIMM, P., Historical and Regional Geology
SCHMIDT-EFFING, R., Geology
TUFAR, W., Mineralogy
VOGLER, ST., Structural Geology
ZANKL, H., Geography and Sedimentology

Department of Geography:

BRÜCKNER, H.
BUCHHOFER, E.
ENDLICHER, W.
MERTINS, G.
MIEHE, G.
NUHN, H.
PLETSCH, A.
SAILER-FLIEGE, U.

Department of Medicine:

ARNOLD, R., Internal Medicine
AUMÜLLER, G., Anatomy
AUSTERMANN, K.-H., Maxillo-Facial Surgery
BASLER, H.-D., Psychology
BAUM, E., General Medicine
BEATO, M., Physiological Chemistry
BERGER, R., Oto-rhino-laryngology
BESEDOVSKY, H., Physiology
BIEN, S., Neurosurgery
CETIN, Y., Anatomy
DAUT, J., Physiology
DIBBETS, J., Dentistry
DOSS, M., Clinical Biochemistry and Biochemical Microbiology
ENGEL, P., Physiology and Rehabilitation Research
ESCHENBACH, C., Child Medicine
FLORES DE JACOBY, L., Paradontology
FRUHSTORFER, H., Physiology
FUHRMANN, G. F., Pharmacology and Toxicology
GARTEN, W., Virology
GEMSA, D., Immunology
GEUS, A., History of Medicine
GÖKE, B., Endocrinology
GOTZEN, L., Surgery
GRESSNER, A., Interdisciplinary Medicine
GRISS, P., Orthopaedics
GRÖNE, H.-J., Pathology
GRUNDNER, H.-G., Radiology
GRZESCKIK, K.-H., Human Genetics
HABERMEHL, A., Medical Data Processing
HAPPLE, R., Dermatology
HARTMANN, K.-U., Immunology
HASILIK, A., Physiological Chemistry
HEBEBRAND, J., Child Psychiatry
HERPERTZ-DAHLMANN, B., Child Psychiatry
HILGERMANN, R., Forensic Medicine
HOFFMANN, G., Child Medicine
JONES, D., Orthopaedics
JOSEPH, K., Experimental Nuclear Medicine
KERN, H. F., Cytobiology and Cytopathology
KLEINE, T. O., Neurobiochemistry and Physiological Chemistry
KLENK, H.-D., Virology
KLOSE, K., Radiology
KRAUSE, W., Andrology
KRETSCHMER, V., Transfusion Medicine
KRIEG, J. C., Psychology

KROLL, P., Ophthalmology
KUNI, H., Experimental Nuclear Medicine
KUSLER, W., Dermatology
LANG, R. E., Experimental Nuclear Medicine
LANGE, H., Internal Medicine
LAUER, H. H., History of Medicine
LEHMANN, K., Dentistry
LENNARTZ, H., Anaesthesiology
LORENZ, W., Experimental Surgery and Pathological Biochemistry
LOTZMANN, K.-U., Dentistry
LÜHRMANN, R., Physiological Chemistry and Molecular Biology
MAISCH, B., Cardiology
MENNEL, H.-D., Pathological Anatomy
MOOSDORF, R., Cardiac Surgery
MÜLLER, R., Molecular Biology
MUELLER, U., Medical Sociology
NIESSING, J., Physiological Chemistry
OERTEL, W., Neurology
PIEPER, K., Dentistry for Children
RADSAK, K., General Medicine
REHDER, H., General Pathology and Pathological Anatomy
REMSCHMIDT, H., Child Psychology
ROTHMUND, M., Surgery
SCHACHTSCHABEL, D., Physiological Chemistry
SCHÄFER, H., Medical Biometry
SCHÜFFEL, W., Psychosomatics
SCHULZ, K.-D., Obstetrics
SCHWARZ, R., Parasitology
SEIFART, K., Physiological Chemistry
SEITZ, J., Anatomy
SEYBERTH, H. W., Child Medicine, Clinical and Theoretical Pharmacology
SLENCZKA, W., Medical Microbiology
STACHNISS, V., Dentistry
STEINIGER, B., Anatomy
STREMPEL, J., Ophthalmology
STURM, G., Clinical Chemistry and Microscopy
THOMAS, C., Institute of Pathology
VOIGT, K.-H., Physiology
WEIHE, E., Anatomy
WESEMANN, W., Physiological Chemistry
WICHERT, P. VON, Internal Medicine

Department of Education:

BECKER, P., Sociology of Sports
BERG, H.-C., Educational Theory
BÜCHNER, P., Sociology of Education
HAFENEGER, B., Extracurricular Education
HILDENBRANDT, E., Sports Education
KUTZER, R., Didactics of Educational Handicaps
LERSCH, R., School Education
NUISSL, E., Adult Education
PROBST, H., Psychology of Special School Education
PROKOP, U., Socialization Theory
ROHRMANN, E., Education
SCHILLING, F., Socio-psychological Basis of Sports and Motional Therapy
SOMMER, H.-M., Sports Medicine
WOLF, W., Empirical Education

LUDWIG-MAXIMILIANS-UNIVERSITÄT MÜNCHEN

80539 Munich, Geschwister-Scholl-Platz 1
Telephone: (89) 2180-0
Telex: 5 29 860
Fax: (89) 2180-2322

Founded 1472
Academic year: October to March, April to September

Rector: Prof. Dr ANDREAS HELDRICH
Pro-Rectors: Prof. Dr LUTZ VON ROSENSTIEL, Prof. Dr Dr DIETER ADAM, Prof. Dr HEINRICH SOFFEL
Chief Administrative Officer: Dr HENDRIK RUST
Director of Library: Dr FRITZ JUNGINGER

Number of teachers: 3,440
Number of students: 58,663

Publications: *Vorlesungsverzeichnis* (2 a year), *Chronik der Ludwig-Maximilians-Universität* (annually), *Informationsdienst* (monthly), *Veranstaltungskalender* (7 a year), *MUM* (7 a year), *'Einsichten'* (2 a year).

DEANS

Department of Catholic Theology: Prof. Dr PETER NEUNER
Department of Evangelical Theology: Prof. Dr Dr MICHAEL VON BRÜCK
Department of Law: Prof. Dr BERND SCHÜNEMANN
Department of Business Administration: Prof. Dr WOLFGANG BOLLWIESER
Department of Economics: Prof. Dr JOHN KOMLOS
Department of Medicine: Prof. Dr Dr KLAUS PETER
Department of Veterinary Science: Prof. Dr WALTER HERRMANNS
Department of History and Art: Prof. Dr HANS-MICHAEL KÖRNER
Department of Philosophy, Science and Statistics: Prof. Dr ECKHARD KESSLER
Department of Mathematics: Prof. Dr RUDOLF FRITSCH
Department of Physics: Prof. Dr AXEL SCHENZLE
Department of Chemistry and Pharmacy: Prof. Dr MEINHART H. ZENK
Department of Biology: Prof. Dr REGINE KOHMANN
Department of Geosciences: Prof. Dr UWE RUST
Department of Forestry: Prof. Dr PETER FABIAN
Department of Psychology and Pedagogics: Prof. Dr HEINZ MANDL
Department of Ancient Cultures: Prof. Dr HANS GEORG MAJER
Department of Language and Literature I: Prof. Dr WULF OESTERREICHER
Department of Language and Literature II: Prof. Dr JAN-DIRK MÜLLER
Department of Social Sciences: Prof. Dr HANS WAGNER

TECHNISCHE UNIVERSITÄT MÜNCHEN

80290 Munich, Arcisstrasse 21
Telephone: (89) 289-01
Telex: 522854
Fax: (89) 289-22000
E-mail: praesident@tu-muenchen.de

Founded 1868
State control
Academic year: October to September

President: Prof. Dr Ing. WOLFGANG A. HERRMANN
Vice-Presidents: Prof. Dr-Ing. JOACHIM HEINZL, Prof. Dr ARNULF MELZER
Chancellor: Dr LUDWIG KRONTHALER
Librarian: Dr phil. HORST WERNER

Number of teachers: 3,575
Number of students: 17,743

Publications: *Personen- und Vorlesungsverzeichnis* (2 a year), *Jahrbuch* (annually), *TU-Mitteilungen* (6 a year).

DEANS

Faculty of Mathematics: Prof. Dr K. H. HOFFMANN
Faculty of Physics: Prof. Dr WINFRIED PETRY
Faculty of Chemistry, Biology and Earth Sciences: Prof. Dr-Ing. OSKAR NUYKEN
Faculty of Economics and Social Sciences: Prof Dr KARL-HEINZ LEIST
Faculty of Civil Engineering and Surveying: Prof. Dr-Ing. THEODOR STROBL
Faculty of Architecture: Prof. Dipl.-Ing. MATTHIAS REICHENBACH-KLINKE
Faculty of Mechanical Engineering: Prof. Dr-Ing. BERND-ROBERT HÖHN
Faculty of Electrical Engineering and Information Technology: Prof. Dr-Ing. KURT ANTREICH
Faculty of Computer Science: Prof. Dr ARNDT BODE
Faculty of Agriculture and Horticulture: Prof. Dr JOHANN BAUER
Faculty of Brewing, Food Technology and Dairy Science: Prof. Dr-Ing. KARL SOMMER
Faculty of Medicine: Prof. Dr JOSEF DUDEL

PROFESSORS

Faculty of Mathematics:

BULIRSCH, R., Mathematics
GIERING, O., Geometry
HOFFMAN, K.-H., Applied Mathematics
KARZEL, H., Geometry
KÖNIGSBERGER, K., Mathematics
RITTER, K., Applied Mathematics and Mathematical Statistics
SCHEURLE, J., Mathematics and Analytical Mechanics

Faculty of Physics:

ABSTREITER, G., Experimental Semiconductor Physics
ANDRES, K., Engineering Physics
BRENIG, W., Theoretical Physics
BURAS, A., Theoretical Physics
DIETRICH, K., Theoretical Physics
FEILITZSCH, F. VON, Experimental Physics
FISCHER, S., Theoretical Physics
GLÄSER, W., Experimental Physics
GÖTZE, W., Theoretical Physics
KALVIUS, G., Physics
KIENLE, P., Experimental Physics
KINDER, H., Experimental Physics
KOCH, F., Physics
KÖRNER, H.-J., Experimental Physics
LAUBEREAU, A., Experimental Physics
MENZEL, D., Physics
MÖSSBAUER, R. L., Experimental Physics
PARAK, F., Experimental Physics, Biophysics
PETRY, W., Experimental Physics
SACKMANN, E., Physics
SCHWABL, F., Theoretical Physics
STUTZMANN, M., Experimental Semiconductor Physics
VOGL, P., Theoretical Physics
WEISE, W., Theoretical Physics

Faculty of Chemistry, Biology and Earth Sciences:

BACHER, A., Organic Chemistry and Biochemistry
BAUMGÄRTNER, F., Radiochemistry
BONDYBEY, V., Physical Chemistry
GIERL, A., Genetic Engineering of Plants
GRILL, E., Botany
HERRMANN, W., Inorganic Chemistry
HOFACKER, G. L., Theoretical Chemistry
KESSLER, H., Organic Chemistry
KÖHLER, F., Inorganic Chemistry
MANLEY, G., Zoology
MORTEANI, G., Applied Mineralogy and Geochemistry
NIESSNER, R., Hydrogeology, Hydrochemistry and Environmental Analysis
NITSCH, W., Chemical Engineering
NUYKEN, O., Macromolecular Substances
SCHIEBERLE, P., Food Chemistry
SCHLAG, E. W., Physical Chemistry
SCHLEIFER, K.-H., Microbiology
SCHMIDBAUR, H., Inorganic and Analytical Chemistry
SPAUN, G., Applied Geology
UGI, I., Organic Chemistry
VEPREK, S., Chemistry of Information Storage

Faculty of Economics and Social Sciences:

BÄUMLER, G., Physical Education (Psychology)
BÜSSING, A., Psychology
EBERLEIN, G. L., Sociology
GRANDE, E., Political Science
GROSSER, M., Science of Movement and Training
HEINRITZ, G., Geography
HOLZHEU, F., Social Economics
KRASSER, R., Private and Patent Law
LEIST, K.-H., Physical Education Teaching
POPP, H., Applied Geography
REICHWALD, R., General and Industrial Management
SCHELTEN, A., Pedagogics
WILDEMANN, H., Business Management

Faculty of Civil Engineering and Surveying:

ALBRECHT, G., Steel-girder Construction
BÖSCH, H.-J., Tunnel Construction, Building Management
EBNER, H., Photogrammetry
EISENMANN, J., Highway Construction
FINSTERWALDER, R., Cartography and Reproduction Technology
FLOSS, R., Soil and Rock Mechanics and Foundation Engineering
GRUNDMANN, H., Building Mechanics
HOISL, R., Site Preparation
KIRCHHOFF, P., Transport and Town Planning
RUMMEL, R., Astronomical and Physical Geodesy
SCHNÄDELBACH, K., Geodesy
SCHUNK, E., Building Construction
SPRINGENSCHMID, R., Technology of Building Materials
STROBL, TH., Hydraulic Engineering and Water Supply
VALENTIN, F., Hydraulics and Hydrography
WILDERER, P., Water Quality and Waste Management
WUNDERLICH, W., Structural Engineering
ZILCH, K., Large-Scale Construction

Faculty of Architecture:

BARTHEL, R., Structural Engineering
COTELO LOPEZ, V., Architectural Design, Preservation of Monuments
DIETRICHS, B., Environmental and Country Planning
HERZOG, T., Building Construction and Design
HUGUES, T., Design, Building Construction and Materials
HUSE, N., History of Art
KIESSLER, U., Building Construction and Design
KOENIGS, W., History of Building
KRAU, I., Town Planning and Design
KURRENT, F., Design, Interior Design and Church Buildings
OSTERTAG, D., House Technology
REICHENBACH-KLINKE, M., Design and Rural Construction
SCHRÖDER, H., Design and Theory of Structures
STRACKE, F., Urban Development and Regional Planning
WIENANDS, R., Design and Method of Presentation
WINKLER, B., Building and Industrial Design
WITTENBORN, R., Design
ZBINDEN, U., Design, Building Construction and Materials

Faculty of Mechanical Engineering:

BENDER, K., Information Technology
BUBB, H., Ergonomics
GREGORY, J. K., Materials
GÜNTHNER, W., Production Technology
HABENICHT, G., Joining Technology
HEIN, D., Thermal Power Plants
HEINZL, J., Precision Mechanics and Gearing
HOFFMANN, H., Distortion Science, Foundry Engineering
HÖHN, B.-R., Machine Elements
LASCHKA, B., Fluid Mechanics
LINDEMANN, U., Construction
MAYINGER, F., Thermodynamics
MERSMANN, A., Process Engineering
MILBERG, J., Machine Tools and Operational Sciences
PFEIFFER, F., Mechanics
REINHART, G., Machine Tools
RENIUS, K. T., Agricultural Engineering
SACHS, G., Flight Mechanics and Control
SCHILLING, R., Hydraulic Engines and Installations
SCHMITT, D., Aviation
SCHMITT-THOMAS, K. G., Metallurgy
STICHLMAIR, J., Process Engineering
STRÄTER, B., Space Technology
STROHMEIER, K., Apparatus and Plant Construction
VORTMEYER, D., Thermodynamics
WENGEROTH, U., History of Technology
WINTER, E., Thermodynamics
WOSCHNI, G., Internal Combustion Vehicles and Motor Vehicles

Faculty of Electrical Engineering and Information Technology:

ANTREICH, K., Computer-aided Design
BIRKHOFER, A., Nuclear Reactor Dynamics and Reactor Safety
BOECK, W., High Voltage Engineering and Power Plants
EBERSPÄCHER, J., Communications Networks
FÄRBER, G., Computer Processing
HAGENAUER, J., Telecommunications
HARTH, W., Electrical Engineering
LANG, M., Man–Machine Communication
LORENZEN, H. W., Electrical Machinery and Equipment
NOSSEK, J. A., Network Theory and Switching Technology
RUGE, I., Integrated Circuits
RUSSER, P., High Frequency Technology
SCHMIDT, G., Control Engineering
SCHRÖDER, D., Electrical Drives
SCHRÜFER, E., Measurement Engineering
SWOBODA, J., Data Processings
WACHUTKA, G., Technical Electrophysics
WAGNER, U., Energy Industry and Power Plant Engineering

Faculty of Computer Science:

BAYER, R., Computer Science
BODE, A., Computer Engineering
BRAUER, W., Computer Science
BROY, M., Computer Science
EICKEL, J., Computer Science
ENDRES, A., Computer Science
HEGERING, H.-G., Computer Science
JESSEN, E., Computer Architecture
MAYR, E., Efficient Algorithms
PAUL, M., Computer Science
RADIG, B., Computer Science
SCHLICHTER, J., Applied Computer Science
SIEGERT, H.-J., Computer Science
SPIES, P. P., Operating Systems, Communications Systems and Computer Networks
ZENGER, C., Computer Science

Faculty of Agriculture and Horticulture:

BAUER, J., Animal Hygiene
ELSTNER, E., Phytopathology
FEUCHT, W., Fruit Growing
FORKMANN, G., Ornamental Plant Cultivation
FRIES, R., Stockbreeding
HEISSENHUBER, A., Agricultural Economics
HOCK, B., Botany
KARG, H., Physiology of Reproduction and Lactation
KETTRUP, A., Environmental Chemistry
KIRCHGESSNER, M., Animal Nutrition
KÖGEL-KNABER, J., Soil Science
LATZ, P., Landscape Architecture and Planning
PFADENHAUER, J., Landscape Ecology
ROTHENBURGER, W., Economics in Horticulture and Land Maintenance
SCHMIDT, H.-L., Chemistry and Biochemistry
SCHNITZLER, W., Vegetable-growing
SCHNYDER, J., Grassland and Growing of Fodder Crops
SCHÖN, J., Land Engineering
TREPL, L., Landscape Ecology
URFF, W. VON, Agricultural Policy
VALENTIEN, CH., Landscape Architecture and Design
WENZEL, G., Plant Cultivation
WOLFRAM, G., Nutrition

Faculty of Brewing, Food Technology and Dairy Science:

BACK, W., Brewing Technology
DELGADO, A., Fluid Mechanics and Process Automation
ENGEL, K. H., Food Technology
FRIEDRICH, J., Physics
GEIGER, E., Brewing Technology
KESSLER, H.-G., Food Technology
KLOSTERMEYER, H., Dairy Science
LÜCK, W., Industrial Management in Brewing and Food Industries
MEYER-PITTROFF, R., Energy and Environmental Science of Food Industry
PARLAR, H., Chemical Technical Analysis and Chemical Food Technology
SOMMER, K., Mechanical Engineering
VOGEL, R., Applied Microbiology
WEISSER, H., Brewery Construction and Packaging Technology

Faculty of Medicine:

ARNOLD, W., Otorhinolaryngology
CLASSEN, M., Internal Medicine
CONRAD, B., Neurology
DUDEL, J., Physiology
EMMRICH, P., Paediatrics
FRUHMANN, G., Industrial Medicine
GÄUSBACHER, B., Experimental Surgery
GERHARDT, P., Radiodiagnostics
GRAEFF, H., Gynaecology
GRATZL, M., Anatomy
GREIM, H., Pharmacology and Toxicology
HARTUNG, R., Urology
HIPP, E., Orthopaedics
HÖFLER, H. K., General Pathology and Pathological Anatomy
HOFMANN, F., Pharmacology and Toxicology
HORCH, H.-H., Dentistry
JESCHKE, D., Internal Medicine
KOCHS, E., Anaesthesiology
LAUTER, H., Psychiatry
MERTZ, M., Ophthalmology
MOLLS, M., Radiotherapy and Radiological Oncology
NEISS, A., Medical Statistics and Epidemiology
NEUMEIER, D., Clinical Chemistry and Pathobiochemistry
RAD, M. VON, Psychosomatic Medicine, Clinical Psychology and Psychotherapy
RING, J., Dermatology
SCHÖMIG, A., Internal Medicine
SCHWAIGER, M., Nuclear Medicine
SIEWERT, J. R., Surgery
TRAPPE, A. E., Neurosurgery
WAGNER, H., Clinical Microbiology and Hygiene

ATTACHED INSTITUTES

Walter Schottky Central Institute for Basic Research in Semiconductor Electronics: Dir Prof. Dr GERHARD ABSTREITER.

Central Institute for Regional Planning and Environmental Research: Dir Prof. Dr HANSJÖRG LANG.

Central Institute for Sports Sciences: Dir Prof. Dr GÜNTHER BÄUMBER.

Central Institute for the History of Technology: Dir Prof. Dr ULRICH WENGENROTH.

Weihenstephan Testing and Experimental Institute for Dairy Science: Dir Prof. Dr HEINRICH KARG.

Weihenstephan Bavarian State Brewery: Dir Prof. Dr HEINZ MIEDANER.

UKRAINISCHE FREIE UNIVERSITÄT

81679 Munich, Pienzenauerstrasse 15
Telephone: (89) 98-69-28
Fax: (89) 981-02-63
E-mail: kdx0101@mail.lrz-muenchen.de

Founded 1921
Private, State recognized
Languages of instruction: Ukrainian, English, German
Academic year: October to August (including Summer Courses July–August)

Rector: Prof. Dr MIROSLAV LABUNKA
Pro-Rector: Prof. Dr L. RUDNYTZKY
General Secretary: Dr NICOLAS SZAFOWAL
Librarian: MIROSLAW FICAK

Number of teachers: 54
Number of students: 185

Publications: *Naukovi Zbirnyky UVU*, *Naukovi Zapysky UVU* (annually), *Specimina dialectorum ucrainorum*, *Studien zu deutsch-ukrainischen Beziehungen*.

DEANS

Faculty of Philosophy: Prof. Dr L. RUDNYTZKY
Faculty of Law and Economics: Prof. Dr A. KAMINSKY
Research Institute for German-Ukrainian Relations: Prof. Dr ZENOWIJ SOKOLUK

PROFESSORS

Faculty of Philosophy (Arts):

BILANIUK, P., History of Ukrainian Church
GERUS-TARNAWECKY, I., Slavonic Philology
GOY, P., History of Ukraine
HOLOWINSKY, I., Psychology
HROMIAK, R., Ukrainian Philology
ISAJIW, V., Sociology
KOPTILOV, V., Ukrainian Philology
KOSYK, W., Contemporary History of the Ukraine
KOZAK, S., Slavonic Literature
KULCHYCKY, J., East European History
LABUNKA, M., Medieval History
LESIW, M., Ukrainian Philology
POHRIBNYJ, A., Ukrainian Philology
RUDNYTZKY, L., Comparative Literature
SHTOHRYN, D., History of Ukrainian Literature
STOJKO, W., History of Eastern Europe
SYSYN, F., History of Eastern Europe
WYNAR, L., History of the Ukraine
ŽUK, R., History of Architecture

Faculty of Law and Economics:

BEJ, E., Political Economy
HAWRYLYSHYN, B., Business Management, Geopolitics
KOSTYCKY, M., Ukrainian Public Law
KUSCHPETA, O., Economics
POTICHNYJ, P. J., Political Science
PYNZENYK, V., Political Economy
SUBTELNY, O., History of Political Ideas
ZLUPKO, S., History of Economic Theories

UNIVERSITÄT DER BUNDESWEHR MÜNCHEN

85579 Neubiberg, Werner-Heisenberg-Weg 39
Telephone: (89) 6004-1
Telex: 05215800
Fax: (89) 60042009

Founded 1973
Academic year: October to September (3 semesters)

President: Dr HANS GEORG LÖSSL
Vice-Presidents: Prof. Dr RUDOLF AVENHAUS, Prof. Dipl.-Jug. THEODOR-WOLFGANG WEISSER
Chancellor: (vacant)
Registrar: INGO FRITZ
Librarian: Dr HANS-JOACHIM GENGE

Library of 773,000 vols
Number of teachers: 200
Number of students: 2,700

Publications: *Forschungsbericht*, *'Der Hochschulkurier'* (3 a year).

DEANS

Faculty of Civil Engineering, Surveying and Geodesy: Prof. Dr-Ing. D. KRAUS
Faculty of Electrical Engineering: Prof. Dr-Ing. K. HOFFMANN
Faculty of Computer and Information Sciences: Prof. Dr rer. nat. S. BRAUN
Faculty of Aviation and Space, Aerospace Engineering: Prof. Dr-Ing. K.-J. SCHWENZFEGER
Faculty of Education: Prof. Dr A. KAISER
Faculty of Social Sciences: Prof. Dr Z. VOIGT
Faculty of Economics and Organizational Sciences: Prof. Dr rer. pol. P. FRIEDRICH
Polytechnical College of Mechanical Engineering: Prof. Dipl.-Ing. J. HERRMANN
Polytechnical College of Civil and Electrical Engineering: Prof. Dr-Ing. G. STICHLER
Polytechnical College of Business Administration: Prof. Dr jur. W. ROTTMANN

WESTFÄLISCHE WILHELMS-UNIVERSITÄT MÜNSTER

48149 Münster, Schlossplatz 2
Telephone: (251) 83-0
Telex: 892529
Fax: (251) 83-24813

Founded 1780; became Academy in 1818; University status again in 1902
State control
Academic year: October to July (two terms)

Rector: Prof. Dr GUSTAV DIECKHEUER
Pro-Rectors: Prof. Dr Dr OTMAR SCHOBER, Prof. Dr RUTH-ELISABETH MOHRMANN, Prof. Dr JÜRGEN SCHMIDT, Prof. Dr RAINER MATTES
Chancellor: Dr KLAUS ANDERBRÜGGE
Librarian: Dr ROSWITHA POLL

Number of teachers: 1,217
Number of students: 45,900

Publications: *Personal- und Vorlesungsverzeichnis der WWU* (2 a year), *Jahresbericht der Gesellschaft zur Förderung der WWU* (annual), *Universitäts-Zeitung* (irregular), *Amtliche Bekanntmachungen der WWU* (irregular), *Forschungsjournal* (2 a year).

DEANS

Faculty of Protestant Theology:
Prof. Dr DIETRICH-ALEX KOCH

Faculty of Catholic Theology:
Prof. Dr FRIEDRICH UDO SCHMÄLZLE

Faculty of Law:
Prof. Dr FRIEDRICH DENCKER

Faculty of Economic Sciences:
Prof. Dr ANDREAS PFINGSTEN

Faculty of Medicine:
Prof. Dr THOMAS LUGER

Faculty of Philosophy: Prof. Dr CHRISTOPH STROSETZKI

Department of Social Sciences: Prof. Dr REINHARD MEYERS

Department of History and Philosophy: Prof. Dr WOLFGANG HÜBNER

Department of Psychology: Prof. Dr CATHARINA ZWITSERLOOD

Department of Education: Prof. Dr HANJÖRG SCHEERER

Department of Philology: Prof. Dr VOLKER HONEMANN

Department of Sport Sciences: : (vacant)

Faculty of Mathematics and Natural Sciences: Prof. Dr NORBERT SCHMITZ

Department of Mathematics and Informatics: Prof. Dr PETER SORGER

Department of Physics: Prof. Dr JOHANNES POLLMANN

Department of Chemistry: Prof. Dr HARTMUT REDLICH

Department of Biology: Prof. Dr ENGELBERT WEIS

Department of Earth Sciences: Prof. Dr JULIUS WERNER

ATTACHED INSTITUTES

Central Institute for Development Planning: Dirs Prof. Dr HANS D. JARASS, Prof. Dr Dr W. KRAWIETZ; Prof. Dr R. THOSS.

Freiher vom Stein Institute: Dir Prof. Dr JANBERND OEBBECKE.

Hornheide Clinic for Tumors, Tuberculosis and Facial and Skin Restoration: Medical Dir Dr H. TILKORN.

Institute for Arteriosclerosis Research: Dir Prof. Dr G. ASSMANN (acting).

Nephrological Institute: Mans Prof. Dr U. GRAFE, Prof. Dr K.-H. RAHN.

Academy for Manipulative Medicine: Dir Dr W. H. M. CASTRO.

Erich Schütz Research Institute for Preventative Medicine and Physiotherapeutic Rehabilitation: Dir Prof. Dr W. MÖNNINGHOFF.

Institute for Comparative Local History: Academic Chair. Prof. Dr P. JOHANEK.

Institute for Chemical and Biological Transmission: Head Prof. Dr K. CAMMANN.

Institute for Informatics in Agriculture: Dirs Prof. Dr H. KONERMANN, Prof. Dr U. STREIT.

Institute for Applied Informatics: Dirs Prof. Dr H. L. GROB, Dr W. HELD, Prof. Dr W.-M. LIPPE.

CARL V. OSSIETZKY UNIVERSITÄT OLDENBURG

26111 Oldenburg, Postfach 2503
Premises at: 26129 Oldenburg, Ammerländer Heerstr. 114-118
Telephone: (441) 798-0
Telex: 25655
Fax: (441) 7983000

Founded 1974
Academic year: October to September (two terms)

President: Prof. Dr MICHAEL DAXNER
Vice-Presidents: Prof. Dr JAST VON HAYDELL, INA GRIEB
Administrative Officer: (vacant)
Librarian: HERMANN HAVEKOST

Number of teachers: 209 professors
Number of students: 11,638

Publications: *Uni-info* (*c.* 7 a year), *Veranstaltungsverzeichnis* (2 a year), *Einblicke* (2 a year), *Schriftenreihe der Universität Oldenburg*.

CHAIRMEN

Department 1 (Educational Sciences): Prof. Dr WOLF-DIETER SCHOLZ
Department 2 (Communications and Aesthetics): Prof. Dr WOLFGANG MARTIN STROH
Department 3 (Social Sciences): Prof. Dr RÜDIGER MEYENBERG
Department 4 (Economics and Law): Prof. Dr REINHARD PFRIEM

Department 5 (Philosophy, Psychology, Sport Science): Prof. Dr ULRIKE ROCKMANN
Department 6 (Mathematics, Computer Science): Prof. Dr GERALD SCHMIEDER
Department 7 (Biology): Prof. Dr ULRICH KATTMANN
Department 8 (Physics): Prof. Dr GOTFRIED HEINRICH BAUER
Department 9 (Chemistry): Prof. Dr JÜRGEN MARTENS
Department 10 (Informatics): Prof. Dr WOLFGANG NEBEL
Department 11 (Literature and Languages): Prof. Dr WINFRIED BOEDER

PROFESSORS

Department 1 (Educational Sciences):

Institute of Educational Sciences 1:
(Head of the Institute: Prof. Dr JOST VON MAYDELL)

BUSCH, F.-W., General and Comparative Education
FLESSNER, H., Social Education
FÜLGRAFF, B., Adult Education
GARZ, D., General Education
HOPF, A., General Education, School Teaching
KAISER, A., Elementary Science, Elementary Social Studies
MAYDELL, J. VON, Theory of Socialization, General Education
MEYER, H., General Education, School Teaching
NITSCH, W., Theory of Knowledge
SCHOLZ, W.-D., Educational Methodology
TOPSCH, W., Primary Education
WISSMANN, A., History of Education
WRAGGE-LANGE, J., Primary Education

Institute of Educational Sciences 2 (Special Education, Prevention and Rehabilitation):
(Head of the Institute: Prof. Dr HEINZ MUHL)

KLATTENHOFF, K., Education for Slow Learners
MÜHL, H., Education for the Mentally Handicapped
NEUKÄTER, H., Education for the Handicapped
NIEHAUS, M., Education for the Handicapped
ORTMANN, M., Education for the Handicapped
SCHRÖDER, U., Education for Slow Learners
SEHRBROCK, P., Education for the Speech Handicapped and for Slow Learners
STRUVE, K., General Education for the Handicapped
THIMM, W., General Education for the Handicapped
WESTPHAL, E., Education for Slow Learners
WIELAND, A., Education for the Mentally Handicapped

Institute of Educational Sciences 3 (Education and Communication in Migration Processes):
(Head of the Institute: Prof. Dr ROLF MEINHARDT)

MEINHARDT, R., Education of and Social Work with Ethnic Minorities
MERGNER, G., Social History of Education, Intercultural Communication
SCHMIDTKE, H.-P., Intercultural Education

Department 2 (Communication and Aesthetics):

Fine Arts, Visual Communication:
HOFFMANN, D., History of Fine Arts
LIPPE, R. ZUR, Theory of Aesthetics
SELLE, G., History of Culture, Art Education
SPRINGER, P., Theory and History of Art
THIELE, J., Fine Arts and Visual Communication
WENK, S., History of Art, Gender Studies

Music:
DINESCU, V., Applied Composition
HEIMANN, W., Music History
HOFFMANN, F., Music Teaching
RITZEL, F., Auditive Communication
STROH, W. M., Theory of Music and Music Pedagogics

Textile Design:
ELLWANGER, K., History of Culture
KÖLLER, I., Textile Education

Department 3 (Social Sciences):

Social Sciences:
AICH, P., Sociology and Social Politics
DRÖGE-MODELMOG, I., Sociology
FLAAKE, K., Women's Studies
HOLTMANN, A., Theory and Practice of Political Structures
KRAFFT, A., Organizational Research and Planning
KRAIKER, G., Social and Political Theory
LENK, K., Administration
MEYENBERG, R., Teaching of Social Sciences
MEYER, A., Political Science and Theory
MÜLLER-DOOHM, S., Sociology of the Mass Media
NASSMACHER, K.-H., Politics
NAVE-HERZ, R., Sociology of Youth, Family and Leisure
PETERS, H., Sociology of Deviating Behaviour and Social Control
RAVASANI, S., Social Economy of Developing Countries
RUDZIO, W., Politics, Political Sociology
SCHMIDT, E., Politics, Parties and Associations
VONDERACH, G., Industrial Sociology
WEISMANN, A., Sociology, Methods of Gupivian Social Research

Planning:
BRAKE, K., Structural Planning
KUMMERER, K., Regional Planning
SCHWIER, V., City and Regional Planning
SIEBEL, W., Sociology, City and Regional Sociology
WINDELBERG, J., Regional Planning
ZILLESSEN, H., Environment Politics and Planning

Vocational Studies:
BERG, D. VOM, Dietetics Teaching
HENSELER, K., Technology Teaching
KAMINSKI, H., Vocational Studies Teaching
LEWALD, A., Economics of Housekeeping

Religion:
GOLKA, F., Protestant Theology, Old Testament
HEUMANN, J., Religious Education
LINK-WIECZOREK, U., Systematic Theology and Religious Education
MESEBERG-HAUBOLD, I., Protestant Theology, Church History
WEISS, W., New Testament

History:
BOLDT, W., History
GÜNTHER-ARNDT, H., Teaching of History
HAHN, H. H., Modern and East European History (esp. History of Poland)
HINRICHS, E., History of Early Modern Times
HOLBACH, R., Medieval History
KNEISSE, P., Ancient History
MÜTTER, B., Didactics of History
SAUL, K., Social History with emphasis on the 19th & 20th centuries

Geography:
JANNSEN, G., Geography and Teaching
JUNG, G., Geography
KRÜGER, R., Geography
STRASSEL, J., Social Geography

Department 4 (Economics and Law):

BLANKE, T., Labour Law
BREISIG, T., Organization and Personnel
CZYCHOLL, R., Dir of Institute of Management II
EBERT, U., Public Finance
FRANK, G., Public Economic Law
KUTSUPIS, A., Planning
LACHNIT, L., Business Economics
LITZ, H.-P., Statistics
OSSORIO-CAPELLA, C., Political Economics
PETERS, H.-R., Political Economy
PFAFFENBERGER, W., Political Economy
PFRIEM, R., Business Management
REINISCH, H., Educational Science (Business Education/Economic Education)
SCHÜLER, K. W., Dir of Institute of Economic
STERZEL, D., Public Law
TAEGER, J., Private Law, Trade Law, Economic Law and Informatics
WELSCH, H., Economic Theory
ZIMMERMANN, G., Finance and Banking

Department 5 (Philosophy, Psychology, Sport):

BELSCHNER, W., Psychology
COLONIUS, H., Psychology
DIECKERT, J., Sport Science and Physical Education
GOTTWALD, P., Psychology
GRUBITZSCH, S., Psychology
LAUCKEN, U., Social Psychology
MEES, U., General Psychology
NACHREINER, F., Applied Psychology
PETERSEN, U., Sport Science and Physical Education
RIGAUER, B., Sport Science and Sociology of Sport
ROCKMANN, U., Sports Science, Motor Behaviour, Motor Learning
SCHICK, A., Psychology
SCHMÜCKER, B., Sport Science and Medicine in Sport
SUKALE, M., Philosophy
SZAGUN, G., Developmental Psychology
VIEBAHN, P., Psychology
WALCHER, K.-P., Psychology

Department 6 (Mathematics):

BESUDEN, H., Mathematics Teaching
DEFANT, A., Mathematics, Functional Analysis
EBENHÖH, W., Mathematics, Analysis
EMRICH, O., Mathematics, Stochastics
FLORET, K., Mathematics, Functional Analysis
HERZBERGER, J., Applied Mathematics, Instrumental Mathematics
KNAUER, U., Mathematics, Algebraic Methods
KUNKEL, P., Applied Mathematics
LEISSNER, W., Mathematics, Geometry
PFLUG, P., Mathematics, Complex Variables
PIEPER-SEIER, I., Mathematics, Algebra
QUEBBEMANN, H.-G., Mathematics, Number Theory
SCHMALE, W., Mathematics, Dynamic Systems
SCHMIEDER, G., Mathematics, Complex Analysis
SPÄTH, H., Applied Mathematics
SPROCKHOFF, W., Mathematics Teaching
VETTER, U., Mathematics, Commutative Algebra
WITTE, H. J., Applied Mathematics, Stochastics
ZAIS, T., Mathematics Teaching

Department 7 (Biology):

BRUMSACK, H.-J., Geomicrobiochemistry
CYPIONKA, H., Palaeomicrobiology
EBER, W., Botany, Morphology
FETZNER, S., Microbiology
GEBHARDT, H., Pedology
HAESELER, V., Zoology, Ecology
HÖPNER, T., Biochemistry, Enzymology
JANIESCH, P., Botany, Physiological Ecology
KATTMANN, U., Biology Teaching
KRUMBEIN, W., Geomicrobiology
RICHTER-LANDSBERG, C., Zoology, Neurochemistry
SCHMINKE, H. K., Zoology, Morphology

STABENAU, H., Plant Physiology
VARESCHI, E., Animal Ecology
WACKERNAGEL, W., Genetics
WEILER, R., Zoology, Neurobiology
WILLIG, A., Zoology, Physiology

Department 8 (Physics):
BAUER, G. H., Experimental Physics
HAUBOLD, K., Theoretical Physics
HILF, E., Theoretical Physics
HINSCH, K., Experimental Physics
KOLLMEIER, B., Applied Physics
KUNZ-DROLSHAGEN, J., Theoretical Physics
MAIER, K. H., Experimental Physics
MELLERT, V., Applied Physics
PARISI, J., Experimental Physics
RAUH, A., Theoretical Physics
RIESS, F., Teaching of Physics
RUTH, V., Teaching of Physics

Department 9 (Chemistry):
GMEHLING, J., Industrial Chemistry
HAMANN, C. H., Applied Physical Chemistry
JANSEN, W., Chemistry, Theory and Practice of School Teaching
KAUPP, G., Organic Chemistry
KÖLL, P., Organic Chemistry
MARTENS, J., Organic Chemistry
METZGER, J. O., Organic Chemistry
RÖSSNER, F., Industrial Chemistry
RULLKÖTTER, J., Organic Geochemistry
SCHULLER, D., Analytical and Physical Chemistry
UHL, W., Inorganic Chemistry
WEIDENBRUCH, M., Inorganic Chemistry
ZEECK, E., General Chemistry and Physical Chemistry

Department 10 (Informatics):
APPELRATH, H.-J., Information Systems and Databases
BEST, E., Theoretical Computer Science
DAMM, W., Computer Architecture, Embedded Systems and Design Tools
GORNY, P., Computer Graphics and Human-Computer Interaction
JENSCH, P., Image Processing and Process Control
KOWALK, W., Computer Networks and Telecommunication
MÖBUS, C., Teaching, Learning Systems
NEBEL, W., VLSI Design, Methodology and Tools
OLDEROG, E.-R., Theoretical Informatics
SONNENSCHEIN, M., Simulation and Programming Languages

Department 11 (Literature and Language):

German, including German as a Foreign Language:
BRANDES, H., Literature
DIERKS, M., Literature
DYCK, J., Literature
EICHLER, W., Didactics and Linguistics
GLOY, J., Linguistics
GRATHOFF, D., Literature
MEVES, U., Old German Literature and Language
ROHDE, W., German Linguistics
STÖLTING-RICHERT, W., German as a Foreign Language

English:
BOEDER, W., Linguistics, Commmunications Theory
CALBERT, J. P., Comparative Linguistics
HILLGÄRTNER, R., English Literature
KOEHRING, K., American Literature and Culture
RAUTENHAUS, H., Didactics
SCHMITT VON MUHLENFELS, A., American Literature

Slavic Language and Literature:
GRÜBEL, R., Slav Philology
GRUTTEMEIER, R., Dutch Literature
HENTSCHEL, G., Slav Philology

Dutch:
STURM, A., Dutch Linguistics

UNIVERSITÄT OSNABRÜCK

49069 Osnabrück, Neuer Graben/Schloss
Telephone: (541) 969-0
Telex: 944850
Fax: (541) 969-4570
E-mail: aaa@uni-osnabrueck.de

Founded 1973, first student intake 1974
Academic year: October to September (two terms)

President: Prof. Dr RAINER KÜNZEL
Vice-Presidents: Prof. Dr GUNNAR BORSTEL, Prof. Dr ARNIM REGENBOGEN
Registrar: CHRISTOPH EHRENBERG
Librarian: Dr EILHARD CORDES

Number of teachers: 500
Number of students: 13,000

Publications: *Veranstaltungsverzeichnis* (1 a term), *Amtliches Mitteilungsblatt* (irregular), *Magazin* (annually), *Universitätszeitung* (7 a year), *Bericht des Präsidenten, Forschungsbericht* (every 2 years).

HEADS OF DEPARTMENTS

Law: Prof. Dr WULF-ECKART VOSS
Economics and Business: Prof. Dr MANFRED NELDER
Social Sciences: GYÖRGY SZÉLL
Education and Culture Sciences: Prof. Dr RENATE ZIMMER
Languages and Literature Sciences: Prof. Dr BERND SCHNEIDER
Psychology: Prof. Dr MATHIAS BARTRAM
Mathematics, Computer Sciences: Prof. Dr WINFRIED BRUNS
Physics: Prof. Dr KLAUS BÄRWINKEL
Biology/Chemistry: Prof. Dr ANSELM KRATOCHWIL
Health Sciences: Prof. Dr RUDOLF MANSTETTEN

UNIVERSITÄT-GESAMTHOCHSCHULE PADERBORN

33098 Paderborn, Warburger Strasse 100
Telephone: (5251) 600
Telex: 936776
Fax: (5251) 602519

Founded 1972
State control
Language of instruction: German
Academic year: October to September

Rector: Prof. Dr WOLFGANG WEBER
Chancellor: ULRICH HINTZE
Librarian: KLAUS BARCKOW

Number of teachers: 850
Number of students: 17,200

Publications: *Paderborner Universitätsreden, Paderborner Universitätszeitung, Amtliche Mitteilungen.*

DEANS

Department of Philosophy, History, Geography, Religious and Social Sciences: Prof. Dr HANS-KARL BARTH
Department of Education, Psychology, Physical Education: Prof. Dr WILHELM HAGEMANN
Department of Languages and Literature: Prof. Dr PETER SCHNEIDER
Department of Fine Arts, Music and Design: Prof. Dr SILKE LEOPOLD
Department of Economics: Prof. Dr WILFRIED FUHRMANN
Department of Physics: Prof. Dr MANFRED EULER
Department of Landscape Architecture and Ecological Planning (Höxter): Prof. Dr BERND GERKEN
Department of Environmental Protection Technology (Höxter): Prof. Dr JOACHIM FETTIG
Department of Agriculture (Soest): Prof. Dr HEINRICH SCHULTE-SIENBECK
Department of Mechanical Engineering: Prof. Dr RAINER KOCH
Department of Data Engineering (Meschede): Prof. Dr WOLFGANG OEVENSCHEID
Department of Automation Engineering (Soest): Prof. Dr FRANZ STEMMER
Department of Chemistry and Chemical Engineering: Prof. Dr KARSTEN KROHN
Department of Electrical Engineering: Prof. Dr JUERGEN VOSS
Department of Telecommunications Technology (Meschede): Prof. Dr FRANZ HUFNAGEL
Department of Electrical Power Engineering (Soest): Prof. Dr FRANZ-JOSEF SCHMITTE
Department of Mathematics and Computer Science: Prof. Dr HANS KLEINE BÜNING

PROFESSORS

Department of Philosophy, History, Geography, Religious and Social Sciences:
BALZER, M., History
BARTH, H.-K., Geography
BENSELER, F., Sociology
DÜSTERLOH, D., Geography and its Teaching
EBACH, J., Protestant Theology
EBELING, H., Philosophy
EICHER, P., Catholic Theology
FLACH, D., History
FRANKEMÖLLE, H., Catholic Theology
FUCHS, G., Geography
GÖTTMANN, F., History
HOFMANN, M., Physical Geography
HÜSER, KL, History
JARNUT, J., History
KLÖNNE, A., Sociology
LANG, B., Catholic Theology
METTE, N., Catholic Theology
PIEPMEIER, R., Philosophy
RIESENBURGER, D., History
SCHLEGEL, W., Geography
SCHUPP, F., Philosophy
WEINRICH, M., Protestant Theology

Department of Education, Psychology and Physical Education:
ENGFER, A., Psychology
FRANK, H., Education
HAGEDORN, G., Sport
HAGEMANN, W., Education
KEIM, W., Adult Education
KOCH, J.-J., Psychology
KÖNIG, E., Education
LIESEN, H., Sports Medicine
SCHNEIDER, P., Education
SCHÖLER, W., Education
TULODZIECKI, G., Education
WEBER, A., Education
WEISS, M., Sport
WETTLER, M., Psychology
ZIELKE, G., Education

Department of Languages and Literature:
APEL, F., German Literature
ASSHEUER, J., German
BREUER, R., English
DURZAK, M., German
ECKER, G., General Literary Research
FELDBUSCH, E., German
FREESE, P., American Studies
GNUTZMANN, C., American Studies
GRUBITZSCH, H., Literature
JUNKER, H., Romance Philology
LANGENBACHER-LIEBGOTT, J., Romance Philology
MICHELS, G., Language and Literature
PASIERBSKY, F., German
SCHLESIER, R., Anthropology
SCHÖWERLING, R., English
STEINECKE, H., Modern German Literature
STEINHOFF, H.-H., German
THOMAS, J., Romance Philology

Department of Fine Arts, Music and Design:
ALLROGGEN, G., Music
BASTIAN, H.-G., Music
BAUER, G., Art and Works of Art

BEDER, J., Textile Design
EHMER, H. K., Art
FISCHER, W., Music
KAMPF-JANSEN, H., Art
KEYENBURG, H.-J., Art
KRAWINKEL, H., Art
LEOPOLD, S., Music
REESE-HEIM, D., Textile Design

Department of Economics:

BARTELS, N. B., Economics
DANGELMAIER, W., Economics
DIETRICH, G., Law
DOBIAS, P., Political Economy
FISCHER, J., Business Administration
FUHRMANN, W., Political Economy
GOLLERS, R., Economics
GRÄFER, H., Business Administration
HARFF, P., Economics
HEROLD, W., Business Administration
KAISER, F.-J., Economics
KLEIBOHM, K., Mathematics for Economics
NASTANSKY, L., Computer Science
NISSEN, H.-P., General Political Economy
PULLIG, K.-K., Business Administration
RAHMANN, B., Political Economy
REISS, W., Political Economy
ROSENBERG, O., Business Administration
ROSENTHAL, K., Business Administration
SCHILLER, B., Economics
SCHMIDT, K.-H., Business Administration
SKALA, H.-J., Economics
WEBER, W., Business Administration
WEINBERG, P., Business Administration
WERNER, T., Business Administration.
WOLFF, R., Computer Science

Department of Physics:

ANTHONY, K.-H., Physics
EULER, M., Physics
HOLZAPFEL, W. B., Experimental Physics
LISCHKA, K., Experimental Physics
MEYER ZUR CAPELLEN, F., Physics
MIMKES, J., Experimental Physics
OSTEN, W. VON DER, Experimental Physics
OVERHOF, H., Theoretical Physics
PRIMAS, D., Physics
SCHNEIDER, L., Physics
SCHRÖTER, J., Theoretical Physics
SCHWERMANN, W., Physics
SOHLER, W., Applied Physics
SPAETH, J.-M., Experimental Physics
WEIGELE, K., Physics
WORTMANN, G., High Pressure Physics, Solid-State Physics
ZIEGLER, H., Applied Physics

Department of Landscape Architecture and Ecological Planning:

BÖTTCHER, H., Land Maintenance
GERKEN, B., Land Maintenance
HAAG, H., Landscape Architecture
HARFST, W., Land Maintenance
RIKUS, N., Architecture
RINGE, H., Architecture
RÖHR, W.-D., Land Maintenance
ROSENBAUM, H., Economics
SCHMIDT, U., Land Maintenance
SEYFANG, V., Land Maintenance
WEDECK, H., Land Maintenance
WOLF, A., Land Maintenance

Department of Environmental Protection Technology:

BIELENBERG, K., Environmental Protection Technology
BITTER, W., Environmental Protection Technology
EWERT, F.-K., Environmental Protection Technology
FETTIG, J., Environmental Protection Technology
GRUPE, M., Environmental Protection Technology
LOHR, H., Mathematics, Data Processing
MIETHE, M., Environmental Protection Technology
MEON, G., Environmental Protection Technology
RATHKE, K., Environmental Protection Technology
REINNARTH, G., Environmental Protection Technology
SIETZ, M., Chemistry
TUMINSKI, R. J., Environmental Protection Technology

Department of Agriculture:

BORGMANN, F., Crop Cultivation
BRELOH, B., Stockbreeding, Statistics
FREITAG, M., Anatomy and Physiology, Animal Nutrition
HENSCHE, H.-U., Agricultural Economics
LÜTKE ENTRUP, N., Agriculture
OEHMICHEN, J., Agriculture
PAUL, V., Crop Cultivation and Protection
SCHÄFERKORDT, H., Agriculture
SCHLAGBAUER, A., Biology
SCHÜTTERT, R., Agriculture
SCHULTE-SIENBECK, H., Agriculture
VOLK, L., Agriculture
WECKE, W., Agriculture

Department of Mechanical Engineering:

ALTMIKS, K., Materials Science, Reshaping Technology
DOHMANN, F., Forming Production Processes
GAUSEMEIER, J., Mechanical Engineering
GORENFLO, D., Thermodynamics and Heat Transfer
HAHN, O., Mechanical Engineering
HERRMANN, K., Mechanical Engineering
HORN, M., Mechanical Engineering
JORDEN, W., Mechanical Engineering
KOCH, R., Design
LÖHE, D., Mechanical Engineering
LÜCKEL, J., Mechanical Engineering
MEIERFRANKENFELD, B., Mechanical Engineering
MÖLLENKAMP, F., Mechanical Engineering
PAHL, M. H., Mechanical Engineering
POTENTE, H., Mechanical Engineering
RENNHACK, R., Mechanical Engineering
RICHARD, H. A., Mechanical Engineering
SCHNEIDER, M., Mechanical Engineering
SIEBEN, E., Mechanical Engineering
WALLASCHEK, J., Mechanical Engineering
ZELDER, U., Mechanical Engineering

Department of Data Engineering:

GRONAU, P., Business Administration
HIPP, K. J., Data Engineering
HÖLKER, R., Data Engineering
KLEIN, H. W., Mechanical Engineering
KNOBLOCH, T., Data Engineering
OEVENSCHEIDT, W. F., Production Engineering
PETRY, H.-P., Data Engineering
REINHART, E., Data Engineering
SCHWEINS, M., Data Engineering
STURMATH, R., Data Engineering
TILLNER, W., Mechanical Engineering
WIEDENROTH, W., Theory of Design
WIRRIES, D., Mechanical Engineering

Department of Automation Engineering:

ELIAS, H.-J., Automation Engineering
HAVENSTEIN, G., Mechanical Engineering
KLEFFMANN, O., Automation Engineering
LINGEMANN, F. K., Automation Engineering
MEIER, F., Automation Engineering
PETUELLI, G., Machine Tools
RICHTER, W., Automation Engineering
SAADAT, M., Mechanical Engineering
SCHULZ-BEENKEN, A. S., Mechanical Engineering
SCHÜRMANN, E., Automation Engineering
STEMMER, F., Mechanical Engineering, Automation Engineering
WITKOP, P., Mechanical Engineering

Department of Chemistry and Chemical Engineering:

BROECKER, H.-C., Chemistry
FELS, G., Chemistry
GOLDSCHMIDT, A., Chemistry
HAUPT, H.-J., Chemistry
HEMPEL, D. C., Chemistry
KLEMM, H., Chemistry
KROHN, K., Chemistry
LENDERMANN, B., Chemistry and Chemical Engineering
MARSMANN, H., Chemistry and Chemical Engineering
MORITZ, H.-U., Chemistry and Chemical Engineering
POLLMANN, P., Chemistry and Chemical Engineering
REININGER, G., Chemistry and Chemical Engineering
RISCH, N., Chemistry
STEGEMEYER, H., Chemistry

Department of Electrical Engineering:

ALDEJOHANN, A., Information Technology
BARSCHDORFF, D., Electrical Engineering
BELLI, F., Information Technology
BICK, G., Electrical Engineering
CAMBEIS, L., Electrical Engineering
DÖRRSCHEIDT, F., Electrical Engineering
DOURDOUMAS, N., Electrical Engineering
EBBESMEYER, G., Electrical Engineering
GROTSTOLLEN, H., Electrical Engineering
HARTMANN, G., Electrical Engineering
HORSTICK, G. J., Electrical Engineering
KUMM, W., Electrical Engineering
LATZEL, W., Electrical Engineering
MAEHLE, E., Electrical Engineering
MEERKÖTTER, K., Electrical Engineering
MROZYNSKI, G., Electrical Engineering
NOÉ, R., Electrical Engineering
RENTZSCH-HOLM, I., Electrical Engineering
TEGETHOFF, F.-J., Electrical Engineering
VOSS, J., Electrical Engineering
WICHERT, H. W., Electrical Engineering

Department of Telecommunications:

DRAEGER, J., Telecommunications
HUFNAGEL, F., Telecommunications
JÄGER, H.-G., Telecommunications
KACZMARCZYK, N., Telecommunications
KEUTER, W., Telecommunications
KLASEN, H., Telecommunications
KRAUSE, K., Telecommunications
MEIERLING, H. D., Telecommunications
MÖLLER, G., Telecommunications
NERZ, K.-P., Telecommunications
OPIELKA, D., Telecommunications
REICHE, S., Telecommunications
RIES, S., Telecommunications
SCHMITT, H., Telecommunications
SCHULZE, H., Telecommunications
SCHWARZ, K.-D., Telecommunications
SCHWEPPE, E.-G., Telecommunications
STAUDT, A., Telecommunications
TIMMERMANN, D., Telecommunications
WÜNSCHE, C., Telecommunications

Department of Electrical Power Engineering:

BECKER, W., Electrical Power Engineering
BITZER, B., Electrical Power Engineering
GIESE, K.-G., Electrical Power Engineering
GRAUEL, A., Electrical Power Engineering
GRÜNEBERG, J., Electrical Power Engineering
HEINATZ, H., Electrical Power Engineering
MAJEWSKI, D., Electrical Power Engineering
MEPPELINK, J., Electrical Power Engineering
MÜLLER, K.-H., Electrical Power Engineering
PFAU, D., Electrical Power Engineering
PREHN, H., Electrical Power Engineering
SACHS, G., Electrical Power Engineering
SCHMITTE, F.-J., Electrical Power Engineering
SCHWARZ, U., Electrical Power Engineering
WEIMAR, R.-J., Electrical Power Engineering

Department of Mathematics and Computer Science:

BENDER, P., Mathematics
BIERSTEDT, K.-D., Mathematics
BRUNS, M., Mathematics
CAMPOSANO, R., Mathematics, Information Science
DEIMLING, K., Mathematics
DIETZ, H.-M., Mathematics, Computer Science
DOMIK, G., Computer Science
FUCHSSTEINER, B., Mathematics
HAUENSCHILD, W., Computer Science
HEMBD, H., Mathematics
INDLEKOFER, K.-H., Mathematics
KANIUTH, E., Mathematics
KASTENS, U., Practical Computer Science
KEIL-SLAWIK, R., Computer Science
KEVEKORDES, F.-J., Computer Science
KIYEK, K.-H., Mathematics
KLEINE BÜNING, H., Computer Science
KÖCKLER, N., Mathematics
KUCK, C., Theory of Computer Science
KÜSPERT, H.-J., Computer Science
LENZING, H., Mathematics
MARTINI, P., Computer Science
MELTZOW, O., Mathematics
MEYER AUF DER HEIDE, F., Computer Science
MONIEN, B., Computer Science
RAMMIG, F. J., Computer Science
RAUTMANN, R., Mathematics
RINKENS, H.-D., Mathematics
SCHNITGER, G., Computer Science
SOHR, H., Mathematics
SPIEGEL, H., Mathematics
SZWILLUS, G., Computer Science
WALDEN, R., Mathematics

UNIVERSITÄT PASSAU

94032 Passau, Dr-Hans-Kapfinger-Str. 22
Telephone: (851) 509-0
Fax: (851) 509-1005

Founded 1972
State control
Language of instruction: German
Academic year: October to September

Rector: Prof. Dr W. SCHWEITZER
Pro-Rector: Prof. Dr I. BAUMGARTNER
Administrative Officer: Dr K. A. FRIEDRICHS
Librarian: Dr H. WIMMER

Number of professors: 100
Number of students: 7,998
Library of 1,650,000 vols

Publications: *Personen- und Vorlesungsverzeichnis* (every term), *Nachrichten und Berichte*, *Passauer Universitätsreden*.

DEANS

Faculty of Catholic Theology: Prof. Dr P. FONK
Faculty of Law: Prof. Dr D. HECKMANN
Faculty of Business Sciences: Prof. Dr J. WILHELM
Faculty of Philosophy: Prof. Dr W. BECKER
Faculty of Mathematics and Computer Sciences: Prof. Dr V. WEISPFENNING

PROFESSORS

Faculty of Catholic Theology:

BAUMGARTNER, I., Christian Social Studies and Pastoral Theology
FONK, P., Moral Theology
HOPPE, R., Preliminary Biblical Studies
HORN, ST., Basic Theology
LANDERSDORFER, A., Church History
LISKE, M.-T., Philosophy
MÜHLEK, K., Religious Education and Catechetics
PREE, H., Church Law
SCHÄFER, PH., Dogmatics and the History of Dogma
SCHLEMMER, K., Liturgy and Homiletics
SCHWANKL, O., New Testament Exegesis
SCHWIENHORST-SCHÖNBERGER, L., Old Testament Exegesis and Hebrew

Faculty of Law:

ALTMEPPEN, H., Civil Law, Commercial Law I
BETHGE, H., State and Administrative Law
BEULKE, W., Penal Law
BRAUN, J., Civil Law, Civil Procedural Law and Philosophy of Law
FINCKE, M., Penal Law
HAFFKE, B., Criminal Law, Criminal Procedural Law, Philosophy and Sociology of Law
HECKMANN, D., Public Law
HROMADKA, W., Civil and Labour Law
KOBLER, M., Civil Law and German Legal History
MANTHE, U., Civil Law and Roman Law
MUSIELAK, H. J., Civil and Civic Law
SCHURIG, K., Civil, International and Comparative Law
SCHWEITZER, M., State, Administrative, International and European Law
SEEWALD, O., State and Administrative Law
SÖHN, H., State and Administrative Law
WILHELM, J., Civic and Commercial Law

Faculty of Business Sciences:

BÜHNER, R., Management, Organization and Personnel
HAASE, K. D., Management and Tax Studies
KLEINHENZ, G., Economic Policy
KLEINSCHMIDT, P., Economics-Related Computer Studies
KROMSCHRÖDER, B., Management, Insurance and Risk Theory
LÜDEKE, R., Economics and Finance
MOOSMÜLLER, G., Statistics
MÜCKL, W., Economics and Business Theory
RÜBEL, G., Economics
SCHILDBACH, TH., Management, Investment and Accounts
SCHMALEN, H., Management and Marketing
SCHWEITZER, W., Statistics
STEINER, J., Finance and Banking
WILHELM, J., Management
ZIEGLER, H., Business Management and Economic Production

Faculty of Philosophy:

BAUER, L., Mathematics Teaching
BECKER, W., Modern History
BENDER, H., Archaeology of the Roman Provinces
BERNERT, W., Teaching of Social Policy
BOSHOF, E., Medieval History
BUCHINGER, H., Primary Education
DIRSCHERL, K., Romance Literature
EITEL, B., Physical Geography
EMONS, R., English Language
EROMS, H.-W., German Language
FELIX, S., General and Applied Linguistics
FRENZ, T., Medieval History and Historical Auxiliary Sciences
GELLNER, W., Politics
HANSEN, K., American Studies
HARTINGER, W., Folk Studies
HEITZER, H., History Teaching
HIERING, P., Biology Teaching
HINZ, M., Romance Literature
HOUBEN, V., Southeast Asian Studies
HUNDIUS, H., Thai and Laotian Language and Literature
JARFE, G., English Language and Literature
KAMM, J., English Literature and Culture
LANZINNER, M., Recent History
LAUFHÜTTE, H., New German Literature
LENZ, B., British Studies
LÜTTERFELDS, W., Philosophy
MIEDL, O., Aesthetic Education
MINTZEL, A., Sociology
MOGEL, H., Psychology
NOLTE, T., Old German Literature
POLLAK, G., Educational Theory
ROTHER, K., Geography
SCHÜSSLER, G., History of Art and Christian Archaeology
SEIBERT, N., Education
SEIFERT, W., Teaching of German Language and Literature
STAMPFL, I., Music
STEFENELLI, A., Romance Philology
TITZMANN, M., History of Modern German Literature and General Literature
WALTER, K.-P., Romance Literary and Regional Studies, with emphasis on France
WOLFF, H., Ancient History

Faculty of Mathematics and Computer Studies:

BRANDENBURG, F.-J., Theoretical Computer Studies
DONNER, K., Mathematics
FREITAG, B., Computer Science
GRAF, S., Mathematics
GRASS, W., Computer Science
HAHN, W., Systems Programming
KALHOFF, F., Mathematics
KEMPER, A., Computer Science and Script-oriented Systems
LEHA, G., Mathematics
LENGAUER, CH., Computer Science and Programming
RITTER, G., Mathematics
SCHMIDT, B., Informatics
SCHWARTZ, N., Mathematics
VOLGER, H., Computer Science
WEISPFENNING, V., Mathematics

ATTACHED INSTITUTES

Institute for Research into East Bavarian History: Dir Prof. Dr EGON BOSHOF.

Institute for the History of Modern Psychology: Dir Prof. Dr WERNER TRAXEL.

Institute for Agricultural Law: Dirs Prof. Dr MICHAEL SCHWEITZER, Prof. Dr HANS-JOACHIM MUSIELAK.

Institute for International and Foreign Law: Dir Prof. Dr KLAUS SCHURIG (acting).

UNIVERSITÄT REGENSBURG

93053 Regensburg, Universitätsstrasse 31
Telephone: (941) 943-01
Fax: (941) 943-2305
E-mail: rudolf.dietze@verwaltung.uni-regensburg.de

Founded 1962
Academic year: October to September

Rector: Prof. Dr H. ALTNER
Pro-Rectors: Prof. Dr JÜRGEN BECKER, Prof. Dr RÜDIGER SCHMITT
Administrative Officer: H.-H. ZORGER
Librarian: Dr F. GEISSELMANN

Number of teachers: 1,179, including 298 professors
Number of students: 16,700

Publications: *Universitäts-Zeitung* (monthly), *Personen und Vorlesungsverzeichnis* (2 a year), *Schriftenreihe*, *research report*, *departmental studies*, etc.

DIRECTORS OF DEPARTMENTS

Catholic Theology: Prof. DDr U. LEINSLE
Law: Prof. Dr J. KOLLER
Economics: Prof. Dr D. BARTMANN
Medicine: Dr M. LANDTHALER
Philosophy, Sport and Arts: Prof. Dr D. ALTENBURG
Pedagogy and Psychology: Prof. Dr A. THOMAS
History, Social Sciences and Geography: Dr. P. SCHAUER
Literature and Language: Dr A. GREULE
Mathematics: Prof. Dr TH. BRÖCKER
Physics: Dr M. MAIER
Biology and Basic Medicine: Dr A. BRESINSKY
Chemistry and Pharmacy: Prof. Dr B. DICK

PROFESSORS

Department of Catholic Theology:

- BAUMGARTNER, K., Practical Theology
- BEINERT, W., Dogmatics
- BROX, N., Ancient Church History and Patrology
- HAUSBERGER, K., Church History
- HILGER, G., Religious Education
- JILEK, A., Practical Theology (Liturgics)
- LEINSLE, U., Philosophical-Theological Propaedeutic
- PETRI, H., Fundamental Theology
- RITT, H. P., New Testament
- SCHLÖGEL, H., Moral Theology
- SCHMITT, A., Old Testament
- SCHMUTTERMAYR, G., Introductory Studies
- SCHNEIDER, L., Christian Social Science
- SEIGFRIED, A., Dogmatics and History of Dogma

Department of Law:

- ARNOLD, R., Public Law, Foreign Public Law, Comparative Law
- BECKER, H.-J., Civil Law, History of European Law and Canon Law
- BECKER, U., Public Law, German and European Social Law
- GOTTWALD, P., Civil Law, Law Procedure and International Private Law
- HABERSACK, M., Civil Law, Law of Economics
- HENDLER, R., Public Law, Environmental Law
- HENRICH, D., Civil Law and Comparative Law
- HOYER, A., Penal Law, Criminal Procedural Law, Theory of Law
- KIMMINICH, O., Civil Law, National Law, State Law and Politics
- KOLLER, I., Civil Law
- MANSSEN, G., Public Law, German and European Administrative Law
- RICHARDI, R., Labour Law, Social Law
- ROLINSKI, K., Penal Law
- SCHROEDER, F.-C., Criminal Law, Criminal Procedural Law, Eastern Law
- SCHUMANN, E., Procedural Law, Civil Law
- SCHWAB, D., Civil Law and History of German Law
- STEINER, U., Public Law, German and Bavarian State and Administration Law
- ZIMMERMAN, R., Civil Law, Roman Law and Historical Comparative Law

Department of Business Administration:

- ALTENBURGER, O., Insurance Management
- BOHR, K., Production and Operations Management
- DRUKARCZYK, J., Finance
- DRUMM, H. J., Human Resources Management
- HRUSCHKA, H., Marketing
- MEYER-SCHARENBERG, D., German Tax System
- SCHERRER, G., Financial Accounting, Auditing
- STECKHAN, H., Applied Operational Research

Department of Economics and Econometrics:

- BUCHHOLZ, W., Public Finance and Environmental Economics
- FALKINGER, J., Political Economy
- HEUBES, J., Political Economy
- MÖLLER, J., Political Economy
- OBERHOFER, W., Econometrics
- VOGT, W., Political Economy
- WIDMAIER, H. P., Political Economy

Department of Statistics and Economic History:

- GÖMMEL, R., History of Economics
- HAMERLE, A., Statistics

Department of Business Informatics:

- BARTMANN, D., Business Informatics
- DOWLING, M., Management of Technology and Innovation
- LEHNER, F., Business Informatics
- LORY, P., Mathematics and Information Science
- NIEMEYER, G., Business Computing and Information Science

Department of Medicine:

- ANDREESEN, R., Internal Medicine I
- BIRNBAUM, D., Heart, Thorax and Cardiovascular Surgery
- BOGDAHN, U., Neurology
- BRAWANSKI, A., Neurosurgery
- EILLES, CHR., Nuclear Medicine (Radiotherapy)
- FEUERBACH, S., Radiology
- GABEL, V.-P., Ophthalmology
- HACKI, T., Otorhinolaryngology, Head and Neck Surgery
- HANDEL, G., Prosthodontics
- HERBST, M., Radiotherapy
- HOBBHAHN, J., Anaesthesiology
- HOFSTÄDTER, F., Pathology
- HOSEMANN, W., Otorhinolaryngology, Head and Neck Surgery
- JAUCH, K.-W., General Surgery
- JILG, W., Medical Microbiology and Hygiene
- KLEIN, H. E., Psychiatry
- KNÜCKEL-CLARKE, R., Pathology
- KROMER, E., Internal Medicine II
- LANDTHALER, M., Dermatology
- LANG, B., Internal Medicine I
- LEHN, N., Medical Microbiology and Hygiene
- LORENZ, B., Ophthalmology
- MÄNNEL, D., Tumour Immunology (Pathology)
- NERLICH, M., General Surgery
- NIEDERDELLMANN, H., Oral and Maxillofacial Surgery
- RIEGGER, G., Internal Medicine II
- RÜSCHOFF, J., Pathology
- SCHMALZ, G., Operative Dentistry and Periodontology
- SCHMITZ, G., Clinical Chemistry and Laboratory Medicine
- SCHÖLMERICH, J., Internal Medicine I
- STOLZ, W., Dermatology
- STRUTZ, J., Otorhinolaryngology, Head and Neck Surgery
- TAEGER, K., Anaesthesiology
- WOLF, H., Medical Microbiology and Hygiene

Department of Philosophy, Sport and Arts:

- ALTENBURG, D., Music
- BALZ, E., Sport (Teaching)
- DITTSCHEID, H.-CHR., Art History
- HILEY, D., Music
- HOMMES, U., Philosophy
- KUTSCHERA, F., Philosophy
- LEBER, H., Art Education
- MEINEL, CHR., History of Science
- SCHNIDER, F., Religion
- SCHÖLLER, W., Art History
- SCHÖNBERGER, R., Philosophy
- SCHWARZ, H., Lutheran Theology
- STURM, W., Religion
- TRAEGER, J., History of Art
- ZINK, J., History of Art

Department of Pedagogy and Psychology:

- DRÖSLER, J., Psychology
- FÖLLING-ALBERS, M., Didactics of the Elementary School
- GROSSMANN, K., Psychology
- HEID, H., Pedagogy
- IPFLING, H.-J., School Education
- LUKESCH, H., Psychology
- MERTENS, G., Pedagogy
- PEKRUN, R., Psychology
- PRENZEL, M., Educational Psychology
- PROKOP, E., Education
- RICHTER, S., Didactics of the Elementary School
- THOMAS, A., Psychology
- VUKOVICH, A., Psychology
- ZIMMER, A., Psychology

Department of History, Social Sciences and Geography:

- BAUER, F., History
- BEILNER, H., Didactics of History
- BREUER, T., Cultural Geography
- EHRIG, F. R., Geography
- FUCHS, F., History
- GOETZE, D., Sociology
- HACKER, J., Politics
- HEINE, K., Geography
- HERZ, P., History
- HETTLAGE, R., Sociology
- HOFMANN, R., Political Science
- KÖHLE, K., Didactics of Social Studies
- LUTTENBERGER, A. P., History
- MANSKE, D., Regional Geography
- RINSCHEDE, G., Didactics of Geography
- SCHAUER, P., Pre- and Early History
- SCHMID, P., History
- SCHMITZ, M., Political Science
- VÖLKL, E., History

Department of Language and Literature:

- BERGER, D. A., English Philology
- BRAUNGART, G., German Philology
- BREKLE, H. E., General Linguistics
- BUNGERT, H., English Philology
- DAXELMÜLLER, C., Folklore
- ERNST, G., Romance Philology
- FRANZ, K., Teaching of German Language and Literature
- GÄRTNER, H., Classical Philology
- GREULE, A., German Philology (Language)
- HAHN, G., German Philology
- KLINGENSCHMITT, G., Indo-Germanic Philology
- KRAUSE, J., Linguistic Computer Studies
- KREUTZER, H. J., German Philology
- LIENERT, E., German Philology
- MAYER, M., German Philology
- MECKE, J., Romance Philology
- NEUMANN-HOLZSCHUH, J., Romance Philology
- SCHNEIDER, E. W., English Philology
- THRAEDE, K., Classical Philology (Latin)
- TIEFENBACH, H., German Philology
- TROST, K., Slavonic Philology
- WEDEL, E., Slavonic Studies
- WESENBERG, B., Archaeology
- WETZEL, H., Romance Philology

Department of Mathematics:

- BINGENER, J.
- BRÖCKER, TH.
- HACKENBROCH, W.
- JÄNICH, K.
- KNEBUSCH, M.
- KNORR, K.
- KUNZ, E.
- MAIER, H.
- MENNICKEN, R.
- SIEDENTOP, H.
- TAMME, G.
- WARLIMONT, R.

Department of Physics:

- BRACK, M.
- CREUZBURG, M.
- GEBHARDT, W.
- GÖRITZ, D.
- HEINZ, U.
- HOFFMANN, H.
- KELLER, J.
- KREY, U.
- MAIER, M.
- MORGENSTERN, I.
- OBERMAIR, G.
- PENZKOFER, A.
- PHILIPSBORN, H. VON
- PRETTL, W.
- RENK, K. F.
- RÖSSLER, U.
- SCHÄFER, A.
- SCHRÖDER, U.
- STRAUCH, D.
- WEISS, D.
- WERNER, E.

Department of Biology and Basic Medicine:
- ALTNER, H., Zoology
- BAUMANN, R., Physiology
- BOECKH, J., Zoology
- BRESINSKY, A., Botany
- DARNHOFER-DEMAR, B., Zoology
- DERMIETZEL, R., Anatomy
- ERNST, K.-D., Zoology
- HANSEN, K., Zoology
- HAUSKA, G., Botany
- HEGEMANN, P., Biochemistry
- JAENICKE, R., Biochemistry
- KALBITZER, H. R., Biophysics
- KRAMER, B., Zoology
- KURTZ, A., Physiology
- LÖFFLER, G., Biochemistry
- LÜDEMANN, H.-D., Biophysics
- MINUTH, W., Anatomy
- MOLITORIS, H. P., Botany
- MOLL, W., Physiology
- OERTEL, W., Genetics
- SCHMÄDEL, D. VON, Medical Sociology
- SCHMITT, R., Genetics
- SCHNELL, K., Physiology
- SCHNEUWLY, S., Zoology
- SPEIERER, G. W., Medical Psychology
- STETTER, K. O., Microbiology
- SUMPER, M., Biochemistry
- TANNER, W., Botany
- WIRTH, R., Microbiology
- WROBEL, K.-H., Morphology and Anatomy

Department of Chemistry and Pharmacy:
- BRUNNER, H., Inorganic Chemistry
- BUSCHAUER, A., Pharmaceutical Chemistry II
- DAUB, J., Organic Chemistry
- DICK, B., Physical Chemistry
- FRANZ, G., Pharmaceutical Biology
- GROBECKER, H., Pharmacology of Natural Sciences
- KOHLER, H.-H., Physical Chemistry
- KRIENKE, H., Theoretical Chemistry
- KUNZ, W., Physical Chemistry
- MANNSCHRECK, A., Organic Chemistry
- MÄRKL, G., Organic Chemistry
- MERZ, A., Organic Chemistry
- RANGE, K.-J., Inorganic Chemistry
- SAUER, J., Organic Chemistry
- SCHMEER, J., Physical Chemistry
- SEEGER, S., Analytical Chemistry
- STEINBORN, O., Theoretical and Physical Chemistry
- VOGLER, A., Inorganic Chemistry
- WIEGREBE, W., Pharmaceutical Chemistry
- WOLFBEIS, O., Analytical Chemistry

UNIVERSITÄT ROSTOCK

18051 Rostock, Universitätsplatz 1
Telephone: 4980
Fax: 4981107

Founded 1419
State control
Academic year: October to September

Rector: Prof. Dr sc. nat. GERHARD MAESS
Vice-Rectors: Prof. Dr phil ANNA KATHARINA SZAGUN, Prof. Dr rer. nat. WOLFGANG RIEDEL
Registrar: JOACHIM WITTERN
Library Director: Dr-Ing. PETER HOFFMANN

Library: see Libraries
Number of teachers: 332
Number of students: 9,757

Publications: *Archiv der Freunde der Naturgeschichte in Mecklenburg, Rostocker Agrar- und Umweltwissenschaftliche Beiträge, Rostocker Beitrage zur Verkehrswissenschaft und Logistik, Rostocker Mathematisches Kolloquium, Rostocker Medizinische Beiträge, Rostocker Meeresbiologische Beiträge, Erziehungswissenschaftliche Beiträge, Rostocker Informatik-Berichte, Rostocker Beiträge zur Regional- und Strukturforschung, Rostocker Informationen zu Politik und Verwaltung, Rostocker Philosophische Manuskripte, Forschungsbericht der Universität Rostock, Rostocker Arbeitspapiere zu Rechnungswesen und Controlling, Rostocker Arbeitspapiere zu Wirtschaftsentwicklung und Human Resource Development, Rostocker Beiträge zur Sprachwissenschaft, Rostocker Schriften zur Bank und Finanzmarktforschung, Schiffbauforschung, Thunen-Reihe Angewandter Volkswirtschftstheorie, Rostocker Forum Theologie, Rostocker Beiträge zur Deutschen und Europäischen Geschichte, Rostocker Studien zur Kulturwissenschaft, Pädagogisches Handeln, Rostocker Materialen für Landschaftsplanung und Raumentwicklung, Rostocker Schriften zum Bankrecht*, and various faculty publs.

DEANS

Faculty of Medicine: Prof. Dr med. habil. GERHARD HENNIGHAUSEN
Faculty of Mathematics and Natural Sciences: Prof. Dr rer. nat. habil. GÜNTHER WILDENHAIN
Faculty of Philosophy: Prof. Dr phil. habil. HANS-JÜRGEN WENDEL
Faculty of Agricultural Science: Prof. Dr-agr. habil. FRITZ TACK
Faculty of Economics and Social Science: Prof. Dr rer. pol. habil. PETER BERGER
Faculty of Theology: Prof. Dr theol. ECKART REINMUTH
Faculty of Technical Sciences: Prof. Dr-Ing. habil. RAINER KOHLSCHMIDT
Faculty of Law: Prof. Dr iur. PETER BYDLINSKI

UNIVERSITÄT DES SAARLANDES

66123 Saarbrücken, Im Stadtwald
Telephone: (681) 3020
Fax: (681) 302-2609
E-mail: praesident@uni-sb.de

Founded 1948
Academic year: October to March, April to September

President: Prof. Dr GÜNTHER HÖNN
Administrator: Dr HARTWIG CREMERS
Librarian: Dr BERND HAGENAU

Number of teachers: 1,000
Number of students: 19,000

Publications: *Annales Universitatis Saraviensis* (quarterly), *Vorlesungsverzeichnis*, *Jahresbibliographie*.

DEANS

Faculty of Law and Economics: Prof. HELMUT RÜSSMANN
Faculty of Medicine (at Homburg/Saar): Prof. HERMANN-JOSEF SCHIEFFER
Faculty of Philosophy: Prof. KARL-HEINZ OHLIG
Faculty of Mathematics and Natural Sciences: Prof. THOMAS WICHERT
Faculty of Technology: Prof. ALEXANDER KOCH

PROFESSORS

Faculty of Law and Economics:
- ALBECK, H., Political Economy
- AUTEXIER, C., French Public Law
- BARATTA, A., Sociology of Law and Social Philosophy
- BAUER, J.-P., Civil Law
- BIEG, H., Business Administration, Banking Economics
- BÜRGE, A., Civil Law, Roman Law
- DINKELBACH, W., Business Administration, Operational Research
- EICHBERGER, J., Economics, Economic Theory
- FIEDLER, W., Public Law
- FRIEDMANN, R., Statistics and Econometrics
- GLASER, H., Industrial Economics
- GRUPP, K., National and Administrative Law, Modern Constitutional History
- HERBERGER, M., Legal Data Processing, Civil Law, Theory of Law
- HOLZMANN, R., Economics, International Business Relations, European Business, International Financing
- HÖNN, G., Civil, Commercial and Industrial Law
- JUNG, H., Penal and Procedural Law
- KEUSCHNIGG, C., Department of Economics, Public-Sector Economics
- KNIES, W., Public Administrative and Financial Law
- KORIATH, H., Criminal Law, Criminal Procedural Law, Philosophy of Law, Theory of Law
- KUSSMAUL, H., Business Administration, Business Management Tax
- KÜTING, K., Business Administration, Auditing
- MARTINEK, M., Civil Law, Corporations, Business Law and Conflicts of Law
- MÜLLER-DIETZ, Penal and Procedural Law, Criminology
- RANIERI, F., European Civil Law
- RESS, G., Public Law
- RÜSSMANN, H., Civil and Procedural Law, Philosophy of Law
- SCHEER, A.-W., Business Management, Business Informatics
- SCHMIDT, G., Business Management, Information Management, Technology Management
- SCHMIDTCHEN, D., Economics, Business Policy, International Business Relations
- SCHOLZ, C., Business Management, Personnel Management, Information Management
- STEIN, T., European Law, European Public Law, International Law
- STEINMETZ, V., Statistics and Econometrics
- WADLE, E., History of German Law, Civil Law
- WEINBERG, P., Marketing and Consumer Research
- WENDT, R., Constitutional and Administrative Law, Revenue and Tax Law
- WETH, S., German and European Procedural and Industrial Law
- WITZ, C., French Public Law
- ZENTES, J., Business Management, Foreign Trade, International Management

Faculty of Medicine:
- AUER, L. M., Neurosurgery
- BALDAUF, J., Pharmacology and Toxicology
- BERG, R., Orthodontics
- BOCK, R., Anatomy
- BÜCH, H. P., Pharmacology and Toxicology
- BUCHTER, A., Occupational Medicine
- FEIDEN, W., Neuropathology
- FEIFEL, G., General Surgery, Abdominal Surgery
- FELDMANN, U., Medical Biometry, Epidemiology and Informatics
- FLOCKERZI, V., Pharmacology and Toxicology
- GERSONDE, K., Medical Technology
- GRILLMAIER, R., Biophysics and Physical Basis of Medicine
- HERRMANN, W., Clinical Chemistry
- HOFMANN, W., Paediatrics
- HÜTTERMANN, J., Biophysics
- IRO, H., Otorhinolaryngology
- KIENECKER, E.-W., Anatomy
- KINDERMANN, W., Sports Medicine
- KIRSCH, C.-M., Nuclear Medicine
- KÖHLER, H., Internal Medicine
- KOHN, D., Orthopaedics
- KONNERTH, A., Physiology
- KRAMANN, B., Diagnostic Radiology
- LARSEN, R., Anaesthesiology
- LINDEMANN, B., Physiology
- MAURER, H. H., Pharmacology and Toxicology
- MEESE, E., Human Genetics and Molecular Biology

MENGER, M., Institute for Clinical and Experimental Surgery
MESTRES, P., Anatomy
MEYERHANS, A., Virology
MONTENARH, M., Medical Biochemistry
MORGENSTERN, E., Biology
MÜLLER-LANTZSCH, N., Virology
MUTSCHLER, W., Accident Surgery
NACIMIENTO, A. C., Experimental Neurosurgery
PEPER, K., Physiology
PFREUNDSCHUH, M., Internal Medicine
REICH, E., Dentistry
REMBERGER, K., Pathology
RUPRECHT, K. W., Ophthalmology
SCHÄFERS, H.-J., Surgery
SCHIEFFER, H.-J., Internal Medicine
SCHIMRIGK, K., Neurology
SCHMEISSNER, H., Dentistry
SCHMIDT, W., Gynaecology and Obstetrics
SCHNABEL, K., Radiation Therapy
SCHONECKE, O., Medical Psychology
SCHULZ, I., Physiology
SITZMANN, F. C., Paediatrics
SPITZER, W. C., Maxillofacial Surgery
STAHL, H., Medical Biochemistry
STEUDEL, W.-I., Neurosurgery
SYBRECHT, G. W., Internal Medicine
THIEL, G., Medical Biochemistry
TILGEN, W., Dermatology and Venereology
TRAUB, W. H., Medical Microbiology
UHLMANN, K., Anatomy
WANKE, K., Neurology, Psychiatry
WENZEL, E., Haemostasiology and Blood Transfusion Medicine
WERNER, G., General Biology
WILSKE, J., Forensic Medicine
ZANG, K., Human Genetics
ZEITZ, M., Internal Medicine
ZEPF, S., Internal Medicine, Psychosomatic Studies
ZIEGLER, M., Urology
ZIMMERMANN, R., Physiological Chemistry

Faculty of Philosophy:

BARRY, W. J., Phonetics, Phonology
BÉHAR, P., German for Francophones
BRÜCHER, W., Geography
DAUGS, R., Sports Science
ENGELKAMP, J., Psychology
FEHRENBACH, E., Modern History
FROBENIUS, W., Musicology
GERZYMISCH-ARBOGAST, H., English Translation
GIL ARROYO, A., Translation Studies, Romance Languages
GIRARDET, K. M., Ancient History
GÖBEL, W., English Philology and Literature
GÖRLER, W., Classical Philology
GÖTZE, L., German as a Foreign Language
GRABAS, M., Economic and Social History
GÜTHLEIN, K., History of Art
HALLER, J., Mechanical Transmission
HASENHÜTTL, G., Systematic Theology
HAUBRICHS, W., Medieval German Literature
HILPERT, K., Practical Theology and Social Ethics
HOENSCH, J. K., East European History
HUDEMANN, R., Modern and Contemporary History
JACOBI, R., Islamic Studies
JÄSCHKE, K.-U., Medieval History
JUNG, K. O., Fine Art and Art Education
KLEINERT, S., Romance Philology
KRÄMER, H.-L., Sociology
KRAUSE, R., Psychology
KUBINIOK, J., Physical Geography
LICHARDUS, J., Pre- and Protohistory
LICHTENSTERN, C., History of Art
LÖFFLER, E. W., Physical Geography
LOHMEIER, A.-M., Modern German Philology and Literature
LORENZ, K., Philosophy
LÜSEBRINK, H.-J., Romance Civilization, Intercultural Communication
MARTENS, K., English Philology, American Literature
MARTI, R., Slavic Philology
MAXEINER, J., Education
MEISTER, H., Educational Psychology
MÜLLER, C. W., Classical Philology
MÜLLER, P., Biogeography
MÜLLER, U. B., Theology, New Testament
NEUSCHÄFER, H.-J., Romance Philology and Literature
NORRICK, N., English Philology, Linguistics
OHLIG, K.-H., Theology
PFISTER, M., Romance Philology
PINKAL, M., Computer Languages
QUASTEN, H., Geography
RAASCH, A., Applied Linguistics
RATH, R., Modern German Language
REINSBURG, C., Classical Archaeology
RICHTER, K., Modern German Philology and Literature
SANDER, A., Education
SANDIG, B., German Linguistics
SAUDER, G., Modern German Philology and Literature
SCHLOBACH, J., Romance Philology
SCHMELING, M., General and Comparative Literature
SCHMITT, R., Comparative Indo-Germanic Languages
SCHNEIDER, H., Musicology
SCHNEIDER, R., Medieval History
SERMAIN, J.-P., Romance Philology
STEIN, F., Pre- and Protohistory
STEINER, E., English Linguistics and Translation
STOCKMANN, R., Sociology
STRITTMATTER, P., Education
TACK, W., Psychology
USZKOREIT, H., Computer Linguistics
VAN DÜLMEN, R., History, especially Regional
WINTERHOFF-SPURK, P., Psychology
WINTERMANTEL, M., Social Psychology
WYDRA, G., Sports Education
ZIMMERMANN, H. H., Information Science

Faculty of Natural Sciences:

ALBRECHT, E., Mathematics
BECK, H. P., Inorganic and Analytical Chemistry, Radiochemistry
BECKER, H., Pharmacognosy and Analytical Phytochemistry
BERGER, R., Mathematics
BERNHARDT, R., Biochemistry
BIRRINGER, R., Physical Engineering
BREUER, H. D., Physical Chemistry
BROSAMLER, G.-A., Mathematics
CHMIEL, H., Process Engineering
DECKER, W., Mathematics
DÜRR, H., Organic Chemistry
EICHER, TH., Organic Chemistry
ENGELHARDT, H., Instrumental Analysis, Environmental Analysis
ESCHMEIER, J., Mathematics
FUCHS, M., Mathematics
GEKELER, E.-U., Mathematics
GIFFHORN, F., Microbiology
GRÜTER, M., Mathematics
HARTMANN, R. W., Pharmaceutical Chemistry
HARTMANN, U., Experimental Physics
HEGETSCHWEILER, K., Inorganic Chemistry
HEINZLE, E., Technical Bioengineering
HEMPELMANN, R., Physical Chemistry
HÜFNER, S., Experimental Physics
KALLMAYER, H.-J., Pharmaceutical Chemistry
KALTWASSER, H., Microbiology
KNORR, K., Physical Engineering
KROEGER, H., Genetics
LEHR, C.-M., Pharmaceutical Technology
LEIBENGUTH, F., Genetics
LOUIS, A. K., Mathematics
LÜCKE, M., Theoretical Physics
MEISSNER, G., Theoretical Physics
NACHTIGALL, W., Zoology
PATT, H.-J., Experimental Physics
PETERSSON, J., Physical Engineering
RJASANOW, S., Mathematics
SCHANK, K., Organic Chemistry
SCHMIDT, G., Mathematics
SCHMITT, M., Microbiology
SCHNEIDER, H.-J., Organic Chemistry
SCHULTE, H., Applied Mathematics
SCHULZE-PILLOT-ZIEMEN, R., Mathematics
SCHUPP, H., Mathematics
SCHWITZGEBEL, G., Physical Chemistry
SIEMS, R., Theoretical Physics
UNRUH, H.-G., Experimental Solid-State Physics
VEITH, M., Inorganic Chemistry
WICHERT, T., Physical Engineering
WITTSTOCK, G., Mathematics
ZEPPEZAUER, M., Biochemistry
ZIMMER, H.-G., Mathematics
ZIMMERMANN, W. J., Theoretical Physics
ZINSMEISTER, H.-D., Botany

Faculty of Technology:

BECKER, K.-D., Theoretical Electronics
BLEY, H., Production Engineering
BLUM, A., Electronics and Semiconductor Components
BREME, J., Metallic Materials
CLASEN, R., Materials Science
GANZINGER, H., Informatics
HOTZ, G., Applied Mathematics and Informatics
ISMAR, H., Mechanical Engineering
JANOCHA, H., Automation
JASCHEK, H., Systems Theory of Electrical Theory
KLIEM, H., Electrical Engineering Physics
KOCH, A., Metrology
KOGLIN, H. J., Energy Supply
KRÖNING, M., Testing and Quality Control
MANOLI, Y., Microelectronics
MAURER, R., High and Ultra High Frequency Engineering
MEHLHORN, K., Informatics
MÜCKLICH, F., Work Materials
PAUL, W., Information Science
PFITZMANN, B., Informatics
POSSART, W., Polymers and Surfaces
SCHEIDIG, H., Informatics
SCHMIDT, H., Nonmetallic-Inorganic Materials Chemistry and Technology
SEIDEL, R., Theoretical Informatics
SIEKMANN, J., Informatics
SMOLKA, G., Information Science
VEHOFF, H., Materials Science, Methodology
WAHLSTER, W., Informatics
WEBER, C., Construction Engineering
WEIKUM, G., Informatics
WILHELM, R., Information Science

ATTACHED INSTITUTES

Institut für Konsum- und Verhaltensforschung (Consumer and Behavioural Research Institute): Dir Prof. Dr PETER WEINBERG.

Institut für Handel und Internationales Marketing (Institute of Commerce and International Marketing): Dir Prof. Dr JOACHIM ZENTES.

Institut für Wirtschaftsinformatik (Institute of Business Informatics): Dir Prof. Dr AUGUST-WILHELM SCHEER.

Institut für Wirtschaftsprufung (Institute of Accountancy): Dir Prof. Dr KARLHEINZ KÜTING.

Institut der Gesellschaft zur Förderung der Angewandten Informationsforschung e.V. an der Universität des Saarlandes: Dirs Prof. Dr JOHANN HALLER, Prof. Dr HARALD ZIMMERMANN.

Fraunhofer-Institut für Zerstörungsfreie Prüfverfahren (Fraunhofer Institute of Non-Destructive Testing): Dir Prof. Dr MICHAEL KRÖNING.

Fraunhofer-Institut für Biomedizinische Technik (Fraunhofer Institute of Biomedical Engineering): Dir Prof. Dr KLAUS GERSONDE.

Institut für Neue Materialen gem. GmbH (Institute for New Materials): Dir Prof. Dr HELMUT SCHMIDT (acting).

Deutsches Forschungszentrum für Künstliche Intelligenz GmbH (German Research Centre for Artificial Intelligence): Dir and CEO Prof. Dr WOLFGANG WAHLSIER.

Max-Planck-Institut für Informatik (Max-Planck-Institute for Informatics): Dir Prof. Dr KURT MEHLHORN (acting).

Internationales Begegnungs- und Forschungszentrum für Informatik gem. GmbH (International Research Centre for Informatics): Dir Prof. Dr REINHARD WILHELM.

Institut für Landeskunde im Saarland (Institute for Regional Studies in Saarland): Dir Prof. Dr HEINZ QUASTEN.

Gesellschaft für umweltkompatible Prozesstechnik mbH (Society for Environmentally Friendly Process Engineering): Dir Prof. Dr HORST CHMIEL.

Institut für Präventivmedizin an der Universität des Saarlandes (Institute for Preventive Medicine): comprises:

Institut für Präventive Kardiologie (Institute for Preventive Cardiology): Dir Prof. Dr HERMANN-JOSEF SCHIEFFER.

Institut für Medizinische Genetik (Institute for Medical Genetics): Dir Prof. Dr KLAUS ZANG.

Institut für Präventive Pneumonologie (Institute for Preventive Pneumonology): Dir Prof. Dr GERHARD SYBRECHT.

Zentrum zur Prävention, Erforschung und Dokumentation von Muskel- und Hirnkreislaufkrankheiten (Centre for Prevention, Research and Documentation of Circulatory Disorders of Muscles and the Brain): Dir Prof. Dr KLAUS SCHIMRIGK.

Präventivmedizinisches Zentrum für arbeitsbedingte Erkrankungen (Preventive Medical Centre for Occupational Diseases): Dir Prof. Dr AXEL BUCHTER.

Institut für Präventive Sportmedizin (Institute for Preventive Sports Medicine): Dir Prof. Dr WILFRIED KINDERMANN.

Institut für Prävention in der Pädiatrie (Institute for Preventive Medicine in Paediatrics): Dir Prof. Dr CARL FRIEDRICH SITZMANN.

Institut für Präventive Zahnheilkunde (Institute of Preventive Dentistry): Dir Prof. Dr ELMAR REICH.

UNIVERSITÄT-GESAMTHOCHSCHULE SIEGEN

57068 Siegen, Am Herrengarten 3

Telephone: (271) 740-1
Fax: (271) 740-4899
E-mail: rektor@rektorat.uni-siegen.de

Founded 1972
State control
Academic year: October to July (2 semesters)

Rector: Prof. Dr ALBERT H. WALENTA
Vice-Rectors: Prof. Dr HANS JÖRG DEISEROTH, Prof. Dr MANFRED GRAUER, Prof. Dr THEODORA HANTOS
Chancellor: Dr JOHANN PETER SCHÄFER
Librarian: Dr WERNER REINHARDT

Library of 1,050,000 vols
Number of teachers: 600
Number of students: 11,500

Publications: Research Report, *Reihe Siegen*, *Siegener Hochschulzeitung*, *Siegener Pädagogische Studien*, *SPIEL Diagonal*.

DEANS

Department of Philosophy, Religion and History: Prof. Dr RICHARD SCHLÜTER
Department of Education, Psychology and Physical Education: Prof. Dr ADOLF KELL
Department of Languages and Literature: Prof. Dr BURKHARD SCHAEDER
Department of Art and Design: Prof. Dr HERMANN J. BUSCH
Department of Economics: Prof. Dr IAN FRANKE-VIEBACH
Department of Mathematics: Prof. Dr WOLFGANG HAIN
Department of Natural Sciences I (Physics): Prof. Dr WOLFRAM WINNENBURG
Department of Natural Sciences II (Chemistry, Biology): Prof. Dr HARALD GÜNTHER
Department of Architecture: Prof. Dr-Ing. HUBERT ZUMBROICH
Department of Construction Engineering: Prof. Dr-Ing. ALFONS GORIS
Department of Mechanical Engineering: Prof. Dr-Ing. HORST WEISS
Department of Electrical Engineering: Prof. Dr EGBERT KRAMP

HOCHSCHULE FÜRVERWALTUNGS-WISSENSCHAFTEN SPEYER

67346 Speyer, Freiherr-vom-Stein-Str. 2

Telephone: (6232) 6540
Fax: (6232) 654208

Founded 1947
State control
Academic year: April to September, October to March

Rector: Prof. Dr KLAUS LÜDER
Vice-Rector: Prof. Dr SIEGFRIED MAGIERA
Administrative Officer: Dr WILFRIED EBLING
Librarian: Prof. Dr HELMUT QUARITSCH

Library of 220,300 vols
Number of teachers: 98 (incl. 78 part-time)
Number of students: 560

A postgraduate institution offering courses in administrative sciences

PROFESSORS

ARNIM, H. H. VON, Public Law and Constitutional Theory
BLÜMEL, W., Public Law
BOHNE, E., Public Administration
BÖHRET, C., Political Science
DUWENDAG, D., Economics
FÄRBER, G., Public Finance and Economics
FISCH, R., Empirical Social Sciences
FISCH, S., Modern History
HILL, H., Public Administration, Public Law
KLAGES, H., Empirical Social Sciences
KÖNIG, K., Public Administration, Public Law, Government
LÜDER, K., Public Finance and Business Administration
MAGIERA, S., Public Law
MERTEN, D., Public Law
PITSCHAS, R., Public Administration, Development Policy and Public Law
QUARITSCH, H., Constitutional Law, Political Theory
REINERMANN, H., Public Administration, Information Technology
SCHRECKENBERGER, W., Philosophy of Law, Legal Policy and Legislative Process
SIEDENTOPF, H., Public Administration, Public Law

ATTACHED INSTITUTE

Forschungsinstitut für öffentliche Verwaltung (Research Institute for Public Administration): Dir Prof. Dr Dr KLAUS KÖNIG.

UNIVERSITÄT STUTTGART

70049 Stuttgart, Postfach 106037

Telephone: (711) 1210
Telex: 721703
Fax: (711) 121-2271

Founded 1829 as Gewerbeschule, attained University status 1967
Academic year: April-July, October-February

Rector: Prof. Dr-Ing. Dres. h.c. G. PRITSCHOW
Vice-Rectors: Prof. Dr rer. nat. H. JESKE, Prof. Dr rer. nat. E. MESSERSCHMID, Prof. Dr phil. E. OLSHAUSEN
Chancellor: H.-J. SCHWARZE
Chief Librarian: W. STEPHAN

Library: see Libraries
Number of teachers: 2,400, including 450 professors
Number of students: 21,500

Publications: *Stuttgarter Uni-Kurier*. (4-5 a year), *Forschungsbericht* (2 a year), *Wechselwirkungen-Aus Lehre und Forschung der Universität Stuttgart* (annually), *Forschung-Entwicklung-Beratung* (annually).

DEANS

Faculty of Architecture and Town Planning: Prof. Dr phil. D. KIMPEL
Faculty of Civil Engineering and Surveying: Prof. Dr-Ing. F. BERNER
Faculty of Chemistry: Prof. Dr rer. nat. H. BERTAGNOLLI
Faculty of Electrical Engineering: Prof. Dr-Ing. J. SPEIDEL
Faculty of Energy Techniques: Prof. Dr-Ing. K. HEIN
Faculty of Construction and Production Technology: Prof. Dr-Ing. K. SIEGERT
Faculty of Biological and Geo-Sciences: Prof. Dr rer. nat. P. KELLER
Faculty of History, Social Sciences and Economics: Prof. Dr rer. pol. O. W. GABRIEL
Faculty of Aerospace Engineering: Prof. Dr-Ing. S. WAGNER
Faculty of Mathematics: Prof. rer. nat. P. WERNER
Faculty of Philosophy: Prof. Dr phil. habil. G. DOZIL
Faculty of Physics: Prof. Dr rer. nat. M. WAGNER
Faculty of Chemical Engineering: Prof. Dr-Ing. M. REUSS
Faculty of Computer Science: Prof. Dr rer. nat. V. CLAUSS

PROFESSORS

Architecture and City Planning:

ADAM, J., Design and Construction
AMINDE, H.-J., Public Buildings
BEHLING, S., Building Construction and Design
BOTT, H., City Planning and Urban Design
CHERET, P., Building Construction and Design
EISENBIEGLER, G., Structures and Constructional Design
ERTEL, H., Building Materials, Building Physics, Mechanical Equipment
HARLANDER, T., Housing and Design
HERRMANN, D., Building Materials
HÜBNER, P., Building Constructions and Design
JESSEN, J., City and Regional Planning
JOCHER, T., Housing and Design
KAULE, G., Landscape Planning and Ecology
KIMPEL, D., History of Architecture
KNOLL, W., Drawing, Drafting and Modelling
KÜSGEN, H., Building Economics
MORO, J., Planning and Construction of High-Rise Constructions
PESCH, F., City Planning and Urban Design
PODRECCA, B., Interior Design and Architectural Design

RIBBECK, E., Planning and Building in Developing Countries
SCHÖNWANDT, W., Foundations of Planning
SCHÜRMANN, P., Building Materials, Building Physics
SZYSZKOWITZ-KOWALSKI, K., Public Buildings
TOKARZ, B., Structures and Constructional Design
TRAUB, H., Drawing, Drafting and Modelling
TRIEB, M., City Planning and Urban Design
ULLMANN, F., Interior Design and Architectural Design

Civil Engineering and Surveying:
BÁRDOSSY, A., Water Management
BERNER, F., Construction Industry
EHLERS, W., Engineering Mechanics
ELIGEHAUSEN, R., Material Science in Structural Engineering
ENGESSER, K.-H., Biological Cleaning of Used Air
FRITSCH, D., Photogrammetry and Land Surveying
GERTIS, K., Building Physics
GIESECKE, J., Hydraulic Engineering and Water Resources
GRAFAREND, E. W., Geodetic Science
HAIDER, G., Applied Limnology and Fish Toxicology
HEIMERL, G., Railroad Engineering and Transportation Planning
HOLZER, S., Information Processing in Structural Engineering
KELLER, W., Geodetic Science
KLEUSBERG, A., Navigation
KOBUS, H., Hydraulics and Ground Water
KRAUTH, K., Wastewater Technology
KUHLMANN, U., Design and Construction
METZGER, D., Hydrochemistry and Hydrobiology
MIEHE, C., Engineering Mechanics
MÖHLENBRINK, W., Applied Geodesy
RAMM, E., Building Statistics
REINHARDT, H.-W., Material Science in Structural Engineering
RESSEL, W., Road and Transport Planning and Engineering
ROTT, U., Water Quality Management, Sanitary Engineering
SCHLAICH, J., Structural Design
SOBEK, W., Interdisciplinary Research, Architecture and Civil Engineering
TABASARAN, O., Sanitary Engineering, Wastewater and Solid Waste Management Technology
TREUNER, P., Regional Development Planning
VERMEER, P. A., Geotechnology

Chemistry:
ALDINGER, F., Non-Metallic Inorganic Materials
ARZT, E., Metallurgy
BECKER, G., Inorganic Chemistry
BERTAGNOLLI, H., Physical Chemistry
BREDERECK, K., Textile and Fibre Chemistry
EFFENBERGER, F., Organic Chemistry, Biochemistry and Radiochemistry
EISENBACH, C., Chemical Engineering
JÄGER, V., Organic Chemistry
KAIM, W., Inorganic Chemistry
KRAMER, H., Physical Chemistry
OPPERMANN, W., Textile Chemistry
RODUNER, E., Physical Chemistry
SCHLEID, T., Inorganic Chemistry
SCHMID, R., Technical Biochemistry
SCHMIDT, A., Inorganic Chemistry
WEIDLEIN, J., Inorganic Chemistry
WEITKAMP, J., Chemical Engineering
WERNER, H.-J., Theoretical Chemistry
WOLF, D., Biochemistry
ZABEL, F., Physical Chemistry

Electrical Engineering:
BERROTH, M., Communications Engineering
BOEHRINGER, A., Power Electronics and Building Technology
FESER, K., Power Transmission and High Voltage
GÖHNER, P., Control Engineering and Process Automation
GUTT, H.-J., Electrical Machines and Drives
KASPER, E., Semiconductor Engineering
KÜHN, P., Communications Switching and Data Techniques
LANDSTORFER, F., Radio Frequency Techniques
LÜDER, E., Network Theory and Systems
LUNK, A., Plasma Research
RUCKER, W., Theory of Electrical Engineering
SCHUMACHER, U., Plasma Research
SPEIDEL, J., Telecommunications
WERNER, J., Physical Electronics
ZOHM, H., Plasma Research

Energy Techniques:
BACH, H., Heating, Ventilation, Air Conditioning
BARGENDE, M., Combustion Engines
GÖDE, E., Fluid Machines and Hydraulic Pumps
HAHNE, E., Thermodynamics and Thermal Engineering
HEIN, K., Process Engineering and Steam Boiler Technology
LAURIEN, E., Nuclear Engineering
LOHNERT, G., Nuclear Engineering and Energy Systems
RÜHLE, R., Data Processing and Numerics
SCHMAUDER, S., Materials Testing, Materials Science and Strength of Materials
SEIFERT, H., Thermal Waste Utilization
STETTER, H., Thermal Turbomachines and Testing Laboratory
VOSS, A., Energy Economics
WELFONDER, E., Power Generation and Automatic Control
WIEDEMANN, J., Motor Vehicle Engineering

Design and Production Engineering:
BERTSCHE, B., Machine Construction
BULLINGER, H.-J., Industrial Science and Technology Management
GADOW, R., Manufacturing Technologies of Ceramic Compounds and Composites
HEISEL, U., Machine Tools
HÜGEL, H., High Power Beam Processing Technology
KÜCK, H., Time Measuring, Precision Engineering and Microengineering
LECHNER, G., Machine Elements (Gear Design–CAD–Sealing Technique)
NAGEL, J., Biomedical Technology
PRITSCHOW, G., Control Technology of Machine Tools and Production Systems
ROOS, H., Stock Technology and Logistics
SCHIEHLEN, W., Applied Mechanics
SCHINKÖTHE, W., Design and Production in Precision Engineering
SEEGER, H., Technical Design
SIEGERT, K., Metal Forming
TIZIANI, H., Applied Optics
WEHKING, K.-H., Conveyer and Transmission Technology, Gear Technology
WESTKÄMPER, E., Industrial Production and Plant

Biological and Geo-Sciences:
BLÜMEL, W. D., Geography
GAEBE, W., Cultural Geography
GHOSCH, R., Bioenergetics
GOERTZ, H. D., Zoology
HAHN, R., Geography
HÜLSER, D., Biophysics
JESKE, H., Molecular Biology and Virology of Plants
KELLER, P., Mineralogy and Crystal Chemistry
KNACKMUSS, H. J., Microbiology
KULL, U., Botany
LEINFELDER, R., Geology and Palaeontology
MASSONNE, H.-J., Mineralogy and Crystal Chemistry
MATTES, R., Industrial Genetics
PFIZENMAIER, K., Cell Biology and Immunology
SCHEURICH, P., Molecular Immunology
SCHNEIDER, G., Geophysics
SEUFERT, W., Industrial Genetics
SEYFRIED, H., Geology and Palaeontology
SYLDATK, C., Bioprocessing Technology
WIELANDT, E., Geophysics
WOLLNIK, F., Animal Physiology

History, Social Sciences and Economics:
ACKERMANN, K.-F., Economics
ARNOLD, U., Economics
BRINKHOFF, K.-P., Sports
BUERGEL, H.-D., Economics
CONRADS, N., Early Modern History
ENGLMANN, F., Economics
FRANKE, S., Economic Policy and Public Law
GABRIEL, O., Political Science
GOLLHOFER, A., Sports
GÖRLITZ, A., Political Science
HEILMANN, H., Business Administration
HERMANN, A., History of Natural Science and Technology
HORVÁTH, P., Economics
KORNBLUM, U., Law
MAJER, H., Economics
OLSHAUSEN, E., Ancient History
QUARTHAL, F., Regional History of Baden-Württemberg
REISS, M., Economics
SCHNABL, H., Economics
SCHODER, G., Sports
STEINER, R., History of Arts
STÜRNER, W., History
URBAN, D., Sociology
WIELAND, H., Physical Education
WYSS, B., History of Arts
ZAHN, E., Economics

Aerospace Engineering:
ARENDTS, F.-J., Aircraft Construction
AUWETTER-KURTZ, M., Space Transportation Technology
BRÜGGEMANN, D., Thermodynamics of Aerospace Engineering
KRÖPLIN, B.-H., Statics and Dynamics of Aerospace Structures
MESSERSCHMID, E. W., Space Systems
MUNZ, C.-D., Air and Gas Dynamics
VOIT-NITSCHANN, R., Aircraft Construction
WAGNER, S., Air and Gas Dynamics
WELL, K. H., Guidance and Control of Aerospace Vehicles

Mathematics:

Mathematical Institute A:
BRÜDERN, J., Mathematics
GEKELER, E., Mathematics
HESSE, C., Mathematics
HÖLLIG, K., Mathematics
KIRCHGÄSSNER, K., Mathematics
KÜMMERER, B., Mathematics
PÖSCHEL, J., Mathematics
STRAUSS, W., Mathematics
TIETZ, H., Mathematics
WALK, H., Mathematics
WENDLAND, W., Mathematics
WERNER, P., Mathematics

Mathematical Institute B:
BLIND, G., Mathematics
DEGEN, W., Mathematics
DIPPER, R., Mathematics
HÄHL, H., Mathematics
KÜHNEL, W., Mathematics
ROGGENKAMP, K.-W., Mathematics

Philosophy:
BARK, J., Modern German Literature
BIEN, G., Philosophy
BLUMENTHAL, P., Romance Linguistics
DOGIL, G., Computational Linguistics
FROMM, M., Educational Theory

HUBIG, C., Theory of Science and Technical Philosophy
KAMP, H., Formal Logic and Philosophy of Language
MAAG, G., Italian Studies
PRIMUS, B., Germanic Linguistics
ROBERTS, I., English Linguistics
ROHRER, CH., Computational Linguistics
ROOTH, M., Computational Linguistics
SCHLAFFER, H., Modern German Literature
SCHRÖDER, G., Romance Literatures
SCHWEIKK, G., German Philology
SEEBER, H. U., Modern English Literature
SOMMER, K.-H., Vocational and Technical Economic Education
THOMÉ, H., Modern German Literature

Physics:

DENNINGER, G., Experimental Physics
DRESSEL, M., Experimental Physics
KNEISSL, U., Experimental Physics
MAHLER, G., Theoretical Physics
MEHRING, M., Experimental Physics
MURAMATSU, A., Theoretical Physics
PILKUHN, M., Experimental Physics
SCHWEITZER, D., Experimental Physics
TREBIN, H.-R., Theoretical Physics
WAGNER, M., Theoretical Physics
WEIDLICH, W., Theoretical Physics
WEISS, U., Theoretical Physics

Chemical Engineering:

BRUNNER, H., Interface Chemistry
BUSSE, G., Non-destructive Testing
EIGENBERGER, G., Chemical Process Engineering
EYERER, P., Polymer Testing and Polymer Science
FRITZ, H.-G., Polymer Processing
GAUL, L., Mechanics
GILLES, E.-D., System Dynamics and Control Systems
HASSE, H., Technical Thermodynamics
KISTNER, A., Engineering Mechanics
MERTEN, C., Chemical Engineering
PIESCHE, M., Mechanical Production Engineering
REUSS, M., Biochemical Engineering
RUNGE, R., Technical Thermodynamics
SORG, H., Engineering Mechanics
WAGNER, M. H., Numerical Fluid Mechanics/Rheology
WEHLAN, H., Process Control Engineering
ZEITZ, M., System Dynamics and Control

Computer Science:

BAITINGER, U., Integrated System Design
CLAUS, V., Formal Concepts of Computer Science
DIEKERT, V., Theoretical Computer Science
EGGENBERGER, O., Real Time Processing
GUNZENHÄUSER, R., Man-Machine-Interaction
LAGALLY, K., Operating Systems
LEHMANN, E., Export Systems
LEVI, P., Computer Vision
LUDEWIG, J., Software Engineering
PLÖDEREDER, E., Programming Languages
ROLLER, D., Computer Science Fundamentals
ROTHERMEL, K., Distributed Systems
WUNDERLICH, H.-J., Computer Architecture

ATTACHED INSTITUTES

Computer Centre, University of Stuttgart: Dir Prof. Dr Ing. ROLAND RÜHLE.

Language Centre: Dirs Prof. Dr BLUMENTHAL, Prof. Dr I. ROBERTS.

Centre for Infrastructural Planning: Dirs Prof. Dr F. ENGELMANN, Prof. Dr agr. GISELHER KAULE, Prof. Dr-Ing. U. ROTT.

Computer Applications: Dirs Prof. Dr H. HERRMANN, Prof. Dr-Ing. R. RÜHLE, Prof. Dr G. WITTUM.

Centre for Civilization Studies and Cultural Theory: Dirs Prof. Dr F. QUARTHAL, Prof. Dr G. SCHRÖDER, Prof. Dr H. THOMÉ.

UNIVERSITÄT TRIER

54286 Trier, Universitätsring 15
Telephone: (0651) 201-0
Telex: 472680
Fax: (0651) 201-4247
E-mail: neyses@olewig.uni-trier.de

Founded 1473, reopened 1970

President: Prof. Dr RAINER HETTICH
Vice-Presidents: Prof. Dr ROLAND BAUMHAUER, Prof. Dr HELGA SCHNABEL-SCHÜLE
Chancellor: IGNAZ BENDER
Librarian: Dr LAURENZ BÖSING

Number of teachers: 676
Number of students: 11,501

Publications: *UNI-Journal* (every 2 months), *Studienführer*, *Vorlesungsverzeichnis*, *Trierer Beiträge*, *Forschungsbericht* (every 2 years), *Jahresbericht*.

DEANS

Faculty of Pedagogy, Philosophy and Psychology: Prof. Dr DIETER BARTUSSEK
Faculty of Language and Literature: Prof. Dr KARL HÖLZ
Faculty of History, Political Sciences, Classical Archaeology, Egyptology, Art History, Papyrology: Prof. Dr BÄRBEL KRAMER
Faculty of Management Economics, Sociology, Political Economy, Applied Mathematics and Ethnology: Prof. Dr WILLY EIRMBTER
Faculty of Law: Prof. Dr GABRIELE BURMESTER
Faculty of Geography and Geosciences: Prof. Dr JEAN-FRANK WAGNER

PROFESSORS

Faculty of Pedagogy, Philosophy and Psychology:

ANTONI, C., Psychology
BARTUSSEK, D., Psychology
BECKER, P., Psychology
BLESS, H., Psychology
BRANDTSTÄDTER, J., Psychology
DRÄGER, H., Pedagogics
FILIPP, S.-H., Psychology
FISCHER, K., Philosophy
HELLHAMMER, D., Psychology
HINSKE, N., Philosophy
HOMFELDT, H.-C., Pedagogy
HONIG, M. S., Pedagogy
MONTADA, L., Psychology
MÜLLER-FOHRBRODT, G., Pedagogy
ORTH, E.-W., Philosophy
SCHELLER, R., Psychology
SCHMIDT, L., Psychology
SCHWENKMEZGER, P., Psychology
SEILER, H., Pedagogy
WENDER, K. F., Psychology

Faculty of Language and Literature:

ALTHAUS, H. P., German Linguistics
ANTONI, K., Japanese Studies
BENDER, K.-H., Romance Literature
BREUER, H., English Literature
BUCHER, H.-J., Media
GÄRTNER, K., German Philology
GELHAUS, H., German Linguistics
GÖSSMANN, H., Japanese Studies
HASLER, J., English and American Literature
HEFTRICH, U., Slavic Literature
HÖLZ, K., Romance Literature
KLOOSS, W., English Literature
KÖHLER, H., Romance Literature
KÖHLER, R., Linguistic Data Processing
KÖSTER, J.-P., Applied Philology, Phonetics
KRAMER, J., Romance Philology
KREMER, D., Romance Philology
KÜHLWEIN, W., English Philology
NIEDEREHE, H.-J., Romance Philology
PIKULIK, L., Modern German Literature
PLATZ, N., English Literature
POHL, K. H., Sinology
REINHARDT, H., Modern German Literature
RESSEL, G., Slavistics
RIEGER, B., Linguistic Data Processing, Computer Languages
RÖLL, W., German Philology
STRAUSS, J., English Philology
STUBBS, M., English Linguistics
THORAU, H.-E., Portuguese Philology
TIMM, E., Yiddish Language
UERLINGS, H., Modern German Literature
WIMMER, R., German Linguistics
WÖHRLE, G., Classical Philology

Faculty of History, Political Science, Classical Archaeology, Egyptology, Art History, Papyrology:

ANTON, H. H., Medieval History
DASZEWSKI, W. A., Classical Archaeology
EBELING, D., Modern Economic and Social History
GESTRICH, A., Modern History
GRIMM, G., Classical Archaeology
HAVERKAMP, A., Medieval History
HEINEN, H., Ancient History
IRSIGLER, F., Cultural History
KIMMEL, A., Politics
KRAMER, B., Papyrology
MANDT, H., Political Science
MAULL, H. W., Political Science
RAPHAEL, L., Modern and Recent History
SCHMIDT-LINSENHOFF, V., Art History
SCHNABEL-SCHÜLE, H., Modern History
STROBEL, K., Ancient History
VLEEMING, S. P., Egyptology
WOLF, G., Art History
ZIEMER, K., Political Science

Faculty of Management Economics, Sociology, Political Economy, Applied Mathematics and Ethnology:

AMBROSI, C. M., Political Economy
ANTWEILER, C., Ethnology
BAUM, D., Computer Science
BRAUN, H., Sociology
CZAP, H., Management Economics
DICKERTMANN, D., Political Economy
DIEROLF, P., Mathematics
ECKERT, R., Sociology
EIRMBTER, W., Sociology
EL-SHAGI, E. S., Political Economy
FILC, W., Political Economy
GAWRONSKI, W., Mathematics
HAHN, A., Sociology
HAMM, B., Sociology
HARDES, H.-D., Political Economy
HECHELTJEN, P., Political Economy
HETTICH, R., Applied Mathematics
HORST, R., Mathematics
JÄCKEL, M., Sociology
JUNKERNHEINRICH, M., Political Economy
KNAPPE, E., Political Economy
KRUG, W., Statistics
LEHMANN, M., Management Economics
LUH, W., Applied Mathematics
LUSCHGY, H., Applied Mathematics
MEINEL, C., Computer Science
MILDE, H., Management Economics
OFFERMANN-CLAS, CH., European Community
RÜCKLE, D., Management Economics
SACHS, E., Mathematics
SADOWSKI, D., Management Economics
SCHERTLER, W., Management Economics
SCHMIDT, A., Management Economics
SEIDL, H., Computer Science
SENDLER, W., Applied Mathematics
SONNEMANN, E., Mathematics
SPEHL, H., Political Economy
STURM, P., Computer Science
TICHATSCHKE, R., Mathematics
WÄCHTER, H., Management Economics
WALTER, B., Computer Science
WEIBER, R., Management Economics
WINDOLF, P., Sociology

Faculty of Law:

BIRK, R., Private Law, Labour Law, Conflict of Laws
BÜLOW, P., Private Law, Mercantile Law, German and European Commercial Law
BURMESTER, G., National and International Finance and Tax Law
DI FABIO, U., Constitutional and Administrative Law
EHMANN, H., Private Law, Labour Law
HOFFMANN, B. VON, Private Law, Conflict of Laws, Comparative Law
KRAUSE, P., Public and Social Law, Philosophy of Law
KREY, V., Criminal Law, Criminal Procedure, Legal Methods
KÜHNE, H.-H., Criminal Law, Criminology, Criminal Procedure
LINDACHER, W., Private Law, Commercial Law, Civil Procedure
MARBURGER, P., Private Law, Commercial Law, Civil Procedure
MÜLBERT, P. O., Private Law, Commercial Law, Corporation Law
REIMANN, M., Private Law, Legal History, Comparative Law
REINHARD, M., Constitutional and Administrative Law
ROBBERS, G., Public Law, Ecclesiastical Law, Philosophy of Law
SCHRÖDER, M., Public, International and EC Law
WIELING, H., Private Law, Roman Law
ZACZYK, R., Criminal Law, Criminal Procedure, Philosophy of Law

Faculty of Geography and Geosciences:

ALEXANDER, J., Physical Geography
BAUMHAUER, R., Physical Geography
BECKER, CHR., Applied Geography and Geography of Tourism
BOLLMANN, J., Cartography
EBERLE, I., Economic and Social Geography
FISCHER, K., Inorganic and Analytical Chemistry
HELBIG, A., Climatology
HERZFELD, U., Geomathematics
HILL, J., Remote Sensing
HORNETZ, B., Cultural and Regional Geography
JÄTZOLD, R., Cultural and Regional Geography
MONHEIM, Applied Geography, Urban and Regional Planning and Development
NEITZKE, M., Geobotany
NIEMEYER, J., Soil Science
RUTHSATZ, B., Geobotany
SCHRÖDER, D., Soil Science
SYMADER, W., Hydrology
VOGEL, H., Communal Science
WAGNER, J.-F., Geology

EBERHARD-KARLS-UNIVERSITÄT TÜBINGEN

72074 Tübingen, Wilhelmstr. 7
Telephone: (7071) 290
Telex: 7262867
Fax: (7071) 295990

Founded 1477
Academic year: October to July

President: HANS-WERNER LUDWIG
Vice-Presidents: Prof. GEORG WIELAND, Prof. HARTMUT GABLER
Chief Administrative Officer: Prof. Dr GEORG SANDBERGER
Librarian: Dr BERNDT VON EGIDY

Number of teachers: 1,825
Number of students: 21,035

Publications: *Amtliche Mitteilungen* (4 a year), *Attempto! Forum der Universität Tübingen* (2 a year), *Tübinger Universitätsnachrichten* (8 a year), *Forschungsnachrichten* (c. 8 a year), *Forschungsbericht* (every 3 years).

PROFESSORS

Department of Protestant Theology:

BAYER, O., Systematic Theology
DREHSEN, V., Practical Theology
HENNIG, G., Practical Theology
HERMS, E., Systematic Theology
HOFIUS, O., New Testament
JANOWSKI, B., Old Testament
JÜNGEL, E., Systematic Theology
KOEPF, U., Church History
LICHTENBERGER, H., New Testament and Ancient Jewish Culture
MEHLHAUSEN, J., Liturgy
MITTMANN, S., Biblical Archaeology
STUHLMACHER, P., New Testament

Department of Catholic Theology:

BIESINGER, A., Educational Religion
ECKERT, M., Fundamental Theology
GROSS, W., Old Testament
HILBERATH, B. J., Systematics
HUNOLD, G. W., Moral Theology
MIETH, D., Moral Theology and Social Sciences
PUZA, R., Church Law
THEOBALD, M., New Testament
VOGT, H. J., Old Church History, Patrology and Christian Archaeology
WIELAND, G., Basic Questions of Theology
WINKLER, G., Comparative Liturgiology

Department of Law:

ASSMANN, H.-D., Civil Law, Trade and Commercial Law
ERNST, W., Roman and Civil Law
GÜNTHER, H.-L., Penal Law
HAFT, F., Penal Law and Procedural Law
HESS, B., Civil Law and Procedural Law
KÄSTNER, K.-H., Civil Law, State Church Law
KERNER, H.-J., Criminology
KIRCHHOF, F., Public Law
KUHL, K., Penal Law and Procedural Law
MAROTZKE, W., Civil Law and Procedural Law
MÖSCHEL, W., Civil, Trade and Commercial Law
NÖRR, K. W., Civil, Roman and Commercial Law
OPPERMANN, T., Public Law
PICKER, E., Civil Law, Labour and Trade Law
PÜTTNER, G., Constitutional, Administrative Law
RONELLENFITSCH, M., Public Law
SCHIEMANN, G., Civil Law
SCHRÖDER, J., Penal and Private Law, History of German Law
VITZTHUM, W. GRAF, Public Law
WEBER, U., Penal and Procedural Law
WESTERMANN, H. P., Civil, Trade and Commercial Law

Department of Economics:

BEA, F. X., Commerce
BERNDT, R., Commerce
CANSIER, D., Economics
JAHNKE, B., Commerce
MOLSBERGER, J., Economics
NEUS, W., Commerce
RONNING, G., Economics and Statistics
SCHAICH, E., Economics and Statistics
SCHÖBEL, R., Commerce
SCHWEITZER, M., Commerce, Business Management, Operations Research
STADLER, M., Economics
STARBATTY, J., Economics
ULLMANN, H.-P., History of Economics and Social History
WAGNER, F. W., Commerce
WALZ, U., Economics
WIEGARD, W., Economics

Department of Medicine:

APITZ, J., Paediatric Cardiology
BAMBERG, M., Radiography
BARES, R., Nuclear Medicine
BECKER, H. D., Surgery
BICHLER, K.-H., Urology
BIRBAUMER, N., Psychology
BOCK, K. W., Toxicology
BOTZENHART, K., Hygiene
BUCHKREMER, G., Psychiatry
BÜLTMANN, B., Pathology
CLAUSSEN, C., Radiography
DICHGANS, H., Neurology
DICKHUTH, H.-H., Medicine of Sports
DIETZ, K., Medical Biometrics
DREWS, U., Anatomy
FICHTNER, G., History of Medicine
GÖZ, G., Dentistry
GREGOR, M., Internal Medicine
GROTE, E., Neurosurgery
HÄRING, H.-U., Internal Medicine
HENSELER, H., Psychoanalysis
HIRSCH, J., Obstetrics and Gynaecology
JAHN, G., Medical Virology
KANZ, L., Internal Medicine
KLOSINSKI, G., Child and Youth Psychiatry
KNOBLOCH, J., Tropical Medicine
KREISSIG, I., Ophthalmology
KÜSSWETTER, W., Orthopaedics
LANG, F., Physiology
LÖST, C., Dentistry
MEYERMANN, R., Neuropathology
MICHAELIS, R., Child Development Problems
NIETHAMMER, D., Paediatrics
NÜSSLIN, F., Medical Physics
OSSWALD, H., Pharmacology
RASSNER, G., Dermatology
RITTER, H., Anthropology and Genetics
RUPPERSBERG, P., Physiology
SCHMAHL, F. W., Social Medicine
SCHWEIZER, P., Child Surgery
SCHWENZER, R. N., Maxillo-Facial Surgery
SEIPEL, L., Internal Medicine
SELBMANN, H.-K., Medical Statistics and Data Processing
THIEL, H.-J., Ophthalmology
UNERTL, K., Anaesthesiology
VOIGT, K., Neuroradiology
WAGNER, H.-J., Anatomy
WEBER, H., Dentistry
WEHNER, H.-D., Forensic Medicine
WEISE, K., Traumatology
WELLER, S., Orthopaedic Surgery
WERNER, H., Medical Microbiology
ZENNER, H.-P., Oto-rhino-laryngology
ZIEMER, G., Thoracic and Cardiovascular Surgery
ZRENNER, E., Ophthalmology

Department of Philosophy:

FRANK, M., Philosophy
HOEFFE, O., Philosophy
KOCH, A. F., Philosophy

Department of Social and Behavioural Sciences and Pedagogics:

BOECKH, A., Political Studies
DEUTSCHMANN, CH., Sociology
DIEHL, M., Psychology
GABLER, H., Theory of Physical Education
GILDENMEISTER, R., Sociology
GÖHNER, U., Physical Education
GRUNDER, H.-U., Pedagogics
GRUPE, O., Theory of Physical Education
HAUTZINGER, M., Psychology
HRBEK, R., Political Studies
HUBER, G., Pedagogics
MÜLLER, S., Social Pedagogics
PRANGE, K., Pedagogics
RITTBERGER, V., Political Studies
SPRONDEL, W., Sociology
STAPF, K., Psychology
THIERSCH, H., Social Pedagogics
ZIFREUND, W., Pedagogics

Department of Modern Languages:

BERGER, T., Slavonic Philology
DRUBIG, H. B., English Philology
ENGLER, B., English Philology
FICHTE, J., English Philology

FIETZ, L., English Philology
HINRICHS, E., Computing Science of Linguistics
HUBER, CH., Medieval German Literature
KEMPER, H.-G., German Philology
KLUGE, R.-D., Slavonic Philology
KOCH, P., German Philology
KOHN, K., English Philology
KORTE, B., English Philology
MOOG-GRUNEWALD, M., Romance Philology
MÜLLER, K.-O., German Philology
REIS, M., German Philology
SCHLIEBEN-LANGE, B., Romance Philology
SCHRÖDER, J., German Language and Literature
STECHOW, A. VON, Theoretical Linguistics
STRASSNER, E., German Philology
UEDING, G., German Philology
WACHINGER, B., German Philology
WERTHEIMER, J., German Philology

Department of History:
BEYRAU, D., East European History
DOERING-MANTEUFFEL, A., Modern and Contemporary History
HARTMANN, W., Medieval and Modern History
KOLB, F., Ancient History
LANGEWIESCHE, D., Medieval and Modern History
LORENZ, S., Medieval and Modern History
SCHINDLING, A., Medieval and Modern History

Department of Cultural Sciences:
EGGERT, M., Pre- and Ancient History
ESS, J. VAN, Semitic and Islamic Studies
GAUER, W., Classical Archaeology
GERÖ, ST., Oriental Christian Philology and Culture
GLADIGOW, B., Comparative Religion
HOFMANN, H., Classical Philology
KANNICHT, R., Classical Philology
KLEIN, P., Art History
SCHENKEL, W., Egyptology
SCHMID, M. H., Music
SCHMIDT, E. A., Classical Philology
STELLRECHT, J., Ethnography
SZLEZÁK, TH., Greek Philology
VOGEL, H.-U., Sinology

Department of Mathematics:
HERING, C.
HEYER, H.
HUISKEN, G.
KAUP, W.
LUBICH, C.
SALZMANN, H.
SCHEJA, G.
WOLFF, M.
YSERENTANT, H.

Department of Physics:
FÄSSLER, A., Theoretical Physics
GÖNNENWEIN, F., Experimental Physics
HÜBENER, R., Experimental Physics
KERN, D., Basic Physical Computer Science
PLIES, E., Applied Physics
PRANDL, W., Crystallography
REINHARDT, H., Theoretical Physics
RUDER, H., Theoretical Astrophysics
SCHOPOLL, N., Theoretical Physics
WAGNER, G. J., Experimental Physics

Department of Chemistry and Pharmacy:
AMMON, H., Pharmacology
GÖPEL, W., Theoretical Chemistry
HAMPRECHT, B., Biochemistry
HANACK, M., Organic Chemistry
HEIDE, L., Pharmacology
JUNG, G., Organic Chemistry
LINDNER, E., Inorganic Chemistry
MAIER, M., Organic Chemistry
MECKE, D., Biochemistry
OBERHAMMER, H., Physical Chemistry
SCHMIDT, P., Pharmaceutical Technology
SEELIG, F. F., Theoretical Chemistry
STRÄHLE, J., Inorganic Chemistry

Department of Biology:
BRAUN, V., Microbiology
ENGELS, E.-M., Development Physiology
ENGELS, W.
FROMMER, W.
GÖTZ, F., Microbiological Genetics
HADELER, F.-P., Biomathematics
HAMPP, R., Botany
JÜRGENS, G.
MAIER, W., Zoology
NORDHEIM, A., Molecular Biology
OBERWINKLER, F., Botany
SCHNITZLER, H.-U., Zoophysiology
SCHÖFFL, F., Genetics
WOHLLEBEN, W.

Department of Geosciences:
CONARD, N., Palaeohistory and Protohistory
EBERLE, D., Geography
FÖRSTER, H., Geography
FRISCH, W., Geology
KOHLHEPP, G., Anthropogeography
LUTERBACHER, H., Micropalaeontology
MOSBRUGGER, V., Palaeontology
PFEFFER, K.-H., Physical Geography
SATIR, M., Geological Chemistry
TEUTSCH, G., Geology

Department of Computing Science:
GÜNTZER, U.
KLAEREN, H.
LANGE, K.-J.
LOOS, R.
ROSENSTIEL, W.
STRASSER, W.
ZELL, A.

ATTACHED INSTITUTES

Deutsches Institut für Fernstudien (German Institute for Distance Studies): 72074 Tübingen; Dir Prof. Dr PETER HAUCK.

Goethe-Wörterbuch: 72074 Tübingen; Dir of Commission Prof. Dr E. A. SCHMIDT.

UNIVERSITÄT ULM

89069 Ulm
Telephone: (731) 502-01
Telex: 712567
Fax: (731) 502-2038

Founded 1967 as Medizinische-Naturwissenschaftliche Hochschule, University charter 1967
State control
Language of instruction: German
Academic year: October to September

Rector: Prof. Dr HANS WOLFF
Pro-Rectors: Prof. Dr JÜRGEN ASCHOFF, Prof. Dr KARL JOACHIM EBELING
Chancellor: Dr DIETRICH EBERHARDT
Chief Librarian: SIEGFRIED FRANKE

Number of teachers: 418
Number of students: 4,612

Publication: *Uni Ulm Intern* (monthly).

DEANS

Faculty of Natural Sciences: Prof. Dr OTHMAR MARTI
Faculty of Medicine: Prof. Dr GUIDO ADLER
Faculty of Engineering: Prof. Dr ERHARD KOHN
Faculty of Information Science: Prof. Dr UWE SCHÖNING
Faculty of Mathematics and Mathematical Economics: Prof. Dr FRANK STEHLING

ATTACHED INSTITUTES

Institut für Lasertechnologien in der Medizin (Institute for Laser Technology in Medicine): Dir Prof. Dr RUDOLF STEINER.

Forschungsinstitut fur anwendungsorientierte Wissensverarbeitung (Research Institute for the Application of Knowledge): Dir Prof. Dr Dr FRANZ JOSEF RADERMACHER.

Zentrum für Sonnenenergie- und Wasserstofforschung (Centre for Research into Solar Energy and Hydrogen): Dir Prof. Dr JÜRGEN GARCHE.

Institut für Diabetestechnologie GmbH (Institute for Diabetes Treatment): Man. Dir Prof. Dr ROLF FUSSGÄNGER.

Institut für dynamische Materialprüfung (Institute for Testing Materials): Chair. Prof. Dr WOLFGANG PECHHOLD.

Institut für Medienforschung und Medienentwicklung (Institute for Media Research and Development): Man. Dirs Prof. G. HÖRMANN, Prof. Dr W. E. REINKE.

BAUHAUS-UNIVERSITÄT WEIMAR

99421 Weimar, Geschwister-Scholl-Str. 8
Telephone: (3643) 58-0
Fax: (3643) 58-1120

Founded 1860
Academic year: October to June

Chancellor: Dr-Ing. HEIKO SCHULTZ
Rector: Prof. Dr-Ing. GERD ZIMMERMANN
Vice-Rectors: Prof. HERBERT WENTSCHER, Prof. Dr-Ing. habil. FRANK WEINER
Librarian: Dip.-Bibl. INGRID KRANZ

Number of teachers: 78
Number of students: 4,200

Publications: *Wissenschaftliche Zeitschrift* (8 a year), *Schriften der Bauhaus-Universität* (irregular), *Der Bogen* (10 a year), *VERSO-Architekturtheorie* (2 a year).

DEANS

Faculty of Architecture and Urban and Regional Planning: Prof. EGON SCHIRMBECK
Faculty of Construction: Prof. Dr-Ing. habil. GERHARD BURKHARDT
Faculty of Arts: Dr KARL SCHAWELKA
Faculty of Media: LORENZ ENGELL

PROFESSORS

Faculty of Architecture and Urban and Regional Planning:
BARZ-MALFATTI, H., Construction and Development
BÜTTNER, H., Sources of Construction
CHRIST, W., Construction and Town Planning I
DONATH, D., Computers in Architecture and Development Planning
GLÜCKLICH, D., Principles of Ecological Construction
GRONAU, H.-J., Building Ecology and Air-conditioning
HAHN, H., Design and Industrial Buildings
HASSENPFLUG, D., Sociology and Social History of Towns
KÄSTNER, A., Methodology of Depiction
KIND, G., Space Research, Development and Land Planning
KLEIN, B., Construction and Town Planning II
KOPPANDY, J., Landscape Architecture
LINDNER, G., Design and Building Construction
RIESS, H., Design and Building I
RUDOLF, B., Building Morphology
SALZMANN, D., Principles of Design
SCHIRMBECK, E., Design and Interior Design
SCHMITZ, K.-H., Design and Building II
STAMM-TESKE, W., Design and House-Building
WENZEL, H., Design and Rural Buildings
WIRTH, H., Care of Historic Monuments
ZIMMERMANN, G., Theory of Architecture

Faculty of Construction:
BENCKE, K., Informatics in Civil Engineering
BIDLINGSMAIER, W., Waste Management
BRASCHEL, R., Planning of Engineering Facilities for the Construction Industry

BRANNOLTE, U., Traffic Planning and Engineering
BUCHER, C., Building Mechanics
BURKHARDT, G., Structural Engineering
FREUNDT, U., Transport-Related Buildings
HACK, H.-P., Hydraulic Engineering
HEMPEL, L., Mathematical Optimization
HILBIG, G., Physics of Building
HOHMANN, G., Computer Technology
HÜBLER, R., Information Processing
KAPS, A., Chemistry for Building
KRANAWETTREISER, J., Current Mechanics
MÜLLER, A., Construction Site Preparation and Development
RAUE, E., Solid Buildings I
RAUTENSTRAUCH, K., Wood and Stone Construction
RUTH, J., Solid Buldings II
STARK, J., General Building Materials
VOIGTLÄNDER, G., Estate Water Supply
WERNER, F., Solid Buildings I

Faculty of Arts:
BACHHUBER, L., Free Art
BARTELS, H., Product Design
FRÖHLICH, E., Free Art
GRONERT, S., History and Theory of Design
HINTERBERGER, N., Free Art
HOLTZWARTH, W., Visual Communication
KUFUS, A., Product Design
NEMITZ, B., Free Art
PREISS, A., History of Architecture
PREY, K., Product Design
RAHMANN, F., Free Art
RUTHERFORD, J., Visual Communication
SATTLER, W., Product Design
SCHAWELKA, K., History and Theory of Art
STAMM, H., Visual Communication
WEBER, O., Aesthetics
WENTSCHER, H., Visual Communication

Faculty of Media:
ENGELL, L., Theory of Communication and Media
HUPFER, P., Data Banks and Communication Systems
WÜTHRICH, C., Graphic Data Processing

HOCHSCHULE WISMAR

23952 Wismar, Postfach 1210
Premises at; 23966 Wismar, Philipp-Müller-Str.

Telephone: (3841) 753-0
Fax: (3841) 753-383

Founded 1969 as Ingenieurhochschule Wismar, renamed 1988 and 1992
Academic year: September to August

Rector: Prof. Dr-Ing. BURCKHARD SIMMEN
Pro-Rectors: Prof. Dr rer. oec. habil. JOACHIM FRAHM, Prof. Dr-Ing. habil. DIETER HEIN
Chancellor: BERND KLÖVER
Librarian: JOHANNES FREYDANK

Number of teachers: 146
Number of students: 3,065

HEADS OF DEPARTMENTS

Architecture: Prof. Dipl.-Ing. HENNER HANNIG
Civil Engineering: Prof. Dr-Ing. OLAF NIEKAMP
Design/Interior Architecture: Prof. Dipl.-Designer KNUT WOLFGANG MARON
Electrical Engineering and Computer Science: Prof. Dr-Ing. habil. WINFRIED SCHAUER
Mechanical Engineering/Process and Environmental Engineering: Prof. Dr-Ing. HANS-RAINER KLEMKOW
Maritime Studies: Prof. Dr-Ing. habil. KNUD BENEDICT
Commerce: Prof. Dr rer. nat. JÜRGEN CLEVE

BERGISCHE UNIVERSITÄT-GESAMTHOCHSCHULE WUPPERTAL

42097 Wuppertal, Gaussstr. 20

Telephone: (202) 439-1
Telex: 8592262
Fax: (202) 439-2901

Founded 1972
State control
Language of instruction: German
Academic year: October to September

Rector: Prof. Dr rer. pol. Dr h.c. ERICH HÖDL
Co-Rectors: Prof. Dr phil. DIETER WOLFF (Academic), Prof. Dr rer. nat. PETER C. MÜLLER (Science and Research), Prof. Dr rer. pol. VOLKER RONGE (Planning and Finance)
Chancellor: Dr KLAUS PETERS
Librarian: Dr DIETER STÄGLICH

Number of teachers: 321
Number of students: 17,500

DEANS

Faculty of Sociology: Prof. Dr phil. M. A. HEINZ SÜNKER
Faculty of Philosophy and Theology: Prof. Dr theol. THOMAS SÖDING
Faculty of Education: Prof. Dr phil. EDUARD KLEBER
Faculty of Languages and Literature: Prof. Dr phil. Dr h.c. PETER SCHERFER
Faculty of Art, Design and Music: Prof. Dr h.c. BAZON BROCK
Faculty of Economics: Prof. Dr rer. pol. WINFRIED MATTHES
Faculty of Mathematics: Prof. Dr rer. nat. ANDREAS FROMMER
Faculty of Physics: Prof. Dr rer. nat. KARL-HEINZ MÜTTER
Faculty of Chemistry: Prof. Dr rer. nat. WOLFGANG PIEPERSBERG
Faculty of Architecture: Prof. ECKHARD GERBER
Faculty of Construction Engineering: apl. Prof. Dr-Ing. DIETRICH HOEBORN
Faculty of Mechanical Engineering: Prof. Dr-Ing. WERNER HOFFMANNS
Faculty of Electrical Engineering: Prof. Dr rer. nat. LUDWIG JOSEF BALK
Faculty of Safety and Accident Prevention: Prof. Dr rer. pol. Dr rer. pol. habil. WOLFGANG KRÜGER

ATTACHED INSTITUTES

Institute for Applied Computer Science: Dir Prof. Dr ANDREAS FROMMER.

Institute for Robotics: Dir Prof. Dr PETER C. MÜLLER.

Institute for European Economic Research: Dir Prof. Dr GERHARD ARMINGER.

Institute for Materials Science: Dir Prof. Dr SIEGFRIED DIETRICH.

Institute for the Environment: Dir Prof. Dr FRANK WERNER.

Institute for Educational Research and Teacher Training: Dir Prof. Dr EDUARD W. KLEBER.

Institute for Economic and Technological Development: Dir Prof. Dr GÜNTHER OUTHMANN.

Institute for Civil Engineering, Waste Processing and Water Supply: Dir Prof. Dr HANS KALDENHOFF.

BAYERISCHE-JULIUS-MAXIMILIANS-UNIVERSITÄT WÜRZBURG

97070 Würzburg, Sanderring 2

Telephone: (931) 310
Fax: (931) 312600
E-mail: universitaet@zv.uni-wuerzburg.de

Founded 1582
State control
Academic year: 1 October to 30 September

President: Prof. Dr phil. Drs h.c. Prof. h.c. TH. BERCHEM
Vice-Presidents: Prof. Dr rer. nat. H. HAGEDORN, Prof. Dr med. J. BÖNING, Prof. Dr rer. pol. W. FREERICKS
Chancellor: B. FORSTER
Chief Librarian: (vacant)

Library of 2,950,000 vols
Number of teachers: 755
Number of students: 19,800

Publications: *Personal- und Vorlesungsverzeichnis* (2 a year), *Jahresbericht*, *Blick* (3 a year), *Würzburg Heute* (2 a year).

DEANS

Faculty of Catholic Theology: Prof. Dr THEODOR SEIDL
Faculty of Law: Prof. Dr JÜRGEN WEITZEL
Faculty of Medicine: Prof. Dr KLAUS VIKTOR TOYKA
Faculty of Philosophy I (Antiquity, Cultural Studies): Prof. Dr KARL-THEODOR ZAUZICH
Faculty of Philosophy II (Philology, History, History of Art): Prof. Dr HELMUT PFOTENHAUER
Faculty of Philosophy III (Philosophy, Education, Social Sciences): Prof. Dr WOLFGANG SCHNEIDER
Faculty of Biology: Prof. Dr MARKUS RIEDEER
Faculty of Chemistry and Pharmacy: Prof. Dr WOLFGANG KIEFER
Faculty of Geosciences: Prof. Dr HERBERT VOSSMERBÄUMER
Faculty of Mathematics and Computer Science: Prof. Dr HERMANN HEINEKEN
Faculty of Physics and Astronomy: Prof. Dr WOLFGANG KINZEL
Faculty of Economics: Prof. Dr PETER BOFINGER

PROFESSORS

Faculty of Catholic Theology:
ARX, W. VON, Science of Liturgy
DROESSER, G., Christian Sociology
GANZER, K., Medieval and Modern Church History
HAERING, B., Church Law, History of Church Law
KLINGER, E., Basic Theology and Comparative Religion
MEUFFELS, O., Dogmatics
MÜLLER, K.-H., Biblical Introduction
SEIDL, TH., Old Testament Exegesis and Biblical Oriental Languages
SIMONIS, W., Dogmatics and History of Dogma
SPEIGL, J., Church History
WEIER, W., Christian Philosophy
WITTSTADT, K., History of the Frankish Church
ZERFASS, R., Pastoral Theology
ZIEBERTZ, H.-G., Religious Instruction

Faculty of Law:
BLUMENWITZ, D., International Law and Political Science
DREIER, H., Philosophy of Law, Political and Administrative Law
DREXL, J., Civil Law and European Economic Law
FORKEL, H., Civil Law, Commercial Law, Industrial Law, Copyright
HERGENRÖDER, C. W., Civil Law and Labour Law
JUST, M., Roman Law, Ancient Law, Civil Law
KEMPEN, B., Public and International Law
KNEMEYER, F.-L., Public and Administrative Law
KREUZER, K., Comparative Law, Civil Law, International Law and Commercial Law
LAUBENTHAL, K., Criminology and Penal Law
SCHERER, I., Civil Law

SCHEUING, D. H., German and Foreign Public Law, Civil and European Law
SCHULZE-FIELITZ, H., Public Law, Environmental Law and Administrative Science
SCHWARZ, G. CH., Civil, Procedural and Comparative Law
SIEBER, U., Criminal Law, Criminal Procedural Law, Information Law and Legal Informatics
TIEDTKE, K., Law of Finance and Economics
WEITZEL, J., Civil Law, History of European Law and Procedural Law
WILLOWEIT, D., History of German Law, Church Law, Civil and Labour Law
WOLLENSCHLÄGER, M., Public Law

Faculty of Medicine:

BARTELS, H., Paediatrics
BECKMANN, H., Psychiatry
BRÖCKER, E.-B., Dermatology and Venereal Diseases
DIETL, J., Obsterics and Gynaecology
DRENCKHAHN, D., Anatomy
ELERT, O., Thoracic and Cardiovascular Surgery
EULERT, J., Orthopaedics
FLENTJE, M., Radiology
FROSCH, M., Hygiene and Microbiology
GREHN, F., Ophthalmology
HACKER, J., Medical Microbiology
HAHN, D., Radiodiagnostics
HELMS, J., Oto-rhino-laryngology
HÖHN, H., Human Genetics
HÜNIG, T., Virology
KEIL, G., History of Medicine
KLAIBER, B., Dentistry
KOCHSIEK, K., Internal Medicine
KOEPSELL, H., Anatomy
LANG, H., Psychotherapy and Medical Psychology
LOHSE, M., Pharmacology and Toxicology
LUTZ, W., Pharmacology and Toxicology
MEULEN, V. TER, Clinical Virology and Immunology
MÜLLER-HERMELINK, H. K., Pathology
PATZELT, D., Forensic and Social Medicine
RAPP, U., Medical Radiology
REINERS, CH., Medical Radiology
REUTHER, J., Dentistry, Maxillo-facial Surgery
RICHTER, E.-J., Dental and Facial Medicine
RIEDMILLER, H., Urology
ROEWER, N., Anaesthesiology
ROOSEN, K., Neurosurgery
SCHARTL, M., Physiological Chemistry
SCHMIDT, R. F., Neurophysiology
SEBALD, W., Physiological Chemistry
SILBERNAGL, S., Physiology
THIEDE, A., Surgery
THULL, R., Experimental Dentistry
TOYKA, K. V., Neurology
WALTER, U., Clinical Biochemistry and Pathobiochemistry
WARNKE, A., Child Psychiatry
WILMS, K., Internal Medicine
WITT, E., Dental and Facial Surgery

Faculty of Philosophy I:

ERLER, M., Classical Philology
HANNICK, CH., Slavic Philology
HETTRICH, H., Comparative Linguistics
KONRAD, U., Musicology
KUHN, D., Oriental Philology
SCHOLZ, U. W., Classical Philology
SINN, U., Classical Archaeology
WILHELM, G., Oriental Philology
ZAUZICH, K.-T., Egyptology

Faculty of Philosophy II:

ABRAHAM, U., German Language and Literature
AHRENS, R., Cultural Studies of English-Speaking Countries and Teaching Methodology of English Language and Literature
BAUMGART, P., Modern History
BERCHEM, TH., Romance Philology
BRANDT, H.-H., Modern and Contemporary History
BRUNNER, H., German Philology
BURGSCHMIDT, E., English Linguistics
HERDE, P., History
HESS, G., History of Modern German Literature
HOFFMANN, G., American Studies
KOHL, ST. M., English Literature and British Cultural Studies
KUMMER, S., History of Art
LAITENBERGER, H., Romance Philology
PFOTENHAUER, H., History of Modern German Literature
RUHE, E., Romance Philology
SPRANDEL, R., History
WOLF, N. R., German Linguistics

Faculty of Philosophy III:

BITTNER, G., Education
BÖHM, W., Education
BUSSHOFF, H., Politics
GÖTZ, M., Elementary Teaching and Education
HOFFMANN, J., Psychology
HOJER, E., Pedagogy
JANKE, W., Psychology
KAPUSTIN, P., Physical Education
KLAES, N., History of Religion
LEMBECK, K.-H., Philosophy
LIPP, W., Sociology
MÜLLER, W., Education
RUPP, H., Protestant Religion and Religious Education
SCHNEIDER, W., Psychology
SCHÖPF, A., Philosophy
STRACK, F., Psychology
THALHAMMER, M., Special Education
VERNOOJI, M. A., Special Education
WEINACHT, P.-L., Didactics of Sociology and Political Science

Faculty of Biology:

CZYGAN, F.-C., Pharmaceutical Biology
GOEBEL, W., Microbiology
HEDRICH, R., Botany
HEISENBERG, M., Genetics
HÖLLDOBLER, B., Zoology and Comparative Physiology
LINSENMAIR, K. E., Zoology
RIEDERER, M., Botany
SCHEER, U., Zoology
ZIMMERMANN, U., Biotechnology

Faculty of Chemistry and Pharmacy:

ADAM, W., Organic Chemistry
BRINGMANN, G., Organic Chemistry
EBEL, S., Pharmaceutical Chemistry
GROSS, H. J., Biochemistry
KIEFER, W., Physical Chemistry
MÜLLER, G., Silicate Chemistry
SCHNEIDER, F., Physical Chemistry
SCHREIER, P., Food Chemistry
TACKE, R., Inorganic Chemistry
WERNER, H., Inorganic Chemistry
ZIMMERMANN, I., Pharmacy

Faculty of Geosciences:

BÖHN, D., Geography Teaching
FÜRSICH, F. T., Palaeontology
HAGEDORN, H., Geography
LÖFFLER, G., Cultural and Economic Geography
LORENZ, V., Geology
OKRUSCH, M., Mineralogy
WAGNER, H.-G., Geography

Faculty of Mathematics and Computer Science:

ALBERT, J., Computer Science
DOBROWOLSKI, M., Applied Mathematics
GRUNDHÖFER, TH., Mathematics
HEINEKEN, H., Mathematics
HELMKE, U., Mathematics
KOLLA, R., Computer Science
NOLTEMEIER, H., Computer Science
PUPPE, F., Computer Science
RUSCHEWYH, S., Mathematics
STOER, J., Applied Mathematics
TRAN-GIA, P., Computer Science
VOLLRATH, H.-J., Mathematics Teaching
WAGNER, K. W., Computer Science

Faculty of Physics and Astronomy:

DEUBNER, F.-L., Astronomy
FORCHEL, A., Semiconductor Technology and Physics
GERBER, G., Experimental Physics
HAASE, A., Experimental Physics (Biophysics)
HANKE, W., Theoretical Physics
HEUER, D., Physics Teaching
KINZEL, W., Computational Physics
LANDWEHR, G., Experimental Physics
RÜCKL, R., Theoretical Physics
SCHÜTZ-GMEINEDER, G., Experimental Physics
UMBACH, E., Experimental Physics

Faculty of Economics:

BERTHOLD, N., Political Economy
BOFINGER, P., Political Economy
FREERICKS, W., Industrial Management
KOLLER, H., Industrial Management
LENZ, H., Industrial Management
MEYER, M., Industrial Management
MONISSEN, H. G., Political Economy
NOLL, W., Economics
SCHULZ, N., Political Economy
THOME, R., Economics and Computer Science
WENGER, E., Industrial Management

Colleges

GENERAL

Schiller International University – Germany: Bergstrasse 106, 69121 Heidelberg; tel. (6221) 49159; fax (6221) 402703; f. 1964 as independent international univ.; campuses in France, Germany, Spain, Switzerland, UK and USA; degrees at Florida (USA) campus conferred under charter granted by State of Florida; degrees at all other campuses conferred under charter granted by State of Delaware (USA); language of instruction at all centres is English; depts of commercial art, computer studies, engineering management, international business, international tourism and hospitality management, international relations and diplomacy, literature, para-legal studies, pre-medicine; 1,519 students (total for all campuses); library of 91,000 vols (total for all campuses); Pres. Dr WALTER W. LEIBRECHT; Vice-President for Academic Affairs C. F. EBERHART.

Schiller International University – Heidelberg Campus: Friedrich-Ebert-Anlage 4, 69121 Heidelberg; tel. (6221) 12046; fax (6221) 164253; Dir LISA EVANS.

Wissenschaftskolleg zu Berlin (Institute for Advanced Study): Wallotstr. 19, 14193 Berlin; tel. (30) 89001-0; fax (30) 89001-300; f. 1980; private institution for international and interdisciplinary post-doctoral research; 40 Fellows; library mainly reference collection; Rector Prof. Dr WOLF LEPENIES; Sec. Dr JOACHIM NETTELBECK.

ART, ARCHITECTURE

Akademie der Bildenden Künste (Academy of Fine Arts): 80799 Munich, Akademiestr. 2; tel. (89) 3852-0; f. 1770 (Charter conferred 1808 and 1953); 35 professors; 600 students; Rector Prof. OLAF METZEL; Chancellor B. MARZOCCA; publ. *Studienführer* (annually).

Akademie der Bildenden Künste in Nürnberg: 90480 Nuremberg, Bingstr. 60; tel. (911) 94040; fax (911) 9404150; f. 1662; 320 students; library of 22,000 vols; Pres. Prof.

HANNS HERPICH; Vice-Pres. Prof. ROLF-GUNTER DIENST.

Deutsche Film- und Fernsehakademie Berlin GmbH (German Film and Television Academy): 14052 Berlin, Heerstr. 18–20; tel. (30) 300904-0; fax (30) 300904-63; f. 1966; 40 teachers; 110 students; library of 80,000 vols; Dir Prof. REINHARD HAUFF.

Hochschule der Künste Berlin: 10595 Berlin, POB 126720; premises at: 10587 Berlin, Ernst-Reuter-Platz 10; tel. (30) 31850; fax (30) 3185-2635; e-mail presse@hdk-berlin.de; f. 1975 by amalgamation of the fmr *Staatliche Hochschule für Bildende Künste* f. 1696 and *Staatliche Hochschule für Musik und Darstellende Kunst* f. 1869; depts of fine arts, architecture, design, visual communication, publicity and communication, art education and art science, music, music education and science, performing arts and drama, educational and social sciences, aesthetic education, art and cultural sciences; 5,500 students; library of *c.* 650,000 vols; Pres. Prof. LOTHAR ROMAIN; publs *HdK Magazin* (2 a year), *HdK-Aktuell* (2–4 a year), *Schriftenreihe der HdK*, *Ausstellungskataloge*.

Hochschule für Bildende Künste: 38118 Brunswick, Johannes-Selenka-Platz 1; tel. (531) 391-9122; fax (531) 391-9292; e-mail hbk@hbk-bs.de; f. 1963; depts of art (painting, graphics, sculpture, film, video, performing arts and photography), design (industrial and graphic), art teaching, art history; institute for media and film studies, institute for art history and visual research; 1,000 students; library of *c.* 26,000 vols; Pres. Prof. Dr MICHAEL SCHWARZ; publs *Vorlesungsverzeichnis/Studienführer* (2 a year), *Schriftenreihe* (3–5 a year).

Hochschule für Bildende Künste: 01307 Dresden, Güntzstr. 34; tel. (351) 4402-0; fax (351) 4590025; f. 1764; stage and theatre design, costume design, painting, sculpture, graphics, restoration; Rector Prof. Dipl. Rest. Dr ULRICH SCHIESSL.

Hochschule für Bildende Künste Hamburg: 22081 Hamburg, Lerchenfeld 2; depts of art, architecture, industrial design, visual communication, education and technology; Pres. ADRIENNE GOEHLER.

Hochschule für Film und Fernsehen 'Konrad Wolf' Potsdam-Babelsberg (Academy of Film Art and Television): 14482 Potsdam, Karl-Marx-Str. 33–34; tel. (331) 7469-0; fax (331) 7469-202; f. 1954; Rector Prof. Dr sc. DIETER WIEDEMANN; 100 lecturers; 400 students; library of 72,000 vols; publ. *BFF (Beiträge zur Film- und Fernsehwissenschaft)* (irregular).

Hochschule für Grafik und Buchkunst Leipzig (Leipzig State Academy of Graphic Arts and Book Design): 04107 Leipzig, Wächterstr. 11; tel. (341) 2135-0; fax (341) 2135-166; e-mail hgb@hgb-leipzig.de; f. 1764; painting, graphic arts, book art, graphic design, photography, media art; 48 teachers; 350 students; library of 30,000 vols; Rector Prof. RUEDI BAUR.

Kunstakademie Düsseldorf, Hochschule für Bildende Künste (Acad. of Art): 40213 Düsseldorf, Eiskellerstr. 1; tel. (211) 1396-0; fax (211) 1396-225; f. 1773; 50 teachers; 700 students; library of 100,000 vols; Rector Prof. MARKUS LÜPERTZ; Librarian HELMUT KLEINENBROICH.

Kunsthochschule Berlin-Weissensee, Hochschule für Gestaltung: 13086 Berlin, Bühringstr. 20; tel. (30) 47705-0; fax (30) 47705-290; f. 1946; fine arts, industrial design, ceramics, fashion design, textile design, communication design, architecture, stage design, sculpture; 550 students; 39 teachers; library of 20,000 vols.

Staatliche Akademie der Bildenden Künste: 76042 Karlsruhe, Postfach 6267; tel. (721) 85018-0; fax (721) 848150; f. 1854; library of 30,000 vols; Rektor Prof. Dr ANDREAS FRANZKE.

Staatliche Akademie der Bildenden Künste: 70191 Stuttgart, Am Weissenhof 1; tel. (711) 2575-0; fax (711) 2575-225; f. 1761; art, graphics, sculpture, architecture, design, conservation, ceramics, textiles, etc.; teaching staff 95; Rector Prof. KLAUS LEHMANN; Pro-Rector Prof. MORITZ BAUMGARTL.

Staatliche Hochschule für Bildende Künste—Städelschule: 60596 Frankfurt, Dürerstr. 10; tel. (69) 605008-0; fax (69) 605008-66; f. 1817; art, architecture, film and cooking, sculpture, painting, drawing, architecture (conceptual design); 12 profs; 150 students; library of 16,000 vols; Rector Prof. KASPER KÖNIG; Chancellor JÜRGEN GRUMANN.

ECONOMICS, POLITICAL AND SOCIAL SCIENCES, PUBLIC ADMINISTRATION

European Business School: Schloss Reichartshausen, 65375 Oestrich-Winkel; tel. (6723) 6-90; fax (6723) 69-133; f. 1971; private, state-recognized; 18 teachers; 750 students; diploma courses; library of 12,000 vols; President WALTHER LEISLER KIEP; Librarian MONIKA FAULSTICH.

HEADS OF DEPARTMENTS

Law: Prof. Dr J. BUNGE
International Management: Prof. Dr R. CASPERS
Data Processing: Dr HARRY MUCKSCH
Finance: Prof. Dr Dr ACHLEITNER
Language: TONY LEE

Hochschule für Politik München: 80539 Munich, Ludwigstr. 8; tel. (89) 285018; fax (89) 283705; f. 1950; 850 students; library of 35,000 vols; Rector Prof. Dr F. KNÖPFLE; publ. *Zeitschrift für Politik* (quarterly).

Hochschule für Wirtschaft und Politik: Von-Melle-Park 9, 20146 Hamburg; tel. (40) 41233245; fax (40) 41234150; f. 1948; economics and politics; 80 teachers; 2,200 students; Pres. Prof. Dr LOTHAR ZECHLIN; Registrar DIETMAR PLUM.

LANGUAGES

Akademie für Fremdsprachen: 10663 Berlin, Nürnberger Str. 38, Postfach 150104; tel. (30) 884302-0; fax 884302-48; f. 1971; translators' and interpreters' courses in German, English, French, Spanish, Italian, Russian, and courses in German as a foreign language; 1,600 students; Sec. NORBERT ZÄNKER.

MEDICINE

Medizinische Akademie Erfurt: 99089 Erfurt, Nordhäuser Str. 74, PSF 595; tel. 790; telex 61384; fax 23697; f. 1954; 121 teachers; 750 students; library of 140,000 vols; Rector Prof. Dr Dr h.c. mult. W. KÜNZEL; Pro-Rector Prof. Dr G. ENDERT; Medical Dir Prof. Dr W. KRAFFT; Librarian Dr B. ADLUNG.

MUSIC AND DRAMA

Hochschule des Saarlandes für Musik und Theater: 66111 Saarbrücken, Bismarckstrasse 1; tel. (681) 96731-0; fax (681) 96731-30; e-mail t.wolter@hmt.uni-sb.de; f. 1947; 110 teachers; 350 students; library of 82,000 vols; Rector Prof. THOMAS KRÄMER.

Hochschule für Musik 'Hanns Eisler': 10117 Berlin, Charlottenstr. 55; tel. 2090-2420; fax 2090-2408; f. 1950; 1,050 students.

Hochschule für Musik Detmold: 32756 Detmold, Neustadt 22; tel. (5231) 975-5; fax (5231) 975-972; f. 1946; 116 teachers; 1,174 students; library of 127,100 items; Rector Prof. MARTIN CHRISTOPH REDEL.

Hochschule für Musik 'Carl Maria von Weber' Dresden: 01001 Dresden, Wettiner Platz 13, Postfach 120039; tel. (351) 492360; fax (351) 4923657; f. 1856; 81 teachers; 820 students; library of 50,000 vols, 7,000 records and CDs; contains Heinrich-Schütz archive; Rector Prof. WILFRIED KRÄTZSCHMAR; Pro-Rector Prof. MANFRED WEISS; publ. *Schriftenreihe der Hochschule für Musik* (irregular).

Hochschule für Musik Köln: 50668 Cologne, Dagobertstr. 38; tel. (221) 912818-0; fax (221) 131204; e-mail johann.kees@uni-koeln.de; f. 1925; instrumental music and musicology; 330 teachers; 1,800 students; library of 136,000 vols, 8,600 records, 400 films; Rector Prof. Dr WERNER LOHMANN; publ. *Journal* (2 a year).

Hochschule für Musik und Theater 'Felix Mendelssohn Bartholdy' Leipzig: PSF 100809, 04008 Leipzig, Grassistr. 8; tel. (341) 214455; fax (341) 2144503; e-mail reichelt@rz.uni-leipzig.de; f. 1843; 504 mems; library of 90,399 vols; Rector Prof. Dr CHRISTOPH KRUMMACHER.

Hochschule für Musik in München: 80333 Munich, Arcisstr. 12; tel. (89) 28927430; fax (89) 28927419; f. 1846; 300 teachers; 900 students; Pres. Prof. ROBERT M. HELMSCHROTT.

Hochschule für Musik 'Franz Liszt' Weimar: 99423 Weimar, Platz der Demokratie 2/3; tel. (3643) 555-0; fax (3643) 61865; f. 1872; 840 students; 132 teachers; library of 65,000 vols and 45,000 tapes; Rector Prof. Dr WOLFRAM HUSCHKE; Pro-Rectors Prof. HANS-CHRISTIAN STEINHÖFEL, Prof. GUNTER KAHLERT; instruction in: keyboard, string and wind instruments, accordion, guitar, jazz/pop instruments and vocal, composition, conducting, singing and music teaching, church music and musicology.

Hochschule für Musik: 97070 Würzburg, Hofstallstr. 6-8; tel. (931) 321870; fax (931) 3218740; f. 1804; Pres. Prof. D. KIRSCH.

Hochschule für Musik und Darstellende Kunst: 60322 Frankfurt a.M., Eschersheimer Landstrasse 29–39; tel. (69) 154007-0; fax (69) 154007-108; f. 1878 as Konservatorium, Hochschule since 1938; Rector Prof. BERNHARD WETZ.

Hochschule für Musik und Theater Hannover: 30175 Hanover, Emmichplatz 1; f. 1961; 280 teachers; 1,160 students; library of 192,500 vols; Pres. Prof. Dr KLAUS-ERNST BEHNE.

Hochschule für Musik und Theater: 20148 Hamburg, Harvestehuder Weg 12; f. 1950; teaching staff of 250; 900 students; Pres. Prof. Dr HERMANN RAUHE.

Internationales Musikinstitut Darmstadt (IMD): 64285 Darmstadt, Nieder-Ramstäder Str. 190; tel. (6151) 133093; telex 4197127; fax (6151) 132405; e-mail tourco@stadt.darmstadt.de; f. 1946; international holiday courses on contemporary music (composition, interpretation); international music lending library (20th-century) of 24,000 scores, 6,000 vols, 3,700 tapes, 1,500 records; Dir SOLF SCHAEFER.

Leopold Mozart Konservatorium: 86150 Augsburg, Maximilianstrasse 59; tel. (821) 324-2891; f. 1873; international college of higher education; concerts, productions, International Leopold Mozart Competition for Young Violinists, Studio for Old and New Music; 70 lecturers; 200 students; Dir (vacant).

Musikhochschule Lübeck: 23552 Lübeck, Gr. Petersgrube 21; tel. (451) 1505-0; fax (451) 1505-300; f. 1933; musical training on all instruments, opera singing and performing, training of music teachers, sacred music (Protestant and Catholic), preparatory training of professional musicians and music teachers; 400 students; 130 teachers; library of 30,000 vols; Rector Prof. INGE-SUSANN RÖMHILD; Admin JÜRGEN CLAUSSEN; publ. *Vorlesungsverzeichnis* (2 a year).

Richard-Strauss Konservatorium: 81667 Munich, Kellerstr. 6; tel. (89) 48098-409; fax (89) 48098-417; f. 1962; courses in vocal and instrumental studies, conducting, composition, jazz; 120 teachers; 500 students; library of 20,000 vols; Dir MARTIN MARIA KRÜGER.

Robert-Schumann-Hochschule Düsseldorf: 40476 Düsseldorf, Fischerstrasse 110; tel. (211) 4918-0; f. 1935; formerly the Staatliche Hochschule für Musik Rheinland; 204 teachers; 760 students; library of 120,000 vols; Rector Prof. H. CALLHOFF.

Staatliche Hochschule für Musik: 79095 Freiburg im Breisgau, Schwarzwaldstr. 141; f. 1946; 160 teachers; 570 students; Rector Prof. Dr MIRJAM NASTASI.

Staatliche Hochschule für Musik Karlsruhe: 76040 Karlsruhe, Postfach 6040; tel. (721) 662950; fax (721) 662966; f. 1884; library of 90,000 vols; 150 teachers; 550 students; Rector Prof. FANY SOLTER.

Staatliche Hochschule für Musik und Darstellende Kunst: 70182 Stuttgart, Urbanstr. 25; f. 1857; 200 teachers; about 800 students; Dir Prof. RAINER WEHRINGER.

Staatliche Hochschule für Musik und Darstellende Kunst Heidelberg-Mannheim: 68161 Mannheim, N7, 18; f. 1899; 200 teachers; 550 students; Rector Prof. R. MEISTER.

PHILOSOPHY, THEOLOGY

Augustana Hochschule: 91564 Neuendettelsau, Waldstr. 11; tel. (9874) 5090; fax (9874) 50995; f. 1947; 30 teachers; 210 students; Rector Prof. Dr WOLFGANG SOMMER.

Hochschule für Philosophie: 80539 Munich, Kaulbachstrasse 31A; tel. (89) 23862300; fax (89) 23862302; e-mail admin@hfph.mwn.de; f. 1925; library of 189,000 vols; Rector H. GOLLER; Librarian J. OSWALD; publ. *Theologie und Philosophie* (quarterly).

Kirchliche Hochschule Bethel: 33544 Bielefeld, Postfach 130140; premises at: 33617 Bielefeld, Remterweg 45; tel. (521) 144-3948; fax (521) 1443961; f. 1905; 27 teachers; 250 students; library of 120,000 vols; Rector Prof. Dr FRANK CRÜSEMANN; publ. *Jahrbuch—Wort und Dienst* (every 2 years).

Kirchliche Hochschule Wuppertal: 42285 Wuppertal, Missionstr. 9B; tel. (202) 2820-0; fax (202) 2820-101; e-mail ua0051@uni-wuppertal.de; f. 1935; library of 100,000 vols; 250 students; Protestant; Rector JOHANNES VON LÜPKE.

Lutherische Theologische Hochschule Oberursel: 61440 Oberursel im Taunus, Altkönigstrasse 150; tel. (6171) 24340; f. 1947; library of 30,000 vols; publ. *Lutherische Theologie und Kirche* (quarterly).

Philosophisch-Theologische Hochschule Sankt Georgen: 60599 Frankfurt am Main, Offenbacher Landstr. 224; tel. (69) 60610; fax (69) 6061307; e-mail rektor-st-georgen-ffm@em.uni-frankfurt.de; f. 1926 (since 1950 combined with Jesuit Theological Faculty, f. 1863); library of 370,000 vols; 43 teachers, including 24 professors; 410 students; Rector Prof. Dr M. SIEVERNICH; Librarian Dr G. MICZKA; publs *Theologie und Philosophie* (quarterly), *Frankfurter Theologische Studien*.

Theologische Fakultät Fulda (Staatlich anerkannte Wissenschaftliche Hochschule): 36037 Fulda, Domplatz 2; tel. (661) 87220; fax (661) 87224; f. 748; 20 teachers; 92 students; Rector Prof. Dr ALOYSIUS WINTER; publs *Fuldaer Studien*, *Fuldaer Hochschulschriften*.

Theologische Fakultät Paderborn: 33098 Paderborn, Kamp 6; f. 1615; 26 teachers; 351 students; Rector Prof. Dr Dr HUBERTUS DROBNER; Pro-Rector Prof. Dr Dr HANS F. FUHS; publ. *Theologie und Glaube* (quarterly).

Theologische Fakultät Trier: 54296 Trier, Universitätsring 19; tel. (651) 201-3520; f. 1950; library of 400,000 vols; 16 ordinary professors; 296 students; Chancellor Dr H. J. SPITAL, Bishop of Trie; Rector Prof. Dr W. LENTZEN-DEIS; publ. *Trierer Theologische Zeitschrift* (quarterly).

TECHNOLOGY

Burg Giebichenstein Hochschule für Kunst und Design: 06108 Halle, Neuwerk 7; tel. (345) 7751-50; fax (345) 7751-569; e-mail burgpost@burg-halle.de; f. 1915; 760 students; Rector Prof. LUDWIG EHRLER.

Fachhochschule Anhalt (Bernburg-Dessau-Köthen): 06366 Köthen, Bernburger Str. 52–57; tel. (3496) 67220; fax (3496) 212152; e-mail quabis@dez-2.koethen.fh-anhalt.d400.de; f. 1891, present status 1992; Köthen: mechanical engineering (plant construction), chemical and environmental engineering, biotechnology and food processing, computer science, electrical engineering; Bernburg: business economics, agriculture, landscape architecture and planning, food and health management; Dessau: architecture, civil engineering, surveying, design; Rector Prof. Dr KLAUS HERTWIG.

Hochschule für Technik und Wirtschaft Mittweida (FH): 09642 Mittweida, Postfach 91; tel. (3727) 580; telex 322710; fax (3727) 58379; f. 1867; electrical engineering, electronics, microelectronics, mechanical engineering, mathematics, physics, computer studies, economic sciences; social sciences; library of 65,000 vols; Rector Prof. Dr-Ing. habil. R. SCHMIDT.

Hochschule für Technik, Wirtschaft und Kultur Leipzig (FH): 04251 Leipzig, Postfach 300066; premises at: 04277 Leipzig, Karl-Liebknecht-Str. 132; tel. (341) 307-60; fax (341) 307-6456; f. 1992; architecture, civil engineering, automatic control and instrumentation, electrical engineering, mechanical engineering, printing technology, multimedia technology, publishing, computer science, business mathematics, business administration, social work, library science, museology, book trade, electrical engineering management, energy engineering management, mechanical engineering management, civil engineering management; 190 teachers; 4,300 students; library of 300,000 vols; Rector Prof. Dr-Ing. KLAUS STEINBOCK.

Hochschule für Technik, Wirtschaft und Sozialwesen Zittau/Görlitz (FH): 02763 Zittau, Theodor-Koerner-Allee 16; tel. (3583) 611401; fax (3583) 611402; e-mail p.dierich@htw-zittau.de; f. 1992; architecture, civil engineering, business management, chemistry, electrical engineering, chemical engineering, energy and environmental technology, real estate and housing management, management engineering, computer science, mechanical engineering, ecology and environmental protection, mechatronics, tourism, translating English and Czech, social work, teacher-training (remedial teaching and teaching of handicapped people), communication psychology, culture and management, utilities and waste-removal technology, business mathematics; 3,049 students; library of 105,000 vols; Rector Prof. Dr-Ing. habil. Dr oec. PETER DIERICH.

Westsächsische Hochschule Zwickau (FH): 08056 Zwickau, Dr-Friedrichs-Ring 2A; tel. (375) 536-0; fax (375) 536-1127; e-mail rektorat@fh-zwickau.de; f. 1969; automotive engineering, traffic systems engineering, mechanical engineering, industrial management and engineering, utilities and environmental engineering, recycling and building machines, electrical engineering, automotive electronics, physical engineering, computer sciences, business administration, industrial engineering, management for public utilities, languages and business administration, healthcare management, textile and leather engineering (Reichenbach), courses of applied arts (Schneeberg), woodwork design, fashion design, textile design, textile art, musical instrument making (Markneukirchen); 164 teachers; 3,000 students; library of 150,000 vols; Rector Prof. Dr-Ing. habil. HORST-DIETER TIETZ; publs *Jahresjournal* (annually), *Hochschulmagazin* (2 a year), *Hochschulführer* (annually), *Hochschulforschungsbericht* (annually).

GHANA

Learned Societies

GENERAL

Centre for National Culture: POB 2738, Accra; f. 1958; tel. 664099; to promote and develop the arts and preserve traditional arts; includes a research section; a regional museum is planned; Chair. NII AYITEY AGBOFU II; Dir M. K. AMOATEY, publ. *DAWURO*.

Ghana Academy of Arts and Sciences: POB M.32, Accra; tel. 777651; fax 777655; f. 1959; sections of Arts (Chair. Prof. J. H. KWABENA NKETIA), Sciences (Chair. Prof. E. Q. ARCHAMPONG); 65 Fellows, 8 hon. Fellows; Pres. Prof. D. A. BEKOE; Sec. Prof. E. V. DOKU; publ. *Proceedings* (annually).

ARCHITECTURE AND TOWN PLANNING

Ghana Institute of Architects: POB M.272, Accra; tel. (21) 75676; f. 1962; 203 Fellows and Associates; Pres. E. L. AKITA; Hon. Sec. H. D. L. YARTEY, publs *Ghana Architect*, *PATO*.

BIBLIOGRAPHY, LIBRARY SCIENCE AND MUSEOLOGY

Ghana Library Association: POB 4105, Accra; tel. 668731; f. 1962; Pres. E. S. ASIEDU; Sec. A. W. K. INSAIDOO; publ. *Ghana Library Journal* (annually).

ECONOMICS, LAW AND POLITICS

Economic Society of Ghana: POB 57, Legon, Accra; f. 1957; 500 mems; publs *Economic Bulletin of Ghana, Social and Economic Affairs* (quarterly).

Ghana Bar Association: POB 4150, Accra; tel. 226748; Nat. Pres. NUTIFAFA KYENYEHIA; Nat. Sec. PAUL ADU-GYAMFI.

EDUCATION

West African Examinations Council: Headquarters Office, POB 125, Accra; tel. (21) 221511; telex 2934; fax (21) 222905; e-mail waechgrs@africaonline.com.gh; national offices in Lagos, Nigeria; Accra, Ghana; Freetown, Sierra Leone; Banjul, The Gambia; Monrovia, Liberia; and a representative office in London, England; f. 1952 by the four West African Commonwealth countries; conducts GCE examinations for The Gambia, Ghana and Sierra Leone, the West African Senior School Certificate Examination (WASSCE) for The Gambia, Nigeria and Sierra Leone, Senior Secondary School Certificate Examinations (SSSCE) for Ghana, and 9th and 12th grade examinations for Liberia; also selection examinations for entry into secondary schools and similar institutions and the Public Services; entrance and final examinations for teacher training colleges, commercial and technical examinations at the request of the various Ministries of Education; holds examinations on behalf of the UK examining authorities and the Educational Testing Service, Princeton, New Jersey, USA; Chair. Dr YAHAYA HAMZA; Registrar S. A. M. BOYE; publs *Annual Report, Regulations and Syllabuses, Research Reports, WAEC News* (2 a year), *Statistics for International Examinations*.

HISTORY, GEOGRAPHY AND ARCHAEOLOGY

Ghana Geographical Association: University of Ghana; f. 1955; Pres. Prof. E. V. T. ENGMANN; Hon. Sec. Dr L. J. GYAMFI-FENTENG; publ. *Bulletin* (annually).

Historical Society of Ghana: POB 12, Legon; f. 1952; formerly Gold Coast and Togoland Historical Soc.; *c.* 600 mems; Pres. T. A. OSAE; Sec. R. ADDO-FENING; publ. *Transactions* (1 a year).

LANGUAGE AND LITERATURE

Ghana Association of Writers: POB 4414, Accra; f. 1957; aims at bringing together all the writers of the country, to protect and champion the interests of Ghanaian writers, to encourage contact with foreign writers, and to foster the development of Ghanaian literature; literary evenings, annual congress, etc.; Pres. ATUKWEI OKAI; Gen. Sec. J. E. ALLOTEY-PAPPOE; publs *Takra* (monthly newsletter), *Angla* (anthology, annually).

MEDICINE

Pharmaceutical Society of Ghana: POB 2133, Accra; tel. 228341; e-mail psgh@ighmail.com; f. 1935; aims to advance chemistry and pharmacy and maintain standards of the profession; 8 regional brs; library of 250 vols; 900 mems; Pres. DELA C. ASHIABOR; Hon. Gen. Sec. DANIEL SEKYERE-MARFO.

NATURAL SCIENCES

General

Ghana Science Association: POB 7, Legon; f. 1959; Nat. Pres. Dr P. A. KURANCHIE; Nat. Sec. I. J. KWAME ABOH; publ. *The Ghana Journal of Science*.

West African Science Association: c/o Botany Dept, POB 7, University of Ghana, Legon; f. 1953; mems: Ghana, Nigeria, Sierra Leone, Côte d'Ivoire, Senegal, Togo, Niger, Benin; observers: Burkina Faso, Liberia; Pres. Prof. ANDRÉ DOVI KUEVI; Sec. Dr J. K. B. A. ATA; publ. *Journal* (annually).

RELIGION, SOCIOLOGY AND ANTHROPOLOGY

Ghana Sociological Association: c/o Dept of Sociology, University of Ghana, Legon; f. 1961; financial aid from the universities and the Academy of Arts and Sciences; academic activities, conferences, etc.; 215 mems; Pres. Prof. J. M. ASSIMENG; Sec. E. H. MENDS; publ. *Ghana Journal of Sociology*.

TECHNOLOGY

Ghana Institution of Engineers: POB 7042, Accra-North; tel. 772005; f. 1968; 1,000 mems; Pres. Ing. K. OFORI-KURAGO; Exec. Sec. Ing. LAURI LAWSON; publ. *The Ghana Engineer* (quarterly).

Research Institutes

GENERAL

Council for Scientific and Industrial Research (CSIR): POB M.32, Accra; tel. 777651; fax 777655; e-mail ghastnet@ncs.ccm.gh; f. 1958; functions include advice to the Government, encouragement of scientific and industrial research relevant to national development and commercialization of research results; co-ordination of research in all its aspects in Ghana, and collation, publication and dissemination of research results; central library: see Libraries; Dir-Gen. Prof. W. S. AL-HASSAN; Sec. E. C. SAKA; Librarian J. A. VILLARS; publs *CSIR Handbook, Ghana Journal of Science, Ghana Journal of Agricultural Science, Annual Report*.

Attached research institutes:

Animal Research Institute: POB 20, Achimota; f. 1957; Dir Dr E. O. OTCHERE.

Building and Road Research Institute: Univ. POB 40, Kumasi; f. 1952; library of 8,000 vols; Dir Dr J. K. OCLOO.

Crops Research Institute: POB 3785, Kumasi; Dir Dr D. B. HEMENG (acting).

Food Research Institute: POB M.20, Accra; f. 1964; food processing, preservation, storage, analysis, marketing, etc.; Dir ABIGAIL ANDAH; publ. *Bulletin*.

Forestry Research Institute of Ghana: POB 65, KNUST, Kumasi.

Oil Palm Research Institute: POB 74, Kade; f. 1964; Dir Dr J. B. WONKYI-APPIAH.

Plant Genetic Resources Centre: Bunso; Dir Dr S. O. BENNETT-LARTEY.

Savanna Agricultural Research Institute: POB 52, Tamale.

Soil Research Institute: PMB, Academy PO, Kwadaso, Kumasi; f. 1951; Dir R. D. ASIAMAH.

Water Research Institute: POB M.32, Accra; Dir C. A. BINEY.

Institute for Science and Technology Information: POB M.32, Accra; Dir J. A. VILLARS (acting).

Science and Technology Policy Research Institute: POB M.32, Accra; Dir Dr J. O. GOGO.

AGRICULTURE, FISHERIES AND VETERINARY SCIENCE

Cocoa Research Institute of Ghana: POB 8, Tafo-Akim; tel. (81) 22221; fax (81) 23257; e-mail crig@ghana.com; f. 1938; research on cocoa, cola, coffee, and shea nut; 3 substations; library of 15,000 vols, 8,100 pamphlets, 200 journals; Exec. Dir Dr G. K. OWUSU (acting); publs *Annual Report, Technical Bulletin, Newsletter*.

MEDICINE

Health Laboratory Services: Ministry of Health, POB 300, Accra; f. 1920; laboratory services, public health reference laboratory, reference haematology laboratory, training of laboratory technicians; research on public health microbiology, abnormal haemoglobins and allied subjects; library of 8,000 vols combined with that of the Ghana Medical School; Head E. C. MARBELL.

NATURAL SCIENCES

Physical Sciences

Geological Survey of Ghana: POB M.80, Accra; tel. (21) 228093; f. 1913; geological mapping and geophysical surveying of the country, research and evaluation of mineral resources; library of 30,216 vols; Dir G. O. KESSE; publs *Annual Report*, memoirs and bulletins.

Ghana Meteorological Services Department: POB 87, Legon; f. 1937; serves civil and military aviation, agriculture, forestry, engineering and medical research; 409 mems; Dir S. E. TANDOH; publs numerous regular and irregular reports.

Libraries and Archives

Accra

Accra Central Library: Thorpe Rd, POB 2362, Accra; tel. 665083; f. 1950; central reference library; central lending library; central children's library; mobile library unit; union catalogues; Regional Librarian SUSANNAH MINYILA.

George Padmore Research Library on African Affairs: POB 2970, Accra; tel. 228402; f. 1961; collection, processing and dissemination of recorded literature, history and culture of all Africa; incl. Ghana National Collection; 48,400 vols, 80 periodicals; Librarian SARAH KANDA; publs *Ghana National Bibliography* (6 a year and 1 a year), special subject bibliographies (irregular).

Ghana Library Board: POB 663, Accra; tel. 662795; f. 1950; comprises Accra Central Library, regional libraries at Kumasi, Sekondi, Ho, Tamale, Bolgatanga, Cape Coast, Koforidua, Sunyani, Research Library on African Affairs (*q.v.*); 37 branch libraries, mobile libraries, children's libraries; research library 35,029 vols, adults' libraries 1,167,653 vols, children's libraries 1,383,712 vols; Dir of Library Services DAVID CORNELIUS.

National Archives of Ghana: Headquarters: POB 3056, Accra; f. 1946, legal recognition 1955; charged with the collection, custody, rehabilitation and reproduction of all Public Archives, including valuable private and family papers; regional offices, which serve as record centres and cater for local history, in Kumasi, Cape Coast, Sekondi, Tamale, Sunyani, Koforidua and Ho; library of 2,000 vols; staff of 116; Chief Archivist J. M. AKITA; publs *Annual Report*, exhibition catalogues, etc.

National Science and Technology Library and Information Centre (NASTLIC): POB M.32, Accra; tel. (21) 778808; fax (21) 777655; e-mail jvillars@ghastinet.gn.apc.org; f. 1964; 20,000 vols, 60 current periodicals; publishes Union List of Serials; Dir J. A. VILLARS; publs *Ghastinet Newsletter* (4 a year), *Ghana Science Abstracts* (6 a year).

Kumasi

Ashanti Regional Library: Bantama Rd, POB 824, Kumasi; tel. 2784; f. 1954; lending, reference and extension services for adults, students and schoolchildren; 20,000 vols, incl. local collection on Ghana of 450 vols; Librarian KOFI S. ANTIRI.

University of Science and Technology Library: University PO, Kumasi; tel. (51) 60133; telex 2555; fax (51) 60137; e-mail ustlib@ust.gn.apc.org; 266,219 vols; 750 periodicals; Librarian G. E. ADDO.

Legon

University of Ghana Library (Balme Library): POB 24, Legon; tel. 302347; telex 2556; fax (21) 667701; e-mail balme@ug.gn.apc.org; f. 1948; 362,000 vols; comprises Arabic, United Nations, World Bank, Africana, Braille, Volta Basin Research Project collections and Students' Reference libraries; Librarian C. O. KISIEDU; publ. *Library Bulletin*.

Sekondi

Western Regional Library: Old Axim Rd, POB 174, Sekondi; f. 1955; 21,000 vols; Librarian S. Y. KWANSA.

Museums and Art Galleries

Accra

Ghana National Museum: Barnes Rd, POB 3343, Accra; tel. (21) 221633; f. 1957; controlled by the Ghana Museums and Monuments Board; archaeological and ethnological finds from all over Ghana and West Africa; modern works by Ghanaian artists; the preservation and conservation of ancient forts and castles and traditional buildings; the achievement of man in Africa; Dir I. N. DEBRAH (acting).

Museum of Science and Technology: POB 3343, Accra; tel. 223963; f. 1965; a temporary exhibition hall with an open-air cinema is used for the display of working models, charts, films and other exhibits on science and technology; collection of exhibits for permanent galleries has begun; temporary exhibitions are taken to the regions, films shown to colleges and schools and regional and national Science Fairs are organized; Officers-in-Charge K. A. ADDISON, J. I. ADAM.

Cape Coast

Cape Coast Castle Museum: POB 281, Cape Coast; tel. (42) 32701; f. 1971; cultural history of Ghana's Central region; Curator RAYMOND O. AGBO.

Universities

UNIVERSITY FOR DEVELOPMENT STUDIES

POB 1350, Tamale
Telephone: (71) 22078
Fax: (71) 23617

Founded 1992
State control
Academic year: October to June

Vice-Chancellor: Prof. R. B. BENING
Pro-Vice-Chancellor: Prof. G. W. K. MENSAH
Registrar: PAUL EFFAH
Librarian: I. K. ANTWI

Library of 8,750 vols
Number of teachers: 58
Number of students: 386

DEANS

Faculty of Agriculture: Dr SAA J. DITTOH
Faculty of Integrated Development Studies: Rev. Dr A. H. K. ABASI (acting)
School of Medicine and Health Sciences: Prof. NII AMON-KOTEI

UNIVERSITY OF CAPE COAST

University PO, Cape Coast
Telephone: (42) 32480
Telex: 2552
Fax: (42) 32485

Founded 1962
Language of instruction: English
State control
Academic year: October to July (2 semesters)

Chancellor: (vacant)
Pro-Chancellor: Dr H. PHILLIPS
Vice-Chancellor: Prof. S. K. ADJEPONG
Pro-Vice-Chancellor: Prof. J. ANAMUAH-MENSAH
Registrar: KWAKU KUNADU
Librarian: RICHARD ARKAIFIE

Library of 183,000 vols, 390 current periodicals
Number of teachers: 220
Number of students: 4,274

Publications: *Bulletin* (fortnightly), *Calendar, Annual Report, University Gazette* (monthly).

DEANS

Faculty of Science: Prof. C. E. AMEYAW-AKUMFI
Faculty of Arts: Prof. Y. S. BOAFO
Faculty of Education: Prof. J. ANAMUAH-MENSAH
Faculty of Social Sciences: Prof. L. A. DEI
School of Agriculture: Prof. A. G. CARSON
Board of Graduate Studies: Prof. D. E. K. AMENUMEY

HEADS OF DEPARTMENTS

Faculty of Science:

Zoology: Prof. C. E. AMEYAW-AKUMFI
Botany: Prof. C. E. STEPHENS
Chemistry: Dr V. P. Y. GADZEKPO
Mathematics: Prof. D. N. OFFEI
Physics: Prof. A. AYENSU
School of Agriculture: Prof. A. G. CARSON
Laboratory Technology: Dr E. C. QUAYE (Co-ordinator)
Computer Centre: D. OBUOBI (acting)

Faculty of Arts:

Religious Studies: Prof. P. J. RYAN
Classics: Dr F. OPEKU (acting)
English: Prof. K. E. YANKSON
French: Prof. Y. S. BOAFO
History: Prof. D. E. K. AMENUMEY
African and General Studies: Dr J. A. SACKEY (acting)
Music: Dr N. N. KOFIE (acting)
Ghanian Languages: Prof. J. O. DEGRAFT HANSON

Faculty of Social Sciences:

Geography: Prof. L. A. DEI
Economics and Business Studies: F. G. GERRAR
Sociology: Dr J. H. ADDAI-SUNDIATA
African and General Studies: Dr J. A. SACKEY (acting)

Faculty of Education:

Educational Foundations: Dr B. A. ESHUN (acting)
Science Education: Prof. J. ANAMUAH-MENSAH
Arts and Social Sciences Education: Prof. E. K. TAMAKLOE
Health, Physical Education and Recreation: F. S. BEDIAKO (acting)
Vocational and Technical Education: Dr G. E. EKUBAN (acting)
Primary Education: Dr D. K. FOBIH (acting)

School of Agriculture:

Department of Crop Science: Prof. A. G. CARSON
Department of Animal Science: Dr F. N. A. ODOI (acting)
Department of Agricultural Engineering: Prof. E. A. BARYEH
Department of Soil Science: Dr MENSAH BONSU
Department of Agricultural Economics and Extension: Dr J. A. KWARTENG (acting)

DIRECTORS

Centre for Development Studies: Prof. C. K. BROWN
Institute of Education: Prof. M. K. ANTWI (acting)
Centre for Research on Improving the Quality of Primary Education in Ghana: Dr B. OKYERE (Co-ordinator)
Institute for Educational Planning and Administration: S. K. ATAKPA

UNIVERSITY OF GHANA

POB 25, Legon, Accra
Telephone: (21) 501967
Fax: (21) 502701
E-mail: addae-mensah@ug.gn.ape.org

Founded 1948 as the University College of Ghana (then Gold Coast); raised to University status 1961
Language of instruction: English
Academic year: September to June
State control

Vice-Chancellor: Prof. IVAN ADDAE-MENSAH
Pro-Vice-Chancellor: Prof. FLORENCE ABENA DOLPHYNE
Registrar: G. F. DANIEL Jr
Librarian: C. O. KISIEDU

Number of teachers: 608
Number of students: 8,495

Publications: *Annual Reports, University of Ghana Reporter, Calendar*, *Newsletter*.

DEANS

School of Administration: Prof. S. A. NKRUMAH
Faculty of Agriculture: Prof. F. K. FIANU
Faculty of Arts: J. N.-D. DODOO
Faculty of Law: Prof. AKUA KUENYEHIA
Faculty of Science: Prof. J. K. A. AMUZU
Faculty of Social Studies: Prof. J. R. ANQUANDAH
Medical School: Prof. S. K. OWUSU

PROFESSORS

ADDAE-MENSAH, I., Chemistry
ADU-GYAMFI, Y., Anaesthesia
AHENKORAH, Y., Crop Science
AKYEAMPONG, D. A., Mathematics
ANTESON, R. K., Microbiology
ANYIDOHO, K., English
ARCHAMPONG, E. Q., Surgery
ASHITEY, G. A., Community Health
ASSIMENG, J. M., Sociology
ASSOKU, R. K. G., Animal Science
BADOE, E. A., Surgery
BAETA, R. D., Physics
BENNEH, G., Geography and Resource Development
BRITWUM, K., French
CLERK, G. C., Botany
COKER, W. Z., Zoology
DOKU, E. V., Crop Science
FYNN, J. K., History
GYEKYE, K., Philosophy
HODASI, J. K. M., Zoology
KROPP DAKUBU, Mary E., Sociolinguistics
LAING, E., Botany
NEEQUAYE, J. E., Child Health
NKRUMAH, F. K., Paediatrics
NUKUNYA, G. K., Sociology
ODURO, K. A., Anaesthesia
OFOSU-AMAAH, S., School of Public Health
OLIVER-COMMEY, J. O., Child Health
OWUSU, S. K., Medicine and Therapeutics
TETTEH, G. K., Physics
YANKAH, K., Linguistics
YEBOAH, E. D., Surgery

ATTACHED INSTITUTES

Institute of Adult Education: POB 31, Legon; Dir J. O. BARNOR (acting).

Institute of African Studies: POB 73, Legon; Dir Prof. G. HAGAN.

School of Communication Studies: POB 53, Legon; Dir A. GADZEKPO (acting).

School of Performing Arts: POB 19, Legon; Dir Prof. K. ANYIDOHO (acting).

School of Public Health: POB 13, Legon; Dir Prof. S. OFOSO-AMAAH.

Institute of Statistical, Social and Economic Research: POB 74, Legon; Dir S. Y. ATSU (acting).

Noguchi Memorial Institute for Medical Research: POB 25, Legon; f. 1979; international centre for basic and applied research; Dir Prof. F. K. NKRUMAH.

Regional Training Centre for Archivists: POB 60, Legon; Head C. O. KISIEDU.

Regional Institute for Population Studies: POB 96, Legon; f. 1972 with UN aid; Dir Dr E. O. TAWIAH (acting).

United Nations University Institute for Natural Resources in Africa: Private Mail Bag, Kotoka International Airport, Accra; Dir Dr UZO MOKWUNYE.

Volta Basin Research Project: Legon; Chair. Prof. E. A. GYASI.

Legon Centre for International Affairs: Legon; Dir Prof. G. K. BLUWEY (acting).

AGRICULTURAL RESEARCH STATIONS

Agricultural Research Station: POB 43, Kade; Officer-in-Charge Dr J. K. OSEI.

Agricultural Research Station: POB 9, Kpong; Officer-in-Charge Dr J. W. OTENG.

Agricultural Research Station: POB 38, Legon; Officer-in-Charge Rev. Dr K. AMANING-KWARTENG.

UNIVERSITY OF SCIENCE AND TECHNOLOGY, KUMASI

University PO, Kumasi
Telephone: (51) 60351
Fax: (51) 60137
E-mail: ustlib@ust.gn.apc.org

Founded 1951 as College of Technology, University status 1961
Language of instruction: English
State control
Academic year: October to June (2 semesters)

Chancellor: (vacant)
Vice-Chancellor: (vacant)
Pro Vice-Chancellor: Prof. A. K. TUAH
Registrar: NANA OSEI BONSU II
Librarian: G. E. ADDO

Number of teachers: 487
Number of students: 7,611

Publications: *University Calendar*, *Annual Report*, *Recorder*, *Newsletter*, *Journal of the University of Science and Technology.*

DEANS

Faculty of Agriculture: Prof. A. K. TUAH
Faculty of Environmental and Development Studies: Dr E. A. TACKIE
College of Art: JOYCE J. STUBER
School of Engineering: Prof. N. K. KUMAPLEY
School of Medical Science: Prof. G. W. BROBBY
Faculty of Pharmacy: Prof. J. S. K. AYIM
Faculty of Science: Prof. K. SINGH
Faculty of Social Sciences: Prof. A. OWUSU-SARPONG
Board of Postgraduate Studies: Prof. A. C. SACKEYFIO

DIRECTORS

Institute of Mining and Mineral Engineering: Prof. K. SRAKU-LARTEY
Institute of Renewable Natural Resources: Dr S. J. QUASHIE-SAM
Institute of Technical Education: Dr S. OTENG-SEIFAH
School of Mines, Tarkwa: Dr J. K. BORSAH (Principal)
Institute of Land Management and Development: Prof. KASIM KASANGA
Technology Consultancy Centre: S. BUATSI
Bureau of Integrated Rural Development: Dr A. OWUSHU-BI
Centre for Cultural Studies: Dr E. OSEI-KOFI
Distance Education: Dr E. BADU

PROFESSORS

BROBBY, G. W., Ear, Eye, Nose and Throat Surgery
OWUSU-SARPONG, A. K., Languages
SARPONG, K., Pharmacy

Colleges

Accra Polytechnic: POB 561, Accra; tel. 662262; f. 1949; technical and vocational education with practical research programmes in manufacturing, commerce, science and technology; from technician to higher national diploma level; 122 teachers; 2,833 students; library of 10,000 vols; Principal Dr N. D. SODZI.

Accra Technical Training Centre: POB M.177, Accra; f. 1966, attached to Ministry of Education; to train tradesmen for industry and civil service; number of students: 350; library of 10,500 vols; Principal T. K. ADZEI.

Ghana Institute of Management and Public Administration: Greenhill, POB 50, Achimota; tel. and fax 667681; telex 2551; f. 1961; research, consultancy, human resource development, strategic studies and policy analysis and postgraduate studies, diploma, certificate and master's degree programmes in management; 42 teachers; library of 33,000 vols; Dir-Gen. T. B. WEREKO; Exec. Sec. E. A. COOPER; publs. *Greenhill Case Studies Book*, *Administrators' Digest*, *Greenhill Journal of Administration* (2 a year), *GIMPA News* (quarterly), *Ghana Economic Outlook* (2 a year).

Government Technical Institute: POB 206, Sunyani; f. 1967; technical and business education; 65 teachers; 1,300 students; library of *c.* 4,500 vols; Pres. E. O. AHULU.

Ho Polytechnic: POB 217, Ho, Volta Region; tel. (91) 456; fax (91) 8398; f. 1968; training of middle-level management personnel and technicians to HND standard; library of 10,000 vols; 90 teachers; 1,800 students; Principal Dr G. M. AFETI; Registrar F. K. DZINEKU.

Takoradi Polytechnic: POB 256, Takoradi; tel. (31) 22178; fax (31) 22643; f. 1955; library of 7,000 vols, 40 periodicals; Principal Dr N. AIDOO-TAYLOR; Sec. KOBINA ANANE-WAE.

Tamale Technical Institute: POB 3, E.R. Tamale.

Koforidua Technical Institute: POB 323, Koforidua; f. 1960; 9 teachers; 206 students; library of 2,000 vols; Principal P. C. NOI.

Kpandu Technical Institute: Technical Division, POB 76, Kpandu, Volta Region; telephone Kpandu 22; f. 1956; 70 teachers; 689 students; library of 4,000 vols; Principal J. Y. VODZI.

National Film and Television Institute (NAFTI): PMB, GPO, Accra; tel. (21) 777610; fax (21) 774522; e-mail nafti@ghana.com; f. 1978 by Government decree; 3-year courses in film and television production with special emphasis on the production of educational programmes, and feature, informative, animation, documentary and industrial films; mem. of CILECT, Int. Asscn. of Film and Television Schools; receives financial help from public funds and technical assistance from NGOs and Unesco; 43 students; specialized library of 51,000 vols; Dir MARTIN LOH; publ. *NAFTI Concept* (2 a year).

West Africa Computer Science Institute: POB 1643, Mamprobi, Accra; tel. (21) 229927; fax (21) 229575; f. 1988; independent college providing training in computers, accounting and related fields; br. in Liberia; Pres. AIKINS BRIGHT KUMI; Principal LAWRENCE NYARKO.

GREECE

Learned Societies

GENERAL

Akadimia Athinon (Academy of Athens): Odos Panepistimiou 28, Athens; tel. 360-1163; f. 1926; sections of Positive Sciences (Pres. C. STEFANIS), Literature and Fine Arts (Pres. C. GROLLIOS), Moral and Political Sciences (Pres. Most Rev. Metropolitan of Pergamon IOANNIS ZIZIOULAS); 42 mems, 33 foreign mems, 137 corresp. mems, 3 hon. mems; attached research institutes: see Research Institutes; library: see Libraries and Archives; Pres. IOANNIS PESMAZOGLOU; Sec.-Gen. P. SAKELLARIDIS; publ. *Praktika* (Proceedings, annually).

BIBLIOGRAPHY, LIBRARY SCIENCE AND MUSEOLOGY

Enosis Hellinon Bibliothekarion (Greek Library Association): Themistocleus 73, 106 83 Athens; tel. and fax (1) 322-6625; f. 1968; 800 mems; Pres. K. XATZOPOULOU; Gen. Sec. E. KALOGERAKY; publ. magazine.

EDUCATION

Hellenic Association of University Women: 44A Voulis St, 105 57 Athens; Pres. IRENE DILARI; Sec.-Gen. FLORA KAMARI.

Syllogos pros Diadosin ton Hellenikon Grammaton (Society for the Promotion of Greek Education): Odos Pindarou 15 (136), Athens; f. 1869; 9 mems; Pres. PHILIP DRAGOUMIS; Sec.-Gen. ALEXANDRATOS PANAYIOTIS.

FINE AND PERFORMING ARTS

Enosis Hellinon Mousourgon (Union of Greek Composers): Odos Mitropoleos 38, Athens; tel. 32-23-302; f. 1931; 135 mems; Pres. THODOROS ANTONIOU; Sec.-Gen. GEORGIOS KOUROUPOS.

Epimelitirion Ikastikon Technon Ellados (Chamber of Fine Arts): Odos Nikis 11, 105 57 Athens; tel. (1) 3231230; fax (1) 3240296; f. 1945; promotion of the fine arts, support for artists, organizes exhibitions in Greece and abroad, organizes conferences, etc.; 3,100 mems; library of 2,000 vols; Pres. EVA MELA; Gen. Sec. MICHALIS PAPADAKIS.

Society for Byzantine Studies: Odos Aristeidou 8, Athens 122; f. 1919; 250 mems; library of 5,000 vols; Pres. A. ORLANDOS; Sec.-Gen. N. B. TOMADAKIS; publ. *Epetiris Etairias Byzantinon Spoudon (EEBS)* (annually).

HISTORY, GEOGRAPHY AND ARCHAEOLOGY

Archaeologiki Hetairia (Archaeological Society): Odos Panepistimiou 22, 106 72 Athens; tel. (1) 3609689; fax (1) 3644996; f. 1837; 418 mems; library of 105,000 vols; Pres. GEORGE DONTAS; Sec.-Gen. BASIL PETRAKOS; publs *O Mentor* (quarterly), *Archaeologiki Ephimeris* (annually), *Praktika* (annually), *Ergon* (annually).

Hellenic Geographical Society: 11 Voucourestiou St, 106 71 Athens; tel. 36-31 112; f. 1919; 148 mems; Pres. DIMITRIOS DIMITRIADIS; Gen. Sec. GEORGE. IVANTCHOS; publ. *Bulletin.*

Historical and Ethnological Society: Old Parliament, Stadiou St, Athens; f. 1882; Pres. ATHANASSIOS K. TOMARAS; Sec.-Gen. I. C. MAZARACIS-AENIAN.

LANGUAGE AND LITERATURE

Hetairia Hellinon Logotechnon (Society of Greek Men of Letters): 8 Gennadiou St and Acadimias, 106 78 Athens; tel. 3634-559; f. 1934; 700 mems; Pres. ILIAS SIMOPOULOS; Sec. PANOS PANAGIOTOUNIS.

Hetairia Hellinon Theatricon Syngrapheon (Greek Playwrights' Assocn): Asklipiou St 33, Athens; f. 1908; 120 mems; Pres. DIMITRI IOANNOPOULOS; Sec. DIMITRI YANOUKAKIS.

NATURAL SCIENCES

Mathematical Sciences

Helliniki Mathimatiki Eteria (Greek Mathematical Society): Odos Panepistimiou 34, 106 79 Athens; f. 1918; 13,000 mems; library of 2,000 vols; seminars, lectures, summer schools, educational policy; Pres. Prof. NIC ALEXANDRIS; Gen. Sec. C. G SALARIS; publs *Euclides* (quarterly), *Mathimatiki Epitheorissi* (Review, every 6 months), *Deltion* (Bulletin, annually), *Enimerossi* (News, quarterly).

Physical Sciences

Enosis Ellinon Chimikon (Association of Greek Chemists): 27 Odos Kanningos, 106 82 Athens; tel. 36-21-524; f. 1924; 5,000 mems; library of 5,000 vols, 100 periodicals; Pres. P. HAMAKIOTIS; Gen. Sec. D. PSOMAS; publ. *Chimika Chronika* (General Edition monthly, new series quarterly).

TECHNOLOGY

Helliniki Epitropi Atomikis Energhias (Greek Atomic Energy Commission): POB 60092, 153 10 Aghia Paraskevi, Athens; tel. 6515194; telex 218254; fax 6533939; f. 1954; Pres. Prof. ANASTASIOS KATSANOS.

Research Institutes

GENERAL

Ethnikon Idryma Erevnon (National Hellenic Research Foundation): 48 Vassileos Constantinou Ave, 116 35 Athens; tel. (30-1) 72-29-811-15; telex 224064; fax 7246618; f. 1958; research in its own institutes (humanities, natural sciences), subsidises research in universities and other centres; 270 staff; library of 2,000 periodicals; Euronet facilities; Man. Dir Prof. B. MAGLARIS; publs monographs, studies, etc.

AGRICULTURE, FISHERIES AND VETERINARY SCIENCE

Benakio Phytopathologiko Institouto (Benaki Phytopathological Institute): 8 Odos Delta, 145 61 Kiphissia, Athens; tel. (1) 8077506; fax 8077506; f. 1930; phytopathology, entomology, agricultural zoology, pesticides; 21 laboratories; library of 25,000 books, 60,000 pamphlets and 930 current periodicals; museum of zoological and entomological specimens, including 22,000 species, and culture collections; Dir Dr A. S. ALIVIZATOS; publs *Annales de l'Institut Phytopathologique Benaki* (irregular), *Activities Report* (annually).

National Centre for Marine Research (formerly the Institute of Oceanographic and Fisheries Research): Aghios Kosmas, 166 04 Hellinikon, Athens; tel. (1) 98-20-214; telex 224135; fax (1) 98-33-095; f. 1965; freshwater and marine fishery and biology, oceanography, marine geology and geophysics, environmental monitoring; hydrobiological research station and aquarium at Rhodes; library of 3,000 vols and 541 periodicals; Dir Prof. D. PAPANIKOLAOU; publ. *Thalassographica* (annually).

ECONOMICS, LAW AND POLITICS

Centre of International and European Economic Law: POB 14, 55102 Kalamaria, Thessaloniki; e-mail cieel@momos.csd.auth.gr; f. 1977; national documentation and research centre, specializing in European Community law; European Documentation Centre by decision of the EEC; library of 45,000 vols, 250 periodicals; Dir and Pres. of Admin. Council Prof. WASSILIOS SKOURIS; Sec. PAROULA NASKOS-PERRAKIS; publ. *Revue hellénique de droit européen*.

Centre of Planning and Economic Research: Hippokratous 22, 106 80 Athens; tel. 3627321; fax 3611136; f. 1961; prepares development plans and conducts economic research; library of 23,000 vols, 730 periodical titles, 270 series of statistical bulletins; Dir. Gen. Prof. VASSILIS DROUCOPOULOS.

Hellenic Centre for European Studies (EKEM): Prassa 1 & Didotou St, 106 80 Athens; tel. 3636880; fax 3631133; e-mail ekem@prometheus.hol.gr; f. 1988; non-profit-making, semi-public organization, linked to the Ministry of Foreign Affairs; advises public administration on matters of European policy; organizes conferences and seminars; maintains Depository Library of the European Community, with 4,500 vols; Pres. of Admin. Council and Dir Prof. ST. PERRAKIS; publs *Balkan Briefing* (monthly), *Report for the Balkans* (2 a year).

Hellenic Institute of International and Foreign Law: 73 Solonos St, 106 79 Athens; tel. 3615646; fax 3619777; e-mail hiifl@ath.forthnet.gr; f. 1939; library of 25,000 vols; Dir Prof. KONSTANTINOS KERAMEUS; publ. *Revue hellénique de droit international* (annually) (English, French, German and Italian).

Hellenikon Kentron Paragochikotitos (Greek Productivity Centre): 28 Kapodistriou St, 106 82 Athens; tel. 360-04-11; telex 219416; aims at dissemination of principles of productivity and their implementation in the national economy; Dir.-Gen. D. PALEOTHODOROS.

Institute of International Public Law and International Relations: Megalou Alexandrou 15 and Hadji, 546 40 Thessaloniki; tel. (31) 841-751; fax (31) 853427; f. 1966; research, documentation and education centre; library and World Bank and UN depository library; summer sessions; Dir Prof. KALLIOPI K. KOUFA; publs *Greek Journal of International Law and Politics* (2 a year), *Thesaurus Acroasium* (annually).

Kentron Erevnis Historias Ellinikou Dikeou (Centre for Research in the History of the Greek Law): Akadimia Athinon Anagnostopoulou 14, 106 73 Athens; tel. and fax (1) 3623565; f. 1929; attached to Acad. of Athens; collects, studies and publishes legal material of Byzantine and post-Byzantine times; Dir Prof. Dr J. KONIDARIS; publ. *Epetiris* (annually).

FINE AND PERFORMING ARTS

Kentro Erevnas Byzantinis kai Metabyzantinis Technis (Research Centre for Byzantine and Post-Byzantine Art): Odos Anagnostopoulou 14, 106 73 Athens; tel. and fax (1) 3645610; f. 1994; attached to Acad. of Athens; Supervisor MANOLIS CHATZIDAKIS.

HISTORY, GEOGRAPHY AND ARCHAEOLOGY

Centre for Asia Minor Studies: Kydathineon 11, 105 58 Athens; tel. 3239225; fax 3229758; f. 1930; independent, private, non-profit organization; research into history and civilization of Greek communities in Asia Minor before 1922; 5 research staff; library of 12,000 vols, 501 MSS; oral history archive of 150,000 MS pages; photographic archive of *c.* 5,000 photographs; folk music archive of 1,000 records, 700 tapes; special collections: Karamanli books, and Greek books, newspapers and periodicals printed in Turkey; Pres. Prof. M. B. SAKELLARIOU; Dir Prof. P. M. KITROMILIDES; publs *Deltio K. M. S.* (annually), *Bibliotheca Asiae Minoris Historica, Exodus,* monograph series.

Institute for Balkan Studies: POB 50932, 540 14 Thessaloniki, tel. (31) 832143; fax (31) 831429; e-mail imxa@hyper.gr; f. 1953; research centre concerned with the historical, literary, political, economic and social development of the Balkan peoples from their early times to the present day; library of 30,000 vols; Dir Prof. Dr BASIL KONDIS; Chair. Prof. KALLIOPI KOUFA; publs *Balkan Studies* (2 a year), *Balkanika Symmeikta*.

International Centre for Classical Research (of the Hellenic Society for Humanistic Studies): 47 Alopekis St, Athens 140; study of and research into ancient Greek culture, scientific research and promotion of popular education through conferences and publications; f. 1959; 700 mems; library of 20,000 vols; Pres. Prof. ARISTOXENOS D. SKIADAS; Sec.-Gen. GEORGE BABINIOTIS; publs *Antiquity and Contemporary Problems, Studies and Research*.

Kentron Erevnis Archaiotitos (Research Centre for Antiquity): Odos Anagnostopoulou 14, 106 73 Athens; tel. (1) 3600040; fax (1) 3602448; f. 1977; attached to Acad. of Athens; Supervisor S. IAKOVIDIS; Dir M. PIPILI.

Kentron Erevnis Messeonikou kai Neou Ellinismou (Centre for Research into Mediaeval and Modern Hellenism (up to 1821)): Odos Panepistimiou 28, Athens; f. 1930; attached to Acad. of Athens; Dir D. SOPHIANOS; publ. *Epetiris* (annually).

Kentron Erevnis Neoterou Ellinismou (Centre for Research in Contemporary Hellenism (from 1821)): Odos Panepistimiou 28, Athens; f. 1957; attached to Acad. of Athens; Dir HELEN BELIA.

LANGUAGE AND LITERATURE

Kentron Ekdoseos Ergon Ellinon Sygrafeon (Centre for the Publication of Greek Texts): Odos Anagnostopoulou 14, 106 73 Athens; tel. (1) 3612541; fax (1) 3602691; f. 1955; attached to Acad. of Athens.

Kentron Syntaxeos Historikou Lexikou (Centre for the compilation of the Historical Dictionary of the Modern Greek Language): Odos Panepistimiou 28, Athens; f. 1914; attached to Acad. of Athens; Dir E. YAKOUMAKI.

MEDICINE

Institut Pasteur Hellénique: 127 Vassilissis Sofias Ave, 11521 Athens; tel. (1) 6462281; telex 221188; fax (1) 6423498; f. 1919; study and research of bacteriology, biochemistry, biotechnology, immunology, microbiology, molecular biology, molecular virology, parasitology, virology; library of 3,500 vols and 155 periodicals; Pres. Prof. C. MIRAS.

NATURAL SCIENCES

Physical Sciences

Institouton Geologikon kai Metalleutikon Ereunon (Institute of Geology and Mineral Exploration): 70 Messoghion St, 115 27 Athens; tel. (1) 7798412; telex 216357; fax 7752211; f. 1952; activities include mineral surveys, mapping and exploration, groundwater exploration, energy resources exploration, engineering geology, geophysical investigation, environmental geology; 1,154 mems; library of 26,500 vols and 7,600 reports; four laboratories; Dir-Gen. Prof. C. KATAGAS; publs *Geological and Geophysical Research* (irregular), *The Geology of Greece, Bulletin*.

Kentron Erevnis Phissikistis Atmospheras kai Climatologias (Research Centre for Atmospheric Physics and Climatology): Odos Panepistimiou 28, Athens; f. 1977; attached to Acad. of Athens; Dir CHR. REPAPIS.

Kentron Erevnon Astronomias kai Ephirmosmenon Mathimatikon tis Akadimias Athinon (Research Centre for Astronomy and Applied Mathematics, Academy of Athens): Odos Panepistimiou 28, Athens; f. 1959; attached to Acad. of Athens; Dir C. POULACOS; publs *Contributions from the Research Centre for Astronomy and Applied Mathematics, Annual Report*.

National Observatory of Athens: POB 22048, 118 10 Athens; tel. (1) 3464161; telex 215530; fax (1) 3421019; f. 1842; library contains 60,000 vols; Pres. of the Administration Board Prof. D. P. LALAS; Directors: Astronomical Institute, Prof. E. KONTIZAS; Meteorological Institute Prof. D. ASIMAKOPOULOS; Geodynamics Institute, Dr G. STAVRAKAKIS (acting); Ionospheric Institute, Prof. E. SARRIS; publs *Annals of the National Observatory of Athens, Memoirs*, Series I—Astronomy, Series II—Meteorology; bulletins of the Astronomical, Meteorological, Ionospheric and Geodynamics Institutes.

PHILOSOPHY AND PSYCHOLOGY

Kentron Erevnis Ellinikis Philosophias (Centre for Research in Greek Philosophy): Odos Panepistimiou 28, Athens; f. 1966; attached to Acad. of Athens; Dir A. KELESSIDOU.

RELIGION, SOCIOLOGY AND ANTHROPOLOGY

Athens Center of Ekistics: 24 Strat. Syndesmou St, 106 73 Athens; tel. 3623-216; fax (1) 3629337; f. 1963; research, education, collaboration and documentation in the development of human settlements; secretariat of World Society for Ekistics; library of 30,000 vols; Dir PANAYOTIS C. PSOMOPOULOS; publs *Ekistics, Ekistic Index*, special research reports and monographs.

Hellenic Folklore Research Centre of the Academy of Athens (Research Centre for Hellenic Folklore): 1 Dipla St and 129 Syngrou Ave, 117 45 Athens; tel. 9344811; f. 1918; folklore, anthropology, ethnology (ethnography), folk music, social, spiritual life, archives of folk material, MSS, tape, video tape, cassette movie, photos, slides; library of 9,000 vols, 4,238 MSS, 23,901 songs, 14,500 proverbs, customs, etc.; Dir Dr AIK. POLYMEROU-KAMILAKIS; publ. *Yearbook*.

Kentron Erevnis Ellinikis Kinonias (Research Centre for Greek Society): Panepistimiou 28, Athens; f. 1978; attached to Acad. of Athens; Dir GR. GIZELIS.

National Centre of Social Research (EKKE): 1 Sophocleous St, 105 59 Athens; tel. 32-12-611; f. 1960; operates under the Ministry of Research and Technology; aims to promote the development of the social sciences in Greece, to organize and conduct social research and to act as a link between Greek and foreign social scientists, to promote international co-operation in this field; Pres. Prof. CONSTANTINOS TSOUKALAS; Scientific Dir Prof. PAVLOS SOURLAS; publ. *Epitheorissis Koinonikon Erevnon* (Greek Review of Social Research, quarterly).

Patriarchal Institute for Patristic Studies: 64 Eptapyrgiou St, Moni Vlatadon, 546 34 Thessaloniki; tel. and fax (31) 203620; f. 1968; research centre with depts of patrology, palaeography, history of Byzantine art, history of worship and ecclesiastical history; library of 15,000 vols, 300 periodicals, 115 codex MSS, 450 rare books, 10,000 MSS on microfilm, colour slides of illuminated MSS; Dir Prof. JOHN FOUNTOULIS; publs *Kleronomia* (2 a year), *Analekta Vlatadon* (monograph series).

TECHNOLOGY

'Demokritos' National Centre for Scientific Research: POB 60228, 153 10 Aghia Paraskevi, Athens; tel. 6503000; telex 216199; fax 6519180; f. 1961; study and research by eight institutes: nuclear physics, materials science, microelectronics, biology, nuclear technology and radiation protection, informatics and telecommunications, physical chemistry, radioisotopes and radiodiagnostic products; 659 mems; library of 15,000 vols and over 1,000 periodicals; Dir Prof. DIONYSIOS S. ITHAKISIOS; Librarian Miss NORIA CHRISTOPHORIDOU; publs *DEMO Reports*.

Libraries and Archives

Athens

Academy of Athens Library: Odos Panepistimiou 28, 106 79 Athens; 500,000 vols.

Benaki Library: Odos Anthimou Gazi, Athens; tel. 3227148; f. 1924; 200,000 vols, 45,000 vols donated by Emmanuel Benakis; Librarian I. KOIS.

Eugenides Foundation Library: Syngrou Ave 387, Paleon Phaleron, 175 64 Athens; tel. 94-11-181; e-mail library@eugenfound.edu.gr; f. 1966; 23,500 vols, 441 periodicals (science and technology); Librarian HARA BRINDESI.

Gennadius Library: Odos Souidias 61, Athens; tel. (1) 7210536; fax (1) 7237767; f. 1926; rare book and research library attached to American School of Classical Studies; 100,000 vols; spec. colln on Greece, the Near East, the Balkans and travel accounts; Dir Dr HARIS KALLIGAS; Librarian SOPHIE PAPAGEORGIOU; publs *Gennadeion Monographs, Catalogues of Travels, Catalogue, The New Griffon* (2 a year).

Greek Chamber of Deputies Library: Parliament Bldg, 100 21 Athens; tel. (1) 323-5030; fax (1) 323-6072; e-mail abadjis@artemis.parl.ariadne-t.gr; f. 1844; burnt 1859, rebuilt 1875; 1,500,000 vols; Dir IRENE CON. ELIOPOULOU.

Library of the Technical Chamber of Greece: Odos Lekka 23–25, 105 62 Athens; tel. (1) 3254590; fax (1) 3237525; f. 1926; 50,000 vols, 1,400 periodicals, on mechanics, engineering and other technical subjects.

National Library: Odos Venizelou 32, 106 79 Athens; tel. 3614-413; f. 1828; 2,500,000 vols; collections of MSS, maps, engravings; Gen. Dir Dr PANAYOTIS G. NICOLOPOULOS.

National Technical University of Athens Library: Odos Polytechniou 9, Zogsafou Campus, 157 75 Athens; 200,000 vols; Librarian MARIA KALAMBALIKI.

Thessaloniki

Aristotelian University of Thessaloniki Library: Thessaloniki; tel. 995325; fax 206433; f. 1927; 2 m. vols; Dir DIMITRIOS DIMITRIOU.

Tripolis

Pan Library ('Circle of the Friends of Progress'): Odos Giorgios 43, Tripolis, Arcadia; vols on all subjects.

Volos

Library of the Three Hierarchs: Demetriados-Ogl, Volos; tel. and fax (421) 25641; f. 1907; 23,000 vols; literature, religion, history, philosophy; Asst Dir K. KONTOSTERGIOS.

Museums and Art Galleries

Athens

Acropolis Museum: Office: Makriyani 2–4, 117 42 Athens; tel. 323-66-65; f. 1878; contains the sculptures discovered on the Acropolis; illustrates the origins of Attic art, pedimental compositions, Korai, sculptures of the Parthenon, Temple of Niké, Erechtheion, etc.; Dir ISMENE TRIANTIS.

Benaki Museum: Odos Koumbari 1, 106 74 Athens; tel. 361-16-17; fax 3622547; f. 1930; Greek art from Neolithic to late Roman period; Byzantine and post-Byzantine; Greek folk art and costumes; historic memorabilia from the War of Independence in 1821 to the politician E. Venizelos in 1936; 18th–19th-century paintings, engravings and drawings; works of art by N. Hadjikyriakos-Ghikas; Coptic and Islamic art; textiles and embroidery from Far East and Western Europe; neolithic to modern Chinese porcelain; library of 30,000 vols, 500 MSS; historical archives dept, photographic archives dept; Dir Prof. ANGELOS DELIVORRIAS. (The museum was expected to be closed to the public until at least 1996.)

Byzantine Museum: 22 Vasilissis Sophias Ave, 106 75 Athens; tel. (1) 7211027; fax (1) 7231883; f. 1914; rich collection of Byzantine and post-Byzantine icons and wall paintings, early Christian and Byzantine sculpture and pottery, mosaic pavements, minor arts in wood, ivory and metal, Coptic textiles, jewellery, vestments of the Orthodox Church, liturgical articles, Greek MSS of the Byzantine and post-Byzantine eras; library and photo-archives on Byzantine art; Dir CHRYSSANTHI BALTOYANNI.

National Archaeological Museum: Odos Patission 44, Athens; tel. 8217724; fax 8213573; f. 1874; contains rich collections of original Greek sculptures of all kinds and Roman copies of Greek originals; sculptures of the Roman period; Neolithic objects from Thessaly; Bronze Age relics from the mainland and the Aegean Islands; Mycenaean treasures; frescoes and pottery from Thera; rich collections of Greek vases and terracottas; collections of jewels and bronzes; Egyptian antiquities; Dir E. ZERVOUDAKI; Curator of Sculpture N. KALTSAS; Curator of Vases E. ZERVOUDAKI; Curator of Prehistoric Collection (vacant); Curator of Bronzes ROSA PROSKYNITOPOULOU; Curator of Egyptian Collection (vacant).

National Art Gallery and Alexander Soutzos Museum: 50 Vassileos Konstantinou Ave, 116 10 Athens; tel. 7211010; telex 222322; fax 7224889; f. 1900; 17th–20th-century Greek paintings, sculptures and prints; 14th–20th-century European paintings, including El Greco, Caravaggio, Jordaens, Poussin, Tiepolo, Delacroix, Mondrian, Picasso; engravings; drawings; library of 8,000 vols; Dir Prof. MARINA LAMBRAKI-PLAKA.

Stoa of Attalos: Athens; tel. 321-01-85; f. as a museum in 1956; the design of the original building of the 2nd century BC has been exactly reproduced in the reconstruction carried out 1953–56 by the American School of Classical Studies; collections include all material found in the excavations of the Athenian Agora, illustrating 5,000 years of Athenian history; Dir P. KALLIGAS.

Zoological Museum of the University of Athens: Panepistimiopolis (Kouponia), 157 84 Athens; tel. (1) 7284619; fax 7284604; f. 1858; permanent and temporary exhibitions on Greek and world fauna: birds, mammals, shells, insects etc.; research in ecology and zoogeography; Dir Prof. C. S. ZAFEIRATOS.

Corinth

Archaeological Museum in Corinth: C/o American School of Classical Studies, 54 Souidias, Athens; tel. (741) 3-12-07; f. 1932; findings from excavations made by the American School; Dir PHANI PACHIYANNI; publs *Hesperia* (annually), *Corinth*.

Delphi

Archaeological Museum: 330 54 Delphi; tel. (265) 82313; fax (265) 82966; f. 1903; findings from the Delphic excavations; continuous excavation; restoration and conservation; library of 4,400 vols; Dir DESPINA SKORDAS.

Heraklion

Archaeological Museum: 2 Xanthoudidou St, 712 02 Heraklion, Crete; tel. (81) 226092; f. 1904; contains rich collection of Minoan art (pottery, sealstones, frescoes, jewellery); traces the development of Cretan art up to the Roman period; Dir AL. KARETSOU.

Nafplion

Peloponnesian Folklore Foundation: Vas. Alexandrou 1, 211 00 Nafplion; tel. (752) 28379; fax (752) 27960; e-mail pff@hol.gr; f. 1974; research, presentation, study and preservation of the material culture of Greece (costume, music and dance); br. in Stathmos; library of 5,500 vols; Pres. JOANNA PAPANTONIOU; Curator KANELLOS KANELLOPOULOS; publ. *Ethnographica*.

Olympia

Archaeological Museum: Olympia; tel. (624) 22-529; contains largest single collection of Greek geometric and archaic bronzes in the world; two pediments from Temple of Zeus, Hermes of Praxiteles, Victory of Paionios; Dir XENI ARAPOYANNI; publs on history and remains of Olympia.

Paiania

Vorres Museum of Greek Art: Paiania, Attica; tel. 6642520; telex 224358; fax 6645775; f. 1982; covers 3,000 years of Greek history; two sections: folk art and architecture (a group of traditional buildings containing artefacts, furniture, etc.) and a museum of contemporary Greek art; Dir IAN VORRES; publ. *Catalogue*.

Rhodes

Archaeological Museum: Rhodes; tel. (241) 75674; in the Hospital of the Knights; f. 1440; library of 27,400 vols; sculpture, vases and other objects from Rhodes, Ialysos, Kamiros and other sites, dating from Mycenean to late Roman times, funerary stelae and weapons dating from Middle Ages; Dir Dr JOHN PAPACHRISTODOULOU.

Thessaloniki

Archaeological Museum of Thessaloniki: 6 Manolis Andronikos St, Thessaloniki; tel. 830538; fax 861306; f. 1962; archaeology of Macedonia, mainly the prefectures of Thessaloniki, Chalkidiki, Pieria and Kilkis; includes finds from the ancient cemetery of Sindos; library of 7,700 vols; branch museums at Kilkis, Dion, Polygyros; Dir Dr D. GRAMMENOS; publs *Thessaloniki Philippou Vassilissan*, *Archeologiko Ergo ste Makedonia kai Thrace* (annual journal).

Universities

ATHINISIN ETHNIKON KAI KAPODISTRIAKON PANEPISTIMION (National and Capodistrian University of Athens)

Odos Panepistimiou 30, 106 79 Athens
Telephone: (1) 3614301
Telex: 223815
Fax: (1) 3602145

Founded 1837
State control
Language of instruction: Greek
Academic year: September to June

Rector: Prof. PETROS A. GAMTOS
Vice-Rectors: Prof. G. PHILOKYPROU, Prof. K. EVANGELIDES
Secretary-General: (vacant)

Number of teachers: 1,709
Number of students: 45,000

DEANS

Faculty of Theology: VASILIOS TSAKONAS
Faculty of Law, Economic and Political Sciences: CHRISTOS ROZAKIS
Faculty of Health Sciences: KONSTANTINOS DIMOPOULOS
Faculty of Arts: IOANNIS PARASKEVOPOULOS
Faculty of Sciences: NIKOLAOS SIMEONIDIS

HEADS OF DEPARTMENTS

Faculty of Theology:

- Theology: CHRISTOS VOULGAKIS
- Pastoral Studies: ILIAS VOULGARAKIS

Faculty of Law, Economics and Political Sciences:

- Law: I. SPYRIDAKIS
- Economic Studies: K. VAITSOS
- Political Sciences and Public Administration: ARGYRIS FATOUROS

Faculty of Health Sciences:

- Medicine: K. DIMOPOULOS
- Dentistry: Z. MANTZAVINOS
- Pharmacology: NICOS HOULIS
- Hospital Care: K. KYRIAKOU

Faculty of Arts:

- Greek Language and Literature: G. BABINIOTIS
- History and Archaeology: E. MIKROYIANNAKIS
- Philosophy, Psychology and Education: I. MARKANTONIS
- English Language and Literature: B. RAIZIS
- French Language and Literature: D. PANTELODEMOS
- German Language and Literature: W. BENNING

Faculty of Sciences:

- Physics: P. LASKARIDIS
- Chemistry: N. HATZICHRISTIDIS
- Mathematics: E. KOUNIAS
- Biology: E. FRANGOULIS
- Geosciences: S. SKOUNAKIS

Computer Sciences: G. PHILOKYPROU
Physical Education and Athletics: V. KLEISSOURAS
Teacher Training for Primary Education: TH. EXARHAKOS
Teacher Training for Pre-school Education: I. PAPACOSTAS
Theatre Studies: The Rector
Communication and Mass Media Studies: G. LAVVAS
Music: The Rector

ARISTOTELEIO PANEPISTIMIO THESSALONIKIS (Aristotle University of Thessaloniki)

University Campus, 540 06 Thessaloniki
Telephone: (31) 996703
Telex: 412181
Fax: (31) 206138
Founded 1925
State University, with autonomous function
Language of instruction: Greek
Academic year: September to August
Rector: Prof. A. MANTIS
Vice-Rectors: Prof. P. LADIS, Prof. M. PAPADOPOULOS
Administrator: DIMITRIOS BATZIOS
Librarian: D. DIMITRIOU
Number of teachers: 2,491
Number of students: 72,000
Publications: catalogue, scientific annals and faculty periodicals.

DEANS

Faculty of Theology: N. MATSOUKAS
Faculty of Philosophy: G. PARASOGLU
Faculty of Law and Economic Sciences: P. GESIOU-FALTSI
Faculty of Science: G. PAPANASTASIOU
Faculty of Geotechnical Sciences: (vacant)
Faculty of Health Sciences: (vacant)
Faculty of Technology: V. PAPATHANASIOU
Faculty of Fine Arts: (vacant)
Faculty of Education in Thessaloniki: E. VARNAVA-SKOURA
Faculty of Education in Florina: A. KAPSALIS

CHAIRMEN OF DEPARTMENTS

Theological Faculty
School of Theology: I. PETROU
School of Pastoral and Social Theology: V. FANOURGAKIS
Faculty of Philosophy
School of Philology: I. KAZAZIS
School of History and Archaeology: A. ZAFRAKA-STAVRIDOU
School of Philosophy and Education: S. DELIVOGIATZIS
School of Psychology: A. KOSTARIDOU-EFKLIDI
School of English Language and Literature: A. KAKOURIOTIS
School of French Language and Literature: Z. SIAFLEKIS
School of German Language and Literature: I. ECONOMOU-AGORASTOU
School of Italian Language and Literature: M. DITSA-ELEFANTI
Faculty of Sciences
School of Physics: I. ANTONOPOULOS
School of Mathematics: G. STAMOU
School of Chemistry: D. NIKOLAIDIS
School of Biology: I. TSEKOS
School of Geology: A. PSILOVIKOS
School of Computer Science: I. TSOUKALAS
Faculty of Law and Economics
School of Law: N. PARASKEVOPOULOS
School of Economics: A. TSAKLAGANOS
Faculty of Geotechnical Sciences
School of Agriculture: CH. KAMENIDIS
School of Forestry and Natural Environment: D. KOTOULAS
School of Veterinary Medicine: CH. CHIMONAS
Faculty of Health Sciences
School of Medicine: P. SYMEONIDIS
School of Dentistry: D. KARAKASSIS
School of Pharmacy: S. MALAMATARIS
Faculty of Technology
School of Civil Engineering: P. LATINOPOULOS
School of Architecture: X. SKARPIA-CHOIPEL
School of Survey Engineering: K. KATSABALOS
School of Mechanical Engineering: A. GOULAS
School of Electrical Engineering: S. PANAS
School of Chemical Engineering: M. ASSAEL
General School of the Faculty of Technology: CH. FRAGAKIS
Faculty of Fine Arts
School of Pictorial and Applied Arts: S. MAKRI
School of Musical Studies: D. THEMELIS
School of Theatre: N. PAPANDREOU
Faculty of Education in Thessaloniki:
School of Education of Infant Teachers: M. TZOURIADOU
School of Education of Primary Teachers: K. ATHANASIOU
Faculty of Education in Florina:
School of Education of Infant Teachers: A. KAPSALIS
School of Education of Primary Teachers: K. FOTIADIS
Independent Schools:
School of Physical Education and Athletics: A. DELIGIANNIS
School of Journalism and Mass Media Communication: N. INTZESILOGLOU
School of Physical Education and Athletics in Serres: I. KALOGEROPOULOS

DIMOKRITEIO PANEPISTIMIO THRAKIS ('Demokritos' University of Thrace)

Demokritos Str. 17, 691 00 Komotini
Telephone: (531) 39000
Telex: 462205
Fax: (531) 26660
Founded 1973
State control
Language of instruction: Greek
Academic year: September to August
Rector: K. SIMOPOULOS
Vice-Rectors: A. CHARALAMBAKIS, PH. TSALIDES
Administrative Officer: P. PAVLIDIS
Librarians: O. PAPOUTSI (Law), M. LEKIDOU (Engineering), TH. KYRKOUDIS (Medicine), EL. CHRISTODOULOU (Pedagogy), A. NAOUMIDOU (History and Ethnology), CH. PETRODASKALAKI (Physical Education and Sports)
Library of 143,000 vols
Number of teachers: 257
Number of students: 8,560

DEANS

Faculty of Law: P. KARGADOS
Faculty of Engineering: ANT. THANAILAKIS
Faculty of the Science of Physical Education and Athletics: G. GODOLIAS
Faculty of Medicine: T. DIMITRIOU
Pedagogical Department of Primary Education: K. OUZOUNIS
Pedagogical Department of Infant School Education: L. BEZE
Department of History and Ethnology: K. GALLIS
Department of Greek Literature: K. SIMOPOULOS
Department of Social Administration: A. CHARALAMBAKIS
Department of Environmental Engineering: PH. TSALIDES

PROFESSORS

Faculty of Law:
ALIPRANDIS, N., Labour Law
CHARALAMBAKIS, A., Penal Law
IOANNOU, KR., Public International Law
KALAVROS, K., Civil Procedural Law
KARGADOS, P., Civil Procedural Law
KONSTANDINIDIS, K., Penal and Procedural Law
POULIS, G., Ecclesiastical Law
SCHINAS, J., Commercial Law
VOULGARIS, J., Private International and Comparative Law

Faculty of Engineering:

Department of Civil Engineering
ATHANASSOPOULOS, CHR., Building Construction
CHALIOULIAS, AN., Geodesy
GALOUSSIS, EV., Steel Construction
GDOUTOS, EM., Technical Engineering and Applied Mechanics
KOGETSOPH, L., Higher Mathematics
KOTSOVINOS, N., Hydraulics
LABRINOS, P., Higher Mathematics
LIOLIOS, AST., Higher Mathematics
PANAGIOTAKOPOULOS, D., Construction Project Management
SAKKAS, J., Hydraulics
SIDERIS, K., Building Materials
STEPHANIS, VAS., Transport Engineering, Survey Engineering

Department of Electrical Engineering
MERTZIOS, V., Computer Science
PAPADOPOULOS, D., Electric Engines
SARRIS, EM., Electromagnetic Theory
SCHINAS, J., Applied Mathematics, Mathematical Analysis
SPARIS, P., Special Mechanical Engineering
THANAILAKIS, A., Electrical and Electronic Materials Technology
TSALIDIS, PH., Computer Science
TSANGAS, N., Nuclear Engineering and Technology
YAKINTHOS, J., General Physics

Faculty of Medicine:
ANASTASSIADIS, P., Obstetrics and Gynaecology
ANDROULAKIS, J., Paediatrics
ANNINOS, PH., Neurology
BOURIKAS, G., Pathology
CHATSERAS, D., Cardiology
CHOURDAKIS, K., Toxicology, Forensic Medicine
DIMITRIOU, TH., Anatomy
GEORGOPOULOS, G., Ear-Nose-Throat Specialist
GERMANIS, J., Orthopaedics
GOTSIS, N., Pathology
KARTALIS, G., Pathology
KONTOLEON-VAKALOPOULOU, E., Physiology
KOUSKOUKIS, A., Dermatology, Venereal Diseases
MANOLAS, K., Surgery
MONOS, P., Biology
PAPADOPOULOS, E., Urology
SIMOPOULOS, K., Surgery
STATHOPOULOS, G., Hygiene
TRIANTAPHYLLIDIS, K., Pharmacology
VARGEMEZIS, V., Pathology
YPSILANTIS, K., Pneumonology

Faculty of the Science of Physical Education and Athletics:
GODOLIAS, G., Sports Medicine
KABITSIS, CH., Classical Athletics
KOUJIOUMTZIDIS, CH., Anatomy, Traumatology
MAVROMATIS, G., Statistics
TAXILDARIS, K., Basketball

Pedagogical Department of Primary Education:
OUZOUNIS, K., Mathematics, Physics
TZOULIS, A., Psychology

VOUGIOUKLIS, TH., Mathematics

Pedagogical Department of Infant School Education:

BEZE, L., Psychology and Sociology of Education
CHATSISSAVAS, J., Education Law
GOGOU-KRITIKOU, L., Sociology of Education
KLADIS, D., Organization and Administration of Education
ZOUMAS, EV., Humanities

Department of History and Ethnology:

CHATZOPOULOS, K., Modern Greek History
GALLIS, K., Prehistoric Archaeology
KOULOURI, CH., Modern History
PAPADRIANOS, J., Balkan History
PAPAZOGLOU, G., History (based on sources such as Codices)
PITSAKIS, K., History of Law
SAMPSARIS, D., Roman History
XIROTYRIS, N., Physical Anthropology

Department of Greek Literature:

DIMITROKALLIS, G., Byzantine Archaeology
POLEMIS, J., Byzantine Literature

Department of Environmental Engineering:

AIVAZIDIS, AL., Environmental Technology

ETHNIKO METSOVIO POLYTECHNEIO (National Technical University of Athens)

Polytechnioupoli, Zografou, 15780 Athens
Telephone: (1) 7721000
Fax: (1) 7722048

Founded 1836
State control
Language of instruction: Greek
Academic year: September to August

Rector: Prof. THEMISTOCLES XANTHAPOULOS
Vice-Rectors: E. GALANIS, E. PAPAGIANNAKIS
Chief Administrative Officer: E. RELAKI
Librarian: M. KALABALIKI

Library: see Libraries
Number of teachers: 566
Number of students: 8,269

Publications: *Scientific Papers, Scientific Year Book, Pyrphoros* (every 2 weeks).

HEADS OF DEPARTMENTS

Civil Engineering: Prof. K. MOUTSOURIS
Mechanical Engineering: Prof. D. KOUREMENOS
Electrical and Computing Engineering: Prof. D. KOUTSOURIS
Architecture: Prof. N. KALOGERAS
Chemical Engineering: Prof. D. MARINOS-KOURIS
Rural Engineering and Surveying: Prof. D. BALODIMOS
Mining and Metallurgical Engineering: Prof. J. KOUMADAKIS
Naval Architecture and Marine Engineering: Prof. N. KIRTATOS
General Studies: Prof. E. GALANIS

DIRECTORS OF SECTIONS

Civil Engineering:

Structural Engineering: J. ERMOPOULOS
Water Resources, Hydraulic and Maritime Engineering: A. ADREADAKIS
Transportation Planning and Engineering: J. FRANTSESKAKIS
Geotechnical Engineering: (vacant)
Engineering Construction and Management: A. ANAGNOSTOPOULOS

Mechanical Engineering:

Fluid Mechanics Engineering: G. BERGELES
Thermal Engineering: K. RAKOPOULOS
Nuclear Engineering: D. LEONIDOU
Mechanical Construction and Automatic Control: P. MAKRIS
Manufacturing Technology: A. MAMALIS
Industrial Management and Operational Research: G. FOKAS-KOSMETATOS

Electrical and Computing Engineering:

Computer Science: G. STASINOPOULOS
Electrical Power: J. STATHOPOULOS
Electroscience: N. OUZOUNOGLOU

Architecture:

Architectural Design: A. BIRIS
Urban and Regional Planning: G. SARIGIANNIS
Design, Visual Studies and Communication: G. PARMENIDIS
Design and Technology: E. KORONEOS

Chemical Engineering:

Chemical Sciences: D. MARINOS-KOURIS
Process Analysis and Plant Design: D. TASIOS
Material Science and Engineering: TH. THEOFANIDES
Synthesis and Development of Industrial Processes: S. STOURNAS

Rural Engineering and Surveying:

Topography: K. PAPAZISIS
Geography and Regional Planning: K. KOUTSOPOULOS
Rural Technology Development: E. MARKETOS

Mining and Metallurgical Engineering:

Geological Sciences: J. KOUMADAKIS
Mining Engineering: A. ECONOMOU
Metallurgy and Materials Technology: E. ZEVGOLIS

General Studies:

Physics: P. PISSIS
Mathematics: K. KYRIAKIS
Applied Mechanics: G. SPATHIS
Humanities, Social Science and Law: V. NIKOLAIDOU

LABORATORIES

Civil Engineering:

Sanitary Engineering
Harbour Works
Applied Hydraulics
Hydrology and Water Resources
Foundation Engineering
Soil Mechanics
Railway Engineering and Transport
Highway Engineering
Traffic Engineering
Steel Structures
Reinforced Concrete
Structural Analysis and Seismic Research
Earthquake Engineering
Earthquake Technology and Engineering Seismology
General and Specialized Mechanical Engineering

Mechanical Engineering:

Refrigeration and Air Conditioning
Steam Boilers and Thermal Plants
Applied Thermodynamics
Internal Combustion Engines
Manufacturing Technology
Nuclear Technology
Mechanical Design and Dynamics
Hydraulic Turbomachines
Aerodynamics
Thermal Turbomachines
Metrology
Organization
Operational Research
Production Management

Electrical and Computing Engineering:

Special Electrotechnology
Wireless and Long-Distance Communications
Electrotechnology
Electrical Machines
Electronics
Electrical Energy Systems
High-Voltage and Electrical Measurements
Digital Systems and Computers
Telecommunications
General Electrotechnology
Intelligent Robotics and Control
Control Systems

Architecture:

Sound Technology (Acoustics)
Building Materials
Paintings
Structural Mechanics (Engineering)
Sculpture
Model Making
Photographic
Drawing Methodology and Space Organization
Descriptive and Projective Geometry
Architecture of the Interior Space
Architectural Morphology and Rythmology
Architectural Design
History of Art
Special Building Design
History of Architectural Research
Building Design
Building Construction
Town Planning Research
Regional Planning and Housing Development
Services and Architectural Environment
Town Planning Design
Archive Documentation Processing
Computer-Simulated Architectural Design, and Town and Regional Planning
Building Construction and Industrial Design
Urban Environment
Geographic Information Systems in Town and Regional Planning

Chemical Engineering:

General Chemistry
Analytical Chemistry
Inorganic Chemical Technology
Industrial and Energy Economics
Thermodynamics and Transport Phenomena
Special Chemical Technology
Polymer Technology
Chemical Processes Engineering
Organic Chemistry
Organic Chemical Technology
Fuels and Lubricants Technology
Physical Chemistry
Food Chemistry and Technology
Process Design and Analysis

Rural Engineering and Surveying:

Reclamation Works and Water Resources Management
Cartography
General Geodesy
Structural Mechanics and Engineering Constructions
Photogrammetry
Remote Sensing
Dionysos Satellite Observatory
Transport Engineering

Mining and Metallurgical Engineering:

Mining Research and Mineral Exploitation
Mineralogy, Petrology, Economic Geology
Mining Technology
Metallurgy
Physical Metallurgy
Mineral Processing
Applied Geophysics
Geology and Applied Geology

Naval Architecture and Marine Engineering:

Ship and Marine Hydrodynamics
Shipbuilding Technology
Marine Engineering
Ship Design

General Studies:

Laboratory for Testing Materials
Applied Mechanics and Photoelasticity
Physics

UNIVERSITY OF THE AEGEAN

Xarilaou Trikoupi kai Faonos, 81100 Mytilene

Telephone: (251) 36001
Fax: (251) 36199

Founded 1984

Rector: THEMISTOCLES D. LEKKAS
Librarian: ELLI VLACHOU

Library of 50,000 vols
Number of teachers: 146
Number of students: 2,495

Departments: Environmental Studies, Social Anthropology, Geography (Mytilene); Business Administration (Chios); Mathematics (Samos); Primary Education, Secondary Education (Rhodes).

TECHNICAL UNIVERSITY OF CRETE

Agiou Markou St, 731 32 Chania

Telephone: (821) 28404
Fax: (821) 28418
E-mail: intoffice@dialup.isc.tuc.g

Founded 1977, first student intake 1984
State control
Academic year: September to January, February to June

President: Prof. DIMITRIOS SOTIROPOULOS
Vice-Presidents: Assoc. Prof. CHRISTOS SKIADAS (Personnel and Academics), Prof. EMM. CHRISTODOULOU (Finance and Planning)
Registrar: EMM. VANDOULAKIS
Librarian: ANTHI KATSIRIKOU

Library of 25,000 vols
Number of teachers: 51 full-time, 35 part-time
Number of students: 1,031

HEADS OF DEPARTMENT

Production Engineering: Assoc. Prof. VASSILIOS MOUSTAKIS
Mineral Resources Engineering: Assoc. Prof. D. MONOPOLIS
Electronic and Computer Engineering: Prof. NIKOLAOS VOULGARIS
Sciences: Prof. YANNIS SARIDAKIS

DIRECTORS OF LABORATORIES

CAD: Assoc. Prof. N. BILALIS
Environmental Technology: Assoc. Prof. E. DIAMANTOPOULOS
Dynamical Systems and Simulation: Asst Prof. M. PAPAGEORGIOU
Decision Support Systems: Prof. Y. SISKOS
Robotics: Asst. Prof. A. POULIEZOS
CAM: Prof. Y. PHILLIS
Inorganic and Organic Geochemistry and Organic Petrography: Prof. A. FOSCOLOS
Petrology and Economic Geology: Prof. TH MARKOPOULOS
Reservoir Engineering: Assoc. Prof. N. VAROTSIS
Applied Geology: Assoc. Prof. D. MONOPOLIS
Automation: Prof. EMM. CHRISTODOULOU
Telecommunications: Prof. ST. CHRISTODOULAKIS
Electronics: Prof. N. VOULGARIS
Software Engineering: Prof. ST. CHRISTODOULAKIS
Distributed Information Systems and Applications: Prof. ST. CHRISTODOULAKIS
Institute of Materials Structure and Laser Physics: Prof. K. SIOMOS
Applied Mechanics: Prof. D. SOTIROPOULOS
Analytical and Environmental Chemistry: Prof. A. KATSANOS
Applied Mathematics: Prof. G. AVDELAS

ATTACHED INSTITUTES

Multimedia Systems Institute of Crete: Dir Prof. S. CHRISTODOULAKIS.

Institute of Telecommunications Systems: Dir Prof. ST. CHRISTODOULAKIS.

UNIVERSITY OF CRETE

741 00 Rethymnon, Crete

Telephone: (831) 77900
Fax: (831) 77909
E-mail rectsecr@cc.uch.gr

Founded 1973
State control
Language of instruction: Greek
Academic year: September to June

Rector: Prof. CHRISTINA SPYRAKI
Vice-Rectors: Prof. IOANNIS PYRGIOTAKIS, Prof. CHRISTOS NIKOLAOU
Administrative Officer: YANNIS TZIKAS
Librarian: MICHALIS TZEKAKIS

Library of 400,000 vols
Number of teachers: 361
Number of students: 6,300

Publications: *Ariadne* (faculty of letters), *Triton* (newsletter), *Mandatoforos* (Modern Greek studies).

AFFILIATED INSTITUTION

Foundation for Research and Technology – Hellas: POB 1527, 711 10 Heraklion; tel. (813) 91500; fax (813) 91555; f. 1983; 254 research and teaching staff; 374 graduate students; Chair. Prof. E. N. ECONOMOU; constituent institutes:

Institute of Molecular Biology and Biotechnology: Dir Prof. G. THIREOS.

Institute of Electronic Structure and Lasers: Dir Prof. C. FOTAKIS.

Institute of Computer Science: Dir Prof. ST. ORPHANOUDAKIS.

Institute of Mediterranean Studies: Dir Prof. A. KALPAXIS.

Institute of Applied and Computational Mathematics: Dir Prof. J. PAPADAKIS.

Institute of Chemical Engineering and High Temperature Chemical Processes: Dir Prof. G. PAPATHEODOROU.

Chemical Process Engineering Research Institute: Dir Prof. I. VASALOS.

UNIVERSITY OF IOANNINA

University Campus, 451 10 Ioannina

Telephone: (651) 42915
Telex: 0322160
Fax: (651) 44112
E-mail: intlrel@cc.uoi.gr

Founded 1964 as a dept of the Aristotle University of Thessaloniki; established as an independent university 1970
State control
Language of instruction: Greek
Academic year: September to January, February to June

Rector: Prof. CH. MASSALAS
Vice-Rectors: Prof. D. GLAROS, Prof. G. DIMOU
Registrar: L.-N. PAPALOUKAS
Librarian: G. ZAHOS

Library of over 310,000 vols
Number of teachers: 384
Number of students: 9,063

Publications: *Epetiris 'Dodoni I'* (History and Archaeology, 1 a year), *Eperitis 'Dodoni II'* (Philology, 1 a year), *Eperitis 'Dodoni III'* (Philosophy, Education and Psychology, 1 a year).

DEANS

School of Philosophy: Prof. G. PLOUMIDIS
School of Natural Sciences and Computer Science: Assoc. Prof. S. GALANIS
School of Medicine: Prof. I. HATZIS
School of Educational Sciences: Prof. G. DIMOU

PROFESSORS

School of Philosophy:

APOSTOLOPOULOU, G., History, Interpretation and Practice of Philosophy
CHRYSOS, E., Byzantine History
GOTOVOS, A., Pedagogics
HADJIDAKI-BACHARA, T., Byzantine Archaeology
ILINSKAJA-ALEXANDROPOULOU, S., Modern Greek Literature
KAPSOMENOS, E., Modern Greek Literature and Literary Theory
KARPOZILOS, A.-D., Medieval Greek Literature
KOLIAS, T., Ancient and Medieval Greek Literature
KONDORINI, B., History and Archaeology
KONSTANDINIDIS, C., Ancient and Medieval Greek Literature
KORDOSIS, M., Ancient and Medieval Greek Literature
MALAKASIS, I., Modern Greek History
MARAGOU, E., Classical Archaeology
MAVROYIORGOS, Y., Pedagogic Educational Policy
NIKOLAIDOU, E., History of Modern Greece
NOUTSOS, CH., History of Education
NOUTSOS, P., Philosophy
PALIOURAS, A., Byzantine Archaeology
PAPACONSTANDINOU, P., Pedagogics
PAPADIMITRIOU, E., Philosophy
PAPADOPOULOS, A., Prehistoric Archaeology
PAPAGEORGIOU, G., Modern History
PAPAPOSTOLOU, J., Classical Archaeology
PLOUMIDIS, G., Venetian History and Historical Geography
PSIMMENOS, N., Modern Greek Philosophy
SAVVANTIDIS, G., Latin Literature
TSANGALAS, K., Folklore
TSIRPANLIS, Z., Medieval and Modern European History
VELOUDIS, G., Modern Greek and Comparative Literature

School of Natural Sciences and Computer Science:

AKRIVIS, G., Computer Science
ALEXANDROPOULOS, N., Physics of Compressed Matter
ALISSANDRAKIS, C., Physics of the Sun and Space
ASSIMAKOPOULOS, P., Nuclear Physics and Radio ecology
BATAKIS, N., Physics
BOLIS, TH., Combinatorial Group Theory
DRAINAS, C., Chemistry
GRAMMATIKOPOULOS, M., Differential Equations
HADJILIADIS, N., Inorganic and General Chemistry
HASANIS, T., Differential Geometry
KAMARATOS, E., Physical Chemistry
KARAKOSTAS, G., Mathematical Analysis and Applications
KARAYANNIS, M., Analytical Chemistry
KATSARAS, A., Functional Analysis
KATSOULIS, V., Meteorology and Climatology
KONDOMINAS, M., Chemistry
KOSMAS, M., Chemistry
MARMARIDIS, N., Algebra
MASSALAS, CH., Continuum Physics and Mechanics
PAPAGEORGOPOULOS, C., Solid State Physics and Surface Science
PAPAIOANNOU, P., Statistical Theory and Applications
PAPAKONSTANTOPOULOS, D., Physics
PHILOS, C., Differential Equations
SAKARELLOS, C., Organic Peptide Chemistry
SDOUKOS, A., Industrial Chemistry
SFIKAS, Y. G., Differential Equations
STAVROULAKIS, I., Differential Equations
TAMVAKIS, K., Elementary Particle Theory and Cosmology
TRIANTIS, F., High-Energy Physics and Related Technological Applications
TSANGARIS, J., Inorganic and General Chemistry
VAGIONAKIS, C., Physics
VERGADOS, J., Theoretical Physics

School of Medicine:

AGNADI-GIRA, N. J., Pathological Anatomy
ANAGNOSTOPOULOS, K.
ANTONIADIS, G., Microbiology
GLAROS, D., Medical Physics
HATZIS, I., Dermatology
KAPPAS, A., Surgery
KONSTANTOPOULOS, S.
KOTOULAS, O., Anatomy and Histology
LIAKOS, A., Psychiatry
LOLIS, D., Obstetrics and Gynaecology
MARSELOS, M.-A., Medical Pharmacology
PAGOULATOS, G., General Biochemistry
PAPADOPOULOU-KOULOUMBI, Z., Paediatric Nephrology
PAVLIDIS, N., Oncology
PSILAS, C., Ophthalmology
SIAMOPOULOS, K.
SIDERIS, D., Cardiology
SKEVAS, A., Oto-rhino-laryngology
SOUCACOS, P., Orthopaedics
TSIANOS, E., Oncology
TSOLAS, O., Biological Chemistry

School of Educational Sciences:

BELLAS, T., Research Methodology
DIMOU, G., Pedagogics and Psychology of Learning Disabilities
KAPSALIS, G.
KARPOZILOU, M.
ZAHARIS, D., Evolutionary Psychology in Education

UNIVERSITY OF MACEDONIA

Egnatia 156, POB 1591, 540 06 Thessaloniki
Telephone: (31) 844-825
Telex: 410497
Fax: (31) 844-536

Founded 1957 as Graduate Industrial School of Thessaloniki
State control

Rector: Prof. MICHALIS HATZIPROUOPIOU
Vice-Rectors: Prof. ARISTOCLIS IGNATIADES, Assoc. Prof. GEORGE TSIOTRAS
Secretary-General: ATHANASIOS TSAPAKIDIS
Librarian: ANNA FRANKOU

Number of teachers: 110
Number of students: 8,000

HEADS OF DEPARTMENT

Department of Economics: Assoc. Prof. STELLA KARAYANNI
Department of Business Administration: Assoc. Prof. G. TSIOTRAS
Department of International and European Economic and Political Studies: Prof. E. THERMOS
Department of Accounting and Finance: Prof. A. IGNATIADES
Department of Applied Informatics: Prof. K. TSOUROS
Department of Educational and Social Policy: Prof. YANNIS TSEKOURAS
Department of Balkan, Slavic and Eastern Studies: Prof. YANNIS TSEKOURAS
Department of Music Science and Art: Prof. YANNIS TSEKOURAS

PROFESSORS

EFTHYMOGLOU, P., Microeconomics
HATZIPROKOPIOU, M., History of Economic Theory
IGNATIADES, A., Business Accounting
KATOS, A., Econometrics
LAZOS, B., Monetary Principles, European Monetary System
MARKIS, D., Contemporary Political Philosophy
NEGREPONTI-DELIVANI, M., Macro- and Microeconomics
PAPADIMITRIOU, I., Statistics and Data Analysis
PAPADOPOULOS, D., Business and Investment
PEKOS, G., Mathematics and Statistics
PIPEROPOULOS, G., Applied Psychology in Business
SKALIDIS, L., Commercial Law
THERMOS, E., Politics
TSEKOURAS, Y., Economic Development
TSOUROS, K., Computer Science
XIARHOS, S., Public Finance, Microeconomics
XOURIS, D., Business Administration

UNIVERSITY OF PATRAS

265 00 Patras
Telephone: (61) 997-608
Telex: 312447
Fax: (61) 991-711

Founded 1964
State control
Language of instruction: Greek
Academic year: September to June

Rector: Prof. STAMATIS N. ALAHIOTIS
Vice-Rectors: Prof. NICHOLAS ZOUMBAS (Academic Affairs and Personnel), Prof. KONSTANTINOS VAGENAS (Finance and Development)
Administrative Officer: SPILIOS PAPATHANASSOPOULOS

Number of teachers: 650
Number of students: 14,000

Publication: *Bulletin* (annually).

DEANS

School of Engineering: Prof. VASSILIOS MAKIOS
School of Health Sciences: Prof. APOSTOLOS VAGENAKIS
School of Natural Sciences: Prof. DIMITRIOS PHOTINOS
School of Social Sciences and Humanities: Prof. JOSEPH BOUZAKIS

PROFESSORS

School of Engineering:

Department of Chemical Engineering

DASSIOS, G.
DONDOS, A.
KOUTSOUKOS, P.
LADAS, S.
NIKOLOPOULOS, P.
LYBERATOS, G.
PAPAMANTELLOS, D. (Head)
PAPATHEODOROU, G.
PAVLOU, S.
PAYATAKES, A.
THEODOROU, T.
TSAHALIS, D.
TSAMOPOULOS, J.
VAGENAS, K.
VERYKIOS, X.
ZYBERATOS, G.

Department of Civil Engineering

ANAGNOSTOPOULOS, S.
ATMATZIDIS, D.
BESKOS, D.
DEMETRACOPOULOS, A.
FARDIS, M.
GRIGOROPOULOS, S.
HATZITHEODOROU, C. (Head)
IKONOMOU, A.
MASTROGIANIS, E.
PAPADEMETRIOU, A.
POLYDORIDES, N.

Department of Computer Engineering and Informatics

CHRISTODOULAKIS, D. (Head)
GALLOPOULOS, E.
KIROUSSIS, E.
MOUSTAKIDES, G.
PAPATHEODOROU, TH.
SPIRAKIS, P.
TSAKALIDIS, A.

Department of Electrical Engineering

BITSIOURIS, G.
GEORGOPOULOS, CH.
GIANNAKOPOULOS, G.
GOUTIS, C.
GRAMMATICOS, A.
GROUMPOS, P.
KING, R.
KOKKINAKIS, G.
MAKIOS, V.
NICOLIS, J.
PAPADOPOULOS, G.
SAFACAS, A. (Head)
TSANAKAS, D.
VOVOS, N.

Department of Engineering Science

HATZIKONSTANTINOU, P. (Head)
IOAKIMIDIS, N.
KOUTROUVELIS, I.
LIANOS, P.
MARKELLOS, V.
POLITIS, C.

Department of Mechanical Engineering

CHRYSSOLOURIS, G.
DRAKATOS, P.
KERMANIDIS, TH. (Head)
MASSOUROS, G.
MISSIRLIS, Y.
PAIPETIS, S.
PAPAILIOU, D.
PAPAIOANNOU, S.
PAPANICOLAOU, G.
PAPANIKAS, D.
SISSOURAS, A.

School of Health Sciences:

Faculty of Medicine

ANDROULAKIS, J.
BARBALIAS, G.
BASSIARIS, H. (Head)
BERATI, S.
BERATIS, N.
BONIKOS, D.
DIMITRAKOPOULOS, G.
DIMOPOULOS, J.
KALLINIKOS-MANIATIS, A.
KOLIOPOULOS, I.
KONDAKIS, X.
KOSTOPOULOS, G.
KOUVELAS, E.
LAMBIRIS, E.
MANIATIS, G.
MANOLIS, A.
MARAGOUDAKIS, M.
PAPADAKIS, N.
PAPAPETROPOULOS, TH.
PAPAPETROPOULOU, M.
TSAMBAOS, D.
TZINGOUNIS, V.
VAGENAKIS, A.
VARAKIS, J.
VLACHOGIANNIS, J.
ZOUMBOS, N.

Faculty of Pharmacy

CORDOPATIS, P.
ITHAKISSIOS, D. (Head)
PAPAIOANNOU, ST.

School of Natural Sciences:

Department of Biology

ALAHIOTIS, ST.
CHRISTODOULOU, C.
DIMITRIADIS, G.
GEORGIADIS, TH. (Head)
KAMARI, G.
LYKAKIS, J.
MANETAS, I.
MARMARAS, V.
VALKANA, TH.
YANNOPOULOS, G.
ZAGRIS, N.

Department of Chemistry

ANTONOPOULOS, CHR.
BARLOS, K.
IOANNOU, P.
KALFOGLOU, N.
KARAISKAKIS, G.
KLOURAS, N.

KOUTINAS, A.
LYCOURGHIOTIS, A.
MAROULIS, G. (Assoc. Prof., Head)
MATSOUKAS, J.
MIKROYIANNIDIS, J.
PAPAIOANNOU, D.
POULOS, C.
STAVROPOULOS, G.
TSIGANOS, C.
VOLIOTIS, S.

Department of Geology

CONTOPOULOS, N.
DOUTSOS, TH.
FERENTINOS, G.
FRYDAS, D.
KALLERGIS, G.
KATAGAS, C.
KOTOPOULI, C. (Assoc. Prof., Head)
KOUKIS, G.
VARNAVAS, S.

Department of Mathematics

BOTSARIS, CH.
BOUNTIS, A.
COTSIOLIS, A.
GOUDAS, C.
IPHANTIS, E.
ILIADIS, S.
IORDANIDIS, K.
KAFOUSSIAS, N.
METAKIDES, G.
PAPANTONIOU, V.
PHILIPPOU, A.
PINTELAS, P.
SIAFARIKAS, P.
STABAKIS, J.
STRATIGOPOULOS, D.
TSERPES, N.
TSOUBELIS, D.
ZAGOURAS, CH. (Head)

Department of Physics

ANTONACOPOULOS, G.
BAKAS, I.
DELIYANNIS, TH.
GEORGALAS, CHR.
GEORGES, A.
GOUDIS, CHR.
KATSIARIS, G.
MANTAS, G.
PAPATHANASOPOULOS, K.
PHOTINOS, D.
PISANIAS, M. (Assoc. Prof., Head)
PRIFTIS, D.
YIANOULIS, P.
ZDETSIS, A.

School of Social Sciences and Humanities:

Department of Elementary Education:

BOUZAKIS, J.
KOSMOPOULOS, A. (Head)
PORPODAS, C.

Department of Pre-School Education:

BAYONAS, A.
KALLERGIS, I.
KOMILIS, E.
PAPAMICHAEL, Y.
PATELLI, I. (Assoc. Prof., Head)
PATINIOTIS, N.

Department of Economics:

DEMIANOS, D.
DEMOUSSIS, M.
SYPSAS, P. (Assoc. Prof., Head)
VERNADAKIS, N.

Department of Theatre Studies

HAAS, D. (Assoc. Prof., Head)
STEFANOPOULOS, T.

Department of Literature

ZOUMBOS, N. (Head)

Colleges of University Standing

Anotati Scholi Kalon Technon (Athens School of Fine Art): Odos Patission 42, 106 82 Athens; tel. 3816930; fax 3816926; f. 1837; comprises sections for painting, sculpture, printmaking, theoretical studies; 30 teachers, 570 students; library of 22,000 vols; brs in Delphi, Hydra, Mykonos, Rhodes, Lesbos and Rethymnon; Rector YANNIS PAPADAKIS.

DIRECTORS OF SECTIONS

Painting: Prof. CHR. BOTSOGLOU
Sculpture: Prof. G. LAPPAS
Printmaking: Prof. G. MILIOS
Theoretical Studies: Prof. M. LAMBRAKI

Deree College of the American College of Greece: 6 Gravias St, Aghia Paraskevi, 153 42 Athens; tel. (1) 600-9800; fax (1) 600-9811; e-mail acg@hol.gr; f. 1875; undergraduate division of the American College of Greece; BA courses in dance, economics, English, history, history of art, music, philosophy, psychology, sociology, BSc course in business administration; incl. Junior College division: 650 teachers, 6,450 students; library of 100,000 vols; Pres. JOHN S. BAILEY; publ. *Catalogue* (annually).

Geoponiko Panepistimio Athinon (Athens Agricultural University): Iera Odos 75, 118 55 Athens; tel. 5294802; fax 3460885; f. 1920; Rector Prof. S. KYRITSIS; Sec.-Gen. (vacant).

Ikonomiko Panepistimio Athinon (Athens University of Economics and Business): Odos Patission 76, 104 34 Athens; tel. (1) 823-7361; telex 225363; fax (1) 822-8419; f. 1920; 118 professors, 11,800 students; economics, business administration, statistics, international and European economic studies, management science and marketing, computer science; library of 70,000 vols, 850 periodicals; Rector Prof. ANDREAS KINTIS; Sec.-Gen. S. BENOS; Librarian G. THEOFANOPOULOU.

Panepistimo Pireos (University of Piraeus): 80 Karaoli and Dimitriou St, 185 34 Piraeus; tel. 4120751; fax (1) 4179064; f. 1938, since 1958 has university status; economics, business administration, statistical and actuarial sciences, banking and financial management, maritime studies, computer studies, industrial and operation management depts; 90 teachers; 11,400 students; library of 27,000 vols, 200 periodicals; Rector T. GAMALETSOS; Sec. A. GOTSIS; publ. *Spoudai* (quarterly).

'Panteios' University of Social and Political Sciences: Leoforos A. Syngrou 136, 176 71 Athens; tel. 9220100; telex 224296; fax 9223690; f. 1930; 7,500 students; Rector D. CONSTAS; Gen. Sec. M. VARELLA.

Colleges

ARCHAEOLOGY, GREEK STUDIES

American School of Classical Studies at Athens: Odos Souidias 54, 106 76 Athens; f. 1881; research institute and postgraduate school for students of classical and post-classical literature, history and archaeology; controlled by a committee representing 150 American and Canadian universities; Blegen library of 90,000 vols; Gennadius library: see Libraries; Dir J. D. MUHLY; publ. *Hesperia*.

British School at Athens: Odos Souedias 52, 106 76 Athens; tel. (1) 7210974; fax (1) 723-65-60; and Senate House, Malet St, London, WC1E 7HU; tel. (171) 862-8732; fax (171) 862-8733; f. 1886; archaeology and Hellenic studies; Fitch Laboratory for research, analysis, etc.; library of over 60,000 vols (ancient, medieval and post-medieval Greek studies and archaeology of all periods) including the Finlay Library (Greek travel and modern Greek studies); Chair. G. CADOGAN; Dir D. J. BLACKMAN; London Sec. S. E. WAYWELL.

Deutsches Archäologisches Institut, Abteilung Athen (German Archaeological Institute): Odos Fidiou 1, 106 78 Athens; tel. 3820270; fax 3814762; f. 1874; library of 66,000 vols; Dirs Prof. Dr K. FITTSCHEN, Dr-Ing. H. KIENAST; publ. *Athenische Mitteilungen* (annually), *Beihefte*.

Ecole Française d'Athènes (French Archaeological School): Odos Didotou 6, 106 80 Athens; tel. (1) 3612518; fax (1) 3632101; f. 1846; excavations, historical and archaeological publications; 15 mems and architects; library of *c.* 80,000 vols; Dir R. ETIENNE; Sec.-Gen. J.-M. SAULNIER; publs *Bulletin de correspondance hellénique* (annually; f. 1877), *Bibliothèque des Ecoles françaises d'Athènes et de Rome, Fouilles de Delphes, Exploration archéologique de Délos, Etudes thasiennes, Etudes crétoises, Travaux et mémoires, Etudes péloponnésiennes, Etudes chypriotes, Recherches franco-helléniques, Etudes épigraphiques.*

Italian School of Archaeology: 14 Parthenonos, 117 42 Athens; tel. (1) 9239163; fax (1) 9224014; f. 1909; post-graduate studies in archaeology, epigraphy and antiquities, ancient architecture, research and excavations; library of 41,000 vols; Dir Prof. ANTONINO DI VITA; Library Dir Dr ALBERTO G. BENVENUTI; publ. *Annuario della Scuola Archeologica di Atene e delle Missioni Italiane in Oriente* (annually).

Svenska Institutet i Athen (Swedish Institute at Athens): 9 Mitseon St, 117 42 Athens; tel. (1) 92-32-102; fax (1) 92-20-925; e-mail sia@otenet.gr; f. 1948; 15 mems; library of 35,000 vols (housed at the Nordic Library, Kavalotti 7, 117 42 Athens); research into Greek antiquity and archaeology, and cultural exchange between Sweden and Greece; Dir Dr BERIT WELLS; publs *Skrifter utgivna av Svenska Institutet i Athen (Acta Instituti Atheniensis Regni Sueciae)*, including *Opuscula Atheniensia*.

ARTS, DRAMA, MUSIC

Dramatiki Scholi (Drama School): National Theatre, Odos Menandrou 65, Athens; f. 1924; open to actors who desire to improve their art and to young people who desire to take up the stage as a career. The staff comprises the Director, 11 professors, and 2 teachers.

Kratiko Odeio Thessaloniki (State Conservatory of Music): Leondos Sofou Str. 16, 546 25 Thessaloniki; tel. (31) 510551; fax (31) 522158;

f. 1914; instrumental, vocal and theoretical studies; 60 teachers, 630 students; library of c.17,000 vols, scores, records, slides, compact discs, video cassettes, including collection in Braille; exhibition of musical instruments; Chair. Prof. P. I. RENTZEPERIS.Odeion Athenon (Odeon of Athens): Odos Rigillis and Vassileos Georgiou 17–19, Athens; f. 1871; comprises a music section, a drama section, a section for military music, and a section for Byzantine Church music; 53 professors, 40 teachers, 1,200 students; Dir A. GAROUFALIS.

Odeion Ethnikon (National Conservatory): Odos Maxer 18, Athens 10438; tel. 5233175; fax 5245291; f. 1926; sections for music and opera; 200 teachers, 5,000 students; Dirs HARA KALOMIRI, VYRON KOLASSIS, PERIKLIS KOUKOS; publ. *Deltio* (annually).

GRENADA

Learned Societies

HISTORY, GEOGRAPHY AND ARCHAEOLOGY

Grenada National Trust and Historical Society: Grenada National Museum, Young St, St George's; tel. 440-3725; f. 1967 to preserve the tangible evidence of the history and growth of the island for the people of Grenada, and to support the Grenada National Museum; 240 mems; Pres. PAUL FINLAY; Sec. JEAN PITT; publ. *Quarterly Newsletter.*

Libraries and Archives

St George's

Grenada Public Library: Carenage, St George's; tel. (809) 440-2506; f. 1853; 60,000 vols; special West Indian and National Archives of Grenada collections; reference, research and lecture facilities; links its activities with other educational agencies; attached to Ministry of Education; Dir RUTH JOHN; Librarian: S. L. SYLVESTER.

Marion Library: St George's University School of Medicine, True Blue, St George's; tel. 444-1467; fax 444-2884; f. 1979; 8,480 vols, 225 periodicals; Dir. GERALDINE GRAVES.

Museums and Art Galleries

St George's

Grenada National Museum: Young St, St George's; tel. 440-3725; f. 1976; history, technology, fauna and flora; Curator HUGH THOMAS; Man. JEAN PITT; publ. *Newsletter*.

Colleges

ST GEORGE'S UNIVERSITY SCHOOLS OF MEDICINE, ARTS AND SCIENCES AND GRADUATE STUDIES

University Centre, St George's

Telephone: (1-809) 444-4357
Fax: (1-809) 444-4823

Founded 1977

Language of instruction: English

Chancellor: CHARLES R. MODICA
Registrar: MARGARET LAMBERT
Librarian: GERALDINE GRAVES

Library: see Libraries

Number of teachers: 76 full-time, 700 part-time

Number of students: 2,000

Publications: *Newsletter, Catalogue, SGU Review, Alumni Quarterly, Chancellor's Report*.

DEANS

Clinical Studies: STEPHEN WEITZMAN
Basic Sciences: A. PENSICK
Dean of Students: C. V. RAO
Arts and Sciences: T. HOLLIS
Graduate Studies: T. HOLLIS

CHAIRMEN OF DEPARTMENTS

Anatomy: ROBERT JORDAN
Behavioural Sciences: Prof. DAVID BROWN
Biochemistry: H. CHADWELL
Histology: BRUCE LIPTON
Medicine: Prof. S. WEITZMAN
Microbiology: A. PENSICK
Nutrition: Prof. KEITH TAYLOR
Obstetrics and Gynaecology: Prof. P. BEAUGARD
Pathology: Prof. S. BHUSNURMATH
Paediatrics: Prof T. POTTER
Pharmacology: Prof. DIANA GAZIS
Physiology: Prof. A. RATNER
Psychiatry: Prof. PETER BOURNE
Surgery: Prof. G. LUTCHMAN

School of Agriculture: Mirabeau.

University of the West Indies School of Continuing Studies: Marryshow House, H. A. Blaize St, POB 439, St George's; tel. 440-2451; fax 440-4985; e-mail rtscsuwi@caribsurf.com; f. 1956; first-year university courses, general courses; library and resource collection of 10,000 vols; folk theatre, telecommunications distance teaching centre; 15 teachers, 150 students; Resident Tutor BEVERLEY A. STEELE.

GUATEMALA

Learned Societies

GENERAL

Academia de Ciencias Médicas, Físicas y Naturales de Guatemala (Academy of Medical, Physical and Natural Sciences): 13 Calle 1–25, Zona 1, Apdo Postal 569, Guatemala City; f. 1945; 125 mems; library of *c.* 4,000 vols; Pres. Dr ROBERTO LEMBKE; Sec. Ing. CARLOS ROLZ ASTURIAS; publs *Annals* (irregular), monographs, research summaries.

FINE AND PERFORMING ARTS

Sociedad Pro-Arte Musical (Musical Society): 12 Calle 2–09, Zona 3, Apdo 980, Guatemala City; f. 1945; 200 mems; Pres. LULÚ C. DE HERRARTE; Exec. Sec. DORA G. DE MENDIZÁBAL.

HISTORY, GEOGRAPHY AND ARCHAEOLOGY

Academia de Geografía e Historia de Guatemala (Geographical and Historical Academy of Guatemala): 3 Avda 8–35, Zona 1, Guatemala City; tel: 535141; f. 1923; 45 mems; library of 30,000 vols; Pres. JORGE LUJÁN MUÑOZ; Sec. ROLANDO RUBIO CIFUENTES; publs *Anales* (annually), *Biblioteca Goathemala, Viajeros, Publicaciones Especiales.*

LANGUAGE AND LITERATURE

Academia de la Lengua Maya Quiché (Academy of the Maya-Quiché Languages and Culture): 7 Calle 11–27, Zona 1, Quezaltenango; f. 1959; to study the philologies of and preserve the most important indigenous languages, especially the Quiché; 20 mems; Pres. Prof. ADRIÁN INES CHÁVEZ; Sec. Prof. VÍCTOR SALVADOR DE LEÓN TOLEDO; publ. *El Idioma Quiché y su Grafía.*

Academia Guatemalteca de la Lengua (Guatemala Academy of Letters): 12 Calle 6–40, Zona 9, Edificio Plazuela, Guatemala City; tel. 322824; f. 1887; corresp. of the Real Academia Española (Madrid); library of 5,000 vols; Dir Lic. DAVID VELA; Sec.-Gen. Lic. MARIO ALBERTO CARRERA.

NATURAL SCIENCES

Biological Sciences

Asociación Guatemalteca de Historia Natural (AGHN): Jardín Botánico, Universidad de San Carlos, Mariscal Cruz 1–56, Zona 10, Guatemala City; f. 1960; 86 mems; Pres. Dr MARIO DARY RIVERA.

TECHNOLOGY

Colegio de Ingenieros de Guatemala: 7 Avda 39–60, Zona 8, Guatemala City; f. 1947; 1,965 mems; Pres. Ing. CARLOS GERARDO BRAN GUZMÁN; publ. *Revista Ingeniería.*

Research Institutes

HISTORY, GEOGRAPHY AND ARCHAEOLOGY

Instituto de Antropología e Historia: 12 Avda 11-11, Zona 1, Guatemala City; tel. (2) 325571; fax (2) 325956; f. 1946; research on Middle-American history, Mayan archaeology, ethnology, philology, and Spanish Colonial history; supervises archaeological sites, monuments and museums; library of 25,000 vols; Dir-Gen. Dr JUAN ANTONIO VALDÉS; publs *Antropología e Historia de Guatemala* (annually), books and special publs.

Instituto Geográfico Militar: Avda Las Américas 5–76, Zona 13, Guatemala City; f. 1983; 411 mems; Dir Col Ing. MARCO ROLANDO ASTURIAS GARCIA-SALAS.

MEDICINE

Instituto de Nutrición de Centro América y Panamá (INCAP) (Institute of Nutrition of Central America and Panama): Carretera Roosevelt, Zona 11, 01901 Guatemala City; tel. 723762; telex 5696; fax 736529; f. 1949; member countries: Belize, Costa Rica, El Salvador, Guatemala, Honduras, Nicaragua, Panama; administered by Pan American Health Bureau Organization (PAHO)/World Health Organization (WHO); Food and Nutrition Security Program considers food systems, nutrition education and communication, and health and nutrition with an emphasis on mother and child; Master programme and short training courses; well documented library; Dir Dr HERNÁN DELGADO; publs scientific articles in Spanish and English, information bulletins, periodic compilations of scientific publications for member governments, annual reports, monographs, various other documents.

NATURAL SCIENCES

Biological Sciences

Centro de Estudios Conservacionistas: Avda La Reforma 0–63, zona 10, Guatemala City; tel. 3310904; fax 3347664; e-mail cecon@usac.edu.gt; f. 1981; studies of woodland flora and fauna and the sustainable management of natural resources; administration of nature reserves; Exec. Dir ISMAEL PONCIANO GÓMEZ.

Physical Sciences

Instituto Nacional de Sismología, Vulcanología, Meteorología e Hidrología (National Institute of Seismology, Vulcanology, Meteorology and Hydrology): Guatemala City; f. 1976; Dir CLAUDIO URRUTIA EVANS; publs *Anuario Hidrológico* (annually), *Boletín Meteorológico* (monthly), *Boletín Sismológico* (annually), *Datos Meteorológicos* (annually), *Reporte Meteorológico* (daily).

RELIGION, SOCIOLOGY AND ANTHROPOLOGY

Instituto Indigenista Nacional (National Institute of Indian Affairs) (Ministerio de Educación Pública): 6 Avda 1–22, Zona 1, Guatemala City; f. 1945; library of 3,500 vols; social research undertaken for the advice of the Government in economic conditions and the education of the Indians; affiliated to the Inter-American Indian Institute, Mexico; Dir EPAMINONDAS QUINTANA; publs *Guatemala Indígena* (quarterly), and special works.

TECHNOLOGY

Dirección General de Energía Nuclear: Diagonal 17 29–78, Zona 11, Apdo postal 1421, Guatemala City; tel. 760679; telex 5516; f. 1978; work concerns peaceful application of nuclear energy in medicine, industry, agriculture, etc.; 50 mems; library of 1,200 vols; Dir Ing. RAÚL EDUARDO PINEDA GONZÁLEZ.

Instituto Centroamericano de Investigación y Tecnología Industrial (ICAITI) (Central American Research Institute for Industry): Avda La Reforma 4–47, Zona 10, Apdo 1552, Guatemala City 01010-01901; tel. 331-0631; fax 331-7470; e-mail general@icaiti.org.gt; f. 1956; research on marketing, development of new industries and manufacturing techniques, establishment of Central American standards, information services to industry, and professional advice; library of 36,000 vols; Dir Lic. LUIS FIDEL CIFUENTES ECHEVERRIA (acting).

Libraries and Archives

Guatemala City

Archivo General de Centro América (National Archives): 4 Avda 7–16, Zona 1, Guatemala City; f. 1846; comprises two sections: La Colonia, with 8,427 files of 99,157 documents relating to Guatemala, Chiapas, El Salvador, Honduras, Nicaragua and Costa Rica; library contains ancient and modern historical volumes; periodicals pertaining to the colonial epoch and the period of independence; microfilm and photocopying service for researchers; Dir ARTURO VALDÉS OLIVA; publ. *Boletín.*

Biblioteca Central de la Universidad de San Carlos de Guatemala: Ciudad Universitaria, Zona 12, Guatemala City; tel. 767117; f. 1965; economics, humanities and multidisciplinary collections; thesis collection; newspaper and magazine collection; Guatemalan collection, Carlos Mérida collection; 205,000 vols; Dir Licda OFELIA AGUILAR (acting).

Biblioteca de la Organismo Judicial: 21 Calle 7-70, Zona 1, Guatemala City; f. 1881; 10,000 vols; Dir DORA CRISTINA GODOY LÓPEZ.

Biblioteca de la Tipografía Nacional (Library of the Government Printers): Guatemala City; f. 1892; the greater part of the contents of the Library was destroyed by the earthquakes of 1917 and 1918; modern works printed by them now form the collection.

Biblioteca del Banco de Guatemala: 7a Avda 22–01, Zona 1, Apdo 365, Guatemala City; tel. 80-9-09; f. 1946; 38,000 vols; Librarian JULIO C. MARISCAL.

Biblioteca del Congreso Nacional: 9 Avda 9–42, Guatemala City; f. 1823; 7,000 vols; Dir CARLOS H. GODOY Z.

Biblioteca Nacional de Guatemala: 5A Avda 7–26, Zona 1, Guatemala City; tel. 253-9071; fax 232-2443; e-mail vicast@biblionet.edu.gt; f. 1879; 200,000 vols; Dir Lic. VICTOR CASTILLO LÓPEZ.

Biblioteca y Sala de Lectura de la Sociedad El Porvenir de los Obreros (Library and Reading Room of the Workmen's Benefit Society): Edif. Social, 24 Avda Sur 13, Guatemala City; f. 1896; 3,018 vols; Dir RICARDO DOMÍNGUEZ P.

Quezaltenango

Biblioteca Pública de Quezaltenango: a/c Casa Cultura Occidente 7a, Calle 11–35, Zona

1, Quezaltenango; reopened 1958; 25,000 vols; Dir JULIO CÉSAR ALVAREZ.

Museums and Art Galleries

Antigua Guatemala

Museo Colonial: 5a Calle O. 5, Antigua Guatemala; f. 1936; housed in the old San Carlos University building; period furniture, paintings, sculpture; Dir-Librarian RAFAEL DE LA HOZ.

Museo del Libro Antiguo: Portal Municipal, Plaza Mayor de Antigua, Antigua Guatemala; f. 1956; controlled by the Instituto de Antropología e Historia; books, documents relating to the history of Guatemala; Sec.-Librarian MANUEL REYES.

Museo de Santiago: Portal Municipal, Plaza Mayor de Antigua, Antigua Guatemala; f. 1956; arms, furniture, Spanish colonial art; Sec.-Librarian JOSÉ F. MÉNDEZ.

Chichicastenango

Museo Regional de Chichicastenango: Plaza Central, Chichicastenango; f. 1950; articles of the Maya-Quiché culture; Dir RAÚL PÉREZ MALDONADO.

Guatemala City

Museo Nacional de Arqueología y Etnología de Guatemala (Archaeological and Ethnographical Museum): Edif. No. 5, La Aurora, Zona 13, Guatemala City; f. 1948; collection of some 3,000 archaeological pieces, mainly Mayan art, and 1,000 ethnological exhibits, all from Guatemala; Dir Licda DORA GUERRA DE GONZÁLEZ; publ. *Revista* (2 a year).

Museo Nacional de Arte Moderno: Edif. No. 6, Finca La Aurora, Zona 13, Guatemala City; f. 1975; paintings, sculpture, engravings, drawings, etc.; Dir J. OSCAR BARRIENTOS.

Museo Nacional de Artes e Industrias Populares: 10 Avda 11–72, Zona 1, Guatemala City; f. 1959; collections of metal, ceramic, textile and wooden objects belonging to indigenous races, also costumes; Dir RICARDO TOLEDO PALOMO.

Museo Nacional de Historia (National Museum of History): 11 Calle 6–33, Zona 1, Guatemala City; tel. 29013; f. 1975; Dir ITALO MORALES HIDALGO.

Museo Nacional de Historia Natural 'Jorge A. Ibarra': 6A Calle 7–30, Zona 13, Apdo 987, Guatemala City; f. 1950; collection of geological, botanical and zoological specimens; library of 2,600 vols; Dir and Founder JORGE A. IBARRA.

Universities

UNIVERSIDAD DE SAN CARLOS DE GUATEMALA

Ciudad Universitaria, Zona 12, 01012 Guatemala

Telephone: 760790
Fax: 767221

Founded 1676 by King Carlos II, established in its present form 1927, autonomous 1944.
Private control
Language of instruction: Spanish
Academic year: January to October

Chancellor: Lic. GONZALO MENÉNDEZ PARK
Rector: Dr JUAN ALFONSO FUENTES SORIA
Director-General of Administration: Lic. MIGUEL ORLANDO GARZA SAGASTUME
Registrar: Lic. EDGAR ABDIEL GRAJEDA ORANTES
Librarian: Licda MERCEDES DE BEECK

Library: see Libraries
Number of teachers: 2,545
Number of students: 70,431 undergraduate, 768 postgraduate

Publications: *Revista de la Universidad de San Carlos de Guatemala* (quarterly), *Universidad* (monthly), *USAC al Día* (fortnightly).

DEANS

Faculty of Law and Social Sciences: Lic. JUAN FRANCISCO FLORES JUÁREZ
Faculty of Medicine: Dr JAFETH ERNESTO CABRERA FRANCO
Faculty of Engineering: Ing. JORGE MARIO MORALES GONZÁLEZ
Faculty of Dentistry: Dr NORMAN AQUINO ESTEBAN
Faculty of Chemistry and Pharmacy: Licda CLEMENCIA DEL PILAR GÁLVEZ PALACIOS DE AVILA
Faculty of Economics: Lic. GILBERTO BATRES PAZ
Faculty of Humanities: Lic. ELEÁZAR AUGUSTO MONROY MEJÍA
Faculty of Veterinary Medicine and Zoology: Dr JUAN PABLO MORATAYA CUEVAS
Faculty of Agriculture: Ing. EFRAÍN MEDINA GUERRA
Faculty of Architecture: Arq. FRANCISCO CHAVARRÍA SMEATON

DIRECTORS

School of Political Science: Lic. EDGAR ROSENDO AMADO SÁENZ
School of Psychology: Lic. WALTER RENÉ SOTO REYES
School of History: Lic. EDELIBERTO EZEQUIEL CIFUENTES MEDINA
School of Social Work: Lic. CÉSAR AUGUSTO ESTRADA OVALLE
School of Communications: Lic. JESÚS MARÍA ALVARADO MENDIZÁBAL

UNIVERSIDAD DEL VALLE DE GUATEMALA

Apdo Postal No. 82, 01901 Guatemala

Telephone: (2) 364-0336
Fax: (2) 364-0052

Founded 1966
Language of instruction: Spanish
Private control
Academic year: February to November

Rector: Ing. HÉCTOR A. CENTENO
Vice-Rector: Dr JORGE R. ANTILLÓN-MATTA
Secretary: Ing. HUGO ROMEO MASAYA
Librarian: Dra MARÍA EMILIA LÓPEZ

Library of 68,000 vols, 130 current periodicals
Number of teachers: 250
Number of students: 2,000

DEANS

School of Science and Humanities: Dr RAÚL GONZÁLES DE PAZ
School of Social Sciences: Dr NELSON AMARO
School of Education: JACQUELINE DE DE LEÓN
Research Institute: Ing. CARLOS ROLZ ASTURIAS
University College: Ing. CÉSAR FERNÁNDEZ FERNÁNDEZ

UNIVERSIDAD FRANCISCO MARROQUIN

6 Calle Final, Zona 10, Guatemala City

Telephone: 334-6886
Fax: 334-6896
E-mail: info@ufm.edu.gt

Founded 1971
Language of instruction: Spanish
Private control
Academic year: January to May, July to November

Rector: Lic. FERNANDO MONTERROSO
Secretary: Ing. GIANCARLO IBÁRGÜEN
Librarian: Licda VICTORIA DE GÓMEZ

Library of 83,000 vols
Number of teachers: 750
Number of students: 16,858

DEANS

School of Law: Dr EDUARDO MAYORA A.
School of Architecture: Arq. ERNESTO PORRAS
School of Economics: Lic. JOSÉ RAÚL GONZÁLES M.
School of Medicine: Dr RODOLFO HERRERA-LLERANDI
School of Dentistry: Dr RAMIRO ALFARO
School of Systems Engineering, Data Processing and Computer Science: Dr EDUARDO SUGER
School of Theology: F. Dr FELIX SERRANO
School of Public Accounting and Auditing: Lic. HUGO ARÉVALO
Graduate School of Economics and Business Administration: Eng. RICARDO ALVARADO

DIRECTORS

Graduate School of Social Science: Dr ARMANDO DE LA TORRE
Department of Political Studies: Licda MARIA EUGENIA DE MASSIS
Department of Philosophy: Lic. MARIO RAFAEL OLMOS
Departments of Education and Art History: Lic. ARTURO HIGUEROS
Department of Psychology: Dr LUIS A. RECINOS
Department of Art: GERALDINA BACA
Departments of Communications and Education: Dr FELIX SERRANO
Department of Religious Studies: F. Dr. EDUARDO AGUIRRE
Institute of Distance Education (IDEA): Dr EDUARDO SUGER

UNIVERSIDAD MARIANO GÁLVEZ DE GUATEMALA

Apdo Postal 1811, Guatemala

Telephone: 53-42-17

Founded 1966
Language of instruction: Spanish
Private control
Academic year: February to November

Rector: Lic. ALVARO R. TORRES MOSS
Vice-Rectors: Lic. HUGO C. MORALES Y MORALES, Dr ALFREDO SAN JOSÉ
Secretary: Licda RUBY SANTIZO DE HERNÁNDEZ
Registrar: Lic. JOSÉ CLODOVEO TORRES MOSS
Librarian: GLORIA MARINA ARROYO

Library of 9,000 vols
Number of teachers: 400
Number of students: 10,000

Publication: *Boletín Mensual* (monthly).

DIRECTORS

Schools of Economics, Public Auditing and Accounting: Lic. OSCAR EUGENIO DUBÓN PALMA
School of Law: Lic. RODERICO SEGURA TRUJILLO
School of Civil Engineering: Ing. HANS JOAQUÍN LOTTMANN
School of Business Administration: Lic. CARLOS F. CÁRDENAS C.
School of Theology: Lic. ADALBERTO SANTIZO ROMÁN
School of Information Systems: Ing. JORGE A. ARIAS TOBAR
School of Education: Lic. VÍCTOR EGIDIO AGREDA GODÍNEZ
School of Humanities: Lic. VÍCTOR EGIDIO AGREDA GODÍNEZ
School of Architecture: Arq. VÍCTOR HUGO HERNÁNDEZ ORDÓÑEZ
School of Odontology: Dr ROLANDO DÍAZ LOZZA
School of Linguistics: Dr DAVID OLTROGGE

School of Languages: Dr NEVILLE STILES
School of Nursing: Licda DELIA LUCILA CHANG CHANG

UNIVERSIDAD RAFAEL LANDÍVAR

Vista Hermosa III, Zona 16, Apdo Postal 39 'C'

Telephone: 3692751
Fax: 3692756
E-mail: info@url.edu.gt

Founded 1961
Language of instruction: Spanish
Private control
Academic year: January to November

Rector: Lic. GABRIEL MEDRANO
General Vice-Rector: Licda. GUILLERMINA HERRERA
Academic Vice-Rector: Dr CHARLES J. BEIRNE
General Secretary: Lic. JORGE ARAUZ
Librarian: Licda REGINA ROMERO DE LA VEGA

Number of teachers: 854
Number of students: 16,882

Publications: *Estudios Sociales* (quarterly), *Cultura de Guatemala* (3 a year), *Vida Universitaria* (monthly), *Boletín de Lingüística* (6 a year), *Aprapalabra, Revista de Literatura.*

DEANS

Faculty of Architecture: Arq. DANIEL BORJA
Faculty of Agriculture and Environmental Sciences: Ing. JAIME CARRERA
Faculty of Economic Sciences: Lic. LUIS ALFREDO CORONADO
Faculty of Humanities: Lic. MANUEL SALAZAR
Faculty of Engineering: Ing. JORGE LAVARREDA
Faculty of Political and Social Sciences: Lic. GONZALO DE VILLA
Faculty of Theology: Dr MARIO MOLINA

ATTACHED INSTITUTES

Institute of Agriculture, Natural Resources and the Environment: Dir Ing. OSWALDO MACZ
Institute of Economic and Social Research: Dir Lic. MIGUEL VON HOEGEN
Institute of Linguistics: Dir Licda GUILLERMINA HERRERA
Institute of Musicology: Dir Dr DIETER LEHNHOFF
Institute of Psychology: Dir Dra BLANCA DELIA LÓPEZ
Institute of Science and Technology: Dir Ing. CARLOS VELA

Schools of Art and Music

Conservatorio Nacional de Música (National Academy of Music): 3a Avda 4-61, Zona 1, 01001 Guatemala City; tel. 28726; f. 1875; 40 teachers; 900 students; Dir LUIS A. LIMA Y LIMA.

Escuela Nacional de Artes Plásticas 'Rafael Rodríguez Padilla': 6 Avda 22-00, Zona 1, Guatemala City; tel. 534872; f. 1920; library of 2,500 vols; Dir ZIPACNÁ DE LEÓN; publ. *Revista de la Escuela Nacional de Artes Plásticas 'Rafael Rodríguez Padilla'.*

Escuela Taller de Artes Plásticas: Quezaltenango; f. 1963; drawing, painting; Dir RAFAEL MORA.

GUINEA

Learned Societies

LANGUAGE AND LITERATURE

PEN Centre de Guinée: BP 440, Conakry; Tel. 44-14-75; telex 627; f. 1989; 32 mems; library of 92 vols; Pres. ABDOULAYE FANYE TOURE; Sec.-Gen. ROGER GOTTO ZOMOU: publ. *Pour Mémoire*.

Research Institutes

GENERAL

Direction Nationale de la Recherche Scientifique et Technique: Conakry, BP 561; telex 22331; f. 1958; 60 mems; two libraries; Dir Dr FODE SOUMAH; publ. *Bulletin*.

AGRICULTURE, FISHERIES AND VETERINARY SCIENCE

Centre de Recherches Rizicoles: Kankan.

Institut de Recherche en Animalculture Pastoria: BP 146, Kindia; tel. 610811; f. 1923; former *Institut Pasteur,* nationalized 1965; research on infectious animal diseases; production of various vaccines; 18 staff; library of 362 vols; Dir Dr ALHASSANE DIALLO.

Institut de Recherches Fruitières: BP 36, Kindia; f. 1961; Dir C. KEITA.

Libraries and Archives

Conakry

Archives Nationales: BP 617, Conakry.

Bibliothèque Nationale: BP 561, Conakry; tel. 46-10-10; f. 1958; 40,000 vols, also special collection on slavery (about 500 books, pamphlets and MSS); 225 current periodicals; courses in librarianship; Dir LANSANA SYLLA.

Museums and Art Galleries

Conakry

Musée National: BP 561, Conakry; f. 1960; Curator MAMADOU SAMPIL.

Universities

UNIVERSITÉ GAMAL ABDEL NASSER DE CONAKRY

BP 1147, Conakry

Telephone: 46-46-89
Fax: 46-48-08

Founded 1962

Rector: Prof. MOHAMED LAMINE KABA
Vice-Rector (Academic): JEAN-MARIE TOURÉ
Vice-Rector (Research): Dr M. KODJOUGOU DIALLO
Secretary-General: GALEMA GUILAVOGUI
Director of Library: MANSA KANTÉ

Library of 4,000 vols
Number of teachers: 824
Number of students: 5,000

Publications: *Guinée Médicale, Horizons*.

DEANS

Faculty of Arts and Humanities: GOUDOUSSY DIALLO
Faculty of Law, Economics and Management: HAWA FOFANA
Faculty of Medicine and Pharmacy: (vacant)
Faculty of Science: Dr DJELIMANDJAN CONDÉ
Polytechnic Institute: Prof. NANAMOUDOU MAGASSOUBA (Director-General)

ATTACHED CENTRES

Computer Centre: Dir Dr BINKO MADY TOURÉ
Environment Study and Research Centre: Dir Prof. AHMED TIDIANE BOIRO

UNIVERSITÉ DE KANKAN

Ministère de l'Éducation Nationale, Kankan

Telephone: 20-93

Founded 1963; university status 1987

Rector: SÉKOU KONATE
Vice-Rector/Secretary-General: Dr SEYDOUBA CAMARA
Librarian: AÏSSATOU DIALLO

Library of 5,962 vols
Number of teachers: 72
Number of students: 1,048

Publication: *Journal* (monthly).

DEANS

Faculty of Social Sciences: ABOUBACAR CISSE
Faculty of Natural Sciences: Dr ALBERT BALAMOU

HEADS OF DEPARTMENTS

Economics: FODÉ TRAORE
Sociology: SALIM FOFANA
Linguistics: SÉKOU BERETE
Modern Literature: AHMADOU DIABY
Philosophy: BOCAR CAMARA
History: KARINKAN DOUMBOUYA
Geography: MANGA KEITA
Mathematics: GBALIPÉ SONOMOU
Physics: ABDOULAYE MOUCTAR DIALLO
Biology: KABINÉ OULARE

Colleges

Ecole Nationale de la Santé: Conakry; Dir M. KADER.

Ecole Nationale des Arts et Métiers: POB 240, Conakry; tel. and fax 46-25-62; f. 1962; industrial automation, electromechanical engineering, electronics, refrigeration and air-conditioning, diesel mechanics, industrial maintenance; Dir MAHMOUDOU BARRY.

Ecole Supérieure d'Administration: Conakry; f. 1964.

Institut Supérieur Agronomique et Vétérinaire 'Valéry Giscard d'Estaing' de Faranah: POB 131, Faranah; tel 81-02-15; fax 81-08-18; f. 1978; undertakes research; library of 4,000 vols, 814 periodicals, 7,351 reports; 164 teachers, 861 students; faculties of agriculture, agricultural engineering, stockbreeding and veterinary medicine, waters and forestry; Dir-Gen. Dr YAZORA SOROPOGUI.

GUYANA

Learned Societies

BIBLIOGRAPHY, LIBRARY SCIENCE AND MUSEOLOGY

Guyana Library Association: c/o National Library, 76–77 Main St, POB 10240, Georgetown; tel. 62690; f. 1968; 35 personal, 13 institutional mems; Pres. HETTY LONDON; Sec. JEAN HARRIPERSAUD; publ. *Bulletin*.

ECONOMICS, LAW AND POLITICS

Guyana Institute of International Affairs: POB 101176, Georgetown; tel. and fax (2) 77768; f. 1965; 100 mems; library of 5,000 vols; Pres. DONALD A. B. TROTMAN; publs *Annual Journal of International Affairs*, occasional papers.

EDUCATION

Adult Education Association of Guyana: POB 101111, Georgetown; tel. (2) 50757; f. 1957; a non-governmental organization which aims to provide opportunities for Guyanese to improve their skills, raise the level of awareness of their culture, acquire a critical understanding of major contemporary issues; programmes: academic, technical, scientific, creative art, commercial and professional development; Pres. ADOLA GRANDSOULT; Exec. Dir NEWTON L. PROFITT.

Research Institutes

AGRICULTURE, FISHERIES AND VETERINARY SCIENCE

Inter-American Institute for Cooperation on Agriculture (IICA): Antilles Zone, Lot 18, Brickdam, Stabroek, POB 10-1089, Georgetown; tel. (2) 68347; telex 2279; fax (2) 58358; f. 1974; Guyana branch of the specialized agency of the OAS for the agricultural sector; aims to stimulate and promote rural development as a means of achieving the general development of the population; library of 1,450 vols, 160 periodicals; Rep. JERRY LA GRA.

MEDICINE

Pan-American Health Organization, Guyana Office: Lot 8, Brickdam, Stabroek, POB 10969, Georgetown; tel. (2) 53000; fax (2) 66654; f. 1949; maternal and child health, environmental health, health services development, human resource development, communicable diseases, management programmes for national development; library of *c.* 3,500 vols (PAHO, WHO, etc.); Rep. VETA BROWN.

Libraries and Archives

Georgetown

Bank of Guyana Library: POB 1003, Georgetown; tel. (2) 63261; telex 2267; fax (2) 72965; f. 1966; provides support for the information needs of the staff; 8,355 vols, 495 periodicals; special collections: staff publs, conference papers, IMF documents, World Bank publs; Librarian PAMELA KNIGHTS; publ. *List of Additions to the Library Catalogue* (quarterly).

Documentation Centre, Caribbean Community Secretariat: 4th floor, Bank of Guyana Bldg, POB 10827, Georgetown; tel. (2) 69281; telex 2263; fax (2) 67816; f. 1980; 12,982 official documents, 16,620 monographs, 7,279 pamphlets, 5,039 microfiches, 91 microfilms, 12 reel tapes, 111 cassettes; collections (documents): CARICOM, UN, UN agencies; Officer-in-Charge: MAUREEN C. NEWTON.

Guyana Medical Science Library: Georgetown Hospital Compound, Georgetown; f. 1966; attached to the Ministry of Health; provides medical information to doctors, nurses, and health personnel; 9,914 vols, 300 journals, 1,000 pamphlets; Librarian Mrs JENNIFER WILSON; publs *Bulletin* (quarterly), *Annual Report*.

National Library: POB 10240, Georgetown; tel. (2) 62699; f. 1909; combines the functions of a National Library and Public Library; legal depository for material printed in Guyana; 197,355 vols; special collections: Caribbeana, library science, A. J. Seymour, Unesco deposit; Chief Librarian GWYNETH BROWMAN (acting); publ. *Guyanese National Bibliography* (quarterly).

University of Guyana Library: POB 101110, Georgetown; tel. (22) 5401; fax (2) 54885; f. 1963; 320,000 book and non-book materials, 4,000 periodicals; special collections: UN deposit collection, Caribbean Research Library, Law Collection; Librarian DUDLEY KISSOORE; publs *Caribbean Additions, Additions in Science and Technology, Additions in the Humanities* (all every 2 months).

Museums and Art Galleries

Georgetown

Guyana Museum: Company Path, North St, Georgetown; f. 1853 by the Royal Agricultural and Commercial Society; subjects covered include Industry, Art, History, Anthropology, Zoology; Curator CLAYTON RODNEY; publ. *Journal* (annually).

Incorporates:

> **Guyana Zoo:** Company Path, North St, Georgetown; specializes in the display, care and management of South American fauna; Dir GEORGE E. BURNHAM.

University

UNIVERSITY OF GUYANA

POB 101110, Turkeyan, Greater Georgetown

Telephone: (22) 4184
Fax: (22) 3596

Founded 1963
State control
Language of instruction: English
Academic year: two terms, beginning September and January

Chancellor: RUDOLPH INSANALLY
Pro-Chancellor: Dr MARTIN BOADHOO
Vice-Chancellor: Prof. HAROLD LUTCHMAN
Deputy Vice-Chancellor: GEM FLETCHER
Registrar: Dr DAVID CHANDERBALLI
Librarian: YVONNE LANCASTER

Number of teachers: 226
Number of students: 3,311

Publications: *University of Guyana Bulletin* (annually), *UG Info* (quarterly newsletter).

DEANS

Faculty of Agriculture: Dr ODHO HOMENAUTH
Faculty of Arts: Dr JAMES ROSE
Faculty of Education: WILBURN WEEVER
Faculty of Health Sciences: DEEN SHARMA
Faculty of Natural Sciences: Dr MARLENE COX
Faculty of Social Sciences: Dr CYRIL SOLOMON
Faculty of Technology: Dr CHARLES GARRETT

PROFESSORS

BRITTON, P., Law
DANNS, G. K., Sociology
LONCKE, J., Creative Arts
MASSIAH, K., Law
PERSICO, A.
ROGERS, D., Creative Arts
THOMAS, C. Y., Economics and Business Administration
VISSWANATHAN, E., History
WESTMOSS, R., Architecture

ATTACHED INSTITUTES

Institute of Development Studies: Dir Prof. C. Y. THOMAS.

Institute of Distance and Continuing Education: Dir SAMUEL SMALL.

Colleges

Linden Technical Institute: Lot 1, New Rd, Constabulary Compound, Mackenzie, Linden; tel. (4) 3333; fax (4) 6719; f. 1958; Guyana Technical Education Examination courses in electrical installation, welding, mechanical fitting, metal machining, instrumentation, motor vehicle work, internal combustion engines, carpentry and joinery, driver training; 10 instructors, 86 full-time students; Principal ISAAC LAMAZON (acting).

E. R. Burrowes School of Art: 96 Carmichael St, Georgetown; tel. (2) 63649; f. 1975; 4-year diploma course; library of 750 vols; 13 teachers; 52 students; Administrator AGNES JONES.

Carnegie School of Home Economics: Durban and High Sts, Werk-en-Rust, Georgetown; tel. 62441; f. 1933; library of 1,040 vols; 11 teachers, 180 students; in-service and technical training.

Critchlow Labour College: Woolford Ave, Non Pareil Park, Georgetown; tel. 62481; f. 1970; library of 2,000 vols; 40 teachers; 600 students; industrial and social studies; Principal T. ANSON SANCHO.

Government Technical Institute: Woolford Ave, Georgetown; tel. 02-62468; f. 1951; library of 3,500 vols; 37 teachers, 2,000 students; Principal LENNOX B. WILLIAMS.

Guyana Industrial Training Centre: Woolford Ave and Albert St, Non Pareil Park, Georgetown; tel., (02) 66196; f. 1966; library of 1,600 vols; 6 teachers; 120 full-time, 90 part-time students; Dir SYDNEY R. WALTERS.

Guyana School of Agriculture Corporation: Mon Repos, East Coast Demerara; tel. (20) 2804; f. 1963; library of 6,000 vols; Principal DESMOND A. NICHOLSON.

Kuru-Kuru Co-operative College: Linden Highway, POB 896; tel. 061-326; f. 1973; library of 5,800 vols; 26 teachers; 270 students; Principal AVRIL BACCHUS (acting); Librarian LINDA CALDER.

COURSE CO-ORDINATORS

Extra-Mural: DERECK BOSTON
Economics: MICHAEL BOBB-SEMPLE
Agriculture: TREVOR CALLENDER (acting)
Accounting: VIBART DUNCAN
English: ASHLEY B. WOOLFORD
Management and Commercial Law: LLOYD STUART
Co-operative Studies: JAMES N. FRASER
Statistics: EMANUEL GILKES

New Amsterdam Technical Institute: POB 50, Garrison Road, Fort Ordnance, New Amsterdam, Berbice; tel. (3) 2702; f. 1971; Guyana Technical Education Examination in electrical trades, radio and electronic servicing, agricultural mechanics, automotive engineering, wood trades, fitting, welding, masonry, plumbing, etc.; secretarial and business studies; Ordinary Technician diploma, Mechanical Engineering Technician course, Agricultural Engineering Technician course; Architectural and Building Construction Technician course; library of 2,186 vols; 32 teachers, 1,000 students; Principal RONALD L. SIMON.

HAITI

Learned Societies

BIBLIOGRAPHY, LIBRARY SCIENCE AND MUSEOLOGY

Bibliophile, Le: Cap Haïtien; f. 1923 to extend and increase knowledge of world literature and love of good books; 28 mems; Pres. SILVIO FASCHI; Sec. LOUIS TOUSSAINT; publs *La Citadelle* (weekly), *Stella* (monthly).

NATURAL SCIENCES

General

Conseil National des Recherches Scientifiques (National Council for Scientific Research): Département de la santé publique et de la population, Port-au-Prince; f. 1963; to co-ordinate scientific development and research, particularly in the field of public health; Pres. Prof. VICTOR NOËL; Sec. M. DOUYON.

Research Institutes

RELIGION, SOCIOLOGY AND ANTHROPOLOGY

Bureau National d'Ethnologie: Angle rue St Honoré and ave Magloire Ambroise, Place des Héros de l'Indépendance, BP 915, Port-au-Prince; tel. 22-5232; f. 1941; departments: African and Haitian ethnography, pre-Columbian archaeology; Dir Dr MAX PAUL; publ. *Bulletin* (2 a year).

Libraries and Archives

Port-au-Prince

Archives Nationales d'Haiti: Angle rues Geffrard et Borgella, BP 1299, Port-au-Prince; tel. 22-8566; fax 22-6280; f. 1860; Dir-Gen. JEAN WILFRID BERTRAND.

Bibliothèque du Petit Séminaire: Port-au-Prince.

Bibliothèque Haitienne des F.I.C.: Saint-Louis de Gonzague, 180 Rue du Centre, BP 1758, Port-au-Prince; tel. 232148; fax 232029; f. 1920; 11,400 vols; 19th- and 20th-century newspapers; Dir ERNEST EVEN.

Bibliothèque Nationale d'Haiti: 193 rue du Centre, Port-au-Prince; tel. 22-0236; fax 23-8773; f. 1940; 22,600 vols, 419 periodicals; 12 brs; Dir FRANÇOISE BEAULIEU THYBULLE.

Museums and Art Galleries

Port-au-Prince

Centre d'Art: 58 rue Roy, Port-au-Prince; tel. 2-2018; f. 1944; Dir FRANCINE MURAT; arranges representative exhibitions of Haitian art in the Americas and Western Europe.

Musée du Panthéon National: Place des Héros de l'Indépendance, Port-au-Prince; f. 1983; historical artefacts, art and craft; Dir GÉRALD ALEXIS.

Universities

UNIVERSITÉ D'ÉTAT D'HAITI

1 rue Dehoux, Port-au-Prince
Telephone: 22-3210
Fax (via Min. of Foreign Affairs): 23-8912

Founded 1920
State control
Language of instruction: French
Academic year: October to July

Rector: ROGER GAILLARD
Vice-Rector (Administrative): MARIE CARMEL AUSTIN
Vice-Rector (Academic): MICHEL HECTOR
Secretary-General: LESLIE DUCHATELLIER
Librarian: (vacant)

Library of 7,000 vols
Number of teachers: 664
Number of students: 10,446

DEANS AND CO-ORDINATORS

Faculty of Law and Economics: JUSTIN CASTEL
Faculty of Medicine and Pharmacy: Dr MARIO ALVAREZ
Faculty of Odontology: Dr ALIX CHATEIGNE
Faculty of Ethnology: PATRICIA MICHEL FOUCAULT, JEAN YVES BLOT
Faculty of Science: CHRISTIAN ROUSSEAU (Administrative), GUICHARD BEAULIEU (Academic)
Faculty of Humanities: JEAN RENOL ELIE
Faculty of Agronomy and Veterinary Medicine: JEAN VERNET HENRY
Faculty of Applied Linguistics: PIERRE VERNET
Institut National d'Administration de Gestion et des Hautes Etudes Internationales (INAGHEI): EDDY CARRÉ
Institut d'Etudes et de Recherches Africaines d'Haiti: ERNST BERNADIN
Ecole Normale Supérieure: BERARD CENATUS, ROGER PETIT-FRÈRE

UNIVERSITÉ QUISQUEYA

Angle rue Chareron et boulevard Harry Truman, BP 796, Port-au-Prince
Telephone: 229002
Fax: 237430
E-mail: uniql@ht.syfed.refer.org

Founded 1988
Private control
Language of instruction: French

Rector: PAUL SAINT-HILAIRE
Vice-Rectors: LIONEL RICHARD (Administration), ARIEL AZAEL (Research and Extension)
General Secretary: EDGARD PREVILON
Librarian: KETTELIE NEMORIN

Library of 24,000 vols
Number of teachers: 153
Number of students: 1,758

Publication: *Revue Juridique de l'UniQ* (quarterly).

DEANS

Faculty of Agriculture and the Environment: GLADYS G. ARCHANGE (Vice-Dean)
Faculty of Economics and Management: DANIEL ALTINE
Faculty of Science and Engineering: ERNST LARAQUE
Faculty of Education: MICHAËLLE SAINT-NATUS
Faculty of Law: BERNARD GOUSSE
Faculty of Health Sciences: KYSS JEAN-MARY

ATTACHED INSTITUTE

Institute of Research, Training and Counselling in Management of Co-operatives and Small Enterprises: Dir Dr JOEL JEAN-PIERRE.

UNIVERSITÉ ROI HENRI CHRISTOPHE

BP 98, Rues 17-18, H-1, Cap-Haïtien

Telephone: 21316

Private control

Rector: Prof. RAOUL REMY
Aministrator: EDGARD BERNARDIN
Librarian: MARIE-MERCIE PREDESTIN

Number of students: 100

DEANS

Faculty of Agriculture: BRUNEL GARÇON
Faculty of Medicine: Dr GUY DUGUÉ
Faculty of Engineering: (vacant)

Colleges

Ecole de Technologie Médicale: Rue Oswald Durand, Port-au-Prince; Dir PAULETTE A. CHAMPAGNE.

Ecole Nationale des Arts: 266 rue Monseigneur Guilloux, Port-au-Prince; tel. 2-9686; f. 1983; Dirs EMERANTE DE PRADINES MORSE, ROBERT BAU DUY.

Institut International d'Etudes Universitaires: c/o Fondation Haitienne de Développement, 106 ave Christophe, Port-au-Prince; Dir Mme Y. ARMAND.

HONDURAS

Learned Societies

GENERAL

Academia Hondureña (Honduran Academy): Apdo 38, Tegucigalpa; f. 1949; corresp. of the Real Academia Española (Madrid); 28 mems; Dir MIGUEL R. ORTEGA; Sec. JORGE FIDEL DURÓN; publ. *Boletín*.

ARCHITECTURE AND TOWN PLANNING

Colegio de Arquitectos de Honduras: Apdo 1974, Tegucigalpa; tel. 33-4768; f. 1979; 140 mems; library; publ. *Bahareque* (2 a year).

BIBLIOGRAPHY, LIBRARY SCIENCE AND MUSEOLOGY

Asociación de Bibliotecarios y Archivistas de Honduras: 11a Calle, 1a y 2a Avdas No. 105, Comayagüela, DC, Tegucigalpa; f. 1951; 53 mems; library of 3,000 vols; Pres. FRANCISCA DE ESCOTO ESPINOZA; Sec.-Gen. JUAN ANGEL AYES R.; publ. *Catálogo de Préstamo* (monthly).

HISTORY, GEOGRAPHY AND ARCHAEOLOGY

Academia Hondureña de Geografía e Historia: Apdo 619, Tegucigalpa; f. 1968; 21 mems; library of 1,535 vols; Pres. Dr RAMÓN E. CRUZ; Sec. PM FERNANDO FERRARI BUSTILLO; publ. *Revista*.

Research Institutes

GENERAL

Instituto Hondureño de Cultura Interamericana (IHCI): Calle Real, 2 Avda Entre 5 y 6 Calle 520, Comayagüela, Apdo 201, Tegucigalpa; tel. 22-07-03; fax 38-00-64; e-mail rosario@ihci.sdnhon.org.hn; f. 1939; courses in English, bilingual secretarial studies; art gallery; library of 8,000 vols (English and Spanish); Dir ROSARIO ELENA CORDOVA.

AGRICULTURE, FISHERIES AND VETERINARY SCIENCE

Instituto Hondureño del Café: POB 40-C, Tegucigalpa; Gen. Man. ARMANDO ZELAYA.

Instituto Nacional Agrario: Tegucigalpa; Dir MARIO ESPINAL ZELAYA.

HISTORY, GEOGRAPHY AND ARCHAEOLOGY

Instituto Geográfico Nacional (IGN) (National Geographic Institute): Barrio La Bolsa, Tegucigalpa, DC; f. 1945; delineates natural and mineral resources, their evaluation and their exploitation; 130 staff; library of 1,250 vols; Dir-Gen. JOSÉ EDMUNDO ALCERRO PRUDOTH; publs *Boletín de la Comisión Geográfica Especial de la Secretaría de Marina y Aviación, Boletín de la Dirección General de Cartografía, Secretaría de Fomento, Boletín de la Dirección General de Cartografía del Ministerio de Comunicaciones y Obras Públicas, Boletín del Instituto Geográfico Nacional.*

Instituto Hondureño de Antropología e Historia: Apdo 1518, Villa Roy, Tegucigalpa; tel. 223470; fax 222552; f. 1952; library of 12,000 vols; research and conservation of cultural property, archaeology, history, ethnography, linguistics, museology; Dir OLGA MARINA JOYA SIERRA; publs *Yaxkin* (2 a year), *Estudios Antropológicos e Históricos* (annually).

Libraries and Archives

Tegucigalpa

Archivo Nacional de Honduras: Avda Cristóbal Colón, Calle Salvador Mendieta 1117, Tegucigalpa; fax 222-8338; f. 1880; 700 linear metres of documents; library of 2,700 vols and 100 periodicals; Dir CARLOS WILFREDO MALDONADO..

Biblioteca Nacional de Honduras: Ave Cristobal Colón, Calle 'Salvador Mendieta', POB 1117, Tegucigalpa; tel. and fax 22-8577; f. 1880; 70,000 vols; co-ordinates national and international exchange; shares legal deposit with other centres; Dir HECTOR ROBERTO LUNA; publ. *Anuario Bibliográfico*.

Biblioteca 'Wilson Popenoe': Escuela Agrícola Panamericana, Apdo 93, Tegucigalpa; tel. 76-6140; telex 1567; fax 766240; f. 1946; tropical agriculture; 20,000 vols, 800 periodicals; Librarian DANIEL F. KAEGI; publ. *Ceiba* (2 a year).

Biblioteca del Ministerio de Relaciones Exteriores: Avda La Paz, Edif. Atala, Tegucigalpa; f. 1913; 5,000 vols; Dir ERNESTO ALVARADO GARCÍA.

Sistema Bibliotecario Universidad Nacional Autónoma de Honduras: Ciudad Universitaria, Tegucigalpa; f. 1847; tel. 32-2204; telex 1289; fax 31-0675; 200,000 vols; Librarian ORFYLIA PINEL; publ. *Boletín del Sistema Bibliotecario* (quarterly).

Museums and Art Galleries

Comayagua

Museo Arqueológico de Comayagua: Frente a Plaza San Francisco, Ciudad de Comayagua; tel. 72-03-86; f. 1946; archaeological collection from the Comayagua Valley; some contemporary items; Dir SALVADOR TURCIOS.

Copán

Museo Regional de Arqueología Maya: Ciudad de Copán; f. 1939; objects relate exclusively to Maya culture; Dir Prof. OSMIN RIVERA.

Cortés

Museo Nacional de Historia Colonial: Puerto de Omoa, Cortés; f. 1959 in former prison; colonial and historical items; Curator RAMÓN ZÚÑIGA ANDRADE.

Quimistán

Museo Histórico 'Miguel Paz Baraona': Aldea de Pinalejo, Municípío de Quimistán; f. 1953; archaeological, colonial and contemporary art items of the region; Dir ESTEBAN MADRID.

Tegucigalpa

Museo de Historia Republicana: Apdo 1518, Villa Roy, Barrio Buenos Aires, Tegucigalpa; tel. 22-14-68; fax 22-25-52; modern political history; Dir Prof. SALVADOR ECHIGOYEN.

Museo Histórico de la República: Tegucigalpa; tel. 37-02-68; fax 22-25-52; f. 1993; political history from 1821 to present; former Presidential house; Dir Prof. SALVADOR ECHIGOYEN; publ. *Cuadernos del Museo*.

Universities

UNIVERSIDAD JOSÉ CECILIO DEL VALLE

Apdo 917, Tegucigalpa, DC

Telephone: 22-8961
Fax: 37-0575

Founded 1978
Private control

Rector: Ing. IRMA ACOSTA DE FORTÍN
Academic Director: Dr. MARCO POLO MICHELETTI
Administrative Director: MARIO ROBERTO GÓMEZ
Librarian: EDA ALICIA MEZA

Number of teachers 48
Number of students: 280

Publications: university catalogues and bulletins.

Departments of engineering, administration, accountancy and computer science.

ATTACHED CENTRE

Centro Ganadero Comayagua: Apdo. 917, Tegucigalpa, DC; Dir MARCO POLO MICHELETTI.

UNIVERSIDAD NACIONAL AUTÓNOMA DE HONDURAS

POB 3560, Tegucigalpa, DC

Telephone: (504) 312110
Telex: 1289

Founded 1847
Autonomous control
Language of instruction: Spanish
Academic year: February to December

Rector: Lic. JORGE OMAR CASCO ZELAYA
Vice-Rector: OCTAVIO SÁNCHEZ MIDENCE
Administrative-Secretary: RAÚL FLORES

General Secretary: AFREDO HAWIT
Librarian: ORFYLIA PINEL

Library: see Libraries
Number of teachers: 2,250
Number of students: 33,000

Publications: *Presencia Universitaria, Revista de la Universidad, Catálogo de Estudios, Memoria Anual,* and various faculty publs.

DEANS

Faculty of Juridical and Social Sciences: RIGOBERTO CHIANG CASTILLO
Faculty of Economics: RAMÓN SARMIENTO
Faculty of Medicine: ANTONIO NUÑEZ
Faculty of Pharmacy: ANA BELÉN DE RODRÍGUEZ
Faculty of Dentistry: FRANCISCO DUBÓN
Faculty of Engineering: ARTHUR BANEGAS-HILL

DIRECTORS

University Centre of the North (San Pedro Sula): JOSÉ MARÍA KURY
Atlantic Coast University Centre (La Ceiba): Ing. JORGE I. SOTO M.
General Studies Centre: ANGEL A. MEJÍA
Graduate School: MARCO A. ZÚNIGA

Colleges

Escuela Nacional de Música: 2a Avda 307, Tegucigalpa.

Zamorano, Escuela Agrícola Panamericana: Apdo 93, Tegucigalpa; tel. 766140; fax 766240; e-mail zamorano@ns.zamorano.edu.hn; f. 1942; private, non-profit international institution; training in tropical agriculture, natural resource management and rural development; student intake from 22 Latin-American countries; 70 teachers, 800 students; library of 20,000 vols, 800 periodicals; Dir Dr KEITH L. ANDREWS; publ. *CEIBA* (3 a year).

ATTACHED CENTRES

International Seed and Grain Science Centre
Centre for Biological Control
Centre for Rural Development
Centre for Meat Science
Centre for Milk Processing
Centre for Evaluation and Management of Pesticides
Centre for Agricultural Policy
Centre for Agribusiness
W. K. Kellogg Training Centre
Centre for Food Technology
Centre for Apiculture
Centre for Natural Resources Economics
Centre for Geographic Information Systems

HUNGARY

Learned Societies

GENERAL

Magyar Tudományos Akadémia (Hungarian Academy of Sciences: 1051 Budapest, Roosevelt tér 9; tel. (1) 1382-344; fax (1) 1328-943; f. 1825; sections of Linguistic and Literary Sciences (Chair. ZSIGMOND RITOÓK), Philosophy and Historical Sciences (Chair. FERENC PATAKI), Mathematical Sciences (Chair. ÁKOS CSÁSZÁR), Physical Sciences (Chair. KÁROLY NAGY), Agricultural Sciences (Chair. PÁL STEFANOVITS), Medical Sciences (Chair. KÁROLY MÉHES), Technical Sciences (Chair. JÁNOS PROHÁSZKA), Chemical Sciences (Chair. ANDRÁS LIPTÁK), Biological Sciences (Chair. PÉTER FRIEDRICH), Economics and Law (Chair. KÁLMÁN KULCSÁR), Earth Sciences (Chair. ERNŐ MÉSZÁROS); 155 hon. mems, 209 ordinary mems, 81 corresp. mems, 88 external mems; attached research institutes: see Research Institutes; library: see Libraries and Archives; Pres. FERENC GLATZ; Gen. Sec. LÁSZLÓ KEVICZKY; publs *Acta Agronomica, Acta Alimentaria, Acta Antiqua, Acta Archaeologica, Acta Biologica, Acta Botanica, Acta Chirurgica, Acta Ethnographica, Acta Geodaetica et Geophysica, Acta Historiae Artium, Acta Historica, Acta Juridica, Acta Linguistica, Acta Mathematica, Acta Medica, Acta Microbiologica et Immunologica, Acta Oeconomica, Acta Orientalia, Acta Physica, Acta Physiologica, Acta Phytopathologica, Acta Technica, Acta Veterinaria, Acta Zoologica, ACH Models in Chemistry, Analysis Mathematica, Studia Musicologica, Studia Scientiarium Mathematicarum Hungarica, Studia Slavica* (all available for exchange), Bulletins of the Sections of the Academy, in five series, *Magyar Tudomány* and *Akadémia* (reviews of the Hungarian Academy of Sciences) and other publications in Hungarian.

Müszaki és Természettudományi Egyesületek Szövetsége (Federation of Technical and Scientific Societies): 1055 Budapest, Kossuth L. tér 6–8; tel. 153-4795; fax 153-0317; e-mail mtesz@mtesz.hu; f. 1948; 42 mem. socs; Pres. MIKLÓS HAVASS; Man. Dir Dr LÁSZLÓ HALMAI; publ. *Műszaki Magazin*.

Széchenyi Irodalmi és Művészeti Akadémia (Széchenyi Academy of Letters and Arts): 1051 Budapest, Roosevelt tér 9; tel. and fax (1) 331-4117; f. 1825 as section of Hungarian Acad. of Sciences, ind. 1992; sections of Letters, of Fine Arts, of Theatre and Film, of Music; 65 mems, 7 corresp. mems; Pres. MIKLÓS JANCSÓ; Exec. Pres. LÁSZLÓ LATOR; Exec. Sec. ANIKÓ KOVÁCS.

AGRICULTURE, FISHERIES AND VETERINARY SCIENCE

Magyar Agrártudományi Egyesület (Hungarian Society of Agricultural Sciences): 1055 Budapest, Kossuth Lajos tér 6–8; tel. (1) 1530-651; fax (1) 1531-950; f. 1951; 8,500 mems; 14 affiliated socs; Pres. Dr PÉTER HORN; Sec.-Gen. Dr VILMOS MARILLAI; publ. *Magyar Mezőgazdaság* (Hungarian Agriculture, weekly).

Magyar Élelmezésipari Tudományos Egyesület (Hungarian Scientific Society for Food Industry): 1027 Budapest, Fő u. 68; tel. (1) 2146-691; fax (1) 2146-692; f. 1949; poultry breeding and processing, viticulture, sugar industry, confectionery, grain processing, meat industry, cold storage, canning, paprika, tobacco, oil, soap, cosmetics, brewery, bakery, distillery; 3,800 mems; Pres. Dr TIBOR DEÁK; Exec. Dir ZOLTÁN HERNÁDI; publs include *Élelmezési Ipar* (Food Industry) and journals on many branches of the food industry.

Országos Erdészeti Egyesület (Hungarian Forestry Association): 1027 Budapest, Fő utca 68; tel. 201-6293; fax 201-7737; f. 1866; forestry, forest industries, environment protection; 5,000 mems; library of 20,000 vols; Pres. ANDRÁS SCHMOTZER; Sec.-Gen. GÁBOR BARÁTOSSY; publ. *Erdészeti Lapok* (Forestry Bulletin).

ARCHITECTURE AND TOWN PLANNING

Építéstudományi Egyesület (Scientific Society for Building): 1027 Budapest, Fő u. 68; tel. 2018416; telex 22-4343; fax 156-1215; f. 1949; 3,500 mems; Pres. Dr CELESZTIN MESZLÉRY; Sec.-Gen. PÁL SEENGER; publs *Magyar Építőipar* (Hungarian Building Industry), *Magyar Épületgépészet* (Hungarian Sanitary and Installation Engineering).

BIBLIOGRAPHY, LIBRARY SCIENCE AND MUSEOLOGY

Magyar Könyvtárosok Egyesülete (Asscn of Hungarian Librarians): 1088 Budapest, Szabó Ervin tér 1; tel. and fax 1182-050; f. 1935; 2,400 mems; Pres. Dr T. HORVÁTH; Sec.-Gen. I. PAPP.

Magyar Levéltárosok Egyesülete (Asscn of Hungarian Archivists); 1014 Budapest, Hess András tér 5; tel. 214-0333; f. 1986; 500 mems; Pres. Dr GYULA ERDMANN; Sec. ÉVA VARGA.

EDUCATION

Magyar Művelődési Intézet (Hungarian Institute of Culture): 1251 Budapest, Corvin tér 8; tel. (1) 201-3766; fax (1) 201-3766; e-mail corvin@c3.hu; f. 1951; centre for life-long education, cultural activities, folk art, minority cultures, amateur artistic and leisure pursuits, community development; library of 50,000 vols; special collection on past and present Hungarian folk high schools; Dir. ANDRÁS FÖLDIÁK.

FINE AND PERFORMING ARTS

Liszt Ferenc Társaság (F. Liszt Society): 1064 Budapest, Vörösmarty u. 35; tel. 3421-573; f. 1893, re-formed 1973; to foster the cult of Liszt, to further the interest of audiences in live music; concerts, competitions, annual Liszt Record Grand Prix, setting up Liszt memorials; 780 mems; Pres. ISTVÁN LANTOS; Gen. Sec. Dr KLÁRA HAMBURGER.

Magyar Zenei Tanács (Hungarian Music Council): 1051 Budapest, Vörösmarty tér 1. 1364, POB 47; tel. (1) 318-4243; fax (1) 337-8267; e-mail hmc@a-m.hu; f. 1990 to replace Magyar Zeneművészek Szövetsége; library of 11,500 scores, 6,600 vols, 7,000 records, 700 tapes with 1,400 Hungarian compositions; Pres. ADRIENNE CSENGERY; Sec.-Gen. ÉVA CSÉBFALVI; Head of the Music Information Centre ESZTER VIDA.

Magyar Zeneművészeti Társaság (Hungarian Music Society): 1025 Budapest, Pusztaszeri ut. 30; tel. and fax (1) 325-7313; f. 1987; 60 mems; aims to foster cultivation of Hungarian music, to promote the interests of musical artists, to educate young people's musical taste, to preserve Hungarian music past and present; Pres. JÁNOS DEVICH.

Országos Magyar Cecilia Társulat (National Hungarian Cecilia Society): 1119, Budapest, Fehérvári út 82; f. 1897; 2,800 mems; aims to foster cultivation of Catholic music; Ecclesiastical Chair. GY. SZAKOS.

Országos Színháztörténeti Múzeum és Intézet (Theatre Institute and Museum): 1013 Budapest, Krisztina-krt. 57; tel. and fax 1751-184; f. 1957; to research into theatre history and theory, information on Hungarian drama and theatre for abroad and on world drama and theatre for Hungarian professionals; 50 mems; Dir. Dr NINA KIRÁLY; publs *Thália könyvek, Prospero könyvek, Magyar színházi hírek, Világszínház, Szinháztudományi szemle, Évkönyv*; controls the theatrical memorial places, and the Bajor Gizi Actors' Museum.

HISTORY, GEOGRAPHY AND ARCHAEOLOGY

Károlyi Mihály Társaság (Mihály Károlyi Society): 1053 Budapest, Károlyi Mihály utca 16; tel. 1173-611; f. 1988; aims to foster the idea of the Danube confederation; 128 mems; Pres. JÁNOS PÉTER; Sec. Ms SARA KARIG.

Magyar Földmérési, Térképészeti és Távérzékelési Társaság (Hungarian Society for Surveying, Mapping and Remote Sensing): 1027 Budapest, Fő utca 68; tel (1) 201-8642; fax (1) 156-1215; f. 1956; 1,000 mems; Pres. ÁKOS DETREKŐI; Sec.-Gen. FERENC BARTOS; publ. *Geodézia és Kartográfia* (Geodesy and Cartography).

Magyar Földrajzi Társaság (Hungarian Geographical Society): 1062 Budapest, Andrássy u. 62; tel. and fax (1) 1117-688; f. 1872, reorg. 1952; 1,300 mems; library of 32,000 vols, 800 periodicals, 5,000 maps; Pres. SANDOR MAROSI; Gen. Sec. ANTAL NEMERKÉNYI; publ. *Földrajzi Közlemények* (English summaries, quarterly).

Magyar Irodalomtörténeti Társaság (Society of Hungarian Literary History): 1052 Budapest, Piarista köz 1; tel. 1377-819; f. 1912; Pres. DEZSŐ KERESZTURY; Gen. Sec. LÓRÁNT KABDEBÓ; publs *Irodalomtörténet* (Literary History, quarterly).

Magyar Régészeti és Művészettörténeti Társulat (Hungarian Society of Archaeology and History of Fine Arts): 1088 Budapest, Múzeum-krt. 14; tel. (1) 1383-918; fax (1) 1177-806; e-mail wollak@hnm.hu; f. 1878; Pres. Dr JENŐ FITZ; Sec. KATALIN WOLLÁK; publs *Archaeológiai Értesítő, Művészettörténeti Értesítő, Henszlmann Lapok*.

Magyar Történelmi Társulat (Hungarian Historical Society): 1014 Budapest, Uri u. 51–53; tel. 1759-011; f. 1867; Pres. ISTVÁN DIÓSZEGI; Gen. Sec. KLÁRA HEGYI; publ. *Századok* (every 2 months).

LANGUAGE AND LITERATURE

Magyar Írószövetség (Union of Hungarian Writers): 1062 Budapest, Bajza u. 18; tel. (1) 3228-840; f. 1945; Pres. BÉLA POMOGÁTS.

Magyar Nyelvtudományi Társaság (Hungarian Linguistic Society): 1052 Budapest,

Piarista köz 1; tel. 1376-819; f. 1904; 660 mems; Pres. LORÁND BENKŐ; Gen. Sec. JENŐ KISS; Sec. ANDRÁS ZOLTÁN; publ. *Magyar Nyelv* (quarterly).

Magyar PEN Club (Hungarian PEN Club): 1056 Budapest, Károlyi Mihály ut. 16; tel. (1) 318-4143; fax (1) 117-1722; f. 1926; 325 mems; Pres. MIKLÓS HUBAY (acting); Gen. Sec. TAMÁS UNGVARI; publs *The Hungarian PEN, Le PEN Hongrois* (yearly bulletin).

Magyar Ujságirók Országos Szövetsége (National Federation of Hungarian Journalists): 1062 Budapest, Andrássy ut. 101; tel. 3221-699; fax 322-1881; 6,800 mems; Pres. ANDRÁS KERESZTY; Gen. Sec. GÁBOR BENCSIK.

MEDICINE

Magyar Gyógyszerészeti Társaság (Hungarian Pharmaceutical Society): 1051 Budapest, Zrinyi u. 3; tel. and fax (1) 1181-573; f. 1924; 1,200 mems; Pres. Dr Z. VINCZE; Gen. Sec. Dr J. LIPTÁK; publs *Acta Pharmaceutica Hungarica*, *Gyógyszerészet*, *Up-to-date problems of Pharmaceutical Sciences.*

Magyar Orvostudományi Társaságok és Egyesületek Szövetsége (MOTESZ) (Federation of Hungarian Medical Societies): 1051 Budapest, Nádor u. 36; tel. (1) 111–6687; fax (1) 183-7918; f. 1966; 69 mem. societies; Pres. Prof. Dr OTTÓ RIBÁRI.

NATURAL SCIENCES

General

Tudományos Ismeretterjesztő Társulat (Society for the Dissemination of Scientific Knowledge): 1088 Budapest, Bródy Sándor u. 16; tel. 1382-496; fax 138-3320; f. 1841; library of 20,000 vols; 17,000 mems; Gen. Dir ESZTER PIRÓTH (acting); publs *Élet és Tudomány* (Life and Science) (weekly), *Természet Világa* (World of Nature) (monthly), *Valóság* (Reality) (monthly).

Biological Sciences

Magyar Biofizikai Társaság (Hungarian Biophysical Society): 1027 Budapest, Fő utca 68; tel. and fax 2021-216; telex 224343; f. 1961; medical physics, ultrasound, radiation biophysics, photo-biophysics; 450 mems; Pres. Dr LAJOS KESZTHELYI; Sec.-Gen. Dr SÁNDOR GYÖRGYI; publ. *Magyar Biofizikai Társaság Értesítője* (every 3 years).

Magyar Biokémiai Egyesület (Hungarian Biochemical Society): 1518 Budapest, POB 7; premises at: 1113 Budapest, Karolina u. 29; tel. and fax (1) 166-5856; f. 1949; Pres. Dr PETER FRIEDRICH; Sec.-Gen. Dr PETER CSERMELY; publ. *Biokémia*.

Magyar Biológiai Társaság (Hungarian Biological Society): 1061 Budapest, Fő u. 68; tel. 201-6484; f. 1952; 1,500 mems; Pres. Dr TAMÁS PÓCS; Sec.-Gen. Dr ERNŐ BÁCSY; publs *Antropológiai Közlemények, Állattani Közlemények, Botanikai Közlemények, Természetvédelmi Közlemények* (all annually).

Magyar Biomassza Társaság (Hungarian Biomass Association): 2103 Gödöllő, Páter Károly u. 1; tel. (28) 410-200; e-mail barotfi.kott.mgk@mgk.gau.hu; f. 1991; Pres. Dr ISTVÁN BARÓTFI (acting).

Magyar Rovartani Társaság (Hungarian Society of Entomology): 1088 Budapest, Baross u. 13; tel. (1) 1850-666; f. 1910; 280 mems; Pres. Dr Z. MÉSZÁROS; Sec. A. PODLUSSÁNY; publ. *Folia Entomologica Hungarica (Rovartani Közlemények).*

Mathematical Sciences

Bolyai János Matematikai Társulat (János Bolyai Mathematical Society): 1027 Budapest, Fő u. 68; tel. 2017-656; fax 2016-974; e-mail bjmt@math-inst.hu; f. 1891; 1,850 mems; Pres. IMRE CSISZÁR; Gen. Sec. GÁBOR FEJES TÓTH; publs *Matematikai Lapok* (Mathematical Gazette, 4 a year), *Combinatorica* (4 a year), *Középiskolai Matematikai Lapok* (Mathematical Gazette for Secondary Schools), *Periodica Mathematica Hungarica.*

Physical Sciences

Eötvös Loránd Fizikai Társulat (Roland Eötvös Physical Society): 1027 Budapest, Fő u. 68; tel. and fax (1) 201-8682; telex 224343; f. 1891; physics and astronomy; 1,800 mems; Pres. GYÖRGY MARX; Gen. Sec. DÉNES LAJOS NAGY; publ. *Fizikai Szemle* (Physics Review, monthly).

Magyar Asztronautikai Társaság (Hungarian Astronautical Society): 1027 Budapest, Fő u. 68; tel. 2018443; telex 22-4343; f. 1956; 450 mems; Pres. Dr IVÁN ALMÁR; Gen. Sec. ANDRÁS VARGA.

Magyar Geofizikusok Egyesülete (Asscn of Hungarian Geophysicists): 1027 Budapest, Fő u. 68 I/113; tel. and fax 2019-815; e-mail geophysic@mtesz.hu; f. 1954; 630 mems; Pres. ZSUZSANNA HEGYBÍRÓ; Sec. LÁSZLÓ VERŐ; publ. *Magyar Geofizika* (Hungarian Geophysics).

Magyar Hidrológiai Társaság (Hungarian Hydrological Society): POB 433, 1371 Budapest; tel. 2017-655; fax 202-7244; f. 1917; 5,000 mems; Pres. Dr ÖDÖN STAROSOLSZKY; Sec.-Gen. ZOLTAN SZÖLLŐSI; publs *Hidrológiai Közlöny* (Hydrological Journal, every 2 months), *Hidrológiai Tájékoztató* (Circular on Hydrology, 1 a year).

Magyar Karszt- és Barlangkutató Társulat (Hungarian Speleological Society): 1027 Budapest, Fő u. 68; tel. and fax 2019-493; e-mail mkbt@mail.matav.hu; f. 1910; 1,000 mems; library of 5,000 vols; Pres. Dr ATTILA HEVESI; Sec.-Gen. PÉTER SZABLYÁR; publ. *Karszt és Barlang* (annually with summaries in English).

Magyar Kémikusok Egyesülete (Hungarian Chemical Society): 1027 Budapest, Fő u. 68; tel. 201-6883; fax 201-8056; e-mail mail1.mke@mtesz.hu; f. 1907; 6,000 mems; Pres. Dr ALAJOS KÁLMÁN; Sec.-Gen. Dr LÁSZLÓ HARSÁNYI; publs *Magyar Kémikusok Lapja* (Hungarian Chemical Journal, monthly), *Magyar Kémiai Folyóirat* (Hungarian Journal of Chemistry, monthly), *Középiskolai Kémiai Lapok* (Secondary School Chemical Papers, 5 a year).

Magyar Meteorológiai Társaság (Hungarian Meteorological Society): 1371 Budapest, Fő u. 68, PO Box 433; tel. 2017-525; telex 224343; fax 156-1215; f. 1925; 450 mems; Pres. Dr PÁL AMBRÓZY; Gen. Sec. Dr GYÖRGY MAJOR.

Magyarhoni Földtani Társulat (Hungarian Geological Society): 1027 Budapest, Fő utca 68; tel. 2019-129; telex 22 4343; fax 1561-215; f. 1848; 1,400 mems; Pres. Dr TIBOR KECSKEMÉTI; Sec.-Gen. Dr JÁNOS HALMAI; publ. *Földtani Közlöny* (Bulletin, quarterly).

Optikai, Akusztikai és Filmtechnikai Tudományos Egyesület (Scientific Society for Optics, Acoustics, Motion Pictures and Theatre Technology): 1027 Budapest, Fő u. 68; tel. 202-0452; telex 22-4343; f. 1933; 1,800 mems; Pres. Dr OLIVER PETRIK; Sec.-Gen. LÁSZLÓ FÜSZFÁS; publs *Kép és Hangtechnika* (Picture and Audio Techniques) (every 2 months), *Elektrónikai Technológia-Mikrotechnika* (Electronic Technology-Microtechnics) (monthly), *Szinháztechnikai Fórum* (Forum of the Technical Theatre) (quarterly).

PHILOSOPHY AND PSYCHOLOGY

Magyar Filozófiai Társaság (Hungarian Philosophical Asscn): 1364 Budapest, Pf. 107; tel. and fax (1) 266-4195; f. 1987; 400 mems; Pres. KRISTÓF NYÍRI; Gen. Sec. ISTVÁN M. BODNÁR; publ. *MFT-Hírek* (Newsletter, 4 a year).

Magyar Pszichológiai Társaság (Hungarian Psychological Association): 1536 Budapest, Pf. 220, Teréz krt 13; tel. 1426-178; f. 1928; 1,225 mems; Pres. ISTVÁN CZIGLER; Gen. Sec. KLÁRA SZILÁGYI; publ. *Magyar Pszichológiai Szemle* (Hungarian Psychological Review).

RELIGION, SOCIOLOGY AND ANTHROPOLOGY

Magyar Néprajzi Társaság (Hungarian Ethnographical Society): 1055 Budapest, Kossuth Lajos tér 12; tel. (1) 332-6340; fax (1) 269-1272; e-mail mnt@post.hem.hu; f. 1889; 1,318 mems; Pres. LÁSZLÓ KÓSA; Sec.-Gen. IMRE GRÁFIK; publs *Ethnographia* (quarterly), *Néprajzi Hírek* (Newsletter).

Magyar Szociológiai Társaság (Hungarian Sociological Association): 1068 Budapest, Benczur u. 33; tel. (1) 322-5265; fax (1) 322-1843; f. 1978; 760 mems; Pres. PÁL TAMÁS; Sec. IMRE KOVÁCH.

TECHNOLOGY

Bőr-, Cipő-, és Bőrfeldolgozóipari Tudományos Egyesület (Scientific Society of the Leather, Shoe and Allied Industries): 1372 Budapest, Pf. 433; premises at 1027 Budapest, Fő u. 68; tel. and fax (1) 2020-182; f. 1930; Pres. Dr TAMÁS KARNITSCHER; publ. *Bőr és Cipőtechnika* (Leather and Shoe News, monthly).

Energiagazdálkodási Tudományos Egyesület (Scientific Society of Energetics): 1055 Budapest, Kossuth Lajos tér 6–8; tel. 1532-751: telex 22-5792; fax 1533-894; f. 1949; 4,300 mems; Pres. Dr TAMÁS ZETTNER; Vice-Pres. GYŐZŐ WIEGAND; publs *Energiagazdálkodás* (Energy Economics) (monthly).

Faipari Tudományos Egyesület (Scientific Society of the Timber Industry): 1027 Budapest, Fő utca 68; tel. 2019-929; telex 22-4343; f. 1950; 1,800 mems; Pres. Dr SÁNDOR MOLNÁR; Sec.-Gen. DEZSŐ LELE; publ. *Faipar* (Timber Industry).

Gépipari Tudományos Egyesület (GTE) (Scientific Society of Mechanical Engineers): 1371 Budapest, Fő u. 68, POB 433; tel. (1) 2020-582; telex 22-4343; fax (1) 2020-252; f. 1949; sciences of mechanical engineering, dissemination of technical culture, assisting the technical and economic development of Hungary; 10,600 mems; library of 1,500 vols; Pres. Prof. Dr JÁNOS TAKÁCS; Sec.-Gen. Ing. ÁDÁM WEIN; publs *Gép* (Machine), *Járművek, Mezőgazdasági Gépek* (Vehicles and Agricultural Machines), *Gépgyártástechnológia* (Production Engineering), *Műanyag és Gumi* (Plastics and Rubber), *Gépipar* (Machinery).

Hiradástechnikai Tudományos Egyesület (Scientific Society for Telecommunication): 1372 Budapest, Pf. 451, Kossuth Lajos tér 6–8; tel. (1) 353-1027; fax (1) 353-0451; e-mail hiradastechnika@mtesz.hu; f. 1949; organization of conferences, discussions, seminars, technical exhibitions, postgraduate courses, study trips, expert advice for official organs and enterprises, recommendations for official organs, public discussion and criticism of technical, economic, scientific and educational matters, engineering activities; 2,500 mems; Pres. Prof. Dr LÁSZLÓ PAP; Sec.-Gen. Dr GÁBOR HUSZTY; publs *Híradástechnika* (Telecommunication, monthly), *Hírlevél* (Newsletter, monthly).

Közlekedéstudományi Egyesület (Scientific Association for Transport): 1055 Budapest, Kossuth Lajos tér 6–8; tel. and fax 153-2005; f. 1949; 4,500 mems; Pres. Dr SÁNDOR GYURKOVICS; Sec.-Gen. ANDRÁS KATONA; publs *Közlekedéstudományi Szemle* (Communications Review), *Közlekedésépitési és Mélyépitéstudományi Szemle* (Civil Engineering Review), *Városi Közlekedés* (Urban Transport).

Magyar Elektrotechnikai Egyesület (Hungarian Electrotechnical Association): 1055 Budapest, Kossuth Lajos tér 6–8; tel. 1530-117; telex 22-5792; fax 1534-069; f. 1900; 6,500 mems; Pres. Dr ISTVÁN KRÓMER; Dir PÉTER LERNYEI; publ. *Electrotechnika* (Electrical Engineering, monthly).

Magyar Iparjogvédelmi Egyesület (Hungarian Association for the Protection of Industrial Property): 1055 Budapest V, Kossuth Lajos tér 6–8; tel. 153-1661; telex 22-5792; fax 153-1780; f. 1962; 2,250 mems; Pres. Dr ENDRE LONTAI; Sec.-Gen. GEORGE MAROSI; publ. *MIE Közleményei* (report).

Méréstechnikai és Automatizálási Tudományos Egyesület (Scientific Society for Measurement and Automation): 1055 Budapest V, Kossuth tér 6–8; tel. 1531-406; telex 22-5792; f. 1952; 3,000 mems; Pres. Prof. Dr ISTVÁN MARTOS; Gen. Sec. Dr JÓZSEF HAJAS; publ. *Mérés és Automatika* (Measurement and Automation).

Neumann János Számitógéptudományi Társaság (John v. Neumann Computer Society): 1054 Budapest, Báthori u. 16; tel. 1329-349; telex 225369; fax 1318-140; f. 1968; to promote the study, development and application of computer sciences; 5,500 mems; library of 3,000 vols; Pres. DEZSŐ SIMA; Man. Dir ISTVÁN ALFOLDI.

Országos Magyar Bányászati és Kohászati Egyesület (Hungarian Mining and Metallurgical Society): 1027 Budapest, Fő utca 68; tel. 201-7337; telex 224343; fax 201-7337; f. 1892; Pres. Dr ISTVÁN TÓTH; Gen. Sec. Dr PÁL TARDY; 6,000 mems; library of 4,000 vols; publs *Bányászat* (Mining), *Kohászat* (Metallurgy), *Öntöde* (Foundry), *Kőolaj és Földgáz* (Oil and Gas) (all monthly).

Papír- és Nyomdaipari Műszaki Egyesület (Technical Association of the Paper and Printing Industry): H-1371 Budapest, Pf. 433, Fő u. 68; tel. 2018-495; fax 2020-256; e-mail mail.pnyme@mtesz.hu; f. 1948; 3,800 mems; Pres. GYÖRGY KARDOS; Sec.-Gen. LÁSZLÓ BURGER; publs *Papíripar* and *Magyar Grafika* (Paper Industry and Hungarian Graphics).

Szervezési és Vezetési Tudományos Társaság (Society for Organization and Management Science): 1027 Budapest, Fő u. 68; tel. 2021-456; telex 22-4343; fax 202-0856; f. 1970; 5,000 mems; Pres. Dr FERENC TRETHON; Sec.-Gen. Dr JÁNOS PAKUCS; publ. *Ipar-Gazdaság* (Industrial Economy, monthly).

Szilikátipari Tudományos Egyesület (Scientific Society of the Silicate Industry): 1027 Budapest, Fő utca 68; tel. and fax 201-9360; telex 224343; f. 1949; 2,300 mems; library of *c.* 2,500 vols; Pres. JENŐ VIG; Sec.-Gen. Dr MÁRTA FODOR; publ. *Építőanyag* (Building Materials).

Textilipari Műszaki és Tudományos Egyesület (Hungarian Society of Textile Technology and Science): 1027 Budapest, Fő utca 68; tel. 2018-782; fax 201-8782; e-mail mail2.tmte@mtesz.hu; f. 1948; 7,200 mems; Pres. Dr FRIGYES GELEJI; Gen. Sec. Dr KATALIN MÁTHÉ; publs *Magyar Textiltechnika* (Hungarian Textile Engineering), *Textiltisztitás* (Textile Cleaning).

Research Institutes

AGRICULTURE, FISHERIES AND VETERINARY SCIENCE

Állattenyésztési és Takarmányozási Kutatóintézet (Research Institute for Animal Breeding and Nutrition): 2053 Herceghalom; tel. and fax (23) 319-082; research into large animal breeding, nutrition, reproductive biology, genetics, nutrition biology and microbiology; library of 4,800 vols; Dir Prof. Dr LÁSZLÓ FÉSÜS; publ. *Állattenyésztés és Takarmányozás* (Animal Breeding and Nutrition, 6 a year, with English summaries).

Gabonatermesztési Kutató Kht. (Cereal Research Non-Profit Co.): 6701 Szeged, POB 391; tel. (62) 435-235; fax (62) 434-163; e-mail h10152mes@ella.hu; f. 1924; wheat, barley, oats, maize, triticale, sunflower, oil-flax, oilrape, red clover; library of 12,000 vols; Dir Dr JÓZSEF FRANK; publ. *Cereal Research Communications* (quarterly).

Magyar Tejgazdasági Kisérleti Intézet (Hungarian Dairy Research Institute): 9200 Mosonmagyaróvár, Lucsony u. 24; tel. (98) 15 711; telex 24 217; f. 1903; brs in Budapest and Pécs; scientific research of raw materials, technology, engineering, chemistry, microbiology, economics; 90 staff; library of 5,700 vols; Dir GYÖRGY BABELLA.

Magyar Tudományos Akadémia Állatorvostudományi Kutatóintézete (Veterinary Medical Research Institute of the Hungarian Academy of Sciences): 1143 Budapest, Hungária krt. 21; tel. 252-2455; fax 2521-069; f. 1949; research in infectious and parasitic diseases of domestic animals; library of 6,500 vols; Dir BELA NAGY.

Magyar Tudományos Akadémia Mezőgazdasági Kutatóintézete (Agricultural Research Institute of the Hungarian Academy of Sciences): 2462 Martonvásár; tel. (22) 460-016; telex 22 4008; fax (22) 460-213; f. 1949; research in plant genetics, plant physiology, plant breeding and plant cultivation of maize and wheat; library of 16,000 vols; Dir ZOLTÁN BEDŐ.

Magyar Tudományos Akadémia Növényvédelmi Kutatóintézete (Plant Protection Institute, Hungarian Academy of Sciences): 1525 Budapest II, Herman Ottó út. 15, Box 102; tel. 1558-722; f. 1880, reorganized 1950; research on plant diseases, insect pests, pesticide chemistry and plant biochemistry, biotechnology, virology; 100 mems; library of 20,000 vols; Dir Dr T. KŐMÍVES.

Magyar Tudományos Akadémia Talajtani és Agrokémiai Kutató Intézete (Research Institute for Soil Science and Agricultural Chemistry of the Hungarian Academy of Sciences): 1022 Budapest, Herman Ottó u. 15; tel. 1564-682; fax 1558-839; f. 1949; research in soil physics, chemistry, geography and cartography, reclamation of salt-affected and sandy soils, irrigation, conservation, fertilization, soil mineralogy, soil microbiology, soil ecology, recultivation; isotope laboratory; library of 27,000 vols; Dir Prof. Dr T. NÉMETH; publs *Agrokémia és Talajtan* (Agrochemistry and Soil Science, quarterly).

Országos Állategészségügyi Intézet (Central Veterinary Institute): 1149 Budapest, Tábornok u. 2; tel. 252-8444; telex 22 4430; fax 252-5177; f. 1928; diagnostic examinations and research work on the infectious, parasitic and metabolic diseases of animals, also veterinary toxicology and diseases of wild animals; 95 mems; library of 5,966 vols; Dir L. TEKES.

Országos Mezőgazdasági Minősítő Intézet (National Institute for Agricultural Quality Control): 1024 Budapest, Keleti Károly u. 24; tel. (1) 2123-127; fax (1) 2122-673; f. 1988 by amalgamation of four orgs.; 700 mems; library of 20,000 vols; Dir-Gen. Dr KÁROLY NESZMÉLYI; publs National Variety List of state-registered plant varieties, Descriptive List of Varieties, List of approved grape and fruit varieties, selections and foreign varieties permitted for propagation (annually), *Yearbook* of cattle, pig, sheep, horse, water fowl, fish breeding and beekeeping.

Szőlészeti és Borászati Kutató Intézet (Research Institute for Viticulture and Oenology): 6000 Kecskemét, Kisfái 182, POB 25; tel. (76) 486-311; telex 26518; fax (76) 327-599; f. 1898; viticulture, oenology, economy; library of 7,200 vols; Dir Dr ERNŐ PÉTER BOTOS; publ. *Magyar Szőlő és Borgazdaság* (Hungarian Viticulture and Oenology, every 6 weeks).

Vízgazdálkodási Tudományos Kutató Rt. (VITUKI) (Water Resources Research Centre plc): 1095 Budapest, Kvassay Jenő ut. 1; tel. (1) 2156-140; telex 224957; fax (1) 2161-514; f. 1952; basic, applied and development research associated with hydrological data collection, processing, storage, information; hydrology of ground-, karstic water, regional soil moisture control; hydromechanics of hydraulic structures; pollution and quality control of water; hydrological and hydraulic problems in agricultural water management (drainage, irrigation); international post-graduate course on hydrology; library of 13,000 vols; Dir-Gen. Dr ÖDÖN STAROSOLSZKY; publs *Hydrological Yearbook of Hungary, Hydrological Atlases of Hungarian Catchments, VITUKI Proceedings* (research reports, etc, mostly with summaries in a world language).

ECONOMICS, LAW AND POLITICS

Magyar Külügyi Intézet (Hungarian Institute of International Affairs): 1125 Budapest, Szilágyi Erzsébet fasor 22/C; tel. (1) 275-2496; fax (1) 275-2497; f. 1972; prepares analytical material and information for foreign policy institutions; research on theoretical issues of international relations; organizes round-table conferences, seminars, lectures; reference library; Dir Dr ANDRÁS BALOGH; publ. *Külpolitika* (Foreign Policy, 4 a year).

Magyar Tudományos Akadémia Állam- és Jogtudományi Intézete (Institute for Legal and Administrative Sciences of the Hungarian Academy of Sciences): 1014 Budapest, Országház u. 30; tel. (1) 355-7384; fax (1) 175-7858; f. 1949; departments of legal theory, international law, constitutional and administrative law, civil law, criminal law, comparative law, human rights, documentation; library of 52,000 vols; Dir Prof. Dr VANDA LAMM.

Magyar Tudományos Akadémia Ipar- és Vállalatgazdaságkutató Intézet (Research Institute for Industrial Economics of the Hungarian Academy of Sciences): 1112 Budapest, Budaörsi ut 45; tel. 319-3164; telex 227030; fax 319-3169; f. 1960; industrial development and policy, structural adaptation, technology and labour, management, productivity and competitiveness; 20 mems; library of 8,000 vols; Dir ÁDÁM TÖRÖK; publ. *Ipargazdasági Szemle* (Review of Industrial Economics, quarterly).

Magyar Tudományos Akadémia Közgazdaságtudományi Intézet (Institute of Economics of the Hungarian Academy of Sciences): 1112 Budapest, Budaörsi ut 45; tel. 185-0777; fax 185-1120; f. 1954; research in economics, economic policy and economic transition, functioning of modern market economies, control theory, stabilization policy, money and credit, labour market, foreign trade, agriculture; 65 research workers; library of 6,000 vols, 1,000 periodicals; Dir Prof. JENŐ KOLTAY; publs *Acta Oeconomica* (4 issues in 2 vols a year, in English), *KTI/IE Papers* (irregular in English and Hungarian).

Magyar Tudományos Akadémia Politikai Tudományok Intézete (Institute for Political Science of the Hungarian Academy of Sciences): 1068 Budapest, Benczúr u. 33; tel. 321-4830; fax 322-1843; f. 1991; study of political systems, party structure, national and local government, political culture, elections, problems of integration with the EU and migration; library of 43,000 vols; Dir Prof. Dr KÁLMÁN KULCSÁR; publs *Hungarian Political Science Review* (quarterly), *European Studies, City Societies, Local Authority and Local Policy, Scientia Humana – Politology, Embourgeoisement, Yearbook of the International Migration Research Team.*

Magyar Tudományos Akadémia Világgazdasági Kutató Intézete (Institute for World Economics of the Hungarian Academy of Sciences): 1124 Budapest, Kálló esperes u. 15; tel. (1) 319-9381; fax (1) 319-9377; e-mail vki@vki3.vki.hu; f. 1965; research in world economics; library of 102,000 vols; Dir ANDRÁS INOTAI; publs *Trends in World Economy*, *Working Papers* (all irregularly, in English), *Kihívások* (Challenges, irregularly), *Mühelytanulmányok* (Workshop Studies, irregularly).

EDUCATION

MTA Szociológiai Intézet Kultúrakutató Műhely (Cultural Research Centre of the Hungarian Academy of Sciences Institute of Sociology): 1014 Budapest, Úri u. 49; tel. and fax (1) 1569-457; f. 1980; centre for scientific research in cultural development, sociology of culture and leisure pursuits; Dirs IVÁN VITÁNYI, PÉTER HIDY; publ. *Kultúra és Közösség* (Culture and Community).

Oktatáskutató Intézet (Hungarian Institute for Educational Research): 1395 Budapest, POB 427, Victor Hugo u. 18–22; tel. and fax (1) 129-7639; e-mail h6229ier@ella.hu; f. 1981; applied social research and postgraduate training on education and higher education systems; library of 20,000 vols; Dir TAMÁS KOZMA; publ. *Educatio* (quarterly review).

FINE AND PERFORMING ARTS

Magyar Tudományos Akadémia Művészettörténeti Kutatóintézet (Research Institute for Art History of the Hungarian Academy of Sciences): 1014 Budapest, Uri-utca 49; tel. 175-9011; f. 1969; research on 10th–20th-century Hungarian art; library of 21,000 vols; Dir ERNŐ MAROSI; publ. *Ars Hungarica* (2 a year).

Magyar Tudományos Akadémia Zenetudományi Intézete (Institute for Musicology of the Hungarian Academy of Sciences): 1014 Budapest, Táncsics M. u. 7; tel. 214-6770; fax 375-9282; f. 1961; incorporates the Bartók Archives, the Museum of History of Music, and depts of Sociology of Music, Folk Music, Folk Dances, Theory of Music, History of Music; library of 150,000 vols; 100,000 recorded melodies; Dir ZOLTÁN FALVY; publs *Corpus Musicae Popularis Hungaricae*, *Musicalia Danubiana*, *Studia Musicologica*.

HISTORY, GEOGRAPHY AND ARCHAEOLOGY

Magyar Tudományos Akadémia Földrajztudományi Kutatóintézete (Geographical Research Institute, Hungarian Academy of Sciences): 1062 Budapest, Andrássy ut. 62; tel. 1116-838; telex 22-6413; fax 131-7991; f. 1950, reorg. 1952; research in physical and human geography; library of 67,000 vols; Dir FERENC SCHWEITZER; publs *Földrajzi Értesítő* (quarterly), *Földrajzi Tanulmányok, Studies in Geography in Hungary, Geographical Abstracts from Hungary.*

Magyar Tudományos Akadémia Régészeti Intézete (Archaeological Institute of the Hungarian Academy of Sciences): 1250 Budapest, Uri u. 49; tel. 1759-011; fax 1564-567; f. 1958; 25 mems; library of 46,000 vols; Dir Dr BÁLINT; publs *Studia Archaeologica* (irregularly in foreign languages), *Magyarország Régészeti Topográfiája* (Archaeological Topography of Hungary), *Antaeus* (yearbook in German and English).

Magyar Tudományos Akadémia Regionális Kutatások Központja (Research Centre for Regional Studies of the Hungarian Academy of Sciences): 7621 Pécs, Papnovelde u. 22; tel. (72) 212-755; fax (72) 233-704; e-mail postmaster@dti.rkk.hu; f. 1943; research into regional planning, geography, economics, government, sociology, ethnography, and history; 45 mems; 60 researchers; library of 40,000 vols; Dir Prof. GYULA HORVÁTH; publs *Tér és Társadalom* (quarterly), *Alföldi Tanulmányok* (irregular), *MTA RKK Kutatási Eredményeit* (irregular), *Területi és települési kutatások* (irregular), regional research reports (annually), discussion papers (irregular).

Magyar Tudományos Akadémia Történettudományi Intézete (Institute of Historical Science of the Hungarian Academy of Sciences): 1014 Budapest, Uri u. 53; tel. 1561-539; fax 1566-373; f. 1949; five depts of Hungarian history and comparative European history, one dept. of documentation and bibliography, historiography; 62 researchers, library of 100,000 vols; Dir ZOLTÁN SZÁSZ; publs *Történelmi Szemle* (quarterly), annual bibliography of historical works published in Hungary.

LANGUAGE AND LITERATURE

Magyar Tudományos Akadémia Irodalomtudományi Intézete (Institute of Literary Studies of the Hungarian Academy of Sciences): 1118 Budapest, Ménesi u. 11–13; tel. (1) 385-8790; fax (1) 185-3876; f. 1956; research in Hungarian and world literature; library of 170,000 vols; Dir Prof. LÁSZLÓ SZÖRÉNYI; publs *Irodalomtörténeti Közlemények, Helikon, Literatura* (quarterly), *Irodalomtörténeti Füzetek* (studies), etc.

Magyar Tudományos Akadémia Nyelvtudományi Intézete (Research Institute of Linguistics of the Hungarian Academy of Sciences): 1014 Budapest, Színház u. 5–9; tel. (1) 1758-285; fax (1) 2122-050; f. 1949; 124 mems; library of 40,000 vols; Dir F. KIEFER; publs *Nyelvtudományi Közlemények* (Linguistic Publications), *Műhelymunkák a nyelvészet és társtudományai köréből* (Working Papers on Linguistics and Related Sciences), *Magyar Fonetikai Füzetek* (Hungarian Papers in Phonetics).

MEDICINE

'Johan Béla' Országos Közegészségügyi Intézet ('B. Johan' National Institute of Public Health): 1097 Budapest, Gyáli út. 2–6; tel. (1) 215-2250; telex 22-5349; fax (1) 215-0148; f. 1927; research in environmental health, epidemiology, microbiology; 160 research staff; library of 30,000 vols; Dir D. PÁPAY; publ. *Évi Működés* (Annual Report).

Magyar Tudományos Akadémia Kísérleti Orvostudományi Kutatóintézete (Institute of Experimental Medicine of the Hungarian Academy of Sciences): 1083 Budapest, Szigony u. 43; tel. 210-0810; fax 210-0813; f. 1952; research work in experimental morphology, pathophysiology, pharmacology, neuroscience, etc.; library of 21,000 vols; Dir Prof. Dr E. SYLVESTER VIZI.

Mozgássérültek Pető András Nevelőképző és Nevelőintézete (András Pető Institute for Conductive Education of the Motor Disabled, and Conductors' College): 1125 Budapest, Kutvölgyi u. 6; tel. (1) 224-1500; fax (1) 155-6649; f. 1945; conductive education for 500 residential motor disabled and 1,900 out-patients; training for 300 professional conductors; Gen. Dir ILDIKÓ KOZMA.

Országos Epidemiológiai Központ, Mikrobiológiai Kutatócsoport (Microbiological Research Group of the National Centre for Epidemiology): 1529 Budapest, Pihenő u. 1; tel. 1760-044; f. 1963; oncogenic viruses, virus tumours, AIDS, interferon, mycobacteria and mycobacteriophages; library of 2,000 vols; Dir JÁNOS MINÁROVITS.

Országos 'Fréderic Joliot-Curie' Sugárbiológiai és Sugáregészségügyi Kutató Intézet (National Research Institute for Radiobiology and Radiohygiene): 1775 Budapest, POB 101; tel. and fax (1) 226-0026; telex 225103; f. 1957; under Min. of Public Welfare; radiohygiene, including protection of workers from radiation; radiobiology research on effects of external ionizing radiation and incorporated radioisotopes; radiation and radioisotope applications including preservation of biological tissue, sterilization or detoxification of drugs, toxins and vaccines as well as preparation of radiopharmaceuticals for in vitro and in vivo uses in nuclear medicine; teaching within the Postgraduate Medical School, Budapest; library of 7,000 vols; Dir Prof. Dr G. J. KÖTELES.

Országos Haematológiai, Vértranszfúziós és Immunologiai Intézet (National Institute of Haematology, Blood Transfusion and Immunology): 1113 Budapest, Daróczi út 24; tel. 1665-822; telex 224283; fax 166-7020; f. 1948; research and clinical activities in haematology and immunology, including bone-marrow transplantation; production of blood components and plasma derivatives; library of *c.* 10,000 vols, 91 periodicals; Dir Dr GY. PETRÁNYI; publs *Haematologia* (int. quarterly in English), *Transzfúzió* (quarterly, in Hungarian).

Országos Onkológiai Intézet (National Institute of Oncology): 1122 Budapest, Ráth György u. 7/9; tel. 1554-411; telex 22-4260; fax 1562-402; f. 1952; experimental and clinical activities; 173 staff; library of 15,973 vols, 164 periodicals, service for reprints of all publs available; Dir Dr M. KASLER; publ. *Magyar Onkológia* (quarterly).

NATURAL SCIENCES

Biological Sciences

Magyar Madártani Intézet (Hungarian Institute for Ornithology): 1121 Budapest, Költő u. 21; tel. 395-2605; fax 1757-457; e-mail bueki.jozsef@ktmdom2.ktm.hu; f. 1893; 6 mems; library of 5,000 vols, 400 periodicals; Dir Dr ZSOLT KALOTÁS; library; publ. *Aquila* (Yearbook).

Magyar Tudományos Akadémia Balatoni Limnológiai Kutatóintézete (Balaton Limnological Research Institute of the Hungarian Academy of Sciences): 8237 Tihany, POB 35; tel. (87) 448-244; fax (87) 448-006; e-mail intezet@tres.blki.hu; f. 1927; research particularly in hydrobiology, and experimental zoology; library of 16,000 vols; Dir Dr SÁNDOR HERODEK; publ. collected reprints, progress report.

Magyar Tudományos Akadémia Ökológiai és Botanikai Kutatóintézete (Ecological and Botanical Research Institute of the Hungarian Academy of Sciences): 2163 Vácrátót; tel. (28) 360-122; fax (28) 360-110; e-mail obki@botanika.botanika.hu; f. 1952; theoretical and experimental research; library of 8,700 vols; Dir Dr ATTILA BORHIDI.

Magyar Tudományos Akadémia Szegedi Biológiai Központja (Biological Research Centre of the Hungarian Academy of Sciences): 6701 Szeged, Temesvári krt. 62, POB 521; tel. (62) 432-232; telex 82-442; fax (62) 432-576; f. 1971; library of 25,000 vols; Dir-Gen. DÉNES DUDITS.

Attached institutes:

Biofizikai Intézet (Institute of Biophysics): C/o Magyar Tudományos Akadémia

Szegedi Biológiai Központja, 6701 Szeged, Temesvári krt. 62, POB 521; tel. (62) 433-465; f. 1971; Dir Pál Ormos.

Biokémiai Intézet (Institute of Biochemistry): C/o Magyar Tudományos Akadémia Szegedi Biológiai Központja, 6701 Szeged, Temesvári krt. 62, POB 521; tel. (62) 433-506; f. 1971; Dir László Vígh.

Enzimológiai Intézet (Institute of Enzymology): 1113 Budapest, Karolina u. 29; tel. (1) 466-5856; fax (1) 466-5465; f. 1957; Dir Péter Friedrich.

Genetikai Intézet (Institute of Genetics): C/o Magyar Tudományos Akadémia Szegedi Biológiai Központja, 6701 Szeged, Temesvári krt. 62, POB 521; tel. (62) 432-232; fax (62) 433-503; f. 1971; Dir István Raskó.

Növénybiológiai Intézet (Institute of Plant Biology): C/o Magyar Tudományos Akadémia Szegedi Biológiai Központja, 6701 Szeged, Temesvári krt. 62, POB 521; tel. and fax (62) 433-434; f. 1970; Dir Dénes Dudits.

Mathematical Sciences

Magyar Tudományos Akadémia Matematikai Kutatóintézete (Mathematical Research Institute of the Hungarian Academy of Sciences): 1053 Budapest, Reáltanoda u. 13–15; tel. 1173-151; fax 1177-166; e-mail mail@math-inst.hu; f. 1950; research in fields of pure and applied mathematics; 80 mems; library of 60,000 vols; Dir G. O. H. Katona; publ. *Studia Scientiarum Mathematicarum Hungarica*.

Physical Sciences

Magyar Állami Eötvös Loránd Geofizikai Intézet (Eötvös Loránd Geophysical Institute of Hungary): 1145 Budapest, Columbus u. 17–23; tel. 2524-999; fax 3637-256; e-mail elgi@elgi.hu; f. 1919; geophysical exploration for hydrocarbons, coal, bauxite, water, ores; engineering geophysics: Dir Dr Tamás Bodoky; library of 31,130 vols; publs *Geophysical Transactions* (quarterly), *Bulletin—Study of the Earth Tides* (annually).

Attached institute:

Geophysical Observatory: 8237 Tihany; tel. (80) 44-029; e-mail h7215obs@ella.hu; f. 1954; Head László Hegymegi; publ. *Annual Report*.

Magyar Állami Földtani Intézet (Hungarian Geological Institute): 1442 Budapest, Pf. 106; located at: 1143 Budapest Stefánia u. 14; tel. (1) 2510-999; fax (1) 2510-703; e-mail geo@mafi.hu; f. 1869; conducts geological survey of Hungary; library of 320,000 vols; Dir Károly Brezsnyánsky; publ. *Évi jelentés* (Annual Report).

Magyar Tudományos Akadémia Atommagkutató Intézete (Institute of Nuclear Research of the Hungarian Academy of Sciences): 4026 Debrecen, Bem-tér 18/c; tel. (52) 417-266; fax (52) 416-181; f. 1954; nuclear physics, atomic physics, materials science and analysis, earth and cosmic sciences, environmental research, biological and medical research, development of methods and instruments; library of 55,000 vols; Dir Dr Rezső G. Lovas; publ. *Annual Report*.

Magyar Tudományos Akadémia Csillagászati Kutatóintézete (Konkoly Observatory of the Hungarian Academy of Sciences): 1121 Budapest, Konkoly Thege Miklós u. 13–17; tel. 1754-122; fax 2754-668; f. 1899; 52 staff; library of 32,000 vols; Mountain Station: Piszkéstető, Galyatető (f. 1962), with Schmidt telescope, Cassegrain-reflector and 100 cm Ritchey-Chretien telescope; Dir Béla Szeidl; publs *Mitteilungen der Sternwarte der Ungarischen Akademie der Wissenschaften* (Communications from the Konkoly Observatory of the Hungarian Academy of Sciences), *Information Bulletin on Variable Stars of Commission 27 of the IAU*.

Magyar Tudományos Akadémia Csillagászati Kutatóintézetének Napfizikai Obszervatóriuma (Heliophysical Observatory of the Hungarian Academy of Sciences): 4010 Debrecen, Egyetem tér 1, POB 30; tel. (52) 311-015; e-mail obs@fenyi.sci.klte.hu; f. 1958; studies of solar activity: sunspots, solar flares, prominences; library of 10,000 vols, 20 periodicals, 5,500 sunspot drawings (1872–1919), 100,000 full-disc solar photographs; Dir B. Kálmán; publ. *Publications*.

Magyar Tudományos Akadémia Geodéziai és Geofizikai Kutató Intézete (Geodetical and Geophysical Research Institute of the Hungarian Academy of Sciences): 9400 Sopron, Csatkai E. u. 6–8; tel. (99) 314-290; fax (99) 313-267; f. 1955 as two separate laboratories, merged as one institute 1972; research in advanced problems of geodesy and geophysics including seismology; library of 34,000 vols; Dir Dr P. Varga; publs *Rapport Microséismique de Hongrie* (annually), *Geophysical Observatory Reports* (annually).

Magyar Tudományos Akadémia Kémiai Kutatóközpont Izotóp- és Felületkémiai Intézet (Institute of Isotope and Surface Chemistry Chemical Research Centre of the Hungarian Academy of Sciences): 1525 Budapest, POB 77; tel. (1) 395-9220; fax (1) 395-9080; e-mail wojn@alpha0.iki.kfki.hu; f. 1959; research in the field of catalysis, surface chemistry, adsorption, radiation chemistry, photochemistry, molecular spectroscopy, nuclear spectroscopy, nuclear safety, radioactive tracer technique; library of 14,000 vols; Dir László Wojnárovits.

Magyar Tudományos Akadémia, KFKI Anyagtudományi Kutató Intézet (Research Institute for Materials Science of the Hungarian Academy of Sciences): 1525 Budapest, POB 49; located at: 1121 Budapest, Konkoly Thege u. 29–33; tel. (1) 395-9253; fax (1) 395-9284; e-mail gyulai@ra.atki.kfki.hu; f. 1992; shares library of 120,000 vols; Dir Prof. Jozsef Gyulai.

Magyar Tudományos Akadémia, KFKI Atomenergia Kutató Intézet (KFKI Atomic Energy Research Institute of the Hungarian Academy of Sciences): 1525 Budapest, Konkoly Thege M. u. 29–33, POB 49; tel. (1) 1696762; fax (1) 1552530; f. 1992; shares library of 120,000 vols; Dir János Gadó.

Magyar Tudományos Akadémia, KFKI Mérés- és Számítástechnikai Kutató Intézet (KFKI Research Institute for Measurement and Computing Techniques of the Hungarian Academy of Sciences): 1525 Budapest, Konkoly Thege M. u. 29–33, POB 49; tel. and fax (1) 1695532; f. 1992; Dir Ferenc Vajda.

Magyar Tudományos Akadémia, Központi Kémiai Kutató Intézet (Central Research Institute for Chemistry of the Hungarian Academy of Sciences): 1025 Budapest, Pusztaszeri u. 59/67; tel. (1) 325-7900; fax (1) 325-7554; f. 1952; fundamental research in organic, bio-organic and physical chemistry, chemistry and structure of biologically active compounds, catalytic reactions of hydrocarbons, polymerization kinetics and polymer degradation, study of molecular structure, photochemistry, corrosion science; library of 45,500 vols; Dir Prof. Dr Ferenc Márta.

Magyar Tudományos Akadémia Műszaki Fizikai Kutató Intézete (Research Institute for Technical Physics of the Hungarian Academy of Sciences): 1047 Budapest, Fóti u. 56; tel. 1692-100; fax 1698-037; f. 1958; fundamental research in the field of technical physics; library of 20,000 vols; Dir László Bartha; publ. *MFKI Yearbook* (every 2 years).

Magyar Tudományos Akadémia Műszaki Kémiai Kutató Intézet (Research Institute for Chemical Engineering of the Hungarian Academy of Sciences): 8200 Veszprém, Egyetem u. 2; tel. (88) 425-206; fax (88) 424-424; f. 1960; fundamental and applied research in traditional chemical engineering, bioengineering and systems engineering; library of 8,500 vols; Dir Dr János Gyenis; publ. *Hungarian Journal of Industrial Chemistry*.

Uránia Csillagvizsgáló (Urania Public Observatory): 1016 Budapest, Sánc u. 3b; tel. 1869-233; fax 2671-391; f. 1947; centre of the Hungarian amateur astronomy movement; 8-inch Heyde refractor, 6-inch Zeiss reflector; library of 1,700 vols; Dir Otto Zombori; publ. *Uránia Füzetek* (Urania Letters, annually).

PHILOSOPHY AND PSYCHOLOGY

Magyar Tudományos Akadémia Filozófiai Intézete (Institute for Philosophy of the Hungarian Academy of Sciences): 1398 Budapest 62, POB 594; tel. and fax (1) 3120-243; f. 1957 for research into problems of epistemology, philosophy of science, social philosophy, methodological problems of social sciences, philosophy of religion, political philosophy, history of philosophical thought; institute library of 26,000 vols; Dir Prof. Dr Kristóf Nyíri; publ. *Magyar Filozófiai Szemle* (6 a year).

Magyar Tudományos Akadémia Pszichológiai Intézete (Institute of Psychology of the Hungarian Academy of Sciences): 1394 Budapest, POB 398; tel. (1) 322-0425; fax (1) 342-0514; f. 1902; basic research on cognitive psychophysiology and neuropsychology, developmental psychology, social psychology and personality, research on educational psychology; library of 19,000 vols; Dir Dr György Karmos; publ. *Pszichológia* (quarterly).

RELIGION, SOCIOLOGY AND ANTHROPOLOGY

Magyar Tudományos Akadémia Néprajzi Kutatóintézete (Institute of Ethnology of the Hungarian Academy of Sciences): 1250 Budapest, POB 29; tel. 1759-011; fax 1759-764; f. 1967; research in ethnology of the Hungarian people, general anthropology, folklore and traditions, study of gypsies; library of 68,000 vols; Dir A. Paládi-Kovács; publs *Népi Kultura—Népi Társadalom*, *Magyar Néprajz*, *Folklór Archivum*, *Documentatio Ethnographica*, *Életmód és Tradició*, *Folklór és Tradició*, *Ciganisztikai tanulmányok*, *Occasional Papers in Anthropology*.

Magyar Tudományos Akadémia Szociológiai Intezete (Institute of Sociology of the Hungarian Academy of Sciences): 1014 Budapest, Uri u. 49; tel. (1) 175-4891; fax (1) 224-0790; f. 1963; study of social structure, social change, effects of economic transformation, social policy, sociology of health, social justice; sociology of women and the family, sociology of culture; library of 8,000 vols; Dir Elemér Hankiss; publ. *Szociológiai tanulmányok* (Social Studies, 3–4 issues a year).

TECHNOLOGY

Magyar Tudományos Akadémia Bányászati Kémiai Kutatólaboratóriuma (Research Laboratory for Mining Chemistry of the Hungarian Academy of Sciences): 3515 Miskolc-Egyetemváros; tel. (46) 367-211; fax (46) 363-349; e-mail lakatos@mta.bkkl.hu; f. 1957; library of 5,000 vols; Dir Istvan Lakatos.

Magyar Tudományos Akadémia Számítástechnikai és Automatizálási Kutató Intézete (Computer and Automation Research Institute of the Hungarian Academy of Sciences): 1111 Budapest, Kende u. 13/17;

tel. 1665-644; telex 225066; fax 1667-503; f. 1964; conducts research in intelligent computing, control and information systems, new computation structures, and computer applications for engineering, production and administration systems; library of 45,600 vols; Dir Dr PÉTER INZELT; publs *Report* (annually), *Transactions* (irregular).

Szilikátipari Központi Kutató és Tervező Intézet (Central Research and Design Institute for the Silicate Industry): 1034 Budapest, Bécsi út 122–124; tel. 250-1311; telex 226827; fax 1687-626; f. 1953; research and technological design in the silicate sciences and building materials industry; library of 25,000 vols, 7,000 periodicals; Dir CSABA ÁRPÁD RÉTI; publs *Tudományos Közlemények* (irregular, summaries in English, German, French, Russian), *Transactions* (irregular, in English, German, French, Russian).

Villamosenergiaipari Kutató Intézet (Institute for Electric Power Research): 1368 Budapest, POB 233; tel. 1183-233; telex 22-5744; fax 1117-9956; f. 1949; research and development on safety assessment of nuclear power plants, combustion technology and environmental management, mechanical and power engineering technology, equipment of the electricity networks, high voltage and high power laboratory testing, systems of control engineering and telemechanics; technical library of 25,000 vols; Gen. Man. Dr ISTVÁN KRÓMER; publ. *VEIKI Publications* (Hungarian, with abstracts in English, annually).

Libraries and Archives

Budapest

Állatorvostudományi Egyetem Központi Könyvtára (Central Library of the University of Veterinary Science): 1078 Budapest, István u. 2; tel. (1) 3220-849; telex 22-4439; fax (1) 3220-849; f. 1787; 130,000 vols, 261 current periodicals; special collections: ancient veterinary literature, historical archives; museum of veterinary history; Dir Mrs MARY CSEREY; publs *Bibliography of Hungarian Veterinary Literature, Az Állatorvostudományi Egyetem Központi Könyvtárának Kiadványai, List of Publications and Scientific Lectures*† (on computer) (all annually).

Budapest Főváros Levéltára (Budapest City Archives): 1052 Budapest, Városház u. 9/11; tel. 1172-033; fax 1183-319; e-mail vargal@ccmail.fph.hu; f. 1901; 23,000 metres of bookshelves; Dir Dr LÁSZLÓ VARGA; publ. *Budapesti Negyed* (quarterly).

Budapesti Közgazdaságtudományi Egyetem Központi Könyvtára (Central Library of Budapest University of Economic Sciences): 1093 Budapest, Zsil u. 2; tel. (1) 2175-827; fax (1) 2174-910; e-mail huszar@puli.lib.bke.hu; f. 1850; economic sciences, world economy, management sciences, etc.; 564,000 vols; Dir-Gen. Dr HEDVIG HUSZÁR.

Budapesti Műszaki Egyetem Könyvtár és Tájékoztatási Központ (Library and Information Centre of the Technical University of Budapest): 1111 Budapest, Budafoki u. 4–6; tel. (1) 463-2441; fax (1) 463-2440; e-mail fonyo@bigmac.cik.bme.hu; f. 1848; library and information services in mathematics, physics, mechanical engineering, transport engineering, chemistry, civil engineering and architecture; 400,000 vols, 140,000 periodicals; Dir Dr PÁL VÁSÁRHELYI.

Eötvös Loránd Tudományegyetem Állam- és Jogtudományi Kar Könyvtára (Faculty of Law Library of Eötvös Loránd University): 1053 Budapest, Egyetem tér 1–3; tel. 2663-005; fax (1) 266-40-91; e-mail kjager@ludens.elte.hu; f. 1903; 42,000 vols, 8,000 periodicals, 21,000 MSS, 3,720 sundry; Dir JÄGERNÉ FÜRSTNER KRISZTINA; publs *Acta Facultatis Politico-Juridicae, Annales Univ. Sci. Budapestinensis Sect. Juridica*.

Eötvös Loránd Tudományegyetem Központi Könyvtára (Loránd Eötvös University Library): 1364 Budapest, Ferenciek tere 6, POB 233; tel. 266-5866; telex 223053; fax 266-4634; f. 1561; Central Library of the University and national scientific library for philosophy, psychology, medieval history and history of Christianity; 1,500,000 vols, 191 codices, 1,100 incunabula, 2,600 old Hungarian printed works (to 1711); Dir-Gen. LÁSZLÓ SZÖGI.

Fővárosi Szabó Ervin Könyvtár (Metropolitan Ervin Szabó Library): 1371 Budapest, Pf. 487, VIII Szabó Ervin tér 1; tel. and fax 118-5815; f. 1904; sociology, humanities; 3,744,000 vols (1,107,000 vols in central library); 78 brs; Dir JENŐ KISS; publs *Yearbook*, current bibliographies of Hungarian sociological literature.

Hadtudományi Könyvtár (Library of Military Science): 1014 Budapest, Kapisztrán tér 2; tel. (1) 1569-770; fax (1) 1569-586; f. 1920; 180,000 vols; Dir LÁSZLÓ VESZPRÉMY; publs *Bibliography* (annually), *Hadtörténelmi Közlemenyek* (Review of Military History, quarterly).

Haynal Imre Egészségtudomanyi Egyetem Központi Könyvtára (Central Library of the Imre Haynal University of Health Sciences): 1135 Budapest XIII, Szabolcs u. 35, POB 112; tel. and fax (1) 270-4763; e-mail ijehoda@lib.hiete.hu; 46,000 vols; Chief Librarian IMOLA JEHODA.

Iparművészeti Múzeum Könyvtára (Library of the Museum of Applied Arts): 1091 Budapest, Üllői u. 33–37; tel. 2175-222; fax 2175-838; f. 1874; scientific research library for the decorative arts; 42,000 vols; 15,000 periodicals; Dir ESTHER TISZAVÁRI; publs *Ars Decorativa* (annually), catalogues.

Kertészeti és Élelmiszeripari Egyetem Könyvtára (Library of the University of Horticulture and Food Technology): 1118 Budapest, Villányi út. 35–43; tel. and fax (1) 1666-220; e-mail ktar@hoya.kee.hu; f. 1860; horticulture, floriculture, nursery, medicinal plants, fruitgrowing, landscape and garden architecture, environmental protection; food industry, canning technology, food fermentation, processing of animal products, processing of cereals and industrial plants, oenology, brewing; 306,000 vols, 800 current periodicals; Dir Dr ÉVA ZALAI-KOVÁCS; publs *'Lippay János' Tudományos Ülésszak Előadásai* (every 2 years), *Universitatis Horticulturae Industriaeque Alimentariae* (every 2 years).

Központi Statisztikai Hivatal Könyvtár és Dokumentációs Szolgálat (Library and Documentation Service of the Central Statistical Office): 1024 Budapest, Pf. 10, II, Keleti Károly u. 5; tel. (1) 345-6105; fax (1) 345-6112; f. 1867; 670,000 books, periodicals, etc.; exchange centre for official statistical publications; Dir-Gen. Dr ISTVÁN CSAHÓK; publs *Statisztikai Módszerek—Témadokumentáció* (Statistical Methods—surveys of literature on various subjects, irregular), *Történeti Statisztikai Tanulmányok* (Studies on Historical Statistics), *Történeti Statisztikai Füzetek* (Papers in Historical Statistics), *Szakbibliográfiák* (Special Bibliographies), *Magyarország Történeti Helységnévtára* (Historical Gazetteer of Hungary), etc.

Liszt Ferenc Zeneművészeti Főiskola Könyvtára (Library of the Ferenc Liszt Academy of Music): 1391 Budapest, Liszt Ferenc tér 8, POB 206; tel. 1220-699; f. 1875; 135,000 musical scores plus 52,000 books and periodicals, 10,000 records; research library for music history; Dir JÁNOS KÁRPÁTI.

Magyar Irók Könyvtára (Library of Hungarian Writers' Union): 1062 Budapest, Bajza u. 18; tel. 1228-840; f. 1950; maintained by the Hungarian Writers Federation; collection of belles-lettres, history of literature, linguistics and allied sciences by Hungarian and foreign authors, translated and/or in original languages; 87,100 vols, 48 foreign and 104 Hungarian periodicals; Dir LÁSZLÓ MEZŐVÁRI.

Magyar Nemzeti Galéria Könyvtára (Library of the Hungarian National Gallery): 1250 Budapest, Budavári Palota, Pf. 31; tel. 1757-533; fax 1758-898; f. 1957; books on art from all over the world, specializing in Hungarian sculpture, wood-carvings, panel paintings, Baroque art, art from the 12th century onwards; 80,000 vols, 27,000 catalogues, 8,800 periodicals, 15,000 slides; Dir Mrs ZSUZSA BERÉNYI; publ. *A Magyar Nemzeti Galéria Évkönyve* (Annals), catalogues.

Magyar Nemzeti Múzeum Régészeti Könyvtára (Archaeological Library of the Hungarian National Museum): 1088 Budapest, Múzeum-körút 14–16; tel. 1134-400; f. 1952; 104,000 vols of Hungarian and foreign archaeology, numismatics and history; Dir Dr ENDRE TÓTH; publs *Folia Archaeologica, Folia Historica, Inventaria Praehistorica Hungariae.*

Magyar Országos Levéltár (Hungarian National Archives): 1014 Budapest, Bécsi-kapu-tér 4; tel. 1565-811; fax 2121-619; f. 1756; 66,500 metres of shelving; records dating from the 12th century to 1989; Gen. Dir Dr LAJOS GECSÉNYI; publ. *Levéltári Közlemények* (Journal of the Hungarian National Archives).

Magyar Testnevelési Egyetem Könyvtára (Library of the Hungarian University of Physical Education): 1123 Budapest, Alkotás utca 44; tel. 156-44-44; fax 156-63-37; f. 1925; collection covers physical education, sport and allied domains, also literature by Hungarian and foreign authors; 89,000 vols; 121 domestic and 92 foreign trade papers; Dir FERENC KRASOVEC; publ *Bulletin of Trade Literature* (in Hungarian, 2 a year).

Magyar Tudományos Akadémia Földrajztudományi Kutató Intézet Könyvtára (Library of the Geographical Research Institute of the Hungarian Academy of Sciences): 1388 Budapest, Andrássy út. 62 (Budapest 62, POB 64); tel. 1116-838; f. 1952; 67,000 vols, 17,500 maps, 8,600 MSS, 7,600 periodicals; Librarian JUDIT SIMONFAI; publs *Geographical Abstracts from Hungary, Földrajzi Értesitő, Elmélet-módszer-gyakorlat, Studies in Geography in Hungary,* occasional papers.

Magyar Tudományos Akadémia Könyvtára (Library of the Hungarian Academy of Sciences): 1245 Budapest V., pf. 1002, Arany J. u. 1; tel. (1) 138-2344; fax (1) 331-6954; e-mail mtak@vax.mtak.hu; f. 1826; 1,075,000 vols, 324,000 periodicals, 692,000 MSS; collection includes oriental manuscripts, old prints and incunabula; depository library for Academy's dissertations; Academy's archives; Dir-Gen. (vacant); publs *Publicationes Bibliothecae Academiae Scientiarum Hungaricae, Catalogi Collectionis Manuscriptorum Bibliothecae Academiae Scientiarum Hungaricae, Oriental Studies, Budapest Oriental Reprints.*

MSZP Politikatörténeti Intézet Könyvtára (Library of the Institute of Political History of the Hungarian Socialist Party): 1054 Budapest, Alkotmány u. 2; tel. 111-5659; f. 1948; 160,000 vols; Dir ÉVA TÓTH.

Művelődési és Közoktatási Minisztérium Levéltári Osztálya (National Board of Archives): 1014 Budapest, Uri u. 54–56; tel. (1) 356-0372; fax (1) 356-0939; f. 1950; functions as supervising board of all archives in Hungary; Gen. Dir JÓZSEF MOLNÁR; publ. *Levéltári Szemle* (quarterly).

Országgyűlési Könyvtár (Library of the Hungarian Parliament): 1357 Budapest, Pf. 3, Kossuth Lajos-tér 1–3; tel. (1) 269-0415; fax (1) 268-4853; e-mail f10ambru@mkogy.hu; f. 1870; parliamentary papers (Hungarian and foreign), contemporary history, administrative and legal sciences, politics, UN depository library; 737,000 vols; Librarian JÁNOS AMBRUS; publ. *INFO-Társadalomtudomány*.

Országos Idegennyelvü Könyvtár (National Library of Foreign Literature): 1056 Budapest, Molnár u. 11; tel. 1183-688; fax 1180-147; e-mail h9126oik@ella.hu; f. 1956; formerly the Gorky State Library; collection of foreign literature and music scores and records; 331,000 vols; Dir JENŐ JUHÁSZ; publs *New Books for Nationalities* (irregularly), *Ethnic Minority Research* (quarterly), *Ethnic Minority Bibliography* (annually).

Országos Műszaki Információs Központ és Könyvtár (National Technical Information Centre and Library): 1428 Budapest, POB 12, Múzeum u. 17; tel. (1) 138-2300; fax (1) 138-2414; e-mail fotitk@omk.omikk.hu; f. 1883; national scientific-technical library; information centre; computerized services; 551,000 vols, 2,700 current periodicals, 512,000 translations; Dir-Gen. Dr ÁKOS HERMAN; publs *Hungarian R & D Abstracts. Science and Technology* (quarterly, in English), *Tudományos és Műszaki Tájékoztatás* (monthly journal of scientific and technical information).

Országos Orvostudományi Információs Intézet és Könyvtár (National Institute for Medical Information and Library—MEDINFO): 1444 Budapest, Szentkirályi u. 21, POB 278; tel. 1176-352; fax 2669-710; f. 1949; centre for medical libraries, training, promotion of interlibrary co-operation; Hungarian and foreign medical bibliographies and reviews compiled; library of 102,000 vols; Dir-Gen. Dr ALEXANDER B. FEDINECZ; publs *Magyar Orvosi Bibliográfia* (Hungarian Medical Bibliography, 6 a year, English edition 2 a year), *Nővér* (Nurse) (quarterly), *Országtanulmányok* (Country profiles).

Országos Pedagógiai Könyvtár és Múzeum (National Educational Library and Museum): 1055 Budapest, Honvéd u. 19; tel. and fax (1) 3126-862; e-mail h6079olv@ella.hu; f. 1877, reorganized 1958; methodological library for education; pedagogical museum; 500,000 vols; Dir Dr TIBOR HORVÁTH; publs *Külföldi Pedagógiai Információ* (Int. Educational Information, quarterly), *Magyar Pedagógiai Irodalom* (Hungarian Educational Literature, quarterly), *A magyar neveléstörténet forrásai* (Sources of Hungarian Educational History), *Magyar pedagógusok* (Hungarian Teachers).

Országos Rabbiképző Intézet Könyvtára (Library of the Jewish Theological Seminary): 1085 Budapest, József-krt. 27; tel. (1) 3342-121; fax (1) 3142-659; f. 1877; 100,000 vols; Chief Librarian Dr L. REMETE.

Országos Széchényi Könyvtár (National Széchényi Library): 1827 Budapest, Budavári Palota F-épület; tel. (1) 224-3700; fax (1) 202-0804; f. 1802; 2,634,000 books and periodicals, 4,750,000 manuscripts, maps, prints, microfilms, etc.; Dir-Gen. GÉZA POPRÁDY; publs include *Magyar Nemzeti Bibliográfia, Könyvek bibliográfiája* (Hungarian National Bibliography, Monographs, fortnightly), *Magyar Nemzeti Bibliográfia. Időszaki kiadványok repertóriuma* (Hungarian National Bibliography, Repertory of Periodicals, monthly), *Magyar Nemzeti Bibliográfia. Zeneművek bibliográfiája* (Hungarian National Bibliography, Musical Works, quarterly), *Magyar Nemzeti Bibliográfia, Időszaki kiadványok bibliográfiája* (Hungarian National Bibliography, Periodicals, annually), *Magyar Nemzeti Bibliográfia* (Hungarian National Bibliography, Books and Periodicals CD-ROM, 2 a year), *Az Országos Széchényi Könyvtár Évkönyve* (Yearbook); *Hungarika Információ* (Hungarica Information, 3 current indexes, 1 cumulative index a year), *Mikrofilmek cimjegyzéke* (lists of microfilms, irregular), *Az Országos Széchényi Könyvtár kiadványai* (Publications of the National Széchényi Library, irregular), *Az Országos Széchényi Könyvtár Füzetei* (Studies of the National Széchényi Library, irregular), *Magyarországi egyházi könyvtárak kéziratkatalógusai* (Catalogues of the Manuscript Collections in Hungarian Church Libraries, irregular).

Affiliated libraries:

Könyvtártudományi és Módszertani Központ (Centre for Library and Information Science): 1827 Budapest, Budavári Palota F-épület; tel. (1) 224-3788; f. 1959; research and development, promotion of inter-library co-operation, literature propaganda, public relations, training and library documentation services; library science; library of 107,000 vols; Dir ERZSÉBET GYŐRI (acting); publs *Könyvtári Figyelő* (Library Review), *A Magyar Könyvtári Szakirodalom Bibliográfiája* (Bibliography of Hungarian Library Literature), *Hungarian Library and Information Science Abstracts* (in English), *Uj Könyvek* (New Books), *Uj Periodikumok* (New Periodicals), *MANCI* (database of library science periodical articles with quarterly updates on floppy disk).

Reguly Antal Historic Library: 8420 Zirc, Rákóczi-tér 1; f. 1720; 68,618 vols.

Pázmány Péter Katolikus Egyetem, Hittudományi Kar Könyvtára (Library of the Péter Pázmány Catholic University's Faculty of Theology): 1053 Budapest, Veres Pálné u. 24; tel. (1) 118-1332; fax (1) 118-4124; f. 1635; history, theology and linguistics; 43,000 vols (books from *c.* 1880, older material kept in the Library of the University); also houses the Collection of the Brothers of St Paul (f. 1775; 12,000 vols; incunabula and MSS from the 15th and 16th centuries), and the Library of the Central Catholic Seminary (Központi Papnevelő Intézet Könyvtára) (f. 1805; 17,300 vols); Dir Dr VILMOS LENHARDT.

Semmelweis Orvostudományi Egyetem Központi Könyvtára (Central Library of Semmelweis Medical University): 1085 Budapest, Üllői út. 26; tel. (1) 117-0948; fax (1) 117-1048; e-mail livia@lib.sote.hu; f. 1828; 501,000 vols; Dir Dr LÍVIA VASAS.

Debrecen

Debreceni Orvostudományi Egyetem Központi Kenézy Könyvtára (Central Kenézy Library of the University Medical School of Debrecen): 4012 Debrecen, Nagyerdei körut 98; tel. and fax (52) 413-847; telex 72-411; f. 1947; 138,000 vols; Librarian Dr MÁRTA VIRÁGOS; publs *Evkönyv, Uj Könyvek* (annually).

Kossuth Lajos Tudományegyetem Egyetemi és Nemzeti Könyvtára (Lajos Kossuth University and National Library): 4010 Debrecen, Egyetem tér 1, Pf. 39; tel. and fax (52) 410-443; e-mail ilevay@giant.lib.klte.hu; f. 1912; 1,402,000 vols and periodicals, 2,516,000 MSS, prints, microfilms, etc.; Dir-Gen. Dr IRÉN LÉVAY; publ. *Könyv és Könyvtár* (annually).

Tiszántúli Református Egyházkerületi és Kollégiumi Nagykönyvtár (Library of the Reformed College and of the Transtibiscan Church District): 4044 Debrecen, Kálvint tér 16, POB 201; tel. (52) 414-744; fax (52) 414-1919; e-mail theca.silver@drk.hu; f. 1538; 570,000 vols; Dir Dr GÁBORJÁNI SZABÓ BOTOND.

Esztergom

Főszékesegyházi Könyvtár (Library of Esztergom Cathedral); 2500 Esztergom, Pázmány Péter u. 2; tel. (33) 411-891; fax (33) 11085; f. in the 11th century; 250,000 items; Fugger, Batthyany and Mayer collections; Dir BÉLA CZÉKLI.

Gödöllő

Gödöllői Agrártudományi Egyetem Központi Könyvtára (Central Library of the Gödöllő University of Agricultural Sciences): 2103 Gödöllő, Páter Károly u. 1; tel. (28) 310-200; telex 22-4892; fax (28) 310-804; e-mail gatekk@kpko.gau.hu; f. 1945; 340,000 vols, 776 current periodicals; Dir Dr TIBOR KOLTAY; publs *Bibliográfia* (every 2 or 3 years), *Information Bulletin* (quarterly).

Keszthely

Pannon Agrártudományi Egyetem Központi Könyvtára (Central Library of the Pannon University of Agricultural Sciences, Keszthely): 8360 Keszthely, Deák F. u. 16, POB 66; tel. 8331-2330; telex 35-282; fax 8331-5105; f. 1797, reorganized 1954; 135,000 vols; Dir Dr ANDRÁS PÉTERVÁRI; publ. *Georgikon for Agriculture* (2 a year).

Miskolc

Miskolci Egyetem Központi Könyvtára (Central Library of the University of Miskolc): 3515 Miskolc-Egyetemváros; tel. (46) 369524; fax (46) 369554; e-mail konzsamb@gold.uni-miskolc.hu; f. 1735; 547,000 vols, 109,000 periodicals; Dir-Gen. Dr LÁSZLÓ ZSÁMBOKI.

Pannonhalma

Főapátsági Könyvtár Pannonhalma (Benedictine Abbey Library): 9090 Pannonhalma, Vár 1; tel. (96) 570-142; fax (96) 470-011; e-mail fokonyvtar@osb.hu; f. 1802; collection of early records, MSS, codices, source material for the Hungarian language; 350,000 vols; Dir P. MIKSA BÁNHEGYI.

Pécs

Janus Pannonius Tudományegyetem Könyvtára (Library of the Janus Pannonius University): 7601 Pécs, Pf. 227; premises at: 7641 Pecs, Szepesy I. u. 1–3; tel. (72) 325-466; fax (72) 324-780; f. 1774; 960,000 vols; Gen. Dir. PÉTER SONNEVEND; publ. *Pécsi Könyv- és Infotár* (8 a year).

Pécsi Orvostudományi Egyetem Központi Könyvtára (Central Library of the Medical University of Pécs): 7643 Pécs, Szigeti u. 12; tel. (72) 324-122; fax (72) 326-244; e-mail fold@lib.pote.hu; f. 1961; collection covers medicine, chemistry, physics and biology; 246,000 vols; Dir RÓZSA FÖLDVÁRI; publ. *Bibliographia Publicationum Universitatis Scientiarum Medicarum Quinqueecclesiensis*.

Sárospatak

Sárospataki Református Kollégium Tudományos Gyűjteményei Nagykönyvtára (Library of the Scientific Collection of the Reformed College of Sárospatak); 3950 Sárospatak, Rákóczy u. 1; tel. (47) 311-057; f. 1531; 394,000 vols; Dir MICHAEL SZENTIMREI.

Sopron

Soproni Egyetem Központi Könyvtára (Central Library of the University of Sopron): 9400 Sopron, Ady E. u. 5; tel. (99) 311-100; fax (99) 311-103; e-mail library@efe.hu; f. 1735; 367,000 vols; Dir Dr MÁRTA MASTALIR.

Szeged

József Attila Tudományegyetem Központi Könyvtára (Central Library of the Attila József University): 6701 Szeged, Dugonics-tér 13; tel. (62) 454-036; fax (62)

312-718; f. 1921; 1,002,000 vols; Dir Dr BÉLA MADER; publs *Acta Bibliothecaria*, *Dissertationes ex Bibliotheca Universitatis de Attila József nominatae*.

Somogyi-Könyvtár (Somogyi Library): 6720 Szeged, Dóm tér 1–4; tel. (62) 322-322; fax (62) 321-921; e-mail gyuris@sk-szeged.hu; f. 1881 with Canon K. Somogyi of Esztergom's bequest of 43,000 vols to township of Szeged; 850,000 vols; Dir GYÖRGY GYURIS; publs *Szegedi Műhely* (Workshop of Szeged), *Csongrád Megyei Könyvtáros* (Librarian of the Csongrád district), *A Somogyi-könyvtár kiadványai* (Publications of the Somogyi library), etc.

Szent-Györgyi Albert Orvostudományi Egyetem Központi Könyvtára (Central Library of the Albert Szent-Györgyi Medical University): 6701 Szeged, Tisza Lajos krt 109; tel. (62) 455-587; fax (62) 455-068; f. 1926; 200,000 vols, 800 current journals; Dir Dr JANOS MARTON.

Veszprém

Veszprémi Egyetem Központi Könyvtára (Library of the University of Veszprém): 8200 Veszprém, Egyetem u. 10; tel. and fax (88) 425-074; e-mail hazitibo@vek.uranus.vein.hu; f. 1949; 170,000 vols; Dir Dr MÁRTA EGYHÁZY; publ. *Hungarian Journal of Industrial Chemistry* (quarterly).

Museums and Art Galleries

Badacsony

Egry József Emlékmúzeum (József Egry Memorial Museum): 8261 Badacsony, Egry Sétány 52; tel. 31-140; f. 1973; art gallery of works by Lake Balaton landscape painter Egry.

Baja

Türr István Múzeum: 6501 Baja, Deák Ferenc u. 1, POB 55; tel. (79) 324-173; f. 1937; archaeological and ethnographic collections, modern Hungarian painters, local history; library of 10,000 vols; Dir ZSUZSA MERK; publs *Türr István Múzeum Kiadványai*, *Bajai Dolgozatok*.

Balassagyarmat

Palóc Múzeum: 2660 Balassagyarmat, Palóc liget 1; f. 1891; ethnography, local folk art and shepherds' art; collections of Nógrád costumes, embroidery, folk religion and folk instruments; library of 12,000 vols; Dir MÁRTA KAPROS.

Békéscsaba

Munkácsy Mihály Múzeum: 5601 Békéscsaba, Széchenyi u. 9; tel. and fax (66) 323-377; f. 1899; archaeological, historical and regional ethnographic collections, modern Hungarian paintings, ornithology, natural science; paintings and legacies of the painter Mihály Munkácsy (1844–1900); library of 15,000 vols; Dir Dr IGOR GRIN; publ. *A Békés Megyei Múzeumok Közleményei* (Publications of Békés County Museums).

Budapest

Bartók Béla Emlékház (Béla Bartók Memorial House): 1025 Budapest, Csalán út. 29; tel. (1) 394-2100; fax (1) 394-4472; f. 1981; organizes musical programmes and concerts; Man. ZSUZSA NYUJTÓ.

Budapesti Történeti Múzeum (Budapest History Museum): 1014 Budapest, Szent György tér 2; tel. (1) 355-8284; fax (1) 355-9175; f. 1887; medieval antiquities, medieval royal castle, Gothic statues; library of 45,700 vols; Dir-Gen. Dr SÁNDOR BODÓ; publs *Budapest Régiségei* (Antiquities of Budapest), *Tanulmányok Budapest Múltjából* (Studies on the History of Budapest), *BTM Műhely* (BTM Workshop), *Pest-budai Hirmondó* (Pest-Buda Courrier), *Monumenta Historica Budapestinensia* (irregular), exhibition catalogues.

Administers:

Kiscelli Múzeum: 1037 Budapest, Kiscelli u. 108; tel. (1) 388-8560; fax (1) 368-7917; f. 1899; history of Budapest from 1686; Dir Dr ANNAMÁRIA S. VÍGH.

Fővárosi Képtár (Municipal Picture Gallery): 1037 Budapest, Kiscelli ut 108; tel. (1) 388-8560; fax (1) 368-7917; fine arts 19th- and 20th-century; Dir PÉTER FITZ.

Budavári Mátyás Templom Egyházművészeti Gyüjteménye (Matthias Church of Buda Castle Ecclesiastical Art Collection): 1014 Budapest, Szentháromság tér 2; tel. 1555-657; f. 1964; permanent collection of Roman Catholic religious objects in the crypt of Matthias Church; Curator Dr JÁNOS FÁBIÁN.

Hadtörténeti Múzeum (Military History Museum): 1250 Budapest, POB 7; 1014 Budapest, Tóth Árpád sétány 40; tel. and fax (1) 1-561-575; f. 1918; arms, medals, uniforms, documents, etc.; library of 49,750 vols; Dir Dr JÓZSEF LUGOSI; publs *Tarsoly* (annually), *Értesitő* (irregular), *Múzeumi Füzetek* (irregular).

Iparművészeti Múzeum (Museum of Applied Arts): 1091 Budapest, Üllői u. 33–37; tel. (1) 2175-222; fax (1) 2175-838; f. 1872; European and Hungarian decorative arts; library: see Libraries; Gen. Dir Dr ZSUZSA LOVAG; publs catalogues, *Ars Decorativa* (annually).

There are three component museums:

Hopp Ferenc Kelet-Ázsiai Művészeti Múzeum (Ferenc Hopp Museum of Eastern Asiatic Arts): 1062 Budapest, Andrássy u. 103; tel. (1) 322-8476; f. 1919; collections of Asiatic arts, exhibition of Chinese Buddhist art; library of 20,000 vols; Chief Curator Dr MÁRIA FERENCZY.

Ráth György Múzeum: 1068 Budapest, Városligeti-fasor 12; tel. (1) 342-3916; f. 1906; exhibition of Chinese and Japanese arts.

Nagytétényi Kastélymúzeum (Castle Museum of Nagytétény): 1225 Budapest, Kastélypark u. 9–11; tel. (1) 2268-547; f. 1948; European furniture of the 15th–17th centuries and Hungarian furniture of the 18th–19th centuries; exhibition of stove pottery, stoves, Roman castrum and stones. (Closed until 2001).

Közlekedési Múzeum (Transport Museum): 1146 Budapest, Városligeti krt 11; tel. 343-0565; fax 344-0322; f. 1896; models of railway locomotives and rolling stock, old vehicles, railway, nautical, aeronautic, road and urban transport collections, road- and bridge-building, etc.; four branch museums including aviation and railway exhibitions with open-air displays; library of 100,000 vols; Dir Dr ANDRÁS KATONA; publs yearbooks, scientific reviews (*c.* every 2 years).

Liszt Ferenc Emlékmúzeum és Kutatóközpont (Ferenc Liszt Memorial Museum and Research Centre): 1064 Budapest VI, Vörösmarty utca 35; tel. and fax (1) 342-7320; e-mail eckhardt@lib.liszt.hu; f. 1986; reconstruction of Liszt's flat in the building of the Old Academy of Music, with his instruments, furniture, library and other memorabilia; permanent and temporary exhibitions; collection of Liszt's music MSS, letters and other documentation, in collaboration with the Research Library for Music History; Dir MÁRIA ECKHARDT.

Magyar Bélyegmúzeum (Stamp Museum): 1400 Budapest, Pf. 86, 1074 Hársfa u. 47; tel. (1) 3415-526; fax (1) 3423-757; f. 1930; collections of 12 million Hungarian and foreign stamps; philatelic history; exhibitions locally and abroad; library of 4,000 vols; Dir ROSALIE SOLYMOSI; publ. *Yearbook*.

Magyar Elektrotechnikai Múzeum (Museum of Electrical Engineering): 1075 Budapest, Kazinczy utca 21; tel. 3220-472; fax 3425-750; f. 1970; historic collection of electrical engineering; library of 10,000 vols; Dir Dr SÁNDOR JESZENSZKY.

Magyar Építészeti Múzeum (Hungarian Museum of Architecture): 1036 Budapest, Mókus u. 20; tel. and fax (1) 1886-170; f. 1968; architecture and history of architecture; library of 5,500 vols; Dir LÁSZLÓ PUSZTAI; publ. *Pavilon* (every 6 months).

Magyar Irodalmi Múzeum (Petőfi Museum of Hungarian Literature): 1053 Budapest, Károlyi M. u. 16; tel. 1173-611; fax 1171-722; f. 1954; 19th–20th-century literature; library of 320,000 vols; archive of 950,000 MSS, 50,000 photographs, 2,200 sound recordings; art collection of 50,000 pieces; Dir MIHÁLY PRAZNOVSZKY; publs *Irodalomismeret* (4 a year), *Irodalomtörténet* (4 a year).

Magyar Kereskedelmi és Vendéglátóipari Múzeum (Hungarian Museum of Commerce and of the Catering Trade): 1014 Budapest, Fortuna-utca 4; tel. 1756-249; catering trade collection f. 1966, covers the subjects of sales and services, particularly in tourism, hotels and hostelry, cuisine, coffee houses, confectionery, shop fittings; commerce collection f. 1970, contains shop fittings, samples, storage pots, packing material, measuring instruments and coins; the two depts also contain documents, photos, posters; Dir Dr BALÁZS DRAVECZKY.

Magyar Mezőgazdasági Múzeum (Museum of Hungarian Agriculture): 1146 Budapest, Városliget Vajdahunyadvár; tel. (1) 343-0573; fax (1) 343-9120; e-mail mmm@mail.matav.hu; f. 1896; collects, exhibits and processes objects, documents, etc., relating to the development of Hungarian agriculture for scientific and educational purposes; 15 permanent exhibitions: domestication, domesticated animals of the ancient Hungarians, pig, cattle, sheep, poultry and small-animal breeding, ploughs, grain and cereal production, horticulture, viticulture, protection of nature, forestry, fishing, hunting, popular farming traditions; several provincial branches; co-ordinates preservation of agricultural monuments in co-operation with the Soc. of Friends of the Hungarian Agricultural Museum; library of 55,000 vols; Dir-Gen. Dr GYÖRGY FEHÉR; publs include *A Magyar Mezőgazdasági Múzeum Közleményei* (Proceedings of the Museum, every 2 years), *Agrártörténeti Szemle* (Agricultural History Review, 4 a year), *Bibliographia Historiae Rerum Rusticarum Internationalis* (every 2 years).

Magyar Nemzeti Galéria (Hungarian National Gallery): 1250 Budapest, Budavári Palota, Pf. 31; tel. (1) 1757-533; fax (1) 1758-898; f. 1957; collections include Hungarian art from 11th to 20th century; paintings, sculptures, drawings, engravings, medals; library of 76,000 vols; Dir Dr LÓRÁND BERECZKY; publs *A Magyar Nemzeti Galéria Évkönyve* (Annals), catalogues.

Magyar Nemzeti Múzeum (Hungarian National Museum): 1088 Budapest, Múzeum krt 14–16; tel. (1) 338-2122; fax (1) 317-7806; e-mail hnm@hnm.hu; f. 1802; history, archaeology, numismatics; library of 240,000 vols; Dir-Gen. Dr ISTVÁN GEDAI; publs *Folia Archaeologica* (annually), *Folia Historica* (annually), *Régészeti Füzetek (Fasciculi Archaeologici)*, *Communicationes Archaeologicae Hungariae* (annually), *Múzeumi Műtárgyvédelem* (Protection of Museum Art Objects, annually), *A* *magyar múzeumok kiadványainak bibliográfiája* (Bibliography of the Hungarian Museum's publications), *Bibliotheca Humanitatis Historica, Inventaria Praehistorica Hungariae*.

Magyar Természettudományi Múzeum (Hungarian Natural History Museum): 1088 Budapest, Baross u. 13; tel. (1) 267-7101; f. 1802; Depts: Mineralogy and Petrography, Geology and Palaeontology, Botany, Zoology, Anthropology; library of 65,000 vols; Chief Dir Dr ISTVÁN MATSKÁSI; publs *Annales Historico-Naturales Musei Nationalis Hungarici, Folia Entomologica Hungarica, Anthropologica Hungarica, Miscellanea Zoologica Hungarica, Studia Botanica, Fragmenta Mineralogica et Palaeontologica* (all annually).

Műcsarnok (Palace of Art): 1406 Budapest, POB 35; tel. 343-7401; fax 343-5205; f. 1896; temporary exhibitions of Hungarian and foreign contemporary art; branch galleries: Ernst Museum, Dorottya Gallery; library of 15,000 vols; Dir Prof. Dr LÁSZLÓ BEKE.

Néprajzi Múzeum (Ethnographical Museum): 1055 Budapest, Kossuth Lajos tér 12; tel. (1) 332-6340; fax (1) 269-2419; f. 1872; collections and research activities cover peasant and tribal folk cultures; Ethnographic Archive with 28,000 MSS and 318,000 photographs, 252 films; Ethnographic Library with 162,000 vols; Folk Music Archive with 62,000 entries; Gen. Dir Dr ZOLTÁN FEJŐS; publs *Néprajzi Értesito* (Yearbook), *Hungarian Folklore Bibliography* (annually), *Fontes Musei Ethnographiae, Series Historica Ethnographiae* (annually).

Öntödei Múzeum (Foundry Museum): 1027 Budapest, Bem József u. 20; tel. 202-5011; f. 1969; attached to the Hungarian Museum of Science and Technology; used by Ábrahám Ganz and others until 1964; original foundry equipment; history of technological development of foundry trade, old mouldings; library of 1,483 vols; Curator KATALIN LENGYEL-KISS.

Országos Műszaki Múzeum (National Museum for Science and Technology): 1502, POB 311, 1117 Budapest, Kaposvár-utca 13/15; tel. (1) 2044-095; fax (1) 2044-088; e-mail vam1337@helka.iif.hu; f. 1954 (collection), 1973 (museum); collection covers inventions and prototypes with reference to natural science and technology, historic exhibits from the early days of industry and its development to the present; library of 20,000 vols; Dir Dr ÉVA VAMOS; publ. *Technikatörténeti Szemle* (Review of History of Technology).

Postamúzeum (Postal Museum): 1061 Budapest, Andrássy út. 3; tel. (1) 268-1997; fax (1) 268-1958; f. 1955; permanent exhibition of the history of post and telecommunications; library of 11,000 vols; Dir Mrs IRÉN KOVÁCS; publ. *Postai és Távközlési Múzeumi Alapítvany Évkönyve* (annually).

Semmelweis Orvostörténeti Múzeum, Könyvtár és Levéltár (Semmelweis Medical Historical Museum, Library and Archives): 1013 Budapest, Apród. u. 1–3 (Museum and Archives); 1023 Budapest, Török u. 12 (Library); tel. 175-35-33 (Museum and Archives), 212-5368 (Library); fax 175-39-36; f. 1951 (Library), 1965 (Museum), 1972 (Archives); administers 12 attached medical museums; total of 112,000 vols, 20,000 periodicals; Gen. Dir Dr MARIA VIDA; Man. Dir Dr KÁROLY KAPRONCZAY; publ. *Orvostörténeti Közlemények / Communicationes de Historia Artis Medicinae*.

Szépművészeti Múzeum (Museum of Fine Arts): 1146 Budapest, Dózsa György ut. 41; tel. (1) 343-97-59; fax (1) 343-82-98; f. 1896, opened 1906; collections and galleries include: Egyptian and Greco-Roman antiquities, foreign paintings, sculptures, drawings and engravings; library of 150,000 vols; Dir Dr MIKLÓS MOJZER; publ. *Bulletin du Musée Hongrois des Beaux-Arts*†.

Administers:

Vasarely Múzeum: 1033 Budapest, Szentlélek tér 1; tel. 1887-551; Dir MARIA EGRI.

Testnevelési és Sportmúzeum (Museum of Physical Education and Sports): 1143 Budapest, Dózsa György u. 3; tel. and fax 252-1696; f. 1963; souvenirs, documents and photos of history of sport in Hungary and abroad; 7,000 books, 35,000 plaques and medals, 4,000 trophies, etc., 200,000 photos; Dir LAJOS SZABÓ.

Textil- és Ruhaipari Múzeum (Museum of the Textile and Clothing Industry): 1036 Budapest III, Lajos u. 138; f. 1972; 3,000 exhibits from Hungary and Central Europe; library of 12,000 vols; Dir M. FEJER; publ. *Évkönyv* (Year Book).

Tűzoltó Múzeum (Fire Brigade Museum): 1105 Budapest, Martinovics tér 12; tel. 1572-190; f. 1955; includes old fire-fighting equipment, pumps and hoses; universal and Hungarian history of fire protection, its means and organization; library of 2,500 vols; Curator Mrs LÁSZLÓ VÁRY.

Zenetörténeti Múzeum (Museum of History of Music): 1014 Budapest, Táncsics M.u.7; tel. (1) 214-6770; fax (1) 375-9282; f. 1969; collection of instruments, MSS, personal objects used by great musicians; Curator Dr ZOLTÁN FALVY.

Zsidó Vallási és Történeti Gyűjtemény (Collection of Jewish Religion and History): 1075 Budapest, Dohány u. 2; tel. (1) 342-8949; e-mail bpjewmus@visio.c3.hu; f. 1916; Jewish pieces of archaeology and art history, religious objects; Dir ROBERT B. TURAN.

Cegléd

Kossuth Lajos Múzeum: 2700 Cegléd, Muzeum u. 5; tel. (53) 310-637; f. 1917; relics of Lajos Kossuth; ethnography, archaeology, arts; library of 11,000 vols; Dir GYULA KOCSIS; publs *Ceglédi Füzetek* (annually).

Debrecen

Déri Múzeum: 4001 Debrecen, Déri tér 1, Pf. 61; tel. (52) 417-577; fax (52) 417-560; e-mail derimuz@amail.datanet.hu; f. 1902; archaeological, ethnographic, fine and applied art, natural history, literary and local history collections and exhibitions; library of 46,000 vols; photographic archive of 100,500 negatives and slides; Dir Dr L. SELMECZI; publs *A Déri Múzeum Évkönyve* (Yearbooks), *A Hajdú-Bihar Megyei Múzeumok Közleményei* (Studies and Monographs), *Múzeumi Kurir* (Review).

Dunaújváros

Intercisa Múzeum: 2400 Dunaújváros, Városháza tér 4; tel. (25) 408-970; fax (25) 411-315; f. 1951; prehistoric, Roman and medieval collections; regional history, archaeology and ethnography; library of 5,000 vols; Curator Mrs MÁRTA MATUSS.

Eger

Dobó István Vármúzeum: 3301 Eger, Vár 1; tel. (36) 312-744; fax (36) 312-450; originally archiepiscopal picture gallery and museum; f. 1872; enlarged by Fort Eger excavation material 1949; local remains of archaeology, ethnography, history of literature and of arts, palaeontology; relics of the Turkish occupation; library of 30,000 vols; Dir Dr TIVADAR PETERCSÁK; publs *Agria* (Yearbook), *Studia Agriensia*.

Esztergom

Balassa Bálint Múzeum: 2500 Esztergom, Mindszenty tér 3; tel. 12-185; f. 1894; history, archaeology, numismatics, applied arts; library of 12,000 vols; Curator Dr ISTVÁN HORVÁTH.

Keresztény Múzeum (Christian Museum): 2501 Esztergom, Mindszenty tér 2; tel. and fax (33) 413-880; f. 1875; Hungarian, Italian, Dutch, Austrian, German and French medieval panels, renaissance and baroque pictures, statues, tapestries, gold and silver artwork, porcelain, miniatures, engravings, medals, etc.; library of 11,000 vols; Pres. PÁL CSÉFALVAY.

Magyar Környezetvédelmi és Vízügyi Múzeum (Hungarian Environmental and Water Management Museum): 2500 Esztergom, Kölcsey u. 2; tel. (33) 411-888; fax (33) 412-395; f. 1973; history of water management; library of 8,900 vols; Curator IMRE KAJÁN; publ. *Vizgazdálkodás* (Water Management).

Vármúzeum: 2500 Esztergom, Szent István tér 1; tel. (33) 415-986; fax (33) 400-103; e-mail varmegom@holop.hu; f. 1967; excavated and reconstructed royal palace from the times of the Hungarian House of the Árpáds; municipal history of Esztergom as royal seat in the Middle Ages; Curator BÉLA HORVÁTH.

Fertőd

Kastélymúzeum: 9431 Fertőd, Bartók Béla u. 2; tel. (99) 370-971; fax (99) 370-120; f. 1959; historic castle of Esterházy family; local documents, furnishings, applied art, memorabilia of composer Haydn; Dir JOLÁN BAK.

Gyöngyös

Mátra Múzeum (Museum Historico-Naturale Matraense): 3200 Gyöngyös, Kossuth u. 40; tel. (37) 311-447; f. 1957; natural history: palaeontology, zoology and botany of Hungary and Europe; history of hunting; library of 12,000 vols; Curator Dr LEVENTE FÜKÖH; publs *Folia Historico-naturalia Musei Matraensis* (annually), *Malacological Newsletter*.

Győr

Xántus János Múzeum: 9022 Győr, Széchenyi tér 5; tel. (96) 310-588; fax (96) 310-731; f. 1854; archaeological collection containing relics of the ancient town of Arrabona (now Győr); history, art, anthropology, Roman lapidarium; picture gallery; library of 34,000 vols; Dir Dr ESZTER SZŐNYI; publ. *Arrabona* (annually).

Gyula

Erkel Ferenc Múzeum (Ferenc Erkel Museum): 5700 Gyula, Kossuth u. 17; tel. 361-236; f. 1868; archaeology, art, local history, musicological and ethnographic collections; library of 9,052 vols; Curator Dr PÉTER HAVASSY.

Hajdúböszörmény

Hajdúsági Múzeum: 4220 Hajdúböszörmény, Kossuth L. u. 1; tel. and fax (52) 371-038; f. 1924; sections: archaeology, ethnography, history and fine arts; library of 15,000 vols; Curator Dr MIKLÓS NYAKAS; publs *Évkönyv* (in Hungarian and German, every 2 years), *Közlemények* (in Hungarian, German, English and Russian, annually).

Herend

Porcelán Múzeum: 8440 Herend, Kossuth-u. 140; tel. (88) 261-159; fax (88) 261-801; e-mail porcelan@c3.hu; f. 1964; exhibits from the famous china factory, est. 1826; library of 4,500 vols.; Dir MAGDOLNA SIMON.

Hódmezővásárhely

Tornyai János Múzeum: 6801 Hódmezővásárhely, Szántó Kovács János-u. 16–18; tel. (62) 344-424; f. 1905; archaeological, ethnographic and folk-art collections, Tornyai paintings and Medgyessy sculptures; pottery and farm-museum; library of 5,500 vols; Curator IMRE NAGY.

Jászberény

Jász Múzeum: 5100 Jászberény, Táncsics-u. 5; tel. 12-753; f. 1873; collections from the later Stone, Copper, Bronze and Iron Ages; ethnography, local history; library 6,593 vols; Curator JÁNOS TÓTH.

Kalocsa

Viski Károly Múzeum: 6300 Kalocsa, Szent István Király u. 25, POB 82; tel. and fax (78) 462-351; f. 1932; regional museum, folk art; library of 9,000 vols; Dir IMRE ROMSICS.

Kaposvár

Somogy Megyei Múzeumok Igazgatósága: 7400 Kaposvár, Fő utca 10; tel. and fax 312-822; f. 1909; archaeological and ethnographic collections, contemporary history, fine arts, natural history; library of 13,000 vols; Dir Dr ISTVÁN S. KIRÁLY; publs *Somogyi Múzeumok Közleményei, Somogyi Múzeumok Füzetei, Múzeumi Tájékoztató.*

Karcag

Győrffy István Nagykun Múzeum: 5300 Karcag, Kálvin u. 4; tel. (59) 312-087; f. 1906; regional museum, ethnography; library of 8,000 vols; Curator Dr MIKLÓS NAGY MOLNÁR.

Kecskemét

Katona József Múzeum: 6001 Kecskemét, Bethlen krt. 15; tel. (76) 481-350; fax (76) 481-122; f. 1894; archaeological, ethnographical, historical and fine art collections; library of 16,600 vols; Dir Dr JÁNOS BÁRTH; publ. *Cumania* (annually).

Kecskeméti Képtár és Tóth Menyhért Emlékmúzeum: 6000 Kecskemét, Pf. 165, Cifrapalota, Rákóczi u. 1; tel. (76) 480-776; f. 1983; Hungarian 19th–20th-century paintings, particularly by Menyhért Tóth; Dir SIMON MAGDOLNA.

Magyar Naiv Művészek Múzeuma (Museum of Hungarian Naive Art): 6000 Kecskemét, Gáspár A. u. 11; tel. 324-767; f. 1976; exhibitions of works of Hungarian primitive painters and sculptors; Dir Dr PÁL BÁNSZKY; publ. *Magyar Naiv Művészek Múzeuma.*

Szórakaténusz Játékmúzeum (Toy Museum): 6000 Kecskemet, Gáspár A. u. 11; tel. (76) 481-469; f. 1981; collection of 15,000 items; library of 2,500 vols; Dir Dr JOZSEF VIZI KRISTON; publs *Exhibition Guides, Methodological Statements, Studies of the History of Play.*

Keszthely

Balatoni Múzeum: 8360 Keszthely, Múzeum-u. 2; tel. and fax 312-351; f. 1898; prehistoric and historic collections relating to Lake Balaton; library of 25,000 vols; Curator Dr RÓBERT MÜLLER.

Helikon Kastélymúzeum: 8360 Keszthely, Kastély u. 1; tel. (83) 312-190; fax (83) 315-039; f. 1974; 18th-century castle of Festetics family; library of 94,000 vols; Dir Dr LÁSZLÓ CZOMA.

Kiskunfélegyháza

Kiskun Múzeum: 6100 Kiskunfélegyháza, Dr Holló L. u. 9; tel. (76) 461-468; fax (76) 462-542; f. 1902; ethnography; library of 20,000 vols; Curator Dr ERZSÉBET MOLNÁR.

Kiskunhalas

Thorma János Múzeum: 6400 Kiskunhalas, Köztársaság-u. 2; tel. and fax (77) 422-864; f. 1874; ethnography, archaeology and history; library of 7,000 vols; Curator AURÉL SZAKÁL.

Kőszeg

Városi Múzeum (Municipal Museum): 9730 Kőszeg, Jurisics tér 6; tel. (94) 360-156; f. 1932; collection of castle and town history; library of 9,000 vols; Dir Prof. Dr KORNÉL BAKAY.

Mátészalka

Szatmári Múzeum: 4700 Mátészalka, Kossuth-u. 54; tel. 11-016; f. 1972; local history and ethnographic collections; Dir LÁSZLÓ CSERVENYÁK.

Miskolc

Herman Ottó Múzeum: 3529 Miskolc, Görgey Artúr ut. 28; tel. (46) 361-411; fax (46) 367-975; f. 1899; collections of archaeology, regional ethnography, fine arts and applied arts, natural science, minerals of Hungary, local history, literary history, history of photography; library of 44,000 vols; Dir Dr LÁSZLÓ VERES; publs *A Herman Ottó Múzeum Évkönyve* (Yearbook), *Officina Musei, A Miskolci Herman Ottó Múzeum Közleményei* (Communications), *Néprajzi Kiadványok* (Ethnographical Studies), *Borsodi Kismonográfiák* (monographs), *Kiállítási Vezetők* (Exhibition guides), *Documentatio Borsodiensis, Natura Borsodiensis.*

Központi Kohászati Múzeum (Central Foundry Museum): 3517 Miskolc-Felsőhámor, Palota-u. 22; tel. 79-375; f. 1949; science and technology; archaeological foundry of the 9th–10th centuries; 18th-century foundry; Curator OSZKÁR SZINVAVÖLGYI.

Mohács

Kamizsai Dorottya Múzeum: 7700 Mohács, Városház u. 1; tel. (69) 311-536; f. 1923; ethnography of the Serbs, Croats and Slavs; library of 2,300 vols; Curator Dr GYÖRGY SAROSÁCZ.

Mosonmagyaróvár

Hansági Múzeum: 9200 Mosonmagyaróvár, Szent István u. 1; tel. (96) 213-834; fax (96) 212-094; f. 1882; regional museum; archaeology, ethnography, lapidarium, local history, paintings by János Szale; library of 7,216 vols; Dir KÁROLY SZENTKUTI.

Nagycenk

Széchenyi István Emlékmúzeum (Széchenyi Memorial Museum): 9485 Nagycenk, Kiscenki-utca 3; tel. (99) 360-023; fax (99) 360-260; f. 1973; history of the Széchenyi family and life (iconography, bibliography) of 19th-century statesman Count István Széchenyi; library of 5,000 vols; Curator Dr ATTILA KÖRNYEI.

Nagykanizsa

Thury György Múzeum: 8801 Nagykanizsa, Erzsébet tér 11; tel. 14-596; f. 1919; archaeological and ethnographical collections, local history displays, numismatics; library of 5,000 vols; Curator Dr LÁSZLÓ HORVÁTH.

Nagykőrös

Arany János Múzeum: 2751 Nagykőrös, Ceglédi-u. 19; tel. and fax (53) 350-810; f. 1928; regional museum; archaeology, ethnography, local history, literary documents of poet J. Arany; library of 17,555 vols; Dir Dr LÁSZLÓ NOVÁK.

Nyirbátor

Báthory István Múzeum: 4300 Nyirbátor, Károlyi-u. 15; tel. 11-341; f. 1955; archaeology, local history and art; library of 2,900 vols; Curator Dr LÁSZLÓ DÁM.

Nyiregyháza

Jósa András Múzeum: 4401 Nyiregyháza, Benczur tér 21, Pf. 57; tel. and fax (42) 315-722; f. 1868; collections of archaeology, ethnography and local history; fine and applied arts, numismatics; library of 17,000 vols; Dir Dr PÉTER NÉMETH; publ. *A nyíregyházi Jósa András Múzeum Évkönyve* (annually).

Pannonhalma

Pannonhalmi Főapátság Gyűjteménye (Abbey of Pannonhalma Collection): 9090 Pannonhalma, Vár 1; tel. (96) 570-142; fax (96) 470-011; f. 1802; paintings, sculptures, applied arts in an ancient Benedictine Abbey.

Pápa

Gróf Esterházy Károly Kastély- és Tájmúzeum (Count Charles Esterházy Castle and Regional Museum): 8501 Pápa, Fő tér 1, Pf. 208, Várkastély; tel. (89) 313-584; f. 1960; ethnographical, archaeological and industrial collections from the town and environment; library of 10,000 vols; Dir Dr PÉTER LÁSZLÓ; publ. *Acta Musei Papensis* (annually).

Pécs

Csontváry Múzeum: 7621 Pécs, Janus Pannonius-u. 11; tel. (72) 310-544; f. 1973; art gallery comprising selected works by the expressionist painter Tivadar Csontváry Kosztka.

Janus Pannonius Múzeum: 7621 Pécs, Káptalan u. 5; tel. (72) 310-172; fax (72) 315-694; f. 1904; natural sciences, archaeology, ethnography, modern Hungarian art, local history; library of 25,000 vols; Dir ISTVÁN ECSEDY; publs *Évkönyv* (Yearbook), *Dunántuli Dolgozatok* (Trans-Danubian Studies), *Füzetek* (Papers), booklets, art publications.

Modern Magyar Képtár I (Modern Hungarian Gallery I, 1900–1950): 7621 Pécs, Káptalan u. 4; tel. 324-822; f. 1957; paintings by Mednyánszky, Gulácsy, Rippl Rónai, Czóbel, Uitz, Kassák, Egry, etc.

Modern Magyar Képtár II (Modern Hungarian Gallery II, 1950–): 7621 Pécs, Szabadság u. 2; tel. 13-058; f. 1957; paintings by Barcsay, Bizse, Korniss, Lantos, Orosz, etc.

Vasarely Múzeum: 7621 Pécs, Káptalan-u. 3; tel. 324-822; f. 1976; art gallery comprising works by Hungarian-born French artist Victor Vasarely.

Rudabánya

Alapítvány Érc- és Ásványbányászati Múzeum (Museum of Mining of Metals and Minerals): 3733 Rudabánya, Petőfi u. 24; f. 1956; history of the industry, exhibitions; Curator BÉLA SZUROMI.

Salgótarján

Nógrádi Történeti Múzeum (Nógrád Historical Museum): 3100 Salgótarján, Múrzeum tér 2; tel. 10-169; f. 1959; 19th- and 20th-century social history, history of art, literary history; library of 11,700 vols; Dir Dr ISTVÁN HORVÁTH.

Sárospatak

Rákóczi Múzeum: 3950 Sárospatak, Kádár Kata-u. 21; tel. 11-083; f. 1950; housed in the Castle of Sárospatak; historical, ethnographic, archaeological and applied art collections; library of 11,000 vols; Curator Dr DANKÓ KATALIN JÓSVAINÉ.

Sárvár

Nádasdy Ferenc Múzeum: 9600 Sárvár, Vár-u. 1; f. 1951; late Renaissance and Baroque Hungarian milieu reconstructed in state rooms of 16th-century castle; library of 3,900 vols; Dir ISTVÁN SÖPTEI.

Sopron

Központi Bányászati Múzeum (Central Mining Museum): 9400 Sopron, Templom u. 2; tel. 12-667; f. 1957; science and technology; history of mining in the Carpathian basin since prehistoric age; Dir LÁSZLÓ MOLNÁR.

Soproni Múzeum: 9400 Sopron, Fő tér 8; tel. (99) 311-327; fax (99) 311-347; e-mail smuzeum@mail.c3.hu; f. 1867; archaeology, folk art, pharmacy, medieval synagogue, local Baroque art and Storno Collections; library of 29,000 vols; Dir Dr ATTILA KÖRNYEI.

Szarvas

Tessedik Sámuel Múzeum: 5540 Szarvas, Vajda P. u. 1; tel. 12-960; f. 1951; archaeology, ethnography and local history collections; Dir Dr JÓZSEF PALOV.

Szécsény

Kubinyi Ferenc Múzeum: 3170 Szécsény, Ady Endre-u. 7; f. 1973; archaeology and local history; library of 8,400 vols; Curator Dr KATALIN SIMÁN.

Szeged

Móra Ferenc Múzeum: 6720 Szeged, Roosevelt tér 1–3; tel. (62) 470-370; fax (62) 312-980; f. 1883; archaeological, ethnographic and biological collections, history of arts and regional collections; library of 30,000 vols; special collection: Sándor Bálint bequest of 5,500 vols on archaic religions and beliefs, old books of prayers and liturgies; Győző Csongor Bequest of 5,500 vols on local history; Dir Dr GABRIELLA VÖRÖS; publ. *Móra Ferenc Múzeum Évkönyve* (Yearbook).

Székesfehérvár

Szent István Király Múzeum: 8002 Székesfehérvár, Fő u. 6; tel. (22) 315-583; fax (22) 311-734; f. 1873; prehistoric, Roman and medieval collections, anthropological collection, regional ethnography, art gallery, musical collection, numismatic collection, stones of the Basilica of King Stephen; library of 50,000 vols; Dir GYULA FÜLÖP; publs *Bulletin of the Szent István Király Museum*, *Alba Regia* (Scientific Almanac).

Szekszárd

Wosinsky Mór Megyei Múzeum: 7101 Szekszárd, Martirok tere 26; tel. and fax (74) 316-222; e-mail wmmm@mail.c3.hu; f. 1896; collections of folk art, archaeology, history, fine arts and applied arts; library of 11,300 vols; Dir Dr ATTILA GAÁL; publ. yearbook.

Szentendre

Ferenczy Múzeum: 2001 Szentendre, Fő tér 6, pf. 49; tel. (26) 310-244; fax (26) 310-790; f. 1951; paintings, drawings, sculptures and Gobelin tapestries; centre for 30 museums in Pest County; library of 24,000 vols, 210 periodicals; Dir SÁNDOR SOÓS; publs *Studia Comitatensia* (yearbook of papers published by the Museums of Pest County), *Pest megyei Múzeumi Füzetek* (Pamphlets of the Museums of Pest County, irregular).

Szabadtéri Néprajzi Múzeum (Hungarian Open Air Museum): 2001 Szentendre, POB 63, Sztaravodai u.; tel. (26) 312-304; fax (26) 310-183; f. 1967; vernacular architecture and furniture; library of 11,000 vols; archive of 90,000 photographs, 13,000 ethnographical, historical, architectural documents, films, maps, drawings, etc.; Dir Dr MIKLÓS CSERI; publs *Téka* (quarterly), *Ház és Ember* (yearbook).

Szentes

Koszta József Múzeum: 6600 Szentes, Alsórét 187; tel. 13-352; f. 1894; archaeological and ethnographical collection and paintings by Koszta; Dir GABRIELLA VÖRÖS.

Szigetvár

Zrínyi Miklós Vármúzeum: 7900 Szigetvár, Vár-u. 1; f. 1917; local history collection, relating particularly to the period of Turkish occupation (16th–17th centuries).

Szolnok

Damjanich János Múzeum: 5001 Szolnok, Kossuth tér 4, Pf. 128; tel. (56) 421-602; f. 1933; archaeology, ethnography, palaeontology, fine arts, applied arts and local history collections; library of 35,600 vols; Dir LÁSZLÓ TÁLAS; publ. *Annual*.

Szombathely

Savaria Múzeum: 9701 Szombathely, Kisfaludy Sándor u. 9; tel. (94) 312-554; f. 1872; natural history, archaeology, local cultural history, ethnography; library of 32,000 vols; Dir Dr CSABA THURÓCZY; publ. *Savaria* (Journal, annually).

Tác

Gorsium Szabadtéri Múzeum (Gorsium Open-Air Museum): 8121 Tác; tel. 363-443; f. 1963; excavations of a Roman city, the ruins showing original shape.

Tata

Kuny Domokos Múzeum: 2892 Tata, Néppark, Kiskastély, POB 224; tel. and fax (34) 487-888; f. 1954; history, archaeology, ethnology, art; library of 27,000 vols; Dir EVE M. FÜLÖP.

Vác

Tragor Ignác Múzeum: 2600 Vác, Múzeum-u. 4; tel. and fax (27) 315-064; f. 1895; archaeology, ethnography, local history and fine arts exhibits; library of 16,070 vols; Dir MÁRTA ZOMBORKA; publ. *Váci Könyvek* (Bulletin).

Várpalota

Magyar Vegyészeti Múzeum (Hungarian Chemical Museum): 8100 Várpalota, Hősök tere 1; tel. (88) 472-391; f. 1963; history of the chemical industry; library of 17,000 vols; Dir ISTVÁN PRÓDER.

Vértesszőllős

Magyar Nemzeti Múzeum Vértesszőllősi Bemutatóhelye: 2837 Vértesszőllős; f. 1975; permanent open-air exhibition; dwelling-place and remains of early man; part of Archaeology Dept of National Museum; Curator Dr VIOLA DOBOSI.

Veszprém

Laczkó Dezső Múzeum: 8201 Veszprém, Erzsébet sétány 1; tel. (88) 424-610; fax (88) 426-081; f. 1903; ethnographic, archaeological, historical, fine and industrial arts, history of literature, numismatic exhibits from Veszprém County; library of 36,000 vols; Dir MARGIT DAX; publs *Veszprém Megyei Múzeumok Közleményei*, *Publicationes Museorum Comitatus Vesprimiensis* (Communications of the Museums of Veszprém County), exhibition catalogues.

Visegrád

Mátyás Király Múzeum (King Matthias Museum): 2025 Visegrád, Fő utca 29; tel. and fax (26) 398-026; f. 1933; managed by Magyar Nemzeti Múzeum of Budapest; ruins of Gothic and Renaissance royal palace; 13th-century upper and lower castle with Roman and medieval archaeological remains; library of 10,000 vols; Curator MÁTYÁS SZŐKE.

Zalaegerszeg

Göcseji Falumúzeum (Village Museum of Göcsej): 8900 Zalaegerszeg, Falumúzeum u. 1; tel. (92) 313-494; f. 1968; open-air ethnographical collection; Dir Dr LÁSZLÓ VÁNDOR.

Göcseji Múzeum: 8900 Zalaegerszeg, Batthyányi u. 2, POB 176; tel. (92) 311-455; f. 1950; collections of regional history, archaeology, ethnography, paintings and sculpture; library of 12,000 vols, exhibition of sculptures by Zs. Kisfaludi-Strobl, etc.; Dir Dr LÁSZLÓ VÁNDOR; publ. *Zalai Múzeum* (1 a year).

Magyar Olajipari Múzeum (Oil Industry Museum): 8900 Zalaegerszeg, Wlassics Gy. u. 13; tel. (92) 313-632; fax (92) 311-081; f. 1969; exhibitions of the history of the professional and technical development of the oil industry; equipment, documents, photos, etc.; library of 9,000 vols; Curator JÁNOS TÓTH.

Zirc

Bakonyi Természettudományi Múzeum (Bakony Mountains Natural History Museum): 8420 Zirc, Rákóczi tér 1, POB 36; tel. and fax (88) 414-157; f. 1972; natural history exhibits from Bakony Mountains; library of 4,000 vols; Curator JÁNOS FUTÓ; publ. *A Bakony természettudományi kutatásának eredményei* (Results of Natural History Research), *Folia Musei Historico-naturalis Bakonyiensis (A Bakonyi Természettudományi Múzeum Közleményei)*.

Universities

EÖTVÖS LORÁND TUDOMÁNYEGYETEM (Loránd Eötvös University)

1364 Budapest, V, Egyetem-tér 1–3, POB 109

Telephone: (1) 267-0820

Fax: (1) 266-9786

Founded 1635

State control

Academic year: September to June (two terms)

Rector: Dr MIKLÓS SZABÓ

Pro-Rectors: Dr ISTVÁN KLINGHAMMER, Dr LÁSZLÓ BOROS, Dr LAJOS IZSÁK

Secretary-General: Dr JÓZSEF FAZEKAS

Head Librarian: Dr L. SZÖGI

Library: see Libraries

Number of teaching staff: 1,363

Number of students: 15,480

Publications: *Annales*, *Egyetemi Értesítő*, *Dissertationes Archaeologicae*, *Az Egyetemi Könyvtár Értesítői*, etc. (all annually), *Tudományos Tájekoztató*.

DEANS

Faculty of Law and Political Science: Dr LAJOS FICZERE

Faculty of Science: Dr ANDRÁS BENCZÚR

Faculty of Arts: Dr KÁROLY MANHERZ

Teacher Training Faculty: Dr GÉZA ZÁVODSZKY (Dir)

Institute and Postgraduate Centre for Sociology and Social Policy: Dr MIHÁLY CSÁKÓ

PROFESSORS

Faculty of Law and Political Science (1053 Budapest, Egyetem tér. 1–3):

BÉKÉS, I., Criminal Law
BERÉNYI, S., Public Administration Law
BIHARI, M., Political Science
DOMÉ, GY., Agricultural Law
ERDEI, Á., Criminal Procedural Law
FICZERE, L., Public Administration Law
FÖLDESI, T., Philosophy
GÖNCZÖL, K., Criminology
HAMZA, G., Roman Law
HARMATHY, A., Civil Law
HORVÁTH, P., Universal Legal and Political History
KOVACSICS, J., Statistics
KULCSÁR, K., Sociology of Law
LŐRINCZ, L., Public Administration Law
MÁDL, F., International Private Law
MOLNÁR, J., Criminal Law
NAGYNE, SZ., Universal Legal and Political History
NÉMETH, J., Civil Procedural Law

Pokol, B., Political Science
Samu, M., Theory of State Law
Sári, J., Constitutional Law
Schlett, I., Political Science
Sólyom, L., Civil Law
Szabó, M., Political Science
Valki, L., International Law
Varga, Cs., Political Science
Vékás, L., Civil Law
Vigh, J., Criminology
Wiener, A., Criminal Law

Faculty of Science (1088 Budapest, Rákóczi út 5.):

Abaffyné Dózsa-Farkas, Á., Systematic Zoology and Ecology.
Balázs, B., Astronomy
Báldi, T., Physical and Historical Geology
Bálint, M., Biochemistry
Barcza, L., Inorganic and Analytical Chemistry
Benczúr, A., Information Systems
Berczik, Á., Systematic Zoology and Ecology
Böröczky, K., Geometry
Buda, Gy., Mineralogy
Csányi, V., Behaviour Genetics
Csikor, F., Theoretical Physics
Csiszár, I., Statistics and Probability Theory
Demetrovics, J., Information Systems
Dörnyeiné Németh, J., Theoretical Physics
Eiben, O., Anthropology
Erdei, A., Immunology
Farsang, Gy., Inorganic and Analytical Chemistry
Fogarasi, G., Theoretical Chemistry
Frank, A., Operational Research
Fried, E., Algebra and Number Theory
Fritz, J., Probability Theory and Statistics
Furka, Á., Organic Chemistry
Galácz, A., Palaeontology
Geszti, T., Physics of Complex Systems
Gráf, L., Biochemistry
Gyurján, I., Plant Anatomy
Hajnal, A., Computer Technology
Halász, G., Analysis
Hámor, G., Regional Geology
Hollósi, M., Organic Chemistry
Horváth, Z., Theoretical Physics
Inzelt, Gy., Physical Chemistry
Iványi, A., General Computer Science
Kapovics, I., Organic Chemistry
Károlyházi, F., Theoretical Physics
Kátai, I., Computer Algebra
Kirschner, I., General Physics
Kiss, Á., Atomic Physics
Kiss, D., Atomic Physics
Klinghammer, I., Cartography
Komjáth, P., Computer Science
Kondor, I., Physics of Complex Systems
Kovács, I., General Physics
Kovács, J., General Zoology
Laczkovich, M., Analysis
Láng, F., Plant Physiology
Lendvai, J., General Physics
Lévay, B., Nuclear Chemistry
Lovász, L., Computer Science
Márton, P., Geophysics
Medzihradszky, K., Organic Chemistry
Meskó, A., Geophysics
Mindszenthy, A., Applied and Environmental Geology
Monostori, M., Palaeontology
Nagy, M., Colloid Chemistry and Technology
Náray-Szabó, G., Theoretical Chemistry
Orbán, M., Inorganic and Analytical Chemistry
Pál, L., Applied Analysis
Pálfy, P., Algebra and Number Theory
Palla, L., Theoretical Physics
Patkós, A., Atomic Physics
Perl, M., Inorganic and Analytical Chemistry
Petruska, Gy., Analysis
Pócsik, Gy., Theoretical Physics
Polonyi, J., Atomic Physics
Prékopa, A., Operational Research
Probáld, F., Regional Geography
Recski, A., Computer Science
Sárközy, A., Algebra and Number Theory
Sármay, I., Immunology
Schipp, F., Numerical Analysis
Sebestyén, Z., Applied Analysis
Simon, L., Applied Analysis
Sohár, P., General and Inorganic Chemistry
Sólyom, J., Physics of Complex Systems
Soós, Gy., Mathematical Methodology
Stoyan, G., Numerical Analysis
Szabó, K., Physical Chemistry
Szalay, S., Atomic Physics
Szathmári, E., Plant Taxonomy and Ecology
Székely, J. G., Statistics and Probability Theory
Szenthe, J., Geometry
Szepes, L., General and Inorganic Chemistry
Szépfalusy, P., Physics of Complex Systems
Tél, T., Theoretical Physics
Tichy, G., Solid State Physics
Ungár, T., General Physics
Varga, L., General Computer Science
Vértes, A., Nuclear Chemistry
Vicsek, T., Biological Physics
Vida, G., Genetics
Vincze, I., Solid State Physics
Záray, Gy., Chemical Technology and Environmental Chemistry
Závodszký, P., Biological Physics
Zsadon, B., Chemical Technology and Environmental Chemistry

Faculty of Arts (1052 Budapest, Piarista köz 1):

Abaffy, E., Hungarian Historical Linguistics and Dialectology
Adamik, T., Latin Language and Literature
Almási, M., Aesthetics
Bábosik, I., Education
Bácskay, V., Economics and Social History
Balogh, A., Modern World History
Banczerowski, J., Polish Language and Literature
Bayer, J., Political Theory
Bécsy, T., Comparative Literature
Bence, Gy., Ethics and Social Philosophy
Bertényi, I., Historical Auxiliary Sciences
Bíró, F., 18th- and 19th-Century Hungarian Literature
Bolla, K., Phonetics
Bóna, I., Prehistory
Czine, M., Modern Hungarian Literature
Diószegi, I., Modern World History
Domokos, P., Finno-Ugric Linguistics
Egri, P., English Studies
Fehér, M. I., History of Philosophy
Fodor, S., Semitic Philology and Arabic Studies
Frank, T., American Studies
Für, L., Medieval and Early Modern Hungarian
Gaál, E., Egyptology
Gergely, J., Modern and Contemporary Hungarian History
Gerics, J., Medieval and Early Modern Hungarian History
Gerő, A., Economic and Social History
Glatz, F., Historical Auxiliary Sciences
Heller, Á., Aesthetics
Hessky, P., German Linguistics
Horváth, I., Old Hungarian Literature
Horváth, M., Education
Hunyady, Gy., Social and Educational Psychology
Illyes, S., Experimental Psychology
Izsák, L., Modern and Contemporary Hungarian History
Kaán, M., Contemporary Hungarian Linguistics
Kákosy, L., Egyptology
Kállay I., Historical Auxiliary Sciences
Kara, Gy., Central Asian Studies
Kelemen, J., Ethics and Social Philosophy
Kenyeres, Z., Modern Hungarian Literature
Kiefer, F., Symbolic Logic and the Methodology of Science
Kis, A., Modern World History
Kiss, J., Hungarian Historical Linguistics and Dialectology
Komoróczy, G., Assyriology and Hebrew Studies
Kósa, L., Cultural History
Kovács, S. I., Old Hungarian Literature
Kubinyi, A., Hungarian Medieval and Early Modern Archaeology
Kulcsár, Zs., Individual and Clinical Psychology
Kulcsár Szabó, E., Comparative Literature
Ludassy, M., Ethics and Social Philosophy
Luft, U., Egyptology
Mádl, A., German Literature
Manherz, K., Germanic Linguistics
Marosi, E., Art History
Masát, A., Scandinavian Languages and Literature.
Medgyes, P., English Teacher Training
Nyíri, J. K., History of Philosophy
Nyomárkay, I., Slavic Philology
Paládi-Kovács, A., Ethnography
Palotás, E., East European History
Passuth, K., Art History
Péter, M., Eastern Slavonic and Baltic Philology
Pölöskei, F., Modern and Contemporary Hungarian History
Poszler, Gy., Aesthetics
Radnóti, S., Aesthetics
Ritoók, Zs., Latin Language and Literature
Romsics, I., Modern and Contemporary Hungarian History
Rónay, L., Modern Hungarian Literature
Sarbu, A., English Studies
Sarkady, J., Ancient Archaeology
Szabics, I., French Language and Literature
Szabó, K., Medieval World History
Szabó, M., Classical Archaeology
Szávai, J., Comparative and World Literature
Szegedy-Maszák, M., Comparative Literature
Szilárd, M., Eastern Slavonic and Baltic Philology
Sziklai, L., Aesthetics
Tarnói, L., Germanic Literature
Tőkei, F., Chinese and East Asian Studies
Töttössy, Cs., Indo-European Linguistics
Urbán, A., Modern World History
Vadász, S., Modern World History
Vargyai, Gy., Historical Auxiliary Sciences
Várkonyi, Á., Medieval and Early Modern Hungarian History
Vásáry, J., Turkish Studies
Voigt, V., Folklore
Vörös, I., French Language and Literature
Wéber, A., 18th- and 19th-Century Hungarian Literature
Zoltai, D., Aesthetics
Zsilka, J., General and Applied Linguistics

Teacher-Training Faculty (1075 Budapest, Kazinczy u. 23–27):

Cs. Varga, I., Hungarian Language and Literature
Demeter, J., Hungarian Language and Literature
Druzsin, F., Hungarian Language and Literature
Dukkon, Á., Hungarian Language and Literature
Estók, J. , History
Fried, I., Italian Language and Literature
Gaizer, F., Chemistry
Gödény, E., Hungarian Language and Literature
Grétsy, L., Hungarian Linguistics
Hajdu, P., Social Theory
Hegyvári, N., Mathematics
Heltai, P., English
Horváth, G., Geography
Madarász, I., Hungarian Linguistics

Milkovits, I., Biology
Németh, A., Educational Science
Salamon, K., History
Sapszon, F., Music
Siposné-Jáger, K., Biology
Uzonyi, P., German
Závodsky, G., History
Zirkuli, P., French Language and Literature

Institute and Postgraduate Centre for Sociology and Social Policy (1088 Budapest, Pollack Mihály tér. 10):

Angelusz, R., Sociology
Csepeli, Gy., Social Psychology
Enyedi, Gy., Sociology
Ferge, Zs., Social Policy
Huszár, T., Historical Sociology
Kolosi, T., Methodology of Social Research
Litván, Gy., Social Theory
Pataki, F., Social Psychology
Somlai, P., Social Theory

ATTACHED INSTITUTE

Postgraduate Institute of Law and Political Science: 1053 Budapest, Egyetem tér 1–3; Dir Dr Rezső Hársfalvi.

PÁZMÁNY PÉTER KATOLIKUS EGYETEM
(Péter Pázmány Catholic University)

1088 Budapest, Szentkirályi u. 28–30
Telephone: (1) 235-8010
Fax: (1) 118-0507
E-mail: rektor@jak.ppke.hu

Founded 1635
Academic year: September to June

Rector: DDr Péter Erdő

Library of 315,000 vols
Number of teachers: 191 full-time, 335 part-time
Number of students: 4,608

DEANS

Faculty of Theology: (vacant)
Faculty of Arts: Miklós Maróth
Faculty of Law: János Zlinszky
Postgraduate Institute of Canon Law: (vacant)

SEMMELWEIS ORVOSTUDOMÁNYI EGYETEM
(Semmelweis University of Medicine)

1085 Budapest VIII, Üllői u. 26
Telephone: (1) 317-2400
Fax: (1) 317-2220
E-mail: rekhiv@rekhiv.sote.hu

Founded 1769 as Medical Faculty of the University of Nagyszombat; independent 1951
State control
Languages of instruction: Hungarian, English and German
Academic year: September to June

Rector: Prof. Dr L. Romics
Vice-Rectors: Prof. Dr T. Tulassay, Prof. Dr V. Ádám, Prof. Dr E. Monos
General Secretary: Dr M. Hári

Library of 250,000 vols
Number of teaching staff: 1,013
Number of students: 3,756

DEANS

Faculty of Medicine: Dr P. Sótonyi
Faculty of Dentistry: Dr T. Zelles
Faculty of Pharmacy: Dr Z. Vincze

PROFESSORS

Faculty of Medicine:

Ádám, V., Medical Biochemistry
Arnold, Cs., Family Medicine
de Châtel, R., Internal Medicine
Faller, J., Surgery
Falus, A., Biology
Fekete, Gy., Paediatrics
Flautner, L., Surgery
Fürst, Zs., Pharmacology
Horváth, A., Dermatology and Venereology
Iván, L., Gerontology
Kádár, A., Pathology
Kopp, M., Behavioural Sciences
Lozsádi, K., Cardiology
Magyar, P., Pulmonology
Makó, E., Radiology
Mandl, J., Medical Chemistry, Molecular Biology and Pathobiochemistry
Monos, E., Physiology and Experimental Laboratory for Clinical Research
Morava, E., Public Health
Nagy, L., Surgery
Nemes, A., Cardiovascular Surgery
Olah, I., Human Morphology and Developmental Biology
Papp, Z., Obstetrics and Gynaecology
Paulin, F., Obstetrics and Gynaecology
Perner, F., Transplantology and Surgery
Pénzes, I., Anaesthesiology and Intensive Therapy
Répássy, G., Otorhinolaryngology, Head and Neck Surgery
Réthelyi, M., Anatomy, Histology and Embryology
Romics, I., Urology
Romics, L., Internal Medicine
Rontó, Gy., Biophysics
Rozgonyi, F., Microbiology
Salacz, Gy., Ophthalmology
Sárváry, A., Traumatology
Sótonyi, P., Forensic Medicine
Spät, A., Physiology
Süveges, I., Ophthalmology
Szende, B., Pathology and Experimental Cancer Research
Szendrői, M., Orthopaedics
Szirmai, I., Neurology
Szollár, L., Pathophysiology
Tringer, L., Psychiatry and Psychotherapy
Tulassay, T., Paediatrics
Tulassay, Zs., Internal Medicine

Faculty of Dentistry:

Dénes, J., Dentistry for Children and Orthodontics
Fábián, T., Prosthetic Dentistry
Fazekas, A., Preservation Dentistry
Gera, I., Periodontics
Szabó, Gy., Oral and Maxillo-Facial Surgery
Zelles, T., Oral Biology

Faculty of Pharmacy:

Marton, S., Pharmaceutics
Mátyus, P., Organic Chemistry
Noszál, B., Pharmaceutical Chemistry
Szőké, E., Pharmacognosy
Török, T., Pharmacodynamics
Vincze, Z., University Pharmacy, Pharmacy Administration

ATTACHED INSTITUTES

Information Technology and Documentation Centre: 1089 Budapest, Kálvária tér 5; tel. 210-0328; Dir A. Sali.

Centre of Educational Resources and Research: 1089 Budapest, Nagyvárad tér 4; tel. 210-2927; Dir F. Hatfaludi.

BUDAPESTI KÖZGAZDASÁGTUDOMÁNYI EGYETEM
(Budapest University of Economic Sciences)

1093 Budapest IX, Fővám tér 8
Telephone: (1) 218-6855
Fax: (1) 217-6714

Founded 1948
State control
Languages of instruction: Hungarian and English
Academic year: September to May

Rector: T. Palánkai
Vice-Rectors: Cs. Forgács, T. Mészáros, J. Temesi
Secretary-General: (vacant)
Registrars: J. Csépai (studies in Hungarian), J. Berács (studies in English)
Librarian: Dr H. Huszár

Number of teachers: 457
Number of students: 5,500

Publications: *AULA, Társadalom és Gazdaság* (AULA, Society and Economy, quarterly), digests, bibliographies.

DEANS

Faculty of Postgraduate Studies: B. Hámori
Faculty of Social-Political Sciences: Zs. Rostoványi
Faculty of Business Administration: M. Virág
Faculty of Economics: J. Száz
Faculty of Undergraduate Economic Studies: B. Szarvas

PROFESSORS

Ábel, J., Business Economics
Ágh, A., Political Theory
Bácskai, T., Finance
Balaton, K., Management and Organization
Ballér, E., Pedagogy
Bánfi, T., Socialist and Credit System
Baricz, R., Accountancy
Bekker, Zs., History of Economic Thought
Berend, T. I., Economic History
Bernát, T., Economic Geography
Bod, P., Mathematics
Bokor, H., International Law
Bora, Gy., Economic Geography
Botos, K., Finance
Búza, J., Economic History
Chikán, A., Business Economics
Csáki, Cs., Agricultural Economics
Dancs, I., Mathematics and Computer Science
Dobák, M., Management and Organization
Erdős, T., Economic Policy
Falus, K., Political Economy
Forgó, F., Operations Research
Galasi, P., Labour Economics
Gálik, M., Business Economics
Gazsó, F., Sociology
Gábor, R., Labour Economics
Gergely, J., Applied Economics
Gyenge, Z., World Economy
Hegedűs, J., Foreign Languages
Hoffmann, M., Marketing
Hoós, J., Futurology
Hunyadi, L., Statistics
Huszár, E., Foreign Trade
Illés, M., Applied Economics
Iványi, A., Industrial Economics
Juhász, Gy., History of Diplomacy
Kerekes, S., Environmental Economics and Technology
Kerékgyártó, Gy., Statistics
Kindler, J., Business Economics
Kollár, Z., World Economy
Kollarik, A., Economic Geography
Kovács, F., Languages
Kovács, G., Planning of National Economy
Kovács, S., Management and Organization
Köves, P., Statistics
Kozma, F., Foreign Trade Economy
Kővári, Gy., Labour Economics
Kupcsik, J., Statistics
László, J., Planning of National Economy
Ligeti, S., Finance
Lőrinc Istvánffy, H., Foreign Trade
Magyar, M., Languages
Magyari-Beck, I., Education
Mandel, M., Economic Policy
Máriás, A., Industrial Economics
Marosi, M., Industrial Economics
Mátyás, A., History of Economic Thought
Mészáros, T., Applied Economics
Meszéna, Gy., Mathematics
Mihalik, I., Political Economics
Móczár, J., Econometrics

MOLNÁR, L., Marketing
MUNDRUCZÓ, GY., Statistics
NOVÁKY, E., Futurology
PACH, ZS. P., Economic History
PALÁNKAI, T., World Economy
RABÁR, F., Agricultural Economics
ROSTOVÁNYI, ZS., International Economy
SAJÓ, A., Law
SÁNDOR, I., Domestic Trade
SÁRKÖZI, T., Law
SIMAI, M., World Economy
SURÁNYI, S., World Economy
SZABÓ, K., Economics
SZABÓ, K., Economics
SZAKÁCS, S., Economic History
SZÁZ, J., Finance
SZENTES, T., International Economy
SZÉP, J., Mathematics
SZIGETI, E., Political Economy
SZILÁGYI, GY., Statistics
SZUHAY, M., Economic History
TIMÁR, J., Labour Economics
TÓTH, T., Foreign Trade
VARGA, GY., Agricultural Economics
VERESS, J., Economic Policy
VITA, L., Statistics
ZALAI, E., Planning of National Economy
ZELKÓ, L., Political Economy

ATTACHED INSTITUTES

Budapest Institute for Graduate International and Diplomatic Studies (BIGIS): 1828 Budapest, POB 489; tel. 117-5316; fax 117-9668; Dir ZSOLT ROSTOVÁNYI.

International Studies Centre (ISC): 1093 Budapest, Fővám tér 8; tel. 117-1153; telex 224186; fax 117-0608; 250 students; Dir JÓZSEF BERÁCS.

CENTRAL EUROPEAN UNIVERSITY

1051 Budapest, Nádor ut. 9
Telephone: (1) 327-3000
Fax: (1) 327-3001
E-mail: main@ceu.hu
Founded 1991
Private control
Language of instruction: English
Academic year: September to June
Postgraduate courses only
President and Rector: Prof. JOSEF JAŘAB
Academic Pro-Rector: Prof. SORIN ANTOHI
Executive Vice-President: Dr ISTVÁN TEPLÁN
Library of 100,000 vols, 800 periodicals
Number of permanent teachers: 100
Number of students: 650
Publication: *CEU Gazette*

DIRECTORS

Central European History: Prof. ALFRED RIEBER
Political Science: Prof. JÁNOS KIS
Medieval Studies: Prof. JOZSEF LASZLOVSKY
Legal Studies: Prof. CSILLA KOLLONAY-LEHOCZKY
Environmental Sciences and Policy: Prof. EDWARD BELLINGER
Economics: Prof. JACEK ROSTOWSKI
Gender and Culture: Prof. JOANNA REGULSKA
International Relations and European Studies: Prof. STEFANO GUZZINI
Nationalism Studies: Prof. MÁRIA KOVACS
Southeast European Studies: Prof. IVO BANAC
Sociology: Prof. EDMUND MOKRZYCKI

KOSSUTH LAJOS TUDOMÁNYEGYETEM
(Lajos Kossuth University)

4010 Debrecen, Egyetem tér 1
Telephone: (52) 316-666
Fax: (52) 416-490
Founded 1912
State control
Academic year: September to June
Rector: Dr G. BAZSA
Vice-Rectors: Dr L. IMRE (Educational Affairs), Dr D. BEKE (Scientific Affairs), Dr J. SZABÓ (Teacher Training), Dr T. MIHÁLYDEÁK (External Relations)
Registrar: Dr ZS. BORBÉLY
Librarian: Dr I. LÉVAY
Number of teachers: 644
Number of students: 9,699
Publication: *Évkönyv* (Yearbook).

DEANS

Faculty of Arts: Dr L. BALOGH
Faculty of Science: Dr GY. BORBÉLY
College Faculty of Engineering: Dr R. HORVÁTH

PROFESSORS

Faculty of Arts:

BALOGH, L., Educational Psychology
BARTA, J., Medieval Hungarian History
BARTHA, E., Ethnography
BEKE, D., German Languages and Cultures
BÉRES, C., Sociology
BITSKEY, I., Old Hungarian Literature
BUGÁN, A., Personality and Clinical Psychology
CSAPÓ, J., English Language and Methodology
CZIEGLER, I., General Psychology
GORETITY, J., Comparative Literature
GÖRÖMBEI, A., Modern and Contemporary Hungarian Literature
GUNST, P., Modern and Contemporary World History
HAJNÁDY, Z., Russian Literature
HAVAS, L., Classical Philology
HOFFMANN, I., Hungarian Linguistics
HOLLÓSY, B., English Linguistics
HUNYADI, L., General Linguistics
HÜLVELY, I., Politology
IMRE, L., 19th-Century Hungarian Literature
KERESZTES, L., Finno-Ugrian Linguistics
KERTÉSZ, A., German Linguistics
KISS, S., French Linguistics and Literature
KOVÁCS, Z., Social and Economic Psychology
KOZMA, T., Pedagogy
LICHTMANN, T., German Literature
MADARÁSZ, I., Italian Linguistics and Literature
MOLNÁR, D. I., Polish Linguistics and Literature
MOLNÁR, J., North American Studies
NAGY, M., History of Art
NÉMETH, GY., Ancient History
OROSZ, I., Modern and Contemporary Hungarian History
PAPP, I., Medieval World History
RÓZSA, N. E., History of Philosophy
RUBOVSZKY, K., Adult and Continuing Education
SOLYMOSI, L., Historical Research and Methodological Studies
SZAFKÓ, P., English Literature
SZIKSZAI, I. N., Hungarian Linguistics
VAJDA, M., Philosophy

Faculty of Science:

ANTUS, S., Organic Chemistry
BÁCSÓ, S., Mathematics
BEKE, D., Solid State Physics
BIRÓ, S., Microbiology and Biotechnology
BORBÉLY, G., Botany
BORBÉLY, J., Colloid Chemistry
DÉVAI, G., Ecology
DRAGÁLIN, A., Computer Science
FAZEKAS, I., Applied Mathematics
FERENCZY, T., Biological Methodology
GYŐRY, K., Algebra and Number Theory
JOÓ, F., Physical Chemistry
KERÉNYI, A., Applied Landscape Geography
KISS, A., Physics
KISS, L., Biochemistry
KÓNYA, J., Isotope Applications
KORMOS, J., Information Technology
LIPTÁK, A., Biochemistry
MEZEY, G., Pharmacy
NAGY, P., Geometry
PÁLES, Z., Mathematical Analysis
PÁLINKÁS, J., Experimental Physics
SAILER, K., Theoretical Physics
SIPICZKI, M., Genetics
SÓVÁGÓ, I., Inorganic and Analytical Chemistry
SÜLI-ZAKAR, I., Social Geography
SZABÓ, J., Physical Geography
SZABÓ, J., Projective Geometry
SZABÓ, M., Botany
SZŐÖR, G., Mineralogy and Geology
SZTARICSKAI, F., Pharmaceutical Chemistry
TAR, K., Meteorology
TERDIK, G., Computer Science
VARGA, V., Comparative Animal Physiology
VARGA, Z., Evolutionary Zoology and Anthropology
ZSUGA, M., Applied Chemistry

College Faculty of Engineering:

BALASSA, B., Architectural Engineering
DÚLL, S., Mechanical and Electrical Engineering
HOMONNAY, G., Building Engineering
KARVALY, E., Civil Engineering
LŐRINCZ, B., Mechanical Engineering
MAKSA, G., Mathematics and Descriptive Geometry
MOLNÁR, I., General and Management Studies
SÁRVÁRI, G., Construction
SZABADOS, M., General Mechanics
ZENTAY, I., Management and Business

Institute of Law:

BALÁZS, I., Constitutional Law
KRÁNITZ, M., Criminal Law
RUSZOLY, F., History of Law
SÜVEGES, M., Civil Law
VÁRNAY, E., European and International Civil Law

Institute of Economics and Business Studies:

MURAKÖZY, L., Economics
PRUGBERGER, T., Economic Law

HAYNAL IMRE EGÉSZSÉGTUDOMÁNYI
(Imre Haynal University of Health Sciences)

1135 Budapest XIII, Szabolcs-u. 35, POB 112
Telephone: 270-2911
Telex: 22 6595
Founded 1910 as Central Commission for postgraduate medical training; re-established 1956 as autonomous institute; university status 1974; became Orvostovábbképző Egyetem 1987; present name 1993
Rector: Prof. Dr L. Z. SZABÓ
Vice-Rectors: Prof. Dr GY. PETRÁNYI, Prof. Dr I. PRÉDA, Prof. Dr I. RÓZSA
Number of teaching staff: 470
Number of students: 10,000

DEANS

Postgraduate Faculty: Prof. Dr M. BODÓ
Faculty of Health Sciences: Dr J. MÉSZÁROS

HEADS OF DEPARTMENTS

Postgraduate Faculty:

BÁNHIDY, F., Head and Neck Surgery
BERENTEY, E., Radiology
BESZNYÁK, Clinical Oncology
BIRKÁS, Medicine for Disasters
BODÓ, M., Oncopathology and Cytology
BÖSZÖRMÉNYI, N, GY., Pulmonology
CZINNER, A., Paediatrics
FORGÁCS, I., Public Health Medicine
FÜREDI, J., Psychiatry and Clinical Psychology
GÖMÖR, B., Rheumatology and Physiotherapy

Halász, P., Neurology
Hatvani, I., Ophthalmology
Jákó, J., Internal Medicine I
Karsza, A., Urology
Kékes, E., Medical Informatics
Kiss, J., Surgery
Köteles, Gy., Radiobiology and Radiohygiene
Magyar, É., Pathology
Nagy, K., Paediatrics
Németh, Gy., Radiotherapy
Nyári, I., Neurosurgery
Paál, T., Pharmaceutics
Pálffy, Gy., Thoracic Surgery
Petrányi, Gy., Immunology
Renner, A., Traumatology
Sas, G., Haematology
Szabó, L. Z., Otorhinolaryngology
Tímár, L., Tropical and Infectious Diseases
Udvarhelyi, I., Orthopaedics
Ungváry, Gy., Labour Hygiene
Vágó, P., Stomatology
Vimláti, L., Anaesthesiology and Intensive Therapy
Vizi, E. Sz., Pharmacology

Faculty of Health Sciences (1046 Budapest, Erkel Gy. u. 26; tel. 1693-039; for the training of physiotherapists, dieticians, public health inspectors, nurses, nursing tutors, ambulance officers):

Bálint, G., Physiotherapy
Bencze, B., Oxyology
Kulcsár, L., Physical Training
Mészáros, J., Psychology and Pedagogy
Molnár, Gy., Faculty in Miskolc
Ormai, S., Morphology and Physiology
Rigó, J., Dietetics
Szarka, G., Sociology
Szél, É., Family Care

DEBRECENI ORVOSTUDOMÁNYI EGYETEM (University Medical School of Debrecen)

4012 Debrecen, Nagyerdei krt 98
Telephone: (52) 417-571
Fax: (52) 419-807

Founded 1912 as the Faculty of Medicine of István Tisza University; independent 1951

Rector: Dr L. Muszbek
Vice-Rectors: Dr Gy. Szegedi, Dr M. Udvardy, Dr L. Fésüs
Dean of the Faculty of Medicine: Dr P. Gergely
Registrar: Dr N. Kapusz
Librarian: Dr M. Virágos

Number of teaching staff: 780
Number of students: 2,408 (full-time), 602 (correspondence)

PROFESSORS

Ádány, R., Hygiene and Epidemiology
Antal, M., Anatomy, Histology, Embryology
Balázs, Gy., Surgery
Balla, Gy., Paediatrics
Barabás, Gy., Medical Biology
Berta, A., Ophthalmology
Biró, V., Traumatology
Borsos, A., Obstetrics and Gynaecology
Buris, L., Forensic Medicine
Csécsei, Gy., Neurosurgery
Csiba, L., Neurology and Psychiatry
Csorba, S., Paediatrics
Damjanovich, S., Biophysics
Degrell, I., Psychiatry
Dombrádi, V., Medical Chemistry
Édes, I., Cardiology and Pulmonology
Fachet, J., Pathophysiology
Fésüs, L., Biochemistry
Furka, I., Experimental Surgery
Gáspár, R., Biophysics
Gergely, L., Medical Microbiology
Gergely, P., Medical Chemistry
Gomba, Sz., Pathology
Hadházy, Cs., Anatomy, Histology, Embryology
Hegedűs, K., Neurology and Psychiatry
Hernádi, F., Pharmacology
Hernádi, Z., Obstetrics and Gynaecology
Horkay, I., Dermatology and Venereology
Hunyadi, J., Dermatology and Venereology
Kakuk, Gy., Internal Medicine
Kertai, P., Hygiene and Epidemiology
Keszthelyi, G., Stomatology
Kovács, L., Physiology
Kovács, P., Pharmacology
Lampé, I., Oto-rhino-laryngology
Lampé, L., Obstetrics and Gynaecology
Lukács, G., Surgery
Maródi, L., Paediatrics
Matesz, K., Anatomy, Histology, Embryology
Mechler, F., Neurology and Psychiatry
Módis, L., Anatomy, Histology, Embryology
Molnár, P., Dept of Behavioural Sciences
Molnár, P., Pathology
Muszbek, L., Clinical Chemistry
Nemes, Z., Pathology
Oláh, É., Paediatrics
Péter, M., Radiology
Péterffy, Á., Surgery
Pintér, J., Urology
Rák, K., Internal Medicine
Rigó, J., Orthopaedics
Sápy, P., Surgery
Sipiczki, M., Medical Biology
Szabó, G., Biophysics
Szegedi, Gy., Internal Medicine
Szepesi, K., Orthopaedics
Sziklai, I., Otorhinolaryngology
Szöllősi, J., Biophysics
Szűcs, G., Physiology
Tóth, Cs., Urology
Tóth, F., Medical Microbiology
Tóth, Z., Obstetrics and Gynaecology
Trón, L., Biophysics
Udvardy, M., Internal Medicine
Uray, É., Anaesthesiology
Varga, S., Central Service Laboratory
Wórum, F., Internal Medicine
Záborszky, Z., Traumatology
Zajácz, M., Ophthalmology
Zs. Nagy, I., Gerontology

JANUS PANNONIUS TUDOMÁNYEGYETEM (Janus Pannonius University)

7633 Pécs, Szántó K. J. u. 1/b

Telephone: (72) 501-509
Fax: (72) 251-527
E-mail: ori@nko.jpte.hu

First founded in 1367, re-founded in 1923
State control
Academic year: September to December, February to May (two terms)

Rector: Prof. József Tóth
Vice-Rectors: Dr Béla Sipos (General and Scientific Affairs), Dr János Bársony (Infrastructure and Development Affairs), Dr László Komlósi (Foreign Affairs), Dr Miklós Vass (Educational and Student Affairs)
Secretary-General: Dr Gyula Kóbor
Chief Administrative Officer: Ferencné Nagy
Chief Librarian: Péter Sonnevend

Number of teaching staff: 742
Number of students: 9,173

Publications: *Studia Iuridica Auctoritatae Universitatis Pécs Publicata, Studia Oeconomica Auctoritatae Universitatis Pécs Publicata, Studia Philosophica et Sociologica Auctoritatae Universitatis Pécs Publicata, Studia Paedagogica Auctoritate Universitatis Pécs Publicata (Scientiae Humanae et Naturales Artesque), Specimina Fennica, Specimina Sibirica, Specimina Nova Dissertationum ex Institutio Historico.*

DEANS

Faculty of Law: Dr Miklós Kengyel
Faculty of Business and Economics: Dr Ferenc Farkas
Faculty of Humanities: Dr Zsolt Visy
Faculty of Science: Dr Mária Csoknya (acting)
Faculty of Fine and Performing Arts: László Vidovszky
Mihály Pollack Engineering College: Dr József Ásványi

PROFESSORS

Faculty of Law:

Andrássy, Gy., Philosophy of Law
Benedek, F., Roman Law
Benkő, A., Agricultural Law
Bruhács, J., International Law
Filó, E., Family Law
Földvári, J., Criminal Law
Ivancsics, I., Administrative Law
Kajtár, I., History of Law
Kecskés, L., Civil Law
Kengyel, M., Civil Procedural Law
Kiss, Gy., Labour Law
Kiss, L., Constitutional Law
Lábady, T., Civil Law
Meleg, Cs., Sociology
Román, L., Labour and Social Security Law
Szita, J., Commercial Law
Szotáczky, M., Legal Theory
Tremmel, F., Criminal Procedural Law
Visegrády, A., Legal Theory
Weisz, J., Philosophy

Faculty of Business and Economics:

Barakonyi, K., Strategic Management
Beke, J., Accounting
Bélyácz, I., Managerial Economics
Csébfalvi, Gy., Management Science
Danyi, P., Operational Research
Dobay, P., Business Informatics
Farkas, F., Management
Hanyecz, L., Agricultural and Environmental Studies
Herich, Gy., Agricultural and Environmental Studies
Herman, S., Statistics and Demography
Hoóz, I., Strategic Management
Komlósi, S., Management Science
László, Gy., Economics
Lehoczky, J., Economics
Mach, P., Economics
Oroszi, S., Economics
Papp, L., Accounting
Rekettye, G., Marketing
Sántha, A., Agricultural and Environmental Studies
Sipos, B., Strategic Management
Szűcs, P., Management
Takács, B., Marketing
Törőcsik, M., Marketing
Tóth, T., Economic History
Varga, J., Management Science
Vörös, J., Management Science
Zeller, Gy., Marketing

Faculty of Humanities:

Aknai, T., Early Modern History
Andrásfalvy, B., Ethnography
Bécsy, T., Literary History
Bókay, A., Literary Theory
Csizmadia, S., Political Science
Font, M., Medieval and Early Modern History
Harsanyi, I., Modern History
Hetesi, I., Literary History
Horányi, Ö., Communication
Katus, L., Medieval and Early Modern History
Kézdi, B., Psychology
Klein, S., Adult Education and Educational Management
Koltai, D., Adult Education and Educational Management
Kulcsár Szabó, E., Literary History
László, J., Psychology

LENDVAI, E., Slavic Philology
MAJOROS, I., Early Modern History
MARTSA, S., English Language and Literature
MEDVE, Z., Slavic Philology
MOLNÁR, P., Psychology
NAGY, E., Social Policy
NAGY, I., Literary History
ORMOS, M., Modern History
PIRNÁT, A., Literary History
SZÉPE, GY., Linguistics
TILKOVSZKY, L., Modern History

Faculty of Science:

ÁNGYÁN, L., Teacher Training
BORHIDI, A., Botany
BOROSS, L., Chemistry and Biochemistry
ERDŐSI, F., Human Geography
FISCHER, E., Zoology
HAJDÚ, Z., Human Geography
HÁMORI, J., Zoology
HIDEG, K., Chemistry and Biochemistry
KÁTAI, I., Applied Mathematics and Informatics
KORPA, CS., Theoretical Physics
KŐSZEGFALVI, G., Human Geography
KOZMA, L., Experimental Physics
LÁZÁR, GY., Teacher Training
LÉNÁRD, L., Zoology
LOVÁSZ, GY., Physical Geography
MAJER, J., Ecology and Zoogeography
PESTI, M., Genetics and Microbiology
SCHIPP, F., Mathematics
SEY, O., Ecology and Zoogeography
SZABÓ, L., Botany
SZLACHÁNYI, K., Theoretical Physics
TOMCSÁNYI, T., Genetics and Microbiology
TÓTH, J., Human Geography

Faculty of Fine and Performing Arts:

BENCSIK, I., Sculpture
KESERŰ, I., Painting
KIRCSI, L., Music
KRAJNIK, J., Painting
RÉTFALVI, S., Sculpture
SCHRAMMEL, I., Sculpture
TILLAI, A., Music
VIDOVSZKY, L., Music

Institute of Teacher Training:

ADERMANN, G.
BÁRDOSSY, I.
BERNÁTH, JÁNOS
BERNÁTH, JÓZSEF
BOHÁR, A.
DÁRDAI, A.
DEME, T.
GÉCZI, J.
KÉRI, K.
KOVÁCS, S.
MOLNÁR, L.
SZILÁGYI, V.
ZÁNKAI, A.

Mihály Pollack Engineering College:

ARADI, L., Public Utilities, Geodesy and Environmental Protection
ÁSVÁNYI, J., Automation
BACHMAN, Z., Planning and Architectural Studies
BÁRSONY, J., Statics and Permanent Structures
FODOR, A. CS., Building Engineering
HELMICH, J., Automation
HÜBNER, M., City Planning
KASSAI, J., Electricity Supply
KISTELEGDI, I., Building Structures
KLINCSIK, M., Mathematics
LENKEI, P., Statics and Permanent Structures
ORBÁN, J., Geotechnics and Transport Engineering
STOJANOVITS, J., Building Engineering
SZAKONYI, L., Technical Engineering
SZVITACS, I., Engineering Management

PÉCSI ORVOSTUDOMÁNYI EGYETEM (Pécs University Medical School)

7624 Pécs, Szigeti u. 12
Telephone: (72) 324-122
Fax: (72) 326-244
E-mail: hivatal@rektori.pote.hu

Founded 1923 as the Faculty of Medicine of the University of Pécs; independent 1951
State control
Languages of instruction: Hungarian and English
Academic year: September to June

Rector: Prof. Dr ÁRPÁD BELLYEI
Vice-Rectors: Prof. Dr LÁSZLÓ LÉNÁRD, Prof. Dr GYÖRGY KOSZTOLÁNYI
Secretary-General: Prof. Dr ERZSÉBET RŐTH
Librarian: Dr RÓZSA FÖLDVÁRI

Number of teachers: 684
Number of students: 3,217

Publication: *Pécsi Orvostudományi Egyetem Évkönyve* (Yearbook).

DEANS

Faculty of Medicine: Prof. Dr BALÁZS SÜMEGI
Faculty of Health Sciences: Dir Dr JÓZSEF BUDA

PROFESSORS

Faculty of Medicine:

ALKONYI, I., Biochemistry
ÁNGYÁN, L., Physiology
BAJNÓCZKY, I., Forensic Medicine
BARTHÓ, L., Pharmacology
BAUER, M., Oto-rhino-laryngology
BELÁGYI, J., Central Research Laboratory
BELLYEI, Á., Orthopaedics
CZIRJÁK, L., Internal Medicine
CZOPF, J., Neurology
DÓCZI, T., Neurosurgery
EMBER, I., Public Health
EMŐDY, L., Microbiology
FARKAS, B., Dermatology
FEKETE, M., Paediatrics
FISCHER, E., Pharmacology
GALLYAS, F., Neurosurgery
GÖTZ, F., Urology
GREGUS, Z., Pharmacology
HIDEG, K., Central Research Laboratory
HORVÁTH, L., Radiology
HORVÁTH, Ö. P., Surgery
KARÁTSON, A., Internal Medicine
KELLERMAYER, M., Clinical Biochemistry
KÉTYI, I., Microbiology
KOSZTOLÁNYI, G., Paediatrics
KOVÁCS, B., Ophthalmology
KOVÁCS, S., Pathophysiology
KRÁNICZ, J., Orthopaedics
KUHN, E., Radiology
LÁZÁR, GY., Anatomy
LÉNÁRD, L., Physiology
LOSONCZY, H., Internal Medicine
MÉHES, K., Paediatrics
MORAVA, E., Public Health
MÓZSIK, GY., Internal Medicine
NAGY, J., Internal Medicine
NAGY, L., Internal Medicine
NÉMETH, P., Immunology and Biotechnology
NYÁRÁDY, J., Traumatology
PAJOR, L., Pathology
PÁR, A., Internal Medicine
PINTÉR, A., Paediatrics
PYTEL, J., Oto-rhino-laryngology
RŐTH, E., Experimental Surgery
SÁNDOR, A., Biochemistry
SCHNEIDER, I., Dermatology
SÉTÁLÓ, GY., Anatomy
SOLTÉSZ, GY., Paediatrics
SOMOGYI, B., Biophysics
SÜMEGI, B., Biochemistry
SZABÓ, GY., Oral Medicine
SZABÓ, IMRE, Behavioural Sciences
SZABÓ, ISTVÁN, Obstetrics and Gynaecology
SZABÓ, J., Oral Medicine
SZEBERÉNYI, J., Biology
SZÉKELY, J., Obstetrics and Gynaecology
SZÉKELY, M., Pathophysiology
SZEKERES, J., Microbiology
SZELÉNYI, Z., Pathophysiology
SZOLCSÁNYI, J., Pharmacology
TEKERES, M., Intensive Therapy and Anaesthesia
TÉNYI, J., Public Health
THAN, G., Obstetrics and Gynaecology
TÓTH, GY., Chemistry
TRIXLER, M., Psychiatry and Medical Psychology
VERECZKEY, L., Behavioural Sciences
VÉRTES, M., Physiology

Faculty of Health Sciences:

BUDA, J., Social Medicine
CHOLNOKY, P., Paediatrics
FARKAS, M., Clinical Laboratory
GYÓDI, GY., Paediatrics
HORVÁTH, B., Obstetrics and Gynaecology
ILLEI, GY., Obstetrics and Gynaecology
KISS, T., Biology
KOMÁROMY, L., Biology
KOVÁCS, L. G., Physiology
LAKY, R., Traumatology
MÉSZÁROS, L., Health Insurance
ROZSOS, I., Surgery
TAHIN, T., Sociology
TÁRNOK, F., Internal Medicine
TÖRÖK, B., Anatomy

JÓZSEF ATTILA TUDOMÁNYEGYETEM (József Attila University)

6720 Szeged, Dugonics tér 13
Telephone: (62) 454-000
Fax: (62) 310-412
E-mail: rektor@jate.u-szeged.hu

Founded 1872, refounded 1921
State control
Academic year: September to June

Rector: Prof. Dr REZSŐ MÉSZÁROS
Vice-Rectors: Prof. Dr BÉLA RÁCZ (General), Dr TIBOR ALMÁSI (Education), Dr ISTVAN KENESEI (Science)
Librarian: Dr BÉLA MADER

Library: see Libraries
Number of teachers: 543
Number of students: 10,388

Publication: *Acta Universitatis Szegediensis de Attila József Nominatae*.

DEANS

Faculty of Law and Political Science: Prof. Dr IMRE MOLNÁR
Faculty of Arts: Dr MIHÁLY BALÁZS
Faculty of Science: Prof. Dr KÁROLY VARGA

PROFESSORS

Faculty of Law and Political Science:

BÉRCZY, I., Civil Law and Civil Procedure
BESENYEI, L., Civil Law and Civil Procedure
BODNÁR, L., International Law
CZÚCZ, O., Social and Labour Law
MOLNÁR, I., Roman Law
NAGY, F., Criminal Law and Criminal Procedure
NAGY, K., International Law
RUSZOLY, J., Legal History
VERES, J., Agricultural and Environmental Law

Faculty of Arts:

ANDERLE, Á., Hispanic Studies
BASSOLA, P., German Linguistics
BERNÁTH, Á., German Literature
BERTA, Á., Altaic Studies
CSAPÓ, B., Education
CSEJTEI, D., Philosophy
CSÚRI, K., Austrian Culture and Literature
FRIED, I., Comparative Literature
JUHÁSZ, A., Ethnography
KENESEI, I., English and American Studies

KRISTÓ, GY., Medieval and Early Modern Hungarian History
MAKK, F., Auxiliary Sciences of History
MIKOLA, T., Finno-Ugrian Studies
NAGY, J., Education
NAGY, L., Modern and Contemporary Hungarian History
OLAJOS, T., Classical Philology
PÁL, J., Italian Language and Literature
RÓNA-TAS, A., Altaic Studies
SOÓS, K., Modern and Contemporary Hungarian History
SZABÓ, J., Hungarian Linguistics
SZIGETI, L., Modern Hungarian Literature
TÓTH, I., Slavic Philology
WOJTILLA, GY., Ancient History

Faculty of Science:

BÁN, M., Physical Chemistry
BARTÓK, M., Organic Chemistry
BECSEI, J., Economic Geography
BOR, ZS., Optics and Quantum Electronics
BURGER, A., Economic Geography
BURGER, K., Inorganic and Analytical Chemistry
CSÁKÁNY, B., Algebra and Number Theory
CSIRIK, J., Computer Science
CSÖRGŐ, S., Applied Analysis
CZÉDLI, G., Algebra and Number Theory
DÉKÁNY, I., Colloid Chemistry
ERDEI, L., Plant Physiology
ERDŐHELYI, A., Solid State Chemistry and Radiochemistry
ÉSIK, Z., Principles of Computer Science
FARKAS, GY., Anthropology
FEJES, P., Applied Chemistry
FERENCZY, L., Microbiology
GALLÉ, L., Ecology
GULYA, K., Zoology and Cell Biology
HATVANI, L., Analysis
HETÉNYI, M., Mineralogy, Geochemistry and Petrography
HEVESI, I., Experimental Physics
KÉRCHY, L., Analysis
KIRICSI, I., Applied Chemistry
KISS, T., Inorganic Chemistry
KOPPÁNY, GY., Climatology
KRAJKÓ, GY., Economic Geography
KRÁMLI, A., Applications of Analysis
LEHOCZKI, E., Botany
LEINDLER, L., Analysis
MARÓTI, P., Biophysics
MÉSZÁROS, R., Economic Geography
MEZŐSI, G., Physical Geography
MOLNÁR, A., Organic Chemistry
MOLNÁR, B., Geology and Palaeontology
MÓRICZ, F., Applications of Analysis
NAGYPÁL, I., Physical Chemistry
NOVÁK, M., Physical Chemistry
RÁCZ, B., Optics and Quantum Electronics
SCHNEIDER, GY., Organic Chemistry
SOLYMOSI, F., Solid State and Radiochemistry
SZABÓ, G., Optics and Quantum Electronics
SZATMÁRI, S., Experimental Physics
SZEDERKÉNYI, T., Mineralogy, Geochemistry and Petrography
SZENDREI, Á., Algebra and Number Theory
SZENDREI, M., Algebra and Number Theory
SZENTE, M., Comparative Physiology
TOLDI, J., Comparative Physiology
TOTIK, V., Set Theory and Mathematical Logic
VARGA, K., Applied Chemistry
VINCZE, I., Organic Chemistry
VISY, CS., Physical Chemistry

SZENT-GYÖRGYI ALBERT ORVOSTUDOMÁNYI EGYETEM (Albert Szent-Györgyi Medical University)

6720 Szeged, Dugonics-tér 13
Telephone: (62) 455-007
Fax: (62) 455-005

Founded 1872, refounded 1921 as the Medical Faculty of Szeged University; independent 1951
State control
Languages of instruction: Hungarian and English
Academic year: September to June
Rector: Prof. ATTILA DOBOZY
Vice-Rectors: Prof. G. TELEGDY, Prof. M. CSANÁDY, Prof. J. GY. PAPP
Secretary-General: Dr B. PRÁGAI
Number of teaching staff: 721, including 45 full professors
Number of students: 2,635
Publications: *Studia Medica Szegedinensia, Évkönyv, Tanrend, University Guide, Curriculum, Contract Research.*

DEANS

Faculty of General Medicine: Prof. T. MÉSZÁROS
Faculty of Pharmacy: Prof. I. ERŐS
Faculty of Nursing and Social Sciences: Prof. E. SZÉL

PROFESSORS

Faculty of General Medicine:

BALOGH, Á., Clinical Surgery
BENEDEK, GY., Physiology
BODOSI, M., Neurological Surgery
BOROS, M., Experimental Surgery
CSANÁDY, M., Internal Medicine
CSERNAY, L., Radiology (acting)
CZÍGNER, J., Otolaryngology
DÉSI, I., Public Health
DOBOZY, A., Dermatology
DUX, L., Biochemistry
GÁL, GY., Blood Transfusion
HANTOS, Z., Medical Informatics
JANKA, Z., Neurology and Psychiatry
JULESZ, J., Endocrinology
KÁSA, P., Alzheimer's Disease Research
KISS, A., Urology
KOLOZSVÁRI, L., Ophthalmology
KOVÁCS, L., Obstetrics and Gynaecology
KRASZKÓ, P., Pulmonology
LIPOSITS, ZS., Anatomy and Histology
LONOVICS, J., Internal Medicine
MARI, A., Dentistry and Stomatology
MÉRAY, J., Anaesthesiology
MÉSZÁROS, T., Orthopaedics
MIKÓ, T., Pathology
NAGY, E., Clinical Microbiology
PAPP, J. GY., Pharmacology
PENKE, B., Medical Chemistry
PINTÉR, S., Paediatrics
SONKODI, S., Nephrology, Dialysis
SZABAD, J., Medical Biology
SZABÓ, J., Medical Genetics
SZÉCSI, J., Cardiac Surgery
SZÉL, E., Nursing and Health Sciences
TELEGDY, GY., Pathophysiology
THURZÓ, L., Oncotherapy
VARGA, T., Forensic Medicine
VÉCSEI, L., Neurology

Faculty of Pharmacy:

BERNÁTH, G., Pharmaceutical Chemistry
ERŐS, I., Pharmaceutical Technology
FALKAY, GY., Pharmacodynamics
MÁTHÉ, I., Pharmacognosy

Technical Universities

GÖDÖLLŐI AGRÁRTUDOMÁNYI EGYETEM (Gödöllő University of Agricultural Sciences)

2103 Gödöllő, Páter Károly u. 1
Telephone: (28) 410-971
Fax: (28) 410-804
E-mail: rector@gau.hu

Founded 1945
State Control
Language of instruction: Hungarian, English, Russian
Academic year: September to May
Rector: Dr CSABA SZÉKELY
Vice-Rectors: Dr MIKLÓS MÉZES, Dr KÁROLY KOCSIS
Secretary-General: Dr LÁSZLÓ GUTH
Librarian: Dr TIBOR KOLTAY
Number of teaching staff (including professors): 480
Number of students: 5,317
Publications: *University Calendar,* scientific publications, faculty publications, etc.

DEANS

Faculty of Agricultural Sciences: Dr GYÖRGY HELTAI
Faculty of Agricultural Engineering: Dr ATTILA VAS
Faculty of Economic and Social Sciences: Dr JÓZSEF MOLNÁR
Institute of Scientific Training: Dr PÉTER SZENDRŐ

DIRECTORS

College Faculty of Agricultural Economics, Gyöngyös: Dr SÁNDOR MAGDA
College Faculty of Agricultural Engineering, Mezőtur: Dr ISTVÁN PATAI
College Faculty of Agriculture, Nyíregyháza: Dr BOTOND SINÓROS-SZABÓ

PROFESSORS

Faculty of Agricultural Sciences:

BEDŐ, S., Animal Breeding
FÜLEKY, GY., Soil Science
HELTAI, GY., Chemistry
HESZKY, L., Plant Genetics
HORNOK, L., Microbiology
HORVÁTH, L., Animal Genetics
KISS, J., Plant Protection
MÁTÉ, A., Crop Production
MENYHÉRT, Z., Crop Production
MÉZES, M., Animal Feeding
OROSZ, L., Biotechnology
PÉCZELY, P., Animal Breeding
PEKLI, J., Tropical Agriculture
SAJGÓ, M., Biochemistry
SZALAI, GY., Water Management
SZEMÁN, L., Grassland Management
TUBA, Z., Botany and Plant Physiology

Faculty of Agricultural Engineering:

BARÓTFY, I., Environmental Engineering
BEER, GY., Agricultural Engineering
FARKAS, I., Physics
GYÜRK, I., Mechanics
JESZENSZKY, Z., Agricultural Engineering
KÓSA, A., Mathematics
SEMBERY, P., Food Engineering
SZENDRŐ, P., Agricultural Mechanization
SZÜLE, ZS., Agricultural Mechanization
VAS, A., Agricultural Engineering

Faculty of Economic and Social Sciences:

BARKÓ, E., Education
BIRÓ, S., Economic Law
HAJÓS, L., Labour Science
KISS, K., Statistics
KULCSÁR, L., Rural Sociology
RATHMANN, J., Philosophy
SZÉKELY, CS., Agricultural Economics
TÓTH, P., Accounting and Finance
VÖLGYESY, P., Psychology

ATTACHED INSTITUTES

Academy of Trading and Enterprise: Dir Dr B. HAUK.
Agricultural Research Institute: Dir Dr A. FEHÉR.
Farm Machinery Historical Museum: Dir GY. PÁLFY.
Environmental and Landscape Management Institute: Dir Dr J. ÁNGYÁN.

Institute of Management and Business Training: Dir Dr F. NEMES.

ÁLLATORVOSTUDOMÁNYI EGYETEM (University of Veterinary Science)

1078 Budapest, István út. 2
Telephone: (1) 322-2660
Fax: (1) 342-7303

Founded 1787
State control
Languages of instruction: Hungarian, German, English
Academic year: September to June

Rector: Prof. Dr V. L. FRENYÓ
Deputy Rectors: Prof. Dr F. HAJÓS, Prof. Dr P. SCHEIBER, Prof. Dr GY. HUSZENICZA
Questor: P. BÁDONFAI
Librarian: Dr M. CSEREY

Library: see Libraries
Number of teachers: 140
Number of students: 665

Publications: *Évkönyv* (Yearbook), *Bibliography of Hungarian Veterinary Literature.*

PROFESSORS

BIRÓ, G., Food Hygiene
BODÓ, I., Animal Husbandry
ÉLIÁS, B., Zoology
FEKETE, S., Animal Nutrition
FRENYÓ, V. L., Immunology and Biochemistry
GAÁL, T., Internal Medicine
HAJÓS, F., Anatomy and Histology
HUSZENICZA, GY., Obstetrics and Reproduction
KISS, A., Social Sciences
RAFAI, P., Animal Hygiene
RUDAS, P., Physiology and Biochemistry
SCHEIBER, P., Chemistry
SEMJÉN, G., Pharmacology
SOLTI, L., Obstetrics and Reproduction
SZENCI, O., Obstetrics and Reproduction
TÓTH, J., Surgery and Ophthalmology
TUBOLY, S., Microbiology
TURY, E., Anatomy and Histology
VARGA, I., Parasitology
VARGA, J., Microbiology
VETÉSI, F., Pathology
VETTER, J., Botany
VÖRÖS, K., Internal Medicine
ZÖLDÁG, L., Obstetrics and Reproduction

ATTACHED INSTITUTE

Research Institute: Dir Dr J. SEREGI.

BUDAPESTI MŰSZAKI EGYETEM (Technical University of Budapest)

1521 Budapest, Műegyetem-Rkp 3
Telephone: (1) 463-1111
Telex: 225931
Fax: (1) 463-1110

Founded in 1782 as Institutum Geometrico-Hydrotechnicum and reorganized as Hungarian Palatine Joseph Technical University in 1871. Építőipari és Közlekedési Műszaki Egyetem (Technical University of Building and Transport Engineering) was incorporated with the university in 1967
State control
Languages of instruction: Hungarian, English, German, French, Russian
Academic year: September to June

Rector: Prof. Dr ÁKOS DETREKŐI
Pro-Rectors: Prof. Dr JÁNOS GINSZTLER, Prof. Dr GYÖRGY HORVAI, Prof. Dr FERENC VÖRÖS
Secretary General: Dr JÓZSEF VAJDA
Librarian: Dr PÁL VÁSÁRHELYI

Number of teachers 1,123
Number of students: 12,950

Publications: *Periodica Politechnica, Chemical, Electrical, Mechanical, Architectural, Civil and Transport Engineering, Physics and Nuclear Sciences, Humanities and Social Sciences Series* (quarterly), *A Budapesti Műszaki Egyetem Évkönyve,* information on research works.

DEANS

Faculty of Civil Engineering: Prof. Dr GYÖRGY FARKAS
Faculty of Mechanical Engineering: Prof. Dr KÁROLY MOLNÁR
Faculty of Architecture: Prof. Dr BÁLINT PETRÓ
Faculty of Chemical Engineering: Prof. Dr MIKLÓS KUBINYI
Faculty of Electrical Engineering and Informatics: Prof. Dr LÁSZLÓ PAP
Faculty of Transport Engineering: Prof. Dr ÉVA KÖVES-GILICZE
Faculty of Natural and Social Sciences: Prof. Dr GYULA CSOM

PROFESSORS

Faculty of Civil Engineering:

ADAM, J., Geodesy
BALÁZS, GY., Building Materials
BÉNYEI, A., Road Construction
BIRÓ, P., Geodesy
BORJÁN, J., Building Materials
DETREKŐI, Á., Photogrammetry
FARKAS, GY., Reinforced Concrete Structures
FARKAS, J., Geotechnique
FÍ, I., Road Construction
GÁLOS, M., Geology
GÁSPÁR, ZS., Mechanics
GRESCHIK, GY., Geology
HASZPRA, O., Hydraulic Engineering
HEGEDŰS, I., Reinforced Concrete Structures
HORVÁTH, K., Surveying
IVÁNYI, M., Steel Structures
KALISZKY, S., Mechanics
KECSKÉS, S., Railway Construction
KLEB, B., Geology
KOLLAR, L., Building Construction
KRAUTER, A., Surveying
KURUTZ KOVÁCS, M., Mechanics
MEGYERI, J., Railway Construction
NEMESDY, E., Road Construction
OROSZ, A., Reinforced Concrete Structures
ÖLLŐS, G., Water Supply and Canalization
PATONAI, D., Building Construction
PLATHY, P., Steel Structures
SÁRKÖZY, F., Surveying
SOMLYODY, L., Water Supply and Canalization
SZALAY, K., Reinforced Concrete Structures
SZÉKELY, J. G., Mathematics
SZOLNOKY, CS., Water Supply and Canalization
SZÖLLŐSI-NAGY, A., Hydraulic Engineering
TARNAI, T., Mechanics
VARGA, I., Hydraulic Engineering
VISONTAI, J., Steel Structures
ZSUFFA, I., Water Management

Faculty of Mechanical Engineering:

ARTINGER, I., Mechanical Technology
BAJCSAY, P., Mathematics
BÁNHIDI, L., Sanitary Engineering
BÉDA, GY., Technical Mechanics
BÜKI, G., Energetics
CZVIKOVSZKY, T., Polymer Engineering and Textile Technology
FARKAS, J., Machine Production
FARKAS, M., Mathematics
FÜZY, O., Hydraulic Machines
GINSZTLER, J., Electrical Materials Technology
HORVÁTH, M., Machine Production
IMRE, L., Energetics
JÁSZAY, T., Energetics
JEDERÁN, M., Polymer Engineering and Textile Technology
KERTÉSZ, V., Mathematics
KONKOLY, T., Mechanical Technology
KULLMANN, L., Hydraulic Machines
LAJOS, T., Fluid Mechanics
LEVAY, A., Energetics
MAGYAR, J., Machine Elements
MOLNÁR, E., Geometry
MOLNÁR, K., Chemical and Food Engineering
NAGY, I., Electrotechnics
PENNINGER, A., Heat Engines
PETRIK, O., Precision Mechanics-Optics
REMENYI, K., Energetics
SOMLÓ, J., Machine Production
STÉPÁN, G., Technical Mechanics
SZABÓ, I., Systems and Control Engineering
SZÁNTAI, T., Mathematics
SZENTGYÖRGYI, S., Chemical and Food Engineering
SZENTMÁRTONY, T., Fluid Mechanics
VAJNA, Z., Fluid Mechanics
VARGA, L., Machine Elements
ZETTNER, T., Systems and Control Engineering
ZIAJA, GY., Mechanical Technology
ZSEBIK, A., Systems and Control Engineering

Faculty of Architecture:

BALOGH, B., Design
BITÓ, J., Housing Design
BONTA, J., History of Architecture
DOMOKOS, G., Structural Mechanics
DULÁCSKA, E., Structural Mechanics
GYULAY, J., Building Management and Organization
HAJNÓCZI, GY., History of Architecture
HARASTA, M., Industrial and Agricultural Architecture
HOFER, M., Design of Public Buildings
ISTVÁNFI, GY., History of Architecture
KERÉNYI, J., Housing Design
KLAFSZKY, E., Building Management and Organization
KUBA, G., Industrial and Agricultural Architecture
LÁSZLÓ, O., Building Construction
LÁZÁR, A., Industrial and Agricultural Architecture
MEGGYESI, T., Urban Studies
PEREDY, J., Descriptive Geometry
PETRÓ, B., Building Constructions
SZENTKIRÁLYI, Z., History of Architecture
TÖRÖK, F., Drawing and Moulding
VÁMOSSY, F., Theory of Architecture
VÖRÖS, F., Building Construction
ZÁDOR, M., Preservation of Monuments and History of Architecture
ZÖLD, A., Sanitary Engineering

Faculty of Chemical Engineering:

BITTER, I., Organic Chemical Technology
FOGASSY, E., Organic Chemical Technology
FONYÓ, ZS., Chemical Unit Operations
GÁL, S., General and Analytical Chemistry
HARGITTAI, I., General and Analytical Chemistry
HENCSEI, P., Inorganic Chemistry
HOLLÓ, J., Agricultural Chemical Technology
HORVAI, GY., Chemical Informatics
KALAUS, GY., Organic Chemistry
KEGLEVICH, GY., Organic Chemical Technology
KEMÉNY, S., Chemical Unit Operations
KÓSA, L., Mechanical Engineering for the Chemical Industry
KUBINYI, M., Physical Chemistry
LÁSZLÓ, E., Agricultural Chemical Technology
LÁSZTITY, R., Biochemistry and Food Technology
LEMPERT, K., Organic Chemistry
LINDNER, E., General and Analytical Chemistry
MANCZINGER, J., Chemical Unit Operations
MIHÁLTZ, P., Chemical Technology
MÓSER, M., Chemical Technology
NAGY, L. GY., Physical Chemistry
NOVÁK, B., Agricultural Chemical Technology
NOVÁK, L., Organic Chemistry
NYITRAI, J., Organic Chemistry

ÖRSI, F., Biochemistry and Food Technology
POKOL, GY., General and Analytical Chemistry
PUKÁNSZKY, B., Plastics and Rubber Industries
PUNGOR, E., General and Analytical Chemistry
RÉFFY, J., Inorganic Chemistry
RUSZNÁK, I., Organic Chemical Technology
SALGÓ, A., Biochemistry and Food Technology
SEVELLA, B., Agricultural Chemical Technology
SZABADVÁRY, F., General and Analytical Chemistry
SZÁNTAY, CS., Organic Chemistry
SZEBÉNYI, I., Chemical Technology
SZÉCHY, G., Chemical Technology
SZEPESVÁRI TOTH, K., General and Analytical Chemistry
TŐKE, L., Organic Chemical Technology
TUNGLER, A., Organic Chemical Technology
VARGA, J., Plastics and Rubber Industries
ZRINYI, M., Physical Chemistry

Faculty of Electrical Engineering and Informatics:

ARATÓ, P., Process Control
BÁN, G., Electric Power Plants and Networks
BENYÓ, Z., Process Control
BERTA, I., High-Voltage Engineering
BOSZNAY, Á., Electromagnetic Theory
CSIBI, S., Telecommunications
CSURGAY, Á., Electromagnetic Theory
FODOR, GY., Electromagnetic Theory
FRIGYES, I., Microwave Telecommunications
GÉHER, K., Telecommunications
GORDOS, G., Telecommunications and Telematics
GYŐRFI, L., Mathematics
HALÁSZ, S., Electrical Machines
HORVÁTH, T., High-Voltage Engineering
ILLYEFALVI-VITÉZ, ZS., Electronic Technology
KEVICZKY, L., Automation
KISS, O., Mathematics
LANTOS, B., Process Control
MOJZES, I., Electronic Technology
NAGY, I., Automation
PAP, L., Telecommunications
PÉCELI, G., Measurement and Instrument Engineering
RECSKI, A., Mathematics
RETTER, GY., Electrical Machines
RÓZSA, P., Mathematics
SCHMIDT, I., Electrical Machines
SELÉNYI, E., Measurement and Instrument Engineering
SIMONYI, K., Telecommunications
SZABÓ, CS., Telecommunications
SZÉKELY, V., Electronic Devices
TARNAY, K., Electronic Devices
TUSCHÁK, R., Automation
VAJK, I., Automation
VARJU, GY., Electric Power Plants and Networks
VESZELY, GY., Automation
ZOMBORY, L., Microwave Telecommunications

Faculty of Transport Engineering:

BENEDEK, Z., Aircraft and Ships
BOKOR, J., Transport Automatics
BOROTVÁS, E., Transport Economics
HANTOS, T., Machine Elements
ILOSVAI, L., Motor Vehicles
KÖVES GILICZE, É., Transport Operation
KULCSÁR, B., Building and Materials-Handling Machines
LÉVAI, Z., Motor Vehicles
MÁRIALIGETI, J., Machine Elements
MICHELBERGER, P., Mechanics
NÁNDORI, E., Mechanics
PALKOVICS, L., Motor Vehicles
PÁSZTOR, E., Aircraft and Ships
ROHÁCS, J., Aircraft and Ships
SCHMIDT, T., Mathematics
SIMONYI, A., Mechanics
TAKÁCS, J., Machine Production Technology
TÁNCZOS, LNÉ., Transport Economics
ZOBORY, I., Railway Vehicles

Faculty of Natural and Social Sciences:

ANTALOVITS, M., Ergonomics and Psychology
BARTHA, L., Psychology
BIRÓ, G., Experimental Physics
BISZTERSZKY, E., Technical Pedagogy
BOROSS, Z., Industrial Business and Management
CSOM, GY., Nuclear Technology
DEÁK, P., Atomic Physics
FARKAS, J., Sociology
FEHÉR, M., Philosophy
FÜZESSY, Z., Physics
GIBER, J., Atomic Physics
GYULAI, J., Experimental Physics
JÁNOSSY, A., Experimental Physics
KERÉKGYÁRTÓ, GY., Economics
KERTÉSZ, J., Physics
MIHÁLY, GY., Physics
NAGY, B., Mathematics
NOSZTICZIUS, Z., Chemical Physics
PETZ, D., Mathematics
RICHTER, P., Atomic Physics
SZAKOLCZAI, GY., Economics
SZATMÁRY, Z., Nuclear Technology
TERPLÁN, Z., History of Science
VASVÁRI, B., Quantum Theory
VERHÁS, J., Chemical Physics
VIROSZTEK, A., Quantum Theory
ZAWADOWSKI, A., Physics

Institute of Postgraduate Engineering Courses:

REUSS, P.

University Information Centre:

MILCSÁK, J.

International Education Centre:

PENNINGER, A.

DEBRECENI AGRÁRTUDOMÁNYI EGYETEM
(Debrecen University of Agricultural Sciences)

4015 Debrecen, POB 36
Telephone: (52) 347-888
Fax: (52) 413-385

Founded 1868
State control
Language of instruction: Hungarian
Academic year: September to June

Rector: Dr J. LOCH
Vice-Rectors: Dr ZS. NEMESSÁLYI, Dr Z. CSIZMAZIA
Registrar: Dr GY. NÁDAS
Librarian: ZS. NÁDAS

Library of 175,000 vols
Number of teachers: 166
Number of students: 3,088

Publication: *A Debreceni Agrártudományi Egyetem Tudományos Közleményei* (annually).

DEANS

Faculty of Agricultural Sciences: Dr A. NÁBRÁDI
College of Water and Environmental Management, Szarvas: Dr F. LIGETVÁRI (Director)
College of Agriculture, Hódmezővásárhely: Dr GY. SINKOVICS (Director)

PROFESSORS

Faculty of Agricultural Sciences:

CSIZMAZIA, Z., Agricultural Engineering
GYŐRI, Z., Food Processing and Quality Testing
KOZMA, A., Accounting and Finance
LOCH, J., Agrochemistry
NAGY, G., Rural Resource Management
NEMESSÁLYI, ZS., Farm Business Management
NYIRI, L., Plant Cultivation and Agriculture
PALOTÁS, G., Zoology and Wildlife Biology; Animal Physiology and Health
PEPÓ, P., Crop Science and Land Use
PETHŐ, M., Botany and Plant Physiology
PFAU, E., Institute of Agricultural Economics and Management
RUZSÁNYI, L., Institute of Crop Production
SZÁSZ, G., Environmental Management and Agrometeorology
SZARUKÁN, I., Plant Protection
SZIKI, G., Agricultural Water Management
THYLL, SZ., Agricultural Water Management

College of Agriculture, Hódmezővásárhely:

FRANK, J., Plant Production
MUCSI, I., Animal Breeding

College of Water and Environmental Management, Szarvas:

HODOSSI, S., Horticulture
LIGETVÁRI, F., Landscape and Water Management

ATTACHED INSTITUTES

Debreceni Agrártudományi Egyetem Kutató Intézete (Research Institute): 5300 Karcag, POB 11; Dir Dr Á. JÓZSA.

Szaktanácsadási és Fejlesztési Intézet (Institute for Extension and Development): 4015 Debrecen, POB 36; Dir S. ESZENYI.

Kutató Központ (Research Centre): 4400 Nyíregyháza, POB 12; Dir Dr J. LAZÁNYI.

KERTÉSZETI ÉS ÉLELMISZERIPARI EGYETEM
(University of Horticulture and Food Technology)

1118 Budapest, XI, Villányi út 35-43
Telephone: (1) 185-0666
Fax: (1) 186-8312
E-mail: rekt@hoya.kee.hu

Founded 1853
State control

Rector: Prof. Dr PÁL SASS
Vice-Rectors: Prof. Dr ÁGOSTON HOSCHKE, Prof. Dr ZOLTÁN LÁNG, Prof. Dr GÁBOR SCHMIDT
Secretary-General: Dr TIBOR JANKOVITS
Librarian: ÉVA ZALAI-KOVÁCS

Library: see Libraries
Number of teachers: 335
Number of students: 2,800

Publication: *Kertészeti és Élelmiszeripari Egyetem Közleményei* (annually).

DEANS

Faculty of Horticulture: Dr JENŐ BERNÁTH
Faculty of Food Industry: Prof. Dr ANDRÁS FEKETE
Faculty of Landscape Architecture: Dr ILONA BALOGH ORMOS
College Faculty of Food Industry, Szeged: Dr GÁBOR SZABÓ
College Faculty of Horticulture, Kecskemét: Dr PÉTER LÉVAI

PROFESSORS

BALÁZS, S., Vegetable Production
BALOGH, S., Food Industry Economics
BÉKÁSSY-MOLNÁR, E., Food Technology
BERNÁTH, J., Medicinal Plants
BOROSS, L., Chemistry and Biochemistry
CSEMEZ, A., Landscape Architecture
CSEPREGI, P., Viticulture
DALÁNYI, L., Landscape Architecture
DEÁK, T., Microbiology
DIMÉNY, I., Agricultural Economics
DINYA, L., Economics and Marketing
EPERJESI, I., Oenology
ERDÉLYI, E., Food Technology
FARKAS, J., Food Preservation
FEKETE, A., Food Physics
FODOR, P., Chemistry and Biochemistry
GLITS, M., Plant Pathology

HARNOS, ZS., Mathematics
HORVÁTH, G., Plant Physiology
HOSCHKE, A., Brewing and Distillation
JÁMBOR, I., Landscape Architecture
KISS, I., Food Preservation
KOSÁRY, J., Chemistry and Biochemistry
KÖRMENDY, I., Food Preservation
LÁNG, Z., Technical Department
MÉSZÁROS, Z., Entomology
MŐCSÉNYI, M., Landscape Architecture
PAIS, I., Chemistry
PAPP, J., Fruit Growing
RIMÓCZI, I., Botany
SÁRAI, T., Food Technology
SÁRKÖZY, P., Agricultural Economics
SASS, P., Fruit Growing
SCHMIDT, G., Floriculture and Dendrology
SZABÓ, S. A., Food Chemistry
VARSÁNYI, I., Food Preservation
VELICH, I., Plant Genetics and Selection
VERMES, L., Agrometeorology and Water Management

ATTACHED INSTITUTES

Kertészeti és Élelmiszeripari Egyetem Kisérleti Üzeme (University Research and Experimental Station): Budapest-Soroksár.
Szarvasi Arborétum (Szarvas Arboretum).

MISKOLCI EGYETEM (Miskolc University)

3515 Miskolc-Egyetemváros

Telephone: (46) 565-111
Fax: (46) 312-842
E-mail: stbes@gold.uni-miskolc.hu

Founded 1735 in Selmecbánya, Academy status 1770; moved 1919 to Sopron; reorganized 1949 in Miskolc
State control
Languages of instruction: Hungarian, English for foreign students
Academic year: September to June

Rector: Prof. Dr LAJOS BESENYEI
Vice-Rectors: Prof. Dr Á. DÖBRÖCZÖNI, Prof. Dr M. SZABÓ, Dr GY. PATKÓ, Prof. Dr A. NAGY
Secretary-General: Dr B. MANG
Librarian: Dr L. ZSÁMBOKI

Number of teachers: 724
Number of students: 9,544

Publications: *Miskolci Egyetem Közleményei* (papers in Hungarian, irregular), *Publications of the University of Miskolc* (papers in German, English and Russian, irregular), *Évkönyv* (yearbook).

DEANS

Faculty of Mechanical Engineering: Dr J. CSELÉNYI
Faculty of Metallurgical Engineering: Dr F. TRANTA
Faculty of Mining Engineering: Dr F. KOVÁCS
Faculty of Law: Dr T. KALAS
Faculty of Economics: Dr I. SZINTAY
Faculty of Arts: Dr L. KABDEBÓ

HEADS OF DEPARTMENT AND PROFESSORS

Faculty of Mechanical Engineering:

AJTONYI, J., Automation
CSELÉNYI, J., Materials Handling and Logistics
CZIBERE, T., Heat and Fluid Engineering
DEMENDY, L., Physics
DÖBRÖCZÖNI, Á., Machine Elements
DUDÁS, I., Production Engineering
GALÁNTAI, A., Applied Mathematics
JÁRMAI, K., Materials Handling and Logistics
KOZÁK, I., Mechanics
NYIRI, A., Heat and Fluid Engineering
ORTUTAY, M., Chemical Machinery
PÁCZELT, I., Mechanics
PATKÓ, GY., Machine Tools
RONTÓ, M., Mathematical Analysis
SCHOLTZ, P., Descriptive Geometry
SZABÓ, SZ., Heat and Fluid Engineering
SZARKA, T., Electrotechnics and Electronics
SZENTIRMAI, L., Electrotechnics and Electronics
TAJNAFŐI, J., Machine Tools
TISZA, M., Mechanical Engineering
TÓTH, T., Information Engineering
VADÁSZ, D., Information Technology
VINCZE, E., Mathematical Analysis

Faculty of Metallurgical Engineering:

BÁRÁNY, S., Analytical Chemistry
BÁRCZY, P., Non-metallic Materials
FARKAS, O., Ferrous Metallurgy
KAPTAY, GY., Ferrous Metallurgy
KÁROLY, GY., Ferrous Metallurgy
KÉKESI, T., Non-ferrous Metallurgy
KOVÁCS, K., Quality Assurance
MIKÓ, J., Combustion Engineering
PALOTÁS, Á., Energy Utilization
ROÓSZ, A., Physical Metallurgy
SZALAI, GY., Foundry Engineering
SZITA, L., Analytical Chemistry
TÓTH, L. A., Ferrous Metallurgy
TRANTA, F., Physical Metallurgy
VOITH, M., Metalworking Machinery and Technology

Faculty of Mining Engineering:

CSETE, J., Gas Engineering
CSŐKE, B., Process Engineering
DEBRECZENI, E., Equipment for Geotechnology
DOBRÓKA, M., Geophysics
EGERER, F., Mineralogy and Petrology
GRACZKA, GY., Geodesy and Mine Surveying
HAHN, GY., Geography and Ecology
JUHÁSZ, J., Hydrogeology and Engineering Geology
KOVÁCS, F., Mining and Geotechnology
LAKATOS, I., Mining Chemistry
NÉMEDI VARGA, Z., Geology and Mineral Deposits
SOMFAI, A., Geology and Mineral Deposits
SOMOSVÁRI, ZS., Mining and Geotechnology
STEINER, F., Geophysics
TAKÁCS, G., Petroleum Engineering
TARJÁN, I., Process Engineering

Faculty of Law:

BIRÓ, GY., Civil Law
FARKAS, Á., Criminal Procedural Law and Law Enforcement
FERENCZY, E., Financial Law
GÁSPÁRDY, L., Civil Procedural Law
KALAS, T., Administrative Law
LAMM, V., International Law
LÉVAI, M., Criminal Law and Criminology
MISKOLCZI BODNÁR, P., Commercial Law
PRUGBERGER, T., Labour Law and Agricultural Law
STIPTA, I., Legal History
SZABÓ, B., Roman Law
SZABÓ, M., Legal Theory and Legal Sociology
SZAMEL, K., Administrative Law
TORMA, A., Administrative Law
VÖRÖS, I., International Private Law, European Law

Faculty of Economics:

BESENYEI, L., Accountancy and Statistics
CZABÁN, J., Business Economics
FEKETE, I., Applied Economics
GYÖNGYÖSY, Z., Finance
KOCZISZKY, GY., Regional Economics
NAGY, A., Economic Theory
PISKÓTI, I., Marketing
SZINTAY, I., Management and Organization
VÉKÁS, I., Finance

Faculty of Arts:

BESSENYEI, J., Ancient History
BIRÓ, F., Literature of the Enlightenment and Romanticism
BORSÁNYI, L., Cultural and Visual Anthropology
BRADEAN-EBINGER N., German Linguistics
FERENCZI, L., Contemporary Hungarian Literature and History of Literature
FORRAI, G., History of Philosophy
FÜGEDI, M., Cultural History and Museology
FÜLÖP, ZS., English Literature
GERGELY, P., Hungarian Linguistics
HÁRSING, L., Social Philosophy and Philosophy of Science
KABDEBÓ, L., Contemporary Hungarian Literature
KILIÁN, I., Old Hungarian Literature
KLAUDY, K., Applied Linguistics
KONTOR, I., German Literature
KOVÁCS, S., Political Science
KULCSÁR, P., Ancient History
LENDVAY, F., Social Philosophy and Philosophy of Science
MIHÁLY, O., Science of Education
Ö. KOVÁCS, J., Hungarian History
PÁLFFY, I., English Literature
PETNEKI, Á., Literature and Culture of Central Europe
POKOL, B., Sociology
RADNAI, ZS., English Linguistics
RINGER, Á., Prehistory
SCHIMERT, P., World History
SZŐKE, GY., Contemporary Hungarian Literature

ASSOCIATE INSTITUTES

Dunaújváros Polytechnic: 2400 Dunaújváros, POB 152; f. 1969; 103 teachers, 2,584 students; Dir Dr ENDRE KISS.

Bela Bartók Music Institute: 3530 Miskole, Bartók tér 1; Dir ZOLTÁN SÁNDOR.

PANNON AGRÁRTUDOMÁNYI EGYETEM (Pannon University of Agricultural Sciences)

8361 Keszthely, Deák Ferenc u. 16

Telephone: (83) 312-257
Telex: 35 282
Fax: (83) 315-405

Founded 1797
State control
Language of instruction: Hungarian
Academic year: September to June

Rector: Prof. PÉTER HORN
Vice-Rectors: Prof. FERENC HUSVÉTH, Prof. JÁNOS SCHMIDT
Head of Rectorate: J. GELENCSÉR
Librarian: A. PÉTERVÁRI

Number of teaching staff: 250
Number of students: 2,800

Publications: *Georgicon for Agriculture*, *Acta Ovariensis.*

DEANS

Georgikon Faculty of Agriculture (Keszthely): Prof. TAMÁS KISMÁNYOKY
Faculty of Agricultural Sciences (Mosonmagyaróvár): Prof. JÁNOS IVÁNCSICS
Faculty of Animal Science (Kaposvár): Prof. JENŐ PAÁL

PROFESSORS

Georgikon Faculty of Agriculture (Keszthely):

ALMÁDI, L., Botany
ANDA, A., Agrometeorology
BARTOS, A., Mathematics
BENET, I., Agricultural Economics, Economics
BUZÁS, GY., Farm Management
DEBRECZENI, K., Agricultural Chemistry
GÁBORJÁNYI, R., Plant Virology
HENÉZI, J., Model and Experimental Farm
HORVÁTH, J., Plant Pathology and Virology
HORVÁTH, S., Potato Research
HUNYADI, K., Botany
HUSVÉTH, F., Zoology and Animal Physiology
IVANCSICS, J. Horticulture
KARDOS, Z., Social Sciences

KÁRPÁTI, L., Computer Science and Information Centre
KISMÁNYOKY, T., Crop Production
KOCSONDI, J., Work Organization
KOVÁCS, J., Animal Husbandry
LÁSZLÓ, A., Agricultural Engineering
LAVOTHA, E., Foreign Languages
LEHOCZKI, E., Agricultural Chemistry
MÁTÉ, F., Soil Science
MÉSZÁROS, L., Physical Education
PALKOVICS, M., Agricultural Economics
RAGASITS, I., Crop Production
SÁRDI, K., Agricultural Chemistry
SÁRINGER, GY., Entomology
SOMOGYI, S., Work Organization
SZABÓ, F., Animal Husbandry
SZABÓ, I., Botany
SZABOLCS, J., Entomology
SZUCS, E., Animal Husbandry
TÓTH, B., Microbiology and Biochemistry
VÁRNAGY, L., Agricultural Hygiene
VINCZE, L., Animal Nutrition

Faculty of Agriculture (Mosonmagyaróvár):

BENEDEK, P., Zoology
CZIMBER, GY., Botany
GERGÁCZ, E., Biotechnology
IVÁNCSICS, J., Animal Breeding
KÉSMÁRKI, I., Crop Production
KUROLI, G., Plant Protection
MÉSZÁROS, M., Physical Education
NEMÉNYI, M., Mechanics
NOSTICZIUS, Á., Chemistry
OLÁH, J., Foreign Languages
ÖRDÖG, V., Plant Physiology
PORPÁCZY, A., Horticulture
SALAMON, L., Farm Economics
SCHMIDT, J., Feeding
SZABÓ, I., Social Sciences
SZABÓ, I., Zoobiology
SZIGETI, J., Food Science
TENK, A., Agricultural Economy
VARGA-HASZONITS, Z., Environment Science, Agrometeorology
VESZELI, T., Work Organization

Faculty of Animal Science (Kaposvár):

ALPÁR, GY., Practice and Work Organization
BABINSZKY, L., Animal Nutrition
BOGENFÜRST, F., Poultry Breeding
CSAPÓ, J., Biochemistry
DÉR, F., Plant Production
ERŐSS, I., Fish-breeding and Environmental Protection
FARKAS, J., Foreign Languages
HECKER, W., Academy of Equitation
HORN, P., Pig Production
HORVÁTH, GY., Social Sciences
KLENOVICS, E., Physical Education
KOVÁCS, M., Physiology and Animal Hygiene
LENGYEL, A., Sheep Production
PAÁL, J., Mathematics and Computer Science
REPA J., CT Biological Centre
SARUDI, J., Chemistry and Biochemistry
STEFLER, J., Cattle Production
SZABÓ, G., Marketing
SZÉLES, GY., Farm Economics
SZENDRŐ, ZS., Animal Breeding
TAKÁTSY, T., Agricultural Engineering

AFFILIATED INSTITUTE

Forage Science Research Institute: 7095 Iregszemcse; Dir LÁSZLÓ TAKÁCS.

SOPRONI EGYETEM
(University of Sopron)

9400 Sopron, Ady E. u. 5

Telephone: (99) 311-100
Telex: 249126
Fax: (99) 311-103

Founded 1735
State control
Academic year: September to December, February to May

Rector: Dr JÓZSEF KOLOSZÁR
Pro-Rectors: Dr K. MÉSZÁROS, Dr ZS. KOVÁCS
Administrative Officer: Dr J. SZITÁS
Librarian: Dr M. MASTALIR
Library of 352,000 vols

Number of teachers: 165
Number of students: 1,777 undergraduate, 164 postgraduate

Publications: *Erdészeti és Faipari Egyetem Tudományos Közleményei, Acta Facultatis Forestalis, Acta Facultatis Ligniensis.*

DEANS

Faculty of Forestry: Dr S. FARAGÓ
Faculty of Wood Technology: Dr L. BORONKAI
College of Surveying and Country Planning (in Székesfehérvár): Dr M. ÁGFALVI

HEADS OF DEPARTMENTS

Architecture: Dr G. WINKLER
Business Management: Dr K. MÉSZÁROS
Chemistry: Prof. K. NÉMETH
Earth Sciences: Prof. P. BENCZE
Environmental Protection: Dr CS. MÁTYÁS
Foreign Languages: Dr I. KRISCH
Forest Development and Hydrology: Dr M. KOSZTKA
Forest Protection: Dr F. VARGA
Forest Site and Soil Classification: Prof. I. SZODFRIDT
Forest Utilization: Dr J. RUMPF
Forestry Management: Dr J. GÁL
Forestry Mechanization: Dr B. HORVÁTH
Geodesy and Remote Sensing: Dr L. BÁCSATYAI
Mathematics and Descriptive Geometry: Prof. J. HORVÁTH
Physics and Electronics: Prof. GY. PAPP
Plant Sciences: Dr D. BARTHA
Product Development: Dr ZS. KOVÁCS
Pulp and Paper Sciences: Prof. J. ERDÉLYI
Sawing Industry: Dr L. HARGITAI
Silviculture: Dr J. KOLOSZÁR
Social Sciences: Dr I. LÜKŐ
Technical Mechanics: Dr J. SZALAI
Technology: Dr J. SZABÓ
Wildlife Management: Dr T. KŐHALMY
Wood Composites: Prof. A. WINKLER
Wood Sciences: Dr S. MOLNÁR
Woodworking Machines: Dr M. LANG

College of Surveying and Country Planning:

Foreign Languages: J. JANURIK
Geodesy: Prof. I. JOÓ
Natural and Social Sciences: Dr H. SZŐCS
Photogrammetry and Remote Sensing: Dr SZ. MIHALY
Spatial Informatics: Dr B. MÁRKUS
Surveying: Prof. GY. SZABÓ

ATTACHED INSTITUTES

Institute of Chemistry: Dir Prof. K. NÉMETH.
Institute of Economics and Management Development: Dir Prof. E. GIDAI.
Institute of Education: Dir Dr M. LANG
Institute of Mathematics: Dir Prof. J. HORVÁTH.
Institute of Product Design and Technology: Dir Dr ZS. KOVÁCS.
Institute of Wood and Paper Technology: Dir Dr L. HARGITAI.

VESZPRÉMI EGYETEM
(University of Veszprém)

8200 Veszprém, Egyetem u. 10

Telephone: (88) 422-022
Fax (88) 423-866

Founded 1949
State controlled
Languages of instruction: Hungarian and English
Academic year: September to June

Rector: Prof. I. GYŐRI
Pro-Rectors: Prof. G. SPEIER, Prof. J. HLAVAY
Librarian: Dr M. EGYHÁZI

Library: see Libraries

Number of teachers: 261
Number of students: 3,068, including 261 on correspondence course and 58 postgraduate

PROFESSORS

BÁRDOS, J., Foreign Languages
BENCZE, L., Organic Chemistry
DEÁK, GY., Hydrocarbon and Coal Processing
FÖLDES, CS., German
FRIEDLER, F., Systems Engineering Computer Science
GAÁL, Z., Management and Economy
GALICZA, J., Pedagogy and Psychology
GYŐRI, I., Mathematics
HEIL, B., Organic Chemistry
HLAVAY, J., Analytical Chemistry
HORVÁTH, A., Inorganic Chemistry
JÓZSA, L., Economics
KANYÁR, B., Radiochemistry
KISS, I., Biology
KOTSIS, I., Silicate Chemistry
KOVÁTS, E., Physical Chemistry
LENGYEL, ZS., Applied Linguistics
LISZI, J., Physical Chemistry
MARKÓ, L., Organic Chemistry
MARTON, GY., Chemical Process Engineering
MÉRAY, L., Physics
MÉSZÁROS, E., Environmental Sciences
MINK, J., Analytical Chemistry
PAPP, S., Inorganic Chemistry
RÉDEY, Á., Chemical Technology, Environmental Engineering
SCHANDA, J., Display Optics, Colour Image Sensing
SPEIER, G., Organic Chemistry
SZEIFERT, F., Cybernetics
SZILÁGYI, I., Social Sciences
TAMÁS, F., Silicate Chemistry
TIMÁR, I., Mechanical Engineering
UNGVÁRY, F., Organic Chemistry
VASS, J., Computer-controlled Systems
VERESS, G., Informatics and Control

ATTACHED INSTITUTES

The Hungarian Academy of Sciences research groups for Petrochemistry, Analytical Chemistry and Air Chemistry.

Colleges of University Standing

LISZT FERENC ZENEMŰVÉSZETI FŐISKOLA
(Ferenc Liszt Academy of Music)

1391 Budapest, POB 206, Liszt Ferenc tér 8

Telephone: 3414-788

Founded 1875
State control
Academic year: September to June

Rector: Prof. SÁNDOR FALVAI
Vice-Rector: Prof. PÉTER PONGRÁCZ
Librarian: Dr. J. KÁRPÁTI

Library of 187,000 vols
Number of teaching staff: 158
Number of students: 767

HEADS OF DEPARTMENTS

Composition: Z. JENEY
Musicology: Prof. T. TALLIÁN
Keyboard Instruments and Harp: Prof. I. LANTOS
Chamber Music: S. DEVICH
Stringed Instruments: A. KISS
Wind Instruments and Percussion: Prof. H. PRŐHLE
Singing and Opera: J. PATKÓ
Secondary School Singing Teachers and Choir Conductors: Prof. T. SZABÓ
Music Theory: Dr K. KOMLÓS

ATTACHED INSTITUTES

Zeneiskolai Tanárképző Intézet (Training Institute for Music Teachers): 1052 Budapest, Semmelweiss u.12; Dir Prof. LEHEL BOTH.

Bartók Béla Zeneművészeti Szakközépiskola (Béla Bartók Conservatory of Music): 1065 Budapest, Nagymező u.1; Dir T. SZABÓ.

MAGYAR IPARMŰVÉSZETI EGYETEM
(Hungarian University of Craft and Design)

1121 Budapest, Zugligeti ut 11-25

Telephone: (1) 176-1722
Fax: (1) 200-8726
E-mail: rektori@mif.mif.hu

Founded 1880, present status 1985
State control
Academic year: September to June

Rector: Prof. IMRE SCHRAMMEL
Vice-Rectors: Prof. Dr FERENC MÜLLER (General), Prof. JOZSEF SCHERER (Academic)
General Secretary: Dr EMŐKE PORDÁN
Librarian: PÁL ZÖLDY

Library of 42,000 vols
Number of teachers: 98
Number of students: 570

Publication: *Magyar Iparművészet* (every 2 months).

DIRECTORS OF INSTITUTES AND HEADS OF DEPARTMENTS

Institute of Foundation Studies: Prof. JÓZSEF SCHERER
Institute of Humanities: Prof. GYULA ERNYEY
Institute of Education: Assoc. Prof. EMIL GAUL
Institute for Manager Training: Prof. Dr FERENC MÜLLER
Department of Product Design: Prof. KÁROLY SIMON
Department of Architecture: Prof. ISTVÁN FERENCZ
Department of Silicate Design: Assoc. Prof. JÁNOS PROBSTNER
Department of Textile Design: Prof. CSABA POLGÁR
Department of Visual Communication: Assoc. Prof. PÉTER VIRÁGVÖLGYI

MAGYAR KÉPZŐMŰVÉSZETI FŐISKOLA
(Hungarian Academy of Fine Arts)

1062 Budapest, Andrássy ut. 69–71

Telephone: (1) 342-1738
Fax: (1) 342-1563

Founded 1871

Rector: ÁRPÁD SZABADOS
Vice-Rector: KÁLMÁN MOLNÁR
International Affairs: RITA ROMÁN
Librarian: KATALIN BLASKÓ

Library of 47,500 vols
Number of teachers: 110
Number of students: 497

PROFESSORS

FARKAS, Á., Sculpture
KOCSIS, I., Graphic Art
MENRÁTH, P., Restoration
MOLNÁR, K., Applied Graphic Art
NAGY, G., Painting
PETERNÁK, M., Multimedia Studies
SZABADI, J., Art History
SZÉKELY, L., Stage and Costume Design
TÖLG-MOLNÁR, Z., Painting

MAGYAR TÁNCMŰVÉSZETI FŐISKOLA
(Hungarian Dance Academy)

1372 Budapest, PO Box 439

Telephone: 267-8646
Fax: 2680-828

Founded 1950

Director: IMRE DÓZSA

Library of 19,000 vols
Number of teachers: 100
Number of students: 750

MAGYAR TESTNEVELÉSI EGYETEM
(Hungarian University of Physical Education)

1123 Budapest, Alkotás u. 44

Telephone: 156-4444
Fax: 156-6337

Founded 1925, University status 1975
Academic year: September to May

Rector: Dr J. TIHANYI
Vice-Rectors: Dr E. BIRÓ NAGY, Dr E. RIGLER
Secretary-General: Dr GY. KÁROLYI
Librarian: F. KRASOVEC

Library of 80,000 vols
Number of teachers: 120
Number of students: 1,250

Publications: *Kalokagathia* (university review, 3 a year), *Évkönyv* (Yearbook).

PROFESSORS

BIRÓ NAGY, E., Pedagogy
FÖLDESINÉ, S. GY., Sociology
FRENKL, R., Medical Sciences
ISTVÁNFI, CS., Theory of Coaching
KERTÉSZ, I., History
NAGY, GY., Psychology
PAVLIK, G., Medical Sciences
SZÉCSÉNYI, J., Athletics
TAKÁCS, F., Philosophy
TIHANYI, J., Kinesiology
ZALKA, A., Sports

ATTACHED INSTITUTE

Postgraduate Centre: Dir I. TAMÁS.

SZINHÁZ- ÉS FILMMŰVÉSZETI FŐISKOLA
(Academy of Drama and Film)

1088 Budapest, Vas u. 2C

Telephone: 1188-111

Founded 1865

Rector: PÉTER HUSZTI
Vice-Rectors: LÁSZLÓ BABARCZY, ÁDÁM HORVÁTH
Secretary-General: L. TISZEKER

Number of teachers: 87
Number of students: 259

HEADS OF DEPARTMENT

Drama: PÉTER HUSZTI
Film: JÁNOS ZSOMBOLYAI

Other Colleges

GENERAL

Collegium Budapest: 1014 Budapest, Szentháromság u. 2; tel. (1) 457-7600; fax (1) 375-9539; f. 1991; centre for interdisciplinary postdoctoral research and international scholarly exchange between East and West; library of 5,000 vols; Rector GÁBOR KLANICZAY, Sec. FRED GIROD.

BUSINESS AND COMMERCE

Kereskedelmi, Vendéglátóipari és Idegenforgalmi Főiskola (College of Commerce, Catering and Tourism): 1054 Budapest, Alkotmány u. 9/11; tel. (1) 3327-150; fax (1) 302-2956; e-mail lcsizmadia@kvif.hu; f. 1969; library of 56,000 vols; 142 teachers, 4,400 students; Dir Dr LASZLÓ CSIZMADIA.

Külkereskedelmi Főiskola (College for Management and Business Studies): 1165 Budapest, Diósy L. u. 22–24; tel. (1) 467-7800; fax (1) 407-1556; f. 1962; 189 teachers, 4,000 students; library of 80,000 vols, 250 periodicals; Gen. Dir Prof. KÁROLY IVÁNYI.

Pénzügyi és Számviteli Főiskola (College of Finance and Accountancy): 1149 Budapest, Buzogány u. 10; tel. and fax (1) 383-4799; telex 226868; f. 1962; 172 teachers, 3,500 students; library of 125,000 vols; Dir Dr JÓZSEF ROÓZ.

TECHNOLOGY

Bánki Donát Gépipari Műszaki Főiskola (Donát Bánki Polytechnic): 1081 Budapest, Népszínház u. 8; tel. 210-1450; fax 1336-761; f. 1969; 95 teachers, 1,340 students; library of 30,000 vols; Dir Dr I. CZINEGE.

Gépipari és Automatizálási Műszaki Főiskola (College of Mechanical Engineering and Automation): 6001 Kecskemét, Izsáki u. 10, Pf. 91; tel. (76) 48-12-91; fax (76) 48-13-04; e-mail gamf@gandalf.gamf.hu; f. 1964; training of production engineers in tool designing, product design, informatics, machine production, plastics production, plastics processing and cybernetics; 80 teachers, 1,300 students; library of 65,000 vols; Dir Dr A. SZABÓ; publ. *GAMF Közlemények*.

Kandó Kálmán Műszaki Főiskola (Kálmán Kandó College of Engineering): 1084 Budapest, Tavaszmező u. 17; tel. 2101-442; fax (1) 269-9425; f. 1969; electrical engineering, computer production engineering, engineering management, higher education quality control; 250 teachers, 1,900 students; library of 75,000 vols; Rector Prof. Dr MIHÁLY TÓTH.

Könnyüipari Műszaki Főiskola (College of Technology for Light Industry): 1034 Budapest, Doberdó u. 6; tel. (1) 250-0333; fax (1) 388-6763; f. 1972; training and research in the textile, clothing, leather, packaging, paper and printing industries; 90 teachers, 1,500 students; library of 45,000 vols; Rector Prof. Dr ISTVÁN SZŰTS.

Széchenyi István Főiskola (István Széchenyi College): 9026 Győr, Hédervári u. 3; tel. (96) 429-722; fax (96) 329-263; e-mail szif@szif.hu; f. 1968; departments of architecture, automation, civil and urban engineering, computing, economics, environment, foreign languages, health, information systems, logistics, materials and manufacturing technology, mathematics, music teacher-training, organization and management, regional studies, social sciences, technical teacher training, telecommunications, transportation, vehicle engineering; 250 teachers, 4,500 students; library of 180,000 vols, 1,000 periodicals; Dir-Gen. P. KERESZTES.

Ybl Miklós Műszaki Főiskola (Miklós Ybl Polytechnic): 1146 Budapest, Thököly u. 74; tel. 343-0890; fax 343-9602; f. 1879; 93 teachers, 1,200 students; library of 88,000 vols; Dir Prof. Dr GEORGE SAMSONDI KISS.

THEOLOGY

Debreceni Református Teológiai Akadémia (Reformed Theological Seminary of Debrecen): 4044 Debrecen, Kálvin tér 16; tel. and fax (52) 414-744; f. 1538; 12 staff, 250 students; library of 600,000 vols; Rector KLÁRA L. SEMSEY.

Evangélikus Hirtudományi Egyetem (Evangelical-Lutheran Theological University): 1141 Budapest, Rózsavölgyi köz 3; tel. (1) 3834-537; fax (1) 3637-454; f. 1557; 140

students; library of 51,000 vols; Rector Dr Lajos Szabó.

Károli Gáspár Református Egyetem, Teológiai Akadémia (Gáspár Károli Reformed Church University Faculty of Theology): 1092 Budapest, Ráday u. 28; tel. and fax (1) 217-2403; f. 1855; 190 students; library of 150,000 vols; Dean Dr Sándor Tenke.

Országos Rabbiképző Intézet (National Rabbinical College): 1084 Budapest, Bérkocsis u. 2; tel. and fax (1) 117-2396; f. 1877; library of 110,000 vols; Rector Rabbi Dr Y. A. Schőner.

ICELAND

Learned Societies

AGRICULTURE, FISHERIES AND VETERINARY SCIENCE

Bændasamtök Íslands (Farmers' Association of Iceland): Baendahöllinni v/Hagatorg, POB 7080, 127 Reykjavík; tel. 563-0300; fax 562-8290; e-mail bi@bi.bondi.is; f. 1995; mems: 4,500 farmers in 192 local agricultural socs; library of 10,000 vols; Chair. ARI TEITSSON; Dir Dr SIGURGEIR THORGEIRSSON; publs *Freyr* (monthly), *Bændablaðið* (Farmers' News, fortnightly).

BIBLIOGRAPHY, LIBRARY SCIENCE AND MUSEOLOGY

Icelandic Library Association: POB 1497, 121 Reykjavík; tel. 564-2050; fax 564-3877; f. 1960; Pres. H. A. HARÐARSON; Sec. A. AGNARSDÓTTIR; publs *Bókasafnið* (1 a year), *Fregnir* (3 a year).

FINE AND PERFORMING ARTS

Bandalag Íslenzkra Listamanna (Union of Icelandic Artists): POB 637,121 Reykjavik; tel. (1) 22620; f. 1928; Pres. HJÁLMAR H. RAGNARSSON; 1,712 mems.

Constituent organizations:

Arkítektafélag Íslands (Icelandic Architects' Association): Freyjugata 41, 101 Reykjavík; tel. (1) 28440; Chair. ORMAR THOR GUDMUNDSSON; 226 mems.

Félag Íslenzkra Leikara (Icelandic Actors' Association): Lindargata 6, 101 Reykjavík; tel. (1) 26040; Chair. EDDA THORARINSDOTTIR; 310 mems.

Félag Íslenzkra Listdansara (Association of Icelandic Dance Artists): POB 8654, 128 Reykjavík; Chair. NANA ÓLAFSDÓTTIR; 55 mems.

Félag Íslenzkra Myndlistarmanna (Association of Icelandic Visual Artists): Chair. KRISTJÁN STEINGRÍMUR JÓNSSON; 263 mems.

Félag Íslenzkra Tónlistarmanna (Icelandic Musicians' Association): POB 3127, 123 Reykjavík; Chair. GUDRIDUR SIGURDARDÓTTIR; 92 mems.

Félag Kvikmyndagerdarmanna (Icelandic Film Makers' Association): POB 5162, Reykjavík; tel. 623225; Chair. EIRÍKUR THORSTEINSSON; 156 mems.

Rithöfundasamband Íslands (Icelandic Writers' Association): POB 949, 121 Reykjavík; tel. (1) 13190; Chair. INGIBJÖRG HARALDSDÓTTIR; 350 mems.

Tónskáldafélag Íslands (Icelandic Composers' Society): Laufásvegi 40, 101 Reykjavík; tel. (1) 24972; Chair. JOHN SPEIGHT; 50 mems.

Félag Leikstjóra á Íslandi (Icelandic Association of Stage Directors): Lindargata 6, 101 Reykjavík; tel. (1) 621025; Chair. PETER EINARSSON; 68 mems.

Samband Íslenzkra Myndlistarmanna: Thorsgata 25, 101 Reykjavík; tel. (1) 11346; Chair. SOLVEIG EGGERTSDÓTTIR; 355 mems.

Samtök Kvikmundaleikstjóra (Guild of Icelandic Film Directors): Sudurgata 14, 101 Reykjavík; tel. (1) 12260; Chair. FRIDRIK THOR FRIDRIKSSON; 50 mems.

Tónlistarfélagið (Music Society): Reykjavík; f. 1930; operates a College of Music; affiliated societies in major towns; Chair. BALDVIN TRYGGVASON; Man. RUT MAGNÚSSON; Headmaster of College HALLDÓR HARALDSSON.

HISTORY, GEOGRAPHY AND ARCHAEOLOGY

Íslenzka fornleifafélag, Hid (Icelandic Archaeological Society): Suðurgötu 41, 101 Reykjavík; f. 1879; Pres. THÓR MAGNÚSSON; Sec. THÓRHALLUR VILMUNDARSON; 700 mems; publ. *Árbók* (Year Book).

Sögufélagið (Icelandic Historical Society): Fischerssundi 3, 101 Reykjavík, POB 1078, R 121; tel. 14620; f. 1902; 1,600 mems; Pres. HEIMIR THORLEIFSSON; Sec. SVEINBJÖRN RAFNSSON; publs *Saga* (annually), *Ný saga* (annually).

LANGUAGE AND LITERATURE

Íslenzka bókmenntafélag, Hid (Icelandic Literary Society): Sídumúli 21, P.O. Box 8935, 128 Reykjavík; e-mail hib@islandia.is; f. 1816; research work and publishing; 2,000 mems; Pres. SIGURDUR LÍNDAL; Sec. REYNIR AXELSSON; publ. *Skírnir* (2 a year).

NATURAL SCIENCES

General

Vísindafélag Íslendinga (Icelandic Academy of Sciences and Letters): Bárugötu 3, 101 Reykjavík; f. 1918; 159 mems; Pres. SIGURDUR STEINTHORSSON; publs *Rit*, *Ráðstefnurit* (irregular).

Biological Sciences

Íslenzka náttúrufrædifélag, Hid (Icelandic Natural History Society): POB 5355, 125 Reykjavík; f. 1889; Pres. FREYSTEINN SIGURÐSSON; 1,600 mems; publ. *Náttúrufrædingurinn* (quarterly journal of natural history).

Physical Sciences

Iceland Glaciological Society: POB 5128, 125 Reykjavík; fax 28911; f. 1951; 550 mems; Pres. HELGI BJÖRNSSON; Sec. ODDUR SIGURDSSON; publ. *Jökull* (annually).

TECHNOLOGY

Verkfrædingafélag Íslands (Association of Chartered Engineers in Iceland): POB 1745, Reykjavík 121; tel. 568-8511; fax 568-9703; f. 1912; c. 1,100 mems; Pres. PETUR STEFANSSON; Sec. LOGI KRISTJÁNSSON; publs *Árbók Verkfrædingafélags Islands* (annually), *Verktækni* (newsletter, 18 times a year).

Research Institutes

ECONOMICS, LAW AND POLITICS

Hagstofa Íslands (Statistics Iceland): Skuggasund 3, 150 Reykjavík; tel. 560-9800; fax 562-8865; f. 1914; Dir-Gen. HALLGRÍMUR SNORRASON; publs *Hagtíðindi* (Statistics Monthly), *Hagskýrslur Íslands* (Statistics of Iceland).

MEDICINE

Rannsóknastofa Háskólans (University Institute of Pathology): POB 1465, 121 Reykjavík; f. 1917; 81 mems; Dir Prof. JONAS HALLGRIMSSON.

Tilraunastöð Háskóla Íslands i meinafræði að Keldum (Institute for Experimental Pathology, University of Iceland): v/Vesturlandsveg, 112 Reykjavík; tel. 567-4700; fax 567-3979; f. 1948; affiliated to University of Iceland; library of 4,000 vols; Dir GUÐMUNDUR GEORGSSON.

NATURAL SCIENCES

General

Rannsóknarrád Íslands (Icelandic Research Council): Laugavegi 13, 101 Reykjavík; tel. 562-1320; fax 552-9814; f. 1994 to advise the Government and Parliament on all aspects of science, technology and innovation, and to promote international co-operation in science and technology; a government institution subordinate to the Ministry of Culture and Education; Chair. Prof. THORSTEINN I. SIGFÚSSON; Dir Dr VILHJÁLMUR LÚDVÍKSSON.

Attached research institutes:

Hafrannsóknastofnunin (Marine Research Institute): C/o Rannsóknarrád Íslands, Laugavegi 13, 101 Reykjavík; research into marine biological and oceanographic sciences; special divisions for pelagic fish, demersal fish, flat-fish, technology and fishing gear, hydrography, phytoplankton, zooplankton and benthos; Government institution subordinate to the Ministry of Fisheries; Chair. BRYNJÓLFUR BJARNASON; Dir JAKOB JAKOBSSON.

Idntæknistofnun Íslands (Technological Institute of Iceland): C/o Rannsóknarrád Íslands, Laugavegi 13, 101 Reykjavík; research and service institution for industry; research on raw materials, machinery and end products to improve quality and competitiveness of Icelandic industrial production; special divisions for training and information, industrial development, technical services and for research; Government institution subordinate to the Ministry of Industry; Chair. MAGNÚS FRIÐGEIRSSON; Dir HALLGRÍMUR JÓNASSON.

Rannsóknastofnun landbúnadarins (Agricultural Research Institute): C/o Rannsóknarrád Íslands, Laugavegi 13, 101 Reykjavík; government-financed research and experimental development in agriculture; special divisions for animal-breeding, ecology and cultivation and farming technology; Government institution subordinate to the Ministry of Agriculture; Chair. PÉTUR HELGASON; Dir THORSTEINN TÓMASSON.

Rannsóknastofnun fiskidnadarins (Fish Industrial Research Institute): C/o Rannsóknarrád Íslands, Laugavegi 13, 101 Reykjavík; research and services for the fish industry, quality control, etc.; divisions for chemistry, bacteriology and technology; Government institution subordinate to the Ministry of Fisheries; Chair. ÁRNI KOLBEINSSON; Dir Dr HJÖRLEIFUR EINARSSON.

Rannsóknastofnun byggingaidnadarins (Building Research Institute): C/o Rannsóknarrád Íslands, Laugavegi 13, 101 Reykjavík; f. 1965; scientific research and services for the construction and building industries; Government institution subordinate to the Ministry of Industry; Chair

MAGNUS FRIÐGEIRSSON; Dir HÁKON ÓLAFSSON.

Surtseyjarfélagið (Surtsey Research Society): POB 352, 121 Reykjavík; f. 1965; to promote and co-ordinate scientific work in geo- and biological sciences on the island of Surtsey; 104 mems; Chair. STEINGRIMUR HERMANNSSON; Sec. SVEINN JAKOBSSON; publ. *Surtsey Progress Reports*.

Biological Sciences

Náttúrufræðistofnun Íslands (Icelandic Institute of Natural History): POB 5320, 125 Reykjavík; tel. 562-9822; fax 562-0815; e-mail ni@nattfs.is; f. 1889 by Hið Íslenzka Náttúrufrædifélag (The Icelandic Natural History Society) and maintained by this Society until 1946; taken over by the State 1947; library of 8,000 vols, 500 periodicals; Dir-Gen. JÓN G. OTTÓSSON; Dir AEVAR PETERSEN (Reykjavík); Dir HÖRÐUR KRISTINSSON (Akureyri); publs *Bliki* (irregularly), *Fjölrit Náttúrufræðistofnunar* (irregularly), *Acta Botanica Islandica*† (2 a year).

Physical Sciences

Vedurstofa Íslands (Icelandic Meteorological Office): Bústadavegi 9, 150 Reykjavík; tel. (354) 560-0600; fax (354) 552-8121; f. 1920; weather forecasts, climatology, aerology, sea ice, seismology; library of 10,000 vols; Dir MAGNÚS JÓNSSON; publs *Sea Ice off the Icelandic Coasts* (annually), *Vedráttan* (monthly and annually).

Libraries and Archives

Reykjavík

Borgarbókasafn Reykjavíkur (City Library of Reykjavík): Thingholtsstraeti 27, 101 Reykjavík; tel. 552-1755; fax 551-4643; e-mail borgarbokasafn@skyrr.is; f. 1923; library of 430,000 vols; Dir THORDIS THORVALDSDOTTIR.

Landsbókasafn Íslands-Háskólabókasafn (National and University Library of Iceland): Arngrímsgötu 3, 107 Reykjavík; tel. 525-5600; fax 525-5615; f. 1994 by amalgamation of the National Library of Iceland (f. 1818) and the University Library (f. 1940); 750,000 printed vols, 15,000 MSS; Dir EINAR SIGURÐSSON.

Thjódskjalasafn Íslands (National Archives of Iceland): Laugavegur 162, POB R5 5390, Reykjavík; tel. 562-3393; f. 1882; collection of historical documents covers 800 years; Dir ÓLAFUR ÁSGEIRSSON.

Museums and Art Galleries

Reykjavík

Listasafn Einars Jónssonar (National Einar Jónsson Museum): Njardargata, POB 1051, 121 Reykjavík; tel. 5513797; fax 5623909; e-mail listsafn@treknet.is; sculpture and paintings by Einar Jónsson; Dir HRAFNHILDUR SCHRAM; publ. catalogue.

Thjódminjasafn (National Museum): Sudurgata 41, 101 Reykjavík; tel. 552-8888; fax 552-8967; f. 1863; the main collection is of Icelandic antiquities; collection of folk art and ethnology; Dir THOR MAGNÚSSON, State Antiquary; publs *Skýrsla um Forngripasafn Islands, Thjódminjasafn Islands, Leidarvísir, Árbók hins islenzka fornleifafélags, Summary Guide, Asa G. Wright Memorial Lectures, Rit Hins íslenska fornleifafélags og Thjódminjasafns Islands*.

University

HÁSKÓLI ÍSLANDS (University of Iceland)

Suðurgata, 107 Reykjavík
Telephone: 525-4000
Fax: 552-1331

Founded 1911
State control
Academic year: September to June

Rector: Prof. SVEINBJÖRN BJÖRNSSON
Vice-Rector: THORGEIR ÖRLYGSSON
Registrar: GUNNLAUGUR H. JÓNSSON
Librarian: EINAR SIGURÐSSON

Library: see Libraries
Number of teachers: 400 tenured, 1,200 non-tenured
Number of students: 5,700
Publications: *Árbók Háskóla Íslands, Ársskýrsla, Sæmundur á selnum, Rannsóknir við Háskóla Íslands*.

DEANS

Faculty of Theology: Prof. BJÖRN BJÖRNSSON
Faculty of Medicine: Prof. HELGI VALDIMARSSON
Faculty of Law: Prof. THORGEIR ÖRLYGSSON
Faculty of Economics and Business Administration: Prof. RAGNAR ÁRNASON
Faculty of Arts: Prof. PÁLL SKÚLASON
Faculty of Engineering: Prof. BJÖRN KRISTINSSON
Faculty of Dentistry: Prof. SIGFÚS THÓR ELÍASSON
Faculty of Social Science: Prof. JÓN TORFI JÓNASSON
Faculty of Natural Sciences: Prof. THORSTEINN VILHJÁLMSSON

ATTACHED RESEARCH INSTITUTES

Árni Magnússon Institute in Iceland: preservation of manuscripts of the Icelandic Sagas.
Centre for International Studies.
Centre for Women's Studies.
Engineering Research Institute.
Ethical Research Institute.
Fisheries Research Institute.
Icelandic Language Institute.
Institute of Anthropology.
Institute of Biology.
Institute of Business Administration.
Institute of Economics.
Institute of Experimental Pathology.
Institute of Foreign Languages.
Institute of History.
Institute of Human Rights.
Institute of Lexicography (Ordabók).
Institute of Linguistics.
Institute of Literary Research.
Institute of Philosophy.
Institute of Theology.
Law Institute.
Library and Information Science Research Institute.
Nordic Volcanological Institute.
Science Institute.
Sigurdur Nordal Institute: medieval and modern Icelandic culture.
Social Science Research Institute.

Colleges

Búnadarskólinn á Hólum i Hjaltadal (Agricultural School): Hólum i Hjaltadal; f. 1882; library of 6,000 vols; 4 professors; 50 students; Dir HAUKUR JØRUNDARSON.

Bændaskólinn á Hvanneyri (Agricultural College): Hvanneyri, 311 Borgarnes; tel. 437-0000; fax 437-0048; f. 1889; BSc degree in agriculture; teaching and research in fields of agriculture, livestock and farm management; 15 teachers; 130 students; library of 13,000 vols; Rector Dr MAGNÚS JÓNSSON; publ. *Fjölrit Bændaskólans* (annually).

Tónlistarskólinn í Reykjavík (Reykjavík College of Music): Skipholti 33, 105 Reykjavík; f. 1930; teaching in piano, organ, harpsichord and orchestral instruments, singing, theory, composition, music history, including aural and music education training; 210 students; Dir HALLDÓR HARALDSSON.

Tækniskóli Íslands (Icelandic College of Engineering and Technology): Höfðabakka 9, 112 Reykjavík; tel. 577-1400; fax 577-1401; f. 1964; B.Sc. programmes in engineering technology (civil, industrial, mechanical and energy, electrical and electronic engineering) and health sciences (medical laboratory technology, radiological technology); B.Sc. degrees in international marketing and logistics; associate degree programmes in construction technology, electrical and electronics technology, mechanical technology, industrial and business administration; 40 full-time and 100 part-time teachers; 550 students; library of 7,000 vols; Rector GUDBRANDUR STEINTHORSSON.

INDIA

Learned Societies

GENERAL

India International Centre: 40 Max Mueller Marg, New Delhi 110003; tel. 4619431; f. 1958; international cultural organization for promotion of amity and understanding between the different communities in the world; programme of lectures, discussions, film evenings, etc.; mems: 3,746 individuals, 256 corporate (including 35 univs); library of 31,000 vols, also houses the India Collection of 3,500 rare documents on British India and the Himalayan Club Library of 900 vols; Pres. Dr KAPILA VATSYAYAN; Dir N. N. VOHRA; Sec. N. H. RAMACHANDRAN; publs *IIC Quarterly*, *IIC Diary* (every 2 months).

Indian Council for Cultural Relations: Azad Bhawan, Indraprastha Estate, New Delhi 110002; tel. 3318303; telex (031) 61860; fax 3712639; f. 1950 to establish and strengthen cultural relations between India and other countries; branch offices in Bombay, Calcutta, Madras, Bangalore, Chandigarh, Lucknow, Trivandrum and Hyderabad; cultural centres in Georgetown (Guyana), Paramaribo (Suriname), Moscow (Russia), Port Louis (Mauritius), Jakarta (Indonesia), Berlin (Germany), Cairo (Egypt), Tashkent (Uzbekistan), Almaty (Kazakhstan) and London (United Kingdom); activities include exchange visits between scholars, artists and men of eminence in the field of art and culture; exchange of exhibitions; international conferences and seminars, lectures by renowned scholars including Azad Memorial Lectures; establishment of chairs and centres of Indian studies abroad and welfare of overseas students in India; administration of Jawaharlal Nehru Award for International Understanding; presentation of books and Indian art objects to universities, libraries and museums in other countries; library of over 75,000 vols on India and other countries; Pres. VASANT SATHE; Dir-Gen. SHIV SHANKER MUKHERJEE; publs interpretations of Indian art and culture and translations of Indian works into foreign languages; publs: *Indian Horizons*, *African Quarterly* (in English, quarterly), *Thaqafat-ul-Hind* (in Arabic, quarterly), *Papeles de la India* (in Spanish, quarterly), *Rencontre avec l'Inde* (in French, quarterly), *Gagananchal* (Hindi, quarterly).

Indian Institute of World Culture: POB 402, 6 Shri B.P. Wadia Rd, Basavangudi, Bangalore 560004; tel. 602581; f. 1945; Mumbai Office: Theosophy Hall, 40 New Marine Lines, Mumbai 400020; 2,400 mems; library of 38,000 vols, 400 periodicals; objects: to provide opportunities for cultural and intellectual development, to promote exchange of thought between India and other countries and to raise the consideration of national and world problems to the plane of moral and spiritual values and to foster a sense of universal brotherhood; Pres. K. R. RAMACHANDRAN; Hon. Sec. M. S. S. MURTHY; publs *Monthly Bulletin*, *Annual Reports*, *Transactions and Reprints*, etc.

Jammu and Kashmir Academy of Art, Culture and Languages: Srinagar, Kashmir; tel. and fax 542640 (Jammu), 32379 (Srinagar); f. 1958; to promote arts, culture and languages of the State; library of 20,000 vols, 650 rare MSS, 250 laminated photographs, 90 opera and folk song recordings; collections of gramophone records, cassettes, paintings, jewellery, calligraphy, costumes, contemporary paintings and sculpture; Pres. Gen. K. V. KRISHNA RAO; Sec. B. THAKUR; publs *Sheeraza* (monthly in Urdu, every 2 months in Kashmiri, Dogri, Punjabi and Hindi, quarterly in Ladakhi, Pahari, Gojri and annually in English and Balti), *Hamara Adab* (annual anthology in Urdu, Kashmiri, Gojri, Pahari, Dogri, Punjabi, Hindi, Ladakhi), *Akademi* (Newsletter), *Encyclopaedia Kashmirana*.

AGRICULTURE, FISHERIES AND VETERINARY SCIENCE

Agri-Horticultural Society of India: Alipore Rd, Calcutta 700027; tel. 479-1713; f. 1820; 1,300 mems; library of 400 vols; Pres. S. G. KHAITAN; Sec. Dr S. K. BASU; publ. *Horticultural Journal* (quarterly).

Agri-Horticultural Society of Madras: Cathedral PO, Chennai 600086; f. 1835; 3,410 mems; Patron H.E. The GOVERNOR OF TAMIL NADU; Chair. R. SADASIVAM; Hon. Sec. Prof. J. RAMCHANDRAN.

Crop Improvement Society of India: Dept of Plant Breeding, Punjab Agricultural University, Ludhiana 141004; tel. 401960, ext. 224; telex 386473; f. 1974; aims to disseminate knowledge on crop improvement through lectures, symposia, publications, to arrange excursions and explorations, and to co-operate with national and international organizations; 200 mems; Pres. Dr P. S. PHUL; Sec. Dr G. S. SANDHA; publ. *Crop Improvement* (2 a year).

Indian Dairy Association: IDA House, Sector IV, R. K. Puram, New Delhi 110022; 3,000 mems; library of 700 vols; 100 periodicals; Pres A. BANERJEE; publs *Indian Journal of Dairy Science* (6 a year), *Indian Dairyman* (monthly).

Indian Society of Agricultural Economics: 46–48 Esplanade Mansions, Mahatma Gandhi Rd, Fort, Mumbai 400001; tel. 2842542; fax 2838790; f. 1939; 1,850 mems and subscribers; library of 18,000 vols; Pres. Dr A. VAIDYANATHAN; Hon. Sec. Dr TARA SHUKLA; publ. *The Indian Journal of Agricultural Economics* (quarterly).

Indian Society of Soil Science: Division of Soil Science and Agricultural Chemistry, Indian Agricultural Research Institute, New Delhi 110012; tel. (11) 5720991; fax (11) 5755529; e-mail soils@nde.vsnl.net.in; f. 1934; aims to cultivate and promote soil science and its allied disciplines and to disseminate knowledge of soil science and its applications; co-operation with Int. Soc. of Soil Science and similar organizations; 2,200 mems; Pres. Dr D. K. DAS; Sec. Dr G. NARAYANASAMY; publs *Journal* (quarterly), *Bulletin* (occasional).

ARCHITECTURE AND TOWN PLANNING

Indian Institute of Architects: Prospect Chambers Annexe, Dr D. N. Rd, Mumbai 400001; tel. 2046972; fax 2832516; f. 1929; aims: to promote aesthetic, scientific and practical efficiency of the architectural profession; to sponsor architectural education; to set qualifying standards for the profession; to provide a forum for discussing related subjects; mems: 1,086 Fellows, 20 Hon. Fellows, 6,974 Assocs, 95 Licentiates, 650 students, 65 retired; library of 3,000 vols; Pres. A. C. DESAI; Hon. Secs N. RANGNEKAR, V. M. PARELKAR; publs *Journal* (monthly), *News Letter* (monthly).

BIBLIOGRAPHY, LIBRARY SCIENCE AND MUSEOLOGY

Indian Association of Special Libraries and Information Centres (IASLIC): P. 291, CIT Scheme No. 6M, Kankurgachi, Calcutta 700054; tel. (33) 3349651; f. 1955 to promote study and research into special librarianship and information science; to conduct short-term training courses on the subject, hold conferences and co-ordinate activities among special libraries and special interest groups; publishes seminar and conference papers and books on information and library science; translation and reprographic services; 1,500 mems; library of 2,500 vols, 50 current periodicals; Hon. Pres. Prof. Dr M. G. SOM; Hon. Gen. Sec. J. N. SATPATHI; publs *IASLIC Bulletin* (4 a year), *Indian Library Science Abstracts (ILSA)* (1 a year), *IASLIC Newsletter* (monthly), etc.

Indian Library Association: A/40-41, Flat 201, Ansal Bldgs, Dr Mukherjee Nagar, Delhi 110009; tel. 711-7743; f. 1933; 2,500 mems; library of 600 vols; Pres. Dr P. S. G. KUMAR; Sec. A. P. GAKHAR; publs *Bulletin* (quarterly), *Newsletter* (monthly).

Museums Association of India: c/o State Museum, Lucknow 226001; f. 1944; professional discussions, seminars, conferences, exhibitions, etc.; 700 individual and institutional mems; Pres. Dr S. D. TRIVEDI; Sec. Dr S. K. SRIVASTAVA; publ. *Journal of Indian Museums*.

National Book Trust, India: A-5, Green Park, New Delhi 110016; tel. 664667; telex (031) 73034; f. 1957; an autonomous body set up by the Government; activities include publishing moderately-priced books for general readers in 12 Indian languages and English, giving assistance to authors, illustrators and publishers for producing books for children, neo-literates and the higher education sector, organizing book fairs, exhibitions, seminars and workshops, and promoting Indian books abroad; Chair. ANAND SARUP; Dir ARVIND KUMAR.

ECONOMICS, LAW AND POLITICS

Bar Association of India: Chamber 93, Supreme Court Bldg, New Delhi 110001; publ. *The Indian Advocate* (quarterly).

Indian Council of World Affairs: Sapru House, Barakhamba Rd, New Delhi 110001; f. 1943; non-governmental institution for the study of Indian and international questions; 2,625 mems; library of 124,122 vols, 523 periodicals, and all UN publs; Pres. HARCHARAN SINGH JOSH; Hon. Sec.-Gen. S. C. PARASHER; publs *India Quarterly, Foreign Affairs* (monthly).

Indian Economic Association: Delhi School of Economics, Delhi 110009; f. 1918; Pres. Prof. V. M. DANDEKAR; Hon. Sec. Prof. K. A. NAQVI; publ. *Indian Economic Journal*.

Indian Law Institute: Opp. Supreme Court, Bhagwandas Rd, New Delhi 110001; tel. (11) 3389429; f. 1956 to promote advanced studies and research in law and reform of administration of law and justice; library of 60,000 vols;

Pres. Chief Justice of India; Registrar K. S. BHATI; publs *Journal* (4 a year), *Annual Survey.*

Institute of Chartered Accountants of India: Indraprastha Marg, New Delhi 110002; tel. 3312055; fax 3721334; f. 1949; 62,000 mems; library of 40,000 vols; Pres. N. P. SARDA; Sec. A. K. MAJUMDAR; publ. *The Chartered Accountant* (monthly).

EDUCATION

Association of Indian Universities: 16 Kotla Marg, New Delhi 110002; tel. and fax (11) 3236105; telex 3166180; e-mail aiu@del2.vsnl.net.in; f. 1925; facilitates exchange of information between universities, organizes meetings, conferences of vice-chancellors, inter-university youth festivals and sports events, researches into contemporary problems and issues relating to higher education and overseas degree equivalence, liaises with foreign universities; mems: 237 universities; library of 30,000 vols, 130 periodicals; Pres. Prof. S. RINPOCHE; Sec.-Gen. Prof. K. B. POWAR; publs *Universities Handbook* (every 2 years), *Handbook of Medical Education, Handbook of Distance Education, Handbook of Engineering Education, Handbook of Management Education, Handbook of Computer Education, Handbook of Library and Information Science, Scholarships for Study Abroad and at Home* (all annually), *University News* (weekly), monographs, research publs, etc.

Hyderabad Educational Conference: 19 Bachelors' Quarters, Jawaharlal Nehru Rd, Hyderabad, Deccan; f. 1913; to promote academic research, assist needy students and further education in Andhra Pradesh; library of over 9,500 vols; Pres. SYED MASOOD ALI; Sec. GHOUSE MOHIUDDIN; publs (in Urdu) *Proceedings of Public Sessions, Educational Annual, Ruh-e-tarraqui.*

Indian Adult Education Association: 17B Indraprastha Estate, New Delhi 110002; tel. (11) 3319282; fax (11) 3355306; f. 1939; recognized by national govt; training, research, publs and field programmes; 1,500 mems; library of 12,000 vols; Pres. B. S. GARG; Sec. K. C. CHOUDHARY; publs *Indian Journal of Adult Education* (quarterly), *Proudh Shiksha* (Hindi monthly), *IAEA Newsletter* (monthly), *Jago Aur Jagao* (Hindi monthly).

National Bal Bhavan: Kotla Rd, New Delhi 110002; f. 1958; an autonomous institution set up by the Ministry of Human Resource Development; provides planned environment and creative activities based on Arts and Science to children between the ages of 5 and 16; provides leadership and guidance to teachers towards fostering a creative approach in teaching of art and science, organizes orientation courses for teachers and parents, runs a repertory theatre for children, the National Children's Museum and a national training resource centre; children's library of 43,347 vols and a reference library of 11,584 vols; Chair. SAROJ DUBEY; Sec. MADHU PANT.

Petit, J. N., Institute: 312 Dr Dadabhoy Naoroji Rd, Fort, Mumbai 400001; f. 1856; organizes lectures and makes accessible literary, scientific and philosophic works; 4,300 mems; library: see Libraries; Pres. J. P. DALAL; Hon. Secs. K. P. DRIVER, K. R. SIRVALLA.

University Grants Commission: Bahadur Shah Zafar Marg, New Delhi 110002; tel. 3319628; telex 3165913; f. 1953 to promote and co-ordinate university education; to determine and maintain the standards of teaching, examination and research in universities; may allocate grants to universities and colleges for these purposes; library of 41,850 vols; receives 50 journals; Chair. Prof. A. S. DESAI; Sec. Dr G. D. SHARMA; publs *Annual Report, University Development in India* (annual statistical review), *Journal of Higher Education, Bulletin of Higher Education,* reports.

FINE AND PERFORMING ARTS

All-India Fine Arts and Crafts Society: Old Mill Rd (Rafi Marg), New Delhi 110001; tel. 3711315; f. 1928; holds art exhibitions including the All India Annual Art Exhibition, exhibitions of Indian art abroad and exhibitions of arts and crafts from foreign countries in India, talks and film shows on art; 600 mems; library of 5,000 vols; Pres. Prof. JAGMOHAN CHOPRA; Sec. S. S. BHAGAT; publs *Roopa Lekha* (annually), *Arts News* (monthly).

Art Society of India: Sandhurst House, 524 S.V.P. Rd, Mumbai 400004; f. 1918; 650 mems; library of 2,000 vols; Pres. P. DAHANUKAR; Hon. Sec. B. R. KULKARNI.

India International Photographic Council: 1 Modern School, Barakhamba Rd, New Delhi 110001; tel. 3327762; f. 1983; promotes art and science of photography; 4,000 mems; publ. *Indian Photography and Cinematography* (monthly).

Indian Society of Oriental Art (Calcutta): 15 Park St, Calcutta 700016; f. 1907; 320 mems; to promote and research all aspects of ancient and contemporary Indian and Oriental art; library of 3,500 vols; Sec. Smt. INDIRA NAG CHAUDHURI; publ. *Journal* (annually).

Mumbai Art Society: Jehangir Art Gallery, Mumbai 400023; tel. 2044058; f. 1888; Pres. K. K. HEBBAR; Hon. Sec. G. S. ADIVREKAR; 450 Life mems, 150 ord. mems, 200 student mems; holds All India Annual Art Exhibition; publs *Art Journal,* illustrated catalogues of exhibitions.

National Academy of Art/Lalit Kala Akademi: Rabindra Bhavan, New Delhi 110001; tel. 387241; f. 1934; autonomous, government-financed; sponsors national and international exhibitions, such as the National Exhibition of Art (annually) and Triennale-India; arranges seminars, lectures, films, etc.; Sec. Prof. C.L. PORINCHUKUTTY; publs art books, brochures and prints; *Lalit Kala* (annual ancient art journal), *Lalit Kala Contemporary* (2 a year).

Sangeet Natak Akademi (National Academy of Music, Dance and Drama): Rabindra Bhavan, Feroze Shah Rd, New Delhi 110001; tel. (11) 3381833; fax (11) 3385715; f. 1953 for the preservation and development of the performing arts of India; governed by a General Council; documents the performing arts through films, tapes and photographs; maintains a museum of musical instruments, costumes, masks and puppets; library of 20,000 vols and audio-visual library of tapes and discs; offers financial assistance to music, dance and theatre institutions; administers the Jawaharlal Nehru Manipur Dance Academy, Imphal, Kathak Kendra, Delhi, and Rabindra Rangashala, Delhi; conducts festivals, seminars; gives awards and fellowships for outstanding work; Chair. JAMSHED J. BHABHA; Sec. SHARBARI MUKHERJEE; publ. *Sangeet Natak* (4 a year).

South India Society of Painters: No. 13, 111 Trust Cross, Chennai 600028.

HISTORY, GEOGRAPHY AND ARCHAEOLOGY

Bharata Itihasa Samshodhaka Mandala: 1321 Sadashiva Peth, Pune, 411030; f. 1910 for collecting, conserving and publishing historical materials; collection of 3,500 coins; 33,000 Persian, Sanskrit and Marathi MSS; 1,600,000 documents, about 1,200 old Indian paintings; 1,000 copperplates, sculptures and other antiquarian objects; 750 mems; library of 22,000 vols; Pres. R. S. WALIMBE; Chair. V. T. SHETE; Sec. Dr USHA RANADE; publs *Journal* (quarterly), *Sviya Granthamala Series, Puraskrita Granthamala.*

Geographical Society of India: c/o Dept of Geography, Calcutta University, 35 Ballygunge Circular Rd, Calcutta 700019; tel. 475-3681; f. 1933; 750 mems; library of 14,200 vols; 5,709 journals; geographical lectures, seminars and exhibitions; encouragement of geographical research and training; Pres. S. P. DASGUPTA; Sec. Prof. H. R. BETAL; publ. *Geographical Review of India* (quarterly).

LANGUAGE AND LITERATURE

Central Hindi Directorate: Department of Education, Ministry of Human Resource Development, West Block 7, R. K. Puram, New Delhi 110022; f. 1960; preparation and publication of bilingual and trilingual dictionaries of Indian and foreign languages; teaching of Hindi by correspondence courses to Indians and foreigners; extension courses; *c.* 300 mems; library of 83,100 vols; Dir Dr G. P. VIMAL; publs *Bhasha* (quarterly), *Varshiki* (annually), *UNESCO DOOT* (monthly).

International Tamil People Promotive Organization: c/o 'Thamizh Nilam', 5 Arunachala St, Chepauk, Chennai 600005, Tamil Nadu; tel. 847829; f. 1968; research and development of Tamil language, literature, culture and history; 20,000 mems; library of 15,000 vols; Founder Pres. PERUNCHITHIRANAR; Gen. Sec. PARAMBAI ARIVAN; publs *Thenmozhi* (monthly), *Thamizh Chittu* (monthly), *Thamizh Nilam* (every 2 weeks).

Linguistic Society of India: c/o Deccan College, Pune 411006; tel. 27231; f. 1928; 700 mems; library of 6,000 vols; Pres. Dr O. N. KOUL; Sec. Dr S. R. SHARMA; publ. *Indian Linguistics* (annually).

Madras Literary Society: College Rd, Chennai 600006; tel. 827966; Pres. M. GOPALAKRISHNAN; Hon. Sec. U. RAMESH RAO.

Mythic Society: 2 Nrupathunga Rd, Bangalore 560002; tel. 2215034; f. 1909 to promote the study of mythology, archaeology, indology and Karnataka history; 400 mems; library of 24,000 vols, incl. special collections of Mysore history; Pres. Dr SURYANATH U. KAMATH; Sec. Dr M. K. L. N. SASTRY; publ. *Journal* (quarterly).

PEN All-India Centre: Theosophy Hall, 40 New Marine Lines, Mumbai 400020; tel. 2032175; e-mail arsirkar@gemb.vsnl.net.in; f. 1933; Founder SOPHIA WADIA; Pres. ANNADA SHANKAR RAY; Sec.-Treas. NISSIM EZEKIEL; publs *The Indian PEN* (quarterly), PEN series on Indian literatures, *PEN Conference Proceedings.*

Sahitya Akademi/National Academy of Letters: Rabindra Bhavan, 35 Ferozeshah Rd, New Delhi 110001; tel. (11) 3387064; fax (11) 3382428; f. 1954 for the development of Indian literature, the co-ordination of literary activities in the Indian languages and research in Indian languages and literature; publication of literary works; promotion of cultural exchanges with other countries; Gen. Council consists of eminent persons in the field of letters, nominees of the Central and State Governments, representatives of the universities and one representative of each of the 22 languages of India recognized by the Academy; awards annual prizes; library of 100,000 vols; Pres. Dr RAMAKANTA RATH; Sec. Prof. K. SATCHIDANANDAN; publs *Indian Literature* (English, 6 a year), *Sanskrita Pratibha* (Sanskrit, 2 a year), *Samakaleena Bharatiya Sahitya* (Hindi, 6 a year), *Encyclopaedia of Indian Literature,* books and translations into Indian languages.

Samskrita Academy: Sanskrit College Buildings, 84 Thiru Vi. Ka. Rd, Mylapore, Chennai 600004; tel. 847320; f. 1927; promotion and propagation of Sanskrit language, publication of studies and expositions of Sanskrit works, organization of oratorical and recitation competitions, regular lectures and seminars in Sanskrit and Tamil on well-known Sanskrit poets and philosophers by eminent scholars, occasional production of Sanskrit drama; 200 mems; Pres. B. MADHAVAN.

Tamil Association: Karanthai Tamil Sangam, Thanjavur 2, Tamil Nadu; tel. 21149; f. 1911; conducts literary research and maintains schools for general education as well as an arts college with Tamil and science depts; 216 mems; library of 25,000 vols; Pres. S. RAMANATHAN; Sec. T. K. P. GOVINDASAMI; publ. *Tamil Pozhil* (monthly).

Tamil Nadu Tamil Development and Research Council: Fort St George, Chennai 600009; f. 1959; development of Tamil in all its aspects, especially as a modern language; library of 27,000 vols, 320 MSS, 85 periodicals; 16 teachers, 50 students; Chair. Chief Minister; Vice-Chair. Minister for Education; Sec. Director of Tamil Development; publ. *Tamil Nadu Tamil Bibliography.*

MEDICINE

All-India Ophthalmological Society: c/o Dr A. K. Gupta, V1/10 Maulana Azad Medical College Campus, Kotla Rd, New Delhi 110002; tel. 3318813; f. 1937; cultivation and promotion of the study and practice of ophthalmic sciences with a view to render service to the community and to promote social contacts among ophthalmologists; 4,690 mems; Pres. Dr C. P. GUPTA; Gen. Sec. Dr A. K. GUPTA; publ. *Indian Journal of Ophthalmology* (quarterly).

Association of Medical Physicists of India: c/o Radiological Physics Division, Bhabha Atomic Research Centre, Mumbai 400085; tel. (22) 5563060 ext. 2201; telex 72322; fax (22) 5560750; e-mail mpssrphd@magnum.bareti.ernet.in; f. 1976; 680 mems representing medical physicists, radiation oncologists and others interested in this field; organizes annual conference, workshops, lectures, awards, research grants, travel fellowships within India; Pres. Dr A. V. LAKSHAMAN; Sec. K. N. GOVINDA RAJAN; publ. *Journal of Medical Physics* (quarterly).

Association of Surgeons of India: 18 Swamy Sivananda Salai (Adams Rd), Chepauk, Chennai 600005; tel. 567095; f. 1938; 6,500 mems; library of *c.* 12,000 vols; Pres. Dr S. S. DESHMUKH J. JOSHI; Hon. Sec. Dr B. KRISHNA RAU; publ. *Indian Journal of Surgery* (monthly).

Federation of Obstetric & Gynaecological Societies of India: Purandare Griha, 31/C Dr N. A. Purandare Marg, Mumbai 400007; tel. 3614011; f. 1950; organizes annual congress for the exchange of views in the various aspects of the subject; organizes workshops on family planning, etc.; medical education programme; holds periodic international seminars; 10,100 mems; Pres. Dr VASANT B. PATWARDHAN; Hon. Sec. Gen. Dr D. K. TANK; publ. *Journal of Obstetrics & Gynaecology of India* (every 2 months).

Helminthological Society of India: Dept of Parasitology, UP College of Veterinary Science and Animal Husbandry, Mathura; Pres. Prof. S. N. SINGH; Treas.-Sec. Prof. B. P. PANDE; publ. *Indian Journal of Helminthology* (2 a year).

Indian Association of Parasitologists: 110 Chittaranjan Ave, Calcutta 700012; Pres. Dr H. N. RAY; Sec. Dr A. B. CHAUDHURY.

Indian Cancer Society: 74 Jerbai Wadia Rd, Parel, Mumbai 400012, and Eucharistic Bldg, 5 Convent St, Mumbai 400039; tel. (22) 204 7642; f. 1951; charitable trust subsisting on donations; objects: to support cancer research, to aid sufferers from cancer, to improve facilities for diagnosis, treatment and rehabilitation, to educate the public and the profession and to organize national conferences; diagnostic, treatment and research centre in South Mumbai (Lady Ratan Tata Medical and Research Centre); Hon. Founder Sec. and Man. Trustee Dr D. J. JUSSAWALLA; publ. *Indian Journal of Cancer* (quarterly).

Indian Medical Association, The: I.M.A. House, Indraprastha Marg, New Delhi 110002; tel. 3319009; fax 3316270; f. 1928; 90,367 mems; Pres. Dr B. C. CHAPARWAL; Hon. Gen. Sec. Dr J. C. SOBTI; publs *Journal* (monthly), *Your Health* (monthly), *I.M.A. News* (monthly); affiliated with the British Medical Asscn, the Nepal Medical Asscn, and the Commonwealth Medical Asscn; mem. South Asian Medical Asscn, World Medical Asscn.

Indian Pharmaceutical Association: Kalina, Santacruz (East), Mumbai 400098; 7,000 mems; Pres. P. D. SHETH; Hon. Gen. Sec. Dr M. K. RAINA; publs *Indian Journal of Pharmaceutical Sciences* (6 a year), *Pharma Times* (monthly).

Indian Public Health Association: 110 Chittaranjan Ave, Calcutta 700073: tel. 241-3831; f. 1957; promotion of public health and allied sciences; 22 state and local brs; holds Annual Convention, meetings, conferences, etc.; 2,350 mems; Pres. Prof. A. K. CHAKRABORTY; Gen. Sec. Dr K. K. DUTTA; publ. *Indian Journal of Public Health* (quarterly).

Indian Society for Medical Statistics: C/o Institute for Research in Medical Statistics (ICMR), Mayor Ramanathan Rd, Chetput, Chennai 600031; tel. (44) 8265308; fax (44) 8264963; e-mail icmrtrc@ren.nic.in; f. 1983 to contribute to the development of medical statistics and strengthen the application of statistics in medicine, health and related disciplines; organizes annual conferences, refresher courses, symposia; 480 mems; Pres. Prof. P. P. TALWAR; Gen Sec. Dr M. KACHIRAYAN; publs *ISMS Bulletin*, proceedings of annual meetings, monographs.

Indian Society of Anaesthetists: c/o Dept of Anaesthesiology, K.E.M. Hospital, Parel, Mumbai 400012; f. 1947; 4,000 mems; Pres. Dr K. P. RAMCHANDRAN; Hon. Sec. Dr D. DAS GUPTA; publ. *Indian Journal of Anaesthesia* (every 2 months).

Medical Council of India: Aiwan-e-Galib Marg, Kotla Rd, New Delhi 110002; tel. (11) 3235178; fax (11) 3236604; f. 1933, maintenance of uniform standards of medical education, reciprocity in mutual recognition of medical qualifications with other countries, maintenance of Indian Medical Register; Pres. Dr KETAN DHIRAJLAL DESAI; Sec. Dr M. SACHDEVA; publs *Indian Medical Register, MCI Bulletin of Information, Report of the Programme on Continuing Medical Education.*

Mumbai Medical Union: Blavatsky Lodge Bldg, Chowpatty, Mumbai 400007; f. 1883; 250 mems; Pres. Dr U. N. BASTODKAR; Sec. Dr Smt. M. K. THACKER.

Pharmacy Council of India: 2nd Floor, Combined Councils' Building, Temple Lane, Kotla Rd, POB 7020, New Delhi 110002; f. 1949 to set and maintain educational standards for qualification and registration in pharmacy and to co-ordinate the practice thereof; Pres. Prof. J. S. QADRY; Asst Sec. ARCHNA MUGDAL.

NATURAL SCIENCES

General

Indian Academy of Sciences: CV Raman Ave, POB 8005, Sadashivanagar, Bangalore 560080; tel. (80) 3344592; telex 845-2178; fax (80) 3346094; e-mail madhavan@ias.ernet.in; f. 1934; 785 Fellows, 47 Hon. Fellows, 32 Associates; Pres. Prof. N. KUMAR; Secs Prof. R. GADAGKAR, Prof. N. BALAKRISHNAN; publs *Proceedings Chemical Sciences* (every 2 months), *Proceedings Earth and Planetary Sciences* (quarterly), *Proceedings Mathematical Sciences* (quarterly), *Pramana* (journal of physics, monthly), *Journal of Biosciences* (quarterly), *Journal of Astrophysics and Astronomy* (quarterly), *Bulletin of Materials Science* (every 2 months), *Sadhana* (Engineering Sciences, every two months), *Journal of Genetics* (quarterly), *Resonance* (monthly), *Current Science* (fortnightly), *Patrika* (newsletter), *Year Book.*

Indian National Science Academy (formerly National Institute of Sciences of India): Bahadur Shah Zafar Marg, New Delhi 110002; tel. (11) 3231038; telex 31-61835; fax (11) 3235648; email insa@giasdlol.vsnl.in; f. 1935 to promote scientific knowledge, coordination between scientific bodies, and safeguard the interests of scientists in India; adhering organization of ICSU; 676 Fellows, 104 Foreign Fellows; library of 21,000 vols; Pres. Dr S. VARADARAJAN; Secs Prof. N. APPAJI RAO, Prof. P. T. MANOHARAN; publs *Proceedings, Monographs, Bulletin, Progress of Science in India, Indian Journal of History of Science, Year Book, Indian Journal of Pure and Applied Mathematics, Biographical Memoirs.*

Indian Science Congress Association: 14 Dr Biresh Guha St, Calcutta 700017; tel. (33) 2402551; fax (33) 2402551; f. 1914 to advance and promote science in India; holds annual congress; 11,928 mems; library of 6,000 vols, 50 periodicals; Pres. P. RAMA RAO; Secs Prof. A. S. MUKHERJEE, Dr Y. PATHAK; publs *Proceedings* (annually, in 4 parts), *Everyman's Science* (4 a year).

National Academy of Sciences: 5 Lajpatrai Rd, Allahabad 211002, UP; f. 1930 for the cultivation and promotion of science in all its branches; 2,580 mems excluding 732 fellows, 48 honorary fellows and 23 foreign fellows; Pres. Prof. U. S. SRIVASTAVA; Secs Dr O. M. PRASAD, Dr SANDEEP K. BASU; Foreign Sec. Prof. ALOK K. GUPTA; publs *Proceedings* in two sections—*Section A: Physical Sciences, Section B: Biological Sciences* (quarterly), *National Academy of Sciences Letters* (monthly), *Annual Number* (annually).

Biological Sciences

Academy of Zoology: Church Rd 2/95, Civil Lines, Agra 282002; f. 1954; 1,500 mems; library of 91,000 vols, exchange service with other zoological institutions; international organization and forum for the advancement of zoology; Pres. and Sec. Dr D. P. S. BHATI; publs *The Annals of Zoology*.

Association of Microbiologists of India: c/o Div. of Microbiology, Indian Agricultural Research Institute, New Delhi 110012; tel. 587649; f. 1938; 1,200 mems; library of 3,000 vols; Pres. Dr S. RAMCHANDRAN; Gen. Sec. Dr K. V. B. R. TILAK; publ. *Indian Journal of Microbiology.*

Bombay Natural History Society: Hornbill House, Shahid Bhagat Singh Rd, Mumbai 400023; tel. (22) 2821811; f. 1883; studies natural history, ecology and conservation in the Indian sub-continent; research programmes in field zoology; 5,000 mems; 17,000 vols; Pres. B. G. DESHMUKH; Hon. Sec. J. C. DANIEL; publs *Journal, Hornbill.*

Indian Association of Biological Sciences: Life Science Centre, Calcutta University, Calcutta 700019; tel. 4753681; f. 1968; 400 mems; Sec. and Editor Prof. T. M. DAS; publ. *Indian Biologist* (2 a year).

Indian Biophysical Society: Saha Institute of Nuclear Physics, 92 Acharya Prafula Chandra Rd, Calcutta 700009; tel. 354281; f. 1965; *c.* 200 mems; Pres. Prof. N. N. SAHA;

Gen. Sec. Prof. D. P. BURMA; publ. *Proceedings* (annually).

Indian Botanical Society: Dept of Botany, University of Madras, Chepauk, Chennai 600005; Pres. K. S. THIND; Sec. Prof. K. S. BHARGAVA; publ. *Journal*.

Indian Phytopathological Society: Indian Agricultural Research Institute, New Delhi 110012; tel. (11) 5781474; telex 3177161; fax (11) 5752006; f. 1947; 1,720 mems; virology, bacteriology, mycology, nematology and plant pathology; holds seminars, symposia, etc.; Pres. Dr A. K. SARBHOY; Sec. Dr DINESH KUMAR; publ. *Indian Phytopathology* (quarterly).

Indian Society of Genetics and Plant Breeding: Indian Agricultural Research Institute, Genetics Division, New Delhi 110012; f. 1941; plant breeding and genetic research; 1,400 mems; Pres. Prof. V. L. CHOPRA; Sec. Dr R. B. MEHRA; publ. *Journal*.

Marine Biological Association of India: Cochin, Kerala (South India); f. 1958; Pres. Dr E. G. SILAS; Vice-Pres. Dr R. R. PRASAD, Dr R. NATARAJAN; publs *Journal* (2 a year), *Memoirs* (irregular), Proceedings of symposia (irregular).

Palynological Society of India: Environmental Resources Research Centre, Thiruvananthapuram 695005, Kerala; tel. 435115; f. 1965; conducts symposia, seminars, annual lectures and the Indian Palynological Conference (every three years); 60 mems; Pres. Dr P. K. K. NAIR; Gen. Sec. Prof. P. M. MATHEW; publ. *Journal of Palynology*.

Society of Biological Chemists, India: Indian Institute of Science, Bangalore 560012; f. 1930; 1,600 mems; Pres. Dr P. M. BHARGAVA; publs *Biochemical Reviews* (annually), *Proceedings and Abstracts* (annually), *News Letter* (quarterly).

Uttar Pradesh Zoological Society: c/o PG-Dept of Zoology, Sanatan Dharm College, Muzaffarnagar, UP 251001; tel. 4936; f. 1981; 125 mems; Pres. Prof. S. C. RASTOGI; Hon. Sec. Dr. S. C. GOEL; publ. *Uttar Pradesh Journal of Zoology* (2 a year).

Zoological Society of India: c/o Zoological Survey of India, 34 Chittaran Ave, Calcutta 700012; f. 1916; library of 37,100 vols, 875 periodicals.

Mathematical Sciences

Allahabad Mathematical Society: 10 C. S. P. Singh Marg, Allahabad 211001; tel. 623553; f. 1958; to further the cause of advanced study and research in various branches of mathematics, including theoretical physics and mathematical statistics; 270 mems; library of 5,000 vols; Pres. Prof. D. P. GUPTA; Sec. U. K. SAXENA; publs *Indian Journal of Mathematics* (3 a year), *Bulletin* (annually), *Lecture Notes* series, *Communications in Theoretical Physics* (2 a year).

Bharata Ganita Parisad (formerly Benares Mathematical Society): Dept of Mathematics and Astronomy, University, Lucknow; tel. (522) 325944; f. 1950; 450 mems; library of 15,500 vols; Pres. Prof. K. D. SINGH; Gen. Sec. Dr D. SINGH; publ. *Ganita*.

Calcutta Mathematical Society: Asutosh Bhavan, AE-374, Sector I, Saltlake City, Calcutta 700064; tel. (33) 3378882; telex 021-5380; fax (33) 376290; f. 1908; special lectures, seminars, symposia, workshop in mathematical sciences; research projects sponsored by various funding agencies; 892 mems; library of 12,000 vols; Pres. Prof. B. K. LAHIRI; Sec. Dr M. R. ADHIKARI; publ. *Bulletin* (6 a year), *News Bulletin* (monthly), *Review Bulletin* (2 a year).

Indian Mathematical Society: Department of Mathematics, Maitreyi College, Bapu Dham Complex, Chanakyapuri, New Delhi 110021; f. 1907; 1,000 mems; library of 4,000 vols; Pres. Prof. B. K. LAHIRI; Admin. Sec. Prof. M. K. SINGAL; publs *Journal*, *Mathematics Student* (4 a year).

Physical Sciences

Astronomical Society of India: Dept of Astronomy, Osmania University, Hyderabad 500007; tel. (80) 3340122; fax (80) 3340492; e-mail dipankar@rri.ernet.in; f. 1973; 750 mems; Pres. Dr V. K. KAPAHI; Sec. Dr D. BHATTACHARYA; publs *Bulletin* (quarterly), *Memoirs* (occasional).

Electrochemical Society of India, The: Indian Institute of Science Campus, Bangalore 560012; tel. (80) 3340977; telex 0845-8349; fax (80) 3341683; e-mail mahesh@cedt.iisc.ernet.in; f. 1964 to promote the science and technology of electrochemistry, electrodeposition and plating, corrosion including high-temperature oxidation, electrometallurgy and metal finishing, semi-conductors and electronics, batteries, solid electrolytes, solid state electrochemistry, and protection of metals and materials against environmental attack; 670 mems; library of 4,000 vols; Pres. M. RAVINDRANATH; Sec. Dr G. ANANDA RAO; publ. *Journal* (quarterly).

Indian Chemical Society: University Science College Bldgs, 92 Acharya Prafulla Chandra Rd, Calcutta 700009; tel. 350-3478; f. 1924; 2,000 mems; library of 10,500 vols; Pres. Dr JAI P. MITTAL; Hon. Sec. Prof. P. L. MAJUMDER; publ. *Journal* (monthly).

Indian Physical Society: 2 & 3 Raja Subodh Mallick Rd, Jadavpur, Calcutta 700032; tel. 4734971; fax 4732805; f. 1934 to promote and uphold the cause of physical science in India; 425 life mems, 150 ordinary mems, 10 assoc. mems, 8 hon. mems; Pres. Prof. D. CHAKRAVORTY; Gen. Sec. Prof. S. P. SEN GUPTA; publs *Physics Teacher* (quarterly), *Proceedings, Reports, Monographs*.

Optical Society of India, The: Applied Physics Dept, Calcutta Univ., 92 Acharya Prafulla Chandra Rd, Calcutta 700009; tel. 350-8386; f. 1965 to promote and diffuse the knowledge of optics in all its branches, pure and applied; 420 mems; library of 100 vols; Pres. Prof. O. P. NIJHAWAN; Gen. Sec. Dr AJAY GHOSH; publ. *Journal of Optics* (4 a year).

RELIGION, SOCIOLOGY AND ANTHROPOLOGY

Anthropological Society of Mumbai: 209 Dr Dadabhai Naoroji Rd, Fort, Mumbai 400001; f. 1886; Pres. Dr. J. F. BULSARA; Hon. Sec. SAPUR F. DESAI.

Asiatic Society, The: 1 Park St, Calcutta 700016; tel. 29-0779; fax 29-0355; f. 1784; to study humanities and sciences in India; 1,292 mems; 64 research Fellows; library of 200,000 vols; 50,000 MSS, 24,000 old coins, 75 oil paintings; research on Indology and Oriental studies; Pres. Dr MANINDRA MOHAN CHAKRABORTY; Gen. Sec. Dr CHANDAN ROYCHAUDHURI; publs *Journal, Year Book, Bibliotheca Indica, Monthly Bulletin*, etc.

Asiatic Society of Mumbai: Town Hall, Mumbai 400023; tel. 2660956; f. 1804 to investigate and encourage sciences, arts and literature in relation to Asia and India in particular; established Dr P. V. Kane Research Institute for Oriental Studies; 2,811 mems; 235,000 vols, 2,357 MSS, 10,443 old coins; Pres. Dr D. R. SARDESAI; Hon. Sec. VIMAL SHAH; publs *Journal*, monographs, reports.

Indian Anthropological Association: Department of Anthropology, University of Delhi, Delhi 110007; f. 1964; 400 mems; Pres. Prof. Dr R. S. MANN; publs *Indian Anthropologist* (2 a year), *News Bulletin* (annually), *Anthropologists in India* (every 2–3 years).

Indian Society for Afro-Asian Studies: 297 Sarswati Kunj, I.P. Ext., New Delhi 110092; tel. 2442920; fax 2425698; e-mail isaas@giasdl01.vsnl.net.in; f. 1980; aims at analysing political, economic, social and cultural situation of Afro-Asian countries; 875 mems; Pres. LALIT BHASIN; Sec.-Gen. Dr DHARAMPAL; publs. *IRAA* (4 a year), *ISAAS Newsletter* (1 a year).

Theosophical Society, The: International Headquarters, Adyar, Chennai 600020; tel. (44) 4912815; e-mail para.vidya@gemsvsnl.net.in; f. in New York 1875; 32,314 mems throughout the world; library of 152,000 vols and 18,000 palm-leaf and paper MSS; aims: to form a nucleus of the Universal Brotherhood of Humanity without distinction of race, creed, sex, caste or colour, to encourage the study of comparative religion, philosophy and science, and to investigate unexplained laws of nature and the powers latent in man; Pres. Mrs RADHA BURNIER; Sec. CONRAD JAMIESON; publs *The Theosophist* (monthly), *Adyar Library Bulletin* (annually), *Adyar Newsletter* (quarterly).

TECHNOLOGY

Aeronautical Society of India, The: 13B, Indraprastha Estate, New Delhi 110002; tel. 3317516; f. 1948 for the promotion and diffusion of knowledge of aeronautical sciences and aircraft engineering, and for the advancement of the aeronautical profession; 2,500 mems; library of over 4,000 vols; Pres. Dr A. P. J. ABDUL KALAM; Hon. Sec. Air Cdre C. M. SINGLA; Admin. Sec. Wing Commdr J. R. BHASKAR; publ. *Journal* (quarterly).

Geological, Mining and Metallurgical Society of India: c/o Geology Dept, University of Calcutta, 35 B.C. Rd, Calcutta 700019; tel. 475-3681; f. 1924; 315 mems; Pres. Prof. A. K. BANERJI; Joint Secs Dr B. K. SAMANTA, Dr A. SENGUPTA; publs *Journal* (quarterly), *Bulletin*.

India Society of Engineers: 12-B Netaji Subhas Rd, Calcutta 700001; f. 1934; library of 20,000 vols; 8,000 mems; Pres. A. C. SINHA; Gen. Sec. D. B. CHOWDHURY; publ. *Science and Engineering* (monthly in English).

Indian Association of Geohydrologists: c/o Geological Survey of India, 4 Chowringhee Lane, Calcutta 700016; f. 1964; 440 mems; Pres. V. SUBRAMANYAM; Hon. Sec. A. K. ROY; publ. *Indian Geohydrology*.

Indian Ceramic Society: Central Glass and Ceramic Research Institute, Calcutta 700032; f. 1928; 2,000 mems; Pres. Dr N. R. SIRCAR; Sec. AMIT KR. DE.; publ. *Transactions* (6 a year).

Indian Institute of Metals: Metal House, Plot 13/4, Block AQ, Sector V, Salt Lake, Calcutta 700091; tel. (33) 3215006; fax (33) 3215325; f. 1946; 10,000 mems; Pres. Dr R. KRISHNAN; Hon. Sec. Dr Sri S. S. DAS GUPTA; publs *Transactions* (every 2 months), *Metal News* (every 2 months).

Indian National Academy of Engineering: 117 Visiting Faculty, Nalanda House, IIT Campus, Hauz Khas, New Delhi 110016; tel. (11) 6968475; fax (11) 6968635; e-mail inae@nda.vsnl.net.in; f. 1987 to promote the general advancement of engineering and technology and related sciences and disciplines; awards Professorship, Fellowship and Scholarship; 299 Fellows; Pres. Prof. P. V. INDIRESAN; Exec. Sec. Maj.-Gen. J. C. AHLUWALIA.

Indian Society of Mechanical Engineers (ISME): c/o Dept of Mechanical Engineering, Indian Institute of Technology, New Delhi 110016; tel. 654187; telex 31-73087; fax 6862037; f. 1975; 480 mems; Pres. Prof. G. S. SEKHON; Sec. Dr S. G. DESHMUKH; publs

Journal of Engineering Production (quarterly), *Journal of Thermal Engineering* (quarterly), *Journal of Engineering Design* (quarterly).

Institution of Electronics and Telecommunication Engineers (IETE): 2 Institutional Area, Lodi Rd, New Delhi 110003; tel. 4631810; telex 31-62747; f. 1953 to promote the advancement of electronics and telecommunications engineering and related fields; 40,000 mems; Pres. Prof. R. K. Arora; Sec. Maj.-Gen. K. B. Jhal Diyal; publs *IETE Journal of Research* (6 a year), *IETE Technical Review* (6 a year), *IETE Journal of Education* (4 a year).

Institution of Engineers (India): 8 Gokhale Rd, Calcutta 700020; tel. (33) 2238311; telex 217885; fax (33) 2238345; e-mail ieihqrs@giascl01.vsnl.net.in; f. 1920; incorp. by Royal Charter 1935; over 300,000 mems; 60 libraries; Pres. A. K. Ghose; Sec. and Dir-Gen. Dr A. Mukherjee; publs *Technorama, Journal, IEI News*.

Mineralogical Society of India: Manasa Gangotri, Mysore 6; f. 1959; objects: to advance knowledge of crystallography, mineralogy, petrology, etc. by means of research and the holding of conferences, meetings and discussions; 400 mems; library of 1,500 vols; Pres. Dr Viswanathiah; Sec. Dr P. N. Satish; publ. *The Indian Mineralogist*.

Research Institutes

GENERAL

Council of Scientific and Industrial Research: Rafi Marg, New Delhi; tel. 3711251; telex (031) 65202; fax 3714788; e-mail csirhq@sirnetd.ernet.in; f. 1942; the national research laboratories described below have been established under the Council, which is itself responsible to the Ministry of Science and Technology (Government of India); National Institute of Science Communication incorporates library of 20,000 vols; Indian National Scientific Documentation Centre: see Libraries and Archives; Pres. The Prime Minister; Dir-Gen. Dr R. A. Mashelkar; Joint Sec. (Admin.) Ajay Kumar; publ. *Technical Manpower Bulletin* (monthly).

Attached research institutes:

Central Building Research Institute: Roorkee 247667, Uttar Pradesh; tel. 72243; telex 059-203; fax (1332) 72272; e-mail cbri@sirnetd.ernet.in; f. 1947; research and development in building science and technology; soil mechanics and foundation engineering; rural building and environment; building processes, plant and productivity; education and health buildings; housing and planning; fire research and building economics and management; *c.* 600 staff; library of *c.* 24,500 vols; Dir Dr R. Narayana Iyenger; publs *Annual Report, CBRI Abstracts, Information Bulletin*, etc.

Central Drug Research Institute: Chattar Manzil Palace, PB 173, Lucknow; tel. (522) 214219; telex 0535-2286; fax (522) 223405; e-mail cdrilk@sirnetd.ernet.in; f. 1951; biochemical, pharmacological, chemical, microbiological, endocrinological, biophysical and medical research; library of 21,300 vols; Dir Dr C. M. Gupta; publ. *Annual Report*.

Central Electrochemical Research Institute: Karaikudi 630006; tel. 22065; telex 0443-211; fax 23088; e-mail cecrik@cscecri.ren.nic.in; f. 1953; electrochemical and allied research; library of 31,755 vols; Dir Dr M. Raghvan; publs *Bulletin of Electro-chemistry, Battery Newsletter, Annual Report*.

Central Electronics Engineering Research Institute: Pilani, Rajasthan; tel. 42111; telex 031-4171; fax 42294; f. 1953; design and construction of electronic equipment, components and test equipment; Dir Dr R. N. Biswas; publ. *Annual Report*.

Central Food Technological Research Institute: Cheluvamba Mansion, V. V. Mohalla PO, Mysore 570013; tel. 565760; telex 0846-241; fax 521713; e-mail prakash@micfos.ernet.in; f. 1950; library of 27,500 vols; food processing; food conservation and preservation; nutritional, dietetic, technological and biochemical studies; microbiology, packaging, quality control and engineering aspects of food technology; information, statistics and extension services; Dir V. Prakash; publs *Food Technology Abstracts, Food Digest, Food Patents Techno-economic News, CFTRI Newsletter*.

Central Fuel Research Institute: PO Fuel Research Institute, Jealgora, Dhanbad 828108, Bihar; tel. 460141; telex 0629-201; fax 469350; e-mail director@cscfri.ren.nic.in; f. 1945; research on technological and industrial aspects of coal; *c.* 1,320 staff; library of 7,855 vols, 15,000 periodicals; Dir Dr K. S. Narasimhan; publs *CFRI Newsletter* (monthly), *Fuel Science and Technology, Annual Report*.

Central Glass and Ceramic Research Institute: Jadavpur, University PO, Calcutta 700032; tel. 4735829; telex 021-7787; fax 4730957; f. 1950; fundamental and applied research on glass, ceramics, vitreous enamels, refractories and mica; technical assistance to the industry, testing and standardization; library of 25,000 vols; Dir Dr H. S. Maity (acting); publs *Documentation List on Glass and Ceramics, Glance, Ceramic Update, Annual Report*.

Central Institute of Medicinal and Aromatic Plants: PO Ram Sagar Misra Nagar, Lucknow; tel. 342683; telex 0535-2298; fax 342666; f. 1959; co-ordination of activities in the development of cultivation and utilization of medicinal and aromatic plants on organized basis; library of 2,688 vols; Dir Dr Sushil Kumar; publs *Farm Bulletin, Current Research on Medicinal and Aromatic Plants* (quarterly), *CIMAP Newsletter* (quarterly), *Annual Report*.

Central Leather Research Institute: Adyar, Chennai 600020; tel. 4912146; telex 041-21014; fax 4912150; e-mail clri@sirnetm.iitm.ernet.in; f. 1953; all aspects of leather research; library of 16,050 vols; Dir Dr T. Ramasami; publ. *Leather Sciences Abstracts*.

Central Mechanical Engineering Research Institute: Mahatma Gandhi Ave, Durgapur 9; tel. 546749; telex 0205-213; fax 546745; f. 1958; materials, mechanisms and machines; heat engines and heat transfer; designs and production; library of 15,139 vols; Dir Shri Hardyal Singh; publs *Mechanical Engineering Bulletin* (quarterly), *Annual Report*.

Central Mining Research Institute: Barwa Rd, Dhanbad, Bihar 826001; tel. 203043; telex 0629-208; fax 205028; f. 1956; research on safety, health and efficiency in mining; library of 21,061 vols; Dir Dr T. N. Singh; publs *Journal of Mining Research, CMRI Newsletter* (quarterly)

Central Road Research Institute: PO Road Research Institute, Delhi-Mathura Rd, New Delhi 110020; tel. 6848917; telex 031-75369; fax 6823437; e-mail root@cscrri.ren.nic.in; f. 1952; research and development in highway engineering, traffic engineering, transportation economics and allied fields; *c.* 500 staff; library of 50,000 vols; Dir Dr A. K. Gupta; publs *Road Abstracts* (2 a year), *Highway Documentation* (monthly), *Annual Report*.

Central Salt and Marine Chemicals Research Institute: Waghawadi Rd, Bhavnagar 364002; tel. 429496; telex 0182-230; fax 426970; e-mail csmcri@sirnetd.ernet.in; f. 1954; preparation of salt, potassium fertilizers, magnesium compounds, bromine and bromides, industrial trace metals; survey and cultivation of marine algae, water desalination by solar distillation, electrodialysis, ion-exchange and reverse osmosis techniques; library of 27,967 vols; Dir Dr C. M. Gomkale (acting); publ. *CSMCRI Newsletter*.

Central Scientific Instruments Organization: Sector 30-C-C, Chandigarh 20; tel. 657027; telex 0395-300; fax 657267; f. 1959; 13,290 vols; 240 periodicals; promotion and development of indigenous manufacture of scientific instruments for teaching, research, industry and essential services; Dir Prof. S. Mohan; publ. *CSIO Communications* (quarterly).

Centre for Biochemicals Technology: Patel Chest Institute, Delhi University Campus, Delhi; tel. 7257298; telex 031-78085; fax 7257471; e-mail cfb@sirnetd.ernetd.in; f. 1966; preparation of biochemicals and antigens required for use for biological research and medicines; Dir Samir K. Brahamchari; publ. *Annual Report*.

Centre for Cellular and Molecular Biology: Hyderabad; tel. 7173487; telex 0425-7046; fax 7171195; e-mail dbala@ccmb.uunet.in; f. 1977; research in frontier areas and multi-disciplinary areas of modern biology with a view to aiding development of biochemical and biotechnological technology in India by providing centralized facilities and training; Dir Dr Lalji Singh; publs *CCMB Highlights, Annual Report*.

Indian Institute of Chemical Biology: 4 Raja S.C. Mullick Rd, Jadavpur, Calcutta 700032; tel. 4735197; telex 021-7108; fax 4735197; e-mail iicb%sirnetc@sirnetd.ernet.in; f. 1956; solution of medical problems through fundamental and applied research in the basic biological sciences, with emphasis on projects bearing directly on the country's current biological and medical needs; library of 30,000 vols; Dir Dr J. Das; publ. *Annual Report*.

Indian Institute of Chemical Technology: Hyderabad 500 007; tel. 7173389; telex 0425-7061; fax 7173387; f. 1944; the first regional laboratory under the Council of Scientific and Industrial Research; research on utilization of regional raw materials and development of industries; physical, analytical, inorganic and organic chemistry; biochemistry; chemical engineering; coal; heavy chemicals and fertilizers; ceramics; essential oils; X-ray crystallography; entomology; library of 40,000 vols, 500 periodicals; Dir Dr K. V. Raghvan; publ. *IICT Bulletin* (quarterly).

Indian Institute of Petroleum: Dehra Dun 248005; tel. 624508; telex 0585-217; fax 671986; f. 1960; research and development in the field of petroleum, natural gas, and petrochemicals and utilisation of petroleum products; trains technical personnel; assists Indian Standards Institution in framing standards for petroleum products; *c.* 700 staff; library of 12,000 vols, 9,000 periodicals; the institute is a Patents Inspection Centre of the Indian Patents Office and is open to the public for studying patent specifications; Dir Prof. T. S. R. Prasada Rao; publs *R & D Newsletter, Petroleum Conservation Abstracts* (quarterly), *Annual Report*.

Industrial Toxicology Research Centre: Mahatma Gandhi Marg, Lucknow, 226001, U.P.; tel. 221856; telex 0535-456; fax 228227; e-mail intox@itrc.sirnetd.ernet.in; f. 1965; studies the effects of industrial pollution; library of 20,205 vols; Dir Dr P. K. SETH.

Institute of Himalayan Bioresources Technology, Palampur: Dist. Kangra, Himachal Pradesh; tel. 30411; fax (1894) 30433; e-mail director@csihbt.ren.nic.in; f. 1983; effective use of the vast resources of Himachal Pradesh, especially the agricultural and forest resources; R&D on forest aspects of tea development technologies and horticulture products, food preserving processes; Dir Dr P. S. AHUJA.

Institute of Microbial Technology: POB 1304, Sector 39A, Chandigarh 160036; tel. 690785; telex 0395-369; fax 690632; e-mail root@csimtech.ren.nic.in; f. 1983; research and development in genetic engineering and microbiology; library of 3,542 vols; Dir Dr AMIT GHOSH.

National Aerospace Laboratories: PB 1779, Kodihalli, Bangalore 560017; tel. 5270584; telex 0845-2279; fax 5260862; e-mail viman@csnal.ren.in; f. 1959; scientific investigations of the problems of flight with a view to their practical application to the design, construction and operation of aircraft in India; library of 58,000 vols; Dir Dr T. S. PRALAHAD; publ. *Newsletter* (quarterly).

National Botanical Research Institute: Rana Pratap Marg, Lucknow 226001; tel. 282879; telex 0535-2315; fax 282881; e-mail manager@nbri.sirnetd.ernet.in; f. 1953; undertakes research into economic botany and collection, introduction, propagation and improvement of ornamental and economic plants; 300 mems; library of 28,600 vols; Dir Dr SUSHIL KUMAR (acting); publs *NBRI Newsletter* (quarterly), *Applied Botany Abstracts* (quarterly).

National Chemical Laboratory: Pune 336151; tel. 336151; telex 0145-7266; fax 330233; e-mail root@csncl.ren.nic.in; f. 1950; physical, inorganic, organic synthesis, polymer chemistries; biochemistry; chemical engineering and process development; houses the National Collection of Industrial Micro-organisms; library of 75,000 vols; Dir Dr PAUL RATNASAMY; publ. *NCL Bulletin* (quarterly).

National Environmental Engineering Research Institute: Nagpur, Maharashtra; tel. 223893; telex 0715-233; fax 225191; e-mail root@csneeri.ren.nic.in; f. 1958; chemical, biological and microbiological research; instrumentation and field investigations; water, sewage, industrial waste, air pollution, industrial hygiene, rural sanitation; library of 20,000 vols; Dir Prof. P. KHANNA; publs. *Paryavaran Patrika, Annual Report*.

National Geophysical Research Institute: Hyderabad 500007; tel. 7171124; telex 0425-7018; fax 7171564; e-mail postmast@ngri.uunet.in; f. 1961; basic and applied research into mineral exploration and investigation of the earth's interior through seismic, geomagnetic, electric, geochemical and paleogeophysical studies; library of 21,300 vols; Dir Dr HARSH K. GUPTA; publs *Bulletin, Observatories Data* (quarterly), *Progress in Geophysics* (annually).

National Institute of Oceanography: Miramar, Panaji, Goa 403004; tel. 221352; telex 0194-216; fax 223340; e-mail ocean@bcgoa.ernet.in; f. 1966; investigates physical, chemical, geological and biological oceanography, also functions as the National Oceanographic Data Centre; research on marine geophysics and instrumentation; maintenance of data pertaining to the Indian Ocean at Planning and Data Division; library of 7,000 vols; Dir Dr E. DESA; publ. *Quarterly Bulletin*.

National Institute of Science, Technology and Development Studies: Hillside Rd, New Delhi 110012; tel. 5746024; telex 031-77182; fax 5787062; e-mail root@csnistad.ren.nic.in; f. 1973 to undertake studies on problems relating to the development of techniques of planning, monitoring and evaluation of research and its utilization; library of 15,000 vols, 250 periodicals; Dir Dr ASHOK JAIN; publ. *Annual Report*.

National Metallurgical Laboratory: Jamshedpur 831007, Singhbhum District, Bihar; tel. 431131; telex 0626-210; fax 426527; f. 1950; ore dressing, production, physical and chemical metallurgy; library of 35,000 vols; Dir Prof. P. R. RAO; publ. *Annual Report*.

National Physical Laboratory: Hillside Rd, New Delhi 110012; tel. 5741440; telex 031-77099; fax 5752678; e-mail root@csnpl.ren.nic.in; f. 1950; fundamental and applied research in physics; maintenance of standards; testing; library of 80,000 vols; Dir Prof. A. K. RAYCHAUDHARY; publs *Sameeksha* (quarterly), *Ionospheric Data* (quarterly), *Annual Report*.

Regional Research Laboratory: Bhubaneswar 4, Orissa; tel. 581126; telex 0675-6275; fax 586126; f. 1964; research in problems relating to the industry and raw materials of the region; Dir Prof. H. S. RAY. publs *RRL Bulletin* (quarterly), *Annual Report*.

Regional Research Laboratory: Canal Rd, Jammu-Tawi, Jammu & Kashmir; tel. 546368; telex 0377-231; fax 548607; f. 1957; drug and medicinal plants; introduction of exotic plants, particularly from temperate zones; plant chemistry, extraction and processing of drugs; library of 18,317 vols; Dir Prof. S. S. HANDA; publ. *Annual Report*.

Regional Research Laboratory: Jorhat, Assam 785000; tel. 320353; telex 0287-204; fax 321158; e-mail director@csrrljt.ren.nic.in; f. 1959; national laboratory, conducting research into such areas as coal, petroleum, pulp and paper, cement, drugs and pharmaceuticals, essential oils and medicinal plants, general and earthquake engineering; library of 6,100 vols; Dir Dr J. S. SANDHU; publs. *RRL News* (monthly), *Annual Report*.

Regional Research Laboratory: Library Building, University of Bhopal, Bhopal 462026; tel. 580836; telex 0287-204; fax 580985; e-mail rrlbho@sirnetd.ernet.in; f. 1981 to undertake research and development projects on minerals and materials with particular focus on aluminium; Dir Prof. T. C. RAO; publ. *Annual Report*.

Regional Research Laboratory: Industrial Estate, Trivandrum; tel. 490324; telex 0435-6232; fax 491712; f. 1976 to develop technologies for the optimal use of regional resources, to help industry in the region through research, development and technology transfer; Dir Dr G. V. NAIR.

Structural Engineering Research Centre: Chennai 600113; tel. 2352139; telex 041-8906; fax 2350508; e-mail sercm@sirnetm.ernet.in; research into steel structures, pressurized vessel structures, large panel prefabrication and welding, structural dynamics, model analysis, shell structures, offshore and marine structures; library of 7,300 vols, 146 periodicals; Dir Dr T. V. S. R. APPA RAO; publ. *Annual Report*.

Structural Engineering Research Centre: Ghaziabad, UP; tel. 721874; telex 0592-204; fax 721882; e-mail root@cssercg.ren.nic.in; f. 1965; research in specialized design and development work in structural problems connected with storage structures, bridges and long span structures, high rise buildings, ferro-cement construction and in problems particular to the terrain of N. India; library of 7,500 vols; Dir V. K. GHANEKAR; publ. *Journal* (quarterly).

AGRICULTURE, FISHERIES AND VETERINARY SCIENCE

Agro-Economic Research Centre: Visva-Bharati University, Santiniketan, West Bengal; tel. (3463) 52751 ext. 338; fax (3463) 52672; e-mail aere@vbharat.ernet.in; f. 1954; conducts research in agricultural economics; library of 6,000 vols; Dir KAZI M. B. RAHIM.

Central Arid Zone Research Institute: Jodhpur 342003; tel. 40584; fax (291) 40706; f. 1959; eight divisions: Resource Survey and Monitoring, Resource Management, Arable Cropping System, Perennial Cropping System, Animal Sciences and Rodent Control, Energy Management, Engineering and Product Processing, Social and Information Science; Outreach programme; regional research stations in Pali, Bikaner, Jaisalmer, Bhuj; library of 17,000 vols, 230 periodicals; Dir Dr A. S. FARODA; publs *Annals of Arid Zone* (quarterly), *Annual Progress Report*.

Central Inland Capture Fisheries Research Institute: PO Barrackpore 743101, West Bengal; tel. (33) 5601190; fax (33) 5600388; f. 1947; research into ecology, fish diseases and their control, fisheries management and exploitation, and fisheries management of selected rivers, small and large reservoirs, ox-bow lakes, estuaries, estuarine wetlands and mangroves; cage culture of carps in reservoirs and lakes; biology and recruitment of important fish and prawns in rivers, reservoirs and estuaries; ecology and production biology of aquatic insects and edible inland molluscs; water pollution studies; extension, information and training programmes in inland fisheries; conservation and environmental monitoring; library of 8,000 vols and 90 journals; Dir Dr M. SINHA; publs *Newsletter* (quarterly), *Indian Fisheries Abstracts* (quarterly).

Central Rice Research Institute: Cuttack, 753006 Orissa; tel. 21887; telex 676220; f. 1946; research on basic and applied aspects of all disciplines of rice culture; 530 mems; library of 12,000 vols, 200 periodicals; Dir Dr H. K. PANDE; publs *Annual Report, Oryza* (quarterly), *Rice Research News* (quarterly).

Central Tobacco Research Institute: Rajahmundry 533105, Andhra Pradesh, SC Rly; tel. (883) 471871; fax (883) 464341; e-mail ctri@x400.nicgw.nic.in; f. 1947; 600 staff; library of 22,000 vols, 173 periodicals; under the Indian Council of Agric. Research (Ministry of Agriculture and Rural Reconstruction, Govt of India); applied and fundamental research on all types of tobacco grown in India; regional stations at Guntur, Vedasandur, Pusa, Hunsur, Dinhata, Jeelugumilli and Kandukur; Dir Dr K. NAGARAJAN; publ. *Newsletter* (4 a year).

Forest Research Institute: New Forest, Dehra Dun 248006; tel. 27021; f. 1906; library of 150,000 vols, 500 periodicals; Dir-Gen. G. P. MAITHANI; publs *Indian Forest Records, Bulletins, Annual Report, FRI Quarterly News Letter*.

Indian Agricultural Statistics Research Institute: Library Ave, New Delhi 110012; tel. 581479; f. 1959; part of ICAR (see below); research in experimental designs, sampling methods and statistical genetics, bio-statistics and statistical economics; conducts postgraduate courses and in-service training; in agricultural statistics and computer application; provides advisory service to agricultural scientists; provides consultancy service in data processing; develops computer software; library of 19,800 vols, 4,500 periodicals; Dir Prof. PREM NARAIN; publs *IASRI Statistical Newsletter* (quarterly), *Technical Reports, Annual Report*.

Indian Council of Agricultural Research (ICAR): Krishi Bhavan, Dr Rajendra Prasad Rd, New Delhi 110001; tel. 388991; telex 031-62249; fax 387293; f. 1929 to promote agricultural and animal husbandry research in conjunction with State Governments, Central and State Research Institutions, etc.; operates through 49 research insts; 30 national research centres; Pres. BAL RAM JAKHAR; Dir-Gen. Dr V. L. CHOPRA; publs *Indian Journal of Agricultural Sciences, Indian Journal of Animal Sciences, Indian Farming, Kheti* (all monthly), *Indian Journal of Fisheries, Indian Journal of Agricultural Engineering, Indian Horticulture, Phal-Phool, Krishi Chayanika* (all quarterly).

Indian Plywood Industries Research Institute: Post Bag No. 2273, Tumkur Rd, Bangalore 560022; tel. 384231; telex 0845-5065; f. 1962; research on sawmilling, plywood manufacturing techniques, preservative treatment of wood and wood-based panels, development of synthetic and natural adhesives; testing of panel products; training in mechanical wood processing technology; library of 8,500 vols; Dir Dr P. M. GANAPATHY.

Indian Veterinary Research Institute: PO Izatnagar 243122, UP; tel. (581) 447069; fax (581) 447284; f. 1889 to undertake research, teaching and extension activities in all aspects of veterinary science and animal husbandry; campuses at Bangalore, Mukteswar and Bhopal; regional stations at Srinagar, Palampur and Calcutta; libraries at Izatnagar and Mukteswar provide 85,000 vols and 547 periodicals; Dir Dr OM SINGH TOMER; publs *Annual Report,* annual scientific reports, bibliographies, catalogues, monographs, etc.

National Dairy Research Institute: Karnal, Haryana 132001; tel. 252800; telex 0396-204; fax 250042; f. 1923; training, research and extension; regional stations at Bangalore, and Kalyani; library of 75,000 vols and 22,000 periodicals; Dir Dr O. S. TOMER; publs *Annual Report, Dairy Samachar* (quarterly).

National Sugar Institute: Kalyanpur, Kanpur 208017, UP; tel: (512) 250541; fax (512) 250247; f. 1936 to undertake research, teaching and consultancy activities in all aspects of sugar technology; library of 7,368 vols; Dir RAM KUMAR; publs *Sharkara, N.S.I. News*.

Rubber Research Institute of India, The: Kottayam 686009, Kerala; tel. 8311; telex 888-285; fax (481) 578317; e-mail rrii-kotm@x400.nicgw.nic.in; f. 1955 to promote the development of the industry; scientific, technological and economic research in improved methods of planting, cultivation, processing and consumption of natural rubber; library of 45,000 vols; Chair. K. J. MATHEW; Rubber Production Commr Dr A. K. KRISHNAKUMAR; Dir of Research Dr N. M. MATHEW; Sec. T. OUSEPH; publs *Indian Journal of Natural Rubber Research, Rubber, Indian Rubber Statistics, Rubber Growers' Companion, Rubber Statistical News, Annual Report.*

Vasantdada Sugar Institute: Manjari (Bk.) 412307, Tal. Haveli, Dist. Pune, Maharashtra; tel. (212) 670650; fax (212) 672735; f. 1975; library of 10,000 vols; Dir-Gen. V. P. RANE.

BIBLIOGRAPHY, LIBRARY SCIENCE AND MUSEOLOGY

Documentation Research and Training Centre (Indian Statistical Institute): 8th Mile, Mysore Rd, R. V. College Post, Bangalore 560059; tel. (8) 8600648; telex 845-8376; fax (8) 8430265; e-mail drtc@isibang.ernet.in; f. 1962; conducts research in the fields of library science, documentation and information science; trains documentalists, provides an advisory service to industry, academic and research institutions; library of 15,000 vols; Head Prof. I. K. RAVICHANDRA RAO; publs *DRTC Annual Seminar, DRTC Refresher Seminar.*

ECONOMICS, LAW AND POLITICS

Gokhale Institute of Politics and Economics: Pune 411004; tel. (212) 350287; fax (212) 352979; e-mail gokhale@pn2.vsnl.net.in; f. 1930; to conduct research into the economic and political problems of India and to train research workers; library of 245,000 vols, 436 periodicals; Dir Prof. V. S. CHITRE; Registrar K. Y. DHAWADE; publs *Artha Vijnana* (quarterly), etc.

Indian Institute of Public Administration, The: Indraprastha Estate, Ring Rd East, New Delhi 110002; tel. 3317309; f. 1954 to promote the study of public administration; research, training, consultancy; library of 185,000 vols, 501 periodicals; Dir M. C. GUPTA; Registrar S. N. SURI; publs *The Indian Journal of Public Administration* (4 a year), *Documentation in Public Administration* (4 a year), *Nagarlok* (4 a year), *Newsletter* (monthly).

Institute for Defence Studies and Analyses, The: Sapru House Annexe, Barakhamba Rd, New Delhi 110001; tel. 3314951; fax 3321851; f. 1965; research on national security, undertakes study on methods of warfare, strategy, disarmament and international relations; library of 45,000 vols, and 1,500 maps; Pres. DINESH SINGH; Dir J. SINGH; publs *Strategic Digest* (monthly), *Strategic Analysis* (monthly), *News Reviews* (monthly).

Institute for Social and Economic Change: Nagarabhavi PO, Bangalore 560072; tel. (80) 3387010; fax (80) 3387008; f. 1972; social and economic development in India; library of 81,000 vols, 300 periodicals; Pres. The Gov. of Karnataka; Dir Dr P. V. SHENOI.

Madras Institute of Development Studies: 79 Second Main Rd, Gandhinagar, Adyar, Chennai 600020; tel. (44) 4412589; fax (44) 4910872; e-mail ssmids@ren.nic.in; f. 1970; aims to contribute to the economic and social development of Tamil Nadu State and India; undertakes studies and research in micro-development problems; aims at upgrading economic research in the South Indian universities through research methodology courses and studies; fosters inter-university co-operation of southern states and promotes inter-disciplinary research; recognized by Univ. of Madras for PhD courses; library of 40,000 vols; Chair Prof. C. T. KURIEN; Dir Dr PAUL P. APPASAMY; publ. *Review of Development and Change* (2 a year).

National Council of Applied Economic Research: Parisila Bhavan, 11 Indraprastha Estate, New Delhi 110002; tel. 3317860; fax 3327164; f. 1956; autonomous research organization to study economic problems for government, international organizations and private business; library of 61,000 vols, 550 periodicals, microfiche collection of census of India 1872–1951; Dir-Gen. Dr RAKESH MOHAN; publs *Margin, Artha Suchi (4 a year), Macro Track* (4 a year).

National Productivity Council: 5–6 Institutional Area, Lodi Rd, New Delhi 110003; tel. (11) 4618480; fax (11) 4615002; e-mail dgnpcind@sansad.nic.in; f. 1958 by the Government of India to help increase productivity in every sector of the national economy; 12 regional directorates (Kanpur, Chandigarh, Calcutta, Madras, Bangalore, Guwahati, Bombay, Ahmedabad, Delhi, Bhopal, Hyderabad, Patna); library of 18,000 vols, 300 journals; Dir-Gen. S. S. SHARMA; publs *Productivity* (quarterly), *Productivity News* (monthly), *Utpadakta* (Hindi, monthly), *Energy Management* (quarterly), *Maintenance* (every 2 months).

EDUCATION

Indian Institute of Advanced Study: Rashtrapati Nivas, Shimla 171005; tel. (177) 230006; fax (177) 231389; f. 1965 to undertake post-doctoral research, especially in the humanities and social sciences; also functions as Inter-University Centre for Humanities and Social Sciences on behalf of the University Grants Commission of India; library of 120,000 vols and 550 periodicals; Dir Prof. MRINAL MIRI; publs two journals.

Indian Psychometric and Educational Research Association: Dept of Education, Patna Training College Campus, Patna 800004; f. 1969 to promote and develop the study of, and undertake research into, psychology, education, statistics, etc.; 330 mems; library of 3,700 vols; Pres. Dr A. K. P. SINHA; Gen. Sec. Dr R. P. SINGH; publ. *Indian Journal of Psychometry and Education.*

National Council of Educational Research and Training: Sri Aurobindo Marg, New Delhi 110016; tel. (11) 666047; telex 31-73024; fax (11) 6868419; e-mail ncert@x400.nicgw.nic.in; f. 1961 with the aim of improving school education; academic adviser to the Ministry of Human Resource Development; co-ordinates research and development in all branches of education; organizes pre- and in-service training; publishes school textbooks, instructional material for teachers and educational surveys; eight major constituent units: National Institute of Education and Central Institute of Educational Technology in New Delhi, Central Institute of Vocational Education in Bhopal and five regional Institutes of Education at Ajmer, Bhopal, Bhubaneswar, Mysore and Shillong; Pres. The Union Minister of Human Resource Development; Dir Dr A. K. SHARMA; publs *Indian Educational Review* (4 a year), *Journal of Indian Education* (6 a year), *Bhartiya Adhunik Shiksha* (4 a year), *Primary Shikshak (4 a year), School Science* (4 a year), *NCERT Newsletter* (monthly), *Primary Teacher* (4 a year).

FINE AND PERFORMING ARTS

National Institute of Design: Paldi, Ahmedabad 380007; tel. 79692; telex 1216322; f. 1961; established by the Government of India as a research, training and service organization in industrial and communication design; Diploma in Design after 2–3 years' training (graduate) or 5 years' training (undergraduate) in Industrial Design or Communication Design; library of 23,000 vols, 130 current periodicals, 75,000 slides, 2,044 tapes and records, 1,545 other audio-visual aids and 600 well-designed objects for reference; Exec. Dir VIKAS SATWALEKAR.

National Research Laboratory for Conservation of Cultural Property: Sector E-3, Aliganj Scheme, Lucknow 226020; tel. and fax (522) 372378; f. 1976 by the Ministry of Human Resource Development, Dept of Culture; conducts research into conservation techniques of objects of art and provides technical assistance to museums and related institutions; training in conservation for Asian countries sponsored by UNESCO; regional laboratory at Mysore; *c.* 50 scientific staff; library of *c.* 12,000 vols, 130 periodical subcriptions; Dir TEJ SINGH.

HISTORY, GEOGRAPHY AND ARCHAEOLOGY

Archaeological Survey of India: Government of India, New Delhi 110011; f. 1902; excavating, preservation, surveying and maintenance of archaeological sites; advanced archaeological training; library of 80,000 vols containing rare material; Dir-Gen. Dr M. S. NAGARAJA RAO; publs *Memoirs, Indian Archaeology—A Review.*

Bihar Research Society: Museum Bldgs, Patna 800001, Bihar; f. 1915; 180 mems; library of 31,000 vols; Pres. Dr J. C. JHA; Sec M. S. PANDEY; publ. *Journal*.

Indian Council of Historical Research: 35 Ferozeshah Rd, New Delhi 110001; tel. 384347; gives grants for doctoral theses, research projects, historical journals, and for bibliographical and documentation works; organizes and supports seminars, workshops and conferences for promotion of historical research; Dir Dr T. R. SAREEN; publ. *The Indian Historical Review.*

Jayaswal, K. P., Research Institute: Patna 800001; f. 1904 to promote historical research; library of 31,650 vols; Dir Dr JATA SHANKAR JHA.

Kamarupa Anusandhana Samiti (Assam Research Society): Gauhati, Assam; f. 1912; historical and archaeological research; 250 mems; Pres. Dr BISWANARAYAN SHASTRI; Joint Sec. ATULANANDA GOSWAMI; publ. *Journal of Assam Research Society* (annually).

Karnatak Historical Research Society: Diwan Bahadur Rodda Rd, Dharwad 1, Karnataka; f. 1914; to promote historical research in the Karnatak; to popularize the study of history and culture by lectures, slides, exhibitions, celebrations of historical events, excursions etc.; sections for research in language, culture and Vedic literature, socio-economic problems; 100 mems; library of 3,000 vols; Pres. RAJA S. G. ACHARYA; Chair. Dr P. R. PANCHAMUKHI; Secs A. R. PANCHAMUKHI, G. G. NADGIR; publs *Karnatak Historical Review* (2 a year in English and Kannada), and research publications.

National Atlas and Thematic Mapping Organisation: 50A Gariahat Rd, Calcutta 700019; tel. 47-9924; telex 21-3287; f. 1956; engaged in cartographical research and preparation of national atlas of India; library of 19,000 vols, 78,000 maps, 350 atlases; Dir A. K. KUNDU; publs *National Atlas of India* (English and Hindi editions), *Irrigation Atlas of India* (in English), *Tourist Atlas of India* (in English), *Atlas of Forest Resources* (in English), *Agricultural Resources Atlas of India* (in English), *Atlas of Water Resources,* other maps and monographs.

Survey of India: Map Record and Issue Office, Hathibarkala, Dehra Dun 248001, UP; f. 1767; engaged in topographical, geographical and geodetic preparation of large scale development project maps; acts as adviser to the Government of India on all survey matters.

LANGUAGE AND LITERATURE

Abul Kalam Azad Oriental Research Institute: Public Gardens, Hyderabad 500004, AP; tel. 230805; f. 1959; research in history, philosophy, culture and languages; Pres. B. PRATAP REDDY; Hon. Sec. and Dir M. K. ALI KHAN; publs various.

Academy of Sanskrit Research: Melkote 571 431, Karnataka State; tel. (8236) 58741; e-mail asrmel@blr.vsnl.net.in; f. 1978; affiliated to Mysore University and Kannada University, Hampi; research and study of Vedas, Agamas and comparative philosophy, with primary focus on Visistadyaita; undergraduate, postgraduate and doctoral courses; library of 23,000 vols, 10,500 palm leaf and paper manuscripts; Pres. M. A. S. RAJAN: Dir M. A. LAKSHMITHATHACHAR; publs *Journal* (2 a year), *Newsletter* (4 a year), critical works in Sanskrit, English and Kannada.

All-India Oriental Conference: Bhandarkar Oriental Research Institute, Pune 411004; f. 1919; 1,350 mems; mem. International Union for Oriental and Asian Studies; academic sessions every two years; Pres. Prof. R. N. DANDEKAR; Sec. Prof. S. D. JOSHI; publs Proceedings of Sessions, *Index of Papers* (in 4 vols).

Anjuman-i-Islam Urdu Research Institute: 92 Dr Dadabhoy Nowroji Rd, Mumbai 400001; tel. 4150177; f. 1947; postgraduate teaching and research in Urdu language and literature, guidance to Ph.D. scholars and organization of lectures and symposia in Urdu; Urdu calligraphy training centre; Urdu teaching for non-Urdu speakers; library of 20,200 vols; Chair. Dr M. J. JAMKHANAWALA; Dir Prof. N. S. GOREKAR; publs *Nawa-e-Adab* (2 a year) and research books (in Urdu).

Bhandarkar Oriental Research Institute: Pune 411004; tel. 356932; f. 1917; Sanskrit, Indological and Oriental studies; library of 94,425 vols, 28,000 MSS; Hon. Sec. Prof. A. M. GHATAGE; publ. *Annals* (annually).

Cama, K. R., Oriental Institute and Library: 136 Mumbai Samachar Marg, Fort, Mumbai 400023; f. 1916; 285 mems; 25,000 vols, 2,000 MSS, 500 journals; Pres. JAMSETJEE JEJEEBHOY; Hon. Sec. H. N. MODI; publ. *Journal* (1 a year).

Deccan College Postgraduate and Research Institute: Yeravada, Pune 411006; tel. 662982; fax (212) 660104; e-mail deccan .college@gems.vsnl.net.in; f. 1939; postgraduate research in linguistics, archaeology, history and Vedic Sanskrit; library of 130,000 vols, 12,000 MSS; Dirs Dr V. N. MISRA, Dr K. PADDAYYA; publ. *Annual Bulletin*.

Ganganatha Jha Kendriya Sanskrit Vidyapeetha (Central Sanskrit Research Institute): Azad Park, Allahabad 211002, UP; tel. 600957; f. 1943; research into Sanskrit and other Indological subjects; library of 60,000 vols, 50,000 MSS; Principal Dr G. C. TRIPATHI; publs *Quarterly Research Journal,* catalogues, bibliographies, Sanskrit texts and studies.

Gujarat Research Society: Dr Madhuri Shah Campus, Ramkrishna Mission Marg, Khar (West), Mumbai 400052; tel. 6462691; fax 6047398; f. 1936 to organize and co-ordinate research in social and cultural activities; teacher-training; library of 10,000 vols; Pres. K. P. HAZARAT; publ. *Journal* (quarterly).

International Academy of Indian Culture: J 22 Hauz Khas Enclave, New Delhi 110016; tel. 6515800; f. 1935 to study India's artistic, literary and historic relations with other Asian countries; library of 80,000 vols, 40,000 MSS; Pres. Dr LOKESH CHANDRA; publ. *Satapitaka Series* (irregular).

Kuppuswami Sastri Research Institute: 84 Thiru V. Kalayanasundaranar Rd, Mylapore, Chennai 600004; tel. 847320; f. 1944; govt-sponsored and affiliated to University of Madras; promotion of Oriental learning especially Indology; lectures, seminars and workshops; 400 mems; library of 30,000 vols (including palm-leaf manuscripts); Dir Dr S. S. JANAKI; publs *Journal of Oriental Research* and numerous research publs.

Mumbai Marathi Granth Sangrahalaya: Dadar, Mumbai 400014; f. 1898; research in Marathi language and literature; library of 185,020 vols; Pres. S. K. PATIL.

Nava Nalanda Mahavihara (Nalanda Institute of Buddhist Studies and Pali): PO Nalanda, Bihar 803111; tel. and fax (6112) 74820; f. 1951; administered by Dept of Culture, Ministry of Human Resources Development; studies and research in Pali, Buddhism, philosophy, ancient Indian and Asian studies; diploma in languages: Chinese, Japanese, Tibetan, Hindi, Sanskrit and Pali; library of 36,000 vols; Dir Prof. Dr DIPAK KUMAR BARUA; publs *Pali Tipitaki, Atthakatha.*

Oriental Institute of Indian Languages: 32 Khorsheed Bldgs, PM Rd, Mumbai 400001; founded to promote inter-regional and intercontinental understanding through the study of languages; Secs A. RAHIM, A. A. ABEDI.

Oriental Research Institute: Mysore, 570005; tel. 23136; library of 28,300 vols and 50 periodicals; collection of 60,000 ancient MSS; Dir K. RAJAGOPALACHAR.

Sri Venkateswara University Oriental Research Institute: Tirupati, Andhra Pradesh 517502; tel. 24166; fax 24111; f. 1939; given by T. T. DEVASTHANAMS to the University in 1956; research in language and literature, philosophy and religion, art and archaeology, ancient Indian history and culture; library of 30,000 vols, 16,948 palm leaf and paper MSS; Dir M. SRIMANNARAYA MURTI; publs *SVU Oriental Journal* and other treatises.

Vishveshvaranand Vedic Research Institute: Sadhu Ashram PO, Hoshiarpur 146021; tel. 23582; f. 1903; 3,230 mems; academic and cultural studies on Indian literatures and religion; Pres. Prof. G. P. CHOPRA; Dir Prof. S. BHASKARAN NAIR; publs *Vishva Jyoti* (cultural, Hindi monthly), *Vishva Samskritam* (cultural research, Sanskrit quarterly), *Vishveshvaranand Indological Series,* etc.

Attached institute:

Vishveshvaranand Vishva Bandhu Institute of Sanskrit and Indological Studies: Hoshiarpur 146021; tel. 21002; f. 1965; postgraduate teaching, research and study in Indology; 37 fellows; library of 77,675 vols, 10,000 ancient MSS; Chair. Dr GIRISH CHANDRA OJHA; publs *Vishveshvaranand Indological Journal* (research, English, 2 a year), *Panjab University Indological Series.*

MEDICINE

B.M. Institute of Mental Health: Ashram Rd, Navragpura, Ahmedabad 380009, Gujarat; tel. (79) 6578256; f. 1951; comprehensive mental health services, teaching, and research; psychiatric clinic for the emotionally disturbed; clinic for children with learning difficulties; occupational therapy and rehabilitation services; speech clinic; postgraduate training in psychodiagnostics and counselling; offers diploma in working with the developmentally handicapped; library of 6,484 vols; Dir Dr RAO DUGGIRALA; publ. *Mental Health Review* (1 a year).

Cancer Research Institute: Tata Memorial Centre, Parel, Mumbai 400012; tel. (22) 4123803; fax (22) 4146089; e-mail cril@ soochak.nest.ernet.in; library of 14,000 vols; Dir Dr A. N. BHISEY.

Central Jalma Institute for Leprosy: Taj Ganj, Agra 282001, UP; tel. 331751; fax 331755; f. 1966; part of Indian Council of Medical Research; treatment, research and training; library of 2,496 books, 40 journals; Dir Dr U. SENGUPTA; publ. *Quarterly Bulletin.*

Central Leprosy Teaching and Research Institute: POB 24, Thirumani, Chingalpattu, Tamil Nadu 603001; tel. (4114) 26274; fax (4114) 26064; f. 1955; a WHO regional training centre; library of 10,000 vols, 52 periodicals; Dir Dr K. V. KRISHNAMOORTHY; publs *News Bulletin* (4 a year), *Annual Report*.

Central Research Institute: Kasauli, Himachal Pradesh; f. 1905; medical research, graduate and postgraduate training, manufacture of biological products; Institute of the Govt of India; library of 30,000 vols; Dir Dr J. SOKHEY; publ. *Annual Scientific Report*.

Haffkine Institute for Training, Research and Testing: Acharya Donde Marg, Parel, Mumbai 400012; tel. (22) 4160847; fax (22) 4150826; f. 1897; principal centre of research in communicable diseases, biomedical and allied sciences in India; library of 40,000 vols; Depts: Bacteriology, Biochemistry, Chemotherapy, Clinical Pathology, Immunology, Pharmacology and Phytochemistry, Radiation Biology Unit, Testing Unit, Zoonosis, Human Pharmacology and Virology, each with its staff of scientists; Dir Dr V. L. YEMUL; publ. *Annual Report*.

Indian Brain Research Association: Dept of Biochemistry Calcutta University, 35 Ballygunge Circular Rd, Calcutta 700019; f. 1964; 300 mems; library of 2,000 vols; Pres. and Ed. Sec. Prof. J. J. GHOSH; publ. *Brain News* (2 a year).

Indian Council of Medical Research: Medical Enclave, Ansari Nagar, POB 4911, New Delhi 110029; tel. 667136; telex 031-73067; fax 6868662; f. 1911; promotes, co-ordinates and funds medical research; maintains the National Institute of Nutrition (Hyderabad), National Institute of Virology (Pune), Tuberculosis Research Centre (Madras), National Institute of Cholera and Enteric Diseases (Calcutta), Institute of Pathology (New Delhi), National Institute of Occupational Health (Ahmedabad), Institute of Immunohaematology (Mumbai), Institute for Research in Reproduction (Mumbai), Entero Virus Research Centre (Mumbai), Vector Control Research Centre (Pondicherry), Central Jalma Institute for Leprosy (Agra), Malaria Research Centre (Delhi), Institutes for Research in Medical Statistics (New Delhi and Madras), Inst. of Cytology and Preventive Oncology (New Delhi), Rajendra Memorial Research Institute of Medical Sciences (Patna), National AIDS Research Institute (Pune), Laboratory Animal Information Service, Food and Drug Toxicology Research Centre (both Hyderabad), Centre for Research in Medical Entomology (Madurai), Genetics Research Centre (Mumbai), and six Regional Medical Research Centres (Bhubaneswar, Dibrugarh, Jabalpur, Jodhpur, Port Blair, Belgaum); library of 5,000 vols; Dir-Gen. G. V. SATYAVATI; publs *Indian Journal of Medical Research* (monthly, with supplements), *ICMR Bulletin* (monthly), *Indian Journal of Malariology* (quarterly), Annual Reports of the Council, Special Reports, etc.

Institute of Child Health: 11 Dr Biresh Guha St, Calcutta 700017; f. 1953; affiliated to College for Child Health, Calcutta University; Dir Dr SISIR KUMAR BOSE; departments of Clinical Paediatrics, Paediatric Surgery, Biochemistry, Radiology, Pathology, Preventive Paediatrics, Physiotherapy, Psychiatry, Dermatology, Ophthalmology and Oto-rhinolaryngology.

King Institute of Preventive Medicine: Guindy, Chennai 600032; f. 1899; postgraduate training in microbiology; library of 20,137 vols; Dir Dr K. V. MURTHY; publ. *Annual Report*.

National Institute of Communicable Diseases: 22 Sham Nath Marg, Delhi 110054; tel. 2913148; fax 2922677; e-mail dir-nicd@x400.nicgw.nic.in; f. 1963; formerly Malaria Institute of India, f. 1909; research and training centre in field of communicable and vector-borne diseases; brs at Alwar (Rajasthan), Coonoor (Tamil Nadu) and Jagdalpur (Madhya Pradesh) (all for research and training in epidemiology), Calicut (Kerala), Rajahmundry (Andhra Pradesh) and Varanasi (Uttar Pradesh) (all for research and training on helminthology), Patna (medical entomology and vector control), Bangalore (zoonosis); library of 32,000 vols, 252 maps, 89 photocopies; Dir Dr JOTNA SOKHEY; publ. *CD Alert* (monthly).

Attached institute:

National Malaria Eradication Programme: 22 Sham Nath Marg, Delhi 110054; tel. 2918576; fax 2518329; f. 1958; co-ordination, technical guidance, planning, monitoring and evaluation of a nation-wide malaria control and eradication programme; library of 4,000 vols; Dir Dr RAM SWAROOP SHARMA.

National Institute of Nutrition: Indian Council of Medical Research, Jamai-Osmania, Hyderabad 500007, Andhra Pradesh; tel. 7018909; fax 7019074; e-mail icmrnin@ren.nic.in; f. 1918; principal research and training centre for South and South-East Asia; includes centres for Food and Drug Toxicology Research and National Centre for Laboratory Animal Sciences; library of 14,000 vols, 23,563 periodicals; Dir Dr KAMALA KRISHNASWAMY; Documentation Officer K. SAMPATHACHARY; publs *Annual Report, Nutrition* (4 a year), *Nutrition News* (6 a year), *NCLAS Newsletter* (2 a year).

National Tuberculosis Institute: Govt of India, 'Avalon', 8 Bellary Rd, Bangalore 560003; tel. 362431; f. 1959; 240 mems; research in epidemiology, applied tuberculosis bacteriology, sociological aspects and systems research with regard to tuberculosis control; training and control programme; Dir K. CHAUDHURI; publ. *Newsletter* (quarterly).

Pasteur Institute and Medical Research Institute: Shillong, Assam; f. 1915; library of 7,311 vols; Dir N. G. BANERJEE.

Pasteur Institute of India: Coonoor 643103 (Nilgiris), Tamil Nadu; tel. (4264) 21250; telex 853-203; fax (4264) 21655; f. 1907; work on virus diseases incl. rabies, development of vaccines; a WHO international reference centre for quality control and production of rabies vaccines; library of 20,000 vols; Dir Dr G. L. N. PRASAD RAO.

Vallabhbhai Patel Chest Institute: POB 2101, University of Delhi, Delhi 110007; tel. (11) 7256180; fax (11) 7257420; e-mail vpic@delnet.ren.nic.in; f. 1951; postgraduate teaching and research in respiratory diseases and allied biomedical sciences; library of 25,000 vols; Dir Prof. H. S. RANDHAWA; publ. *Indian Journal of Chest Diseases and Allied Sciences* (quarterly).

Vector Control Research Centre: Medical Complex, Indira Nagar, Pondicherry 605006; tel. 37896; telex 0469202; f. 1975; part of Indian Ccl of Medical Research, and affiliated with Central Univ., Pondicherry; research and postgraduate training; 20 students; library of 10,000 vols, 104 periodicals and 2,700 reprints; Dir Dr V. DHANDA; publs *Annual Reports*.

NATURAL SCIENCES

General

Bose Institute: 93/1 Acharya Prafulla Chandra Rd, Calcutta 700009; tel. 350-7073; f. 1917; research in biology, cytogenetics, mutation, physiological genetics, antibiotics, biochemistry, molecular biology, biotechnology, microbiology, immunology, environmental sciences, chemistry of plant products, physical chemistry, radiation and nuclear physics, solid state physics, biophysics; experimental stations at Falta, Shamnagar, Madhyamgram and Darjeeling; library of 24,883 vols; Dir Prof. P. K. RAY; publs *Transactions, Annual Report, News Letter*.

Indian Association for the Cultivation of Science (IACS): Jadavpur, Calcutta 700032; tel. 473-4971; telex 021-5501; fax 73-2805; f. 1876; research in theoretical physics, spectroscopy, material science, solid state physics, physical chemistry, biological chemistry, energy research unit, polymer science unit, organic and inorganic chemistry; 1,600 mems; library of 57,000 vols; Pres. Prof. A. K. SHARMA; Dir Prof. D. CHAKRABORTY; publs *Indian Journal of Physics, Bulletin of the IACS* and special publications.

Raman Research Institute: C. V. Raman Ave, Sadashivanagar, Bangalore 560080; tel. (80) 3340122; fax (80) 3340492; e-mail root@rri.ernet.in; f. 1948; liquid crystals, astrophysics, radio astronomy, theoretical physics and optics; library of 19,000 vols and 22,000 periodicals; Dir Prof. N. KUMAR.

Tata Institute of Fundamental Research: Homi Bhabha Rd, Mumbai 400005; tel. 215-2971; telex 011-83009; fax 215-2110; f. 1945; nat. govt research centre; fundamental research in pure and applied mathematics, theoretical physics, astronomy and astro-physics, experimental high-energy physics and gravitation, nuclear and atomic physics, condensed-matter physics and materials science, chemistry and biology, epidemiology and dental science; National Centre for Radio Astrophysics, National Centre for Biological Sciences, Homi Bhabha Centre for Science Education; library of 100,000 vols; Dir Prof. S. S. JHA.

Unesco New Delhi Office: 8 Poorvi Marg, Vasant Vihar, New Delhi 110057; tel. (11) 6147310; telex 3165896; fax (11) 6143351; e-mail in!unesco.newdelhi@unesco.org; f. 1948; covers countries of South and Central Asia, working in co-operation with national and regional organizations; activities in all areas of Unesco competence: special focus on science and technology for development, science for progress and the environment, environment and natural resources management; documentation centre of 31,000 Unesco documents, reports, etc.; special collections: science and technology, education, social sciences, culture and communication; films library, posters; Dir Prof. M. DE GIADI; publ *UNESCO New Delhi Fact Sheet* (quarterly), *Library Accession List, Select List of Periodicals* (monthly).

Biological Sciences

Birbal Sahni Institute of Palaeobotany: 53 University Rd, Lucknow 226007; tel. (522) 324291; fax (522) 381948; e-mail bsip@bsip.sirnetd.ernet.in; f. 1946; scientific research on the fundamental and applied aspects of fossil plants and their bearing on the origins of life; evolutionary linkages; biostratigraphy; fossil fuel exploration; phytogeography and biodiagenesis; repository of fossil plants; library of 5,000 vols, 10,000 current periodicals, 35,000 reprints and 300 microfilms, etc; Dir Dr G. RAJAGOPALAN (acting); publ. *The Palaeobotanist* (3 a year).

Botanical Survey of India: P/8 Brabourne Rd, Calcutta 700001; tel. 2424922; fax (33) 2429330; f. 1890; botanical surveys and research; Headquarters: Central National Herbarium and Indian Botanic Garden at Howrah; Industrial Section, Indian Museum at Calcutta; regional circles at Allahabad, Pune, Coimbatore, Jodhpur, Port Blair, Shillong, Dehra Dun, Itanagar and Gangtok; library of over 2.5 lakhs vols; 491 scientific staff; Dir Dr B. D. SHARMA; publs *Bulletin* (quarterly), *Reports* (annually), *Indian Floras*, etc.

Indian Association of Systematic Zoologists: c/o Zoological Survey of India, 34 Chittaranjan Ave, Calcutta 700012; f. 1947; Pres. Dr A. P. KAPUR.

Institute of Plant Industry: Indore, Madhya Pradesh; f. 1924; research in cotton genetics, and in crop improvement of cotton and rotation crops; Dir RAI BAHADUR R. L. SETHI.

Tropical Botanic Garden and Research Institute: Pacha-Palode, Trivandrum 695562, Kerala; tel. (472) 84236; fax (471) 437230; f. 1979; to establish a botanical garden, an arboretum, a medicinal plant garden and laboratories for botanical, horticultural, plant biotechnical ethnomedicinal, ethnopharmacological and phytochemical research; conservation of rare and endangered tropical plant species; promotion of research and development studies of plants of medicinal and economic importance; library of 5,000 vols, 65 journals; herbarium of 17,800 mounted specimens and 30,000 duplicates of vascular plants; museum; Dir Dr P. PUSHPANGADAN; publs *Annual Report, Index Seminum, Information Brochures, Quarterly Newsletter.*

Zoological Survey of India: M Block, New Alipur, Calcutta 700053; f. 1916; activities include maintenance of National Zoological Collections, conduct of faunistic surveys and research on systematic zoology, wildlife, environmental conservation, etc; regional stations at Berhampur, Canning, Dehra Dun, Digha, Hyderabad, Itanagar, Jabalpur, Jodhpur, Kozhikode, Madras, Patna, Port Blair, Pune, Shillong, Solan; library of 60,000 vols, 800 periodicals; Dir Dr ASISH K. GHOSH; publs *Records* (quarterly), *Memoirs, Annual Reports, Fauna of India, Occasional Papers, Handbooks, State Fauna Series, Bibliography of Indian Zoology, and a series of monographs.*

Mathematical Sciences

Indian Statistical Institute: 203 Barrackpore Trunk Rd, Calcutta, 700035; tel. (33) 5778085; fax (33) 5776680; f. 1931 to promote knowledge of and research on statistics and other subjects relating to national development and social welfare and to provide for, and undertake, the collection of information, investigations, projects and operational research for planning and the improvement of the efficiency of management and production; departments of theoretical statistics, applied statistics and computing, social sciences, physical and earth sciences, statistical quality control and operational research, biological sciences, library, documentation and information science; maintains research units, laboratories; conducts courses leading to the Bachelor's, Master's and doctorate degrees; specialized library of 200,000 vols and 2,500 current periodicals; Chair. P. N. HAKSAR; Dir Prof. S. B. RAO; publs *Sankhya: The Indian Journal of Statistics, Technical Reports, Memoranda*.

Institute of Mathematical Sciences: CIT Campus, Taramani, Chennai 600113; tel. (44) 2351856; telex 0418960; fax (44) 2350586; e-mail postmaster@imsc.ernet.in; f. 1962; research in pure and applied mathematics, theoretical physics and theoretical computer science; library of 37,000 vols, 250 periodicals; Dir Prof. R. RAMACHANDRAN; publs *I.M.Sc. Reports*, etc.

Physical Sciences

Alipore Observatory and Meteorological Office: Calcutta; f. 1877; publ. *The India Meteorological Department.*

Astronomical Observatory: Presidency College, Calcutta; f. 1898; Dir Dr P. CHOUDHURY.

Astronomical Observatory of St Xavier's College: 30 Park St, Calcutta 700016; f. 1875; Dir Rev. F. GOREUX.

Bhabha Atomic Research Centre: Trombay, Mumbai 400085, Maharashtra; tel. (22) 5563060; telex 011-61017; fax (22) 5560750; f. 1957; national centre for research in and development of nuclear energy for peaceful purposes; facilities include: three research reactors; Van de Graaff accelerator; laboratories at Srinagar, Gulmarg, and Gauribidanur; isotope production unit; central workshops; pilot plants for production of heavy water, zirconium, titanium, etc.; uranium metal plant; food irradiation and processing laboratory; reactor engineering laboratory and test facilities; library of 160,000 vols, 1,600 technical journals, over 800,000 technical reports; Dir ANIL KAKODKAR; publs. *Newsletter* (monthly), *Annual Report*.

Central Seismological Observatory: Shillong; headquarters at New Delhi.

Geodetic and Research Branch, Survey of India: POB 77, Dehra Dun 248001; f. 1800; geodetic and allied geophysical activities, including development and research of instrumentation; library of 55,000 vols; Dir Dr M. G. ARUR; publs reports and technical publications.

Geological Survey of India: 29 J. L. Nehru Rd, Calcutta 700016; tel. 2497645; f. 1851; devoted to study of geology, geophysics, engineering geology, mineral resources, exploration and research; library of 500,500 vols; Dir-Gen. D. B. DIMRI; Dir S. GHOSH; publs *News, Bulletin, Indian Geoscience Abstracts,* etc.

India Meteorological Department: Lodi Rd, New Delhi 110003; tel. (11) 4619415; telex 31-66494; fax (091-11) 4669216; e-mail rrkelkar@imd.ernet.in; f. 1875; six regional offices at New Delhi, Mumbai, Calcutta, Madras, Nagpur and Guwahati; 11 meteorological centres at Thiruvananthapuram, Bangalore, Hyderabad, Bhubaneshwar, Lucknow, Jaipur, Srinagar, Ahmedabad, Patna, Chandigarh and Bhopal; 10 cyclone detection radars; Positional Astronomy Centre at Calcutta; provides weather service; scientific activities cover research in all branches of meteorology, including agricultural and hydrometeorology, radio-meteorology, satellite and environmental meteorology, atmospheric electricity, seismology; New Delhi is Regional Telecommunication Hub and Regional Meteorological Centre under WMO World Weather Watch; Regional Specialised Meteorological Centre for Tropical Cyclones; also Regional Area Forecast Centre under ICAO; Dir-Gen. Dr R. R. KELKAR (acting); publs *Indian Astronomical Ephemeries* (annually), *Mausam* (quarterly), *Indian Weather Review, Regional / State Daily Weather Reports,* occasional Memoirs, Monographs and Reviews.

Indian Bureau of Mines: 'Indira Bhavan', Civil Lines, Nagpur 440001; tel. (712) 524500; fax (712) 533041; f. 1948; Government dept responsible for the conservation and development of mineral resources and protection of mining environment; aid in mine and mineral development, technical consultancy in mining and mineral processing, collection and dissemination of mineral statistics and information, preparation of feasibility reports of mining projects, including benefication plants, and preparation of environmental management plans; conducts market surveys on minerals and mineral commodities; regional offices at Ajmer, Bangalore, Calcutta, Chennai, Dehradun, Goa, Hyderabad, Jabalpur, Nagpur, Ranchi, Udaipur; library of 50,000 vols, 300 periodicals; Controller-Gen. A. N. BOSE (acting); publs *Indian Minerals Yearbook, Monthly Statistics of Mineral Production,* bulletins.

Indian Institute of Astrophysics: Bangalore 560034; tel. (80) 5530672; fax (80) 5534043; f. 1786 as private observatory in Madras; specializes in the study of solar physics, stellar physics, solar system objects, theoretical astrophysics including ionosphere, cosmology, solar-terrestrial relationship and instrumentation; library of more than 10,000 vols; field stations at Kavalur, Kodaikanal and Gauribidanur; Dir Prof. R. COWSIK; publs *Bulletins, Annual Reports, Reprints*.

Indian Institute of Geomagnetism: Colaba, Mumbai 400005; tel. 2150293; telex 1185928; fax 2189568; f. 1971; observatories in Alibag, Annamalainagar, Trivandrum, Jaipur, Nagpur, Ujjain, Gulmarg, Shillong, Pondicherry, Tirunelveli, Vishakapatnam; World Data Centre WDC-C2 for geomagnetism; operates geomagnetic observatory over Antarctica, records geomagnetic pulsations and ionospheric scintillations, airglow observations, study of atmospheric tides in 60–100 km height range with partial reflection radar, crustal magnetic anomalies, palaeomagnetic studies and magnetic petrology, magnetotelluric studies, geomagnetic depth sounding, deep electrical sounding, equatorial electrojet studies, ocean bottom geoelectromagnetism, physics of ionospheric-magnetospheric processes, globalelectric circuit, electrodynamics of the middle atmosphere, crustal deformation studies through global positioning satellites; library of 15,000 vols (books, bound periodicals and magnetic data); Dir Prof. B. P. SINGH; publs *Newsletter, Indian Magnetic Data, Annual Report.*

Indian Space Research Organization (ISRO): Antariksh Bhavan, New BEL Rd, Bangalore 560094; f. 1969; development of satellites, launch vehicles and ground stations for satellite-based communications, resources survey and meteorological services; operates Vikram Sarabhai Space Centre, Space Applications Centre at Ahmedabad, ISRO Satellite Centre at Bangalore, SHAR Centre at Sriharikota Island, Liquid Propulsion System Unit at Trivandrum and Bangalore, Development & Educational Communications Unit at Ahmedabad, ISRO Telemetry Tracking and Command Network at Bangalore, ISRO Inertial Systems Unit, Trivandrum, INSAT Master Control Facility, Hassan; the Nat. Remote Sensing Agency at Hyderabad, the Physical Research Laboratory at Ahmedabad and the Nat. Mesosphere-Stratosphere-Troposphere Radar Facility at Gadanki are grant-in-aid instns; Chair. Dr K. KASTURIRANGAN; Scientific Sec. K. R. SRIDHAR MURTHY.

Indira Gandhi Centre for Atomic Research: Kalpakkam 603102, Tamil Nadu; tel. (4114) 40240; fax (4114) 40360; e-mail dir@igcar.ernet.in; f. 1969; attached to Dept of Atomic Energy, Govt of India; research in Fast Reactor technology and related disciplines; library of 62,000 vols, 655 journals, 195,000 research reports; Dir Dr PLACID RODRIGUEZ; publs *Newsletter* (6 a year), *IGC Highlights* (2 a year).

Institute for Plasma Research: Bhat, Gandhinagar 382428; tel. (79) 2864690; telex 121-7016; fax (79) 2864310; f. 1986; research in plasma physics; library of 12,000 vols, 7,800 technical reports, 950 reprints, 119 periodicals; Dir P. K. KAW; publ. *Plasma Processing Update*.

Inter-University Centre for Astronomy and Astrophysics: Post Bag 4, Ganeshkhind, Pune 411 007; tel. (212) 351414; fax (212) 350760; e-mail root@iucaa.ernet.in; f. 1988; fundamental research and training in all aspects of astronomy and astrophysics; MSc and PhD, refresher courses, research workshops, etc.; Dir Prof. JAYANT V. NARLIKAR; publs *Khagol* (quarterly), *Annual Report, Lecture Notes*.

Mining, Geological and Metallurgical Institute of India: 29 Chowringhee Rd, Calcutta 700016; tel. 2491751; f. 1906; library of *c.* 3,500 vols; Pres. U. KUMAR; Hon. Sec. R. P. BHATNAGAR; publs *Transactions* (2 a year), *Newsletter* (every 2 months).

National Institute of Rock Mechanics: Champion Reefs P.O., Kolar Gold Fields 563117, Karnataka; tel. (8153) 61169; telex 0843215; fax (8153) 60937; e-mail nirm@giasbg01.vsnl.net.in; f. 1989; library of 1,400 vols; Dir Dr N. M. RAJU; publs *Bulletin* (3 a year), *Annual Report*.

Nizamiah and Japal-Rangapur Observatories and Centre of Advanced Study in Astronomy: Osmania University, Hyderabad 500007; tel. (40) 7017306; e-mail pies@ouastr.ernet.in; f. 1908, transferred to control of Osmania Univ. 1919; library of 15,000 vols, 4,000 periodicals; Dir Prof. P. V. SUBRAHMANYAM; publ. *Astronomical*.

Physical Research Laboratory: Ahmedabad 380009; tel. 462129; telex 0121-6397; fax 6560502; f. 1947; 500 mems; library of 50,000 vols, 2,500 scientific reports and 1,200 maps; centre for space research and postgraduate studies leading to Ph.D. degree; research in atmospheric sciences and planetary aeronomy, optical, infrared and radio astronomy (interplanetary scintillations), astrophysics, atomic and molecular physics, nuclear and particle physics, laser physics and quantum optics, plasma theory and experiment, oceanography and climate studies, solar systems and geochronology; Dir Prof. G. S. AGARWAL.

Saha Institute of Nuclear Physics: 1/AF, Bidhannagar, Calcutta 700064; tel. (33) 33753459; fax (33) 3374637; e-mail public@lib163.saha.ernet.in; f. 1951; library of 60,000 books and journals and 21,000 reports; research and teaching in nuclear and allied sciences; Dir Prof. BIKASH SINHA.

PHILOSOPHY AND PSYCHOLOGY

Pratap Centre of Philosophy: Dept of Philosophy, University of Poona, Amalner, District Jalgaon, Maharashtra 425401; tel. Amalner 280; f. 1916 as Indian Inst. of Philosophy, taken over by Univ. and renamed 1972; comparative study of Indian and European philosophy; 12 mems; library of 6,000 vols; 3 fellowships awarded yearly for research; Dir J. V. JOSHI; publs *Indian Philosophical Quarterly* (English), *Paramarsh* (Marathi, Hindi).

Yoga Institute, The: Santa Cruz, Mumbai 400055; tel. 6122185; f. 1918 to promote self-education, physical, mental, moral and psychic, aided by the science of Yoga; to conduct academic and scientific research in Yoga culture and technique; conducts teacher training Institute of Yoga and a Clinical and Psychosomatic Hospital based on Yoga; library of 3,000 vols; Dir Dr J. YOGENDRA; publs *Yoga Studies, Cyclopaedia Yoga, Yoga and Total Health* (monthly), and other literature.

RELIGION, SOCIOLOGY AND ANTHROPOLOGY

Anjuman-i-Islam Islamic Research Association: 92 Dadabhoy Nowroji Rd, Mumbai 400001; library of 5,000 vols; Pres. Dr M. ISHAQUE JAMKHANAWALA; Dir Prof. N. S. GOREKAR; publs 12 vols of research work on Islamic studies.

Anthropological Survey of India: 27 Jawaharlal Nehru Rd, Calcutta 700016; tel. (33) 249-8731; fax (33) 249-7696; f. 1945; research in cultural and physical anthropology, human ecology, linguistics, psychology, folklore, biochemistry and radiology; library of 40,935 vols; Dir Dr R. K. BHATTACHARYA publ. *Journal* (quarterly).

Applied Interdisciplinary Development Research Institute: 10 Nelson Manickam Rd, 2nd floor, Choolaimedu, Chennai 600094; f. 1985; interdisciplinary development education, training, research, consultancy, information dissemination; Exec. Dir Dr A. PETER.

Ethnographic and Folk Culture Society: POB 209, L-11/31 Sector B, Aliganj Housing Scheme, Lucknow 226024; tel. 372362; fax 338872; f. 1945; research in anthropological sciences; museum of Folk Life and Culture; library; 575 life mems; Pres. Prof. B. SINGH; Hon. Gen. Sec. Dr NADEEM HASNAIN; publs *The Eastern Anthropologist* (quarterly), *Manav* (Hindi, quarterly), *Indian Journal of Physical Anthropology and Human Genetics* (2 a year), Monographs, Folk Culture Series, Rural Profiles, Human Genetics, Pre-history, Museology, Man and Society, etc.

Indian Council of Social Science Research: JNU Institutional Area, Asuna Asaf Ali Marg, New Delhi 110067; tel. (11) 6176771; telex 3160183; fax (11) 6179836; regional centres in Mumbai, Calcutta, Chandigarh, Delhi, Hyderabad, and Shillong; f. 1969; sponsors and co-ordinates research in social science, provides financial assistance for research programmes, awards fellowships and grants; sponsors conferences, seminars, training programmes and publications; provides partial support to 28 social science research institutes; collaborates with international bodies in research programmes; National Social Science Documentation Centre (NASSDOC: see Libraries); Data Archives; library of 35,000 monographs, 150,000 serial vols; Chair. Dr D. M. NANJUNDAPPA; Member-Sec. Dr R. BARMAN CHANDRA; publs *Surveys of Research in Social Sciences, Newsletter* (quarterly), *ICSSR Journal of Abstracts and Reviews, ICSSR Research Abstracts Quarterly, Indian Psychological Abstracts and Reviews,* etc.

Indian Institute of Population Studies: Gandhinagar, Chennai 600020; Dir Dr S. CHANDRASEKHAR; publ. *Population Review* (2 a year).

Institute of Applied Manpower Research: Indraprastha Estate, Ring Rd, New Delhi 110002; tel. (11) 3317849; fax (11) 3319909; e-mail iamr@del2.vsnl.net.in; f. 1962; autonomous body under Planning Commission; studies and disseminates information on the nature, characteristics and utilization of human resources in India; develops methodologies for forecasting demand and supply; organizes seminars, conferences, study courses and training programmes in techniques of manpower planning at nat. and int. levels and provides consultancy services; library of 21,000 vols, 150 journals; Pres. Hon. JASWANT SINGH; Dir Prof. ASHOKA CHANDRA; publs *Manpower Journal, Manpower Documentation* (4 a year), *Manpower Profile, India* (1 a year), *Technical Manpower Profile, India and the States*(1 a year).

Institute of Economic Growth: University Enclave, Delhi 110007; f. 1958; an autonomous body recognized by the University of Delhi as a national-level multidisciplinary centre for advanced research and training, including Ph.D. supervision in the fields of economic and social development; specialized library and documentation service; Dir Prof. S. N. MISHRA; publs *Contributions to Indian Sociology: New Series* (2 a year), *Studies in Asian Social Development* (occasionally), *Studies in Economic Development and Planning.*

National Institute of Rural Development: Rajendranagar, Hyderabad 500030; tel. (40) 4015001; telex 0425-6510; fax (40) 4015277; f. 1958; autonomous servicing and consultancy agency for central and state governments; training for government and non-government officials; a Centre on Rural Documentation (CORD) provides computerized library services; development research into all facets of rural life; offers consultancy service to national and international organizations; aims to repackage govt and other literature on rural development for wider dissemination; library of 85,000 vols; Dir-Gen. R. C. CHOWDHURY; publs *CORD Index* (monthly), *Journal of Rural Development* (quarterly), *Newsletter, CORD Abstracts* (every 2 months), *CORD Alerts* (fortnightly), *Research Highlights, Handbook of Rural Development Statistics* (annually), etc.

National Labour Institute: AB–6, Safdarjang Enclave, New Delhi 110029; f. 1964 as Indian Inst. of Labour Studies; research, training and consultancy; library of 22,000 vols; Dir Dr H. PAIS; publs *Bulletin, Awards Digest* (monthly).

Rural Development Organization: Lamsang Bazar, PO Lamsang, Manipur; tel. (85) 310961; f. 1975; research, socio-economic development programme for the rural poor, skill training programme; Library and Documentation Centre, AIDS Prevention and Control Programme, Community Health Centre, Micro-credit scheme, rural bank, all set up with govt aid; library of 10,000 vols; Gen. Sec. W. BRAJABIDHU SINGH; publ. *Loyalam* (monthly).

Sikkim Research Institute of Tibetology: Gangtok, Sikkim; f. 1958; research centre for study of Mahayana (Northern Buddhism); library of Tibetan literature (canonical of all sects and secular) in MSS and xylographs; museum of icons and art objects; Dir J. K. RECHUNG; publs in Tibetan, Sanskrit and English, including *Bulletin of Tibetology* (quarterly).

Sinha, A. N., Institute of Social Studies: Patna 800001, Bihar; f. 1958 to undertake teaching and research in the social sciences, especially economics, sociology, social psychology and political science; library of 46,047 vols; Dir Prof. M. N. KARNA; Sec B. PRASAD; publ *Journal of Social and Economic Studies* (quarterly).

Sri Aurobindo Centre: Adhchini, Junction of Sri Aurobindo Marg and Qutab Hotel Rd, New Delhi 110017; multi-disciplinary research and training in the integral study of Man; research in comparative religions, Indian cultural values; lectures, seminars, study groups, summer programmes; homeopathic dispensary; research facilities; library; Chair. DHARMA VIRA; Hon. Sec. K. M. AGARWALA.

TECHNOLOGY

Ahmedabad Textile Industry's Research Association: PO Ambavadi Vistar, Ahmedabad 380015; tel. (79) 442671; telex 121-6571; fax (79) 6569874; f. 1949; textile consultation, training and research; library of 37,000 vols; Dir A. R. GARDE; publs *ACT (ATIRA Communications on Textiles)* (quarterly), *UPDATIRA-ATIRA Newsletter* (6 a year), *TEXINCON* (quarterly).

Automotive Research Association of India: POB 832, Vetal Hill, Pune 411004; tel. (212) 337180; fax (212) 334190; e-mail pune.arai@sm3.sprintrpg.ems.vsml.net.in; f. 1966; research institution of the Automotive Industry with the Ministry of Industry; provides facilities for research and development, product design, evaluation of equipment and standardization, compilation and dissemination of technical information to the automotive and engineering industry; testing laboratories; library of 10,000 vols, 75 periodicals; Dir Brig. (retd) S. R. PURANIK; publs *Automotive Abstracts* (monthly), *ARAI Newsletter* (quarterly).

Bengal Ceramic Institute: Calcutta 10; f. 1941.

Bengal Tanning Institute: Calcutta; f. 1919.

Bengal Textile Institute: Serampore; f. 1904.

Berhampore Textile Institute: Berhampore; f. 1925.

Birla Research Institute for Applied Sciences: Birlagram 456331, Nagda, MP; f. 1965; registered society to help national industrial growth; research in pulp, paper, cellulose fibre and pollution abatement; Pres. D. P. MANDELIA; Dir-Gen. S. K. ROY MOULIK; publs *Annual Report, Bulletin* (quarterly).

Bombay Textile Research Association: Lal Bahadur Shastri Marg, Ghatkopar (West), Mumbai 400086; tel. (22) 5003651; fax (22) 5000459; e-mail btra@bom3.vsnl.net.in; f. 1957; research in all aspects of processing cotton, silk and other natural and man-made fibres; training/communication and library services, seminars, etc.; recognized for postgraduate studies by Univ. of Bombay; 131 institutional mems; library of 19,000 vols; Dir Dr B. N. BANDYOPADHYAY; publ. *BTRA Scan* (quarterly).

Bureau of Indian Standards (BIS) 9 Bahadur Shah Zafar Marg, New Delhi 110002; tel. 3230131; telex (031) 65870; fax (11) 3234062; f. 1947; library of 720,000 standards and technical publications and 416 periodicals; Dir-Gen. P. S. DAS; Dir (Library Services) A. SINHA; publs *Current Published Information on Standardization, Standards Worldover – Monthly Additions to Library, Standards India.*

Central Institute for Research on Cotton Technology: Adenwala Rd, Matunga, Mumbai 400019; tel. 4127273; telex 011-71594; f. 1924; part of Indian Council of Agricultural Research; library of 11,800 vols; Dir Dr K. R. KRISHNA IYER.

Central Water and Power Research Station: PO Khadakwasla Research Station, Pune 411024; tel. (212) 802551; telex 0145-7390; fax (212) 802004; e-mail root@wapis .nic.in; f. 1916; basic and applied research in hydraulic engineering and allied subjects; hydrology and water resources analysis; activities in eight disciplines: River Engineering, Reservoir and Appurtenant Structures, Coastal and Offshore Engineering, Ship Hydrodynamics, Hydraulic Machinery, Foundations and Structures, Mathematical Modelling, Instrumentation and Control; library of 61,000 vols, 392 periodicals; Dir Dr B. U. NAYAK; publs *Annual Reports, Newsletter.*

Indian Lac Research Institute: Namkum, Ranchi 834010, Bihar; tel. (651) 520117; fax (651) 520202; e-mail ilri@x400.nicgw.nic.in; f. 1924; library of 36,000 vols; Dir Dr S. C. AGARWAL; publs *Annual Report, Newsletter.*

Indian Rubber Manufacturers Research Association: Plot No. B–88, Rd U–2, Wagle Industrial Estate, Thane 400604, Maharashtra; f. 1959; research and development relating to rubber and allied industries; 45 staff; Dir Dr W. MILLNS.

Institute of Hydraulics and Hydrology: Poondi 602023, (Via) Trivellore, Chingleput District, Tamil Nadu; f. 1945; library of 8,000 vols and 5,870 journals; Dir K. SUBRAMANIAM; publ. *Annual Report.*

Irrigation and Power Research Station: Amritsar; conducts research in fields of irrigation and hydraulic engineering; Dir J. NATH.

National Council for Cement and Building Materials: P–21, South Extension II, New Delhi 110049; tel. 6440133; telex 031-70071; fax 6468868; e-mail nccbm@gi.asdl01.vsnl.net.in; f. 1966; fmrly Cement Research Institute of India; provides intensive and planned research and development support to the cement and allied industries in the fields of new materials, technology development and transfer, continuing education and industrial services; *c.* 400 staff; library of 42,000 vols, reports, etc, 216 periodicals; Dir-Gen. Dr S. P. GHOSH; publs *CRI Current Contents* (documentation list, every 2 months), *CRI Abstracts* (research and development digest, quarterly), *Research Reports, Annual Reports, Cement Standards of the World.*

National Institute of Hydrology: Jal Vigyan Bhawan, Roorkee, UP 247667; tel. (1332) 72106; telex 0597-205; fax (1332) 72123; f. 1979; under Min. of Water Resources; research in all aspects of water resources; library of 7,000 vols, 3,000 technical reports, 87 periodicals, etc.; Dir Dr SATISH CHANDRA; publs *Jal Vigyan Sameeksha, NIH Newsletter, Research Reports.*

Pulp and Paper Research Institute: Jaykaypur 765017, Orissa; tel. (6856) 22050; telex 6602201; fax (6856) 22238; f. 1974; research in pulp and paper technology, forestry, environment and pigment; library of 6,000 vols, periodicals, etc; Deputy Dir A. K. BISWAL; publs *Abstract Index of Periodicals* (6 a year), *PAPRI Information Bulletin* (6 a year).

Research Designs and Standards Organization: Ministry of Railways, Government of India, Manak Nagar, Lucknow 226011; tel. (522) 451200; telex 5352424; fax (522) 458500; f. 1957; conducts studies on the design and standardization of all railway infrastructure and equipment and tests and trials of new railway stock and other assets, and research into the economic and effective maintenance of operating practices; library of 154,000 vols, 130 periodicals; Dir-Gen. HARI MOHAN; publs *Annual Report, RDSO Highlights, Indian Railway Technical Bulletin* (4 a year), Research Reports, Technical Papers, etc.

Silk and Art Silk Mills' Research Association: Sasmira, Sasmira Marg, Worli, Mumbai 400025; tel. 4935351; fax 4930225; f. 1950; research and development in man-made textiles; technical education (postgraduate and diploma courses) in the field of man-made fibres, textile technology, textile chemistry, knitting technology and marketing and management of man-made textiles; library of 26,000 vols; Dir M. K. BARDHAN; publ. *Man Made Textiles in India.*

Telecommunications Research Centre: c/o Indian Posts and Telegraphs Dept, New Delhi 110001; tel. 320252; telex 2222; f. 1956; library of 33,300 vols; Dir K. R. NAYAR.

Libraries and Archives

Ahmedabad

Gujarat Vidyapith Granthalaya: Ahmedabad 380014; tel. (79) 7541148; fax (79) 7542547; e-mail gujvi@adinet-emet.in; f. 1920; University, State Central and Public Library combined; 460,000 vols; depository collection; Librarian K. K. BHAVSAR.

Sheth Maheklal Jethabhai Pustakalaya (Free Public Library): Ellis Bridge, Ahmedabad, Gujarat State; f. 1933; 25,012 mems; 178,317 vols; UNESCO programmes for children's libraries; Librarian M. M. PATEL.

Allahabad

Allahabad Public Library: Rajkeeya Public Library, Alfred Park, Allahabad 211002; tel. 52386; f. 1864; 72,601 vols; Librarian Dr K. K. SAXENA.

Bangalore

Bangalore State Central Library: Cubbon Park, Bangalore 1, Karnataka; f. 1914; 140,000 vols; State Librarian and Head of Public Libraries N. D. BAGERI.

Karnataka Government Secretariat Library: Vidhana Soudha, Bangalore 560 001; tel. 2257686; e-mail bngvslib@kar.nic.in; f. *c.* 1919; 106,000 vols, 193 periodicals; Chief Librarian M. N. EARE-GOWDA.

Bankipore

Khuda Bakhsh Oriental Public Library: Bankipore, Patna 800004, Bihar; tel. and fax (612) 670109; f. 1891; annual symposia and seminars; extension lectures and workshops; contains over 19,800 MSS in Arabic, Persian, Urdu, Turkish and Sanskrit, many illuminated, 117,000 prints, 34,600 periodicals, over 1,200 audio and video cassettes, research library specializing in Arabic and Persian MSS and Mughal and Rajput paintings; Dir HABIBUR RAHMAN CHIGHANI; publs *Journal* (quarterly), catalogues, proceedings, research publications.

Baroda

Central Library: Baroda 390006, Gujarat; tel. 540133; f. 1910; 280,000 vols; State Librarian BAKULESH BHUTA; publ. *Granth Deep* (quarterly).

Calcutta

Centre for Asian Documentation: K-15, CIT Bldgs, Christopher Rd, POB 11215, Calcutta 700014; provides reference services; Dir S. CHAUDHURI; publs *Index Indo-Asiasticus* (quarterly), *Index Internationalis Indicus* (every 3 years), *Index Asia Series in Humanities* (irregular), *Indian Science index* (every 2 years), *Indian Biography* (annually).

National Library: Belvedere, Calcutta 700027; tel. 479-1381; fax 479-1462; f. 1903 by the amalgamation of the Calcutta Public Library and the Imperial Library; depository and research library; 2,186,500 vols, 84,952 maps, 3,127 MSS; 4,145 microfilms, 94,500 microfiches, 17,650 periodicals; ind. Central Reference Library, at the same address, compiles *Indian National Bibliography*, but does not hold a book colln; Dir HARJIT SINGH; publs *India's National Library—Systematization and Modernization, The National Library and Public Libraries in India, Conservation of Library Materials, Rabindra Grantha Suchi* (vol 1 part 1), *Bibliographical Control in India, Indological Studies and South Asia Bibliography, General Collection Author and Subject Catalogues, Bibliographies, Reports, Newsletter* (quarterly) etc.

Chennai

Adyar Library and Research Centre: Adyar, Chennai 600020; tel. 4913528; f. 1886; research in Indology; library of 160,000 vols, 18,000 MSS; specializes in religion, philosophy, civilization; Dir K. KUNJUNNI RAJA; Librarian Mrs PARVATI GOPALARATNAM (acting); publ. *Brahmavidya* (annually).

Connemara (State Central) Public Library: Pantheon Road, Egmore, Chennai 600008; tel. 8261151; f. 1896; deposit library from 1954 for all Indian publications; information centre for UN and allied agencies and for Asian Development Bank; 63,397 mems; 525,000 vols; Librarian N. AVUDAIAPPAN; publ. *Tamil Nadu State Bibliography* (in Tamil, monthly).

Indian Institute of Technology Central Library: Chennai 600036; tel. (44) 2351365 telex 041-8926; fax (44) 2350509; e-mail lib@iitm.ernet.in; f. 1959; includes collection of technical and scientific books (German and English); partial archive of scientific films;

264,097 vols, 700 current periodicals, 400 films, 1,600 microfilms and microfiches; user education programmes; Chief Librarian Dr HARISH CHANDRA; publ. *New Additions to the Library*.

Madras Literary Society Library: Chennai 600006; f. 1812; 105,000 vols; Man. P. N. BALASUNDARAM; Hon. Sec. S. V. B. ROW.

Tamil Nadu Government Oriental Manuscripts Library: University Bldg, Chepauk, Chennai 600005; f. 1869; acquisition, preservation and publication of rare and important collection of MSS in Sanskrit, Islamic and South Indian languages; 23,000 vols, 71,000 MSS; Curator Dr S. SOUNDARAPANDIAN; publs *Bulletin*, catalogues, etc.

Delhi

Central Archaeological Library: Annexe bldg of National Archives of India, Janpath, New Delhi 110001; tel. 3387475; telex (031) 66242; attached to Archaeological Survey of India; 100,000 vols, 5,776 maps, 250 current periodicals; Dir-Gen. AJAY SHANKER.

Central Secretariat Library: Department of Culture, Govt of India, G Wing, Shastri Bhavan, New Delhi 110001; tel. (11) 3389684; fax (11) 3384846; e-mail root%csl@delnet.ren.nic.in; f. 1890; lending, reference, reprographic divisions, background material on selected topics and biographies; 810,000 vols, 730 periodicals; special collections: area study, Indian official documents, foreign official documents, Hindi and Indian regional languages publs; Dir KALPANA DASGUPTA.

Delhi Public Library: S. P. Mukherjee Marg, Delhi 110006; tel. (11) 2916881; fax (11) 2943990; f. 1951 in association with UNESCO; established as a model for public library development in south-east Asia; among its depts, the central library has an adult lending and reference dept, a children's dept, gramophone lending library, and an extension services dept serving 102 areas through 5 mobile vans and 19 deposit stations; one prison library, and a Braille dept; 3 sports libraries; 1 zonal library, 3 brs and 53 sub-brs; community and resettlement colony libraries; 1,481,000 vols in Hindi, English, Urdu, Punjabi, Bengali, Sindhi and Braille; Dir Dr BANWARI LAL.

Indian Council of World Affairs Library: Sapru House, Barakhamba Rd, New Delhi 110001; tel. 3317246; f. 1950; research collections on social sciences with special reference to international relations, international law and international economics; 127,265 vols, 523 periodicals, 2,458,000 press clippings, 157,000 documents; Press library; maps, microfilms and microfiches; United Nations and EEC documents; Librarian MAN SINGH DEORA (acting); publ. *Documentation on Asia* (annually).

Indian National Scientific Documentation Centre (INSDOC): 14 Satsang Vihar Marg, POB 10513, New Delhi 110067; tel. (11) 6863617; telex 031-73099; fax (11) 6862228; e-mail teevee@sirnetd.ernet.in; f. 1952; attached to Council of Scientific and Industrial Research; national science library; 138,000 vols, 8,000 current periodicals; provides networking services and network-based online services; bibliographical information retrieval from national or international online/CD-ROM databases; Dir Prof. T. VISHWANATHAN; publs *Annals of Library Science and Documentation* (quarterly), *Indian Science Abstracts* (fortnightly); Regional Centres at Indian Institute of Science, Bangalore 560012, Indian Institute of Chemical Biology, Calcutta 700032 and CSIR Complex, Madras 600115.

Indira Gandhi National Centre for the Arts: Central Vista Mess, Janpath, 3 Dr Rajendra Prasad Rd, New Delhi 110001; tel. (11) 3385277; fax (11) 3383911; e-mail ignca@doe.ernet.in; f. 1986; resource centre with reference material relating to Indian arts and culture; Academic Dir Dr KAPILA VATSYAYAN.

National Archives of India: Janpath, New Delhi 110001; tel. (11) 3383436; fax (11) 3384127; f. 1891; valuable collections of public records, maps, private papers and microfilm covering 35km of shelf space; library of 200,000 vols; Dir-Gen. S. SARKAR; publs *Indian Archives* (2 a year), *Annual Report, Bulletin of Research Theses and Dissertations* (every 2 years).

National Social Science Documentation Centre: 35 Ferozshah Rd, POB 712, New Delhi 110001; tel. (11) 3385959; telex 3161083; fax (11) 3381571; e-mail postmast@nassdoc.delnet.ernet.in; f. 1970; division of Indian Council of Social Science Research; provides information and documentation service in social sciences, international collaboration in documentation activities, document delivery and reprographic services, consultancy service, select bibliography service, training courses; library of 2,500 current periodicals, 150,000 serial vols, 40,000 monographs including Ph.D. theses, research project reports and reference books, conference papers, working papers; Dir Dr K. G. TYAGI; publs *Union Catalogues, Bibliographies, Indexing and Abstracting Journals, Conference Alert, Current Contents in Social Sciences.*

Nehru Memorial Museum and Library: Teen Murti House, New Delhi 110011; tel. 3015333; f. 1964; archival collections on modern Indian history with emphasis on Indian nationalism; research centre for studies in 20th-century Indian history and social sciences; 194,000 vols; large collection of newspapers, microfilms, private papers, institutional records, photographs and oral history recordings; Dir Prof. RAVINDER KUMAR.

Dharamsala

Library of Tibetan Works and Archives: Gangchen Kyishong, Dharamsala 176215; tel. 22467; fax 23723; e-mail ltwa@dsala.tibet.net; f. 1971; 80,000 vols; 10,000 photographs, 15,000 hours of audio/video tape, 1,200 icons and artifacts; Dir GYATSHO TSHERING; publ. *The Tibet Journal*.

Hyderabad

State Central Library: Afzalgunj, Hyderabad 500012, AP; tel. 43107; f. 1891; 347,000 vols; Librarian T. V. VEDAMRUTHAM.

Attached library:

> **Government Oriental Manuscripts Library:** 5-8-599 Ratan Mahal Bldgs, Hyderabad 500001, AP; tel. 202487; f. 1975; 23,968 MSS; Dir N. R. V. PRASAD; publ. *Vijnana Saraswati* (in English and Telugu, quarterly).

Lucknow

Acharya Narendra Dev Pustakalaya: 10 Ashoka Marg, Lucknow; f. 1959; public library, with special emphasis on social sciences; 79,636 vols; 150 periodicals; Librarian T. N. MISRA.

Ludhiana

Panjab University Extension Library: Civil Lines, Ludhiana, Punjab; tel. 449558; f. 1960; serves educational institutions within a radius of 60 km; 138,000 vols; Librarian Dr K. C. AHUJA (acting).

Mumbai

Petit, J. N., Institute Library: 312 Dr Dadabhoy Naoroji Rd, Fort, Mumbai 400001; f. 1856 as 'Fort Improvement Library'; moved 1898 to own building; 160,000 vols; Admin. J. R. MODY.

Patna

Bihar Secretariat Library: Patna 800015; f. 1885; 106,300 vols; Chief Librarian P. N. SINHA DOSHI.

Shrimati Radhika Sinha Institute and Sachchidananda Sinha Library (State Central Library, Bihar): G.P.O., Patna 800001; tel. 221674; f. 1924; 141,000 vols, 497 periodicals; Librarian Dr R. S. P. SINGH.

Rajahmundry

Gowthami Regional Library: Rajahmundry 533104, Andhra Pradesh; tel. 76908; f. 1898; management transferred to Andhra Pradesh Government in 1979; research library of 58,643 vols, 428 palm leaf MSS; special collection of rare 19th-century periodicals in English and Telugu, rare collection of old Telugu books; Librarian VENNA POLI REDDY.

Trivandrum

Trivandrum Public Library (State Central Library): Trivandrum, Kerala State; tel. 62895; f. 1829; 240,044 vols; Librarian KURSHID AHAMED.

Museums and Art Galleries

Ahmedabad

Calico Museum of Textiles: Sarabhai Foundation, Shahibag, Ahmedabad 380004; tel. (79) 2868172; fax (79) 2865759; f. 1948; collection of 17th–18th-century Indian textiles and costumes, and reconstructed 17th–19th-century carved wooden façades; Sec. D. S. MEHTA; publs *Historic Textiles of India in the Calico Museum, Contemporary Textile Crafts of India* (series).

Ajmer

Rajputana Museum: Ajmer 305001, Rajasthan; f. 1908; archaeology; rare sculptures, architectural carvings, old coins, epigraphs, Rajput paintings, arms and armour of Rajasthan; Curator R. D. SHARMA.

Banares

Bharat Kala Bhavan: Banaras Hindu University, Varanasi 221005; tel. 316337; f. 1920, attached to univ. 1950; art objects, miniature paintings, sculpture, textiles, archaeology, seals; library of *c.* 14,000 vols and periodicals, 26,511 MSS; Dir Prof. R. C. SHARMA; publs *Chhavi*, catalogues, etc.

Bangalore

Government Museum: Kasturba Rd, Bangalore 560001, Karnataka; f. 1866; art, archaeology, industrial art and natural history; library of 2,000 vols; Curator (vacant); publ. *Annual Report.*

Visvesvaraya Industrial and Technological Museum: Kasturba Rd, PMB 5216, Bangalore 560001, Karnataka; tel. (80) 2864563; telex 0845-8016; fax (80) 2864114; f. 1962; aims to stimulate interest in science and technology, and to portray the application of technology in industry and human welfare; library of 9,600 vols; also a/v materials; Dir M. PARVATHINATHAN.

Baroda

Baroda Museum and Picture Gallery: Baroda 390005, Gujarat; f. museum 1894 and picture gallery 1920; Indian archaeology; prehistoric and historic; Indian art: ancient, medieval and modern; numismatic collections; modern Indian paintings; industrial art; Asiatic and Egyptian collections; Greek, Roman, European civilizations and art; European paintings; ethnology, zoology, geology, economic botany; library of 19,000 vols; Dir S. K. BHOWMIK; Curators: R. K. MAKWANA (Art and Archaeology), G. M. PATHAK (Natural History); publ. *Bulletin*.

Bhubaneswar

Orissa State Museum: Bhubaneswar 751006, Orissa; f. 1932; archaeology, epigraphy, numismatics, armoury, arts and crafts, anthropology, palmleaf MSS, natural history; library of 22,000 vols, 2,000 periodicals; Dir Dr H. C. DAS; publ. *Orissa Historical Research Journal*.

Bikaner

Government Museum: Bikaner 334001, Rajasthan; tel. (151) 528894; f. 1937; collection of terracottas, sculptures, bronzes, coins, inscriptions, Rajasthani paintings, documents, arms and costumes, specimens of folk-culture; Superintendent P. C. BHARGAVA.

Bodh Gaya

Archaeological Museum: Bodh Gaya, Bihar State; stone and bronze sculpture, etc.; Curator S. SINGH.

Calcutta

Asutosh Museum of Indian Art: Centenary Building, University of Calcutta, Calcutta 700073; f. 1937; library of over 2,000 vols and periodicals; Curator NIRANJAN GOSWAMI; publs catalogues.

Birla Industrial and Technological Museum: 19A Gurusaday Rd, Calcutta 700019; tel. 247-7241; telex 21-7723; f. 1959; administered by the National Council of Science Museums; portrays the history and development of science and technology; four regional science centres and six mobile science exhibition buses in rural areas; educational programmes for students and teachers; library of 14,000 vols incl. periodicals; film library; archives; special collections on history and development of science and technology, arts, painting museology etc.; Dir S. GOSWAMY.

Indian Museum: 27 Jawaharlal Nehru Rd, Calcutta 700016; tel. (33) 2495699; fax (33) 2495696; f. 1814; collections of archaeology, art, coins, anthropology, geology, botany, zoology; library; herbarium; Dir Dr S. K. CHAKRAVARTI; publs *Bulletin* (1 a year), monographs, etc.

Victoria Memorial Hall: 1 Queens Way, Calcutta 700071; tel. and fax (33) 2235142; f. 1906; museum of medieval Indian history and culture, and British Indian history of the late 18th and early 19th centuries; wide collection of oil-paintings, water-colours, miniatures, engravings, photographs, sculptures, maps, MSS, furniture, stamps, coins, medals, textiles, arms and armour; library of almost 10,000 vols; Sec. and Curator Prof. C. PANDA.

Chennai

Fort Museum: Fort St George, Chennai 600009; tel. 561127; f. 1948; exhibits belong mainly to the days of the East India Co.; Dir Dr D. JITHENDRADAS.

Government Museum and National Art Gallery: Pantheon Rd, Egmore, Chennai 600008; tel. 869638; f. 1851; archaeology, ancient and modern Indian art, South Indian bronzes, Buddhist sculptures, numismatics, philately, anthropology, botany, zoology, geology, chemical conservation education, contemporary art, design and display; Dir M. RAMAN; publs *Madras Museum Bulletins*, *Newsletter* (2 a year).

Delhi

Archaeological Museum Red Fort Delhi: Mumtaz Mahal, Red Fort; tel. 267961; f. 1909; 420 vols; historical collections of the Mughal period; old arms, seals and signets, letters, MSS, coins, miniatures, Mughal dresses and relics of India's War of Independence; Curator S. K. SHARMA.

Crafts Museum: Pragati Maidan, Bhairon Rd, New Delhi 110001; tel. (11) 3371641; fax (11) 3371515; f. 1952; Indian traditional crafts and tribal arts; library of 11,000 vols; Dir Dr JYOTINDRA JAIN.

Gandhi National Museum and Library: Rajghat, New Delhi 110002; tel. (11) 3310168; fax (11) 3311793; e-mail gandhimk.@nda.vsnl.net.in; f. 1953 by the Gandhi Memorial Museum Society to collect and display Gandhi's records and mementos and to promote the study of his life and work; library of 45,000 vols, 50,000 documents and 91 periodicals; 130 films and recordings; 9,000 photographs; large picture gallery; Chair. SADIQ ALI; Dir Dr Y. P. ANAND.

National Gallery of Modern Art: Jaipur House, India Gate, Sher Shah Rd, New Delhi 110003; tel. 382835; f. 1954; contemporary art (paintings, sculpture, drawings, graphics, architecture, industrial design, photography, prints and minor arts); Dir Dr ANIS FAROOQI.

National Museum of India: Janpath, New Delhi 110011; tel. 3018159; fax 3019821; f. 1949; Departments of Art, Archaeology, Anthropology, Modelling, Presentation, Preservation, Publication, Library and Photography; Indian prehistoric tools, protohistoric remains from Harappa, Mohenjodaro, etc., representative collections of sculptures, terracottas, stuccos and bronzes from 2nd century BC to 18th century AD; illustrated MSS and miniatures; Stein Collection of Central Asian murals and other antiquities; decorative arts; textiles, coins and illuminated epigraphical charts; armour; copper-plate etchings; woodwork; library of 43,400 vols; Dir-Gen. Dr R. C. SHARMA; publs *Bulletin* (annually), special publs on art and archaeology.

National Museum of Natural History: FICCI Museum Bldg, Barakhamba Rd, New Delhi 110001; f. 1978; exhibits on natural history, ecology, environment, conservation; educational programmes for children and other groups, school loan service, mobile museum for rural extension service; library of 25,000 vols, etc.; Dir K. SETHURAMAN.

National Rail Museum: Chanakyapuri, New Delhi 110021; tel. (11) 6881816; fax (11) 6880804; e-mail nrm@nrm.nrm.cmc.net.in; f. 1977; library of 5,000 vols; Dir A. LOHANI; publ. *Newsletter* (2 a year).

Rabindra Bhavan Art Gallery: 35 Ferozeshah Rd, New Delhi; f. 1955; permanent gallery of the Lalit Kala Akademi (National Academy of Art), and venue of the National Exhibition of Art and Triennale-India (international art); Chair. ANAND DEV; publs *Lalit Kala* (annually), *Lalit Kala Contemporary* (2 a year).

Shankar's International Dolls Museum: Nehru House, 4 Bahadur Shah Zafar Marg, New Delhi 110002; tel. 3316970; fax 3721090; f. 1965; 6,000 exhibits from all over the world; Curator SHANTA SRINIVASAN.

Gauhati

Assam State Museum: Gauhati 781001, Assam; f. 1940; indological and archaeological studies; library of 5,850 vols; Dir Dr R. D. CHOUDHURY; publ. *Bulletin* (annually).

Guntur

Archaeological Museum: Nagarjunakonda, Guntur, Andhra Pradesh; f. 1966; prehistoric and historical antiquities, mainly sculptures, Buddhist and Hindu; Curator K. VEERABHADRA RAO.

Hyderabad

Andhra Pradesh State Museum: Hyderabad 500034; f. 1930; sculpture, epigraphy, arms and weapons, Bidriware, bronze objects, miniatures and paintings, MSS, numismatics, European paintings (prints), decorative and modern arts, textiles; excavations at Yeleswaram Pochampal, Peddabankur; Dir Dr V. V. KRISHNA SASTRY; publs various on numismatics.

Salarjung Museum: Hyderabad 500002, AP; tel. 523211; f. 1951; paintings, textiles, porcelain, jade, carpets, MSS, antiques, ivory, glass, silver- and bronze-ware; children's section; library of 60,000 vols incl. Persian, Arabic and Urdu MSS; Dir Dr I. K. SARMA; publs *Research Journal* (2 a year), Guide Book and Manuscript Catalogue.

Imphal

Manipur State Museum: Polo-ground, Imphal, Manipur; general collection.

Jaipur

Maharaja Sawai Man Singh II Museum: City Palace, Jaipur 302002, Rajasthan; tel. 48146; f. 1959; textiles and costumes, armoury, Mughal and Rajasthani miniature paintings, Persian and Mughal carpets, transport accessories, regalia, manuscript library of 10,000 Sanskrit, Persian, Hindi and Rajasthani MSS; Dir YADUENDRA SAHAI; publs catalogues, etc.

Lucknow

Uttar Pradesh State Museum: Banarasibagh, Lucknow, UP; tel. and fax 273146; f. 1863; collections of sculptures, terracottas, copper plates, numismatics, paintings, manuscripts, textiles and natural history specimens; library of 15,000 vols; Dir S. D. TRIVEDI; publ. *Bulletin* (2 a year).

Mathura

Government Museum: Dampier Nagar, Mathura 281001, UP; f. 1874; 40,000 items, dominated by sculptures, terracottas of Mathura School to Kushana and Gupta period; coins, paintings, etc.; reference library of 20,000 vols.

Mumbai

Dr Bhau Daji Lad Museum: 91A Dr B. Ambedkar Rd, Byculla, Mumbai 400027; tel. 3757943; f. 1855; reference library on Indian and foreign art, archaeology, ethnology, geology, history, numismatics and museology; exhibits of agriculture and village life, armoury, cottage industries, ethnology, fine arts, crafts, fossils, Indian coins, minerals, miscellaneous collection, Old Mumbai, collection; Curator M. GANDHI; publs catalogues, etc.

Prince of Wales Museum of Western India: Mahatma Gandhi Rd, Fort, Mumbai 400023; tel. 2844484; fax (22) 2045430; f. 1905; sections: Art, Painting, Archaeology, Natural History; library of 15,000 vols; Dir Dr K. DESAI; publs *Bulletin*, catalogues.

Nagpur

Central Museum: Nagpur 440001, Maharashtra; f. 1863; miscellaneous collection of objects relating to archaeology, art, ethnology, cottage industry, megalithic sites, copper implements, Buddhist sculptures, aboriginal tribal remains; Dir P. M. MULEY.

Nalanda

Archaeological Museum: Nalanda, Bihar State; f. 1958; collections of antiquities, specializing in Buddhist sculptures; Curator S. K. SHARMA.

Patna

Patna Museum: Patna-Gaya Rd, Buddha Marg, Patna 800001, Bihar; tel. 235731;

f. 1917; archaeology, ethnology, geology, arms and armour, natural history, art, coins, Tibetan paintings; Additional Dir Dr P. K. JAYASWAL.

Rajahmundry

Sri Rallabandi Subbarao Government Museum (formerly the Andhra Historical Research Society): Godavari Bund Rd, Rajahmundry, East Godavari District, Andhra Pradesh 533101; f. 1967; art, archaeology, epigraphy, history and numismatics; collection of coins, sculpture, pottery, terra cotta, palm-leaf MSS, inscriptions, etc.; Dir Dr V. V. KRISHNA SASTRY; publ. *Journal of the AHRS*

Santiniketan

Rabindra Bhavana (Tagore Museum and Archives): Visva-Bharati, PO Santiniketan 731235; tel. (3463) 52773; f. 1942; collection of MSS, letters, newspaper clippings, gramophone records, photographs, cine-film, paintings by Tagore and tape recordings of his voice; library of 41,000 vols; inside the Uttarayana Campus where the poet spent the last days of his life; publs *Rabindra Jijnasa, Rabindra-Viksa* (2 a year), *Tagoreana* (3 a year), *Rabindra-Bhavana* (4 a year).

Sarnath

Sarnath Museum: District Varanasi Pin 221007, UP; archaeological site museum; f. 1904; Buddhist and Hindu collection from 3rd century BC to 12th century AD; Superintending Archaeologist: Dr B. BANDYOPADHYAY.

Srinagar

Sri Pratap Singh Museum: Lalmandi, Srinagar 190008, Jammu and Kashmir; tel. 32374; f. 1898; general collection of Jammu and Kashmir; library of 1,300 vols about cultural subjects; Curator M. S. ZAHID.

Trichur

Kerala State Museums, Zoos, Art Galleries and Government Gardens: include: (1) State Museum and Zoo, Trichur, f. 1885; (2) Govt Museums and Zoological and Botanical Gardens, Trivandrum, f. 1857; tel. (471) 62275; natural history collections, Indian arts and crafts; (3) Art Gallery and Krishna-Menon Museum, Calicut; tel. (485) 51253; f. 1976; (4) Govt Botanical Garden, Olavanna; f. 1991.

Trivandrum

Sri Chitra Art Gallery, Gallery of Asian Paintings: Trivandrum 695001, Kerala; f. 1935; sections: Pure Indian Art, Rajput, Mughal and Persian, Tanjore, Tibetan, Chinese, Japanese, Balinese, Indo-European (water and oil), etchings and woodcuts; Modern Indian Contemporary Art and Murals; library of 736 vols; Dir K. RAJENDRA BABU; publ. *Administration Report*.

Universities

There are in India three types of university: Affiliating and Teaching (most teaching done in colleges affiliated to the university, but some teaching, mostly postgraduate, undertaken by the university); Residential and Teaching (all teaching done on one campus); Federal (a number of university or constituent colleges are closely associated with the university's work). It is not possible, for reasons of space, to give details of affiliated colleges.

AGRA UNIVERSITY

Paliwal Park, Agra 280004, Uttar Pradesh

Telephone: 352135

Founded 1927

Affiliating and Teaching

Languages of instruction: English and Hindi

Academic year: July to April (one term)

Chancellor: HE THE GOVERNOR OF UTTAR PRADESH

Vice-Chancellor: Prof. MOHAMMD ISMULLAH KHAN

Registrar: Shri RAKESH

Hon. Librarian: Dr S. V. PANDEY

Library of 155,879 vols

Number of students: 20,000

DEANS

Faculty of Arts: Dr S. V. PANDEY
Faculty of Science: Dr B. K. LEHRI
Faculty of Law: Dr J. C. GUPTA
Faculty of Commerce: Dr R. P. GUPTA
Faculty of Agriculture: Dr V. SINGH
Faculty of Medicine: Dr U. C. MISRA
Faculty of Home Science: Dr H. KUMAR
Faculty of Education: Dr M. C. SHARMA

CONSTITUENT INSTITUTES

Institute of Social Sciences: Agra; 14 teachers; Dir Dr B. K. LEHRI.

K.M. Institute of Hindi Studies and Linguistics: Agra; 9 teachers; Dir Dr RAJNESH (acting).

Institute of Household Art and Home Science: Agra; 10 teachers; Dir Smt. H. KUMAR (acting).

Institute of Basic Science: Agra; Dir Dr G. C. SHARMA (acting).

Seth Padam Chandjain Institute of Commerce, Business Management and Economics: Agra; Dr G. C. SHARMA (acting).

There are 45 affiliated colleges.

UNIVERSITY OF AGRICULTURAL SCIENCES

G.K.V.K., Bangalore 560065, Karnataka

Telephone: (80) 3330153

Telex: 8458393

Fax: (80) 3330277

Founded 1964

Residential

Languages of instruction: English and Kannada

State control

Academic year: September to August (two terms)

Chancellor: HE THE GOVERNOR OF KARNATAKA

Pro-Chancellor: THE MINISTER OF AGRICULTURE, KARNATAKA

Vice-Chancellor: Dr S. BISLAIAH

Dean: Dr M. C. DEVAIAH

Registrar: Dr. K. M. JAYARAMAIAH

Administrative Officer: Shri B. GANGADHAR

Librarian: K. T. SOMASHEKHAR

Libraries of 168,000 vols

Number of teachers: 1,082

Number of students: 2,214

Publications: *Dairy* (monthly), *Annual Report, Calendar, Mysore Journal of Agricultural Sciences* (4 a year), *Current Research* (monthly), *Krishi Vijana* (4 a year, in Kannada), Technical Series, Extension Series, Research Series, Miscellaneous Series (irregular).

PROFESSORS

ABDUL RAHMAN, S., Parasitology
ANANTHANARAYANA, R., Chemistry and Soils
ANILKUMAR, T. B., Plant Pathology
ASHOK, T. H., Horticulture
AVADHANI, K. K., Genetics and Plant Breeding
BHAT, G. S., Dairy Chemistry
CHALLAIAH, Agricultural Extension
CHANDRAKANTH, M. G., Agricultural Economics
CHANDRAMOULI, K. N., Anatomy
CHANDRAPPA, H. M., Plant Breeding
CHANDRASHEKAR GUPTA, T. R., Fishery Oceanography
CHANNAPPA, T. C., Agricultural Engineering
CHENGAPPA, P. G., Agricultural Marketing
CHIKKADEVAIAH, Seed Processing Engineering
CHOWDEGOWDA, M., Agricultural Engineering
DAS, T. K., Animal Nutrition
DEVEGOWDA, G., Poultry
ESHWARAPPA, G., Agricultural Extension
FAROOQ MOHAMMED, Veterinary Physiology
FAROOQI, A. A., Medicinal and Aromatic Plants
GANGADHAR, K. S., Gynaecology and Obstetrics
GEETHA RAMACHANDRA, Biochemistry
GIRIJA, P. R., Psychology
GOPALA GOWDA, H. S., Agricultural Microbiology
GOPALAKRISHNA HEBBAR, Agricultural Economics
GOPALAKRISHNA RAO, Agricultural Extension
GOVINDAIAH, M. G., Animal Genetics and Breeding
GOVINDAN, R., Entomology
GOWDA, H., Pharmacology
GUNDURAO, D. S., Mathematics
GURUMURTHY, Statistics
GURURAJ HUNSIGI, Agronomy
HEGDE, S. V., Microbiology
HONNEGOWDA, Pharmacology
HUDDAR, A. G., Horticulture
JAGADISH, A., Entomology
JAGADISH KUMAR, Pharmacology
JAGANNATH, M. S., Parasitology
JANARDHANA, K. V., Crop Physiology
JAVAREGOWDA, S., Agricultural Engineering
JAYADEVAPPA, S. M., Surgery
JAYARAMAIAH, M., Sericulture
JOSEPH BHAGYARAJ, D., Agricultural Microbiology
JOSHI SHAMASUNDAR, Botany
KAILAS, M. M., Dairy Production
KARUNASAGAR, I., Fishery Microbiology
KATTEPPA, Y., Agricultural Extension
KESHAVAMURTHY, K. V., Plant Pathology
KESHAVANATH, P., Aquaculture
KHAN, M. M., Horticulture
KRISHNA, K. S., Agricultural Extension
KRISHNAPPA, A. M., Soil Science
KRISHNAPRASAD, Agricultural Entomology
KRISHNAPRASAD, P. R., Pathology
KRISHNEGOWDA, K. T., Agronomy
KULAKARNI, R. S., Agricultural Botany
KUMARASWAMY, A. S., Water Management and Plant Breeding
LAKKUNDI, N. H., Agricultural Entomology
LOKANATH, G. R., Poultry for Meat
MALLIK, B., Acarology
MALLIKARJUNAIAH, R. R., Microbiology
MANJUNATH, A., Plant Breeding
MELANTA, R., Horticulture
MOHAN JOSEPH, Fishery Biology
MUNI LAL DUBEY, B., Gynaecology and Obstetrics
MUNIYAPPA, V., Plant Pathology
MUNIYAPPA, T. V., Agricultural Extension
MUSHTARI BEGUM, J., Home Science
NAGARAJA SETTY, M. V., Plant Breeding
NAGARAJU, Animal Sciences
NANJEGOWDA, D., Nematology
NARASIMHAMURTHY, S., Mathematics
NARAYANA, K., Pharmacology
NARAYANA GOWDA, K., Agricultural Extension
NARAYANAGOWDA, J. V., Horticulture
NARENDRANATH, R., Physiology
PANCHAKSHARAIAH, S., Agronomy
PARAMASHIVAIAH, B. M., Animal Science
PARAMESWAR, N. S., Plant Breeding
PARASHIVAMURTHY, A. S., Soil Science
PARVATHAMMA, S., Mathematics
PARVATHAPPA, H. C., Soil Science and Agricultural Chemistry
PRABHAKAR HEGDE, B., Dairy Production
PRABHAKAR SETTY, T. K., Agronomy
PRABHUSWAMY, H. P., Agricultural Entomology
PRASAD, T. G., Crop Physiology
PRATAP KUMAR, K. S., Poultry Science
PUTTASWAMY, Entomology
RAGHAVAN, R., Veterinary Microbiology
RAJ, J., Microbiology

RAJAGOPAL, D., Apiculture
RAMACHANDRAPRASAD, T. V., Agronomy
RAMANJANEYULU, G., Dairy Technology
RAMAPRASANNA, K. P., Seed Technology
RANGANATHAIAH, K. G., Plant Pathology
RAVI, P. C., Agricultural Marketing
SAMIULLA, R., Horticulture
SATHYAN, B. A., Plant Breeding
SATHYANARAYANA RAO, G. P., Agricultural Extension
SESHADRI, V. S., Agricultural Extension
SHAKUNTALA SRIDHARA, Zoology
SHANBHOGUE, S. L, Fishery Biology
SHANKAR, P. A., Dairy Microbiology
SHANKAREGOWDA, B. T., Plant Sciences
SHANTHA JOSEPH, Fishery Economics
SHANTHA R. HIREMATH, Plant Breeding
SHANTHAMALLAIAH, N. R., Crop Production
SHARIEF, R. A., Plant Science
SHESHAPPA, D. S., Fishery Engineering
SHIVAPPA SHETTY, K., Microbiology
SHIVARAJ, B., Agronomy
SHIVASHANKAR, K., Agronomy
SHIVANNA, H., Plant Breeding and Genetics
SIDDARAMAIAH, A. L., Plant Pathology
SIDDARAMAIAH, B. S., Agricultural Extension
SIDDARAMAPPA, R., Soil Science
SIDDARAMEGOWDA, T. K., Biotechnology
SINGLACHAR, M. A., Agronomy
SOMASHEKARAPPA, G., Agricultural Extension
SRIHARI, K., Zoology
SRINIVASA GOWDA, M. V., Economics
SRINIVASA GOWDA, R. N., Poultry Pathology
SRIKAR, L. N., Biochemistry
SUSHEELA DEVI, L., Soil Science and Agricultural Chemistry
SURYA PRAKASH, S., Agricultural Economics
THIMME GOWDA, S., Agronomy
UDAYAKUMAR, M., Crop Physiology
UPADHYA, A. S., Veterinary Microbiology
UTTAIAH, B. C., Horticulture
VAIDEHI, M. P., Home Science
VAJRANABAIAH, S. N., Crop Physiology
VASUDEVAPPA, Inland Fisheries
VEERABHADRAIAH, V., Agricultural Extension
VENKATASUBBAIAH, K., Botany
VENKATESH REDDY, T., Post-Harvest Technology
VENUGOPAL, Agricultural Extension
VENUGOPAL, N., Agricultural Meteorology
VIDYACHANDRA, B., Plant Breeding
VIJAYASARATHI, S. K., Veterinary Microbiology
VIRAKTHAMATH, C. A., Agricultural Entomology
VISHWANATH, D. P., Soil Science
VISWANATH, S., Virology
VISWANATHA, S. R., Plant Breeding
VISWANATHA REDDY, V. N., Gynaecology and Obstetrics
VISWANATHA SASTRY, K. M., Veterinary Medicine
YADAHALLI, Y. H., Agronomy

CONSTITUENT COLLEGES

College of Agriculture: G.K.V.K., Bangalore; f. 1946; Dir Dr M. B. CHANNEGOWDA.

Veterinary College: Hebbal, Bangalore; f. 1957; Dir Dr S. ABDUL REHMAN.

College of Basic Sciences and Humanities: Bangalore; f. 1967; Dir Dr R. V. RAMA MOHAN.

College of Post-Graduate Education: G.K.V.K., Bangalore; f. 1967; Dir Dr J. V. VENKATARAM.

College of Fisheries, Mangalore: f. 1970; Dir Dr S. L. SHANBHOGUE.

Dairy Science College: Hebbal, Bangalore; f. 1979; Dir Dr P. A. SHANKAR.

College of Agriculture, Shimoga: f. 1990; Dir Dr K. SHIVAPPA SHETTY.

College of Horticulture: Mudigere; f. 1991; Dir Dr N. VIJAYAKUMAR.

College of Agriculture: Mandiya; f. 1991; Dir S. KUMARASWAMY.

College of Forestry: Ponnampet; f. 1995; Dir Dr N. SWAMY RAO.

College of Sericulture: Chinthamani; f. 1995; Dir Dr D. K. NAGESHCHANDRA.

College of Agriculture: Hassan; f. 1996; Dir Dr M. B. CANNEGOWDA.

UNIVERSITY OF AJMER

Ajmer

Founded 1987; in process of formation

Vice-Chancellor: Prof. R. B. UPADHYAYA
Registrar : Dr J. P. GUPTA

PROFESSORS

BHARDWAJ, T. N., Botany
DUBE, S. N., Mathematics
JOSHI, R. P., Political Science
VASHISHTHA, V. K., History

ALAGAPPA UNIVERSITY

Alagappa Nagar, Karaikudi 630003, Tamil Nadu

Telephone: 35205

Founded 1985

Chancellor: HE THE GOVERNOR OF TAMIL NADU
Vice-Chancellor: Dr P. RAMASAMY
Registrar: Dr R. DHANASEKARAN

Number of teachers: 101
Number of students: 1,545

PRINCIPALS

College of Education: Karaikudi 630003; T. N. SHAMALA
College of Physical Education: Karaikudi 630004; Dr E. K. CHINNAMA REDDY

HEADS OF DEPARTMENTS

Commerce: Dr M. A. ARULANADAM
Computer Applications: Dr S. SAKTHIVEL
Corporate Secretaryship: Dr R. NEELAMEGAM
Education: Dr S. MOHAN
Industrial Chemistry: Dr T. VASUDEVAN
Physical Education: Dr A. M. MOORTHY
Mathematics: Dr K. C. RAO
Physics: Dr R. SABESAN
Tamil: Dr A. VISVANATHAN
Women's Studies: Dr S. GOKILAVANI
Alagappa Institute of Management: Dr A. R. UMAMAHESWAR
Crystal Research Centre: Dr R. DHANASEKARAN

ALIGARH MUSLIM UNIVERSITY

Aligarh, UP 202002

Telephone: 400220
Fax: 400528

Founded as Anglo-Mohamedan Oriental College, 1875; raised to university status, 1920
Residential and Teaching
Language of instruction: English
Indian govt control
Academic year: July to May

Chancellor: HAKIM ABDUL HAMEED SAHEB
Vice-Chancellor: MAHMOOD UR REHMAN
Registrar: Dr H.A.S. JAFRI
Librarian: Prof. NOORUL HASAN KHAN

Library of 680,597 vols; MSS in Arabic, Persian, Urdu and Hindi
Number of teachers: 1,169
Number of students: 19,194

Publications: *News and Views, Tehzibul Akhlaq.*

DEANS

Faculty of Theology: Prof. ABDUL ALEEM
Faculty of Arts: Prof. K. P. SINGH
Faculty of Engineering and Technology: Prof. ASLAM QADEER
Faculty of Law: Prof. S. S. HASANAT AZMI
Faculty of Science: Prof. M. S. Z. CHAGTAI
Faculty of Medicine: Prof. M. ARIF SIDDIQUI
Faculty of Commerce: Prof. A. FAROOQ KHAN
Faculty of Social Sciences: Prof. IQTIDAR H. SIDDIQUI
Faculty of Life Sciences: Prof. M. M. AGRAWAL
Faculty of Unani Medicine: Prof. ANIS AHMAD ANSARI
Faculty of Management Studies and Research: Prof. S. M. OZAIR.

ATTACHED RESEARCH INSTITUTES

Institute of Agriculture: Dir GHULAM NABI BHATT.
Institute of Biotechnology: Dir Prof. SALAHUDDIN.
Centre of West Asian Studies: Dir Prof. AKHTAR MAJEED.
Institute of Petroleum Studies and Chemical Engineering: Dir Prof. HAMID ALI.

UNIVERSITY OF ALLAHABAD

Allahabad 211002, Uttar Pradesh

Telephone: 50668

Founded 1887
Residential and Teaching
Languages of instruction: English and Hindi
Academic year: July to April

Chancellor: HE THE GOVERNOR OF UTTAR PRADESH
Vice-Chancellor: Prof. R. C. MEHROTRA
Registrar: D. N. S. YADAVA
Librarian: R. S. SAXENA

Library of 528,000 vols
Number of students: 37,694

DEANS

Faculty of Arts: Prof. JANAK PANDEY
Faculty of Commerce: Prof. S. K. MITTAL
Faculty of Engineering: Prof. S. K. BHATTACHARYA
Faculty of Law: Prof. RAM SINGH
Faculty of Medicine: Prof. S. K. BAPAT
Faculty of Engineering: Prof. Y. V. N. RAO

UNIVERSITY COLLEGES

Kali Prasad University College: Allahabad; Principal Dr D. K. SAXENA.

Madan Mohan Malaviya College: Allahabad; Principal Prof. M. P. SINGH.

William Holland University College: Allahabad; Principal Dr E. S. K. GHOSH.

CONSTITUENT COLLEGE

Moti Lal Nehru Medical College: Allahabad; f. 1961; Principal Prof. S. K. BAPAT.

There are 11 associated colleges.

AMRAVATI UNIVERSITY

Amravati, Maharashtra 444604

Telephone: 3279

Founded 1983
Teaching and affiliating
Languages of instruction: English, Marathi and Hindi
Academic year: June to April

Chancellor: HE THE GOVERNOR OF MAHARASHTRA
Vice-Chancellor: Dr RAM T. DESHMUKH
Registrar: G. L. JAGTAP

Library of 16,500 vols
Number of students: 90,000

Faculties of arts, ayurvedic medicine, commerce, education, engineering and technology, home science, law, science, social sciences, medicine

There are 100 affiliated colleges

ANDHRA PRADESH AGRICULTURAL UNIVERSITY

Hyderabad 500030, Andhra Pradesh

Telephone: (40) 4015011

Fax: (40) 4015031

Founded 1964
Language of instruction: English
Academic year: July to June

Chancellor: HE THE GOVERNOR OF ANDHRA PRADESH
Vice-Chancellor: Dr I. V. SUBBA RAO
Registrar: Dr V. PRABHAKAR RAO
Librarian: Dr D. B. ESWARA REDDY

Library of 83,000 vols
Number of teachers: 1,565
Number of students: 3,894

Publication: *Research Journal* (English, quarterly).

DEANS

Faculty of Agriculture: Dr P. RAGHAVULU
Faculty of Veterinary Science: Dr V. JAYARAMA KRISHNA
Faculty of Home Science: Dr R. VATSALA
Faculty of Postgraduate Studies: Dr M. V. SHANTARAM

CONSTITUENT COLLEGES

College of Agriculture: Bapatla; Principal Dr N. SREERAM REDDY.

College of Agriculture: Rajendranagar; Principal Dr Y. N. REDDY.

College of Agriculture: Naira; Principal Dr V. T. RAJU.

College of Agriculture: Aswaraopet; Principal Dr I. V. SUBBA RAO.

College of Agriculture: Tirupati; Principal Dr B. LAKSHMI REDDY.

College of Agriculture: Mahanandi; Principal S. RAMI REDDY (acting).

College of Agricultural Engineering: Bapatla; Principal Dr D. APPA RAO (acting).

College of Veterinary Science: Tirupati; Principal Dr K. NARASAIAH NAIDU.

College of Veterinary Science: Rajendranagar; Principal Dr B. YADAGIRI.

College of Home Science: Hyderabad; Principal Dr S. RENUKA.

College of Home Science: Bapatla; Principal Dr D. SHARADA.

Agricultural Polytechnic College: Palem; Principal Dr T. BAPIREDDY.

College of Fishery Science: Muthukur; Principal Dr K. GOPALA RAO.

Extension Education Institute: Hyderabad; Head Dr P. VENKATA RAMAIAH.

Agricultural Polytechnic College: Jagtial; Principal Dr N. VENKATA REDDY (acting).

College of Veterinary Science: Gannavaram; Principal Dr M. V. SUBBA RAO.

ANDHRA UNIVERSITY

Waltair 530003, Andhra Pradesh

Telephone: 63324

Founded 1926
Teaching and Affiliating
Languages of instruction: English and Telugu
Academic year: July to June

Chancellor: THE GOVERNOR OF ANDHRA PRADESH
Vice-Chancellor: Dr R. RADHAKRISHNA
Registrar: Prof. P. U. S. RAMA RAS
Librarian: Prof. GUSLNARASIMHA RAJU

Library of 341,505 vols
Number of teachers: 883
Number of students: 53,137

Publications: *Annual Report, Handbook.*

The faculties are in the process of reorganization.

CONSTITUENT COLLEGES

Erskine College of Natural Sciences: Waltair; f. 1941; Principal Prof. V. LAKSHMINARAYANA.

J.V.D. College of Science and Technology: Waltair; f. 1932; Principal Prof. V. LAKSHRINARAYANA.

University College of Arts and Commerce: Waltair; f. 1931; Principal Prof. B. V. KISHAN.

University College of Engineering: Waltair; f. 1955; Principal Prof. R. P. RANGANADNA RAO.

University College of Law: Waltair; f. 1945; Principal Prof. B. V. KISHAN.

There are 109 affiliated colleges. The University also runs postgraduate courses at Nuzvid, Srikakulam and Kakinada.

ANNA UNIVERSITY

Sardar Patel Rd, Guindy, Chennai 600025

Telephone: (44) 2351445
Fax: (44) 2350397

Founded 1978 as Perarignar Anna University of Technology, name changed 1982
Autonomous control
Language of instruction: English
Academic year: July to July

Vice-Chancellor: Prof. R. M. VASAGAM
Registrar: Dr R.JEGATHEESAN
Librarian: Dr M. SREENIVASAN

Library of 169,000 vols
Number of teachers: 470
Number of students: 5,818

Publications: *Annual Report, Calendar, News Bulletin.*

DEANS

Civil Engineering: Dr A. R. SANTHAKUMAR
Mechanical Engineering: Dr G. RAMAIYAN
Electrical Engineering: Dr M. ABDULLAH KHAN
Engineering (Madras Institute of Technology): Dr S. GANAPATHY
Technology: Dr KUNTHALA JAYARAMAN
Architecture and Planning: Dr A. N. SACHITHANANDAN
Science and Hamanities: Dr S. NATARAJAN

HEADS OF DEPARTMENT

Civil Engineering: Dr M. LAKSHMIPATHY
Mechanical Engineering: Dr C. P. SARATHY
Printing Technology: Dr LALITHA JAYARAMAN
Mining Engineering: Dr L. AJAYKUMAR
Management Studies: THIRU V. NAGESWARAN
Centre for New and Renewable Sources of Energy: Dr A. N. RAO
Centre for Appropriate Technology: Prof. K. ARUNAGIRI
Mathematics: Dr M. SREENIVASN
Physics: Dr R. ASOKAMANI
Geology and Geophysics: Dr C. MOHANA DOSS
Chemistry: Dr V. MURUGESAN
Humanities and Social Sciences: Prof. V. JALAJAMANI
Chemical Engineering: Dr V. MOHAN
Textile Technology: Dr J. VENKATA RAO
Leather Technology: Dr T. RAMASAMI
Aeronautical Engineering: Dr P. BASKARAN
Automobile Engineering: Dr S. SUBRAMANIYAM
Production Technology: Dr S. VENKATASWAMY
Rubber Technology (Division): Dr V. SIVASANKARAN
Centre for Water Resources and Ocean Management: Dr N. V. PUNDARIKANTHAN
Centre for Environmental Studies: Dr K. R. RANGANATHAN
Institute of Remote Sensing: Dr T. NATARAJAN
Electrical and Electronics Engineering: Dr S. R. PARANJOTHI
Electronics and Communication Engineering: Dr F. F. PAPA
Computer Science and Engineering: Dr K. M. MEHATA
Ramanujan Computer Centre: Dr V. SANKARANARAYANAN
Audio Visual Research Centre: Dr R. S. RAMASWAMY
Centre for Biotechnology: Dr P. KALIRAJ
Crystal Growth Centre: Dr C. SUBRAMANIAM
Architecture and Planning: Prof. A. MOHAMMED HARIS
Instrumentation and Electronics: Dr C. N. KRISHNAN

ANNAMALAI UNIVERSITY

Annamalai Nagar PO, Tamil Nadu 608002

Telephone: (4144) 22249
Telex: 04602-201
Fax: (4144) 23080

Founded 1929
Languages of instruction: Tamil and English
Academic year: July to June

Chancellor: Dr JUSTICE MS FATHIMA BEEVI
Pro-Chancellor: Dr M. A. M. RAMASWAMY
Vice-Chancellor: Dr M. G. MUTHUKUMARASAMY
Registrar: Dr P. L. SABARATHINAM
Librarian: Dr M. SURIYA

Library of 428,000 vols, 1,140 MSS
Number of teachers: 877
Number of students: 8,972

Publications: *Annamalai University Research Journal, Annamalai University Magazine, Annamalai University Newsletter.*

DEANS

Faculty of Arts: Dr K. KARUPPIAH
Faculty of Science: Dr P. R. KARPAGAGANAPATHY
Faculty of Engineering and Technology: Prof. G. AMBALAVANAN
Faculty of Education: Dr MAMOTA DAS
Faculty of Indian Languages: Dr A. ANANTHANATARAJAN
Faculty of Fine Arts: (vacant)
Faculty of Agriculture: Dr P. BASKARAN
Faculty of Medicine: Dr S. VEMBAR
Faculty of Dentistry: Dr B. SRINIVASAN

ARUNACHAL UNIVERSITY

Rono Hills, Itanagar 791112

Telephone: (360) 47252
Fax: (360) 47317

Founded 1984
State control
Language of instruction: English

Chancellor: Shri MATA PRASAD
Vice-Chancellor: Prof. A. C. BHAGABATI
Registrar: JORAM BEGI
Librarian: (vacant)

Number of teachers: 46
Number of students: 385

Publications: *Newsletter* (1 a year), *Research Journal* (1 a year).

DEAN

Faculty of Social Sciences: Prof. S. DUTTA

HEADS OF DEPARTMENTS

History: Prof. S. DUTTA
Political Science: Prof. A. C. TALUKDAR
Education: Prof. J. C. SONI
English: Dr B. N. SINGH
Economics: Dr A. MITRA
Geography: Dr R. S. YADAV
Tribal Studies: Prof. TAMO MIBANG
Commerce: Dr RANJIT TAMULI

ASSAM AGRICULTURAL UNIVERSITY

Jorhat 785013, Assam

Telephone: 320989

Founded 1969

Teaching, research and extension at undergraduate and postgraduate levels in agriculture (Jorhat campus and Biswanath Chariali), home science (Jorhat campus), animal husbandry and veterinary science (Khanapara campus and Azad, North Lakhimpur) and fisheries (Raha)
Language of instruction: English
Autonomous control

Chancellor: HE THE GOVERNOR OF ASSAM
Vice-Chancellor: Dr U. C. UPADHYAY
Registrar: Dr M. N. CHETIA
Librarian: Sri MAHENDRA NATH BORAH

Library of 90,000 vols (main campus)
Number of teachers: 530
Number of students: 2,500

Publications: *Newsletter* (English, fortnightly), *Ghare-Pathare* (Assamese, monthly), *Krishibikshan* (Assamese, quarterly), *Package of Practices for Rabi Crops* (English, 2 a year), *Package of Practices for Kharif Crops* (English, 2 a year), *Journal of Research.*

DEANS

Faculty of Agriculture: Dr D. N. DUTTA
Faculty of Veterinary Science: Dr A. R. GOGOI
Faculty of Home Science: Dr LABONYA MAJUMDER

HEADS OF DEPARTMENTS

Faculty of Agriculture:

Genetics and Plant Breeding: Dr P. K. DUARA (acting)
Horticulture: Dr A. SADEQUE
Extension Education: Dr R. C. SARMA (acting)
Agronomy: Dr S. R. BAROOVA
Botany and Plant Pathology: Dr A. C. THAKUR
Zoology and Entomology: Dr J. N. KHOUND
Animal Production and Management: Dr H. GOGOI
Agricultural Economics and Farm Management: Shri R. N. SARMA
Tea Husbandry and Technology: A. K. NEOG
Physics and Meteorology: Dr K. K. NATH (acting)
Language: Dr M. N. CHOUDHURY
Agricultural Engineering: Dr P. K. DUTTA
Biochemistry and Agricultural Chemistry: Dr C. R. SARKAR
Crop Physiology and Agricultural Botany: Dir S. C. DEY
Agricultural Statistics: Dr B. K. BHATTACHARYYA
Nematology: Dr P. N. PHUKAN

Faculty of Veterinary Science:

Medicine: Dr C. C. KALITA
Surgery: Dr S. C. PATHAK
Gynaecology: Dr B. N. BORGOHAIN
Extension Education: Dr K. SAHARIAH
Nutrition: Dr P. C. DAS
Animal Production and Management: Dr N. N. BORA
Microbiology: Dr G. P. PATGIRI (acting)
Pathology: Dr A. MUKIT
Physiology: Dr B. N. CHAKRAVARTTY
Pharmacology: Dr H. N. KHANIKAR
Anatomy: Dr C. C. BORDOLOI
Parasitology: Dr B. C. LAHKAR
Animal Breeding and Genetics: Dr D. DAS
Poultry Science: Dr K. K. DUTTA

Faculty of Home Science:

Clothing and Textiles: Dr AMIYA GOGOI
Child Development and Family Relations: Dr M. PHUKON
Home Management: Dr M. PATHAK
Food and Nutrition: Dr B. BAROOVA
Extension Education: Dr S. SIDDIQUI

AVADH UNIVERSITY

PB 17, Faizabad, UP 224001
Telephone: 814230
Founded 1975
Teaching and Affiliating
Languages of instruction: English, Hindi
Academic year: July to June

Chancellor: HE THE GOVERNOR OF UTTAR PRADESH
Vice-Chancellor: Prof. K. P. NAUTIYAL
Registrar: A. N. SETH
Librarian: S. K. SINGH

Number of teachers: 19 (university), 2006 (affiliated colleges)
Number of students: 45,220 (university and affiliated colleges)

DEANS

Arts: Prof. V. K. PANDEY
Commerce: Dr S. M. VERMA
Education: Dr S. P. SINGH
Law: Dr K. N. PANDEY
Science: Prof. L. K. SINGH

There are 33 affiliated colleges.

AWADHESH PRATAP SINGH UNIVERSITY

Rewa 486003, Madhya Pradesh
Telephone: 22277
Founded 1968
Affiliating and Teaching
Languages of instruction: Hindi and English
Autonomous control
Academic year: July to March

Chancellor: HE THE GOVERNOR OF MADHYA PRADESH
Vice-Chancellor: Prof. J. S. RATHORE
Registrar: Shri N. K. TIWARI
Librarian: (vacant)

Library of 517,229 vols
Number of students: 53,196

Publication: *Vindhya Bharati* (quarterly).

DEANS

Faculty of Life Science: Prof. G. P. SHRIVASTAVA
Faculty of Social Science: Prof. R. K. VERMA
Faculty of Arts: (vacant)
Faculty of Law: (vacant)
Faculty of Medicine: Dr M. L. GUPTA
Faculty of Engineering: Dr PARANJPE
Faculty of Education: (vacant)
Faculty of Commerce: Prof. R. P. NAMDEO
Faculty of Science: Dr K. C. MATHUR
Faculty of Ayurveda: Dr R. B. SOHGAURA
Faculty of Sanskrit: (vacant)

HEADS OF DEPARTMENT

Environmental Biology: Dr S. BHATNAGAR
Physics: Prof. S. P. AGRAWAL
Psychology: Dr A. K SRIVASTAVA
Chemistry: Dr K. C. MATHUR
Ancient Indian History: Dr R. K. VARMA
Russian Language: RANI MATHUR
Hindi: Dr K. PRASAD
English: (vacant)
Business Economics: Dr V. C. SINHA
Management: Dr V. C. SINHA
Mathematics and Statistics: Dr R. B. MISHRA

There are 11 constituent colleges and 43 affiliated colleges.

BABASAHEB BHIMRAO AMBEDKAR BIHAR UNIVERSITY

Muzaffarpur, Bihar 843001
Telephone: 3066
Founded 1952, re-established 1960
Teaching and Affiliating
Languages of instruction: English and Hindi
Academic year: June to May (three terms)

Chancellor: HE THE GOVERNOR OF BIHAR
Vice-Chancellor: Prof. (Mrs) SHKIL AHMED
Registrar: Dr SHASTRI BHUSHAN VERMA
Librarian: R. ROY (acting)

Library of 98,395 vols
Number of students: 84,000

Publications: *Calendar, Journal.*

DEANS

Faculty of Arts: K. N. SINHA
Faculty of Commerce: (vacant)
Faculty of Education: N. K. PRASAD
Faculty of Engineering: R. K. GARG
Faculty of Law: N. P. SINGH
Faculty of Medicine: R. N. THAKUR
Faculty of Science: S. C. PRASAD
Faculty of Social Science: B. P. SINHA

There are 20 constituent colleges, two government colleges and 38 affiliated colleges.

BANARAS HINDU UNIVERSITY

Varanasi 221005, UP
Telephone: (542) 311558
Telex: 0545-304
Fax: (542) 312059
Founded 1915
Residential and Teaching
Languages of instruction: Hindi and English
Central control
Academic year: July to April (three terms)

Visitor: PRESIDENT OF THE REPUBLIC OF INDIA
Chancellor: Dr VIBHUTI NARAIN SINGH
Vice-Chancellor: Dr HARI GAUTAM
Registrar: Prof. K. M. PANDEY
Librarian: RAMJI SINGH

Library of 870,000 vols
Number of teachers: 1,157
Number of students: 14,812

Publications: *BHU Journal, Prajna, BHU News.*

DEANS

Faculty of Arts: Prof. V. C. SRIVASTAVA
Faculty of Agriculture: Prof. A. N. MAURYA
Faculty of Indian Medicine (Ayurveda): Prof. G. P. DUBEY
Faculty of Commerce: Prof. D. N. SINGH
Faculty of Education: Prof. KAMALA RAI
Faculty of Engineering and Technology: Prof. M. PRASAD
Faculty of Law: Prof. G. P. VERMA
Faculty of Management Studies: Prof. R. M. SRIVASTAVA
Faculty of Medicine: Prof. S. MOHANTI
Faculty of Oriental Learning and Theology: Prof. S. S. SHASTRI
Faculty of Performing Arts: Prof. C. R. JYOTISHI
Faculty of Science: Prof. SURESH CHANDRA
Faculty of Social Sciences: Prof. A. S. UPADHYAY
Faculty of Visual Arts: Prof. B. S. KATT

HEADS OF DEPARTMENTS

Faculty of Arts:

Ancient Indian History Culture, Archaeology: Prof. V. C. SRIVASTAVA
History of Art: Dr M. N. P. TIWARI
Arabic: Dr N. FARUQUI
Bengali: Dr K. B. CHAKRAVORTY
English: Prof. M. K. CHAUDHURY
Foreign Languages: Dr KAMAL SHEEL
Hindi: Prof. SRINIVAS PANDEY
Indian Languages: GHANSHYAM NEPAL
Journalism and Mass Communication: Dr B. R. GUPTA
Library and Information Science: Dr S. N. SINGH
Persian: Dr S. AKHTAR
Philosophy and Religion: Prof. R. R. PANDEY
Urdu: Dr S. H. A. NAQAVI
Physical Education: Dr D. K. DUREHA
Sanskrit: Prof. K. P. SINGH
Pali and Buddhist Studies: Dr P. DUBEY

German Studies: Dr Indu Bhave
French Studies: Prof. V. C. Srivastava
Marathi: Dr Sunanda Das
Telugu: Dr G. Trivikramaiah
Linguistics: Dr R. B. Mishra

Faculty of Social Sciences:

Economics: Prof. P. K. Bhargava
History: Dr Aruna Sinha
Political Science: Prof. R. R. Jha
Psychology: Dr A. P. Singh
Sociology: Prof. O. P. Gupta

Faculty of Medicine:

Anatomy: Prof. M. Singh
Anaesthesiology: Prof. A. Lal
Biochemistry: Prof. S. Mohauti
Biophysics: Prof. S. Mohauti
Cardiology: Dr P. R. Gupta
Cardiothoracic Surgery: Prof. T. K. Lahiri
Dentistry: Prof. B. P. Singh
Dermatology and Venereology: Dr Lata Sharma
Endocrinology: Prof. J. K. Agrawal
Forensic Medicine: Prof. C. B. Tripathi
Gastroenterology: Prof. A. K. Jain
Medicine: Prof. K. K. Tripathi
Microbiology: Prof. A. K. Gulati
Nephrology: Prof. R. G. Singh
Neurology: Prof. Surendra Mishra
Neurosurgery: Prof. S. Mohanti
Obstetrics and Gynaecology: Prof. L. K. Pandey
Ophthalmology: Prof. Rajendra Singh
Otorhinolaryngology: Prof. M. K. Agrawal
Orthopaedics: Prof. S. K. Saraf
Paediatric Surgery: Prof. S. Chooramami Gopal
Physiology: Prof. R. K. Sharma
Pharmacology: Prof. S. K. Bhattacharya
Pathology: Prof. P. K. Shukla
Plastic Surgery: Prof. F. M. Tripathi
Preventive and Social Medicine: Prof. J. Tadon
Psychiatry: Prof. Indra Sharma
Paediatrics: Prof. P. N. Singla
Radiology: Prof. A. K. Agrawal
Surgery: Prof. H. S. Shupla
Radiotherapy and Radiation Medicine: Dr A. K. Asthana
Tuberculosis and Chest Diseases: Dr S. C. Matah
Urology: Dr B. P. Singh

Faculty of Ayurveda:

Ayurveda Samhita: Prof. G. B. Dubey
Dravya Guna: Dr V. K. Joshi
Basic Principles: Prof. I. P. Singh
Kaya Chikitsa: Prof. R. H. Singh
Prasuti Tantra: Dr M. Dwivedi
Shalya Shalakya: Dr M. Sahu
Medicinal Chemistry: Dr Mahendra Sahai
Rasa Shastra: Dr C. B. Jha

Faculty of Science:

Botany: Prof. K. P. Singh
Chemistry: Prof. R. Balaji Rao
Geology: Prof. V. K. Gairola
Geophysics: Prof. T. Lal
Geography: Prof. Onkar Singh
Mathematics: Prof. S. N. Lal
Physics: Prof. O. N. Srivastava
Zoology: Prof. A. K. Mittal
Statistics: R. C. R. Yadav
Biochemistry: Dr R.-S. Dubey
Home Science: Prof. P. Srivastava
Computer Science: Prof. A. N. Mantri
Biotechnology: Prof. A. Sadhi

Faculty of Agriculture:

Agronomy: Prof. H. C. Sharma
Agricultural Economics: Prof. R. S. Dixit
Entomology and Agricultural Zoology: Prof. H. N. Singh
Horticulture: Prof. A. M. Maurya
Genetics and Plant Breeding: Prof. Bhupendra Rai
Mycology and Plant Pathology: Prof. D. C. Pant
Plant Physiology: Prof. C. P. Singh
Soil Science and Agricultural Chemistry: Prof. R. C. Tiwari
Extension Education: Prof. K. N. Pandey
Animal Husbandry and Dairying: Prof. R. K. Yadava
Farm Engineering: Prof. S. Singh

Faculty of Engineering and Technology:

Applied Chemistry: Prof. D. C. Rupainwar
Applied Mathematics: Prof. V. V. Menon
Applied Physics: Prof. S. P. Ojha
Chemical Engineering: Prof. P. Mishra
Civil Engineering: Prof. V. P. Mishra
Ceramic Engineering: Prof. S. P. Singh
Electrical Engineering: Prof. G. K. Rao
Electronics Engineering: Prof. S. K. Srivastava
Mechanical Engineering: Prof. B. B. Bansal
Metallurgical Engineering: Prof. V. Singh
Mining Engineering: Prof. D. P. Singh
Pharmaceutics: Prof. S. K. Patnaik
Computer Engineering: Dr A. K. Tripalhi

Faculty of Oriental Learning and Theology:

Dharmashastra and Mimamsa: Dr N. R. Srinivasan
Vaidic Darshan: Prof. K. K. Sharma
Jyotish: Dr R. C. Pandey
Dharmagam: Prof. K. D. Tripathi
Sahitya: Dr C. M. Dwivedi
Veda: V. Mishra
Vyakaran: Dr R. C. Panda
Bauddha and Jain Darshan: Prof. S. S. Shashtri

Faculty of Performing Arts:

Vocal Music: Prof. C. R. Jyolishi
Instrumental Music: Prof. R. P. Shashtri
Musicology: Prof. C. R. Jyotishi

Faculty of Visual Arts:

Painting: Dr R. N. Mishra
Plastic Arts: Prof. B. S. Katt
Applied Arts: S. Dasgupta

CONSTITUENT COLLEGE

Mahila Maha Vidyalaya: Varanasi; f. 1929; Principal Prof. K. R. Ranganayakalu.

ATTACHED INSTITUTES

Institute of Agricultural Sciences: Dir Prof. C. B. S. Rajput
Institute of Medical Sciences: Dir Prof. V. P. Singh
Institute of Technology: Dir Prof. M. Bhattacharya

There are four affiliated colleges.

BANASTHALI VIDYAPITH

PO Banasthali Vidyapith, Rajasthan 304022

Telephone: (1438) 8324
Fax: (1438) 8365

Founded 1935 as college, university status 1983
Autonomous control
Languages of instruction: Hindi and English

President: Shrimati Ratan Shastri
Vice-President: Dr Sushila Nayyar
Director: Prof. (Miss) Sushila Vyas
Secretary: Prof. D. Shastri

Library of 200,000 vols
Number of teachers: 306
Number of students: 2,875

DEANS

Faculty of Education: Dr T. K. S. Lakshmi
Faculty of Fine Arts: Prof. R. C. S. Nadkarni
Faculty of Home Science: Prof. Sushila Vyas
Faculty of Humanities: Dr C. K. Goswami
Faculty of Science: Dr D. Kishore
Faculty of Social Sciences: Prof. Diwakar Shastri

BANGALORE UNIVERSITY

Jnana Bharathi, Bangalore 560056, Karnataka State

Telephone: (80) 3303172
Fax: (80) 3389295

Founded 1964
Affiliating
Languages of instruction: Kannada and English
Academic year: June to March

Chancellor: HE The Governor of Karnataka
Vice-Chancellor: Dr N. R. Shetty
Registrar: B. R. Jayaramaraj Urs
Librarian: Pattan Shetty

Central Library of 271,098 vols
Number of teachers: 456
Number of students: 142,697

Publications: *Sadhane* (Kannada, quarterly), *Vignana Bharathi, Vidya Bharathi, Bash Bharathi* (2 a year), *Janapriya Vignana* (monthly).

DEANS

Faculty of Arts: Prof. Srinivasa Rao
Faculty of Commerce: Dr P. N. Reddy
Faculty of Education: Dr M. Khajapeer
Faculty of Engineering: Dr K. Ranga
Faculty of Law: Prof. V. B. Coutinho
Faculty of Medicine: Dr B. M. Jayaram
Faculty of Science: Dr S. Ravichandra Reddy
Faculty of Technology: Prof. B. G. Srinivasalu
Faculty of Oncology: Dr N. Anantha
Faculty of Communication: Dr Leela Rao

HEADS OF DEPARTMENTS

English: Dr Vimala Rao
Kannada: Dr K. Marulasiddappa
Telugu: Dr G. S. Mohan
Sanskrit: Dr M. Shivakumaraswamy
Hindi: Dr T. G. Prabha Shankar
Urdu: Dr M. Nooruddin
Drama, Dance and Music: Rajalakshmi Tirunarayanan
History: Dr Shadakshariah
Political Science: R. L. M. Patil
Geography: Dr B. Eshwarappa
Economics: S. N. Nanje Gowda
Sociology: Dr Srinivasa Rao
Social Work: Dr L. S. Gandhi Doss
Philosophy: Dr Srinivasa Rao
Psychology: Dr Indira Jai Prakash
Physics: Dr C. Raghavendra Rao
Chemistry: Dr N. M. Nanje Gowda
Mathematics: Dr H. T. Rathod
Botany: Dr B. H. M. Nijalingappa
Zoology: Dr S. Ravichandra Reddy
Geology: K. G. Gubbaiah
Statistics: Dr K. Harischandra
Library Science: Dr A. Y. Asundi
Civil Engineering: Dr K. Ranga
Mechanical Engineering: Dr V. K. Basalalli
Electrical Engineering: Prof. K. Mallikarjun Chetty
Law: Prof. V. B. Coutinho
Commerce: Dr P. N. Reddy
Education: M. S. Talawar
Physical Education: L. R. Vydyanathan
Communication: Dr Leela Rao
Centre for Rural Development Studies: K. Rangaswamy
Electronics and Computer Engineering: Prof. H. N. Shivashankar
Architecture: K. V. Guruprasad
Sericulture: S. R. Ananthanarayana

UNIVERSITY COLLEGES

University College of Physical Education: Bangalore; Principal Dr K. B. Chinnappa.

University Law College: Bangalore; Principal Prof. V. B. Coutinho.

University Visvesvaraya College of Engineering: Bangalore; Principal Dr P. NARAYANA REDDY.

There are 315 affiliated colleges.

BARKATULLAH VISHWAVIDYALAYA

Bhopal 462026, MP

Telephone: 547151

Founded 1970 as Bhopal University, name changed 1989

Teaching and Affiliating

Languages of instruction: English and Hindi

Chancellor: HE THE GOVERNOR OF MADHYA PRADESH

Vice-Chancellor: Prof. I. S. CHAUHAN

Registrar: Dr N. S. VERMA

Librarian: R. K. MISHRA

Library of 52,700 vols

Number of teachers: 1,100

Number of students: 40,000 (incl. affiliated colleges)

DEANS

Faculty of Arts: Dr ARIFA SIMMIN

Faculty of Commerce: Dr D. P. SHARMA

Faculty of Education: P. K. KHANNA

Faculty of Engineering: Dr C. S. BHATNAGAR

Faculty of Home Science: Dr MADHU MISHRA

Faculty of Law: H. L. JAIN

Faculty of Medicine: Dr N. R. BHANDARI

Faculty of Science: (vacant)

Faculty of Social Science: Dr I. S. CHAUHAN

Faculty of Life Science: Dr SANTOSH KUMAR

Faculty of Technical Education: Prof. G. S. CHANDARAN

There are 43 affiliated colleges.

MAHARAJA SAYAJIRAO UNIVERSITY OF BARODA

Baroda 390002, Gujarat

Telephone: 795600

Founded 1949

Residential and Teaching

Language of instruction: English

Academic year: June to April (two terms)

Vice-Chancellor: PADMA RAMACHANDRAN

Pro-Vice-Chancellor: Prof. DIPAK KUMAR

Registrar: D. P. CHHAYA

Librarian: Prof. M. K. R. NAIDU

Library of 404,043 vols

Number of teachers: 1,230

Number of students: 32,609

Publications: *Handbook, Annual Report, Journal of Oriental Institute, Journal of Education and Psychology, Journal of Animal Morphology and Physiology, Journal of Education and Psychology, Swadhyaya, Pavo, Journal of Technology and Engineering* (annually).

DEANS

Faculty of Arts: Prof. D. H. MOHITE

Faculty of Science: Prof. L. J. PAREKH

Faculty of Commerce: Prof. B. S. PATEL

Faculty of Education and Psychology: Prof. S. M. YOSHI

Faculty of Medicine: Dr KAMAL J. PATHAK

Faculty of Technology and Engineering: Prof. H. V. BHAVNANI

Faculty of Fine Arts: Prof. P. D. DHUHAL

Faculty of Home Science: Dr ANUPAMA SHAH

Faculty of Social Work: Prof. S. B. SAXENA

Faculty of Law: Prof. L. J. PAREKH

Faculty of Management Studies: Prof. M. M. DADI

Faculty of Performing Arts: Prof. D. K. BHONSALE

Faculty of Journalism and Communication: Dr H. N. DESAI

PROFESSORS

Faculty of Arts:

JUNEJA, O. P., English
KAR, P., English
MEHTA, S. Y., Gujarati
MOHITE, D. H., Political Science
PANDYA, N. M., Economics
PANTHAM, T., Political Science
PAREKH, V. S., Archaeology
PATEL, K. H., Environmental Archaeology
PATEL, P. J., Sociology
REDE, L. A., Economics
SHAH, M. N. (Mrs), Economics
SIDDIQI, M. H., Persian
SONAWANE, V. H., Archaeology

Faculty of Science:

AMBADKAR, P. M., Zoology
BHATTACHARYA, P. K., Chemistry
CHATTOO, B., Microbiology
CHHATPAR, H. S., Microbiology
DESAI, N. D., Geology
DESAI, S. J., Geology
DEVI, S. G., Chemistry
GOYAL, O. P., Mathematics
KATYARE, S. S., Biochemistry
MEHTA, T., Biochemistry
PADH, H., Biochemistry
PAREKH, L. J., Biochemistry
PATEL, H. C., Statistics
PATEL, M. P., Geology
PATEL, N. V., Mathematics
PILO B., Zoology
RAKSHIT, A. K., Chemistry
RAMCHANDRAN, A. V., Zoology
RANGASWAMY, V. C., Geography
RAO, K. K., Microbiology
SHAH, A. C., Chemistry
SHREEHARI, M., Statistics
SOMAYAJULU, D. R. S., Physics
TELANG, S. D., Biochemistry

Faculty of Medicine:

BHOTI, S. J., Ophthalmology
BONDRE, K. V., Anatomy
BUCH, V. P., Radiology
CHANDWANI, S., Physiology
CHAUHAN, L. M., Obstetrics and Gynaecology
DESAI, M. R., Obstetrics and Gynaecology
GHOSH, S., Biochemistry
HATHI, G., Physiology
HEMAVATI, K. G., Pharmacology
JHALA, D. R., Paediatrics
JOSHI, G. D., Preventative and Social Medicine
KARELIA, L. S., Pathology
MAZUMDAR, U., Dentistry
MEHTA, J. P., Surgery
MEHTA, N. C., Medicine
PATHAK, K., Medicine
PATRA, B. S., Surgery
PATRA, S. B., Pathology
RAWAL, H. H., Anaesthesia
SAINATH, M., Ophthalmology
SANGHVI, N. G., Medicine
SAXENA, S. B., Microbiology
SHAH, A. U., Preventative and Social Medicine
SHAH, D. N., Preventative and Social Medicine
SHAK, K. D., Surgery
SHARMA, S. N., Plastic Surgery
SHETH, R. T., Ophthalmology
SHUKLA, G. N., Surgery
TIWARI, R. S., Ear, Nose and Throat
VAISHNAVI, A. J., Orthopaedics
VANKAR, G. K., Psychiatry
VOHRA, P. A., Radiology
VYAS, D. C., Anatomy

Faculty of Technology and Engineering:

AGRAWAL, S. K., Metallurgical Engineering
AGRAWAL, S. R., Applied Mathematics
BALARAMAN, R., Pharmacy
BANGLORE, V. A., Textile Engineering
BASA, D. K., Metallurgical Engineering
BHAGIA, R. M., Applied Mechanics
BHATT, G. D., Mechanical Engineering
BHATT, R. D., Civil Engineering
BHAVNANI, H. V., Civil Engineering
BHAVSAR, N., Electrical Engineering
BIYANI, K. R., Applied Mechanics
CHUDASAMA, U. V., Applied Chemistry
DE, D. K., Textile Engineering
DESAI, P. B., Mechanical Engineering
DESHPANDE, S. V., Architecture
DIVEKAR, M. H., Chemical Engineering
ETHIRAJULU, K., Chemical Engineering
GADGEEL, V. I., Metallurgical Engineering
GOROOR, S. P., Water Management
GUHA, S., Textile Chemistry
GUPTE, S. G., Electrical Engineering
JOSHI, S. M., Electrical Engineering
JOSHI, T. R., Applied Physics
KANITKAR, S. A., Electrical Engineering
KAPADIA, V. H., Textile Engineering
LOIWAL, A. S., Mechanical Engineering
MISHRA, A. N. R., Pharmacy
MISHRA, S. H., Pharmacy
MODI, P. M., Water Management
MOINUDDIN, S., Chemical Engineering
MORTHY, R. S. R., Pharmacy
NANAVATI, J. I., Mechanical Engineering
PAI, K. B., Metallurgical Engineering
PAREKH, B. S., Computer Science
PARMAR, N. B., Civil Engineering
PATEL, A. A., Mechanical Engineering
PATEL, B. A., Electrical Engineering
PATEL, H. J., Computer Science
PATEL, N. M., Applied Mechanics
PATHAK, V. D., Applied Mathematics
PATODI, S. C., Applied Mechanics
POTBHARE, V. N., Applied Physics
PRAJAPATI, J. J., Civil Engineering
PURANIK, S. A., Chemical Engineering
PUTHANPURAYIL, P., Mechanical Engineering
RAJPUT, H. G., Training and Placement
SAVANI, A. K., Civil Engineering
SHAH, A. N., Civil Engineering
SHAH, D. L., Applied Mechanics
SHAH, S. G., Electrical Engineering
SHROFF, A. V., Applied Mechanics
SUKLA, H. J., Mechanical Engineering
SUBRAMANYAM, N., Chemical Engineering
SUNDAR MORTI, N. S., Metallurgical Engineering
SUTARIA, P. N., Civil Engineering
THAKUR, S. A., Electrical Engineering
TRIVEDI, A. I., Electrical Engineering
VASDEV, S., Chemical Engineering
VORA, R. A., Applied Chemistry
VYAS, J. K., Applied Mechanics
YADAV, R., Pharmacy

Faculty of Education and Psychology:

GOEL, D., Education
JOSHI, S. M., Educational Administration
YADAV, M. S., Education

Faculty of Commerce:

BHATT, A. S., Commerce and Business Administration
MOHITE, M. D., Co-operation
PANCHOLI, P. R., Business Economics
PATEL, B. S., Commerce and Business Administration
SANDHE, A. G., Commerce and Business Administration
SHAH, K. R., Economics
SINGH, S. K., Business Economics
SYAN, J. K., Banking and Business Finance
VYAS, I. P., Commerce and Business Administration

Faculty of Management Studies:

DADI, M. M., Management
DHOLAKIA, M. N., Management
JOSHI, K. M., Management
MAHESHWARI, G. C., Management

Faculty of Fine Arts:

PANCHAL, R. R., Sculpture
PATEL, V. S., Graphic Arts

Faculty of Home Science:

BALKRISHNAIH, B., Clothing and Textiles
MANI, U. V., Foods and Nutrition
SARASWATI, T. S., Human Development and Family Studies
SHAH, A., Home Science Extension and Communication

Faculty of Social Work:

ANJARIA, V. N., Social Work
NAVALE, A. S., Social Work
SAXENA, S. B., Social Work

Faculty of Law:

PARIKH, S. N., Law
RATHOD, J. C., Law

Faculty of Performing Arts:

BHONSLE, D. K., Vocal Music
SHAH, P., Dance

Oriental Institute:

NANAVATI, R. I.
WADEKAR, M. L

Centre for Continuing and Adult Education and Community Services:

PARALIKAR, K. R.

CONSTITUENT COLLEGES

Baroda Sanskrit Mahavidyalaya: Baroda; f. 1915; Principal U. H. SHUKLA.

Manibhai Kashibai Amin Arts and Science College and College of Commerce: Padra; f. 1965; Principal Dr W. V. AHIRE.

Oriental Institute: Baroda; see under Research Institutes; Dir Dr R. I. NANAVATI.

Polytechnic: Baroda; f. 1957; Principal A. G. TELPANDE.

ATTACHED CENTRE

Women's Studies Research Centre: Dir Prof. AMITA VERMA.

BERHAMPUR UNIVERSITY

Berhampur 760007, Orissa

Telephone: 3404

Founded 1967
Teaching and Affiliating
Language of instruction: English
State control
Academic year: June to May

Chancellor: HE THE GOVERNOR OF ORISSA
Vice-Chancellor: Prof. M. I. KHAN
Registrar: R. N. MISHRA
Librarian: B. PANDA

Library of 73,000 vols
Number of teachers: 168
Number of students: 31,550

Publication: *Research Journal* (annually).

PROFESSORS

ACHARYA, S., Oriya
BARAL, J. K., Political Science
DAS, D., Oriya
DAS, G. N., Linguistics
DAS, H. H., Political Science
DAS, N. C., Physics
KHAN, P. A., Botany
MAJHI, J., Electronics
MISHRA, S. K., English
MISRA, B. N., Botany
MISRA, D.
MISRA, P. M., Marine Science
MOHANTY, S. P., Physics
MOHAPATRA, N. C., Physics
PADHISHARMA, R., Economics
PANDA, C. S., Chemistry
PANDA, G. P., Law
PANDA, G. S., Business Administration
PANDA, J., Commerce
PANDA, P., Economics
PANIGRAHY, G. P., Chemistry
PARHI, N., Mathematics
PATI, S. C., Chemistry
PATNAIK, B. K., Zoology
PATRA, G. C., Industrial Relations and Labour Welfare
PRASAD, R., Zoology
RAO, E. R., English
RATH, D., Mathematics
SAHU, P. K., Commerce
SAMAL, J. K., History
VERMA, G. P., Zoology

There are 48 affiliated colleges.

BHAGALPUR UNIVERSITY

Bhagalpur 812007, Bihar

Telephone: 22100

Founded 1960
Teaching and Affiliating

Chancellor: HE THE GOVERNOR OF BIHAR
Vice-Chancellor: Dr SUNIL SHARAN
Registrar: Dr MAHENDRA THAKUR
Librarian: (vacant)

Library of 84,350 vols
Number of teachers: 2,038
Number of students: 43,500

DEANS

Faculty of Social Science: Dr LALA INDU BHUSHAN
Faculty of Science: Dr P. L. SRIVASTAVA
Faculty of Commerce: Dr B. K. KEJRIWAL
Faculty of Humanities: Dr V. N. MISHRA
Faculty of Law: Dr S. B. PRASAD
Faculty of Education: USHA RANI KISHKI
Faculty of Engineering: Prof. N. K. P. MISHRA
Faculty of Medicine: Dr A. P. VERMA

There are 42 constituent colleges and 30 affiliated colleges.

BHARATHIAR UNIVERSITY

Coimbatore, Tamil Nadu 641046

Telephone: 422222
Telex: (0855) 488

Founded 1982
Teaching and Affiliating

Chancellor: HE THE GOVERNOR OF TAMIL NADU
Vice-Chancellor: Dr S. SUBRAMANYAN
Registrar: Prof. M. MUTHASAMY
Librarian: M. NARASIMHALU

Library of 66,000 vols
Number of teachers: 78
Number of students: 343

DEANS

Arts: Dr S. PERUMALSAMY
Social Sciences: Prof. P. MUTHUSAMY
Sciences: Dr M. R. RAGHAVACHAR

HEADS OF DEPARTMENTS

Botany: Dr K. UDAIYAN
Computer Science: Dr K. CHELLAPPAN (acting)
Chemistry: Dr K. NATARAJAN
Economics: Dr S. PERUMALSAMY
Environmental Sciences: Dr V. GOPAL
Linguistics: Dr C. SHANMUGOM (acting)
Mathematics: Dr M. R. RAGHAVACHAR
Physical Education: K. R. MUTHUSAMY
Physics: Dr SA. K. NARAYANDASS
Psychology: Dr S. NARAYANAN
Sociology: Dr M. LAKSHMANASINGH
Statistics: Dr V. SOUNDARARAJAN
Tamil: Dr P. BALASUBRAMANIAM
Zoology: Dr R. MANAVALALARAMANUJAM (acting)
School of Management and Entrepreneur Development: Dr P. MUTHUSAMY

There are 62 affiliated colleges.

BHARATHIDASAN UNIVERSITY

Palkalaiperur, Tiruchirappalli, Tamil Nadu 620024

Telephone and fax: (431) 660245

Founded 1982
Teaching and Affiliating
Languages of instruction: English and Tamil
State control
Academic year: July to June

Chancellor: HE THE GOVERNOR OF TAMIL NADU
Vice-Chancellor: Dr P. JAGADEESAN
Registrar: Dr P. SUBAS CHANDRA BOSE (acting)
Librarian: P. SEETHARAMAN (acting)

Library of 52,500 vols
Number of teachers: 2,779
Number of students: 50,007

Publications: *Annual Report, BARD News Letter, Information Bulletin.*

HEADS OF DEPARTMENTS

Mathematics: Dr N. RAMANUJAM
Physics: Dr M. LAKSHMANAN
Chemistry: Dr M. KRISHNA PILLAY
English: Dr A. JOSEPH
Economics: Dr C. THANGAMUTHU
Tamil: Dr M. RAMALINGAM
Earth Sciences: Dr S. M. RAMASWAMY
Educational Technology: Dr S. PURUSHOTHAMAN
Animal Sciences: Dr M. R. CHANDRAN
Biotechnology: Dr M. VIVEKANANDAN
Microbiology: Dr G. SUBRAMANIAN
Plant Science: Dr K. V. KRISHNAMURTHY
Centre for History: Dr N. RAJENDRAN
Sociology: Dr R. SHANKAR
Social Work: Dr S. PALANISAMY
Physical Education: Dr P. MARIAYYAH
Adult, Continuing Education and Extension: Dr K. PARTHASARATHY

There are 68 affiliated colleges, eight approved institutions and two Schools of Excellence.

ATTACHED INSTITUTES

Bharathidasan Institute of Management: Tiruchirappalli 620014; Dir Dr N. JAYASANKARAN.

Bharathidasan School of Energy: Tiruchirappalli 620023; Dir Dr R. VASUDEVAN.

Centre for Distance Education: Tiruchirappalli 620024; Dir Dr V. AYOTH.

BHAVNAGAR UNIVERSITY

Gaurishanker Lake Rd, University Campus, Bhavnagar 364002, Gujarat

Telephone: 20006

Founded 1978
Teaching and Affiliating
Language of instruction: Gujarati
State control
Academic year: June to March (two terms)

Chancellor: HE THE GOVERNOR OF GUJARAT
Vice-Chancellor: Prof. G. H. BHATT
Registrar: D. A. VAISHNAV
Librarian: K. M. VYAS

Library of 77,000 vols
Number of teachers: 391
Number of students: 12,788

DEANS

Faculty of Arts: Dr VINOD JOSHI
Faculty of Science: Dr H. C. DUBE
Faculty of Commerce: Dr. B. K. OZA
Faculty of Education: Dr D. J. MODI
Faculty of Law: D. A. BHATT
Faculty of Rural Studies: R. H. PANDYA
Faculty of Engineering: Prof. G. J. RAVAL

ATTACHED INSTITUTE

Central Salt and Marine Chemicals Research Institute: see under Research Institutes.

BIDHAN CHANDRA KRISHI VISWAVIDYALAYA

PO Krishi Viswavidyalaya, Mohanpur 741252, Nadia, West Bengal

Telephone: (33) 829772
Fax: (3473) 22275
Founded 1974
Residential

Chancellor: The Governor of West Bengal
Vice-Chancellor: Dr S. P. Sarkar
Registrar: Dr S. K. Brahmachari

Library of 65,000 vols
Number of students: 1,082

DEANS

Faculty of Agriculture: Prof. N. Mukherjee
Faculty of Horticulture: Prof. T. P. Mukhopadhyay
Faculty of Agricultural Engineering: Prof. R. K. Ghosh
Postgraduate Studies: Prof. D. K. Dutta

BIRLA INSTITUTE OF TECHNOLOGY

Mesra, Ranchi

Telephone: 301565
Fax: 300615

Founded 1955, university status 1986

Vice-Chancellor: Dr B. Kanta Rao
Registrar: Prof. G. Sahay (acting)
Librarian: Dr U. N. Singh

Library of 60,000 vols
Number of teachers: 149
Number of students: 1,650

HEADS OF DEPARTMENTS

Applied Chemistry: Dr J. Paul
Applied Mechanics: Prof N. R. Rao
Applied Physics: Dr J. Ram
Civil Engineering: Prof. B. S. Rajeevalochanam
Computer Science: Dr P. K. Mahanti
Electrical and Electronic Engineering: Prof. S. H. Kekre
Electronics and Communication Engineering: Prof. S. C. Goel
Management: Prof. A. Prasad
Mathematics: B. B. Mishra
Mechanical Engineering: Prof. K. M. Sirbhaya
Pharmaceutical Sciences: Dr A. K. Sharma
Polymer Engineering: Dr M. Mukherjee
Production Engineering: Dr S. Kumar
Space Engineering and Rocketry: Dr N. L. Munjal

ATTACHED INSTITUTE

Technology Centre, Lalpur: I/C Dr B. B. Mishra.

BIRLA INSTITUTE OF TECHNOLOGY AND SCIENCE

Pilani, Rajasthan 333031

Telephone: Pilani 42192
Fax: 44183
E-mail: jlarora@bits-pilani.ac.in

Founded 1964
Private control
Language of instruction: English
Academic year: July to May (two semesters)

Chairman: Shri K. K. Birla
Director: Prof. S. Venkateswaran
Registrar: Prof. J. L. Arora
Librarian: Shri U. K. Bhargava

Library of 201,030 vols
Number of teachers: 246
Number of students: 4,677

Publication: *Bulletin.*

GROUP LEADERS

Biological Sciences: Dr S. K. Ray
Chemical Engineering: Prof. R. K. Gupta
Chemistry: Prof. G. Sundu
Civil Engineering: Dr Rajiv Gupta
Computer Science and Information Systems: K. Venkatasubramanian
Electrical and Electronics Engineering: Prof. Shivendra N. Sharan
Economics and Finance: Dr N. V. M. Rao
Engineering Technology: Dr V. Rao Raghupatruni
Hospital and Health Systems Management: Dr Nirupama Prakash
Instrumentation: S. Gurunarayanan
Humanistic Studies: Dr Chhana Chakraborti
Management: Subhash Chandra
Mathematics: Prof. M. Ganesh
Mechanical Engineering: Prof. Kodali Rambabu
Museum Studies: Prof. M. K. Kashiramka
Pharmacy: Prof. Ranendra N. Sala
Physics: Prof. R. Mehrotra
Languages, and Science and Technology Development: Prof. Meera Banerji

BIRSA AGRICULTURAL UNIVERSITY

Kanke, Ranchi 834006, Bihar

Telephone: (651) 455850
Fax: (651) 304451
E-mail: bau@bitsmart.com

Founded 1981
Languages of instruction: English and Hindi
Academic year: July to June

Chancellor: HE The Governor of Bihar
Vice-Chancellor: Dr M. A. Mohsin
Registrar: Dr K. P. Singh
Librarian: (vacant)

Library of 70,000 vols
Number of students: 700

Publication: *Journal of Research, BAU* (2 a year)

DEANS

Faculty of Agriculture: Dr M. F. Haque
Faculty of Forestry: (vacant)
Faculty of Veterinary Science and Animal Husbandry: Dr K. G. Narayan
Postgraduate Studies: Dr G. S. Dubey

CHAIRMEN OF DEPARTMENTS

Faculty of Agriculture:
- Plant Breeding and Genetics: Dr F. M. Haque
- Soil Science and Agricultural Chemistry: Dr A. K. Sarkar
- Horticulture: Dr B. P. Jain
- Plant Pathology: Dr D. K. Jha
- Agronomy: Dr V. C. Srivastava
- Agricultural Physics: Dr P. K. Roy
- Entomology: (vacant)
- Agricultural Extension: (vacant)
- Agricultural Engineering: (vacant)

Faculty of Veterinary Science and Animal Husbandry:
- Parasitology: Dr M. Z. Ansari
- Gynaecology: Dr A. K. Sinha
- Pharmacology: Dr R. C. P. Singh
- Medicine: Dr D. K. Thakur
- VPHE: Dr K. G. Narayan
- Physiology: Dr S. P. Prasad
- Anatomy: Dr Gaya Prasad
- Pathology: (vacant)
- Nutrition: Dr J. P. Srivastava
- Surgery: (vacant)
- Animal Production: (vacant)
- Microbiology: Dr J. P. Soman
- Animal Breeding and Genetics: Dr C. S. P. Singh

UNIVERSITY OF BOMBAY

University Rd, Fort, Mumbai 400032

Telephone: (22) 2652819
Fax: (22) 2652832

Founded 1857
Teaching and Affiliating
Language of instruction: English
Academic year: June to April (two terms)

Chancellor: HE The Governor of Maharashtra
Vice-Chancellor: Dr Snehalata S. Deshmukh
Pro Vice-Chancellor: A. P. Pradhan
Registrar: Dr J. D. Chavan
Librarian: Dr S. R. Ganpule

Library of 661,039 vols
Number of students: 262,350

Publications: *Journal of the University of Bombay, University Handbook Parts I–IV, University Series in Monetary and International Economics, University Economics Series, University Sociology Series, University of Bombay Studies, Sanskrit, Prakrit and Pali.* The university Publications Section publishes textbooks and research works done by students and teachers of the university.

DEANS

Faculty of Arts: Dr V. R. Belaporia
Faculty of Science: (vacant)
Faculty of Technology: Prof. S. Sundaram
Faculty of Law: Dr P. V. Mehta
Faculty of Medicine: (vacant)
Faculty of Commerce: (vacant)
Faculty of Dentistry: Dr J. N. I. N. Khanna
Faculty of Fine Arts: Prof. M. G. Rajadhyaksha
Faculty of Ayurvedic Medicine: Vaidya M. G. Naravane

PROFESSORS

Faculty of Arts:
- Antarkar, S. S., Philosophy
- Annakutty, V. K., German Literature
- Arunachalam, B., Geography
- Bandivadekar, C. M., Comparative Literature
- Bhagwatar, P. A., Psychology
- Bharadwaj, M. A., Econometrics
- Bharucha, N., Post-Colonial Literature
- Bhat Nayak, V., Mathematics
- Bhougle, N., 20th-Century Indian Literature in English
- Bokit, S. V., Industrial Policy and Development Banking
- Bhowmik, S. K., Sociology
- Chawathe, P. D., Graphs Theory
- Cowsik, R. C., Mathematics
- Dalvi, A. M. I., Urdu
- Dange, S. S., Sanskrit
- David, A. M., History
- Deshmukh, U. M., Marathi
- Deshpande, C. G., Clinical Psychology
- Deshpande, J. V., Mathematics
- Deshpande, L. K., Economics
- Ganpule, S. R., Library Science
- Gidadhubli, R. G., Economics and Politics of USSR
- Gummadi, N., General Economics
- Janwa, H. L., Algebra
- Joshi, S. A., Philosophy
- Joshi, S. M., Statistical Inference
- Kamath, P. M., American Studies
- Kerawalla, G. J., Education
- Khokle, V. S., Socio-linguistics
- Kumaresan, S., Mathematics
- Lukmani, V. M., English
- Mody, N. B., Civics and Politics
- Mohanty, S. P., Social Demography
- Momin, A. R., Cultural Anthropology
- Nabar, V., Indo-English Literature
- Nachane, D. N., Quantitative Economics
- Nadkarni, M. G., Mathematics
- Nemade, B. V., Comparative Literature
- Phadke, V. S., Geography
- Pinto, M., Public Administration
- Prasad, K. N., Planning and Development
- Pratap, R., Physics
- Ramesh Babu, B., American Political Institutions
- Rao, M. J. M., General Economics
- Sabnis, R. S., Monetary and Industrial Economics
- Sandesara, J. C., Industrial Economics
- Sane, S. S., Mathematics
- Sarang, V. G., English
- Sawant, A. B., African Studies

SAWANT, S. D., Agricultural Economics
SEN, M., Experimental Psychology
SRIRAMAN, S., Transport Economics
TIKEKAR, A. C., Library Science
TIWARI, R., Hindi
VAIDYA, S. S., Marathi
VANAJA, N., Algebra
VASANTKUMAR, T., Kannada Literature

Faculty of Science:
GAJBHIYE, N. S., Physics
GOGAVALE, S. V., Experimental Electronic and Plasma Physics
HOSANGADI, B. D., Organic Chemistry
JOSHI, V. N., Computer Science
KULKARNI, A. R., Plant Sciences
NARAYANAN, P., Life Sciences
PATEL, S. B., Experimental Nuclear Physics
PRATAP, R., Electronics
RANGWALA, A. A., Theoretical Physics
SHETHNA, Y. I., Life Sciences
SIVAKAMI, S., Life Science

Faculty of Commerce:
ANAGOL, M., Banking
GHOSH, P. K., Personnel Management
IYER, V. R., Management
MANERIKAR, V. V., Research Methodology
MURTHY, G. N., Finance and Accounts
SANTANAM, H., Operational Research

Faculty of Technology:
AKMANCHI, K. G., Pharmaceutical Chemistry
BHAT, N. V., Physics
CHANDALIA, S. B., Chemical Engineering
DIXIT, S. G., Physics
JOSHI, J. B., Chemical Engineering
KALE, D. D., Polymer Technology
KULKARNI, P. R., Food Science and Technology
KULKARNI, V. M., Medicinal Chemistry
LOKHANDE, H. T., Fibre Science
MALSHE, V. C., Paint Technology
NYAYADHISH, V. B., Mathematics
PAI, J. S., Biochemical Engineering
PANGARKAR, V. G., Chemical Engineering
RAJADYAKSHA, R. A., Physical Chemistry
RAO, H. M., Engineering
SESHADRI, S., Dyestuffs Technology
SHARMA, M. M., Chemical Engineering
SHENAY, V. A., Textile Chemistry
SUBRAMANIAN, V. V. R., Oil Technology
TELI, M. D., Fibre Science
TIWARI, K. K., Chemical Engineering
TUNGARE, S. A., Architecture
VENKATESEN, T. K., Oil Chemistry
VARADARAJAN, T. S., Applied Physics

Faculty of Law:
CHITNIS, V. S., Criminal Law
KHODIE, N., Mercantile Law

There are 263 constituent colleges and 76 recognized postgraduate institutions (mostly listed under Research Institutes).

BUNDELKHAND UNIVERSITY

Jhansi, UP 284003

Telephone: 1561, 1578

Founded 1975
Affiliating

Vice-Chancellor: Dr SATYAVATI PANDEY RAHGIR
Registrar: Dr RADHEY SHYAM BANSAL
Librarian: Dr S. C. SROTIA

Library of 10,000 vols
Number of teachers: 434
Number of students: 38,000

DEANS

Faculty of Arts: Dr V. S. SHUKLA
Faculty of Science: Dr R. K. DIXIT
Faculty of Commerce: Dr N. S. SRIVASTAVA
Faculty of Education: Dr TAQDIR SINGH
Faculty of Agriculture: Dr G. N. LODHI
Faculty of Law: M. P. DIXIT
Faculty of Medicine: Dr R. N. SRIVASTAVA

There are 20 affiliated colleges.

UNIVERSITY OF BURDWAN

Burdwan 713104, West Bengal

Telephone: Burdwan 2371

Founded 1960
Teaching and Affiliating
Languages of instruction: English and Bengali
Academic year: June to May

Chancellor: HE THE GOVERNOR OF WEST BENGAL
Vice-Chancellor: Prof. DILIP K. BASU
Registrar: M. K. CHATTERJEE
Librarian: (vacant)

Library of 147,000 vols
Number of teachers: 310 (University), 3,411 (Colleges)
Number of students: 72,525

PROFESSORS

ACHARYYA CHAUDHURY, M., Botany
AGARWALA, N., Economics
BAISNAL, A. P., Mathematics
BANDYOPADHYAY, P. C., Sanskirt
BANERJEE, A. K., Botany
BANERJEE, D., History
BANERJEE, R. N., Commerce
BANERJEE, S., Physics
BARUA, D. K., English
BARUA, P. B., Library Science
BASU, A. S., Chemistry
BASU, D. K., Philosophy
BASU, P. S., Botany
BASU, S., Philosophy
BHANJA, P., Botany
BHAR, G. C., Physics
BHATTACHARYA, A. J., Chemistry
BHATTACHARYYA, G. N., Sanskrit
BHATTACHARYYA, R. P., Sanskrit
BISWAS, B. N., Physics
CHAKRABORTY, R. K., History
CHAKRABORTY, S. C., Physics
CHAKRABORTY, S. K., Mathematics
CHAKRABORTY THAKAR, R. M., Economics
CHANDRA, M. C., Law
CHATTERJEE, B., History
CHATTERJEE, P. K., History
CHATTERJEE, S. S., Commerce
CHATTOPADHYAY, P. N., Business Administration
CHATTOPADHYAY, S. P., Botany
CHAUDHURI, A. K., Chemistry
CHAUDHURI, D. K., Zoology
CHAUDHURY, S. B., Mathematics
CHAUDHURY, T. K., Mathematics
DAS, J, Chemistry
DAS, P., Commerce
DAS, T. K., Physics
DE, G. S., Chemistry
DE, N. K., Geography
DE, S. B., Bengali
DUTTA, B. K., Bengali
DUTTA, J. G., Chemistry
DUTTA, R. L., Chemistry
GHOSH, H. C., Law
GHOSH, S. B., Bengali
GHOSH MAJUMDAR, S., Chemistry
GHOSHAL, S. K., Zoology
HAQUE, A., Philosophy
KHAN, G. C., Philosophy
MAJUMDAR, G., Zoology
MAJUMDAR, K. K., Economics
MALLIK, A. K., Commerce
MEDDA, J. N., Zoology
MITRA, C., Geography
MONDAL, K. K., Mathematics
MUKHOPADHYAY, A. K., Botany
MUKHOPADHYAY, M. C., Zoology
MUKHOPADHYAY, R., Commerce
MUKHERJEE, S. N., Mathematics
NANDI, B., Botany
NEOGI, D., Physics
PARASURAM, L., English
RAKSHIT, S. C., Chemistry
ROY, A. B., Political Science
ROY, R. K., Physics
ROY, S., History
ROY, S., Zoology
ROY, S. K., Botany
ROY S. K., Physics
ROY, S. K., Political Science
ROY CHOUDHURY, K. C., Economics
ROY CHOUDHURY, S. K., Mathematics
SAMANTA, B. C., Physics
SAMANTA, L. K., Physics
SARKAR, A. K., Zoology
SARKAR, G. K., Economics
SARMA, P., Botany
SEAL, B. K., Chemistry
SEN, D., Physics
SEN, H., Mathematics
SEN, M. K., English
SEN, P. K., Geography
SENGUPTA, P. K., Physics

There are 63 affiliated colleges.

ATTACHED INSTITUTE

Institute of Science Education: Golapbag, Burdwan; Dir Dr S. K. BANERJEE.

UNIVERSITY OF CALCUTTA

Senate House, 87/1, College St, Calcutta, West Bengal 700073

Telephone: 38-0071
Telex: 0212752

Founded 1857
Teaching and Affiliating
Language of instruction: English
Academic year: July to June

Chancellor: Prof. SAYEED NURAL HASSAN
Vice-Chancellor: Prof. RATHINDRANARAYAN BASU
Pro-Vice-Chancellors: Prof. BHARATI ROY (Academic Affairs), Prof. SUNIL KUMAR LAHIRI (Business Affairs and Finance)
Registrar: Dr TAPAN KUMAR MUKHERJEE
Librarian: (vacant)

Library of 679,001 vols
Number of teachers: 667
Number of students: 300,000

Publications: *Calcutta Review*, *CU Newsletter*, *UNICAL* (all quarterly).

DEANS

Faculty of Agriculture: Prof. B. BHATTACHARYYA
Faculty of Arts: Prof. P. N. RAY
Faculty of Commerce, Social Welfare and Business Management: Prof. B. K. BASU
Faculty of Education, Journalism and Library Science: Prof. B. K. BASU
Faculty of Fine Arts, Music and Home Science: Prof. H. MUKHERJEE
Faculty of Law: A. SEN
Faculty of Medicine: Dr A. CHAUDHURI
Faculty of Science: Prof. J. M. MANDAL
Faculty of Technology: Prof. S. C. SOM

PROFESSORS

University College of Agriculture:
ADHIKARI, M.
BANERJEE, S. P.
BASU, R. N.
BHATTACHARYYA, B.
DAS GUPTA, D. K.
GUPTA, S. K.

University College of Arts:
ALQUADRI, S. M., Arabic and Persian
BANDYOPADHYAY, S., Ancient Indian History and Culture
BANERJEE, A., Economics
BANERJEE, D., Sociology
BANERJEE, S., Linguistics
BANERJEE, S. P., Philosophy
BARUA, D. K., Pali
BASU, S. P., Bengali
BHATTACHARYA, B., Political Science
BHATTACHARYA, M., Political Science
BHATTACHARYA, S., Museology

Bhattacharya, S. C., Ancient Indian History and Culture
Bhattacharya, S. K., Sociology
Chatterjee, A., Sansksrit
Chatterjee, R., Political Science
Chaudhuri, A. K., Economics
Chaudhuri, B., South and South-East Asian Studies
Chowdhuri, B., History
Chowdhuri, K. C., Political Science
Chowdhuri, S., Islamic History and Culture
Das, S. K., English
Dasgupta, A. K., English
Dasgupta, B. K., Economics
Dasgupta, K., Ancient Indian History and Culture
Dutta, R., Economics
Ganguli, B., Political Science
Ganguli, M., Political Science
Ganguli, M. K., Sanskrit
Ghosh, A., Economics
Ghosh, J., Bengali
Goswami, K. R., Philosophy
Hanifi, M., Urdu
Mahapatra, R., Tamil
Majumder, U. K., Bengali
Mallik, A., Economics
Mukherjee, A. K., Bengali
Mukherjee, A. K., Political Science
Mukherjee, B. N., Ancient History and Culture
Mukherjee, N., History
Mukherjee, S. K., Museology
Niyogi, P., Ancient History and Culture
Pal, A. C., Archaeology
Pramanik, S. K., Sociology
Quamruddin, S. M., Islamic History and Culture
Rahatullah, M., Arabic and Persian
Ray, A., Archaeology
Ray, A., South and South-East Asian Studies
Ray, A., Islamic History and Culture
Ray, B., History
Ray, D. K., Museology
Ray, J. K., South and South-East Asian Studies
Ray, P. N., Economics
Sanyal, S., History
Sen, P. K., Philosophy
Sen, R., Philosophy
Sen, S., History
Shastri, V., Hindi
Uganwi, M. Z., Urdu

University College of Commerce:

Banerjee, B.
Basu, B. K.
Datta, K. L.
Dattagupta, A. K.
Dhar, S.
Ganguli, S. K.
Ghob, K.
Khasnobis, R. D.
Mukherjee, S. P.
Ray, A. K.
Sengupta, S. K.
Sinha, G. C.

University College of Law:

Sen, A.

University College of Medicine:

Chakraborti, A. N., Medical Microbiology
Chatterjee, P. C., Pathology
Datta, A. K., Anatomy
Datta, S. K., Pathology
Ganguli, A. K., Physiology
Ghosh, A., Biochemistry
Goswami, M., Physiology
Mukherjee, B. P., Pharmacology
Mukherjee, M. M., Anatomy
Roy, N., Pathology
Sikdar, S., Pharmacology

University College of Science:

Bandhyopadhyay, B., Geography
Bandhyopadhyay, D., Chemistry
Bandhyopadhyay, M. K., Geography
Bandhyopadhyay, P., Chemistry
Banerjee, A., Chemistry
Banerjee, A. B., Biochemistry
Banerjee, A. N., Applied Psychology
Banerjee, A. R., Anthropology
Basu, B., Applied Mathematics
Basu, R., Chemistry
Basu, S., Applied Psychology
Basu, S. C., Applied Mathematics
Basu, S. R., Geography
Betal, H. R., Geography
Bhattacharya, A. K., Biochemistry
Bhattacharya, A., Zoology
Bhowmik, P. K., Anthropology
Biswas, K. M., Chemistry
Chakrabarti, C. G., Applied Mathematics
Chandra, A. K., Botany
Chatterjee, G. C., Biochemistry
Chatterjee, I. B., Biochemistry
Chatterjee, N. B., Zoology
Chatterjee, S. K., Pure Mathematics
Chattopadhyay, S. K., Statistics
Choudhuri, U., Biophysics
Chowdhuri, A., Marine Science
Chowdhuri, R. K., Botany
Das, J., Pure Mathematics
Das, J. N., Applied Mathematics
Das, K. C., Physics
Das, T. K., Physics
Dasgupta, C. K., Biophysics
Datta, N. C., Zoology
Datta, P. C., Botany
Datta, S. C., Botany
Datta Gupta, A. K., Zoology
De, A., Geology
Deb, C. C., Physiology
Deb, M., Psychology
Deb, S., Applied Psychology
Ganguli, S., Pure Mathematics
Ghosh, A., Zoology
Ghosh, A. K., Anthropology
Ghosh, C. K., Biochemistry
Ghosh, P. N., Physics
Ghosh, S., Botany
Gupta, A., Applied Mathematics
Gupta, M. R., Applied Mathematics
Koley, B. N., Physiology
Kundu, R., Psychology
Maiti, A. K., Physiology
Maity, B. R., Zoology
Mondal, J. N., Applied Psychology
Mukherjee, D. P., Anthropology
Mukherjee, M., Biochemistry
Mukherjee, S., Botany
Mukherjee, S., Geology
Mukherjee, S. P., Statistics
Mukhopadhyay, A. S., Zoology
Mukhopadhyay, D. J., Geology
Mukhopadhyay, S. C., Geography
Mullick, D. D., Applied Mathematics
Nanda, D. K., Zoology
Pal, S. G., Zoology
Pan, N. R., Physics
Paramanik, A. K., Applied Mathematics
Poddar, R. K., Biophysics
Purakayastha, R. P., Botany
Ray, A., Applied Mathematics
Ray, M. K., Physics
Raychaudhuri, P., Applied Mathematics
Saha, G. B., Psychology
Saha, H. K., Chemistry
Saha, M., Physics
Saha, N. N., Chemistry
Samajpati, N., Botany
Samanta, B. K., Geology
Sanyal, A. B., Biophysics
Sarkar, S. K., Physics
Sen, B. K., Chemistry
Sen, R. N., Physiology
Sen, R. N., Applied Mathematics
Sen, S., Botany
Sengupta, M., Pure Chemistry
Sharma, A., Botany
Sinha, D. K., Applied Mathematics
Talapatra, B., Chemistry
Talapatra, S. K., Chemistry

University College of Technology:

Bandyopadhyay, S., Computer Science
Banik, A. K., Chemical Engineering
Barman, B., Chemical Engineering
Basu, M. S., Radiophysics and Electronics
Basu, P. K., Radiophysics and Electronics
Basu, S. K., Applied Physics
Basu, S. P., Applied Physics
Bhattacharyya, A. K., Computer Science
Bhattacharyya, D. K., Chemical Technology
Chakrabarti, A. N., Radiophysics and Electronics
Chakrabarti, B. N., Chemical Engineering
Chakrobarti, A. K., Applied Physics
Chatterjee, M. K., Chemical Technology
Chattopadhyay, D., Radiophysics and Electronics
Das, B., Plastics and Rubber Technology
Dasgupta, A. K., Radiophysics and Electronics
Datta, A. K., Radiophysics and Electronics
Datta, A. N., Radiophysics and Electronics
Datta, B. K., Chemical Engineering
Datta, S. N., Applied Physics
Daw, A. N., Radiophysics and Electronics
Dutta, A. K., Applied Physics
Ghosh, A. K., Applied Physics
Ghosh, P., Plastics and Rubber Technology
Lahiri, C. R., Chemical Technology
Majumder, R. N., Chemical Technology
Mitra, N. K., Chemical Technology
Mitra, T. K., Applied Physics
Mukherjee, A. K., Applied Physics
Nag, B. R., Radio Physics and Electronics
Nath, N. J., Radiophysics and Electronics
Paria, B. B., Chemical Engineering
Paria, H., Radiophysics and Electronics
Purkait, N. N., Radiophysics and Electronics
Rakshit, P. C., Radiophysics and Electronics
Roy, P., Chemical Engineering
Roy, S. K., Radiophysics and Electronics
Saha, P. K., Radiophysics and Electronics
Sen, A. K., Radiophysics and Electronics
Sen, D., Chemical Technology
Sen, S., Electronics Science
Sengupta, P. K., Plastics and Rubber Technology
Shom, S. C., Applied Physics

UNIVERSITY COLLEGES

University Colleges of Agriculture: Calcutta; Sec. Prof. A. K. Banik.

University Colleges of Arts: Calcutta; f. 1954; Sec. Dr S. C. Banerjee.

University Colleges of Commerce, Social Welfare and Business Management: Calcutta; f. 1954; Sec. Dr S. C. Banerjee.

University Colleges of Education, Journalism and Library Science: Sec. A. K. Sengupta.

University Colleges of Fine Arts, Music and Home Science: Sec. A. K. Sengupta.

University Colleges of Law: Calcutta; f. 1909; Sec. M. K. Nag.

University Colleges of Medicine: Calcutta; f. 1957; Sec. Dr D. Bagchi.

University Colleges of Science: Calcutta; f. 1954; Sec. Prof. A. K. Banik.

University Colleges of Technology: Calcutta; f. 1954; Sec. Prof. A. K. Banik.

CONSTITUENT COLLEGES

All India Institute of Hygiene and Public Health: Dir Dr B. N. Ghosh; see under Colleges.

Institute of Post-Graduate Medical Education and Research: 244 Acharyya J. C. Bose Rd, Calcutta 700020; Dir Prof. D. Sen.

Presidency College: 86/1 College St, Calcutta; f. 1817; Principal Dr S. Roychowdhury.

Sanskrit College: Bankim Chatterjee St, Calcutta; f. 1824; Principal B. P. Bhattacharyya.

School of Tropical Medicine: Calcutta; Dir Dr B. D. Chatterjee.

There are also 37 professional colleges and 207 affiliated colleges.

UNIVERSITY OF CALICUT

PO Calicut University, Thenhipalam 673635, Kerala

Telephone: 801144
Fax: (493) 800269

Founded 1968
Teaching and Affiliating
State control
Languages of instruction: English and Malayaam
Academic year: June to March

Chancellor: HE The Governor of Kerala
Vice-Chancellor: Dr M. Abdul Rahiman
Pro-Vice Chancellor: Prof. G. K. Sasidharan
Registrar: Prof. T. K. Ummer
Librarian: M. Bavakutty

Library of 84,000 vols
Number of teachers: 175 (University Depts), 5,920 (Affiliated Colleges)
Number of students: 2,823 (University Depts), 119,006 (Affiliated Colleges)

Publication: *University News* (quarterly).

DEANS

Faculty of Science: Dr K. Unnikrishnan
Faculty of Dentistry: Dr N. S. Rajeevan
Faculty of Medicine: Dr P. C. Easaw
Faculty of Education: Prof. M. Khajapeer
Faculty of Law: Prof. M. Ramakrishnan
Faculty of Fine Arts: Smt. J. Ammal
Faculty of Languages and Literature: Dr C. P. Achuthanunni
Faculty of Homeopathy: Dr Jagakumar
Faculty of Commerce: Dr K. C. Vijagakumar
Faculty of Ayurveda: Dr A. P. Haridasan
Faculty of Engineering: Dr Venkataramani
Faculty of Humanities: Dr P. P. Pillai
Faculty of Journalism: S. A. Ahamad

HEADS OF DEPARTMENTS

Arabic: Dr S. E. A. Nadvi
Biotechnology: Dr M. V. Joseph
Journalism: Dr S. A. Ahamed
Malayalam: Dr C. P. Achuthan Unni
Psychology: Dr C. B. Asha
Mathematics: Dr V. Krishna Kumar
Sanskrit: Dr C. Rajemdran
Hindi: Dr I. Ahamed
Commerce and Management Studies: Dr K. C. Vijayakumar
Physics: Dr K. Neelakandan
History: Dr K. K. N. Kurup
Economics: D. Prabhakaran Nair
English: Dr R. Viswanathan
Chemistry: Dr T. D. Radhakrishnan Nair
Philosophy: V. C. Narayanadas
Russian: S. Hirmala
Statistics: N. Raju
Botany: Dr K. Unnik
Applied Zoology: Dr U. V. K. Mohamed
Life Science: Dr V. K. Sasidharan
Library Science: M. Paramesararan
Education: Dr P. Kelu
Drama and Fine Arts: Dr V. Vasinderan Pollai

Academic Staff College: C. P. Achuthanunny (Dir).

School of Distance Education: K. Kunhikrishnan (Dir).

Adult Education and Extension Services: Dr K. Karunakaran (Dir).

Physical Education: S. Muralichkaran (Coach in Charge).

There are 102 affiliated colleges.

CHANDRA SHEKHAR AZAD UNIVERSITY OF AGRICULTURE AND TECHNOLOGY

Nawabganj, Kanpur 208002, UP

Telephone: 244466

Founded 1975
State control
Languages of instruction: Hindi and English
Academic year: July to June

Chancellor: HE The Governor of Uttar Pradesh
Vice-Chancellor: Dr S. P. Tewari
Registrar: Dr S. P. Tewari
Librarian: Dr U. Singh

Library of 55,442 vols
Number of teachers: 318
Number of students: 1,187

DEANS

Faculty of Agriculture: Dr H. G. Singh
Faculty of Veterinary Science: Dr J. N. Dwivedi

HEADS OF DEPARTMENTS

Agriculture:

- Agricultural Biochemistry: Dr G. P. Srivastava
- Agricultural Economics: Dr R. I. Singh
- Agricultural Extension: Dr J. P. Yadav
- Agronomy: Dr V. Singh
- Animal Husbandry and Dairying: Dr C. Singh
- Entomology: Dr N. D. Pandey
- Horticulture: Dr A. Prasad
- Plant Breeding and Genetics: Dr C. N. Chaubey
- Plant Pathology: Dr J. Swarup
- Plant Physiology: Dr H. K. Saxena
- Seed Technology: Dr R. P. Katiyar
- Soil Conservation: Dr Suraj Bhan
- Soils and Agricultural Chemistry: Dr H. G. Singh

Veterinary Science:

- Anatomy: Dr G. Chandra
- Animal Genetics and Breeding: Dr B. P. Singh
- Animal Nutrition: (vacant)
- Biochemistry: Dr R. K. Srivastava
- Bacteriology: Dr R. C. Pathak
- Gynaecology: Dr H. C. Pant
- Medicine: Dr B. P. Joshi
- Parasitology: Dr P. P. S. Chauhan
- Pathology: Dr D. N. Sharma
- Pharmacology: Dr N. D. Sharma
- Physiology: Dr M. D. Pandey
- Poultry Science: Dr R. K. Srivastava
- Surgery: Dr Y. S. Bhatia

COCHIN UNIVERSITY OF SCIENCE AND TECHNOLOGY

Cochin University P.O., Cochin, Kerala 682022

Telephone: (484) 555181
Telex: 885-5019
E-mail: register@cochin.ernet.in

Founded 1971
State control
Language of instruction: English
Academic year: July to April

Chancellor: HE The Governor of Kerala
Pro-Chancellor: The Minister for Education, Kerala State
Vice-Chancellor: Dr K. Babu Joseph
Pro-Vice-Chancellor: V.J. Pappoo
Registrar: Dr K. G. Balakrishnan
Librarian: Dr Baby

Library of 66,669 vols, 226 periodicals
Number of teachers: 197
Number of students: 2,100

Publications: *Law Review*, *Marine Sciences Bulletin*, *Indian Manager*, *Management Information Service*, *Anuseelam*, *Cochin University News*.

DEANS

Faculty of Law: Dr Chandrasekharan Pillai
Faculty of Social Science: Prof. P. Ramachandra Poduval
Faculty of Science: Dr N. Unnikrishnan Nair
Faculty of Marine Science: Dr N. Ravindranatha Menon
Faculty of Humanities: Dr P. V. Vijayan
Faculty of Technology: Dr K. Gopalakrishnan Nair
Faculty of Engineering: Dr N. P. Chandrasekharan
Faculty of Environmental Studies: Dr A. Mohandas

PROFESSORS

Aliyar, S., Hindi
Aravindakshnan, A., Hindi
Babu, J. K., Physics
Babu, T. J., Civil Engineering
Balakrishnan, K. G., Electronics
Chacko, J., Chemical Oceanography
Chandrasekharan, N. S., Legal Studies
Chandrasekharan Pillai, K. N., Legal Studies
Chandrasekharan Pillai, N., Management Studies
Damodaran, K. T., Marine Sciences
Damodaran, R., Marine Sciences
Easwari, M., Hindi
George, K. K., Management Studies
George, P., Marine Sciences
Girijavallabhan, C. P., Physics
Gopalakrishnan Nair, K., Electronics
Gopalakrishna Kurup, P., Marine Sciences
Hridayanathan, C., Industrial Fisheries
Jacob, P., Physics
Jathavedan, M., Mathematics
Jose, T. P., Management Studies
Joseph Francis, D., Polymer Science and Rubber Technology
Krishna Menon, A., Computer Science
Krishnamoorthy, A., Mathematical Sciences
Kuriakose, A. P., Polymer Science and Rubber Technology
Leelakrishnan, P., Law
Madhavan Pillai, P., Applied Chemistry
Mathai, E., Physics
Mohammed Yussuf, K., Applied Chemistry
Mohandas, A., Environmental Studies
Nandakumaran, V. M., International School of Photonics
Narayanan Nampoori, V. P., Physics
Payyappilly, J.T., Management Studies
Philip, B., Marine Biology, Microbiology and Biochemistry
Philip, J., Instrumentation
Rajappan Nair, K. P., Physics
Rajappan Nair, K., Physics
Rajasenan, D., Applied Economics
Ramachandra, P., Management Studies
Ravindra-Natha Menon, N. R., Marine Sciences
Ram Mohan, H. S., Marine Sciences
Sabir, M., Physics
Sadasivan Nair, G., Legal Studies
Sankara-Narayanan, K. C., Applied Economics
Sasindran Pillai, P.R., Electronics
Sebastian, K. L., Applied Chemistry
Seralathan, P., Marine Geology and Geophysics
Shahul Hameed, M., Industrial Fisheries
Shajahan, S., Hindi
Sivasankara Pillai, V. N., Applied Chemistry
Sridhar, C. S., Electronics
Sugunan, S., Applied Chemistry
Sukumaran Nair, M.K., Applied Chemistry
Suneetha Bai, L., Hindi
Thrivikraman, T., Mathematical Sciences
Unnikrishnan Nair, N., Mathematical Sciences
Vasudevan, K., Electronics
Vijayakumar, E.P., Physics
Vijayan, P. V., Hindi

DAYALBAGH EDUCATIONAL INSTITUTE

Dayalbagh, Agra 282005, UP
Telephone: (562) 350059
Fax: (562) 351845
E-mail: rmms@dei.ernet.in

Founded 1981

President: Justice G. D. SAHGAL
Director: Prof. P. S. SATSANGI
Registrar: Dr R. M. M. SINGH

Library of 107,500 vols
Number of teachers: 156
Number of students: 2,172

DEANS

Arts: Dr U. ANAND
Education: Dr J. C. SINHA
Commerce: Dr D. N. KAPOOR
Engineering: Dr P. R. PRASAD
Science: Dr A. K. SINHA
Social Sciences: Dr L. R. KULSHRESTHA

ATTACHED INSTITUTES

DEI Technical College: Principal P. P. DUA.

DEI Prem Vidyalaya Intermediate College: M. DAS.

UNIVERSITY OF DELHI

Delhi 110007
Telephone: 2521521

Founded 1922
Teaching and Affiliating
Languages of instruction: English and Hindi
Academic year: July to April (three terms)

Chancellor: VICE-PRESIDENT OF INDIA
Pro-Chancellor: CHIEF JUSTICE OF INDIA
Vice-Chancellor: Prof. VRAJENDRA RAJ MEHTA
Registrar: J. C. KOCHHAR
Librarian: A. L. KAPOOR

Library of 1,029,723 vols
Number of professors: 270
Number of students: 101,493

DEANS

Faculty of Arts: Prof. T. N. BALI
Faculty of Science: MANOHAR LAL
Faculty of Law: Prof. P. S. SANGAL
Faculty of Medical Sciences: Prof. D. S. DUSAI
Faculty of Education: Prof. KRISHNA KUMAR
Faculty of Social Sciences: Prof. A. CHAKRAVARTI
Faculty of Technology: Prof. RAJNISH PARKASH
Faculty of Music and Fine Arts: Prof. V. K. AGGARWAL
Faculty of Mathematics: Prof. S. P. AGGARWAL
Faculty of Management: Prof. B. C. TANDON
Faculty of Ayurvedic and Unani Medicine: Prof. K. K. PANDEY
Faculty of Interdisciplinary and Applied Sciences: Prof. B. K. BACHAWAT
Faculty of Applied Sciences and Humanities: Prof. K. D. GANGRADE
Faculty of Planning and Administrative Reforms: Prof. S. NILAMEGHAM

CONSTITUENT COLLEGES

Atma Ram Sanatan Dharam College: New Delhi; f. 1959.

Bharati Mahila College: New Delhi; f. 1971.

Daulat Ram College: Delhi 7; f. 1960.

Gargi College: New Delhi; f. 1967.

Guru Gobind Singh College of Commerce: Delhi; f. 1984.

Gyan Devi Salwan College: New Delhi; f. 1970.

Hamdard College of Pharmacy: New Delhi; f. 1972.

Hamdard Tibbi College: Delhi; f. 1977.

Hans Raj College: Delhi; f. 1948.

Hindu College: Delhi; f. 1922.

Indraprastha College for Women: Delhi; f. 1925.

Institute of Home Economics: Delhi; f. 1969.

Janki Devi Mahavidyalaya: New Delhi; f. 1959.

Jesus and Mary College: New Delhi; f. 1968.

Kalindi College: New Delhi; f. 1967.

Kamla Nehru College: New Delhi; f. 1964.

Lady Irwin College: New Delhi; f. 1950.

Lady Shri Ram College for Women: New Delhi; f. 1956.

Lakshmibai College: Delhi; f. 1965.

Maitreyi College: New Delhi; f. 1967.

Mata Sundri College: New Delhi; f. 1967.

Moti Lal Nehru College: New Delhi; f. 1964.

P.G.D.A.V. College: New Delhi; f. 1957.

Rajdhani College: New Delhi; f. 1964.

Ramjas College: Delhi; f. 1917.

Satyawati Co-educational College: Delhi; f. 1972.

Shaheed Bhagat Singh College: New Delhi; f. 1967.

Shivaji College: New Delhi; f. 1961.

Shri Aurobindo College: New Delhi; f. 1972.

Shri Guru Teg Bahadur Khalsa College: Delhi; f. 1951.

Shri Ram College of Commerce: Delhi; f. 1926.

Shyam Lal College: Delhi; f. 1964.

Shyama Prasad Mukherjee College: New Delhi; f. 1969.

Sri Venkateswara College: New Delhi; f. 1961.

St Stephen's College: Delhi; f. 1922.

Swami Shardhanand College: Delhi; f. 1967.

Vivekanand Mahila College: Delhi; f. 1970.

Zakir Hussain College: Delhi; f. 1948.

UNIVERSITY MAINTAINED COLLEGES

Deshbandhu College: Kalkaji, New Delhi; f. 1952.

Dyal Singh College: New Delhi; f. 1959.

Kirori Mal College: Delhi; f. 1954.

Miranda House for Women: Delhi; f. 1948.

School of Correspondence Courses and Continuing Education: Delhi; f. 1962.

University College of Medical Sciences: Delhi; f. 1971.

Vallabhbhai Patel Chest Institute: see under Research Institutes.

College of Vocational Studies: New Delhi; f. 1972.

GOVERNMENT MAINTAINED COLLEGES

Ayurvedic and Unani Tabbia College: New Delhi; f. 1974.

College of Art: New Delhi; f. 1972.

College of Nursing: New Delhi; f. 1946.

College of Pharmacy: New Delhi; f. 1971.

Delhi College of Engineering: Kashmeri Gate, Delhi 6; f. 1959.

Delhi Institute of Technology: Delhi; f. 1983.

Lady Hardinge Medical College: New Delhi; f. 1949.

Maulana Azad Medical College: New Delhi; f. 1958.

DEVI AHILYA VISHWAVIDYALAYA

Nalanda Parishar, Indore 452001, Madhya Pradesh
Telephone: 433615

Founded 1964 as University of Indore
Teaching and Affiliating
Languages of instruction: Hindi and English
Private control
Academic year: July to May (three terms)

Chancellor: HE THE GOVERNOR OF MADHYA PRADESH
Vice-Chancellor: Prof. A. A. ABBASSI
Registrar: Dr S. K. BEGDE
Librarian: Dr G. H. S. NAIDU (deputy)

Library of 117,210 vols
Number of teachers: 1,251
Number of students: 35,394

DEANS

Faculty of Arts: Dr C. DEOTALE
Faculty of Ayurved: Dr P. P. AGRAWAL
Faculty of Science: Dr K. K. PANDEY
Faculty of Education: Dr S. VAIDYA
Faculty of Engineering: (vacant)
Faculty of Commerce: Dr D. D. MUNDRA
Faculty of Social Sciences and Law: Dr B. Y. LALITHAMA
Faculty of Medicine: Dr K. BHAGAWAT
Faculty of Life and Home Sciences: Dr R. BHARADWAJ
Faculty of Management Studies: Dr R. D. PATHAK
Faculty of Dentistry: Dr H. C. NEEMA
Faculty of Engineering Sciences: (vacant)
Faculty of Pharmacy: Dr S. C. CHATURVEDI
Faculty of Electronics: Dr RAJKAMAL
Faculty of Physical Education: (vacant)

There are 65 affiliated colleges.

DIBRUGARH UNIVERSITY

Dibrugarh 786004, Assam
Telephone: (373) 70231
Fax: (373) 70323

Founded 1965
Affiliating and Teaching
State control
Languages of instruction: Assamese and English
Academic year: July to June

Chancellor: HE THE GOVERNOR OF ASSAM
Vice-Chancellor: Prof. M. M. SHARMA
Registrar: B. K. GOGOI
Academic Registrar: Dr K.K. DEKA
Librarian: (vacant)

Library of 140,186 vols
Number of teachers: 210 (University Depts)
Number of students: 58,850 (including affiliated colleges)

Publications: *The North Eastern Research Bulletin* (sociology, irregular), *Padartha Vigyan Patrika* (physics, in Assamese, annually), *Dibrugarh University Journal of English Studies, Assam Economic Journal, Anthropology Bulletin, Assam Statistical Review, Life Sciences Bulletin, Mathematical Forum, Journal of Education, Journal of Historical Research, Pharmray* (pharmaceutical sciences).

HEADS OF DEPARTMENTS

Anthropology: Prof. I. BARUA
Applied Geology: Prof. K. GOSWAMI
Assamese: Prof. B. K. BARUAH
Chemistry: Prof. S. SEN
Commerce: Dr P. BEZBORAH
Economics: Dr K.C. BORA
Education: Dr G. L. BOROOAH
English: Dr A.D. MAHANTA
History: Prof. S. BORA
Life Sciences: Prof. P. BARUA
Mathematics: Dr G.C. HAZARIKA
Petroleum Technology: R. S. LADIA

Pharmaceutical Sciences: Dr S. K. GHOSH
Physics: Prof. A. RAJPUT
Political Science: Dr D. BHAGAWATI
Sociology: Dr C.K. GOGOI
Statistics: Dr S. DAS

There are 76 affiliated colleges.

DR B. R. AMBEDKAR OPEN UNIVERSITY

6-3-645 Somajiguda, Hyderabad 500482, Andhra Pradesh

Telephone: 211391
Fax: 211391

Founded 1982
Study centres throughout the state

Chancellor: Sri KRISHAN KANT
Vice-Chancellor: Prof. S. BAHIRUDDIN
Registrar: C. N. V. SUBBA REDDY
Asst Librarian: G. SUJATHA

Library of 29,912 vols
Number of teachers: 63
Number of students: 63,575

DEANS

Faculty of Arts: Prof. C. SUBBA RAO
Faculty of Sciences: Prof. K. KUPPUSWAMY RAO
Faculty of Commerce: Prof. V. NAGARAJA NAIDU
Faculty of Social Sciences: Prof. M. SATYANARAYANA RAO

PROFESSORS

KUPPUSWAMY RAO, K., Mathematics
NAGARAJA NAIDU, V., Commerce
PRASAD, V. S., Public Administration
RAMAIAH, P., Economics
SATYANARAYANA RAO, M., Political Science
SUBBA RAO, C., English
UMAPATHI VARMA, Y. V., Educational Technology
VENKAIAH, V., Business Management
VISWANATHA REDDY, K., Telugu

DR BABASAHEB AMBEDKAR MARATHWADA UNIVERSITY

Aurangabad (Deccan), Maharashtra 431004

Telephone: (2432) 334431
Fax: (2432) 334291

Founded 1958
Teaching and Affiliating
Languages of instruction: English and Marathi
Academic year: June to April (two terms)

Chancellor: HE THE GOVERNOR OF MAHARASHTRA
Vice-Chancellor: Dr S. B. NAKADE
Registrar: Dr P. M. BORA
Librarian: Dr SNEHLATA M. MOHAL

Library of 294,000 vols
Number of teachers (incl. affiliated colleges): 3,275
Number of students: 87,973

Publications: *Annual Report, University Journal, University Handbook, Rabindranath Tagore Lecture Series.*

FULL PROFESSORS

BHISE, V. B., Economics
BORA, P. M., Public Administration
DHULE, D. G., Chemistry
FAROOQUI, M. N., Zoology
GANGAVANE, L. V., Botany
GANI, H. A., Political Science
GAWALI, P. A., History
KALYANKAR, G. S., Economics
KAWADE, C. B., Hindi
KHILLARE, Y. K., Zoology
LOMTE, V. S., Environmental Science
NIKAM, P. K., Zoology
PACHPATTE, B. G., Mathematics
PRASAD, V. R. N., English
RANVEER, K. G., English
SAPRE, A. B., Botany
SHAH, S. S., Physics
SHAMKUWAR, N. R., Physics
SHINDE, G. B., Zoology
SHINGARE, M. S., Chemistry
VYAWHARE, S. B., Marathi
WAGH, S. B., Environmental Science

There are 144 affiliated colleges, including five medical colleges, four law colleges, 32 teachers' training colleges, two Ayurvedic colleges, a science institute, seven engineering colleges, four homeopathy colleges, two pharmacy colleges, and four research institutes.

DR HARI SINGH GOUR UNIVERSITY

Gour Nagar, University Campus, Sagar, Madhya Pradesh 470003

Telephone: 22417
Fax: 07582

Founded 1946
Teaching, Affiliating and Residential
Languages of instruction: Hindi and English
Private control
Academic year: July to April (two terms)

Chancellor: HE THE GOVERNOR OF MADHYA PRADESH
Vice-Chancellor: Dr D. VERMA
Registrar: Dr M. P. AGNIHOTRI
Librarian: Shri G. P. RAI

Library of 278,260 vols
Number of teachers: 192
Number of students: 5,984

Publications: *Madhya Bharti—Research Journal* (annually, Hindi and English).

DEANS

Faculty of Arts: Prof. B. D. MISHRA
Faculty of Science: Prof R. S. KASANA
Faculty of Law: (vacant)
Faculty of Education: Prof. B. B. SINGH
Faculty of Life Sciences: Prof. Y. N. SAHAI
Faculty of Social Sciences: Prof. R. MEHROTRA
Faculty of Commerce: Prof. R. K. BHARTI
Faculty of Technology: Prof. V. K. DIXIT
Faculty of Ayurved: Prof. V. K. DIXIT
Faculty of Engineering: (vacant)
Faculty of Management Studies: Prof. H. C. SAINI

There are 98 affiliated colleges.

DR PANJABRAO DESHMUKH AGRICULTURE UNIVERSITY

Krishi Nagar, Akola 444104, Maharashtra

Telephone: (724) 58200
Fax: (724) 58219

Founded 1969
Languages of instruction: English and Marathi
State control

Chancellor: HE THE GOVERNOR OF MAHARASHTRA
Pro-Chancellor: THE MINISTER FOR AGRICULTURE, MAHARASHTRA
Vice-Chancellor: Dr G. M. BHARAD
Registrar: R. K. GAIKWAD
Librarian: Prof. S. P. DESHPANDE

Library of 135,000 vols
Number of teachers: 650
Number of students: 3,650

Publications: *PKV Research Journal* (2 a year), *Post Graduate Institute Research Journal* (annually), *Krishi Patrika* (Marathi, monthly), *PKV Newsletter* (monthly).

DEANS

Faculty of Agriculture: Dr V. B. SHEKAR
Faculty of Veterinary Science: Dr S. D. HARNE
Faculty of Agricultural Engineering and Technology: Prof. G. K. MUZUMDAR

CONSTITUENT COLLEGES

College of Agriculture: Akola; f. 1955; Principal Dr V. B. SHEKAR.

College of Horticulture: Akola; f. 1985; Principal Dr V. B. SHEKAR.

College of Forestry: Akola; f. 1986; Principal Dr V. B. SHEKAR.

College of Agriculture: Nagpur; f. 1906; Principal Dr S. V. DIXIT.

College of Agricultural Engineering and Technology: Akola; f. 1970; Principal G. K. MUZUMDAR.

Nagpur Veterinary College: Nagpur; f. 1958; Principal Dr V. R. BHAMBURKAR.

College of Dairy Technology: Warud (Pusad); f. 1992; Principal Dr R. B. SARODE.

Postgraduate Institute: Akola; f. 1970; Principal Dr K. B. GAHUKAR.

There are two affiliated colleges and 18 research stations.

DR YASHWANT SINGH PARMAR UNIVERSITY OF HORTICULTURE AND FORESTRY

Nauni (Solan) 173230, HP

Telephone: (1792) 52219

Founded 1985
State control
Academic year: July to June

Chancellor: V. S. RAMA DEVI
Vice-Chancellor: Prof. L. R. VERMA
Registrar: P. S. KUTLAHRIA
Librarian: Dr A. S. CHANDEL

Library of 48,000 vols
Number of teachers: 287
Number of students: 577

DEANS

College of Horticulture: Dr R. P. AWASTHI
College of Forestry: D. C. THAKUR

PROFESSORS

AGNIHOTRI, R. P., Regional Horticultural Research Station, Jachh
AMIT NATH, Entomology
ANANDA, S. A., Pomology
ARYA, S. P., Silviculture and Agroforestry
BADALYA, S. D., K.V.K., Chamba
BHANDARI, A. R., Soil and Water Management
BHARDWAJ, L. N., Mycology and Plant Pathology
BHARDWAJ, S. D., Silviculture and Agroforestry
BHARDWAJ, S. P., Entomology
BHARGAVA, J. N., Regional Horticultural Research Station, Dhaulakuan
BHUTANI, V. P., Pomology
CHAUHAN, J. M. S., Pomology
CHAUHAN, P. S., Silviculture and Agroforestry
CHOPRA, S. K., Regional Horticulture Research Station, Dhaulakuan
CHOWFLA, S. C., Mycology and Plant Pathology
DHAR, R. P., Regional Horticultural Research Station, Bajaura
DINABANDHOO, C. L., Entomology and Apiculture
DWIVEDI, M. P., Pomology
FARMAHAN, H. L., Pomology
GAUTAM, D. R., Horticultural Research Station, Kotkhai
GULERIA, D. S., Mycology and Plant Pathology
GUPTA, P. R., Entomology and Apiculture
JANDAIK, C. L., Mycology and Plant Pathology
JULKA, N. K., Pomology
KANWAR, B. S., Basic Science
KAUL, J. L., Mycology and Plant Pathology
KAUSHAL, A. N., Forest Products
KAUSHAL, B. B. L., Postharvest Technology
KHOKHAR, U. U., Pomology
KHURANA, D. K., Tree Improvement and Genetic Resources
KOHLI, U. K., Vegetable Crops
KORLA, B. N., Vegetable Crops
MEHTA, B. S., Vegetable Crops
MISHRA, V. K., Silviculture and Agroforestry
NAYITAL, R. K., Silviculture and Agroforestry

RASTOGI, J. M. SINGH, Forest Products
RASTOGI, K. B., Vegetable Crops
SAMBHAR, O. P., Social Science
SARSWAT, C. V., Seed Technology Centre
SEHGAL, O. P., Floriculture and Landscaping
SEHGAL, R. N., Tree Improvement and Genetic Resources
SHANDILYA, T. R., Mycology and Plant Pathology
SHARMA, A. K., Basic Sciences
SHARMA, D. R., Biotechnology
SHARMA, N. K., Regional Horticultural Research Station, Jachh
SHARMA, O. P., Extension Education
SHARMA, R. D., Regional Horticultural Research Station, Mashobra
SHARMA, R. K., Fruit Breeding and Genetic Resources
SHARMA, S. D., Fruit Breeding and Genetic Resources
SHARMA, S. K., Vegetable Crops
SHARMA, Y. P., Extension Education
SINGH, B. P., Extension Education
SOOD, G., Regional Horticultural Research Station, Jachh
SRIVASTAVA, L. J., Forest Products
SUSHEEL KUMAR, Mycology and Plant Pathology
THAKUR, G. C., Extension Education
THAKUR, J. R., Entomology and Apiculture
TIWARI, S. C., Social Sciences
VERMA, A. K., Entomology and Apiculture
VERMA, H. S., Regional Horticultural Research Station, Bajaura
VERMA, K. D., Extension Education
VERMA, K. L., Extension Education

GANDHIGRAM RURAL INSTITUTE

Gandhigram 624302, Dindigul District, Tamil Nadu

Telephone: (451) 52371
Fax: (451) 52323

Founded 1956, university status 1976
Central Government control
Language of instruction: English
Academic year: July to June

Chancellor: Dr K. R. NARAYANAN
Vice-Chancellor: Dr M. MARKANDAN
Registrar: Dr A. SURIAKANTHI
Librarian: N. ARUMUGAM (Deputy Librarian)

Library of 79,000 vols, 320 periodicals
Number of teachers: 118
Number of students: 1,172

Publications: *GRI News* (monthly), *Annual Report.*

DEANS

Tamil, Indian Languages and Rural Arts: Dr M. KURUVAMMAL (acting)
Rural Social Sciences: Dr A. AROCKIASAMY
Rural Oriented Sciences: Dr C. THILAGAVATHI DANIEL
English and Foreign Languages: Dr M. A. JEYARAJU
Agriculture and Animal Husbandry: Dr T. RENGANATHAN
Rural Health and Sanitation: Dr S. PONNURAJ
Student Affairs: Dr M. JOSEPH
Rural Development: Dr P. ARUMUKHAM

HEADS OF DEPARTMENTS

Co-operation: Dr M. JOSEPH
Economics: Dr A. AROCKIASAMY
Rural Industries and Management: Dr N. MEENAKSHISUNDARAM
Sociology: Dr S. JANAKIRAMAN
Gandhian Thought and Peace Science: S. NARAYANASAMY (acting)
Home Science: Dr N. KAMALAMMA
Chemistry: Dr G. KARTHIKEYAN
Physics: Dr S. RAMAMURTHY
Mathematics: Dr S. SIVARAMAN
Futurology: S. SIVARAMAN
Biology: Dr C. THILAGAVATHI DANIEL
Computer Science and Applications: Dr K. SOMASUNDARAM (acting)
Rural Development: Dr P. ARUMUKHAM
Agriculture and Animal Husbandry: Dr T. RENGANATHAN
Rural Health and Sanitation: Dr S. PONNURAJ
Tamil: Dr M. KURUVAMMAL
English: Dr M. A. JEYARAJU
Political Science and Development Administration: Dr G. PALANITHURAI
Physical Education: M. A. SUBBIAH
Adult and Continuing Education and Extension Education: Dr B. S. NAGARAJAN
Applied Research: Dr M. A. SUDHIR
Rural Technology Centre: Dir Dr R. BALASUBRAMANIAN

GAUHATI UNIVERSITY

Gauhati 781014, Assam

Telephone: (361) 570415
Fax: (361) 570133

Founded 1948
Teaching, Residential and Affiliating
Language of instruction: English
Academic year: July to June (three terms)

Chancellor: HE THE GOVERNOR OF ASSAM
Vice-Chancellor: Dr H. L. DUORAH
Registrar: Dr M. C. SARMA
Librarian: A. K. TALUKDAR

Library of 243,000 vols
Number of students: 3,411

DEANS

Faculty of Arts: Dr H. N. GOHAIN
Faculty of Commerce: Dr S. SIKIDAR
Faculty of Science: (vacant)
Faculty of Medicine: Dr S. K. BHATTACHARYYA
Faculty of Law: (vacant)
Faculty of Engineering: Dr H. K. DAS

HEADS OF DEPARTMENTS

Anthropology: Dr H. CH. SARMA
Arabic: A. B. A. MARTIN
Assamese: Dr P. HAZARIKA
Bengali: U. R. BHATTACHARJEE
Biotechnology: Dr G. BHOWMIK
Botany: Dr C. K. BASUAH
Chemistry: Dr S. K. BHATTACHARYYA
Commerce: Dr S. SIKIDAR
Computer Science: (vacant)
Economics: Dr K. BARMAN
Education: Dr P. DAS
Electronics Science: (vacant)
English: Dr H. N. GOHAIN
English Language Teaching: A. TAMULI
Environmental Science: Dr D. C. GOSWAMI
Folklore: (vacant)
Foreign Languages: Dr G. JHA
Geography: Dr R. BONMAN
Geology: Dr P. C. DAS
Hindi: Dr D. TIWARI
History: Dr R. BEZBARUA
Journalism: Dr A. MAJUMDAR
Law: Dr K. N. SARMA
Library and Information Science: Dr N. SAYMA
Linguistics: R. CHOUDHURY
Management of Business Administration: Dr U. R. DHAR
Mathematics: Dr B. C. KALITA
Modern Indian Languages: Dr M. DEVI
Philosophy: Dr S. SARMA
Physics: Dr M. BORA
Political Science: Dr A. DATTA
Psychology: Dr M. SINGH
Sanskrit: Dr R. SARMA
Statistics: Dr H. K. BARVAH
University Science of Instrumentation Centre: Dr G. DUTTA MUJUMDAR
Zoology: Dr P. C. BHATTACHARYYA

CONSTITUENT COLLEGE

University Law College: Gauhati; Prin. A. HUSSAIN.

ATTACHED CENTRE

University Science of Instrumentation Centre: Dir Dr G. K. D. MAJUNDAR.

There are 105 affiliated colleges.

GOA UNIVERSITY

Sub Post Office Goa University, Taleigao Plateau, 403203

Telephone: 53375

Founded 1985

Vice-Chancellor: Prof. B. S. SONDE
Registrar: G. V. KAMAT

GORAKHPUR UNIVERSITY

Gorakhpur, UP 273009

Telephone: 5201, 3060

Founded 1957
Teaching and Affiliating
Languages of instruction: Hindi and English
Academic year: July to April (two terms)

Chancellor: HE THE GOVERNOR OF UTTAR PRADESH
Vice-Chancellor: K. C. PANDYA
Registrar: R. C. PANT
Librarian: Prof. U. R. RAI

Library of 223,400 vols
Number of teachers: 300
Number of students: 115,000, including students of the colleges

DEANS

Faculty of Agriculture: Prof. G. S. SHUKLA
Faculty of Arts: Prof. M. ILLAHI
Faculty of Science: Prof. S. N. DIXIT
Faculty of Commerce: Prof. B. K. SINGH
Faculty of Law: Prof. U. R. RAI
Faculty of Engineering: Prin. B. B. LAL

There are one constituent college and 36 affiliated colleges.

GOVIND BALLABH PANT UNIVERSITY OF AGRICULTURE AND TECHNOLOGY

Pantnagar, Udham Singh Nagar, 263145 Uttar Pradesh

Telephone: (5944) 33640
Fax: (5944) 33473
E-mail: vc@gbpuat.ren.nic.in

Founded 1960
Languages of instruction: English and Hindi
State control
Academic year: July to June (two terms)

Chancellor: HE THE GOVERNOR OF UTTAR PRADESH
Vice-Chancellor: Dr S. B. SINGH
Registrar: Dr T. S. DWIVEDI
Librarian: Dr R. C. PANT

Library of 319,000 vols
Number of teachers: 783
Number of students: 2,774

Publications: *Indian Farmers Digest* (monthly), *Kisan BHARTI* (monthly), *Pantnagar Journal of Research* (2 a year).

DEANS

Faculty of Agriculture: Dr R. V. SINGH
Faculty of Basic Sciences and Humanities: Dr G. K. GARG
Faculty of Veterinary Sciences: Dr H. SINGH
Faculty of Technology: Dr B. SINGH
Faculty of Home Science: Dr S. RAM
Faculty of Fisheries: Dr H. SINGH
Faculty of Forestry: Dr M. C. NAUTIYAL
Faculty of Postgraduate Studies: Dr S. RAM.
Faculty of Agribusiness Management: Dr V. P. S. ARORA

There are nine constituent colleges and 70 teaching departments.

GUJARAT AGRICULTURAL UNIVERSITY

Sardar Krushinagar 385506, District Banaskantha

Telephone: 222

Founded 1972

Chancellor: HE The Governor of Gujarat
Vice-Chancellor: Dr V. M. Jhala
Registrar: V. P. Macwan (acting)

Library of 113,131 vols
Number of teachers: 954
Number of students: 2,413

DEANS

Faculty of Agriculture: Dr K. A. Patel
Faculty of Home Sciences: Dr K. N. Vyas (acting)
Faculty of Veterinary Science: Dr K. N. Vyas
Faculty of Dairy Science: Dr J. M. Dave
Post-Graduate Research: Dr K. Janakiraman
Faculty of Agricultural Engineering and Technology: Dr J. C. Patel (acting)
Faculty of Home Economics: Dr K. A. Patel
Faculty of Forestry and Horticulture: Dr B. S. Chundavat

CONSTITUENT COLLEGES

College of Agriculture, Sardar Krushinagar: Prin. Dr K. A. Patel.

Gujarat College of Veterinary Science and Animal Husbandry: Sardar Krushinagar; Prin. Dr K. N. Vyas.

Mansukhlal Chhaganlal College of Dairy Science: Anand; Prin. Dr J. M. Dave.

Aspee College of Nutritional Science and College of Home Science and Food Technology: Prin. Dr K. N. Vyas (acting).

GUJARAT AYURVED UNIVERSITY

Jamnagar, Gujarat 361008

Telephone: 76854

Founded 1966
Affiliating and Teaching
Languages of instruction: Gujarati, Hindi, English and Sanskrit
Academic year: June to April (two terms)

Chancellor: HE The Governor of Gujarat
Vice-Chancellor: B. T. Trivedi
Registrar: L. H. Maharishi (acting)
Director of Pharmacy: S. N. Mishra
Dean of Faculty: Dr G. Singh
Librarian: S. M. Jani

Library of 27,000 vols
Number of teachers: 231
Number of students: 1,185

GUJARAT UNIVERSITY

Navrangpura, Ahmedabad 380009, Gujarat

Telephone: 6440341
Fax: 6441654

Founded 1949
Teaching and Affiliating
Languages of instruction: Gujarati, Hindi and English
Academic year: June to March (two terms)

Chancellor: HE The Governor of Gujarat
Vice-Chancellor: Prof. S. B. Vora
Pro-Vice-Chancellor: Prof. K. S. Shastri
Registrar: M. P. Jadia
Librarian: Ramanbhai L. Patel

Libraries of 323,000 vols
Number of teachers: 3,075
Number of students: 153,379

DEANS

Faculty of Arts: Prof. N. A. Parikh
Faculty of Science: Prof. Y. K. Agrawal
Faculty of Commerce: Prof. D. M. Sikh
Faculty of Education: Prin. Dr B. M. Modi
Faculty of Law: Prin. A. N. Karia
Faculty of Medicine: Dr C. A. Desai
Faculty of Technology: Dr H. M. Desai
Faculty of Dentistry: (vacant)

There are 152 affiliated colleges and 10 recognized institutions (mostly listed under Research Institutes).

GUJARAT VIDYAPITH

Ashram Rd, Ahmedabad 380014, Gujarat

Telephone: (79) 7541148
Fax: (79) 7542547
E-mail: gujvi@adinet.ernet.in

Founded 1920, university status 1963
Languages of instruction: Gujarati and Hindi
Academic year: June to April

Chancellor: Prof. Ramlal Parikh
Vice-Chancellor: Govindbhai Raval
Registrar: Shailesh Patel (acting)
Librarian: Kiritbhai Bhavsar

Library of 450,000 vols
Number of teachers: 84
Number of students: 1,887

Publication: *Vidyapith* (6 a year).

DEANS

Social Sciences: K. Naik
Education: M. K. Patel (acting)

PROFESSORS

Desai Pankaj, T., History and Culture
Dube, M., Hindi
Nagar, A., Hindustani
Naik, I. L. A., AC/CE and Extension
Parikh Ramlal, Peace Studies
Pathak, D. N., Gandhian Thought and Peace Research

GULBARGA UNIVERSITY

Gulbarga, Karnataka 585106

Telephone: (8472) 21446
Telex: 0895-208
Fax: (8472) 21632

Founded 1980
State (Govt of Karnataka) control
Language of instruction: English/Kannada
Academic year: June to March

Chancellor: Sri Kursheed Alam Khan
Vice-Chancellor: Prof. M. Muniyamma
Registrar: Raj Kamal
Librarian: R. B. Gaddagimath

Library of 146,000 vols
Number of teachers: 201
Number of students: 1,089

DEANS

Faculty of Commerce: Dr V. Santosh Pai
Faculty of Science and Technology: Dr B. S. Krishna Murthy
Faculty of Arts: Dr S. D. Soudattimath
Faculty of Law: J. S. Patil
Faculty of Education: Dr S. Akhtar
Faculty of Engineering: Prof. N. Ravindranath Reddy
Faculty of Medicine: Dr S. Shankar
Faculty of Social Science: Dr S. G. Ghatapanadi

HEADS OF DEPARTMENTS

Kannada: Dr S. D. Soudattimath
English: Dr Balaram Gupta
Hindi: Dr Senapathy Katake
Urdu and Persian: Dr Laik Qatiza
Sanskrit: Dr P. G. Santappanavar
Marathi: Dr Vijay Telang
Economics: Dr M. S. Kallur
History: Dr S. G. Ghatapanadi
Political Science: Dr B. M. Baen
Sociology: Dr L. S. Hiremath
Social Work: Konnur
Psychology: S. S. Chengati
Statistics: Dr S. S. Nayak
Library and Information Science: Dr Maheshwarappa
Commerce: Dr Ramesh Agadi
Mathematics: Dr M. S. Maleshetty
Botany: Dr N. C. Reddy
Physics: Dr B. Krishnamurthy
Chemistry: Dr H. A. Pujar
Microbiology: Dr M. S. Gaddad
Applied Electronics: Dr A. B. Kulkarni
Biochemistry: Dr V. H. Mulimani
Zoology: Dr Ravindra Paul
Earth Sciences: Dr R. Nijagunappa
Law: S. S. Patil
Education: Dr Syeda Akhtar

ATTACHED INSTITUTE

Postgraduate Centre: Krishnadevaraya Nagar, Sandur, Bellary District; Dir Dr G. S. Patel.

GURUKULA KANGRI VISHWAVIDYALAYA

Hardwar, Dist. Hardwar, UP 249404

Telephone: 7366

Founded 1900, university status 1962
Residential

Chancellor: Prof. Sher Singh
Vice-Chancellor: Dr D. R. Dharam Pal
Registrar: Dr Virendra Arora
Librarian: J. P. Vidyalankar

Number of teachers: 69
Number of students: 690

Publications: *Gurukula Patrika* (monthly), *Prahlad* (quarterly), *Arya Bhatt* (quarterly), *Vedic Path* (quarterly).

CONSTITUENT COLLEGES

Ved and Arts College: Principal R. P. Vedalankar

College of Science: Principal Dr V. S. Saxena

Kanya Gurukul Mahavidyalaya: Dehradun; Principal Smt. Indira Shankar Bhargava

HEADS OF DEPARTMENTS

Psychology: S. C. Dhamija
Ancient Indian History: Dr J. S. Sengar
English: S. S. Bhagat
Hindi: Prof. V. D. Rakesh
Philosophy: J. D. Vedalankar
Ved: Dr Bharat Bhushan Vedalankar
Sanskrit: Dr Mahavir Agarwal
Botany: Prof. V. Shanker
Zoology: T. R. Seth
Chemistry: Dr A. K. Indrayan
Physics: Dr B. P. Shukla
Mathematics: Dr S. L. Singh

GURU NANAK DEV UNIVERSITY

Amritsar 143005

Telephone: 258802
Fax: (183) 258819

Founded 1969
Affiliating and Teaching
State control
Languages of instruction: Punjabi, Hindi and English
Academic year: July to April

Chancellor: HE The Governor of Punjab
Vice-Chancellor: Dr Harbhajan Singh Soch
Registrar: R. S. Bawa
Librarian: S. Singh

Library of 322,215 vols
Number of teachers: 3,251
Number of students: 94,080

Publications: *University Samachar* (quarterly), *Khoj Darpan* (2 a year), *Journal of Sikh Studies* (English, 2 a year), *Law Journal* (English, quarterly), *Economics Analyst* (English, 2 a year), *Punjab Journal of Politics, Calendar* (annually), *Guru Nanak Journal of Sociology* (2 a year), *Journal of Regional History* (annually), *Personality Study and Group Behaviour* (2 a year), *Punjab Journal of English Studies* (annually), *Pradhikrit* (2 a year), *Annual Report*.

DEANS

Faculty of Agriculture and Forestry: (vacant)
Faculty of Applied Sciences: Dr S. S. Parmar
Faculty of Arts and Social Sciences: Dr G. Singh
Faculty of Ayurvedic Medicine: (vacant)
Faculty of Dental Sciences: Dr O. P. Nar
Faculty of Economics & Business: Dr H. S. Sandhu
Faculty of Education: Dr R. S. Kumar
Faculty of Engineering & Technology: Dr I. S. Hudiara
Faculty of Fine Arts and Music: Dr S. Arora
Faculty of Humanities and Religious Studies: Dr Madanjit Kaur
Faculty of Languages: (vacant)
Faculty of Law: Dr K. Singh
Faculty of Life Sciences: S. P. Sharma
Faculty of Medical Sciences: Dr S. Khanna
Faculty of Music and Fine Arts: Dr P. S. Kinot
Faculty of Physical Education: Dr K. Singh
Faculty of Physical Planning and Architecture: S. N. Misra
Faculty of Sciences: Dr B. Singh

HEADS OF DEPARTMENTS

Applied Physics: Dr S. S. Bhatti
Architecture: Prof. S. S. Behl
Biotechnology: Dr G. Kaur
Botanical Sciences: Dr A. K. Thukral
Business and Commerce: Dr S. Chander
Chemistry: Dr M. Singh
Computer Science and Engineering Science: S. H. Singh
Electronics Technology: Dr D. Engles
English: Dr B. L. Chackoo
Food Science and Technology: Dr A. S. Bawa
Foreign Languages: Dr P. S. Sharma
Guru Nanak Studies: Dr S. J. S. Sagar
Guru Ram Dass Postgraduate School of Planning: Prof. S. Singh
Hindi: Dr H. S. Bedi
History: Dr S. Singh
Human Genetics and Human Biology: Dr Jai Rup Singh
Laws: Dr Kirpal Singh
Library and Information Science: Dr M. P. Satiza
Mathematics: Dr S. Sharma
Microbiology: Dr D. S. Arora
Molecular Biology and Biochemistry: Dr B. Singh
Music: Dr B. Kaur
Pali, Sanskrit and Prakrit: Dr S. Sharma
Pharmaceutical Sciences: Dr M. Pal
Physical Education: H. Shargill
Physics: Dr R. K. Bedi
Political Science: Dr S. S. Narang
Psychology: Dr S. Singh
Punjab School of Economics: Dr A. S. Dhindsa
School of Punjabi Studies: Dr B. S. Ghuman
Sociology: Dr J. S. Sandhu
Sugar Technology: Dr M. Singh
Textile Technology: Dr S. S. Parmar
Zoology: Dr P. Kaur
Jullundur Regional Centre: Dr T. Singh

There are 86 affiliated colleges.

HARYANA AGRICULTURAL UNIVERSITY

Hissar 125004, Haryana

Telephone: 73313
Telex: 0345 216
Fax: 73552

Founded 1970
State control
Languages of instruction: English and Hindi
Academic year: July to June

Chancellor: HE The Governor of Haryana
Vice-Chancellor: Dr S. Arya
Registrar: S. N. Roy
Librarian: Prem Singh

Number of teachers: 1,277
Number of students: 2,268
Library of 157,568 vols, 75,389 periodicals

Publications: *Journal of Research* (quarterly), *Haryana Veterinarian* (2 a year), *Thesis Abstracts* (quarterly), *Haryana Kheti* (monthly), *Haryana Farming* (monthly).

DEANS

College of Agriculture: Dr D. P. Singh
College of Agriculture, Kaul: Principal Dr O. P. Singh
College of Animal Sciences: Dr R. A. Singh
College of Basic Sciences and Humanities: Dr S. K. Arora
College of Home Science: Dr A. C. Kapoor
College of Veterinary Science: Dr B. D. Garg
Postgraduate Studies: Dr K. S. Panwar
Sports College: Dr T. C. Kundu

UNIVERSITY OF HEALTH SCIENCES, ANDHRA PRADESH

Vijayawada, Andhra Pradesh 520008

Telephone: 477206
Telex: 475269

Founded 1986
Residential and Teaching
Language of instruction: English
State control
Academic year: June to June

Chancellor: HE The Governor of Andhra Pradesh
Vice-Chancellor: Prof. Gurnurkar Sham Sunder
Registrar: Dr M. John Appa Row
Librarian: K. Srinivasa Rao

Library in process of formation
Number of teachers: 3,000
Number of students: 9,000 undergraduate, 3,000 postgraduate

Publications: *UHS News* (quarterly), *University Information and Employment*.

UNIVERSITY COLLEGE

Siddhartha Medical College: Vijayawada; Principal Dr Y. Sri Hari Rao.

There are 24 affiliated colleges.

HEMVATI NANDAN BAHUGUNA GARHWAL UNIVERSITY

Srinagar, Dist. Pauri Garhwal, UP 246174

Telephone: 2167
Fax: 2174

Founded 1973, formerly Garhwal University, renamed 1989
Teaching and Affiliating
State control
Languages of instruction: Hindi and English
Academic year: July to June

Chancellor: HE The Governor of Uttar Pradesh
Vice-Chancellor: Prof. K. P. Nautiyal
Registrar: S. C. Sharma
Librarian: Prof. R. N. Singh

Library of 100,000 vols
Number of teachers: 280
Number of students: 100,000 (incl. colleges)

DEANS

Faculty of Arts: Prof. S. S. Deo
Faculty of Science: Prof. P. S. Thapliyal
Faculty of Commerce: Prof. K. S. Negi
Faculty of Education: Dr K. B. Budhori
Faculty of Law: S. K. Mittal
Faculty of Adult and Continuing Education: Dr Arun Misra

There are three constituent and 23 affiliated colleges.

HIMACHAL PRADESH KRISHI VISHVAVIDYALAYA (Himachal Pradesh Agricultural University)

Palampur 176062, Kangra

Telephone: (1894) 30521
Fax: (1894) 30511

Founded 1978; formerly Faculty of Agriculture of Himachal Pradesh University
State control
Language of instruction: English
Academic year: July to June

Chancellor: HE The Governor of Himachal Pradesh
Vice-Chancellor: Prof. P. K. Khosla
Registrar: O. P. Sharma
Librarian: D. R. Sharma

Library of 36,000 books, 21,806 bound periodicals
Number of teachers: 337
Number of students: 567

Publications: *HPKV Newsletter* (quarterly), *Annual Report, Himachal Journal of Agricultural Research* (2 a year), *Parvatiya Khetibari* (4 a year).

DEANS

College of Agriculture (Palampur): Dr B. M. Singh
College of Veterinary and Animal Sciences: Dr J. M. Nigam
College of Basic Sciences: Dr A. C. Kapoor (acting)
College of Home Science: Dr Manoranjan Kalia (acting)
Postgraduate Studies: Dr V. Gupta

DIRECTORS

Director of Research: Dr B. M. Singh (acting)
Director of Extension Education: Dr C. M. Singh

ATTACHED REGIONAL RESEARCH STATIONS

Regional Research Station, Dhaulakuan, Sirmour 173001: Assoc. Dir Dr L. N. Singh.

Regional Research Station, Bajaura, Kullu 175125: Assoc. Dir Dr S. K. Bhalla.

Regional Research Station, Kukumseri (Lahoul and Spiti): Scientist-in-charge Dr J. J. Sharma.

HIMACHAL PRADESH UNIVERSITY

Summer Hill, Shimla 171005

Telephone: (177) 230778
Fax: (177) 230775
E-mail: h.p.university@x400nicgw.nic.in

Founded 1970
Affiliating and Teaching
State control
Languages of instruction: English and Hindi
Academic year: July to June

Chancellor: HE The Governor of Himachal Pradesh
Vice-Chancellor: Prof. C. L. Kundu
Registrar: Padam Singh Chauhan
Librarian: M. S. Garga

Library of 171,000 vols
Number of teachers: 258
Number of students: 3,678

DEANS

Faculty of Physical Science: Prof. M. B. Banerjee
Faculty of Law: Prof. C. L. Anand
Faculty of Education: Prof. Lokesh Koul
Faculty of Commerce and Management Studies: Prof. B. Dogra
Faculty of Medical Sciences: Dr D. J. Dasgupta
Faculty of Languages: Prof. B. S. Pathania
Faculty of Performing and Visual Arts: Dr Indrani Chakravarti
Faculty of Ayurveda: Dr S. Kumar

Faculty of Engineering and Technology: Dr R. L. CHAUHAN
Faculty of Life Sciences: Prof. R. K. MALHOTRA
Faculty of Social Sciences: Dr R. D. SHARMA

There are 58 affiliated colleges/institutes and 18 Sanskrit associated colleges.

UNIVERSITY OF HYDERABAD

Central University PO, Hyderabad 500046, Andhra Pradesh
Telephone: (40) 3010500
Fax: (40) 3010145
E-mail: pmsh@uohyd.ernet.in
Founded 1974
Teaching
State control
Language of instruction: English
Academic year: July to June

Chancellor: Prof. ROMILA THAPAR
Vice-Chancellor: Prof. GOVERDHAN MEHTA
Registrar: T. R. VIG
Librarian: E. RAMA REDDY

Library of 240,000 vols
Number of teachers: 200
Number of students: 2,000

Publications: *Newsletter* (2 a year), *Annual Report*.

DEANS

School of Life Sciences: Prof. R. P. SHARMA
School of Chemistry: Prof. P. S. ZACHARIAS
School of Physics: Prof. A. K. BHATNAGAR
School of Humanities: Prof. K. K. RANGANADHACHARYULU
School of Mathematics and Computer/Information Sciences: Prof. C. MUSILI
School of Social Sciences: Prof. T. R. SHARMA
School of Performing Arts, Fine Arts and Communication: Prof. B. P. SANJAY

INDIRA GANDHI NATIONAL OPEN UNIVERSITY

Maidan Garhi, New Delhi 110068
Telephone: (11) 6862598
Telex: (031) 73023
Fax: (11) 6862312
Founded 1985
Autonomous
Languages of instruction: English and Hindi
Academic year: January to October

Vice-Chancellor: Prof. A. W. KHAN
Pro-Vice-Chancellors: Dr S. K. GANDHE, Prof. RAKESH KHURANA, Dr JANARDAN JHA
Registrar: Dr TILAK R. KEM
Librarian: Dr NEELA JAGANNATHAN

Number of teachers: 239
Number of students: 310,000

Publications: *Newsletter* (3 a year), *Indian Journal of Open Learning* (2 a year).

DIRECTORS

School of Education: (vacant)
School of Humanities: Prof. ASHA S. KANWAR
School of Sciences: Prof. B. S. SARASWAT
School of Engineering and Technology: Prof. V. V. MANDKE
School of Management Studies: Prof. MADHULIKA KAUSHIK
School of Continuing Education: Prof. PRABHA CHAWLA
School of Social Sciences: Prof. S. K. SINGH
School of Health Sciences: Prof. A. K. AGARWAL
School of Computer and Information Science: Prof. M. M. PANT

INDIRA KALA SANGIT UNIVERSITY

Khairagarh 491881, Madhya Pradesh
Telephone: (7820) 44534
Founded 1956
Teaching and Affiliating
Languages of instruction: Hindi and English
Academic year: July to April (two terms)

Chancellor: HE THE GOVERNOR OF MADHYA PRADESH
Vice-Chancellor: HAFEEZ AHMAD KHAN
Registrar: Dr S. P. SINGH
Deputy Librarian: K. B. SUNDARESAN

Library of 36,000 vols, 292 periodicals, 97 MSS
Number of teachers: 586
Number of students: 9,680

Publications: *Shiv Mangalam, Bharat Bhashyam, Bhatkhande Smriti Granth, Kala Saurabh, Sangit Suryodaya, Meri Dakshin Bharat, Ki Sangit Yatra.*

DEANS

Faculty of Music: A. N. MALLIK
Faculty of Dance: Dr MADHURIMA CHANDRASHEKHAR
Faculty of Fine Arts and Arts: Dr R. K. SHRIVASTAVA
Faculty of Painting: Dr U. C. MISHRA
Faculty of Folk Music and Art: SHARIEF MOHAMMED

There are 38 affiliated colleges.

JADAVPUR UNIVERSITY

PO Jadavpur University, Calcutta 700032
Telephone: 473-4044
Telex: 214160
Founded 1955
Residential and Teaching
Language of instruction: English
Academic year: July to June (two terms)

Chancellor: HE THE GOVERNOR OF WEST BENGAL
Vice-Chancellor: Prof. P. K. MUKERJEE
Registrar: B. BANERJEA
Chief Librarian: R. K. SAHA

Library of 361,381 vols, including periodicals
Number of teachers: 736
Number of students: 6,315

DEANS

Faculty of Engineering and Technology: Prof. Dr A. K. PAL
Faculty of Science: Prof. Dr A. N. BASU
Faculty of Arts: Prof. Dr A. K. DEV

HEADS OF DEPARTMENTS

Architecture: A. N. DAS
Bengali: Dr B. RAY
Chemical Engineering: Prof. Dr S. K. SANYAL
Chemistry: Prof. Dr A. DAS
Civil Engineering: Prof. Dr B. N. GHOSH
Comparative Literature: Prof. S. K. MAJUMDER
Construction Technology: Prof. T. RAY
Computer Science and Engineering: Prof. Dr D. GHOSH DASTIDAR
Economics: Prof. JABA GUHA
English: Dr S. LAHIRI CHAUDHURI
Electrical Engineering: Prof. Dr S. K. BASU
Electronics and Telecommunications Engineering: Prof. Dr A. K. MONDAL
Film Studies: Prof. M. R. BHATTACHARYYA
Food Technology and Biochemical Engineering: P. CHATTOPADHYAY
Geological Sciences: Prof. A. BHATTACHARYYA
History: B. K. GHOSH
International Relations: Dr P. BHATTACHARYYA
Instrumentation Engineering: S. GHOSH
Library and Information Science: Prof. P. ROY CHAUDHURI
Mathematics: Prof. Dr K. S. CHAUDHURI
Mechanical Engineering: Prof. Dr M. BHATTACHARYYA
Metallurgical Engineering: Dr S. MUKHERJEE
Philosophy: Prof. Dr S. R. SAHA
Physical Education: G. CHAKRABORTY
Physics: Prof. Dr A. BANERJEE
Power Plant Engineering: Prof. S. DATTA GUPTA
Production Engineering: Prof. Dr S. K. SORKHEL
Pharmaceutical Technology: Prof. Dr S. C. LAHIRI
Printing Engineering: S. CHANDA ROY
Sanskrit: Dr M. BANERJEE

CO-ORDINATORS OF INTERDISCIPLINARY COURSES

Biotechnology Programme: Prof. Dr S. CHATTOPADHYAY
Environmental Sciences (M.Phil.): Prof. Dr A. D. MUKHERJEE

There are two affiliated colleges.

JAMIA MILLIA ISLAMIA

Jamia Nagar, New Delhi 110025
Telephone: 6831717
Founded 1920
Autonomous control (government financed)
Languages of instruction: Urdu, Hindi and English
Academic year: July to July

Chancellor: KHURSHEED ALAM KHAN
Vice-Chancellor: Lt-Gen. M. A. ZAKI
Registrar: Prof. ANISUR REHMAN
Librarian: V. K. NANDA

Library of 254,288 vols
Number of teachers: 548
Number of students: 8,820

Publications: *Jamia Monthly* (in Urdu), *Islam and the Modern Age* (quarterly, English), *Islam Aur Asr-i-Jadeed* (quarterly, Urdu), student magazines (in Urdu, Hindi, English).

DEANS

Faculty of Education: Prof. R. S. KHAN
Faculty of Humanities and Languages: Prof. R. A. KHAN
Faculty of Social Sciences: Prof. S. J. R. BILGRAMI
Faculty of Natural Sciences: Prof. S. K. WASAN
Faculty of Engineering and Technology: Prof. R. A. KHAN
Faculty of Law: Prof. V. K. GUPTA

HEADS OF DEPARTMENTS

Faculty of Humanities and Languages:

- History and Culture: Prof. S. M. AZIZUDDIN
- Urdu: Prof. Q. O. R. HASHMI
- Islamic Studies: Prof. AKHTARUL WASEY
- Hindi: Prof. A. S. WAJAHAT
- English: Prof. S. N. H. JAFRI
- Arabic: Prof. S. Z. H. NADVI
- Persian: Dr QAMAR GHAFFAR

Faculty of Social Sciences:

- Social Work: Prof. H. Y. SIDDIQUI
- Economics: Prof. NAUSHAD A. AZAD
- Political Science: Prof. S. J. R. BILGRAMI
- Sociology: Prof. S. M. RIZVI
- Psychology: Dr NAZIRUL HASNAIN
- Commerce: Prof. K. M. UPADHYAY
- Adult and Continuing Education: Prof. S. K. BHATI

Faculty of Natural Sciences:

- Physics: Prof. M. Y. KHAN
- Chemistry: Prof. M. A. KHAN
- Mathematics: Prof. IQBAL AHMAD
- Geography: Prof. S. M. RASHID
- Bio-Sciences: Prof. ARIF ALI

Faculty of Education:

- Foundations of Education: Prof. MOHD. MIYAN
- Teacher Training and Non-Formal Education: Prof. R. S. KHAN
- Fine Arts: Prof. RIAZ MUNIR AHMAD

Faculty of Engineering and Technology:

- Civil Engineering: Prof. I. H. KHAN
- Mechanical Engineering: Prof. R. A. KHAN
- Electrical Engineering: Prof. MOINUDDIN
- Electronics: Prof. M. R. KHAN
- University Polytechnic: IQBAL AZAM (Principal)

ATTACHED INSTITUTES

Dr Zakir Husain Institute of Islamic Studies: Dir Prof. I. H. AZAD.

Mass Communication Research Centre: Dir Prof. H. R. KIDWAI.

State Resource Centre: Dir NISHAT FAROOQUI.

Coaching/Career Planning: Dir Prof. A. SHARFUDDIN.

Academy of Third World Studies: Dir Prof. ZAHID HUSSAIN ZAIDI.

Academic Staff College: Dir Prof. M. AKHTAR SIDDIQUI.

UNIVERSITY OF JAMMU

Baba Saheb Ambedkar Rd, Jammu (Tawi) 180004

Telephone: 535248

Founded 1969

Affiliating and Teaching

Language of instruction: English

Academic year: July to March

Chancellor: HE THE GOVERNOR OF JAMMU AND KASHMIR

Vice-Chancellor: Prof. R. R. SHARMA

Registrar: (vacant)

Librarian: (vacant)

Library of 293,244 vols

Number of teachers: 205

Number of students: 22,796

DEANS

Faculty of Arts: Prof. RAM PARTAP

Faculty of Commerce: Prof. M. M. MISRA

Faculty of Education: Prof. S. P. SURI

Faculty of Law: Prof. K. L. BHATIA

Faculty of Science: Prof. A. K. KOUL

Faculty of Social Sciences: Prof. A. N. SADHU

Faculty of Music and Fine Arts: Prof. B. S. BALI

Faculty of Oriental Learning: Prof. DEVINDER SINGH

Faculty of Medicine: Dr KASTURI LAL

PROFESSORS

ABROL, P. N., Commerce
AHMED, N., Law
BHATIA, K. L., Law
BHUSHAN, I., Chemistry
BHUSHAN, V., Political Science
CHIB, S. S., Geography
DHAR, B. L., Geology
GUPTA, B., Punjabi
GUPTA, J. S., Mathematics
GUPTA, O. P., Hindi
GUPTA, V. P., Physics
GUPTA, Y. P., Geology
HARI OM, History
JASWAL, I. S., Home Science
JYOTI, M. K., Zoology
KALRA, S. L., Urdu
KALSOTRA, B. L., Chemistry
KANT, S., Botany
KOTRU, P. N., Physics
KOTWAL, O. P., Economics
KOUL, A. K., Botany
MAGOTRA, L. K., Physics
MISRA, M. M., Management Studies
MUNSHI, C. L., Geology
PARTAP, R., Sanskrit
RAIZADA, V. K. V., Management Studies
RAO, N. K., Physics
SADHU, A. N., Economics
SEGHAL, S. K., Geology
SHAH, S. K., Geology
SHARMA, B., Zoology
SHARMA, C., Dogri
SHARMA, M. C., Botany
SHARMA, N. K., Chemistry
SHARMA, O. P., Zoology
SHARMA, O. P., Economics
SHARMA, R. D., Commerce
SINGH, A., Economics
SINGH, R. K., Mathematics
SINGH, Y. B., History
SURI, S. P., Education
TRISAL, P. N., Hindi
WADAN, D. S., Punjabi
WALLI, K., Sanskrit
ZAHUR-UD-DIN, Urdu

CONSTITUENT COLLEGES

Government Medical College: Jammu; f. 1971; Principal Dr KASTURI LAL.

Government College of Education: Jammu; f. 1961; Principal Prof. Smt. B. K. SAWHNEY (acting).

MIER College of Education: Jammu; f. 1981; Principal Dr ARUN GUPTA.

M. C. Khalsa College of Education: Jammu; f. 1989; Principal Dr MADHU SINGH (acting).

Institute of Music and Fine Arts: Jammu; f. 1963; Principal Prof. B. S. BALI (acting).

There are 13 affiliated colleges.

JAWAHARLAL NEHRU AGRICULTURAL UNIVERSITY

PB 80, Krishnagar, Jabalpur 482004, MP

Telephone: 343771

Fax: (761) 343606

E-mail: psingh@jnaump.nic.in

Founded 1964

Languages of instruction: Hindi and English

Academic year: July to June

Chancellor: HE THE GOVERNOR OF MADHYA PRADESH

Vice-Chancellor: Dr P. SINGH

Registrar: Sri A. B. L. BHAGOLIWAL

Assistant Librarian: J. S. BHATTA

Library of 202,000 vols, including periodicals

Number of students: 2,282

Publications: *JNKVV News* (quarterly), *JNKVV Research Journal* (quarterly).

DEANS

Faculty of Agriculture: Dr A. S. TIWARI

Faculty of Veterinary Science and Animal Husbandry: Dr K. S. JOHAR

Faculty of Agricultural Engineering: Dr M. C. SHRIVASTAVA

DIRECTORS

Instruction: Dr A. S. TIWARI
Research: Dr R. K. GUPTA
Extension: Dr B. L. MISHRA
Instrumentation: Dr S. N. MURTHY
Farms: Dr R. K. GUPTA

HEADS OF DEPARTMENTS

Faculty of Agriculture:

- Agricultural Economics: Dr A. K. CHENDHARY
- Agronomy: Dr K. L. TIWARI
- Entomology: Dr S. M. VAISAMPAYAN
- Extension: Dr B. D. RAI
- Food Science: Y. K. SHARMA
- Plant Breeding and Genetics: C. B. SINGH
- Plant Pathology: Dr N. D. SHARMA
- Pomology and Fruit Preservation: Dr G. S. RATTUSE
- Soil Science and Agrochemistry: Dr M. K. MEMA
- Vegetable Crops and Floriculture: Dr R. P. PANDY

Faculty of Veterinary Science and Animal Husbandry:

- Anatomy: Dr G. P. TIWARI
- Animal Breeding: Dr H. K. B. PAREKH
- Animal Nutrition: (vacant)
- Animal Production: Dr V. P. SINGH
- Biochemistry: Dr H. S. KUSHWALS
- Medicine: K. N. P. RAO
- Parasitology: Dr V. K. SHAHANSHRISUDHE
- Poultry Science: (vacant)
- Veterinary Pathology: (vacant)

Faculty of Agricultural Engineering:

- Farm Machinery and Power: (vacant)
- Post Harvest Process and Food Engineering: Dr C. K. TECKCHANDANI
- Soil and Water Engineering: Dr M. C. SHRIVASTAVA

Basic Science:

- Mathematics and Statistics: Dr M. L. CHANDAK
- Physics: V. K. GUPTA

CONSTITUENT COLLEGES

College of Agriculture, Gwalior: Dean Dr J. S. RAGHU.

College of Agriculture, Indore: Dean Dr R. M. SARAN.

College of Agriculture, Jabalpur: Dean Dr C. B. SINGH.

College of Agriculture, Khandwa: Dean Dr K. C. MANDLAI.

College of Agriculture, Rewa: Dean Dr R. A. KHAN.

College of Agriculture, Sehore: Dean Dr V. S. TOMAR.

College of Veterinary Science and Animal Husbandry, Jabalpur: Dean Dr H. K. B. PAREKH.

College of Veterinary Science and Animal Husbandry, Mhow: Dean Dr G. P. TIWARI.

College of Agricultural Engineering, Jabalpur: Dean Dr M. C. SHRIVASTAVA.

JAWAHARLAL NEHRU TECHNOLOGICAL UNIVERSITY

Mahaveer Marg, Hyderabad 500028

Telephone: 391442

Fax: 397648

Founded 1972

State control

Chancellor: HE THE GOVERNOR OF ANDHRA PRADESH

Vice-Chancellor: Dr P. DAYARATNAM

Registrar: Dr N. SREERAMULU

Librarian: B. SATYANARAYANA

Library of 128,000 vols

Number of teachers: 457

Number of students: 8,980

DIRECTORS

Institute of Postgraduate Studies and Research: Dr K. V. K. NEHRU

School of Continuing and Distance Education: Dr K. RAMA SASTRY

School of Planning and Architecture: P. S. SHINDE

Bureau of Industrial Consultancy, Research and Development: E. ANJANEYULU

PROFESSORS

Institute of Postgraduate Studies and Research:

- PEDDY, D. V., Water Resources
- ANJANEYULU, Y., Chemistry
- LAKSHMI NARAYANA, P., Hydraulics
- MURALIKRISHNA, I. V., Remote Sensing
- NARASIMHA MURTHY, D., Mathematics
- PRATAP REDDY, S., Industrial Engineering
- SRINIVAS BHATT, M., Management Science
- SAMBASIVA RAO, I., Placement and Training
- VENKATA SESHAIAH, P., Energy

School of Continuing and Distance Education:

- JAGMOHAN DAS, G., Civil Engineering
- PURUSHOTHAM, G., Mathematics
- GOPAL REDDY, P., Electronics and Communication Engineering
- RADHAKRISHNA, C., Mechanical Engineering
- PRABHAKARA RAO, S. S., English

School of Planning and Architecture:

KOLHATKAR, R. V., Professional Practice

College of Fine Arts:

DASARATHA RED., K., Applied Art
GOURISHANKAR, P., Painting
PRAKASH, N., Photography
SADANAND, P., Applied Art

Examination Cell:

SATYANARAYANA MURTHY, N., Geotechnical Engineering

Bureau of Industrial Consultancy, Research and Development:

RADHAKRISHNA, C., Electrical Engineering

College of Engineering, Anantapur:

BALARAMI REDDY, G., Refrigeration and Air Conditioning
DESIKACHAR, K. V., Electrical Power Systems
KAMAKSHAIAH, S., High Voltage Engineering
KAMESWARA RAO, P., Electronics, Molecular Spectroscopy
KESAVA RAO, P. S., Electronics Space Physics
KRISHNAMACHARYULU, J., Chemistry
LAKSHMI PRAKASH, M. V., Refrigeration and Air Conditioning
MOULY, V. S. R., Optimization and Electrical Machine Design
RAGHUPRASAD RAO, V., Biomechanics, Bio-Fluid Mechanics
RAJA REDDY, K., Power Systems, Operation and Control
RANGAIAH, N., Structural Engineering
RAZAQ, S. A., Production Engineering, Electrical Discharge Machining
SUBBRAYUDU, M., Telecommunications Electronics Instrumentation, Digital Signal Processing
VEMGOPALA RAO, P., Environmental Engineering
VENKATA RAMI REDDY, Y., Electrics Control Systems

College of Engineering, Hyderabad:

CHAKRAVARTHY, G., Production Engineering
JINGA, B. C., Digital Signal Processing
KRISHNA MURTHY, C. B., Thermal Engineering
KUMAR, S. P., Molecular Physics
LALKISHORE K., Microelectronics and Instrumentation
MURTHY, H. S. N., Advanced Electronics
NARASIMHA MURTHY, D., Fluid Dynamics
NARASINHA RAO, P., Social Engineering
NARAYANA, T. S., Advanced Electronics
PARADESI RAO, D. V., Digital Systems Design and Microprocessors
PRASADA RAO, A., Structural Engineering
RAMA DURGAIAH, D., Hydraulics and Water Resources
RAMA RAO, P., Solid State Physics
RAMANA, I. V., Control and Computers
RAMASASTRY, K., Geotechnical Engineering
RAMI REDDY, B., Power Systems Reliability
RAMI REDDY, P., Refrigeration of Air Conditioning
SANJEEVA RAO, B., Control Systems
SANKARA RAO, G., Heat Power Engineering
SREEHARI RAO, V., Stability of Motion under Impulsive Perturbation
SRINIVASAN, G., Computer Control of Power Systems
SYAMSUNDER, K., Co-ordination Chemistry (Analytical).
VARAPRASADA RAO, R., Thermal Engineering
VENUGOPALA RAO, P., Environmental Engineering

College of Engineering, Kakinada:

GUPTA, L. S. N., Machine Design
KAILASA RAO, A., Power Systems Control Engineering
KAMARAJU, V., High Voltage Engineering, Liquid Die, Electronics and Partial Discharges
KRISHNA MURTHY, H., Soil Mechanics and Foundation Engineering
MADEENA SAHEB, S., Structural Engineering
MALLIKARJUNA RAO, D., Microwaves
MURTHY, G. R. K., Electrical Engineering
PENCHALAIAH, Ch., Machine Design
RAMA RAO, K. S., Power Electronics, Electrical Machine Design
RAMANA, B. V., Fluid Dynamics
RAMANA SASTRY, M. V. B., Soil Mechanics and Foundation Engineering
RANGA RAO, V., Applied Electronics and Servo Mechanism
RAO, V. S., Theory of Elasticity
SARVARAYUDU, G. P. R., Control Systems
SATYANARAYANA MURTHY, P., Production Planning and Control
SESHAGIRI RAO, A., Nuclear Physics
SRI RAMA RAO, A., Soil Mechanics
SURAYYA, K., Structural Engineering
VARADARAJULU, S., Organic and Inorganic Synergistic Extractions and Solvent Extractions
VENKATA NARSAIAH, P., Coastal Engineering Hydraulic
VENKATA RAO, M., Power Systems Control, Stability and Control

JAWAHARLAL NEHRU UNIVERSITY

New Mehrauli Rd, New Delhi 110067
Telephone: (11) 6167557
Telex: 031-73167
Fax: (11) 6198234

Founded 1969
Teaching and Residential
Academic year: May to December, January to May

Chancellor: Prof. M. S. GORE
Vice-Chancellor: Prof. ASIS DATTA
Registrar: MOTI RAM (acting)
Librarian: B. N. RAO

Library of 460,000 vols
Number of teachers: 371
Number of students: 3,843

Publications: *International Studies* (4 a year), *Studies in History* (2 a year), *Hispanic Horizon* (2 a year), *Journal of School of Languages* (2 a year), *JNU News* (6 a year).

DEANS

School of International Studies: Prof. G. D. DESHPANDE
School of Languages: Prof. KAPIL KAPOOR
School of Social Sciences: Prof. ANJAN MUKHERJEE
School of Life Sciences: Prof. RAJENDRA PRASAD
School of Environmental Sciences: Prof. V. RAJAMANI
School of Computer and Systems Sciences: Prof. P. C. SAXENA
School of Physical Sciences: Prof. A. PANDEY
Special Centre for Biotechnology: Prof. KUNAL B. ROY

HEADS OF CENTRES

School of International Studies:

Centre for American and West European Studies: Prof. C. S. RAJ
Centre for Studies in Diplomacy, International Law and Economics: Prof. S. K. DAS
Centre for West Asian and African Studies: Dr G. C. PANT
Centre for East Asian Studies: Prof. R. R. KRISHNAN
Centre for International Politics, Organization and Disarmament: Dr K. D. BAJPAI
Centre for Soviet and East European Studies: Prof. N. M. JOSHI
Centre for South, Central South-East Asian and South-West Pacific Studies: Prof. I. N. MUKHERJI

School of Languages:

Centre for Arabic and African Studies: Prof. M. A. ISLAHI
Centre for Persian and Central Asian Studies: Prof. M. ALAM
Centre for Japanese and North-East Asian Languages: Prof. RAJENDER TOMAR
Centre for Chinese and South-East Asian Languages: Dr P. MUKHERJI
Centre of French Studies: Prof. C. SIVAM
Centre of German Studies: Prof. REKHA VAIDYARAJAN
Centre for Indian Languages: Prof. MANAGER PANDEY
Centre of Russian Studies: Prof. A. K. BASU
Centre of Spanish Studies: Prof. S. P. GANGULY
Centre of Linguistics and English: Prof. H. C. NARANG

School of Social Sciences:

Centre for Political Studies: Prof. BELVEER ARORA
Centre for the Study of Regional Development: Prof. SUDESH NANGIA
Centre of Social Medicine and Community Health: Dr MOHAN RAO
Centre for the Study of Social Systems: Prof. DIPANKAR GUPTA
Centre for Historical Studies: Prof. M. K. PALAT
Zakir Husain Centre for Educational Studies: Prof. KARUNA CHANANA
Centre for Economic Studies and Planning: Prof. PRABHAT PATNAIK
Centre for Studies in Science Policy: Prof. ANJAN MUKHERJEE (acting)

There are 12 attached degree-granting institutions.

JIWAJI UNIVERSITY

Vidya Vihar, Gwalior 474002, Madhya Pradesh

Telephone: 341348

Founded 1964
Teaching and Affiliating
Languages of instruction: Hindi and English
Academic year: July to June

Chancellor: HE THE GOVERNOR OF MADHYA PRADESH
Vice-Chancellor: Dr R. R. DASS
Registrar: S. S. DIKSHIT
Librarian: (vacant)

Library of 57,000 vols
Number of students: 47,358

Publications: *Humanities, Science* (2 a year).

DEANS

Faculty of Arts: Dr H. C. GUPTA
Faculty of Social Sciences: Dr P. L. SABLOOK
Faculty of Science: (vacant)
Faculty of Law: S. P. SHARMA
Faculty of Education: Dr D. S. SHUKLA
Faculty of Engineering: Dr R. N. SAPRE
Faculty of Medicine: Dr Smh S. OPOHAYA
Faculty of Ayurved: Dr B. M. GUPTA
Faculty of Commerce: Dr D. C. SHARMA
Faculty of Physical Education: (vacant)
Faculty of Home Science: Dr Smh VEENA SHIRASTAM

There are 71 affiliated colleges.

UNIVERSITY OF JODHPUR

Jodhpur 342001, Rajasthan

Telephone: 31413

Founded 1962
Languages of instruction: English and Hindi

Chancellor: THE GOVERNOR OF RAJASTHAN (ex officio)
Vice-Chancellor: (vacant)
Registrar: D. D. JOSHI
Librarian: R. K. DAVE

Library of 256,833 vols
Number of teachers: 459
Number of students: 13,926

Publications: *Jodhpur University Gazette and News Bulletin, The Beacons* (Engineering), *Annals of Economics, The University Times* (Students' Union).

DEANS

Faculty of Arts, Social Sciences and Education: Prof. J. N. SHARMA
Faculty of Commerce: Prof. U. L. GUPTA
Faculty of Engineering: Prof. B. C. PUNAMIA
Faculty of Law: S. R. BHANSALI
Faculty of Science: Prof. R. K. SAXENA

DIRECTORS

Institute of Evening Studies: Dr R. C. DIXIT
K. Nehru College for Women: Mrs KAMINI DINESH

PROFESSORS

AGARWAL, G. K., Mechanical Engineering
AGARWALA, R. K., Commerce
ANGRISH, A. C., Economics
BANSAL, V. S., Electrical Engineering
BHADADA, R., Mining Engineering
BHANDARI, M. M., Botany
BHANDARI, S., Mining Engineering
BHANSALI, S. R., Mining Engineering
BHANSALI, V. K., Electrical Engineering
BHARGAVA, D. N., Sanskrit
BHATIA, P. K., Mathematics
CHANDRA JAGDISH, Civil Engineering
CHANDRA, R., Structural Engineering
CHETANYA, English
DINESH, K., English
DIVAKARAN, S., Structural Engineering
DIXIT, R. C., Psychology
GOYAL, S. R., History
GUPTA, K. S., Mechanical Engineering
GUPTA, N. P., Physics
GUPTA, S. P., Structural Engineering
GUPTA, U. L., Commerce
HUKKU, V. N., Commerce
JAIN, K. S., Engineering
JOHNSON, S., Zoology
JOSHI, I., Hindi
JOSHI, M. C., Psychology
KANT, K., Chemistry
KAPOOR, B. G., Zoology
KUMAR, S., Mining Engineering
LAL, S. K., Sociology
MATHUR, M. L., Mechanical Engineering
MATHUR, N. K., Chemistry
MEHTA, F. S., Mechanical Engineering
MEHTA, R. K., Chemistry
MURTY, S. K., Electrical Engineering
NIGAM, A. N., Physics
PHATAK, M. B., Civil Engineering
PUNMIA, B. C., Civil Engineering
RAO, S. P., Chemistry
RATHORE, L. S., Political Science
SANKHLA, N. S., Botany
SAXENA, R. K., Mathematics
SEN, D. N., Botany
SHARMA, C. S., Mechanical Engineering
SHARMA, D. P., Structural Engineering
SHARMA, J. N., English
SINGH, S. S., Mining Engineering
SURANA, D. C., Electronics and Communications Engineering
SURANA, D. M., Mining
TALWAR, D. V., Civil Engineering
TANDON, S. P., Physics
TEWARI, A. K., Geography
TEWARI, P. S., Electronics and Communications Engineering

There are six affiliated colleges.

KAKATIYA UNIVERSITY

Vidyaranyapuri, Warangal 506009
Telephone: (8712) 77687
Fax: (8712) 78935
E-mail: kakatiya@ap.nic.in

Founded 1976
Teaching and Affiliating
Languages of instruction: English, Telugu, Urdu

Chancellor: HE THE GOVERNOR OF ANDHRA PRADESH
Vice-Chancellor: Prof. VIDYAVATI
Registrars: Prof. G. SREENIVAS REDDY, M. UPENDER RAO
Librarian: K. RAMANAIAH (Deputy Librarian)

Library of 104,000 vols
Number of students: 72,000

Publications: *Syllabus, University Act, Kakatiya Journal of English Studies and Vimarshini.*

DEANS

Faculty of Arts: Prof. P. SHIV KUMAR
Faculty of Science: Prof. D. V. KRISHNA REDDY
Faculty of Social Sciences: Prof. G. SREENIVAS REDDY
Faculty of Education: Prof. G. RAMESH
Faculty of Commerce: Prof. O. GHANSHYAMDAS
Faculty of Pharmaceutical Sciences: Prof. C. K. KOKATE
Faculty of Law: Justice S. V. MARUTHI
Faculty of Engineering and Technology: Prof. K. KISHAN RAO

KALYANI UNIVERSITY

Kalyani 741235, Nadia, West Bengal
Telephone: (33) 828220
Fax: (33) 828282
E-mail: klyuniv@giasc.lol.vsnl.net.in

Founded 1960
Teaching and Research
Language of instruction: English
Academic year: June to May

Chancellor: THE GOVERNOR OF WEST BENGAL
Vice-Chancellor: Prof. BASUDEB BARMAN
Registrar: R. K. ROY
Librarian: (vacant)

Library of 115,000 vols
Number of teachers: 238
Number of students: 4,000

DEANS

Faculty of Science: Prof. ASIT GUHA
Faculty of Arts and Commerce: Prof. P. K. BHATTACHARYYA
Faculty of Education: Prof. A. K. BANERJEE

PROFESSORS

Botany

BISWAS, A. K.
SAHA, S. P.
SAMADDAR, K. R.
SARKAR, A. R.

Zoology

BHATTACHARYYA, S. P.
HALDER, D. P.
JANA, B. B.
KONAR, S. K.
SAHA, A. K.

Chemistry

CHAKRABORTY, B. N.
DEY, K.
DUTTA, C. P.
GUPTA, A.
LAHIRI, S. C.
MAJUMDER, K. C.
MAJUMDER, M. N.
MUKHERJEE, S.
PRAMANIK, D.
SANYAL, G. S.
SARKAR, A. R.

Physics

CHAUDHURI, S.
DASGUPTA, P.
DEB, S. K.
RUDRA, P.

Mathematics

BHATTACHARYYA, P.
JANA, R. N.
MAJUMDER, N. C.
SENGUPTA, P. R.

Biophysics and Biochemistry

GHOSH, N.
PAL, M. K.

Bengali

BANERJEE, R.
SHAW, R.

English

DEB, P. K.

Economics

BHATTACHARYYA, R. N.
CHATTERJEE, P. K.
MUKHOPADHYAY, S.
SEN, A.

Commerce

BHATTACHARYYA, P. K.
LAHIRI, R. K.
MAJI, M. M.

History

NATH, R. C.

Education

PURKAIT, B.

Physical Education

BANERJEE, A. K.
GHOSH, S. R.
KHANNA, S. N.

KAMESHWARA SINGH DARBHANGA SANSKRIT UNIVERSITY

Darbhanga, Bihar 846004
Telephone: 2340 and 2178

Founded 1961
Teaching and Affiliating
Autonomous control
Languages of instruction: Sanskrit and Hindi
Academic year: July to June

Chancellor: H.E. THE GOVERNOR OF BIHAR
Vice-Chancellor: Dr MUNISHWAR JHA
Registrar: KANHALYA JEE CHOUBEY
Librarian: J. MAHTO

Library of 100,000 vols, 15,000 periodicals, 10,000 MSS
Number of students: 515,000

Publication: *Vishwa Maneesha* (quarterly).

DEANS

Faculty of Darshan: R. S. JHA
Faculty of Jyotish: R. C. JHA
Faculty of Samaj Shstra: K. MISHRA
Faculty of Vyakaran: V. MISHRA
Faculty of Puran: (vacant)
Faculty of Veda: S. MISHRA

There are 38 constituent colleges and 37 affiliated colleges.

KANPUR UNIVERSITY

Kalyanpur, Kanpur 208024, UP
Telephone: 250301

Founded 1966
Affiliating
State control
Languages of instruction: English and Hindi
Academic year: July to June

Chancellor: HE THE GOVERNOR OF UTTAR PRADESH
Vice-Chancellor: Prof. SARVAGYA S. KATIYAR
Registrar: Dr R. S. BANSAL
Librarian: Dr S. D. MISRA

Library of 47,000 vols
Number of students: 220,000

DEANS

Faculty of Agriculture: Dr D. P. SHARMA
Faculty of Arts: Dr M. M. SAXENA
Faculty of Ayurvedic and Unani Medicine: Dr K. K. THAKRAL
Faculty of Commerce: Dr A. NARAIN
Faculty of Education: Dr K. M. RAI SAXENA

Faculty of Law: Sri RAMESH CHARAN
Faculty of Medicine: Dr R. K. SRIVASTAVA
Faculty of Science: Dr R. K. NIGAM
Faculty of Engineering and Technology: Dr A. K. VASHISTHA
Faculty of Advanced Studies in Life Sciences: Dr L. C. MISRA
Faculty of Advanced Studies in Social Sciences: Dr S. S. AWASTHI
Faculty of Advanced Studies in Commerce, Business and Industrial Management: Dr A. P. GUPTA

KARNATAKA UNIVERSITY

Dharwad, Karnataka 580003
Telephone: (836) 747121
Fax: (836) 747884
E-mail: unikard@ren.nic.in

Founded 1949, incorporated 1950
Teaching and Affiliating
Language of instruction: English
Academic year: June to March

Chancellor: HE THE GOVERNOR OF KARNATAKA
Vice-Chancellor: Dr ABDULJALEELKHAN M. PATHAN
Registrar: Dr S. RAJASEKHARA
Librarian: Dr S. C. KENDADMATH

Library of 350,000 vols
Number of students: 3,779 (postgraduate)
Number of students in affiliated and constituent colleges: 100,562
Number of postgraduate teachers: 310
Number of college teachers: 5,556

Publications: *Journal of the Karnataka University—Science, Humanities, Social Sciences; Karnataka Bharati* (4 a year), *Bharati Vidyarthi* (4 a year).

DEANS

Faculty of Arts: Dr S. G. IMRAPUR
Faculty of Commerce: Dr S. S. HUGAR
Faculty of Education: Dr SHASHIKALA DESHPANDE
Faculty of Engineering: Prof. R. P. JOSHI
Faculty of Medicine: Dr B. N. BIRADAR
Faculty of Law: Dr S. S. VISHWESHWARAIAH
Faculty of Science and Technology: Dr B. NEELAKANTHAN
Faculty of Social Sciences: Dr LEELASHANTAKUMARI
Faculty of Indian System of Medicine: Dr H. B. KARIGOUDAR
Faculty of Management: M. S. SUBHAS

CHAIRMEN OF POSTGRADUATE DEPARTMENTS

Faculty of Arts:

- Institute of Kannada Studies: Dr B. R. HIREMATH
- English: Dr G. A. GIRADDIYAVAR
- Sanskrit: Dr M. B. PARADDI
- Foreign Languages: Dr M. S. MULLA
- Hindi: Dr T. R. BHAT
- Music, Dance and Painting: Dr S. G. IMRAPUR
- Marathi: Dr B. D. GIAKWAD
- Janapad: Dr S. G. IMRAPUR

Faculty of Commerce:

- Commerce: Dr S. S. HUGAR

Faculty of Education:

- Education: Dr SHASHIKALA DESHPANDE
- Physical Education: (vacant)

Faculty of Law:

- Law: Dr S. S. VISHWESHWARAIAH

Faculty of Science and Technology:

- Statistics: Dr S. H. KUNCHUR
- Chemistry: Prof. A. H. H. SIDDHALINGAIAH
- Physics: Dr T. S. MUDHOLE
- Geology: Dr S. G. TENGINKAI
- Mathematics: Dr P. S. NEERALAGI
- Zoology: Dr R. D. KANAMADI
- Botany: Dr S. C. HIREMATH
- Geography: Dr S. G. KADARAMANDALGI
- Marine Biology, Karwar: Dr B. NEELAKANTHAN
- Sericulture: Dr C. J. SAVANURMATH
- Biochemistry: Dr S. R. HINCHIGERI

Faculty of Social Sciences:

- History and Archaeology: Dr M. T. KAMBLE
- Economics: Dr R. V. DADIBHAVI
- Political Science: Dr S. Y. GUBBANNAVAR
- Sociology: Dr K. M. GOUDAR
- Philosophy: Dr B. P. SHIDDASHRAM
- Anthropology: Dr P. B. GAI
- Library and Information Science: Prof. B. V. RAJASHEKHAR
- Psychology: Dr P. S. HALYAL
- Ancient Indian History and Epigraphy: Dr LEELASHANTAKUMARI
- Social Work: Dr N. A. GANIHAR
- Criminology: A. S. INAMDAR
- Yoga Studies: Dr LEELASHANTAKUMARI
- Gandhian Studies: Dr V. S. HEGDE
- Mass Communication and Journalism: Dr A. S. BALASUBRAMANYA

Faculty of Management:

- Business Management: M. S. SUBHAS

CONSTITUENT COLLEGES

Karnatak Arts College: Dharwad; f. 1917; Prin. Dr VEENA SHANTESHWAR.

Karnatak Science College: Dharwad; f. 1919; Prin. S. D. DESHPANDE.

University College of Education: f. 1962; Prin. R. T. JANTLI.

University College of Law: f. 1962; Prin. Dr S. S. VISHWESHWARAIAH.

University College of Music: f. 1975; Prin. Dr VEENA SHANTESHWAR.

There are 275 affiliated colleges.

UNIVERSITY OF KASHMIR

Hazratbal, Srinagar 190006, Jammu and Kashmir
Telephone: Hazratbal 72745, 72333

Founded 1969
Teaching and Affiliating

Vice-Chancellor: Dr MOHAMMAD Y. QADRI
Registrar: Prof. G. N. SIDDIQUI
Librarian: J. A. WAJID

Library of 199,585 vols
Number of teachers: 1,456
Number of students: 11,900

DEANS

Faculty of Arts: Prof. SHAKEEL-UR-REHMAN
Faculty of Science: Prof. J. MOHAMMED
Faculty of Social Science: Dr A. Q. RAFIQUI
Faculty of Education: Dr H. N. PARIMOO
Faculty of Medicine: Dr (Mrs) GIRJA DHAR
Faculty of Engineering: Dr O. N. WAKHLOO
Faculty of Oriental Learning: Prof. SHAMAS-UD-DIN AHMAD
Faculty of Commerce: Dr A. R. MATOO
Faculty of Music and Fine Arts: T. K. JALALI
Student Welfare: Dr M. I. KHAN
Faculty of Non-Formal Education: R. PUNJABI

PROFESSORS

AHMED, S., Persian
BOKADIA, M. M., Chemistry
FOTEDAR, D. N., Zoology
GIRDHAR, H. L., Chemistry
HAMIDI, H. U., Urdu
JAVLID, G. N., Botany
KHAN, N. H., Library and Information Science
KAUL, V., Botany
KHERA, M. K., Physics
MAJID, H., Geography
MAQBOOL, A., Central Asian Studies
MATTOO, A. R., Commerce
MOHAMMAD, J., Mathematics
PARIMOO, H. N., Education
QAZI, G. M., Mathematics
ROWLAND, R., Home Science
SAROOR, A. A., Iqbal Institute
SHAKEEL-UR-REHMAN, Urdu
SHARMA, B. D., Economics
SHARMA, R. K., Hindi
SHIRWANI, R. R., Arabic and Islamic Studies
SIDDIQUI, M. A., Biochemistry
SIDDIQI, Z. M., Law
WAHID, A., Economics
WAMI, A. A., Law

UNIVERSITY OF KERALA

Thiruvananthapuram 695034, Kerala
Telephone: (471) 445738
Fax: (471) 447158
E-mail: reg@uni-ker.ernet.in

Established 1937
Teaching and Affiliating
Language of instruction: English
Academic year: June to March

Chancellor: HE THE GOVERNOR OF KERALA
Pro-Chancellor: THE MINISTER FOR EDUCATION, GOVERNMENT OF KERALA
Vice-Chancellor: Prof. Dr N. BABU
Pro-Vice-Chancellor: Prof. M. SALIHU
Registrar: Smt S. SUSLEELAKUMARIA
Librarian: Smt MARY GEORGE (Deputy Librarian)

Library of 264,000 vols, 16,000 MSS
Number of teachers: 5,799
Number of students: 123,310

DEANS

Faculty of Arts: Dr K. RADHA
Faculty of Education: Dr VASANTHA RAMKUMAR
Faculty of Engineering Technology: P. O. J. LEBBA
Faculty of Law: Dr N. NARAYANAN NAIR
Faculty of Oriental Studies: Dr V. R. PRABADHACHANDRAN NAIR
Faculty of Science: Dr P. K. RAJENDRAN NAIR
Faculty of Social Sciences: Dr N. JOSE CHANDER
Faculty of Commerce: Dr M. SARNGADHARAN
Faculty of Medicine: Dr P. SIVASANKARA PILLAI
Faculty of Ayurveda: Dr J. R. LEELA
Faculty of Fine Arts: Prof. K. OMANAKUTTY AMMA
Faculty of Physical Education: Dr PATHROS P. MATHAI
Faculty of Homoeopathic Medicine: Dr P. MURALEEDHARAN
Faculty of Applied Sciences: Dr A. K. POOJARI
Faculty of Management Studies: Dr M. N. V. NAIR
Faculty of Dentistry: Dr THRESIAMMA JOSEPH

HEADS OF DEPARTMENT

English: Dr K. RADHA
German: Dr S. SANTHAKUMARI
Russian: Dr R. GOPI
Journalism: Dr M. THANGADORAI
Sanskrit: Dr T. DEVARAJAN
Oriental Research Institute: Dr K. VIJAYAN
Law: Dr N. K. JAYAKUMAR
Library and Information Science: Dr G. DEVARAJAN
Botany: Dr B. VIJAYAVALLI
Chemistry: Dr P. INDRASENAN
Physics: Dr S. DEVANARAYANAN
Zoology: Dr OOMMEN V. OOMMEN
Demography: Dr P. SADASIVAN NAIR
Sociology: Dr M. INDUKUMARI
Psychology: Dr B. DHARMANGADAN
Philosophy: Dr K. SARATCHANDRAN
Economics: Dr K. RAMACHANDRAN NAIR
History: Dr K. K. KUSUMAN
Islamic Studies and Culture: Dr K. T. MUHAMMED ALI
Politics: Dr M. BHASKARAN NAIR
Aquatic Biology and Fisheries: Dr R. KALEYSA RAJ
Biochemistry: Dr P. R. SUDHAKARAN
Geology: Dr P. K. RAJENDRAN NAIR

Mathematics: Dr M. I. Jinnah
Statistics: Dr T. S. Krishnan Moothathu
Hindi: Dr N. Ravindranath
Linguistics: Dr V. R. Prabodhachandran Nair
Malayalam: Dr M. R. Gopinatha Pillai
Tamil: Prof. Dr C. Subramonia Pillai
Commerce: Dr K. Sarngadharan
Education: Dr Vasantha Ramkumar
Computer Science: Dr M. R. Kaimal
Futures Studies: Dr V. Nanda Mohan
Management Studies: Dr M. K. Ramachandran Nair
Environmental Science: Dr V. Sobha
Opto-Electronics: Dr V. Unnikrishnan Nayar
Biotechnology: Dr V. Thankamani

There are 77 affiliated colleges.

KERALA AGRICULTURAL UNIVERSITY

Vellanikkara 680654, Trichur, Kerala

Telephone: (487) 370432
Telex: 887-268
Fax: (487) 370019

Founded 1972
Language of instruction: English

Chancellor: HE The Governor of Kerala
Vice-Chancellor: Dr K. N. Syamasundaran Nair
Registrar: A. K. Dharni
Librarian: Prof. R. Raman Nair

Library of 98,000 vols
Number of teachers: 823
Number of students: 2,445

CONSTITUENT COLLEGES

College of Agriculture: Vellayani, Thiruvananthapuram (formerly affiliated to University of Kerala); Dean Dr Balakrishna Pillari.

College of Cooperative Banking and Management: Mannuthy, Thrichur; f. 1981; Dean Dr M. Mohandas.

College of Fisheries: Panangad; f. 1979; Dean Dr D. M. Thampi.

College of Horticulture: Vellanikkara, Thrichur; f. 1972; Dean Dr A. I. Jose (acting).

College of Veterinary and Animal Sciences: Mannuthy, Thrichur (formerly affiliated to University of Calicut); Dean Dr S. Sulochana.

Kelappaji College of Agricultural Engineering and Technology: Tavanur, Malappuram; Dean Dr K. John Thomas.

College of Forestry: Vellanikkara, Thrichur; Dean Dr Luckins C. Babu.

College of Agriculture: Nilesaher; Dean Dr P. A. Wahid.

KONKAN AGRICULTURAL UNIVERSITY

Dapoli 415712, Ratnagiri, Maharashtra

Telephone: (2358) 2064
Fax: (2358) 2074

Founded 1972
State control
Language of instruction: English

Chancellor: HE The Governor of Maharashtra
Vice-Chancellor: Dr A. G. Sawant
Registrar: Prof. D. R. Ghag

Library of 23,000 vols
Number of teachers: 239
Number of students: 1,170

Publication: *Newsletter.*

DEANS

Faculty of Agriculture: Dr R. B. Dumbre
Faculty of Veterinary Science: Dr M. D. Chauhan
Faculty of Fisheries: Dr P. C. Raje

HEADS OF DEPARTMENTS

Faculty of Agriculture:

Agricultural Botany: Dr S. P. Birari
Agricultural Chemistry: Dr A. S. Chavan
Agricultural Economics: Dr G. G. Thakare
Agricultural Engineering: Dr G. R. More
Agricultural Extension: Dr S. A. Khanvilkar
Agricultural Entomology: R. B. Dumbre
Agronomy: Dr S. A. Khanvilkar
Animal Husbandry and Dairy Science: Dr S. G. Kshirsagar
Horticulture: Dr R. T. Gunjate
Plant Pathology: Dr A. M. Mandokhot

Faculty of Fisheries:

Fresh Water Fisheries: Dr G. A. Shirgur
Marine Biology: Dr P. C. Raje

Faculty of Veterinary Science:

Anatomy, Histology, Animal Nutrition, Embryology: Dr P. M. Puntambekar
Animal Production: Dr S. G. Narayankhedkar
Bacteriology, Immunology, Pharmacology, Toxicology, Clinical and Preventive Medicine: Dr V. S. Narsapur
Veterinary Jurisprudence: Dr S. Jagdish
Surgery and Anaesthesiology: Dr V. L. Deopurkar

CONSTITUENT COLLEGES

College of Agriculture: Dapoli; Prin. Dr A. S. Chavan.

Veterinary College: Mumbai; Prin. Prof. M. D. Chauhan.

College of Fisheries: Ratnagiri; Prin. Dr P. C. Raje.

KUMAUN UNIVERSITY

Nainital 263001, Uttar Pradesh

Telephone: 2068, 2563

Founded 1973
Teaching and Affiliating
Languages of instruction: Hindi and English
Academic year: July to December, February to June (two terms)

Chancellor: HE The Governor of Uttar Pradesh
Vice-Chancellor: Dr M. D. Upadhyay
Registrar: N. C. Pande

Library of 90,000 vols
Number of teachers: 485
Number of students: 29,000

DEANS

Faculty of Science: Dr S. P. Singh
Faculty of Arts: Dr V. K. Pant
Faculty of Commerce: Dr R. M. Saxena
Faculty of Law: Dr K. C. Joshi
Faculty of Education: Dr D. C. Upreti

PROFESSORS

Faculty of Arts:

Dixit, H. N., Sanskrit
Gupta, R. K., Hindi
Pande, G. C., Economics
Pande, P. C., Economics
Pant, V. K., Sociology
Ruwali, K. D., Hindi
Sharma, B. D., English
Singh, O. P., Geography

Faculty of Commerce:

Saxena, R. M., Commerce

Faculty of Science:

Durgapal, M. C., Physics
Pant, M. C., Zoology
Pathak, H. D., Chemistry
Rajput, B. S., Physics
Singh, S. P., Botany
Valdiya, K. S., Geology

Faculty of Education:

Upreti, D. C.

Faculty of Law:

Joshi, K. C.

There are two constituent colleges and 15 affiliated colleges.

KURUKSHETRA UNIVERSITY

Kurukshetra 136119, Haryana

Telephone: 20026

Founded 1956
Teaching and Affiliating
State control
Languages of instruction: English and Hindi
Academic year: July to June

Chancellor: HE The Governor of Haryana
Vice-Chancellor: Dr M. L. Ranga
Pro-Vice-Chancellor: (vacant)
Registrar: I. A. S. Neerja
Librarian: R. D. Mehla

Library of 261,550 vols, 5,074 MSS, 666 periodicals and 591 Braille books
Number of teachers: 390
Number of students: 5,584.

Publications: *Annual Report, Handbook of Information, Digest of Indological Studies, Research Journal for Arts and Humanities, Sambhawana* (Hindi), *Calendar, Prospectus, Kurukshetra Law Journal, Journal of Haryana Studies.*

DEANS

Faculty of Science: Dr M. L. H. Kaul
Faculty of Arts and Languages: Dr S. L. Paul
Faculty of Social Sciences: Prof. Ranbir Singh
Faculty of Education: Dr S. P. Malhotra
Faculty of Indic Studies: Dr M. B. Saxena
Faculty of Law: Prof. S. K. Singh
Faculty of Commerce and Management: Dr. A. S. Chaudhary
Faculty of Ayurvedic: Dr S. K. Verma (acting)
Faculty of Medicine and Dentistry: Dr S. S. Dua
Faculty of Engineering and Technology: Dr N. P. Mehta

PROFESSORS

Faculty of Science:

Arya, S. P., Chemistry
Asthana, V. K., Geography
Chaturvedi, D. K., Physics
Chopra, G., Zoology
Dhawan, S. N., Chemistry
Dubey, S. N., Chemistry
George, P. J., Electronics Science
Gupta, S. C., Chemistry
Gur, I. S., Chemistry
Handa, R. N., Chemistry
Kakkar, L. R., Chemistry
Kaul, M. L. H., Botany
Krishan Lal, Chemistry
Kundu, B. S., Microbiology
Lunkad, S. K., Geology
Mahesh,K. , Physics
Mehta, J. R., Chemistry
Mittal, I. C., Zoology
Mukherji, D., Botany
Nand, Lal, Geophysics
Ram Raj, Physics
Rohtash, C., Zoology
Sharda Kumari, Statistics
Sharda Rani, Botany
Sharma, C. L., Statistics
Sharma, H. C., Physics
Sharma, N. D., Physics
Sharma, R. L., Geography
Sharma, V. K., Geography
Singh, N., Mathematics
Singh, S. P., Chemistry
Singhal, R. N., Zoology
Sinha, S. P., Geography
Suri, P. K., Computer Science
Takkar, G. L., Zoology
Trehan, K., Botany
Vinod Kumar, Mathematics

Virmani, L. R., Mathematics
Yadav, J. S., Zoology

Faculty of Arts and Languages:
Dwivedi, D. S., Linguistics
Grewal, O. P., English
Gupta, L. C., Hindi
Kaang, A. S., Punjabi
Paul, S. L., English
Sharma, S. D., English
Singh, R. D., Hindi

Faculty of Social Sciences:
Chauhan, I. S., Political Science
Kaushil, S., Economics
Kundu, T. R., Economics
Khurana, G., History
Rana, R. K., Economics
Sharma, P. D., Political Science
Sharma, R. K., History
Singh, A., Psychology
Singh, H., Public Administration
Singh, R., Political Science
Sunita Pathania, History
Tanwar, R., History
Tuteja, K. L., History
Upadhyaya, R. K., Social Work
Vashist, B. K., Economics

Faculty of Education:
Malhotra, S. P.
Mavi, N. S.
Verma, K. K., Physical Education
Yadav, D. S.

Faculty of Law:
Aggarwal, V. K.
Kumari, D.
Singh, S. K.
Srivastava, S. C.
Varandani, G.

Faculty of Commerce and Management:
Bansal, M. L., Commerce
Bhardwaj, D. S., Tourism
Chaudhary, A. S., Management
Dwivedi, R. S., Management
Gupta, S. L., Management
Hooda, R. P., Commerce
Jain, M. K., Commerce
Mittal, R. K., Commerce
Sharma, V. D., Management

Faculty of Indic Studies:
Jain, D. C., ISIS
Kushwaha, S. K., Fine Arts
Saxena, Madu Bala, Music
Shakla, S. P., Ancient Indian History, Culture and Archaeology
Shankar, V., Philosophy
Sharma, Indu Bala, ISIS
Singh, A., Sanskrit
Singh, M., Sanskrit
Verma, S. P., Philosophy

There are 871 affiliated colleges and two maintained colleges.

KUVEMPU UNIVERSITY

BR Project, Shimoga District, Karnataka 577 115

Founded 1989; in process of formation

Vice-Chancellor: Prof. P. Venkataramaiah
Registrar: Dr H. J. Lakkappa Gowda

Number of teachers: 24

LALIT NARAYAN MITHILA UNIVERSITY

Kameshwarnagar, POB 13, Darbhanga 846004, Bihar

Telephone: 2047, 2582

Founded 1972
Teaching and Affiliating
Languages of instruction: Hindi and English
Academic year: June to May

Chancellor: HE The Governor of Bihar
Vice-Chancellor: Dr Janardan Kumar
Registrar: B. L. Das
Librarian: K. K. Kamal

Library of 168,854 vols
Number of teachers: 1,251
Number of students: 110,355

DEANS

Faculty of Arts: Prof. R. N. Thakur
Faculty of Commerce: Dr Gopal Lal
Faculty of Education: (vacant)
Faculty of Law: Prof. D. K. Jha
Faculty of Medicine: Dr S. N. Singh
Faculty of Science: Prof. S. Pandey

PROFESSORS

Jha, B. N., Mathematics
Jha, S. M., Maithili
Lall, G., Commerce
Pandey, S., Zoology
Pathak, R. K., Hindi
Prasad, A. B., Botany
Rahman, M., Urdu
Roy, B. K., History
Thakur, B., Economics
Thakur, R. N., Political Science
Thakur, Y., Chemistry

UNIVERSITY OF LUCKNOW

Badshah Bagh, Lucknow 226007, UP

Fax: (522) 330065

Founded 1921
Residential and Teaching
Languages of instruction: English and Hindi
Academic year: July to April

Chancellor: HE The Governor of Uttar Pradesh
Vice-Chancellor: Prof. Ramesh Chandra
Pro Vice-Chancellor: Prof. H. N. Verma
Registrar: R. S. Ram
Librarian: Prof. P. C. Misra

Library of 510,000 vols
Number of teachers: 661
Number of students: 48,625

DEANS

Faculty of Arts: Prof. S. N. Misra
Faculty of Science: Prof. V. K. Srivastava
Faculty of Medicine: P. K. Mishra
Faculty of Law: K. C. Srivastava
Faculty of Commerce: Dr S. B. Singh
Faculty of Ayurveda: Dr B. N. Singh
Faculty of Fine Arts: J. K. Agarwal
Faculty of Architecture: Nehru Lal
Faculty of Dental Sciences: Prof. D. N. Kapoor
Faculty of Education: R. J. Singh
Faculty of Engineering Technology: Prof. G. N. Pandey

HEADS OF DEPARTMENTS

English & Modern European Languages: Dr M. S. Kushwah
Philosophy: Dr R. R. Verma
Psychology: Dr Neelima Misra
Library Science: Dr N. R. Satyanarayana
Ancient Indian History and Archaeology: Dr S. N. Misra
Med. & Mod. Indian History: Dr N. K. Zutshi
Western History: Dr R. N. Mehra
Political Science: Dr S. M. Sayeed
Public Administration: Dr C. P. Barthwal
Economics: Dr A. K. Sengupta
Sociology: Dr A. Awasthi
Anthropology: Dr B. R. K. Shukla
Social Work: Dr Surendra Singh
Persian: Dr Asifa Zamani
Urdu: Dr S. Sulaiman Husain
Arabic: Dr U. Farahi
Sanskrit & Prakrit Languages: Dr Navjeeran Rastogi
Hindi: Dr S. P. Dikshit
Linguistics: Dr V. P. Jain
Education: Dr R. J. Singh
Physics: Dr L. M. Bali
Chemistry: Dr A. Khare
Zoology: Dr Vinod Gupta
Geology: Dr I. B. Singh
Botany: Dr N. K. Mehrotra
Mathematics & Astronomy: Dr S. Dutta
Statistics: Dr V. K. Srivastava
Commerce: Dr S. B. Singh
Applied Economics: Dr R. Sharma
Business Administration: Dr B. L. Bajpai
Law: Sri K. C. Srivastava
Anatomy: Dr D. R. Singh
Physiology: Dr S. Singh
Pharmacology & Therapeutics: Dr R. C. Saxena
Pathology: Dr Pramod Nath
Forensic Medicine: Dr B. Singh
Social & Preventive Medicine: Dr R. Chandra
Medicine: Dr A. R. Sircar
Surgery: Dr K. N. Sinha
Ophthalmology: Dr V. B. Pratap
Tuberculosis: Dr P. K. Mukerji
Paediatrics: Dr P. K. Mishra
Orthopaedic Surgery: Dr U. K. Jain
Otorhinolaryngology: Dr S. C. Misra
Anaesthesiology: Dr B. K. Singh
Obstetrics & Gynaecology: Dr Chandrawati
Psychiatry: Dr A. K. Agarwal
Plastic Surgery: Dr Ramesh Chandra
Neurology: Dr Devika Nag
Cardiology: Dr V. K. Puri
Biochemistry: Dr R. K. Singh
Microbiology: Dr U. C. Chaturvedi
Radiotherapy: Dr H. R. Mali
Radio Diagnosis: Dr V. K. Tandon
Kaya Chikitsa: Dr C. C. Pathak
Shalya Shalakya: Dr Pramod Kumar
Prasuti Stri Avam Balrog: Dr D. N. Mishra
Dravya Gun: Dr R. A. Gupta
Ras Shastra: Dr K. K. Srivastava
Sharir: Dr J. R. Yadav
Maulik Siddhant and Sanhita: Dr S. Srivastava
Sculpture: R. N. Mahapatra
Commercial Art: P. C. Little
Fine Arts: J. K. Agarwal
Architecture: N. Lal
Electrical Engineering: Smt. B. Dwivedi
Electronics: Dr N. Malaviya
Computer Science: Dr S. K. Bajpai
Mechanical Engineering: Dr R. C. Gupta
Applied Sciences: Dr S. K. Srivastava
Civil Engineering: A. K. Shukla

CONSTITUENT COLLEGES

King George's Medical College: Lucknow; f. 1911; 4-year postgraduate medical courses have been established; Prin. Dr P. K. Mishra.

State College of Ayurveda: Lucknow; f. 1954; Prin. Prof. B. N. Singh.

College of Arts and Crafts: Lucknow; Prin. J. K. Agarwal.

Government College of Architecture: Lucknow; Prin. Prof. N. Lal.

Institute of Engineering and Technology: Lucknow; Dir Prof. G. N. Pandey.

There are 20 associated colleges.

UNIVERSITY OF MADRAS

Chepauk, Triplicane PO, Chennai 600005, Tamil Nadu

Telephone: 568778
Telex: 41-6376
Fax: 566693

Founded 1857
Teaching and Affiliating
Languages of instruction: English and Tamil
Academic year: June to March (three terms)

Chancellor: HE The Governor of Tamil Nadu
Vice-Chancellor: Dr P. K. Ponnusamy
Registrar: Dr P. Govindarajulu
Librarian: C. Srinath (acting)

Library of 473,850 vols and 2,261 maps
Number of students: 107,518

Publications: *University Calendar, University Journals, Annals of Oriental Research, University Bulletin* (monthly).

FACULTY PRESIDENTS

Faculty of Science: Dr G. J. SRINIVASAN
Faculty of Law: Prof. R. V. DHANAPALAN
Faculty of Teaching: Dr P. S. BALASUBRAMANIAN
Faculty of Medicine: (vacant)
Faculty of Engineering: (vacant)
Faculty of Indian and Other Languages: Dr C. BALASUBRAMANIAN
Faculty of Commerce: Dr N. VINAYAGAM
Faculty of Arts: Dr K. CHOCKALINGAM

There are 124 affiliated colleges.

MADURAI-KAMARAJ UNIVERSITY

Palkalai Nagar, Madurai 625021, Tamil Nadu
Telephone: 858471
Founded 1966
Teaching and Affiliating
Languages of instruction: English and Tamil
Academic year: July to April

Chancellor: HE THE GOVERNOR OF TAMIL NADU STATE
Vice-Chancellor: Prof. K. ALUDIAPILLAI
Registrar: Dr A. RAMASAMY
Librarian: Dr A. R. BALASUBRAMANIAN

Library of 230,000 vols
Number of teachers: 377 (excluding affiliated colleges)
Number of students: 133,100 (including affiliated colleges)

Publication: *Journal of Biology Education* (quarterly).

There are 82 affiliated colleges.

MAGADH UNIVERSITY

Bodh-Gaya 824234, Bihar
Telephone: 835, 836
Founded 1962
Teaching and Affiliating
Languages of instruction: English and Hindi
Academic year: June to May

Chancellor: HE THE GOVERNOR OF BIHAR
Vice-Chancellor: Justice SURESH C. MOOKHERJI
Pro-Vice-Chancellor: Dr B. N. SINGH
Registrar: Dr B. N. PANDEY
Librarian: (vacant)

Library of 220,000 vols
Number of teachers: 5,000
Number of students: 170,500

Publications: *Annual Report, Handbook.*

DEANS

Faculty of Humanities: Dr C. N. MISHRA
Faculty of Science: Prof. G. P. SINGH
Faculty of Commerce: Dr N. C. AGRAWAL
Faculty of Social Science: Dr K. B. SINGH
Faculty of Medicine: Dr M. P. SINGH
Faculty of Business Management: (vacant)

PROFESSORS

AGRAWAL, N. C., Commerce
AGRAWAL, B. N., Political Science
AMBASHTHA, A. V., Commerce
GUPTA, L. N., Commerce
JHA, B. K., Political Science
LAL, B. K., Philosophy
MISHRA, C. N., Sanskrit
NATH, B., Philosophy
PRASAD, B. K., Philosophy
PRASAD, B. N., Mathematics
PRASAD, N., English
ROY, L. M., Economics
ROY, P., Hindi
SAHAI, S., Ancient Indian and Asian Studies
SHRIVASTAVA, J. P., Chemistry
SINGH, A. N., Physics
SINGH, B. K., Psychology
SINGH, B. P., Political Science
SINGH, G. P., Physics
SINGH, H. G., Economics
SINGH, J. P., English
SINGH, R. C. P., Ancient Indian and Asian Studies
SINGH, S., Mathematics
SINGH, S. B., Zoology
SINHA, D. P., Zoology
SINHA, H. P., Philosophy
SINHA, N. C. P., Psychology
SINHA, S. P., Economics
SINHA, V. N., Philosophy
THAKUR, U., Ancient Indian and Asian Studies
TIWARY, P., Mathematics
VERMA, B. B., Commerce
VISHESHWARAM, S., Mathematics

ATTACHED INSTITUTES

Mishra, L. N., Institute of Economic Development and Social Change: Hon. Dir Dr CHAKERDHAR SINGH.

Nava Nalanda Mehavihar: Nalanda; postgraduate teaching in Pali and research in Pali literature with special reference to Buddhism; Dir Dr U. THAKUR.

Rajendra Memorial Research Institute of Medical Science: postgraduate research in conjunction with the Faculty of Medicine; Dir Dr LALA SURAYNANDAN PRASAD.

Sri D. K. Jain Orient Research Institute: Arrah; postgraduate research in Prakrit, Jain philosophy and religion; Hon. Dir Dr RAJA RAM JAIN.

There are 50 constituent colleges and 60 affiliated colleges.

MAHARSHI DAYANAND UNIVERSITY, ROHTAK

Rohtak 124001, Haryana
Telephone: 42639
Founded 1976
Affiliating
Languages of instruction: English and Hindi
Academic year: June to May

Chancellor: MAHAVIR PRASAD
Vice-Chancellor: Lt-Gen. O. P. KAUSHIK (Retd)
Pro-Vice-Chancellor: Dr L. N. DAHIYA
Registrar: SH. SHRIKANT WALGAD
Librarian: Dr P. N. SHARMA

Library of 218,580 vols, 700 periodicals
Number of teachers: 385
Number of students: 90,999

Publications: *Sahityanushilan, MDU* (quarterly).

DEANS

Faculty of Management Sciences: Dr DALIP SINGH
Faculty of Humanities: Dr S. S. SANGWAN
Faculty of Physical Sciences: Prof. R. S. CHOUDHARY
Faculty of Social Sciences: Prof. R. D. DIKSHIT
Faculty of Medical Sciences: Dr D. S. DUBEY
Faculty of Ayurvedic and Unani System of Medicine: Dr SHAKUNTLA CHAUDHARY
Faculty of Life Sciences: Prof. RAVI PARKASH
Faculty of Law: Prof. C. P. SHEORAN
Faculty of Commerce: Prof. L. N. DAHIYA
Faculty of Education: Prof. D. K. CHADDA

HEADS OF DEPARTMENTS

English: Dr S. S. SANGWAN
Hindi: Dr R. N. MISHRA
Sanskrit: Dr S. K. BHARDWAJ
History: Dr NEELIMA DAHIYA
Economics: Dr SURINDER KUMAR
Political Science: Dr M. G. GANDHI
Mathematics: Dr S. K. AGGARWAL
Physics: Dr NATHI SINGH
Management Studies and Research: Dr DALIP SINGH
Chemistry: Dr ISHWAR SINGH
Commerce: Dr S. N. MITTAL
Law: Dr L. C. DHINGRA
Sociology: Dr K. S. SANGWAN
Psychology: Dr PROMILA BATRA
Geography: Dr S. H. ANSARI
Education: Dr D. K. CHADDA
Biosciences: Dr K. V. SHASHTRI
Music: Dr C. M. SHARMA
Journalism and Mass Communication: Dr ISHWAR SINGH
Computer Science: Dr MANOHAR LAL
Public Administration: Dr R. K. PARBHAKAR
Statistics: Dr R. K. TETEJA
Fine Arts: Dr DALIP SINGH (acting)
Defence and Strategic Studies: Dr HARVIR SHARMA
Rural Development: Dr S. R. AHLAWAT
Physical Education: Dr B. S. DAGAR
Pharmaceutical Sciences: Dr A. K. MADAN

There are 85 affiliated colleges and one maintained college.

MAHATMA GANDHI UNIVERSITY

Kottayam 686 560, Kerala
Telephone: 597605
Telex: 888-288

Founded 1983 as Gandhiji University
State control
Language of instruction: English
Academic year: June to March

Chancellor: HE THE GOVERNOR OF KERALA
Vice-Chancellor: Prof. V. N. RAJASEKHARAN PILLAI
Pro-Vice-Chancellor: Dr C. A. ABDUSSALAAM
Registrar: Dr M. C. CHACKO
Librarian: R. RAVINDRAN ASARI

Number of teachers: 5,000
Number of students: 125,000

Publications: *Newsletter, Annual Report.*

DEANS

Education: Dr P. M. JALEEL
Fine Arts: Dr V. S. SHARMA
Science: Dr SHANKAR SHASIDHAR
Social Science: Dr A. K. CHIRAPPANATH
Commerce: Dr C. N. PURUSHOTHAMAN NAIR
Language and Literature: Dr P. N. VISWAMBARAN
Law: Dr K. VIKRAMAN NAIR
Medicine (Modern): Dr SHERIFA BEEVI
Medicine (Ayurveda): Dr J. R. LEELA

HEADS OF DEPARTMENT

Bio-Sciences: Dr SHANKAR SHASHIDHAR
Behavioural Science: Dr K. A. KUMAR
Chemical Sciences: (vacant)
Gandhian Studies and Peace Science: Dr A. K. CHIRAPPANATH
International Relations: Dr C. P. RAMACHANDRA
Law: Dr K. VIKRAMAN NAIR
School of Letters: Prof. R. NARENDRA PRASAD
Mathematics and Computer Science: Dr K. N. RAMACHANDRAN NAIR
Pure and Applied Physics: Dr M. A. ITTYACHEN
Social Sciences: Dr RAJAN GURUKKAL
School of Distance Education: Dr P. K. JOSE
School of Pedagogical Science: Dr P. M. JALEEL
Adult Continuing Education and Extension: C. THOMAS ABRAHAM

There are 69 affiliated colleges.

MAHATMA PHULE KRISHI VIDYAPEETH

Rahuri 413722, Ahmednagar District, Maharashtra
Telephone: 8, 16
Founded 1968
Academic year: July to May

Chancellor: HE The Governor of Maharashtra
Pro-Chancellor: The Minister for Agriculture
Vice-Chancellor: Dr Y. S. Nericar
Registrar: D. K. Jaddale
Librarian: A. G. Karande

Library of 51,000 vols
Number of students: 2,200

DEANS

Faculty of Agricultural Engineering: Prof. G. B. Bangal
Faculty of Agriculture: Dr S. S. Magar

CONSTITUENT COLLEGES

Agricultural College: Dhulia; f. 1960; Assoc. Dean Dr R. S. Patil.

Agricultural College: Kolhapur; f. 1963; Assoc. Dean Dr A. M. Kale.

Agricultural College: Pune; f. 1906; Assoc. Dean Prof. A. V. Tendulkar.

College of Agricultural Engineering: Rahuri; f. 1969; Assoc. Dean Prof. G. B. Bangal.

Postgraduate Agricultural Institute: Rahuri; f. 1972; Assoc. Dean Dr V. M. Pawar.

MANGALORE UNIVERSITY

Mangalagangotri 574199, D.K., Karnataka

Telephone: 80276

Founded 1980
Languages of instruction: English and Kannada
Academic year: June to April

Chancellor: HE The Governor of Karnataka
Vice-Chancellor: Prof. S. Gopal
Registrar: Dr K. M. Kaveriappa
Librarian: Dr Jayarama Hegde (acting)

Library of 83,734 vols
Number of teachers: 2,849
Number of students: 50,023

Publication: *Newsletter* (quarterly).

DEANS

Faculty of Arts: Prof. C. N. Ramachandran
Faculty of Science and Technology: Prof. N. Lingappa
Faculty of Engineering: Prof. M. N. Channabasappa
Faculty of Commerce: Prof. M. P. Subramanian
Faculty of Medicine: Prof. C. R. Kamath
Faculty of Education: Prof. B. R. Sharathchandra
Faculty of Law: Prof. N. J. Kadamba

CHAIRMEN OF DEPARTMENTS

English: Prof. C. N. Ramachandran
History: Prof. H. V. Sreenivasa Murthy
Economics: Prof. N. S. Bhat
Political Science: (vacant)
Mathematics: Dr Sampath Kumar
Physics: Prof. N. Lingappa
Materials Science: Prof. Jayagopal Uchil
Statistics: Dr K. K. Acharya
Commerce: Prof. M. P. Subramanian
MBA: Prof. M. P. Subramanian
Chemistry: Prof. B. Thimme Gowda
Marine Geology: Prof. K. R. Subramanya
Sociology: (vacant)
Kannada: Prof. B. A. Vivek Rai
Biosciences: Prof. M. Abdul Rahiman
Applied Zoology: Prof. S. N. Hegde
Applied Botany: Prof. K. M. Kaveriappa
Library and Information Science: Dr A. K. Baradol
Mass Communication and Journalism: G. P. Shivaram

There are 70 affiliated colleges

MANIPUR UNIVERSITY

Canchipur, Imphal, Manipur 795003
Telephone: 220756
Fax: (385) 221429
E-mail: manipur@shakti.ncst.ernet.in

Founded 1980
Teaching and Affiliating
State control
Language of instruction: English
Academic year: August to May

Chancellor: HE The Governor of Manipur
Vice-Chancellor: Prof. I. S. Khaidem
Registrar: Th. Joychandra Singh
Librarian: Ch. Radheshyam Singh

Library of 95,000 vols
Number of teachers: 184 (postgraduate depts only)
Number of students: 1,834 (postgraduate depts only)

Publications: *Manipur University Bulletin* (4 a year), *Manipur University Magazine* (1 a year), *Manipur University Annual Report.*

DEANS

Humanities: Prof. S. Shyamkishore Singh
Science: Prof. H. Nandakamur Sarma
Social Sciences: Prof. M. Iboton Singh

There are 60 affiliated colleges.

MARATHWADA AGRICULTURAL UNIVERSITY

Parbhani 431402, Maharashtra

Telephone: 45002

Founded 1972
State control
Language of instruction: English
Academic year: June to May

Chancellor: HE The Governor of Maharashtra
Vice-Chancellor: Dr V. K. Patil
Registrar: Dr. D. N. Kulkarni
Librarian: R. Subbaiah

Number of teachers: 282
Number of students: 2,017

Publications: *News Letter* (English and Marathi, monthly), *Sheti Bhati* (Marathi, monthly), *Research Bulletin* (English, monthly).

PROFESSORS

Faculty of Agriculture:

Adkine, B. D., Agricultural Engineering
Dhanorkar, B. K., Entomology
Dhoble, M. V., Agronomy
Malewar, G. U., Agricultural Chemistry
Mali, V. R., Plant Pathology
Nandapurkar, G. G., Extension Studies
Patil, G. R., Animal Husbandry and Dairy Farming
Patil, H. N., Economics
Patil, V. D., Botany
Shinde, N. N., Horticulture

Faculty of Agricultural Technology:

Kadam, P. S., Food Microbiology
Kulkarni, D. N., Food Science and Cereal Technology
Rathi, S. D., Animal Products Technology
Sawate, A. R., Food Engineering
Wankhede, D. B., Biochemistry

Faculty of Home Science:

Ekale, J. V., Home Science and Extension Education
Murali, D., Home Management
Reddy, N. S., Foods and Nutrition
Visala, P., Child Development and Family Relationship

Faculty of Veterinary and Animal Sciences:

Bhokre, A. P., Surgery
Dhoble, R. L., Gynaecology
Gujar, M. B., Microbiology
Sakhare, P. G., Animal Management
Vadlamudi, V. P., Pharmacology

CONSTITUENT COLLEGES

College of Agriculture: Parbhani; Principal Dr M. V. Dhoble.

College of Agriculture: Latur; Principal Dr U. S. Raut.

College of Agricultural Engineering Parbhani; Principal Dr S. A. Quadri.

College of Agricultural Technology: Parbhani; Principal Dr D. B. Wankhede.

College of Home Science: Parbhani; Principal S. M. Harode.

College of Veterinary and Animal Sciences: Parbhani; Principal Dr B. B. Deshpande.

College of Veterinary and Animal Sciences: Ugdir; Principal Dr M. A. Gaffar.

There are 16 affiliated research stations.

MEERUT UNIVERSITY

Meerut 250005, Uttar Pradesh

Telephone: 75454

Founded 1966
Affiliating and Teaching
Languages of instruction: Hindi and English

Chancellor: HE The Governor of Uttar Pradesh
Vice-Chancellor: Dr B. B. L. Saxena
Registrar: Dr V. B. Bansal

Library of 102,064 vols
Number of students: 125,365

DEANS

Faculty of Arts: Dr S. S. Sharma
Faculty of Science: Dr D. Banerjee
Faculty of Commerce: Dr K. N. Nagar
Faculty of Education: Dr K. G. Sharma
Faculty of Agriculture: Dr P. K. Gupta
Faculty of Law: O. P. Garg
Faculty of Medicine: Dr J. S. Mathur

There are one constituent college and 61 affiliated colleges.

MOHAN LAL SUKHADIA UNIVERSITY

Pratap Nagar, Udaipur 313001, Rajasthan
Telephone: (294) 414166
Fax: (294) 413150

Founded 1962 as Rajasthan Agricultural University, present name 1981
Teaching and Affiliating
Autonomous control
Languages of instruction: English and Hindi
Academic year: July to June

Chancellor: Bali Ram Bhagat
Vice-Chancellor: Prof. R. K. Rai
Registrar: H. M. Chandalia
Librarian: S. L. Dave

Library of 249,000 vols
Number of teachers: 264
Number of students: 47,209

Publications: *Information Bulletin* (annually), Annual Report.

DEANS

Faculty of Commerce: Dr K. R. Sharma
Faculty of Law: Dr R. L. Jain (Assoc. Dean)
Faculty of Science: Dr C. M. Joshi
Faculty of Humanities and Social Sciences: Dr P. S. Jain (Assoc. Dean)

PROFESSORS

Faculty of Commerce:

Sharma, K. R.
Singh, A. K.

Faculty of Science:

Choudhary, B. L., Mathematics
Joshi, C. M., Mathematics
Mehta, O. P., Chemistry

PUROHIT, D. N., Chemistry
ROY, A. B., Geology
SUD, K. K., Physics
UPADHYAYA, U. N., Physics

Faculty of Humanities and Social Sciences:

MEHTA, G. M., English

CONSTITUENT COLLEGES

College of Science: Udaipur; Dean C. M. JOSHI.

College of Law: Udaipur; Dean Dr R. L. JAIN (Assoc. Dean).

College of Social Sciences and Humanities: Udaipur; Dean Dr P. S. JAIN (Assoc. Dean).

College of Commerce and Management Studies: Udaipur; Dean Prof. K. R. SHARMA.

MOTHER TERESA WOMEN'S UNIVERSITY

Kodaikanal 624102

Telephone: 41122

Founded 1984
State government and University Grants Commission control
Languages of Instruction: English and Tamil
Academic year: August to June

Chancellor: HE Dr M. CHANNA REDDY
Vice-Chancellor: Dr P. SUNDARAM
Registrar: Dr SATHYAVATHI MANUEL
Assistant Librarians: Ms K. P. PADMAVATHI, Ms SEMBIANMADEVI

Library of 41,000 vols
Number of teachers: 34
Number of students: 1,000

Courses in economics, education, English, family life management, historical studies, sociology, Tamil, computer science, music, women's studies, guidance and counselling, population studies, business economics, history and tourism, entrepreneurship and industrial training, health and family welfare.

PROFESSORS

BAI, N. S., Economics
DAVID, M. T., English
DEVADATTA, V. P., Tamil
SUBBAMMAL, K., Education
SURYAKUMARI, A., Historical Studies

UNIVERSITY OF MYSORE

POB 407, Mysore 570005, Karnataka

Telephone: 438666
Fax: 421263

Founded 1916
Teaching and Affiliating
Languages of instruction: English and Kannada
Academic year: June to March (two terms)

Chancellor: HE THE GOVERNOR OF KARNATAKA
Vice-Chancellor: Dr S. N. HEGDE
Registrar: Dr V. G. TALAWAR
Registrar (Evaluation): Dr K. N. UDAYA KUMAR
Librarian: Dr H. R. ACHYUTHA RAO

Library of 650,000 vols (undergraduate library)
Number of students: 62,966 undergraduate, 11,589 postgraduate

DEANS

Faculty of Arts: Dr DAYANANDA MANE
Faculty of Science and Technology: Dr P. NAGABHUSHAN
Faculty of Engineering: Dr T. R. SEETHARAM
Faculty of Education: Dr N. VENKATAIAH
Faculty of Law: Dr H. K. NAGARAJ
Faculty of Commerce: Dr VIJAYA KUMAR

UNIVERSITY COLLEGES

Maharaja's College; Yuvaraja's College; University College of Physical Education; College of Fine Arts for Women; University Evening College.

There are 100 affiliated colleges, 2 evening colleges and 3 postgraduate centres.

NAGARJUNA UNIVERSITY

Nagarjuna Nagar 522510, Andhra Pradesh

Telephone: (863) 293378

Founded 1976
Language of instruction: English
Academic year: July to April

Chancellor: HE THE GOVERNOR OF ANDHRA PRADESH
Vice-Chancellor: Prof. S. V. J. LAKSHMAN
Principal: Prof. V. L. NARASIMHAM
Registrar: Prof. LAM PRAKASA
Librarian: J. RAMA RAO

Library of 86,000 vols
Number of teachers: 148
Number of students: 1,700

DEANS

Faculty of Commerce: Prof. D. DAKSHINA MURTHY
Faculty of Engineering: Prof. V. V. SUBBA RAO
Faculty of Humanities: Prof. B. R. SUBRAHMANYAM
Faculty of Law: Prof. D. VIJAYANARAYANA REDDY
Faculty of Natural Sciences: Prof. P. NARASIMHAM
Faculty of Physical Sciences: Prof. V. L. NARASIMHAM
Faculty of Social Sciences: Prof. C. V. RAGHAVULU
Faculty of Education: Dr M. SHYAM SUNDAR

PROFESSORS

Faculty of Commerce:

BRAHMANANDAM, G. N., Commerce
DAKSHINA MURTHY, D., Commerce
GANJU, M. K., Commerce
HANUMANTHA RAO K., Commerce
NARASIMHAM, V. V. L., Commerce
PRASAD, G., Commerce
UMAMAHESWARA RAO, T., Commerce
VIYYANNA RAO, K., Commerce

Faculty of Humanities:

BALAGANGADHARA RAO, Y., Telugu and Languages
KRUPACHARY, G., Telugu and Languages
KUMARASWAMY, Y., Ancient History and Archaeology
NIRMALA, T., Telugu and Oriental Languages
PUNNA RAO, A., Telugu and Oriental Languages
RAMA SASTRY, N. A., Telugu and Languages
RAMALAKSHMI, P., Ancient History and Archaeology
BHASKARA MURTHY, D., Ancient History and Archaeology
SARASWATHI, R., English
SUBRAHMANYAM, B. R., Ancient History and Archaeology

Faculty of Law:

HARAGOPAL REDDY, Y. R.
RANGAIAH, N., Law
VIJAYANARAYANA REDDY, D.

Faculty of Natural Sciences:

BALAPARAMESWARA RAO, M., Aquaculture
DURGA PRASAD, M. K., Zoology
GOPALAKRISHNA REDDY, T., Zoology
LAKSHMI, N., Botany
MALLAIAH, K. V., Botany
NARASIMHA RAO, P., Botany
NIRAMALA MARY, T., Botany
RAMAMOHANA RAO, P., Botany
RAMAMURTHY NAIDU, K., Botany
RANGA RAO, V., Geology
SANTHA KUMARI, D., Botany
SHARMA, S. V., Zoology

Faculty of Physical Sciences:

ANJANEYULU, Y., Chemistry
GOPALA KRISHNA MURTHY, P. V., Physics
HARANADH, C., Physics
KOTESWARA RAO, G., Mathematics
NARASIMHAM, V. L., Statistics
NARAYANA MURTHY, P., Physics
PRAKASA RAO, L., Mathematics
PRAKASA RAO, N. S., Chemistry
RAMA BADRA SARMA, I., Mathematics
RAMAKOTAIAH, D., Mathematics
RANGACHARYULU, H., Physics
SATYANANDAM, G., Physics
SATYANARAYANA, P. V. V., Chemistry
SHYAM SUNDAR, B., Chemistry
SIVA RAMA SARMA, B., Chemistry
VENKATACHARYULU, P., Physics
VENKATESWARA REDDY, Y., Mathematics

Faculty of Social Sciences:

ASHEERVADH, N., Political Science
BAPUJI, M., Political Science
BHAVANI, V., Political Science
NARAYANA RAO, C., Political Science
RAGHAVULU, C. V., Political Science and Public Administration
RAJA BABU, K., Economics
RAJU, C. S. N., Economics
SUDHAKARA RAO, N., Economics

Faculty of Engineering:

THRIMURTY, P., Computer Science and Engineering

There are 174 affiliated colleges.

UNIVERSITY OF NAGPUR

Rabindranath Tagore Marg, Nagpur 440001, Maharashtra

Telephone: 525417

Founded 1923
Teaching and Affiliating
Languages of instruction: English, Hindi and Marathi
Academic year: June to March (two terms)

Chancellor: HE THE GOVERNOR OF MAHARASHTRA
Vice-Chancellor: M. T. GABHE
Registrar: P. B. MISTRI
Librarian: Dr P. S. G. KUMAR

Library of 319,000 vols, including 14,313 MSS
Number of teachers: 4,074
Number of students: 95,664

DEANS

Faculty of Arts: A. K. DEY
Faculty of Law: SUNDARAM
Faculty of Medicine: Dr W. B. TAYADE
Faculty of Ayurvedic Medicine: S. SHARMA
Faculty of Science: Dr T. M. KARDE
Faculty of Education: R. S. DAGAR
Faculty of Commerce: N. H. KHATRI
Faculty of Engineering and Technology: H. THAKARE
Faculty of Social Sciences: V. H. GHORPADE
Faculty of Home Science: Dr A. G. MOHARIL

CHAIRMEN OF BOARDS OF STUDIES

Faculty of Arts (including Fine Arts):

Arabic: Dr A. MAJID
English: K. SATYANARAYANA
Fine Arts: A. S. MOREY
Hindi: H. CHAURASIA
Linguistics: Dr R. P. SAXENA
Marathi: Prof. S. W. SWAN
Music: S. S. PALDHIKAR
Other Foreign Languages: P. R. DEO
Other Indian Languages: Dr R. N. ROY
Pali and Prakrit: Prof. M. S. WAGHMARE
Persian: Q. JOHAN
Sanskrit: Dr M. GULAB
Urdu: Dr ARSHAD JAMAL

Faculty of Science:

Biochemistry: Dr S. Chari
Botany: Dr K. M. Makde
Chemistry: Dr V. G. Deshmukh
Electronics: Dr A. A. Sakale
Geology: Dr N. K. Mohobey
Languages: K. M. Thomas
Mathematics: Dr T. M. Karde
Microbiology: A. V. Gomase
Physics: S. R. Bajaj
Statistics: C. P. Cholkar
Zoology: Dr P. G. Puranik

Faculty of Law:

V. R. Manohar

Faculty of Education:

Education: Dr P. B. Gupta
Physical Education and Recreation: R. S. Dagar

Faculty of Commerce:

Accounts and Statistics: Prof. T. D. Lodhi
Business Administration and Business Management: Prof. V. M. Chopde
Business Economics: B. A. Megde
Commerce: V. S. Ainchwar
Languages: D. Jog

Faculty of Engineering and Technology:

Applied Science and Humanities: V. S. Gogulwar
Architecture: Prof. A. L. Chhatre
Chemical Engineering: Dr R. L. Sonulikar
Chemical Technology: Dr J. D. Dhake
Civil Engineering: R. S. Bais
Electrical Engineering: Dr N. T. Khobragade
Electronics Engineering: J. B. Helonde
Fire Engineering: (vacant)
Mechanical Engineering: Prof. I. K. Chopde
Metallurgical Engineering: Dr S. U. Pathak
Mining Engineering: L. L. Muthreja
Production Engineering: Prof. V. M. Kriplani

Faculty of Medicine:

Dentistry (Clinical): Dr P. V. Hazare
Dentistry (Preclinical): V. K. Hazare
Clinical Medicine: (vacant)
Clinical Medicine II: Dr N. D. Wasudev
Homoeopathy: Dr V. P. Mishra
Modern Medicine (OT and PT): Dr G. J. Ramteke
Paraclinical Medicine: Dr B. D. Paranjape
Preclinical Medicine: Dr V. M. Sathe
Pharmaceutical Sciences: Dr K. P. Bhusari
Surgery: Dr R. Narang

Faculty of Home Science:

Dr P. Akhani

Faculty of Ayurvedic Medicine:

Clinical: Dr G. N. Tiwari
Paraclinical: H. B. Deshpande
Preclinical: J. T. Chotai
Pharmaceutical Surgery: M. M. Jumale

Faculty of Social Sciences:

Ancient Indian History, Culture and Archaeology: Dr C. S. Gupta
Economics: M. K. Gurpude
Geography: V. H. Ghorpade
Gandhian Thought: B. M. Mandeokar
History: Dr Y. N. Gujar
Home Economics: P. Dhoble
Library and Information Science: Dr P. S. G. Kumar
Mass Communication: (vacant)
Philosophy: Dr B. Y. Deshpande
Political Science: Dr B. L. Bhole
Psychology: Dr A. V. Kulkarni
Public Administration: Dr P. L. Joshi
Rural Services: R. B. Ghate
Social Work: A. W. Dhage
Sociology: M. B. Bute

CONSTITUENT COLLEGES

Laxminarayan Institute of Technology: Nagpur; f. 1942; 50 teachers; 510 students; Dir Dr G. D. Nageshwar.

University College of Law: Nagpur; f. 1925; 10 teachers; 2,571 students; Principal V. D. Thakare.

University College of Education: Nagpur; f. 1945; 16 teachers; 320 students; Principal C. K. Nagose.

There are 218 affiliated colleges.

NARENDRA DEVA UNIVERSITY OF AGRICULTURE & TECHNOLOGY

Narendranagar, Kumarganj 224229, Faizabad, Uttar Pradesh

Telephone: (2023) 814947

Founded 1974
State control
Languages of instruction: Hindi and English

Chancellor: The Governor of Uttar Pradesh
Vice-Chancellor: Dr B. R. Tripathi
Registrar: S. M. Shamim
Librarian: B. K. Singh

Library of 33,000 vols
Number of teachers: 67
Number of students: 432

Publication: *NDUAT News Bulletin*.

HEADS OF DEPARTMENTS

Genetics and Plant Breeding: Dr D. M. Maurya
Horticulture: Dr I. S. Singh
Entomology: Dr S. M. A. Rizvi
Agronomy: Dr R. S. Dixit
Animal Science: Dr D. N. Verma
Crop Physiology: Dr B. B. Singh
Agricultural Engineering: Dr P. M. Singh
Agricultural Economics: J. N. Singh
Soil Science: Dr Room Singh
Plant Pathology: Dr R. V. Singh
Biochemistry: Dr A. B. Abidi
Extension Education: Dr R. K. Shukla
Vegetable Science: Dr R. D. Singh
Nematology: Dr A. C. Verma
Microbiology: Dr Raman Rai
Food Technology: Dr I. S. Singh
Fisheries: Dr Ram Singh
Agricultural Statistics: Dr B. V. S. Sisodia
Forestry: Dr B. P. Singh
Home Science: Dr Suman Bhanot

UNIVERSITY OF NORTH BENGAL

PO North Bengal University, Raja Rammohunpur, Darjeeling District, West Bengal 734430

Telephone: (353) 450255

Founded 1962
Teaching and Affiliating

Chancellor: HE The Governor of West Bengal
Vice-Chancellor: Prof. R. G. Mukherjee
Registrar: Dr T. K. Chatterjee

Library of 119,000 vols
Number of students: 30,000

DEANS

Faculty of Arts, Commerce and Law: Prof. J. C. Debnath
Faculty of Science and Medicine: Prof. B. Bhattacharjee

PROFESSORS

Arts, Commerce and Law:

Banerjee, A., English
Bhadra, R. K., Sociology and Social Anthropology
Bhattacharyya, P. K., History
Bhowmick, D. J., Political Science
Chakraborty, U., English
Dasgupta M., Economics
Deb, K., Commerce
Debnath, J. C., Economics
Kar, J., History
Kundu, P. K., Bengali
Misra, B. P., Centre for Himalayan Studies
Roy, K. K., English
Roy S. N., Political Science
Roy Choudhury, T. K., History
Sengupta, P. K., Political Science

Science and Medicine:

Basu, P. K., Botany
Bhattacharjee, B., Physics
Bhattacharyya, A., Geography and Applied Geography
Bose, S. C., Mathematics
Chakraborty, A. K., Zoology
Chakraborty, P. K., Geography and Applied Geography
Chowdury, N., Physics
Das, B. K., Chemistry
Dasgupta, D., Physics
Dutta, K. B., Botany
Ghosh, M. L., Mathematics
Hazra, D. K., Chemistry
Karanjai, S. B., Mathematics
Majee, B., Chemistry
Majumdar, S. K., Chemistry
Mukherjee, S., Physics
Murthi, G. S. S., Chemistry
Pal, A., Geography and Applied Geography
Pal, B. C., Zoology
Pal, S. P., Mathematics
Pal, R., Physics

There are three university colleges and 55 affiliated colleges.

NORTH-EASTERN HILL UNIVERSITY

PO NEHU Campus, Shillong 793002

Telephone: (364) 250705
Fax: (364) 250076

Founded 1973
Teaching and Affiliating
Language of instruction: English
Academic year: July to June

Chancellor: Dr K. R. Narayanan
Vice-Chancellor: Prof. Barrister Pakem
Pro-Vice Chancellors: Prof. Lalthantluanga, Prof. M. S. Sangma, Prof. K. S. Lyngdoh.
Registrar: P. S. Rynjah
Librarian: Dr Lalit P. Pathak

Library of 187,000 vols
Number of teachers: 271
Number of students: 23,709

Publications: *NEHU News* (monthly), *NEHU Journal of Social Sciences and Humanities* (quarterly).

DEANS

School of Life Sciences: Prof. A. Raghuverman
School of Social Sciences: Prof. J. P. Singh
School of Physical Sciences: Prof. S. N. Bhatt
School of Human and Environmental Sciences: Prof. A. C. Mohapatra
School of Economics, Management and Information Science: Prof. S. K. Mishra
School of Humanities and Education: (vacant)

There are 54 affiliated colleges.

NORTH GUJARAT UNIVERSITY

University Rd, POB 21, Patan 384265, North Gujarat

Telephone: (2766) 30427

Founded 1986
State control
Language of instruction: Gujarati
Academic year: June to April

Chancellor: Hon. Krushnapalsingh
Vice-Chancellor: Prof. N. R. Dave
Registrar: B. N. Shah
Librarian: M. K. Prajapati

Library of 19,000 vols
Number of teachers: 1,319

Number of students: 52,349

Publications: *Udichya* (fortnightly), *Anart* (annually), *Uttara*.

DEANS

Faculty of Arts: Dr JAGDISH DAVE
Faculty of Commerce: Prin. J. R. PATEL
Faculty of Science: Prin. M. D. KOTAK
Faculty of Law: SURESHCHANDRA C. SHAH
Faculty of Pharmacy: Prin. NATVARLAL PATEL
Faculty of Engineering and Technology: JANARDAN V. DAVE
Faculty of Education: Prin. Dr RATILAL PATEL
Faculty of Management Studies: Dr BALULAL A. PRAJAPATI

NORTH MAHARASHTRA UNIVERSITY

PB No. 80, Jalgaon 425001, Maharashtra
Telephone: (257) 222187
Fax: (257) 222183

Founded 1990
State control
Vice-Chancellor: Dr SOMAJI FAKIRA PATIL
Registrar: Dr SAMBHAJI NILKANTH DESAI
Librarian: T. R. BORSE (Assistant Librarian)

Library of 11,000 vols
Number of teachers: 3,174
Number of students: 47,974

DEANS

Faculty of Arts: Prof. SHRIPAL SABNIS
Faculty of Education: Prin. M. L. NANKAR
Faculty of Commerce: Prof. R. H. GUPTA
Faculty of Science: Prin. Dr K. B. PATIL
Faculty of Mental, Moral and Social Sciences: Prof. T. T. MAHAJAN
Faculty of Engineering: Prof. G. S. PATIL
Faculty of Medicine: Dr A. B. SOLPURE
Faculty of Law: Adv. UJJWAL NIKAM
Ayurveda Faculty: Vd. T. N. PATIL

ORISSA UNIVERSITY OF AGRICULTURE AND TECHNOLOGY

Bhubaneswar 751003, District Khurda, Orissa
Telephone: 402719

Founded 1962
Teaching and Research
State control
Language of instruction: English
Academic year: July to July

Chancellor: C. RANGARAJAN
Vice-Chancellor: R. K. BHUJABALA
Registrar: Dr S. MOHANTY
Librarian: S. K. ROUT

Library of 175,000 vols
Number of teachers: 294
Number of students: 3,046

DEANS

College of Agriculture (Bhubaneswar): Dr U. N. DIXIT
College of Agriculture (Chiplima): Dr S. C. PANDA (Assoc. Dean)
College of Veterinary Science and Animal Husbandry: Dr SARAT CHANDRA MISHRA
College of Engineering and Technology: Dr SUBASH CHANDRA MISHRA
College of Agricultural Engineering and Technology: Dr N. S. SWAIN
Postgraduate Faculty: Dr S. MOHANTY

DIRECTORS

College of Basic Science and Humanities: Dr D. PRATIHARI
College of Fisheries: Dr P. C. THOMAS
College of Home Science: Dr S. D. SHARMA

OSMANIA UNIVERSITY

Hyderabad 500007, Andhra Pradesh
Telephone: 868951

Founded 1918
Teaching, Residential and Affiliating
Languages of instruction: English, Hindi, Telugu, Urdu and Marathi
Academic year: June to April (two terms)
Chancellor: HE THE GOVERNOR OF ANDHRA PRADESH
Vice-Chancellor: Prof. V. RAMAKISTAIAH
Registrar: Prof. H. POLASA
Librarian: D. ISSAC

Library of 422,000 vols
Number of students: 78,212

Publications: *Journal of Osmania University, Syllabuses, University Act, University Diary, List of Recognized Examinations of Other Universities, University Hand Book, Osmania Journal of English Studies, Research Bulletin of Department of Psychology,* etc.

DEANS

Faculty of Arts: Prof. C. RAMA RAO
Faculty of Science: Prof. P. RAMCHANDER RAO
Faculty of Social Sciences: Prof. N. Y. REDDY
Faculty of Commerce: Prof. P. SUBRAHMANYAM
Faculty of Engineering: Prof. D. C. REDDY
Faculty of Education: Prof. V. EASHWAR REDDY
Faculty of Law: Justice BHASKAR RAO
Faculty of Medicine: Dr P. S. RAO
Faculty of Ayurvedha and Unani: Dr K. G. K. SASTRY
Faculty of Technology: Prof. P. SADASHIVA RAO

HEADS OF DEPARTMENTS

Faculty of Arts:

Ancient Indian History, Culture & Archaeology: Dr S. DHARESWARI
Arabic: Prof. SULTAN MOHIUDDIN
English: Prof. M. SIVARAMA KRISHNA
French: Dr PRAMILA VENKAT RAO
German: Dr D. SATYANARAYANA
Hindi: Dr T. MOHAN SINGH
Islamic Studies: Dr SULEMAN SIDDIQUI
Journalism: ABDUR RAHIM
Kannada: Dr K. G. NARAYAN PRASAD
Linguistics: Dr A. K. SHARMA
Marathi: Dr KAVITA KATKE
Persian: Dr SYEDA BASHEERUNNISA BEGUM
Philosophy: Prof. P. SITARAM REDDY
Russian: MADHAV MARURKAR
Sanskrit: Prof. K. KAMALA
Tamil: G. PRABALAMBAL
Telugu: Prof. V. SITA KALYANI
Theatre Arts: Dr PRADEEP KUMAR
Urdu: Prof. S. YOUSUF SHARIFUDDIN

Faculty of Social Sciences:

Economics: Prof. H. VENKATESWARA RAO
Geography: Prof. RAM MOHAN RAO
History: Prof. P. JHANSI LAXMI
Library Science: N. LAXMAN RAO
Political Science: Prof. S. D. JATKAR
Psychology: Prof. N. YADAGIRI REDDY
Public Administration: Prof. M. A. ALEEM
Sociology: Prof. J. V. RAGHVENDER RAO

Faculty of Science:

Astronomy: Prof. B. LOKANADHAM
Biochemistry: Dr. G. VENKATESWALU
Botany: Prof. M. NUSRATH
Chemistry: Prof. P. K. SAI PRAKASH
Genetics: Prof. T. POPI REDDY
Geology: Prof. M. VENKATESHWARA RAO
Geophysics: Prof. J. B. RAMAPRASADA RAO
Mathematics: Prof. V. SHIVA RAMA PRASAD
Microbiology: Prof. G. SEENAYYA
Physics: Prof. K. RAMA REDDY
Statistics: Dr Y. SIVARAMA KRISHNA
Zoology: Prof. T. SATYANARAYAN SINGH

Faculty of Commerce:

Commerce: Prof. S. RAMA MURTHY
Business Management: Prof. A. V. SATYANARAYAN RAO

Faculty of Education:

Education: Prof. R. KRISHNA RAO

Faculty of Law:

Law: Prof. P. SHESHADRI

Faculty of Engineering:

Civil Engineering: Prof. D. SHANTA RAM
Electrical Engineering: Prof. P. ETHIRAJULU
Electronics and Communication Engineering: Prof. SADASIV SHARMA
Computer Science Engineering: Prof. K. V. CHALAPATTI RAO
Mechanical Engineering: Prof. M. KOMARAIAH
Mining Engineering: Prof. VEERENDER SINGH

Faculty of Technology:

Chemical Engineering and Technology: Prof. M. BHAGWANTH RAO

UNIVERSITY COLLEGES

University College of Arts: Hyderabad; f. 1918; Principal Prof. K. SUBHASHCHANDRA REDDY.

University College of Commerce and Business Management: Hyderabad; f. 1975; Principal Prof. B. GOVERDHAN REDDY.

University College of Education: Hyderabad; f. 1928; Principal Prof. R. KRISHNA RAO.

University College of Engineering: Hyderabad; f. 1929; Principal Prof. P. S. R. MURTHY.

University College of Law: Hyderabad; f. 1960; Principal V. KRISHNAMA CHARY.

University College of Science: Hyderabad; f. 1918; Principal Prof. M. GOVIND RAM REDDY.

University College of Technology: Hyderabad 7; f. 1969; Principal M. BHAGAWANTHA RAO.

CONSTITUENT COLLEGES

Postgraduate College of Law: Hyderabad; f. 1954; Principal G. MANCHAR RAO.

Nizam College: Hyderabad; f. 1887; Principal Prof. G. GOPALA KRISHNA.

Kothagudem School of Mines: Kothagudem 507101; f. 1976; Principal Prof. G. S. N. RAJU.

Satavahana P. G. Centre: Karimnagar; f. 1976; Head Prof. V. SURENDER.

Postgraduate Centre: Kothagudem; f. 1976; Head Prof. A. A. MOIZ (acting).

Postgraduate Centre: Godavari Khani; f. 1976; Head Prof. M. LAKSHRIPATHI RAO (acting).

Postgraduate Centre: Biknoor; f. 1976; Head Prof. Dr D. MALLESHWAR.

Postgraduate Centre: Mahaboobnagar; f. 1987; Head Prof. C. R. ANAND RAO.

Postgraduate Centre: Mirzapur, Medak District; f. 1980; Head Dr K. S. K. RAO PATNAIK.

Postgraduate Centre: Nalgonda; f. 1987; Head Prof. D. O. REDDY.

Postgraduate College: Secunderabad; f. 1947; Principal Prof. N. UMAPATHY.

Postgraduate College of Science: Saifabad, Hyderabad; f. 1951; Principal Prof. K. SHANKARAIAH.

University College for Women: Hyderabad; f. 1924; Principal Prof. V. R. LALITHA.

There are 120 affiliated colleges and 16 Oriental colleges.

PANDIT RAVISHANKAR SHUKLA UNIVERSITY, RAIPUR

Raipur 492010, Madhya Pradesh
Telephone: 23957
Fax: 534283

Founded 1964
Teaching and Affiliating
Languages of instruction: Hindi and English
Private control
Academic year: July to June (two terms)

Chancellor: HE THE GOVERNOR OF MADHYA PRADESH
Vice-Chancellor: Prof. R. K. THAKUR
Registrar: Prof. H. L. GUPTA
Librarian: R. SINGH

Library of 93,000 vols
Number of students: 28,496

DEANS AND PRINCIPALS

Faculty of Arts: R. C. MEHROTRA
Faculty of Law: R. L. YADAV
Faculty of Education: P. R. GAHINE
Faculty of Medicine: Dr T. N. MEHROTRA
Faculty of Ayurved: P. K. JAIN
Faculty of Commerce: A. K. SHUKLA
Faculty of Social Sciences: R. D. HELODE
Faculty of Engineering: D. N. KHANDELWAL
Faculty of Life Science: S. S. ALI
Faculty of Home Science: Smt. KUMUD NAGARIYA
Faculty of Science: V. K. GUPTA

There are 92 affiliated colleges.

PANJAB UNIVERSITY

Chandigarh 160014, Union Territory
Telephone: 541945
Founded 1947
Teaching and Affiliating
Languages of instruction: English, Punjabi, Urdu and Hindi
Academic year: July to April

Chancellor: THE VICE-PRESIDENT OF INDIA
Vice-Chancellor: Prof. T. N. KAPOOR
Registrar: S. P. DHAWAN
Librarian: A. R. SETHI

Libraries of 590,000 vols
Number of teachers: 746
Number of students: 20,554

Publications: *Research Bulletin* (Arts), *Parakh, Parishodh, Social Sciences Research Journal, P.U. News, Research Bulletin* (science).

DEANS

Faculty of Arts: Dr MADAN MOHAN PURI
Faculty of Languages: Dr ANIRUDH JOSHI
Faculty of Science: Prof. K. N. PATHAK
Faculty of Engineering and Technology: Prof. D. K. VOHRA
Faculty of Education: NIRMAL KAUR
Faculty of Business Management and Commerce: Prof. S. P. SINGH
Faculty of Law: GOPAL KRISHAN CHATRATH
Faculty of Medical Sciences: Dr K. S. CHUGH
Faculty of Dairying, Animal Husbandry and Agriculture: Dr JOGINDER SINGH YADAV
Faculty of Design and Fine Arts: JOGINDER SINGH
Faculty of Pharmaceutical Sciences: Prof. V. K. KAPOOR

There are 104 affiliated colleges.

UNIVERSITY OF PATNA

Patna 800005, Bihar State
Telephone: 52500, 50352
Founded 1917: re-founded 1952
Residential and Teaching
Languages of instruction: Hindi and English
Academic year: June to May (three terms)

Chancellor: HE THE GOVERNOR OF BIHAR
Vice-Chancellor: Dr R. K. AWASTHI
Registrar: K. K. TRIPATHI
Librarian: B. P. MISHRA

The library contains 220,560 vols
Number of students: 17,850

Publications: *University of Patna Journal, Patna University News Bulletin* (monthly).

DEANS

Faculty of Arts: V. P. VERMA
Faculty of Education: R. R. SINGH
Faculty of Engineering: B. B. CHAKRAVARTY
Faculty of Law: B. N. SRIVASTAVA
Faculty of Medicine: S. P. VERMA
Faculty of Commerce: P. N. SHARMA
Faculty of Science: Prof. D. MISHRA

PROFESSORS

AHMAD, M., Urdu
AHMAD, Z., Sociology
AHSAN, S. N., Zoology
CHATERJEE, J. N., Chemistry
HINGORANI, R. C., Law
JHA, J. C., History
JHA, S. K., Mathematics
KARIMI, S. M., Geography
MEHTA, A. S., Botany
MISHRA, S. K., Mathematics
MUKHERJEE, P. C., Economics
NADDA, N. L., Commerce
NARAIN, V. A., History
NATH, B., Geology
OJHA, D. N., Geology
PRASAD, B., Economics
PRASAD, M. M., Economics
PRASAD, R. C., English
PRASAD, R. S., Physics
ROY, R. K., Hindi
ROY, R. P., Botany
SAHAY, B., Ancient Indian History and Archaeology
SAHAY, S. N., Applied Economics and Commerce
SHARAN, R. K., Zoology
SIDDIQUE, M., Persian
SINGH, L. S., Physics
SINHA, L. N. K., Psychology
SINHA, R. C., Geology
SINHA, R. P., Botany
SINHA, U., Botany
VARMA, B. P., Political Science
TIWARI, K. M., English
VERMA, A. K., Philosophy

The university maintains 12 constituent colleges and 40 postgraduate departments.

CONSTITUENT COLLEGES

Arts and Crafts College: Patna 800001; f. 1938; 14 teachers; 100 students; Principal P. S. NATHSINHA.

Bihar College of Engineering: Mahendru, Patna; f. 1924; 4-year course; 51 teachers; 450 students; Principal B. B. CHAKRAVARTY.

Bihar National College: Bankipur, Patna 4; f. 1917; 89 teachers; 3,000 students; Principal S. ALAM.

Commerce College: Patna 4; f. 1953; 26 teachers; 1,300 students; Principal Dr P. N. SHARMA.

Magadh Mahila College: Patna; f. 1946; 52 teachers; 1,000 students; Principal M. BOSE.

Patna College: PO Bankipur, Patna, Bihar; f. 1863; the oldest college in the province, and the parent institution of three other colleges; 105 teachers; 1,583 students; Principal Dr C. JHA.

Patna Law College: PO Mahendru, Patna, Bihar; f. 1906; 29 teachers; 1,400 students; Principal B. N. SRIVASTAVA.

Patna Training College: Patna; f. 1908; 8 teachers; 264 students; Principal R. R. SINGH.

Patna Women's College: Patna; f. 1940; 55 teachers; 950 students; Principal Sister M. LUCILE.

Prince of Wales' Medical College: Bankipur, Patna; f. 1925; 60 teachers; 900 students; Principal Dr M. SINGH.

Science College: Bankipur, Patna; f. 1927; 104 teachers; 1,541 students; Principal Dr L. S. SINGH.

Women's Training College: Patna; f. 1951; 8 teachers; 420 students; Principal Mrs UMA BASU.

PONDICHERRY UNIVERSITY

R. Venkataraman Nagar, Kalapet, Pondicherry 605014
Telephone: (413) 65105
Fax: (413) 65255
Founded 1985
State control
Languages of instruction: English, French, Tamil, Hindi, Malayalam, Telegu and Sanskrit
Academic year: July to June

Chancellor: HE THE VICE-PRESIDENT OF INDIA
Vice-Chancellor: Dr A. GNANAM
Chief Rector: HE THE LT-GOVERNOR OF PONDICHERRY
Registrar: Dr V. NATARAJAN
Librarian: Thiru P. RAMANATHAN

Number of teachers: 140
Number of students: 1,217 (University), 11,673 (affiliated colleges and institutes)

Publications: *Handbook, Annual Report, Quarterly Newsletter.*

DEANS

School of Management: Dr M. T. THIAGARAJAN
School of International Studies: Dr SALOMON GABRIEL (acting)

HEADS OF DEPARTMENTS:

Sri Aurobindo School of Eastern and Western Thought: Dr V. C. THOMAS (acting)
Sri Sankaradass Swamigal School of Performing Arts: Dr K. A. GUNASEKARAN (acting)
Sri Subramania Bharathi School of Tamil Language and Literature: Dr K. P. ARAVAANAN
English: Dr P. MARUDANAYAGAM
Sanskrit: Dr V. KUTUMBA SASTRI
French: Dr R. KITCHENAMOURTHY
History: Dr L. S. VISHWANATH
Economics (Pondicherry): Dr K. RAMACHANDRAN
Economics (Mahe): Dr P. IBRAHIM
Sociology: Dr S. GUNASEKARAN
Ecology and Environmental Sciences: Dr K. V. DEVIPRASAD (acting)
Computer Science: Dr S. KUPPUSWAMI
Commerce: Dr D. RAJAGOPALAN
Mathematics: Dr P. JOTHILINGAM
Physics: Dr S. MOHAN
Chemistry: Dr A. G. RAMACHANDRAN NAIR
Life Science: Dr E. VIJAYAN
Earth Science: Dr M. S. PANDIAN (acting)
Sports and Physical Education: Dr N. GOVINDARAJULU (acting)

ATTACHED INSTITUTES

Centre for Biotechnology: Dr S. JAYACHANDRAN
Centre for Mutagen Studies: Dir Dr C. B. S. R. SHARMA.
Centre for Pollution Control and Biowaste Energy: Dir Dr S. A. ABBASI.
Centre for Tourism Studies: Dir Dr S. V. NARAYANAN.
Centre for Future Studies: Dir Dr A. M. S. RAMASAMY.

UNIVERSITY OF POONA

Ganeshkhind, Pune 411007, Maharashtra
Telephone: 56061/9
Founded 1949
Teaching and Affiliating
Languages of instruction: English and (optional) Marathi
Academic year: June to March (two terms)

Chancellor: HE THE GOVERNOR OF MAHARASHTRA
Vice-Chancellor: Dr VASANT GOWARIKAR
Registrar: V. S. POL
Librarian: Dr S. G. MAHAJAN

Library of 272,000 vols

Number of students 96,000 (including affiliated colleges)

DEANS

Faculty of Arts: Prof. SUDHAKER PANDEY
Faculty of Law: Shri VIJAYRAO MOHITE
Faculty of Medicine: Dr M. J. JOSHI
Faculty of Science: Dr S. C. GUPTE
Faculty of Engineering: Prof. H. M. GANESHRAO
Faculty of Mental, Moral and Social Science: Dr D. B. KERUR
Faculty of Ayurvedic Medicine: Shri P. H. KULKARNI
Faculty of Commerce: Dr J. R. GODHA
Faculty of Education: Prof. S. V. KHER

HEADS OF DEPARTMENTS

Chemistry: Dr N. S. NARASIMHAN
Physics: Dr A. S. NIGVEKAR
Mathematics: Dr S. S. ABHYANKAR
Botany: Dr S. B. DAVID
Zoology: Dr S. MODAK
Geography: Dr K. R. DIKSHIT
Sanskrit and Prakkrit Languages: Dr S. D. JOSHI
Marathi: Dr M. S. KANADE
Experimental Psychology: Dr M. N. PALSANE
Politics: Dr N. R. INAMDAR
Geology: (vacant)
Sociology: (vacant)
Modern European Languages: Prof. S. R. SALKAR
English: Dr SUDHAKAR PANDEY
Hindi: Dr A. P. DIKSHIT
Archaeology: Dr V. N. MISRA
Linguistics: Dr P. BHASKARRIO
Philosophy: Dr M. P. MARATHE
History: Dr A. R. KULKARNI
Journalism: Shri P. N. PARANJPE
Defence Studies: Maj. GANTAM SEN
Law: Dr S. K. AGRAWALA
Anthropology: Prof. B. V. BHANU
Statistics: Dr S. R. ADKE

CONSTITUENT COLLEGES

Adarsha College of Education: Erandawana, Karve Rd, Pune 4; f. 1970.

Adhyapak Mahavidyalaya College of Education: Aranyeshwar, Pune 9; f. 1970.

Armed Forces Medical College: Pune 1; f. 1948.

Arts and Commerce College: Hadapsar, Pune 28; f. 1971.

Ashtang Ayurved Mahavidyalaya: Pune 30.

Bharati Vidyapeeth Pune College of Pharmacy: Pune 4.

Bharati Vidyapeeth New Law College: Pune 4.

Chandrasekhar Agashe College of Physical Education: Pune 9.

B.J. Medical College: Pune 1; f. 1946.

Brihan Maharashtra College of Commerce: Pune 4; f. 1943.

College of Architecture: Pune 30.

College of Engineering: Pune 4; f. 1854.

Fergusson College: Pune 4; f. 1885.

Jain College of Arts and Commerce: Chinchwad, Pune 19; f. 1971.

Law College: Pune 4; f. 1924.

M.E. Society's Abasaheb Garware College of Commerce: Pune 4; f. 1967.

M.E. Society's Abasaheb Garware College of Arts and Sciences: Pune 4; f. 1945.

Modern College of Arts, Science and Commerce: Shivajinagar, Pune 5.

Ness Wadia College of Commerce: Pune 1; f. 1969.

Nowrosjee Wadia College: 19 Bund Rd, Pune 1; f. 1932.

Pune College of Arts, Science and Commerce: Compound of Anglo-Urdu High School, Shankarsheth Rd, Pune 1; f. 1970.

St Mira's College for Girls: Pune 1; f. 1962.

Shahu Mandir Mahavidyalaya: Pune 9; f. 1960.

Sir Parashurambhau College: Pune 30; f. 1916.

St Vincent College: 2004 St Vincent St, Pune 1; f. 1970.

Symbiosis Institute of Management: Senapati Bapat Marg, Pune 411004.

Tilak College of Education: Pune 30; f. 1941.

Tilak Ayurveda Mahavidyalaya: 583/2 Rasta Peth, Pune 11; f. 1933.

Yeshwantrao Mohite Arts, Science and Commerce College: Pune 4.

There are 117 affiliated colleges.

PUNJAB AGRICULTURAL UNIVERSITY

Ludhiana 141004, Punjab

Telephone: (161) 401960

Fax: (161) 401221

Founded 1962

Teaching, Research and Extension

Autonomous control

Languages of instruction: English and Punjabi

Academic year: August to July (two terms)

Chancellor: HE THE GOVERNOR OF PUNJAB
Vice-Chancellor: Dr G. S. KALKAT
Registrar: SH. A. VENU PRASAD
Librarian: S. R. VERMA

Library of 305,700 vols
Number of teachers: 1,428
Number of students: 2,555

Publications: *Progressive Farming* (in English, monthly), *PAU News* (monthly), *Changi Kheti* (in Punjabi, monthly), *Journal of Research* (quarterly), *Package of Practices for Crops* (every 6 months).

DEANS

College of Agriculture: Dr PAUL SINGH SIDHU
College of Agricultural Engineering: Dr H. S. SEKHON
College of Veterinary Science: Dr R. P. SAIGAL
Postgraduate Studies: Dr M. S. BAJWA
College of Basic Science and Humanities: Dr H. S. GARCHA
College of Home Science: Dr S. K. MANN
College of Home Science (Kaoni): Dr R. S. DHALIWAL

HEADS OF DEPARTMENTS

College of Agriculture:

- Agronomy: Dr K. S. SANDHU
- Entomology: Dr D. R. C. BAKHETIA
- Vegetable Crops: Dr SURJAN SINGH
- Floriculture and Landscaping: Dr J. S. ARORA
- Extension Education: (vacant)
- Food Science and Technology: (vacant)
- Plant Pathology: Dr INDERJIT SINGH
- Horticulture: Dr A. S. BINDRA
- Plant Breeding: Dr G. S. NANDA
- Soils: Dr N. S. PASRICHA
- Agricultural Meteorology: Dr S. S. HUNDAL
- Forestry and Natural Resources: Dr D. S. SIDHU
- Seed Science and Technology: (vacant)

College of Basic Sciences and Humanities:

- Botany: Dr D. S. BHATIA
- Business Management: Dr O. P. SAHNEY
- Chemistry: Dr BALBIR SINGH PANNU
- Biochemistry: Dr A. P. S. MANN
- Economics and Sociology: Dr K. C. DHAWAN
- Genetics: Dr R. G. SAIMI
- Agricultural Journalism, Languages and Culture: Dr K. S. GILL
- Mathematics and Statistics: Dr TEJWANT SINGH
- Microbiology: Dr R. P. GUPTA
- Physics: Dr S. S. BEDI
- Zoology: Dr M. L. SOOD
- Fisheries: Dr P. K. SAXENA

College of Veterinary Science:

- Veterinary Anatomy and Histology: Dr R. P. SAIGAL
- Veterinary Microbiology: Dr M. S. OBEROI
- Veterinary Parasitology: Dr A. K. SRIVASTVA
- Veterinary Pathology: Dr B. S. GILL
- Veterinary Pharmacology and Toxicology: Dr A. K. SRIVASTVA
- Veterinary Physiology: Dr S. P. S. SODHI
- Veterinary Surgery and Radiology: Dr V. K. SOBTI
- Animal Reproduction, Gynaecology and Obstetrics: Dr G. R. PANGAONKAR
- Veterinary Medicine and Animal Husbandry Extension: Dr S. N. S. RANDHAWA
- Veterinary Clinical Medicine, Ethics and Jurisprudence: Dr S. N. S. RANDHAWA
- Veterinary Epidemiology and Preventative Medicine: Dr K. B. SINGH
- Veterinary Public Health: Dr D. V. JOSHI
- Veterinary Biochemistry: Dr S. P. S. SODHI
- Animal Breeding and Genetics (including Biostatistics): Dr J. S. DHILLON
- Livestock Production and Management: Dr S. C. GUPTA
- Animal Nutrition: Dr G. S. MAKKAR
- Livestock Products Technology: (vacant)
- Veterinary Clinical Services: (vacant)

College of Agricultural Engineering:

- Civil Engineering: (vacant)
- Computer Science and Electrical Engineering: Dr JOGISHWAR SINGH SOHAL
- Farm Power and Machinery: Dr A. M. CHAUHAN
- Mechanical Engineering: Dr Y. P. GUPTA
- Processing and Agricultural Structures: Dr V. K. SEHGAL
- Soil and Water Engineering: Dr S. K. SONDHI

College of Home Science:

- Home Science Education and Extension: Dr SUMITA ROY
- Foods and Nutrition: Dr B. L. KWATRA
- Human Development: Dr SUSHMA JASWAL
- Family Resources Management: Dr MANJIT KAUR
- Clothing and Textiles: Dr O. P. SINGH

PUNJABI UNIVERSITY

Patiala 147002, Punjab

Telephone: 822461

Founded 1962

Languages of instruction: Punjabi and English

State control

Academic year: July to May (three terms)

Chancellor: HE THE GOVERNOR OF PUNJAB
Vice-Chancellor: Dr J. SINGH PUAR
Registrar: Dr R. SINGH
Librarian: D. KAUR

Library of 312,192 vols
Number of students: 53,399

Publications: *Punjabi University Bulletin*, *Journal of Religious Studies* (quarterly), etc.

DEANS

Faculty of Arts and Social Sciences: Prof. G. S. BHATNAGAR
Faculty of Life Sciences: Prof. T. SINGH
Faculty of Physical Sciences: Prof. M. SINGH
Faculty of Medicine: Dr S. SINGH
Faculty of Business Administration and Commerce: Prof. M. S. BEDI
Faculty of Languages: Prof. G. SINGH
Faculty of Law: Prof. S. NALWA

Faculty of Education: Dr AMRIT KAUR
Faculty of Humanities and Religious Studies: Prof. J. SINGH
Faculty of Vocational Courses: Prof. S. C. GUPTA

There are 65 affiliated colleges.

RABINDRA BHARATI UNIVERSITY

56A Barrackpore Trunk Road, Calcutta 700050

Telephone: 5568019
Fax: 5568079

Founded 1962
Languages of instruction: Bengali and English
State control
Academic year: June to May (three terms)

Chancellor: HE THE GOVERNOR OF WEST BENGAL
Vice-Chancellor: Dr SUBHANKAR CHAKRABORTY
Registrar: O. S. ADHIKARI
Librarian: B. B. DAS

Library of 83,500 vols
Number of teachers: 165
Number of students: 6,759

Publications: *Rabindra Bharati Journal* (English, annually), *Rabindra Bharati University Patrika* (Bengali, annually), *R.B.U. Newsletter,* departmental journals (annually: Bengali, Sanskrit, English, Education, Economics, Library and Information Science, Vedic Studies, Study and Research on Tagore, Rabindra Sangeet).

Departments of Bengali, English, Sanskrit, philosophy, history, economics, political science, dance, drama, vocal music, instrumental music, Rabindra Sangeet, painting, graphics, applied art, sculpture, history of art, education, library and information science.

RAJASTHAN AGRICULTURAL UNIVERSITY, BIKANER

Beechwal, Bikaner 334002, Rajasthan

Telephone: 6276

Founded 1988, in process of formation

Vice-Chancellor: Dr RAM KISHORE PATEL
Registrar: K. SINGH
Librarian: (vacant)

Library of 200,000 vols
Number of teachers: 425
Number of students: 2,250

DEANS

Faculty of Agriculture: Dr R. C. MEHTA
Faculty of Veterinary and Animal Science: Dr P. R. JATKAR
Faculty of Agricultural Engineering: Y. V. HUPRIKAR
Faculty of Home Science: (vacant)
Faculty of Dairy Science: Dr V. V. SHARMA

There are nine affiliated colleges.

UNIVERSITY OF RAJASTHAN

Gandhi Nagar, Jaipur 302004

Telephone: 511070

Founded 1947
Teaching and Affiliating
Languages of instruction: English and Hindi
Academic year: July to May (two terms)
Independent control

Chancellor: HE THE GOVERNOR OF RAJASTHAN
Vice-Chancellor: Prof. T. K. N. UNNITHAN
Registrar: R. S. SHARMA
Librarian: Prof. K. D. TRIVEDI

Library of 305,000 vols, 59,000 periodicals
Number of university teachers: 575
Number of students: 175,000

DEANS

Faculty of Arts: B. PAHI
Faculty of Fine Arts, Music and Drama: (vacant)
Faculty of Science: Prof. N. CHANDRA
Faculty of Commerce: Dr K. C. SHARMA
Faculty of Law: Prof. T. BHATTACHARYA
Faculty of Medicine and Pharmacy: Dr B. BHANDARI
Faculty of Education: (vacant)
Faculty of Engineering and Technology: Prof. S. C. AGARWAL
Faculty of Social Sciences: Dr L. S. TIWARI
Faculty of Ayurveda: (vacant)
Faculty of Sanskrit Studies: Dr G. MISRA
Faculty of Management Studies: Prof. R. N. SINGH

PROFESSORS

ACHARYA, H. R., Sanskrit
AGARWAL, H. L., Statistics
ARCRA, R. K., Public Administration
ASOPA, S. K., Political Science
BANSAL, J. L., Mathematics
BARLA, C. S., Economics
BHANDARI, C. S., Chemistry
BHATTACHARYA, T., Law
BHAWANI SINGH, Political Science
DIXIT, V. P., Zoology
DUBE, S. N., History and Indian Culture
GARG, J. C., Physics
GARG, K. B., Physics
GERWA, R. K., Hindi
GOYAL, A. N., Mathematics
GUPTA, V. P., Statistics
JACOB, D., Zoology
JAIN, J., English
JEDIA, S. L., Sociology
MATHUR, I., Sociology
MEHROTRA, R. C., Chemistry
MEHTA, C. S., Drawing and Painting
MEHTA, V. R., Political Science
MISHRA, S. K., Chemistry
NARESH CHANDRA, Botany
PAHI, B., Philosophy
RAI, A. K., Chemistry
RAMAKANT, South Asia Studies Centre
SAXENA, M. P., Physics
SHARMA, B. K., Physics
SHARMA, S. R., Physics
SHARMA, V. K., Chemistry
SHASTRI, P., Sanskrit
SHUKLA, L., Geography
SINGH, R. N., Business Administration
SINGHI, N. K., Social Science Research Methodology
SISODIA, Y. S., University Science Instrumentation Centre
SURANA, P., Modern European Languages
TRIVEDI, K. D., Public Administration
UMA KANT, Botany
VERMA, B. L., Law
VYAS, P. C., Chemistry

UNIVERSITY COLLEGES

Commerce College: Jaipur; f. 1956.
Maharaja's College: Jaipur; f. 1944.
Maharani's College: Jaipur; f. 1944.
Rajasthan College: Jaipur; f. 1956.

RAJENDRA AGRICULTURAL UNIVERSITY

Pusa, Samastipur 848125, Bihar

Telephone: (6274) 74226
E-mail: rau@bih.nic.in

Founded 1970
Languages of instruction: Hindi and English
Academic year: July to June (two terms)

Chancellor: H.E. THE GOVERNOR OF BIHAR
Vice-Chancellor: Dr K. S. CHAUHAN
Registrar: Dr R. P. ROY SHARMA
Librarian: Dr B. N. VERMA

Library of 42,000 vols and 2,000 MSS
Number of teachers: 400
Number of students: 1,200

Publications: *Adhunik Kisan* (monthly), *Research Journal* (quarterly).

DEANS

Faculty of Agriculture: Dr P. N. JHA
Faculty of Veterinary Science: Dr R. R. P. SINHA
Faculty of Basic Science: Dr A. K. SRIVASTAVA
Faculty of Agricultural Engineering: Dr A. P. MISHRA
Postgraduate Faculty: Dr T. P. SINGH
Faculty of Home Science: Dr A. P. MISHRA

PROFESSORS

Faculty of Agriculture:

CHOUDHARY, L. B., Plant Breeding
MISHRA, S. S., Agronomy
OJHA, K. L., Plant Pathology
PRASAD, B., Soil Science
SAKAL, R., Soil Science
SHARMA, R. P. ROY, Agronomy
SINGH, B. K., Agronomy
SINGH, R. K., Seed Technology
THAKUR, R., Plant Breeding
YAZDANI, S. S., Entomology and Agricultural Zoology

Faculty of Veterinary Science:

MANI MOHAN, Animal Breeding and Genetics
PRASAD, C. B., Veterinary Microbiology
SINGH, M. K., Veterinary Pharmacology
SINHA, R. R. P., Animal Nutrition
SRIVASTAVA, P. S., Veterinary Parasitology

Faculty of Agricultural Engineering:

KUMAR, A., Soil Conservation
RAM, R. B., Farm Machinery

There are eight constituent colleges.

RANCHI UNIVERSITY

Ranchi 834008, Bihar

Telephone: 23600, 22553

Founded 1960
Teaching and Affiliating

Chancellor: HE THE GOVERNOR OF BIHAR
Vice-Chancellor: Dr L. S. SINGH
Registrar: M. ORAON

Library of 70,100 vols
Number of teachers: *c.* 2,000
Number of students: 67,500

Publications: *The University Journal, Journal of Social Research, The Geographical Outlook, Journal of Historical Research, Research Journal of Philosophy, Political Scientist, Journal of Agricultural Science.*

DEANS

Faculty of Social Sciences: Dr S. M. PATHAK
Faculty of Humanities: Dr A. P. SINGH
Faculty of Science: Dr G. JHA
Faculty of Commerce: Dr V. L. SRIVASTAVA
Faculty of Law: Prin. B. K. PRASAD
Faculty of Engineering: Prin. Dr S. N. SINHA
Faculty of Education: Dr N. DATKEOLYAR
Faculty of Medicine: Prin. N. L. DAS

There are 53 constituent colleges and 34 affiliated colleges.

RANI DURGAVATI UNIVERSITY

Saraswati Vihar, Jabalpur, MP 482001

Telephone: (761) 320785
Fax: (761) 323752

Founded 1957 as Jabalpur University, name changed 1983
Teaching and Affiliating
Languages of instruction: Hindi and English
Academic year: July to April (three terms)

Chancellor: HE THE GOVERNOR OF MADHYA PRADESH

Vice-Chancellor: Dr J. P. Shukla
Registrar: Dr M. P. Agnihotri
Librarian: Y. L. Chopra

Library of 164,000 vols
Number of teachers: 1,053
Number of students: 95,000

DEANS

Faculty of Arts: (vacant)
Faculty of Science: Dr B. P. Chandra
Faculty of Commerce: (vacant)
Faculty of Education: Prof. Rajendra Tiwari
Faculty of Law: Dr M. A. Qureshi
Faculty of Engineering: (vacant)
Faculty of Ayurveda: Dr G. S. Kalchuri
Faculty of Home Science: (vacant)
Faculty of Medicine: Dr B. M. Arora
Faculty of Life Science: Dr R. C. Rajak
Faculty of Social Sciences: (vacant)
Faculty of Mathematical Science: Dr B. L. Mishra
Faculty of Management: Y. S. Teja

There are 46 government and 35 affiliated colleges.

ROHILKHAND UNIVERSITY

Bareilly, UP 243001

Telephone: 73541

Founded 1975
State control
Languages of instruction: Hindi and English
Academic year: July to June

Chancellor: HE The Governor of Uttar Pradesh
Vice-Chancellor: Dr Murlidhar Tiwary
Registrar: S. M. Srivastava

Number of teachers: 1,062
Number of students: 65,000

DEANS

Faculty of Agriculture: Dr S. K. Rajput
Faculty of Arts: Dr U. P. Arora
Faculty of Commerce: Dr P. K. Yadav

There are 32 affiliated colleges.

UNIVERSITY OF ROORKEE

Roorkee, UP 247667

Telephone: (1332) 72349
E-mail: regis@rurkiu.ernet.in

Founded in 1847 as Thomason College; inaugurated as a university 1949
Residential and Teaching; specializes in all branches of engineering
Language of instruction: English
Academic year: July to May (two terms)

Chancellor: HE The Governor of Uttar Pradesh
Vice-Chancellor: Dr. N. C. Nigam
Registrar: G. G. Chhabra
Librarian: Yogendra Singh

Library of 260,000 vols
Number of teachers: 400
Number of students: 2,860

SAMBALPUR UNIVERSITY

PO Jyoti Vihar, Burla, Sambalpur 768017, Orissa

Telephone: (663) 430158

Founded 1967
Teaching and Affiliating
Language of instruction: English
Academic year: June to May

Chancellor: The Governor of Orissa
Vice-Chancellor: Dr Hrushikesh Panda
Registrar: B. Behera
Librarian: Dr B. P. Mohapatra

Library of 93,000 books, 15,000 vols of periodicals
Number of teachers: 1,653
Number of students: 36,225

Publications: *Saptarshi* (monthly), *Journal* (Science, annually), *Journal of Humanities* (annually).

DEANS

Faculty of Arts: Prof. S. Nanda
Faculty of Science: Dr M. K. Behera
Faculty of Commerce: Prof. D. P. Nayak
Faculty of Education: (vacant)
Faculty of Law: Prof. G. K. Rath
Faculty of Medicine: Prof. A. K. Sarangi
Faculty of Engineering: Dr R. K. Mishra

There are 128 affiliated colleges and two constituent colleges.

SAMPURNANAND SANSKRIT UNIVERSITY

Varanasi 221002, UP

Telephone: 64011, 64089

Founded 1958
Teaching and Affiliating

Chancellor: The Governor of Uttar Pradesh
Vice-Chancellor: Dr Mandan Mishra
Registrar: Ram Prasad Ambast
Librarian: V. N. Misra

Library of 262,000 vols
Number of students: 35,000

There are two affiliated colleges on-campus, and 1,998 off-campus.

SARDAR PATEL UNIVERSITY

Vallabh Vidyanagar 388120, Kaira, Gujarat

Telephone: (2692) 46545
Fax: (2692) 46475
E-mail: root@patelernate.in

Founded 1955
Teaching and Affiliating
Languages of instruction: Hindi, English or Gujarati
Academic year: June to April (two terms)

Chancellor: HE The Governor of Gujarat
Vice-Chancellor: Prof. V. S. Patel
Registrar: K. M. Patel
Librarian: Dr S. M. Charan

Number of teachers: 1,050, including 241 postgraduate
Number of students: 21,629, including 3,606 postgraduate

Publications: *Journal of Education and Psychology, Arth-Vikas* (Economics Journal), *Pragna* (Journal of Engineering and Technology), *Prasna* (Journal of Social Sciences), *Mimansa* (Journal of English Literature), *Sheel Shrutam*.

DEANS

Faculty of Arts: Prin. R. C. Talati
Faculty of Science: Dr H. K. Patel
Faculty of Engineering and Technology: Prin. B. P. Swadas
Faculty of Home Science: Dr S. S. Sail
Faculty of Business Studies: Prof. D. M. Shah
Faculty of Law: Prin. M. A. Vohra
Faculty of Education: Prof. J. K. Dave
Faculty of Medicine: Dr N. Desai
Faculty of Pharmaceutical Science: Dr B. G. Patel
Faculty of Homoeopathy: Prin. S. S. Patel
Faculty of Management: Prin. B. A. Shuh

PROFESSORS IN POSTGRADUATE DEPARTMENTS

Agrawal, M. K., Physics
Arora, S. K., Physics
Baxi, M. J., Political Science
Bhatt, S. J., Mathematics
Bhide, B. H., Chemistry
Dave, J. K., Education
Dave, Y. S., Biosciences
Gadit, J. G., Gujarati
Gupta, B. C., Mathematics
Jani, A. R., Physics
Jani, H. J., MBA course
Joshipura, K. N., Physics
Kothari, I. L., Biosciences
Manocha, L. M., Materials Science
Marchant, A. M., Sociology
Mishra, D. S., English
Panwar, J. S., MBA course
Parmar, J. S., Chemistry
Patel, A. S., Economics
Patel, H. G., Economics
Patel, M. D., Mathematics
Patel, M. M., Chemistry
Patel, N. G., Electronics
Patel, P. D., Physics
Patel, P. G., USIC
Patel, R. G., Chemistry
Patel, R. M., Chemistry
Patel, S. M., Computer Science
Patel, V. G., Business Studies
Prabhakar, R. K., MBA course
Pramodkumar, Psychology
Raj, M. S., Economics
Sail, S. S., Home Science
Shah, D. M., Business Studies
Shah, J. R., Chemistry
Sharma, R. M., History
Shukla, B. G., Sanskrit
Singh, P. K., Economics
Srivastav Ramji, Physics
Trivedi, H. C., Chemistry
Vyas, S. R., Hindi

There are 26 affiliated colleges and one constituent college.

SAURASHTRA UNIVERSITY

University Campus, University Rd, Rajkot 360005, Gujarat

Telephone: 78501

Founded 1967
Teaching and Affiliating
State control
Languages of instruction: Gujarati, Hindi and English
Academic year: June to March/April (two terms)

Chancellor: HE The Governor of Gujarat State
Vice-Chancellor: Prof. H. M. Joshi
Pro-Vice-Chancellor: K. T. Trivedi
Registrar: V. H. Joshi
Librarian: (vacant)

Library of 136,000 vols
Number of teachers: 2,266 (inc. affiliated colleges)
Number of students: 63,548 (inc. affiliated colleges)

Publications: *Annual Report, Annual Budget, Vol, Syllabus, Samachar Patrika.*

DEANS

Faculty of Arts: Prin. D. M. Acharya
Faculty of Science: Prof. U. V. Manavar
Faculty of Commerce: Prin. C. D. Patel
Faculty of Education: Prin. D. A. Uchat
Faculty of Law: Prof. D. G. Modi
Faculty of Technology and Engineering: Prin. D. B. Desai
Faculty of Medicine: Dr H. M. Mangal
Faculty of Home Science: Prof. Vasuben Trivedi
Faculty of Rural Studies: P. S. Gajera

HEADS OF DEPARTMENTS

Biosciences: Dr S. M. Pandya
Chemistry: Dr A. R. Parikh
Physics: Prof. R. G. Kulkarni
Mathematics: (vacant)
Sociology: H. V. Rao
Education: Dr D. A. Uchat
Economics: Dr K. K. Khakhkhar
Hindi: Dr S. P. Sharma
Statistics: Dr D. K. Ghosh

History: Dr A. M. KIKANI
Gujarati: Dr B. S. JANI
Commerce: Dr N. M. KHANDELWAL
Law: Dr N. K. INDRAYAN
Home Science: (vacant)
English: Dr AVDHESH SINGH
Sanskrit: Dr M. V. JOSHI
Psychology: Dr D. J. BHATT
Post-Graduate Centre in Business Management: Dr D. G. NAIK
Library and Information Science: (vacant)
A. D. Sheth Department of Journalism: Dr Y. A. DALAL
Postgraduate Centre in Computer Science and Application: Dr N. N. JANI
Electronics: Dr H. N. PANDYA
Computer Centre: Dr V. R. RATHOD

There are 108 affiliated colleges.

SHIVAJI UNIVERSITY

Vidyanagar, Kolhapur 416004, Maharashtra
Telephone: 655571

Founded 1962
Teaching and Affiliating
Languages of instruction: English and Marathi
Academic year: June to April (two terms)

Chancellor: HE THE GOVERNOR OF MAHARASHTRA
Vice-Chancellor: Prof. DATTATREYA N. DHANAGARE
Registrar: B. P. SABALE
Librarian: SUMITRA JADHAV (acting)

Library of 231,000 vols
Number of teachers: 7,075
Number of students: 149,427

Publication: *University Journal* (Humanities and Social Sciences sections).

DEANS

Faculty of Arts: Dr A. H. SALUNKHE
Faculty of Social Sciences: A. B. PATIL
Faculty of Science: Dr M. V. BHOSALE
Faculty of Commerce: G. L. DHARMADHIKARI
Faculty of Education: Dr S. K. WAGH
Faculty of Engineering: (vacant)
Faculty of Law: Prin. V. T. CHOUSURE
Faculty of Medicine: Dr C. S. NATH
Faculty of Ayurvedic Medicine: Smt. A. P. DESHPAISDE
Faculty of Fine Arts: Dr BHARATI VAISHAMPAYAN
Faculty of Inter-Disciplinary Studies: (vacant)

There are 196 affiliated colleges and 9 recognized institutes.

SHREEMATI NATHIBAI DAMODAR THACKERSEY WOMEN'S UNIVERSITY

1 Nathibai Thackersey Rd, Mumbai 400020 (BR)
Telephone: 2031879
Telegraphic Address: Uniwomen

Founded 1916
Teaching and Affiliating
State control
Languages of instruction: English, Gujarati, Marathi and Hindi
Academic year: June to March (two terms)

Chancellor: HE THE GOVERNOR OF MAHARASHTRA
Vice-Chancellor: MARIAMMA VARGHESE
Registrar: Dr HEMLATA PARASNIS
Librarian: HARSHA PAREKH

Library of 280,000 vols
Number of teachers: 744 full-time, 238 part-time
Number of students: 44,525 including 7,906 distance education students and 16,549 senior college students

DEANS

Faculty of Arts: MAHENDRA ODHARIA
Faculty of Commerce: Dr G. B. NAGPURWALA
Faculty of Education: Dr S. V. JOGLEKAR
Faculty of Fine Arts: M. R. KELKAR
Faculty of Home Sciences: NILIMA CHITALE
Faculty of Library Science: HARSHA PAREKH
Faculty of Nursing: A. JOYKUTTY
Faculty of Science: Dr A. Y. SATHE
Faculty of Social Science: P. S. TRIVEDI
Faculty of Technology: Dr PARVATI RAJAN

CONSTITUENT COLLEGES

Sir Vithaldas Thackersey College of Home Science: Sir Vithaldas Vidyavihar, Juhu Rd, Mumbai 400049; f. 1962; Principal Dr NINA S. DODD.

Leelabai Thackersey College of Nursing: Nathibai Thackersey Rd, Mumbai 400020; f. 1964; Principal Dr NAINA S. POTDAR.

Premcoonverbai Vithaldas Damodar Thackersey College of Education for Women: Nathibai Thackersey Rd, Mumbai 400020; f. 1959; Principal Dr A. G. BHALWANKAR.

Shree Hansraj Pragji Thackersey School of Library Science: 1 Nathibai Thackersey Rd, Mumbai 400020; f. 1961; Principal HARSHA PAREKH.

Shree Hansraj Pragji Thackersey College of Science: 1 Nathibai Thackersey Rd, Mumbai 400020; f. 1978; Dir Dr A. Y. SATHE.

Shreemati Nathibai Damodar Thackersey College of Arts and Commerce for Women: Karve Rd, Maharshi Karve Vidyavihar, Pune 411038; f. 1916; Principal Dr ASHWINI DHONGDE.

Shreemati Nathibai Damodar Thackersey College of Arts, and Smt. Champaben Bhogilal College of Commerce and Economics for Women: 1 Nathibai Thackersey Rd, Mumbai 400020; f. 1931; Principal ARUN N. KAMBLE.

Shreemati Nathibai Damodar Thackersey College of Education for Women: Karve Rd, Maharshi Karve Vidyarihar, Pune 411038; f. 1964; Principal Dr V. V. DATAR.

Shreemati Nathibai Damodar Thackersey College of Home Science: Karve Rd, Maharshi Karve Vidyarihar, Pune 411038; f. 1968; Principal S. R. KUKADE.

Premlila Vithaldas Polytechnic: Sir V. Vidyavihar Juhu Rd, Mumbai 400049; f. 1976; Principal RADHA SINHA.

C.U. Shah College of Pharmacy: Sir Vithaldas Vidyavihar Juhu Rd, Mumbai 400049; f. 1980; Principal Dr S. G. DESHPANDE.

Department of Postgraduate Studies and Research: 1 Nathibai Thackersey Rd, Mumbai 400020; f. 1983; Dir Dr S. K. Q. SUNDARAM.

Centre of Education: PVDT College of Education, 1 Nathibai Thackersey Rd, Mumbai 400020; Co-ordinator Dr S. S. JOGIEKAV.

Department of Postgraduate Studies and Research in Domestic Science: Sir Vithaldas Vidyavihar Juhu Rd, Mumbai 400049; Dir (vacant).

There are 21 affiliated colleges.

SOUTH GUJARAT UNIVERSITY

PB 49, Surat 395007, Gujarat
Telephone: 227141

Founded 1967
Teaching and Affiliating
State control
Language of instruction: Gujarati
Academic year: June to March (two terms)

Chancellor: HE THE GOVERNOR OF GUJARAT
Vice-Chancellor: Dr A. S. KAPADIA
Registrar: V. B. YADAV
Librarian: A. I. PATEL

Library of 137,000 vols
Number of teachers: 110 (University), 1,666 (colleges)
Number of students: 61,234

Publication: *University Journal.*

DEANS

Faculty of Arts: Prin. G. J. DESAI
Faculty of Science: Dr N. A. PANDYA
Faculty of Commerce: J. B. SHAH
Faculty of Education: K. R. GOHIL
Faculty of Law: Shri P. D. GANDHI
Faculty of Medicine: Dr G. AGRAWAL
Faculty of Rural Studies: Prof. S. B. SHAH
Faculty of Engineering and Technology: Dr J. C. VYAS

There are 64 affiliated colleges.

SRI KRISHNADEVARAYA UNIVERSITY

Sri Venkateswarapuram PO, Anantapur 515003, Andhra Pradesh
Telephone: 21192

Founded 1967, university status 1981
Postgraduate Teaching and Research
Language of instruction: English
Academic year: December to October

Chancellor: HE THE GOVERNOR OF ANDHRA PRADESH
Vice-Chancellor: Prof. P. R. NAIDU
Principal (University College): Prof. D. V. KRISHNA
Registrar: B. LAKSHMIPATHY
Librarian: Dr P. KAMAIAK

Library of 63,000 vols, *c.* 500 periodicals
Number of teachers: 154
Number of students: 1,500

DEANS

Faculty of Arts: Prof. V. T. NAIDU
Faculty of Commerce: Prof. T. SUBBI REDDY
Faculty of Law: Prof. T. P. SUDARSHANA RAO
Faculty of Science: Prof. R. SEETHARMASWAMY

PROFESSORS

ANKI REDDY, K. C., Mathematics
BASHA MOHIDEEN, M., Zoology
BRAHMAJI RAO, S., Chemistry
ENOCK, K., Telugu
GHOUSE, M., Law
GOPAL, B. R., History
KAMESWARA RAO, A.
KANTHA RAO, M. L., Economics
KOTESWARA RAO, T., Telugu
KRISHNA, D. V., Mathematics
MANOHARA MURTHY N., Physics
NAIDU, V. T., Rural Development
NARAYANA, N., Economics
PRAKASHA RAO, C. G., Botany
RAGHUNATHA, SARMA, S., Telugu
RAJGOPAL E.
RAMA MURTHY, V., Physics
RAMAKRISHNA RAO, A., English
RAMAKRISHNA RAO, P., Biochemistry
RAMAKRISHNA RAO, T. V., Physics
RAMAVATHARAM, S. I., Law
SEETHARAMASWAMY R., Mathematics
SHARMA, D. P., Commerce
SUBBA RAO, C., English
SUBBARAMAIAH, S., Economics
SUBBI REDDY, T., Commerce
SUBRAHMANYAM, S. V., Physics
SUDARSHAN RAO, T. P., Law
SWAMINATHAN, E., Geography
SWAMINIATHAN E.
TIRUPATHI NAIDU, V., Rural Development
VENKATA REDDY, C., Economics
VENKATA REDDY, D., Chemistry
VENKATA REDDY, K., English
VENKATA REDDY, K., Rural Development
VENKATASIVA MURTHY, K. N., Mathematics

SRI SATHYA SAI INSTITUTE OF HIGHER LEARNING

Prasantinilayam, Anantapur District, Andhra Pradesh 515134

Telephone: (8555) 87239

Founded 1981
Private control
Language of instruction: English
Academic year: June to March (two terms)

Chancellor: BHAGWAN SATHYA SAI BABA
Vice-Chancellor: Prof. G. VENKATARAMAN
Registrar: Prof. A. V. LAKSHMINARASIMHAM
Librarian: Dr K. TATA RAO

Libraries (3 campuses) of 150,000 vols
Number of teachers: 115
Number of students: 1,100

DEANS

Arts: Prof. J. HEMALATHA
Business Management and Finance: Prof. U. S. RAO
Science: Prof. K. SRINIVASAN

HEADS OF DEPARTMENTS

Bioscience: Prof. P. V. BHIRAWA MURTHY
Chemistry: Prof. P. SATYANARAYANA
Commerce: Prof. M. RADHASWAMI
Home Science: Dr R. KAPOOR
Mathematics: Prof. K. B. NAIDU
Physics: Prof. K. SRINIVASAN
Telugu Language and Literature: Prof. J. HEMALATHA
Philosophy: Dr C. KUPPUSAMY
Political Science: Dr R. GANGADHAR SASTRY
Education: Dr M. KAPANI
Business Management, Finance and Accounting: Prof. U. S. RAO

SRI VENKATESWARA UNIVERSITY

Tirupati 517502, District Chittoor, Andhra Pradesh 2166

Telephone: Tirupati 20166

Founded 1954 as Residential and Teaching; Affiliating since 1956
Languages of instruction: English and Telugu
Academic year: June to April (two terms)

Chancellor: HE THE GOVERNOR OF ANDHRA PRADESH
Vice-Chancellor: Prof. RALLAPALLI RAMAMURTHI
Registrar: K. JAYADEVA REDDY (acting)
Librarian: Dr M. R. CHANDRAN

Libraries of 278,974 vols
Number of teachers: 498
Number of students: 3,259

Publications: *Annual Report, College Magazine, SV University News, SV University Central Journal, Research Bulletin,* etc.

DEANS

Faculty of Arts: Prof. G. NAGESWARA RAO
Faculty of Science: (vacant)
Faculty of Commerce: Prof. M. CHANDRASEKHAR
Faculty of Engineering: Prof. T. RANGASWAMY
Faculty of Education: Prof. A. VENKATARAMI REDDY
Faculty of Teaching: (vacant)
Faculty of Medicine: (vacant)
Faculty of Oriental Learning: (vacant)
Faculty of Law: Prof. P. KOTESWARA RAO
School of Humanities and Extension: Prof. V. ANJANEYA SARMA
School of Biological and Earth Sciences: Prof. M. V. NAYUDU
School of Mathematical and Physical Sciences: Prof. M. S.R. NAIDU
School of Social and Behavioural Sciences: Prof. V. RAMI REDDY

HEADS OF DEPARTMENTS

School of Biological and Earth Sciences:

- Zoology: (vacant)
- Botany: Prof. P. M. SWAMY
- Virology: Prof. M. V. NAYUDU
- Geology: Prof. K. R. REDDY
- Home Science: B. DEVAKI
- Geography: Dr. P. NARAYANAMMA
- Biochemistry: Dr K. THYAGARAJU

School of Humanities and Extension Studies:

- Philosophy: Dr K. MUNIRATHNAM CHETTY
- English: Prof. G. NAGESWARA RAO
- Hindi: Dr T. RAJESWARANDA SARMA
- Sanskrit: Dr K. PRATAP
- Telugu Studies: Prof. K. SARVOTNAMA RAO
- Urdu, Arabic and Persian: Dr K. BASHEER AHMED
- Tamil: Dr R. MANUVEL
- Education: Dr B. RAMACHANDRA REDDY
- Adult Education: Dr M. C. REDDEPPA REDDY
- Population Studies: Prof. K. MAHADEVAN
- Indian Culture: Prof. S. S. RAMACHANDRA MURTHY
- Linguistics: Prof. P. C. NARASIMHA REDDY

School of Mathematical and Physical Sciences:

- Chemistry: Prof. Y. KRISHNA REDDY
- Mathematics: Dr L. NAGAMUNI REDDY
- Physics: Dr B. JAGANNADHA REDDY
- Statistics: Dr P. BALASIDDAMUNI

School of Social and Behavioural Sciences:

- Economics: Dr Y. JAYASIMHULU NAIDU
- History: Sri A. R. RAMACHANDRA REDDY
- Psychology: Dr B. NAGARATHNAMMA
- Commerce: Dr B. BHAGAVAN REDDY
- Political Science and Public Administration: Prof. K. V. NARAYANA RAO
- Social Anthropology: Prof. A. MUNIRATHNAM REDDY
- Sociology: Dr M. HANUMANTHA RAO
- Library Science: Prof. N. GURUSWAMY NAIDU
- Physical Anthropology and Prehistoric Archaeology: Prof. V. RAMI REDDY
- Econometrics: Prof. L. KANNAIAH NAIDU
- Law: Prof. P. KOTESWARA RAO
- Business Management: Prof. B. V. V. N. MURTHY
- Indo-China: Prof. A. LAKSHMANNA CHETTY

College of Engineering:

- Chemical Engineering: Prof. D. CHENGAL RAJU
- Civil Engineering: Prof. K. SRINIVASA RAO
- Electrical and Electronics Engineering: Prof. B. SUBRAMANYAM
- Mechanical Engineering: Dr G. GURUNADHAN
- Chemistry: Prof. S. JAYARAMA REDDY
- Mathematics and Humanities: Dr M. SUNDARA MURTHY
- Physics: Dr M. KRISHNAIAH
- Computer Applications: Dr M. MUNIRATHNAM NAIDU

There are also three university postgraduate centres, three oriental colleges, two engineering colleges, three training colleges, six law colleges, four physical education colleges, one music college, one inst. of research in yoga and allied sciences, and 55 affiliated degree colleges.

TAMIL UNIVERSITY

New Campus, Trichy Rd, Thanjavur, Tamil Nadu 613005

Telephone: 40740

Founded 1981
Languages of instruction: Tamil and English
Academic year: July to June

Chancellor: HE THE GOVERNOR OF TAMIL NADU
Vice-Chancellor: Dr K. KARUNAKARAN
Registrar: Dr K. JEYARAMAN
Library Director: T. PADMANABAN

Number of teachers: 76
Number of students: 68

Publications: *Tamil Civilization, Tamil Kalai* (quarterly), *News Bulletin, Seithi Malar* (monthly).

DEANS

Arts: Prof. RAJU KALIDOS
Developing Tamil: Prof. R. M. SUNDARAM
Languages: Dr S. RAJARAM
Manuscript Studies: Dr P. SUBRAMANIYAN
Science: Prof. G. DEIVANAYAGAM

ATTACHED INSTITUTES

Tribal Research Institute: Muthorai Palada, Uthagamandalam, Tamil Nadu 643004; Dir Dr R. PERIYALWAR (acting).

School of Philosophy: New Campus, Trichy Rd, Thanjavur 613005; research in philosophy; Dir Dr G. BASKARAN (acting).

Centre for Underwater Archaeology: New Campus, Trichy Rd, Thanjavur, Tamil Nadu 613005; Dir Thiru N. ATHIAMAN (acting).

TAMIL NADU AGRICULTURAL UNIVERSITY

Coimbatore 641003, Tamil Nadu

Telephone: 431222
Telex: (422) 855-8360
Fax: (422) 431672

Founded 1971
Federal
State control
Language of instruction: English
Academic year: July to April (two semesters)

Chancellor: HE THE GOVERNOR OF TAMIL NADU
Pro-Chancellor: THE MINISTER OF AGRICULTURE, GOVERNMENT OF TAMIL NADU
Vice-Chancellor: Dr A. ABDUL KAREEM
Registrar: Dr S. PURUSHOTHAMAN
Librarian: Shri R. BORAIYAN

Library of 150,000 vols
Number of teachers: 1,100
Number of students: 2,451

Publications: *TNAU News Letter* (monthly), *Valarum Velanmai, Ulazvar Thunaivan* (Tamil, monthly), *Annual Report.*

DEANS

Agricultural College and Research Institute, Coimbatore: Dr S. KANNAIYAN
Horticultural College and Research Institute, Coimbatore: Dr S. THAMBURAJ
College of Agricultural Engineering, Coimbatore: Prof. Dr V. V. SREE NARAYANAN
Agricultural College and Research Institute, Trichy: Dr A. RAJAKANNU
Horticultural College and Research Institute, Periyakulam: Dr R. S. AZHAKIAMANAVALAN
Postgraduate Studies, Coimbatore: Dr P. P. RAMASAMY
Forest College and Research Institute, Mettupalayam: S. BALAJI
Agricultural College and Research Institute, Madurai: Dr A. REGHUPATHI
Agricultural College and Research Institute, Killikulam: Dr A. MOHAMMED ALI

HEAD OF DEPARTMENTS

Coimbatore Campus:

- Agricultural Extension and Rural Sociology: Dr R. ANNAMALAI
- Bio-Chemistry: Dr THAYUMANAVAN
- Soil Science and Agricultural Chemistry: Dr K. K. MATHAN
- Agricultural Entomology: Dr K. ASAFALI
- Agricultural Nematology: Dr C. V. SIVAKUMAR
- Plant Pathology: Dr V. NARASIMHAN
- Seed Technology: Dr V. KRISHNASWAMY
- Environmental Science: Dr K. RAMASWAMY
- Agricultural Microbiology: Dr P. SANTHANAKRISHNAN
- Crop Physiology: Dr M. THANGARAJ
- Agricultural Economics: Dr N. SRINIVASAN
- Horticulture (Spices and Plantation Crops): Dr T. THANGARAJ

Floriculture: Dr P. Rangasamy
Olericulture: Dr D. Veeraragava
Pomology: Dr N. Kumar
Soil and Water Conservation: O. Padma Kumari
Zonal Research Centre: Er G. Duraiswamy
Bio-Energy: Prof. M. Ramanathan
Farm Machinery: Prof. K. Rangaswamy
Agricultural Processing: Dr R. Kailappan
Agronomy: Dr J. Krishnarajan
Forage: Dr A. K. Fazullakan
Sericulture: Dr Chandramohan
Statistics: Dr M. K. Ayyasamy

Madurai Campus:
Agricultural Extension (KVK): Dr Ranachandra Boopathy
Agricultural Extension: Dr M. Manoharan
Agricultural Microbiology: Dr S. Anthoniraj
Agricultural Entomology: Dr M. S. Venugopal
Plant Pathology: Dr. M. Muthuswamy
Agricultural Engineering: Th. G. Chinnanchetty
Soil Science: Dr K. Kumaraswamy
Agronomy: Dr P. Subramanian
Botany: Dr P. Rangaswamy
Agricultural Economics: Dr S. Kombairaj
Food Science: Dr A. Susheela Thirumaran
Horticulture: Dr N. Ramasamy
Physical Science: Dr K. Jayaprakasam
Home Science: Selvi Dr G. Manimegalai

Killikulam Campus:
Agronomy: Dr V. Veerabadran
Genetics: (vacant)
Soil Science: Dr A. Chandrasekaran
Plant Pathology: Dr R. Jegannathan
Entomology: Dr N. R. Mohavalavan
Horticulture: Dr V. Ponnuswamy
Agricultural Engineering: Dr D. Asoken

DIRECTORS

Agricultural Research: Dr T. V. Karivaratharaju
Centre for Agricultural and Rural Development Studies: Dr C. Ramasamy
School of Genetics: Dr R. Sethupathi Ramalingam (acting)
Centre for Plant Protection Studies: Dr P. C. Sundarababu
Centre for Soil and Crop Management Studies: Dr T. V. Karivaradaraaju (acting)
Water Technology Centre: Dr A. Rajagopal
Extension Education: Dr K. Chandrakanthan
Tamil Nadu Rice Research Institute: Dr M. Subramanian
Centre for Plant Molecular Biology: Dr S. Sadasivam

THAPAR INSTITUTE OF ENGINEERING AND TECHNOLOGY

Patiala 147001
Telephone: (175) 393021
Telex: 394207
Fax: (175) 214498

Founded 1956

President: L. M. Thapar
Director: Dr M. P. Kapoor
Registrar: Prof. A. Juneja
Librarian: Dr Janak Raj

Library of 38,000 vols
Number of teachers: 102
Number of students: 1,340

HEADS OF DEPARTMENTS

Computer Science and Engineering: Dr G. K. Sharma
Civil Engineering: Dr V. S. Batra
Electrical and Electronics Engineering: Dr P. S. Bimbhra
Mechanical and Industrial Engineering: Dr T. P. Singh
Chemical Engineering: Dr P. K. Bajpai

HEADS OF SCHOOL

School of Basic and Applied Sciences: Dr K. K. Raina
School of Biotechnology: Dr V. Ramamurthy
School of Management Studies: Dr D. S. Bawa

TILAK MAHARASHTRA VIDYAPEETH

Vidyapeeth Bhavan, Gultekdi, Pune 411037
Telephone: (212) 461856
Fax (212) 466068

Founded: 1921
Languages of instruction: Marathi, English
Academic year: July to April

Chancellor: Shri S. B. Chavan
Vice-Chancellor: Dr V. M. Bachal
Registrar: R. K. Dhavalikar
Librarian: Smt. R. P. Deshmukh

Library of 51,000 vols
Number of teachers: 35
Number of students: 5,508

DEANS

Faculty of Arts: Dr M. G. Dhadphale
Faculty of Moral and Social Sciences: Dr H. B. Adyanthaya
Faculty of Ayurveda: Dr B. P. Nanal
Distance Education Board: Dr A. V. Gadgil

HEADS OF DEPARTMENTS

Nehru Institute of Social Studies: Dr H. B. Adyanthaya
Shree Balmukund Lomiya Centre of Sanskrit and Asian Studies: Dr S. S. Bamulkar
Mukta Vidya Kendra (Open University Centre): V. P. Deshpande (acting)
Department of Ayurveda: Vd. D. P. Gadgil

TRIPURA UNIVERSITY

PO Agartala College, Agartala 799004, Tripura
Telephone: (381) 225434
Fax: (381) 225434

Founded 1987
State control
Languages of instruction: English and Bengali
Academic year: April to May

Chancellor: HE The Governor of Tripura
Vice-Chancellor: Prof. A. K. Chakrabarti
Registrar: Dr D. K. Chaudhuri
Librarian: (vacant)

Library of 35,000 vols
Number of teachers: 63
Number of students: 800
Publication: *News Letter* (quarterly).

PROFESSORS

Ahmed, S., Bengali
Chakrabarti, A. K., Chemistry
Chakrabarti, M., History
Dinda, B., Chemistry
Mukherjee, L. M., Chemistry
Saha, A., Economics
Srivastava, R. C., Life Science

There are 20 affiliated colleges.

UTKAL UNIVERSITY

PO Vani Vihar, Bhubaneswar 751004, Orissa
Telephone and fax: (674) 581850

Founded 1943
Teaching and Affiliating
State control
Language of instruction: English and Oriya
Academic year: July to June

Chancellor: HE The Governor of Orissa
Vice-Chancellor: Prof. G. K. Das
Registrar: Dr A. K. Paul (acting)
Librarian: Dr Nilakantha Sarangi (acting)

Library of 233,000 vols, 256 periodicals
Number of teachers: 8,521
Number of students: 200,000

DEANS

Faculty of Arts: Prof. K. M. Patra
Faculty of Education: M. Das
Faculty of Law: Indrajit Ray
Faculty of Science: Dr. P. K. Jesthi
Faculty of Commerce: Dr. Gunanidhi Sahoo
Faculty of Medicine: Dr R. N. Dash
Faculty of Engineering: Dr Nilakantha Pattanaik

CONSTITUENT COLLEGES

Madhusudan Law College: Cuttack; f. 1949; Prin. Dr D. P. Kar.

University Law College: Vani Vihar, Bhubaneswar 751004; f. 1975; Prin. Dr P. K. Padhi

There are 362 affiliated colleges.

VIDYASAGAR UNIVERSITY

P.O. Vidyasagar University, Midnapore 721102, West Bengal
Telephone: (3222) 62297
Fax: (3222) 62329
E-mail: root@viduni.ren.nic.in

Founded 1981
State control
Languages of instruction: English and Bengali
Academic year: July to June

Chancellor: HE The Governor of West Bengal
Vice-Chancellor: Prof. A. K. Dev
Registrar: Dr J. Debnath (acting)
Librarian: S. Gupta (Deputy Librarian)

Library of 44,000 vols
Number of teachers: 85
Number of students: 35,650 (incl. affiliated colleges)
Publications: journals of physical science, library science, life science, economics, commerce, political science, geography.

DEANS

Faculty of Arts and Commerce: Prof. T. J. Banerjee
Faculty of Science: Prof. M. Maiti

VIKRAM UNIVERSITY

University Rd, Ujjain 456010, Madhya Pradesh
Telephone: (734) 552072
Fax: (734) 552076

Founded 1957
Teaching and Affiliating
Languages of instruction: Hindi and English
Academic year: July to June

Chancellor: HE The Governor of Madhya Pradesh
Vice-Chancellor: Dr R. K. S. Chauhan
Registrar: Dr S. K. Begde
Librarian: (vacant)

Library of 140,000 vols
Number of students: 31,472

DEANS

Faculty of Arts: Dr K. N. Joshi
Faculty of Science: Dr S. N. Gupta
Faculty of Life Science: Dr O. P. Mall
Faculty of Commerce: Prof. T. L. Jain
Faculty of Law: Dr K. N.Joshi
Faculty of Engineering: Dr M. G. Sharma
Faculty of Education: Dr R. R. Mishra
Faculty of Social Sciences: (vacant)
Faculty of Ayurveda: Dr. S. L. Sharma

There are 55 affiliated colleges

VISVA-BHARATI

PO Santiniketan, Birbhum, West Bengal 731235
Telephone: (3463) 52751
Telex: 203201

Fax: (3463) 52672

Founded 1951 (previously 1921)
Teaching and Residential
Central Government control
Languages of instruction: English and Bengali
Academic year: July to April (three terms)

Rector: HE THE GOVERNOR OF WEST BENGAL
Chancellor: I. K. GUJRAL
Vice-Chancellor: Prof. D. K. SINHA
Registrar: D. MUKHOPADHYAY
Librarian: Prof. S. MISHRA (acting)

Library of 639,866 vols
Number of teachers: 486
Number of students: 6,116

HEADS OF DEPARTMENTS

English and Other Modern European Languages: S. BASU
Sanskrit, Pali and Prakrit: Dr A. BANERJEE
Bengali: Dr J. BOSE
Hindi: H. MISHRA
Oriya: Prof. S. MAHAPATRA
Chinese: Dr A. NAYAK
Japanese: Dr P. MUKHERJEE
Indo-Tibetan Studies: Dr N. K. DAS
Arabic, Persian and Islamic Studies: Dr HAFIZ MOHAMMED T. ALI
Philosophy and Religion: Prof. R. ROY
History: Dr B. BASU
Geography: Dr V. C. JHA
Ancient Indian History and Culture: Prof. P. JASH
Economics and Politics: A. K. MAJUMDAR
Mathematics: Prof. S. K. SAMANTA
Chemistry: Prof. G. P. SENGUPTA
Physics: Prof. R. CHOWDHURY
Zoology: Prof. P. NATH
Botany: Dr S. MANDAL
Education: Prof. D. K. MUKHOPADHYAY
Painting: Prof. J. CHOUDHURY
Sculpture: Prof. S. K. GHOSH
Graphic Art: Dr N. DAS
History of Art: R. SIVAKUMAR
Rabindra Music and Dance: G. SARBADHIKARY
Classical Music: I. BHATTACHARYA
Social Work: Dr S. DEV KANUNGO
Agronomy, Soil Science, Agricultural Engineering, Plant Physiology and Animal Science: Prof. S. K. KHAN
Agricultural Extension, Economics and Statistics: Prof. S. CHAKRABORTY
Crop Improvement, Horticulture and Agricultural Botany: P. S. MUNSHI
Plant Protection: K. BARAL
Palli Charcha Kendra: Dr M. CHOUDHURY

There are eight constituent colleges.

Institutes with University Status

All-India Institute of Medical Sciences: Ansari Nagar, New Delhi 110029; tel. 661123; f. 1956; undergraduate and postgraduate training; research in all brs of medicine; library of 100,000 vols; *c.* 1,000 students; Dir Dr S. K. KACKER; Registrar B. S. DHINGRA; Librarian Dr R. P. KUMAR; publ. *Annual Report*.

Central Institute of English and Foreign Languages: Hyderabad, AP 500007; tel. (40) 7018131; fax (40) 7018402; f. 1958; academic year: June to May; postgraduate and research degrees, diplomas, certificates; correspondence course; library of 117,000 vols; 1,142 students; Vice-Chancellor Prof. PRAMOD TALGERI; Registrar Dr G. VENKATESHWER RAO.

Indian Agricultural Research Institute: New Delhi 110012; tel. (11) 5782081; fax (11) 5766420; f. 1905; postgraduate courses in all major branches of agriculture; library of 600,000 vols; 360 teachers; 600 students; Dir Prof. RAM BADAN SINGH; Registrar NAMARTA SHARMA; Dean Prof. ANUPAM VARMA; Librarian CHHOTEY LAL; publs *Agricultural Press Bulletin* (monthly), *Current Contents in Agriculture* (fortnightly).

HEADS OF DEPARTMENTS

Agricultural Chemicals: Dr B. S. PARMAR
Agricultural Economics: Dr PARMATNA SINGH
Agricultural Engineering: Dr J. S. PAWAR
Agricultural Extension: Dr B. P. SINHA
Agricultural Physics: Dr D. K. DAS
Agronomy: Dr MAHENDRA PAL
Biochemistry: Dr M. L. LODHA
Biotechnology Centre: Dr R. P. SHARMA
Central Seed Testing Laboratory: Dr M. AHLUWALIA
Entomology: Dr O. P. LAL
Floriculture: (vacant)
Fruits and Horticulture: Dr A. M. GOSWAMI
Genetics: Dr V. ARUNACHALAM
Microbiology: Dr K. V. B. R. TILAK
Mycology and Plant Pathology: Dr J. P. VARMA
Blue-Green Algae: Dr P. K. SINGH
Nematology: Dr EKRAMULLAH KHAN
Nuclear Research Laboratory: Dr D. R. DASGUPTA
Plant Physiology: Dr G. C. SRIVASTAVA
Seed Science and Technology: Dr S. P. SHARMA
Soil Science and Agricultural Chemistry: Dr S. K. GHOSH
Vegetables: Dr NARINDER SINGH
Water Technology Centre: Dr P. B. S. SARMA

Indian Institute of Science: Bangalore, Karnataka 560012; tel. 3344411; telex 0845-8349; fax (812) 3341683; f. 1909; library of 400,000 vols; 1,589 postgraduate students; Dir Prof. GOVINDRAJAN PADMANABAN; Registrar B. S. SRINIVASA MURTHY; Librarian N. M. MALWAD; publ. *Journal*.

DEANS

Faculty of Science: Prof. G. S. R. SUBBA RAO
Faculty of Engineering: Prof. A. V. KRISHNAMURTHY

CHAIRMEN OF DIVISIONS

Biological Science: Prof. M. VIJAYAN
Chemical Sciences: Prof. S. S. KRISHNAMURTHY
Electrical Sciences: Prof. M. A. L. THATHACHAR
Mechanical Sciences: Prof. S. RANGANATHAN
Mathematical and Physical Sciences: Prof. S. V. SUBRAMANYAM

HEADS OF DEPARTMENTS

Aerospace Engineering: Prof. H. S. MUKUNDA
Astronomy and Astrophysics: Prof. CHANDA J. JOG
Biochemistry: Prof. R. MAHESHWARI
Central Animal Facility: Prof. R. NAYAK
Centre for Cryogenic Facility: Dr SUBHASH JACOB
Central Workshop: Prof. K. S. SRINIVASA MURTHY
Centre for the Application of Science and Technology to Rural Areas: Prof. U. SRINIVASA
Centre for Atmospheric and Oceanic Sciences: Prof. J. SRINIVASAN
Centre for Continuing Education: Prof. T. S. MRITHYUNJAYA
Centre for Ecological Sciences: Prof. RAGHAVENDRA GADAGKAR
Centre for Electronic Design Technology: Prof. H. S. JAMADAGNI
Centre of Excellence in Chemistry: Prof. C. N. R. RAO
Centre for Reproductive Biology and Molecular Endocrinology: Prof. A. J. RAO
Centre for Scientific and Industrial Consultancy: Prof. B. DATTAGURU
Centre for Sponsored Schemes and Projects: Prof. H. S. MUKUNDA
Centre for Theoretical Studies: Prof. J. PASUPATHY
Chemical Engineering: Prof. K. S. GANDHI
Civil Engineering: Prof. K. S. SUBBA RAO
Computer Science and Automation: Prof. U. R. PRASAD
Education and Research in Computer Networking: Prof. ANURAG KUMAR
Electrical Communication Engineering: Prof. A. SELVARAJAN
Electrical Engineering: Prof. V. RAMANARAYANAN
Foreign Languages: Prof. THOMAS CHACKO
High Voltage Engineering: Prof. M. S. NAIDU
IISc-ISRO Space Technology Cell: Prof. K. P. RAO
Inorganic and Physical Chemistry: Prof. K. KISHORE
Instrumentation: M. V. KRISHNAMURTHY
Management Studies: Prof. K. B. AKHILESH
Materials Research Centre: Prof. T. R. N. KUTTY
Mathematics: Prof. PHOOLAN PRASAD
Mechanical Engineering: Prof. V. H. ARAKERI
Metallurgy: Prof. D. H. SASTRY
Microbiology and Cell Biology: Prof. K. P. GOPINATHAN
Molecular Biophysics Unit: Prof. P. BALARAM
National Centre for Science Information: Prof. N. BALAKRISHNAN
Organic Chemistry: Prof. S. CHANDRASEKARAN
Physics: Prof. ANIL KUMAR
Primate Research Laboratory: Prof. A. JAGANNADDHA RAO
Solid State and Structural Chemistry: Prof. M. S. HEGDE
Sophisticated Instruments Facility: Prof. C. L. KHETRAPAL
Supercomputer Education and Research Centre: Prof. N. BALAKIRSHNAN

Indian Institute of Technology, Mumbai: Powai, Mumbai 400076, Maharashtra; tel. (22) 5782545; fax (22) 5783480; f. 1958; residential; library of 324,000 vols, 1,500 periodicals; 374 teachers; 3,045 students; Dir Prof. SUHAS P. SUKHATME; Registrar D. K. GHOSH; Librarian V. S. SUBBARAO (acting).

HEADS OF DEPARTMENTS

Aerospace Engineering: Prof. S. SURYANARAYAN
Chemical Engineering: Prof. K. C. KHILAR
Chemistry: Prof. S. S. TALWAR
Civil Engineering: Prof. S. L. DHINGRA
Computer Science and Engineering: Prof. D. M. DHAMDHERE
Earth Sciences: Prof. S. D. SHAH
Electrical Engineering: Prof. T. ANJANEYULU
Humanities: Prof. AMITABHA GUPTA
Industrial Design Centre: Prof. K. MUNSHI
Mathematics: Prof. V. D. SHARMA
Mechanical Engineering: Prof. D. P. ROY
Metallurgical Engineering and Metallurgical Science: Prof. N. B. BALLAL
Physics: Prof. SHIVA PRASAD

Indian Institute of Technology, Delhi: Hauz Khas, New Delhi 110016; tel. and fax 6861977; f. 1961; first degree courses in manufacturing science and engineering, civil, mechanical, electrical, chemical engineering, textile technology, computer science and engineering; postgraduate courses in physics, chemistry, mathematics, textile technology, electrical, mechanical, chemical and civil engineering, humanities and social sciences, applied mechanics, biochemical engineering, biotechnology, energy studies, polymer science and technology, etc.; offers research facilities and registration for PhD in various engineering and science departments; library of 285,000 vols; 488 teachers; 2,851 students; Dir Dr V. S. RAJU; Registrar A. S. MALHOTRA.

DEANS

Industrial Research and Development: Prof. M. L. GULURAJANI
Postgraduate Studies and Research: Prof. L. K. MALHOTRA
Undergraduate Studies: Prof. S. N. MAHESHWARI
Students: Prof. G. V. RAO.
Alumni Affairs and International Programmes: Prof. ASHOK MISRA

Indian Institute of Technology, Kanpur: IIT PO, Kanpur 208016, UP; tel. 250151; telex 0325-296; f. 1960; state control; language of instruction: English; library of 390,000 vols and 900 periodicals; 319 teachers; 2,061 students; Dir Prof. R. C. Malhotra; Registrar V. Narasimhan; Librarian Dr Bhooshan Lal; publs *Courses of Study* (annually), *Research, Design and Development Capabilities* (annually), *Research Reports.*

DEANS

Faculty Affairs: Prof. S. S. Prabhu
Research & Development: Prof. Sachchidanand
Academic Affairs: Prof. Vijay Gupta
Student Affairs: Prof. Kripa Shankar
Planning and Resource Generation: Prof. A. K. Mittal

HEADS OF DEPARTMENT

Aerospace Engineering: Prof. Krishna Kumar
Chemical Engineering: Prof. D. P. Rao
Chemistry: Prof. P. K. Ghosh
Civil Engineering: Prof. S. Surya Rao
Computer Science and Engineering: Prof. S. Biswas
Electrical Engineering: Prof. M. U. Siddiqui
Humanities & Social Sciences: Prof. R. R. Barthwal
Industrial and Management Engineering: Prof. A. P. Sinha
Materials and Metallurgical Engineering: Prof. R. K. Dube
Mathematics: Prof. S. K. Gupta
Mechanical Engineering: Prof. S. G. Dhande
Nuclear Engineering Technology: Prof. S. G. Dhande
Physics: Prof. A. K. Majumdar
Laser Technology: Dr Anjan K. Ghosh

Indian Institute of Technology, Kharagpur: PO Kharagpur Technology, Kharagpur 721302, Dist. Midnapore, West Bengal; tel. (3222) 55221; telex 6401-201; fax (3222) 55303; f. 1950; academic year: July to June; library of 320,000 vols; 435 teachers; 2,633 students; Dir Prof. Amitabha Ghosh; Registrar M. N. Gupta; Deputy Librarian M. Das Gupta; publ. *Newsletter* (monthly).

HEADS OF DEPARTMENTS

Aerospace Engineering: Prof. P. K. Sinha
Agricultural and Food Engineering: Prof. S. Bal
Architecture and Regional Planning: Prof. Mridula Banerji
Chemical Engineering: Prof. D. S. De
Chemistry: Prof. C. R. Saha
Civil Engineering: Prof. P. J. Pise
Computer Science and Engineering: Prof. A. K. Majumdar
Electrical Engineering: Prof. P. B. Dattagupta
Electronics and Electrical Communication Engineering: Prof. D. Bhattacharya
Geology and Geophysics: Prof. H. C. Dasgupta
Humanities and Social Sciences: Prof. Bani Chatterjee
Industrial Engineering and Management: Prof. P. K. J. Mahapatra
Mathematics: Prof. J. C. Mishra
Mechanical Engineering: Prof. A. B. Chattopadhyay
Metallurgical and Materials Engineering: Prof. S. K. Pabi
Mining Engineering: Prof. S. C. Roy
Ocean Engineering and Naval Architecture: Prof. S. K. Satsangi
Physics and Meteorology: Prof. M. L. Mukherjee

HEADS OF CENTRES

Biotechnology Centre: Prof. S. C. Kundu
Cryogenics Engineering Centre: Prof. S. S. Bandyopadhyay
Computer Centre: Prof. A. K. Majumdar
Educational Technology Centre: Prof. A. K. Ray
Materials Science Centre: Prof. S. Basu
Rubber Technology Centre: Prof. S. K. De
Rural Development Centre: Prof. R. N. Chattopadhyay

Indian Institute of Technology, Madras: Chennai 600036; tel. (44) 2351365; telex 041-8926; fax (44) 2350509; f. 1959; state control; language of instruction: English; academic year: July to April; library: see Libraries; 400 teachers; 2,968 students; Dir Prof. R. Natarajan; Registrar Prof. R. C. Janakarajan; Librarian Dr H. Chandra; publs *Annual Report, Handbook.*

HEADS OF DEPARTMENTS

Aerospace Engineering: Prof. E. G. Tulapurkara
Applied Mechanics: Prof. B. S. Prabhu
Chemical Engineering: Prof. C. Durgaprasada Rao
Chemistry: Prof. M. Ramakrishna Udupa
Civil Engineering: Prof. K. Elango
Computer Science and Engineering: Prof. S. V. Raghavan
Electrical Engineering: Prof. G. Sridhara Rao
Humanities and Social Sciences: Profr. R. Rajagopalan
Mathematics: Prof. S. N. Majhi
Mechanical Engineering: Prof. K. A. Bhaskaran
Metallurgical Engineering: Prof. D. R. G. Achar
Ocean Engineering Centre: Prof. M. R. Pranesh
Physics: Prof. G. Rangarajan

Indian School of Mines: Dhanbad 826004, Bihar; tel. (326) 202381; fax (326) 202380; f. 1926; residential; language of instruction: English; academic year: July to June; degree courses, postgraduate and research degrees; 140 teachers; 760 students; library of 97,000 vols; Dir Dr D. K. Paul; Registrar Prof. B. L. Jha; Librarian N. Suryanarayana; publs *ISM News Letter* (4 a year), *Annual Report*.

HEADS OF DEPARTMENTS

Applied Geology: Prof. Y. R. Dhar
Applied Geophysics: Prof. B. N. P. Agarwal
Applied Chemistry: Dr A. Sarkar
Applied Mathematics: Prof. A. Chattopadhyay
Applied Physics: Prof. A. R. Chetal
Computer Science and Engineering: K. K. Rao
Electronics and Instrumentation: Prof. D. Chandra
Engineering and Mining Machinery: Prof. S. Dey
Fuel and Mineral Engineering: Prof. R. Venugopal
Humanities and Social Sciences: Prof. R. K. Singh
Management Studies: Prof. K. Mukherjee
Mining Engineering: Prof. B. K. Kejriwal
Petroleum Engineering: Prof. N. Choudhary
Continuing Education: Prof. P. K. Banik

HEADS OF CENTRES

Mine Mechanization: Prof. S. N. Mukherjee
Mine Environment: Prof. N. C. Saxena

International Institute for Population Sciences: Govandi Station Rd, Deonar, Mumbai 400088; tel. 5563254; fax 5563257; f. 1956; a 'deemed university'; 30 teachers; 120 students; library of 60,000 vols; Dir Prof. K. B. Pathak; publ. *Newsletter.*

HEADS OF DEPARTMENTS

Mathematical Demography and Statistics: Dr G. Rama Rao
Fertility Studies: Dr F. Rem
Public Health and Mortality Studies: Dr S. Lahiri
Migration and Urban Studies: Dr Shekhar Mukherji
Population Policies and Development Programme: Dr T. K. Roy
Development Studies: Dr S. Kulkarni

National Law School of India University: Nagarbhavi, PB 7201, Bangalore 560072; tel. 3303160; fax (80) 3387858; f. 1987; library of 21,000 vols; 30 teachers; 400 students; Dir Dr N. L. Nitra; Registrar Prof. V. S. Mallar; publs *National Law School Journal* (1 a year), *March of the Law* (1 a year), *Law and Medicine* (1 a year), *Gender Justice Reporter* (1 a year).

School of Planning and Architecture: 4 Block B, Indraprastha Estate, New Delhi 110002; tel. (11) 3317892; fax (11) 3319435; f. 1955; library of 64,000 vols; 70 teachers; 750 students; Dir A. K. Maitra; Registrar D. R. Bains.

HEADS OF DEPARTMENTS

Architecture: Prof. S. Grover
Architectural Conservation: Prof. Nalini M. Thakur
Environmental Planning: Prof. A. K. Maitra
Urban Planning: Prof. T. M. Vinod Kumar
Transport Planning: A. K. Sharma
Housing: Prof. Subir Shah
Industrial Design: Prof. Vinai Kumar
Landscape Architecture: Prof. M. Shaheer
Urban Design: Prof. K. T. Ravindran
Building Engineering and Management: Dr V. Thiruvengadam
Physical Planning: Prof. J. H. Ansari
Regional Planning: Prof. H. B. Singh

ATTACHED CENTRES

Centre for Advanced Studies in Architecture: Prof. V. P. Raori
Centres for Analysis and Systems Studies: Dir Prof. T. M. Vinod Kumar
Centre for Housing Studies: Prof. H. P. Bahri
Centre for Rural Development: Dir Prof. R. C. Gupta
Centre for Transport Studies: Prof. N. Ranganathan
Centre for Environmental Studies: Dir Prof. A. K. Maitra
Centre for Conservation Studies: Dir Prof. H. D. Chhaya
Centre for Urban Studies: Prof. B. Misra

Sree Chitra Tirunal Institute for Medical Sciences and Technology: Thiruvananthapuram, Kerala 695011; tel. (471) 443152; fax (471) 446433; f. 1981; postgraduate courses; includes a hospital complex, a centre for health science studies and a biomedical technology wing; Pres. Dr N. H. Wadia; Dir Dr K. Mohandas; Registrar A. V. George.

HEADS OF DIVISIONS

Anaesthesiology: Dr R. C. Rathod
Artificial Internal Organs: Dr G. S. Bhuvaneshwar
Biochemistry: Dr K. Subramonia Iyer
Biomaterials Technology: Dr R. Sivakumar
Biosurface Technology: Dr C. P. Sharma
Blood Transfusion: Dr Jaisy Mathai
Cardiology: Dr K. G. Balakrishnan
Cardiovascular Thoracic Surgery: Dr M. P. Mohansingh
Cellular and Molecular Cardiology: Dr C. C. Kartha
Clinical Engineering: K. Vijhyakumar
Engineering Services: Neelakantan Nair
Microbiology: Dr J. Shanmugham
Neurology: Dr K. Radhakrishnan
Neurosurgery: Dr D. Rout
Pathology: Dr V. V. Radhakrishnan
Pathophysiology: Dr Mohanty Mira
Polymer Chemistry: Dr A. Jayakrishnan
Radiology: Dr A. K. Gupta
Toxicology: Dr K. Rathinam
Vivarium: A. Vijayanlal

Tata Institute of Social Sciences: POB 8313, Deonar, Mumbai 400088, Maharashtra; tel. 5563289; fax 5562912; e-mail tissbom@ren.nic.in; f. 1936; postgraduate courses and professional training in social work and personnel management and industrial relations;

health and hospital administration; research; library of 88,000 vols; 375 students; Dir Dr P. N. MUKHERJI; Registrar Dr S. K. BANDYOPADHYAY; publs *Indian Journal of Social Work, Research Abstracts, Sociology and Education Papers.*

Colleges

BUSINESS

Administrative Staff College of India: Bella Vista, Hyderabad 500082; tel. (40) 3310952; fax (40) 3312954; e-mail ascilib@hd1.vsnl.net.in; 212954; f. 1956; conducts post-experience management development programmes in general management and in specific fields; specialized programmes for education, hospital and government administrators and R & D managers; library of 68,000 vols, 500 periodicals; Principal T. L. SANKAR; Librarian N. K. GOPALAKRISHNAN; publ. *ASCI Journal of Management* (2 a year).

Indian Institute of Management, Ahmedabad: Vastrapur, Ahmedabad 380015; tel. (79) 407241; telex 121-6351; fax (79) 6568345; e-mail director@iimahd.ernet.in; f. 1962; 2-year postgraduate, 4-year doctoral programme in management; general and functional management programmes for practising managers, and special programmes for government officials, university teachers and sectors such as agriculture, public systems; undertakes project research and consulting in the field of management; 80 faculty members, 400 postgraduate programme students, 50 Ph.D. level students; library of 148,300 vols; Dir JAHAR SAHA; publs *Vikalpa* (4 a year), *Alumnus* (3 a year).

Indian Institute of Management, Bangalore: Bannerghatta Rd, Bangalore 560076; tel. 6632450; fax 6644050; f. 1973; postgraduate programmes; 80 teachers; 425 students; Dir Prof. M. RAMMOHAN; publs *IIMB Management Review* (2 a year), *IIMB Campus News* (6 a year), *IIBM Alumni* (6 a year).

Indian Institute of Management, Calcutta: Joka, Diamond Harbour Rd, POB 16757, PO Alipore, Calcutta 700027; tel. 4678310; telex 021-2501; fax 4678307; e-mail director@iimcal.ernet.in; f. 1961 to promote improvement in management through education, research and consultancy; two-year MBA course in CAM, three-year part-time MBA in business management; fellowship and extension courses; centres for studies in human values, public enterprises, project management, rural development and environment management; executive development; faculty development through research and consulting services; Dr B. C. Roy Memorial library of 125,000 vols; Dir Dr AMITAVA BOSE; publs *Decision, Journal on Human Values* (2 a year), etc.

Indian Institute of Management, Lucknow: Prabandh Nagar, Off Sitapur Rd, Lucknow 226013; tel. 361891; telex 0522-2226; fax 361843; f. 1984; 2-year postgraduate programme, exec. development programmes; undertakes project research and consulting in the field of management; main areas: health, education, rural development, state public enterprises, int. management, corporate management, entrepreneurship; 37 faculty mems, 360 postgraduate students; library of 52,000 documents; Dir Dr J. L. BATRA; Librarian Dr R. RAINA; publ. *IIML Newsletter* (every 2 weeks).

EDUCATION

National Institute of Educational Planning and Administration: 17-B Sri Aurobindo Marg, New Delhi 110016; tel. 665472; f. 1962; diploma courses for education personnel of developing countries and district education officers; other in-service training courses; research in various aspects of educational planning and management; consultancy service for developing countries, State govts and other organizations; collaboration with UNESCO and other foreign agencies; library of 45,963 vols, 350 current journals; Dir Prof. KULDEEP MATHUR; publs *Journal of Educational Planning and Administration* (quarterly), *Pariprakshya* (in Hindi).

LANGUAGES

Central Institute of Indian Languages: Ministry of Human Resource Development, Department of Education, Government of India, Manasagangotri, Mysore 570006; tel. (821) 515820; telex 0846-268; fax (821) 515032; f. 1969; assisting and co-ordinating the development of Indian languages; preparation of grammars and dictionaries of tribal and border languages; inter-disciplinary research; preparation of materials for teaching and learning; 290 academic and technical staff; 7 Regional Language Centres in Mysore (languages: Kannada, Telugu, Malayalam, Tamil), Bhubaneswar (languages: Assamese, Bengali, Oriya), Pune (languages: Marathi, Gujarati, Sindhi), Patiala (languages: Urdu, Punjabi, Kashmiri), Solan (Urdu), Lucknow (Urdu) and Guwahati (north-eastern languages); library of 65,000 vols and 400 periodicals in 75 Indian and 30 foreign languages; Dir Dr N. RAMASWAMI; publ. *New Language Planning Newsletter* (quarterly).

LAW

Indian Academy of International Law and Diplomacy: 9 Bhagwan Dass Rd, New Delhi 110001; tel. (11) 3384458; e-mail rpanand@giasdl01.vsnl.net.in; f. 1964; part of the Indian Society of International Law; includes a research institute and library; Sec.-Gen. Prof. V. S. MANI; publ. *Indian Journal of International Law* (4 a year).

MEDICINE

All India Institute of Hygiene and Public Health: 110 Chittaranjan Ave, Calcutta 700073; tel. (33) 2413831; f. 1932; constituent college of University of Calcutta; administered by Directorate-General of Health Services and Ministry of Health and Family Welfare; facilities for postgraduate work and medical research; depts of Behavioural Sciences, Biochemistry and Nutrition, Epidemiology and Health Education, Maternal and Child Health, Microbiology, Occupational Health, Public Health Administration, Public Health Nursing, Sanitary Engineering, Social and Preventive Medicine; Statistics and Demography, Veterinary Public Health, Rural Health and Training Centre, Urban Health and Training Centre; offers diploma, certificate, and orientation courses; academic year: July to June; 112 teachers (incl. 14 professors); 300 students; library of 85,000 vols, 250 current periodicals; Dir Prof. K. J. NATH; publs *Annual Report, Prospectus.*

National Institute of Health and Family Welfare (NIHFW): New Mehrauli Rd, Munirka, New Delhi 110067; tel. 6850057; fax 6851623; f. 1977; in-service training, MD course in community health administration, biomedical research, research and consultancy; regional centre for health management; documentation and reprographic services; specialized library of 35,000 vols; Dir Dr H. HELEN; publs *Dharna—Health and Population Perspectives and Issues, Alumni Newsletter* (quarterly, in English), *NIHFW News Bulletin* (quarterly), and Technical Report series.

TECHNOLOGY

Institute of Radiophysics and Electronics: 92 Acharya Prafulla Chandra Rd, Calcutta 700009; tel. 3509115; f. 1949; houses postgraduate teaching and research dept of Univ. of Calcutta, Faculty of Technology; 3-year post-B.Sc. integrated course leading to BTech. degree, and 1½-year post-BTech./BE course leading to MTech. degree in radiophysics and electronics; conducts training programmes; research facilities in ionosphere, radio wave propagation, radio astronomy, solid state and microwave electronics, millimetre wave technology, solid state devices, plasma and quantum electronics, optoelectronics, control systems and micro-computers, communication theory and systems, microelectronics and VLSI technology; maintains ionosphere field station at Haringhata and radio astronomy field station at Kalyani; 36 teachers; library of 15,000 vols; Head Prof. N. PURKAIT; publ. *Yearbook.*

National Institute of Fashion Technology: Hauz Khas, Near Gulmohar Park, New Delhi 110016; tel. (11) 6965080; fax (11) 6851198; f. 1986; undergraduate and postgraduate diploma courses relevant to the textiles and clothing industries; library of 17,000 books and documents; campuses in New Delhi, Mumbai, Calcutta, Gandhinagar, Hyderabad and Madras; Exec. Dir L. V. SAPTHARISHI.

Seshasayee Institute of Technology: Industrial Colony P.O., Tiruchirapalli 620010, Tamil Nadu; tel. 491211; f. 1952; training to diploma level in civil, mechanical and electrical engineering, computer technology, instrumentation technology, pulp and paper technology; post-diploma course in plant maintenance; 36 teachers, 695 students; library of 14,000 vols; Pres. V. K. SESHASAYEE; Principal V. NAGARAJAN; publ. *SITMAG.*

Schools of Art and Music

Academy of Architecture: Plot No. 278, Shankar Ghanekar Marg, next to Tyresoles Co., Prabhadevi, Mumbai 400025; f. 1955; five-year Govt Diploma courses in architecture; library of 5,600 vols and 2,000 slides; Principal P. P. AMBERKAR.

Bharatiya Vidya Bhavan: Kulapati Munshi Rd, Mumbai 400007; tel. (22) 3634462; f. 1938; aims to revitalize ancient Indian values to suit modern needs; postgraduate courses in Indology; colleges of arts, science, commerce and engineering; runs schools, Academy of Foreign Languages, College of Sanskrit; dept of Ancient Insights and Modern Discoveries; Ayurveda Research Centre; Institute of Communication and Management; Institute of Management and Research; schools of music, dancing, dramatic art; library of 76,688 vols and 1,404 MSS; 31,450 mems; Pres. C. SUBRAMANIAM; Hon. Dir Prof. J. H. DAVE; Dir-Gen. and Exec. Sec. S. RAMAKRISHNAN; publs *Bharatiya Vidya* (quarterly), *Samvid* (Sanskrit, quarterly), *Bhavan's Journal* (fortnightly), *Navaneet* (Hindi, monthly), *Navaneet-Samarpan* (Gujarati, monthly), 11 vols of the *History and Culture of the Indian People,* and various series.

Kalakshetra Foundation: Tiruvanmiyur, Chennai 600041; tel. (44) 4911836; fax (44) 4914359; f. 1936; centre for education in classical music, dancing, theatrical art, painting and handicrafts; maintains a weaving-centre for the production of silk and cotton costumes in traditional design and a Kalamkari Unit for dyeing and hand-block printing with vegetable dyes; Dr U. V. Swaminatha Aiyar library noted for classical MSS and literature in Tamil; Dir S. RAJARAM; Sec R. V. RAMANI.

Music Academy: 306 T.T.K. Rd, Royapettah, Chennai 600014; tel. 8275619; f. 1927; research and study of Indian music; directs the Teachers' College of Music; library of 5,300 vols; Pres. T. T. VASU; Secs T. S. PARTHASARATHY, M. RAMADURAI, M. S. VENKATARAMAN, N. RAMJI; publs *Journal* and books.

National School of Drama: Bahawalpur House, Bhagwandas Rd, New Delhi 110001; tel. 3389402; f. 1959; three-year diploma course for a maximum of 20 students in each class, short-term theatre training workshops; library of 26,000 vols, 2,500 slides, records, etc.; Dir Prof. RAM GOPAL BAJAJ; Librarian ANIL SRIVASTAVA; publ. *N.S.D. Newsletter* (every 6 months).

Sri Varalakshmi Academies of Fine Arts: Ramavilas, Kashipathy Agarahar, Chamaraja Double Rd, Mysore 4; f. 1945; educational and cultural research institution; gives advanced courses of study in Karnataka music; library of 5,000 vols; Prin. VIDWAN C. V. SRIVATSA; Head Research Dept Prof. R. SATHYANARAYANA.

INDONESIA

Learned Societies

GENERAL

Jajasan Kerja-Sama Kebudajaan (Foundation for Cultural Co-operation): Jl. Gajah Mada 13, Bandung; to promote co-operation and mutual understanding between the countries of Western Europe and Indonesia; Rep. for Indonesia A. KOOLHAAS

BIBLIOGRAPHY, LIBRARY SCIENCE AND MUSEOLOGY

Indonesian Library Association: Jl. Imam Bonjol 1, POB 3624, Jakarta 10002; tel. 34-25-29; f. 1954; Pres. M. H. PRAKOSO; Sec.-Gen. SOEMARNO.

MEDICINE

Ikatan Dokter Indonesia (Indonesian Medical Association): Jl. Dr Sam Ratulangi 29, Jakarta; f. 1950; 12,650 mems; Chair. Dr KARTONO MOHAMAD; Sec.-Gen. Dr IHSAN OETAMA; publ. *Majalah Kedokteran Indonesia* (monthly).

NATURAL SCIENCES

General

Balai Pengetahuan Umum Bandung (Popular Science Society): Universitas Bandung, Jl. Merdeka 27, Bandung; f. 1946; to promote the cultural development of Indonesia; Pres. Prof. Dr L. VAN DER PIJL; Vice-Pres. Prof. Dr C. O. SCHAEFFER; Sec. F. J. SUYDERHOUD.

Unesco Regional Office for Science and Technology for South-East Asia: UN Bldg, Jl. Thamrin 14, Tromol Pos 1273/JKT, Jakarta 10012; tel. (21) 3141308; telex 61464; fax (21) 3150382.

Physical Sciences

Astronomical Association of Indonesia: Jakarta Planetarium, Cikini Raya 73, Jakarta; f. 1920; to promote the advancement of astronomical science; Chair. Prof. Dr BAMBANG HIDAYAT; Sec. Drs S. DARSA; Treas. Dr WINARDI SUTANTYO.

TECHNOLOGY

Persatuan Insinyur Indonesia (Indonesian Institute of Engineers): Kompleks Pertamina, Simprug Staff Houses R-08, Jl. Sinabung II, Terusan, Kebayoran Baru, Jakarta 12120; tel. (21) 739-8858; fax (21) 739-2255; 27,000 mems; Pres. ABURIZAL BAKRIE; Sec.-Gen. I. SUCIPTO UMAR.

Research Institutes

GENERAL

Lembaga Ilmu Pengetahuan Indonesia (Indonesian Institute of Sciences): Jl. Jendral Gatot Subroto no. 10, POB 250, Jakarta; tel. (21) 5251542; telex 62554; fax (21) 5207226; f. 1967; government agency to promote the development of science and technology, to serve as the national centre for regional and international scientific co-operation, to organize national research centres; library of 150,000 titles; Chair. Dr SOEFJAN TSAURI; publs *Berita Ilmu Pegetahuan dan Teknologi* (2 a year), *Sari Karangan Indonesia (SKI)* (2 a year), *Teknologi Indonesia* (2 a year), *Bulletin LIPI* (annually), *Masyarakat Indonesia* (2 a year).

AGRICULTURE, FISHERIES AND VETERINARY SCIENCE

Badan Penelitian dan Pengembangan Kehutanan (Agency for Forestry Research and Development): Gedung Manggala Wanabakti Lt. 11, Jl. Gatot Subroto, POB 51/JKWB, Jakarta 10270; tel. 583034; telex 45996; f. 1983; 114 research scientists; library of 25,000 vols; Dir Gen. Ir WARTONO KADRI; publs *Jurnal Penelitian dan Pengembangan Kehutanan* (Forestry Research and Development Journal), *Warta Penelitian dan Pengembangan Kehutanan* (Forestry Research and Development News), *Buletin Penelitian Hutan* (Forest Research Bulletin), *Jurnal Penelitian Hasil Hutan* (Forest Products Research Journal), *Pengumuman, Penelitian Hasil Hutan* (Communication, Forest Products Research).

Balai Penelitian Veteriner (Research Institute for Veterinary Science, Agency of Agricultural Research and Development, Ministry of Agriculture): Jl. R.E. Martadinata 30, POB 151, Bogor 16114; tel. (251) 331048; fax (251) 336425; e-mail balivet@indo.net.id; f. 1908; depts of bacteriology, pathology and epidemiology, toxicology, parasitology, mycology, virology, balitvet culture collection; library of 12,545 vols and periodicals; Dir Dr SJAMSUL BAHRI; publs *Annual Report, Newsletter* (2 a year).

Pusat Penelitian dan Pengembangan Hortikultura (Central Research Institute for Horticulture): Jl. Ragunan 19, Pasarminggu, Jakarta; tel. (21) 7890990; fax (21) 7805135; research and development of horticultural crops; Dir Dr PRABOWO TJITRO PRANOTO.

Attached institutes:

Balai Penelitian Tanaman Hias (Research Institute for Ornamental Flowers): Jl. Ragunan 29, Pasarminggu, Jakarta 12540; tel. (21) 7805087; Dir Dr TOTO SUTATER.

Balai Penelitian Tanaman Sayur (Research Institute for Vegetables): Jl. Tangkuban Perahu 517, Lembang; tel. (22) 2786245; Dir Dr ATI SRIE DURIAT.

Balai Penelitian Tanaman Buah (Research Institute for Fruit): Jl. Raya Aripan Km 8, Kotak Pos No 5, Solok 27301, Sumatera Barat; tel. (755) 20137; Dir Dr L. SETYOBUDI.

Pusat Penelitian dan Pengembangan Peternakan (Central Research Institute for Animal Sciences): Jln. Raya Pajajaran, Bogor, West Java; tel. 322185; fax 328382; e-mail criansci@indo.net.id; f. 1950; research into farm animals and animal parasites and diseases; library of 14,000 vols, 1,199 periodicals; Dir Drh. M. RANGKUTI; publs *Ilmu Peternakan dan Veteriner, Wartazoa* (both irregular).

Pusat Penelitian dan Pengembangan Tanaman Pangan (Central Research Institute for Food Crops): Jl. Merdeka 147, Bogor 16111; tel. (251) 334089; telex 46432; fax (251) 312755; f. 1961; food crops research and development; library of 3,000 vols; Dir Dr ACHMAD M. FAGI; publ. *Contributions of CRIFC* (4–6 a year).

Attached institutes:

Balai Penelitian Tanaman Pangan Lahan Rawa (Research Institute for Food Crops on Swampy Areas): Jl. Kebun Karet, Lok Tabat, Kotak Pos 31, Banjarbaru 70712, Kalimantan Selatan; tel. (511) 92534; fax (511) 93034; Dir YUSUF MAMUN; publ. *Pemberitaan Penelitian* (2–4 a year, in Indonesian and English).

Balai Penelitian Bioteknologi Tanaman Pangan (Research Institute for Biotechnology of Food Crops): Jl. Tentara Pelajar 3A, Bogor 1611; tel. (251) 337975; fax (251) 338820; Dir Dr DJOKO S. DAMARDJATI; publs *Penelitian Pertanian* (Agricultural Research, 3–4 a year, in Indonesian and English), *Buletin Penelitian* (Research Bulletin, 2–4 a year).

Balai Penelitian Tanaman Kacang-kacangan dan Umbi-umbian Malang (Research Institute for Legumes and Root Crops): Jl. Raya Kendal Payak, Kotak Pos 66, Malang 65101, Jawa Timur; tel. (341) 81468; fax (341) 318148; Dir Dr SUYAMTO; publ. *Penelitian Palawija* (Palawija Research, 2 a year, in Indonesian, and abstract in English).

Balai Penelitian Tanaman Jagung dan Serealia Lain (Research Institute for Maize and Other Cereals): Jl. Ratulangi, Kotak Pos 173, Maros 90511, Ujung Pandang, Sulawesi Selatan Telp; tel. (411) 371016; fax (411) 318148; Dir Dr MARSUM DAHLAN; publ. *Agrikam: Buletin Penelitian Pertanian* (Agricultural Research Bulletin, 2–4 a year, with English summary).

Balai Penelitian Tanaman Padi (Research Institute for Rice): Jl. Raya 9, Sukamandi – Tromol Pos 11, Cikampek Subang 41255, Jawa Barat; tel. (264) 520157; fax (264) 520158; Dir Dr ANDI HASANUDDIN; publ. *Media Sukamandi* (Research at Sukamandi, 2–4 a year, with English summary).

Pusat Penelitian Kelapa Sawit (Indonesian Oil Palm Research Institute): POB 104, Medan; f. 1916; to promote agricultural improvement on the member estates; 500 mems; 11,000 vols, 20,000 periodicals; Dir Dr H. ADLIN U. LUBIS; publs *Bulletin* (quarterly, in Indonesian with English summaries), *Berita* (in Indonesian), *Annual Report* (in Indonesian), *Oil Palm Statistics* (in Indonesian), *Rainfall Records* (in Indonesian).

Pusat Penelitian Perkebunan Gula Indonesia (Indonesian Sugar Research Institute): Jl. Pahlawan 25, Pasuruan 67126; tel. (343) 421086; fax (343) 421178; e-mail isri@mlg.mega.net.id; f. 1887; library of 15,000 vols; 150 staff; Dir Dr Ir GUNAWAN SUKARSO; publs *Majalah Penelitian Gula* (Sugar Journal, quarterly), *Berita* (Communications), *Laporan Tahunan* (Annual Report), etc.

Pusat Penelitian Tanah Dan Agroklimat (Soil and Agricultural Climate Research Centre): Jl. Ir. H. Juanda 98, Bogor 16123; f. 1905; library of 4,000 vols; Dir Dr SYARIFUDDIN KARAMA.

Unit Penelitian Bioteknologi Perkebunan (Indonesian Biotechnology Research

Unit for Estate Crops): Jl. Taman Kencana 1, POB 179/Bgr 16001, Bogor 16151; tel. (251) 324048; fax (251) 328516; e-mail briec@indo.net.id; f. 1933; supportive research in molecular biology and immunology, and microbes and bioprocessing; library of 12,000 vols, 1,533 periodicals; Head of Unit Ir BASUKI; publs *Menara Perkebunan* (4 a year, with English summary), *Warta Bioteknologi Perkebunan*.

ARCHITECTURE AND TOWN PLANNING

Research Institute for Human Settlements and United Nations Regional Centre for Research on Human Settlements: Jl. Panyawungan, Cileunyi, Wetan, Kab. Bandung 40393; tel. (22) 798393; fax (22) 798392; f. 1953; research on housing, building etc.; library of 29,000 vols; Dir SUTIKUI UTORO; publs *Masalah Bangunan* (quarterly, in English), *Jurnal Penelitian Pemutiman* (4 a year, in Bahasa Indonesian), *Buku Petunjuk Pedesaan* (in Bahasa Indonesian).

ECONOMICS, LAW AND POLITICS

Biro Pusat Statistik (Central Bureau of Statistics): Jl. Dr Sutomo 8, Jakarta 10010; f. 1925; library of 25,000 vols and 1,100 periodicals; Dir SUGITO SOEWITO.

Centre for Strategic and International Studies: Jl. Tanah Abang III/27, Jakarta; tel. 3865532; fax (21) 3847517; f. 1971; library of 25,000 vols; policy-oriented studies in international and national affairs in collaboration with industry, commerce, and the political, legal and journalistic communities; Chair. DAOED JOESOEF; publs *The Indonesian Quarterly*, *Analisis CSIS* (4 a year).

Indonesian Institute of World Affairs: c/o University of Indonesia, Jakarta; Chair. Prof. SUPOMO; Sec. Mr SUDJATMOKO.

Lembaga Administrasi Negara (National Agency for State Administration): Jl. Veteran 10, Jakarta 10110; tel. 3868208; fax 375743; f. 1958; library of 26,000 vols; Chair. Dr J. B. KRISTIADI; publ. *Manajemen Pembangunan*.

Lembaga Pers dan Pendapat Umum (Press and Public Opinion Institute, Ministry of Information): Pegangsaan Timur 19B, Jakarta; f. 1953; audience research of press, film and radio; library of *c.* 4,500 vols; Dir Dr MARBANGUN.

HISTORY, GEOGRAPHY AND ARCHAEOLOGY

Dinas Intelijen Medan & Geografi Jawatan Topografi TNI-AD (Geographical Institute): Jl. Dr Wahidin 1/11, Jakarta; Dir Capt. AMARUL AMRI.

Direktorat Perlindungan dan Pembinaan Peninggalan Sejarah dan Purbakala (Directorate for the Protection and Development of the Historical and Archaeological Heritage): Jl. Cilacap 4, POB 2533, Jakarta; Dir UKA TJANDRASASMITA.

Pusat Penelitian Arkeologi Nasional (National Research Centre of Archaeology): Jl. Raya Condet Pejaten 4, Pasar Minggu, Jakarta; tel. 798187; brs in Yogyakarta and Denpasar; library of 15,000 vols; Dir R. P. SOEJONO; publs *Bulletin*, reports, monographs, *Aspects*, *Amerta*, *Kalpataru*.

LANGUAGE AND LITERATURE

Pusat Pembinaan dan Pengembangan Bahasa (National Centre for Language Development): POB 2625, Jl. Daksinapati Barat IV, Rawamangun, Jakarta 13220; tel. (21) 4894564; fax (21) 4750407; e-mail kapusba@server.pdk.qo.id; f. 1975; attached to the Ministry of Education and Culture; language planning policies, research in linguistics and vernaculars, co-ordinating and supervising language development and cultivation, applied research in language education; branches in Yogyakarta, Denpasar,Ujungpandang; library of 60,000 vols; Dir HASAN ALWI; publs *Bahasa dan Sastra* (quarterly), *Lembar Komunikasi* (every 2 months), *Informasi Pustaka Kebahasaan* (quarterly).

MEDICINE

Central Institute for Leprosy Research: Jl. Kimia 17, Jakarta; f. 1935; Institute includes a clinic and laboratory; Dir MOH. ARIF.

Direktorat Jenderal Pengawasan Obat dan Makanan (Directorate General for Drug and Food Control): Jl. Percetakan Negara 23, Jakarta; tel. 413605; f. 1963; controls drugs, food, cosmetics, indigenous drugs, narcotics and hazardous material; Dir-Gen. Dr MIDIAN SIRAIT.

Attached institute:

Direktorat Pengawasan Makanan dan Minuman (Directorate for Food and Beverage Control): Jl. Percetakan Negara 23, Jakarta; tel. 411781; f. 1974; Dir Drs WISNU KATIM.

Laboratorium Kesehatan Daerah (Pathological Laboratory, Ministry of Health): Jl. Laboratorium 5, Medan; f. 1906; investigation and control of contagious and endemic diseases in Sumatra; *c.* 3,000 vols; Dir Dr ISKAK KOIMAN.

Laboratorium Kesehatan Pusat Lembaga Eijkman (Eijkman Institute): Library, Clinical Pathology Dept, Medical Faculty of the University of Indonesia, Ciptomangunkusumo Hospital, Jl. Diponegoro 69–71, Jakarta 10010; tel. 332265; fax 3147713; f. 1888; bacteriological-serological department, chemical department and virus division; Head Dr HENDRO JOEWONO; publs Reports, Papers.

Lembaga Malaria (Malaria Institute, Ministry of Health): Jl. Percetakan Negara 29, Jakarta; tel. (21) 417608; fax (21) 4207807; f. 1920; Dir Dr P. R. ARBANI.

Perusahaan Negara Bio-Farma (Pasteur Institute): Jl. Pasteur 9, POB 47, Bandung; Dir M. S. NASUTION.

Pusat Penelitian dan Pengembangan Pelayanan Kesehatan (Health Services Research and Development Centre): Jl. Indrapura 17, Surabaya 60176; tel. (31) 3528748; fax (31) 3528749; e-mail agus-p4k@surabaya.wasantara.net.id; Jl. Percetakan Negara 23A, Jakarta 10560; tel. (21) 4243314; fax (21) 4211013; f. 1975; library of 12,000 vols, 543 journals; Dir Dr AGUS SUWANDONO.

Unit Diponegoro (Nutrition Institute): c/o Nutrition Centre, Seameo Tropmed–U.I., Campus University of Indonesia, Salemba 4, Jakarta; f. 1937; Dir Dradjat D. PRAWIRANEGARA.

NATURAL SCIENCES

General

Institut Français de Recherche Scientifique pour le Développement en Coopération (ORSTOM): Wisma Anugraha, Jalan Taman Kemang 32B, Jakarta 12730; geography, agroforestry, anthropology, entomology, virology, aquaculture, agronomy, fishery; Dir Dr PATRICE LEVANG. (See main entry under France.)

Biological Sciences

Pusat Penelitian dan Pengembangan Biologi (Research and Development Centre for Biology): Jl. Raya Juanda 18, POB 110, Bogor 16122; f. 1817; 156 mems; library of 14,995 vols, 4,393 bound periodicals, *c.* 600 current periodicals, 24,587 reprints, 4,377 unpubl. reports, 7,155 newspaper clippings, 2,463 maps; Dir Dr SOETIKNO WIRJOATMODJO; publs *Berita Biologi, Reinwardtia, Treubia* (all irregular), *Laporan Tahunan, Laporan Teknik* (annually), *Laporan Kemajuan* (quarterly), *Warta Biologi* (every 2 months), pamphlets.

Attached institutes:

Balai Penelitain dan Pengembangan Botani (Research and Development Institute for Botany): Jl. Raya Juanda 22, Bogor; f. 1884; Head Dr JOHANIS PALAR MOGEA.

Balai Penelitian dan Pengembangan Mikrobiologi (Research and Development Institute for Microbiology): c/o Kebun Raya Indonesia; f. 1884; Head Dr SUBADRI ABDULKADIR.

Balai Penelitian dan Pengembangan Zoologi (Research and Development Institute for Zoology): Jl. Raya Juanda 3, Bogor; Head Drs MOHAMAD AMIR.

UPT Balai Pengembangan Kebun Raya (Bogor Botanical Gardens): f. 1817; Head Dr SUHIRMAN; publs *Buletin Kebun Raya* (quarterly), *Index Seminum* (annually), *Alphabetical List of Plant Species, Warta Kebun Raya* (irregular), pamphlets.

Physical Sciences

Badan Meteorologi dan Geofisik (Meteorological and Geophysical Agency): Jl. Aarif Rahman Hakim 3, Jakarta; Dir Drs C. SOETRISNO.

Balai Besar Penelitian dan Pengembangan Industri Hasil Pertanian (Institute for Research and Development of Agro-Based Industry): Jl. Ir. H. Juanda 11, Bogor 16122; tel. (251) 324068; fax (251) 323339; f. 1909; attached to Min. of Industry and Trade; library of 8,000 books, 21,000 periodicals; research and development on agriculture-based industry, including treatment of waste materials; Dir A. BASRAH ENIE; publs *Warta IHP* (Journal of agro-based industry, 2 a year), *Komunikasi IHP*†.

Dinas Geodesi, Jawatan Topografi TNI-AD (Geodetic Section, Army Topographic Service): Jl. Bangka 1, Bandung; f. 1855; library of *c.* 2,000 vols, 2,500 periodicals; Dir Ir. MOH TAWIL.

National Atomic Energy Agency: Jl. Kuningan Barat, Mampang Prapatan, POB 4390, Jakarta 12043; tel. 5204246; telex 62354; fax 511110; Dir-Gen. Ir. DJALI AHIMSA.

Observatorium Bosscha (Bosscha Observatory): Lembang, Java; tel. Lembang 1; f. 1925; since 1951 the observatory has been part of the Dept of Astronomy, Bandung Institute of Technology, Bandung; Dir Dr BAMBANG HIDAYAT; publs *Annals* (irregular), *Contributions* (irregular), *Annual Report*.

Pusat Penelitian dan Pengembangan Geologi (Geological Research and Development Centre): Jl. Diponegoro 57, Bandung 40122; tel. (22) 72601; telex 28167; fax (22) 702669; f. 1978; geological and geophysical research and systematic mapping; library: see Libraries; geological research and systematic museum; Dir Dr Ir. IRWAN BAHAR; publs *Publikasi Teknik* (Technical Papers: Geophysics, Palaeontology Series), *Publikasi Khusus* (Special Publications), *Buletin*, *Laporan Tahunan* (Annual Reports), *Geosurvey Newsletter*, *Journal of Geology and Mineral Resources, Peta Geologi, Geofisika dan Tematik*.

Pusat Penelitian dan Pengembangan Oseanologi (Research and Development Centre for Oceanology): Jl. Pasir Putih 1, Ancol Timur, POB 4801/JKTF, Jakarta 11048; tel. 683850; telex 62875; fax 681948; f. 1905; library of 2,000 vols, 250 periodical titles; Dir Prof. Dr KASIJAN ROMIMOHTARTO; publs *Marine Research in Indonesia* (irregular), *Oseanologi di Indonesia* (irregular), *Oseana* (quarterly),

Indonesian Marine Information Journal (2 a year).

TECHNOLOGY

Akademi Teknologi Kulit (Academy of Leather Technology): Jl. Diponegoro 101, Yogyakarta; Dir P. SUKARBOWO.

Balai Besar Penelitian dan Pengembangan Industri Barang Kulit, Karet dan Plastik (BBKKP) (Institute for Research and Development of Leather and Allied Industries): Jl. Sokonandi 9, Yogyakarta 55166; tel. (274) 563939; fax (274) 563655; e-mail marsam-k@pusdata.dprin.go.id; f. 1927; library of 4,000 vols; Dir Drs MARSAM KARDI.

Balai Fotogrametri (Institute of Photogrammetry, Ministry of Defence): Jl. Gunung Sahar 90, Jakarta; f. 1937; research on problems relative to photogrammetry, aerotriangulization, topographical maps, etc.; library of *c.* 1,500 books and periodicals; Head Maj. R. E. BEAUPAIN.

Balai Penelitian Batik & Kerajinan (Batik and Handicraft Research Institute): Jl. Kusumanegara 2, Yogyakarta; f. 1951; research, testing, and training courses; 108 mems; library of 1,792 vols; Dir SOEPARMAN S. TEKS.

Dinas Hidro-Oseanografi (Naval Hydro-Oceanographic Office): Jalan Pantai KutaV1, Jakarta 14430; f. 1947; hydrographical survey of Indonesia; staff of 700; Dir Col. P. L. KATOPPO; publs Tide Tables, etc.

Institut Teknologi Tekstil (Institute of Textile Technology): Jl. Jond. A. Yani 318, Bandung; f. 1922; Dir Maj. JON SEORJOSEOJARSO.

Jajasan Dana Normalisasi Indonesia (Indonesian Standards Institution): Jl. Braga 38, (Atas) Bandung; f. 1920; Chair. Prof. Ir. R. SOEMONO; Sec. GANDI.

Lembaga Research dan Pengujian Materiil Angkatan Darat (Military Laboratory for Research and Testing Material, Ministry of Defence): Jl. Ternate 6–8, Bandung; f. 1865; library of 1,500 vols; Dir Brig.-Gen. N. A. KUSOMO.

Panitya Induk untuk Meter dan Kilogram (Institute of Standards): Jl. Pasteur 27, Bandung; Dir of Metrology G. M. PUTERA.

Pusat Penelitian dan Pengembangan Pengairan (Research Institute for Water Resources Development): attached to Agency for Research and Development, Ministry of Public Works; Jl. Ir. H. Juanda 193, POB 841, Bandung 40135; tel. (22) 2504053; fax (22) 2500163; e-mail pusair@bdg.centrin.net.id; f. 1966; survey, investigation and research in the field of water resources development; library of 6,000 vols, 3,000 reports, 9,000 periodicals; Dir Dr BADRUDDIN MACHBUB; publs *Jurnal Penelitian dan Pengembangan Pengairan* (4 a year), *Bulletin Penelitian dan Pengenbangan Pengairan* (4 a year), *Technical and Research Report* (1 a year).

Libraries and Archives

Bandung

Perpustakaan Pusat Institut Teknologi Bandung (Central Library, Bandung Institute of Technology): Jl. Ganesya 10, Bandung; tel. (22) 2500089; fax (22) 2500089; f. 1920; science and technology and fine arts; 196,000 vols, 951 current periodicals, 40,000 bound vols; rare books, pamphlets and reports on Indonesia, collection on fine arts; Librarian Drs I. NYOMAN SUSILA; publ. *ITB Proceedings*.

Perpustakaan Pusat Penelitian dan Pengembangan Geologi (Library of Geological Research and Development Centre): Jl. Diponegoro 57, Bandung 40122; 10,096 vols, 887 periodicals, 3,985 maps, 10,671 reports, 8,965 reprints, 400 microfiches; Chief Librarian RINI H. MARINO.

Pusat Perpustakaan Angkatan Darat (Central Military Library): Jl. Kalimantan 6, Bandung; 36,000 vols in Central Library, and about 20,000 vols in departmental, territorial and college and office libraries; Dir Brig.-Gen. SOESATYO.

Bogor

Pusat Perpustakaan Pertanian dan Komunikasi Penelitian (Centre for Agricultural Library and Research Communication): Jl. Ir. Haji Juanda 20, Bogor 16122; tel. (251) 321746; fax (251) 326561; f. 1842; 400,000 vols; Dir Dr PRABOWO TJITROPRANOTO; publs *Bibliography* (irregular), *Indek Biologi Pertanian Indonesia* (6 a year), *Abstrak Hasil Penelitian Pertanian* (2 a year), *Indonesian Agricultural Bibliography* (annually), *Daftar Tambahan Koleksi* (quarterly), *Indonesian Journal of Crop Science* (2 a year), *Indonesian Agricultural Research and Development Journal* (quarterly), *Journal Penelitian dan Pengembangan Pertanian* (quarterly), *Warta Penelitian dan Pengembangan Pertanian* (6 a year).

UPT Perpustakaan Institut Pertanian Bogor (Bogor Agricultural University Library): Kampus Darmaga, POB 199, Bogor; tel. and fax (251) 621073; f. 1963; 153,000 vols; 3,185 periodicals; Chief Officer Ir. ABDUL RAHMAN SALEH; publs *Forum Pasca Sarjana*, *Indonesian Journal of Tropical Agriculture*.

Jakarta

Arsip Nasional Republik Indonesia (National Archives): Jl. Ampera Raya, Cilandak Timur, Jakarta 12560; tel. (21) 7805851; fax (21) 7805812; e-mail anrinet@indosat.net.id; f. 1892; preservation of documents as a national heritage and national account of the planning, execution and performance of the national life; to provide records for government and public activities; supervises the management of current operational records and the collection, storage, preservation, safe-keeping and use of historical archives; *c.* 25 km archives; 8,437 vols of books and other publications, 48,000 films, 10,000 video recordings, 4,000 oral history recordings, 1,600,000 photographs; Dir Dr NOERHADI MAGETSARI; publs *Penerbitan Sumber Sejarah* (irregular), *Penerbitan Sumber Sejarah Lisan* (irregular), *Lembaran Berita Sejarah Lisan Arsip Nasional RI* (irregular), *Berita Arsip Nasional RI* (2 a year).

Central Documentation and Library of the Ministry of Information: Medan Merdeka Barat 9, Jakarta; f. 1945; specializes in mass communication, social and political subjects, and supplies regional branch offices; press-cutting service from Indonesian newspapers since 1950; temporarily acting as Exchange Centre for government publications and official documents; 10,000 vols; Head Drs P. DALIMUNTHE; Librarian Mrs SAMPOERNO.

Library of Political and Social History: Medan Merdeka Seletan 11, Jakarta; f. 1952; 65,000 vols; includes the National Bibliographic Centre (Kantor Bibliografi Nasional) deposit library; Librarian Drs SOEKARMAN; publs *Berita Bulanan* (Monthly Bulletin), *Regional Bibliography of Social Sciences, Publications—Indonesia, Checklist of Serials in the Libraries of Indonesia.*

Perpustakaan Bagian Pathologi Klinik R. S. Dr Tjipto Mangunkusumo (Dr Tjipto Mangunkusumo Hospital Library): Jl. Diponegoro 69, Jakarta; 3,000 vols; medicine, public health; Dir Prof. Dr JEANNE LATU.

Perpustakaan Dewan Perwakilan Rakyat Republik Indonesia (Library of Indonesian Parliament): Jl. Jenderal Gatot Subroto, Jakarta 10270; tel. 5715220; fax 584804; f 1946; 200,000 vols; Librarian Mrs ROEMNINGSIH.

Perpustakaan Nasional (National Library of Indonesia): Jl. Salemba Raya 28, POB 3624, Jakarta 10002; tel. 3101411; f. 1980 by a merger of four libraries; depository library of Indonesia; *c.* 750,000 vols; special collections: Indonesian newspapers since 1810, Indonesian periodicals since 1779, Indonesian maps since 17th century, Indonesian dissertations, Indonesian monographs since 17th century; Dir Ms MASTINI HARDJO PRAKOSO; publs *Bibliografi Nasional Indonesia* (quarterly), *Indexs artikel suratkabar* (Press Index, quarterly), subject bibliographies, catalogues, etc.

Pusat Dokumentasi dan Informasi Ilmiah – Lembaga Ilmu Pengetahuan Indonesia (Centre for Scientific Documentation and Information of the Indonesian Institute of Sciences): Jl. Jendral Gatot Subroto 10, POB 4298, Jakarta 12042; tel. 5733465; fax 5733467; f. 1965; 147,175 vols, 1,200 periodicals, 3,125 theses and dissertations, 56,717 microforms; Head BLASIUS SUDARSONO; publs *Index of Indonesian learned periodicals* (2 a year), *Baca* (Read, every 2 months), *Accessions List* (books and microforms, irregular), *Annual Report, Directory of special libraries and information sources in Indonesia* (irregular), *Union Catalogue of dissertations on Indonesia* (irregular), *Index of research and survey reports* (annually), *Index to papers submitted to seminars, workshops and meetings held in Indonesia* (annually), bibliographies on various technical topics.

UPT Perpustakaan dan Dokumentasi, Biro Pusat Statistik (Library and Statistical Documentation, Central Bureau of Statistics): POB 1003, Jl. Dr Sutomo 8, Jakarta; tel. (21) 3810291; fax (21) 3857046; 60,000 vols, Librarian DAME MUNTHE.

Ujung Pandang

Hasanuddin University Library: Kampus UNHAS Tamalanrea, Jl. Perintis Kemerdekaan km 10, Ujung Pandang 90245; tel. (411) 512026; fax (411) 510088; f. 1956; open to public; 122,000 vols, 3,821 periodicals, 23,421 dissertations and theses; Head Dra ROSDIANI RACHIM; publs *Warta Perpustakan, Iaporan Tahunan, Info Pustaka*.

Perpustakaan Umum Makassar (Makassar Public Library): Jl. Madukelleng 3, POB 16, Ujungpandang 90112; f. 1969; organizes lending library services in brs throughout South Sulawesi Province; film and music programmes; foreign language courses; children's library services; exhibitions and talks; 42,000 vols; Dir (vacant).

Yogyakarta

Perpustakaan Islam (Islamic Library): Jl. P. Mangkubumi 38, Yogyakarta; tel. 2078; f. 1942; under the Ministry of Religion; 70,000 vols; MSS and periodicals; Dir Drs H. ASYHURI DAHLAN; Librarian MOH. AMIEN MANSOER.

Perpustakaan Jajasan Hatta (Hatta Foundation Library): Malioboro 85, Yogyakarta; 43,000 vols; Librarian R. SOEDJATMIKO.

Perpustakaan Wilayah (Regional Library): Malioboro 175, Yogyakarta; f. 1949; 120,000 vols; Librarian ST. KOSTKA SOEGENG.

Museums and Art Galleries

Denpasar

Museum Bali: Jl. Letnan Kolonel Wisnu 1, Denpasar, Bali; f. 1932; exhibits of Bali culture; library of 1,970 vols, 1,605 magazines,

1,023 transcriptions of lontars (palm leaves); Dir Drs PUTU BUDIASTRA; publs *Majalah Saraswati, Karya Widia tak berkala*, reports, etc.

Jakarta

Museum Nasional (National Museum): Jl. Merdeka Barat 12, Jakarta Pusat; tel. 360796; f. 1778, formerly Museum Pusat; library of 360,000 vols (now part of National Library); departments of ceramics, ethnography, prehistory, classical archaeology, anthropology, manuscripts and education; Dir Drs BAMBANG SUMADIO; publs subject catalogues.

State Universities

UNIVERSITAS AIRLANGGA

Jl. Airlangga 4–6, Surabaya 60286
Telephone: (31) 5341348
Fax: (31) 5342557
Founded 1954
Language of instruction: Indonesian
Academic year: September to February, March to August

Rector: Prof. Dr H. BAMBANG RAHINO SETOKOESOEMO
Vice-Rector for Academic Affairs: Prof. Dr H. SOEDARTO
Vice-Rector for General Administration: Dr Ec. H. EFFENDIE
Vice-Rector for Student Affairs: Dr H. ZAENAL EFFENDI
Vice-Rector for Co-operation: Prof. Dr H. SAJID HOOD ALSAGAFF
Chief, Bureau for General Academic Administration and Student Affairs: NUR ALI
Chief, Bureau for General Administration: H. KOENARDI
Chief, Bureau for Planning Administration and Information Systems: Dra Hj. SOENARSASI
Librarian: Hj. ENDANG SOEMARSIH

Number of teachers: 1,404
Number of students: 15,139

Publications: *Majalah Kedokteran Tropis Indonesia* (4 a year), *Majalah Kedokteran Surabaya* (4 a year), *Majalah Kedokteran Gigi* (4 a year), Yuridika (4 a year), *Majalah Masyarakat Kebudayaan dan Politik* (4 a year), Jurnal (2 a year).

DEANS

Faculty of Medicine: Prof. Dr Dr ASKANDAR TJOKROPRAWIRO
Faculty of Dentistry: Dr Drg. BOEDIHARTO
Faculty of Law: ISMED BASWEDAN
Faculty of Economics: Prof. Dr SUROSO IMAM ZADJULI
Faculty of Pharmacy: Dr PURWANTO
Faculty of Veterinary Medicine: Prof. Dr Drh. ROCHIMAN SASMITA
Faculty of Social and Political Sciences: MACHSUN ALI
Faculty of Mathematics and Natural Sciences: Drs HARJANA
Faculty of Psychology: Dr Dr HANAFI MOELJOHARDJONO
Faculty of Public Health: Dr Dr RIKA SOEBARNIATI
Postgraduate Programmes: Prof. Dr Dr SOEDIJONO

ATTACHED INSTITUTES

Research Institute: Dir Prof. Dr Drs NOOR CHOLIES ZAINI.

Research Institute for Public Services: Dir Prof. Dr FARIED KASPAN.

UNIVERSITAS ANDALAS

Kampus Limau Manis, Padang, 26163 West Sumatra
Telephone: (751) 71389
Fax: (751) 71085
E-mail: uwand@padang.wasantara.net.id
Founded 1956
Language of instruction: Indonesian
Academic year: September to June

Rector: MARLIS RAHMAN
Vice-Rector for Academic Affairs: AMIRMUSLIM MALIK
Vice-Rector for Administration and Finance: DJASWIR ZEIN
Vice-Rector for Student Affairs: FIRMAN HASAN
Head Librarian: RUSDA SYARIEF GANI

Number of teachers: 1,396
Number of students: 13,009

Publications: *Jurnal Penelitian Andalas, Warta Pengabdian Andalas, Jurnal Pembangunan dan Perubahan Sosial Budaya, Jurnal Ekonomi Manajemen, Jurnal Peternakan dan Lingkungan, Jurnal Matematika dan Ilmu Pengetahuan Alam, Jurnal Teknologi Pertanian* (Journal of Agricultural Technology), *Potetika, Teknika, Justisia, Andalas Medical Journal.*

DEANS

Faculty of Law and Social Science: FIRMAN HASAN
Faculty of Medicine: RUSDAN DJAMIL
Faculty of Mathematics and Natural Sciences: HAZLI NURDIN
Faculty of Agriculture: BUJANG RUSMAN
Faculty of Animal Husbandry: AZINAR KAMARUDDIN
Faculty of Economics: SJAFRIZAL
Faculty of Arts: SYAFRUDDIN SULAIMAN
Faculty of Engineering: DAHNIL ZAINUDDIN
Faculty of Political and Social Sciences: DAHRUL DAHLAN
Polytechnic of Engineering: ALIZAR HASAN
Polytechnic of Agriculture: MASRUL JALAL

ATTACHED INSTITUTES

Research Centre: NURZAMAN BACHTIAR.

Social Research Centre: RUSJI DJAMAL.

Institute for Regional Economic Research: Dir SYAHRUDDIN.

Institute for Management: Dir KHAIDIR ANWAR.

Institute for Demography: Dir SYAHRUDDIN.

Sumatra Nature Study: Dir ANAS SALSABILA.

Environmental Study: Dir ARDINIS ARBAIN.

Women's Studies: LAURA SYAHRUL.

Irrigation Study: SJOFJAN ASNAWI.

Forestry Study: ANWAR KASIM.

Environmental Law Study: SUKANDA HUSIN.

Centre for Manpower Research: AZHAR MAKMUR.

Centre for Human Resources Research: ROSDIWATI.

INSTITUT TEKNOLOGI BANDUNG (Bandung Institute of Technology)

Jl. Tamansari 64, Bandung 40132
Telephone: (22) 2503147
Fax: (22) 431792

Founded 1920, present form 1959 as a merger of the faculties of mathematics, natural sciences and engineering of the University of Indonesia
State control
Language of instruction: Indonesian
Academic year: August to July

Rector: Prof. Ir LILIK HENDRAJAYA
Vice-Rector for Academic Affairs, Research and Community Service: Prof. Dr Ir WIDIADNYANA MERATI
Vice-Rector for General Administration: Prof. Dr Ir DJOKO SANTOSO
Vice-Rector for Student Affairs: Dr Ir ISNUWARDIANTO
Vice-Rector for Communication and Culture: Dr Ir TRESNA DERMAWAN KUNAEFI
Vice-Rector for Administration, Planning and Information Systems: Dr Ir RIZAL ZAINUDDIN TAMIN
Librarian: Prof. Dr Ir WIDIADNYANA MERATI

Number of teachers: 1,500
Number of students: 13,000

DEANS

Faculty of Mathematics and Natural Sciences: Dr MAMAN A. DJAUHARI
Faculty of Civil Engineering and Regional City Planning: Prof. Dr Ir DJOKO SUJARTO
Faculty of Industrial Technology: Prof. Dr Ir DJOKO SUJARTO
Faculty of Mineral Technology: Ir PUDJO SUKARNO
Faculty of Fine Arts and Design: Drs HARRY K. LUBIS

PROFESSORS

ACHMAD, S. A., Chemistry
AGOES, G., Pharmacy
ALGAMAR, K., Environmental Engineering
AMIRUDDIN, A., Chemistry
ANSJAR, M., Mathematics
ARIFIN, A., Mathematics
ARISMUNANDAR, W., Mechanical Engineering
AROEF, M., Industrial Engineering
ASIKIN, S., Geology
BARMAWI, M., Physics
BESARI, M. S., Civil Engineering
BROTOSISWOJO, B. S., Physics
CHATIB, B., Environmental Engineering
DANISWORO, M., Architecture
DIRAN, O., Mechanical Engineering
DJAJADININGRAT, A. H., Environmental Engineering
DJAJAPUTRA, A. A., Civil Engineering
DJALARI, Y. A., Design
DJOJODIHARDJO, H., Mechanical Engineering
GANI, A. Z., Industrial Engineering
HARAHAP, F., Mechanical Engineering
HARJOSUPARTO, S., Chemical Engineering
HARSOKOESOEMO, D., Mechanical Engineering
HIDAJAT, B., Astronomy
KAHAR, J., Geodesy
KANA, J. C., Petroleum Engineering
KARSA, K., Electrical Engineering
KOESOEMADINATA, R. P., Geology
KROMODIHARDJO, H. K., Mathematics
KUKUH, A., Chemical Engineering
KUSBIANTORO, City Planning
LIANG, O. B., Chemistry
LIONG, T. H., Physics
LOEKSMANTO, W., Physics
MANGUNWIDJAJA, A., Mining Engineering
MARDIHARTANTO, F. X., Industrial Engineering
MARDISEWOJO, P., Petroleum Engineering
MARTODIPUTRO, M., Civil Engineering
MARTODJOJO, S., Geology
MARTOJO, W., Mining Engineering
MERATI, I. G. W., Civil Engineering
MIRA, S., Geodesy
ON, T. M., Physics
PADMAWINATA, K., Pharmacy
PIROUS, A. D., Design
PRAMUTADI, S., Chemistry
PRAWIROWARDOJO, S., Meteorology and Geophysics
PRINGGOPRAWIRO, H., Geology
PRINGGOPRAWIRO, M., Physics
PRODJOSOEMARTO, P., Mining Engineering
PULUNGGONO, A., Geology
RAHAYU, S. I., Chemistry
RELAWATI, S. E., Geology
SAMADIKUN, S., Electrical Engineering
SAMPURNO, Geology
SANTOSO, D., Geophysics
SAPIIE, S., Electrical Engineering
SASMOJO, S., Chemical Engineering
SASTRAMIHARDJA, I., Chemical Engineering
SASTRODIHARDJO, S., Chemistry
SATIADARMA, K., Pharmacy

SILABAN, P., Physics
SIRAIT, K. T., Electrical Engineering
SIREGAR, C., Pharmacy
SJUIB, F., Pharmacy
SLAMET, J. S., Environmental Engineering
SOEDIGDO, S., Chemistry
SOEDIRO, I., Pharmacy
SOEDJITO, B. B., City Planning
SOEDJOKO, Fine Arts
SOEGIJANTO, R. M., Engineering Physics
SOEGONDO, T., Civil Engineering
SOELARSO, Mechanical Engineering
SOEMARTO, S., Environmental Engineering
SOEMINTAPOERA, K., Electrical Engineering
SOEMODINOTO, W., Mining Engineering
SOEPANGKAT, H. P., Physics
SOERIA-ATMADJA, R., Geology
SOERIAATMADJA, R. E., Biology
SUDARWATI, S., Biology
SUHARTO, D., Mechanical Engineering
SUHUD, R., Civil Engineering
SUJARTO, D., City Planning
SUKARMADIJAYA, H., Environmental Engineering
SULE, D., Mining Engineering
SUMAWIGANDA, S., Civil Engineering
SURAATMADJA, D., Civil Engineering
SURDIA, N. M., Chemistry
SURDIA, T., Metallurgical Engineering
TAROEPRATJEKA, H., Industrial Engineering
TJAHJATI, S. B., City Planning
UMAR, F., Mining Engineering
WANGSADINATA, W., Civil Engineering
WARDIMAN, A., Engineering Physics
WIDAGDO, Design
WIDODO, R. J., Electrical Engineering
WIRASONJAYA, S., Architecture
WIRJOMARTONO, S. H., Mechanical Engineering
WIRJOSUDIRDJO, S., Mathematics
WIRJOSUMARTO, H., Mechanical Engineering
WISJNUPRAPTO, Environmental Engineering
ZAINUDDIN, I. M., Design
ZEN, M. T., Geology

UNIVERSITAS BENGKULU

Jl. Raya Kandang Limun, Bengkulu
Telephone: (736) 32105
Founded 1982
Rector: Dr Ir SOEKOTJO
Chief Administrative Officer: SYAIFUL AKHMAD
Librarian: Mrs ROSDIANAH ASSAUDI
Library of 20,600 vols
Number of teachers: 444
Number of students: 3,320

DEANS
Faculty of Agriculture: TOEKIDJO MARTOREJO
Faculty of Economics: ILYAS YAKUB
Faculty of Social Sciences: HASNUL BASRI
Faculty of Law: HIDJAZIE K.
Faculty of Education: AZNAM YATIM

INSTITUT PERTANIAN BOGOR (Bogor Agricultural University)

Jl. Lingkar Akademik, Kampus IPB Darmaga, Bogor
Telephone: (251) 622642
Fax: (251) 622708
Founded 1963
State control
Languages of instruction: Indonesian and English for foreign visiting professors
Academic year: September to June (two semesters)
Rector: Prof. Dr SOLEH SOLAHUDDIN
Vice-Rectors: Prof. Dr R. M. AMAN WIRAKARTAKUSUMAH (Academic Affairs), Dr B. SANIM (Administration), Dr PALLAWARUKA (Student Affairs), Dr ROKHMIN DAHURI (Co-operative Affairs), KAMARUDDIN ABDULLAH (Planning and Development)
Registrar: ABUBAKAR BURNIAT
Administrator: ANSHARY CHAERUDDIN
Librarian: ABDURAHMAN SALEH
Number of teachers: 1,299
Number of students: 12,708

Publications: *Indonesian Journal of Tropical Agriculture, Jurnal Ilmu Pertanian Indonesian, Forum Pasca Sarjana, Media Peternakan, Media Veteriner, Communication Agriculture, Buletin Hama dan Penyakit Tumbuhan, Gema Penelitian, Buletin Ilmu Tanah, Media Konservasi, Teknologi, Bibliografi Karya Ilmiah Staf Pengajar, Bibliografi Disertasi IPB, Jurnal Primatologi, Feed and Nutrition Journal.*

DEANS
Faculty of Agriculture: Dr SJAFRI MANGKUPRAWIRA
Faculty of Veterinary Medicine: Prof. Dr EMIR A. SIREGAR
Faculty of Animal Science: Dr KOOSWARDHONO MUDIKDJO
Faculty of Forestry: Dr ZACHRIAL COTTO
Faculty of Fisheries and Marine Science: Dr DARNAS DANA
Faculty of Agricultural Technology: Dr M. BAMBANG PRAMUDYA NOORACHMAT
Faculty of Mathematics and Natural Sciences: Prof. Dr AHMAD ANSORI MATTJIK

ATTACHED INSTITUTES AND CENTRES
Research Institute: Chair. Dr DUDUNG DARUSMAN; comprises:
- Environmental Studies Centre
- Engineering Applications in Tropical Agriculture Research Centre
- Tropical Biology Studies Centre
- Tropical Biodiversity Studies Centre
- Primates Studies Centre
- Food and Nutrition Policy Studies Centre
- Women's Studies Centre
- Development Studies Centre
- Tropical Fruits Studies Centre
- Marine Commodities Studies Centre
- Coastal and Marine Resources Studies Centre
- Traditional Food Studies Centre

Institute for Community Service: Dr RIZAL SYARIEF.
Institute for Information Resource: Dr DIDIN S. DAMANHURI.
Institute for the Assessment and Development of Education: SUHADI HARDJO.
Inter-University Centre for Food and Nutrition: Dir Prof. Dr DEDY FARDIAZ.
Inter-University Centre for Life Sciences: Dir Prof. Dr DUDUNG DARUSMAN.
Inter-University Centre for Biotechnology: Dir Dr ABDUL AZIS DARWIS.

UNIVERSITAS BRAWIJAYA

Jl. Mayor Jendral Haryono 169, Malang, 65143 Jawa Timur
Telephone: (341) 51611
Telex: 31873
Fax: (341) 65420
Founded 1963
State control
Language of instruction: Indonesian
Academic year: September to August
Rector: Prof. Drs H.M. HASYIM BAISOENI
Vice-Rectors: Prof. Dr M. KAFWARI, Dra MURYATI, Dr R. HARIJANTO POERWITO HUSODO, Prof. Dr BAMBANG GURITNO
Head of General Administration: Drs ACHMAD SAID
Head of Student and Academic Administration: Dra INDAH WINARNI
Head of Planning and Information System Bureau: Drs MINARTO SYAIFUDDIN
Librarian: SOEJONO
Number of teachers: 1,279
Number of students: 15,219

Publications: *Mimbar Universitas Brawijaya* (6 a year), *Siaran Universitas Brawijaya* (weekly), *Febra* (monthly), *Administrator* (monthly), *Agrivita* (monthly), *Jurnal Ilmu Peternakan* (2 a year), *Jurnal Brawijaya* (quarterly), *Prasetya* (monthly), *Dian* (monthly), *Indikator* (monthly), Canopy (monthly).

DEANS
Faculty of Law: MASRUCHIN RUBA'I
Faculty of Economics: Drs ABIDIN LATING
Faculty of Administrative Sciences: Prof. Dr MOCH. ICHSAN
Faculty of Engineering: Ir. BUDIONI MISMAIL
Faculty of Agriculture: Dr Ir. YOGI SUGITO
Faculty of Animal Husbandry: Dr Ir. SOEBARINOTO
Faculty of Fishery: Ir. SAHRI MUHAMAD
Faculty of Medicine: Dr M. HIDAYAT
Faculty of Basic Science and Mathematics: Drs SUTIMAN BAMBANG SUMITRO
Polytechnic: Drs UMAR NIMRAN
Postgraduate Studies Programme: Dr Ir. IKSAN SEMAOEN

PROFESSORS
ACHMADY, Z. A., Administration
AMAN, S., Education
BISOENI, H., Mathematics
DARMODIHARDJO, D., Law
DJAMHURI, A., Medicine
EFFENDI, M., Law
GURITNO, B., Agriculture
KALIM, H., Medicine
HARSONO, Economics
HASTUTI, H., Economics
ICHSAN, M., Administration
ISMANI, X., Administration
KAFRAWI, M., Law
KARTASASMITA, G., Administration
RASMINAH, S., Agriculture
SOEDARMANTO, Agriculture
TAMPUBOLON, M., Agriculture
WIDODO, W., Animal Husbandry

UNIVERSITAS CENDERAWASIH

Jl. Perumnas III, Waena, POB 422, Jayapura 99351, Irian Jaya
Telephone: (967) 72101
Telex: 76138
Fax: (967) 81674
Founded 1962
Language of instruction: Indonesian
Rector: Ir FRANS A. WOSPAKRIK
Vice-Rectors: Drs ISAAK AJOMI, Drs DAAN DIMARA, Ir ROBERT LALENOH
General Administration Officer: Ir H. SUMANTO
Academic and Student Administration Officer: Drs M. HATTU
Librarian: Drs A. C. SUNGKANA HADI
Library of 53,000 vols
Number of teachers: 527
Number of students: 4,593

Publication: *Bulletin of Irian Jaya Development*.

Faculties of law, social and political sciences, education and teacher training, economics, mathematics, natural sciences, agriculture.

UNIVERSITAS DIPONEGORO

Jl. Imam Barjo, Sh. 1-3, POB 270, Semarang 50241, Central Java
Telephone: (24) 311520
Telex 22315
Fax: (24) 318381
Founded 1956
Academic year: September to August
Rector: Prof. Dr H. MULADI

Vice-Rector (Academic Affairs): Prof. Dr SOEDARSONO
Vice-Rector (Administration and Finance): Prof. Dr SOEWITO
Vice-Rector (Student Affairs): Prof. Dr H. SARJADI
Vice-Rector (Development and Co-operation): Dr Dr H. M. ROFIQ ANWAR
Head of Administration and Academic Bureau: SOESANTO MOELJOATMOJO
Head of General Administration Bureau: SOEHARDJONO
University Librarian: Drs TONO SUHARTONO

Library of 194,860 vols
Number of teachers: 1,559
Number of students: 20,354

Publications *Manunggal, UNDIP Newsletter, Forum, Berita Penelitian, Teknis, Media, Info, Media Ekonomi & Bisnis, Masalah-Masalah Hukum, Masalah Teknik, Buletin Fekom, Berita UNDIP, Transient, Opini, Gema Teknologi, Bhakti, Cakrawala, Prasasti, Pulsa, Publica, Mahaprika, Nuansa, Konsolidasi, Kinetika, Gallery, Respect, Zigma, Gema, Majalah, Ilmiah Politeknik, Gema Keadilan, Edent, Majalah Kedokteran, Bulletin Fakultas Peternakan & Perikanan, Lembaran Imu Sastra, Hayam Wuruk, Warta Perpustakaan, Bulletin Dharma Wanita.*

DEANS

Faculty of Law: Prof. Dr BARDA NAWAWI
Faculty of Engineering: Prof. Ir. EKO BUDIHARDJO
Faculty of Medicine: Dr ANGGORO D. B. SACHRO
Faculty of Economics: Dr SUYUDI MANGUNWIHARDJO
Faculty of Animal Husbandry: Dr Ir. DIDIEK RACHMADI
Faculty of Letters: Drs ANHARI BASUKI
Faculty of Social and Political Sciences: Dr ABDUL KAHAR BADJURI
Faculty of Mathematics and Natural Sciences: Dr SRIANI HENDARKO
Faculty of Public Health: Dr ISTIANA HARSOJO
Faculty of Fisheries and Marine Science: Prof. Dr LACHMUDDIN SYA'RANI

DIRECTORS

Research Institute: Prof. Dr Dr Ag. SOEMANTRI HARDJOJUWONO
Community Service Institute: Drs H. DARYONO RAHARDJO
Polytechnic Diploma Programmes: BAMBANG SETYOKO

PROFESSORS

BRODJOHOEDOJO, S., Microbiology
BUDIHARDJO, E., Architecture
DARMOJO, R. B., Internal Medicine
GUNAWAN SETIARDJO, A., Philosophy
HADIHARDAJA, J., Steel Construction
HADISAPUTRO, S., Public Health
HADISOETIKNO, S., Sociology
HANITYO SOEMITRO, R., Criminal Law
HARDJOJUWONO, S., Paediatrics
HARIJONO SOEJITNO, R., Paediatrics
HARTADI, Skin and Venereal Diseases
HARTONO, D., Law
HARTONO, S. R., Commercial Law
HARTOWO, Economics
KELIB, A., Islamic Law
KOESOEMOPRADONO, M., Chemistry
LOKOLLO, D. M., Parasitology
MOELJANTO, D., Internal Medicine
MULADI, H., Criminal Law
MURYONO, S., Anatomy
NAWAWI ARIEF, B., Criminal Law
NURDJAMAN, Histology
PARSUDI ABDULROCHIM, I., Internal Medicine
PATRIK, P., Civil Law
PRAPTOHARDJO, U., Gynaecology and Obstetrics
RAHARDJO, S., Social and Development Law
RAHARDJO, S., Cultural Psychology
REKSOPRODJO, R. H., Oto-rhino-laryngology
ROMIMOHTARTO, K., Oceanography
SARJADI, H., Anatomy, Pathology
SASTROSOEBROTO, H., Paediatrics
SASTROSOEHARDJO, S., Constitutional Law
SIDHARTA, Architecture
SOEBOWO, Anatomy, Pathology
SOEDARSONO, Animal Production
SOEDIRO, R., Civil Engineering
SOEDJARWO, Indonesian Literature
SOEDJATI, Linguistics
SOEGENG SOENARSO, B., Otorhinolaryngology
SOEHARDI, Public Finance
SOEHARDJO, Personnel Management
SOEHERMAN, Spatial Law
SOEJOENOES, A., Obstetrics and Gynaecology
SOENARTO, S., Internal Medicine
SOEPARDJO, H., Otorhinolaryngology
SOETOMO, I., Linguistics
SOEWITO, Industrial Economics
SUDIGBIA, Paediatrics
SYA'RANI, L., Fishery
TJOKRO, HADI K., Anaesthesiology
TJOKROWINOTO, S., Philology and Indonesian Literature
TRASTOTENOJO, M. S., Paediatrics
WIDAGDO, Ophthalmology

ATTACHED INSTITUTES

Coastal Region Ecodevelopment Laboratory: Jepara; Chair. Dr Drs Ign. BUDI HENDRARTO.

Centre for Educational Systems and Development: Chair. Drs YUSMILARSO.

Computer Centre and Data Processing: Chair. Prof. Drs SOEHARDJO.

UNIVERSITAS GADJAH MADA

Bulaksumur, Yogyakarta 55281

Telephone: (274) 90-1109
Fax: (274) 563-974

Founded 1949
Language of instruction: Indonesian
Academic year: September to June

Rector: Prof. Dr SUKANTO REKSOHADIPRODJO
Vice-Rector for Academic Affairs: Prof. Dr Ir. BOMA WIKAN TYOSO
Vice-Rector for General Administration: Dr ZAKI BARIDWAN
Vice-Rector for Student Affairs: Ir. BAMBANG KARTIKA
Vice-Rector for Co-operation: Dr Ir. JOEDORO SOEDARSONO
Vice-Rector for Planning and Development: Dr SOFIAN EFFENDI
Librarian: Dra MURYANTI PRANOWO

Number of teachers: 2,122
Number of students: 31,156

DEANS

Faculty of Biology: Prof. Dr ISSIREP SUMARDI
Faculty of Economics: Dr NOPIRIN
Faculty of Philosophy: Dr Sri SOEPRAPTO
Faculty of Pharmacy: Dr ACHMAD MURSYIDI
Faculty of Geography: Prof. Dr SUTIKNO
Faculty of Law: Dr MARIA SRI WULANI SUMARDJONO
Faculty of Mathematics and Natural Sciences: Dr SURYO GURITNO
Faculty of Medicine: Dr SOENARTO SASTROWIJOTO
Faculty of Dentistry: Drg SUBAGYO HARDJOWIJOTO
Faculty of Veterinary Medicine: Drh DJOKO PRANOWO
Faculty of Forestry: Dr Ir. HASANU SIMON
Faculty of Agriculture: Prof. Dr Ir. TUMARI JATILEKSONO
Faculty of Animal Husbandry: Dr Ir. KRISHNA AGUNG SANTOSA
Faculty of Psychology: Dr DALIL ADISUBROTO
Faculty of Letters: Dr DJOKO SURYO
Faculty of Social and Political Science: Dr ICHLASUL AMAL
Faculty of Engineering: Prof. Dr Ir. Sri HARTO BROTOWIRYATMO
Faculty of Agricultural Technology: Dr Ir. SUPRODJO PUSPOSUTARDJO

ATTACHED INSTITUTES

Institute of Community Service: Dir Prof. Dr A. SAMIK WAHAB.
Centre for Study Service Activities (KKN): Dir Drg M. MASYKUR RAHMAT.
Centre for Public Service: Dir Dr HADIANTO ISMANGOEN.
Centre for Public Adult Education: Dir Dr SABIKIS.
Centre for Integrated Rural Development: Dir Ir. DARMADI.
Centre for Appropriate Technology: Dir Ir. SUNARTO CIPTOHADIJOYO.
Centre for 'Mangunan Girirejo' Conservation Management: Dir Dr Ir. DJUWANTOKO

Institute of Research: Dir Prof. Dr Ir. PRAYOTO.
Research Centre for Population Studies: Dir Dr AGUS DWIYANTO.
Research Centre for Rural and Regional Development: Dir Prof. Dr LOEKMAN SOETRISNO.
Research Centre for Culture: Dir Dr SYAFRI SAIRIN.
Research Centre for National Development Planning: Dir Dr BUDIONO SRIHANDOKO.
Research Centre for Environmental Studies: Dir Dr Ir. HARYADI.
Research Centre for Traditional Medicine: Dir Dr SUDARSONO.
Research Centre for Economics and Business Studies: Dir Dr HARSONO.
Research Centre for Tourism Development: Dir Prof. Dr MOELJARTO TJOKROWINOTO.
Centre for Japanese Studies: Dir Dr Ir. NUGROHO MARSOEM.
Centre for Sports Studies: Dir Dr EDDY MOELJONO.
Centre for Women's Role Studies: Dr Ir. MARY ASTUTI.

Centre for Asia-Pacific Studies: Dir Dr DIBYO PRABOWO.

Language Training Centre: Dir Drs MULYONO.

UNIVERSITAS HALUOLEO

Kampus Bumi Tridharma Anduonohu, Kendari 93232

Telephone: (401) 25104
Fax: (401) 22006

Founded 1981
Academic year: September to June

Rector: Prof. Dr Ir. H. SOLEH SOLAHUDDIN
Vice-Rectors: Drs SULEMAN, Drs H. AHMAD BAKKARENG, Drs LA ODE MUH. ARSYAD TENO, Drs H. ALIBAS YUSUF
Librarian: Drs L. HAISU

Library of 43,342 vols
Number of teachers: 452
Number of students: 9,029

Publications: *Journal Haluoleo* (quarterly), *Agri Plus* (6 a year), *Gema Pendidikan* (6 a year), *Sosial Politik* (6 a year), *Majalah Ekonomi* (6 a year).

DEANS

Faculty of Education: Drs H. MUHAMMAD GAZALI
Faculty of Economics: HASAN AEDY
Faculty of Social and Political Sciences: Drs H. M. NUR RAKHMAN
Faculty of Agriculture: Ir. H. MAHMUD HAMUNDU

ATTACHED INSTITUTES

Institute of Social Research: Dir Prof. H. USMAN D. MASIKI.
Institute of Community Service: Dir Prof. Dr H. ABDURRAUF TARIMANA.

Centre for Ecological Studies: Dir Ir. ABDUL MANAN.
Centre for Population Studies: Dir Drs ABD. AZIS RASAKE.
Centre for Women's Studies: Dra Ny. Hj. SAARTJE DJARUDJU ROMPAS.
Centre for Computer Science and Information Systems: Dir Ir. GATOT ILHAMTO.
Small Earth Station and Electronic Classroom for Distance Learning: Dir Drs H. AHMAD BAKKARENG.
Centre for Rural Areas Development: Dir MUH. IDRUS MUFTI.
Open University: Dir Drs SULEMAN.
Centre for Dry Land Area: Dir Dr Ir. Y. B. PASOLON.
Centre for Education and Humanities: Dir Drs GUSARMIN SOFYAN.
Centre for Economics and Social Research: Dir ABD. AZIS ABD. MUTHALIB.

UNIVERSITAS HASANUDDIN

Jl. Perintis Kemerdekaan, Kampus Tamalanrea, Ujung Pandang 90245
Telephone: (411) 510102
Fax: (411) 510088
Founded 1956
Rector: Prof. Dr H. BASRI HASANUDDIN
Vice-Rectors: Prof. Dr Ir. RADI A. GANY (Academic Affairs), Prof. Dr Ir. H. M. NATSIR NESSA (General Administration), Prof. SYARIFUDDIN WAHID (Student Affairs)
Registrar: H. A. RIVAI MUSLANG
Librarian: Dra ROSDIANA RAHIM
Number of teachers: 1,596
Number of students: 20,428
Publications: *Majallah Universitas Hasanuddin, Identitas* (weekly newspaper), *Lontara.*

DEANS

Faculty of Law: ACHMAD ALI
Faculty of Medicine: Prof. MUH. FARID
Faculty of Agriculture: Dr AMBO ALA
Faculty of Letters: Drs. MUSTAFA MAKKAH
Faculty of Economics: Dr DJABIR HAMZAH
Faculty of Social and Political Science: Prof. Dr MAPPA NASRUN
Faculty of Public Health: Prof. Dr M. RUSLI NGATIMIN
Faculty of Dentistry: Drg. M. HATTA HASAN S.
Faculty of Animal Sciences: Dr THAMRIN IDRIS
Faculty of Mathematics and Physics: Dr NUR DJALALUDDIN
Faculty of Engineering: Prof. Dr Ir. ARIFUDDIN RESSANG
Faculty of Marine Sciences and Fishery: Ir. SYAMSUL ALAM ALI

DIRECTORS

Postgraduate Studies Programme: Prof. Dr SUMALI WIRYOWIDAGDO
Polytechnic of Technological Science: Ir. MAURAGA MACHMUD
Polytechnic of Agricultural Science: Dr Ir. ACHMAR MALLAWA

UNIVERSITAS INDONESIA

Jl. Salemba Raya 4, Jakarta Pusat
Telephone: (21) 330343
Fax: (21) 330343
E-mail: rector@makara.cso.ui.ac.id
Founded 1950
Language of instruction: Indonesian
Academic year: August to June (two semesters)
Rector: Prof. Dr ASMAN BOEDISANTOSO RANAKUSUMA
Deputy Rector for Academic Affairs: Dr USMAN CHATIB WARSA
Deputy Rector for General Administration: MUHAMMAD NAZIF
Deputy Rector for Student Affairs: Drs UMAR MANSUR
Librarian: LILY IRAWATI ROESMA
Number of teachers: 2,664
Number of students: 32,222
Publications: various faculty bulletins.

DEANS

Faculty of Medicine: Prof. Dr ALI SOELAIMAN
Faculty of Dental Medicine: Drg FARUK HOESIN
Faculty of Mathematics and Natural Sciences: Dr ENDANG ASIJATI WIDIJANINGSIH
Faculty of Technology: Prof. Dr Ir. DJOKO HARTANTO
Faculty of Law: Prof. Dr. SRI SETIANINGSIH SUWARDI
Faculty of Economics: Prof. Dr ANWAR NASUTION
Faculty of Letters: Prof. Dr SAPARDI DJOKO DAMONO
Faculty of Psychology: Prof. Dr SARLITO WIRAWAN SARWONO
Faculty of Social and Political Sciences: Prof. Dr KAMANTO SUNARTO
Faculty of Public Health: Dr ASCOBAT GANI
Faculty of Computer Sciences: Ir. BAGYO Y. MOELIODIHARDJO
Faculty of Nursing Sciences: Prof. Dr AZRUL AZWAR
Non-degree Faculty of Technology: Ir. BAGIO BUDIARDJO
Programme of Postgraduate Studies: Prof. Dr FARID ANFASA MOELOEK

ATTACHED RESEARCH INSTITUTES

Institute for Research: Dir Prof. Dr UMAR FAHMI ACHMADI.

Institute of Social Services: Dir Prof. MARDJONO REKSODIPUTRO.

Centre for Studies of the Environment and Human Resources: Dir Prof. RETNO SUTARJONO.

Centre for Health Research: Dir Dr BUDI UTOMO.

Centre for Research in Society and Culture: Dir Dr RAHAYU SURTIATI HIDAYAT.

Centre for Research in Science and Technology: Dir Prof. Dr SOLEH KOSELA.

Centre for Research Development: Dir Drs ASLAM SUMHUDI.

Centre for Family Welfare: Dir Dr ALEX PAPILAYA.

Centre for Studies and Research in Higher Education: Dir Dr SITI OETARINI S. WIDODO.

Centre for American Studies: Dir Dra PIA ALISJAHBANA.

Centre for Australian Studies: Dir Dra RENI WINATA.

Centre for Japanese Studies: Dirs Dr BACHTIAR ALAM, Drs SUTOPO SUTANTO.

Centre for European Studies: Dir Dr OKKE K. S. ZAIMAR.

Regional Centre for Nutrition (in co-operation with SEAMEO Tropmed): Dir Prof. Dr SOEMILAH SASTROAMIDJOJO.

Centre for Middle Eastern and Islamic Studies: Dir ACHMAD RAMZY TADJOEDIN.

APEC Study Centre: Dir Prof. Dr B. S. MULYANA.

AFFILIATED COLLEGES AND INSTITUTES

Lembaga Demografi (Institute of Demography): Kampus UI-Depok; Dir Dr MURTININGSIH ADITOMO.

Lembaga Ekonomi dan Penelitian Masyarakat (Institute of Economic and Social Research): Jl. Salemba 4, Jakarta; Dir Dr MULYANI INDRAWATI.

Lembaga Management (Institute of Management): Jl. Salemba 4, Jakarta; Dir BUDHI SUGARDHA.

Lembaga Konsultasi Hukum dan Bantuan Hukum (Legal Consultation and Legal Aid Department): Kampus UI-Depok; Dir RETNO MURNIATI.

Pusat Dokumentasi Hukum (Legal Documentation Centre): Jl. Cirebon 5, Jakarta; Dir WAHYONO DARMABRATA.

Lembaga Psikologi Terapan (Institute of Applied Psychology): Jl. Salemba 4, Jakarta; Dir Dr SOESMALIJAH SOEWONDO.

Lembaga Teknologi (Institute of Technology): Jl. Salemba 4, Jakarta; Dir Ir. SYAHRIL A. RAHMIN.

Pusat Kajian Ilmu Komunikasi (Centre for Communications Studies): Kampus UI-Depok; Dir Drs ZULHASRIL NASIR.

Pusat Pelayanan Bahasa (Language Service Centre): Jl. Salemba 4, Jakarta; Dir GRACE WIRADISASTRA.

UNIVERSITAS JAMBI

Jl. Prof. Dr Sri Soedewi Maschun Sofwan SH Jambi
Telephone: (741) 25122
Fax: (741) 62774
Founded 1963
Language of instruction: Indonesian
Academic year: September to August
Rector: Prof. Dr Ir. SOEDARMADI
Vice-Rector (Academic Affairs): Dr Ir. ALI M. A. RACHMAN
Vice-Rector (Administration): Drs AMIN SAIB
Vice-Rector (Student Affairs): Drs H. RASMAN ADIWIJAYA
Registrar: A. R. KASIM
Librarian: Drs SYAHRIL ZAWIR
Library of 99,000 vols
Number of teachers: 567
Number of students: 6,000
Publication: *Berita UNJA* (monthly).

DEANS

Faculty of Law: Prof. ROZALI ABDULLAH
Faculty of Economics: Dra SETYANINGSIH
Faculty of Agriculture: Ir. ROSYID
Faculty of Animal Husbandry: Drh. MOHD. TOHA
Faculty of Education: Drs EKA WARNA

UNIVERSITAS JEMBER

Jl. Kalimantan III/24, Jember, East Java
Telephone: 21270, 41500, 41422
Founded 1957
State control
Languages of instruction: Indonesian (English and French in Faculty of Letters, Foreign Languages division)
Rector: Prof. Dr SIMANHADI WIDYAPRAKOSA
Vice-Rector (Academic Affairs): Ir. SOEBROTO WIJAHNO
Vice-Rector (Administration and Finance): ARIE SOEDJATNO
Vice-Rector (Student Affairs): Drs SANDJAJA
Registrar: Drs MADE PEDUNGAN SARDHA
Librarians: Drs WIBOWO, Drs MARYONO
Library of 109,015 vols
Number of teachers: 718
Number of students: 10,706
Publications: *Gema Universitas, Argopuro, Dian Wanita.*

DEANS

Faculty of Law: SOEHARSONO
Faculty of Social and Political Sciences: Drs SOENARJO
Faculty of Agriculture: Ir. SUSIJOHADI
Faculty of Economics: Drs SUGIHARTO
Faculty of Teacher Training & Educational Sciences: Drs IDA BAGUS ALIT ANA
Faculty of Letters: Drs SUNDHORRO

DIRECTORS

University Planning and Development: Prof. Ir. I. MADE SEDHANE
University Research Institute: Ir. WAGITO
Public Service: Ir. SUTJIPTO
Language Training and Development Institute: Dra SRI KUSTIATI
Agricultural Polytechnic: Ir. SUTRISNO WIJAYA
Computer Centre: Drs KASWARI
Central Library: Drs MARYONO

HEADS OF DEPARTMENT

Faculty of Law:

Criminal Law: SOENARJATI
Civil Law: H. ACHMAD LINOCH
Basic Law: I. KETUT SUANDRA
Constitutional Law: Dr TJUK WIRAWAN

Faculty of Social and Political Science:

International Relations: Drs UMAIDI RADI
Administration: Drs RADLIA KEMAL WIJADI
General Studies: Drs BAWI FATHONI
Social Welfare: Drs UUNG NASDIA

Faculty of Agriculture:

Soil Science: Ir. WUSTAMIDIN
Social Economics: Ir. RIJANTO
Agronomy: Ir. SOETILAH
Plant Protection: Ir. SUKARTO
Agricultural Technology: Ir. SITI HARTANTI

Faculty of Teacher Training & Educational Sciences:

General Education: Drs SOEDARWOTO
Social Science Education: Drs AMIN SOEJANTO
Mathematics and Physics Education: Drs TITIK SUGIARTI
Language and Art: Drs H. SOEPARTO

Faculty of Letters:

Indonesian Literature: Drs SOEDJADI
English Literature: Drs M. BUSJAIRI
Indonesian History: Drs SOEDIRO

Faculty of Economics:

Economics and Development: Drs KADIMAN
Management: Drs SUKUSNI

UNIVERSITAS JENDERAL SOEDIRMAN

Kampus UNSOED Grendeng, POB 15, Purwokerto 53122, Central Java

Telephone: (281) 35292
Fax: (281) 31802

Founded 1963
Language of instruction: Indonesian
Academic year: September to August (two semesters)

Rector: (vacant)
Vice-Rector (Academic Affairs): Ir. DJOKO ADISUWIRJO
Vice-Rector (Administration Affairs): Prof. SHOWAM MASJHURI
Vice-Rector (Student Affairs): Drs MOELJONO
Chief Administrative Officer: Drs H. ADAN MULYONO
Chief Registrar: Drs SOETRISNO
Librarian: Drs INDRATMO YUDONO

Number of teachers: 700
Number of students: 8,977

Publication: *Majalah Ilmiah Unsoed* (quarterly).

DEANS

Faculty of Agriculture: Ir. SUDARMONO
Faculty of Biology: Prof. Dr SOEMARJANTO
Faculty of Animal Husbandry: Ir. MACHFUDIN BUDIONO
Faculty of Economics: Prof. H. MOCH THOLIB.
Faculty of Law: NOOR AZIZ SAID
Faculty of Social Sciences and Politics: Prof. Drs SOEMARDI

UNIVERSITAS LAMBUNG MANGKURAT

Kampus UNLAM, Jl. Brigjen H. Hasan Basry, POB 219, Banjarmasin 70123, South Kalimantan

Telephone and fax: (511) 54177

Founded 1958 as private university, state control 1960
Language of instruction: Indonesian

Rector: (vacant)
Vice-Rector (Administrative Affairs): Prof. H. ALFIAN NOOR
Vice-Rector (Student Affairs): Prof. H. DARMANSYAH DJAMAIN
Head of Academic Administration, Student Affairs, Planning and Information Systems: Drs H. M. SYACHRIAR ACHMAD
Head of General Administration, Financial and Employee Affairs: Drs Hj. SUNDUSIAH
Librarian: Drs Haji SAFWAN IDERIS

Number of teachers: 803
Number of students: 8,084

Publications: *Kalimantan Scientiae* (2 a year), *Orientasi* (quarterly), *Vidya Karya* (monthly), *Studi Hukum Tanah* (monthly).

DEANS

Faculty of Teaching Training and Education: Drs H. AZIZ TAMJID
Faculty of Law: Hj. YURLIANI
Faculty of Economics: Drs H. YUSRIANSYAH AZIS
Faculty of Social and Political Sciences: Drs H. ISRAN SYAM
Faculty of Agriculture: Ir. RASMADI
Faculty of Forestry: Dr Ir. H. M. RUSLAN
Faculty of Fisheries: Ir. Gt. CHAIRUDDIN
Faculty of Engineering: Ir. ZAIN HERNADY
Faculty of Medicine: Dr HARYONO SOEHARTO

UNIVERSITAS LAMPUNG

Kampus UNILA, Gedong Meneng, Kedaton, Bandar Lampung

Telephone: 52673

Founded 1965
State control
Languages of instruction: Indonesian and English
Academic year: August to June (two terms)

Rector: Prof. Dr R. MARGONO SLAMET
Vice-Rector (Academic Affairs): Dr BAMBANG SUMITRO
Vice-Rector (Finance and Administration): Drs MAS'UD YUSUF
Vice-Rector (Student Affairs): RIZANI PUSPAWIDJAJA
Registrar: ZEN SALIM
Library Director: Dra DIANA AMISANI

Number of teachers: 650
Number of students: 10,000

Publications: *Buletin Penelitian*, *Warta Pengabdian pada Masyarakat.*

DEANS

Faculty of Law: M. PULUNG
Faculty of Economics: A.T. SYAMSUDDIN
Faculty of Education and Teacher Training: Drs HIFNI MUKODAM
Faculty of Agriculture: Dr Ir. MINTARSIH ADIMIHARDJA
Faculty of Technology: Ir. SITI SUDJALMI

DIRECTORS

Bureau of Legal Consultation and Aid: M. PULUNG
Centre of Public Services: Drs KANTAN ABDULLAH
Research Centre: Dr FADDEL DJAUHAR
Institute of Environmental Studies: Ir. SUGENG HARJANTO
Institute of Demography: MUCHSIN BADAR
Institute of Management: SUDANAR
Institute of Languages: Dra ROSITA S. PANJAITAN

UNIVERSITAS MATARAM

Jl. Majapahit, Mataram 83125, Nusa Tenggara Barat

Telephone: (364) 33007
Fax: (364) 36041

Founded 1962
Academic year: July to January, January to July

Rector: Prof. Dr Ir. Sri WIDODO
Vice-Rectors: Dr Ir. MANSUR MA'SHUM (Academic Affairs), A. M. RESAD (Administrative Affairs), Ir. SOEKARDONO (Student Affairs)
Registrar: SYUKUR MUSTAKIM
Administrative Officer: ABDURRAHMAN ANDY
Librarian: Drs I GUSTI BAGUS NGURAH HARRY

Library of 64,000 vols
Number of teachers: 635
Number of students: 5,167

DEANS

Faculty of Economics: Drs MAR'I FAUZI
Faculty of Agriculture: Ir. SUDARMADJI RAHARDJO
Faculty of Law: SALIM BASIR
Faculty of Animal Science: Dr Ir. M. ICHSAN
Faculty of Education: BADRUN
Faculty of Engineering: Dr Ir. MORISCO

ATTACHED INSTITUTES

Research Centre: Dir Prof. Ir. M. QAZUINI.
Community Service Department: Dir Ir. SYAHIBUDDIN R.

UNIVERSITAS MULAWARMAN

Kampus Gn. Kelua, Samarinda

Telephone: (541) 21118

Founded 1962
Academic year: September to August

Rector: Prof. Dr H. M. YUNUS
Vice-Rector: Dr Ir. RIYANTO
Registrar: M. YAMIN
Librarian: RAFIDHAH ILHAM

Number of teachers: 412
Number of students: 4,603

Publication: *Frontir* (2 a year).

DEANS

Faculty of Economics: Drs DARMINTO
Faculty of Social and Political Sciences: Drs KUSOSI
Faculty of Agriculture: Prof. Ir. RACHMAT HERNADI
Faculty of Forestry: Dr Ir. SOEYITMO SOEDIRMAN
Faculty of Teacher Training: Drs H. NURDIN EFFENDI

UNIVERSITAS NUSA CENDANA

Jl. Adi Sucipto, Penfui, Kupang, Nusa Tenggara Timur

Telephone: (380) 21680
Fax: (380) 21674

Founded 1962
State control
Languages of instruction: Indonesian, English
Academic year: July to June

Rector: Prof. Dr A. BENU
Vice-Rector (Academic Affairs): Drs I. LATUNUSSA
Vice-Rector (Administration Affairs): Drs ANSGAR DIAHIMO
Vice-Rector (Student Affairs): Drs P. CH. MAUKO
Chief Administrative Officer (Finance and Facilities): Drs KAREL TAHITOE
Chief Administrative Officer (Academic, Students and Information System): Drs I. PUTO SUENDA

Librarian: Drs PORAT ANTONIUS
Number of teachers: 813
Number of students: 4,853
Publication: *Sinergia.*

DEANS

Faculty of Teacher Training and Education: Drs M. ULY
Faculty of Administration: Drs B. TOBE
Faculty of Animal Husbandry: Ir. KUNENG M. ARSYAD
Faculty of Agriculture: Dra A. P. PELLO-DE HAAN
Faculty of Law: B. PASARIBU
Polytechnic Education for Agriculture: Ir. RETNO NUNINGSIH
Polytechnic Education for Engineering: Drs I. IAMBAK

UNIVERSITAS PADJADJARAN

Jl. Dipati Ukur 35, Bandung 40132, Java
Telephone: (22) 2503271
Fax: (22) 2501977
Founded 1957
State control
Languages of instruction: Indonesian, English
Academic year: August to July (two semesters)
Rector: Prof. Dr H. MAMAN P. RUKMANA
Vice-Rector for Academic Affairs: Prof. Dr TANWIR Y. MUKAWI
Vice-Rector for Administration: Hj. DAIDUMI DARMAWAN
Vice-Rector for Student Affairs: Prof. Dr H. A. D. SAEFULLAH
Vice-Rector for International Relations: Prof. Dr H. LILI RASJIDI
Vice-Rector for Planning Information Systems: Prof. A. HIMENDRA W.
Librarian: Dra Hj. ATI MURNIATI
Library of 158,000 vols
Number of teachers: 1,778
Number of students: 30,000
Publications: *Journal of Padjadjaran University,* several faculty journals.

DEANS

Faculty of Law: Prof. Dr MIEKE KOMAR
Faculty of Social Science and Politics: Prof. Dr KUSNAKA ADIMIHARDJA
Faculty of Economics: Prof. Dr H. SUTARYO SALIM
Faculty of Medicine: Prof. Dr H. PONPON S. IDJRADINATA
Faculty of Dentistry: Dr SETIAWAN NATASAMITA
Faculty of Letters: Prof. Dr H. EDI SUHARDI EKADJATI
Faculty of Agriculture: Dr Ir. TUHPAWANA PRIATNA SENDJAJA
Faculty of Animal Husbandry: Prof. Dr NASIPAN USRI
Faculty of Psychology: Dr WISNUBRATA HENDROYUWONO
Faculty of Mathematics and Natural Sciences: Dr SUPRIYATNA
Faculty of Communication Science: Drs SOLEH SOEMIRAT

ATTACHED INSTITUTES

Research Institute: Dr R. OTJE SALMAN SOEMADININGRAT
Public Service Institute: H. MOH. ENDANG DAUD

UNIVERSITAS PALANGKARAYA

Kampus UNPAR, Tunjung Nyaho, Jl. Yos Sudarso, Palangkaraya, Kalimantan Tengah
Telephone: (514) 21492
Fax: (514) 21722
Founded 1963
Language of instruction: Indonesian
Academic year: July to June
Rector: Prof. Dr Ir. H. ALI HASYMI
Vice-Rector (Academic Affairs, and Co-operative and Institutional Development Affairs): Dr AHIM S. RUSAN
Vice-Rector (Administrative Affairs): Drs DIARSYAD ISAM
Vice-Rector (Student Affairs): Drs M. O. HASIBUAN
General Administrative Officer: Drs BOLANG G. SYAWAL
Academic and Students' Administrative Officer: Drs LEUNHARD BAN YEN
Librarian: Dra ISTIRAHAYU
Number of teachers: 501
Number of students: 5,265
Publications: *Suara Tunjung Nyaho* (monthly), *Garantung* (monthly), *Optimal* (monthly), *Wahana* (monthly).

DEANS

Faculty of Economics: Drs EFENDY D. TIMBANG
Faculty of Education and Teacher Training: Drs HENRY SINGARASA
Faculty of Agriculture: Ir. SINTO R. NOEHAN

HEADS OF DEPARTMENT

Faculty of Economics:

Public Economics: Drs SUFRIDSON
Management: Drs Y. KALVIN ANGGEN
General Subjects: Drs BERLIE A. LABIH

Faculty of Education and Teacher Training:

Education Science: Dra DALIKAH
Educational Technology and Curriculum: Drs SARLES
Non-formal Education: Drs HANNES M. B. HAMUN
Educational Administration: Drs SITJAI MANDAGIE
Guidance and Counselling: Drs SUNARYO
Civics: Drs EDDY
English: Drs SURYA TAIB
Indonesian: Drs MARIYEDIE
Mathematics: Drs WALTER PUNDING
Accountancy: Drs TIMBUL
Business: Drs DEHEN ERANG
Social Science: Drs ARNIANSYAH
Art and Language: Drs RUS ANDIANTO
Mathematic Natural Science: Dra UMINASTUTI
Biology: Dra YULA MIRANDA
Co-operation: Drs MIDDAY
Physics: Drs KOMANG GDE SWASTIKA
Chemistry: Drs ABDUL MUM'IN

Faculty of Agriculture:

Agriculture (Social Economics): Ir. NYELONG I. SIMON
Agriculture (Agronomy): (vacant)
Forestry: Ir. BAMBANG WALDY
Civil Engineering: Ir. MOH. AMIN
Fishery: Ir. PETRUS SENAS

UNIVERSITAS PATTIMURA AMBON

POB 95, Jl. Ir. M. Putuhena, Kampus Poka, Ambon
Telephone: 53560
Founded 1956, became university 1962
Language of instruction: Indonesian
Academic year: August to July
Rector: Dr Ir. J. L. NANERE
Vice-Rector for Academic Affairs: Prof. P. J. SIWABESSY
Vice-Rector for Administration and Finance: J. LEIWAKABESSY
Vice-Rector for Student Affairs: Ir. J. J. TUHUMURY
Registrar: Drs E. LEUWOL
Librarian: ALI ZAWAWI
Number of teachers: 636
Number of students: 7,516
Publication: *Media Unpatti* (monthly).

DEANS

Faculty of Law: C. M. PATTIRUHU
Faculty of Social and Political Sciences: Drs M. RENUR
Faculty of Agriculture: Ir. J. PUTINELLA
Faculty of Economics: Drs L. A. RASJID
Faculty of Teacher Training and Education: Drs T. J. A. UNEPUTTY
Faculty of Fishery: Ir. J. M. NANLOHY
Faculty of Technology: Ir. J. ASTHENU

DIRECTORS

Institute of Research: Dr Ir. P. SITIAPESSY
Institute of Community Service: Dr MUS. HULISELAN

UNIVERSITAS RIAU

Kampus Bina Widya Km 12.5, Simpang Baru, Pekanbaru 28293, Sumatra
Telephone: (761) 63266
Fax: (761) 63279
E-mail: rektor@unri.ac.id
Founded 1962
Academic year: September to July
Rector: Prof. Dr MUCHTAR AHMAD
Vice-Rectors: Prof. Dr MOCHAMMAD SAAD (Academic Affairs), Prof. Dr MUCHTAR RACHMAN (Administration), Ir. ARIFFIEN MANSYOER (Student Affairs)
Registrar: Dr MOCHAMMAD SAAD
Librarian: Drs WUSONO INDARTO
Number of teachers: 846
Number of students: 12,128
Publication: *Terubuk* (Fisheries Bulletin, quarterly), *Jurnal Penelitian* (General Scientific Research, quarterly), *Dawat* (Journal of Malay Language and Culture), *Jurnal Ilmu Sosial dan Ilmu Politik* (Social and Political Sciences, quarterly), *Jurnal Ekonomi* (Economics), *Jurnal Agritek* (Agricultural Technology), *Jurnal Perikanan dan Ilmu Kelautan* (Fisheries and Marine Science).

DEANS

Faculty of Politics and Social Science: Drs R. SYOFYAN SAMAD
Faculty of Economics: Drs AMIR HASAN
Faculty of Natural Sciences and Mathematics: Dr DADANG ISKANDAR
Faculty of Fisheries: Dr Ir. ADNAN KASRY
Faculty of Teacher Training and Education: Drs M. ZEIN MAADAP
Faculty of Agriculture: Ir. A. Z. FACHRI YASIN
Faculty of Engineering: Ir. HARTONO

PROFESSORS

ADAM, D., Government and Law
AHMAD, M., Marine Sciences and Fisheries
DAHRIL, T., Planktonology and Water Quality
HASAN, K., Education
IMRAN, A., Islamology
KASMY, M. F., Physics
KASRY, A., Aquatic Resources Management
MARZUKI, S., History
RAB, T., Enzymology
RAHMAN, M., Mathematics
SAAD, M., Rural Sociology
SALEH, M. B., Economics
SAMAD, R., Education
SUWARDI, History
UMAR, S. M., Education
USMAN, F., Agriculture
ZEIN, Z., Education

UNIVERSITAS SAM RATULANGI

Kampus UNSRAT Bahu, Manado 95115
Telephone: 63786
Founded 1961
State control
Language of instruction: Indonesian
Academic year: starts September
Rector: Prof. Drs R. S. TANGKUDUNG

Vice-Rectors: Ir. J. L. PALENEWEN, Prof. Drs J. A. RACO, D. ALING
Librarian: Dra S. A. G. TANGKERE-PAMURU

Number of teachers: 1,496
Number of students: 12,526

Publication: *Palakat-Inovasi.*

DEANS

Faculty of Letters: Dra J. KARISOH-NAJOAN
Faculty of Education: Drs HUSAIN JUSUF
Faculty of Law: M. G. M. MAMAHIT
Faculty of Social Sciences and Politics: Prof. Drs W. T. PALAR
Faculty of Economics: Drs R. P. L. KAKAUHE
Faculty of Agriculture: Dr Ir. J. WAROUW
Faculty of Animal Husbandry: Prof. A. F. WILAR
Faculty of Fisheries: Prof. Drh Ir. M. RONDO
Faculty of Medicine: Dr R. S. M. RAMPEGAN
Faculty of Engineering: Ir. BONNY F. SOMPIE

PROFESSORS

ALAMSJAH, Soil Physics
BUDIARSO, Technology
DUNDU, B., Microbiology
JAN, H., Statistics
KAKAUHE, R. P. L., Management Accounting
KAPOJOS-MONGULA, I. C. R., Civil Law
KARINDA, D. S., English and Dutch
KASINEM-S., Commercial Law
KORAH, M. W., Marketing Management Science
MANDANG, J. H. A., Ahli Mata
MUNIR, M., Paediatrics
MUSA, A., Modern Indonesian History
MUSA KARIM, Indonesian Literature
PALAR, W. T., Agrarian Studies
PALENEWEN, J. L., Ecology
PANDA, H. O., Surgery
PUNUH-GO, S., Civil Law
ROGI, M., Economic Development
SALEH, M., Indonesian Government System
SINOLUNGAN, J. M., Medical Psychology
SOEPENO, Customary Law
SUPIT, J. T., Sociology
TANGKUDUNG, R. S., Civil Administration
TIMBOELENG, K. W., Physics and Research Methodology
TUSACH, N. A., Civil Law
WANTASEN, D., Soil Physics
WAWOROENTOE, S. A., Physics
WAWOROENTOE, W. J., Urban and Regional Planning
WILAR, A. F., Veterinary Science
WOKAS, F. H. M., Plant Protection
WOWOR, G. E., Gynaecology
WUMU, J., History of Economics

UNIVERSITAS SEBELAS MARET

Jl. Ir. Sutami 36A, Surakarta 57126
Telephone: 46994
Fax: 46655

Founded 1976
State control
Language of instruction: Indonesian

Rector: Prof. Drs HARIS MUDJIMAN
Vice-Rector (Academic Affairs): Dr AMBAR MUDIGDO
Vice-Rector (Administration Affairs): Drs BACHTIAR EFFENDI
Vice-Rector (Student Affairs): Drs SUPARNADI
Academic Affairs Bureau Officer: Drs SEHAT SINURAYA
Administrative General Bureau Officer: MOEKIYO
Planning and Information Systems Bureau Officer: Drs SUNARDI
Student Affairs Bureau Officer: Drs SARSITO
Librarian: Drs H. TARJANA

Library of 96,000 vols
Number of teachers: 1,339
Number of students: 18,145

Publications: *Widya Bhawana, Varia Budaya, Buletin UNS.*

DEANS

Teacher-Training and Education: Dr SOEDJARWO
Letters and Arts: Drs D. EDI SUDADI
Social and Political Science: Drs H. ZAINUDIN
Law: SOENARYO
Economics: Drs KASIMAN TJILIK SUWITO
Medicine: Dr SUROTO
Agriculture: Ir. ZAINAL DJAUHARI FATAWI
Engineering: Ir. DJOKO KUNTJORO
Mathematics and Natural Sciences: SOETOMO

UNIVERSITAS SRIWIJAYA

Jl. Jaksa Agung R. Suprapto, Palembang, South Sumatra
Telephone: 26004, 26388, 23155

Founded 1960
State control
Language of instruction: Indonesian
Academic year: July to June

Chancellor: HE THE GOVERNOR OF SOUTH SUMATRA
Vice-Chancellor and Rector: Drs SJAFRAN SJAMSUDDIN
Vice-Rectors: Ir. BAKRY HAMID, Drs M. BASIR KIMIN, Dr MUNGGANA SASMITAPURA
Registrar: Drs H. ZAHRUDDIN ABDULLAH
Librarian: Dra CHUZAIMAH DIEM

Number of teachers: 540 full-time, 617 part-time
Number of students: 8,427

Publications: *Majalah Universitas Sriwijaya* (3 a year), and faculty bulletins.

DEANS

Faculty of Economics: Drs SOEBEDJO
Faculty of Law: M. ABDULLAH
Faculty of Engineering: Ir. I. NAZIR ACHMAD
Faculty of Agriculture: Ir. Z. SYAHRUL
Faculty of Medicine: Dr A. MERDJANI
Faculty of Teacher Training: Drs Z. ABIDIN GAFFAR
Faculty of Education: Drs A. MUIS (acting)

PROFESSORS

HALIM, A., Linguistics
HARDJOWIJONO, G., Paediatrics
MUKTI, H. D., Advanced Management
MUSLIMIN, A., Administrative Law
SOELAIMAN, M., Adat Law

ATTACHED INSTITUTES

Institute of Research: Chair. Ir. BUCHORI RAHMAN.
Institute of Community Service: Chair. Drs DJAKFAR MUROD.
University Planning and Development Board: Chair. Dr A. BAGHOWI BACHAR.

UNIVERSITAS SUMATERA UTARA (University of North Sumatra)

Jl. Dr. T. Mansur No. 9, Campus USU, POB 641, Medan 20155
Telephone: (61) 814210
Telex: 51753
Fax: (61) 811633

Founded 1957
State control
Language of instruction: Indonesian
Academic year: August to July

Rector: Prof. CHAIRUDDIN P. LUBIS
Vice-Rector (Academic Affairs): Dr Ir. A. FAIZ ALBAR
Vice-Rector (Administrative Affairs): Dr LUHUR SOEROSO
Vice-Rector (Student Affairs): Ir ISMAN NURIADI
Vice-Rector (Information, Planning, Co-operation and Foreign Affairs): Drs SOBAT SEMBIRING
Librarian: Drs A. RIDWAN SIREGAR

Number of teachers: 1,795
Number of students: 19,887

DEANS

Faculty of Medicine: Dr SUTOMO KASIMAN
Faculty of Dentistry: Drg SORIMUDA HARAHAP
Faculty of Agriculture: Ir. T. MARZUKI YACOB
Faculty of Engineering: Ir. RACHMAN SIREGAR
Faculty of Mathematics and Sciences: Drs YUSRAN
Faculty of Economics: Prof. Dr AMRIN FAUZI
Faculty of Law: REHNGENA PURBA
Faculty of Letters: Drs A. SAMIN SIREGAR
Faculty of Political and Social Science: Drs AMRU NASUTION
Faculty of Public Health: Dr ACHSAN HARAHAP
Polytechnic Faculty: Ir. PINTORO WIRJODIHARDJO

ATTACHED INSTITUTES

Institution of Research: Dir Prof. Dr HSR. PARLINDUNGAN SINAGA.
Institution of Community Service: Dir Dr DARWIN DALIMUNTHE.

UNIVERSITAS SYIAH KUALA

Jl. Darussalam, Banda Aceh 23111
Telephone and Fax: (651) 52721

Founded 1961
State control
Language of instruction: Indonesian
Academic year: August to June

Rector: Prof. Dr DAYAN DAWOOD
Vice-Rector for Academic Affairs: Dr ABDI A. WAHAB
Vice-Rector for Financial Affairs: Drs FACHRURRAZI ZAMZAMI
Vice-Rector for Student Affairs: Drs HAIDAR PANJI INDRA
Vice-Rector for Co-operation Affairs: Prof. Drs UTJU ALI BASYAH
Chief Academic Administrative Officer: Drs ABDUL GANI HANAFIAH
Chief Administrative Officer: Drs MOHD YACOB YUSUF
Librarian: Drs DAMRIN LUBIS

Number of teachers: 1,095
Number of students: 11,068

Publications: *Warta Unsyiah, Mon Mata* (3 a year).

DEANS

Faculty of Economics: Dr CHAIRUL ICHSAN
Faculty of Law: Dr AMIRUDDIN A. WAHAB
Faculty of Veterinary Science: Dr DJEMAAT MANAN
Faculty of Agriculture: Ir. M. JAMIL ALI
Faculty of Engineering: Ir. THANTAWI JAUHARI
Faculty of Teacher Training and Education: Drs MUHAMMAD IBRAHIM
Faculty of Medicine: Dr T. MAKMUR MOHD. ZEIN
Faculty of Mathematical and Natural Sciences: Dr A. DAMHOERI

UNIVERSITAS TADULAKO

Kampus Bumi Tadulako Tondo, Palu, Sulawesi
Telephone: 22611

Founded 1981

Rector: Prof. Dr H. MUSJI AMAL PAGILING
Vice-Rectors: Prof. Drs H. AMINUDDIN PONULELE (Academic Affairs), Prof. Dra NURHAYATI NAINGGOLAN (Administration and Finance), BUSTAMIN NONGTJI (Student and Alumni Affairs)
Head of General Administration Bureau: RAFIGA PONULELE
Librarian: Drs MUH. ASRI HENTE

Library of 30,042 vols
Number of teachers: 660
Number of students: 6,500

DEANS

Faculty of Teacher Training: Drs H. A. GHANI HALI
Faculty of Political Sciences: Drs M. RASYID
Faculty of Law: A. RAHMAN BADONG
Faculty of Economics: THAHA ALDJUFRI
Faculty of Agricultural Sciences: Ir. MASRIL BUSTAMI
Diploma Programme for Technical Sciences: Ir. T. A. M. TILAAR

UNIVERSITAS TANJUNGPURA

Jl. Jenderal Achmad Yani, POB 1049, Pontianak 78124

Telephone: (561) 36439
Fax: (561) 39636

Founded 1959
Language of instruction: Indonesian
Academic year: begins September

Chancellor: Prof. MAHMUD AKIL
First Vice-Chancellor: Prof. Dr HENDRO S. SUDAGUNG
Registrar: RADJALI HADIMASPUTRA
Head of General Administration Bureau: MAYARANA RANITA
Librarian: SUTARMIN

Number of teachers: 734
Number of students: 9,305

DEANS

Faculty of Law: Prof. ANWAR SALEH
Faculty of Social and Political Sciences: Prof. Dr Sy. IBRAHIM ALKADRIE
Faculty of Engineering: Ir. Hj. PONY SEDYANINGSIH
Faculty of Economics: ASNIAR SUBAGYO
Faculty of Agriculture: Prof. Ir. ALAMSYAH
Faculty of Teaching and Education: Prof. Drs JAWADI HASID

HEADS OF DEPARTMENTS

Civil Law: Ny. WIWI WIDARSIH KARSUM
Criminal Law: SAMPUR DONGAN SIMAMORA
State Law: MASLEH M. YAMAN
State Administration Science: Drs BACHTIAR
Sociology: Dra ROHANI YAHYA
Civil Engineering: Ir. HERRY SANTOSO
Electrical Engineering: Ir. DASRIL
Management: EVI ASMAYADI
Economics and Developmental Study: ZAINAL SYAMSU
Forestry: Dr HERUYONO HADISUPARTO
Agriculture: Ir. SURYADI ALIMIN
Language and Arts Teaching: Drs SUKAMTO
Educational Science: Dra H. SUTIAH ANY ADWAN
Social Studies Teaching: Drs BACHTIAR A. WAHAB

UNIVERSITAS TERBUKA
(Indonesian Open Learning University)

Jl. Cabe Raya, Pondok Cabe, Ciputat Tangerang 15418, POB 6666, Jakarta 10001

Telephone: (21) 7490941
Fax: (21) 7490147
E-mail: info@p2m.ut.ac.id

Founded 1984
State control

President: Prof. Dr Ir. BAMBANG SUTJIATMO
Registrar: Drs AHMAD RASYAD
Librarian: Drs EFFENDI WAHYONO

Library of 25,000 vols
Number of teachers: 766
Number of students: 397,552

Publications: *Journal of Indonesian Studies* (2 a year), *Komunika* (4 a year), *Suara Terbuka* (monthly).

DEANS

Faculty of Economics: Prof. Dr NURIMANSYAH HASIBUAN
Faculty of Education: Drs UDIN S. WINATAPUTRA
Faculty of Mathematics and Natural Science: Dr DJATI KERAMI
Faculty of Social and Political Science: Dra NURBAEDAH DAHLAN

INSTITUT SENI INDONESIA YOGYAKARTA
(Indonesia Institute of the Arts Yogyakarta)

Jl. Parangtritis Km 6, 5, POB 210, Yogyakarta

Telephone: (274) 71233

Founded 1984; university status
Language of instruction: Indonesian

Rector: Prof. Dr R. M. SOEDARSONO
Vice-Rectors: VICTOR GANAP (Academic Affairs), Y. SUMANDIYO HADI (Administrative Affairs), Drs. NARNO S. (Student Affairs)
Registrar: VICTOR GANAP
Librarian: Dra SITI KOLIMAH SUBALIDINATA

Library of 12,238 vols
Number of teachers: 219
Number of students: 2,200

DEANS

Faculty of Performing Arts: BEN SUHARTO
Faculty of Fine Arts: Drs SUN ARDI
Faculty of Art of Recorded Media: Drs RISMAN MARAH

HEADS OF DEPARTMENT

Faculty of Performing Arts:
- Dance: I. WAYAN DANA
- Traditional Music: DJOKO MADUWIYOTO
- Western Music: Drs SURYANTO WIJAYA
- Drama: Drs SOEPRAPTO SOEDJONO
- Ethnomusicology: I. WAYAN SENEN
- Puppetry: Drs MARSONO

Faculty of Fine Arts:
- Fine Art: Drs BAMBANG DWIANTORO
- Crafts: Drs SUPRIASWOTO
- Design: Drs B. SUPARTO

INSTITUT TEKNOLOGI SEPULUH NOPEMBER
(Tenth of November Institute of Technology)

POB 900/SB, Surabaya 60008, East Java; located at: Kampus ITS, Sukolilo, Surabaya 60111, East Java

Telephone: (31) 5947274
Fax: (31) 5947845
E-mail: massan@indo.net.id

Founded 1960
State control
Language of instruction: Indonesian
Academic year: September to June

Rector: Prof. SOEGIONO
Vice-Rector for Academic Affairs: Dr SOEPENO DJANALI
Vice-Rector for Administration: Ir. MOESDARJONO SOETOJO
Vice-Rector for Student Affairs: SOEMARTOJO
Vice-Rector for Co-operation: Dr MAS SANTOSA
Head of the Academic Administration and Student Affairs Bureau: Drs LUKMAN SULAIMAN
Head of the General Administration and Finance Bureau: Dra SUBAIDAH
Librarian: Drs ACHMAD

Library of 93,200 vols
Number of teachers: 730
Number of students: 10,282

Publications: *Berita ITS, Iptek,* various faculty bulletins.

DEANS

Faculty of Civil Engineering and Planning: Ir. NADJADJI ANWAR
Faculty of Mathematics and Sciences: Drs HASTO SUNARNO
Faculty of Industrial Technology: Ir. SRITOMO WIGNYOSUBROTO
Faculty of Ocean Engineering: DIGUL SISWANTO

DIRECTORS

Research Institute: Prof. Ir. DJATI NURSUHUD
Public Service Institute: Prof. Ir. A. BACHTIR
Polytechnic of Ship Building: Ir. SUGIANTO
Polytechnic of Electronics: Dr Ir. MOHAMMAD NUH

PROFESSORS

BAKTIR, A., Chemical Engineering
DJOERIAMAN, O., Chemical Engineering
KUSTALAM, P., Transport Engineering
NURSUHUD D., Mechanical Engineering
PURWONO, R., Structural Engineering
RACHIMOELLAH, M., Chemistry
SILAS, J., Architecture
SOEGIONO, Naval Architecture
SOEWARNO, J., Chemical Engineering
SUKARDJONO, S., Electrical Engineering
SUTRISNO, H., Electrical Engineering
WAHYU WINATA, S., Physics
ZAKI, M., Physics

UNIVERSITAS UDAYANA

Universitas Udayana, Bukit Jimbaran, Badung 80361, Bali

Telephone: (361) 701139
Fax: (361) 701907
E-mail: rektorunud@denpasar.wasantara.net.id

Founded 1962
State control
Language of instruction: Indonesian

Rector: Prof. Dr I. KETUT SUKARDIKA
Deputy Rector for Academic Affairs: Prof. Dr I. KETUT NEHEN
Deputy Rector for Administrative Affairs: Prof. Dr IDA BAGUS TJITARSA
Deputy Rector for Student Affairs: Prof. Dr Ir. I. GEDE SUYATNA
Librarian: Drs I. GUSTI NYOMAN TIRTAYASA

Number of teachers: 1,702
Number of students: 10,853

Publications: *Majalah Ilmiah Universitas Udayana* (4 a year), *Majalah Kedokteran Unud* (4 a year), *Berita Udayana* (monthly).

DEANS

Faculty of Letters (Arts): Drs A. A. BAGUS WIRAWAN
Faculty of Medicine: Prof. Dr I. KETUT SUATA
Faculty of Animal Husbandry: Prof. I. MADE MASTIKA
Faculty of Law: Prof. Dr DEWA GEDE ATMAJA
Faculty of Engineering: Ir. MADE DANA
Faculty of Economics: Dr KOMANG GEDE BENDESA
Faculty of Agriculture: Dr Ir. NYOMAN SUTJIPTA
Faculty of Sciences: Ir. I. DPP. SASTRAWAN
Faculty of Veterinary Science: Dr Drh. NYOMAN SADRA DHARMAWAN

PROFESSORS

ADIPUTRA, N., Occupational Health
ARDANA, G. G., History
ARDIKA, W., Archaeology
ARGA, Agricultural Economics
ARHYA, N., Biochemistry
ARKA, B., Veterinary Science
ARYANTA, W. R., Food Microbiology
ASTININGSIH, K., Poultry Production
ASTITI, T I. P., Custom Law
ATMAJA, D. G., Law
BAGUS, G. N., Social Anthropology
BAGUS, G. N., Indonesian Language
BAKTA, M., Internal Medicine
BAWA, W., Indonesian Language
BHINAWA, N., Animal Production
BUDHA, K., Surgery
BUNGAYA, G., Management

DJAGRA, I. B., Animal Production
KALAM, A. A. R., Arts and Design
LANA, K., Animal Nutrition
LANANG, O., Genetics
MANIK, G., Animal Husbandry
MANUABA, I. B. A., Human Physiology
MARDANI, N. K., Biology (Environmental Studies)
MASTIKA, M., Animal Nutrition
MATRAM, R. B., Veterinary Physiology
NALA, G. N., Human Physiology
NEHEN, K., Economic Development
NETRA SUBADIYASA, N., Soil Science
NITIS, M., Animal Nutrition
OKA, I. B., Pharmacology
PANGKAHILA, J. A., Sexology
PUTHERA, G. A. G., Human Histology
PUTRA, D. K. H., Animal Physiology
RATA, I. B., Archaeology
RIKA, K., Forage Science
SAIDI, H. S., Islamology
SIRTA, N., Custom Law
SOEWIGIONO, S., Gastroenterology
SUARNA, I. M., Forage Science
SUATA, I. K., Microbiology
SUDHARTA, T. R., Sanskrit Language
SUDJATHA, W., Food and Technology
SUKARDI, E., Human Anatomy
SUKARDIKA, K., Microbiology
SURAATMAJA, S., Paediatrics
SURYADHI, N. T., Public Health
SUTAWAN, N., Social and Agricultural Economics
SUTER, K., Food Technology
SUTHA, G. K., Law
SUTJIPTA, N., Social and Agricultural Economics
SUWETA, G. P., Veterinary Science
SUYATNA, G., Social Economics
TJITARSA, I. B., Public Health
WIDNYANA, M., Law
WINAYA, P. D., Soil Fertility
WIRAWAN, D. N., Public Health
WITA, W., Cardiology

CHAIRMEN OF STUDY PROGRAMMES

Veterinary Science: Drh I GUSTI MADE GEDE
Tourism: Drs MADE SUKARSA
Fine Arts and Design: Drs NYOMAN SUKAYA
Agricultural Technology: Prof. I. WAYAN REDI ARYANTA

Private Universities

UNIVERSITAS 17 AGUSTUS 1945

Jl. Teuku Cik Ditiro 46, Jakarta
Telephone: 343901

Founded 1962
Language of instruction: Indonesian

Rector: Dr SADJARWO
Vice-Rectors: Dr THOMAS N. PEEA (Academic Affairs), Dr CHRISTOFFEL S. (Administrative Affairs), Dr DJOKOPITOJO (Student Affairs)

Number of teachers: 224
Number of students: 5,000
Publication: *Untag Induk Bulletin.*

DEANS

Faculty of Business and Public Administration: Dr BAMBANG HARIANTO
Faculty of Law: Dr KARYOSO
Faculty of Political and Social Sciences: Dr KUSLING ALIMIN
Faculty of Technology: Ir. SARBINI
Faculty of Pharmacy: Drs Apt. SIRAD ADMODJO
Faculty of Economics: KARNA RADJASA

UNIVERSITAS HKBP NOMMENSEN

Jl. Sutomo 4A, POB 1133, Medan
Telephone: 522922
Fax: 511426

Founded 1954
Private control: Batak Protestant Church (HKBP)
Language of instruction: Indonesian
Academic year: September to July

Rector: FIRMAN P. A. SIREGAR
Vice-Rector (Academic Affairs): Ir. HOTMAN MANURUNG
Vice-Rector (Financial Affairs): Dr Ir. PARULIAN SIMANJUNAK
Vice-Rector (Student Affairs): Ir. RICKSON SIMARMATA
Director of Community Service: Ir. MARINGAN SIREGAR
Director of Research: Ir. B. TAMPUBOLON

Number of teachers: 205 (permanent), 255 (part-time)
Number of students: 10,500

Publications: *Warta Nommensen* (students' bulletin), *VISI* (scientific magazine).

DEANS

Faculty of Economics: Dra JULIANA L. TOBING
Faculty of Public and Business Administration: Drs MARULI PANGGABEAN
Faculty of Engineering: Ir. PAIMA SIMBOLON
Faculty of Law: REGINA HUTABARAT
Faculty of Animal Husbandry: Ir. HENRI HUTABARAT
Faculty of Agriculture: Dr BINNEN SARAGIH
Faculty of Education: Drs P. H. SIMAREMARE
Faculty of Arts: Drs BEN M. PASARIBU

UNIVERSITAS IBN KHALDUN

Jl. Pemuda, Kav. 97, POB 1224, Rawamangun, Jakarta, Timur 13220
Telephone and Fax: (21) 4702564

Founded 1956
Languages of instruction: Indonesian, English and Arabic

Rector: Prof. Drs H. AMURA
Vice-Rectors: Drs TWK. ABBAS ABDULLAH, MUHSIN SOLEMAN, Drs H.M. ZIDNI NURI
Registrar: Drs M. UMAR BAAY
Librarian: Drs H. AIDIL FITRI M. HATTA

Number of teachers: 115
Number of students: 3,000
Publication: *Media UIC.*

DEANS

Faculty of Communication: Drs HAMID SUCHAS
Faculty of Social and Political Science: (vacant)
Faculty of Law: ZULFATLI
Faculty of Economics: Ir. DJADID ASSEGAF
Faculty of Theology: ABD. KHALIK NUR ALI
Faculty of Agriculture: Ir. WASIS GUNADI
Institute of Islamic Mass Communication: Drs H. MOH. ALI
Institute of Social Research: Ir. RUSLI DJOHAN

UNIVERSITAS IBN KHALDUN BOGOR

Jl. Martadinata 4, POB 172, Bogor 16162
Telephone and fax: (251) 321112

Founded 1961
Private control
Language of instruction: Indonesian

Chancellor: K. H. DADUN A. QOHHAR
Rector: H. CHAERUDDIN A. NAWAWI
Head of Academic Administration: Drs PARNO SISWANTO
Head of General Administration: Drs DJAMIRUDDIN
Librarian: TATI TARSITI

Number of teachers: 300
Number of students: 3,000

DEANS

Faculty of Education: Drs T. ABDUL MADJID
Faculty of Economics: Drs H. SYAMSU YUSUF
Faculty of Law: MUHYAR NUGRAHA
Faculty of Islamic Studies: Drs KH. DIDIN HAFIDUDDIN
Faculty of Technology: Ir. YOYO TACHYA

UNIVERSITAS ISLAM INDONESIA
(Islamic University of Indonesia)

Jl. Cik Ditiro 1, POB 56, Yogyakarta 55223, Java
Telephone: (274) 513091
Fax: (274) 563207

Founded 1945
An independent and private Islamic university
Language of instruction: Indonesian
Academic year: July to June

Rector: Prof. H. ZAINI DAHLAN
Vice-Rector (Academic Affairs): Dr H. MOCH. MAHFUD
Vice-Rector (Administrative and Financial Affairs): Drs H. SUPARDI
Vice-Rector (Student Affairs): Ir. H. HARSOYO
Chief Administrative Officer: Alhaj MOH. FACHRUR ROZI
Librarian: Ir. M. SIGIT

Library of 73,000 vols
Number of teachers: 630
Number of students: 11,762

Publications: *Himmah* (every 2 months), *Unisia* (Science Quarterly), *Warta Kampus* (Campus News).

DEANS

Faculty of Economics: Drs H. KUMALA HADI
Faculty of Law: Hj. MURYATI MARZUKI
Faculty of Civil Engineering and Planning: Ir. SUSASTRAWAN
Faculty of Islamic Law: Drs M. ARSYAD KUSASY
Faculty of Islamic Education: Drs HUJAIR A. H. SANAKY
Faculty of Industrial Technology: Dr H. SUHARNO RUSDI
Faculty of Psychology: Dr H. DJAMALUDDIN ANCOK
Faculty of Mathematics and Science: Dr H. SURHARNO RUSDI

HEADS OF DEPARTMENT

Centre for Research: H. E. ZAINAL ABIDIN
Centre for Computerization and Statistics: Ir. A. KADIR ABOE
Centre for Public Service: Drs H. AMIR MUALIM
Centre for Islamic Guidance and Development: Drs H. DARWIN HARSONO
Language Centre: Dr H. MOCH. MAHFUD

PROFESSORS

AHMAD ANTONO, Concrete Structures
ASYMUNI, H., Islamic Court
ATMADJA, M. K., International Law
BAHARUDDIN LOPA, Criminal Law
BERNADIB, S. I., Methods of Educational Evaluation, Educational Philosophy
CHOTIB, H. A., Ushl al-Fiqh
DAHLAN, H. Z., Principles of Islamic Law
FATKHURRAHMAN, History of Islam and Islamic Law
HADITONO, S. R., Individual Psychology
HARDJOSO, R., Irrigation
HASAN POERBOHADIWIDJAJA, Environmental Planning
KOESNOE, H. M., Private Procedural Law
KUSNADI HARDJOSUMANTRI, Environment Law
MOCHTAR YAHYA, H., General Philosophy
MUH ZEIN, Method and Evaluation of Islamic Education
MULADI, Politics of Law
PARLINDUNGAN, A. P., Agrarian Law
PARTADIREDJA, H. A., Indonesian Economy
PRAGNYONO, R., Fluid Mechanics
PURNOMO, B., Criminal Law
RIYANTO, B., Development Economy
SATJIPTO RAHARDJO, Sociology of Law
SITI RAHAYU, Psychology

SOEDIKNO MERTOKOESOEMO, Civil Law, Jurisprudence
SOEDIRDJO, Educational Counselling, Curriculum Advancement
SOEKANTO, Business Policy
SOELISTYO, International Economy
SOEPARNO, Analytical Geometry
SRI SUMANTRI, Constitutional Law
SUNARDJO, R., Irrigation Technology
SUYUTI, H. Z., Statistics
SYACHRAN BASAH, Administrative Law
SYAFI'I MA'ARIF, A., Islamic Cultural History
TUGIMAN, N., Indonesian Language
UMAR, H. M., Modern Islamic Ideology
UMAR ASSASUDDIN, English
WARSITO, Polymer Chemistry
YUSUF, H. H., Hadits I, II, III

UNIVERSITAS ISLAM INDONESIA CIREBON
(Islamic University of Indonesia in Cirebon)

Jl. Kapten Samadikun 31, Cirebon
President: SA'DILLAH FATHONI
Secretary: M. Z. ABIDIEN

DEANS
Faculty of Law: S. PRAWIRO
Faculty of Economics: Drs ROSYADI
Faculty of Theology: H. MAS'OED

UNIVERSITAS ISLAM JAKARTA

Jl. Prof. Muh. Yamin 57, Jakarta
Telephone: 45286
Founded 1951
President: Prof. Dr SOEMEDI
Rector: SOEDJONO HARDJOSOEDIRO
Registrar: RASJIDI OESMAN
Librarian: ZAINAL ABIDIN
Number of teachers: 34
Number of students: 309

DEANS
Faculty of Law and Social Sciences: Drs H. NAZARUDIN
Faculty of Economics: TAHER IBRAHIM
Faculty of Education: H. M. NUR ASJIK

UNIVERSITAS ISLAM NUSANTARA

Jl. Soekarno-Hatta 530, POB 1579, Bandung 40286
Telephone and fax: (22) 764143
E-mail: sanusi@bm.net
Founded 1959 as Universitas Nahdlatul Ulama; present name 1976
Academic year: August to July
Chancellor: Mayjen H. ACHMAD RUSTANDI
Rector: Ir. H. KUSMAN KUSUMANEGARA
Deputy Rectors: ERFANTO SANAF (Academic Affairs), TONNY LEGIMAN (Personnel and Finance), Drs H. SYARIF MUHAMMAD (Student Affairs)
Registrar: Drs BARNAS
Librarian: Drs UNDANG SUDAR SANA
Number of teachers: 402
Number of students: 6,574
Publications: *Suara UNINUS* (4 a year), *Literat* (4 a year).

DEANS
Faculty of Law: Prof. H. R. E. DJAELANI
Faculty of Economics: Prof. Dr SURACHMAN SUMAWIHARDJA
Faculty of Education: Drs H. MAHMUDIN
Faculty of Literature: Drs SUHENDRA YUSUF
Faculty of Engineering: Ir. BUDI SETIAWAN
Faculty of Agriculture: Ir. USMAN DAHLAN
Faculty of Communication Sciences: Drs SUMARNO
Faculty of Islamology: K. H. SALIMUDDIN

PROFESSORS
Faculty of Law:
BASYAH, S., Public Administration Law
RASYIDI, L., Family Law
SANUSI, H. A., Law, Public Administration and Education

Faculty of Economics:
SURACHMAN, H., Management Economics

Faculty of Education:
EFFENDY, E. R., Mathematics
ENGKOSWARA, Curriculum Development and Methodology
FAISAL, Y. A., Indonesian Literature
SLAMET, H. A., Indonesian Language
SOEHARTO, B., Non-Formal Education

Faculty of Literature:
EMUH, Arabic
RUSYANA, Y., Indonesian Literature

Faculty of Engineering:
HANDALI, D., Mathematics

Faculty of Agriculture:
AISYAH, H., Pedology

Faculty of Communication Sciences:
EFFENDI, O. U., Communications Sciences

Faculty of Islamology:
DJATNIKA, H. R., Islamology
HELMY, H., Islamology
MUSSADDAD, A., Islamology

UNIVERSITAS ISLAM RIAU
(Islamic University of Riau)

Jl. Raya Teratak Buluh Km. 11, Perhentian, Marpoyan, Pekanbaru, Riau
Telephone: 33664
Founded 1962
Rector: Dr Ir. TENGKU DAHRIL
Vice-Rector for Academic Affairs: H. A. KADIR ABAS
Vice-Rector for Student Affairs: Drs AMBIAR BOER
Librarian: FIRDAUS
Library of 5,150 vols
Number of teachers: 87 full-time, 500 part-time
Number of students: 7,391

DEANS
Faculty of Islamic Theology: Drs S. MUCHTARUDDIN
Faculty of Law: SH. RAMLI ZEIN
Faculty of Engineering: Ir. ANWAR KHATIB
Faculty of Agriculture: Dr Ir. TENGKU DAHRIL
Faculty of Economics: Drs YULIFAR
Faculty of Political and Sociological Sciences: Drs ALI MANDAN
Faculty of Education: Drs UU HAMIDY
Faculty of Medicine: Dr KUSMEDI

HEADS OF DEPARTMENT
Faculty of Islamic Theology:
Islamic Aqidah and Philosophy: Drs MAWARDI AHMAD

Faculty of Law:
Civil Law: SUNIMAR MARBUN
Criminal Law: YULIDA ARYANTI
State Law: H. SYAFRINALDI

Faculty of Engineering:
Civil Engineering: Ir. ABDUL KUDUS
Petroleum Engineering: Ir. OON SYAHRONI
Mechanical Engineering: Ir. N. PERANGIN ANGIN

Faculty of Agriculture:
Agronomy: Ir. ZULKIFLI
Aquaculture: Ir. T. ISKANDAR JOHAN
Agricultural Economics: Drs Ir. ILMI SENAWAN

Faculty of Economics:
Management: Dra EKA NURAINI RAHMAWATI
Economic Development Study: Drs ARMIS
Accounting: Dra ENY WAHYUNINGSIH
Co-operation: Drs SYAHDANUR

Faculty of Social Sciences and Politics:
Government Sciences: Drs AZAM AWANG
Public and Business Administration: Drs A. TARMIZI

Faculty of Education:
Administration of Education: Drs H. ARIFIN
Indonesian Teaching: Drs NAZIRUN
English Teaching: Dra SYOFIANIS
Biology Teaching: Dra SURYANTI
Mathematics and Physics Teaching: Dra Hj. HANIFAH BOER

Faculty of Medicine:
General Medicine: Dr H. TABRANI RAB

ATTACHED INSTITUTES
Centre for Rural Development Studies: Perhentian Marpoyan, Pekenbaru, Riau; Dir Ir. T. ISKANDAR JOHAN.

Management Development Centre: c/o Faculty of Economics, Perhentian Marpoyan, Pekanbaru, Riau; Dir Drs YULIFAR.

Centre for South-East Asian Studies (ASEAN): Jl. Teratai No. 23, Pekanbaru, Riau; Dir Drs SUTAN BALIA.

Legal Aid Institution: Jl. Teratai No. 27, Pekanbaru, Riau; Dir SH. RAMLI ZEIN.

Institute for Social Services: Jl. Prof. M. Yamin SH No. 69, Pekanbaru, Riau; Dir Drs ALI IMRAN.

Institute for Research: Jl. Perhentian Marpoyan, Pekanbaru, Riau; Dir Dr MUCHTAR AHMAD.

UNIVERSITAS ISLAM SUMATERA UTARA
(Islamic University of North Sumatra)

Campus Munawarah, Teladan, Medan 20217, Sumatra
Telephone and fax: (61) 716790
Founded 1952
Private control
Language of instruction: Indonesian
Academic year: July to June
Chancellor: Brig.-Gen. (retd) H. A. MANAF LUBIS
Rector: Drs H. M. YAMIN LUBIS
Registrar: Drs ABDUL HAKIM SIREGAR
Librarian: Drs SUDIAR SUDARGO
Number of teachers: 808
Number of students: 10,000
Publications: *Al Jamiah-UISU* (3 a year), *Buletin Fakultas Pertanian* (quarterly), *Buletin Fakultas Hukum* (6 a year).

DEANS
Faculty of Law: AMRIZAL PULUNGAN
Faculty of Islamic Law: Drs SAID ALHINDUAN
Faculty of Economics: Drs AHMAD GHAZALI
Faculty of Education and Teaching: Drs H. ADLIN AHMAD
Faculty of English: Drs MISRAN SUDIONO
Faculty of Islamic Education: H. MAHMUD AZIZ SIREGAR
Faculty of Islamic Communication: Drs MUSTAFA KAMIL
Faculty of Political Science: Drs DANAN JAYA
Faculty of Agriculture: Ir. MEIZAL
Faculty of Medicine: Prof. Dr H. HABIBAH HANUM NASUTION
Faculty of Engineering: Ir. H. M. ICHWAN NASUTION

UNIVERSITAS JAYABAYA

Jl. Jenderal A. Yani By-Pass, Jakarta
Telephone 414904

Founded 1958

Rector: Dr H. MOESLIM TAHER
Executive Rector: Drs M. O. TAMBUNAN
Registrar: R. AZHARI A. KUSUMAHBRATA
Vice-Rector for Academic Affairs: MOH. SOEDJIMAN
Vice-Rector for Administration: Drs W. SILALAHI
Vice-Rector for Students: RAZAINI D.

Number of teachers: 782
Number of students: 15,000

DEANS

Faculty of Law: Dr MAS SUBAGIO
Faculty of Economics: Drs RACHMAT
Faculty of Social Sciences: Dr BUCHARI ZAINUN
Faculty of Technology: Ir. PURWOKO HADI

ATTACHED RESEARCH INSTITUTES

Research and Development Institute: Dir Drs M. O. TAMBUNAN.
Business Research and Development: Dir CHALID ISMAIL.
Law Research and Legal Aid Bureau: Dir Mrs IDA.
Business Administration Aid Bureau: Dir Drs SUTRISNO.

UNIVERSITAS KATOLIK INDONESIA ATMA JAYA

POB 2639 Jakarta 10001, Jl. Jendral Sudirman 51, Jakarta 12930

Telephone: (21) 5703306
Fax: (21) 5708811

Founded 1960
Language of instruction: Indonesian

Chairman of Board: Prof. Dr HARIMURTI KRIDALAKSANA
Rector: THOMAS SUYATNO
Vice-Rectors: Prof. Dr Dr H. H. B. MAILANGKAY (Academic Affairs), Dra MARGARETHA SUMARYATI (Administration and Finance), Drs YOHANES TEMALURU (Student and Alumni Affairs), Dra M. B. WIDYARTO (Development and Co-operation)
Librarian: Drg ELLY WIRIAWAN

Library of 37,000 vols
Number of teachers: 802
Number of students: 11,353

DEANS

Faculty of Economics: S. E. WIDODO
Faculty of Business Administration: Dr A. AGUS NUGROHO
Faculty of Education: Dra GERDA K. WANEI
Faculty of Technology: Dr Ir. YOSEPH SEDYONO
Faculty of Law: DJOKO SUDYATMIKO
Faculty of Medicine: Dr LILIANA SUGIHARTO
Faculty of Psychology: Prof. Dr SUDIRGO WIBOWO
Graduate School: Prof. Dr B. S. MULJANA (Dir)

ATTACHED CENTRES

Centre for Studies in Societal Development: Dir Dr. IRWANTO
Centre for Studies in Culture and Lanaguage: Dir Prof. Dr SOENJONO D.
Centre for the Development of Ethics: Dir Drs ANDRE ATA UJAN
Centre for Health Research: Dir Drg YVONE SUSY HANDAYANI
Centre for Langage Teaching: Dir Dra VONNY DJIWAMDONO
Centre for Human Resources Development: Dir Drs FRANS SISU ODJAN
Centre for the Development of Integrated Small Business: Dir Ir. C. SRI WIDAYATI

UNIVERSITAS KATOLIK PARAHYANGAN (Parahyangan Catholic University)

Jl. Ciumbuleuit 94, Bandung 40141

Telephone: (22) 230918
Fax: (22) 231110

Founded 1955
Private control
Language of instruction: Indonesian
Academic year: August to June

Chancellor: Prof. Dr BENNY SUPRAPTO BROTOSISWOJO
Rector: A. P. SUGIARTO
Vice-Rector (Academic Affairs): JOHANNES GUNAWAN
Vice-Rector (Administration): Ir. R. W. TRIWEKO
Vice-Rector (Student Affairs): F. X. BUDI WIDOLO P.
Vice-Rector (Domestic Affairs and International Co-operation): Drs SUGIE J. HAMBALI
Librarian: Dra MELINA L. TARDIA

Number of teachers: full-time 441, part-time 495
Number of students: 10,181

Publications: *Research Journal* (2 a year), *Bina Ekonomi* (4 a year), *Pro Justitia* (4 a year), *Potensia* (4 a year), *Profil, Melintas* (4 a year), *Integral* (4 a year), *Rekasaya* (4 a year).

DEANS

Faculty of Economics: Drs ARTHUR PURBOYO
Faculty of Law: B. ARIEF SIDHARTA
Faculty of Industrial Technology: Prof. Dr. IGN. SUHARTO
Faculty of Social and Political Sciences: ULBERT SILALAHI
Faculty of Philosophy: F. VERMEULEN
Faculty of Engineering: Prof. Dr WIMPY SANTOSA
Faculty of Mathematics and Natural Sciences: Dr A. RUSLI
Graduate School: Dir Prof. Dr JOHN S. NIMPOENO

PROFESSORS

AFFENDY, Y., Art Design
ANSIAR, M., Mathematics
HARTONO, S., Law
KARTODIRJO, A. S., Economics
MOEDOMO, R., Mathematics
NIMPOENO, J. S., Psychology
ON, T. M., Mathematics
SAMPURNO, Mathematics
SOEDJONO, D., Civil Law
SOELARNOSIDJI, D., Geotechnology in Civil Engineering
SUHARTO, IGN., Biotechnology
SUNDJAJA, R. S., Management
SYAFRUDDIN, A., Law
WINARDI, Economics
WIRJOSUDIRDJO, S., Mathematics

ATTACHED INSTITUTE

Research Institute: Dir. Dr MAURO P. RAHARDJO.

UNIVERSITAS KRISNADWIPAJANA

Jl. Tegal 10, Jakarta

Telephone: 51249

Founded 1952
Language of instruction: Indonesian
Academic year: February to December

Chancellor: Prof. R. S. KARTANEGARA
Vice-Chancellor: Brig.-Gen. MOEHONO
Rector: Prof. R. SOEBEKTI
Secretary: S. WIRONEGORO
Registrar: E. DIMONTI
Librarian: Dr DASPAN

Number of teachers: 128
Number of students: 2,000

UNIVERSITAS KRISTEN INDONESIA (Christian University of Indonesia)

Jl. Mayjen Sutoyo, Cawang, Jakarta 13630

Telephone: (21) 8092425

Founded 1953

Rector: Prof. Dr K. TUNGGUL SIRAIT
Vice-Rector for Academic Affairs: Dr A. S. L. RAMPEN
Vice-Rector for Administration Planning and Development: E. GUNAWAN
Vice-Rector for Student Affairs: A. SIREGAR

Number of teachers: 739
Number of students: 7,024

Publications: *UKI Bulletin, Logos, Jurnal Ekonomi, Honeste Vivere, Dialektika, Dinamika Pendidikan, Emas.*

DEANS

Faculty of Education: TOGAP LINANJUNTAK
Faculty of English Language and Literature: Dr L. S. BANGUN
Faculty of Economics: Drs A. ZABUA
Faculty of Law: Dr BERNARD HUTABARAK
Faculty of Medicine: Dr S. M. L. TORUAN
Faculty of Technology: Dr A. SOEBAGIO
Faculty of Social and Political Science: Prof. Dr PAYUNG BANGUN

ATTACHED INSTITUTES

Department of Languages
Department of Legal Aid
Department of Educational Research
Computer Centre
Educational Technology Centre
Centre for Guidance and Counselling
Community Development Centre
Institute of Management

UNIVERSITAS KRISTEN MARANATHA (Maranatha Christian University)

Jl. Suria Sumantri 65, Bandung 40164

Telephone: (22) 2003450
Fax: (22) 215154
E-mail: humas@maranatha.edu

Founded 1965
Language of instruction: Indonesian
Academic year: September to August

President: DANIEL S. WIBOWO
Vice-Presidents: ANITA SUPARTONO (Academic Affairs), L. TEDJARUTJIANTA (Finance and Administration), HENRY HERU LESMANA (Student Affairs)

Number of teachers: 806
Number of students: 5,822

Publications: various bulletins.

DEANS

Faculty of Medicine: SULAIMAN SASTRAWINATA
Faculty of Psychology: SAWITRI SUPARDI
Faculty of Engineering: IBRAHIM SURYA
Faculty of Literature: JUSAK SUPARDJAN
Faculty of Economics: R. SANUSI

HEADS OF DEPARTMENT

Civil Engineering: NOEK SULANDARI
Electrical Engineering: AAN DARMAWAN
Industrial Engineering: IMAM ISTIYANTO
English: TRISNOWATI TANTO
Japanese: ENDAH S. SATARI
Management: TEDY WAHYUSAPUTRA
Accounting: Ec. SODDIN MANGUNSONG

UNIVERSITAS KRISTEN SATYA WACANA (Satya Wacana Christian University)

Jl. Diponegoro 52–60, Salatiga 50711, Central Java

Telephone: (298) 21212
Fax: (298) 21433
E-mail: purek_iv@uksw.ac-id.net

Founded 1956
Languages of instruction: Indonesian and English (for special programmes only)
Academic year: August to July
Rector: Dr JOHN J. O. I. IHALAUW
Deputy Rector for Academic Affairs: Dr KRIS HERMAWAN TIMOTIUS
Deputy Rector for Finance and Administration: HARI SUNARTO
Deputy Rector for Student Affairs: KRISHNA DJAJA NDARUMURTI
Deputy Rector for External Affairs: KONTA INTAN DAMANIK
Registrar: Drs SUMIYARSO
Librarian: DAVID SAMIYONO
Number of teachers: 287 (full-time)
Number of students: 6,000
Publications: *Bulletin Satya Wacana* (weekly), *Gita Kampus* (monthly), *Citra Wacana* (4 a year), *Wacana Newsletter* (4 a year), *Kritis* (4 a year), *Annual Report*.

DEANS

Faculty of Law: SOEWANDI
Faculty of Economics: ROOS KITIES ANDADARI
Faculty of Biology: Drs ADJAR SUBADI
Faculty of Agriculture: Dr Ir. RUKMADI WARSITO
Faculty of Electronic Engineering: SUDIGNO
Faculty of Science and Mathematics: Dr CHR. SUMARGO
Faculty of Theology: DRIE SUTANTYO BROTOSUDARMO
Faculty of Education and Teacher Training: Drs KUSYADI
Postgraduate Programmes: JOHN TITALEY
Professional Programmes: Dra Dra NORA ZAKARIAS

UNIVERSITAS MUHAMMADIJAH

Jl. Limau 1, Keb. Baru, Jakarta
Faculties of education, law, literature, sociology.

UNIVERSITAS MUHAMMADIYAH MALANG
(Muhammadiyah University of Malang)

Jl. Raya Tlogomas km 8, Malang 65144
Telephone: (341) 52318
Fax: (341) 802060
Founded 1966
Language of instruction: Indonesian
Rector: Drs H. A. MALIK FADJAR
Vice-Rector for Academic Affairs: MUHADJIR EFFENDY
Vice-Rector for Financial Affairs: WAKIDI
Vice-Rector for Student Affairs: MOCH. HAMZAH
Vice-Rector for Religious Affairs: ABDULLAH HASYIM
Chief of Public Administration: MANSYUR, M.
Chief of Academic Administration: Drs SHOBARI
Librarian: WAHJOE DWI PRIJONO
Number of teachers: 768
Number of students: 18,278

DEANS

Faculty of Agriculture: ARMAND SUDIYONO
Faculty of Economics: RATIH JUHATI
Faculty of Engineering: MARSUDI
Faculty of Islamic Education: ISHOMUDDIN
Faculty of Law: MUSLAN ABDURRAHMAN
Faculty of Psychology: DIAH KARMIATI
Faculty of Social and Political Science: AHMAD HABIB
Faculty for Teacher Training and Education: DWI PRIYO UTOMO
Faculty of Animal Husbandry: SULTAWI

UNIVERSITAS NASIONAL

Jl. Sawo Manila, Pasar Minggu, Jakarta Selatan
Telephone: 7806700
Fax: 7802719
Founded 1949
Academic year: September to August
Rector: Prof. AHMAD BAIQUAI
Vice-Rectors: BAMBANG PERMADI (Academic Affairs), DJAKARIAH SALEH (Financial and General Administrative Affairs), ROESTAMADJI (Student and Alumni Affairs)
Chief Administrative Officer: Ir. SJAHROEL SJARIF
University Librarian: Drs ROZALI SAID
Number of teachers: 611
Number of students: 5,500
Publication: *Ilmu Dan Budaya* (monthly).

DEANS

Faculty of Social and Political Science: Drs DWISUSANTO
Faculty of Biology: Dra NYOMAN AYU RATMINI
Faculty of Economics: Drs UMAR BASALIM
Faculty of Engineering: Ir. SOEWARNO SOEWARDJO
Faculty of Mathematics and Natural Science: Dr. AHYAR UMRI
Faculty of Letters: Prof. Dr. Y.S. BADUDU
Faculty of Agriculture: Dr Ir. SATTA WIGENASANTANA
Faculty of Law: DAHLAN RANOEWIHARDJO.

UNIVERSITAS PAKUAN

Jl. Pakuan, POB 353, Bogor
Telephone: 26226
Founded 1961
Chancellor: R. SURATNO WIRJOATMODJO
Rector: ACHMAD SUBROTO
Secretary: R. H. NATANEGARA
Number of teachers: 60
Number of students: 350

DEANS

Faculty of Law: ACHMAD SUBROTO
Faculty of Economics: Drs USMAN ZAKARIA

UNIVERSITAS PANCASILA

Srengseng Sawah, Jagakarsa, Jakarta Selatan 12640
Telephone: 7270086
Founded 1966
Language of instruction: Indonesian
Academic year: September to August
Chairman: ACHMAD TAHIR
Rector: Prof. Dr SUBROTO
Vice-Rectors: Prof. Ir. SOEWARDI (Academic Affairs), Drs SEDIA OETOMO (Finance and Administration), LEO SIMANDJUNTAK (Student Affairs), Dra Hj AMIARTI SUGIARTO (Domestic Affairs and Foreign Co-operation)
Registrar: R. SOEGIJONO
Librarian: Dra FERRIAL
Library of 52,000 vols
Number of teachers: 915
Number of students: 11,878
Publications: *Media Humas, Buletin Farmasi, Suara Ekonomi, Retorika, Jurnal FTUP.*

DEANS

Faculty of Pharmacy: Drs M. SOEMITRO
Faculty of Economics: Drs B. D. SURADI
Faculty of Law: KOENARTHO
Faculty of Engineering: Prof. N. SOENARTO

PETRA CHRISTIAN UNIVERSITY

Jl. Siwalankerto 121–131, POB 1991, Surabaya 60238
Telephone: (31) 839040
Fax: (31) 836418
Founded 1961
Private control
Language of instruction: Indonesian
Academic year: September to August
Rector: Drs WASIS
Vice-Rectors:
Academic Affairs: Ir. PAUL NUGRAHA
Finance and Administration: Ir. GUANA TANDJUNG
Student Affairs: Ir. F. JONES SYARANAMUAL
Research, Development and Co-operation: Ir. TAKIM ANDRIONO
Registrar: Dra WIDIARTI SUPRAPTO
Librarian: ARLINAH IMAM RAHARDJO
Library of 49,420 vols
Number of teachers: 356 (155 full-time)
Number of students: 7,784
Publications: *Dimensi* (scientific magazine, quarterly), *Dwi Pekan* (newsletter, fortnightly).

DEANS

Faculty of Letters: Dra J. DJUNDJUNG
Faculty of Engineering: Ir. M. I. ADITJIPTO
Faculty of Business Management: Dra M. SULASTRI

ATTACHED INSTITUTE

English Language Institute: Dir Dra DIANAWATI SUTOMO.

UNIVERSITAS TRISAKTI

Jl. Kyai Tapa, Grogol, Jakarta 11440
Telephone: (21) 5663232
Fax: (21) 5673001
Founded 1965
Language of instruction: Indonesian
Academic year: September to August
Rector: Prof. Dr R. MOEDANTON MOERTEDJO
Vice-Rectors: Ir. SEMIAWAN (Academic Affairs), Drs H. YUSWAR Z. BASRI (Personnel, Administration and Finance), I. KOMANG SUKA'ARSANA (Student Affairs), Ir. N. SUTAN ASSIN (Co-operation and Human Resources)
University Librarian: Dra SURATNI DJAJA
Number of teachers: 2,382
Number of students: 30,590
Publication: *Warta Usakti* (monthly).

DEANS

Faculty of Dentistry: Drg. BAMBANG S. TRENGGONO
Faculty of Medicine: Dr YULIUS E. SURYAWIDJAJA
Faculty of Law: H. ADI ANDOJO SUTJIPTO
Faculty of Economics: Dr CHAIRUMAN ARMIA
Faculty of Civil Engineering and Planning: Ir. SOERJATMO WREKSOATMODJO
Faculty of Industrial Technology: Prof. Dr Ing. H. FARAZ UMAR
Faculty of Landscape Architecture and Environmental Technology: Prof. Dr Ir. SOEPANGAT SOEMARTO
Faculty of Mineral Technology: Ir. ASRI NUGRAHANTI IRDJIANTO
Faculty of Art and Design: Dra J. PAMUDJI SUPTANDAR
Postgraduate Programme: Prof. Dr THOBY MUTIS

HEADS OF DEPARTMENTS

Faculty of Law:
Civil Law: HASNI
Criminal Law: ERIYANTOU WAHID
International Law (Public): G. P. H. HARYO MATARAM

Faculty of Economics:
Management: Dra Hj. NIDJAT IBRAHIM
Accountancy: Drs BAMBANG SUDARYONO
Economics and Developmental Studies: Dra TIKTIK S. PRATOMO

Faculty of Civil Engineering and Planning:
Civil Engineering: Dr Ir. BUDI WIBAWA

Architectural Engineering: Ir. DJOKO SANTOSO

Faculty of Industrial Technology:

Electrical Engineering: Ir. MAULA SUKMAWIDJAJA
Mechanical Engineering: Ir. TRIYONO
Industrial Engineering: Ir. DOCKY SARASWATI
Computer Engineering: Ir. DJASLI DJAMARUS

Faculty of Landscape Architecture and Environmental Technology:

Landscape Architecture: Ir. RUSTAM HAKIM
Environmental Technology: Ir. WIDYO ASTONO
Planning Engineering: Ir. AIDAD A. GAFAR

Faculty of Mineral Technology:

Petroleum Engineering: Ir. SITI NURAINI SIBUEA
Geological Engineering: Ir. HIDARTAN
Mining Engineering: Ir. ATMOSO SOEHOED

Faculty of Art and Design:

Art: Drs UDANARTO
Design: Dra TETTY SEKARYATI

ATTACHED INSTITUTES

Research Institute: Dr Ir. DADAN UMAR DAIHANI.
Institute for Community Service: Ir. ADHY R. THAHIR.

ATTACHED COLLEGES AND ACADEMIES

Academy of Tourism: Dir MARYAM MIHARDJO.
College of Economics: Dir HANDOKO KARYANTORO.
College of Transport Management: Dir H. SJAHRIR SOELAIMAN.
Academy of Insurance: Dir Drs SAFRI AYAT.
Academy of Graphical Engineering: Dir Drs FAREL SITANGGANG.

UNIVERSITAS VETERAN REPUBLIK INDONESIA

Jl. G. Bawakaraeng 72, Ujungpandang
Faculties of history, law and education.

Schools of Art and Music

Sekolah Tinggi Seni Indonesia Surakarta (Ex ASKI Surakarta) (College of Traditional Indonesian Arts): Kampus STSI, Surakarta, Jl. ki Hajar Dewantara 19, Kentingan, Jebres, Surakarta Jawa Tengah 57126; tel. (271) 47658; fax (271) 46175; f. 1964; diploma and master's degree courses; library of 30,000 vols; 181 teachers; 754 students; Dir Dr SRI HASTANTO; Vice Dirs SUMANTO, Dr SUTARNO, I. NYOMAN CHAYA, Drs ACHMAD SUMIYADI; Librarian SULISTYOWATI.

HEADS OF DEPARTMENTS

Music: DJOKO PURWANTO
Puppetry: I. NYOMAN MURTANA
Dance: SUTARNO HARYONO
Fine Arts: Drs SUGENG TOEKIO

Academi Seni Karawitan Indonesia Padang Panjang (Academy for Traditional Music and Dance): Jl. Puti Bungsu 35, Padang Panjang, Sumatera Barat; tel. 77; f. 1966; diploma courses; library of 6,196 vols; 62 teachers; 428 students; Dir Prof. MARDJANI MARTAMIN; Registrar BAHRUL PADEK; Librarian Drs ANNAS HAMIR.

HEADS OF DEPARTMENTS

Traditional Music: Drs DJARUDDIN AMAR
Traditional Dance: NIRWANA MURNI
School Music: DIRWAN WAKIDI

Akademi Seni Tari Indonesia: Jl. Buahbatu 212, Bandung; tel. 421532; f. 1970; degree courses in traditional music and dance; library of *c.* 5,113 vols; *c.* 74 teachers; *c.* 342 students; Dir Drs MA'MUR DANASASMITA; Librarian R. OETJE ROEKMIATI.

HEADS OF DEPARTMENTS

Dance: IYUS RUSLIANA
Traditional Music: TATANG SURYANA
Theatre: YOYO C. DURACHMAN

IRAN

Learned Societies

GENERAL

National Association for Cultural Relations: Ministry of Higher Education and Culture, Bldg No. 3, Taleghani Ave, Teheran; f. 1966 to create facilities in the field of cultural and artistic relations and exchanges; Sec.-Gen. Dr Z. HACOBIAN.

ECONOMICS, LAW AND POLITICS

Iran Management Association: POB 15855-359, Teheran; premises at: Karimkhan Blvd 1/53 corner of Asjodi St, Teheran; tel. (21) 8827878; fax (21) 8835278; f. 1960 to promote sound management principles and techniques for the improvement of management in Iran, and to create understanding and co-operation among managers in Iran and other countries; 1,000 individual and 300 institutional mems; library of 8,000 vols; Sec.-Gen. PARVIZ BAYAT; publ. *Management Magazine* (monthly, in Persian, with summary in English).

HISTORY, GEOGRAPHY AND ARCHAEOLOGY

Ancient Iran Cultural Society, The: Jomhorie Eslamie Ave, Shahrokh St, Teheran; f. 1961; Man. Dir A. QUORESHI.

British Institute of Persian Studies: POB 11365-6844, Khiaban Dr Ali Shariati, Kucheh Alvand, Gholhak, Teheran 19396; f. 1961; cultural institute, with special emphasis on history and archaeology; library of over 10,000 books and MSS; 650 mems; Hon. Sec. Dr ROBERT GLEAVE; publ. *Iran* (annually).

LANGUAGE AND LITERATURE

PEN Club of Iran: 55 Kechvardoust St, Djomhoury Ave, Teheran; tel. 641828; Founder Pres. Z. RAHNAMA; Gen. Sec. Dr S. VAHIDNIA.

MEDICINE

Iranian Society of Microbiology: Department of Microbiology and Immunology, Faculty of Medicine, University of Teheran; f. 1940; 185 mems; Gen. Sec. G. H. NAZARI.

NATURAL SCIENCES

Mathematical Sciences

Iranian Mathematical Society: POB 13145-418, Teheran; f. 1971; mem. of IMU; 2,300 mems; Sec. R. ZAARE–NAHANDI; publs *Bulletin, Mathematical Thought, Newsletter.*

Research Institutes

GENERAL

Institute for Humanities and Cultural Studies (IHCS): 64 St, Seyyed Jamal-eddin Ave, Teheran 14374; tel. 8048037; fax 8036317; f. 1981 by merging 12 cultural research centres; is now the largest research centre in Iran; research faculties: literature, history, history and philosophy of science, religious studies, linguistics, social sciences, cultural studies; 143 full-time researchers; library of 120,000 vols; Dir Prof. MEHDI GOLSHANI; publs *The Farhang* (quarterly), *Journal of Historical Research* (quarterly), *Iran and Central Asia* (annually).

AGRICULTURE, FISHERIES AND VETERINARY SCIENCE

Animal Husbandry Research Institute: POB 31585-1483, Teheran; tel. 22012; f. 1933; research on cattle, water buffalo, sheep, goats, poultry and honey-bees, also animal nutrition and physiology; 181 staff; library of 3,515 vols; Gen. Dir. H. MOGHADAMNIA; publ. *Animal Husbandry Research Institute*, etc.

Plant Pests and Diseases Research Institute: POB 1454, Teheran 19395; f. 1961; research on pests and diseases of agricultural crops; botany, entomology, biological control, pesticides and agricultural zoology; library of 13,000 vols; Dir Dr H. BAYAT ASSADI; publs *Entomologie et Phytopathologie Appliquées* (annually), and publication from Botany Department (irregular).

Razi State Institute: POB 11365-1558, Karadj, Hesarak; tel. (261) 72005; fax (261) 74658; f. 1930; epizootological and ecological studies of animal diseases and human and animal biology; research and preparation of all veterinary vaccines, some human vaccines and therapeutic sera; library of 7,390 vols; Gen. Dir Dr ALI AKBAR MOHAMMADI; publs *Archives of the Razi Institute* (annually in English and French), annual and quarterly reports.

ECONOMICS, LAW AND POLITICS

Institute for Political and International Studies (IPIS): POB 19395/1793, Tajrish, Teheran; tel. (21) 2571010; fax (21) 270964; f. 1983; acts as a research and information centre on international relations, law, economics and Islamic studies, with emphasis on the Middle East, the Persian Gulf and Central Asia; holds conferences and seminars on contemporary international issues; library of 25,000 vols; Pres. ABBAS MALEKI; Dir-Gen. AHMAD HAJIHOSSEINI; publs *Siyasat-e Khariji / Journal of Foreign Policy* (quarterly), *Iranian Journal of International Affairs* (quarterly), *Asyaye Markazi va Ghafghaz* (Central Asia and Caucasia Review (quarterly), *Journal of African Studies* (2 a year).

HISTORY, GEOGRAPHY AND ARCHAEOLOGY

Institut Français de Recherche en Iran: Ave Shahid Nazari, 52 rue Adib, POB 15815-3495, Teheran 13158; tel. (21) 640-11-92; fax (21) 6405501; f. 1897, present name 1983; research into Iranian civilization, contact between French and Iranian scholars; library of 27,000 vols; Dir RÉMY BOUCHARLAT; publs. *Abstracta Iranica* (annually), *Cahiers de la DAFI, Bibliothèque Iranienne.*

Iranian Cultural Heritage Organization: Azadi Ave, Zanjan Int., POB 13445-719, Teheran; tel. 601-7071; fax 601-3498; f. 1986; conservation, promotion and education concerning the cultural heritage of Iran; Pres. SERAJEDDIN KAZEROUNI; publs *Asar Magazine* (quarterly), *Miras-e Farhangi Magazine* (quarterly), *Muzehha Magazine* (quarterly).

National Cartographic Centre: POB 13185-1684, Azadi Sq., Meraj Ave, Teheran; tel. (21) 600-0031; fax (21) 600-1971; f. 1953; library of 4,000 vols, 2,500 reports; Dir Dr M. MADAD; publ. *Journal* (4 a year).

MEDICINE

Institut Pasteur: Pasteur Ave, Teheran; tel. (21) 6469871; fax (21) 6465132; f. 1921; vaccine production, research in microbiology, biochemistry, virology, medicine and epidemiology, teaching and postgraduate training; Dir Dr M. AZARNOUSH.

RELIGION, SOCIOLOGY AND ANTHROPOLOGY

Islamic Research Foundation, Astan Quds Razavi: POB 91735-366, Mashhad; tel. 821033; fax 827081; f. 1984; research into Islamic subjects, Quran, hadith, jurisprudence, scholastic theology, Islamic text editing, translating Islamic books, study of Islamic arts; library of 40,000 vols; Dir ALI AKBAR ELAHI KHORASANI; publ. *Meshkat* (quarterly).

TECHNOLOGY

Electric Power Research Centre: POB 15745–448, Shahrak Ghods, Pounak Bakhtari Blvd, Teheran; tel. (21) 8079401; fax (21) 8094774; e-mail eprc@dci.iran.com; f. 1983; attached to Min. of Energy; library of 12,000 vols, 151 periodicals; Pres. S. M. TABATABAEE; publ. *Journal of Electrical Science and Technology* (quarterly).

Libraries and Archives

Isfahan

Municipal Library: Shahied Nikbakht St, POB 81638, Isfahan; tel. (31) 621200; fax (31) 621100; f. 1991; 60,000 vols.

University of Isfahan Library: Isfahan; 112,150 vols, half in Persian and Arabic, the remainder in European languages; Persian MSS and incunabula; Dir Dr MEHDI JAMSHIDIAN.

Mashhad

Central Library and Documentation Centre of Astan Quds Razavi: POB 91735-177, Mashhad; tel. (51) 836555; fax (51) 20845; dates from *c.* 15th century; general library and assistance for researchers; 927,000 vols and 46,500 MSS; 40,000 vols of foreign books (in 50 languages); 12 br. libraries; Gen. Dir Dr SEYYED ALI ARDALAN JAVAN.

Ferdowsi University of Mashhad Central Library and Documentation Centre: POB 1163-91375, Mashhad; 250,000 vols; Gen. Dir Prof. Dr M. T. EDALATI.

Tabriz

Central Library and Documentation Centre, University of Tabriz: Tabriz; tel. (41) 344705; fax (41) 342199; f. 1967; 93,000 vols; 6,231 microfiches, 2,200 maps, 1,151 microfilms, 2,000 periodicals, 647 tapes; Librarian A. ADINE GHAHRAMANI; publs *New Books* (monthly), catalogue.

Tabriz Public Library (*Ketabkhaneh Melli Tabriz*): Tabriz; 12,816 vols; Dir MAJID FARHANG.

Tarbiat Library: Atesh Neshani Ave, Tabriz; 18,972 vols; Dir ABDOLLAH ABDOLELAHI FARD.

Teheran

Central Library and Documentation Centre of Shahid Beheshti University: Evin, Teheran 19834; tel. 293155; f. 1960; 120,000 vols, 700 periodicals; Librarian ALI AKBAR TORABI-FARD; publs *Tazehaye Ketabkhaneh, Sourat Ketabhaye Fehrest Shodeh*.

Central Library and Documentation Centre of Teheran University: Enghelab Ave, Teheran; f. 1949, re-housed 1970; 650,000 vols (central library), 700,000 vols (faculty libraries); Librarian Dr F. HARIRCHI; various publs.

Central Library and Documentation Centre of the Iran University of Medical Sciences and Health Services: POB 14155-6439, Teheran; tel. (21) 8269196; fax (21) 8278503; f. 1975; 33,000 books, 1,351 current periodicals, 10,000 theses, 3,000 audiovisual titles; Dir Dr MEHRANGIZ HARIRI.

Centre for Socio-Economic Documentation and Publications: Baharestan Sq., Teheran 11365; tel. 3271; telex 212642; fax 301135; f. 1962, reorganized 1982; attached to Planning and Budget Organization; branches in 6 divisions: technical services, information services and network affairs, libraries (Central Library, Archive for Development Maps and Projects and 25 regional libraries), editing, graphics and production, distribution; libraries: 49,000 vols, 576 periodicals, 1,627 titles microforms, 16,000 titles development projects, 18,000 maps and plans, databases of selected articles; Dir MEHDI PAZOUKI; publs *Plan and Budget* (6 a year), *Periodical Index to Socio-Economic Articles* (quarterly), *List of Acquisitions* (monthly), *Informatics Newsletter* (monthly), subject bibliographies and catalogues, technical reports.

Documentation Centre of the Iranian Cultural Heritage Organization: POB 13445-1594, Teheran; tel. (1) 6035293; fax (1) 6014027; f. 1994; 25,000 vols, 14,000 research reports, 1,500 films; 12,000 maps, 150,000 photographs, 15,000 slides, 200 cassettes, 1,000 traditional designs; Head FARIBA FARZAM.

Institute for Political and International Studies Library and Documentation Centre: POB 19395-1793, Tajrish, Teheran; tel. 2571010; telex 212324; f. 1983; attached to the Foreign Ministry; special library and assistance for researchers; 20,000 vols on Islamic science, history, politics, economics, law, geography, diplomacy, military studies; 400 periodicals; Dir A. S. ELAHI; publ. *New Books Review* (monthly).

Iran Bastan Museum Library: Khiaban-e Imam Khomeini, Khiaban-e Sium-e Tir, Teheran 11365; f. 1964; 17,000 vols; Dir M. R. RIYAZI KESHE.

Iran National Archives: Behjatabad, 66 Bahafarin Ave, Teheran 15938; Dir M. ABBASSI.

Iranian Information and Documentation Centre (IRANDOC): POB 13185/1371, Teheran; tel. (21) 6462548; fax (21) 6462254; f. 1968; work in the fields of basic sciences, agriculture, medical sciences, humanities and technology; advises and assists in the establishment of specialized information centres and acts as the national reference centre; part of the Ministry of Culture and Higher Education; library of 33,000 vols, 4,200 periodicals, 34,000 student dissertations; Dir H. GHARIBI; publs *Directory of Scientific Meetings held in Iran* (quarterly), *Current Research in Iranian Universities and Research Centres* (quarterly), *Iranian Dissertation Abstracts* (quarterly), *Abstracts of Scientific/Technical Papers* (quarterly), *Iranian Government Reports* (quarterly), *Dissertation Abstracts of Iranian Graduates Abroad* (quarterly), *Iranian Scholars and Experts* (annually), *Ettela s Resani* (Technical Bulletin, quarterly).

Library of the Bank Markazi Jomhouri Islami Iran (Central Bank of the Islamic Republic of Iran): POB 11365/8531, Ferdowsi Ave, Teheran; tel. (21) 3119381; fax (21) 64463362; f. 1339; 59,000 vols; Dir B. B. ESHAGZADEH.

Malek Library: Boozarjomehri Ave, Bazar-e-Beinolharamein, Teheran; 25,000 vols; Dir ALI-REZA PAHLAWANI.

National Library of the Islamic Republic of Iran: Anahita Alley, Africa St, POB 11365-9597, Teheran 19176; tel. and fax (21) 8788950; f. 1937; 340,000 Persian and Arabic vols, 8,600 lithographic prints, 19,000 Persian and Arabic MSS, 117,000 vols in other languages, 500,000 Persian and Arabic periodicals, 40,000 periodicals in other languages, 45,000 manuscript documents and patchworks, 1,000 maps, 100,000 pamphlets, slides, photographs, microfilms, microfiches and CDs; maintains library higher education centre for library science; Dir Dr KAZEM MOOSAVI BOJNOURDI; publs *Iranian National Bibliography* (2 a year), *Directory of Iranian Periodicals* (annually), *Directory of Iranian Newspapers* (annually), *Faslname-ye ketab* (National Library of Iran Quarterly).

Parliament Library (1): Ketabkhaneh Majles-e Shoraye Eslami 1, Baharestan Sq., Teheran 11564; tel. and fax (21) 3124339; f. 1924; 197,000 vols; Dir GHOLAMREZA FADAIE ARAGHI.

Attached library:

Parliament Library (2): Ketabkhaneh Majles-e Shoraye Eslami 2, Eman Khomeyni Ave, Teheran 13174; tel. (21) 6467930; fax (21) 3124339; f. 1950; 46,000 vols; Dir GHOLAMREZA FADAIE ARAGHI.

Museums and Art Galleries

Isfahan

Armenian Museum of All Saviour's Cathedral: POB 81735-115, Julfa, Isfahan; tel. (31) 243471; fax (31) 270999; f. 1930; rehoused 1971 with additions; under the supervision of the Diocesan Council of the Armenians in Isfahan; 750 ancient MSS, 570 paintings, miniatures and antique church vestments, tomb portraits; a library of 25,000 vols; Dir L. G. MINASSIAN.

Chehel Sotun Museum: Isfahan; Dir KARIM NIKZAD.

Mashhad

Astan-i-Qods Museums: Sahn-e-Imam, Mashhad; tel. (51) 24570; f. 1945; four depts: Central Museum, Koran Museum, Stamp Museum, Religious Anthropological Museum; Dir MOHAMMAD MALEK JAFARIAN.

Qom

Qom Museum: Eram St, Qom; tel. 32333; f. 1936; under the supervision of the Archaeological Service; Dir M. FOTOGHI.

Shiraz

Pars Museum: Shiraz; f. 1938; exhibits include manuscripts, earthenware, ancient coins; Dir MOHAMMED HOSSEIN ESTAKHR; Curator HASRAT ZADEH SORUDE.

Teheran

Golestan Palace Museum: Maidan Panzdah Khordad, POB 11365-9595, Teheran 11149; f. 1894; Dir ALI REZA ANISI.

Iran Bastan Museum: Khiaban-e Imam Khomeini, Khiaban-e Sium-e Tir, Teheran 11364; tel. 672061; f. 1946; archaeological and cultural research; conservation, repair and exhibition of cultural material; four departments; library of 15,924 vols; Dir J. GOLSHAN; publ. *Catalogue*.

Mardom Shenassi Museum (Ethnological Museum): Maidan Panzdah Khordad, POB 11365-9595, Teheran 11149; f. 1888; Dir ALI REZA ANISI.

Teheran Museum of Modern Art: Karegar Ave, Laleh Park, Teheran; f. 1977; library of 20,000 vols in formation; Dir KAMRAN DIBA.

Universities

AHWAZ UNIVERSITY OF MEDICAL SCIENCES

Ahwaz

Telephone: (61) 39092
Fax (61) 335200

Founded 1988; previously part of Shahid Chamran University

President: Dr HAYAT MAMBINI
Registrar: Mr JALALI
Librarian: H. FATHI MOGHADAM

Number of teachers: 231
Number of students: 2,675

DEANS

Medical College: Dr H. NAHVI
Sub-medical College: Dr T. JALAL
College of Pharmacology: Dr MORTAZAVI
College of Nursing: Mrs ABBAS ZADEH
Physiotherapy Centre: (vacant)

AZ-ZAHRA UNIVERSITY

Vanak, Teheran 19934

Telephone: 684051
Fax: 685187

Founded 1965, name changed 1981
State control
Language of instruction: Farsi
Academic year: September to June

Chancellor: Dr A. KOOHIAN
Vice-Chancellor for Academic Affairs: MORTEZA AMINFAR
Vice-Chancellor for Administration and Finance: KARIM FATHAL IZADEH
Vice-Chancellor for Research: ZAHRA KHAVANIN SHIRAZI
Vice-Chancellor for Student Affairs: FOROGH SHOJANOORI
Librarian: MAHMOOD SHAMSBOD

Number of teachers: 259
Number of students: *c.* 5,000
Library of *c.* 43,000 vols

Publications: *Journal of Art 'Jelveye Honar', Journal of Humanities, Journal of Science*.

DEANS

College of Sciences: SHAYESTEH SEPEHR
College of Theology, Literature and Humanities: ABDOL-KARIM BI-AZAR-E-SHIRAZI
College of Social Sciences and Economics: SEIED ALI ALAVI
College of Art: ALI ASGHAR FARAMARZIAN

HEADS OF DEPARTMENTS

College of Sciences:

- Chemistry: FAEZEH FARZANEH
- Physics: GOHAR ABDOL RASHIDI
- Mathematics: HASAN MALEK MUHAMDI
- Biology: FATIMA MOBASHERI

College of Social Sciences and Economics:

- Accountancy: HOSSEIN BOLOORCHI
- Management: AHMAD JAFARNEJAD
- Economics: SEIED JAVAD POURMOGHIM
- Social Sciences: SEIED YAGHOOB MOOSAVI

College of Theology, Literature and Humanities:
- English: Azam Sazvar
- French: Muhamad Kari
- Persian: Fatima Rakei
- Psychology: Dr Kianoosh Hashemian

College of Fine Arts:
- Drawing: Fatima Honarimehr
- Graphics: Fahimeh Daneshgar
- Handicrafts: Khadijeh Kazemi
- Design and Sewing: Fatima Mehrinfar
- Industrial Design: Bahar Mosavi Hejazi

ALLAMEH TABATABA'I UNIVERSITY

POB 15815/3487, Teheran

Telephone: 891521
Telex: 215372
Fax: 892536

Founded 1984, by merger of the University Complex for Literature and Humanities and the University Centre for Public and Business Administration
State control
Languages of instruction: English, Persian
Academic year: September to June

President: Dr M. Khaliji
Vice-Presidents: Dr Ali Reza Shirani (Research Affairs), Dr Jalil Mesgar Nejad (Academic Affairs), Hamid Khaleghi Moghaddam (Administration and Finance), Javad Kashani (Student Affairs)
Registrar: H. Shabani
Chief Librarian: N. Afnani

Number of full-time teachers: 330
Number of students: 11,252

Faculties of Persian literature and foreign languages, economics, psychology and education, social sciences, accounting and management, and law and politics.

ATTACHED INSTITUTE

International Centre for Insurance Education and Research (ICIER).

AMIRKABIR UNIVERSITY OF TECHNOLOGY

Hafez Ave 424, Teheran

Telephone: 61390
Fax: 6413969

Founded 1958 as Teheran Polytechnic
State control
Academic year: September to June

Chancellor: Dr A. R. Rahaie
Deputy Vice-Chancellor: Dr Jafar Millimonfared
Chief Administrative Officer: Dr M. Saddighi
Librarian: Dr S. M. Safavi

Number of teachers: 400
Number of students: 7,000

Publication: *Amir Kabir Journal of Science and Technology.*

HEADS OF DEPARTMENT

Aerospace Engineering: Dr M. Mani
Chemical Engineering: Dr S. M. Alaie
Civil Engineering: Dr A. Fahimifar
Computer Engineering: Dr R. Safabakhsh
Electrical Engineering: Dr M. Karrari
Foreign Languages: B. Maleki
Industrial Engineering: Dr M. Amin Nayeri
Islamic Theology and Humanities: M. H. Karami
Mathematics: Dr M. Dehghan
Mechanical Engineering: Dr M. H. Ghafari Saadat
Medical Engineering: Dr H. Taheri
Mining and Metallurgical Engineering: Dr B. Rezaie
Physics: Dr S. Nourazar
Polymer Engineering: Dr A. A. Katbab
Shipbuilding Engineering: Dr M. H. Salimi Namin
Textile Engineering: Dr M. Safajohari

ATTACHED INSTITUTES

Automation and Robotics Research Centre: Dir Dr M. Bahrami.
Electrical and Electronics Research Centre: Dir Dr A. Tavakoli.
Food Industry Research Centre: Dir Dr M. Sanati.
Industrial Engineering and Productivity Research Centre: Dir Dr M. A. Kimiyagari.
Textile Industry and Synthetic Fibre Research Centre: Dir Dr A. Ayatollahi.

UNIVERSITY OF ART

42 First St, Parvin Etesami St, Dr Fatemi Ave, POB 14155-6434, Teheran

Telephone: (21) 8864606
Fax (21) 8864609

Founded 1980 from five existing colleges
State control
Language of instruction: Farsi
Academic year: September to July

Chancellor: Dr Akbar Zargar
Vice-Chancellor for Administration and Finance: S. Javad Salimi
Vice-Chancellor for Instruction: S. Saeid Zavieh
Vice-Chancellor for Research: Parvin Partovi
Vice-Chancellor for Student Affairs: Ahmad Tondi

Library of 50,000 vols
Number of teachers: 170 part-time, 82 full-time
Number of students: 2,200

DEANS

Visual and Applied Arts: Mr Eskandari
Cinema and Theatre: Mr Kashan-Fallah
Music: Mr Lotfi
Pardis College of Isfahan: Mr Pustinduz
Graduate Studies: Mr Hosseini

BU-ALI SINA UNIVERSITY

Shariati Ave, University Square, Hamadan 65174

Telephone: (81) 226041
Fax: (81) 225046

Founded 1973
State control
Academic year: September to July

President: Dr M. Gholami
Vice-Presidents: Dr A. Afkhami (Education), Dr N. Mirazi (Research), Dr A. Karegar (Administration and Finance), A. Yalfani (Student Affairs), M. Esna-Ashary (Development)
Librarian: Dr M. G. Ghalechian

Number of teachers: 221
Number of students: 7,450

Publication: *Bulletin.*

DEANS

Faculty of Engineering: Dr M. Nili
Faculty of Science: Dr J. S. Sabounchi
Faculty of Agriculture: D. Mansouri-Rad
Faculty of Letters and Humanities: Dr F. Mirzaii
Faculty of Teacher Training (Malayer): S. Ghanbary

HEADS OF DEPARTMENT

Faculty of Engineering:
- Mechanical Engineering: Dr G. Majzoubi
- Civil Engineering: Dr M. Nili
- Industrial Engineering: A. Khodayvandi
- Architecture: M. R. Araghchian

Faculty of Science:
- Chemistry: Dr M. A. Kharkhanehei
- Physics: M. Farshchi
- Mathematics: Dr A. Ansari
- Geology: Dr G. Khanlari
- Biology: Dr B. E. Malayeri

Faculty of Agriculture:
- Soil Science Engineering: Dr A. Jalali
- Plant Protection Engineering: Dr M. J. Soleimani
- Crop Production and Plant Breeding Engineering: Dr A. Deljou
- Agricultural Machinery: D. Mansouri-Rad
- Agricultural Education and Extension: D. Aazami
- Veterinary Science: Dr N. Mirazi
- Horticulture: Dr M. Gholami

Faculty of Letters and Humanities:
- Social Science: A. Mohammadi
- Economics: Dr A. Salimian
- Persian Literature: Dr A. Nosrati
- Educational Science: A. Yaghubi
- Library Science: A. Zareie
- Law: H. Savari
- Arabic Literature: H. Fatehi
- Physical Education: Dr F. Nazem
- Foreign Languages: Fazelmaniea

Faculty of Teacher Training:
- Training Technology: M. Asgary
- Mathematics: S. Baghery

FERDOWSI UNIVERSITY OF MASHHAD

Shariati Circle, Ahmadabad St, POB 91764, Mashhad

Telephone and fax: (051) 827079
Telex: 512271

Founded 1956
State control
Language of instruction: Farsi
Academic year: September to June (two semesters)

Chancellor: Dr A. Sarafraz Yazdi
Vice-Chancellor for Academic Affairs: Dr J. Abrishami
Registrar: Taghi Assadollahi
Librarian: Dr M. T. Edalati Sherbaf

Number of teachers: 550
Number of students: 12,000

Publications: Journals of literature, agriculture and engineering (all quarterly).

DEANS

Faculty of Letters and Humanities: Dr M. M. Rokni
Faculty of Sciences: Dr A. R. Ashori
Faculty of Theology: Dr A. Abdolahi Nejad
Faculty of Education and Psychology: Dr H. A. Koohestani
Faculty of Agriculture: Dr R. Valizadeh
Faculty of Veterinary Science: Dr G. Mohamedi
Faculty of Engineering: Dr B. Sharifi
Faculty of Administration and Economics: Dr Gh. Mahdavi Adeli
Faculty of Physical Education: A. Marefati

UNIVERSITY OF GILAN

PO 401, Rasht

Telephone: (231) 35035
Telex: 232100

Founded 1977
State control
Language of instruction: Farsi
Academic year: September to June (two semesters)

IRAN UNIVERSITY OF MEDICAL SCIENCES AND HEALTH SERVICES

Shahid Hemmat Highway/Shahid Chamran Crossroads, POB 15875-6171, Tehran

Telephone: (21) 8270060

Fax: (21) 8278514

Founded 1974 as Iran Medical Centre
State control
Language of instruction: Persian
Academic year: September to June

Chancellor: Dr GH. H. SHAHOSSEINI
Vice-Chancellors: Dr H. FARAHINI (Academic Affairs), S. SAMADI (Administrative and Financial Affairs), Dr R. FARASATKISH (Student and Cultural Affairs), Dr S. A. EMAMI (Research)
Registrar: Dr HOSEIN KABIR ANARAKI
Head of Central Library: Dr MEHRANGIZE HARIRI

Library of 33,000 vols

Number of teachers: 627
Number of students: 5,890

Publications: *Iran Journal of Nursing and Midwifery* (quarterly), *University Journal* (quarterly), *Thought and Behaviour* (quarterly), *Students* (monthly), *University Bulletin* (monthly), *Medical Management* (quarterly).

DEANS

School of Medicine: Dr MADHI MODARRESZADEH
School of Nursing and Midwifery: Dr FATEMEH HAGHDOOST OSKOUI
School of Public Health: Dr S. AHMAD AMERI
School of Rehabilitation Sciences: Dr E. EBRAHIMI TAKAMJAI
School of Paramedical Sciences: Dr E. NOURMOHAMMADI
School of Management and Medical Information: Dr S. JAMELEDDIN TABIBI

HEADS OF DEPARTMENT

Anaesthesiology: Dr H. HASANI
Anatomy: Dr M. JOGHATAEE
Biochemistry: Dr M. FIROOZ RAAY
Biophysics: Dr ALI A. SHARAFI
Community Medicine: Dr S. A. ABTAHI
Dermatology: Dr M. MOSHIR
Internal Medicine: Dr A. EHTESHAMI AFSHAR
Microbiology and Immunology: Dr A. SALEK MOGHADAM
Neurosurgery: Dr M. AZAR
Obstetrics and Gynaecology: Dr A. AKBARIAN
Ophthalmology: Dr M. HASHEMI
Orthopaedics: Dr GH. SHAH-HOSSEINI
Otorhinolaryngology: Dr H. ZADANFARROKH
Paediatrics: Dr A. A. MOHAMMAD HOSSEINI
Parasitology: Dr H. OURMAZDI
Pathology: Dr SH. YOUSEFI
Pharmacology: Dr M. MAHMOUDIAN
Physiology: Dr HOMAYUNFAR
Psychiatry: Dr F. MEHRABI
Radiology: Dr P. ALIPOOR
Reconstructive Surgery: Dr A. EMAMI
Surgery: Dr M. MOSHKGOO
Urology: Dr K. KARIMI

IRAN UNIVERSITY OF SCIENCE AND TECHNOLOGY

Narmak, Teheran 16844

Telephone: (21) 7451120
Telex: 212965
Fax: (21) 7451143

Founded 1928

State control
Language of instruction: Persian
Academic year: September to July

President: Dr SEYED JAVAD AZHARI
Vice-Presidents: Dr M. SALEHI (Administration and Finance), Dr A. GHOLAMI (Education), Dr S. M. SHAHRTASH (Research), Dr M. KHANSADI (Students), Dr S. M. M. BASSIR (Graduate Studies)
Registrar: Dr M. KHANSADI
Librarian: Dr A. DAVAEE MARKAZI

Library of 112,000 vols

Number of teachers: 289 (full-time), 235 (part-time)
Number of students: 6,182

Publications: *International Journal of Engineering* (4 a year, in Persian and English), *Research News* (1 a year, in Persian), *University Bulletin* (1 a year, in English), *Newsletter* (monthly, in Persian and English).

DEANS

Faculty of Architecture and Urban Design: A. NOGHREHKAR
Faculty of Electrical Engineering: Dr A. AYATULLAHI
Faculty of Chemical Engineering: Dr H. KARIMPOOR
Faculty of Civil Engineering: Dr H. BEHBAHANI
Faculty of Industrial Engineering: Dr A. MOEINI
Faculty of Metallurgical Engineering: Dr M. ABOUTALEBI
Faculty of Mechanical Engineering: Dr M. BIDABADI
Faculty of Physics: Dr H. MAJIDI
Faculty of Railway Engineering: A. NOUROUZI
Faculty of Computer Engineering: Dr M. R. JAHED MOTLAGH
Faculty of Mathematics: Dr B. JAZBI

PROFESSORS

ESRAFILIAN, E., Mathematics
HOJAT KASHANI, F., Electrical Engineering
JAFAR ALI JASBI, A., Industrial Engineering
KAVEH, A., Civil Engineering
MAJIDI ZULBANIN, H., Physics
SHIDFAR, A., Mathematics
SOLEIMANI, M. R., Electrical Engineering

UNIVERSITY OF ISFAHAN

Isfahan, Darvazeh Shiraz 81744

Telephone: (31) 681070
Telex: 312295
Fax: (31) 687396
E-mail: uisf@math.ui.ac.ir

Founded 1950

State control
Language of instruction: Persian
Academic year: September to June

Chancellor: Dr HOSHANG TALEBI
Vice-Chancellor for Finance and Administration: ALIREZA FIRUZ
Vice-Chancellor for Research Affairs: Dr REZA ENSHAIE
Vice-Chancellor for Student Affairs: Dr SAYYED EBRAHIM JAFARI
Vice-Chancellor for Academic Affairs: Dr HOSSEIN FAGHIHIAN
Office of International and Scientific Relations: Dr RAHIM DALLALI ISFAHANI
Librarian: Dr HOSSEIN HARSIJ

Number of teachers: 545
Number of students: 16,950

Publications: *Research Bulletin* (quarterly, in Persian and English), *Payame Daneshgah* (Message of the University, monthly).

DEANS

Faculty of Administrative Sciences and Economics: Dr SADEGH BAKHTIARI
Faculty of Educational Sciences: Dr HASSAN ALI BAKHTIAR NASR ABADI
Faculty of Engineering: Dr AHMAD BARAANI
Faculty of Foreign Languages: Dr NASROLLAH SHAMELI
Faculty of Letters and Humanities: Dr ALI ASGHAR MIR-BAGHERI-FARD
Faculty of Pure Sciences: Dr SAYYED HOSSEIN LOGHMANI
Faculty of Physical Education: MASOUD NADERIAN
Faculty of Technology: Dr AHMAD BARAANI

HEADS OF DEPARTMENTS

Faculty of Administrative Sciences and Economics:

- Accountancy: Dr MIR SHAMS SHAHSHAHANI
- Economics: Dr HOSHANG SHAJARI
- Management: Dr ALI KAZEMI
- Political Science: Dr SAYED JAVAD IMAM JOMEH ZADEH

Faculty of Educational Sciences:

- Education: Dr ABDUOL RASOOL JAMSHIDIYAN
- Library Science: MOHAMMAD TAGHI DARBEEMAMIEH
- Psychology: KOUROSH-NAMDARI
- Educational Counselling: Dr SAYYED AHMAD AHMADI

Faculty of Foreign Languages:

- Arabic: Dr S. A. MIRLOHI
- Armenian and German Languages: Dr JAHANGIR FEKRI ERSHAD
- English: Dr AKBAR AFGHARI
- French: MOHAMMAD JAVAD SHOKRIAN

Faculty of Letters and Humanities:

- Geography: Dr M. H. RAMESHT
- History: Dr MORTAZA DEGHAN NAJAD
- Persian Literature: Dr ESHAGH TOGHYANI ESFARJANI
- Philosophy: Dr MORTAZA HAJ HOSSEINI
- Social Sciences: Dr MAJID KARSHENAS
- Theology and Islamic Studies: SAYYED MAHMOD FAGHIHI

Faculty of Pure Sciences:

- Biology: Dr MANSOUR SHARIATI
- Chemistry: Dr IRAJ MOHAMMAD POOR
- Geology: Dr RASSOUL AJALLOCIAN
- Mathematics: Dr ALI AKBAR MOHAMMADI HASSANABADI
- Physics: Dr AHMAD KIASAT POOR

Faculty of Engineering:

- Computing: Dr KAMRAN ZAMANIFAR
- Surveying: HOSSEIN MOSSAVI AL-KAZEMI
- Chemical Engineering: Dr SHAHRAM TANGESTANI NEZAD
- Technology: Dr KAMAL JAMSHIDI

ISFAHAN UNIVERSITY OF MEDICAL SCIENCES

Hezar-Jerib Avenue, Isfahan

Telephone: (31) 685141
Fax: (31) 275145

Founded 1950
State control
Language of instruction: Persian
Academic year: September to June
Chancellor: Dr HAMIDREZA JAMSHIDI
Vice-Chancellor for Finance and Administration: Dr GH. ASGHARI
Vice-Chancellor for Student Affairs: M. HARIRCHIAN
Vice-Chancellor for Academic Affairs: Dr B. SHAMS
Vice-Chancellor for Research Affairs: Dr R. LABBAF GHASSEMI
Registrar: M. MARDANI
Head of Libraries: Dr A. ASLANI

Number of teachers: 530
Number of students: 9,724

Publication: *Journal of Isfahan Medical School* (quarterly).

DEANS

Faculty of Medicine: Dr A. MORTAZAVI
Faculty of Dentistry: Dr B. MUSAVI
Faculty of Pharmacy: Dr E. SADJADI
Faculty of Health: (vacant)
Faculty of Nursing: Dr T. CHANGIZ
Faculty of Management, Information and Rehabilitation Sciences: Dr M. ZAREH

HEADS OF DEPARTMENTS

Faculty of Medicine:

Anaesthesiology: Dr H. Soltani
Applied Pathology: Dr P. Rajabi
Basic Sciences: Dr R. Salehi
Community-Oriented Medicine: Dr H. Taban
Dermatology: Dr M. Meghdadi
ENT: Dr M. Sonbolastani
Gynaecology and Obstetrics: Dr T. Allameh
Infectious Diseases: Dr I. Karimi
Internal Medicine: Dr M. Pourmoghaddas
Microbiology, Virology and Immunology: Dr A. Nafissi
Mycology and Parasitology: Dr Sh. Shadzi
Neurology: Dr M. Sheerzadi
Neurosurgery: Dr H. Moin
Ophthalmology: Dr H. Razmjoo
Paediatrics: Dr B. Shams
Pharmacology: Dr H. R. Jamshidi
Physiology: Dr H. Alai
Psychiatry: Dr G. Asadollahi
Radiology: Dr M. Khadjavi
Surgery: Dr N. Nejat-Bakhsh

Faculty of Pharmacy:

Biochemistry: Dr H. Orooji
Medicinal Chemistry and Toxicology: Dr M. A. Jalili
Pharmaceutics: Dr N. Tavakoli
Pharmacognosy: Dr A. Ghanadi

Faculty of Dentistry:

Dental Diseases Diagnosis: Dr P. Ghaliani
Dental Pathology: Dr Gh. Jahanshahi
Dental Surgery: Dr A. Hosein-Zadeh
Endodontics: Dr A. Khademi
Orthodontics: Dr A. Kalantar-Motamedi
Paediatric Dentistry: Dr M. Haj-Noruzali Tehrani
Periodontics: Dr M. Shah Abuei
Permanent and Temporary Prosthesis: Dr M. Dakhil Alian
Prosthetics: Dr H. Vakili
Radiology: Dr M. Sheikhi
Restoration: Dr K. Khosravi

AFFILIATED CENTRE

Amin Research Centre: Dr R. Labbaf Ghassemi

ISFAHAN UNIVERSITY OF TECHNOLOGY

Isfahan

Telephone: (31) 891-2505
Telex: 312764
Fax: (31) 8913112
E-mail: isco@cc.iut.ac.ir

Founded 1977
State control
Language of instruction: Persian
Academic year: September to July

President: Dr Ali Ahoonmanesh
Vice-President for Academic Affairs: Dr Mojtaba Azhari
Vice-President for Research: Dr Ebrahim Shirani
Vice-President for Student Affairs: Dr Ali Akbar Alem Rajabi
Vice-President for Finance and Administration: Dr Mohammad Hassan Abbasi
Registrar: Dr Soroush Alimoradi
Library Director: Dr Mostafa Karimian Eghbal

Library of 88,000 vols, 2,500 periodicals
Number of teachers: 440
Number of students: 9,338

Publications: *Esteghlal* (Journal of Engineering, 2 a year), *Journal of Agricultural Engineering and Natural Resources, Peyke Ryazy, Iranian Journal of Physics Research.*

DEANS

Faculty of Mathematics: Dr Z. Hamedani
Faculty of Physics: Dr Ali A. Babaee
Faculty of Electrical and Computer Engineering: Dr M. A. Montazeri
Faculty of Civil Engineering: Dr M. M. Saadatpour
Faculty of Mechanical Engineering: Dr M. S. Saeidi
Faculty of Materials Engineering: Dr M. A. Golozar
Faculty of Industrial Engineering: Dr S. H. Saghaian Nejad
Faculty of Agriculture: Dr Mohammad Shahedi
Faculty of Mining Engineering: Dr A. R. Hajipour
Faculty of Textile Technology: Dr S. H. Amirshabi
Faculty of Chemical Engineering: Dr Gh. Etemad
Faculty of Chemistry: Dr Mehdi Amirnasr
Faculty of Natural Resources: Mohammad R. Vahabi

PROFESSORS

Amini, S. M., Computational Physics
Aref, M. R., Telecommunications
Bassir, H., Mining Engineering
Haghany, A., Pure Mathematics
Hajrasooliha, Sh., Soil Science
Kalbasi, M., Soil Science
Molki, M., Mechanical Engineering
Parsafar, Gh., Chemistry
Rezaei, A., Plant Breeding, Cytogenetics

ISLAMIC AZAD UNIVERSITY

POB 19585/466, 9th Nayestan, Pasdaran Ave, Tehran

Telephone: (21) 2588168
Fax: (21) 249606

Founded 1982
Academic year: September to September

President: Dr A. Jassbi
Vice-Presidents: Dr A. Abbaspour (Research), Dr K. Zare (Academic Affairs), Dr J. Azizian (Student Affairs), Dr H. Yahyavi (Medical Affairs), M. S. Kalhor (Financial Affairs), A. Shahraki (Construction and Development)
Librarian: P. Mahasti Shotorbani

Library of 1,300,000 vols
Number of teachers: 15,000
Number of students: 521,472

Colleges of Agricultural Engineering, Arts, Civil Engineering, Humanities, Medicine and Basic Sciences. Each of the University's 115 branches, which are located throughout Iran, offers a selection of the courses run by the University.

K. N. TOOSSI UNIVERSITY OF TECHNOLOGY

POB 15875-4416, 322 West Mirdamad Ave, 19697 Teheran

Telephone: (21) 8882991
Telex: 214230
Fax: (21) 8797469

Founded 1980; present name 1985
State control
Language of instruction: Persian
Academic year: September to June

Chancellor: Dr R. Amrolahi
Vice-Chancellors: Dr S. Zokaee (Education), Dr. A. Ghafari (Research), Dr M. Zia-Bashar-Hagh (Administration and Finance), A. Abdul Hassani (Student Affairs)
Registrar: Dr T. Zargar Irshadi
Librarian: Dr H. Chegini

Library of 79,000 vols
Number of teachers: 167 full-time, 35 part-time
Number of students: 2,580

Faculties of electrical engineering, mechanical engineering, civil engineering, and science.

KERMANSHAH UNIVERSITY OF MEDICAL SCIENCES AND HEALTH SERVICES

Building No. 2, POB 67147-1688, Bolvar-e-shahid Dr Beheshti, Kermanshah

Telephone: (831) 59795
Fax: (831) 50013
E-mail: contacts@kums.ac.ir

Founded 1986; previously part of Razi University
State control
Academic year: September to July

Chancellor: Dr Mohammad Reza Saeedi
Vice-Chancellor for Financial and Administrative Affairs: Dr Ali Soroosh
Head of Educational and Research Affairs: Dr Masood Naseripoor
Librarian: Fayzollah Frouybi

Library of 36,000 vols
Number of teachers: 183
Number of students: 1,883

DEANS

Faculty of Medicine: Dr Mohammad Reza Abbasi
Faculty of Health: Dr Ali Almasi
Faculty of Nursing and Midwifery: Dr Mojdeh Asarehzadegan
Night Faculty of Nursing and Midwifery: Sayed Galal Kazemi

MASHHAD UNIVERSITY OF MEDICAL SCIENCES

POB 91735-588, Mashhad

Telephone: (51) 813007
Telex: 512015
Fax: (51) 813006

Founded 1945

Chancellor: Dr A. Bahrami
Vice-Chancellor: Dr A. Shamsa
Principal: Dr A. Bahrami
Librarians: A. Bakhtiarnia, F. Asadpour

Library of 100,000 vols
Number of teachers: 554
Number of students: 5,688

DEANS

Faculty of Medicine: Dr M. T. Rajabi Mashhadi
Faculty of Dentistry: Dr H. Hosseinpour Jajarm
School of Pharmacy: Dr Orafai
School of Nursing: Dr M. R. Hajzadeh

MAZANDARAN UNIVERSITY

POB 416, Babolsar

Telephone: (1291) 32091
Fax: (1291) 33707
E-mail: mazanuni1@www.dci-co.ir

Founded 1975 as Reza Shah Kabir University, name changed 1980

State control
Language of instruction: Persian
Academic year: September to June

Chancellor: Dr Abdol-Reza Sheikh El-Eslami
Vice-Chancellors: Dr Susan Ghahramani Ghagar (Research), Dr Mohsen Soriani (Education), Ali Reza Poorfarag (Student Affairs), Dr Jahanbakhsh Raoof (Administration and Finance)
Registrar: Dr Abdol-Ali Neamati
Librarian: Dr Reza Ojani

Number of teachers: 228
Number of students: 5,835

DEANS

Faculty of Basic Sciences: Dr A. Rostami
Faculty of Humanities and Social Sciences: Dr K. Piraee
Faculty of Engineering: Dr H. Mohammadi Doostdar

Faculty of Agricultural Sciences: Dr M. A. Bahmanyar

PAYAME NOOR UNIVERSITY

Lashkarak Rd, POB 19395-4697, Tehran

Telephone: (21) 2440925
Fax: (21) 2441511

Founded 1987
State control
Distance education; 130 study centres in Iran
Language of instruction: Persian
Academic year: September to July (two terms)

Chancellor: Prof. Hassan Zohoor
Vice-Chancellors: Prof. Mohammad Hassan Bijanzadeh (Research), Dr Masood Shafiee (Academic), Dr Isa Ebrahimzadeh (Student Affairs), Dr Mohammed Reza Nasiri (Financial and Administrative Affairs), Vahid Afshinmehr (Constructional Plans)
Librarian: Mahmoud Hormozi

Library of 500,000 vols (total for all centres)
Number of teachers: 499 (full-time), 4,346 (part-time)
Number of students: 147,815

Publication: *Newsletter* (monthly)

DEANS

Faculty of Science: Dr Mehrdad Farhoodi
Faculty of Humanities: Dr Arsalan Sabet Saeidi
Faculty of Persian Language and Literature (exclusively for external students): Dr Reza Mostafavi Sabzevari

HEADS OF DEPARTMENT

Accountancy: M. Taghavi
Applied Physics: M. M. Tehranchi
Biology: F. Seyed Mozafari
Business Administration: (vacant)
Chemistry: T. Partovi
Computer Engineering: (vacant)
Education: I. Ebrahimzadeh
English Language Translation: Prof. R. Nilipour
Geography: A. Nazari
Geology: A. Chehrazi
Islamic Theology: M. Mirdamadi
Mathematics: A. Jamali
Persian Language and Literature: T. Hashempour Sobhani
Physical Education: A. Azizabadi Farahani
Psychology: M. A. Ahmadvand
Public Administration: T. Feizi
Social Sciences: (vacant)
Statistics: M. Vahidi Asl

PETROLEUM UNIVERSITY OF TECHNOLOGY

569 Hafez Ave, Teheran 15996

Telephone: (21) 6151
Telex: 212514
Fax: (21) 8807687

Founded 1939 as Abadan Institute of Technology
State control, under Ministry of Petroleum
Languages of instruction: English and Farsi
Academic year: September to June (two semesters)

Chancellor: Dr M. H. Salimi
Vice-Chancellors: Dr M. R. Shishesaz (Academic), Dr M. Akhlaghi (Research and Postgraduate Studies), Mr Gayem (Student Affairs), Dr M. Izadi (Finance and Administration), Dr A. A. Sohrabi (Planning)
Registrar: Gh. Rashed

Number of teachers: 150
Number of students: 1,100

Publication: *P.U.T. Monthly News.*

DEANS

Faculty of Petroleum Engineering (in Ahwaz): Dr R. Kharrat
Faculty of Chemical and Petrochemical Engineering (in Abadan): Dr J. Hashemi
Faculty of Nursing (in Ahwaz): Dr Gh. Naseri
Faculty of Accounting and Finance (in Teheran): Dr A. Emamzadeh
Faculty of Nautical Studies (in Mahmood-Abad): A. Taherdin

ATTACHED INSTITUTES

Mahmood-Abad Engineering and Technology Institute: POB 161, Mahmood-Abad; Dir Dr N. Nabhani.

Isfahan Engineering and Technology Institute: POB 196, Isfahan; Dir Dr Peykari.

Ahwaz Engineering and Technology Institute: 63 Ameri Ave, Ahwaz; Dir Dr Shahvarani.

RAZI UNIVERSITY

Kermanshah Azadi Square, Kermanshah

Telephone: 28050
Fax: 26183

Founded 1974
State control
Academic year: January to September

Chancellor: Dr M. Mehdi Khodaei
Vice-Chancellor: Dr M. Motalebi
Administrative Officer: Mr Ghahramani
Librarian: Dr Ghasempor

Number of teachers: 175
Number of students: 3,550

DEANS

College of Agriculture: Mr A. Popzan
College of Engineering: Dr G. Shiesi
College of Letters: Mr V. Sabzianpoor
College of Science: Dr M. Elahi
College of Veterinary Sciences: Dr A. Chalehchaleh

SHAHED UNIVERSITY

115 North Kargar Ave, POB 15875-5794, Teheran

Telephone: (21) 6419568
Fax: (21) 6419752

Founded 1989
Private control
Academic year: September to June

Chancellor: Dr A. A. Noorballa
Vice-Chancellors: Dr Ahmad Zavvaran Hosseini (Research), Dr Mohammad Taghikhani (Academic), Dr Hossein Ghosian Moghaddam (Student Affairs), Asghar Norouzi (Administrative and Financial Affairs), Meysam Amroudi (Cultural Affairs), Seiyed Ali Akbar Mirlowhi (Development)
Registrar: Rezwan'ollah Sadeghi
Librarian: Parvin Rahnema

Library of 120,000 vols
Number of teachers: 120
Number of students: 1,289

Publication: *Daneshvar* (quarterly)

DEANS

Faculty of Medical Sciences: Dr Mahmood Noorisafa
Faculty of Art: Ali Asghar Shirazi
Faculty of Dentistry: Dr Fereshte Baghaie
Faculty of Agriculture: Eng. Hassan Habbibi
Faculty of Basic Sciences: Dr Iraj Rasooli
Faculty of Open Learning: Dr Mohammad Nassiri
Faculty of Humanities and Literature: Mohammad Ali Moshfegh
Faculty of Engineering: Dr Hamid Reza Hassani

SHAHID BAHONAR UNIVERSITY OF KERMAN

POB 76169-133, Kerman

Telephone: (341) 235391
Fax: (341) 237001

Founded 1974, courses began 1976
State control
Languages of instruction: Persian and English
Academic year: September to June

Chancellor: A. Mostafavi
Registrar: H. Rooholamini
Librarian: K. Saidi

Number of teachers: 410
Number of students: 12,000

Faculties of engineering, sciences, mathematics and computer sciences, arts, economics, literature and human sciences, agriculture, physical education and sports science.

SHAHID BEHESHTI UNIVERSITY

Evin, 19834 Teheran

Telephone: 21411
Fax: 2403003

Founded 1959 as National University of Iran, present name 1983
State control
Language of instruction: Farsi
Academic year: September to June

President: Dr Hadi Nadimi
Vice-President for Research: Dr Zahra Sabbaghian
Vice-President for Academic Affairs: Dr Bahman Honary
Vice-President for Student Services: Dr Sadegh Mahdavi
Vice-President for Complementary Education: Dr Ahmad Shemirani
Vice-President for Administrative and Financial Affairs: Farshid Jahedi
Registrar: A. Shahvarani Semnani

Library: see Libraries
Number of teachers: 453
Number of students: 13,576

Publications: various faculty journals.

DEANS

Faculty of Letters and Humanities: Dr Mohammad Ali Sheikh
Faculty of Law: Dr Goodarz Eftekhar Jahromi
Faculty of Sciences: Dr Naser Safari
Faculty of Economics and Political Sciences: Dr Mohammad Naser Sherafat
Faculty of Architecture: Dr Ali Ghaffari
Faculty of Education and Psychology: Mohammad Hassan Pardakhtchi
Faculty of Administrative Sciences: Dr Ali Jahnkhani
Faculty of Earth Sciences: Dr Mohsen Pourker Mani
Faculty of Computer and Electrical Engineering: Dr Javad Esmaili
Faculty of Mathematical Sciences: Dr Syamak Nourbalouchi

SHAHID BEHESHTI UNIVERSITY OF MEDICAL SCIENCES AND HEALTH SCIENCES

Shahid Chamran Highway, Evin, POB 4139-19395, Tehran

Telephone: (21) 2401022
Fax: (21) 2400052

Founded 1961 as Melli University; present name 1986
State control
Language of instruction: Farsi
Academic year: September to June

Chancellor: Prof. S. Mahmood Tabatabaie
Vice-Chancellors: Dr S. Mohsen Mahmoodi (Academic Affairs), Dr Mohammad Haidarian (Administration and Finance), Dr Ali Fat-

TAHI (Student Affairs), Dr FARSHAD ROSHANZAMIR (Research)
Director of Scientific and International Relations Bureau: MAHBOOB RIAZI
Librarian: AGHDAS TAGHIZADIEH

Library of 9,000 vols, 880 journals
Number of teachers: 988
Number of students: 8,761

Publications: *Research in Medical Subjects* (in Farsi, 4 a year), *Pejouhandeh* (4 a year).

DEANS

Faculty of Medicine: Dr A. HAERI
Faculty of Dentistry: Dr M. JAFAR DALAIE
Faculty of Pharmacy: Dr GH. REZA FANAIE
Faculty of Allied Medicine: Dr F. SHARAFI
Faculty of Rehabilitation: Dr HOSSEINI KHAMENE
School of Nursing and Midwifery: Dr S. MOHSEN MAHMOODI
School of Public Health: Dr S. JAMAL NIATTI

ATTACHED INSTITUTE

Institute of Nutrition and Food Industrial Sciences: Dir Dr M. KIMIAGAR.

SHAHID CHAMRAN UNIVERSITY

Ahwaz, Khuzestan
Telephone: (61) 330011
Telex: 612075
Fax: (61) 338048

Founded 1955 as Jundi Shapur University, present name 1983
State control
Language of instruction: Farsi
Academic year: September to June

Chancellor: Dr MANSOUR SAYYARI
Vice-Chancellors: Dr ALIZADEH (Academic Affairs), Dr SHAFAEE BAJESTAN (Research), Mr BASIRZADEH (Student Affairs), Dr BAKHSHANDEH (Administration and Finance), Dr MOHAMMAD VALI SAMANI (Development)
Registrar: M. NAMAKI
Librarian: Dr A. FARAJPAHLOU

Number of teachers: 454
Number of students: 13,500

Publications: *Scientific Journal of Agriculture, University Journal of Science, Journal of Education and Psychology.*

DEANS

Faculty of Agriculture: Dr FARROKHI-NEJAD
Faculty of Science: Dr ROAYAIE
Faculty of Economic and Social Science: Dr SINAIE
Faculty of Engineering: Dr TABATABAIE
Faculty of Veterinary Science: Dr MAYAHI
Faculty of Education and Psychology: Dr PAKSERESHT
Faculty of Literature and Humanities: Dr FIROUZI
Faculty of Theology and Islamic Studies: Dr SHOJALPOURIAN
Faculty of Physical Education: M. SHAKERIAN
Education and Research Centre in Ramin: Dr DABIRI
Junior College of Engineering: Dr RASHIDIAN
Faculty of Marine Science and Oceanography: Dr ALIZADEH

SHAHID SADOUGHI UNIVERSITY OF MEDICAL SCIENCES

POB 89195-734, Yazd
Telephone: (351) 41751

Founded 1983
State control
Language of instruction: Persian
Academic year: September to June

Chancellor: Dr SYED MOHAMMAD KAZIMENI

Number of teachers: 185
Number of students: 2,029

Faculties of medicine, nursing and obstetrics, and health, and pre-medical faculty.

SHAHREKORD UNIVERSITY OF MEDICAL SCIENCES

Kashany Ave, POB 88184, Shahrekord
Telephone: (381) 34590
Fax (381) 34588

Founded in 1986
State control
Language of instruction: Persian

President: Dr M. HASHEMZADEH
Vice-Chancellor for Education and Research: Dr M. R. SAMIEY NASAB
Vice-Chancellor for Curative, Drug and Food Affairs: Dr E. NOORIAN
Vice-Chancellor for Student and Cultural Affairs: Dr H. DAVOODPOUR
Vice-Chancellor for Administrative and Financial Affairs: F. SHARAFATI
Librarian: Dr A. AMINI

Library of 33,000 vols
Number of teachers: 130
Number of students: 1,357

DEANS

Faculty of Medicine: Dr M. ROGHANY
Faculty of Nursing and Midwifery: M. RAHIMY
Broujen Faculty of Nursing: SH BANAEYAN

SHARIF UNIVERSITY OF TECHNOLOGY

POB 11365-8639, Teheran
Telephone: (21) 6005419
Fax: (21) 6012983
E-mail: scientia@alborz.sharif.ac.ir

Founded 1965 as Aryamehr University, present name 1979
State control
Languages of instruction: Farsi and English
Academic year: September to June

President: Prof. SAEED SOHRABPOUR
Vice-President of Education: Prof. MEHDI EHSAN
Vice-President of Research: Dr MOHAMMAD KERMANSHAH
Vice-President of Student Affairs: Dr SAEED ADIB-NAZARI
Vice-President of Administration and Finance: ALI ASGHAR ESKANDAR-BAYATI
Dean of Graduate School: Prof. MOHAMMAD SOLTANIEH
Librarian: Dr HAMID MEHDIGHOLI

Number of teachers: 300 full-time, 430 part-time
Number of students: 8,000

Publications: *Scientia Iranica* (4 a year, in English), *Sharif* (scientific research, 4 a year, in Farsi), *Sharif Research Proceedings* (1 a year, in Farsi and English).

CHAIRMEN OF DEPARTMENTS

Chemical Engineering: Dr DARYOUSH BASTANI
Chemistry: Dr FIROUZ MATLOUBI-MOGHADDAM
Civil Engineering: Dr NADER TABATABAEE
Computer Engineering: Dr GHASEM SANI
Electrical Engineering: Dr KASRA BARKESHLI
Industrial Engineering: Dr MOHAMMAD-TAGHI AKHAVAN-NIAKI
Mathematical Sciences: Dr YAHYA TABESH
Mechanical Engineering: Dr ALI MEGHDARI
Metallurgical Engineering: Dr HOSSEIN YOUZBASHI-ZADEH
Physics: Dr ABBAS ANVARI

ATTACHED RESEARCH CENTRES

Biochemical and Bio-environmental Research Centre: Dir Dr MANOUCHEHR VOSSOUGHI.

Electronics Research Centre: Dir Dr MAHMOUD TABIANI.

Water, Energy and Ocean Engineering Research Centre: Dir Dr SEYED JAMALIDDIN HASHEMIAN.

Advanced Industrial Systems Research Centre: Dir MOJTABA TAHMOURESS.

SHIRAZ UNIVERSITY

Zand Ave, Shiraz
Telephone: (71) 59220
Telex: 332169
Fax: (71) 332227

Founded 1946 as Pahlavi University, present name 1979
State control
Languages of instruction: Farsi and English
Academic year: October to July (two semesters)

Chancellor: Dr MAHMOOD MOSTAFAVI
Vice-Chancellors: Dr S. REZA GHAZI (Research), Dr MAJID ERSHAD (Academic Affairs), Dr ALI KHALAFINEJAD (Administrative and Financial Affairs), Dr MORTEZA AKHOND (Student Affairs), Dr KHOSVOW JAFARPOOR (Development Affairs)
Librarian: Dr S. M. M. JAHFARY

Number of teachers: 497
Number of students: 12,000

Publications: *Iranian Journal of Science and Technology, Iran Agricultural Research Journal of Social Sciences and Humanities.*

DEANS

College of Agriculture: Dr S. MOHSEN TAGHAVI
College of Education: Dr MOHSEN KHADEMI
College of Electronic Industry: Dr S. A. AKBAR SAFAVI
College of Engineering: Dr A. JAHANMIRI
College of Law: Dr M. HADI SADEGHI
College of Literature and Human Sciences: CH. KAKAIE
College of Science: Dr HAMID NADGARAN
College of Veterinary Medicine: Dr M. MALEKI
Junior Agricultural College, Darab: Dr A. HASANLIE

UNIVERSITY OF SISTAN AND BALUCHISTAN

POB 98135-987, Zahedan
Telephone: (541) 445981
Fax: (541) 26888

Founded 1974
State control
Language of instruction: Persian
Academic year: September to July (two semesters)

Chancellor: Dr HABIBOLLAH DAHMARDEH
Vice-Chancellor for Academic Affairs: PARVEEZ AZIMI
Vice-Chancellor for Finance and Administration: ESMAIL ZARE-BEHTASH
Vice-Chancellor for Research: M. H. KARIMKOSHTEH
Vice-Chancellor for Student Affairs: DANESH SHAHRAKI
Registrar: M. H. SANGTARASH
Director of Central Library: RAHMATOLLAH LASHKARIPOUR

Number of teachers: 449
Number of students: 17,500

DEANS

Engineering College: Dr ABDOL-ALI FARZAD
Faculty of Nautical Science: Y. KAHKHAEI
Agricultural College: Dr MOHAMMAD GALAVI
Science College: Dr HASAN MANSOORI
College of Humanities (Zahedan): BADRUDDIN YAZDANI
Fine Arts College: M. TAJERI (Sub-Dean)
College of Humanities (Iranshar): SYYED FARID KHALIFA NOAH

PROFESSORS

ATASHI, H., Chemical Engineering
AZIMI, P., Mathematics
DAHMARDEH, H., Mathematics
FARZAD, A. A., Mechanics
HASHEMI, B. H., Civil Engineering
JABBARZADEH, A., Fine Arts
KHOSHNOODI, M., Chemical Engineering
MOBASHERI, M. R., Physics
NOORA, A. A., Mathematics
RAHIMI, R., Chemical Engineering
RANJBARAN, A. R., Civil Engineering
REZVANI, A. R., Chemistry
SARDASHTI, A. R., Chemistry
SHARIATI, H., Mathematics
TORMANZAHI A., Agriculture
TORSHIZI, H. M., Chemistry
VALIZADEH, J., Agriculture
YAZDANI, B.-O., Humanities

TABRIZ UNIVERSITY OF MEDICAL SCIENCES

Golgasht Ave, Tabriz
Telephone: (41) 346147
Telex: 412045
Fax: (41) 342761

Founded 1986, fmrly part of University of Tabriz
State control
Languages of instruction: Persian, English
Academic year: October to July (two semesters)

Chancellor: Dr M. PEZESHKIAN
Deputy Chancellor: Dr M. NOURI DOLAMA
Academic Vice-Chancellor: Dr N. PIRMOAZZEN
Vice-Chancellor for Research: Dr K. MADAIN
Vice-Chancellor for Administration and Finance: A. RAHMANI
Vice-Chancellor for Therapy and Drugs: Dr A. JODATI
Vice-Chancellor for Health Services: Dr A. NIKNIAZ
Vice-Chancellor for Culture and Student Affairs: Dr J. PANAHI
Registrar: Dr F. SALEHPOUR
Librarian: Mrs AKRAMI

Number of teachers: 637
Number of students: 5,669

Publications: *Medical Journal, Journal of Basic Science in Medicine, Research Journal, Pharmaceutical Sciences, Journal of Nursing and Obstetrics* .

DEANS

Faculty of Medicine: Dr J. VAEZ
Faculty of Pharmacy: Dr A. GARJANI
Faculty of Dentistry: Dr S. DIBAJ
Faculty of Nursing and Obstetrics: A. MORADI
Faculty of Paramedical Sciences: Dr A. RAFI
Faculty of Public Health and Nutrition: Dr S. A. MAHBOOB
Faculty of Medical Rehabilitation Sciences: Dr S. MOSTOFI

UNIVERSITY OF TABRIZ

Tabriz 711-51664

Telephone: (41) 340081
Fax: (41) 344272
E-mail tabriz-u@vax.ipm.ac.ir

Founded 1946, formerly University of Azarabadegan
State control
Language of instruction: Farsi
Academic year: September to June (two semesters)

Chancellor: Dr M. A. HOSSEINPOUR FEIZI
Academic Vice-Chancellor: Dr M. B. BEHESHTI
Vice-Chancellor for Research Affairs: Prof. SAMAD SOBHANIAN
Vice-Chancellor for Student Affairs: M. T. AALAMI
Vice-Chancellor for Finance and Administrative Affairs: Dr S. P. T. ANVARIAN
Registrar: Dr SAMAD KARIMZADEH
Librarian: A. A. GHAHRAMANI

Library: see Libraries
Number of teachers: 444
Number of students: 13,678

Publications: *Pazhoohesh* (research, 2 a year), *Journal of Agricultural Science, Journal of the Faculty of Engineering, Journal of the Faculty of Humanities and Social Sciences.*

DEANS

Faculty of Agriculture: SHOJE GHIAS
Faculty of Agriculture (Maragheh): Dr A. R. HOSSEINPOUR SONBOLY
Faculty of Chemistry: Dr MANZOORI
Faculty of Education and Psychology: Dr E. FATHI-AZAR
Faculty of Engineering: Prof. JAVAD FAIZ
Faculty of Humanities and Social Sciences: Dr A. SADEGZADEH
Faculty of Mathematics: Dr A. A. MEHRVARZ
Faculty of Natural Sciences: Dr A. A. MOGHADDAM
Faculty of Persian Literature and Foreign Languages: Dr M. AKRAMI
Faculty of Physics: Dr B. SALEHPOUR

ATTACHED COLLEGES

College of Engineering (Bonab): Dir M. R. A. PARSA.

College of Engineering (Marand): Dir S. HOSSEINI.

College of Veterinary Medicine: Dir Dr M. H. MOOSAVI.

ATTACHED RESEARCH CENTRES

Centre for Applied Physics Research: Dir Dr M. KALAFI.

Centre for Geographical Research: Dir Dr F. JAMALI.

Khajeh Nassir-Alddin Toussi Observatory.

Teaching and Research Centre for Agriculture (Khalat-Poushan).

UNIVERSITY OF TEHERAN

Enghelab Ave, Teheran 14174
Telephone: (21) 6111-2500
Telex: 222966
Fax: (21) 640-9348

Founded 1934
Language of instruction: Persian
Academic year: September to July (two semesters)

Chancellor: Dr MOHAMMAD REZA AREF
Vice-Chancellors: Dr EBADI (Academic Affairs), Dr MOUSAVI MOVAHEDI (Research), Dr MOZAFAR (Administration and Finance), Dr PISHBIN (Student Affairs)
Director-General: Dr M. FAEZIPOUR
University Librarian: Dr TAJLIL

Library: see Libraries
Number of teachers: 1,271
Number of students: 30,000

DEANS

Faculty of Literature and Humanities: Dr SHIKHOLSLAMI
Faculty of Science: Dr MAGHARI
Faculty of Engineering: Dr MOOSAVI MASHHADI
Faculty of Agriculture: Dr SADLOL ASHRAFI
Faculty of Natural Resources: Dr PARSAPAJOOH
Faculty of Law and Political Science: Dr TAKHSHID
Faculty of Education: Dr SADJADI
Faculty of Theology and Islamic Studies: S. ABOULFAZL MIRMOHAMMADI
Faculty of Social Science: Dr M. MIRZAEE
Faculty of Economics: Dr KHALILI ARAGHI
Faculty of Management and Business Administration: Dr A. REZARIAN
Faculty of Fine Arts: Dr JABINI
Faculty of Veterinary Medicine: Dr KIAEE
Faculty of Foreign Languages: Dr AFKHAMI
Faculty of Physical Education: Dr BAYAT

DIRECTORS

Institute of Geophysics: Dr JAVAHERIAN
Institute of Psychology: Dr MOHAMMAD ALI KARDAN
Institute of Dehghoda Encyclopaedias: Dr S. JAFAR SHAHEIDI
Institute of Geography: Dr MOSHIRI
Institute of Desert Regions and Arid Zones: Dr ZEHTABIAN
Institute of Comparative Law: Dr HABIBI
Institute of Biophysics and Chemistry: Dr SEMNANIAN
Centre for Environmental Studies: Dr BAHRINI
Centre for International Studies: Dr HABIBI
Aboureihan Educational Complex: Dr SAFARI
Ghom Higher Educational Complex: M. ELLAHIAN

URMIA UNIVERSITY

POB 165, Urmia 57153
Telephone: (441) 45409
Telex: 442081
Fax: (441) 43442

Founded 1967

Chancellor: Dr M. RAZAVI-ROHANI
Vice-Chancellors: Dr R. KHODABAKHSH, Dr H. SEDGHI, Dr R. HOBBEH-NAGHI, Dr M. MAHAM
Registrar: H. HEIDARNEZHAD
Librarians: A. TALEBI, G. DARABNEZHAD

Library of 50,000 vols
Number of teachers: 240
Number of students: 3,300

DEANS

Agriculture: Dr J. FARHOUDI
Veterinary Science: Dr R. SADRKHANLOU
Technical Science: Dr H. SHOWKATI
Science: Dr N. ARDABILCHI
Literature and Humanities: M. TALEI

UNIVERSITY OF YAZD

POB 89195-741, Yazd
Telephone: (351) 662111
Fax: (351) 25777

Founded 1988
State control
Languages of instruction: Persian and English
Academic year: September to June

Chancellor: Dr MOHAMMAD ALI BARKHORDARI
Vice-Chancellors: AHMAD JAMALI (Finance and Administration), Dr MEHDI NAVABPOUR (Research), ALI TORABI (Development and Construction), Dr ABBAS BEHJAT (Student Affairs), Dr MOHAMMAD ALI VAHDAT (Registrar)
Librarian: Dr MOHAMMAD KAZEM KAHDOUEI

Number of teachers: 259
Number of students: 5,700

Publication: *Bulletin.*

DEANS

School of Humanities: Dr JALIL BAHARESTAN
School of Basic Sciences: Dr JAFAR QUAISARI
School of Engineering: Dr KHODADAD
Faculty of Natural Resources and Arid Zones: MOHAMMAD HUSSEIN EMTHANI
Faculty of Architecture and Urban Planning: MOHAMMAD HUSSEIN MASOUDI

HEADS OF DEPARTMENT

School of Humanities:

English Language: Dr ANOUSHE
History: Dr SASAN ASHTARI
Geography: Mr ZIYARI
Education: Dr JALIL BAHARESTAN
Industrial Management: Dr ABBAS QAZAEI

Social Science and Anthropology: Dr MOHSEN SAEIDI MADANI

School of Basic Sciences:

Mathematics: Dr SAYED MEHDI KARBASI

Physics: Dr SALEHI

Chemistry: Dr SHAYESTE DADFARNIYA

School of Engineering:

Civil Engineering: Dr NOSRATOLLA AMANIAN

Industrial Engineering: Dr MOHAMMAD SALEH OWLYA

Electronic Engineering: Dr BEHZAD ASAEI

Textile Engineering: AHMAD JAMALI

Mining Engineering: Dr AMIR HUSSEIN KOOHSARI

Mechanical Engineering: Dr MOHAMMAD BOZORG

Colleges

(There are *c.* 50 colleges of higher education in Iran, and *c.* 40 technological institutes, of which the following are a selection only.)

Iran Banking Institute: 205 Pasdaran Ave, POB 19395/4814, Teheran; tel. 238000; telex 212503; fax 232618; f. 1963; four-year BA degree course in banking, approved by Ministry of Culture and Higher Education, and MA degree course in banking; 990 students; Principal Dr MEHDI EMRANI.

Military Academy: Sepah Ave, Teheran; depts of military history, military science and tactics, international relations and treaties, general engineering science, physics and electronics, military armaments, nuclear warfare.

College of Surveying: POB 1844, Azadi Sq., Teheran; f. 1965; national training centre for surveyors; 210 students; affiliated to National Geographic Organization; Dir Col (retd) BABA MODAGHAM.

IRAQ

Learned Societies

EDUCATION

Arab Literacy and Adult Education Organization (ARLO): POB 3217, Al Saadoon, Baghdad; tel. 7186246; telex (21) 2564; f. 1966 by ALECSO to promote co-operation in all aspects of literacy and adult education between the Arab states; all Arab states are mems; library of 14,700 vols; Dir HASHIM ABU ZEID EL SAFI (acting); publ. *The Education of the Masses* (2 a year).

FINE AND PERFORMING ARTS

Society of Iraqi Artists: Damascus St, Baghdad; f. 1956; exhibitions and occasional publs; Pres. NOORI AL RAWI; Sec. AMER ALUBIDI.

LANGUAGE AND LITERATURE

Iraqi Academy: Waziriya, Baghdad; f. 1947 with the aims of maintaining the Arabic language and heritage, supporting research in Arabic and Muslim history, the history of Iraq and Arabic language and heritage, maintaining Kurdish and Assyrian languages; 37 mems; Pres. Prof. Dr NAJAH M. K. EL-RAWI; Sec.-Gen. Prof. Dr AHMED MATLOUB; publ. *Majallat Al Mejmah Al Ilmi* (literary quarterly).

MEDICINE

Iraqi Medical Society: Maari St, Al Mansoor, Baghdad; f. 1920; 871 mems; Pres. F. H. GHALI; Sec. A. K. AL KHATEEB.

NATURAL SCIENCES

General

Federation of Arab Scientific Councils: POB 13027, Baghdad; tel. 8881709; telex 212466; f. 1976; aims to strengthen collaboration among scientific research councils, institutions, centres and universities in all Arab states; to adopt the Arabic language in scientific research and technology and to encourage the use of Arabic in scientific research and promote the Arabization of scientific terminology; to plan joint research projects among Arab states, especially those related to Arab development plans; 15 mem. states; library of 800 vols, 600 periodicals, 1,100,000 patent documents from USA, EPO, WIPO; Sec.-Gen. Prof. Dr TAHA T. AL-NAIMI; publs *Journal of Computer Research*, *Federation News*.

Research Institutes

GENERAL

Scientific Research Council: POB 2441, Jadiriya, Baghdad; telex 2187; f. 1963; Pres. Dr NAJIH M. KHALIL.

Attached research centres:

Petroleum Research Centre: Jadiriya; Dir Dr A. H. A. K. MOHAMMED.

Building Research Centre: Jadiriya; Dir Dr M. AL-IZZI.

Biological Research Centre: Jadiriya; Dir Dr AZWAR N. KHALAF.

Scientific Documentation Centre: Jadiriya; see under Libraries.

Space Research Centre: Jadiriya; Dir Dr ALI AL-MASHAT.

Solar Energy Research Centre: Jadiriya; Dir Mrs N. I. AL-HAMDANY.

Agriculture and Water Resources Research Centre: Fudhailiyah; Dir Dr SAMIR A. AL-SHAKER.

Electronics and Computer Research Centre: Jadiriya; Dir Dr M. N. BEKIR.

Genetic Engineering and Biotechnology Research Centre: Jadiriya; Dir Dr FARUQ YASS AL-ANI.

Psychological Research Centre: Jadiriya; Dir Dr ALHARITH A. H. HASSAN.

Scientific Affairs Office: Jadiriya; Dir Dr RADHWAM K. A. HALIM.

AGRICULTURE, FISHERIES AND VETERINARY SCIENCE

Agriculture and Water Resources Research Centre: POB 2416, Karada Al-Sharkiya, Baghdad; tel. 7512080; telex 214012; f. 1980 to carry out research to improve and develop water and agricultural resources; 75 researchers; library of 6,000 vols, 450 periodicals; Dir-Gen. Dr SAMIR A. H. AL-SHAKIR; publ. *Journal of Agriculture and Water Resources Research*.

EDUCATION

Centre for Educational and Psychological Research: University of Baghdad, 9 Waziriya, Baghdad; f. 1966; educational and psychological research studies to make education an effective power for the acceleration of economic and social development; library of *c.* 6,000 vols; Dir Dr MOHAMMED ALI KHALAF; publ. *Journal of Educational Psychological Research* (2 a year).

HISTORY, GEOGRAPHY AND ARCHAEOLOGY

British School of Archaeology in Iraq (Gertrude Bell Memorial): 31–34 Gordon Square, London WC1H 0PY, England; f. 1932; Pres. Prof. D. J. WISEMAN; Chair. Prof. NICHOLAS POSTGATE; publ. *Iraq* (annually).

TECHNOLOGY

Department of Scientific and Industrial Research: Directorate-General of Industry, Baghdad; f. 1935; staff 42; Dir-Gen. of Industry SHEETH NA'AMANN; publs *Technical Bulletin, Annual Report*.

Nuclear Research Centre: Tuwaitha, Baghdad; f. 1967; main establishment of Iraq Atomic Energy Commission; research activities with emphasis on the applications of radio-isotopes to problems in the areas of medicine, agriculture and industry; includes nuclear research reactor, radioisotope production facilities; research in nuclear and solid state physics, analytical and radio-chemistry, biology and agriculture, health physics, computer system and services.

Libraries and Archives

Arbil

University of Salahaddin Central Library: Arbil; tel. 23102; telex 218510; f. 1968; 118,000 vols, 530 current periodicals; Dir Dr ABDULL S. ABBAS.

Baghdad

Al-Awqaf Central Library: (Library of Waqfs): POB 14146, Baghdad; f. 1928; emphasis on Islamic religion and Islamic-Arabic history and literature; 30,000 vols, 300 periodical titles, 8,500 original MSS, 1,000 microfilms and copies of MSS; Dir AFAF ABIDUL LATIF; publ. *Al-Rissala-Al-Islamiya*.

Al-Mustansiriya University Library: POB 14022, Waziriya, Baghdad; f. 1963; 174,000 vols (30,000 vols of periodicals, 330 rolls of film, 280 current periodicals; also 11 college libraries with 33,000 vols, 850 periodicals; Dir FAISAL ANWAN AL-TAEE.

Arab Gulf States Information and Documentation Center: POB 5063, Baghdad; tel. 5433914; telex 213267; f. 1981; affiliated to the Board of Ministers of Information of the Arab Gulf States; aims to gather information from many sources, and to systematize, analyse and exchange it; supports the basic structure of existing information services; seven mem. states; provides a consultancy service; databases, microfilms; specialized library of 8,000 vols; Dir-Gen. HAYFA A. JAJAWI.

Educational Documentation Library: Ministry of Education, Educational Campus, Baghdad; tel. 8860000-2178; telex 2259; f. 1921; 37,000 vols, 73 periodicals; Librarian Dr KADHIM G. AL-KHAZRAJI.

Ibn Hayyan Information House: Iraqi Atomic Energy Commission, POB 765, Tuwaitha, Baghdad; up-to-date references, reports, pamphlets, microcards, magazines and film reels; Dir ISAM ATTA AJAJ.

Iraqi Academy Library: Waziriya, Baghdad; f. 1947; 60,000 vols, 32 original MSS, 1,600 copied MSS, 1,500 microfilms; Librarian SABAH NOAH.

Iraqi Museum Library: Salhiya Quarter, Baghdad West; tel. 8879687; f. 1934; archaeology, history of civilization, art, architecture, cultural heritage; 229,000 vols; 34,000 MSS; Dirs Dr MUYAD SAID DAMERJI, ZAINAB SADIQ; publ. *Al-Maskukat*.

National Centre of Archives: POB 594, National Library Building, 2nd Floor, Bab-el-Muaddum, Baghdad; f. 1964; attached to the Ministry of Culture and Information; divisions of research and statistics, technical photography, palaeography and sigillography; library of 5,333 vols; Dir-Gen. SALIM AL-ALOUSI.

National Library: Bab-el-Muaddum, Baghdad; tel. 4164190; f. 1961; legal deposit centre and national bibliographic centre; 417,000 vols, 2,618 periodicals, 4,412 rare books; Dir ABDUL HAMEED AL-ALAWCHI.

Scientific Documentation Centre: Abu Nuas Rd, POB 2441, Baghdad; tel. 7760023; telex 2187; f. 1972; scientific information services to researchers at the institutes/centres of the Scientific Research Council (*q.v.*), and to others working in Iraqi laboratories, including UNDP experts; seven libraries are being developed, each attached to a research centre of the Council, including the Central Science Library; in-service training for students of Library Science and Documentation and librarians; 20 staff mems; Dir Dr FAIK ABDUL S. RAZZAQ.

University of Baghdad Central Library: POB 47303, Jadiriya, Baghdad; f. 1960; govt and UN depository library; acts as Exchange and governmental Bibliographical Centre; 560,000 vols, 6,197 current periodicals, 4,324 maps, 2,242 Arabic MSS on microfilm; indexes issued on various subjects; Librarian Dr ZEKI AL-WERDI; publ. *Current Contents of Iraqi Universities' Journals* (2 a year).

Basrah

University of Basrah Central Library: Basrah; f. 1964; 190,000 vols, 700 MSS, 1,400 current periodicals; Librarian Dr TARIK AL-MANASSIR; publ. catalogue (irregular).

Mosul

University of Mosul Central Library: Mosul; tel. 810162; telex 8011; fax 814765; f. 1967; 890,000 vols, 2,500 periodicals, depository of UN and Iraqi Govt publications; Dir-Gen. Dr ADNAN S. NATHEEV; publs *Adab Al-Rafidarn* (irregular), *Research Work of University Faculty Members* (annually), *Catalogue* (annually), *Mesopotamia Journal of Agriculture, Journal of Rafidain Development, Annals of the College of Medicine-Mosul, Al-Rafidain Engineering, Iraqi Journal of Veterinary Sciences, Journal of Education and Science* (all irregular).

Museums and Art Galleries

Arbil

Arbil Museum: Arbil; objects from Iraqi history up to Arabic-Islamic period.

Babylon

Babylon Museum: Babylon; f. 1949; contains models, pictures, and paintings of the remains at Babylon; the museum is situated amongst the ruins.

Baghdad

Abbasid Palace Museum, The: Baghdad; a restored palace dating back to the late Caliphs of the Abbasid dynasty (13th century AD); an exhibition of Arab antiquities and scale models of important Islamic monumental buildings in Iraq. Opened as a Museum in 1935.

Baghdad Museum: Sahat Al-Risafi, Baghdad; tel. 4165317; f. 1970; museum of folklore and costumes, natural history; photographic exhibition on history of Baghdad; Memorial Exhibition, containing the royal relics of King Faisal I; picture gallery; Dir ALAE AL-SHIBLI.

Iraq Military Museum: A'dhamiya, Baghdad; f. 1974 combining Arms Museum (f. 1940) and Museum of War (f. 1966); contains old Arabian weapons, Othmanic firearms and contemporary Iraqi weapons.

Iraq Natural History Research Centre and Museum: Bab Al-Muadham, Baghdad; f. 1946; attached to the University of Baghdad; includes sections on zoology, botany and geology; research work in Natural History; exhibitions of animals, plants, rocks and minerals pertaining to Iraq; organizes cultural, educational and scientific training programmes; library of 31,000 vols, 850 periodicals; Dir H.-A. ALI; publs scientific papers in English (with Arabic summaries) dealing with the natural history of Iraq and neighbouring countries in the series *Iraq Natural History Research Centre Publications, Bulletin of the Iraq Natural History Research Centre* and *Annual Report*.

Iraq Museum: Salhiya quarter, Baghdad West; f. 1923; antiquities dating from the early Stone Age to the beginning of the 18th century AD, including Islamic objects in almost uninterrupted sequence; Al-Sarraf gallery, containing Islamic coins; library: see Libraries; Dir RABIE AL-QAISY; publs *Sumer* (annually), *Al-Maskukat* (2 a year), *Iraq Museum Guide, Treasures of the Iraq Museum*.

National Museum of Modern Art: Al-Nafoura Square, Bal Al-Sharqi, Baghdad; f. 1962; Supervisor AMER AL-UBAIDI.

Basrah

Natural History Museum of the University of Basrah: Corniche St, POB 432, Basrah; tel. 213494; telex 7025; f. 1971; study of flora and fauna of the marshes of South Iraq and the Arabian Gulf; sections on mammals, birds, reptiles and amphibia, and fishes; scientific collections in all sections accessible to specialists and exhibits open to public; Dir Dr KHALAF AL-ROBAAE; publ. *Bulletin*.

Mosul

Mosul Museum: Dawassa, Mosul; f. 1951; collections of Assyrian antiquities of the 9th and 8th centuries BC found at Nimrud, objects uncovered in the ruins of Hatra dating back to the 2nd century BC and 2nd century AD, agricultural tools and pottery vessels from the 5th and 4th millennia BC, photographs of excavated buildings at Tepe Gawra, maps of the Assyrian Empire, Nimrud and Hatra; Prehistoric and Islamic exhibits; assists in discovery and maintenance of several archaeological sites; library of *c.* 2,000 vols; Dir HAZIM A. AL HAMEED.

Nasiriya

Nasiriya Museum: Nasiriya; Sumerian and other archaeological objects found in Ur, Al-Abeed and Aridu.

Samarra

Samarra Museum: Samarra; f. 1936; it is housed in one of the old city gates, and contains objects excavated in the ruins of ancient Samarra; also historic maps, writings, pictures.

Universities

AL-MUSTANSIRIYA UNIVERSITY

14022, Waziriya, Baghdad
Telephone: (1) 4168500
Fax: (1) 4165521

Founded 1963
State control
Languages of instruction: Arabic and English
Academic year: September to June

President: Dr RIYADH HAMID AL-DABBAGH
Assistant President: Prof. Dr MOHAMAD JAWAD KADHIM
Registrar: YOUSIF RABIE YOUSIF
Librarian: FAISAL ALWAN AL-TAEE

Library: see Libraries
Number of teachers: 1,340
Number of students: 23,748

Publications: *Al-Mustansiriya Literary Review, Al-Mustansiriya Journal of Science, Journal of Administration and Economics, Journal of the College of Education, Journal of the College of Teachers, Journal of Engineering and Pollution, Journal of Medical Research, Journal of Dialah Education, Journal of the Founding Leader for National and Socialist Studies, Journal of Middle Eastern Studies.*

DEANS

College of Science: Asst Prof. RA'AD K. AL-MUSLIH
College of Arts: Dr SAMI M. AL-ANI
College of Administration and Economics: Prof. Dr JAMAL D. SALMAN
College of Medicine: Dr SABAH AL-OBEIDI
First College of Education: Dr SABAH MAHMOOD-MUHAMMAD
Second College of Education: Asst Prof. Dr SAAD MOHAMMAD AL-MASHHADANI
College of Engineering: Dr ADIL IBRAHIM AL-HADITHI
First College of Teachers: Asst Prof. Dr ABDUL MUNAF SHUKIR AL-NADAWI
Second College of Teachers: Asst Prof. Dr JASSIM MOHAMMAD AL-NADAWI

ATTACHED INSTITUTES

Institute for National and Socialist Studies: Dir Dr AZMI S. AL-SALIHI

Environment Research Centre: Dir Asst Prof. Dr MUTHANNA KHALIS AL-DOORI

Centre for Middle East Studies: Dir Asst Prof. Dr KHALIL AL-AZZAWA

National Diabetes Centre: Asst Prof. Dr MAJEED ABDUL AMIR SAEED

Polymer Units Centre: Prof. Dr SALAH MOHSIN ALEIWI

UNIVERSITY OF BAGHDAD

POB 17635, Jadiriya, Baghdad
Telephone: 7763091
Telex: 2197
Fax: 7763592

Founded 1957
State control
Languages of instruction: Arabic and English
Academic year: September to June

President: Dr ABDUL-ILAH Y. AL-KHASHAB
Registrar: TUMADHR ABDULLAH
Librarians: YUSRA R. ZAHAWI, AMIR ABID MAJBOUR

Library: see Libraries. Each institute and college has its own library of Arabic and foreign books
Number of teachers: 3,000
Number of students: 50,000

Publications: *Bulletin of the College of Arts* (quarterly), *Journal of the College of Education for Women* (every 6 months), *The Iraqi Journal of Veterinary Medicine* (every 6 months), *Journal of Political Science* (quarterly), *Iraqi Journal of Science* (quarterly), *Iraqi Journal of Pharmaceutical Sciences* (quarterly), *Journal of the College of Dentistry* (irregular), *Journal of the Faculty of Medicine* (quarterly), *Journal of Engineering* (irregular), *Journal of Sports Education* (irregular), *Journal of Agricultural Sciences* (every 6 months), *The Professor* (quarterly), *The Academic* (quarterly), *Journal of the College of Sharia* (every 6 months), *Statistical Bulletin* (annually), *Current Awareness* (quarterly), *Journal of the College of Languages* (annually), *Ibn Al-Haitham Journal for Pure and Applied Sciences* (every 6 months), *Journal of Legal Sciences* (quarterly), *Journal of the College of Administration and Economics* (quarterly), *Iraqi Natural History Museum Bulletin* (annually).

COLLEGE DEANS

Islamic Sciences: Dr ABDUL MUNIM AHMED SALIH
Law: Dr MUHAMMED AL-DOURI
Engineering: Dr LAITH ISMAIL
Education (Ibn Rushd): Dr MALIK IBRAHIM SALIH
Education (Ibn Al-Haitham); Dr FAROUK ABDUL SALAM AWNI
Medicine: Dr FAKHRI M. AL-HADITHI
Pharmacy: Dr WALEED R. A. SULAIMAN
Administration and Economics: Dr ADIL H. SALIH
Arts: Dr NOURI HAMMOUDI AL-QAYSI

Science: Dr Farouk Al-Ani
Agriculture: Dr Baqir Abid Khalaf
Dentistry: Dr Isam Abdul Aziz Ali
Veterinary Medicine: Dr Khalil Ibrahim Altayif
Sports Education: Dr Ali Turki
Nursing: Badia Al-Daghstani
Fine Arts: Dr Abdul Mursil Al-Zaydi
Education for Women: Dr Fadhil Al-Saqi
Languages: Dr Adnan Al-Jubouri
Political Science: Dr Shafik Al-Samarraie

AFFILIATED CENTRES

Educational and Psychological Research Centre (attached to the College of Education (Ibn Rushd)): Dir Mahdi Al-Samarrae.

Centre for Urban and Regional Planning (Post-graduate studies): Dir Dr Wadhah Said Yahya.

Centre for the Revival of Arab Scientific Heritage: Dir Nabila Abdul Munim.

Centre for Palestinian Studies (attached to the College of Political Science): Dir Dr Khldoun Naji Marouf.

Centre for International Studies (attached to the College of Political Science): Dir Dr Abdul Ghafour Karim Ali.

Astronomical Research Unit (attached to the College of Science): Dir Dr Hameed Mijwil Al-Niaimi.

UNIVERSITY OF TECHNOLOGY

POB 35010, Tel Mohammad, Baghdad
Telephone: (1) 7182336
Telex: 212149
Fax: (1) 7184826
Founded 1975; formerly the College of Engineering Technology of the University of Baghdad
State control
Languages of instruction: Arabic and English
President: Dakhil H. Jerew
Assistant President: Dr Ramzi B. Ardul-Ahad
Registrar: Abdul Sattar W. Al-Hadithy
Librarian: Ayad J. Shamis Elden
Number of teachers: 449 full-time, 170 part-time
Number of students: 7,550 (480 postgraduate)

PROFESSORS

Hammudi, Walleed Khalaf, Applied Sciences
Al-Mutalib Ibrahim, Abdu, Applied Sciences
Al-Hadeethi, Aadil, Structural Engineering
Khorseed, Nameer, Structural Engineering
Al-Samaaui, Adnaan, Structural Engineering
Khairi, Wallaa, Computer and Control Engineering
Al-Haidary, Jaafar Tahir, Production Engineering and Metallurgy
Al-Rezaaq, Muneer Abdu, Production Engineering and Metallurgy
Al-Toornaji, Muhammed, Mechanical Engineering
Tawfick, Husham, Mechanical Engineering
Majeed, Jawameer, Mechanical Engineering

UNIVERSITY OF BASRAH

POB 49, Basrah
Telephone: 417954
Telex: 207025
Fax: 8868520
Founded 1964
State control
Languages of instruction: Arabic and English
Academic year: September to June
President: Prof. Dr Akram Mohammad Subhi Mahmood
Vice-President: Prof. Dr Anis Abdul Khudhur Mohammad Ali
Director of Scientific Affairs and Postgraduate Studies: Dr Riyad S. Haddad
Director of Administration: Mageed H. Yaseen
Librarian: Dr Raheem A. Jassim
Number of teachers: 998
Number of students: 15,652
Publications: *Arab Gulf Journal, Marina Mesopotamica, Economic Studies, Medical Journal of Basrah University, Basrah Journal of Sciences, Basrah Journal of Agricultural Sciences, Journal of Basrah Research, Gulf Economics Journal, Basrah Journal of Surgery, Journal of Arts, Iraqi Journal of Polymers, Journal of Physical Education.*

DEANS

Faculty of Medicine: Dr Alim Abdulhamid Yacoub
Faculty of Engineering: Dr Abdulamir S. Resan
Faculty of Science: Prof. Dr Gourgis Abidal Adam
Faculty of Arts: Dr Abdulmahdi Saleem Almudhaffar
Faculty of Administration and Economics: Dr Jalil S. Thamad
Faculty of Agriculture: Dr Nazar A. Shukri
Faculty of Education: Dr Galib Bakir M. Galib
Faculty of Physical Education: Prof. Dr Najah M. Shalash
Faculty of Law: Dr Jassim L. Salman
Faculty of Fine Arts: Muayad Abdulsamad
Faculty of Veterinary Science: Dr Abdulmuttalib Y. Yousif

DIRECTORS

Centre for Arab Gulf Studies: Dr Owda Sultan
Medical Centre: Dr Abdulkhaliq Z. Bnayan
Centre for Marine Sciences: Dr Abdulrazak Mahmood
Computer Centre: Dr Waleed A. J. Mohammad Ali

UNIVERSITY OF MOSUL

Mosul
Telephone: (60) 810733
Fax: (60) 815066
Founded 1967 as a separate university; formerly part of the University of Baghdad
State control
Languages of instruction: Arabic and English
Academic year: September to June (two terms)
President: Kubais S. Abdul-Fatah Fahady
Assistant to the President: Wadeh Yaseen
Librarian: Adnan Sami
Number of teachers: 1,705
Number of students: 18,500
Publications: *Journal of Tanmiat al-Rafidain* (quarterly), *Adab Al-Rafidian* (quarterly), *Annals of The Medical College* (quarterly), *Mesopotamia Agriculture & Forestry* (quarterly), *Journal of Education and Science* (quarterly), *Iraqi Journal of Veterinary Medicine* (quarterly), *Al-Rafidian Engineering Sciences* (quarterly), *Al-Rafidain Physical Education* (quarterly).

DEANS

College of Agriculture: Saad-Alla al-Nieme
College of Arts: Salah Ameen al-Jubouri
College of Engineering: Hisham Mustafa al-Anaaz
College of Medicine: Jamal Shareef M. Abed
College of Science: Khalid al-Yamour
College of Administration: Adil Flayih al-Ali
College of Education: Zuhair al-Sharook
College of Veterinary Medicine: Khair al-Deen Mohe al-Deen
College of Physical Education: Muaid Abdulla
College of Dentistry: Tariq Kassab Bashi
College of Law: Sallah al-Hadeethi
College of Pharmacy: Raad al-Bakua'
College of Teaching: Mahdi al-Aubadi
College of Nursing: Hamad Jindari
College of Fine Arts: Mahdi al-Aubadi

ATTACHED INSTITUTES

Computer Centre: Dir Subhi Humaadi al-Munasiri

Turkish Studies Centre: Dir Ebraheem Khaleel al-Alaaf

Research Centre for Saddam Dam: Dir Hameed Rasheed al-Jabari

Centre for the Development of Teaching Methods: Dir Mwafaq Hyawi

Remote Sensing Centre: Dir Hikmet Subhi al-Daghastemi

SADDAM UNIVERSITY

POB 47077, Jadiriyah, Baghdad
Telex: 214417
Fax: (1) 7760297
Founded 1993
Director: Prof. Laith Ismail Namiq
Registrar: Dr Amir A. Amir
Librarian: Zainab H. Rashid
Library of 12,000 vols
Number of teachers: 165
Number of students: 1,180

DEANS

Saddam College of Law: Dr Basim M. Saleh
Saddam College of Medicine: Dr Mahmood H. Hamash
College of Engineering: Dr Mazin A. Kadhim
College of Science: Dr Falah A. Attawi
College of Political Sciences: Dr Mazin I. al-Ramadani

HEADS OF DEPARTMENT

Chemistry and Biochemistry: Dr Kanan M. Jameel
Human Anatomy: Dr Mahmood H. Hamash
Bacteriology: Dr Tariq I. al-Juboori
Pathology: Dr Raji H. Mohammed
Physiology: Dr Nabeel A. Antewan
Pharmacology: Dr Farouq Hassan al-Jawad
Paediatrics: Dr Najim Aldin al-Roznamaji
Community Medicine: Dr Amjad D. Niazi
Surgery: Dr Usama N. Rafaat
Obstetrics and Gynaecology: Dr Qais A. Kobaa
Medicine: Khalid A. Mohammed
Civil Engineering: Dr Hani M. Fahmi
Electronics: Dr Fawzi M. Munir al-Naama
Mechanics: Dr Muayid D. Hanna
Chemical Engineering: Dr Talib B. Kashmoola
Physics: Dr Shakir J. Shakir
Chemistry: Dr Amir A. Tobia
Mathematics and Computer Applications: (vacant)
Computer Sciences: Dr Mohamed A. Shallal

UNIVERSITY OF SALAHADDIN

Arbil
Telephone: (0566) 21422
Telex: 218510
Founded 1968 as University of Sulaimaniya
State control
Languages of instruction: Arabic, English, Kurdish
Academic year: September to June (two terms)
President: Khusrow Ghani Shali
Library: see Libraries
Number of teachers: 560
Number of students: 7,000
Publications: *University News* (monthly, Arabic), *Statistical Abstract* (annually), *Zanco* (scientific journal, Arabic and English).

DEANS

College of Engineering: Dr M. Tayib
College of Agriculture: H. Shubar
College of Science: Dr Dia Al-Rawi
College of Arts: Abdul Karim Nassar
College of Administration: M. Karadagi

College of Education: ABBAS ALI ATTAR
College of Medicine: ABDUL MAJEED YOUNIS

UNIVERSITY OF TIKRIT

POB 42, Tikrit

Telephone: (01) 5434161
Telex: 216700
Fax: 825730

Founded 1987
State control
Languages of instruction: Arabic and English
Academic year: September to June

Chancellor: Dr AWNI K. SHAABAN
Vice-Chancellor: Dr AMIN S. BADAWI
Chief Administrative Officer: FAUK MUSHAL ADORY
Librarian: SABAH S. KHALEFE

Number of teachers: 364
Number of students: 2,296

DEANS

College of Medicine: Dr GHANIM Y. MUSTAFA-ALSHEIKH
College of Education for Women: Dr SABAH A. HAISHAN
College of Education: Dr ABDUL-MUNIM HAMAD
College of Engineering: Dr BASIM KADHEM GERIO
College of Agriculture: Dr R. A. LATIF

PROFESSORS

AL-OMER, A. K., Arabic Language
ALJUBURI, M. M.
AZIZ, A. A., Chemistry
GHANIM, Y. M.-A., Medicine
HAMAD, G. K., Arabic Language
HUSEIN, M. H., Civil Engineering
ISSAM, M. A. SH., Chemistry
LATIF, R. A., Crops
MAHMOOD, Y., History

Colleges

Al-Imam Al-A'dham College: Karkh, Baghdad; f. 1967, affiliated to Baghdad University 1978; degree course in Islamic studies; 34 teachers, 516 students; Dean Dr SUBHI MOHAMMAD JAMIL AL-KHAYYAT; publ. *Journal* (annually).

Foundation for Technical Institutes: Baghdad; f. 1972; attached to the Ministry of Higher Education; groups all the institutes of technology; Pres. H. M. S. ABDUL WAHAB.

INCORPORATED INSTITUTES

Institute of Technology: Baghdad; f. 1969; Dean N. S. MUSTAFA.

Technical Institute, Basrah: f. 1973; UNDP/Unesco project; technology and administration; 1,660 students; Dean H. I. MOHAMMED.

Technical Institute of Agriculture: Abu-Ghraib, Baghdad; f. 1964; Dean S. A. HASSAN.

Technical Institute of Medicine: Baghdad; f. 1964; Dean A. S. AL-MASHAT.

Technical Institute in Sulaimaniya: f. 1973; medical technology and administration; Dean R. M. ABDULLAH.

Institute of Administration: Rissafa, Baghdad; f. 1964; Dean A. S. AL-MASHAT.

Institute of Applied Arts: Baghdad; f. 1969; Dean A. NOOR-EDDIN.

Technical Institute in Mosul: f. 1976; technology and administration; Dean M. S. SAFFO.

Technical Institute in Kirkuk: f. 1976; technology and administration; Dean M. ABDUL RAHMAN.

Technical Institute of Agriculture: Aski-Kalak, Arbil; f. 1976; Dean M. S. ABBASS.

Technical Institute of Agriculture: Kumait, Missan; f. 1976; Dean H. L. SADIK.

Technical Institute in Hilla: f. 1976; technology and administration; Dean S. B. DERWISH.

Institute of Administration in Karkh (Baghdad): f. 1976; Dean T. SHAKER.

Technical Institute in Ramadi: f. 1977; technology and administration; Dean J. M. AMIN.

Technical Institute in Najaf: f. 1978; technology and administration; Dean M. A. JASSIM.

Technical Institute in Missan: f. 1979; technology and administration.

Technical Institute of Agriculture: Mussaib-Babylon; f. 1979.

Technical Institute of Agriculture: Shatra-Thi Qar; f. 1979.

IRELAND

Learned Societies

GENERAL

Royal Dublin Society: Ballsbridge, Dublin 4; tel. 6680866; fax 6604014; f. 1731 for the advancement of agriculture, industry, science and the arts; this Society is responsible for the annual Dublin Horse Show; 6,000 mems; the Society contains a scientific library; Pres. LIAM CONNELLAN; Chief Exec. SHANE CLEARY; Registrar KEVIN BRIGHT; library: see Libraries.

Royal Irish Academy: Academy House, 19 Dawson St, Dublin 2; tel. 6762570; fax 6762346; e-mail admin@ria.ie; f. 1785; cttees of Science (Sec. R. P. KERNAN), Polite Literature and Antiquities (Sec. R. FANNING); 277 mems, 60 hon. mems; library of 35,000 vols, 31,000 pamphlets, 1,800 sets of current periodicals, 2,500 MSS; Pres. M. HERITY; Sec. E. SAGARRA; Exec. Sec. PATRICK BUCKLEY; publs *Proceedings* (Section A, Mathematical and Physical Sciences; Section B, Biology and the Environment; Section C, Archaeology, Celtic Studies, History, Linguistics, Literature), *Annual Report*, *Eriu*, *Irish Journal of Earth Sciences*, *Irish Studies in International Affairs*.

AGRICULTURE, FISHERIES AND VETERINARY SCIENCE

Royal Horticultural Society of Ireland: Swanbrook House, Bloomfield Ave, Morehampton Rd, Donnybrook, Dublin 4; f. 1830; 1,100 mems; Pres. GEORGE A. F. HARRISON; Sec. MONICA NOLAN.

Society of Irish Foresters: c/o Royal Dublin Society, Ballsbridge, Dublin 4; f. 1942; aims to advance and spread the knowledge of forestry in all its aspects, to promote professional standards in forestry and the regulation of the forestry profession in Ireland; annual study tour, field days, annual symposium, lectures; 612 mems; Pres. EUGENE HENDRICK; Sec. PAT O'SULLIVAN; publ. *Irish Forestry* (2 a year).

Veterinary Council: 53 Lansdowne Rd, Dublin 4; tel. (1) 6684402; fax (1) 6604373; f. 1931; 2,024 registered names; Registrar M. FENLON.

ARCHITECTURE AND TOWN PLANNING

Architectural Association of Ireland: 8 Merrion Sq., Dublin 2; tel. 6761703; f. 1896 for the promotion of architecture by lectures, exhibitions, visits to buildings, etc.; 450 mems; Pres. SEAN MAHON; publs *The Green Book* (annually), *AAI Newsletter* (monthly), *New Irish Architecture* (annually).

Royal Institute of the Architects of Ireland: 8 Merrion Sq., Dublin 2; tel. 6761703; fax 6610948; f. 1839; 1,700 mems; Pres. EOIN O'COFAIGH; Hon. Sec. ANTHONY BRABAZON; Dir JOHN GRABY; publs *RIAI Year Book*, *Irish Architect* (monthly).

Society of Chartered Surveyors in the Republic of Ireland, The: 5 Wilton Place, Dublin 2; tel. (1) 6765500; constituent body of the Royal Institution of Chartered Surveyors; Dir A. P. SMITH.

BIBLIOGRAPHY, LIBRARY SCIENCE AND MUSEOLOGY

Library Association of Ireland (Cumann Leabharlann na hÉireann): 53 Upper Mount St, Dublin 2; tel. (1) 6619000; fax (1) 6761628; f. 1928, incorporated 1952; 650 mems; Pres. LIAM RONAYNE; Hon. Sec. BRENDAN TEELING; publs *An Leabharlann / The Irish Library* (quarterly), *Directory of Libraries in Ireland* (jointly with Northern Ireland Branch of the Library Association).

ECONOMICS, LAW AND POLITICS

Incorporated Law Society of Ireland: Blackhall Place, Dublin 7; tel. 6710711; telex 31219; fax 6710704; f. 1841; 5,000 mems; library of 12,000 vols; Dir-Gen. NOEL C. RYAN; Librarian MARGARET BYRNE; publs *Law Directory* (annually), *Gazette* (monthly).

Institute of Chartered Accountants in Ireland: Offices and Library: 87/89 Pembroke Rd, Ballsbridge, Dublin 4; Belfast Office: 11 Donegall Sq. South, Belfast, BT1 5JE; tel. 6680400; fax 6680842; e-mail charternet@icai.ie; inc. by Royal Charter 1888; 10,000 mems; library of 20,000 vols; Dir SEAN DORGAN; Sec. BRIAN WALSH; publ. *Accountancy Ireland* (6 a year).

Irish Society of Arts and Commerce: c/o Miss A. von Muntz, 55 Fairview Strand, Dublin; f. 1911; Pres. Rt Rev. Mgr EDWARD KISSANE; Sec. Miss A. VON MUNTZ.

King's Inns, Honorable Society of: Henrietta St, Dublin 1; tel. (1) 8744840; fax (1) 8726048; f. 1542; 62 Benchers; degree students and barristers are members of the Inns; library of over 115,000 vols; Under-Treas. CAMILLA MCALEESE; Education Dir J. K. WALDRON; Librarian J. ARMSTRONG; publ. *Irish Student Law Review* (annually).

Statistical and Social Inquiry Society of Ireland: c/o AIB Group, Bankcentre, Ballsbridge, Dublin 2; tel. 6600311; f. 1847 to promote the study of social and economic developments; *c.* 500 mems; Pres. Prof. DERMOT MCALEES; Hon. Secs E. JARDINE, B. M. WALSH, D. DE BUITLEIR; publ. *Journal* (annually).

EDUCATION

Church Education Society: 28 Bachelor's Walk, Dublin 1; f. 1839; Hon. Sec. Rev. W. J. BRIDCUT; publ. *Annual Report*.

National Council for Educational Awards: 26 Mountjoy Square, Dublin 1; tel. (1) 8556526; fax (1) 8554250; f. 1972; develops higher education outside the universities in the Republic of Ireland, approves and recognizes courses, grants and confers national awards, (degrees, diplomas, certificates), coordinates courses within and between institutions; Dir S. PÚIRSÉIL; publs *Annual Report*, *Directory of Approved Courses in Higher Education*, newsletters, etc.

FINE AND PERFORMING ARTS

Aosdána: 70 Merrion Sq., Dublin 2; tel. (1) 6611840; fax (1) 6761302; f. 1981; attached to the Arts Council; an affiliation of artists engaged in literature, music and visual arts; 200 mems; Dir TOSCAIRÍ; Registrar ADRIAN MUNNELLY.

Arts Council: 70 Merrion Square, Dublin 2; tel. (1) 6611840; fax (1) 6761302; e-mail info@artscouncil.ie; f. 1951; the statutory body appointed by the Minister for Arts, Culture and Gaeltacht to promote and assist the arts; in addition to organizing and promoting exhibitions and other activities itself, the Council gives grant-aid to many organizations including the theatre, opera, arts centres, arts festivals, exhibitions and publishers; also awards bursaries and scholarships to individual artists; Dir PATRICIA QUINN.

Music Association of Ireland Ltd, The: Waltons School of Music, 69 South Great Georges St, Dublin 2; tel. (1) 4785368; fax (1) 4754426; f. 1948; organises schools recital and workshop scheme, composer workshops, and Irish auditions for the European Union Youth Orchestra; Chair. RODNEY SENIOR; publs *Music Events Diary*, *Policy Statement of Music Education*, *Annual Report*.

Royal Hibernian Academy of Arts: 15 Ely Place, Dublin 2; tel. 6766212; f. 1823; 30 acads28 hon. mems, 10 assoc. mems; Pres. ARTHUR GIBNEY; Sec. BRETT MCENTAGART.

HISTORY, GEOGRAPHY AND ARCHAEOLOGY

Cork Historical and Archaeological Society: c/o Ballysheehy Lodge, Clogheen, Cork; f. 1891; 400 mems; Pres. JOHN J. SHEEHAN; Hon. Sec. PATRICK HOLOHAN; publ. *Journal* (annually).

Folklore of Ireland Society: University College, Belfield, Dublin 4; f. 1927; Pres. ANRAÍ Ó BRAONÁIN; Sec. DÉIRDRE HENNIGAN; Patrons SEÁN Ó SÚILLEABHÁIN, CAOIMHÍN Ó DANACHAIR; Editor SÉAMAS Ó CATHÁIN; publ. *Béaloideas* (annually).

Geographical Society of Ireland: c/o Hon. Sec., Dept of Geography, Trinity College, Dublin; tel. 7021143; fax 6713397; f. 1934; seeks to provide information and promote discussion about a wide range of topics of geographical interest, within Ireland and abroad; organizes lectures and seminars, field trips; *c.* 200 mems; Pres. Dr P. DUFFY; Sec. MICHAEL QUIGLEY; publs *Irish Geography* (2 a year), *Geonews* (2 a year).

Military History Society of Ireland: University College Dublin, Newman House, 86 St Stephen's Green, Dublin 2; f. 1949; 1,000 mems; Hon. Secs Dr PATRICK MCCARTHY (Correspondence), R. O'SHEA (Membership); publ. *The Irish Sword* (2 a year).

Old Dublin Society: City Assembly House, 58 South William St, Dublin 2; f. 1934; promotes study of history and antiquities of Dublin; 15,000 mems; library of 1,300 vols; Pres. ANTHONY P. BEHAN; Sec. SHEILA SMITH; publ. *Dublin Historical Record* (quarterly).

Royal Society of Antiquaries of Ireland: 63 Merrion Sq., Dublin 2; tel. (1) 6761749; fax (1) 6761749; f. 1849; 1,100 mems; library of 13,000 vols; Hon. Gen. Sec. Dr DOROTHY KELLY; publ. *Journal* (annually).

LANGUAGE AND LITERATURE

Conradh na Gaeilge (Gaelic League): 6 Sráid Fhearchair, Dublin 2; tel. (1) 4757401; fax (1) 4757402; f. 1893; 200 brs; Pres. GEARÓID Ó CAIREALLÁIN; Gen. Sec. SEÁN MAC MATHÚNA; publs *Feasta*, *An tUltach* (monthlies), pamphlets.

Irish PEN: 26 Rosslyn, Killarney Rd, Bray, Co. Wicklow; f. 1921; 62 mems; Chair. Fr J. A. GAUGHAN; Hon. Sec. ARTHUR FLYNN.

Irish Texts Society: c/o Royal Bank of Scotland, 49 Charing Cross Rd, London, SW1A

2DX, England; f. 1898 to advance public education by promoting the study of Irish literature, and to publish texts in the Irish language, with translations, notes, etc.; 640 mems; library of 57 vols in print, and dictionary; Pres. Prof. PÁDRAIG Ó RIAIN; Hon. Sec. SEÁN HUTTON.

MEDICINE

Apothecaries' Hall: 95 Merrion Sq., Dublin 2; tel. 6762147; Gov. Dr MALACHY POWELL; Registrar Dr BRENDAN POWELL.

Dental Council: 57 Merrion Sq., Dublin 2; tel. (1) 6762069; f. 1928 as the Dental Board, superseded by the Dental Council in 1985; registration of dentists and controls standards of education and conduct among dentists in Ireland; Pres. DANIEL I. KEANE; Registrar THOMAS FARREN.

Irish Medical Organisation: 10 Fitzwilliam Place, Dublin 2; tel. 6767273; fax 6612758; f. 1936; CEO GEORGE MCNEICE; 4,000 mems; publ. *Irish Medical Journal* (8 a year).

Medical Council: Lynn House, Portobello Court, Lower Rathmines Rd, Dublin 6; tel. (1) 496-5588; fax (1) 496-5972; f. 1978; Pres. Prof. G. P. BURY; Registrar BRIAN V. LEA.

Pharmaceutical Society of Ireland: 37 Northumberland Rd, Dublin 4; tel. (1) 6600699; f. 1875; Pres. MICHAEL DURCAN; Registrar and Sec. EUGENIE CANAVAN; publ. *Calendar*.

Royal Academy of Medicine in Ireland: 6 Kildare St, Dublin 2; f. 1882; 1,500 Fellows; Pres. Prof. KEVIN O'MALLEY; Gen. Sec. and Treas. Prof. BRIAN L. SHEPPARD; publ. *Irish Journal of Medical Science* (quarterly).

NATURAL SCIENCES

Biological Sciences

Dublin University Biological Association: Trinity College, Dublin; f. 1874; 400 mems; Pres. Prof. IAN TEMPERLEY; Hon. Sec. EMER LOUGHREY.

Zoological Society of Ireland: Phoenix Park, Dublin 8; tel. (1) 6771425; fax (1) 6771660; f. 1830; 9,000 mems; Pres. JOSEPH MCCULLOUGH; Hon. Sec. DOROTHY KILROY; Dir PETER WILSON; publ. *Annual Report*.

Physical Sciences

Institute of Chemistry of Ireland, The: c/o Royal Dublin Society, Science Section, Ballsbridge, Dublin 4; f. 1950; 850 mems; Pres. B. GERAGHTY; Hon. Sec. J. P. RYAN; publ. *Irish Chemical News* (2 a year).

Institute of Physics (Irish Branch): c/o Dr J. McLaughlin, NIBEC, University of Ulster, Newtownabbey, Co. Antrim, BT37 0QB, Northern Ireland; tel. (1232) 368933; fax (1232) 366863; e-mail jao.mclaughlin@ulst.ac.uk; f. 1964; Chair. Dr R. MCCULLOUGH; Hon. Sec. Dr J. MCLAUGHLIN.

Irish Astronomical Society: P.O. Box 2547, Dublin 14; tel. (1) 820-2135; f. 1937; 110 mems; video and book libraries; Sec JAMES O'CONNOR; publ. *Orbit* (every 2 months).

PHILOSOPHY AND PSYCHOLOGY

Psychological Society of Ireland: 13 Adelaide Rd, Dublin 2; tel. (1) 4783916; f. 1970 to advance psychological knowledge and research in Ireland, to ensure maintenance of high standards of professional training and practice, to seek the development of psychological services; 1,000 mems; Pres. Dr JOAN TIERNAN; Hon. Sec. JOSEPHINE GLEESON; publs *The Irish Journal of Psychology*, *The Irish Psychologist*.

Theosophical Society in Ireland: 31 Pembroke Rd, Dublin 4; f. 1919; Pres. Rep. W. WOODS.

University Philosophical Society: Trinity College, Dublin 2; tel. (1) 7022089; fax (1) 6778996; f. 1684, re-f. 1854; 'Major Society' for composition, reading and discussion of papers on literary, political, philosophical and scientific subjects; 1,150 mems; Pres. JOSEPH GUERIN; Sec. NICK ROYLE; publs *Laws*, *Phil-in* (occasional).

TECHNOLOGY

Engineering and Scientific Association of Ireland: Green Hills, 13 Mather Rd South, Mount Merrion, Co. Dublin; f. 1903; 100 mems; Pres. T. A. MCINERNEY; Hon. Sec. and Treas. M. J. HIGGINS; publ. *Annual Report*.

Forbairt: Glasnevin, Dublin 9; tel. (1) 8082000; fax (1) 8082020; f. by the govt to facilitate the development of Irish business and to provide a range of science and technology services and programmes for enterprise in Ireland.

Institution of Civil Engineers (Republic of Ireland Division): 2 Putland Rd, Bray, Co. Wicklow; tel. 2860517; f. 1818; *c.* 550 mems; Chair. DON N. MCENTEE; Hon. Sec. GABRIEL DENNISON; publs *New Civil Engineer* (weekly), *Municipal Engineer* (quarterly).

Institution of Electrical Engineers, The (Irish Centre): c/o Hon. Sec. J. A. Lysaght, Telecom Eireann, St Stephen's Green West, Dublin 2; Chair. P. ROCHE; Hon. Sec. J. A. LYSAGHT.

Institution of Engineers of Ireland, The: 22 Clyde Rd, Ballsbridge, Dublin 4; tel. 6684341; fax 6685509; f. 1835; promotes knowledge and advancement of the engineering profession, conducts examinations and confers the designation 'Chartered Engineer'; 14,700 mems; Pres. JACK KAVANAGH; Dir-Gen. FRANK BURKE; publs *Transactions*, *Monthly Journal*.

Irish Society for Design and Craftwork, The: c/o Miss Angela O'Brien, 112 Ranelagh, Dublin 6; f. 1894; Chair. Prof. DOMNALL O'MURCADA; Hon. Sec. Miss ANGELA O'BRIEN.

Research Institutes

GENERAL

Science Policy Research Centre: Faculty of Commerce, University College, Belfield, Dublin 4; tel. (1) 7068263; fax (1) 7061132; f. 1969 to carry out research and to undertake commissioned studies in areas related to science and technology policy; 6 staff; small private library; Dir Prof. DENIS J. COGAN.

AGRICULTURE, FISHERIES AND VETERINARY SCIENCE

Teagasc (Agriculture and Food Development Authority): 19 Sandymount Avenue, Ballsbridge, Dublin 4; tel. (1) 6688188; telex 30459; fax (1) 6688023; f. 1988; national body providing advisory, research, education and training services to the agriculture and food industry; activities are integrated and managed through six divisions; Dir Dr LIAM DOWNEY.

Divisions:

Grange Research and Development Division (Teagasc): Dunsany, Co. Meath; tel. (46) 25214; fax (46) 25187; national beef division; headquarters for advisory and training services in Teagasc North; Dir DONAL CAREY.

Kildalton College of Agriculture: Piltown, Co. Kilkenny; tel. (51) 643105; fax (51) 643446; national crops division and headquarters for advisory and training services in Teagasc South; Dir MICHAEL GALVIN.

Moorepark Research and Development Division (Teagasc): Fermoy, Co. Cork; tel. (25) 31422; fax (25) 32498; national centre for research, advice and training in dairying and pig production; Head of Dairy Husbandry Dr KEVIN O'FARRELL; Head of Pig Husbandry BRENDAN LYNCH.

Rural Development Division (Teagasc): Athenry, Co. Galway; tel. (91) 44473; fax (91) 44296; national centre for rural development; Dir PETER SEERY.

National Food Centre: Dunsinea, Castleknock, Dublin 15; tel. (1) 8383222; fax (1) 8383684; centre providing research, development and consultancy services for all aspects of food production (except dairy products); Dir Dr VIVION TARRANT.

National Dairy Products Research Centre: Moorepark, Fermoy, Co. Cork; tel. (25) 31422; fax (25) 32563; national centre providing research, development and consultancy services for the dairy industry; Dir Dr LIAM DONNELLY.

BIBLIOGRAPHY, LIBRARY SCIENCE AND MUSEOLOGY

Irish Manuscripts Commission: 73 Merrion Sq., Dublin 2; f. 1928; 17 mems; Chair. Dr BRIAN TRAINOR; Research Officer Dr MICHAEL J. HAREN; Business Records Surveyor BRIAN DONNELLY; 166 published vols of historical interest.

ECONOMICS, LAW AND POLITICS

Economic and Social Research Institute: 4 Burlington Rd, Dublin 4; tel. 6671525; fax 6686231; f. 1960; 130 individual mems and 400 corporate mems; library of 40,000 vols; Pres. M. F. DOYLE; Chair. J. F. HARFORD; Dir B. J. WHELAN; Sec. J. ROUGHAN; numerous publications.

HISTORY, GEOGRAPHY AND ARCHAEOLOGY

Genealogical Office (incorporating Office of the Chief Herald and State Heraldic Museum): 2 Kildare Street, Dublin; tel. (1) 6030305; f. 1552; granting, confirming, registering of armorial bearings, genealogy consultancy service, in-house research service; 1,000 MSS from 1350 to the present, 100,000 archive items from *c.* 1800 to the present; Chief Herald of Ireland (vacant).

LANGUAGE AND LITERATURE

Institiúid Teangeolaíochta Éireann/ Linguistics Institute of Ireland: 31 Fitzwilliam Place, Dublin 2; tel. (1) 6765489; fax (1) 6610004; f. 1972; research in applied linguistics with special reference to the Irish language and teaching and learning of languages generally; 23 mems; library of 10,000 monographs, 151 periodicals; Chair. CLÍONA DE BHALDRAITHE MARSH; Dir EOGHAN MAC AOGÁIN; publs *Teangeolas* (2 a year), *Annual Report*, *Language, Culture and Curriculum* (3 a year).

MEDICINE

Health Research Board: 73 Lower Baggot St, Dublin 2; tel. (1) 6761176; fax (1) 6611856; f. 1987, fmrly Medical Research Ccl of Ireland; Chief Exec. Dr J. V. O'GORMAN.

NATURAL SCIENCES

Physical Sciences

Dunsink Observatory: Dublin 15; tel. (1) 8387959; telex 31687; fax (1) 8387090; e-mail astro@dunsink.dias.ie; f. 1785; part of Dublin Institute for Advanced Studies; 12 staff; library of 5,000 vols, 75 periodicals.

Libraries and Archives

Cork

University College Cork Library: The Boole Library, University College, Cork; tel. (21) 276871; fax (21) 903119; e-mail library@ucc.ie; f. 1849; 500,000 vols, including Irish Manuscript collection (microfilm), Senft (philosophy), Torna (Irish), Cooke (travel), John E. Cummings Memorial Collection (humour), Langlands Collection (Africa); EEC documentation centre; Irish copyright privilege; Librarian JOHN FITZGERALD.

Dublin

An Chomhairle Leabharlanna (Library Council): 53–54 Upper Mount St, Dublin 2; tel. (1) 6761167; fax (1) 6766721; e-mail libcounc@iol.ie; f. 1947 by Public Libraries Act; advises local authorities and the Min. for the Environment on the development of public library services; provides an information service on libraries and librarianship; operates the inter-library lending system for Ireland, and provides the Secretariat for the Cttee on Library Co-operation in Ireland; Dir NORMA MCDERMOTT; publs *Annual Report, Irish Library News, Serials Informations News, TIPS, Region K* (Ireland), *ISBN List*.

Central Catholic Library: 74 Merrion Sq., Dublin 2; tel. (1) 6761264; f. 1922; controlled by the Central Catholic Library Association; open to the public; lending and reference depts containing material on every aspect of Catholicism; audio and video cassettes; 130,000 vols, incl. large journal collection, special collection of 2,000 vols on Christian art, Ireland Collection; Librarian TERESA WHITINGTON.

Chester Beatty Library: 20 Shrewsbury Rd, Dublin 4; tel. 2692386; fax 2830983; donated to the Irish nation by Sir Chester Beatty in 1968; contains one of the world's leading collections of Islamic and Far Eastern art, and important Western and Biblical MSS and miniatures; incunabula and other printed books; Librarian MICHAEL RYAN.

Dublin Public Libraries: Cumberland House, Fenian St, Dublin 2; tel. 6619000; telex 33287; fax 6761628; 2.4 m. vols; special collections include early Dublin printing and fine binding, incunabula, political pamphlets and cartoons, Dublin periodicals and 18th-century plays, Abbey Theatre material, Swift and Yeats material; extensive local history collection in books, newspapers and pictures; representative holdings of modern Dublin presses; special music library; language learning centre; City Librarian DEIRDRE ELLIS-KING.

Irish Theatre Archive: C/o Dublin City Archives, City Assembly House, 58 South William St, Dublin 2; tel. (1) 6775877; fax (1) 6775954; f. 1981 to collect and preserve Ireland's theatre heritage; large collection of material: programmes, posters, play-scripts, prompt-books, etc.; organizes lecture series, exhibitions; Archivist MARY CLARK.

Law Library: Four Courts, Dublin 7; tel. 8720622; fax 8720455; controlled by the Council of the Bar of Ireland; open to mems of the Irish Bar only; 100,000 vols; Librarian JENNEFER ASTON; Dir JOHN DOWLING.

Marsh's Library: St Patrick's Close, Dublin 8; tel. 4543511; fax 4543511; e-mail marshlib@iol.ie; f. 1707; 25,000 vols and 300 MSS; Keeper MURIEL MCCARTHY.

National Archives: Bishop St, Dublin 8; tel. (1) 4072300; fax (1) 4072333; f. 1988 (merger of Public Record Office, f. 1867, and State Paper Office, f. 1702), under the National Archives Act, to preserve and make accessible the records of Departments of State, courts, other public service organizations, and private donors; 25,000 linear metres of archives; Dir Dr DAVID CRAIG; publ. *Reports of Director and Advisory Council* (annually).

National Library of Ireland: Kildare St, Dublin 2; tel. 6030200; fax 6766690; f. 1877; 500,000 vols including Irish printing collection, pamphlets, newspapers, 55,000 MSS, including 1,200 Gaelic MSS, 50,000 photographic negatives; also maps, prints and drawings, microforms; serves as a national bibliographical centre; Dir BRENDAN O'DONOGHUE (acting).

Oireachtas Library: Leinster House, Dublin; tel. (1) 6183412; fax (1) 6184109; selective works of parliamentary interest, the nucleus of which was the Chief Secretary's Office, Dublin Castle; Librarian MAURA CORCORAN.

Representative Church Body Library: Braemor Park, Rathgar, Dublin 14; tel. 4923979; fax 4924770; e-mail library@ireland.anglican.org; f. 1932; theological library controlled by the Representative Body of the Church of Ireland; 40,000 vols, mainly theology, history, ethics and education; Church of Ireland archives; MSS collection, mainly ecclesiastical; Librarian and Archivist Dr RAYMOND REFAUSSÉ.

Royal College of Surgeons in Ireland Library: The Mercer Library, Mercer St Lower, Dublin 2; tel. (1) 4022411; fax (1) 4022457; e-mail library@rcsi.ie; f. 1784; 75,000 vols; special collections: archives of RCSI and Dublin hospitals, 20,000 rare books, medical pamphlets from 17th century; Librarian BEATRICE M. DORAN.

Royal Dublin Society Library: Ballsbridge, Dublin 4; tel. 6680866; fax 6604014; f. 1731; scientific collection of 105,000 vols, general collection of 120,000 vols, and an agricultural collection of 11,000 vols and pamphlets; Librarian MARY KELLEHER.

Trinity College Library: College St, Dublin 2; tel. (1) 6081665; telex 93782; fax (1) 6719003; f. 1592; University and British/Irish legal deposit library; 3,500,000 printed books, 5,000 MSS, including the Book of Kells and an extensive collection of music scores and maps; Librarian W. G. SIMPSON; publ. *Long Room* (annually).

University College Dublin Library: Belfield, Dublin 4; tel. 7067777; fax 2837667; f. 1908; 975,000 vols, 5,000 periodicals; special collections include Baron Palles (Law) Library of 2,500 vols, Zimmer (Celtic) Library of 2,000 vols, C. P. Curran (Irish literature), McCormack (music), Ó Lochlainn and O'Kelley (Irish printing) collections; Librarian SEAN PHILLIPS.

Galway

Galway County Libraries: Island House, Cathedral Square, Galway; tel. (91) 562471; fax (91) 565039; e-mail gallibr@indigo.ie; f. *c.* 1927; 350,000 vols; County Librarian PATRICK MCMAHON; publs *Annual Reports*; publ. *Annual Reports*.

University College Galway, James Hardiman Library: Galway; tel. (91) 524809; fax (91) 522394; f. 1849; 257,000 vols; extensive collection of books in Irish published since 1890; EEC Documentation Centre; enjoys Irish copyright privilege; Librarian MARIE REDDAN.

Maynooth

Library of the National Univeristy of Ireland, Maynooth, and of St Patrick's College, Maynooth: Maynooth, Co. Kildare; tel. (1) 7083884; fax (1) 6286008; f. 1795; 300,000 vols incl. EC Documentation Centre; special collections: Russell Library with incunabula, pre-1850 imprints, Irish MSS, Salamanca Collection letters, 18th-century pamphlets, bibles, Furlong Historical and Theological Collection; Librarian Dr THOMAS KABDEBO.

Museums and Art Galleries

Cork

Cork Public Museum: Fitzgerald Park, Cork; tel. (21) 270679; fax (21) 270931; f. 1945; sections devoted to Irish history and archaeology, also municipal, social and economic history, Cork glass, silver and lace; items of special interest include the Cork helmet horns, the Garryduff gold bird, the Roche silver collar, civic maces, municipal oar, freedom boxes and Grace Cup of Cork Corporation; Curator STELLA CHERRY.

University College Zoological Museum: Lee Maltings, Prospect Row, Cork; tel. 276871; fax 270562; Curator TRICHA J. MURPHY.

Dublin

Civic Museum: 58 South William St, Dublin; tel. (1) 6794260; f. 1953; original exhibits of antiquarian and historical interest pertaining to Dublin; prints, photographs, tapestries, maps, glass and silverwork, coins, medals; Curator THOMAS P. O'CONNOR.

Dublin Writers Museum: 18 Parnell Square, Dublin 1; tel. (1) 8722077; f. 1991; history of Irish literature; library; Administrator FIONA MCKIERRAN.

Hugh Lane Municipal Gallery of Modern Art, The: Charlemont House, Parnell Sq. North, Dublin 1; tel. (1) 8741903; fax (1) 8722182; e-mail hughlane@iol.ie; works of Irish, English and Continental schools of painting, and pictures from the Sir Hugh Lane collection; sculptures; Dir BARBARA DAWSON.

James Joyce Museum: Martello Tower, Sandycove, Co. Dublin; tel. (1) 2809265; f. 1962; relics of the writer and critical works on him; Curator ROBERT NICHOLSON.

National Botanic Gardens Glasnevin: Glasnevin, Dublin 9; tel. (1) 8374388; fax 8360080; f. 1795; includes Irish National Herbarium; 60 staff; library of 40,000 vols, including collection of illustrated botanical works; Dir DONAL SYNNOTT; publs *Glasra, Occasional Papers*.

National Gallery of Ireland: Merrion Sq. West, Dublin 2; tel. 6615133; fax 6615372; f. 1854; national, historical and portrait galleries; continental European, British and Irish masters since 1250; 2,500 oil paintings, 300 sculptures, 5,200 drawings and watercolours, 3,000 prints; Dir RAYMOND KEAVENEY; publ. illustrated catalogues.

National Museum of Ireland: Kildare St, Dublin 2; tel. 6777444; fax 6766116; f. 1731 by Royal Dublin Society; includes (1) Irish Antiquities Division (Keeper EAMONN P. KELLY); (2) Art and Industrial Division (Keeper MAIREAD DUNLEVY); (3) Irish Folklife Division (vacant); (4) Natural History Division, which includes zoological and geological sections (Dr J. P. O'CONNOR); Dir Dr PATRICK F. WALLACE.

Royal College of Surgeons in Ireland Museum: St Stephen's Green, Dublin 2; f. 1820; Curator Prof. MARY LEADER.

Strokestown

Famine Museum: Strokestown Park, Strokestown, Co. Roscommon; tel. (78) 33013; fax (78) 33712; f. 1994; Irish famine of 1840s; Dir DECLAN JONES.

Universities

DUBLIN CITY UNIVERSITY

Dublin 9
Telephone: (1) 7045000
Telex: 30690
Fax: (1) 8360830
Founded 1980 as National Institute for Higher Education, Dublin; University status 1989
State control
Academic year: September to May
President: Dr DANIEL O'HARE
Registrar: Prof. JOHN CARROLL
Secretary: MARTIN CONRY
Librarian: Dr ALAN MACDOUGALL
Number of teachers: 270
Number of students: 8,012
Publications: annual report, undergraduate and postgraduate prospectuses, *NewsLink* (3 a year).

DEANS

Dublin City University Business School: Prof. B. LEAVY
Faculty of Computing and Mathematical Sciences: Prof. A. SMEATON
Faculty of Science and Paramedical Studies: Prof. M. SMYTH
Faculty of Engineering and Design: Prof. C. MCCORKELL
Faculty of Distance Education: Prof. C. CURRAN
Joint Faculty of Humanities: Dr P. TRAVERS
Joint Faculty of Education: J. CANAVAN
Research: Dr C. LONG

HEADS OF SCHOOLS

Faculty of Computing and Mathematical Sciences:
  Mathematical Sciences: Prof. A. WOOD
  Computer Applications: Prof. M. RYAN
Faculty of Distance Education:
  Distance Education: Prof. C. CURRAN
Faculty of Science and Paramedical Studies:
  Biological Sciences: Prof. R. O'KENNEDY
  Chemical Sciences: Prof. H. VOS
  Physical Sciences: Prof. E. KENNEDY
  Nursing Studies: (vacant)
Faculty of Engineering and Design:
  Electronic Engineering: Prof. C. MCCORKELL
  Mechanical and Manufacturing Engineering: Prof. M. S. HASHMI
Joint Faculty of Humanities:
  Communications: Prof. F. CORCORAN
  Applied Languages and Intercultural Studies: Prof. M. TOWNSON
Joint Faculty of Education:
  Education Studies: (vacant)

RESEARCH CENTRES

Centre for Laser Plasma Research: Dir Prof. E. KENNEDY.

Inorganic Chemistry Research New Materials and Molecular Devices Centre: Dir Prof. H. VOS.

National Cell and Tissue Culture Centre: Dir Prof. M. CLYNES.

Telecommunications Centre: Dir Dr T. CURRAN.

Optronics Ireland Laboratory: Dir Prof. M. HENRY.

National Centre for Technology in Education: Dir J. MORRISSEY.

Materials Processing Research Centre: Dir Prof. S. HASHMI.

Centre for Power Electronics: Dir J. DOWLING.

Environmental Research Monitoring and Consultancy Centre: Dir Dr B. QUILTY.

Sensor Technology Instrumentation and Process Analysis Centre: Dir Dr D. DIAMOND.

National Centre for Software Engineering: Dir R. COCHRAN.

National Centre for Language Technology: Dir J. PEARSON.

Communication Technology and Culture Research Centre: Dir P. PRESTON.

Surface Engineering Centre: Dir Dr M. HOPKINS.

ATTACHED INSTITUTE

National Distance Education Centre: Dublin 9; a faculty of the university; f. 1982; the executive arm of the Nat. Distance Education Ccl; Dir Prof. CHRIS CURRAN.

ATTACHED COLLEGE

St Patrick's College: Drumcondra, Dublin 9; tel. (1) 8376191; fax (1) 8376197; f. 1875; joint faculties, with Dublin City University, of Education and of Humanities; 58 academic staff; 1,033 students; library of 100,000 vols; Pres. Very Rev. SIMON CLYNE; Registrar Dr LIAM MACMATHÚNA; publs *Studia Hibernica* (annually), *The Irish Journal of Education* (2 a year).

UNIVERSITY OF DUBLIN TRINITY COLLEGE

Dublin 2
Telephone: (1) 6772941
Telex: 93782
Fax: (1) 6772694
Founded 1592
Chancellor: (vacant)
Pro-Chancellors: W. J. L. RYAN, R. P. WILLIS, Sir PETER FROGGATT, A. J. F. O'REILLY, S. J. G. DENHAM
Provost: T. N. MITCHELL
Vice-Provost: A. D. H. MAYES
Registrar: D. J. MCCONNELL
Secretary to the College: M. GLEESON
Librarian: W. G. SIMPSON
Library: see Libraries
Number of teachers: 539
Number of students: 12,600 (including postgraduate)
Publications: *Hermathena*, *University of Dublin Calendar*.

DEANS

Faculty of Arts (Humanities): L. A. CAMERON
Faculty of Arts (Letters): V. J. SCATTERGOOD
Faculty of Business, Economic and Social Studies: N. T. KEARNEY
Faculty of Engineering and Systems Sciences: J. B. GRIMSON
Faculty of Health Sciences: D. COAKLEY
Faculty of Science: (vacant)
Graduate Studies: J. A. N. PARNELL

PROFESSORS

Faculty of Arts (Humanities):
  BINCHY, W., Law
  CLARKE, A., Modern History
  CULLEN, L. M., Modern Irish History
  DUNCAN, W. R., Law and Jurisprudence
  FREYNE, S. V., Theology
  LYONS, W. E., Philosophy
  MAYES, A. D. H., Hebrew
  RICE, J. V., Education
  STALLEY, R. A., History of Art
Faculty of Arts (Letters):
  BREATNACH, L. P., Early Irish
  BROWN, T. P. MCC., Anglo-Irish Literature
  DILLON, J. M., Greek
  DIXON, V. F., Spanish
  KENNEDY, D., Drama and Theatre Studies
  KENNELLY, T. B., Modern Literature (English)
  Ó HÁINLE, C. G., Irish
  SCATTERGOOD, V. J., Medieval and Renaissance Literature (English)
  SCOTT, D. H. T., French (Textual and Visual Studies)
  TATLOW, A. T., Comparative Literature
  WRIGHT, B., French Literature
Faculty of Business, Economic and Social Studies:
  HILL, R. J., Comparative Government (Political Science)
  KEATINGE, N. P., European Integration (Political Science)
  LAVER, M. J., Political Science
  MCALEESE, D. F., Political Economy
  MURRAY, J. A., Business Studies
Faculty of Engineering and Systems Sciences:
  BOLAND, F. M., Electronic and Electrical Engineering
  BYRNE, J. G., Computer Science
  FITZPATRICK, J. A., Mechanical and Manufacturing Engineering
  HARRIS, N. R., Computer Science
  HASLETT, J., Statistics
  NEELAMKAVIL, F., Computer Science
  PERRY, S. H., Civil Engineering
Faculty of Health Sciences:
  BELL, C., Physiology
  BONNAR, J., Obstetrics and Gynaecology
  CLAFFEY, N. M., Periodontology
  CLARE, A. W., Clinical Psychiatry
  CLARKSON, J., Public Dental Health
  COAKLEY, D., Medical Gerontology
  FEELY, J., Pharmacology and Therapeutics
  FITZGERALD, M., Child and Adolescent Psychiatry
  HOEY, H. M. C. V., Paediatrics
  HOLLYWOOD, D. P., Clinical Oncology
  MCCANN, S. R., Haematology
  MCDEVITT, W. E. A., Prosthetic Dentistry
  MCKENNA, P., Clinical Obstetrics and Gynaecology
  MALONE, J. F., Medical Physics
  O'BRIEN, M., Anatomy
  O'DOWD, T. C., General Practice
  SCOTT, J. M., Experimental Nutrition
  SHANLEY, D. B., Oral Health
  TIMON, C. V. I., Clinical Otolaryngology
  WEBB, M. G. T., Psychiatry
  WEIR, D. G., Clinical Medicine
Faculty of Science:
  ALLEN, P. A., Geology
  COEY, J. M. D., Experimental Physics
  CORISH, J., Physical Chemistry
  CORRIGAN, O. I., Pharmaceutics
  CUNNINGHAM, E. P., Animal Genetics
  DORMAN, C. J., Microbiology
  FOSTER, T. J., Molecular Microbiology
  HEGARTY, J., Laser Physics
  HUMPHRIES, P., Medical Molecular Genetics
  JONES, M. B., Botany
  LLOYD, D. R., General Chemistry
  MCBRIERTY, V. J., Polymer Physics
  MCCONNELL, D. J., Genetics
  MCMURRY, T. B. H., Organic Chemistry
  ROBERTS, B. L., Zoology
  SCOTT, J. M., Experimental Nutrition
  SHAW, G. G., Pharmacology
  TIPTON, K. F., Biochemistry
  WATTS, W. A., Quaternary Ecology
  WEAIRE, D. L., Physics
  WHITEHEAD, A. S., Medical Genetics

HEADS OF DEPARTMENTS

(Non-Professorial)

Faculty of Arts (Humanities):
  Education: S. M. PARKES
  Hebrew, Biblical and Theological Studies: M. JUNKER-KENNY
  Medieval History: C. E. MEEK
  Music: S. J. TREZISE

Philosophy: D. BERMAN
Psychology: H. V. SMITH

Faculty of Arts (Letters):
Centre for Language and Communication Studies: D. G. LITTLE
English: E. NÍ CHUILLEANÁIN
French: R. F. COX
Germanic Studies: T. R. JACKSON
Italian: C. S. LONERGAN
Russian: P. J. O'MEARA
Spanish: J. F. WHISTON

Faculty of Business, Economic and Social Studies:
Economics: F. P. RUANE
Social Studies: R. H. GILLIGAN
Sociology: B. M. BRADBY

Faculty of Health Sciences:
Clinical Speech and Language Studies: M. LEAHY
Histopathology and Morbid Anatomy: E. C. SWEENEY
Nursing and Midwifery Studies: C. M. BEGLEY
Occupational Therapy: G. O'NEILL
Oral Surgery, Oral Medicine and Oral Pathology: H. J. BARRY
Physiotherapy: P. YUNG

Faculty of Science:
Chemistry: J. M. KELLY
Geography: A. C. MACLARAN
Mathematics: S. SEN
Pharmacognosy: I. L. I. HOOK
Pharmaceutical Chemistry: M. J. MEEGAN
Physics: W. J. BLAU

RECOGNIZED COLLEGES

Church of Ireland College of Education: Upper Rathmines Rd, Dublin 6; tel. 4970033; 3-year course leading to BEd pass degree; Principal SYDNEY BLAIN.

Froebel College of Education: Sion Hill, Blackrock, Co. Dublin; tel. 2888520; 3-year course leading to BEd pass degree; Principal Sister DARINA HOSEY.

St Catherine's College of Education for Home Economics: Sion Hill, Blackrock, Co. Dublin; tel. 2884989; f. 1929; 4-year course leading to BEd (Home Econ.) honours degree; Principal CLARE O'BRIEN.

St Mary's College, Marino: Griffith Ave, Dublin 9; tel. 8335111; 3-year course leading to BEd pass degree; Principal Br S. NOLAN.

NATIONAL UNIVERSITY OF IRELAND

49 Merrion Sq., Dublin 2
Telephone: 6767246-7
Fax: 6621574

Founded 1908

Chancellor: (vacant)
Vice-Chancellor: Dr P. FOTTRELL
Registrar: Dr JOHN NOLAN

Publication: *Calendar*.

CONSTITUENT COLLEGES

University College Dublin

Belfield, Dublin 4
Telephone: (1) 7067777
Telex: 32693
Fax: (1) 2694409

Founded 1908

President: ART COSGROVE
Registrar: CAROLINE HUSSEY
Secretary: GERARD A. WRIGHT
Librarian: SEAN PHILLIPS

Library: see Libraries
Number of teachers: 818 full-time, 1,355 part-time
Number of students: 17,282

Publications: *President's Report*, prospectuses, etc.

DEANS

Faculty of Arts: Dr FERGUS D'ARCY
Faculty of Philosophy and Sociology: Prof. PATRICK CLANCY
Faculty of Celtic Studies: Dr SEOSAMH WATSON
Faculty of Science: Dr GERARD DOYLE
Faculty of Law: PAUL A. O'CONNOR
Faculty of Medicine: Prof. RONAN G. O'REGAN
Faculty of Commerce: Prof. PHILIP BOURKE
Faculty of Engineering and Architecture: Prof. VINCENT A. DODD
Faculty of General Agriculture: Prof. P. JOSEPH MANNION
Faculty of Veterinary Medicine: Dr MICHAEL MONAGHAN

PROFESSORS

(Many professors are members of more than one faculty; entry here is shown under one faculty only)

Faculties of Arts, Philosophy and Sociology and Celtic Studies:
ALMQVIST, B., Irish Folklore
BARNES, J. C., Italian
BARTLETT, T., Modern Irish History
BENSON, C., Psychology
BOLAND, P. J., Statistics
BREATNACH, P., Classical Irish
BURKE, M., Library and Information Studies
BUTTIMER, A., Geography
BYRNE, F. J., Early (incl. Medieval) Irish History
CALDICOTT, C. E. J., French
CATHCART, K., Near Eastern Languages
CONVERY, F. J., Environmental Studies
DINEEN, S., Mathematics
FANNING, J. R., Modern History
GALLAGHER, P., Spanish
GARVIN, T. C., Politics
HAYES, M., Mathematical Physics
KIBERD, D., Anglo-Irish Literature and Drama
LAFFAN, B., European Politics
MCCARTHY, M. J., History of Art
MCQUILLAN, D., Mathematics
MAYS, J. C. C., Modern English and American Literature
MENNELL, S., Sociology
MORAN, D., Philosophy
NEARY, J. P., Political Economy
NÍ CHATHÁIN, M., Early (incl. Medieval) Irish Language and Literature
RAFTERY, B., Celtic Archaeology
RIDLEY, H. M., German
SMITH, A., Classics
WALSH, B., National Economics of Ireland and Applied Economics
WHITE, H., Music

Faculty of Science:
DAWSON, K. A., Physical Chemistry
DUKE, E., Zoology
ENGEL, P. C., Biochemistry
FOGARTY, W. M., Industrial Microbiology
HEGARTY, A. F., Organic Chemistry
KENNEDY, M. J., Geology
MONTWILL, A., Experimental Physics
RYAN, M. P., Pharmacology
STEER, M., Botany

Faculty of Law:
BRADY, J. C., Law of Property and Equity
CASEY, J. P., Law
OSBOROUGH, W. N., Law

Faculty of Medicine:
BANNIGAN, J. G., Anatomy
BRADY, H. R., Medicine and Therapeutics
BRESNIHAN, B., Rheumatology
BURY, G., General Practice
CASEY, P., Clinical Psychiatry
DERVAN, P., Pathology
DRUMM, B., Paediatrics
ENNIS, J. T., Radiology
EUSTACE, P., Ophthalmology
FITZGERALD, M. X., Medicine
FITZPATRICK, J. M., Surgery
GERAGHTY, M. T., Medical Genetics
GREEN, A., Medical Genetics.
HERITY, B., Public Health Medicine and Epidemiology
MACERLEAN, D., Radiology
MCKENNA, T. J., Investigative Endocrinology
MORIARTY, D. C., Anaesthesiology
O'HERLIHY, C., Obstetrics and Gynaecology
O'HIGGINS, N. J., Surgery
O'REGAN, R., Physiology and Histology
PARFREY, N. A., Pathology
POWELL, D., Research Medicine
WALSH, N., Clinical Psychiatry

Faculty of Commerce:
BOURKE, P., Banking and Finance
BRADLEY, M. F., International Marketing
CROWLEY, J. A., Transport Policy and Logistics
HALLY, D. L., Accounting
HESSION, E., Corporate Planning
HOURIHAN, A. P., Management of Financial Institutions
KELLY, W. A., Business Administration
O'BRIEN, F. J., Accountancy

Faculty of Engineering and Architecture:
BANNON, M. J., Regional and Urban Planning
BYRNE, G., Mechanical Engineering
DEPAOR, A. M., Electrical Engineering
HAMER, G., Chemical Engineering
KEALY, L., Architecture
MCNULTY, P. B., Agricultural Engineering
O'BRIEN, E. J., Civil Engineering
SCANLAN, J. O., Electronic Engineering

Faculty of Agriculture:
BOLAND, M. P., Animal Husbandry
CURRY, J., Agricultural Zoology
GARDINER, J. J., Forestry
HENNERTY, M. J., Horticulture
KAVANAGH, J. A., Plant Pathology
MCKENNA, B., Food Science
SHEEHY, S. J., Applied Agricultural Economics

Faculty of Veterinary Medicine:
BELLENGER, C. R., Veterinary Surgery
JONES, B. R., Small Animal Clinical Studies
QUINN, P. J., Veterinary Microbiology and Parasitology
ROCHE, J. F., Animal Husbandry and Production
SHEAHAN, B., Veterinary Pathology

University College

Cork
Telephone: (021) 903000
Fax: (21) 273428
E-mail: eodriscoll@ucc.ie

Founded 1845 as Queen's College, Cork; changed to above in 1908

Academic year: October to September

President: M. P. MORTELL
Vice-Presidents: Prof. D. I. F. LUCEY, Very Rev. Prof. B. E. O'MAHONEY
Registrar: Prof. M. A. MORAN
Finance Officer and Secretary: MICHAEL F. KELLEHER
Librarian: JOHN A. FITZGERALD

Number of teachers: 400
Number of students: 9,890 full-time

Publications: many and various through the Cork University Press

DEANS

Faculty of Arts: Prof. P. C. WOODMAN
Faculty of Celtic Studies: Prof. M. R. M. HERBERT

Faculty of Commerce: Prof. E. P. CAHILL
Faculty of Law: B. M. C. FENNELL
Faculty of Science: Prof. P. BRINT
Faculty of Food Science and Technology: Prof. C. DALY
Faculty of Engineering: Prof. J. P. J. O'KANE
Faculty of Medicine: Prof. D. M. JENKINS

PROFESSORS

(Some professors also have responsibilities in other faculties.)

Faculties of Arts and Celtic Studies:
- COX, D. H., Music
- HOWARD, M. P., German
- HYLAND, A., Education
- KEARNEY, C. J., Modern English
- KEOGH, D. F., Modern History (European Integration Studies)
- LEE, J. J., Modern History
- MAGUIRE, J. M., Sociology
- Ó CARRAGÁIN, E., Old and Middle English
- Ó COILEÁIN, S., Modern Irish Language
- O'DONOVAN, P. T., French
- O'MAHONY, Very Rev. B. E., Philosophy
- Ó RIAIN, P. S., Early Irish Language and Literature
- SACCONE, E., Italian
- SMYTH, W. J., Geography
- TAYLOR, M., Applied Psychology
- WOODMAN, P. C., Archaeology

Faculty of Commerce:
- CAHILL, E. P., Accounting and Finance
- FANNING, C. M., Economics
- GREEN, S., Management and Marketing

Faculty of Law:
- CARROLL, B. A., Law
- MORGAN, D. G., Law

Faculty of Science:
- BARRY, P. D., Mathematics
- BOWEN, J. A., Software Engineering
- BRÜCK, P. M., Geology
- CASSELLS, A. C., Plant Science
- COTTER, T. G., Biochemistry
- CUNNINGHAM, J., Physical Chemistry
- GUILBAULT, G. G., Analytical Chemistry
- JENNINGS, W. B., Organic Chemistry
- MCINERNEY, J. G., Physics
- MORAN, M. A., Applied Statistics
- MULCAHY, M. F., Zoology
- O'REGAN, P. G., Computer Science
- SPALDING, T. R., Inorganic Chemistry

Faculty of Food Science and Technology:
- BUCKLEY, D. J., Food Technology
- CONDON, J. J., Microbiology
- FOLEY, J., Food Technology
- FOX, P. F., Food Chemistry
- LUCEY, D. I. F., Food Economics
- MORRISSEY, P. A., Nutrition
- MULVIHILL, D. M., Food Chemistry
- RAFTERY, T. F., Agriculture
- SYNNOTT, E. C., Food Engineering

Faculty of Engineering:
- O'KANE, J. P. J., Civil Engineering
- WRIXON, G. T., Microelectronics
- YACAMINI, R., Electrical Engineering

Faculty of Medicine:
- BRADY, M. P., Surgery
- DALY, R. J., Psychiatry
- DOYLE, C. T., Pathology
- FRAHER, J. P., Anatomy
- HALL, W. J., Physiology
- HEGARTY, M., Orthodontics
- JENKINS, D. M., Obstetrics and Gynaecology
- KEARNEY, P. J., Paediatrics
- MCCONNELL, R. J., Restorative Dentistry
- MURPHY, M. B., Clinical Pharmacology
- O'MULLANE, D. M., Preventive and Paediatric Dentistry
- PERRY, I. J., Public Health
- SHANAHAN, F. L. J., Medicine
- SLEEMAN, D., Dental Surgery

National University of Ireland, Galway

Galway
Telephone: (91) 524411
Fax: (91) 525700

Founded 1845 as Queen's College, Galway; became University College, Galway in 1908; present name 1997
Languages of instruction: English, Irish
Academic year: September to June

President: Dr P. F. FOTTRELL
Vice-Presidents: Prof. G. F. IMBUSCH, Dr RUTH M. CURTIS
Registrar: Prof. I. Ó MUIRCHEARTAIGH
Secretary for Academic Affairs: Dr S. MAC MATHÚNA

Library: see Libraries
Number of teachers: 330
Number of students: 7,984

DEANS

Faculty of Arts: Prof. N. MAC CONGÁIL
Faculty of Celtic Studies: Dr D. Ó HAODHA
Faculty of Science: Dr P. MORGAN
Faculty of Law: Prof. C. CAMPBELL
Faculty of Medicine: Dr P. A. CARNEY
Faculty of Engineering: Prof. J. J. BROWNE
Faculty of Commerce: Prof. J. F. COLLINS

PROFESSORS

Faculties of Arts and Celtic Studies:
- BARRY, K., English
- BOURKE, T. E., German
- BRADLEY, D., Spanish
- CANNY, N. P., History
- CURTIN, C. A., Political Science and Sociology
- IRVINE, D. G., Education
- JAMES J., Psychology
- LUIBHÉID, C., Ancient Classics
- MACAODHA, B. S., Geography
- MAC CRAITH, M., Modern Irish
- NÍ DHONNCHADHA, N., Old and Middle Irish and Celtic Philology
- Ó GORMAILE, P., French
- O'HEALY, Á., Italian
- RYNNE, E., Archaeology
- WORNER, M. H., Philosophy

Faculty of Science:
- BROCK, A., Applied Geophysics
- BUTLER, R., Chemistry
- FLAVIN, J. N., Mathematical Physics
- GUIRY, M. D. R., Botany
- HURLEY, T. C., Mathematics
- IMBUSCH, G. F., Experimental Physics
- KANE, M. T., Physiology
- Ó CÉIDIGH, P., Zoology
- ORREN, M. J., Oceanography
- RYAN, P. A., Geology
- WALKER, B., Biochemistry
- WALTON, P. W., Applied Physics

Faculty of Law:
- CAMPBELL, C., Law
- MCMAHON, B. M. E., Common Law
- O'MALLEY, W. A., Business Law

Faculty of Medicine:
- FAHY, T. J., Psychiatry
- FLYNN, J., Bacteriology
- FOLAN-CURRAN, J., Anatomy
- GIVEN, H. F., Surgery
- KEANE, P. W., Anaesthesia
- KELLEHER, C., Health Promotion
- LEONARD, B. E., Pharmacology
- LOFTUS, B. G., Paediatrics
- MCCARTHY, C. F., Medicine
- MCCARTHY, P. A., Radiology
- MORRISON, J., Obstetrics and Gynaecology
- MURPHY, A., General Practice

Faculty of Commerce:
- COLLINS, J. F., Accountancy and Finance
- CUDDY, M. P., Economics
- WARD, J. J., Marketing

Faculty of Engineering:
- CUNNANE, C., Hydrology
- MCNAMARA, J. F., Mechanical Engineering
- O'DONOGHUE, P. E., Civil Engineering
- O'KELLY, M. E. J., Industrial Engineering
- WILCOX, D., Electronic Engineering

National University of Ireland, Maynooth

Maynooth, Co. Kildare
Telephone: (1) 6285222
Fax: 6289063

Founded 1795 as St Patrick's College, Maynooth, which divided in 1997 into National University of Ireland, Maynooth, and a continuing St Patrick's College, Maynooth
State control
Languages of instruction: Irish, English
Academic year: September to June

President: Dr W. J. SMYTH
Vice-President: Dr F. J. MULLIGAN
Registrar: Prof. PETER CARR
Librarian: Dr THOMAS KABDEBO

Library: see Libraries
Number of teachers: 165
Number of students: 4,500

Publications: *Social Studies* (4 a year), *Archivium Hibernicum* (1 a year), *Irisleabhar Mhá Nuad* (1 a year), *Maynooth University Record* (1 a year).

DEANS

Faculty of Arts: Dr MICHAEL O'DWYER
Faculty of Philosophy: Rev. Prof. JAMES MCEVOY
Faculty of Science: Dr KINGSTON H. G. MILLS
Faculty of Celtic Studies: Dr MUIREANN NÍ BHROLCHÁIN
Postgraduate Studies: Dr TOM MCCARTHY

RECOGNIZED COLLEGES OF THE UNIVERSITY

National College of Art and Design: see below.

Royal College of Surgeons in Ireland: see below.

St Angela's College of Education for Home Economics: Lough Gill, Sligo; tel. (71) 42051; fax (71) 44585; 4-year BEd degree courses in Home Economics and Biology or Home Economics and Catechetics; BA in Economic and Social Studies; 2-year diploma course in Home Economics for overseas students; other certificate and diploma programmes; Pres. Sr MARIANNE O'CONNOR.

UNIVERSITY OF LIMERICK

Limerick
Telephone: (61) 202700
Telex: 70609
Fax: (61) 330316

Founded 1970 as National Institute for Higher Education, Limerick; University status 1989
State control
Language of instruction: English
Academic year: September to May

President: Prof. ROGER G. H. DOWNER
Vice-President (Academic Affairs): Prof. KIERAN R. BYRNE
Vice-President: Prof. NOEL WHELAN
Registrar: P. LEO COLGAN
Director of Information Systems and Services, and Librarian: (vacant)

Library of 169,000 vols
Number of teachers: 450
Number of students: 9,211

Publications: *Degree Programmes* (undergraduate brochure, annually), *Prospectus* (every 2 years), *University of Limerick News* (5 a year).

DEANS

College of Business: Prof. NOEL WHELAN
College of Humanities: Prof. COLIN TOWNSEND
College of Engineering: Prof. EAMONN MCQUADE
College of Informatics and Electronics: Prof. KEVIN T. RYAN
College of Science: Prof. JULIAN ROSS
College of Education: Dr JOHN O'BRIEN (acting)

HEADS OF DEPARTMENTS

College of Business:
- Accounting and Finance: THOMAS KENNEDY
- Management and Marketing: JAMES DALTON
- Economics: Prof. DONAL A. DINEEN
- Personnel and Employment Relations: JOSEPH WALLACE

College of Engineering:
- Manufacturing and Operations Engineering: Prof. MICHAEL T. HILLERY
- Materials Science and Technology: Prof. MARTIN BUGGY
- Mechanical and Aeronautical Engineering: Prof. PATRICK J. MALLON

College of Humanities:
- Arts: Dr JOHN HAYES, Prof. NICHOLAS REES
- Government and Society: JOHN J. STAPLETON
- Languages and Cultural Studies: Prof. SERGE RIVIÈRE
- Law: RAYMOND FRIEL

College of Science:
- Chemical and Environmental Science: Dr JOHN MULLANE
- Life Sciences: Prof. DAVID O'BEIRNE
- Physical Education and Sports Science: Prof. PHILIP JAKEMAN
- Physics: Dr NOEL BUCKLEY

College of Informatics and Electronics:
- Computer Science and Information Systems: Dr RICHARD SUTCLIFFE
- Electronic and Computer Engineering: Prof. CYRIL BURKLEY
- Mathematics and Statistics: Prof. MICHAEL WALLACE

College of Education:
- Education and Professional Studies: Dr JOHN O'BRIEN
- Primary-Level Education: PEADAR CREMIN

ATTACHED INSTITUTES

Irish Peace Institute: research into conflict resolution; Dirs Prof. D. MURRAY, T. O'DONNELL.

National Microelectronics Applications Centre: Dir Dr JOHN O'FLAHERTY.

National Centre of Environmental Education: Dir PEADAR CREMIN.

Irish World Music Centre: research into Irish traditional music studies and ethnomusicology; Dir Prof. MICHAEL Ó SÚILLEABHÁIN.

National Centre for Tourism Policy Studies: Dir J. DEEGAN.

AMT Ireland: provides consultancy and training support in all aspects of manufacturing technology; Dir Dr EAMONN MURPHY.

Materials Ireland: research and development in industrial materials technologies; Dir Prof. STUART HAMPSHIRE.

Multimedia Technologies Ireland: Dir DERMOT MCQUILLAN.

Power Electronics Ireland: research into thermal design, and power electronics and analog design; Dir Prof. PHILIP BURTON.

TELTEC Ireland: research and development in telecommunications; Dir Prof. CYRIL BURKLEY.

National Centre for Quality Management: Dirs Prof. MICHAEL WALLACE, Dr EAMONN MURPHY.

Institute of Incareer Development: Dir Prof. KIERAN BYRNE.

Marketing Centre for Small Business: Dirs Prof. BARRA Ó CINNÉIDE, Dr PATRICIA FLEMING.

International Equine Institute: education, training, incareer development, research, development and internationalization of the horse industry; Dir Mgr FRANK MCGOURTY.

Centre for Project Management: education, training and research in project management; Dir Prof. BERT HAMILTON.

National Coaching and Training Centre: Dir PAT DUFFY.

PEI Technologies Thermofluids Research Centre: Dir Dr MARK DAVIES.

University Level Institutions

DUBLIN INSTITUTE FOR ADVANCED STUDIES

10 Burlington Rd, Dublin 4
Telephone: (1) 6140100
Fax: (1) 6680561
E-mail: registrar@admin.dias.ie

Founded 1940

Chairman of Council: Prof. D. M. X. DONNELLY
Registrar: JOHN DUGGAN

CONSTITUENT SCHOOLS

School of Celtic Studies: Chair. Prof. B. Ó MADAGÁIN.

SENIOR PROFESSORS

Ó MURCHÚ, M.

School of Theoretical Physics: Chair. Prof. C. S. MORAWETZ.

SENIOR PROFESSORS

Ó RAIFEARTAIGH, L. S.
LEWIS, J. T.

School of Cosmic Physics: Chair. Prof. M. A. KHAN.

SENIOR PROFESSORS

DRURY, L. O'C.
JACOB, A. W. B.
MEURS, E. J. A.

DUBLIN INSTITUTE OF TECHNOLOGY

Fitzwilliam House, 30 Upper Pembroke St, Dublin 2
Telephone: (1) 6611688
Fax: (1) 6611696

Founded 1978 by bringing together six established colleges; formally established 1993

President: Dr B. GOLDSMITH
Registrar: T. J. DUFF

Number of teachers: 1,500 (incl. part-time)
Number of students: 25,000 (incl. part-time)

CONSTITUENT CENTRES

DIT Kevin Street: Kevin St, Dublin 8; tel. (1) 4757541; fax (1) 4780282; Dir F. M. BRENNAN; Sec./Registrar DAMIEN GALLANAGH.

HEADS OF DEPARTMENTS

Mathematics, Statistics and Computer Science: J. M. GOLDEN
Physics: M. HUSSEY
Chemistry: N. RUSSELL
Biological Sciences: B. A. RYAN
Electrical Engineering: J. FISHER
Electronic and Communications Engineering: C. COWLEY
Languages and Industrial Studies: D. CAMPBELL (acting)
Electrical Installation: J. O'DONNELL

DIT College of Music: Adelaide Rd, Dublin 2; tel. (1) 4784393; fax (1) 4784738; Dir I. BEAUSANG (acting).

HEADS OF DEPARTMENTS

Musicianship: E. FARRELL
Keyboard: M. LENNON
Orchestral Studies: B. MOONEY-MCCARTHY
Vocal, Operatic and Dramatic Studies: A. M. O'SULLIVAN

DIT Rathmines: Rathmines, Dublin 6; tel. (1) 970666; fax (1) 970647; Dir E. HAZELKORN; Sec./Registrar C. G. LYNCH.

HEADS OF SCHOOL

Professional and Social Studies: F. P. LANE
Accountancy and Business Studies: N. TIMONEY (acting)
Management Studies: R. BURNS

DIT Mountjoy Square: 40-45 Mountjoy Square, Dublin 1; tel. (1) 363000; fax (1) 8740505; Dir P. O'SULLIVAN; Sec./Registrar T. GROGAN (acting).

HEADS OF SCHOOL

Art and Design: J. F. CREAGH
Business and Management: K. UI GHALLACHOIR (acting)
Distribution: P. J. O'NEILL

DIT Bolton Street: Bolton St, Dublin 1; tel. (1) 8727177; fax (1) 8727879; Dir M. MURPHY (acting); Sec./Registrar T. FOLEY.

HEADS OF SCHOOL/DEPARTMENT

Department of Architecture and Town Planning: J. HORAN
Department of Surveying and Building Technology: T. DUNNE (acting)
Department of Engineering Technology: O. MCNULTY
Department of Transport Engineering: D. TUITE
Department of Science, Mathematics and General Studies: G. LAWLOR (acting)
Department of Engineering Trades: R. EUSTACE
School of Construction Trades: J. BERNIE
Department of Building Trades: P. KELLY
School of Printing: J. P. B. KENNEDY

DIT Cathal Brugha Street: Cathal Brugha St, Dublin 1; tel. (1) 8747886; fax (1) 8743634; Dir F. MCMAHON (acting); Sec./Registrar M. FITZPATRICK (acting).

HEADS OF SCHOOL

Hotel, Tourism and Catering Management: M. MULVEY (acting)
Hotel and Catering Operations: J. HEGARTY
Social Sciences: N. HAYES
Food Science and Environmental Health: M. PROCTOR

ROYAL COLLEGE OF PHYSICIANS OF IRELAND

6 Kildare St, Dublin 2
Telephone: 6616677
Fax: 6763989

Founded 1654

Awards a Fellowship, a Membership, and a Diploma in Obstetrics

President: Dr J. A. B. KEOGH
Registrar: Dr T. J. MCKENNA
Secretary: J. W. BAILEY

Faculties of obstetrics and gynaecology, paediatrics, public health medicine, occupational medicine, pathology

ROYAL COLLEGE OF SURGEONS IN IRELAND

123 St Stephen's Green, Dublin 2
Telephone: (1) 4022100
Telex: 30795
Fax: (1) 4022458
Founded 1784; recognized College of the National University of Ireland
Private control
President: P. McLean
Vice-President: B. O'Donnell
Hon. Secretary: T. P. J. Hennessy
Registrar: Prof. K. O'Malley
Library: see Libraries
Number of teachers: 125
Number of students: 900
Publication: *Journal* (quarterly).

DEANS OF POSTGRADUATE FACULTIES

Faculty of Anaesthetists: Dr J. Cooper
Faculty of Dentistry: T. Holland
Faculty of Radiologists: D. MacErlaine
Faculty of Nursing: G. Redmond

PROFESSORS

Bouchier-Hayes, D., Surgery
Cahill, K. M., Tropical Medicine
Collins, P. B., Biochemistry
Collum, L., Ophthalmology
Conroy, R. T. W. L., Physiology
Cunningham, A., Anaesthesia
Docherty, J., Clinical Physiology
Gill, D. G., Paediatrics
Graham, I., Epidemiology and Preventive Medicine
Green, V., Psychiatry
Harbison, J., Forensic Medicine and Toxicology
Harrison, R., Obstetrics and Gynaecology
Johnson, A. H., Biochemistry
Leader, M., Pathology
Lyons, J. B., History of Medicine
Monkhouse, S., Anatomy
Moorhouse, E., Microbiology
Nolan, K., Chemistry
O'Boyle, C., Psychology
Shannon, W., General Practice
Waddington, J., Clinical Neuroscience
Walsh, M., Otolaryngology

AFFILIATED INSTITUTE

Institute of Clinical Science and Research: Dublin.

Other Higher Education Institutions

Athlone Institute of Technology: Dublin Rd, Athlone, Co. Westmeath; tel. (902) 24400; fax (902) 24417; f. 1970; two-year Nat. Certificate courses, three- and one-year Nat. Diploma courses, four-year degree/professional courses, one-year post-Diploma degree courses, graduate Diploma courses, master's degree courses, postgraduate research; library of 50,000 vols; 300 teachers; 4,000 students; Dir Dr David F. Fenton; Registrar J. Coyle.

HEADS OF SCHOOLS

Business Studies: J. Cusack
Engineering: E. Ambikairajah
Science: (vacant)

Carlow Institute of Technology: Kilkenny Rd, Carlow; tel. (503) 70400; fax (503) 70500; f. 1970; national certificate, diploma, degree and postgraduate courses; library of 25,000 vols; 4,000 students; Dir John J. Gallagher; Registrar Brian L. Bennett.

HEADS OF SCHOOLS

Engineering: F. Dawe
Business: F. Quinn
Science: Dr S. Cawley

Cork Institute of Technology: Rossa Ave, Cork; tel. (21) 326100; fax (21) 545343; f. 1912; library of 65,000 vols, 550 periodicals; 1,050 teachers; 12,200 students; Dir P. Kelleher; Registrar B. Goggin.

HEADS OF DEPARTMENTS

Applied Physics and Instrumentation: Dr E. M. Cashell
Biological Sciences: Dr J. O'Mullane
Building and Civil Engineering: L. F. Hodnett
Business Studies: T. J. Rigney
Chemical and Process Engineering: J. T. O'Shea
Chemistry: Dr J. O. Wood
Electrical and Electronics Engineering: L. J. M. Poland
Mathematics and Computing: Dr B. J. Brendan Murphy
Mechanical and Manufacturing Engineering: D. A. Fitzpatrick
Nautical Studies: D. C. Burke
Printing, Graphics and Editorial Studies: D. Power
Social and General Studies: D. A. Courtney
Tourism and Catering Studies: J. Killilea
Transport and Automobile Engineering: D. Dempsey
Continuing Adult Education: P. Mahony
Attached Centres:

Centre for Clean Technology: Dir D. Cunningham.

Centre for Advanced Manufacturing and Management Systems: Dir M. Cotterell.

Centre for Surface and Interface Analysis: Dirs L. McDonnell, E. M. Cashell.

Centre for Nautical Enterprise: Dir G. Trant.

Centre for Educational Opportunities: Dir M. Bermingham.

Centre for Innovation in Education: Dir R. P. Coughlan.

Constituent Schools:

Cork School of Music: Union Quay, Cork; tel. (21) 270076; fax (21) 276595; f. 1878; Principal G. Spratt.

Crawford College of Art and Design: Sharman Crawford St, Cork; tel. (21) 966343; fax (21) 962767; f. 1884; Principal Geoffrey Steiner-Scott.

Dun Laoghaire Institute of Art, Design and Technology: Carraiglea Park, Kill Ave, Dun Laoghaire, Co. Dublin; tel. 2144600; fax 2144700; certificate, diploma and degree programmes; Dir Roisin Hogan; Registrar Jim Devine.

Dundalk Institute of Technology: Dundalk; tel. (42) 34785; fax (42) 33505; f. 1970; certificate, diploma and degree courses; library of 30,000 vols; Dir Sean McDonagh; Registrar S. McManus.

HEADS OF SCHOOLS

Business Studies: Peter Fuller
Engineering: John Connolly
Science: Dr Simon O'Brien

Galway Mayo Institute of Technology: Dublin Rd, Galway; tel. (91) 753161; fax (91) 751107; f. 1972; degree, diploma and certificate courses; library of 48,000 vols; 222 teachers; 4,000 full-time, 1,860 part-time students; Dir J. G. Corr.

HEADS OF SCHOOLS

Science: Dr B. Place
Engineering: G. MacMichael
Business Studies: B. O'Hara
Hotel and Catering: L. Hanratty
Adult Continuing Education: Michael J. O'Reilly
Art and Design and Humanities: Marion Coy

Institute of Public Administration: 57-61 Lansdowne Rd, Ballsbridge, Dublin 4; tel. (1) 6686233; fax (1) 6689135; e-mail info@ipa.ie; f. 1957; training, research, publishing, educational courses: Bachelor of Business Studies (BBS), BA, MA and Graduate Diploma in Public Management; 1,500 individual and 100 corporate mems; library of 40,000 vols, 330 periodicals; Dir-Gen. John Gallagher; publs *Administration* (quarterly), *Administration Yearbook & Diary* (annually), *Personnel & Industrial Relations Directory* (every two years).

Institute of Technology, Sligo: Ballinode, Sligo; tel. (71) 55222; fax (71) 44096; f. 1970; national certificate and diploma courses; degree courses; professional courses; library of 23,000 vols; 140 teachers; 2,127 full-time students, 500 part-time students; 250 apprentices; Dir Breandán MacConamhna.

HEADS OF SCHOOLS

Business and Humanities: D. M. Finan
Engineering: J. P. Cox
Science: J. P. Timpson
Development: D. McConville

Institute of Technology, Tralee: Clash, Tralee, Co. Kerry; tel. (66) 45600; fax (66) 25711; f. 1977; full-time Nat. Certificate courses, Nat. Diploma courses, bachelor's and master's degrees and doctorates, part-time degree courses; library of 30,000 vols; 160 teachers; 3,500 students; Dir Dr Sean McBride.

HEADS OF SCHOOL

Science: Seamus O'Shea
Engineering: Kevin Lynch
Business Studies: Brian O'Connor

Letterkenny Institute of Technology: Port Rd, Letterkenny, Co. Donegal; tel. (74) 64100; fax (74) 64111; courses at certificate, diploma and degree levels in engineering, science, design and business studies; library of 30,000 vols; 170 teachers; 1,300 students; Dir Paul Hannigan; Registrar Daniel Brennan.

HEADS OF SCHOOLS

Business Studies: S. Ó Cnáimhsí
Science: W. J. W. Hines
Engineering: C. Ó Somacháin

Limerick Institute of Technology: Moylish Park, Limerick; tel. (61) 208208; fax (61) 208209; e-mail mcadm@lit.ie; Dir J. P. MacDonagh; Registrar V. N. McCarthy.

HEADS OF SCHOOLS AND DEPARTMENTS

School of Art and Design: R. Ruth
School of Professional and Management Studies: G. Fleming
Department of Communications: Bill Hurley
Department of the Built Environment: G. O. Loughlin
Department of Information Technology: M. Guerin
Department of Electrical and Electronic Engineering: B. Callan
Department of Mechanical and Automobile Engineering: P. Ryan
Department of Science: Ruaidhri Neavyn

National College of Industrial Relations: Sandford Rd, Ranelagh, Dublin 6; tel. (1) 44972917; fax (1) 44972200; f. 1951; Ph.D., masters degree, diploma and certificate courses, full-time and part-time; also short courses; specialist areas; human resource management, personnel management, industrial relations, trade union studies, accountancy, business management, languages and European studies; Pres. Prof. Joyce O'Connor.

St Patrick's College: Maynooth, Co. Kildare; tel. (1) 6285222; fax (1) 6289063; f. 1795; comprises National Seminary and Pontifical University; Bachelor's, Master's and Doctoral degrees, and Diplomas and Licentiates; library of 65,000 vols; 24 teachers; 392 students; Pres. Mgr DERMOT FARRELL.

Waterford Institute of Technology: Cork Rd, Waterford; tel. (51) 302000; fax (51) 378292; f. 1969; degree courses, doctorates, Diplomas, Certificates; library of 55,000 vols, 215 periodicals; 200 full-time teachers; 4,200 full-time, 3,500 part-time students; Dir M. R. GRIFFIN; Registrar P. DOWNEY.

HEADS OF SCHOOLS

Accountancy and Business: B. M. ROWE
Engineering: D. MORAN
Science and Information Technology: Dr E. MARTIN
Humanities: J. P. ENNIS

Schools of Art and Music

NATIONAL COLLEGE OF ART AND DESIGN

100 Thomas St, Dublin 8

Telephone: (1) 6711377
Fax: (1) 6711748

Founded 1746, reconstituted as an autonomous semi-state body 1971

Director: Prof. NOEL SHERIDAN
Registrar: KEN LANGAN

HEADS OF FACULTIES

Design: Prof. ANGELA WOODS
Education: (vacant)
Fine Art: Prof. THEO MCNAB
History of Art and Design and Complementary Studies: Prof. JOHN TURPIN

ROYAL IRISH ACADEMY OF MUSIC

36 Westland Row, Dublin 2

Telephone: (1) 6764412
Fax: (1) 6622798
E-mail: info@riam.iol.ie

Founded 1848, incorporated 1889

Director: JOHN O'CONOR
Secretary: DOROTHY SHIEL
Registrar: TONY MADIGAN

Number of teachers: 75
Number of students: 1,000

ISRAEL

Learned Societies

GENERAL

Israel Academy of Sciences and Humanities: POB 4040, 91 040 Jerusalem; tel. (2) 5676222; fax (2) 5666059; f. 1959; sections of Humanities (Chair. SHAUL SHAKED), Sciences (Chair. RUTH ARNON); 69 mems; Pres. JACOB ZIV; Exec. Dir MEIR ZADOK.

BIBLIOGRAPHY, LIBRARY SCIENCE AND MUSEOLOGY

Israel Librarians' Association: POB 303, 61 002 Tel Aviv; f. 1952; general organization of librarians, archivists and information specialists; promotes the interests and advances the professional standards of librarians; professional and examining body; 850 mems; Chair. BENJAMIN SCHACHTER; Sec. NAAMA RAVID; publs *Yad-La-Kore* (Libraries and Archives Magazine), *Meida La Sefran*.

Israel Society of Special Libraries and Information Centers (ISLIC): 31 Ha-Barzel St, Ramat Ha-Hayal, 69 710 Tel-Aviv; tel. (3) 6480592; f. 1966 to promote the utilization of recorded knowledge by disseminating information in the fields of science, technology and the humanities, and to facilitate written and oral communication; 900 mems; Chair. KAREN SITTON; publs *Bulletin* (monthly), *Information and Librarianship* (2 a year).

Israeli Center for Libraries: POB 242, 91002 Jerusalem; tel. (2) 6252949; fax (2) 6250620; est. in 1965 by the Israel Library Asscn, Ministry of Education and Culture and Graduate Library School of the Hebrew University; provides centralized processing and other services for libraries; organizes non-academic librarianship courses; Chair. JACOB AGMON; Dir IRIS CHAI; publs *Leket* (on New Books) (monthly), *Yad Lakore* (Journal) (1 a year), *Basifriyot* (quarterly), *Tamar* (abstracts, 6 a year), monographs.

Museums Association of Israel: POB 71117, 91710 Jerusalem; tel. (2) 6708811; fax (2) 5631833; f. 1964 to foster public interest in museums and cooperation among association members; affiliated to International Council of Museums (ICOM); 55 mems; Dir Dr MARTIN WEYL.

ECONOMICS, LAW AND POLITICS

International Association of Jewish Lawyers and Jurists: 10 Daniel Frish St, 64 731 Tel-Aviv; tel. (3) 6910673; fax (3) 6953855; f. 1969 to contribute towards establishing international order based on law and the promotion of human rights; examines legal problems related to Jewish communities; holds international congresses and seminars; 10 centres (in Israel and abroad); affiliated with the World Jewish Congress (WJC); 10,000 mems; Pres. Judge HADASSA BEN-ITTO; Exec. Dir O. KIDRON; publ. *Justice* (quarterly).

Israel Bar Association: POB 34022, 10 Daniel Frish St, Tel-Aviv 64731; 16,000 mems; Pres. DROR HOTER-ISHAI; Sec.-Gen. SHOSHANA GLASS; Exec. Dir HAIM KLUGMAN; publs *Hapraklit, Orech Hadin* (4 a year).

Israel Political Science Association: c/o Dept of Political Studies, Bar-Ilan University, 52 900 Ramat Gan; tel. (3) 5318578; fax (3) 9234511; e-mail wilzis@ashur.cc.biu.ac.il; 100 mems; Chair. Prof. SAM LEHMAN-WILZIG; publ. *Research Newsletter.*

Israel Society of Criminology: Mount Scopus, Jerusalem 91905; tel. 882502; fax (2) 881725; f. 1972; 250 mems; Pres. Justice MOSHE TALGAM.

EDUCATION

Council for Higher Education: POB 4037, 91 040 Jerusalem; tel. (2) 5663131; fax (2) 5660625; f. 1958; recommends to the government granting a licence to higher education institutes, accreditation, and authorizes awarding of degrees; 25 mems; Chair. The Minister of Education and Culture; Dir-Gen. GURY ZILKHA; publ. *Report*.

FINE AND PERFORMING ARTS

ACUM Ltd. (Society of Authors, Composers and Music Publishers in Israel): ACUM House, 118 Rothschild Blvd, POB 14220, Tel Aviv 61140; tel. (3) 6841414; fax (3) 6850119; e-mail acum@acum.org.il; f. 1936; copyright; promotion of music and literature; 2,700 mems; Dir-Gen. RAN KEDAR; publ. *ACUM News* (quarterly).

Israel Music Institute: POB 3004, 61030 Tel-Aviv; tel. (3) 5246475; fax (3) 5245276; e-mail 035245275@doar.net; f. 1961; publishes and promotes Israeli music and musicological works throughout the world; mem. of the Int. Asscn of Music Information Centres and Int. Fed. of Serious Music Publishers; Chair. Judge RUTH TALGAM; Dir PAUL LANDAU; publ. *IMI News* (quarterly).

Israel Painters and Sculptors Association: 9 Alharizi St, Tel-Aviv 64244; tel. (3) 5246685; f. 1934 to advance plastic arts in Israel and protect artists' interests; affiliated to the International Association of Art; organizes group exhibitions and symposia; provides assistance to immigrant artists; maintains a gallery for members' exhibitions; graphic arts workshop and materials supply store; 3 branches; 2,000 mems; Chair. RACHEL SHAVIT.

Wilfrid Israel House for Oriental Art and Studies: Kibbutz Hazorea, 30 060 Post Hazorea; f. 1947; opened 1951 in memory of the late Wilfrid Israel; a cultural centre for study and art exhibitions; houses the Wilfrid Israel collection of Near and Far Eastern art and cultural materials; local archaeological exhibits from neolithic to Byzantine times; art library; Dir EHUD DOR.

HISTORY, GEOGRAPHY AND ARCHAEOLOGY

Historical Society of Israel, The: POB 4179, 91041 Jerusalem; tel. (2) 5637171; fax (2) 5662135; f. 1926 to promote the study of general and Jewish history; 1,000 mems; Library of Jewish History, Judaica, 7,000 vols; Chair. Prof. YOSEF KAPLAN; Sec.-Gen. ZVI YEKUTIEL; publs *Zion* (in Hebrew, with summary in English, 4 a year), *Historia* (Hebrew journal).

Israel Antiquities Authority: POB 586, 91 004 Jerusalem; tel. (2) 6204622; fax (2) 6289066; e-mail harriet@israntique.org.il; Offices: Rockefeller Museum Compound; f. 1948; engages in archaeological excavations and surveys, inspection and preservation of antiquities and ancient sites, scientific publications; has custodianship of all antiquities; see also Israel Museum, Rockefeller Museum, Israel Antiquities Authority Documentation Department and Library; Dir of Antiquities A. DRORI; Sec. H. MENAHEM; publs *Atiqot*, *Hadashot Arkheologiyot* (Archaeological Newsletter, with English version *Excavations and Surveys in Israel*), *Archaeological Survey of Israel*.

Israel Association of Archaeologists: POB 586, Jerusalem; f. 1955; a professional organization; Chair. DAVID ILAN.

Israel Geographical Association: c/o Dept of Geography, Bar-Ilan University, 52900 Ramat-Gan; f. 1961; 650 mems; Pres. Prof. AMIRAM GONEN; Sec. Dr GABI LIPSHITZ; publ. *Ofakim*.

Israel Prehistoric Society: POB 1502, Jerusalem; f. 1958; 100 mems; includes the 'M. Stekelis' Museum of Prehistory; Chair A. GOPHER; Sec. N. GOREN; publ. *Mitekufat Haeven* (annually).

Jerusalemer Institut der Görres-Gesellschaft (Jerusalem Institute of the Görres Society): Notre Dame of Jerusalem Center, POB 4595, Jerusalem; tel. (72-2) 271170; f. 1908; fmrly Orientalisches Institut der Görres-Gesellschaft; art, history, archaeology, biblical studies, Christian iconography; library, photo archive, computerized index of Christian monuments in the Holy Land; Exec. Dir GUSTAV KÜHNEL.

LANGUAGE AND LITERATURE

Academy of the Hebrew Language: POB 3449, 91 034 Jerusalem; tel. (2) 5632242; fax (2) 5617065; f. 1953; 29 full mems, 15 advisory mems; studies the vocabulary, structure and history of the Hebrew language and is the official authority for its development; is compiling a historical dictionary of the Hebrew language; special library: Hebrew and Semitic languages; Pres. Prof. M. BAR-ASHER; Chief Scientific Sec. G. BIRNBAUM; publs *Zikhronot*, *Leshonenu* (quarterly), *Leshonenu La'am*, studies, dictionaries.

Association of Religious Writers: POB 7440, Jerusalem; tel. and fax (2) 5660478; f. 1963; Chair. Dr ZAHAVA BEN-DOV; publ. *Mabua*.

Hebrew Writers Association in Israel: POB 7111, Tel-Aviv; tel. (3) 6953256; fax (3) 6919681; f. 1921; 400 mems; publ. *Moznayim* (monthly).

Mekize Nirdamim Society: POB 4344, Jerusalem; tel. (2) 636072; f. 1861; the society publishes Hebrew MSS of Jewish literature; 600 mems; Pres. Prof. S. ABRAMSON; Sec. Prof. I. TA-SHMA.

Palestinian PEN Centre: Wadi al-Juz, Al-Khaldi St 4, Jerusalem; tel. (2) 6262970; fax (2) 6264620; Pres. HANAN AWWAD.

MEDICINE

Israel Gerontological Society: POB 1105, 52 111 Ramat Gan; tel. (3) 5755010; fax (3) 5756748; f. 1956; 800 mems; Chair. Prof. A. GLOBERSON; Vice-Chair. Prof. I. LOMERANZ; publs *Gerontology* (quarterly), *Surveys and Reviews in Gerontology* (quarterly).

Israel Medical Association: POB 33003, 61 330 Tel Aviv; Central Committee, Hadar Dafna Building, 39 Shaul Hamelech, Tel-Aviv; f. 1912; 18 brs in Israel; 10,000 mems in Israel,

10,000 mems abroad; Pres. Dr M. ZANGEN; publs *Harefuha* (fortnightly in Hebrew, abstracts in English), *Mikhtav Lekhaver* (monthly in Hebrew), *Quarterly Medical Review* (English), *Israel Journal of Medical Science* (monthly in English).

Israel Society of Allergology: 23 Balfour St, Tel-Aviv; f. 1949; about 30 mems; Pres. Dr N. LASS.

Israel Society of Clinical Pediatrics: c/o J. Sack, Dept of Pediatrics A, Sheba Medical Centre, Ramat Gan 52621; tel. (3) 710111; f. 1953 to promote research and cooperation among hospitals and paediatricians; holds monthly meetings, annual presentations of cases and original studies; 200 mems; Chair. J. SACK; publ. abstracts of reports from Israel Journal of Medicine.

Israel Society of Geriatric Medicine: Sheba Medical Centre, Ramat Gan 52621; tel. ((03) 753171; f. 1963; affiliated to the Israel Medical Association (IMA), the Association for the Advancement of Science in Israel and the Israel Gerontological Society; holds an annual scientific convention; 100 mems; Chair. M. FISHER.

Israel Society of Internal Medicine: Division of Medicine, Sapir Medical Centre, Meir Hospital, Kfar Sava 44281; tel. (9) 7472591; fax (9) 7472671; e-mail mlahav@post.tau.ac.il; f. 1958; four regional centres; a division of the Israel Medical Association (IMA), and affiliated to the International Society of Internal Medicine (ISIM); organizes scientific meetings and congresses; participates in the planning of postgraduate education in internal medicine and improving conditions of internal medicine practitioners; 750 mems; Chair. Prof. MORDECHAI RAVID; Sec. Dr MEIR LAHAV.

Society for Medicine and Law in Israel: POB 6451, Haifa 31063; tel. and fax (4) 8381587; f. 1972; 3 branches; affiliated to the World Association for Medical Law (WAML); examines and recommends amendments to medical laws; organizes international conferences; 2,300 mems; Pres. A. CARMI; publ. *Refuah U Mishpat* (Medicine & Law, in Hebrew, quarterly).

NATURAL SCIENCES

General

Association for the Advancement of Science in Israel: f. 1953; 5,200 mems; Pres. Prof. M. JAMMER, Dept of Physics, Bar-Ilan University, 52100 Ramat-Gan; tel. 5318433; telex 342290; fax 344622; publ. *Proceedings of Congress of Scientific Societies.*

Biological Sciences

Botanical Society of Israel: c/o Dept of Biology, Technion-Israel Institute of Technology, Haifa 32000; tel. (4) 294211; fax (4) 225153; f. 1936; aims to promote the advancement of the fundamental and applied branches of botanical science; conducts research, organizes lectures and field work; over 300 mems; Pres. Prof. SHIMON GEPSTEIN; Sec. Prof. PETER NEWMANN.

Entomological Society of Israel: POB 6, 50 250 Bet-Dagan; tel. (3) 9683520; fax (3) 9604180; e-mail manesw@netvision.net.il; f. 1965 to promote, improve and disseminate the science of entomology (incl. acarology) in Israel; holds four bi-monthly half-day meetings and one full-day meeting per year; *c.* 120 mems; Pres. Dr MANES WYSOKI; Chair. Dr DAVID BEN-YAKIR; publs *Israel Journal of Entomology,* newsletters.

Israel Society of Biochemistry and Molecular Biology: POB 9095, 52 190 Ramat Efal; tel. (3) 6355038; fax (3) 5351103; e-mail mrgzur@ibm.net; 350 mems; Pres. Prof. A. LEVITZKI.

Society for the Protection of Nature in Israel: 4 Hashfela St, Tel-Aviv 66183; tel. (03) 375063; fax. (03) 377695; f. 1953 to promote nature conservation and quality of the environment; operates 24 local branches, 26 field-study centres, 7 biological information centers; research centres on birds, mammals, reptiles, insects, plants and caves; maintains close cooperation with the Nature Reserves Authority, the Environmental Protection Service and the Council for Beautiful Israel; organizes international seminars on nature conservation education; 45,000 mems; Chair. YOAV SAGI; Exec. Dir EITAN GEDALIZON; publ. *Teva Va'aretz* (Nature & Land, in Hebrew, every 2 months), *Eretz Magazine* (in English, 6 a year), *Pashosh* (children's in Hebrew, monthly).

Zoological Society of Israel: c/o Dept of Zoology, Tel-Aviv University, Ramat Aviv; f. 1940; 300 mems; Chair. B. S. GALIL.

Mathematical Sciences

Israel Mathematical Union: C/o Bar-Ilan University, Dept of Mathematics and Computer Science, Ramat Gan 52900; fax (3) 5353325; e-mail imu@wisdom.weizmann.ac.il; f. 1953; 210 mems; Pres. Prof. L. ZALCMAN; Sec. Dr J. SCHIFF.

Physical Sciences

Israel Chemical Society: 66 Nordau Blvd, 62 381 Tel-Aviv; a scientific and professional association; holds two conventions each year and organizes lectures and symposia in various parts of Israel; the society represents Israel in the International Union of Pure and Applied Chemistry; Chair. Exec. Council Dr HERBERT BERNSTEIN; Gen. Sec. Dr I. BLANK.

Israel Geological Society: POB 1239, Jerusalem; f. 1951; 400 mems; Pres. Y. EYAL; Sec. H. RON; publ. *Israeli Journal of Earth Sciences.*

Israel Physical Society: c/o Dept of Physics, Bar-Ilan University, 52900 Ramat-Gan; tel. (3) 5318431; fax (3) 5353298; e-mail havlin@ophir.ph.biu.ac.il; f. 1954; 250 mems; Pres. Prof. S. HAVLIN; Sec. Prof. V. HALPERN; publs *IPS Bulletin* (annually), *Annals of the IPS.*

PHILOSOPHY AND PSYCHOLOGY

Israel Psychological Association: 74 Frishman St, POB 65244, 61 652 Tel-Aviv; tel. (3) 5239393; fax (3) 5230763; e-mail psycho@inter.net.il; f. 1958; 2,623 mems; Chair. NIRIT APELOIG-ESHKAR; publ. *Bulletin* (quarterly).

RELIGION, SOCIOLOGY AND ANTHROPOLOGY

Hechal Shlomo: King George St, Jerusalem; tel. (2) 6241865; fax (2) 6231810; f. 1958; seat of Chief Rabbinate; centre for Rabbinic research and religious information; contains Central Rabbinical Library of Israel and museum.

Israel Oriental Society, The: The Hebrew University, Jerusalem; f. 1949; aims to promote interest in and knowledge of history, politics, economics, culture and life in the Middle East; arranges lectures and symposia to study all aspects of contemporary Middle Eastern, Asian and African affairs; Chair. NEHEMIA LEVTZION; Sec. IDO SHAHAR; publ. *Hamizrah Hehadash* (The New East, 1 a year).

TECHNOLOGY

Association of Engineers and Architects in Israel: 200 Dizengoff Rd, 63 462 Tel-Aviv, POB 3082; tel. (3) 5240274; telex 371690; fax (3) 5235993; f. 1922; brs in Tel-Aviv, Jerusalem, Haifa, Beersheba; 20,000 mems; Pres. A. BRAUNSTEIN; Chair. S. SOREK; publ. *Journal* (monthly, in Hebrew with English summaries).

Israel Society of Aeronautics and Astronautics: POB 2956, 61 028 Tel-Aviv; f. 1951 as Israel Society of Aeronautical Sciences, merged 1968 with Israel Astronautical Society; lectures and conferences to foster the growth of aerospace science; *c.* 400 mems; Chair. DOV SA'AR; Sec. YEHUDA BOROVIK; publ. *BIAF-Israel Aviation and Space Magazine* (quarterly).

Society of Municipal Engineers of Israel: 200 Dizengoff St, Tel-Aviv; f. 1937; 120 mems; Pres. Ing. J. KOEN; Sec. Ing. J. KORNBLUM.

Research Institutes

GENERAL

Samuel Neaman Institute for Advanced Studies in Science and Technology: Technion-Israel Institute of Technology, Technion City, Haifa 32000; tel. (72-4) 237145; fax (72-4) 231889; f. 1978; independent public policy institute researching national problems in science and technology, education, and economic, health and social development; Dir Prof. A. SEGINER; publ. *S. Neaman Institute Bulletin.*

Technion Research and Development Foundation Ltd: Senate House, Technion City, 32000 Haifa; tel. (4) 231219; fax (4) 323056; f. 1952; operates Industrial Testing Laboratories (building materials, geodetic research, soils and roads, hydraulics, chemistry, metals, electro-optics, vehicles); administers sponsored research at Technion—Israel Institute of Technology (see under Universities) in aeronautical, agricultural, biomedical, chemical, civil, computer, electrical, food and biotechnology, industrial, management and mechanical engineering; biology, chemistry, mathematics, and physics (sciences); and architecture and town planning, education in technology and science, general studies, medicine; 22 subsidiaries in fields of electronics, energy, agriculture, food and medicine; Man. Dir RAN KOBO.

AGRICULTURE, FISHERIES AND VETERINARY SCIENCE

Agricultural Research Organization: Volcani Center, POB 6, 50 250 Bet-Dagan; tel. (3) 9683111; fax (3) 9665327; f. 1921; fundamental and applied research in agriculture; numerous scientific projects at 7 institutes and 3 experiment stations; part of the Min. of Agriculture; library 30,000 vols and periodicals; Dir Prof. N. SNAPIR; publs *Israel Agresearch* (Hebrew with English summaries and captions), bulletins, special publications.

Attached institutes:

Institute of Field and Garden Crops: C/o Agricultural Research Organization, Volcani Center, POB 6, 50 250 Bet-Dagan; Dir D. LEVY.

Institute of Horticulture: C/o Agricultural Research Organization, Volcani Center, POB 6, 50 250 Bet-Dagan; Dir Y. ESHDAT.

Institute of Animal Science: C/o Agricultural Research Organization, Volcani Center, POB 6, 50 250 Bet-Dagan; Dir A. BAR.

Institute of Soils and Water: C/o Agricultural Research Organization, Volcani Center, POB 6, 50 250 Bet-Dagan; Dir Z. GERSTEL.

Institute of Plant Protection: C/o Agricultural Research Organization, Volcani Center, POB 6, 50 250 Bet-Dagan; Dir I. SHEPIGEL.

Institute for Technology and the Storage of Agricultural Products: C/o Agricultural Research Organization, Volcani Center, POB 6, 50 250 Bet-Dagan; Dir Y. KANER.

Institute of Agricultural Engineering: C/o Agricultural Research Organization, Volcani Center, POB 6, 50 250 Bet-Dagan; Dir Eng. U. PEIPER.

Beth Gordon, The A.D. Gordon Agriculture, Nature and Kinnereth Valley Study Institute: Deganya A, 15 120 Emeq Ha-Yarden; tel. (6) 750040; f. 1935; inaugurated 1941; regional and research centre and museum of natural history and agriculture and history of the Kinneret (Lake of Galilee) Region; Dir S. BEN-NOAM; Curator of Natural History S. LULAV; Curator of Archaeology Z. VINOGRADOV (see library).

ECONOMICS, LAW AND POLITICS

Development Study Centre: POB 2355, 76 122 Rehovot; tel. (72-8) 9474111; fax (72-8) 9475884; f. 1963; research, training and planning activities related to the promotion of rural regional development in Israel and the developing world; library of 50,000 vols, World Bank depository library; Head Prof. RAANAN WEITZ; Gen. Dir Dr DAFNA SCHWARTZ; publs research reports, summaries, working papers, occasional publs.

Israel Institute of Productivity: 4 Henrietta Szold St, POB 33010, 61 330 Tel-Aviv; tel. (3) 6920230; fax (3) 6916892; f. 1951; research, consultation and training in management, administration, technology, marketing, industrial relations, etc.; library of 15,000 vols; Dir RAMI GABISON; publ. *Hamif'al* (monthly), *Maydaon* (6 a year).

Jerusalem Institute for Israel Studies: 20a Radak St, 92 186 Jerusalem; tel. (02) 5630175; fax (2) 5639814; f. 1981; independent non-profit organization to study policy issues and social, economic and political processes in Israel in order to facilitate and improve public policy making; Dir ORA AHIMEIR; Exec. Dir Prof. ABRAHAM FRIEDMAN; publ. *Israel Studies* (2 a year).

Research Institute of the Yitzhak Rabin Center for Israel Studies: 26 Chaim Levanon St, POB 17538, 61 175 Tel Aviv; tel. (3) 6436545; fax (3) 6436546; f. 1997; history, society and culture of the State of Israel; associated Rabin archive, library and museum; Head of Research Institute Prof. ANITA SHAPIRA; Exec. Dir of Research Institute IRIT KEYNAN.

EDUCATION

Henrietta Szold Institute—National Institute for Research in the Behavioural Sciences: 9 Columbia St, Kiryat Menachem, Jerusalem; tel. (2) 6494444; fax (2) 6437698; e-mail szold@szold.org.il; f. 1941; non-profit organization to undertake research on psychology, psychometry, sociology and education; information retrieval centre for the social sciences in Israel; database of 40,000 records; Dir Prof. ISAAC FRIEDMAN; publs research reports, *Megamot—Behavioral Sciences Quarterly.*

HISTORY, GEOGRAPHY AND ARCHAEOLOGY

Albright, William Foxwell, Institute of Archaeological Research in Jerusalem: 26 Salah ed-Din St, Jerusalem, POB 19096; tel. (2) 6288956; fax (2) 6264424; f. 1900; 2,000 mems; library of 25,000 vols; research projects in Semitic languages, literatures, and history; archaeological surveys and excavations; Pres. P. GERSTENBLITH; Dir S. GITIN.

Archaeological Survey of Israel: c/o Israel Antiquities Authority, POB 586, Jerusalem 91004; tel. (2) 6204622; fax (2) 6289066; e-mail harriet@israntique.org.il; f. 1964, to carry out a general archaeological survey of Israel; develop archives of maps, photographs and other documents pertaining to historical sites, for the benefit of researchers and the interest of the public; sponsored by the Israel Antiquities Authority; Chair. R. COHEN; publs series of archaeological maps and surveys (in Hebrew and English, irregular).

Israel Exploration Society: Avida St 5, POB 7041, 91 070 Jerusalem; tel. (2) 6257991; fax (2) 6247772; e-mail ies@vms.huji.ac.il; f. 1913; aims (*a*) to engage in excavations and allied research into the history and geography of Israel; (*b*) to publish the results of such research; (*c*) to educate the public in these matters by means of congresses, general meetings, etc.; 4,000 mems; Chair. of Exec. Cttee Prof. A. BIRAN; Dir J. AVIRAM; publs *Eretz-Israel* (Hebrew, English, every 2 years), *Qadmoniot* (Hebrew, quarterly), *Israel Exploration Journal* (English quarterly).

Joe Alon Centre for Regional and Folklore Studies: Kibbutz Lahav, 85335 D.N. Negev; tel. (7) 913322; fax (7) 919889; f. 1972; centre for research, study and survey of the Southern Shefelah (the hilly region between Jerusalem and Beersheba); includes an Archaeological Museum, the Museum of Bedouin Culture, the Fehalin Exhibit, housed in a restored dwelling cave complex, at the foot of a major site; awards grants for research in the region; library of 900 vols, 3,500 slides; Exec. Dir UZZI HALAMISH.

MEDICINE

Rogoff-Wellcome Medical Research Institute: Beilinson Medical Center, Petah-Tikva; tel. (3) 9376742; f. 1955; attached to Tel-Aviv University; Dir Prof. A. NOVOGRODSKY.

NATURAL SCIENCES

Biological Sciences

Israel Institute for Biological Research: POB 19, 74 100 Ness-Ziona; tel. (8) 9381656; fax (8) 9401404; f. 1952; conducts biomedical research in drug design, synthesis of fine chemicals and development of newly-advanced products and processes in biotechnology; three research divisions: Chemistry, Biology and Environmental Sciences; 320 scientists and supporting staff; library of 50,000 vols and 800 periodicals; Dir A. SHAFFERMAN; publ. *OHOLO Annual International Scientific Conference*.

National Institute for Psychobiology in Israel: Hebrew University, Givat Ram Campus, Jerusalem; f. 1971 with funds from the Charles E. Smith Family Foundation, to create a network of scientists engaged in research in psychobiology, to further co-operative programmes between existing institutions, and to train personnel in the field of psychobiology; administers Charles E. Smith Family Laboratory for Collaborative Research in Psychobiology; operates through the Research and Development Authority of the Hebrew University; Dir Prof. BERNARD LERER; Sec. HADASSAH FINDLEY-SHARON.

Physical Sciences

Earth Sciences Research Administration: Ministry of National Infrastructure, Energy and Infrastructure, POB 1442, 91 130 Jerusalem; tel. (2) 5316130; fax (2) 5373470; e-mail beyth@netvision.net.il; defines R & D needs in natural resources; plans and directs the research institutes under its jurisdiction; Dir M. BEYTH.

Directs the following institutions:

Geophysical Institute of Israel: 1 Hamashbir St, POB 2286, 58 122 Holon; tel. (3) 5576050; fax (3) 5502925; f. 1957; activities devoted chiefly to the exploration of petroleum, water and mineral resources and to engineering studies in Israel and abroad, using geophysical methods; documentation unit; data processing centre; Dir Y. ROTSTEIN.

Geological Survey of Israel: 30 Malkhei Israel St, 95 501 Jerusalem; tel. (2) 5314220; fax (2) 5380688; f. 1949; geological mapping, research and exploration of mineral, water and energy resources; environmental geology; Dir G. STEINITZ.

Israel Oceanographic and Limnological Research: POB 1793, 31 000 Haifa; tel. (4) 8515202; fax (4) 8511911; f. 1967; physical, chemical and biological oceanography and limnology; aquaculture; Dir J. KOHEN.

Israel Meteorological Service: POB 25, 50250 Bet Dagan; tel. (3) 9682121; telex 0341764; fax (3) 9682176; f. 1936; provides general service to public and detailed service to various orgs; library; various publications; Dir Z. ALPERSON.

RELIGION, SOCIOLOGY AND ANTHROPOLOGY

Harry Fischel Institute for Research in Talmud and Jewish Law: Bucharim Quarter, 14 David St (Corner Fischel St), POB 5289, Jerusalem 91052; tel (2) 5322517; fax (2) 5326448; f 1932; seminary for Rabbis and Rabbinical Judges; legislation and research publications; codification of Jewish law; Jewish adult education centre; 80 mems; Chancellor Chief Rabbi SHEAR-YASHUV COHEN.

Louis Guttman Israel Institute of Applied Social Research: 19 George Washington St, POB 7150, 91071 Jerusalem; tel. (72-2) 231421; fax (72-2) 231329; f. 1948; conducts research in sociology, psychology, management, communications and related fields; 25 mems; Scientific Dir Prof. ELIHU KATZ; Exec. Dir AHARON DISHON; publs biennial research report (in English) and research monographs (mostly in Hebrew).

World Jewish Bible Center: POB 7024, Jerusalem; tel. (2) 6255965; aims to disseminate a knowledge of the Bible and of Bible research by publications, lectures and exhibitions; Chair. S. J. KREUTNER; publ. *Beit Mikra* (Hebrew, quarterly).

Yad Izhak Ben-Zvi: POB 7660, 91 076 Jerusalem; tel. (2) 5639201; fax (2) 5638310; f. 1964 as a non-profit foundation by the Government to honour the memory of Israel's second President; aims to foster research into the history of the land of Israel and into that of Jerusalem, to promote the study of the Jewish communities of the Middle Eastern countries, to reflect the involvement of Izhak Ben-Zvi in the Jewish community, and the Zionist and Labour Movements of Israel; library and historical archive; Dir Dr ZVI ZAMERET.

Administers the following:

Institute for Research of Eretz Israel: POB 7660, 91 076 Jerusalem; tel. (2) 5637268; e-mail mahonzvi@hum.huji.ac.il; promotes research on the history of Eretz Israel from Biblical times to the mid-twentieth century and studies on history and culture of the Jewish people in Israel from the destruction of the Second Temple to the first years of the State of Israel's existence; research and studies based on the work of scientists at the main universities; Dir Prof. DAVID ROSENTHAL; publs *Shalem* (irregular), *Cathedra* (quarterly, in Hebrew) and monographs in Hebrew and English.

Ben-Zvi Institute for the Study of Jewish Communities in the East: POB 7660, 91 076 Jerusalem; tel. (2) 5639204;

fax (2) 5638310; e-mail mahonzvi@hum.huji.ac.il; f. 1947; operated jointly with the Hebrew University of Jerusalem; sponsors research in the history and culture of Jewish communities in Muslim countries from the seventh century to the present day; maintains a large collection of MSS, and other historical documents; Dir Prof. HAGGAI BEN-SHANMAI; publs *Sefunot* (irregular, in Hebrew), *Pe'amim* (quarterly in Hebrew), numerous books and documents.

TECHNOLOGY

Israel Atomic Energy Commission: POB 7061, 61 070 Tel-Aviv; premises at: 26 Rehov Chaim Levanon, Ramat Aviv, Tel Aviv; tel. (3) 6462922; telex 33450; fax (3) 6462974; f. 1952; advises the Government on long-term policies and priorities in the advancement of nuclear research and development; supervises the implementation of policies approved by the Government, including the licensing of nuclear power plants; promotion of technological industrial applications; represents Israel in relations with scientific institutions and organizations abroad (Israel is a mem. of IAEA); Chair. The PRIME MINISTER; Dir-Gen. G. FRANK.

Attached research centres:

Soreq Nuclear Research Centre: 81800 Yavne; tel. (8) 9434290; f. 1958; swimming-pool research reactor IRR-1 of 5 MW thermal; Dir. URI HALAVEE.

Negev Nuclear Research Centre: Dimona; natural uranium fuelled and heavy water moderated reactor IRR-2 of 26 MW thermal; Dir MICHA DAPHT.

Office of the Chief Scientist—Industrial Research Administration, Ministry of Industry and Trade: POB 2197, 91 021 Jerusalem; tel. (72-2) 256368; fax (72-2) 248159; f. 1970; promotes industrial research and development in industry, research institutes and higher education institutes by financing projects; encourages establishment of science-based industrial parks near universities and research institutes; proposes policies to promote innovative industry through legislation, developing physical and technical infrastructure and intergovernmental industrial R&D agreements; Chief Scientist YIG'AL ERLICH.

Associated institutions:

Institutes for Applied Research, Ben-Gurion University of the Negev: POB 1025, 84 110 Beer-Sheva; tel. (72-57) 78382; telex 5379; f. 1956; engage in applied research in water desalination, membrane and ion-exchange technologies, chemical technologies, irrigation with brackish and seawater, development of salt- and drought-resistant crops and ornamentals, natural products from higher plants and algae, development of mechanical and electro-mechanical products, utilization of non-conventional energy sources; 120 staff; library of 13,200 vols; Dir Prof. A. SHANI; publ. *Scientific Activities* (2 a year).

Israel Ceramic and Silicate Institute: Technion City, 32 000 Haifa; tel. (72-4) 222107; telex 46406; f. 1962; provides the local ceramic industry with technical assistance and with research and development into advanced and new fields in ceramics technology; 18 staff; Dir Dr RUDICA FISCHER.

Israel Fiber Institute: POB 8001, Jerusalem; tel. (72-2) 707377; fax (2) 245110; f. 1953; to advance textile, polymer, paper, leather and related industries; applied R&D, testing services, quality control, training courses for engineers and technicians, M.Sc. and Ph.D. courses in conjunction with the Hebrew University; 45 staff; library of 4,000 vols and 30 periodicals; Dir Dr HILDA GUTTMAN.

Israel Institute of Metals: Technion City, 32 000 Haifa; tel. (72-4) 294473; telex 46406; f. 1962; serves industry in metallurgy and powder technology, foundry, corrosion and coating technology, vehicle and mechanical engineering; Dir Prof. A. ROSEN.

Israel Institute of Plastics: POB 7293, 31 072 Haifa; tel. (72-4) 225174; fax (72-4) 225173; f. 1981; R&D and information centre for promoting the plastic industry; Dir Dr S. ABRAHAMI.

Israel Wine Institute: POB 2329, 4 Ha-Raz St, 76 310 Rehovot; tel. (72-8) 475693; f. 1957 to improve the country's wines by means of quality control and applied research and promote their export; Dir SHLOMO COHEN.

National Physical Laboratory: Hebrew University, Danziger A Bldg, Givat Ram Campus, 91 904 Jerusalem; tel. (72-2) 584475; fax (72-2) 520797; attached to Min. of Industry and Trade Dept; f. 1950; basic physical standards, energy saving, ecology, solar energy, applied research with industrial orientation; Dir Dr A. SHENHAR.

Rubber Research Association Ltd: Technion City, 32 000 Haifa; tel. (72-4) 222124; fax (72-4) 227582; f. 1951; the advancement of the rubber industry in Israel; Dir D. CZIMERMAN.

Standards Institution of Israel: POB 39020, 61390 Tel-Aviv; tel. (72-3) 5454154; telex 35508; fax (72-3) 419683; f. 1923; tests the compliance of commodities with the requirements of standards and specifications; grants standards mark; conducts technological research; publishes the National Standards Specifications and Codes; 550 staff; library of 300,000 standards; Dir-Gen. ELI HADAR; publ. *Mati* (quarterly).

Libraries and Archives

Be'ersheva

Ben Gurion University of the Negev Library: POB 653, 84 105 Be'ersheva; tel. (7) 6461401; fax (7) 6472940; f. 1966; 720,000 vols, 5,000 current periodicals, 1,300 microfilms, 15,000 microfiche; Dir AVNER SHMUELEVITZ.

Emeq Ha-Yarden

Beth Gordon, The A.D. Gordon Agriculture, Nature and Kinnereth Valley Study Institute Library: Deganya A, 15 120 Emeq Ha-Yarden; tel. (6) 750040; 60,000 vols of which 23,500 in Hebrew; also periodicals and maps; Librarian T. LOEWENKOPF.

Haifa

Borochov Library: c/o Haifa Labour Council, POB 5226, Haifa; f. 1921; 40,000 vols, in central library, 60,000 in 24 brs; Chief Librarian EZECHIEL OREN.

Haifa AMLI Library of Music: 23 Arlosoroff St, Haifa; tel. (72-4) 644485; f. 1958; affiliated to the Haifa music and ethnology museum (*q.v.*); lending library including books, scores, records and cassettes; Librarian LEAH MARCUS.

Pevsner Public Library: 54 Pevsner St, POB 5345, Haifa; tel. (72-4) 66-77-66; f. 1934; 200,000 vols covering all fields of literature and science, in Hebrew, English and German; 15 brs; Chief Librarian Dr S. BACK.

Technion—Israel Institute of Technology, Library System: Technion City, Haifa 32000; tel. (4) 8292507; fax (4) 8233501; f. 1925; science, technology, architecture and medicine; Elyachar (Central) Library, 21 departmental libraries; 900,000 vols, 5,000 current periodicals; Dir NURIT ROITBERG.

University of Haifa Library: Mount Carmel, 31905 Haifa; tel. (4) 8240289; fax (4) 8257753; f. 1963; 780,000 vols; 19,500 periodical titles; 8,000 current periodicals; 480,000 micro-fiches and -films; 27,000 maps; 168,000 slides; 5,600 films (incl. videos); special collections include integrated law collection, rare books, media centre, laboratory for children's librarianship; Dir SHMUEL SEVER; publ. *Index to Hebrew Periodicals* (also in CD-ROM).

Jerusalem

Awkaf Supreme Council Library: The Haram Area, Jerusalem; f. 1931; contains Arabic and Islamic MSS.

Bibliothèque de l'Ecole Biblique et Archéologique Française: POB 19053, 91 190 Jerusalem; tel. (2) 6264468; fax (2) 6282567; f. 1890; 115,000 vols; archaeology and epigraphy of the ancient Near East, biblical studies; Librarian KEVIN MCCAFFREY; publ. *Revue biblique* (quarterly), *Cahiers de la Revue biblique, Etudes bibliques*.

Central Archives for the History of the Jewish People, The: (formerly Jewish Historical General Archives); POB 1149, 91 010 Jerusalem; tel. (72-2) 635716; f. 1969; Dir HADASSAH ASSOULINE; this institution is intended to serve as the central archives of Jewish history; publ. *Newsletter-Ginzei Am Olam*.

Central Rabbinical Library of Israel: Hechal Shlomo, Jerusalem; f. 1953; 50,000 vols on Rabbinica and Judaica.

Central Zionist Archives, The: POB 92, Jerusalem; tel. (2) 6526155; fax (2) 6527029; e-mail cza@shani.net; f. 1919; 125,000 vols; 8,180 metres of files; 8,430 newspapers; 545,000 pictures; 1,000 private archives and collections; 490 magnetic tapes; 240,000 items of small printed matter; Dir Y. MAYOREK; Librarian S. PALMOR; publs *Zionist Literature* (bibliographic bulletin, annually).

Gulbenkian Library: Armenian Patriarchate, POB 14106, 91 140 Jerusalem; tel. (2) 287862; f. 1929; donated by the late CALOUSTE GULBENKIAN; the library is one of the three great Armenian libraries in the diaspora, the others being the Mekhitarist Fathers' Library in Venice and another in Vienna; public library *c.* 100,000 vols of which one-third are Armenian and the rest in foreign languages, primarily English and French; receives over 360 newspapers, magazines, periodicals (of which more than half are Armenian) from foreign countries; collections of newspapers and magazines dating from the 1850s; a copy of the first printed Armenian Bible (1666); 3,890 Armenian MSS; Sec. and Librarian SAHAG KALAYDJIAN; Manuscripts Librarian Archbishop DAVID SAHAGIAN; publs *Sion* (monthly, official organ of the Armenian Patriarchate).

Israel Antiquities Authority Archives Branch: POB 586, 91 004 Jerusalem; tel. (2) 292614; fax (2) 292628; f. 1948; written, computerized and photographic records, maps and plans; Archivist A. ROCHMAN-HALPERIN.

Israel State Archives: Prime Minister's Office, Kiryat Ben-Gurion, 91 919 Jerusalem; tel. (2) 5680680; fax (2) 6793375; f. 1949; comprises seven sections: Department of Files and Manuscripts, Library Department, Records Management, Supervision Department of Public and Private Archives, Services to the Public, Technical Services Department and Publication of State Papers; holdings include files occupying 30 kilometres of shelving, 150,000 printed items and 25,000 books; administrative records, including foreign relations, are available after 30 years and records on defence after 50 years; State Archivist E. FRIESEL; Dir M. MOSSEK; publs *Israel Government Publications* (bibliography, annually), *Documents on the Foreign Policy of Israel*.

Jerusalem City (Public) Library: POB 1409, Jerusalem; tel. (2) 256785; fax (2) 255785; f. 1961; 750,000 vols; 20 brs and 2 Bookmobiles; Dir ABRAHAM VILNER.

Jerusalem International YMCA Library: PO Box 294, 26 King David St, Jerusalem; tel. (2) 257111; fax (2) 253438; f. 1933; *c.* 25,000 vols; Librarian RITA MOUCHABECK.

Jewish National and University Library: POB 34165, 91 341 Jerusalem; tel. (2) 6584651; fax (2) 6511771; f. 1892; 4,000,000 vols, including those in departmental libraries; 10,000 MSS; 49,000 microfilmed Hebrew MSS; microfilms of Jewish and Israeli newspapers; 200 incunabula (120 Hebrew and 80 in other languages); 15,000 current periodicals; special collections include the Abraham Schwadron Collection of Jewish Autographs and Portraits, the Harry Friedenwald Collection on the History of Medicine, the National Sound Archives and the Jacob Michael Collection of Jewish Music, the Sidney M. Edelstein Collection on the History of Chemistry, the Eran Laor Cartographic Collection, the Archives of Albert Einstein Dir Prof. SARA JAPHET; publs *Kiryat Sefer* (bibliography, quarterly), *Index of Articles on Jewish Studies* (annually).

Library of the Central Bureau of Statistics: POB 13015, 91 130 Jerusalem; tel. (72-2) 6553484; f. 1948; *c.* 40,000 vols; special collection: all publs of (British) Palestine Dept of Statistics; Librarian Mrs C. ZIEGLER; most publs available for exchange.

Library of the Israel Antiquities Authority: POB 586, 91 004 Jerusalem; tel. (2) 6204685; fax (2) 6289066; e-mail giovanna@isantique.org.il; f. 1935; collections mainly on the archaeology, ancient history and civilizations of Israel and the ancient Near East; 100,000 vols; Librarian GIOVANNA BAROUCH.

Library of the Knesset: Knesset, 91 950 Jerusalem; tel. (2) 753333; fax (2) 662733; f. 1949; principally for members' use; 150,000 vols, including books, bound periodicals and collection of all Israeli Government publications, UN publications and foreign parliamentary papers; Librarian SANDRA FINE.

Library of the Ministry of Foreign Affairs: Ha-Kirya, Romema, 91 950 Jerusalem; tel. (72-2) 303451; f. 1948; 44,000 vols, 300 periodicals; Librarian MOSHE ALUF.

Library of the Ministry of Justice: POB 1087, 29 Saladin Rd, 91 010 Jerusalem; tel. ((02) 708628; f. 1922; including 19 branch libraries, 60,000 vols.

Library of the Ministry of Science: Government Offices, Building 3, Hakirya Hamizrachit, POB 18195, 91 181 Jerusalem; tel. (2) 826459; fax (2) 323576; f. 1969; 7,000 vols, 200 periodicals; Librarian JUDITH RUDMAN.

Library of the Studium Biblicum Franciscanum: POB 19424, Monastery of the Flagellation, Via Dolorosa, 91 193 Jerusalem; tel. (2) 6282936; fax (2) 6264519; e-mail sbfnet@netvision.net.il; f. 1924; 40,000 vols chiefly on archaeology, judaeo-christianism, biblical and patristic studies; 20 mems; Librarian D. ROBAERT.

Muriel and Philip Berman National Medical Library: POB 12272, 91 120 Jerusalem; tel. (2) 6758795; fax (2) 6757106; e-mail libinfo@mdlib.huji.ac.il; f. 1919; 62,000 book titles, 6,000 periodicals; Dir DAFNA YUDELEVITCH.

Schocken Library: 6 Balfour St, 92 102 Jerusalem; tel. (2) 631288; f. 1900; 55,000 vols, 200 MSS, 20,000 photostats (Hebrew Liturgy and Poetry); Dir Dr SHMUEL GLICK.

Supreme Court Library: Supreme Court of Israel, Rehov Sha'arei Mishpat, Kiryat Ben Gurion, 91 909 Jerusalem; tel. (2) 759663; f. 1949; 45,000 vols; Librarian MICHAEL RUDA.

Kfar Giladi

Kfar Giladi Library: Kfar Giladi, 12 210 Upper Galilee; f. 1934; 35,000 vols, 110 periodicals; Librarian SHULAMIT ROSENTHAL.

Kiryat Shmona

Library of Tel-Hai Regional College: Upper Galilee, 12 210 nr Kiryat Shmona; tel. (6) 6900904; fax (6) 6900906; 65,000 vols, 500 periodicals, 1,200 videotapes; includes the Calvary Collection, the Ofer Collection, the Kapeliuk Middle East collection, Dvir Collection in Environmental Studies, the Lubin art collection and the Gail Chasin art collection, Littauer Judaic Collection; Library Dir Dr CAROL HOFFMAN; publ. *Index to articles in Israeli daily newspapers* (on-line and microfiche).

Nahariya

Municipal Library in Memory of William and Chia Boorstein: 61 Herzl St, Nahariya; tel. (4) 9879870; f. 1946; under the supervision of the Ministry of Education and Culture, Jerusalem; 70,000 vols; Chief Librarian SHOSHANA GIBLEY.

Ramat-Gan

Bar-Ilan University Library: POB 90000, Ramat-Gan 52900; tel. (3) 5318486; fax (3) 5349233; f. 1955; serves faculties of Humanities, Judaica, Law, Natural Sciences and Social Sciences; 850,000 vols and 4,500 current journals; special collections include the Mordecai Margulies collection of rare 16th- and 17th-century Hebrew books and 800 Hebrew Oriental MSS, Berman collection of early Eastern European Hebrew books, rare Latin and German edns of books on Jewish studies, Old Testament criticism, material on the Dead Sea Scrolls and the Samaritans; a collection of material on the development of Religious Zionism; collection of Responsa and Jewish studies; Librarian YA'AKOV ARONSON; publ. *Index to Articles in the Literary Supplements of the Daily Hebrew Newspapers* (annually), online *Index to Israeli Legal Periodicals, Hebrew Subject Headings,* (2 a year).

'Dvir Bialik' Municipal Central Public Library: Hibat-Zion St 14, Ramat-Gan; f. 1945; 400,000 vols, including special Rabbinic literature and Social Sciences collection; maintains 11 branches; Chief Librarian HADASSAH PELACH.

Rehovot

Hebrew University of Jerusalem, Central Library of Agricultural Science: POB 12, 76 100 Rehovot; tel. (72-8) 481270; f. 1960; National Agricultural Library, operated jointly by the Volcani Centre of the Ministry of Agriculture's Agricultural Research Organization and the Hebrew University's Faculty of Agriculture; maintains exchange relations all over the world; 300,000 vols, 3,200 current periodicals and serials, 180,000 documents; regional libraries at Gilath, Dor and N've Ya'ar; Dir N. BARZELY.

Weizmann Archives: POB 26, 76 100 Rehovot; tel. (8) 9343486; fax (8) 9344146; f. 1950; contains assembled letters, papers, and other documents relating to political and scientific activities of late First President of Israel; approx. 180,000 items; Dir MERAV SEGAL.

Weizmann Institute of Science Libraries: POB 26, 76 100 Rehovot; tel. (8) 9343583; fax (8) 9344176; e-mail rapinsk@wis.weizmann.ac.il; f. 1934; Wix Central Library, 4 faculty libraries, 1 departmental library and *c.* 50 departmental collections; computerized information retrieval unit; 250,000 vols, incl. bound periodicals and 1,450 current periodicals in science and technology; Chief Librarian Mrs I. POLLACK.

Tel-Aviv

Felicja Blumental Music Centre and Library: 26 Bialik St, 65 241 Tel-Aviv; tel. (3) 5250499; fax (3) 5281032; e-mail irit_s@tzion.tel-aviv.gov.il; f. 1950; 74,600 vols, 64 periodicals, 18,000 records, 2,055 compact discs, 123 video cassettes; Bronislav Huberman archive, Joachim Stutschewsky archive, Shulamith Conservatory (1910), Beit Levi'im (1919), etc.; Dir IRIT SCHÖNHORN.

General Archives of the City of Tel-Aviv-Yafo: City Hall, Kikar Malkhei Israel, 64 162 Tel-Aviv; tel. (72-3) 438554; f. 1967; Archivist JUDITH Z. FASTOVSKY.

Library of the Kibbutzim College of Education: State Teachers' College, Tel-Aviv; 72,000 vols; Librarian EDNA NAAMAN.

Rambam Library: 25 King Saul Blvd, Tel-Aviv; tel. (3) 6910141; fax (3) 6919024; f. 1935; 80,000 vols; specializes in Judaica; Librarian Rabbi A. ELBOIM.

Sourasky Central Library, Tel-Aviv University: POB 39038, Ramat-Aviv, 69 978 Tel-Aviv; tel. (3) 6408745; fax (3) 6409598; f. 1954; 880,000 vols, 4,800 current periodicals and 96,000 microforms; 7 specialized br. libraries with a further 788,000 vols; includes the Pevsner Collection of Hebrew Press, the Faitlovitch collection, the Collection of Yiddish Literature and Culture in memory of Benzion and Pearl Margulies, the Wiener Library collection, which concerns the Second World War, especially the Holocaust, and the history of antisemitism, the Herbert Cohen collection of rare books, the Dr Horodisch collection on the history of books and the Jaffe collection of Hebrew poetry; Dir Dr DAN SIMON.

Tel-Aviv Central Public Library 'Shaar Zion': 25 King Saul Blvd, POB 33235, Tel-Aviv; f. 1891; 900,000 vols (in 23 branches); General Library in 8 languages; special collections: Rambam Library (*q.v.*, Judaica), Ahad ha-Am Library (history and geography of Eretz Israel), Dance Library; Dir ORA NEBENZAHL.

Museums and Art Galleries

Acre

Akko Municipal Museum: Old City of Akko (Acre), El- Jazz'ar St; tel. (72-4) 911-764; fax (72-4) 811-611; f. 1954; old Turkish bathhouse; Crusader excavations including the once famous quarter of the Knights of St John (Hospitalers), the Knights' Halls, the Grand Maneir, the Refectory (Crypt), the Tunnel and the Domus Infirmorum; Dir YOSSI ADAR.

Be'ersheva

Negev Museum: POB 5188, 84 100 Be'ersheva; tel. (57) 239105; f. 1954; exhibits from regional excavations, mainly from the Chalcolithic, Israelite, Roman and Byzantine periods; exhibitions of Israeli contemporary art; Dir GALIA GAVISH.

Beit Shean

Local Museum of Beit Shean: Local Council of Beit Shean, 10 900 Beit Shean; tel. (72-65) 86221; f. 1949; housed in a 15th-century mosque; prehistoric flint, pottery, bronze, etc.; finds from all periods particularly Canaanite, Israelite, Roman and Byzantine, including a 6th-century monastery and several new excavations; Roman villa mosaics and funerary busts, artefacts and floor mosaics from secular and religious structures of the Jewish and Christian communities in Scythopolis—Beit Shean of the Byzantine period; outstanding selection of Roman and Byzantine decorated capitals in museum garden; Roman theatre from Severian period, eliptical amphitheatre; library of 1,000 vols; Dir ARIE EIZENBERG.

Gilboa district

Beit Chaim Sturman: Centre for Science and Education, MP Gilboa; tel. (6) 531605; fax (6) 532751; f. 1941; museum and institute of centre for science and education of the District Council of Gilboa; depts of archaeology, history of Zionist settlement, natural history; Dir KIENAN OFRA.

Haifa

Haifa Museum of Art: 26 Shabbetai Levy St, Haifa; tel. (4) 8523255; fax (4) 8552714; f. 1951; collections of Israeli and world contemporary art, prints, art posters, paintings and sculptures; library of 10,000 vols; Curator Dir NISSIM TAL.

Haifa Music and Ethnology Museum: 26 Shabbetai Levy St, Haifa; tel. (4) 523255; fax ((04) 552714; f. 1956; ethnographical material from all countries; large collection of musical instruments from all continents; reconstructed instruments from the time of the Bible; library: see Libraries; Curator (vacant); publs exhibition catalogues (bilingual Hebrew and English). (In 1998 the museum was reported to be temporarily closed.)

National Maritime Museum: 198 Allenby Rd, POB 44855, 31447 Haifa; tel. (4) 536622; fax (4) 539286; f. 1954; large collection of artefacts and ship models illustrating 5,000 years of navigation and shipbuilding, old maps and engravings, undersea archaeology, a Hellenistic bronze ram, and stamps and ancient coins connected with seafaring and maritime symbols; archaeology and civilizations of ancient peoples; scientific instruments; research library of 6,000 vols; Chief Curator AVSHALOM ZEMER; publs *Sefunim, Bulletin* (irregular).

Tikotin Museum of Japanese Art: 89 Hanassi Ave, 34 642 Haifa; tel. (4) 8383554; fax (4) 8379824; f. 1960; 6,500 items; paintings, prints, drawings, textiles, netsuke, lacquer work, ceramics, metalwork, collection of Mingei (folk art); library of 2,500 vols.

Jerusalem

Archaeological (Rockefeller) Museum: Rockefeller Bldg, Suleiman Rd, POB 586, Jerusalem 91004; tel. (2) 6282251; fax (2) 6292628; f. 1938; formerly Palestine Archaeological Museum; archaeology of Israel from earliest times up until end of Islamic period; largely material found in excavations before 1948; Curator ORNIT ILAN.

Beit Ha'Omanim (Jerusalem Artists' House): 12 Shmuel Hanagid St, Jerusalem; tel. (2) 6253653; fax (2) 6258594; f. 1965; exhibitions and permanent gallery of works by Jerusalem artists.

Bible Lands Museum Jerusalem: POB 4670, 91 046 Jerusalem; premises at: 25 Granot St, 93 706 Jerusalem; tel. (2) 5611066; fax (2) 5638228; e-mail biblelnd@netvision .net.il; f. 1992; ancient Near Eastern history and Biblical archaeology; Dir BATYA BOROWSKI.

Israel Museum: POB 71117, 91 710 Jerusalem; tel. (2) 6708811; fax (2) 5631833; f. 1965; incl. Bezalel National Art Museum (Jewish general and ceremonial works of art; Curators YIGAL ZALMONA (Arts), Dr IRIS FISHOF (Judaica and Ethnography)), Billy Rose Art Garden (European, American and Israeli sculpture), Bronfman Biblical and Archaeological Museum (Chief Curator (Archaeology) Prof. YA'AKOV MESHORER), Shrine of the Book (D. Samuel and Jeanne H. Gottesman Center for Biblical Manuscripts; incl. Dead Sea Scrolls; Curator Dr ADOLFO ROITMAN); library of 65,000 vols; Dir JAMES S. SNYDER; publ. *Journal* (annually).

Mayer, L.A., Museum for Islamic Art: POB 4088, 2 Hapalmach St, 92 542 Jerusalem; tel. (2) 5661291; fax (2) 5619802; f. 1974; collection of Islamic art: metalwork, glass, miniatures, ceramics, ivories, jewellery; Sir David Salomons collection of antique clocks and watches; educational activities in Jewish and Arab sectors; library of 14,000 vols, 50 periodicals; photographs and slides; Dir RACHEL HASSON.

Museum of Prehistory, Institute of Archaeology, Hebrew University: Mt Scopus Campus, Jerusalem; tel. (72-2) 882-430; f. 1955; large collection of objects from prehistoric sites in Israel; library.

Museum of Taxes: POB 320, 91 002 Jerusalem; tel. (2) 6258978; f. 1964; four sections: artifacts from the Land of Canaan and neighbourhood, taxes levied specifically on Jews in Diaspora, general section for tax-related items from all over the world, taxation in Israel; Dir M. DROR.

Museum of the Studium Biblicum Franciscanum: POB 19424, Monastery of the Flagellation, Via Dolorosa, Jerusalem; tel. (2) 282936; f. 1923; Palestinian archaeology: city coins of Palestine, Roman-Byzantine-Crusader pottery and objects; Curator M. PICCIRILLO; publ. *S.B.F. Museum*.

Sir Isaac and Lady Edith Wolfson Museum: Hechal Shlomo, POB 7440, Jerusalem 91073; tel. 6247112; fax 231810; f. 1958; modern Judaica, archaeological exhibits, glass, coins and manuscripts; Dir ESTELLE FINK.

Yad Vashem, the Holocaust Martyrs' and Heroes' Remembrance Authority: POB 3477, Mount Herzl, Jerusalem 91034; tel. (2) 6751611; fax 6433511; e-mail info@yad-vashem.org.il; the Jewish people's national memorial to the Holocaust; world's largest repository of archival and documentary information on the Holocaust: 50 million pages of documents, microfilms, testimonies, diaries, memorabilia; library of 70,000 vols; Int. Centre for Holocaust Studies is responsible for expanding academic and research activities; seminars and provision of teaching materials; museum: permanent exhibition of photographs and documents; Hall of Remembrance; Children's Memorial; Valley of the Communities; Memorial to the Deportees; Chair. AVNER SHALEV.

Kibbutz Kfar Menahem

Shephela Museum: Kibbutz Kfar Menahem, 79 875 Post Kfar Menahem; tel. (72-8) 501827; f. 1949; educational museum for creative activity and instructive exhibitions; collections of regional antiquities, fine arts and children's art; reconstruction of first stage of settlement; library; Dir M. ISRAEL; publs *Museum News, Chronicle* (6–10 a year) (in Hebrew), *For the Young Visitor* (in Hebrew), catalogues, guides.

Kibbutz Lahav

Museum of Bedouin Culture: Joe Alon Centre, Kibbutz Lahav, 85 335 D.N. Negev; tel. (7) 918597; f. 1985; part of the Colonel Joe Alon Centre for Regional and Folklore Studies; exhibition of contemporary arts and crafts, educational lectures and guided tours, photographs, demonstrations of Bedouin life (weaving, cooking, etc.); library of *c.* 100 vols, 3,000 slides; awards grants for research.

Kibbutz Sedot Yam

Caesarea Museum: Kibbutz Sedot Yam 38805; tel. (6) 6364367; f. 1950; collection of antiquities from the region of ancient Caesarea; Dir RINA ANGERT.

Kiryat Shmona

Tel Hai Museum: Tel Hai, 12 210 Upper Galilee; reconstruction of a Jewish settlement from the beginning of the 20th century; documents of Joseph Trumpeldor and his defence of the region in 1920.

Ma'ayan Baruch

Ma'ayan Baruch Prehistory Museum of the Huleh Valley: Ma'ayan Baruch, 12 220 Upper Galilee; tel. (6) 6954611; fax (6) 6950724; f. 1952; regional antiquities including implements from all prehistoric periods, exhibits from Middle Bronze Age tombs and from Roman and Byzantine periods; ethnographic section; Dir A. ASSAF.

Nazareth

Terra Sancta Museum: Terra Sancta Monastery, POB 23, Nazareth; f. 1920; Byzantine (and later) remains, coins, Roman and Byzantine glass; collection of antiquities from excavations made in the monastery compound; Vicar of Monastery Rev. P. JOSÉ MONTALVERNE DE LANCASTRE.

Safad

Israel Bible Museum: C/o POB 1396, Safad; tel. (6) 973472; f. 1984; exhibition of the biblical art of Phillip Ratner; permanent and changing exhibitions including Kabbalah and art for children.

Sha'ar Ha-Golan

Museum of Prehistory: Sha'ar Ha-Golan, Jordan Valley; f. 1950; large number of exhibits from the neolithic Yarmukian culture excavated in the region; Dir Y. ROTH.

Tel-Aviv

Ben-Gurion House: 17 Ben-Gurion Blvds, Tel-Aviv 63454; tel. (3) 5221010; residence of David Ben-Gurion, first Prime Minister of the State of Israel; opened to the public 1974 as a museum and research and study centre; library of 20,000 vols and periodicals on history of Zionist movement, land and state of Israel, ancient peoples, cultures, religions and philosophies, general and military history; Dir MALKA LIF.

Beth Hatefutsoth (The Nahum Goldmann Museum of the Jewish Diaspora): POB 39359, 61 392 Tel-Aviv; tel. (3) 6462020; fax ((03) 6462134; e-mail bhmuseum@post.tau.ac.il; f. 1978; permanent exhibition tells the story of Jewish survival and life in the Diaspora; temporary exhibitions portray Jewish communities all over the world; seminars and youth educational activities; photo and film archives; Jewish Genealogy and music centre; Dir Dr DAVID ALEXANDER.

Eretz-Israel Museum: 2 Chaim Levanon St, POB 17068, Ramat Aviv, 61 170 Tel-Aviv; tel. (3) 6415244; fax (3) 6412408; Tel-Aviv region archaeology and history, Jewish ethnography and folklore, ceramics, ancient glass, numismatics, history of Jewish theatre, tools and technology, planetarium; library of 40,000 vols; Gen. Man. SHILO SASSON.

Jabotinsky Institute in Israel: 38 King George St, POB 23110, 61 230 Tel-Aviv; modern history.

Tel-Aviv Museum of Art: 27 Shaul Hamelech Blvd, POB 33288, 61 332 Tel-Aviv; tel. (3) 6957361; fax (3) 6958099; also at Helena Rubinstein Pavilion for Contemporary Art, 6 Tarsat Blvd, Tel-Aviv; f. 1932; art collection consisting of works from the 16th century to the present day; collection of Israeli art; temporary exhibitions of fine arts, design, photography; art library of 50,000 vols, periodicals, microfiches; concerts, lectures and films on art; workshops, educational activities and circulating exhibitions service; Dir and Chief Curator Prof. MORDECHAI OMER.

Tiberias

Municipal Museum of Antiquities: Lake Front, Tiberias; f. 1953; collection of antiquities from Tiberias and region, mainly of the Roman, Byzantine and Arab periods; Dir ELISHEVA BALLHORN.

Universities

BAR-ILAN UNIVERSITY

52 100 Ramat-Gan

Telephone: (3) 5318111

Founded 1953; inaugurated 1955
State control
Language of instruction: Hebrew
Academic year: October to June

Chancellor: Prof. E. RACKMAN
President: Prof. M. KAVEH
Rector: Prof. Y. FRIEDLANDER
Pro-Rector: Prof. M. KAVEH
Vice-President for Research: Prof. S. HOZ
Director-General: S. LUBEL
Academic Registrar: M. MISHAN
Librarian: Y. ARONSON
Library: see Libraries
Number of teaching staff: 1,500
Number of students: 20,000

Publications: *Bar-Ilan Annual*, *Philosophia* (quarterly).

DEANS

Faculty of Jewish Studies: Prof. M. GARSIEL
Faculty of Humanities: Prof. R. KATZOFF
Faculty of Social Sciences: Prof. H. LAVEE
Faculty of Natural Sciences: Prof. E. MARZBACH
Faculty of Law: Dr D. SCHWARTZ

PROFESSORS

Faculty of Jewish Studies:

COHEN, M., General History
DAR, S., Land of Israel Studies
ELSTEIN, Y., Literature of the Jewish People
FRIEDLANDER, Y., Literature of the Jewish People
GARSIEL, M., Bible
GENIZI, H., General History
HAZAN, E., Literature of the Jewish People
KLEIN, J., Hebrew and Semitic Languages
KOGEL, J., Bible
LANDAU, D., Literature of the Jewish People
LUZ, Z., Literature of the Jewish People
SAFRAI, Z., Land of Israel Studies
SCHWARTZWALD, O., Hebrew Language
SHARVIT, S., Hebrew Language
SOKOLOFF, M., Hebrew and Semitic Languages
SPERBER, D., Talmud
SPIEGEL, Y., Talmud
STEINFELD, A., Talmud
TABORI, Y., Talmud
TOAFF, A., Jewish History
WEISS, H., Literature of the Jewish People
ZIMMER, A. Y., Jewish History and Talmud

Faculty of Humanities:

HAJDU, A., Musicology
HALAMISH, M., Philosophy
HASSINE, J., Comparative Literature
KATZOFF, R., Classical Studies
REICHELBERG, R., Comparative Literature
SILMAN, J., Philosophy
SPOLSKY, B., English
SPOLSKY, E., English

Faculty of Social Sciences:

ADAD, M., Criminology
ALPEROVITCH, G., Economics
BABKOFF, H., Psychology
COHEN, S., Political Science
DON, Y., Economics
DON-YEHIEH, E., Political Science
ECKSTEIN, S., Economics and Business Administration
ELAZAR, D., Political Studies
ETZIONI-HALEVI, H., Sociology and Anthropology
FLORIAN, Y., Psychology
FRIEDMAN, M., Sociology
GOLDREICH, Y., Geography
GREILSAMMER, I., Political Studies
GROSSMAN, D., Geography
HALEVY-SPIRO, M., Social Work
HILLMANN, A., Economics and Business Administration
IRAM, Y., Education
KATZ, J., Geography
KATZ, S., Psychology
KLEIN, P., Education
KRAUSZ, E., Sociology
LAPIDOT, A., Economics
LAVEE, H., Geography
LIEBMAN, Y., Political Sciences
LIPSCHITZ, G., Geography
MENIS, J., Education
MIKULINCER, M., Psychology
NACHSHON, I., Criminology
NITZAN, S., Economics
ORBACH, I., Psychology
PAROUSH, Y., Economics and Business Administration
PHILLIPS, B., Sociology
RUBIN, N., Sociology and Anthropology
SCHWARZWALD, J., Psychology
SILBER, J., Economics
SUNIS, M., Geography
WEISSENBERG, M., Psychology
WELLER, L., Sociology
YANOOV, B., Social Work
YEHUDA, S., Psychology
YIZRAELI, D., Sociology and Anthropology
ZEIDERMAN, A., Economics
ZISSER, B., Political Science

Faculty of Natural Sciences and Mathematics:

ACHITUV, Y., Life Sciences
AGRONOVSKY, M., Mathematics
ALBECK, M., Chemistry
AMIR, A., Mathematics and Computer Science
ARAD, Z., Mathematics
AVIEZER, N., Physics
AVTALION, R., Life Sciences
BEITNER, R., Life Sciences
BASCH, H., Chemistry
BRAVERMAN, S., Chemistry
BREITBART, H., Life Sciences
COHEN, Y., Life Sciences
CHOVEKA, Y., Mathematics
DEUTSCH, M., Physics
DUBINSKY, Z., Life Sciences
DUNIN, Y., Mathematics and Computer Science
EHRENBERG, B., Physics
EISENBERG, L., Mathematics
FREULIKHER, V., Physics
FREUND, Y., Physics
FRIEDMAN, H., Chemistry
FRIMER, A., Chemistry
GARBER, N., Life Sciences
GEDANKEN, A., Chemistry
GITTERMAN, M., Physics
GOLDSCHMIDT, Z., Chemistry
GOLOMBIK, M., Mathematics and Computer Science
GROSSMAN, S., Life Sciences
HALPERN, H., Physics
HAAS, E., Life Sciences
HASSNER, A., Chemistry
HAVLIN, S., Physics
HOCHBERG, K., Mathematics and Computer Science
HOZ, S., Chemistry
KANTOR, I., Physics
KANTOROVITZ, S., Mathematics
KAVEH, M., Physics
KAY, K., Chemistry
KESSLER, D., Physics
KRUPNIK, N., Mathematics and Computer Science
KRUSHKAL, S., Mathematics
LESHEM, Y., Life Sciences
MALIK, Z., Life Sciences
MARGEL, S., Chemistry
MARGOLIS, S., Mathematics and Computer Science
MARZBACH, E., Mathematics and Computer Science
MAYEVSKY, A., Life Sciences
MEKER-LIMINOV, L., Mathematics
NUDELMAN, A., Chemistry
ORBACH, D., Chemistry
PERSKY, A., Chemistry
PINCHUK, B., Mathematics
RABIN, I., Physics
RAPPAPORT, D., Physics
ROSENBLAU, M., Physics
ROWEN, L., Mathematics
SALZBERG, S., Life Sciences
SAMPSON, S., Life Sciences
SHAINBERG, A., Life Sciences
SHAPIRA, B., Physics
SHLIMAK, I., Physics
SHNIDER, S., Mathematics
SHOHAM, Y., Life Sciences
SPRECHER, M., Chemistry
SREDNI, B., Life Sciences
STEINBERGER, J., Life Sciences
SUKENIK, H., Chemistry
SUSSWEIN, A., Life Sciences
YESHURUN, Y., Physics
ZALCMAN, L., Mathematics and Computer Science

Faculty of Law:

ALBECK, S.
ENKER, A.
LERNER, S.

AFFILIATED SCHOOLS AND INSTITUTES

School of Education: Dir Dr Y. KATZ.

School of Social Work: Dir Prof. R. SCHINDLER.

Institute for the History of Jewish Bible Research: Dirs Prof. R. KASHER.

Institute for Post-Talmudic Research: Dir Prof. Z. A. STEINFELD.

Kramer Institute of Assyriology: Dir Prof. Y. KLEIN.

S. Daniel Abraham School of Economics and Business Administration: Dir Prof. D. TEENI.

B. Kurzweil Institute for the Literature of the People of Israel: Dir Prof. B. BAR-TIKVA.

Institute for Research in the History of Oriental Jewry: Dir Prof. A. TOAFF.

Naftal Centre for the Study of Oral Law and its Dissemination; Dir Prof. Z. A. STEINFELD.

J.M. Kaplan Centre for Legal Research, Praxis and Theory: Dir Prof. P. H. BARIS.

Finkler Institute for Research of the Holocaust: Dir Prof. D. MICHMAN.

Institute for the Study of Jews in Diaspora: Dir Prof. D. MICHMAN.

Institute for Advanced Torah Studies: Dir Rabbi M. RAZIEL.

Rena Costa Yiddish Centre: Dir Dr A. LIPSKER.

Institute for Research into Religious Zionism: Dir Dr G. BACON.

Institute for Information Retrieval and Computational Linguistics: Dir Dr U. SHIELD.

Centre for Lexicography: Dir Prof. S. SHARVIT.

Menachem Begin Institute for Research in Resistance Movements: Dir Prof. H. GENIZI.

David and Batya Kotler Institute for Judaism and Contemporary Thought: Dir Dr G. BACON.

Pasternak Institute: Dir (vacant).

Rivlin Institute for the History of Israel and its Settlements: Dir Prof. A. BAUMGARTEN.

Institute for Computerized Data in Jewish Studies: Dir Prof. S. FRIEDMAN.

Institute for the Study of Tiberias: Dir Dr M. HILDESHEIMER.

Kukin Center for Study of the Family (social work): Dir Prof. R. SCHINDLER.

Lechter Institute for Literary Research: Dir Prof. E. SPOLSKY.

Latin America Research Institute: Dir Prof. S. ECKSTEIN.

William Farber Centre for Alzheimer's Research: Dir Prof. S. YEHUDA.

Dr Joseph H. Lookstein Institute for Jewish Education in the Diaspora: Dir Prof. J. PLENIS.

Institute for Social Integration in the Educational System: Dir Dr R. BEN-ARI.

Institute for Sociological Research of Ethnic Groups: Dir Prof. E. KRAUSZ.

Institute for the Research and Advancement of Religious Education: Dir Prof. Y. RICH.

Institute for Research in Jewish Economic History: Dir Prof. Y. DON.

Centre for Documentation of Contemporary Jewish Communities: Dir Prof. M. FRIEDMAN.

Shlomo Argov Centre for Israel–Diaspora Relations: Dir Prof. C. LIEBMAN.

Institute for Economic Research: Dir Prof. A. HILLMAN.

Midrasha for Women: Dir Rabbi YITZCHAK COHEN.

Institute for Local Government: Dr H. KALCHEIM.

Center for Retail Management.

Institute for International and Comparative Law: Prof. A. ENKER.

Abraham Gelbart Research Institute in Mathematical Sciences: Prof. B. PINCHUK.

Dr Jaime Lusinchi Center for Applied Research in the Life Sciences: Prof. B. SREDNI.

Haddad Centre for Research in Dyslexia and Reading Disorders: Dir Prof. S. SIMPSON.

Centre for the Study of Mountainous Areas in Judea and the Ezion Bloc: Dir Prof. J. KATZ.

The Cancer, AIDS and Immunology Research Institute: Dir Prof. B. SREDNI.

The David J. Azrieli Institute for Research on the Economy of Israel: Dir Dr A. WEISS.

The Edward I. and Fannie Baker Center for the Study of Developmental Disorders in Infants and Young Children: Dir Prof. PNINA KLEIN.

The Institute for Research on the European Community: Dir Prof. I. GREILSAMMER.

The Center for International Policy and Communication: Dir Prof. S. SANDLER.

The Center for Commercial Law: Dir Dr D. SCHWARTZ.

Emmy Noether Mathematics Institute in Algebra, Geometry, Function Theory and Summability: Dir Prof. Z. ARAD.

Center for Strategic Studies: Dir Prof. G. STEINBERG.

Rehabilitation Center for IDF Head-Injured Disabled Veterans: Dir Prof. S. KATZ.

Rabbi Joseph Carlebach Institute for Studies in Jewish Thought: Dir Dr MIRIAM GILLIS.

Institute for Education and Community Research: Dir Dr Y. KATZ.

Otto Meyeroff Center for Study of Drug Receptor Interactions: Dir Prof. A. NUDELMAN.

Health Sciences Research Center: Dir Prof. S. R. SAMPSON.

Pearl and Jack Resnick Institute for Advanced Technology: Dir Prof. M. KAVEH.

Joseph Tanenbaum Centre for Judaic Values and Moral Education: Dir Prof. M. ORFALI.

Jacob Taubes Centre for Religious Anthropology: Dir Prof. A. BAUMGARTEN.

J. M. Kaplan Program for American Literature: Dir Dr SHARON BARIS.

Sal van Gelden Centre for Teaching and Research of Holocaust Literature: Dir Prof. HANNA MAOZ.

Lewis Family Foundation for International Conferences in the Humanities.

Arnold and Anita Lorber Entrepreneurial Award Program: Dir Dr R. ALDOR.

Schnitzer Foundation for Research on the Israeli Economy and Society: Dir Prof. H. BABHOFF.

Philip Slomowitz Program in Public Communications: Dir Prof. S. SANDLER.

Pollack Foundation in Basic and Applied Research in the Natural Sciences.

Samuel M. and Helene K. Soref Young Scientist Endowment Program: Dir Prof. M. KAVEH.

Jerome Schottenstein Cell Scan Centre for the Early Detection of Cancer: Dir Prof. M. DEUTSCH.

Edith Wolfson Instrumentation Research Centre: Dir Prof. H. BASCH.

Fanya Gottesfeld Heller Centre for the Study of Women in Judaism: Dir Prof. T. COHEN.

Ingeborg Rennert Centre for Jerusalem Studies: Dir Prof. Y. SCHWARTZ.

Helene and Paul Schulman Centre for Basic Jewish Studies: Dir NAFTALI STERN.

Pasternak Institute for Furthering Studies and Publication in the Field of the Hebrew Language: Dir Prof. M. Z. KADDARI.

Gerson and Judith Leiber Jewish Art Exhibition Centre: Dir Prof. D. SPERBER.

Institute for Electro-Acoustic Music.

Gonda-Goldschmied Medical Diagnostic Research Centre: Dir Prof. S. HAVLIN.

Language Policy Research Centre: Dir Prof. B. SPOLSKY.

Bernard W. Marcus Centre for Pharmaceutical and Medicinal Chemistry: Dir Prof. A. NUDELMAN.

Science and Mathematical Education Centre: Dir Prof. J. MENIS.

Minerva Centre for Physics of Mesoscopics, Fractals and Neutral Networks: Dir Prof. M. KAVEH.

Minerva Centre for High-Temperature Superconductivity (in collaboration with Tel Aviv University and the Technion): Bar-Ilan Dir Prof. Y. YESHURUN.

BEN GURION UNIVERSITY OF THE NEGEV

POB 653, Beersheva 84105
Telephone: (7) 6461111
Telex: 5253
Fax: (7) 6237682

Founded 1965
Language of instruction: Hebrew
Academic year: October to June

President: Prof. AVISHAY BRAVERMAN
Rector: Prof. NACHUM FINGER
Director-General: ISRAEL GERMAN
Vice-President and Dean for Research and Development: Prof. LECHAIM NAGGAN
Academic Secretary: AVRAHAM BAR-ON
Librarian: AVNER SCHMUELEVITZ

Library: see Libraries

Number of teachers: 900
Number of students: 13,000

DEANS

Engineering Sciences: Prof. GABI BEN-DOR
Natural Sciences: Prof. AMOS ALTSHULER
Humanities and Social Sciences: Prof. JIMMY WEINBLATT
Health Sciences: Prof. SHRAGA SEGAL
Management: Prof. AMOS DRORI

PROFESSORS

Faculty of Engineering Sciences:

AHARONI, H., Electrical and Computer Engineering
ALFASSI, Z., Nuclear Engineering
APELBLAT, A., Chemical Engineering
ARAZI, B., Electrical and Computer Engineering
BEN-DOR, G., Mechanical Engineering
BEN-YAAKOV, S., Electrical and Computer Engineering
BORDE, I., Mechanical Engineering
BRANOVER, H., Mechanical Engineering
CENSOR, D., Electrical and Computer Engineering
COHEN, A., Electrical and Computer Engineering
DARIEL, M., Materials Engineering
DINSTEIN, I., Electrical and Computer Engineering
DUBI, A., Nuclear Engineering
ELIEZER, D., Materials Engineering
ELPERIN, T., Mechanical Engineering
FINGER, N., Industrial Engineering and Management
GALPERIN, A., Nuclear Engineering
GOLENKO-GINZBURG, D., Industrial Engineering and Management
GOTTLIEB, M., Chemical Engineering
GUTMAN, E., Materials Engineering
HERSKOWITZ, M., Chemical Engineering
IGRA, O., Mechanical Engineering
JACOB, I., Nuclear Engineering Management
KAPLAN, B., Electrical and Computer Engineering
KOPEIKA, N., Electrical and Computer Engineering
KOST, J., Chemical Engineering
LADANY, S., Industrial Engineering and Management
LANG, S. B., Chemical Engineering
LETAN, R., Mechanical Engineering
MEHREZ, A., Industrial Engineering and Management
MERCHUK, J., Chemical Engineering
MOND, M., Mechanical Engineering
PERL, M., Mechanical Engineering
PLISKIN, J., Industrial Engineering and Management
PREISS, K., Mechanical Engineering
RONEN, Y., Nuclear Engineering
ROTMAN, S., Electrical and Computer Engineering
SANDLER, B., Mechanical Engineering
SCHULGASSER, K.,Mechanical Engineering
SEGEV, M., Nuclear Engineering
SHACHAM, M., Chemical Engineering
SHAI, I., Mechanical Engineering
SHANI, G., Nuclear Engineering
SHER, E., Mechanical Engineering
SHINAR, D., Industrial Engineering and Management
SHUVAL, P., Industrial Engineering and Management
SINUANI-STERN, Z., Industrial Engineering and Management
SLONIM, M., Electrical and Computer Engineering
STERN, H., Industrial Engineering and Management
TAMIR, A., Chemical Engineering
WISNIAK, J., Chemical Engineering
WOLF, D., Chemical Engineering

Faculty of Natural Sciences:

Abramsky, Z., Life Sciences
Alfai, D., Mathematics and Computer Sciences
Altshuler, A., Mathematics and Computer Sciences
Avishai, Y., Physics
Bahat, D., Geological and Environmental Sciences
Band, Y., Chemistry
Becker, J., Chemistry
Belitski, H., Mathematics and Computer Sciences
Berenstein, J., Chemistry
Bittner, S., Chemistry
Carmeli, M., Physics
Chipman, D., Life Sciences
Cohen, M., Mathematics and Computer Sciences
Davidson, A., Physics
Efrima, S., Chemistry
Eichler, D., Physics
Eisenberg, T., Mathematics and Computer Sciences
Feintuch, A., Mathematics and Computer Sciences
Freidlander, M., Life Sciences
Fuhrmann, A. P., Mathematics and Computer Sciences
Gersten, A., Physics
Gertsbakh, I., Mathematics and Computer Sciences
Gill, D., Physics
Glaser, R., Chemistry
Goren, S., Physics
Gorodetsky, G., Physics
Horovitz, B., Physics
Horowitz, Y., Physics
Kisch, H., Geological and Environmental Sciences
Kost, D., Chemistry
Lichtenstein, G., Chemistry
Lin, M., Mathematics and Computer Sciences
Markus, A., Mathematics and Computer Sciences
Mizrahi, Y., Life Sciences
Moalem, A., Physics
Mordechai, S., Physics
Moreh, R., Physics
Owen, D., Physics
Priel, Z., Chemistry
Pross, A., Chemistry
Rabinovitsch, A., Physics
Rosenwaks, S., Physics
Rubin, M., Mathematics and Computer Sciences
Scharf, B., Chemistry
Shaked, H., Physics
Shani, A., Chemistry
Shoshan-Barmatz, V., Life Sciences
Tal, M., Life Sciences
Thiberger, R., Physics
Voltera, V., Physics
Weiss, S., Chemistry
Zaritsky, A., Life Sciences

Faculty of Humanities and Social Sciences:

Bar-On, D., Behavioural Sciences
Bar-Yosef, H., Hebrew Literature
Blidstein, G., History
Blumenthal, T., Economics
Bowman, D., Geography and Environmental Development
Braverman, A., Economics
Gelman, Y., History
Gordon, D., Education
Gordon, H., Education
Gradus, Y., Geography
Henik, A., Behavioural Sciences
Hochman, O., Economics
Laskar, D., History
Lazin, F., Behavioural Sciences
Meir, A., Geography and Environmental Development
Pery, T., Foreign Languages and Literature
Qimron, E., Hebrew Language
Redlich, S., History
Sharot, S., Behavioural Sciences
Shinar, D., General Studies
Spivak, A., Economics
Stern, E., Geography
Tobin, I., Foreign Languages and Literature
Troen, I., History
Tsahor, Z., History
Tzelgov, Y., Behavioural Sciences
Vinner, S., Education
Weinblatt, J., Economics
Weingrod, A., Behavioural Sciences
Zoar, H., Geography and Environmental Development

Faculty of Health Sciences:

Abud, M., Microbiology
Alkan, M.
Appelbaum, A., Cardiology
Apte, R., Microbiology
Batler, A., Cardiology
Belmaker, R. H., Psychiatry
Carmi, R., Paediatrics
Chaimovitz S., Nephrology
Cohen, Y., Oncology
Danon, A., Pharmacology
Galinsky, D., Geriatrics
Grossman, Y., Physiology
Gutnick, M., Physiology
Halevi, S., Dermatology
Harishanu, Y., Neurology
Isakov, N., Microbiology and Immunology
Katz, M., Gynaecology
Levy, Y., Biochemistry
Maresh, A., Surgery
Margulis, C.
Mazoz, M., Gynaecology
Meyerstein, N., Physiology
Moran, A., Physiology
Naggan, L., Epidemiology
Ovsyshcheher, I., Internal Medicine
Potashnik, G., Gynaecology
Segal, S., Microbiology
Sofer, S., Paediatrics
Sukenik, S., Internal Medicine
Weinstein, J., Microbiology
Weitzman, S.
White, E., Morphology
Yagil, R., Physiology

School of Management:

Menipaz, E., Business Administration
Reichel, A., Hotel and Tourism Management

Blaustein Institute for Desert Research:

Abeliovich, A.
Ben-Asher, J.
Degan, A.
Feiman, D.
Gordon, J.
Gutterman, Y.
Issar, A.
Kressel, G.
Lips, H.
Oron, G.
Pinshow, B.
Richmond, A.
Rubinstein, I.
Safriel, U.
Zarmi, Y.

Institute for Applied Research:

Arad, S.
Forgacs, C.

Ben-Gurion Research Centre:

Gal, A.
Pinkus, B.

UNIVERSITY OF HAIFA

Mount Carmel, 31 905 Haifa
Telephone: (4) 8240111
Fax: (4) 8342104

Founded 1963
Independent

Language of instruction: Hebrew
Academic year: October to June

President: Prof. Yehuda Hayuth
Rector: Prof. Gad Gilbar
Vice-President (Administration): Prof. Aharon Kellerman
Vice-President (Public Relations and Resource Development): Yael Metser
Registrar: Giora Lehavi
Head of Research Authority: Prof. Aaron Ben-Zeev
Librarian: Prof. Shmuel Sever

Number of teachers: 964
Number of students: 13,000

Publications: *Jewish History* (2 a year), *Dappim – Research in Literature* (annually, Hebrew, with English abstracts), *Studies in Education* (2 a year, Hebrew), *Studies in Children's Literature* (annually, Hebrew), *JTD Haifa University Studies in Theatre and Drama* (annually), *Mishpat Umimshal Law and Government in Israel* (2 a year, Hebrew).

DEANS AND HEADS OF SCHOOLS

Graduate School: Prof. Abraham Sagi
Faculty of Humanities: Prof. Joseph Chetrit
Faculty of Social Science and Mathematics: Prof. Arie Melnik
Faculty of Law: Prof. Joseph Edrey
Faculty of Social Welfare and Health Studies: Prof. Arik Rimmerman
School of Education: Prof. Rachel Seginer
Graduate School of Business: Prof. Nahum Biger

PROFESSORS

Faculty of Humanities:

Avishur, Y., Hebrew Language
Azar, M., Hebrew Language
Chetrit, J., French
David, E., General History
Dolgopolsky, A., Hebrew Language
Eldar, I., Hebrew Language
Freedman, W., English
Gelber, Y., Land of Israel Studies
Gilbar, G., Middle-East History
Ginat, J., Land of Israel Studies
Gooditch, M., General History
Grabois, A., History
Heltzer, M., Bible
Hoffman, J., Hebrew Language
Kellner, M., Jewish History
Mansour, Y., Hebrew Language
Michel, J., French
Oded, B., Jewish History
Rappaport, U., Jewish History
Ronen, A., Archaeology
Rozen, M., Jewish History
Schatzker, C., Jewish History
Shenhar, A., Hebrew and Comparative Literature
Sobel, M., History
Stow, K., Jewish History
Warburg, G., Middle Eastern History
Yardeni, M., History
Yehoshua, A. B., Hebrew and Comparative Literature
Zinguer, I., French

Faculty of Social Sciences and Mathematics:

Arazy, J., Mathematics and Computer Science
Arian, A., Political Science
Bar-Lev, S., Statistics
Beit-Hallahmi, B., Psychology
Ben-Dor, G., Political Science
Biger, N., Business Administration
Braun, A., Mathematics and Computer Science
Breznitz, S., Psychology
Butnario, D., Mathematics
Caro, Y., Mathematics, Physics
Censor, Y., Mathematics and Computer Science

DAFNI, A., Biology
EDEN, B., Economics
FELZENTAL, D., Political Science
FISHMAN, G., Sociology
GOLAN, J., Mathematics and Computer Science
GORDON, A., Physics
GUIORA, A. Z., Psychology
HAIM, A., Biology
HAYUTH, Y., Geography
ISHAI, Y., Political Science
KELLERMAN, A., Geography
KEREN G., Psychology
KIPNIS, B., Geography
KLIOT, N., Geography
KORIAT, A., Psychology
KOROL, A., Evolutionary Biology
LANDSBERGER, M., Economics
LANGBERG, N., Statistics
MATTRAS, Y., Sociology
MELNIK, A., Economics
MINTZ, A., Political Science
MORAN, G., Mathematics and Computer Science
NAVON, D., Psychology
NEVO, B., Psychology
NEVO, E., Evolutionary Biology
ROSENFELD, H., Sociology
ROSNER, M., Sociology
RUBINSTEIN, Z., Mathematics and Computer Science
SAGI, A., Psychology
SHECHTER, M., Economics
SHLIFER, E., Business Administration
SKOLNICK, A., Biology
SMOOHA, S., Sociology
SOBEL, Z., Sociology
SOFFER, A., Geography
STERNFELD, Y., Mathematics and Computer Science
STRELITZ, S., Mathematics and Computer Science
VAISMAN, I., Mathematics and Computer Science
WEIMAN, G., Sociology and Communication
WEISS, G., Statistics
WEIT, I., Mathematics and Computer Science
ZAKS, J., Mathematics and Computer Science
ZOLLER, U., Biology

Faculty of Social Welfare and Health Studies:

RIMMERMAN, A., Social Work

School of Education:

BEN-PERETZ, M., Education
NESHER, P., Education
SALOMON, G.

ATTACHED RESEARCH INSTITUTES, CENTRES, LABORATORIES

Bertha von Suttner Research Program for Peace Studies and Conflict Resolution in the Middle East

Bund Institute for the Study of the History of the Bund, the History of Jewish Labor in Eastern Europe, and Yiddish Culture

Center for Advanced Studies

Center for Alternatives in Education

Center for Children's Literature

Center for Administration and Evaluation

Center for the Research and Study of Aging

Center for the Interdisciplinary Study of Emotions

Center for Jewish Education in the Diaspora

Center for Research and Study of the Family

Center for the Study of Israel and its Settlement (jointly with the Ben-Zvi Foundation)

Center for Rehabilitation Research and Human Development

Center for the Study of Child Development

Center for the Study of Crime and Society

Center for the Study of Jewish Culture in Spain and Islamic Lands

Center for the Study of Pilgrimage, Tourism and Recreation

Center for National Security Studies

Golan Research Institute

Gottlieb Schumacher Institute of Research of Christian Activity in Palestine in the 19th Century

Gustav Heinemann Institute for Middle Eastern Studies

Haifa and Galilee Research Institute

Herzl Institute for the Study of Zionism and Israel

Institute for Public Policy

Center for Educational Research and Multi-Culturalism

Institute for the Study of French History and Culture

Institute for the Study of the Kibbutz and the Cooperative Idea

Institute of Evolution

Institute of Information Processing and Decision-Making

International Centre for Health Law and Ethics

Jewish-Arab Center

Laboratory for Audio-Visual Productions

Laboratory for Experimental Research in Education

Laboratory for Learning and Teaching

Leon Recanati Center for Maritime Studies

Max Wertheimer Minerva Center for Cognitive Processes and Human Performance

Minerva Center for Youth Studies

Natural Resources and Environmental Research Center

Ray D. Wolfe Center for the Study of Psychological Stress

Rubin Zimmerman Foundation for the Study of Banking and Finance

Shlomo Zalman Strochlitz Institute of Holocaust Studies

Wydra Institute of Shipping and Aviation Research

Zinman Institute of Archaeology

AFFILIATED INSTITUTIONS AND REGIONAL COLLEGES:

Hadera Menashe College

Oranim—School of Education of the Kibbutz Movement: Dir Prof. YAIR CARO

Zinman College of Physical Education and Sports Sciences at the Wingate Institute

HEBREW UNIVERSITY OF JERUSALEM

Mount Scopus, 91 905 Jerusalem
Telephone: (2) 882111
Telex: 26458
Fax: (2) 322545

Founded 1918; inaugurated 1925
Private control, partially supported by the Government
Academic year: October to June
Language of instruction: Hebrew

Chairman, Board of Governors: ALEX BRASS
President: Prof. MENACHEM MAGIDOR
Rector: Prof. MENACHEM BEN-SASSON
Vice-Presidents: Prof. ILAN CHET, MOSHE ARAD, MOSHE VIGDOR
Academic Secretary: JOEL ALPERT
Library Director: Prof. SARA JAPHET

Library: see Jewish National and University Library
Number of teachers: 1,400
Number of students: 24,637

Publications include: *Scopus* (in English), *Ba-Universita* (in Hebrew), *News from the Hebrew University* (in Spanish, French, English and German), *Research* (in English), faculty handbooks, etc.

DEANS AND DIRECTORS

Faculty of Humanities: Prof. YAIR ZAKOVITCH
Faculty of Mathematics and Natural Science: Prof. MICHA SPIRA
Faculty of Medicine: Prof. GAD GLASER
Faculty of Law: Prof. URIEL PROCACCIA
Faculty of Agricultural, Food and Environmental Science: Prof. HAIM D. RABINOWITCH
Faculty of Social Sciences: Prof. JACOB METZER
Faculty of Dental Medicine: Prof. ADAM STABHOLZ
School of Education: Prof. DAN INBAR
Paul Baerwald School of Social Work: Prof. URI AVIRAM
School of Library, Archive and Information Studies: Prof. BLUMA PERITZ
Nadine and Fredy Herrmann Graduate School of Applied Science: Prof. JOSEPH SHAPPIN
School of Nutritional Sciences: Prof. MICHA NAIM
Jerusalem School of Business Administration: Prof. ABRAHAM MESHULACH
Rothberg School for Overseas Students: Prof. MICHEL ABITBOL
School of Pharmacy: Prof. JEHOSHUA KATZHENDLER
Centre for Pre-Academic Studies: Prof. SHMUEL SHILO
Dean of Students: Prof. AVIGDOR SHINAN
Hebrew University—Hadassah School of Public Health and Community Medicine: Prof. YECHIEL FRIEDLANDER
Henrietta Szold-Hebrew University—Hadassah School of Nursing: Dr MIRI ROM
Hebrew University—Hadassah School of Occupational Therapy: Prof. NAOMI KATZ

PROFESSORS

Faculty of Humanities:

(The Joseph and Ceil Mazer Center for the Humanities, including the Institutes of: Jewish Studies; Contemporary Jewry; Asian and African Studies; Archaeology, Philosophy and History; Languages, Literatures and Art; School of Education)

ABITBOL, M., Contemporary Jewry and African Studies
ALTSCHULER, M., Contemporary Jewry
AMISHAI-MAISELS, Z., History of Art
ARAZI, A., Arabic Language and Literature
ASSIS, Y.-T., Jewish History
BABAD, E., Education
BAR ASHER, M., Hebrew Language
BARAG, D., Archaeology
BARTAL, I., Jewish History
BARTFELD, F., French Language and Literature
BELLER, M., History and Philosophy of Science
BEN-SASSON, M., Jewish History
BEN-SHAMMAI, H., Arabic Language and Literature
BEN-TOR, A., Archaeology
BLUM-KULKA, S., Education, Communication
BONFIL, R., Jewish History
BRINKER, M., Hebrew Literature
BUDICK, S., English Literature
CHAZAN, N., African Studies and Political Science
COHEN, A., History of Muslim Countries
COHEN, R., Jewish History
COTTON, H., History and Classics
DAN, J., Jewish Thought
DELLA PERGOLA, S., Contemporary Jewry
ELBOIM, Y., Hebrew Literature
ELIOR, R., Jewish Thought
EPH'AL, I., History of the Jewish People

ETKES, I., Education and History of the Jewish People
FRENKEL, J., Russian Studies
FRIEDGUT, T., Russian and Slavic Studies
FRIEDMAN, Y., Islamic Studies
GAFNI, I., Jewish History
GATI, I., Education
GEIGER, J., Classical Studies
GERBER, H., Islamic Studies
GILULA, D., Theatre Studies
GOREN-INBAR, N., Archaeology
GROSSMAN, A., History of the Jewish People
HACKER, J. R., History of the Jewish People
HARRAN, D., Musicology
HASAN-ROKEM, G., Literature and Folklore
HERR, M. D., History of the Jewish People
HEYD, D., Philosophy
HEYD, M., History
HIRSHBERG, J., Musicology
HOCHMAN, B., English Literature
HOPKINS, S. A., Arabic
HOROWITZ, A., Bible and Hebrew Language
IDEL, M., Jewish Thought
INBAR, D., Education
JAPHET, S., Bible
KAHANG, R., Sociology and Education
KAPLAN, Y., History of the Jewish People
KARK, R., Geography
KARTUN-BLUM, R., Modern Hebrew Literature
KEDAR, B., History
KOHLBERG, E., Arabic Language and Literature
KULKA, O., History of the Jewish People
LAISH, A., Islamic Studies
LEVIN, A., Arabic Language and Literature
LEVTZION, N., African and Islamic History
LEWIN, I., Archaeology
LIEBES, Y., Jewish Thought
LINDER, A., History
MAOZ, M., History of Islamic Countries
MARGALIT, A., Philosophy
MAZAR, A., Archaeology
MEDDING, P., Contemporary Jewry and Political Science
MEGGED, N., Spanish and Latin American Studies
MENDELS, D., History
MENDELSOHN, E., Contemporary Jewry and Russian Studies
MENDES-FLOHR, P., Jewish Thought
MILSON, M., Arabic Language and Literature
MIRON, D., Hebrew Literature
MOREH, S., Arabic Language and Literature
MOSKOVICH, W., Russian and Slavic Studies
NETZER, A., Iranian Studies
NIR, R., Education and Communication
NISSAN, M., Education
PAUL, S., Bible
PITOWSKY, I., History and Philosophy of Science
RAVITZKY, A., Jewish Thought
RICCI, D., American Studies and Political Science
RIMMON-KENAN, S., English Literature
ROFÉ, A., Bible
ROJTMAN, B., French Language and Literature
ROKEAH, D., History
ROSEN, H., Classical Studies
ROSENBERG, S., Jewish Thought and Philosophy
ROSENHAK, M., Education
ROSENTHAL, D., Talmudic Studies
SANDBANK, S., English and Comparative Literature
SCHEFER, A., Assyriology
SCHULMAN, D., Indian Studies and Comparative Religion
SCHWARTZ, D., History of the Jewish People
SEGAL, D., Russian and Slavic Studies and Comparative Literature
SELLA, A., International Relations and Russian Studies
SHAKED, S., Iranian Studies and Comparative Religion
SHARON, M., Islamic Studies
SHATZMAN, I., History
SHESHA-HALEVY, A., General and Egyptian Philology
SHILLONY, B. A., Japanese History
SHINAN, A., Hebrew Literature
SIVAN, E., History
SOLOTOREVSKY, M., Spanish and Latin-American Studies
STEINER, M., Philosophy
STEWART, F., Islamic Studies
STONE, M., Indo-Iranian and Armenian Studies
STROUMSA, G., Comparative Religion
SUSSMAN, Y., Talmudic Studies
TOV, E., Bible
TURNIAVSKY, C., Yiddish
TZAFRIR, Y., Archaeology
VAN CREVELD, M., History
WISTRICH, R., History, and History of the Jewish People
YAHALOM, Y., Hebrew Literature
YOVEL, J., Philosophy
ZAKOVITCH, Y., Bible
ZEMACH, E. M., Philosophy

Faculty of Social Sciences:
(the Eliezer Kaplan School of Economics and Social Sciences)

AVINERI, S., Political Science
BAR-HILLEL, M., Psychology
BAR-SIMAN-TOV, Y., International Relations
BEN-SHAKHAR, G., Psychology
BEN-YEHUDA, N., Sociology
BENTIN, S., Psychology and Education
BIENSTOCK, M., Economics
BILO, Y., Psychology and Sociology
BLEJER, M., Economics
BLUM-KULKA, S., Communication and Education
COHEN, E., Sociology
COHEN, R., International Relations
DANET, B., Communications and Sociology
GALNOOR, I., Political Science
GALOR, O., Economics
GATI, I., Psychology and Education
GILULA, Z., Statistics and Social Work
GOLAN, G., Political Science and Russian Studies
GOLDBERG, H., Sociology
GONEN, A., Geography and Urban Studies
GREENBAUM, C. W., Psychology, Levin Centre
GRONAU, R., Economics
HAITOVSKY, Y., Statistics and Economics
HANDELMAN, D., Sociology
HANOCH, G., Economics
HART, S., Economics
HASSON, S., Geography and Urban Studies
JOFFE, E., International Relations and Chinese Studies
JOSSELSON, R., Psychology
KAHANE, R., Sociology and Education
KARK, R., Geography
KELLA, O., Statistics
KEREN, M., Economics
KLEIMAN, E., Economics
LAPIDOT, R., International Relations and Law
LEVHARI, D., Economics
LIEBLICH, A., Psychology
MEDDING, P., Political Science and Contemporary Jewry
METZER, J., Economics
NATHAN, G., Statistics
NINIO, A., Psychology
OFER, G., Economics
POLLAK, M., Statistics
POMERANCE, M., International Relations
RICCI, D., Political Science
RITOV, Y., Statistics
ROB, R., Economics
ROSE, N., International Relations
SALOMON, I., Geography and Urban Studies
SAMUEL-COHEN, E., Statistics
SCHICK, A. P., Physical Geography
SCHWARTZ, S., Psychology
SCHWARZ, G., Statistics
SELLA, A., International Relations and Russian Studies
SHACHAR, A., Geography
SHANON, B., Psychology
SHARKANSKY, I., Political Science
SHESHINSKY, E., Economics
STERNHELL, Z., Political Science
TEUBAL, M., Economics
VERTZBERGER, Y., International Relations
YAHAV, J., Statistics
YAIR, A., Geography
YITZHAKI, S., Agricultural Economics
ZAMIR, S., Statistics

Paul Baerwald School of Social Work:
AVIRAM, U.
BAR-HILLEL, M.
DORON, A.
GILULA, Z.
JAFFE, E.
ROTENBERG, M.

Jerusalem School of Business Administration:
BAR-LEV, B., Business Admnimistration
GALAI, D., Banking
KORNBLUTH, J., Business Administration
LEVY, H., Business Administration
PELES, Y., Business Administration
VENEZIA, I., Business Administration
ZUCKERMAN, D., Business Administration

School of Library, Archive and Information Studies:
BEIT-ARIE, M., Palaeography and Codicology

Faculty of Law:
(including the Harry Sacher Institute for Legislative Research and Comparative Law, the Israel Matz Institute for Research in Jewish Law)

BLUM, Y., International Public Law
GAVISON, R., Philosophy of Law
GOLDSTEIN, S., Civil Procedure
HARNON, E., Criminal Procedure and Criminal Evidence
KLEIN, C., Constitutional Law
KRETZMER, D., Public Law
LAPIDOTH, R., International Law and International Relations
LIFSCHITZ, B., Jewish Law
PROCACCIA, U., Corporate Law
RABELLO, A., Comparative Law
RADAY, F., Labour Law
SCHOCHETMAN, E., Jewish Law
SHALEV, G., Contract Law
SHIFMAN, P., Family Law and Succession Law
SHILO, S., Jewish Law
WEISMAN, J., Property Law

Faculty of Science:
(including the Institute of Mathematics; Institute of Computer Science; Racah Institute of Physics; Institute of Chemistry; Alexander Silberman Institute of Life Sciences; Institute of Earth Sciences; Fredy and Nadine Herrmann Graduate School of Applied Science and Technology; Amos de Shalit Science Teaching Centre; Heinz Schteinitz Interuniversity Institute for Marine Biological Research)

ADIN, A., Environmental Science
AGRANAT, I., Inorganic Chemistry
AIZENSHTAT, Z., Applied Chemistry
ARDON, M., Inorganic and Analytical Chemistry
ATLAS, D., Biological Chemistry
AVNIR, D., Organic Chemistry
BALBERG, Y., Experimental Physics
BARAK, A., Computer Science
BARKAT, Z., Physics
BECKENSTEIN, Y., Theoretical Physics
BEERI, C., Computer Science
BEN-ARTZI, M., Mathematics
BEN-DOR, L., Inorganic and Analytical Chemistry

Ben-Naim, A., Physical Chemistry
Ben-Or, M., Computer Science
Ben-Shaul, A., Theoretical Chemistry
Ben-Yosef, N., Applied Physics
Biali, S., Organic Chemistry
Bino, A., Theoretical and Analytical Chemistry
Blum, J., Organic Chemistry
Cabantchik, Y., Biophysics
Camhi, J. M., Cell and Animal Biology
Cohen, A., Atmospheric Sciences
Cohen, D., Botany
Cohen, M., Theoretical Chemistry
Czapski, G., Physical Chemistry
Davidov, D., Experimental Physics
Dekel, A., Theoretical Physics
Devor, M., Zoology
Dolev, D., Computer Science
Dror-Farjoun, E., Mathematics
Elber, R., Physical Chemistry, Biological Chemistry
Elitzur, S., Theoretical Physics
Farkas, H., Mathematics
Felner, I., Experimental Physics
Friedland, L., Theoretical Physics
Friedman, E., Experimental Physics
Friedmann, A., Genetics
Furstenberg, H., Mathematics
Gal, A., Theoretical Physics
Gale, J., Plant Sciences
Garfunkel, Z., Geology
Garti, N., Applied Chemistry
Gerber, R. B., Theoretical Chemistry
Gilon, C., Organic Chemistry
Ginsburg, H., Biological Chemistry
Glaberson, W., Experimental Physics
Goldstein, Y., Physical Chemistry
Grushka, E., Inorganic and Analytical Chemistry
Gutfreund, H., Theoretical Physics
Haas, Y., Physical Chemistry
Harel, E., Plant Sciences
Hart, S., Mathematics
Hirschberg, J., Genetics
Hochberg, A., Biological Chemistry
Hochstein, S., Neurobiology
Hrushovski, E., Mathematics
Kalai, G., Mathematics
Kaniel, S., Mathematics
Kaplan, A., Plant Sciences
Kaplan, N., Physics
Katz, A., Geology
Kifer, Y., Mathematics
Kolodny, Y., Geology
Kosloff, A., Physical Chemistry
Kulka, R., Biological Chemistry
Laikhtman, B., Physics
Lehmann, D., Computer Science
Levanon, H., Physical Chemistry
Levine, R., Theoretical Chemistry
Levitski, A., Biological Chemistry
Levy, A., Mathematics
Lewis, A., Applied Physics
Lifshitz, A., Physical Chemistry
Lifshitz, C., Physical Chemistry
Lindenstrauss, J., Mathematics
Linial, N., Computer Science
Lozinskii, E., Computer Science
Loyter, A., Biological Chemistry
Lubotzky, A., Mathematics
Luria, M., Applied and Environmental Science
Magidor, M., Mathematics
Mandelzweig, V., Theoretical Physics
Mann, A., Mathematics
Marcus, Y., Inorganic and Analytical Chemistry
Marom, G., Applied Chemistry
Matthews, A., Geology
Meerson, B., Experimental Physics
Nebenzahl, I., Physics
Neyman, A., Mathematics and Economics
Nisan, N., Computer Science
Nowik, I., Experimental Physics
Ohad, I., Biological Chemistry
Ottolenghi, M., Physical Chemistry
Ovadyahu, Z., Experimental Physics
Padan, E., Microbiological Ecology
Parnas, H., Neurobiology
Parnas, I., Neurobiology
Paul, M., Experimental Physics
Pazi, A., Mathematics
Peleg, S., Computer Science
Pener, M. P., Cell and Animal Biology
Perles, M. A., Mathematics
Piran, Z., Theoretical Physics
Plitman, V., Plant Sciences
Rabani, J., Physical Chemistry
Rabin, M., Computer Science
Rabinovici, E., Theoretical Physics
Rabinowitz, M., Organic Chemistry
Rappoport, Z., Organic Chemistry
Reisfeld, R., Inorganic and Analytical Chemistry
Rips, E., Mathematics
Rogawski, J. D., Mathematics
Rokni, M., Physics
Sachs, T., Plant Sciences
Safriel, U., Zoology
Sagiv, Y., Computer Science
Sass, E., Geology
Sasson, Y., Applied Chemistry
Schuldiner, S., Microbial Ecology
Schwob, J. L., Experimental Physics
Selinger, Z., Biological Chemistry
Sever, M., Mathematics
Shaik, S. S., Organic Chemistry
Shalev, A., Mathematics
Shamir, E., Computer Science
Shappir, Y., Applied Physics
Shelah, S., Mathematics
Sheradsky, T., Organic Chemistry
Shmida, A., Botany
Simchen, G., Genetics
Soller, M., Genetics
Solomon, S., Theoretical Physics
Sompolinsky, H., Physics
Soreq, H., Biological Chemistry
Sperling, R., Genetics
Spira, M., Neurobiology
Stein, W. Z., Biological Chemistry
Steinberg, M., Inorganic Chemistry
Tchernow, E., Zoology
Tikochinsky, Y., Physics
Tzafriri, L., Mathematics
Wagschal, J. J., Physics
Weger, M., Experimental Physics
Weiss, B., Mathematics
Werner, Y., Zoology
Wigderson, A., Computer Science
Willner, I., Organic Chemistry
Yacobi, Y., Experimental Physics
Yariv, S., Inorganic and Analytical Chemistry
Yarum, Y., Neurobiology
Zilkha, A., Organic Chemistry
Zippin, M., Mathematics
Zlotkin, E., Cell and Animal Biology

Faculty of Agricultural, Food and Environmental Science:
(the Levi Eshkol School of Agriculture, including the School of Nutritional Sciences and the School of Veterinary Medicine)

Altman, A., Horticulture
Applebaum, S. W., Entomology
Banin, A., Soil and Water Sciences
Bravdo, B., Horticulture
Cahaner, A., Field Crops, Vegetables and Genetics
Chen, Y., Soil and Water Sciences
Chet, I., Microbiology
Chorev, M., Pharmaceutical Chemistry
Cohen, E., Entomology
Dinoor, A., Plant Pathology and Microbiology
Gertler, A., Agricultural Biochemistry
Goldschmidt, E. E., Horticulture
Goren, R., Horticulture
Hadar, Y., Plant Pathology and Microbiology
Heller, D. A., Animal Sciences
Hillel, J., Field Crops, Vegetables and Genetics
Hochman, E., Agricultural Economics
Hod, Y., Animal Sciences
Johnston, D., Veterinary Medicine
Kafkafi, U., Field and Vegetable Crops
Katan, Y., Plant Pathology
Kislev, Y., Agricultural Economics
Ladizinsky, G., Field and Vegetable Crops (Genetics)
Lavee, S., Horticulture
Madar, Z., Agricultural Biochemistry
Mahrer, Y., Soil and Water Sciences
Mayak, S., Horticulture
Mualem, Y., Soil and Water Sciences
Naim, H., Food Science and Nutrition
Nir, S., Soil and Water Sciences
Noy-Meir, I., Horticulture
Okon, Y., Plant Pathology and Microbiology
Paperna, I., Animal Sciences
Perk, K., Animal Anatomy and Physiology
Rabinowitch, H. D., Field Crops, Vegetables and Genetics
Riov, J., Horticulture
Rubin, B., Field Crops, Vegetables and Genetics
Sela, I., Virology
Singer, A., Soil and Water Sciences
Sklan, D., Animal Sciences
Snapir, N., Animal Sciences
Tel-Or, E., Agricultural Economics
Yahav, J., Agricultural Economics
Zamir, D., Field Crops, Vegetables and Genetics
Zehavi, U., Agricultural Biochemistry
Zislin, N., Horticulture

Faculty of Medicine:
(the Hebrew University-Hadassah Medical School, including the School of Pharmacy, School of Social Medicine and Public Health, the Hadassah-Henrietta Szold School of Nursing, the School of Occupational Therapy)

Abeles, M., Physiology
Abraham, A. S., Medicine
Abramsky, O., Neurology
Anteby, S. O., Obstetrics and Gynaecology
Atlan, H., Medical Biophysics
Bach, G., Genetics
Bar-On, H., Medicine
Bar-Tana, J., Biochemistry
Bar-Ziv, J., Diagnostic Radiology
Barenholz, Y., Biochemistry
Becker, Y., Virology
Ben-David, M., Pharmacology
Ben-Ezra, D., Ophthalmology
Ben-Neriah, Y., Immunology
Ben-Sasson, Z., Immunology
Benita, S., Pharmacy
Bentwich, Z. H., Medicine
Bercovier, H., Clinical Microbiology
Bialer, M., Pharmacology
Bransky, D., Paediatrics
Brautbar, C., Microbiology
Breuer, E., Pharmaceutical Chemistry
Brezis, M., Medicine
Cedar, H., Molecular Biology
Cerasi, E., Chemical Endocrinology
Chajek-Shaul, T., Medicine
Cohen, A., Molecular Genetics
Cotev, S., Anaesthesiology
Dikstein, S., Cell Pharmacology
Durst, A., Surgery
Eilat, D., Immunology
Engelberg-Kulka, H., Molecular Biology
Epstein, L. M., Social Medicine
Fibach, E., Experimental Haematology
Floman, Y., Orthopaedic Surgery
Freund, H., Surgery
Friedman, M., Pharmacy
Glaser, G., Biochemistry
Godfrey, S., Paediatrics
Goldberg, I., Microbiology
Gotsman, M., Medicine
Greenblatt, C., Parasitology

GROVER, N., Experimental Medicine and Cancer Research
GUTMAN, A., Clinical Biochemistry
GUTMAN, Y., Pharmacology
HANSKY, E., Microbiology
HASIN, Y., Cardiology
HERSHKO, CH., Haematology
KAEMPFER, R., Molecular Virology
KAHANE, I., Microbiology
KANNER, B. I., Biochemistry
KAPLAN-DENOUR, A., Psychiatry
KARK, J., Social Medicine
KATZHENDLER, J., Pharmaceutical Chemistry
KEDAR, E., Immunology
KEREN, A., Cardiology
KESHET, E., Virology
KLAUS, S., Dermatology
LASKOV, R., Experimental Physics
LAUFER, N., Obstetrics and Gynaecology
LEITERSDORF, E., Medicine
LERER, B., Psychiatry
LEVY, M., Medicine
LICHTENSTEIN, D., Physiology
LOEBENTHAL, E., Paediatrics
MANNY, J., Surgery
MATZNER, Y., Haematology
MAYER, M., Clinical Biochemistry
MECHOULAM, R., Medicinal Chemistry (Natural Products and Pharmacognosy)
MERIN, G., Cardiothoracic Surgery
MERIN, S., Ophthalmology
MINKE, B., Physiology
NAOR, D., Immunology
NAPARSTEK, J., Medicine
OPPENHEIM, A., Experimental Haematology
OPPENHEIM, A. B., Microbiological Chemistry
ORNOY, A., Anatomy
PALTI, H., Social Medicine
PANET, A., Virology
PENCHAS, S., Organization and Management of Health Services
POLLAK, A., Haematology
POPOWTZER, M., Nephrology
RACHMILEWITZ, D., Medicine
RACHMILEWITZ, E. A., Haematology
RAHAMIMOFF, H., Biochemistry
RAHAMIMOFF, R., Physiology
RAZIN, A., Cell Biochemistry
RAZIN, E., Biochemistry
RAZIN, S., Clinical Microbiology
RECHES, A., Neurology
RESHEF, L., Biochemistry
ROTEM, S., Clinical Microbiology
ROTSHENKER, S., Anatomy
SAMUNI, S., Molecular Biology
SCHENKER, J., Gynaecology and Obstetrics
SCHILLER, M., Paediatric Surgery
SCHLEIN, Y., Parasitology
SCHLESINGER, M., Experimental Medicine and Cancer Research
SEGAL, D., Orthopaedic Surgery
SHALEV, A., Psychiatry
SHANI, J., Pharmacology
SHAPIRA, Y., Paediatrics
SHLOMAI, J., Molecular Biology
SHOUVAL, D., Medicine
SIEGAL, T., Neurology and Neuro-Oncology
SILVER, J., Nephrology
SLAVIN, S., Medicine
SOHMER, H., Physiology
SPIRA, D., Parasitology
SPRUNG, CH. L., Medicine
TZIVONI, D., Medicine
VLODAVSKY, I., Oncology
WEIDENFELD, J., Experimental Neurology
WEINSTEIN, D., Obstetrics and Gynaecology
WEINSTOCK-ROSIN, M., Pharmacology
WEISSMAN, CH., Anaesthesiology
WESHLER, Z., Oncology
WEXLER, M. R., Plastic Surgery
YAGEN, B., Natural Products
YATZIV, S., Paediatrics
ZAKAI-RONES, Z., Virology
ZAUBERMAN, H., Ophthalmology

Faculty of Dental Medicine:
(Hebrew University-Hadassah School of Dental Medicine)

BAB, I., Oral Pathology
BIMSTEIN, E., Pedodontics
CHEVION, M., Biochemistry
CHOSACK, A., Pedodontics
DEUTSCH, D., Oral Biology
EIDELMAN, A., Pedodontics
FUKS, A., Pedodontics
GARFUNKEL, A., Oral Medicine
HOROWITZ, M., Physiology
MANN, J., Community Dentistry
MUHLRAD, A., Oral Biology
SCHWARTZ, Z., Periodontics
SELA, J., Oral Pathology
SELA, M., Maxillofacial Rehabilitation
SELA, M., Oral Biology
SHARAV, Y., Oral Medicine
SMITH, P., Anthropology
STABHOLZ, A., Endodontics
SHTEYER, A., Oral Surgery
STERN, N., Oral Rehabilitation

RESEARCH CENTRES AND INSTITUTES

Institute for Advanced Studies: Dir Prof. DAVID SHULMAN.

Harry S. Truman Research Institute for the Advancement of Peace: Dir Prof. MOSHE MAOZ.

Ben-Zion Dinur Institute for Research in Jewish History: Dir Dr AHARON KEDAR.

Center for Research on Dutch Jewry: Dir Prof. YOSEF KAPLAN.

Center for Research on the History and Culture of Polish Jews: Dir Prof. ISRAEL BARTAL.

Center for the Study of Jewish Languages and Literature: Dir Prof. MOSHE BAR-ASHER.

Folklore Research Center: Dir Prof. GALIT HASAN-ROKEM.

Vidal Sassoon International Center for the Study of Antisemitism: Dir Dr SIMON EPSTEIN.

Orion Center for the Study of the Dead Sea Scrolls: Dir Prof. MICHAEL STONE.

Philip and Muriel Berman Center for Biblical Archaeology: Dir Prof. TRUDE DOTHAN.

S. H. Bergman Center for Philosophical Studies: Dir Prof. DAVID HEYD.

Sidney M. Edelstein Center for the History and Philosophy of Science, Technology and Medicine: Dir Prof. YEMIMA BEN-MENAHEM.

Richard Koebner Center for German History: Dir Prof. MOSCHE ZIMMERMAN.

Center for Literary Studies: Dir Prof. SANFORD BUDICK.

Franz Rosenzweig Center for the Study of German Culture and Literature: Dir Prof. GABRIEL MOTZKIN.

Center for Slavic Languages and Literatures: Dir Prof. WOLF MOSCOWICH.

Center for Jewish Art: Dir Dr ALIZA COHEN-MUSHLIN.

Robert H. and Clarice Smith Center for Art History: Dir Prof. ZIVA AMISHAI-MAISELS.

Jewish Music Research Center: Dir Prof. DON HARRAN.

Paul Desmarais Centre for the Study of French Culture: Dir Prof. BETTY ROJTMAN.

Center for the Study of Sephardi and Oriental Jewry: Dir Prof. ZEEV HARVEY.

Center for Research and Documentation of East European Jewry: Chair. Prof. MORDECHAI ALTSHULER.

Bernard Cherrick Center for the Study of Zionism, the Yishuv and the History of Israel: Dir Prof. HAGIT LAVSKY.

Ben-Zvi Institute for the Study of Jewish Communities in the East: Chair. Prof. HAGGAI BEN-SHAMAI.

Center for the Study of the History of Eretz Israel and its Population: Chair Prof. DAVID ROSENTHAL.

National Council of Jewish Women Research Institute for Innovation in Education: Dir Prof. ELITE OLSHTAIN.

Goldie Rotman Center for Cognitive Science in Education: Dir Dr YAACOV KAREEV.

Leonard Davis Institute for International Relations: Dir Prof. YAACOV BARSIMAN TOV.

Levi Eshkol Institute for Economic, Social and Political Research: Dir Prof. YORAM BILU.

Pinhas Lavon Labor History Research Institute: Dir Prof. SHLOMO AVINERI.

Lewin Center for the Study of Normal Child and Adolescent Development: Dir Prof. AMIA LIEBLICH.

Scheinfeld Center for Human Genetics in the Social Sciences: Dir Dr ADA ZOHAR.

Sigmund Freud Center for Study and Research in Psychoanalysis: Dir Prof. SHMUEL EHRLICH.

Sturman Center for Human Development: Dir Prof. ANAT NINIO.

Harvey L. Silbert Center for Israel Studies: Dir Prof. ARIE SHACHAR.

Brian Y. Davidson Center for Agribusiness: Dir Dr CHEZY OFIR.

Lafer Center for Women's Studies: Chair. Prof. GALIA GOLAN.

Shaine Center for Research in the Social Sciences: Dir Prof. EYAL BEN-ARI.

Krueger Center for Finance: Dir Prof. HAIM LEVY.

K Mart International Retail and Marketing Center: Dir Prof. DAVID MAZURSKY.

Gal-Edd Center for Industrial Development: Dir Prof. AVRAHAM MESHULAH.

Center for Management Development: Dir ORA ALTMAN.

Recanati Center for Research in Business Administration: Dir Prof. AVRAHAM FRIEDMAN.

Mordechai Zagagi Center for Finance and Accounting: Dir Prof. AVRAHAM MESHULACH.

Center for Rationality and Interactive Decision Theory: Dir Prof. SERGIU HART.

Smart Family Foundation Communication Institute: Dir Prof. TAMAR LIEBES.

Institute for European Studies: Dir Prof. SHLOMO AVINERI.

Marjorie Mayrock Center for Russian, Eurasian and East European Research: Dir Dr STEFANIE HOFFMAN.

Israel Matz Institute for Research in Jewish Law: Dir Prof. HANINA BEN-MENAHEM.

Harry and Michael Sacher Institute for Legislative Research and Comparative Law: Dir Prof. MORDECHAI RABELLO.

Center for Human Rights: Dir Prof. DAVID KRETZMER.

Minerva Center for the Study of Arid Ecosystems: Dir Prof. AHARON KAPLAN.

Moshe Shilo Center for Marine Biogeochemistry: Dir Prof. AHARON OREN.

G. W. Leibnitz Minerva Center for Research in Computer Sciences: Dir Prof. MICHAEL BEN-OR.

Edmund Landau Minerva Center for Research in Mathematical Analysis: Dir Prof. HERSHEL FARKAS.

Fritz Haber Research Center for Molecular Dynamics: Dir Prof. RONNIE KOSLOFF.

Minerva Avron Center of Photosynthesis Research: Dir Prof. YITZHAK OHAD.

Knune Minerva Farkas Center for the Study of Light Induced Processes: Dir Prof. HAIM LEVANON.

Center for the Study of Visual Transduction: Dir Prof. ZVI SELINGER.

James Frank Laser–Matter Interaction Research Center: Dir Prof. RAPHAEL LEVINE.

Otto Loewi Center for Cellular and Molecular Neurobiology: Dir Prof. ITZCHAK PARNAS.

Wolfson Center for Applied Structural Biology: Dir Prof. BOAZ SHAANAN.

Minerva Center for Computational Quantum Chemistry: Dir Prof. SASSON SHAIK.

Yad Ha-Nadiv Center for Computer Science and Discrete Mathematics: Dir Prof. AVI WIGDERSON.

National Institute for Psychobiology in Israel: Dir Prof. BERNARD LERER.

Harry Stern National Center for the Study and Treatment of Alzheimer's Disease and Related Disorders: Dir Prof. BERNARD LERER.

Da'at Consortium for Developing Generic Technologies for Drugs and Diagnostic Kits Design and Development: Dir Prof. RACHEL NECHUSHTAI.

Center for Geographical Information Systems: Dir Dr RONEN KADMON.

National Center for Human Genome Diversity: Dir Dr. BATHSHEBA KEREM.

Israel Academy of Science Center of Biophysics: Dir Prof. AHARON LEWIS.

Herbarium of Middle Eastern Flora (Israel National Herbarium): Dir Prof. UZI PLITMANN.

Interdisciplinary Center for Neural Computation: Dir Prof. MOSHE ABELES.

Center for the Study of Bone Metabolism: Dir Prof. JUSTIN SILVER.

Alpha Omega Dental Research and Postgraduate Center: Dir Prof. DAN DEUTSCH.

D. Walter Cohen Middle East Center for Dental Education: Dir Prof. A. GARFUNKEL.

Sanford F. Kuvin Center for the Study of Infectious and Tropical Diseases: Dir Prof. DAN SHAPIRA.

Lautenberg Center for General and Tumour Immunology: Dir Prof. EITAN YEFE-NOF.

Hubert H. Humphrey Center for Experimental Medicine and Cancer Research: Dir Prof. ZUI BAR-SHAVIT.

Center for Diabetes Research: Chair. Prof. ASHER OR-NOY.

Center for the Study of Pain: Dir Prof. MARSHALL DEVOR.

Bernard Katz Center for Cell Biophysics: Dir Prof. RAMI RAHAMIMOFF.

Center for Agricultural Economic Research: Dir Prof. ELI FEINERMAN.

Nutrition Research Center: Dir Prof. ZECHARIA MEDAR.

Seagram Center for Soil and Water Sciences: Dir Prof. ARIE SINGER.

Benjamin Triwaks Bee Research Center: Dir Prof. YAACOV LENSKY.

Leo Picard Groundwater Research Center: Dir Prof. YITZHAK MAHRER.

Otto Warburg Center for Agricultural Biotechnology: Dir Prof. ARIE ALTMAN.

Herb and Frances Brody Center for Food Sciences: Dir Prof. HAIM A. RABINOWITCH.

Center for Agricultural Research in Desert and Semi-Arid Zones: Dir Prof. UZI KAFKAFI.

Kennedy Leigh Center for Agricultural Research: Dir Prof. RAPHAEL GOREN.

OPEN UNIVERSITY OF ISRAEL

16 Klausner St, Ramat Aviv, POB 39328, 61 392 Tel Aviv

Telephone: (3) 6460460
Fax: (3) 6423639

Founded 1974, formerly Everyman's University, present name 1989; a distance-learning open university serving students on a nationwide basis. Academic and general adult education using a multimedia self-study system supplemented by tutorial instruction. Offers 400 courses in life sciences, natural sciences, mathematics, computer studies, management, social sciences, humanities, education, behavioural sciences, Judaic studies, music and the arts

Language of instruction: Hebrew
Academic year: September to June (two semesters) and summer semester

Chancellor: Sir CLAUS MOSER
Deputy Chancellor: Lord ROTHSCHILD
Vice-Chancellor: Prof. ABRAHAM GINZBURG
President: Prof. MENAHEM E. YAARI
Vice-President: Prof. RUTH BEYTH-MAROM
Director General: GIORA ULMAN
Dean of Teaching: Dr RUTH ARAV
Dean of Students: Prof. NACHMAN ESHEL
Director, Centre for the Design of Distance Teaching Methods: Dr MICHAEL BELLER
Librarian: ANAT EIDINGER

Library of 50,000 vols
Number of teachers: 250 academic staff members and 1,000 tutors throughout Israel teaching in 100 study centres
Number of students: 26,000

TEL-AVIV UNIVERSITY

Ramat-Aviv, 69 978 Tel-Aviv

Telephone: (3) 6408111
Fax: (3) 6408601

Founded 1953; inaugurated 1956
Private control, partially supported by the Government
Language of instruction: Hebrew
Academic year: October to June (two terms)

President: Prof. Y. DINSTEIN
Rector: Prof. N. COHEN
Vice-Rector: Prof. Y. EISENBERG
Vice-President (Research and Development): Prof. E. MAROM
Vice-President (Foreign Relations): Y. BEN-ZVI
Director-General: D. LANIR
Academic Secretary: Mrs H. BEN-SHEFFER

Library: see Libraries
Number of teachers: 1,792
Number of students: 24,700

Publications: *Hasifrut, Iunei Mishpat, Poetics Today, Zemanim, Mideast File* (all quarterly), *Middle East Contemporary Survey, Jahrbuch des Instituts für Deutsche Geschichte, Dinei Israel, Israel Yearbook in Human Rights, Tel-Aviv University Studies in Law* (all annually), *Studies in Zionism* (every 6 months), *Mediterranean Historical Review* (every 6 months), *Michael* (8 every 18 months), *Shvut* (9 a year).

DEANS

Faculty of Humanities: Prof. M. DASCAL
Faculty of Social Sciences: Prof. A. NADLER
Faculty of Management (Leon Recanati Graduate School of Business Administration): Prof. I. ZANG
Buchmann Faculty of Law: Prof. E. LEDERMAN
George S. Wise Faculty of Life Sciences: Prof. I. BARASH
Raymond and Beverly Sackler Faculty of Exact Sciences: Prof. A. NITZAN
Iby and Aladar Fleischman Faculty of Engineering: Prof. U. SHAKED
Sackler Faculty of Medicine: Prof. E. KAPLINSKY
Yolanda and David Katz Faculty of Arts: Prof. E. ROZIK-ROZEN

HEADS OF SCHOOLS

School of Education: Prof. D. CHEN
Aranne School of History: Prof. B. ISAAC
Chaim Rosenberg School of Jewish Studies: Prof. Y. NINI
Shirley and Leslie Porter School of Cultural Studies: Prof. G. TOURY
School of Health Professions: Prof. H. MONITZ
School of Continuing Medical Education: Prof. M. FAINARU
Maurice and Gabriella Goldschleger School of Dental Medicine: Prof. H. JUDES
School of Mathematical Sciences: Prof. M. SHARIR
School of Physics and Astronomy: Prof. S. YANKIELOWICZ
School of Chemistry: Prof. S. ROZEN
Bob Shapell School of Social Work: Prof. Y. WOZNER
Eitan Berglas School of Economics: Prof. CH. FERSHTMAN

PROFESSORS

AARONSON, J., Mathematics
ABARBANEL, S., Applied Mathematics
ABOUDI, J., Mechanical Engineering
ABRAMOVICI, A., Pathology
ABRAMOVICI, F., Applied Mathematics
ADAR, R., Surgery
AHARONOV, Y., Physics
AHARONOWITZ, Y., Microbiology
AHARONY, A., Physics
AHITUV, N., Management
AKSELROD, S., Physics
ALEXANDER, G., Physics
ALGOM, D., Psychology
ALON, N., Mathematics
ALONI, R., Botany
ALSTER, J., Physics
AMIR, D., Mathematics
AMIRAV, A., Chemistry
AMOSSY, R., French Literature
ANBAR, M., Bible
ANDELMAN, D., Physics
APPELBAUM, J., Electrical and Electronic Engineering
APTER, A., Psychiatry
AR, A., Zoology
ARBEL, A., Industrial Engineering
ARENSBURG, B., Anatomy and Anthropology
ASHERY, D., Physics
ASHKENAZI, Y., Human Genetics
ATZMON, A., Mathematics
AUERBACH, N., Physics
AVIRAM, I., Biochemistry
AZBEL, M., Physics
BANKS-SILLS, L., Mechanical Engineering
BAR-ELI, K., Chemistry
BAR-KOCHVA, B., History of the Jewish People
BAR-MEIR, S., Medicine
BAR-NAVI, E., History
BAR-NUN, A., Planetary Sciences
BAR-TAL, D., Education
BARASH, I., Botany
BARNEA, A., Management
BARNEA, D., Mechanical Engineering
BDOLAH, A., Zoology
BECHLER, Z., History of Science and Ideas
BEJA, A., Management
BELKIN, M., Ophthalmology
BEN-AMI, S., History
BEN-AVRAHAM, Z., Geophysics
BEN-BASSAT, I., Haematology
BEN-DAVID, Y., Anatomy and Anthropology
BEN-ISRAEL, R., Law
BEN-JACOB, E., Physics
BEN-RAFAEL, E., Sociology and Anthropology
BEN-RAFAEL, Z., Gynaecology and Obstetrics
BEN-REUVEN, A., Chemistry
BEN-SHAHAR, H., Economics
BEN-SHAUL, Y., Cell Biology
BEN-ZVI, A., Political Science
BENVENISTE, Y., Mechanical Engineering
BERAN, M. J., Engineering
BERECHMAN, J., Urban Planning
BERGMAN, D., Physics
BERMAN, R., Linguistics
BERNHEIM, J., Medicine
BERNSTEIN, J., Mathematics

BINDERMAN, I., Dentistry
BITAN, A., Geography
BIXON, M., Chemistry
BLUMBERG, SH., Biochemistry
BLUMENTHAL, M., Ophthalmology
BOICHIS, H., Paediatrics
BONNE, B., Human Genetics
BOROVITS, I., Management
BOXMAN, R., Electrical and Electronic Engineering
BRAUNER, N., Mechanical Engineering
BRAUNSTEIN, A., Electrical and Electronic Engineering
BRIN, G., Bible
BUCHNER, A., Oral Pathology
CARMELI, CH., Biochemistry
CASHER, A., Physics
CHEN, M., Education
CHESNOVSKY, O., Chemistry
COHEN, A., Communication
COHEN, G., Molecular Microbiology and Biotechnology
COHEN, N., Law
CUKIERMAN, A., Economics
DAGAN, G., Engineering
DAGAN, S., Physics
DASCAL, M., Philosophy
DASCAL, N., Physiology
DESHEN, S., Social Anthropology
DEUTSCHER, G., Physics
DINBAR, A., Surgery
DINER, D., History
DINSTEIN, Y., Law
DYN, N., Applied Mathematics
EDEN, D., Management
EIN-DOR, P., Management
EINAV, S., Biomedical Engineering
EISENBERG, J., Physics
ELDOR, A., Haematology
ELIZUR, A., Psychiatry
ELKANA, Y., History of Science and Ideas
ENTIN, O., Physics
EPEL, B. L., Botany
ERLICH, H., History of the Middle East and Africa
ERSHKOVICH, A., Planetary Studies
ESHEL, I., Statistics
EVEN, U., Chemistry
EVEN-ZOHAR, I., Theory of Literature
EVIATAR, A., Geophysics
EVRON, Y., Political Science
EYAL, Z., Botany
FABIAN, I., Cell Biology and Histology
FAIN, B., Chemistry
FAINARU, M., Medicine
FARBER, M., Mathematics
FELDON, J., Psychology
FERSHTMAN, CH., Economics
FINKELSTEIN, I., Archaeology
FLEXER, A., Geology
FRANKENTHAL, S., Electrical and Electronic Engineering
FRANKFURT, L. L., Physics
FREEMAN, A., Biotechnology
FRENK, H., Psychology
FRENKEL, J., Economics
FRENKEL, N., Cell Research and Immunology
FRIEDLAND, N., Psychology
FRIEDLANDER, S., History
FRIEDMAN, D., Law
FRIEDMAN, J., Botany
FRIEDMAN, M. A., Talmud
FUCHS, B., Chemistry
GAATONE, D., French Linguistics
GADOTH, N., Neurology
GAFTER, U., Medicine
GAZIT, A., Human Microbiology
GAZIT, E., Paediatrics
GERLING, D., Zoology
GERSHONI, I., History of the Middle East
GILAT, T., Medicine
GILEADI, E., Chemistry
GITIC, M., Mathematics
GLASNER, S., Mathematics
GLOBERSON, SH., Management
GLUCKER, J., Philology and Classical Philosophy
GLUSKIN, E., Mathematics
GOLANI, I., Zoology
GOLDBERG, I., Chemistry
GOLDBOURT, U., Preventive and Social Medicine
GOLDHIRSCH, I., Mechanical Engineering
GOLDMAN, B., Genetics
GOLDSMITH, S., Physics
GOLDWASSER, B., Surgery
GOOR, D., Surgery
GORNY, Y., History of the Jewish People
GORODETSKY, G., History
GOTSMAN, A., Physics
GOVER, A., Electrical and Electronic Engineering
GOVRIN, N., Hebrew Literature
GOZES, I., Clinical Biochemistry
GREEN, M., Epidemiology and Preventive Medicine
GREENSTEIN, E., Bible
GROSS, J., Law
GROSU, A., Linguistics
GRUENWALD, I., Jewish Philosophy
GRUNHAUS, J., Physics
GUTMAN, M., Biochemistry
GUTNIK, D., Microbiology
HALKIN, H., Medicine
HARDY, A., Electrical and Electronic Engineering
HAREL, SH., Paediatrics
HASSIN, R., Statistics
HAZAN, H., Sociology and Anthropology
HEFETZ, A., Zoology
HELPMAN, E., Economics
HENIS, Y., Biochemistry
HERZOG, M., Mathematics
HEYMAN, E., Electrical Engineering
HIZI, A., Cell Biology
HOCHBERG, Y., Statistics
HOFFMAN, Y., Bible
HORN, D., Physics
HORNIK, J., Management
HOROWITZ, A., Geology
HORWITZ, L. P., Physics
HUPPERT, D., Chemistry
ISAAC, B., Classics
ISHAY, J., Physiology
ITZCHAK, Y., Diagnostic Radiology
JARDEN, M., Mathematics
JORTNER, J., Chemistry
JOSEPH, J., Atmospheric Sciences
KAHANE, Y., Management
KALDOR, U., Chemistry
KALINA, M., Cell Biology and Histology
KAMIN, S., Mathematics
KANDEL, SH., Management
KANTOR, Y., Physics
KAPLINSKY, E., Cardiology
KARLINER, M., Physics
KASHER, A., History of the Jewish People
KASHER, A., Philosophy
KASHMAN, Y., Chemistry
KATZ, D., History
KATZIR, A., Physics
KAUFMANN, G., Biochemistry
KELSON, I., Physics
KENAAN-KEDAR, N., History of Arts
KEREN, G., Cardiology
KISSEBERTH, CH., Linguistics
KIT, E., Mechanical Engineering
KLAFTER, J., Chemistry
KLEIN, A., Mathematics
KLIEMAN, A., Political Science
KLOOG, Y., Biochemistry
KORCZYN, A., Neurology
KORENSTEIN, R., Physiology
KOSLOFF, D., Geophysics
KOVETZ, A., Geophysics
KOZLOVSKY, B. Z., Physics
KRAEMER, J., History of Islam
KRAICER, P., Endocrinology
KREITLER, S., Psychology
LANGHOLZ, G., Electrical Engineering
LANIADO, S., Cardiology
LASS, Y., Physiology
LAVI, S., Cell Biology
LAZAR, A., Mathematics
LAZAR, M., Ophthalmology
LEIBOWITZ, E., Physics and Astronomy
LEIDERMAN, L., Economics
LEVANON, N., Electrical and Electronic Engineering
LEVIATAN, D., Mathematics
LEVIN, D., Applied Mechanics
LEVIN, E. M., Physics
LEVIN, I., Education
LEVIN, Z., Atmospheric Sciences
LEVO, Y., Medicine
LEVY, A., Physics
LEWIN, L., Chemical Pathology
LIBERMAN, U., Physiology
LIBERMAN, U., Statistics
LICHTENBERG, D., Pharmacology
LICHTENSTADT, J., Physics
LIPTSER, R., Electrical and Electronic Engineering
LIVSHITS, Z., Anatomy and Anthropology
LOMRANZ, J., Psychology
LOYA, Y., Zoology
LUBIN, E., Nuclear Medicine
LUBOW, R., Psychology
MALKIN, I., Ancient History
MAOR, U., Physics
MAOZ, Z., Political Science
MARGALIT, M., Education
MARGALIT, R., Biochemistry
MAROM, E., Engineering
MAROM, Z., Medicine
MASHIAH, S., Gynaecology and Obstetrics
MATSAEV, V., Mathematics
MAZEH, T., Physics
MEDIN, Z., History
MEGIDO, N., Statistics
MEILIJSON, I., Statistics
MEIR, E., Psychology
MEKLER, Y., Planetary Sciences
MEKORY, Y., Medicine
MELAMED, E., Neurology
MICHAELI, D., Medicine
MICHAELSON, D., Biochemistry
MILGRAM, N. A., Psychology
MILMAN, V., Mathematics
MILOH, T., Engineering
MOALEM-MARON, D., Mechanical Engineering
MODAN, B., Preventive and Social Medicine
MOINESTER, M., Physics
MOROZ, CH., Human Microbiology
MULLER, E., Management
MYSLOBOTSKY, M., Psychology
NA'AMAN, N., History of the Jewish People
NACHMIAS, D., Political Science
NADLER, A., Psychology
NAOR, Z., Biochemistry
NAVON, G., Chemistry
NAVON, R., Human Genetics
NELSON, N., Biochemistry
NETZER, H., Physics
NEUMAN, J., Botany
NEUMAN, Z., Business Administration
NEVO, D., Education
NEVO, Z., Clinical Biochemistry
NINI, Y., History of the Jewish People
NISSENKORN, I., Surgery
NITZAN, A., Chemistry
NITZAN, M., Paediatrics
NOVOGRODSKY, A., Immunology
NUSSINOV, R., Biochemistry
NUSSINOV, S., Physics
OFEK, I., Human Microbiology
OFER, A., Management
OLEVSKII, A., Mathematics
OPPENHEIMER, A., History of the Jewish People
ORDA, R., Surgery
OREN, J., Physics
ORGLER, Y., Business Administration
ORON, Y., Pharmacology
OVADIAH, A., Archaeology and History of Arts
PARNES, R., Mechanical Engineering
PASTERNAK (PAZ), M., Physics
PASWELL, I., Paediatrics

PAZ, G., Physiology
PELED, E., Chemistry
PICK, E., Immunology
PINES, D., Economics
PINKHAS, J., Medicine
PODOLACK, M., Planetary Science
PORTUGALI, J., Geography
PRAS, M., Medicine
RABINOVICH, I., History of the Middle East
RAINEY, A., Cultures of the Ancient East
RAVID, M., Medicine
RAZ, Y., East Asian Studies
RAZI, Z., History
RAZIN, A., Economics
REINHART, T., Theory of Literature and Linguistics
REPHAELI, Y., Physics
RO'I, Y., History
RON, E., Microbiology
RONEN, A., History of Art
RONEN, S., Management
ROSENAU, PH., Applied Mathematics
ROSENBERG, E., Microbiology
ROSENTHAL, T., Medicine
ROSS, I. J., Philosophy
ROSSET, SH., Mathematics
ROZEN, M., History of the Jewish People
ROZEN, P., Medicine
ROZEN, S., Chemistry
ROZIK, E., Theatre Arts
RUBIN, U., Arabic Language and Literature
RUBIN, Z., History
RUBINSTEIN, A., Economics
RUBINSTEIN, E., Medicine
RUSCHIN, SH., Electrical Engineering
SACK, J., Paediatrics
SADAN, J., Islamic Culture, Arabic Literature
SADKA, E., Economics
SAFRA, Z., Management
SAHAR, A., Neurosurgery
SAMET, D., Management
SAMIR, U., Planetary Sciences
SARNE, Y., Physiology
SAVION, N., Clinical Biochemistry
SCHEJTER, A. B., Biochemistry
SCHMEIDLER, D., Statistics and Economics
SCHUSS, Z., Applied Mathematics
SCHWARTZ, M., Physics
SEGAL, E., Human Microbiology
SEGEV, E., Management
SEIDMAN, A., Engineering
SELIGSON, U., Medicine
SEMYONOV, M., Sociology
SERVADIO, C., Surgery
SHAI, A., History
SHAKED, H., History of the Middle East
SHAKED, U., Electrical and Electronic Engineering
SHALGI, R., Embryology
SHAMIR, S., History of the Middle East
SHANI, M., Health Systems Management
SHAPIRA, A., Law
SHAPIRA, A., History of the Jewish People
SHAPIRA, R., Sociology of Education
SHAPIRA, Y., Electrical and Electronic Engineering
SHAPIRO, Y., Physiology
SHARAN, S., Educational Psychology
SHARIR, M., Computer Sciences
SHAVA, M., Law
SHAVIT, U., Hebrew Literature
SHAVITT, Y., History of the Jewish People
SHELEFF, L., Law, Sociology and Anthropology
SHEMER, L., Mechanical Engineering
SHENKAR, O., Management
SHENKMAN, L., Medicine
SHILOH, Y., Human Genetics
SHIROM, A., Labour Studies
SHOENFELD, Y., Medicine
SHOHAM, S., Law
SHOKEID, M., Sociology and Anthropology
SHUSTIN, E., Mathematics
SHVO, Y., Chemistry
SINGER, I., Ancient Near Eastern Culture
SINGER, S., Electrical Engineering
SIVASHINSKY, G., Applied Mathematics
SKUTELSKY, E., Pathology
SMORODINSKY, M., Statistics
SNEH, B., Botany
SOKOLOV, M., Mechanical Engineering
SOKOLOVSKY, M., Biochemistry
SOLOMON, Z., Social Work
SOMEKH, S., Arabic Literature
SPERLING, O., Chemical Pathology
SPIRER, Z., Paediatrics
STERNBERG, M., Theory of Literature
STRAUSS, S., Educational Psychology
TADMOR, E., Applied Mathematics
TAITEL, Y., Mechanical Engineering
TAL, A., Hebrew Language
TAL, H., Periodontology
TAMARKIN, M., History of Africa
TAMIR, A., Statistics
TAUMAN, Y., Management
TEBOULE, M., Operation Research and Statistics
TERKEL, J., Zoology
TODER, V., Embryology
TOURY, G., Theory of Literature and Comparative Literature
TREISTER, G., Ophthalmology
TROPE, Y., Psychology
TSINOBER, A., Engineering
TSIRELSON, B., Statistics
TSUR, R., Hebrew Literature
TUR, M., Electrical and Electronic Engineering
TURKEL, E., Mathematics
TYANO, S., Psychiatry
UNGURU, S., History of Science and Ideas
USSISHKIN, D., Archaeology
VIDNE, B., Surgery
VISHKIN, V., Computer Sciences
VOLKOV, S., History
VORONEL, A., Physics
WAISEL, Y., Botany
WASSERSTEIN, D., History of Islam
WEINSTEIN, E., Electrical and Electronic Engineering
WEISMAN, Y., Paediatrics
WEISS, Y., Economics
WEIZMAN, A., Psychiatry
WEIZMAN, R., Psychiatry
WEXLER, P., Linguistics
WIENTROUB, S. H., Orthopaedic Surgery
WINTER, M., History of the Middle East, History of Islam
WITZ, I., Immunology
WOLLBERG, Z., Zoology
WOOL, D., Zoology
WYGNANSKI, I., Engineering
YAAR, E., Sociology
YAGIL, E., Biochemistry
YAKAR, J., Archaeology
YANIV, A., Human Microbiology
YANKIELOWICZ, S., Physics
YARON, M., Medicine
YARON, Z., Zoology
YASSIF, E., Hebrew Literature
YASSUR, Y., Ophthalmology
YECHIALI, U., Statistics
YINON, U., Physiology
YOM-TOV, Y., Zoology
ZADOK, R., History of the Jewish People and Cultures of the Ancient East
ZAGAGI, N., Classical Studies
ZAIZOV, R., Paediatrics
ZAKUTH, H., Gynaecology and Obstetrics
ZANG, I., Management
ZILCHA, I., Economics
ZISAPEL, N., Biochemistry
ZIV, A., Educational Psychology
ZWAS, G., Science Instruction

ATTACHED RESEARCH INSTITUTES

Chaim Weizmann Zionist Research Institute
Diaspora Research Institute
Benzion Katz Institute for Research in Hebrew Literature
Sonia and Marco Nadler Institute of Archaeology
Dayan Center for Middle Eastern and African Studies
Cummings Center for Soviet and East European Studies
Institute for German Studies
Porter Institute for Poetics and Semiotics
Jaffee Center for Strategic Studies
Foerder Institute for Economic Research
Institute for Social Research
David Horowitz Research Institute for Developing Countries
Golda Meir Institute for Labor and Social Research
Israel Institute of Business Research
Operations Research Center
Florence and George S. Wise Observatory
Cohn Institute for the History and Philosophy of Sciences and Ideas
Institute for Nature Preservation Research
Institute for Cereal Crops Improvement
Rogoff-Wellcome Medical Research Institute: see under Research Institutes
B. Gattegno Research Institute of Human Reproduction and Fetal Development
Center for Nuclear Research, Nahal Soreq
Center for Research in the Biology of Cancer
Institute for Petroleum Research and Geophysics: see Research Institutes
Interdisciplinary Center for Technological Analysis and Forecasting
Pinchas Sapir International Center for Development
Eva and Marc Besen Institute for the Study of Contemporary Historical Consciousness
Marcel and Annie Adams Institute for Business Management Information Systems
Joseph Kasirer Institute for Research in Accounting
Institute of Occupational Health
Djerassi-Elias Institute of Oncology
Neufeld Cardiac Research Institute
Institute for Petroleum and Energy
Raymond and Beverly Sackler Institute of Theoretical Physics
Vladimir Schreiber Institute of Mathematical Sciences
Max and Betty Kranzberg Institute for Electronic Devices Research
Prof. Dr Raphael Taubenschlag Institute of Criminal Law
Institute for Continuing Legal Studies
Cegla Institute of Comparative and Private International Law
Mortimer and Raymond Sackler Institute of Advanced Studies
Gordon Center for Energy Studies
Kovens Health Systems Management Center
Ruth and Albert Abramson Center for Medical Physics
Institute for Research of the Jewish Press
Sackler Institute for Economic Studies
Dead Sea Research Center
Interdisciplinary Institute of Biotechnology
Tami Steinmetz Center for Peace Research
Raymond and Beverly Sackler Institute for Physical Chemistry
Ela Kodesz Institute for Research on Cancer Development and Prevention
Herczeg Institute on Aging
David and Anne Warsaw Center for Entrepreneurial Studies
Morris E. Curiel Center for International Studies
Adams Super-Center for Brain Studies
Ela Kodesz Institute for Cardiac Physical Sciences and Engineering
Stanly Steyer Institute for Cancer Epidemiology and Research
Porter Super-Center for Environmental and Ecological Studies
Raymond and Beverly Sackler Institute of Astronomy
Center for Material Sciences
Sackler Institute of Molecular Medicine
Zwitzerland Institute of Developmental Biology
Shalom and Varda Yoran Institute for Human Genome Research

Elizabeth and Nicholas Slezak Center for Cardiac Research and Medical Engineering
Science and Technology Education Center
Maurice and Gabriela Goldschleger Eye Research Institute
Sackler Institute of Molecular Medicine
Minerva Research Center on Cholesterol Gallstones and Lipid Metabolism in the Liver
Julius F. Cohnheim Center of Cellular and Molecular Phagocyte Research
Felsenstein Medical Research Center
Institute for Environmental Research (Ministry of the Environment and Sackler School of Medicine)
Minerva Center for Human Rights
Erhard Center for Higher Studies and Research in Insurance
Max Perlman Center for Global Business
B. I. Cohen Institute for Public Opinion Research
Deutsch Institute of Computer Sciences
Reymond and Beverly Sackler Institute of Scientific Computation
Heinrich Herts Minerva Center for High Temperature Superconductivity
Hermann Minkowski Center for Geometry

TECHNION—ISRAEL INSTITUTE OF TECHNOLOGY

32 000 Haifa
Telephone: (4) 8292111
Telex: 46406
Fax: (4) 8221581

Founded 1912; inaugurated 1924
Language of instruction: Hebrew
Academic year: October to July

Chairman of Board of Governors: H. TAUB
President: Prof. ZEHEV TADMOR
Senior Vice-President: Prof. URI KIRSCH
Vice-President for Academic Affairs: Prof. NADAV LIRON
Vice-President for Research: Prof. ARNON BENTUR
Vice-President for Finance and Administration: Prof. MICHAEL RUBINOVITCH
Dean of Undergraduate Studies: Prof. RAPHAEL SIVAN
Dean of Graduate School: Prof. DANIEL WEIHS
Dean of Students: Prof. MENAHEM KAFTORY

Library: see Libraries
Number of teachers: 1,100
Number of students: 8,369 undergraduates, 3,428 graduates

Publications: *The Joseph Wunsch Lectures* (annually), *Shlomo Kaplansky Memorial Series* (incorporated in *Israel Journal of Technology), Synopses of DSc and MSc Theses* (annually), *Catalogue* (annually), *Research Report* (annually), *Technion* (2 a year), *Bulletin* (weekly).

DEANS

Faculty of Aerospace Engineering: Prof. A. ROSEN
Faculty of Agricultural Engineering: Prof. I. RAVINA
Faculty of Architecture and Town Planning: Prof. R. OXMAN
Faculty of Biology: Prof. D. GERSHON
Faculty of Chemical Engineering: Prof. M. SHEINTUCH
Faculty of Chemistry: Prof. Y. APELOIG
Faculty of Civil Engineering: Prof. M. STIASSNIE
Faculty of Computer Science: Prof. A. PAZ
Faculty of Electrical Engineering: Prof. Y. ZEEVI
Faculty of Food Engineering and Biotechnology: Prof. S. MIZRAHI
Faculty of Industrial Engineering and Management: Prof. M. EREZ
Faculty of Materials Engineering: Prof. M. EIZENBERG
Faculty of Mathematics: Prof. R. AHARONI
Faculty of Mechanical Engineering: Prof. G. GROSSMAN
Faculty of Medicine: Prof. P. LAVIE
Faculty of Physics: Prof. M. MOSHE
Department of Biomedical Engineering: Prof. U. DINNAR (Head)
Department of Education in Technology and Science: Prof. R. LAZAROWITZ (Head)
Department of General Studies: Prof. S. SHAPIRA (Head)

PROFESSORS

Faculty of Aerospace Engineering:

BAR-ITZHACK, I., Navigation, Guidance and Control
DURBAN, D., Aircraft Structures
GAL-OR, B., Jet Engines Fluid Dynamics
GANY, A., Rocket Propulsion
GREENBERG, B., Combustion Theory
GUELMAN, M., Space Engineering
NISSIM, E., Aeroelasticity, Aerodynamics
ROSEN, A., Rotary Wings, Aircraft Structures
SEGINER, A., Fluid Dynamics
SHINAR, J., Analytical Flight Mechanics
STAVSKY, Y., Mechanics of Structures
TAMBOUR, Y., Combustion of Fuel Sprays
WEIHS, D., Fluid Mechanics, Bio-Mechanics and Stability Theory
WELLER, T., Aircraft Structures
WOLFSHTEIN, M., Fluid Mechanics

Faculty of Agricultural Engineering:

AVNIMELECH, Y., Soil Chemistry
GALILI, N., Applied Mechanics
PELEG, K., Post Harvesting
RAVINA, I., Irrigation
SEGINER, I., Agricultural Micrometeorology
WOLF, D., Field Machinery
ZASLAVSKY, D., Soil Physics

Faculty of Architecture and Town Planning:

ALTERMAN, R., Land Development
AMIR, S., Regional Planning
BURT, M., Structural Morphology
OXMAN, M. R., Theory and Methodology of Architecture
SHAVIV, E., Energy and Architecture
SHEFER, D., Urban and Regional Economics
WACHMAN, A., Architecture and Planning

Faculty of Biology:

GERSHON, D., Gerontology
LIFSCHYTZ, E., Genetics and Cytogenetics
MANOR, H., Molecular Biology
WARBURG, H., Physiological Ecology of Animals

Department of Biomedical Engineering:

DINNAR, U., Cardiovascular Fluid Dynamics, Minimal Invasive Diagnosis
GATH, I., Signal Processing and Pattern Recognition Biological Symbols
LANIR, Y., Tissues Mechanics and Structure, Cardiac Mechanics, Coronary Circulation
LOTAN, N., Biomaterials and their Medical Applications
MAROUDAS, A., Structure and Functions of Articular Cartilage
MIZRAHI, J., Orthopaedic and Rehabilitation Biomechanics

Faculty of Chemical Engineering:

LAVIE, R., Process Control and Resource Management
MARMUR, A., Surfaces and Colloids
NARKIS, M., Polymers and Plastic Materials
NIR, A., Fluid Mechanics
PISMAN, L., Chemical Engineering
SHEINTUCH, M., Chemical and Biochemical Reaction Engineering, Reactor Stability
TADMOR, Z., Polymer Engineering
TALMON, Y., Electron Microscopy, Interfacial Phenomena, Colloidal Systems

Faculty of Chemistry:

APELOIG, Y., Organosilicon and Computational Chemistry
KAFTORY, M., Chemical Crystallography
KATRIEL, J., Theoretical Chemistry
KEINAN, E., Biocatalysis, Organic Synthesis
MANDELBAUM, A., Organic Chemistry
MOISEYEV, N., Quantum Chemistry
NIKITIN, E. E., Theory of Molecular Dynamics
OREF, Y., Molecular Dynamics, Energy Transfer
RON, A., Spectroscopy of Semiconductor Structures
SPEISER, S., Laser Photophysics
YARNITZKY, C., Electrochemistry

Faculty of Civil Engineering:

ARGAMAN, Y., Water and Waste Treatment
BENTUR, A., Cementitious and Composite Building Materials
BRAESTER, C., Groundwater Hydrology
FRYDMAN, S., Geotechnical Engineering
GLUCK, J., Structural and Earthquake Engineering
KIRSCH, U., Structural Engineering
LAUFER, A., Construction Management
LIVNEH, M., Transport and Engineering
MURAVSKI, G., Soil Structure Interaction
NARKIS, N., Water Treatment Chemistry
POREH, M., Environmental Fluid Mechanics and Wind Engineering
RUBIN, H., Contaminant Hydrology
RUTENBERG, A., Structural Dynamics and Stability
SHAMIR, U., Water Resources Systems
SHEINMAN, I., Post-buckling, Dynamics, Static Damage
SHELEF, G., Waste Water Treatment and Reclamation
STAIASSNIE, M., Water Waves
UZAN, J., Pavement Engineering
WARSZAWSKI, A., Construction Management
ZIMMELS, Y., Environmental and Process Engineering

Faculty of Computer Science:

BERRY, D. M., Software Engineering
BRUCKSTEIN, A., Image Processing
EVEN, S., Algorithms and Cryptography
FRANCEZ, N., Semantics and Verification, Computational Linguistics
HEYMANN, M., Control Theory
ISRAELI, M., Scientific Computing, Numerical Methods
ITAI, A., Analysis of Algorithms and Data Structures
KOHAVI, Z., Computational Model Switching and Automata Theory
LEMPEL, A., Information Theory
MORAN, S., Distributed Algorithms
PAZ, A., Theory of Algorithms
RODEH, M., Theory of Compilation, Computer Systems
SEGALL, A., Computer Communication Networks
SIDI, A., Theoretical Numerical Analysis and Scientific Computing
UNGARISH, M., Modelling and Numerical Simulation of Fluid Flows

Faculty of Electrical Engineering:

ALEXANDROVITZ, A., Electro-mechanical Energy Converters
CIDON, I., Communication Networks
DEMBO, A., Large Deviations Theory
EISENSTEIN, G., Optoelectronics
FISCHER, B., Opto-Electronics
INBAR, G., Biosignal Analysis
KATZENELSON, J., Circuits and Systems
LEVIATAN, V., Electromagnetic Waves
MALAH, D., Digital Signal Processing of Speech and Images
PORAT, B., Random Signal Processing
RAZ, S., Sonar and Communication System
SCHIEBER, D., Energy Conversion
SHAMAI, S.,Information Theory
SHAMIR, J., Electro-optics

SIDI, M., Computer Networks
SIVAN, R., Automatic Control
ZEEVI, Y., Vision and Image Sciences
ZEHEV, E., Filters
ZEITOUNI, Z., Large Deviations Theory
ZIV, J., Statistical Communication, Information Theory

Faculty of Food Engineering and Biotechnology:

BERK, Z., Food Process Development
COGAN, U., Food Chemistry
KOPELMAN, I., Food Technology
MILTZ, J., Packaging Engineering
MIZRAHI, S., Food Engineering
MOKADY, S., Nutrition Proteins
ULITZUR, S., Food Microbiology

Faculty of Industrial Engineering and Management:

ADIRI, I., Stochastic Processes
ADLER, R., Stochastic Processes
AVRIEL, M., Mathematical Programming, Energy Policy
BEN-TAL, A., Non-linear Optimization
DAR-EL, E., Production Planning, Human Factors and Safety Research
EREZ, M., Organizational Psychology
FEIGIN, P., Probability Theory
GOPHER, D., Human Factors
KASPI, H., Probability and Stochastic Processes
MANDELBAUM, A., Operations Research, Stochastic Processes and their Applications
MAYTAL, S., Economic Psychology
MESHOULAM, I., Management and Human Resources Management
NEMIROVSKY, A., Optimization Complexity Theory
NOTEA, A., Non-Destructive Testing
PASSY, U., Mathematical Programming
ROSENBLAT, M., Production Planning and Control Facility Layout and Design
ROTHBLUM, U. G., Operations Research
RUBINOVITCH, M., Operations Research
RUBINSTEIN, R., Stochastic Systems
WEISSMAN, I., Probability and Statistics

Department of Materials Engineering:

BRANDON, D., Metallurgy
EIZENBERG, M., Electronic Materials
GUTMANAS, E., Processing of High-Performance Materials
KOMEM, Y., Electronic Materials
SHECHTMAN, D., Properties and Microstructure of Intermetallic Compounds
SIEGMANN, A., Polymers and Plastic Structuring
YAHALOM, J., Corrosion, Electrodeposition

Faculty of Mathematics:

AHARONI, R., Combinatories
AHARONOV, D., Theory of Functions
BENYAMINI, Y., Banach Spaces
BROOKS, R., Differential Geometry
BERMAN, A., Matrix Theory
BRUDNYI, Y., Approximation and Interpolation
CHILLAG, D., Algebra Group Theory
CWIKEL, M., Interpolation of Linear Operators
DYNKIN, E., Function Theory
GOLDBERG, M., Numerical Analysis
GORDON, Y., Functional Analysis
HERSHKOWITZ, D., Matrix Theory
IOFFE, A., General Theory of Subdifferentials
KATCHALSKI, M., Combinatorial Geometry
LERER, L., Linear Algebra
LIN, V., Functional Analysis
LIRON, N., Applied Mathematics
LOEWY, R., Linear Algebra
LONDON, D., Matrix Theory
LYUBICH, Y., Analysis
MARCUS, M., Functional Analysis
NEPOMNYASHCHY, A., Fluid Mechanics
PANEAH, B., Partial Differential Equations
PINKUS, A., Approximation Theory
REICH, S., Non-linear Analysis
RUBINSTEIN, J., Applied Mathematics
SAPHAR, P., Functional Analysis
SOLEL, B., Operator Theory, Functional Analysis
SONN, J., Algebraic Number Theory
SREBRO, U., Complex Analysis Quasi-Regular Functions
VOLPERT, A., Partial Differential Equations
ZAKS, A., Semi-Primary Rings
ZIEGLER, Z., Theory of Approximation

Faculty of Mechanical Engineering:

ADLER, D., Aero-Thermodynamics of Turbomachinery
BAR-YOSEPH, P., Finite Element Analysis
BEN-HAIM, Y., Decisions under Uncertainty, Reliability
BRAUN, S., Vibration Signal Processing
DEGANI, D., Computational Fluid Dynamics
ELIAS, E., Thermohydraulics, Nuclear Engineering
ETSION, I., Tribology, Lubrication
GROSSMAN, G., Thermodynamics, Heat Pumps
GUTFINGER, E. H., Fluid Mechanics
GUTMAN, S., Relative Stability of Linear Dynamic Systems
HETSRONI, G., Two Phase Flow, Transport Dynamics
PALMOR, Z., Digital Control of Industrial and Mechanical Systems
PNUELI, D., Fluid Mechanics, Heat Transfer, Aerosols, Thermodynamics, Mechanics
ROTEM, A., Composite Materials
RUBIN, M., Continuum Mechanics
SHITZER, A., Bio-Heat Transfer
SHPITALNI, M., CAD/CAM, Manufacturing
SOLAN, A., Fluid Mechanics, Heat Transfer
TIROSH, J., Fracture Mechanics
WOLBERG, J., Computer Applications in Engineering
YARIN, A., Rheology, Fluid Mechanics
YARIN, L. P., Two-Phase Flow, Combustion
ZVIRIN, Y., Solar Energy

Faculty of Medicine:

BEYAR, R., Invasive Cardiology
BROOK, G., Internal Medicine
CIECHANOVER, A., Intercellular Breakdown of Proteins
FINBERG, J., Neuropharmacology
FRONT, D., Neurology and Nuclear Medicine
FRY, M., Enzymology of DNA Replication
HERSHKO, A., Biochemical Mechanisms of Intracellular Protein Degradation
KRAUSZ, M., General Surgery
LAVIE, P., Psychobiology, Sleep Research
LEWIS, B., Cardiology
PALTI, Y., Physiology
PERLMAN, I., Vision Physiology
PRATT, H., Electro-Physiology of the Auditory System
ROWE, J., Haematology, Bone Transplantation
SILBERMAN, M., Teratology, Ageing
SKORECKI, K., Nephrology, Molecular Medicine
URETZKY, G., Cardiovascular Surgery
YOUDIM, M., Psychopharmacology and Neochemistry

Faculty of Physics:

AVRON, J., Mathematical Physics
BEN-GUIGUI, L., Liquid Crystals
BESERMAN, R., New Materials for Solid-State Opto-Electronics Devices
COHEN, E., Spectroscopic Properties of Laser Materials
DAR, A., Astroparticle Physics
ECKSTEIN, Y., Low Temperature Physics
EHRENFREUND, E., Low dimensional Metallic and Magnetic Solids
EILAM, G., Elementary Particle Physics
FELSTEINER, J., Condensed Matter Physics, Plasma Physics
FISHER, B., High-Temperature Oxide Superconductors
FISHMAN, S., Quantum Chaos
GRONAU, M., Theoretical High Energy Physics
KALISH, R., Ion-Implantation—Hyperfine Interactions
KOREN, G., Superconductivity and Lasers
LIPSON, S., Low Temperature Physics
MANN, A., Theoretical Physics
MARINOV, M., Theoretical and Mathematical Physics
MOSHE, M., Theoretical High Energy Physics
PERES, A., Theoretical Physics
PITAEVSKI, L., Condensed Matter
REGEV, O., Astrophysics
REVZEN, M., Solid State Physics
RIESS, I., Solid State Electrochemistry
ROSNER, B., Nuclear Physics
SHAPIRO, B., Theory of Condensed Matter
SHAVIV, G., Astrophysics
SHECHTER, H., Surface Physics
SINGER, P., Elementary Particles Physics

Department of Education in Technology and Science:

LAZAROWITZ, R., Biology Education
LERON, U., Mathematics Education
MOVSHOVITZ-HADAR, N., Mathematics Education

AFFILIATED INSTITUTES

Technion Research and Development Foundation Ltd: see under Research Institutes.

Aeronautical Research Center.
Agricultural Engineering Research Center in Water and Soil.
Agricultural Machinery Research Center.
Architectural Heritage Research Center.
Center for Architectural Research and Development.
Norman and Helen Asher Space Research Center.
Center for Biological Research.
Center for Chemical Research.
Center for Research in Energy and Environmental Conservation Engineering.
Center for Research in Environmental and Water Resources Engineering.
Chemical Engineering Research Center.
Electrical Engineering Research Center.
Food Industries Research and Development Center.
Philip M. and Ethel Kluznik Center for Urban and Regional Studies.
Izhak Kidron Microelectronics Research Center.
Materials Engineering Research Center.
National Building Research Institute.
Quality and Reliability Research Center.
Research Center for Intelligent Systems.
Research Center for Mapping and Geodesy.
Research and Development Center for Education in Technology and Science and for Vocational Training.
Research Center for Very Large Scale Integrated Systems (VLSI).
Research Center for Work Safety and Human Engineering
J. Silver Institute of Bio-Medical Engineering.
Solid State Institute.
Transportation Research Institute.
J. W. Ullman Center for Manufacturing Systems and Robotics.
Water Research Institute.

Coastal and Marine Engineering Research Institute.

Israel Institute of Metals: see under Research Institutes.

Samuel Neaman Institute for Advanced Studies in Science and Technology: see under Research Institutes.

Rappaport Family Institute for Research in Medical Science.

WEIZMANN INSTITUTE OF SCIENCE

POB 26, 76 100 Rehovot

Telephone: (8) 9343111
Fax: (8) 9466966

Founded 1949; includes the Daniel Sieff Research Institute (f. 1934).

The Institute is a private non-profit corporation for fundamental and applied research in the natural and exact sciences. The Feinberg Graduate School offers MSc and PhD courses

Chairman, Board of Governors: G. KEKST
President: Prof. HAIM HARARI
Chairman, Scientific Council: Prof. A. FRIESEM
Vice-President: Prof. YORAM GRONER
Vice-President, Finance and Administration: YAAKOV NAAN
Vice-President for International Affairs and Public Relations: Dr HANAN ALON
Vice-President for Technology Transfer: Prof. DAVID MIRELMAN
Chief Librarian: Mrs I. POLLACK

Library: see Libraries
Number of teachers: 300
Number of graduate students: 700

Publications: *President's Annual Report, Annual Report of Scientific Activities*, *Rehovot Magazine Interface Research*, *List of Current Research Activities.*

DEANS

Faculty of Mathematical Sciences: Prof. D. HAREL
Faculty of Physics: Prof. DAVID MUKAMEL
Faculty of Chemistry: Prof. ITAMER PROCACCIA
Faculty of Biochemistry: Prof. MEIR WILCHEK
Faculty of Biology: Prof. YOSEF YARDEN
Feinberg Graduate School: Prof. SAMUEL SAFRAM

HEADS OF DEPARTMENTS

Faculty of Mathematical Sciences:

Applied Mathematics and Computer Science: Prof. S. ULLMAN
Theoretical Mathematics: Prof. G. SCHECHTMAN

Faculty of Physics:

Condensed Matter Physics: Prof. S. LEVIT
Particle Physics: Prof. Y. FRISHMAN
Physics of Complex Systems: Prof. E. DOMANY
Physics Services: Prof. I. BAR-JOSEPH

Faculty of Chemistry:

Chemical Physics: Prof. R. NAAMAN
Environmental Sciences and Energy Research: Prof. A. SHEMESH
Materials and Interfaces: Prof. M. LAHAV
Organic Chemistry: Prof. D. MILSTEIN
Structural Biology: Prof. L. ADDADI
Solar Energy Facilities Unit: M. EPSTEIN
Chemical Services: Prof. M. SHEVES

Faculty of Biochemistry:

Biological Chemistry: Prof. H. GARTY
Molecular Genetics: Prof. B. Z. SHILO
Plant Sciences: Prof. R. FLUHR
Biological Services: Prof. M. RUBINSTEIN

Faculty of Biology:

Molecular Cell Biology: Prof. B. GEIGER
Immunology: Prof. Z. ESHHAR
Biological Regulation: Prof. S. SHALTIEL
Neurobiology: Prof. E. YAVIN

Feinberg Graduate School:

Science Teaching: Prof. U. GANIEL

DIRECTORS OF CENTERS

Faculty of Biology:

Belle S. and Irving E. Meller Center for Biology of Ageing: Prof. B. GEIGER
Nella and Leon Benoziyo Center for Neurosciences: Prof. I. SILMAN
Leo and Julia Forchheimer Center for Molecular Genetics: Prof. M. OREN
Murray H. and Meyer Grodetsky Center for Research of Higher Brain Functions: Prof. A. GRINVALD
Robert Koch Minerva Center for Research in Autoimmune Diseases: Prof. I. COHEN
Carl and Micaela Einhorn-Dominic Institute for Brain Research: Prof. A. GRINVALD

Faculty of Biochemistry:

Dr Joseph Cohn Minerva Center for Biomembrane Research: Prof. M. EISENBACH
Mel Dobrin Center for Nutrition: Prof. R. FLUHR
Charles W. and Tillie K. Lubin Center for Plant Biotechnology: Prof. R. FLUHR
Avron-Wilstätter Minerva Center for Research in Photosynthesis: Prof. A. SCHERZ
Harry and Jeanette Weinberg Center for Plant Molecular Genetics Research: Prof. R. FLUHR

Faculty of Chemistry:

Energy Research Center: Prof. A. YOGEV
Gerhard M. J. Schmidt Minerva Center for Supermolecular Architecture: Prof. M. LAHAV
Fritz Haber Center for Physical Chemistry: Prof. R. NAAMAN
Helen and Milton A. Kimmelman Center for Biomolecular Structure and Assembly: Prof. A. E. YONATH
Joseph and Ceil Mazer Center for Structural Biology: Prof. A. E. YONATH
Sussman Family Center for the Study of Environment Sciences: Prof. S. WEINER
Helen and Martin Kimmel Center for Archaeological Sciences: Prof. S. WEINER

Faculty of Physics:

Joseph H. and Belle R. Braun Center for Submicron Research: Prof. M. HEIBLUM
Albert Einstein Minerva Center for Theoretical Physics: Prof. V. IMRY
Nella and Leo Benoziyo Center for High Energy Physics: Prof. G. MIKENBERG
Minerva Center for Non-linear Physics of Complex Systems: Prof. U. SMILANSKY

Faculty of Mathematics:

Arthur and Rochelle Belfer Institute of Mathematics and Computer Science: Prof. D. HAREL
Carl F. Gauss Minerva Center for Scientific Computation: Prof. A. BRANDT

Feinberg Graduate School:

Aharon Kafzir-Katchalsky Center: Prof. S. SAFRAN

Colleges and Higher Institutes

Bezalel Academy of Arts and Design: Mount Scopus, POB 24046, Jerusalem 91240; tel. (2) 5893333; fax (2) 5823094; f. 1906; degree courses in fine arts, graphic design, gold- and silver-smithing, architecture, industrial design, ceramics design, photography; interdepartmental units of video and film animation; library of 35,000 vols; 220 lecturers, 1,100 students; Dir Dr RAN SAPOZNIK.

British School of Archaeology in Jerusalem: POB 19283, Jerusalem; tel. (2) 5828101; fax (2) 5323844; e-mail bsaj@vms.huji.ac.il; f. 1920; conducts archaeological excavation, survey and research; library of 10,000 vols; Pres. Dr P. R. S. MOOREY; Chair. P. G. DE COURCY IRELAND; Dir (in Jerusalem) R. P. HARPER; publ. *Levant* (annually).

Conservatory of Music: 2 Hatomor St, 58 352 Holon; tel. 842847; f. 1942; general musical and instrumental training provided; public concerts organized for charity; mem. of ISME (Int. Soc. for Music Educ.) and approved by the Ministry of Education and Culture; 25 teachers, 300 students; library of nearly 1,400 vols; Dir Mrs NADIVA SHOR.

Ecole Biblique et Ecole Archéologique Française: POB 19053, 91 190 Jerusalem; tel. (2) 6264468; fax (2) 6282567; e-mail ebaf@netvision.net.il; f. 1890; research, Biblical and Oriental studies, exploration and excavation in Palestine; 17 professors; Dir CLAUDE GEFFRÉ; library, see Libraries; publs *Revue Biblique* (quarterly), *Etudes Bibliques, Cahiers de la Revue Biblique, Etudes Annexes, Littératures anciennes du Proche Orient.*

Etz Hayim, General Talmud, Torah and Grand Teshivah: POB 300, Jerusalem; f. 1841; 1,400 students; library of 10,000 vols; Pres. Rabbi I. Z. MELTZER.

Hebrew Union College—Jewish Institute of Religion, Jerusalem School: 13 King David St, 94 101 Jerusalem; tel. (2) 6203333; f. 1963; branch of the same institution in the United States of America; the first year of graduate rabbinic studies, Jewish education, cantorial training and programme in biblical archaeology, including summer excavations; Rabbinic programme for Israel Reform (Progressive); Hebrew and English 'Lehrhaus' study programmes in classical Jewish Literature for general public (Bet Midrash); Abramov Library of 40,000 vols; microfilm collection from American Jewish Archives; Skirball Museum of Biblical Archaeology; Pres. SHELDON ZIMMERMAN; Dean MICHAEL MARMUR.

International Institute for Development, Co-operative and Labour Studies (Afro-Asian Institute of the Histadrut): Neharde'a St 7, POB 16201, 64 235 Tel-Aviv; tel. (3) 5229195; telex 361480; fax (3) 5229195; f. 1958 to train labour and co-operative movement leadership in Asia, Africa, Caribbean and Pacific; candidates nominated by trade unions, co-operatives, universities, international labour organizations, etc.; courses and seminars in fields of labour, development and co-operative studies in English and French; courses also in other countries; library of 15,000 vols, and monographs and periodicals; 21,000 graduates from 115 countries; Dir and Prin. Dr YEHUDAH PAZ.

Jerusalem College of Technology: 21 Havaad Haleumi St, POB 16031, 91 160 Jerusalem; tel. (2) 6751111; fax (2) 6422075; e-mail pr@brachot.jct.ac.il; f. 1969; 4-year first degree courses; library of 20,000 vols; 60 full-time teachers, 700 full-time students; Pres. Prof. JOSEPH BODENHEIMER; Rector Prof. YAAKOV ZEISEL; Librarian ZVI SOBEL.

CHAIRMEN OF DEPARTMENTS

Applied Physics/Electro-Optics: Prof. MEIR NITZAN
Computer Science: Prof. RAPHAEL YEHAZKEL
Electronics: Dr ARYEH WEISS
Managerial Accounting: Prof. ALAN STOLMAN
Technology Management and Marketing: Dr GERSHON MILES
Science Teaching: Dr REUVEN FREEMAN
Basic Studies: Prof. Y. FRIEDMAN
Applied Mathematics: Prof. Y. FRIEDMAN

Jerusalem Rubin Academy of Music and Dance: Givat Ram Campus, Jerusalem 91904; tel. (2) 6759911; fax (2) 6527713; f. 1947; performing arts, composition, conducting and theory, music education, dance; awards B. Mus., B.Ed.Mus., B. Dance and Artists' Diplomas; courses leading to B.A.Mus., M.A.Mus. and M.Mus. in co-operation with the Hebrew University; Conservatory and High School (Music and Dance); 190 teachers, 1,500 students; library of 55,000 vols; collection of musical instruments; electroacoustic laboratory; Head AVNER BIRON; publs *Music In Time, Calendar of Events* (monthly), *Bulletin of Information, Notes.*

Jerusalem University College: POB 1276, Mount Zion, Jerusalem 91012; tel. (2) 6718628; fax (2) 6732717; f. 1957; Christian study centre at university level; graduate and undergraduate courses in the history, languages, religions and cultures of Israel in the Middle East context; field trips and archaeological excavation programme; Pres. Dr SIDNEY DEWAAL; publ. *From Mount Zion* (newsletter, 2 a year).

Mosad Harav Kook: POB 642, Jerusalem; tel. (2) 526231; fax (2) 526968; f. 1937 to educate and train young men for research in the field of Torah Literature and to infuse the original Hebrew culture in all classes of the people; Dir YITZCHAK RAPHAEL; publs Torah-Science books, including the printing of MSS of previously unpublished *Rishonim* works that are still retained in Genizah form.

Pontifical Biblical Institute: POB 497, 3 Paul-Emile Botta St, Jerusalem; tel. (2) 6252843; fax (2) 6241203; e-mail pbijer@netvision.net.il; f. 1913 as a branch of the Pontifical Biblical Institute of Rome; fosters the study of Biblical geography and archaeology; provides courses for students and graduates of Roman Institute; library of 20,000 vols for biblical studies; Prehistorical Museum containing discoveries of Teleilat Ghassul, a chalcolithic site in the Jordan valley, excavated by the Institute; Dir Rev. JOHN R. CROCKER.

Ruppin Institute: PO Ruppin Institute, Emek Hefer 40250; tel. (9) 8983030; fax (9) 8983090; f. 1949; three-year degree courses in economics, accounting, business administration and the behavioural sciences; two-year courses in basic trades, electrical engineering, industrial management, soil and water engineering; short courses in basic economics, accounting, agriculture and mechanics; Coventry University Programme of Engineering Studies in Israel; School of Hotels and Tourism; library of 40,000 vols; Dir ELIEZER LEVIN.

Shenkar College: 12 Anna Frank St, Ramat-Gan 52526; tel. (72-3) 7521133; fax (72-3) 7521141; e-mail info@mail:shenkar.ac.il; f. 1970; bachelors' degrees and research in industrial management and marketing, computer science, plastics engineering, industrial chemistry, textile engineering, fashion design, textile and interior design, jewellery design; MSc programme in global textile marketing; library of 20,000 vols, 250 periodicals; 50 teachers; 680 full-time, 1,500 part-time students; Pres. Prof. AMOTZ WEINBERG; Man. Dir BARUCH SAGIV.

Studium Biblicum Franciscanum: POB 19424, Monastery of the Flagellation, 91 193 Jerusalem; tel. (2) 6282936; fax (2) 6264519; e-mail sbfnet@netvision.net.il; f. 1927; centre of archaeological research sponsored by the Franciscan Custody of the Holy Land, biblical faculty of the *Pontificium Athenaeum Antonianum,* Rome, for degrees of Bachelor, Licentiate and Doctorate in Biblical Theology, and diploma in biblico-oriental sciences; 30 mems; Dir F. MANNS; publs *Liber Annuus, Collectio Maior, Collectio Minor, Analecta, Museum.*

Swedish Theological Institute: 58 Rehov Hanevi'im, POB 37, 91 000 Jerusalem; tel. (2) 6253822; fax (2) 6254460; e-mail sti@netvision.net.il; f. 1951; biblical, interreligious, ecumenical and Jewish Studies; Dir Rev. ÅKE SKOOG.

Tel Hai Regional College: 12 210 Upper Galilee; tel. (6) 6900888; fax (6) 6950697; e-mail telhai@telhai.ac.il; f. 1957; bachelor degree courses in agriculture, biotechnology, education, economics and management, environmental sciences, humanities, social sciences, social work, languages, computer science; associate degree courses in architecture, construction, electronics and electricity, computers, mechanics and machinery; Art Institute courses in sculpture, drawing, ceramics, photography and ethnic crafts; library: see Libraries; 6,500 students; Dir Dr AMOS LEVIN.

Ulpan Akiva Netanya, International Hebrew Study Centre: POB 6086, 42 160 Netanya; tel. (9) 8352312; fax (9) 8652919; e-mail ulpanakv@netvision.net.il; f. 1951; basic and supplementary courses in Hebrew and Arabic; cultural studies; 45 teachers; Dir EPHRAIM LAPID.

Yeshivat Dvar Yerushalayim (Jerusalem Academy of Jewish Studies): 53 Katzenellenbogen, Har Nof, POB 5454, 91 053 Jerusalem; tel. (2) 6522817; fax (2) 6522827; e-mail dvar@netmedia.net.il; f. 1970; runs courses in English, French, Russian and Hebrew on the Bible, Hebrew, Talmud, philosophy, ethics and Halacha; 70 mems; library of 5,000 vols; Dean Rabbi B. HOROVITZ; Vice-Prin. Rabbi A. CARMELL; publ. *Jewish Studies Magazine* (annually), *Jerusalem Academy Publications* (Hebrew, English, quarterly).

Zinman College of Physical Education and Sport Sciences at the Wingate Institute: 42 902 Netanya; tel. (9) 8639222; fax (9) 8650960; e-mail zinman@wincol.macam98.ac.il; four-year B.Ed programme, M.A. programme in conjunction with Haifa Univ.; in-service training; 200 teachers; 850 regular students, 1,000 students on other courses; library of 52,000 vols, 180 periodicals; Rector Dr ZVI ARTZI.

ISRAELI-OCCUPIED TERRITORIES AND EMERGING PALESTINIAN AUTONOMOUS AREAS

Libraries and Archives

Nablus

Public Library: Nablus, West Bank, via Israel; tel. (9) 383356; fax (9) 374690; f. 1960; 65,000 vols, mainly in Arabic and English; Librarian ALI MUHAMMED WASEF TUQAN.

Ramallah

Public Library: Ramallah, West Bank, via Israel; f. 1962; 3,500 vols; Librarian ADEL UWAIS.

Universities

BETHLEHEM UNIVERSITY

POB 9, Bethlehem, West Bank, via Israel
Telephone: (2) 74-1241/2/3
(2) 74-4440
Founded 1973
Private control (Roman Catholic)
Languages of instruction: Arabic and English
Academic year: September to June

Chancellor: Archbishop ANDREA DI MONTEZEMOLO
Vice-Chancellor: Rev. Br RONALD GALLAGHER
President: Msgr RAOUFF NAJJAR
Executive Vice-President: Dr ANTON SANSOUR
Academic Vice-President: Rev. Br NEIL KIEFFE
Financial Vice-President: Rev. Br CYRIL LITECKY
Vice-President for Development: Rev. Br THOMAS COONEY
Registrar: MARY JUHA
Librarian: ELSA HAZBOUN

Library of 100,000 vols
Number of teachers: 132 full-time, 52 part-time
Number of students: 1,842 (day and evening)
Publication: *University Journal*.

DEANS AND DIRECTORS

College of Arts: Dr MANUEL HASSASSIAN
- Department of Arabic: Dr IBRAHIM EL-ALAM
- Department of English: Dr HANNA TUSHYEH
- Department of Social Sciences: Dr BERNARD SABELLA
- Department of Humanities: Dr MANUEL HASSASSIAN

College of Sciences: Dr ALFRED ABED RABBO
- Department of Chemistry: Dr ALFRED ABED RABBO
- Department of Mathematics: KARIM ABDUL NOUR
- Department of Life Sciences: Dr NAIM IRAQI

College of Business Administration: JAMIL KOUSSA
College of Education: Dr VIOLET FASHEH
Faculty of Nursing: DIANNE ABRAHAM
Institute of Hotel Management: A. WALID DAJANI

BIRZEIT UNIVERSITY

POB 14, Birzeit, West Bank, via Israel
Telephone: (2) 9982000 via Israel
Fax: (2) 9957656 via Israel

(Also Birzeit University Liaison Office, POB 950666, Amman, Jordan; tel. (6) 5527181; fax (6) 5527202)

Founded 1924 as school, 1951 college, present status 1975
Private autonomous control
Languages of instruction: Arabic and English
Academic year: September to June (two semesters), summer session July–August

President: Dr HANNA NASIR
Vice-President for Academic Affairs: Dr AHMAD BAKER
Vice-President for Administrative Affairs: ISA MASRIEH
Vice-President for Financial Affairs: Dr CARMELLA ARMANIUS-OMARI
Head Librarian: AFAF HARB

Library of 109,000 vols, 250 periodicals
Number of teachers: 255
Number of students: 3,646

Publications: University catalogues (in Arabic and English, every 2 years), *Afaq Filistiniyyah Birzeit Research Review* (in Arabic and English, 4 a year), *Birzeit University Newsletter* (in English), *Birzeit Human Rights Record* (in English).

DEANS

Arts: Dr SAID ZEEDANI
Science: Dr ABDEL-LATIF ABU HIJLEH
Commerce and Economics: Dr MOHAMMAD NASR
Engineering: Dr HANI NIJIM
Graduate: Dr GEORGE GIACAMAN

ATTACHED RESEARCH INSTITUTES

Centre for Research and Documentation of Palestinian Society: Dir Dr SALEH ABDUL JAWAD.

Palestinian Institute of Archaeology: Dir Dr KHALED NASHEF.

HEBRON UNIVERSITY

POB 40, Hebron, West Bank, via Israel
Telephone: (2) 9920995
Fax (2) 9929303
E-mail: huplann@palnet.com
Founded 1971
Independent national university
Languages of instruction: Arabic and English
Academic year: October to June

Chancellor: Dr NABEEL AL-JABARI
President: Dr ALI AMRO
Vice-President (Academic Affairs): Dr AWNI KHATIB
Vice-President (Planning and Development): Dr AKRUM TAMIMI
Registrar: M. ZIAD JA'BARI
Librarian: NO'AMAN SHAHEEN

Library of 40,000 vols
Number of teachers: 95
Number of students: 1,994

DEANS

Arts: Dr AHMAD AHAWNAH
Islamic Studies: Dr HAFAZ JAABARI
Agriculture: AAYAD MOHAMMAD
Science: Dr FAHAD TAKRURI
Finance and Management: Dr SAMIR ABUZNAID
Scientific Research: MUSA AJWEH

HEADS OF DEPARTMENTS

Arabic: Dr HASSAN FLAFEL
English: Dr AHMAD ATTAWNEH
History: Dr ABED AL-QADER JABARIN
Education: Dr ALAM DEEN KHATEEB
Biology: JAMIL RABBA
Chemistry: Dr FAHED TAKRURI
Mathematics: Dr MOHAMMED ABU EIDEH
Animal Husbandry: Dr AYED GHALEB
Plant Production and Protection: Dr RADWAN BARAKAT
Figh: Dr HANI SAID
Islamic Law: Dr HAFEZ JAABARI

AN-NAJAH NATIONAL UNIVERSITY

POB 7,707, Nablus, West Bank, via Israel
Telephone: (9) 381113
Fax: (9) 387982

(For communications from the Arab countries: An-Najah National University Liaison Office, POB 254, Al-Jubeiha, Jordan; tel. and fax 845886)

Founded 1977
Private control
Languages of instruction: Arabic; English for Sciences and Engineering
Academic year: October to June

Chairman: ABDEL GHANI ANABTAWI
President: Prof. MUNTHIR SALAH
Vice-Presidents (Academic Affairs): Dr RAMI HAMDALLAH, Dr MOHAMMAD HANNOUN
Vice-President (Administrative Affairs): Prof. BAHJAT SABRI
Vice-President (Cultural and University Affairs): (vacant)
Registrar: SADEQ ANABTAWI
Librarian: ADEL AL-HAJ HAMAD

Library of 88,000 vols
Number of teachers: 284
Number of students: 7,400 (excluding Community College)

Publications: *An-Najah Journal of Research (Natural Sciences)*, *An-Najah Journal of Research (Humanities)*, *Risalet An-Najah*.

DEANS

Faculty of Agriculture: Dr JAMAL ABU-OMER
Faculty of Islamic Studies: Dr MARWAN QADUMI
Faculty of Law: Dr AWNI BADER
Faculty of Economics and Administrative Sciences: Dr NASER ABDEL KARIM
Faculty of Arts: Dr KHALIL ODEH
Faculty of Fine Arts: Dr GHAWI M. GHAWI
Faculty of Engineering: Dr MARWAN HADDAD
Faculty of Education: Dr ALI HABAYEB
Faculty of Science: Dr MOHAMMED S. ISHTAYYEH
Faculty of Graduate Studies: Dr ALI ZIEDAN
Scientific Research: Dr KHALIL AL-SHAQAQI
Community College: Dr ANAN ABU ZAHRA

HEADS OF DEPARTMENTS

Faculty of Science:
- Chemistry: Dr SHOKRI KHALAF
- Biology: Dr SAMI YAISH
- Medical Sciences: Dr SOLIMAN KHALIL
- Physics: Dr MOUSA ABU-AL-HASSAN
- Mathematics: Dr TAHA ABU-KAF

Faculty of Education:
- Education and Psychology: Dr FAROUQ EL-SAAD
- Teaching Methods: Dr SOUZAN ARAFAT
- Physical Education: Dr ABDEL NASER KADOUMI

Faculty of Engineering:
- Civil Engineering: Dr WAEL ABU-ASAB
- Architecture: Dr KHALED QAMHIEH
- Electronics: Dr MAHER KHAMMASH
- Industrial Engineering: Dr AMJAD AL-GHANEM

Chemical Engineering: Dr AMER AL-HAMMOUZ

Faculty of Arts:

Arabic: Prof. MOHAMMED QASEM NOFAL
English: ODEH ODEH
Geography: Dr TAHA SALAMEH
Sociology: Dr MAHER ABU ZANET
History: Dr TAYSIR JBARA
Archaeology: Dr JALAL QAZZOUH

Faculty of Economics and Administrative Sciences:

Economics: Dr QASEM JUDEH
Business Administration: Dr NOUR ABO AL-RUB
Political Science: Dr OTHMAN OTHMAN
Accounting: Dr NAFEZ ABU BAKER
Journalism: Dr ATEF SALAMEH

Faculty of Agriculture:

Animal Husbandry and Animal Health: Dr HASSAN ABU-QAUD
Plant Production and Plant Protection: Dr MOHAMMAD AJJOUR

Faculty of Fine Arts:

Music: AHMED MOUSSA
Painting and Art Decoration: AHMED AL-HAJ HAMAD

ATTACHED INSTITUTES

Water and Environmental Studies Centre: Dir Dr ANAN JAYYOUSI.
Centre for Renewable Energy: Dir Dr MARWAN MAHMOUD.
Centre for Earth Sciences and Earthquakes: Dir Dr JALAL DABIK.

AL-QUDS UNIVERSITY

POB 51000, Jerusalem, via Israel
Telephone: (2) 274980 via Israel
Fax: (2) 277166 via Israel
Founded 1979
Private control
Language of instruction: English
Academic year: October to August
President: Dr SARI NUSSEIBEH
Vice-President: Dr TOUFIK SHAKHASHIR
Assistant to the President for Academic Affairs: Dr KHALED KANAN
Dean of Research and Academic Studies: Dr ZIAD ABDEEN
Registrar: Dr HANNA ABDUL NUR
Librarian: RANDA KAMAL
Library of 100,000 vols
Number of teachers: 244
Number of students: 2,800

DEANS

Faculty of Science and Technology: Prof. ADNAN RASHID
Faculty of Allied Health Professions: Prof. VARSEEN SHAHEEN
Faculty of Arts: Prof. HASAN SILWADI
Faculty of Law: Prof. ALI KHASHAN
Faculty of Medicine: Prof. NA'EL SHIHABI
Faculty of Jurisprudence: Prof. HAMZEH THEEB
Faculty of Quran and Islamic Studies: Prof. ISMAIL NAWAHDAH

ATTACHED INSTITUTES

Higher Institute of Islamic Archaeology: Dir Prof. MARWAN ABU-KHALAF.
Islamic Research Centre: Dir Prof. HASAN SILWADI.
Centre for Area Studies: Dir Prof. MUSA BUDEIRI.
Centre for Commerce and Economic Science: Dir Prof. MAHMOUD JAFARI.
Language Centre: Dir Prof. OMAR ABU-HOMMOS.
Institute of Phonetics and Language Sciences: Dir Prof. YOUSEF EL-HALLIS.
Institute of Modern Media: Dir DAOUD KUTTAB.

Colleges

Tulkarm Community College: West Bank, Via Israel; f. 1931; library of 30,000 vols; 27 teachers; 400 students; a teacher-training college preparing teachers of agriculture, science, mathematics, computer science, Arabic, Islamic and social studies, English and physical education; Dean Dr M. Z. GHAZALEH.

ITALY

Learned Societies

GENERAL

Accademia delle Scienze dell'Istituto di Bologna: Via Zamboni 31, 40126 Bologna; tel. 051-222596; f. 1711; 60 mems, 200 corresp. mems; Pres. Prof. DARIO GRAFFI; Sec. Prof. SILVANO LEGHISSA.

Accademia delle Scienze di Ferrara: Via Romei 3, 44100 Ferrara; tel. 0532-205209; fax 0532-205209; f. 1823; 270 mems; library of 12,000 vols; Pres. Prof. ITALO BARRAI; Sec. Avv. V. CAPUTO; publ. *Atti*.

Accademia delle Scienze di Torino (Turin Academy of Sciences): Via Maria Vittoria 3, 10123 Turin; tel. 011-5620047; fax 011-5620047; f. 1783; 250 mems; all fields of learning; publications, congresses and lectures; library: see Libraries; Pres. Prof. ELIO CASETTA; publs *Memorie*, *Atti* (annually), *Quaderni* (irregular).

Accademia Etrusca: Palazzo Casali, Piazza Signorelli, 52044 Cortona-Arezzo; tel. 0575-630415; f. 1727; 80 mems, 50 hon. mems, 80 corresp. mems; Pres. Dott. GUGLIELMO MAETZKE; Vice-Pres./Sec. Dott. Prof. EDOARDO MIRRI; publs *Annuario*, *Note e Documenti*.

Accademia Gioenia di Scienze Naturali: Corso Italia 55, 95129 Catania; f. 1824; 136 mems; library of 20,000 vols, 400 periodicals; Pres. Prof. A. ARCORIA; Gen. Sec. Prof. F. FURNARI; publs *Bollettino delle Sedute della Accademia Gioenia di Scienze Naturali in Catania*, *Atti della Accademia Gioenia di Scienze Naturali in Catania*.

Accademia Ligure di Scienze e Lettere (Academy of Sciences and Letters): Piazza G. Matteotti 5, 16123 Genoa; tel. 010-565570; fax 010-566080; f. 1798; library of 50,000 vols; 20 hon. mems, 160 mems (30 ordinary, 50 corresp. in each class); Pres. Prof. E. BENVENUTO; Sec.-Gen. Dr G. P. PELOSO; publs *Atti* (annually), *Studi e Ricerche*, *Monografie*.

Accademia Nazionale dei Lincei: Palazzo Corsoni, Via della Lungara 10, 00165 Rome; tel. 06-6838831; fax 06-6893616; e-mail lincei@axcasp.caspur.it; f. 1603; sections of Physical, Mathematical and Natural Sciences (Academic Secs Prof. GIUSEPPE GRIOLI, Prof. ANTONIO ASCENZI), Moral, Historical and Philological Sciences (Academic Secs Prof. GIANNINO PARRAVICINI, Prof. GIANCARLO SUSINI); 180 mems, 180 corresp. mems, 180 foreign mems; library: see Libraries and Archives; Pres. Prof. SABATINO MOSCATI; Academic Administrators Prof. SUGELO FALZEA, Prof. LUIGI A. RADICATI DI BROZOLO.

Accademia Nazionale di San Luca: Piazza dell'Accademia di San Luca 77, 00187 Rome; tel. 06-6798850; fax 06-6789243; f. 14th century; sections of Painting, of Sculpture, of Architecture; 54 mems, 90 corresp. mems, 30 foreign mems, 47 cultural and hon. mems; library: see Libraries and Archives; Pres. CARLO AYMONINO; Sec.-Gen. GIORGIO CIUCCI.

Accademia Nazionale di Santa Cecilia: Via Vittoria 6, 00187 Rome; tel. 06-3611068; fax 06-3611402; f. 1566; 70 national mems and 30 foreign mems; Pres. BRUNO CAGLI.

Accademia Nazionale di Scienze, Lettere ed Arti: Palazzo Coccapani, Corso Vittorio Emanuele II 59, 41100 Modena; tel. 059-225566; f. 1683; 40 mems, 60 corresponding mems, 30 honorary mems; library of 120,000 vols; Pres. Prof. GUSTAVO VIGNOCCHI; publ. *Atti e Memorie*.

Accademia Nazionale di Scienze, Lettere ed Arti (Academy of Sciences, Letters and Arts): Piazza Indipendenza 17, 90129 Palermo; tel. 091-420862; library of 14,000 vols; Pres. Prof. GIUSEPPE LE GRUTTE; Gen. Sec. Prof. ROMUALDO GIUFFRIDA.

Accademia Nazionale Virgiliana di Scienze, Lettere e Arti: Via dell' Accademia 47, 46100 Mantua; tel. 0376-320314; fax 0376-222774; f. early 17th century, present name 1981; 90 mems, 20 hon. mems, 60 corresp. mems; library: see Libraries; Pres. Prof. CLAUDIO GALLICO; Sec. Dott. A. ZANCA; publ. *Atti e Memorie N.S.* (periodical, annually).

Accademia Petrarca di Lettere, Arti e Scienze (Petrarch Academy of Letters, Arts and Science): Via dell' Orto, 52100 Arezzo; tel. 0575-24700; f. 1810; 413 mems; library of 16,000 vols; Pres. Prof. ALBERTO FATUCCHI; Sec. Rag. LUCIANO NOCENTI; publs *Atti e Memorie*, *Studi Petrarcheschi*.

Accademia Pugliese delle Scienze: Palazzo dell'Ateneo, Piazza Umberto I, 70121 Bari; tel. 080-5714578; fax 080-5714578; f. 1925; divided into two classes: Physical, Medical and Natural Sciences, and Moral Sciences, with 120 ordinary mems, 200 corresp. mems and 20 hon. mems; Pres. Prof. MICHELE DELL' AQUILA; publ. *Atti e Relazioni* (1 a year).

Accademia Roveretana degli Agiati: Via Canestrini 1, 38068 Rovereto (Trento); tel. 0464-436663; f. 1750; fosters the development of sciences, literature and art; 319 mems; library of 43,000 vols; Pres. Prof. LIVIO CAFFIERI; Sec. Dr GIANFRANCO ZANDONATI; publ. *Proceedings* (annually).

Accademia Spoletina: Palazzo Ancaiani, Piazza della Libertà 12, 06049 Spoleto; tel. 0743-261321; f. 1477; 10 honorary mems, 40 mems, and 150 corresponding mems; library of 10,000 vols; Pres. Avv. FILIPPO DE MARCHIS; publs *Spoletium*, *Rivista di Arte Storia Cultura* (annually).

Accademia Tiberina: Via del Vantaggio 22, 00186 Rome; tel. 06-3619305; f. 1813; 200 mems and 2,000 assoc., corresp., resident and hon. mems; applied sciences, psychology, arts, hygiene and health, anthropology, Yoga-Vedanta centre; library of 10,000 vols; Pres. Prof. Dott. IGOR ISTÓMIN-DURANTI; Sec. SILVIA RAMINI.

Accademia Toscana di Scienze e Lettere 'La Colombaria' (La Colombaria Tuscan Academy of Science and Letters): Via S. Egidio 23, 50122 Florence; tel. 055-2396628; fax 055-2396628; e-mail colombaria@dada.it; f. 1735; library of 30,000 vols; Pres. Prof. FRANCESCO ADORNO; Gen. Sec. Prof. FRANCESCO MAZZONI; publs *Atti e Memorie* (annually), *Studi* (4–5 a year).

Istituto Lombardo Accademia di Scienze e Lettere: Via Brera 28, 20121 Milan; tel. 02-864087; fax 02-86461388; f. 1802; Pres. Prof. ANTONIO PADOA SCHIOPPA; Vice-Pres. Prof. LUIGI AMERIO; it is divided into two classes: Mathematics and Natural Sciences (Sec. Prof. GIUSEPPE CASSINIS; 42 mems, 82 corresponding associates, 30 foreign mems); Moral Sciences (Sec. FRANCESCO MATTESINI; 40 mems, 80 corresponding associates, 30 foreign mems); library of 400,000 vols, 330 Italian periodicals, 600 foreign periodicals; publs *Rendiconti, Parte Generale e Atti Ufficiali*, *Rendiconti della Sezione di Scienze Matematiche e Naturali*, *Rendiconti della Sezione di Scienze Biologiche e Mediche Chimica e Fisica*, *Rendiconti della Classe di Scienze Morali*, *Memorie della Classe di Scienze Matematiche e Naturali*, *Memorie della Classe di Scienze Morali*, *Cicli di Conferenze*, Proceedings of Symposiums.

Istituto Veneto di Scienze, Lettere ed Arti (Venetian Institute of Sciences, Letters and Arts): San Marco 2945, 30124 Venice; tel. 041-5210177; fax 041-5210598; e-mail ivsla@unive.it; f. 1838; functions as academy; also organizes postdoctoral courses; 60 mems, 120 assoc. mems; library of 200,600 vols; Pres. Prof. BRUNO ZANETTIN; publs *Atti*, *Memorie*.

Società di Letture e Conversazioni Scientifiche (Scientific Society): Palazzo Ducale, Am. to Ala Sud Matteotti 5, Genoa; f. 1866; library of 15,310 vols; Dir P. BOZZO-COSTA.

Società Nazionale di Science, Lettere ed Arti: Via Mezzocannone 8, 80100 Naples; library of 35,000 vols; Pres. Prof. A. VALLONE; Sec.-Gen. Prof. F. TESSITORE.

AGRICULTURE, FISHERIES AND VETERINARY SCIENCE

Accademia dei Georgofili (Academy of Georgofili): Logge degli Uffizi, 50122 Florence; tel. 055-212114; fax 055-2302754; e-mail accademia@georgofili.it; f. 1753; 139 ordinary mems, 193 corresp. mems; library of 50,000 vols; Pres. Prof. FRANCO SCARAMUZZI; publs *Atti*, *Quaderni*, *Rivista di Storia della Agricoltura*.

Accademia di Agricoltura di Torino (Academy of Agriculture of Turin): Via Andrea Doria 10, 10123 Turin; tel. 011-511689; f. 1785; library of 16,000 vols; Pres. Dott. Prof. PIER LUIGI GHISLENI.

Accademia Italiana di Scienze Forestali: Piazza Edison 11, 50133 Florence; tel. 055-570348; fax 055-575724; f. 1952; 240 mems; library of 5,000 vols; Pres. Prof. A. MANCINI; publs *Annali* (annually), *L'Italia Forestale e montana* (every 2 months).

Accademia Nazionale di Agricoltura: Via Castiglione 11, 40124 Bologna; tel. 051-268809; f. 1807; 80 mems and 140 corresponding mems; library of 10,000 vols and 14,000 pamphlets; Pres. Prof. GIUSEPPE MEDICI; Sec. Dott. TULLIO ROMUALDI; publ. *Annali* (quarterly).

Associazione Forestale Italiana: Via Guido d'Arezzo 16, 00198 Rome; Pres. Dott. ALFONSO FRONCILLO.

Istituto Agronomico per l'Oltremare (Agronomic Institute for Overseas): Via Antonio Cocchi 4, 50131 Florence; tel. 055-50611; telex 574549; fax 055-5061333; e-mail iao@iao.florence.it; f. 1904; 50 mems; library of 124,000 vols; Dir-Gen. Dott. ALICE PERLINI; publ. *Rivista di Agricoltura Subtropicale e Tropicale* (quarterly).

Società Italiana delle Scienze Veterinarie: Via A. Bianchi 1, 25124 Brescia; tel. 030-223244; fax 030-2420569; f. 1947; 1,700 mems; Pres. Prof. MONTI FRANCO; publ. *Atti*.

Società Italiana di Economia Agraria: Istituto di Zooeconomia, Coviolo, 42100 Reggio Emilia; tel. 0522-21745; f. 1962; 300 mems;

Pres. Prof. GIULIO ZUCCHI; publ. *Atti* (annually).

ARCHITECTURE AND TOWN PLANNING

Centro Internazionale di Studi di Architettura 'Andrea Palladio': Palazzo Barbaran da Porto, contra' Porti 11, CP 835, 36100 Vicenza; tel. 0444-323014; fax 0444-322869; f. 1959 to make known the work of Andrea Palladio, b. Padua 1508, and to encourage the study of Palladianism and of Venetian architecture of all ages; Pres. MARINO QUARESIMIN.

Istituto Nazionale di Architettura (IN-ARCH): Via Catalana 5, 00186 Rome; tel. 06-68802254; f. 1959; organizes meetings, debates and exhibitions; 2,000 mems; Pres. Ing. PAOLO BARATTA.

Istituto Nazionale di Urbanistica (INU): Via S. Caterina da Siena 46, 00186 Rome; tel. 06-6793559; fax 06-6780929; f. 1930; 960 mems, 1,211 assoc. mems; Pres. Prof. Arch. STEFANO STANGHELLINI; Sec. Prof. Arch. PAOLO AVARELLO; publs *Urbanistica* (quarterly), *Urbanistica Informazioni* (every 2 months).

Italia Nostra—Associazione Nazionale per la Tutela del Patrimonio Storico Artistico e Naturale della Nazione (Italia Nostra—National Association for the Preservation of the Historical, Artistic and Natural Heritage of the Nation): Via Nicolò Porpora 22, 00198 Rome; tel. 06-8542333; f. 1955; 20,000 mems, subscribers, delegates; library of 4,500 vols; brs in 206 towns; Pres. FLORIANO VILLA; Sec.-Gen. GAIA PALLOTTINO; publ. *Italia Nostra* (9 a year).

BIBLIOGRAPHY, LIBRARY SCIENCE AND MUSEOLOGY

Associazione Italiana Biblioteche: CP 2461, 00100 Rome A-D; tel. 06-4463532; fax 06-4441139; e-mail aib@aib.it; f. 1930; 3,200 mems; library of 6,000 vols; Pres. Dr L. POGGIALI; Sec. Dr E. FRUSTACI; publs *Bollettino d'informazioni* (quarterly), *AIB notizie* (monthly).

Associazione Nazionale dei Musei Italiani: Piazza San Marco 49, 00186 Rome; tel. 06-6791343; fax 06-6791343; Pres. Prof. D. BERNINI; Sec. Dott. L. BARBACINI; publ. *Musei e Gallerie d'Italia*.

Centro Di (International Documentation Centre): Piazza de'Mozzi 1, 50125 Florence; f. 1968; documentation, distribution of books and catalogues in the field of art, architecture, visual communication; library of 8,000 vols; Dir F. MARCHI; publs bulletin of catalogues, indexes.

Istituto Centrale per la Patologia del Libro (Central Institute of Book Pathology): Via Milano 76, 00184 Rome; tel. 06-482911; fax 06-4814968; e-mail patolo@mbox.vol.it; f. 1938; book restoration and preservation; 77 mems; library of 12,000 vols; Dir Prof. CARLO FEDERICI; publs *Bollettino* (annually), *Cabnewsletter* (every 2 months).

ECONOMICS, LAW AND POLITICS

Accademia Italiana di Economia Aziendale (Academy of Business Economics): Via Cairoli 11, 40121 Bologna; tel. 051-558798; fax 051-6492446; f. 1813; divided into 3 classes; 375 national mems, 50 foreign mems, 10 hon. mems; reps from all Italian universities; Pres. UMBERTO BERTINI; Vice-Pres VITTORIO CODA, GIANNI LORENZONI.

Associazione Italiana di Diritto Marittimo (Italian Maritime Law Association): Via Po 1, Palazzo Assitalia, Rome; Sec.-Gen. CAMILLA DAGNA.

Cenacolo Triestino: Piazza della Borsa 14, 34121 Trieste; tel. 040-64210; f. 1946; academy of economic and social studies; Pres. BENIAMINO ANTONINI; Sec.-Gen. SPIRIDIONE NICOLAIDI; publ. *Observatore Economico e Sociale*.

CIRGIS (International Centre for Juridical Research and Scientific Initiatives): Via Manzoni 45, 20121 Milan; tel. 02-6552167; f. 1979 to promote cultural relations between scholars of Italian and foreign law; aims for the realization of exchanges of thought and experience between Italian and foreign jurists, the knowledge of laws and institutions of different countries through meetings, publications etc.; *c.* 400 mems; Pres. Avv. Prof. FRANCESCO OGLIARI; International Sec. Avv. GIUSEPPE AGLIALORO.

Istituto di Diritto Romano e dei Diritti dell'Oriente Mediterraneo: Facoltà di Giurisprudenza, Piazzale Aldo Moro 5, 00185 Rome; tel. 06-49910608; fax 06-49910241; f. 1937; library of 45,000 vols; Dir Prof. ANDREA DI PORTO.

Istituto per il Rinnovamento Economico (IRE): Via Petronio Arbitro 4, 00136 Rome; f. 1924; promotes international economic and monetary reform; Pres. G. DI DOMENICO.

Istituto per l'Economia Europea: Via C. Colombo 70, 00147 Rome; f. 1960; 62 mems; library of 1,500 vols; Pres. Sen. Prof. GAETANO STAMMATI; Sec.-Gen. Dr SILVANO PALUMBO; publs *Europa: Fatti e Idee*, *Europa Selezione* (2 a year).

Società Italiana degli Economisti: Via Pizzecolli 68, 60121 Ancona; f. 1950; 594 mems; Pres. Prof. S. LOMBARDINI; Sec.-Gen. Prof. M. CRIVELLINI; publ. *Bollettino-Lettera*.

Società Italiana di Economia, Demografia e Statistica: c/o Dip. di Teoria Economica e Metodi Quantitativi per le Scelte Politiche, Università 'La Sapienza', Piazzale Aldo Moro 5, 00185 Rome; tel. 06-4462991; f. 1938; *c.* 600 mems; Pres. Prof. ORNELLO VITALI; Sec. Gen. Prof. FRANCO VACCINA; publs *Rivista Italiana di Economia, Demografia e Statistica* (quarterly), *Collana di Studi e Monografie* (irregular).

Società Italiana di Filosofia Giuridica e Politica: c/o Ist. di Filosofia del Diritto, Facoltà di Giurisprudenza, Università La Sapienza, 00185 Rome; tel. 06-490489; fax 06-49910951; f. 1936; 200 mems; Pres. LUIGI LOMBARDI VALLAURI; Sec. MAURIZIO BASCIU; publ. *Rivista internazionale di filosofia del diritto* (quarterly).

Società Italiana di Statistica: Salita de' Crescenzi 26, 00186 Rome; tel. 06-6869845; fax 06-68806742; f. 1939; 1,000 mems; statistics and demography; Pres. Prof. LUIGI BIGGERI; Gen. Sec. Prof. MAURIZIO VICHI; publs Proceedings of the Scientific Meetings, *SIS-Bollettino* (quarterly), *SIS-Informazioni* (monthly), *Journal of the Italian Statistical Society* (quarterly).

Società Italiana per l'Organizzazione Internazionale (SIOI) (UN Asscn for Italy): Piazza Di S. Marco 51, Palazzetto di Venezia, 00186 Rome; tel. 06-6920781; fax 06-6789102; e-mail sioi@mclink.net; f. 1944; sections in Florence, Milan, Naples, Turin; library: see Libraries; Pres. UMBERTO LA ROCCA; Sec.-Gen. LUIGI VITTORIO FERRARIS; publ. *La Comunità Internazionale* (quarterly).

EDUCATION

Associazione Pedagogica Italiana: Via Zamboni 34, 40126 Bologna; tel. 051-258442; fax 051-228847; f. 1950; aims to promote the development of schools in general and all other institutions of education, also studies and research in education; 50 brs; *c.* 5,000 mems; Pres. SIRA SERENELLA MACCHIETTI; Sec.-Gen. ALDO D'ALFONSO; publ. *Bollettino* (quarterly).

Istituto per la Cooperazione Universitaria: Viale G. Rossini 26, 00198 Rome; tel. 06-85300722; fax 06-8554646; e-mail icu.roma@agore.stm.it; f. 1967; to promote cultural relations between different countries, chiefly through university co-operation, international meetings and study groups; international technical co-operation by sending volunteers and experts to developing countries; Pres. Prof. UMBERTO FARRI; Dir Ing. ENNIO DI FILIPPO; Sec.-Gen. Dr PIER GIOVANNI PALLA; publs *SIPE—Servizio Stampa Educazione e Sviluppo* (6 a year), *Educazione e Sviluppo* (irregular).

FINE AND PERFORMING ARTS

Academia Española de Bellas Artes en Roma (Spanish Fine Arts Academy in Rome): Piazza San Pietro in Montorio 3 (Gianicolo), 00153 Rome; f. 1873; Dir Prof. FELIPE V. GARIN LLOMBART.

Consiglio Nazionale per i Beni Culturali e Ambientali (National Council for Culture and the Environment): Ministry of Culture and the Environment, Via del Collegio Romano 27, 00186 Rome; tel. 06-6789529; six committees: environment and architecture (Pres. Prof. ROBERTO DI STEFANO); archaeology (Pres. Prof. ATTILIO STAZIO); history of art (Pres. Prof. FRANCESCO NEGRI ARNOLDI); archives (Pres. Prof. GIUSEPPE PANSINI); books (Pres. Dott. LETIZIA VERGNANO PECORELLA); cultural institutes (Pres. Prof. AURELIO RIGOLI); Pres. of the Council, Minister for Culture and the Environment; Sec. Dott. MARILISA CORDONE CAMETTI.

Istituto Italiano di Arti Grafiche SpA (Italian Institute of Graphic Art): Via Zanica 92, 24100 Bergamo; library of 15,000 vols; Dir ROMANO MONTANARI.

Istituto Italiano per la Storia della Musica (Italian Institute for the History of Music): c/o Accademia Nazionale di Santa Cecilia, Via Vittoria 6, 00187 Rome; tel. 06-36000146; f. 1938; Pres. Prof. BRUNO CAGLI; publ. *Bollettino*.

Istituto Nazionale di Studi Verdiani (National Institute of Verdi Studies): Strada della Repubblica 56, 43100 Parma; tel. 0521-286044; fax 0521-287949; f. 1960 under the patronage of the International Music Council and the Italian Ministry of Cultural Affairs and Education; to study the life and works of Giuseppe Verdi; library of 12,000 vols, archives of 15,000 documents; Pres. ALBERTO CARRARA VERDI; Dir PIERLUIGI PETROBELLI; publs *Verdi Bulletin*, *Quaderni*, *Proceedings of Congresses*, *Studi Verdiani*, *Carteggi Verdiani*.

Istituto Universitario Olandese di Storia dell'Arte (Dutch University Institute for the History of Art): Viale Torricelli 5, 50125 Florence; tel. 055-221612; f. 1955; library of 50,000 vols; Dir BERT W. MEIJER.

Kunsthistorisches Institut/Istituto di Storia dell'Arte (Institute for the Study of History of Art): Via Giuseppe Giusti 44, 50121 Florence; tel. 055-249111; fax 055-2491155; f. 1897; 32 mems; library of 200,000 vols, 2,450 periodicals and 530,000 reproductions; special collections: art in Northern Italy, 19th- and 20th-century Italian art; Dir Prof. Dr MAX SEIDEL; publs *Mitteilungen* (annually), *Monographienreihe: Italienische Forschungen* (every 2 years), *Jahresbericht* (annually).

Società d'Incoraggiamento d'Arti e Mestieri (Society for the Encouragement of Arts and Crafts): Via Santa Marta 18, 20123 Milan; tel. 02-86450125; fax 02-86450125; f. 1838; education in mechanics, electronics, electrotechnics, chemistry, computer studies; library of *c.* 6,000 vols; Pres. MASSIMO SCORTECCI; Gen. Sec. DANILO CANCELLIERI.

Società Italiana di Musicologia: Piazza S. Croce in Gerusalemme 9A, 001825 Rome; tel.

06-7886486; e-mail s.vallef@iol.it; f. 1964; 800 mems; Pres. Prof. CAROLYN GIANTURCO; publs *Rivista Italiana di Musicologia*, *Quaderni della Rivista Italiana di Musicologia*.

Società Italiana Musica Contemporanea: Piazza Buenos Aires 20, 00198 Rome; tel. 06-868012; Pres. M. PERAGALLO; Sec. M. R. MANN.

HISTORY, GEOGRAPHY AND ARCHAEOLOGY

Accademia Archeologica Italiana: Via Archimede 139, 00197 Rome; tel. 06-8072575; f. 1952; 60 academicians in five classes: archaeology, history, art, literature, science; Pres. Prof. LEO MAGNINO; Sec. Prof. VITALIANO ROCCHIERO; publ. *La Cultura nel Mondo* (quarterly).

Associazione Archeologica Romana (Roman Archaeological Society): Piazza B. Cairoli 117, 00186 Rome; tel. 06-6865647; f. 1902; 400 mems; library of 3,000 vols; Pres. Dott. V. SANTA MARIA SCRINARI; Sec. Dott. LEANDRO SPERDUTI; publ. *Romana Gens* (quarterly).

Istituto Geografico Militare: Via C. Battisti 10, 50122 Florence; tel. 055-27751; fax 055-282172; f. 1872; geodetic and topographical surveying; official cartography; library of 200,000 vols; Dir-Gen. MATTEO FACCIORUSSO; publs *L'Universo* (6 a year), *Bollettino di Geodesia e Scienze Affini* (quarterly).

Istituto Italiano di Numismatica: Palazzo Barberini, Via Quattro Fontane 13, 00184 Rome; tel. 06-4743603; fax 06-4743603; f. 1936; numismatics; library of 15,000 vols; Pres. Prof. ATTILIO STAZIO; Dir Prof. SARA SORDA; publ. *Annali* (annually).

Istituto Italiano di Paleontologia Umana: Piazza Mincio 2, 00198 Rome; f. 1913; quaternary environment, geology, palaeontology, palaeoanthropology, archaeology; 250 mems; library of 5,800 vols, 31 periodicals; extensive offprints series; Pres. Prof. Dr A. ASCENZI; Sec.-Gen. Prof. A. BIETTI; publs *Memorie* (irregular), *Quaternaria* (annually).

Istituto Italiano per la Storia Antica: Via Milano 76, 00184 Rome; tel. 06-4880597; f. 1935; library of 17,000 vols; Pres. Prof. S. ACCAME; publs *Miscellanea Greca e Romana*, *Dizionario Epigrafico di Antichità Romane*.

Istituto Nazionale di Archeologia e Storia dell'Arte: Piazza San Marco 49, 00186 Rome; tel. 06-6780817; fax 06-6798804; f. 1922; library of 500,000 vols; Pres. ALESSANDRO BETTAGNO; Chief Officer PAOLO PELLEGRINO; publ. *Rivista* (annually).

Istituto Nazionale di Studi Etruschi ed Italici (Institute for Etruscan and Italic Studies): Via Ricasoli 31, 50122 Florence; tel. 055-2396846; f. 1932; 207 mems; library of 14,000 vols; Pres. Prof. GIOVANNANGELO CAMPOREALE; Sec. Prof. LUIGI DONATI; publ. *Studi etruschi* (annually).

Istituto per la Storia del Risorgimento Italiano (Institute for the History of the Italian Revival): Vittoriano, Piazza Venezia, Rome; tel. 06-6793598; fax 06-6782572; f. 1935; 3,400 mems; Pres. Prof. GIUSEPPE TALAMO; Sec.-Gen. SERGIO LA SALVIA; publs *Rassegna storica del Risorgimento*, *Biblioteca Scientifica* (3 series).

Istituto Storico Italiano per il Medio Evo (Italian Institute of Medieval History): Piazza dell' Orologio 4, 00186 Rome; tel. 06-68802075; fax 06-6877059; f. 1883; library of 120,000 vols; Pres. Prof. GIROLAMO ARNALDI; publs *Bullettino*, *Fonti per la storia dell' Italia medievale*, *Nuovi Studi Storici*, *Repertorium Fontium Historiae Medii Aevi*.

Istituto Storico Italiano per l'Età Moderna e Contemporanea: Via Michelangelo Caetani 32, 00186 Rome; tel. 06-68806922; fax 06-6875127; f. 1934; historical research and publications; Pres. LUIGI LOTTI; publ. *Annuario*.

Società di Minerva: Piazza Hortis 4, 34123 Trieste; f. 1810 for the study of the history, art and culture of Trieste, Istria and Gorizia; 150 mems; Pres. Prof. arch. LUIGI PAVAN; Secs Prof. BRUNO MAIER, Capt. SERGIO DEGLI IVANISSEVICH; publ. *Archeografo Triestino* (annually).

Società di Studi Geografici (Society for Geographical Studies): Via San Gallo 10, 50129 Florence; tel. 055-2757956; e-mail capineri@unisi.it; f. 1895; 600 mems; library of 18,000 vols; Pres. PAOLO ROBERTO FEDERICI; Sec. CRISTINA CAPINERI; publ. *Rivista Geografica Italiana* (quarterly).

Società Geografica Italiana: Villa Celimontana, Via della Navicella 12, Rome; tel. 06-7008279; fax 06-77079518; e-mail geomail@tin.it; f. 1867; library: see Libraries; Pres. Prof. FRANCO SALVATORI; publs *Bollettino*, *Memorie*.

Società Napoletana di Storia Patria (Neapolitan Society of Italian History): Piazza Municipio Maschio Angioino, 80133 Naples; f. 1876; 650 mems; Pres. Prof. GIUSEPPE GALASSO; Vice-Pres. Prof. RAFFAELE AJELLO; publ. *Archivo Storico per le Province Napoletane*.

Società Romana di Storia Patria: Piazza della Chiesa Nuova 18, 00186 Rome; tel. 06-68307513; f. 1876; *c.* 100 mems; Pres. LETIZIA ERMINI PANI; Sec. PASQUALE SMIRAGLIA; publs *Archivio della Società* (annually), *Miscellanea della Società* (irregular), *Codice diplomatico di Roma e della Regione Romana* (irregular).

Società Storica Lombarda: Via Morone 1, 20121 Milan; tel. 02-860118; fax 02-72002108; f. 1874; 344 mems; library of 27,000 vols; Pres. Co. Ing. GAETANO BARBIANO DI BELGIOJOSO; Sec. Dott. LUIGI OROMBELLI; publ. *Archivio Storico Lombardo* (1 a year).

LANGUAGE AND LITERATURE

Accademia della Crusca: Villa Medicea di Castello, Via di Castello 46, 50141 Florence; tel. 055-454277; fax 055-454279; f. 1583; library of 160,000 vols; Pres. Prof. GIOVANNI NENCIONI; Dir of Philological Studies DOMENICO DE ROBERTIS; Dir of Lexicographical Studies D'ARCO SILVIO AVALLE; Dir of Grammatical Studies GIOVANNI NENCIONI; Sec. SEVERINA PARODI; publs *Autori classici e documenti di lingua*, *Vocabolari e Glossari*, *Studi di Filologia Italiana*, *Studi di Grammatica Italiana*, *Studi di Lessicografia Italiana*, etc.

Keats-Shelley Memorial Association: Piazza di Spagna 26, Rome; tel. 06-6784235; fax 06-6784167; e-mail ksmhrome@tin.it; f. 1907; library of 9,000 vols; Dir CATHERINE PAYLING; publ. *Review*.

PEN International Centre: Via Daverio 7, 20122 Milan; Pres. MARIO LUZI; Sec.-Gen. MARIA BRUNELLI.

Società Dante Alighieri: Palazzo di Firenze, Piazza Firenze 27, 00186 Rome; tel. 06-6873694; f. 1889; promotes Italian language and culture throughout the world; Sec.-Gen. Dr GIUSEPPE COTA; publ. *Pagine della Dante* (quarterly).

Società Dantesca Italiana (Italian Dante Society): Via dell'Arte della Lana 1, 50123 Florence; tel. 055-287134; fax 055-211316; e-mail sdi@leonet.it; f. 1888; library of 20,000 vols, 1,500 microfilms; Pres. Prof. FRANCESCO MAZZONI; publs *Studi Danteschi*, *Quaderni degli 'Studi Danteschi'*, *Quaderni del Centro di Studi e Documentazione Dantesca e Medievale*, *Edizione Nazionale delle Opere di Dante Alighieri*.

Società Filologica Romana: Città Universitaria, Rome; f. 1901; library of 8,000 vols; Pres. AURELIO RONCAGLIA; publ. *Studi Romanzi*.

Società Italiana degli Autori ed Editori (SIAE): Viale della Letteratura 30, 00144 Rome (EUR); tel. 06-59901; telex 611423; fax 06-59647050; f. 1882; protects authors' and publishers' rights; 50,000 mems; administers the Museo e Biblioteca Teatrale del Burcardo (35,000 vols); Pres. LUCIANO VILLEVIEILLE BIDERI; Gen. Man. FRANCESCO CHIRICHIGNO; publs *Il Diritto d'Autore*, *Lo Spettacolo* (quarterly), *Bollettino SIAE*, *Teatro in Italia* (annually), *Lo Spettacolo in Italia* (annually).

Società Letteraria (Literary Society): Piazzetta Scalette Rubiani 1, 37100 Verona; tel. 045-8030641; fax 045-595949; e-mail slvr01@chiostro.univr.it; f. 1808; library of 200,000 vols; Pres. Dott. GIOVANNI BATTISTA RUFFO; publ. *Bollettino* (annually).

MEDICINE

Accademia delle Scienzi Mediche di Palermo: Clinica Chirurgica B, Via Liborio Giuffrè 5, 90127 Palermo; tel. 091-230808; f. 1621; library; Pres. Prof. P. LI VOTI; Sec. Prof. P. BAZAN; publ. *Atti* (annually).

Accademia di Medicina di Torino (Academy of Medicine): Via Po 18, 10123 Turin; tel. 011-8179298; fax 011-8179298; f. 1846; 120 mems; library of 7,100 vols; Pres. Prof. MARIO UMBERTO DIANZANI; Sec.-Gen. Prof. NAPOLEONE MASSAIOLI; publ. *Giornale* (2 a year).

Accademia Medica di Roma: Policlinico Umberto I, 00161 Rome; tel. 06-4957818; f. 1875; *c.* 400 mems; Pres. Prof. ANDREA SCIACCA; Sec. Prof. MARIO STEFENINI; publ. *Bolletino ed Atti* (annually).

Associazione Italiana di Dietetica e Nutrizione Clinica: Via dei Penitenzieri 13, 00193 Rome; f. 1950; education and training; application of research in nutrition; 200 mems; Pres. Prof. P. MONTENERO.

Associazione Italiana di Medicina Aeronautica e Spaziale: Via Piero Gobetti 2A, Rome; Sec.-Gen. Prof. ARISTIDE SCANO.

Associazione Italiana di Radiologia Medica e Medicina Nucleare: III Cattedra di Radiologia, Instituto di Radiologia, Policlinico Umberto I, 00161 Rome; Pres. Prof. CARISSIMO BIAGINI; Sec. Prof. VINCENZO CAVALLO.

Centro di Studi e Ricerche di Medicina Aeronautica e Spaziale dell'Aeronautica Militare: Via Piero Gobetti 2A, 00185 Rome; f. 1951; library of 4,300 vols; Dir Col. GIORGIO MEINERI.

Fondazione Luigi Villa: Via Pace 9, 20122 Milan; tel. 02-5510709; fax 02-54100125; f. 1969; research in molecular biology; library of 9,000 vols; Pres. Prof. GIUSEPPE SIMONI; Sec.-Gen. Dott. OLGA MOSCA.

Società Italiana di Anestesiologia e Rianimazione: Ist. An. Rean. Nuovo Policlinico, Viale Bracci 53, 53100 Siena; tel. 0577-50103; f. 1934; 2,000 mems; Pres. Prof. GUALTIERO BELLUCCI; Sec. Dott. ANDREA DI MASSA; publ. *Minerva Anestesiologica*.

Società Italiana di Cancerologia: Istituto di Anatomia, Università di Napoli, Via L. Armanni 5, 80100 Naples; Pres. Prof. P. VERGA; Sec. Prof. P. BUCALOSSI.

Società Italiana di Chirurgia: Viale di Villa Massimo 21, 00161 Rome; tel. 06-4881818; Pres. Prof. G. DI MATTEO; Sec.-Gen. Prof. L. ANGELINI.

Società Italiana di Farmacologia: Via Giorgio Jan 18, 20129 Milan; tel. 02-29520311; fax 02-29520179; e-mail sifcse@imiucca.csi.unimi.it; f. 1939; 1,113 ord. mems, 13 hon. mems, 33 assoc. mems; Pres. Prof. GIANCARLO PEPEU; Sec. Prof. VINCENZO CUOMO; publs *SIF Notizie* (3 a year), *Pharmacological Research* (monthly).

Società Italiana di Ginecologia ed Ostetricia: Via dei Soldati 25, 00186 Rome; tel. 06-6875119; fax 06-6868142; f. 1892; 5,300 mems; Pres. Prof. V. GIAMBANCO; Sec. Dr G. VITTORI; publs *Atti*, *Bollettino* (quarterly), *Italian Journal of Gynaecology and Obstetrics* (quarterly).

Società Italiana di Medicina Interna: Via Savoia 37, 00198 Rome; tel. 06-8559067; fax 06-8559067; f. 1887; 2,166 mems; Pres. Prof. FRANCO DAMMACCO; Sec. Prof. GIUSEPPE LICATA; publ. *Journal Annali Italiani di Medicina Interna* (quarterly in Italian and English, annual special supplements).

Società Italiana di Medicina Legale e delle Assicurazioni: Via Falloppio 50, 35100 Padua; tel. 049-8272200; fax 049-663155; Pres. Prof. FRANCESCO INTRONA; Pres. Prof. A. FORMARI; Sec. G. UMANI ROMCHI.

Società Italiana di Neuroradiologia: Via Gen. Orsini 40, 80100 Naples; Sec. Prof. ENZO VALENTINO.

Società Italiana di Odontostomatologia e Chirurgia Maxillo-Facciale: Via Verdi 28 Clinica Odontostomatologica, 67100 L'Aquila; tel. 0862-411176; fax 0862-411176; f. 1957; 2,000 mems; Pres. Prof. SERGIO TARTARO; Sec.-Gen./Treas. Prof. FRANCO MARCI; publ. *Minerva Stomatologica* (monthly).

Società Italiana di Ortopedia e Traumatologia: presso Clinica Ortopedica, Università, Piazzale Aldo Moro 5, Rome; f. 1906; 3,100 mems; Pres. Prof. MARIO GANDOLFI; Sec. Prof. MARCELLO PIZZETTI; publ. *Giornale Italiano di Ortopedia e Traumatologia* (quarterly).

Società Italiana di Reumatologia: Via Gramsci 14, Ospedale Maggiore, 43100 Parma; Pres. Prof. U. CARCASSI; Sec.-.Gen. Prof. U. AMBANELLI.

Società Italiana di Scienze Farmaceutiche: Via Giorgio Jan 18, 20129 Milan; tel. 02-29513303; fax 02-29520179; f. 1953; 350 mems; Pres. Prof. RODOLFO PAOLETTI; Exec. Sec. Prof. FRANCO BONATI; publ. *Cronache Farmaceutiche* (every 2 months).

Società Italiana di Traumatologia della Strada: Istituto di Clinica Ortopedica e Traumatologica dell' Universita La Sapienza, Piazzale A. Moro 5, 00185 Rome; tel. 06-491672; fax 06-49914846; f. 1984; 150 mems; Pres. ANDREA COSTANZO; Sec.-Gen. Dr ROBERTO SAPIA.

Società Medica Chirurgica di Bologna (Society of Medicine and Surgery): Piazza Galvani 1, 40124 Bologna; tel. 051-231488; f. 1823; holds scientific meetings; 330 mems; library of 15,000 vols; Pres. Prof. EMILIO PISI; Sec. Prof. MICHELE FIORENTINO; publ. *Bullettino delle Scienze Mediche*.

NATURAL SCIENCES

General

Accademia Nazionale delle Scienze, detta dei XL (National Academy of Sciences, known as the Forty): Via Cassia Antica 35, 00191 Rome; tel. 06-3297667; fax 06-36300057; f. 1782 as the Italian Society of Sciences; 40 Italian, 25 foreign mems; Pres. Prof. G. T. SCARASCIA MUGNOZZA; Sec. Prof. M. CUMO; publs *Rendiconti: Memorie Scienze Fisiche e Naturali*, *Memorie di Matematica* (annually), *Scritti e Documenti*, *Annuario*.

Federazione delle Associazioni Scientifiche e Tecniche: Piazzale R. Morandi 2, 20121 Milan; tel. 02-76015672; fax 02-782485; f. 1897; aims at fostering cultural debate and scientific diffusion in the fields of science policy, technological and industrial research and development, with particular reference to: energy and resources, chemistry and materials, electronics and information, biotechnology, technological research and innovation, ecology and environment, training, professionalism and job organization; mems: 37 scientific orgs, 50,000 individuals; Pres. Prof. R. MANIGRASSO; Gen. Sec. Dr ALBERTO PIERI.

Società Adriatica di Scienze (Adriatic Society of Sciences): Via Orsera 3, CP1029, 34145 Trieste; f. 1874; 200 mems; library of 27,000 vols; Pres. Prof. DULIO LAUSI; Sec. Dr TIZIANA CUSMA VELARI; publ. *Bollettino* (annually).

Società Italiana di Scienze Naturali (Italian Society of Natural Sciences): Museo Civico di Storia Naturale, Corso Venezia 55, 20121 Milan; tel. 02-795965; f. 1857; 1,000 mems; library of 1,600 periodicals; Pres. B. PARISI; Sec. BONA BIANCHI POTENZA; publs *Atti* (2 a year), *Natura* (2 a year), *Memorie*, *Rivista di Ornitologia* (2 a year), *Paleontologia Lombarda*.

Società Italiana per il Progresso delle Scienze: Viale Regina Margherita 202, 00198 Rome; tel. 06-855-41-56; f. 1839; library of 30,000 vols; Pres. Prof. ARNALDO M. ANGELINI; Sec. Prof. ROCCO CAPASSO; publs *Atti delle Riunioni della SIPS*, *Scienza e Tecnia* (monthly).

Società Toscana di Scienze Naturali (Tuscan Society of Natural Sciences): Via S. Maria 53, 56100 Pisa; f. 1847; 412 mems; library of 50,000 vols; Sec.-Gen. Prof. MARCO TONGIORGI; publ. *Atti* (2 a year).

Biological Sciences

Società Botanica Italiana (Italian Botanical Society): Via Giorgio La Pira 4, 50121 Florence; tel. 055-2757379; fax 055-2757379; f. 1888; 1,200 mems; library of 9,000 vols; Pres. Prof. CARLO BLASI; Sec. Prof. DONATO CHIATANTE; publs *Plant Biosystems* (3 a year), *Informatore Botanico Italiano* (3 a year).

Società Entomologica Italiana (Italian Entomological Society): c/o Museo Civico di Storia Naturale, Via Brigata Liguria 9, 16121 Genoa; f. 1869; pure and applied entomology; 900 mems; Pres. Prof. A. VIGNA TAGLIANTI; publs *Bollettino* (3 a year), *Memorie* (annually).

Società Italiana di Biochimica: Dipartimento di Scienze Biochimiche 'A. Rossi Fanelli', Università di Roma 'La Sapienza', Piazzale Aldo Moro 5, 00185 Rome; f. 1951; 1,300 mems; Pres. Prof. SANDRO PONTREMOLI, tel. 010-3538162; Sec Prof. SERGIO PAPA, tel. 080-5478428; publs *Biochimica in Italia*, *Bioit* (2 a year).

Società Italiana di Biochimica Clinica e Biologia Molecolare Clinica: Via C. Farini 70, 20159 Milan; tel. 02-6887556; fax 02-6887026; f. 1969; 2,500 mems; mem. of Int. Fed. of Clinical Chemistry; Pres. M. PAZZAGLI; publ. *Biochimica Clinica* (monthly).

Società Italiana di Ecologia: c/o Dip. Scienze Ambientali, Viale delle Scienze, 43100 Parma; tel. 0521-905609; fax 0521-905402; f. 1976; aims to promote theoretical and applied ecological research, to disseminate knowledge of ecology, encourage the development of cultural exchange among researchers, and to facilitate national and international co-operation; operates working groups, congresses, etc.; 544 mems; Pres. IRENEO FERRARI; Sec.-Gen. EROS BACCI; publ. *SITE Notizie* (annually).

Società Italiana di Microbiologia: c/o Istituto di Microbiologia, Via Androne 81, 95124 Catania; tel. 095-312633; f. 1962; Pres. Prof. GIOVANNI A. MELONI; Sec.-Gen. Prof. GIOVANNI RUSSO.

Physical Sciences

Associazione Geofisica Italiana: c/o Istituto di Fisica dell' Atmosfera, Piazzale Luigi Sturzo 31, 00144 Rome; tel. 06-59293011; fax 06-5915790; f. 1951; 300 mems; library of 1,500 vols; Pres. Ing. M. PAGLIARI; Sec. Dr M. AVERSA; publ. *Bollettino Geofisico*.

Associazione Geotecnica Italiana: Piazza Bologna 22, 00162 Rome; tel. 06-44249272; fax 06-44249274; f. 1947; independent; aims to encourage, carry out and support geotechnical studies and research in Italy through publications, conferences, scholarships, etc.; 1,100 mems; Pres. Prof. G. BARLA; publ. *Rivista Italiana di Geotecnica* (quarterly).

Società Astronomica Italiana (Italian Astronomical Society): Largo E. Fermi 5, 50125 Florence; tel. 055-2752270; fax 055-220039; f. 1920; 700 mems; Pres. Prof. MASSIMO CAPACCIOLI; Sec. Dr MAZZUCCONI FABRIZIO; publs *Memorie* (quarterly), *Giornale di Astronomia* (quarterly).

Società Chimica Italiana: Viale Liegi 48/C, 00198 Rome; tel. 06-8549691; fax 06-8548734; f. 1909; 4,800 mems; library of 2,300 vols; Pres. Prof. BRUNO SCROSATI; publs *Gazzetta Chimica Italiana* (monthly), *Annali di Chimica* (6 a year), *Il Farmaco* (monthly), *La Chimica e l'Industria* (monthly), *Chimica nella Scuola* (5 a year).

Società Geologica Italiana: c/o Dipartimento di Scienze della Terra, Università La Sapienza, Piazzale Aldo Moro 5, 00185 Rome; tel. 06-4959390; f. 1881; 2,400 mems; Sec. Dott. ACHILLE ZUCCARI; publs *Bollettino* (quarterly), *Memorie* (irregular).

Società Italiana di Fisica (Italian Physics Society): Via Castiglione 101, 40136 Bologna; tel. 051-331554; fax 051-581340; 1,500 mems; library of 6,500 vols; Pres. Prof. R. A. RICCI; publs *Il Nuovo Cimento A* (monthly), *Il Nuovo Cimento B* (monthly), *Il Nuovo Cimento C* (every 2 months), *Il Nuovo Cimento D* (monthly), *Europhysics Letters* (2 a month), *Rivista del Nuovo Cimento* (monthly), *Bollettino* (every 2 months), *Giornale di Fisica* (quarterly).

PHILOSOPHY AND PSYCHOLOGY

Associazione Internazionale Filosofia, Arti e Scienze: Via Oberdan 15, 40126 Bologna; f. 1957; Pres. Prof. SILVIO CECCATO; Sec.-Gen. Prof. C. GENOVESE; publ. *Quaderni FAS*.

Società Filosofica Italiana: C/o Prof. Emidio Spinelli, V. C. Bertinoro 13, 00162 Rome; tel. 06-8604360; e-mail sfi@getnet.it; f. 1902; independent organization to promote philosophical research on a scientific level, to safeguard the professional status of philosophy lecturers, to encourage contact and collaboration in Italy and internationally between philosophic disciplines; helps set up local centres of study; 1,420 mems; Pres. Prof. GIOVANNI CASERTANO; Gen. Sec. Prof. EMIDIO SPINELLI; publ. *Bollettino* (3 a year).

Società Italiana per gli Studi Filosofici e Religiosi: presso l'Università Cattolica del Sacro Cuore, Piazza S. Ambrogio 9, 20123 Milan; library of 25,618 vols; Pres. Prof. GUSTAVO BONTADINI; Gen. Sec. Prof. LUCIANA VIGONE; Librarian Dott. VALENTINO FOFFANO.

RELIGION, SOCIOLOGY AND ANTHROPOLOGY

Fondazione Internazionale Premio E. Balzan – 'Premio': Secretariat: Piazzetta U. Giordano 4, 20122 Milan; tel. 02-76002212; fax 02-76009457; f. 1957; annual prizes for the world-wide promotion of the arts and sciences and for the most meritorious actions in the cause of humanity; Pres. Amb. C. GUAZZARONI.

Fondazione Marco Besso (Marco Besso Foundation): Largo di Torre Argentina 11, Rome; tel. 06-6865611; fax 06-68804078; f. 1918; promotes development of Roman cultural world; library: see Libraries; Pres.

GLORIA SONAGLIA LUMBROSO; Dir ANTONIO MARTINI.

Gruppo Interdisciplinare per la Ricerca Sociale: Facoltà di Scienze Statistiche Demografiche e Atluariale, Piazza Aldo Moro 5, 00185 Rome; tel. 06-4453828; f. 1937; Italian section of Int. Institute of Sociology; Pres. Prof. AMMASSARI.

Società di Etnografia Italiana: Via Tacito 50, 00193 Rome; tel. 06-359512; f. 1911 to investigate the folklore of Italy; library of 4,000 vols; 170 mems; Pres. Prof. PABLO TOSCHI; publ. *Lares* (quarterly).

Società Italiana di Antropologia e Etnologia: Via del Proconsolo 12, 50122 Florence; tel. 055-2396449; fax 055-219438; f. 1871; 200 mems; library of 5,760 vols, 70 periodicals; Pres. Prof. CLETO CORRAIN; Librarian CATERINA SCARSINI.

TECHNOLOGY

Associazione Elettrotecnica ed Elettronica Italiana (AEI) (Italian Electrical and Electronics Association): Piazzale Morandi 2, 20121 Milan; tel. 02-777901; fax 02-798817; e-mail presid@aci.it; f. 1896; Pres. U. DE JULIO; publs *AEI—Automazione Energia Informazione* (monthly), *L'Energia Elettrica* (6 a year), *European Transactions on Telecommunications* (6 a year, in English), *Alta Frequenza Rivista di Elettronica* (6 a year).

Associazione Idrotecnica Italiana: Via Nizza 53, 00198 Rome; tel. 06-8845064; fax 06-8852974; f. 1923; study of problems concerning the utilization and management of water resources, and the safeguarding of the environment; 1,500 mems; library of 200 vols; Pres. Dr. Ing. UMBERTO UCELLI; Sec.-Gen. Dott. Ing. PASQUALE PENTA; publ. *L'Acqua* (every 2 months).

Associazione Italiana di Aeronautica e Astronautica: Via Po 50, 00198 Rome; tel. 06-8845894; f. 1920; promotes and co-ordinates research in aeronautical and space sciences, co-operates with nat. and int. bodies in this field; *c.* 1,000 mems in eight sections; Pres. Prof. Ing. ERNESTO VALLERANI; Sec.-Gen. Dott. Ing. ANTONIO CASTELLANI; publ. *Aerotecnica Missili e Spazio* (quarterly).

Associazione Italiana di Metallurgia: Piazzale R. Morandi 2, 20121 Milan; tel. 02-76021132; fax 02-76020551; e-mail aim@fast.mi.it; f. 1946; promotes and develops all aspects of science, technology and use of metals and materials closely related to metals; 2,000 mems; Pres. Ing. LUIGI IPERTI; Gen. Sec. Ing. Dr PIERO BUFALINI; publ. *La Metallurgia Italiana* (monthly).

Associazione Nazionale di Ingegneria Nucleare: Piazza Sallustio 24, 00187 Rome; tel. 06-486415; Pres. MAURIZIO CUMO; Sec.-Gen. GUIDO BOTTA.

Associazione Termotecnica Italiana: Piazzale Morandi 2, 20121 Milan; tel. 02-2367330; fax 02-2363927; e-mail ati@clausius.energ.polimi.it; f. 1947; thermal engineering; Pres. Prof. UMBERTO RUGGIERO; Sec.-Gen. GIOVANNI RIVA; publs *La Termotecnica* (monthly), *Ricerche di Termotecnica* (occasional), *Atti Congressi Nazionali*.

Comitato Elettrotecnico Italiano (CEI) (Italian Electrotechnical Committee): Viale Monza 259, 20126 Milan; tel. 02-257731; fax 02-25773210; Pres. Dr Ing. GERMANO BONANNI.

Comitato Termotecnico Italiano (CTI) (Italian Thermotechnical Committee): c/o Dipartimento de Energetica, Politecnico di Milano, Piazzale Leonardo da Vinci 32, 20133 Milan; tel. 02-257731; fax 02-25773210; f. 1933; Pres. Prof. PIERANGELO ANDREINI; Gen. Sec. Prof. GIOVANNI RIVA; publ. *La Termotecnica* (monthly).

Ente Nazionale Italiano di Unificazione (UNI) (Italian National Standards Association): Via Battistotti Sassi 11, 20123 Milan; tel. 02-70105955; telex 312481; f. 1921; Pres. Dr Ing. GIACOMO ELIAS; Exec. Vice-Pres. Dr Ing. ENRICO MARTINOTTI; publ. *Unificazione* (quarterly).

Istituto di Studi Nucleari per l'Agricoltura (ISNA): Via IV Novembre 152, 00187 Rome; tel. 06-6784964; f. 1959; Pres. Avv. Prof. GIUSEPPE GESUALDI; Sec.-Gen. Prof. M. L. SCARSELLI; publs *Agricoltura d'Italia* (monthly), *Il Corriere di Roma*, *Quaderni ISNA*.

Istituto Elettrotecnico Nazionale 'Galileo Ferraris' (Galileo Ferraris National Electrotechnical Institute): Corso Massimo d'Azeglio 42, 10125 Turin; tel. 011-39191; telex 211553; fax 011-6507611; f. 1934; 123 mems; library of 11,000 vols, 340 current journals, CEI standards; Pres. SIGFRIDO LESCHIUTTA; publ. annual scientific report.

Istituto Italiano del Marchio di Qualità (IMQ) (Italian Institute of the Quality Mark): Via Quintiliano 43, 20138 Milan; tel. 02-50731; telex 310494; fax 02-5073271; f. 1951; tests electrical and gas products to grant the IMQ safety mark and certifies company quality and management systems according to the CSQ system; Pres. Ing. LORENZO TRINGALI CASANUOVA; publs *Guida agli Acquisti IMQ* (list of products and companies approved by IMQ, 2 a year), *IMQ Notizie* (News, quarterly).

Istituto Italiano della Saldatura (Italian Welding Institute): Lungobisagno Istria 15, 16141 Genoa; tel. 010-83411; fax 010-8367780; f. 1948; consultancy training, research, standardization, certification, laboratory tests and diploma courses in welding; 800 mems; library of 15,000 vols; Sec.-Gen. Ing. FRANCESCO MASETTI; publ. *Rivista Italiana della Saldatura*.

Research Institutes

GENERAL

Consiglio Nazionale delle Ricerche (CNR) (National Research Council of Italy): Piazzale Aldo Moro 7, 00185 Rome; tel. 06-49931; fax 06-4957241; f. 1923; research is supervised by 15 National Advisory Committees and is undertaken in (a) institutes, which are permanent bodies, (b) study centres, which are attached to universities and to public and private scientific institutions, and (c) research groups, which are temporary institutions, of no more than 5 years' duration, undertaking research for individuals and scientific institutions; National Advisory Committees on Mathematical Sciences (Chair. Prof. CARLO CERCIGNANI), Physical Sciences (Chair. Prof. MARCELLO FONTANESI), Chemical Sciences (Chair. Prof. ROMANO CIPOLLINI), Biological and Medical Sciences (Chair. Prof. GIORGIO BERNARDI), Geological and Mineralogical Sciences (Chair. Prof. PIERO MANETTI), Agricultural Sciences (Chair. Prof. FRANCESCO BONCIARELLI), Engineering and Architectural Sciences (Chair. Prof. VITO ANTONIO MONACO), Historical, Philosophical and Philological Sciences (Chair. Prof. MARIO MAZZA), Juridical and Political Sciences (Chair. Prof. LUIGI LABRUNA), Economic, Sociological and Statistical Sciences (Chair. Prof. LUIGI PAGANETTO), Technological Research and Innovation Sciences (Chair. Dott. CLAUDIO BATTISTONI), Information Science and Technology (Chair. Dott. FRANCO DENOTH), Environmental Science and Technology (Chair. Dott. ALFREDO LIBERATORI), Molecular Biology and Biotechnology (Chair. Prof. GAETANO SALVATORE), Cultural Heritage (Chair. Dott. ANGELO GUARINO); Pres. LUCIO BIANCO; Dir-Gen. Dott. NUNZIO DE RENSIS; publs *Bollettino Ufficiale* (5 parts), *Annuario*.

Institutes and study centres in mathematical sciences:

Istituto per le Applicazioni del Calcolo 'Mauro Picone': Viale del Policlinico 137, 00161 Rome; tel. 06-884701; fax 06-4404306; Dir Prof. A. TESEI.

Istituto per la Matematica Applicata: Area di Ricerca di Genova, Via de Marini 6, Torre di Francia, 16149 Genoa; tel. 010-64751; fax 010-6475660; f. 1970; Dir Dottssa BIANCA FALCIDIENO.

Istituto di Analisi Numerica: C/o Dipartimento di matematica, Università, Via Abbiategrosso 209, 27100 Pavia; tel. 0382-21185; fax 0382-28079; f. 1970; Dir Prof. FRANCO BREZZI.

Istituto di Analisi Globale ed Applicazioni: Via S. Marta 13A, 50139 Florence; tel. 055-474389; fax 055-475915; f. 1975; Dir Prof. C. PUCCI.

Istituto per le Applicazioni della Matematica e dell'Informatica: Via Ampère 56, 20131 Milan; tel. 02-70643201; fax 02-2663030; f. 1981; Dir Prof. E. REGAZZINI.

Istituto per Applicazioni della Matematica: Via P. Castellino 111, 80131 Naples; tel. 081-5608101; fax 081-5608288; f. 1981; Dir Prof. M. R. OCCORSIO.

Istituto per Ricerche di Matematica Applicata: Via Giovanni Amendola 116/124, 70126 Bari; tel. 080-330719; fax 080-5588235; f. 1983; Dir Prof. R. PELUSO.

Istituto di Matematica Computazionale: Via S. Maria 46, 56126 Pisa; tel. 050-593400; Dir Dott. B. CODENOTTI.

Centro di Ricerche per il Calcolo Parallelo e i Supercalcolatori: C/o Dip. di Matematica e Applicazioni, Università 'Federico II', Complesso Monte Sant'Angelo, Via Cintia, 80126 Naples; tel. 081-675624; fax 081-7662106; Dir Prof. A. MURLI.

Institutes and study centres in physical sciences:

Istituto di Acustica 'O. M. Corbino': Via Cassia 1216, 00189 Rome; tel. 06-30365776; fax 06-30365741; Dir Dott. E. VERONA.

Istituto di Elaborazione della Informazione: Via S. Maria 46, 56126 Pisa; tel. 050-593400; fax 050-554342; f. 1968; Dir Prof. P. MAESTRINI.

Istituto di Fisica dell' Atmosfera: Piazzale Luigi Sturzo 31, 00144 Rome; tel. 06-5910941; fax 06-5915790; f. 1961; Dir Dott. A. MUGNAI.

Istituto di Ricerca sulle Onde Elettromagnetiche 'Nello Carrara': Via Panciatichi 64, 50127 Florence; tel. 055-4378512; fax 055-410893; Dir Prof. N. RUBINO.

Istituto di Studio e Tecnologie sulle Radiazioni Extraterrestri: Area di ricerca di Bologna, Via P. Gobetti 101, 40129 Bologna; tel. 051-6398688; fax 051-6398724; f. 1968; Dir Dott. N. MANDOLESI.

Istituto di Radioastronomia: Area di ricerca di Bologna, Via P. Gobetti 101, 40129 Bologna; tel. 051-6399111; fax 051-6399431; f. 1970; Dir. Dssa LUCIA PADRIELLI.

Istituto per lo Studio dei Fenomeni Fisici e Chimici della Bassa e Alta Atmosfera: Area di ricerca di Bologna, Via P. Gobetti 101, 40129 Bologna; tel. 051-6399619; fax 051-6399658; Dir Dott. C. TOMASI.

Istituto di Elettronica Quantistica: Via Panciatichi 56/30, 50127 Florence; tel. 055-416128; fax 055-414612; f. 1970; Dir Dott. RENZO SALIMBENI.

Istituto di Cibernetica e Biofisica: c/o Area di ricerca di Genova, Via De Marini 6,

Torre di Francia, 16149 Genoa; tel. 010-64751; f. 1969; Dir Dott. FRANCO GAMBALE.

Istituto per Ricerche in Fisica Cosmica e Tecnologie Relative: Via Bassini 15, 20133 Milan; tel. 02-23699302; fax 02-2362946; f. 1968; Dir Dott. E. G. TANZI.

Istituto di Fisica del Plasma: Via Bassini 15, 20133 Milan; tel. 02-70638646; fax 02-2663212; f. 1970; Dir Dott. GIAMPIETRO LAMPIS.

Istituto di Cibernetica: Via Toiano 6, 80072 Arco Felice (Naples); tel. 081-8534111; fax 081-5267654; Dir Dott. A. MASSAROTTI.

Istituto di Materiali Speciali per l'Elettronica e Magnetismo: Via Chiavari 18A, 43100 Parma; tel. 0521-269227; fax 0521-269206; f. 1969; Dir Dott. L. ZANOTTI.

Istituto di Biofisica: Via San Lorenzo 26, 56127 Pisa; tel. 050-513111; fax 050-553501; f. 1969; Dir Dott. F. LENCI.

Istituto di Fisica Atomica e Molecolare: Via del Giardino 3, 56127 Pisa; tel. 050-542346; fax 050-906072; f. 1969; Dir Dott. M. MARTINELLI.

Istituto di Fisica dello Spazio Interplanetario: Via G. Galilei, 00044 Frascati (Rome); tel. 06-94186236; fax 06-9417757; f. 1981; Dir Dott. M. CANDIDI.

Istituto di Elettronica dello Stato Solido: Via Cineto Romano 42, 00156 Rome; tel. 06-415221; fax 06-41522220; f. 1969; Dir Dott. P. DE GASPERIS.

Istituto di Astrofisica Spaziale: Via E. Fermi 23, 00044 Frascati (Rome); tel. 06-9425651; fax 06-9416847; f. 1970; Dir Dott. A. PREITE MARTINEZ.

Istituto di Cosmo-Geofisica: Corso Fiume 4, 10133 Turin; tel. 011-6604066; fax 011-6604056; f. 1968; Dir Prof. P. PICCHI.

Istituto per lo Studio della Dinamica delle Grandi Masse: Palazzo Papadopoli 1364, San Polo, 30125 Venice; tel. 041-5216830; fax 041-5216892; f. 1969; Dir Dott. G. DALLAPORTA.

Istituto di Tecniche Spettroscopiche: C/o Università, Contrada Papardo, Salita Sperone 31, 98166 Villaggio S. Agata (Messina); tel. 090-392281; fax 090-392855; f. 1981; Dir Dott. CIRINO S. VASI.

Istituto per le Applicazioni Interdisciplinari della Fisica: C/o Istituto di Fisica Università, Via Archirafi 36, 90123 Palermo; tel. 091-6233111; fax 091-6162480; f. 1981; Dir Prof. S. L. FORNILI.

Istituto di Fisica Cosmica con Applicazioni all'Informatica: Via Mariano Stabile 172, 90139 Palermo; tel. 091-332903; fax 091-332889; f. 1981; Dir Dott. B. SACCO.

Istituto di Struttura della Materia: Via E. Fermi 38, 00044 Frascati (Rome); tel. 06-9426335; fax 06-9417003; f. 1981; Dir Dott. P. PERFETTI.

Istituto per l'Elaborazione di Segnali ed Immagini: Via G. Amendola 166/5, 70126 Bari; tel. 080-481154; fax 080-484311; Dir Dott. ARCANGELO DISTANTE.

Istituto per lo Studio delle Metodologie Geofisiche Ambientali: Via Emilia Est 770, 41100 Modena; tel. 059-362388; fax 059-374506; Dir Dott. F. TAMPIERI.

Istituto di Tecnologia Informatica Spaziale: c/o Agenzia Spaziale Italiana, Centro di Geodesia Spaziale, Località Terlecchia, 75100 Matera; tel. 0835-339027; fax 0835-339027; Dir Dott. P. TOMASI.

Istituto Nazionale di Metodologie e Tecnologie per la Microelettronica: c/o SGS Thomson Microelettronica Srl, Stradale Primo sole 50, 95121 Catania; tel. 095-591912; fax 095-7139154; Dir Prof. SALVATORE UGO CAMPISANO.

Istituto per lo Studio dei Nuovi Materiali per l'Elettronica: c/o Dipartimento di Scienza dei Materiali, Università, Via Arnesano, ex Collegio Fiorini, 73100 Lecce; tel. 0832-320242; fax 0832-320525; Dir Prof. L. VASANELLI.

Centro di Elettronica Quantistica e Strumentazione Elettronica: c/o Istituto di Fisica, Politecnico, Piazza Leonardo da Vinci 32, 20133 Milan; tel. 02-2664711; fax 02-23996126; Dir Prof. O. SVELTO.

Centro per l'Astronomia Infrarossa e lo Studio del Mezzo Interstellare: c/o Osservatorio Astrofisico di Arcetri, Largo Enrico Fermi 5, 50125 Florence; tel. 055-27521; fax 055-220039; Dir Prof. GIANNI TOFANI.

Centro di Fisica degli Stati Aggregati ed Impianto Ionico: c/o Istituto per la Ricerca Scientifica e Tecnologica, 38050 Povo (Trento); tel. 0461-881682; fax 0461-810628; Dir Dott. S. IANNOTTA.

Centro di Studio di Fisica delle Superfici e delle Basse Temperature: c/o Dipartimento di Fisica, Università, Via Dodecaneso 33, 16146 Genoa; tel. 010-3536261; fax 010-3622790; Dir Prof. UGO VALBUSA.

Institutes and study centres in chemical sciences:

Istituto di Chimica delle Macromolecole: Via Bassini 15, 20133 Milan; tel. 02-70636333; fax 02-2362946; f. 1970; Dir Dott. GUIDO AUDISIO.

Istituto di Spettroscopia Molecolare: Area di ricerca di Bologna, Via P. Gobetti 101, 40129 Bologna; tel. 051-6398531; fax 051-6398540; f. 1968; Dir Dott. CARLO TALIANI.

Istituto di Fotochimica e Radiazioni d'Alta Energia: Area di ricerca di Bologna, Via P. Gobetti 101, 40129 Bologna; tel. 051-6399784; fax 051-6399844; f. 1968; Dir Dott. P. G. DI MARCO.

Istituto dei Composti del Carbonio Contenenti Eteroatomi e loro Applicazioni: Area di ricerca di Bologna, Via P. Gobetti 101, 40129 Bologna; tel. 051-6398294; fax 051-6398349; f. 1968; Dir Dott. G. SECONI.

Istituto di Chimica e Tecnologia dei Materiali e dei Componenti per l'Elettronica: Area di ricerca di Bologna, Via P. Gobetti 101, 40129 Bologna; tel. 051-6399141; f. 1968; Dir Dott. PIER GIORGIO MERLI.

Istituto per lo Studio della Stereochimica ed Energetica dei Composti di Coordinazione: Via Jacopo Nardi 39–41, 50132 Florence; tel. 055-243990; fax 055-2478366; f. 1968; Dir Dott. CLAUDIO BIANCHINI.

Istituto di Chimica di Molecole di Interesse Biologico: Via Toiano 2, 80072 Arco Felice (Naples); tel. 081-8671255; fax 081-8041770; f. 1968; Dir Dott. G. CIMINO.

Istituto di Ricerca e Tecnologia delle Materie Plastiche: Via Toiano 6, 80072 Arco Felice (Naples); tel. 081-8661446; fax 081-8663378; f. 1968; Dir Prof. E. MARTUSCELLI.

Istituto di Ricerche sulla Combustione: c/o Dipartimento di Ingegneria Chimica, Università Federico II, Piazzale V. Tecchio, 80125 Naples; tel. 081-616227; fax 081-5936936; f. 1968; Dir Prof. G. RUSSO.

Istituto di Chimica e Tecnologie Inorganiche e dei Materiali Avanzati: Area di Ricerca di Padova, Corso Stati Uniti 4, 35020 Padua; tel. 049-8295611; fax 049-8702911; f. 1968; Dir Dott. P. ZANELLA.

Istituto di Polarografia e Elettrochimica Preparativa: Area di Ricerca di Padova, Corso Stati Uniti 4, 35020 Padua; tel. 049-8295611; fax 049-8295649; f. 1968; Dir Dott. S. DAOLIO.

Istituto di Chimica Quantistica ed Energetica Molecolare: Via Risorgimento 35, 56126 Pisa; tel. 050-918111; fax 050-502270; f. 1968; Dir Dott. R. AMBROSETTI.

Istituto di Chimica dei Materiali: Area di Ricerca di Roma-Montelibretti, Via Salaria Km 29,300, CP 10, 00016 Monterotondo Stazione (Rome); tel. 06-90625407; fax 06-90625849; f. 1968; Dir Dott. SESTO VITICOLI.

Istituto di Cromatografia: Area di Ricerca di Roma-Montelibretti, Via Salaria Km 29,300, CP 10, 00016 Monterotondo Stazione (Rome); tel. 06-90625328; fax 06-90625849; f. 1968; Dir Dssa L. OSSICINI.

Istituto di Strutturistica Chimica 'Giordano Giacomello': Area di Ricerca di Roma-Montelibretti, Via Salaria Km 29,300, CP 10, 00016 Monterotondo Stazione (Rome); tel. 06-906721; fax 06-90625849; f. 1968; Dir Dott. S. CERRINI.

Istituto di Chimica Nucleare: Area di Ricerca di Roma-Montelibretti, Via Salaria Km 29,300, CP 10, 00016 Monterotondo Stazione (Rome); tel. 06-90625111; fax 06-90672238; f. 1968; Dir Dott. G. ANGELINI.

Istituto di Metodologie Avanzate Inorganiche: Area di Ricerca di Roma-Montelibretti, Via Salaria Km 29,300, CP 10, 00016 Monterotondo Stazione (Rome); tel. 06-906721; fax 06-90672238; f. 1969; Dir Dott. M. PAGANNONE.

Istituto per l'Applicazione delle Tecniche Chimiche Avanzate ai Problemi Agrobiologici: Via Vienna 2, 07100 Sassari; tel. 079-210162; fax 079-218497; f. 1981; Dir Dott. GIANLUIGI CASALONE.

Istituto per la Chimica e la Tecnologia dei Materiali Polimerici: c/o Dipartimento di Scienze Chimiche, Università, Viale A. Doria 6, 95125 Catania; tel. 095-339926; fax 095-221541; f. 1981; Dir Prof. G. MONTAUDO.

Istituto per lo Studio delle Sostanze Naturali di Interesse Alimentare e Chimico-Farmaceutico: Via del Santuario 110, 95028 Valverde (Catania); tel. 095-7212139; fax 095-7212141; f. 1981; Dir Prof. M. PIATTELLI.

Istituto di Ricerche sui Metodi e Processi Chimici per la Trasformazione e l'Accumulo dell'Energia: c/o Cattedra di Chimica Industriale, Università, Via Salita S. Lucia sopra Contesse 39, Pistunina, 98126 Messina; tel. 090-624200; fax 090-601011; f. 1981; Dir Dott. GAETANO CACCIOLA.

Istituto di Chimica Fisica Applicata dei Materiali: Area di Ricerca di Genova, Via de Marini 6, Torre di Francia, 16149 Genoa; tel. 010-64751; f. 1982; Dir Dott. A. PASSERONE.

Istituto di Chimica Analitica Strumentale: c/o Dipartimento di Chimica e Chimica Industriale, Università, Via Risorgimento 35, 56126 Pisa; tel. 050-501224; fax 050-502589; f. 1983; Dir Prof. GIORGIO RASPI.

Istituto di Chimica e Tecnologia dei Prodotti Naturali: c/o Dipartimento di Chimica Inorganica, Università, Via Archirafi 26/28, 90123 Palermo; tel. 091-6162920; Dir Prof. G. DEGANELLO.

Istituto per i Materiali Speciali: Area di Ricerca di Potenza, CP 27, 85050 Tito Scalo

(Potenza); tel. 0971-427211; fax 0971-427222; Dir Profa A. GIARDINI.

Istituto di Ricerca su Membrane e Modellistica di Reattori Chimici: c/o Dipartimento di Chimica, Università della Calabria, 87030 Arcavacata di Rende (Cosenza); tel. 0984-402101; fax 0984-402103; Dir Prof. E. DRIOLI.

Istituto per la Tecnologia dei Materiali Compositi: c/o Facoltà di Ingegneria, Università 'Federico II', Piazzale Tecchio, 80125 Naples; tel. 081-7682201; Dir Prof. L. NICOLAIS.

Istituto di Studi Chimico-Fisici di Macromolecole Sintetiche e Naturali: Area di ricerca di Genova, Via De Marini 6, Torre di Francia, 16149 Genoa; tel. 010-64751; fax 010-6475880; Dir Dott. A. PERICO.

Centro di Studio sulle Sostanze Organiche Naturali: c/o Dipartimento di Chimica, Politecnico, Via L. Mancinelli 7, 20131 Milan; tel. 02-23993044; fax 02-23993080; Dir Prof. P. BRAVO.

Centro di Studio sulla Sintesi e la Struttura dei Composti dei Metalli di Transizione nei Bassi Stati di Ossidazione: c/o Dipartimento di Chimica Inorganica, Metallorganica e Analitica, Università, Via Venezian 21, 20133 Milan; tel. 02-70600163; fax 02-2362748; Dir Dott. R. PSARO.

Centro di Studio per la Sintesi e la Stereochimica di Speciali Sistemi Organici: c/o Istituto di Chimica Industriale, Università, Via Camillo Golgi 19, 20133 Milan; tel. 02-2666352; fax 02-2364369; Dir Prof. FERNANDO MONTANARI.

Centro di Studio sui Processi Elettrodici: c/o Dipartimento di Chimica Fisica Applicata, Politecnico, Via L. Mancinelli 7, 20131 Milan; tel. 02-23993172; fax 02-23993180; Dir Profa LUISA PERALDO BICELLI.

Centro per lo Studio sulle Relazioni tra Struttura e Reattività Chimica: c/o Istituto di Chimica Fisica, Università, Via Camillo Golgi 19, 20133 Milan; tel. 02-26603273; fax 02-70638129; Dir Dott. STEFANIN POLEZZO.

Centro di Studio per la Chimica dei Composti Cicloalifatici ed Aromatici: c/o Istituto di Chimica Organica, Università, Palazzo delle Scienze, Corso Europa, 16132 Genoa; tel. 010-3538201; fax 010-3538218; Dir Prof. GIUSEPPE GUANTI.

Centro di Studio per la Chimica e Tecnologia dei Composti Metallorganici degli Elementi di Transizione: c/o Istituto di Chimica Industriale, Università, Via Marzolo 9, 35131 Padua; tel. 049-35205; fax 049-831680; Dir Dotta ROBERTA BERTANI.

Centro di Studio sui Meccanismi di Reazioni Organiche: C/o Dipartimento di Chimica Organica, Università, Via Marzolo 1, 35131 Padua; tel. 049-831237; fax 049-831222; Dir Prof. GIORGIO MODENA.

Centro di Studio sulla Stabilità e Reattività dei Composti di Coordinazione: c/o Dipartimento di Chimica Inorganica, Metallorganica e Analitica, Università, Via Marzolo 1, 35131 Padua; tel. 049-831307; fax 049-831249; Dir Prof. EUGENIO TONDELLO.

Centro di Studio sulla Chimica del Farmaco e dei Prodotti Biologicamente Attivi: c/o Dipartimento di Scienze Farmaceutiche, Università, Via Marzolo 5, 35131 Padua; tel. 049-831623; fax 049-831660; Dir Prof. F. DALL'ACQUA.

Centro di Studio Sugli Stati Molecolari Radicalici ed Eccitati: c/o Dipartimento di Chimica Fisica, Università, Via Loredan 2, 35131 Padua; tel. 049-8755456; fax 049-8275135; Dir Prof. GIOVANNI GIACOMETTI.

Centro di Studio per la Fisica delle Macromolecole: C/o Dipartimento di Chimica "G. Ciamician", Università, Via Selmi 2, 40126 Bologna; tel. 051-259450; fax 051-259456; Dir Profa GIULIANA CARDILLO.

Centro di Studio su Fotoreattività e Catalisi: c/o Dipartimento di Chimica, Università, Via Luigi Borsari 46, 44100 Ferrara; tel. 0532-291180; fax 0532-40709; Dir Prof. ORAZIO TRAVERSO.

Centro di Studio sulla Chimica e Struttura dei Composti Eterociclici e Loro Applicazioni: c/o Dipartimento di Chimica Organica, Università, Via Gino Capponi 9, 50121 Florence; tel. 055-2479985; fax 055-2476964; Dir Prof. FRANCESCO DE SARLO.

Centro di Studi sui Processi Ionici di Polimerizzazione e Proprietà Fisiche e Tecniche di Sistemi di Macromolecole: c/o Dipartimento di Ingegneria Chimica, Università, Via Diotisalvi 2, 56126 Pisa; tel. 050-511111; fax 050-511266; Dir Prof. ENZO BUTTA.

Centro di Studio per l'Elettrochimica e la Chimica Fisica delle Interfasi: C/o Dipartimento di Ingegneria Chimica, Università "La Sapienza", Via del Castro Laurenziano 7, 00161 Rome; tel. 06-49766744; fax 06-49766749; Dir Prof. ITALO CARELLI.

Centro di Studio sulla Struttura e Attività Catalitica dei Sistemi di Ossidi: c/o Dipartimento di Chimica, Università "La Sapienza", Piazzale Aldo Moro 5, 00185 Rome; tel. 06-4451242; fax 06-44661954; Dir Prof. DANTE CORDISCHI.

Centro di Studio per la Termodinamica Chimica alle Alte Temperature: c/o Dipartimento di Chimica, Univ. "La Sapienza", Piazzale Aldo Moro 5, 00185 Rome; tel. 06-4462950; fax 06-4462950; Dir Prof. GIOVANNI DE MARIA.

Centro di Studio per la Chimica delle Sostanze Organiche Naturali: c/o Dipartimento di Chimica, Univ. "La Sapienza", Piazzale Aldo Moro 5, 00185 Rome; tel. 06-490422; fax 06-490631; Dir Dott. PAOLO BOVICELLI.

Centro di Studio per la Chimica del Farmaco: c/o Dipartimento di Studi Farmaceutici, Università "La Sapienza", Piazzale Aldo Moro 5, 00185 Rome; tel. 06-49913654; fax 06-491491; Dir Prof. AURELIO ROMEO.

Centro di Studio sui Meccanismi di Reazione: c/o Dipartimento di Chimica, Università "La Sapienza", Piazzale Aldo Moro 2, 00185 Rome; tel. 06-4957808; fax 06-490631; Dir Prof. LUIGI MANDOLINI.

Centro di Studio per la Strutturistica Diffrattometrica: c/o Istituti di Strutturistica Chimica e Chimica Generale, Università, Viale delle Scienze, 43100 Parma; tel. 0521-905552; fax 0521-905556; Dir Prof. GIOVANNI DARIO ANDREETTI.

Centro di Studio per la Chimica dei Plasmi: c/o Dipartimento di Chimica, Università, Via Re David 200, Traversa 4, 70126 Bari; tel. 080-5580707; fax 080-5442024; Dir Prof. MARIO CAPITELLI.

Centro di Studio per la Sintesi, le Proprietà Chimiche e le Proprietà Fisiche di Macromolecole Stereordinate ed Otticamente Attive: c/o Dipartimento di Chimica e Chimica Industriale, Università, Via Risorgimento 35, 56126 Pisa; tel. 050-918111; fax 050-918260; Dir Prof. PIERO SALVADORI.

Centro di Studio sui Biopolimeri: c/o Dipartimento di Chimica Organica, Università, Via Marzolo 1, 35131 Padua; tel. 049-831232; fax 049-831222; Dir Prof. MARIO MAMMI.

Centro di Studio per la Radiochimica ed Analisi per Attivazione: c/o Dipartimento di Chimica Generale ed Inorganica, Università, Viale Taramelli 12, 27100 Pavia; tel. 0382-526252; fax 0382-423578; Dir Dott. MARIO GALLORINI.

Centro di Studio per la Termodinamica e l'Elettrochimica dei Sistemi Salini Fusi e Solidi: c/o Istituto di Chimica Fisica, Università, Viale Taramelli 16, 27100 Pavia; tel. 0382-392216; fax 0382-392575; Dir Prof. ALDO MAGISTRIS.

Centro di Studio sulle Metodologie Innovative di Sintesi Organiche: c/o Dipartimento di Chimica, Università, Via Amendola 173, 70126 Bari; tel. 080-242072; fax 080-242129; Dir Prof. FRANCESCO NASO.

Centro di Studio sulla Chimica e le Tecnologie per l'Ambiente: C/o Dipartimento di Scienze Ambientali, Università, Calle Larga Santa Marta 2137, Dorsoduro, 30123 Venice; tel. 041-5298564; Dir Prof. PAOLO CESCON.

Centro di Studi Chimico-Fisici Sull' Interazione Luce/Materia: C/o Dipartimento di Chimica, Università, Via Orabona 4, 70126 Bari; Dir Prof. MARIO DELLA MONICA.

Institutes and study centres in biological and medical sciences:

Istituto de Neuroscienze e Bioimmagini: Via Mario Bianco 9, 20131 Milan; tel. 02-2840227; fax 02-2610846; Dir Prof. F. FAZIO.

Istituto di Psicologia: Viale Marx 15, 00137 Rome; tel. 06-8292626; fax 06-824737; Dir Prof. D. PARISI.

Istituto di Fisiopatologia Respiratoria: c/o Ospedale 'V. Cervello', Via Trabucco 180, 90146 Palermo; tel. 091-6882879; fax 091-6882165; Dir Prof. G. BONSIGNORE.

Istituto di Fisiologia Clinica: Via P. Savi 8, 56126 Pisa; tel. 050-583111; fax 050-553461; f. 1968; Dir Prof. L. DONATO.

Istituto di Neurofisiologia: Via San Zeno 51, 56127 Pisa; tel. 050-559711; fax 050-559725; f. 1968; Dir Prof. L. MAFFEI.

Istituto di Mutagenesi e Differenziamento: Via Svezia 10, 56124 Pisa; tel. 050-574161; fax 050-576661; f. 1968; Dir Prof. R. PAOLO REVOLTELLA.

Istituto di Biologia Cellulare: Viale Marx 43, 00137 Rome; tel. 06-8293879; fax 06-8273287; f. 1969; Dir Prof. G. TOCCHINI VALENTINI.

Istituto di Psicobiologia e Psicofarmacologia: Via Reno 1, 00198 Rome; tel. 06-85353772; fax 06-8553561; f. 1969; Dir Prof. A. OLIVERIO.

Istituto di Ricerche sulle Talassemie ed Anemie Mediterranee: c/o Istituto di Clinica Medica, Università, Via Ospedale 107, 09124 Cagliari; tel. 070-656937; f. 1981; Dir Prof. ANTONIO CAO.

Istituto di Biologia dello Sviluppo: C/o Dipartimento di Biologia Cellulare e dello Sviluppo, Università, Via Archirafi 20, 90123 Palermo; tel. 091-6165752; fax 091-6165665; f. 1981; Dir Prof. D. GERACI.

Istituto di Citomorfologia Normale e Patologica: C/o Ist. di Anatomia Umana Normale, Facoltà di Medicina e Chirurgia, Università, Località Madonna delle Piane, 66100 Chieti; tel. 0871-59541; f. 1981; Dir Prof. N. MARALDI.

Istituto sulla Tipizzazione Tissutale e Problemi della Dialisi: C/o Ente Ospedaliero 'S. Maria di Collemaggio', 67100 l'Aquila; tel. 0862-27129; fax 0862-410758; f. 1981; Dir Prof. D. ADORNO.

Istituto di Medicina Sperimentale e Biotecnologie: Via F. Cervi 1, 87100 Cosenza; tel. 0984-391106; fax 0984-391106; f. 1981; Dir Prof. ALDO QUATTRONE.

Istituto di Medicina Sperimentale: Viale Marx 15, 00137 Rome; tel. 06-86894953; fax 06-822203; f. 1984; Dir Prof. G. RAVAGNAN.

Istituto di Fisiopatologia Respiratoria: C/o Ospedale 'V. Cervello', Via Trabucco 180, 90146 Palermo; tel. 091-6882879; fax 091-6882165; Dir Prof. G. BONSIGNORE.

Istituto di Tecnologie Biomediche Avanzate: Via Ampère 56, 20131 Milan; tel. 02-70643351; fax 02-2663030; Dir Prof. P. CERRETELLI.

Istituto di Neurobiologia: Viale Marx 15, 00137 Rome; tel. 06-86090246; fax 06-86090370; Dir Prof. PIETRO CALISSANO.

Istituto di Scienze e Tecnologia dello Sport: c/o Ospedale 'V. Cervello', Via Trabucco 180, 90146 Palermo; tel. 091-6882879; fax 091-6882165; Dir Prof. GIUSEPPE LA GRUTTA.

Istituto di Metodologie Diagnostiche Avanzate: c/o Istituto di Patologia Generale, Università, Corso Tukory 211, 90134 Palermo; tel. 091-598474; fax 091-598474; Dir Prof. A. SALERNO.

Istituto di Bioimmagini e Fisiopatologia del Sistema Nervoso Centrale: Area di ricerca di Catania, Piazza Roma 2, 95123 Catania; tel. 095-551580; fax 095-551582; Dir Prof. V. ALBANESE.

Istituto di Biotecnologie Applicate alla Farmacologia: C/o Facoltà di Farmacia, Complesso 'Ninì Barbieri', 88021 Roccelletta di Borgia (Catanzaro); tel. 0961-391157; fax 0961-391490; Dir Prof. DOMENICANTONIO ROTIROTI.

Istituto per lo Studio della Patologia del Sangue e degli Organi Emopoietici: c/o Istituto di Ematologia ed Endocrinologia, Università, Viale S. Pietro 12, 07100 Sassari; tel. 079-228282; Dir Prof. M. LONGINOTTI.

Centro di Studio dell'Immunogenetica e l'Oncologia Sperimentale: C/o Dipartimento di Genetica, Biologia e Chimica Fisica, Università, Via Santena 19, 10126 Turin; tel. 011-6960532; fax 011-6960147; Dir Prof. GUIDO FORNI.

Centro di Studio sulla Biologia Cellulare e Molecolare delle Piante: c/o Dipartimento di Biologia, Università, Via Celoria 26, 20133 Milan; tel. 02-26604390; fax 02-2361070; Dir Prof. GIORGIO FORTI.

Centro per lo Studio della Farmacologia Cellulare e Molecolare: c/o Dipartimento di Farmacologia, Chemioterapia e Tossicologia Medica, Università, Via Vanvitelli 32, 20129 Milan; tel. 02-70146254; fax 02-7490574; Dir Prof. FRANCESCO CLEMENTI.

Centro di Studio per le Ricerche Cardiovascolari: c/o Cattedra di Cardiologia, Università, Via C. Parea 4, 20138 Milan; tel. 02-58011039; fax 02-504667; Dir Prof. MAURIZIO GUAZZI.

Centro di Studio sulla Patologia Cellulare: c/o Istituto di Patologia Generale, Università, Via Mangiagalli 31, 20133 Milan; tel. 02-2367484; fax 02-26681092; Dir Prof. UGO DEL MONTE.

Centro di Studio sulla Patologia della Mammella e la Produzione Igienica del Latte: c/o Ist. di Malattie Infettive, Profilassi e Polizia Veterin., Università, Via Celoria 10, 20133 Milan; tel. 02-235338; fax 02-2367788; Dir Prof. GIANFRANCO RUFFO.

Centro di Studio per la Neurofisiologia Cerebrale: c/o Clinica Neurologica, Università, Via de Toni 5, 16132 Genoa; tel. 010-509058; fax 010-354180; Dir Prof. MICHELE ABBRUZZESE.

Centro di Studio per la Biologia e Fisiopatologia Muscolare: c/o Dipartimento di Scienze Biomediche Sperimentali, Università, Via Trieste 75, 35121 Padua; tel. 049-8286538; fax 049-8286576; Dir Prof. STEFANO SCHIAFFINO.

Centro di Studio per la Fisiologia e Biochimica delle Metalloproteine: c/o Dipartimento di Biologia, Università, Via Trieste 75, 35121 Padua; tel. 049-8276345; fax 049-8276344; Dir Profa ANNA MAGALDI.

Centro di Studio sulla Fisiologia Mitocondriale: c/o Dipartimento di Scienze Biomediche Sperimentali, Università, Via Trieste 75, 35121 Padua; tel. 049-8276073; fax 049-8276049; Dir Prof. GIOVANNI FELICE AZZONE.

Centro di Studio per la Faunistica ed Ecologia Tropicali: c/o Dipartimento di Biologia Animale e Genetica, Università, Via Romana 17, 50125 Florence; tel. 055-222389; fax 055-222565; Dir Dott. FRANCO FERRARA.

Centro di Studio sulla Genetica Evoluzionistica: c/o Dip. di Genetica e Biologia Molecolare, Università "La Sapienza", Piazzale Aldo Moro 5, 00185 Rome; tel. 06-49912594; fax 06-4456866; Dir Dssa PAOLA LUCARELLI.

Centro di Studio sulla Biologia Molecolare: C/o Dipart. di Scienze Biochimiche, Università "La Sapienza", Piazzale Aldo Moro 5, 00185 Rome; tel. 06-4450349; fax 06-4440062; Dir Profa EMILIA CHIANCONE.

Centro di Studio per gli Acidi Nucleici: c/o Dip. di Genetica e Biologia Molecolare, Università "La Sapienza", Piazzale Aldo Moro 5, 00185 Rome; tel. 06-491183; Dir Prof. ERNESTO DE MAURO.

Centro di Studio per la Fisiopatologia dello Shock: c/o Istituto di Clinica Chirurgica, Policlinico "Agostino Gemelli", Largo Agostino Gemelli 8, 00168 Rome; tel. 06-3385446; fax 06-3385446; Dir Prof. MARCO CASTAGNETO.

Centro di Studio per la Endocrinologia e l'Oncologia Sperimentale: Dipartimento di Biologia e Patologia Cellulare e Molecolare, Università 'Federico II', Via Sergio Pansini 5, 80131 Naples; tel. 081-5453028; fax 081-7701016; Dir Prof. EDUARDO CONSIGLIO.

Centro di Studio sui Mitocondri e Metabolismo Energetico: c/o Istituto di Chimica Biologica, Facoltà di Scienze MM.FF.NN., Università, Via Amendola 165/A, 70126 Bari; tel. 080-243390; fax 080-243317; Dir Profa ERSILIA MARRA.

Centro di Studio per l'Istochimica: c/o Dipartimento di biologia animale, Università, Piazza Botta 10, 27100 Pavia; tel. 0382-22347; Dir Prof. GIOVANNI BOTTIROLI.

Centro di Fisiologia Clinica: c/o Reparto Nefrologico "G. Monasterio", Ospedali Riuniti, Via Sbarre Inferiori 39, 89131 Reggio Calabria; tel. 0965-57048; fax 0965-56005; Dir Dott. CARMINE ZOCCALI.

Centro per lo Studio delle Cellule Germinali: c/o Università, Via Tommaso Pendola 62, 53100 Siena; tel. 0577-287006; fax 0577-44474; Dir. Prof. BACCIO BACCETTI.

Centro per lo Studio dell' Invecchiamento: C/o Istituto di Medicina Interna, Università, Via Nicolò Giustiniani 2, 35128 Padua; tel. 049-8212150; Dir Prof. GAETANO CREPALDI.

Centro di Studio per la Medicina Nucleare: C/o Istituto di Scienze Radiologiche, Facoltà di Medicina e Chirurgia, Università 'Federico II', Via Sergio Pansini 5, 80131 Naples; Dir Prof. MARCO SALVATORE.

Centro per la Neurofarmacologia: C/o Dipartimento di Neuroscienze, Università, Via Porcell 4, 09100 Cagliari; tel. 070-669014; Dir. Prof. GIAN LUIGI GESSA.

Institutes and study centres in geological and mineralogical sciences:

Istituto di Ricerca per la Protezione Idrogeologica nell'Italia Meridionale ed Insulare: Via Verdi 1, 87030 Roges di Rende (Cosenza); tel. 0984-839131; fax 0984-837382; Dir Dott. MARIO GOVI.

Istituto Internazionale per le Ricerche Geotermiche: Piazza Solferino 2, 56126 Pisa; tel. 050-41503; fax 050-47055; Dir Dott. P. SQUARCI.

Istituto Internazionale di Vulcanologia: Piazza Roma 2, 95123 Catania; tel. 095-448746; fax 095-435801; Dir Prof. LETTERIO VILLARI.

Istituto di Geocronologia e Geochimica Isotopica: Via Cardinale Maffi 36, 56127 Pisa; tel. 050-560430; fax 050-589008; f. 1970; Dir Prof. G. FERRARA.

Istituto per il Trattamento dei Minerali: Via Bolognola 7 (Via Salaria Km 11,600), 00138 Rome; tel. 06-8804361; fax 06-8804463; f. 1968; Dir Profa A. M. MARABINI.

Istituto di Ricerca per la Protezione Idrogeologica nel Bacino Padano: Area di Ricerca di Torino, Strada delle Cacce 73, 10135 Turin; tel. 011-343428; fax 011-343574; f. 1970; Dir Dott. DOMENICO TROPEANO.

Istituto di Geologia Marina: Area di ricerca di Bologna, Via P. Gobetti 101, 40129 Bologna; tel. 051-6398891; fax 051-6398940; f. 1968; Dir Prof. ENRICO BONATTI.

Istituto di Ricerca sul Rischio Sismico: Via A. M. Ampere 56, 20131 Milan; tel. 02-70643624; fax 02-26680987; f. 1969; Dir Prof. V. PETRINI.

Istituto di Ricerca per la Protezione Idrogeologica nei Bacini dell'Italia Nord-Orientale: Area di Ricerca di Padova, Corso Stati Uniti 4, 35020 Padua; tel. 049-8295803; fax 049-8295827; f. 1969; Dir Dott. S. SILVANO.

Istituto di Ricerca per la Protezione Idrogeologica nell'Italia Centrale: Via Madonna Alta 126, 06128 Perugia; tel. 075-5006730; fax 075-5051325; f. 1970; Dir Prof. L. UBERTINI.

Istituto di Geochimica dei Fluidi: Via Torino 27D, 90133 Palermo; tel. 091-6167936; fax 091-6168703; f. 1981; Dir Prof. M. VALENZA.

Istituto di Ricerca 'Geomare Sud': Via Amerigo Vespucci 9, 80142 Naples; Dir Prof. B. D'ARGENIO.

Istituto di Ricerca per lo Sviluppo di Metodologie Cristallografiche: c/o Dipartimento Geomineralogico, Università, Via Re David 200, IV Traversa, 70125 Bari; tel. 080-242556; Dir Prof. C. GIACOVAZZO.

Istituto di Ricerca sulle Argille: Area di ricerca di Potenza, CP 27, 85050 Tito Scalo (Potenza); tel. 0971-485106; fax 0971-427222; Dir Prof. G. PICCARRETA.

Centro di Studi per la Fisica delle Rocce e le Geotecnologie: c/o Dipartimento Georisorse e Territorio, Politecnico, Corso Duca degli Abruzzi 24, 10129 Turin; tel. 011-5647617; fax 011-5647679; Dir Prof. RENATO MANCINI.

Centro di Studi sulla Geodinamica delle Catene Collisionali: C/o Dipartimento di Scienze della Terra, Università,

Via Accademia delle Scienze 5, 10123 Turin; tel. 011-518928; Dir Dott. RICCARDO POLINO.

Centro di Studio per la Geodinamica Alpina e Quaternaria: c/o Dipartimento di Scienze della Terra, Università, Via Mangiagalli 34, 20133 Milan; tel. 02-236981; fax 02-70638261; Dir Dott. PIETRO MARIO ROSSI.

Centro di Studio sulla Cristallochimica e Cristallografia: c/o Dipartimento di Scienze della Terra, Università, Via Abbiategrasso 209, 27100 Pavia; tel. 0382-505753; fax 0382-505887; Dir Prof. ELIO CANNILLO.

Centro di Studio per la Geodinamica Alpina: C/o Dipartimento di Mineralogia e Petrologia, Università, Corso Garibaldi 37, 35122 Padua; tel. 049-651156; fax 049-8753813; Dir Prof. F. PAOLO SASSI.

Centro di Studio per la Minerogenesi e la Geochimica Applicata: c/o Dipartimento di Scienze della Terra, Università, Via G. La Pira 4, 50121 Florence; tel. 055-2757309; Dir Prof. GIAMPIERO BERNARDINI.

Centro di Studio di Geologia dell'Appennino e delle Catene Premediterranee: c/o Dipartimento di Scienze della Terra, Università, Via G. La Pira 4, 50121 Florence; tel. 055-2757515; fax 055-2302302; Dir Dotta GIOVANNA MORATTI.

Centro di Studio per la Geologia Strutturale e Dinamica dell'Appennino: c/o Dipartimento di Scienze della Terra, Università, Via Santa Maria 53, 56126 Pisa; tel. 050-847111; fax 050-500932; Dir Dott. ANTONIO RAU.

Centro di Studio per il Quaternario e l'Evoluzione Ambientale: C/o Dipartimento di Scienze della Terra, Università 'La Sapienza', Piazzale Aldo Moro 5, 00185 Rome; tel. 06-4463508; fax 06-4468632; Dir Dott. GIUSEPPE CAVARRETTA.

Centro di Studio per la Geologia Tecnica: c/o Istituto di Geologia Applicata, Facoltà di Ingegneria, Università "La Sapienza", Via Eudossiana 18, 00184 Rome; tel. 06-44585829; fax 06-44585016; Dir Prof. CARLO BOSI.

Centro di Studio per gli Equilibri Sperimentali in Minerali e Rocce: c/o Istituto di Petrografia, Università 'La Sapienza', Piazzale Aldo Moro 5, 00185 Rome; tel. 06-4463731; fax 06-4454729; Dir Prof. RAFFAELLO TRIGILA.

Centro di Studi Geominerari e Mineralurgici: c/o Dipartimento di Ingegneria Mineraria e Mineralurgica, Università, Piazza d'Armi, 09123 Cagliari; tel. 070-280233; fax 070-272031; Dir Dott. MICHELE AGUS.

Centro di Studio sulle Risorse Idriche e la Salvaguardia del Territorio: c/o Istituto di Geologia Applicata e Geotecnica, Facoltà di Ingegneria, Politecnico, Via Re David 200, 70125 Bari; tel. 080-228137; Dir Prof. VINCENZO COTECCHIA.

Institutes and study centres in agricultural sciences:

Istituto di Nematologia Agraria Applicata ai Vegetali: Via G. Amendola 168/5, Traversa 174, 70126 Bari; tel. 080-484185; fax 080-484165; f. 1970; Dir Prof. F. LAMBERTI.

Istituto del Germoplasma: c/o Fac. di Agraria, Università, Via G. Amendola 165A, 70126 Bari; tel. 080-5583463; fax 080-5587566; f. 1970; Dir Dott. ALVARO DONADIO.

Istituto per lo Studio dei Problemi Agronomici dell'Irrigazione nel Mezzogiorno: Via Cupa Patacca 85, 80056 Ercolano (Naples); tel. 081-7717325; fax 081-7718045; f. 1970; Dir Prof. P. TEDESCHI.

Istituto di Ricerche sull'Adattamento dei Bovini e dei Bufali all'Ambiente del Mezzogiorno: c/o Ist. Tecnico Agrario Statale 'E. de Cillis', Via Argine 1085, 80147 Ponticelli (Naples); tel. 081-5771471; fax 081-5965291; f. 1970; Dir Dott. L. FERRARA.

Istituto per le Biosintesi Vegetali nelle Piante di Interesse Agrario: Via E. Bassini 15, 20133 Milan; tel. 02-2365330; fax 02-2362946; f. 1974; Dir Prof. A. BERTANI.

Istituto per la Chimica del Terreno: Via Corridoni 78, 56125 Pisa; tel. 050-48337; fax 050-500631; f. 1969; Dir Dott. G. VIGNA GUIDI.

Istituto di Biochimica ed Ecofisiologia Vegetali: Area di Ricerca di Roma, Montelibretti, Via Salaria Km 29,300, CP 10, 00016 Monterotondo Stazione (Rome); tel. 06-906721; fax 06-9064492; f. 1968; Dir Dott. G. DI MARCO.

Istituto per la Fisiologia della Maturazione e della Conservazione del Frutto delle Specie Arboree Mediterranee: Via dei Mille 48, 07100 Sassari; tel. 079-233466; fax 079-232047; f. 1981; Dir Prof. M. AGABBIO.

Istituto di Fitovirologia Applicata: Area di Ricerca di Torino, Strada delle Cacce 73, 10135 Turin; tel. 011-39771; fax 011-343809; f. 1968; Dir Prof. M. CONTI.

Istituto per l'Agrometeorologia e l'Analisi Ambientale Applicata all'Agricoltura: c/o Istituto di Agronomia Generale e Coltivazioni Erbacee, Facoltà di Agraria, Università, Piazzale delle Cascine 18, 50144 Florence; tel. 055-354895; fax 055-332472; f. 1981; Dir Prof. G. MARACCHI.

Istituto Tossine e Micotossine da Parassiti Vegetali: Viale Luigi Einaudi 51, 70125 Bari; tel. 080-338968; f. 1970; Dir Dott. A. VISCONTI.

Istituto di Ecologia e Idrologia Forestale: Via Alessandro Volta 106/C, 87030 Castiglione Scalo (Cosenza); tel. 0984-837323; fax 0984-838625; f. 1981; Dir Prof. FRANCESCO IOVINO.

Istituto sulla Propagazione delle Specie Legnose: Via Ponte di Formicola 76, 50018 Scandicci (Florence); tel. 055-754718; fax 055-755121; f. 1970; Dir Prof. GIANCARLO ROSELLI.

Istituto Miglioramento Genetico delle Piante Forestali: Via A. Vannucci 13, 50134 Florence; tel. 055-461071; fax 055-486604; f. 1983; Dir Prof. R. GIANNINI.

Istituto per l'Agroselvicoltura: Via G. Marconi 2, Villa Paolina, 05010 Porano (Terni); tel. 0763-65122; fax 0763-65330; f. 1983; Dir Dott. E. BRUGNOLI.

Istituto per la Difesa e la Valorizzazione del Germoplasma Animale: c/o Ist. di Zootecnia Generale, Fac. Medicina Veterinaria, Università, Via Celoria 10, 20133 Milan; tel. 02-26680350; f. 1983; Dir Prof. G. PAGNACCO.

Istituto di Ricerche sull'Olivicoltura: Zona C.A.I., Madonna Alta, 06128 Perugia; tel. 075-754271; fax 075-5000286; Dir Dott. G. FONTANAZZA.

Istituto di Ricerche sul Miglioramento Genetico delle Piante Foraggere: Via Madonna Alta 130, 06128 Perugia; tel. 075-5003074; fax 075-5005228; Dir Dott. SERGIO ARCIONI.

Istituto di Orticoltura e Colture Industriali: Area di Ricerca di Potenza, CP 27, 85050 Tito Scalo (Potenza); tel. 0971-427211; Dir Prof. V. LATTANZIO.

Istituto sull' Orticoltura Industriale: C/o Istituto di Agronomia, Università, Via G. Amendola 165/A, 70126 Bari; tel. 080-242976; Dir Prof. V. V. BIANCO.

Istituto di Ecofisiologia delle Piante Arboree da Frutto: Area di ricerca di Bologna, Via P. Gobetti 101, 40129 Bologna; tel. 051-6399013; Dir Dotta G. CRISTOFERI.

Istituto di Ricerca sulle Biotecnologie Agro-alimentari: c/o Dipartimento di Biologia, Università, Provinciale Lecce/Monteroni, 73100 Lecce; tel. 0832-420000; fax 0832-320602; Dir Dott. G. ZACHEO.

Istituto di Ricerca per il Monitoraggio degli Agro-ecosistemi: Via Funtana di Lu Colbu 4/A, Loc. Lu Traineddu, 07100 Sassari; tel. 079-268246; fax 079-268248; Dir Dott. F. BENINCASA.

Centro di Studio sulla Micologia del Terreno: c/o Dipartimento di Biologia Vegetale, Università, Viale P.A. Mattioli 25, 10125 Turin; tel. 011-6502927; fax 011-655839; Dir. Profa PAOLA BONFANTE.

Centro di Studio per il Miglioramento Genetico e la Biologia della Vite: C/o Dipartimento di Colture Arboree, Università, Via Pietro Giuria 15, 10126 Turin; tel. 011-6503757; fax 011-6508577; Dir Dotta GIULIANA GAY.

Centro di Studio per l'Alimentazione degli Animali in Produzione Zootecnica: C/o Dipartimento di Produzioni Animali, Epidemiologia ed Ecologia, Università, Via Nizza 52, 10126 Turin; tel. 011-6504980; fax 011-655445; Dir Prof. SILVANO MALETTO.

Centro di Studio sulla Biologia ed il Controllo delle Piante Infestanti: C/o Istituto di Agronomia Generale e Coltivazioni Erbacee, Università, Via Gradenigo 6, 35131 Padua; tel. 049-8071348; fax 049-8070850; Dir Prof. GIUSEPPE ZANIN.

Centro di Studio sulla Gestione dei Sistemi Agricoli e Territoriali: C/o Istituto di Estimo Rurale e Contabilità, Università, Via Filippo Re 10, 40126 Bologna; tel. 051-243204; fax 051-252187; Dir Prof. MAURIZIO GRILLENZONI.

Centro di Studio dei Fitofarmaci: C/o Dip. di Protezione e Valorizzazione Agroalimentare, Università, Via Filippo Re 8, 40126 Bologna; tel. 051-351407; fax 051-351364; Dir Prof. AUGUSTO CESARI.

Centro di Studio per la Conservazione dei Foraggi: c/o Istituto di Agronomia Generale e Coltivazioni Erbacee, Università, Via Filippo Re 8, 40126 Bologna; tel. 051-351515; fax 051-351511; Dir Prof. ALLEGRO GIARDINI.

Centro di Studio per la Patologia delle Specie Legnose Montane: c/o Istituto di Patologia e Zoologia Forestale e Agraria, Facoltà di Agraria, Università, Piazzale delle Cascine 28, 50144 Florence; tel. 055-360546; fax 055-354786; Dir Prof. FRANCESCO MORIONDO.

Centro di Studio per i Colloidi del Suolo: C/o Dipartimento di Scienza del Suolo e Nutrizione delle Piante, Università, Piazzale delle Cascine 28, 50144 Florence; tel. 055-364491; fax 055-321148; Dir Prof. GIUSEPPE GABRIEL RISTORI.

Centro di Studio dei Microorganismi Autotrofi: c/o Dip. di Scienze e Tecnologie Alimentari e Microbiologiche, Università, Piazzale delle Cascine 27, 50144 Florence; tel. 055-360506; Dir Prof. RICCARDO MATERASSI.

Centro di Studio per la Genesi, Classificazione e Cartografia del Suolo: c/o Istituto di Geopedologia e Geologia Applicata, Facoltà di Agraria, Università, Piazzale delle Cascine 15, 50144 Florence; tel. 055-360517; fax 055-321148; Dir Dott. ERMANNO BUSONI.

Centro di Studio per la Microbiologia del Suolo: c/o Istituto di Microbiologia Agraria e Tecnica, Università, Via del Borghetto 80, 56124 Pisa; tel. 050-571561; Dir Prof. GIOVANNI PICCI.

Centro di Studio sulla Chimica e Biochimica dei Fitofarmaci: c/o Istituto di Chimica Agraria, Università, Borgo XX Giugno 72, 06121 Perugia; tel. 075-5856228; fax 075-5856239; Dir Prof. LUCIANO SCARPONI.

Centro di Studio sulle Colture Erbacee Strategiche per l'Ambiente Mediterraneo: c/o Istituto di Agronomia Generale e Coltivazioni Erbacee, Università, Via Valdisavoja 5, 95123 Catania; tel. 095-351361; fax 095-351420; Dir Prof. SALVATORE FOTI.

Centro di Studio per il Miglioramento Genetico degli Agrumi: c/o Istituto di Coltivazioni Arboree, Università, Viale delle Scienze, 90128 Palermo; tel. 091-484482; Dir Prof. FRANCESCO GIULIO CRESCIMANNO.

Centro per lo Studio Tecnologico, Bromatologico e Microbiologico del Latte: C/o Dipartimento Scienze e Tecnologie Alimentari e Microbiologiche, Università, Via Celoria 2, 20133 Milan; tel. 02-2666257; fax 02-70638625; Dir Dott. LUCIANO CECCHI.

Centro di Studio sui Pascoli Mediterranei: c/o Istituto di Agronomia Generale e Coltivazioni Erbacee, Università, Via E. De Nicola, 07100 Sassari; tel. 079-229332; fax 079-212490; Dir Prof. SALVATORE CAREDDA.

Centro di Studio sul Miglioramento Genetico degli Ortaggi: c/o Istituto di Agronomia e Coltivazioni Erbacee "Il Castello", Parco Gussone, Via Università 133, 80055 Portici (Napoli); tel. 081-7753579; fax 081-7753579; e-mail cnrmontiinacriai.criai .it; Dir Prof. LUIGI MONTI.

Centro di Studio sui Virus e Virosi delle Colture Mediterranee: C/o Dipartimento di Protezione delle Piante dalle Malattie, Università, Via Amendola 165/A, 70126 Bari; tel. 080-330244; fax 080-242813; Dir Prof. GIOVANNI MARTELLI.

Centro di Studio per il Miglioramento Sanitario delle Colture Agrarie: c/o Istituto di Patologia Vegetale, Università, Via Celoria 2, 20133 Milan; tel. 02-2666081; fax 02-70631287; Dir Prof. GIUSEPPE BELLI.

Centro di Ricerche sui Ruminanti Minori: C/o Dipartimento di Produzione Animale, Campus Universitario, Via Amendola 165/A, 70126 Bari; Dir (vacant).

Centro di Studio sulle Tecniche di Lotta Biologica: C/o Dipartimento di Entomologia e Zoologia Agraria, Universita 'Federico II', Via Università 133, 80055 Portici (Napoli); tel. 081-274766; Dir GENNARO VIGGIANI.

Institutes and study centres in engineering and architectural sciences:

Istituto per i Circuiti Elettronici: Area di ricerca di Genova, Via De Marini 6, Torre di Francia, 16149 Genoa; tel. 010-64751; fax 010-6475200; f. 1970; Dir Ing. CLAUDIO MARTINI.

Istituto per l'Automazione Navale: Area di Ricerca di Genova, Via de Marini 6, Torre di Francia, 16149 Genoa; tel. 010-64751; fax 010-6475600; f. 1970; Dir Ing. FILIPPO ALDO GRASSIA.

Istituto Motori: Piazza Barsanti e Matteucci 1, 80125 Naples; tel. 081-7177111; fax 081-2396097; f. 1968; Dir Prof. A. DI LORENZO.

Istituto per la Tecnica del Freddo: Area di Ricerca di Padova, Corso Stati Uniti 4, 35020 Padua; tel. 049-8295701; fax 049-8295649; f. 1968; Dir Ing. R. CAMPORESE.

Istituto di Sistemistica e Bioingegneria: Area di Ricerca di Padova, Corso Stati Uniti 4, 35020 Padua; tel. 049-8295702; fax 049-8295649; f. 1973; Dir Ing. GIOVANNI PACINI.

Istituto 'CNUCE': Via S. Maria 36, 56126 Pisa; tel. 050-593111; fax 050-589354; f. 1974; Dir Prof. LUCA SIMONCINI.

Istituto di Analisi dei Sistemi ed Informatica: Viale Manzoni 30, 00185 Rome; tel. 06-77161; fax 06-7716461; f. 1970; Dir Prof. L. BIANCO.

Istituto per la Sistemistica e l'Informatica: c/o Dipartimento di Sistemi, Università della Calabria, 87030 Arcavacata di Rende (Cosenza); tel. 0984-839259; Dir Prof. DOMENICO SACCA.

Istituto per la Pianificazione e la Gestione del Territorio: Via P. Castellino 111, 80131 Naples; tel. 081-7701918; f. 1981; Dir Prof. U. CARDARELLI.

Istituto per la Residenza e le Infrastrutture Sociali: Strada Crocifisso 2/B, 70126 Bari; tel. 080-481265; fax 080-482533; f. 1981; Dir Prof. G. TORTORICI.

Istituto per l'Edilizia ed il Risparmio Energetico: Via Cardinale Mariano Rampolla 8/d, 90142 Palermo; tel. 091-6374666; fax 091-6374601; f. 1981; Dir Prof. G. FRANZITTA.

Istituto per le Macchine Movimento-Terra e Veicoli Fuori Strada: Via Canal Bianco 28, 44044 Cassana (Ferrara); tel. 0532-731571; fax 0532-732250; f. 1981; Dir Ing. G. RIGAMONTI.

Istituto di Ricerca per l'Elettromagnetismo e i Componenti Elettronici: Via Diocleziano 328, 80124 Naples; tel. 081-5707999; fax 081-5705734; f. 1981; Dir Prof. G. FRANCESCHETTI.

Istituto Gas Ionizzati: Area di Ricerca di Padova, Corso Stati Uniti 4, 35020 Padua; tel. 049-8295611; fax 049-8700718; f. 1983; Dir Prof. G. MALESANI.

Istituto per la Ricerca sui Sistemi Informatici Paralleli: Via P. Castellino 111, 80131 Naples; tel. 081-5454195; fax 081-5454593; f. 1990; Dir Prof. R. VACCARO.

Centro di Studio sull'Ingegneria dei Sistemi per l'Elaborazione dell'Informazione: c/o Dipartimento di Elettronica, Politecnico, Piazza Leonardo da Vinci 32, 20133 Milan; tel. 02-23993405; fax 02-23993587; Dir Prof. RENATO STEFANELLI.

Centro di Studio per l'Interazione Operatore–Calcolatore: c/o Dipartimento di Elettronica, Informatica e Sistemistica, Università, Viale Risorgimento 2, 40136 Bologna; tel. 051-6443548; fax 051-6443540; Dir Prof. ORESTE ANDRISANO.

Centro di Studio sulle Cause di Deperimento e sui Metodi di Conservazione delle Opere d'Arte: c/o Dipartimento di Chimica Organica, Università, Via Gino Capponi 9, 50121 Florence; tel. 055-2757651; fax 055-214777; Dir Prof. FRANCO PIACENTI.

Centro di Studio per Metodi e Dispositivi per Radiotrasmissioni: C/o Dipartimento di Ingegneria dell'Informazione, Università, Via Diotisalvi 2, 56126 Pisa; tel. 050-550100; fax 050-555057; Dir Prof. MARIO MANCIANTI.

Centro di Studio sulle Cause di Deperimento e dei Metodi di Conservazione delle Opere d'Arte: c/o Dipartimento di Tecnica Edilizia, Università "La Sapienza", Via di Monte d'Oro 28, 00186 Rome; tel. 06-6878071; Dir Prof. PIERLUIGI TESTA.

Centro di Studio per la Elaborazione Numerale dei Segnali: c/o Dipartimento di Automatica e Informatica, Politecnico, Corso Duca degli Abruzzi 24, 10129 Turin; tel. 011-5647036; fax 011-541713; Dir Prof. ANGELO RAFFAELE MEO.

Centro di Studio per la Propagazione ed Antenne: c/o Dipartimeno di Elettronica, Politecnico, Corso Duca degli Abruzzi 24, 10129 Turin; tel. 011-5644020; fax 011-5644089; Dir Ing. CORRADO CUGIANI.

Centro di Studio per la Dinamica dei Fluidi: c/o Dipartimento di Ingegneria Aeronautica e Spaziale, Politecnico, Corso Duca degli Abruzzi 24, 10129 Turin; tel. 011-5646832; fax 011-5656859; Dir Dotta M. SANDRA OGGIANO.

Centro di Studio per la Televisione: c/o Istituto Elettrotecnico Nazionale "Galileo Ferraris", Strada delle Cacce 91, 10135 Turin; tel. 011-341882; fax 011-341882; Dir Prof. ERMANNO NANO.

Centro di Studio sulle Telecomunicazioni Spaziali: c/o Dipartimento di Elettronica, Politecnico, Piazza Leonardo da Vinci 32, 20133 Milan; tel. 02-23993407; fax 02-23993587; Dir Prof. GUIDO TARTARA.

Centro di Studio sulla Teoria dei Sistemi: c/o Dipartimento di Elettronica e Informazione, Politecnico, Piazza Leonardo da Vinci 32, 20133 Milan; tel. 02-23993400; fax 02-23993587; Dir Prof. ARTURO LOCATELLI.

Centro di Studio delle Cause di Deperimento e sui Metodi di Conservazione delle Opere d'Arte "Gino Bozza": c/o Dipartimento di Energetica, Politecnico, Piazza Leonardo da Vinci 32, 20133 Milan; tel. 02-23993806; fax 02-23993940; Dir Profa GIOVANNA ALESSANDRINI.

Centro di Studi sulla Affidabilità, Sicurezza e Diagnostica dei Sistemi Elettrici di Potenza: c/o Centro Universitario di Calcolo, Viale delle Scienze, 90128 Palermo; Dir Prof. VITTORIO CECCONI.

Centro di Studio sulle Reti di Elaboratori: c/o Dip. di Ingegneria Elettrica, Università, Viale delle Scienze, 90128 Palermo; tel. 091-595735; Dir Profa MARIA TORTORICI.

Institutes and study centres in historical, philosophical and philological sciences:

Istituto per gli Studi Micenei ed Egeoanatolici: Via Giano della Bella 18, 00162 Rome; tel. 06-44232313; fax 06-44237724; Dir Prof. MIROSLAVO SALVINI.

Istituto di Linguistica Computazionale: Via della Faggiola 32, 56126 Pisa; tel. 050-560481; fax 050-589055; f. 1981; Dir Prof. A. ZAMPOLLI.

Istituto per la Civiltà Fenicia e Punica: Area di Ricerca di Roma, Montelibretti, Via Salaria Km 29,300, CP 10, 00016 Monterotondo Stazione (Roma); tel. 06-90627564; f. 1983; Dir Prof. E. ACQUARO.

Istituto sui Rapporti Italo-Iberici: Via G. B. Tuveri 128, 09129 Cagliari; tel. 070-403635; fax 070-498118; f. 1983; Dir Prof. F. C. CASULA.

Istituto per l'Archeologia Etrusco-Italica: Viale di Villa Massimo 29, 00161 Rome; tel. 06-85301926; f. 1990; Dir Prof. M. CRISTOFANI.

Centro di Studi del Pensiero Filosofico del '500 e del '600 in Relazione ai Problemi della Scienza: c/o Dipartimento di Filosofia, Università, Via Albricci 9, 20122 Milan; tel. 02-8052538; fax 02-8052424; Dir Dott. GUIDO CANZIANI.

Centro di Studio sulla Filosofia Contemporanea: C/o Dipartimento di Filosofia, Università, Via Lomellini 8, 16124 Genoa; tel. 010-293511; fax 010-2471184; Dir Prof. EVANDRO AGAZZI.

Centro di Studio sulla Storia della Tecnica: c/o Istituto di Storia Moderna e Contemporanea, Università, Via Balbi 6, 16126 Genoa; tel. 010-280816; fax 010-3539826; Dir Prof. CARLO MACCAGNI.

Centro di Studio per la Dialettologia Italiana "Oronzo Parlangeli": c/o Istituto di Glottologia e Fonetica, Fac. di Lettere, Università, Via Beato Pellegrino 1, 35137 Padua; tel. 049-651688; Dir Prof. ALBERTO MIONI.

Centro di Studio per le Ricerche di Fonetica: c/o Dipartimento di Linguistica, Università, Via G. Anghinoni 10, 35121 Padua; tel. 049-8274418; fax 049-8274416; Dir Prof. ALBERTO ZAMBONI.

Centro di Studio per il Lessico Intellettuale Europeo: c/o Villa Mirafiori, Via Nomentana 118, 00161 Rome; tel. 06-86320527; Dir Prof. TULLIO GREGORY.

Centro di Studio del Pensiero Antico: c/o Villa Mirafiori, Via Nomentana 118, 00161 Rome; tel. 06-49917235; fax 06-49917237; Dir Prof. GABRIELE GIANNANTONI.

Centro di Studio sull'Archeologia Greca: c/o Istituto di Archeologia, Università, Via Antonino di Sangiuliano 262, 95124 Catania; tel. 095-316821; fax 095-326583; Dir Prof. G. RIZZA.

Centro di Studi Vichiani: C/o Dipartimento di Filosofia A. Aliotta, Università 'Federico II', Via Porta di Massa 1, 80133 Naples; tel. 081-5420276; Dir Prof. GIUSEPPE CACCIATORE.

Centro di Studi Opera del Vocabolario Italiano: C/o Accademia della Crusca, Villa Medicea di Castello, Via di Castello 46, 50141 Florence; tel. 055-452841; fax 055-4250678; Dir Prof. PIETRO BELTRAMI.

Centro per lo Studio delle Letterature e delle Culture delle Aree Emergenti: C/o Centro Linguistico Audiovisivi Universitario, Università, Via Sant' Ottavio 20, 10124 Turin; Dir Profa ANNA PAOLA MOSSETTO.

Institutes and study centres in juridical and political sciences:

Istituto per la Documentazione Giuridica: Via Panciatichi 56/16, 50127 Florence; tel. 055-431722; fax 055-4221637; Dir Prof. NICOLA PALAZZOLO.

Istituto di Studi sulle Regioni: Lungotevere delle Armi 22, 00195 Rome; tel. 06-3216061; fax 06-3216071; Dir Prof. T. MARTINES.

Istituto per lo Studio Comparato sulle Garanzie dei Diritti Fondamentali: Viale Gramsci 5, 80122 Naples; tel. 081-7611575; fax 081-7612309; f. 1981; Dir Prof. GIOVANNI MOTZO.

Istituto di Ricerca sui Sistemi Giudiziari: Via Giuseppe Petroni 33, 40126 Bologna; tel. 051-265349; fax 051-237044; Dir Prof. GIUSEPPE DI FEDERICO.

Istituto di Studi Giuridici sulla Comunità Internazionale: Corso Vittorio Emanuele II 251, 00186 Rome; tel. 06-6893009; fax 06-68308307; Dir Prof. SERGIO MARCHISIO.

Centro di Studio e Ricerche di Diritto Comparato e Straniero: c/o Istituto Internazionale per l'Unificazione del Diritto Privato, Via Panisperna 28, 00184 Rome; tel. 06-6783189; Dir Prof. MICHAEL J. BONELL.

Institutes and study centres in economic, sociological and statistical sciences:

Istituto Ricerche sull' Impresa e lo Sviluppo: Via Avogadro 8, C.P. 1381 Ferrovia, 10121 Turin; tel. 011-5601111; fax 011-5626058; f. 1972; Dir Dotta MARISA GERBI.

Istituto di Ricerche sulla Economia Mediterranea: Via Gramsci 5, 80122 Naples; tel. 081-681530; fax 081-7611157; f. 1981; Dir Dssa MARIA ROSARIA CARLI.

Istituto di Ricerche sulle Attività Terziarie: Via Michelangelo Schipa 115, 80122 Naples; tel. 081-7612130; fax 081-667318; f. 1981; Dir Prof. GIUSEPPE VITO.

Istituto di Ricerche sulla Popolazione: Viale Beethoven 56, 00144 Rome; tel. 06-5914277; fax 06-5925308; f. 1981; Dir Prof. A. GOLINI.

Istituto di Ricerche sulle Dinamiche della Sicurezza Sociale: Via Vittorio Emanuele 9/11, 84080 Penta di Fisciano (Salerno); tel. 089-891850; fax 089-958365; f. 1981; Dir Prof. ENZO BARTOCCI.

Istituto di Studi sull'Economia del Mezzogiorno nell'Età Moderna: Via Gramsci 5, 80122 Naples; tel. 081-664553; fax 081-7613993; Dir Dotta ILARIA ZILLI.

Istituto di Ricerca sulla Dinamica dei Sistemi Economici: Via Ampère 56, 20131 Milan; tel. 02-70643501; fax 02-70602807; Dir Prof. GILBERTO ANTONELLI.

Istituto di Studi sulle Strutture Finanziarie e lo Sviluppo Economico: Via Gramsci 5, 80122 Naples; Dir Prof. ANTONIO MARIA FUSCO.

Institutes and study centres in technological research and innovation sciences:

Istituto Centrale per l'Industrializzazione e la Tecnologia Edilizia: Via Lombardia 49, Fraz. Sesto Ulteriano, 20098 San Giuliano Milanese (Milan); tel. 02-98061; fax 02-98280088; Dir Prof. G. BALLIO.

Istituto per la Ricerca sul Legno: Via Barazzuoli 23, 50136 Florence; tel. 055-661886; fax 055-670624; f. 1954; Dir Prof. STEFANO BERTI.

Istituto di Metrologia 'Gustavo Colonnetti': Area di ricerca di Torino, Strada delle Cacce 73, 10135 Turin; tel. 011-39771; fax 011-346761; Dir Dott. SERGIO SARTORI.

Istituto di Studi sulla Ricerca e sulla Documentazione Scientifica: Via C. De Lollis 12, 00185 Rome; tel. 06-4452351; fax 06-4463836; f. 1968; Dir Prof. P. BISOGNO.

Istituto di Tecnologie Biomediche: Via G.B. Morgagni 30E, 00161 Rome; tel. 06-44230121; fax 06-44230229; f. 1970; Dir Profa ANGELA SANTONI.

Istituto per la Meccanizzazione Agricola: Area di Ricerca di Torino, Strada delle Cacce 73, 10135 Turin; tel. 011-346288; fax 011-3489218; f. 1968; Dir Ing. SANDRO POTECCHI.

Istituto di Ricerche Tecnologiche per la Ceramica: Via Granarolo 64, 48018 Faenza (Ravenna); tel. 0546-46147; fax 0546-46381; f. 1970; Dir Dott. G. N. BABINI.

Istituto per la Corrosione Marina dei Metalli: Area di Ricerca di Genova, Via de Marini 6, Torre di Francia, 16149 Genoa; tel. 010-64751; fax 010-6475400; f. 1968; Dir Prof. A. NICOLIN.

Istituto di Tecnologie Industriali e Automazione: Area di ricerca di Milano, Viale Lombardia 20/A, 20131 Milan; tel. 02-70643901; fax 02-70643915; f. 1968; Dir Prof. F. JOVANE.

Istituto per la Tecnologia dei Materiali Metallici non Tradizionali: Via Induno 10, 20092 Cinisello Balsamo (Milan); tel. 02-66013243; fax 02-66011921; f. 1968; Dir Dott. E. OLZI.

Istituto de Ricerche e Sperimentazione Laniera 'Oreste Rivetti': Corso Giuseppe Pella 16, 13051 Biella; tel. 015-8493043; fax 015-8353523; Dir Ing. GIORGIO MAZZUCCHETTI.

Istituto per la Lavorazione dei Metalli: Via Frejus 127, 10043 Orbassano (Turin); tel. 011-9003565; fax 011-9018055; f. 1968; Dir Prof. R. CHIARA.

Istituto per le Tecnologie Didattiche: Area di ricerca di Genova, Via De Marini 6, Torre di Francia, 16149 Genoa; tel. 010-64751; fax 010-6475300; f. 1970; Dir Prof. G. OLIMPO.

Istituto per la Tecnologia del Legno: Via Biasi 75, 38010 San Michele all'Adige (Trento); tel. 0461-660111; fax 0461-650045; f. 1981; Dir Dott. O. DELMARCO.

Istituto sulla Propulsione e sull'Energetica: Viale Baracca 69, 20068 Linate di Peschiera Borromeo (Milan); tel. 02-715015; fax 02-714063; Dir Dott. ALBERTO QUARANTA.

Istituto di Tecnologie Didattiche e Formative: Via Ruggiero VII 55, 90139 Palermo; tel. 091-6113370; fax 091-6114616; Dir Prof. A. M. GRECO.

Istituto per le Tecnologie Informatiche Multimediali: Area di ricerca di Milano, Via Ampère 56, 20131 Milan; tel. 02-70643003; fax 02-2663030; Dir Profa ANNA DELLA VENTURA.

Institutes and study centres in environmental science and technology:

Istituto di Ricerca sulle Acque: Via Reno 1, 00198 Rome; tel. 06-8841451; fax 06-8417861; Dir Prof. R. PASSINO.

Istituto di Ricerche sulla Pesca Marittima: Largo Fiera della Pesca, 60125 Ancona; tel. 071-51280; fax 071-55313; f. 1968; Dir Dott. ANTONIO ARTEGIANI.

Istituto per lo Studio degli Ecosistemi Costieri: Via Pola 4, 71010 Lesina (Foggia); tel. 0882-91166; fax 0882-91352; f. 1968; Dir Prof. GIUSEPPE MAGAZZÙ.

Istituto di Tecnologia della Pesca e del Pescato: Via Luigi Vaccara 61, 91026 Mazara del Vallo (Trapani); tel. 0923-948723; fax 0923-906634; f. 1981; Dir Prof. D. LEVI.

Istituto sull'Inquinamento Atmosferico: Area di Ricerca di Roma, Montelibretti, Via Salaria Km 29,300, CP 10, 00016 Monterotondo Stazione (Rome); tel. 06-906721; fax 06-90625849; f. 1968; Dir Dott. I. ALLEGRINI.

Istituto di Biologia del Mare: Riva 7 Martiri 1364/A, 30122 Venice; tel. 041-5207622; fax 041-5204126; Dir Dott. PAOLO FRANCO.

Istituto Italiano di Idrobiologia 'Marco de Marchi': Largo V. Tonolli 50/52, 28048 Pallanza (NO); tel. 0323-556571; fax 0323-556513; f. 1938; Dir Prof. R. DE BERNARDI.

Istituto Sperimentale Talassografico: Viale R. Gessi 2, 34123 Trieste; tel. 040-305312; fax 040-308941; Dir Prof. D. BREGANT.

Istituto Sperimentale Talassografico: Spianata S. Raineri 86, 98122 Messina; tel. 090-669003; fax 090-669007; f. 1981; Dir Dott. ERMANNO CRISAFI.

Istituto Sperimentale Talassografico: Via Roma 3, 74100 Taranto; tel. 099-4542111; fax 099-4542215; f. 1981; Dir Dott. M. PASTORE.

Istituto di Metodologie Avanzate di Analisi Ambientale: Area di Ricerca di Potenza, CP 27, 85050 Tito Scalo (Potenza); tel. 0971-427211; fax 0971-427222; Dir Prof. V. CUOMO.

Istituto per lo Studio dell'Inquinamento Atmosferico e l'Agrometeorologia: c/o Dipartimento di Scienze dei Materiali, Università, Via Arnesano, ex Collegio

Fiorini, 73100 Lecce; tel. 0832-320554; fax 0832-320475; Dir Prof. FERRUCIO ZVANNI.

Istituto di Ricercha sul Controllo Biologico dell'Ambiente: c/o Istituto di Entomologia Agraria, Facoltà di Agraria, Università, Via Enrico De Nicola, 07100 Sassari; tel. 079-216370; fax 079-229329; Dir Prof. R. PROTA.

Institutes and study centres in molecular biology and biotechnology:

Istituto di Chimica degli Ormoni: Via M. Bianco 9, 20131 Milan; tel. 02-2847737; fax 02-2841934; f. 1969; Dir Prof. L. FERRARA.

Istituto di Biochimica delle Proteine ed Enzimologia: Via Gugliemo Marconi 10, 80125 Naples; tel. 081-7257111; fax 081-7257240; Dir Prof. M. ROSSI.

Istituto Internazionale di Genetica e Biofisica: Via Marconi 10, 80125 Naples; tel. 081-7257111; fax 081-5936123; f. 1962; Dir Dott. J. GUARDIOLA.

Istituto di Genetica Biochimica ed Evoluzionistica: Via Abbiategrasso 207, 27100 Pavia; tel. 0382-527967; fax 0382-422286; f. 1970; Dir Prof. S. RIVA.

Istituto di Genetica Molecolare: Casella Postale, 07040 Santa Maria la Palma (Sassari); tel. 079-998518; fax 079-998409; Dir. Dott. M. PIRASTU.

Istituto di Scienze dell'Alimentazione: Via Roma, Angolo Via Rubilli, 83100 Avellino; tel. 0825-781600; fax 0825-781600; Dir Prof. V. ZAPPIA.

Centro di Studio per la Chimica dei Recettori e delle Molecole Biologicamente Attive: c/o Istituto di Chimica, Facoltà di Medicina e Chirurgia, Università Cattolica "Sacro Cuore", Largo Francesco Vito 1, 00168 Rome; tel. 06-33054215; Dir Prof. BRUNO GIARDINA.

Centro di Studio di Biocristallografia: C/o Dipartimento di Chimica, Università 'Federico II', Via Mezzocannone 4, 80134 Naples; tel. 081-205730; Dir Prof. C. PEDONE.

Institutes and study centres in cultural heritage:

Istituto per le Tecnologie Applicate ai Beni Culturali: Area di Ricerca di Roma, Montelibretti, Via Salaria Km 29,300, CP 10, 00016 Monterotondo Stazione (Rome); tel. 06-90625274; fax 06-90625849; f. 1981; Dir Prof. DOMENICO PATELLA.

Istituto Internazionale di Studi Federiciani: Area di ricerca di Potenza, CP 27, 85050 Tito Scalo (Potenza); tel. 0971-427211; fax 0971-427222; Dir Prof. COSIMO DAMIANO FONSECA.

Istituto per la Conservazione delle Opere Monumentali: C/o Dipartimento di Scienza dei Materiali, Università, Via Arnesano, ex Collegio Fiorini, 73100 Lecce; tel. 0832-320561; fax 0832-320559; Dir Dotta P. ROTA.

AGRICULTURE, FISHERIES AND VETERINARY SCIENCE

Istituto Sperimentale per la Cerealicoltura: Via Cassia 176, 00191 Rome; tel. 06-3295705; fax 06-36306022; e-mail isc.sede@iol.it; f. 1919; cereal crops improvement; 40 scientific staff; library of 15,000 vols; Dir Prof. N. POGNA; publs *Annali*, *Journal of Genetics and Breeding*, *Maydica* (quarterly).

Istituto Sperimentale per la Zoologia Agraria (Experimental Institute of Agricultural Zoology): Via Lanciola-Cascine del Riccio, 50125 Florence; tel. 055-24921; fax 055-209177; f. 1875; library of 53,000 vols; Dir Dott. MARCO VITTORIO COVASSI; publ. *Redia* (annually).

Ufficio Centrale di Ecologia Agraria e difesa delle Piante coltivate dalle Avversità Meteoriche (Meteorological and Ecological Centre): Ministero per le Politiche Agricole, Via del Caravita 7A, 00186 Rome; tel. 06-6793376; f. 1876; controls *c.* 100 observatories; 18 mems; Dir Dott. DOMENICO VENTO.

ECONOMICS, LAW AND POLITICS

Centro di Ricerche Economiche e Sociali (CERES): Via Nomentana 201, 00161 Rome; tel. 06-8541016; f. 1970 as an autonomous body promoted by a trade union (CISL); aims to improve economic and social conditions of workers; fosters contact and collaboration between national and international centres and institutes interested in problems of economic and social development; Pres. Prof. LUIGI FREY; Sec.-Gen. Prof. RENATA LIVRAGHI; publ. *Tendenze della occupazione* (monthly).

Fondazione Giangiacomo Feltrinelli: Via Romagnosi 3, 20121 Milan; tel. 02-874175; fax 02-86461855; f. 1949; history of international socialism, communism and labour movement; library of 400,000 vols, 20,000 periodicals; Pres. SALVATORE VECA; publ. *Annali*.

Istituto Affari Internazionali: Via Angelo Brunetti 9, 00186 Rome; tel. 06-3224360; fax 06-3224363; f. 1965; library of 17,000 vols; Pres. CESARE MERLINI; Dir GIANNI BONVICINI; publ. *The International Spectator* (quarterly in English).

Istituto di Studi Europei 'Alcide De Gasperi': Via Poli 29, 00187 Rome; tel. 06-6784262; fax 06-6794101; f. 1955; scientific and teaching activities; library of 5,000 vols; Pres. Prof. Dr GIUSEPPE SCHIAVONE; Sec. CESARE SELVA.

Istituto Italiano di Studi Legislativi: Via del Corso 267, 00186 Rome; tel. 06-6789488; fax 06-69941306; f. 1925 to promote the scientific and technical studies of legislation; Pres. Prof. GIAN PIERO ORSELLO; Gen. Sec. Dssa FRANCA CIPRIGNO; publs *Yearbook of Comparative Law and Legislative Studies*, *L'Italia e l'Europa*.

Istituto Nazionale di Statistica (National Institute of Statistics): Via Cesare Balbo 16, 00184 Rome; tel. 06-46731; telex 610338; fax 06-46733107; f. 1926; library of 300,000 books, 2,500 periodicals; Pres. ALBERTO ZULIANI; Dir-Gen. P. GARONNA; publs *Annuario statistico italiano*, *Bollettino mensile di statistica* (monthly).

Istituto per gli Studi di Politica Internazionale: Palazzo Clerici, Via Clerici 5, 20121 Milan; tel. 02-878266; fax 02-8692055; f. 1933; public and private funding; aims to provide information and analysis of the great global issues of today, to identify opportunities for more effective Italian participation in int. affairs, to identify the domestic factors which constrain or enhance Italy's int. role; research in int. politics and economics, strategic problems and the history of foreign relations, European integration, int. economic co-operation, consolidation of peace and security among nations, strengthening of political freedoms and democratic institutions; library of *c.* 100,000 vols, historical archive, press archive; postgraduate training courses; organizes conferences, lectures etc.; Pres. Amb. MARCELLO GUIDI; Man. Dir Dott. ENZO CALABRESE; publs *Relazioni Internazionali* (6 a year), *Rapporto sullo Stato del Sistema Internazionale*, *Papers* (20 a year).

Istituto per le relazioni tra l'Italia e i paesi dell'Africa, America Latina e Medio Oriente (IPALMO) (Institute for relations between Italy and the countries of Africa, Latin America and the Middle East): Via del Tritone 62b, 00187 Rome; tel. 06-679-23-21; fax 06-6797849; f. 1971 to promote and develop political, economic and cultural relations between these countries; research and promotion of information at all levels of Italian society; to organize conferences, seminars, etc.; library of 15,000 vols, 500 periodicals; Pres. GILBERTO BONALUMI; Dir CARLO GUELFI; publ. *Politica Internazionale* (6 a year).

EDUCATION

Centro Europeo dell'Educazione: Villa Falconieri, 00044 Frascati, Rome; tel. 06-941851; fax 06-94185205; e-mail cede@bdp.it; f. 1974; library of 16,000 vols; research on planning and funding educational systems, permanent and recurrent education, learning processes, educational innovation and in-service training, educational technology; nat. agency for the evaluation of quality in education; Pres. Prof. BENEDETTO VERTECCHI; Dean Isp. LINO LAURI.

Fondazione Rui: Viale XXI Aprile 36, 00162 Rome; tel. 06-86321281; fax 06-86322845; e-mail info@fondazionerui.it; f. 1959; promotes the training of university students and researchers; manages international halls of residence and cultural centres in nine cities; awards scholarships; carries out research in the international educational field in collaboration with local and national authorities, the EEC, etc.; holds international conferences on secondary and higher education; library: specialized 3,000 vols; Pres. Prof. VINCENZO LORENZELLI; Dir Dr. Ing. ALFREDO RAZZANO; publs reports and working documents.

Istituto per ricerche ed attività educative: Via Luca Giordano 56, 80127 Naples; tel. 081-5580090; fax 081-5788276; f. 1979; aims to give young people access to education, culture and jobs; offers grants, promotes study and research in education; 32 mems; library of 6,500 vols; Pres. Prof. ROBERTO MARRAMA; Sec.-Gen. Prof. LUCIO IANNOTTA.

FINE AND PERFORMING ARTS

Istituto Centrale per il Restauro (Central Institute for the Restoration of Works of Art): Piazza S. Francesco di Paola 9, 00184 Rome; tel. 06-488961; fax 06-4815704; f. 1939; research on the influence of environment on cultural property and on prevention of deterioration; studies formulation of rules on theory of conservation and restoration and on techniques to be used; advises institutes of the Min. of Cultural Property, and regional organizations; in-service teaching and refresher courses; carries out restoration of complex works or those of interest in research and teaching; library of 36,000 vols, 675 periodicals; archive of 46,000 negatives, 4,664 X-rays, 22,850 slides on restoration; Dir Prof. MICHELE CORDARO; publs *Raccomandazioni NORMAL* (quarterly), *DIMOS* (series), preprints of International Conferences on non-destructive testing, micro-analytical methods and environment evaluation for study and conservation of works of art (quinquennial).

Villa I Tatti/Harvard University Center for Italian Renaissance Studies: Via di Vincigliata 26, 50135 Florence; tel. 06-603251; fax 06-603383; e-mail vit@vit.iris.firenze.it; f. 1961 for the post-doctoral study of the Italian Renaissance: history of art, political, economic and social history, history of philosophy and religion, history of literature, music and science; the Villa is the former residence of Bernard Berenson, who left his library and art collection to Harvard; *c.* 15 fellows, 30 staff; library of *c.* 100,000 vols, *c.* 300,000 photographs; Dir WALTER KAISER; publs *I Tatti Studies* (every 2 years), other monographs.

HISTORY, GEOGRAPHY AND ARCHAEOLOGY

Academia Belgica: Via Omero 8, 00197 Rome; tel. 06-3201889; fax 06-3208361; f. 1939; library of 96,000 vols; research centre and residence; Dir Prof. JACQUELINE HAMESSE; publ. *Bulletin de l'Institut Historique Belge de Rome*.

Accademia di Danimarca (Danish Institute of Science and Art in Rome): Via Omero 18, 00197 Rome; tel. 06-3265931; fax 06-3222717; f. 1956; archaeology, philology, art, history of art, history of music, literature; library of 24,000 vols; Dir Prof. Dr. phil. JAN ZAHLE; Sec. and Librarian Dr KAREN ASCANI; publ. *Analecta Romana Instituti Danici*.

Accademia di Francia: Villa Medici, Viale Trinità dei Monti 1, 00187 Rome; tel. 06-67611; fax 06-6761305; f. 1666; library of 26,000 vols; Dir BRUNO RACINE; Sec.-Gen. GÉRARD FONTAINE.

Accademia Tedesca (German Academy in Rome): Villa Massimo, Largo di Villa Massimo 1–2, 00161 Rome; tel. 06-44236394; fax 06-44290771; Dir Dr JÜRGEN SCHILLING.

American Academy in Rome: Via Angelo Masina 5, 00153 Rome; tel. 06-58461; fax 06-5810788; f. 1894; fellowships for independent study and advanced research in fine arts, classical studies, art history, Italian studies and archaeology; library of 116,000 vols; Pres. ADELE CHATFIELD-TAYLOR; Dir CAROLINE BRUZELIUS; Librarian CHRISTINA HUEMER.

British Institute of Florence: Piazzi Strozzi 2, 50123 Florence; tel. 055-284031; fax 055-287071; e-mail british@fol.it; f. 1917; courses in Italian language and culture, English as a second language, TEFL; centre for art history studies; cultural activities; 2,000 students; library of 60,000 vols; Pres. HM Ambassador to Italy; Dir CHRISTINE WILDING.

British Institute of Rome: Via Quattro Fontane 109, 00184 Rome; tel. 06-4881979; 2,000 students; Dir PATRICK CLARE.

British School at Rome: Piazzale Winston Churchill 5, 00197 Rome; tel. 06-3230743; fax 06-3221201; f. 1901, inc. by Royal Charter 1912; postgraduate residential centre for higher research in the humanities and for the practice of the fine arts and architecture; *c.* 40 residents; library of *c.* 72,000 vols; Dir Prof. A. WALLACE-HADRILL; publs *Papers* (annually), *Supplementary Publications* (occasional).

Canadian Academic Centre in Italy: Via Tacito 50, 00193 Rome; tel. 06-6873677; fax 06-6873693; f. 1978; assists Canadian researchers and scholars in Italy and promotes their work through lectures, conferences and publications; fosters academic exchanges between Italy and Canada; library of 3,000 vols; Dir EGMONT LEE.

Centro Camuno di Studi Preistorici: 25044 Capo di Ponte Valcamonica; tel. 0364-42091; fax 0364-42572; e-mail ccsp@globalnet.it; f. 1964; research centre specializing in prehistoric rock art; archaeological research, primitive religions, anthropology and ethnology; seminars, int. symposia, individual tutoring in prehistoric and primitive art, summer school; co-ordinator of World Archives of Rock Art; provides advisers and consultants on conservation, exhibition and evaluation of prehistoric and primitive art, park and museum planning; library of 45,000 vols, 500,000 photographs; Dir Prof. EMMANUEL ANATI; publ. *BCSP: The World Journal of Prehistoric and Primitive Art*.

Centro Italiano di Studi sul Basso Medioevo Accademia Tudertina: Via Ciuffelli 31, 06059 Todi; tel. 075-8942521; all aspects of late medieval civilization; Pres. Prof. TULLIO GREGORY; Dir Prof. ENRICO MENESTÒ.

Centro Italiano di Studi sull'Alto Medioevo: Palazzo Ancaiani, Piazza della Libertà 12, 06049 Spoleto; tel. 0743-23271; fax 0743-232701; f. 1951; promotes research, conferences and scientific publications on all aspects of early medieval civilization; library of 3,000 vols; Pres. Prof. ENRICO MENESTÒ; Dir Prof. STEFANO BRUFANI.

Deutsches Archäologisches Institut (German Archaeological Institute): Via Sardegna 79, 00187 Rome; tel. 06-4888141; f. 1829; library of 200,000 vols; Dir Prof. Dr PAUL ZANKER; Librarian Dr HORST BLANCK; publ. *Römische Mitteilungen*.

Ecole Française de Rome/Scuola Francese di Roma: Piazza Farnese 67, 00186 Rome; tel. 06-686011; fax 06-6874834; f. 1873; French school of archaeology and history; library of 180,000 vols, 1,650 periodicals and 32,000 off-prints; Dir ANDRÉ VAUCHEZ; Dirs of Studies CATHERINE VIRLOUVET, CATHERINE BRICE, FRANÇOIS BOUGARD; Librarian CHRISTIANE BARYLA; publ. *Mélanges de l'Ecole Française de Rome* (series *Antiquité, Moyen Age, Italie et Méditerranée*).

Escuela Española de Historia y Arqueología, CSIC Roma: Via di Torre Argentina 18-3°, 00186 Rome; tel. 06-68309043; fax 06-68309047; e-mail csic@giannutri.caspur.it; f. 1910; history of Italian-Spanish interaction; organizes conferences, seminars; 8 mems; library of 20,000 vols; special collections: Monumenta Albornotiana, documents on Spanish music in Italy; Dir Prof. MANUEL ESPADAS BURGOS.

Institutum Romanum Finlandiae: Villa Lante, Passeggiata del Gianicolo 10, 00165 Rome; tel. 06-68801674; fax 06-68802349; e-mail irfrome@librsek.vatlib.it; f. 1938; Classical and Italian studies; library of 14,000 vols; Dir Prof. CHRISTER BRUUN; publs *Acta Instituti Romani Finlandiae*, *Opuscula Instituti Romani Finlandiae*.

Istituto di Norvegia in Roma di Archeologia e Storia dell'Arte: Viale Trenta Aprile 33, 00153 Rome; tel. 06-58391007; fax 06-5880604; f. 1959; library of 22,000 vols; Dir Prof. J. RASMUS BRANDT; publ. *Acta ad Archaeologiam et Artium Historiam Pertinentia* (irregular).

Istituto di Studi Adriatici (Institute of Adriatic Studies): 1364-A Riva 7 Martiri, 30122 Venice; f. 1946; Pres. Prof. G. FERRO; publ. *Memorie di Biogeografica Adriatica*.

Istituto Ellenico di Studi Bizantini e Postbizantini di Venezia (Hellenic Institute of Byzantine and Post-Byzantine Studies of Venice): Castello 3412, 30122 Venice; tel. 041-5226581; fax 041-5238248; f. 1951; library of 20,000 vols, and archives containing 200,000 documents of 16th to 19th centuries relating to the Greek Orthodox community of Venice; Dir (vacant); Sec. ATHOS MOUROUSSIAS; publs *Thesaurismata* (annually), monograph series.

Istituto Italiano di Studi Germanici (Italian Institute for Germanic Studies): Via Calandrelli 25, 00153 Rome; tel. 06-5812465; fax 06-5835929; f. 1932; library of 70,000 vols; Dir Prof. PAOLO CHIARINI; publs *Studi Germanici* (quarterly), *Wissenschaftliche Reihen: Materiali e documenti*, *Atti*, *Studi e ricerche*, *Poeti e prosatori tedeschi*, *Strumenti*.

Istituto Italiano per gli Studi Storici: Via Benedetto Croce 12, 80134 Naples; tel. 081-5517159; fax 081-5512390; f. 1947; scientific studies and teaching in the humanities; awards 16 student grants annually; library of 100,000 vols; Pres. SERGIO SIGLIENTI; Dir Prof. GENNARO SASSO; publs *Annali*, *Collana delle monografie* (annually), *Carteggi di Benedetto Croce*, etc.

Istituto Nazionale di Studi Romani: Piazza dei Cavalieri di Malta 2, 00153 Rome; tel. 06-5743442; fax 06-5743447; e-mail studiromani@mclink.it; f. 1925; promotes the study of Rome from ancient to modern times in all aspects; 120 mems; library of 25,000 vols, 1,435 periodicals; Pres. Prof. MARIO PETRUCCIANI; Dir Dott. FERNANDA ROSCETTI; publs *Studi Romani* (quarterly), *Rassegna d'Informazioni* (monthly).

Istituto Nazionale di Studi sul Rinascimento: Palazzo Strozzi, 50123 Florence; tel. 055-287728; fax 055-280563; f. 1938; publishes critical texts and results of research; 10-mem. council; library of 45,000 vols, 500 periodicals, special collection 'Machiavelli-Serristori', art photo library of 78,000 items, 700 micro-films; Pres. Prof. MICHELE CILIBERTO; publ. *Rinascimento* (annually).

Istituto Olandese di Roma (Netherlands Institute): Via Omero 10–12, 00197 Rome; tel. 06-3200751; fax 06-204971; e-mail general@nir_roma.it; f. 1904; classical archaeology, modern history, history of art; cultural centre and residence; library of 30,000 vols; Dir Prof. Dr HERMAN GEERTMAN; publs *Mededelingen*, *Studien*, *Scripta Minora*, *Scrinium*.

Istituto Papirologico 'Girolamo Vitelli': Via degli Alfani 46/48, 50121 Florence; tel. 055-2478969; fax 055-2480722; f. 1908; study of Greek and Latin papyri; library of 18,000 vols; collection of papyri; Scientific Dir Prof. MANFREDO MANFREDI; Curators Dr GIOVANNA MENCI, Dr ISABELLA ANDORLINI; publs *Papiri Greci e Latini della Società Italiana* (PSI), *Studi e Testi di Papirologia*, *Comunicazioni*, *Notizario di Studi e Ricerche in Corso*.

Istituto Siciliano di Studi Bizantini e Neoellenici: Via Noto 34, 90141 Palermo; tel. 6259541; fax 6259541; f. 1952; 60 ordinary mems, 60 corresponding mems; library of 10,000 vols; Pres. Prof. VINCENZO ROTOLO; Sec.-Gen. Prof. RENATA LAVAGNINI.

Istituto Storico Germanico (German Historical Institute): Via Aurelia Antica 391, 00165 Rome; tel. 06-6604921; fax 06-6623838; f. 1888; medieval and modern history, history of music; library of 180,000 vols; Dir Prof. A. ESCH; publs *Quellen und Forschungen aus italienischen Archiven und Bibliotheken*, *Bibliothek des Deutschen Historischen Instituts*.

Istituto Storico presso l'Istituto Austriaco di Cultura a Roma (Austrian Historical Institute at the Austrian Cultural Institute in Rome): Viale Bruno Buozzi 113, Rome; tel. 06-3224793; fax 06-3224296; e-mail iarom@librs6k.vatlib.it; f. 1881; Dir Prof. Dr OTTO KRESTEN; publs *Römische Historische Mitteilungen*, *Publikationen*.

Real Colegio de San Clemente de los Españoles (Royal College of Spain): Via del Collegio di Spagna 4, 40123 Bologna; tel. 330408; f. 1364 under Will of Cardinal Don Gil de Albornoz; study centre for 20 Spanish postgraduates; library of 12,000 vols; Rector Prof. Dr JOSÉ GUILLERMO GARCÍA VALDECASAS; publ. *Studia Albornotiana* (irregular).

Svenska Institutet i Rom (Swedish Institute in Rome): Via Omero 14, 00197 Rome; tel. 06-3201966; fax 06-3230265; f. 1926; library of 53,000 vols; Swedish courses for students of classical archaeology and history of art; fellowships in classical philology, archaeology, architecture, history of art and conservation; excavations at San Giovenale, Acquarossa, Luni sul Mignone and the Temple of the Dioscuroi, Forum Romanum; Dir Prof. ANNE-MARIE LEANDER TOUATI; publs *Acta Instituti Romani Regni Sueciae*, *Opuscula Romana*, *Suecoromana*.

MEDICINE

Centro di Ricerche sulle Attività Umane Superiori: Istituto Fisica, Università di Ferrara, 44100 Ferrara; f. 1964; research on normal, mental and pathological phenomena concerned in experiences of graphic activity; Pres. Prof. A. DRIGO; Dir Prof. F. FLARER; Sec. Dott. C. GENOVESE.

Istituto di Ricerche Farmacologiche 'Mario Negri': Via Eritrea 62, 20157 Milan; tel. 02-390141; fax 02-3546277; f. 1961; non-profit org. for research and education in pharmacology and biomedicine; library of 8,000 vols, 725 periodicals; Pres. Dr PAOLO MARTELLI; Dir Prof. SILVIO GARATTINI; publs *Negri News* (monthly), *Research and Practice* (every 2 months), *Lettera in Psichiatria* (2 a year).

Istituto Nazionale della Nutrizione: Via Ardeatina 546, 00178 Rome; tel. 06-5032412; fax 06-5031592; f. 1936 as part of CNR, independent 1958 on budget of Min. of Agricultural Resources, supported by contracts and grants from Min. of Health, CNR and int. bodies; biological research in human nutrition, analyses and surveys on composition and nutritive value of foods; Pres. GIUSEPPE ROTILIO; Dir-Gen. E. CIALFA.

Istituto Nazionale per la Ricerca sul Cancro (National Institute for Cancer Research): Largo Rosanna Benzi 10, 16132 Genoa; tel. 010-56001; fax 010-352888; e-mail admin@hp380.ist.unige.it; f. 1978; research in all fields of cancer prevention, diagnosis, cure and rehabilitation; holds conferences, seminars, training courses; library of 2,000 vols, 195 periodicals; Chief Exec. Prof. GIORGIO DELLACASA; Scientific Dir Prof. LEONARDO SANTI.

Istituto Sieroterapico Milanese (Milan Serum Institute): Via Darwin 22, 20100 Milan; tel. 02-8397441; telex 325649; f. 1896; research on immunological products and pharmaceuticals; library of 32,487 vols; Dir Prof. S. CANESCHI; publs *Bollettino*, *La Clinica Veterinaria*.

Istituto Superiore di Sanità: Viale Regina Elena 299, 00161 Rome; tel. 06-49901; telex 610071; fax 06-4469938; f. 1934; aims to promote public health through scientific research, surveys, controls and analytical tests in the various fields of health sciences; library of 175,000 vols, 3,500 periodicals; Dir-Gen. Prof. GIUSEPPE BENAGIANO; publs *Annali dell' Istituto Superiore di Sanità* (quarterly), *Notiziario dell' Istituto Superiore di Sanità* (monthly), *ISTISAN Congressi*, *Serie Relazioni*, *Rapporti interni*, *Rapporti ISTISAN*, *Strumenti di Riferimento*.

NATURAL SCIENCES

General

Istituto per l'Interscambio Scientifico (Institute for Scientific Interchange): Viale Settimo Severo 65, 10133 Turin; tel. 011-6502679; f. 1982; promotes basic research in molecular biology, chemistry, computer sciences, economics, mathematics, theoretical physics; Pres. Prof. TULLIO REGGE; Dir Prof. MARIO RASETTI.

Biological Sciences

Herbarium Universitatis Florentinae—Museo Botanico: Via G. La Pira 4, 50121 Florence; tel. 055-2757462; f. 1842; systematic botany, plant geography; Dir Prof. GUIDO MOGGI; publs *Pubblicazioni del Museo Botanico*, *Webbia*.

Stazione Zoologica 'Anton Dohrn' di Napoli (Zoological Station of Naples): Villa Comunale, 80121 Naples; tel. 081-5833111; fax 081-7641355; e-mail segrszn@alpha.szn.it; f. 1873; conducts biological research on marine organisms and marine ecosystems; library of over 1,000 journals and 80,000 vols; Pres. Prof. GIORGIO BERNARDI; Dir Dr LUCIO CARIELLO; publs *History and Philosophy of Life Sciences*, *Marine Ecology*.

Mathematical Sciences

Istituto Nazionale di Alta Matematica Francesco Severi: Piazzale Aldo Moro 5, 00185 Rome; tel. 06-490320; fax 06-4462293; f. 1939; Pres. Prof. CARLO PUCCI; publs *Rendiconti di Matematica*, *Symposia Mathematica*.

Physical Sciences

Comitato Glaciologico Italiano (Italian Glaciological Committee): Via Accademia delle Scienze 5, 10123 Turin; tel. 011-658813; fax 011-6707155; f. 1895; glaciology and alpine climatology; *c.* 50 mems; library of 700 books, 15,000 photographs; Pres. Prof. G. OROMBELLI; Gen. Sec. Prof. A. CARTON; publ. *Geografia Fisica e Dinamica quaternaria* (2 a year).

Dipartimento di Ingegneria Nucleare, Centro Studi Nucleari Enrico Fermi (CESNEF) (E. Fermi Centre for Nuclear Studies): Politecnico di Milano, Via Ponzio 34/3, 20133 Milan; tel. 02-23996300; telex 333467; fax 02-23996309; f. 1957; one of the Institutes of the Politecnico di Milano; trains technical personnel in the fields of nuclear energy, physics of materials, and electronics; library of 5,000 vols.

Istituto Gemmologico Italiano: Viale A. Gramsci 228, 20099 Sesto S. Giovanni-Milan; tel. 02-2409354; fax 02-2406257; f. 1973; courses in gemmology, laboratory analysis, research; *c.* 1,500 mems; Pres. GIAN-MARIA BUCCELLATI.

Istituto Idrografico della Marina (Naval Institute of Hydrography): Passo Osservatorio 4, 16134 Genoa; f. 1872; library of 36,000 vols; Library Dir Mrs P. PRESCIUTTINI BELLEZZA.

Istituto Italiano di Speleologia: Castellana-Grotte, 70013 Bari; f. 1929; exploration and scientific research in natural caves; 5 mems; library of 1,250 vols; Dir V. MANCHISI; publ. *Le Grotte d'Italia* (2 a year).

Istituto Italiano di Storia della Chimica: Via G. B. Morgagni 32, 00161 Rome; Pres. Prof. M. TALENTI; Sec.-Gen. Prof. A. VITOLO.

Istituto Nazionale di Fisica Nucleare (INFN) (National Institute of Nuclear Physics): CP 56, 00044 Frascati, Rome; f. 1951; promotes and undertakes research in fundamental nuclear physics; consists of: Central Administration (Frascati), 19 sections, 4 National Laboratories (Frascati, Legnaro, Gran Sasso (L'Aquila), Catania), the National Centre for Informatics and Networking (CNAF Bologna) and 7 groups; the sections are at the Institutes of Physics at the Universities of Turin, Milan, Padua, Genoa, Trieste, Bologna, Pisa, Pavia, Florence, Rome, Naples, Bari, Catania, Cagliari, Ferrara, Perugia, Lecce, Tor Vergata (Rome), and at the Istituto Superiore di Sanità in Rome; the groups are at the Institutes of Physics at the Universities of Parma, Trento, Udine, Salerno, Messina, Aquila, Cosenza; Pres. Prof. LUCIANO MAIANI.

Istituto Nazionale di Geofisica (National Institute of Geophysics): Via di Vigna Murata 605, 00143 Rome; tel. 06-518601; telex 610502; fax 06-5041181; f. 1936; seismology, geomagnetism, ionospheric physics; library of 4,000 vols, 100 periodicals; Pres. Prof. ENZO BOSCHI; publs *Annali di Geofisica* (6 a year), *Bollettino sismico* (quarterly), *Bollettino macrosismico* (annually), *Annuario geomagnetico*, *Bollettino indici K* (monthly), *Bollettino dei valori istantanei alle ore 0, 2* (3 a year), *Bollettino ionosferico* (monthly), *Tavole di previsione ionosferica* (fortnightly).

Istituto Nazionale di Ottica (National Institute of Optics): Largo Enrico Fermi 6, 50125 Florence; tel. 055-23081; telex 572570; fax 055-2337755; f. 1927; quantum, instrumental and physiological optics; 35 staff; library of 7,000 vols; Pres. Prof. F. TITO ARECCHI.

Laboratori Nazionali di Frascati dell' INFN (National Laboratories of INFN, Frascati): CP 13, 00044 Frascati, Rome; tel. 06-94031; telex 614122; fax 06-9403-427; f. 1953; 450 MeV Linear accelerator for electrons and positrons, 1.5 GeV electron positron storage ring; theoretical research group, high energy and nuclear physics research, electronics and radio-frequency laboratory, laboratory of technology and vacuum; library of 20,000 vols; Dir Dr P. LAURELLI.

Osservatorio Astronomico di Capodimonte: Via Moiariello 16, 80131 Naples; f. 1819; 12 astronomers; library of 24,000 vols; Dir Prof. MASSIMO CAPACCIOLI; publs *Memorie Astronomiche*, *Contributi*.

Osservatorio Astronomico di Padova: Vicolo dell' Osservatorio 5, 35122 Padua; tel. 049-8293411; fax 049-8759840; f. 1767; library of 10,000 vols; Dir Prof. GIANFRANCO DE ZOTTI; publs various papers.

Osservatorio Astronomico di Roma: Viale del Parco Mellini 84, 00136 Rome; tel. 06-35347056; fax 06-35347802; and at Via Frascati 33, 00040 Monteporzio Catone (RM); tel. 06-9428641; fax 06-9447243; f. 1923; library of 25,000 vols, 51 astronomical and astrophysical periodicals; astronomical museum; attached astronomical station at Campo Imperatore; Dir Prof. R. BUONANNO; publ. *Solar Phenomena*.

Osservatorio Astronomico di Trieste (Astronomical Observatory of Trieste): Via Tiepolo 11, 34131 Trieste; tel. 040-3199111; fax 040-309418; f. 1753; research in astrophysics, astrophysical techniques, computer science; library of 9,500 vols; Dir Prof. FABIO MARDIROSSIAN; publs *Pubblicazioni*, *Solar Observations*, *Astronet Documentation Notes*, *Preprints*.

Osservatorio Geofisico Sperimentale (Experimental Geophysics Observatory): CP 2011, 34016 Trieste; tel. 040-21401; telex 460329; fax 040-327307; f. 1958; 200 staff; library of 3,000 vols; Pres. Prof. RINALDO NICOLICH; publ. *Bollettino di Geofisica Teorica e Applicata* (quarterly).

Osservatorio Vesuviano: Ercolano, 80056 Naples; f. 1841; chiefly concerned with research on geophysical warning of Mount Vesuvius, Campi Flegrei Caldera and other active volcanic areas in Southern Italy; Dir Prof. GIUSEPPE LUONGO; publs *Wovo News*, *Stop Disasters*, annual report.

Servizio Geologico d'Italia (Italian Geological Survey): Via Curtatone 3, Rome; tel. 06-4465188; fax 06-4465622; f. 1873; library of over 150,000 vols, 800 current serials, 40,000 geological maps; Dir ANDREA TODISCO; publs *Bollettino* (annually), *Memorie per servire alla descrizione della Carta geologica d'Italia*, *Memorie descrittive della Carta geologica d'Italia* (irregular), *Quaderni*, *Miscellanea* (all irregular).

PHILOSOPHY AND PSYCHOLOGY

Centro Superiore di Logica e Scienze Comparate: Gall. del Leone 3, 40125 Bologna; f. 1969; promotes the study of Logic and contributes to research in this field; 1,250 mems; library and archives; Pres. Prof. F. SPISANI; Research Dirs Prof. I. M. COPI, Prof. C. G. HEMPEL, Prof. A. MARTINET, Prof. E. NAGEL, Prof. K. POPPER, Prof. P. RICOEUR, Prof. P. SUPPES; publ. *International Logic Review—Rassegna Internazionale di Logica* (2 a year).

Istituto di Studi Filosofici 'Enrico Castelli': Via Nomentana 118, c/o Facoltà di Filosofia, Università, 00161 Rome; tel. 06-4403077; f. 1939; Dir Prof. M. M. OLIVETTI; publs *Edizione Naz. dei Classici del pensiero italiano*, *Settimana di studi filosofici internazionali* (annually), *Archivio di Filosofia* (quarterly), *Bibliografia filosofica Italiana*, *Edizione Naz. A. Rosmini*, *Edizione Naz. V. Gioberti*, *Studi Filosofici e Religiosi*.

RELIGION, SOCIOLOGY AND ANTHROPOLOGY

Fondazione di Ricerca 'Istituto Carlo Cattaneo': Via Santo Stefano 11, 40125 Bologna; tel. 051-239766; fax 051-262959; e-mail catt@bo.nettuna.it; f. 1965; study and research in the field of social science with particular regard to education, electoral behaviour, politics, crime, terrorism and family; Pres. Prof. RAIMONDO CATANZARO; Dir Prof. PIERGIORGIO CORBETTA; Sec. ADRIANA GUELFI; publs *Cattaneo* (irregular), *Misure/Materiali di ricerca dell'Istituto Carlo Cattaneo* (irregular), *Polis-Ricerche e studi su società e politica in Italia* (3 a year), *Italian Politics — A Review* (annually).

Istituto Italiano di Antropologia (Italian Institute of Anthropology): Università di Roma 'La Sapienza', Dipart. di Biologia Animale e dell'Uomo, P.le Aldo Moro 5, 00185 Rome; tel. 06-49912273; fax 06-49912273; f. 1893; Pres. Prof. A. OLIVERIO; Technical Dir and Sec. Prof. P. PASSARELLO; publ. *Rivista di Antropologia* (annually).

Istituto Italiano per il Medio ed Estremo Oriente (ISMEO) (Italian Institute for the Middle and Far East): Palazzo Brancaccio, Via Merulana 248, 00185 Rome; tel. 06-4874273; fax 06-4873138; f. 1933; Pres. Prof. GHERARDO GNOLI; a library and museum of oriental art are attached to the Institute; publs *East and West* (quarterly), *Rome Oriental Series*, *Nuovo Ramusio*, *Archaeological reports*, *Cina*, *Il Giappone* (annually).

Istituto Luigi Sturzo: Via delle Coppelle 35, 00186 Rome; tel. 06-6875528; fax 06-6864704; e-mail ils@pronet.it; f. 1951; sociological and historical research; library of 65,000 vols; Pres. Prof. GABRIELE DE ROSA; Sec.-Gen. Dott. FLAVIA NARDELLI; publ. *Sociologia* (3 a year).

Istituto per l'Oriente C. A. Nallino: Via Alberto Caroncini 19, 00197 Rome; tel. 06-8084106; f. 1921; research on modern and ancient Near East; library of 30,000 vols; Pres. Prof. F. CASTRO; Scientific Dir Prof. C. BAFFIONI; publs *Oriente Moderno*, *Rassegna di Studi Etiopici*.

TECHNOLOGY

Centro Radioelettrico Sperimentale 'Guglielmo Marconi' (Marconi Experimental Radio-electric Centre): Viale Europa 190, 00144 Rome; tel. 06-5942484; fax 06-5410904; f. 1937; attached to the Istituto Superiore delle Poste e Telecomunicazioni; experimental research on radio waves; Pres. Prof. G. C. CORAZZA.

Centro Sviluppo Materiali SpA: Via di Castel Romano 100-102, 00129 Rome; f. 1963; library of over 40,000 vols; Man. Dir Dr R. BRUNO; Gen. Man. Dr A. MASCANZONI.

CISE S.p.A.: Via Reggio Emilia 39, CP 12081, 20134 Milan; tel. 02-21671; telex 311643; fax 02-21672620; f. 1946; field of activity: development of innovation technologies and their transfer to industry; includes technologies for electric power plants, the environment, manufacturing industries, energy and space, and innovative instrumentation; acts as consultant; library of 24,000 vols, 700 journals; Chair. Dott. FRANCO TATÓ; publs *CISE Newsletter*, *Azienda CISE*.

Ente per le Nuove Tecnologie, l'Energie e l'Ambiente (ENEA) (Agency for New Technology, Energy and the Environment): Lungotevere Thaon di Revel 76, 00196 Rome; tel. 06-36271; fax 06-36272591; e-mail com@sede .enea.it; f. 1960; scientific research and technological development, implementing advanced research programmes and conducting complex projects for Italy's social and economic development; library of 250,000 vols; Pres. NICOLA CABIBBO; publ. *Energia ambiente e innovazione* (fortnightly).

Fondazione Guglielmo Marconi (Guglielmo Marconi Foundation): Via Celestini 1, 40044 Pontecchio Marconi (Bologna); tel. 051-846121; fax 051-846951; f. 1938; research in telecommunications; library of 3,500 vols.

Istituto Nazionale per gli Studi ed Esperienze di Architettura Navale (National Institute of Naval Architecture Studies and Experiments): Via Vallerano 139, Rome; tel. 06-5071580; fax 06-5070619; e-mail secretary@mail.insean.it; f. 1927; library of 3,500 vols; Pres. Adm. ULDERICO GRAZIOLI; Dir Ing. PAOLINO MANISCALCO; publ. *Quaderni* (annually).

SORIN Biomedica SpA: 13040 Saluggia, Vercelli; tel. 0161-4871; telex 200064; fax 0161-487545; f. 1956; applied research in biomedicine; production and development of radiopharmaceuticals and immunodiagnostic kits (using radioactive and enzymatic tracers), pace-makers, artificial cardiac valves (mechanical and biological), oxygenators, dialysers, haemodialysis and haemoperfusion accessories; 2,112 staff; Pres. UMBERTO ROSA; Chief Exec. EZIO GARIBALDI; Gen. Man. ENNIO DENTI.

Libraries and Archives

Alessandria

Biblioteca Civica: Via Tripoli 16, 15100 Alessandria; tel. 0131-253708; fax 0131-254681; f. 1806; 125,000 vols; Dir (vacant).

Ancona

Archivio di Stato di Ancona: Via Maggini 80, 60127 Ancona; tel. 071-2802053; fax 071-2800356; f. 1941; provincial archives dating from before Unification; library of 8,000 vols, 280 periodicals; Dir Dott. ALESSANDRO MORDENTI; publ. *Archivio di Stato-Ancona* (series, irregular).

Biblioteca Comunale Luciano Benincasa: Via Bernabei 32, 60121 Ancona; tel. 071-222-5020; fax 071-222-5015; f. 1669; 140,000 vols, 62 incunabula, 118 periodicals, 347 MSS, 3,000 *cinquecentine*; Dir ALESSANDRO L. AIARDI.

Arezzo

Biblioteca della Città di Arezzo: Via dei Pileati-Palazzo Pretorio, 52100 Arezzo; tel. 0575-353916; fax 0575-370419; f. 1603; 237,000 vols, pamphlets and miscellanea, 578 MSS and 180 incunabula; Dir L. MELANI.

Ascoli Piceno

Biblioteca Comunale 'Giulio Gabrielli': Piazza Arringo 6, 63100 Ascoli Piceno; tel. 0736-298212; fax 0736-298232; f. 1849; 180,000 vols, 265 incunabula, 644 MSS, 2,000 *cinquecentine*, 340 periodicals; Dir Dssa EMANUELA IMPICCINI.

Avellino

Biblioteca Provinciale Scipione e Giulio Capone: Corso Europa, 83100 Avellino; f. 1885; 101,500 vols; Dir Dott. MARIO SARRO.

Bari

Archivio di Stato di Bari: Via Demetrio Marin 3, 70125 Bari; tel. 080-363173; f. 1835; library of 6,192 vols, 224 periodicals, 139 MSS; Dir Dr GIUSEPPE DIBENEDETTO.

Biblioteca Nazionale 'Sagarriga-Visconti-Volpi': Palazzo Ateneo, Piazza Umberto, 70121 Bari; tel. 080-5212534; fax 080-5212667; f. 1865; 300,000 vols; Dir Dssa MARIA TERESA TAFURI DI MELIGNANO.

Bergamo

Biblioteca Civica A. Mai: Piazza Vecchia 15, 24129 Bergamo; tel. 035-399430; f. 1760; 650,000 vols, 9,380 MSS, 37,478 documents, 1,640 incunabula; Dir GIULIO ORAZIO BRAVI.

Bologna

Archivio di Stato di Bologna: Piazza dei Celestini 4, 40123 Bologna; tel. 051-223891; f. 1874; library of 23,000 vols, 331 periodicals; Dir Dr CLAUDIA SALTERINI.

Biblioteca Carducci: Piazza Carducci 5, 40125 Bologna; given to the commune of Bologna in 1907 by Marguerite of Savoy, inaugurated in 1921; the library preserves the surroundings of the poet Giosuè Carducci and contains his collected works, as well as many rare editions of other works; 60,000 vols; Dir Dr PAOLO MESSINA.

Biblioteca Comunale dell'Archiginnasio: Piazza Galvani 1, 40124 Bologna; tel. 051-276811; fax 051-261160; e-mail archiginnasio@comune.bologna.it; f. 1801; contains 750,000 vols, including 2,500 incunabula and *c.* 20,000 rare editions of the 16th century; 12,000 MSS, 500,000 letters and documents; Dir Dr PIERANGELO BELLETTINI; publs *L'Archiginnasio*, *Bollettino della Biblioteca Comunale di Bologna* (annually).

Biblioteca dell'Istituto Giuridico 'Antonio Cicu': Via Zamboni 27–29, 40126 Bologna; tel. 051-259626; fax 051-259624; f. 1925; 292,000 vols; Dir Prof. GIORGIO GHEZZI; publs *Pubblicazioni del Seminario Giuridico della Università di Bologna* (8–10 a year), *Miscellanee*, *Ristampe*.

Biblioteca della Cassa di Risparmio in Bologna S.p.A.: Via Farini 22, 40124 Bologna; tel. 051-6454111; fax 051-6454366; f. 1837; 20,000 vols; Dir Dott. LEONE SIBANI.

Associated library:

Biblioteca Della Fondazione Cassa di Risparmio in Bologna: Via Morgagni 3, 40122 Bologna; tel. 051-230727; fax 051-232676; 100,000 vols, 15 incunabula, 545 vols of MSS; Curator Dssa FRANCA VARIGNANA.

Biblioteca 'Studium' S. Domenico: Piazza San Domenico 13, 40124 Bologna; tel. 051-6400493; fax 051-6400492; e-mail biblsand@ iperbole.bologna.it; f. 1218; 78,000 vols, incunabula and MSS; special collection: philosophy and theology; Dir P. ANGELO PIAGNO.

Biblioteca Universitaria di Bologna: Via Zamboni 35, 40126 Bologna; tel. 051-243420; fax 051-252110; f. 1712; 818,000 vols, 300,000 pamphlets, 7,624 MSS, 1,022 incunabula, 63,000 microforms, 8,000 periodicals; Dir Dr STEFANIA MURIANNI.

Brescia

Civica Biblioteca Queriniana: Via Mazzini 1, 25121 Brescia; tel. 030-2978200; f. 1747; 482,832 vols; Dir ALDO PIROLA.

Cagliari

Archivio di Stato di Cagliari: Via Gallura 2, 09125 Cagliari; tel. 070-669450; fax 070-653401; f. 19th century; library of 27,000 vols, 2,690 periodicals, 407,000 microfiches; Dir Dott. MARINELLA FERRAI COCCO ORTU.

Biblioteca Universitaria: Via Università 32A, 09100 Cagliari; tel. 070-660017; f. 1792; 460,470 vols; 1,033 MSS, 5,469 letters and documents, 241 incunabula, 2,784 magazines; Gabinetto delle Stampe 'Anna Marongiu Pernis' contains 4,541 etchings; Dir Dott. GRAZIELLA SEDDA DELITALA.

Campobasso

Archivio di Stato di Campobasso: Via Orefici 43, 86100 Campobasso; tel. 0874-411488; fax 0874-411525; f. 1818; library of 17,000 vols, 746 periodicals, 29 MSS; Dir Dssa RENATA DE BENEDITTIS.

Catania

Archivio di Stato di Catania: Via Vittorio Emanuele 156, 95131 Catania; tel. 095-7159860; fax 095-7150465; f. 1854; 161,790 items; library of 10,702 vols; Dir CRISTINA GRASSO.

Biblioteca Regionale Universitaria: Piazza Università 2, 95124 Catania; tel. 095-7366111; f. 1755; 306,700 vols, 117 incunabula, 418 MSS; Dir UGO GIOVALE.

Biblioteche Riunite Civica e A. Ursino Recupero: Via Biblioteca 13, 95124 Catania; tel. 316883; f. 1931 as municipal library, fmrly a Benedictine monastery library, nationalized in 1867; *c.* 180,000 vols, specializing in Sicily and Catania; Dir Prof. MARIA SALMERI.

Cesena

Istituzione Biblioteca Malatestiana: Piazza Bufalini 1, Cesena; tel. 0547-610892; fax 0547-21237; f. 1452; 400,000 vols, 286 incunabula, 2,180 MSS; Dir Dr LORENZO BALDACCHINI.

Como

Biblioteca Comunale: Via Indipendenza 87, 22100 Como; tel. 031-270187; fax 031-240183; f. 17th century; 365,000 vols; Dir R. TERZOLI.

Cremona

Biblioteca del Seminario Vescovile: Via Milano 5, 26100 Cremona; f. 1592; 138,450 vols, 400 MSS, 18 incunabula; Dir Prof. Dr Don GIUSEPPE GALLINA.

Biblioteca Statale e Libreria Civica: Via Ugolani Dati 4, 26100 Cremona; tel. 0372-495611; fax 0372-495615; f. *c.* 1600; 680,000 vols, 2,380 MSS, 18,600 letters and documents, 394 incunabula, 6,000 16th-century editions; Dir Dott. EMILIA BRICCHI PICCIONI; publs *Annali*, *Mostre*, *Fonti e Sussidi*.

Fermo

Biblioteca Comunale: Piazza del Popolo 63, Fermo; tel. 0734-284310; fax 0734-224170; e-mail biblioteca.fermo@sapienza.it; f. 1688; 350,000 vols; Dir MARIA CHIARA LEONORI.

Ferrara

Biblioteca Comunale Ariostea: Via Scienze 17, 44100 Ferrara; tel. 0532-206977; fax 0532-204296; e-mail ariostea.comfe@fe.nettuno.it; f. 1753; 350,000 vols; Dir Dott. A. CHIAPPINI.

Florence

Archivio di Stato di Firenze: Viale G. Italia 6, 50122 Florence; tel. 055-263201; fax 055-2341159; f. 1852; 81 staff; 604,580 items; library of 41,000 vols; Dir Dssa ROSALIA MANNO TOLU.

Biblioteca del Gabinetto Scientifico Letterario G. P. Vieusseux: Palazzo Strozzi, Piazza Strozzi, 50123 Florence; tel. 055-288342; fax 055-2396743; also Archivio Contemporaneo 'A. Bonsanti' (Palazzo Corsini-Suarez, via Maggio, 50125 Florence; tel. 055-213295; f. 1819; 600,000 vols; f. 1975; 50,000 vols, 500,000 records); Dir Prof. ENZO SICILIANO; publ. *Antologia Vieusseux* (quarterly).

Biblioteca della Galleria degli Uffizi: Via della Ninna 5, 50100 Florence; f. 1770; 40,000 vols; Dir Dr EMME MICHELETTI.

Biblioteca di Lettere e Filosofia dell' Università: Piazza Brunelleschi 4, 50121 Florence; tel. 055-2757811; fax 055-243471; e-mail biblet@eesit1.unifi.it; f. 1959; 1,600,000 vols; Librarian-in-Chief ANGELO MARINO.

Biblioteca Marucelliana: Via Cavour 43, 50100 Florence; tel. 055-210602; f. 1752; 543,000 vols; 2,549 MSS; 489 incunabula, 2,000 drawings, 20,000 prints, 8,000 16th century editions, 16,636 letters and documents, 2,046 periodicals; Dir MARIO CISCATO.

Biblioteca Medicea-Laurenziana: Piazza S. Lorenzo 9, 50123 Florence; tel. 055-210760; fax 055-2302992; f. 1571; contains the private Medici Library, collections of MSS from the Grand Dukes of Lorena, S. Croce, S. Marco, Badia Fiesolana, cathedral of Florence, and private family collections; 15th- and 16th-century first editions; 13,000 MSS of the 5th–19th centuries; 2,000 papyri, 80 ostraca, 150,000 vols; Dir Dott. FRANCA ARDUINI.

Biblioteca Moreniana: Via dei Ginori 10, 50100 Florence; tel. 055-2760334; f. 1869; 34,000 vols, about 2,000 MSS, specializing in ancient Tuscan history; Dir Dott. ANNA MARIA OGNIBENE.

Biblioteca Nazionale Centrale: Piazza Cavalleggeri 1B, 50122 Florence; tel. 055-249191; fax 055-2342482; f. 1747; 5,300,000 vols, pamphlets, 24,000 MSS, 4,000 incunabula; Dir Dr ANTONIA IDA FONTANA; publ. *Bibliografia nazionale italiana* (monthly, annual accumulations, printed cards).

Biblioteca Pedagogica Nazionale: c/o Biblioteca di Documentazione Pedagogica, Palazzo Gerini, Via M. Buonarroti 10, 50122 Florence; tel. 055-23801; fax 055-2380330; f. 1941; 98,000 vols, 543 periodicals, rare books, drawings, etc.; data banks on education; Pres. Prof. IVAN FASSIN; publs *Schedario* (review of children's literature, 3 a year), *Segnalibro* (review of literature for young people, annually).

Biblioteca Riccardiana: Via dei Ginori 10, 50129 Florence; tel. 055-212586; fax 055-211379; f. 1815; 70,000 vols and about 6,000 MSS; Dir Dott. GIOVANNA LAZZI.

Forlì

Biblioteca Comunale 'A. Saffi': Corso della Repubblica 72, 47100 Forlì; tel. 0543-712600; fax 0543-712616; 450,000 vols; Dir Dr FRANCO FABBRI.

Genoa

Archivio di Stato di Genova: Via T. Reggio 14, 16123 Genoa; tel. 010-2468373; fax 010-2468992; f. 1817; library of *c.* 13,000 vols, 145 periodicals; Dir Prof. Dott. CARLO BITOSSI.

Biblioteca di Storia dell'Arte: Largo Pertini 4, 16121 Genoa; tel. 010-583836; f. 1908; 50,000 vols; Italian and Genoese art from 11th century to the present; Curator ELISABETTA PAPONE.

Biblioteca Durazzo Giustiniani: Via XXV Aprile 12, 16123 Genoa; tel. 010-2476232; fax 010-2474122; f. 1760–1804; 20,000 18th-century vols, 1,000 *cinquecentine*, 448 incunabula, 300 MSS; Curator Dr SANDRA MACCHIAVELLO.

Biblioteca Universitaria: Via Balbi 3, 16126 Genoa; f. 18th century; 512,423 vols, 1,037 incunabula, 1,861 MSS; 14,148 letters and documents; Dir Reg. Dssa MARIA SANSEVERINO COSTAMAGNA.

Gorizia

Biblioteca Statale Isontina di Gorizia: Via Mameli 12, 34170 Gorizia; tel. 0481-531802; fax 0481-530230; f. 1629; lending and reference library, bibliographical information service; 613 MSS, 229,103 vols, 60,936 pamphlets, 39 incunabula, 675 *cinquecento*, 542 current periodicals; Dir Dott. MARCO MENATO; publ. *Studi Goriziani* (2 a year).

Imola

Biblioteca Comunale: Via Emilia 80, 40026 Imola; tel. 0542-602636; fax 0542-602602; f. 1761; 400,000 vols, 487 current periodicals, 1,692 MSS, 140 incunabula; Dir Dott. GRAZIA-VITTORIA GURRIERI.

L'Aquila

Biblioteca Provinciale 'Salvatore Tommasi': Piazza Palazzo 30, 67100 L'Aquila; tel. 0862-299263; fax 0862-61964; f. 1848; 211,000 vols; 128 incunabula, 880 MSS, 3,232 *cinquecentine* (rare 16th-century editions); Dir Dott. WALTER CAPEZZALI.

Livorno

Biblioteca Comunale 'Labronica' Francesco Domenico Guerrazzi: Villa Fabbricotti, Viale della Libertà 30, 57100 Livorno; tel. 0586-808176; fax 0586-806089; f. 1816; 400,000 vols including 2,000 15th- and 16th-century editions, various MSS and 56,000 letters and documents; Dir Dott MASSIMO LAPI; publ. *Quaderni della Labronica* (quarterly).

Lucca

Biblioteca del Giardino Botanico: 55100 Lucca; contains very rare books on natural sciences.

Biblioteca Statale di Lucca: Via S. Maria Corteorlandini 12, 55100 Lucca; f. 17th century; 461,000 vols, 835 incunabula, 4,321 MSS; musical collection of 68 MSS and *c.* 500 scores; Dir Dott. ROBERTO SIGNORINI.

Macerata

Biblioteca Comunale Mozzi-Borgetti: Piazza Vittorio Veneto 2, 62100 Macerata; tel. 0733-256360; fax 0733-256338; f. 1773; library of 350,000 vols; Dir Dott. ALESSANDRA SFRAPPINI.

Mantua

Biblioteca Comunale: Via Roberto Ardigò 13, 46100 Mantua; tel. 0376-321515; fax 0376-222556; f. 1780; 330,000 vols, 1,375 MSS, 1,425 incunabula, 8,500 *cinquecentine*; Dir Dssa IRMA PAGLIARI.

Biblioteca dell'Accademia Nazionale Virgiliana: Via dell' Accademia 47, 46100 Mantua; f. early 17th century; 30,000 vols; Librarian Prof. MARIO VAINI; publs *Atti e Memorie*, *Nuova Serie* (annually).

Messina

Biblioteca Regionale: Via dei Verdi 71, 98122 Messina 1; tel. 090-663332; fax 090-771909; f. 1731; 400,000 vols, 1,307 MSS, 423 incunabula, 3,637 *cinquecentine*; Dir Dr SANDRA CONTI.

Milan

Archivio di Stato di Milano: Via Senato 10, 20121 Milan; tel. 02-76000369; fax 02-76000986; f. 1782; library of 18,250 vols and pamphlets, 6,500 periodicals, etc.; Dir Dssa GABRIELLA CAGLIARI POLI.

Biblioteca Ambrosiana: Piazza Pio XI 2, 20123 Milan; tel. 02-806921; fax 02-80692210; f. 1609; 850,000 vols and rare prints, 35,000 MSS mostly Latin, Greek, and Oriental, 2,100 incunabula, 12,000 parchments, 20,000 prints, 10,000 drawings; Dir Dott. GIANFRANCO RAVASI.

Biblioteca Centrale della Facoltà di Ingegneria del Politecnico di Milano: Piazza Leonardo da Vinci 32, 20133 Milan; tel. 02-23992550; fax 02-23992560; 175,500 vols, 350 MSS, 3,400 periodicals, 525 current periodicals.

Biblioteca Comunale: Palazzo Sormani, Corso di Porta Vittoria 6, 20122 Milan; tel. 02-795480; fax 02-76006588; e-mail bibcommi@isanet.it; f. 1886; 606,000 vols, 2,500 current periodicals, 62,000 audio and video items; Dir Pietro Florio.

Biblioteca d'Arte: Castello Sforzesco, 20122 Milan; f. 1930; art library and Leonardo da Vinci Collection; Librarian Dott. Lia Gandolfi.

Biblioteca degli Istituti Ospedalieri: Piazza Ospedale Maggiore 3, 20100 Milan; f. 1842; 90,000 vols; Dir Dott. Giulio Brunetti.

Biblioteca del Centro Nazionale di Studi Manzoniani: Via Morone 1, 20121 Milan; tel. 02-86460403; f. 1937; 20,000 vols; Pres. Prof. Giancarlo Vigorelli; publs *Annali*, *Edizione Nazionale Opere di A. Manzoni*, *Bollettino Bibliografico*.

Biblioteca del Conservatorio di Musica G. Verdi: Via Conservatorio 12, 20122 Milan; f. 1808; 450,000 vols; books on music, scores and MSS of 16–20th centuries; Dir Prof. Agostina Zecca Laterza; publs *Annuario del Conservatorio*, catalogues, guide.

Biblioteca della Facoltà di Agraria: Via G. Celoria 2, 20100 Milan; 43,500 vols; Dir Prof. R. Locci; Librarian Iside Marenghi Marchetti.

Biblioteca delle Facoltà di Giurisprudenza e di Lettere e Filosofia dell' Università: Via Festa del Perdono 7, 20122 Milan; tel. 02-58352273; fax 02-58306817; f. 1923; 851,879 vols; Dir Maria Alessandra Dall'Era.

Biblioteca dell' Istituto Lombardo Accademia di Scienze e Lettere: Via Borgonuovo 25, 20121 Milan; tel. 02-864087; fax 02-86461388; f. 1802; 400,000 vols; Dir Dr A. Bianchi Robbiati.

Biblioteca dell' Università Cattolica del S. Cuore: Largo Gemelli 1, 20123 Milan; f. 1921; 1,125,000 vols and pamphlets, 17,450 publications in series; Dir Dott. Ellis Sada.

Biblioteca dell' Università Commerciale Luigi Bocconi: Via Sarfatti 25, 20136 Milan; tel. 02-58365092; fax 02-58365100; f. 1903; 700,000 vols and 6,500 periodical publs; Librarian Dr Marisa Santarsiero.

Biblioteca Nazionale Braidense: Via Brera 28, 20121 Milan; tel. 02-86460907; f. 1770; 965,183 vols, 17,149 periodicals, 26,455 autographs, 2,107 MSS; Dir Dr Goffredo Dotti.

Biblioteca Trivulziana: Castello Sforzesco, 20121 Milan; f. 18th century; 150,000 vols, 1,500 codices, including MSS from the 8th century, 2,000 incunabula, and rare editions of works on history and literature; Dir Dr Giovanni M. Piazza.

Raccolte Storiche del Comune di Milano, Biblioteca e Archivio: Palazzo De Marchi, Via Borgonuovo 23, 20121 Milan; tel. 02-8693549; fax 02-72001483; f. 1884; 250,000 vols, newspapers and pamphlets, 3,825 files of documents of the period 1750 to the present day; Dir Dott. Roberto Guerri.

Modena

Biblioteca Estense Universitaria: Palazzo dei Musei, Largo Porta S. Agostino 337, 41100 Modena; tel. 059-222248; fax 059-230195; e-mail estense@kril.cedoc.unimo.it; 519,000 vols, 11,066 MS vols, 153,300 loose MSS, 1,661 incunabula, 15,966 *cinquecentine*, 124,690 pamphlets, 4,071 periodicals; Dir Dott. Ernesto Milano.

Naples

Archivio di Stato di Napoli: Piazzetta Grande Archivio 5, 80138 Naples; tel. 081-204046; f. 1808; 544,000 items; library of 16,840 vols; Dir Giulio Raimondi.

Biblioteca del Conservatorio di Musica S. Pietro a Maiella: Via S. Pietro a Maiella 35, 80100 Naples; f. 1791; 300,000 vols, 4 incunabula; Dir Francesco Melisi.

Biblioteca della Facoltà di Scienze Agrarie dell' Università degli Studi di Napoli Federico II: Via dell' Università 100, 80055 Portici, Naples; f. 1872; 63,496 vols, 3,000 periodicals; Dir O. Petriccione.

Biblioteca della Pontificia Facoltà Teologica dell' Italia Meridionale, sezione 'San Tommaso d'Aquino': Viale Colli Aminei 2, Capodimonte, 80131 Naples; tel. 081-7413166; f. 1687; 110,000 vols; Dir Russo Francesco.

Biblioteca della Società Napoletana di Storia Patria: Piazza Municipio, Maschio Angiono, 80133 Naples; f. 1876; 270,000 vols, 3,000 MSS, 5,000 periodicals, 15,000 pamphlets; Dir Dr Silvana Musella; publ. *Archivio Storico per le Province Napoletane*.

Biblioteca di Castelcapuano: Piazza dei Tribunali, Palazzo di Giustizia, 80138 Naples; tel. 081-269416; f. 1848; 40,000 vols; Dir Dott. Rossi Bussola Raffaello.

Biblioteca Nazionale 'Vittorio Emanuele III': Palazzo Reale, 80132 Naples; tel. 081-7819111; fax 081-403820; f. 1804; 1,425,000 vols, 33,973 MSS and documents, 4,563 incunabula, 1,788 papyri from Herculaneum; Dir Dott. Mauro Giancaspro; publ. *I Quaderni*.

Biblioteca Oratoriana del Monumento Nazionale dei Girolamini: Via Duomo 142, 80138 Naples; tel. 081-294444; f. 1586; 150,000 vols, 104 incunabula, 482 MSS; Dir P. Giovanni Ferrara.

Biblioteca Universitaria di Napoli: Via G. Paladino 39, 80138 Naples; tel. 081-5517025; fax 081-5528275; f. 1816; 750,000 vols; open to the public; Dir Dr Maria Sicco.

Novara

Biblioteca Comunale Negroni: Corso Felice Cavallotti 4, 28100 Novara; tel. 0321-623040; fax 0321-628068; f. 1906; 250,000 vols, 3,052 periodicals, 5,540 records, 131 incunabula, 771 microfilms, 420 MSS, maps, etc.; Dir Dr M. Carla Uglietti.

Padua

Biblioteca Antoniana: Basilica del Santo, 35100 Padua; f. 1352; 75,000 vols, 800 MS; Dir Prof. Giovanni M. Luisetto.

Biblioteca Civica: Via Orto Botanico 5, 35123 Padua; tel. 049-656375; fax 049-8753207; e-mail biblioteca.civica@padovanet.it; f. 1852; art, history, local history; 500,000 vols, 5,500 MSS, 385 incunabula, 2,000 periodicals; Dir Dr D. Banzato; publ. *Bollettino*.

Biblioteca del Seminario Vescovile: Via Seminario 29, 35100 Padua; f. 1671; 400,000 vols, 1,135 MSS, 417 incunabula; Dir Pierantonio Gios.

Biblioteca Universitaria: Via S. Biagio 7, 35121 Padua; tel. 049-8751090; fax 049-8762711; f. 1629; 636,000 vols, 2,704 MSS, 1,280 incunabula, 1,530 music scores, 1,055 maps, 6,344 periodicals; Dir Dott. Antonio Antonioni.

Palermo

Archivio di Stato di Palermo: Corso Vittorio Emanuele 31, 90133 Palermo; tel. 091-589693; fax 091-6110594; f. 1814; 386,918 items; library of 22,000 vols; Dir Dssa Giuseppina Giordano.

Biblioteca Centrale della Regione Siciliana: Corso Vittorio Emanuele 429–431, 90134 Palermo; tel. 091-6967642; fax 091-6967644; f. 1782; 580,000 vols; 1,930 MSS and 1,044 incunabula, 5,907 periodicals, 15,000 letters and documents, 5,066 rare books, 4,125 maps, prints and engravings, 47,664 microforms, 3,541 photographs and slides; Dir Dssa Carmela Perretta.

Biblioteca Comunale: Piazza Brunaccini 1, 90134 Palermo; f. 1760; 350,000 vols; Dir Dott. Filippo Guttuso.

Biblioteca dell' Università: Via Maqueda 175, 90100 Palermo; tel. 091-230127; 120,000 vols; Dir (vacant).

Parma

Biblioteca Palatina: Palazzo della Pilotta, 43100 Parma; tel. 0521-282217; fax 0521-235662; f. 1761; 708,000 vols, 6,668 MSS; 3,044 incunabula, 320 periodicals, 52,482 engravings and drawings; Dir Dr Leonardo Farinelli, musical section: Via Conservatorio 27, tel. 0521-289429; library of 93,224 vols; 30,340 MSS; 45 periodicals; Librarian Dssa Daniela Moschini.

Biblioteca Palatina—Sezione Musicale presso il Conservatorio di Musica 'A. Boito': Via del Conservatorio 27, 43100 Parma; f. 1889; 72,449 vols, 16,288 MSS, 30 periodicals; Dir Dr Leonardo Farinelli; Librarian Dr Daniela Moschini.

Pavia

Biblioteca Civica: Piazza Petrarca 2, 27100 Pavia; Dir Dott. Felice Milani.

Biblioteca Universitaria: Palazzo dell' Università, 27100 Pavia; f. 1763; 478,601 vols, 1,945 MSS, 669 incunabula, 834 periodicals; Librarian Dott. Maria Anfossi.

Perugia

Biblioteca Augusta del Comune di Perugia: Palazzo Conestabile della Staffa, Via delle Prome 15, 06122 Perugia; tel. 075-5772500; fax 075-5722231; e-mail augusta@comune.perugia.it; f. 1615; 320,000 vols; Dir Dott. Maria Fop.

Pesaro

Biblioteca e Musei Oliveriani: Via Mazza 97, 61100 Pesaro; f. 1793; 250,000 vols on general culture and local history; Librarian Prof. Dott. Antonio Brancati; publ. *Studia Oliveriana* (annually).

Piacenza

Biblioteca Cardinale Giulio Alberoni: Collegio Alberoni—Frazione S. Lazzaro Alberoni, Via Emilia Parmense 77, 29100 Piacenza; tel. 0523-613198; fax 0523-613342; f. 1751; 150,000 vols; Dir Prof. Giuseppe Strinati; publ. *Monografie del Collegio Alberoni*.

Biblioteca Comunale Passerini Landi: Via Carducci 11, 29100 Piacenza; tel. 0523-337912; f. 1774; 200,000 vols; Dir Dott. Carlo Emanuele Manfredi.

Pisa

Biblioteca Universitaria: Via Curtatone e Montanara 15, 56100 Pisa; tel. 050-913411; fax 050-42064; e-mail webmaster@pisa.sbn.it; f. 1742; 428,000 vols, 1,375 MSS, 23,203 documents, 153 incunabula, 1,030 current periodicals; Dir Dr Marco Paoli.

Pistoia

Biblioteca Comunale Forteguerriana: Piazza della Sapienza 5, POB 177, 51100 Pistoia; tel. 0573-24349; fax 0573-24348; f. 1696; 300,000 vols; Dir Dr Daniele Danesi.

Portici

Biblioteca del Dipartimento di Entomologia e Zoologia Agraria, Università degli Studi di Napoli Federico II: Via Università 100, 80055 Portici; f. 1872; applied entomology and biological control; 100,000 vols; Dirs Prof. E. Tremblay, Prof. G. Viggiani; publ. *Bollettino del Laboratorio di Entomologia Agraria 'Filippo Silvestri'*.

Potenza

Archivio di Stato: Corso Garibaldi 4A, 85100 Potenza; tel. 0971-411686; fax 0971-410708; f. 1818; administrative and judicial archives from 1687; notarial archives from 1524; archives of religious houses dissolved in the 19th century; private and feudal archives from 1500; collections of parchments and municipal statutes; also archives of ecclesiastical bodies incl. those of the Venosa cathedral chapter (from 11th century); library of 5,723 vols, 1,643 periodicals; Dir Dott. GREGORIO ANGELINI.

Biblioteca Nazionale: Via del Gallitello, 85100 Potenza; tel. 0971-54829; f. 1985; functions as univ. library (Univ. della Basilicata) and regional library; 256,000 vols, 1,681 periodicals; Dir Dott. MAURIZIO RESTIVO.

Ravenna

Biblioteca Comunale Classense: Via Baccarini 3, 48100 Ravenna; tel. 0544-482149; fax 0544-482104; f. 1707–1711; 650,000 vols; Dir Dott. DONATINO DOMINI; publs *Letture Classensi*, *Bollettino Classense*.

Reggio Emilia

Biblioteca Municipale 'A Panizzi': Via Farini 3, 42100 Reggio Emilia; tel. 0522-456078; fax 0522-456081; f. 1796; 500,000 vols, 10,000 MSS; Dir Dr MAURIZIO FESTANTI.

Rimini

Biblioteca Civica Gambalunga: Via Gambalunga 27, Rimini; tel. 0541-51105; fax 0541-26167; f. 1619; 220,000 vols (7,000 16th-century), 384 incunabula, 1,350 MSS, 350 current periodicals, 1,960 bound periodicals, 8,000 drawings and engravings, 40,000 photographs; Dir Prof. MARCELLO DI BELLE.

Rome

Archivio Centrale dello Stato: Piazzale degli Archivi, EUR, 00144 Rome; tel. 06-5920371; fax 06-5413620; f. 1861; library of 130,000 vols, also periodicals, etc.; political, administrative, cultural and judicial archives of the Kingdom of Italy and Italian Republic; Dir Prof. PAOLA CARUCCI.

Archivio di Stato di Roma: Corso del Rinascimento 40, 00186 Rome; tel. 06-6819081; fax 06-68190851; f. 1871; conservation of archives produced by the central offices of the Papal State from the Middle Ages to 1870, together with documents produced by other agencies in the Rome area; papal provincial treasuries (incl. Avignon and Benevento); archives of religious orders from the 14th century onwards and of brotherhoods, academies, corporate bodies, the University of Rome and notary registers from the 13th century onwards; conservation of government office records of the Italian State with seat in Rome; School of Archival Science, Latin Palaeography and Diplomatics; library of 50,000 vols, with three important collections: Statutes, MSS, Decrees; Dir LUIGI LONDEI.

Biblioteca Angelica: Piazza S. Agostino 8, 00186 Rome; tel. 06-6875874; fax 06-6832312; f. 1605; 200,000 vols, 2,704 MSS, 1,156 incunabula; 15th–18th-century literature; Augustinian, Jansenist, Reformation and Counter-reformation collections; Dir Dssa ARMIDA BATORI.

Biblioteca Casanatense: Via S. Ignazio 52, 00186 Rome; tel. 06-6798855; fax 06-6790550; e-mail casanatense.polosbn@inroma.roma.it; f. 1701; 305,254 vols, 6,459 MSS, 2,183 incunabula; Dir Dr ANGELA A. CAVARRA.

Biblioteca Centrale del Consiglio Nazionale delle Ricerche (Central Library of National Research Council): Piazzale Aldo Moro 7, 00185 Rome; tel. 06-49933221; fax 06-49933834; f. 1927; 1,000,000 vols, 10,000 periodicals, EU depository; scientific and technical subjects; Dir Prof. ENZO CASOLINO.

Biblioteca Centrale Giuridica presso il Ministero di Grazia e Giustizia: Palazzo di Giustizia, Piazza Cavour, 00192 Rome; f. 1866; 200,000 vols; Dir Dr ORAZIO FRAZZINI.

Biblioteca del Ministero degli Affari Esteri: Farnesina, 00194 Rome; f. 1850; 200,000 vols; international relations, contemporary history; Dir Dott. RAFFAELLA MAINIERI.

Biblioteca del Ministero dell'Interno: Palazzo del Viminale, Via Agostino Depretis, 00100 Rome; f. 1872; 170,000 vols; Dir ARTURO LETIZIA.

Biblioteca del Ministero delle Finanze e del Tesoro: Palazzo del Ministero delle Finanze, Via XX Settembre, 00100 Rome; f. 1857; 160,000 vols; Dir Prof. WALTER D'AVANZO.

Biblioteca del Ministero delle Risorse Agricole, Alimentari e Forestali: Via XX Settembre 20, 00187 Rome; tel. 06-4743482; f. 1860; 800,000 vols.

Biblioteca del Senato: Palazzo Madama, Via Dogana Vecchia 27, 00186 Rome; f. 1848; 600,000 vols; chiefly works on law, history and politics; medieval statutes; Dir (vacant).

Biblioteca dell' Accademia Nazionale dei Lincei e Corsiniana: Via della Lungara 10, 00165 Rome; tel. 06-6838831; fax 06-6877195; f. 1754; 552,000 vols, 4,600 MSS, 2,307 incunabula; Dir Dr ANNA M. CAPECCHI.

Biblioteca Archeologia e Storia dell'Arte: Piazza Venezia 3, 00187 Rome; tel. 06-6789965; fax 06-6781167; f. 1922; 511,000 vols, 1,489 MSS, 16 incunabula, 20,000 prints; Dir Dott. ARIANNA JESURUM; publs *Annuario bibliografico di storia dell' arte*, *Annuario bibliografico di archeologia*.

Biblioteca della Camera dei Deputati: Via del Seminario 76, 00186 Rome; f. 1848 in Turin; 900,000 vols; Dir Dssa E. LAMARO; publs *Catalogo Metodico*, *Bollettino Nuove Accessioni*, *Bollettino Legislazione Straniera*.

Biblioteca della Fondazione Marco Besso: Largo di Torre Argentina 11, 00186 Rome; tel. 06-68806290; 60,000 vols and 5,000 pamphlets; special collections: Rome, Dante, Proverbs, Tuscia; Cur. ANNA MARIA AMADIO.

Biblioteca della Società Geografica Italiana: Villa Celimontana, Via della Navicella 12, 00100 Rome; tel. 06-7008279; fax 06-77079518; e-mail geomail@tin.it; f. 1867; 300,000 vols; Library Counsellor Prof. GIORGIO SPINELLI.

Biblioteca della Società Italiana per l'Organizzazione Internazionale (SIOI): Piazza di S. Marco 51, Palazzetto di Venezia, 00186 Rome; tel. 06-6920781; fax 06-6789102; e-mail sioi@mclink.net; f. 1944; 500,000 UN documents; 70,000 vols, 800 periodicals; Librarian Dr SARA CAVELLI.

Biblioteca della Soprintendenza Speciale alla Galleria Nazionale d'Arte Moderna e Contemporanea: Viale delle Belle Arti 131, 00196 Rome; tel. 06-32298410; fax 06-3221579; f. 1945; 65,000 vols, 1,030 periodicals, on 19th- and 20th-century art; Librarian Dott. MASSIMINA CATTARI; publ. *Catalogo dei periodici della biblioteca*.

Biblioteca di Storia Moderna e Contemporanea: Via M. Caetani 32, 00186 Rome; tel. 06-68806624; fax 06-68807662; f. 1917; 300,000 vols; Dir Dr F. PRINZI.

Biblioteca Istituto Italo-Latino Americano: Piazza B. Cairoli 3, 00186 Rome; tel. 06-68492; fax 06-6872834; specializes in contemporary Latin-American life; 80,000 vols, 1,500 periodicals; services: offsets of any item in library, in-service library loans, information service; audio-visual collection; Librarian Prof. RICCARDO CAMPA; publs annotated bibliographical catalogues, lists of book exhibits.

Biblioteca Lancisiana: Borgo S. Spirito 3, 00193 Rome; tel. 06-68352449; fax 06-68352442; f. 1711; history of medicine; 17,932 vols; Librarian Dr MARCO FIORILLA.

Biblioteca Medica Statale: Viale del Policlinico 155, 00161 Rome; tel. 06-490778; fax 06-4457265; f. 1925; 130,000 vols, 8 MSS, 1,193 periodicals; Dir Dr GIOVANNI ARGANESE; publ. *Bollettino bimestrale nuove accessioni*.

Biblioteca Musicale S. Cecilia: Via dei Greci 18, 00187 Rome; f. 1584; 145,367 MSS and printed works; Dir Dott. DOMENICO CARBONI.

Biblioteca Nazionale Centrale Vittorio Emanuele II: Viale Castro Pretorio 105, 00185 Rome; tel. 06-4989; fax 06-4457635; f. 1876; 4,500,000 vols; 6,511 MSS; Dir Dott. PAOLO VENEZIANI; publ. *Bollettino delle opere moderne straniere acquisite dalle Biblioteche pubbliche statali italiane* (annually).

Biblioteca Romana A. Sarti: Piazza dell'Accademia di S. Luca 77, 00187 Rome; tel. 06-6798848; fax 06-6789243; f. 1877; 40,000 vols on architecture and modern decorative art, with particular regard to Rome; 255 MSS, 200 periodicals; Librarian Dott. FABRIZIO AMBROSI DE MAGISTRIS.

Biblioteca Universitaria Alessandrina: Piazzale Aldo Moro 5, 00185 Rome; tel. 06-4474021; fax 06-447402222; f. 1661; 1,062,000 vols; Dir MARIA CONCETTA PETROLLO.

Biblioteca Vallicelliana: Piazza della Chiesa Nuova 18, 00186 Rome; tel. 06-68802671; f. 1581; 150,000 vols, 2,558 MSS, 403 incunabula; also contains library of 'Società Romana di Storia Patria', 50,000 vols; Dir Dr BARBARA TELLINI SANTONI.

Bibliotheca Hertziana (Max-Planck-Institut): Palazzo Zuccari, Via Gregoriana 28, 00187 Rome; tel. 06-699931; fax 06-69993333; f. 1913; 200,000 vols on the history of Italian art; 465,000 photographs of Italian art; Dirs Prof. Dr CHRISTOPH LUITPOLD FROMMEL, Prof. Dr MATTHIAS WINNER; Librarian Dr FRITZ-EUGEN KELLER.

Cineteca Nazionale: Via Tuscolana 1524, 00173 Rome; tel. 06-722941; fax 06-7211619; f. 1935; includes the National Film Archive and the Luigi Chiarini Library; Pres. LINO MICCICHE; Dir-Gen. ANGELO LIBERTINI; publ. *Bianco e Nero* (4 a year).

Discoteca di Stato (State Gramophone Record Library): Via M. Caetani 32, 00186 Rome; tel. 06-6879048; fax 06-6865837; e-mail discoteca@dds.it; f. 1928; collection of recordings of eminent Italians; 190,000 records of classical and light music, jazz; records and tapes on anthropology and folklore; library of 55,000 vols; Dir Dott. MARIA CARLA CAVAGNIS SOTGIU.

Istituto Centrale per il Catalogo Unico delle Biblioteche Italiane e per le Informazioni Bibliografiche (Central Institute of the Union Catalogue of Italian Libraries and Bibliographical Information): Viale del Castro Pretorio 105, 00185 Rome; tel. 06-4454701; fax 06-4959302; f. 1951; Dir Dr GIOVANNA MAZZOLA MEROLA.

Library and Documentation Systems Division, Food and Agriculture Organization of the United Nations (David Lubin Memorial Library): Viale delle Terme di Caracalla, 00100 Rome; tel. 06-52253703; telex 610181; fax 06-52252002; f. 1946; 1,000,000 vols, 7,000 current serials, 32 incunabula, 140,000 microforms, 184 audiovisual items; collection of former International Institute of Agriculture includes the Library of the Centre International de Sylviculture; Chief Librarian JANE M. WU.

Rovigo

Biblioteca dell' Accademia dei Concordi: Piazza V. Emanuele II 14, 45100 Rovigo; tel. 0425-21654; fax 0425-27993; f. 1580; 200,000 vols.

Sassari

Biblioteca Universitaria: Piazza Università 22, 07100 Sassari; tel. 079-235179; fax 079-235787; f. between 1558 and 1562; 250,000 vols, 1,385 MSS, 1,431 microfilms, 71 incunabula; Dir Dr TOMMASO STRACQUALURSI.

Siena

Biblioteca Comunale degli Intronati: Via della Sapienza 5, 53100 Siena; tel. 0577-280079; f. 1758; 500,000 vols, 5,375 vols MSS, 938 incunabula; Dir Dott. CURZIO BASTIANONI.

Teramo

Biblioteca Provinciale Melchiorre Delfico: Convitto Nazionale, Via del Nardo, 64100 Teramo; f. 1816; 130,906 vols; Dir M. MUZII.

Trento

Biblioteca Comunale: Via Madruzzo 26, 38100 Trento; tel. 0461-232171; fax 0461-985166; f. 1856; 327,000 vols, 533 incunabula and 6,000 16th-century editions, music section of 18,000 volumes; 25,000 MSS, 300,000 letters and documents, 4,000 periodicals, 5,000 maps; collection on history and culture of Trentino-Alto Adige; Austrian Library (4,800 vols); Dir Dr FABRIZIO LEONARDELLI; publ. *Studi trentini di scienze storiche*.

Biblioteca dell' Archivio di Stato di Trento: Via Roma 51, Trento; tel. 0461-984105; f. 1919; administered by the Ministero per i Beni Culturali e Ambientali; cultural function and to promote historical research; 5,070 vols, 100 periodicals, holds archives of state offices from pre-unification Italy and single documents and archives belonging to or deposited with the State; Dir Dr SALVATORE ORTOLANI.

Treviso

Biblioteca Comunale: Borgo Cavour 18, 31100 Treviso; tel. 0422-545342; fax 0422-583066; f. 1770; 450,000 vols, 4,000 MSS, 810 incunabula; Dir EMILIO LIPPI; publ. *Studi Trevisani*.

Trieste

Archivio di Stato di Trieste: Via Lamarmora 17, 34139 Trieste; tel. 040-390020; fax 040-394461; f. 1926; library of 37,000 vols, 1,030 periodicals; Dir Dott. UGO COVA.

Biblioteca Civica 'A. Hortis': Piazza Attilio Hortis 4, 34123 Trieste; tel. 040-301108; fax 040-301108; e-mail bibcivica@comune.trieste.it; f. 1793; 400,000 vols; 401 MSS, drawings and maps; Petrarch, Piccolomini and Svevo sections and historical archives; Dir Dott. ANNA ROSA RUGLIANO.

Biblioteca Statale di Trieste: Via del Teatro Romano 17, 34100 Trieste; tel. 040-631679; fax 040-369449; f. 1956; 173,000 vols; Dir CLAUDIO CALTANA (acting).

Narodna in študijska knjižnica v Trstu (Slovene National Study Library): Via S. Francesco 20/1, 34133 Trieste; tel. 040-635629; f. 1947; 92,000 vols.

Turin

Archivio di Stato di Torino: 10100 Turin Centro; tel. 011-540382; fax 011-546176; f. 12th century, building 1731; houses documents of the House of Savoy up to 1861, and those of the provincial State administrations of the 19th century; archives: 70 shelf-kms; library of 45,000 vols, MS collections; Dir Dr ISABELLA MASSABÒ RICCI.

Biblioteca del Politecnico di Torino: Castello del Valentino, 10128 Turin; 15,000 vols; Librarian GIACOMO TRIVERO.

Biblioteca dell' Accademia delle Scienze di Torino: Via Maria Vittoria 3, 10123 Turin; tel. 011-5620047; f. 1783; all fields of learning; 250,000 vols including periodicals, 40,000 letters, MSS; Heads of Library Cttee Prof. AURELIO BURDESE, Prof. ELIO CASETTA.

Biblioteca Matematica dell' Università di Torino: Via Carlo Alberto 10, 10123 Turin; fax 011-534497; f. 1883; 50,000 vols; Dir Prof. L. RODINO.

Biblioteca Nazionale Universitaria: Piazza Carlo Alberto 3, 10123 Turin; tel. 011-889737; fax 011-8178778; f. 1723; 817,657 vols, 171,700 vols of periodicals, 4,209 MSS, 1,603 incunabula, 10,063 *cinquecentine*, 12,440 drawings and prints; Dir Dr LEONARDO SELVAGGI.

Biblioteca Reale: Piazza Castello 191, 10100 Turin; tel. 011-545305; fax 011-543855; f. 1831; 186,000 vols, 4,358 MSS, 1,491 parchments, 3,003 drawings, 187 incunabula, 1,104 periodicals; library of the Savoy family; historical documents on heraldry, military matters, the Sardinian States, the *Risorgimento* and the Piedmont; Dir GIOVANNA GIACOBELLO BERNARD.

Biblioteche Civiche e Raccolte Storiche: Via Cittadella 5, 10122 Turin; tel. 011-4423900; f. 1869; library of 433,000 vols, 61 incunabula, 2,375 MSS, 1,360 *cinquecentine*, 1,105 rare vols, 4,376 microfilms, 2,933 periodicals; 12 br. libraries; Dir GISELDA RUSSO.

Udine

Biblioteca Civica 'Vincenzo Joppi': Piazza Marconi 8, 33100 Udine; tel. 0432-271583; fax 0432-271580; f. 1864; 423,945 vols; 10,000 MSS, 124 incunabula; Dir Dott. ROMANO VECCHIET.

Urbino

Biblioteca Universitaria: Via Aurelio Saffi 2, 61029 Urbino; tel. 0722-305212; fax 0722-305286; e-mail bibhum@uniurb.it; f. 1720; library of 436,755 vols; Dir GOFFREDO MARANGONI.

Venice

Biblioteca del Civico Museo Correr: Piazza S. Marco 52, Procuratie Nuove, 30100 Venice; tel. 041-5225625; fax 041-5200935; f. 1830; specializes in history of art and Venetian history; 116,933 vols, 1,022 periodicals, 13,018 MSS, 700 MSS on microfiche; Dir GIANDOMENICO ROMANELLI.

Biblioteca dell'Accademia Armena di S. Lazzaro dei Padri Mechitaristi: Isola S. Lazzaro, 30126 Venice; tel. 041-5260104; fax 041-5268690; f. 1701; 100,000 vols, 4,000 MSS; Dir Dr SAHAK DJEMDJEMIAN.

Biblioteca Nazionale Marciana: Piazzetta, San Marco 7, 30124 Venice; tel. 041-5208788; fax 041-5238803; f. 1468; 900,000 vols; 13,000 MSS; Dir Dott MARINO ZORZI.

Fondazione Scientifica Querini-Stampalia: Castello 4778, 30122 Venice; tel. 041-2711411; fax 041-2711445; f. 1869; 300,000 vols; Dir Dr GIORGIO BUSETTO.

Verona

Biblioteca Civica: Via Cappello 43, 37121 Verona; tel. 045-8079710; fax 045-8005701; f. 1792; 540,000 vols; 1,188 incunabula; 3,477 MSS; Dir Dott. ENNIO SANDAL.

Vicenza

Biblioteca Civica Bertoliana: Via Riale 5–13, 36100 Vicenza; tel. 0444-323832; fax 0444-546347; e-mail bertoliana@goldnet.it; f. 1696; 447,100 vols, 961 incunabula, 3,556 MSS; Librarian GIORGIO LOTTO.

Museums and Art Galleries

Ancona

Museo Archeologico Nazionale delle Marche: Palazzo Ferretti, Via Ferretti 6, 60100 Ancona; tel. 071-202602; fax 071-202134; f. 1906 (1860); pre-historic and Roman archaeology; large collection from Iron Age Picene and Celtic Cultures; Dir Prof. Dr GIULIANO DE MARINIS.

Aquileia

Museo Archeologico: Via Roma 1, 33051 Aquileia; tel. 0431-91016; fax 0431-919537; f. 1882; collection of Roman architecture, sculpture, inscriptions, mosaics, etc. from excavations in the town; library of 9,000 vols; Dir Dott. FRANCA MASELLI SCOTTI; publ. *Aquileia Nostra* (annually).

Attached museum:

Museo Paleocristiano: Piazza Pirano, Monastero, 33051 Aquileia; tel. 0431-91131; fax 0431-919537; f. 1961; mosaics and inscriptions from the palaeo-Christian era.

Ardea

Raccolta Manzù: 00040 Ardea; f. 1969; paintings and sculptures by Giacomo Manzù (b. 1908 in Bergamo); part of Nat. Gallery of Modern Art in Rome.

Arezzo

Museo Archeologico: Via Margaritone 10, 52100 Arezzo; tel. 0575-20882; f. 1832; Etruscan, Greek and Roman antiquities, coralline vases of Augustan period, sarcophagi, mosaics, coins and bronzes; Management: Superintendent of Antiquities, Florence.

Museo Statale d'Arte Medievale e Moderna: Palazzo Bruni Ciocchi, Via San Lorentino, 52100 Arezzo; tel. 0575-300301; fax 0575-29850; f. 1957; Italian paintings from 13th century to 19th century, Majolica ware, glass, ivories, seals and coins; Curator Dott. STEFANO CASCIU.

Assisi

Museo-Tesoro della Basilica di S. Francesco: 06082 Assisi; tel. 075-819001; fax 075-816187; f. 1927; historical and artistic collections relating to the Basilica church of St Francis, F. M. Perkins colln of 14th- and 15th-century Florentine art; Dir Fr PASCHAL M. MAGRO.

Bari

Museo Archeologico: Palazzo dell'Ateneo, 70100 Bari; tel. 080-5211559; f. 1882; library of 2,500 vols; Dir Dott. GIUSEPPE ANDREASSI.

Pinacoteca Provinciale: Via Spalato 19, 70121 Bari; tel. 080-5412421; f. 1928; Apulian, Venetian and Neapolitan paintings and sculpture from 11th century to 19th century; library of *c*. 3,000 vols; Dir Dott. CLARA GELAO.

Bergamo

Galleria dell' Accademia Carrara: Piazza Giacomo Carrara 82/A, 24100 Bergamo; tel. 035-399643; fax 035-224510; f. 1796; collection includes paintings by Bellini, Raffaello, Pisanello, Mantegna, Botticelli, Beato Angelico, Previtali, Tiepolo, Dürer, Brueghel, Van Dyck, etc.; Pres. Avv. IGNAZIO BONOMI; Dir Dr F. ROSSI.

Bologna

Museo Civico Archeologico: Via Archiginnasio 2, 40124 Bologna; tel. 051-233849; fax 051-266516; e-mail mca@comune.bologna.it; f. 1881; prehistoric, Egyptian, Greek, Roman, Villanovan, Etruscan, Celtic antiquities;

library of 28,000 vols; Dir Dott. CRISTIANA MORIGI GOVI.

Pinacoteca Nazionale: Via Belle Arti 56, 40100 Bologna; tel. 051-243222; fax 051-251368; f. 1808; 14th–18th-century Bolognese paintings and other Italian schools. German and Italian engravings; Dir Prof. ANDREA EMILIANI.

Bolzano

Museo Civico di Bolzano: Via Cassa di Risparmio 14, 39100 Bolzano; tel. 0471-974625; fax 0471-980144; f. 1902; Dir Dr REIMO LUNZ.

Brescia

Direzione Civici Musei d'Arte e Storia: Via Musei 81, 25121 Brescia; Dir Dssa RENATA STRADIOTTI.

Responsible for:

Pinacoteca Tosio Martinengo: Piazza Moretto 4, Brescia; f. 1906; art from the 13th to 18th centuries.

Museo di Santa Giulia: Via Piamarta 4; f. 1882; art and archaeology and three churches.

Museo Romano: Via Musei 57/A, Brescia; f. 1830; prehistoric, pre-Roman and Roman remains.

Museo del Risorgimento: Castello, Brescia; f. 1959; 19th century historical exhibits.

Museo delle Armi 'Luigi Marzoli': Castello, Brescia; f. 1988, armoury from the 14th to 18th centuries.

Museo Civico di Scienze Naturali: Via Ozanam 4, 25128 Brescia; tel. 030-2978661; fax 030-3701048; e-mail museoscienze.bs@intelligenza.it; f. 1949; botanical, geological, zoological and palaeoethnographical collns; library of 60,000 vols; Dir MARCO TONON; publs *Natura Bresciana*, *Annuario Civica Specola Cidnea*.

Museo Diocesano d'Arte Sacra: Via Gasparo da Salò 13, 25121 Brescia; tel. 030-3751064; f. 1978; Dir IVO PANTEGHINI.

Cagliari

Museo Archeologico Nazionale: Piazza Indipendenza, 09124 Cagliari; tel. 070-654237; f. 1806; Sardinian antiquities (prehistorical, Punic, Roman periods); library of 8,000 vols; Dir Dr VINCENZO SANTONI.

Capua

Museo Provinciale Campano: Via Roma, 81043 Capua; tel. 0823-961402; fax 0823-961402; f. 1870; library of 50,000 vols, 2,956 MSS; Dir Dott. DOMENICO D'ANGELO.

Chieti

Museo Archeologico Nazionale: Villa Comunale 3, 66100 Chieti; tel. 0871-403295; fax 0871-330946; Dir Dott. MARIA RUGGERI.

Cividale

Museo Archeologico Nazionale: Piazza del Duomo 13, 33043 Cividale; tel. 0432-700700; fax 0432-700751; f. 1817; prehistoric, Roman and medieval archaeology, jewellery and miniatures; library of 12,000 vols and archives; Dir Dott. PAOLA LOPREATO; publ. *Forum Iulii* (1 a year).

Cosenza

Museo Civico: Piazza XV Marzo, 87100 Cosenza; tel. 0984-73387; f. 1898; history and archaeology; Dir Dr VINCENZO ZUMBINI; publ. *Guide*.

Faenza

Museo Internazionale delle Ceramiche: Via Campidori 2, 48018 Faenza; tel. 0546-21240; fax 0546-27141; e-mail micfaenza@provincia.ra.it; f. 1908; history, art and techniques of ceramics; library of 50,000 vols; Dir Dr GIAN CARLO BOJANI; publ. *Faenza* (every 2 months).

Ferrara

Civiche Gallerie d'Arte Moderna e Contemporanea: Corso Ercole I d'Este 21, 44100 Ferrara; Dir Dott. ANDREA BUZZONI.

Include:

Palazzo dei Diamanti: Corso Ercole I d'Este 21, 44100 Ferrara; tel. 0532-204092; incorporates Galleria d'Arte Moderna e Contemporanea, Museo M. Antonioni.

Palazzo Massari: Corso Porta Mare 5–9, 44100 Ferrara; tel. 0532-248303; fax 0532-205035; incorporates Museo d'Arte Moderna e Contemporanea, Museo G. Boldini, Padiglione d'Arte Contemporanea, Galleria Massari.

Museo Archeologico Nazionale di Spina: Via XX Settembre 124 (Palazzo di Ludovico il Moro), 44100 Ferrara; tel. 0532-66299; f. 1935; Greco-Etruscan vases, statuettes, bronzes and gold ornaments from the graves of Spina; Dir Dr FEDE BERTI.

Florence

Appartamenti Reali: Palazzo Pitti, 50125 Florence; furniture of the 17th, 18th and 19th centuries; Dir MARCO CHIARINI.

Comune di Firenze, Direzione Cultura Servizio Musei: Via Ghibellina 30, 50122 Florence.

Museums and galleries under its control:

Museo di Palazzo Vecchio: Piazza della Signoria, 50122 Florence; tel. 055-27681; paintings, furnishings; frescoes by Ghirlandaio, Salviati, Bronzino, Vasari; Michelangelo's 'Victory' statue.

Museo di Santa Maria Novella: Piazza S. Maria Novella, 50123 Florence; tel. 055-282187; museum built in part of a Dominican church; 15th-century frescoes of the Genesis story by Paolo Uccello, Dello Delli; 14th-century frescoes by Andrea di Bonaiuto depicting the Dominican order and the Church Triumphant.

Museo Bardini: Piazza dei Mozzi 1, 50125 Florence; tel. 055-2342427; f. 1925; paintings by Pollaiolo, Beccafumi, Luca Cranach, Mirabello Cavalori, Giovanni da S. Giovanni, Cecco Bravo, Guercino, Carlo Dolci, Luca Giordano, Il Volterano; sculptures by Nicola and Giovanni Pisano, Tino di Camaino, Andrea della Robbia, Donatello, Michelozzo; oriental rugs, bronzes, arms, furniture, medals, etc.

Raccolta d'Arte Contemporanea 'Alberto della Ragione': Piazza della Signoria 5, 50122 Florence; tel. 055-283078; *c.* 250 works donated by Alberto della Ragione in 1970; Italian art 1914-60.

Museo storico topografico 'Firenze com' era': Via dell'Oriolo 24, 50122 Florence; tel. 055-2616545; depicts the history of the city.

Fondazione Romano nel Cenacolo di Santo Spirito: Piazza Santo Spirito 29, 50125 Florence; tel. 055-287043; collection of sculptures given by Salvatore Romano; includes two pieces by Tino di Camaino, and two fragments attributed to Donatello.

Galleria Rinaldo Carnielo: Piazza Savonarola 3, 50132 Florence; works by the sculptor Rinaldo Carnielo (1853–1910).

Gabinetto Disegni e Stampe degli Uffizi: Via Ninna 5, 50122 Florence; tel. 055-2388671; fax 055-2388699; Dir Dott. ANNAMARIA PETRIOLI TOFANI.

Galleria d'Arte Moderna di Palazzo Pitti: Piazza Pitti 1, 50125 Florence; tel. 055-2388601; f. 1914; paintings and sculptures of the 19th and 20th centuries; Dir Dott. CARLOC SISI.

Galleria degli Uffizi: Piazzale degli Uffizi, 50122 Florence; tel. 055-2388651; fax 055-2388694; f. 16th century; the finest collection of Florentine Renaissance painting in the world; Dssa ANNAMARIA PETRIOLI TOFANI.

Galleria dell' Accademia: Via Ricasoli 60, 50122 Florence; tel. 055-2388609; fax 055-2388609; f. 1784; contains the most complete collection of Michelangelo's statues in Florence and works of art of 13th–19th-century masters, mostly Tuscan; Dir Dssa FRANCA FALLETTI.

Galleria Palatina: Palazzo Pitti, Piazza Pitti, 50125 Florence; tel. 055-2388611; f. 17th century; contains a fine collection of paintings of 16th and 17th centuries; Dir Dott. MARCO CHIARINI.

Istituto e Museo di Storia della Scienza di Firenze: Piazza dei Giudici 1, 50122 Florence; tel. 055-293493; fax 055-288257; e-mail imss@galileo.imss.firenze.it; f. 1930; library of 80,000 vols; Dir Prof. PAOLO GALLUZZI; publs *Nuncius, Annali di Storia della Scienza* (every 6 months), *Bibliografia italiana di storia della scienza* (annually), *Archivio della corrispondenza degli scienzati italiani*, *Biblioteca di Nuncius. Studi e testi*, *Biblioteca della Scienza Italiana*.

Museo Archeologico: Via della Colonna 38, 50121 Florence; tel. 055-23575; fax 055-242213; f. 1870; Egyptian, Etruscan and Greco-Roman archaeology; Dir Dott. FRANCESCO NICOSIA.

Museo degli Argenti: Palazzo Pitti, 50100 Florence; summer state apartments of the Medici Grand Dukes; collections of gold, silver, enamel, *objets d'art*, hardstones, ivory, amber, cameos and jewels, principally from the 15th to the 18th centuries; Dir Dr MARIA MADDALENA MOSCO.

Attached gallery:

Galleria del Costume: Palazzo Pitti, 50125 Florence; period costumes, principally from the 18th to 20th centuries, shown in the neo-classical Meridiana wing of the palace; Dir Dr CARLO SISI.

Museo dell' Opera del Duomo: Piazza del Duomo 9, 50122 Florence; tel. 055-2398796; fax 055-2302898; f. 1891; Dir PATRIZIO OSTICRESI.

Museo della Casa Buonarroti: Via Ghibellina 70, 50100 Florence; tel. 055-241752; e-mail casabuonarroti@theta.it; f. 1858; works by Michelangelo and others; large collection of drawings, sculptures, majolica and archaeological items from the Buonarroti family collections; Dir P. RAGIONIERI.

Museo delle Porcellane: Boboli Gardens, 50100 Florence; collection of European porcelain from *c.* 1720 to 1850; Dir Dr MARIA MADDALENA MOSCO.

Museo di Palazzo Davanzati (Casa Fiorentina Antica): Via Porta Rossa 13, 50123 Florence; tel. 055-2388610; f. 1956; applied arts, specializing in lace and ceramics; Dir Dott. STEFANO FRANCOLINI; (The museum was expected to remain closed to the public until October 1998.).

Museo di S. Marco o dell' Angelico: Piazza San Marco 3, 50121 Florence; tel. 055-2388608; fax 055-2388699; f. 1869; contains the largest existing collection of paintings by Fra Angelico; Dir Dssa MAGNOLIA SCUDIERI.

Museo Horne: Fondazione Horne, Via dei Benci, 50100 Florence; furniture and works of art of the 14th, 15th and 16th centuries; Pres. Dr UMBERTO BALDINI.

Museo Mediceo: Palazzo Medici-Riccardi, Via Cavour 1, 50100 Florence; chapel built by Michelozzo and frescoed by Benozzo Gozzoli (1459); gallery with frescoes by Luca Giordano (1680).

Museo Nazionale (Bargello): Via del Proconsolo 4, 50122 Florence; tel. 055-2388606; f. 1859; medieval and modern sculpture and *objets d'art*; Dir GIOVANNA GAETA BERTELÀ; publ. *Lo Specchio del Bargello*.

Museo Stibbert: Via F. Stibbert 26, 50134 Florence; tel. 055-486049; fax 055-486049; f. 1908; Etruscan, Roman and medieval arms and armour; 15th–19th-century European and Oriental arms; holy objects and vestments; 18th and 19th-century European and Oriental costumes, etc.; 15th–17th-century Flemish tapestries, 14th–19th-century Italian and foreign paintings and furniture; library of 3,500 vols.

Forlì

Istituti Culturali ed Artistici: Corso della Repubblica 72, 47100 Forlì; tel. 0543-712600; fax 0543-712616; comprises a picture gallery, collection of prints and engravings, archaeological and ethnographical museums, ceramics, sculpture and local history; Piancastelli collection of paintings, medals and coins; Dir Dr FRANCO FABBRI.

Pinacoteca e Musei Comunali: Corso Repubblica 72, 47100 Forlì; tel. 0543-712606; fax 0543-712616; Dir Dr FRANCO FABBRI.

Genoa

Galleria Nazionale di Palazzo Spinola: Piazza Pelliceria 1, 16123 Genoa; tel. 010-2705300; fax 010-2705322; f. 1958; Dir Dssa FARIDA SIMONETTI; publ. *Quaderni*.

Museo Civico di Storia Naturale 'G. Doria': Via Brigata Liguria 9, 16121 Genoa; tel. 010-564567; f. 1867; research in natural history; zoological, mineralogical, geological and botanical collections; library of 50,000 vols; Dir Dr ROBERTO POGGI; publs *Annali* (every 2 years), *Doriana*.

Servizio Beni Culturali: Via Garibaldi 18, 16124 Genoa; tel. 010-2476368; fax 010-206022; f. 1908; library of 40,000 vols; Dir LAURA TAGLIAFERRO; publ. *Bollettino dei Musei Civici Genovesi* (quarterly).

Museums and galleries under its control:

Galleria di Palazzo Rosso: Via Garibaldi 18, 16124 Genoa; tel. 010-282641; f. 1874; paintings and sculpture, frescoes and stuccos, nativity models, coins, weights and measures, Ligurian ceramics; Curator PIERO BOCCARDO.

Galleria di Palazzo Bianco: Via Garibaldi 11, 16124 Genoa; tel. 010-2476377; f. 1889; paintings by Genoese and Flemish masters and other schools; Curator CLARIO DI FABIO.

Museo Navale: Villa Doria, Piazza Bonavino 7, 16156 Genoa-Pegli; tel. 010-6969885; f. 1930; models of ships, nautical instruments, navigation maps, prints; Curator PIERANGELO CAMPODONICO.

Galleria di Arte Moderna: Villa Serra, Via Capolungo 3, Nervi, 16167 Genoa; tel. 010-3726025; f. 1928; 19th and 20th century paintings; Curator MARIA FLORA GIUBILEI.

Museo Giannettino Luxoro: Via Aurelia 29, Nervi, 16167 Genoa; tel. 010-322673; f. 1945; Flemish and Genoese paintings of the 17th and 18th centuries, furniture, ceramics; Curator (vacant).

Museo del Tesoro di San Lorenzo: Cattedrale di San Lorenzo, 16123 Genoa; tel. 010-208627; f. 1892; relics, copes and goldsmiths' work; Curator CLARIO DI FABIO.

Museo del Risorgimento e Istituto Mazziniano: Casa di Mazzini, Via Lomellini 11, 16124 Genoa; tel. 010-207553; f. 1934; exhibits illustrating life and work of Mazzini, 19th century documents and arms, specialized library containing works from the 18th to the 20th century; Curator LEO MORABITO.

Museo di Architettura e Scultura Ligure di S. Agostino: Piazza Sarzano 35r., 16128 Genoa; tel. 010-2511263; f. 1938; 6th to 18th century sculpture; Curator CLARIO DI FABIO.

Museo Etnografico del Castello d'Albertis: Corso Dogali 18, 16136 Genoa; tel. 010-2476360; f. 1932; non-European archaeology and ethnology; Curator MARIA CAMILLA DE PALMA.

Museo d'Arte Orientale 'Edoardo Chiossone': Villetta di Negro, Piazzale Mazzini, 16122 Genoa; tel. 010-542285; f. 1905; Japanese works of art from 11th to 19th century; Chinese bronzes; Curator DONATELLA FAILLA.

Museo Civico di Archeologia Ligure: Villa Durazzo-Pallavicini, Via Pallavicini 1, 16155 Genoa; tel. 010-6981048; fax 010-206022; f. 1892; Ligurian archaeology of the periods up to the Roman era; collection of Greek vases; Curator ANNA MARIA PASTORINO.

Archivio Storico del Comune di Genova: Palazzo Ducale, Piazza Matteotti 5, 16121 Genoa; tel. 010-543793; f. 1906; documents from 15th to 19th centuries; Curator LIANA SAGINATI.

Archivio Fotografico del Comune di Genova: Via Garibaldi 18, 16124 Genoa; tel. 010-282641; fax 010-206022; f. 1910; 200,000 photographs (1860–1946) on Genoese customs and history, 19th-century landscapes, war damage, Genoese art and architecture; current art; Curator ELISABETTA PAPONE.

Gabinetto Disegni e Stampe: Via Garibaldi 18, 16124 Genoa; tel. 010-282641; fax 010-206022; f. 1893; 10,000 drawings of Italian schools and 6,000 prints; Curator PIERO BOCCARDO.

Civico Museo di Storia e Cultura Contadina Genovese e Ligure: Salita al Garbo 47, 16159 Genoa; tel. 010-7401243; collection of objects relating to local rural life in the 19th and 20th centuries; Curator PATRIZIA GARIBALDI.

Raccolte Frugone in Villa Grimaldi: Villa Grimaldi, Via Capolungo 9, 16167 Nervi-Genoa; tel. 010-322396; collection of sculpture and paintings by 19th- and 20th-century Italian artists; Curator MARIA FLORA GIUBILEI.

Soprintendenza ai Beni Archeologici della Liguria: Palazzo Reale, Via Balbi 10, 16126 Genoa; tel. 010-27181; fax 010-2465925; f. 1939; preservation of monuments and excavations of Liguria (prehistoric, Roman and medieval) and ancient city of Luni and prehistoric caves of Balzi Rossi; library of 10,000 vols; Superintendent Dott. GIUSEPPINA SPADEA.

Grosseto

Museo Archeologico e d'Arte della Maremma: Piazza Baccarini 3, 58100 Grosseto; tel. 0564-455132; f. 1865; archaeological and medieval findings from the Maremma; library of 3,000 vols; Dir Dssa MARIAGRAZIA CELUZZA.

L'Aquila

Museo Nazionale d'Abruzzo: Piazza Castello, 67100 L'Aquila; tel. 0862-6331; fax 0862-413096; f. 1949; art from the early Middle Ages to contemporary times; Dir Dott. CALCEDONIO TROPEA.

Lecce

Museo 'Sigismondo Castromediano': Viale Gallipoli 28, 73100 Lecce; tel. 0832-307415; fax 0832-304435; f. 1868; archaeology and art gallery; library of 1,900 vols; 2,500 pamphlets and off-prints; Dir ANTONIO CASSIANO.

Lucca

Museo di Villa Guinigi: Villa Guinigi, Via della Quarquonia, 55100 Lucca; tel. 0583-46033; collection of Roman and late Roman sculptures and mosaics; Romanesque, Gothic, Renaissance and Neoclassical sculpture; paintings from 12th to 18th century including Fra Bartolomeo and Vasari; wood inlays, textiles, medieval goldsmiths' art; Dir Dr MARIA TERESA FILIERI.

Museo e Pinacoteca Nazionale di Palazzo Mansi: Via Galli Tassi 43, 55100 Lucca; tel. 0583-55570; f. 1868; paintings by Titian, Tintoretto, etc., and Tuscan, Venetian, French and Flemish Schools; Dir Dr MARIA TERESA FILIERI.

Mantua

Palazzo Ducale: Piazza Sordello, 46100 Mantua; tel. 0376-352111; fax 0376-366274; e-mail museo.ducale@soprintmn.inet.it; incorporates Museo e Galleria di Pittura (13th- to 18th-century paintings) and Museo Statuario d'Arte Greca e Romana; Dir Dott. ALDO CICINELLI; publ. *Catalogue* (fully illustrated).

Matera

Museo Nazionale D. Ridola: Via D. Ridola 24, 75100 Matera; tel. 0835-311239; Dir Dr MARIA GIUSEPPINA CANOSA.

Messina

Museo Regionale: Via della Libertà 465, 98121 Messina; tel. 090-361292; f. 1953; Dir Dssa FRANCESCA CAMPAGNA CICALA.

Milan

Civiche Raccolte Archeologiche e Numismatiche: Via B. Luini 2, 20123 Milan; tel. 02-8053972; fax 02-86452796; prehistoric, Roman, Etruscan, Greek and Egyptian archaeology; coins and medals; library of 30,000 vols; Dir ERMANNO A. ARSLAN; publ. *Rassegna di Studi* (2 a year).

Galleria d'Arte Moderna: Villa Reale, Via Palestro 16, 20121 Milan; tel. 02-86463054; fax 02- 86463054; painting and sculpture from Neo-Classical period to end of 19th century: includes the Grassi and Vismara collections and Museo Marino Marini; attached galleries of contemporary art; Dir Dott. MARIA TERESA FIORIO.

Museo Civico di Storia Naturale di Milano: Corso Venezia 55, 20121 Milan; tel. 02-781312; fax 02-76022287; f. 1838; all branches of natural history; depts of Vertebrate Palaeontology, Invertebrate Palaeontology, Mineralogy, Vertebrate Zoology, Invertebrate Zoology, Entomology, Botany; library of 115,000 vols; Dir Dr LUIGI CAGNOLARO.

Museo d'Arte Antica: Castello Sforzesco, 20121 Milan; f. 1893; sculpture from Middle Ages to 16th century, including the *Pietà* of Michelangelo; paintings, including works by Mantegna, Foppa, Lippi, Bellini, Lotto, Tintoretto, Tiepolo, Guardi, etc.; furniture, silver, bronzes, ivories, ceramics, musical instruments, tapestries by Bramantino, Bertarelli stamp collection; library of 41,000 vols; Dirs Dr MARIA TERESA FIORIO (painting and sculpture), Dr CLAUDIO SALSI (decorative art).

Museo Nazionale della Scienza e della Tecnica 'Leonardo da Vinci': Via San Vittore 21, 20123 Milan; tel. 02-485551; fax 02-48010016; f. 1953; scientific and technical activities, displaying relics, models and designs, with particular emphasis on Leonardo's work; library of 32,000 vols, mostly history of science and technology, 150 16th-century vols, large section on Leonardo, including facsimile of every MS; Pres. CARLO CAMERANA; Dir Dr ARCH DOMENICO LINI; publ. *Museoscienza* (2 a year).

Museo Poldi Pezzoli: Via A. Manzoni 12, 20121 Milan; tel. 02-796334; fax 02-8690788; f. 1881; paintings from 14th–19th centuries; armour, tapestries, rugs, jewellery, porcelain, glass, textiles, furniture, clocks and watches, etc.; library of 5,500 vols; Dir Dott. ALESSANDRA MOTTOLA MOLFINO.

Pinacoteca Ambrosiana: Piazza Pio XI 2, 20123 Milan; tel. 02-806921; fax (02-80692210; f. 1618; paintings by Raphael, Botticelli, Titian, Bramante, Luini, etc.; drawings by Leonardo, Dürer, Rubens, etc.; miniatures, enamels, ceramics and medallions; Dir Dott. GIANFRANCO RAVASI.

Pinacoteca di Brera: Via Brera 28, 20121 Milan; tel. 02-722631; f. 1809; pictures of all schools, especially Lombard and Venetian; paintings by Mantegna, Bellini, Crivelli, Lotto, Titian, Veronese, Tintoretto, Tiepolo, Foppa, Bergognone, Luini, Piero della Francesca, Bramante, Raphael, Caravaggio, Rembrandt, Van Dyck, Rubens; also 20th-century works, mostly Italian; Dir Dott. PIETRO PETRAROIA.

Raccolte Storiche del Comune di Milano, Museo del Risorgimento: Palazzo De Marchi, Via Borgonuovo 23, 20121 Milan; tel. 02-8693549; fax 02-72001483; f. museum 1884; documents, relics, etc., of the period 1796 to 1870; Dir Dott. ROBERTO GUERRI.

Modena

Galleria, Museo e Medagliere Estense: Palazzo dei Musei, Piazza S. Agostino 337, 41100 Modena; tel. 059-222145; fax 059-230196; f. 15th century in Ferrara, transferred to Palazzo Ducale, Modena, 1598, to Palazzo di Musei 1854; collections include about 2,000 paintings and drawings of 14th to 18th centuries, sculpture, engravings, medals, etc.; library of 5,000 vols; Dir JADRANKA BENTINI.

Museo Civico Archeologico Etnologico: Piazza S. Agostino 337, 41100 Modena; tel. 059-243263; fax 059-224975; f. 1871; prehistory and ethnology; library of 4,000 vols, 2,000 pamphlets; Dir Dr ANDREA CARDARELLI; publ. *Quaderni*.

Museo Civico di Storia e Arte Medievale e Moderna: Largo Porta Sant'Agostino 337, 41100 Modena; tel. 059-223892; telex 522338; fax 059-224795; f. 1871; paintings, sculpture, decorative arts; library of 5,000 vols, 2,000 pamphlets; Dir Dr ENRICA PAGELLA.

Museo Lapidario Estense: Piazza S. Agostino 337, 41100 Modena; tel. 059-235004; fax 059-230196; f. 1808; Roman and medieval archaeological collections; Dir JADRANKA BENTINI.

Naples

Museo Archeologico Nazionale: Piazza Museo 19, 80135 Naples; tel. 081-440166; fax 081-440013; f. 18th century; Greek, Roman, Italian and Egyptian antiquities; Curator Dr STEFANO DE CARO.

Museo Civico 'Gaetano Filangieri': Via Duomo 288, 80138 Naples; tel. 081-203175; fax 081-203175; f. 1888; paintings, furniture, archives, photographs, majolica, arms and armour; library of 15,000 vols, and coin collection of Neapolitan history; Dir ANTONIO BUCCINO GRIMALDI.

Museo 'Duca di Martina' alla Floridiana: Via Cimarosa 77, 80100 Naples; tel. 081-5788418; ceramics; exhibits donated by the Duke; Dir Dr PAOLA GIUSTI.

Museo e Gallerie Nazionali di Capodimonte: 80100 Naples; tel. 081-7441307; f. 1738; paintings from 13th to 18th centuries; paintings and sculptures of 19th century; collection of arms and armour; medals and bronzes of the Renaissance; porcelain; library of 50,000 vols; Dir Prof. NICOLA SPINOSA.

Museo Nazionale di S. Martino: 80129 Naples; tel. 081-5781769; f. 1872; ancient church of S. Martino with 16th- to 18th-century pictures, 13th- to 19th-century sculpture, majolica and porcelain, Neapolitan historical records and topographical collection, naval collection, arms and military costumes, opaline glass, section of modern painting, prints and engravings; Dir Dssa ROSSANA MUZII.

Soprintendenza Archeologica di Pompei: 80045 Pompei; tel. 081-8575301; fax 081-8613183; Supt Prof. PIETRO GIOVANNI GUZZO.

Supervises:

Antiquarium Nazionale di Boscoreale: 80041 Boscoreale; tel. 081-5368796; Dir Dott. GRETE STEFANI.

Scavi di Ercolano: 80056 Ercolano; tel. 081-7390963; fax 081-7777167; Dir Dott. MARIO PAGANO.

Scavi di Oplontis: 80058 Torre Annunziata; tel. 081-8624081; Dir Dott. LORENZO FERGOLA.

Scavi di Pompei: 80045 Pompei; tel. 081-8575238; Dir Dott. ANTONIO D'AMBROSIO.

Scavi di Stabia: 80053 Castellammare di Stabia; tel. 081-8714541; Dirs Dott. ANNA MARIA SODO, Dott. GIOVANNA BONIFACIO.

Padua

Musei Civici di Padova: Piazza Eremitani 8, 35121 Padua; tel. 049-8204550; fax 049-8204566; Dir DAVIDE BANZATO; publ. *Bollettino del Museo Civico di Padova*.

Consist of:

Museo Archeologico: Piazza Eremitani, Padua; f. 1825; pre- and early historic and Roman finds; Curator Dott. G. ZAMPIERI.

Museo d'Arte Medioevale et Moderna: c/o Musei Civici, Piazza Eremitani, Padua; f. 1825; paintings, sculptures, bronzes, ceramics, industrial arts; Curator (vacant).

Museo Bottacin: Piazza Eremitani, Padua; Graeco-Roman, Paduan, Venetian, Italian, Napoleonic coins and medals; Curator Dott. BRUNO CALLEGHER.

Cappella degli Scrovegni: Piazza Eremitani, Padua; Giotto frescoes.

Sala della Ragione: Via 8 Febbraio, Padua; tel. 049-8205006; fax 049-8204566; f. 1218; works by Fra Giovanni degli Eremitani, frescoes by Nicolò Miretto.

Palermo

Museo Archeologico Regionale A. Salinas: Piazza Olivella, 90133 Palermo; tel. 091-6116805; fax 091-6110740; f. 1866; prehistoric, Egyptian, Greek, Punic, Roman and Etruscan antiquities; library of 25,000 vols and pamphlets; Dir Prof. Dssa CARMELA ANGELA DI STEFANO.

Parma

Galleria Nazionale: Palazzo Pilotta 15, 43100 Parma; tel. 0521-233309; fax 0521-206336; f. 1752, later reconstructed and added to; paintings from 13th to 19th centuries, including works by Correggio, Parmigianino, Cima, El Greco, Piazzetta, Tiepolo, Holbein, Van Dyck, Mor, Nattier, and several painters of the school of Parma; 19th-century paintings by Parmesan painters; library of history of art; Dir LUCIA FORNARI SCHIANCHI.

Museo Archeologico Nazionale: Via della Pilotta 4, 43100 Parma; tel. 0521-233718; f. 1760; archaeological collection of sculptures and other monuments from Veleia; Pre-Roman and Roman monuments from province of Parma; Egyptian, Greek, Etruscan and Roman art documents; Dir Dr MARIA BERNABÒ BREA.

Museo Bodoniano: c/o Biblioteca Palatina, Palazzo della Pilotta 3/A, 43100 Parma; tel. 0521-282217; fax 0521-235662; f. 1963; one of the richest museums of the art of printing: punches, original matrices and moulds (*c.* 80,000) from Bodoni's printing works; rare editions, technical manuals, press and tools of 'the prince of printers'; Commr Dott. LEONARDO FARINELLI; Curator LUIGI PELIZZONI; publ. *Bollettino*.

Pavia

Civici Musei—Castello Visconteo: Piazza Castello, 27100 Pavia; tel. 0382-33853; fax 0382-303028; f. 1838; library of 16,500 vols; Dir Dott. DONATA VICINI.

Perugia

Galleria Nazionale dell' Umbria: Palazzo dei Priori, Corso Vannucci, 06100 Perugia; tel. 075-5741257; fax 075-5720316; f. 1863; paintings of Umbrian school, 13th–19th centuries; also sculptures and jewellery; library of 5,300 vols; Dir Dssa VITTORIA GARIBALDI.

Museo Archeologico Nazionale dell' Umbria: Piazza Giordano Bruno 10, 06121 Perugia; tel. 075-5720345; fax 075-5728200; Dir A. E. FERUGLIO.

Pesaro

Museo Civico: Piazza Toschi Mosca 29, 61100 Pesaro; tel. 0721-67815; f. 1936; Dir Dott. CLAUDIO GIARDINI.

Pisa

Museo Nazionale di S. Matteo: Convento di S. Matteo, Lungarno Mediceo, 56100 Pisa; tel. 050-23750; sculptures by the Pisanos and their school; important collection of the Pisan school of the 13th and 14th centuries, and paintings and sculpture of the 15th, 16th and 17th centuries, ceramics, important collection of coins and medals, etc.; Dir Dott. MARIAGIULIA BURRESI.

Portoferraio

Museo Napoleonico di S. Martino: 57037 Portoferraio.

Ravenna

Museo Nazionale di Ravenna: Via Benedetto Fiandrini, 48100 Ravenna; tel. 0544-34424; fax 0544-37391; State property since 1885; art and archaeology; Dir Dott. LUCIANA MARTINI.

Reggio Calabria

Museo Nazionale: Piazza De Nava 26, 89100 Reggio Calabria; tel. 0965-22005; fax 0965-25164; f. 1958; archaeological objects from Calabria from prehistoric era to Roman times; also *Antiquarium di Locri* (Locri), *Museo Archaeologico* (Vibo Valentia), *Museo Archaeologico* (Crotone), *Museo della Sibaritide* (Sibari); library of 10,000 vols; art gallery; Dir Dr ELENA LATTANZI; publ. *Klearchos* (annually).

Rome

Galleria Borghese: Villa Borghese, 00197 Rome; f. *c.* 1616; picture gallery, collections of classical and Baroque sculpture; Dir Dr ALBA COSTAMAGNA.

Galleria Nazionale d'Arte Moderna-Arte Contemporanea: Viale delle Belle Arti 131,

00197 Rome; tel. 06-322981; fax 06-3221579; f. 1883; art of 19th and 20th centuries; Dir Dr SANDRA PINTO.

Galleria Nazionale Palazzo Barberini: Via Quattro Fontane 13, 00184 Rome; tel. 06-4824184; 12th–18th-century Italian and European paintings, Baroque architecture; Dir Dssa LORENZA MOCHI ONORI; Corsini collection at Galleria Corsini, Via della Lungara 10; Dir Dr SIVIGLIANO ALLOISI.

Istituto Nazionale per la Grafica: Calcografia, Via della Stamperia 6, 00187 Rome; tel. 06-699801; fax 06-69921454; f. 1895; Italian and foreign prints and drawings from 14th century to present time; collection of matrices from 16th century to present time; Dir Dott. SERENITA PAPALDO.

Musei Capitolini: Piazza del Campidoglio 00186 Rome; tel. 06-67102071; fax 06-67103118; f. 1471; archaeology, art history; Dir Dssa A. SOMMELLA.

Museo Barracco: Corso Vittorio Emanuele 168, 00186 Rome; tel. 06-6540848; f. 1905; evolution of sculpture from Egyptian to Roman styles; Dir MARESITA NOTA.

Museo della Civiltà Romana: Piazza G. Agnelli 10, 00144 Rome; tel. 06-5926135; f. 1952; Curator Dssa ANNA MURA SOMMELLA.

Museo di Palazzo Venezia: Via del Plebiscito 118, 00186 Rome; tel. 06-69994318; Dir MARIA LETIZIA CASANOVA UCCELLA.

Museo di Roma: Piazza S. Pantaleo 10, 00186 Rome; tel. 06-6865696; fax 06-67103118; Dir Dott. LUCIA CAVAZZI.

Museo Nazionale d'Arte Orientale: Palazzo Brancaccio, Via Merulana 248, 00185 Rome; tel. 06-735946; f. 1957; Dir Dott. DONATELLA MAZZEO; library of 6,273 vols.

Museo Nazionale delle Arti e Tradizioni Popolari: Piazza Marconi 8/10, 00144 Rome; tel. 06-5926148; fax 06-5911848; e-mail mnatp@nexus.it; f. 1923; library of 30,000 vols; archives of musical, spoken and photo-cinematographic material; Dir Dott. STEFANIA MASSARI.

Museo Nazionale di Castel Sant'Angelo: Lungotevere Castello 50, 00193 Rome; tel. 06-6819111; fax 06-68191196; f. 1925; ancient armoury; architectural and monumental remains, frescoes, sculptures, pictures and period furniture; library of 11,000 vols, 60 periodicals; Dir Arch. RUGGERO PENTRELLA.

Museo Nazionale di Villa Giulia: Piazzale di Villa Giulia 9, 00196 Rome; tel. 06-3201951; fax 06-3202010; f. 1889; Etruscan and Italian antiquities; Dir Dr FRANCESCA BOITANI.

Museo Nazionale Preistorico Etnografico 'Luigi Pigorini': Piazzale G. Marconi 14, Rome; tel. 06-549521; fax 06-54952310; f. 1875; prehistory and ethnology; library of 63,000 vols; Superintendent Dr MARIA ANTONIETTA FUGAZZOLA; publ. *Bullettino di Paletnologia Italiana* (annually).

Scavi di Ostia: Roman antiquities, monuments, paintings, sculpture, mosaics, etc.; Curator Dssa ANNA GALLINA ZEVI.

Soprintendenza Archeologica di Roma: Piazza S. Maria Nova 53, 00186 Rome; tel. 06-6990110; fax 06-6787689; Superintendent Prof. ADRIANO LA REGINA.

Supervises:

Foro Romano e Palatino: Rome; Dir Dr IRENE IACOPI.

Museo Nazionale Romano: Piazza dei Cinquecento 79, 00185 Rome; tel. 06-483617; fax 06-4814125; f. 1889; Greek, Hellenistic and Roman sculpture and bronzes, paintings and mosaics, numismatics; archaeological collection; Dir Prof. ADRIANO LA REGINA.

Villa della Farnesina: Via della Lungara 230, 00165 Rome; now the property of the Accademia Nazionale dei Lincei; built 1509 by Peruzzi; decorated by Raphael, Peruzzi and others.

Rovigo

Museo dell'Accademia dei Concordi: Piazza V. Emanuele II 14, 45100 Rovigo; tel. 0425-21654; fax 0425-27993; Protovillanovian, Egyptian and Roman antiquities; numismatic collection of 4,500 items.

Pinacoteca dell'Accademia dei Concordi: Piazza V. Emanuele II 14, 45100 Rovigo; tel. 0425-21654; fax 0425-27993; f. 1833; contains 650 Venetian paintings (14th–18th centuries), including work by Seminario Vescovile di Rovigo.

Sarsina

Museo Archeologico Nazionale: Via Cesio Sabino 39, 47027 Sarsina; tel. 0547-94641; f. 1890; exhibition of archaeological remains from the Roman age; Dir Dott. JACOPO ORTALLI.

Sassari

Museo Nazionale G. A. Sanna: Via Roma 64, 07100 Sassari; tel. 079-272203; f. 1932; archaeology, medieval and modern art, ethnography; Dir Dott. F. LO SCHIAVO.

Siena

Museo Archeologico: Via della Sapienza, 53100 Siena; tel. 0577-44293; Dir ELISABETTA MANGANI.

Museo Aurelio Castelli: Via dell'Osservanza 7, 53100 Siena.

Pinacoteca Nazionale: Via San Pietro 29, 53100 Siena; tel. 0577-286143; fax 0577-270508; f. 1930; 650 paintings exhibited; Dir Dr Ssa ANNA MARIA GUIDUCCI.

Syracuse

Museo Archeologico Regionale: Viale Teocrito 66, 96100 Syracuse; tel. 0931-464022; f. 1886; prehistory, statuary and antiques from the excavations of the Greco-Roman city and from prehistoric and classical sites of Eastern Sicily; Dir GIUSEPPE VOZA.

Taranto

Museo Nazionale: Corso Umberto 41, 74100 Taranto; tel. 099-4532113; fax 099-4594946; Dir Dr GIUSEPPE ANDREASSI.

Tarquinia

Museo Nazionale Tarquiniense: Palazzo Vitelleschi, 01016 Tarquinia; f. 1924; Etruscan sarcophagi 4th and 3rd centuries BC, Etruscan and Greek vases, bronzes, ornaments; Etruscan paintings; Dir Dr MARIA CATALDI.

Trento

Castello del Buonconsiglio – Monumenti e Collezioni Provinciali: Via B. Clesio 5, 38100 Trento; tel. 0461-233770; fax 0461-239497; ancient, medieval and modern art; Dir Dott. FRANCO MARZATICO.

Trieste

Musei Civici di Storia ed Arte: Via Cattedrale 15, 34121 Trieste; tel. 040-310500; fax 040-311301; Dir Dott. ADRIANO DUGULIN.

Comprise:

Civico Museo di Storia ed Arte e Orto Lapidario: Via Cattedrale 15, 34121 Trieste; tel. 040-308686.

Castello di San Giusto e Civico Museo del Castello: Piazza Cattedrale 3, 34121 Trieste; tel. 040-313636.

Civico Museo Sartorio e Collezione Artistiche Stavropulos: Largo Papa Giovanni XXIII 1, 34123 Trieste; tel. 040-301479.

Civico Museo di Storia Patria—Museo Morpurgo de Nilma: Via Imbriani 5, 34122 Trieste; tel. 040-636969.

Civico Museo del Risorgimento e Sacrario Oberdan: Via XXIV Maggio 4, 34133 Trieste; tel. 040-361675.

Civico Museo de Guerra per la Pace 'Diego de Henriquez': Via Revoltella 29, 34139 Trieste; tel. 040-948430; fax 040-948430.

Civico Museo Teatrale di Fondazione Carlo Schmidl: Via Imbriani 5, 34122 Trieste; tel. 040-66030.

Civico Museo della Risiera di S. Sabba: Ratto della Pileria 43, 34148 Trieste; tel. 040-826202.

Turin

Armeria Reale: Piazza Castello 191, 10122 Turin; tel. 011-543889; f. 1837; considered as one of the best collections of arms in Europe; includes the famous equestrian armour of Otto Heinrich and works by Pompeo della Chiesa, Etienne Delaune and the famous engravers of the Monaco de Baviera school, Emanuel Sadeler, Daniel Sadeler and Caspar Spät; Dir Dr PAOLO VENTUROLI.

Galleria Sabauda: Via Accademia delle Scienze 6, 10123 Turin; tel. 011-5641755; fax 011-549547; f. 1832; one of principal Flemish and Dutch collections, and early Italian, also Bronzino, Veronese, Tiepolo and Lombard and Piedmontese schools, furniture, sculpture and jewellery; Dir Dssa PAOLA ASTRUA.

Musei Civici di Torino: Via Magenta 31, 10128 Turin; Curators for the artistic collections Dott. SILVANA PETTENATI (ancient art), Dott. PIER GIOVANNI CASTAGNOLI (modern and contemporary art); Curator for Coins Dssa SERAFINA PENNESTRÌ.

Comprise:

Museo Civico d'Arte Antica e Palazzo Madama: Piazza Castello, 10122 Turin; tel. 011-543823; fax 011-540249; closed until 1998.

Museo di Numismatica, Etnografia, Arti Orientali: Via Bricherasio 8, 10128 Turin; tel. 011-541557.

Galleria Civica d'Arte Moderna e Contemporanea: Via Magenta 31, 10128 Turin; tel. 011-5629911; fax 011-5628637.

Borgo e Castello Medioevale: Parco del Valentino, 10126 Turin; tel. 011-6699372.

Museo Pietro Micca: Via Guicciardini 7, 10121 Turin; tel. 011-546317.

Museo di Antichità: Corso Regina Margherita 105, 10123 Turin; tel. 011-5212251; fax 011-5213145; Dir Dott. LILIANA MERCANDO.

Museo Egizio: Via Accademia delle Scienze 6, 10123 Turin; tel. 011-5617776; fax 011-5623157; e-mail egizi@arti.beniculturali.it; f. 1824; sarcophagi, mummies, stele, statues, papyri, Ptolemaic and Coptic antiquities; entire furnishings of the tomb of architect Kha and his wife, reconstructed Nubian temple of 18th dynasty, presented by the Egyptian Government; Dir ANNA MARIA DONADONI ROVERI.

Udine

Civici Musei e Gallerie di Storia e Arte: Castello, Piazza Libertà, 33100 Udine; tel. 0432-501824; fax 0432-501681; f. 1866; history, art; Dir Dr GIUSEPPE BERGAMINI.

Urbino

Galleria Nazionale delle Marche—Palazzo Ducale: 61029 Urbino; f. 1912; medieval and Renaissance works of art originating in the town of Urbino and the provinces of Marche; Dir Prof. PAOLO DAL POGGETTO.

Venice

Biennale di Venezia: S. Marco, Ca' Giustinian, 30124 Venice; tel. 041-5218711; telex 410685; fax 041-5236374; f. 1895; an autonomous body; organizes artistic and cultural events throughout the year: visual arts, architecture, cinema, theatre, music, special projects, etc.; the Biennale owns historical archives of contemporary art; library of 100,000 vols and catalogues, photographs, etc.; Pres. GIAN LUIGI RONDI.

Civici Musei Veneziani d'Arte e di Storia: S. Marco 52, 30100 Venice; tel. 041-5225625; fax 041-5200935; Dir Prof. GIANDOMENICO ROMANELLI.

Comprise:

Museo Correr: Piazza San Marco, 30100 Venice; f. 1830 by Teodoro Correr who bequeathed his collections to the City; Venetian art (13th–16th centuries) and history of the Serenissima, Renaissance coins, ceramics; publ. *Bollettino* (quarterly).

Ca' Rezzonico: S. Barnaba-Fondamenta Rezzonico, Canal Grande, 30100 Venice; f. 1935; 18th-century Venetian art, sculpture, etc.

Museo Vetrario di Murano: Fondamenta Giustiniani 8, 30121 Murano; f. 1861; Venetian glass from middle ages to the present; also collections of 1st-century Roman glass, Spanish, Bohemian and English collections; archives and photographic collection; special exhibitions and educational projects.

Museo del Risorgimento: S. Marco 52, 30100 Venice; history of Venice from 1797 to First World War.

Museo Fortuny: San Marco 3780, 30124 Venice; tel. 041-5200995; fax 041-5223088; closed for restoration in 1995.

Palazzo Mocenigo: 30100 Venice; palace of the noble Venetian family which provided several of the doges; collection of fabrics and costumes; library on history of fashion.

Gabinetto delle Stampe e Disegni: 30100 Venice.

Casa Goldoni: Venice; house of the comic playwright (1707–93).

Galleria Internazionale d'Arte Moderna di Ca' Pesaro: Santa Croce, San Stae, 30100 Venice; tel. 041-721127; 19th-and 20th-century works of art.

Galleria dell'Accademia: Campo della Carità 1059A, 30100 Venice; f. 1807; Venetian painting, 1310–1700; Dir Dott. GIOVANNA SCIRÈ NEPI.

Galleria 'G. Franchetti': Calle Ca d'Oro, Canal Grande, 30100 Venice; f. 1927; sculpture and paintings; Dir Dott. ADRIANA AUGUSTI.

Museo Archeologico: Piazza S. Marco 17, 30122 Venice; tel. 041-5225978; f. 1523, reorganized 1923–26 and again after 1945; Greek and Roman sculpture, gems and coins, mosaics and sculptures from the 5th century BC to the 11th AD; library of *c.* 3,000 vols; Dir Dott. GIOVANNA LUISA RAVAGNAN.

Museo Civico di Storia Naturale: Fontego dei Turchi-S. Croce 1730, 30135 Venice; tel. 041-5240885; fax 041-5242592; f. 1921; marine fauna of the Adriatic, ornithology, entomology; collections of plants and algae of the world; library: scientific 15,000 vols, 2,350 periodicals; Dir Dr E. RATTI; publ. *Bollettino* (annually).

Museo d'Arte Moderna: Ca' Pesaro, Canal Grande, 30100 Venice; tel. 041-24127; f. 1897; 19th- and 20th-century works of art; Dir Prof. GIANDOMENICO ROMANELLI.

Museo d'Arte Orientale: Ca' Pesaro, Canal Grande, 30100 Venice; 17th–19th- century decorative arts from the Far East; Dir Dott. ADRIANA RUGGERI.

Museo della Fondazione Querini Stampalia: Palazzo Querini Stampalia, Castello 4778, 30122 Venice; tel. 041-2711411; fax 041-2711445; f. 1869; 14th–19th-century Italian paintings; Dir Dr GIORGIO BUSETTO.

Museo Storico Navale: Campo San Biagio, Castello 2148, 30122 Venice; tel. 041-5200276; f. 1923; library of 3,000 vols; Dir Adm. LORENZO SFERRA.

Palazzo Ducale: Piazza S. Marco, 30100 Venice; tel. 041-5224951; fax 041-5285028; Dir Prof. GIANDOMENICO ROMANELLI.

Peggy Guggenheim Collection (Solomon R. Guggenheim Foundation, New York): Palazzo Venier dei Leoni, 701 Dorsoduro, 30123 Venice; tel. 041-5206288; fax 041-5206885; e-mail pgcven@tin.it; f. 1980; art from 1911 to the 1970s; Dir THOMAS KRENS.

Pinacoteca Manfrediniana: Campo della Salute 1, 30123 Venice; tel. 041-5225558; fax 041-5237951; f. 1827; paintings and sculpture of the Roman, Gothic, Renaissance, Baroque, Neo-classical periods; library of 80,000 vols; Dir LUCIO CILIA.

Verona

Musei Civici d'Arte di Verona: Corso Castelvecchio 2, 37121 Verona; tel. 045-594734; fax 045-8010729; Dir Dssa PAOLA MARINI.

Comprise:

Art Library and Graphic Collections: Corso Castelvecchio 2, 37121 Verona; library of 28,000 vols; Dir Dott. GIORGIO MARINI.

Museo Archaeologico al Teatro Romano: Regaste Redentore, 37129 Verona; tel. 045-8000360; Dir Dssa MARGHERITA BOLLA.

Museo di Castelvecchio: Corso Castelvecchio 3, 37121 Verona; tel. 045-8005817; Dir Dssa PAOLA MARINI.

Museo Lapidario Maffeiano: Piazza Brà, 37121 Verona; tel. 045-590087; Dir Dr MARGHERITA BOLLA.

Museo degli Affreschi e Tomba di Giulietta: Via del Pontiere, 37122 Verona; tel. 045-8000361; Dir Dr PAOLA MARINI.

Galleria Comunale d'Arte Moderna e Contemporanea: Via Forti 1, 37121 Verona; tel. 045-8001903; fax 045-8003524; Dir Dott. G. ROSSI CORTENOVA.

Vicenza

Museo Civico: Palazzo Chiericati, Piazza Matteotti 39, 36100 Vicenza; tel. 0444-321348; fax 0444-546619; Dir Dssa MARIA ELISA AVAGNINA.

Attached museums:

Museo del Risorgimento e della Resistenza: Villa Guiccoli, Viale X Guigno 115, 36100 Vicenza; tel. 0444-322998; fax 0444-326023.

Museo di Archaeologie e Scienze Naturali: Contrà S. Corona, 36100 Vicenza; tel. 0444-320440.

Viterbo

Museo Civico: Piazza Crispi 2, 01100 Viterbo; tel. 0761-348275; fax 0761-348276; f. 1912; archaeology, art history; Dir Dssa ADRIANA EMILIOZZI.

Volterra

Museo Diocesano d'Arte Sacra: Palazzo Vescovile, Via Roma 13, 56048 Volterra; sculpture, paintings, costumes, ornaments, etc.

Museo Etrusco: Via Don Minzoni 15, 56048 Volterra; f. 1761; Roman and Etruscan coins, urns, bronzes, etc.; Dir Dott. GABRIELE CATENI.

State Universities

UNIVERSITÀ DEGLI STUDI DI ANCONA

Piazza Roma 22, 60121 Ancona

Telephone: 071-2201
Fax: 071-2202324

Founded 1969

Academic year: November to October

Rector: Prof. MARCO PACETTI
Vice-Rector: Prof. MARIO GOVERNA
Director: Dott. SANDRO FERRI
Librarian: Dssa SILVIA SOTTILI

Library of 26,000 vols
Number of teachers: 430
Number of students: 13,000

DEANS

Faculty of Engineering: Prof. GIOVANNI LATINI
Faculty of Medicine and Surgery: Prof. TULLIO MANZONI
Faculty of Economics: Prof. PAOLO ERCOLANI
Faculty of Agronomy: Prof. EDOARDO BIONDI
Faculty of Sciences: Prof. ETTORE OLMO

UNIVERSITÀ DEGLI STUDI DI BARI

Palazzo Ateneo, 70121 Bari

Telephone: 080-311111

Founded 1924

Rector: Prof. ATTILIO ALTO
Registrar: Dott. M. NATALE

Number of teachers: 700
Number of students: 42,439

DEANS

Faculty of Agriculture: Prof. E. BELLITTI
Faculty of Economics and Commerce: Prof. G. CHIASSINO
Faculty of Pharmacology: Prof. V. TORTORELLA
Faculty of Jurisprudence: Prof. G. PIEPOLI
Faculty of Engineering : Prof. B. MAIONE
Faculty of Letters and Philosophy: Prof. F. TATEO
Faculty of Foreign Languages: Prof. V. MASIELLO
Faculty of Education: Prof. M. DELL'AQUILA
Faculty of Medicine: Prof. V. MITOLO
Faculty of Veterinary Medicine: Prof. G. O. MARCOTRIGIANO
Faculty of Science: Prof. A. COSSU

UNIVERSITÀ DEGLI STUDI DELLA BASILICATA

Via Nazario Sauro 85, 85100 Potenza

Telephone: 0971-474111
Fax: 0971-474102

Founded 1982

Rector: Prof. GIANFRANCO BOARI
Vice-Rector: Prof. PASQUALE PIAZZOLLA
Administrative Director: Dr MARIO ROSARIO CAVALIERE
Librarians: Prof. CARLO MARIA SIMONETTI, Prof. GABOR KORCHMAROS

Library of 85,000 vols
Number of teachers: 307
Number of students: 4,845

Publications: *Basilicata Università*, *Collana 'Atti e Memorie'*, *Collana 'Strutture e Materiali'*, *Quaderni*.

DEANS

Faculty of Agriculture: Prof. F. BASSO
Faculty of Engineering: Prof. V. COPERTINO

Faculty of Letters and Philosophy: Prof. A. DE FRANCESCO
Faculty of Sciences: Prof. A. M. TAMBURRO

HEADS OF DEPARTMENTS

Faculty of Sciences:
- Mathematics: Prof. G. M. MASTROIANNI
- Chemistry: Prof. A. S. FRACASSINI

Faculty of Engineering:
- Structures, Geotechnology, Geology applied to Engineering: Prof. M. DOLCE
- Architecture, Planning and Transport Infrastructure: Prof. A. CAPPELLI
- Engineering and Environmental Physics: Prof. B. DE BERNARDINIS

Faculty of Letters and Philosophy:
- Literature and Philology: Prof. E. GIACCHERINI
- History, Linguistics and Anthropology: Prof. C. M. SIMONETTI

Faculty of Agriculture:
- Plant Biology, Protection and Biotechnology: Prof. P. RICCIO
- Animal Production: Prof. MICHELE LANGELLA
- Plant Production: Prof. C. XILOYANNIS
- Forest Economics: Prof. E. BOVE

UNIVERSITÀ DEGLI STUDI DI BERGAMO

Via Salvecchio 19, 24129 Bergamo
Telephone: 035-227111
Fax: 035-243054

Founded 1968

Rector: Prof. PIETRO ENRICO FERRI
Administrative Director: Dott. DOMENICO DANISI
Librarian: Dott. ENNIO FERRANTE

Library of 142,000 vols
Number of teachers: 211
Number of students: 6,317

DEANS

Faculty of Economics: Prof. MARIA IDA BERTOCCHI
Faculty of Foreign Languages and Literature: Prof. ALBERTO CASTOLDI
Faculty of Engineering: Prof. ANTONIO PERDICHIZZI

PROFESSORS

Faculty of Economics:
- AMADUZZI, A., Business Administration
- ARCUCCI, F., International Trade and Finance
- BERTOCCHI, M. I., Financial Mathematics
- BIFFIGNANDI, S., Statistics Applied to Economics
- FENGHI, F., Commercial Law
- FERRI, P. E., Economic Analysis
- GAMBARELLI, G., General Mathematics
- GRAZIOLA, G., Economics of Enterprise
- LEONI, R., Labour Economics
- MASINI, M., Banking
- RENOLDI, A., Value Management
- SACCHETTO, C., Tax Law
- SPEDICATO, E., Operations Research
- TAGI, G., Industrial Operations Management
- TAGLIARINI, F., Commercial Penal Law

Faculty of Foreign Languages and Literature:
- BELLER, M., German Language and Literature
- CASTOLDI, A., French Language and Literature II
- CERUTI, M., Epistemology
- CORONA, M., Anglo-American Languages and Literature
- GOTTI, M., History of the English Language
- LOCATELLI, A., English Language and Literature
- MARZOLA, A., English Language and Literature
- MIRANDOLA, G., French Language and Literature I
- MOLINARI, M. V., Germanic Philology
- MORELLI, G., Spanish Language and Literature
- PAPA, E., Modern and Contemporary History
- VILLA, C., Medieval and Humanist Philology

Faculty of Engineering:
- BUGINI, A., Industrial Management of Quality
- COLOMBI, R., Statistics and Probability
- PERDICHIZZI, A., Energetic Powerplants
- RIVA, R., Theoretical and Applied Mechanics
- SALANTI, A., Economics

UNIVERSITÀ DEGLI STUDI

Via Zamboni 33, 40126 Bologna
Telephone: 051-259111
Fax: 051-259034

Founded 11th century

Rector: Prof. FABIO ROVERSI-MONACO
Administrative Director: Dssa INES FABBRO

Number of teachers: 2,694
Number of students: 101,800

DEANS

Faculty of Jurisprudence: Prof. MARCO CAMMELLI
Faculty of Political Science: Prof. CARLO GUARNIERI
Faculty of Economics: Prof. GIORGIO NICOLETTI
Faculty of Arts and Philosophy: Prof. WALTER TEGA
Faculty of Education: Prof. FRANCESCA BOCCHI
Faculty of Medicine: Prof. VITTORIO BONOMINI
Faculty of Mathematics, Physics and Natural Sciences: Prof. PAOLO PUPILLO
Faculty of Industrial Chemistry: Prof. LUIGI BUSETTO
Faculty of Pharmacy: Prof. GIORGIO CANTELLI FORTI
Faculty of Engineering: Prof. ARRIGO PARESCHI
Faculty of Agriculture: Prof. GUALTIERO BARALDI
Faculty of Veterinary Medicine: Prof. ERALDO SEREN
Faculty of Statistics and Demography: Prof. PAOLA MONARI
Faculty of Cultural Heritage Conservation: Prof. ANTONIO CARILE
Faculty of Foreign Languages and Literature: Prof. VITA FORTUNATI
Faculty of Psychology: Prof. GUIDO SARCHIELLI
School of Modern Languages for Interpreters and Translators: Prof. MARCELLO SOFFRITTI

UNIVERSITÀ DEGLI STUDI DI BRESCIA

Piazza Mercato 15, 25121 Brescia
Telephone: 030-29881
Telex: 304116
Fax: 030-2988329

Founded 1982

Rector: AUGUSTO PRETI
Vice-Rector: PIER LUIGI MAGNANI
Administrative Officer: ANGELO BRESCIANI
Librarians: RICCARDO FAINI (Economics and Law), FRANCESCO GENNA (Engineering), PIER FRANCO SPANO (Medicine and Surgery)

Number of teachers: 355
Number of students: 12,020

DEANS

Faculty of Economics: GIANCARLO PROVASI
Faculty of Engineering: ANDREA TARONI
Faculty of Law: VINCENZO ALLEGRI
Faculty of Medicine and Surgery: LUIGI CAIMI

HEADS OF DEPARTMENTS

Faculty of Economics and Commerce:
- Business Management: ANTONIO PORTERI
- Quantitative Methods: LIVIA DANCELLI
- Economics: FRANCESCO SPINELLI
- Social Studies: GIUSEPPE STALUPPI
- Foreign Languages: CAMILLO MARAZZA

Faculty of Engineering:
- Mechanical Engineering: PIERLUIGI MAGNANI
- Civil Engineering: BALDASSARE BACCHI
- Electronics for Automation: DANIELE MARIOLI
- Materials Chemistry and Physics: EVANDRO LODI RIZZINI

Faculty of Law:
- Law Studies: SALVATORE PROSDOCIMI

Faculty of Medicine and Surgery:
- Experimental and Applied Medicine: GIUSEPPE NARDI
- Mother and Child Unit and Biomedical Technology: PIERGIOVANNI GRIGOLATO
- Medical Sciences: VITTORIO GRASSI
- Biomedical Sciences and Biotechnology: DANIELA COCCHI
- Surgical Sciences: GIOVANNI MARINI
- Surgical Pathology: CARLO ALBERTO QUARANTA

UNIVERSITÀ DI CAGLIARI

Via Università 40, 09124 Cagliari, Sardinia
Telephone: 070-662493
Telex: 790269

Founded 1606 by Pope Paolo V

Rector: Prof. DUILIO CASULA
Administrative Director: Dott. E. TOXIRI
Librarian: Dott. GRAZIELLA SEDDA DELITALA

Number of teachers: *c.* 1,000
Number of students: *c.* 18,000

Publications: *Studi economico-giuridici* and publications from each faculty.

DEANS

Faculty of Economics and Commerce: Prof. G. USAI
Faculty of Pharmacy: Prof. A. MACCIONI
Faculty of Law: Prof. F. SITZIA
Faculty of Engineering: Prof. CARLO VIVANET
Faculty of Letters and Philosophy: Prof. G. RESTAINO
Faculty of Education: Prof. S. TAGLIAGAMBE
Faculty of Medicine: Prof. A. BALESTRIERI
Faculty of Science: Prof. F. RAGA
Faculty of Political Science: Prof. G. SOTGIU

UNIVERSITÀ DI CALABRIA

Via P. Bucci, 87030 Arcavacata di Rende
Telephone: 0984-4911
Telex: 800044
Fax: 0984-493616

Founded 1972

Academic year: November to October

Rector: Prof. GIUSEPPE FREGA
Administrative Officer: Dott. GAETANO PRINCI

Number of teachers: 500
Number of students: 20,000

DEANS

Faculty of Letters and Philosophy: Prof. FRANCO CRISPINI
Faculty of Economics: Prof. GIOVANNI LATORRE
Faculty of Mathematical, Physical and Natural Sciences: Prof. ROBERTO BARTOLINO
Faculty of Engineering: MARIA LAURA LUCHI
Faculty of Pharmacy: SEBASTIANO ANDÒ

HEADS OF DEPARTMENTS

Arts: Prof. LUIGI SPEZZA FERRO
Cellular Biology: Prof. GIOVANNA DE BENEDICTIS
Chemistry: Prof. GIOVANNI SINDONA
Soil Conservation: Prof. FRANCESCO CALOMINO
Ecology: Prof. ANNA MARIA INNOCENTI
Political Economy: Prof. GIUSEPPE DE BARTOLO
Philology: Prof. FRANCA ELA CONSOLINO
Philosophy: Prof. DANIELE GAMBARARA
Physics: Prof. GIOVANNI FALCONE
Linguistics: Prof. FRANCESCO ALTIMARI
Mathematics: Prof. ESPEDITO DE PASCALE
Mechanics: Prof. GAETANO FLORIO
Management and Public Administration: Prof. IVAR MASSABÒ
Land Planning: Prof. GIOVANNI GIANNATTASIO
Education: Prof. GIUSEPPE SPADAFORA
Earth Sciences: Prof. FRANCO RUSSO
Electronics: Prof. GIUSEPPE DI MASSA
Sociology: Prof. ADA CAVAZZANI
History: Prof. GIOVANNA DE SENSI
Structures: Prof. DOMENICO BRUNO
Chemical Engineering: Prof. GABRIELE IORIO
Pharmaceutical Sciences: Prof. FRANCESCO MENICHINI
Pharmacology and Biology: Prof. GIACINTO BAGETTA

UNIVERSITÀ DI CAMERINO

Via del Bastione, 62032 Camerino
Telephone: 0737-4011
Fax: 0737-402085

Founded 1336; University status 1727
Academic year: November to October

Rector: Prof. IGNAZIO BUTI
Administrative Director: Dr SERGIO SABBIETI

Number of teachers: 269
Number of students: 8,227

Publications: *Annuario, Notiziario, Studi geologici camerti, Index—International Survey of Roman Law, Quaderni Camerti, Università Rassegna, Documents Phytosociologiques, Laboratorio di Studi linguistici, Quaderni dell'Istituto di studi economici e sociali, Medicina legale — Quaderni camerti.*

DEANS

Faculty of Architecture: Prof. GIOVANNI GUAZZO
Faculty of Jurisprudence: Prof. ANTONIETTA DI BLASE
Faculty of Science: Prof. GIOVANNI MATERAZZI
Faculty of Pharmacy: Prof. MARIO GRIFANTINI
Faculty of Veterinary Medicine: Prof. FRANCO POLIDORI

DIRECTORS

Faculty of Jurisprudence:
- Institute of Private Law: Prof. ANTONIO FLAMINI
- Institute of Public Law: Prof. JEAN PIERRE BERARDÒ
- Institute of Forensic Medicine: Prof. GASTONE PASQUI
- Institute of Economics and Social Studies: Prof. ROBERTO SCHIATTARELLA
- Institute of Historico-Legal, Philosophical and Political Studies: Prof. ALBERTO FILIPPI

Faculty of Science:
- Department of Botany and Ecology: Prof. FRANCO PEDROTTI
- Department of Earth Sciences: Prof. MAURIZIO CHICOCCHINI
- Department of Mathematics and Physics: Prof. P. TOMBESI
- Department of Comparative Morphology and Biochemistsry: Prof. GIOVANNI MATERAZZI

Faculty of Pharmacy:
- Department of Pharmacology and Experimental Medicine: Prof. GIUSEPPE DE CARO
- Department of Hygiene and Sanitation: Prof. MARIO COCCHIONI
- Department of Biology: Prof. FRANCO PETRELLI
- Department of Chemistry: Prof. MARIO GIANNELLA

Faculty of Architecture:
- Department of Environmental Planning and Construction: Prof. GIOVANNI GUAZZO

ATTACHED INSTITUTES

School of Postgraduate Studies in Civil Law: Dir Prof. V. RIZZO.

School of Clinical-Chemical Research: Dir Prof. E. FIORETTI.

School of Specialization in Hospital Pharmacy: Dir Prof. MAURIZIO MASSI.

UNIVERSITÀ DEGLI STUDI DI CASSINO

Via G. Marconi, 03043 Cassino (Frosinone)
Telephone: 0776-2991
Fax: 0776-310562

Founded 1979
State control

Rector: Prof. FEDERICO ROSSI
Administrative Director: Dott. LUIGI PELUSO CASSESE

Number of teachers: 160
Number of students: 9,500

DEANS

Faculty of Letters and Philosophy: GIANFRANCO RUBINO
Faculty of Economics and Commerce: Prof. MARIA CLAUDIA LUCCHETTI
Faculty of Engineering: Prof. GUIDO CARPINELLI
Faculty of Education: Prof. GIANFRANCO RUBINO

UNIVERSITÀ DEGLI STUDI DI CATANIA

Piazza dell' Università 2, 95124 Catania
Telephone: 095-310355
Telex: 970255
Fax: 095-325194

Founded 1434

Rector: Prof. ENRICO RIZZARELLI
Pro-Rector: Prof. ROMILDA RIZZO
Administrative Director: Dr ETTORE GILOTTA

Number of teachers: 1,517
Number of students: 53,674

DEANS

Faculty of Jurisprudence: Prof. VINCENZO ZAPPALA
Faculty of Political Science: Prof. VINCENZO SCIACCA
Faculty of Economics and Commerce: Prof. EMILIO GIARDINA
Faculty of Literature and Philosophy: Prof. GIUSEPPE GIARRIZZO
Faculty of Medicine: Prof. GIOVANNI RUSSO
Faculty of Mathematics, Physics, Chemistry and Natural Sciences: Prof. RENATO PUCCI
Faculty of Architecture: Prof. UGO CANTONE
Faculty of Pharmacy: Prof. GIUSEPPE RONSISVALLE
Faculty of Agriculture: Prof. GIUSEPPE PERROTTA
Faculty of Engineering: Prof. GIUSEPPE COZZO
Faculty of Education: Prof. ROSARIO SORACI

UNIVERSITÀ DEGLI STUDI DI FERRARA

Via Savonarola 9, 44100 Ferrara
Telephone: 0532-293111
Telex: 510850
Fax: 0532-248927
E-mail: mgn@dns.unife.it

Founded 1391

Rector: Prof. FRANCESCO CONCONI
Pro-Rector: (vacant)
Administrative Director: Dott. ALESSANDRO FABBRI

Number of teachers: 586
Number of students: 13,545

Publications: *Annali dell' Università, Annuario, Ateneo.*

DEANS

Faculty of Law: Prof. L. COSTATO
Faculty of Letters and Philosophy: Prof. LAURA BALBO
Faculty of Medicine and Surgery: Prof. F. M. AVATO
Faculty of Mathematical, Physical and Natural Sciences: Prof. G. FIORENTINI
Faculty of Pharmacy: Prof. G. POLLINI
Faculty of Engineering: Prof. P. RUSSO
Faculty of Architecture: Prof. P. CECCARELLI
Faculty of Economics: Prof. P. BIANCHI

PROFESSORS

Faculty of Law:
- ADAMI, F. E., Canon Law
- BALANDI, G. G., Labour Law
- BATTAGLINI, G.
- BIANCHI, P.
- BIN, R., Constitutional Law
- CASAROTTO, G., EU Agrarian Law
- CIAN, G., Civil Law
- COSTATO, L., Agrarian Law
- GIANFORMAGGIO, L., Philosophy of Law
- GIUNTA, F., Penal Law
- GRIPPO, G., Commercial Law
- MANFREDINI, A., Foundations of Roman Law
- MICCINESI, M., Tax Law
- PELLIZZER, F.
- POLA, G., Finance
- SCARANO USSANI, V., History of Roman Law
- ZAMORANI, P., Roman Law

Faculty of Letters and Philosophy:
- BALBO CECCARELLI, L., Sociology
- BOLLINI, M., Roman History
- CARABELLI, G., History of Philosophy
- CARILE, P., French Language and Literature
- FABBRI, P., Modern and Contemporary Music
- GENOVESI, G., Education
- MIEGGE, M., Theoretical Philosophy
- MONDADORI, M., Philosophy of Science
- MORETTI, W., Italian Literature
- PANCERA, C., History of Schools and Educational Institutions
- SECHI, S., Contemporary History
- TROVATO, P., History of the Italian Language
- VENTURINI, A., Psychology

Faculty of Medicine and Surgery:
- AVATO, F. M., Forensic Medicine
- AZZENA, G. F., General Surgery
- BARBANTI BRODANO, G., Clinical Microbiology
- BEANI, L., Clinical Pharmacology
- BENASSI, G., General Pathology
- BERGAMINI, C., Chemistry and Introductory Biochemistry
- BERTI, G., General Pathology
- BODO LUMARE, M., Histology
- BOREA, P. A., Pharmacology
- CALEARO, C. V., Otorhinolaryngology
- CALIFANO, A., Dermatology
- CALZOLARI, E., Human Genetics
- CAPITANI, S., Human Anatomy
- CARRERAS, M., Neurology
- CASNATI, E., Physics

CASTAGNARI, L., Infectious Diseases
CASTOLDI, G. L., Haematology
CAVAZZINI, L., Anatomy and Pathological Histology
CIACCIA, A., Diseases of the Respiratory Tract
CONCONI, F., Applied Biochemistry
DE ROSA, E., Industrial Medicine
DEGLI UBERTI, E., Endocrinology
DI VIRGILIO, F., General Pathology
DONINI, I. G., General Surgery
FELLIN, R., Internal Medicine
FERSINI, C., Internal Medicine
GANDINI, E., Medical Genetics
GRAZI, E., Biological Chemistry
GREGORIO, P., Hygiene
GRITTI, G., Anaesthesiology and Resuscitation
LIBONI, A., General Surgery
MANNELLA, P., Radiology
MIGLIORE, A., Neurosurgery
MOLINARI, S., Psychology
MOLLICA, G., Obstetrics and Gynaecology
NENCI, I., Anatomy and Pathological Histology
PERRI, V., Human Physiology
PIFFANELLI, A., Nuclear Medicine
PINAMONTI, S., Cellular Biology
RAMELLI, E., Psychiatry
RIPPA, M., Introductory Biochemistry
ROSSI, A., Ophthalmology
SCARPA, P., Preventive and Social Paediatrics
SEBASTIANI, A., Ophthalmology
SPIDALIERI, G., Human Physiology
TRAINA, G. C., Orthopaedics and Traumatology
TURINI, D., Urology
VIGI, V., Neonatology
VOLPATO, S., Paediatrics

Dentistry Course:

CALURA, G., Odontostomatology
CARUSO, A., Histology
CASSAI, E., Microbiology
DALLOCCHIO, F., Chemistry and Biochemistry
DEL SENNO, L., Biological Chemistry
FAVILLA, M., Human Physiology
GRANIERI, E., Neurology
LONGHINI, C., Internal Medicine
REGOLI, D., Pharmacology
SICILIANI, G., Orthognathism

Faculty of Mathematical, Physical and Natural Sciences:

ALBERTI, A., Mineralogy
BARRAI, I., Genetics
BECCALUVA, L., Petrography
BIASINI, L., Numerical Analysis
BOSELLINI, A., Geology
BROGLIO, A., Human Palaeontology
CANESCHI, L., Foundations of Theoretical Physics
CIMIRAGLIA, R., Physical Chemistry
DALPIAZ, P., General Physics
DEL CENTINA, A., Foundations of Advanced Geometry
DEL GUERRA, A., Medical Physics
DI CAPUA, E., Experimental Physics
DISTEFANO, G., Physical Chemistry
DONDI, F., Analytical Chemistry
DONDONI, A., Organic Chemistry
ELLIA, P., Geometry
FAGIOLI, F., Analytical Chemistry
FASULO, M. P., Botany
FIORENTINI, G., Foundations of Nuclear and Subnuclear Physics
FOA, A., Zoology
GERDOL, R., Botany
GILLI, G., Physical Chemistry
LASCU, A., Geometry
LORIGA, C., Palaeontology
LOVITCH, L., Nuclear Physics
MANTOVANI, G., Industrial Organic Chemistry
MARZIANI, M., Rational Mechanics
MASSARI, U., Mathematical Analysis
MENINI, C., Algebra
NIZZOLI, F., Solid-State Physics
PEPE, L., History of Mathematics
PICCOLINO, M., General Physiology
PRODI, F., Experimental Physics
PULIDORI, F., Analytical Chemistry
ROSSI, R., Ecology
SACCHI, O., General Physiology
SACERDOTI, M., Mineralogy
SALVATORELLI, G., Cytology and Histology
SCANDOLA, F., General and Inorganic Chemistry
SCHIFFRER, G., Mathematical Methods of Physics
SEGALA, F., Mathematical Analysis
SEMENZA, E., Applied Geology
SIENA, F., Petrography
TRABANELLI, G., Corrosion and Protection of Metals
TRAVERSO, O., General and Inorganic Chemistry
ZAFFAGNINI, F., Comparative Anatomy
ZANGHIRATI, L., Mathematical Analysis

Faculty of Pharmacy:

BARALDI, P. G., Pharmaceutical Chemistry and Toxicology
BIANCHI, C., Pharmacology and Pharmacognosy
BIONDI, C., General Physiology
BRIGHENTI, L., General Physiology
BRUNI, A., Pharmocognosy
MANSERVIGI, R., Microbiology
MENEGATTI, E., Socio-Economic Technology and Pharmaceutical Legislation
MENZIANI, E., Chemistry of Nutrition
POLLINI, G. P., Organic Chemistry
SALVADORI, S., Pharmaceutical Chemistry and Toxicology
SCATTURIN, A., Applied Pharmaceutical Chemistry
SIMONI, D., Pharmaceutical Chemistry and Toxicology
TANGANELLI, S., Pharmacology and Pharmacognosy
TOMATIS, R., Pharmaceutical Chemistry and Toxicology
TRANIELLO, M. S., Biological Chemistry

Faculty of Engineering:

BEGHELLI, S., Electronic Engineering
BETTOCCHI, R., Mechanical Engineering
DAL CIN, R., Lithology and Geology
DEL PIERO, G., Construction Theory
FERRETTI, P.
GALDI, G. P., Rational Mechanics
MELLO, P., Computer Science
OLIVO, P., Electronics
PADULA, M., Rational Mechanics
POMPOLI, R., Technical Physics
RUSSO, P., Topography
TRALLI, A., Construction Theory
ZUCCHI, F., Chemistry

Faculty of Architecture:

CECCARELLI, P., Urban System Analysis
DI FEDERICO, I., Technical Physics
LAUDIERO, F., Construction Technology
TRIPPA, G., Architectural Technology

Faculty of Economics:

PINI, P., Political Economy

UNIVERSITÀ DEGLI STUDI DI FIRENZE

Piazza San Marco 4, 50121 Florence
Telephone: 055-27571
Fax: 055-264194

Founded 1321

Academic year: September to August

Rector: Prof. PAOLO BLASI
Vice-Rector: Prof. GIANCARLO ZAMPI
Registrar: Dott. GAETANO SERAFINO
Librarian: Dott. A. M. TAMMARO

Number of teachers: 2,236
Number of students: 59,847

DEANS

Faculty of Jurisprudence: Prof. PAOLO CARETTI
Faculty of Political Sciences: Prof. CLAUDIO FRANCHINI
Faculty of Economics: Prof. CARLO VALLINI
Faculty of Letters and Philosophy: Prof. PAOLO MARRASSINI
Faculty of Education: Prof. PAOLO OREFICE
Faculty of Medicine and Surgery: Prof. GIOVANNI ORLANDINI
Faculty of Mathematical, Physical and Natural Sciences: Prof. P. MALESANI
Faculty of Pharmacy: Prof. SERGIO PINZAUTI
Faculty of Architecture: Prof. FRANCESCO GURRIERI
Faculty of Agriculture and Forestry: Prof. AUGUSTO MARINELLI
Faculty of Engineering: Prof. ENNIO CARNEVALE

DIRECTORS OF INSTITUTES

Faculty of Agriculture and Forestry:

Forestry Management and Technology: Prof. O. CIANCIO
Forestry Pathology and Zoology: Prof. G. SURICO
Silviculture: Prof. G. BERNETTI

Faculty of Architecture:

Mathematics: Prof. O. ARENA

Faculty of Economics:

Law: Prof. R. ALESSI
Linguistics: Prof. R. E. SCHMIDT
Economic History: Prof. G. MORI

Faculty of Education:

Germanic and Oriental Languages and Literature: Prof. I. HENNEMANN
English and North American Language and Literature: Prof. A. SERPIERI

Faculty of Letters and Philosophy:

Germanic, Slav and Ugro-Finnish Languages and Literatures: Prof. C. CORTI

Faculty of Medicine and Surgery:

Anatomy and Pathological Histology: Prof. G. ZAMPI
Anaesthesiology and Resuscitation: Prof. G. P. NOVELLI
Dermosyphilopathy: Prof. B. GIANNOTTI
General Surgery: Prof. C. CORTESINI
General Surgery and Surgical Therapy I: Prof. M. PACE
General Medicine and Cardiology: Prof. G. G. NERI SERNERI
Internal Medicine: Prof. P. GENTILINI
Internal Medicine and Immunoallergology: Prof. S. ROMAGNANI
General Clinical Medicine and Medical Therapy IV: Prof. M. CAGNONI
Ophthalmology: Prof. G. SALVI
Orthopaedics and Traumatology: Prof. G. STRINGA
Obstetrics and Gynaecology: Prof. G. B. MASSI
Otorhinolaryngology: Prof. O. FINI STORCHI
Gerontology and Geriatrics: Prof. A. D'ALESSANDRO
Labour Medicine: Prof. G. GIULIANO
Microbiology 'Renzo Davoli': Prof. G. GARGANI
Odonto-stomatology: Prof. P. PIERLEONI

Faculty of Mathematical, Physical and Natural Sciences:

Anthropology: Prof. G. ARDITO

Interfaculty:

Geography: Prof. L. ROMBAI
Forensic and Insurance Medicine: Prof. C. FAZZARI
General Pathology: Prof. A. FONNESU

UNIVERSITÀ DEGLI STUDI DI GENOVA

Via Balbi 5, 16126 Genoa
Telephone: 010-20991
Telex: 271114
Founded 1471
Academic year: November to October
Rector: Prof. S. Pontremoli
Vice-Rector: Prof. A. E. Calcagno
Administrative Director: Dott. D. Pellitteri
Number of teachers: 1,810
Number of students: 44,844

DEANS

Faculty of Jurisprudence: Prof. G. Visintini
Faculty of Political Sciences: Prof. G. Casale
Faculty of Economics and Commerce: Prof. L. Caselli
Faculty of Letters and Philosophy: Prof. F. Bertini
Faculty of Education: Prof. L. Puncuh
Faculty of Medicine and Surgery: Prof. U. Marinari
Faculty of Mathematics, Physics and Natural Science: Prof. S. Giammarino
Faculty of Pharmacy: Prof. G. Bignardi
Faculty of Engineering: Prof. A. Squarzoni
Faculty of Architecture: Prof. E. Benvenuto
Faculty of Foreign Languages: Prof. G. De Piaggi

UNIVERSITÀ DEGLI STUDI DELL' AQUILA

Piazza Rivera 1, 67100 L'Aquila
Telephone: 0862-4311
Telex: 600213
Fax: 0862-412948
Founded 1952
Rector: Prof. Giovanni Schippa
Administrative Director: Dott. Laura Paoni
Library of 171,356 vols
Number of teachers: 509
Number of students: 8,260

DEANS

Faculty of Sciences: Prof. Armando Reale
Faculty of Engineering: Prof. Luigi Bignardi
Faculty of Education: Prof. Enrico Montanari
Faculty of Medicine: Prof. Ferdinando di Orio
Faculty of Business Economics: Stelio Valentini

UNIVERSITÀ DEGLI STUDI DI LECCE

Via dell'Università 1, C.P. 193, 73100 Lecce
Telephone: 0832-4061
Telex: 860830
Fax: 0832-406204
Founded 1956
Academic year: November to October
Rector: Prof. Angelo Rizzo
Administrative Director: Dott. Stanislao Natali
Librarian: Dott. M. G. D'Aloisio
Library of 150,000 vols
Number of teachers: 351
Number of students: 15,000
Publication: *Annuario.*

DEANS

Faculty of Education: Prof. O. Bianco
Faculty of Letters: Prof. S. Alessandri
Faculty of Science: Prof. M. Carriero
Faculty of Banking and Insurance: Prof. B. Leoci
Faculty of Engineering: Prof. S. Mongelli

UNIVERSITÀ DEGLI STUDI DI MACERATA

Piaggia Università 2, 62100 Macerata
Telephone: 0733-2581
Fax: 0733-232639
E-mail: rettore@unimc.it
Founded 1290
Rector: Prof. Dott. Alberto Febbrajo
Administrative Director: Dott. Gianni Crosta
Librarian: Dott. Maria Teresa Vitali
Number of teachers: 220
Number of students: 12,882
Publication: *Annali.*

DEANS

Faculty of Law: Prof. Glauco Giostra
Faculty of Literature and Philosophy: Prof. Pierluigi De Vecchi
Faculty of Political Science: Prof. Mauro Marconi
Faculty of Training Sciences: (vacant)

DIRECTORS OF INSTITUTES

Faculty of Law:
- International and Private Law: Prof. Vincenzo Cannizzaro
- Civil Procedural Law: G. Tomei
- Law and Penal Procedure: G. Insolera
- Roman Law: S. Serangeli
- Legal Institutions: F. Bolognini
- Legal Medicine and Insurance: R. Froldi
- History and Philosophy of Law, Ecclesiastical Law: G. Mantuano
- Historical Studies: M. Sbriccoli

Faculty of Literature and Philosophy:
- Classical Philology: R. Palla
- Glottology and General Linguistics: D. Maggi

DIRECTORS OF DEPARTMENTS

Archaeological and Historical Studies of Antiquity: Prof. G. Paci
Historical, Documentary, Artistic and Territorial Studies: Prof. R. Paci
Private Law, Italian and Comparative Labour Law: Prof. C. A. Graziani
Public Law and Theory of Government: Prof. C. Pinelli
Economic and Financial Institutions: Prof. G. Galeazzi
Studies on Social Change, Legal Institutions and Communication: Prof. D. Nelken
Philosophy and Human Sciences: Prof. J. Petofi
Modern Languages and Literatures: Prof. D. Mugnolo

DIRECTORS OF CENTRES

Modern Language Teaching: (vacant)
'A. Barnave' Constitutional History Laboratory: Prof. R. Martucci
Legal, Sociological and Economic Studies on the State and Public Institutions: Prof. R. Bin
'Luigi Piccinato' Laboratory of Government of Territory: Prof. P. Paolillo
'Fausto Vicarelli' Laboratory for the Study of Relations between Banks and Industry: (vacant)
Studies and Documentation on the History of the University of Macerata: Prof. S. Serangeli
Studies on Means of Mass Communication and Information Law: (vacant)
'Alberico Gentili' Centre for Legal Studies: (vacant)

UNIVERSITÀ DEGLI STUDI

Piazza Salvatore Pugliatti, 98100 Messina
Telephone: 090-6761
Telex: 980075
Founded 1548
Rector: Prof. Giacomo Ferrau
Pro-Rector: Prof. Giacomo Ferrau
Administrative Director: Dr Vincenzo Ferluga
Number of teachers: 1,216
Number of students: 41,500

DEANS

Faculty of Jurisprudence: Prof. A. Metro
Faculty of Literature and Philosophy: Prof. G. Ferrau
Faculty of Medicine: Prof. F. Tomasello Francesco
Faculty of Mathematics, Physics and Natural Sciences: Prof. S. Giambo
Faculty of Pharmacy: Prof. G. Lamonica
Faculty of Economics: Prof. G. Calabrò
Faculty of Education: Prof. A. Mazzarino
Faculty of Veterinary Medicine: Prof. O. Catarsini
Faculty of Politics: Prof. A. Romano
Faculty of Engineering: Prof. F. Basile
Faculty of Statistical Sciences: M. Teresa Di Maggio

UNIVERSITÀ DEGLI STUDI DI MILANO

Via Festa del Perdono 7, 20122 Milan
Telephone: 02-58351
Telex: 320484
Fax: 02-58304482
Founded 1923
Academic year: November to October
Rector: Prof. P. Mantegazza
Vice-Rector: Prof. F. Pocar
Administrative Director: Dott. Filippo Sori
Librarian: Dott. Giuliana Giustino
Number of teachers: 729
Number of students: 96,155
Publications: *Statuto dell' Università*, *Annuario* (1 a year), *Guida dello Studente* (annually), *Guida alle scuole di specializzazione* (1 a year), *Ricerca Scientifica ed Educazione Permanente* and various faculty publications.

DEANS

Faculty of Law: Prof. A. Padoa Schioppa
Faculty of Law II: Prof. Aldo Chiancone
Faculty of Political Sciences: Prof. A. Martinelli
Faculty of Economics: Prof. M. Zenga
Faculty of Letters and Philosophy: Prof. E. Decleva
Faculty of Medicine: Prof. A. Scala
Faculty of Sciences: Prof. M. Fontanesi
Faculty of Sciences (in Como): Prof. G. Casati
Faculty of Sciences (in Varese): Prof. G. Lanzavecchia
Faculty of Pharmacy: Prof. R. Paoletti
Faculty of Agriculture: D. Casati
Faculty of Veterinary Medicine: Prof. G. Ruffo

PROFESSORS

Faculty of Law:
- Alessandri, A., Commercial Penal Law
- Amodio, E., Procedural Penal Law
- Angiolini, V., Constitutional Law
- Benatti, F., Institutions of Private Law
- Bognetti, G., Comparative Public Law
- Cantarella, E., Institutions of Roman Law
- Carnevali, U., Institutions of Private Law
- Casuscelli, G., Ecclesiastical Law
- Cattaneo, G., Civil Law
- Cattaneo, M. A., Philosophy of Law
- Cavallone, B., Procedural Civil Law
- Conetti, G., International Law
- De Nova, G., Civil Law
- Denozza, F., Commercial Law
- Di Renzo Villata, M. G., History of Italian Law
- Dolcini, E., Penal Law

DOMINIONI, O., Procedural Penal Law
FERRARI, S., Canon Law
FERRARI, V., Sociology of Law
GAFFURI, G., Tributary Law
GAMBARO, A., Comparative Private Law
GNOLI, F., Institutions of Roman Law
GOISIS, G., Political Economy
GUERCI, M., Political Economy
JAEGER, P., Commercial Law
JORI, M., Philosophy of Law
LANCELLOTTI, E., Financial Science
LURASCHI, G., Institutions of Roman Law
LUZZATTO, R., International Law
MARINUCCI, G., Penal Law
MASSETTO, G., History of Italian Law
MOR, G., Constitutional Law
NASCIMBENE, B., European Community Law
ONIDA, V., Constitutional Law
PADOA SCHIOPPA, A., History of Italian Law
PASTORI, F., Roman Law
PELOSI, A. C., Institutions of Private Law
PERICU, G., Administrative Law
PISANI, M., Procedural Penal Law
POCAR, F., International Law
POLARA, G., History of Roman Law
POTOTSCHNIG, U., Administrative Law
RICCI, E., Bankruptcy Law
SACCHI, R., Commercial Law
SANTA MARIA, A., International Law
SCOVAZZI, T., International Law
SENA, G., Industrial Law
SICA, M., Administrative Law
SPAGNUOLO VIGORITA, L., Labour Law
TALAMONA, M., Political Economy
TARZIA, G., Civil Procedural Law
TREVES, T., International Private and Procedural Law
TRIMARCHI, F., Administrative Law
TRIMARCHI, P., Civil Law
VILLATA, R., Administrative Law
VITALI, E. G., Ecclesiastical Law

Faculty of Law II:

ALBISETTI, A., Ecclesiastical Law
BARDUSCO, A., Constitutional Law
BARIATTI, S., European Community Law
CASELLA, P., Commercial Law
CENDERELLI, A., Institutions of Roman Law
CHIANCONE, A., Political Economy
GALANTINI, M. N., Procedural Penal Law
GRECO, A., Administrative Law
LANZILLO, R., Civil Law
PULITANÒ, P., Penal Law
SALETTI, A., Civil Procedural Law
SBISÀ, G., Institutions of Private Law
TESAURO, F., Tax Law

Faculty of Political Sciences:

ALBERTONI, E., History of Political Doctrines
BAGLIONI, G., General Sociology
BERNAREGGI, G., Public Economy
BLANGIARDO, G., Demography
BOGNETTI, G., Financial Sciences
CELLA, G. P., Economic Sociology
CHIARINI, R., History of Political Parties and Political Movements
CLERICI, R., International Private Law
DE LILLO, A., Sociology
DONZELLI, F., Political Economy
FERRARI, P. A., Statistics
GARAVELLO, O., Economic Politics
ICHINO, P., Labour Law
INZITARI, B., Private Law
ITALIA, V., Institutions of Public Law
LACAITA, G., Modern History
LAMBERTI ZANARDI, P., International Law
LANDENNA, G., Statistics
LOSANO, M. G., General Theory of Law
MARASINI, D., Statistics
MARTINELLI, A., Political Science
MARTINI, M., Economic Statistics
MARTINOTTI, G., Urban Sociology
MAURI, A., Economics of Credit Institutions
MELUCCI, A., Sociology of Cultural Processes
MOIOLI, A., Economic History
OLLA BRUNDU, M., History of International Relations
PANZARINI, G., Institutions of Private Law
PISCEL COLLOTTI, E., History and Institutions of Africa and Asia
PREDETTI, A., Economic Statistics
RAINERO, R., Contemporary History
REGINI, M., Industrial Relations
RIOSA, A., Contemporary History
RIVOLTA, G. C., Commercial Law
RUFFINI GANDOLFI, M., Comparative Private Law
SALVATI, M., Political Economy
SANDULLI, M.A., Institutions of Public Law
SANTORO, C.M., International Relations
SCARPAT, O., Economics of Development
SPRANZI, A., Economy and Management of Companies
VENTURINI, G., International Law

Faculty of Economics:

BRONDONI, S., Marketing
CIVARDI, M., Sample Analysis and Public Opinion Polls
FRANCESCHELLI, V., Institutions of Private Law
LANZI, A., Criminal Law and Economics
PORTA, P. L., Political Economics
PROSPERETTI, L., Politics of Industrial Economics
SAITA, M., Business Economics
TRAVERSO, C., Institutions of Public Law
TREZZI, G. L., Economic History
ZAMBRUNO, G., Financial Mathematics
ZENGA, M., Statistics

Faculty of Letters and Philosophy:

AGNOLETTO, A., History of Christianity
ALBONICO, P., Hispano-American Language and Literature
ANZI, A., History of the English Theatre
ARENA, R., Glottology
BARBARISI, G., Italian Literature
BASTIANINI, G., Papyrology
BIGALLI, D., History of Philosophy
BIGNAMI, M. L., English Language and Literature
BONOMI, A., Philosophy of Language
BRIOSCHI, F., History of Literary Criticism
BROGI, G., History of the Russian Language
CAIZZI, F., History of Ancient Philosophy
CAPRA, C., Modern History
CASTELFRANCHI, G., History of Medieval Art
CATTANEO, M. T., Spanish Language and Literature
CERCIGNANI, F., German Language and Literature
CHIERCHIA, G., General Linguistics
CHIESA, G., Archaeology and History of Greek and Roman Art
CHITTOLINI, G., Medieval Institutions
CIANCI, G., English Language and Literature
CICALESE, M. L., Theory and History of Historiography
CLERICI, N., French Language and Literature
COMBA, R., Medieval History
COMETTA, M., German Philology
CONCA, F., History of the Greek Language
CORDANO, F., Greek History
CORNA PELLEGRINI SPANDRE, G., Geography
D'AGOSTINO, A., Romance Philology
DE ANGELIS, V., Humanistic Philology
DECLEVA, E., Contemporary History
DEGRADA, F., History of Music
DEL CORNO, D., Greek Literature
DELLA CASA, C., Sanskrit
DELLA PERUTA, F., History of the Risorgimento
DE STASIO, C., English Language and Literature
DI SALVO, M. G., Slavonic Philology
DONATI, C., History of the Ancient Italian States
DONINI, P., History of Ancient Philosophy
FINOLI, A. M., History of French Language
FORABOSCHI, D., Roman History
FUMAGALLI, M., History of Medieval Philosophy
FUNARI, E., Psychology
GIORELLO, G., Philosophy of Science
GORI, G., History of Modern and Contemporary Philosophy
GUALANDRI, I., Latin Literature
IOVINO, M., Etruscan Studies and Italic Archaeology
LAMBERTI, M., History of Contemporary Art
LARIZZA, M., History of Political Doctrine
LEGRENZI, P., History of Psychology
LEHNUS, L., Classical Philology
MALCOVATI, F., Russian Language and Literature
MANGIONE, C., Logic
MASSA, R., Pedagogy
MERLO, G., History of the Medieval Church and Heresy
MILANINI, C., Italian Literature
MOISO, F., History of Philosophy
MORGANA, S., Italian Language History
MOSCONI, G., Psychology
NISSIM, L., French Language and Literature
ORLANDI, G., Medieval Latin Literature
PAGETTI, C., English Language and Literature
PIANA, G., Theoretical Philosophy
PLATONE, R., Russian Language and Literature
RAMBALDI, E., Moral Philosophy
RICCOMINI, E., History of Modern Art
RUMI, G., Contemporary History
SAMPIETRO, L., Anglo-American Literature
SAPELLI, G., Economic History
SCARAMELLINI, G., Geography
SCARAMUZZA, G., Aesthetics
SINI, C., Theoretical Philosophy
SOLDI RONDININI, G., Medieval History
SPERA, F., Italian Literature
SPINAZZOLA, V., History of Modern and Contemporary Italian Literature
VALOTA, B., History of Eastern Europe
VARIN, D., Evolutionary Psychology
VELLI, G., Italian Literature
VIGEZZI, B., Modern History
ZECCHI, S., Aesthetics
ZERBI, M., Geography

Faculty of Medicine:

AGOSTONI, A., Internal Medicine
AGOSTONI, E., Human Physiology
AGRIFOGLIO, G., Vascular Surgery
ALBANO, A., Hygiene
ALESSI, E., Dermatology
ALLEGRA, L., Diseases of the Respiratory System
ALTAMURA, C., Psychiatry
ANASTASIA, M., Chemistry and Biochemical Propaedeutics
AZZOLINI, A., Plastic Reconstructive Surgery
BALDISSERA, F., Human Physiology
BASILE, L., Forensic Medicine
BEK PECCOZ, P., Endocrinology
BERGAMINI, F., Hygiene
BERNELLI ZAZZERA, A., General Pathology
BERTELLI, A., Clinical Pharmacology
BERTI, F., Pharmacology
BERTOLINI, M., Child Neuropsychiatry
BIANCHI, G., Nephrology
BIANCHI, P., Gastroenterology
BIANCO, S., Respiratory Physiopathology
BIGLIOLI, P., Cardiac Surgery
BORTOLANI, E., General Surgery
BRANCATO, R., Ophthalmology
BRUSATI, R., Maxillo-facial Surgery
CABITZA, P., Orthopaedics and Traumatology
CAINELLI, T., Dermatology
CAJONE, F., General Pathology
CALDERARI, G., Conservative Dentistry
CANAL, N., Neurology
CANTABONI, A., Pathological Anatomy and Histology
CANTALAMESSA, L., Internal Medicine
CAPETTA, P., Obstetrics and Gynaecology

CAPUTO, R., Dermatology
CARACCIOLO, E., Clinical Psychology
CARANDENTE, F., Internal Medicine
CAREDDU, P., Paediatrics
CARRASSI, A., Special Odontostomatological Pathology
CARRUBA, M., Pharmacology
CARTA, I., Psychiatry
CAVAGNA, G., Human Physiology
CAVAGNINI, F., Endocrinology
CERRETELLI, P., Human Physiology
CESA BIANCHI, M., General Psychology
CESTARO, B., Biological Chemistry
CHIAPPINO, G., Labour Medicine
CHIESARA, E., Toxicology
CHIUMELLO, G., Paediatrics
CIANCAGLINI, R., Clinical Gnathology
CLEMENTI, F., Cellular and Molecular Pharmacology
CLERICI, E., Immunology
COCUZZA, G., Virology
COGGI, G., Pathological Anatomy and Histology
COLOMBO, M., Internal Medicine
CONTI, A., General Genetics
CORNEO, G. M., Internal Medicine
CORTI, M., Medical Physics
COSTANZI, G., Pathological Anatomy and Histology
CROSIGNANI, P. G., Obstetrics and Gynaecology
CROSTI, C., Dermatology
D'ANGELO, E., Human Physiology
DEL MONTE, U., General Pathology
DI CARLO, V., General Surgery
DI NARO, C., Clinical Psychology
DONATI, L., Plastic Reconstructive Surgery
DUBINI, F., Microbiology
FAGLIA, G., Endocrinology
FARNETI, A., Forensic Medicine
FAZIO, F., Nuclear Medicine
FERRARI, A., Obstetrics and Gynaecology
FERRARIO, V., Human Anatomy
FINZI, A., Dermatology
FIORELLI, G., Internal Medicine
FOÀ, V., Industrial Hygiene
FRASCHINI, F., Chemotherapy
FRATTOLA, L., Neurology
GAINI, S., Neurosurgery
GAJA, G., General Pathology
GALLI, M. G., Hygiene
GALLUS, G., Medical Statistics and Biometrics
GATTINONI, L., Anaesthesiology and Resuscitation
GHIDONI, R., Biological Chemistry
GINELLI, E., General Biology
GIOVANELLI BARILARI, M., Neurosurgery
GIOVANNINI, M., Paediatrics
GRANDI, M., Forensic Medicine
GRIECO, A., Preventive Medicine for Workers and Psychotechnicians
GROPPETTI, A., Pharmacology
GROSSI, A., Cardiac Surgery
GUARESCHI CAZZULLO, A., Child Neuropsychiatry
GUAZZI, M., Cardiology
INVERNIZZI, F., Internal Medicine
INVERNIZZI, G., Psychiatry
KIENLE, M., Chemistry and Biochemical Propaedeutics.
LAMBERTENGHI DELILIERS, G., Internal Medicine
LANZETTA, A., Orthopaedics and Traumatology
LARIZZA, L., Medical Genetics
LEONETTI, G., Medical Semiology and Methodology
LIBRETTI, A., Internal Medicine
LODI, F., Forensic Toxicology
LOMBARDO, A. E., Biological Chemistry
LONGO, T., General Surgery
LUVONI, R., Forensic Medicine
MAIOLO, A. T., Haematology
MALCOVATI, M., Molecular Biology
MALLIANI, A., Internal Medicine
MANCIA, G., Internal Medicine
MANCIA, M., Human Physiology
MANGILI, F., Forensic Medicine
MANGIONI, C., Obstetrics and Gynaecology
MANGONI, A., Neurology
MANNUCCI, P. M., Internal Medicine
MANTEGAZZA, P., Pharmacology
MARINI, A., Neo-natal Pathology
MARTINI, L., Endocrinology
MARUBINI, E., Medical Statistics and Biometrics
MASERA, G., Paediatrics
MASSIMINI, F., General Psychology
MATTINA, R., Microbiology
MATTURRI, L., Pathological Anatomy and Histology
MELDOLESI, J., Pharmacology
MEZZETTI, M., Thoracic Surgery
MIGLIOR, M., Ophthalmology
MILANESI, G., Cellular Biology
MILANESI, S., Human Anatomy
MILANI, F., Radiotherapy
MISEROCCHI, G., Human Physiology
MORONI, M., Infectious Diseases
MÜLLER, E., Pharmacology
ORECCHIA, R., Radiotherapy
ORZALESI, N., Ophthalmology
OTTAVIANI, A., Oto-rhino-laryngology
PAGANI, M., Medical Therapy
PAGANO, A., Hygiene
PANNESE, E., Neurocytology
PARDI, G., Obstetrics and Gynaecology
PARRINI, L., Orthopaedics and Traumatology
PECILE, A., Pharmacology
PENATI, G., Psychiatry
PERACCHIA, A., General Surgery
PERETTI, G., Orthopaedics and Traumatology
PERIN, A., General Pathology
PERRELLA, M., Physical Biochemistry
PETRUCCIOLI, M. G., Human Anatomy
PIETRI, P., General Surgery
PIGNANELLI, H., Odontostomatology
PIGNATARO, O., Oto-rhino-laryngology
PISANI, E., Urology
PIZZINI, G., Human Anatomy
PODDA, M., Internal Medicine
POLI, M., General Psychology
PONTI, G., Forensic Psychopathology
PONTIROLI, A., Internal Medicine
POZZA, G., Internal Medicine
PRINCIPI, N., Paediatrics
RAGNOTTI, G., General Pathology
REMOTTI, G., Obstetrical and Gynaecological Pathology
ROCCO, F., Urology
RONCHETTI, F., Chemistry and Biochemical Propaedeutics
ROSSI BERNARDI, L., Biological Chemistry
ROSSI, R., General Surgery
RUBERTI, U., General Surgery
RUGARLI, C., Internal Medicine
SALVAGGIO, L., Hygiene
SALVATO, A., Orthognathodontics
SALVINI, A., Emergency Surgery and First Aid
SAMBATARO, G., Oto-rhino-laryngology
SANTANIELLO, E., Chemistry and Biochemical Propaedeutics
SANTORO, F., Odontostomatology
SCALA, A. E., Chemistry and Biochemical Propaedeutics
SCALABRINO, G., General Pathology
SCARLATO, G., Neurology
SCORZA, R., Clinical Immunology and Allergology
SCORZA, R., General Surgery
SEMENZA, G., Biological Chemistry
SERENI, F., Paediatrics
SICCARDI, A., General Biology
SMERALDI, E., Psychiatry
SONNINO, S., Biological Chemistry
SPINNLER, H., Neurology
STEFANI, M., Anatomy and Pathological Histology
STROHMENGER, L., Pedodontics
SURACE, A., Orthopaedics and Traumatology
TALLONE, L., Medical Physics
TAROLO, G., Nuclear Medicine
TASCHIERI, A., General Surgery
TESSARI, L., Orthopaedics and Traumatology
TETTAMANTI, G., Human Systematic Biochemistry
TIBERIO, G., Emergency Surgery and First Aid
TORRI, G., Anaesthesiology and Resuscitation
TRABUCCHI, E., General Surgery
TRAZZI, R., Anaesthesiology and Resuscitation
TREDICI, G., Neuroanatomy
USLENGHI, C., Radiology
VEGETO, A., Organ Transplant and Replacement Surgery
VENERANDO, B., Biological Chemistry
VERGANI, C., Gerontology and Geriatrics
VIALE, G., Pathological Anatomy and Histology
VIGNALI, M., Obstetrics and Gynaecology
VILLA, M. L., Immunology
VILLANI, R., Neurosurgery
VINCRE, G., General Surgery
VOGEL, G., Odontostomatology
WEINSTEIN, R., Parodontology
ZANCHETTI, A., Internal Medicine
ZANETTI, A., Hygiene
ZANOBIO, B., History of Medicine

Faculty of Sciences:

ACERBI, E., Physics, Experiments
ALBERGHINA, L. F. A., Comparative Biochemistry
ALBERTONI, S., Numerical and Graphic Calculations
ANGOLETTA, M., General and Inorganic Chemistry
ARCHETTI, F., Operating Logic
BAIRATI, A., Human Anatomy
BALDINI, G., Biophysics
BELLINI, G., Physics, Experiments
BELLOBONO, I. R., General and Inorganic Chemistry
BELLON, P., General and Inorganic Chemistry
BELLONI, S., Geomorphology
BELLOTTI, E., Physics, Experiments
BELTRAME, P., Industrial Chemical Processes and Systems
BENEDEK, G., Structure of Matter
BERTINO, E., Database and Information Systems
BERTONI, A., Theoretical Computer Science
BIANCHETTI, R., Plant Physiology
BIRATTARI, C., Physics
BISIANI, R., Computer Architecture Module
BLASI, A., Mineralogy
BLASI, F., Genetics
BOELLA, G., Physics, Experiments
BONIFACIO, R., Institutions of Theoretical Physics
BONOMETTO, S., General Physics
BORGHESI, A., Laboratory of General Physics
BORIANI, A., Petrography
BOZZINI, M. T., Numerical Calculation
BRIGO, L., Geomining Prospecting
BROGLIA, R., Theory of Nuclear Structures
CAMATINI, M., Cellular Biology
CANCELLI, A., Applied Geology
CANTONI, V., Pure Mechanics
CANUTO, G., Geometry
CAPASSO, V., Mathematical Statistics
CARBONI, A., Algebra
CARIATI, F., Analytical Chemistry
CATTI, M., Structural Chemistry
CAVALLIN, A., Physical General Geography
CAVALLINI, G., General Pedagogy
CELLINI, A., Institutions of Mathematics
CENINI, S., General and Inorganic Chemistry

CHINCARINI, G., Astronomy
CIANI, G. F., Laboratory Chemistry
CINQUINI, M., Organic Chemistry
CIRELLI, R., Mathematical Methods of Physics
COLOMBO, R., Cytology and Histology
COLZANI, L., Institutions of Mathematics
COMOLLI, R., General Pathology
COTTAFAVA, G., Computer Architecture Module
COZZI, F., Organic Chemistry
CREMASCHI, D., General Physiology
CURTI, B., Biological Chemistry
D'ESTE, G., Algebra
DANIELI, B., Physical Methods in Organic Chemistry
DE BERNARDI, F., Zoology
DE FALCO, D., Calculus of Probability and Mathematical Statistics
DE MICHELE, L., Mathematical Analysis
DE MICHELIS, M., Plant Physiology
DE SOCIO, M., Pure Mechanics
DEDÒ, M., Geometry
DEGLI ANTONI, G., Applied Computer Science
DESTRO, R., Physical Chemistry
DI CORATO, M., General Physics
DI FRANCESCO, D., General Physiology
DI MARTINO, L., Institutions of Advanced Algebra
FACCHINI, U., General Physics
FAELLI, A., General Physiology
FANTUCCI, P. C., General and Inorganic Chemistry
FERRARI, R., Statistical Mechanics
FERRARIO, A., Mineral Deposits
FERRONI, A., General Physiology
FERRUTI, P., Macromolecular Chemistry
FIORINI, E., Institutions of Nuclear and Subnuclear Physics
FONTANESI, M., General Physics
FORTI, G., Plant Biochemistry
GADIOLI, E., Nuclear Physics
GAETANI, M., Geology
GALGANI, L., Pure Mechanics
GALLI FOSSATI, E. A., General Microbiology
GARANTI, L., Organic Chemistry
GELATI, R., Geology
GHIDONI, A., Cytogenetics
GIACCONI, R., Astrophysics
GIANINETTI, E., Theoretical Chemistry
GIAVINI, E., Comparative Anatomy
GIGLIO, M., Physics, Experiments
GIRARDELLO, L., Quantum Theory
GNACCOLINI, M., Sedimentology
GORLA, M., Genetics
GOSSO, G., Structural Geology
GRAMACCIOLI, C., Physical Chemistry
GREGNANIN, A., Petrography
GUERRITORE, A., Biological Chemistry
GUZZI, M., Laboratory of General Physics
HANOZET, G., Biological Chemistry
IORI, I., General Physics
ITALIANI, M., Software Engineering
JADOUL, F., Regional Geology
JENNINGS, R., Photobiology
LANDINI, D., Special and Organic Synthesis and Method
LANTERI, A., Geometry
LANZ, L., Elements of Theoretical Physics
LEVI, S., Mathematical Analysis
LONGHI, P., Electrochemistry
LONGO, C., Botany
LORENZI, A., Mathematical Analysis
LUCCHINI, G., Genetics
LUGIATO, L., Quantum Electronics
LUNELLI, M., Data Processing Systems
MAGRI, F., Institutions of Mathematical Physics
MAIORANA, S., Organic Chemistry
MANDELLI, L., Physics
MANITTO, P. M., Chemistry of Natural Organic Substances
MARANESI, P., Electronics
MARCHESINI, G., Theoretical Physics
MARTELLA, G., Information Systems
MAURI, G., Theoretical Computer Science
MAZZA, F., Corrosion and Protection of Metals
MAZZOTTI, A., Geophysical Prospecting
MICHELETTI, S., Physics
MIGLIOLI, P., Theoretical Computer Science
MILAZZO, M., Physical Methodology in the Arts
MONTALDI, E., Thermodynamics
MONTANARI, F., Industrial Chemistry
MUNDICI, D., Theoretical Computer Science
MUSSINI, T., Electrochemistry
NARDELLI, G., Physics
NEGRI, P., Experimental Physics
NICOLA, P. C., Mathematical Economics
OROMBELLI, G., Physical Geography
OTTOLENGHI, S., Molecular Genetics
PAGANI, G., Heterocyclic Chemistry
PAGANONI, L., Mathematical Analysis
PALLESCHI, M., Institutions of Advanced Geometry
PANERAI, A., Pharmacology
PASQUARÈ, G., Geology
PAVERI, S., Institutions of Mathematics
PELIZZONI, F., Organic Chemistry
PEROTTI, M. E., Cytology and Histology
PICCININI, F., Applied Pharmacology
PICCININI, R., Algebraic Topology
PIGNANELLI, M., Institutions of Nuclear and Subnuclear Physics
PITEA, D., Physical Chemistry
PIZZINI, S., Physical Chemistry of Materials
PLEVANI, P., Molecular Biology
PREMOLI SILVA, I., Micropalaeontology
PREPARATA, G., Theories of Subnuclear Interactions
PROSPERI, G. M., Institutions of Theoretical Physics
PROVINI, A., Ecology
PULLIA, A., General Physics
RAGAINI, V., Chemical Industrial Processes and Systems
RAIMONDI, M., Physical Chemistry
RANZI, M., Chemistry of Fermentation and Industrial Microbiology
REATTO, L., General Physics
RICCI, R., Pure Mechanics
RINDONE, B., Organic Chemistry
ROBBA, E., Palaeontology
ROSSI, M., General and Inorganic Chemistry
ROUX, D., Institutions of Advanced Analysis
RUF, B., Mathematical Analysis
RUSSO, G., Organic Chemistry
SABADINI, N., Programming Languages
SABADINI, R., Terrestrial Physics
SALA, F., Botany
SANNICOLÒ, F., Organic Chemistry
SCATTURIN, V., General and Inorganic Chemistry
SCOLASTICO, C., Organic Chemistry
SINDONI, E., General Physics
SIRONI, G., Micro-organism Genetics
SIRONI, G., Radioastronomy
SOARDI, P. M., Mathematical Analysis
SOAVE, C., Plant Physiology
SPINOLO, G., General Physics
STURANI, E. P., Cellular Biochemistry
TERRENI, B., Mathematics
TERZI, N., Solid State Physics
TISATO, F., Operating Systems
TRASATTI, S., Electrochemistry
TRAVAGLINI, G., Institutions of Mathematics
TUBINO, R., General Physics
TUCCI, P., History of Physics
UGO, R., General Inorganic Chemistry
VALLE, G., Computer Science
VEGNI, G., Elementary Particle Physics
VERDI, C., Institutions of Mathematics
WANKE, E., General Physiology
WOESS, W., Probability and Statistical Methods, Stochastic Processes
ZAMBELLI, V., Algebra
ZANETTI, G., Biological Chemistry
ZULLINI, A., Zoology

Faculty of Sciences (in Como):

ANDREONI, A., General Physics
CASATI, G., Institutions of Theoretical Physics
GAMBA, A., Physical Chemistry
GENNARI, C., Organic Chemistry
GORINI, V., Institutions of Theoretical Physics
LA MONICA, G., General and Inorganic Chemistry
TREVES, A., Astrophysics

Faculty of Sciences (in Varese):

CALAMARI, D., Ecology
GEROLA, P., Botany
LANZAVECCHIA, G., Comparative Anatomy
MARTEGANI, E., Molecular Biology
PERES, A., General Physiology
PILONE, M., Biological Chemistry
TARAMELLI, R., Genetics
VALVASSORI, R., Zoology

Faculty of Pharmacy:

ASDENTE, M., Physics
BERRA, B., Biological Chemistry
BOLIS, C., General Biology
BOMBIERI, G., Drug Analysis
CASTANO, P., Human Anatomy
CATTABENI, F., Applied Pharmacology
CIGNARELLA, G., Pharmaceutical and Toxicological Chemistry
COLONNA, S., Organic Chemistry
DA RE, P., Pharmaceutical and Toxicological Chemistry
DALLA CROCE, P., Heterocyclic Chemistry
DE MICHELI, C., Pharmaceutical and Toxicological Chemistry
DEL PRA, A., General and Inorganic Chemistry
FERRI, V., Pharmaceutical and Toxicological Chemistry
FOLCO, G., Pharmacology and Pharmacognosy
FRENI, M., General and Inorganic Chemistry
FUMAGALLI, R., Pharmacology and Pharmacognosy
GALLI, C., Pharmacological Tests and Measuring
GALLI, G., Applied Biochemistry
GAVEZZOTTI, A., Physical Chemistry
MAFFEI FACINO, R., Drug Analysis
MARCHESINI, A., Organic Chemistry
MAROZZI, E., Toxicological Chemistry
MARTINI, L., Endocrinology
MONTANARI, L., Pharmaceutical Technology, Socioeconomy and Legislation
MOTTA, M., General Physiology
NICOSIA, S., Cellular and Molecular Pharmacology
PAOLETTI, R., Pharmacology and Pharmacognosy
POCAR, D., Organic Chemistry
PUGLISI, C., Pharmacology and Pharmacognosy
RACAGNI, G., Pharmacology and Pharmacognosy
SIRTORI, C., Clinical Pharmacology
STRADI, R., Physical Methods in Organic Chemistry
VILLA, L., Pharmaceutical and Toxicological Chemistry

Faculty of Agriculture:

ALBONICO, F., Agricultural Industry
ARAGOZZINI, F., Fermentation Chemistry
BASSI, D., Fruit Farming
BELLI, G., Plant Pathology
BISIACH, M., Phytotherapy
BODRIA, L., Agricultural Mechanics
CASATI, D., Agrofood Economy
CASTELLI, G., Agricultural Mechanics
CAVAZZONI, V., Industrial Microbiology
CERLETTI, P., Alimentary Biochemistry
CERUTTI, G., Additives and Residues in Food Products

CICOGNA MOZZONI, M., General Animal Husbandry
COCUCCI, M., Physiology of Farmed Plants
DAGHETTA, A., Chemical Analysis of Foodstuffs
DE WRACHIEN, D., Irrigation and Drainage
DESIMONI, E., Analytical Chemistry
ECCHER, T., General Arboriculture
ELIAS, G., Environmental Technical Physics
FERRARI, A., Soil Microbiology
GALLI, A., Foods Microbiology
GASPARETTO, E., Agricultural Mechanization
GAVAZZI, G., Plant Genetic Improvement
GENEVINI, P., Soil Chemistry
GIURA, R., Agricultural Hydraulics
GREPPI, M., Hydraulic Systems, Forestry
LECHI, F., Agricultural Politics
MAGGIORE, T., Herbaceous Farming
MANACHINI, P., General Microbiology
MANNINO, S., Chemico-Physical and Sensory Analysis of Food
MERLINI, L., Organic Chemistry
MONDELLI, R., Organic Chemistry
OTTOGALLI, G., Microbiology of Food Products
PAGANI, S., Enzymology
PELLIZZI, G., Agricultural Mechanics
PERI, C., Unit Operations in Food Technology
POLELLI, M., Rural Evaluation
POMPEI, C., Food Technology Processes
RESMINI, P., Agricultural Industry
RIGONI, M., Animal Feedstuffs and Nutrition
ROMITA, P. L., Agricultural Hydraulics
SANGIORGI, F., Rural and Forest Constructions
SCHIRALDI, A., Physical Chemistry
SORLINI, C., Agricultural and Forest Microbiology
SUCCI, G., Special Animal Husbandry
SÜSS, L., Agricultural Entomology
TANO, F., Herbaceous Farming
TESTOLIN, G., Human Food and Nutrition
VOLONTERIO, G., Agricultural Industry

Faculty of Veterinary Medicine:
ADDIS, F., Clinical Veterinary Surgery
AGNES, F., General Veterinary Pathology
BELLOLI, A., Medical Veterinary Semiology
BERETTA, C., Pharmacology, Pharmacodynamics and Veterinary Pharmacy
CAIROLI, F., Clinical Obstetrics and Veterinary Gynaecology
CAMMARATA, G., Veterinary Autopsy
CANTONI, C. A., Animal Food Products Inspection and Control
CARENZI, C., Morpho-Functional Evaluation of Animal Production
CLEMENT, C., Veterinary Physiology
CORINO, C., Animal Feedstuffs and Nutrition
CORSICO, G., Animal Food Products Inspection and Control
CRIMELLA, C., Special Animal Husbandry
DE GRESTI DI SAN, L. A., Surgical Veterinary Semiology
DELL' ORTO, V., Animal Foodstuffs and Nutrition
FERRANDI, B., Systematic and Comparative Veterinary Anatomy
FINAZZI, M., Veterinary Pathological Anatomy
GENCHI, C., Parasitic Diseases
GUIDOBONO CAVALCHINI, A., Mechanization of Farming Processes.
GUIDOBONO CAVALCHINI, L., Aviculture
LANFRANCHI, P., Veterinary Parasitology
LAURIA, A., Veterinary, Systematic and Comparative Anatomy
LEONARDI, L., Veterinary Radiology and Nuclear Medicine
MAFFEO, G., Physiology of Domestic Animals
MANDELLI, G., Veterinary Pathological Anatomy
MORTELLARO, C., Veterinary Surgical Pathology
PAGNACCO, G., Animal Genetic Improvement and General Husbandry
POLI, G., Veterinary Microbiology and Immunology
POMPA, G., Veterinary Toxicology
PORCELLI, F., General and Special Histology and Embryology
POZZA, O., Pathology of Domestic Animals
REDAELLI, G. L., Public Veterinary Health
RONCHI, S., Biochemistry
RUFFO, G., Infectious Diseases, Prophylaxis and Veterinary Inspectors
SECCHI, O., Biochemistry
TRADATI, F., Veterinary Medical Pathology
VACIRCA, G., Veterinary Clinical Medicine
VALFRÈ, F., Supply, Markets and Rural Industries

UNIVERSITÀ DEGLI STUDI DI MODENA

Via Università 4, 41100 Modena
Telephone: 059-329216
Telex: 520355
Fax: 059-245156
E-mail: rettore@casa.unimo.it

Founded 1175
Academic year: November to October

Rector: Prof. C. CIPOLLI
Administrator: Dott. A. SALVINI

Library of 294,000
Number of teachers: 653
Number of students: 14,100

Publications: *Annuario*, *Notiziario*.

DEANS

Faculty of Jurisprudence: Prof. R. LAMBERTINI
Faculty of Economics: Prof. A. FERRARI
Faculty of Medicine and Surgery: Prof. N. CARULLI
Faculty of Mathematics, Physics and Natural Sciences: Prof. C. JACOBONI
Faculty of Pharmacy: Prof. F. FORNI
Faculty of Engineering: Prof. G. C. PELLACANI

PROFESSORS

Faculty of Jurisprudence:
ALESSANDRINI, S., Economic Policy
ANTONINI, A., Navigation Law
BIONE, M., Commercial Law
BONFATTI, S., Banking Law
BORGHESI, D., Law of Civil Procedure
CALANDRA BUONAURA, V., Commercial Law
GALANTINO, L., Labour Law
GASPARINI CASARI, V., Administrative Law
GIANOLIO, R. C., Administrative Law
GUERZONI, L., Ecclesiastical Law
LAMBERTINI, R., Institutions of Roman Law
LUBERTO, S., Anthropology and Criminology
MARANI, F., General Private Law
RONCO, M., Penal Law
SILINGARDI, G., Transport Law
VIGNUDELLI, A., Constitutional Law

Faculty of Economics:
BIAGI, M., Labour Law
BISONI, C., Professional and Banking Procedures
BOSI, P., Finance and Financial Law
BRUSCO, S., Economics and Industrial Policy
BURSI, T., Industrial and Commercial Techniques
CANOVA, F., Economic Policy
FERRARI, A., Stock Exchange Techniques
GINZBURG, A., Economic and Financial Policy
GOLZIO, L. E., Work Study
GRANDORI, A., Personnel Management
LANE, D. A., Statistics
RICCI, G., Financial Mathematics
VELLA, F., Commercial Law

Faculty of Medicine and Surgery:
AGGAZZOTTI, G., Hygiene and Dentistry
AGNATI, L. F., Human Physiology
ALBERTAZZI, A., Nephrology
ARTIBANI, W., Urology
BAGGIO, G. G., Pharmacology
BALLI, R., Otorhinolaryngology
BARBIERI, G. C., Anaesthesiology
BARBOLINI, G., Anatomy, Histology and Pathology
BEDUSCHI, G., Forensic Medicine
BERGOMI, M., Hygiene and Odontology
BERNASCONI, S., Paediatrics
BERTOLINI, A., Pharmacology
BLASI, E., Microbiology
BOBYLEVA, V., General Pathology
BON, L., Human Physiology
BONATI, B., General Clinical Medicine and Medical Therapy
CALANDRA BUONAURA, S., General Pathology
CANÉ, V.
CARULLI, N., Medical Pathology and Clinical Methodology
CAVAZZUTI, G. B., Clinical Paediatrics
CELLI, L., Orthopaedics and Traumatology
CIPOLLI, C., Psychology
CONSOLO, U., Odontostomatological Special Surgery
CORAZZA, R., Human Physiology
CORTESI, N., General Clinical Surgery and Surgical Therapy
CORTI, A., Biological Chemistry
CURCI, P., Psychiatry
DE BERNARDINIS, G., General Surgery
DE FAZIO, F. A., Forensic and Insurance Medicine
DE GAETANI, C., Foundations of Medicine and Histological Pathology
DELLA CASA, L., Infectious Diseases
DE RENZI, E., Neurology
FABIO, U., Microbiology
FAGLIONI, P., Clinical Neurology
FERRARI, F., Pharmacology
FERRARI, S., Biological Chemistry
FORABOSCO, A., Histology and Embryology
FRANCESCHI, C., Immunology
GALETTI, G., Clinical Otorhinolaryngology
GIANNETTI, A., Clinical Dermatology
GUARALDI, G. P., Clinical Psychiatry
GUERRA, R., Clinical Ophthalmology
JASONNI, V. M., Obstetrics and Gynaecology
LODI, R. G., Thoracic Surgery
MANENTI, F., Gastroenterology
MANZINI, E., Rheumatology
MAROTTI, G., Human Anatomy
MARRAMA, P., Endocrinology
MATTIOLI, G., Cardiology
MODENA, M. G., Cardiology
MONETA CAGLIO, E., Clinical Obstetrics and Gynaecology
MONTI, M. G., Biological Chemistry
MORUZZI, M. S., Chemical Biology
MUSCATELLO, U., General Pathology
PONZ DE LEON, M., Internal Medicine
PORTOLANI, M., Virology
ROMAGNOLI, R., Radiology
SALVIOLI, G., Surgical Pathology
SAVIANO, M., Surgical Pathology
SEIDENARI, S., Allergological Dermatology
SILINGARDI, V., Special Medical Pathology and Clinical Methodology
STERNIERI, E., Clinical Pharmacology
TAMPIERI, A., Medical Statistics and Biometry
TOMASI, A., General Physiopathology
TORELLI, G., Haematology
TORELLI, U., General Clinical Medicine and Therapy
TRENTINI, G. P., Anatomy and Pathological History
VENTURA, E., General Clinical Medicine and Therapy
VERNOLE, B., Clinical Dentistry
VIVOLI, G., Hygiene

VOLPE, A., Physiopathology of Human Reproduction
ZENEROLI, M. L., Semiotics
ZINI, I., Human Physiology

Faculty of Mathematics, Physics and Natural Sciences:

ACCORSI, C. A., Phytogeography
BERTOLANI, R., Zoology
BERTONI, C. M., Theoretical Physics
BIANCHI, U., Genetics
BISI, O., Mathematical Methods of Physics
BONI, M., Mathematical Analysis
BORTOLANI, V., Solid State Physics
CALANDRA BUONAURA, C., Structure of Materials
CAPEDRI, S., Petrography
CAVICCHIOLI, A., Institutes of Advanced Geometry
CHITI, G., Mathematical Analysis
CREMA, R., Ecology
DEL PRETE, C., Botany
DIECI, G., Micropalaeontology
FANTIN, A. M., Histology and Embryology
FAZZINI, P., Geology
FERRARI, I., Mathematical Methods in Physics
FUNARO, D., Numerical Analysis
GAGLIARDI, C., Geometry II
JACOBONI, C., Atomic Physics
LARATTA, A., Numerical Analysis and Programming
LAZZERETTI, P., Physical Chemistry
LEVONI, S., Foundations of Mathematical Physics
MAGHERINI, P.C., General Physiology
MARINI, M., Comparative Anatomy
MENABUE, L., General and Inorganic Chemistry
MESCHIARI, M., Geometry
MIRONE, P., Physical Chemistry
MOMICCHIOLI, F., Physical Chemistry
OTTAVIANI, G., Physics (Preparation of Experiments)
PAGLIAI, A. M., Zoology
PAGNONI, U. M., Organic Chemistry
PALYI, G., Chemical Composition
PANIZZA, M., Physical Geography
PAREA, G. C., Sedimentology
PASSAGLIA, E., Mineralogy
PELLEGRINI, M., Applied Geology
PRUDENZIATI, M., Applied Electronics
QUATTROCCHI, P., Advanced Elementary Mathematics
RIVALENTI, G., Metamorphic Petrography
RONCHETTI, I., General Pathology
RUSSO, A., Palaeo-ecology
SANTANGELO, R., Terrestrial Physics
SEGRE, U., Electrochemistry
SERPAGLI, E., Palaeontology
SIGHINOLFI, G., Geochemistry
TADDEI, F., Advanced Organic Chemistry
TONGIORGI, P., Ethnology
TORRE, G., Organic Chemistry

Faculty of Pharmacy:

ALBASINI, A., Applied Pharmaceutical Chemistry and Toxicology
BARALDI, M., Pharmacology
BERNABEI, M. T., Pharmaceutical Procedures and Legislation
BRASILI, L., Pharmaceutical and Toxicological Chemistry
CAMERONI, R., Applied Pharmaceutical Chemistry
FORNI, F., Pharmaceutical Procedures and Legislation
GALLI, E., Mineralogy
GAMBERINI, G., Pharmaceutical Chemical Analysis
MELEGARI, M., Pharmaceutical Chemical Analysis II
MONZANI, V. A., Pharmaceutical Chemical Analysis
PECORARI, P., Pharmaceutical Chemical Analysis
PIETRA, P., General Physiology
QUAGLIO, G., Hygiene

Faculty of Engineering:

ALBERIGI, A., Electronics
ANDRISANO, A. O., Industrial Design
ANICHINI, G., Mathematical Analysis
BAROZZI, G. S., Technical Physics
CAMPI, S., Mathematical Analysis
CANALI, C., Applied Electronics
CANNAROZZI, M., Construction Theory
CANTORE, G.
CECCHI, R.
FANTINI, F., Industrial Electronics
FRANCESCHINI, V., Rational Mechanics
IMMOVILLI, G., Electronic Communications
NANNARONE, S., Physics
PELLACANI, G. C., General and Inorganic Chemistry
PILATI, F., Macromolecular Chemistry
SCARABOTTOLO, N., Foundations of Information Science
STROZZI, A.

UNIVERSITÀ DEGLI STUDI DEL MOLISE

Via Mazzini 8/12, 86100 Campobasso
Telephone: 0874-4041
Fax: 0874-63968

Founded 1982

Rector: Prof. LUCIO D'ALESSANDRO
Administrative Director: Dr GIUSEPPE PATRIZI

DEANS

Faculty of Agriculture: Prof. RAIMONDO CUBADDA
Faculty of Economics and Social Sciences: Profa LUCIANA FRANGIONI
Faculty of Law: Prof. ANTONIO PROCIDA MIRABELLI DI LAURO

UNIVERSITÀ DI NAPOLI

Corso Umberto I, 80138 Naples
Telephone: 081-5477111

Founded 1224

Rector: Prof. CARLO CILIBERTO
Administrative Director: Dott. T. PELOSI

Number of teachers: 1,833
Number of students: 100,000

DEANS

Agriculture: C. NOVIELLO
Architecture: U. SIOLA
Economics: F. LUCARELLI
Pharmacy: (vacant)
Law: A. PECORARO ALBANI
Political Science: G. CUOMO
Engineering: G. VOLPICELLI
Letters and Philosophy: F. TESSITORE
Mathematics and Natural Sciences: L. MANGONI
Medicine I: D. MANCINO
Medicine II: G. SALVATORE
Veterinary Medicine: G. PELAGALLI

UNIVERSITÀ DEGLI STUDI DI PADOVA

Via 8 Febbraio 2, 35122 Padua
Telephone: 049-8275111
Telex: 430176
Fax: 049-8273009

Founded 1222

Rector: Prof. GIOVANNI MARCHESINI
First Pro-Rector: Prof. VINCENZO MILANESI
Pro-Rectors: Prof. ACHILLE PESSINA, Prof. P. N. BISOL, Prof. F. BOMBI, Prof. G. ZACCARIA
Secretary: Dott. D. ARTMANN
Librarian: Prof. P. DEL NEGRO

Number of teachers: 1,382
Number of students: 65,579

Publications: *Annuario*, *Bollettino-Notiziario* (1 a year), *Guida dello Studente*.

DEANS

Faculty of Jurisprudence: Prof. A. BURDESE
Faculty of Political Science: Prof. G. ZACCARIA
Faculty of Statistical Sciences: Prof. L. BERNARDI
Faculty of Letters and Philosophy: Prof. S. COLLODO
Faculty of Education: Prof. M. CHIARANDA
Faculty of Medicine and Surgery: Prof. A. GATTA
Faculty of Psychology: Prof. V. RUBINI
Faculty of Veterinary Medicine: Prof. B. BIOLATTI
Faculty of Mathematics, Physics, and Natural Sciences: Prof. C. PECILE
Faculty of Pharmacy: Prof. F. DALL' ACQUA
Faculty of Engineering: Prof. G. B. GUARISE
Faculty of Agriculture: Prof. U. ZILIOTTO
Faculty of Economics: (vacant)

HEADS OF DEPARTMENTS

Physics: Prof. L. PERUZZO
Biology: Prof. G. CASADORO
Pharmacology: Prof. L. CIMA
Paediatrics: Prof. F. ZACCHELLO
Pharmaceutical Science: Prof. M. NICOLINI
Geography: Prof G. BRUNETTA
Developmental Psychology: Prof. A. MAZZOCCO
Statistical Sciences: Prof. S. RIGATTI LUCCHINI
Linguistics: Prof. M. MELI
Education Science: Prof. F. ANTINORI
Inorganic, Metallorganic and Analytical Chemistry: Prof. M. VIDALI
Organic Chemistry: (vacant)
Physical Chemistry: Prof. R. BOZIO
Sociology: Prof. T. R. MINGIONE
General Psychology: Prof. E. GIUS
International Studies: Prof. E. DEL VECCHIO
History: Prof. A. RIGON
Astronomy: Prof. F. LUCCHIN
History of the Fine Arts and Music: Prof. G. CATTIN
Pure and Applied Mathematics: Prof. G. B. DI MASI
Agrarian Biotechnology: Prof. P. SPETTOLI
Electronics and Information Science: Prof. G. TONDELLO
Anglo-Germanic Languages and Literature: Prof. G. BRUNETTI
Electrical Engineering: Prof. S. LUPI
Mechanical Engineering: Prof. G. SCARINCI
Land and Forest Management: Prof. F. VIOLA
Biological Chemistry: Prof. A. RIGO
Mineralogy and Petrology: Prof. A. DAL NEGRO
Geology, Palaeontology and Geophysics: Prof. D. RIO
Mathematical Methods and Models for the Applied Sciences: Prof. M. PITTERI
New Technology and Management Restructuring: P. BARIANI
Biomedical Sciences: Prof. T. POZZAN
Economics: Prof. F. FAVOTTO
Ancient History: Prof. M. PERI
Zootechnical Sciences: Prof. I. ANDRIGHETTO
Agronomy: Prof. G. MOSCA
Italian Studies: Prof. G. CAPOVILLA
Comparative Law: Prof. N. OLIVETTI RASON
Clinical and Experimental Medicine: Prof. A. TIENGO
Psychology and Neurological Sciences: Prof. G. TESTA
Construction and Transport: Prof. B. SCHREFLER
Philosophy: Prof. E. BERTI
Oncology: Prof. L. CHIECO BIANCHI

There are 50 attached Institutes.

UNIVERSITÀ DEGLI STUDI

Piazza Marina 61, 90133 Palermo
Telephone: 091-270111
Telex: 910170
Founded 1777
Rector: Prof. I. M. GIAMBERTONI
Administrative Director: Dr FILIPPO GUAGLIARDO
Number of teachers: *c.* 1,300
Number of students: *c.* 20,000
Publications: *Annali del Seminario Giuridico, Circolo Giuridico L. Sampolo, Annali della Facoltà di Economia e Commercio.*

DEANS

Agriculture: G. FIERROTTI
Architecture: M. DE SIMONE
Economics: V. FAZIO
Pharmacy: S. GIAMMANCO
Law: S. MAZZAMUTO
Engineering: E. OLIVIERI
Letters and Philosophy: A. BUTTITA
Education: G. A. PUGLISI
Medicine: A. GULLOTTI
Mathematics: F. MAGGIO

UNIVERSITÀ DEGLI STUDI

Via Università 12, 43100 Parma
Telephone: 0521-2041
Telex: 530327
Fax: 0521-20437
Founded 962
Rector: Prof. NICOLA OCCHIOCUPO
Administrative Director: Dott. M. CASTELLI
Number of teachers: 1,100
Number of students: 30,214

DEANS

Faculty of Jurisprudence: Prof. G. UBERTIS
Faculty of Medicine: Prof. A. NOVARINI
Faculty of Pharmacy: Prof. G. PELIZZI
Faculty of Physical, Mathematical and Natural Sciences: Prof. E. ONOFRI
Faculty of Veterinary Medicine: Prof. E. TAMANINI
Faculty of Economics and Commerce: Prof. C. GIACOMINI
Faculty of Arts: Prof. A. C. QUINTAVALLE
Faculty of Engineering: Prof. G. PRATI
Faculty of Agricultural Science: Prof. R. MARCHELLI

UNIVERSITÀ DEGLI STUDI DI PAVIA

Corso Strada Nuova 65, 27100 Pavia
Telephone: 0382-5041
Fax: 0382-21389
Founded 1361 by Emperor Charles IV
Academic year: November to October
Rector: Prof. ROBERTO SCHMID
Vice-Rector: Prof. PAOLA VITA-FINZI
Administrative Director: Dr GESUINO PIGA
Number of teachers: 1,055
Number of students: 28,867
Publications: *Annuario, Guida dello Studente* (for each faculty), *Guida dello Studente Straniero* and many faculty publs.

DEANS

Faculty of Law: Prof. G. ZANARONE
Faculty of Political Sciences: Prof. P. SCARAMOZZINO
Faculty of Economics: Prof. F. ROSITI
Faculty of Arts and Philosophy: Prof. G. GIORGI
Faculty of Medicine and Surgery I: Prof. E. ROMERO
Faculty of Medicine and Surgery II (Varese): Prof. R. DIONIGI
Faculty of Mathematics, Physics and Natural Science: Prof. G. GERZELI
Faculty of Pharmacy: Prof. U. CONTE
Faculty of Engineering: Prof. U. MOISELLO
School of Musical Palaeography and Philology: Prof. G. PRATO

HEADS OF DEPARTMENTS AND INSTITUTES

Law:
Economics: Prof. E. GERELLI
Private and Procedural Law: Prof. V. DENTI
Public Law: Prof. F. MOSCONI
Law and Penal Procedure: Prof. V. GREVI
Roman Law and History of Law: Prof. F. BONA

Political Science:
Economics: Prof. E. GERELLI
Political and Social Studies: Prof. G. SANI
Statistics: Prof. P. SCARAMOZZINO
Legal-Political Studies: Prof. P. G. GRASSO
Foreign Languages: Prof. R. CARPANINI

Economics:
Business Research: Prof. G. GIORGI
History and Geography: Prof. G. VIGO
Economics, Politics and Quantitative Methods: L. RAMPA

Arts and Philosophy:
Philosophy: Prof. M. VEGETTI
Modern Languages: Prof. G. CARAVAGGI
Antiquities: Prof. O. CARRUBA
Medieval and Modern Literature and Art: Prof. A. STELLA
History and Geography: Prof. G. GUDERZO
Psychology: Prof. O. ANDREANI DENTICI
Linguistics: Prof. P. RAMAT

Medicine and Surgery:
Biochemistry: Prof. C. BALDUINI
Surgery: Prof. A. ZONTA
Internal Medicine: Prof. A. CREMA
Occupational and Community Preventive Medicine: Prof. M. T. TENCONI
Human Pathology: Prof. L. TIEPOLO
Anatomy: Prof. A. FAZZI
Pharmacology: Prof. F. BERTE
Physiology: Prof. U. VENTURA
Histology and Embryology: Prof. A. CALLIGARO
Legal Medicine and Insurance: Prof. G. PIERUCCI
Institute of General Surgery and Organ Transplant: Prof. M. VIGANO
Microbiology: Prof. E. ROMERO
General Pathology: Prof. V. VANNINI
Clinical Psychiatry: Prof. D. DE MARTIS
Radiology: Prof. L. DI GUGLIELMO
Applied Health Sciences: Prof. A. MARINONI
Respiratory Diseases: Prof. C. GRASSI
Clinical Surgery: Prof. E. FORNI
Paediatrics: Prof. F. SEVERI
Ophthalmology: Prof. F. TRIMARCHI
Dentistry: Prof. C. BRUSOTTI
Orthopaedics and Traumatology: Prof. L. CECILIANI
Obstetrics and Gynaecology: Prof. C. ZARA
Otorhinolaryngology: Prof. E. MIRA
Infectious Diseases: Prof. L. MINOLI
Neurology: Prof. V. COSI
Traumatology II (Varese): Prof. P. CHERUBINO
Public Medicine (Varese): Prof. M. TAVANI

Mathematics, Physics and Natural Sciences:
Biochemistry: Prof. C. BALDUINI
Animal Biology: Prof. A. GRIGOLO
Physical Chemistry: Prof. G. FLOR
General Chemistry: Prof. L. FABBRIZZI
Organic Chemistry: Prof. P. V. VITA FINZI ZALMAN
General Physics: Prof. G. GUIZZETTI
Nuclear and Theoretical Physics: Prof. A. PIAZZOLI
Genetics and Microbiology: Prof. A. GALIZZI
Mathematics: Prof. G. GILARDI
Earth Sciences: Prof. R. CASNEDI
Pharmacology: Prof. G. BENZI
Botany: Prof. A. PIROLA
Medical Mycology: Prof. G. CARETTA
Agricultural Entomology: Prof. M. PAVAN
General Physiology: Prof. C. CASELLA

Pharmacology:
Pharmaceutical Chemistry: Prof. G. CACCIALANZA
Pharmacology: Prof. E. GRANA

Engineering:
Electronics: Prof. V. DE GIORGI
Computer Science: Prof. V. CANTONI
Civil Engineering: Prof. R. GALETTO
Hydraulic and Environmental Engineering: Prof. M. GALLATI
Structural Mechanics: Prof. C. CINQUINI
Electrical Engineering: Prof. A. SAVINI

UNIVERSITÀ DEGLI STUDI DI PERUGIA

Piazza dell' Università, 06100 Perugia
Telephone: 075-5851
Telex: 662078
Fax: 075-5852067
Founded 1200
State control
Academic year: November to October
Rector: Prof. G. CALZONI
Administrative Director: Dott. P. SANTINI
Pro-Rector: Prof. A. TATICCHI
Librarian: Dott. M. PIERONI
Number of teachers: 312
Number of students: 31,746
Publications: *L'Università, Rivista di Idrobiologia, Rivista di Dermatologia, Rivista di Biologia, La Salute Umana.*

DEANS

Faculty of Jurisprudence: Prof. S. CAPRIOLI
Faculty of Political Science: Prof. M. RAVERAIRA
Faculty of Economic Science: Prof. T. SEOIARI
Faculty of Letters and Philosophy: Prof. A. PIERETTI
Faculty of Education: Prof. E. MIRRI
Faculty of Medicine and Surgery: Prof. R. ROSSI
Faculty of Mathematical, Physical and Natural Sciences: Prof. C. MANTOVANI
Faculty of Pharmacy: Prof. C. M. FIORETTI CECCHERELLI
Faculty of Agrarian Science: Prof. B. ROMANO
Faculty of Veterinary Medicine: Prof. A. GAITI
Faculty of Engineering: Prof. R. SORRENTINO

DIRECTORS OF DEPARTMENTS

Plant Biology: Prof. A. MENGHINI
Chemistry: Prof. F. FRINGUELLI
Physics: Prof. F. SACCHETTI
Hygiene: Prof. A. M. IORIO
Mathematics and Computer Science: Prof. G. COLETTI
Experimental Medicine and Biochemical Science: Prof. R. F. DONATO
Earth Sciences: Prof. L. PASSERI
Linguistic and Philological-literary Science of the Anglo-Germanic Area: Prof. S. RUFINI
Statistical Science: Prof. G. CICCHITELLI
Historical Science: Prof. L. TOSI
Historical Science (Antiquity): Prof. F. RONCALLI DI MONTORIO
Internal Medicine and Endocrinology: Prof. P. BRUNETTI
Surgery: Prof. A. DELOGU
Surgery and Emergency Surgery: Prof. L. MOGGI
Cellular Biology: Prof. A. ORLACCHIO
Clinical and Experimental Medicine: Prof. C. RICCARDI

PROFESSORS

Faculty of Jurisprudence:
AZZARITI, G., Constitutional Law
BADIALI, G., International Law

BARBERINI, G., Ecclesiastical Law
CAPRIOLI, S., History of Modern Italian Law
CARDI, E., Procedural Law
CAVALAGLIO, A., Bankruptcy Law
CAVALLO, B., Administrative Law
CINELLI, M., Labour Law
DALLERA, G. F., Finance and Financial Law
GAITO, A., Penal Law
MIGLIORINI, L., Administrative Law
MORSELLI, E., Penal Law
PALAZZO, A., Institutions of Private Law
PALAZZOLO, N., History of Roman Law
PEPPE, L., Roman Law
SALVI, C., Civil Law
SASSANI, M., Civil Procedural Law
TALAMANCA, A., Canon Law
TINELLI, G., Tax Law
VOLPI, M., Constitutional Comparative Law

Faculty of Letters and Philosophy:

AGOSTINIANI, L., Linguistics
BONAMENTE, G., Roman History
CARANCINI, G. L., European Protohistory
COARELLI, F., Greek and Roman Antiquity
DI PILLA, F., French Language and Literature
FALASCHI, G., Italian Literature
FROVA, C., Medieval History
GIORDANI, R., Christian Archaeology
ISOLA, A., Ancient Christian Literature
MADDOLI, G., Greek History
MELELLI, A., Geography
MENESTÒ, E., Medieval Latin Literature
MORETTI, G., Italian Dialectology
PICCINATO, S., Anglo-American Literature
PIERETTI, A., Theoretical Philosophy
PIZZANI, U., Latin Literature
PRIVITERA, G. A., Greek Literature
RONCALLI DI MONTORIO, F., Etruscan Studies and Italic Antiquity
RUFINI, S., English Language and Literature
SANTACHIARA, U., Church History
SCARPELLINI PANCRAZI, P., History of Medieval Art
SEPPILLI, T., Cultural Anthropology
SPAGGIARI PERUGI, B., Romance Philology
TORELLI, M., Archaeology and History of Greek and Roman Art
TORTI, A., English Language and Literature

Faculty of Political Science:

BONO, S., History and Institutions of Afro-Asian Countries
CARINI, C., History of Political Doctrine
COMPARATO, V. I., Modern History
CRESPI, F., Sociology
D'AMOJA, F., History of International Relations
DI GASPARE, G., Economic Law
GALLI DELLA LOGGIA, E., History of Political Parties and Movements
GROHMANN, A., Economic History
MARCHISIO, S., International Law
MELOGRANI, P., Contemporary History
MERLONI, F., Administrative Justice
RAVERAIRA, M., Institutions of Public Law
TEODORI, M., American History
TOSI, L., History of Treaties and International Politics
TRAMONTANA, A., Finance

Faculty of Economics:

BORGIA, R., Institutions of Private Law
BRACALENTE, B., Economics Statistics
CALZONI, G., Political Economy
CAVAZZONI, G., Accountancy
CHIARELLE, R., Institutions of Public Law
CICCHITELLI, G., Statistics
CORALLINI, S., Banking
FORCINA, A., Statistics
GRASSELLI, P. M., Political Economy
MEZZACAPO, V., Banking Legislation
MORICONI, F., Mathematics
PAGLIACCI, G., General Mathematics
PERONI, G., Marketing
RIDOLFI, M., Political Economy
SEDIARI, T., Agrarian Economics and Politics
SEVERINO, P., Commercial Penal Law

Faculty of Medicine and Surgery:

ABBRITTI, G., Industrial Medicine
AMBROSIO, G., Cardiology
ARIENTI, G., Biological Chemistry
BARTOLI, A., General Surgery
BECCHETTI, E., Histology
BINAGLIA, L., Chemistry and Biomedicine
BISTONI, F., Microbiology
BOLIS, G. B., Anatomy and Pathological Histology
BOLLI, G., Metabolic Diseases
BORRI, P. F., Psychiatry
BRUNETTI, P., Internal Medicine
BUCCIARELLI, E., Anatomy and Pathological Histology
CALANDRA, P., Dermatology
CAPRINO, G., Radiology
CASALI, L., Diseases of the Respiratory System
DADDI, G., Surgical Pathology and Clinical Propaedeutics
DELOGU, A., Ophthalmology
D'ERRICO, P., Dental Prosthesis
DONATO, R. F., Neuroanatomy
FABRONI, F., Forensic Medicine
FALORNI, A., Paediatrics
FIORE, C., Physiopathological Optics
FRONGILLO, R. F., Infectious Diseases
FURBETTA, M., Preventive and Social Paediatrics
GALLAI, V., Neurology
GIOVANNINI, E., General Biology
GORACCI, G. F., Biological Chemistry
GRIGNANI, F., Internal Medicine
LATINI, P., Radiotherapy
LAURO, V., Gynaecology and Obstetrics
LIOTTI, F. S., General Biology
LISI, P., Dermatology
MAGNI, F., Human Physiology
MAIRA, G., Neurosurgery
MANNARINO, E., Internal Medicine
MARCONI, P., Immunology
MARTELLI, M. F., Haematology
MASTRANDREA, V., Hygiene
MODOLO, M. A., Hygiene
MOGGI, L., General Surgery
MORELLI, A., Gastroenterology
NEGRI, P. L., Paradontology
NENCI, G. G., Internal Medicine
NORELLI, G. A., Forensic Medicine
PALUMBO, R., Nuclear Medicine
PAULUZZI, S., Infectious Diseases
PECORELLI, F., Orthopaedics and Traumatology
PEDUTO, V. A., Anaesthesia and Resuscitation
PETTOROSSI, V. E., Human Physiology
PORENA, M., Urology
PUXEDDU, A., Internal Medicine
RIBACCHI, R., Anatomy and Pathological Histology
RICCARDI, C., Pharmacology
RINONAPOLI, E., Orthopaedics and Traumatology
ROSI BARBERINI, G., Cellular Biology
ROSSI, R., General Pathology
SALVADORI, P., Physics
SANTEUSANIO, F., Endocrinology
SENIN, U., Geriatrics and Gerontology
STAFFOLANI, N., Oral Surgery
STAGNI, G., Infectious Diseases
TRISTAINO, B., General Surgery
VACCARO, R., Paediatrics
VALORI, C., Internal Medicine
VILLANI, C., Oncological Gynaecology
VIOLA MAGNI, M. P., General Pathology

Faculty of Pharmacy:

CORSANO LEOPIZZI, S., Pharmaceutical and Toxicological Chemistry
COSTANTINO, U., General and Inorganic Chemistry
DAMIANI, P., Food Science Chemistry
FIORETTI CECCHERELLI, M. C., Pharmacology and Pharmacognosy
FLORIDI, A., Biochemistry
FRAVOLINI, A., Pharmaceutical and Toxicological Chemistry
GRANDOLINI, G., Socioeconomic Technology and Pharmaceutical Legislation
MENGHINI, A., Pharmaceutical Botany
PELLICCIARI, R., Pharmaceutical and Toxicological Chemistry
PUCCETTI, P., Pharmacology
ROSSI, C., Applied Pharmaceutical Chemistry
SCASSELLATI, S. G., Hygiene
TESTAFERRI, L., Organic Chemistry
TIECCO, M., Organic Chemistry
VECCHIARELLI, A., Microbiology

Faculty of Agrarian Science:

ABBOZZO, P., Farm Evaluation
BENCIVENGA, M., Systematic Agricultural Botany
BERNARDINI BATTAGLINI, M., Animal Husbandry
BIANCHI, A. A., Herbaceous Cultivation
BIN, F., Biological Techniques
BONCIARELLI, F., Cultivation of Special Herbaceous Plants
BUSINELLI, M., Soil Chemistry
CIRICIOFOLO, E., Biology, Production and Technology of Seeds
COSTANTINI, F., Animal Nutrition and Feeding
COVARELLI, G., Weed Control
DURANTI, E., Physiology of Animals in Stockbreeding
FALCINELLI, M., Genetic Improvement in Cultivated Plants
FANTOZZI, P., Alimentation
FATICHENTI, F., Agrarian and Arboreal Microbiology
GIOVAGNOTTI, C.
LORENZETTI, F., Agrarian Genetics
MANNOCCHI, F., Agrarian Hydraulics
MARTE, M., Plant Pathology
MARTINI, A., Agrarian Microbiology
MARUCCHINI, C., Introductory Agrarian Chemistry
MENNELLA, V. G., Agricultural and Forestry Planning
MONOTTI, M., General Agriculture
MONTEDORO, G., Agricultural Industries
PENNACCHI, F., Agrarian Economics
RAGGI, V., Plant Pathology
ROMANO, B., Morphology and Plant Physiology
ROSSI, A. C., Economics and Agrarian Policy
ROSSI, J., Dairy Food Microbiology
SARTI, D. M., Stockbreeding
SCARPONI, L., Agrarian Biochemistry
SOLINAS, M., Agricultural Entomology
STANDARDI, A., Specialist Fruit Growing
TOMBESI, A., General Fruit Growing
VERONESI, F., Genetic Biotechnology
ZAZZERINI, A., Phytotherapy

Faculty of Veterinary Medicine:

ASDRUBALI, G., Pathology of Birds
AVELLINI, G., Clinical Veterinary Medicine
BATTISTACCI, M., Clinical Veterinary Surgery
BEGHELLI, V., Veterinary Physiology and Ethology
BELLUCCI, M., Veterinary Radiology and Nuclear Medicine
BOITI, C., Veterinary Physiology and Ethology
CASTRUCCI, G., Infectious Diseases and Prophylaxis
CECCARELLI, P., Topographical Veterinary Anatomy
CHIACCHIARINI, P., Obstetrics and Gynaecology
DEBENEDETTI, A., Endocrinology of Domestic Animals
DI ANTONIO, E., Inspection and Control of Foodstuffs of Animal Origin

FRUGANTI, G., Veterinary Medical Pathology
GAITI, A., Biochemistry
GARGIULO BERSIANI, A. M., Histology and General Embryology
LORVIK, S., Anatomy of Domestic Animals
MALVISI, J., Pharmacology and Pharmacodynamics
MANGILI PECCI, V., Laboratory Diagnosis
MANOCCHIO, I., Pathological Anatomy
MORICONI, F., Veterinary Surgical Pathology
OLIVIERI, O., Animal Nutrition
POLIDORI GIROLAMO, A. B., Veterinary Parasitology
RANUCCI, S., Veterinary Medical Semiology and Clinical Methodology
SILVESTRELLI, M., Special Stockbreeding
VALENTE, C., Infectious Diseases
VITELLOZZI, G., Veterinary Pathological Anatomy

Faculty of Mathematical, Physical and Natural Sciences:

ALBERTI, G., Inorganic Chemistry
AMBROSETTI, P. L., Palaeontology
ANTONIELLI, M., Plant Physiology
AQUILANTI, V., General and Inorganic Chemistry
AVERNA, A.
BARSI, F., Theory and Application of Mechanical Calculation
BARTOCCI, U., Geometry
CATALIOTTI, R. S., Physical Chemistry
CIOFI DEGLI ATTI, C., Institutions of Nuclear Physics
CIONINI, P. G., Botany
CIROTTO, C., Cytology and Histology
CLEMENTI, S., Organic Chemistry
COLETTI, G., Institutions of Mathematics
DE TOLLIS, B. A., Institutions of Theoretical Physics
DI GIOVANNI, M. V., Zoology
FAINA, G., Geometry
FAVARO MAZZUCATO, G., Physical Chemistry
FRINGUELLI, F., Organic Chemistry
GAINO, E., Zoology
GIANFRANCHESCHI, G. L., General Physiology
GRANETTI, B., Botany
GUAZZONE, S., Algebra
IORIO, A. M., Virology
LAGANÀ, A., General and Inorganic Chemistry
LARICCIA, P., Physics Laboratory
MAFFEI, P., Astrophysics
MANTOVANI, G., General Physics
MARINO, G., Organic Chemistry
MAZZUCATO, U., Physical Chemistry
MONTANINI MEZZASOMA, I., Biochemistry
MOROZZI, G., Hygiene
MORPURGO, G. P., Genetics
NAPPI, A., General Physics
ONORI, G., Physics
ORLACCHIO, A., Biochemistry
PASCOLINI, R., Comparative Anatomy
PASSERI, L., Sedimentology
PECCERILLO, A., Petrography
PERUZZI, M. I., General Physics
PIALLI, G., Geology
PIOVESANA, O., General and Inorganic Chemistry
PUCCI, P., Mathematical Analysis
RINALDI, R., Mineralogy
SACCHETTI, F., Solid State Physics
SANTUCCI, S., Physics Laboratory
SAVELLI, G., Organic Chemistry
SGAMELLOTTI, A., Inorganic Chemistry
SRIVASTAVA YOGENDRA, N., Quantum Theory
TATICCHI, A., Organic Chemistry
TATICCHI, M. I., Ecology
TULIPANI, S., Computer Science
VERDINI, L., Structure of Matter
VOLPI, G., General and Inorganic Chemistry
ZANAZZI, P. F., Crystallography

Faculty of Education:

BALDINI, M., History of Philosophy
BUCCI, S., General Education
DOTTI, U., Italian Language and Literature
FINZI, C., History of Political Doctrine
FISSI MIGLIORINI, R., Dantesque Philology
FURIOZZI, G. B., History of Umbria
MANCINI, F. F., History of Umbrian Art
MIRRI, E., Philosophy
PERUGI, M., Romance Philology
PETRONI, F., History of Modern and Contemporary Italian Literature
RICCIOLI, G., French Language and Literature
ROSATI, L., Teaching
SANTINI, C., Latin Language and Literature
SETAIOLI, A., Latin Grammar
UGOLINI, R., Contemporary History
ZURLI, L., Latin Philology

Faculty of Engineering:

BALLI, R., Applied Mechanics
BASILI, P., Electromagnetic Fields
BATTISTON, R., Physics
BERNA, L., Urban Technology
BIDINI, G., Machines
BORRI, A., Construction Theory
BRANDI, P., Mathematical Analysis
BURRASCANO, P., Electrotechnology
CANDELORO, D., Mathematical Analysis I
CONTI, P., Industrial Technical Drawing
CORRADINI, C., Technical Hydrology
FELLI, M., Technical Physics
LA CAVA, M., Automatic Controls
LIUTI, G., Chemistry
MAZZOLAI, F. M., Physics
PALMIERI, L., Physics
PARDUCCI, A., Construction Technology
PUCCI, E., Advanced Mechanical Engineering
SOCINO, G., Physics
SOLETTI, A. C., Design
SORRENTINI, R., Electromagnetic Fields
TACCONI, P., Applied Geology
VECCHIOCATTIVI, F., Chemistry

UNIVERSITÀ DEGLI STUDI

Lungarno Pacinotti 43–45, 56100 Pisa
Telephone: 050-920115
Fax: 050-42446
E-mail: rettore@unipi.it

Founded 1343
State control
Academic year: November to October

Rector: Prof. LUCIANO MODICA
Chief Administrative Officer: Dott. GIORGIO COLUCCINI
Librarian: Dott. RENATO TAMBURRINI

Number of teachers: 300
Number of students: 47,000

DEANS

Faculty of Law: Prof. E. RIPEPE
Faculty of Economics: Prof. T. FANFANI
Faculty of Political Science: Prof. A. PALAZZO
Faculty of Letters and Philosophy: Prof. E. GUARINI FASANO
Faculty of Foreign Languages and Literature: Prof. R. AJELLO
Faculty of Medicine and Surgery: Prof. M. CAMPA
Faculty of Mathematical, Physical and Natural Sciences: Prof. M. PASQUALI
Faculty of Pharmacy: Prof. B. MACCHIA
Faculty of Engineering: Prof. P. CORSINI
Faculty of Agrarian Science: A. ALPI
Faculty of Veterinary Medicine: D. CIANCI

HEADS OF DEPARTMENTS

Agronomy and Management of the Agro Ecosystem: Prof. E. BONARI
Anatomy, Biochemistry and Veterinary Physiology: Prof. F. MARTELLI
Anglistics: Prof. F. GOZZI
Biology of Agricultural Plants: Prof. M. DURANTE
Experimental, Infective and Public Biomedicine: Prof. M. BARGAGNA
Cardiology, Angiology and Pneumology: Prof. M. MARINI
Bio-organic Chemistry: Prof. I. MORELLI
Chemistry and Industrial Chemistry: Prof. F. CIARDELLI
Surgery: Prof. C. A. ANGELETTI
Cultivation and Protection of Ligneous Species: Prof. F. LORETI
Mechanical and Nuclear Engineering: Prof. E. VITALE
Private Law: Prof. L. BRUSCUGLIA
Public Law: Prof. R. ROMBOLI
Business Economics: Prof. L. ANSELMI
Agricultural and Agro-Forestal Economics: Prof. F. CAMPUS
Energetics: Prof. S. FAGGIANI
Ethology, Ecology and Evolution: Prof. N. E. BALDACCINI
Classical Philology: Prof. A. PERUTELLI
Philosophy: Prof. M. CILIBERTO
Physics: Prof. A. STEFANINI
Physiology and Biochemistry: Prof. B. GELARDUCCI
Computer Science: Prof. F. TURINI
Aerospace Engineering: Prof. C. CASAROSA
Chemical Engineering, Industrial Chemistry and the Science of Materials: Prof. G. CENCETTI
Production Engineering: (vacant)
Engineering and Information Systems: Prof. M. MANCIATI
Constructional and Hydraulic Engineering: Prof. N. GUCCI
Structural Engineering: Prof. L. S. DE FALENA
Institutions, Business Enterprise and the Market: Prof. R. BARSOTTI
Romance Languages and Literature: Prof. G. FASANO
Linguistics: Prof. R. AMBROSINI
Mathematics: Prof. M. NACINOVICH
Applied Mathematics: Prof. H. B. DA VEIGA
Medieval Studies: Prof. M. TANGHERONI
Neuroscience: Prof. A. MURATORIO
Oncology: Prof. G. BEVILACQUA
Animal Pathology, Disease Prevention and Food Hygiene: Prof. S. RINDI
Animal Products: Prof. B. COLOMBANI
Public and Biostatistic Health: Prof. G. CAROLI
Archaeology: Prof. C. TOZZI
Botany: Prof. P. MELETTI
Man and the Environment: Prof. R. BARALE
Political Science: Prof. D. MARRARA
Earth Sciences: Prof. M. FRANZINI
Economics: Prof. M. AUGELLO
Pharmaceutical Science: Prof. A. DA SETTIMO PASSETTI
Social Science: Prof. M. TOSCANO
Historical Sciences and the Ancient World: Prof. U. LAFFI
Electrical and Automotive Systems: Prof. R. GIGLIOLI
Statistics and Mathematics applied to Economics: Prof. C. SODINI
History of Art: Profssa G. DALLI REGOLI
Modern and Contemporary History: Profssa R. POZZI
Roads and Transport: Prof. F. LANCIERI

UNIVERSITÀ DI REGGIO CALABRIA

Via Zecca 4, 89125 Reggio Calabria
Telephone: 0965-331701
Fax: 0965-332201

Founded 1982

Rector: Prof. ROSARIO PIETROPAOLO
Pro-Rector: Prof. ANTONIO ROMANO

DEANS

Faculty of Agriculture: Prof. M. C. SINATRA
Faculty of Architecture: Prof. S. PETRUCCIOLI
Faculty of Law: S. CICCARELLO
Faculty of Engineering: V. COCCORESE

Faculty of Medicine and Surgery: S. VENUTA
Faculty of Pharmacy: Prof. D. ROTIROTI

UNIVERSITÀ DEGLI STUDI DI ROMA 'LA SAPIENZA'

Piazzale Aldo Moro 5, 00185 Rome

Telephone: 06-49911

Founded 1303 by Pope Boniface VIII, with the Papal Bull 'In Supremae praeminentia dignitatis'

Rector: Prof. GIUSEPPE D'ASCENZO
Director: A. FRATTAROLI
Librarian: A. SERRAI

Number of teachers: 4,312
Number of students: 189,000

DEANS

Faculty of Jurisprudence: Prof. M. TALAMANCA
Faculty of Political Science: F. GIUSTI
Faculty of Economics and Commerce: Prof. E. CHIACCHIERINI
Faculty of Statistics, Demography and Actuarial Science: Prof. G. ALVARO
Faculty of Letters and Philosophy: Prof. E. PARATORE
Faculty of Medicine: Prof. L. FRATI
Faculty of Mathematics, Physics and Natural Science: (vacant)
Faculty of Pharmacy: Prof. R. CIPOLLINI
Faculty of Engineering: Prof. G. ORLANDI
School of Aerospace Engineering: Prof. U. PONZI
Faculty of Architecture: Prof. M. DOCCI
Faculty of Sociology: G. STATERA
Faculty of Psychology: V. DAZZI
School of Librarianship and Archivists: Prof. E. LODOLINI

ATTACHED CENTRE

Interuniversity Research Centre on Developing Countries.

UNIVERSITÀ DEGLI STUDI DI ROMA 'TOR VERGATA'

Via Orazio Raimondo, 00173 Rome

Telephone: 06-72591
Fax: 06-7234368

Founded 1985

Rector: Prof. ALESSANDRO FINAZZI AGRÒ
Administrative Director: Dr ERNESTO NICOLAI

Publications: *L'Osservatorio*, *I Quaderni di Tor Vergata*.

DEANS

Faculty of Law: Prof. FILIPPO CHIOMENTI
Faculty of Engineering: Prof. FRANCO MACERI
Faculty of Literature and Philosophy: Prof. FRANCO SALVATORI
Faculty of Medicine and Surgery: Prof. RENATO LAURO
Faculty of Mathematics, Physics and Natural Sciences: Prof. PAOLO LULY
Faculty of Economics: Prof. LUIGI PAGANETTO

HEADS OF DEPARTMENTS

Biology: Prof. F. AUTORI
Surgery: CARLO UMBERTO CASCIANI
Law and Civil Procedure: Prof. G. GALLONI
Public Law: Prof. A. ANZON
Physics: Prof. S. TAZZARI
Civil Engineering: Prof. A. NUZZOLO
Electronic Engineering: Prof. R. LOJACONO
Mechanical Engineering: Prof. F. GORI
Modern Languages: Prof. F. BEGGIATO
Mathematics: Prof. A. PICARDELLO
Internal Medicine: Prof. G. FEDERICI
Experimental Medicine: Prof. C. FAVALLI
Philosophical Research: Profssa M. CRISTIANI
Public Health: Prof. G. SIRACUSA
Chemical Science and Technology: Prof. G. PALLESCHI
History: Profssa V. VON FALKENHAUSEN
History and Theory of Law: Prof. F. CASTRO
Finance and Quantitative Methods: Prof. MARTINO LO CASCIO
Business Studies: Prof. ERICO CAVALIERI
Physical Science and Technology and Energy Sources: Prof. S. MARTELLUCCI
Data Processing, Systems and Production: Prof. A. LA BELLA
Economics and Institutions: Prof. M. BAGELLA
Neuroscience: Profssa M. G. MARCIANI
Biopathology and Diagnosis through Imaging: Prof. L. G. SPAGNOLI

UNIVERSITÀ DEGLI STUDI DI SALERNO

Strada Provinciale, Ponte don Melillo 24, 84084 Fisciano (Salerno)

Telephone: 089-961111

Founded 1970

Rector: GIORGIO DONSÌ
Administrative Director: FRANCO LUCIANI

DEANS

Faculty of Economics and Commerce: Prof. N. POSTIGLIONE
Faculty of Law: Prof. M. PANEBIANCO
Faculty of Letters and Philosophy: Prof. A. TRIMARCO
Faculty of Education: Prof. A. MANGO
Faculty of Science: Prof. G. SODANO
Faculty of Engineering: Prof. R. PASQUINO
Faculty of Political Science: Prof. A. MUSI

UNIVERSITÀ DEGLI STUDI DI SASSARI

Piazza Università 21, 07100 Sassari, Sardinia

Telephone: 079-228211
Telex: 790299
Fax: 079-228820

Founded 1562
State control
Academic year: November to October
Rector: Prof. ALESSANDRO MAIDA
Administrative Director and Secretary: Dott. GIOVANNINO SIRCANA
Librarian: Dott. ELISABETTA PILIA

Number of teachers: 658
Number of students: 15,907

Publication: *Annuario*.

DEANS

Faculty of Law: Prof. FRANCESCO ANGIONI
Faculty of Medicine and Surgery: Prof. GIULIO ROSATI
Faculty of Pharmacy: Prof. RICCARDO CERRI
Faculty of Veterinary Medicine: Prof. ANTONELLO LEONI
Faculty of Agronomy: Prof. GAVINO DEL RIO
Faculty of Mathematics, Physics and Natural Sciences: Prof. BRUNO MASALA
Faculty of Economics and Commerce: Prof. PASQUALE BRANDIS
Faculty of Political Science: Prof. VIRGILIO MURA
Faculty of Letters and Philosophy: Prof. ATTILIO MASTINO
Faculty of Languages: Prof. SIMONETTA SANNA

UNIVERSITÀ DEGLI STUDI

Banchi di Sotto 55, 53100 Siena

Telephone: 0577-298000
Fax: 0577-298202

Founded 1240

Rector: Prof. PIERO TOSI
Vice-Rector: Prof. FRANCESCO FRANCIONI

Number of teachers: 514
Number of students: 19,093

Publication: *Annuario Accademico*.

DEANS AND DIRECTORS

Faculty of Law: R. MARTINI
- Institute of Economics and Statistics: Prof. R. CAMAITI
- Institute of Forensic Medicine and Criminology: Prof. I. PIVA
- Institute of Modern History and International Relations: Prof. G. BUCCIANTI
- Institute of Penal Law: Prof. L. MAZZA
- Institute of Private Law: Prof. M. COMPORTI
- Institute of Procedural Law: Prof. P. MOSCARINI
- Institute of Public and International Law: Prof. A. L. RAVÀ BAGNOLI
- Institute of Roman Law: Prof. R. MARTINI

Faculty of Medicine and Surgery: L. ANDREASSI
- Institute of General Histology and Embryology: Prof. R. GERLI
- Institute of Labour Medicine: Prof. E. SARTORELLI
- Institute of General Pathology: Prof. M. COMPORTI
- Institute of Special Medical Pathology: Prof. C. GENNARI
- Institute of Social Paediatrics and Puericulture: Prof. M. DETTORI
- Institute of Rheumatology: Prof. F. R. MARCOLONGO
- Institute of Radiology: Prof. P. STEFANI
- Institute of Pharmacology: Prof. A. TAGLIAMONTE
- Institute of Medical Semiotics and Geriatrics: Prof. S. FORCONI
- Institute of Surgical Sciences: Prof. A. CARLI
- Institute of Human Anatomy: Prof. L. COMPARINI
- Institute of Thoracic and Cardiovascular Surgery and Biomedical Technology: Prof. M. TOSCANO
- Institute of General and Specialist Surgery: Prof. L. LORENZINI
- Institute of General Medicine and Medical Therapy: Prof. T. DI PERRI
- Institute of Clinical Obstetrics and Gynaecology: Prof. N. D'ANTONA
- Institute of Clinical Paediatrics: A. FOIS
- Institute of Anaesthesiology: Prof. G. BELLUCCI
- Institute of Neurological Sciences: G. GUAZZI
- Institute of Orthopaedics and Traumatology: Prof. L. BOCCHI
- Institute of Oto-Rhino-Laryngology: D. PASSALI
- Institute of Infectious Diseases: Prof. A. ROSSOLINI
- Institute of Hygiene: Prof. G. BOSCO
- Institute of Clinical Dermosyphilopathy: Prof. L. ANDREASSI
- Institute of General and Clinical Psychology: Prof. M. A. REDA
- Institute of Psychiatry: Prof. N. BATTISTINI
- Institute of Phthisiology and Respiratory Diseases: Prof. M. VAGLIASINDI
- Institute of Human Physiology: Prof. G. CARLI
- Institute of General Surgery and Surgical Therapy: Prof. S. ARMENIO
- Institute of Pathological Anatomy and Histology: Prof. P. TOSI
- Institute of Biochemistry and Enzymology: Prof. E. MARINELLO

Faculty of Mathematics, Physics and Natural Sciences: R. DALLAI
- Institute of Mineralogy and Petrography: Prof. G. SABATINI
- Institute of General Physiology: Prof. A. PACINI BRANDANI
- Institute of General Biology: Prof. B. BACCETTI

Faculty of Pharmacy: C. PELLERANO
- Institute of General Physiology and Alimentation: Prof. V. BOCCI

Institute of Organic Chemistry: G. ADEMBRI
Institute of Pharmacology: G. P. SCARAGLI
Faculty of Economics: G. ROLLA
Institute of Economic Technology: Prof. F. CAPARRELLI
Faculty of Education: F. ABBRI
Faculty of Letters and Philosophy: M. BETTINI
Institute of Ancient History: Prof. F. FABBRINI
Faculty of Arts and Humanities: T. DETTI
Faculty of Engineering: R. TIBERIO

UNIVERSITÀ DEGLI STUDI DI TORINO

Via Verdi 8, 10124 Turin
Telephone: 011-6706111
Telex: 220225
Founded 1404
Rector: Prof. MARIO UMBERTO DIANZANI
Pro-Rector: Prof. ALBERTO CONTE
Administrative Director: Dssa FRANCA VERCELLI FISICARO
Number of teachers: 2,050
Number of students: 65,000

DEANS

Agriculture: Prof. ANGELO GARIBALDI
Economics: Prof. DANIELE CIRAVEGNA
Pharmacy: Prof. ALBERTO GASCO
Law: Prof. GASTONE COTTINO
Arts and Philosophy: Prof. MARZIANO GUGLIELMINETTI
Education: Prof. LUIGI MARINO
Medicine: Prof. FRANCESCO DI CARLO
Veterinary Medicine: Prof. GIUSEPPE LADETTO
Mathematics, Physics and Natural Sciences: Prof. ENZO BORELLO
Political Sciences: Prof. GIAN MARIO BRAVO

UNIVERSITÀ DEGLI STUDI DI TRENTO

Via Belenzani 12, 38100 Trento
Telephone: 0461-881111
Telex: 400674
Fax: 0461-881299
Founded 1962
State control (since 1982)
Academic year: November to October
President: Dott. CARLO ANDREOTTI
Rector: Prof. MASSIMO EGIDI
Administrative Director: Dott. MARCO TOMASI
Librarian: Dott. PAOLO BELLINI
Library of 280,000 vols and 8,700 periodicals
Number of teachers: 430
Number of students: 14,000
Publication: *Unitn*.

DEANS

Faculty of Sociology: Prof. ANTONIO COBALTI
Faculty of Mathematics, Physics and Natural Sciences: Prof. GABRIELE ANZELLOTTI
Faculty of Economics: Prof. GIANFRANCO CEREA
Faculty of Law: Prof. ROBERTO TONIATTI
Faculty of Engineering: Prof. ARONNE ARMANINI
Faculty of Literature and Philosophy: Prof. EMANUELE BANFI

HEADS OF DEPARTMENTS

Physics: Prof. MAURIZIO MONTAGNA
Mathematics: Prof. LUCIANO TUBARO
Materials Engineering: Prof. CLAUDIO MIGLIARESI
Civil and Environmental Engineering: Prof. PAOLO BERTOLA
Structural Mechanics and Design: Prof. RODOLFO PAUABAZZER
Economics: Prof. GEREMIA GIOS
Sociology and Social Research: Prof. ANTONIO SCAGLIA
Social Theory, History and Research: Prof. IGINO FAGIOLI
Law: Prof. DIEGO QUAGLIONI
Philology and History: Prof. FABRIZIO CAMBI
Computer and Management Science: Prof. ALESSANDRO ZORAT

UNIVERSITÀ DEGLI STUDI DI TRIESTE

Piazzale Europa 1, 34127 Trieste
Telephone: 040-6767111
Fax: 040-6763093
Founded 1924
Rector: G. BORRUSO
Vice-Rector: M. POLICASTRO
Administrative Director: G. PAFUMI
Librarian: G. LUZENBERGER PIAN
Number of teachers: 1,200
Number of students: 24,500

DEANS

Faculty of Law: F. TOMMASEO
Faculty of Political Science: D. COCCOPALMERIO
Faculty of Economics: L. COSSAR
Faculty of Humanities: S. MONTI
Faculty of Education: L. LAGO
Faculty of Medicine: A. LEGGERI
Faculty of Natural Sciences: L. FONDA
Faculty of Pharmacy: G. STEFANCICH
Faculty of Engineering: L. DELCARO
Faculty of Psychology: W. GERBINO
Modern Languages for Interpreters and Translators: J. M. DODDS
Data Processing Centre: Dr M. GREGORI (Dir)

DIRECTORS OF DEPARTMENTS

Applied Chemistry and Materials Engineering: S. MERIANI
Applied Mathematics and Actuarial Sciences: S. HOLZER
Archaeology: S. SCONOCCHIA
Biology: P. L. NIMIS
Human Morphology: P. NARDUCCI
Human Sciences: G. GIORIO
Chemistry: G. DE ALTI
Energetics: S. TOMMASI
Theoretical Physics: G. GHIRARDI
Astronomy: M. HACK
Economic and Statistical Sciences: R. FINZI
Economics and Business: V. NANUT
Economics and the Commodity Studies of Natural Resources and Production: L. FAVRETTO
Electrical and Electronic Engineering: M. POLICASTRO
Education: C. DESINAN
Mathematics: G. TIRONI
Physics: E. CASTELLI
Biochemistry, Biophysics and Macromolecular Chemistry: G. SANDRI
Political Science: C. BONVECCHIO
Psychology: W. GERBINO
Italian Studies, Linguistics, Communication and Performing Arts: E. GUAGNINI
Pharmaceutical Sciences: L. VIO
Philosophy: M. C. GALAVOTTI
Geography and History: G. BATTELLI
Medieval and Modern History: G. TODESCHINI
Biomedical Sciences: C. MONTI BRAGADIN
Chemical Engineering, the Environment and Raw Materials: P. ALESSI
Civil Engineering: A. AMODEO
Languages and Literature of the Mediterranean: G. TRISOLINI
Naval Architecture, Ocean and Environmental Engineering: R. NICOLICH
Earth Sciences: C. EBBLIN
Geological, Environmental and Marine Sciences: A. BRAMBATI
Physiology and Pathology: P. P. BATTAGLINI
Anglo-German Literature and Civilization: R. S. CRIVELLI
Law Sciences: G. SPANGHER

ATTACHED INSTITUTES

Institute of History of Medieval and Modern Art: Dir R. GIORDANI.
Institute of Law: Dir P. CENDON.
Institute of Physiology: Dir A. BAVA.
Institute of General Pathology: Dir L. PATRIARCA.
Institute of Hygiene: Dir C. CAMPELLO.
Institute of Forensic Medicine: Dir B. M. ALTAMURA.
Institute of Pathological Anatomy: Dir L. DI BONITO.
Institute of Radiology: Dir L. DALLA PALMA.
Institute of General Clinical Medicine: Dir G. GUARNIERI.
Institute of Medical Pathology: Dir L. CAMPANACCI.
Institute of General Surgery: Dir A. LEGGERI.
Institute of Surgical Pathology: Dir A. NEMETH.
Institute of Ophthalmology: Dir G. RAVALICO.
Institute of Orthopaedics: Dir F. MAROTTI.
Institute of Otorhinolaryngology: Dir M. RUSSOLO.
Institute of Venereal Diseases and Dermatology: Dir C. SCARPA.
Institute of Paediatrics: Dir F. PANIZON.
Institute of Obstetrics and Gynaecology: Dir S. GUASCHINO.
Institute of Nervous and Mental Diseases: Dir G. CAZZATO.
Institute of Surgical Semiotics: Dir E. TENDELLA.
Institute of Anaesthesiology and Intensive Care: Dir A. GULLO.
Institute of Dentistry: Dir M. SILLA.
Institute of Psychiatry: Dir E. AGUGLIA.
Institute of Industrial Medicine: Dir F. GOBBATO.
Institute of Urology: Dir E. BELGRANO.

UNIVERSITÀ DEGLI STUDI DELLA TUSCIA

Via S. Giovanni Decollato 1, 01100 Viterbo
Telephone: 0761-3571
Fax: 0761-325785
Founded 1979
State control
Academic year: November to October
Rector: Prof. G. T. SCARASCIA MUGNOZZA
Vice-Rector: Prof. G. GIOVANNOZZI SERMANNI
Administrative Director: Dr FRANCO FRACASSA
Number of teachers: 300
Number of students: 5,800

DEANS

Faculty of Agriculture: Prof. C. PERONE PACIFICO
Faculty of Modern Languages: Prof. G. MANACORDA
Faculty of Mathematics, Physics and Natural Sciences: Prof. M. MAZZINI
Faculty of Conservation of Cultural Heritage: Prof. R. MERCURI
Faculty of Economics and Commerce: Prof. G. BENEDETTI

HEADS OF DEPARTMENTS

Agrobiology and Agrochemistry: Prof. G. GIOVANNOZZI SERMANNI
Economics and Appraisal: Prof. L. ANGELI

Forestry-Environment Sciences and Resources: Prof. E. GIORDANO
Plant Protection: Prof. M. OLMI
Environmental Sciences: Prof. S. CANNISTRARO
Crop Production: Prof. B. LO CASCIO
History of Writing and Documents: Prof. P. INNOCENTI

UNIVERSITÀ DEGLI STUDI DI UDINE

Via Palladio 8, 33100 Udine
Telephone: 0432-556111
Fax: 0432-507715
Founded 1978
State control
Rector: Prof. MARZIO STRASSOLDO
Pro-Rector: Prof. LORENZO AGNOLETTO
Administrative Director: Dr FRANCESCO SAVONITTO
Librarian: Dr DE FRANCESCHI SORAVITO
Library of 200,000 vols
Number of teachers: 700
Number of students: 11,000
Publications: *NUSU*, *News*.

DEANS

Faculty of Modern Languages: Prof. GUIDO BARBINA
Faculty of Engineering: Prof. STEFANO DEL GIUDICE
Faculty of Science: Prof. F. HONSELL
Faculty of Literature: Prof. M. A. CAPRONI
Faculty of Agriculture: Prof. P. BONFANTI
Faculty of Medicine and Surgery: Prof. FABRIZIO BRESADOLA
Faculty of Economics: Prof. GIAN NEREO MAZZOCCO

DIRECTORS OF DEPARTMENT

Biomedical Science and Biotechnology: Prof. F. QUADRIFOGLIO
Chemical Science and Technology: Prof. R. PORTANOVA
Biology applied to Crop Protection: Prof. F. FRILLI
Economics, Society and Environment: Prof. R. STRASSOLDO
Germanic and Romance Languages and Literatures: Prof. A. D'ARONCO
Physics: Prof. F. WALDNER
Historical and Documentary Science: Prof. P. C. I. ZORATTINI
Economics: Prof. G. BRUNELLO
Statistics: Prof. R. GUSEO
Linguistics and Classical Philology: Prof. V. ORIOLES
Eastern European Languages, Civilization and Literatures: Prof. R. FACCANI
Food Science: Prof. C. CORRADINI
Law: Prof. M. D'ADDEZIO
Clinical and Experimental Medicine: Prof. F. S. AMBESI IMPIOMBATO
Animal Production Science: Prof. M. PINOSA
Land Resources and Environment: Prof. G. LIBERATORE
Business Administration and Financial Markets: Prof. M. RUTIGLIANO
History and the Protection of the Cultural Heritage: Prof. C. FURLAN
Electrical and Mechanical Engineering: Prof. A. STELLA
Civil Engineering: Prof. L. ARLOTTI
Mathematics and Computer Science: Prof. C. TASSO
Philosophy, History and Social Sciences: Prof. M. MAMIANI
Vegetable Production and Agricultural Technologies: Prof. R. GIOVANARDI
Medical and Morphological Research: Prof. M. BAZZOCCHI
Surgical Sciences: Prof. A. PASETTO
Energy and Machinery: Prof. G. COMINI

ATTACHED INSTITUTES

Institute of History of Italian Language and Literature: Dir Prof. G. GRONDA.

Institute of Philosophy, Education and Modern Language Teaching: Dir Prof. C. GIUNTINI.

UNIVERSITÀ DEGLI STUDI DI URBINO

Via Saffi 2, 61029 Urbino
Telephone: 0722-3051
Founded 1506
Rector: Prof. Dott. C. BO
Administrative Director: Dott. G. ROSSI
Library: see Libraries
Number of teachers: 800, including 500 professors
Number of students: 23,792
Publications: *Studi Urbinati—A* (Law and Economics), *Studi Urbinati—B* (History, Philosophy and Literature), *Studi Urbinati—C* (Pharmacy), *Notizie da Palazzo Albani* (Art Review), *Annuario*, *L'Università Urbinate* (monthly).

DEANS

Faculty of Jurisprudence: G. PANSINI
Faculty of Economics: GIANCARLO POLIDORI
Faculty of Letters and Philosophy: RAFFAELE MOLINELLI
Faculty of Education: NANDO FILOGRASSO
Faculty of Pharmacy: M. DACHÀ
Faculty of Mathematics, Physics and Natural Sciences: MAURO MAGHANI
Faculty of Languages: G. B. BOGLIOLO
Faculty of Sociology: E. MASCILLI MIGLIORINI
Faculty of Political Science: VITTORIO PARLATO
Faculty of Environmental Science: GABRIELLA GALLO

PROFESSORS

(Some staff serve in more than one faculty)

Faculty of Jurisprudence:

BALDINI, V., Regional Law
CALCAGNINI, G., Political Economy
CASSIANI, M., Bankruptcy Law
CASTALDO, A., Penal Commercial Law, Criminology
CICIRIELLO, M. C., European Community Law
CLARIZIA, R., Civil Law
CODINI, E., Administrative Law
COTTIGNOLA, G., Navigational Law
DEGRASSI, L., Constitutional Law
ESPOSITO, G., Penal Law
FABRONI, F., Forensic and Insurance Medicine
FANTAPPIÈ, C., History of Canon Law
FERRONI, L., Civil Law
GILIBERTI, G., History of Roman Law, Roman Law
GIOMARO, A. M., Institutions of Roman Law, Comparative Private Law
GUALTIERI, P., Constitutional Law
MARI, L., Private International Law
MERLIN, E., Procedural Civil Law
MODICA, R., Land Law
MONACO, L., Penal Law
MORONI, E., Philosophy of Law
NUZZO, A., Commercial Law, Financial Market Law
PALANZA, A., State Accountancy
PALAZZOLO, S., General Principles of Law
PANSINI, G., Procedural Civil Law, Penal Procedure, General Principles of Law
PANSOLLI, L., History and Interpretation of Italian Law
PARLATO, V., Canon and Ecclesiastical Law
PERUZZI, P., Public Law, Law of San Marino
PIACINTINO, D., Financial Law
PITTALIS, M., Family Law
RINALDI, R., Tributary Law
ROSSI, L., International Law
ROZO ACUNA, E., American Public Law
RUDAN, M., Labour Law
TENELLA SILLANI, C., Private Institutional Law

Faculty of Letters and Philosophy:

ARBIZZONI ARTUSI, G., Humanist Literature and Italian Literature
ARENA, L., History of Philosophical Historiography
BACCHIELLI, L., Archaeology, History of Greek and Roman Art
BALDUCCI, S., Italian Dialects, History of Italian Language
BARATTA, G., History of Moral Philosophy, Theory and Practice of Communication
BARTOLONI, P., Archaeology of the Near East
BELPASSI, P., Pedagogics
BERNARDELLI, R., Epigraphy and Roman Antiquities
BERNARDINI, P., History of Greek Language and Theatre
BERTINI, M. A., History of Cartography
BIGLIARDI, R., Library Science
BOGLIOLO, G., French Language and Literature
BOLDRINI, S., Latin Metre
BOZZI, S., Logic
BRUSCIA, M., Critical History
BULTRIGHINI, U., Greek History
CANTILENA, M., Greek Civilization
CARAZZI, M., Geography
CAVAZZANI, G., Sociology, Economics
CECCHINI, E., History of Medieval Latin Literature, Medieval Philology
CECCHINI, F. M., Contemporary History, History of the Risorgimento
CERBONI BAIARDI, G., Italian Literature
CIPOLLONI, M.
CLERI, B., Art History and Criticism
CONSIGLIO, F., Philosophy of Law
CONVERSAZIONI, E., Diplomacy
CUBEDDU, I., Theoretical Philosophy, Aesthetics
CUPPINI, S., History of Contemporary Art
DANESE, R., History of Latin Theatre
DE MARZI, G., Modern History
DE MATTEIS, S., Cultural Anthropology
DEL TUTTO, L., Linguistics
DELLA FORNACE, A. M., Classification Theory and Practice
DONDI, A., Book Restoration
DONNICI ROCCO, A., Moral Philosophy
FALIVENE, M. R., Greek Palaeography
FERRI, M., Cataloguing and Classification Theory and Practice
FERRI, T., Literary Theory
FILENI, M. G., Greek Grammar
FRANCHI, A., Glottology, Italic Philology
GALLI, F., Latin Epigraphy, Roman History
GATTUCCI, A., Medieval History
GHINI, G. G., Russian Language and Literature
GIACOMINI, C., Bibliography
GIANFRANCESCHI, M., Computerization of Libraries and Archives
GORI, F., History of Christianity
GRASSI, P., Philosophy of Religion
GUARDAMAGNA, D., English Language and Literature
HAMILTON, A., English Language and Literature
IACOBINI, A., History of Byzantine Art
ILLUMINATI, A., History of Political Philosophy
KAMMERER, P., Sociology
LANCIOTTI, S., Latin Grammar
LEONE, S., Russian Language and Literature
LOSURDO, D., History of Modern and Contemporary Philosophy
LUISI, F., History of Music, Musical Palaeography
LUNI, M., Archaeology of Roman Africa, Ancient Topography

MANCINI, A. M., Italian Linguistics
MARCHI, D., History of Modern and Contemporary Italian Literature
MARIANI, F., History of Books and Printing
MARTELLI, M., Philosophy of History
MERCATANTI, R., Italian Philology
MINIATI, M. V., History of Popular Tradition
MORANTI, M., History of Libraries
MORDENTI, A., General Archives, Archival History
MOSCI, G., French Language and Literature
NONNI, G., Humanist and Medieval Philology
OSSANIA, A. T., Literature of Italian Theatre
PANSOLLI, L., History of Italian Law
PERSI, P., Geography
PERUSINO, L., Greek Literature
PICCININI, G., Theory and History of Historiography
PICCIONI, L., History of Italian Philosophy
PIERSANTI, U., Sociology of Literature
PRETAGOSTINI, R., Greek Philology, Greek Metrical Verse
PURCARO, V., Archaeology of the Roman Provinces
QUESTA, E., History the Prosperity of Ancient Civilizations
RAFFAELLI, R., Latin Literature
RIZZO, A., Etruscology and Italic Archaeology
RUGGERI, R., Medieval and Modern Church History
SASSI, M. G., Latin Philology
SAURIN DE LA IGLESIA, M. R., Spanish
SCIANNA, N., Conservation of Library Materials
SCODITTI, G., Ethnology
SICHIROLLO, L., Moral Philosophy
SPAGNA MUSSO, S., Cultural and Environmental Law
STARACE, G., Psychology
TAROZZI, G., Philosophy of Science, Epistemology
TONTINI, A., Latin Palaeography
VARESE, R., History of Medieval and Modern Art
VECCHIOTTI, I., Indian and Oriental Religions and Philosophy, History of Philosophy
VENERI, A., Greek Dialectology
VENTURELLI, A., German Language and Literature
VITALI, R., History of Ancient Philosophy
ZAGANELLI, G., Romance Philology

Faculty of Education:

ALBANO, A., Hygiene
ARENA, L. V., Psychology
AURELI, T., Evolutionary Psychology
BERTI, C., Methodology of Social-Psychological Research
BONVINI, M., Modern History
CASTIELLO, U., Psychometric Statistics, Techniques of Research Psychology and Data Analysis
CATANI, E., English Language and Literature
CECCARELLI, G., History of Psychology
CERBONI BAIARDI, G., Italian Literature and Language, Information Technology
CERRATO, R., Social History
CHIARANTINI, L., Biology
COMUNE, A., French Language and Literature
CRINELLA, G., Philosophy of Religion
CUPPINI, S., History of Contemporary Art
D'ERME, P., Clinical Psychology
DE FELICE, F., Occupational Psychology
DEI, M., Sociology of Education
DE SANCTIS, N., Logic
DE SIMONE, A., Methodology of Social Research
DI CARO, A., History of Political Doctrine
DONADI, P., Psychology of Mass Communications
DORICCHI, F., Physiological Psychology
FICCADENTI, B., History of the Risorgimento
FILOGRASSO, N., Pedagogy, Developmental Psychology
FLEBUS, G. B., Theory and Techniques of Testing
FONTANA, W., Medieval and Modern Art
GALLI, F., Roman History
GASPARI, P., Special Education
GIALLONGO, A., History of Education
GOCCI, G., Social Psychology
GORI, F., History of Christianity
LABBROZZI, E., Methodology and Education, History of Educational Institutions
LORENZETTI, L. M., Psychology of Individual Difference
LOSURDO, D., History of Modern and Contemporary Philosophy
MARINI, C., Children's Literature
MEAZZINI, P., Methodology of Behavioural Science
MERIGGI, A., Medieval History
MENGOZZI, D., Modern History
NICOLETTI, R., Psychology
NISI, C., Experimental and Social Education
PAPA, S., Foundations of Anatomical and Physiological Psychic Activity
PANICHI, N., History of Philosophical Historiography
PASCOCCI, M., Educational Research Statistics
PERSI, P., Geography
PIRANI, P., Educational Psychology
POZZI, E., History of the Theatre
RAFFAELLI, L., Latin Language and Literature
RICCIO, A., Structural Psychology
RIPANTI, G., Philosophy, Structural Philosophy
RIZZARDI, M., Social Psychology
ROSSI, S., Psychology
SALA, G., Psychology
SALVUCCI, P., History of Philosophy
SAURIN DE LA IGLESIA, M. R., Spanish Language and Literature
SIMONE, G., German Philology
TABONI, P., History of Political Philosophy, Cultural Anthropology
TROMBINI, E., Child Development Observation Techniques
VARDABASSO BENVENUTI, F., Social Psychology
VENDITTI, P., Moral Philosophy, Sociology
VOGT, U., German Language and Literature
ZAGANELLI, G., Romance Philology

Faculty of Pharmacy:

ACCORSI, A., Biological Chemistry Enzymology
ALBANO, A., Hygiene
BAFFONE, W., Microbiology
BALDONI, F., Hydrology
BALSAMINI, C., Organic Chemistry
BONIFAZI, P., Medicine Analysis
BRUNER, F., Analytical Chemistry
BRUSCIOTTI, B., International Pharmacological Legislation
CANTONI, O., Pharmacology and Pharmacognosy
CAPPELLINI, O., Human Anatomy
CARPI, C., Applied Pharmacology
CASTAGNINO, E., Experimental Pharmaceutical Chemistry
CATTABENI, F., Applied Pharmacology
DACHA, M., Applied Biochemistry
DESIDERI, D., Physical Chemistry
DIAMANTINI, G., Applied Pharmaceutical Chemistry
GALLO, G., General Physiology
GHIANDONI, G., Higher Mathematics and Basic Mathematics
GIANOTTI, M., Experimental Chemistry, Pharmaceutical Chemistry and Toxicology
MANUNTA, A., Pharmaceutical Botany
MARRAS, O., Industrial Toxicology
MICHELI, M., Chemistry of Heterocyclic Compounds
PALMA, F., Comparative Biochemistry, Clinical Chemical Analysis
PENNA, M., Microchemistry
PERUZZI, G., Chemotherapy, Pharmacology and Pharmacognosy
PETRUCCIANI, P., General Pathology
PIATTI, E., Alimentation, Genetics
QUAGLIA STRANO, M. G., Pharmaceutical Plant and Machinery
RICCI, D., General Biology
SALVATORI, A., Experimental Chemistry
SAMMARTINO, V., Hydrology
STACCIOLI, L., Experimental Chemistry
TARZIA, G., Pharmaceutical Chemistry and Toxicology
TESTA, C., General and Inorganic Chemistry
VETRANO, F., Physics
VILLA, M., Physics

Faculty of Economics:

ANTONELLI, G., Agrarian Economics and Politics
BOIDIN, K., French Language
BONAZZOLI, V., Economic History
CANESTRARI, S., Auditing
CASTALDO, A., Penal Commercial Law
CENSONI, P., Bankruptcy Law
CIAMBOTTI, M., Accountancy
CIASCHINI, M., Economic Analysis
COMITO, V., Finance
DI CIACCIO, A., Statistics
DE NARDIS, S., International Economics
FAVARETTO, I., Territorial Economy and Politics
FERRERO, G., Economics of Marketing, Business Organization
GAMBARDELLA, A., Economics and Management
GARDINI, L., Financial Mathematics
GIAMPAOLI, A., Banking
MANCINELLI, L., Professional Techniques
MARCHINI, I., General and Applied Accountancy
MONTANARI, G. E., Statistics
MORGANTE, A., Marketing Productivity Technology
PAOLONI, M., General and Applied Accountancy
PELLIZZER, F., Administrative and Public Law
PEPE, C., Techniques of International Trade
PERSI, P., Economic Geography
PETROSELLI, F., Mechanographic Systems
PIACENTINO, D., Finance and Financial Law
POLIDORI, G., Transport Economics
PREVIATI, D., Economics of Financial Intermediaries
RINALDI, R., Financial Law
RODANO, G., Political Economy, Economic Institutes
ROMAGNOLI, G. C., Regional Economic Politics
SALTARI, E., Political Economy, Economic Analysis
SARALE, M., Commercial Law
SAURIN DE LA IGLESIA, M. R., Spanish Language
SCHIATTARELLA, R., Economic Financial Politics
STEFANINI, L., General Mathematics
TARIGO, P., General and Applied Accountancy
TULLINI, P., Employment Law
VENTURELLI, A., German Language
WORTHINGTON, B. A., English
ZAGNOLI, P., Commercial and Industrial Techniques
ZANFEI, A., Industrial and Political Economics

Faculty of Mathematics, Physics and Natural Sciences:

ATTANASI, O. A., Organic and Experimental Chemistry
BALDINI, W., Toxicology

BATTISTELLI, S., Analytical and Experimental Biology
BELLAGAMBA, M., Experimental Palaeontology
BERETTA, E., Mathematical Methods applied to Biology, Mathematical Methods and Statistics
BONIFAZI, P., Chemistry, Toxicology
BORGIA, G. C., Mineral Geophysics
BOSSÙ, M., Clinical Chemical Analysis and Food Science
BRANDI, G., Hygiene
BRUNER, F., Analytical Chemistry
BRUNO, C., General Physiology
BRUSCOLINI, F., Microbiology, Virology
CANESTRARI, F., Cellular Biochemistry, Clinical Chemistry
CAPACCIONI, B., Mineralogy
CAPPIELLO, A., Instrumental Analytical Chemistry
CAPUANO, N. P., Geology of the Apennines
CECCHETTI, G., Applied Ecology
CECCHINI, T., Experimental Microscope Techniques
CIARONI, S., Cytology
CIMINO, M., Pharmacology
COCCIONI, R., Micropalaeontology
COLANTONI, P., Sedimentology, Marine Geology
CONFORTO, G., Physics and Experimental Physics
CUCCHIARINI, L., Histology, Biochemical Methodology
CUPPINI, R., General Physiology, Neurobiology
DALLAPICCOLA, B., Genetics
DEL GRANDE, P., Comparative Anatomy
DIDERO, M., Hydrogeology
FANUCCI, F., Geodynamics, Geology
FAZI, A., Enzymology, Biological Chemistry
FILIPPONE, , Organic Chemistry
FRANCHI, R., Geochemistry
FRANCI, A., Statistics
GAZZANELLI, G., Histochemistry, Cytology and Histology
GIOMARO, G. M., Botany
GORI, U., Applied Geology
GRANDI, G., Zoology
GRIANTI, F., Physics, Biophysics
GUERRERA, F., Geological Survey
LAZZARI, C., Basic Mathematics
MAGNANI, M., Biological Chemistry, General Biology
MANGANI, F., Atmospheric Chemistry
MANICASTRI, C., Zoology
MARTELLI, G., Regional Geology
MICHELONI, M., General and Inorganic Chemistry, Principles of Organic Chemistry
MONTECCHIA, F., Experimental Physics
MORETTI, E., Experimental Geology
MUSCO, A., General Inorganic Chemistry
NAPPI, G., Vulcanology
NESCI, O., Physical Geography
NINFALI, P., Comparative Biochemistry, Molecular Biology
NOVELLI, G., Genetics
OTTAVIANI, F., Physical Chemistry
PANDOLFI, M., Ecology
PAPA, S., Human Anatomy, Immunology
PERRONE, V., Geology and Stratigraphy
PERSI, P., Geography, Physical Geography
PIANETTI, A., Atmospheric Hygiene
RAFFI, S., Palaeontology
RENZULLI, A., Experimental Mineralogy
RICCI, A., Botany
SANTINI, S., Geophysics
SANTONI, A., General Pathology
SAVELLI, D., Quaternary Geology
SCOCCIANTI, V., Plant Physiology
SERRAZANETTI, F., Organic Chemistry
SERRI, G., Petrography
SOLIMANO, F., Mathematical Institutions
STOCCHI, V., Molecular Biology, Applied Biochemistry
TOMADIN, L., Sedimentology
TONELLI, G., Geotechnology
TRAMONTANA, M., Tectonics
VETRANO, F., Experimental Physics
WEZEL, F. C., Geology

UNIVERSITÀ DEGLI STUDI DI VENEZIA

Dorsoduro 3246, Ca' Foscari, 30123 Venice
Telephone: 041-2578111
Telex: 410638
Fax: 041-52101112

Founded 1868, formerly Istituto Universitario di Economia e Commercio e di Lingue e Letterature Straniere

Academic year: November to October

Rector: Prof. PAOLO COSTA
Pro-Rector: Prof. FRANCESCO GATTI
Administrative Director: Dott. FRANCESCO COSTANZI
Librarian: Sig. ALESSANDRO BERTONI

Number of teachers: 494
Number of students: 17,427

Publications: *Cafoscarinotizie* (quarterly), *Cafoscariappuntamenti* (every 2 months), *Annuario*.

DEANS

Faculty of Economics and Commerce: Prof. F. MASON
Faculty of Foreign Languages and Literature: Prof. M. CICERI
Faculty of Letters and Philosophy: Prof. G. LEVI
Faculty of Mathematical, Physical and Natural Sciences: Prof. G. A. MAZZOCCHIN

DIRECTORS OF DEPARTMENTS

Faculty of Economics and Commerce:
- Applied Mathematics and Computer Science: Prof. E. CANESTRELLI
- Economics: Prof. D. SARTORE
- Business Economics and Management: Prof. M. RISPOLI
- Statistics: Prof. P. MANTOVAN
- Economic History: Prof. U. MEOLI
- Law: Prof. M. L. PICCHIO FORLATI

Faculty of Foreign Languages and Literature:
- Anglo-Germanic Literature and Civilization: Prof. F. MARUCCI
- French Literature: Prof. G. CACCIAVILLANI
- Iberian Literature: Prof. E. PITTARELLO
- History of Art: Prof. A. BETTAGNO
- Indology and Far Eastern Studies: Prof. A. BOSCARO
- Linguistics and Language Teaching: Prof. G. CINQUE

Faculty of Letters and Philosophy:
- Classical Studies: Prof. A. MARINETTI
- History and Criticism of Art: Prof. L. PUPPI
- Philosophy and Theory of Science: Prof. M. RUGGENINI
- Archaeology and Eastern Studies: Prof. F. G. TRAVERSARI
- History: Prof. M. ISNENGHI
- Italian Studies and Romance Philology: Prof. F. BRUNI
- Eurasian Studies: Prof. R. ZIPOLI

Faculty of Mathematical, Physical and Natural Sciences:
- Chemistry: Prof. G. MARANGONI
- Environmental Sciences: Prof. P. GHETTI
- Physical Chemistry: Prof. S. GHERSETTI

UNIVERSITY CENTRES AND SCHOOLS

Interfaculty Linguistics Centre: Santa Croce 2161, 30125 Venice; tel. 5241642; Dir Prof. G. CINQUE.

Statistical Documentation Centre: Dorsoduro 3246, 30123 Venice; tel. 5298111; Dir Prof. R. VEDALDI.

Computer Centre: Dorsoduro 3861, 30123 Venice; tel. 5229823; Pres. Prof. G. PACINI.

Interuniversity Centre for Venetian Studies: San Marco 2945, Ca' Loredan, 30124 Venice; tel. 5200996; Dir Prof. G. PADOAN.

Administrative Computer Centre: Dorsoduro 2169, Santa Marta, 30123 Venice; Pres. Dott. G. BUSETTO.

Interdepartmental Experimental Centre: Dorsoduro 2137, 30123 Venice; tel. 5298111; Pres. Prof. G. A. MAZZOCCHIN.

UNIVERSITÀ DEGLI STUDI DI VERONA

Via dell'Artigliere 8, 37129 Verona
Telephone: 045-8098111
Telex: 481106
Fax: 045-8098255

Founded 1982

Rector: Prof. MARIO MARIGO
Pro-Rector: Prof. GIUSEPPE BRUNI
Administrative Director: Dott. RENZO PICCOLI

Number of teachers: 258
Number of students: 13,087

DEANS

Faculty of Economics and Commerce: Prof. G. BORELLI
Faculty of Arts and Philosophy: Prof. L. SECCO
Faculty of Medicine and Surgery: Prof. R. CORROCHER
Faculty of Languages and Foreign Literature: Prof. E. MOSELE
Faculty of Mathematics, Physics and Natural Sciences: Prof. E. BURATTINI

POLITECNICO DI MILANO

Piazza Leonardo da Vinci 32, 20133 Milan
Telephone: 02-23991
Telex: 333467
Fax: 02-23992206

Founded 1863

Academic year: November to October

Rector: Prof. ADRIANO DE MAIO
Pro-Rector: Prof. GIAMPIO BRACCHI
Vice-Rector: Prof. MARIA VALERIA ERBA
Administrative Director: Dott. PIERO ZANELLO
Librarians: Prof. MARIO CAIRONI, Prof. MAURIZIO BORIANI

Number of teachers: 953
Number of students: 45,337

DEANS

Faculty of Architecture: Prof. CESARE STEVAN
Faculty of Engineering: Prof. OSVALDO DE DONATO

HEADS OF DEPARTMENTS

Chemistry: Prof. FRANCESCO MINISCI
Applied Physical Chemistry: Prof. PIETRO PEDEFERRI
Industrial Chemistry and Chemical Engineering: Prof. ELISEO RANZI
Energetics: Prof. GIANCARLO FERRARI
Electronics and Computing: Prof. CARLO GHEZZI
Electrical Engineering: Prof. IVO VISTOLI
Aerospace Engineering: Prof. LUIGI PUCCINELLI
Nuclear Engineering: Prof. CARLO LOMBARDI
Planning and Building Engineering: Prof. CONSTANTINO CORSINI
Structural Engineering: Prof. ANTONIO MIGLIACCI
Bioengineering: Prof. ANTONIO PEDOTTI
Economics and Production: Prof. EMILIO BARTEZZAGHI
Hydraulic, Environmental and Surveying Engineering: Prof. CONSTANTINO FASSÓ
Mathematics: Prof. CLAUDIO CITRINI
Mechanics: Prof. SERGHIO SIRTORI

Conservation and History of Architecture: Prof. VITTORIO UGO
Architectural Projects: Prof. ANTONIO ACUTO
Regional and Urban Planning: Prof. PIERCARLO PALERMO
Physics: Prof. RINALDO CUBEDDUL
Transport and Motion Systems: Prof. ARRIGO VALLATTA

POLITECNICO DI TORINO

Corso Duca degli Abruzzi 24, 10129 Turin
Telephone: 011-5646111
Telex: 220646
Fax: 011-5646329
Founded 1859
Higher Institute of Engineering and Architecture
Academic year: November to October
Vice-Chancellor: Prof. R. ROSCELLI
Rector: Prof. R. ZICH
Administrative Director: Dssa A. M. GAIBISSO
Librarian: Prof. C. NALDI
Library facilities with 175,000 vols
Number of teachers: 774
Number of students: 23,000

DEANS

Faculty of Architecture (Turin): Prof. V. COMOLI
Faculty of Engineering (Turin): Prof. P. APPENDINO
Faculty of Engineering (Vercelli): Prof. A. GUGLIOTTA

HEADS OF DEPARTMENTS

Faculty of Engineering:
- Computer and Control Engineering: Prof. S. RIVOIRA
- Electronics: Prof. F. CANAVERO
- Industrial Electrical Engineering: Prof. A. VAGATI
- Energetics: Prof. M. MASOERO
- Physics: Prof. R. D'AURIA
- Georesources and Land: Prof. G. GECCHELE
- Aeronautical and Space Engineering: Prof. S. CHIESA
- Building and Territorial Systems: Prof. V. BORASI
- Structural Engineering: Prof. P. MARRO
- Mathematics: Prof. G. MONEGATO
- Mechanics: Prof. G. BELFORTE
- Materials Science and Chemical Engineering: Prof. B. DE BENEDETTI
- Hydraulics, Transportation and Civil Infrastructures: Prof. L. BUTERA
- Manufacturing Systems and Economics: Prof. R. LEVI

Faculty of Architecture (at Viale Mattioli 39, 10125 Turin):
- Town and Housing: Prof. M. VIGLINO DAVICO
- Architectural Design: Prof. C. OLMO
- Technical Science for Settlement Processes: Prof. B. ASTORI
- Regional Urban and Environmental Studies and Planning: Prof. R. GAMBINO

Other Universities, Colleges and Institutes

EUROPEAN UNIVERSITY INSTITUTE

C.P. No 2330, 50100 Florence Ferrovia; Via dei Roccettini 9, 50016 San Domenico di Fiesole, Florence
Telephone: 055-4685379
Telex: 571528
Fax: 055-4685444
Founded 1972 by the member states of the European Communities
Academic year: October to July
Languages of instruction: EC languages
President: PATRICK MASTERSON
Secretary-General: ANTONIO ZANARDI LANDI
Librarian: PILAR ALCALÁ
Library of 500,000 vols
Number of teachers: (full-time): 44
Number of students: 400 (postgraduate)
Publications: *Yearly Information Booklet, EUI Working Papers, European Journal of International Law, European Foreign Policy Bulletin, President's Annual Report, European Law Journal, EUI Review, Robert Schuman Centre Newsletter*.

HEADS OF DEPARTMENTS

Economics: Prof. M. ARTIS
History: Prof. R. ROMANELLI
Law: Prof. M.-J. CAMPANA
Political Science: Prof. S. BARTOLINI

ATTACHED INSTITUTIONS

Academy of European Law: Dirs P. ALSTON, R. DEHOUSSE, J. WEILER.

European Forum: Dir Y. MÉNY.

Robert Schuman Centre: Dir Y. MÉNY.

UNIVERSITÀ DEGLI STUDI 'G. D'ANNUNZIO'

Via dei Vestini, 66013 Chieti Scalo
Telephone: 0871-3551
Fax: 0871-3556007
Founded 1965
Rector: Prof. FRANCO CUCCURULLO
Administrator: Dr MARCO NAPOLEONE
Faculties of architecture, economics, literature and philosophy, mathematical, physical and natural sciences, foreign languages and literature, medicine, pharmacy.

UNIVERSITÀ CATTOLICA DEL SACRO CUORE (Catholic University of the Sacred Heart)

Largo A. Gemelli 1, 20123 Milan
Telephone: 02-72341
Telex: 321033
Fax: 02-72342210
Founded 1920; recognized by the Government 1924
Rector: Prof. A. BAUSOLA
Administrative Officer: Dott. G. MOLINARI
Librarian: Dr ELLIS SADA
Number of teachers: 3,000
Number of students: 39,103
Publications: various, published by individual faculties.

DEANS

Faculty of Jurisprudence: Prof. G. PASTORI
Faculty of Political Sciences: Prof. A. QUADRIO CURZIO
Faculty of Economics (Milan): Prof. A. COVA
Faculty of Economics (Piacenza): Prof. V. MORAMARCO
Second Faculty of Economics (Banking, Finance, and Insurance): Prof. B. V. FROSINI
Faculty of Letters and Philosophy: Prof. G. PICASSO
Faculty of Higher Education: Prof. G. VICO
Faculty of Agrarian Sciences: Prof. G. PIVA
Faculty of Medicine: Prof. P. MARANO
Faculty of Mathematical, Physical and Natural Sciences: Prof. C. BANFI
Faculty of Modern Languages and Literature: Prof. S. CIGADA

HEADS OF DEPARTMENTS

Religious Sciences: Prof. A. ACERBI
Private and Public Law of Economics: Prof. E. BALBONI
Philosophy: Prof. A. GHISALBERTI
Foreign Languages and Literature: Prof. G. PORCELLI
Mathematics and Physics: Prof. M. DEGIOVANNI
Pedagogy: Prof. L. PATI
Psychology: Prof. F. DOGANA
Economic Sciences: Prof. D. P. GIARDA
Political Sciences: Prof. V. F. PIACENTINI
Medieval, Humanistic and Renaissance Studies: Prof. A. AMBROSIONI
Sociology: Prof. V. CESAREO

UNIVERSITÀ COMMERCIALE LUIGI BOCCONI

Via R. Sarfatti 25, 20136 Milan
Telephone: 02-58361
Telex: 316003
Fax: 02-58362000
Founded 1902; private control
Academic year: November to October
President: Prof. MARIO MONTI
Rector: Prof. ROBERTO RUOZI
Chief Exec.: Prof. L. GUATRI
General Manager: Dott. GIOVANNI PAVESE
Librarian: MARISA SANTASIERO
Number of teachers: 670
Number of students: 12,400
Publications: *Giornale degli Economisti e Annali di Economia, Economia delle Fonti di Energia, Finanza Marketing e Produzione, Sviluppo e Organizzazione, Economia e Management, Economia e Politica Industriale, Commercio, Azienda Publica.*

DEANS

Department of Economics: Prof. A. PREDETTI
Department of Business Administration: Prof. PAOLO MOTTURA

DIRECTORS

Department of Economics:
- 'Ettore Bocconi' Institute of Economics: Prof. F. BRUNI
- Institute of Quantitative Methods: Prof. D. M. CIFARELLI
- Institute of Economic History: Prof. A. M. ROMANI
- 'Angelo Sraffa' Institute of Comparative Law: Prof. P. MARCHETTI
- Institute of Economic and Social Studies of East Asia: Prof. C. FILIPPINI
- Centre for the Study of Labour Economics: Prof. A. PREDETTI
- Research Centre on Entrepreneurship 'Furio Cicogna': Prof. G. MUSSATI
- Research Centre for Comparative Politics: Prof. G. URBANI
- Institute of Energy Economics: Prof. S. VACCÀ
- Institute of Latin-American Studies: Prof. C. SECCHI
- Research Centre for Public Sector Economics: Prof. R. ARTONI
- Centre of Monetary and Financial Economics 'Paolo Baffi': Prof. A. PORTA
- Centre for Research on Business Taxation: Prof. A. PROVASOLI
- Centre of Research on Internationalization Processes: Prof. F. MALERBA
- Centre of Research on Analysis and Systematic Use of Information: Prof. D. M. CIFARELLI
- Innocenzo Gasparini Institute for Economic Research: Prof. G. TABELLINI

Department of Business Administration:
- 'Gino Zappa' Institute of Business Administration: Prof. V. CODA
- Institute of Economics of Industrial and Commercial Companies Management: Prof. L. GUATRI

'Giordano Dell'Amore' Institute of Financial Intermediaries: Prof. G. FORESTIERI
Centre for Research on the Distributive Trades: Prof. A. SPRANZI
Research Centre for Health Care Management: Prof. E. BORGONOVI
Centre for Research on Business Organization: Prof. R. C. D. NACAMULLI
Business Administration Research Centre: Prof. F. AMIGONI
Centre for Research on Innovation and Industrial Reorganization: Prof. G. BRUGGER
Research Institute on the Stock Exchange 'A. Lorenzetti': Prof. S. PIVATO
Centre for Research on Financial Innovation: Prof. P. MOTTURA
Centre for Research on Markets and the Industrial Sector: Prof. S. PODESTÀ
Centre for Research on Insurance and Social Security: Prof. S. PACI
Centre for Research on Security and Protection against Crime and Emergencies: Prof. S. PIVATO
Centre for Economics and Financial Information: Prof. S. SALVEMINI
Centre for Economic and Business Research: Prof. A. BERTONI
Graduate School of Business Administration: Prof. E. BORGONOVI
Computer-Assisted Education and Research Development Centre: Prof. A. PROVASOLI
Language Centre: Prof. L. SCHENA
Centre for Teaching and Learning: Prof. V. CODA
Centre for Regional Economics, Transport and Tourism: Prof. L. SENN

PROFESSORS

AIROLDI, G., Business Administration
AMIGONI, F., Cost Accounting and Management Control Systems
ARTONI, R., Public Finance
BERTONI, A., Capital Budgeting
BIANCHI, T., Banking
BINI, M., Business Finance
BORGONOVI, E., Public Administration
BRUGGER, G., Industrial Administration
BRUNETTI, G., Business Administration
BRUNI, F., International Monetary Theory and Policy
CASTAGNOLI, E., Mathematics
CATTINI, M., Economic History
CIFARELLI, D. M., Statistics
CODA, V., Business Administration
DEMATTÈ, C., Financial Intermediaries
FABRIZI, P. L., Securities Market
FILIPPINI, C., Economics Development
FORESTIERI, G., Financial Intermediaries
GIAVAZZI, F., Economics
GUATRI, L., Management of Industrial Companies
IUDICA, G., Civil Law
MARCHETTI, P., Industrial Law
MASSARI, M., Capital Budgeting
MONTESANO, A., Economics
MONTI, M., Economics
MOTTURA, P., Financial Intermediaries
ONIDA, F., International Economics
PECCATI, L., Mathematics for Economics and Finance
PEDRAZZI, C., Business and Corporate Criminal Law
PEZZANI, F., Public Management Programming and Control
PIVATO, S., Management of Industrial Companies
PODESTÀ, S., Management of Commercial Companies
PORTA, A., Monetary Theory and Policy
PREDETTI, A., Economic and Financial Policy
PROVASOLI, A., Cost Accounting and Management Control Systems
REGAZZINI, E., Statistics
ROMANI, A., Economic History
ROSSI, G., Commercial Law
RUGIADINI, A., Organizational Analysis
RUOZI, R., Banking
SACERDOTI, G., International Law
SALVEMINI, S., Organization of Labour
SECCHI, C., Economics of the European Communities
SENN, L., Regional Economics
SITZIA, B., Econometrics
TABELLINI, G., Economics
URBANI, G., Political Science
VACCÀ, S., Energy Economics
VALDANI, E., Marketing
VICARI, S., Management of Industrial Companies
VIGANO, A., Cost Accounting and Management Control Systems

UNIVERSITÀ ITALIANA PER STRANIERI

Palazzo Gallenga, 06100 Perugia
Telephone: 075-57461
Fax: 075-62014
Founded 1921
Academic year: January to December

Founded for the diffusion abroad of Italian language and culture; courses in Italian language and civilization for foreigners of all nationalities. There are courses in advanced culture on Italian institutions, literature, pedagogy, history of art, the geography of Italy, Italian history, and Italian thought throughout the centuries; also courses in Italian language and culture, divided into three sections: Preparatory, Intermediate, Advanced; there are also in the summer term special courses in Etruscology, History of Art and Modern Italian and a course for teachers of Italian abroad. Lectures and classes are given by professors of Italian universities, leading members of academies, etc.

Rector: Prof. GIORGIO SPITELLA
Pro-Rector: ALBERTO MAZZETTI
Administrator: Dott. CARMELO SAETTA
Library of 70,000 vols
Number of teachers: *c.* 100
Number of students: *c.* 7,000 annually
Publication: *Annali dell'Università*.

ISTITUTO UNIVERSITARIO DI STUDI EUROPEI

Via Maria Vittoria 26, 10123 Turin
Telephone: 011-5625458
Fax: 011-530235
E-mail: iuse@arpnet.it
Founded 1952
President: Prof. ANDREA COMBA
Library of *c.* 12,000 vols; 20,000 documents from int. orgs.

Postgraduate courses and research in law and international economics

ISTITUTO UNIVERSITARIO DI ARCHITETTURA

Tolentini 191, 30135 Venice
Telephone: 041-2571111
Telex: 420024
Fax: 041-2571760
Founded 1926
State control
Academic year: November to October
Rector: Prof. M. FOLIN
Administrative Director: Dott. G. SERAFINO
Librarian: Dott. A. DI GUAROLO
Library of 42,000 vols, 625 current periodicals
Number of teachers: 236
Number of students: 11,644

ISTITUTO UNIVERSITARIO NAVALE

Via Ammiraglio Acton 38, 80133 Naples
Telephone: 081-5475111
Telex: 710417
Fax: 081-5521485
Founded 1920
Rector: Prof. GENNARO FERRARA
Administrative Director: Dr FERDINANDO FIENGO
Library of 50,000 vols
Number of teachers: 102
Number of students: 5,689
Publication: *Annali*.

DEANS

Faculty of nautical science: Prof. A. PUGLIANO
Faculty of maritime economics: Prof. C. QUINTANO

ISTITUTO UNIVERSITARIO ORIENTALE

Largo San Giovanni Maggiore 30, 80134 Naples
Telephone: 081-5526948
Telex: 721089
Fax: 081-5526928
Founded 1732
Rector: Prof. ADRIANO ROSSI
Administrative Director: Dr M. R. CAVALIERE

DEANS

Faculty of Letters and Philosophy: Prof. G. D'ERME
Faculty of Political Science: Prof. P. FRASCANI
Faculty of Foreign Languages and Literatures: Prof. G. DE CESARE
School of Islamic Studies: Prof. L. SERRA

LIBERA UNIVERSITÀ INTERNAZIONALE DEGLI STUDI SOCIALI GUIDO CARLI IN ROMA (Independent International University of Social Studies in Rome)

Viale Pola 12, 00198 Rome
Telephone: 06-852251
Fax: 06-85225300
Founded 1945, recognized by the Government 1966
President: Dr LUIGI ABETE
Rector: Prof. MARIO ARCELLI
Registrar: Dott. MARIO TEANE PANUNEI
Library of 118,000 vols and 2,133 periodicals
Number of teachers: 515
Number of students: 4,800

DEANS

Faculty of Law: Prof. M. FOSCHINI
Faculty of Political Science: Prof. G. C. DE MARTIN
Faculty of Economics: Prof. F. FONITANE

LIBERA UNIVERSITÀ MARIA SS. ASSUNTA

Via Traspontina 21, 00193 Rome
Telephone: 06-6865945
Founded 1939
President: GIUSEPPE DALLA TORRE DEL TEMPIO DI SANGUINETTO
Registrar: Dott. NICOLINA JORIO
Librarian: Dott. GIUSEPPINA D'ALESSANDRO
Library of 55,000 vols
Number of teachers: 70
Number of students: 1,480
Faculties of Law and of Letters and Philosophy

BOLOGNA CENTER OF THE JOHNS HOPKINS UNIVERSITY PAUL H. NITZE SCHOOL OF ADVANCED INTERNATIONAL STUDIES

Via Belmeloro 11, 40126 Bologna

Telephone: 051-232185
Fax: 051-228505
E-mail: registrar@jhubc.it

Founded 1955
Academic year: September to May

Graduate courses in international relations

Director: ROBERT H. EVANS
Registrar: HANNELORE ARAGNO
Librarian: GAIL MARTIN

Library of 75,000 vols
Number of teachers: 25
Number of students: 150

Publications: *Bologna Center Catalogue*, *Occasional Papers Series*, *Rivista* (alumni newsletter).

SCUOLA INTERNAZIONALE SUPERIORE DI STUDI AVANZATI IN TRIESTE

Via Beirut 2–4, 34013 Trieste

Telephone: 040-37871
Telex: 460269
Fax: 040-3787528

Founded 1978; sponsored by the Italian Government
Languages of instruction: English and Italian
Academic year: November to October

Director: Prof. DANIELE AMATI
Administrator: GIULIANA ZOTTA VITTUR

Library of 10,000 vols
Number of teachers: 45
Number of students: 130

Higher degrees in physics and mathematics; research; fellowships for students from developing countries

SCUOLA NORMALE SUPERIORE DI PISA

Piazza dei Cavalieri 7, 56100 Pisa

Telephone: 050-509111
Telex: 590548

Founded 1813
State control

Director: Prof. FRANCO BASSANI
Chief Administrative Officer: Dssa GIOVANNA GIOVANNINI
Librarian: Dssa SANDRA DI MAJO

Library of 500,000 vols
Number of teachers: 36
Number of students: 279

Publications: *Annali* (Arts series, Science series), *Studi e Testi*, *Studi Linguistici e Filologici*, *Quaderni di Matematica*, *Testi umanistici inediti o rari*, *Italia dialettale*.

SCUOLA SUPERIORE ENRICO MATTEI ENI

Piazza S. Barbara 7, 20097 San Donato Milanese

Telephone: 02-52023960
Fax: 02-52023937

Founded 1957

President: Prof. GUSTAVO DE SANTIS
Vice President: Prof. PIERANGELO CIGNOLI

Economic and management studies; higher degree in energy and environmental economics

Library of 15,000 vols
Number of teachers: 50
Number of students: annual intake of 55

ISTITUTO REGIONALE DI STUDI E RICERCA SOCIALE

Piazza S. Maria Maggiore 7, 38100 Trento

Telephone: 0461-220110
Fax: 0461-233821
E-mail: dir@irsrs.tn.it

Founded 1947; until *c.* 1993, Scuola Superiore Regionale di Servizio Sociale

President: Prof. CARLO FAIT
Director: Dott. GIAMPIERO GIRARDI

Library of 15,000 vols
Number of teachers: 350
Number of students: 6,000

Publication: *Annali* (annually).

CONSTITUENT INSTITUTES

Scuola per Educatore Professionale (School for Professional Educators).

Scuola per Operatore Socio-Assistenziale (School for Social Service Workers).

Università della Terza Età e del Tempo Disponibile (Open University): training for social workers, and adult education.

Schools of Music and Art

MUSIC

Accademia Filarmonica Romana (Rome Philharmonic Academy): Via Flaminia 118, 00196 Rome; tel. 06-3201752; fax 06-3210410; f. 1821; library of 1,500 vols; Pres. ROMAN VLAD.

Accademia Musicale Chigiana: Via di Città 89, 53100 Siena; tel. 0577-46152; f. 1932; master classes, lectures, concerts; Pres. Prof. GIOVANNI GROTTANELLI DE' SANTI.

Conservatorio di Musica 'Santa Cecilia': Via dei Greci 18, 00187 Rome; tel. 06-6784552; Dir Maestro GIORGIO CAMBISSA.

Conservatorio Statale di Musica G. B. Martini: Piazza Rossini 2, 40126 Bologna; tel. 051-221483; f. 1804; Dir (vacant).

Conservatorio di Musica G. Verdi: Via Conservatorio 12, 20122 Milan; tel. 02-76001755; fax 02-76014814; f. 1808; library: see Libraries; Dir MARCELLO ABBADO.

Conservatorio di Musica 'Gioacchino Rossini': Piazza Olivieri 5, 61100 Pesaro; tel. 0721-33670; f. 1882; library of *c.* 25,000 vols; Dir MARIO PERRUCCI.

Conservatorio Statale di Musica 'Giuseppe Verdi': Via Mazzini 11, 10123 Turin; tel. 011-8178458; fax 011-885165; f. 1867; Dir GIORGIO FERRARI.

Conservatorio Nazionale di Musica 'Benedetto Marcello': Palazzo Pisani, San Marco 2809, 30124 Venice; tel. 041-5225604; fax 041-5239268; f. 1877; 90 teachers; 480 students; library of 50,000 vols, 70 periodicals; Dir GIOVANNI UMBERTO BATTEL.

Conservatorio di Musica Niccoló Piccinni: Via Brigata Bari 26, 70124 Bari; tel. 080-347962; f. 1959; library of 11,000 vols; Dir G. ROTA; Sec. Dr V. A. DELLEGRAZIE.

Conservatorio Statale di Musica 'C. Monteverdi': Piazza Domenicani 19, 39100 Bolzano; tel. 0471-978764; f. 1940; library of 10,000 vols; international Busoni Piano Competition held annually; Dir Prof. V. BRUNETTI; Admin. Dir Dott. N. MARCHESONI.

Conservatorio Statale di Musica 'G. Pierluigi da Palestrina': Piazza Porino 1, 09100 Cagliari; tel. 070-493118; f. 1939; Dir NINO BONAVOLONTÁ.

Conservatorio di Musica 'L. Cherubini': Piazzetta delle Belle Arti 2, 50121 Florence; tel. 055-292180; fax 055-2396785; f. 1861; Dir Maestro G. GIGLIO; Sec. Dssa M. POLLICINA.

Conservatorio di Musica 'S. Pietro a Majella': Via S. Pietro a Majella 35, 80138 Naples; tel. 081-459255; Dir Dr A. COLLUCCI.

Conservatorio di Musica 'V. Bellini': Via Squarcialupo 45, 90133 Palermo; tel. 091-580921; fax 091-586742; f. 1721; library of 40,000 vols, collection of 18th- and 19th-century MSS; Pres. A. ALESSI; Dir A. SCARLATO; publ. *Quaderni del Conservatorio* (irregular).

Conservatorio di Musica 'A. Boito': Via Conservatorio 27, 43100 Parma; tel. 0521-282320; f. 1825; library of 70,000 vols; Dir CLAUDIA TERMINI.

Conservatorio di Musica Giuseppe Tartini: Via Carlo Ghega 12, 34132 Trieste; tel. 040-363508; fax 040-370205; Dir GIORGIO BLASCO.

ART

Accademia Albertina di Belle Arti: Via Accademia Albertina 6, 10123 Turin; tel. 011-889020; fax 011-8125688; f. 1652; Pres. Dott. Proc. A. M. MAROCCO; Dir Prof. CARLO GIULIAMO.

Accademia di Belle Arti (Academy of Fine Arts): Via Belle Arti 54, 40126 Bologna; tel. 051-243064; f. 1710; library of 15,000 vols; Dir Prof. A. BACCILIERI; Librarian Prof. M. V. RICCARDI SCASSELLATI; publ. *Prontuario* (annually).

Accademia di Belle Arti e Liceo Artistico (Academy of Fine Arts): Via Roma 1, 54033 Carrara; tel. 0585-71658; courses in painting, sculpture and scene-painting.

Accademia di Belle Arti (Academy of Fine Arts): Via Ricasoli 66, 50122 Florence; tel. 055-215449; f. 1801; library of 22,000 vols; Pres. Sen. L. BAUSI; Dir Prof. D. VIGGIANO.

Accademia di Belle Arti (Academy of Fine Arts): Via Libertini 3, 73100 Lecce; Dir Prof. S. SPEDICATO.

Accademia di Belle Arti (Academy of Fine Arts): Palazzo di Brera, Via Brera 28, 20121 Milan; tel. 02-86461929; fax 02-86403643; f. 1776; library of 25,000 vols; Pres. Sen. WALTER FONTANA; Dir Dott. DANIELA PALAZZOLI.

Accademia di Belle Arti (Academy of Fine Arts): Via S. M. Constantinopoli 107A, 80138 Naples; f. 1838; library of 7,000 vols; Dir Prof. C. LORENZETTI.

Accademia di Belle Arti (Academy of Fine Arts): Via Papireto 20, 90134 Palermo; tel. 091-580876.

Accademia di Belle Arti (Academy of Fine Arts): Piazza S. Francesco al Prato 5, 06123 Perugia; tel. 075-5730631; fax 075-5730632; f. 1573; 96 Academicians, 143 Hon. Academicians; collections of paintings, engravings, drawings, etc.; library of 13,330 vols; Pres. CLAUDIO SPINELLI; Dir Prof. EDGARDO ABBOZZO.

Accademia di Belle Arti (Academy of Fine Arts): Loggetta Lombardesca, Via di Roma 13, 48100 Ravenna; tel. 0544-482874; fax 0544-213641; f. 1827; library of 10,000 vols; Dir VITTORIO D'AUGUSTA; Sec.-Gen. PATRIZIA POGGI.

Accademia di Belle Arti (Academy of Fine Arts): Via Ripetta 222, 00186 Rome; tel. 06-3227025; fax 06-3218007; f. 1873; Dir Prof. ANTONIO PASSA.

Accademia di Belle Arti (Academy of Fine Arts): Campo della Carità 1050, 30123 Venice; tel. 041-5225396; fax 041-5230129; f. 1750; Dir Prof. ANTONIO TONIATO.

Istituto Statale d'Arte: Piazza d'Armi 16, CP 105, 07100 Sassari; tel. 079-234466; woodwork, metalwork, weaving, painting, ceramics, graphic art and architecture; Pres. Prof. NICOLÒ MASIA.

Istituto Statale d'Arte per la Ceramica: Corso Baccarini 17, 48018 Faenza; tel. 0546-21091; basic courses in ceramic art and technology; higher courses in stoneware, porcelain, restoration, ceramic building coatings, traditional ceramics, technology of special ceramics.

Istituto Statale d'Arte 'Enrico e Umberto Nordio': Via di Calvola, 34143 Trieste; tel. 040-300660; f. 1955; courses in architecture, interior decorating, design and printing of textiles; library of 5,450 vols; Dir Prof. TEODORO GIUDICE.

Istituto Statale d'Arte: Piazza Duca Federico 1, 61029 Urbino; tel. 0722-329892; fax 0722-4830; f. 1865; engraving techniques, cartoon drawing, ceramics, photography, editorial graphics, publicity art; library of 20,000 vols; 110 teachers; 714 students; Pres. Prof. NICOLÒ NICOSIA.

DANCE AND DRAMA

Accademia Nazionale di Arte Drammatica 'Silvio d'Amico': Via Vincenzo Bellini 16, 00198 Rome; tel. 06-8543680; fax 06-8542505; f. 1935; Dir Prof. LUIGI MARIA MUSATI.

Accademia Nazionale di Danza: Largo Arrigo VII 5, Castello dei Cesari (Aventino), 00153 Rome; tel. 06-5743284; fax 06-5780994; f. 1948; Pres. CARLO SCARASCIA MUGNOZZA; Dir LIA CALIZZA.

JAMAICA

Learned Societies

GENERAL

Institute of Jamaica: 12-16 East St, Kingston; tel. 922-0620; fax 922-1147; f. 1879; comprises the National Library of Jamaica (see Libraries); two Junior Cultural Centres; Natural History Division; Arawak (Indian) Museum; Jamaica Folk Museum; Military Museum; Maritime Museum; the National Gallery of Jamaica; the African-Caribbean Institute/Jamaica Memory Bank; Institute of Jamaica Publications; Exec. Dir. Dr Elaine Fisher (acting); publs *Bulletin (Science Series)*, *Sloanea* (occasional papers in natural history), *Jamaica Journal*.

AGRICULTURE, FISHERIES AND VETERINARY SCIENCE

Jamaican Association of Sugar Technologists: c/o Sugar Industry Research Institute, Mandeville; tel. 962-2241; fax 962-1288; f. 1937 by the Local Sugar Industry to conduct research and investigate technical problems of the Jamaican sugar industry; 266 mems; uses library of Sugar Industry Research Institute; Pres. Michael G. Hylton; Sec. H. M. Thompson; publ. *JAST Journal* (annually).

ARCHITECTURE AND TOWN PLANNING

Jamaican Institute of Architects: POB 251, Kingston 10; tel. 926-8060; fax 920-3589; f. 1957; 88 mems; Pres. Arch. Douglas Stiebel; Hon. Sec. Arch. Maurice Burnside; publ. *Jamaica Architect* (1 a year).

BIBLIOGRAPHY, LIBRARY SCIENCE AND MUSEOLOGY

Jamaica Library Association: POB 58, Kingston 5; f. 1949; 215 mems; Pres. P. Kerr; Sec. F. Salmon; publs *JLA Newslink* (monthly), *JLA News* (2 a year), *JLA Bulletin* (annually).

HISTORY, GEOGRAPHY AND ARCHAEOLOGY

Jamaica National Heritage Trust: POB 8934, 79 Duke St, Kingston CSO; f. 1959; restoration and preservation of monuments of national, historical and architectural importance; Chair. Herbert D. Repole.

MEDICINE

Medical Association of Jamaica: 3A Paisley Ave, Kingston 5; tel. (92) 95829; f. 1966; for the promotion of medical and allied sciences and of the medical profession; 707 mems; Pres. Dr K. Orrin Barrow; Hon. Sec. Dr M. Green; publ. *Newsletter* (quarterly), *Journal* (annually).

TECHNOLOGY

Jamaica Institution of Engineers: 2 3/4 Ruthven Rd, Kingston 10; f. 1960, present name 1977; to promote and encourage the general advancement of the engineering profession and the practice and science of engineering, and to facilitate the exchange of information and ideas on those subjects among the mems and others; Exec. Ccl of 16 mems; Pres. Dr Rae Davis; publ. *JIE News* (monthly).

Research Institutes

AGRICULTURE, FISHERIES AND VETERINARY SCIENCE

Sugar Industry Research Institute (Agricultural Division): Kendal Rd, Mandeville; f. 1973; formerly Sugar Research Dept, Sugar Manufacturers' Association (of Jamaica) Ltd; research in sugar cane production; laboratories; 50 staff; library of 660 vols, 2,500 bound vols of periodicals; Dir of Research M. Hylton; publs *Annual Report*, *Annual Sugar Cane Production Cost Survey*, *Sugar Cane* (quarterly), various technical bulletins.

ECONOMICS, LAW AND POLITICS

Planning Institute of Jamaica: Ministry of Finance and Planning, POB 634, Kingston Mall; tel. 967-36-89; fax 967-36-88; f. 1955; for social and economic development projects; Dir-Gen. Dr Wesley Hughes; publs *Economic and Social Survey of Jamaica* (1 a year), *Economic Update and Outlook* (4 a year), *Jamaica Survey of Living Conditions* (1 a year), *People Magazine* (4 a year), *The Labour Market Information Newsletter* (4 a year).

MEDICINE

Caribbean Food and Nutrition Institute (CFNI): Jamaica Centre, POB 140, Mona, Kingston 7; tel. 9271540; telex 3705; fax (809) 927-2657; f. 1967; conducts research and training courses and provides technical advisory services to 16 governments of the English-speaking Caribbean on matters relating to food and nutrition; library of 4,500 vols; there is a centre in Trinidad; Dir Dr Fitzroy Henry; publs *Cajanus*, *Nyam News*, *Nutrient-Cost Tables* (quarterly).

Medical Research Council Laboratories: University of West Indies, Mona, Kingston 7; tel. 927-2471; fax 927-2984; e-mail grserjnt@uwimona.edu.jm; f. 1974; attached to Medical Research Council, London; research on sickle cell disease; 20 staff; Dir. G. R. Serjeant.

NATURAL SCIENCES

General

Scientific Research Council: POB 350, Kingston 6; tel. 92-71771; telex 3631; fax 927-5347; e-mail adminsrc@toj.com; f. 1960; undertakes, fosters and co-ordinates scientific research in the island; divisions: Information and Co-ordination Services, Finance and Administration, Research and Development; library of 10,000 vols; Council of 10 mems; Exec. Dir Dr Jean Dixon; publs *Focus on Science and Technology* (quarterly newsletter), *Jamaican Journal of Science and Technology* (1 a year), *Conference Proceedings* (1 a year), *Insights* (4 a year), *Agrolink* (6 a year).

Libraries and Archives

Kingston

Jamaica Library Service: POB 58, 2 Tom Redcam Drive, Kingston 5; tel. 92-63310; fax 92-62188; f. 1948; provides an island-wide network of 615 service points, including 13 parish libraries, and 114 branch libraries; offers Community Information Service and Service to the Blind; total bookstock 2,711,000 vols, 70 periodicals; a Schools Library Service operates to 820 primary and 114 secondary schools, with a bookstock of 1,121,000 and 428,000 vols respectively; Dir Gloria Salmon; publ. *Statistical Report of the Jamaica Library Service* (annually).

National Library of Jamaica: 12 East St, POB 823, Kingston; tel. 922-0620; fax 922-5567; e-mail natlibja@uwimona.edu.jm; f. 1979; 46,000 printed items, 29,571 maps and plans, 4,200 serials, 207,000 photographs, 3,000 manuscripts, 2,500 items of audio-visual material on Jamaica and the West Indies; Dir John Aarons; publs *Jamaica National Bibliography* (quarterly), *Gleaner Index* (quarterly), *Occasional Bibliography Series* (irregular), *Gleaner Index* (monthly).

University of the West Indies Library: Mona, Kingston 7; tel. 927-2123; fax 927-1926; e-mail manlibry@uwimona.edu.jm; f. 1948; 493,000 vols including 6,700 current and 4,805 non-current periodicals in the Main Library and two branch libraries for the Medical (35,279 vols) and Scientific (90,592 vols) Collections; Librarian Stephney Ferguson. (See also Barbados and Trinidad and Tobago.)

Spanish Town

Jamaica Archives: King and Manchester Streets, Spanish Town PO; tel. 984-2581; fax 984-8254; f. 1659; national archives of Jamaica; special collection of ecclesiastical records; Government Archivist Elizabeth Williams.

Museums and Art Galleries

Kingston

Institute of Jamaica Museum: (see above).

University

UNIVERSITY OF THE WEST INDIES, MONA CAMPUS

Mona, Kingston 7

Telephone: 92-71661–9
Telex: 2123
Fax: (809-92) 72765

Founded 1948, University 1962

Serves 14 territories: Jamaica, Bahamas, Belize, British Virgin Islands, Cayman Islands; Barbados, Antigua & Barbuda, Dominica, Grenada, Montserrat, St Christopher and Nevis, St Lucia, St Vincent and the Grenadines; Trinidad and Tobago. The faculties of arts and general studies, medical sciences, natural sciences, social sciences and education are located on all three campuses. The faculty of law is in Barbados, agriculture and engineering in Trinidad

Chancellor: Sir Shridath Ramphal
Vice-Chancellor: Sir Alister McIntyre
Principal, Mona: Prof. G. C. Lalor
University Registrar: Gloria Kirton
Campus Registrar: G. E. A. Falloon

Librarian (Mona): Mrs A. A. JEFFERSON

Number of teachers: 373
Number of students: 6,385

Publications: *Calendar*, *Caribbean Quarterly*, *Vice-Chancellor's Report*, *Departmental Reports*, *Social and Economic Studies*, *West Indian Medical Journal*, *Caribbean Journal of Education*.

DEANS AT MONA

Faculty of Arts and General Studies: Dr P. CHRISTIE
Faculty of Education: Dr H. EVANS
Faculty of Medical Sciences: D. RAJE
Faculty of Natural Sciences: Prof. K. E. MAGNUS
Faculty of Social Sciences: Dr D. ROBOTHAM

PROFESSORS

ALLEYNE, M. C., Sociolinguistics
AUGIER, R., History
BALL, I., Zoology
BAUGH, E., English
BAXTER-GRILLO, D., Anatomy
BROOKS, S. E. H., Pathology
BROWN, A., Mass Communication
CAMPBELL, C., History
DASGUPTA, T., Inorganic Chemistry
DOUGLAS, D., Library Studies
FLETCHER, P., Clinical Surgery
GIRVAN, N., Social Sciences
GRAY, R. H., Child Health
GREENE, J. E., Social and Economic Research
HAGLEY, K., Social and Preventive Medicine
HIGMAN, B., History
JONES, E., Public Administration
KEAN, E. A., Biological Chemistry
KING, S. D., Microbiology
LALOR, G. C., Chemistry
LEO-RHYNIE, E., Women and Development Studies
MAGNUS, K. E., Applied Chemistry
MCGREGOR, S., Child Health and Nutrition
MEYER-ROCHOW, V. B., Experimental Zoology
MILLER, E., Teacher Education
MORGAN, O., Medicine
NETTLEFORD, R. N., Continuing Studies
PERSAUD, B., Caribbean Development
PERSAUD, V., Anatomical Pathology
REICHGELT, J., Computer Science
ROBINSON, E., Geology
ROBINSON, L. R. B., Mathematics
ROGERS-JOHNSON, P., Experimental Medicine
SHIRLEY, G., Production and Operations Management
SIVAPRAGASAM, S., Anaesthetics and Intensive Care
STONE, C., Political Sociology
WEST, M., Pharmacology
WILLIAMS, R. L., Accounting
WRAY, S. R., Neuropsychology
WYNTER, H. H., Obstetrics and Gynaecology
YOUNG, R., Physiology

ATTACHED INSTITUTES

School of Continuing Studies: Mona; Dir R. M. NETTLEFORD.

Creative Arts Centre: Mona; f. 1967; term-to-term activity in painting, sculpture, dance, theatre, writing, exhibitions, readings, etc.; acting as the home for ICC Week activities; the mounting of a small Caribbean Arts Festival; Sec. JEAN SMITH.

Consortium Graduate School of Social Sciences: Mona; offers multi-disciplinary higher degree programme undertaken jointly by Univ. of West Indies and Univ. of Guyana; Dir N. GIRVAN.

Institute of Social and Economic Research: Mona; tel. (92) 72409; applied research relating to the Caribbean; brs in Barbados, Leeward and Windward Islands; Dr ELSIE LEFRANC.

Trade Union Education Institute: Mona; Dir of Studies R. M. NETTLEFORD.

Tropical Metabolism Research Unit: Kingston 7; Dir Dr TERRENCE FORRESTER.

Medical Research Council: Dir Prof. G. SERJEANT.

Biotechnology Centre: Dir M. AHMAD.

Education Research Centre: Dir Dr H. EVANS.

Centre for Marine Sciences: Dir Prof. I. BALL.

Centre for Nuclear Sciences: Dir G. C. LALOR.

Institute of Business: Dir C. SAMPSON.

Women and Development Studies: Dir Prof. E. LEO-RHYNIE.

Institute of Caribbean Studies: Dir J. PEREIRA.

AFFILIATED INSTITUTIONS

United Theological College of the West Indies: Mona; awards degrees and licentiates of the Univ. of the West Indies; Pres. Rev. Dr HOWARD GREGORY.

St Michael's Seminary: Mona; awards degrees of the Univ. of the West Indies; Rector Mgr ROBERT HAUGHTON-JAMES.

Colleges

College of Agriculture, Science and Education: POB 170, Passley Gardens, Port Antonio, Portland; tel. 993-3246; fax 993-2208; f. 1995 by merger of College of Agriculture and Passley Gardens Teachers College; two-year degree course in all aspects of agriculture; 47 faculty mems; 533 full-time students, 86 part-time, 24 evening; library of 35,000 vols, special collections: UN publs, West Indian works, Jamaica Govt publs; Pres. Dr ISMAIL BIN YAHYA; Registrar PATRICIA WRIGHT-CLARKE.

College of Arts, Science and Technology: 237 Old Hope Rd, Kingston 6; tel. 927-1680; fax 927-1925; f. 1958; full-time and part-time diploma and certificate programmes; BA, BSc, BBA, BEd, BEng and BTech courses, also MArchitecture; 219 full-time, 220 part-time lecturers; 2,621 full-time, 3,953 part-time students; library of 50,000 vols; President Dr A. W. SANGSTER; Registrar DIANNE MITCHELL; publ. *CAST Review* (2 a year).

JAPAN

Learned Societies

GENERAL

Nihon Gakujutsu Kaigi (Science Council of Japan): 22–34 Roppongi 7-chome, Minato-ku, Tokyo 106; tel. (3) 3403-6291; fax (3) 3403-6224; f. 1949; governmental org. co-ordinating Japan's scientific research; divisions of Literature, Philosophy, Pedagogy, Psychology, Sociology and History (Chair. Yasunao Nakada), Law and Political Science (Chair. Kazuhisa Nakayama), Economics, Commerce and Business Administration (Chair. Toshinosuke Kashiwazaki), Pure Science (Chair. Muneyuki Date), Engineering (Chair. Moriya Uchida), Agriculture (Chair. Teitaro Kitamura), Medicine, Dentistry and Pharmacology (Chair. Kazuhiko Atsumi); 210 mems; library: see Libraries and Archives; Pres. Masao Ito; Sec.-Gen. Yasuhiko Nagashima

Nihon Gakujutsu Shinko-kai (Japan Society for the Promotion of Science): 5-3-1, Kojimachi, Chiyoda-ku, Tokyo 102-0083; tel. (3) 3263-1721; fax (3) 3222-1986; f. 1967; quasi-governmental org. under the jurisdiction of the Minister of Education, Science and Culture; provides 1,000 fellowships annually for foreign scientists for co-operative study in Japan; conducts bilateral programmes with 59 foreign organizations, exchanging 3,400 scientists annually; operates JSPS overseas liaison offices in 7 cities; administers several domestic programmes including those for postdoctoral fellowships, university/industry co-operation, etc.; Pres. Hiroyuki Yoshikawa; Dir-Gen. Hitoshi Osaki; publs *Japan Society for the Promotion of Science, Annual Report, Japanese Scientific Monthly, JSPS Newsletter* (6 a year).

Nippon Gakushiin (Japan Academy): 7-32 Ueno Park, Taito-ku, Tokyo 110-0007; tel. (3) 3822-2101; fax (3) 3822-2105; f. 1879; sections of Humanities and Social Sciences (Chair. Prof. Mikio Sumiya), Pure and Applied Sciences (Chair. Prof. Setsuro Ebashi); 150 mems; Pres. Prof. Yoshio Fujita; Sec.-Gen. Prof. Teiji Ichiko; publs *Proceedings* (2 series, 10 a year), *Nippon Gakushiin Kiyo* (3 a year).

AGRICULTURE, FISHERIES AND VETERINARY SCIENCE

Danchi-Nogaku Kenkyu-Kai (Southern Agricultural Society): Miyazaki University, Faculty of Agriculture, Gakuen Kibanadai Nishi, 1-1, Miyazaki 889-21; f. 1947; 200 mems; Pres. Taiji Adachi; publ. *Danchi-Nogaku*.

Engei Gakkai (Japanese Society for Horticultural Science): Business Center for Academic Societies Japan, 16–9 Honkomagome 5-chome, Bunkyo-ku, Tokyo 113; tel. (3) 5814-5801; fax (3) 5814-5820; f. 1923; 2,814 mems; Pres. Shuichi Iwahori; Sec. Nobuo Sugiyama; publ. *Journal* (quarterly).

Gyogyo Keizai Gakkai (Fisheries Economic Society): Tokyo-Suisan University, 4-5-7 Kohnan, Minato-ku, Tokyo 108; f. 1953; 220 mems; Pres. Ryuzo Takayama; publ. *Journal* (quarterly).

Nihon Ikushu Gakkai (Japanese Society of Breeding): c/o Faculty of Agriculture, University of Tokyo, Bunkyo-ku, Tokyo 113; f. 1951; 2,000 mems; Pres. Genkichi Takeda; publ. *Breeding Science* (quarterly).

Nihon Ju-í Gakkai (Japanese Society of Veterinary Science): Rakuno-Kaikan Bldg, 1-37-20, Yoyogi, Shibuya-ku, Tokyo 151; tel. and fax (3) 3379-0636; f. 1885; e-mail ahkrki@hongo.ecc.u-tokyo.ac.jp; veterinary medical science; 4,400 mems; Pres. Michio Takahashi; publ. *The Journal of Veterinary Medical Science* (monthly).

Nihon Oyo Toshitsu Kagaku Kai (Japanese Society of Applied Glycoscience): c/o National Food Research Institute, 2-1-2 Kannondai, Tsukuba, Ibaraki 305; tel. (298) 38-7991; fax (298) 38-8005; f. 1952; 1,147 mems; Pres. Keiji Kainuma; Sec. Takafumi Kasumi; publ. *Oyo Toshitsu Kagaku*† (Journal of Applied Glycoscience, 4 a year).

Nihon Seibutsu-kogaku Kai (Society for Fermentation and Bioengineering, Japan): c/o Faculty of Engineering, Osaka University, 2-1 Yamadaoka, Suita, Osaka 565-0871; tel. (6) 876-2731; fax (6) 879-2034; f. 1923; 4,500 mems; Pres. Prof. Takeishi Kobayashi; publs *Journal of Fermentation and Bioengineering* (monthly, English), *Seibutsu-kogaku Kaishi* (monthly, in Japanese).

Nippon Chikusan Gakkai (Japanese Society of Zootechnical Science): 201 Nagatani Corporas, Ikenohata 2-9-4, Taito-ku, Tokyo 110-0008; tel. (3) 3828-8409; fax (3) 3828-7649; f. 1924; animal science; 2,706 mems; Pres. Shigeru Sugano; publ. *Animal Science and Technology*† (monthly).

Nippon Dojo-Hiryo Gakkai (Japanese Society of Soil Science and Plant Nutrition): 26-10-202 Hongo, 6 chome, Bunkyo-ku, Tokyo; f. 1914; 2,300 mems; Pres. Toshiaki Tadano; publs *Journal* (every 2 months), *Soil Science and Plant Nutrition* (quarterly).

Nippon Nogei Kagaku Kai (Japan Society for Bioscience, Biotechnology and Agrochemistry): 4–16 Yayoi 2-chome, Bunkyo-ku, Tokyo 113-0033; fax (3) 3815-1920; f. 1924; 13,412 mems; Pres. Akinori Suzuki; publs *Bioscience, Biotechnology and Biochemistry* (in English, monthly), *Journal* (in Japanese, monthly).

Nippon Ringakukai (Japanese Forestry Society): c/o Japan Forest Technical Asscn, Rokubancho 7, Chiyoda-ku, Tokyo; tel. and fax (3) 3261-2766; f. 1914; forestry research; 2,900 mems; Pres. Kazumi Kobayashi; publs *Journal* (every two months), *Shinrin Kagaku* (bulletin, 3 a year).

Nippon Sakumotsu Gakkai (Crop Science Society of Japan): c/o Faculty of Agriculture, University of Tokyo, Hongo, Bunkyo-ku, Tokyo 113-8657; fax (11) 706-3878; e-mail iwama@res.agr.hokudai.ac.jp; f. 1927; 1,900 mems; Pres. Dr Tetsuro Taniyama; Sec. Kazuto Iwama; publs *Japanese Journal of Crop Science* (quarterly), *Plant Production Science* (quarterly).

Nippon Sanshi Gakkai (Japanese Society of Sericultural Science): c/o National Institute of Sericultural and Entomological Science, Tsukuba, Ibaraki 305; tel. (298) 38-6056; f. 1930; 1,127 mems; Pres. A. Shimazaki; publ. *Journal* (every 2 months).

Nippon Shokubutsu-Byori Gakkai (Phytopathological Society of Japan): Shokubo Bldg, Komagome 1-43-11, Toshima-ku, Tokyo 170; tel. and fax (3) 3943-6021; f. 1916 to promote research on plant diseases; 1,880 regular mems; Pres. S. Ouchi; publ. *Annals* (6 a year).

Nippon Suisan Gakkai (Japanese Society of Fisheries Science): Tokyo University of Fisheries, 4-5-7 Konan, Minato-ku, Tokyo; tel. (3) 3471-2165; fax (3) 3471-2054; f. 1932; research in food and fishing science, mariculture, aquaculture and marine environmental science; 4,790 mems; library of 61 vols; Pres. Prof. K. Hashimoto; publs *Fisheries Science* (every 2 months), *Nippon Suisan Gakkaishi* (every 2 months).

Nogyokikai Gakkai (Japanese Society of Agricultural Machinery): c/o BRAIN, 1-40-2 Nisshin-cho, Omiya, Saitama 331; f. 1937; 1,677 mems; Pres. Osamu Kitani; publ. *Journal* (every 2 months).

Sapporo Norin Gakkai (Sapporo Society of Agriculture and Fisheries): Faculty of Agriculture, Hokkaido University, Kita-ku, Kita 9, Nishi 9, Sapporo 060-8589; tel (11) 706-2417; fax (11) 716-0879; f. 1908; 300 mems; library of 289,000 vols; Pres. Dr Akira Ogoshi; publ. *Journal* (irregular).

ARCHITECTURE AND TOWN PLANNING

Kansai Zosen Kyokai (Kansai Society of Naval Architects): C/o Dept of Naval Architecture & O.E., Osaka University, 2-1 Yamada-oka, Suita, Osaka 565; tel. (6) 879-7593; fax (6) 878-5364; f. 1912; 2,400 mems; Pres. S. Furuta; publs *Journal* (2 a year), *Bulletin* (quarterly).

Nihon Zoen Gakkai (Japanese Institute of Landscape Architects): c/o Faculty of Architecture, University of Tokyo, Hongo, Bunkyo-ku, Tokyo 113; f. 1924; 1,800 mems; Pres. Akira Homma; publ. *Journal*.

Nihon Zosen Gakkai (Society of Naval Architects of Japan): Sempaku-Shinko Building, 15–16 Toranomon 1-chome, Minato-ku, Tokyo 105; f. 1897; 4,400 mems; Pres. K. Yoshida; publs *Journal* (2 a year), *Bulletin* (monthly), *Journal of Marine Science and Technology* (quarterly).

Nippon Toshi Keikaku Gakkai (City Planning Institute of Japan): Ichibancho-West Building 6F, Ichibancho 10, Chiyoda-ku, Tokyo 102; f. 1951; 5,322 mems; Pres. Kazuo Yoda; publ. *City Planning Review* (every 2 months).

BIBLIOGRAPHY, LIBRARY SCIENCE AND MUSEOLOGY

Gakujutsu Bunken Fukyu-Kai (Association for Science Documents Information): c/o Tokyo Institute of Technology, 2-12-1 O-okayama, Meguro-ku, 152 Tokyo; f. 1933; Pres. Shu Kanbara; publs *Reports on Progress in Polymer Physics in Japan* (English, annually), *Proceedings*, etc.

Information Processing Society of Japan: Shibaura-Maekawa Bldg, 7F, 3-16-20, Shibaura, Minato-ku, Tokyo 108-0023; tel. (3) 5484-3535; fax (3) 5484-3534; e-mail somu@ipsj.or.jp; f. 1960; 30,000 mems; Pres. Dr Iwao Toda; publs *Joho Shori* (monthly), *Transactions* (monthly).

Joho Kagaku Gijutsu Kyokai (Information Science and Technology Association): Sasaki Bldg, 5–7 Koisikawa 2, Bunkyo-ku, Tokyo;

f. 1950; 2,020 mems; Pres. T. GONDOH; publ. *Journal* (monthly).

Nihon Hakubutsukan Kyokai (Japanese Association of Museums): Shoyu-Kaikan 3-3-1, Chiyoda-ku, Tokyo; publ. *Museum Studies* (monthly).

Nihon Toshokan Kyokai (Japan Library Association): 1-10, 1-chome, Taishido, Setagaya-ku, Tokyo 154; tel. (3) 3410-6411; f. 1892; all aspects of library development; 8,500 mems; library of *c.* 3,000 vols; Sec.-Gen. REIKO SAKAGAWA; publs *Toshokan Zasshi* (monthly), *Gendai no Toshokan* (quarterly), *Nihon no Sankotosho Shikiban* (quarterly), *Nihon no Toshokan* (annually), *Toshokan Nenkan* (annually).

Nippon Kagaku-Gijutsu Joho Sentah (Japan Information Center of Science and Technology—JICST): POB 1478, Tokyo; f. 1957; preparation of abstracts, on-line and manual search services, translation and photo-duplication service, library service, computer processing; 330 mems; Pres. M. NAKAMURA; publs *Current Bibliography on Science and Technology* (Abstracts from about 16,200 journals; 12 series); *Journal of Information Processing and Management, JICST Thesaurus, Current Science and Technology Research in Japan* (in English and Japanese), *JICST Holding List of Serials and Proceedings.*

Nippon Toshokan Gakkai (Japan Society of Library Science): c/o Faculty of Sociology, Toyo University, 28-20 Hakusan 5-chome, Bunkyo-ku, Tokyo 112-8606; tel. (3) 3945-7444; f. 1953; 570 mems; Pres. MASAO NAGASAWA; publs *Annals* (quarterly), *Bibliography of Library and Information Science* (annually).

ECONOMICS, LAW AND POLITICS

Ajia Seikei Gakkai (Japan Association for Asian Political and Economic Studies): c/o Prof. S. AMAKO, School of International Politics, Economics and Business, Aoyama Gakuin University, 4-4-25 Shibuya, Shibuya-ku, Tokyo 150; f. 1953; 900 mems; Pres. T. WATANABE; publ. *Aziya Kenkyu* (Asian Studies, quarterly).

Hikaku-ho Gakkai (Japan Society of Comparative Law): c/o Faculty of Law, Tokyo University, Hongo, Bunkyo-ku, Tokyo 113; f. 1950; studies in comparative law; holds conferences; issues publications; 780 mems; Pres. H. TANAKA; publ. *Hikakuhô Kenkyû* (Comparative Law Journal, annually).

Hogaku Kyokai (Jurisprudence Association): Faculty of Law, University of Tokyo, Hongo, Bunkyo-ku, Tokyo; tel. (3) 3812-2111; f. 1884; 600 mems; Pres. YOSHIMITSU AOYAMA; publs *Hogaku Kyokai Zasshi, Journal.*

Hosei-shi Gakkai (Japan Legal History Association): Tohoku University, Kawauchi, Aoba-ku, Sendai 980-8576; tel. (22) 217-6237; fax (22) 217-6249; f. 1949; 495 mems; Pres. S. KOYAMA; publ. *Legal History Review* (annually).

Hosokai (Lawyers' Association): 1, 1-chome, Kasumigaseki, Chiyoda-ku, Tokyo; f. 1891; 20,000 mems; library of 30,000 vols; Pres. RYOHACHI KUSABA; Dir ISAO IMAI; publ. *Hoso Jiho.*

Keizai Riron Gakkai (Japan Society of Political Economy): Faculty of Economics, Rikkyo University, 3 Ikebukuro, Toshima-ku, Tokyo; f. 1959; 865 mems; Pres. H. OOUCHI.

Keizai-ho Gakkai (Association of Economic Jurisprudence): Hitotsubashi University, Kunitachi, Tokyo 186; f. 1951; 280 mems; publ. *Journal* (annually).

Keizaigaku-shi Gakkai (Japan Society for the History of Economic Thought): Dept of International Economics, Aoyama Gakuin University, Shibuya, Tokyo; tel. (3) 3409-8111; fax (3) 5485-0782; f. 1949; 810 mems; Pres. TAKASHI NEGISHI; publs *Annual Bulletin, History of Economic Thought Society Newsletter.*

Kinyu Gakkai (Financial Science Association): c/o Toyo Keizai, Motoishi 1–4 Nihonbashi, Chuo-ku, Tokyo; f. 1943; 459 mems; Pres. T. TAKAGAKU; publ. *Report* (2 a year).

Kokusaiho Gakkai (Association of International Law): Faculty of Law, University of Tokyo, Hongo, Bunkyo-ku, Tokyo; tel. (3) 3812-2111; f. 1897; 804 mems; Pres. SHIGERU KOZAI; publs *Kokusaiho Gaiko Zasshi, Journal of International Law and Diplomacy.*

Minji Soshoho Gakkai (Japanese Association of Civil Procedure Law): c/o Faculty of Law, Chuo University, 742–1 Higashinakano, Hachioji-shi, Tokyo; tel. (426) 74-2111; fax (426) 74-3301; f. 1949; 690 mems; Pres. T. KOJIMA; publ. *Journal of Civil Procedure* (annually).

Nichibei Hogakkai/Japanese American Society for Legal Studies: c/o Faculty of Law, University of Tokyo, Hongo, Bunkyo-ku, Tokyo 113; (American branch: c/o Asian Law Program, University of Washington School of Law, JB-20, Seattle, Wash. 98105, USA); f. 1964; promotion of comparative study of Japanese and American law and co-operation among the lawyers of both countries; 980 mems; Rep. Dirs D. F. HENDERSON, T. KINOSHITA; publs *Amerika Hō* (Law in the United States, 2 a year), *Law in Japan* (annually).

Nihon Koho Gakkai (Japan Public Law Association): University of Tokyo, Hongo, Bunkyo-ku, Tokyo; f. 1948; 1,100 mems; Pres. H. SHIONO; publ. *Koho-Kenkyu* (Public Law Review, annually).

Nihon Tokei Gakkai (Japan Statistical Society): c/o The Institute of Statistical Mathematics, 4-6-7 Minami-azabu, Minato-ku, Tokyo 106; f. 1931; 1,312 mems; Pres. KIYOSHI TAKEUSHI; publ. *Journal* (2 a year).

Nihon Zaisei Gakkai (Japanese Association of Fiscal Science): Hitotsubashi University, Kunitachi, Tokyo 186; f. 1940; 195 mems.

Nippon Gyosei Gakkai (Japanese Society for Public Administration): Meiji University, Kanda-surugadai 1-1, Chiyoda-ku, Tokyo; f. 1945; 400 mems; Pres. A. SATO; publ. *Nenpo* (Annals, annually).

Nippon Hoshakai Gakkai (Japan Association of Sociology of Law): University of Tokyo, Hongo, Bunkyo-ku, Tokyo; f. 1947; 805 mems; Pres. N. TOSHITANI; publ. *Sociology of Law* (annually).

Nippon Hotetsu-Gakkai (Japan Association of Legal Philosophy): Faculty of Law, Kyoto University, Yoshida Honmachi, Sakyo-ku, Kyoto 606-01; tel. (75) 753-3204; fax (75) 753-3290; f. 1948; 486 mems; Pres. Prof. SHIGEAKI TANAKA; publ. *The Annals of Legal Philosophy.*

Nippon Keiei Gakkai (Japan Society of Business Administration): Hitotsubashi University, 2-1 Naka, Kunitachi, Tokyo 186; tel. (425) 80-8571; f. 1926; 2,075 mems; Pres. A. MORI; publ. *Journal of Business Management.*

Nippon Keiho Gakkai (Criminal Law Society of Japan): University of Tokyo, Hongo, Bunkyo-ku, Tokyo; f. 1949; 1,000 mems; Pres. K. SHIBAHARA; publ. *Journal* (quarterly).

Nippon Keizai Seisaku Gakkai (Japan Economic Policy Association): Keio University, Mita, Minato-ku, Tokyo; f. 1940; 862 mems; Pres. T. YAMANAKA; publ. *Annals.*

Nippon Kokusai Seiji Gakkai (Japan Association of International Relations): Hosei University, Fujimi-cho, Chiyoda-ku, Tokyo; f. 1956; 512 mems; Pres. H. KAMIKAWA; publ. *International Relations* (quarterly).

Nippon Rodo-ho Gakkai (Japanese Labour Law Association): University of Tokyo, 7-3-1 Hongo, Bunkyo-ku 113, Tokyo; tel. (3) 3812-2111, extn 3243; fax (3) 3816-7375; f. 1950; 595 mems; Pres. Y. YAMAMOTO; publ. *Journal* (2 a year).

Nippon Seizi Gakkai (Japanese Political Science Association): Faculty of Law, Rikkyo University, 3-34-1, Nishi-Ikebukuro, Toshima-ku, Tokyo 171; 820 mems; Pres. JIRO KAMISHIMA.

Nippon Shiho Gakkai (Japan Association of Private Law): University of Tokyo, Hongo, Bunkyo-ku, Tokyo 113; f. 1948; 688 mems; Pres. T. SUZUKI; publ. *Journal* (annually).

Nippon Shogyo Gakkai (Japan Society of Commercial Sciences): Meiji University, Surugadai Kanda, Chiyoda-ku, Tokyo; f. 1951; 429 mems; Pres. K. FUKUDA.

Nogyo-Ho Gakkai (Japan Agricultural Law Association): c/o Faculty of Law, University of Nihon, Chiyoda-ku, Tokyo 101; f. 1956; 200 mems; Pres. TAKEKAZU OGURA; publ. *Nogyo-ho Kenkyu* (annually).

Riron Keiryou Keizai Gakkai (Japanese Association of Economics and Econometrics): c/o The Institute of Statistical Research, 1-18-16 Shimbashi, Minato-ku, Tokyo 105; fax (3) 3595-2220; f. 1934; 2,248 mems; Pres. MASAHIKO AOKI.

Tokyo Daigaku Keizai Gakkai (Society of Economics): Faculty of Economics, University of Tokyo, Bunkyo-ku, Tokyo 113-0033; f. 1922; 200 mems; Pres. HIROSHI MIYAJIMA; publ. *Journal of Economics* (quarterly).

EDUCATION

Asia-Pacific Cultural Centre for UNESCO (ACCU): 6 Fukuromachi, Shinjuku-ku, Tokyo 162; tel. (3) 3269-4435; fax (3) 3269-4510; e-mail general@accu.or.jp; f. 1971; children's books, music, audio-visual and literacy materials development, training programmes, campaigns for cultural heritage, photo contest and other regional cultural activities; library of 29,000 vols; Pres. KAZUO SUZUKI; Dir-Gen. MUNEHARU KUSABA; publs *Activity Report, ACCU News* (Japanese, monthly), *Asian/Pacific Book Development* (English, quarterly).

Kyoiku Tetsugakkai (Society of Educational Philosophy): Sophia University, Kioi-cho, Chiyoda-ku, Tokyo; f. 1957; 510 mems; Pres. T. OURA; publ. *Studies in the Philosophy of Education.*

Nihon Gakko-hoken Gakkai (Japanese Association of School Health): Dept of Health Education, Faculty of Education, University of Tokyo, Hongo 7-3-1, Bunkyo-ku, Tokyo 113; tel. (3) 3812-2111; f. 1954; 1,500 mems; Pres. ATSUHISA EGUCHI; publ. *Gakko-hoken Kenkyu* (Japanese Journal of School Health, monthly).

Nihon Hikaku Kyoiku Gakkai (Japan Comparative Education Society): c/o NIER, 6-5-22, Shimomeguro, Meguro-ku, Tokyo 153; tel. (3) 5721-5040; fax (3) 3714-3653; f. 1965; 663 mems; Pres. S. KAWANOBE; Sec. Gen. T. YAMADA; publs *Comparative Education Research Bulletin* (annually), *Newsletter* (annually).

Nihon Kyoiku Gakkai (Japan Society for the Study of Education): 2-29-3-3F Hongo, Bunkyo-ku, Tokyo 113-0033; tel. (3) 3818-2505; fax (3) 3816-6898; f. 1941; 3,200 mems; Pres. TERUHISA HORIO; publ. *The Japanese Journal of Educational Research* (quarterly).

Nihon Kyoiku-shakai Gakkai (Japan Society of Educational Sociology): Faculty of Education, University of Tokyo, Hongo 7-3-1, Bunkyo-ku, Tokyo 113; tel. (3) 5800-6813; fax (3) 5800-6814; f. 1949; 1,200 mems; Pres.

MORIKAZU USHIOGI; publ. *Journal of Educational Sociology* (2 a year).

Nihon Kyoiku-shinri Gakkai (Japanese Association of Educational Psychology): Faculty of Education, University of Tokyo, Hongo 7-3-1, Bunkyo-ku, Tokyo 113; f. 1955; 5,200 mems; Pres. SEIJUN TAKANO; publs *Japanese Journal of Educational Psychology* (quarterly), *Annual Report of Educational Psychology in Japan*.

Nihon Shiritsu Daigak Kyokai (Association of Private Universities of Japan): 4-2-25 Kudan-kita, Chiyoda-ku, Tokyo 102; tel. (3) 3261-7048; fax (3) 3261-0769; f. 1946; 266 mem. universities; Pres. Dr SHIGEYOSHI KITTAKA; Sec. Gen. Dr YUKIYASU HARANO; publs *Annual Activity Plan*, *Annual Report*, *Kyoikugakujutsu*.

Nippon Kagaku Kyoiku Gakkai (Japan Society for Science Education): National Institute for Educational Research, 6-5-22 Shimomeguro, Meguro-ku, Tokyo 153-0064; f. 1977; science and mathematics education and educational technology; 1,200 mems; Pres. S. KIMURA; publs *Journal* (quarterly), *Letter* (every 2 months).

Nippon Sugaku Kyoiku Gakkai (Japan Society of Mathematical Education): POB 18, Koishikawa, Tokyo 112-8691; f. 1919; 3,334 mems; Pres. Prof. Y. SUGIYAMA; publs *Journal* (monthly), *Supplementary issue, Report on Mathematical Education* (2 a year).

Nippon Taiiku Gakkai (Japanese Society of Physical Education): Kishi Memorial Hall (Rm 508), Jinnan 1-1-1, Shibuya-ku, Tokyo 150; tel. (3) 3481-2427; fax (3) 3481-2428; f. 1950; 6,752 mems; Pres. Dr JUJIRO NARITA; publs *Research Journal* (quarterly), *Journal of Health and Physical Education* (monthly).

FINE AND PERFORMING ARTS

Bijutsu-shi Gakkai (Japanese Art History Society): c/o Tokyo National Research Institute of Cultural Properties, 13–27 Ueno Park, Taito-ku, Tokyo 110; f. 1949; 665 mems; publ. *Journal* (quarterly).

Nihon Engeki Gakkai (Japanese Society for Theatre Research): Waseda University, 1-6-1 Nishi-Waseda, Shinjuku-ku, Tokyo; f. 1949; Pres. T. MORI; publ. *Kiyō* (News Bulletin, annually).

Nippon Ongaku Gakkai (Musicological Society of Japan): Tokyo National University of Fine Arts and Music, Ueno Park, Taito-ku, Tokyo; tel. (3) 5685-7500; f. 1952; 1,350 mems; Pres. I. SUMIKURA; publ. *Ongaku Gaku* (Journal, 3 a year).

HISTORY, GEOGRAPHY AND ARCHAEOLOGY

Keizai Chiri Gakkai (Japan Association of Economic Geographers): Institute of Economic Geography, Faculty of Economics, East Bldg, Hitotsubashi University, Naka 2-1, Kunitachi-shi, Tokyo 186; tel. (425) 72-1101, ext 5374; fax (425) 71-1893; f. 1954; 700 mems; Pres. K. TAKEUCHI; publ. *Annals* (quarterly).

Kokushi-Gakkai (Society of Japanese Historical Research): Kokugakuin University, 10–28, Higashi 4-chome, Shibuya-ku, Tokyo; f. 1910; Sec. H. ROMIE TSUBAKI; publ. *Kokushi-gaku* (Journal of Japanese History).

Nihon Kokogakkai (Archaeological Society of Japan): c/o Tokyo National Museum, Ueno Park, Taito-ku, Tokyo; f. 1895; Pres. Dr SEKINO TAKESHI; publ. *Kokogaku Zasshi* (quarterly).

Nippon Chiri Gakkai (Association of Japanese Geographers): c/o Building of Japan Academic Societies Center, Yayoi 2-4-16 Bunkyo-ku, Tokyo 113-0032; f. 1925; 3,100 mems; Pres. S. YAMAMOTO; publ. *Geographical Review of Japan, Series A* (monthly, Japanese and English), *Series B* (2 a year, English).

Nippon Kokogaku Kyokai (Japanese Archaeological Association): 5-15-5, Hirai, Edogawa-ku, Tokyo 132; tel. (3) 3618-6608; f. 1948; 3,382 mems; library of 22,000 vols; Pres. T. IWASAKI; publ. *Archaeologia Japonica* (Annual Report), *Nihon Kōkogaku* (Journal).

Nippon Oriento Gakkai (Society for Near Eastern Studies in Japan): Tokyo-Tenri-kyokan 9, 1-chome, Kanda Nishiki-cho, Chiyoda-ku, Tokyo 101; tel. and fax (3) 3291-7519; f. 1954; 910 mems; Pres. Dr HIDEO OGAWA; publ. *Oriento* (2 a year in Japanese), *Orient* (1 a year in European languages).

Nippon Seibutsuchiri Gakkai (Biogeographical Society of Japan): 2-26-12 Sendagi, Bunkyo-ku, Tokyo 113; tel. (3) 3828-0445; f. 1928; 300 mems; Pres. SEIROKU SAKAI; publs *Bulletin*, *Biogeographica*, *Fauna Japonica*.

Nippon Seiyoshi Gakkai (Japanese Society of Western History): Machikaneyama-cho 1–5, Toyonaka-shi, Osaka-fu 500; tel. and fax (6) 850-5105; f. 1948; 800 mems; Pres. Prof. S. AISAKA; publ. *Studies in Western History* (4 a year).

Shigaku-kai (Historical Society of Japan): University of Tokyo, Hongo, Bunkyo-ku, Tokyo 113; f. 1889; *c.* 2,470 mems; Pres. OSAMU NARUSE; publ. *Shigaku-Zasshi* (Historical Journal of Japan).

Tokyo Chigaku Kyokai (Tokyo Geographical Society): 12-2 Nibancho, Chiyoda-ku, Tokyo 102; f. 1879; 810 mems; Pres. ISAMU KOBAYASHI; publ. *Journal of Geography* (6 a year, and one special issue annually).

Toyoshi-Kenkyu-Kai (Society of Oriental Researches): Kyoto University, Sakyo-ku, Kyoto City; tel. (75) 753-2790; f. 1935; 1,400 mems; Pres. I. MIYAZAKI; publ. *Toyoshi-Kenkyu* (Journal of Oriental Researches) (quarterly).

LANGUAGE AND LITERATURE

Japan PEN Club: Room 265, Syuwa Residential Hotel, 9-1-7 Akasaka, Minato-ku, Tokyo; tel. (3) 3402-1171; fax (3) 3402-5951; f. 1935; 1,485 mems; library of 1,500 vols; Pres. MAKOTO OOKA; Sec. HOTSUKI OZAKI; publ. *Japanese Literature Today* (annually).

Kokugogakkai (Society for the Study of Japanese Language): Faculty of Letters, University of Tokyo, Hongo, Bunkyo-ku, Tokyo 113; f. 1944; 1,500 mems; Pres. ETSUTARO IWABUCHI; publ. *Studies in the Japanese Language* (quarterly).

Manyo Gakkai (Society for Manyo Studies): Kansai University, Senriyama Suita-shi, Osaka; f. 1951; 810 mems; publ. *The Manyo* (quarterly).

Nihon Dokubungakkai (Japanese Society of German Literature): c/o Ikubundo, Hongo 5-30-21, Bunkyo-ku, Tokyo 113-0033; f. 1947; 2,600 mems; Pres. Prof. TAKAO TSUNEKAWA; publ. *Doitsu Bungaku* (German Literature, 2 a year).

Nihon Eibungakkai (English Literary Society of Japan): 501 Kenkyusha Bldg, 9 Surugadai 2-chome, Kanda, Chiyoda-ku, Tokyo 101; tel. (3) 3293-7528; fax (3) 3293-7539; f. 1928; 4,000 mems; Pres. YOSHIYUKI FUJIKAWA; publ. *Studies in English Literature* (3 a year).

Nihon Esperanto Gakkai (Japan Esperanto Institute): Waseda-mati 12-3, Sinzyuku-ku, Tokyo 162; tel. (3) 3203-4581; fax (3) 3203-4582; e-mail chb71944@biglobe.ne.jp; f. 1919; 1,435 mems; linguistics; Pres. YAMASAKI SEIKÔ; Sec. ISINO YOSIO; publ. *La Revuo Orienta* (monthly).

Nihon Gengogakkai (Linguistic Society of Japan): Shimotachiuri Ogawa Higashi, Kami Kyoku, Kyoto 602-8048; fax (75) 415-3662; f. 1938; 2,050 mems; Pres. MASAYOSHI SHIBATANI; publ. *Gengo Kenkyu* (Journal, 2 a year).

Nihon Mass Communication Gakkai (Japanese Society for Studies in Journalism and Mass Communication): C/o Institute of Socio-Information and Communication Studies, University of Tokyo, 7-3-1 Hongo, Bunkyo-ku, Tokyo 113-0033; tel. (3) 3812-2111 ext. 5921; f. 1951; 1,300 mems; Pres. I. TAKEUCHI; publ. *Journal of Mass Communication Studies* (2 a year).

Nippon Bungaku Kyokai (Japanese Literature Association): 2-17-10 Minami-otsuka, Toshima-ku, Tokyo; tel. and fax (3) 3941-2740; f. 1946; 1,500 mems; library of 2,000 vols; Pres. KUNIAKI MITANI; publ. *Japanese Literature* (monthly).

Nippon Hikaku Bungakukai (Comparative Literature Society of Japan): Aoyamagakuin University, Shibuya-ku, Tokyo; f. 1948; 400 mems; Pres. K. NAKAJIMA; Gen. Sec. SABURO OTA; publs *Journal* (annually), *Bulletin* (quarterly).

Nippon Onsei Gakkai (Phonetic Society of Japan): 3-1 Sarugaku 1-chome, Chiyoda-ku, Tokyo 101; tel. (3) 3292-1718; f. 1926; study of sound phenomena of human speech; 780 mems; library of 30,000 vols; Pres. MIYOKO SUGITO; publ. *Bulletin* (3 a year).

Nippon Rosiya Bungakkai (Russian Literary Society in Japan): c/o Baba-ken, Tokyo Institute of Technology, 2-12-1 O-okayama, Meguro-ku, Tokyo 152; 380 mems; Pres. MASANOBU TOGO; Sec.-Gen. General T. EGAWA; publ. *Bulletin*.

Nippon Seiyo Koten Gakkai (Classical Society of Japan): Dept of Classics, Faculty of Letters, Kyoto Univ., Kyoto 606; f. 1950; 550 mems; Pres. NORIO FUJISAWA; publ. *Journal of Classical Studies* (annually).

MEDICINE

Japanese Society for the Study of Pain: Dept of Anaesthesia, Kyoto University, 54 Kawahara-cho Syogoin, Sakyo-ku, Kyoto 606-01; tel. (75) 751-3433; fax (75) 752-3259; f. 1973; research into pain mechanism and pain management; 698 mems; Sec.-Gen. Prof. K. MORI; publ. *Pain Research* (quarterly).

Nihon Eisei Gakkai (Japanese Society for Hygiene): Dept of Preventive Medicine and Public Health, Keio University School of Medicine, 35 Shinanomachi, Shinjuku-ku, Tokyo 160-8582; tel. (3) 3353-1211; fax (3) 3358-0614; f. 1902; 2,750 mems; Chief Officer Prof. HARUHIKO SAKURAI; publ. *Japanese Journal of Hygiene* (in Japanese, 4 a year), *Environmental Health and Preventive Medicine* (in English, 4 a year).

Nihon Hinyokika Gakki (Japanese Urological Association); Taisei Bldg, Hongo 3-14-10, Bunkyo-ku, Tokyo; f. 1912; 6,200 mems; Pres. Prof. KAZUKI KAWABE; publs *Japanese Journal of Urology* (monthly), *International Journal of Urology* (6 a year).

Nihon Ishi-Kai (Japan Medical Association): Bunkyo-ku, Tokyo 113; f. 1916; 121,514 mems; Pres. E. TSUBOI; publs *Journal* (in Japanese, fortnightly), *Asian Medical Journal* (in English, monthly).

Nihon Kakuigakukai (Japanese Society of Nuclear Medicine): c/o Japan Radioisotope Association, 28-45 Hon-Komagome 2-chome, Bunkyo-ku, Tokyo; f. 1963; 3,500 mems; Pres. JUNJI KONISHI; publ. *Japanese Journal of Nuclear Medicine* (monthly).

Nihon Koko Geka Gakkai (Japanese Society of Oral Surgeons): Tokyo Joshi Ika Daigaku, 10 Kawada-cho, Shinjuku-ku, Tokyo; f. 1952; 2,000 mems; Gen. Sec. M. MURASE; publ. *Japanese Journal of Oral Surgery* (quarterly).

Nihon Koku Eisei Gakkai (Japanese Society for Dental Health): c/o Koku Hoken Kyokai 44-2, Komagome 1-chome Toshima-ku, Tokyo 170; f. 1952; 2,000 mems; Pres. Y. SAKAKIBARA; publ. *Journal* (quarterly).

Nihon Kokuka Gakkai (Japanese Stomatological Society): Department of Oral Surgery, School of Medicine, University of Tokyo, 7-3-1 Hongo, Bunkyo-ku, Tokyo; tel. (3) 3815-5411; f. 1947; 3,600 mems; Dir ICHIRO YAMASHITA; publ. *Journal* (quarterly).

Nihon Kyosei Shikagakkai (Japan Orthodontic Society): c/o Koku Hoken Kyokai, 1-44-2 Komagome, Toshima-ku, Tokyo 170; tel. (3) 3947-8891; fax (3) 3947-8341; f. 1932; 4,200 mems; Pres. KAZUO YAMAUCHI; Vice-Pres. MASAYAKI SEBATA; publ. *Journal of the Japan Orthodontic Society* (every 2 months).

Nihon Masui Gakkai (Japan Society of Anaesthesiology): TY Bldg, 18-11 Hongo 3-chome, Bunkyo-ku, Tokyo 113; f. 1954; 3,711 mems; Pres. K. SHIMOJI; Sec. T. SATO; publs *Japanese Journal of Anaesthesiology* (monthly), *Journal of Anaesthesia* (quarterly).

Nihon Naika Gakkai (Japanese Society of Internal Medicine): Hongo Daiichi Bldg, 34-3, Hongo 3-chome, Bunkyo-ku, Tokyo 113; f. 1903; 73,000 mems; Chief Dir ICHIRO KANAZAWA; publs *Journal* (monthly in Japanese), *Internal Medicine* (monthly, English).

Nihon Ronen Igakukai (Japan Geriatrics Society): Kyorin Bldg No 702, 4-2-1 Yushima, Bunkyo-ku, Tokyo 113; f. 1959; 4,500 mems; Chair. Prof. H. ORIMO; publ. *Japan Journal of Geriatrics* (every 2 months).

Nihon Seishin Shinkei Gakkai (Japanese Society of Psychiatry and Neurology): c/o Hongo Sky Bldg 38-11, 3-chome, Hongo, Bunkyo-ku, Tokyo 113; 8,200 mems; Pres. MASAHIRO ASAI; publ *Seishin Shinkeigaku Zasshi* (Japanese, monthly).

Nihon Shika Hoshasen Gakkai (Japanese Society for Oral and Maxillofacial Radiology): C/o Hitotsubashi Printing Co. Ltd, Gakkai Business Center, 3-12-15 Kami-ohsaki, Shinagawa-ku, Tokyo 141-0021; tel. (3) 3441-3284; fax (3) 3441-3472; f. 1951; 1,200 mems; Sec.-Gen. H. FUCHIHATA; publs *Dental Radiology* (quarterly, in Japanese), *Oral Radiology* (in English, every 6 months).

Nihon Shonika Gakkai (Japan Paediatric Society): 4F Daiichi Magami Bldg, 1-1-5 Koraku, Bunkyo-ku Tokyo; tel. (3) 3818-0091; f. 1896; 16,100 mems; Pres. M. NISHIDA; publs *Pediatrics International* (in English every 2 months), *Journal of the Japan Paediatric Society* (in Japanese, monthly).

Nihon Syoyakugakkai (Japanese Society of Pharmacognosy): Business Center for Academic Societies, 4–16, Yayoi 2-chome, Bunkyo-ku, Tokyo 113; f. 1946; 1,027 mems; Pres. M. KONOSHIMA; publ. *Japanese Journal of Pharmacognosy* (quarterly).

Nihon Yakuri Gakkai (Japanese Pharmacological Society): Yayoi 2-4-16, Bunkyo-ku, Tokyo 113; tel. (3) 3814-4828; fax (3) 3814-4809; e-mail pharmacology@hi-ho.ne.jp; f. 1927; 6,500 mems; Chair. EISHICHI MIYAMOTO; publs *Folia Pharmacologica Japonica* (monthly), *Japanese Journal of Pharmacology* (monthly, in English).

Nippon Bitamin Gakkai (Vitamin Society of Japan): Nippon Italy Kyoto-Kaikan 3rd floor, 04-Ushinomiya-cho, Yoshida, Sakyo-ku, Kyoto 606-8302; f. 1947; 2,000 mems; Pres. Dr M. MINO; publs *Journal of Nutritional Science and Vitaminology* (English, every 2 months), *Vitamins* (Japanese, monthly).

Nippon Byorigakkai (Japanese Society of Pathology): New Akamon Bldg 4F, 2-40-9 Hongo, Bunkyo-ku, Tokyo 113-0033; f. 1911; 4,200 mems; Chair. RIKUO MACHINAMI; publs *Pathology International* (monthly in English), *Proceedings* (Japanese), *Annual of Pathological Autopsy Cases in Japan* (Japanese).

Nippon Gan Gakkai (Japanese Cancer Association): c/o Cancer Institute, Kami-Ikebukuro 1-37-1, Toshima-ku, Tokyo 170; tel. (3) 3918-0111, ext. 4231; fax (3) 3918-5776; f. 1907; 16,976 mems; Pres. Dr FUMIMATO TAKAKU; publs *Japanese Journal of Cancer Research (Gann,* monthly), *Gann Monograph on Cancer Research* (irregular).

Nippon Ganka Gakkai (Japanese Ophthalmological Society): 2-4-11-402, Sarugaku-cho, Chiyoda-ku, Tokyo 101; f. 1897; 8,800 mems; Pres. YASUO UEMURA; publ. *Acta Societatis Ophthalmologicae Japonicae* (monthly).

Nippon Geka Gakkai (Japan Surgical Society): Hakuoh Bldg, 2-3-10 Koraku, Bunkyo-ku, Tokyo; f. 1899; 37,405 mems; Pres. K. SUGIMACHI; publ. *Journal* (monthly).

Nippon Hifu-ka Gakkai (Japanese Dermatological Asscn): Taisei Bldg, 14-10 3-chome, Hongo, Bunkyo-ku, Tokyo; tel. (3) 3811-5099; fax (3) 3812-6790; f. 1901; 8,567 mems; Pres. S. HARADA; publs *Japanese Journal of Dermatology* (Japanese, 14 a year), *Journal of Dermatology* (English, monthly).

Nippon Hoi Gakkai (Medico-Legal Society of Japan): Department of Forensic Medicine, Faculty of Medicine, University of Tokyo, 7-3-1 Hongo, Bunkyo-ku, Tokyo 113; tel. (3) 5800-5416; f. 1914; 1,400 mems; Pres. SHOGO MISAWA; publ. *Japanese Journal of Legal Medicine* (every 2 months).

Nippon Hoshasen Eikyo Gakkai (Japan Radiation Research Society): National Institute of Radiological Sciences, 9-1 Anagawa-4, Inage-ku, Chiba 263-8555; tel. (43) 251-2111; fax (43) 251-9231; f. 1959; 1,095 mems; Pres. M. SASAKI; publ. *Journal of Radiation Research* (4 a year).

Nippon Hotetsu Shika Gakkai (Japan Prosthodontic Society): c/o Koku Hoken Kyokai, 1-44-2 Komagome, Toshima-ku, Tokyo; f. 1931; 6,000 mems; Pres. YOSHINORI KOBAYASHI; publ. *Journal* (every 2 months).

Nippon Igaku Hōshasen Gakkai (Japan Radiological Society): Room 301 Akamon Habitation, 5-29-13 Hongo, Bunkyo-ku, Tokyo; tel. (3) 3814-3077; fax (3) 5684-4075; f. 1923; 5,986 mems; Pres. Y. ONOYAMA; publ. *Nippon Acta Radiologica* (monthly).

Nippon Jibi-Inkoka Gakkai (Oto-Rhino-Laryngological Society of Japan): c/o Chateau-Takanawa 23-14, 3-chome Takanawa, Minato-ku, Tokyo; tel. (3) 3443-3085; fax (3) 3443-3037; f. 1893; 10,000 mems; Pres. ATSUSHI KOMATSUZAKI; publ. *Journal of Otolaryngology of Japan* (monthly).

Nippon Junkan-ki Gakkai (Japanese Circulation Society): Kinki Invention Center, 14 Yoshida Kawahara-cho, Sakyo-ku, Kyoto 606-8305; tel. (75) 751-8643; fax (75) 771-3060; f. 1935; cardiology; 19,828 mems; Chief Dir YOSHIO YAZAKI; publ. *Japanese Circulation Journal* (monthly in English, 2 or 3 a year in Japanese).

Nippon Kaibo Gakkai (Japanese Association of Anatomists): c/o Business Center for Academic Societies Japan, 5-16-9 Honkomagome, Bunkyo-ku, Tokyo 113; f. 1893; 2,700 mems; Pres. Dr SHIGEO UCHINO; publ. *Kaibogaku Zasshi, Acta Anatomica Nipponica* (every 2 months).

Nippon Kansenshoh Gakkai (Japanese Association for Infectious Diseases): Sankei 8 Bldg 6F, 1-8-7 Ebisu, Shibuya-ku, Tokyo 150; tel (03) 3473-5095; fax (3) 3442-1196; f. 1926; 5,300 mems; Pres. KAORU SHIMADA; publ. *The Journal* (monthly).

Nippon Kekkaku-byo Gakkai (Japanese Society for Tuberculosis): 1-24, Matsuyama 3-chome, Kiyose-shi, Tokyo 204-0022; tel. 0424-92-2091; fax 0424-91-8315; f. 1925; 2,750 mems; Chair. Dr K. AOKI; publ. *Kekkaku* (monthly).

Nippon Ketsueki Gakkai (Japanese Society of Haematology): C/o Kinki Chiho Invention Center, 14 Kawahara-cho, Yoshida, Sakyo-ku, Kyoto 606; tel. (75) 752-2844; fax (75) 752-2842; f. 1937; 6,066 mems; Pres. F. TAKAKU; publ. *International Journal of Hematology* (8 a year with 2 supplements).

Nippon Kikan-Shokudo-ka Gakkai (Japan Broncho-Esophagological Society): 5th Floor, Hakuo Bldg, 2-3-10 Koraku, Bunkyo-ku, Tokyo 112-0004; tel. (3) 3818-3030; fax (3) 3815-2810; e-mail kishoku@hi-ho.ne.jp; f. 1949; 3,600 mems; Dir Dr Y. MURAKAMI; publ. *Journal* (every 2 months).

Nippon Kisei-chu Gakkai (Japanese Society of Parasitology): Institute of Medical Science, University of Tokyo, Minato-ku, Tokyo 108; f. 1926; 998 mems; Sec. Prof. S. KOJIMA; publ. *Parasitology International* (4 a year).

Nippon Koshu-Eisei Kyokai (Japan Public Health Asscn): Koei Building, 29–8, Shinjuku 1-chome, Shinjuku-ku, Tokyo; f. 1883; 5,000 mems; Pres. MINORU SEIJO; publs *Japanese Journal of Public Health, Public Health Information* (monthly).

Nippon Naibumpigaku-Kai Tobu-bukai (Eastern Branch of Japan Endocrinological Society): c/o Department of Urology, School of Medicine, Gumma University, Maebashi; f. 1954; 1,300 mems; Pres. K. SHIDA; publ. *Endocrinologia Japonica* (every 2 months in English, German, French).

Nippon No-Shinkei Geka Gakkai (Japan Neurosurgical Society): Akamon-mae Iwata Bldg 2F, 5-27-8 Hongo, Bunkyo-ku, Tokyo; tel. (3) 3812-6226; fax (3) 3812-2090; f. 1948; 6,700 mems; Chair. T. HAYAKAWA; publs *Neurologia medico-Chirurgica* (monthly in English).

Nippon Rai Gakkai (Japanese Leprosy Association): 4-2-1, Aoba-cho, Higashi-murayama-shi, Tokyo 189; tel. (423) 91-8211; fax (423) 94-9092; f. 1927; 355 mems; Pres. TOSHIHARU OZAWA; publ. *Japanese Journal of Leprosy* (every 4 months).

Nippon Saikingakkai (Japanese Society for Bacteriology): C/o Oral Health Association of Japan, 1-44-2 Komagome, Toshima-ku, Tokyo 170; f. 1927; 3,400 mems; Pres. Dr MASANOSUKE YOSHIKAWA; publ. *Japanese Journal of Bacteriology* (4 a year), *Microbiology and Immunology* (monthly).

Nippon Sanka-Fujinka Gakkai (Japan Society of Obstetrics and Gynaecology): c/o Hoken Kaikan Bldg, 1-1, Sadohara-cho, Ichigaya, Shinjuku-ku, Tokyo 162; f. 1949; 16,100 mems; Pres. Prof. AKIRA YAJIMA; publ. *Acta Obstetrica et Gynaecologica Japonica* (monthly).

Nippon Seikei Geka Gakkai (Japanese Orthopaedic Association): 2-40-17, Hongo, Bunkyo-ku, Tokyo 113-8418; f. 1926; 18,000 mems; Pres. Prof. TAKAHIDE KUROKAWA; publs *Journal* (6 a year), *Journal of Orthopaedic Science* (in English, 6 a year).

Nippon Seiri Gakkai (Physiological Society of Japan): Fuse Bldg, Hongo 3-30-10, Bunkyo-ku, Tokyo 113; f. 1922; 3,700 mems; Pres. M. ITO; publ. *Journal*.

Nippon Shika Hozon Gakkai (Japanese Society of Conservative Dentistry): Tokyo Dental Univ., 1 Misaki-cho Kanda, Chiyoda-ku, Tokyo; f. 1955; 826 mems; Pres. E. SEKINE; publ. *Journal* (2 a year).

Nippon Shika Igakkai (Japanese Association for Dental Science): 4-1-20 Kudan-kita, Chiyoda-ku, Tokyo; tel. (3) 3262-9214; fax (3) 3262-9885; f. 1949; 80,000 mems; 14 mem. societies; Pres. Prof. H. SEKINE; publs *Journal* (annually, in Japanese), *Dentistry in Japan* (annually).

Nippon Shinkei Gakkai (Japanese Society of Neurology): Ichimaru Building 2-31-21 Yushima, Bunkyo-ku, Tokyo 113; f. 1960; 6,895 mems; Chair. NOBUO YANAGISAWA; publ. *Clinical Neurology* (monthly).

Nippon Shinkeikagaku Gakkai (Japan Neuroscience Society): Business Center for Academic Societies, 5-16-9 Honkomagome, Bunkyo-ku, Tokyo 113; f. 1974; 2,750 mems; Pres. M. ITO; publs *News, Neuroscience Research* (6 a year).

Nippon Shokaki-byo Gakkai (Japanese Society of Gastroenterology): Ginza Orient Bldg, Ginza 8-9-13, Chuo-ku, Tokyo; tel. (3) 3573-4297; fax (3) 3289-2359; f. 1898; 25,000 mems; Pres. TADASU TSUJII; publs *Nihon Shokaki-byo Gakkai Zasshi* (Japanese, monthly), *Journal of Gastroenterology* (English, 6 a year).

Nippon Teiinoshujutsu Kenkyukai (Japanese Society for Stereotactic and Functional Neurosurgery): Dept of Neurological Surgery, Nihon University, 30-1 Ohyaguchi Kamimachi, Itabashi-ku, Tokyo 173; tel. (3) 3972-8111, ext. 2481; fax (3) 3554-0425; f. 1963; 484 mems; Sec.-Gen. Prof. T. TSUBOKAWA; publ. *Functional Neurosurgery* (annually).

Nippon Tonyo-byo Gakkai (Japan Diabetes Society): 3-38-11 Hongo Sky Bldg, Room 403, Hongo, Bunkyo-ku, Tokyo 113; f. 1958; 9,750 mems; Pres. KAHEJIRO YAMASHITA; publ. *Journal* (monthly).

Nippon Uirusu Gakkai (Society of Japanese Virologists): Business Centre for Academic Societies, 5-16-9 Honkomagome, Bunkyo-ku, Tokyo 113; f. 1953; 3,000 mems; Pres. Dr HIROSHI YOSHIKURA; publs *Virus* (Japanese text with English summary, 2 a year), *Microbiology and Immunology* (monthly).

Nippon Yakugaku-Kai (Pharmaceutical Society of Japan): 12-15-201, Shibuya 2-chome, Shibuya-ku, Tokyo; tel. (3) 3406-3321; fax (3) 3498-1835; e-mail gigy_win@pharm.or.jp; f. 1880; 21,541 mems; Pres. O. YONEMITSU; Exec. Dir M. OHZEKI; publs *Farumashia* (monthly), *Chemical and Pharmaceutical Bulletin* (monthly), *Japanese Journal of Toxicology and Environmental Health* (6 a year), *Biological and Pharmaceutical Bulletin* (monthly).

Nippon Yuketsu Gakkai (Japan Society of Blood Transfusion): Nisseki Chuo-Ketsueki Center, 1-31 4 Hiroo, Shibuya-ku, Tokyo; f. 1954; 1,969 mems; Pres. H. TOHYAMA; publ. *Journal* (every 2 months).

NATURAL SCIENCES

General

Nihon Kagakushi Gakkai (History of Science Society of Japan): c/o West Pine Bldg 201, 2-15-19 Hirakawa-cho, Chiyoda-ku, Tokyo 102; f. 1941; 1,000 mems; Pres. T. KIKUCHI; publs *Kagakushi Kenkyu* (quarterly), *Historia Scientiarum* (3 a year).

Biological Sciences

Hassei Seibutsu Gakkai (Japanese Society of Developmental Biologists): Department of Life Science (Biology), University of Tokyo, 3-8-1 Komaba, Meguro-ku, Tokyo 153; tel. (3) 5454-6632; fax (3) 3485-2904; f. 1968; 1,320 mems; Pres. M. OKADA; publ. *Development, Growth and Differentiation* (every 2 months, English).

Nihon Jinrui Iden Gakkai (Japan Society of Human Genetics): Dept of Human Genetics, Tokyo Medical and Dental University, 1-5-45 Yushima, Bunkyo-ku, Tokyo; tel. (3) 3813-6111; f. 1956; 1,046 mems; Pres. E. MATSUNAGA; publ. *Journal* (quarterly).

Nihon Kairui Gakkai (Malacological Society of Japan): National Science Museum, 3-23-1, Hyakunin-cho, Shinjuku-ku, Tokyo 169-0073; tel. (3) 3364-7124; f. 1928; scientific research on molluscs; 900 mems; Pres. T. OKUTANI; publs *Venus* (quarterly), *Chiribotan* (in Japanese with English abstract, quarterly).

Nihon Kontyû Gakkai (Entomological Society of Japan): c/o Dept of Zoology, National Science Museum (Natural History), 3-23-1 Hyakunin-chô, Shinjuku, Tokyo 169; f. 1917; 1,300 mems; Pres. M. SASAKAWA; publ. *Japanese Journal of Entomology* (quarterly).

Nihon Mendel Kyokai (Japan Mendel Society): Editorial and Business Office, Cytologia, c/o Toshin Bldg, Hongo 2-27-2, Bunkyo-ku, Tokyo 113; f. 1929; 1,100 mems; Pres. T. IINO; publ. *Cytologia* (4 a year).

Nippon Chô Gakkai (Ornithological Society of Japan): C/o Laboratory of Wildlife Ecology, University of Agriculture and Veterinary Medicine, Inada, Obihiro 080-8555; f. 1912; 1,000 mems; library of 600 vols; Pres. Y. FUJIMAKI; publ. *Japanese Journal of Ornithology* (quarterly).

Nippon Dobutsu Gakkai (Zoological Society of Japan): Toshin Bldg, Hongo 2-27-2, Bunkyo-ku, Tokyo 113; f. 1878; 2,610 mems; Pres. KOSCAK MARUYAMA; publ. *Zoological Science* (6 a year).

Nippon Eisei-Dobutsu Gakkai (Japanese Society of Medical Entomology and Zoology): C/o Dept of Environmental Biology, Japan Environmental Sanitation Center 10-6 Yotsuyakami-cho, Kawasaki-ku, Kawasaki 210; tel. (44) 288-4878; fax (44) 288-5016; f. 1943; 650 mems; Pres. Dr YOSHITO WADA; publ. *Medical Entomology and Zoology* (4 a year).

Nippon Iden Gakkai (Genetics Society of Japan): National Institute of Genetics, 1, 111 Yata, Mishima 411-8540, Shizuoka; f. 1920; 1,500 mems; Pres. M. SEKIGUCHI; publs *Fukuoka Dental College* (6 a year).

Nippon Kin Gakkai (Mycological Society of Japan): c/o Business Center for Academic Societies Japan, 16-9 Honkomagome 5-chome, Bunkyo-ku, Tokyo 113; tel. (3) 5814-5801; fax (3) 5814-5820; f. 1956; 1,600 mems; Pres. MAKOTO MIYAJI; publs *Mycoscience* (quarterly), *Nippon Kingakukai Kaiho* (quarterly).

Nippon Kumo Gakkai (Arachnological Society of Japan): c/o Biological Laboratory, Otemon Gakuin University, 2-1-15, Nishi-Ai, Ibaraki, Osaka 567; tel. (726) 43-5421; fax (726) 43-5427; f. 1936; 340 mems; Pres. Dr Y. NISHIKAWA; publ. *Acta Arachnologica* (2 a year).

Nippon Oyo-Dobutsu-Konchu Gakkai (Japanese Society of Applied Entomology and Zoology): c/o Japan Plant Protection Asscn, 43-11, 1-chome, Komagome, Toshima-ku, Tokyo 170; f. 1957; 2,000 mems; Pres. YOSHIO TAMAKI; publs *Applied Entomology and Zoology* (in English, quarterly), *Japanese Journal of Applied Entomology and Zoology* (Japanese with English synopsis, quarterly).

Nippon Rikusui Gakkai (Japanese Society of Limnology): Nagoya Women's University, 3-40 Shioji-cho, Mizuho-ku, Nagoya 467; tel. (52) 852-1111 ext. 254; fax (52) 852-7470; f. 1931; 1,300 mems; Pres. Prof. T. OKINO; Gen. Sec. Prof. A. YAGI; publ. *Japanese Journal of Limnology* (4 a year).

Nippon Seibutsu Kankyo Chosetsu Kenkyukai (Japanese Society of Environment Control in Biology): Faculty of Agriculture, University of Tokyo, Yayoi 1-1-1, Bunkyo-ku, Tokyo 113; fax (3) 3813-2437; f. 1963; 1,090 mems; Pres. T. TAKAKURA; publ. *Seibutsu Kankyo Chosetsu* (quarterly).

Nippon Seitai Gakkai (Ecological Society of Japan): C/o Dept of Biology, University of Tokyo, Komaba, Meguro-ku, Tokyo 153; tel. and fax (3) 5454-4322; e-mail cmatsu@komaba.ecc.u-tokyo.ac.jp; f. 1949; research in all aspects of ecology; 2,500 mems; Pres. Y. OSHIMA; Sec.-Gen. M. NISHIHIRA; publs *Japanese Journal of Ecology* (3 a year, in Japanese with English summary), *Ecological Research* (3 a year, in English).

Nippon Shokubutsu Gakkai (Botanical Society of Japan): c/o Toshin Building, 2-chome 27-2 Hongo, Bunkyo-ku, Tokyo; tel. (3) 3814-5675; f. 1882; 2,300 mems; Pres. A. KOMAMINE; publs *Journal of Plant Research* (4 a year).

Nippon Shokubutsu Seiri Gakkai (Japanese Society of Plant Physiologists): Shimotachiuri Ogawa Higashi, Kamikyoku, Kyoto 602; f. 1959; 3,170 mems; Pres. KOZI ASADA; publ. *Plant and Cell Physiology* (monthly).

Shokubutsu Bunrui Chiri Gakkai (Phytogeographical Society): Kyoto University Museum, Kyoto 606-8501; tel. (75) 753-3284; fax (75) 753-3276; e-mail nagamasu@inet.museum.kyoto-u.ac.jp; f. 1932; 500 mems; plant taxonomy and phytogeography; Pres. NOBUYUKI FUKUOKA; Sec. HIDETOSHI NAGAMASU; publ. *Acta Phytotaxonomica et Geobotanica* (2 a year).

Mathematical Sciences

Nippon Sugaku Kai (Mathematical Society of Japan): 25-9-203, Hongo 4-chome, Bunkyo-ku, Tokyo 113-0033; f. 1877; 5,000 mems; Pres. YUKIHIKO NAMIKAWA; publs *Journal, Sugaku, Sugaku-Tsushin* (4 a year), *Publications of the Mathematical Society of Japan* (irregular), *Japanese Journal of Mathematics* (2 a year), *MSJ Memoirs* (irregular).

Physical Sciences

Butsuri Tansa Gakkai (Society of Exploration Geophysicists of Japan): San-es Bldg, 2-2-18 Nakamagome, Ota-ku, Tokyo; f. 1948; 1,420 mems; Pres. T. KAWAMURA; publ. *Butsuri Tansa* (Geophysical Exploration, every 2 months).

Chigaku Dantai Kenkyu-kai (Association for Geological Collaboration in Japan): Kawai Bldg, 2–24–1, Minami-Ikebukuro, Toshima-ku, Tokyo 171; tel. (3) 3983-3378; fax (3) 3983-7525; e-mail chidanken@tokyo.email.ne.jp; f. 1947; study of geology, mineralogy, palaeontology and related earth sciences; 2,800 mems; Pres. TAKAYUKI KAWABE; Sec. TADAO KOBAYASHI; publs *Sokuhō* (News, monthly), *Chikyu-Kagaku* (Earth Science, 6 a year) *Senpō* (Monograph, irregular).

Chikyu-Denjiki Chikyu-Wakuseiken Gakkai (Society of Geomagnetism and Earth, Planetary and Space Science): c/o Business Centre for Academic Societies, 5-16-9 Honkomagome, Bunkyo-ku, Tokyo 113; f. 1947; frmly Nippon Chikyu Denki Ziki Gakkai; 750 mems; Pres. Prof. MASARU KONO; publ. *Earth, Planets and Space* (monthly).

Ikomasan Tenmon Kyokai (Ikomasan Astronomical Society): Ikoma-Sanzyo, Ikoma-gun, Nara Ken; f. 1942; 705 mems; Pres. JOE UETA; Sec. H. HAMANE; publ. *Tenmon Kyositu* (Astronomical Class, monthly).

Japan Weather Association: Research Institute, Kaiji Center Bldg, 5, 4-chome, Kojimachi, Chiyoda-ku, Tokyo; f. 1950; Pres. NAOSHI MACHIDA; publs *Kisho, Daily Weather Maps, Journal of Meterological Research* (monthly), *Geophysical Magazine, Oceanographical Magazine* (quarterly).

Kaiyoo Kisho Gakkai (Oceanographical and Meteorological Society): 7-chome, Ikutaku, Kobe; f. 1921; 310 mems; Pres. HAYATO OIDA; publ. *Sea and Sky* (every 2 months).

Kobunshi Gakkai (Society of Polymer Science, Japan): 3 Nagaoka Building, 2-4-2 Tsukiji, Chuo-ku, Tokyo 104-0045; tel. (3) 3543-

3765; fax (3) 3545-8560; e-mail kokusai@spsj.or.jp; f. 1951; 12,680 mems; Pres. M. KAMACHI; publs *Kobunshi* (monthly), *Kobunshi Ronbunshu* (monthly), *Polymer Journal* (monthly in English), *Polymer Preprints, Japan* (2 a year).

Nihon Bunseki Kagaku-Kai (Japan Society for Analytical Chemistry): Gotanda Sanhaitsu, 26-2, Nishigotanda 1-chome, Shinagawa-ku, Tokyo 141; f. 1952; 9,108 mems; Pres. M. TANAKA; Sec.-Gen. Dr TADASHI FUJINUKI; publs *Bunseki Kagaku* (monthly), *Bunseki* (monthly), *Analytical Sciences* (every 2 months).

Nihon Ganseki Kobutsu Kosho Gakkai (Japanese Association of Mineralogists, Petrologists and Economic Geologists): Faculty of Science, Tohoku University, Sendai 980-8578; tel. and fax (22) 224-3852; e-mail kyl04223@nifty.ne.jp; f. 1929; 1,000 mems; library of 17,000 vols; Pres. SATOSHI KANISAWA; publ. *Journal of Mineralogy, Petrology and Economic Geology* (monthly).

Nihon Nensho Gakkai (Combustion Society of Japan): c/o Department of Aeronautics and Astronautics, Faculty of Engineering, University of Tokyo, Bunkyo-ku, Tokyo 113-8656; tel. (3) 3812-2111; f. 1953; 558 mems; Pres. T. NIIOKA; publ. *Nensho Kenkyu* (4 a year).

Nihon Nogyo-Kisho Gakkai (Society of Agricultural Meteorology of Japan): C/o Dept of Agricultural Engineering, University of Tokyo, Yayoi, Bunkyo, Tokyo 113; tel. (3) 3812-2111, ext. 5355; fax (3) 3813-2437; f. 1942; study of protected cultivation, agricultural meteorology and resources of food production; 1,300 mems; Pres. ZENBEI UCHIJIMA; publ. *Nogyo-Kisho* (Journal of Agricultural Meteorology, quarterly).

Nihon Seppyo Gakkai (Japanese Society of Snow and Ice): Room 207, Belvedere-kudan, Fujimi 2-15-5, Chiyoda-ku, Tokyo 102; tel. (3) 3261-2339; fax (3) 3262-1923; f. 1939; 1,150 mems; Pres. Dr GOROW WAKAHAMA; publs *Seppyo* (Journal of the Japanese Society of Snow and Ice, 6 a year in Japanese and English), *Bulletin of Glacier Research* (annually in English), occasional papers and bibliography.

Nippon Bunko Gakkai (Spectroscopical Society of Japan): c/o Industrial Hall, 1-13, Kanda-Awaji-cho, Chiyoda-ku, Tokyo 101; tel. (3) 3253-2747; fax (3) 3253-2740; f. 1951; 1,200 mems; Pres. M. TASUMI; Sec. Y. F. MIBUGAI; publ. *Journal* (every 2 months).

Nippon Butsuri Gakkai (Physical Society of Japan): Room No. 211, Kikai-Shinko Bldg, 3-5-8 Shiba-Koen, Minato-ku, Tokyo 105; tel. (3) 3434-2671; fax (3) 3432-0997; f. 1946; 19,284 mems; Pres. K. SATO; publs *Butsuri* (monthly, in Japanese), *Journal of the Physical Society of Japan* (monthly), *Japanese Journal of Applied Physics* (Part 1: monthly, Part 2: fortnightly), *Progress of Theoretical Physics* (monthly).

Nippon Chishitsu Gakkai (Geological Society of Japan): Maruishi Bldg, 10-4, Kajicho 1-chome, Chiyoda-ku, Tokyo 101; tel. (3) 3252-7242; fax (3) 5256-5676; f. 1893; stratigraphy, petrology, tectonics, volcanology, etc; 5,278 mems; 10,000 vols; Pres. HAKUYU OKADA; publ. *Journal* (monthly).

Nippon Dai-Yonki Gakkai (Japan Association for Quaternary Research): c/o Business Center for Academic Societies, Honkomagome 5-16-9, Bunkyo-ku, Tokyo 113; tel. (3) 5814-5801; fax (3) 5814-5820; f. 1956; 2,000 mems; Pres. KIYOTAKA CHINZEI; publ. *Quaternary Research* (5 a year).

Nippon Denshi Kenbikyo Gakkai (Japanese Society of Electron Microscopy): c/o Business Centre for Academic Societies, 4-16 Yayoi 2-chome, Bunkyo-ku, Tokyo 113; f. 1949; 2,690 mems; Pres. KAZUO OGAWA; publ. *Journal* (quarterly).

Nippon Kagakukai (Chemical Society of Japan): 5, 1-chome, Kanda-Surugadai, Chiyoda-ku, Tokyo 101-0062; f. 1878; 39,000 mems; Pres. TADASU TACHI; Exec. Dir ATSUO NAKANISHI; publs *Kagaku to Kogyo, Kagaku to Kyoiku, Nippon Kagaku Kaishi, Chemistry Letters, Bulletin of the Chemical Society of Japan* (monthly).

Nippon Kaisui Gakkai (Society of Sea Water Science, Japan): c/o Japan Salt Industry Association, 7-15-14, Roppongi, Minato-ku, Tokyo; f. 1950; 485 mems; Pres. SHOJI KIMURA; publ. *Journal*.

Nippon Kaiyo Gakkai (Oceanographic Society of Japan): MK Bldg No. 202, 1-6-14 Minamidai, Nakano-ku, Tokyo 164; tel. (3) 3377-3951; fax (3) 3378-9419; f. 1941; 2,044 mems; Pres. KEISUKE TAIRA; publs *Journal of Oceanography* (6 a year), *Umi no Kenkyu* (6 a year).

Nippon Kazan Gakkai (Volcanological Society of Japan): Earthquake Research Institute, University of Tokyo, 1 Yayoi-cho, Bunkyo-ku, Tokyo; tel. (3) 3813-7421; f. 1932; 1,086 mems; Pres. KENICHIRO AOKI; publs *Bulletin* (quarterly), *Bulletin of Volcanic Eruptions* (annually).

Nippon Kessho Gakkai (Crystallographic Society of Japan): Cosmos Hongo Bldg 8F, 4-1-4 Hongo, Bunkyo-ku, Tokyo 113; tel. (3) 3815-8514; fax (3) 3815-8529; f. 1950; 1,000 mems; Pres. HITOSHI IWASAKI; publ. *Journal* (every 2 months).

Nippon Kisho Gakkai (Meteorological Society of Japan): c/o Japan Meteorological Agency, Ote-machi, Chiyoda-ku, Tokyo; f. 1882; 4,300 mems; Pres. T. ASAI; publs *Tenki* (monthly), *Journal* (every 2 months).

Nippon Kokai Gakkai (Japan Institute of Navigation): c/o Tokyo University of Mercantile Marine, 2-1-6 Etchujima, Koto-ku, Tokyo; f. 1948; 933 mems; Pres. Prof. T. YAMADA; publs *Journal* (2 a year), *Navigation* (quarterly).

Nippon Koseibutsu Gakkai (Palaeontological Society of Japan): c/o Business Centre for Academic Societies, 5-16-9 Honkomagome, Bunkyo-ku, Tokyo 113; f. 1935; 1,050 mems; Pres. NORIYUKI IKEYA; publs *Paleontological Research* (4 a year), *Fossils* (2 a year).

Nippon Onkyo Gakkai (Acoustical Society of Japan): 4th Floor, Ikeda Bldg 7-7, Yoyogi 2 chome, Shibuya-ku, Tokyo; tel. (3) 3379-1200; fax (3) 3379-1456; f. 1936; 3,600 mems; Pres. T. SONE; publs *Journal* (monthly), *Reports of Spring and Autumn Meetings* (2 a year).

Nippon Sokuchi Gakkai (Geodetic Society of Japan): Geographical Survey Institute, 1 Kitasato, Tsukuba-shi, Ibaraki 305-0811; f. 1954; studies astronomy, crustal activity, earth tide, geodesy, geomagnetism, gravity, etc; 600 mems; library of 5,000 vols; Pres. TORAO TANAKA; publ. *Journal* (4 a year).

Nippon Temmon Gakkai (Astronomical Society of Japan): National Astronomical Observatory, Osawa Mitaka, Tokyo; f. 1908; 2,640 mems; Pres. Y. UCHIDA; publs *Publications* (every two months), *The Astronomical Herald* (monthly in Japanese).

Nippon Yukagaku Kai (Japan Oil Chemists' Society): 7th Floor, Yushi Kogyo Kaikan, 13-11, Nihonbashi 3-chome, Chūo-ku, Tokyo 103-0027; tel. (3) 3271-7463; fax (3) 3271-7464; e-mail yukagaku@blue.ocn.ne.jp; f. 1951; 2,426 mems; Pres. TORU TAKAGI; publ. *Journal* (monthly).

Sen-i Gakkai (Society of Fibre Science and Technology, Japan): 3-3-9-208 Kamiosaki, Shinagawa-ku, Tokyo 141; f. 1943; *c.* 3,000 mems; Pres. HIROSHI INAGAKI; publ. *Journal* (monthly).

Shokubai Gakkai (Catalysis Society of Japan): Shin-Ikeda-yama Mansions, Room 302, 5-21-13, Higashi-Gotanda, Shinagawa-ku, Tokyo 141; tel. (3) 3444-2126; fax (3) 3444-8794; f. 1958; 2,370 mems; Pres. Y. MOROOKA; publ. *Shokubai* (Catalyst, 8 a year).

Zisin Gakkai (Seismological Society of Japan): Earthquake Research Institute, The University of Tokyo, Yayoi 1-1-1 Bunkyo-ku, Tokyo; tel. (3) 3813-7421; fax (3) 5684-2549; f. 1929; 1,700 mems; Chair. MASATAKA AMDO; publs *Zisin* (Journal, quarterly), *Journal of Physics of the Earth* (every 2 months).

PHILOSOPHY AND PSYCHOLOGY

Bigaku-Kai (Japanese Society for Aesthetics): Faculty of Arts and Letters, Seijo University, Seijo 6-1-20, Setagaya-ku, Tokyo 157; f. 1950; 1,500 mems; Pres. KEIJI ASANUMA; publ. *Bigaku* (quarterly, in Japanese), *Aesthetics* (every 2 years).

Moralogy Kenkyusho (Institute of Moralogy): 1-1, 2-chome, Hikarigaoka, Kashiwa-shi, Chiba-ken; f. 1926; Pres. M. HIROIKE; publs *Studies in Moralogy* (2 a year).

Nihon Oyo Shinri-gakkai (Japan Association of Applied Psychology): Dept of Psychology, College of Humanities and Sciences, Nihon University, 3-25-40 Sakurajosui, Setagaya-ku, Tokyo; tel. (3) 3329-1151; f. 1931; Pres. HARUO YAMAMOTO; Sec. KENSUKE MURAI.

Nihon Rinrigakukai (Japanese Society for Ethics): Department of Ethics, Faculty of Letters, The University of Tokyo, Bunkyo-ku, Tokyo 113; f. 1950; 800 mems; Pres. YÔKICHI YAZIMA; publs *Rinrigakunenpo* (Annals), *Rinrigakukaironshu* (Transactions of annual meeting).

Nippon Dobutsu Shinri Gakkai (Japanese Society for Animal Psychology): Institute of Psychology, University of Tsukuba, 1-1-1 Tennoudai, Tsukuba-shi 305-8572; tel. and fax (298) 53-4720; f. 1933; 450 mems; Pres. SHIGEHISA SEKIGUCHI; publ. *The Japanese Journal of Animal Psychology* (2 a year).

Nippon Shakai Shinri Gakkai (Japanese Society of Social Psychology): Department of Psychology, Tokyo Woman's Christian University, 2-6-1, Zempukuji, Suginami-ku, Tokyo 167-8585; f. 1960; 1,450 mems; Pres. T. KINOSHITA; publs *Japanese Journal of Social Psychology, Bulletin* (4 a year).

Nippon Shinrigakkai (Japanese Psychological Association): 5-23-13-7F, Hongo, Bunkyo-ku, Tokyo 113; tel. (3) 3814-3953; fax (3) 3814-3954; f. 1927; 5,700 mems; Pres. TOSHITAKA TANAKA; publs *Japanese Journal of Psychology* (every 2 months), *Japanese Psychological Research* (quarterly).

Tetsugaku-kai (Philosophical Society): Faculty of Letters, University of Tokyo, Hongo, Bunkyo-ku, Tokyo 113; f. 1884; 500 mems; Pres. JUICHI KATSURA; publ. *Tetsugaku-zasshi* (annually).

RELIGION, SOCIOLOGY AND ANTHROPOLOGY

Nihon Indogaku Bukkyôgakukai (Japanese Association of Indian and Buddhist Studies): c/o Dept of Indian Philosophy and Buddhist Studies, Graduate School of Humanities and Sociology, University of Tokyo, Bunkyo-ku, Tokyo 113; f. 1951; 2,350 mems; Pres. YASUNORI EJIMA; publ. *Indogaku Bukkyôgaku Kenkyû* (Journal of Indian and Buddhist Studies).

Nihon Shūkyō Gakkai (Japanese Association for Religious Studies): 1-29-7-205 Hongo, Bunkyo-ku, Tokyo 113; tel. (3) 5684-5473; fax (3) 5684-5474; f. 1930; 2,000 mems; Pres. FUJIO IKADO; publ. *Journal of Religious Studies* (4 a year).

Nippon Dokyo Gakkai (Japan Society of Taoistic Research): Kansai University, Faculty of Letters, 3-35 Yamate-cho 3-chome, Suita-shi, Osaka 564-8680; tel. (6) 368-0326; f. 1950; 650 mems; Pres. Y. SAKADE; publ. *Journal of Eastern Religions* (2 a year).

Nippon Jinruigaku Kai (Anthropological Society of Nippon): Business Center for Academic Societies, 5-16-9 Honkomagome, Bunkyo-ku, Tokyo 113; tel. (3) 5814-5801; fax (3) 5814-5820; f. 1884; 1,050 mems; Pres. HIDEMI ISHIDA; publ. *Anthropological Science* (6 a year).

Nippon Shakai Gakkai (Japanese Sociological Society): Department of Sociology, Faculty of Letters, The University of Tokyo, Bunkyo-ku, Tokyo 113-0033; tel. (3) 3812-2111; f. 1923; 2,800 mems; Pres. OTOHIKO HASUMI; publs *Shakaigaku Hyóron* (quarterly), *International Journal of Japanese Sociology* (annually in English).

Shibusawa, K., Memorial Foundation for Ethnological Studies: Higashicho 3-1-17, Hoya-shi, Tokyo; f. 1935; 900 mems; library of 14,000 vols; Dir NAKANE CHIE; publs *Newsletter, Cultural Anthropology.*

Tōhō Gakkai (Institute of Eastern Culture): 4-1, Nishi Kanda 2-chome, Chiyoda-ku, Tokyo 101-0065; tel. (3) 3262-7221; fax (3) 3262-7227; f. 1947; Asian studies; 1,600 mems; Chair. MASAAKI HATTORI; Sec.-Gen. HIROSHI YANASE; publs *Acta Asiatica* (2 a year), *Tōhōgaku* (2 a year), *Transactions of the International Conference of Eastern Studies* (1 a year).

TECHNOLOGY

Denki Gakkai (Institute of Electrical Engineers of Japan): 1-12-1, Yurakucho, Chiyoda-ku, Tokyo 100; tel. (3) 3201-0983; f. 1888; 26,000 mems; 9 brs; Pres. HISAO OKA; publs *Journal* (monthly), *Transactions* (section J, monthly, Japanese).

Denshi Joho Tsushin Gakkai (Institute of Electronics, Information and Communication Engineers): Kikai-Shinko-Kaikan Bldg, 5-8, Shibakoen 3-chome, Minato-ku, Tokyo 105; tel. (3) 3433-6691; fax (3) 3433-6659; f. 1917; 40,000 mems; Pres. HISASHI KANEKO; publs *Journal, Transactions* (11 series, incl. *Original Contributions in English and Abstracts in English from the Transactions,* monthly).

Doboku-Gakkai (Japan Society of Civil Engineers): Yotsuya 1-chome, Shinjuku-ku, Tokyo; tel. (3) 3355-3441; fax (3) 5379-0125; f. 1914; 38,278 mems; library of 45,000 vols; Pres. Prof. Dr HIROSHI OKADA; Exec. Dir. ITSUJI MIYOSHI; publs *Journal, Coastal Engineering in Japan* (in English, 2 a year), *Proceedings* (monthly).

Doshitsu Kogakkai (Japanese Society of Soil Mechanics and Foundation Engineering): Sugayama Bldg 4F, Kanda Awaji-cho 2-23, Chiyoda-ku, Tokyo; tel. (3) 3251-7661; fax (3) 3251-6688; f. 1949; 13,000 mems; Pres. YOSHIAKI YOSHIMI; publs *Soils and Foundations* (quarterly), *Tsuchi to Kiso* (monthly).

Keikinzoku Gakkai (Japanese Institute of Light Metals): Nihonbashi Asahiseimei Bldg, 1-3, Nihonbashi 2 chome, Chuo-ku, Tokyo 103; tel. (3) 3275-3688; fax (3) 3213-2918; f. 1951; 1,985 mems; Pres. KENICHI HIRANO; publ. *Journal* (monthly in Japanese and synopsis in English).

Keisoku Jidouseigyo Gakkai SICE (Society of Instrument and Control Engineers): 35-28-303, Hongo 1-chome, Bunkyo-ku, Tokyo 113; f. 1962; tel (03) 3814-4121; fax (3) 3814-4699; 9,183 mems; Pres. MAKOTO IBUKA; Sec.-Gen. YASUTAKA SAITO; publs *Journal* (monthly), *Transactions* (monthly).

Kogyo Kayaku Kyokai (Industrial Explosives Society of Japan): Gunma Bldg, 2-3-21 Nihonbashi, Chuo-ku, Tokyo 103; tel. (3) 3271-6715; f. 1939; 971 mems; Pres. IKUO FUKUYAMA; publ. *Journal* (every 2 months).

Kuki-Chowa Eisei Kogakkai (Society of Heating, Air-conditioning and Sanitary Engineers of Japan): 8-1, 1-chome, Kitashinjuku, Shinjuku-ku, Tokyo; f. 1917; 18,000 mems; library of 10,000 vols; Pres. S. YOSHIZAWA; publs *Journal* (monthly), *Transactions* (3 a year).

Nihon Kasai Gakkai (Japanese Asscn for Fire Science and Engineering): Business Center for Academic Science, 2-chome 4-16 Yayoi, Bunkyo-ku, Tokyo 113; f. 1951; 2,000 mems; Pres. TAKAO WAKAMATU; publs *Kasai* (Fire, every 2 months), *Bulletin* (2 a year).

Nihon Kikai Gakkai (Japan Society of Mechanical Engineers): Shinanomachi-Rengakan 5F, 35 Shinanomachi, Shinjuku-ku, Tokyo; tel. (3) 5360-3500; f. 1897; 47,000 mems; Pres. AKIHIRO WADA; publs *Journal, Transactions* (monthly), *JSME International Journal* (in English, monthly).

Nihon Shashin Sokuryo Gakkai (Japan Society of Photogrammetry and Remote Sensing): Daichi Honan Bldg 502, 2-8-17 Minami Ikebukoro, Toshima-ku, Tokyo 171; f. 1962; 1,067 mems; Pres. K. OTAKE; publ. *Journal* (every 2 months).

Nippon Genshiryoku Gakkai (Atomic Energy Society of Japan): 1-1-13 Shimbashi, Minato-ku, Tokyo 105; tel. (3) 3508-1261; fax (3) 3581-6128; f. 1959; peaceful uses of atomic energy; 7,500 mems; Pres. M. HAYASHI; Sec.-Gen. H. ISHIKAWA; publs *Nihon-Genshiryoku-Gakkai Shi* (monthly), *Journal of Nuclear Science and Technology* (monthly).

Nippon Kinzoku Gakkai (Japan Institute of Metals): Aoba Aramaki Aoba-ku, Sendai 980; tel. (22) 223-3685; fax (22) 223-6312; f. 1937; 11,000 mems; Pres. HIROSHI OIKAWA; publs *Journal* (monthly), *Bulletin* (monthly), *Transactions* (monthly, in English).

Nippon Kogakukai (Japan Federation of Engineering Societies): Nogizaka Bldg, 6-41, Akasaka 9-chome, Minato-ku, Tokyo 107; f. 1879.

Nippon Koku Ūchu Gakkai (Japan Society for Aeronautical and Space Sciences): 18-2 Shinbashi 1-chome, Minato-ku, Tokyo 105; tel. (3) 3501-0463; f. 1934; 4,400 mems; Pres. Prof. KANICHIROU KATO; publs *Journal* (monthly), *Transactions* (quarterly).

Nippon Seramikkusu Kyokai (Ceramic Society of Japan): 22-17, 2-chome, Hyakunincho, Shinjuku-ku, Tokyo 169-0073; fax (3) 3362-5714; f. 1891; 7,360 mems; Pres. ISAMI AKIMOTO; publs *Journal of the Ceramic Society of Japan, Ceramics Japan* (Bulletin).

Nippon Shashin Gakkai (Society of Photographic Science and Technology of Japan): Tokyo Polytechnic Institute, 2-9-5 Hon-cho, Nakano-ku, Tokyo 164; f. 1925; 1,550 mems; Pres. T. WAKABAYASHI; publ. *Journal* (every 2 months).

Nippon Tekko Kyokai (Iron and Steel Institute of Japan): Keidanren Kaikan (3rd Floor) 9-4, Otemachi, 1-chome, Chiyoda-ku, Tokyo; f. 1915; 10,455 mems; Pres. TERUO KISHI; publs *Tetsu-to-Hagané* (Iron and Steel, monthly, Japanese), *ISIJ International* (monthly, English), *Ferrum* (bulletin, monthly, Japanese).

Nippon Tribologi Gakkai (Japanese Society of Tribologists): c/o Kikai Shinko Kaikan No. 407-2, 3-5-8, Shibakoen, Minato-ku, Tokyo 105-0001; tel. (3) 3434-1926; fax (3) 3434-3556; f. 1956; 3,044 mems; Pres. K. KIMURA; publ. *Tribologists* (monthly).

Nogyo-Doboku Gakkai (Japanese Society of Irrigation, Drainage and Reclamation Engineering): Nogyo Doboku-Kaikan, 34-4 Shinbashi 5-chome, Tokyo 105; tel. (3) 3436-3418; fax (3) 3435-8494; f. 1929; 13,000 mems; Pres. Prof. HASEGAWA TAKASHI; publs *Journal* (monthly), *Transactions* (every 2 months), *Journal of Rural and Environmental Engineering* (2 a year, English).

Seisan Gijutsu Kenkyusho (Institute of Industrial Science): The University of Tokyo, 7-22-1 Roppongi, Minato-ku, Tokyo; f. 1949; Dir Prof. Dr MASAO SAKAUCHI; publs *Seisan-Kenkyu* (monthly), *Annual Report.*

Shigen Sozai Gakkai (Mining and Materials Processing Institute of Japan): Nogizaka Bldg, 9-6-41 Akasaka, Minato-ku, Tokyo 107; tel. (3) 3402-0541; fax (3) 3403-1776; f. 1885; 2,627 mems; Sec.-Gen. YAMAGUCHI TAKASHI; publs *Journal* (monthly), *Metallurgical Review* (2 a year), *MMIJ Proceedings* (2 a year).

Sisutemu Seigyo Jyouhou Gakkai (Institute of Systems, Control and Information Engineers): 14 Yoshidakawaharacho, Sakyo ward, Kyoto City, Kyoto 606; f. 1957; 2,744 mems; Pres. MINORU ABE; publ. *Systems, Control and Information* (monthly).

Yosetsu Gakkai (Japan Welding Society): 1-11 Sakuma-cho, Kanda, Chiyoda-ku, Tokyo; tel. (3) 3253-0488; fax (3) 3253-3059; f. 1925; 5,000 mems; Pres. Prof. Dr YOSHIHIKO MUKAI; publ. *Journal* (monthly).

Research Institutes

GENERAL

Kokusai Nihon Bunka Kenkyu Center (International Research Center for Japanese Studies): 3–2 Oeyama-cho, Goryo, Nishikyo-ku, Kyoto 610-1192; tel. (75) 335-2222; fax (75) 335-2091; f. 1987; national inter-university institute of the Ministry of Education, Science, Sports and Culture; interdisciplinary and comprehensive research on Japanese studies, and research co-operation; library of 172,000 vols; Dir-Gen. HAYAO KAWAI; publs *Nihon Kenkyu* (Japanese), *Japan Review* (English).

Sogo Kenkyu Kaihatsu Kiko (National Institute for Research Advancement): 34F Yebisu Garden Place Tower, 4-20-3 Ebisu, Shibuya-ku, Tokyo 150; tel. (3) 5448-1700; fax (3) 5448-1743; f. 1974 under parliamentary legislation to promote and conduct inter-disciplinary research that focuses on the problems facing modern society and their alleviation; conducts its own research, also commissions and subsidizes research by other bodies; promotes international exchange of research affecting policy-making around the world; research results are made public through lectures, symposia or publication of reports; Chair TAKASHI ISHIHARA; Pres. SHINYASU HOSHINO; Dirs MASASHI NAMEKAWA (Gen. Affairs), NORIKI HIROSE (Research and Planning), SHIN-ICHI ITO (Int. Co-operation), MICHIO ITO (Centre for Public Activities), HAJIME ISHIDA (Centre for Policy Research Information); publs *NIRA News, NIRA Seisaku Kenkyu, NIRA Kenkyu Hokokusho, Almanac of Think Tanks in Japan, NIRA Research Output* (in English), *NIRA Review* (in English), *NIRA's World Directory of Think Tanks* (in English).

AGRICULTURE, FISHERIES AND VETERINARY SCIENCE

Forest and Forest Products Research Institute: POB 16, Tsukuba Norin Kenkyu Danchi-nai, Ibaraki 305; f. 1878; library of 383,000 vols (including Br. Stations); Dir ITSUHITO OHNUKI; publ. *Bulletin* (irregular).

National Agriculture Research Center: Kannondai, Tsukuba, Ibaraki 305-8666; tel. (298) 38-8481; fax (298) 38-8484; f. 1981; library of 172,000 vols; Dir HIROSHI FUJIMAKI; publ. *Bulletin* (2 a year).

National Food Research Institute: Kannondai, Tsukuba, Ibaraki 305-8642; f. 1934;

food processing, chemistry, technology, storage, engineering, distribution, nutrition; applied microbiology, analysis, radiation, etc.; 138 mems; library of 40,000 vols; Dir Dr S. TANIGUCHI; publs *Report*, *Food, its Science and Technology*.

National Institute of Agro-Environmental Sciences: 3-1-1 Kannondai, Tsukuba, Ibaraki 305-8604; tel. (298) 38-8143; fax (298) 38-8199; f. 1983; library of 130,000 vols; Dir-Gen. TOORU NAGATA; publ. *Bulletin* (irregular).

National Institute of Animal Health: 3-1-1, Kannondai, Tsukuba-shi, Ibaraki 305-0856; tel. (298) 38-7707; fax (298) 38-7907; f. 1921; veterinary medicine, animal husbandry, biology; 3 branch laboratories; library of 20,399 vols, 2,054 serial titles; Dir Dr MAMORU KASHIWAZAKI; publs *Bulletin* (1 a year), *Animal Health* (research report, 1 a year).

National Institute of Animal Industry: POB 5, Tsukuba Norindanchi, Ibaraki 305; f.1916; library of 48,000 vols; Dir (vacant); publs *Bulletin* (irregular), *Summaries* (irregular, in English), *Annual Report.*

National Institute of Fruit Tree Science: 2-1 Fujimoto, Tsukuba, Ibaraki 305-8605; tel. (298) 38-6416; fax (298) 38-6437; e-mail kikaku@fruit.affrc.go.jp; f. 1902; 2 branches; research on fruit tree cultivation, breeding of fruit trees, and disease and pest control; library of 60,000 vols; Dir Dr TORU MAOTANI; publ. *Bulletin* (2 a year).

National Institute of Sericultural and Entomological Science: 1-2, Ohwashi, Tsukuba, Ibaraki 305-8634; tel. (298) 38-6011; f. 1988; research on development of new techniques for the promotion of sericulture, and use of functions of other insects and invertebrates; 184 mems; library of 75,000 vols; Dir S. KIMURA; publs *Bulletin* (1–2 a year), *Acta Sericologica et Entomologica* (2 or 3 a year), *Annual Report, News* (4 a year).

National Research Institute of Agricultural Economics: 2-2-1 Nishigahara, Kita-ku, Tokyo; f. 1946; library of 312,000 vols; Dir K. NONAKA; publ. *Quarterly Journal of Agricultural Economy* (in Japanese).

National Research Institute of Agricultural Engineering: 2-1-2 Kannondai, Tsukuba-shi, Ibaraki-ken 305; tel. (298) 38-7513; fax (298) 38-7609; f. 1961; tests, research, investigation, analysis, identification and training with regard to irrigation, drainage, reclamation, farm facilities, rural planning; 115 mems; library of 38,000 vols; Dir K. IWASAKI; publs *Bulletin* (monthly), *Technical Report* (irregular).

National Research Institute of Vegetables, Ornamental Plants and Tea: 2769 Kanaya, Shizuoka 428; tel. (547) 45-4101; fax (547) 46-2169; f. 1986; Dir M. AMANO; publ. *Bulletin* (annually).

ECONOMICS, LAW AND POLITICS

Ajia Keizai Kenkyusho (Institute of Developing Economies): 42 Ichigaya-Hommura-cho, Shinjuku-ku, Tokyo 162-8442; f. 1960; library of 333,000 vols; Chair. YOTARO IIDA; Pres. KATSUHISA YAMADA; publs *Ajia Keizai* (monthly), *The Developing Economies* (quarterly, in English).

Asia Pacific Association of Japan: Rm No. 2306, World Trade Center Bldg., Hamamatsu-cho 2-4-1, Minato-ku, Tokyo 105; tel (03) 3578-0949; fax (3) 3438-4749; f. 1966; research and study on international affairs and diplomatic problems; 70 mems; library of *c.* 1,000 vols; Pres. TOSHIAKI OGASAWARA; Gen. Man. MASARU TANIMOTO; publs occasional reports.

Chemical Economy Research Institute: 13-7, 1-chome, Uchikanda, Chiyoda-ku, Tokyo 101; f. 1954; Dir (Chair.) SEIJI SUZUKI; publ. *Kagaku-Keizai* (monthly).

Chuto Chosakai (Middle East Institute of Japan): 802, 15th Mori Bldg, 2-8-10, Toranomon, Minato-ku, Tokyo; f. 1960; government-aided; exchanges information with other countries; research activities in four areas: political and diplomatic affairs, industry, economy, natural resources; library in process of formation; Chair. WASUKE MIYAKE; publs *Chuto Kenkyu* (Journal of Middle East Studies, monthly), *Chuto Kitaafurika Nenkan* (Yearbook of the Middle East and North Africa).

Institute of Local Government: 2-2-4, Hirakawa-cho, Chiyoda-ku, Tokyo 102; tel. (3) 3234-2901; fax (3) 3234-2946; f. 1946; independent research institute which undertakes self-initiated and contractual projects in the fields of development of local government and improvement of welfare and democratic politics; 41 research staff; library of 5,000 vols; Chair. KOKICHI YAMANO; Sec.-Gen. KUNIYOSHI MUKAI.

Institute of Population Problems: 1-2-2 Kasumigaseki, Chiyoda-ku, Tokyo 100-45; tel. and fax (3) 3591-4816; f. 1939; part of Ministry of Health and Welfare; library of 16,000 vols; Dir Dr MAKOTO ATOH; publs *The Journal of Population Problems* (quarterly), *Annual Reports, Research Series, Field Survey Report* (annually), *Latest Demographic Statistics* (annually), *Working Paper Series* (irregular), *Reprint Series* (irregular).

Japan Center for International Exchange: 9-17 Minami-Azabu 4-chome, Minato-ku, Tokyo 106; tel. (3) 3446-7781; fax (3) 3443-7580; f. 1971 to promote dialogue between Japan and the rest of the world; international conferences and seminars, overseas programme planning, promotion of policy studies and exchange programmes among philanthropic organizations; Japanese Secretariat of the Trilateral Commission; Pres. TADASHI YAMAMOTO.

Japan Economic Research Institute: Kowa 35 Bldg, 14-14 Akasaka 1-chome, Minato-ku, Tokyo 107-0052; tel. (3) 3582-0541; fax (3) 3582-0542; f. 1962; research and study of domestic and foreign economic and business management; library of *c.* 8,000 vols; Exec. Dir HIROSHI KIYASU; Sec-Gen. ITSUROU ARIMITSU; publs *Annual Report*, research reports.

Kabushikikaisha Mitsubishi Sogo Kenkyusho (Mitsubishi Research Institute, Inc.): 3-6, Otemachi 2-chome, Chiyoda-ku, Tokyo 100; tel. (3) 3270-9211; fax (3) 3279-1308; f. 1970; aims to meet new social, economic and industrial requirements in an age of advanced information systems and internationalization; research on national and international scale to serve the needs of government agencies and industry in the fields of economic, political, industrial and management affairs, techno-economics, social engineering, technology and data processing; 800 mems; library of 63,000 vols, 1,000 periodicals; Pres. SADAMI TAKAHASHI; publs *Chart for Brighter Business*, *Outlook for the Japanese Economy* (2 a year), *MRI Newsletter, Journal* (annually), *Hit Products of the Year* (1 a year), *MRI Analysis of Japanese Corporations* (2 a year).

Kaiji Sangyo Kenkyusho (Japan Maritime Research Institute): Kaiun Bldg, 6-4, 2-chome, Hirakawa-cho, Chiyoda-ku, Tokyo; tel. (3) 3265-5231; e-mail jamri003@infotokyo.ne.jp; f. 1966; library of 34,000 vols; Pres. MINORU TOYODA; publs *Bulletin* (monthly), *JAMRI Report* (2 a year), *Overseas Maritime Information* (every 10 days).

Keidanren (Japan Federation of Economic Organizations): 1-9-4, Otemachi, Chiyoda-ku, Tokyo 100; tel. (3) 3279-1411; f. 1946; an independent body which aims to maintain contact with various economic sectors, to sound out opinions in business circles on economic problems, domestic and international, and to obtain practical solutions to these problems thereby promoting sound development of the national economy; carries out surveys, research studies; gives assistance in the exchange of information, dissemination of materials, etc.; 1,192 mems; library of 100,000 vols; Chair. TOYODA SHOICHIRO; Pres. and Dir-Gen. KOZO UCHIDA.

Nihon Keizai Kenkyu Center (Japan Center for Economic Research): Nikkei Kayaba-cho Bldg, 2-6-1 Nihombashi-kayabacho, Chuo-ku, Tokyo 103; tel. (3) 3639-2801; fax (3) 3639-2839; f. 1963; 372 institutional, 280 individual mems; library of 45,813 vols, 920 periodicals; Pres. S. TOSHIDA; publs *Keizai Kenkyu Center Kaiho* (fortnightly), *Quarterly Forecast of Japan's Economy, Five-year Economic Forecast, Long-term Economic Forecast* (1 a year).

Nikko Research Center Ltd: 2-5 Nihonbashi, Kayabacho 1-chome, Cyuo-ku, Tokyo 103; f. 1970; provides investment information for Nikko Securities Ltd and its clients; economic research on Japanese economy; business research on Japanese companies; projects research sponsored by governments and corporations; *c.* 200 mems; library of 20,000 vols; Pres. TAKAO FURUMI; Dir-Gen. MASAO YOKOMIZO; publs various monthly reports, *Nikko Monthly Bulletin* (in English), *NRC Chartroom—A Graphic Survey of the Japanese Economy and Securities Market* (monthly, in English).

Nippon Research Center Ltd: Shuwa-Sakurabashi Bldg, 4-5-4 Hatchobori, Chuo-ku, Tokyo 104; f. 1960 by interdisciplinary researchers and business men to meet the needs of industrial and economic circles; marketing and public opinion research, marketing consultancy, public relations, economic forecasting and urban and regional development; 96 staff; library of *c.* 3,000 vols; Chair. MATSUO SUZUKI; Pres. KOHJI NIKI; publ. *Bulletin of Marketing Research* (annually, in Japanese).

Rôdô Kagaku Kenkyusho (Institute for Science of Labour): 2-8-14, Sugao, Miyamae-ku, Kawasaki-shi, Kanagawa-ken 216-8501; e-mail isl.info@isl.or.jp; f. 1921; work stress, human-technology interaction, systems safety, human work environment management, chemical health risk management, occupational epidemiology, employment and working life conditions, local industries and welfare support; Chair. ISAO AMAGI; Dir of Research KAZUTAKA KOGI; publs *Rôdô Kagaku* (Journal of Science of Labour, monthly), *Rôdô no Kagaku* (Digest of Science of Labour, monthly), *Reports and Monographs.*

Seisaku Kagaku Kenkyusho (Institute for Policy Sciences, Japan): Friend Bldg, 2-4-11, Nagata-cho, Chiyoda-ward, Tokyo; tel. (3) 3581-2141; fax (3) 3581-2143; f. 1971; independent institute authorized by the Ministries of Finance and International Trade and Industry; undertakes its own and contractual research in the problems of advanced societies caused by technological innovation, industrialization, urbanization, etc.; research in the fields of regional development, environmental problems, energy and natural resources, economic and social problems, etc.; Chair. and Exec. Dir. SHIGERU WATANABE; publs research reports, *The 21st Century Forum* (quarterly).

EDUCATION

National Institute for Educational Research: 6-5-22 Shimomeguro, Meguro-ku, Tokyo 153; f. 1949; library: see Libraries; Dir-Gen. SHIGERU YOSHIDA; publs *Bulletin* (in Japanese, annually; in English, irregularly), *Koho* (Japanese, 6 a year), *Unesco-NIER*

Newsletter (in English, 3 a year), *Kenkyushu-roku* (Japanese, 2 a year).

FINE AND PERFORMING ARTS

Tokyo Kokuritsu Bunkazai Kenkyu-jo (Tokyo National Research Institute of Cultural Properties): 13–27 Ueno Park, Taito-ku, Tokyo 110-8713; tel. (3) 3823-2241; fax (3) 3828-2434; f. 1930; five research depts: fine arts, performing arts, conservation science, restoration techniques, archives; also Japan Centre for International Co-operation in Conservation and Division of General Affairs; special collection of works of Seiki Kuroda; library of 57,032 vols; Dir-Gen. AKIYOSHI WATANABE; publs *Bijutsu Kenkyu* (Journal of Art Studies, quarterly), *Bijutsu Nenkan* (Year Book of Japanese Art), *Geinoh no Kagaku* (Science of Performing Arts, annually), *Hozon Kagaku* (Science for Conservation, annually), *Proceedings of the International Symposium on the Conservation and Restoration of Cultural Property* (annually), reports.

Tōyō Ongaku Gakkai (Society for Research in Asiatic Music): c/o Seiha Hogaku Kaikan, 3 Sanai-cho, Ichigaya, Shinjuku-ku, Tokyo 162; f. 1936; aims to promote research in Japanese and other Asian music and ethnomusicology; 750 mems; Pres. SATOAKI GAMOU; publ. *Tōyō Ongaku Kenkyū* (annually).

HISTORY, GEOGRAPHY AND ARCHAEOLOGY

Geographical Survey Institute: Kitasato-1, Tsukuba-shi, Ibaraki-ken 305-0811; tel. (298) 64-1111; fax (298) 64-8087; f. 1869; part of Ministry of Construction; library of 32,000 vols; Dir KUNIO NONOMURA; publ. *Bulletin* (irregular).

LANGUAGE AND LITERATURE

Gengo Bunka Kenkyujo (Research Institute for Linguistic Culture): 16-26 Nampeidai-machi, Shibuya-ku, Tokyo; Pres. MORITO NAGANUMA; publ. *Nippongo Kyoiku Kenkyu* (2 a year, Japanese).

Kokubungaku Kenkyu Siryokan (National Institute of Japanese Literature): 16-10 Yutaka-cho 1-chome, Sinagawa-ku, Tokyo 142; tel. (3) 3785-7131; f. 1972 by the Ministry of Education, Science and Culture at the recommendation of the Japan Science Council and in response to requests for a centre for the preservation of Japanese classical literature; surveys, collects (largely in microfilm), studies, processes, preserves and provides access to MSS and old printed books relating to Japanese literature before 1868; also undertakes research in this field; provides scholarly community with facilities for consultation and reproduction of materials; historical documents division collects and preserves documents of *kinsei* (1600–1867); library: see Libraries; Dir-Gen. Dr AKIHIRO SATAKE; publs *Bulletin* (annually), *NIJL Technical Report* (irregular), *NIJL Report* (2 a year), *Bibliographic Reports* (annually), *Bibliography of Research in Japanese Literature* (annually), *Proceedings of the International Conference on Japanese Literature in Japan* (annually), *Bulletin of Research of the Dept. of Historical Documents* (annually).

Kokuritu Kokugo Kenkyuzyo (National Language Research Institute): 3-9-14, Nisigaoka, Kita-ku, Tokyo 115; tel. (3) 3900-3111; fax (3) 3906-3530; f. 1948; library of 105,000 vols; Dir O. MIZUTANI; publs *Annual Report, Report, Linguistic Atlas of Japan* (6 vols).

MEDICINE

Cancer Institute, Japanese Foundation for Cancer Research: Kami-Ikebukuro, Toshima-ku, Tokyo, 170; tel. (3) 3918-0111; telex 2722810; fax (3) 5394-3893; f. 1908; departments of pathology, experimental pathology, cell biology, viral oncology, biochemistry, gene research, physics, cancer chemotherapy, molecular biotherapy and human genome analysis; library of 5,000 vols, 10,000 periodicals; Cancer Institute Hospital and Cancer Chemotherapy Centre attached; Dir TOMOYUKI KITAGAWA; publ. *Japan Journal for Cancer Research* (monthly).

Fujisawa Foundation: Doshomachi 3-4-7, Chuo-ku, Osaka 541; tel. (6) 201-5894; f. 1946; fmrly Foundation for the Promotion of Research on Medicinal Sources; Chair. Dr T. FUJISAWA; publ. *ZAIDANHO* (2 a year).

Institute of Brain and Blood Vessels: 6-23 Ootemachi, Isezaki-city, Gumma; tel. (270) 25-0112; fax (270) 23-5522; f. 1963; clinical and basic research on cerebrovascular disease; 95 mems; Dir Dr TATSURU MIHARA; publ. *Nosotchu No Kenkyu* (Studies on Apoplexy).

Institute of Chemotherapy: 6-1-14 Kohnodai, Ichikawa-city, Chiba; tel. (473) 75-1111; fax (473) 73-4921; f. 1939; Dir Prof. TSUGUO HASEGAWA; publ. *Bulletin of the Institute of Chemotherapy.*

Institute of Public Health: 4-6-1 Shirokanedai, Minato-ku, Tokyo; tel. (3) 3441-7111; fax (3) 3446-4314; f. 1938; part of Ministry of Health and Welfare; postgraduate education and research in public health; library of 68,000 vols, 1,500 periodicals; Dir K. FURUICHI; publ. *Bulletin* (quarterly).

Kekkaku Yobo Kai Kekkaku Kenkyujo (Research Institute of Tuberculosis, Japan Anti-Tuberculosis Association): 1-24 Matsuyama 3-chome, Kiyose-shi, Tokyo 204; tel. (424) 93-5711; fax (424) 92-4600; f. 1939; research on tuberculosis and respiratory diseases; information, surveillance and training centre; health education campaign against tuberculosis; 56 mems; library of 15,000 vols; Dir Dr T. MORI; publs *Information and Review of Tuberculosis and Respiratory Disease Research* (quarterly), *Red Double-Barred Cross* (every 2 months), *Review of Tuberculosis for Public Health Nurses* (2 a year), Medical Conference series (all in Japanese).

Kitasato Institute: 9-1 Shirokane 5-chome, Minato-ku, Tokyo 108; tel. (3) 3444-6161; telex 2423378; f. 1914; research on the cause, prevention and therapy of various diseases; 1,100 mems; library of 86,000 vols; Dir S. OMURA.

Kohno Clinical Medicine Research Institute: 1-28-15 Kita-Shinagawa, Shinagawa-ku, Tokyo; tel. (3) 474-1351; f. 1951; 62 staff; library of 3,000 vols; Dir M. KOHNO; publs *Archives, Bulletin.*

Leprosy Research Centre: 4-2-1, Aoba-cho, Higashi-murayama-city, Tokyo; tel. (423) 91-8211; fax (423) 94-9092; f. 1955; part of Ministry of Health and Welfare; Dir S. YAMAZAKI; publ. *Japanese Journal of Leprosy* (4 a year).

Miyake Medical Institute: 1-3 Tenjin-mae, Takamatsu-city, Kagawa; f. 1949; Dir T. MIYAKE.

National Cancer Centre: 1-1 Tsukiji 5-chome, Chuo-ku, Tokyo 104; tel. (3) 3542-2511; fax (3) 3542-3567; f. 1962; diagnosis, treatment and research of cancer and allied diseases; Dept. of Ministry of Health and Welfare; 800 staff; library of 56,000 vols, 17,000 monographs, 500 periodicals; Pres. K. SUEMASU; Dirs T. KAKIZOE (Hospital) and M. TERADA (Research Inst.); publs (distributed free to libraries) *Collected Papers of Research Inst.* (in English, annually), *Collected Papers of Hospital* (in Japanese and English, annually), *Tumour Registration of Bone, Lung, Stomach, Blood, Brain, etc.* (in Japanese).

National Institute of Genetics: 1, 111 Yata, Mishima-city, Shizuoka 411-8540; tel. (559) 81-6707; fax (559) 81-6715; f. 1949; part of Ministry of Education, Science, Sports and Culture; library of 20,000 vols; Dir Y. HOTTA; publ. *Annual Report*.

National Institute of Health and Nutrition: 1-23-1 Toyama, Shinjuku-ku, Tokyo; tel. (3) 3203-5721; fax (3) 3202-3278; f. 1920; part of Ministry of Health and Welfare; library of 30,000 vols; Dir S. KOBAYASHI; publs *Annual Report, Japanese Journal of Nutrition* (in Japanese, every 2 months).

National Institute of Health Sciences: 1-18-1 Kamiyoga, Setagaya, Tokyo 158; tel. (3) 3700-1141; fax (3) 3707-6950; f. 1874; research in connection with the regulation of foods, drugs, medical devices, cosmetics and environmental chemicals; Dir MITSURU UCHIYAMA; publ. *Bulletin* (annually).

National Institute of Health Services Management: 1 Toyama-cho, Shinjuku-ku, Tokyo 162; tel. (3) 3203-5327; fax (3) 3202-6853; f. 1948; part of Ministry of Health and Welfare; Dir. S. KITAGAWA; publs *Annual Report* and *Report in Research* (9 a year).

National Institute of Industrial Health: 21-1, Nagao 6-chome, Tama-ku, Kawasaki-city 214, Kanagawa; tel. (44) 865-6111; fax (44) 865-6116; f. 1956; part of Ministry of Labour; library of 25,000 vols; Dir HARUHIKO SAKURAI; publ. *Industrial Health* (quarterly).

National Institute of Infectious Diseases: Toyama 1-23-1, Shinjuku-ku, Tokyo 162; tel. (3) 5285-1111; fax (3) 5285-1150; f. 1947; part of Ministry of Health and Welfare; research on communicable diseases, including an AIDS Research Centre; assay of biological products and antibiotics; library of 30,000 vols; Dir SHUDO YAMAZAKI; publ. *The Japanese Journal of Medical Science and Biology* (6 a year).

National Institute of Mental Health, National Centre of Neurology and Psychiatry: 1-7-3 Kohnodai, Ichikawa, Chiba 272; f. 1952; part of Ministry of Health and Welfare; Dir A. FUJINAWA; publ. *Journal of Mental Health* (annually).

Neuropsychiatric Research Institute: 91 Benten-cho, Shinjuku-ku, Tokyo; tel. (3) 3260-9171; fax (3) 3235-0961; f. 1951; research on sleep disorders, mood disorders; art therapy; Chief Dir Y. SHIMAZONO; Exec. Dir Y. HONDA.

Nukada Institute for Medical and Biological Research: 5-18 Inage-cho, Chiba-city, Chiba; f. 1939; Dir Dr H. NUKADA; publ. *Report* (irregular).

Ogata Institute for Medical and Chemical Research: 2-10-14 Higashi-Kanda, Chiyoda-ku, Tokyo 101; f. 1962; library of 12,000 vols; Pres. MASAHIDE ABE; publ. *Igaku to Seibutsugaku* (Medicine and Biology, monthly).

Pharmaceutical Research Institute: 2-7 Daigaku-cho, Takatsuki-city, Osaka; f. 1947; Dir S. MATSUMOTO; publ. *Bulletin* (3–6 a year).

Tokyo Metropolitan Institute of Medical Science: Honkamagome 3-18, Bunkyo-ku, Tokyo 113; tel. (3) 3823-2591; fax (3) 3823-2202; e-mail ui@rinshoken.or.jp; f. 1975; research in aetiology and pathogenesis of intractable diseases and application of molecular and cellular biology to the aetiology of these diseases; library of 30,000 vols; Dir MICHIO UI; publs (in Japanese) *Rinshoken News* (monthly), *Annual Report.*

NATURAL SCIENCES

General

Kokuritsu Kyokuchi Kenkyujyo (National Institute of Polar Research): 9-10 Kaga 1-chome, Itabashi-ku, Tokyo 173; tel. (3) 3962-4712; telex 2723515; fax (3) 3962-2529; e-mail shomu@nipr.ac.jp; f. 1973; replaces the frmr Polar Research Centre of the National Science Museum; government-sponsored; implements programmes of the Japanese Antarctic Research Expeditions (JARE), organizes postgraduate courses in polar subjects, offers research facilities to national and foreign universities and individual researchers; library of 39,000 vols and bound periodicals; 129 full-time staff; Dir Prof. TAKEO HIRASAWA; publs include *Namkyoku Shiryo* (Antarctic Record, 3 a year), *Memoirs of the National Institute of Polar Research, JARE Data Reports* (10 a year), *Proceedings* (annually), *Catalog, Antarctic Geological Map Series.*

Biological Sciences

Kihara Institute for Biological Research: Mutsukawa, 3-122-21, Minami-ku, Yokohama 232; f. 1942; 10 staff; library of 20,000 vols; Dir M. UMEDA; publs *Seiken Ziho* (annually), *Wheat Information Service* (2 a year).

Mitsubishi Kasei Institute of Life Sciences: 11 Minamiooya, Machida-shi, Tokyo 194-8511; tel. 427-24-6226; fax 427-29-1252; f. 1971; research in human and general life science; library of over 5,000 vols; Pres. YOSHITAKA NAGAI; publ. *Annual Report.*

Research Institute for Chemobiodynamics: Chiba University, 1-8-1, Inohana, Chiba; tel. 0472-22-7171; f. 1946; 53 mems; library of 200,000 vols; Dir TADASHI ARAI; publ. *Annual Report.*

Tokyo Biochemical Research Institute: 41-8 Takada, 3-chome, Toshima-ku, Tokyo; f. 1950; Dir M. OKADA; publ. *Report* (annually).

Mathematical Sciences

Institute of Statistical Mathematics: 4-6-7 Minami Azabu, Minato-ku, Tokyo 106-8569; tel. (3) 3446-1501; fax (3) 3443-3552; f. 1944; National Inter-University Research Institute; research in statistics; library of 43,497 vols, 2,100 periodicals; Dir Dr R. SHIMIZU; publs *Annals* (quarterly), *Proceedings* (2 a year), *Computer Science Monographs.*

Physical Sciences

Fukada Geological Institute: 2-13-12 Hon-Komagome, Bunkyo-ku, Tokyo; tel. (3) 3944-5825; f. 1954; Dir ATSUO FUKADA; publ. *Nenpo* (annually).

Institute of Physical and Chemical Research (RIKEN): 2-1 Hirosawa, Wako-shi, Saitama 351-01; tel. (48) 462-1111; telex 02962818; fax (48) 462-4714; f. 1917; studies related to science and technology; 621 mems; library of 100,000 vols; Pres. AKITO ARIMA; publs *RIKEN Review* (3 a year), *Annual Report of Research Activities of RIKEN* (annually), *List of Papers IPCR* (annually), *RIKEN Accelerated Progress Report* (annually), *Laser Science Progress Report of RIKEN* (annually).

Japan Atomic Energy Research Institute (JAERI): Fukoku-Seimei Bldg, 2-2-2 Uchisaiwai-cho, Chiyoda-ku, Tokyo; f. 1956; library of 36,000 vols; Pres. MASAJI YOSHIKAWA; publs *Nuclear Science Information of Japan* (irregular), *JAERI Reports* (irregular), *JAERI Research* (irregular), *JAERI-Data / Code* (irregular), *JAERI-Tech* (irregular), *JAERI-Review* (irregular), *JAERI-Conf* (irregular).

Kobayasi Institute of Physical Research: 3-20-41 Higashi-Motomachi, Kokubunji, Tokyo 185; tel. (423) 21-2841; fax (423) 22-4698; f. 1940; acoustics (noise and vibration, acoustic material, piezoelectric material, audiology); Pres. J. IGARASHI; Dir M. YAMASHITA; publ. *Bulletin* (annually).

Meteorological Research Institute: 1-1 Nagamine, Tsukuba, Ibaraki 305; tel. (298) 51-5111; fax (298) 51-1449; f. 1942; meteorology, geophysics, seismology, oceanography, geochemistry; Dir S. KADOWAKI; publ. *Papers in Meteorology and Geophysics* (quarterly).

National Astronomical Observatory, Earth Rotation Division, and Mizusawa Astrogeodynamics Observatory: 2-12 Hoshigaoka, Mizusawa, Iwate 023; tel. (197) 22-7111; telex 837628; fax (197) 22-7120; f. 1899; astronomy, geophysics, geodesy; part of Ministry of Education, Science, Sports and Culture; library of 68,400 vols; Chair. of Earth Rotation Division Prof. K. YOKOYAMA; Dir of Mizusawa Astrogeodynamics Observatory Assoc. Prof. S. MANABE; publs *Annual Report of the Mizusawa Astrogeodynamics Observatory—Time Service and Geophysical Observations, National Astronomical Observatory Technical Reports of the Mizusawa Kansoku Centre.*

National Institute for Research in Inorganic Materials: Namiki 1-1, Tsukuba-shi, Ibaraki; f. 1966; part of Science and Technology Agency; synthesis of high purity inorganic materials and their physical analysis; 163 mems; library of 24,000 vols; Dir Dr Y. INOMATA.

National Research Institute for Metals: 1-2-1 Sengen, Tsukuba-shi, Ibaraki-ken 305; Dir K. NII; publs *Report* (annually), *Research Activities* (annually), *Kinzaigiken News* (monthly), *NRIM Research Activities* (annually), *NRIM Special Report* (irregular), *Creep Data Sheets* (irregular).

Space Activities Commission: 2-2-1 Kasumigaseki, Chiyoda-ku, Tokyo 100-8966; tel. (3) 3581-5271; fax (3) 3503-2570; f. 1968; contributes to a comprehensive and streamlined execution of government programmes on space development, including organization of administrative agencies, planning of general policies and outlining training programmes for researchers and technicians; Chair. SADAKAZU TANIGAKI; publ. *Monthly Report.*

RELIGION, SOCIOLOGY AND ANTHROPOLOGY

Okura Institute for the Study of Spiritual Culture: 706 Futoo-cho, Kohoku-ku, Yokohama; tel. (45) 542-0050; fax (45) 542-0051; f. 1929; Dir N. SASAI; publ. *Okuravama Ronshu.*

Zinbun Kagaku Kenkyusho (Institute for Research in Humanities): 1 Ushinomiyacho, Yoshida, Sakyo-ku 606-8501, Kyoto; f. 1939; 54 staff; library: see Libraries; attached to Kyoto University; Pres. YUZO YAMAMOTO; the Institute is divided into three sections, dealing with Japanese, Oriental and Western Culture; publs *Zinbun Gakuho* (1 a year), *Toho Gakuho* (1 a year), *Annual Bibliography of Oriental Studies, Social Survey Reports* (1 a year), *Annales Zinbun* (1 a year), *News Letter Zinbun* (1 a year).

TECHNOLOGY

Agency of Industrial Science and Technology (AIST): C/o Ministry of International Trade and Industry, 1-3-1 Kasumigaseki, Chiyoda-ku, Tokyo 100; tel. (3) 3501-1511; fax (3) 3501-2081; f. 1948; attached to Ministry of International Trade and Industry; government-sponsored research and development in public and private sectors; Dir Dr S. ISHIZAKA.

Attached institutes:

National Research Laboratory of Metrology: 1-1-4 Sakurama Umezono, Niihari-gun, Ibaraki-ken 305; tel. (298) 54-4148; f. 1903; co-operates with the Int. Bureau of Weights and Measures and similar insts. in other countries; *c.* 250 staff; library of 20,000 vols; Dir M. KAWATA; publs *Bulletin* (2 a year), *Report* (quarterly).

Mechanical Engineering Laboratory: 1-2 Namiki, Sakuramura, Niihari-gun, Ibaraki-ken 305; tel. (298) 54-2501; f. 1937; work on systems engineering for the machine industry, space development, pollution prevention technology.

National Chemical Laboratory for Industry: Higashi 1-1-4, Yatabe-cho, Tsukuba-gun, Ibaraki-ken 305; tel. (298) 54-4451; f. 1900; *c.* 300 staff; library of 60,000 vols; research in 5 main fields: technology of energy and resources, knowledge-intensive technology, future technology, standardization technology, prevention of environmental damage and industrial hazards; Dir Dr J. KATO; publs *Journal* (monthly), *Annual Report.*

Government Industrial Research Institute, Osaka: Midorigaoka 1-8-31, Ikeda-shi, Osaka 563; tel. (727) 51-8531; f. 1918; research mainly to do with the chemical industry; development of new materials and related measuring technology.

Government Industrial Research Institute, Nagoya: Hirate-cho 1-1, Kita-ku, Nagoya-shi 462; tel. (52) 911-2111; f. 1952; research in six main fields: machinery, metals, chemicals, radiation chemistry, ceramics, pottery.

Fermentation Research Institute: Higashi 1-1-3, Yatabe-cho, Tsukuba-gun, Ibaraki-ken 305; tel. (298) 54-6000; f. 1940 to contribute to the progress and development of industries involved with microorganisms; publ. *Report.*

Research Institute for Polymers and Textiles: Higashi 1-1-4, Yatabe-cho, Tsukuba-gun, Ibaraki-ken 305; tel. (298) 54-6203; f. 1918; *c.* 100 staff; library of 20,000 vols; Dir Dr A. OKADA; publs *Bulletin* (quarterly), *News* (every 2 months), *Annual Report, Survey* (annually).

Geological Survey of Japan: Higashi 1-1-3, Yatabe-cho, Tsukuba-gun, Ibaraki-ken 305; tel. (298) 54-3513; f. 1882; 405 staff; library of 16,000 vols; Dir J. SUYAMA; publs *Report* (irregular), *Bulletin* (monthly), geological maps.

Electrotechnical Laboratory: 1-1-4 Umezono, Sakuramura, Niihari-gun, Ibaraki-ken 305; tel. (298) 54-5022; f. 1891; fundamental electronic technology, information and computer technology, energy technology, standards and measurements technology.

Industrial Products Research Institute: Higashi 1-1-4, Yatabe-cho, Tsukuba-gun, Ibaraki-ken 305; tel. (298) 54-6621; f. 1928; application of human engineering and materials to areas closely related to everyday life.

National Research Institute for Pollution and Resources: Onogawa 16-3, Yatabe-cho, Tsukuba-gun, Ibaraki-ken 305; tel. (298) 54-3017; f. 1920; development of resources and energy, including recyling, conservation, heat utilization; industrial safety in mines; environmental pollution research.

Government Industrial Development Laboratory, Hokkaido: 17-2 Higashi 2-jo, Tsukisamu, Toyohira-ku, Sapporo-shi 061-01; tel. (11) 851-0151; f. 1960; development and research in mining and manufacturing technology in Hokkaido; processes for direct liquefaction and gasification of coal, establishment of a technological base for utilization of coal ash, development of technology for utilization of non-metallic resources.

Government Industrial Research Institute, Kyushu: Shuku-machi, Tosu-shi, Saga-ken 841; tel. (9428) 2-5161; f. 1964; development and research in mining and manufacturing in Kyushu.

Government Industrial Research Institute, Shikoku: 2-3-3 Hananomiya-cho, Takamatsut-shi 760; tel. (878) 67-3511; f. 1967; research necessary for the development of industrial technology in the Shikoku region: ocean development and the pulp and paper industry.

Government Industrial Research Institute, Tohoku: Nigatake, Haranomachi, Sendai-shi 983; tel. (222) 57-5211; f. 1967; development and research in mining and manufacturing technology in the Tohoku region; automation of iron-ore separation process, development of new flocculating materials for treatment of industrial waste water, foam treatment.

Government Research Institute, Chugoku: 15000 Hiromachi, Kure-shi 737-01; tel. (823) 72-1111; f. 1971; research in industrial technology in Chugoku district, and pollution prevention of the Seto Inland Sea; depts of Marine Environment and Machinery and Metals.

Applied Science Research Institute: 49 Tanaka Ohi-cho, Sakyo-ku, Kyoto 606; tel. (75) 701-3164; fax (75) 701-1217; f. 1916; metals engineering, surface modification, heat treatment, chemical engineering; Pres. B. KONDO.

Building Research Institute: 1 Tachihara, Tsukuba-shi, Ibaraki Pref.; tel. (298) 64-2151; fax (298) 64-2989; e-mail bri@kenken.go.jp; f. 1946; town planning, building economics, building materials, construction techniques, structural engineering, earthquake engineering, fire safety, environmental engineering, building design and use; library of 50,000 vols; Dir-Gen. Y. YAMAZAKI; publs *Annual Report, BRI Research Papers.*

Civil Engineering Research Institute (Hokkaido Development Agency): Hiragishi, Sapporo-city; f. 1951; 36,000 vols in library; Dir T. OHTA; publs *Monthly Report* and *Report* (quarterly), *Annual Report.*

Communications Research Laboratory, Ministry of Posts and Telecommunications: 2-1 Nukui-Kitamachi 4-chome, Koganei-shi, Tokyo 184; tel. (423) 21-1211; telex 2832611; fax (423) 27-7586; f. 1952; highly intelligent communications, human and biological informatics, space and earth system science, materials science and quantum devices, communications technology in manned space era; 425 staff; library of 140,000 vols; Dir K. YOSHIMURA; publs *CRL News* (in Japanese, monthly), *CRL Annual Bulletin* (in Japanese), *Review* (in Japanese, quarterly), *Journal* (3 a year), *Standard Frequency and Time Service Bulletin* (monthly), *Ionospheric Data in Japan* (monthly).

Doboku Kenkyujo (Public Works Research Institute, Ministry of Construction): 1, Asahi, Tskuba-shi, Ibaraki-ken 305-0804; tel. (298) 64-2211; telex 3652574; fax (298) 64-2840; f. 1921; has 35 research divisions and one experimental laboratory; 477 staff; research on roads and traffic, rivers and coast, dam and water resources, geology, chemistry, materials, structures, sewage, environment, disaster prevention, etc.; library of 134,000 vols; Dir YASUTAKE INOUE; publs *Journal of Research* (in English), *Technical Note, Technical Memorandum, Civil Engineering Journal, Annual Report, Newsletter,* and others.

Engineering Research Institute: Faculty of Engineering, University of Tokyo, 11-16, Yayoi, 2 chome, Bunkyo-ku, Tokyo; f. 1939; 67 staff; library of 6,747 vols; Dir YOICHI GOSHI; publ. *Annual Report.*

Fire Research Institute (Fire Defence Agency): 14-1 Nakahara, 3-chome, Mitaka-city, Tokyo; tel. (422) 44-8331; fax (422) 42-7719; f. 1948; fire science and technology; 53 staff; library of 6,000 vols; Dir KAZUO HASEGAWA; publs *Shobokenkyujohokoku, Shoken Syuho*(annually).

Institute for Fermentation, Osaka: 17-85, Juso-honmachi 2-chome, Yodogawaku, Osaka 532; tel. (6) 302-7281; fax (6) 300-6814; f. 1944; preservation and distribution of micro-organisms and animal cells; 23 staff; library of 800 vols; Dir Dr TORU HASEGAWA; publs *List of Cultures, IFO Research Communications* (every 2 years).

Institute for Future Technology: Tomioka-bashi Bldg, 2-6-11 Fukagawa, Koto-ku, Tokyo; f. 1971 as an independent institute under the auspices of AIST (*q.v.*); research in the fields of technology forecasting, technology assessment and other socio-economic research in future technologies (electronics, telecommunications, space and energy); library of 15,000 vols; Pres. HIROEI FUJIOKA; Chief Sec. TAKAMITSU KOSHIKAWA; publ. *Kenkyu Seika Gaiyo* (research results, annually, in Japanese).

Institute of Energy Economics, Japan: Shuwa Kamiyacho Bldg, 3-13 Toranomon 4-chome, Minato-ku, Tokyo; tel. (3) 5401-4311; telex 2225427; fax (3) 5401-4310; inc. 1966; co-ordinates information related to energy, its use, supply, conservation and economic aspects; provides material as basis for planning and policy formation by government and private business; int. co-operation on energy projects; 155 mems incl. energy-related industries and research institutions; library of 33,000 vols; Pres. TOYOAKI IKUTA; Man. Dirs MITSURU MIYATA, HIROSHI HAGIWARA, TADARAKI TOKUNAGA, KAZUYA FUJIME, HIDEO OBA, TSUTOMU TOICHI, KEIICHI YOKOBORI; publs *Energy in Japan* (6 a year in English), *Energy Economy* (monthly, in Japanese), *International Energy News Abstracts* (fortnightly, in Japanese), *International Energy Analysis* (monthly, in Japanese), *Energy Balance Table* (1 a year, in Japanese), *Energy Statistics* (1 a year, in Japanese).

Institute of Research and Innovation, Japan: 1-6-8 Yushima, Bunkyo-ku, Tokyo 113; tel. (3) 5689-6356; fax (3) 5689-6350; f. 1959; fmrly Industrial Research Institute, Japan; independent; innovative research and development on technology and socio-technology, including alternative energy sources, nuclear technologies and related innovative problems; 70 research staff; library of *c.* 2,000 vols; Pres. SHO NASU; Dir. YOICHI TAKASHIMA; publ. *Bulletin* (quarterly, in Japanese).

International Association of Traffic and Safety Sciences: 6-20, 2-chome, Yaesu, Chuo-ku, Tokyo 104; f. 1974; aims to contribute to the realization of a better traffic society through the practical application of research conducted in a variety of fields; research surveys on traffic and its safety; collection and retrieval of information on traffic-related sciences; sponsorship of domestic and international symposia and study meetings; provision of awards; IATSS Forum, human resource development programme for S.E. Asian countries; Exec. Dir HIDEO KUNIEDA; publs *IATSS Review* (quarterly, in Japanese with English abstracts), *IATSS Research* (2 a year, in English), *White Paper on Transportation Safety* (annually, in English), *Statistics of Road Traffic Accidents in Japan* (annually, in English), reports, proceedings of symposia, etc.

Japan Construction Method and Machinery Research Institute: 3154 Obuchi, Fuji-shi, Shizuoka-ken; tel. (545) 35-0212; fax (545) 35-3719; f. 1964; construction machine testing and environmental assessment; 60 staff; Dir KOMIN UEHIGASHI; publs *Nenpo* (annually), *Kensetsu Kikaika Kenkyujo Hokokusho* (irregular), *Seino Shiken Hokokusho* (irregular).

National Aerospace Laboratory: 7-44-1 Jindaiji Higashi-machi, Chofu-City, Tokyo; tel. (422) 47-5911; fax (422) 47-3290; e-mail wwwadmin@nal.go.jp; f. 1955; part of Science and Technology Agency; library of 157,000 vols; Dir M. EBIHARA; publ. *Technical Report* (irregular).

National Research Institute for Earth Science and Disaster Prevention (NIED): 3-1 Tennodai, Tsukuba-shi, Ibaraki-ken 305; f. 1963; library of 71,232 vols; Dir SHIGETSUGU UEHARA; publs *Report of NIED* (2 a year), *Major Disaster Field Study* (irregular), *NIED Research Notes* (irregular), *NIED Bulletin* (2 a year), *Strong-motion Earthquake Records in Japan* (annually), *Prompt Report of Strong-motion Earthquake Records* (irregular).

Branches:

Nagaoka Institute of Snow and Ice Studies: 187-16, Maeyama, Suyoshi Omachi, Nagaoka-shi, Niigata-ken 940; study of techniques for the prevention of snow damage.

Shinjyo NIED Branch of Snow and Ice Studies: 1400, Takadan, Toka-machi, Shinjo-shi, Yamagata-ken 996; study of the prevention of disasters caused by snow and ice.

National Research Institute of Brewing: 2-6-30 Takinogawa, Kita-ku, Tokyo; f. 1904; Dir H. MURAKAMI; publ. *Report* (annually).

Noguchi Institute: 1-8-1 Kaga, Itabashi-ku, Tokyo 173-0003; tel. (3) 3961-3255; fax (3) 3964-4071; e-mail noguchik@mb.infoweb.or.jp; f. 1941; research into carbohydrate chemistry, solid-state catalysts for ecoprocess; Pres. ITSUHO AISHIMA; publ. *Annual Report*.

Port and Harbour Research Institute: 3-1-1 Nagase, Yokosuka, Kanagawa 239; fax (468) 42-9265; f. 1962; attached to Ministry of Transport; research on harbour and coastal hydraulic engineering; library of 20,000 vols; Dir S. NODA; publs *Report* (quarterly), *Technical Notes* (quarterly), *Annual Report.*

Railway Technical Research Institute: 2-8-38 Hikari-cho, Kokubunji-shi, Tokyo 185-8540; tel. (425) 73-7258; fax (425) 73-7356; f. 1907; research in railway engineering and magnetic levitated vehicles; library of 350,000 vols; Chair. YOSHINOSUKE YASOSHIMA; Pres. HIROUMI SOEJIMA; publ. *Quarterly Report of RTRI.*

Research Institute for Production Development: 15 Shimo Kamomori Honmachi, Sakyo-ku, Kyoto; f. 1947; Dir A. OKUDA.

Research Institute of Printing Bureau: 1-6-1 Ooji, Kita-ku, Tokyo; f. 1891; Dir H. NONAKA; publ. *Research Bulletin* (2 a year).

Ship Research Institute: 38-1, 6-chome, Shinkawa, Mitaka, Tokyo 181-0004; tel. (422) 41-3015; fax (422) 41-3026; e-mail bunsho@srimot.go.jp; f. 1916; attached to Ministry of Transport; shipbuilding and marine engineering; library of 68,000 vols; Dir NOBUTAKA NANBU; publs *Papers* (6 a year).

Tensor Society: c/o Kawaguchi Institute of Mathematical Sciences, Matsu-ga-oka 2-7-15, Chigasaki 253; fax (467) 86-4713; f. 1937; undertakes original research in the field of Tensor Analysis and its applications; 700 mems world-wide; library of 23,000 vols; Pres. Prof. Dr T. KAWAGUCHI; Sec. Prof. Dr H. KAWAGUCHI; publ. *Tensor* (3 a year).

Uchu Kagaku Kenkyusho (Institute of Space and Astronautical Science): 3-1-1, Yoshinodai, Sagamihara, Kanagawa 229; tel. (427) 51-3911; f. 1981; government sponsored central institute for organization of scientific space research; facilities in all fields: implements research, development and operation of balloons, sounding rockets, satellites and launch vehicles; 290 mems; library of 60,000 vols; Dir Prof. ATSUHIRO NISHIDA; publs *Uchuken Hokoku* (Japanese, irregular), *ISAS Report* (English, irregular), *ISAS Research Note* (English, irregular).

Libraries and Archives

Akita

Akita Prefectural Library: 2-52 Senshume-itoku-cho, Akita-shi; tel. (188) 33-5411; f. 1899; 403,162 vols; Librarian N. FUJITA.

Chiba

Chiba Prefectural Central Library: 26 Ichiba-machi, Chiba City; 268,488 vols; Librarian S. TATEISHI.

Hakodate

Hakodate City Library: 23 Aoyagi-cho, Hakodate City; 122,500 vols (including branch library); Librarian I. FUKUDA.

Hiroshima

Hiroshima Prefectural Library: 3-7-47 Senda-machi, Naka-ku, Hiroshima City; tel. (82) 241-4995; fax (82) 241-9799; f. 1951; public library; 399,957 vols; Librarian K. HATAKEYAMA.

Kagoshima

Kagoshima Prefectural Library: 1-1 Shiroyama-machi, Kagoshima City, 222,357 vols; Librarian H. KUBOTA.

Kanazawa

Kanazawa City Library: 2-20 Tamagawa-cho, Kanazawa City 920; 510,000 vols; Librarian N. YOSHIMOTO.

Kanazawa Municipal Izumino Library: 22-22, 4-chome Izumino-machi, Kanazawa City 921-8034; tel. (76) 280-2345; fax (76) 280-2342; e-mail lib@kanazawa.or.jp; 360,000 vols; Dir N. SHIGA.

Kobe

Kobe City Library: 7-2 Kununoki-cho, Ikuta, Kobe; f. 1911; 240,000 vols; Librarian S. AKAI.

Kobe University Library: Rokkodai-cho, Nada-ku, Kobe; tel. (78) 803-0420; fax (78) 803-0436; f. 1908; 2,900,000 vols; Dir T. KOBAYASHI.

Kochi

Kochi Prefectural Library: 3 Marunouchi, Kochi City: 141,927 vols; Librarian N. SHIMESHINO.

Kyoto

Institute for Research in Humanities Library: 1 Ushinomiyacho, Yoshida, Sakyo-ku, Kyoto 606-8501; attached to Kyoto University; 493,000 vols; Dir Prof. YUZO YAMAMOTO.

Kyoto Prefectural Library: Okazaki Park, Kyoto-shi, Kyoto; tel. (75) 771-0069; fax (75) 771-2743; f. 1898; 350,000 vols; Dir MINORU SHIBATA; publs *Toshokan Kyoto* (bulletin, annually), *Jigyou Gaiyou* (annual report).

Kyoto University Library: Yoshida Hon-machi, Sakyo-ku, Kyoto 606-8501; tel. (75) 753-2613; fax (75) 753-2629; f. 1899; general library and 30 libraries of 10 faculties and 20 research institutes; 5,550,000 vols; Dir KOZO KIKUCHI.

Ryukoku University Library: 67 Tsukamoto-cho, Fukakusa, Fushimi-ku, Kyoto 612; tel. (75) 645-7885; fax (75) 641-7955; f. 1639; 1,180,367 vols; Librarian JITSUZO SHIGETA.

Matsuyama

Matsuyama University Library: 4-2 Bunkyo-cho, Matsuyama 790; f. 1923; 540,000 vols; collection of rare books, including first editions of eighteenth- and nineteenth-century works on political economy; Librarian Prof. K. MOCHIZUKI.

Nagoya

Nagoya University Library: Furo-cho, Chikusa-ku, Nagoya; f. 1939; central library and 9 school and 3 institute libraries; 2,542,000 vols; Dir Dr M. USHIOGI.

Tsurumai (Nagoya) Central Library: 43 Tsurumai-cho; Showa-ku, Nagoya City; 201,519 vols; Librarian M. WATANABE.

Naha

Ryukyu Islands Central Library: Central Library Building, Naha, Okinawa; f. 1950; 45,926 vols; central deposit library.

Nara

Nara Prefectural Library: 48 Nobori Oojicho, Nara City 630; f. 1909; 296,000 vols; Librarian KATSUKO TOYODA; publ. *Untei*.

Niigata

Niigata Prefectural Library: 2066 Meike, Niigata City; tel. (25) 284-6001; fax (25) 284-6832; f. 1915; 456,147 vols; Librarian K. SHIBUYA.

Niigata University Library: Ikarashi 2-Nocho, Niigata City 950-21; f. 1949; 1,397,560 vols; Dir S. KOBAYASHI.

Nishinomiya

Kwansei Gakuin University Library: 1-1-155 Uegahara, Nishinomiya, Hyogo; f. 1889; 1,200,000 vols, nearly 40 per cent in foreign languages; branch libraries for 8 schools and the Institute for Industrial Research; Niwa, Sato and Shibata collections; Dir A. MARUMO; publ. *Tokeidai* (Bulletin).

Okayama

Okayama University Library: 1-1 Naka 3-chome, Tsushima, Okayama City 700; f. 1949; 2 br. libraries; 1,720,000 vols; Dir H. KANDATSU; publ. *Kai* (Library News, 2 a year).

Osaka

Kansai University Library: 3-3-35 Yamate-cho, Suita-shi, Osaka; tel. (6) 368-1121; fax (6) 330-1464; f. 1914; 1,528,962 vols (including 567,775 foreign), 21,168 periodicals; Librarian K. URANISHI.

Osaka Prefectural Nakanoshima Library: 1-2-10 Nakanoshima, Kita-ku, Osaka; tel. (6) 203-0474; fax (6) 203-4914; f. 1903; 913,836 vols; Head Librarian SHIGEMITSU NAKAYAMA; publ. *Osaka Furitsu Tosyokan Kiyou* (annually).

Sapporo

Hokkaido University Library: Kita 8 Nishi 5, Kita-ku, Sapporo 060; tel. (11) 716-2111; fax (11) 746-4595; f. 1876; 18 br. libraries; 2,971,000 vols (including 1,408,000 foreign); special collections on Slavic studies and North Eurasian culture studies; Librarian Prof. T. SANBONGI; publ. *Yuin* (quarterly).

Sendai

Tohoku University Library: Kawauchi, Aoba-ku, Sendai 980-77; f. 1911; 2,247,000 vols, including Kano Collection (108,000 vols) in Japanese and Chinese, the Tibetan Buddhist Canons (6,652 vols), Wundt Collection (15,800 vols) and several other special collections; Dir S. KOYAMA; publs *Annual Report*, *Bulletin*.

Shizuoka

Shizuoka Prefectural Central Library: 53-1 Yada, Shizuoka City; tel. (54) 262-1242; fax (54) 264-4268; f. 1925; 430,000 vols, 7,500 periodicals, 4,000 films and videotapes; Librarian YOSHIHIKO SUZUKI; publs *Aoi* (1 a year), *Toshokan-Dayori* (6 a year).

Tenri

Tenri Central Library: Tenri City, Nara; tel. (743) 63-1515; fax (743) 63-7728; f. 1930; Tenri University Library also open to the public; 1,754,000 vols (including 445,489 foreign); Chief Librarian TERUAKI IIDA; special libraries: Yorozuyo Library on Christian Missions (including Jesuit mission printings in Japan), Kogido Library of Ito Jinsai on Confucian Studies, Wataya Library on Renga and Haikai Works (*c.* 20,000 items), Africana Collection (6,000 vols); publ. *Biblia* (2 a year, Japanese).

Tokyo

Chuo University Library: 742 Higashi-nakano, Hachioji-shi, Tokyo 192-03; f. 1885; 1,365,024 vols (577,826 in foreign languages), 14,561 periodicals; Librarian Prof. NOBUO YASUI.

Hitotsubashi University Library: Naka 2-1, Kunitachi-city, Tokyo 186; tel. (425) 72-1101; f. 1887; 1,518,000 vols (including Kodaira branch); Librarian MASANORI NAKAMURA; houses branch library for Institute of Economic Research; f. 1940; 242,500 vols; Dir Y. KIKOKAWA.

Imperial Household Agency Library: 1-1 Chiyoda, Chiyoda-ku, Tokyo; tel. (3) 3213-1111; fax (3) 3214-2792; f. 1948; 87,946 vols; Librarian Mr MOMOTA.

International Christian University Library: 10-2 Osawa 3-chome, Mitaka-city, Tokyo 181; 462,000 vols (including 225,000 foreign), 5,561 periodicals; Dir YUKI NAGANO.

Japan Meteorological Agency, Office of Archives and Library: 1-3-4 Ote-machi, Chiyoda-ku, Tokyo 100; f. 1875; 110,000 vols; Chief Librarian SHINJIRO KATO.

Keio University MediaNet—Library and Computer Services: 2-15-45 Mita, Minato-ku, Tokyo 108; Chair. Y. KURASAWA.

Kokugakuin University Library: 4-10-28 Higashi, Shibuya-ku, Tokyo; f. 1882; 1,087,663 vols; Librarian Prof. TOSHIO SAWANOBORI; publ. *Kokugakuin Daigaku Toshokan Kiyo* (Library Journal).

Kokuritsu Kobunshokan (National Archives): 3-2 Kitanomaru Park, Chiyoda-ku, Tokyo; tel. (3) 3214-0621; fax (3) 3212-8806; f. 1971; attached to the Prime Minister's office; archives, Cabinet Library of 574,000 vols, and br. of the National Diet Library; Dir-Gen. KAZUMASA INAHASHI; publs *Annual Report*, *Kitanomaru*.

Kokuritsu Kyoiku Kenkyusho Kyoiku Toshokan (National Institute for Educational Research Library): 6-5-22 Shimomeguro, Meguro-ku, Tokyo 153-8681; f. 1949; 424,000 vols; publ. *Kyoiku Kenkyu Ronbun Sakuin* (Education Index, 1 a year).

Ministry of Education Library: 3-2-2 Kasumigaseki, Chiyoda-ku, Tokyo 100; 120,000 vols; Librarian TARO SUZUKI.

Ministry of Foreign Affairs Library: 2-2 Kasumigaseki, Chiyoda-ku, Tokyo 100; 90,638 vols and 175 periodicals; Librarian S. UCHIDA.

Ministry of Justice Library: 1-1, 1-chome, Kasumigaseki, Chiyoda-ku, Tokyo 100; f. 1928; 278,000 vols; Chief Librarian FUSAO MURATA.

National Diet Library: 10-1, Nagatacho 1-chome, Chiyoda-ku, Tokyo 100-8924; tel. (3) 3581-2331; fax (3) 3597-9104; e-mail kokusai@ndl.go.jp; f. 1948; deposit library for Japanese publs and publs of US Government, UN, UNESCO, ILO, WHO, ICAO, WTO, etc.; IFLA PAC centre for Asia, ISSN centre, international book exchange and information centre of Japan; is divided into one bureau and six departments: Administrative, Research and Legislative Reference, Acquisitions, Books, Serials, Special Materials and Library Co-operation; consists of the Main Library, Detached Library in the Diet and Ueno Library (6,767,000 vols, 157,000 periodicals), Toyo Bunko (Oriental) Library and 35 branch libraries in the Executive and Judicial agencies of the Government; Librarian SHIN-ICHIRO OGATA; publs *Japanese National Bibliography* (weekly), *National Diet Library Monthly Bulletin*, *General Index to the Debates* (each Diet Session), *Index to the Japanese Laws and Regulations in Force* (annually), *Reference* (monthly), *Annual Report of the National Diet Library*, *National Diet Library Newsletter* (in English, quarterly), *CDN LAO Newsletter* (3 a year), etc.

National Institute of Japanese Literature Library: 16-10 Yutaka-cho 1-chome, Sinagawa-ku, Tokyo 142; f. 1972; microforms of woodcuts, old printed books and MSS; 28,452 reels microfilm, 52,987 sheets microfiche, 60,566 vols paper copy; 94,736 vols old and current books; 4,313 titles of serials; Archives for Japanese Historical Documents: 500,000 items (holdings), 8,879 items deposited, 3,256 reels microfilm, 5,000 articles of folk material, 94,665 vols current books, 1,213 titles of serials; Dir of Bibliographic and Reference Services H. ONISHI; Historical Documents Division Y. MORI; publs catalogues.

Norin Suisansho Toshokan (Ministry of Agriculture, Forestry and Fisheries Library): 2-1, Kasumigaseki, 1-chome, Chiyoda-ku, Tokyo 100; f. 1948; 275,000 vols; Librarian TATEKI ARAI; publs *Norin Suisan Tosho Shiryo Geppo* (monthly review of publs on agriculture, forestry and fisheries), *Norin Suisan Bunken Kaidai* (annual annotated bibliography).

Ochanomizu University Library: 1-1 Otsuka 2-chome, Bunkyo-ku, Tokyo 112-8610; tel. (3) 5978-5835; fax (3) 5978-5849; f. 1874, reorganized 1949; 563,000 (including 179,000 foreign) vols; Dir YUJIRO OGUCHI.

Patent Office Library: 1-1 Sannen-cho, Chiyoda-ku, Tokyo; 144,502 vols; Librarian T. NAKASHIBA.

Science Council of Japan Library: 22-34, Roppongi 7-chome, Minato-ku, Tokyo 106; tel. (3) 3403-6291; f. 1949; 54,000 vols; Librarian MASATO OKAMOTO.

Seikado Bunko Library: 2-23-1 Okamoto, Setagaya-ku, Tokyo; 200,000 vols of Chinese and Japanese classics.

Sophia (Jôchi) University Library: 7-1 Kioi-cho, Chiyoda-ku, Tokyo 102; tel. (3) 3238-3511; telex 24140; fax (3) 3238-3268; f. 1913; 840,000 vols, 12,000 periodicals; Librarian MASATAKA SO.

Statistical Library, Statistics Bureau, Management and Co-ordination Agency: 19-1, Wakamatsu-cho, Shimjuku-ku, Tokyo 162; tel. (3) 3202-1111; f. 1946; *c.* 400,000 vols; Librarian KENJI OKADA; publs numerous reports and statistical handbooks.

Supreme Court Library: 4-2 Hayabusacho, Chiyoda-ku, Tokyo 102; f. 1949; 240,000 vols; Librarian Y. SIRAKI.

Tokyo Geijutsu Daigaku Toshokan (Tokyo National University of Fine Arts and Music Library): Ueno Park, Taito-ku, Tokyo; over 175,108 vols, 1,747 microfilm reels; also music and gramophone record collections (83,168 scores, 18,421 records); Librarian T. NARUKAWA.

Tokyo Metropolitan Central Library: 5-7-13 Minami-Azabu, Minato-ku, Tokyo 106-0047; tel. (3) 3442-8451; fax (3) 3447-8924; f. 1972; research and reference centre, centre of library co-operation in Tokyo; 1,471,000 vols and 10,000 periodicals; Yedo Collection, Kaga Collection (rare books of the Yedo Era), Morohashi Collection (Chinese classics), Sanetoh Collection (Chinese literature) and others; Dir TETSUYA SAITO; publs *Hibiya*, *Library Science Bulletin* (1 a year), *Annual Report*.

Tokyo University of Fisheries Library: Konan 4-5-7, Minato-ku, Tokyo 108; tel. (3) 5463-0444; f. 1888; 258,000 vols (including 69,000 foreign); Librarian KO MATUDA; publs *Report* (1 a year), *Transactions* (irregular).

Tokyo University of Foreign Studies Library: 4-51-21 Nishigahara, Kita-ku, Tokyo 114-8580; f. 1899; 482,000 vols (including 355,000 foreign); Dir S. TAKAHASHI.

Toyo Bunko/Oriental Library: Honkomagome 2-28-21, Bunkyo-ku, Tokyo 113-0021; tel. (3) 3942-0121; fax (3) 3942-0258; e-mail webmaster@toyo-bunko.or.jp; f. 1924; research library specializing in Asian studies; 800,000 vols; special collections: Morrison collection of Western books on Asia, Iwasaki collection of old and rare Japanese and Chinese books and manuscripts, Kawaguchi collection of Tibetan and Buddhist classics; Dir HAJIME KITAMURA; publs *Toyo Gakuho* (4 a year), *Memoirs of the Research Department of the Toyo Bunko* (annually) (see also National Diet Library).

Has attached:

Centre for East Asian Cultural Studies for UNESCO (CEACS): Honkomagome 2-28-21, Bunkyo-ku, Tokyo 113-0021; tel. (3) 3942-0124; fax (3) 3942-0120; affiliated to Toyo Bunko; information centre providing research material on Asia (excluding Japan) in the humanities and social sciences; UNESCO microfilm collection; Dir YONEO ISHII.

University of Tokyo Library System: Hongo 7-3-1, Bunkyo-ku, Tokyo 113-0033; f. 1877; general library and libraries of 10 faculties and 17 institutes; 7,386,000 vols, including Nanki collection (96,000 vols) and several other special collections; Dir K. ROKUMOTO; publ. *The University of Tokyo Library System Bulletin*.

Waseda University Library: 1-6-1 Nishiwaseda, Shinjuku-ku, Tokyo 169-50; fax (3) 5272-2061; f. 1882; 1,796,000 vols; Librarian N. OKAZAWA; publ. *Bulletin* (1 a year).

Toyonaka

Osaka University Library: 1-4, Machikaneyama-cho, Toyonaka, Osaka 560; tel. (6) 850-5045; fax (6) 850-5052; f. 1931; 2,800,000 vols; Main library and 2 branch libraries; Dir TAKESHI HAYASHI.

Ujiyamada

Mie Shinto Library: Kushimoto-machi, Kanda, Ujiyamada, Mie Prefecture; 189,000 vols; Librarian MASAATSU NOGAMI.

Utsunomiya

Tochigi Prefectural Library: 357 Bandacho, Utsunomiya City; 196,579 vols; Librarian T. IZUMI.

Yamaguchi

Yamaguchi Prefectural Library: 150-1 Matsue, Ushirogawa, Yamaguchi City; f. 1903; 389,104 vols; Librarian TANAKA HIROSHI; publ. *Toshokan Yamaguchi*.

Yamaguchi University Library: Yoshida, Yamaguchi City 753; f. 1949; 2 br. libraries; 1,414,000 vols.

Yokohama

Kanagawa Prefectural Library: 9-2 Momijigaoka, Nishi-ku, Yokohama City; f. 1954; 76 mems; 540,875 vols; Librarian M. ANDO; publ. *Kanagawa Bunka* (every 2 months).

Yokohama National University Library: 156 Tokiwadai, Hodogaya-ku, Yokohama City 240; tel. (45) 335-1451; fax (45) 341-9880; f. 1949; 1,018,000 vols; Dir Prof. T. OKUMURA.

Museums and Art Galleries

Abashiri

Abashiri Kyodo Hakubutsukan (Abashiri Municipal Museum): Katsuramachi 1-1-3, Abashiri-shi, Hokkaido 093; tel. (152) 43-3090; f. 1936; 600 local products, 25,000 articles of historical, geographical and archaeological interest, and 1,800 ethnological objects; Dir M. TATEWAKI.

Asahikawa

Asahikawa Kyodo Hakubutsukan (Asahikawa Folk Museum): 1 Ichijo, 4-ku, Asahikawa City, Hokkaido 070; f. 1952; cultural objects of Ainu race, many archaeological items.

Atami

MOA Museum of Art: 26-2, Momoyama, Atami 413; tel. (557) 84-2511; fax (557) 84-2570; f. 1957, reorganized 1982 by Mokichi Okada Asscn; Oriental fine arts: paintings, ceramics, lacquers, calligraphy and sculptures; library of 25,000 vols; Dir YOJI YOSHIOKA; publs *MOA Art*, *Selected Catalogue* (5 vols), *Digest Catalogue*.

Gora

Hakone Museum of Art: Gora, Kanagawa Pref.; f. 1952; private collection of Okada Mokichi (founder of the Church of World Messianity) of Japanese ceramic works of art; Dir YOJI YOSHIOKA.

Hakodate

Hakodate City Museum: Hakodate Park, 17-1 Aoyagi-cho, Hakodate City; f. 1879; oldest local museum in Japan; Dir M. ISHIKAWA.

Hiraizumi

Chuson-ji Sanko-zo (Chuson-ji Temple Sanko Repository): Hiraizumi-machi, Nishi-Iwai-gun; f. 1955 to preserve treasures and possessions of the Fujiwara family who were important in the late period of Heian (801–1185).

Hiroshima

Hiroshima Children's Museum: 5-83, Moto-machi, Naka-ku, Hiroshima City 730; tel. (82) 222-5346; fax (82) 222-7020; f. 1980; scientific and cultural programmes; planetarium; exhibits on industry, science, transport, astronomy; Dir EIJI HIGAKI; publs guides, *Kagakukan Dayori* (monthly), *Planetarium* (4 a year), *Report of Activities* (annually).

Ikaruga

Hōryuji (Hōryūji Temple): Aza Hōryūji, Ikaruga-cho, Ikoma-gun, Nara Prefecture; a large number of Buddhist images and paintings; the buildings date from the Asuka, Nara, Heian, Kamakura, Ashikaga, and Tokugawa periods.

Ise

Jingu Chokokan (Jingu Historical Museum): Kuratayama, Ise-city; 1,734 exhibits, including treasures of the Grand Shrine of Ise (Naiku Shrine and Geku Shrine) and many objects of historical interest; library of 1,082 vols, MSS and pictures; Dir and Chief of Cultural Section of the Grand Shrine of Ise YASUJI AKIOKA.

Jingu Nogyokan (Agricultural Museum): Kuratayama, Ise-city; f. 1905; 9,583 exhibits connected with agriculture, forestry, and fishing (including collection of over 40 species of shark); Dir YASUJI AKIOKA.

Itsukushima

Itsukushima Jinja Homotsukan (Treasure Hall of the Itsukushima Shinto Shrine): Miyajima-cho, Saeki-gun; f. 1934; 4,000 exhibits of paintings, calligraphy, sutras, swords, and other ancient weapons; Curator and Chief Priest MOTOYOSHI NOZAKA.

Kamakura

Kamakura Kokuhokan (Kamakura Museum): 2-1-1 Yukinoshita, Kamakura City; tel. (467) 22-0753; fax (467) 23-5953; f. 1928; Japanese art and history in the Middle Ages; 3,521 valuable specimens of Japanese fine arts; 12 mems; library of 6,587 vols; Dir TATSUTO NUKI; publ. *Kokuhokan-zuroku*.

Museum of Modern Art, Kamakura: 2-1-53 Yukinoshita, Kamakura 248; tel. (467) 22-5000; fax (467) 23-2464; f. 1951; modern and contemporary art in Japan and Europe; Dir TADAYASU SAKAI; publ. *Kanagawa Bijutsu Fudoki*.

Kawaguchi

Museum of Ethnology and Nature: Kawaguchi, Yamanashi-ken; f. 1987; entomological research centre containing the largest collection of exotic Coleoptera in Japan; Dir HIKARU NAKAMURA.

Kobe

Hakutsuru Bijitsukan (Hakutsuru Fine Art Museum): 6-1-1 Sumiyoshiyamate, Higashinada-ku, Kobe 658; tel. (78) 851-6001; fax (78) 851-6001; f. 1934; 1,300 specimens of fine art, including noted Chinese ceramics, old bronze vases and silver ware, and oriental carpets; library of 10,000 vols; Dir HIDEO KANO.

Kobe City Museum: 24 Kyo-machi, Chuoku, Kobe 650; tel. (78) 391-0035; fax (78) 392-7054; f. 1982; theme of museum is the historical view of "international cultural intercourse", especially contact between eastern and western cultures; 32,000 items including 21 national treasure items, 71 important collections of Namban and Kohmoh arts, 17th–19th century maps, also historical and archaeological items; library of 30,000 vols; Dir Dr TATSUO MIYAZAKI; publs *Yearbook, Museum Tayori* (news letter, quarterly), catalogues.

Kochi

Kochi Koen Kaitokukan (Museum in Kochi Park): 1-2-1 Marunouchi, Kochi City; tel. (888) 24-5701; fax (888) 24-9931; 1913; 800 exhibits, including autographs and material of interest in Japanese historical research; Dir TAKESHI IKEGAMI.

Kotohira

Kotohira-gü Hakubutsukan (Museum in the Kotohira Shrine): Kotohira-gü Shrine, Kotohira-machi, Nakatado-gun; 3,011 exhibits; Chair. MITSUSHIGE KOTOOKA; Sec. HAZIME HIRAO KOTOHIRA.

Kumamoto

Kumamoto Museum: 3-2 Furukyōmachi, Kumamoto City 862; tel. (96) 324-3500; fax (96) 351-4257; f. 1952; 10,000 books; 80,000 items of natural scientific interest (sea shells, minerals, rocks etc.) and 30,000 items of historical interest (folklore, archaeology etc.); Chief Officer NOBUO TOMOZOE; publ. *Gazette*.

Kurashiki

Ohara Bijutsukan (Ohara Museum of Art): 1-1-15 Chuo, Kurashiki-city; f. 1930; 19th- and 20th-century Western paintings and contemporary arts; Japanese modern ceramics and fabrics; modern Japanese oil paintings; Dir TADAO OGURA.

Kushiro

Kushiro-shiritsu Hakubutsukan (Kushiro City Museum): Harutori Park 1-7, Shunkodai, Kushiro; tel. (154) 41-5809; fax (154) 41-5809; f. 1936; 12,130 earthenware articles, natural history museum; Curator YASHUTOSHI ISHIGURO; publs *Memoirs of the Kushiro City Museum* (annually), *Science Report of the Kushiro City Museum* (quarterly).

Kyoto

Chishakuin (Treasure Hall of the Chishakuin Temple): Higashi-Kawaramachi, Higashiyama-ku, Kyoto; Buddhist equipment and utensils, old documents, paintings, calligraphy, sutras, and books in Japanese and in Chinese.

Daigoji Reihokan (Treasure Hall of the Daigoji Temple): Daigo, Fushimi-ku, Kyoto; f. 1936; contains 1,500 old art objects and 120,000 historical documents relating chiefly to Buddhism.

Jishoji (Ginkakuji) (Silver Temple): Ginkakuji-cho, Sakyo-ku, Kyoto; f. 1482 by Soami, a Shogun of Ashikaga, as twelve separate buildings in the grounds of his villa; only the Ginkaku or Silver Hall, and the Togudo are now left; Curator R. ARIMA.

Kitano Temmangu Homotsuden (Treasure Hall of Kitano-Temmangu shrine): Kitano Bakuro-cho, Kamigyo-ku, Kyoto; shrine dedicated to Michizane Sugawara, statesman and great scholar of Heian period; exhibits of treasure hall include the 'Kitano-Tenjin' history picture scrolls and an ancient copy of the 'Nihon Shoki'.

Korūji Reihōden (Treasure Museum of the Koryuji Temple): Koryuji Temple, Uzumasa, Ukyo-ku, Kyoto; f. 1922; many Buddhist images and pictures, including the two images of 'Miroku Bosatsu'; Curator EIKO KIYOTAKI.

Kyoto Daigaku Bungakubu Hakubutsukan (Kyoto University Museum): Yosida Honmachi, Sakyō-ku, Kyoto; f. 1997; geology, natural history, archaeology, scientific instruments, maps, historical documents.

Kyoto Kokuritsu Hakubutsukan (Kyoto National Museum): 527 Chaya-machi, Higashiyama-ku, Kyoto; tel. (75) 541-1151; f. 1889 as Imperial Kyoto Museum; renamed Kyoto City Museum in 1924; reorganized in 1952 as National Museum; 47 mems; 43,296 books and 100,108 research photographs; 9,832 exhibits, including fine art and handicraft exhibits and historical materials of Asia, chiefly of Japan; Dir NORIO FUJISAWA; Chief Curator HIROSHI KANAZAWA; publ. *Gakuso* (annually).

Kyoto-shi Bijutsukan (Kyoto Municipal Museum of Art): Okazaki Park, Sakyo-ku, Kyoto; tel. (75) 771-4107; f. 1933 for exhibitions of contemporary art; a collection of contemporary fine arts objects, including 939 Japanese pictures (of which 320 are oils), 48 Japanese sculptures, 260 craftworks, 84 Japanese prints and 21 items of calligraphy; Dir MITSUGI UEHIRA; publs *Annual Report*, Exhibition Catalogues, *Museum Newspaper, The Arts of Kyoto* (series), etc.

Myōhōin (Treasure House of the Myōhōin Temple): Myohoin-maegawa-cho, Higashiyama-ku, Kyoto; possessions of Toyotomi-Hideyoshi and many other national treasures.

National Museum of Modern Art, Kyoto: Enshoji-cho, Okazaki, Sakyo-ku, Kyoto; tel. (75) 761-4111; fax (75) 752-0509; f. 1963; modern art, crafts, design, photography; Dir TAKEO UCHIYAMA; Chief Curator YASUHIRO SHIMADA; publs *Museum News, Annual Report*.

Ninnaji Reihóden (Treasure Hall of the Ninnaji Temple): Ninnaji Temple, Omuro Daimoncho, Ukyo-ku, Kyoto.

Rengeoin (Sanjusangendo) (Treasure House of the Rengeoin Temple): Mawari-cho, Higashiyama-ku, Kyoto; 'One Thousand Images' and many other Buddhist images.

Rokuonji (Treasures of the Rokuonji Temple): Kinkakuji-cho, Kita-ku, Kyoto; famed for its garden and gold pavilion.

Shoren-in (Treasure House of the Shōren-in Temple); Sanjōbō-machi, Awadaguchi, Higashiyama-ku, Kyoto; f. 1153: Dir JIKO HIGASHIFUSHIMI; library of 5,000 vols; rare books, writings, paintings, etc.

Taiten Kinen Kyoto Shokubutsuen (Kyoto Prefectural Museum Botanical Garden): Hangi-machi, Shimogamo, Sakyô-ku, Kyoto; 70,000 plants and 5,500 botanical specimens.

Toyokuni Jinja Hómotsuden (Treasure Hall of the Toyokuni Shrine): Shomen Chayamachi Yamato-Ooji, Higashiyama-ku, Kyoto; treasures and possessions of Toyotomi-Hideyoshi, including paintings, painted screens, swords, etc.

Yogen-In (Treasure Hall of the Yōgen-In Temple): Sanju-sangendō-mae, Yamato-ōji Shichijō Higashi Iru, Higashiyama-ku, Kyoto.

Yūrinkan (Yurinkan Collection): 44 Okazaki-Enshōjichyô, Sakyō-ku, Kyoto; f. 1926; some 30,000 exhibits of rare antique Chinese fine arts and curios, including bronze and jade ware, porcelain, seals, Buddhist images, pictures, and calligraphy; Dir Z. FUJII. The collection is privately owned by the Fujii Foundation.

Matsue

Koizumi-Yakumo Kinenkan (Lafcadio Hearn Memorial Hall): 322 Okudani-machi, Matsue City; tel. and fax (852) 21-2147; f. 1933; collection of items belonging to Lafcadio Hearn; library of 492 vols (works by and on Hearn); Dir KAZUO KIMURA.

Shimane Prefectural Museum: 1 Tonomachi, Matsue City; tel. (852) 22-5750; f. 1959; Japanese arts; Shinjo ukiyoe collections of Utamaro, Hirosige, Hokusai and other famous ukiyoe painters' works; Dir KAZUO SAKAMOTO; publ. *Museum News* (quarterly).

Matsumoto

Japan Folklore Museum (Matsumoto City Museum): 4-1 Marunouchi, Matsumoto City; 92,000 exhibits of geological, historical and archaeological interest; 45 star festival dolls; 293 popular belief tools; fine art.

Minobu

Minobusan Homotsukan (Treasury of the Kuonji Temple): Kuonji Temple, Minobumachi, Minami-Koma-gun; 300 articles, examples of the fine arts, and materials connected with the history of the Nichiren Sect of Buddhism, the biography of Saint Nichiren.

Miyazaki

Miyazakijingū Chókokan (Historical Museum in the Miyazaki Shrine): 360 Jingumachi, Miyazaki City; 4,000 objects of historical and archaeological interest; Dir H. YANAGHI.

Mount Koya

Kōyasan Reihōkan (Museum of Buddhist Art on Mount Kōya): Kōyasan, Kōya-cho, Itogun; f. 1926; 50,000 exhibits, including Buddhist paintings and images, sutras and old documents, some of them registered National Treasures and Important Cultural Properties; a centre of Buddhism in Japan; Dir CHIKYŌ YAMAMOTO.

Nagoya

Nagoya Castle Donjon: 1-1 Hon-maru, Naka-ku, Nagoya; tel. (52) 231-1700; built in 1612 by Ieyasu Tokugawa; destroyed by fire

1945; restored to its original form 1959; exhibition rooms, galleries and observatory; 331 frescoes painted by Tan-yu Kano and his successors.

Nara

Kasugataisha Homotsuden (Treasure Hall of the Kasugataisha Shrine): Kasugataisha Shrine, Kasugano-cho, Nara City; f. 1934; the ancient, curvilinear style of architecture is called 'Kasuga Zukuri' after this shrine; Shrine Master CHIKATADA KASANNOIN.

Museum Yamato Bunkakan: 1-11-6 Gakuen-minami, Nara City; tel. (742) 45-0544; f. 1960; art objects of East Asia, chiefly Japan, China and Korea; library of 20,000 vols; Dir Prof. ITSUJI YOSHIKAWA; publs *Yamato Bunka* (2 a year), *Catalogues* (English).

Nara National Museum: 50 Nobori-oji-cho, Nara-shi 630; tel. (742) 22-7771; f. 1895; Buddhist sculptures, paintings, applied arts, calligraphy, archaeological objects, etc.; also special exhibitions; Dir HIROYASU UCHIDA.

Neiraku Museum: Isuien Park, 74 Suimon-cho, Nara City; tel. (742) 22-2173; fax (742) 25-0781; f. 1939; ancient Chinese bronze mirrors, seals, etc., and Korean potteries; Dir JUNSUKE NAKAMURA.

Todaiji: 406-1 Zōshi-cho, Nara City; tel. (742) 22-5511; fax (742) 22-0808; f. 752; headquarters of Kegonshū Buddhist sect; 25 Buddhist priests, 90 staff; Daibutsuden: Main Hall of the Todaiji Temple, the largest wooden edifice in the world, the world-famous Great Image of Buddha and two Bodhisattvas; attached buildings are the Hokkedō, Kaidan-in, Nigatsudō, which contain many famous images of Buddha and Bodhisattva; library of 50,000 vols, 10,000 manuscripts; Dir M. KOSAI; publ. *Nanto Bukkyō: Journal of the Nanto Society for Buddhist Studies* (1 a year).

Yakushiji (Yakushiji Temple): Nishi-no-Kyō-machi, Nara City; tel. (742) 33-6001; fax (742) 33-6004; e-mail yksj8@mahoroba.or.jp; famous bronze images of the Yakushi Trinity; a pagoda 1,300 years old; Dir K. TAKADA.

Narita

Naritasan Reikokan Museum (Treasure Hall of the Naritasan-Shinshoji Temple): Narita Park, Narita-City, Chiba Pref.; f. 1947; contains treasures dedicated to the shrine and archaeological pieces from the region, 12,113 MSS and books, sculptures, botanical specimens; Curator SHOSEKI TSURUMI.

Omishima

Oyamazumi Jinja Kokuhokan (Treasure Hall of the Oyamazumi Shrine): Oyamazumi Shrine, Omishima town, Ochigun; f. AD 1; 2,000 exhibits, including a large collection of ancient armour, swords, and the oldest mirrors in Japan; library of 20,000 vols; Curator YASUHISA MISHIMA.

Osaka

National Museum of Ethnology: 10-1 Senri Expo Park, Suita, Osaka 565; tel. (6) 876-2151; fax (6) 875-0401; f. 1974; library of 393,000 books, 11,000 journals; Dir-Gen. KOMEI SASAKI; publs *Bulletin* (quarterly), *Minpaku Tsushin* (newsletter), *Gekkan Minpaku* (monthly).

Osaka Municipal Museum of Art: 1-82 Chausuyama-cho, Tennoji-ku, Osaka 543; tel. (6) 771-4874; fax (6) 771-4856; f. 1936; Chinese, Korean and Japanese fine art; library of *c.* 11,000 vols; Dir YUTAKA MINO; publ. *Bulletin* (1 a year).

Osaka Museum of Natural History: Nagai Park, Higashisumiyoshi-ku, Osaka 546; f. 1952; entomology, zoology, botany, geology and palaeontology; Dir YOKIO MIYATAKE; Head Curator TAKAYOSHI NASU; publs *Bulletin*, *Occasional Papers*, *Special Publications*, *Annual Report*, *Nature Study*.

Tenri

Tenri University Sankokan Museum: 1 Furu, Tenri City, Nara Prefecture 632-8540; tel. and fax (743) 63-7721; f. 1930; attached to Tenri University; ethnographic and archaeological items from all parts of the world.

Tokyo

Ancient Orient Museum: 1-4 Higashi Ikebukuro 3-chome, Toshima-ku, Tokyo 170; tel. (3) 3989-3494; fax (3) 3590-3266; f. 1978; archaeology and ancient history of Middle and Near East, Egypt, India and Central Asia; library of 9,000 vols; Dir Prof. NAMIO EGAMI; publs *Bulletin* (annually), research reports.

Art Museum of the Tokyo National University of Fine Arts and Music: Ueno Park, Taito-ku, Tokyo 110-8714; tel. (3) 5685-7744; fax (3) 5685-7805; paintings, sculptures and applied art of Japan, China and Korea.

Bridgestone Museum of Art, Ishibashi Foundation: 10-1, Kyobashi 1-chome, Chuo-ku, Tokyo 104; tel. (3) 3563-0241; fax (3) 3561-2130; f. 1952 by Shojiro Ishibashi; private museum of 19th- and 20th-century French paintings and modern Western-style Japanese paintings; Dir HIDEO TOMIYAMA; publ. *Annual Report of Bridgestone Museum of Art and Ishibashi Museum of Art*.

Gotoh Museum: 9-25 3-chome Kaminoge, Setagaya-ku, Tokyo; f. 1960; Japanese, Chinese and Korean art; about 2,000 exhibits, including the 'Tales of Genji' scroll and the 'Diary of Lady Murasaki' scroll.

Inokashira Onshi Koen Shizen Bunkaen (Natural Science Park in Inokashira Park): 1-17-6 Gotenyama, Musashinoshi, Tokyo; zoo, botanical garden, research room, marine biology room.

Kokuritsu Kagaku Hakubutsukan (National Science Museum): Ueno Park 7-20, Taito-ku, Tokyo 110-8718; tel. (3) 5814-9898; e-mail webmaster@kahaku.go.jp; f. 1877; merged with Research Institute for Natural Resources in 1971; exhibits of natural history, physical science and engineering; library of 80,000 vols; Dir HIRONAO SAKAMOTO; publs *Bulletin* (in 5 series), *Memoirs* (1 a year).

Kotsu Hakubutsukan (Transport Museum): 25 1-chome, Kanda-Sudacho, Chiyoda-ku, Tokyo; f. 1921; 235,000 articles, including locomotives, electric equipment, motor-cars, aircraft, ships, etc.; Dir NOBUO OHASHI (acting).

Meiji Jingu Homotsuden (Meiji Shrine Treasure Museum): Yoyogi, Shibuya-ku, Tokyo; f. 1921; 102 treasures and possessions of Emperor Meiji and 74 objects belonging to Empress Shoken; there is also a Memorial Picture Gallery.

National Museum of Modern Art, Tokyo: 3 Kitanomaru Koen, Chiyoda-ku, Tokyo 102-8322; tel. (3) 3214-2561; fax (3) 3213-1340; f. 1952; collection of Japanese-style paintings, oil paintings, prints, sculpture, drawings, watercolours and photographs, and European and American works; includes a Crafts Gallery and Film Centre; Dir KIYOHISA NISHIZAKI; publs *Gendai no Me* (6 a year, Japanese), *National Film Centre Newsletter* (6 a year, Japanese).

National Museum of Western Art, The: 7-7 Ueno-koen, Taito-ku, Tokyo 110-0007; tel. (3) 3828-5131; fax (3) 3828-5135; f. 1959 (designed by Le Corbusier); 19th-century European paintings and sculptures collected by the late Kojiro Matsukata and new acquisitions of old masters; Dir SHUJI TAKASHINA; publs *Annual Bulletin of the National Museum of Western Art, Journal of the National Museum of Western Art*.

Nezu Institute of Fine Arts: 6-5 Minami-Aoyama, Minato-ku, Tokyo 107; tel. (3) 3400-2536; fax (3) 3400-2436; f. 1940; private collection by Kaichiro Nezu of 7,195 paintings, calligraphy, sculpture, swords, ceramics, lacquerware, archaeological exhibits; 184 items designated as national treasures; Dir HISAO SUGAHARA.

Nippon Mingeikan (Japan Folk Crafts Museum): 4-3-33 Komaba, Meguro-ku, Tokyo 153; tel. (3) 3467-4527; fax (3) 3467-4537; f. 1936; Japanese traditional folk craft and craft from around the world; special collections from founding members of Mingei Movement: Kanjiro Kawai, Shoji Hamada, Keisuke Serizawa, Bernard Leach, Shiko Munakata; Dir SORI YANAGI; publ. *Mingei* (monthly).

Okura Cultural Foundation Okura Shukokan Museum: 2-10-3, Toranomon, Minato-ku, Tokyo; f. 1917; 1,700 articles of fine arts; 36,000 vols Chinese classics; Pres. NOBORU NISHITANI.

Shitamachi Museum: 2–1 Ueno-koen, Taito-ku, Tokyo; tel. (3) 823-7451; f. 1980; re-creation of the old commercial district of Tokyo; includes a typical street, wooden houses, life-size figures, furniture, pictures, books and letters, religious material, domestic utensils, Second World War items, games and musical instruments, cosmetics and accessories, etc.; Dir HIDENOBU HIROSE.

Shodo Hakubutsukan (Calligraphy Museum): 125 Kaminegishi, Daito-ku, Tokyo; f. 1936; collection of the calligrapher, the late F. Nakamura; 1,000 rubbed copies of the stone tablets and 'hōjō', ancient texts of calligraphy (10,000 articles).

Tokyo Daigaku Rigakubu Fuzoku Shokubutsuen (Botanical Gardens, Faculty of Science, University of Tokyo): 7-1, Hakusan 3, Bunkyo-ku, Tokyo 112; tel. (3) 3814-2625; fax (3) 3814-0139; f. 1684, transferred to University 1877; Nikko branch; f. 1902; research in systematic botany and conservation of plants; 6,000 kinds of plants; 2,500 in Nikko; library of 20,000 vols; Dir Prof. Dr TOSHIYUKI NAGATA.

Tokyo Kokuritsu Hakubutsukan (Tokyo National Museum): 13-9 Ueno Park, Taito-ku, Tokyo 110; tel. (3) 3822-1111; f. 1871; largest art museum in Japan; Eastern fine arts, including paintings, calligraphy, sculpture, metal work, ceramic art, textiles, lacquer ware, archaeological exhibits, etc.; Dir-Gen. BUNICHIRÔ SANO; publs *National Museum News* (monthly) and *Museum* (monthly).

Tokyo-to Bijutsukan (Tokyo Metropolitan Art Museum): Ueno Park 8–36, Taito-ku, Tokyo; tel. (3) 3823-6921; telex (03) 3823-6920; f. 1926; ancient and modern art exhibition, educational service, art library and gallery for group exhibitions; Dir YOSHITAKE MAMURO; publs *Bijutsukan News* (irregular), *Bulletin* (1 a year).

Waseda Daigaku Tsubouchi Hakase Kinen Engeki Hakubutsukan (Tsubouchi Memorial Theatre Museum, Waseda University): 1-6-1 Nishi-Waseda, Shinjuku-ku, Tokyo 169-8050; tel. (3) 5286-1829; f. 1928; 92,000 (Japanese), 30,000 (foreign) books on drama, 46,000 wood-block colour prints, 23,000 pictures and 518 costumes, properties, and other items used on the stage; Dir BUNZO TORIGOE; publs *News Bulletin, Catalogues, Studies in Dramatic Art*.

Ueno

Iga Bungyó Kyokai (Iga Art and Industry Institute): 6, 1-Marunouchi, Ueno, Ueno City; 3,000 articles.

Yokohama

Kanazawa Bunko Museum Kanagawa Prefectural: 142 Kanazawa-cho, Kanagawa-ku, Yokohama; library f. 1275; 680 articles, including various specimens of Japanese fine arts, 20,000 old books and 4,149 documents; 36 collections including 4,362 national treasures (figure of Hojo-Sanetoki, etc.); Curator ISAKICHI KUTSUKAKE.

Yonago

San-in Rekishikan (San-in Historical Museum): Ooshinozu, Yonago-shi, Shimoneken; f. 1940; 23,500 exhibits, including specimens and material of value in historical and archaeological research.

National Universities

AKITA UNIVERSITY

1-1 Tegata Gakuenmachi, Akita City 010-8502
Telephone: (18) 889-2207
Fax: (18) 889-2219

Founded 1949
Academic year: April to March

President: HIROSHI TOKUDA
Director of Administration Bureau: TOSHIO UENO
Dean of Student Administration: SABURO MINATO
Librarian: TADASHI SAWADA

Number of teachers: 513
Number of students: 4,758

Publication: *Bulletin*.

DEANS

Faculty of Education and Human Studies, and Graduate School of Education: TATSUO TSUSHIMA
School of Medicine and Graduate School of Medicine: AKIRA MIUMA
Faculty of Engineering and Resource Science, and Graduate School of Mining: NOBORU YOSHIMURA
College of Allied Medical Sciences: TOMIO NARISAWA

ATTACHED INSTITUTES

Center for Educational Research and Practice: Dir KENZI TERAI.

University Hospital: Dir KOZO SATO.

Animal Facilities for Experimental Medicine: Dir HIROTAKE MASUDA.

Central Research Laboratory: Dir KATSUHIKO ENOMOTO.

Research Institute of Materials and Resources: Dir ETSURO YAMADA.

Mineral Industry Museum: Dir TAKAHIKO MARUYAMA.

ASAHIKAWA MEDICAL COLLEGE

4-5 Nishikagura, Asahikawa 078-8510
Telephone: (166) 65-2111
Telex: 922492

Founded 1973
Academic year: April to March

President: YOSHIHIKO KUBO
Vice-Presidents: MAKOTO KATAGIRI, ISAO MAKINO
Secretary-General: TAKASHI TAKAHASHI
Librarian: JORO IWABUCHI

Library of 128,000 vols
Number of teachers: 257
Number of students: 805 undergraduate, 74 postgraduate

Publication: *Asahikawa Medical College* (1 a year).

HEADS OF DEPARTMENTS

Anatomy 1: Prof. HIROSHI KIYAMA
Anatomy 2: Prof. SHOJI MATSUSHIMA
Physiology 1: Prof. AKIHIRO KUROSHIMA
Physiology 2: Prof. TAKASHI SAKAMOTO
Biochemistry 1: Prof. HITOSHI FUJISAWA
Biochemistry 2: Prof. TORU KANAZAWA
Pharmacology: Prof. MASANOBU AZUMA
Pathology 1: Prof. KATSUHIRO OGAWA
Pathology 2: KEISUKE SATO
Microbiology: Prof. MASANOBU AZUMA
Hygiene: Prof. KOHTAROH YAMAMURA
Public Health: Prof. KOHTAROH YAMAMURA
Parasitology: Prof. AKIRA ITO
Legal Medicine: Prof. HIROSHI SHIONO
Internal Medicine 1: Prof. KENJIRO KIKUCHI
Internal Medicine 2: Prof. ISAO MAKINO
Internal Medicine 3: Prof. YUTAKA KOGO
Psychiatry and Neurology: Prof. SHIGERU CHIBA
Paediatrics: Prof. AKIMASA OKUNO
Surgery 1: Prof. TADAHIRO SASAJIMA
Surgery 2: Prof. SHINICHI KASAI
Orthopaedic Surgery: Prof. TAKEO MATSUNO
Dermatology: Prof. HAJIME IIZUKA
Urology: Prof. SUNAO YACHIKU
Ophthalmology: Prof. AKITOSHI YOSHIDA
Otorhinolaryngology: Prof. TAKEO MATSUNO
Obstetrics and Gynaecology: Prof. MUTSUO ISHIKAWA
Radiology: Prof. TAMIO ABURANO
Anaesthesiology and Critical Care Medicine: Prof. MUTSUO ISHIKAWA
Neurosurgery: Prof. TATSUYA TANAKA
Laboratory Medicine: Prof. HISAMI IKEDA
Dentistry and Oral Surgery: Prof. SHINICHI KITA
Principles of Nursing 1: Prof. JUN IWAMOTO
Principles of Nursing 2: Prof. SHOJI KIMURA
Clinical Nursing 1: Prof. NORIKO NOMURA
Clinical Nursing 2: Prof. YOKO OKADA
Public Health Nursing: Prof. YOSHIKATSU MOCHIZUKI
Philosophy: Prof. MASAKATSU OKADA
History: Prof. HITOSHI KONDOH
Psychology: Prof. JIRO IWABUCHI
Sociology: Asst Prof. ETSUKO MATSUOKA
Mathematics: Prof. KAZUNARI YAMAUCHI
Mathematical Information Science: Asst Prof. TAMOTSU MITAMURA
Physics: Prof. MITSUHO TANIMOTO
Chemistry: Prof. MASAO NAKAMURA
Biology: Prof. YUJIROH KAMIGUCHI
English: HISASHI NAITOH
German: Asst Prof. TSUYOSI TANAKA

ATTACHED INSTITUTES

Animal Laboratory for Medical Research: Dir TAKASHI SAKAMOTO.
Central Laboratory for Research and Education: Dir KATSUHIRO OGAWA.

CHIBA UNIVERSITY

1–33 Yayoi-cho, Inage-ku, Chiba 263-8522
Telephone: (43) 251-1111
Fax: (43) 290-2041

Founded 1949

President: K. MARUYAMA
Vice-Presidents: K. NOGUCHI, T. SAWAI
Secretary-General: K. NOZUMI
Librarian: S. TUTIYA

Number of full-time teachers: 1,245
Number of students: 15,928

Publications: Each faculty publishes a *Journal* or *Bulletin*.

DEANS

Faculty of Letters: K. GORYO
Faculty of Education: H. MIZUUCHI
Faculty of Law and Economics: H. HAYAMA
Faculty of Science: M. TAGURI
School of Medicine: M. TANIGUCHI
Faculty of Pharmaceutical Sciences: T. IMANARI
School of Nursing: M. NOGUCHI
Faculty of Engineering: Y. YAMAGUCHI
Faculty of Horticulture: K. NAKAYAMA
Graduate School of Science and Technology: M. MURAKAMI
Graduate School of Humanities and Social Sciences: M. IWATA

DIRECTORS

University Hospital: A. YAMAURA
Health Sciences Center: K. NAGAO
Chemical Analysis Center: T. UEMATSU
Center for Environmental Remote Sensing: Y. YASUDA
Center for Frontier Science: Y. HARADA
Information Processing Center: S. SHIMAKURA
International Student Center: Y. IKEDA
Radioisotope Research Center: K. OHASHI
Research Center for Pathogenic Fungi and Microbial Toxicoses: M. MIYAJI
Center for Foreign Languages: S. MINAMIZUKA
Center of Co-operative Research: Y. YOSHIDA
Laboratory Waste Treatment Plant: M. YAMAGUCHI

PROFESSORS

Faculty of Letters:

AKIYAMA, K., Basic Linguistics and Literature
AOKI, T., Psychology
FUJIMOTO, T., Philosophy and Axiology
GORYO, K., Psychology
HARA, S., History of Ancient Japan
HAYASHIDA, R., French Literature
IIDA, N., Philosophy
INUZUKA, S., Sociology
JITSUMORI, M., Comparative Cognition
KANEKO, T., Basic Linguistics and Literature
KAWAHARA, S., Archaeology
KINOSHITA, T., Russian Literature
KURACHI, T., Basic Linguistics and Literature
MAEDA, S., Austrian Literature
MINAMIZUKA, S., History
MITSUI, Y., French Thought
MIURA, S., Ancient Japanese Literature
MIYAKE, A., Modern Japanese Labour History
MIYANO, H., Psychology
MIZUNOE, Y., English and American Literature
NAKAMURA, M., Cultural Anthropology
NEUSTUPNY, J., Linguistics
OGATA, T., Sociology
OGIHARA, S., Basic Linguistics and Literature
OGURA, M., English Philology
OKAMOTO, T., Japanese Archaeology
ONO, K., English and American Literature
ONO, M., Japanese History
SAKURAI, A., Sociology
SATO, H., History
SUGAHARA, K., Japanese History
SUZUKI, H., Sociology
TAKAHASHI, K., Ancient Philosophy
TAKEI, H., Medical Anthropology
TAKITO, M., Modern Japanese Literature
TAMAIZUMI, Y., English Renaissance Literature
TOCHIGI, Y., Japanese Linguistics and Literature
TSUCHIYA, S., Philosophy
UCHIMA, T., Japanese Linguistics and Literature
UEMURA, Y., Experimental Psychology
WAKAKUWA, M., History of Art

Faculty of Education:

ABE, A., Physical Education and School Health Education
AKASHI, Y., Educational Sociology
AKIYAMA, M., Vocal Music
AMAGASA, S., School Management
FUJII, T., Constitutional Law
FUJISAWA, H., Art Education
HIROHASHI, G., Physical Education
HIRONAKA, M., Clinical Psychology
IKEDA, Y., American and European History

IMAMURA, H., Sociology of Physical Education and Sport
INABA, H., Chemistry
INAGAKI, K., Early Childhood Education
ISOBE, K., Orthopaedics
IWAGAKI, O., Classroom Teaching Methods
KAMO, H., Philosophy
KATAOKA, Y., Sports Physiology
KATAYAMA, T., Sports Management
KAWAGUCHI, K., Instrumental Music
KENMOCHI, N., Analysis and Applied Mathematics
KIKUCHI, T., Teaching Methods of Physical Education and Sports
KIMURA, S., Japanese Language
KOBAYASHI, S., Theory of School Nursing and School Health
KOMIYA, T., English and American Literature
KUMABE, T., Mechanics
KURANO, M., Analysis and Applied Mathematics
KUSAKARI, H., Nuclear Physics
MAEJIMA, M., Clothing Science
MIURA, K., Cognitive Development and Instruction
MIURA, Y., Teaching of Physical Education
MIWA, S., School Management
MIYAHARA, T., Teaching of Social Studies
MIYAMOTO, M., Home Management
MIYANO, M., Teaching of Music
MIZUNO, S., Composition and Teaching of Music
MIZUUCHI, H., Curriculum Development
MURAMATSU, S., Sports and Nutrition
NAGASHIMA, K., Food and Nutrition
NAGATA, K., Comparative Theory of Art
NAKAMA, M., Home Economics Education
NUKUI, M., Teaching of Science
OHGAMA, T., Wood Science and Technology
OKAMOTO, K., Solid State Physics
OKI, T., Industrial Design
ONODERA, T., Psychology of School Learning
OTSUKA, T., English Linguistics
SASAKI, M., Japanese Literature
SATO, K., Ethics
SHIMA, H., Economics
SHIMADA, K., Teaching of Mathematics
SHIMIZU, M., Personal and Group Counselling
SHIMIZU, T., English and American Literature
SHIMOMURA, Y., Theory and History of Music
SHUTOU, H., Japanese Language Education
SUEYOSHI, K., Neurosurgery
SUNADA, J., Physics of Solid Surfaces
SUZUKI, A., Physiology and Ecology of Fungi
TAJIMA, Y., Physical Education
TAKATA, M., Agronomy
TAKEFUTA, Y., English Linguistics
TERAKADO, Y., Housing
TOKUYAMI, I., Sports Pedagogy
TOYOTA, H., Teaching Methods of Physical Education and Sports
UENO, H., Sculpture
UESHIBA, Y., Clinical Psychology
UMETANI, T., Psychology of Handicapped Children
URANO, T., Teaching of Calligraphy
USAMI, H., Teaching Method and Curriculum
UTSUMI, S., Plant Genetics
UZAWA, M., Analysis and Applied Mathematics
YAMAMURA, J., Human Geography
YAMANO, Y., Electrical Engineering
YAMAZAKI, Y., Geology
YODA, A., Technology Education

Faculty of Law and Economics:

ABE, K., History of Comparative Economic Systems
ABIKO, S., Contemporary Economic Theory
AKIMOTO, E., Comparative Economic Systems
AMANO, M., Applied Economics
AMEMIYA, A., German Socio-Economic History
ARAI, M., Civil Law, Trust Law
BANNO, J., Political History of Modern Japan
ENDO, Y., Commercial Law, Anti-monopoly Law
FUJII, R., Social Policy
FURUUCHI, H., European Economic History
HANDA, Y., Civil Law
HATA, I., Diplomatic History
HAYAMA, H., Applied Economics
HOMMA, T., Intellectual Property Law and International Trade Law
INABA, H., Econometrics
INOUE, R., Financial Accounting
IWATA, A., Constitutional Law, Parliamentary System
IWATA, M., Comparative Economic Systems
KAKIHARA, K., Macroeconomics
KAMANO, K., Civil Law, Environmental Law
KOGURE, A., Statistics and its application to Finance
KOMATSU, K., Applied Economics
KOMORI, T., Law of Treaties, Jurisdiction, Law of Armed Conflict
KUDO, H., History of Social Thought
MAEDA, Y., Political Studies
MARUYAMA, E., Condominium Law, Housing Law, Urban Law, Property Law
MATSUDA, T., Applied Economics
MIYAZAKI, R., Japanese Government and Politics
MURAYAMA, M., Business Administration
MURAYAMA, M., Sociology of Law
MUSASHI, T., Applied Economics
NAKAKUBO, H., Labour and Employment Law
NOMURA, Y., Microeconomics
NOZAWA, T., Theoretical Economics
OKUMOTO, Y., Economic Statistics
SAITO, Y., Criminal Law, Criminal Justice Policy
SASAKI, Y., Comparative Economics Systems and History
SHIMAZU, I., Philosophy of Law
SUZUKI, T., Administrative Procedure, Private Law, Local Government
TAKAHASHI, K., Theoretical Jurisprudence
TAGAYA, K., Information Law, Administrative Law
TEZUKA, K., Foreigners and Law, Employment Security in Japan, Germany and USA
WATANABE, T., German Studies
YAMASHINA, T., Middle High German
YUMOTO, K., Political Consciousness in Republican China

Faculty of Science:

FUNABASHI, M., Carbohydrate Chemistry
HINO, Y., Mathematical Analysis
HIROI, Y., Metamorphic Petrology
IMAMOTO, T., Organic Chemistry
INABA, T., Topology
INOUE, A., Clay Mineralogy
ISEZAKI, N., Geophysics
ITO, T., Structural Geology
KANEKO, K., Surface Solid State Chemistry, Molecular Science, Adsorption Science
KIMURA, T., High Energy Physics
KOBAYASHI, K., Cell Biology
KOMORI, Y., Mathematical Logic
KOSHITANI, S., Algebra
KOYAMA, N., Biochemistry
KURASAWA, H., Nuclear Physics
KURITA, S., Plant Systematics
MATSUMOTO, R., Astrophysics
MIYAZAKE, T., Aquatic Ecology
MIZUTANI, T., Geomorphology
NAKAGAMI, J., Statistics, Mathematical Programming
NAKAMURA, Y., Mathematical Analysis
NAKANO, M., Biochemistry
NATSUME, Y., Solid State Physics
NISHIDA, T., Mineralogy
NOZAWA, S., Algebra
OBINATA, T., Developmental Biology
OGAWA, K., Nuclear Physics
OGAWA, T., History of Physics
OHARA, S., Environmental Geology
OHASHI, K., Cell Physiology
OSAWA, M., Ecology
SAKURA, Y., Hydrogeology
SATO, T., Analysis
SHIGA, H., Theory of Manifolds and Numbers
TAGURI, M., Statistics
TAKAGI, R., Geometry
TAKEDA, Y., Co-ordination Chemistry, Solution Chemistry
TSUJI, T., Computer Software, Theory of Programmes
YAMADA, I., Solid State Physics
YAMAGUCHI, T., Palaeobiology
YAMAMOTO, K., Molecular Physiology
YASUDA, M., Statistics
YOKOYAMA, M., Organic Reaction and Synthesis
YOSHIDA, H., Analysis

School of Medicine:

ADACHI, E., Ophthalmology
ADACHI, M., Public Health
CHIBA, T., Anatomy
FUJIMURA, S., Biochemistry
FUJISAWA, T., Pulmonary Surgery
FUKUDA, Y., Physiology
HARIGAYA, K., Pathology
HATTORI, T., Neurology
HIRASAWA, H., Emergency and Critical Care Medicine
ICHINOSE, M., Plastic and Reconstructive Surgery
ITO, H., Radiology
ITO, H., Urology
KIMURA, S., Cardiovascular Biology
KITADA, M., Pharmaceutical Services
KITAHARA, H., Radiological Services
KIUCHI, M., Legal Medicine
KONDO, Y., Pathology
KONNO, A., Otorhinolaryngology
KOSEKI, H., Molecular Embryology
KOUNO, Y., Paediatrics
KURIYAMA, T., Chest Medicine
MASUDA, Y., Internal Medicine
MORIYA, H., Orthopaedic Surgery
NAKAJIMA, N., Surgery
NAKAJIMA, Y., Physiology
NAKAYA, H., Pharmacology
NISHINO, T., Anaesthesiology
NODA, M., Microbiology
NOGAWA, K., Hygiene
ONUMA, N., Paediatric Surgery
OWADA, H., Pathology of the Lung
SAISHO, H., Internal Medicine
SAITO, T., Molecular Genetics
SAITO, Y., Internal Medicine
SATO, T., Psychiatry
SATOMURA, Y., Medical Informatics
SEINO, S., Molecular Medicine
SEKIYA, S., Obstetrics and Gynaecology
SHIMADA, Y., Anatomy
SHINKAI, H., Dermatology
SHIRASAWA, H., Microbiology
SUZUKI, N., Biochemistry
TANIGUCHI, M., Molecular Immunology
TANZAWA, H., Oral Surgery
TOKUHISA, T., Developmental Genetics
WAKASHIN, M., Postgraduate Education Center
YAMAURA, A., Neurological Surgery
YANO, A., Parasitology
YONEMITSU, H., Laboratory Medicine
YUASA, S., Anatomy

Faculty of Pharmaceutical Sciences:

AIMI, N., Molecular Structure and Biological Function
CHIBA, K., Biochemical Pharmacology and Toxicology
HAMADA, Y., Pharmaceutical Chemistry
HORIE, T., Biopharmaceutics
IGARASHI, K., Clinical Biochemistry

Imanari, T., Analytical Chemistry
Ishibashi, M., Natural Products Chemistry
Ishikawa, H., Medicinal Organic Chemistry
Kobayashi, H., Biochemistry
Nakagawa, M., Synthetic Organic Chemistry
Ohashi, K., Radiopharmaceutical Chemistry
Saitoh, K., Molecular Biology and Biotechnology
Sawai, T., Microbial Chemistry
Suzuki, K. T., Toxicology and Environmental Health
Tsuda, M., Physical Chemistry
Ueda, S., Drug Information and Communication
Unemoto, T., Membrane Biochemistry
Watanabe, K., Chemical Pharmacology
Yamamoto, K., Pharmaceutical Technology
Yano, S., Molecular Pharmacology and Pharmacotherapeutics

School of Nursing:

Hirayama, A., Community Health Nursing
Kanematsu, Y., Child Nursing
Kimizuka, G., Pathobiology
Kusakari, J., Nursing Administration
Noguchi, M., Gerontological Nursing
Nojiri, M., Health Science
Saito, K., Psychiatric Nursing
Sato, R., Adult Nursing
Sugimori, M., Nursing Education
Yamada, S., Biophysics and Biochemistry
Yokota, M., Clinical Nursing Practice

Faculty of Engineering:

Amari, T., Printing Materials
Ando, Y., Architectural Design
Aoki, H., Materials Planning for Design
Aoyagi, S., Bio-Organic Chemistry
Fukasawa, A., Communication and Information Networks
Harada, Y., Advanced Molecular Assemblies
Hattori, M., Architectural Planning
Hattori, T., Ceramic Sciences
Hirohashi, M., Materials Science
Hisida, M., Heat Engine Engineering
Honda, T., Optical Engineering, Image Processing
Hori, Y., Environmental Energy Chemistry
Hotta, A., Industrial Design
Ikeda, H., Computer Sciences
Imiya, M., Computer Science
Ito, H., Computer Systems
Ito, K., Antenna Engineering
Kato, H., Optimization of Manufacturing
Katsuura, T., Ergonomics
Kawarada, H., Mathematics for Engineering
Kawase, T., Robot and Energy Engineering
Kitahara, T., City Planning
Kitamura, A., Fundamentals of Materials Science
Kitamura, T., Electronic Image Processing
Kobayashi, H., Organic Memory and Display Materials
Kotera, H., Printing Image Processing
Kudo, K., Physical Electronics
Kuryu, A., Architectural Design
Machida, S., Fracture Mechanics
Matsuba, I., Engineering of Information Processing
Mii, N., Imaging Chemistry
Miyake, Y., Measurement and Analysis of Image Information
Miyata, T., Interior Design
Miyazaki, K., Philosophy and History of Design
Miyazaki, M., Visual Communication Design
Morita, K., Structural Planning
Murakami, M., Structural Mechanics
Nakahira, T., Polymer Chemistry
Nakai, S., Disaster Prevention
Nakamura, M., Plastic Working
Nishikawa, N., Fluids Engineering
Noguchi, H., Building Material and Structural Engineering
Noguchi, K., Visual Perception
Nonami, K., Control and Robotics
Ochiai, Y., Advanced Device Materials
Oguma, K., Analytical Chemistry
Ogura, K., Synthetic Organic Chemistry
Okamoto, H., Optical Properties of Semiconductors
Okawa, S., Microwave Theory and Techniques
Otaka, K., Applied Physics
Saito, O., Semiconductor Rhotonics
Sasaki, Y., Industrial Inorganic Chemistry
Shimizu, T., Environmental Design
Shirai, R., Fundamentals of Materials Science
Sugita, K., Information Recording Materials
Takanashi, K., Structural Analysis
Tamai, T., History of Architecture
Tanaka, K., Physical Electronics
Tateda, M., Opto-electronics
Tatsumoto, H., Systems Design in Water and Wastewater Treatment
Uematsu, T., Industrial Physical Chemistry
Watanabe, T., Micro-machine Elements
Yaguchi, H., Visual Science
Yamaguchi, M., Electrical Circuits
Yamamoto, M., Synthetic Organic Chemistry
Yamaoka, T., Imaging Materials
Yashiro, K., Microwave Theory and Technology
Yasuda, Y., Pattern Processing
Yoshida, Y., Precision Machining
Yoshikawa, A., Quantum Electronics

Faculty of Horticulture:

Amano, H., Applied Entomology and Zoology
Amemiya, Y., Green Space Environmental Technology
Amemiya, Y., Plant Pathology
Ando, T., Ornamental Plant Science
Fujii, T., Microbial Engineering
Harada, K., Genetics and Plant Breeding
Iimoto, M., Plant Production Engineering
Inubushi, K., Soil Science
Ito, T., Vegetable Science
Keino, S., Agricultural Marketing
Kikuchi, M., Agricultural Economics
Kon, H., Green Space Meteorology
Kozai, T., Environmental Control Engineering
Maruta, Y., Planting Design
Masada, M., Biochemistry
Matsui, H., Fruit Science
Mii, M., Plant Cell Technology
Minamida, S., International Agricultural Studies
Motoyama, N., Pesticide Toxicology
Nagae, H., Farm Management
Nagata, Y., Molecular Biology
Nakagawa, H., Biotechnology of Agroresources
Nakamura, O., Town and Country Planning
Nakayama, K., Environmental Science of Plants
Noma, Y., University Farms
Ohmuro, M., Humanistic Study of the Environment
Sanada, H., Food and Nutrition
Sato, T., Biotechnology of Agroresources
Takahashi, E., University Farms
Takasaki, Y., Crop Science
Tashiro, Y., Urban Landscape Design
Watanabe, Y., Plant Nutrition
Yabashi, S., Green Space Environmental Technology
Yamauchi, S., Humanistic Study of the Environment
Yoshida, M., Agricultural Information Science
Yui, M., Landscape Planning

Graduate School of Science and Technology:

Ando, A., Proteins Engineering
Fujikawa, T., XAFS Theory
Fukukawa, Y., Planning Systems
Fukasawa, A., Information Systems
Furuya, T., Applied Geomorphology
Hirata, H., Systems Engineering
Honma, H., Shock Waves
Ichikawa, A., Knowledge Engineering
Kohmoto, S., Organic Photochemistry
Majima, T., Mechanics of Materials Grip Strength
Nishikawa, K., Physical Chemistry
Noguchi, H., Building Materials
Ohno, T., Fundamental Imaging Materials
Sato, T., Plant Molecular Biology
Shimakura, S., Fundamentals of Electrical and Electronic Engineering
Sugiyama, K., Design Systems Planning
Tamura, T., Molecular Biology
Uesugi, H., Fireproofing of Buildings
Yahagi, T., Information Systems

Health Sciences Center:

Nagao, K., Internal Medicine

Center for Environmental Remote Sensing:

Miwa, T., Dept of Geoinformation Analysis
Shindo, S., Dept of Database Research
Sugimori, Y., Dept of Geoinformation Analysis
Takamura, T., Dept of Sensor and Atmospheric Radiation
Takeuchi, N., Dept of Sensor and Atmospheric Radiation

Research Center for Pathogenic Fungi and Microbial Toxicoses:

Akao, M., Division of Molecular Biology and Therapeutics
Miyaji, M., Division of Fungal Infection
Nishimura, K., Division of Fungal Systematics
Takeo, K., Division of Ultrastructure and Function

International Student Center:

Hata, H., Teaching Japanese as a Second Language

Center for Foreign Languages:

Boswell, P. D., Linguistics
Kubota, M., English Linguistics
Mikoshiba, M., Russian Intellectual History
Murata, M., Lexicography
Nakazato, C., Applied Linguistics
Sakaino, J., German Literature
Yamaoka, K., French Literature

ATTACHED INSTITUTES

Center for Research, Training and Guidance in Educational Practice.

Marine Ecosystems Research Center.

University Hospital.

Institute of Pulmonary Cancer Research.

Center for Biomedical Science.

Laboratory Animal Center.

Institute for Training Nurses.

Institute for Training Midwives.

Institute for Training Radiological Technicians.

Research Center of Medicinal Resources.

Center for Education and Research in Nursing Practice.

University farms.

EHIME UNIVERSITY

10-13 Dogo-Himata, Matsuyama City 790-8577

Telephone: (89) 927-9000
Fax: (89) 927-9025

Founded 1949

Academic year: April to March (two terms)

President: K. Ayukawa
Administrative Officer: I. Tanaka
Dean of Students' Affairs Office: H. Watanabe
Library Director: E. Konishi

Library of 1,086,000 vols
Number of full-time teachers: 967
Number of students: 10,130

DEANS

Faculty of Law and Literature: K. KOMATSU
Faculty of Education: Y. MUKAI
Faculty of Science: M. KOMATSU
Faculty of Medicine: N. UEDA
Faculty of Engineering: K. ARII
Faculty of Agriculture: T. SAITO
United Graduate School of Agricultural Sciences: M. SIRAISHI

FUKUI UNIVERSITY

9-1 Bunkyo 3-chome, Fukui City 910

Telephone: (776) 23-0500
Fax: (776) 27-8518

Founded 1949

President: HIROSHI JINNO
Director of Administration: KOUNI KITAGAWA
Librarian: HIROYUKI SASAZI
Library of 407,000 vols
Number of teachers: 351
Number of students: 4,214

DEANS

Faculty of Education: TAKASHI CHIBA
Faculty of Engineering: YOSHIYUKI SYONO

GIFU UNIVERSITY

1-1 Yanagido, Gifu-shi, Gifu-ken

Telephone: (58) 230-1111
Fax: (58) 230-2021

Founded 1949

President: T. KINJOH
Secretary-General: Y. KIJIMA
Librarian: T. UNO

Library of 822,409 vols, 13,000 periodicals
Number of full-time teachers: 738
Number of students: 5,995

Publications: Research Bulletins and Reports from each faculty (annually).

DEANS

Faculty of Education: Y. KINOSITA
School of Medicine: Y. NOZAWA
Faculty of Engineering: H. SHIMIZU
Faculty of Agriculture: T. NAKAMURA
Faculty of Regional Studies: Y. MATSUDA

ATTACHED INSTITUTES

Curriculum Research and Development Center: Dir Prof. G. CHUMAN.

Institute of Equilibrium Research: Dir Prof. K. MATSUNAMI.

Institute of Anaerobic Bacteriology: Dir Prof. K. WATANABE.

Institute of Basin Ecosystem Studies: Dir Prof. A. YUASA.

Center for Cooperative Research: Dir Prof. S. YAMASHITA.

Molecular Genetics Research Center: Dir Prof. K. WAWAI.

GUNMA UNIVERSITY

4-2 Aramaki-machi, Maebashi

Telephone: (27) 220-7111

Founded 1949

Academic year: April to March

President: H. AKAIWA
Administrator: K. KIBE
Librarian: S. OZAWA

Number of full-time teachers: 844
Number of students: 6,479

Publication: *Journal of Social and Information Studies* (1 a year).

DEANS

Faculty of Education: H. MUTO
Faculty of Social and Information Studies: S. NOMURA
Faculty of Medicine: M. SUZUKI
Faculty of Engineering: H. SHIZUKA
Institute of Molecular and Cellular Regulation: K. WAKABAYASHI

HIROSAKI UNIVERSITY

1 Bunkyo-cho, Hirosaki-shi 036-8560

Telephone: (172) 36-2111

Founded 1949
State control
Academic year: April to March

President: Y. YOSHIDA
Registrar: M. SUGAWARA
Librarian: K. UCHIDA
Director of the Hospital: I. HASHIMOTO

Number of teachers: 660
Number of students: 5,361

Publications: *School Outline* (annually), *Student Handbook* (1 a year), Faculty Bulletins.

DEANS

Faculty of Humanities: T. TANNO
Faculty of Education: H. OZAWA
Faculty of Science and Technology: H. OHNUKI
School of Medicine: M. ENDO
Faculty of Agriculture and Life Science: K. TOYOKAWA

PROFESSORS

Faculty of Humanities:

ARAI, K., System of Management Accounting
CARPENTER, V., English
FUJINUMA, K., Japanese Archaeology
FUJITA, M., Behaviour of Enterprises
FUNAKI, Y., Statistics
HAMADA, M., Western History
HAMADA, T., Organizational Behaviour
HASEGAWA, S., Japanese History
HORIUCHI, T., Law
HOSHINO, Y., Accounting Information
IGARASHI, Y., Ethics
ISHIDOU, T., English
IWAI, T., Western History
KATORI, K., Management Science
KITAMURA, K., Human Behavioural Studies
MATSUI, M., Greek and Medieval Philosophy
MOROOKA, M., Ethics
MURAMATSU, K., Politics
MURATA, S., English and American Literature
NAKAYASHIKI, H., Asian Culture Studies
NAKAZAWA, K., World Economic History
NITTA, S., English
OGASAWARA, S., German Literature
OKAZAKI, E., Philosophy
SAITOH, Y., History of Political Economy
SATO, N., English
SHINOMIYA, T., Business History
SIMUZU, A., Philosophy
SUZUKI, K., Principles of Political Economy
SYOJI, S., German
TANAKA, I., German Literature
TANAKA, S., Urban Sociology
TANNO, T., Cultural Anthropology
TERADA, M., French Literature
UEKI, H., Chinese Literature
USUDA, S., Japanese Literature
WARASHINA, K., Japanese Language

Faculty of Education:

ADACHI, H., Instrumental Music
ANDO, F., Education of Handicapped Children
ANNO, M., History
EZURE, T., Japanese Language Education
FUKUSHIMA, M., Surgical Nursing
FUMOTO, N., Health and Physical Education
GION, Z., Social Studies Education
HAGA, T., Clothing Science
HAYAKAWA, M., Basic Medical Science
HORIUCHI, H., Soil Science
HOSHI, K., Art Education
HOSCHINO, H., Physics
ISHIKAWA, S., Developmental Psychology
IWAI, Y., Painting
KAMADA K., Soil Science
KAMIYA, K., Sociology
KATO, Y., Food Science
KITADA, T., Analysis and Applied Mathematics
KON, M., Mathematics Education
KURIHARA, O., Philosophy
MARUYAMA. M., Japanese Literature
MATSUSHITA, K., Health and Physical Education
MENZAWA, M., Basic Medical Science
MIZUNO, Y., Geography
MORI, A., Clinical and Nursing Science
MORI, R., Home Economics
MORIKAWA, Y., Home Economics
MURAKAMI, O., Biology
MURAYAMA, M., Educational Method
MURAYAMA, H., Instrumental Music
NAGANO, T., Japanese Literature
NISHIZAWA, Y., Construction and Design
NOGUCHI, I., Education of Preschool Children
OGURA, H., Japanese Language
OGUSHI, Y., Nursing
OHSAWA, Y., Health and Sports Science
OKADA, K., Sculpture
OKUNO, T., English Language
ONODA, O., Economics
OYAMA, S., Teaching of Health and Physical Education
OZAWA, H., Educational Administration
SAITO, S., Psychology of Disabled Children
SAITO, S., Natural Sciences Education
SAITO, T., History
SATO, K., Physiology and Hygiene
SATO, S., Educational Sociology
SATO, T., Wood Processing
SATO, Y., School Health
SATOH, Y., Electricity
SEKI, H., Chemistry
SOTOKAWA, J., Mechanics
TAKANASHI, Y., English Language Education
TANDO, S., Educational Psychology
TOYOSHIMA, A., Student Guidance
WATANABE, K., Vocal Music
YAJIMA, T., Philosophy
YAMABE, H., Medical Nursing
YOSHIKAWA, Y., Mathematics Education
YOSHINO, H., Developmental Psychology

Faculty of Science and Technology:

ARAXI, T., Computer Engineering
FUKASE, M., Computer Engineering
GOTO, T., Molecular Design Engineering
INAMURA, T., Materials Science and Device Physics
ITO, S., Chemistry
KAWAGUCHI, S., Communications Technology
KURAMATA, S., Astrophysics
KURATSUBO, S., Applied Mathematics and Optimization
MASHITA, M., Physics and Technology of Quantum Effect Materials
MOTOSE, K., Structures
NAKAZATO, H., Analysis
NANJO, H., Astrophysics
OHNUKI, H., Natural Disaster Prevention Technology
OHZEKI, K., Chemistry
RIKIISHI, K., Environmental Science of the Atmosphere and Hydrosphere
SAITO, M., Cognitive Science and Bioinformatics
SAKISAKA, Y., Materials Science and Device Physics
SASAKI, K., Solid State Physics
SATO, T., Solid State Physics
SATO, T., Solid Earth Sciences
SHIMIZU, T., Cognitive Science and Bioinformatics
SUDOH, S., Molecular Design Engineering
SUTO, S., Functional Material Technology
TAJIRI, A., Functional Material Technology
TAKAGUCHI, M., Analysis

TAKEGAHARA, K., Physics and Technology of Quantum Effect Materials
TANAKA, K., Natural Disaster Prevention Technology
TANAKA, T., Applied Mathematics and Optimization
TSURUMI, M., Environmental Science of the Atmosphere and Hydrosphere
UCHIDA, K., Molecular Design Engineering
UJIIE, Y., Solid Earth Sciences
YOSHIOKA, Y., Communications Technology

School of Medicine:

ABE, Y., Radiology
ENDO, M., Biochemistry
FUKUDA, M., Rehabilitation
HARATA, S., Orthopaedic Surgery
HASHIMOTO, I., Dermatology
KACHI, T., Anatomy
KAMIYA, H., Parasitology
KANEKO, S., Neurology and Psychiatry
KIMURA, H., Dentistry and Oral Surgery
KOYA, G., Pathology
KUDO, H., Pathology
KURATA, K., Physiology
KURODA, N., Legal Medicine
MATSUKI, A., Anaesthesiology
MATSUNAGA, M., Neurology
MITA, R., Public Health
MIZUSHIMA, Y., Geriatrics
MOTOMURA, S., Pharmacology
MUNAKATA, A., Internal Medicine
NAKANE, A., Bacteriology
NAKAZAWA, M., Ophthalmology
OKUMURA, K., Internal Medicine
SAITOH, Y., Obstetrics and Gynaecology
SASAKI, M., Surgery
SATOH, K., Pathological Physiology
SAWADA, Y., Plastic Surgery
SHINKAWA, H., Otorhinolaryngology
SHOMURA, K., Anatomy
SUDA, T., Internal Medicine
SUGAWARA, K., Hygiene
SUZUKI, S., Neurosurgery
SUZUKI, S., Surgery
SUZUKI, T., Urology
TUTIDA, S., Biochemistry
YAGIHASI, S., Pathology
YASUJIMA, M., Laboratory Medicine
YOKOYAMA, M., Paediatrics
WAKUI, M., Physiology

Faculty of Agriculture and Life Science:

ANDO, Y., Bioenvironmental Sciences
ASADA, Y., Bioscience and Biotechnology
BEKKI, E., Agricultural Machinery and Process Engineering
BOKURA, T., Bioenvironmental Sciences
FUKUDA, H., Horticultural Science
HARADA, Y., Bioenvironmental Sciences
KANDA, K., Agricultural Economics
KUDO, A., Regional Environmental Engineering
MAKITA, H., Regional Environmental Planning
MIYAIRI, K., Biochemistry and Molecular Biology
MOTOMURA, Y., Science of Bioproducts
MUTO, A., Genetic Engineering
NAKAMURA, S., Science of Bioproducts
NIIZEKI, M., Bioscience and Biotechnology
OBARA, Y., Systematics and Morphology
OHMASHI, T., Cell Technology
OKUNO, T., Bioscience and Biotechnology
SAWADA, S., Environmental Biology
SAWARA, Y., Environmental Biology
SUGIYAMA, K., Physiology and Developmental Biology
TAKAHASHI, H., Agricultural Economics
TAKAMURA, K., Division of Life Science
TAKEDA, K., Bioscience and Biotechnology
TANIGUCHI, K., Irrigation, Drainage and Reclamation Engineering
TOYOKAWA, K., Horticultural and Agricultural Sciences
UNO, T., Agricultural Economics

ATTACHED INSTITUTES

Gene Research Centre: 3 Bunkyo-cho, Hirosaki-shi 036-8561; Dir M. NIIZEKI.

Centre for Computing and Communications: 3 Bunkyo-Cho, Hirosaki-shi 036-8561; Dir Y. YOSHIOKA.

Centre for Education and Research of Lifelong Learning: 1 Bunkyo-cho, Hirosaki-shi 036-8560; Dir S. SATO.

Centre for Joint Research: 1 Bunkyo-cho, Hirosaki-shi 036-8560; Dir. A. TAJIRI.

Centre for Educational Research and Practice: 1 Bunkyo-cho, Hirosaki-shi 036-8560; Dir K. FUKIGAI.

Earthquake and Volcano Observatory: 3 Bunkyo-cho, Hirosaki-shi 036-8561; Dir K. TANAKA.

Institute of Neurological Diseases: 5 Zaifucho, Hirosaki-shi 036-8562; Dir M. ENDO.

Institute for Experimental Animals: 5 Zaifucho, Hirosaki-shi 036-8562; Dir H. KAMIYA.

University Farms: 7-1 Shitafukuro, Fujisakimachi, Aomori-ken 038-3802; Dir T. NOMURA.

HIROSHIMA UNIVERSITY

3-2, Kagamiyama 1-chome, Higashi-Hiroshima 739-8511

Telephone: (82) 22-7111
Fax: (82) 24-6020

Founded 1949
State control
Academic year: April to March (two semesters)

President: Y. HARADA
Vice-Presidents: M. OGASAWARA, K. MORI
Director-General: T. NISHIMURA
Library Director: K. ITOH

Library of 2,848,000 vols, including 1,161,000 in foreign languages
Number of teachers: 1,975, including 568 professors
Number of students: 17,027, including 3,384 graduates

Publications: *Journal of Science of Hiroshima University: Hiroshima Mathematical Journal, Physics and Chemistry, Earth and Planetary Sciences, Hiroshima University Studies—Faculty of Letters, Bulletin of the Faculty of Education–Hiroshima University, Hiroshima Journal of Mathematics Education, Bulletin of the Hiroshima University Faculty of School Education, Journal of Educational Research into School Bullying, Hiroshima Journal of School Education, Hiroshima Journal of Medical Sciences, The Journal of Hiroshima University Dental Society, Bulletin of the Faculty of Engineering, Proceedings of the Research Institute for Radiation Biology and Medicine, Hiroshima Economic Studies, Hiroshima Economic Review, Economic Studies, Hiroshima Law Journal, Journal of the Faculty of Applied Biological Science, Studies in Area Culture, Studies in Social Sciences, Studies in Culture and the Humanities, Science Reports, Studies in Language and Culture, Journal of International Development and Cooperation, Bulletin of the Institute for Cultural Studies of the Seto Inland Sea, Annual Report of Research Centre for Regional Geography, Reports of the Miyajima Natural Botanical Garden.*

DEANS AND DIRECTORS

Faculty of Integrated Arts and Sciences: H. SEIWA
Faculty of Letters: H. MUKAIYAMA
Faculty of Education: T. TOSHIJIMA
Faculty of School Education: Y. MADA
Faculty of Law: C. MIZUKAMI
Faculty of Economics: K. MAEKAWA
Faculty of Science: T. MUTA
School of Medicine: F. YOSHINAGA
University Medical Hospital: Y. MATSUURA (Director)
School of Dentistry: N. NAGASAKA
University Dental Hospital: H. SHINTANI (Director)
Faculty of Engineering: M. MATSUMURA
Faculty of Applied Biological Science: H. MIKUNI
Graduate School for International Development and Co-operation: S. YAMASHITA
Research Institute for Nuclear Medicine and Biology: N. KAMADA (Director)

PROFESSORS

Faculty of Integrated Arts and Sciences:

Division of Culture and the Humanities

HARA, M., Comparative Philosophy and Music Aesthetics
INADA, K., American Literature, Gender Studies
KANATA, S., Comparative Studies in Art
KOJIMA, H., Comparative Literature
KOTHO, T., Comparative Philosophy
MURASE, N., French Theatre
NARISADA, K., History and Sociology of Science
NISHIMURA, M., Austrian Culture
SAITO, T., Mysticism, the Brain and Consciousness
SATO, M., History of German Customs and Manners

Division of Area Studies

ASAKURA, H., Medieval Japanese Literature
CHOE, K., Historical Anthropology (East Asia)
FUJII, M., Chinese Thought and Literature
KANO, T., History of US Foreign Trade Policy
KASHIHARA, O., Modern Japanese Literature
KOHATA, F., Biblical Studies
KUSUNOSE, M., Chinese Modern History
OKAMOTO, M., American Studies
TOMODA, T., English History

Division of Social Sciences

FUNAHASHI, Y., History of Political and Social Thoughts
HAMAUZU, T., Oil Economics
ITOH, M., Sociology of Law
IWATA, K., International Politics (USSR and Russia)
KAI, S., Labour Law
MORI, T., Peace Studies in South Asia, International Politics
OKUMURA, K., International Economics
TAMURA, K., Administrative Law
TOMII, T., Civil Law
TOMIOKA, S., Economic History

Division of Foreign Languages

GOLDSBURY, P., Ancient Greek Philosophy
HIGUCHI., M., English Philology
IIDA, M., English Literature
IMAZATO, C., History of the English Language
INOUE, K., Russian Studies
ITOH, S., American Literature
IWAKURA, K., English Linguistics
KOBAYASHI, H., Applied Linguistics
NISHIDA, T., Applied Linguistics
OKAZAKI, T., History of the German Language
TAKESHIMA, T., Linguistics, German Studies, Greek Studies
TANJI, N., German Literature
YAMADA, J., Psycholinguistics
YOON, K., Korean Literature

Division of Mathematical and Information Sciences

EGUCHI, M., Harmonic Analysis
FURUSHIMA, M., Algebraic Geometry
HARADA, K., Computational Geometry
KUWADA, M., Experimental Design
MIZUKAMI, K., Information and System Control
MIZUTA, Y., Potential Theory

NARA, S., Information and Complex Dynamics
NISHII, R., Statistical Image Analysis
SHOHOJI, T., Applied Statistics
YAMAGATA, K., Computer-Aided Design
YOSHIDA, K., Partial Differential Equations
YOSHIDA, T., Topology

Division of Material and Life Sciences

AKABORI, K., Bioinorganic Chemistry
FUJII, H., Materials Sciences
FUKAMIYA, N., Bio-Constituents Chemistry
HIKOSAKA, M., Soft Materials and Polymer Physics
HOSHINO, K., Condensed Matter Physics
KOMINAMI, S., Biophysical Chemistry
MATSUDA, M., High Energy Particle Physics
NAGAI, K., Low Temperature Physics
OKANO, M., Bio-Constituents Chemistry
TAMURA, K., Semiconductor Physics
UDAGAWA, M., Condensed Matter Physics
UTSUMI, K., Astrophysics
WATANABE, K., Developmental Biology and Species Biology
YAMASHITA, K., Physical Chemistry

Division of Environmental Sciences

FUJIWARA, K., Inorganic Analytical Chemistry
HAYASHI, N., Chemical Ecology
HONDA, K., Chemical Ecology
HORIKOSHI, T., Microbial Ecology
KAIHOTSU, I., Hydrology
NAKAGOSHI, N., Landscape Ecology
NAKANE, K., Ecosystem Ecology
NEHIRA, K., Plant Phylogeny
OHO, Y., Basal Geology
SAKURAI, N., Environmental Physiology
YOSHIKAWA, T., Environment Meteorology

Division of Behavioural and Biological Sciences

ANDO, M., Animal Physiology
CHOSHI, K., Psychology of Motor Behaviour
HORI, T., Psychophysiology
KAMIRYO, T., Molecular Biology
KIKUCHI, K., Physiology (Exercise)
KOMURA, T., Health Science
KUROKAWA, M., Group Dynamics
KUSUDO, K., History of Sport
NANBA, K., Human Pathology
NIIHATA, S., Training Theory
SEIWA, H., Psychology of Personality
TSUTSUI, K., Brain Science

Faculty of Letters:

HARANO, N., French Language and Literature
ITO, K., Ancient and Medieval Japanese Literature
KANO, M., Chinese Linguistics
KATSURA, S., Indian Philosophy
KAWAGOE, T., Archaeology
KAWASE, M., Study of Cultural Properties
KISHIDA, H., Ancient and Medieval Japanese History
KONDO, Y., History of Ethical Thought
KOURA, T., Linguistics
MAKIBAYASHI, K., Modern and Contemporary Japanese Literature
MATSUMOTO, M., Japanese Language Studies
MATSUMOTO, Y., French Language and Literature
MIZUTA, H., History of Philosophy
MUKAIYAMA, H., Ancient and Medieval Western History
MUROYAMA, T., Japanese Language Studies
NAKATA, T., Physical Geography, Regional Geography
NOMA, F., History of Ancient and Medieval Chinese Thought
OCHI, M., Ethics
OKAHASHI, H., Human Geography, Regional Geography
OKAMOTO, A., Modern and Contemporary Western History
RAI, K., Modern Japanese History
TAKAYANAGI, H., Philosophy
TAKEDA, T., German Literature
TANAKA, H., Contemporary English and American Literature
TANAKA, T., English Language Studies
TERAJI, J., Chinese History
TOMINAGA, K., Chinese Literature
UEDA, Y., Linguistics
UEKI, K., English Literature
UEMURA, Y., Asian History
YAMASHIRO, H., Ancient and Medieval Western History
YOSIDA, K., History of Modern Chinese Thought

Faculty of Education:

Department of Education

HARADA, A., Sociology of Education
IKEHATA, J., History of Western Education
NINOMIYA, A., Comparative Education
OGASAWARA, M., Philosophy of Education
OKATO, T., Educational Management
SATO, H., History of Japanese and Eastern Education
SEMBA, K., Educational Administration

Department of Psychology

HABU, Y., Learning Psychology
ICHIMARU, T., Clinical Psychology
IMAIZUMI, N., Developmental Psychology
MATSUDA, F., Educational Psychology
TOSHIMA, T., Experimental Psychology
YOSHIMORI, M., Social Psychology

Department of Curriculum and Instruction

AKIYAMA, M., Science Education
EBATA, Y., Japanese Language
ESASHI, Y., Physical Education
FUKUDA, K., Home Economics Education
FURUTA, S., Clothing Construction
HARADA, H., Musicology
HASEGAWA, S., Chinese Literature
ICHIHARA, T., Violin
IKEDA, H., Biology and Biology Education
IMAOKA, M., Geometry
INAMIZU, T., Sports Medicine
IWADARE, Y., Clothing Storage and Care
IWASHIGE, H., House Environment Science
KATAKAMI, S., Social Studies Education
MARUO, O., Algebra
MATSUHASHI, Y., Child Health
MATSUMOTO, N., English Philology (Middle English)
MATSUOAKA, S., Physical Education
MIURA, S., English Language Education
MORIWAKE, T., Social Studies Education
NAKAHARA, T., Mathematics Education
NISHIMURA, K., Ball Games
OCHIAI, H., Chemistry and Chemistry Education
OKUDA, M., Vocal Music
OTSUKI, K., Japanese Language Education
SAKATE, T., Psychology of Physical Education
SATO, K., Food Science
SATO, K., Piano
TAKEMURA, S., Science Education
YOSHITOMI, K., Music Education
WATANABE, K., Physiology, Sports Biomechanics

Department of Teaching Japanese as a Second Language

AIHARA, K., Modern Japanese Literature
IMADA, S., Teaching Methodology of Japanese as a Second Language
KISAKA, M., Study of Japanese Composition and Style
MIZUMACHI, I., Educational Language Technology
MIZUSHIMA, H., Comparative Cultures
NUIBE, Y., Teaching Methodology of Japanese as a Second Language
NUMOTO, K., Historical Study of Japanese Language
OKUDA, K., Teaching Methodology of Japanese as a Second Language

Graduate School of Early Childhood Study Course

YAMAZAKI, A., Child Psychology

Graduate School of Learning and Curriculum Development:

KISHI, M., Educational Research on Learning
MORI, T., Psychology of Learning

Faculty of School Education:

BANSHOYA, K., Woodworking
CHII, A., Housing
DANJO, M., Japanese Literature (Classical Japanese Literature)
FUNATU, M., Psychology of the Disabled
HAMAGUCHI, O., American Literature
HAYASHI, T., Clothing
HIRAI, S., Developmental Psychology
HIROSE, T., Educational Methods
ISHIBASHI, Y., Algebra
ISHII, S., Child Psychology
IWASAKI, F., Japanese Literature
KAGEYAMA, S., Statistics and Combinatorics
KANATA, S., Clinical Pathology of the Disabled
KOBARA, T., Social Studies Education
KOBAYASHI, K., Teaching Methods of Physical Education
KODAIRA, Y., Sculpture and Modelling
KONO, M., Design and Construction
KUROSE, M., Keyboard Music
MADA, Y., Teaching of Industrial Arts
MATSUDA, Y., Psychology of Physical Education
MIYAKE, T., Modern Japanese History
MIYAMOTO, S., Clothing Science
MORITA, N., Japanese Language Education
NAGASAWA, T., Methods of Teaching the Disabled
NAKANISHI, M., Taxonomy and Evolution
NAMBA, H., Drawing and Painting
NISHINE, K., Sociology of Education
NOMURA, K., Music Education
OBI, T., Eastern History
OKADA, Y., Mathematics Education
OZASA, T., Teaching English as a Foreign Language
SATO, S., Western History
SHIBA, K., Science Education
SHIRANE, F., Organic Chemistry
SUZUKI, M., Petrology
TAINOSHO, J., Home Economics Education
TAKAHASHI, S., Social Psychology
TAKASUGI, H., Methods of Teaching the Disabled
TAMURA, S., Food Science
TANAKA, H., Inorganic Chemistry
TOKUNAGA, T., Applied Physics
UEDA, K., Teaching of Industrial Arts
WAKAMOTO, S., Art Education
WAKAO, Y., Composition
YAMANASHI, M., Methods of Teaching the Disabled
YANAGIHARA, E., Sports Science (Ball Games)

Faculty of Law:

AIZAWA, Y., Private International Law
CHIKUMA, M., Criminal Procedure
FUJITA, K., Political Economy
HIRANO, T., Legal Philosophy
KAI, K., Criminal Law
KATAGI, H., Commercial Law
KAMITANI, Y., Civil Law
KAWASAKI, N., Public Administration
KONTANI, K., Civil Procedure
MAKINO, M., Political History
MIZUKAMI, C., International Law
NISHITANI, H., International Law
OTANI, T., Sociology of Law
PICKRON, J. E., Anglo-American Law
SAKAMOTO, M., Constitutional Law
TAKAHASHI, H., Civil Law
TANABE, M., Civil Procedure
TORIYABE, S., Civil Law
TSUJI, H., Labour Law
WATANABE, M., Social Policy

YAMADA, S., History of Political Ideas
YOSHIHARA, T., Legal History

Faculty of Economics:

ENOMOTO, S., International Management
FUKIHARU, T., Microeconomics
GINAMA, I., Macroeconometrics
HIRAKI, S., Management Information Systems
KAN, T., Fiscal Policy
KATO, F., Occidental Economic History
KITAOKA, T., Monetary Policy
MAEKAWA, K., Econometrics
MATSUMIZU, Y., Market Economic Systems
MORIOKA, T., Labour Economics
MORITA, K., Comparative Economic Systems
NOMOTO, R., Industrial Organization
SAKAGUCHI, K., Accounting
SAKANE, Y., Economic History of Japan
SANO, S., International Economics
TODA, T., Urban and Regional Planning
TSUBAKI, Y., Data Processing
UEDA, Y., Public Economics
UNO, Y., Organization Theory
YANO, J., Macroeconomics

Faculty of Science:

Mathematics

FUJIKOSHI, Y., Mathematical Statistics
KUBO, I., Probability Theory and Ergodic Theory
MATUMOTO, T., Topology
MIMURA, M., Applied Analysis
OHARU, S., Functional Analysis
SUMIHIRO, H., Algebraic Geometry
TANISAKI, T., Algebraic Groups
UMEHARA, M., Differential Geometry

Physical Sciences

ENDO, I., Photon Physics
FUJITA, T., Low Temperature Physics
GEKKO, K., Physical Chemistry of Biopolymers
HIRAYA, A., Synchrotron Radiation Science, Particle Beam Science
INOUE, M., Semiconductor Physics, Low Temperature Physics
ITOH, K., Physics of Structural Phase Transition
JO, T., Theory of Condensed Matter
KOJIMA, Y., Astrophysics and General Relativity
MIYAMURA, O., High-Energy, Nuclear and Particle Physics
MUTA, T., Elementary Particle Physics and Quantum Field Theory
OGUCHI, T., Electron Theory of Solids
SUMI, Y., Intermediate and High Energy Physics
TANIGUCHI, M., Optical Properties of Solids, Synchroton Radiation Spectroscopy
TAKABATAKE, T., Magnetism, Strongly Correlated Electron Systems
TANAKA, K., Photochemistry Synchrotron Radiation Chemistry

Chemistry

AKIBA, K.-Y., Reaction Mechanism of Organic Molecules, Organic Main Group Chemistry
FUKAZAWA, Y., Organic Stereochemistry
HANAZAKI, I., Nonlinear Chemical Reactions
HIRATA, T., Biological Chemistry and Biotechnology
KUMAMARU, T., Analytical Chemistry and Solution Chemistry
MATSUURA, H., Colloid Chemistry and Molecular Spectroscopy
MIYOSHI, K., Coordination and Organometallic Chemistry
OHKATA, K., Synthesis and Isolation of Natural Products
OKUDA, T., Solid State Chemistry, Magnetic Resonance Spectroscopy
SAITO, K., Chemical Kinetics and Dynamics
TANIMOTO, Y., Laser Photochemistry and Magnetochemistry

Biological Sciences

DEGUCHI, H., Plant Taxonomy and Ecology, Bryology
HOSOYA, H., Cell Biology, Signal Transduction
MATSUSHIMA, O., Adaptation Physiology, Neurobiology
SATOH, T., Plant Physiology, Microbial Physiology
YOSHIDA, K., Plant Molecular Biology, Gene Technology, Amphibian Biology
YOSHIZATO, K., Molecular Cell Science

Earth and Planetary Systems Science

HONDA, S., Geodynamics, Physics of the Earth's Interior
SANO, Y., Isotope Geochemistry
SHIMIZU, H., Trace Element Geochemistry
TAKENO, S., Experimental Mineralogy, Geochemistry
TAKESHITA, T., Structural Geology, Structural Petrology

Gene Science

GEKKO, K., Physical Chemistry of Biopolymers
IDE, H., Molecular Aspects of DNA Damage and Repair
KONDO, K., Plant Demography and Gene Resources
MICHIBATA, H., Marine Molecular Biology
MORIKAWA, H., Molecular Plant Biology
SHIMADA, H., Molecular Genetics

Marine Biological Laboratory

MICHIBATA, H., Marine Molecular Biology

Miyajima Natural Botanical Garden

SATOH, T., Symbiontology and Taxonomy of Aerial Algae

Laboratory for Amphibian Biology

NAKAMURA, M., Biochemistry and Molecular Biology
YOSHIZATO, K., Developmental Biology, Metamorphosis, Regeneration

Laboratory of Plant Chromosome and Gene Stock

KONDO, K., Plant Demography and Gene Resources

School of Medicine, Institute of Pharmaceutical Science and Institute of Health Sciences:

Basic Medicine

INAI, K., Pathology, Tumour Pathology
KANNO, M., Immunology and Parasitology, Molecular Immunology
KATAOKA, K., Anatomy (II), Histology, Histochemistry and Cell Biology of the Digestive Organs
KIKUCHI, A., Biochemistry (I), Intracellular Signal Transduction
KOJIMA, T., Legal Medicine, Forensic Toxicology
OGATA, N., Physiology (II), Neurophysiology
SASA, M., Pharmacology, Psychoneuropharmacology
SEYAMA, I., Physiology (I), Membrane Physiology, Cardiac Cellular Physiology
TAHARA, E., Pathology (I), Oncology of the Gastrointestinal Tract, Molecular Diagnosis
TAKEDA, M., Biochemistry (II), Metabolic Regulation (Protein Phosphorylation and Dephosphorylation)
YASUDA, M., Anatomy (I), Developmental Toxicity of Chemicals
YOSHIDA, T., Virology, Paramyxovirus, Bacteriology
YOSHINAGA, F., Public Health, Industrial Health
YOSHIZAWA, H., Hygiene, Seroepidemiology of Viral Hepatitis

Clinical Medicine

DOHI, K., Surgery, Transplant Surgery and Immunology, Hepatobiliary Surgery, Vascular Surgery
IKUTA, Y., Orthopaedic Surgery, Hand Surgery, Microsurgery, Traumatology
ISHIKAWA, K., Medical Informatics and Systems Management, Medical Systems Management
ITO, K., Radiology, Diagnostic Imaging, Interventional Radiology
KAJIYAMA, G., Internal Medicine (I), Gastroenterology, Lipid and Bile Acid Metabolism
KAMBE, M., Clinical Laboratory Medicine, Clinical Physiology, ME, Medical Informatics, Gene Engineering
KIHIRA, K., Pharmaceutics and Therapeutics, Clinical Pharmacy
KURISU, K., Neurosurgery, Neuro-Oncology, Neuroradiology, Surgery of Brain Tumours and Cerebro-vascular Disease, Skull Base Surgery
MATSUURA, Y., Surgery (I), Thoracic and Cardiovascular Surgery, Artificial Organs
MISHIMA, H. K., Ophthalmology, Glaucoma, Ocular Cell Biology, Ocular Pharmacology, Retinal Disease
NAKAMURA, S., Internal Medicine, Neurology, Geriatric Medicine
OHAMA, K., Obstetrics and Gynaecology, Clinical Genetics, Prenatal Medicine, Postmenopausal Gynaecology
OHTANI, M., Emergency and Critical Care Medicine, Emergency Medicine, Critical Care Medicine, Pathophysiology of Burns, Clinical Toxicology
UEDA, K., Paediatrics, Hematology and Pathology, Cancer Treatment
USUI, T., Urology, Andrology, Oncology
YAJIN, K., Otorhinolaryngology, Head and Neck Oncology, Rhinology
YAMAKIDO, M., Internal Medicine, COPD Lung Cancer, Allergy and Immunology
YAMAMOTO, S., Dermatology, Allergology and Immunopharmacology in Skin
YAMAWAKI, S., Psychiatry, Biological Psychiatry, Psychopharmacology, Affective Disorders, Neuroleptic Malignant Syndrome, Psychosomatic Medicine, Liaison Psychiatry, Psycho-Oncology
YOKOYAMA, T., General Medicine, General Surgery, Paediatric Surgery
YUGE, O., Anaesthesiology, Immunology in Anaesthesia, Biotransformation of Anaesthetics, Malignant Hyperthermia, Defence Mechanism of Surgical Patients, Critical Care Medicine

Institute of Pharmaceutical Science

FUJIMURA, K., Pharmacobiodynamics (I), Biochemistry, Clinical Pharmacotherapeutics, Clinical Cell Biology
HAZEKI, O., Pharmacobiodynamics (II), Cellular Signal Transduction
IDE, T., Cellular and Molecular Biology
KIMURA, E., Medicinal Chemistry, Chemistry of Biologically and Functionally Active Macrocyclic Compounds
MASUJIMA, T., Analytical Chemistry, Videonanoscopes, Cell Dynamics, Pharmacodynamics, Bioanalysis
NAKATA, Y., Pharmacobiodynamics (III), Neuropharmacology
OHTA, S., Public Health Chemistry, Neurochemistry, Drug Metabolism
SUGIYAMA, M., Genetic Engineering, Antibiotics, Enzymology, Molecular Genetics, Applied Microbiology
TAKANO, M., Biopharmaceutics, Drug Transport in Biological Membrane, Drug Delivery Systems
YAMASAKI, K., Department of Medicinal Chemistry, Medical Chemistry of Natural Products

Institute of Health Sciences

ANDREW, P. D., Physical Therapy, Kinesiology
KAJIHARA, H., Cardiovascular Pathology, Ultrastructural Pathology, Pathology of Shock

KAKEHASHI, M., Health Science, Health Statistics, Mathematical Modelling, Public Health
KAMAKURA, N., Occupational Therapy, Neuropsychological Rehabilitation
KAWAMATA, S., Histology of the Inner Ear, Anatomy of Calcified Tissue, Anatomy of Musculoskeletal System
KISHIMOTO, S., Internal Medicine, Gastroenterology, Brain–gut Regulatory Peptides, Gastrointestinal Pathophysiology
KONISHI, M., Community Health Nursing, Occupational Health Nursing, Geriatric Nursing
MATSUKAWA, K., Physiology, Neural Control of the Cardiovascular System, Motor Control
MIYAMAE, T., Occupational Therapy, Neurological Dysfunction, Occupational Therapy Education
MURAKAMI, T., Rheumatoid Surgery, Elbow Surgery, Sports Medicine
NARA, I., Physical Therapy, Postural Control, Central Nervous Disorders
NISHIKI, M., Chest Surgery, Health Science, Nursing Education
NISHIMURA, R., Child and Adolescent Psychiatry, Psychotherapy, Mental Health
NOJIMA, Y., Philosophy and Theory of Nursing
OKADA, K., Internal Medicine, Haematology, Oncology, Environmental and Health Sciences
ONARI, K., Sports Science and Medicine, Sports Injury and Disturbance, Exercise Prescription
SHIMIZU, H., Science of Occupational Therapy
SUZUKI, M., Nursing Methodology, Nurse–Client Interaction, Terminal Care in Adults with Cancer, Recovery Care in Clinical Nursing
TANAKA, Y., Paediatrics, Health Science, Nursing Education
TOMIKAWA, T., Psychiatric-Mental Health Nursing
YAMAMURA, Y., Internal Medicine, Neurology, Neuropathology
YOKOO, K., Maternal Health Behaviour in the Prenatal Period
YOSHIMURA, O., Rehabilitation Medicine, Stroke Amputation and Prosthesis, Spinal Cord Injury

School of Dentistry:

AKAGAWA, Y., Removable Prosthodontics, Implantology
DOHI, T., Pharmacology, Dental Pharmacology
HAMADA, T., Gerodontics, Prosthodontics, Stomatognathic Dysfunction
ISHIKAWA, T., Oral and Maxillofacial Surgery, Plastic Surgery
IWAMOTO, Y., Preventive Dentistry, Behavioural Science
KATO, Y., Biochemistry and Oral Biology
KAWAHARA, M., Anaesthesiology, Pain Clinic
KURIHARA, H., Periodontology, Endodontology
MAEDA, N., Oral Anatomy, Development of Masticatory System
NAGASAKA, N., Paediatric Dentistry
NIKAI, H., Pathology, Oral Pathology
OKAMOTO, T., Oral and Maxillofacial Surgery, Molecular Oral Medicine
SHIBA, Y., Physiology, Oral Physiology
SHINTANI, H., Operative Dentistry, Dental Materials
SUGINAKA, H., Microbiology, Oral Bacteriology
TANIMOTO, K., Oral and Maxillofacial Radiology, Dysphagia
TANNE, K., Orthodontics, Craniofacial Growth and Function, Biomechanics
UCHIDA, T., Anatomy, Oral Anatomy

Faculty of Engineering:

Engineering Fundamentals

HIROKAWA, T., Analytical Chemistry
ITO, S., Physical Chemistry
IWASE, K., Mathematical Statistics
KANEKO, A., Environmental Oceanography
NASU, M., Symbolic Dynamics
ODA, T., Optical Spectroscopy
OKADA, M., Environmental Chemical Engineering
SETO, N., Engineering Mathematics
SHIBA, M., Complex Analysis and its Applications
SHIMOMURA, Y., Radiation Damage and Lattice Defects
SHIZUMA, K., Applied Nuclear Physics

Mechanical Engineering

FUKUNAGA, H., Composites Science and Engineering
KIKUCHI, Y., Heat Transfer
KUROKI, H., Welding, Powder Metallurgy and Ceramics
NAGAMURA, K., Machine Elements, Gear Design and Vibration
NAKAGAWA, N., Dynamics of Machines
NAKASA, K., Functional Materials for Machine Structures
NARUTAKI, N., Machining Technology and Science
OBA, F., Manufacturing Systems
SAEKI, M., Automatic Control
SUDO, K., Fluid Mechanics
TAKI, S., Reactive Gas Dynamics
TSUTA, T., Computational Mechanics and Biomechanics
YAMANE, Y., Machine Tool and Mechatronics
YANAGISAWA, O., Property Control of Materials
YOSHIDA, F., Engineering Elasto-Plasticity

Electrical and Industrial Engineering

AE, T., Computer Engineering
BABA, E., Human Science
HINAMOTO, T., Electronic Control Engineering, Digital Signal Processing
HIROSE, M., Microelectronics
ICHIKAWA, T., Information Systems
ISAWA, Y., Solid State Physics
IWATA, A., Integrated Electronics
KANEKO, M., Human Factors Engineering
MIURA-MATTAUSCH, M., Device Physics
MORITA, K., Knowledge Engineering
NAKAMURA, N., Production Engineering
OSAKI, S., Mathematical System Engineering
SAKAWA, M., Systems Engineering
SASAKI, H., Power System Engineering
TAKAHAGI, T., Materials Science
WATANABE, T., Computer Science
YAMANISHI, M., Quantum Electronics
YAMASHITA, H., Electrical Machinery

Chemical Engineering and Bioengineering

ASAEDA, M., Membrane Separation
KUNAI, A., Organometallic Chemistry
MASUOKA, H., Chemical Engineering Thermodynamics
MATSUMURA, M., Chemical Plant Materials
MIYAKAWA, T., Biophysical Chemistry
OHTAKE, H., Bioinformation Engineering
OKUYAMA, K., Heat Transfer
OTSUBO, T., Organic Chemistry
SAKOHARA, S., Polymer Technology
SHIOTANI, M., Physical Chemistry
SUZUKI, O., Industrial Biochemistry
TAKEHIRA, K., Catalysis
TSUCHIYA, E., Molecular Biology
YAMADA, T., Industrial Microbiology
YAMANAKA, S., Inorganic Chemistry
YASUDA, H., Polymer Chemistry
YOSHIDA, H., Powder Technology

Structural Engineering and Architecture

FUJIMOTO, Y., Reliability of Structures and Systems
FUJITANI, Y., Structural Mechanics
FUKUOKA, S., River Engineering
FUKUSHIMA, T., Environmental Engineering
ISHIMARU, N., City and Architectural Planning
KITAGAWA, Y., Prevention of Building Disasters
KOSE, K., Dynamics and Control of Systems
MORI, K., Marine Hydrodynamics and Propulsion
MURAKAWA, S., Community Environmental Science
NAKAMURA, Y., Structural Engineering
NOBUKAWA, H., Design Technology of Transport Systems
SASAKI, Y., Geotechnical Earthquake Engineering
SHIMAZU, T., Earthquake-resistant Engineering
SUGIMOTO, T., Architectural Design
TAKAKI, M., Ocean Space Engineering
TAZAWA, E., Concrete and Concrete Structure Engineering
YAJIMA, H., Welding and Production Systems
YAO, T., Strength of Structures
YOKOSHI, S., Hydraulics
YONEKURA, A., Concrete and Concrete Structures Engineering

Faculty of Applied Biological Science:

Fisheries Science

GUSHIMA, K., Feeding Ecology of Reef Fishes
IKEGAMI, S., Molecular Biology of Blastulation in Echinoderms
IMABAYASHI, H., Larval Settlement of Benthic Organisms
MATSUDA, O., Biogeochemical Cycle of Nutrients
MUROGA, K., Bacterial Diseases of Cultured Fish
NAKAGAWA, H., Fish Nutrition
NANBA, K., Respiration and Circulation in Fishes
RAJENDRAN, N., Responses of Microbial Communities to Environmental Perturbation
UEMATSU, K., Neural Basis of Fish Swimming
UYE, S., Production Ecology of Marine Zooplankton

Animal Science

ANDO, T., Interactions between Plants and Soils
FUJITA, K., Carbon-Nitrogen Interaction in Crop Production
ITO, T., Effects of Behavioural Activity and Feeding Levels on Heat Production and Heart Rate in Growing Pigs
MATSUDA, H., Ontogeny of Chicken B Lymphocytes
MIKUNI, H., Marketing System Analysis of Agricultural Products
OKAMOTO, T., Morphological Studies of the Avian Gastrointestinal Endocrine Cells
TANIGUCHI, K., Digestion of Nutrients in the Rumen and Small Intestine
TERADA, T., Nuclear Transfer in the Bovine and Porcine Embryo
YAMAMOTO, S., Environmental Physiology of Farm Animals
YAMAMOTO, Y., Immunogenetic Analysis for Resistance to Marek's Disease
YAMAO, M., Community-Based Approaches to Rural Resource Management

Food Science

KAWAKAMI, H., Pathogenicity and Cell Function of Food-Borne Disease-Causing Bacteria
KUBOTA, K., Physical Properties of Foods
KUTSUKAKE, K., Control of Gene Expression in Bacteria
MIYAZAWA, K., Marine Biotoxins, Food Science
OHTA, Y., Application of Lipase and Related Enzymes to Food Processing
OHTA, Y., Microbial Deodorization and Utilization of Agricultural Wastes

Sato, K., Physical Chemistry of Lipids
Suzuki, K., Emulsifying Characteristics and Properties of Food Emulsions
Yoshida, S., Isolation of Milk Minor Proteins
Yoshimoto, A., Microbial Origin of Bioactive Substances

Graduate School of Biosphere Science
Fujita, M., Productive Physiology in Farm Animals

Graduate School for International Development and Co-operation:

Division of Development Science
Iwata, M., Welding Technology and Materials Science
Kinbara, T., Corporate Strategy
Komatsu, M., Development Finance
Nohara, H., Comparative Study of Industrial Organizations
Saito, K., Marine Hydrodynamics and Transport
Sugie, Y., Transport Engineering
Tominaga, K., Soil Mechanics and Foundation Engineering
Yamashita, S., Development Economics
Yoshimura, Y., Physiology of Domestic Animals

Division of Educational Development and Cultural and Regional Studies
Inoue, S., Theory of International Education
Kasai, T., Human Neurophysiology
Murakami, M., Economic Geography
Nakayama, S., Geography and Teaching of Geography
Tabata, Y., Human Resource Development in Education
Uehara, A., Intercultural Communication

Graduate School of Advanced Sciences of Matter:

Department of Quantum Matter
Endo, I., Photon Physics
Fujita, T., Low Temperature Physics
Inoue, M., Semiconductor Physics, Low Temperature Physics
Jo, T., Theory of Condensed Matter
Oguchi, T., Computational Physics
Tabatake, T., Magnetism, Strongly Correlated Electron Systems

Department of Molecular Biotechnology
Hasegawa, T., Molecular Cell Chemistry
Itoh, K., Metabolic Chemistry
Kinashi, H., Cell Biochemistry
Nishio, N., Metabolic Engineering Chemistry
Ono, K., Molecular Biochemistry

Research Institute for Radiation Biology and Medicine:
Hayakawa, N., Epidemiology
Hoshi, M., Radiation Biophysics
Ito, A., Experimental Pathology, Tumour Biology
Kamada, N., Molecular Cytogenetics
Kamiya, K., Experimental Pathology, Molecular Carcinogenesis
Kimura, A., Internal Medicine, Haematology
Komatsu, K., Radiation Biology
Miyagawa, K., Molecular Oncology
Nishiyama, M., Molecular Oncology, Preclinical Development
Ohtaki, M., Biometrics, Environmetrics
Suzuki, F., Radiation Biology
Toge, T., Surgical Oncology
Watanabe, H., Experimental Pathology, Radiation Biology

ATTACHED INSTITUTES

Research Institute for Higher Education: 2-2 Kagamiyama 1-chome, Higashi-Hiroshima 739-8521; Dir A. Arimoto.

Information Processing Center: 4-2 Kagamiyama 1-chome, Higashi-Hiroshima 739-8526; Dir T. Matsumoto.

Research Center for Nanodevices and Systems: 4-2 Kagamiyama 1-chome, Higashi-Hiroshima 739-8527; Dir M. Hirose.

Center for Gene Science: 4-2 Kagamiyama 1-chome, Higashi-Hiroshima 739-8527; Dir T. Miyakawa.

Institute for International Education: 1-2 Kagamiyama 1-chome, Higashi-Hiroshima 739-8523; Dir S. Tawata.

Instrument Center for Chemical Analysis: 3-1 Kagamiyama 1-chome, Higashi-Hiroshima 739-8526; Dir H. Matsuura.

Cryogenic Center: 3-1 Kagamiyama 1-chome, Higashi-Hiroshima 739-8526; Dir H. Fujii.

Radioisotope Center: 4-2 Kagamiyama 1-chome, Higashi-Hiroshima 739-8526; Dir H. Ide.

Center for Technology Research and Development: 10-31 Kagamiyama 3-chome, Higashi-Hiroshima 739-0046; Dir E. Tazawa.

Health Service Center: 7-1 Kagamiyama 1-chome, Higashi-Hiroshima 739-8511; Dir S. Nakamura.

Institute for Peace Science: 1-89, Higashisenda-machi 1-chome, Naka-ku, Hiroshima 730-0053; Dir M. Matsuo.

Saijo Seminar House: Misonou, Saijo-cho, Higashi-Hiroshima 739-0024; Dir K. Nishimura.

Institute for Waste Water Treatment: 5-3 Kagamiyama 1-chome, Higashi-Hiroshima 739-8513; Dir M. Okada.

Hiroshima Synchrotron Radiation Center: 313 Kagamiyama 2-chome, Higashi-Hiroshima 739-8526; Dir M. Taniguchi.

Center for the Study of International Co-operation in Education: 3-2 Kagamiyama 1-chome, Higashi-Hiroshima 739-8529; Dir A. Ninomiya.

Research Center for Regional Geography: 2-3 Kagamiyama 1-chome, Higashi-Hiroshima 739-8522; Dir M. Murakami.

Venture Business Laboratory: 313 Kagamiyama 2-chome, Higashi-Hiroshima 739-8527; Dir M. Matsumura.

Research Institute for Information Science and Education: 7-1 Kagamiyama 1-chome, Higashi-Hiroshima 739-8521; Dir K. Nagai.

Institute for Foreign Language Research and Education: 7-1, Kagamiyama 1-chome, Higashi-Hiroshima 739-8521; Dir H. Mukaiyama.

HITOTSUBASHI UNIVERSITY

2-1 Naka, Kunitachi-city, Tokyo 186-8601
Telephone: (42) 580-8000
Fax: (42) 580-8006

Founded 1875
Academic year: April to March

President: Kinya Abe
Director-General: Yukihisa Kitamura
Dean of Students: Susumu Yamauchi
Librarian: Hiromitsu Ishi

Library of 1,590,000 vols
Number of full-time teachers: 373
Number of students: 5,898

Publications: *Hitotsubashi Review* (monthly), *Journal of Commerce and Management* (annually), *Journal of Economics* (2 a year), *Journal of Law and Politics* (1 a year), *Journal of Social Studies* (2 a year), *Hitotsubashi Arts and Sciences* (1 a year), *Gengo Bunka* (1 a year).

DEANS

Faculty of Commerce: H. Ando
Faculty of Economics: A. Yamazaki
Faculty of Law: M. Kawamura
Faculty of Social Sciences: M. Hamatani

ATTACHED INSTITUTES

Institute of Economic Research: Tokyo; f. 1940; 34 teachers; Dir J. Teranishe; publ. *Economic Research Review* (4 a year).

Institute of Innovation Research: Tokyo; f. 1997; 12 teachers; Dir H. Kataoka: publ. *Business Review* (4 a year).

HOKKAIDO UNIVERSITY

Nishi 5, Kita 8, Kita-ku, Sapporo 060-0808
Telephone: (11) 716-2111
Fax: (11) 746-9488

Founded 1876
State control
Academic year: April to March

President: Norihito Tambo
Vice-Presidents: Ichiro Azuma, Mutsuo Nakamura
Director-General, Administration Bureau: Toshimichi Nishimura
Director, University Library: Teruyuki Hara

Number of teachers: 2,143
Number of students: 19,418

Publications: various faculty bulletins.

DEANS

Faculty of Letters: A. Kitahara
Faculty of Education: Y. Kimura
Faculty of Law: K. Nakamura
Faculty of Economics: K. Uchida
Graduate School of Science: T. Sambongi
School of Medicine: Y. Inoue
School of Dentistry: Y. Totsuka
Graduate School of Pharmaceutical Sciences: S. Nagasawa
Graduate School of Engineering: S. Fukusako
Faculty of Agriculture: A. Ogoshi
Graduate School of Veterinary Medicine: Y. Maede
Faculty of Fisheries: K. Yamauchi
Graduate School of Environmental Earth Science: N. Nishi
Institute of Language and Culture Studies: K. Namita

PROFESSORS

Faculty of Letters:
Abe, J., Psychology
Adachi, A., History and Cultural Anthropology
Akashi, M., European History
Ando, A., Western Literature
Anzai, M., Western Literature
Fujii, K., Cultural Sciences
Haiya, K., Western Literature
Hatano, M., Regional Sciences
Hayashi, K., Northern Cultures
Hishitani, S., Psychology
Inoue, K., Japanese History
Irimoto, T., Northern Cultures
Ishizuka, H., Linguistics and Information Sciences
Ito, T., Chinese Philosophy
Kadowaki, S., Linguistics and Information Sciences
Kajiwara, K., History and Cultural Anthropology
Kamei, H., Japanology
Kamiya, T., Japanology
Kaneko, I., Sociology
Kasai, S., Linguistics and Western Languages
Kikuchi, T., Asian History
Kitahara, A., History and Cultural Anthropology
Kochi, S., Japanese History
Koyama, K., Asian History
Kuryuzawa, T., European History
Misaki, H., Japanology
Miyazawa, T., Japanology
Nagao, T., Western Literature
Nambu, N., Japanese History
Nishikawa, Y., Psychology

NITTA, T., Ethics and Applied Philosophy
ONO, Y., Linguistics and Information Science
OTSU, T., Behavioural Sciences
SAKAI, A., Ethics and Applied Philosophy
SEKI, T., Regional Sciences
SINOTSUKA, H., Behavioural Sciences
SUTO, Y., Sinology
TAKAHASHI, H., Linguistics and Western Languages
TAKAHEI, H., Philosophy
TAKIGAWA, T., Psychology
TANAKA, T., Philosophy
TSUCHIYA, H., Cultural Sciences
TSUMAGARI, T., Northern Cultures
TUDA, Y., Asian History
UEKI, M., Linguistics and Western Languages
URAI, Y., Linguistics and Western Languages
UTSUNOMIYA, T., Cultural Sciences
YAMADA, T., Philosophy
YAMADA, T., Western Literature
YAMAGISHI, T., Behavioural Sciences

Faculty of Education:

FUKUCHI, Y., Public Health
HEMMI, M., History of Education
ISERI, T., Physical Education
KIMURA, Y., Vocational Education
KOIDE, T., Educational Administration
MORIYA, K., Adaptation Physiology
MOROTOMI, T., Educational Psychology
SUDA, K., Teaching Methods for Mathematics
SUDA, T., Exercise Physiology
SUGIMURA, H., Educational Planning
SUZUKI, T., Adult Education
SUZUKI, T., Physical Education
TAKEDA, M., History of Education
YOKOYU, S., Clinical Psychology in Education

Faculty of Law:

ATSUYA, J., Economic Law
DOKO, T., Labour Law
FUJIWARA, M., Civil Law
FURUYA, J., Political History
HASEGAWA, K., Philosophy of Law
HATAKEYAMA, T., Administrative Law
HAYASHI, T., Commercial Law
HAYASHIDA, S., Sociology of Law
HIENUKI, T., Economic Law
HOBARA, K., Labour Law
IMAI, H., Philosophy of Law
KANBARA, M., Public Administration
KAWASAKI, O., Political Science
KISA, S., Administrative Law
MATSUHISA, M., Civil Law
MATSUMURA, Y., Sociology of Law
NAKAGAWA, A., Educational Law
NAKAMURA, K., International Politics
NAKAMURA, M., Constitutional Law
NANKI, T., Public Administration
NOSE, H., Law of Criminal Procedure
OGAWA, K., History of Law
OKADA, N., Constitutional Law
OKUDA, Y., Private International Law
OTSUKA, R., Commercial Law
OZAWA, N., Administrative Law
SAINO, H., Criminal Law
SEGAWA, N., Civil Law
SHINKAWA, T., Political Science
SHIRATORI, Y., Law of Criminal Procedure
SHOJI, K., Civil Law
TAGUCHI, A., Political History
TAKAMI, K., Constitutional Law
TAKAMI, S., Law of Civil Procedure
TSUNEMOTO, T., Constitutional Law
USUKI, T., International Law
WATARI, I., Administrative Law
YAMAGUCHI, J., Public Administration
YOSHIDA, KATSUMI, Civil Law
YOSHIDA, KUNIHIKO, Civil Law

Faculty of Economics:

HAMADA, Y., Business Finance, Banking
HASHIMOTO, T., Statistics
HAYAKAWA, Y., Accounting
INOUE, H., Industrial Policy
ISHIZAKA, A., European Economic History
KANAI, K., Business Organization and Corporate Strategy
KARATO, O., Principles of Economics
KIMURA, T., Operations Research
KOJIMA, H., Management
KURODA, S., Marketing
MIYAMOTO, K., Economic History of Asia
ONO, H., Microeconomics
SASAKI, T., World Economy, European Integration
SEKIGUCHI, Y., Management Engineering and Information Systems
SHIRAI, T., Principles of Economics
SUZUKI, Y., Comparative Japanese Economy
TANAKA, S., Agrarian History
UCHIDA, K., Macroeconomics
YONEYAMA, K., Industrial Management
YOSHIDA, F., Industrial Technology and Environmental Economics
YOSHINO, E., Comparative Economic Systems

Graduate School of Science:

AGEMI, R., Partial Differential Equations
ARAI, A., Mathematical Physics
FUJIMOTO, M., Theoretical Physics
FUJINO, K., Mineralogy
FUKUNAGA, N., Microbiology and Biochemistry
GIGA, Y., Partial Differential Equations
HARIMAYA, T., Meteorology
HAYASHI, M., Function Theory
HAYASHI, Y., Geophysical Fluid Dynamics
HIKICHI, K., Polymer Physics
HINATSU, Y., Solid State Chemistry
ICHIMURA, T., Evolution of Sexuality in Algae
IDO, M., Solid State Physics
IKAWA, S., Structural Chemistry
INABE, T., Solid State Physics
INOUE, J., Functional Analysis
ISHIGAKI, T., Philosophy of Science
ISHIKAWA, K., Theoretical Physics
IZUMIYA, S., Differential Topology
KATAKURA, H., Speciation of Terrestrial Invertebrates
KAWAMOTO, N., Theoretical Physics
KISHIMOTO, A., Operator Algebra
KITAMURA, N., Analytical Chemistry
KOIKE, T., Molecular and Cellular Neurobiology
KOIZUMI, I., Micropalaeontology
KOMEDA, Y., Plant Molecular Genetics
KONAKA, S., Structural Chemistry
KOYAMA, J., Solid Earth Science
KUBOTA, K., Partial Differential Equations
KUMAGAI, K., Solid State Physics
MARUOKA, K., Organometallic Chemistry
MASUDA, M., Plant Systematics
MAWATARI, S., Taxonomy of Invertebrates
MIYAKE, T., Number Theory
MIYASHITA, M., Organic Chemistry
MUKAI, H., Marine Ecology
MURAI, A., Organic Chemistry
NAKAHARA, J., Experimental Physics
NAKAMURA, I., Algebraic Geometry
NAKAMURA, Y., Physical Chemistry
NAKASHIMA, S., Experimental Physical Geochemistry
NAKAZI, T., Functional Analysis
NISHIDA, Y., Solid Earth Physics
NISHIMURA, S., Bio-organic Chemistry
NITTA, K., Protein Chemistry
NOMURA, K., Solid State Physics
OCHIAI, H., Cell Biology
OHKAWA, F., Theoretical Physics
OKADA, H., Micropalaeontology
ONO, K., Geometry
OSADA, Y., Polymer Chemistry
OZAWA, T., Partial Differential Equations
SAKAKIBARA, T., Solid State Physics
SAMBONGI, T., Solid State Physics
SASAKI, Y., Co-ordination Chemistry
SHIMAMURA, H., Geophysics
SHIOZAKI, Y., Solid State Physics
SUGANO, K., Algebra
SUGIMOTO, K., Biochemistry
SUGIYAMA, S., History of Science
SUWA, T., Algebraic Geometry
SUZUKI, N., Developmental Biology
TAKAHASHI, T., Cellular Biochemistry
TAKAHATA, M., Behavioural Physiology
TANAKA, I., Protein Crystallography
TANIGUCHI, K., Biological Chemistry
TOKUNAGA, M., Theoretical Physics
TSUDA, I., Applied Mathematics
TSUJI, T., Organic Chemistry
TSUJISHITA, T., Applied Mathematics
UI, T., Volcanology
UOSAKI, K., Physical Chemistry
URAKAMI, K., Hydrology
URANO, A., Neuroendocrinology
WADA, K., Theoretical Physics
WATANABE, S., Planetary Atmosphere
WATANABE, T., Structural Geology
YAMAGISHI, A., Inorganic Chemistry
YAMAGUCHI, K., Differential Geometry
YAMAMOTO, T., Planetary Science
YAMASHITA, M., Reproductive Biology
YAZAWA, M., Biochemistry
YOGOMIDA, K., Seismology
YOSHIDA, M. C., Somatic Cell Genetics
YOSHIDA, T., Algebra

School of Medicine:

ABE, H., Neurosurgery
ABE, K., Cytology and Histology
ARIKAWA, J., Laboratory Animals
ASAKA, M., Internal Medicine
FUJIMOTO, S., Obstetrics and Gynaecology
FUKUSHIMA, K., Sensorimotor and Cognitive Research
HONMA, K., Chronobiology
HONMA, Y., Internal Medicine
HOSOKAWA, M., Pathology
IMAMURA, M., Gerontology and Oncology
INOUE, Y., Molecular Neuroanatomy
INUYAMA, Y., Otolaryngology
ISHIBASHI, T., Molecular Chemistry
KANEDA, K ., Orthopaedic Surgery
KANNO, M., Cellular and Molecular Pharmacology
KATO, H., Surgery
KAWAGUCHI, H., Laboratory Medicine
KAWAKAMI, Y., Internal Medicine
KEMMOTSU, O., Anaesthesiology
KISHI, R., Public Health
KITABATAKE, A., Cardiovascular Medicine
KOBAYASHI, K., Paediatrics
KOIKE, T., Internal Medicine
KOYAMA, T., Psychiatry
KOYANAGI, T., Urology
KUZUMAKI, N., Molecular Genetics
MANO, Y., Rehabilitation and Physical Medicine
MATSUDA, H., Ophthalmology
MINAGAWA, T., Microbiology
MIYASAKA, K., Radiology
MORIUCHI, T., Cell Biology
NAGASHIMA, K., Molecular and Cellular Pathology
NISHI, S., Molecular Biology
OHKAWARA, A., Dermatology
SUGIHARA, T., Plastic Surgery
TAKADA, K., Virology
TAMAKI, N., Nuclear Medicine
TASHIRO, K., Neurology
TERAZAWA, K., Legal Medicine
TODO, S., Surgery
YASUDA, K., Medical Biomechanics
YOSHIKI, T., Pathology
YOSHIOKA, M., Applied Pharmacology and Experimental Therapeutics

School of Dentistry:

AKAIKE, T., Oral Physiology
FUKUDA, H., Oral Diagnosis and Oral Surgery
FUKUSHIMA, K., Dental Anaesthesiology

KATO, H., Periodontology and Endodontology
KAWASAKI, T., Removable Prosthetic Dentistry I
KOHGO, T., Oral Pathology
KUBOKI, Y., Oral Biochemistry
MATSUMOTO, A., Dental Pharmacology
NAKAMURA, M., Dental Radiology
NAKAMURA, S., Orthodontics
OGUCHI, H., Paediatric Dentistry
OHATA, N., Crown and Bridge Prosthodontics
SANO, H., Operative Dentistry
TANI, H., Preventive Dentistry
TOTSUKA, Y., Oral and Maxillofacial Surgery
WAKITA, M., Oral Histology and Embryology
WATANABE, T., Oral Microbiology
WATARI, F., Dental Materials and Engineering
YOSHIDA, S., Oral Anatomy

Graduate School of Pharmaceutical Sciences:
ARIGA, H., Molecular Biology
HASHIMOTO, S., Synthetic and Industrial Chemistry
IGARASHI, Y., Biomembrane and Biofunctional Chemistry
KAMATAKI, T., Drug Metabolism
KAMO, N., Biophysical Chemistry
KOBAYASHI, J., Natural Products Chemistry
KURIHARA, K., Pharmaceutics
MATSUDA, A., Medicinal Chemistry
MIYAZAKI, K., Pharmaco-kinetics
MORI, M., Fine Synthetic Chemistry
NAGASAWA, S., Hygienic Chemistry
NOMURA, Y., Pharmacology
OHTSUKA, E., Gene Organic Chemistry
TOKUMITSU, Y., Physiological Chemistry
YOKOSAWA, H., Biochemistry

Graduate School of Engineering:
AMEMIYA, Y., Semiconductor Devices
AOKI, Y., Multimedia
BABA, N., Astronomical Optics
DATE, T., Intelligence-Oriented Computer Engineering
ENAI, M., Measurement and Analysis of Buoyant Air Circulation
ENOTO, T., Plasma Physics
FUJITA, M., Hydrology
FUKUSAKO, S., Convective Heat and Mass Transfer with and without Phase Change
FURUICHI, R., Reaction Chemistry of Inorganic Solids
FURUICHI, T., Environmental Systems Planning
HARAGUCHI, M., Knowledge Representation
HASEGAWA, H., Semiconductor Devices and Integrated Electronics
HASEGAWA, J., Electric Power Engineering
HIGUCHI, K., Mine Planning
HINO, T., Plasma Wall Interactions in Nuclear Fusion Devices
HISHINUMA, Y., Plasma-surface Interactions in Nuclear Fusion Devices
HONMA, T., Computational Electromagnetics
ICHIKAWA, T., Magnetic Resonance Spectroscopy
IGARASHI, S., Computer Vision
IGUCHI, M., Transport Phenomena and Materials Processing
IIDA, S., Fluid Mechanics and Machinery
IKEDA, M., High-power Laser Processing
INAGAKI, M., Inorganic Materials Chemistry
INO, S., Structural Engineering
INOUE, Y., Theoretical Non-linear Acoustics
ISHII, K., Physical Chemistry of Iron and Steel Making
ISHIJIMA, Y., Design and Evaluation of CAES and Geological Disposal
ISHIKAWA, H., Constitutive Modelling for Viscoplastic Deformation
ISHIYAMA, Y., Structural Dynamics
ITAKURA, T., Hydraulics
ITO, H., Chemical Reaction Engineering
ITO, K., Combustion Engineering
ITO, K., Communication Systems, Electromagnetic Waves and Transmission
JOH, O., Earthquake-Resistant Design of Reinforced Concrete
KAGAMI, H., Earthquake Engineering
KAGAYA, S., Regional, City and Transport Planning
KAGIWADA, T., Theories of Material Cutting and Grinding
KAKAZU, Y., Autonomous Systems
KAKUTA, Y., Structural Engineering
KAMADA, E., Engineering of Concrete and Other Building Materials
KAMIDATE, T., Bioanalytical Chemistry
KANEKO, K., Rock Mechanics
KINOSHITA, S., Applied Biochemistry
KISHIDA, M., Theory of Elasticity and Plasticity
KISHINAMI, T., Manufacturing Information Modelling
KITAJIMA, H., Image Coding
KIYA, M., Turbulent Shear Flows
KIYANAGI, Y., Neutron Scattering
KOBAYASHI, H., Urban Planning and Design
KODAIRA, K., Inorganic Materials Chemistry
KOSHIBA, M., Opto- and Wave-Electronics
KOSHINO, T., Architectural History
KOSHIZAWA, A., Environmental Planning
KUDO, I., Spacecraft Design
KUDO, K., Analytical Study of Radiation and other Heat Transfer
KUDO, M., Solidification
KUMADA, T., Nuclear Reactor Safety
MAE, S., Crystal Lattice Defects
MAGARA, Y., Environmental Risk Management
MAJIMA, J., Mechanism of Housing Demand and Supply
MARUKAWA, K., Metal Physics
MIKAMI, T., Structural Mechanics
MISHIMA, T., Optoelectronics and Nonlinear Optics
MITACHI, T., Geotechnical Engineering
MITAMURA, Y., Biomedical Engineering
MIYAKOSHI, M., Functional Analysis and Fuzzy Set Theory
MIYAMOTO, E., Programming Languages
MIYAMOTO, N., Combustion and Thermodynamics
MIYANAGA, Y., Intelligent Communication Systems and Signal Processing
MIYAURA, N., Synthetic Organic Chemistry
MOCHIDA, T., Human-Thermal Environmental System
MOHRI, T., Computational Materials Science
MORIYOSHI, A., Highway Engineering
MUKASA, K., Applied Solid State Physics
MUNEKATA, M., Cell Technology
MUTO, S., Physics of Superlattices and Quantum Devices
NAKAJIMA, I., Mining Machinery
NAKAYAMA, T., Very-Low-Temperature Physics
NARITA, M., Nuclear Radiation Physics and Measurements
NARITA, T., Applied Materials Science of Ceramics
NOGUCHI, T., Structural Materials and Foundry Engineering
OCHIFUJI, K., Heating, Ventilation and Air Conditioning
OGAWA, Y., Communication Engineering
OGAWA, Y., Integrated Devices
OHASHI, H., Nuclear Fuels and Reactor Materials
OHBA, R., Data Processing
OHNISHI, T., Superconducting Machines and Power Devices
OHNUKI, S., Radiation Damage
OHNUMA, H., Materials Engineering
OHTA, S., Air Pollution Modelling
OHTSUKA, T., Corrosion Science
OHUCHI, A., Computer-supported Co-operative Work
OKADA, A., Crystal Imperfections
SAEKI, H., Harbour and Coastal Engineering
SAEKI, N., Concrete Engineering
SAKAI, Y., Plasma Processing
SATO, J., Metallic and Non-Metallic Ore Deposits
SATO, K., Bridge Engineering
SATO, K., Regional, City and Transport Planning
SATO, Y., Computational Statistics
SAWAMURA, S., Quantum Beam Science and Engineering
SEO, M., Surface Electrochemistry
SHIMA, M., Theory of Systems and Control
SHIMADA, S., Solid State Chemistry
SHIMBO, M., Speech Recognition
SHIMIZU, K., Biological Measurement
SHIMIZU, T., Water Quality Engineering
SHINOHARA, K., Chemical Engineering
TAKAHASHI, H., Anodizing of Aluminium
TAKAI, M., Polysaccharide Chemistry
TAKAKUWA, T., Design of Hydraulic Networks
TAKEZAWA, N., Catalyst Design
TAMURA, S., Condensed Matter Physics
TANAKA, K., Amorphous Materials
TANAKA, N., Sanitary Landfill Engineering
TANAKA, Y., Media Architecture
TOCHINAI, K., Natural Language Understanding
TOKUDA, M., Synthetic Chemistry
TOKUDA, N., Theoretical Solid State Physics
TSUCHIYA, T., Control Engineering
TSUNEKAWA, M., Flotation of Salt-Type Minerals
TSUTSUMI, A., Polymer Physics
UCHIYAMA, T., Structural Mechanics
UKAI, T., Mechanical Systems Design
WADA, M., Human Informatics and Robotics
WATANABE, Y., Water and Sewage Works
WRIGHT, O., Phonon Physics
YAMADA, G., Machine Dynamics
YAMAMOTO, K., Non-invasive Measurement
YAMASHITA, M., Femtosecond Optical-Pulse Technology
YAMAYA, K., Solid State Physics
YAMAZAKI, I., Molecular Photophysics on Molecular Assemblies
YOKOTA, K., Polymer Chemistry
YONEDA, N., Industrial and Synthetic Organic Chemistry

Faculty of Agriculture:
AOYAMA, Y., Food Biochemistry
ARAYA, T., Erosion Control
ASAKAWA, S., Ornamental Plants and Landscape Architecture
CHIBA, S., Comparative Molecular Enzymology
DEMURA, K., Agricultural Policy
HARADA, T., Horticultural Science
HATANO, R., Soil Science
HIRAI, T., Timber Engineering
HONMA, M., Biochemistry
HORIGUCHI, I., Environmental Information concerning Land
IIZUKA, T., Applied Molecular Entomology
ISHII, Y., Forest Policy
ITO, K., Agricultural Process Engineering
KASAI, T., Nutritional Biochemistry
KIKUTA, Y., Crop Physiology
KOBAYASHI, K., Plant Functions Development
KONDO, K., Animal Byproduct Science
KUROKAWA, I., Farm Management
MATSUDA, J., Agricultural Systems Engineering
MATSUDA, Y., Soil Amelioration
MIKAMI, T., Genetic Engineering
MIKAWA, K., Food Hygiene Science
MISHIMA, T., Agricultural Marketing
MIURA, K., Forest Resource Biology
NAGASAWA, T., Land Improvement and Management
NAITO, S., Molecular Biology
NAKASEKO, K., Crop Science
NIGI, T., Forest Management
OGOSHI, A., Plant Pathology
OHTAHARA, T., Agricultural Co-operatives

OHTANI, J., Wood Biology
OKUBO, M., Animal Production System
SAITO, Y., Applied Zoology
SANO, Y., Wood Chemistry
SANO, Y., Plant Breeding
SHIMAMOTO, Y., Plant Genetics and Evolution
SHIMAZAKI, K., Dairy Science
SHIMIZU, H., Animal Breeding and Reproduction
SUWA, M., Systematic Entomology
TADANO, T., Plant Nutrition
TAHARA, S., Ecological Chemistry
TAKAHASHI, K., Meat Science
TAKAHASHI, K., Silviculture
TAKAI, M., Crop Production Engineering
TANAKA, K., Animal Nutrition
TERAO, H., Agricultural Vehicle Systems Engineering
TERAZAWA, M., Forest Chemistry
TOMITA, F., Applied Microbiology
URANO, S., Agricultural Physics
UYEDA, I., Plant Virology and Mycology
YOSHIHARA, T., Bioorganic Chemistry

Graduate School of Veterinary Medicine:

FUJINAGA, T., Veterinary Clinical Sciences
FUJITA, S., Environmental Veterinary Sciences
HABARA, Y., Biomedical Sciences
HASHIMOTO, A., Veterinary Clinical Sciences
IWANAGA, T., Biomedical Sciences
KAMIYA, M., Disease Control
KIDA, H., Disease Control
KUWABARA, M., Environmental Veterinary Sciences
MAEDE, Y., Veterinary Clinical Sciences
NAKAZATO, Y., Biomedical Sciences
OHTAISHI, N., Environmental Veterinary Sciences
ONUMA, M., Disease Control
SAITO, M., Biomedical Sciences
TAKASHIMA, I., Environmental Veterinary Sciences
UMEMURA, T., Veterinary Clinical Sciences
WATANABE, T., Disease Control

Faculty of Fisheries:

AMAGAI, K., Fishing Boat Seamanship
AMAOKA, K., Marine Zoology
ANMA, G., Training Ship 'Oshoro-Maru'
EZURA, Y., Microbiology
HARA, A., Comparative Biochemistry
HASHIMOTO, S., Marine Production System, Electronics Instrumentation and Control
HAYASHI, K., Chemistry of Marine Biogenic Lipids
HIROYOSHI, K., Fisheries Business Economics
IKEDA, T., Zooplankton Ecology
INOUE, N., Freeze Denaturation of Fish Muscular Proteins
KANNO, Y., Biology of Fish Population
KARASUNO, K., Fishing Boat Engineering
KISHI, J. M., Numerical Modelling of Marine Ecosystems
MAITA, Y., Marine Biochemical Science
MATSUNAGA, K., Marine Chemistry
MIURA, T., Operational Technology of Fishing
MUGIYA, Y., Animal Physiology
NAKAO, S., Mariculture
NASHIMOTO, K., Fishing Gear Engineering
NISHITA, K., Biopolymer Chemistry
OGI, H., Ecology of Seabirds
OHTANI, K., Oceanography
OTA, T., Marine Lipid Chemistry
SEKI, N., Food Biochemistry
SHIMAZAKI, K., Marine Ecology
SUZUKI, A., Chemical Engineering
SUZUKI, T., Food Wholesomeness
TAKAHASHI, K., Food Science and Technology
TAKAHASHI, T., Fisheries Ecology
TAKAMA, K., Food Hygiene
YAMAMOTO, H., Marine Botany
YAMAMOTO, K., Fishing Gear Engineering
YAMAUCHI, K., Freshwater Fish Culture
YAMAZAKI, F., Developmental Genetics
YOSHIMIZU, M., Viral and Bacterial Fish Diseases

Graduate School of Environmental Earth Science:

ARAKI, Y., Biochemistry
ASHIDA, M., Insect Defence Mechanisms
FUJIYOSHI, Y., Mesoscale Meteorology
FUKUDA, M., Cryolithology
HARA, T., Mathematical Modelling and Plant Ecology
HASEBE, K., Analytical Chemistry
HIGASHI, S., Behavioural Ecology and Sociobiology
HIRAKAWA, K., Geomorphology
HIRAO, K., Synthetic Organic Chemistry
HONDOH, T., X-ray Crystallography
ICHIKAWA, K., Inorganic Physical Chemistry and Bioinorganic Chemistry
IKEDA, M., Numerical Modelling and Remote Sensing of Ocean and Sea Ice
IWAKUMA, T., Freshwater Ecology
KAWAMURA, K., Atmospheric Chemistry and Organic Geochemistry
KIMURA, M., Ecological and Physiological Genetics
KOBAYASHI, D., Snow Hydrology
KOHYAMA, T., Ecosystem Ecology and Plant Ecology
KOUCHI, A., Planetary Science
KUBOKAWA, A., Physical Oceanology
MAENO, K., Physics of Snow and Ice
MATSUSHIMA, T., Dynamics of Surface Reactions
MINAGAWA, M., Isotope Biogeochemistry
NAKAMURA, H., Photochemistry and Analytical Chemistry
NAKAMURA, T., Physical Chemistry
NISHI, N., Biopolymer Chemistry
NORIKI, S., Chemical Oceanography
OBA, T., Palaeo-oceanography
OHATA, T., Cryosphere and Climate
OKUHARA, T., Catalytic Chemistry
ONO, Y., Enviromental Geography
OSAWA, M., Surface Electrochemistry
TAKAGI, N., Cytogenetics
TAKASUGI, M., Natural Products Chemistry
TAKEUCHI, K., Air–Sea Interactions in the Cryosphere and their Roles in Climate Change
TANAKA, A., Plant Physiology
TODA, M. J., Ecology and Taxonomy of Drosophilid Flies
TSUNOGAI, S., Geochemistry of Atmosphere and Hydrosphere
WAKATSUCHI, M., Polar Oceanography
YAMAMOTO, K., Plant Physiology and Molecular Biology
YAMAMURA, E., Geographic Information Systems
YAMAZAKI, K., Atmospheric General Circulation Model for Climate Change
YOSHIDA, M., Somatic Cell Genetics and Cytogenetics

Institute of Language and Culture Studies:

FUJIIE, S., Russian
FUJIMOTO, K., Chinese
HASHIMOTO, H., English
IKEZAWA, K., French
INOUE, K., English
ISHIBASHI, M., German
ITOH, A., English
KAJINO, K., French
KANOH, K., German
KIKUCHI, M., French
KOGA, H., Italian
KUDOH, M., Russian
KURIHARA, T., English
NAGANO, K., English
NAKATA, K., German
NAMITA, K., English
NISHIHORI, Y., English
NOSAKA, M., English
NOZAWA, T., Chinese
OGAWA, Y., English
OHHIRA, T., French
SATOH, T., German
TAKAHASHI, N., English
TAKAHASHI, Y., German
TANAKA, T., Greek
TSUKUWA, M., German
WATANABE, H., English
YAMADA, K., Russian
YAMANAKA, S., German
YANADA, N., English
YOSHIDA, T., German

ATTACHED INSTITUTES

Institute of Low Temperature Science: f. 1941; Dir T. HONDOH; publs *Contributions from the ILTS, Series A* (irregular).

Institute of Immunological Science: f. 1950; Dir K. ONOUE; publ. *Collected Papers* (1 a year).

Research Institute for Electronic Science: f. 1943; Dir K. INOUE.

Catalysis Research Center: f. 1989; Dir M. IWAMOTO; publ. *Annual Report*.

Slavic Research Center: f. 1955; Dir K. INOUE; publ. *Acta Slavica Iaponica* (1 a year).

Research Center for Interface Quantum Electronics: f. 1991; Dir H. HASEGAWA.

Computing Center: f. 1970; Dir E. MIYAMOTO.

Central Institute of Radioisotope Science: f. 1978; Dir S. NISHI.

Center for Information Processing Education: f. 1979; Dir Y. SHIOZAKI.

Center for Instrumental Analysis: f. 1979; Dir H. YOKOSAWA.

Center for Experimental Plants and Animals: f. 1981; Dir M. YOSHIDA.

Research Center for Molecular Genetics: f. 1985; Dir N. TAKAGI.

Center for Advanced Research in Energy Technology: f. 1994; Dir R. FURUICHI.

Center for Research and Development in Higher Education: f. 1995; Dir M. NAKAMURA.

College of Medical Technology; f. 1980; Dir Y. MORITA.

Centre for Advanced Science and Technology: f. 1996; Dir Y. KAKAZU.

IBARAKI UNIVERSITY

1-1, Bunkyo 2-chome, Mito-Shi, Ibaraki-ken 310-8512

Telephone: (29) 228-8111
Fax: (29) 228-8019

Founded 1949
State control
Academic year: April to March

President: K. HASHIMOTO
Administrator: H. HASHIMOTO
Librarian: M. HIRAYAMA

Library of 834,000 vols
Number of full-time teachers: 558
Number of students: 8,750

Publications (in Japanese): bulletins and journals of the faculties.

DEANS

Student Affairs: Y. USUI
Faculty of Education: R. KIKUCHI
Faculty of Humanities: K. SUZUKI
Faculty of Science: Y. IKEDA
Faculty of Engineering: T. MIYATA
School of Agriculture: M. NIWA

PROFESSORS

Faculty of Humanities:

AIZAWA, Y., English and American Culture
AMEMIYA, S., Politics
AOKI, K., French
ARIIZUMI, S., Economic Structure
ARITOMI, M., Psychology
ASANO, Y., Regional Sciences
EGUCHI, H., Foreign Media

FUKASAWA, Y., European History
FUKAYA, N., Law
FUSHIMI, K., German
HASEGAWA, S., Japanese Culture
IIZUKA, K., Law
IMAHASHI, M., Local Administration
KAMATA, A., Social Structure
KAMIYA, T., Social Structure
KANOU, Y., Asian Culture
KATAYAMA, Y., Philosophy
KIMURA, K., German
KINBARA, M., Finance and Banking
KOIDO, M., European Culture
KOMIYAMA, E., Communication and Media
MATSUMURA, N., Social Structure
MAYANAGI, M., Oriental History
MOGI, M., Comparative Culture
MORIYA, S., Logic
MORIYA, T., Sociology
MURANAKA, T., Sociology
NAKURA, B., Economic Structure
NISHIMURA, M., Philosophy
NOGAMI, K., International Culture Communication
NOSAKA, M., Law
OHATA, K., English and American Culture
OKUBO, N., French Culture
OKUBO, Y., Human Science
SAITO, N., Regional Societies
SAITO, Y., Local Administration
SASAKI, H., History
SASAKURA, S., English
SATO, K., Economic Structure
SATO, K., German Culture
SHIMAOKA, S., English
SUZUKI, K., Japanese Literature
SUZUKI, K., German
SUZUKI, T., Communication
TAKAGI, A., Regional Sciences
TAKAHASHI, T., English
TAKASHIMA, H., Media and Communication
TAMURA, T., Law
TANAKA, S., Regional Societies
TANAKA, Y., Comparative Culture
TATEWAKI, I., Regional Societies
TATEYAMA, Y., International Comparative Study
TOKUE, K., International Comparative Study
UMEDA, T., Law
WATANABE, K., European Culture
YOSHII, M., English and American Culture
YOSHIZAWA, M., Asian Culture

Faculty of Education:

ADACHI, K., School Education
ARAKAWA, C., Housing and Domestic Science
ASAI, S., Mechanical Engineering
EBATA, H., School Education
GASHA, T., Biochemistry
HASEGAWA, S., Vocal Music
HATTORI, K., Physical Activity Science
HONDA, T., Information Education
IKEYA, F., European History
INAMI, Y., Computer Science
KAIZU, S., Applied Mathematics
KAJIWARA, S., Instrumental Music
KANEKO, K., Art Education
KANO, K., School Health
KAWAMATA, T., Japanese Language Teaching
KIKUCHI, R., Adult Education
KOJIMA, H., Information Education
KUSAKA, Y., Physical Education
KUSHIDA, M., Home Economics Education
MAKINO, Y., Geology
MATSUDA, M., Art Education
MATSUI, M., Information Sciences
MATSUMURA, T., Education for Handicapped Children
MIURA, T., Health and Physical Education
MIZUNO, A., Health Education
MORI, A., Philosophy
MORITA, Y., Art Education
NAGASAWA, K., English Language Teaching
NAGASHIMA, T., Technical Education
NAKAMURA, T., Health Education
NAMIKI, T., English Morphology
NODA, Y., Health and Physical Education
OGATA, T., Health and Physical Education
OGUMA, H., School Education
OKAMOTO, K., Physical Education
OSHIMA, K., Earth Science
OTA, S., Physical Education
OTANI, H., School Nursing
OTSUKI, I., Economic History of Modern Japan
OZAKI, H., Physiology for Children with Handicap
SAKAI, H., Family Studies and Women's Studies
SASAKI, Y., Japanese Language Teaching
SATO, E., Mathematical Education
SATO, H., Technical Education
SHOJI, M., English and American Literature
SOGA, H., Mathematical Science
SOGOU, M., Painting
SUZUKI, E., Social Studies Teaching
TAGUCHI, M., Japanese Language Teaching
TAKAHASHI, N., Electrical Engineering
TANAKA, Y., Astrophysics
TANIGUCHI, T., School Education
TASHIRO, T., School Education
TATSUMI, N., Physical Education
TOYAMA, T., English Language Teaching
USUI, H., Instrumental Music
WATANABE, M., Health and Physical Education
YAMAMOTO, H., Organic Chemistry
YAMANE, S., Insect Ecology
YAMASHITA, T., School Education
YANAGITA, N., Mathematics
YAZAWA, CH., Music Education
YOSHIDA, H., Home Economics Education
YOSHIDA, T., School Education
YOSHIZAWA, T., Solid State Physics

Faculty of Science:

AMANO, K., Geology
AMANO, T., Science of Cosmic Matter
FUJII, Y., Co-ordination Chemistry
HATSUSE, K., Differential Geometry
HIAI, H., Analysis
HIRAYAMA, M., Structural Chemistry
HORIUCHI, T., Analysis
ICHIMASA, M., Cell Biology
ICHIMASA, Y., Physiology
IKEDA, Y., Geochemistry
IMURA, H., Analytical Chemistry
ISHIZUKA, T., Astrophysics
KANEKO, M., Chemistry
KANNO, S., Atomic Physics
KAWADA, Y., Chemistry
MATSUDA, R., Algebra
MIMURA, N., Urban Systems
MISHIMA, S., Biology
MIWA, I., Biology
MORINO, H., Systematics
NAKANO, Y., Structural Chemistry
NIREI, H., Environmental Geology
NISHIHARA, Y., Magnetism and Superconductivity
NODA, F., Theoretical High Energy
OHASHI, K., Analytical Chemistry
ONISHI, K., Applied Mathematics
ONOSE, H., Statistics
OSHIMA, H., Topology
SAKATA, F., Mathematical Science
SAKUMA, T., Solid-State Physics
SHIOMI, M., Ecology
TAGIRI, M., Earth and Planetary Physics
TAKAHASHI, M., Synthetic Chemistry
TAKANO, K., Mathematics
TOYODA, A., Physics
USUI, Y., Structural Chemistry
WATANABE, T., Earth Science
YAMADA, M., Physics
YANAGITA, S., Cosmic Ray Physics
YOKOSAWA, M., Astrophysics

Faculty of Engineering:

AGU, M., Field and Information
ARAKI, T., Computer Science
ASANO, N., Industrial Engineering
BETSUYAKU, H., Simulations
EDA, H., Production Engineering and Machine Tools
ENOMOTO, M., Materials Physics
FUJII, K., Laser and Plasma
FUKUZAWA, K., Concrete Engineering
HAMAMATSU, Y., Modelling and Simulation
HARIU, T., Electronic Material Systems
HOSHI, T., Systems Information and Remote Sensing
ICHIMURA, M., Materials Physics
IKEHATA, T., Plasma Science
ISHIGURO, M., Computer Applications
KAGOSHIMA, K., Antennae
KAJITANI, S., Energy Conversion
KAMINAGA, H., Energy Conversion
KANO, M., Discrete Mathematics and its Application
KATO, H., Coastal Engineering
KIKUMA, I., Electronic Materials
KISHI, Y., Intelligent Systems
KOBAYASHI, M., Systems Information
KOBAYASHI, M., Electromagnetic Systems
KOYAMADA, Y., Photonic Systems
KOYANAGI, T., Landscape Planning and Design
MASE, H., Plasma Science
MASUI, M., Electronic Materials
MIYATA, T., Electronic Circuits
MOMOSE, Y., Surface Chemistry
MOTOHASHI, Y., Materials Science and Engineering
MURANOI, T., Electronic Materials for New Functionality
NAITO, K., Analytical Chemistry
NAKAMOTO, R., Functional Analysis
NARA, K., Electrical Power Systems
NOGITA, S., Urban Systems
OGUCHI, K., Power Electronics
OKADA, Y., Dynamics of Machines
OKU, T., Design Engineering
OMORI, M., Manufacturing Technology
ONO, K., Polymer Science
OZAWA, S., Applied Physics
SAGAWA, N., Design Engineering
SASAKI, Y., Foundation and Design of Precision Engineering
SENBA, I., Computer Science
SHIDA, T., Manufacturing Technology
SHIMOJO, M., Human Interface
SHIRAISHI, M., Systems and Controls
SHIRAKI, M., Photo-electric Conversion Systems
SUZUKI, H., Mechanical Design
SUZUKI, T., Energy Conversion
TAKAHASHI, M., Organic Chemistry
TAKAMURA, S., Material Systems
TAKEUCHI, M., Electrical Materials
TAZUKE, Y., Applied Physics
TOMOTA, Y., Mechanical Metallurgy
TOZUNE, A., Electric Machines
TSUJIMOTO, T., Materials Processing
TSURUTA, K., High Voltage and Plasma Science
TSUTSUMI, Y., Fuel Cells
URAO, R., Metallurgy and Plasma Treatment
YAMAGATA, K., Transport Planning
YAMAGUCHI, H., Metallurgy
YAMANAKA, K., Control Theory
YASUHARA, K., Geotechnical Engineering
YOKOYAMA, K., Structural Engineering

School of Agriculture:

ADACHI, Y., Animal Microbiology and Immunology
AKUTSU, K., Plant Pathology
HAYASHI, N., Farm Machinery, Farm Work Science
HIRANO, Y., Modern History of Japanese Agriculture
KINOSE, K., Hydraulic Engineering
KODAMA, O., Bio-regulation Chemistry
KONO, Y., Chemical Ecology
KOSUGIYAMA, M., Animal Breeding

KUBOTA, M., Soil Science and Plant Nutrition
MACHIDA, T., Agricultural Systems
MASAKI, T., Enzymatic Chemistry
MATSUDA, T., Plant Production Science
MATSUDA, T., Horticultural Science
MATSUZAWA, Y., Animal Husbandry and Behaviour
MINATO, H., Feed Science
MORIIZUMI, S., Agricultural Machinery
NAGATA, T., Entomology
NAKAJIMA, M., Food Economics and Policy Sciences
NAKASONE, H., Agricultural and Environmental Engineering
NIWA, M., Plant Breeding
SHIO, K., Information Science
SHIRAI, M., Molecular Microbiology
TAKAHARA, H., Bioresource Engineering
TAKAMURA, Y., Applied and Environmental Microbiology
TANNO, S., Agricultural Management
TSUKIHASHI, T., Crop Production
TSUTSUMI, M., Applied Biological Chemistry

ATTACHED INSTITUTES

Centre for Research and Development in Higher Education: Dir T. OKU.

Centre for Co-operative Research and Development: Dir Y. TSUTSUMI.

Centre for Educational Research and Training: Dir M. TAGUCHI.

Centre for Water Environment Studies: Dir K. AMANO.

Experimental Farm: Dir T. MATSUDA.

Centre for Instrumental Analysis: Dir Y. KAWADA.

Centre for Education and Research of Lifelong Learning: Dir Y. ASANO.

Information Processing Centre: Dir S. OZAWA.

Izura Institute of Arts and Culture: Dir Y. MORITA.

International House: Dir Y. USUI.

Institute of Regional Studies: Dir O. TATEWAKI.

IWATE UNIVERSITY

3-18-8 Ueda, Morioka, Iwate

Telephone: (19) 621-6000
Fax: (19) 621-6014

Founded 1949
State control

President: NORIHIKO KAIZUMA
Chief Administrative Officer: YOSHIHIRO NAKAYAMA
Librarian: NORIAKI KUBOTA

Library of 696,000 vols
Number of teachers: 477
Number of students: 6,572

Publications: *Journal of the Faculty of Agriculture, Report on Technology of Iwate University, Annual Report of the Faculty of Education, Artes Liberales.*

DEANS

Faculty of Agriculture: T. TAKAHASHI
Faculty of Technology: K. HIRAYAMA
Faculty of Education: M. FUKUI
College of Humanities and Social Sciences: N. FUJIWARA

KAGAWA UNIVERSITY

1-1 Saiwai-cho, Takamatsu-shi 760

Telephone: (878) 36-1607

Founded 1949

President: TOMOTOSHI OKAICHI
Secretary-General: TERUO MOROHASHI
Librarian: KAZUO OYABU

Library of 694,589 vols
Number of teachers: 334
Number of students: 4,961

DEANS

Faculty of Agriculture: KOUICHI OKUTANI
Faculty of Economics: SUSUMU HOSOKAWA
Faculty of Education: KOJI KONDO
Faculty of Law: KIICHI GOTO

KAGOSHIMA UNIVERSITY

21–24, 1-chome, Korimoto, Kagoshima-shi 890-8580

Telephone: (992) 85-7111

Founded 1949

President: HIROMITSU TANAKA
Secretary-General: MASUMI TOBITA

Library of 1,247,000 vols
Number of full-time teachers: 1,061
Number of students: 10,620

DEANS

Faculty of Law, Economics and the Humanities: T. ISHIDA
Faculty of Education: T. SAKAO
Faculty of Science: M. HOTTA
Faculty of Medicine: Y. OHI
Faculty of Dentistry: Y. KASAHARA
Faculty of Engineering: H. AKASAKA
Faculty of Agriculture: T. HORIGUCHI
Faculty of Fisheries: H. ICHIKAWA

KANAZAWA UNIVERSITY

Kakuma-machi, Kanazawa-shi 920-1192

Telephone: (76) 262-5111
Fax: (76) 264-5111

Founded 1949

Academic year: April to March

President: A. OKADA
Director-General: A. NAKAMURA
Dean of Student Affairs: Y. HIROSE
Director-General of Library: T. HASHIMOTO

Libraries of 1,459,000 vols
Number of teachers: 1,025
Number of students: 10,761

DEANS

Faculty of Letters: J. TSUCHIYA
Faculty of Education: S. KANEKO
Faculty of Law: Y. KAMONO
Faculty of Economics: M. MIYATA
Faculty of Science: Y. HIWATARI
Faculty of Medicine: I. NAKANISHI
Faculty of Pharmaceutical Sciences: O. NIKAIDO
Faculty of Engineering: Y. HAYASHI
Graduate School of Socio-Environmental Studies: M. FUKAYA
Graduate School of Natural Science and Technology: M. HANAOKA

DIRECTORS

Cancer Research Institute: M. MAI
University Hospital: Y. WATANABE
Extension Institute: A. KIYOTA
Health Service Center: M. TAKAMORI
Radioisotope Center: H. MORI
Institute for Gene Research: K. YAMAGUCHI
General Information Processing Center: H. ISHIDA
Center for Co-operative Research: S. ISHIDA
International Student Center: N. OHASHI
Foreign Language Institute: T. OTAKI

PROFESSORS

Faculty of Letters:

FUJITA, S., English Literature
FURUYA, A., Japanese Language
HASHIMOTO, K., Sociology
HONMA, T., American Literature
KAJIKAWA, J., Geography
KANO, K., Cultural Anthropology
KASAI, J., Japanese History
KASHIWAGI, H., Linguistics
KIKUTA, M., Chinese Language
KOMAI, M., Geography
KOMAKI, J., Psychology
KUBOTA, I., German Literature
KUBUKI, S., Comparative Culture
KUNO, Y., Psychology
MORIYA, I., Geography
NAKABAYASHI, N., Cultural Anthropology
OHTAKI, S., Chinese Language
OHTAKI, T., German Language
SASAKI, T., Archaeology
SUGIMOTO, T., Comparative Culture
SUNAHARA, Y., Philosophy
TANABE, K., Archaeology
TSUCHIYA, J., Philosophy
TSUGE, Y., Linguistics
UCHIDA, H., French Literature
UEDA, M., Japanese Literature
USUI, T., Sociology
WAJIMA, S., Cultural Studies
YAMANOUCHI, K., French Language

Faculty of Education:

DEMURA, S., Lifelong Sports
EDO, K., Science of Physical Movement (Kendo)
EMORI, I., Pedagogy
FUJISAWA, H., Social Science Education
FUKAGAWA, H., Japanese Language Teaching
GOMI, T., Geography
HATANAKA, H., Physics
IKEGAMI, K., Developmental Psychology
IMAI, H., Painting
ISHIMURA, U., Physical Education
KANEKO, S., Developmental Psychology
KATAGIRI, K., Developmental Neuropsychology of Mental Retardation
KUJIRA, Y., Crop Science
KUROBORI, T., Laser Technology
MAEDA, H., Japanese Literature
MATSUDAIRA, M., Clothing Science
MATSUNAKA, H., Instrumental Music
MATSUURA, N., Construction
MITSUI, T., Musicology
MIYAGI, Y., Chemistry
MIYAGUCHI, H., Science of Physical Movement (Track and Field)
MIYASHITA, T., Theory of Formative Arts
MIYOSHI, Y., Information Science
MORI, E., Japanese Literature
MORI, G., Psychology of Speech Disorder and Mental Retardation
MOROOKA, K., Methods of Education
MURATA, S., Technology Education
NAGASAWA, R., Algebra
OHHASHI, Y., Education of Mentally Retarded Children
OHKAWA, M., Principles of Crop Production
OHTSUKA, I., English Linguistics
OI, M., Communication Disorders
OKAZAKI, F., Philosophy
OKUBO, H., History of Physical Education and Sports
OKUDA, H., Japanese History
SAITO, K., Geometry
SANADA, M., Vocal Music
SHIGETA, T., Sculpture
SUGIMOTO, M., Geology
TAKANO, N., Physiology
UEDA, J., Chemistry
YAKURA, K., Biology
YAMAMOTO, H., Japanese Classic Literature
YAMAOKA, T., Learning Psychology
YAMASHITA, H., Western History
YAMASHITA, S., Musical Composition and Conducting
YASUKAWA, I., History of Education
YOSHIDA, S., Center for Educational Research and Training

Faculty of Law:

AONO, T., History of Legal Theory
ENDO, K., Civil Procedure
FUKAYA, M., Civil Law
FURITSU, T., Criminal Law
HATA, Y., Comparative Constitutional Law
IGARASHI, M., International Law

IKUTA, S., English Literature
INOUE, H., Social Security Law
KAMONO, Y., Constitutional Law
KANEKO, Y., German Language
KASHIMA, M., International Relations
KASHIMI, Y., Civil Law
KATO, K., History of Social and Political Thought
KIYOTA, A., Civil Procedure
KUGA, M., Criminology
KUSUNE, S., International Communication
MAEDA, T., Labour Law
MATSUNO, M., Cross-cultural Understanding and French
NAKAMURA, S., English Literature
NAKASHIMA, F., Commercial Law
NAKO, M., Labour Law
NISHIMURA, S., Political Sociology
NISHIYAMA, Y., Commercial Law
OIKAWA, M., Anglo-American Law
SAKURAI, T., European Legal History
SASADA, E., Constitutional Law
TOKUMOTO, S., Civil Law
UENO, H., German Literature
UMEDA, Y., Japanese Legal History
URABE, H., Tax Law
YAMAGATA, K., Developmental Psychology
YASUMURA, T., Criminal Procedure

Faculty of Economics:

AIZAWA, K., German Literature and Thought
FUJITA, A., Economic Theory and Political Economy
GOKA, K., Labour Economics
HASHIMOTO, T., Economic History of Japan
HAYASHI, Y., Economic History of Japan
HIRADATE, M., Statistics and Econometrics
HIRATA, M., English Literature
HORIBAYASHI, T., Theory of Economic Planning
KAMIJO, I., History of Economic Thought
KOBAYASHI, A., Public Finance
KUWANO, H., British Poetry
MAEDA, T., Modern Economics
MARUKAMA, K., Comparative Social Philosophy
MIYATA, M., Banking and Financial Systems
MURAKAMI, K., Principles of Economics
NAKAZAWA, M., History of Social Thought
OHNO, H., Accountancy
SAKARI, D., Sports Science
SASAKI, M., Regional Economics
TSURUZONO, Y., Korean History
UNNO, Y., Economic Policy
WATANABE, T., Mathematical Methods for Economic Science
YAMANOBE, T., History of Political Economy
YOKOYAMA, T., Social Security
YOSHIMURA, F., Management Accounting
YOSHINO, Y., Sports Science

Faculty of Science:

ANDO, T., Biophysics
FUJIMAGARI, T., Mathematical Analysis
FUJIMOTO, H., Complex Analysis
FUJISHITA, H., Quantum Physics of Condensed Matter
FUKUMORI, Y., Physiological Chemistry
HIROSE, Y., Theory of Material Physics
HIWATARI, Y., Theory of Material Physics
HONJO, T., Analytical Chemistry
IKEDA, O., Electrochemistry
ISHIHARA, Y., Quantum Physics of Condensed Matter
ISHIMOTO, H., Geometry
ITAGAKI, E., Biochemistry
ITO, T., Algebraic Combinatorics
KASHIWAYA, K., Hydro-Geomorphology
KATO, M., Stratigraphy and Palaeontology
KAWADA, S., Crystal Physics
KIHARA, K., Mineralogy and Crystallography
KINOSHITA, H., Organic Chemistry
KITAHARA, H., Geometry
KOBAYASHI, O., Geometry
KODAMA, A., Geometry
KOMURA, K., Nuclear Geochemistry
KUBO, J., Theoretical Physics
MASUZAKI, M., Plasma Physics
NAKAO, S., Applied Mathematics
NISHIKAWA, K., Theoretical Chemistry
OHASHI, N., Molecular Physics
OMURA, A., Stratigraphy and Palaeontology
SAKAMOTO, K., Radiochemistry
SAKURAI, S., Developmental Biology
SASAYAMA, Y., Biochemistry
SUGANO, T., Algebra
SUHARA, M., Theoretical Chemistry
SUZUKI, M., Co-ordination Chemistry
SUZUKI, T., Nuclear Physics
TAGO, Y., Computational Science
TAZAKI, K., Environmental Earth Science
UEDA, K., Systematic Botany
UEHARA, A., Inorganic Chemistry
WADA, K., Plant Physiology and Biochemistry
YAJIMA, T., Ecology
YAMADA, M., Combinatorics

Faculty of Medicine:

AMANO, R., Medical Radiological Science
ANDO, A., Medical Radiological Science
AOKI, M., Basic Medical Science
FUKUDA, R., Biochemistry 1
FURUKAWA, M., Otorhinolaryngology
HAIDA, N., Clinical Physical Therapy
HASHIMOTO, T., Laboratory Medicine
HIGASHIDA, H., Molecular Neurobiology
HOSO, M., Basic Physical Therapy
HOSONO, R., Physical Information
IKUTA, M., Clinical Occupational Therapy
INOUE, M., Obstetrics and Gynaecology
ISEKI, S., Anatomy 1
IWASAKI, T., Clinical Occupational Therapy
IZUMI, K., Adult and Gerontological Nursing
KANOU, M., Physiology 2
KASUGA, T., Medical Radiological Science
KATO, S., Biophysical Genetics, Molecular Medicine and Bioinformatics
KAWAHARA, E., Physical Information
KAWASAKI, K., Ophthalmology
KIDO, T., Community Health Nursing
KIKUCHI, Y., Clinical Radiological Technology
KOBAYASHI, K., Internal Medicine 1
KOBAYASHI, N., Basic Occupational Therapy
KOBAYASHI, T., Anaesthesiology and Intensive Care Medicine
KOIZUMI, S., Paediatrics
KOJIMA, K., Medical Radiological Science
KOSHINO, Y., Neuropsychiatry
KOYAMA, M., Adult and Gerontological Nursing
MABUCHI, H., Internal Medicine 2
MAKIMOTO, K., Community Health Nursing
MATUDA, T., Internal Medicine 3
MIWA, K., Surgery 2
MIZUKAMI, M., Basic Nursing
MIZUKAMI, Y., Clinical Radiological Technology
NAGAI, M., Basic Medical Science
NAGAKAWA, T., Adult and Gerontological Nursing
NAKAMURA, S., Microbiology
NAKANISHI, I., Pathology 1 (Molecular and Cellular)
NAKANUMA, Y., Pathology 2
NAKASHIMA, H., Basic Medical Science
NAMIKI, M., Urology
OGINO, K., Public Health
OHSHIMA, T., Legal Medicine
OHTAKE, S., Physical Information
SAIJO, K., Hygiene
SAKAI, A., Maternal and Child Nursing and Midwifery
SEKI, H., Maternal and Child Nursing and Midwifery
SOMEYA, F., Basic Occupational Therapy
SUZUKI, M., Clinical Radiological Therapy
TACHINO, K., Basic Physical Therapy
TAKAMORI, M., Neurology
TAKASHIMA, T., Radiology
TAKATA, S., Physical Information
TAKAYAMA, T., Clinical Radiological Technology
TAKEHARA, K., Dermatology
TANAKA, J., Clinical Laboratory Science
TANAKA, S., Anatomy 2
TANISHIMA, K., Clinical Laboratory Science
TAWARA, T., Basic Nursing
TOMITA, K., Orthopaedic Surgery
TONAMI, N., Nuclear Medicine
WATANABE, Y., Surgery 1
YACHIE, A., Clinical Laboratory Science
YAMAGISHI, T., Clinical Laboratory Science
YAMAMOTO, E., Oral and Maxillofacial Surgery
YAMAMOTO, H., Biochemistry 2
YAMASHITA, J., Neurosurgery
YOSHIMOTO, T., Pharmacology

Institute for Experimental Animals:

HAYAKAWA, J.

Faculty of Pharmaceutical Sciences:

GOMI, Y., Pharmacology
HANAOKA, M., Pharmaceutical Chemistry
HAYAKAWA, K., Hygiene Chemistry
ISHIBASHI, H., Synthetic Organic Chemistry
ITAYA, T., Bio-organic Chemistry
MIKAGE, M., Pharmacology and Medicinal Plants
NAKAGAKI, R., Physical Chemistry
NAKANISHI, Y., Biology
NIKAIDO, O., Radiation Biology
OHTA, H., Pharmacognosy and Natural Products Chemistry
SEKIZAKI, M., Physical Chemistry of Crystals
SOMEI, M., Chemistry
TSUJI, A., Pharmaceutics
YOKOI, T., Drug Metabolism

Faculty of Engineering:

CHATANI, A., Strength of Materials
EMI, H., Aerosol Engineering
FUJIWARA, N., Vehicle Automation
FUNADA, T., Speech Information Processing
GYAKUSHI, N., Thermal Engines
HASEGAWA, S., Thin Film Technology
HASHIMOTO, H., Visual Communication, Video Coding, Multimedia Processing
HATA, T., Electron Devices
HAYASHI, Y., Separation Engineering
HAYASHI, Y., Heat Transfer
HOJO, A., Strength of Materials
INABE, K., Radiation and Solid States
ISHIDA, H., Coastal Engineering
ISHIDA, S., Solution Properties of Condensing Polymers
IWAHARA, M., Power Electronics, Applied Magnetics
IWAKI, N., Textile Engineering
KAJIKAWA, Y., Structural Engineering
KAMIYA, Y., Robotics
KANAGAWA, S., Stochastic Numerics
KANAOKA, C., Aerosol Engineering, Powder Technology, Environmental Technology
KANJIN, Y., Harmonic Analysis
KAWAKAMI, M., Urban and Regional Planning
KAWAMURA, M., Construction Materials
KIMATA, N., Infrastructure Planning, System Simulation
KIMURA, H., Artificial Intelligence
KIMURA, S., Fluid Mechanics and Thermal Sciences
KITAGAWA, K., Engineering Materials
KITAGAWA, M., Deformation and Strength of Engineered and Naturally-Produced Materials
KITAURA, M., Earthquake Engineering
KOMORI, T., Agricultural Meteorology, Environmental and Construction Engineering, Phytotronic Engineering Science
KOMURA, A., Electrochemistry
KUMEDA, M., Electronic Materials
KUROBE, T., Manufacturing Systems
MAEGAWA, K., Structural Engineering
MAGAI, T., Defects in Solids
MASADA, H., Organic Chemistry

MATSUMURA, F., Control Engineering
MATSUURA, K., Instrumentation by Image Processing
MIYAE, S., Hydraulic Machinery
MIYAGISHI, S., Applied Physical Chemistry
MORI, S., Heat and Mass Transfer
MOTOI, M., Synthetic Chemistry of Polymers
MURAMOTO, K., Image Information Systems
NAGANO, I., Radio Wave Engineering
NAKAJIMA, T., Physical Organic Chemistry
NAKAMOTO, Y., Polymer Materials
NAKAYAMA, K., Adaptive Systems
NAOE, S., Optical Properties of Materials
NISHIKAWA, K., Digital Signal Processing
ODA, J., Bionic Design
OGAWA, S., Stochastic Analysis and Numerics
OHTA, H., Soil Mechanics
OKABE, S., Automated Mechanics
OKAJIMA, A., Fluid Dynamics, Flow-Induced Vibration
RYU, C., Coastal Engineering
SAKUTA, T., Electric Power Engineering
SATO, H., Non-Linear Vibration
SAWADA, T., Environmental Systems Engineering
SENDA, H., Co-ordination Chemistry
SHIMIZU, N., Information Processing in Biological Systems
SHIMIZU, T., Electronic Materials
SHINTAKU, S., Textile Machinery
SUGITA, T., Precision Machining
SUMITA, H., Ancient Western Philosophy
SUZUKI, M., Microelectronics, Devices and Fabrication Processes
TAKAMIYA, S., Microwave/Opto Semiconductor Devices
TAKASHIMA, T., Electric Power Engineering
TAKAYAMA, J., Traffic Engineering and Transport Planning
TAKIMOTO, A., Heat and Mass Transfer
TANAKA, I., History of Science and Technology
TORII, K., Civil Engineering Materials
TSUCHIYA, M., Mathematics (Theory of Stochastic Processes)
UCHIYAMA, Y., Tribology (Friction and Wear Mechanisms of Polymers)
UEDA, H., German Articles (Definite, Indefinite and Without)
UEDA, K., Separation and Analytical Chemistry
UEDA, T., Precision Machining, Laser Processing
UENO, H., Fluid Machinery, Fluid Power
WATANABE, A., Utopian Literature
WATANABE, I., Materials Science
YAMADA, M., Opto-electronics
YAMADA, S., Applied Magnetics
YAMADA, T., Polymer Processing, Reaction Engineering and Phase Equilibria
YAMAKOSHI, K., Biomechatronics
YAMAZAKI, K., Structural Optimization
YASUI, T., Manufacturing Systems
YASUMURA, N., Classics (Greek and Latin Literature)
YATOMI, C., Non-linear Continuum Mechanics

Graduate School of Natural Science and Technology:

ARAI, S., Petrology
FUJIWARA, N., Vehicle Automation
HASEGAWA, S., Physics of Thin Films
HAYASHIDA, K., Differential Equations
ICHINOSE, T., Functional Analysis
INOMATA, K., Organic Chemistry
KAJIKAWA, Y., Structural Engineering
KANAOKA, C., Aerosol Engineering, Power Technology Engineering, Environmental Engineering
KANJIN, Y., Harmonic Analysis
KOMURA, T., Electrochemistry
KONO, Y., Geophysics and Geodynamics
KUROBE, T., Manufacturing Systems
MASAMUNE, Y., Microbiology
MIYAMOTO, K., Pharmacology
MOTOI, M., Synthetic Chemistry of Polymers
MUKAI, C., Pharmaceutical Chemistry
NAKAMURA, K., Ecology
NAKAYAMA, K., Adaptive Systems
OHKUMA, S., Biochemistry
SHIMADA, K., Analytical Chemistry
SUZUKI, H., Solid State Physics
SUZUKI, N., Physiology
TAKIMOTO, A., Thermal Energy Conversion

Cancer Research Institute:

HARADA, F., Cellular and Molecular Biology
MAI, M., Basic and Clinical Oncology
MURAKAMI, S., Laboratory of Molecular Oncology
OHNO, S., Basic and Clinical Oncology
SASAKI, T., Basic and Clinical Oncology
SAWABU, N., Basic and Clinical Oncology
SATO, H., Laboratory of Molecular Oncology
TAKAHASHI, M., Cellular and Molecular Biology
YAMAMOTO, K., Cellular and Molecular Biology

Center for the Development of Molecular Target Drugs:

SUDA, T.

Extension Institute:

UCHIDA, T., Adult Education (Life-long Education)

Foreign Language Institute:

KIKUCHI, E., German
SANBAI, R., English
YABUCHI, T., Chinese

Health Service Center:

NAKABAYASHI, H., Endocrinology and Metabolism

Institute for Gene Research:

YAMAGUCHI, K.

International Student Center:

MIURA, K., Japanese Education
OKAZAWA, T., Animal Ecology
YAEZAWA, M., Psychology

University Hospital:

SATO, T., Department of Medical Informatics
ICHIMURA, F., Department of Hospital Pharmacy
KOIZUMI, J., Department of General Medicine

Radioisotope Center:

MORI, H.

KITAMI INSTITUTE OF TECHNOLOGY

165 Koen-cho, Kitami, Hokkaido 090
Telephone: (157) 24-1010
Fax: (157) 26-9117

Founded 1960
State Control
Academic year: April to March (2 semesters)

President: I. ATSUYA
Administrator: S. KATAKURA
Library Director: K. AYUTA

Number of full-time teachers: 137
Number of students: 2,028

Publications: *Memoirs of Kitami Institute of Technology.*

KOBE UNIVERSITY

1–1 Rokkodai-cho, Nada-ku, Kobe 657-8501
Telephone: (78) 881-1212

Founded 1949
Academic year: April to March

President: Y. NISHIZUKA
Director of Administration: K. OGUCHI
Dean of Students' Affairs: F. HAMADA
Library Director: T. KOBAYASHI

Library of 2,896,000 vols

Number of full-time teachers: 1,296
Number of students: 15,520

Publications: *Outline of Kobe University* and various faculty publs.

DEANS

Faculty of Letters: T. MAGATA
Faculty of Cross-Cultural Studies: T. HASHIMOTO
Faculty of Human Development: M. TSUCHIYA
Faculty of Law: M. YASUNAGA
Faculty of Economics: H. ADACHI
Faculty of Business Administration: T. KAGONO
Faculty of Science: T. TONEGAWA
Faculty of Medicine: M. YAMAMOTO
Faculty of Engineering: S. KITAMURA
Faculty of Agriculture: S. KATO
Research Institute for Economics and Business Administration: K. IGAWA
Graduate School of Humanities and Social Sciences: T. MAGATA
Graduate School of Science and Technology: T. SASAKI
Graduate School of International Co-operation Studies: T. TOYODA

PROFESSORS

Faculty of Letters:

DONOHASHI, A., History of Art
EDAGAWA, M., Comparative Literature
HACHIYA, Y., Social Psychology
HAMADA, M., Ancient and Medieval History of Asia
HASEGAWA, K., Geography
IKEGAMI, J., Japanese Literature
IWASHAKI, N., Empirical Sociology
KITAHARA, A., Social Anthropology
KURIHARA, M., Modern History of Europe and America
MAGATA, T., History of European Philosophy
MATSUSHIMA, T., Psychology
MORI, M., History of Science
MORI, N., Modern History of Asia
NAKAGAWA, Y., English Philology
NISHIMITSU, Y., English Philology
NOGUCHI, T., Modern Japanese Literature
OHNO, M., Theoretical Sociology
RINBARA, S., Japanese Language
SAITO, S., English Literature
SHIBATANI, M., Theoretical Linguistics
SUZUKI, M., Modern History of Japan
SUZUKI, T., Ancient and Medieval History of Europe
TAKAHASHI, M., Ancient and Medieval History of Japan
WATANABE, K., American Literature
YAMADA, K., Chinese Language and Literature
YAMAGATA, H., Science of Art
YAMAGUCHI, K., German Language and Literature
YAMAMOTO, M., Ethics

Faculty of Cross-cultural Studies:

FUROMOTO, T., American Cultures
GODA, T., Intercultural Communication
HASHIMOTO, T., European Cultures
HAYASHI, H., Linguistics
HIRANO, M., European Cultures
HIROTA, M., Cultural Interaction
INAZUMI, K., Communication
ISHIHARA, K., Cultural Interaction
KABURAGI, M., Computer Studies
KAGEYAMA, S., Japanese Culture
KASHIWAGI, T., European Cultures
KATAYANAGI, E., Cultural Norms
KIBA, H., Intercultural Communication
KINOSHITA, M., Japanese Culture
KOMURASAKI, S., European Cultures
MATSUBARA, R., Linguistics
MIKIHARA, H., European Cultures
MITSUSUE, N., European Cultures
MIURA, N., Cultural Norms
MIZUTA, K., Cultural Systems
MORI, Y., Cultural Interaction

MUNAKATA, S., Cultural Norms
MURAI, T., Cultural Interaction
NAKAGAWA, M., Linguistics
NISHIGAKI, T., Cultural Systems
OKIHARA, K., Communication
ONO, A., Computer Studies
SHIDA, I., Japanese Culture
SONE, H., Japanese Culture
SUDO, K., Asia-Pacific Cultures
SUZAKI, S., Japanese Culture
TAKIGAMI, Y., Communication
UCHIDA, M., European Cultures
UEDA, K., American Cultures
UOZUMI, K., Asia-Pacific Cultures
UTSUKI, N., Communication
YASUI, S., Asia-Pacific Cultures
YODA, H., Intercultural Communication
YOKOO, Y., Computer Studies
YOKOYAMA, M., Cultural Norms
YOKOYAMA, R., American Cultures
YOSHIOKA, M., International Communication

Faculty of Human Development:

AMAKAWA, T., Sciences for Natural Environment
AOKI, T., Human Life Environment
DOI, S., Educational Science
EGAWA, J., Mathematics and Computer Studies
FUKAWA, K., Studies of Social Environment
FUNAKOSHI, S., Childhood Development and Education
HAMAGUCHI, H., Human Life Environment
HAMAMOTO, J., Childhood Development and Education
HIGASHIYAMA, A., Childhood Development and Education
IMATANI, N., Studies of Social Environment
ISHIKAWA, T., Health Education
IWAI, M., Music
JOH, H., Human Life Environment
KANKI, K., Adult Learning
KANOU, T., Sports Performance
KISHIMOTO, H., Childhood Development and Education
KODERA, E., Sciences for Natural Environment
MARUYA, N., Human Life Environment
MASUMI, K., Human Life Environment
MERA, T., Music
MINAMI, S., Health Education
MISAKI, N., Health Education
MORII, T., Sciences for Natural Environment
MURAKAMI, S., Art and Design
MUROMATSU, A., Sciences for Natural Environment
NAKABAYASHI, T., Developmental Psychology
NAKAMURA, M., Mathematics and Computer Studies
NAKAYAMA, A., Studies of Social Environment
NINOMIYA, A., Studies of Social Environment
NOGAMI, T., Educational Science
NOMURA, H., Sports Performance
ODA, T., Social Gerontology
OGURA, T., Developmental Psychology
OKUYAMA, A., Mathematics and Computer Studies
ONISHI, N., Art and Design
SAITO, S., Art and Design
SAWADA, M., Developmental Psychology
SHIMIZU, S., Sports Performance
SHIMIZU, T., Childhood Development and Education
SHIRAKAWA, Y., Childhood Development and Education
SHIRAKURA, A., Mathematics and Computer Studies
SUGINO, K., Developmental Psychology
SUZUKI, M., Educational Science
TAKEUCHI, Y., Mathematics and Computer Studies
TAKEYA, Y., Music
TSUCHIYA, M., Educational Science
UCHIDA, A., Sciences for Natural Environment
UEZI, S., Sciences for Natural Environment
WATANABE, H., Human Life Environment

Faculty of Law:

ABE, Y., Administrative Law
FUJITA, H., International Law
FUJIWARA, A., Japanese Legal History
FUKUNAGA, A., Civil Procedure
HAMADA, F., Labour Law
HASUNUMA, K., Philosophy of Law
HATSUSE, R., International Relations
INOUE, N., Constitutional Law
IOKIBE, M., Political and Diplomatic History
ISOMURA, T., Civil Law
ITO, M., Political and Diplomatic History
JI, W. D., Chinese Law and Sociology of Law
KANZAKI, K., Commercial Law
KASHIMURA, S., Sociology of Law
KIKKAWA, G., International Relations
KISHIDA, M., Commercial Law
KOIZUMI, N., Intellectual Property Law
KOMURO, N., International Economic Law
KONDO, M., Commercial Law
KUBOTA, A., Civil Law
KUME, I., Public Administration
KURONUMA, E., Commercial Law
MARUYAMA, E., Anglo-American Law
MATSUOKA, H., Civil Law
MITSUI, M., Criminal Law and Procedure
MIYAZAWA, S., Sociology of Law and Criminology
MORISHITA, T., Soviet Law
MUNESUE, T., Constitutional Law
NAKANO, S., Private International Law
NEGISHI, A., Economic Law
SAKAMAKI, T., Criminal Law and Procedure
SATO, H., Tax Law
TAKIZAWA, E., Western Legal History
TAKATA, H., Civil Procedure
TSUKIMURA, T., International Political History
URABE, N., Constitutional Law
YAMADA, S., Civil Law
YAMASHITA, A., Administrative Law
YASUNAGA, M., Civil Law

Faculty of Economics:

ADACHI, H., Theoretical Economics
ADACHI, M., Social Policy
AMANO, M., Modern Economic History
BODART-BAILY, B. M., Pre-Modern Japanese Economic History
FUJITA, S., International Finance
FUKUDA, W., Economic Systems
HAGIWARA, T., Economics of Innovation
HARA, M., International Investment
IRITANI, J., Theory of Public Finance
ISHIGURO, K., International Political Economy
KATO, H., Chinese Economy
KISHIMOTO, T., Public Economics
MARUYA, R., Principles of Economic Policy
MINO, K., Economic Theory
MITANI, N., Labour Economics
NAGATANI, K., Economic Theory
NAKATANI, T., Mathematical Economics
OTANI, K., Statistics
OTSU, S., Russian Economy
SHINJO, K., Industrial Policy
SUZUKI, T., Southeast Asian Economics
TAKAHASHI, H., Economic History (General)
TAKAHASHI, S., Economic Geography
TAKIGAWA, Y., Monetary Economics
TANAKA, Y., Economic Theory
UEMATU, T., Japanese Economy
UEMIYA, S., History of Economic Doctrines
URANAGASE, T., Japanese Economic History
WASHIDA, T., Environmental Economics
YAMAGUCHI, M., Agricultural Policy

Faculty of Business Administration:

DEI, F., Finance
FUTATSUGI, Y., Finance
GOTO, M., Business Environment
ISHII, J., Marketing
KAGONO, T., Business Strategy
KANAI, T., Business Systems
KATO, Y., Management Accounting
KOBAYASHI, T., Management Accounting
KOGA, T., International Business
KURAMITSU, H., Marketing
KURODA, M., Management Accounting
KUWAHARA, T., International Business
MARUYAMA, M., International Environment
MIYASHITA, K., International Environment
MUNAKATA, M., International Business
NAITO, F., International Environment
NAKANO, T., Financial Accounting
OKABE, T., Financial Accounting
OKUBAYASHI, K., Business Systems
SAKAKIBARA, S., Business Systems
SAKASHITA, A., Business Systems
SAKURAI, H., Financial Accounting
SASAKI, H., Business Systems
SHOJI, K., Marketing
TAKAO, A., Finance
TAKASHIMA, K., Marketing
TAMURA, M., Marketing
TANI, T., Management Accounting
TOKUTSU, I., Management Information Science
YAMADA, A., Management Information Science
YOSHIDA, J., Culture, Consumption and Product Macromarketing

Faculty of Science:

FUKE, K., Condensed Matter Physics
FUKUDA, Y., Condensed Matter Physics
HAYASHI, F., Biology of Living Functions
HIGUCHI, Y., Applied Mathematics
HIMENO, S., Inorganic Chemistry
IKEDA, H., Applied Mathematics
ISONO, K., Biology of Living Functions
ITO, K., Planetary Science
KATO, H., Physical Chemistry
KAWAMOTO, Y., Inorganic Chemistry
KUNITOMO, M., Condensed Matter Physics
MATSUDA, T., Planetary Science
MATSUDA, Y., Biology of Living Structures
MIYAKAWA, T., Analysis
MIYATA, T., Earth Science
NAKAMURA, N., Planetary Science
NAKANISHI, Y., Algebra and Geometry
OISHI, K., Biology of Living Structures
ONO, Y., Biology of Living Functions
OTOFUJI, Y., Earth Science
RIN, S., Theoretical Physics
SAITO, M., Algebra and Geometry
SATO, H., Earth Science
SASAKI, T., Algebra and Geometry
SOTANI, N., Physical Chemistry
TAKANO, K., Analysis
TAKAYAMA, N., Analysis
TAKEDA, H., Particle Physics
TOMEOKA, K., Planetary Science
TONEGAWA, T., Theoretical Physics
TSUCHIYA, T., Biology of Living Functions
WADA, S., Condensed Matter Physics
WATANABE, K., Biology of Living Structures
YAMAMURA, K., Organic Chemistry
YAMAZAKI, T., Algebra and Geometry

Faculty of Medicine:

AMATSU, M., Otorhinolaryngology, Head and Neck Surgery
ANDO, H., Basic Allied Medicine
ASHITAKA, Y., Maternal Nursing and Midwifery
CHIHARA, K., Internal Medicine
FUJIWARA, Y., Radiation Biophysics and Genetics
FURUKAWA, H., Applied Occupational Therapy
HISAMA, K., Community Nursing
HOTTA, H., Microbiology
ICHIHASHI, M., Dermatology
ISHII, N., Disaster and Emergency Medicine
ISHIKAWA, H., Applied Physical Therapy
ISHIKAWA, Y., Basic Nursing
ITO, H., Pathology
KAMIDONO, S., Urology

KANEKO, T., Basic Occupational Therapy
KASUGA, M., Internal Medicine
KATAOKA, T., Physiology
KAWABATA, M., International Health
KINOSHITA, I., Basic Occupational Therapy
KURODA, Y., Surgery
KUMAGAI, S., Laboratory Medicine
MAEDA, K., Psychiatry and Neurology
MAEDA, S., Surgical Pathology
MARUO, T., Obstetrics and Gynaecology
MATSUMURA, S., Basic Allied Medicine
MATSUMURA, T., Medical Zoology
MATSUO, M., Genetics
MIKI, A., Basic Physical Therapy
MIZUNO, K., Orthopaedic Surgery
MURATA, K., Clinical Nursing
NAKAMURA, H., Paediatrics
NAKAMURA, S., Biochemistry
NISHIYAMA, K., Basic Medical Technology
OBARA, H., Anaesthesiology
ODAIRA, N., Applied Occupational Therapy
OKADA, M., Surgery
OKADA, Y., Physiology
OKAMURA, H., Anatomy and Brain Science
OKUMURA, K., Pharmaceutics
RYOU, R., Applied Medical Technology
SAKO, M., Medical Information
SATO, E., Basic Medical Technology
SATO, S., Hygiene
SHIMADA, T., Applied Physical Therapy
SHINDO, S., Maternal Nursing and Midwifery
SHINFUKU, N., Epidemiology, International Health
SHIOZAWA, S., Basic Medical Technology
SUMINO, K., Public Health
TABUCHI, Y., Clinical Nursing
TAHARA, S., Plastic Surgery
TAMAKI, N., Neurosurgery
TANIGUCHI, H., Community Nursing
TATSUNO, Y., Legal Medicine
TERASHIMA, T., Anatomy
TSUTOU, A., Basic Allied Medicine
UCHIYAMA, S., Applied Medical Technology
USAMI, M., Basic Allied Medicine
WATANABE, M., Applied Medical Technology
YAMAGUCHI, M., Applied Occupational Therapy
YAMAMOTO, M., Ophthalmology
YAMAMURA, H., Biochemistry
YOKONO, K., Geriatric Medicine
YOKOTA, Y., Clinical Nursing
YOKOYAMA, M., Internal Medicine
YOSHIKAWA, N., Maternal Nursing and Midwifery

Faculty of Engineering:

ABE, S., Systems Modelling and Control
AKAZAWA, K., Biomedical Engineering
DEKI, S., Applied Inorganic Chemistry
FUJII, S., Production Systems Engineering
FUJII, T., Steam Power Engineering
HANEDA, H., Computer Engineering
HAYASHI, S., Mesoscopic Materials Science
HAYASHI, S., Mathematical Theory of Programming
HORIE, T., Coastal Engineering
IWATSUBO, T., Engineering Mechanics and Machine Design
KAKUDA, Y., Mathematical Logic and Set Theory
KANDA, T., Hydraulic Engineering
KANKI, H., Machine Dynamics and Control
KANOU, T., Architectural Design and Theory
KATAOKA, K., Transport Science and Engineering
KATOU, S., Biochemical Engineering
KAWAMURA, H., Structural Planning and Control
KAYA, N., Space Solar Power Systems
KITAMURA, S., Control Engineering
KITAMURA, Y., Vibration Engineering
KUBOTA, H., Physico-chemical Properties of Fluids under High Pressure
KURODA, K., Transportation Engineering and Infrastructure Planning
KUSAKABE, K., Earthquake Resistant Design
MINEMOTO, T., Optical Image Processing
MITANI, I., Ultimate Design of Steel and Composite Structures
MIYOSHI, T., Semiconductor Devices
MORIMOTO, M., Environmental Acoustics
MORITA, Y., Repair and Maintenance Technology
MORIWAKI, T., Manufacturing Systems
MOTOOKA, I., Inorganic Chemistry
MUROSAKI, M., Urban Spatial Safety Planning
NAKAI, Y., Fatigue and Fracture of Engineering Materials
NAKAGIRI, S., Control of Distributed Systems
NAKAJIMA, T., Thermal Fluid Engineering
NAKAMAE, K., Polymer Chemistry
NANBU, T., Analysis
NISHINO, T., Electronic Materials Science
OHKUBO, M., Polymer Colloid Chemistry
OHMAE, N., Micro- and Nano-Tribology and Surface Engineering
OHSAWA, Y., Electrical Power Systems Engineering
OHTA, Y., Control Engineering
SAKAGUCHI, T., Multiphase Flow Science and Engineering
SAKURAI, S., Rock Engineering
SIGEMURA, T., Architectural Design
TABUCHI, M., Steel Structures
TADA, Y., Optimum Design of Systems
TAKADA, S., Earthquake Engineering
TAKAMORI, T., Robotics and Mechatronics
TAKEUCHI, H., Organic Reaction
TAKI, K., Computer and Systems Engineering
TAMURA, A., Computational Fluid Dynamics
TANAKA, H., Information Theory, Coding and Cryptography
TANAKA, Y., High Pressure Physical Chemistry
TOMITA, Y., Solid Mechanics
TSURUYA, S., Catalytic Chemistry
UEDA, K., Manufacturing Systems and Intelligent Machines
USUI, H., Non-Newtonian Fluid Mechanics
YAMAMOTO, K., Fundamental Electronics of Mesoscopic Materials
YASUDA, C., Architectural Planning and Urban Design
YOSHIDA, K., New Metal Alloys and Structure Analysis by X-ray and Electron Diffraction

Faculty of Agriculture:

AIZONO, Y., Biofunctional Molecules
AOKI, K., Applied Biofunctional Chemistry
DANNO, G., Biofunctional Molecules
HATA, T., Environmental Information and Regional Engineering
HATAYAMA, H., Biofunctional Molecules
HORIO, H., Systems and Information Engineering of Bioproduction
INAGAKI, N., Horticultural Science
KAKO, T., Food and Environmental Economics
KAMIJIMA, O., Plant Breeding and Crop Production
KANNAN, Y., Laboratory of Animal Breeding and Reproduction
KATO, S., Laboratory of Animal Breeding and Reproduction
KISHIHARA, S., Applied Biofunctional Chemistry
MAYAMA, S., Plant Protection
NAITO, T., Plant Protection
NAKAMURA, T., Genetics and Tropical Botany
NAKANISHI, T., Horticultural Science
NAKANO, M., Environmental Information and Regional Engineering
OJI, Y., Soil Science and Plant Nutrition
OKAWA, H., Plant Protection
OKAYAMA, T., Applied Biofunctional Chemistry
OTSUKA, H., Soil Science and Plant Nutrition
SHIMIZU, A., Laboratory of Animal Nutrition, Physiology and Immunology
TOYOSAWA, K., Laboratory of Animal Nutrition, Physiology and Immunology
TSUCHIDA, H., Horticultural Science
TSUGAWA, H., Plant Breeding and Crop Production
TSUJI, S., Laboratory of Animal Breeding and Reproduction
UCHIDA, K., Environmental Information and Regional Engineering
UCHIDA, Y., Food and Environmental Economics
YAMAMOTO, H., Systems and Information Engineering of Bioproduction
YASUDA, S., Food and Environmental Economics
YASUDA, T., Genetics and Tropical Botany

Research Institute for Economics and Business Administration:

ABE, S., International Environmental Studies
GOTO, J., International Environmental Studies
HINO, H., International Economics
IGAWA, K., International Economic Studies
ISHIGAKI, K., Comparative Economic Studies
ITO, K., Management Information Systems
KATAYAMA, S., Comparative Economic Studies
KONISHI, Y., Management Information Systems
MIYAGIWA, K., International Economic Studies
NAKANO, I., Management Information Systems
SHIMOMURA, M., International Economic Studies
YAMAJI, H., International Business
YOSHIHARA, H., International Business

Graduate School of International Co-operation Studies:

ALEXANDER, R. B., International Relations
HATSUSE, R., International Relations
HONDAI, S., Economics
KAGAWA, K., Law
KATAYAMA, Y., Politics
KIMURA, M., Economics
MATSUSHITA, H., Politics
NAKAMURA, O., International Law
NISHIJIMA, S., Economics
NISHIZAWA, N., Economics
SERITA, K., International Law
TOYADA, T., Economics
TSUCHIYA, H., Law
UCHIDA, Y., Development Aid Management

Graduate School of Science and Technology:

AKASAKA, K., Functional Molecular Assembly
ANDO, Y., Environmental Planning
BOKU, S., Environmental Science of Bioresource Production
FUKUDA, H., Applied Molecular Assembly
HASEGAWA, S., Functional Biology
HIRANO, K., Information and Instrumentation
KANAZAWA, Y., Bioresource and Energy Creation
KANEDA, Y., Computer and Computational Systems
KARUBE, T., Space Formation Engineering
MATSUMURA, T., Molecular Structure and Function
NAKAYAMA, A., Regional Environment
TAKAHASHI, N., Information and Systems
TAKEDA, M., Molecular Cellular Science
TANAKA, K., Media Technology and its Production
TSUTAHARA, M., Energy and Power Systems
YAMANAKA, M., Earth Sciences
WELCH, P., Mathematical Information Science and Technology

Biosignal Research Centre:

KIKKAWA, U., Biochemistry

SAITO, N., Pharmacology
YONEZAWA, K., Biochemistry

Research Institute for Higher Education:
HADA, S., Geology

Research Centre for Inland Seas:
KAWAI, H., Marine Biology

Research Centre for Urban Safety and Security:
ISHIBASHI, K., Seismotectonics
KAMAE, I., Health Informatics and Decision Sciences
KAWATANI, T., Groundwater Hydraulic Engineering
NISHI, M., Geotechnical Engineering
OKIMURA, T., Geotechnical Engineering
UEHARA, K., Artificial Intelligence, Machine Learning

International Student Centre:
NISHIDE, I., Comparative Education

Medical Centre for Student Health:
BABA, H., Internal Medicine

KUMAMOTO UNIVERSITY

39–1, Kurokami 2-chome, Kumamoto-shi 860
Telephone: (96) 344-2111
Fax: (96) 342-3110

Founded 1949
State control
Academic year: April to March (two terms)

President: Dr GORO EGUCHI
Director of Administration Bureau: MICHTOSHI URABE
Dean of Students: Prof. MASANAO EBATA
Librarian: Prof. TADASHI KIMPARA

Number of teachers: 931
Number of students: 8,289

Publications: Faculty Journals (annually or quarterly).

DEANS

Faculty of Letters: Prof. SADAMI MARUYAMA
Faculty of Education: Prof. YASUO OSAKO
Faculty of Law: Prof. HIROSHI SEISHO
Faculty of Science: Prof. MASUYUKI HITSUDA
School of Medicine: Prof. MASARU YOSHINAGA
Faculty of Pharmaceutical Sciences: Prof. TAKEHISA KUNIEDA
Faculty of Engineering: Prof. YOSHFUSA SATO

PROFESSORS

Faculty of Letters:
ADACHI, K., Oriental History
AGARI, M., English Language
IKAI, T., Japanese History
IHARA, S., Japanese Language
KAMIMURA, N., German Language
KIMPARA, T., Comparative Literature
KOGA, Y., German Language
KOMOTO, M., Archaeology
KUDO, K., Japanese History
KUWAHARA, K., Occidental History
MARUYAMA, S., Regional Sociology
MATSUMOTO, S., Japanese History
MORI, M., Japanese Literature
NAKAYAMA, S., Aesthetics
NISHIDA, K., Japanese Literature
NOGUCHI, K., Chinese Language and Literature
OKABE, T., Aesthetics
OOKUMA, K., French Literature
SAKATA, M., German Literature
SAKURAI, T., Cultural Anthropology
SHIGEOKA, K., Psychology
SHIMIZU, K., Linguistics
SHIMIZU, T., German Literature
SHINOZAKI, S., Philosophy
SHUTO, M., Japanese Literature
TAGUCHI, H., Sociology
TAKAHASHI, T., Philosophy
TANAPA, Y., German Literature
TANIKAWA, N., English Literature
TOKIWA, K., Philosophy
TONE, T., Psychology
YAMAGUCHI, M., Anthropogeography

Faculty of Education:
AKUTAGAWA, M., Chemistry
ASAKAWA, M., Food
BABA, K., Biology
EBIHARA, H., History of Education
FUJIWARA, T., Classical Chinese Literature
FUKUDA, S., English and American Literature
HIGUCHI, M., Education
HIRAMINE, Y., Algebra
ICHIKADO, K., Education of Handicapped Children
ISHIHARA, S., Sculpture
IWASAKI, K., Sports Psychology
KAMIDE, K., Clothing
KANEMARU, T., Analysis
KATSUMATA, T., Clinical Psychology
KAWAMINAMI, H., Teaching of Social Studies
KAWASAKI, J., Theory and History of Physical Education
KIHARA, S., Surgical Nursing
KIKUKAWA, K., Human Geography
KIMURA, M., School Health
KIYOZUMI, M., School Health
KOJIMA, K., Painting
KUBOTA, J., German Philosophy
KUWAHATA, M., Teaching of Domestic Sciences
MATUMOTO, K., Teaching of School Health
MISHIMA, T., Teaching of Science
MIYAMOTO, M., Teaching of Social Studies
MOMOI, T., Physics
MORIYAMA, H., Calligraphy
NAGATA, N., Teaching of School Health
NAKAMOTO, T., Japanese Literature
NAKAMURA, S., Japanese Literature
NISHIKAWA, M., English Language
NIWAKI, M., Teaching of Health and Physical Education
OGO, K., Exercise and Hygiene
OSAKO, Y., Teaching of Industrial Technology
OTOMO, N., Psychology of Handicapped Children
SATO, M., Economics
SATO, S., Educational Psychology
SHINOZAKI, K., Education of Handicapped Children
SHINOHARA, H., Educational Psychology
SOHGUCHI, H., Teaching of English
SUZUKI, K., Developmental Psychology
SUZUKI, R., English and American Literature
TAKAMORI, H., Clothing
TANIGUCHI, K., Psychology of Exercise
TSUZINO, T., Mechanics
WATANABE, K., Earth Science
WATANABE, M., Teaching of Music
YAMASAKI, T., Instrumental Music
YANAGI, H., Educational Sociology
YASUTAKE, R., Fundamental Medicine
YOKOYAMA, S., Geography
YONEMURA, K., Clinical Medicine and Nursing
YOSHIKAWA, N., Theory and History of Art

Faculty of Law:
AMARI, K., Private Law
EBISAWA, T., Public Law
ETOH, T., Criminal Law
IHARA, T., Economics
ISHIBASHI, H., Social Law
IWAOKA, N., Politics
KAWAMOTO, T., English Literature
KITAGAWA, K., Philosophy
KITAMURA, S., Public Law
KIZAKI, Y., Private Law
MATSUBARA, H., Private Law
MORI, M., German Literature
NAKAGAWA, Y., Administrative Law
NAKAMURA, N., Legal Theory and History
NAKAMURA, S., Criminal Law
ONO, Y., Private Law
SEISHO, H., Social Law
SINOKURA, M., Criminal Law
SUZUKI, K., Politics
TAKIZAWA, S., Politics
TOGASHI, S., Private Law
WAKASONE, K., Legal Theory and History
YAMAMOTO, E., Constitutional Law
YAMANAKA, I., Legal Theory and History
YAMANAKA, S., Anthropogeography
YAMASHITA, T., Economics
YOSHIDA, I., Legal Theory and History
YOSHINAGA, Y., Social Law

Faculty of Science:
ABE, S., Laboratory of Biological Regulation
FUJII, A., Solid State and Optical Physics
HARA, K., Solid State and Optical Physics
HIDAKA, T., Biology Laboratory
HITSUDA, M., Integrated Mathematics
ICHIMURA, K., Organic and Inorganic Chemistry
IMAFUKU, K., Physical Chemistry
ISHIDA, A., Dynamics of Environments
IWASAKI, Y., Geology, Palaeontology and Environmental Earth Science
KAI, F., Physical Chemistry
KAMIYA, M., Solid State and Optical Physics
KIMURA, H., Analysis and Applied Analysis
KOHNO, M., Analysis and Applied Analysis
KUROSAWA, K., Department of Environmental Science
MAEBASHI, T., Algebra and Geometry
MAEKAWA, T., Basic Physics
MATSUMOTO, N., Physical Chemistry
MATSUOKA, M., Solid State and Optical Physics
MATSUSAKA, T., Dynamics of Environments
MATSUZAKI, S., Organic and Inorganic Chemistry
OBATA, M., Petrology, Mineralogy and Geodynamics
ODA, M., Geology, Palaeontology and Environmental Earth Science
OHWAKI, S., Integrated Mathematics
ONO, K., Laboratory of Biological Regulation
SAKAMOTO, N., Organic and Inorganic Chemistry
SANEMASA, I., Department of Environmental Science
SHIMIZU, H., Department of Environmental Science
SHIODA, M., Biology Laboratory
SUZUKI, A., Laboratory of Biological Regulation
TAKAHASHI, T., Petrology, Mineralogy and Geodynamics
TAKEMIYA, T., Basic Physics
YAMAKI, H., Algebra and Geometry
YOSHITAMA, K., Biology Laboratory

School of Medicine:
AIZAWA, S., Morphogenesis
ANDO, M., Internal Medicine I
FUTATSUKA, M., Public Health
HARADA, S., Biodefence and Medical Virology
HIRAGA, S., Molecular Cell Biology
HORIUCHI, S., Biochemistry II
ISHIKAWA, T., Otorhinolaryngology
KAWAMURA, S., Morphological Neural Science
KITAMURA, N., Surgery I
KODAMA, K., Anatomy I
MAEDA, H., Microbiology
MATSUDA, I., Pediatrics
MIIKE, T., Child Development
MITSUYA, H., Internal Medicine II
MIURA, R., Biochemistry I
MIYAKAWA, T., Neuropsychiatry
MIYAMOTO, E., Pharmacology I
MORI, M., Molecular Genetics
NAKANO, M., Pharmacy
NEGI, A., Ophthalmology
NISHI, K., Pharmacology II
NISHIMURA, Y., Immunogenetics
OGAWA, H., Physiology II
OGAWA, M., Surgery II
OHKUBO, H., Gene Regulation
OKABE, H., Laboratory Medicine

OKAMURA, H., Obstetrics and Gynaecology
ONO, T., Dermatology
SAKAGUCHI, N., Immunology
SAYA, H., Tumour Genetics and Biology
SERA, Y., Paediatric Surgery
SHICHIRI, M., Metabolic Medicine
SHIGA, K., Physiology I
SUDA, T., Cell Differentiation
TAEN, A., Oro-dental Surgery
TAKAGI, K., Orthopaedic Surgery
TAKAHASHI, K., Pathology II
TAKAHASHI, M., Radiology
TANAKA, H., Developmental Neurobiology
TERASAKI, H., Anaesthesiology
TOMITA, K., Internal Medicine III
TSUNENARI, S., Forensic Medicine
UCHINO, M., Neurology
UEDA, A., Hygiene
UEDA, S., Urology
USHIO, Y., Neurosurgery
YAMAIZUMI, M., Cell Genetics
YAMAMOTO, T., Molecular Pathology
YAMAMURA, K., Developmental Genetics
YASUE, H., Cardiology
YOSHINAGA, M., Pathology I

Faculty of Pharmaceutical Sciences:

GOTO, M., Pharmacological Sciences
HARANO, K., Medicinal Chemistry
KUNIEDA, T., Medicinal Chemistry
MIYATA, T., Pharmacological Sciences
NAKAYAMA, H., Hygienic Chemistry
NOHARA, T., Medicinal Chemistry
OHTSUKA, M., Medicinal Chemistry
OTAGIRI, M., Pharmaceutics
SHOJI, S., Hygienic Chemistry
TAKAHAMA, K., Hygiene Chemistry
UEDA, M., Pharmacological Sciences
UEKAMA, K., Pharmaceutics
UNO, T., Hygiene Chemistry

Faculty of Engineering:

AKIYOSHI, T., Disaster Prevention Engineering
AKIYAMA, H., Electrical Energy Systems
CHIBA, A., Materials Development Systems
EBATA, M., Intelligent Systems Engineering
EBIHARA, K., Electrical Energy Systems
FUJITA, M., High Pressure Science and Materials Processing
FURUKAWA, K., Water Environmental Engineering
HIRAYAMA, C., Materials Chemistry
HIROE, T., High-Pressure Science and Materials Processing
HIROSE, T., Biochemical Engineering
HIYAMA, T., Electrical Energy Systems
HONDA, T., Materials Development Systems
IHARA, H., Chemistry for Materials Science
IKI, K., Disaster Prevention Engineering
IKUNO, H., Electronic and Communication Systems
IMURA, H., Thermal and Fluid Energy Systems
INOUE, T., Electronic and Communication Systems
ISHIHARA, O., Regional Planning and Management
ISHITOBI, M., Intelligent Systems for Measurement and Control
IWAI, Z., Intelligent Systems for Measurement and Control
JYO, A., Chemistry of Molecular Engineering
KASHIWAGI, H., Intelligent Systems for Measurement and Control
KAWAHARA, M., Advanced Materials Technology
KAWAJI, S., Intelligent Systems Engineering
KIDA, K., Biochemical Engineering
KITANO, T., Regional Planning and Management
KOBAYSI, I., Water Environmental Engineering
MAKINO, Y., Architectural Planning and Design
MATSUMOTO, Y., Chemistry for Materials Science
MATSUO, H., High-Pressure Science and Materials Processing
MITA, N., Electronic and Communication Systems
MITSUI, Y., Architectural Planning and Design
MIURA, H., Advanced Materials Technology
MIYAHARA, K., Electronic and Communication Systems
MOROZUMI, M., Regional Planning and Management
MURAYAMA, N., Advanced Technology of Electrical and Computer Systems
NAITOU, K., Mathematical Science
NAKAMURA, R., Intelligent Systems Engineering
NONAKA, T., Chemistry for Materials Science
OBARA, Y., Geotechnical Engineering
ODA, I., Intelligent Machine Design and Manufacturing
OGAWA, K., Architectural Planning and Design
OHBA, H., Thermal and Fluid Energy Systems
OHMI, G., High-Pressure Science and Materials Processing
OHMI, M., Geotechnical Engineering
OHNO, Y., Materials Development Systems
OHTSU, M., Structural Engineering
OKUNO, Y., Advanced Technology of Electrical and Computer Systems
OSHIMA, Y., Mathematical Science
SAIKI, H., High-Pressure Science and Materials Processing
SAISHO, M., Disaster Prevention Engineering
SAKAKI, S., Chemistry for Molecular Engineering
SAKIMOTO, T., Structural Engineering
SAKURADA, K. , Disaster Prevention Engineering
SATO, Y., Thermal and Fluid Energy Systems
SATONAKA, S., Intelligent Machine Design and Manufacturing
SHIMOTU, M., Water Environmental Engineering
SHOSENJI, H., Chemistry for Molecular Engineering
SONODA, Y., Electronic and Communication Systems
SUGAWARA, K., Geotechnical Engineering
SUZUKI, A., Geotechnical Engineering
TAKIKAWA, K., Water Environmental Engineering
TANIGUCHI, I., Biorelated Molecular Science
TONDA, H., Materials Development Systems
UCHIYAMA, O., Architectural Planning and Design
WATANABE, A., Intelligent Systems Engineering
YAMAO, T., Structural Engineering
YANO, T., Regional Planning and Management
YASUI, H., Intelligent Machine Design and Manufacturing
YOKOI, Y., Mathematical Science

KYOTO INSTITUTE OF TECHNOLOGY

Hashigami-cho, Matsugasaki, Sakyo-ku, Kyoto 606-8585
Telephone: (75) 724-7111
Fax: (75) 724-7010

Founded 1949

President: KOSUKE KIMURA
Director-General: SHOGO SUGAYA
Librarian: MINORU HAMAZAKI

Library of 332,564 vols
Number of teachers: 311
Number of students: 4,300

Publications: *Bulletin, Outline of KIT, Memoirs.*

DEANS

Student Affairs: HIROSHI ZAINO
Faculty of Engineering and Design: NOBUYUKI SATOFUKA
Faculty of Textile Science: SHUNJI NOMURA

KYOTO UNIVERSITY

Yoshida-Honmachi, Sakyo-ku, Kyoto 606-8501
Telephone: (75) 753-7531

Founded 1897
Academic year: April to March

President: MAKOTO NAGAO
Vice-Presidents: IWAO FURUSAWA, IKUO MIYOSHI
Director-General: SUSUMU KUROKAWA
Dean of Students: TADAYUKI IWAMOTO

Library: see Libraries
Number of teachers: 2,809 (891 profs)
Number of students: 21,533

Publications include faculty memoirs and reviews.

DEANS

Faculty of Integrated Human Studies: T. HAYASHI
Graduate School of Letters and Faculty of Letters: H. KOZEN
Graduate School of Education and Faculty of Education: T. TAKEUCHI
Graduate School of Law and Faculty of Law: S. TANAKA
Graduate School of Economics and Faculty of Economics: H. WATANABE
Graduate School of Science and Faculty of Science: K. OIKE
Graduate School of Medicine and Faculty of Medicine: T. HONJO
Graduate School of Pharmaceutical Sciences and Faculty of Pharmaceutical Sciences: T. KAWASAKI
Graduate School of Engineering and Faculty of Engineering: K. TOKI
Graduate School of Agriculture and Faculty of Agriculture: A. MIYAZAKI
Graduate School of Human and Environmental Studies: Y. TOYOSHIMA
Graduate School of Energy Science: Y. ITO
Graduate School of Asian and African Area Studies: Y. TSUBOUCHI
Graduate School of Informatics: K. IKEDA

PROFESSORS

Faculty of Integrated Human Studies:

AOYAMA, H., Theory of Elementary Particles
ARIFUKU, K., Ontology, Epistemology, Ethics
BECKER, C., Comparative Religion, Ethics, Death and Dying
FUKUI, K., Cultural Anthropology of Ethiopia
FUKUOKA, K., American Literature
FUNAHASHI, S., Neurophysiology
HANADA, T., Inorganic Materials Chemistry
HAYASHI, T., Solid State Spectroscopy
IKEDA, H., Popular Literature and Mass Culture under Fascist Regimes
IMANISHI, H., Differential Topology
INADA, I., German Literature
INAGAKI, N., Modern French Literature
ISHIDA, A., Modern German Philology and Literature
ISHIKAWA, M., German and Norse Philology
IWAI, A., Homological Algebra
KAMATA, H., Volcanology
KATAGIRI, A., Electrochemistry
KIMURA, T., Russian Literature
KIWAMOTO, Y., Plasma Physics
KOGISHI, A., 20th-century German Literature
KONO, N., Probability Theory
MARUYAMA, K., Cytology
MATSUDA, K., History of Western Learning in Japan
MATSUDA, S., Theory of Elementary Particles
MATSUMARA, M., Neurophysiology

MATSUSHIMA, T., French Literature
MATSUURA, S., History of North-Eastern Asia
MICHIHATA, T., German Literature
MIHARA, O., German Literature
MIYAMOTO, M., History of Political Thought
MIYAMOTO, M., Probability Theory
MIYOSHI, I., French Literature
MURAKATA, A., American Studies, Comparative Art and Literature
MURANAKA, S., Solid State Chemistry
NAGAYA, M., History and Theory of Social Statistics
NAKAMURA, E., Sports Medicine; the Study of Aging
NAKANISHI, T., International Relations
NISHIMOTO, Y., German Language
NISHIMURA, K., Labour and Social Law
NISHIWADA, K., Theory of Partial Differential Equations
NISHIWAKI, T., History of Chinese Philosophy
NISHIYAMA, R., Ancient History of Japan
NIWA, T., American Literature
OKA, Y., Solid State Chemistry
OKADA, K., Pedagogy
OKI, M., French Language
ONO, S., Middle High German Literature
OTAGI, H., History of Medieval China
OTANI, S., Carbohydrate Chemistry
SAKURAI, S., Renaissance and Modern English Poetry
SHIKAYA, T., Philosophy of Aesthetics
SHIMADA, M., Contemporary History of the United States
SHINOHARA, M., Aesthetics, Art Criticism
SONODA, M., Comparative Religion
SUGAWARA, K., Social Anthropology and Communication
SUGIMAN, T., Group Dynamics
SUIKO, M., English Language
SUZUKI, M., 18th-Century English Culture and Literature
TAKAHASHI, S., Sociology
TAKAHASHI, Y., Sociology
TAKEYASU, K., Molecular Biology
TOBE, H., Plant Taxonomy and Morphology
TOMITA, H., Statistical Physics
TSUDA, K., Internal Medicine
UCHIDA, M., Grammar of the Japanese Language
UEDA, T., Theory of Functions of Several Complex Variables
UEMATSU, T., Theory of Elementary Particles
YAMADA, M., Urban Geography
YAMAGUCHI, R., Organic Synthesis, Organometallic Chemistry
YAMANASHI, M., Cognitive Linguistics
YAMAUCHI, M., Number Theory
YODA, Y., Shakespeare

Graduate School of Letters and Faculty of Letters:

CRAIK, E. M., Greek and Latin Classics
FUJII, J., Japanese History
FUJITA, M., Japanese Philosophy
FUMA, S., Oriental History
HASE, S., Philosophy of Religion
HATTORI, Y., European History
HINO, T., Japanese Language and Literature
HIROTA, M., French Language and Literature
HOGETSU, M., Sociology
IKEDA, S., History of Chinese Philosophy
INOUE, S., Sociology
ISHIHARA, H., Geography
ITO, K., Philosophy
IWAKI, K., Aesthetics and Art History
KAMADA, M., Japanese History
KASHIWAKURA, Y., Twentieth-Century Studies
KATAYANAGI, E., Christian Studies
KATO, H., Ethics
KAWAI, K., Chinese Language and Literature
KIDA, A., Japanese Language and Literature
KIHIRA, E., Contemporary History
KINDA, A., Geography
KISHI, T., English Language and Literature
KOZEN, H., Chinese Language and Literature
MANO, E., West Asian History
MIMAKI, K., Buddhist Studies
MINAMIKAWA, T., European History
MIYAOKA, O., Linguistics
NAGAI, K., Contemporary History
NAKAMURA, K., American Literature
NAKATSUKASA, T., Greek and Latin Classics
NARITA, K., Geography
OSAKA, N., Psychology
SAITO, K., Italian Language and Literature
SASAKI, J., Aesthetics and Art History
SATO, A., Slavic Languages and Literature
SHIMIZU, M., Psychology
SHOGAITO, M., Linguistics
SONODA, T., History of Western Philosophy
SUGIYAMA, M., Oriental History
TANIGAWA, M., European History
TOKUNAGA, M., History of Indian Philosophy
TONAMI, M., Oriental History
TOYOTA, M., English Language and Literature
TSUTSUI, K., Sociology
UCHII, S., Philosophy and History of Science
UCHIYAMA, K., History of Western Philosophy
UEHARA, M., Archaeology
YAMAGUCHI, T., German Language and Literature
YAMAMOTO, K., History of Western Philosophy
YOSHIDA, J., French Language and Literature
YOSHIDA, K., Linguistics

Graduate School of Education and Faculty of Education:

AMANO, M., Theories of Instruction
EHARA, T., Comparative Education
FUZIWARA, K., Clinical Psychology
HIGASHIYAMA, H., Clinical Pedagogy
KAWASAKI, Y., Library and Multimedia Science
KOYASU, M., Educational Cognitive Psychology
OKADA, Y., Clinical Personality Psychology
SAITO, K., Clinical Personality Psychology
SHIRAISHI, Y., Educational Finance
SUMERAGI, N., Clinical Pedagogy
TAKEUCHI, Y., Sociology of Education
TUJIMOTO, M., Japanese History of Education
UESUGI, T., Adult Education and Out-of-School Activities of Youth and Children
YAMADA, Y., Developmental Psychology
YAMANAKA, Y., Educational Clinical Psychology
YAMAZAKI, T., Education

Graduate School of Law and Faculty of Law:

IDA, R., Law of International Organizations
ITO, Y., Political and Diplomatic History of Japan
KAWAHAMA, N., Economic Law
KAWAKAMI, R., European Legal History
KIMURA, M., Comparative Politics
KINAMI, A., Anglo-American Law
MAEDA, M., Commercial Law
MAEDA, T., Civil Law
MATOBA, T., Political Science
MORIMOTO, S., Commercial Law
MURAMATSU, M., Public Administration
MURANAKA, T., Labour Law
NAKAMORI, Y., Criminal Law
NISHIGORI, S., Civil Law
OISHI, M., Constitutional Law
OKAMURA, S., Administrative Law
OKUMURA, T., Tax Law
ONO, N., History of Political Thought
OTAKE, H., Political Process
SAKURADA, Y., Private International Law
SATO, K., Constitutional Law
SHIBAIKE, Y., Administrative Law
SHIBATA, M., Roman Law
SHIOMI, J., Criminal Law
SHIYAKE, M., Constitutional Law
SUGIHARA, T., International Law
SUZAKI, H., Commercial Law
SUZUKI, S., Law of Criminal Procedure
TAKAKUWA, A., International Trade Law
TANAKA, S., Legal Philosophy
TANASE, T., Sociology of Law
YAMAMOTO, K., Law of Civil Procedure
YAMAMOTO, K., Civil Law
YOSHIOKA, K., Criminology

Graduate School of Economics and Faculty of Economics:

AKAOKA, I., Business Administration
FUJII, H., International Accounting
FURUKAWA, A., Money and Finance
HIOKI, K., Organization Theory
HISAMOTO, N., Labour Economics
HORI, K., Economic History
IMAKUBO, S., Economic Policy
KAZUSA, Y., Managerial Accounting
KIKUCHI, K., Social Policy
KOJIMA, H., Principles of Economics
KONDO, F., Marketing
MOTOYAMA, Y., World Economy
NAKAI, B., Accounting
NAKANO, I., Agricultural Economics
NARIU, T., Applied Economics
NISHIMURA, S., Applied Economics
NISHIMUTA, Y., Business History
OHNISHI, H., Economic Statistics
OKADA, T., Regional Economy
SADAMICHI, H., Information Systems
SECHIYAMA, S., Economic Theory
SHIMOTANI, M., Japanese Economy
TANAKA, H., History of Social Thought
TAO, M., Business Policy
UETA, K., Public Finance
WATANABE, H., Economic Policy
YAGI, K., Economic Theory
YAMAMOTO, H., Chinese Economy
YOSHIDA, K., Contemporary Economics

Graduate School of Science and Faculty of Science:

ARAKI, T., Geomagnetism and Space Physics
AWAJI, T., Physical Oceanography
FUJIYOSHI, Y., Molecular Biophysics
FUKAYA, K., Differential Geometry
GO, N., Theoretical Chemistry
HAYASHI, T., Organic Chemistry
HIJIKATA, H., Number Theory
HIRAI, T., Functional Analysis
HIRANO, T., Neurobiology
HIROTA, I., Meteorology and Atmospheric Physics
HIROTA, N., Physical Chemistry
HORI, M., Animal Ecology
HORIUCHI, H., Theoretical Nuclear Physics
IMAI, K., Experimental Nuclear Physics
IMASATO, N., Physical Oceanography
INAGAKI, S., Astrophysics
INOUE, T., Biochemistry and Molecular Biology
ISHIDA, H., Anthropology
ISHIGURO, T., Physics of Low-Dimensional Material
JIMBO, M., Mathematical Physics
KAJIMOTO, O., Physical Chemistry
KATO, S., Theoretical Chemistry
KAWANO, S., Plant Taxonomy
KIDA, H., Climate Physics
KITAMURA, M., Mineralogy
KONO, A., Algebraic Topology
KOSUGE, K., Solid State Chemistry
KOYAMA, K., Cosmic Ray Physics
KUGO, T., Theoretical Particle Physics
KURAMOTO, Y., Nonlinear Dynamics
KUROKAWA, H., Solar Physics
MACHIDA, Y., Molecular Biology
MARUYAMA, M., Algebraic Geometry
MASUDA, F., Stratigraphy and Sedimentology

MIKI, K., Structural Biochemistry and Protein Crystallography
MIYATA, T., Molecular Evolution
MIZUSAKI, T., Low-Temperature Physics
NAGATANI, A., Plant Physiology
NISHIDA, E., Biochemistry
NISHIDA, G., Algebraic Topology
NISHIDA, T., Nonlinear Equations
NISHIDA, T., Anthropology
NISHIJIMA, M., Surface Science
OBATA, M., Petrology
OHTANI, H., Astrophysics
OIKE, K., Seismology and Physics of the Earth's Interior
OKADA, A., Neotectonics and Geomorphology
OKADA, K., Plant Molecular Genetics
ONUKI, A., Statistical Physics
OSUKA, A., Organic Chemistry
SAITO, G., Organic Solid State Chemistry
SAITO, M., Astrophysics
SASAO, N., Experimental High Energy Physics
SATO, H., Astrophysics and Relativity
SATOH, N., Developmental Biology
SETOGUCHI, T., Vertebrate Palaeontology
SHICHIDA, Y., Molecular Physiology
SHIDA, T., Physical Chemistry
SHIMAMOTO, T., Structural Geology and Rock Rheology
SHIRAYAMA, Y., Marine Biology
SUZUKI, H., Organic Chemistry
TAKEICHI, M., Cell Biology
TAKEMOTO, S., Geodesy
TATSUMI, Y., Magmatology and Geothermal Science
TERAO, T., Chemical Physics
TERUMICHI, Y., Plasma Physics
UENO, K., Theory of Manifolds
WATANABE, S., Probability Theory
YABUZAKI, T., Laser Spectroscopy
YAMADA, K., Theory of Condensed Matter
YAMAGISHI, S., Ethology and Ornithology
YANAGIDA, M., Molecular Biophysics
YONEI, S., Radiation Biology
YOSHIDA, H., Number Theory
YOSHIKAWA, K., Chemical Physics
YUSA, Y., Hydrology and Geothermal Sciences

Graduate School of Medicine and Faculty of Medicine:

CHIBA, T., Gastroenterology and Hepatology
FUJII, S., Obstetrics and Gynaecology
FUJITA, J., Clinical Molecular Biology
FUKUI, T., General Medicine
FUKUI, Y., Legal Medicine
HASHIMOTO, N., Neurosurgery
HIAI, H., Pathology and Biology of Diseases
HIRAOKA, M., Therapeutic Radiology and Oncology
HITOMI, S., Thoracic Surgery
HONDA, Y., Ophthalmology and Visual Science
HONJO, I., Hearing and Speech Science
HONJO, T., Medical Chemistry
ICHIYAMA, S., Laboratory Medicine
IDE, C., Anatomy and Neurobiology
IIZUKA, T., Oral and Maxillofacial Surgery
IMAMURA, M., Surgery and Basic Surgical Science
INUI, K., Pharmacy
ITO, K., Transfusion Medicine
IZUMI, T., Respiratory Medicine
KAWAGUCHI, S., Integrative Brain Science
KITA, T., Geriatric Medicine
KOMEDA, M., Cardiovascular Surgery
KONISHI, J., Nuclear Medicine and Diagnostic Imaging
MINATO, N., Immunology and Cell Biology
MITSUYAMA, M., Microbiology
MIYACHI, Y., Dermatology
MIYOSHI, K., Neuropsychiatry
MORI, K., Anaesthesia
NABESHIMA, Y., Pathology and Tumour Biology
NAKAHARA, T., Public Health
NAKAMURA, T., Orthopaedic and Musculoskeletal Surgery
NAKANISHI, S., Biological Sciences
NAKAO, K., Medicine and Clinical Science
NARUMIYA, S., Cell Pharmacology
NISHIKAWA, S., Molecular Genetics
NISHIMURA, Y., Plastic and Reconstructive Surgery
NODA, M., Molecular Oncology
NOMA, A., Physiology and Biophysics
OHMORI, H., Physiology and Neurobiology
SASAYAMA, S., Cardiovascular Medicine
SEINO, Y., Metabolism and Clinical Nutrition
SERIKAWA, T., Laboratory Animals
SHIBASAKI, H., Brain Pathophysiology
SHIOTA, K., Anatomy and Developmental Biology
TAKAHASHI, T., Medical Informatics
TANAKA, K., Transplantation and Immunology
TSUKITA, S., Cell Biology
UCHIYAMA, T., Haematology and Oncology
YAMABE, H., Diagnostic Pathology
YAMAOKA, Y., Gastroenterological Surgery

Graduate School of Pharmaceutical Sciences and Faculty of Pharmaceutical Sciences:

AKAIKE, A., Pharmacology
FUJII, N., Bio-organic Medicinal Chemistry
HANDA, T., Biosurface Chemistry
HASHIDA, M., Pharmaceutics
HONDA, G., Pharmacognosy
IBUKA, T., Organic Chemistry
ICHIKAWA, A., Physiological Chemistry
ITOH, N., Genetic Biochemistry
KAWAI, A., Molecular Microbiology
KAWASAKI, T., Biochemistry
NAKAGAWA, T., Analytical Chemistry
NEGISHI, M., Molecular Neurobiology
SAJI, H., Radiopharmaceutical Chemistry
SATOH, M., Molecular Pharmacology
TAGA, T., Structural Chemistry
TAKAKURA, Y., Biopharmaceutics
TOMIOKA, K., Synthetic Organic Chemistry

Graduate School of Engineering and Faculty of Engineering:

ADACHI, H., Quantum Theory of Materials Design
ADACHI, T., Foundation Engineering
AOKI, K., Rarefied Gas Dynamics
AOYAMA, Y., Urban and Regional Planning
ARAKI, M., Control Engineering
ASAKI, Z., Processing Engineering
ASHIDA, Y., Exploration Geophysics
AWAKURA, Y., Materials Electrochemistry
CHUJO, Y., Polymerization Chemistry
FUJIMOTO, H., Quantum Molecular Science and Technology
FUJIMOTO, T., Atomic and Plasma Spectroscopy
FUJITA, S., Optoelectric Materials and Properties
HANASAKI, K., Non-destructive Evaluation
HASHIMOTO, I., Process Control and Process Systems Engineering
HASHIMOTO, K., Chemical Reaction Engineering
HASHIMOTO, T., Polymer Mechanics
HIGASHI, K., Nuclear Materials
HIGASHITANI, K., Surface Control Engineering
HIYAMA, T., Organic Chemistry of Natural Products
HOKOI, S., Thermal Analysis and Design
IEMURA, H., Earthquake Engineering
IIDA, Y., Traffic Engineering
IMANAKA, T., Biotechnology
IMANISHI, N., Quantum Beam Engineering
INOUE, K., Systems Control
ISHIKAWA, J., Charged Particle Devices
ITO, Y., Organometallic Chemistry
KAKINO, Y., Numerical Control
KAKIUCHI, T., Functional Solution Chemistry
KATO, K., History of Architectural Theory
KATO, N., Architectural Information Systems
KAWAHARA, T., Continuum Mechanics
KAWASAKI, M., Photochemistry
KIKUCHI, K., Geological Engineering
KIMURA, I., Neutron Reaction Engineering
KITAMURA, R., Transport Planning and Engineering
KOBAYASHI, K., Civil Engineering Systems Analysis
KOBAYASHI, K., Nuclear Reactor Physics
KOBAYASHI, M., Environmental Design
KOBAYASHI, S., Geosphere Engineering
KOBAYASHI, S., Biomaterials Chemistry
KOIWA, M., Physical Metallurgy
KOKUBO, T., Industrial Solid State Chemistry
KOMAI, K., Engineering Materials
KOMORI, S., Fluids Engineering
KUBO, A., Machine Design
MAKI, T., Mechanical Properties of Steel
MAKINO, T., Thermophysical Properties of Materials
MASUDA, H., Powder Technology
MASUDA, T., Transition Metal-Catalysed Polymerization
MASUDA, T., Polymer Physics and Rheology
MATSUHISA, H., Vibration Engineering
MATSUI, S., Control of Micropollutants
MATSUMOTO, M., Wind Engineering
MATSUNAMI, H., Energy Conversion Devices
MATSUOKA, Y., Integrated Assessment Modelling
MATSUSHIGE, K., Molecular Nano-electronics
MITSUDO, T., Catalysis
MIURA, K., Environmental Process Engineering
MIYAGAWA, T., Durability of Reinforced Concrete
MORISAWA, S., Environmental Risk Analysis
MORISHIMA, I., Molecule Design
MUNEMOTO, J., Architectural Planning
MURAKAMI, M., Thin Film Metallurgy
MURAMOTO, Y., River Engineering
MUTA, I., Applied Superconductivity
NAGAOKA, H., Building Construction
NAITO, M., Environmental Management Plan
NAKAMURA, Y., Urban Environmental Engineering
NAKAMURA, Y., Processor Systems Design
NAKATSUJI, H., Quantum Chemistry
NEZU, I., Fluid Mechanics and Hydraulics
NISHIMOTO, S., Excited-state Hydrocarbon Chemistry
OCHIAI, S., Characterization of Microstructures
OGINO, F., Transport Phenomena
OGUMI, Z., Electrochemistry
OHNISHI, Y., Rock Mechanics
OHTANI, R., Mechanical Behaviour of Materials
OKA, F., Soil Mechanics
OKAZAKI, S., Architectural Planning Theory
OKAZAKI, S., Instrumental Analytical Chemistry
OKUMURA, K., Nonlinear Electric and Electronic Circuits
ONO, K., Lining Concrete
OSAMURA, K., Science of Materials
OSHIMA, K., Chemistry of Functional Materials
SAITO, I., Bio-organic Chemistry
SAITO, T., Mining and Rock Mechanics
SAKAI, A., Mesoscopic Materials Science
SAKAI, T., Coastal Engineering
SAWAMOTO, M., Living Cationic Polymerization
SERIZAWA, A., Nuclear Reactor Engineering
SHIBA, M., Hydrology
SHIBATA, T., Elasticity
SHIGA, M., Magnetism of Metals and Metallic Compounds
SHIMA, S., Engineering Plasticity
SHIMASAKI, M., Computational Electromagnetic Field Analysis
SOMIYA, I., Water Quality Control Engineering

SONE, Y., Fluid Dynamics
SUMITOMO, H., Environmental Planning
SUNAMOTO, J., Biorelated Polymers
SUZUKI, K., Heat Transfer
TACHIBANA, A., Quantum Theory of Condensed Matter
TACHIBANA, K., Plasma Physics and Technology
TAKAGI, K., Effects of Noises on Man and the Human Environment
TAKAHASHI, H., Architectural Design and Theory
TAKAHASHI, Y., History of Architecture
TAKAMATSU, S., Architectural Design
TAKEDA, N., Solid Waste Management
TAKEUCHI, K., Hydrocarbon Chemistry Fundamentals
TAKUMA, T., High-Voltage Engineering
TAMON, H., Separation Engineering
TAMURA, T., Applied Mechanics
TANAKA, A., Biotechnology
TANAKA, F., Polymer Core Physical Chemistry
TANAKA, K., Molecular Energy Conservation
TANIGAKI, M., Materials Processing Engineering
TERASHIMA, Y., Environmental Design
TOKI, K., Earthquake Engineering
TSUCHIYA, K., Dynamics and Control of Space Vehicles
TSUJI, B., Steel Structures
TSUNO, H., Water Quality Conservation
UEDA, Y., Electrical Power System Engineering
UEMURA, S., Organic Chemistry
UETANI, K., Mechanics of Building Structures
UTIMOTO, K., Organic Reaction Chemistry
WASHIZU, M., Micromachines
WATANABE, E., Structural Mechanics
WATANABE, F., Reinforced and Pressed Concrete Structures
YABE, H., Machine Elements
YAMABE, T., Statistical Thermodynamics
YAMADA, I., Ion Beam Engineering
YAMAGUCHI, M., Lattice Defects and Crystal Plasticity
YAMAOKA, H., Characteristic Properties of Polymer Materials
YAMASHINA, H., Computer-integrated Manufacturing
YOSHIDA, J., Organic Chemistry
YOSHIDA, S., Molecular Science and Technology of Catalysis
YOSHIKAWA, T., Robotics
YOSHIZAKI, T., Polymer Statistical Mechanics

Graduate School of Agriculture and Faculty of Agriculture:

AMACHI, I., Biochemistry
AMANO, T., Plant Production Systems
AZUMA, J., Biomass Recycling System
ENDO, T., Plant Genetics
FUJITA, M., Wood Structure of Plant Cells
FURUSAWA, I., Plant Pathology
FUSHIKI, T., Nutritional Chemistry
HAYASHI, I., Marine Benthic Biology
HAYASHI, R., Biomacromolecular Chemistry
HORIE, T., Crop Science
IKEDA, T., Biomolecular Physical Chemistry
IKEDA, Y., Farm Processing Machinery
IKEHASHI, H., Plant Breeding
IMAI, H., Animal Reproduction
INAMOTO, S., Farm Managerial Information and Accounting
INOUE, K., Enzyme Chemistry
ITO, M., Weed Science
IWAI, Y., Forest Management
IWAMURA, H., Biofunction Chemistry
IZUI, K., Plant Molecular Physiology
KADA, R., Food and Environmental Policy
KAGATSUME, M., Regional Environmental Economics
KATO, N., Microbial Biotechnology
KAWACHI, T., Water Resources Engineering
KAWANABE, S., Forest Biology
KAWASE, K., Plant Production Control
KOBAYASHI, S., Regional Planning
KOSAKI, T., Soil Science
KUMAGAI, H., Industrial Microbiology
KUNO, E., Entomology
KUWAHARA, Y., Chemical Ecology
MASUDA, M., Wood Technology
MATSUMOTO, T., Natural Fibrous Materials
MATSUNO, R., Bioengineering
MITSUNO, T., Irrigation, Drainage and Hydrological Environmental Engineering
MIYAMOTO, H., Anatomy and Physiology
MIYAZAKI, A., Animal Husbandry Resources
MIZUYAMA, T., Erosion Control
MURASHIMA, Y., Forest Policy and Economics
NAKATSUBO, F., Chemistry of Biomaterials
NAKAHARA, H., Marine Microbial Ecology
NISHIOKA, T., Insect Physiology
NODA, K., Comparative Agricultural History
OHIGASHI, H., Organic Chemistry in Life Science
OHNISHI, O., Crop Evolution
OHYAMA, K., Plant Molecular Biology
OKUMURA, S., Wood Machining
OOHATA, S., Silviculture
SAKAGUCHI, M., Fisheries Chemistry
SAKAI, H., Forestry Engineering
SAKAMOTO, W., Fisheries Oceanography
SAKURATANI, T., Tropical Agriculture
SASAKI, R., Biosignals and Response
SASAKI, Y., Animal Breeding and Genetics
SATO, F., Molecular and Cellular Biology
SEKIYA, J., Plant Nutrition
SHIMIZU, S., Fermentation Physiology and Applied Microbiology
SHIRAISHI, N., Materials for Wood Improvement
SODA, O., Agricultural Science Principles
SUGIURA, A., Pomology
TAKAFUJI, A., Population Biology and Acarology
TAKAHASHI, T., Rural Planning
TAKEDA, H., Forest Ecology
TAKEUCHI, M., Forest Engineering
TANAKA, M., Fish Biology
TSUDA, M., Mycology
TSUJII, H., International Rural Development
UCHIDA, A., Marine Microbiology
UENO, T., Bioregulation Chemistry
UMEDA, M., Farm Machinery
WATANABE, H., Tropical Forest Resources
YAMAZAKI, M., Agricultural Systems Engineering
YANO, H., Animal Nutrition
YAZAWA, S., Vegetable and Ornamental Horticulture
YOSHIDA, H., Landscape Architecture

Graduate School of Human and Environmental Studies:

ADACHI, Y., Socio-Cultural Environments
ASANO, K., Environmental Information Processing
ASHIKAGA, K., Socio-cultural Environments
EJIMA, Y., Environmental Information Processing
GOTO, T., Analysis for Environmental Material Sciences
HORI, T., Natural Environments
ISHIZAKA, K., Natural Environments
KANASAKA, K., Human Societies
KITABATAKE, Y., Environmental Conservation and Development
KUJIRAOKA, T., Human Development
MAMIYA, Y., Common Environmental System
MATSUMOTO, K., Environmental Dynamic Behaviour
MIYAZAKI, K., Human Societies
NISHII, M., Environmental Conservation and Development
OGAWA, T., Co-existing Systems of Nature and Human Beings
SAEKI, K., Social-environmental System
SAGARA, N., Co-existing Systems of Nature and Human Beings
SAITO, H., Environmental Conservation and Development
TAGUCHI, S., Co-existing Systems of Nature and Human Beings
TAKAHASHI, Y., Environmental Conservation and Development
TAMADA, O., Environmental Conservation and Development
TOYOSHIMA, Y., Bio-environmental System
UMIHARA, T., Human Development
USHIKI, S., Co-existing Systems of Nature and Human Beings
YAMAMOTO, N., Environmental Conservation and Development
YAMAUCHI, J., Molecular Environments of Life and Nature
YAMORI, Y., Environmental Conservation and Development
YASUI, K., Human Development

Graduate School of Energy Science:

HATTA, N., Computational Heat Transfer and Fluid Mechanics
IKEGAMI, M., Internal Combustion Engineering
INOUE, T., Material Design for Energy Machinery
ITO, Y., Energy Process Chemistry
IWASE, M., Physical Chemistry of Iron- and Steelmaking and Related High-Temperature Processes
KASAHARA, M., Atmospheric Environmental Engineering
KONDO, K., Plasma Diagnostics
MAEKAWA, T., Plasma Physics
MATSUMOTO, E., Non-linear Continuum Mechanics
NISHIYAMA, T., Resources Geology
NOZAWA, H., Physics and Technology of VLSI
ONO, K., Extractive Metallurgy
SAKA, S., Ecosystems of Biomass for Energy Use
SAWA, T., Econometrics
SHINGU, H., Social Engineering
SHIOJI, M., Combustion Science and Engineering
SHIOTSU, M., Thermal Hydraulics in Energy Systems
WAKATANI, M., Fusion Plasma Physics
YAO, T., Solid-State Energy Chemistry
YOSHIDA, K., Materials Science
YOSHIKAWA, H., Man–Machine Systems

Graduate School of Asian and African Area Studies:

ARAKI, S., Agricultural Ecology in Africa
FURUKAWA, H., Natural History of Southeast Asia
ICHIKAWA, M., Socio-Ecological History of Africa
ISHIDA, N., Environmental Ecology in Southeast Asia
KAIDA, Y., Asian Ecotechnology Development
KAKEYA, M., Livelihood and Economy in Africa
KATO, T., Dynamics of Social Configuration in Southeast Asia
KOSUGI, Y., The Islamic World
KOYAMA, N., Natural History of Africa
OHJI, T., The Hindu World
SHIMADA, S., Socio-Cultural Integration in Africa
SHIRAISHI, T., Comparative State Formation in Southeast Asia
TACHIMOTO, N., Social Structure and Cultural Dynamics in Southeast Asia
TANAKA, J., Culture and Ethnicity in Africa
TSUBOUCHI, Y., Comparative Social Transformation in Southeast Asia
YAMADA, I., Environment and Society in Southeast Asia
YOSHIHARA, K., Social Institutions and Economic Development in Southeast Asia

Graduate School of Informatics:

ADACHI, N., Systems Theory

DOSHITA, S., Information Processing
EIHO, S., Digital Image Processing Systems
FUJISAKA, H., Non-equilibrium Statistical Physics
FUKUSHIMA, M., Optimization
FUNAKOSHI, M., Non-linear Dynamics
IBARAGI, T., Discrete Mathematics
IKEDA, K., Informatics
INUI, T., Computational Neuroscience
ISHIDA, T., Social Information Systems
ISO, Y., Numerical Analysis
IWAI, T., Dynamic Systems
IWAMA, K., Algorithms and Complexity Theory
KAMBAYASHI, Y., Data Engineering
KATAI, O., Intelligent Systems Engineering
KATAYAMA, T., Control Theory
KOBAYASHI, S., Neuroscience
KUMAMOTO, H., Intelligent Transport Systems
MATSUYAMA, T., Image Understanding
MORIYA, K., Genetic Evaluation
MUNAKATA, T., Physical Statistics
NAKAMURA, Y., High-Level Synthesis Design
NOGI, T., Fundamentals of Complex Systems
SAKAI, H., Signal Processing
SAKAI, T., Geographic Information Systems
SATO, M., Computer Science Theory
SATO, T., Radar Signal Processing
SUGIE, T., Control Theory
TAMARU, K., Logic Circuits Design
TOMITA, S., Computer Architecture
YABUSHITA, S., Computational Physics
YAMAMOTO, Y., Intelligent and Control Systems
YOSHIDA, S., Digital Communications
YUASA, T., Symbolic Processing Languages

ATTACHED INSTITUTES

Center for African Area Studies: Shimoadachi-cho 46, Yoshida, Sakyo-ku, Kyoto; f. 1986; Dir Prof. J. TANAKA; publ. *African Study Monographs* (quarterly, in English).

Center for Archaeological Operations: Yoshida Honmachi, Sakyo-ku, Kyoto; f. 1977; Dir Prof. Dr I. YAMANAKA; publs *Annual Report, Excavation Reports* (irregular).

Center for Information and Multimedia Studies: Yoshida Honmachi, Sakyo-ku, Kyoto; f. 1997; Dir Prof. Dr S. TOMITA; publ. *Bulletin* (1 a year, in Japanese).

Center for Molecular Biology and Genetics: Kawahara-cho Shogoin, Sakyo-ku, Kyoto; f. 1988; Dir Prof. Dr A. SHIMIZU.

Center for Southeast Asian Studies: Shimoadachi-cho 46, Yoshida, Sakyo-ku, Kyoto; f. 1965; Dir Prof. Dr N. M. TACHIMOTO; publs *Southeast Asian Studies* (quarterly), *Monographs* (irregular), *Reprint Series* (irregular), *Discussion Papers* (irregular).

Center for Student Exchange: Yoshida Honmachi, Sakyo-ku, Kyoto; f. 1990; Dir Prof. Dr A. MIYAZAKI.

Center for Student Health: Yoshida Honmachi, Sakyo-ku, Kyoto; f. 1966; Dir Prof. Dr R. MORISHITA.

Data Processing Center: Yoshida-Honmachi, Sakyo-ku, Kyoto; f. 1969; Dir Prof. S. DOSHITA; publ. *Bulletin* (every 2 months, in Japanese).

Disaster Prevention Research Institute: Gokasho, Uji City, Kyoto; f. 1951; Dir Prof. H. IMAMOTO; publs *DPRI Newsletter* (3 a year, in English and Japanese) and *Annuals*.

Environment Preservation Center: Yoshida Honmachi, Sakyo-ku, Kyoto; f. 1977; Dir Prof. K. UCHIMOTO.

Institute of Advanced Energy: Gokasho, Uji City, Kyoto; f. 1941; Dir Prof. N. INOUE; publs *Annual Report, Research Report* (irregular), *Newsletter* (quarterly).

Institute for Chemical Research: Gokasho, Uji City, Kyoto; f. 1926; library of 40,000 vols; Dir Prof. Y. SUGIURA; publ. *ICR Annual Report*.

Institute for Frontier Medical Sciences: Kawahara-cho, Shogoin, Sakyo-ku, Kyoto; f. 1998; Dir Prof. Y. YAMAOKA; publ. *Annual Report*.

Institute for Virus Research: Kawara-cho, Shogoin, Sakyo-ku, Kyoto; f. 1956; Dir Prof. Y. ITO; publ. *Annual Report*.

Institute of Economic Research: Sakyo-ku, Kyoto; f. 1962; library of 72,000 vols; Dir Prof. Dr T. SAWA.

Primate Research Institute: Inuyama City, Aichi Prefecture; f. 1967; Dir Prof. Y. SUGIYAMA; publ. *Annual Report* (in Japanese).

Radiation Biology Center: Yoshida Konoecho, Sakyo-ku, Kyoto; f. 1976; research and postgraduate training in radiation biology; Dir Prof. M. IKENAGA; publ. *Annual Report*.

Radio Atmospheric Science Center: Gokasho, Uji City, Kyoto; f. 1981; Dir Prof. S. FUKAO.

Radioisotope Research Center: Yoshida Konoecho, Sakyo-ku, Kyoto; f. 1971; Dir Prof. Dr Y. TERASHIMA.

Research Center for Higher Education: Yoshida Honmachi, Sakyo-ku, Kyoto; f. 1994; Dir Prof. E. KAJITA.

Research Center for Sports Science: Yoshida Honmachi, Sakyo-ku, Kyoto; f. 1972; Dir Prof. Dr I. MIYOSHI.

Research Institute for Food Science: Gokasho, Uji City, Kyoto; f. 1946; research and postgraduate training in food science; Dir Prof. T. MORI; publ. *Bulletin* (annually).

Yukawa Institute for Theoretical Physics: Kitashirakawa, Sakyo-ku, Kyoto; f. 1953; Dir Prof. T. MASKAWA; publs *Progress of Theoretical Physics* (monthly), *Supplement* (quarterly).

Institute for Research in Humanities Ushinomiyacho, Sakyo-ku, Kyoto; f. 1939; Dir Prof. Y. YAMAMOTO; publs *Journal of Oriental Studies* (annually), *Journal of Humanities Studies* (in Japanese, annually), *Social Survey Report* (in Japanese, annually), *Annual Bibliography of Oriental Studies, Annals ZINBUN* (in European languages, irregularly), *News Letter ZINBUN* (in Japanese, annually).

Research Institute for Mathematical Sciences: Kitashirakawa, Sakyo-ku, Kyoto; f. 1963; research and postgraduate training in mathematical sciences; library of 74,000 vols; Dir Prof. M. MORI; publs *Publications* (6 a year), *Seminar Reports 'Kokyuroku'* (47 a year, in Japanese).

Research Reactor Institute: Kumatori-cho, Sennan-gun, Osaka; f. 1963; library of 44,000 vols; Dir Prof. Y. MAEDA; publs *KUR Report* (in Japanese), *KUR Technical Report* (in Japanese), *Progress Report* (in English, annually).

Wood Research Institute: Uji, Kyoto; f. 1944; Dir Prof. M. KUWAHARA; publs *Wood Research* (in English, annually), *Wood Research and Technical Notes* (in Japanese, annually).

Center for Ecological Research: Shimosakamoto, Otsu City, Shiga Prefecture; f. 1991; Dir Prof. E. WADA.

ATTACHED COLLEGE

College of Medical Technology: 53 Shogoin Kawahara-cho, Sakyo-ku, Kyoto 606-8507; f. 1975; Dean Prof. T. SHIMONO; publ. *Annual Report* and its supplement *Health Anthropology* (in Japanese and English).

KYUSHU INSTITUTE OF DESIGN

Shiobaru 4-9-1, Minami-ku, Fukuoka-shi 815-8540
Telephone: (92) 553-4407
Fax: (92) 553-4593
Founded 1968
Academic year: April to March (two semesters)
President: SHO YOSHIDA
Director-General: MAKOTO OHYA
Dean of Students: MASAMICHI OHKUBO
Library Director: RYUZO TAKIYAMA
Number of teachers: 95
Number of students: 901 undergraduate, 228 postgraduate
Publication: *Annual Bulletin*.

PROFESSORS

Department of Environmental Design:
HIROKAWA, S., Theory of Environmental Design
ISHI, A., Environmental Systems
KATANO, H., Environmental Systems
MIYAMOTO, M., Environmental Planning and Design
OHKUBO, M., Environmental Systems
SHIGEMATSU, T., Theory of Environmental Design
SUGIMOTO, M., Environmental Planning and Design

Department of Industrial Design:
FUKADA, S., Intelligent Mechanics and Control
ISHIMURA, S., Industrial Design
ITOI, H., Industrial Design
KAWAKITA, K., Intelligent Mechanics and Control
SAKAMOTO, T., Intelligent Mechanics and Control
SATO, H., Ergonomics
TOCHIHARA, Y., Ergonomics

Department of Visual Communication Design:
GENDA, E., Visual Image Design
NAGASHIMA, K., Image Engineering
SATO, M., Visual Image Design
TAKIYAMA, R., Image Engineering
URAHAMA, K., Image Engineering
YAMASHITA, S., Vision Science

Department of Acoustic Design:
FUJIWARA, K., Science of Acoustical Environment
IWAMIYA, S., Science of Acoustical Environment
KAWABE, T., Science of Acoustical Environment
MATSUNAGA, K., Science of Sound Culture
MIZUNO, T., Science of Sound Culture
TSUMURA, T., Science of Acoustical Information
YOSHIKAWA, S., Science of Acoustical Information

Department of Art and Information Design:
FUJIMURA, N., Media Design
KUROSAWA, S., Media Art and Culture
OHNISHI, S., Media Art and Culture
OHTA, S., Information Environment Sciences
SUZUKI, T., Information Environment Sciences

Division of Audio and Visual Communication Studies:
FUKUSHIMA, S., Applied Science of Audio and Visual Communication

KYUSHU INSTITUTE OF TECHNOLOGY

1-1 Sensui-sho, Tobata-ku, Kitakyushu-shi, Fukuoka 804-8550
Telephone: (93) 884-3000
Founded 1909

State control
Language of instruction: Japanese
Academic year: April to March

President: KUNISUKE HOSOKAWA
Registrar: ISAO SUNAGA
Librarian: YASUHIKO KATO

Library of 450,900 vols
Number of full-time teachers: 379
Number of students: 6,265

Publications: *Bulletin, Memoirs*.

ATTACHED INSTITUTES

Information Science Center: f. 1987; Dir NAOYUKI OKADA.

Center for Co-operative Research: f. 1989; Dir YASUSUKE JINNOUCHI.

Center for Microelectronic Systems: f. 1990; Dir HITOSHI FUJII.

Center for Instrumental Analysis: f. 1993; Dir TORU MINAMI.

Satellite Venture Business Laboratory: f. 1995; Dir KUSUHIRO MUKAI.

KYUSHU UNIVERSITY

Hakozaki, Higashi-ku, Fukuoka-shi 812-8581
Telephone: Fukuoka (092) 642-2111

Founded 1911
Academic year: April to March

President: Y. SUGIOKA
Vice-Presidents: T. YADA, Y. SHIBATA
Administrator: I. ITABASHI
Librarian: S. ARIKAWA

Library of 3,297,000 vols
Number of teachers: 2,246, including 637 professors
Number of students: 16,233

Publications: numerous faculty and institute journals and reports.

DEANS

Faculty of Letters: J. KIKUTAKE
Faculty of Education: M. SUMIDA
Faculty of Law: M. KAWANO
Faculty of Economics: H. ITO
Faculty of Science: K. TAKADA
Faculty of Medicine: K. SUGIMACHI
Faculty of Dentistry: M. NAKATA
Faculty of Pharmaceutical Sciences: S. WATANABE
Faculty of Engineering: T. OZAKI
Faculty of Agriculture: N. YAMASAKI
Graduate School of Information Science and Electrical Engineering: K. USHIJIMA
Graduate School of Social and Cultural Studies: M. ARIMA
Graduate School of Mathematics: M. KATO
Interdisciplinary Graduate School of Engineering Sciences: K. MURAOKA
Graduate School of Human–Environment Studies: H. OHNO

DIRECTORS

Medical Institute of Bioregulation: T. SASAZUKI
Institute of Advanced Material Study: H. HONDA
Research Centre for Higher Education: T. INAZU
Research Institute for Applied Mechanics: M. OHKUSA
Institute of Health Science: M. TOKUNAGA
Institute of Languages and Cultures: M. IWASA
Research Centre for Coal Mining Materials: N. TOJO
Computer Centre: F. MATSUO
KITE Network Operation Centre: F. MATSUO

PROFESSORS

Faculty of Letters:

AKAMATSU, A., Indian Philosophy
ANDO, T., Japanese History
HAMADA, K., Korean History
HARAGUCHI, S., American Literature
HOSOKAWA, R., Ethics
IKEDA, K., German Literature
IMANISHI, Y., Japanese Literature
INADA, T., Applied Linguistics
KAN, T., Linguistics
KIKUTAKE, J., Aesthetics and History of Fine Arts
NAKANO, M., Japanese Literature
NISHITANI, T., Archaeology
NOZAWA, H., Geography
SAKONO, F., Japanese Literature
SHIBATA, A., Chinese Philosophy
SHIMIZU, K., History of Islamic Civilization
SHINPO, H., Occidental History
SONOI, E., English Literature
SUEMATSU, H., French Literature
TAKEMURA, N., Chinese Literature
TAKUBO, Y., Linguistics
TANI, R., Occidental Philosophy

Faculty of Education:

HARIZUKA, S., Clinical Psychology for Disabled Children
NOJIMA, K., Counselling Psychology

Faculty of Law:

AGO, S., International Economic Law
ANDO, T., Comparative Constitutional Law
DOI, M., Criminology and Criminal Policy
IMASATO, S., Public Administration
ISHIDA, M., International Political History
ISHIKAWA, S., Political History
ISOGAWA, N., Civil Law
ITOU, S., Civil Law
KAWANO, M., Social Security Law
KIKUCHI, T., Social Law
KITAGAWA, T., International Trade Law
KOCHI, H., Civil Law
KODAMA, H., Comparative Private Law
KONO, T., International Private Law
MORI, J., Commercial Law, Company Law
NAOE, S., Western Legal History
NISHIMURA, S., Roman Law
NODA, S., Labour Law
OHKUMA, Y., Constitutional Law
OHKAWARA, N., Comparative Politics
OODE, Y., Law of Criminal Procedure
OYAMA, T., History of Political Thought
SAKO, I., Philosophy of Law
SEKIGUCHI, M., History of Political Thought
SHIMIZU, I., Commercial Law I, Consumer Law
UCHIDA, H., Criminal Law
UEDA, N., Japanese Legal History
WADA, Y., Science of Judicial Process
YABUNO, Y., Contemporary Japanese Politics
YANAGIHARA, M., International Law

Faculty of Economics:

ARAI, M., Economic Analysis and Policy
FUJITA, M., Business Accounting
FUKUDOME, H., Economic Theory
HAMASUNA, K., Economic Analysis and Policy
HISANO, K., Industrial Planning
HORIE, Y., Economic Analysis and Policy
HOSOE, M., Econometrics
ITO, H., Economic Analysis and Policy
IWAMOTO, S., Economic Mathematics
KAKU, S., Business Administration
KAWANAMI, Y., Economic Theory
KON, A., Economic Analysis and Policy
MUROYAMA, Y., Economic Theory
NAKAI, T., Economic Mathematics
NISHIMURA, A., Business Accounting
OGINO, Y., Economic History
OISHI, M., Insurance
OKABE, T., Management Engineering
OSUMI, K., Econometrics
SAEKI, C., Econometrics
SAKAGUCHI, K., Economic Mathematics
SEKI, G., Economic Theory
SHIOTSUGU, K., Business Administration
TAKA, T., Economic Theory
TAKITA, H., Economic History
TODA, K., Industrial Planning
TOKINAGA, S., Management Engineering
TOKUMASU, F., Business Accounting
TOKUNAGA, S., Economic Analysis and Policy
USHIYAMA, M., Business Administration
YADA, T., Industrial Planning

Faculty of Science:

ACHIWA, N., Diffraction Physics
AJIRO, Y., Solid-state Physics
AOKI, Y., Mineralogy
AOMINE, T., Semiconductor Physics
ARATONO, M., Physical Chemistry
FUJIKI, Y., Molecular Cell Biology
FUJIMORI, Y., Low-temperature Physics
GONO, Y., Experimental Nuclear Physics
IBA, K., Plant Physiology and Plant Molecular Biology
IIJIMA, T., Space Physics
INAZU, T., Organic Chemistry
INOUE, K., Elementary Particles and Fields
INOUE, S., Solid-state Physics
ISHIGURO, S., Solution Chemistry
ITO, A., Enzyme Chemistry
ITOH, H., Large-Scale Atmospheric Dynamics
IWASA, Y., Theoretical Biology
KAMIMURA, M., Theoretical Nuclear Physics
KANATOMI, H., Molecular Designing Chemistry
KATSUKI, T., Synthetic Organic Chemistry
KAWAGUTI, T., Low-dimensional Systems
KAWATO, T., Molecular Designing Chemistry
KOYAMA, H., Molecular Designing Chemistry
MAEDA, H., Polymer Chemistry
MAEDA, Y., Radiochemistry
MATSUBARA, A., Molecular Dynamic Chemistry
MATSUDA, Y., Inorganic Chemistry
MATSUOKA, O., Molecular Dynamic Chemistry
MIYAHARA, S., Middle Atmosphere Dynamics
MORINOBU, S., Experimental Nuclear Physics
MURAE, T., Organic Geoscience
NAKADA, M., Mantle Dynamics
NAKANISHI, H., Statistical Physics
NAKASHIMA, T., Experimental Nuclear Physics
NAKAYAMA, M., Environmental Science
NISHI, N., Structural Chemistry
ODAGAKI, T., Condensed Matter Theory
OHSHIMA, Y., Molecular Genetics
OKAWA, H., Co-ordination Chemistry
OKAYAMA, S., Cell Biology
SAGATA, N., Molecular Biology
SEKIYA, H., Structural Chemistry
SHIMADA, N., Metallogenic Geochemistry
SHIMAZAKI, K., Plant Physiology
SHIMIZU, H., Seismology, Volcanic Seismology
SHIMOHIGASHI, Y., Biochemistry
SHINOZAKI, B., Low-dimensional Systems
SIRATORI, K., Physics of Magnetism
SUGIYAMA, H., Physical Biology
SUZUKI, S., Seismology
TAKADA, K., Theoretical Nuclear Physics
TAKAHASHI, K., Marine Geology
TAKAOKA, N., Isotope Cosmochemistry
TAKEDA, S., Liquids and Disordered Systems
TANAKA, T., Quantum Chemistry
TAWADA, K., Biophysics and Biochemistry
TOH, Y., Animal Physiology
TOKESHI, M., Aquatic Ecology
TOMOKIYO, A., Low-temperature Physics
YAHARA, T., Ecology and Systematics
YAMAZAKI, T., Cytogenetics and Population Genetics
YANAGI, T., Chemical Geodynamics
YOSHIMURA, K., Molecular Dynamic Chemistry
YUMOTO, K., Solar-Terrestrial Physics

Faculty of Medicine:

AKAIKE, N., Physiology II
FUJISHIMA, M., Internal Medicine II
FUKUI, M., Neurosurgery
FURUE, M., Dermatology

HAMASAKI, N., Clinical Chemistry and Laboratory Medicine
HARA, N., Respiratory Diseases
HARA, T., Paediatrics
HORI, T., Physiology I
IKEDA, N., Forensic Medicine
INOMATA, H., Ophthalmology
INOUE, N., Hygiene
ITO, Y., Pharmacology
IWAKI, T., Neuropathology
IWAMOTO, Y., Orthopaedic Surgery
KANAIDE, H., Molecular Cardiology
KASHIWAGI, S., General Medicine
KATO, M., Clinical Neurophysiology
KAWABUCHI, Y., Anatomy I
KOMIYAMA, S., Oto-rhino-laryngology
KONO, S., Public Health
KOSAKA, T., Anatomy III
KUBO, C., Psychosomatic Medicine
KUWANO, M., Biochemistry I
MASUDA, K., Radiology
MOURI, S., Animal Experiments Laboratory
NAKANO, H., Obstetrics and Gynaecology
NAWATA, H., Internal Medicine III
NIHO, Y., Internal Medicine I
NOSE, Y., Medical Data Processing
OHTSUKI, I., Clinical Pharmacology
OISHI, R., Pharmacy
SHIBATA, Y., Anatomy II
SUEISHI, K., Pathology I
SUGIMACHI, K., Surgery II
SUITA, S., Paediatric Surgery
TADA, I., Parasitology
TAKAHASHI, S., Anaesthesiology, Clinical Care Medicine
TAKESHIGE, K., Biochemistry II
TAKESHITA, A., Angiocardiology
TANAKA, M., Surgery I
TASHIRO, N., Neuropsychiatry
TAWADA, K., Biophysics, Molecular Physiology
TSUNEYOSHI, M., Pathology II
TSUZUKI, T., Experimental Radiology
YANAGI, Y., Virology
YASUI, H., Cardiac Surgery

Division of Medical Science, Graduate School:

MIHARA, K., Protein Engineering
NISHIMOTO, T., Molecular Cell Biology
NOBUTOMO, K., Medical System

Institute of Genetic Information:

FUKUMAKI, Y., Gene Regulation
HAYASHI, K., Genome Analysis

Faculty of Dentistry:

AKAMINE, A., Conservative Dentistry 2
HIRATA, M., Oral Biochemistry
IJIMA, T., Oral Anatomy 2
IKEMOTO, Y., Dental Anaesthesiology
KANDA, S., Oral and Maxillofacial Radiology
KOGA, T., Preventive Dentistry
KOYANO, K., Prosthetic Dentistry 2
MAEDA, K., Conservative Dentistry 1
NAKASIMA, A., Orthodontics
NAKATA, M., Paediatric Dentistry
NAKAYAMA, H., Oral Bacteriology
OHISHI, M., Oral and Maxillofacial Surgery 1
OHTA, M., Dental Materials Engineering
OHTA, M., Oral Physiology
SAKAI, H., Oral Pathology
SHIRASUNA, K., Oral and Maxillofacial Surgery 2
TANAKA, T., Oral Anatomy 1
TERADA, Y., Prosthetic Dentistry 1
YAMAMOTO, K., Dental Pharmacology

Faculty of Pharmaceutical Sciences:

HIGUCHI, R., Plant Chemistry
HIGUCHI, S., Clinical Pharmaco-kinetics
HIMENO, M., Physiological Chemistry
IMOTO, T., Immunobiochemistry
KOGA, N., Pharmaceutical Chemistry
MAEDA, M., Radiopharmaceutical Chemistry
OGURI, K., Hygienic and Forensic Chemistry
SAWADA, Y., Pharmaceutics
SEKIMIZU, K., Microbiology
SHOYAMA, Y., Pharmacognosy
SUEMUNE, H., Pharmaceutical Synthetic Chemistry
UTSUMI, H., Physical Chemistry
WATANABE, S., Pharmacology
ZAITSU, K., Analytical Chemistry

Faculty of Engineering:

AOYAMA, Y., Supramolecular Chemistry
ARAI, Y., Molecular Systems Chemistry
ARIURA, Y., Precision Machining
CHISHAKI, T., City Planning and Management
EHARA, S., Geothermics
ESAKI, T., Environmental Geotechnology
FUJITA, Y., Heat Transfer
FUJIWARA, Y., Applied Organic Chemistry
FUKANO, T., Multi-phase Flow, Aerodynamic Noise
FUKUCHI, N., Functional Design of Marine Systems
FUKUDA, K., Heat Transfer and Hydrodynamics in Nuclear Reactors
FUKUDA, M., Geothermal Reservoir Engineering
FUKUSHIMA, H., Electrochemistry of Materials
FUNAKI, K., Applied Superconductivity
FUNATSU, K., Biochemical Engineering, Polymer Processing, Rheology
FURUKAWA, A., Fluid Mechanics
FURUSAKI, S., Bioprocess Chemistry
FURUYA, H., Nuclear Fuel Technology, Nuclear Energy Environment
GOTO, N., Aircraft Guidance and Control
HAYASHI, Y., Surface Science and Thin Film Technology
HIKOSAKA, H., Structural Mechanics
HIRAKAWA, K., Mechanical Engineering
HIRANO, M., River Engineering
HIROKAWA, S., Graphic Science, Biomechanics
HISAEDA, Y., Artificial Enzyme Chemistry
HOJO, J., Applied Inorganic Chemistry
ICHIMARU, K., Machine Design and Tribology
IDOGAKI, T., Applied Physics
IMASAKA, T., Applied Analytical Chemistry
IMATO, T., Electroanalytical Chemistry
IMURA, H., Environmental Systems Analysis and Planning
INOUE, M., Turbomachinery
IRIE, I., Coastal Engineering
IRIE, M., Advanced Materials Chemistry
ISHIBASHI, K., Radiation Measurement and Safety
ISOGAI, K., Aircraft Strength and Vibration
ITO, T., Thermodynamics
IZAWA, E., Economic Geology
JINNO, K., Water Resources Engineering
KAGAWA, K., Ship Vibration
KAI, S., Applied Physics
KAJIYAMA, T., Advanced Surface Chemistry
KANAYAMA, H., Computational Mechanics
KANEMITSU, Y., Sound and Vibration Control
KAWAKAMI, K., Bioreaction Engineering
KIDO, H., Reactive Gas Dynamics
KIJIMA, K., Hydrodynamics and Ship Dynamics
KINOSHITA, C., Science and Technology of Radiation Effects
KOMATSU, T., Environmental Hydraulics
KOMORI, S., Fluid Mechanics and Transport Phenomena
KONDO, E., Systems Mathematics and Engineering
KONDOU, T., Mechatronics
KUDO, K., Reactor Engineering
KUNITAKE, T., Molecular Assembly
KUNOO, K., Aerospace Structural System Engineering
KUSUDA, T., Environmental Engineering
MAEDA, M., Biomolecular Systems Chemistry
MASUOKA, T., Heat Transfer
MATOBA, M., Nuclear Physics and Instrumentation
MATSUI, K., Rock Engineering and Mining Machinery
MATSUMOTO, H., Theoretical Plasticity and Rolling
MATSUMURA, S., Irreversible Processes in Materials
MATSUSHITA, H., Construction Materials and Concrete Structure
MATSUYAMA, H., Process Systems Engineering
MIURA, Y., Materials Characterization and Evaluation
MIYATAKE, O., Thermal Engineering
MIYAZAKI, N., Mechanical Strength of Materials, Computational Mechanics
MOHRI, A., Systems Control
MORI, K., Physical Chemistry of Materials
MORI, S., Resources Processing
MOROOKA, S., Functional Materials Engineering
MOTOOKA, T., Materials Science
MURAKAMI, T., Machine Design, Biomechanics and Biotribology
MURAKAMI, Y., Fatigue and Fracture
MURAYAMA, T., Reaction Engineering for Materials Processing
NAGAYAMA, K., Applied Physics
NAKAO, Y., Fusion Plasma Science
NAKATAKE, K., Resistance and Propulsion of Ships
NAMBA, M., Aerospace Propulsion Systems
NEMOTO, M., Microstructure Analysis and Control
NISHIDA, M., Fluid Mechanics
OCHIAI, H., Geotechnical and Geoenvironmental Engineering
OHGI, K., Processing of Composite Materials
OHTA, T., Bridge Engineering and Aesthetic Design
ONIKURA, H., Machining Systems
ONO, S., Combustion
ONODERA, R., Plasticity and Metal Working
OTSUKA, H., Earthquake Engineering
OZAKI, T., Metal Forming
SAKURAI, A., Flight Mechanics
SHINKAI, A., Ship Design and Maritime Intelligence Technology
SHINKAI, S., Molecular Recognition Chemistry
SUEOKA, A., Dynamics of Machinery
SUMI, T., Transport Planning
TAKAGI, M., Molecular Information Chemistry
TAKAKI, S., Phase Transformation
TAKEDA, K., Applied Physics
TOMOKIYO, Y., Nano-characterization of Materials
TOYOSADA, M., Fracture and Welding Mechanics
UCHINO, K., Mining Technology and Safety Engineering
USHIJIMA, K., Exploration Geophysics
WAKABAYASHI, K., Chemical Reaction Engineering
YAMADA, S., Molecular Photochemistry
YAMAJI, T., Applied Oxygen Chemistry
YAMAMOTO, Y., Tribology
YANAGI, K., Control of Heat and Fluid Flow Transport Phenomena
YASAKA, T., Space Systems Dynamics
YOSHIDA, S., Thermal Energy Conversion

Faculty of Agriculture:

AKIMOTO, K., Agricultural Process Engineering
EGASHIRA, K., Soil Chemistry and Mineralogy
FUJIHARA, N., Animal Breeding and Reproduction
FUJII, H., Insect Genetic Resources
FUJIO, Y., Food Process Engineering
FUKUYAMA, M., Agricultural Energy
FURUICHI, M., Aquaculture and Fish Nutrition
FURUKAWA, K., Applied Microbiology
HASHIGUCHI, K., Agricultural Machinery

HATANO, S., Food Hygienic Chemistry
HIGUCHI, M., Polymer Chemistry of Wood Materials
HIROSE, Y., Insect Natural Enemies
HONJO, T., Fisheries Environmental Science
IKEDA, M., Plant Nutrition and Soil Fertility
IMADA, M., Forest Management
IMAIZUMI, K., Nutrition Chemistry
ISHIGURO, M., Protein Chemistry and Engineering
ISHIZAKI, A., Microbial Technology
ITO, T., Chemistry and Technology of Animal Products
IWAMOTO, H., Functional Anatomy of Domestic Animals
KAI, S., Agricultural Marketing
KANAZAWA, S., Microbiological Biochemistry of Soils
KAWAGUCHI, T., Quantitative Analysis of Agricultural Economics
KAWARABATA, T., Insect Pathology and Microbial Control
KOGA, K., Sericultural Science
KUBOTA, F., Practical Botany
KUHARA, S., Molecular Genetics
KURODA, M., Irrigation and Water Utilization
KUWANO, E., Pesticide Chemistry
MASUDA, Y., Animal Feed Science
MATAKI, Y., Wood Technology
MATSUMOTO, K., Food Analysis
MATSUO, E., Horticultural Science
MATSUYAMA, M., Marine Biology
MATSUYAMA, N., Plant Pathology
MORI, T., Zoology
MURATA, T., Agricultural Policy
NAKAMURA, T., Fisheries Technology
NAKAZONO, A., Fisheries Biology
OGATA, S., Microbial Genetics
OGAWA, S., Forest Environment
OKUMA, M., Wood Science
OMURA, H., Erosion Control
SAITO, A., Silviculture
SAKAI, K., Wood Chemistry
SAKAI, M., Forest Resources Management
SATOH, H., Plant Genetic Resources
SHIKASHO, S., Land-drainage and Reclamation Engineering
SHIRAHATA, S., Cellular Regulation Technology
SUZUKI, Y., Agricultural Meteorology
TAKANAMI, Y., Plant Virology
TAKAYAMA, M., Soil Science and Engineering
TANAKA, H., Industrial Chemistry of Wood
TSUJI, M., Farm Management
YAMADA, K., Food Chemistry
YAMASAKI, N., Biochemistry
YANO, T., Fisheries Chemistry
YOKOGAWA, H., Agricultural Economics
YOSHIMURA, A., Plant Breeding
YUKAWA, J., Entomology

Graduate School of Information Science and Electrical Engineering:

AKAIWA, Y., Digital Radio Communications
AMAMIYA, M., Intelligent Systems Architecture
ARAKI, K., Software Engineering and Internetworking
ARIKAWA, S., Machine Learning and Machine Discovery
CHENG, J., Knowledge Engineering, Software Engineering
FUNAKI, K., Applied Superconductivity
HARA, M., Electric Power Engineering
HASEGAWA, R., Machine Intelligence and Systems Architecture
HASEGAWA, T., Robotics
HIRASAWA, K., Control and Systems Engineering
HIROKAWA, S., Advanced Information Processing Systems
HITAKA, T., Computational Linguistics
KAWAHARA, Y., Theoretical Computer Science
KOHDA, T., Systems Communication
KUROKI, Y., Microelectronics
MAEDA, M., Optical and Quantum Electronic Devices
MAKINOUCHI, A., Data and Knowledge
MATSUNAGA, K., Cognitive Science
MATSUO, F., Data Science
MATSUYAMA, K., Solid-State Functional Devices
NIIJIMA, K., Numerical Synthesis
NINOMIYA, T., Electronic Circuits and Systems
NISHI, T., Circuits and Systems
OKADA, T., Laser Engineering
SAKOE, H., Media Signal Recognition
TAKEO, M., Superconducting Magnet and Device Technology
TANIGUCHI, R., Computer Vision
TATEIBA, M., Electromagnetic Wave Engineering
TOKO, K., Advanced Biomimetic Materials and Sensors
TSURUSHIMA, T., Solid State Technology and Integrated Systems
USHIJIMA, K., Computer Science
WADA, K., Control Engineering
WATANABE, Y., Plasma Processing
YAMASHITA, M., Theoretical Computer Science
YASUMOTO, K., Microwave Engineering and Photonics
YASUURA, H., VLSI Systems Design
YOSHIDA, K., Electrical Machinery and Control
YOSHIDA, K., Optical and Microwave Devices
ZEUGMANN, TH., Algorithmic Learning Theory

Graduate School of Social and Cultural Studies:

ARIMA, M., Japanese History
EBII, E., Modern Japanese Literature
FUKUDOME, H., Socioeconomics
GOYAMA, K., Chinese Classical Literature
HANADA, T., Modern Japanese Literature
HATTORI, H., History
HISANO, K., Economics of Technology
HONMA, Y., Urban Policy
ISHII, N., Nature Conservation Policy
IWASA, M., Modern Chinese Literature
KAN, H., American History and International Relations
KOIKE, H., Prehistoric Ecology
MATSUBARA, T., Asian Languages and Cultures
MICHEL, W., Comparative Culture and Language
MIYAKAWA, Y., Regional Studies
MORI, T., Greek Philosophy
MORIKAWA, T., Asian History
NAKAYAMA, M., Environmental Physics
NISHITANI, T., Archaeology
OHKAWARA, N., Comparative Politics
SAIGUSA, T., Environmental Biology
SAKAI, H., Sedimentological Sciences
SHIMA, H., Environmental Biology
SHIMIZU, H., Cultural Anthropology
SHINNO, I., Optical Mineralogy
TAJIMA, M., English and Sociolinguistics
TAKADA, K., International Relations
TAKAHASHI, K., History of Science
TANAKA, Y., Archaeology
TANIGUCHI, H., Earthquake Engineering
TERAZONO, Y., Occidental Religious Thought
TOJO, N., Japanese Socioeconomic History
YAHATA, H., Forest Ecophysiology
YOGO, T., Comparative Social Studies in Development
YOKOTA, K., Constitutional Law
YONEDA, M., Nature Conservation Information
YOSHIDA, M., Modernization of Japan
YOSHINO, M., English Literature
YOSHIOKA, H., Political Economy of Sciences

Graduate School of Mathematics:

BANNAI, A., Algebra and Combinatorics
HAMACHI, T., Dynamic Systems
ISHIKAWA, N., Topology
IWASAKA, K., Differential Equations
KAMATA, M., Topology
KATO, H., Mathematical Analysis
KATO, M., Topology
KAWASHIMA, S., Applied Mathematics
KAZAMA, H., Complex Analysis
KOIKE, M., Number Theory
KONISHI, S., Mathematical Statistics
KOSAKI, H., C-Algebra
KUNITA, H., Stochastic Analysis
MATSUI, T., Mathematical Analysis
MIYAWAKI, I., Number Theory
NAKAO, M. T., Computational Mathematics
NAKAO, M., Mathematical Analysis
SATO, E., Algebraic Geometry
SATO, H., Functional Analysis
SUZUKI, M., Complex Analysis
TABATA, M., Numerical Analysis
TANAKA, S., Mathematics of Complex Systems
WAKAYAMA, M., Representation Theory
WAKIMOTO, M., Infinite-dimensional Lie Algebra
WATATANI, Y., Operator Algebra
YAMAGUCHI, T., Differential Geometry
YAMAGUCHI, T., Differential Geometry
YANAGAWA, T., Mathematical Statistics
YOSHIDA, M., Complex Analysis
YOSHIKAWA, A., Mathematical Analysis

Interdisciplinary Graduate School of Engineering Sciences:

ABE., H., Structural Materials Science
HAYASHI, T., Thermal Environment Systems
HONJI, H., Environmental Fluid Dynamics
HONJO, H., Non-linear Physics
KATAYAMA, T., Urban and Architectural Environment Engineering
KAWAI, Y., Fundamental Plasma Physics
KYOZUKA, Y., Coastal Environmental Research
MASUDA, M., Laser-Aided Fluid Diagnostics
MATSUO, K., High-Speed Gas Dynamics
MORINAGA, K., Inorganic Optoelectronic Materials Engineering
MURAOKA, K., Ionized Gas Dynamics
NAKASHIMA, H., Advanced Energy Conversion Engineering
NEMOTO, N., Polymer Physical Chemistry
NISHIKAWA, M., Energy Chemical Engineering
OGAWA, T., Molecular Spectroscopy
OHTA, S., Complex Dynamic Systems
OKI, K., Crystal Physics and Engineering
SAKAI, Y., Theoretical Materials Science
SASADA, I., Applied Electromagnetics
SHIMIZU, A., Thermal Hydraulics in Extreme Conditions
SUGISAKI, M., Materials Science under Severe Conditions
TAKASAKI, K., Engine Systems
TANAKA, T., Energy Storage
TOCHIHARA, H., Surface Science
TSUTSUI, T., Organic Materials Chemistry
UCHINO, K., Plasma and Quantum Electronics
UEDA, K., Electric Energy Systems
YAMAZOE, N., Theory of Functional Materials

Graduate School of Human Environment Studies:

FUJIMOTO, K., Environmental Planning in Architecture
FUKUDA, S., History of Architecture
FURUKAWA, H., Social and Organizational Psychology
HAGISHIMA, S., Urban Design and City Planning
HAKODA, Y., Cognitive Psychology
INABA, T., Comparative and International Education III
KIKUCHI, S., Housing Design and Planning
KITAYAMA, O., Psychoanalysis
MAEDA, J., Wind Disaster Mitigation
MARUNO, S., Cognitive Developmental Psychology
MARUYAMA, K., Cultural Anthropology

MATSUFUJI, Y., Building Materials and Construction Methods
MATSUI, C., Steel Structures and Structural Mechanics
MINAMI, H., Environmental Psychology
MIURA, K., Psychology of Art and Cognition
MOCHIDA, K., Comparative and International Education I
MURATA, T., Lifespan Developmental Psychology
NAKADOME, T., School Management
NAKAMIZO, S., Psychology and Visual Perception
NANRI, Y., Planning of Adult and Community Education
OGAWA, T., Sociology
OHGAMI, H., Developmental Psychology
OHNO, H., Clinical Psychology of Human Development
OKAMOTO, H., Philosophy of Education I
SAKINO, K., Reinforced Concrete Structures and Structural Mechanics
SINYA, Y., History of Japanese Education
SUMIDA, M., Sociology of Community Education
SUZUKI, Y., Sociology
TAGA, N., Urban Disaster Management
TAKESHITA, T., Architectural Planning
TAKEZAWA, S., Religious Anthropology
TOMOEDA, T., Sociology
TSUCHIDO, T., Philosophy of Education II
WATANABE, T., Environmental Engineering in Architecture

Medical Institute of Bioregulation:

AKIYOSHI, T., Surgical Oncology
KIMURA, G., Virology
MORI, M., Surgical Oncology
NAKABEPPU, Y., Biochemistry
NAKAYAMA, K., Molecular and Cellular Biology, and Laboratory of Embryonic and Genetic Engineering
NISHIMURA, J., Clinical Immunology
NOMOTO, K., Immunology
SASAZUKI, T., Genetics
SUZUKI, T., Clinical Genetics
WAKE, N., Reproductive Physiology and Endocrinology
WATANABE, T., Laboratory of Embryonic and Genetic Engineering
WATANABE, T., Molecular Immunology
YAMAMOTO, K., Clinical Immunology

Institute of Advanced Material Study:

FUJII, M., New Energy Systems
HAYAMI, H., Advanced Energy Systems
HONDA, H., Cooling Technology
IMAISHI, N., Interfacial Reaction
KANEMASA, S., Synthetic Design
KOYAMA, S., Phase Transformation
MATAKA, S., Structural Design of Functional Molecules
MOCHIDA, I., Molecular Engineering on Functional Materials
MORI, A., Chemistry of Photofunctional Substances
NAGASHIMA, H., Electronic Functional Substances
NISHIMURA, Y., Control of Molecular Functions
OZOE, H., Mathematical Modelling of Transport Phenomena
YAMAKI, J., Measurement of Physical Properties

Research Institute for Applied Mechanics:

IMAWAKI, S., Ocean Eddy Dynamics
ITOH, S., Advanced Fusion Research Center
ITOH, S.-I., Plasma Physics and Fusion Physics
KOTERAYAMA, W., Ocean Engineering
KURAMOTO, E., High Energy Solid State Physics
MASUDA, A., Dynamics Simulation Research Center
NAKAMURA, K., Advanced Fusion Research Center
OHKUSU, M., Free Surface/Interface Problems
OHYA, Y., Wind Engineering
OIKAWA, M., Nonlinear Dynamics
SATO, K., Advanced Fusion Research Center
TAKAHASHI, K., Fracture Mechanics and Materials
TAKAO, Y., Heterogeneous Solid Mechanics
TAKEMATSU, M., Ocean Circulation Dynamics
UNO, I., Atmospheric Dynamics
WAKATA, Y., Geophysical Fluid Dynamics
YANAGI, T., Dynamics Simulation Research Center
YOON, J.-H., Dynamics Simulation Research Center
YOSHIDA, N., Radiation Damage of Materials
ZUSHI, H., Advanced Fusion Research Center

Institute of Health Science:

FUJISHIMA, K., Exercise Physiology
HASHIMOTO, K., Sports Psychology
KAWASAKI, T., Health Care
KOMIYA, S., Exercise Physiology
SONODA, G., Psychology
TOKUNAGA, M., Sports Psychology
YAMADA, H., Mental Health

Institute of Languages and Cultures:

AOYAMA, T., Russian
ARIMURA, T., German
FUJISAKI, M., English
HAGA, K., French
HIROTA, M., English
IWASA, M., Chinese
MATSUBARA, T., Korean
MICHEL, W., German
OHTA, K., English
ONO, K., English
SHIMBO, S., German
TAJIMA, M., English
TAKATO, F., French
TANAKA, T., German
TANAKA, Y., French
TANASE, A., German
TOKUMI, M., English
TSUNEYOSHI, N., German
YAMAUCHI, S., English
YOSHINO, M., English

Biotron Institute:

EGUCHI, H., Environment Control and Environmental Botany

Institute of Tropical Agriculture:

HIROTA, O., Tropical Crops and Environment
YAMATA, H., Land-water Resources and Environment Conservation

Radioisotope Centre:

OSAKI, S., Radiation Protection

International Student Centre:

KASHIMA, E., Japanese Language Teaching and Linguistics
MITO, T., International and Japanese Political Economy
MORIYAMA, H., Advising

Institute for Fundamental Research in Organic Chemistry:

AOYAMA, Y., Supramolecular Chemistry
MATSUMURA, Y., Organic Synthesis
NARUTA, Y., Organic Synthesis
NISHINO, N., Structure-Activity Relationship in Artificial Enzymes
TOKITOH, N., Hetero-Atomic Chemistry

Research Centre for Higher Education:

OSHIKAWA, M., Mathematics

Advanced Science and Technology Center for Co-operative Research:

MAEDA, M., Optical and Quantum Electronic Devices

Computer Centre:

HIROKAWA, S.

MIE UNIVERSITY

1515 Kamihama-cho, Tsu-shi, Mie 514
Telephone: (592) 32-1211
Fax: (592) 31-9000
Founded 1949
State Control
Academic year: April to March

President: YASUO TAKEMURA
Chief Administration Officer: KATSUYUKI KUROSAKI
Librarian: HIROYUKI NODA

Library of 783,000 vols
Number of teachers: 788
Number of students: 7,012

Publications: *Outline of Mie University* (every 2 years), *The Journal of Law and Economics* (Hōkei Ronsō), various faculty bulletins.

DEANS

Faculty of Humanities and Social Sciences: HIDEKAZU HIROSE
Faculty of Education: TAKESHI KINOSHITA
School of Medicine: RYUICHI YATANI
Faculty of Engineering: GORO SAWA
Faculty of Bioresources: TAKAO TAKAHASHI
College of Medical Sciences: KATSUMI DEGUCHI

MIYAZAKI UNIVERSITY

Gakuen Kibanadai Nishi 1-1, Miyazaki 889-21
Telephone: (985) 58-2811
Fax: (985) 58-2886
Founded 1949

President: K. FUTAGAMI
Registrar: Y. SUZUKI
Librarian: K. SHIMOKAWA

Number of teachers: 411, including 146 professors
Number of students: 4,156

Publications: Bulletins and memoirs of the faculties.

DEANS

Faculty of Agriculture: M. UENO
Faculty of Education: N. KAWANO
Faculty of Engineering: T. HASEGAWA

ATTACHED INSTITUTES

Co-operative Research Center: Dir S. SUGIO.
Education and Research Center for Lifelong Learning: Dir K. KUSANO.
Materials Research Center: Dir K. IMADA.
Gene Research Center: Dir S. TATEYAMA.
Radioisotope Center: Dir T. TAKAMATSU.
Information Processing Center: Dir T. SAKUDA.

MURORAN INSTITUTE OF TECHNOLOGY

Mizumoto-cho 27, Muroran 050, Hokkaido
Telephone: (143) 44-4181
Fax: (143) 47-3126
Founded 1949

President: KIYOTO IZUMI
Administrative Officer: SHUICHI MIZUKAMI
Chief Librarian: KENICHI MACHUOKA

Library of 229,000 vols
Number of teachers: 213
Number of students: 3,520

Publication: *Memoirs.*

HEADS OF DEPARTMENT

Electrical and Electronic Engineering: TAKESHI SAKAGUCHI
Civil Engineering and Architecture: KAZUO OCHUKI
Mechanical Systems Engineering: HIROMU SUGIYAMA

Computer Science and Systems Engineering: YASHUHIKO DOTE
Materials Science and Engineering: KAZUNORI SHIMAKAGE
Applied Chemistry: TOSHIKACHU KOGA
Faculty of Engineering II: YUTAKA HANAOKA
Common Subject Division: AKIO TERADA

NAGAOKA UNIVERSITY OF TECHNOLOGY

1603-1 Kamitomioka, Nagaoka, Niigata 940-21

Telephone: (258) 46-6000
Fax: (258) 47-9000

Founded 1976
State control

President: YASUZO UCHIDA
Administrator: REIKI KIZIMA
Librarian: MASA HAYASHI

Library of 127,000 vols
Number of teachers: 206
Number of students: 2,182

Departments of Mechanical Engineering, Electrical Engineering, Chemistry, Civil and Environmental Engineering, Bioengineering, and Planning and Management Science.

NAGASAKI UNIVERSITY

1-14 Bunkyo-machi, Nagasaki 852-8521

Telephone: (958) 47-1111

Founded 1949
Academic year: April to March
State control

President: TETSUO YOKOYAMA
Director-General: HARUSHIGE NAGASUE
Dean of Student Bureau: TOSHIHIDE SATO
Library Director: HIROYOSHI TOGASHI

Library of 1,001,000 vols
Number of full-time teachers: 947
Number of students: 8,305

Publications: *Bulletin of the Faculty of Education, Journal of Business and Economics* (4 a year), *Annual Report of the Research Institute of South East Asia, Annual Review of Economics, Nagasaki Medical Journal* (4 a year), *Acta Medica Nagasakiensia* (2 a year), *Annual Report of Nagasaki University School of Dentistry, Report of the Faculty of Engineering* (2 a year), *Bulletin of the Faculty of Environmental Studies, Bulletin of the Faculty of Fisheries, Bulletin of the Faculty of Liberal Arts, Bulletin of the School of Allied Medical Sciences, Nagasaki, University* (in Japanese and English), various faculty journals.

DEANS

Faculty of Education: Prof. YOSHIZOU MURONAGA
Faculty of Economics: Prof. MASAMITSU KANKE
School of Medicine: Prof. TAKAYOSHI IKEDA
School of Dentistry: Prof. YUZO KATO
School of Pharmaceutical Sciences: Prof. TADASHI YOSHIMOTO
Faculty of Engineering: Prof. EIJI YAMADA
Faculty of Environmental Studies: Prof. YOSHIHIKO INOUE
Faculty of Fisheries: Prof. OSAME TABETA
Institute of Tropical Medicine: Prof. AKIRA IGARASHI
Graduate School of Marine Science and Engineering (Doctorate Course): Prof. MITSUYOSHI TSUCHIMOTO
Junior College of Commerce: Prof. TADASHI IMADA
School of Allied Medical Sciences: Prof. TOMITAROU AKIYAMA

PROFESSORS

Faculty of Education:

ADACHI, K., Analysis and Applied Mathematics
AIKAWA, K., Education of Mentally Retarded Children
AKIYAMA, H., Study of Living
ARITA, Y., Teaching of Social Studies
AZUMA, M., Biology
FUKUI, A., Music Education
FUKUYAMA, Y., Physics
FUNAKOE, K., Law
GOTO, Y., Early Childhood Education and Care
HAMASAKI, K., German Literature
HARANO, T., Philosophy of Education
HASHIMOTO, T., Science Education
HAYASHIMA, O., Philosophy
HORINO, S., Physical Sport
INOUE, I., American Literature
IKAWA, S., Painting
ITOYAMA, K., Teaching of Technology
KAMIZONO, K., Moral and Philosophy Education
KANESHIGE, M., Art History and Theory of Art
KAWASE, H., Instrumental Music
KITAMURA, Y., Analysis
KIYOTA, I., English and American Literature
KOGA, M., Solid State Physics
KOTEGAWA, A., Vocal Music
MATSUSHIMA, A., Meteorology
MATUNAGA, J., Teaching of Health and Physical Education
MINO, E., Teaching of Mathematics
MIYAMOTO, M., Methodology of Education
MIYAZAKI, M., Developmental Psychology
MURATA, Y., Developmental Psychology
MURONAGA, Y., History
NAKAMURA, M., American Literature
NAKAMURA, Y., English and American Literature
NISHIZAWA, S., Physical Fitness
OTSUBO, Y., Teaching of English
SATO, K., Sculpture
SINNO, T., Psychological Study of Preschool Children's Play
SINOHARA, S., Philosophy
SUGAWARA, M., Exercise Physiology
SUGAWARA, T., Geometry
SUGIYAMA, S., Wood Working
SUZUKI, A., Clothing Science
TAHARA, Y., School Health and Sports Physiology
TAKAHASHI, S., International Law, Constitutional Law
TAKENOSHITA, H., Electrical Technology
TAMARI, M., Food and Nutritional Chemistry
WASHIO, T., Algebra
YAMAGUCHI, Y., Japanese Linguistics
YAMANO, S., Theory of Music
YASUKOUCHI, Y., Teaching of Japanese
YONEDA, A., Teaching of Art
YOSHIOKA, H., Educational Psychology

Faculty of Economics:

AHMED, M., Portfolio Theory
AIZAWA, K., Public Finance
ARAMAKI, K., International Economic Policy
BASU, D., International Economics
FUJINO, T., Japanese Business Management
GOTTINGER, H., Applied Statistics
GUNN, G., International Relations
IDE, Y., Business Management
IMADA, T., Accounting
KAJIHARA, Y., Market Research
KANKE, M., Business Management
KOREEDA, M., Microeconomics
MIHARA, Y., Human Resource Management
MIYAIRI, K., Local Public Finance
MIYAMICHI, K., Risk and Insurance
MURATA, S., Microeconomics
MURATA, Y., Applied Mathematics
SHIBATA, K., Japanese Economic History
SUGIHARA, T., Management Engineering
TAGUCHI, N., International Investment
TAKAHASHI, Y., Intellectual Property and Licensing
TAKAKURA, Y., Political Economy
TAKASHIMA, M., Economic Policy
TAKEYAMA, S., Business Enterprises and Asian Economics
TSUNO, H., International Finance
UCHIDA, S., Monetary Economics
UENO, K., Financial Accounting
YAJIMA, K., Derivative Securities
YAMASHITA, M., Principles of Bookkeeping

School of Medicine:

AIKAWA, T., Physiology
AYABE, H., Surgery
AMEMIYA, T., Ophthalmology
EGUCHI, K., Internal Medicine
FUJII, T., Plastic and Reconstructive Surgery
HAYASHI, K., Radiology
ICHIKAWA, M., Hospital Pharmacy
IKEDA, T., Pathology
ISHIMARU, T., Obstetrics and Gynaecology
IWAHORI, N., Anatomy
KAMIHIRA, S., Laboratory Medicine
KANEMATSU, T., Surgery
KATAMINE, S., Bacteriology
KATAYAMA, I., Dermatology
KOBAYASHI, T., Otorhinolaryngology
KOHNO, S., Internal Medicine
KONDO, T., Biochemistry and Molecular Biology in Disease
MAITA, T., Biochemistry
MATSUDA, Y., Physiology
MATSUYAMA, T., Oncology
NAGASHIMA, S., Anatomy
NAKANE, Y., Neuropsychiatry
NAKASONO, I., Forensic Medicine
NIIKAWA, N., Human Genetics
NIWA, M., Pharmacology
OKUMURA, Y., Radiation Biophysics
SAITO, H., Preventive Medicine and Health Promotion
SAITO, Y., Urology
SEKINE, I., Molecular Pathology
SHIBATA, S., Neurosurgery
SHINDO, H., Orthopaedic Surgery
SUMIKAWA, K., Anaesthesiology
TAGUCHI, T., Pathology
TAKEMOTO, T., Public Health
TANIYAMA, K., Pharmacology
TOMONAGA, M., Haematology
YAMASHITA, S., Natural Medicine
YANO, A., Medical Zoology
YANO, K., Internal Medicine
YUI, K., Medical Zoology

School of Dentistry:

ATSUTA, M., Fixed Prosthodontics
FUJII, H., Removable Prosthodontics
GOTO, G., Paediatric Dentistry
HAYASHI, Y., Endodontics and Operative Dentistry
HISATSUNE, K., Dental Materials Science
INOKUCHI, T., Maxillofacial and Oral Surgery II
KATO, I., Periodontology
KATO, Y., Dental Pharmacology
KOBAYASHI, K., Orthodontics
MIZUNO, A., Maxillofacial and Oral Surgery I
NAKAMURA, T., Radiology and Cancer Biology
OI, K., Dental Anaesthesiology
ROKUTANDA, A., Oral Anatomy
SATO, T., Oral Physiology
TAKAGI, O., Preventive Dentistry
TAKANO, K., Oral Histology
YAMADA, T., Oral Bacteriology

School of Pharmaceutical Sciences:

FUJITA, K., Pharmaceutical Chemistry
HATAKEYAMA, S., Pharmaceutical Manufacturing Chemistry
KAI, M., Chemistry of Functional Macromolecules
KOBAYASHI, N., Molecular Biology of Diseases
KOHNO, M., Cell Regulation
KOUNO, I., Pharmacognosy
MATSUMURA, Y., Synthetic Chemistry for Pharmaceuticals
NAKAMURA, J., Pharmaceutics
NAKASHIMA, K., Hygienic Chemistry and Toxicology

UEDA, H., Molecular Pharmacology and Molecular Neuroscience
WATANABE, M., Radiation and Life Science
YOSHIMOTO, T., Biotechnology

Faculty of Engineering:

AOYAGI, H., Biochemistry
ASANABE, Tribology
EGASHIRA, M., Materials Chemistry
FUJIYAMA, H., Plasma Science
FUKUNAGA, H., Magnetics
FURUKAWA, M., Materials Science of Polymers
FURUMOTO, K., Hydraulics
GOTOH, K., Remote Sensing
HARADA, T., Reinforced and Prestressed Concrete Structures
HASAKA, M., Materials Physics and Engineering
IMAI, Y., Fracture Mechanics
ISHIDA, M., Combustion Engineering in Diesel Engines
ISHIMATSU, T., Measurement and Control Engineering
IWANAGA, H., Analysis of Crystal Structure
IWAO, M., Synthetic Organic Chemistry
KAGAWA, S., Industrial Physical Chemistry
KANEMARU, K., Heat Transfer
KISU, H., Computational Mechanics
KODAMA, Y., Fluid Dynamics
KOMORI, K., Structural Analysis
KUDO, A., Algebra
KURODA, H., Computer and Communication Systems
MATSUMOTO, H., Catalysis
MATSUO, H., Electronic and Digital Control
MATSUO, H., High-Voltage Engineering
MIYAHARA, S., Pattern Recognition and Information Retrieval Systems
MORIKAWA, R., Number Theory
NAKASHIMA, N., Membrane Chemistry
NISHIDA, N., Manufacturing Systems
NOGUCHI, M., Hydraulics
OKABAYASHI, T., Hydrology
ONISHI, M., Co-ordination Chemistry
OYAMA, J., Electrical Machinery
SAKAMOTO, Y., Metal Science
SAKIYAMA, T., Structural Analysis
SETOGUCHI, K., Fatigue
SHIGECHI, T., Thermal Engineering
SHUGYO, M., Inelastic Behaviour of Steel Structures
SUEOKA, T., Structural Mechanics
TAKAHASHI, K., Structural Vibration
TAKENAKA, T., Electromagnetic Wave Theory
TAMARU, Y., Organic Chemistry
TANABASHI, Y., Soil Mechanics
TANAKA, K., Engineering Optics
TOGASHI, H., Coastal Engineering
TSUJI, T., Structural Engineering
URA, A., Tribology
YAMADA, E., Power Electronics
YOSHITAKE, Y., Vibrations of Structures

Faculty of Environmental Studies:

ARAO, K., Meteorology and Climatology
FUKUSHIMA, K., Anthropology of Religion
GOTO, N., Solid State Physics
HAMA, T., Labour Environment
HAYASE, T., Environmental Policy
HIMENO, J., History of Economics
IDE, Y., Environmental Business Management
IKUNO, M., Civil Law
INOUE, Y., Philosophy
ISIZAKI, K., Environmental Engineering
MASAKI, H., Oriental Philosophy and Bioethics
MATSUDA, Y., Environmental Chemistry
MIYA, Y., Crustacean Taxonomy
MIYAMOTO, Y., English Literature
NAKAMURA, T., Biostatistics
SAKUMA, T., Japanese Intellectual History
SONODA, N., German Literature
TAIMURA, A., Exercise Physiology
TAKAKURA, T., Bio-environmental Engineering
TAKAZANE, Y., French Literature
TAKEMASA, T., Soil Physics
TSUCHIYA, K., Environmental Physiology
UEDA, K., Peptide Chemistry
UMEDA, H., English Literature
WAKAKI, T., Japanese Literature
YOSHIDA, M., Greek Philosophy
YOSHIKAWA, I., Radiation Genetics

Faculty of Fisheries:

FUJISAWA, H., Ocean Biostatistics
FUJITA, Y., Algal Biotechnology, Protoplast Fusion, Tissue Culture
HAGIWARA, A., Marine Invertebrate Zoology
HARA, K., Biochemistry
ISHIHARA, T., Aquatic Biochemistry
ISHIMATSU, A., Fish Physiology
KATAOKA, C., Marine Social Science
KITAMURA, H., Marine Chemical Ecology, Effects of Pollution on Marine Life
MATSUBAYASHI, N., Colloid and Interface Science
MATSUNO, T., Mixing Process in the Ocean, Internal Tides, Coastal Oceanography
MATSUOKA, K., Micropalaeontology and Coastal Environment Science
MATSUYAMA, M., Limnology and Oceanography
MURAMATSU, T., Biophysical Chemistry and Biochemistry
MORII, H., Ecology and Physiology of Marine and Food Bacteria
NATSUKARI, Y., Fisheries Biology, Invertebrates, Cephalopoda
NISHINOKUBI, H., Fishing Boat Seamanship, Fishing Gear Engineering
NOGUCHI, T., Marine Toxins
NOZAKI, Y., Chemistry and Technology of Marine Food Materials
SHIOTANI, S., Computational Fluid Dynamics, Naval Ship Hydrodynamics
TAKITA, T., Ichthyology, Early Life History of Fishes, Estuarine Biology
TAKEMURA, A., Acoustical Behaviour of Marine Animals, Life History of Marine Mammals and Sharks
TABETA, O., Ichthyology, Early Stages of Fishes, Fin Fish Culture, Fish Ecology
TSUCHIMOTO, M., Adaptability of Fishes to Water Temperature, Improvement of Flesh Flavour in Cultured Fish, Rigor Mortis
YADA, S., Fishing Boat Seamanship, Fishing Boat Handling
YOSHIKOSHI, K., Fish Pathology

Institute of Tropical Medicine:

AOKI, Y., Parasitology
HIRAYAMA, T., Bacteriology
IGARASHI, A., Virology
ITAKURA, H., Pathology
KAMBARA, H., Protozoology
KOSAKA, M., Environmental Physiology
MIZOTA, T., Social Environment
NAGATAKE, T., Internal Medicine
NAKAMURA, M., Biochemistry
TAGAKI, M., Medical Entomology
YAMAMOTO, N., Preventive Medicine and AIDS Research

Junior College of Commerce:

HAMA, T., Labour Law, Labour Economics
IMADA, T., Accounting
KOREEDA, M., Microeconomics
MIYAIRI, K., Public Finance
TAKAKURA, Y., Marxian Economics
TATEYAMA, S., Forms of Business Organization, Asian Economics

School of Allied Medical Sciences:

AKIYAMA, T., Rehabilitation Medicine, Orthopaedic Surgery
FUNASE, K., Human Motor Control, Exercise Physiology
ISHIHARA, K., Adult Nursing
KATO, K., Anatomy of Locomotor System, Physical Anthropology
KAWASAKI, C., Developmental and Behavioural Paediatrics
KISHI, E., Maternal and Child Health Care, Midwifery
KUBOTA, K., Obstetrics and Gynaecology
MATSUSAKA, N., Rehabilitation Medicine, Orthopaedic Surgery
NAKAMURA, T., Biostatistics, Mathematical Information Science
ODA, T., Parasitology and Medical Zoology
OHTA, T., Psychiatry, Mental and Physical Health
TAGAWA, Y., Thoracic Surgery and Cytometry
TASHIRO, T., Respirology, Infectious Diseases
TOMIOKA, T., Gastroenterological Surgery, Surgery of Liver, Biliary Tract and Pancreas
YOSHIMURA, T., Neurology (Morphology in Neuromuscular Diseases)
YOSHITANI, S., Infection Control in Nursing

DIRECTORS

Center for Educational Research and Training: Prof. TATEO HASHIMOTO
University Hospital attached to School of Medicine: Prof. YUTAKA SAITO
Atomic Bomb Disease Institute: Prof. ICHIRO SEKINE
Laboratory Animal Center for Biomedical Research: Prof. TAKAHITO KONDO
University Hospital attached to School of Dentistry: Prof. AKIO MIZUNO
Experimental Institute for Medicinal Plant Garden: Assoc. Prof. TOSHIHIKO IKENAGA
Information and Research Center of Tropical Medicine: Prof. MASAAKI SHIMADA
Animal Research Center: Prof. MISHIO NAKAMURA
Marine Research Institute: Prof TORU TAKITA
Education and Research Center of Marine Resources: Prof. TORU TAKITA
Health Center: Prof. NOBUKO ISHII
Educational Research Center for Life-long Learning: Prof. KATSUTOSHI IYAMA
Science Information Center: Prof. HIDEO KURODA
Joint Research Center: Prof. SADAO ASANABE
Environmental Protection Center: Prof. MASAYUKI HASAKA
Radioisotope Center: Prof. YUTAKA OKUMURA
Center for Instrumental Analysis: Prof. ISAO KONO
International Student Center: Prof. NORITERU NISHIDA
Shimabara Training Center: Prof. TOSHIHIDE SATO

NAGOYA INSTITUTE OF TECHNOLOGY

Gokiso-cho, Showa-ku, Nagoya
Telephone: (52) 732-2111
Fax: (52) 735-5009

Founded 1949
State control
Language of instruction: Japanese
Academic year: April to March

President: TATSUO OKAJIMA
Vice-President: TORU MIYAZAKI
Secretary-General of Administration: KAZUHIRO TANIGUCHI

Library of 446,000 vols
Number of teachers: 357
Number of students: 6,711

Publication: *Bulletin* (annually).

HEADS OF DEPARTMENTS

Applied Chemistry: TADYOSHI YOSHIDA
Materials Science and Engineering: MASAYUKI NOGAMI
Mechanical Engineering: HIDEO FUJIMOTO
Systems Engineering: KAZUYUKI OHE

Electrical and Computer Engineering: AKIRA IWATA
Intelligence and Computer Science: HIDENORI ITOH
Architecture and Civil Engineering: YASUNAGA FUKUCHI
Systems Management and Engineering: HITOSHI TATEMITSU
General Studies: KOJI KAKITA

ATTACHED INSTITUTES

Ceramic Research Laboratory: 6–29 Asahigaoka 10-chome, Tajimi, Gifu; Dir SUGURU SUZUKI.
Educational Center for Information Processing: Gokiso-cho, Showa-ku, Nagoya; Dir TATSUYA HAYASHI.
Instrument and Analysis Center: Gokiso-cho, Showa-ku, Nagoya; Dir YOSHIHARU TSUJITA.
Center for Co-operative Research: Gokiso-cho, Showa-ku, Nagoya; Dir NOBUYUKI MATSUI.
Research Center for Micro-structure Devices: Gokiso-cho, Showa-ku, Nagoya; Dir UMENO MASAYOSI.
Manufacturing and Experimental Center: Gokiso-cho, Showa-ku, Nagoya; Dir TOMIO MATSUBARA.

NAGOYA UNIVERSITY

Furo-cho, Chikusa-ku, Nagoya 464-8601
Telephone: (52) 781-5111
Fax: (52) 780-2045
E-mail: intl@post.jimu.nagoya-u.ac.jp

Founded 1939
State control
Language of instruction: Japanese
Academic year: April to March (two semesters)

President: M. MATSUO
Vice-Presidents: K. TSUJI, O. YAMASHITA
Director-General for Administration: T. FUKUSHIMA
Director of the Library: M. KAINO

Library: see Libraries
Number of full-time teachers: 1,784
Number of students: 15,678

Publications: *Nagoya University Bulletin*, various School publs.

DEANS

School of Letters: H. YAMADA
School of Education: M. KAJITA
School of Law: Y. SASAKI
School of Economics: N. OKUNO
School of Informatics and Sciences: M. ITO
School of Science: R. NOYORI
School of Medicine: I. NAKASHIMA
School of Engineering: Y. INAGAKI
School of Agricultural Sciences: T. NAMIKAWA
Graduate School of Letters: H. YAMADA
Graduate School of Education: M. KAJITA
Graduate School of Law: Y. SASAKI
Graduate School of Economics: N. OKUNO
Graduate School of Science: R. NOYORI
Graduate School of Medicine: I. NAKASHIMA
Graduate School of Engineering: Y. INAGAKI
Graduate School of Bioagricultural Sciences: T. NAMIKAWA.
Graduate School of International Development: N. CHUJO
Graduate School of Human Informatics: T. MITSUI
Graduate School of Mathematics: H. UMEMURA
Graduate School of Languages and Culture: K. HIRAI

DIRECTORS

Research Institute of Environmental Medicine: T. MANO
Solar-Terrestrial Environment Laboratory: S. KOKUBUN
Institute for Hydrospheric-Atmospheric Sciences: H. TANAKA
Radioisotope Research Center: K. NISHIZAWA
Chemical Instrument Center: K. TATSUMI
Research Center for Advanced Energy Conversion: F. TAKAGI
Center for Gene Research: M. SUGIURA
Center for Co-operative Research in Advanced Science and Technology: H. HAYAKAWA
Dating and Materials Research Center: M. ADACHI
Bioscience Center: Y. KITAGAWA
Education Center for International Students: M. ISHIDA
Center for Integrated Research in Science and Engineering: M. HASATANI
Research Center for Advanced Waste and Emissions Management: C. YAMAUCHI
Research Centre for Materials Science: O. YAMAUCHI
Centre for Studies in Higher Education: T. UMAKOSHI
Centre for Information Media Studies: K. MOHRI
Computation Center: J. TORIWAKI
Faculty of Language and Culture: T. OGURI
Research Center of Health, Physical Fitness and Sports: Y. SATO
University Hospital: T. HAYAKAWA

PROFESSORS

School and Graduate School of Letters:

ABE, Y., Comparative Study of Cultures
AMANO, M., English Linguistics
EMURA, H., Oriental History
HIROSE, Y., Psychology
INABA, N., Japanese History
ISHII, K., Psychology
KAMIO, M., English Literature
KANEKO, S., German Literature
KATO, J., Indian Philosophy
KUGINUKI, T., Japanese Linguistics
KUROZUMI, T., Philosophy
MACHIDA, K., Linguistics
MIKI, S., Japanese History
MIYAJI, A., Aesthetics and Art History
MIZOGUCHI, T., Geography
MURAKAMI, M., Japanese Literature
NAKANO, H., English Linguistics
OGAWA, M., Western Classics
ORIHARA, H., Sociology
SANO, K., Chinese Philosophy
SATO, S., Occidental History
SHIMIZU, S., German Literature
SHINODA, T., French Literature
SUGIYAMA, H., Chinese Literature
SUZUKI, S., Japanese History
TAJIMA, I., Japanese Linguistics
TAMURA, H., Philosophy
TSUJI, K., Psychology
UMITSU, M., Geography
WAKAO, Y., Occidental History
WATANABE, M., Archaeology
YAMADA, H., Philosophy
YANO, M., Linguistics

School and Graduate School of Education:

ABIKO, T., Curriculum Planning
HAYAKAWA, M., Philosophy of Education
HAYAMIZU, I., Child Psychology: Human Relations and Motivation
HIBI, Y., Methods of Education
HONJO, S., Clinical Study for Family Development
IMAZU, K., Sociology of Education
KAGEYAMA, H., Research Seminar on Clinical Development Help, Resource Methods in Clinical Psychology
KAJITA, M., Educational Psychology
KATOH, S., History of Education
KOJIMA, H., Clinical Study for Family Development
MATOBA, M., Methods of Education
MURAKAMI, T., Educational Statistics
NOGUCHI, H., Educational Statistics
SAKAKI, T., Educational Administration
SHINKAI, H., Adult Education and Lifelong Learning
SHINODA, H., History of Education
TABATA, O., Clinical Study for Developmental Help
TERADA, M., Technical and Technological Education
UMAKOSHI, T., Comparative and International Education
YOSHIDA, T., Social Psychology

School and Graduate School of Law:

FUKE, T., Public Finance Law and Tax Law
HAMADA, M., Corporate Law
HIRAKAWA, M., Criminal Law
ICHIHASHI, K., Administrative Law
ISHIDA, M., Sociology of Law
ISOBE, T., History of Western Political Thought
ITO, K., Criminal Law
ITO, T., Civil Code
JIMBO, F., Japanese Legal History
KAGAYAMA, S., Civil Code
KAINO, M., Anglo-American Law
KAISE, Y., Civil Procedure
KAMINO, K., Administrative Law
KATO, H., Environmental Law
KATO, M., Civil Code
KITAZUMI, K., Western Political History
KOBAYASHI, R., Commercial Law
MASUDA, T., Japanese Political History
MATSUI, Y., International Law
MORI, H., Constitutional Law
MORIGIWA, Y., Jurisprudence
OKUBO, Y., Western Legal History
ONO, K., Political Science
SABURI, H., International Law
SADAKATA, M., International Politics
SASAKI, Y., International History
SUGIURA, K., Russian Law
TANABE, M., Commercial Law
TOKUDA, K., Civil Procedure
USHIRO, F., Public Administration
WADA, H., Labour Law

School and Graduate School of Economics:

ANDO, T., History of European Economic Thought
IIDA, A., Financial Accounting of Business Enterprises
KANAI, Y., British Monetary History during the Inter-war Period
KINOSHITA, S., Econometrics of the Japanese Economy
KISIDA, T., Organization
MAKIDO, T., International Competitiveness of Japanese Enterprises
MINAGAWA, T., Microeconomic Foundations of Macroeconomics
MURAOKA, T., Studies on East Asia Capitalism
OHASHI, I., Japanese Employment System
OKOMURA, R., Open-economy Macroeconomics
OKUNO, N., Public Economics
SAKURAI, K., Management Study on Social Responsibility in Business
SENDA, J., Monetary Economics
TAKAKUWA, S., Business Administration
TAKEUCHI, J., Comparative Study on Economic Development
TAKEUCHI, N., Stabilization Policy
TOMOSUGI, Y., Management Audit
TSUKADA, H., Pricing Mechanism of Financial Derivatives
YAMADA, T., Institutional Economics

School of Informatics and Sciences:

AKAMATSU, H., Creativity and Informatics
HATTA, T., Behaviour and Information Processing
HAYASHI, N., Regional Systems
HOSHINO, M., Environmental Systems
IHARA, S., Mathematical Analysis and Informatics
IKADATSU, Y., Formation of Culture and Society
ISHII, K., Biological Systems
ITO, M., Environmental Systems

ITO, M., Mathematical Analysis of Social Information
IWAIKAWA, Y., Biological Systems
KAINUMA, J., Information and Society
KAMIYA, N., Mathematical Analysis and Informatics
KANEYOSHI, T., Material Physics and Informatics
KATOU, K., Biological Systems
KAWADA, M., Formation of Culture and Society
KAWASAKI, S., Mathematical Analysis of Social Informatics
KOGISO, M., Material Physics and Informatics
KUMANO, S., Formation of Culture and Society
KURODA, T., Mathematical Analysis of Social Information
MATSUBARA, T., Environmental Systems
MATSUO, S., Material Physics and Informatics
MORI, M., Material Physics and Informatics
ODA, Y., Regional Systems
OKAWA, M., Information and Society
OSADA, M., Behaviour and Information Processing
OZAWA, M., Mathematical Analysis and Informatics
SANO, M., Design for Functional Materials
SASAKI, K., Design for Functional Materials
SHINODA, K., Information and Society
SINODA, K., Information and Society
SUGIMOTO, T., Design for Functional Materials
TANAKA, K., Creativity and Informatics
TANAKA, M., Design for Functional Materials
TEZUKA, T., Environmental Systems
TSUBOI, H., Creativity and Informatics
YOKOSAWA, H., Methodologies for Information Processing

School and Graduate School of Science:

ADACHI, M., Sedimentology and Tectonics
AIBA, H., Molecular Biology
ENDO, T., Biochemistry
FUJII, N., Physical Volcanology and Planetary Physics
FUJISAWA, H., Developmental Neurobiology
FUKUI, Y., Astrophysics
FUNAHASHI, S., Analytical Chemistry
GÔ, M., Computational Structural Biology
HAYASHI, H., Cell Biology, Biochemistry
HIRAHARA, K., Seismology
HOMMA, M., Bioenergetics
HORI, H., Evolutionary Genetics
HOTANI, H., Biophysics
IKEUCHI, S., Astrophysics
KAKITANI, T., Biophysics
KAWABE, I., Geochemistry
KIJIMA, H., Biophysics
KITAKADO, S., Nuclear and Particle Physics
KONDO, T., Plant Physiology
KONTANI, M., Solid State Physics
KOUYAMA, T., Biophysics
KURODA, Y., Solid State Physics
KUROIWA, A., Developmental Biology
KUSUMI, A., Cellular Biophysics
MAMIYA, T., Solid State Physics
MATSUMOTO, K., Molecular Biology
MATSUURA, T., Solid State Physics
MORI, K., Nuclear and Particle Physics
NAKANISHI, T., Nuclear and Particle Physics
NISHIDA, Y., Animal Development
NIWA, K., Nuclear and Particle Physics
NOYORI, R., Organic Reaction Chemistry
NOZAKI, K., Nonlinear Physics
OGAWA, K., Earth Physics
OHMINE, I., Physical Chemistry
OHSHIMA, T., Nuclear and Particle Physics
OZAWA, T., Geobiology
SAITO, S., Nuclear and Particle Physics
SANDA, I., Nuclear and Particle Physics
SATO, M., Solid State Physics
SATO, S., Astrophysics
SHIBAI, H., Astrophysics
SHICHI, R., Gravity and Geodynamics
SUGAI, S., Solid State Physics
SUGIHARA, R., Plasma Physics
SUZUKI, K., Petrology
TANAKA, T., Cosmochemistry and Isotope Geology
TANIMURA, K., Solid State Physics
TOMIMATSU, A., Gravity and General Relativity
UEMURA, D., Organic Chemistry
YAMADA, I., Seismology and Planetary Physics
YAMASHITA, K., Astrophysics
YAMAUCHI, O., Inorganic Chemistry
YAMAWAKI, K., Nuclear and Particle Physics

School and Graduate School of Medicine:

AOYAMA, T., Radiological Technology
FURUKAWA, K., Biochemistry
GOTO, S., Nursing and Nursing Administration
HAMAGUCHI, M., Molecular Pathogenesis
HASEGAWA, T., Medical Technology
HAYAKAWA, T., Internal Medicine
HIDAKA, H., Pharmacology
HOTTA, N., Internal Medicine
IDA, K., Physical Therapy
IGUCHI, A., Geriatrics
ISHIGAKI, T., Radiology
ISHIGURO, A., Developmental Nursing and Midwifery
ISOMURA, S., Medical Zoology
ITO, T., Public Health and Home Nursing
IWATA, H., Orthopaedic Surgery
KATSUMATA, Y., Legal Medicine
KAWAMURA, M., Physical Therapy
KAWATSU, Y., Nursing and Nursing Administration
KIKUCHI, A., Medical Mycology
KOBAYASHI, K., Physical Therapy
KODERA, Y., Medical Radiological Therapy
KOIKE, Y., Medical Laboratory Technology
KUBA, K., Physiology
MAEKOSHI, H., Radiological Technology
MATSUMURA, Y., Clinical Nursing
MIYAHARA, H., Medical Radiological Technology
MIYAKE, Y., Ophthalmology
MIZUTANI, M., Clinical Nursing
MIZUTANI, S., Obstetrics and Gynaecology
MORI, N., Pathology
MORISHIMA, T., Nursing and Nursing Administration
MORITA, S., Developmental Nursing and Midwifery
MURAMATSU, T., Biochemistry
NAGASE, E., Medical Laboratory Technology
NAKAKI, T., Nursing and Nursing Administration
NAKASHIMA, I., Immunology
NAKASHIMA, N., Laboratory Medicine
NAKASHIMA, T., Otorhinolaryngology
NIMURA, Y., Surgery
NISHIYAMA, Y., Virology
OBATA, Y., Medical Radiological Technology
OHNO, Y., Preventive Medicine
OHSHIMA, S., Urology
OHTA, M., Bacteriology
OHTA, T., Psychiatry
SAITO, H., Internal Medicine
SAKAKIBARA, H., Public Health and Home Nursing
SHIBATA, S., Applied Occupational Therapy
SHIMADA, Y., Anaesthesiology
SOBUE, G., Neurology
SOKABE, M., Physiology
SUGIMURA, K., Occupational Therapy
SUGIURA, Y., Anatomy
SUZUKI, K., Occupational Therapy
TABUSHI, K., Radiological Technology
TAKAGI, H., Surgery
TAKAGI, K., Medical Technology
TAKAHASHI, M., Pathology
TAKEUCHI, Y., Hygiene
TAKEZAWA, J., Emergency Medicine
TOMITA, Y., Dermatology
TOMODA, Y., Obstetrics and Gynaecology
TOYOSHIMA, H., Public Health
TSUJII, Y., Applied Physical Therapy
UEDA, M., Oral Surgery
WAKABAYASHI, T., Anatomy
WATANABE, K., Paediatrics
YASUDA, M., Nursing and Nursing Administration
YOSHIDA, J., Neurosurgery
YOSHIDA, S., Cancer Cell Biology
YOSHIKAI, Y., Germfree Life

School and Graduate School of Engineering:

ABE, H., Solid State Physics
ASAI, S., Electromagnetic Processing of Materials
ASAOKA, A., Soil Mechanics
CHOH, T., Composite Materials Engineering
DOI, M., Computational Physics
EGUCHI, S., Applied Organic Chemistry
FUJITA, H., Thermal Energy Engineering
FUJIWARA, T., Space Precision Engineering
GOTO, S., Chemical Reaction Engineering
GOTO, T., Optical Electronics
HARAGUCHI, H., Analytical Chemistry
HASATANI, M., Energy Conversion Engineering
HATTA, I., Biophysics and Biotechnology
HAYAKAWA, H., Electronic Device Engineering
HAYAKAWA, Y., Intelligent Electronic-Mechanical Engineering
HAYASHI, Y., Sustainable Transport and Spatial Development
HIRAIDE, M., Analytical Science
HIRANO, S., Chemistry of Inorganic Materials
HIRATA, T., Design and Analysis of Algorithms
HOSOE, S., Control of Electronic-Mechanical Systems
ICHIMIYA, A., Surface Physics
IGUCHI, T., Nuclear Radiation Measurement and Instrumentation
IIDA, T., Radiation and Environmental Safety Engineering
IIJIMA, S., Genetic Engineering
IKEBE, Y., Nuclear and Functional Materials
IKUTA, K., Biomedical Micro Systems
INAGAKI, Y., Logics of Information Systems
INOUE, J., Theory of Solid State Physics
ISHIBASHI, Y., Crystal Physics
ISHIDA, Y., Intelligent Manufacturing Technology
ISHIKAWA, K., Deformation Processing of Materials
ITOH, K., Selective Organic Synthesis
IWADARE, Y., Information Engineering Science
IWATA, K., Coastal Engineering
IZUMI, Y., Materials Conversion Chemistry
KADOTA, K., Electronic Process Engineering
KAJZER, J., Impact Biomechanics
KANEDA, Y., Computational Physics of Fluids
KANETAKE, N., Composite Materials Engineering
KASHIWAMURA, S., Statistical Physics
KATAGI, A., Architectural Design and Theory
KAWADE, K., Applied Nuclear Physics
KAWAKAMI, S., Transport Engineering
KIKUYAMA, K., Fluid Transport Engineering
KOBAYAKAWA, H., High Energy Accelerator Physics
KOBAYASHI, K., Polymer Biomaterials Chemistry
KOBAYASHI, T., Bioprocess Engineering
KONDOH, K., Manufacturing Process Technology
KOUMOTO, K., Chemistry of Inorganic Reactions
KUKITA, Y., Nuclear Energy Systems Engineering
KUNO, S., Architectural Environmental Engineering
KURODA, K., Material Physics and Electron Microscopy

KURODA, S., Solid State Physics
MATSUI, M., Magnetism and Magnetic Materials
MATSUI, T., Quantum Materials Engineering
MATSUI, T., Structural Mechanics
MATSUMURA, T., Energy Conversion Systems
MATSUZAKI, Y., Structure Mechanics
MINAMOTO, K., Applied Bio-organic Chemistry
MITSUYA, Y., Micromechatronics and Micromeasurements Engineering
MIYATA, T., Strength and Fracture of Materials
MIYAZAKI, T., Radiation Chemistry
MIZUTANI, T., Compound Semiconductor Devices
MIZUTANI, T., Functional Materials and Devices
MIZUTANI, U., Electronic Physics of Condensed Matter
MOHRI, K., Intelligent Control Systems
MORI, C., Radiation Measurement
MORI, S., Materials and Energy Process Technology
MORINAGA, M., Materials Design
MORITA, K., Surface and Interface Co-ordination Engineering
MURAKAMI, S., Continuum Mechanics
MURASE, T., Mechanical Separation and Membrane Separation Technology
NAGAFUJI, T., Hydraulic Machinery
NAKAMURA, I., Turbulence Research
NAKAMURA, M., Resources and Environment
NAKAMURA, Y., Fluid Mechanics
NISHI, J., Underground Space Design
NODA, I., Physical Chemistry of Macromolecules
NOMURA, HIROYASU, Chemical Physics of Condensed Matter
NOMURA, HIROYUKI, Phase Transformation and Solidification Processing
OGAWA, A., Information and Communication Systems
OHNISHI, N., Human Information Processing
OHNO, N., Microsystems in Materials
OKAMOTO, Y., Polymer Synthesis
OKUBO, H., Energy System and Environment
OKUMA, S., Intelligent Systems
ONOGI, K., Process Systems Engineering
OTA, H., Dynamics of Machinery
SAKA, H., Interface Engineering
SAKABE, T., Programming Languages
SAKATA, M., Maximum Entropy Method
SANO, M., Materials Reaction Processing Engineering
SATO, K., Micromachining and Micromechanics
SATOH, K., Plasma Diagnostics Engineering
SAWADA, Y., Earthquake Engineering
SAWAKI, N., Semiconductor Electronics
SAWAKI, Y., Mechanistic Organic Chemistry
SHIMADA, T., Computer Engineering
SHIMIZU, H., Facility Planning
SHOBATAKE, K., Material Design Chemistry
SOGA, T., Kinetic Theory, Rarefied Gas Dynamics
SUEMATSU, Y., Integrated Mechanical Engineering
SUENAGA, Y., Media Engineering
SUGAI, H., Plasma Science
SUGIHARA, M., Mathematical Engineering
SUZUKI, M., Control Systems Engineering
TAKAGI, F., Hydraulics and Hydrology
TAKAGI, K., Functional Crystal Chemistry
TAKAGI, N., Information Engineering Science
TAKAHASHI, K., Diffusional Separation Technology
TAKAI, O., Instrumentation and Analysis
TAKAI, Y., Superconducting Engineering
TAKAMURA, S., Basic Plasma Engineering
TAKEDA, Y., Intelligent Materials
TAKENO, T., Environmental Engineering Science and Systems
TAKEUCHI, H., Extraction and Membrane Separation
TANABE, T., Concrete Mechanics
TANAKA, E., Biomechanics
TANAKA, K., Continuum Mechanics
TANIGAWA, Y., Building Materials and Construction Systems
TANIGUCHI, G., Architectural Planning
TANIMOTO, M., Fundamentals of Information Electronics
TOKUNAGA, Y., Physical Metallurgy of Steel
TORIWAKI, J., Image Processing Graphics and Pattern Recognition
TSUBAKI, J., Function Development Technology
TSUGE, S., Instrumental Analysis
TSUJI, T., Nuclear and Functional Materials
TSUJIMOTO, M., Disaster Prevention and Safety Engineering
TSUNASHIMA, S., Magnetic Materials
UCHIKAWA, Y., Complex Systems Engineering
UMEMURA, A., Thermo Fluid Dynamics
USAMI, T., Structural Mechanics
VATCHKOV, G., Intelligent Control and Simulation
WATANABE, T., Knowledge Information Systems
YAMADA, K., Structural Engineering
YAMAGUCHI, K., Ultra Precision Technology
YAMAMOTO, H., Bioorganic and Biomimetic Chemistry
YAMAMOTO, I., Isotope Separation, Fission and Fusion Nuclear Fuel Cycle
YAMANE, T., Protein Crystallography, Structural Biology
YAMANE, Y., Control Engineering of Collective Neutron
YAMASHITA, H., Human Systems Engineering
YAMAUCHI, C., Physicochemical Processing of Materials
YASHIMA, E., Macromolecular Science
YASUDA, K., Knowledge-Based Design Technology
YASUDA, Y., Semiconductor Materials and Device Science

School of Agricultural Sciences and Graduate School of Bioagricultural Sciences:

DOKE, N., Bioresource Functions
EBIHARA, S., Biomodelling
FUKUTA, K., Biofunctions Development
HATTORI, K., Biosource Functions
HIRASHIMA, Y., Biomaterial Enginering
IMAI, T., Dynamics of Biomolecular Functions
ISOBE, M., Biofunctional Chemistry
KIMURA, M., Bioresource Functions
KIMURA, S., Mechanical Engineering for Biologists
KOBAYASHI, M., Biodynamics
MAKI, M., Applied Biochemistry
MAKINO, S., Applied Biochemistry
MATSUDA, T., Applied Biochemistry
MIYATA, T., Biofunctions Development
MIZUNO, T., Molecular and Cellular Biology
NAKAMURA, H., Biomodelling
MORIOKA, N., Forest Resources Utilization
NAKAMURA, H., Biomodelling
NAKAMURA, K., Molecular and Cellular Biology
NAMIKAWA, T., Genetics and Physiology
NIWA, H., Biofunctions Development
NOGUCHI, T., Applied Biochemistry
OKADA, M., Biofunctional Chemistry
OKUMURA, J., Genetics and Physiology
OKUYAMA, T., Biomaterial Physics
OMATA, T., Molecular and Cellular Biology
OSAWA, T., Biofunctional Chemistry
SAKAGAMI, Y., Biofunctional Chemistry
SASAKI, Y., Developmental and Genetic Regulation
SHIBATA, E., Forest Protection
SHIMADA, K., Genetics and Physiology
SUGIYAMA, T., Biodynamics
TAKEDA, Y., Forest Hydrology and Erosion Control
TAKEOKA, Y., Plant Resources and Environment
TAKESUE, S., Genetics and Physiology
TAKEYA, H., Socioeconomic Science of Food Production
TATSUMI, J., Crop Science
TSUKAGOSHI, N., Molecular and Cellular Biology
UMEMURA, T., Forest Environment and Resources
WAKASUGI, N., Genetics and Physiology
YAMAKI, S., Bioresource Functions
YAMAMOTO, S., Forest Ecology and Physiology
YAMANE, T., Molecular and Cellular Biology
YAMASHITA, O., Biofunctions Development
YASUDA, S., Forest Chemistry
YOKOTA, H., University Farm
YOSHIDA, S., University Farm

Graduate School of International Development:

AIKYO, M., Comparative Law and Vietnamese Law
CHUJO, N., Russian Language, Linguistics
EZAKI, M., Development Economics
IWASAKI, K., International Business Law, Commercial Dispute Regulation
KATO, H., International Environmental Co-operation, Environmental Law and Policy
KIMURA, H., International Relations, Regional Politics of Southeast Asia
MATSUMURA, Y., Computational Linguistics
NISHIMURA, Y., Agricultural and Rural Development, Development Project Management
OSADA, H., International Trade and Economic Development
TAKAHASHI, K., Japanese History, Maritime History
TSUDA, Y., International and Intercultural Communication
WAKABAYASHI, M., Organization Behaviour, International Human Resources Development, Educational Development
YAMADA, M., English Literature
YASUDA, N., Law and Development in Asia

Graduate School of Human Informatics:

HAYAKAWA, Y., Biological Informatics
ITAKURA, T., Informatics for Organizations
KAKEHI, K., Cognitive Informatics
KASUGA, Y., Informatics for Organizations
KOTANI, Y., Humanities in Informatics
MINEMURA, K., Informatics Models for the Natural Environment
MITSUI, T., Theoretical Foundations of Informatics
MORIMOTO, H., Electronic Society Systems
NISHIKAWA, T., Environment Informatics
SAITO, H., Cognitive Informatics
SASAI, M., Informatics Models for the Natural Environment
SHIBATA, H., Environmental Informatics
SHINODA, J., Theoretical Foundations of Informatics
TAKAHASHI, T., Humanities in Informatics
YAMASHITA, M., Chemical Physics of Complex Systems
YOKOI, S., Electronic Society Systems

Graduate School of Mathematics:

ACCARDI, L., Quantum Probability and Infinite Dimensional Analysis
AOMOTO, K., Analysis
GYOJA, A., Representation Theory
HASEGAWA, K., Computer Science, Physics of the Brain
ITO, H., Number Theory
KANAI, M., Geometry and Dynamic Systems
KIMURA, Y., Fluid Dynamics
KITAOKA, Y., Number Theory
KOBAYASHI, R., Differential Geometry
MATSUGI, T., Applied Econometrics
MIHASHI, K., Biophysics

MIYAKE, M., Partial Differential Equations
MIYAO, M., Public Health and Medical Mathematics
MUKAI, S., Algebraic Geometry
NAMIKAWA, Y., Algebraic Geometry
OHSAWA, T., Complex Analysis
OSADA, H, Probability Theory
SATO, H., Geometry
SHIOTA, M., Real Algebraic Geometry
TAKAHASHI, M., Polymathematical Analysis of Educational Finance
TSUCHIYA, A., Geometry and Mathematical Physics
UMEMURA, H., Algebraic Geometry

NARA WOMEN'S UNIVERSITY

Kita-Uoya-Higashi-Machi, Nara City 630-8506

Telephone: (742) 20-3330

Founded 1908

President: MASAKO NIWA
Secretary-General: YOSHIMI MORISAWA
Librarian: MINORU ISHIKAWA

Library of 485,000 vols
Number of teachers: 210
Number of students: 2,436

Publications: *Annual Report of Studies in Humanities and Social Sciences, Studies in Home Economics, Graduate School of Human Culture.*

DEANS

Department of Literature: Prof. S. SATO
Department of Science: Prof. K. YABUTA
Department of Human Life and Environment: Prof. H. KAWAI
Graduate School of Human Culture (Doctorate Course): Prof. M. ATARASHI

NIIGATA UNIVERSITY

8050 Ikarashi 2-no cho, Niigata City 950-2181

Telephone: (25) 223-6161
Fax: (25) 262-6539

Founded 1949
State control
Academic year: April to March

President: M. ARAKAWA
Chief Administrative Officer: K. KITAGAWA
Librarian: T. OKUMA

Library: see Libraries
Number of teachers: 1,251
Number of students: 12,849

Publications: faculty journals, reports, etc.

DEANS

Faculty of Humanities: S. FUKASAWA
Faculty of Education and Human Sciences: A. SATAKE
Faculty of Law: T. YAMASHITA
Faculty of Economics: T. FUJII
Faculty of Science: A. HASEGAWA
School of Medicine: M. IWAFUCHI
School of Dentistry: H. OZAWA
Faculty of Engineering: Y. SAITO
Faculty of Agriculture: M. KOJIMA
Graduate School of the Study of Modern Society and Culture: T. SATO
Graduate School of Science and Technology: K. IKEDA

ATTACHED INSTITUTE

Brain Research Institute: R. TANAKA

OBIHIRO UNIVERSITY OF AGRICULTURE AND VETERINARY MEDICINE

Inada-cho, Obihiro, Hokkaido 080-8555

Telephone: (155) 49-5111
Fax: (155) 49-5229
E-mail: sym@obihiro.ac.jp

Founded 1941
Academic year: April to March

President: Y. KUBO
Director of Administration Bureau: M. KIMURA
Director of University Library: S. ITOH

Library of 156,000 vols
Number of teachers: 146
Number of students: 1,448

Publications: *Research Bulletin* (on Natural Sciences and on Humanities and Social Sciences, each 2 a year).

ATTACHED RESEARCH INSTITUTE

Research Centre for Protozoan Molecular Immunology

OCHANOMIZU UNIVERSITY

1–1, Otsuka, 2-chome, Bunkyo-ku, Tokyo 112

Telephone: (3) 3943-3151

Founded 1874; reorganized 1949 as National University

President: J. OHTA
Administrator: S. DOH

Number of teachers: 300
Number of students: 2,314

DEANS

Faculty of Letters and Education: Y. TOKUMARU
Faculty of Science: Y. OGAWA
Faculty of Human Life and Environmental Science: N. ARAKAWA

OITA UNIVERSITY

700 Dannoharu, Oita City

Telephone: (975) 69-3311

Founded 1949
State control
Language of instruction: Japanese
Academic year: April to March (two semesters)

President: ARATA NOMURA
Director of Administration: KOICHI TSUJI
Librarian: HARUO FUKAMICHI

Library of 522,000 vols
Number of teachers: 381
Number of students: 5,103

DEANS

Faculty of Education: KANZO TOYOTA
Faculty of Economics: KATSUHIKO YOSHIME
Faculty of Engineering: KOICHI UTSUMIYA
General Education: HIROSHI KUSUMOTO

ATTACHED INSTITUTE

Tsurumi Seaside Research Institute: Aza-Hirama, Oaza-Ariakeura, Tsurumi-mati, Minamiamabe-gun, Oita 876-12; tel. (9723) 3-1133.

OKAYAMA UNIVERSITY

1–1, Naka 1-chome, Tsushima, Okayama 700–8530

Telephone: (86) 252-1111
Fax: (86) 254-6104

Founded 1949
State control
Academic year: April to March (2 semesters)

President: F. KOSAKA
Director-General: T. FUJII
Dean of Students: S. IZAWA
Library Director: H. KANDACHI

Library: see Libraries
Number of full-time teachers: 1,311
Number of students: 12,975

Publication: *Okayama University Bulletin.*

DEANS

Faculty of Letters: T. NARITA
Faculty of Law: H. ISHIJAMA
Faculty of Education: N. MORIKAWA
Faculty of Economics: K. TATEBE
Faculty of Science: K. SATOH
Medical School: T. UBUKA
Dental School: T. MATSUMURA
Faculty of Pharmaceutical Sciences: T. HARAYAMA
Faculty of Engineering: H. OSAKI
Faculty of Environmental Science and Technology: I. KONO
Faculty of Agriculture: S. UCHIDA
Graduate School of the Humanities and Social Sciences (Doctorate Course): K. IWAMA
Graduate School of Natural Science and Technology (Doctorate Course): M. IWAMI

PROFESSORS

Faculty of Letters:

ATSUMI, R., Cross-Cultural Social Psychology
FURUKAWA, T., English Literature
INADA, T., Archaeology
INAMURA, S., Ethics
ISHIDA, Y., History of Asia
KAIHARA, Y., English Philology
KANO, H., Japanese History
KINOSHITA, T., French Literature
KOBAYASHI, T., Sociology
KUDO, S., Japanese Literature
KURACHI, K., History of Japanese Culture
MITANI, K., Psychology
MORITAKI, K., Geography
MOTOIKE, R., European History
MUROYA, Y., English
NAGATA, R., European History
NARITA, T., Philosophy
NISHIMAE, T., American Literature
OGAWA, H., German
OKAMOTO, F., Chinese Language and Literature
SAITO, T., Japanese Art History
SCANLON, P., English
SHIMIZU, K., German Language
SHIMOKOBE, Y., Japanese Linguistics
TAKAHASHI, F., Ethics
TAKAHASHI, T., German Language and Literature
TAYA, R., Psychology
TSUJI, S., Linguistics
UCHIDA, K., Geography
UMEKI, E., French
WATANABE, M., Japanese Literature
WILKS, J., English

Faculty of Law:

ARAKI, M., Western Political History
ASADA, M., International Law
FUJITA, H., Civil Law
FUKAI, S., International Politics
HARANO, A., Administrative Law
HAYASE, T., Public Administration
IGUCHI, F., Constitutional Law
IMAMURA, Y., Civil Law
ISHIJIMA, H., Tax Law
IWAMA, K., History of Asian Political Ideas
KAMIYAMA, T., Penal Law
MATSUBAYASHI, K., Labour Law
MORIYA, A., Sociology of Law
NISHIHARA, J., Civil Law
NISHIMURA, M., Western Legal History
OBATA, T., Japanese Political History
OKADA, M., Administrative Law
OTSUKA, H., Penal Law
SANO, H., Private International Law
TAGASHIRA, S., Civil Procedure Law
TAKECHI, M., Commercial Law
TAMURA, U., Commercial Law
TANI, S., Political Process
TONAI, K., Labour Law
TSUNEMITSU, T., Criminology
UEMATSU, H., Philosophy of Law
UKON, T., Civil Law
YAMAGUCHI, K., Constitutional Law

Faculty of Economics:

FUJIMOTO, T., Theoretical Economics

FUJIMOTO, T., Econometrics
GENKA, T., Comparative Economic Systems
HARUNA, S., Microeconomics
ICHINOSE, A., Economic Policy
KANDACHI, H., Economic History of Japan
KUROKAWA, K., Economic History of the United States
MATSUMOTO, T., Economic History of Asia
MATSUO, N., Economic History
NAGATA, Y., Economic Statistics
NAKAMURA, R., Urban and Regional Economics
NIIMURA, S., History of Economic Thought
OOTA, Y., History of Economic Thought
SAKAMOTO, C., Local Public Finance
SATO, M., Accounting
SHIMIZU, K., Economic Dynamics
SHIMONO, K., Economic History of Modern Japan
TAKEMURA, S., Microeconomics
TATEBE, K., International Finance
WAKABAYASHI, M., Theory of Japanese Firms
WAKISAKA, A., Public Economics
YOSHIDA, T., Economic Statistics

Faculty of Education:

ARAKI, I., Physical Education
ARIMICHI, M., Instrumental Music
FUJII, T., Education of the Disabled
HIRASA, K., Industrial Design
HIRATA, K., Jurisprudence
IDO, K., Music Education
IKEDA, A., Geometry
INADA, T., Japanese Literature
INOUE, J., Electricity
INOUE, S., Educational Psychology
ISHIHARA, M., Education of School Health Care
ITAMI, T., Student Teaching
IZAWA, S., Psychology of Handicapped Children
KAMISHIMA, Y., Biology
KANETA, Y., Composition
KANI, K., Material Engineering
KASAI, Y., Science of Food Preparation
KOHARA, N., Physical Education
KOIDE, Y., Medicine for School Health Care
KONDO, I., Information Technology
KOSAKO, M., English Philology
KUSACHI, I., Mineralogy
MATSUHATA, K., English Language Education
MINAMOTO, Y., Japanese Language Education
MIYOSHI, T., Music Education
MIZUNO, M., Developmental Psychology
MORI, K., Chinese Philosophy
MORIKAWA, N., Pedagogy
MURATA, Y., Physical Education
NAKAO, Y., Chemistry
NII, I., Arts and Crafts Education
NISHIYAMA, M., Paintings
OGAWA, T., Paintings
OHASHI, Y., Physical Education
SAKATA, N., Physical Education
SANEKATA, N., Mathematical Analysis
SASAKI, M., Social Education
SUGIHARA, R., Clothing Science
TAKAHASHI, K., Fundamental Medicine
TAKAHASHI, T., Mathematics Education and Geography
TAKAHATA, M., School Management
TAKAYAMA, Y., Social Studies Education
TANAKA, F., Social Studies Education
TANAKA, K., Social Psychology
TARA, M., Natural Science Education
TOKUNAGA, T., Sport Education
TOMITA, F., Calligraphy
UEHARA, K., History
YAMAGUCHI, S., Psychology of Pre-school Children
YAMAMOTO, H., Systems Engineering
YAMASHITA, N., Solid State Spectroscopy
YAMAUCHI, M., History
YANAGAWA, K., Educational Health
YANAGIHARA, M., Psychology of Handicapped Children
YOSHIDA, N., Japanese Language
YOSHIDA, Y., Vocal Music

Faculty of Science:

ABUKU, S., Physics of Measurement
ASAMI, M., Petrology
ENOMOTO, M., Molecular Genetics
FUJII, M., Topology
HARADA, I., Theoretical Physics
INOMATA, N., Cytogenetics
IWACHIDO, T., Separation Chemistry
IWAMI, M., Thin Films and Surface Physics
KAGAWA, H., Molecular Biology
KAMADA, T., Molecular Cell Biology
KASE, K., Resources Geology
KASHINO, S., Structural and Polymer Chemistry
KIMURA, M., Synthetic and Physical Organic Chemistry
KOJIMA, M., Co-ordination Chemistry
KURATANI, S., Evolutionary Developmental Biology
MACHIDA, K., Mathematical Physics
MAEDA, H., XAFS
MIMURA, M., Topology
MOTOMIZU, S., Analytical Chemistry
NAGAO, M., Surface Chemistry
NAKAMURA, K., Solid State Spectroscopy
NAKANO, I., High Energy Physics
NAKASHIMA, H., Chronobiology
OHARA, H., Radiobiology
OSHIMA, K., Physics of Quantum Material
ONO, F., Physics of Material under Extreme Conditions
SAKAI, M., Neuroethology
SAKAI, T., Differential Geometry
SATO, R., Analysis
SATOH, K., Bioenergetics and Photobiology
SAWADA, A., Quantum Electromagnetic Physics
SHIBATA, T., Geology
SUZUKI, I., Geophysics
TAKAGI, K., Synthetic Organic Chemistry
TAKAHASHI, S., Endocrinology
TAKAMURA, H., Analysis
TANAKA, H., Theoretical Chemistry
TASAKA, T., Algebra
TSUKAMOTO, O., Atmospheric Science
YAMAMOTO, H., Organic Chemistry
YAMAMOTO, M., Geochemistry
YAMAMOTO, M., Marine Biology
YAMAMOTO, S., Physical Chemistry
YAMAMOTO, Y., Plant Physiology and Biochemistry
YAMAZAKI, H., Magnetism
YOSHIKAWA, Y., Inorganic Chemistry

Medical School:

ABE, K., Neurology
AKAGI, T., Pathology
AOYAMA, H., Hygiene
ARATA, J., Dermatology
HARADA, H., Laboratory Medicine
HARADA, M., Internal Medicine
HIRAKAWA, M., Anaesthesiology and Resuscitation
HIRAKI, Y., Radiology
INOUE, H., Orthopaedic Surgery
ISHIZU, H., Legal Medicine
KIRA, S.
KUDO, T., Obstetrics and Gynaecology
KUMON, H., Urology
KURODA, S., Neuropsychiatry
MAKINO, H., Internal Medicine
MASUDA, Y., Otorhinolaryngology
MATSUI, H., Physiology
MURAKAMI, T., Anatomy
NAKAYAMA, E., Parasitology and Immunology
NANBA, M., Cell Biology
NINOMIYA, Y., Molecular Biology and Biochemistry
OHE, T., Cardiovascular Medicine
OGAWA, N., Neuroscience
OGUMA, K., Bacteriology
OHMOTO, T., Neurological Surgery
OHTSUKI, H., Ophthalmology
OKA, E., Child Neurology
OKADA, S., Pathology
SAEKI, K., Pharmacology
SANO, S., Cardiovascular Surgery
SASAKI, J., Anatomy
SEINO, Y., Paediatrics
SEKI, S., Molecular Biology
SHIMIZU, K., Molecular Genetics
SHIMIZU, N., Surgery
SUGA, H., Physiology
TANAKA, N., Surgery
TOKUNAGA, A., Anatomy
TSUJI, T., Internal Medicine
UBUKA, T., Biochemistry
YAMADA, M., Virology
YASUDA, T., Cell Chemistry

Dental School:

FUKUI, K., Microbiology
FURUTA, H., Pharmacology
INOUE, K., Operative Dentistry
KISHI, K., Oral Radiology
MATSUMURA, T., Oral and Maxillofacial Surgery II
MURAYAMA, Y., Periodontology and Endodontology
NAGAI, N., Oral Pathology
SATO, T., Removable Prosthodontics
SHIMONO, T., Paediatric Dentistry
SUGAHARA, T., Oral and Maxillofacial Surgery I
SUGIMOTO, T., Oral Anatomy II
SUZUKI, K., Dental Materials
TAKIGAWA, M., Biochemistry and Molecular Dentistry
WATANABE, T., Preventive Dentistry
YAMASHITA, A., Fixed Prosthodontics
YAMAMOTO, T., Orthodontics

Faculty of Pharmaceutical Sciences:

HARAYAMA, T., Synthetic and Medicinal Chemistry
HAYATSU, H., Bio-organic Chemistry
HIROTA, T., Pharmaceutical Chemistry
KAMEI, C., Pharmacology
KAWASAKI, H., Clinical Pharmacy
KIMURA, T., Pharmaceutics
NAKAYAMA, T., Pharmaceutical Fundamental Science
NARIMATSU, S., Health Chemistry
SAITO, Y., Pharmaceutical Analytical Chemistry
SHINODA, S., Environmental Hygiene
TAMAGAKE, K., Pharmaceutical Physical Chemistry
TSUCHIYA, T., Microbiology
WATAYA, Y., Medicinal Information
YAMAMOTO, I., Immunochemistry
YOSHIDA, T., Pharmacognosy

Faculty of Engineering:

ABE, T., Elasticity and Plasticity
AKAGI, H., Power Electronics
HASHIGUCHI, K., Information Engineering Fundamentals
HIDA, M., Engineering Materials
INABA, H., Heat Transfer Engineering
INOUE, A., Systems Engineering
KAGAWA, Y., Computational Engineering
KAMIURA, Y., Materials Science
KANAZAWA, H., Genetic Engineering
KOGA, R., Electronic Systems
KONISHI, T., Information Procreation
MASAKI, A., VLSI Computer
MIYAZAKI, S., Engineering Mathematics
MORIKAWA, Y., Signal Processing and Transmission
NAKAJIMA, T., Precision Machining Technology
NAKANISHI, K., Biochemical Engineering
NOGI, S., Electronic Circuits
NORITSUGU, T., Mechanical Control and Robotics
OKAMOTO, T., Computer Systems
OMORI, H., Applied Cell Biology

OSAKA, A., Biomaterials
OSAKI, H., Industrial Management Systems
SAITO, S., Organic and Bio-organic Chemistry
SAKATA, Y., Chemical Reaction Engineering
SHAKUNAGA, T., Computer Vision and Artificial Intelligence
SHIMAMURA, K., Organic Materials
SHISHIDO, M., Bioelectric and Biophotonic Molecules
SUGIYAMA, Y., Computer Software
SUZUKI, K., Reliability and Safety Engineering
TAKADA, J., Advanced Ceramics
TAKAHASHI, N., Electrical Machines
TAKAI, K., Organic and Organometallic Chemistry
TANAKA, Y., Man–Machine Systems
TANAKA, Z., Separation Engineering
TARI, I., Inorganic Electrochemistry
TORAYA, T., Enzyme Science and Technology
TORII, T., Strength of Materials
TOTSUJI, H., Intelligent Electronic Devices and Electronic Materials
UNEYAMA, K., Molecular Design and Synthesis
UNO, Y., Non-traditional Machining
UTAKA, M., Synthetic Organic Chemistry
WASHIO, S., Oil Hydraulic Engineering
YAMADA, H., Protein Engineering
YAMAMOTO, K., Fluid Engineering
YAMASAKI, S., Computational Logic
YOSHIDA, A., Machine Design and Tribology

Faculty of Environmental Science and Technology:

ADACHI, T., Soil Technology
AKAE, T., Land Conservation and Consolidation
BABA, S., Historical Studies in Civil Engineering
FUJII, H., Geotechnical and Structural Engineering in Rural Areas
ICHIMINAMI, F., Agricultural and Rural Geography
IKEHATA, S., Ring Theory
ISHIKAWA, H., Number Theory
KASHIWASE, S., English
KAWABATA, A., German Literature
KAWABATA, C., Computer Science
KAWARA, O., Management of Water Environment
KITAMURA, S., Regional Development
KITAMURA, Y., Chemical Engineering
KONO, I., Geotechnology
MIURA, Y., Environmental Inorganic Materials
MIYAKE, M., Environmental Inorganic Materials
MYOJIN, S., Urban Transport Planning
MOROKAWA, S., American Literature
NAGAI, A., Applied Hydrology
NAGO, H., Hydraulics
NAKAJIMA, A., Ring Theory
NISHIGAKI, M., Geo-Environmental Engineering
NODA, R., Combinatorics
OHTAKI, E., Environmental Physics
OKUMURA, T., Geotechnical Engineering
OTAKE, M., Applied Statistics
SAKATA, K., Concrete Technology
SASAOKA, E., Catalytic Reaction Engineering
SHINABE, Y., Agricultural Economics
TAKEMIYA, H., Seismic Analysis of Soils and Structures
TANAKA, Y., Multivariate Statistical Analysis
TANIGUCHI, T., Computational Mechanics
TARUMI, T., Statistical Expert Systems
TONOMURA, N., German
TSUBOI, S., Environmental Organic Chemistry
WATANABE, M., Applied Mathematics
YAMASHITA, Y., Polymer Science and Technology
YOMOTA, A., Irrigation and Drainage
YOSHIO, T., Environmental Durability of Materials

Faculty of Agriculture:

BABA, N., Chemistry of Biocatalysts
CHIBA, K., Applied Plant Ecology
FUJISAKI, K., Applied Population Ecology
HIGASHIDE, E., Research and Evaluation of Microbial Products
INABA, A., Postharvest Physiology and Biochemistry
IZUMIMOTO, M., Animal Foods Technology
KAGEYAMA, Y., Nutritional Management of Horticultural Crops
KATAOKA, K., Animal Products Technology
KONDO, Y., Animal Physiology and Pharmacology
KUBOTA, N., Management of Intensive Horticulture
KURODA, T., Cropping Systems
MASUDA, M., Vegetable Propagation
MIYAMOTO, T., Animal Products Technology
MOHRI, K., Agricultural Machinery
NAKAJIMA, S., Chemistry of Biological Reactions
NAKASUJI, F., Integrated Pest Management
NIWA, K., Animal Reproduction
OKAMOTO, G., Control of Fruit Development
SATO, K., Laboratory Animals Science
SATO, T., Resources Management
SHIRAISHI, T., Plant Pathology
SUGIO, T., Applied and Environmental Microbiology
TADA, M., Cell Physiology
TANAKA, H., Applied Biochemistry and Biotechnology
UCHIDA, S., Animal Feed Science and Technology
YAMADA, T., Applied Genetic Engineering
YOSHIKAWA, K., Revegetation Ecology

ATTACHED INSTITUTES

Research Institute for Bioresources: 20-1, Chuo 2-chome, Kurashiki, Okayama 710-0046; tel. (86) 424-1661; fax (86) 421-0699; f. 1914; affiliated 1951; Dir Prof. F. MOTOYOSHI.

Institute for Study of the Earth's Interior: 827, Yamada, Misasa-cho, Tohaku-gun, Tottori 682-0193; tel. (858) 43-1215; fax (858) 43-2184; f. 1985; Dir Prof. I. KUSHIRO.

School of Health Sciences: 5-1, Shikata-cho 2-chome, Okayama 700-8558; tel. (86) 223-7151; fax (86) 222-3717; f. 1986; Dean Prof. H. ENDO.

OSAKA UNIVERSITY

1-1 Yamadaoka, Suita, Osaka 565-0871

Telephone: (6) 6877-5111
Fax: (6) 6879-7039
E-mail: w60195a@center.osaka-u.ac.jp

Founded 1931
Academic year: April to March

President: Dr TADAMITSU KISHIMOTO
Vice-Presidents: MASAAKI HOMMA, TADANORI MAYUMI
Director: MITSUO MIMURA
Librarian: HIROSHI NISHIHARA

Libraries: see Libraries
Number of teachers: 2,479, including 684 professors
Number of students: 18,947

Publications include: *Osaka Journal of Mathematics, Medical Journal, Law Review, Osaka Economic Papers, Dental School Journal, Memoirs of the Faculty of Pharmaceutical Sciences, Science Reports, Technology Reports, Memoirs of the Institute of Scientific and Industrial Research, Studies in Language and Culture,* reprint series, discussion papers, etc.

DEANS

Faculty of Letters: MINORU KAWAKITA
Faculty of Human Sciences: YOSHIAKI NAKAJIMA
Faculty of Law: ISAO NAKAYAMA
Faculty of Economics: HIDEO HASHIMOTO
Faculty of Science: MASAYOSHI MIYANISHI
Faculty of Medicine: YUKIHIKO KITAMURA
Faculty of Dentistry: TOSHIFUMI MORIMOTO
Faculty of Pharmaceutical Sciences: AKEMICHI BABA
Faculty of Engineering: MASAHIRO JONO
Faculty of Engineering Science: HIDEO MIYAHARA
Graduate School of Language and Culture: TOSHINORI TAMAI
Osaka School of International Public Policy: MITSURU KUROSAWA
Faculty of Language and Culture: MITSUNORI IMAI
School of Health and Sport Sciences: KAZUYUKI YOSHIZAKI

PROFESSORS

Faculty of Letters:

AISAKA, S., Western History
AMANO, F., Theatre Studies
ASANO, R., Philosophy, Modern Thought and Cultural Studies
EGAWA, A., Western History
FUJII, H., English Literature
FUKUSHIMA, Y., Chinese Literature
GOTO, A., Japanese Language and Literature
HACHIYA, M., Japanese Language and Literature
HAMASHIMA, A., Asian Studies
HAYASHI, M., German Literature
II, H., Japanese Language and Literature
IKAI, T., Japanese History
ISHIDA, H., English Literature
KAJI, N., Chinese Philosophy
KAMBAYASHI, T., Aesthetics
KAMIKURA, T., Aesthetics
KASHIWAGI, T., French Literature
KATAYAMA, T., Asian History
KAWAKAMI, S., English Linguistics
KAWAKITA, M., Western History
KAWAMURA, K., Historical Studies of Cultural Exchanges
KOBAYASHI, S., Human Geography
KOEZUKA, T., Art History
KUDO, M., Japanese Linguistics
MAEDA, T., Japanese Language and Literature
MIZOGUCHI, K., Philosophy, Modern Thought and Cultural Studies
MORITANI, U., Science of Literary Arts
MORIYASU, T., Central Asian History
MURATA, S., Japanese History
NAITO, T., Comparative Literature
NAKAMURA, I., Historical Studies of Cultural Exchanges
NAKAMURA, M., German Literature
NAKAOKA, N., Clinical Philosophy and Ethics
NEGISHI, K., Musicology
OKUDAIRA, S., Art History
SANADA, S., Japanese Linguistics
SATOMI, G., Philosophy and History of Philosophy
SUGIHARA, T., Historical Studies of Cultural Exchanges
TAIRA, M., Japanese History
TOKI, S., Japanese Linguistics
TONO, H., Japanese History
TSUDE, H., Archaeology
WAKAYAMA, E., Art History
WASHIDA, K., Clinical Philosophy and Ethics
YAMAGATA, Y., Philosophy and History of Philosophy
YAMAGUTI, O., Musicology

Faculty of Human Sciences:

ABE, A., Educational Organization and Administration
HASHIMOTO, M., Historical Sociology
HATA, M., Sociological Study of Educational Planning
HINOBAYASHI, T., Developmental Psychology

HIRANO, M., Educational Study of Human Development
HIRASAWA, Y., Human Rights Education
IKEDA, H., Comparative Study of Education and Culture
INOUE, M., Educational Technology Development
ITO, K., Communication Studies and Cultural Sociology
KASHIWAGI, T., Clinical Psychiatry and Geriatric Behavioural Science
KASUGA, N., Cultural Anthropology
KIKUCHI, J., Sociology of Education
KIMAE, T., History of Social Thought
KOIZUMI, J., Cultural Anthropology
KONDO, H., Educational Demography
KOTO, Y., Theoretical Sociology and History of Sociological Thought
KURAMITSU, O., Clinical Psychology of Education
KUWANO, S., Environmental Psychology
MAESAKO, T., Educational Technology
MIKI, Y., Educational Psychology
MINAMI, T., Comparative and Developmental Psychology
MISHIMA, K., Comparative Study of Civilizations
MIURA, T., Applied Cognitive Psychology
NAKAJIMA, Y., General Psychology
NAKAMURA, T., Psychology of Human Information Processing
NAKAYAMA, Y., Foundations of Human Sciences
NIGI, H., Biological Anthropology
OKU, M., Foundations of Human Sciences
OKUMA, K., Sociology of Volunteer Activity
OMORI, M., Traffic Psychology
OMURA, E., Clinical Sociology
SHIRAKASHI, S., Social Psychology
SHIRAKURA, Y., Empirical Sociology and Social Research Methodology
SUGAI, K., Educational Technology
SUGENO, T., Philosophical Anthropology
TOMODA, Y., Adult Education and Out-of-School Education for Youth
TOYAMA, M., Social Psychology
UTSUMI, S., International Co-operation in the Field of Education
YAMAGUCHI, S., Studies of Post-Industrial Society
YAMAMOTO, T., Behavioural Physiology
YOSHIDA, M., Behaviourmetrics

Faculty of Law:

EGUCHI, J., International Economic Law
HAYASHI, T., Western Legal History
HIRATA, K., Civil Law III
IKEDA, T., Civil Procedure Law
KAWATA, J., Political Science
KOJIMA, N., Labour Law
KUNII, K., Civil Law I
MATSUI, S., Comparative Constitutional Law
MATSUOKA, H., International Business Transactions
MATSUURA, Y., Jurisprudence
MITSUNARI, K., Western Legal History
MURAKAMI, T., Administrative Law
NAKAO, T., Japanese Legal History
NAKAYAMA, I., Constitutional Law
NISHIMURA, K., Asian Law and Politics
OKABE, Y., Criminal Procedural Law
ROSLER, A. C. E., Local Government Law and Tax Law
SAKAMOTO, K., International Relations
SHIOMI, Y., Civil Law II
SUENAGA, T., Commercial Law I
TAGO, K., Political History
TANAKA, S., Comparative Legal Cultures
TAKENAKA, Y., Comparative Legal and Political Systems
WATANABE, S., International Civil Procedural Law
YOSHIMOTO, K., Commercial Law II

Faculty of Economics:

ABE, T., Management Theory
AMAKO, T., Management Theory
ASADA, T., Management Science
BAN, K., Economic Policy
HASHIMOTO, H., Economic Policy
HONMA, M., Applied Economics
HONDA, Y., Applied Economics
INOKI, T., Economic Policy
MIYAMOTO, M., Economic History
NAGATANI, H., Economic Theory
NAKAJIMA, N., Management Science
NISHINA, K., Management Science
OMORI, T., Economic Policy
SAITO, S., Economic Policy
SAMURA, T., Economic History
SANADA, H., Management Science
SAWAI, M., Economic History
SUGIHARA, K., Economic Policy
TABATA, Y., Management Science
TAKAGI, S., Economic Theory
TAKAO, H., Management Theory
TAKEDA, E., Management Science
TSUTSUI, Y., Applied Economics
YAMADA, M., Economic Policy

Faculty of Science:

ADACHI, K., Polymer Physical Chemistry
AKAI, H., Quantum Physics
AKUTSU, Y., Quantum Physics
DATE, E., Applied Mathematics
FUKUYAMA, K., Structural Biology
FUJIKI, A., Global Mathematics
HARADA, A., Supermolecular Science
HASE, S., Organic Biochemistry
HIBI, T., Experimental Mathematics
HIGASHIJIMA, K., Fundamental Physics
HIRATA, M., Condensed Matter Physics
IBUKIYAMA, T., Algebra
IKAWA, M., Applied Mathematics
IKEYA, M., Quantum Geophysics
KAIZAKI, S., Inorganic Chemistry
KANAZAWA, H., Molecular Biology
KASAI, T., Reaction Dynamics
KATAKUSE, I., Mesoscopic Physics
KATORI, K., Laboratory of Nuclear Studies
KAWAKUBO, K., Geometry
KAWANAKA, N., Algebra
KAWAMURA, S., Sensory Physiology
KAWARAZAKI, S., Solid State Physics
KIKKAWA, K., Fundamental Physics
KINOSHITA, S., Interdisciplinary Physics
KISHIMOTO, T., Physics of Particles and Nuclei
KOTANI, S., Analysis
KOISO, N., Geometry
KURAMITSU, S., Physical Biochemistry
KUSHI, Y., Co-ordination Chemistry
KUSUMOTO, S., Natural Products Chemistry
MABUCHI, T., Global Mathematics
MATSUDA, J., Planetary Science
MATSUMURA, A., Applied Mathematics
MATSUO, T., Physical Chemistry of Condensed Matter
MATSUO, T., Interdisciplinary Physics
MINAMISONO, T., Physics of Particles and Nuclei
MIYAKO, Y., Condensed Matter Physics
MIYANISHI, M., Algebra
MIYASHITA, S., Condensed Matter Physics
MORISHIMA, Y., Macromolecular Functions
MURASE, K., Condensed Matter Physics
NAGASE, M., Analysis
NAGASHIMA, Y., Physics of Particles and Nuclei
NAKAMURA, N., Structural Physical Chemistry
NAKANISHI, Y., Developmental Biology
NAKASUJI, K., Physical Organic Chemistry
NAMBA, M., Geometry
NISHITANI, T., Analysis
NORISUYE, T., Polymer Solutions
ODA, M., Structural Organic Chemistry
OGURA, A., Comparative Physiology
OHNO, T., Laser Photochemistry
OHTSUBO, H., Fundamental Physics
OHYAMA, T., Condensed Matter Physics
ONUKI, Y., Condensed Matter Physics
SAITOH, M., Condensed Matter Physics
SAKANE, Y., Global Mathematics
SASAKI, M., Cosmology
SORAI, M., Microcalorimetry Research Center
SUNAMURA, T., Geomorphology
SUZUKI, S., Bioinorganic Chemistry
SUZUKI, T., Experimental Mathematics
TAKAHARA, F., Theoretical Astrophysics
TAKAHASHI, N., Physics of Particles and Nuclei
TAKASUGI, E., Fundamental Physics
TAKEI, H., Materials Science
TASHIRO, K., Polymer Structure
TERASHIMA, I., Plant Ecophysiology
TOKUNAGA, F., Extreme-Environmental Biology
TSUNEKI, K., Animal Morphology
TSUNEMI, H., Astrophysics
USUI, S., Algebra
WATARAI, H., Analytical Chemistry
YAMAGUCHI, K., Quantum Chemistry
YAMAMOTO, Y., Experimental Mathematics
YAMANAKA, T., Physics of Matter

Faculty of Medicine:

AMINO, N., Laboratory Medicine
AOZASA, K., Molecular Pathology
ASO, Y., Basic Nursing
BEPPU, S., Medical Physics
DOHI, Y., Community Health
EGAWA, T., Adult and Geriatric Nursing
FUJIWARA, H., Medical Engineering
FUKUDA, Y., Physiology
HAMAOKA, T., Oncogenesis
HARADA, T., Reproductive and Paediatric Nursing
HARUNA, M., Medical Engineering
HASEGAWA, T., Medical Engineering
HAYAKAWA, K., Community Health
HIRANO, T., Molecular Oncology
HORI, M., Internal Medicine I
INAGAKI, S., Basic Laboratory Sciences
INAMOTO, K., Medical Physics
INAMURA, K., Medical Engineering
INOUE, O., Medical Physics
INOUE, T., Multidisciplinary Radiotheraphy
ISHIMOTO, A., Adult and Geriatric Nursing
IWATANI, Y., Clinical Laboratory Sciences
KANAKURA, Y., Haematology and Oncology
KANOSUE, K., Basic Laboratory Sciences
KIDO, Y., Adult and Geriatric Nursing
KITAMURA, Y., Pathology
KONO, N., Basic Laboratory Sciences
KUBO, T., Otorhinolaryngology
KURACHI, Y., Pharmacology II
KUROKAWA, N., Pharmacy
MATSUDA, H., Surgery I
MATSUURA, N., Clinical Laboratory Sciences
MATSUZAWA, Y., Internal Medicine II
MIKAMI, H., Community Health
MIKI, N., Pharmacology I
MIYASAKA, M., Organ Bioregulation
MIYAZAKI, J., Nutrition and Physiological Chemistry
MONDEN, M., Surgery II
MORIMOTO, K., Environmental Health and Preventive Medicine
MURATA, Y., Obstetrics and Gynaecology
NAGATA, S., Genetics
NAKAMURA, H., Radiology
NAKAMURA, T., Biochemistry
NAKAMURA, Y., Clinical Genetics
NISHIMURA, T., Tracer Analysis
NOGUCHI, S., Surgical Oncology
NOMURA, T., Radiation Biology
OCHI, T., Orthopaedic Surgery
OGASAWARA, C., Fundamental Nursing
OGIHARA, T., Medicine and Geriatrics
OGINO, S., Adult and Geriatric Nursing
OHNO, Y., Fundamental Nursing
OKADA, A., Paediatric Surgery
OKADA, S., Paediatrics
OKAMOTO, M., Physiological Chemistry
OKANO, H., Functional Neuroanatomy
OKUYAMA, A., Urology

ORITA, Y., Clinical Laboratory Sciences
SIRAKURA, R., Organ Transplantation
SOBUE, K., Neurochemistry and Neuropharmacology
SUGIMOTO, H., Traumatology and Emergency Medicine
SUGIYAMA, H., Clinical Laboratory Sciences
SUZUKI, A., Reproductive and Paediatric Nursing
TADA, M., Molecular Pathology
TAKAGI, Y., Reproductive and Paediatric Nursing
TAKAI, Y., Molecular Biology and Biochemistry
TAKEDA, H., Medical Information Science
TAKEDA, J., Environmental Health and Preventive Medicine
TAKEDA, M., Neuropsychiatry
TAMURA, S., Functional Diagnostic Imaging
TANIGUCHI, N., Biochemistry
TANO, Y., Ophthalmology
TATARA, K., Public Health
TOYAMA, M., Anatomy and Neuroscience
TSUJIMOTO, Y., Medical Genetics
TSUMOTO, T., Neurophysiology
UCHIYAMA, Y., Anatomy I
WATANABE, S., Adult and Geriatric Nursing
YAMAJI, K., Reproductive and Paediatric Nursing
YAMANISHI, K., Bacteriology
YAMATODANI, A., Medical Physics
YANAGIDA, T., Physicochemical Physiology
YANAGIHARA, T., Neurology
YONEDA, Y., Anatomy III
YORIFUJI, S., Basic Laboratory Sciences
YOSHIKAWA, K., Dermatology
YOSHIYA, I., Anaesthesiology

Faculty of Dentistry:

EBISU, S., Conservative Dentistry
FUCHIHATA, H., Oral and Maxillofacial Radiology
HAMADA, S., Oral Microbiology
IJUIN, N., Oral Pathology
KURISU, K., Oral Anatomy, Developmental Biology
MAEDA, Y., Division for Interdisciplinary Dentistry
MARUYAMA, T., Prosthetic Dentistry I
MATSUURA, H., Dental Anaesthesiology
MATSUYA, T., Oral and Maxillofacial Surgery I
MORIMOTO, T., Oral Physiology
NOKUBI, T., Prosthetic Dentistry II
OKADA, H., Periodontology and Endodontology
SAKUDA, M., Oral and Maxillofacial Surgery II
SHIGENAGA, Y., Oral Anatomy
SHIZUKUISHI, S., Preventive Dentistry
SOBUE, S., Pedodontics
TAKADA, K., Orthodontics
TAKAHASHI, J., Dental Materials Science and Technology
WADA, T., Division for Oral-Facial Disorders
YONEDA, T., Molecular and Cellular Biochemistry, Biomedicine and Biodentistry

Faculty of Pharmaceutical Sciences:

AZUMA, J., Clinical Evaluation of Medicines and Therapeutics
BABA, A., Molecular Neuropharmacology
DOI, T., Protein Molecular Engineering
IMANISHI, T., Bio-organic Chemistry
KITA, Y., Synthetic Organic Chemistry
KOBAYASHI, M., Natural Product Chemistry
KOBAYASHI, Y., Biophysical Chemistry
MAEDA, M., Biochemistry and Molecular Biology
MATSUDA, T., Medicinal Pharmacology
MAYUMI, T., Biopharmaceutics
MIYAMOTO, K., Environmental Bioengineering
MIZOGUCHI, T., Bio-Functional Molecular Chemistry
NASU, M., Environmental Science and Microbiology
NISHIHARA, T., Environmental Biochemistry
OHMORI, H., Analytical Chemistry
TAKAGI, T., Pharmaceutical Information Science
TANAKA, K., Toxicology
YAMAMOTO, H., Immunology

Faculty of Engineering:

Department of Material and Life Science:

FUKUZUMI, S., Physical Chemistry for Life Science
ICHIOKA, Y., Photonic Information Technology
KANAYA, S., Biological Extremity Engineering
MIYATA, M., Molecular Recognition Chemistry
UMENO, M., Applied Surface Science
YANAGIDA, S., Molecular Process Engineering
YOKOYAMA, M., Molecular System Engineering

Department of Molecular Chemistry:

BABA, A., Resources Chemistry
IKEDA, I., Industrial Organic Chemistry
INOUE, Y., Molecular Interaction Chemistry
KUROSAWA, H., Inorganic Synthetic Chemistry
MATSUBAYASHI, G., Chemistry of Physical Properties
MURAI, S., Molecular Design
NOMURA, M., Applied Molecular Chemistry

Department of Materials Chemistry:

ADACHI, G., Inorganic Materials Chemistry
HIRAO, T., Materials Synthetic Chemistry
KAI, Y., Structural Physical Chemistry
KOMATSU, M., Synthetic Organic Chemistry
NOJIMA, M., Structural Organic Chemistry
OSHIMA, T., Theoretical Organic Chemistry
SHIROTA, Y., Organic Materials Chemistry
YONEYAMA, H., Applied Electrochemistry

Department of Biotechnology:

HARASHIMA, S., Molecular Genetics
KOBAYASHI, A., Cell Technology
MUROOKA, Y., Biological Resources
SHIOYA, S., Ecosystems Technology
SUGA, K., Biochemical Engineering
URABE, I., Enzyme Engineering
YAMADA, Y., Biomaterial Chemistry

Department of Precision Science and Technology:

AONO, M., Atomically Controlled Processes
HIROSE, K., Computational Physics
KATAOKA, T., Quantum Measurement and Instrumentation
KISHIDA, K., Applied Mechanics
MORI, Y., Ultra-precision Machining
MORITA, M., Scientific Hardware Systems
YOSHII, K., Functional Materials

Department of Applied Physics:

ISHII, H., General Applications of Statistical Inferences and Operations Research
ITOH, K., Applied Optics and Optical Information Processing
KAWAKAMI, N., Theory of Condensed Matter Physics
KAWATA, S., Scientific Instrumentation and Optics
KINOSHITA, K., Computer Engineering
MASUHARA, H., Laser Photochemistry and Microspectroscopy
NAKASHIMA, S., Solid State Physics and Optical Properties of Solids
SHIMIZU, R., Applied Solid State Physics, Surface and Interface Physics and Electron Microscopy
YAGI, A., Applied Mathematical Analysis

Department of Adaptive Machine Systems:

ASADA, M., Emergent Robotics
KITAGAWA, H., Microdynamics
MINAMINO, Y., Intelligent Materials
OHJI, T., Advanced Materials Processing
OHNAKA, I., Materials Processing and Devices

Department of Mechanophysics Engineering:

INABA, T., Morphology in Machine Phenomena
KATAOKA, I., Fluid Engineering and Thermohydrodynamics
KATSUKI, M., Energy Science and Engineering
MIYAKE, Y., Fluid Engineering and Thermohydrodynamics
NAKAMURA, K., Complex Fluid Mechanics
TAKAGI, T., Energy Science and Engineering
TSUJI, Y., Complex Fluid Mechanics

Department of Mechanical Engineering and Systems:

HANASAKI, S., Production and Measurement Systems Engineering
JONO, M., Materials and Structures Evaluation
KUBO, S., Materials and Structures Evaluation
MIYOSHI, T., Production and Measurement Systems Engineering

Department of Computer-controlled Mechanical Systems:

AKAGI, S., Design and Manufacturing Engineering
FURUSHO, J., Real World Active Intelligence
IKEDA, M., Control Engineering
SHIRAI, Y., Real World Active Intelligence

Department of Materials Science and Processing:

HARA, S., Interface Science and Technology
IIDA, T., Thermophysics of Materials
NAGAI, H., Science and Processing of Powder Materials
OTSUKA-YAO-MATSUO, S., Purification and Synthesis of Materials
SHIBATA, T., Environmental Materials and Surface Processing
USUI, T., Materials Processing and Metallurgy

Department of Materials Science and Engineering:

SABURI, T., Physics of Solids
SAITO, Y., Control of Materials Function and Morphology
SHIRAI, Y., Nanoscale Characterization of Structure-Sensitive Properties
UMAKOSHI, Y., Lattice Defects and Crystal Plasticity
YAMAMOTO, M., Physics of Surface and Interface

Department of Manufacturing Science:

ARAI, E., Integrated Manufacturing Systems
KOBAYASHI, K., Smart Materials Processing
MIYAMOTO, I., Intelligent Materials Processing Systems
NAKATA, S., Micro-Nano Systems
NISHIMOTO, K., Materials Joining
TOYODA, M., Strength/Fracture Evaluation for Manufacturing
ZAKO, M., Design in Advanced Materials and Reliability

Department of Electronic, Information Systems and Energy Engineering:

HORIIKE, H., Electromagnetic Fluid Engineering
IIDA, T., Fusion Engineering
KISHINO, F., Human Interface Engineering
NAKAI, S., Laser Engineering
NISHIKAWA, M., Supra-High-Temperature Engineering
TANIGUCHI, K., Quantum Devices
TANINO, T., Systems Analysis and Optimization

Department of Electrical Engineering:

HIRAO, T., Thin Film Engineering
KUMAGAI, S., Control Engineering
MATSUURA, K., Electric Power Engineering
SASAKI, T., Applied Electro-Physics
TSUJI, K., Systems Engineering

Department of Communications Engineering:
IKEDA, H., Telecommunications Network Engineering
KODAMA, Y., Mathematical Modelling of Optical Communication Systems
KOMAKI, S., Microwave and Optical Communication Systems
MAEDA, H., Systems Technology in Communication Engineering
MORINAGA, N., Telecommunication Systems and Technologies
SHIOZAWA, T., Electromagnetic Wave Theory and Applications

Department of Electronic Engineering:
HAMAGUCHI, C., Semiconductor Electronics
MORITA, S., Microscopic Quantum Engineering
NISHIHARA, H., Integrated Optoelectronics
OURA, K., Surface and Interface Electronics
YOSHINO, K., Electronic Material Engineering

Department of Information Systems Engineering:
FUJIOKA, H., Integrated Systems Engineering
KOMODA, N., Intelligent Information Systems Engineering
MURAKAMI, K., Fundamentals of Information Systems
NISHIO, S., Information Base Engineering
SHIRAKAWA, I., Information Systems Synthesis

Department of Nuclear Engineering:
KATSURA, M., Thermodynamics of Nuclear Materials
MIYAZAKI, K., Nuclear Reactor Engineering
TAKAHASHI, A., Neutronics and Nuclear Instrumentation
TAKEDA, T., Reactor Physics
YAMAMOTO, T., Nuclear Chemical Engineering
YAMANAKA, S., Solid State Physics of Nuclear Fuel

Department of Global Architecture:
IMAI, K., Regional Environment and Global Transport
SUZUKI, T., Regional Environment and Global Transport
TANIMOTO, C., Sustainable Development and Strategy

Department of Naval Architecture and Ocean Engineering:
FUNAKI, T., Naval Architecture
HAMAMOTO, M., Naval Architecture
NAITO, S., Marine Systems Engineering
TOMITA, Y., Marine Systems Engineering

Department of Civil Engineering:
MATSUI, S., Structural and Geotechnical Engineering
MATSUI, T., Structural and Geotechnical Engineering
MORI, Y., Social Systems Engineering
MURAOKA, K., Social Systems Engineering
NAKATSUJI, K., Social Systems Engineering
NISHIMURA, N., Structural and Geotechnical Engineering

Department of Architectural Engineering:
FUNAHASHI, K., Architectural Design
INOUE, Y., Structural Engineering
KASHIHARA, S., Architectural Design
OHNO, Y., Structural Engineering
TACHIBANA, E., Structural Engineering
YOSHIDA, K., Architectural Design

Department of Environmental Engineering:
FUJITA, M., Water Science and Environmental Biotechnology
MIZUNO, M., Energy and Environmental Systems
MORIOKA, T., Environmental Systems Management
NARUMI, K., Urban Environmental Design
SASADA, T., Information Engineering for Urban Design
YAMAGUCHI, K., Atmospheric Environmental Engineering

Plasma Physics Laboratory:
GOTO, S., Plasma Production
OKADA, S., Plasma Diagnostics

Faculty of Engineering Science:

Department of Physical Science:
AMAYA, K., High Pressure Physics
CHO, K., Solid State Theory
GAMO, K., Nanofabrication and Nanodevices
HIYAMIZU, S., Semiconductor Physics
ITOH, T., Photophysics
KITAOKA, Y., Low Temperature Physics
KOBAYASHI, TA., Superconducting Electronics
KOBAYASHI, TE., Ultrafast Quantum Electronics
MIYAKE, K., Condensed Matter Theory
NASU, S., Metal Physics
OKAMOTO, H., Semiconductor Electronics
OKUYAMA, M., Dielectrics and Sensor Electronics
SUGA, S., Spectroscopy
SUZUKI, N., Theory of Magnetism
YAMAMOTO, S., Microwave and Optical Electronics

Department of Chemical Science and Engineering:
HIRATA, Y., Transport Phenomena
KANEDA, K., Design of Metal Catalysts
KITAYAMA, T., Polymer Chemistry
KOMASAWA, I., Chemical Process Engineering
KUBOI, R., Biofunctional Material Design
MURAHASHI, S.-I., Organic Chemistry
NAKATO, Y., Physical Chemistry
NITTA, T., Molecular Chemical Engineering
OKADA, T., Physical Chemistry
TANI, K., Organometallic Chemistry
TAYA, M., Biochemical Reaction Engineering
TONE, S., Chemical Reaction Engineering
UEYAMA, K., Chemical Engineering Fundamentals

Department of Systems and Human Science:
ARAI, T., Intelligent Systems
ARAKI, T., Applied Optics
FUJII, T., Systems Theory
FUJISHIGE, S., Systems Theory
FUJITA, I., Cognitive Neuroscience
FUKUSHIMA, K., Neuroinformation Science
HAYASHI, K., Biomechanics
HIRAO, M., Solid Mechanics
INOKUCHI, S., Intelligent Systems
KASAI, M., Molecular Biology
KIMOTO, H., Thermomechanics
MIYAZAKI, F., Robotics
MURAKAMI, F., Neurophysiology
NAKANO, K., Bio-informatics
NISHIDA, S., Intelligent Systems
OGURA, K., Fracture Mechanics
OSAKADA, K., Manufacturing Systems
SATO, S., Mathematical Neurobiology
SUGIMOTO, N., Nonlinear Mechanics
TAMURA, H., Systems Theory
TANAKA, M., Mechanical Systems
TONOIKE, M., Non-invasive Measurements and Analyses of the Human Brain
TSUJIMOTO, Y., Fluid Mechanics
USHIO, T., Human Information Science
YACHIDA, M., Intelligent Systems
YOSHIKAWA, T., Mechanical Science

Department of Informatics and Mathematical Science:
FUJII, M., Systems Software
FUJIWARA, T., Coding Theory and Information Security
GOTO, M., Statistical Science
HAGIHARA, K., Parallel Processing
HASHIMOTO, A., Bioinformatics and Knowledge Bases
IMAI, M., VLSI Systems Design
INAGAKI, N., Statistical Inference
INOUE, K., Software Engineering
KAMETAKA, Y., Differential Equations
KASHIWABARA, T., Analysis of Information Systems
KIKUNO, T., Fault-Tolerant Computing
MIYAHARA, H., Information Network Architecture
NAGAI, H., Controlled Stochastic Processes
NAKAMURA, Y., Integrable Dynamic Systems
SIRAHATA, S., Statistical Inference
TANIGUCHI, K., Formal Approach for Software Design
TOKURA, N., Programming Languages

Graduate School of Language and Culture:
FUJIMOTO, W., Relationship between Language and Culture and the International Environment
NAKANISHI, H., Language and Information Technology
TSUDA, A., Language and Communication

Osaka School of International Public Policy:
ATODA, N., Public Finance
BAN, K., Economic Policy
EGUCHI, J., International Economic Law
HASHIMOTO, H., Economic Policy
HASHIMOTO, Y., Economics
HAYASHI, T., Public Policy
HORIOKA, C. Y., Macroeconomics, Consumer Economics, the Japanese Economy
ITO, K., Constitution and Law
KOHSAKA, A., International and Development Economics
KUROSAWA, M., International Law
MATSUOKA, H., International Business Transactions
MORIMOTO, M., Constitution and Law
NOMURA, Y., International Business Law
OGAWA, K., Applied Econometrics
TSUJI, M., Economic Theory

Faculty of Language and Culture:
FUKAZAWA, K., Chinese
GUNTI, T., Linguistic Theory
IMAI, M., English
KANASAKI, H., French
KANEKO, M., German
KIMURA, K., Classical Languages
MIYAGAWA, K., English
MIZOBE, K., German
MORIZUMI, M., English
NAKANO, Y., German
NARITA, H., English
SENBA, Y., English
TAKAOKA, K., French
TAKEUCHI, A., English Language and Culture
TAMAI, T., English
TANAKA, M., German
TSUKUI, S., Russian
WATANABE, S., English
YAMAMOTO, M., German

School of Health and Sport Sciences:
ANDO, A., Health Science
IKUTA, K., Sports Science
KASAI, T., Sports Science
KIMURA, M., Sports Science
KURODA, E., Sports Science
SATO, H., Sports Science
SUGITA, Y., Health Science
YOSHIDA, T., Sports Science
YOSHIZAKI, K., Health Science

ATTACHED INSTITUTES

Research Institute for Microbial Diseases: Suita Campus, Yamadaoka, Suita; Dir AKIRA HAKURA.

Institute of Scientific and Industrial Research: Suita Campus, Mihogaoka, Ibaraki; Dir TOICHI OKADA.

Institute for Protein Research: Suita Campus, Yamadaoka, Suita; Dir YOSHIMASA KYOGOKU.

Institute of Social and Economic Research: Suita Campus, Mihogaoka, Ibaraki; Dir TATSUO HATTA.

Joining and Welding Research Institute: Suita Campus, Mihogaoka, Ibaraki; Dir KATSUNORI INOUE.

OSAKA UNIVERSITY OF FOREIGN STUDIES

8-1-1 Aomatani-higashi, Minoo City, Osaka 562

Telephone: (727) 30-5111

Founded 1949

President: OSAMU IKEDA
Librarian: Prof. MASAOKI MIYAMOTO

Library of 544,000 vols
Number of teachers: 201
Number of students: 3,550 day course, 847 evening course, 101 day school, 181 evening school
There is also a Graduate School (232 students)

OTARU UNIVERSITY OF COMMERCE

3-5-21, Midori, Otaru, Hokkaido 047

Telephone: (134) 27-5200
Fax: (134) 27-5213

Founded 1949

President: IEMASA YAMADA
Chief Administrative Officer: TADAATSU YAMAGUCHI
Librarian: MINORU KURATA

Library of 379,000 vols
Number of teachers: 205
Number of students: 2,560

Depts of economics, commerce, law, information and management sciences, teacher-training programme in commerce and graduate school.

UNIVERSITY OF THE RYUKYUS

1, Senbaru, Nishihara-cho, Okinawa 903-0213

Telephone: (98) 895-2221
Fax: (98) 895-8037

Founded 1950
Academic year: April to March
State control
Language of instruction: Japanese

President: KOSHO KATSURA
Administrator: HIROYASU TERAJIMA
Dean of Students: RISHUN SHINZATO
Librarian: AKIO KINJO

Library of 873,000 vols
Number of teachers: 893
Number of students: 8,574

DEANS

Faculty of Law and Letters: K. YOGI
Faculty of Education: T. TAIRA
Faculty of Science: K. KATO
Faculty of Medicine: K. FUKIYAMA
Faculty of Engineering: K. MIYAGI
Faculty of Agriculture: S. MURAYAMA

PROFESSORS

Faculty of Law and Letters:

AKAMINE, K., American Literature
AKAMINE, M., Modern Chinese History, Modern Okinawa History
ARAKAKI, S., Civil Law
ASHITOMI, T., Civil Law
CHINEN, S., Monetary Economics
CHINEN, Y., Public Finance
EGAMI, T., Science of Public Administration, Comparative Politics
GABE, M., International Relations
HAMASAKI, M., Greek Philosophy
HESHIKI, T., International Marketing
HIGA, Y., Philosophy and Ethics
HIYANE, T., History of Political Thought, Political Science
HOSAKA, H., Journalism
IHA, M., Marketing
IKEDA, Y., Japanese Archaeology, Museography
IKEMIYA, M., Ryukyuan Literature
IMURA, O., Clinical Psychology
IREI, T., Human Resources Management, Business Administration
ISHIKAWA, T., Regional Geography, Human Geography
ISHIMINE, K., Constitutional Law
JENKINS, A. P., British Culture
KAKINOHANA, H., Criminology, Criminal Procedure
KAWASOE, M., Social Services for the Aged
KINJO, S., Modern History of East Asia
KISHABA, K., Study of Relations between Japan and Ryukyu
KOMATSU, M., Economic History
MAEKADO, A., Geomorphology
MATSUDA, Y., Socio-Economic History
MATSUOKA, Y., Clinical Psychology
MIYARA, S., Linguistics
MORITA, M., French Literature
NAKAHODO, M., Modern Japanese Literature
NAKACHI, H., Administrative Law
NAKACH, K., American Literature
NAKAHARA, T., Business and Corporation Laws
NAKAMURA, T., Social Psychology
NAMIHIRA, T., Political Philosophy and Theory, Political Science
NISHIKAWA, H., Contemporary Philosophy
OKAMOTO, K., Modern Japanese Literature
OSHIRO, H., International Economics
OSHIRO, I., Theoretical Economics
OSHIRO, M., Managerial Finance
OSHIRO, T., Regional Development Policy
OYAKAWA, T., Linguistics
SAKIMA, N., European History
SHIMABUKURO, S., Human Geography
SHIMABUKURO, T., Commercial Law, Law of Securities Regulation
SHIMIZU, K., Criminal Law
SHIMOJI, Y., English Linguistics
SHIMURA, K., Quality Management
TAIRA, M., American Literature
TAIRA, T., Applied Linguistics
TAKARA, K., Ryukyuan History
TAKARA, T., Constitutional Law, Administrative Law
TAMAKI, I., Civil Procedure Law
TAMAKI, M., Ryukyuan Literature
TANAKA, H., Economic Statistics
TOMA, S., Theoretical Economics
TOMINAGA, H., Econometrics
TOYOOKA, T., Accounting Information Theory, Accounting Systems
TSUHA, T., Social Anthropology
UEZATO, K., Chinese Literature
UEZU, Y., Accounting
YAGI, S., English Literature
YAMAZATO, J., Japanese History
YAMAZATO, K., American Literature
YOGI, K., Linguistics
YONAKUNI, N., Sociology
YONOHARA, T., Strategic Management
YOSHIMURA, K., English Literature
YOSHIZAWA, T., Sociology of Education

Faculty of Education:

AHAGON, C., History of Education
AIZAWA, T., Chinese Literature
ARATA, Y., Biophysics Engineering
EJIRI, A., Solid State Physics
FUJIWARA, Y., Didactics
GIBO, M., Home Economics
HAMAMOTO, M., Sports Methodology
HIGA, Z., Technical Education
HIGASIMORI, K., Food Science
HIRATA, E., Education for the Handicapped
IKEDA, J., Judo
INOUE, K., Lifelong Education
ISHIGURO, E., Optics
ISHIKAWA, K., Social Development in Children
ITOKAZU, T., Educational Music of Wind Instruments
IZUMI, K., Vocal Music
KAKAZU, T., Psychology
KAMIYAMA, T., Woodcut
KATO, M., Complex Analysis
KAMIZONO, S., Developmental Psychology of Mentally Retarded and Handicapped Children
KAWANA, T., Physical Geography
KINJO, M., Mathematics Education
KINJO, S., Culinary Science
KINJO, Y., Inorganic Chemistry
KOBASHIGAWA, H., Sports Psychology
KOBAYASHI, M., Theory and History of Art
KOJIMA, Y., Japanese Literature
KOYANAGI, M., Physical Chemistry
MAEHARA, H., Discrete Geometry
MAEHARA, T., Psychology
MATSUMOTO, S., Mathematical Physics
MIYAGI, M., Geography
MIZUNO, M., Criminal Law
NAGAYAMA, T., Piano Playing
NAKA, J., Dialectology
NAKAMA, M., Japanese Linguistics
NAKAMURA, I., Meteorology
NAKAMURA, T., Education for the Handicapped
NAKAMURA, T., Theory of Music
NAKASONE, Y., Ecology
NAKAZATO, H., Algebra
NISHIMURA, S., Sculpture
NISHIZATO, K., History of East Asia
NOHARA, T., Palaeontology
OKUDA, M., Ceramic Art
ONAGA, J., Visual Design
SEKINE, H., Electricity and Electrical Engineering
SHIMABUKURO, Z., English Linguistics
SHINZATO, R., Clinical Psychology
SHINZATO, S., Kinematics and Dynamics of Mechanisms
SIMABUKURO, T., Psychology of Personality
SUZUKI, M., Home Science
TAIRA, K., Health Promotion
TAIRA, T., Physical Education
TAKASHIMA, N., Social Studies
TAKEDA, H., International Peace Studies
TAMAKI, A., Physical Education
TOMINAGA, D., Psychophysiology
UEZU, E., Nutrition and Physiology
YAMAUTI, S., TESL/TEFL
YONEMORI, T., Educational Information Technology

Faculty of Science:

BURKOV, A., Solid State Physics
FUKUHARA, C., Inorganic Chemistry
GINOZA, M., Condensed Matter Physics
GOYA, E., Functional Analysis
HAGIHARA, A., Forest Ecophysiology
HAYASHI, D., Structural Geology
HENNA, J., Mathematical Statistics
HIDAKA, M., Coral Biology
HIGA, T., Marine Natural Products Chemistry
HOSOYA, M., Computer Physics
IKEHARA, N., Physiology and Biochemistry
ISA, Y., Calcification
ISHIJIMA, S., Atmospheric Science
KAKAZU, K., Mathematical Physics
KATO, Y., Petrology
KIMURA, M., Marine Geology
KINJO, A., Physical Chemistry
KODAKA, K., Functional Analysis
KUNIYOSHI, M., Marine Natural Products Chemistry
MAEHARA, R., Topology
MATAYOSHI, S., Quantum Physics
MIYAGI, Y., Molecular Spectroscopy
NAKAMURA, S., Cytology
NIKI, H., Solid State Physics
NISHISHIRAHO, T., Approximation Theory
OHOMURA, Y., Condensed Matter Physics

ONUMA, K., Experimental Petrology
OOMORI, T., Marine Geochemistry
SHIGA, H., Topology
SHOKITA, S., Fisheries Biology
SUZUKI, T., Number Theory
TAIRA, H., Analytical Chemistry
TAKUSHI, E., Solid State Optics
TEZUKA, M., Topology
TOKUYAMA, A., Environmental Chemistry
TOMOYOSE, T., Solid State Physics
TSUCHIYA, M., Ecology
UEHARA, T., Embryology
UEHARA, Y., Physical Chemistry
YAGASAKI, K., Solid State Physics
YAMAGUCHI, M., Coral-Reef Biology
YAMAMOTO, S., Sedimentology
YAMAZATO, M., Probability Theory
YOGI, S., Organic Chemistry
YONASHIRO, K., Condensed Matter Physics

Faculty of Medicine:
ANIYA, Y., Biochemical Pharmacology
ARAKI, K., Haematology
ARIIZUMI, M., Preventive Medicine
FUKIYAMA, K., Internal Medicine
FUKUNAGA, T., Virology
FUTENMA, H., Adult Health
HOKAMA, T., Health Care
IBARAKI, K., Orthopaedic Surgery
IMAMURA, T., Bacteriology
ISHIKI, K., Child Nursing, Family Nursing
ISHIZU, H., Mental Health Science
ISIDA, H., Anatomy
ITO, E., Pathology
IWAMASA, T., Pathology
IWANAGA, M., Bacteriology
KANAZAWA, K., Gynaecological Oncology, Reproductive Immunology
KOJA, K., Surgery
KONO, S., Obstetrics and Gynaecology, Endocrinology
KOSUGI, T., Physiology, Haematology
MIYAGI, I., Medical Entomology
MIYAZAKI, T., Forensic Medicine
MUTO, Y., Digestive Surgery
NAKA, K., Health Administration
NODA, Y., Otorhinolaryngology, Head and Neck Surgery
NONAKA, S., Dermatology, Photobiology
OGAWA, Y., Urology
OGURA, C., Neuropsychiatry
OHTA, T., Paediatrics
OKUDA, Y., Anaesthesiology
SAITO, A., Internal Medicine
SAKANASHI, M., Pharmacology
SAKIHARA, S., Health Sociology, Community Health
SATO, Y., Parasitology
SAWADA, S., Radiation Oncology
SAWAGUCHI, S., Ophthalmology
SHIMADA, K., Human Pathology
SUNAGAWA, Y., Adult Nursing, Geriatric Nursing
SUNAKAWA, H., Oral and Maxillofacial Surgery
SUZUKI, M., Comprehensive Medicine
TAKASU, N., Internal Medicine
TAKEI, H., Biochemistry
TANAKA, T., Biochemistry
TERASHIMA, S., Physiology
UZA, M., Health Care
YAMANE, N., Laboratory Medicine
YASUZUMI, F., Anatomy
YOSHII, Y., Neurosurgery

Faculty of Engineering:
AMANO, T., Wind Engineering for Building Structures
ASHARIF, M. R., Adaptive Digital Signal Processing, Speech in Images
FUKUSHIMA, S., Architectural Planning
IKEDA, T., Urban and Regional Planning
ITOMURA, S., Materials and Processing
KANESHIRO, H., Fatigue Fracture
KINA, S., Sanitary Engineering
KODAMA, M., Microwave
MAEDA, G., Fluid Machine
MEKARU, S., Plastic Working
MIYAGI, H., Intelligent Systems
MIYAGI, K., High Velocity Impact
MORITA, D., Conservation Science and Environmental Planning for Architecture
NAGAI, M., Mechanics and Fluid Engineering
NAGATA, T., Thermal Engineering
NAKAMURA, I., Electronic Circuits
NAKAO, Z., Mathematical Informatics
ONAGA, K., Intelligence-enhancing Algorithms
OSHIRO, T., Structural Analysis and Materials
OYAKAWA, K., Heat Transfer Augmentation
SHINZATO, T., Thermal Engineering
TAKAHASHI, H., Power Systems Engineering and Surge Analysis
TAKARA, T., Spoken Language Processing
TAMAKI, S., Digital Control
TERUYA, K., Computer Networks
TOGUCHI, M., Electronic Materials
TSUKAYAMA, S., Coastal Engineering
TSUTSUI, S., Coastal Engineering
UEHARA, H., Environmental Geotechnical Engineering
UEMA, K., Highway Traffic Planning
UEZATO, K., Electric Machinery
YABUKI, T., Bridge and Structural Engineering
YAFUSO, T., Strength of Materials
YAMAKAWA, T., Reinforced Concrete Structures
YAMAMOTO, T., Neuro-control
YAMASHIRO, Y., Electrical Materials
YAMASHITA, K., Control and Signal Processing
YARA, H., Welding Engineering
YOSHIYA, K., Intelligent Information Processing
ZUKERAN, C., Multiple-valued Logic Circuit

Faculty of Agriculture:
AKINAGA, T., Postharvest Handling
AZUMA, S., Entomology
CHINEN, I., Applied Biochemistry
FUKUNAKA, K., Farm Management
GIBO, S., Land Conservation
HAYASHI, H., Woody Materials and Processing
HIGA, T., Tropical Horticulture
HIGOSHI, H., Animal Hygiene
HIRATA, E., Forestry Measurement
HONGO, F., Chemistry of Animal Products and Applied Bioresource Utilization
ISHIMINE, Y., Economic Plants
KAWASHIMA, Y., Comparative Anatomy
KOBAMOTO, N., Applied Biophysics
KOKI, Z., Preventive Forestry Engineering
KURODA, T., Environmental Information Sciences
MIYAGI, E., Pasture Science
MIYAGI, N., Soil Engineering
MURAYAMA, S., Crop Science
NAKASONE, Y., Food Chemistry
ONAGA, K., Soil Conservation
OYA, K., Soil Science
SATO, S., Genetics and Breeding of Rice Plants
SHINJO, A., Animal Breeding
SHINJO, T., Geomechanics
SHINOHARA, T., Forest Policy and Economics
TAWATA, S., Pesticide Chemistry
TOYAMA, S., Applied Microbiology
UENO, M., Agricultural Engineering
YAGA, S., Wood Chemistry and Wood Preservation
YAMASHIRO, S., Agricultural Engineering
YASUDA, M., Food Microbiology
YONAHA, T., Plant Pathology
YOSHIDA, S., Agricultural Marketing Theory

Tropical Biosphere Research Center:
ARAMOTO, M., Terrestrial Resources
FUJIMORI, K., Cell Biology
KUMAZAWA, N., Environmental Microbiology Epidemiology
MURAI, M., Animal Ecology
TAKANO, K., Fisheries Biology
TAKASO, T., Plant Morphology

ATTACHED INSTITUTES

Tropical Biosphere Research Center: Senbaru, Nishihara-cho, Okinawa; Dir K. FUJIMORI.

Sesoko Station: Sesoko Motobu-cho, Okinawa; Chief M. MURAI.

Iriomote Station: Uehara Taketomi-cho, Yaeyama Okinawa; Chief M. T. TAKASO.

Gene Research Center: Senbaru, Nishihara-cho, Okinawa; Dir H. TAKEI.

Center for Co-operative Research: Senbaru, Nishihara-cho, Okinawa; Dir T. OSHIRO.

Instrumental Research Center: Senbaru, Nishihara-cho, Okinawa; Dir H. TAIRA.

Education and Research Center for Lifelong Learning: Senbaru, Nishihara-cho, Okinawa; Dir T. YOSHIZAWA.

Center for Integrated Information Processing: Senbaru, Nishihara-cho, Okinawa; Dir K. ONAGA.

Health Administration Center: Senbaru, Nishihara-cho, Okinawa; Dir S. TAKENAKA.

Radioisotope Laboratory: Senbaru, Nishihara-cho, Okinawa; Dir Y. UEHARA.

Language Center: Senbaru, Nishihara-cho, Okinawa; Dir M. MORITA.

Academic Museum (Fujukan): Senbaru, Nishihara-cho, Okinawa; Dir S. AZUMA.

Environmental Science Center: Senbaru, Nishihara-cho, Okinawa; Dir Y. MIYAGI.

Low Temperature Center: Senbaru, Nishihara-cho, Okinawa; Dir K. YAGASAKI.

University Education Center: Senbaru, Nishihara-cho, Okinawa; Dir M. MORITA.

Center for Educational Research and Training: Senbaru, Nishihara-cho, Okinawa; Dir T. MAEHARA.

Center for Educational Research and Training of Handicapped Children: Senbaru, Nishihara-cho, Okinawa; Dir S. KAMIZONA.

University Hospital: Uehara, Nishihara-cho, Okinawa; Dir C. OGURA.

Okinawa—Asia Research Center of Medical Science: Uehara, Nishihara-cho, Okinawa; Dir T. IWAMASA.

Research Laboratory Center: Uehara, Nishihara-cho, Okinawa; Dir Y. ANIYA.

Institute for Animal Experiments: Uehara, Nishihara-cho, Okinawa; Dir E. ITO.

Engineering Manufacture Laboratory: Senbaru, Nishihara-cho, Okinawa; Dir K. OYAKAWA.

University Experimental Farm: Senbaru, Nishihara-cho, Okinawa; Dir E. MIYAGI.

University Experimental Forest: Yona, Kunigami-son, Okinawa; Dir E. HIRATA.

SAGA UNIVERSITY

Honjo-machi 1, Saga City 840
Telephone: (952) 24-5191
Fax: (952) 28-8118

Founded 1949
Academic year: April to March

President: NOBUMICHI SAKO
Administrative Officer: TAKAHIRO NISHIMURA
Librarian: SADAMI MIYAZAKI

Library of 539,000 vols
Number of teachers: 471
Number of students: 595 graduate, 5,808 undergraduate

Publications: various faculty reports and bulletins.

DEANS

Faculty of Education: SUSUMA TOKUMURA
Faculty of Economics: MASAYOSHI TSUTAGAWA
Faculty of Science and Engineering: HARUO UEHARA
Faculty of Agriculture: AKIRA MURATA
College of Liberal Arts: RYO SUZUKI

SAITAMA UNIVERSITY

255 Shimo-Okubo, Urawa City 338-8570

Telephone: (48) 852-2111
Fax: (48) 856-3677

Founded 1949
State control
Academic Year: April to March

President: TSUTOMU HYODO
Secretary-General: TAKASABUROU MAKINO
Director of Library: OSAMU TASHIRO

Library of 690,000 vols, 8,000 periodicals
Number of teachers: 561
Number of students: 8,518

Publications: *Saitama University Bulletin* (1 a year), faculty reports.

DEANS

Faculty of Liberal Arts: TOSHIHARU ABE
Faculty of Education: HIROHIKO KAGAYA
Faculty of Economics: TADANOBU OKUYAMA
Faculty of Science: MITSUO TASUMI
Faculty of Engineering: HIROYUKI NOHIRA
Graduate School of Cultural Science: TOSHIHARU ABE
Graduate School of Education: HIROHIKO KAGAYA
Graduate School of Synthetic Science of Economics: TADANOBU OKUYAMA
Graduate School of Science and Engineering: HIROYUKI NOHIRA
Graduate School of Policy Science: FUMIO NISHINO

ATTACHED INSTITUTES

Chemical Analysis Center: Dir SUMIO TOKITA

Information Processing Center: Dir HIROYUKI WATANABE

Co-operative Research Center: Dir KOJI YAMADA

SHIGA UNIVERSITY

1-1-1 Banba, Hikone-shi, Shiga-ken 522

Telephone: (749) 27-1005
Fax: (749) 27-1129

Founded 1949
Academic year: April to March

President: MIKITA KATO
Administrative Director: HIROYOSHI SHIMIZU
Dean of Students: NOBUO IBUKA
Librarian: AKIRA MISAKI

Library of 492,493 vols
Number of teachers: 225
Number of students: 3,813

Publications: *Monthly Report, Shigadai-Dayori, New University Report, Hikone Ronso* (irregular), *Kyoiku-Gakubu Kiyo* (annually).

DEANS

Faculty of Education: KENTARO KOBAYASHI
Faculty of Economics: NOBUYUKI KADOWAKI
Graduate School of Education: KENTARO KOBAYASHI
Graduate School of Economics: NOBUYUKI KADOWAKI
Health and Medical Sciences Center: MASAO KADO
Research Center for Lifelong Learning: HIDEKI SUMIOKA

ATTACHED INSTITUTES

Research Institute for Lake Science: 5-1 Hiratsu 2-chrome, Otsu, Shiga Pref. 520; Dir MUNETSUGU KAWASHIMA.

Center for Teacher In-Service Training: 5-1 Hiratsu 2-chome, Otsu, Shiga Pref. 520; Dir TAKESHIRO SHIMIZU.

Institute for Economic and Business Research: 1-1-1 Banba, Hikone, Shiga Pref. 522; Dir MITSUHIKO TOMITA.

Information Processing Center: 1-1-1 Banba, Hikone, Shiga Pref. 522; Dir MASAAKI MORI.

Archives Museum: 1-1-1 Banba, Hikone, Shiga Pref. 522; Dir ISAO OGAWA.

Joint Research Center: 1-1-1 Banba, Hikone, Shiga 522; Dir MITSUHIKO TOMITA.

SHIMANE UNIVERSITY

1060 Nishikawatsu-cho, Matsue-shi, Shimane-ken 690-8504

Telephone: (852) 32-6100
Fax: (852) 32-6019

Founded 1949
State control
Academic year: April to March

President: I. KITAGAWA
Registrar: Y. ITO
Librarian: M. YAMASAKI

Library of 663,000 vols
Number of teachers: 520
Number of students: 5,330

DEANS

Faculty of Law and Literature: T. KITAMURA
Faculty of Education: M. NAKAGAWA
Faculty of Science and Engineering: T. ITO
Faculty of Life and Environmental Sciences: Y. HONDA

SHINSHU UNIVERSITY

Asahi 3-1-1, Matsumoto, Nagano-ken

Telephone: (263) 35-4600

Founded 1949

President: AKIMI OGAWA
Administrator: SHIGERU WATANABE

Number of full-time teachers: 1,075
Number of students: 10,699

DEANS

Faculty of Arts: T. AKAMATSU
Faculty of Science: H. NAGAI
Faculty of Education: T. KOBAYASHI
Faculty of Economics: H. WATANABE
Faculty of Medicine: N. YANAGISAWA
Faculty of Engineering: T. YANAGISAWA
Faculty of Agriculture: A. HOSONO
Faculty of Textiles: H. SHIRAI

SHIZUOKA UNIVERSITY

Ohya 836, Shizuoka-shi 422

Telephone: (54) 237-1111
Fax: (54) 237-0089

Founded 1949

President: H. SATOH
Head of Secretariat: H. OHSHIMA

Number of full-time teachers: 718
Number of students: 10,372

DEANS

Faculty of Humanities and Social Sciences: T. NAWA
Faculty of Education: H. TUNOGAE
Faculty of Information Sciences: K. ABE
Faculty of Science: Y. OHTA
Faculty of Engineering: N. OKAMOTO
Faculty of Agriculture: H. NAKAI
Graduate School of Science and Engineering: N. NODA
Graduate School of Electronic Science and Technology: T. ANDOH
Research Institute of Electronics: M. KUMAGAWA

TOHOKU UNIVERSITY

1-1-2-chome, Katahira, Aoba-ku, Sendai 980-8577

Telephone: (22) 217-4844
Fax: (22) 217-4846

Founded 1907

President: HIROYUKI ABE
Vice-Presidents: SADAO KOYAMA, YOSHIO EHARA
Director-General: HIROYUKI ITO
Director of Main Library: TADAO ODA

Library: see Libraries
Number of teachers: 2,513
Number of students: 11,325 undergraduate, 5,351 graduate

Publications: *Tohoku University Bulletin, Tohoku Psychological Folia, Science Report of Tohoku University, Tohoku Journal of Experimental Medicine, Annual Research Bulletin of the Faculty of Pharmaceutical Sciences, Technology Report of Tohoku University, Tohoku Journal of Agricultural Research, Journal of Language and Culture, Journal of the Graduate School of International Cultural Studies, Advances in Materials Research, Annual Report of the Research Institute for Scientific Measurement, Report of the Institute of Fluid Science, Record of Electrical and Communication Engineering Conversazione, Annual Report of the Research Center for Higher Education, CYRIC Annual Report, Annual Report of the Education Center for Information Processing.*

DEANS

Faculty of Arts and Letters: HIDESHI OHASHI
Faculty of Education: KAZUHIKO FUWA
Faculty of Law: HITOSHI OHNISHI
Faculty of Economics: SHOKEN MAWATARI
Faculty of Science: (vacant)
School of Medicine: SHIGERU HISAMICHI
School of Dentistry: HIDEO MITANI
Faculty of Pharmaceutical Sciences: SUSUMU SATOH
School of Engineering: TAKAO YOTSUYANAGI
Faculty of Agriculture: SHIGEKI MIZUNO
Faculty of Language and Culture: KYOJI OIDE
Graduate School of International Cultural Studies: SATOSHI IHARA
Graduate School of Information Sciences: OSAMU KOKUBUN

PROFESSORS

Faculty of Arts and Letters:

AKOSHIMA, K., Japanese History and Archaeology
ARIGA, Y., History of Fine Arts
CHIGUSA, S., Linguistics
GOTO, T., Indology and History of Indian Buddhism
HANATO, M., Sinology
HANAZONO, T., Cultural Anthropology and Science of Religions
HARA, E., Western Literature and Languages
HARA, J., Behavioural Science
HARA, K., Western Literature and Languages
HASEGAWA, K., Sociology
HATAYAMA, T., Psychology
HIRANO, H., Linguistics
IMAIZUMI, T., Japanese History and Archaeology
ISODA, H., Indology and History of Indian Buddhism
KASHIWABARA, K., Philosophy and Ethics
KAWAMOTO, T., Philosophy and Ethics
KUMAMOTO, T., Oriental History
MASAMURA, T., Sociology
MATSUMOTO, N., European History
MATSUO, H., History of Fine Arts
MORI, Y., Western Literature and Languages
MURAKAMI, M., Japanese Linguistics
NAKAJIMA, R., Sinology

NAKAMURA, M., Western Literature and Languages
NIHEI, M., Japanese Literature and History of Japanese Philosophy
NIHEI, Y., Psychology
NOE, K., Philosophy and Ethics
OHASHI, H., Psychology
OHBUCHI, K., Psychology
OHTO, O., Japanese History and Archaeology
ONO, Y., European History
OZAWA, H., Western Literature and Languages
SAITA, I., Applied Japanese Linguistics
SAITO, M., Japanese Linguistics
SAITO, Y., Western Literature and Languages
SATO, M., European History
SATO, M., Western Literature and Languages
SATO, N., Japanese Literature and History of Japanese Philosophy
SHIMA, M., Cultural Anthropology and Science of Religions
SHIMIZU, T., Philosophy and Ethics
SHINO, K., Philosophy and Ethics
SUTO, T., Japanese History and Archaeology
SUZUKI, I., Cultural Anthropology and Science of Religions
TAKAGI, K., Sociology
TAMAKAKE, H., Japanese Literature and History of Japanese Philosophy
TANAKA, H., History of Fine Arts
UMINO, M., Behavioural Science
YASUDA, J., Chinese History
YOSHIHARA, N., Sociology

Faculty of Education:

FUWA, K., Adult Education
HAGIHARA, T., Adult Education
HASEGAWA, K., Clinical Psychology
HOSOKAWA, T., Mental Retardation Research
KIKUCHI, T., Psychology of Childhood and Adolescence
MASUBUCHI, Y., Philosophy of Education
MIZUHARA, K., School Curriculum and Teaching Method
MURAI, N., Mental Retardation Research
NAKAZIMA, N., Sports Science
NUMATA, H., History of Education
SHINTANI, H., Science for the Visually Handicapped
SUGAI, K., Speech Pathology and Audiology
UNO, S., Psychology of Personality and Learning

Faculty of Law:

AOI, H., Jurisprudence
FUJITA, T., Administrative Law
HAYAKAWA, S., Civil Law
KAWAKAMI, S., Civil Law
KAWANO, M., Civil Procedure
KAWASAKI, H., Criminal Procedure
KAWATO, S., Political Theory
KOBAYASHI, N., Commercial Law
KOYAMA, S., European Legal History
MIZUNO, N., Civil Law
MORITA, K., Administrative Law
ODANAKA, T., Criminal Procedure
OKAMOTO, M., Criminal Law
OHNISHI, H., International Politics
SEKI, T., Commercial Law
TERADA, H., Chinese Legal History
YAGYU, K., History of Political Theory
YOSHIDA, M., Japanese Legal History
YOSHIHARA, K., Commercial Law

Faculty of Economics:

AKITA, J., International Finance
AOKI, K., Comparative Economic Systems
FUJII, A., Non-Profit Organizations
FUKUSHIMA, M., Regional Enterprises
HAYASHIYAMA, Y., Environmental Economics
HINO, S., Welfare Economy
HIRAMOTO, A., Japanese Economy
HORI, H., Macroeconomics
HOSOYA, Y., Econometrics
IINO, M., Business Analysis
IZUMIYAMA, S., Industrial Organization
KAMOIKE, O., Money and Banking
KANAZAKI, Y., Financial Management
KAWABATA, N., Industrial Economics
KIKUCHI, K., Accounting Information
KOHNO, D., Management
KOHNO, S., Personnel Administration
KON, K., Research and Development Management
KURIYAMA, T., Economic Statistics
MASUDA, S., Regional Planning
MAWATARI, S., History of Political Economy
MIYAKE, M., Theoretical Economics
NAKAGAWA, T., International Corporate Strategy
NISHIZAWA, A., Policy for Venture Business
NOMURA, M., Social Policy
ODANAKA, N., History of Social Thought
OHTAKI, H., Business Policy
OMURA, I., Political Economy
OZAKI, H., Economic Growth Theory
SAKAKIBARA, M., Tax Accounting
SAKAMAKI, K., Industrial History
SARUWATARI, K., Comparative Business Studies
SASAKI, N., Public Finance
SATO, H., International Economics
SEKITA, Y., Welfare Information Systems
SHIBATA, S., Political Economy II
SUGIMOTO, N., Accounting Theory
SUZUKI, K., Decision Making
TAKADA, T., Auditing
TANAKA, S., Economic Policy
TANIGUCHI, A., Types of Business Enterprise
TERUI, N., Marketing
TSUGE, N., Agricultural Economics
TSUKUDA, Y., Business Statistics
WAKABAYASHI, N., Organization and Management
YAMASHITA, H., Operations Research
YASUDA, K., Information in Management
YOSHIDA, H., Ageing Economy

Faculty of Science:

ABE, K., Experimental High Energy Physics
AKIZUKI, M., Mineralogy
ARAI, H., Harmonic Analysis and Complex Analysis
BANDO, S., Differential Geometry
EBATA, T., Theoretical High Energy Physics
ENDOH, Y., Neutron Scattering and Magnetism
FUJII-KURIYAMA, Y., Biochemistry and Molecular Biology
FUJIMAKI, H., Geochemistry and Petrology
FUJIMURA, Y., Theoretical Chemistry
FUKUNISHI, H., Upper Atmosphere Physics
FUTAMASE, T., Cosmology, General Relativity
GOTO, T., Solid State Physics
HAMAGUCHI, H., Physical Volcanology
HANAWA, K., Physical Oceanography
HASEGAWA, A., Seismology
HASHIMOTO, O., Experimental Nuclear Physics
HIKASA, K., Theoretical High Energy Physics
HINO, M., Human Geography
HIRAMA, M., Organic Chemistry
HIRASAWA, T., Seismology
HIROSE, T., Plant Ecology
HORINO, H., Organometallic Chemistry
IDE, H., Developmental Biology
IGARI, S., Real Analysis
ISHIDA, M., Algebraic Geometry
ITO, T., Co-ordination Chemistry
IWASAKI, I., Atmospheric Science
KABUTO, K., Organic Chemistry
KAIHO, K., Palaeontology
KAMIMURA, T., High Pressure and Magnetism
KANISAWA, S., Petrology
KASAGI, J., Nuclear Physics
KASAYA, M., Solid State Physics
KATO, H.
KATO, J., Differential Equations
KAWAMURA, H., Satellite Oceanography
KENMOTSU, K., Differential Geometry
KIRA, M., Organometallic Chemistry
KOBAYASHI, N., Low Temperature Physics
KOBAYASHI, N., Functional Molecular Chemistry
KOBAYASHI, T., Experimental Nuclear Physics
KOMATSUBARA, T., Experimental Low Temperature Solid State Physics
KUDO, H., Radiochemistry
KURAMOTO, Y., Theoretical Condensed Matter Physics
MAEDA, Y., Cellular and Developmental Biology
MASUDA, K., Functional Analysis
MIKAMI, N., Physical Chemistry
MINOURA, K., Palaeontology
MIYASE, H., Experimental Nuclear Physics
MIYASHI, T., Organic Chemistry
MORIOKA, A., Planetary Space Science
MORITA, N., Organic Chemistry
MORITA, Y., Number Theory
NAGASE, K., Inorganic Chemistry
NAKAGAWA, T., Experimental Nuclear Physics
NAKAMARU, Y., Physiological Chemistry
NAKAMURA, T., Number Theory
NAKAZAWA, T., Atmospheric Physics
NIIZEKI, K., Theoretical Condensed Matter Physics
NISHIHIRA, M., Marine and Animal Ecology
NISHIKAWA, S., Differential Geometry
NISHITANI, K., Plant Physiology
ODA, T., Algebraic Geometry
OGINO, H., Inorganic Chemistry
OHASHI, H., Plant Taxonomy and Morphology
OHKI, K., Biophysics
OHNO, K., Physical Chemistry
OHTAKE, M., Seismology
OHTANI, E., Geochemistry and Planetology
OTSUKI, K., Tectonics and Structural Geology
OYA, H., Cosmic Electrodynamics and Planetary Space Physics
SAIKAN, S., Non-linear Laser Spectroscopy
SAIO, H., Astrophysics
SAITO, T., Palaeontology
SATO, H., Seismology
SATO, S., X-ray Photoemission and Solid State Physics
SATOH, T., Experimental Ultra Low Temperature Physics
SEKI, M., Astrophysics
SHIKAMA, K., Physical Biochemistry and Physiology
SHIMADA, I., Neuroethology
SHIMAKURA, N., Partial Differential Equations
SUNADA, T., Global Analysis
SUZUKI, A., Experimental Particle Physics
SUZUKI, M., Plant Anatomy
TAKAGI, F., Theoretical Nuclear Physics
TAKAGI, I., Partial Differential Equations
TAKAHASHI, T., Number Theory
TAMURA, S., Astronomy
TAMURA, T., Physical Geography
TANAKA, K., Mathematical Logic and Foundations of Mathematics
TANAKA, M., Physical Climatology
TANAKA, T., Mathematical Logic and Foundations of Mathematics
TERAMAE, N., Analytical Chemistry
TOSA, M., Astronomy
TOYOTA, N., Molecular Metals
TSUBOTA, H., Experimental Nuclear Physics
TSUZUKI, T., Theoretical Condensed Matter Physics
UCHIDA, W., Surface Physics
WATANABE, T., Cell Biology
YAMAGUCHI, A., Solid State Physics
YAMAGUCHI, Y., Magnetism and Neutron Diffraction
YAMAMOTO, K., Molecular Genetics

YAMAMOTO, Y., Organic Chemistry
YASUDA, N., Meteorology
YASUHARA, H., Theoretical Condensed Matter Physics
YOSHIFUJI, M., Organic Chemistry
YOSHIMURA, M., Theoretical High Energy Physics
YOSHINO, T., Operator Theory

School of Medicine:

DODO, Y., Anatomy I
FUNAYAMA, M., Forensic Medicine
HANDA, Y., Physical Disability Rehabilitation
HASHIMOTO, Y., Anaesthesiology
HAYASHI, N., Biochemistry II
HISAMICHI, S., Public Health
HONGO, M., Primary Care Unit (University Hospital)
HORII, A., Pathology I
IINUMA, K., Paediatrics
ITOH, S., Internal Medicine II
ITOH, T., Anatomy III
ITOYAMA, Y., Neurology
IWAYA, T., Physical Disability Rehabilitation
KASAI, N., Experimental Animals
KITAMOTO, T., Neuropathology
KOINUMA, N., Hospital Administration
KOKUBUN, S., Orthopaedic Surgery
KONDO, H., Anatomy II
MATSUNO, S., Surgery I
MIZUGAKI, M., Pharmacy (University Hospital)
MURAYAMA, Y., Physiology
NAGURA, H., Pathology II
NARISAWA, K., Biochemical Genetics
NODA, T., Molecular Genetics
OHI, R., Paediatric Surgery
OHMORI, H., Sport and Exercise
OKAMOTO, H., Biochemistry I
ONO, T., Radiation Research
ORIKASA, S., Urology
OTSUKI, M., Medical Informatics
SASAKI, H., Geriatric Medicine (University Hospital)
SASAKI, T., Clinical and Laboratory Medicine
SASANO, H., Anatomic Pathology
SATO, H., Environmental Health
SATO, M., Psychiatry
SATO, T., Cardiopulmonary Rehabilitation
SATOMI, S., Surgery II
SHIBAHARA, S., Applied Physiology
SHIRATO, K., Internal Medicine I
SUGAMURA, K., Microbiology
TABAYASHI, K., Thoracic and Cardiovascular Surgery
TAGAMI, H., Dermatology
TAKASAKA, T., Otorhinolaryngology
TAMAI, M., Ophthalmology
TANJI, J., Physiology II
TOYOTA, T., Internal Medicine III
UEHARA, N., International Health
WATANABE, T., Pharmacology I
YAJIMA, S., Obstetrics and Gynaecology
YAMADA, S., Radiology
YAMADORI, A., Cardiopulmonary Rehabilitation
YANAGISAWA, T., Pharmacology II
YAO, H., Neurophysiology
YOSHIMOTO, T., Neurosurgery

School of Dentistry:

ECHIGO, S., Oral and Maxillofacial Surgery II
HAYASHI, H., Oral Physiology
HORIUCHI, H., Endodontics and Periodontics
IWATSUKI, N., Anaesthesiology (Dental Hospital)
KAGAYAMA, M., Oral Anatomy II
KANUMA, A., Prosthetic Dentistry II
KIKUCHI, M., Oral Anatomy I
KIMURA, K., Prosthetic Dentistry I
MAYANAGI, H., Paediatric Dentistry
MITANI, H., Orthodontics
MOTEGI, K., Oral and Maxillofacial Surgery I
OKUDA, R., Operative Dentistry
OKUNO, O., Dental Materials Science
ŌOYA, K., Oral Pathology
SAKAMOTO, S., Preventive Dentistry
SASANO, T., Oral Diagnosis and Radiology
SHINODA, H., Dental Pharmacology
TAKADA, H., Oral Bacteriology
WATANABE, M., Geriatric Dentistry
YAMADA, T., Oral Biochemistry

Faculty of Pharmaceutical Sciences:

ANZAI, J., Physical Chemistry
ENOMOTO, T., Molecular Cell Biology
GOTO, J., Analytical Chemistry
IHARA, M., Organic Chemistry
NAGANUMA, A., Molecular and Biochemical Toxicology
OGASAWARA, K., Synthetic Organic Chemistry
OHIZUMI, Y., Pharmaceutical Molecular Biology
OHUCHI, K., Pathophysiological Biochemistry
OSHIMA, Y., Natural Products Chemistry
SAKAMOTO, T., Heterocyclic Chemistry
SATOH, S., Cardiovascular Pharmacology
TAKEUCHI, H., Biostructural Chemistry
TERASAKI, T., Pharmaceutics
YAMAGUCHI, M., Organic Chemistry
YAMOZOE, Y., Drug Metabolism and Molecular Toxicology

School of Engineering:

ABE, K., Control Systems Theory
ABE, K., Nuclear Engineering
ABE, K., Fusion Reactor Materials
ARAI, K., Separation Process Engineering
ARASHI, H., Energy Conversion
ASO, H., Information and Communication Network
BERGLUND, L. G., Heating, Ventilation and Air Conditioning Systems
CHIDA, T., Environmental Systems Engineering
CHONAN, S., Dynamics Measurement and Control
EBISAWA, H., Applied Mathematics
EMURA, T., Mechatronics
ENDO, T., Synthetic Chemistry of Advanced Materials
ENOMOTO, H., Energy Resources Engineering
FUKAMICHI, K., Applied Solid State Physics
FUKUNAGA, H., Space Structures
HANE, K., Applied Optics
HARA, H., Dynamics and Control of Complex Systems
HATAKEYAMA, R., Basic Plasma Engineering
HATTA, A., Solid Surface Science
HIGUCHI, T., Electronic Control Systems
HINO, M., Ferrous Process Metallurgy
HIRAKAWA, N., Nuclear Reactor Physics
HOMMA, M., Magnetic Materials
HORIGUCHI, T., Mathematical and Statistical Physics
HOSHIMIYA, N., Biomedical Electronics
ICHINOKURA, O., Power Electronics
IIBUCHI, K., History of Architecture
IIJIMA, Y., Atomic Materials Science
IKEDA, K., Deformation Processing of Materials
INOMATA, H., Chemical Engineering Thermodynamics
INOOKA, H., Control Engineering
INOUE, K., Machine Elements
INOUE, Y., Applied Organic Synthesis
INUTAKE, M., Plasma Physics and Fusion Engineering
ISHII, K., Quantum Science and Nuclear Engineering
ITAYA, K., Manipulation of Atoms and Molecules
ITO, K., Architectural Design
ITO, K., Computational Mechanics and Materials
ITO, T., Foundations of Software Science
IWAKUMA, T., Mechanics of Solids and Structures
KAJITANI, T., Applied X-ray and Neutron Spectroscopy
KAMEYAMA, M., Intelligent Integrated Systems
KANNO, M., Architectural Planning
KATO, K., Tribology
KATO, M., Precision Forming
KAWAMATA, M., Digital Signal and Image Processing
KAWASAKI, A., Architecture of Material Systems
KIKUCHI, A., Materials Process Engineering for Environmental Consciousness
KISHINO, Y., Mechanics of Materials
KITAHARA, M., Non-Destructive Evaluation
KITAMURA, M., Safety Engineering of Nuclear Systems
KIYONO, S., Ultra Precision Measurement and Control
KOIKE, Y., Applied Low Temperature Physics
KOKAWA, H., Welding and Joining Technology
KONDO, T., Engineering Performance of Materials
KONNO, M., Material Processing
KOSUGE, K., Robotics
KOYANAGI, M., Intelligence System Design
KUBO, H., Liquid Phase Processing
KUMAGAI, I., Applied Life Chemistry
KUROKAWA, Y., Sol-Gel Science and Materials Chemistry
KUSHIBIKI, J., Ultrasonics
MANO, A., Hydraulics
MARUOKA, A., Theory of Computing
MARUYAMA, K., Structural Materials
MASUYA, G., Propulsion Engineering
MATSUBARA, F., Applied Mathematical Physics
MATSUKI, H., Bioelectromagnetic Engineering
MATSUKI, K., Geomechanics
MATSUOKA, I., Mineral Processing and Designing
MATSUMOTO, S., Process Control
MIHASHI, H., Building Engineering and Materials Science
MIURA, T., Energy Process Engineering
MIURA, T., Concrete Engineering
MIYAGI, M., Infrared Wave Technology
MIYAMOTO, A., Molecular Materials Design
MIYAMOTO, K., Infrastructure Planning
MIYANO, S., Organic and Bio-organic Synthesis
MIYASHITA, T., Polymer Chemistry
MIYAZAKI, T., Applied Solid State Physics
NAKAHASHI, K., Aircraft Design
NAKAMURA, K., Piezoelectrics and Ultrasonics
NAKAMURA, T., Computer Science
NAKANO, E., Robotics
NAKATSUKA, K., Informatics for Geotechnology
NEMOTO, Y., Communication Science
NIITSUMA, H., Surface and Subsurface Instrumentation
NISINO, T., Applied Biological Chemistry
NISHIZEKI, T., Algorithms
NOIKE, T., Environmental Engineering
NOZAWA, T., Applied Biophysical Chemistry
OGAWA, J., Structural Engineering
OHMI, T., Urban Analysis
OKADA, M., Special Functional Materials
OKUWAKI, A., Recycling Chemistry
OMURA, K., Urban Design
OMURA, T., Water Quality Engineering
OTA, T., Thermo-Fluid Mechanics
SAITOH, T., Energy Systems and Environment
SAKA, M., Solid Mechanics
SATO, M., Biomechanics
SATO, N., Gaseous Electronics and Plasma Physics
SAWADA, K., Computational Fluid Dynamics
SAWAMOTO, M., Hydraulic Engineering

SAWAYA, K., Electromagnetic Wave Engineering
SEKINE, H., Aerospace Materials and Structure Systems
SHIBATA, A., Earthquake Engineering
SHIMAKAWA, T., Electronic Control Engineering
SHIMAMOTO, S., Superconducting Magnet and Power Engineering
SHINDO, Y., Mechanics of Composite Materials
SHOJI, K., Precision Machining
SHOJI, T., Fracture Physics and Chemistry
SUDO, R., Ecological Engineering
SUGIMOTO, K., Device Materials Chemistry
SUGIMURA, Y., Soil Mechanics and Foundation Engineering
SUTO, K., Electronics and Opto-Electronics Materials
SUZUKI, M., Systems Engineering
SUZUKI, M., Bio-Materials
SUZUKI, M., Physical Chemistry of Biomolecules and Materials
SUZUKI, M., Structural Design Engineering
TAKAHASHI, M., Magnetism and Magnetic Material
TAKANAKA, K., Engineering Mechanics
TANAKA, H., River Hydraulics
TANAKA, M., Quantum Physical Chemistry
TANIGUCHI, S., Process Engineering of Functional Materials
TODA, S., Nuclear Thermal-Hydraulics
TOYODA, J., Power Systems Engineering
UCHIDA, I., Electrochemical Science and Technology
UCHIYAMA, M., Spacecraft Systems
WADA, H., Biomechanical Engineering
WAKITA, S., Optical Materials
WATANABE, H., Plasma Physics and Fusion Engineering
WATANABE, R., Powder Process Technology
WATANABE, T., Materials Design and Interface Engineering
YAMADA, M., Organic Resources Chemistry
YAMADA, M., Space Structures
YAMADA, Y., Thin Films and Surfaces
YAMAMOTO, M., Neurophysiology and Bioinformatics
YAMAMURA, T., Electrochemistry of Materials
YAMANAKA, K., Materials Evaluation
YANAGISAWA, E., Soil Mechanics
YONEMOTO, T., Reaction Process Engineering
YOSHINO, H., Building Environmental Engineering
YOTSUYANAGI, T., Analytical Chemistry and Separation Sciences

Faculty of Agriculture:

AKIBA, Y., Animal Nutrition
EHARA, Y., Plant Pathology
FUJIMOTO, K., Lipid Chemistry
FUJIO, Y., Fish Genetics and Breeding Science
FURUKAWA, Y., Nutrition
GOMI, K., Molecular Mycology, Applied Microbiology
HASHIBA, T., Environmental Biotechnology
HATA, M., Marine Biotechnology
ITOH, T., Animal Products Chemistry
KAMIO, Y., Molecular and Applied Microbiology
KANAHAMA, K., Horticultural Science
KATSUMATA, R., Animal Microbiology and Parasitology
KIJIMA, A., Ecological and Population Genetics
KUDO, A., Economics of Food Policy
MAE, T., Plant Nutrition and Function
MIYAZAWA, T., Biodynamic Chemistry
MIZUNO, S., Molecular Biology
MORI, K., Aquacultural Biology
MURAMOTO, K., Food Protein Chemistry
NAKAJIMA, T., Enzymology
NISHIO, T., Plant Breeding and Genetics
NISHIYAMA, I., Crop Science
OBARA, Y., Animal Physiology
OHKAMA, K., Social Decision Making
OHRUI, H., Analytical Bio-Organic Chemistry
OKUBO, K., Chemistry of Food Protein and Glycoside
OMORI, M., Aquatic Ecology
ORITANI, T., Applied Bio-organic Chemistry
OSHIMA, Y., Bio-Organic Chemistry
OTA, M., Livestock Management
SAIGUSA, M., Agronomy (University Farm)
SAKAI, J., Resource Management and Economics
SASAKI, Y., Animal Physiology
SATO, E., Animal Reproduction
SEIWA, K., Plant Ecology
SUGAWARA, K., Grassland Science
SUYAMA, K., Molecular Technology of Animal Products
SUZUKI, A., Functional Morphology
TAKEUCHI, M., Marine Biochemistry
TAMAKI, Y., Entomology
TANIGUCHI, A., Restoration Ecology and Aquatic Biology
TANIGUCHI, K., Applied Aquatic Botany
YAMAGISHI, T., Animal Breeding
YAMAYA, T., Plant Cell Biochemistry
YAMASAKI, S., Soil Science

Faculty of Language and Culture:

ADACHI, Y., Language Art
AOYAMA, T., Regional Language
FUJIWARA, I., Lingual Expression
FUSHIMI, T., Lingual Expression
HATANAKA, M., Lingual Expression
HIRATA, M., Language Art
KUSUDA, I., Linguistic Application
MIZOKOSHI, A., Linguistic Application
NONAKA, K., Lingual Expression
OIDE, K., Language Art
OTOMO, Y., Regional Languages
SEKIMOTO, E., Language Art
TANAKA, T., Regional Languages

Graduate School of International Cultural Studies:

ASANO, Y., Asian Cultural Studies
HAKOGI, M., International Economic Relations
HARADA, S., Asian Cultural Studies
HASHIDA, T., Technology Co-operation
HIRANO, A., International Economic Relations
HIRATA, R., European Cultural Studies
IHARA, S., Technology Co-operation
IKI, Y., European Cultural Studies
KIMURA, Y., Islamic Area and Cultural Studies
KOIKE, M., American Studies
SASAKI, K., Linguistic Communication
SATAKE, M., International Economic Relations
TAKENAKA, K., American Studies
YONEYAMA, C., Linguistic Function

Graduate School of Information Sciences:

ABE, S., Political Analysis of the Information Society
ADACHI, Y., Non-verbal Semiotics
ASANO, N., Method of Logical Analysis
EBISAWA, H., Condensed Matter Theory
FUKUCHI, H., Language and Information Science
HIGUCHI, T., Intelligent Systems Science
HIRATA, M., Nonverbal Semiotics
HORIGUCHI, T., Statistical Physics
INAMURA, H., International and Intermodal Transport
INOOKA, H., Intelligent Control Systems
ITO, K., Computational Mechanics and Materials
ITO, T., Foundations of Software Science
KAMEYAMA, M., Intelligent Integrated Systems
KANEKO, M., Mathematical Structures II
KATO, T., Cognitive Psychology
KOKUBUN, O., Human Learning and Memory
MAKINO, S., Computer Networks
MARUOKA, A., Computation Theory
MIURA, Y., Information Science for Pathologic Physiology
MORISUGI, H., Regional and Urban Planning
NAKAJIMA, K., Advanced Integration Systems
NAKAMURA, T., Computer Architecture
NAKAMURA, Y., Information Storage Systems
NAKANO, E., Advanced Robotics
NEMOTO, Y., Communication Science
NISHIZEKI, T., Algorithm Theory
OIDE, K., Verbal and Cultural Information Analysis
OKADA, M., Mathematical Structures III
SASAKI, K., Socioeconomic Analysis of Urban Systems
SAWADA, Y., Information Physics
SEKIMOTO, E., Verbal and Cultural Information Analysis
SHIRATORI, N., Communication Theory
SHIZUYA, H., Programming Languages
SOEYA, Y., Theory of Social Structure and Change
SONE, T., Logic for Information Science
SUZUKI, A., Econometric System Analysis
SUZUKI, Y., Mathematical System Analysis II
TSUKAHARA, Y., Information Biology
UCHIDA, K., Mathematical Structures I
URAKAWA, H., Mathematical System Analysis I
WADA, M., Philosophy of Human Information
YAMAMOTO, M., Neurophysiology and Bioinformatics

Institute for Materials Research:

FUJIMORI, H., Magnetic Materials
FUJIMORI, H., Chemical Physics of Non-Crystalline Materials
FUKASE, T., Low-temperature Condensed State Physics
FUKUDA, T., Crystal Physics
GOTO, T., Solidification and Casting Metallurgy
HANADA, S., Deformation Processing
HASEGAWA, M., Irradiation Research of Nuclear Materials
HASHIMOTO, K., Surface Materials Chemistry
HIRAGA, K., Structural Science of Non, stoichiometric Compounds
HIRAI, T., High-temperature Materials Science
INOUE, A., High Purity Metallic Materials
INOUE, A., Non-equilibrium Materials
KAWAZOE, Y., Materials Design by Computer Simulation
KOBAYASHI, N., Low-temperature Physics
MAEDA, H., Superconductivity
MAEKAWA, S., Theory of Solid State Physics
MATSUI, H., Irradiation Research of Nuclear Materials
MATSUI, H., Nuclear Materials Engineering
MOTOKAWA, M., Magnetism
SAKURAI, T., Surface Science
SHIOKAWA, Y., Radiochemistry of Metals
SUEZAWA, M., Defect Physics
SYONO, Y., Solid State Chemistry under High Pressure
YAMAGUCHI, S., Nuclear Material Science
YAMAGUCHI, Y., Neutron and Gamma-Ray Spectroscopy of Condensed Matter
YAO, T., Physics of Electronic Materials

Institute for Advanced Materials Processing:

AKIBA, K., Separation Chemistry
FUJINO, T., Solid State Chemistry
HIRASAWA, M., Chemical Process Engineering
ISSHIKI, M., High Purity Materials
ITAGAKI, K., Nonferrous Chemical Metallurgy
NAKAMURA, T., Physical Process Engineering
SAITO, F., Chemical Engineering
SHIMADA, M., Advanced Ceramic Materials

SHINDO, D., Atomic Scale Morphology Analysis
SUGIMOTO, T., Colloid Science
SUITO, H., Ferrous Chemical Metallurgy
UMETU, Y., Mineral Processing, Surface Chemistry
WASEDA, Y., Applied Mineralogy, High Temperature Physical Chemistry
YAGI, J., Transport Phenomena

Institute of Development, Ageing and Cancer:
FUJIMURA, S., Thoracic Surgery, Lung Cancer, Lung Transplantation
FUKUDA, H., Radiation Medicine
FUKUMOTO, M., Pathology
KANAMARU, R., Clinical Oncology
KUDO, T., Tumour Immunology
MATSUZAKI, F., Neurochemistry and Molecular Biology
NAKAMURA, H., Developmental Neurobiology
NITTA, S., Artificial Organs, Cardiology
NUKIWA, T., Chest Physician, Molecular Biology
OBINATA, M., Cell Biology
SATAKE, M., Molecular Biology
SATO, Y., Vascular Biology
TAKAI, T., Experimental Immunology
TAMURA, S., Biochemistry and Molecular Biology
TSUCHIYA, S., Paediatrics
YASUI, A., Molecular Biology

Research Institute for Scientific Measurements:
IKEZAWA, M., Infrared Physics
ISIGAME, M., Solid State Ion Physics
KONO, S., Surface Physics
KUSUNOKI, I., Surface Chemistry
MIZUSAKI, J., Solid State Ion Devices
NODA, Y., Electronic Properties of Solids
OKA, Y., Solid State Spectroscopy
SATO, Y., Ultraviolet Spectroscopy
SHIMADA, Y., Magnetic Properties and Devices
TANAKA, M., Electron Microscopy and Spectroscopy
UDAGAWA, Y., X-Ray Physics
WATANABE, M., Soft X-Ray Optics
YAMAMOTO, M., Soft X-Ray Microscopy

Institute of Fluid Science:
HAYASHI, K., Molten Geomaterials Science
HAYASHI, S., Biofluid Control
IKOHAGI, T., Complex Flow Systems
INOUE, O., Computational Fluid Dynamics
KAMIJO, K., Cryogenic Flow
KOHAMA, Y., Experimental Fluid Dynamics
MARUYAMA, S., Heat Transfer Control
NANBU, K., Gaseous Electronics
NIIOKA, T., Reactive Flow
NISHIYAMA, H., Electromagnetic Intelligent Fluids
TAKAGAKI, T., Advanced Systems Evaluation
TAKAYAMA, K., High Enthalpy Flow
TANI, J., Intelligent Systems

Research Institute of Electrical Communication:
ARAI, K., Spin Electronics
ITO, H., Optoelectronics and Quantum Electronics
KAWAKAMI, S., Optoelectronics
MASUOKA, F., Integrated Circuit
MIZUNO, K., Terahertz Engineering
MUROTA, J., Atomically Controlled Processing
NAKAJIMA, K., Intelligent Integrated Systems
NAKAMURA, Y., Information Storage Engineering
NIWANO, M., Electronic Quantum Devices
OHNO, H., Semiconductor Electronics
SAWADA, Y., Information Physics
SHIRATORI, N., Computer Networks
SONE, T., Acoustics
SUGITA, Y., Magnetic Materials and Devices
TSUBOUCHI, K., Electronics
USHIODA, S., Surface Physics
YAMANOUCHI, K., Phonon Device Engineering
YANO, M., Bioinformatics
YOKOO, K., Vacuum Electronics
YONEYAMA, T., Electromagnetic Wave Transmission

Institute for Chemical Reaction Science:
HARADA, N., Chemistry
HOZAWA, M., Chemical Engineering
IINO, M., Applied Chemistry
ITO, O., Chemistry
KAINO, T., Materials Chemistry
KATO, M., Biochemistry and Engineering
KOYAMA, T., Chemistry
KURIHARA, K., Chemical Engineering
MIYASHITA, T., Materials Chemistry
NAKANISHI, H., Chemistry
NISHIYAMA, Y., Materials Chemistry
SAITO, M., Chemistry
SATO, T., Applied Chemistry
SHIMIZU, T., Chemistry
TERO, S., Chemistry
TOMITA, A., Applied Chemistry
YAMAUCHI, S., Chemistry
YOKOYAMA, C., Chemical Engineering

Institute of Genetic Ecology:
KAMEYA, T., Plant Breeding
KUMAGAI, T., Photobiology
MINAMISAWA, K., Molecular Microbial Ecology
OOTAKI, T., Fungal Morphogenesis
TAKAHASHI, H., Plant Physiology

Computer Center:
MAKINO, S., Computer Communication Engineering

Cyclotron Radioisotope Center:
FUJIOKA, M., Nuclear Physics
IDO, T.,Radioisotope Production and Radiopharmaceutical Chemistry
ITOH, M., Nuclear Medicine
NAKAMURA, T., Health Physics
ORIHARA, H., Nuclear Physics

Education Center for Information Processing:
SHIZUYA, H., Theoretical Computer Science, Cryptology

Gene Research Center:
YAMAMOTO, T., Molecular Genetics

Research Center for Higher Education:
SAITOH, K., Applied Research Section
SEKIUCHI, T., Basic Research Section

International Student Center:
FUJINO, Y., Development of the Short-Term Student Exchange Programme
FUKUSHIMA, E., Japanese Language
HORIE, K., Linguistic Typology and Japanese–Korean Comparative Linguistics
KATO, H., Japanese Language Teaching
SATO, S., Generation of Prose Structure
SATO, S., Japanese Language Teaching
SUKEGAWA, Y., Acquisition of Japanese Speech Sounds by Learners of Japanese as a Second Language
TAGUCHI, Y., Multicultural Health Theory
UEHARA, S., Linguistics
YOSHIMOTO, K., Formal Syntax and Japanese Intonation

Center for Interdisciplinary Research:
KASUYA, A., Materials Science

Center for Northeast Asian Studies:
HIRAKAWA, A., Political Economy
IRUMADA, N., Social Formation
ISOBE, A., Cultural Studies
KIKUCHI, E., Regional Ecosystem Studies
MIYAMOTO, K., Socio-economic Studies on the Environment
NARISAWA, M., East Asian Societies
SATO, M., Environmental and Resources Survey
SEGAWA, M., Social Ecology
TANIGUCHI, H., Geochemistry
TOKUDA, M., North Asian Societies
YAMADA, K., Social Structure
YOSHIDA, T., Science and Technology

Center for Low-temperature Science:
AOKI, H., Low-temperature Physics

New Industry Creation Center:
ESACHI, M., Micromachines
IGUCHI, Y., Physical Chemistry of Materials
INOUE, A., High Purity Metallic Materials
ISHIDA, K., Microstructure Science
OHMI, T., Solid State Electrochemical Science and Technology
YAMADA, M., Architectural Disaster Prevention Engineering
YAMASITA, T., Superconducting Electronics

Tohoku University Museum:
MORI, K., Invertebra Palaeontology
YANAGIDA, T., Archaeology

College of Medical Sciences:
HAYASHI, H., Renal Physiology
ITAGAKI, K., Medical Nursing
KOBAYASI, T., Solid Physics
KUROKAWA, T., Microbiology
MARUOKA, S., Nuclear Medicine
MASUDA, T., Pathology
NAWATA, T., Cell Physiology
OGINO, K., Inorganic Chemistry
SHINDOH, C., Respiratory Physiology
SUNOUCHI, C., Functional Analysis
SUZUKI, S., Generators, X-Ray Images
TAKABAYASHI, T., Obstetrics and Gynaecology
WATANABE, Y., History of Religions
ZUGUCHI, M., Diagnostic Radiology

ATTACHED RESEARCH INSTITUTES

Institute for Materials Research: Dir HIROYASU FUJIMORI.

Institute for Advanced Materials Processing: Dir (vacant).

Institute of Development, Ageing and Cancer: Dir SHIGEFUMI FUJIMURA.

Research Institute for Scientific Measurements: Dir MICHIYOSHI TANAKA.

Institute of Fluid Science: Dir JUNJI TANI.

Research Institute of Electrical Communication: Dir YASUJI SAWADA.

Institute for Chemical Reaction Science: Dir HACHIRO NAKANISHI.

Institute of Genetic Ecology: TAMOTSU OOTAKI.

Research Center for Higher Education: Dir TAKESHI EBATA.

Cyclotron and Radioscope Center: Dir HIKONOJYO ORIHARA.

Education Center for Information Processing: Dir TATSUO HIGUCHI.

Gene Research Center: Dir SHIGEKI MIZUNO.

Research Center for Higher Education: Dir NOZOMU HOSHIMIYA.

Center for Interdisciplinary Research: Dir HIROYASU FUJIMORI.

Center for Northeast Asian Studies: Dir TADASHI YOSHIDA.

Center for Low Temperature Science: Dir HIROYASU FUJIMORI.

New Industry Development Center: Dir TAKAO YOTSUYANAGI.

UNIVERSITY OF TOKUSHIMA

24 Shinkura-cho 2-chome, Tokushima-shi, Tokushima-ken 770-8501
Telephone: (886) 56-7000
Fax: (886) 56-7012

Founded 1949
State control
Academic year: April to March

President: S. SAITO
Director-General: T. MIURA
Bureau of Student Affairs: M. KUMAGAI

Librarian: H. TERADA

Number of full-time teachers: 910

Number of students: 5,813

Publications: scientific papers, faculty journals.

DEANS

Faculty of Integrated Arts and Sciences: A. YOSHIMORI

School of Medicine: T. IKATA

School of Dentistry: M. SATO

Faculty of Pharmaceutical Sciences: M. SHIBUYA

Faculty of Engineering: T. MORIYOSHI

PROFESSORS

Faculty of Integrated Arts and Sciences:

AKIYOSHI, H., Functional Biochemistry
ANDO, M., Chinese Literature
ARAKI, H., Motor and Behavioural Physiology
AZUMA, K., Calligraphy
AZUMA, U., Archaeology
BABA, T., German Language and Literature
FUJIMURA, T., Commercial Law
GOTO, T., Comparative Biochemistry and Physiology
HAMADA, J., Visual Perception
HARAMIZU, T., Japanese Literature
HATTORI, T., Elementary Particle Physics
HAYASHI, H, Environmental Biology
HAYASHI, K., Constitutional Law
HIOKI, Z., Theoretical High Energy Physics
HIRAI, S., Historical Geography
ISHIDA, K., Microfossil Geology
ISHIDA, M., Philosophy
ISHIHARA, T., Differential Geometry
ISHII, K., Digital Imaging
ISHIKAWA, E., German Language and Literature
ITO, M., Visual Perception
ITO, Y., Functional Analysis
IWATA, O., Environmental Psychology
KATAOKA, K., Musicology
KATSURA, S., German Language and Literature
KAWAKAMI, S., German Language and Literature
KAWASAKI, Y., Sculpture
KONDO, S., Developmental Biology
KOORI, N., Nuclear Physics
KORENAGA, T., Environmental Dynamic Analysis
KOTO, K., Mineralogy
KUMAGAI, M., Philosophy
KURODA, H., Sports Psychology
KUWABARA, R., Global Analysis
MAEDA, S., Applied Mathematics
MATOBA, H., Exercise Physiology
MARUYAMA, S., Developmental Psychology
MARUYAMA, Y., History of Japan
MATSUMOTO, M., Physical Chemistry
MATSUSHITA, M., English Literature
MIKI, M., Financial Accounting
MITSUDA, M., Educational Psychology
MITSUI, A., Industrial Technology
MIURA, T., Physical Education
MIYAZAWA, K., Composition, Music using Computers
MIZUNO, K., Solid State Physics
MORIOKA, Y., English Linguistics
MOTOKI, Y., English Linguistics
NAKAGAWA, H., Marine Physiology and Biochemistry
NAKAJIMA, M., Economic History
NAKAMURA, H., Physical Education
NAKAMURA, J., English Linguistics
NAKATANI, T., Theories of Fiscal Reform
NAKAYAMA, S., Nuclear Physics
NISHIDE, K., American History
NISHIMURA, K., International Business
NODA, K., Agricultural Chemistry
OBARA, S., Exercise Physiology
OHASHI, M., Mathematical Programming
OHASHI, M., Immunobiology
OKUYAMA, H., Commutative Algebra
OMURA, Y., Living Environment
OYAMA, Y., Analytical Cytology
SANO, K., Physiological Psychology
SENBA, M., Japanese Linguistics
SEO, I., English Literature
SHIOTA, T., Geology
TACHIBANA, Y., Economic Theory
TAKEDA, Y., Natural Products Chemistry
TERAO, H., Inorganic Chemistry
TODA, H., Indian Philosophy
TOEDA, O., Pedagogy
TOKUTSU, S., German Linguistics and Literature
URUSHIHARA, Y., Agricultural Economics
WADA, M., Organic Chemistry
YAMADA, K., Labour Law
YOSHIDA, H., Theoretical Sociology
YOSHIDA, S., Philosophy
YOSHIMORI, A., Vocal Music and Chorus
YOSHIMORI, K., Chinese Medieval History

School of Medicine:

ADACHI, A., Virology
AONO, T., Gynaecology and Obstetrics
ARASE, S., Dermatology
FUKUI, Y., Anatomy II
HIMENO, K., Parasitology
HISASHIGE, A., Hygiene
IKATA, T., Orthopaedic Surgery
ISHIMURA, K., Anatomy I
ITAKURA, M., Clinical and Molecular Nutrition
ITO, S., Internal Medicine II
IZUMI, K., Pathology II
KAGAWA, S., Urology
KISHI, K., Nutritional Physiology
KOIKE, Y., Otorhinolaryngology
KUBO, S., Forensic Medicine
KURODA, Y., Paediatrics
MATSUMOTO, T., Internal Medicine I
MONDEN, Y., Surgery II
MORITA, Y., Physiology II
NAGAHIRO, S., Neurosurgery
NAKAHORI, Y., Public Health
NAKAYA, Y., Nutrition for Special Physiological Needs
NATORI, Y., Nutritional Chemistry
NISHITANI, H., Radiology
OGAWA, T., Foods Science
ONISHI, Y., Bacteriology
OSHITA, S., Anaesthesiology
OTA, F., Food Microbiology
SANO, T., Pathology I
SHIMA, K., Laboratory Medicine
SHIOTA, H., Ophthalmology
SONE, S., Internal Medicine III
TAKEDA, E., Clinical Nutrition
TAMAKI, T., Pharmacology
TASHIRO, S., Surgery I
YAMAMOTO, S., Applied Nutrition
YAMAMOTO, S., Biochemistry
YOSHIZAKI, K., Physiology I

School of Dentistry:

ASAOKA, K., Dental Engineering
BANDO, E., Fixed Prosthodontics
HAYASHI, Y., Pathology
HOSOI, K., Physiology
ICHIKAWA, T., Removable Prosthodontics
INOUE, H., Biochemistry
ISHIDA, H., Pharmacology
ISHIZUKA, H., Anatomy and Histology
KITAMURA, S., Anatomy
MATSUO, T., Conservative Dentistry
MIYAKE, Y., Microbiology
MORIYAMA, K., Orthodontics
NAGATA, T., Periodontology and Endodontology
NAGAYAMA, M., Oral and Maxillofacial Surgery
NAKAJO, N., Dental Anaesthesiology
NAKAMURA, R., Preventive Dentistry
NISHINO, M., Paediatric Dentistry
SATO, M., Oral and Maxillofacial Surgery and Oncology
UEMURA, S., Oral and Maxillofacial Radiology

Faculty of Pharmaceutical Sciences:

BABA, Y., Physical Chemistry
FUKUI, H., Pharmacology
FUKUZAWA, K., Health Chemistry
HIGUCHI, T., Microbial Chemistry
KIHARA, M., Pharmaceutical Information Science
KIWADA, H., Biopharmaceutics
NAGAO, Y., Pharmaceutical Chemistry
OCHIAI, M., Pharmaceutical Organic Chemistry
SHIBUYA, M., Synthetic Pharmaceutical Chemistry
SHIMABAYASHI, S., Physical Pharmacy
TAKAISHI, Y., Pharmacognosy
TERADA, H., Medicinal Biochemistry
YAMAUCHI, T., Biochemistry
YOKOTA, M., Clinical Pharmacology

Institute for Medicinal Resources:

KUSUMI, T., Marine Medicinal Resources
NIWA, M., Medicinal Biotechnology
SHISHIDO, K., Plant Medicinal Resources

Faculty of Engineering:

AKAMATSU, N., Information and Computer Science
AOE, J., Intelligent Systems Engineering
FUKUI, M., Optical Materials and Devices
FUKUTOMI, J., Mechanical Systems
HANABUSA, T., Production Systems Engineering
HASHIMOTO, C., Concrete Engineering
HASHINO, M., Environmental Engineering
HAYASHI, H., Chemical Process Engineering
HIRAO, K., Structural Engineering and Design
HORI, H., Biological Science
IKEDA, S., Physico-Chemical and Materials Science
IMAEDA, M., Intelligent Mechanics
IMAI, H., Mathematics and Applied Mathematics
INOKO, T., Mechanical Science
IRITANI, T., Communications and Controls
ISAKA, K., Electric Energy Engineering
KANASHIRO, T., Solid State Physics
KANESHINA, S., Biological Science
KAWAKAMI, H., Communications and Controls
KAWASHIRO, K., Biochemical Engineering
KINOUCHI, Y., Communication and Controls
KITAYAMA, S., Telecommunications Engineering
KONDO, A., Geotechnical Engineering
KORAI, N., Biophysical Science
KONISHI, K., Intelligent Mechanics
KUNUGI, A., Physico-chemical and Material Science
MASUDA, S., Synthetic and Polymer Chemistry
MATSUDA, Y., Biochemical Science
MISAWA, H., Mechanical Science
MITSUI, H., Environmental Engineering
MIWA, K., Mechanical System
MIZUGUCHI, H., Urban Planning and Landscape Design
MOCHIZUKI, A., Foundations Engineering
MORI, I., Materials Science and Devices
MORII, M., Information and Computer Science
MORIOKA, I., Mechanical System
MORIYOSHI, T., Physico-chemical and Material Science
MURAKAMI, H., Environmental Engineering
MURAKAMI, R., Production Systems Engineering
NAKABAYASHI, I., Chemical Process Engineering
NAKASE, Y., Mechanical System
NAGATA, M., Electrical Energy Engineering
NAGAMACHI, S., Mathematics and Applied Mathematics
NIKI, N., Optical Information Science

NISHIDA, N., Optical Information Science
NISHIOKA, K., Optical Materials and Devices
NOJI, S., Biochemical Science
OE, S., Intelligent Systems Engineering
OKABE, T., Hydraulic Engineering
ONISHI, T., Electrical Energy Engineering
ONO, N., Information and Computer Science
OOSHIMA, T., Biochemical Science
OUSAKA, A., Mechanical Systems
OYA, K., Materials Science and Devices
SAKAI, S., Materials Science and Devices
SAKAMAKI, K., Mechanical Science
SATO, T., Production Systems Engineering
SATO, T., Synthetic and Polymer Chemistry
SAWADA, T., Geotechnical Engineering
SHIMADA, R., Information and Computer Science
SHIMOMURA, T., Intelligent Systems Engineering
SHINOHARA, Y., Mathematics and Applied Mathematics
SHINTANI, Y., Materials Science and Devices
SUEDA, O., Rehabilitation Engineering
SUZUKI, T., Electric Energy Engineering
TAKI, T., Solid State Physics
TAMESADA, T., Intelligent Networks and Computer Science
TANAKA, H., Optical Materials and Devices
TOMIDA, T., Chemical Processes Engineering
TSUKAYAMA, M., Synthetic and Polymer Chemistry
USHIDA, A., Communication and Controls
UTSUNOMIYA, H., Structural Engineering and Design
YAMADA, K., Mechanical Science
YAMAGAMI, T., Geotechnical Engineering
YAMANAKA, H., Geotechnical Engineering
YANO, Y., Intelligent Systems Engineering
YOSHIMURA, T., Intelligent Mechanics

Center for University Extension:

FUJIOKA, H., Adult Education
HIROWATARI, S., Adult and Continuing Education
KONDO, Y., Educational Engineering
MATSUNAGA, K., Welfare Engineering

Institute for Enzyme Research:

EBINA, Y., Molecular Genetics
FUKUI, K., Gene Regulatorics
KIDO, H., Molecular Enzyme Chemistry
MIYAZONO, T., Engineering for Life Science
MOTOKAWA, Y., Molecular Enzyme Physiology
SUGINO, H., Molecular Cytology

Institute for Genome Research:

ITAKURA, M., Division of Genetic Information

UNIVERSITY OF TOKYO

7-3-1 Hongo, Bunkyo-ku, Tokyo 113
Central Telephone: (3) 3812-2111
Fax: (3) 5689-7344

Founded 1877

President: SHIGEHIKO HASUMI
Director-General: K. NAKANISHI

Library: see Libraries
Number of teachers: 4,110
Number of students: 27,389

DEANS

College of Arts and Sciences: W. OMORI
Graduate School of Law and Politics and Faculty of Law: T. SASAKI
Graduate School of Economics and Faculty of Economics: H. MITAJIMA
Graduate School of Humanities and Sociology and Faculty of Letters: K. KABAYAMA
Graduate School of Education and Faculty of Education: Y. SAEKI
Graduate School of Engineering and Faculty of Engineering: N. NAKAJIMA
Graduate School of Science and Faculty of Science: H. SUEMATSU
Graduate School of Agriculture and Life Sciences and Faculty of Agriculture: M. KOBAYASHI
Graduate School of Medicine and Faculty of Medicine: T. ISHIKAWA
Graduate School of Pharmaceutical Sciences and Faculty of Pharmaceutical Sciences: K. INOUE
Graduate School of Mathematical Sciences: K. OKAMOTO

PROFESSORS

College of Arts and Sciences:

ABE, K., Graphics
AKANUMA, H., Biochemistry
AOKI, M., German
ARAI, Y., Human Geography
ASANO, S., Theory of Solid State Physics
ASASHIMA, M., Developmental Biology
ASO, K., German and German Philosophy
ATOMI, Y., Sports Sciences
BOCCELARI, J., English, Comparative Literature
ENDO, Y., Physical Chemistry
ERIGUCHI, Y., Astrophysics
FUJII, S., Japanese Literature
FUKUBAYASHI, T., Sports Medicine
FUKUNAGA, T., Sports Sciences
FUNABIKI, T., Cultural Anthropology
FURUTA, M., Vietnamese Studies
GOTO, N., Environmental Economics
HATANO, A.,Theoretical Polymer Physics
HAYASHI, F., American Literature
HAYASHI, T., Biophysical Chemistry
HIKAMI, S., Statistical Physics
HIROMATSU, T., Statistics
HOSAKA, K., German
HYODO, T., Physics
ICHIMURA, M., Theoretical Nuclear Physics
IKEDA, N., German
IMAI, T., Philosophy
INOGUCHI, H., German
ISHI, H., Environmental Studies
ISHIDA, H., French Literature
ISHII, A., International Relations
ISHII, Y., French
ISHIMITSU, Y., German Literature
ITO, A., Cultural Anthropology
IWASA, T., French, Contemporary Art
IWASAWA, Y., International Law
IWATA, K., Economics
KAGOSHIMA, S., Solid State Physics
KAJI, T., German
KANEKO, K., Nonlinear Physics, Statistical Physics
KARIMA, F., Chinese
KAWACHI, J., Psychology
KAWAGUCHI, A., Plant Biochemistry
KAWAI, S., Graphics
KAWAMOTO, K., English, Comparative Literature
KAWANAGO, Y., German, History of Christian Thought
KAWATO, S., Biophysics
KAZAMA, Y., Theory of Elementary Particles
KIBATA, Y., English, British History
KIMURA, H., Anthropology
KOBAYASHI, K., Organic Chemistry, Organic Solid State Chemistry
KOBAYASHI, K., Sports Sciences
KOBAYASHI, Y., French, Modern Thought
KODA, K., German
KOJIMA, N., Chemistry
KOMAKI, K., Radiation Physics
KOMIYAMA, S., Theory of Solid State Physics
KOMORI,Y., Japanese Literature
KONOSHI, T., Japanese Literature
KOTERA, A., International Law
KUBOUCHI, T., English
KUDO, Y., French
KUNISHIGE, J., English
KURODA, R., Biochemistry of DNA
KUROZUMI, M., Ethics, Japanese Intellectual History
KUSAMITSU, T., English, British Socioeconomic History
KUWANO, T., Russian
MABUCHI, I., Biochemistry and Biophysics
MATSUBARA, N., Statistics, Decision-making Theory
MATSUMOTO, T., Entomological Ecology
MATSUNO, K., English
MISUMI, Y., Japanese Literature
MITANI, H., Japanese History
MIYAMOTO, H., Philosophy
MIYASHITA, S., French
MIZUTANI, T., Classical Languages
MOTOMURA, R., European History
MURATA, J., Philosophy
NAGANO, S., Graphics
NAGATA, T., Physical Chemistry
NAKAI, K., International Relations
NAKAMURA, K., Russian
NAKAMURA, Y., Geology
NAKAZAWA, H., Crosscultural Communication
NAMAIZAWA, H., Theoretical Low Temperature Physics
NAMIKI, Y., Chinese History
NARITA, A., English
NIWA, K., Research Management
NOBUHIRO, S., Japanese Literature
NOTOJI, M., American Literature
OGAWA, H., Far Eastern Intellectual History
OGAWA, H., English
OKA, H., English
OKABE, Y., German, Comparative Literature
OKOSHI, Y., Criminal Law
OMORI, M., Plant Biochemistry, Cell Biology
OMORI, W., Law, Political Science
ONISHI, N., Theory of Nuclear Physics
ONUKI, T., Hellenistic and Early Christian Literature
OSAWA, Y., English, Comparative Literature
OTA, K., Theoretical Nuclear Physics
OTSUKI, T., Sports Sciences
SAKAHARA, S., French
SAKANASHI, R., Japanese History
SAKURAI, K., Quantum Electronics and Spectroscopy
SASAKI, C., History and Philosophy of Science
SATO, Y., American Literature
SHIBA, N., Serbo-Croat, History
SHIGEMASU, K., Bayesian Statistics
SHIMOI, M., Inorganic Chemistry, Co-ordination Chemistry
SUGAWARA, T., Physical Organic Chemistry
SUGIHASHI, Y., German, Literature and Aesthetics
SUTO, M., Molecular Cell Biology
SUZUKI, H., English and Music
SUZUKI, K., French
SUZUKI, K., Graphics
TAJIRI, M., German
TAKADA, Y., English Literature
TAKAGI, Y., International Economic Co-operation
TAKAHASHI, M., Aquatic Plant Ecology
TAKAHASHI, M., Chinese, Chinese Economy
TAKAHASHI, N., Political Science
TAKAMURA, T., English
TAKANO, B., Geochemistry
TAKATSUKA, K., Theoretical Molecular Science
TAKEUCHI, N., French, Comparative Literature
TAKITA, Y., English
TAMAI, T., Software Engineering
TANIUCH, T., Human Geography
TANJI, A., English Literature
TOMODA, S., Organic Chemistry
TSUKAMOTO, A., English
TSUNEKAWA, K., Political Science
UCHIDA, R., Contemporary Society
UEDA, H., Spanish
URA, M., Russian Literature
USUI, R., German
WAKABAYASHI, M., Chinese, Modern History of East Asia

YAMAKAGE, S., International Relations
YAMAMOTO, S., English
YAMAMOTO, T., Philosophy
YAMAMOTO, Y., Culture and Social Change
YAMAMOTO, Y., International Relations
YAMANAKA, K., English
YAMASHITA, S., Cultural Anthropology
YAMAUCHI, M., Asian History
YAMAWAKI, N., History of Social Thought
YAMAZAKI, Y., Atomic Physics
YOKOYAMA, T., Graphics
YONEYA, T., Theoretical Physics
YOSHIE, A., Japanese History
YOSHIJIMA, S., German
YOSHIOKA, D., Theory of Solid State Physics
YUASA, H., French
YUI, D., American and International History

Graduate School of Law and Politics and Faculty of Law:

AOYAMA, Y., Civil Procedure
BABA, Y., European Political History
CHEN, P. H.-C., Principles of Comparative Law, Chinese Legal System
DOGAUCHI, M., International Civil Procedure
EBIHARA, A., German Law
EGASHIRA, K., Commercial Law
HASEBE, Y., Constitutional Law
HIBINO, T., Constitutional Theory
HIGUCHI, N., Anglo-American Law
HIROSE, H., Consumer Law
IGARASHI, T., American History and Government
INOUYE, M., Criminal Procedure
INOUE, T., Philosophy of Law
ISHIGURO, K., Private International Law, Conflict of Laws
ITO, M., Civil Procedure
IWAHARA, S., Corporations Law, Regulation of Financial Institutions
IWAMURA, M., Social Security Law
KABASHIMA, I., Political Process
KANDA, H., Commercial Law
KASHIWAGI, N., Law of International Business Transactions
KITAMURA, I., French Law
KITAOKA, S., Japanese Political and Diplomatic History
KOBA, A., Roman Law
KOBAYAKAWA, M., Administrative Law
MORITA, A., Public Administration
NAKAYAMA, N., Intellectual Property
NAKAZATO, M., Tax Law
NISHIDA, N., Criminal Law
NISHIKAWA, Y., Occidental Legal History
NISHIO, M., Local Public Administration
NOMI, Y., Civil Law, Trust Law
OCHIAI, S., Commercial Law
ONUMA, Y., International Law
OTA, S., Sociology of Law
ROKUMOTO, K., Sociology of Law
SAEKI, H., Criminal Law
SASAKI, T., History of Political Theory
SHIOKAWA, N., Russian Politics
SUGENO, K., Labour Law
TAKAHASHI, H., Civil Procedure
TAKAHASHI, K., Constitutional Law
TAKAHASHI, S., History of International Politics
TERAO, Y., Anglo-American Law
UCHIDA, T., Civil Law
UGA, K., Administrative Law
USUI, M., Public Finance Law
WATANABE, H., History of Japanese Political Thought
YAMAGUCHI, A., Criminal Law
YAMASHITA, T., Commercial Law
YOKOTA, Y., International Economic Law

Graduate School of Economics and Faculty of Economics:

BABA, S., Economic History of Germany
DAIGO, S., Accounting
DAITO, E., Business History
FUJIWARA, M., Micro-Economies, Public Economics
HARA, A., Economic History of Modern Japan
HAYASHI, F., Statistics and Econometrics
HIROTA, I., Economic History of Modern France
HORIUCHI, A., Monetary Theory
IHORI, T., Economic Policy
ISHIKAWA, T., Income Distribution
ITOH, MASANAO, Japanese Economy
ITOH, MOTOSHIGE, International Economy
IWAI, K., Economic Theory
IWAMI, T., Economic Policy
JINNO, N., Public Finance
KANEMOTO, Y., Economic Policy
KATAHIRA, H., Marketing
KOBAYASHI, T., Business Economics
KUNITOMO, N., Statistics
MIWA, Y., Industrial Organization
MIYAJIMA, H., Public Finance
MOCHIDA, N., Finance
MORI, T., History of Agriculture
NAKAGANE, K., Chinese Economy
NISHIMURA, K., Economic Theory, Economics and Statistics
OBATA, M., Economic Theory
OKUDA, H., Economic History of the USSR
SAITO, S., Accounting
SHIBATA, T., Economic Theory
TAKEDA, H., Economic History of Japan
TAKEMURA, A., Mathematical Statistics
TAKENOUCHI, M., International Economics
UMEZAWA, Y., Management Science
WADA, K., Business History
WAKASUGI, T., Business Finance and Capital Market
YAJIMA, T., Statistics and Economics
YOSHIKAWA, H., Economic Theory

Graduate School of Humanities and Sociology and Faculty of Letters:

AKIYAMA, H., Social Psychology
AMANO, M., Philosophy
AOYAGI, M., Institute for the Study of Cultural Exchange
ASAI, K., German Literature
EJIMA, Y., Indian Buddhism
FUJII, S., Modern Chinese Literature
FUJIKAWA, Y., English Literature
FUJITA, K., Aesthetics
FUJITA, S., Early Modern Japanese History
FUKASAWA, K., Modern History of Europe
FUNATSU, M., Sociology
GE, X., Chinese Language and Literature
GOMI, F., Medieval Japanese History
GOTO, T., Archaeology
HASEMI, K., Russian and Polish Literature
HIRAISHI, T., American Literature
HIRANO, Y., German Language and Literature
IKEDA, T., Chinese Philosophy
IMAMURA, K., Japanese and Asian Archaeology
IMANISHI, N., English Linguistics and Syntax Theory
INAGAMI, T., Sociology
ISHII, N., Modern History of Europe
ITUMI, K., Classical Language and Literature
KABAYAMA, K., Medieval History of Europe
KANAI, S., History of Religion
KANAZAWA, M., Russian Literature
KATAYAMA, H., Classical Languages and Literature
KAWAHARA, H., Chinese Philosophy
KIMURA, K., Chinese Buddhism
KIMURA, S., Contemporary History of Europe
KISHIMOTO, M., Chinese History
KOJIMA, T., Japanese Literature
KOMATSU, H., Central Asian History
KONDO, K., Modern History of Europe
KONO, M., History of Japanese Art
KUMAMOTO, H., Indo-European Linguistics
MATSUMURA, K., Uralic Linguistics
MATSUNAGA, S., Philosophy
MATSUURA, J., German Language
MIZUSHIMA, T., History of South Asia
MURAI, S., Medieval Japanese History
NAKAJI, Y., French Language and Literature
NITAGAI, K., Urban Sociology
OSANO, S., History of Western Art
SAKURAI, M., Ancient Greek History
SAKURAI, Y., Southeast Asian History
SASAKI, K., Aesthetics
SATO, M., Ancient Japanese History
SATO, S., Chinese Philosophy
SATO, T., West Asian History
SATO, T., Visual Perception
SATO, Y., Ethics and Social Thought
SEIYAMA, K., Mathematical Sociology
SEKINE, S., Occidental Ethical Thoughts
SHIMAZONO, S., Japanese Religious Thought
SHIOKAWA, T., French Language and Literature
SHITOMI, Y., West Asian History
SHOJI, K., Social Theories
SIRAFUJI, N., Japanese Language
STEINGRABER, S., History of Art
SUEKI, F., Japanese Buddhism
SUZUKI, H., Ancient Japanese Literature
TACHIBANA, M., Physiological Psychology
TADA, K., Ancient Japanese Literature
TAKAYAMA, M., Philosophy
TAKAHASHI, K., English Literature
TAKESHITA, M., Islamic Studies
TAKEUCHI, S., Japanese Ethical Thought
TAMURA, T., French Language and Literature
TOKURA, H., Chinese Language and Literature
TSUCHIDA, R., Indian Language and Literature
TSUKIMURA, T., French Language and Literature
TSUNODA, T., Linguistics
UENO, C., Family and Gender Studies
UTAGAWA, H., Archaeology
UWANO, Z., Accentology and Dialectology
YABUUCHI, M., Social Psychology
YAMAGUCHI, S., Experimental Social Psychology
YONESHIGE, F. Slav Languages and Literature
YOSHIDA, M., Korean History
YOSHIDA, N., Early Modern Japanese History
YUKAWA, Y., Theoretical Linguistics, Bantu Language

Graduate School of Education and Faculty of Education:

ETO, T., Health Sciences
FUJIOKA, N., Curriculum
FUJITA, H., Sociology of Education
HIJIKATA, S., History of Japanese Education
KAMEGUCHI, K., Clinical Psychology
KANEKO, M., Higher Education
KONDO, K., Clinical Psychology
MINOURA, Y., Comparative Education
MIURA, I., Library and Information Science
MUTOH, Y., Physical Education
NAKADA, M., Methods of Education
OGAWA, M., Educational Administration
OMURA, A., Educational Psychology
SAEKI, Y., Methods of Education
SASAKI, M., Methods of Education
SATOH, K., Adult Education and Youth Services
SATOH, M., Action Research on Teaching
URANO, T., Educational Administration
WATANABE, H., Educational Measurement

Graduate School of Engineering and Faculty of Engineering:

AIDA, T., Macromolecular Chemistry, Supramolecular Chemistry
AIHARA, K., Chaos Engineering, Non-linear Neuroscience
AIZAWA, T., Technology of Plasticity
AKIYAMA, H., Structural Engineering, Steel Structures
AMEMIYA, Y., X-ray instrumentation, X-ray Physics, Small-angle X-ray Scattering

ANDO, S., Sensors, Image Processing
ANDO, T., Architectural Planning and Design
AOYAMA, S., Communication Engineering
AOYAMA, T., Communication Technology, Multimedia Networking
ARAI, T., Advanced Robotics with Artificial Intelligence
ARAKAWA, C., Computational Fluid Dynamics
ARAKAWA, Y., Electric Propulsion
ASADA, Y., Continuum Mechanics, Plasticity Creep, Fatigue and Elevated Temperature Design
CHIKAYAMA, T., Information Engineering
DOHI, T., Medical Precision Engineering and Rehabilitation Engineering
FUJIMOTO, K., Energy Reaction and Catalysis Engineering
FUJIMURA, S., Measurement Science and Sensing Technology
FUJINO, M., Motion of Ships and Offshore Structures, Marine Environmental Engineering
FUJINO, Y., Structural Engineering and Dynamics
FUJISHIMA, A., Photo-functional Materials
FUJITA, K., Petroleum and Natural Gas Engineering
FUJITA, K., Sanitary Engineering
FUJIWARA, T., Solid-State Physics, Electronic Structure in Periodic and Aperiodic Systems
FUSHIMI, A., Merchant Ship Design
FUSHIMI, M., Mathematical Engineering
HANAKI, K., Urban and Global Environmental Management
HARA, H., Urban Design, Architectural Design
HARASHIMA, H., Communication Theory and Systems, Digital Signal Processing, Image Coding and Processing
HATAMURA, Y., Materials Processing, Force Sensors and Micro-actuator, Nano-manufacturing, Micro-tools for Medicine, Principles of Creative Design
HATORI, M., Communication Technology
HAYAKAWA, R., Polymer Physics, Biophysics
HIDAI, M., Organometallic Chemistry
HIDAKA, K., High Voltage Engineering
HIGUCHI, T., Micro-mechatronics, Robotics and Actuators
HIRANO, T., Combustion Environment and Safety Science
HIRAO, K., Quantum Chemistry, Computational Chemistry and Electronic Structure Theory
HIROSE, K., Speech Information Processing
HIROTSU, C., Statistical Engineering
HISADA, T., Nonlinear Finite Element Method
HORI, K., Artificial Intelligence
HORIE, K., Polymer Chemistry, Photochemistry in Solution and Polymer Solids, PHB and Optical Information Materials
HORII, H., Applied Mechanics, Rock Mechanics
HOTATE, K., Photonic Sensing, Photonic Signal Processing
ICHINOSE, H., Interface Science, Electron Microscopy
IEDA, H., Transport Planning and Policy, Infrastructure Development
IIZUKA, Y., Systems Analysis, Systems Design, Software Quality Applied Statics
IKUHARA, Y., Ceramic Materials
INOUE, H., Robotics
INOUE, H., Glass Science and Engineering
INOUE, S, Inorganic Materials in Microgravity
ISHIGURE, K., Applied Radiation Chemistry, Nuclear Reactor Chemistry and Water Chemistry
ISHIHARA, K., Biomaterials
ISHITANI, H., Modelling and Analysis of Resource Systems.
ISHIZUKA, M., Artificial Intelligence, Intelligent Information Systems
ISOBE, M., Coastal Engineering
ITAO, K., Information and Microdynamics
ITO, K., Preferred Orientation of Materials
ITOH, R., Photonics, Nonlinear Optics, Semiconductor Device and Materials Physics
KAGEYAMA, K., Composite Materials Engineering
KAJI, S., Aeroengines, Aeroacoustics
KAMATA, M., Equipment and Environmental Engineering
KAMIYA, T., Semiconductors, Lasers and Optoelectronics
KANDA, J., Wind and Earthquake Engineering, Probabilistic Load Models, Reliability-based Structural Design
KANNO, M., Precipitation Mechanism of Aluminium and Copper-based Alloys
KASAGI, N., Simulation, Prediction and Control of Turbulence and Heat Transfer
KATAOKA, K., Biomaterials
KATO, H., Cavitation, Control of Turbulent Flow
KATSUMURA, Y., Radiation Chemistry, Applied Radiation Chemistry
KATSURAI, M., Plasma Physics and Engineering
KAWAMURA, M., Environmental Chemistry
KIMPARA, I., Composite Materials and Structures
KIMURA, F., Production Engineering, CAD/CAM
KIMURA, H., Systems and Control Theory
KIMURA, K., Applied Solid State Physics
KIMURA, S., Membrane Separation Processes
KISHIO, K., High Temperature Superconductivity and Materials
KITAZAWA, K., Superconducting Materials, Magneto-Chemistry, Conductive Polymers
KODA, S., Chemical Reaction Engineering, Laser Chemistry, Reaction Chemistry
KODAMA, F., Science and Technology Studies, Science and Technology Policy
KOIBUCHI, K., Industrial Innovation, Fatigue Design
KOIDE, O., Evaluation of Regional Risks and Multimedia Database System for Historical Disasters
KOMIYAMA, H., Global Environmental Engineering, Chemical Reaction Engineering, Materials Science and Engineering
KOMIYAMA, M., Bio-organic Chemistry, Bioinorganic Chemistry, Host-Guest Chemistry
KONDO, K., Mechanics of Aerospace Structures
KONDO, S., Nuclear Reactor Design, Probabilistic Risk Assessment, Application of Artificial Intelligence to Human-Interface Design, Nuclear Energy Policy Analysis
KONDO, T., Non-linear Optics
KONO, M., Combustion of Propulsion Systems, Aerospace Propulsion
KOSHI, M., Chemical Reaction Kinetics, Laser Induced Chemistry
KOYAMA, T., Merchant Ship Design, Application of Artificial Intelligence
KUBOTA, H., Aerodynamics
KUDO, T., Solid State Electrochemistry, Inorganic Materials Science
KUDO, T., Intelligent Materials
KUNISHIMA, M., Construction Management and Project Engineering
KUWABARA, M., Preparation and Properties of Electronic Ceramics
MADARAME, H., Thermal Hydraulics, Flow-Induced Oscillations
MAEDA, H., Dynamics of Floating Structures and Underwater Vehicles
MAEDA, K., Defects in Solids
MAEKAWA, K., Concrete Engineering and Thermo-Physics
MAKISHIMA, A., Glass Science and Technology
MATSUI, H., Laser and Combustion Chemistry
MATSUMOTO, Y., Fluid Mechanics, Multiphase Flows, Molecular Dynamics
MATSUO, T., Biological Wastewater Treatment, Global Environmental Issues
MATSUO, Y., Air Conditioning
MINO, T., Applied Environmental Microbiology, Wastewater Treatment
MISONO, M., Catalytic Chemistry, Environmental Catalysis
MIYA, K., High Tc Superconductors and their Application to Nuclear Fusion Reactors and Energy Storage, Applied Electromagnetics and Mechanics
MIYANO, K., Surface Chemical Physics and LB Films
MIYATA, H., Ship System Development, Computational Fluid Dynamics
MIYAZAWA, K., Structure of Materials
MORICHI, S., Infrastructure Planning
MORISHITA, E., High-speed Gas Dynamics
MORITA, K., Iron and Steel Manufacture
NAGAMUNE, T., Biotechnology, Biochemical Engineering, Protein Engineering
NAGAO, T., Materials Processing and Machine Tools, Industrial Economics
NAGASAWA, Y., Architectural Planning and Design
NAGASHIMA, T., Aerospace Propulsion
NAKAJIMA, N., Artifactual Engineering, Micro Machines, Design Engineering
NAKAMURA, Y., Robotics, Automatic Control, Nonlinear Dynamics
NAKAO, S., Membrane Science and Technology
NAKAZAWA, M., Radiation Measurement, Quantum Beam Engineering
NISHI, T., Physics and Chemistry of Solid Polymers and Composite Materials
NISHIMURA, Y., Urban Conservation Planning, Urban Design
NISHINAGA, T., Electronic Materials, Crystal Growth and Electronic Properties
NITTA, T., Applied Superconductivity, Electrical Machinery, Power Systems
NOMOTO, T., Production Engineering, CIM Welding Dynamics
ODA, T., Electrostatics and Magnetic Separation
OHASHI, H., Thermal Hydrodynamics, Advanced Models for Complex Phenomena
OHGAKI, S, Environmental and Sanitary Engineering
OHNISHI, T., National and Regional Development Planning
OHTA, K., Urban Transport Planning
OHTSUBO, H., Structural Mechanics, CAE
OKA, Y, Nuclear Reactor Engineering
OKABE, A., Urban and Regional Analysis, Geographical Information Science
OKABE, Y., Theory of Probability, Time Series Analysis and Statistical Physics
OKAMURA, H., Concrete Engineering and Management
OKANO, Y., Resource Processing
OKUBO, S., Mining Machinery, Rock Mechanics
ONABE, K., Semiconductor Materials
OSHIMA, M., Semiconductor Surface Chemistry
OTANI, S., Structural Engineering and Dynamics, Reinforced Concrete Structures
OZONO, S., Engineering Metrology
SADAKATA, M., Combustion Engineering, Environmental Technology
SAIGO, K., Organic Synthesis, Polymer Synthesis
SAITO, T., Digital Communication and Computer Network
SAKAI, H., Internal Combustion Engines
SAKAI, S., Reliability Analysis, Fatigue under Random Loading

SAKAMOTO, I., Building Construction, Timber Structures
SAKAMOTO, Y., Environmental Engineering, Thermal Environment
SAKUMA, T., Ceramic Materials
SATO, J., Aircraft Design
SATO, J., Recycling and Re-use Systems for Iron and Steel Materials
SATO, T., Intelligent Robot Systems
SAWADA, T., Analytical Chemistry, Laser Spectroscopy, Photothermal Spectroscopy
SHIBATA, K., Control of Microstructures and Properties of Steel
SHIBATA, T., Semiconductor Devices and Integrated Circuits, Integrated Human Intelligence Systems
SHIMIZU, E., Geoinformatics, Regional Planning
SHIMOGAKI, Y., Device Processing
SHIOYA, T., Aerospace Materials, Mechanical Behaviour of Materials
SHOJI, M., Heat Transfer
SHOJI, T., Mining Geology and Industrial Mineralogy
SHINOHARA, O., Landscape Planning, Civic Design
SHINOHARA, T., Surface Technology
SONE, S., Transportation Systems Engineering
SUGAWARA, S., Fire Protection Engineering, Building Materials
SUGIHARA, K., Mathematical Engineering and Computational Geometry
SUGIHARI, S., Planning of Building Materials and Fire Protection Engineering
SUZUKI, A., Engineering Design for Nuclear Fuel Cycles, Environmental Science of Nuclear Energy, Energy Systems Science
SUZUKI, H., History of Architecture, History of Modern Architecture
SUZUKI, S., Flight Mechanics, Control Engineering
SUZUKI, T., Computer Application to Materials Processing
TACHI, S., Robotics, Cybernetics and Virtual Reality
TAKANO, M., Dynamics of Mechanisms
TAKEDA, N., Composite Materials and Structures, Smart Health Monitoring Systems
TAKEDA, T., Brain Science
TAKEICHI, M., Computer Science and Software Engineering
TAMAI, N., River Engineering and Environmental Hydraulics
TAMURA, M., Chemistry of Energetic Materials
TANAKA, H., Computer Architecture and Knowledge Engineering
TANAKA, M., Tribology, Rotordynamics and Security Design
TANAKA, S., Fusion Engineering, Radio Chemistry
TATSUOKA, F., Soil Mechanics, Geotechnology
TERASHIMA, K., Plasma Materials Engineering
TOKURA, Y., Materials Physics
TOMOSAWA, F., Building Materials, Concrete Engineering, Design for Durability
TOWHATA, I., Soil Mechanics, Soil Dynamics
TSUJIKAWA, S., Surface Technology
TSUKIHASHI, F., Chemistry of Materials Processing
TSUKIO, Y., Flexible Manufacturing, Virtual Reality and Social Infrastructure Systems
UCHIDA, S., High-Temperature Superconductivity, Metal-insulator Transition in Solids
UCHINOKURA, K., Superconductivity, Physics of Low-dimensional Spin Systems, Solid State Physics
UMEDA, T., Solidification Processing
WATANABE, A., Coastal Engineering
WATANABE, K., Molecular Biology of the Genetic Systems of Mitochondria, Development of *in Vitro* Translation Systems
WATANABE, S., Computational Science
YAGAWA, G., Computational Mechanics, Structural and Solid Mechanics and Nuclear Engineering
YAMADA, K., Global Environmental Engineering
YAMAJI, K., Energy Systems Analysis, Energy Modelling
YAMASHITA, K., Theoretical Chemistry and Chemical Reaction Dynamics
YAMATO, H., Design Systems, Automatic Control and Guidance
YAMATOMI, J., Rock Engineering and Mining Engineering
YAMAWAKI, M., Fusion and Fission Reactor Fuel and Materials, Chemical Thermodynamics, Solid State and Surface Chemistry
YASUOKA, M., Sound and Vibration Control, Room Acoustics
YOSHIDA, K., Ocean Engineering
YOSHIDA, T., Infrastructure Development and Management Systems for Developing Countries
YOSHIDA, T., Plasma Materials Engineering
YOSHIMOTO, K., Manual and Automatic Control
YOSHIZAWA, S., Bio-cybernetics

Graduate School of Science and Faculty of Science:

AMEMIYA, S., Developmental Biology
AOKI, H., Solid State Physics
AOKI, K., Population Biology
EGUCHI, T., Theoretical Particle Physics
FUJIKAWA, K., Elementary Particle Physics
FUKADA, Y., Biochemistry and Molecular Biology
FUKUDA, H., Plant Cell Biology
FUKUYAMA, H., Condensed Matter Physics
HAGIYA, M., Automated Deduction, Functional Programming, User Interface
HAMAGUCHI, H., Physical Chemistry
HAMANO, Y., Solid Earth Dynamics
HAYANO, R., Experimental Nuclear Physics
HIRAI, M., Human Cytogenetics
HIRAKI, K., Parallel Processing, Computer Architecture
HOTTA, Y., Biophysics, Molecular Biology
IIJIMA, T., Magnetospheric Physics
ISHIHARA, M., Nuclear Physics
ISHIKAWA, H., Insect Physiology and Molecular Biology
IWASAWA, Y., Chemical Kinetics and Catalysis
KAMAE, T., Experimental High Energy Physics
KAMBE, T., Fluid Mechanics
KAMIYA, R., Cell Biology
KATAYAMA, I., Nuclear Physics
KATO, M., Plant Systematics
KAWASHIMA, T., Organic Chemistry
KIMURA, G., Tectonics, Structural Geology
KIMURA, T., Morphological Anthropology and Biomechanics
KOBAYASHI, S., Low Temperature Physics
KOBAYASHI, T., Experimental Particle Physics
KOMA, A., Inorganic Chemistry
KONDO, N., Plant Physiology
KONO, M., Geomagnetism and Geodynamics
KUROIWA, T., Developmental Morphology
MAKISHIMA, K., X-ray Astrophysics
MASUDA, T., Operating Systems, Systems Software
MATSUMOTO, R., Sedimentology and Geochemistry
MATSU'URA, M., Seismology
MIYAMOTO, M., Planetary Material Science
MORI, T., Endocrinology
MORISAWA, M., Cell Biology
NAGAMINE, K., Meson Science
NAGAO, K., Geochemistry
NAGASAWA, N., Solid State Spectroscopy Physics
NAGATA, T., Plant Physiology and Plant Molecular Biology
NAKADA, Y., Astrophysics
NAKAMURA, E., Organic Chemistry
NARASAKA, K., Synthetic Organic Chemistry
NISHIHARA, H., Inorganic Chemistry
NOMOTO, K., Theoretical Astrophysics
NONAKA, M., Molecular Immunology
NOTSU, K., Geochemistry
OGAWA, T., Atmospheric Physics and Chemistry
OHMORI, H., Physical Geography, Climatic Geomorphology
OHTA, T., Physical Chemistry
OKAMURA, S., Extragalactic Astronomy
ORITO, S., Experimental Elementary Particle Physics, Astro-particle Physics
OSAKI, Y., Theoretical Astrophysics
OTSUKA, T., Nuclear Physics
OYANAGI, Y., Numerical Analysis, Parallel Processing
SAIGO, K., Molecular Biology
SAKAI, H., Nuclear Physics
SAKANO, H., Molecular Biology and Molecular Immunology
SATO, K., Astrophysics and Cosmology Physics
SEKIGUCHI, M., Nuclear Physics
SHIMA, A., Radiation Biology
SHIMAZAKI, H., Economic Geology and Chemical Geology
SHIOKAWA, K., Developmental Biology
SOFUE, Y., Radio Astronomy
SUEMATSU, H., Solid State Physics
SUGIURA, N., Planetary Science
TACHIBANA, K., Organic Chemistry of Natural Products
TAJIMA, F., Molecular Population Genetics
TAKASE, Y., Plasma Physics and Nuclear Fusion
TANABE, K., Palaeontology
TANABE, T., Nuclear Physics
TARUCHA, S., Solid State Physics
TERASAWA, T., Space Physics
TOH-E, A., Yeast Genetics
TOKURA, Y., Solid State Physics
TOYAMA, H., Plasma Physics
TSUJII, J., Computational Linguistics, Natural Language Processing
TSUKADA, M., Solid State Physics and Surface Physics
UMEZAWA, Y., Analytical Chemistry
WADATI, M., Statistical Physics and Condensed Matter Physics
WAKABAYASHI, T, Biophysics
WARREN, P. H., Planetary Material Science
WATANABE, A., Plant Physiology
YAMAGATA, T., Physical Oceanography
YAMAMOTO, M., Molecular Genetics
YAMANOUCHI, K., Physical Chemistry
YAMASAKI, M., Meteorology
YANAGIDA, T., Elementary Particle Physics
YAZAKI, K., Nuclear Physics
YOKOYAMA, S., Biophysics, Biochemistry and Molecular Biology
YONEKURA, N., Physical Geography, Quaternary Research, Tectonic Geomorphology, Active Tectonics
YONEZAWA, A., Foundation of Computer Software, Programming Language
YOSHII, Y., Galactic Astronomy

Graduate School of Agriculture and Life Sciences and Faculty of Agriculture:

ABE, H., Biochemistry of Aquatic Animals
ABE, K., Biological Function Development
AIDA, K., Fish Physiology
AKITA, S., Crop Ecology and Morphology
ARIMA, T., Wood Physics, Wood-based Materials and Timber Engineering
ARAI, T., Physics of Biomaterials
DOI, K., Veterinary Pathology
FUJITA, N., Agricultural and Development Economics
FUKUI, Y., Biological Chemistry
FURUTA, K., Forest Entomology and Zoology

FUSETANI, N., Aquatic Natural Products Chemistry
HAYASHI, Y., Veterinary Anatomy
HIGUCHI, H., Wild Life Biology
HINO, A., Aquaculture Biology
HIBI, T., Plant Pathology
HIRAI, A., Radiation Genetics
HORINOUCHI, S., Microbiology and Fermentation
IDE, Y., Forestry Gene Science
IGARASHI, Y., Applied Microbiology
ISHII, R., Crop Physiology
IZUMIDA, Y., International Food System
KAJI, M., Forest Ecosystem
KAMINOGAWA, S., Food Biochemistry
KARAKI, H., Veterinary Pharmacology
KITAHARA, T., Organic Chemistry
KITAMOTO, K., Microbiology
KOBAYASHI, H., Forest Utilization
KOBAYASHI, M., Sericultural Science
KUMAGAI, Y., Forest Landscape Planning and Design
KURATA, K., Bio-environmental Engineering
KUROKURA, H., Aquatic Biology
MATSUMOTO, S., Soil Science
MATSUZAWA, H., Enzymology
MESHIZUKA, G., Wood Chemistry and Pulping Chemistry
MINOWA, M., Forest Management and Mensuration
MIZUMACHI, H., Science of Polymeric Materials
MORI, S., Plant Molecular Physiology
NAGASAWA, H., Bio-organic Chemistry
NAGATA, S., Forest Ecology and Society
NAGATO, Y., Plant Breeding and Genetics
NAMBA, S., Bioresource Technology
NISHIZAWA, N. K., Plant Nutrition and Biotechnology
NOGUCHI, T., Nutritional Biochemistry
OGAWA, H., Veterinary Surgery
OHTA, M., Wood-based Materials and Timber Engineering, Wood Physics
OHTA, T., Forest Hydrology and Erosion Control
OHTSUKA, H., Biochemical Virology
OKAMOTO, T., Biological and Mechanical Engineering
OKANO, T., Structural Biopolymers
ONABE, F., Pulp and Paper Science
ONO, K., Veterinary Clinical Pathobiology
ONODERA, T., Molecular Immunology
OYAIZU, H., Soil Science
SABURI, Y., Forest Chemistry
SAKA, H., Plant Physiology
SAKAI, S., Animal Breeding
SAKIYAMA, R., Horticultural Science
SASAKI, N., Veterinary Surgery
SATO, Y., Land Environmental Engineering
SAWAZAKI, T., Livestock Biotechnology
SEO, Y., Agricultural Process Engineering and Processing Machinery
SHIMIZU, M., Food Chemistry
SHOGENJI, S., Food and Resource Economics
SUGIYAMA, K., Horticultural Science
SUZUKI, K., Forest Botany and Forest Health
TAKAGI, M., Cellular Genetics
TAKAHASHI, E., Veterinary Public Health
TAKAHASHI, M., Veterinary Physiology
TAKEUCHI, K., Landscape Ecology and Planning
TANAKA, M., Agricultural History
TANIGUCHI, N., Agricultural Structure and Policy
TANIUCHI, T., Fisheries Biology
TATSUKI, S., Applied Entomology
TOJO, H., Applied Genetics
UOZUMI, T., Molecular and Cellular Breeding
WAKABAYASHI, H., Fish Pathology
WATABE, S., Aquatic Molecular Biology and Technology
WATANABE, S., Environmental Bioresource Development
YAGI, H., Silviculture
YAGI, H., Farm Business Management
YAMAZAKI, S., Analytical Chemistry
YODA, K., Microbiology Biotechnology
YOSHIKAWA, Y., Laboratory Animal Science

Graduate School of Medicine and Faculty of Medicine:

ARAIE, M., Ophthalmology
ARAKI, S., Public Health
FUJITA, T., Internal Medicine
HAGA, T., Neurobiochemistry
HANAOKA, K., Anaesthesiology
HARII, K., Plastic Surgery
HASHIZUME, K., Paediatric Surgery
HIROKAWA, N., Anatomy
IGA, T., Pharmacy
IHARA, Y., Neuropathology
IINO, M., Pharmacology
IMACHI, K., Medical Engineering
ISHIKAWA, T., Pathology
KAGA, K., Oto-laryngology
KAI, I., Health Sociology
KAMINISHI, M., Surgery
KAMIYA, A., Medical Electronics
KANAGAWA, K., Community Health Nursing
KANAZAWA, I., Neurology
KAWANA, T., Obstetrics and Gynaecology
KIMURA, S., Internal Medicine, Infectious Diseases and HIV Infection
KIRINO, T., Neurosurgery
KIRITANI, S., Logopaedics and Phoniatrics
KITA, K., Biomedical Chemistry
KITAMURA, T., Urology
KOJIMA, M., Adult Nursing
KUBOKI, T., Psychosomatic Medicine
KURITA, H., Mental Health and Nursing
MAEKAWA, K., Traumatology and Critical Care Medicine
MAKUUCHI, M., Surgery
MATHINAMI, R., Pathology
MATSUSHIMA, K., Inflammation, Immunology, Host Defence Mechanism and Molecular Preventive Medicine
MISINA, M., Pharmacology
MIYASHITA, Y., Physiology
MUTO, T., Surgery
NAKAHARA, K., Laboratory Medicine
NAKAMURA, K., Orthopaedic Surgery
NIIMI, S., Logopaedics and Phoniatrics
OHASHI, Y., Epidemiology and Biostatistics
OHE, K., Medical Informatics
OHTOMO, K., Diagnostic Radiology
OHTSUKA, R., Human Ecology
OKAYAMA, H., Biochemistry
OMATA, M., Internal Medicine
OUCHI, Y., Geriatric Medicine and Cardiovascular Diseases
SEYAMA, Y., Nutrition and Physiological Chemistry
SHIBATA, Y., Transfusion Medicine and Immunohaematology
SHIMIZU, T., Biochemistry
SHINOHARA, K., Radiation Biology and X-ray Microscopy
SUGISHITA, C., Family Health Care Nursing
SUGISHITA, M., Neuropsychology
SUZUKI, N., Radiation Biophysics
TAKAHASHI, T., Neurophysiology
TAKAHASHI, Y., Basic Nursing
TAKAMOTO, S., Thoracic Surgery
TAKATO, T., Oral and Maxillofacial Surgery
TAKATORI, T., Forensic Medicine
TAKETANI, Y., Obstetrics and Gynaecology
TAMAKI, K., Dermatology
TANIGUCHI, T., Signal Transduction and Gene Regulation in Host Defence Mechanisms
TOKUNAGA, K., Human Immunogenetics
TOYOOKA, T., Internal Medicine
UENO, S., Biomedical Engineering
UMENAI, T., Health Policy and Economics
USHIJIMA, H., Maternal and Child Health, Developmental Medicine Virology
WONGKHOMTHONG, S., Primary Health Care, AIDS and Health Services in Developing Countries
YAMAMOTO, K., Physical Therapy
YANAGISAWA, M., Paediatrics
YAZAKI, Y., Internal Medicine

Graduate School of Pharmaceutical Sciences and Faculty of Pharmaceutical Sciences:

EBIZUKA, Y., Natural Products Chemistry
FUKUYAMA, T., Synthetic Natural Products Chemistry
IMAI, K., Bio-Analytical Chemistry
INOUE, K., Health Chemistry
IRIMURA, T., Cancer Biology and Molecular Immunology
KATADA, T., Physiological Chemistry
KIRINO, Y., Neurobiophysics
KOBAYASHI, S., Synthetic Medicinal Chemistry
MATSUKI, N., Chemical Pharmacology
NAGANO, T., Bio-organic and Medicinal Chemistry
NAGAO, T., Pharmacology and Toxicology
NATORI, S., Developmental Biochemistry
SATOH, Y., Protein Structural Biology
SHIBASAKI, M., Synthetic Organic Chemistry
SHIMADA, I., Physical Chemistry
SHUDOH, K., Organic and Medicinal Chemistry
SUGIYAMA, Y., Biopharmaceutics
TAKETO, M., Biomedical Genetics

Graduate School of Mathematical Sciences:

FUNAKI, T., Probability Theory
HORIKAWA, E., Algebraic Geometry
KATAOKA, K., Partial Differential Equations
KATO, K., Number Theory
KATSURA, T., Algebraic Geometry
KAWAMATA, Y., Algebraic Geometry and Complex Manifolds
KIKUCHI, F., Numerical Analysis
KOHNO, T., Three-manifolds, Quantum Groups
KUSUOKA, S., Probability Theory and its Application
MATANO, H., Nonlinear Partial Equations, Dynamical Systems
MATSUMOTO, Y., Topology
MORITA, S., Topology of Manifolds
NAKAMURA, S., Differential Equations and Mathematical Physics
NAMBA, K., Axiomatic Set Theory
NOGUCHI, J., Complex Analysis in Several Variables, Complex Geometry
OCHIAI, T., Differential Geometry
ODA, T., Number Theory
OKAMOTO, K., Differential Equations Complex Analysis
OSHIMA, T., Algebraic Analysis, Theory of Unitary Representations
SATSUMA, J., Mathematical Physics
TSUBOI, T., Foliations, Diffeomorphism Groups
YAJIMA, K., Functional Analysis, Differential Equations
YAMADA, M., Fluid Mechanics

ATTACHED INSTITUTES

Institute of Medical Science: 4-6-1 Shirokanedai, Minato-ku, Tokyo 108-8639; f. 1892; Dir K. ARAI.

Earthquake Research Institute: 1-1-1 Yayoi, Bunkyo-ku, Tokyo 113-0032; f. 1925; Dir T. FUJII; publ. *Bulletin* (quarterly).

Institute of Oriental Culture: 7-3-1 Hongo, Bunkyo-ku, Tokyo 113-0033; f. 1941; Dir Y. HARA; publs *Memoirs* (2 a year), *Oriental Culture* (annually).

Institute of Social Science: 7-3-1 Hongo, Bunkyo-ku, Tokyo 113-0033; f. 1946; Dir S. HIROWATARI; publs *Journal of Social Science* (every 2 months), *Social Science Japan Journal* (2 a year), *Social Science Japan* (newsletter, 3 or 4 a year).

Institute of Socio-Information and Communication Studies: 7-3-1 Hongo, Bunkyo-ku, Tokyo 113-0033; f. 1949; Dir J. HAMADA; publs *Bulletin* (annually), *ISICS* series (irregular).

Institute of Industrial Science: 7-22-1 Roppongi, Minato-ku, Tokyo 106-8558; f. 1949; Dir M. SAKAUCHI; publs *Seisan-Kenkyu* (monthly), *Annual Report*.

Historiographical Institute: 3-1 Hongo 7-chome, Bunkyo-ku, Tokyo 113-0032; f. 1869; Dir H. KURODA; publs *Annual Report, Shoho*.

Institute of Molecular and Cellular Biosciences: 1-1-1 Yayoi, Bunkyo-ku, Tokyo 113-0032; f. 1953; Dir K. SUZUKI; publs *Reports* (annually).

Institute for Cosmic Ray Research: 3-2-1, Midori-cho, Tanashi-shi, Tokyo 188-8502; f. 1953; Dir Y. TOTSUKA; publs *ICRR Report* (irregularly), *ICRR News* (quarterly), *ICRR Hokoku, Annual Report*.

Institute for Solid State Physics: 22-1 Roppongi 7-chome, Minato-ku, Tokyo 106-8666; f. 1957; Dir H. YASUOKA; publ. *Technical Report* (100 a year).

Ocean Research Institute: 1-15-1, Minamidai, Nakano-ku, Tokyo 164-8639, f. 1962; Dir K. TAIRA; publs *Bulletin, Preliminary Cruise Report* (irregular).

TOKYO INSTITUTE OF TECHNOLOGY

2-12-1, O-okayama, Meguro-ku, Tokyo 152

Telephone: (3) 3726-1111

Founded 1881

President: T. KIMURA
Director-General of Administration Bureau: K. ITO
Dean of Students: K. OGAWA
Library Director: T. TSUKADA

Library of 780,000 vols
Number of full-time teachers: 1,104
Number of students: 9,811

DEANS

Faculty of Science: Y. HATANO
Faculty of Engineering: H. MATSUMOTO
Faculty of Bioscience and Biotechnology: M. HOSHI
Interdisciplinary Graduate School of Science and Engineering: T. NONAKA
Graduate School of Information Science and Engineering: H. TANAKA
Graduate School of Decision Science and Technology: H. KONNO

DIRECTORS

Research Laboratory of Resources Utilization: T. ENDO
Precision and Intelligence Laboratory: K. IGA
Materials and Structures Laboratory: A. SAWAOKA
Research Laboratory for Nuclear Reactors: A. MORIKAWA

PROFESSORS

Faculty of Science:

ENOKI, T., Physical Chemistry
FUJITA, T., Algebraic Geometry
FUKUDA, T., Singularity and Topology
FUTAKI, A., Differential Geometry
HATANO, Y., Physical Chemistry
HIKIDA, T., Physical Chemistry
HONKURA, Y., Geophysics
HOSOYA, A., Theoretical Cosmology
IGUCHI, I., Material Science
IIO, K., Experimental Solid State Physics, Magneto-Optics
INOUE, A., Global Analysis on Two-Dimensional Manifolds
KAIZU, Y., Coordination Chemistry
KAKIMOTO, F, Experimental Cosmic Ray Physics
KAKINUMA, K., Bioorganic Chemistry
KAWAMURA, K., Geochemistry
KITAHARA, K., Statistical Physics
KUROKAWA, N., Number Theory
KUWAJIMA, I., Synthetic Organic Chemistry
MARUYAMA, S., Tectonics
MINAMI, F., Materials Science and Laser Spectroscopy
MURAI, T.
MURATA, M., Differential Equations
NAGAI, Y., Experimental Nuclear Physics
NAKAZAWA, K., Planetary Science
NISHIDA, N., Experimental Solid State Physics, Low Temperature Physics
NISHIMORI, H., Theoretical Solid State Physics, Neural Networks
NOGUCHI, J., Complex Analysis and Complex Geometry
OBI, K., Physical Chemistry
ODA, T., Theoretical Nuclear Physics
OGUNI, M., Physical Inorganic Chemistry
OHASHI, Y., Crystal Chemistry
OHMURA, Y., Theoretical Solid State Physics
SAITO, M., Geophysics
SAKAI, N., Theoretical Particle Physics
SHIBA, H., Theoretical Solid State Physics
SHIGA, T., Stochastic Processes and Applied Probabilities
SUZUKI, K., Organic Chemistry
TAKAHASHI, E., Experimental Mineralogy
TANIMOTO, T., Earth and Planetary Sciences
TANNO, S., Differential Geometry
TSUNASHIMA, S., Physical Chemistry
WATANABE, Y., Experimental High Energy Physics
YAGI, K., Experimental Solid State Physics, Crystal and Surface Physics
YASHIMA, T., Chemistry
YOSHINO, J., Experimental Solid State Physics

Faculty of Engineering:

ABE, M., Electronic Properties of Matter
ANDO, I., Properties of Polymers
ANDO, M., Antennas, Electromagnetic Wave Theory
AOKI, Y., Urban Planning
ARAKI, K., Coding Theory, Digital Communication Systems
DAIMON, M., Cement Chemistry
ENDO, M., Solid Vibrations
FUJII, N., Electronic Circuits and Networks
FUJIOKA, H., History of Architecture, Architectural Design
FUKAO, T., Power Electronics
FUNAHASHI, H., Machine Elements, Kinematics
FURUYA, K., Optical and Quantum Electronics
HANNA, Z., Imaging Materials
HARASHINA, S., Environmental Planning and Conflict Resolution
HAYASHI, I., Silent Engineering, Micro-Robotics
HIGUCHI, Y., Exercise Physiology
HIROSE, S., Robotics, Biomechanics
IKARIYA, T., Homogeneous Catalysis, Synthetic Organic Chemistry
IKEDA, S., Hydraulics and Applied Hydromechanics
INOUE, T., Physical Chemistry of Polymer Materials
ISEKI, T., Materials for Nuclear and Fusion Reactors, Ceramics
ISHII, S., Electric Power Engineering, Plasma
ISHIZU, K., Polymer Synthesis, Polymer Reactions
ITO, Y., Machine Tool Engineering, Design Methodology, Metal Cutting, Production System
IWAMOTO, M., Electronic Materials
KAJIMOTO, M., Polymer Synthesis, Polymer Thin Films
KAJITANI, Y., Theory of Networks
KAJIUCHI, T., Biochemical Engineering
KAMIO, A., Metallurgy of Non-Ferrous Metals and Alloys
KAMIMOTO, T., Thermal-Fluid Engineering
KATO, K., Mechanics of Plastic Solids
KAWASAKI, J., Mass Transfer Operations
KAWASHIMA, K., Earthquake Engineering
KISHIMOTO, K., Strength of Materials, Computational Mechanics
KITAGAWA, A., Fluid Power Control
KOBAYASHI, A., Industrial Measurement
KOBAYASHI, H., Fracture Mechanics and Fatigue
KONAGAI, M., Semiconductors
KUNIEDA, H., Integrated Circuits, Signal Processing
KUROSAKI, Y., Thermal Engineering, Heat Transfer
KUSAKABE, O., Geotechnical Engineering
MARUYAMA, T., Crystal Technology, Physical Chemistry in Advanced Materials
MATSUMOTO, H., Strength of Materials
MATSUMURA, M., Electronic Devices
MATSUO, T., Physical Metallurgy of Iron and Steels, High Temperature Deformation in Alloys
MATSUO, Y., Mechanical Properties of Ceramics
MIKI, C., Structural Mechanics and Engineering
MITA, T., Control Theory, Applications of Control Theory, Robotics
MIYAUCHI, T., Fluid Dynamics, Reactive Gas Dynamics
MIZUTANI, N., Advanced Ceramics
MOCHIMARU, Y., Computational Fluid Dynamics
MORI, K., Autonomous Decentralized Systems
MORIIZUMI, T., Bioelectronics
NAGAMATSU, A., Dynamics, Numerical Analysis
NAGATA, K., Ferrous Metallurgy and Sensor Technology
NAKAHAMA, S., Polymer Synthesis
NAKAHARA, T., Lubrication Technology, Two-Phase Flow, Oil Hydraulics
NAKAI, T., Synthetic Organic Chemistry, Organosulphur Chemistry
NAKANO, M., Control Machinery
NAOE, M., Electronic Materials
NIIYAMA, H., Chemical Reaction Engineering
NITTONO, O., Metal Physics
NOSE, T., Properties of Polymers
OGAWA, K., Mechanical Operations
OGAWA, T., Steel and Shell Structures
OHKAMI, Y., Space Mechanical Systems
OHYAMA, N., Medical Imaging and Processing
OKADA, K., Ceramic Raw Materials, Mineralogical Science
OKUI, N., Organic Thin Films, Physical Properties of Polymers
ONO, H., Building Materials
ONO, K., Dynamics of Machinery
ONO, Y., Heterogenous Catalysis
ONZAWA, T., Welding and Material Science
OTSUKA, K., Heterogeneous Catalysis, Electrocatalysis
OTSUKI, N., Construction Materials
SAITO, A., Thermal Engineering
SAKAI, Y., Communication Systems
SAKAMOTO, K., Architectural Design
SAKANIWA, K., Communication Theory
SATO, T., Materials Development, Magnetic Materials, Amorphous Metals
SENDA, M., Environmental Design
SHIBUYA, T., Strength of Materials
SHIMOJIMA, H., Motion Analysis and Control
SHIRAKASHI, T., Machining, High Speed Plastic Performance, Material Science
SUMITA, M., Solid Structure and Physical Properties of Organic Materials, Polymer Composites
SUZUKI, H., Organometallic Chemistry
SUZUMURA, A., Joining, High Temperature Materials
TAKAHASHI, T., Synthetic Organic Chemistry, Synthetic Processes for Natural Products
TAKEZOE, H., Optical and Electrical Properties of Organic Materials
TOKIMATSU, K., Geotechnical Engineering

TOKURA, H., Processing Technologies
TSUDA, K., Chemical Plant Materials
TSURU, T., Chemistry of Metal Surfaces, Electrochemistry, Corrosion and Passivity of Metals
UCHIKAWA, K., Visual Information Processing, Colour Vision
UEDA, M., Waves Information Processing
UENO, S., Theory of Parallel and VLSI Computation
WAKIHARA, M., Inorganic Solid State Chemistry
WATANABE, J., Structure and Properties of Polymer Liquid Crystals
YAGI, K., Architectural Design
YAMAJI, A., Materials Science
YAMANE, M., Glass, Inorganic Materials
YAMANE, R., Fluid Engineering

Faculty of Bioscience and Biotechnology:

AIZAWA, M., Biosensors
AKAIKE, T., Medical Polymers
FUJIHIRA, M., Electrochemistry
HAMAGUCHI, Y., Cell Biology
HANDA, H., Biosystems
HASHIMOTO, H., Biochemistry
HIROSE, S., Biochemistry
HIROTSU, S., Biophysics
HOSHI, M., Biochemistry
IKAI, A., Biological Kinetics
INOUE, Y., Physical Chemistry
KISHIMOTO, T., Developmental Biology
KITAMURA, N., Molecular Biology
KUDO, A., Molecular Immunology, Bone Biology
MOTOKAWA, T., Animal Physiology
NAGAI, K., Cell-Engineering
OKADA, N., Molecular Evolution
OKAHATA, Y., Fundamentals of Biomolecules
OKURA, I., Biophysical Chemistry, Enzyme Chemistry
SATO, F., Biological Activated Materials
SHISHIDO, K., Molecular Biology
TAKAMIYA, K., Plant Physiology
TANAKA, N., Structural Studies on Protein by X-Ray Diffraction Methods
UENO, A., Bioorganic Chemistry, Molecular Recognition
UNNO, H., Biochemistry

Interdisciplinary Graduate School of Science and Engineering: (4259 Nagatsuta-cho, Midori-ku, Yokohama 227; tel. (45) 922-1111)

AIKA, K., Catalysis and Reaction Engineering
FORTMANN, C. M., Photo Voltaic Solar Energy
HARA, S., Control Systems Theory
HIROTA, K., Information Systems
HOTTA, E., Plasma Engineering, Pulsed Power Technology
HOYANO, A., Urban and Building Environment
INOUE, A., Reactor Thermal Engineering
ISHIKAWA, T., Hydraulics and Hydrology
ITO, K., Computational Brain Science, Design and Control of Robotics and Prostheses
KABASHIMA, S., Energy Conversion Physics and Low Temperature Engineering
KATO, M., Fracture and Deformation
KAWARADA, H., Information Processing, Pattern Recognition
KIDA, T., Network Theory, Signal Theory, Multi-Dimensional Signal Theory
KITAZAWA, H., Nuclear Physics, Nuclear Engineering, Plasma Physics
KIYA, F., Environmental Equipment
KOBAYASHI, S., Knowledge Information Processing
KUROKAWA, T., Urban Facility Planning, Urban Transport Planning
MIDORIKAWA, S., Earthquake Engineering
MISHIMA, Y., Physical Metallurgy and Alloy Design
NAKAMURA, K., Computational Neuroscience
NAKANO, B., Organizational Decision Making, General Systems Theory, Mathematical Economics
NITTA, K., Artificial Intelligence, Regal Reasoning
NAKANO, Y., Environmental Engineering, Separation Process Engineering
NONAKA, T., Organic Electrochemistry
ODAWARA, O., Electrochemistry of Metals
OHMACHI, T., Earthquake Engineering
OHNO, R., Architectural Design and Planning, Environmental Psychology
OHTSU, M., Opto-quantum Electronics
OKADA, I., Molten Salt Chemistry
SAKATA, T., Physical Chemistry
SATO, A., Strengthening Mechanism and Lattice Imperfections
SEO, K., Engineering Seismology
SHIMIZU, I., Material Science, Imaging Science and Engineering
SUGENO, M., Fuzzy Systems Theory
TAKAYANAGI, K., Diffraction and Crystal
TAKEI, H., Organic Chemistry
TOKUDA, K., Electrochemistry
YABE, T., Laser Fusion, Computational Mathematics
YAMASAKI, H., Energy Conversion Engineering
YAMAZAKI, Y., Solid State Physics and Chemistry
YOKOYAMA, M., Automated Machine Design
YOSHIKAWA, M., Manufacturing Processes

Graduate School of Information Science and Engineering:

AOKI, S., Computational Mechanics
FUJII, S., Environmental Engineering
FUJIWARA, E., Coding Theory, Computer Systems
FURUI, S., Speech Recognition, Human Interfaces
FURUTA, K., Control Theory and its Application, Robot Control
HORAI, M., Theoretical Computer Science
KOJIMA, M., Mathematical Programming
KOJIMA, S., Geometry and Topology
NADAOKA, K., Environmental Systems Analysis, Coastal and Ocean Engineering, Mesoscale Meteorology, Applied Remote Sensing, Coastal-Space Design, Applied Fluid Dynamics
NAKAJIMA, M., Computer Graphics, Image Processing
OGAWA, H., Pattern Recognition, Image Processing
SASSA, M., Computer Software, Programming Environments
SATO, T., Artificial Intelligence and Logic Programming
SHIMIZU, M., Biomechanics, Fluid Dynamics
TAKAHASHI, Y., Applied Probability, Operations Research
TAKAHASHI-HORAI, M., Lambda–Calculus, Type Theory
TAKIGUCHI, K., Mechanics of Building Structures, Disaster Prevention Systems, Concrete Engineering
TANAKA, H., Natural Language Processing
TOKUDA, T., Software Engineering
TSUKADA, T., Precision Engineering, Data Processing
UJIHASHI, S., Biomechanics, Sports Engineering, Safety Engineering
UKAI, S., Nonlinear Partial Differential Equations
WATANABE, T., Regional Planning, City Planning, Planning for Tourism and Recreation
YONEZAKI, N., Applied Logic, Software Science
YOSHIDA, Y., Computational Mechanics and Scientific Computation

Graduate School of Decision Science and Technology:

ENKAWA, T., Production Management
FUKAMI, T., City Planning
FURUKAWA, K., Financial Management
HASHIZUME, D., Sociology
HAYASAKA, M., History of Politics (Slavic Studies)
HIDANO N., Regional Planning and Infrastructure Project Appraisal
IGUCHI, T., Japanese Literature
IIJIMA, J., Systems Theory
IMADA, T., International Relations
ISHII, M., Sports Psychology
ITO, K., Ergonomics, Production Control
KIJIMA, K., Management Systems
KIMOTO, T., History of Technology
KONNO, H., Operations Research (Mathematical Programming)
KUMATA, Y., City Planning, Urban Systems Analysis
KUWAKO, T., Philosophy
MIYAJIMA, M., Industrial Management
MORI, M., Operations Research, Applied Probabilities
MURAKI, M., Process Management
MUTA, H., Educational Planning, Economics of Education
NAKAGAWA, M., Educational Psychology
NAKAHARA, Y., Exercise Physiology
NAKAMURA, Y., Landscape Planning, Regional Planning
ONO, Y., Economic Theory
SAITO, T., Sociometrics
SHIMIZU, Y., Educational Technology, Electromagnetic Wave
TANAKA, Z., Political Science
WARAGAI, T., Philosophy, Logic
WATANABE, C., Technology Policy, Technology Management
WATANABE, T., Political Economy
YAMAZAKI, M., History of Science
YANO, M., Social Planning

Research Laboratory of Resources Utilization:

DOMEN, K., Surface Chemical Reaction
ENDO, T., Polymer Chemistry, Organic Synthesis
HIROSE, C., Molecular Spectroscopy
ICHIMURA, K., Organic Photochemistry
IKEDA, T., Polymer Chemistry and Photochemistry
ISHIDA, M., Chemical Engineering and Chemical Environmental Process Design
MORO-OKA, Y., Catalysis and Organic Synthesis
NAKA, Y., Chemical Environmental Systems Engineering
SHODA, M., Biochemical Engineering, Applied Microbiology
YAMAMOTO, T., Inorganic and Organometallic Chemistry
YAMASE, T., Photochemistry and Photoelectrochemistry
YOSHIDA, M., Biochemistry

Precision and Intelligence Laboratory:

HIGO, Y., Physical Metallurgy, Nondestructive Evaluation
HOUJOH, H., Acoustic Measurement, Machine Dynamics
IGA, K., Opto-Quantum Electronics
IKEGAMI, K., Solid Mechanics
ISHIWARA, H., Semiconductor Electronics
KAGAWA, T., Process Control
MARUYAMA, K., Precision Machine Elements, Metrology
OHTSUKI, S., Bio-medical Ultrasonics, Acoustic Engineering
SATO, M., Pattern Recognition Image Processing
SIMOKOBE, A., Dynamics and Control of Precision Mechanisms
UEHA, S., Ultrasonic Engineering, Applied Optics
UMEZAWA, K., Mechanical Vibration and Sound Control, Gear Engineering
WAKASHIMA, K., Materials Science, Micromechanics of Composites
YOKOTA, S., Fluid Power Control

Materials and Structures Laboratory:

ATAKE, T., Solid State Physical Chemistry
HASHIZUME, H., Diffraction Physics, Characterization and Structure Analysis of Materials
HAYASHI, S., Building Structural Materials
KASAI, K., Structural Engineering, Steel Structures, Dynamic Control
KAWAZOE, H., Opto-electronic Properties of Inorganic Materials
KOINUMA, H., Quantum Functional Materials, Thin Films
KONDO, K., High Pressure and Temperature Science and Technology
SAWAOKA, A., High Pressure and Temperature for Materials Science and Technology
WADA, A., Structural Engineering
WAKAI, F., Physical Ceramics
YAMAUCHI, H., Materials Science, Oxide Superconductors, Phase Transformations in Materials
YASUDA, E., Mechanical Properties of Ceramics
YOSHIMURA, M., Synthesis and Evaluation of Ceramics

Research Laboratory for Nuclear Reactors:

ARITOMI, M., Nuclear Thermal Engineering
FUJII, Y., Fusion Fuel Chemistry, Tritium Chemistry
MORIKAWA, A., Photocatalytic Chemistry
NINOKATA, H., Reactor Safety, Reactor Physics
OGAWA, M., Beam Plasma Sciences, Nuclear Fusion, Nuclear Physics
SEKIMOTO, H., Neutronics, Nuclear Reactor Design
SHIMADA, R., Fusion Reactor Control, Plasma Engineering
TAKAGI, R., Radiation Damage, Molten Salt Chemistry
TOMIYASU, H., Nuclear Chemistry, Co-ordination Chemistry
YOSHIZAWA, Y., Thermal Engineering, Energy System, Combustion

ATTACHED INSTITUTES

Imaging Science and Engineering Laboratory (at Nagatsuta): Dir N. OHYAMA.
Health Service Center: Dir A. NAGAMATSU.
Center for Research and Development of Educational Technology: Dir Y. SHIMIZU.
Computer Center: Dir R. SHIMADA.
International Cooperation Center for Science and Technology: Dir M. NIIYAMA.
Research Center for the Very Low Temperature System: Dir M. YOSHIKAWA.
Center for Research Cooperation and Information Exchange (at Nagatsuta): Dir H. I. SHIMIZU.
Research and Development Center for Educational Facilities: Dir H. ONO.
Kusatsu-Shirane Volcano Observatory: Dir Y. HONKURA.
Gene Research Center (at Nagatsuta): Dir N. OKADA.
Research Center for Carbon Recycling and Utilization: Dir T. HIKITA.
Research Center for Quantum Effect Electronics: Dir T. MORIIZUM.
Research Center for Experimental Biology (at Nagatsuta): Dir S. HIROSE.
Centre for Environment Preservation: Dir T. KAMIMOTO.
Foreign Language Research and Teaching Center: N. MAKOSHI.

TOKYO MEDICAL AND DENTAL UNIVERSITY

5–45, Yushima 1-chome, Bunkyo-ku, Tokyo 113

Telephone: (3) 3813-6111

Founded 1946

Academic year: April to March (two semesters)

President: H. YAMAMOTO
Director-General: O. KIKUKAWA
Director, University Library: A. SATO

Library of 291,000 vols
Number of teachers: 667
Number of students: 2,921

Publications: *Bulletin, Bulletin of the Department of General Education, Reports of the Medical Research Institute, Reports of the Institute for Medical and Dental Engineering.*

DEANS

Faculty of Medicine: T. SATO
Faculty of Dentistry: Y. NAKAMURA
Department of General Education: T. MURAMATU

HEADS OF DEPARTMENTS

Faculty of Medicine:

Anatomy 1: K. WAKE
Anatomy 2: T. SATO
Anatomy 3: Y. NAKAMURA
Physiology 1: G. SINODA
Physiology 2: K. KAMINO
Biochemistry: S. HANDA
Pharmacology: T. TANABE
Pathology: K. NAKAMURA
Microbiology: N. YAMAMOTO
Hygiene: Y. YUASA
Public Health: T. TAKANO
Medical Zoology: K. FUJITA
Forensic Medicine: H. HASEKURA
Internal Medicine 1: N. MIYASAKA
Internal Medicine 2: F. MARUMO
Internal Medicine 3: F. NUMANO
Neurology: (vacant)
Neuropsychiatry: M. TOORU
Paediatrics: J. YATA
Surgery 1: M. ENDO
Surgery 2: Y. MISHIMA
Neurosurgery: K. HIRAKAWA
Thoracic Surgery: (vacant)
Orthopaedic Surgery: K. FURUYA
Dermatology: K. NISIOKA
Urology: H. OSHIMA
Ophthalmology: T. TOKORO
Oto-Rhino-Laryngology: A. KOMATSUZAKI
Radiology: (vacant)
Obstetrics and Gynaecology: T. ASO
Anaesthesiology and Intensive Care Medicine: K. AMAHA
Laboratory Medicine: N. NARA

Faculty of Dentistry:

Oral Anatomy 1: Y. YAMASHITA
Oral Anatomy 2: (vacant)
Oral Physiology: Y. NAKAMURA
Biochemistry: (vacant)
Oral Pathology: M. TAKAGI
Oral Microbiology: N. TSUCHIDA
Dental Pharmacology: K. OHYA
Dental Technology 1: F. NISHIMURA
Dental Technology 2: A. SATO
Preventive Dentistry and Oral Hygiene: S. OKADA
Conservative Dentistry 1: J. TAGAMI
Conservative Dentistry 2: I. ISHIKAWA
Conservative Dentistry 3: H. SUDA
Oral Surgery 1: M. AMAGASA
Oral Surgery 2: S. ENOMOTO
Prosthodontics 1: M. AI
Prosthodontics 2: S. HASEGAWA
Orthodontics 1: K. SOMA
Orthodontics 2: T. KURODA
Paedodontics: H. ONO
Dental Radiology: T. SASAKI
Dental Anaesthesiology: M. UMINO
Stomatognathic Dysfunction: T. OYAMA

Department of General Education:

Literature: T. HIOKI
History of Social Thought: T. SASAKI
Mathematics 1: K. KERA
Mathematics 2: K. NOMURA
Physics 1: G. IMADATE
Physics 2: T. CHIBA
Chemistry 1: K. MURAMATSU
Chemistry 2: H. FUNAKOSHI
Biology 1: G. IMADATE
Biology 2: M. WADA
English: K. MATSUOKA
German: T. SUZUKI
Health and Physical Education: Y. FUSE
Science History: T. SATO
Sociology: S. ITABASHI

ATTACHED INSTITUTES

Institute for Medical and Dental Engineering: 3-10, Kandasurugadai 2-chome, Chiyoda-ku, Tokyo 101; Dir T. TOGAWA.

Medical Research Institute: 3-10, Kandasurugadai 2-chome, Chiyoda-ku, Tokyo 101; Dir A. SAKUMA.

TOKYO NATIONAL UNIVERSITY OF FINE ARTS AND MUSIC

12-8 Ueno Park, Taito-ku, Tokyo

Telephone: (3) 5685-7500
Fax: (3) 5685-7760

Founded 1949

President: KIICHI SUMIKAWA

Library: see Libraries
Number of full-time teachers: 212
Number of students: 2,785

TOKYO UNIVERSITY OF AGRICULTURE AND TECHNOLOGY

2-8-1 Harumi-cho, Fuchu-shi, Tokyo 183

Telephone: (423) 64-3311
Fax: (423) 60-7376

Founded 1949
State control
Language of instruction: Japanese
Academic year: April to March

President: I. S. SAKANOUE
Administrator: K. HAGA
Library Director: I. OHISHI

Library of 346,639 vols
Number of teachers: 405
Number of students: 4,482

Publications: *Report* (every 2 years), faculty bulletins (annually).

DEANS

Faculty of General Education: N. YAGISHITA
Faculty of Agriculture: I. KAJII
Faculty of Technology: S. NISHIMURA

TOKYO UNIVERSITY OF FISHERIES

5–7 Konan 4, Minato-ku, Tokyo 108-8477

Telephone: (3) 5463-0400
Fax: (3) 5463-0359

Founded 1888

President: Dr C. KOIZUMI
Administrative Director: K. UEOKA
Librarian: Dr K. MATSUDA

Publications: *Journal of the TUF* (2 a year), *Report of the TUF* (1 a year).

HEADS OF DEPARTMENTS AND LABORATORIES

Ocean Sciences:

Marine Ecosystem Studies: Dr A. KAMATANI, Dr A. OTUKI, Dr T. ISHIMARU, Dr Y. YAMAGUCHI
Physics and Environmental Modelling: Dr M. MATSUYAMA, Dr S. TAKEUCHI, Dr H. NAGASHIMA, Dr T. MORINAGA, Dr K. KIHARA, Dr N. SHIOTANI, Dr Y. ANDO

Marine Science and Technology:

Fishing Science and Technology: Dr. M. ARIMOTO, Dr H. KANEHIRO, Dr K. MATSUDA

Ocean Systems Engineering: Dr Y. HAMADA, Dr K. SATO, Dr S. YADA, Dr Y. NAKAMURA, Dr T. AKITA, Dr S. MURAMATSU

Aquatic Biosciences:

Aquatic Biology: Dr K. FUJITA, Dr S. SEGAWA, Dr S. WATANABE, Dr M. OMORI

Aquaculture: Dr T. TAKEUCHI, Dr M. NOTOYA, Dr N. OKAMOTO, Dr T. WATANABE, Dr H. FUKUDA, Dr F. TAKASHIMA

Genetics and Biochemistry: Dr T. AOKI

Fisheries Resource Management:

Fisheries Resource Management System: Dr T. KITAHARA, Dr S. YAMADA, Dr K. TAYA, Y. SATO, Dr. K. UENO

Ecology and Economics of Fisheries Resources: Dr Y. NAKAI, Dr S. ONO, Dr R. ISEDA, Dr N. KOIWA

Food Science and Technology:

Food Chemistry: Dr N. ISO, Dr T. SUZUKI, Dr T. FUJII, Dr S. WADA, Dr M. TANAKA

Food Engineering: Dr T. MIHORI, Dr H. WATANABE, Dr R. TAKAI

Marine Biochemistry: Dr S. KIMURA, Dr K. SHIOMI, Dr H. YAMANAKA, Dr T. HAYASHI, Dr T. WATANABE

Applied Microbiology: Dr E. WATANABE

Interdisciplinary Studies:

Pedagogy: Dr N. KAGEYAMA
Psychology: K. NAKAMURA
Logic: T. FUJIMURA
Philosophy: A. HASEGAWA
English: Dr K. KONDO
French: T. SHIMANO
Health and Physical Education: Dr T. AKITA, Dr S. MURAMATSU

TOKYO UNIVERSITY OF FOREIGN STUDIES

4-51-21 Nishigahara, Kita-ku, Tokyo 114

Telephone: (3) 3917-6111

Founded 1899. Reorganized 1949

President: M. NAKAJIMA
Director-General: F. YOSHIZAWA
Library Director: M. IKEGAMI

Library: see Libraries
Number of full-time teachers: 250
Number of students: 4,280

Publication: *Area and Culture Studies* (every 6 months).

ATTACHED INSTITUTE

Institute for the Study of Languages and Cultures of Asia and Africa: Tokyo; f. 1964; library of 82,378 vols; Dir S. IKEHATA; publs *Journal of Asian and African Studies* (annually), *Newsletter* (3 a year).

TOKYO UNIVERSITY OF MERCANTILE MARINE

2-1-6 Etchujima, Koto-ku, Tokyo

Telephone: (3) 5245-7300

Founded 1875

President: AKIO M. SUGISAKI
Director of Administration Bureau: TAKAO OKA
Library Director: SUUSHIN SATO

Number of full-time teachers: 110
Number of students: 1,093

Publications: *Journals* (natural sciences, humanities and social sciences).

HEADS OF DEPARTMENTS

Marine Systems Engineering: HAYAMA IMAZU
Information Engineering and Logistics: YOUJI TAKAHASHI
Electronic and Mechanical Engineering: ISAO MINE

UNIVERSITY OF ELECTRO-COMMUNICATIONS

1-5-1 Chōfugaoka, Chōfu City, Tokyo 182

Telephone: (424) 83-2161
Fax: (424) 81-3612

Founded 1949

State control

President: M. ARIYAMA
Director of Secretariat: S. KASUI
Library Director: H. YASUNAGA

Number of full-time teachers: 345
Number of students: 4,782 undergraduate, 1,004 graduate

Publication: *Bulletin* (2 a year).

DEANS

Faculty of Electro-Communications: E. YAMASHITA
Graduate School of Electro-Communications: E. YAMASHITA
Graduate School of Information Systems: M. YASUHARA

HEADS

Institute for Laser Science: K. UEDA
Information Processing Center: S. ITOH
Co-operative Research Center: S. MIKOSHIBA
Center for Instrumental Analysis: F. IWASAKI

TOTTORI UNIVERSITY

Minami 4-101, Koyama-cho, Tottori City

Telephone: (857) 28-0321
Fax: (857) 31-5018

President: S. HAYASHI
Director-General of Administration: T. SAITO
Librarian: S. AKAGI

Number of full-time teachers: 656
Number of students: 5,672

DEANS

Faculty of Education: S. SASADA
Faculty of General Education: K. TAKASHINA
Faculty of Medicine: K. TAKAHASHI
Faculty of Engineering: M. MICHIUE
Faculty of Agriculture: Y. TSUNO

TOYAMA UNIVERSITY

3, 190 Gofuku, Toyama City 930

Telephone: (764) 41-1271

Founded 1949

Academic year: April to March (two terms)

President: T. OGURO
Chief Administrative Officer: O. IMADA
Librarian: H. FUJITA

Number of full-time teachers: 445
Number of students: 6,547

DEANS

Faculty of Humanities: N. KOTANI
Faculty of Education: M. KASE
Faculty of Economics: S. YOSHIHARA
Faculty of Science: K. MATSUMOTO
Faculty of Engineering: M. TOKIZAWA

ATTACHED INSTITUTES

Hydrogen Isotope Research Center: Dir K. MATUMOTO.
Center for Co-operative Research: Dir C. TATUYAMA.
Health Administration Center: Dir K. INAZAWA.
Center for Research and Training in Teacher Education: Dir S. NAGAI.

TOYOHASHI UNIVERSITY OF TECHNOLOGY

Tempaku, Toyohashi, Aichi 441

Telephone: (532) 47-0111
Fax: (532) 44-6509

Founded 1976

State control

Academic year: April to March

President: KEISHI GOTO
Vice-Presidents: TAKESHI ANAYAMA, KAZUO TSUTSUMI
Director-General of Administration Bureau: TSUTOMU TOMIMURA
Librarian: TAKESHI TERASAWA

Library of 137,000 vols
Number of teachers: 169
Number of students: 1,879

Publications: bulletins.

Departments of Mechanical Engineering, Production Systems Engineering, Electrical and Electronic Engineering, Information and Computer Sciences, Materials Science, Architecture and Civil Engineering, Knowledge-based Information Engineering, Ecological Engineering, and Humanities and Social Engineering

UNIVERSITY OF TSUKUBA

1-1-1 Tennodai, Tsukuba-shi, Ibaraki-ken 305-8577

Telephone: (298) 53-2111
Fax: (298) 53-6019

Founded 1973

State control

Language of instruction: Japanese

Academic year: April to March

President: YASUO KITAHARA
Vice-Presidents: MAKOTO NATORI (Academic Affairs), YOICHI IWASAKI (Research Development), TOSHIAKI KUWAHRA (Administrative Affairs), TAMIO HIRABAYASHI (University Reform), SHIZUO HASEGAWA (Student Affairs)
Provosts: HIROSHI NODA (1st Cluster of Colleges), TETSUYA OHAMA (2nd Cluster of Colleges), SHUICHI ITAHASHI (3rd Cluster of Colleges), TOSHIO MITSUI (School of Medicine), SHINJI TOCHIBORI (School of Health and Physical Education), SHUNYU MITAMURA (School of Art and Design)
Secretary-General: KUNIO OGATA
Library Director: TAKEO SAITO

Library of 1,996,000 books, 18,000 periodicals
Number of teachers: 1,570
Number of students: 14,077

DEANS

First Cluster of Colleges:

College of Humanities: TATSUO MIZUNO
College of Natural Sciences: OSAMU KIKUCHI
College of Social Sciences: HIROSHI KOMAI

Second Cluster of Colleges:

College of Agrobiological Resources: TADAATSU NAKAHARA
College of Biological Sciences: YUZURU OGUMA
College of Comparative Culture: SHIGEYOSHI MUKOUJIMA
College of Human Sciences: NOBUO OTA
College of Japanese Language and Culture: TADAYUKI YUZAWA

Third Cluster of Colleges:

College of Engineering Sciences: MITSUO KAWABE
College of Engineering Systems: KEINOSUKE NAGAI
College of Information Sciences: NAOTO SAKAMOTO
College of International Studies: HIROKO AYABE
College of Policy and Planning Sciences: RYOSUKE HOTAKA

Master's Degree Programmes: NORIO OHSHIMA
Doctor's Degree Programmes: SHO-ICHIRO KUSUMOTO

CHAIRS OF RESEARCH INSTITUTES

Philosophy: MICHIO ARAKI
History and Anthropology: HIROSHI WADA
Literature and Linguistics: CHIKAFUMI HAYASHI
Modern Languages and Cultures: GUNJI ABE
Education: MITSURU YAMAGUCHI
Psychology: JUNSHIRO MAKINO
Special Education: TOMOYOSHI YOSHINO
Social Sciences: EIICHI SHINDO
Policy and Planning Sciences: HIDEHIKO TANIMURA
Biological Sciences: KUNIO YAMANE
Agriculture and Forestry: HARUYUKI MOCHIDA
Agricultural and Forest Engineering: TAKAAKI AMADA
Applied Biochemistry: EISUKE MUNEKATA
Mathematics: MITSUHIRO TAKEUCHI
Physics: SATOSHI TAKADA
Chemistry: AKIRA SHIMOYAMA
Geoscience: YOSHIMICHI KAJIWARA
Applied Physics: HIROMOTO UWE
Materials Science: KOKI TAKITA
Engineering Mechanics: HITOSHI NISHIMURA
Information Sciences and Electronics: KOZO ITANO
Health and Sport Sciences: SHIGERU KATSUTA
Art and Design: HIROSHI KAKUI
Basic Medical Sciences: KATSUTOSHI GOTO
Clinical Medicine: TAKESHI KUBO
Community Medicine: MASATAKA MURAKAMI

DIRECTORS OF CENTRES

Center for Tsukuba Advanced Research Alliance: NAOMICHI FURUKAWA
Foreign Language Center: KEIZO SUZAKI
Sport and Physical Education Center: MASASHI MIYAMARU
Agricultural and Forestry Research Center: TOSHIO SHONO
Educational Media Center: MITSUO WATANABE
Tandem Accelerator Center: KOHEI FURUNO
Cryogenics Center: RYOZO YOSHIZAKI
Science Information Processing Center: YOSHIHIKO EBIHARA
Radioisotope Center: AKIRA HOSOMI
Chemical Analysis Center: TAKUJI KAWASHIMA
Machining Center: SADAO AOKI
Environmental Research Center: FUJIO KIMURA
Laboratory Animal Research Center: HARUO OHKAWA
Shimoda Marine Research Center: YASUTSUGU YOKOHAMA
Sugadaira Montane Research Center: ICHIROKU HAYASHI
Plasma Research Center: KIYOSHI YATSU
International Student Center: MAKOTO TAKADA
Gene Experiment Center: HIROSHI KAMADA
Research Center for University Studies: SHINICHI YAMAMOTO
Proton Medical Research Center: YASUYUKI AKINE
School for Teachers of Acupuncture and Physical Therapy: HIDEKI NAKANO
Center for Computational Physics: AKIRA UKAWA
Health Center: HIROSHI MUTO

DIRECTORS

University Hospital: KATASHI FUKAO
School Education Center: YASUO SEKIOKA
Office of Planning: TSUNEO IWASAKI

UTSUNOMIYA UNIVERSITY

350 Mine-machi, Utsunomiya-shi, Tochigi
Telephone: (286) (36) 1515
Founded 1949
State control
Language of instruction: Japanese
Academic year: April to March
President: KIYOJI THUBURA
Director-General of Administration: TOSHIMICHI NISHIMURA
Librarian: FUJIO TAKAHASHI
Number of teachers: 464
Number of students: 4,793 undergraduates, 143 graduates

DEANS

College of Education: HIROSHI IRIE
College of Engineering: (vacant)
College of Agriculture: KAZUYUKI WATANADE
College of General Education: KAZUO NAKAMURA

WAKAYAMA UNIVERSITY

Sakaedani 930, Wakayama-shi
Telephone: (734) 54-0361
Founded 1949
Academic year: April to March
President: A. ONO
Chief Administrative Officer: M. SAKAMOTO
Librarian: I. MAKI
Library of 618,926 vols
Number of teachers: 178
Number of students: 3,000
Publications: *Bulletin of the Faculty of Education*, *The Wakayama Economic Review*.

DEANS

Faculty of Education: S. MORIYA
Faculty of Economics: M. NISHIKADO

YAMAGATA UNIVERSITY

1-4-12, Koshirakawa-machi, Yamagata City 990
Telephone: (236) 31-1421
Founded 1949
State control
Academic year: April to March (two semesters)
President: SYOZO TUBOI
Secretary-General: YOSHIKATSU NAKAMURA
Librarian: FUICHI UCHIDA
Number of teachers: 880
Number of students: 9,609

DEANS

Faculty of Literature and Social Sciences: MAKOTO NUMAZAWA
Faculty of Education: AKIO SAWAI
Faculty of Science: KAZUO ONITAKE
School of Medicine: KATSUHIKO DOI
Faculty of Engineering: TAKAO AKATSUKA
Faculty of Agriculture: UEKI KATSUJI

YAMAGUCHI UNIVERSITY

1677-1 Yoshida, Yamaguchi 753-8511
Telephone: (839) 33-5000
Fax: (839) 33-5029
Founded 1949
Academic year: April to March
President: HEISUKE HIRONAKA
Chief Administrative Officer: M. TAKAISHI
Librarian: M. KAWAGUCHI
Library: see Libraries
Number of teachers: 884
Number of students: 9,788 undergraduates, 1,265 graduates
Publications: faculty and student society journals and bulletins.

DEANS

Faculty of Humanities: K. YAMAMOTO
Faculty of Education: M. KANEDA
Faculty of Economics: M. HIRANO
Faculty of Science: K. IISHI
School of Medicine: H. KATO
Faculty of Engineering: H. OSAKA
Faculty of Agriculture: T. MARUMOTO

ATTACHED INSTITUTES

Centre for Collaborative Research: Dir M. MATSUURA.
Centre of Instrumental Analysis: Dir H. MASHIYAMA.
Centre for Gene Research: Dir T. NAKAZAWA.

ASSOCIATED COLLEGE

School of Allied Health Sciences: Dir S. TOMONAGA.

YAMANASHI UNIVERSITY

Takeda 4-chome, Kofu 400
Telephone: (552) 52-1111
Fax: (552) 20-8799
Founded 1949
State control
Academic year: April to March
President: T. ITO
Registrar: OSAMU NAKANISHI
Librarian: ASAO HASHIMOTO
Library of 445,640 volumes
Number of teachers: 305
Number of students: 3,970
Publications: *Memoirs of the Faculty of Liberal Arts and Education*, *Bulletin of the Faculty of Education*, *Reports of the Faculty of Engineering*.

DEANS

Faculty of Education: S. MENJU
Faculty of Engineering: HIRONAO KOJIMA

ATTACHED INSTITUTES

Co-operative Research and Development Center.
Center for Instrumental Analysis.
Center for Educational Research and Teacher Development (attached to the Faculty of Education).
Institute of Oenology and Viticulture (attached to the Faculty of Engineering).
Institute of Inorganic Synthesis (attached to the Faculty of Engineering).

YOKOHAMA NATIONAL UNIVERSITY

79-1 Tokiwadai, Hodogaya-ku, Yokohama 240
Telephone: (45) 339-3019
Fax: (45) 341-2582
Founded 1949
State control
Language of instruction: Japanese
Academic year: April to March (2 semesters)
President: H. ITAGAKI
Administrator: M. HOMMA
Librarian: K. SEKIGUCHI
Library: see Libraries
Number of full-time teachers: 680
Number of students: 10,782
Publications: bulletins.

DEANS

Faculty of Education: H. HIRAIDE
Graduate School of Education: H. HIRAIDE
Faculty of Economics: Y. TASHIRO
Graduate School of Economics: Y. TASHIRO
Faculty of Business Administration: H. SASAI
Graduate School of Business Administration: T. YOSHIKAWA
Faculty of Engineering: M. HIROTA
Graduate School of Engineering: M. HIROTA
Graduate School of International and Business Law: T. KUROSHIMA
Graduate School of International Development Studies: K. KOSHIRO

ATTACHED INSTITUTE

Institute of Environmental Science and Technology: Dir S. OKUDA.

University of the Air

UNIVERSITY OF THE AIR

2-11 Wakaba, Mihama-ku, Chiba City 261-8586

Telephone: (43) 276-5111
Fax: (43) 298-4378

Founded 1981

President: Hiroyuki Yoshikawa
Vice-Presidents: Moto-o Kaji, Ryuzo Abe
Director-General: Yukio Osawa
Librarian: Sadio Ito

Library of 580,000 vols
Number of teachers: 67 full-time, 371 part-time
Number of students: 66,730

HEADS OF DEPARTMENTS

Living and Welfare: Toyoko Sakai
Human Development and Education: Makoto Aso
Social and Economic Studies: Hitoshi Abe
Industry and Technology: Masanori Moritani
Humanities: Jiro Watanabe
Natural Sciences: Toru Nakazawa

Municipal Institutions

FUKUSHIMA MEDICAL COLLEGE

1 Hikariga-oka, Fukushima City

Founded 1950

President: H. Wakasa
Director of Library: N. Sugai
Secretary: M. Shishido
Hospital Director: R. Abe

Library of 138,738 vols
Number of teachers: 247
Number of students: 547

Publications: *Fukushima Igaku Zasshi* (Fukushima Medical Journal, quarterly), *Fukushima Journal of Medical Science* (2 a year).

Faculty of medicine, postgraduate research institute, hospital and nurses' school.

GIFU PHARMACEUTICAL UNIVERSITY

5–6–1, Mitahora-higashi, 5-chome, Gifu 502

Telephone: (58) 237-3931
Fax: (58) 237-5979
E-mail: Kuzuya@gifu-pu.ac.jp

Founded 1932
Municipal Control
Academic year: April to March

President: Prof. Masayuki Kuzuya
Chief Administrative Officer: Takashi Shinoda
Library Director: Prof. Hiroichi Nagai

Library of 59,000 vols
Number of teachers: 70
Number of students: 649

Publications: *Proceedings* (annually), *Bulletin of Liberal Arts.*

DEANS

Public Health: Prof. Kazuyuki Hirano
Manufacturing Pharmacy: Prof. Tadashi Kataoka

PROFESSORS

Furukawa, S., Molecular Biology
Goto, M., Pharmaceutical Analytical Chemistry
Hanai, K., Instrument Centre
Hara, A., Biochemistry
Hino, S., Liberal Arts
Hirano, K., Pharmaceutics
Hirota, K., Medicinal Chemistry
Inoue, K., Pharmacognosy
Kataoka, T., Pharmaceutical Chemistry
Kawashima, Y., Pharmaceutical Engineering
Kuzuya, M., Pharmaceutical Physical Chemistry
Masaki, Y., Pharmaceutical Synthetic Chemistry
Nagai, H., Pharmacology
Osada, A., Liberal Arts
Nagase, H., Hygiene

HIMEJI INSTITUTE OF TECHNOLOGY

2167 Shosha, Himeji City, Hyogo 671-22

Telephone: (792) 66-1661
Fax: (792) 66-8868

Founded 1944 as Hyogo Prefectural Special College of Technology, 1949 under present name
Academic year: April to March

President: Chiyoe Yamanaka
Dean of Students: Motoyoshi Hasegawa
Director of Administration: Kentaro Nishio
Library Director: Kazuhiko Sato

Library of *c.* 205,000 vols
Number of teachers: 260
Number of students: 2,525

Publication: *Reports of Himeji Institute of Technology.*

DEANS

Faculty of Engineering: Osamu Sangen
Faculty of Science: Akira Tai
Faculty of General Education: Gakushu Kakimi

ATTACHED INSTITUTES

Laboratory of Advanced Science and Technology for Industry: Dir Michitaka Terasawa.

Institute of Natural and Environmental Sciences: Dir Isao Nakase.

KITAKYUSHU UNIVERSITY

4-2-1 Kitagata, Kokuraminami-ku, Kitakyushu-shi, Fukuoka 802

Telephone: (93) 962-1837

Founded 1946, university status 1950

Library of 379,000 vols
Number of students: 5,456

KOBE CITY UNIVERSITY OF FOREIGN STUDIES

9-1 Gakuen-higashi-machi, Nishi-ku, Kobe 673

Telephone: (78) 794-8111

Founded 1949

President: Yoshio Yukida
Registrar: Yoshio Watanabe
Librarian: Susumu Kuranaka

Library of 218,320 vols
Number of teachers: 84
Number of students: 1,678

KOBE UNIVERSITY OF COMMERCE

Gakuen-nishimachi, Nishi-ku, Kobe 651-2197

Telephone: (78) 794-6161
Fax: (78) 794-6166

Founded 1929
State control
Language: Japanese
Academic year: April to March

President: Shin-ichi Miki
Registrar: Nobuhide Fujiwara
Librarian: Kentaro Nomura

Library of 395,000 vols
Number of teachers: 104
Number of students: 1,964

HEADS OF DEPARTMENTS

Economics: Prof. H. Okamoto
Business Administration: Prof. S. Toribe
Management Science: Prof. M. Fujisaki
Marketing and International Business: Prof. N. Kawanabe.

Graduate schools of economics, business administration and management science.

KYOTO PREFECTURAL UNIVERSITY OF MEDICINE

465 Kajii-cho, Kawaramachi, Hirokoji, Kamikyo-ku, Kyoto 602

Telephone: (75) 251-5111

Founded 1873

President: K. Kuriyama
Librarian: T. Takahashi

Library of 218,000 vols
Number of teachers: 304
Number of students: 649 undergraduate, 193 postgraduate

Publication: *Kyoto Furitsu Ikadaigaku Zasshi* (Journal).

NAGOYA CITY UNIVERSITY

1 Kawasumi, Mizuho-cho, Mizuho-ku, Nagoya

Telephone and fax: (52) 841-6201

Founded 1950

President: N. Ito
Secretary-General: S. Isobe
Library Director: S. Saito

Library of 502,973 vols
Number of teachers: 493
Number of students: 2,361

Publications: *Nagoya Medical Journal* (quarterly, English), *Annual Report of the Faculty of Pharmaceutical Sciences, NCU* (Japanese), *Oikonomika* (quarterly, Japanese).

DEANS

Medical School: M. Sasaki
Faculty of Pharmaceutical Sciences: H. Ikezawa
Faculty of Economics: Y. Naito
School of Humanities and Social Sciences: T. Kido
School of Design and Architecture: T. Yanagisawa

OSAKA CITY UNIVERSITY

3-3-138, Sugimoto, Sumiyoshi-ku, Osaka 558

Telephone: (6) 605-2031
Fax: (6) 692-1295

Founded 1949

President: T. Kodama
Vice-President: T. Takahashi
Director-General: Y. Matsuda
Dean of Bureau for Students' Affairs: G. Endo
Dean of Bureau for Matriculation and Education: S. Togahashi
Dir of Media Centre: T. Ishihara

Library of 1,991,000 vols
Number of teachers: 853, including 272 professors
Number of students: 8,177

Publications: *Business Review, Journal of Economics, Economic Review, Series of Law and Politics, Journal of Law and Politics, Studies in the Humanities, Osaka Journal of Mathematics, Journal of Geosciences, Memoirs of the Faculty of Engineering, Osaka City Medical Journal, Journal of the Osaka City Medical Centre, Annual Report of Human Life Science, Quarterly Journal of Economic Studies, IER Annual Report, Journal of Dowa-Mondai, Annuals of Health Sciences and Physical Education, Annual of Health Science, Annual of Physical Education, Annual Report of the Securities Research Centre.*

DEANS

Faculty of Business: K. KATO
Faculty of Economics: Y. MIYAMOTO
Faculty of Law: N. IKUMA
Faculty of Literature: S. KANEKO
Faculty of Science: M. TANIGUCHI
Faculty of Engineering: H. NISHIMURA
Faculty of Human Life Science: Y. KURATO
Faculty of Medicine: S. OTANI
College of Nursing: M. NAGAYAMA

ATTACHED INSTITUTES

Institute for Economic Research: Dir T. MATSUZAWA.

University Hospital: Dir H. KINOSHITA.

Institute of Health and Physical Education: Dir I. SHIMADA.

Dowa Problem Research Institute: Dir M. NOGUCHI.

OSAKA PREFECTURE UNIVERSITY

1-1 Gakuen-cho, Sakai, Osaka 593

Telephone: (722) 52-1161
Fax: (722) 52-1272

Founded 1949 as Naniwa University; present name 1955
Prefectural control
Academic year: April to March

President: TAKAO HIRASA
Administrator: MASAHIKO MOURI
Director of Library and Science Information Centre: TSUTOMU KANEKO

Library of 1,205,000 vols
Number of teachers: 707
Number of students: 5,898

Publications: *University Bulletin* (series A: Engineering and Natural Sciences; series B: Agriculture and Life Sciences; series C: Humanities and Social Sciences; series D: Economics, Business Administration and Law), *Mathematica Japonicae, Journal of Economic Studies, Studies in British and American Literature.*

DEANS

College of Engineering: TSUTOMU MINAMI
College of Agriculture: SINICHI SAWADA
College of Economics: HIDEAKI MAEDA
College of Integrated Arts and Sciences: TOSHIKATSU YOSHIDA
College of Social Welfare: YOSHIHIRO OHTA

ATTACHED INSTITUTE

Research Institute for Advanced Science and Technology: Dir MICHIO HIMENO

SAPPORO MEDICAL UNIVERSITY

Nishi 17-chome, Minami 1-jo, Chuo-ku, Sapporo, Hokkaido 060

Telephone: (11) 611-2111
Fax: (11) 612-5861

Founded 1945 as Hokkaido Prefectural School of Medicine; became Sapporo Medical College 1950; present name 1993.

Academic year: April to March

President: A. YACHI
Chief Administrative Officer: M. WATANABE
Librarian: S. URASAWA

Library of 214,000 vols
Number of teachers: 373
Number of students: 1,026

Publication: *Sapporo Igaku Zassi* (Sapporo Medical Journal, with English summaries, 6 a year).

DEANS

School of Medicine: M. MORI
School of Health Sciences: T. SATO

ATTACHED INSTITUTES

Cancer Research Institute: Dir K. FUJINAGA.
Marine Biomedical Institute: Dir M. MORI.

TOKYO METROPOLITAN UNIVERSITY

Minami-Ohsawa 1-1, Hachioji-shi, Tokyo 192-0397

Telephone: (426) 77-1111
Fax: (426) 77-1221

Founded 1949
Municipal control
Language: Japanese
Academic year: April to March (two terms)

President: M. YAMAZUMI
Director of Administrative Bureau: S. OTSUKA
Librarian: T. MIZUBAYASI

Library: see Libraries
Number of teachers: 637
Number of students: 6,649

Publication: *Hongaku no Genkyo* (University Information), *Tokyo Metropolitan University Bulletin* (annually).

DEANS

Faculty of Social Sciences and Humanities: K. OHKUBO
Faculty of Law: R. SASAKI
Faculty of Economics: T. TAMURA
Faculty of Science: K. OGIUE
Faculty of Engineering: Y. FURUKAWA

PROFESSORS

Faculty of Social Sciences and Humanities:

FUKUI, A., French Philosophy
FUKUMOTO, Y., German Linguistics
HORI, N., French Poetry of the 19th Century
IDE, H., English Novels
IIJIMA, N., Environmental Sociology, Theory of Social Movement
ISHIHARA, K., Family Studies, Social Research
JIN, K., Comparative Linguistics
KAWAKAMI, M., Modern Literature
KEIYA, T., Chinese Phonology
KOBAYASHI, K., History of Japanese Language
KOBAYASHI, R., Social Studies and Administration
KOTANI, H., Indian History
KUBO, H., Theory and Practice of Social Work
KUROSAKI, I., Educational Administration
MANZAWA, M., Modern German Literature
MARUYAMA, T., German Theatre of the 20th Century
MATSUZONO, M., Social Anthropology, Social Organization, Ethnology of East Africa
MINEGISHI, K., History of Tokugawa Period
MOGI, T., Educational Psychology
MURAYAMA, K., American Novels
NAGUMO, S., Modern Chinese Literature
NAKAJIMA, H., Theoretical Linguistics
NOMOTO, K., Philosophy of Logic and Language
OHGUSHI, R., Adult Education
OHKUBO, K., Studies of Th. W. Adorno
OKABE, H., Modern German Literature
OKADA, N., German Philosophy
OKAZAWA, S., Contemporary German Literature
ORISHIMA, M., American Novels
OZAWA, Y., Discrimination and Education
PEARSON, H. E., Applied Linguistics, TESOL
SANUI, T., Chinese Grammar
SASAKI, R., Modern Japanese History
SATAKE, Y., Federal Chinese History
SATO, S., Chinese Philology
SHINOHARA, S., Psychology of Learning and Memory
SUGIURA, K., Contemporary Austrian Literature
SUZUKI, T., Contemporary Austrian Literature
TAKAYAMA, H., English Poetry of the 17th Century
UENO, Y., Shakespearian Studies
WATANABE, Y., Social Anthropology
YAMANOUCHI, K., Old and Middle English
YOSHIKAWA, K., French Literature of the 20th century

Faculty of Law:

ASAKURA, M., Labour Law, Social Security Law
FUCHI, M., European Legal History
IKEDA, T., Civil Law, Law of Land Property
ISOBE, T., Administrative Law
KIMURA, M., Criminal Law
MAEDA, M., Criminal Law
MIKURYIA, T., Political History of Modern Japan
MIYAMURA, H., History of Japanese Political Thought
MIZUBAYASHI, T., Japanese Legal History
NOMURA, Y., Civil Law, Environmental Law
SHIBUYA, T., Commerical Law, Intellectual Property Law, Competition Law

Faculty of Economics:

ASANO, S., Econometrics
CHIBA, J., Financial Accounting
MIYAKAWA, A., Marxian Economic Theory, History of Economic Thought
NAKATSUKA, T., Business Administration, Operations Research
OHTSUKA, K., Economic Policy, Development Economics
TAMURA, T., Economic Policy
YANAGISAWA, O., European Economic History

Faculty of Science:

ACHIBA, Y., Laser Chemistry
AJHARA, Y., Ageing and Temperature Regulation
AOKI, N., Ergodic Theory
HIROSE T., Experimental High-Energy Physics
HORI, N., Environmental Geography
HUYAMA, Y., Genetics
IKEMOTO, I., Solid State Chemistry
ISHIWATARI, R., Organic Geochemistry
IWATA, S., Glacial Geomorphology
IYODA, M., Organic Chemistry
KAINOSHO, M., Biochemistry
KAMIGATA, N., Organic Chemistry
KATADA, M., Physical Inorganic Chemistry
KITAGAWA, S., Metal Cluster Chemistry, Organometallic Chemistry, Magnetic Resonance
KOBAYASHI, N., Atomic and Molecular Physics (Experimental)
KOMANO, T., Molecular Genetics
KUBO, K., Theoretical Nuclear Physics
KUWASAWA, K., Neurobiology
MIKAMI, T., Climatology, Climate Change, Urban Climate
MINAMIKAWA, T., Plant Biochemistry
MIYAKE, K., Number Theory
MOCHIZUKI, K., Partial Differential Equations
NAKAHARA, H., Nuclear Chemistry
NOGAMI, M., South American Mathematical Modelling
OGIUE, K., Differential Geometry
OHTSUKI, F., Human Growth and Development
OKABE, Y., Theoretical Condensed-Matter Physics
SAKAI, M., Analytic Functions
SATO, H., Electron Theory of Metals
SHINODA, T., Biochemistry
SUGIURA, Y., Human Geography
TAKAHASHI, T., Fluid Mechanics
WADA, M., Photobiology
YAMASAKI, T., Systematic Zoology
YASUGI, S., Developmental Biology

Faculty of Engineering:
- ANDO, Y., River Engineering, Applied Hydrology
- ASAKO, Y., Heat and Mass Transfer
- CHIKAZAWA, M., Physical Chemistry of Solid Surfaces
- FURUKAWA, Y., Precision Machining and Computer-Aided Manufacturing Systems
- HARADA, T., Precision Instruments and Metrology
- HOBO, T., Analytical Chemistry and Instrumental Analysis
- IGOSHI, M., Computer-Aided Design and Manufacturing
- ISHINO, H., Building Service Engineering
- ITO, D., Superconductors and their Applications
- ITO, E., Physical Properties of Polymers
- ITO, N., Environmental Engineering
- IWATATE, T., Geomechanics
- KATAKURA, M., Traffic Engineering and Infrastructure Planning
- KAWAHARA, M., Strength of Materials, Design of Composite Materials
- KIMURA, G., Electrical Machinery and Power Electronics
- KOIZUMI, A., Sanitary Engineering
- KOKUBU, K., Concrete Technology
- KONDA, T., Applied Mechanics and Rock Mechanics
- MORIYA, T., Applications of Ultrasonics
- NAGAHAMA, K., Chemical Engineering, Phase Equilibrium and Related Properties
- NAGAOKA, S., Functional Materials
- NISHIKAWA, T., Structural Engineering
- NISHIMURA, H., Plasticity and New Material Processing
- OKUMURA, T., Semiconductor Physics, Optoelectric Devices
- SAKAKI, T., Strength of Metals and Alloys
- SAKAMOTO, M., Energy Conversion, Heat Transfer
- SEKIMOTO, H., Piezo-electrical Vibrations and their applications
- SHIMADA, R., Building Economics
- SUZUKI, K., Structural Dynamics
- TAKAMIZAW, K., City Planning
- UENO, J., Architectural Planning
- UMEGAKI, T., Ceramics, Inorganic Phosphate Chemistry
- WATANABE, A., Control Systems Engineering
- WATANABE, K., Hydrodynamics, Hydraulic Machinery
- WATANABE, T., Environment and Energy Saving
- YAMADA, A., Computer Systems Design and Design Automation
- YAMAGISHI, T., Synthetic Organic Chemistry
- YAMAMOTO, Y., Building Materials
- YAMAZAKI, S., Structural Engineering
- YASUKAWA, H., Hydraulics
- YOKOYAMA, R., Control and Optimization of Large-Scale Systems

Center for Urban Studies:
- FUKUOKA, S., Urban Public Administration
- HAGIHARA, K., Urban and Regional Economics
- MOCHIZUKI, T., Disaster Prevention
- NAKABAYASHI, I., Urban Geography and City Planning
- TAKAHASHI, Y., Urban Sociology, Community

WAKAYAMA MEDICAL COLLEGE

9 Kyuban-cho, Wakayama City

Founded 1945

President: H. MATSUSHITA

Library of 63,250 vols
Number of teachers: *c.* 260
Number of students: *c.* 399

Publications: *Wakayama Medical Reports* (in English, quarterly), *Wakayama Igaku* (in Japanese, quarterly).

YOKOHAMA CITY UNIVERSITY

22-2 Seto, Kanazawa-ku, Yokohama 236

Telephone: (45) 787-2311
Fax: (45) 787-2316

Founded 1928
Municipal control
Academic year: April to March

Chancellor and President: MAKOTO UMEDA
Chief Administrative Officer: NORIO SUZUKI
Library Director: NOBUYOSHI SHINOHARA

Library of 602,000 vols
Number of teachers: 340
Number of students: 3,850

Publications: *Yokohama Shiritu Daigaku Ronso* (Bulletin, 1 a year), *Yokohama Shiritu Daigaku Kiyo* (Journal, 1 a year), *Keizai-to-Boeki* (Industry and Trade, 4 a year) *Yokohama Medical Bulletin* (English, 6 a year), *Yokohama Igaku* (Medical Journal, 6 a year), *Yokohama Mathematical Journal* (English, 2 a year).

DEANS

Faculty of Economics and Business Administration: MASAHISA HAYASHI
Department of International Culture and Humanities: YUZO KATO
Department of Science: KENNICHI KOJIMA
School of Medicine: MASAHIKO HOSAKA

ATTACHED INSTITUTES

Economics Research Institute: Dir KATSUHIKO MURAHASI.

Kihara Biological Institute: Dir HIDEKI KOYAMA.

University Hospital: Dir TOMIHISA KOSHINO.

Private Universities and Colleges

AICHI UNIVERSITY

1-1 Machihata-cho, Toyohashi-shi, Aichi-ken 441-8522

Telephone: (532) 47-4131
Fax: (532) 47-4144

Founded 1946

President: YOSHIYA ISHII
Registrar (for Foreign Students): TOSHIHIKO HOZUMI
Librarian: HITOSHI ASAO

Library of 1,036,000 vols
Number of teachers: 580
Number of students: 11,294

DEANS

Graduate School of Law: TEIJI MAKI
Graduate School of Business Administration: MITSUO FUJIMOTO
Graduate School of Economics: TOSHIHIKO HOZUMI
Graduate School of Humanities: ICHIRO SUGIMOTO
Graduate School of Chinese Studies: JUNTARO IMAIZUMI
Faculty of Law: TAKASHIGE KURONO
Faculty of Business Administration: TATSUHISA MINAMI
Faculty of Modern Chinese Studies: MITSUYUKI KAGAMI
Faculty of Economics: HIDEYUKI KATSURA
Faculty of Letters: SATOSHI OKUMURA
Faculty of International Communication: SHIN KONO
Junior College: TOSHIKO TAKAKUWA
Junior College Japanese Language Course for Foreign Students: AKIRA TANI

ATTACHED INSTITUTES

Community Research Institute: Dir KAZUTOSHI WATANABE.

Research Institute of Industry in Chubu District: Dir MIKIHIKO FUKUI.

Comprehensive Chinese-Japanese Dictionary Editing Centre: Dir JUNTARO IMAIZUMI.

Institute of International Affairs: Dir MASAHIRO MIYOSHI.

Managerial Research Institute: Dir KATSUKI TAGAWA.

AICHI GAKUIN UNIVERSITY

Iwasaki, Nisshin-cho, Aichi-gun, Aichi-ken 470-01

Telephone: (5617) 3-1111
Fax: (5617) 3-4449

Founded 1876
Private control
Language of instruction: Japanese
Academic year: April to March

President: TADATAKA KOIDE
Registrar: SHINJI SUGIHARA
Librarian: TOYOHIKO ASHIKAWA

Library of 578,383 vols
Number of teachers: 415
Number of students: 12,380

Publications: *Transactions of the Institute for Cultural Studies* (annually), *Business Review of Aichi Gakuin University* (quarterly), *Aichi Gakuin Law Review* (quarterly), *Journal of the Research Institute of Zen* (annually), *The Journal of Aichi Gakuin University* (quarterly), *Foreign Languages and Literature* (annually), *Journal of Aichi Gakuin University Dental Society* (quarterly), *Regional Analysis* (2 a year).

DEANS

Faculty of Letters: NORIAKI AKAIKE
Faculty of Commerce: ISAO KATO
Faculty of Management: TADAKATSU INOUE
Faculty of Law: MASAHARU NAKANO
Faculty of Dentistry: KENJI HIRANUMA
Faculty of General Education: TAKEO TAURA
Japanese Language Course for Foreign Students: TAKEO TAURA

AOYAMA GAKUIN UNIVERSITY

4-4-25 Shibuya, Shibuya-ku, Tokyo 150-8366

Telephone: (3) 3409-8111
Fax: (3) 3409-0927

Founded 1874
Academic year: April to March

Chancellor: M. FUKAMACHI
President: Dr A. KUNIOKA
Vice-Presidents: K. TEZUKA, Y. KAMO
Administrative Officer: K. KASAI
Library Director: S. KOGA

Library of 1,221,000 vols, 15,000 periodicals
Number of full-time teachers: 424
Number of students: 20,339

Publications: *Aoyama Journal of Business, Aoyama Journal of Economics, Aoyama Law Review* (all 4 a year), *Aoyama Journal of General Education, Thought Currents in English Literature, Journal of Education Research, KIYO* (Journal of Literature), *Aoyama Gobun* (Journal of Japanese Literature), *Aoyama Shigaku* (Journal of History), *Aoyama Business Review, Aoyama Journal of International Politics, Economics and Business* (all 1 a year).

DEANS

College of Literature: M. MUTO
College of Economics: A. KUMAGAI
College of Law: H. SERIZAWA
School of Business Administration: M. SUGIYAMA

School of International Politics, Economics and Business Administration: Dr F. ITO
College of Science and Engineering: Dr H. IDE

CHAIRMEN

College of Literature:
Department of Education: M. IKEDA
Department of Education (Evening Division): C. MARUYAMA
Department of English: Dr M. AKIMOTO
Department of English (Evening Division): T. SAITO
Department of French: M. TORII
Department of Japanese: N. YASUDA
Department of History: S. ITO

College of Economics:
Department of Economics: I. HORIBA
Department of Economics (Evening Division): Y. YONEZAWA

College of Law:
Department of Private Law: Dr M. NISHIZAWA
Department of Public Law: S. KUBO

School of Business Administration:
Department of Business Administration: Y. KOBAYASHI
Department of Business Administration (Evening Division): Dr K. TAMAKI

School of International Politics, Economics and Business:
Department of International Politics: Dr S. AMAKO
Department of International Economics: S. HONDA
Department of International Business: Dr A. ISHIKAWA

College of Science and Engineering:
Department of Physics: Dr I. NISHIO
Department of Chemistry: Dr H. ITO
Department of Mechanical Engineering: Dr K. HAYASHI
Department of Electronics and Electrical Engineering: Dr Y. HAYASHI
Department of Industrial and Systems Engineering: M. TSUJI

ASIA UNIVERSITY

5-24-10 Sakai, Musashino-shi, Tokyo 180
Telephone: (422) 54-3111
Fax: (422) 36-4869
Founded 1941
Academic year: April to March (two terms)
President: SHINKICHI ETO
Librarian: YOSHIO SUZUKI
Library of 377,000 vols
Number of teachers: 205 full-time, 291 part-time
Number of students: 8,029

DEANS

Graduate School of Business Administration: H. YASUKUNI
Graduate School of Economics: K. SEKIGUCHI
Graduate School of Law: S. SAKURAI
Faculty of Business Administration: Y. KAMIMURA
Faculty of Economics: J. TSUKUI
Faculty of Law: T. AOYAMA
Faculty of International Relations: S. MAOTANI
Faculty of Liberal Arts: T. KAKIYAMA
Asia University Junior College: YUTAKA SUZUKI

ATTACHED INSTITUTES

Institute for Asian Studies: f. 1973; Dir S. SAITO; publs *Journal* (annually), *Bulletin* (quarterly).

Research Institute of Information Sciences: f. 1988; Dir T. UETAKE; publ. *Journal* (annual).

English Language Education Research Institute: f. 1989; Dir H. KAWAGUCHI; publ. *Journal* (2 a year).

Institute for Japanese Studies: f. 1992; Dir T. ITO; publ. *Journal* (annually).

Physical Education Research Institute: f. 1992; Dir Y. URAGO; publ. *Journal* (2 a year).

Special Course for Foreign Students: f. 1953; Dir K. SAGA.

AZABU UNIVERSITY

1-17-71 Fuchinobe, Sagamihara City, Kanagawa Ken 229-8501
Telephone: (427) 69-1068
Founded 1890
President: TSUNENORI NAKAMURA
Librarian: HIDEO FUJITANI
Library of 135,000 vols
Number of teachers: 182
Number of students: 2,300
Publication: *Bulletin*.

DEANS

School of Veterinary Medicine: TOSHIO MASAOKA
College of Environmental Health: TSUYOSHI HIRATA

BUKKYO UNIVERSITY

96 Kitahananobo-cho, Murasakino, Kitaku, Kyoto
Telephone: (75) 491-2141
Fax: (75) 495-5273
Founded 1868
Private control
Academic year: April to March
President: K. TAKAHASHI
Vice-Presidents: T. YOSHIDA, S. NAKAI
Registrar: S. SATO
Librarian: R. KUNIEDA
Library of 647,000 vols
Number of teachers: 163
Number of students: 6,412

DEANS

Faculty of Letters: M. SHIMIZU
Faculty of Education: T. YOSHIOKA
Faculty of Sociology: E. NAKAMURA

CHUBU UNIVERSITY

1200 Matsumoto-cho, Kasugai-shi, Aichi-ken 487-8501
Telephone: (568) 51-1111
Fax: (568) 51-1141
Founded 1964
Language of instruction: Japanese
Academic year: April to March
President: KAZUO YAMADA
Library of 413,000 vols
Number of teachers: 474 (including 246 part-time teachers)
Number of students: 7,925 (including 182 graduate students)
Publications: *Memoirs of the College of Engineering* (annually), *Sogo Kogaku* (Research Institute for Science and Technology, annually), *Journal of the College of Business Administration and Information Science* (2 a year), *Journal of the College of International Studies* (annually), *International Studies* (annually), *Journal of the Research Institute for Industry and Economics* (annually), *Journal of Information Science* (annually).

DEANS

College of Engineering: MAKOTO WATANABE
College of Business Administration and Information Science: NOBUO KAMATA
College of International Studies: KAORI KAWABATA
Graduate School of Engineering: MAKOTO WATANABE
Graduate School of International Studies: KAORI KAWABATA
Graduate School of Business Administration and Information Science: NOBUO KAMATA

HEADS OF DEPARTMENTS

College of Engineering:
Mechanical Engineering: TOSHIYUKI SAKATA
Electrical Engineering: KEIJU MATSUI
Electronic Engineering: KENJI OTA
Civil Engineering: NAOKI MATSUO
Architecture: KOZO IKE
Industrial Chemistry: HIDEHIKO MORI
Engineering Physics: TAKASHI AOKI
Science Laboratory: HIROLYUKI UEDA

College of Business Administration and Information Science:
Business Administration and Information Science: HIROKAZU TSUJIMURA

College of International Studies:
International Relations: MASAO TODA
Comparative Cultures: NOBUAKI KAWAUCHI

College of Humanities:
Japanese Language and Culture: KAZUYOSHI FUJIKAKE
English Language and Culture: HIROSHI TANAKA
Communication Studies: YOTARO KONAKA

Graduate School of Engineering:
Mechanical Engineering: AKIRA KATO
Electrical Engineering: TOSHIYUKI IDO
Architecture and Civil Engineering: TAKEHISA ODERA
Industrial Chemistry: TOUGO KOUKETSU
Engineering Physics: TAKATOSHI IZUMI

Graduate School of International Studies:
International Studies: MASAO YOSHIDA

Graduate School of Business Administration and Information Science:
Business Administration and Information Science: TOSHIO YOSHIDA

Other Academic Programmes:
Liberal Arts and Sciences: SEIICHI OYAMA
Faculty of Social Sciences: SUMITAKA MAEKAWA
Natural Science and Mathematics: YOSHITAKA OKUMURA
Information Science: SHOJI MIZUSHIMA
Modern Languages: NOBUAKI YAMADA
Health Science: MASATOSHI YAMAZAKI
Course for Teacher Certification: SADAO OKIDO

ATTACHED INSTITUTES AND CENTRES

Research Institute for Science and Technology
Research Institute for Industry and Economics
Research Institute for Regional Studies
Research Institute for Information Science
Chubu Institute for Advanced Studies
Education Center for Information Data Processing
Center for International Programs
Language Center
Education Engineering Center
Innovation Center for Production Engineering
Lifelong Learning Center

CHUO UNIVERSITY

742-1 Higashinakano, Hachioji-shi, Tokyo 192-03
Telephone: (426) 74-2111
Fax: (426) 74-2214
Founded 1885
Academic year: April to March (two semesters)

President and Chancellor: HIROSHI HOKAMA
Secretary-General: KUNIHIKO MIYAKE
Dean of Students: FUMIO NAGAMI
Library Director: SHOJI KANEDA

Library: see Libraries
Number of teachers: 1,988
Number of students: 31,046 (6,216 evening course), 967 graduates

Publications: various faculty bulletins and journals.

DEANS

Faculty of Law: T. OSANAI
Faculty of Economics: Y. YONEDA
Faculty of Commerce: K. KITAMURA
Faculty of Science and Engineering: T. NOKUBO
Faculty of Literature: S. HYASHI
Faculty of Policy Studies: A. MIZUNO
Correspondence Division, Faculty of Law: K. NAGAI
Graduate School of Law: T. KOJIMA
Graduate School of Economics: H. OBUCHI
Graduate School of Commerce: M. TATEBE
Graduate School of Science and Engineering: S. SHINODA
Graduate School of Literature: S. MUTO

DIRECTORS

Institute of Comparative Law in Japan: T. SHIBASHI
Institute of Accounting Research: M. NEMOTO
Institute of Economic Research: S. OSU
Institute of Business Research: M. HAYASHI
Institute of Social Science: T. FURUKI
Institute of Cultural Science: S. FUKAZAWA
Institute of Health and Physical Science: Y. ISHIBE
Institute of Science and Engineering: M. IRI
Computer Center: T. SENNAMI
International Center: K. SATO
Health Center: M. TUKADA

DAITO BUNKA UNIVERSITY

1-9-1 Takashimadaira, Itabashi-ku, Tokyo 175
Telephone: (3) 3935-1110
Fax: (3) 5399-7310

Founded 1923
Academic year: April to March

Chairman of Board: T. SUZUKI
President: Y. SUWA
Registrar: S. KOBAYASHI
Librarian: U. MIZOGUCHI

Library of 849,000 vols
Number of teachers: 328 full-time, 532 part-time
Number of students: 15,165

Publications: *Daito Bunka Daigaku* (Bulletins), various university publs.

DEANS

Faculty of Literature: T. SUTO
Faculty of Economics: H. ISHIBASHI
Faculty of Foreign Languages: T. KUBOTA
Faculty of Law: H. TANAKA
Faculty of International Relations: M. HATTORI

HEADS OF DEPARTMENT

Faculty of Literature:

Japanese Literature: M. NARITA
Chinese Literature: O. OKADA
Anglo-American Literature: T. IIDA
Education: M. OTA

Faculty of Economics:

Economics: S. WATABE
Business Administration: M. HANAOKA

Faculty of Foreign Languages:

Chinese Language: R. SETOGUCHI
English Language: S. KUMAZAWA
Japanese Language: M. TAMAI

Faculty of Law:

Law: S. KOMATSU

Faculty of Political Science: M. WADA

Faculty of International Relations:

International Relations: H. MATSUI
International Cultures: H. KATAOKA

HEADS OF GRADUATE SCHOOLS

Literature: Y. SUZUKI
Economics: A. OKOUCHI
Law: K. NAKAMURA

JAPANESE LANGUAGE PROGRAMME FOR OVERSEAS STUDENTS

Japanese Language Course: D. HIROI

ATTACHED INSTITUTES

Institute for Oriental Studies: Dir M. ENDO.

Institute of Legal Studies: Dir Y. ETO.

Accounting and Management Research Institute: Dir A. YAMANOUCHI.

Institute for Calligraphy: Dir N. MURAKAMI.

Institute of Economic Research: Dir M. YAMADA.

Institute of International Comparative Political Studies: Dir S. YASU.

DOKKYO UNIVERSITY

1-1 Gakuen-cho, Soka-shi, Saitama-ken 340-0042

Telephone: (489) 42-1111
Fax: (489) 41-6621
E-mail: www-admin@dokkyo.ac.jp

Founded: 1964
Private control

President: KOICHI KINOSHITA
Head Administrator: IKUO TOI
Librarian: KO KAJIYAMA

Library of 636,000 vols
Number of teachers: 410
Number of students: 9,143

DEANS

Faculty of Foreign Languages: YUJI NAKAJIMA
Faculty of Economics: MASAMICHI CHIYOURA
Faculty of Law: SHOICHI KOSEKI
Graduate School of Foreign Languages: YUJI NAKAJIMA
Graduate School of Law: SHOICHI KOSEKI
Graduate School of Economics: MASAMICHI CHIYOURA

HEADS OF DEPARTMENTS

German: YOSHITAKA KAKIMIMA
English: KEIICHI SHIMADA
French: TAKAKO INOUE
Economics: TAKESHI MORI
Management Science: TETSU HOSODA

ATTACHED INSTITUTES

Research Institute of Foreign Language Teaching: Dir YOSHISABURO HONDA.

Center for Data Processing and Computer Science: Dir MASARU HONDA.

International Center: Dir YASUO KUWAHARA.

DOSHISHA UNIVERSITY

Karasuma Imadegawa, Kamigyo-ku, Kyoto 602-80

Telephone: (75) 251-3110
Fax: (75) 251-3075

Founded 1875

Chancellor: Y. MATSUYAMA
President: T. IWAYAMA
Dean of Academic Affairs: Y. SAKAMOTO
Dean of Student Affairs: N. KAWAI
Administrative Officer: A. NISHIMURA

Libraries of 1,617,000 vols
Number of full-time teachers: 424
Number of students: 22,851

University publications: *Studies in the Christian Religions, Studies in Humanities, Doshisha Studies in English, Doshisha Studies in Foreign Literature, Social Science Review, Doshisha Law Review, Doshisha Economic Review, Doshisha Business Review, Science and Engineering Review of Doshisha University, Doshisha American Studies, The Social Sciences, The Humanities, The Study of Christianity and Social Problems.*

DEANS

Faculty of Theology: K. MORI
Faculty of Letters: T. OKAMOTO
Faculty of Law: M. UMEZU
Faculty of Economics: E. HATTA
Faculty of Commerce: M. KATO
Faculty of Engineering: K. KANO
Graduate School of American Studies: T. KAMATA
Graduate School of Policy and Management: M. OYA

DIRECTORS

Institute for the Study of Humanities and Social Sciences: T. YAMANAKA
Center for American Studies: T. KAMATA
Science and Engineering Research Institute: A. AMETANI
Institute for Language and Culture: A. NAKAI

DOSHISHA WOMAN'S COLLEGE OF LIBERAL ARTS

Kodo, Kyotanabe-shi, Kyoto-fu 610-0395

Telephone: (774) 65-8411
Fax (774) 65-8461
E-mail: somu-t@adms.dwc.doshisha.ac.jp

Founded 1876
Academic year: April to March

Chancellor: Y. MATSUYAMA
President: S. OHASHI
Registrar: T. MORI
Librarian: K. FUKUDA

Library of 343,000 vols
Number of teachers: 473
Number of students: 4,270

Publication: *Annual Reports of Studies*.

DEANS

Liberal Arts: A. MORITA
Home Economics: S. KUROSAWA

FUKUOKA UNIVERSITY

8-19-1, Nanakuma, Jonan-ku, Fukuoka 814-0180

Telephone: (92) 871-6631
Fax: (92) 862-4431
E-mail: fupr@adm.fukuoka-u.ac.jp

Founded 1934
Private control
Academic year: April to March

President: S. ISHIDA
Vice-Presidents: T. MIYAMOTO, M. MIYOSHI, T. SHINSEKI
Secretary-General: K. SUETSUGU
Librarian: H. NAGATA

Library of 1,300,000 vols
Number of full-time teachers: 928
Number of students: 22,319

Publications: *Reviews, Bulletin, Reports.*

DEANS

Faculty of Humanities: S. MAMOTO
Faculty of Law: N. ASANO
Faculty of Economics: T. TANAKA
Faculty of Commerce: T. ETO
Faculty of Science: M. SAIGO
Faculty of Engineering: H. YAMASHITA
School of Medicine: Y. IKEHARA
Faculty of Pharmaceutical Sciences: H. SHIMENO
Faculty of Sports and Health Science: K. KANAMORI

DIRECTORS

Takamiya Evening School: M. MORI
Central Research Institute: Y. TOMINAGA
Computer Centre: K. SHUDO
Radioisotope Centre: S. TASAKI
Animal Care Unit: S. KASHIMURA
Language Training Centre: K. TACHIBANA
Fukuoka University Hospital: A. ARIYOSHI
Fukuoka University Chikushi Hospital: T. YAO

GAKUSHUIN UNIVERSITY

1-5-1 Mejiro, Toshima-ku, Tokyo 171-8588
Telephone: (3) 3986-0221
Fax: (3) 5992-1005

Founded 1949
Private control
Language of instruction: Japanese
Academic year: April to March

Chancellor: H. SHIMAZU
President: Y. OGURA
Chief Administrative Officer: K. MAEDA
Librarian: M. KOTANI

Number of full-time teachers: 180
Number of students: 9,338, undergraduate 8,898, graduate 440

Publications: *Gakushuin Daigaku Kenkyusosho* (Gakushuin University Studies, 1 a year), *Gakushuin Daigaku Hogaku-Bu Kenkyu Nenpo* (Gakushuin Review of Law and Politics, 1 a year), *Gakushuin Daigaku Keizai Ronshu* (Gakushuin Economic Papers, 4 a year), *Gakushuin Daigaku Bungaku-Bu Kenkyu Nenpo* (Annual collection of Essays and Studies, Faculty of Letters).

DEANS

Faculty of Law: H. TOMATSU
Faculty of Economics: K. IMANO
Faculty of Letters: T. TAKANO
Faculty of Sciences: S. KAWAJI
Dean of Students: M. KAMIYA

CHAIRMEN

Graduate School of Law: T. OHTSUKA
Graduate School of Politics: I. SUNADA
Graduate School of Economics: K. ARAI
Graduate School of Management: A. KOYAMA
Graduate School of Humanities: T. TAKANO
Graduate School of Sciences: S. KAWAJI

HEADS OF DEPARTMENTS

Faculty of Law:
- Law: H. TAKAGI
- Politics: M. MURANUSHI

Faculty of Economics:
- Economics: K. ARAI
- Management: T. UCHINO

Faculty of Letters:
- Philosophy: H. ARIKAWA
- History: K. HORIKOSHI
- Japanese: H. YOSHIOKA
- English: Y. TERAKADO
- German: H. KAWAGUCHI
- French: T. SAEKI
- Psychology: A. SHINODA
- Teachers' Training Course: M. HASHIMOTO

Faculty of Sciences:
- Physics: A. KAWABATA
- Chemistry: K. ISHII
- Mathematics: D. FUJIWARA

PROFESSORS

Faculty of Law:
- FUJITAKE, A., Sociology
- FUKUMOTO, K., Principles of Political Science
- HASEBE, Y., Law of Civil Procedure
- HATANO, R., International Law
- IIDA, Y., Political History of Europe
- INOUE, T., History of Politics and Diplomacy in Japan
- ISOZAKI, N., Political Change in East Asia
- KAMIYA, M., Anglo-American Law
- KANEKO, H., Tax Law
- KANSAKU, H., Commercial Law
- KANZAKI, T., Private International Law
- KAWAI, H., Comparative Politics
- KITAMURA, K., Government (Public Administration and Politics)
- MAEDA, H., Commercial Law
- MATSUSHITA, J., Law of Civil Procedure, Law of Bankruptcy
- MITSUFUJI, K., Civil Law
- MIYAJIMA, H., Labour Law
- MORINAGA, T., History of Western Political Thought
- MURANUSHI, M., International Politics
- NOMURA, T., Civil Law
- NONAKA, N., Principles of Political Science
- NOSAKA, Y., Constitutional Law
- OHTSUKA, T., Civil Law, Environmental Law
- OKINO, M., Civil Law
- SAKAMOTO, K., Political Process of Japan
- SAKAMOTO, T., Political Ideas in Japan
- SHIBAHARA, K., Criminal Law
- SUDO, H., Sociology
- SUNADA, I., American Government and Politics
- SUZUKI, S., Criminal Law
- TAKAGI, H., Administrative Law
- TANAKA, Y., Social Psychology
- TOMATSU, H., Constitutional Law
- TSUMURA, M., Law of Criminal Procedure
- TSUNEOKA, T., Administrative Law

Faculty of Economics:
- AOKI, Y., Consumer Behaviour
- ARAI, K., Statistical Theory, Stochastic Process
- ASABA, S., Business Economics and Strategic Management
- ENDO, H., Health Economics and Business Ethics
- EZAWA, T., Microeconomics and Firms' Growth
- GENDA, Y., Labour Economics and Macroeconomics
- IMANO, K., Human Resource Management
- ISHII, S., Economic History
- ITSUMI, Y., Public Finance
- IWATA, K., Japanese Economic Studies, Land and Housing Economics
- KAMBE, S., Microeconomic Theory and Game Theory
- KAWASHIMA, T., Econometrics and Regional Science
- KOYAMA, A., Business Finance
- MIYA, H., Management Accounting
- MORITA, M., Management Science and Strategic Management
- NAKAMURA, A., Labour Economics
- NAMBU, T., Industrial Economics
- NEBASHI, T., Global Management
- OKUMURA, H., Japanese Economic Studies, International Finance
- OSAWA, M., Environmental Economics, Energy Economics
- SHIMANO, T., Economic Policy
- SUDA, M., International Economics
- SUGITA, Y., Marketing Science
- SUZUKI, T., Business History
- TAJIMA, Y., Marketing and Distribution
- TANAKA, N., Systems and Simulation
- TATSUMI, K., Financial Markets and Investment
- UCHINO, T., Management and Organization Theory
- UEDA, T., Marketing
- WAKOH, J., Game Theory, Mathematical Economics
- YAMAGAMI, T., Financial Accounting
- YONEYAMA, M., Financial Accounting
- YUZAWA, T., Business History

Faculty of Letters:
- AOKI, J., Modern German Literature
- ARIKAWA, H., History of European Art
- ASAWA, S., American Philosophy, Trends of Thought in Modern Japan
- CHINO, K., Japanese Art History and Gender Studies
- CHUJOH, S., 19-Century French Novel
- DOI, Y., Middle Japanese
- FUKUI, N., Contemporary European History
- GOODHEW, LINDA, Feminism in English Literature
- HARADA, Y., Modern and Contemporary French Philosophy
- HARASHIMA, H., Chinese Language
- HASHIMOTO, M., Modern English Literature, Science Fiction
- HAYAKAWA, T., Syntax of Modern German Language
- HORIKOSHI, K., Medieval European History
- HOSAKA, Y., Semantics, Pragmatics
- INAZAWA, H., American Literature
- IMAI, K., Phonetics, Relevance Theory
- INOMATA, H., Elizabethan Drama and Poetry, English Renaissance
- INOUE, I., Modern Japanese History
- IWASAKI, H., 20th-century French Novel
- KAWAGUCHI, H., German Semasiology, German Syntax
- KAWAGUCHI, Y., Educational Methodology
- KAWASAKI, Y., Clinical Psychology
- KISHIDA, T., Historical Linguistics
- KITAJIMA, M., History of Greek Thought
- KOBAYASHI, T., History of Japanese Art
- KOMATSU, E., Linguistics
- KUDŌ, A., English Literature
- KUTSUWADA, O., Modern German Literature, Theory of Literature
- MARÉ, T., French Literature
- MATSUSHIMA, S., English Romantic Poetry
- MAYUZUMI, H., Ancient Japanese History
- MIYASHITA, S., German Poetry
- MURASE, T., Clinical Psychology and Focusing
- MURATA, T., Modern and Contemporary German Literature, Text Linguistics
- NAGASHIMA, Y., Linguistics (Semantics)
- NAGATA, Y., Social Psychology
- NINOMIYA, R., 17th- and 18th-century French Literature
- OHNUKI, A., Theory of Literature
- SAEKI, T., French Drama
- SAIGA, H., Developmental Psychology
- SAITOH, T., Educational History
- SAKAI, K., Philosophy
- SAKONJI, S., Ancient Greek Philosophy
- SASAKI, T., Phonological History of Japanese
- SASAYAMA, H., Ancient Japanese History
- SHIMADA, M., Ancient Roman History
- SHIMBO, M., German Language, Middle High German
- SHIMOMIYA, T., Germanic Linguistics
- SHINKAWA, T., Medieval Thought and Buddhism in Japan
- SHINODA, A., Comparative Psychology
- SHINOZAWA, H., Stylistics, Regional Culture and Literature
- SHIOTANI, K., 18th-century English Novel
- SOMA, T., Clinical Psychology
- SUGIYAMA, M., French Poetry, Prosody, 19th-century Literature, French Cartoons
- SUWA, H., Literature of the Edo Period
- SUWA, T., Cultural Geography
- TAKAHASHI, H., History of European Art
- TAKANO, T., Early Modern Japanese History
- TAKAYANAGI, N., Chinese Language
- TAKEDA, C., American Literature
- TAKETSUNA, S., Educational Psychology
- TAKEUCHI, F., Modern Chinese History
- TANAKA, A., Modern Japanese Language
- TERAKADO, Y., Contemporary American Literature, Jewish Writers
- TOGAWA, S., Modern Japanese Literature
- TOKUGAWA, M., Sociolinguistics
- TSURUMA, K., Ancient Chinese History
- YAHAGI, S., 19th-century American Literature
- YAMASAKI, Y., 20th-century French Literature and Thought
- YAMAMOTO, Y., Modern Japanese Literature
- YOSHIDA, A., Mythology

YOSHIDA, K., Contemporary French Poetry and Poets
YOSHIOKA, H., Literature of the Heian Period

Faculty of Science:
AKAO, K., Algebraic Geometry
AKAOGI, M., Science of the Earth's Materials under High Pressure
AKIYAMA, T., Synthetic Organic Chemistry
ARAKAWA, I., Surface and Vacuum Science
EZAWA, H.
FUJIWARA, D., Functional Analysis, Theory of Partial Differential Equations
GOTO, M., Ecotoxicology
HIRANO, T., Quantum Optics
IIJIMA, T., X-ray and Electron Diffraction, Studies of Gases and Liquids
IITAKA, S., Algebraic Geometry, Birational Geometry
IRISAWA, T., Computer Science
ISHII, K., Vibrational Spectroscopy of Molecular Systems
KATASE, K., Differential Topology, Complex Dynamic Systems
KAWABATA, A., Theory of Solid State Physics, Mesoscopic Physics
KAWAJI, S., Semiconductor Physics, Electronic Properties of Semiconductor Interfaces
KAWASAKI, T., Differential Geometry, Topology
KOJIMA, S., Molecular Biology, Biochemistry
KOTANI, M., Photochemistry and Photophysics of Organic Solids
KURODA, S. T., Functional Analysis, Theory of Partial Differential Equations
MIURA, K., Molecular Biology, Biochemistry
MIZOGUCHI, T., Materials Science, Spin-polarized Electron Spectroscopy, Magnetism, Amorphous Materials
MIZUTANI, A., Numerical Analytics, Functional Analysis
MOCHIDA, K., Organometallic Chemistry of Group 14 Elements
NAGASAWA, H., Geo- and Cosmo-chemistry of Trace Elements
NAKAJIMA, S., Number Theory
NAKANO, S., Algebraic Number Theory
OGAWA, T., Characterization and Growth of Electron Crystals
TAKAHASHI, T., Electronic Properties of Small-dimensional Conductors, Organic Conductors and Superconductors
TAKAMOTO, S., Design and Synthesis of Ligands and Stability Measurements of Chelate Compounds
TASAKI, H., Theoretical Physics and Mathematical Physics

Physical Education:
HAKOZAKI, Y.
HIRO, N.
ONO, T.
SAITO, S.
SATOH, Y.
YAGI, Y.

ATTACHED INSTITUTES

Gakushuin Daigaku Toyo Bunka Kenkyu-Jo (Gakushuin University Research Institute for Oriental Cultures): f. 1952; Dir A. FUJITAKE.

Gakushuin Daigaku Shiryokan (Gakushuin University Archives): f. 1975; Dir T. SAKAMOTO.

Gakushuin Daigaku Keisanki Sentah (Gakushuin University Computer Centre): f. 1974; Dir M. MORITA.

Gakushuin Daigaku Gaikokugo Kyoiku Kenkyu Sentah (Gakushin University Foreign Language and Research Centre): f. 1997; Dir T. SHIMANO.

Gakushuin Daigaku Kokusai Kouryu Sentah (Gakushuin University Centre for International Exchange): f. 1990; Dir T. YUZAWA.

Gakushuin Daigaku Sports Kenkoh Kagaku Sentah (Gakushuin University Centre for Sports and Health Sciences): f. 1994; Dir Y. YAGI.

Gakushuin Daigaku Keizai Keiei Kenkyujo (Gakushuin University Research Institute of Economics and Management): f. 1984; Dir T. NAMBU.

Gakushuin Daigaku Gengo Kyodo Kenkyujo (Language Institute of Gakushuin University): f. 1976; Dir T. SHIMOMIYA.

Gakushuin Daigaku Seimei Bunshi Kagaku Kenkyujo (Gakushuin University Institute for Biomolecular Science): f. 1991; Dir K. MIURA.

HIROSHIMA JOGAKUIN COLLEGE

4-13-1, Ushita-higashi, Higashi-ku, Hiroshima 732-0063
Telephone: (82) 228-0386
Fax: (82) 227-4502
E-mail: hju-inter-center@mvb.biglobe.ne.jp

Founded 1886, as college 1949
Academic year: April to March

President: KEIZO NISHI
Vice-President: ICHIRO IWAUCHI
Registrar: KATSUMASA YAMAMOTO
Chief Administrative Officer: SHIGENOBU HATAKEYAMA
Librarian: IWAO OSATO

Library of 156,000 vols
Number of teachers: 75
Number of students: 2,062

Publication: *Bulletin* (1 a year).

Departments of English and American literature, Japanese literature, Environmental Culture, Environmental Science, Graduate School of Language and Culture.

HIROSHIMA UNIVERSITY OF ECONOMICS

5-37-1 Gion, Asaminami-ku, Hiroshima City 731-0192
Telephone: (82) 871-1002
Fax: (82) 871-1666
E-mail int-sc@hue.ac.jp

Founded 1967
Academic year: April to March

Chancellor: MASAO ISHIDA
President: TSUNEO ISHIDA
Chief Administrative Officer: SHIGEMITSU ARICHI
Librarian: HIROSHI SEIKE

Library of 219,000 vols
Number of teachers: 92 full-time, 106 part-time
Number of students: 4,800

DEANS

Faculty of Economics: TOSHIYUKI MIZOGUCHI
Graduate School of Economics: TOSHIYUKI MIZOGUCHI

HOKKAI GAKUEN UNIVERSITY

4-1-40, Asahimachi, Toyohiraku, Sapporo, 062-8605
Telephone: (11) 841-1161
Fax: (11) 824-3141

Founded 1950

President: N. KUMAMOTO
Librarian: N. NISHIKAWA

Library of 580,000 vols
Number of full-time teachers: 198
Number of students: 7,976

Publications: *Keizai Ronshu* (Journal of Economics, quarterly), *Hogaku Kenkyu* (Law Journal, 3 a year), *Gakuen Ronshu* (Gakuen Review: Journal of Humanities and Science, 2 a year), *Kogakubu Kenkyu Hokoku* (Bulletin of the Faculty of Engineering, annually), *Kaihatsu Ronshu* (Journal of Development Research, annually).

DEANS

Faculty of Economics: M. UCHIDA
Faculty of Law: S. YAMAMOTO
Faculty of Engineering: H. YAMAGUCHI

CHAIRMEN

Graduate School of Economics: H. IKEDA
Graduate School of Law: S. YAMAMOTO

ATTACHED INSTITUTE

Development Research Institute: f. 1957; Dir K. KODA; publ. *Kaihatsu Ronshu* (Journal of Development Research).

HOKURIKU UNIVERSITY

1-1 Taiyogaoka, Kanazawa City, Ishikawa Prefecture 920-1180
Telephone: (76) 229-1161
Fax: (76) 229-1393
E-mail: koho@hokuriku-u.ac.jp

Founded 1975
Academic year: April to March

President: Y. SASAKI
Librarian: E. HIRAI

Library of 167,000 vols
Number of teachers: 175
Number of students: 3,936

Publications: *Hokuriku Daigaku Kiyo* (bulletin, 1 a year), *Hokuriku Hogaku* (journal of law and political science, 4 a year).

DEANS

Faculty of Pharmaceutical Science: I. YAMAMOTO
Faculty of Foreign Languages: K. TAKATA
Faculty of Law: Y. HATSUTANI
Graduate School of Pharmaceutical Research: I. YAMAMOTO (Chairperson)

HOSEI UNIVERSITY

17-1, Fujimi 2-chome, Chiyoda-ku, Tokyo 102-8160
Telephone: (3) 3264-9662
Fax: (3) 3238-9873
E-mail: ic@i.hosei.ac.jp

Founded 1880
Private control
Language of instruction: Japanese

President: TADAO KIYONARI
Vice-Presidents: TOYOKICHI ONIZUKA, TADAO KAWAKAMI, ETSUO ISHIZAKA, TARO INADA
Registrar: SAKAE TSUKAMOTO
Librarian: TADAO OKAMURA

Library of 1,610,000 vols
Number of full-time teachers: 534
Number of part-time teachers: 1,454
Number of students: 27,999
Number of graduate students: 1,201
Number of correspondence education students: 16,311

Publications (all 1 a year): *Hogaku-Shirin* (Law and Political Sciences Review), *Hosei Daigaku Bungakubu Kiyo* (Bulletin of Faculty of Letters), *Keizai-Shirin* (Economic Review), *Shakai Rodo Kenkyu* (Society and Labour), *Keiei Shirin* (Business Journal), *Hosei Daigaku Kogakubu Kenkyu Shuho* (College of Engineering Bulletin), *Daigakuin Kiyo* (Graduate School Bulletin).

DEANS

Faculty of Law: M. KANEKO
Faculty of Letters: H. NAKANO
Faculty of Economics: N. KASUYA
Faculty of Engineering: G. SHIRAI
Faculty of Social Sciences: S. SAMIZO
Faculty of Business Administration: T. SUZUKI

General Education (Daytime): A. TAKEUCHI (Evening): T. INOUE
Graduate Division: C. HIRABAYASHI

ATTACHED INSTITUTES

Nogami Memorial Noh Theatre Research Institute: 17-1 Fujimi 2-chome, Chiyoda-ku, Tokyo 102-8160; f. 1952; Dir A. OMOTE; publ. *Catalogue Noh Drama Collections.*

Ohara Institute for Social Research: 4342 Aihara-machi, Machida-shi, Tokyo 194-0298; f. 1919; Dir S. HAYAKAWA; publs *Labour Yearbook of Japan* (annually), *Report* (monthly).

Institute of Okinawan Studies: 17-1 Fujimi 2-chome, Chiyoda-ku, Tokyo 102-8160; f. 1972; Dir E. MUSHA; publs *Bulletin, Report* (annually).

Boissonade Institute of Modern Laws and Politics: 17-1 Fujimi 2-chome, Chiyoda-ku, Tokyo 102-8160; f. 1977; Dir T. IIDA.

Japan Statistics Research Institute: 4342 Aihara-machi, Machida-shi, Tokyo 194-0298; f. 1946; Dir Y. ITO; publ. *Bulletin* (annually).

Research Center of Ion Beam Technology: 3-7-2 Kajino-cho, Koganei-shi, Tokyo 184-8584; f. 1979; Dir K. KURIYAMA; publ. *Report* (annually).

Computational Science Research Center: 3-7-2 Kajino-cho, Koganei-shi, Tokyo 184-8584; f. 1969; Dir Y. SATO.

Athletics Research Center: 17-1 Fujimi 2-chome, Chiyoda-ku, Tokyo 102-8160; f. 1976; Dir N. ANDO.

Institute of Comparative Economic Studies: 4342 Aihara-machi, Machida-shi, Tokyo 194-0298; f. 1984; Dir M. TSURUMI; publ. *Journal* (annually).

Center for Business and Industrial Research: 17-1 Fujimi 2-chome, Chiyoda-ku, Tokyo 102-8160; Dir K. OGAWA; publ. *Newsletter* (quarterly).

INTERNATIONAL CHRISTIAN UNIVERSITY

10-2, Osawa 3-chome, Mitaka-shi, Tokyo 181-8585

Telephone: (422) 33-3038

Founded 1949

An ecumenical university, accepting students of high academic ability from all countries.
Languages of instruction: Japanese and English
Academic year: April to March or September to June
President: MASAKICHI KINUKAWA
Vice-President for Financial Affairs: HIKARU MIYABE
Vice-President for Academic Affairs: KAZUAKI SAITO
Library Director: YUKI NAGANO
Library: see Libraries
Number of teachers: 155 (full-time)
Number of students: 2,857

Publications: *Humanities-Christianity and Culture*, *Educational Studies*, *Language Research Bulletin*, *Asian Cultural Studies*, *Social Science*, also occasional books and monographs.

DEANS

College of Liberal Arts: G. SCHEPERS
Graduate School: S. KAWASHIMA
Student Affairs: A. AOI

ATTACHED INSTITUTES

Institute of Asian Cultural Studies: f. 1971, replacing Committee f. 1958; Dir W. STEELE; publ. *Asian Cultural Studies* (annually).

Institute of Educational Research and Service: f. 1953; Dir A. CHIBA; publ. *Educational Studies* (annually).

Institute for the Study of Christianity and Culture: f. 1963; Dir Y. MURAKAMI; publ. *Humanities-Christianity and Culture* (annually).

Social Science Research Institute: f. 1958; Dir M. OMORI; publ. *The Journal of Social Science* (2 a year).

Hachiro Yuasa Memorial Museum: f. 1982; collections of Japanese archaeology and folk art; Dir K. SAITO; publ. *Annual Report*.

Peace Research Institute: f. 1991; Dir M. HIROSE.

Research Center for Japanese Language Education: f. 1991; Dir Y. HIDA.

IWATE MEDICAL UNIVERSITY

19-1 Uchimaru, Morioka, Iwate 020
Telephone: (196) 51-5111

Founded 1928, University 1952
Private control
Academic year begins April
President: TSUTOMU OHORI
Librarian: SIGERU ONO

Library of 194,902 vols
Number of teachers: 477
Number of students: 1,015

Publications: *Journal of the Iwate Medical Association, Annual Report of the School of Liberal Arts and Sciences, Dental Journal.*

DEANS

School of Medicine: SHIGERU ONO
School of Dentistry: TAKASI A. SUZUKI
Premedical Course: KAGEHIDE SHIRAISHI

HEADS OF DEPARTMENTS

School of Medicine:

Anatomy I: Prof. MASAHARU HORIGUCHI
Anatomy II: (vacant)
Physiology I: Prof. MAKOTO SATO
Physiology II: Prof. NAOKI YASUDA
Biochemistry: Prof. SHIGERU ONO
Pharmacology: Prof. TAKESHI KASHIMOTO
Pathology I: Prof. KOHSUKE SASAKI
Pathology II: Prof. RYOICHI SATODATE
Bacteriology: Prof. RINJI KAWANA
Bacteriology: Prof. MASAO YOSHIDA
Hygiene and Public Health: Prof. HUMIO TSUNODA
Legal Medicine: Prof. SYUSAKU KATSURA
Medicine I: Prof. SHUNICHI SATO
Medicine II: Prof. YOSHISUKE MATUHAMA
Medicine III: Prof. SHINICHIRO KURIYA
Neurology: Prof. HIDEO TOHGI
Psychiatry: Prof. TOSHIO MITA
Paediatrics: Prof. TETSURO FUJIWARA
Surgery I: Vice-Prof. KAZUYOSHI SAITO
Neurosurgery: Prof. HARUYUKI KANAYA
Surgery III: Prof. KATSUHIRO NIITSU
Orthopaedic Surgery: Prof. MASATAKA ABE
Dermatology: Vice-Prof. SAIICHI KON
Urology: Prof. TAKASHI KUBO
Ophthalmology: Prof. YUTAKA TAZAWA
Otolaryngology: Prof. TAKASHI TSUIKI
Radiology: Prof. TORU YANAGISAWA
Obstetrics and Gynaecology: Prof. IWAO NISHIYA
Anaesthesiology: Prof. REIJI WAKUSAWA
Plastic Reconstructive Surgery: Prof. TAKU NARA
Laboratory Medicine: Prof. CHUICHI ITO
Clinical Pathology: Prof. KAZUO TAKAYAMA
Critical Care and Emergency Center: Prof. SYUITSU HOSHI
Pharmacy: Prof. MAKOTO IKEDA

School of Dentistry:

Oral Anatomy I: Prof. YOHICHIRO NOZAKA
Oral Anatomy II: Prof. TOKIO NAWA
Oral Physiology: Prof. TAKASA SUZUKI
Biochemistry: Prof. HIROYA KAWASAKI
Oral Biochemistry: Prof. MINORU OTA
Oral Pathology: Prof. ATSUMI SUZUKI
Oral Microbiology: Prof. MASARU KANEKO
Dental Pharmacology: Prof. TADANOBU ITO
Dental Technology: Prof. TSUTOMU KAMEDA
Oral Hygiene: Prof. TSUYOSHI KATAYAMA
Conservative Dentistry I: Prof. MASUMI ISHIBASHI
Conservative Dentistry II: Prof. MINORU KUBOTA
Periodontology: Prof. KAZUYUKI UENO
Oral Surgery I: Prof. YUKIO FUZIOKA
Oral Surgery II: Prof. SABURO SEKIYAMA
Prosthetic Dentistry I: Prof. HISATOSHI TANAKA
Prosthetic Dentistry II: Prof. KANJI ISHIBASHI
Orthodontics: Prof. FUJIRO ISHIKAWA
Pedodontics: Prof. EIICHI AMARI
Dental Radiology: Prof. KIMIO SAKAMAKI
Oral Diagnosis: Prof. MORIO TOTSUKA
Medicine: Prof. EIJI TAKAHASI
Surgery: Prof. JUN SASAKI
Dental Anaesthesiology: Prof. SHIGEHARU JOH.

Premedical Course:

Philosophy: Prof. RYUJI ISHIWATA
Jurisprudence: Prof. KOKI KANNO
Mathematics: Prof. TAKAKATSU ICHINOHE
Physics: Prof. HIROSHI ISOBE
Chemistry: Prof. KOICHI NAKADATE
Biology: Prof. KAGEHIDE SHIRAISHI
German: Prof. HISATO OSAWA

JIKEI UNIVERSITY SCHOOL OF MEDICINE

3-25-8 Nishi-Shinbashi, Minato-ku, Tokyo 105
Telephone: (3) 3433-1111
Telex: 2424596
Fax: (3) 3435-1922

Founded 1881
Private control
Academic year: April to March
President: TETSUO OKAMURA

Library of 311,452 vols
Number of teaching and research staff: 2,475
Number of students: 821

Publications: *Tokyo Jikeikai Medical Journal* (6 a year, in Japanese), *Jikeikai Medical Journal* (4 a year, in English), *Kyoiku Kenkyu Nenpo* (1 a year, in Japanese), *Research Activities* (1 a year, in English).

DEANS

School of Medicine: T. OKAMURA
School of Nursing: R. SAITO

ATTACHED INSTITUTE

Institute of DNA Medicine: Dir N. OHNO.

KANSAI UNIVERSITY

3-35, Yamate-cho 3-chome, Suita-shi, Osaka 564-8680

Telephone: (6) 368-1121
Fax: (6) 330-3027

Founded 1886
Academic year: April to March
President: AKIRA ISHIKAWA
Chairman of Board of Trustees: AKIO OHNISHI
Director of Educational Affairs Bureau: KIYOSHI KITADA
Librarian: HIROSHI YAMANO

Library: see Libraries
Number of teachers: 1,616, including 421 professors
Number of students: 28,996

Publications: *Bungaku Ronshu* (Literary Essays, 3 a year), *Hogaku Ronshu* (Law Review, quarterly), *Shakaigaku Ronshu* (Journal of Sociological Research, 2 a year), *Keizai Ronshu* (Economic Review, every 2 months), *Shogaku Ronshu* (Business Review, 5 a year), *Kogaku Kenkyu Hokoku* (Technology Reports, annually), *Keizai-Seiji Kenkyusho*

Kenkyu Shoho (Economic and Political Studies), *Tozaigakujutsu Kenkyusho Kiyo* (Bulletin of Institute of Oriental and Occidental Studies), *Kogaku to Gijutsu* (Engineering and Technology), *Keizai-Seiji Kenkyusho Sangyo-Seminar Nenpo, Hogaku Kenkyusho Kenkyu Sosho, Nomosu, Review of Law and Politics, Review of Economics and Business,* etc.

DEANS

Graduate School: Prof. MASUMI FUJIYOSHI
Faculty of Law: Prof. KEIICHI YAMANAKA
Faculty of Economics: Prof. HIROSHI IWAI
Faculty of Letters: Prof. TATSUO OKAMURA
Faculty of Commerce: Prof. HIROMICHI NAGANUMA
Faculty of Engineering: Prof. YASUO NOMURA
Faculty of Sociology: Prof. MASAO ASADA
Faculty of Informatics: Prof. TOSHIYUKI MIZUKOSHI

PROFESSORS

Faculty of Law:

Department of Law

FUKUTAKI, H., Commercial Law
HAYAKAWA, T., Law of Bills and Notes
HISHIDA, M., Commercial Law
ICHIHARA, Y., History of Legal Thought
ICHIKAWA, K., Japanese Legal History
IKEDA, T., Administrative Law
IMANISHI, Y., Civil Law
IWASAKI, K., Insurance Law and Shipping Law
KAMEDA, K., Administrative Law
KISHII, S., Labour Law
KOCHU, N., Constitutional Law
KOKUBU, T., Family Law and Succession Law
KURITA, K., Maritime Law
KURITA, T., Debtors' and Creditors' Rights
MORII, A., Law of Criminal Procedure
MURAI, T., Law of Taxation
MURATA, H., Constitutional Law
NAGATA, S., Civil Law
OHNUMA, K., Labour Law
OKA, T., European Legal History
OKUMURA, I., Chinese Legal History
SAKAMOTO, S., International Law
SAWADA, Y., Local Government
SENTO, Y., Family Law and Succession Law
SONODA, H., Criminal Law
TAKAMORI, H., Civil Law
TAKEMOTO, M., International Law
TAKESHITA, K., Legal Philosophy
TSUKIOKA, T., Law of Real Property
UEKI, S., Civil Law
UENO, Y., Law of Civil Procedure
YAMANAKA, K., Criminal Law
YAMATO, M., Company Law
YOSHIDA, E., Comparative Constitutional Law
YOSHIDA, N., Emancipation of Buraku

Department of Political Science

HAZAMA, T., Political and Governmental Organization
KOBAYASHI, K., International Politics
MANABE, S., Diplomatic History
TOKURA, K., European Politics
WAKATA, K., Political Psychology
YAMAKAWA, K., Political Theory
YAMAMOTO, K., Information Processing
YAMANO, H., Political History of Modern Japan

Faculty of Letters:

Department of English Language and Literature

AKAI, Y., Audio-lingual English Training
AOYAMA, T., Linguistics
AUGUSTINE, M. J., American and Comparative Literature
FUJITA, M., English Renaissance Drama
GIBBS, A. S., Stylistics
HASEGAWA, A., English Linguistics
HIGUCHI, K., British Novels
IRIKO, F, Introductory Seminar
ISHIHARA, T., British and American Prose
ISHIZAKA, K., Middle English
JOHNSON, G. S., British and American Drama
KAMIMURA, T., Modern British Novels
KOBAYASHI, H., Audio-lingual English Training
KOSHIKAWA, S., History of English Literature
MAKIN, P. J., Modern British and American Poetry
NAKAYAMA, K., Contemporary American Literature
NIWA, Y., British and American Prose
ODA, M., Linguistics and English Grammar
OKUMURA, T., Modern British Novels
SAKAMOTO, T., British and American Prose
SAKAMOTO, Y., Contemporary American Novels
SHIMAZAKI, M., British and American Prose
TAKAHASHI, T., Methods of English Teaching
TANIGUCHI, Y., Modern American Literature
TOYONAGA, A., English Philology
TSUTSUI, O., British and American Drama
USAMI, T., English
YASUKAWA, A., British and American Drama

Department of Japanese Language and Literature

AOKI, A., Tales from the Muromachi Period
ENDO, K., Japanese Linguistics
HAYASHI, S., Early Modern Japanese Fiction
INUI, H., Early Modern Japanese Literature
KAMBORI, S., Early Ancient Japanese Literature
KAMITANI, E., Japanese Linguistics
KATAGIRI, Y., Literature in the Heian Period
OHHAMA, M., Early Ancient Japanese Literature
SEKIYA, T., Textual Criticism of Noh Plays
TANAKA, N., Literature of the Heian Period
URANISHI, K., Modern and Contemporary Japanese Literature
YOSHIDA, N., History of Modern Japanese Literature

Department of Philosophy

AJISAKA, M., Ethics
INOUE, K., Japanese Traditional Thought
KASHIWAGI, T., History of European Art
KAWASAKI, Y., Philosophy
KIOKA, N., Philosophy
MONOBE, K., Aesthetics and History of Art
NAKATANI, N., History of Art in the Far East
NISHIMURA, K., History of European Art
ODA, Y., History of Religions
TANJI, T., Buddhist Studies
UESHIMA, K., History of Religions
YAMAMOTO, I., History of Philosophy
YAMAOKA, T., History of Art in the Far East

Department of French Language and Literature

HIRATA, S., Modern French Literature
HONDA, T., French Linguistics
IJICHI, H., French Classic Literature and Theatre
ITOH, M., French Philology
KAWAKAMI, M., Modern French Literature
MAEHARA, Y., French Catholic Novels
MARUO, K., French Literature
NONAMI, T., French Literature
OKATA, A., French Linguistics
OKU, J., History of French Literature
YAMAMURA, Y., Modern French Literature

Department of German Language and Literature

FUKUOKA, S., German Linguistics
HAMAMOTO, T., German Cultural Studies
MARUYAMA, M., German Literature
MOROSAWA, I., Modern German Literature
NINOMIYA, M., German Literature
OGAWA, S., Modern German Literature
SCHAUWECKER, D. F., Drama (Europe and Japan)
SUGITANI, M., Intercultural Communication
TAKEICHI, O., German Linguistics
UEMATSU, K., Modern German Literature
USAMI, Y., Modern German Literature
WATANABE, Y., German Linguistics
YAKAME, T., German Literature
YOSHIHARA, M., German Literature

Department of History and Geography

ASAJI, K., European Medieval History
FUJIYOSHI, M., History of Medieval China
HASHIMOTO, S., Human Geography
ITOH, O., Human Geography
IZUMI, C., History of Medieval Japan
KAKIMOTO, N., Geography
KOBA, M., Physical Geography
KOYAMA, H., History of Modern Japan
MATSUURA, A., History of Early Modern China
MURAKAMI, M., Human Geography
NAKAMURA, H., History of Modern Russia
SHIBAI, K., History of Modern and Contemporary Europe
SONODA, K., History of Early Japan
TAKAHASHI, S., Human Geography
TAKAHASHI, T., History of Medieval Japan
UWAI, H., History of Early Japan
YABUTA, Y., History of Early Modern Japan

Department of Chinese Language and Literature

AZUMA, J., History of Chinese Philosophy
HAGINO, S., Modern Chinese Literature
INOUE, T., Early Modern Chinese Literature
KAWATA, T., History of Chinese Philosophy
KITAOKA, M., Modern Chinese Literature
KUSAKA, T., Chinese Linguistics
MORISE, T., Classical Chinese Poetry
NISHIKAWA, K., Introduction to Chinese Philosophy
OZAKI, M., Chinese Linguistics
SAKADE, Y., History of Chinese Philosophy
TORII, K., Chinese Linguistics
UCHIDA, K., Chinese Linguistics

Department of Education

FUJII, M., Psychology
HAGA, H., Clinical Psychology
HATASE, N., Psychology
MATSUMURA, N., Developmental Psychology
NAKAJIMA, I., Psychology
NOMURA, Y., Experimental Psychology
OGAWA, T., Introduction to Pedagogy
OKAMURA, T., Public Administration of Education
OZAKI, M., History of Education
TAMADA, K., Pedagogy
TANAKA, T., Psychology
TANAKA, Y., Sociology of Education
YAMAMOTO, F., Pedagogy
YAMASHITA, E., Psychology

General Education

AOKI, S., Health and Physical Education
BAN, Y., Health and Physical Education
FUKUI, N., Japanese
HIRATA, W., Spanish
IWATA, I., Health and Physical Education
KAWAMOTO, T., Health and Physical Education
KIMURA, S., Health and Physical Education
KURAHASHI, E., Library and Information Science
MIURA, T., Health and Physical Education
MIZOHATA, K., Health and Physical Education
OITA, K., Health and Physical Education
SHIBAYAMA, R., Spanish
SHIRAFUJI, I., Health and Physical Education
SUEYOSHI, T., Health and Physical Education
TAKECHI, H., Health and Physical Education
TAMURA, N., Health and Physical Education
UEDA, Y., Liberation of Buraku

Faculty of Economics:

HARADA, S., Socio-Economic History of the West
HASHIMOTO, J. S., History of Economic Theories
HASHIMOTO, N., Econometrics

HIROE, M., Economics of Money and Finance
HORIE, T., Principles of Economics
ICHIEN, M., Social Security
ICHIKAWA, K., Commercial Economics
ISHIDA, H., Economics of Modern China
IWAI, H., Economic Statistics
JIMBO, I., Principles of Economics
KAIDA, I., Public Finance
KASEDA, H., Economic History
KASHIHARA, M., Agricultural Economics
KASUGA, J., Principles of Economics
KITAGAWA, K., European Economic History
KOBAYASHI, H., Labour Economics
KOIKE, H., Principles of Economics
KOSUGI, T., Economic Geography
KUSUNOKI, S., International Economics
MATSUOKA, T., History of Social Thought
MORIOKA, K., Principles of Economics
MORIYA, M., Economic Policy
MOTOKI, H., Macrodynamics
MURATA, Y., Macroeconomics and Econometrics
NAGAHISA, R., Social Choice
ODA, M., International Economics
OHTSUKA, T., Social Policy
OTANI, K., Demography
SATO, M., Macro-Economics
TAKESHITA, K., Economic Policy
TANAKA, M., Industrial Economics
TSUNOYAMA, Y., Japanese Economic History
UEMURA, K., History of Social Thought
WAKAMORI, F., Principles of Economics
YAMAMOTO, S., International Economics
YASUKI, H., Industrial Organization

Faculty of Commerce:

ABE, S., Public Sector Economics
FUJITA, A., Production and Operations Management
HABARA, K., Non-Life Insurance
HATORI, Y., International Relations
HIROSE, M., General Management
HIROTA, T., Corporate Strategy
IKEJIMA, M., Securities Markets
INOUE, S., Business History
ITO, K., Personnel and Labour Relations
IWASA, Y., Financial Intermediation and Institutions
KAMEI, T., Principles of Insurance
KATO, Y., Distribution Theory
KONISHI, Y., Personnel Management in Ageing Society
MATSUO, N., Financial Accounting
MATSUTANI, T., Research Seminar
MIKAMI, H., Economics of Transport and Communication
MIZUNO, I., Management Accounting
MYOJIN, N., Book-keeping
NAGANUMA, H., History of Commerce
NAGASUNA, M., Russian Economy
NAKAMA, K., English for International Business
OHASHI, S., Business Administration
SASAKURA, A., International Accounting
SHIBA, K., Accounting Information Theory
SUDA, K., Corporate Finance
SUGINO, M., International Marketing
SUYAMA, K., Marketing Management
TAKAHASHI, N., International Transport
TAKAYANAGI, T., Auditing
TANAKA, S., International Finance
TSURUTA, H., Public Finance
YASUDA, Y., Marketing Theory
YOKOTA, S., European and American Economy
YOSHIDA, T., Management of International Trade

Faculty of Sociology:

AMEMIYA, T., Ergonomics
ASADA, M., Policy for Economic Stabilization
FUJIOKA, S., Journalism
FUJISAWA, H., Social Psychology
FUNABA, T., Human Resource Studies
HASHIMOTO, K., Philosophy of Science
HAYASHI, H., Marketing Research
HIGASHIMURA, T., Information Processing
IIDA, N., Psychiatry
IKEDA, S., Experimental Psychology
ISHIKAWA, A., Psychology of Personality
IWAMI, K., Japanese Studies
KAKEGAWA, T., History of Mass Communication
KAMIYA, K., Urban Sociology
KATAGIRI, S., Theoretical Sociology
KIMURA, Y., Social Communication
KOTANI, S., Industrial Economics
MAEDA, T., Family Sociology
MATSUHARA, I., Social Policy
MIYASITA, S., Socio-Technology
OGAWA, H., Media and Culture
OH, Y., Industrial Information Theory
OISHI, J., Advertising Theory
OKADA, Y., Social Research
OKUDA, K., Management
ONISHI, M., Labour-Management Relations
SASAKI, T., Industrial Psychology
SENO, G., Human Communication
SHIBATA, M., Information Processing
SHIMIZU, K., Psychometrics
TAKAGI, O., Applied Social Psychology
TAKASE, T., Industrial Sociology
TAKI, H., Media Technology and Society
TAMIYA, T., Theory of Broadcasting
TERASHIMA, S., Clinical Psychology
TOKUOKA, H., Social Problems
TOMITA, M., Cultural Anthropology
TSUCHIDA, S., Social Psychology
TSUNEKI, T., Communication Behaviour
UEDA, T., Small Business Problems
UEJYO, N., Creativity of Advertising
YAMAMOTO, Y., Sociology
YANO, H., Economic Theory

Faculty of Informatics:

AOYAMA, C., Computer Science
ATSUJI, S., Decision Making
COOK, N., General Systems Theory
EZAWA, Y., Computer Science
FUKADA, Y., Image Processing and Pattern Recognition
FURUTA, H., Fuzzy Information Processing and Fuzzy Logic (Theory and Application)
HOSOKAWA, F., Mathematics
IIDA, N., Introduction to Computer Systems Architecture
INOUE, H., Communication
KATO, T., Cognitive Science
KATO, T., Computer Crime
KITAMURA, Y., English
KITANI, S., Public Administration
KOMATSU, Y., Business Administration
KUBOTA, K., Audiovisual Media
KUROKUZU, H., Accounting Information Systems
MIKAYE, I., Micro-political Analysis
MIYASHITA, F., Computer Science
MIZUKOSHI, T., Information and Human Behaviour
NAKAGAWA, Y., Data Structure and Algorithms
NAWA, K., Computer-based Communication
NOGUCHI, H., Business Information
SANO, M., Computers and the Information Society
TAKAGI, N., Communication
TAKAHASHI, H., International Networks
UESHIMA, S., Principles of Language and Programming
UKAI, Y., Economic Policy
WADA, Y., English
YAJIMA, S., Information Systems Management
YAMAMOTO, E., English
YAMANA, T., Economics
YAMAUCHI, A., Information Systems Management
YOSHIDA, N., Principles of Computer Electronics

Faculty of Engineering:

Department of Mechanical Engineering

ISHIHARA, I., Thermal Engineering
KITAJIMA, K., Manufacturing Processes
NAKAGIRI, A., Strength of Materials
SHINKE, N., Strength of Materials
TAGAWA, N., Micromechatronics
YANO, A., Production and Processing Systems

Department of Mechanical Systems Engineering

FUJITA, T., Analytical Dynamics
HIGUCHI, M., Production Engineering
MORI, A., Machine Design and Engineering Tribology
OHBA, K., Fluids Engineering and Biomechanics
OZAWA, M., Engineering Thermodynamics
SHIRAKI, K., Vibration Engineering
UCHIYAMA, H., Control Engineering

Department of Electrical Engineering

HARA, T., Theory of Electricity and Magnetism
HAYASHI, S., Circuit Theory and Systems Engineering
HIRANE, Y., Power Electronics and Machine Control
KANATA, Y., Electronic Circuits
OKADA, T., Electric Power Systems Engineering

Department of Electronics

IIDA, Y., Microwave Electronics
IMANISHI, S., Computers
KOJIMA, T., Electromagnetic Theory
NOMURA, Y., Information Systems and Engineering
OKADA, H., Information Networks
OMURA, Y., Device Physics and Modelling
YAMASHITA, K., Communication Systems Engineering
YOKOTA, K., Semiconductor Physics

Department of Chemical Engineering

MIYAKE, Y., Separation Engineering
MUROYAMA, K., Chemical Reaction Engineering
NAKANISHI, E., Process Systems Engineering
ODA, H., Physical Chemistry
SHIBATA, J., Physical Chemistry
SUZUKI, T., Catalyst Engineering
TAKEHARA, Z., Electrochemical Engineering
UEMURA, T., Chemical Engineering Thermodynamics

Department of Applied Chemistry

ARAKAWA, R., Physical Chemistry
ISHII, Y., Organometallic Chemistry
MATSUDA, Y., Electrochemistry
MATSUMOTO, A., Polymer Chemistry
NISHIYAMA, T., Organic Chemistry
OCHI, M., Polymer Engineering
OUCHI, T., Functional Polymers
SONODA, N., Organic Chemistry

Department of Materials Science and Engineering

AKAMATSU, K., Functional Materials
KOBAYASHI, T., Processing of Molten Metals
KOMATSU, S., Strength of Materials
MATSUMURA, Y., Welding Engineering
MIYAKE, H., Foundry Engineering
OISHI, T., Physical Chemistry of Materials Processing
SUGIMOTO, K., Physical Properties of Materials
SUGIMOTO, T., Nonferrous Metallic Materials
YAKUSHIJI, M., Physical Metallurgy of Steels

Department of Industrial Engineering

FUYUKI, M., Production Systems Engineering
HORII, K., Human Factors Engineering
MORI, K., Production Management
NAKAI, T., Operations Research
TAKANO, M., Mechatronics
UEMURA, T., Visual Information Engineering

Department of Civil Engineering

DOGAKI, M., Structural Mechanics
INOUE, M., Coastal Engineering

MIKAMI, I., Design of Civil Engineering Structures
NISHIDA, K., Soil Mechanics
NORITAKE, M., Transportation Engineering
TOYOFUKU, T., Construction Materials
WADA, Y., Sanitary Engineering
YOSHIKAWA, K., Regional Planning

Department of Architecture

ARAKI, H., Architectural Planning
ASANO, K., Structural Dynamics
KAWAMICHI, R., Architectural Planning and Design
MARUMO, H., City Planning
NAGAI, N., History of Architecture
NOGUCHI, T., Environmental Planning
YAMADA, M., Structural Materials and Design
YAO, S., Structural and Geotechnical Mechanics

Department of Biotechnology

OBATA, H., Microbial Technology
OSHIMA, Y., Genetics and Molecular Biology
SODA, K., Biomolecular Engineering
TOKUYAMA, T., Genetic Engineering
TSUCHIDO, T., Biocontrol Technology
UESATO, S., Pharmaceutical Technology
YAGI, H., Biochemical Engineering

General Education in Natural Sciences

FUKUSHIMA, M., Probability Theory
ISII, K., Mathematical Analysis
KURISU, T., Game Theory
KURIYAMA, A., Physics
KUROKAWA, H., Chemistry
NAGAOKA, Y., Physics
OHIGASHI, N., Physics
SHIRAIWA, T., Chemistry
TATSUMI, M., Chemistry
TETSUKAWA, T., Biology
TOKURA, S., Chemistry
URAGAMI, T., Chemistry
YAMAMOTO, N., Application of Topology to Differential Geometry
YAMAMURA, M., Physics
YANAGAWA, T., Knot Group Theory

KEIO UNIVERSITY

2-15-45 Mita, Minato-ku, Tokyo 108

Telephone: 3453-4511
Telex: 34532
Fax: 3769-2047

Founded 1858
Private control
Academic year: April to July, September to February

President: Y. TORII
Vice-Presidents: R. KOMATSU, Y. UEMURA, T. KOYAZU, J. TAKAHASHI, T. KURIBAYASHI, A. NAGASHIMA
Secretary General: S. KANEDA
Registrar: M. KAMOSHITA
Director of Libraries: K. UCHIIKE

Library: see Libraries
Number of full-time teachers: 1,506
Number of students: 31,032 (regular course); 19,395 (correspondence courses)

Publications: *Keio University Bulletin* (in English), *Jukusei Annai* (Student's Guide), and various faculty and institute publs.

DEANS

Faculty of Letters: T. SEKIBA
Faculty of Economics: H. IIDA
Faculty of Law: T. YAMADA
Faculty of Business and Commerce: M. KURODA
Faculty of Science and Technology: Y. ANZAI
School of Medicine: T. SARUTA
Graduate School of Business Administration: T. YAHAGI
Faculty of Policy Management: K. UNO
Faculty of Environmental Information: N. SAITO
Junior College of Nursing: K. HIRABAYASHI

CHAIRPERSONS

Graduate School of Letters: T. SEKIBA
Graduate School of Economics: H. IIDA
Graduate School of Law: T. YAMADA
Graduate School of Human Relations: S. AOIKE
Graduate School of Business and Commerce: M. KURODA
Graduate School of Medicine: T. SARUTA
Graduate School of Science and Technology: Y. ANZAI
Graduate School of Media and Governance: H. AISO

DIRECTORS

International Center: T. TANAKA
Institute of Cultural and Linguistic Studies: M. SATO
Institute for Communications Research: M. SEKINE
Keio Economic Observatory: G. IWATA
Institute of Physical Education: R. TAKAMINE
Institute of Oriental Classics: T. SEKIBA
Fukuzawa Memorial Center for Modern Japanese Studies: S. NISHIKAWA
Teacher Training Center: M. YAMAGUCHI
Center for Area Studies: M. OKONOGI
Institute of Audio-Visual Education: K. NAKAYA
Centre for Japanese Studies: T. TANAKA
Sports Medicine Research Center: Y. UEMURA
Research Centre for Arts Administration: Y. SUMI
Institute of Computer Education: N. DOI
Keio Institute of Policy Management: K. UNO
Keio Institute of Environmental Information: N. SAITO
Keio Institute of Languages and Communication: I. SEKIGUCHI

KINKI UNIVERSITY

Kowakae 3–4–1, Higashiosaka-shi, Osaka 577-8502
Telephone: (6) 721-2332
Fax: (6) 721-2353
E-mail: postmaster@kindai.ac.jp

Founded 1925

Private control
Language of instruction: Japanese
Academic year: April to March

Chancellor: MASATAKA SEKOH
President: KIICHIROH NODA

Number of teachers: 1,147
Number of students: 32,852

Publications: *Acta Medica Kinki University, Kindai Hogaku* (law review), *Shokei-Gakuso* (Journal of Business and Economics), *Science and Technology, Annual Report of Kinki University Atomic Energy Research Institute, Bulletin of the Pharmaceutical and Technology Institute,* etc.

DEANS

School of Law: HIROYUKI HATA
School of Commerce and Economics: HIDEO VENO
School of Science and Engineering: MEGUMU MUNAKATA (Deputy Dean)
School of Pharmacy: SATORU SUNANO
School of Literature, Arts and Cultural Studies: AKIMASA GOTOH
School of Agriculture: TOSHIO MITSUNAGA
School of Biology-Oriented Science and Technology: JUNYA ISHII
School of Medicine: SEISUKE TANAKA
Hiroshima School of Engineering: TOSHIA SHIOTA
Kyushu School of Engineering: YASUMI SONE

ATTACHED RESEARCH INSTITUTES

Fisheries Laboratory: Dir HIDEMI KUMAI.
Experimental Farms: Dir TAKASHI TOMANA
Atomic Energy Research Institute: Dir TOSHIKAZU SHIBATA.
Environmental Science Laboratory: Dir TOSHIHISA MAESHIMA.
Ethnology Research Centre: Dir (vacant).
General Research Laboratory for Science and Engineering: Dir YOSHIRO MATSUOKA.
Pharmaceutical Research and Technology Institute: Dir MOTOME TERAO.
Agricultural Research Institute: Dir SEISHI OUCHI.
Centre for Legal and Industrial Information: Dir (vacant).
Centre for Human Rights Research: Dir (vacant).
Research Institute of Animal Development Biotechnology: Dir SIROH TAKEUCHI.
Research Institute for Biology-Oriented Science and Technology: Dir (vacant).
Research Institute of Industrial Technology: Dir HIROYUKI HIROYASU.
Institute of Resource Recycling: Dir SHIROH TAKEUCHI.
Life Science Research Institute: Dir KIICHIROH NODA.
Research Institute of Oriental Medicine: Dir (vacant).
Research Institute of Hypertension: Dir TOSHIFUMI OHTORI.
Institute of Immunotherapy for Cancer: Dir MASAYUKI YASUTOMI.

KOBE GAKUIN UNIVERSITY

Ikawadani, Nishiku, Kobe 651-2180
Telephone: (78) 974-1551
Fax: (78) 974-5689
Founded 1966
President: TAKAO HAMA
Administrative Officer: SHIGERU TAKAMUNE
Librarian: YOSHIKIMI MORISHITA
Library of 670,000 vols
Number of teachers: 472
Number of students: 9,562
Publications: *Kobe Gakuin Hogaku* (Law and Politics Review), *Kobe Gakuin Economic Papers, Annual Publication Report of the Faculty of Nutrition, Memoirs of the Faculty of Pharmaceutical Sciences, Faculty Bulletin of Humanities and Sciences.*

DEANS

Faculty of Law: HIROSHI NAKAMURA
Faculty of Economics: GENRI HISATOMI
Faculty of Nutrition: TAKASHI UEDA
Faculty of Pharmaceutical Sciences: KOICHI KAWASAKI
Faculty of Humanities and Sciences: HIRONORI MIZUMOTO
Graduate School of Law: HIROSHI NAKAMURA
Graduate School of Economics: GENRI HISATOMI
Graduate School of Humanities and Sciences: HISAO KAKEHI
Graduate School of Nutrition: TAKASHI UEDA
Graduate School of Pharmaceutical Sciences: KOICHI KAWASAKI
Graduate School of Food and Medicinal Sciences: TAKASHI UEDA

KOGAKUIN UNIVERSITY

1-24-2, Nishi-shinjuku, Shinjuku-ku, Tokyo 163-8677
Telephone: (3) 3342-1211
Fax: (3) 3345-0228
Founded 1887, university status 1949
President: HIDEO OHASHI

Registrar: YUJI KIMURA
Librarian: TAKAHISA OHTA

Library of 240,000 vols
Number of teachers: 208
Number of students: 7,369 undergraduates (5,677 full-time, 1,692 evening), 411 graduates

Publications: *Kogakuin Daigaku Kenkyu Hokoku* (Research Reports, 2 a year), *Ronso* (Journal).

HEADS OF DEPARTMENT

Mechanical Engineering: Prof. SHINJI YAMAKAWA
Mechanical Systems Engineering: Prof. NAOTAKE NIWA
Applied Chemistry: Prof. YASUKAZU OHKATSU
Chemical Engineering: Prof. ICHIRO SHIOTA
Electrical Engineering: Prof. YOSHIO SAWADA
Electronic Engineering: Prof. ISAO OHTOMO
Information Engineering Course: Prof. KAZUNORI MIYOSHI
Architecture: Prof. MAKOTO MOCHIZUKI, Prof. TOHRU HATSUDA

KOKUGAKUIN UNIVERSITY

4-10-28, Higashi, Shibuya-ku, Tokyo
Telephone: (3) 5466-0111
Founded 1882
President: K. UEDA
Registrar: Y. SHIBASAKI
Librarian: T. SAWANOBORI

Library: see Libraries
Number of teachers: 742
Number of students: 9,399

Publications: *Kokugakuin Zasshi* (Journal of Kokugakuin University), *Kokugakuin Keizaigaku* (Kokugakuin University Economic Review), *Kokugakuin Hogaku* (Journal of the Faculty of Law and Politics), *Kokugakuin Daigaku Kiyo* (Transactions of Kokugakuin University).

DEANS

Faculty of Literature: K. FUTAKI
Faculty of Economics: M. IKI
Faculty of Law: M. YOKOYAMA
Graduate School: A. HARUTA

KOKUSHIKAN UNIVERSITY

4-28-1 Setagaya, Setagaya-ku, Tokyo 154
Telephone: (3) 3422-5341
Telex: 32336
Founded 1917
Private control
Academic year: April to March
Chairman: SHIGEYUKI SHIMIZU
President: HIROSHI MATSUSHIMA
General Director: SHOICHI SASAKI
Librarian: KUNIO NISHIO

Library of 709,052 vols
Number of teachers: 278
Number of students: *c.* 13,000

Publications: *Politics and Economics Review*, *Kokushikan Law Review*, various faculty journals and reviews.

DEANS

Faculty of Politics and Economics: TOSHIO SATO
Faculty of Politics and Economics (Evening Session): NOBUYUKI MIURA
Faculty of Physical Education: HACHIRO SUZUKI
Faculty of Engineering: TOSHIO MATSUMOTO
Faculty of Law: MANABU YABE
Faculty of Literature: YUKIO HIRONO
College of General Education: YUICHI YOSHIOKA
Junior College: NOBUO MATSUMOTO

HEADS OF DEPARTMENT

Faculty of Politics and Economics:
- Politics: SHIGEMITSU ICHIKURA
- Economics: KINSHIRO NISHIE
- Management: TOSHIRO MAEDA

Faculty of Politics and Economics (Evening Session):
- Economics: TAKASHI SENO
- Politics: YUKIO FUKUJU

Faculty of Physical Education:
- Physical Education: TOYOJI HASHIMOTO

Faculty of Engineering:
- Mechanical Engineering: TERUO MIYAZAKI
- Electrical Engineering: KATSUTOSHI KAMAKURA
- Civil Engineering: YUKIO KIKUTA
- Architectural Engineering: KENJI TAKIZAWA

Faculty of Law:
- Law: NORIYOSHI WATANABE

Faculty of Literature:
- Education: TAKAO AMANO
- History and Geography Ethics: TERUO NAGASHIMA
- Elementary Education: MUTSUHIKO IKEDA
- Japanese: KIYOSHI OKAWA
- Oriental History: TADASHI FUJITA
- Geography: AKIRA OSAKI
- Chinese Literature: SUSUMU KOSE
- Japanese Language: SHOICHI YAMAMOTO

College of General Education:
- General Education: RYOICHI EDAMURA

Junior College: NAOKO MAESHIRO

ATTACHED INSTITUTES

Institute for the Study of Politics: Dir HIROSHI MATSUSHIMA.

Institute for Cultural Studies of Ancient Iraq: Dir HIDEO FUJII.

Institute for Research on Martial Arts and Ethics: Dir MASAKAZU TAKAHASHI.

Institute for the Study of Religion and Culture: Dir SHINEI SHIGEFUJI.

Centre for Information Science: KIYOSHI OTA.

KOMAZAWA UNIVERSITY

1-23-1 Komazawa, Setagaya-ku, Tokyo 154
Telephone: (3) 3418-9010
Fax: (3) 3418-9017

Founded 1882

President: YASUAKI NARA
Vice-Presidents: MASAYA AMEMIYA
Registrar: OTANI TETSUO
Librarian: RIKIO TOKORO

Number of teachers: 284
Number of students: 14,659

Publications: *Journal of Faculty of Buddhism, Journal of Buddhist Studies, Journal of Buddhist Economic Research, Journal of Religious Studies, Journal of Faculty of Letters, Japanese Literature of Komazawa Univ., Studies in British & American Literature, Komazawa Journal of Geography, Journal of Historical Assn of Komazawa Univ., Journal of Komazawa Sociology, Journal of Faculty of Economics, Economic Review of Komazawa Univ., Journal of Faculty of Law, Law Review of Komazawa Univ., Political Science of Komazawa Univ., Journal of Management Faculty, Journal of Faculty of Foreign Languages, Review of Foreign Languages, Bunka* (Culture), *Journal of Health Education.*

DEANS

Faculty of Buddhist Studies: KANJI KUROMARU
Faculty of Humanities: KAZUO NAKAMURA
Faculty of Economics: TSUNESHI SATONAKA
Faculty of Law: MASAO SEKIGUCHI
Faculty of Business Administration: TOMONORI NAGATA

CHAIRMEN

Graduate Division of Buddhist Studies: SHUDO ISHII
Graduate Division of Arts and Sciences: KIKUO ANDO
Graduate Division of Economics: NAGAO KOSAKA
Graduate Division of Commerce: SHUJI ISHII
Graduate Division of Law: TOMOTSUGU SUGIURA
Graduate Division of Business Management: SADAO KONDO

ATTACHED INSTITUTES

Institute of Zen Buddhism
Institute of Buddhist Economics
Institute of Law
Institute of Population
Institute of Applied Geography
Institute of Mass Communication

KONAN UNIVERSITY

8-9-1, Okamoto, Higashinada-ku, Kobe
Telephone: (78) 431-4341
Fax: (78) 435-2306
E-mail: shomubu@adm.konan-u.ac.jp

Founded 1918

President: H. YOSHIZAWA

Library of 745,000 vols
Number of full-time teachers: 208
Number of students: 10,188

Publications: *Journal of Konan University Faculty of Letters* (irregular), *Memoirs of Konan Univ., Science Series* (irregular), *Konan Economic Papers* (irregular), *Konan Hogaku* (Konen Law Review, irregular), *Konan Business Review* (irregular), *Journal of the Institute for Language and Culture* (irregular).

DEANS

Faculty of Letters: N. YAKAME
Faculty of Science: T. TAGUCHI
Faculty of Economics: T. FUJIMOTO
Faculty of Law: T. WATANABE
Faculty of Business Administration: T. FUKUSIMA

KURUME UNIVERSITY

67 Asahi-Machi, Kurume 830
Telephone: 0942-35-3311
Founded 1928
President: KYOZO KOKETSU
Director of Administrative Office: KATSUMI YOSHIHISA

Library of 375,904 vols
Number of teachers: 534
Number of students: 5,808

Publications: *The Kurume Medical Journal* (quarterly), *The Journal of the Kurume Medical Association* (monthly), *The Journal for Studies on Industrial Economics* (quarterly).

Faculties of Commerce, Medicine and Law.

KWANSEI GAKUIN UNIVERSITY

1-1-155 Uegahara, Nishinomiya, Hyogo
Telephone: (798) 51-0952
Fax: (798) 51-0954

Founded 1889
Academic year: April to March

Chancellor: I. YAMAUCHI
President: H. IMADA
Vice-Presidents: K. INOUE, M. NAKANISHI
Library Director: T. TANAKA

Library: see Libraries
Number of full-time teachers: 368
Number of students: 17,008

Publications: *Theological Studies, Humanities Review, Sociology Department Studies, Journal of Law and Politics, Journal of Econo-*

mics, Journal of Business Administration, Law Reviews, Annual Studies, and others.

DEANS

School of Theology: T. MUKAI
School of Humanities: M. HATA
School of Sociology: M. MAKI
School of Law: N. HAYASHI
School of Economics: S. YASUI
School of Business Administration: Y. IMAI
School of Policy Studies: A. AMANO
School of Science: N. SANO

KYOTO PHARMACEUTICAL UNIVERSITY

5, Misasagi-nakauchi-cho, Yamashina-ku, Kyoto

Telephone: (75) 595-4600

Founded 1884

President: Dr KATSUYA OHATA
Registrar: Dr NORIAKI FUNASAKI
Librarian: Dr TAKESI NISINO

Library of 91,260 vols
Number of teachers: 104
Number of students: 1,821

PROFESSORS

FUJIMOTO, S., Environmental Biochemistry
FUNASAKI, N., Physical Chemistry
HATAYAMA, T., Biochemistry
HIRAYAMA, T., Public Health
IKEDA, M., Pharmaceutical Organic Chemistry
KIM, J., Cell Biology
KISO, Y., Medicinal Chemistry
KITAMURA, K., Analytical Chemistry
KOHNO, S., Pharmacology
MURANISHI, S., Pharmaceutics
NISHINO, T., Microbiology
NODE, M., Pharmaceutical Manufacturing Chemistry
OHTA, S., Chemistry of Functional Molecules
OKABE, S., Applied Pharmacology
SAKURAI, H., Analytical and Bioinorganic Chemistry
SATO, T., Pathological Biochemistry
TAKADA, K., Pharmacokinetics
TAKEUCHI, K., Pharmacology and Experimental Therapeutics
TANIGUCHI, T., Neurobiology
YOKOYAMA, T., Hospital Pharmacy
YOSHIKAWA, M., Pharmacognosy

ATTACHED INSTITUTE

Institute of Molecular and Cellular Biology for Pharmaceutical Sciences.

MATSUYAMA UNIVERSITY

4–2 Bunkyo-cho, Matsuyama 790, Ehime

Telephone: (899) 25-7111

Founded 1923

President: Prof. S. KAMIMORI
Registrar: T. YAMASAKI

Library: see Libraries
Number of teachers: 244
Number of students: 6,171

Publications: *Matsuyama Daigaku Ronshu* (every 2 months), *Studies in Language and Literature* (2 a year).

DEANS

College of Economics: Prof. K. MURAKAMI
College of Business Administration: Prof. S. KURATA
College of Humanities: Prof. Y. MASUDA
College of Law: Prof. S. MAEDA
Graduate School of Economics: Prof. K. TANABE
Graduate School of Business Administration: Prof. T. TAKAZAWA
Junior College: Prof. S. NAKAHARA

MEIJI UNIVERSITY

1-1 Kanda-Surugadai, Chiyoda-ku, Tokyo 101
Telephone: (3) 3296-4545
Fax: (3) 3296-4339
Founded 1881
Private control
Academic year: April to March (two semesters)
Chancellor: KEN KURITA
President: MITSUNORI TOZAWA
Director of Library: SOICHIRO GOTO
Library of 1,630,000 vols
Number of teachers: 1,999 (697 full-time, 1,302 part-time), including 438 professors
Number of students: 34,581, including 32,451 undergraduates, 1,125 graduates, 1,005 women's junior college
Publications: various faculty and institute bulletins, etc.

DEANS

School of Law: KASUO SAEGUSA
School of Commerce: TAKEE ASADA
School of Political Science and Economics: MITSUO KANEKO
School of Arts and Letters: TAKASHI KOAZE
School of Science and Technology: KOKI MATSUSE
School of Agriculture: NOBUYUKI TSUSAKA
School of Business Administration: TAIKICHI GON
Graduate School: HIROSHI NAGASAWA
Women's College: KUNIHIKO KANEKO

GRADUATE SCHOOL CHAIRMEN

Department of Law: SUSUMU ITO
Department of Commerce: MARI NISHINO
Department of Political Science and Economics: JOKICHI SATOMI
Department of Arts and Letters: ISAMU TAKATA
Department of Engineering: MASAO MUKAIDONO
Department of Agriculture: KAZUE INOUE
Department of Business Administration: KATSUHIKO HIRAI

ATTACHED INSTITUTES

Institute of Humanities: Dir MASAKI KONDO.
Institute of Social Sciences: Dir HITOSHI TAGAKI.
Institute of Sciences and Technology: Dir KOKICHI TANIGUCHI.
Criminological Museum: Dir HIROSHI KAWABATA.
Archaeological Museum: Dir SABURO KOBAYASHI.
Commodity Museum: Dir TAKEHARU TONE.
Computer Centre: Dir HARUO SHIMOSAKA.
Centre for International Programmes: Dir SHIGEHIKO ARAI.

MEIJI GAKUIN UNIVERSITY

1-2-37 Shirokanedai, Minato-ku, Tokyo 108-8636
Telephone: (3) 5421-5152
Fax: (3) 5421-5458
E-mail: cicet@mguad.meijigakuin.ac.jp
Founded 1877
Private control
Language of instruction: Japanese
Academic year: April to July, September to March
Chancellor: Prof. SATORU KUZE
President: Prof. KENJI OBA
Vice-Presidents: Prof. MIKIKO YAMAZAKI, Prof. YOSHIKAZU WAKITA, Prof. TOMOYOSHI KOIZUMI
Administrative Officer: SHUJI SHIBASAKI
Librarian: Prof. TOSHIMARO AMA
Library of 825,000 vols
Number of teachers: 256
Number of students: 13,639
Publications: *Meiji Gakuin Review, English Language and Literature, Papers and Proceedings of Economics, Proceedings of Integrated Arts and Sciences, Law Review* (3 a year), *International and Regional Studies* (2 a year), *French Literature, Art Studies, Psychology, Sociology and Social Welfare Review* (1 a year).

DEANS

Faculty of Literature: Prof. NOBUO MATSUMOTO
Faculty of Economics: Prof. KOICHI MASHIYAMA
Faculty of Sociology and Social Work: Prof. TOSHIO HASHIMOTO
Faculty of Law: Prof. NORIHISA KYOTO
Faculty of International Studies: Prof. KEI TAKEUCHI
Faculty of General Education: Prof. HIROGOSHI UDONO
Graduate School of Literature: Prof. YASUSHI SATO
Graduate School of Economics: Prof. YUKIHIKO UEHARA
Graduate School of Sociology and Social Work: Prof. KATSUYOSHI KAWAI
Graduate School of Law: Prof. FUMITOSHI TAMAKUNI
Graduate School of International Studies: Prof. SHIGEMOCHI HIROSHIMA

MEIJO UNIVERSITY

1-501 Shiogamaguchi, Tempaku-ku, Nagoya, Aichi 468
Telephone: (52) 832-1151
Fax: (52) 833-9494
E-mail: kikaku@meijo-u.ac.jp
Founded 1949
Private control
Academic year: April to March
President: MASAKI AMINAKA
Administrative Officer: TOSHITADA IKEHARA
Library Director: HIROSHI KOYAMA
Library of 615,000 vols, 7,300 periodicals
Number of teachers: 374 (full-time)
Number of students: 14,462
Publications: *Meijo Hogaku, Meijo Shogaku,* faculty bulletins and reports.

DEANS

Faculty of Law: SHIROU SHINODA
Faculty of Commerce: TOSHIHARU NAKANE
Faculty of Science and Technology: TAKEYUKI HIDA
Faculty of Agriculture: AKIRA HARA
Faculty of Pharmacy: YOSHIO SUZUKI
Faculty of Urban Science: MAKOTO TERADA
Faculty of Education: IKUJI KAMIYA
Junior College: TAKESHI TANIE

MEISEI UNIVERSITY

2-1-1 Hodokubo, Hino-shi, Tokyo 191; campuses at Hino and Ome
Telephone: Hino: (425) 91-5111; Ome: (428) 25-5111
Fax: Hino: (425) 91-8181; Ome: (428) 25-5182
Founded 1964
Private control
Academic year: April to March
President: SHIGEYUKI TANAKA
Director of General Affairs: Prof. MASAYUKI HASHIMOTO (Hino and Ome)
Director of Educational Affairs: Prof. YASUMITSU MORISHITA (Hino), Prof. YUHKICHI SUZAKI (Ome)
Director of Student Affairs: KAZUYOSHI YAMANAKA
Library Director: JUNSHIRO YAMASHITA
Library of 610,000 vols, 6,000 periodicals
Number of teachers: 400
Number of students: 8,350 (correspondence courses 8,000)
Publication: *General Information* (English).

DEANS

College of Physical Sciences and Engineering (Hino): Prof. EIJIRO HIEI
College of Humanities (Hino): Prof. YASUMITSU KANBE
College of Informatics (Ome): Prof. HIROSHI SATO
College of Japanese Culture (Ome): Prof. EIMEI INOUE

CHAIRMEN OF DEPARTMENTS

College of Physical Sciences and Engineering:
Physics: Prof. HIROFUMI SAKUYAMA
Chemistry: Prof. SATORU IWASHIMA
Mechanical Engineering: TAKASHI JINGU
Electrical Engineering: KUNIHIKO OKAMOTO
Civil Engineering: MORIYUKI HIROSE

College of Humanities and Social Sciences:
English Language and American Literature: Prof. MORIO KIDA
Sociology: Prof. HIDEKI TAKASHIMA
Psychology: TAKASHI OMINO
Pedagogy: TOSHIHIKO KUJIRAI
Economics: Prof. YOSHIKO NISHINO
Correspondence Course in Education: KOICHI TSUKADA

College of Informatics:
Electronics and Computer Science: Prof. JUNICHI UJIIE
Management Information: Prof. TOSHIO OOHI

College of Japanese Culture:
Japanese and Comparative Literature: Prof. EIMEI INOUE
Arts: Prof. MASAKI ISEKI

ATTACHED INSTITUTES

Tokyo Lincoln Center.
Shakespeare Center.
Post-war Educational History Research Center.
High Resolution Analytical Electron Microscopy Research Center.
Information Science Research Center.
International Studies Center.

MIYAGI GAKUIN WOMEN'S COLLEGE

1-1 Sakuragaoka 9-chome, Aoba-ku, Sendai Miyagi 981-8557
Telephone: (22) 279-1311
Fax: (22) 279-7566
Founded 1886; first degree courses
Private control
Language of instruction: Japanese
Academic year: April to March
Chancellor: K. MATSUZAKI
President: M. ANBE
Librarian: T. ONODERA
Library of 290,000 vols
Number of teachers: 306
Number of students: 2,551
Publications: *Bulletin of English Department* (1 a year), *Christianity and Culture* (1 a year), *Japanese Literature Note* (1 a year), *Journal of Miyagi College for Women* (1 a year).

DEANS

Department of Music: T. SUMIKAWA
Department of English Literature: Y. HONDA
Department of Japanese Literature: K. TANAKA
Department of Home Economics: F. TAKEHISA
Department of Cultural Studies: N. KOGA

NAGOYA UNIVERSITY OF COMMERCE AND BUSINESS ADMINISTRATION

Sagamine, Nisshin-cho, Aichi-gun, Aichi 470-01
Telephone: (5617) 3-2111
Telex: 4496002
Founded 1953
Private control
Language of instruction: Japanese
Academic year: April to February (2 terms)
President: HIROSHI KURIMOTO
Director: MASAHIDE KURIMOTO
Director of Library: Prof. MASATAKA YAMADA
Library of 70,000 vols
Number of teachers: 63 full-time, 74 part-time
Number of students: 3,000
Publication: *Bulletin* (2 a year).

HEADS OF DEPARTMENTS

Commerce: Prof. ISHIGOKA
Business Administration: Prof. KOBASHI
Decision Sciences and MIS: Prof. TANAHASHI
International Economics: Prof. ITAYA

NANZAN UNIVERSITY

18 Yamazato-cho, Showa-ku, Nagoya 466-8673
Telephone: (52) 832-3111
Fax: (52) 833-6985
Founded 1949
President: H. J. MARX
Vice-Presidents: K. SAWAKI, H. KOIKE, K. MURAMATSU
Chief of General Affairs Section: M. GOTO
Librarian: M. HAMANA
Library of 781,000 vols
Number of teachers: 206 full-time, 300 part-time
Number of students: 6,875
Publications: *Academia* series (Literature and Language, Humanities, Social Science, Natural Science and Physical Education) (Japanese), *Nanzan Journal of Economic Studies* (Japanese and English), *Nanzan Management Review* (Japanese and English), *Nanzan Law Review* (Japanese), *Nanzan Journal of Theological Studies, Nanzan Kokubun Ronshu.*

DEANS

Faculty of Arts and Letters: K. YAMAMOTO
Faculty of Foreign Studies: I. IWANO
Faculty of Economics: H. KONDO
Faculty of Business Administration: S. FUJII
Faculty of Law: H. NAKAYA

ATTACHED INSTITUTES

Center for Japanese Studies: a one-semester or one-year programme for foreign students who wish to study all aspects of Japanese language, culture and area studies.

Nanzan Anthropological Institute: research in cultural anthropology, mainly in SE, East and South Asia; publs *Nanzan Studies in Cultural Anthropology* (Japanese), *Asian Folklore Studies* (English), *Newsletter.*

Nanzan Institute for Religion and Culture: research in the area of world religions with special reference to the religions of Asia and to the dialogue between religions; publs *Bulletin* (Japanese and English), *Japanese Journal of Religious Studies* (English), *Nanzan Studies in Asian Religions* (English), *Nanzan Studies in Religion and Culture* (English).

Center for American Studies: study of American politics, economics, diplomacy, culture and society and US relationship with Japan; publ. *Nanzan Review of American Studies* (English).

Centre for Australian Studies: study of contemporary Australian society and its relationship to Japan; publs *Newsletter* (Japanese), *Reference Paper* (Japanese or English), *Working Paper* (Japanese or English).

Institute for Social Ethics: research on the ethical problems in the modern and post-industrial society; publ. *Nanzan Forum for Social Ethics* (Japanese).

Center for Latin American Studies: study of Latin America and Iberian Peninsula, mainly social sciences; publ. *Cuadernos de Investigación del Mundo Latino.*

Centre for European Studies: interdisciplinary study of European politics, economics and society; publ. *Bulletin of the Nanzan Centre for European Studies* (Japanese).

Center for Management Studies: specializing in the study of management issues of firms.

Center for Audio-Visual Education: care and development of all facilities and equipment of audio-visual education in language and non-language fields.

NIHON UNIVERSITY

8–24, Kudan-Minami 4-chome, Chiyoda-ku, Tokyo 102
Telephone: (3) 5275-8116
Fax: (3) 5275-8315
Founded as Nihon Law School 1889, University status 1903
Private control
Academic year: April to March
Chairman of Board: K. MORITA
President: Y. SEZAI
Vice-Presidents: S. KADOTA, M. TAKEUCHI, N. YAGI
Library of 5,199,000 vols
Number of full-time teachers: 2,853
Number of students: 87,157
Publications include various periodicals from all departments.

DEANS

College of Law: H. YANAGISAWA
College of Humanities and Sciences: T. OYAMA
College of Economics: M. TAKEUCHI
College of Commerce: H. SUGII
College of Science and Technology: K. KOJIMA
College of International Relations: M. AKIYAMA
College of Industrial Technology: C. HIRAI
College of Engineering: K. YOMOGITA
School of Medicine: I. SAKURAI
School of Dentistry: I. KUDO
School of Dentistry at Matsudo: S. FURUYAMA
College of Art: N. YAGI
College of Bioresource Sciences: S. KADOTA
Correspondence Division: Y. KATO
College of Pharmacy: T. KOYAMA
Junior College: Y. SEZAI

NIPPON DENTAL UNIVERSITY

1-9-20 Fujimi, Chiyoda-ku, Tokyo 102
Telephone: (3) 3261 8311
Fax: (3) 3264-8399
Founded 1907
Academic year: April to March
President: SOH NAKAHARA
Deans: YUKIHIKO MISHIRO (Tokyo Faculty), SEN NAKAHARA (Niigata Faculty)
Registrars: TAMETOSI KADOWAKI (Tokyo), KENEI OHBA (Niigata)
Librarians: SHOICHI SUGA (Tokyo Faculty), TAIZO MASUHARA (Niigata Faculty)
Library of 96,822 vols (Tokyo Faculty), 89,217 vols (Niigata Faculty)
Number of teachers: 474 full-time, 264 part-time
Number of students: 1,580
Publications: *Odontology* (every 2 months), *Annual Publications*, *Bulletin* (annually).

PROFESSORS

Tokyo:
AIYAMA, S., Anatomy
FURUMOTO, K., Radiology
FURUTA, Y., Anatomy

Furuya, H., Anaesthesiology
Kamoi, K., Periodontology
Katsuyama, S., Conservative Dentistry
Kikuchi, S., Paedodontics
Kobayashi, Y., Prosthodontics
Mishiro, Y., Biochemistry
Motohashi, K., Orthodontics
Nakahara, S., Dentistry in Society
Nakamura, Y., Conservative Dentistry
Niwa, M., Hygiene
Sato, T., Anatomy
Sonoyama, N., Oral Surgery
Suga, S., Pathology
Suzuki, T., Surgery
Tsutsui, T., Pharmacology
Uchida, M., Oral and Maxillofacial Surgery
Ushiyama, J., Physiology
Watanabe, T., Microbiology
Yokozuka, S., Prosthodontics
Yoshida, T., Dental Materials Science

Niigata:
1-8 Hamauracho, Niigata-shi, Niigata 951; tel. (25) 267-1500; fax (25) 267-1134

Hasegawa, A., Periodontology
Hata, Y., Prosthodontics
Hatate, S., Prosthodontics
Ishikawa, K., Otorhinolaryngology
Kameda, A., Orthodontics
Kanri, T., Anaesthesiology
Katagiri, M., Oral Pathology
Katoh, J., Oral Surgery
Katoh, Y., Conservative Dentistry
Kawasaki, K., Conservative Dentistry
Kobayashi, K., Oral Anatomy
Maeda, K., Radiology
Masuhara, T., Dental Pharmacology
Matsuki, H., Surgery
Morita, O., Prosthodontics
Murakami, T., Oral Physiology
Nakahara, S., Dentistry in Society
Nakamura, K., Dental Materials Science
Nishimura, K., Oral Surgery
Saito, K., Oral Microbiology
Sanada, K., Oral Biochemistry
Shibazaki, K., Internal Medicine
Shimooka, S., Paedodontics
Suetaka, T., Oral Hygiene
Teraki, Y., Oral Anatomy

NOTRE DAME WOMEN'S COLLEGE

1–2 Minami Nonogami-cho, Shimogamo, Sakyo-ku, Kyoto 606-0847
Telephone: (75) 781-1173
Fax: (75) 702-4060

Founded 1961
Private control
Language of instruction: Japanese
Academic year: April to March

President: M. Honda
Secretary-General: K. Toi
Librarian: Y. Okazaki

Library of 133,000 vols
Number of teachers: 36 full-time, 69 part-time
Number of students: 1,443

Publications: *Kiyo*, *Insight* (1 a year).

Departments of English Language and Literature and Cultural Living.

OSAKA MEDICAL COLLEGE

2–7 Daigakumachi, Takatsuki City, Osaka 569
Telephone: (726) 83-1221
Fax: (726) 81-3723

Founded 1927
Private control
Language of instruction: Japanese
Academic year: April to July, September to December, January to March

Chairman: Tadahiro Tanaka
President: Mamoru Fujimoto
Secretary-General: Kazuyoshi Tada
Librarian: Kimihiro Kiyokane

Library of 184,000 vols
Number of teachers: 329
Number of students: 618

Publications: *Journal* (1 a year, in Japanese), *Bulletin* (1 a year, in English).

HEADS OF DEPARTMENTS

Anatomy I: Prof. Dr Yoshinori Otsuki
Anatomy II: Prof. Dr Masahisa Shimada
Physiology I: Prof. Dr Yūsuke Imai
Physiology II: Takahiro Kubota
Medical Chemistry: Prof. Dr Hiroyuki Kagamiyama
Pathology I: Prof. Dr Yuro Shibayama
Pathology II: Prof. Dr Hiroshi Mori
Microbiology: Prof. Dr Koichi Sano
Pharmacology: Prof. Dr Mizuo Miyazaki
Forensic Medicine: Prof. Dr Koichi Suzuki
Hygiene and Public Health: Prof. Dr Koichi Kouno
Internal Medicine I: Prof. Dr Nakaaki Ohsawa
Internal Medicine II: Prof. Dr Ken-ichi Katsu
Internal Medicine III: Prof. Dr Keishirô Kawamura
General Gastrointestinal Surgery: Prof. Dr Nobuhiko Tanigawa
Thoracic and Cardiovascular Surgery: Prof. Dr Shinjiro Sasaki
Neurosurgery: Prof. Dr Tomio Ohta
Orthopaedic Surgery: Prof. Dr Muneaki Abe
Paediatrics: Prof. Dr Hiroshi Tamai
Obstetrics and Gynaecology: Prof. Dr Minoru Ueki
Dermatology: Prof. Dr Kimihiro Kiyokane
Urology: Prof. Dr Yohji Katsuoka
Otorhinolaryngology: Prof. Dr Hiroshi Takenaka
Ophthalmology: Prof. Dr Ikuo Azuma
Neuropsychiatry: (vacant)
Radiology: Prof. Dr Isamu Narabayashi
Anaesthesiology: Prof. Dr Hidemaro Mori
Clinical Pathology: Prof. Dr Akira Shimizu
Oral Surgery: Prof. Dr Masashi Shimahara
Plastic Surgery: Prof. Dr Sadao Tajima

RIKKYO UNIVERSITY
(St Paul's University)

Nishi-Ikebukuro, Toshima-ku, Tokyo 171
Telephone: 3985-2204
Fax: 3986-8784

Founded 1874
Private control
Academic year: April to March

Chancellor: The Right Revd Takashi Yashiro
President: Rev. Dr David Osamu Tsukada
Registrar: S. Gotoh
Librarian: Y. Matsudaira

Library of 1,093,000 vols
Number of teachers: 927
Number of students: 13,020

Publications: *Rikkyo* (quarterly), *Rikkyo Daigaku Toshokan Dayori* (library news), *Rikkyo Daigaku Shokuin Kiyo* (administrative staff research proceedings, annually), *Kiristokyo Kyoiku Kenkyu* (Studies in Christian Education), *Rikkyo University Bulletin* (every 2 years), *Rikkyo Koho* (Rikkyo news bulletin every 2 months), and numerous faculty journals.

DEANS

Faculty of Arts: O. Tsukada
Faculty of Economics: H. Ohashi
Faculty of Science: R. Hoshi
Faculty of Social Relations: Y. Honma
Faculty of Law and Politics: T. Awaji
Faculty of General Education: Y. Sensui

RISSHO UNIVERSITY

4-2-16 Osaki, Shinagawa-ku, Tokyo 141
Telephone: (3) 3492-5262
Fax: (3) 5487-3343

Founded 1872
Private control
Language of instruction: Japanese
Academic year: April to March

Chancellor: N. Tanaka
President: H. Sakazume
Vice-President: Z. Kitagawa
Registrar: (vacant)
Chief Librarians: H. Fujita (Osaki), Y. Ikoma (Kumagaya)

Number of teachers: 217 full-time, 483 part-time
Number of students: 11,185

Publications: *Journal of Nichiren Buddhism* (annually), *Journal of Buddhist Studies*, *Bulletin* (annually), *Quarterly Report of Economics*, etc.

DEANS

Faculty of Buddhist Studies: K. Mitomo
Faculty of Letters: S. Tegawa
Faculty of Economics: K. Fukuoka
Faculty of Business and Management: Y. Kato
Faculty of Law: S. Iwai
Faculty of Social Wefare: T. Hoshino
Faculty of Geo-Environmental Science: Y. Yoshida
Graduate School (Economics): K. Fukuoka
Graduate School (Literature): Y. Takagi
Graduate School (Business Administration): T. Okumura
Graduate School (Law): T. Suzuki

ATTACHED INSTITUTES

Institute for the Comprehensive Study of the Lotus Sutra: Dir K. Sasaki.

Institute for Nichiren Buddhist Studies: Dir H. Watanabe.

Institute of Humanistic Sciences: Dir T. Nakao.

Institute of Economic Studies: Dir M. Takumi.

Institute of Business and Management: Dir S. Abe.

Institute of Legal Studies: Dir K. Ochiai.

Institute of Environmental Sciences: Dir T. Arai.

RITSUMEIKAN UNIVERSITY

56-1 Tojiin Kitamachi, Kita-ku, Kyoto 603
Telephone: 075-465-1111
Telex: 5423171
Fax: 075-465-8219

Founded 1900
Private control
Academic year: April to March

President: M. Ohnami
Vice-President: F. Ashida
Chairman: S. Nishimura
Dean (Academic Affairs): M. Kohga
Dean (Student Affairs): K. Hatanaka
Director of Library: A. Nakahara

Library of 1,573,420 vols
Number of full-time teachers: 1,495
Number of students: 24,610

Publications: *Ritsumeikan Law Review* (in English and Japanese), *Ritsumeikan Economic Review* etc.

DEANS

Faculty of Law: T. Nakatani
Faculty of Economics: M. Sakano
Faculty of Business Administration: M. Nakata
Faculty of Social Sciences: Y. Sato
Faculty of International Relations: T. Saito
Faculty of Letters: T. Nagata
Faculty of Science and Engineering: Y. Ohno

PROFESSORS

Faculty of Law:

Akazawa, S., Political History
Arakawa, S., Civil Law, Sociology of Law
Aruga, I., Physical Education
Deguchi, M., Civil Procedure Code
Fukui, H., Political Science
Hatanaka, K., Foreign Law, Constitutional Law
Hisaoka, Y., Criminal Law, Criminal Action Law
Idota, A., Criminal Action Law, Criminal Law
Ikuta, K., Criminal Law
Ise, T., Philosophical Naturalism
Ishihara, H., English Literature
Kawakami, T., French Language and Literature
Kidana, S., International Private Law
Kikui, R., International Politics
Matsumiya, T., Criminal Law
Matsuoka, M., Economic Law
Miyamoto, T., Political Culture
Miura, M., Physical Education
Murakami, H., German Politics
Nagao, J., Civil Law
Nakai, Y., Civil Law
Nakajima, S., Constitutional Law
Nakatani, Y., Political Science
Nakatani, T., Political Thought and History
Nakamura, Y., Western Legal Thought
Ninomiya, S., Family Law
Noguchi, M., Japanese Literature, Bilingualism
Ohashi, K., English Language and Literature
Ohira, Y., Japanese Legal History
Okawa, S., Civil Law
Okubo, S., Constitutional Law
Sagami, Y., Civil Procedure Code
Sato, K., Problems of Working People
Sato, M., Political Policy
Shimura, H., Commercial Law
Shioda, C., Commercial Law
Tabayashi, Y., American Literature
Takehama, O., Insurance
Takeharu, S., German, German Literature
Tamura, Y., Administrative Law
Tsuji, Y., German, German Literature
Tsukuma, Y., Comparative Phonetics
Ueda, K., Criminal Law, Criminology
Unoki, Y., The Cultural Revolution of China
Wada, S., Tort
Yakushiji, K., International Guarantees of Human Rights
Yamaguchi, K., Japanese Language
Yamamoto, I., American Literature
Yamashita, K., Constitutional Law
Yasumoto, N., Public Administrative Law
Yoshida, M., Labour Law
Yoshimura, R., Civil Law
Yoshioka, K., American Literature

Faculty of Economics:

Asada, K., Financial Dealings between Governments
Ashida, F., Socialist Economics
Dohme, T., Classical and Contemporary Economics
Fujioka, A., American Economics
Fukumitsu, H., Theory and History of Finance
Futagami, K., General Economics
Hatanaka, T., Modern Japanese History
Hida, S., German
Hidaka, M., English
Hirata, J., Japanese and American Economy
Honda, Y., Japanese Economy
Inaba, K., Japanese and American Economy
Inada, Y., Development of Japan–US Link-model and Simulation Analysis
Ishiguro, K., International Economics
Itani, H., English
Iwata, K., International Finance
Izawa, H., Analysis of Industrial Organization
Kakuta, S., General Economics
Kawamoto, K., Western Economic History
Kobayashi, S., English
Kohga, M., Economic Fluctuation
Matsubara, T., Canadian and Japanese Economy
Matsuda, T., English
Matsukawa, S., Keynes's Economic Policies
Matsuno, S., External Economic Relations of Contemporary China
Matsuno, S., Socialist Economics
Miyoshi, M., Social Policy
Mukai, T., Hegelian Philosophy
Nishiguchi, K., Economic Theory of Developing Nations
Ohkusa, Y., Labour Economics and Theory of Prices
Okazaki, E., General Economics
Okumura, I., French
Okumura, K., Russian
Okuchi, S., Japanese Economy
Ono, S., General Economics
Oyabu, T., Agricultural Economics
Saito, T., Modern Chinese Literature
Sakamoto, K., Industrial Economics
Sakano, M., Public Finance
Shibata, H., Public Finance
Shibata, S., Linguistic Policy
Sugino, K., Regional Economics
Suzuki, N., National Income
Takagi, A., Contemporary Capitalism
Tanaka, H., The Structure of Contemporary Capitalism
Tsuji, E., American Novels
Ueno, T., Economic History
Wakabayashi, H., Economic Policy
Yamada, H., Econometrics
Yamai, T., German Economy
Yamamura, T., Contemporary German Literature
Yamashita, T., Sociology of Sports and Leisure
Yokoyama, M., International Economy

Faculty of Business Administration:

Chiyoda, K., Auditing
Doi, Y., Transportation
Fujimura, K., English
Futaba, K., Medium Enterprises, Trade Unions
Hara, Y., International Corporations
Hashimoto, T., Business Administration History
Hattori, Y., Modern Financial Markets
Ho, W., European Philosophy
Ida, T., English
Ide, K., Socialist Corporate Theory
Imada, O., Production Management
Ito, T., Politics and Literature of the Weimar Republic
Jido, Y., Industrial Technology
Kinoshita, A., Distribution Process
Kosaka, K., English
Kotaki, R., Contemporary Industry
Matsui, T., Medium Enterprises
Matsumura, K., Business Financial Management
Miura, I., Japanese Retail Business
Miyosawa, T., Managerial Accounting
Mukai, J., Analysis of Global Money Circulation
Nagashima, O., Japanese Economy
Nakagami, K., Preservation of the World Environment
Nakamura, F., History
Nakanishi, I., Internationalization of Industry
Nakata, M., General Business Administration
Namie, I., Labour Problems
Okamoto, M., United States Industries and Corporations
Okamoto, N., Athletic Ability Evaluation Tests
Okao, K., Physical Education
Okumura, Y., Business Strategies
Ozaki, A., Spanish
Saito, M., Service Industry Strategy and Management Systems
Sakai, J., Financial Statements
Sasabe, A., Technological Development
Sato, T., Contemporary Capitalism
Shinkai, T., Theoretical Study of Economics
Suto, Y., English
Suzuki, Y., French
Tai, S., Cost Accounting
Tamamura, H., Non-profit Corporations
Tanaka, T., History of Business Thought
Tanaka, T., Social Statistical Study of Statistical Surveys
Taneda, Y., Accounting
Tonegawa, K., System Simulation
Toyohara, N., Japanese Economy
Urano, H., Tax Accounting
Watanabe, T., Business Management
Yamane, H., German Literature
Yamashita, T., Production Management
Yanagase, K., Contemporary Capitalism
Yatabe, S., Linguistics
Yoshida, H., Shakespearean Tragedy
Yoshida, K., Investigation of the Mechanism of Intelligent Information Processing in Humans

Faculty of Social Sciences:

Akai, S., Sociology
Araki, H., Human Development
Endo, A., Urban Problems
Fujiwara, S., Social Policy Labour Problems
Fukai, J., Regional Economics
Hayashi, K., Contemporary Industry
Hihara, M., American Women Writers
Iida, T., Family Sociology
Ikeuchi, Y., American Playwrights
Ito, T., Industrial History
Kaji, R., German Literature
Kanomata, N., Stratification and Mobility
Kato, N., Human Development
Kato, S., Social Welfare
Kawaguchi, K., Economic Statistics and Policy
Kawai, Y., Social Security
Kawamata, J., Science and Technology
Kida, A., Japanese
Kizugawa, K., Art and Aesthetics
Kunihiro, T., French State
Kusafuka, N., Physical Education
Kutsunai, K., French Literature
Lim, B., Urban Planning Policy
Matsuba, M., German Capitalism
Matsuda, H., History of Modern Social Thought
Matsuda, H., Mass Communication Sociology
Miyamoto, K., Regional Economic Theory, Finance
Miyashita, S., History of Science and Technology
Morita, K., Social Psychology
Nagasaki, T., German Language and Literature
Nagasawa, K., Japanese Economy
Nakagawa, J., Lifestyle of the Worker Family
Nakagawa, K., Regional Society
Nakamura, T., Sociology
Okugawa, O., Quantitive Sociology
Otani, R., Industrial Technology
Sanada, N., Social Problems, Social Welfare
Sasaki, K., Social Pathology
Sato, H., Sociology Theory
Sato, Y., World Lifestyles
Seino, M., Sociology Theory
Shinoda, T., Modern Capitalism
Suda, M., Black Literature in America
Sudo, Y., Boundary of Sociology, Economics, and Philosophy
Suzuki, R., Japanese Social History
Takada, S., Urban and Regional Planning
Takagi, M., Sociology
Takeda, H., American Literature

TAKEHAMA, A., Postwar Japan
TSUJI, K., Labour Sociology
UCHIKIBA, T., English
YANAGISAWA, S., Mass Communication
YOSHIDA, M., Contemporary English Novel

Faculty of International Relations:

ANDO, T., Western Political History
ANZAI, I., Nuclear Engineering
ASAHI, M., Contemporary Global Economics
BRUNET, A., History of Cultural Exchange
CHANG, W., International Business Management
HOTTA, M., Rural Legal Systems in the United States
INOUE, J., Cultural Sociology
ITAKI, M., International Trade
ITO, E., International Marketing
KANAI, J., Physical Education
KARASAWA, K., Natural Resources
KATAOKA, S., Contemporary Literature
KATO, S., Japanese Culture
KATO, T., American Black Female Writers
KOBAYASHI, M., International Politics
MATSUOKA, H., History of American Politics
MIYAKE, M., Linguistic Analysis
MORINO, K., Developing Nations' Economies
MORIOKA, M., Theoretical Economics
NAKAMURA, M., International Economic Development
NAKANO, M., American Studies
NISHIKAWA, N., Comparative Literature
OGI, H., Chinese Language
OIKAWA, M., American Literature
OKAMURA, R., Comparative Socio-historical Study of Mass Media
OKUDA, H., Establishment and Development of the Dollar System
OKUYAMA, S., Modern Technology
OUCHI, M., Third World Politics
RYU, S., Contemporary Economics
SAITO, T., Commercial Law
SATO, M., African Politics
SEKI, H., International Relations
SHERARD, M., Linguistics
SHIMIZU, S., International Economics
SMOKER, P., World Peace Study
SUMIZAWA, T., German History
TAKEUCHI, M., Contemporary China
TAKEUCHI, T., Historical Structural Analysis of the Japanese Family
TOKUHISA, S., International Organizations
WAKANA, M., American Literature
YAMADA, H., Japanese Language
YAMADA, S., American Political History
YAMATE, H., International Law
YOSHINARI, T., Soviet and Eastern European Studies

Faculty of Letters:

AKAMA, R., Study of 'Kabuki'
AKITA, K., Learning Psychology
ASAI, M., English Literature
ASHIYA, N., Modern Japanese Literature
BAN, T., Medieval Japanese Literature
EGUCHI, N., Tourist Anthropology
FOX, C., English Literature
FUJI, K., Animal Psychology
FUKUDA, A., Medieval Japanese Literature
HATTORI, K., Philosophy
HAYASHI, N., Educational Anthropological Study
HIKOSAKA, Y., Japanese Literature
HIRAO, H., English
HONDA, O., History of Chinese Agriculture
IKEDA, Y., Study of Transcendental Problems
ISHI, F., German Literature
JIMBO, S., English Literature
KAKEHI, F., Modern and Contemporary Chinese Literature
KATAHIRA, H., Classical Geography
KAWASHIMA, K., Geography
KAWASHIMA, M., Japanese History
KIMURA, K., Japanese Literature
KINUGASA, Y., Modern Japanese History
KITAMURA, M., Chinese Language
KOBAYASHI, K., English Literature
KODAMA, T., English Language and Linguistics
KODERA, M., Philosophy of Education
KOGA, S., Urban Structure in relation to Office Location
KOYAMA, S., Training Education
KUSAKABE, Y., Classical Philosophy
MACLEAN, R. L., English and American Literature
MARUYAMA, M., American Literature
MASHIMO, A., Ancient Japanese Literature
MASUDA, T., Philosophy
MATSUDA, K., English Romantic Poets
MATSUDA, T., Cognitive Psychology
MATSUMIYA, H., Modern German Literature
MATSUMOTO, H., Modern and Contemporary Chinese History
MATSUMOTO, Y., Ancient and Medieval Chinese Literature
MOMOTA, J., Physical Education
MONDEN, K., Social Attitudes
MORIYA, K., Cognitive Psychology
MUROFUSHI, Y., Animal Psychology
NAGAI, K., Modern Japanese Politics
NAGATA, T., American History
NAKAHARA, A., Modern English Literature
NAKAMURA, T., Chinese Cultural History
NOGUCHI, T., English Renaissance Drama
ODAUCHI, K., Western History
OHTO, C., Ancient Greek History
OKADA, H., Chinese Literature
OSAWA, T., History of Chinese Ethnicity
PEATY, D., English Education
SAITO, T., Personality Psychology
SAKAKIBARA, T., Phenomenology
SANO, M., Linguistics
SASAKI, Y., Modern French Literature
SATO, Y., Perception
SHIMA, H., Tang Dynasty Thought
SHIMIZU, Y., Medieval and Modern Chinese Literature
SHIMOKAWA, S., French Literature
SUEKAWA, K., Modern European History
SUGAI, Y., Comparative Education
SUGIHASHI, T., Medieval Japanese History
SUHARA, F., Commercial Geography
SUZUKI, F., Urban Geography
SUZUKI, S., History of Japan
TAKAGI, K., Developmental Psychology
TAKAHASHI, M., Natural Geography
TAKASHIMA, K., American Literature
TERASAKI, S., Ethics
TODOKORO, T., Urban Geography
TSUCHIDA, N., Philosophy
UEDA, H., Modern Japanese Literature
WADA, S., Archaeological Research
WELLS, K., American Poetry
YAGI, Y., Psychology of Self
YAMAO, Y., Ancient Japanese History
YANE, Y., Ancient Japanese History
YANO, K., Theoretical and Metrical Study of Urban Systems

Faculty of Science and Engineering:

Department of Mathematics and Physics

ARAI, M., Mathematics
DOI, K., Algebra
FUJIMURA, S., Geometry
FUKUYAMA, T., Particle Physics
HAKAMADA, S., Analysis and Probability Theory
HARAMI, T., Alkali Halide Crystals
ISHI, H., Automorphic Forms
KAITO, C., Physics
KIDO, Y., Formation and Control of Hetero-Interfaces
KURATSUJI, H., Nuclear Physics
NAKAJIMA, H., Theoretical Analysis
NAKAJIMA, K., Geometry
NAKAJIMA, S., Algebraic Structure of Semigroups
NAKAYAMA, T., Statistical Thermodynamics
NAKAYAMA, Y., Nuclear Physics
NARUKI, I., Mathematics
ONO, R., Positron Life Time in Semiconductors
SHIMAOKA, K., Crystal Physics
SHIN'YA, H., Functional Analysis
SUGANUMA, R., Electromagnetics
TAKENAKA, A., Elemental Particles
TANAKA, Y., Crystal growth of Sb using vapour deposition
TSUDA, N., Derivatives, Phase Transfer
YAMADA, O., Operator Theory
YAMADA, T., Probability Statistics
YOSHMURA, Y., Alkali Metal Cyanide

Department of Chemistry

FUKAMI, H., Interaction of Ecosystem and Chemical Control Factors
HAYASHI, A., High Polymer Chemistry
HAYASHI, T., Organic Chemistry
KANEKO, Y., Synthesis of Inorganic Materials
KITAMURA, K., Physical Chemistry
KOJIMA, K., Synthesis
MATSUDA, J., Inorganic Chemistry
MATSUDA, T., Environmental Analysis Chemistry
MORISAKI, H., Biological Physics
NAGAI, T., Analytical Chemistry
NAKAMURA, N., Ionomers and Liquid Crystals
OGASAWARA, H., The Great Earthquake
OHTAKI, H., Solution Chemistry
OKADA, Y., Synthesis
SAWAMURA, S., Physical Chemistry
SHINODE, J., Organic and Fermentation Chemistry
SHIRAISHI, H., Electro-chemical Restoration
TACHIKI, T., Biochemistry
TAMIAKI, H., Chemistry
TANIGUCHI, Y., Physical Chemistry
TANIKAGA, R., Synthesis
YAMAMOTO, Y., Chemical Batteries

Department of Electrical and Electronic Engineering

ARAKI, Y., Development of Educational Software
KARIYA, K., Instrumentation Engineering
KAWABATA, T., Power Electronics
KOMATSU, Y., Synchronous Machines
MIKI, H., Electrical Engineering
MIZOSHIRI, I., Electrical Mathematics
NAKANISHI, T., Measurement
OKADA, T., Electrical Engineering
SUGIMOTO, S., Systems and Control
TAKAYAMA, S., Intuitive CAI System
TSUDAGAWA, M., Space Filters
TSUJIMURA, H., Electrical Theory
URAYAMA, T., Electrical Apparatus

Department of Mechanical Engineering

AKISHITA, S., Control Engineering
AMEYAMA, K., Physical Property
ISONO, Y., Production Technology
IWASHIMIZU, Y., Solid State Engineering
KAWAMURA, S., Intelligent Movement Control of Robots
NISHIWAKI, K., Internal Combustion Engines
NODA, Y., Biped Locomotion Robots
ONAMI, M., Strength of Materials
SAKAI, T., Reliability Engineering
SAKANE, M., Strength of Materials
TANAKA, T., Machinery Construction Methods
TANAKA, T., Strength of Materials
YAMAMOTO, S., Strength Characteristics of Fine Ceramics
YOSHIHARA, Y., Formation Mechanism

Department of Civil Engineering

AMASAKI, S., Concrete Engineering
DAIDO, A., River Engineering
FUKUMOTO, T., Road Engineering
HARUNA, T., Urban Planning
HAYAKAWA, K., Traffic Systems
ITO, M., Bridge Engineering
IZUNO, K., Structural Engineering
KOBAYASHI, H., Structural Mechanics
KOJIMA, T., Concrete Engineering
MAKIGAMI, Y., Civil Planning
NISHIMOTO, Y., Runoff Mechanisms
OZAWA, K., Meandering Channels

TAKAGI, N., Concrete Utilizing Silica Fume
TAKESHITA, S., Soil Mechanics
TSUKAGUCHI, H., Urban Transport Planning
YAMADA, K., Safety Engineering
YAMAZAKI, M., City Planning

Department of Computer Science and Systems Engineering

IKEDA, N., Probability Theory
INOUE, K., Control Engineering
HAYASHI, T., System Programming
KAMEI, K., Vehicle Control
MAEDA, H., Modelling and Control of Robots
NAGAI, K., Robot Engineering
NISHIKAWA, I., Neural Network
OGAWA, H., Systems Engineering
OHNO, Y., Software Engineering
OKUBO, E., Operating Systems
SATO, Y., Computer Engineering
TAKAYAMA, Y., Mathematical Theory and Application of Functional Parallel Programming
TOKUMARU, H., Random Data Processing
WATANABE, T., Production Systems
YAMAZAKI, K., Computer Engineering

General Education:

ENDO, A., Bio- and Geoscience
HAYASHI, S., English Language and Literature
ISAKA, T., Physical Education
KANEKO, H., German Poetry
KUDO, K., English Language and Literature
MINO, K., Earth Science
NAKAMURA, Y., French Language and Literature
OGASAWARA, H., Geology
SATOMI, J., Physiology
TANAKA, H., English Language and Literature
YAJIMA, M., German Language and Linguistics
YAMAMOTO, S., American Drama
YAMAUCHI, Y., English Language and Literature
YOSHIDA, M., Ecological Research

ATTACHED INSTITUTES

Research Institute of Cultural Sciences: Dir K. MORINO.

Research Institute of Science and Engineering: Dir Y. TANIGUCHI.

Data Processing Centre: Dir T. WATANABE.

International Centre: ANDRÉ BRUNET.

Institute of International Relations and Area Studies: Dir H. SEKI.

Institute of Foreign Languages and Culture Studies: Dir N. NISHIKAWA.

Institute of Educational Sciences: Dir T. MUKAI.

RYUKOKU UNIVERSITY

67 Tsukamoto-cho, Fukakusa, Fushimi-ku, Kyoto 612-77
Telephone: (75) 642-1111
Fax: (75) 642-8867
E-mail: ric@rnoc.fks.ryukoku.ac.jp

Founded 1639
Private control
Academic year: April to March

President: TENSEI KITABATAKE
Vice-Presidents: MORIHIDE AKIMOTO, SHIGEYOSHI YOSHIDA
Secretary-General: CHIKO IWAGAMI
Librarian: JITSUZO SHIGETA

Library: see libraries
Number of teachers: 394
Number of students: 17,890

Publications: *Bulletin of Buddhist Cultural Institute* (annually), *Annual Bulletin of Research Institute for Social Science* (annually), *Ryukoku Law Review* (quarterly), *Journal of Economic Studies* (quarterly), *Journal of Ryukoku University* (2 a year), *Ryukoku Journal of Humanities and Sciences* (2 a year), etc.

DEANS

Faculty of Letters: KOJU FUGEN
Faculty of Economics: FUMITAKA NISHIBORI
Faculty of Business Administration: MITSUHIRO MASAOKA
Faculty of Law: TAKAYOSHI YOROI
Faculty of Science of Technology: KIYOTSUGU OHJI
Faculty of Sociology: MATSUO KUCHIBA
Faculty of Intercultural Communication: MASANORI HIGA
Junior College: WAKAHARA DOSHOI
Japanese Culture and Language Programme: HIROMI YOSHIMURA

PROFESSORS

Faculty of Letters:

AKIMOTO, M., Japanese Language and Literature of the Middle Ages
AMAGASAKI, T., Meaning of Platonism and its Tradition
ASADA, M., Japanese Tendai Sect
ASAEDA, Z., Early History of Japanese Buddhism
ASAI, N., Shin Buddhism
ASANO, K., Teachings of Shinran
CHIN, K., Chinese Language and Literature
DOI, J., Modern Japanese Literature
FUGEN, K., History of Japanese Jodo Sect Thought
FUKUMA, K., History of Japanese Buddhism
FUKUSHIMA, H., Modern Japanese History
HAYASHIDA, Y., Eastern History
HIGASHINAKA, I., English Romantic Literature
ICHIMURA, T., Philosophy
ITOI, M., Japanese Language
IZUMOZI, O., Japanese Language and Literature of the Middle Ages
KAGOTANI, M., Japanese History
KATSUBE, M., Japanese Archaeology
KAWAMORI, K., Philosophy
KODAMA, D., History of Indian Buddhism
KODANI, S., English Language
KOJIMA, M., Intercultural Pedagogy
LAZARIN, M., Philosophy
MARUYAMA, T., Philosophy
MASUDA, R., English Literature
MIKOGAMI, E., Modern Western Philosophy
MIKOGAMI, E., Indian Philosophy
MITSUKAWA, T., Indian Buddhism
MIYAMA, Y., Japanese Literature of the Edo Period
MIYAMOTO, S., Modern English Novels
MIZOGUCHI, K., Philosophy
MORIMOTO, T., Educational Technology
NAGAKAWA, H., American Literature (Novels)
NAGAKAWA, S., History of Chinese Buddhism
NISHIYAMA, R., Mathematics
ODA, Y., Eastern History
OHMINE, A., Philosophy
OHTA, R., Shin Buddhist Theology
OHTORI, K., Tanka Poetry in the Middle Ages
OKA, R., Thought of Shiran
SHOBE, T., English Linguistics
TAKAYAMA, S., Pedagogic Sociology
TANAKA, M., Educational Psychology
TANAKA, S., Psychology
TATSUGUCHI, M., Buddhist Theology
TSUNEYOSHI, K., Methods and Curriculum of Education
TSUZUKI, A., Eastern History
UMITANI, N., Philosophy of Education
UWAYOKOTE, M., Japanese History
WATANABE, K., History of Sports Philosophy
WATANABE, T., Chinese Buddhist Theory
YAMADA, Y., English Literature
YAMAMOTO, H., Modern Japanese Literature
YATA, R., Shin Buddhism History

Faculty of Economics:

HIGUCHI, M., Middle Spanish Literature
IGUCHI, T., Industrial Organization
ISHIKAWA, K., History of the Japanese Economy
ITO, T., Mathematics
KAGO, T., Japanese Literature
KANEKO, H., Economic Theory
KAWAMURA, T., German Literature
KAWAMURA, Y., Development Sociology
KISHIDA, O., History of Economics
MATSUOKA, T., Theory of Modern Capitalism
MISAKI, S., Economic Theory
MIYANAGA, M., Economic Policy
MIZUHARA, S., Economic Thought
NAGAHO, S., Japanese Language
NAKAMURA, H., Regional Economics
NISHIBORI, F., Theoretical Economics
OBAYASHI, M., African Economic Development
OISHI, M., English Language
OTSUKI, M., German Economic History
SHIMUZU, K., American Literature
TAKENAKA, E., Labour Economics
TANAKA, K., Public Finance
TSUBOUCHI, R., Sociology
TSURUMI, Y., Economic History of Southeast Asia
YAMADA, T., American Literature
YOSHIMURA, H., Indian Mahayanist Buddhist Thought

Faculty of Business Administration:

ABE, T., Theoretical Economics
FUJITA, N., Japanese Business History
HARA, M., International Accounting Theory
HATA, N., Service Industry Economics
HAYASHI, A., Corporate Accounting
HAYASHI, K., Cost Accounting
HITOMI, K., Manufacturing Systems Engineering
HONDA, H., Corporate Finance Theory
INOUE, H., Business Management
INOUE, K., Finance Theory
INOUE, Y., English Language
KAMEI, M., International Business Management
KANEKO, A., Insurance Theory
KATAGIRI, M., Marketing Theory
KATAOKA, S., Business Administration
KITAZAWA, Y., Management of Small Businesses
KOIKE, T., Business Management Information Processing
KUDARA, K., Buddhism
MASAOKA, M., Managerial Accounting
MISHIMA, R., Business Administration Psychology
MORIYA, H., Merchandise Studies
MOTOOKA, A., Marketing
NAKAYAMA, J., German Literature
NATSUME, K., International Business Strategy
NISHIHARA, J., Japanese Language Education
NISHIKAWA, K., Labour Management
ONISHI, K., Information Industry
ONO, K., Accounting
OSUGI, M., International Finance Theory
SATO, K., Marketing
SHIMEGOTO, N., Business Organization Theory
SUGIMURA, M., French Literature
TAKADA, S., Religion
TAKAYANAGI, K., Astronomy
TOGAMI, M., Sociology
TOYOSHIMA, M., Engineering Management
YOKOYAMA, K., Regional Sociology
YUI, H., Industrial Engineering

Faculty of Law:

FUJIWARA, H., Civil Law
HAYASHI, T., Buddhism
HIGASHI, F., Physical Education
HIRANO, T., Political Processes
HIRANO, T., The Constitution; Religious Law
HOMMA, Y., Civil Proceedings Act
INUI, S., Civil Law
ISHIDA, T., Political Theory

ISHII, K., Philosophy of Law
KATSURA, F., English Language and Literature
KAWABATA, M., African Politics
KAWASUMI, Y., Civil Law
KIM, D., International Public Law
KISAKA, J., Japanese Political History
MATSUOKA, H., Civil Law
MIKAMI, T., Administrative Law
MIZUGUCHI, N., Public Administration
NAGARA, K., Administrative Law
NAKAGAWA, S., Criminal Law
NISHIO, Y., Commercial Law
OBATA, Y., Commercial Law
SAKAI, S., Current Middle East Politics
SAKAMOTO, M., Administration
SHIGETA, J., Criminal Law
TAKAHASHI, S., Italian Fascism
TAKEHISA, S., Commercial Law
TAKITA, R., Commercial Politics
TANAKA, N., International Law
TSUJITA, J., Astrophysics
UEDA, K., Constitutional Law
USHIO, H., Civil Law
WAKITA, S., Labour Law
YAMAUCHI, S., Philosophy of Religion
YOROI, T., Labour Law

Faculty of Science and Technology:
ABE, H., Plasma Physics
ARIKI, Y., Pattern Recognition
ENAMI, K., Materials Science and Engineering
FUJIMOTO, Y., Information Engineering
GOTO, Y., Materials Science
HARADA, T., Catalytic Chemistry
HAYASHI, H., Polymer Science
HORIKAWA, T., Mechanical Engineering and Materials Science
IKEDA, T., Applied Analysis and Computational Science
IWAMOTO, T., Robot Engineering
KAIYOH, H., Communications Engineering
KAMIJO, E., Inorganic Functional Materials
KATO, K., Multivariable Functions
KAWASHIMA, H., Mechanical Engineering
KOBAYASHI, K., Metallic Materials Chemistry
KOBUCHI, Y., Information Science
KOIZUMI, M., Ceramic Science
KONDO, H., Germanic Literature and Languages
KUME, S., Inorganic Solid Materials Chemistry
KUNIHIRO, T., Nuclear and Elementary Particle Physics
KUTSUNA, H., Mechanical Engineering
MATSUMOTO, W., Mathematics (Analysis)
MATSUSHITA, T., Co-ordination Chemistry
MIYASHITA, T., Mechanical Physics
NAKAGAWA, T., Mechanical Engineering
NAKAMURA, T., Computer Science
NAKANISHI, S., Mechanical Engineering
OHJI, K., Mechanical Engineering
OHTSUKA, N., Materials Strength and Fracture Mechanics
OKADA, Y., Information Processing
OKAMOTO, Y., Anglo-Irish Literature
ONISHI, S., Physical Chemistry
OZAWA, T., Information Technology
SAITO, M., Optics
SAKAI, T., Informatics
TAGUCHI, T., Health and Physical Education
TAKAHASHI, T., Science Education and Educational Technology
TAKEMOTO, K., Functional Polymer Chemistry
TSUBOI, Y., Mechatronics and Electronic Control
TSUNETO, T., Theoretical Physics
UDO, A., Systems Engineering
URABE, K., Ceramics
YAMAGUCHI, M., Applied Mathematics
YOTSUTANI, S., Mathematics (Analysis)
YUKIMOTO, Y., Semiconductor Electronics

Faculty of Sociology:
FUKUZAKI, S., Health Science; Mental Health Studies
HAYASHI, Y., High School Sociology Education
IYASU, T., Politics of Sociology
KAMEYAMA, Y., Sociology
KODAMA, N., Sociology
KUCHIBA, M., Comparative Sociology
KUWABARA, Y., Law and Systems Related to Social Welfare
MATSUNANI, N., Administrative Data Processing
MUKAI, M., Social Science
MUKAI, T., Rural Sociology
NAKA, H., Sociological Theory
NAKAGAKI, M., Studies in Social Welfare
NORIKUMO, S., Information Engineering
OGASAWARA, M., Theoretical Sociology
SHIMIZU, H., Everyday Life and Religion
TAKASHIMA, S., Political Sociology
TAKATSU, H., Social Issues
TANO, T., Health and Physical Education
TERAKAWA, Y., Religious Psychology
WATARI, H., English Philology

Faculty of Intercultural Communication:
AKAGI, H., Japanese Industrial Arts
FUKUDA, K., The United Nations and Japan
HAMANO, S., Human Rights Law, Western Political Thought
HIGA, M., Applied Linguistics
KIGLICS, I., Economics
KOIZUMI, T., Comparative Study of Civilizations
KWON, O., Education
MACADAM, J., Comparative Culture
MATSUBARA, H., Western History
MATSUI, K., Energy Economics
MIYAKAWA, C., French Literature and Language
MURATA, S., Comparative Study of Educational Systems
PANG, C., Chinese Language
SAKAMOTO, S., Food Culture, Ethnobotany
SIMPSON, J., World Agriculture
SUDO, M., Comparative Study of Folklore
SUEHARA, T., Cultural Anthropology, Economic Anthropology
SUGIMURA, T., History of Middle Eastern Art
TOH, L., International Communications and Relations
UEYAMA, D., Buddhist Studies

Junior College:
HAMAGAMI, Y., Child Welfare
IHARA, K., Nursing Technology
INAGAKI, H., Pure Land Buddhism
KOBAYASHI, H., Pedagogy
OHTSUKA, Y., Psychology
ONISHI, M., Community Health
SHIMIZU, K., Social Welfare
WAKAHARA, D., Pedagogy
YAMADA, M., Indian Buddhism
YAMADA, Y., Shin Buddhism
YOSHIDA, K., Discrimination Problems

ATTACHED RESEARCH INSTITUTES

Institute of Buddhist Cultural Studies: Shichijo Ohmiya, Shimogyo-ku, Kyoto 600; Dir KYOSHIN ASANO.

Research Institute for the Social Sciences: 67 Tsukamoto-cho, Fukakusa, Fushimi-ku, Kyoto; Dir TAKESHI HIRANO.

Socio-cultural Research Institute: 1-5 Yokoya, Seta Ohe-cho, Ohtsu, Shiga 520-21; Dir KENICHI MATSUI.

Joint Research Centre for Science and Technology: 1-5 Yokoya, Seta Ohe-cho, Ohtsu, Shiga 520-21; Dir KEISUKE KOBAYASHI.

UNIVERSITY OF THE SACRED HEART, TOKYO

Hiroo 4 chome 3-1, Shibuya-ku, Tokyo
Telephone: (3) 3407-5811
Fax: (3) 5485-3884
E-mail: webmaster@u-sacred-heart.ac.jp

Founded 1948
Private control
Academic year: April to March

President: Prof. TETSUKO NAKAGAWA
Business Chief: M. KODERA
Registrar: S. KAWASHIMA
Librarian: Prof. I. HORIGUCHI

Library of 317,000 vols
Number of teachers: 359
Number of students: 2,232

DEANS

Dean of Studies: R. AOKI
Dean of Students: R. KOBORI

Publications: *Seishin Ronso* (Seishin Studies, 2 a year), *Kiyo* (Publications of the Research Institute for the Study of Christian Culture, 1 a year).

SANNO INSTITUTE OF MANAGEMENT

6-39-15 Todoroki, Setagaya, Tokyo 158-8630
Telephone: (3) 3704-9551
Fax: (3) 3704-9553

Founded 1925

Consists of SANNO Graduate School (MBA Programme), SANNO College Isehara (4-year degree course in Management and Informatics, and distance education course), SANNO College Jiyugaoka (2-year degree course, and distance education course)

President: ICHIRO UENO

Library of 323,000 vols
Number of teachers: 185
Number of students: 5,264 (excluding distance education course students)

SAPPORO UNIVERSITY

3-Jo 7-chome, Nishioka, Toyohira-ku, Sapporo 062-8520
Telephone: (11) 852-1181

Founded 1967
Private Control
Academic year: April to March

President: MASAYUKI KIMURA
Head Administrator: K. KUROSAWA
Librarian: N. TAKAMATSU

Library of 426,000 vols
Number of teachers: 162
Number of students: 6,129

Publications: *Sapporo Law Review* (2 a year), *Journal of Comparative Cultures* (2 a year), *Sapporo University Journal* (2 a year), *Industrial and Business Journal* (2 a year).

DEANS

Faculty of Foreign Languages: M. KATO
Faculty of Economics: K. MOTODA
Faculty of Business Administration: J. ARAKAWA
Faculty of Law: H. TANAKA
Faculty of Cultural Studies: M. YAMAGUCHI
Women's Junior College: A. TODA
Graduate School of Law: K. SAKAI

SEIJO UNIVERSITY

6-1-20 Seijo, Setagaya-ku, Tokyo 157
Telephone: (3) 3482-1181
Fax: (3) 3484-2698

Founded 1950
Private control

President: H. MINAMI
Administrative Secretary: M. FUKUSHIMA
Librarian: S. KIMURA

Library of 750,000 vols
Number of teachers: 141 full-time, 277 part-time

Number of students: 4,809

DEANS

Faculty of Economics: T. MURAMOTO
Faculty of Arts and Literature: M. MOURI
Faculty of Law: A. YOKOKAWA

ATTACHED INSTITUTES

Institute of Folklore Studies.

Institute of Economic Studies.

SEIKEI UNIVERSITY

3-3-1, Kichijoji-Kitamachi, Musashino City, Tokyo 180-8633

Telephone: (422) 37-3531

Founded 1949
Academic year: April to March

President: MICHIO YANAI
Librarian: S. TAKAGI

Library of 600,000 vols
Number of full-time teachers: 176
Number of students: 8,547 undergraduate, 228 graduate

Publications: *Seikei Daigaku Ippankenkyu Hokoku* (Bulletin), *Seikei Daigaku Kogaku Hokoku* (Technology Report), *Journal of Asian and Pacific Studies*, faculty bulletins.

DEANS

Faculty of Economics: K. WATANABE
Faculty of Engineering: Y. KAWADA
Faculty of Humanities: H. ENDO
Faculty of Law: T. KATO

DIRECTORS

Information Processing Center: Y. OZAKI
Center for Asian and Pacific Studies: C. KOMURA

SENSHU UNIVERSITY

8, Kandajimbo-cho, 3-chome, Chiyoda-ku, Tokyo 101

Telephone: (44) 911-1252
Fax: (44) 900-7803

Founded 1880
Academic year: April to March

President: M. DEUSHI
Librarian: (vacant)

Library of 1,110,000 vols
Number of full-time teachers: 376
Number of students: 21,238

Publications: Various faculty and institute publs.

DEANS

School of Economics: T. IZUMI
School of Law: K. ONUMA
School of Business Administration: S. KATO
School of Commerce: T. KOJIMA
School of Literature: T. SHIBATA
Graduate School of Economics: S. NIHEI
Graduate School of Law: H. KAMATA
Graduate School of Literature: T. KITAGAWA
Graduate School of Business Administration: S. ASAJIMA
Graduate School of Commerce: M. HAGIWARA

ATTACHED INSTITUTES

Institute of Social Sciences
Imamura Institute of Legal Studies
Law Institute
Institute of Business Administration
Institute of Commercial Sciences
Institute of Accounting Studies
Institute for Humanities
Institute of Sports, Physical Education and Research
Institute of Information Science

SOKA UNIVERSITY

1-236, Tangi-cho, Hachioji, Tokyo 192

Telephone: (426) 91-2211
Fax: (426) 91-2039

Founded 1971
Private control
Academic year: April to March

Rector: Prof. Dr KAZUO TAKAMATSU
President: Prof. Dr KINNOSUKE KOMURO
Vice-Presidents: AKIRA ONISHI, MASASUKE NIHEI
Librarian: Prof. YUKIO ITAGAKI

Library of 650,000 vols
Number of teachers: 310
Number of students: 7,586

Publication: *SUN* (Soka University News, quarterly).

DEANS

Faculty of Economics: Prof. Dr KATSUHIKO FUKUSHIMA
Faculty of Law: KAZUO KAWASAKI
Faculty of Letters: OSAMU NAKANISHI
Faculty of Business Administration: YUJIRO EGUCHI
Faculty of Education: Prof. YOSHIHIKO MORIMASA
Faculty of Engineering: SHINTARO SUGAI
Division of Correspondence Education:
Faculty of Economics: Prof. MASASUKE NIHEI
Faculty of Law: Prof. KAZUO KAWASAKI
Faculty of Education: Prof. KAZUNORI KUMAGAI
Graduate School of Economics: Prof. TEN ISHINO
Graduate School of Law: Prof. IKUO ITABASHI
Graduate School of Letters: Prof. KAZUNORI KUMAGAI
Graduate School of Engineering: Prof. AKIRI ONISHI
Institute of Japanese Language: Prof. KENJI DOI

DIRECTORS

Institute of Peace Studies: T. TAKAMURA
Institute of Asian Studies: E. IMAGAWA
Institute for the Study of Comparative Culture: G. ITASAKA
Institute of Life Science: Y. TSUKADA
Institute of Systems Science: A. ONISHI

SOPHIA UNIVERSITY (Jôchi University)

Chiyoda-ku, Kioicho 7-1, Tokyo 102-8554

Telephone: (3) 3238-3111
Fax: (3) 3238-3885

Founded 1913
Private control (Society of Jesus)
Academic year: April to March
Languages of instruction: Japanese and English

Chancellor: J. YAMAMOTO
President: K. OTANI
Vice-Presidents: H. AOYAMA, J. KOBAYASHI, T. KASUYA
Registrar: T. SUGAWARA

Library: see Libraries
Number of teachers: 955
Number of students: 9,459 in Japanese Language Programmes, 697 in English Programmes, 922 in Graduate Programmes

Publications: *Monumenta Nipponica* (4 a year in English), *Sophia* (4 a year in Japanese), departmental journals (1 or 2 a year).

DEANS

Faculty of Humanities: A. OSHIMA
Faculty of Law: H. MACHINO
Faculty of Economics: T. TANAKA
Faculty of Foreign Studies: Y. ISHIZAWA
Faculty of Science and Technology: S. IKEO
Faculty of Theology: T. IWASHIMA
Faculty of Comparative Culture: W. CURRIE

DIRECTORS

Institute of International Relations: M. NAYA
Institute of Medieval Thought: K. RIESENHUBER
Iberoamerican Institute: K. KOBAYASHI
Institute of Christian Culture and Oriental Religions: K. MATSUOKA
Counselling Institute: Y. YAMANAKA
Life Science Institute: K. AOKI
Institute of Asian Cultures: Y. AOYAGI
Institute for the Culture of German-speaking Areas: S. IIZUKA
Linguistic Institute for International Communication: H. MINAMIDATE
Institute of American and Canadian Studies: K. MATSUO
Institute of Comparative Culture: H. ICHIKAWA
Institute for the Study of Social Justice: K. YAMADA

HEADS OF DEPARTMENTS

Faculty of Theology:

Theology: T. IWASHIMA

Faculty of Humanities:

Philosophy: K. RIESENHUBER
Education: Y. KATO
Psychology: J. CUSUMANO
History: K. TOYOTA
Japanese Literature: Y. KOBAYASHI (acting)
English Literature: N. TSUCHIYA
German Literature: S. KOIZUMI
French Literature: M. ODAGIRI
Journalism: Y. SUZUKI
Sociology: M. SONOBE
Social Welfare: Y. YAMAZAKI

Faculty of Law:

Law: Y. YAMAMOTO
International Legal Studies: S. MURASE
Legal Studies of the Global Environment: Y. SAKAGUCHI

Faculty of Economics:

Economics: H. URUSHI
Management: T. SUGIMOTO

Faculty of Foreign Studies:

English Language and Studies: J. KASAJIMA
German Language and Studies: J. MAUZ
French Language and Studies: M. NAKAMURA
Spanish Language and Hispanic Studies: M. SILGO
Russian Language and Studies: K. EZAWA
Portuguese Language and Luso-Brazilian Studies: C. MITA

Faculty of Comparative Culture:

Comparative Culture: V. OZAKI
Japanese Language and Studies: N. KAGAMI

Faculty of Science and Technology:

Mechanical Engineering: A. NOZUE
Electrical and Electronics Engineering: M. KATO
Mathematics: K. SHINODA
Physics: T. SEKINE
Chemistry: K. SANUI

TAKUSHOKU UNIVERSITY

3-4-14 Kohinata, Bunkyo-ku, Tokyo 112

Telephone: (3) 3947-2261

Founded 1900
Campuses at Hachioji and Bunkyo

Chancellor: S. ODAMURA
President: T. OSAKAI
Chairman of Board of Directors: T. FUJITO
Librarian: S. KORI

Library of 390,000 vols
Number of teachers: 528
Number of students: 10,377

Publications: *Takushoku Daigaku Ronshu* (every 2 months), *Kaigai Jijo* (Journal of World Affairs, monthly), *Hokoku* (annually).

DEANS

Faculty of Commerce: T. TAKAHASHI
Faculty of Political Science and Economics: K. KOBAYASHI
Faculty of Foreign Languages: T. WADA
Faculty of Engineering: M. SAKATA
Special Japanese Language Course for Foreign Students: M. ARAKI
Takushoku Junior College: T. GOTO
Hokkaido Takushoku Junior College: T. ISHIKAWA
Graduate School: T. OSAKAI

TAMAGAWA UNIVERSITY

1-1 Tamagawa Gakuen 6-chome, Machida, Tokyo 194-8610

Telephone: (427) 39-8111
Fax: (427) 39-1181

Founded 1929
Private control
Language of instruction: Japanese
Academic year: April to March

President: YOSHIAKI OBARA
Registrar: TAKASHI URATA
Librarian: HARUA TODA

Library of 775,000 vols
Number of teachers: 351 full-time, 436 part-time
Number of students: 7,774

Publications: *Zenjin Education* (monthly), *Shoho* (1 a year), *Mitsubachi Kagaku* (4 a year).

DEANS

Faculty of Agriculture: TADAYUKI ISHIYAMA
Faculty of Engineering: HIDETAKE TANIBAYASHI
Faculty of Arts and Education: HIROSHI YONEYAMA
Department of Education by Correspondence: HIROSHI YONEYAMA
Junior College for Women: MICHIAKI NAGAI
Graduate School for Education and Letters: YASUTADA TAKAHASHI
Graduate School for Agriculture: MITSUO MATSUKA
Graduate School of Engineering: TAKURO KOIKE
Graduate School for Engineering: TAKURO KOIKE
Associate Degree Junior College for Women: TOMIO OZAWA

TOHOKU GAKUIN UNIVERSITY

1-3-1 Tsuchitoi, Aoba-ku, Sendai 980

Telephone: (22) 264-6411
Fax: (22) 264-3030
E-mail: ico@tscc.tohoku-gakuin.ac.jp

Founded 1886
Private control
Language of instruction: Japanese
Academic year: April to March

President: ISAO KURAMATSU
Vice-Presidents: SHOZO AKAZAWA, AKIRA DEMURA

Number of teachers: 344
Number of students: 13,557

Publications: *Tohoku Gakuin University Review English Language and Literature* (2 a year), *History and Geography* (2 a year), *Economics* (3 a year), *Church and Theology* (2 a year), *Jurisprudence* (2 a year), *Human, Linguistic and Information Sciences* (3 a year), *Science and Engineering Report* (2 a year).

DEANS

Faculty of Letters: KIYOSHI TSUCHIDO
Faculty of Economics: SHIN-ICHI YAMAMOTO
Faculty of Law: HIROSHI UEDA
Faculty of Engineering: RISABURO SATO
Faculty of Liberal Arts: NORIO MIURA
Evening School: KAZUO ENDO

DEPARTMENTAL CHAIRMEN

Faculty of Letters:
- English: M. SHIKODA
- Christian Studies: S. OSAKI
- History: M. KOSAKA

Faculty of Economics:
- Economics: Y. SAITO
- Commerce: S. SAITO

Faculty of Law:
- Law: H. NAKAMURA

Faculty of Engineering:
- Mechanical Engineering: R. OSHIMA
- Electrical Engineering: N. MIYAMOTO
- Applied Physics: M. SATO
- Civil Engineering: S. HIWATASHI

Faculty of Liberal Arts:
- Human Science: A. OHE
- Linguistics: M. IWAYA
- Information Science: S. WATANABE

Evening School:
- English: K. HIRAKOUJI
- Economics: T. KOSHIBA

TOKAI UNIVERSITY EDUCATIONAL SYSTEM

2-28-4 Tomigaya, Shibuya-ku, Tokyo 151

Telephone: (3) 3467-2211
Telex: 2423402
Fax: (3) 3467-0197

Founded 1942

Chairman and President: TATSURO MATSUMAE

DIRECTORS

Strategic Peace and International Affairs Research Institute: TATSURO MATSUMAE
Research Institute of Faculty Development: SOUNOSUKE KATORI
Research Institute of Science and Technology: SHOJI YOSHIDA
Tokai University Research and Information Center: TOSHIBUMI SAKATA
Tokai University Space Information Center: TOSHIBUMI SAKATA
Okinawa Regional Research Center: SHOJI YOSHIDA
Tokai University European Center (Denmark): IWAO MAESHMA
Tokai University Pacific Center (Hawaii): KIYOSHI YAMADA

Tokai University

Shonan Campus: 1117 Kitakaname, Hiratsuka-shi, Kanagawa 259-1207; tel. (463) 58-1211; fax (463) 35-2458

Yoyogi Campus: 2-28-4 Tomigaya, Shibuya-ku, Tokyo 151-0063; tel. (3) 3467-2211

Shimizu Campus: 3-20-1 Orido, Shimizu-shi, Shizuoka 424-0902; tel. (543) 34-0411

Isehara Campus: Bouseidai, Isehara-shi, Kanagawa 259-1143; tel. (463) 93-1121

Numazu Campus: 317 Nishino, Numazu-shi, Shizuoka 410-0321; tel. (559) 68-1111

Founded 1942
Academic year: April to September, October to March

President: SHUROKU TANAKA
Librarian: TASUKU HAYAMI

Library of 1,660,000 vols
Number of full-time teachers: 1,499
Number of students: 31,305

Publications: *Tokai Journal of Experimental and Clinical Medicine,* bulletins of the various schools, etc.

CHAIRMEN

Graduate School of Letters: NOBUYUKI WATASE
Graduate School of Political Science: YOSHITERU MAKITA
Graduate School of Economics: OSAMU TAKENAKA
Graduate School of Law: SHIN UTSUGI
Graduate School of Arts: TAKEO YOSHIDA
Graduate School of Physical Education: SUKETSUNE IWAGAKI
Graduate School of Science: KATSUMI UJIIE
Graduate School of Engineering: HIROMASA TAKEUCHI
Graduate School of High Technology for Human Welfare: MASAAKI SHINJI
Graduate School of Marine Science and Technology: KENICHI NUMACHI
Graduate School of Medicine: KIYOSHI KUROKAWA
Advanced Course in Shipboard Training: MUNEO IKEDA

DEANS

School of Letters: NOBUYUKI WATASE
School of Political Science and Economics: KAZUMOTOSHI SHIMA
School of Law: SHIN UTSUGI
School of Humanities and Culture: TETSUO WATANABE
School of Physical Education: MASARU SAITO
School of Science: KATSUMI UJIIE
School of Engineering: HIROMASA TAKEUCHI
School of Engineering II (Evening Session): HIROMASA TAKEUCHI
School of High Technology for Human Welfare: MASAAKI SHINJI
School of Marine Science and Technology: TOSHITSUGU SAKO
School of Medicine: KIYOSHI KUROKAWA
School of Health Sciences: HAJIME YAMABAYASHI

HEADS OF DEPARTMENTS

School of Letters:
- Civilization: MASAYUKI USUDA
- Japanese History: MOTI ASAI
- Oriental History: MOTI ASAI
- Occidental History: MITSUO SHINOZAKI
- Archaeology: HIDEO KONDO
- Japanese Literature: KOICHIRO KOIZUMI
- English Literature: MASASHI FUJIMOTO
- Nordic Studies: YASUFUMI YAMASHITA
- Mass Communication: TAKAO MATSUMURA

School of Political Science and Economics:
- Political Science: SHOGO MOCHIZUKI
- Economics: TADAO YAMAGASHI
- Business Administration: KAZUHIRO YOSHIKAWA

School of Law:
- Law: CHIHIRO NUNOI

School of Humanities and Culture:
- Human Development: HISAYOSHI KATSUMATA
- Arts: YUJI ISA
- International Studies: HIDETAKA MIYAZAKI

School of Physical Education:
- Physical Education: KAZUYOSHI MIZUTA
- Judo and Kendo: TADAHIRO AJIRO
- Physical Recreation: MICHINORI MIYAZAKI

School of Science:
- Mathematics: SEIJI NEMOTO
- Mathematical Science: TATEMASA OHYA
- Physics: KENZO NANRI
- Chemistry: TAKASHI YASUOKA

School of Engineering:
- Electrical Engineering: SHOZO OKABE
- Control Engineering: YASUZUMI OCHIAI
- Communications Engineering: SHIGENORI TOMIYAMA
- Electronics: NOBUAKI TAKAHASHI
- Applied Physics: TOSHIO NAKASHITA
- Nuclear Engineering: AKIRA YOKOSHI
- Electro Photo Optics: KENICHIRO NAKAMURA
- Industrial Chemistry: TAKAO HONMA
- Metallurgical Engineering: SACHIO SETO
- Architecture and Building Engineering: TOMOYA NAGASAKA
- Civil Engineering: YOJI SHIMAZAKI

Prime Mover Engineering: MORIHITO HAYASHI
Production Engineering: TAKANE ITO
Precision Mechanics: MASARU SATO
Aeronautics and Astronautics: MASAHISA HANZAWA
Management Engineering: TAKAO HADA
School of Engineering II (Evening Session):
Electrical Engineering: SHOZO OKABE
Communications Engineering: SHIGENORI TOMIYAM
Construction Engineering: TOMOYA NAGASAKA
Mechanical Engineering: MORIHITO HAYASHI
School of High Technology for Human Welfare:
Information and Communication Technology: YASUZO SUTO
Material Science and Technology: AKINORI KATSUI
Biological Science and Technology: MANABU SAKAKIBARA
Bio-Medical Engineering: MUNEYUKI HORIKAWA
School of Marine Science and Technology:
Ocean Engineering: MASAO KIMURA
Marine Civil Engineering: SHIGEMI SAKODA
Marine Mineral Resources: JIRO SEGAWA
Fisheries: RYOHEI AMANO
Marine Design and Engineering: MICHIHISA MIYAGAWA
Marine Science: HIDEO INABA
Nautical Engineering: MUNEO IKEDA
School of Medicine:
Medicine: KIYOSHI KUROKAWA
School of Health Sciences:
Nursing: REIKO SHIMAZAKI
Social Work: SEIJI KITAZAWA
Japanese Language Course for Foreign Students: FUSATO TANIGUCHI
Foreign Language Center: KIYOICHI ONO
Group I (English): SHIGETO SATO
Group II (German, French, Chinese, Korean, Spanish, Russian): EIICHI KANAI
Licensed Professional Training Center: TAKASHI INOUE
Teacher Training Program: YUKO MIYASAKA
Librarian Training Program: TAKASHI INOUE
Curator Training Program: SHINICHI OSAKA
Foreign Student Education Center: MORITO TAKAHASHI
Intensive Japanese Language Program: HISAE WAKAMATSU
Foreign Student Program: HISAE WAKAMATSU

DIRECTORS

Research Institute of Civilization: YOGORO WATANABE
Research Institute of Social Sciences: FUKASHI UTSUNOMIYA
Institute of Oceanic Research and Development: KENICHI NUMACHI
Research Institute of Arts: MASAMICHI TEZENI
Institute of Research and Development: SHOJI YOSHIDA
Medical Research Institute: KIYOSHI KUROKAWA
Research Institute of Education: GINJI YAMAMOTO
Research Institute of Sports Medical Science: SUKETSUNE IWAGAKI

Kyushu Tokai University

Kumamoto Campus: 9-1-1 Toroku, Kumamoto-shi, Kumamoto 862-0970; tel. (96) 382-1141; fax (96) 381-7956

Aso Campus: Kawayou, Choyo-son, Aso-gun, Kumamoto 869-1404; tel. (9676) 7-0611

Founded 1973
Academic year: April to September, October to March

President: KANAU KUWASHIMA
Librarian: NOBUO OHYAMA
Library of 192,000 vols
Number of full-time teachers: 140
Number of students: 3,618

CHAIRMEN

Graduate School of Engineering: MASAMORI IIDA
Graduate School of Agriculture: TAKAO TORIKATA

DEANS

School of Engineering: MASAMORI IIDA
School of Agriculture: YOSHIHIRO TODA

HEADS OF DEPARTMENT

School of Engineering:
Electrical Engineering: YOSHITO SONODA
Electronics and Information Technology: MITSUMI FUJISHITA
Information and Systems Engineering: NORIO YAMAGUCHI
Mechanical Engineering: YOICHI NAKAZONO
Architecture: MITSUHIRO KASHIWAGI
Civil Engineering: MASAFUMI KATO
Management Engineering: NAOTOSHI SUMIKURA
School of Agriculture:
Agronomy: TATSURO MURATA
Animal Science: TAKESHI SHIBATA
General Education Research Center: HEIMA HAYASHI

DIRECTORS

Institute of Industrial Science and Technical Research: SUKEYO SATO
Agricultural Research Institute: TAKEO YAMAGUCHI

Hokkaido Tokai University

Sapporo Campus: 5-1-1-1 Minamisawa, Minami-ku, Sapporo 005-0825; tel. (11) 571-5111; fax (11) 571-7879

Asahikawa Campus: 224 Chuwa, Kamui-cho, Asahikawa 070-8021; tel. (166) 61-5111; fax (166) 62-8180

Founded 1977
Academic year: April to September, October to March

President: TSUNEO NISHIYAMA
Librarian: MIZUHIKO KIYOHARA

Library of 167,000 vols
Number of full-time teachers: 109
Number of students: 2,510

CHAIRMEN

Graduate School of Arts: JIRO OHYA
Graduate School of Science and Engineering: TETSUO SHIMONO

DEANS

School of Art and Technology: JIRO OHYA
School of International Cultural Relations: KOJI BANDO
School of Engineering: TETSUO SHIMONO

HEADS OF DEPARTMENT

School of Art and Technology:
Design: JUN MIKAMI
Architecture: HIROSHI KITAJIMA
School of International Cultural Relations:
Comparative Culture: KAZUSHI TANIMOTO
Intercultural Communications: TOSHIHIKO HARA
School of Engineering:
Electronic and Information Technology: MINORU KOTAKI
Marine Science and Technology: KENICHIRO HAMANAKA
Bioscience and Technology: HIDETOSHI MATSUYAMA

DIRECTORS

Research Institute for Higher Education Program: YASUNARI KURIHARA
Cultural Institute of Northern Region: TSUTOMU KOKAWA
Environmental Research Institute: HIROYUKI NISHIMURA

TOKYO COLLEGE OF PHARMACY

1432-1 Horinouchi, Hachioji, Tokyo 192-03
Telephone: (426) 76-5111
Founded 1880
President: Dr T. YAMAKAWA
Librarian: Prof. A. OHTA
Library of 85,000 vols
Number of teachers: *c.* 200
Number of students: *c.* 2,200
Publication: *Annual Report.*

Departments of pharmaceutical sciences, biopharmacy and pharmaceutical technology.

TOKYO KEIZAI UNIVERSITY

1-7 Minami-cho, Kokubunji, Tokyo 185-8502
Telephone: (42) 328-7711
Founded 1900 as Ohkura School of Commerce
Private control
Academic year: April to March
President: BUNTARO TOMIZUKA
Chief Administrative Officer: YOSHIHIRO NAKAJIMA
Librarian: SHINKEI RYU
Library of 545,000 vols
Number of teachers: 433
Number of students: 8,100

Publications: *Journal of Tokyo Keizai University* (6 a year), *Journal of Humanities and Natural Sciences* (3 a year), *Journal of Communication Studies* (2 a year), and various faculty and institute publs.

DEANS

Faculty of Economics: KAZUO SHIMADA
Faculty of Business Administration: ATSUMO HIMENO
Faculty of Communication Studies: MICHIYO TAKIZAWA
Junior College Business Course: IKUO MURATA
Graduate School of Economics: KAZUO SHIMADA (Chair.)
Graduate School of Business Administration: ATSUMU HIMENO (Chair.)

TOKYO UNIVERSITY OF AGRICULTURE

1-1-1 Sakuragaoka, Setagaya-ku, Tokyo 156
Telephone: (3) 5477-2560
Fax: (3) 5777-2635
E-mail: tuacip@nodai.ac.jp
Founded 1891
Academic Year: April to March
President: Dr TOSHIRO MATSUDA
Chief Administrative Officer: YUTAKA NABAE
Librarian: Dr TSUNEO MAKI
Library of 580,000 vols
Number of teachers: 368
Number of students: 12,303

Publication: *Nogyo Daigaku* (Agricultural Science Journal, 1 a year).

DEANS

Faculty of Agriculture: Dr IKUDO DOMEKI
Faculty of Applied Bioscience: Dr ISOYA SHINJI
Faculty of Regional Environmental Science: Dr SHOICHI MASUSHIGE
Faculty of International Agriculture and Food Studies: Dr KATSUTOSHI NIINUMA
Faculty of Bioindustry: Dr YOSHIRO ISHIJIMA
Graduate School of Agriculture: Dr KANJU OHSAWA

Graduate School of Bioindustry: Dr KATSUHIRO INOUE
Junior College: Dr KOTOYOSHI NAKANISHI

TOKYO DENKI UNIVERSITY (Tokyo University of Electrical Engineering)

2-2 Kanda-Nishiki-cho, Chiyoda-ku, Tokyo 101
Telephone: (3) 5280-3555
Fax: (3) 5280-3623
Founded 1907
President: Dr MAKOTO KOTANI
General Director of Multimedia Resource Centre and Libraries: Dr Y. FUKUI
Library of 285,000 vols, 79,000 periodicals
Number of teachers: 313 full-time, 98 part-time
Number of students: 9,356 undergraduates (7,328 daytime, 2,028 evening), 528 graduates

DEANS

Graduate School of Engineering: S. ARAI
College of Engineering: H. KOYAMA
College of Engineering (Evening Programme): S. MIWA
Graduate School of Science and Engineering: Y. FUKUI
College of Science and Engineering: A. KINOSHITA

DIRECTORS

Research Institute for Technology: T. FUJIMAKI
Superconductivity Research Centre: M. SAITO
Research Institute for Construction Technology: S. NAKANO
Centre for Research Collaboration: S. TAKEUCHI

SCIENCE UNIVERSITY OF TOKYO

1–3 Kagurazaka, Shinjuku-ku, Tokyo 162-8601
Telephone: (3) 3260-4271
Founded 1881
Private control
Academic year begins April
President: TETSUJI NISHIKAWA
Deputy Presidents: KEIGO NAGASAKA, YUKIMASA NISHIMURA
Librarian: NOBUO TSUDA
Library of 760,000 vols
Number of teachers: 750
Number of students: 21,344
Publications: *SUT Bulletin* (monthly), *SUT Journal of Mathematics* (2 a year).

DEANS

Faculty of Science (1st Division): YASUSHI MIYAHARA
Faculty of Science (2nd Division): SHOICHI KONDO
Faculty of Pharmaceutical Sciences: HIROSHI NAKAMURA
Faculty of Engineering (1st Division): SYOUHEI INOUE
Faculty of Engineering (2nd Division): TATSUO TANI
Faculty of Science and Technology: HIROYUKI OKAMURA
Faculty of Industrial Science and Technology: MICHITERU YOSHIDA
School of Management: YOUICHI KATAOKA

HEADS OF DEPARTMENTS

Faculty of Science (1st Division):
- Mathematics: SEIICHI YAMAGUCHI
- Physics: CHIKARA ISHII
- Chemistry: YUKO HASEGAWA
- Applied Mathematics: TADAHIRO UESU
- Applied Physics: SATOSHI KANEKO
- Applied Chemistry: MINORU UENO
- General Education: KENJI MAKINO

Faculty of Science (2nd Division):
- Mathematics: HIROSHI NIIZUMA
- Physics: MITSUNORI YANAGIZAWA
- Chemistry: KENJI MORI
- General Education: HARUO KIZUKA

Faculty of Pharmaceutical Sciences:
- Pharmaceutical Sciences: KEN TAKEDA
- Pharmaceutical Technology: HIROYUKI OSHIMA

Faculty of Engineering (1st Division):
- Architecture: TSUNEHIRO MANABE
- Industrial Chemistry: YASUKAZU SAITO
- Electrical Engineering: MASAM AKAIKE
- Management Science: NAOTO NIKI
- Mechanical Engineering: SHIGEKA YOSHIMOTO
- General Education: MASAYUKI SHIMIZU

Faculty of Engineering (2nd Division):
- Architecture: HIDEKI SHIMIZU
- Electrical Engineering: TOSHIHIDE KIOKA
- Management Science: RYUICHI HIRABAYASHI
- General Education: RYOSUKE KANESASHI

Faculty of Science and Technology:
- Mathematics: NOBUKAZU OTSUKI
- Physics: YASUHIKO HUTAMI
- Information Sciences: SHINICHI YAMADA
- Applied Biological Sciences: HIROYUKI SETO
- Architecture and Building Engineering: HITOSHI TAKEDA
- Industrial and Chemical Engineering: YOSHITOMO ABE
- Electrical Engineering: HIDEAKI IKOMA
- Industrial Administration: YASUHIRO HIRAKAWA
- Mechanical Engineering: RYOJI MURATA
- Civil Engineering: SHIGEAKI MORICHI
- General Education: HISASHI SAITO

Faculty of Industrial Science and Technology:
- Applied Electronics: KOJI ITO
- Materials Science and Technology: SHIN TAKEUCHI
- Biological Science and Technology: JOU CHIBA

ATTACHED INSTITUTES

TRD Research Center for Science and Technology: 2641 Yamazaki, Noda-shi, Chiba-ken 278-8510; tel. 0471-24-1501; Principal TERUAKI MUKAIYAMA.

Research Institute for Biosciences Science University of Tokyo: 2641 Yamazaki, Noda-shi, Chiba-ken 278-8510; tel. (471) 24-1501; Principal TOMIO TADA.

Life-long Education Center: 1–3 Kagurazaka, Shinjuku-ku, Tokyo 162; tel. (3) 3267-9462.

TOKYO WOMAN'S CHRISTIAN UNIVERSITY

2–6–1, Zempukuji, Suginami-ku, Tokyo 167-8585
Telephone: (3) 3395-1211
Fax: (3) 3399-3123
Founded 1918
Private control
Language: Japanese
Academic year: April to March
President: HIROKI FUNAMOTO
Librarian: SHINSUKE MUROFUCHI
Library of 557,000 vols
Number of teachers: 142
Number of students: 4,208, including 78 graduates
Publications: *Japanese Literature* (2 a year), *Essays and Studies in British and American Literature* (2 a year), *Historica* (1 a year), *Sociology and Economics* (1 a year), *Annals of Institute for Comparative Studies of Culture* (1 a year), *Science Reports* (1 a year), *Essays and Studies* (2 a year), *University Bulletin* (monthly).

DEANS

Graduate School: HIROSHI IMAI
College of Arts and Sciences: SANAE INOUE
College of Culture and Communication: YUKO KOBAYASHI

CHAIRMEN

Graduate School of Humanities: HIROSHI IMAI
Graduate School of Science: MASAHIKO SHINOHARA
Graduate School of Culture and Communication: RYOICHI SATO

DIRECTORS

Institute for Comparative Studies of Culture: AIKO KOZAKI
Center for Women's Studies: HIROKO SATO

HEADS OF DEPARTMENTS

College of Arts and Sciences:
- Philosophy: MITSUSHI KUBO
- Japanese Literature: AKIRA KANEKO
- English: YUTAKA KURONO
- History: TESSEI MATSUZAWA
- Sociology and Economics: NOZOMU KAWAMURA
- Psychology: HIROTADA HIROSE
- Mathematics: MASAHIKO SHINOHARA

College of Culture and Communication:
- Communication: MEIKO SUGIYAMA
- Cross-Cultural Studies: AKIRA TAKEDA
- Languages: TAZUKO UENO

TOKYO WOMEN'S MEDICAL UNIVERSITY

8–1 Kawada-cho, Shinjuku-ku, Tokyo 162-8666
Telephone: (3) 3353-8111
Telex: 2322317
Fax: (3) 3353-6793
Founded 1900
Private control
Language: Japanese
Academic year: April to March
President: K. TAKAKURA
Registrar: H. YOSHIOKA
Librarian: E. AIKAWA
Library of 204,000 vols
Number of teachers: 1,134
Number of students: 606
Publication: *Journal of Tokyo Women's Medical College* (monthly, abstracts only in English).

ATTACHED INSTITUTES

Heart Institute of Japan: Dir Y. IMAI.
Institute of Gastroenterology: Dir N. HAYASHI.
Neurological Institute: Dir M. IWATA.
Kidney Center: Dir T. AGISHI.
Diabetes Center: Dir Y. IWAMOTO.
Maternal and Perinatal Center: Deputy Dir T. ISHII.
Institute of Clinical Endocrinology: Dir H. DEMURA.
Critical Care Medical Center: Dir T. SUZUKI.
Institute of Geriatrics: Dir K. YAMASHITA.
Institute of Rheumatology: Dir N. KAMATANI.
Chest Institute: Dir S. NITTA.
Institute of Oriental Medicine: Dir F. SHIROTA.

TOYO UNIVERSITY

28-20 Hakusan 5-chome, Bunkyo-ku, Tokyo 112-8606
Telephone: (3) 3945-7557
Fax: (3) 3942-2489
Founded 1887

Private control
Academic year: April to March
President: TAKUO SUGANO
Director of Academic Affairs: MIZUO OHNO
Librarian: IKURO TAKEUCHI
Library of 987,000 vols
Number of teachers: 515 full-time, 643 part-time
Number of students: 27,996
Publications: faculty bulletins, journals, etc.

DEANS

Faculty of Literature: RIJIKI SAKAZUME
General Education Courses: YOSHIYUKI KITAMURA
Faculty of Economics: KIYOSHI ASANO
Faculty of Business Administration: YASUHIRO OGURA
Faculty of Law: MASUO IMAGAMI
Faculty of Sociology: SHIGERU NISHIYAMA
Faculty of Engineering: MOTOHIKO HAKUNO
Faculty of Regional Development Studies: YUZO AKATSUKA
Faculty of Life Sciences: KOKI HORIKOSHI
Graduate School of Literature: TAKEHIKO OHSHIMA
Graduate School of Sociology: HIDEHIKO HIROSE
Graduate School of Law: MASURA MIZUNO
Graduate School of Business Administration: HIROYUKI SAITOH
Graduate School of Engineering: YUKIO OKAMOTO
Graduate School of Economics: HIROYA AKIMOTO

ATTACHED INSTITUTES

Institute of Asian Studies: Dir HIROYUKI OHKUBO.
Institute of Economics: Dir TORU NAKAKITA.
Institute of Business Administration: Dir YUMIO ONO.
Institute of Social Relations: Dir KYOICHI SONODA.
Institute of Comparative Law: Dir AKIRA MORITA.
Institute of Industrial Technology: Dir FUMIYATA KIYOSAWA.
Institute for Asian and African Culture: Dir KIYOTO HARIU.
Bio-Nanoelectric Research Centre: Dir YOICHI MURAYAMA.

TSUDA COLLEGE

2-1-1 Tsuda-machi, Kodaira-shi, Tokyo 187-8577
Telephone: (42) 342-5111
Fax: (42) 341-2444
E-mail: info-admin@tsuda.ac.jp
Founded 1900
Academic year: April to March
President: HISAKO SHIMURA
Library of 240,000 vols, 2,500 periodicals
Number of full-time teachers: 85
Number of students: 2,676 (98 postgraduate)
Publications: *The Tsuda Review* (1 a year), *Journal of Tsuda College* (1 a year), *The Study of International Relations* (1 a year).

Faculty of Liberal Arts, departments of English language and literature, mathematics and computer science, international and cultural studies.

WASEDA UNIVERSITY

1-104 Totsuka-machi, Shinjuku-ku, Tokyo 169-8050
Telephone: (3) 3203-4141
Telex: 2323280
Fax: (3) 3203-7051
E-mail: intl-ac@mn.waseda.ac.jp
Founded 1882
Private control
Academic year: April to July, September to February
President: TAKAYASU OKUSHIMA
Vice-Presidents: TSUMORU USHIYAMA (Academic and International Affairs), HIROSHI ISHIZUKA (Student and Personnel Affairs), SUNAO KAWAI (General Planning)
Director of Library: NORIO OKAZAWA
Library: see Libraries
Number of teachers: 3,736
Number of students: 42,794 undergraduates (36,806 daytime division, 5,988 evening division), 4,670 graduates
Publications: *Waseda University Bulletin, Memoirs of the School of Science and Engineering, Zaiken: Annual Report of Kagami Memorial Laboratory for Materials Science and Technology, Technical Report of the Advanced Research Institute for Science and Engineering, Report of Materials Science and Technology, Studies in Egyptian Culture, Technical Report, Waseda Bulletin of Comparative Law, Waseda Business and Economic Studies, Waseda Economic Papers, Waseda Political Studies, Waseda Journal of Asian Studies*, etc.

DEANS

School of Political Science and Economics: K. YORIMOTO
School of Law: H. SATO
School of Literature I: T. NISHIMOTO
School of Literature II (evening division): K. ANZAI
School of Education: S. WATANABE
School of Commerce: K. TSUBAKI
School of Science and Engineering: S. USAMI
School of Social Sciences (evening division): K. KOYAMA
School of Human Sciences: H. HAMAGUCHI
Graduate School of Political Science: H. KATAOKA
Graduate School of Economics: H. KOGA
Graduate School of Law: T. MIYASAKA
Graduate School of Literature: Y. SATO
Graduate School of Commerce: N. MIYAZAWA
Graduate School of Science and Engineering: H. OZAKI
Graduate School of Education: N. ICHIMURA
Graduate School of Human Sciences: Y. HARUKI
Graduate School of Social Sciences: S. TAMURA
Graduate School of Asia–Pacific Studies: K. GOTO

HEADS OF DEPARTMENT

School of Literature I:

Department of Philosophy

Philosophy: M. KITAMURA
Asian Philosophy: T. IWATA
Psychology: H. KIMURA
Sociology: H. NASU
Education: Y. SUZUKI
Humanities: S. IGETA

Department of Literature

Japanese: M. TAKEMOTO
Chinese: T. MATSUURA
English: K. OSHIMA
French: H. KURAKATA
German: A. FUJII
Russian: M. TAKANO
Theatre Arts: T. TAKEDA
Creative Writing: N. ENAKA

Department of History

Japanese History: K. FUKAYA
Asian History: J. YOSHIDA
Western History: K. OGURA
History of Art: S. HOSHIYAMA
Archaeology: R. TAKAHASHI

School of Literature II:

Majors

Oriental Culture: K. KONDO
Western Culture: M. KOJIMA
Social Studies: K. OSADA
Japanese: T. TANAKA
English: H. RUSU
Art: Y. MURASHIGE
Dramatic Arts: T. TAKEDA
Creative Writing: T. TAKAHASHI
Philosophy and Religion: M. SATO
Literature and Linguistics: T. KAWASE
History and Folklore: T. EBISAWA
Human and Social Sciences: M. ODA
Arts in Performance: K. IWAMOTO

School of Education:

Education: T. YAMASHITA
Education: T. YAMASHITA
Social Education: I. ASAKURA
Educational Psychology: H. NAMAKI
Japanese Language and Literature: T. KUWAYAMA
English Language and Literature: H. MATSUZAKA
Social Studies: T. MIYAGUCHI
Geography and History: T. HOKAZONO
Social Science: T. OHNISHI
Science: H. HIRANO
Mathematics: Y. HINOHARA
Biology: S. ISHII
Earth Science: H. OGASAWARA

School of Science and Engineering:

Mechanical Engineering: K. NAGATA
Electrical, Electronics and Computer Engineering: S. IWAMOTO
Mineral Resources Engineering: N. ARIHARA
Architecture: N. KANO
Applied Chemistry: T. OSAKA
Materials Science and Engineering: N. ICHINOSE
Electronics, Information and Communication Engineering: F. TAKAHARA
Industrial and Management Systems Engineering: M. AZUMA
Civil Engineering: H. SEKI
Applied Physics: Y. TSUNODA
Mathematical Sciences: K. HASHIMOTO
Physics: S. ISHIWATA
Chemistry: K. MATSUMOTO
Information and Computer Science: S. OHSUGA
Division of Multidisciplinary Studies: H. AKIBA

School of Human Sciences:

Basic Human Sciences: I. KIMURA
Human Health Sciences: E. NOJIMA
Sports Sciences: K. YAMAZAKI

ATTACHED INSTITUTES

Advanced Research Centre for Science and Engineering: Dir T. OTSUKI.
Kagami Memorial Laboratory for Materials Science and Technology: Dir I. OHDOMARI.
Institute of Comparative Law: Dir A. OSUGA.
Institute of Language Teaching: Dir M. KOYASU.
Institute for Research in Business Administration: Dir S. KOBAYASHI.
Institute for Research in Contemporary Political and Economic Affairs: Dir M. UCHIDA.
Advanced Research Centre for Human Sciences: Dir H. SAGAZA.
Centre for Japanese Language: Dir A. NAKAMURA.
Extension Centre: Dir T. HARA.
Media Network Centre: Y. MURAOKA.
Tsubouchi Memorial Theatre Museum: Dir B. TORIGOE.
Aizu Museum: Dir E. TAKAHASHI.
Institute of Asia–Pacific Studies: Dir O. NISHIZAWA.

Global Information and Telecommunication Institute: Dir H. TOMINAGA.

Centre for International Education: Dir T. KAWASE.

Environmental Safety Centre: Dir H. SAKURAI.

Schools of Art and Music

Elizabeth University of Music: 4–15 Noboricho, Naka-ku, Hiroshima; tel. (82) (221) 0918; fax (82) 221-0947; f. 1952; library of 88,750 vols, 15,000 sound recordings; 47 full-time, 70 part-time teachers; 656 undergraduates, 53 postgraduates; Pres. J. M. BENÍTEZ; Dean of Academic Affairs K. NAGAI; publ. *Kenkyuu Kiyoo* (annually).

Kanazawa College of Art: 5-11-1, Kodatsuno, Kanazawa, Ishikawa 920-8656; tel. (76) 262-3531; fax (76) 262-6594; e-mail admin@kanazawa-bidai.ac.jp; f. 1946; depts of Fine Art, Design, Crafts; Graduate School; Research Institute of Art and Craft, f. 1972; 67 full-time staff, 200 part-time staff, 665 students; library of 72,000 vols; Pres. YOSHIAKI INUI; publ. *Bulletin* (annually).

Kunitachi College of Music: 5-5-1 Kashiwa-cho, Tachikawa-shi, 190 Tokyo; tel. (425) 36-0321; fax (425) 35-2313; f. 1950; 433 teachers; 3,275 students; library of 310,000 vols; Pres. Prof. B. EBISAWA; publs *Kenkyu Kiyo* (Memoirs), *Daigakuin Nempo* (annual publication of the postgraduate school), *Ongaku Kenkyujo Nempo* (annual publication of the research institute).

Kyoto City University of Arts: 13-6 Kutsukake-cho, Ohe, Nishikyo-ku, Kyoto 610-11; 500 students.

Musashino Academia Musicae: 1-13-1 Hazawa, Nerima-ku, Tokyo; tel. (3) 3992-1121; fax (3) 3991-7599; f. 1929; 438 staff, 3,766 students; library of 180,000 vols; Pres. N. FUKUI, Dean N. FUKUI; Librarian T. FURUSHO; publ. *Review of Studies* (in Japanese, annually).

Osaka College of Music: 1-1-8, Saiwaimachi, Shonai, Toyonaka City, Osaka 561; tel. (6) 334-2131; f. 1915; courses in composition, vocal music and instrumental music; 372 teachers, 1,406 students; library of 109,000 vols; Pres. YUZURU NAGAI; publs *Bulletin, Hand Book.*

Tama Art University: 3-15-34 Kaminoge, Setagaya-ku, Tokyo 158; tel. (3) 3702-1141; fax 03-702-2235; f. 1935; undergraduate division established 1953; painting, sculpture, architecture, design, art sciences; 237 teachers, 2,662 undergraduates; 162 graduates; Pres. K. GOTO.

Toho-Gakuen School of Music: 41-1, 1-chome, Wakaba-cho, Chofu-shi, Tokyo 182-8510; fax (3) 3307-4354; f. 1961; 84 teachers, 1,100 students; library of 130,000 vols; Pres. T. ETO.

Tokyo College of Music: 3-4-5, Minami, Ikebukuro, Toshimaku, Tokyo 171; f. 1907; 1,697 students; library of 90,000 vols, 11,000 CDs; Pres. YASUKAZU UEMURA.

Ueno Gakuen University: Faculty of International Cultural Studies, 3-1 Haracho 2-chome, Sohka-shi, Saitama 340-0048; tel. (489) 41-3121; fax (489) 41-3039; e-mail ugi-kokusai@ma3.justnet.ne.jp; f. 1995; studies in English Language and British and Irish Culture, and in Spanish Language and Iberian and Latin American Culture; Faculty of Music, 24-12, Higashi-Ueno 4-chome, Taito-ku, Tokyo 110-8642; tel. (3) 3842-1021; fax (3) 3843-7548; f. 1958; 188 teachers; 828 students; library of 170,000 vols; Pres. Prof. HIRO ISHIBASHI; Dean of ICS Prof. K. IKI; Dean of Music Prof. N. FUNAYAMA.

JORDAN

Learned Societies

GENERAL

Islamic Academy of Sciences: POB 830036, Amman; tel. 5522104; fax 5511803; e-mail ias@go.com.jo; f. 1986; international, independent, non-political, non-governmental organization of scientists and technologists, linked to COMSTECH (Committee on Scientific and Technological Co-operation among Islamic Countries) working to promote science, technology and development in the Islamic and developing worlds; organizes conferences and seminars; supervises training workshops; commissions research; 77 Fellows (26 nationalities); Pres. Prof. M. A. KAZI; Deputy Exec. Dir MOUNEEF R. ZOUBI; publs *Journal* (quarterly), *Newsletter* (quarterly), *Islamic Thought and Scientific Creativity* (quarterly), *Proceedings* (annually).

Royal Academy for Islamic Civilization Research (Al Albait Foundation): POB 950361, Amman 11195; tel. 5539471; fax 5526471; f. 1980; 102 mems from 40 countries; research is divided into 2 main categories: long-term projects such as the issuing of the *Encyclopedia of Islamic Civilization*, the *Comprehensive Catalogue of Arab Islamic MSS* and the *Annotated Bibliographies of Islamic Economy and Islamic Education*; and medium-term projects dealing with contemporary Muslim life and thought; library of 23,148 vols, 474 periodicals, 120 microfilms; special collections: Hashemite and Jordanian Collections; Pres. Dr NASSIR EL-DIN EL-ASSAD; Librarian TAROUB KHAYYAT.

BIBLIOGRAPHY, LIBRARY SCIENCE AND MUSEOLOGY

Jordan Library Association: POB 6289, Amman; tel. 629412; f. 1963; 600 mems; Pres. ANWAR AKROUSH; Sec. YOUSRA ABU AJAMIEH; publs *Rissalat al-Maktaba* (The Message of the Library) (quarterly), *Palestinian-Jordanian Bibliography, Directory of the Libraries in Jordan, Jordanian National Bibliography 1979–, Directory of Periodicals in Jordan, Palestinian Bibliography,* etc.

Research Institutes

AGRICULTURE, FISHERIES AND VETERINARY SCIENCE

Department of Agricultural and Scientific Research and Extension: POB 226 and POB 2178, Amman; f. 1958; covers all branches of agricultural research, information and extension; staff of 52; library of 18,500 vols; Dir SAID GHEZAWI.

EDUCATION

Unesco Regional Office for Education in the Arab States/Bureau Régional de l'Unesco pour l'Education dans les Pays Arabes: POB 2270, Amman; tel. 606559; telex 24304; fax 682183; f. 1973; carries out Unesco activities in the Arab region in the field of education; training of personnel, advisory services to Arab countries, studies and research, information and documentation; 19 professional staff; Dir ABDULGADER EL-ATRASH; publs *L'Education Nouvelle* (3 a year), *Education and Development Series* (Arabic and English, monthly).

TECHNOLOGY

Royal Scientific Society: POB 925819, Amman; tel. (962-6) 844701; telex 2127; fax 844806; f. 1970; independent, non-profit industrial research and development centre; electronic services and training centre, computer systems, mechanical engineering, chemical industry, building research centre, economics, wind and solar energy research centre; library: see libraries; Pres. Dr HANI MULKI; publs *Monthly Accession List, Current List of Periodicals Holdings*.

Libraries and Archives

Amman

Abdul Hameed Shoman Public Library: POB 940255, Amman 11194; tel. (6) 5679182; fax (6) 5607368; f. 1986; 120,000 vols, 1,200 periodicals; Librarian YUSRA ABU AJAMIEH.

Greater Amman Public Library: POB 182181, Amman; tel. 627718; telex 21969; fax 649420; f. 1960; 257,179 vols in Arabic and English; 572 current periodicals (15 for children); 11 brs for adults and children (72,579 vols), Deposit Library for UNESCO (5,000 vols); Jordanian publications; Chief Officer MOHAMED AL-KFAWIN.

National Library: POB 6070, Amman; tel. (6) 610311; fax (6) 616832; f. 1990; prepares and issues the national bibliography and union catalogue; responsible for copyrights and legal deposits; depository for national, UNESCO and WIPO publications; 55,000 vols; Dir-Gen. OUSAMA MIKDADI.

Scientific and Technical Information Centre: POB 925819, Amman; tel. (962-6) 844701; telex 21276; fax 844806; f. 1986; core collection includes energy, civil engineering, construction, industrial chemistry, mechanical engineering, computer science, economics, electronics; 47,000 vols, 1,670 periodicals, 200 theses, 2,000 non-pront media, 450 maps, 15,000 specifications; on-line service from Dialog, BRS, Infoline; Dir Dr YOUSEF NUSSEIR.

University of Jordan Library: University of Jordan, Amman; tel. 843555; telex 21629; fax 832318; f. 1962; 560,000 vols, 1,400 current periodicals; 10 faculty reading rooms; legal deposit for UN, WHO, FAO, World Bank, UNESCO, SIPRI, UNU, ILO, Institute for Peace Research documents; legal deposit for dissertations from all Arab universities; Dir Dr SALAH JARRAR ; publs A classified list of books catalogued (monthly), list of theses (2 a year), *Library Guide* (annually), *Reader's Guide* (annually), *Bibliographical list and indexes* (irregular).

Irbid

Irbid Public Library: POB 348, Irbid; f. 1957; 30,000 vols; Librarian ANWAR ISHAQ AL-NSHIWAT.

Museums and Art Galleries

Amman

Folklore Museum: POB 88, Amman; housed by the Department of Antiquities; f. 1972; collection of national traditional costumes; Curator Mrs SA'DIYA AL-TEL.

Jordan Archaeological Museum: POB 88, Amman; f. 1951; 10 staff; library of 3,560 vols; Curator MOSA ZAYAT.

Mosaic Gallery: POB 88, Amman; f. 1972; pieces from the Byzantine era found in Jarash and Madaba; Curator Miss NUHA ABSI.

Popular Life Museum: POB 88, Amman; f. 1973; local domestic history; brs in Petra, Madaba, Salt and Kerak; Curator Miss IMAN QUDA.

Universities

UNIVERSITY OF JORDAN

Amman 11943

Telephone: (6) 844595
Telex: 21629
Fax: (6) 836446

Founded 1962
Languages of instruction: Arabic and English
State and autonomous control
Academic year: September to August (two semesters and a summer session)

President: Dr FAWZI GHARAIBEH
Vice-President for Academic Affairs: Dr MOHAMMAD MAQUSI
Vice-President for Administrative Affairs: Dr WALID ALMAANI
Director of Registration and Admission: GHALEB AL-HOURANI
Director of the Library: Dr SALAH JARRAR

Number of teachers: 950
Number of students: 23,000

Publications: *Dirasat* (scientific research), *Al-Majallah al-Thaqafiyyah* (quarterly), *The University* (newsletter, in Arabic, monthly), *University News / Anba' al-Jami'ah* (in Arabic, monthly), *Yearbook, Statistical Yearbook, Facts and Figures* (annually), *Prospectus* (in Arabic and English), *Campus News* (in English, monthly).

DEANS

Faculty of Arts: Dr ABDUL-RAHMAN SHAHIN
Faculty of Economics and Administrative Sciences: Dr MUHSEN MAKHAMREH
Faculty of Science: Dr ADEL MAHASNEH
Faculty of Shari'a (Islamic Studies): Dr MAHMOUD SARTAWI
Faculty of Medicine: Dr MAHMOUD ABU-KHALAF
Faculty of Nursing: Dr RAGHDA SHUKRI
Faculty of Agriculture: Dr BASSAM SNOBER
Faculty of Education: Dr SULAIMAN RIHANI
Faculty of Engineering and Technology: Dr KHALED TOUQAN
Faculty of Law: Dr MOHAMMAD AL-GHAZWI
Faculty of Physical Education: Dr HASHEM IBRAHIM
Faculty of Pharmacy: Dr FATMA AFIFI
Faculty of Dentistry: Dr GHAZI BAKA'EEN
Postgraduate Studies: Dr ANWAR AL-BATTIKHI

JORDAN UNIVERSITY OF SCIENCE AND TECHNOLOGY (JUST)

POB 3030, Irbid
Telephone: (2) 295111
Telex: 55545
Fax: (2) 295123

Founded 1986
State control
Languages of instruction: Arabic, English
Academic year: September to September

President: Prof. SA'AD HIJAZI
Vice-Presidents: Prof. AHMAD ABU EL-HAIJA, Prof. ANWAR BATIKHI
Registrar: FAISAL AL-RIFAIE
Librarian: ISSA LELLO

Library of 90,000 vols
Number of teachers: 452
Number of students: 7,934

DEANS

Faculty of Medicine: Assoc. Prof. IBRAHIM BANI-HANI (acting)
Faculty of Dentistry: Asst Prof. MOHAMMAD AL-OMARI (acting)
Faculty of Engineering: Prof. TAISIR KHEDAYWI
Faculty of Pharmacy: Prof. MUTAZ SHEIKH SALEM
Faculty of Agriculture: Assoc. Prof. MARWAN MUWALLA (acting)
Faculty of Science: Prof. NABIL AL-BASHIR (acting)
Faculty of Nursing: Assoc. Prof. ROWAIDA AL-MAAITAH (acting)
Faculty of Veterinary Medicine: Prof. ORHAN ALPAN (acting)
Scientific Research: Prof. ABDULRAHMAN TAMIMI
Graduate Studies: Prof. NAJI NAJIB
Student Affairs: Assoc. Prof. ZIAD QUDAH (acting)

ATTACHED CENTRES

Computer Centre: Dir Asst Prof. ALI SHATNAWI.
Centre for Agricultural Research and Production: Dir Asst Prof. RIDA SHIBLI.
Consultative Centre for Science and Technology: Dir Prof. ABDULRAHMAN TAMIMI.
Centre for Environmental Sciences and Technology: Dir Asst Prof. WAIL ABU-EL-SHA'R.

MU'TAH UNIVERSITY

POB 7, Mu'tah, Al Karak
(Amman Liaison Office: POB 5076, Amman)
Telephone: 617860
Telex: 63003
Fax: (6) 654061

Founded 1981
State control
Languages of instruction: Arabic and English
Academic year: October to June

President: Prof. ABDULRAHMAN ATTIYAT
Vice-President for Academic Affairs: Prof. SHAHIR EL-HASSAN AL-RASHDAN
Vice-President for Administration and Construction: Prof. ABDELRAHIM HUNAITI
Registrar: TAHA AL-ADAILA
Librarian: AMIN AL-NAJDAWI

Library of 240,000 vols
Number of teachers: 279
Number of students: 7,193

Publication: *Mu'tah Journal for Research and Studies* (Humanities and Social Sciences series and Natural and Applied Sciences series, both quarterly).

DEANS

Engineering: Dr FOU'AD GHARAIBEH
Sciences: Dr AHMAD ABUSHAMLEH
Arts: Dr MAHMUD AL-QUDAH
Law: Dr NIZAM AL-MAJALI
Economics and Administrative Sciences: Dr AHMAD QATAMIN
Education: Dr ABDULLAH ABABNEH
Scientific Research and Graduate Studies: Prof. ABDULFATTAH AL-HMOUZ
Student Affairs: Dr NO'MAN AL-KHATIB

AL-QUDS OPEN UNIVERSITY

POB 77, Um Summaq, Amman
Telephone: 822561
Telex: 24051
Fax: 962-6-823460

Founded 1985; first phase began 1988

President: Dr MUNTHER SALAH
Directors: Dr TAISEER KAILANI (Academic Affairs, acting), Dr ABDUL-LATIF AKEL (Production, acting), AHMAD TAQI (Student Affairs, acting), MUSTAFA HOURANI (Administration Affairs), Dr AHMAD ABU SHEIKHA (Planning)
Librarian: FADEL KLAIB

Library of 6,000 vols
Number of teachers: 95
Number of students: 3,000 (first phase)

PROGRAMME CO-ORDINATORS

Land and Rural Development: Dr FUAD KAWASMI (acting)
Home and Family Development: Dr TAISEER KAILANI (acting)
Computer Information Systems: Dr MOHAMMAD AL-FAYOMI (acting)
Education: Dr TAISEER KAILANI
Management and Entrepreneurship: Dr ABDEL MOUTIE ASSAF (acting)
Foundation Courses: Dr KHALIL WISHAH

YARMOUK UNIVERSITY

POB 566, Irbid
Telephone: (2) 271100
Telex: 51566
Fax: (2) 274725

Founded 1976
National and autonomous control
Languages of instruction: Arabic and English
Academic year: 2 semesters (October to January, February to June), and summer session (June to August)

President: Prof. Dr MARWAN R. KAMAL
Vice-Presidents: Prof. Dr YASER M. ADWAN (Administrative Affairs), Prof. Dr AHMED S. SALEH (Academic Affairs)
Registrar: FAROUQ AL-MUFTI
Librarian: ANWAR AKROUSH

Library of 340,000 vols, 1,150 current periodicals
Number of teachers: 676
Number of students: 14,518

Publications: *Abhath al-Yarmouk* (Yarmouk Research Journal), *Majallat al-Yarmouk* (Yarmouk Magazine), *Jaridat al-Talabah* (Student Newspaper), *Sahafat al-Yarmouk* (Yarmouk Newspaper), *Al'anba* (Newsletter), *University Academic Catalogue* (annually), *Al'anba* (Institute of Archaeology and Anthropology Newsletter), *Al-Sanabel* (Yearbook).

DEANS

Faculty of Science: Prof. Dr WAJIH OWEIS
Faculty of Arts: Prof. Dr FARIS MASHAGBEH
Faculty of Economics and Administrative Sciences: Prof. Dr ZOHEIR N. EL-SABBAGH
Faculty of Education and Fine Arts: Prof. Dr SHADIA E. TEL
Faculty of Shari'a (Islamic Law): Dr ISMAIL ABU SHARI'A (acting)
Faculty of Physical Education: Prof. Dr ZIAD AL-KURDI
Graduate Studies and Research: Prof. Dr MOHAMMAD AWWAD
Student Affairs: Dr ATEF ODIBAT (acting)
Hijjawi Faculty of Applied Engineering: Dr WAJIH QASSEM (acting)

PROFESSORS

ABDUL-HAFEZ, S., Biology
ABDUL-RAHMAN, A., Arabic
ABU AL-JARAYESH, I., Physics
ABU DAYYE, S., Political Science
ABU HELOU, Y., Education
ABU-HILAL, A., Geology
ABU-SALEH, M., Statistics
ABUL-UDOUSS, Y., Arabic
ADWAN, Y., Public Administration
AL-ADWAN, S., Chemistry
AL-ALOUSI, A., Statistics
AL-ARAB, M., Chemistry
AL-HASSAN, K., Chemistry
AL-MUBARAK, S., Law
AL-MUHEISEN, Z., Archaeology
AL-NOURI, Q., Anthropology
AL-SALEM, H., Physical Education
AL-TELL, SH., Education
ALI, A., Business Administration
ALI JAWAD, A., Geology
ARAJI, A., Public Administration
ATIYYAT, A., Chemistry
AWAD, A., History
AWWAD, M., English
AYYOUB, N., Physics
BAKKAR, Y., Arabic
BANI HANI, A., Economics
BARQAWI, K., Chemistry
BATAYNEH, M., History
DABABNEH, M., Physics
DAIRY, A., Physical Education
EL-KHADRA, B., Public Administration
ESMADI, F., Chemistry
FATAFTAH, Z., Chemistry
FORA, A., Mathematics
GHAWANMEH, Y., History
GHAZAWI, F., Sociology
HADDAD, H., Arabic
HAILAT, Q., Mathematics
HAJ-HUSSEIN, A.T., Chemistry
HAMADANI, R., Chemistry
HAMAM, A., Music
HAMMAD, KH., Economics
HIJJEH, M., Mathematics
HUNAITI, A., Biology
JBOURI, A., Fiqh and Islamic Studies
JIBRIL, I., Chemistry
KAFAFI, Z., Archaeology
KAMAL, M., Chemistry
KHARBUTLI, M., English
KHASSAWNEH, I., Chemistry
KHATEEB, A., Education
KHAWALDEH, M., Education
KURDI, Z., Physical Education
LAHHAM, N., Physics
MAHMOUD, H., Arabic
MAHMOUD, S., Physics
MAKKI, A., Electrical Power Engineering
MARI, T. A., Education
MASHAGBAH, F., English
MOMANI, Q., Arabic
NUSAIR, N., Public Administration
ODEH, A., Education
OGLAH, A., Biology
OLAIMAT, M., Education
OLWAN, M., Law
OMAR, M. K., Sociology
OMARI, K., Education
OWEIS, W., Biology
RABBA'I, A., Arabic
RABBA'I, M., Arabic
RAMADAN, M., Arabic
RASHDAN, SH., English
RASHID, M., Chemistry
RAYYAN, M., History
SABBAGH, Z., Business Administration
SADEDDIN, W., Geology
SAFA, F., Arabic
SALAHUDDIN, A., Statistics
SALEH, S., Mathematics
SALEM, A., Physics
SALHIYYEH, M., History
SHARE', M., Economics
SHARI, A., Arabic

SHAYEB, F., Arabic
Sheikh SALEM, F., Business Administration
STATIYYEH, S., Arabic
SUBBARINI, M., Education
SULEIMAN, I., Journalism
TABBA', H., Chemistry
TALAFHA, H., Economics
TALEB, M., Chemistry
TASHTOUSH, H., Chemistry
TAWARAH, K., Chemistry
THAHER, A., Political Science
UGAILI, S., Computer Science
UGLAH, M., Fiqh and Islamic Studies
WAZARMAS, I., Physical Education
YUSUF, N., Physics
ZAGHAL, A., Sociology
ZUBI, A., Arabic
ZUGHOUL, M., English

ATTACHED INSTITUTES

Institute of Archaeology and Anthropology: Dir Prof. Dr ZEIDAN KAFAFI.

Language Center: Dir Dr HUSSEIN OBEIDAT (acting).

Jordanian Studies Center: Dir Dr RASLAN BANI YASIN (acting).

Educational Research and Development Center: Dir Prof. Dr MOHAMMED KHWALDEH.

Center for Consultation and Community Service: Dir Dr AHMAD HAIAJNA.

Marine Sciences Station (jointly with Univ. of Jordan): Aqaba; Dir Prof. Dr AHMAD ABU-HILAL.

Center for Theoretical and Applied Physics: Dir Prof. Dr SAMI MAHMOUD (acting).

Computer and Information Center: Dir Prof. Dr SALEH UGAILI (acting).

Colleges

Al-Husn Polytechnic: POB 50, Al-Husn; tel. (2) 210397; f. 1981; library of 10,000 vols; 60 teachers; 800 students; 2-year diploma courses; Dean Dr HUSEIN SARHAN.

Amman University College for Applied Engineering: POB 15008, Marka, Amman; tel. 892345; f. 1975; two-year diploma course; four-year Bachelor of Applied Engineering; library of 17,000 vols; 91 teachers; 2,000 students; Dean MOHAMMAD A. K. ALIA.

HEADS OF DEPARTMENTS

Electrical Engineering: Dr RATIB ISA
Mechanical Engineering: Dr SALAMA AHMAD
Chemical Engineering: Dr ADNAN MUSTAFA
Civil Engineering: Dr MOHAMAD KHARABSHI

Jordan Institute of Public Administration: POB 960383, Amman; tel. 664155; telex 23009; fax 680731; f. 1968; administrative training, research and consultation; library of 5,386 vols; Dir-Gen. ABDULLAH ELAYYAN.

Jordan Statistical Training Centre: POB 2015, Amman; tel. 842171; telex 24117; fax 833518; f. 1964 for the training of government employees and other applicants in statistical methods; library of *c.* 700 vols; Dir ABDULHADI ALAWIN; publs *Annual Report, Students' Reports*.

Jordan University for Women: POB 961343, Amman; tel. 715546; fax 715570; f. 1991; library of 34,700 vols, 295 periodicals; 124 teachers; 1,350 students; Pres. Prof. MAHMOUD SAMRA; publ. *Al-Basair*.

Princess Sumaya University College for Technology: POB 925819, Amman; tel. 844701; telex 21276; fax 844806; f. 1991; BSc courses in computer studies; 10 teachers, 120 students; Dean Dr MOHAMMAD QASEM AL-QUARYOTY; Registrar MOHAMMAD HARB ATIYEH.

KAZAKHSTAN

Learned Societies

GENERAL

Kazakhstan Academy of Sciences: 480021 Almaty, Ul. Shevchenko 28; tel. (3272) 69-51-50; fax (3272) 69-61-16; depts of Physics and Mathematics (Academician-Sec. SH. M. AITALIEV), Earth Sciences (Academician-Sec. S. M. KOZHAKHMETOV), Chemical Sciences (Academician-Sec. K. A. ZHUBANOV), Biological Sciences (Academician-Sec. ZH. AKHANOV), Social Sciences (Academician-Sec. A. KOSHANOV), Medical Sciences (Academician-Sec. S. B. BALMUKHANOV), Central Kazakhstan (Academician-Sec. Z. M. MULDAKHMETOV), South Kazakhstan (Academician-Sec. S. BALABEKOV); 45 mems, 94 corresp. mems; attached research institutes: see Research Institutes; library: see Libraries and Archives; Pres. V. S. SHKOLNIK; Academician Sec.-Gen. M. K. SULEIMENOV; publs *Vestnik* (Herald), *Izvestiya* (bulletins: Physics and Mathematics, Geology, Chemistry, Biology, Philology, Social Science).

Research Institutes

AGRICULTURE, FISHERIES AND VETERINARY SCIENCE

Agricultural Research Institute: Almaty obl., Kaskelensky raion, Pos. Almalybak; Dir I. A. ABUGALIEV.

Fisheries Research Institute: Zhezkazgan obl., Balkhash.

Institute of Soil Science: 480032 Almaty, PO 32, Akademgorodok; tel. 48-04-00; attached to Kazakhstan Acad. of Sciences; Dir ZH. U. AKHANOV.

Kazakh Research Institute of Grain Farming: 474070 Akmolinskaya obl., Shortandy 1; tel. (31730) 2-10-80; f. 1956; library of 56,000 vols; Dir A. K. KURISHBAYEV.

Kochetau Agricultural Research Institute: Kochetau obl., Zerendinsky raion, Selo Charlinka.

Northern Research Institute of Livestock Raising: 643150 North Kazakhstan obl., Pos. Bishkul; tel. 2-13-70; f. 1962; library of 41,000 vols; Dir M. A. KINEEV.

Research and Technological Institute of Livestock Raising: 483143 Almaty obl., Kaskelensky raion, Tausamaly; tel. (3272) 34-16-45; f. 1974; library of 18,000 vols, 3,300 journals; Dir A. M. MELDEBEKOV.

Research Institute for Plant Protection: 483117 Almaty obl., Kaskelensky raion, Selo Rakhat; tel. 29-56-09; f. 1958; library of 29,134 vols; Dir T. N. NURMURATOV.

Research Institute of Forestry and Agroforestry Reclamation: Kochetau obl., Shchuchinsk, Ul. Kirova 58; tel. 2-14-62; f. 1957; library of 140,000 vols; Dir V. M. KOSTROMIN.

Research Institute of Potato and Vegetable Growing: Almaty obl., Kaskelensky raion, Pos. Kainar.

Research Institute of Sheep Raising: Almaty obl., Zhambulsky raion, Mynbaevo; tel. 2-20-02; f. 1933; sheep, goat, horse and camel breeding; library of 100,000 vols; Dir K. U. MEDEUBEKOV; publ. *Proceedings* (annually).

ECONOMICS, LAW AND POLITICS

Institute of Economics: 480021 Almaty, Kurmangazy 29; tel. 62-87-88; attached to Kazakhstan Acad. of Sciences; Dir A. K. KOSHANOV.

Institute of State and Law: Almaty, Kurmangazy 29; tel. 69-59-11; attached to Kazakhstan Acad. of Sciences; Dir E. K. NURPEISOV.

HISTORY, GEOGRAPHY AND ARCHAEOLOGY

Institute of Archaeology: Almaty; attached to Kazakhstan Acad. of Sciences; Dir K. M. BAIPAKOV.

Institute of Geography: 480100 Almaty, Ul. Kalinina 69A; tel. 61-81-29; attached to Kazakhstan Acad. of Sciences; Dir N. K. MUKITANOV.

Valikhanov, Ch. Ch., Institute of History and Ethnology: 480021 Almaty, Ul. Shevchenko 28; tel. 62-92-37; attached to Kazakhstan Acad. of Sciences; Dir M. K. KOZYBAEV.

LANGUAGE AND LITERATURE

Auezov, M. O., Institute of Literature and Arts: 480021 Almaty, Ul. Kurmangazy 29; tel. 62-88-23; attached to Kazakhstan Acad. of Sciences; Dir S. S. KIRABAEV.

Institute of Linguistics: 480021 Almaty, Ul. Kurmangazy 29; tel. 69-10-34; attached to Kazakhstan Acad. of Sciences; Dir A. T. KAIDAROV.

MEDICINE

Central Asian Plague Prevention Research Institute: 480034 Almaty, Kopalskaya ul. 14; tel. 35-75-48; Dir V. M. STEPANOV.

Dermatovenereological Research Institute of the Committee for Health: Ministry of Education, Culture and Health, 480002 Almaty, Ul. Raimbeka 60; tel. (3272) 30-40-85; fax (3272) 50-23-77; f. 1931; library of 250,000 vols; Dir ZURA B. KESHILEVA.

Institute of Microbiology, Epidemiology and Infectious Diseases: 480002 Almaty, Ul. Pastera 34; tel. 33-04-26; Dir I. K. SHURATOV.

Institute of Nutrition: 480008 Almaty, Ul. Klochkova 66; tel. 42-92-03; fax 42-97-20; f. 1974; attached to Kazakhstan Acad. of Sciences; Dir T. SH. SHARMANOV; publs *Voprosy pitaniya, Zdravookhranenie Kazakhstana* (8–10 a year).

Institute of Physiology and Labour Hygiene: 470061 Karaganda, Pr. Lenina 71; tel. 52-10-21; attached to Kazakhstan Acad. of Sciences; Dir G. A. KULKYBAEV.

Kazakhstan Paediatrics Research Institute: Almaty, Al-Farabi 146; tel. 48-81-21; telex 251232; fax 63-12-07; f. 1932; library of 36,000 vols; Dir A. K. MASKAKEYEV.

Research Institute of Clinical and Experimental Surgery: 480003 Almaty, Ul. Mira 62; telex 251287; Dir M. A. ALIEV.

Research Institute of Tuberculosis: Almaty, Gorodskaya ul. 5; tel. 61-87-58; f. 1932; library of 11,000 vols, 15 periodicals; Dir Prof. A. D. DJUNUSBEKOV.

NATURAL SCIENCES

Biological Sciences

Aitkhozhin, M.A., Institute of Molecular Biology and Biochemistry: 480012 Almaty, Ul. Michurina 80; tel. 67-18-52; attached to Kazakhstan Acad. of Sciences; Dir N. A. AITKHOZHIN (acting).

Institute of Botany: 480100 Almaty, Ul. Kirova 103; tel. 61-80-19; attached to Kazakhstan Acad. of Sciences; Dir S. A. BEDAREV.

Institute of Experimental Biology: 480072 Almaty, Pr. Abaya 38; tel. 67-23-03; attached to Kazakhstan Acad. of Sciences; Dir A. M. MURZAMADIEV.

Institute of Microbiology and Virology: 480100 Almaty, Ul. Kirova 103; tel. 61-84-97; telex 131391; attached to Kazakhstan Acad. of Sciences; Dir A. N. ILYALETDINOV.

Institute of Physiology: 480032 Almaty, Akademgorodok; tel. 48-04-88; attached to Kazakhstan Acad. of Sciences; Dir KH. D. DUISEMBIN.

Institute of Zoology: 480034 Almaty, Akademgorodok; tel. 48-19-32; attached to Kazakhstan Acad. of Sciences; Dir T. N. DOSZHANOV.

Mathematical Sciences

Institute of Applied Mathematics: Karaganda; attached to Kazakhstan Acad. of Sciences; Dir M. OTELBAEV.

Institute of Theoretical and Applied Mathematics: 480021 Almaty, Ul. Pushkina 125; tel. 61-37-40; attached to Kazakhstan Acad. of Sciences; Dir N. K. BLIEV.

Physical Sciences

Akhmedsafin, U.M., Institute of Hydrogeology and Hydrophysics: 480100 Almaty, Ul. Krasina 94; tel. 61-50-51; attached to Kazakhstan Acad. of Sciences; Dir V. V. VESELOV.

Astrophysical Institute: 480068 Almaty, Kamenskoe plato; tel. 65-00-40; attached to Kazakhstan Acad. of Sciences; Dir B. T. TASHENOV.

Bekturov Institute of Chemical Sciences: 480100 Almaty, Ualikhanov 106; tel. 61-23-89; fax 61-57-65; e-mail adm@chem.academ .alma-ata.su; f. 1945; attached to Kazakhstan Acad. of Sciences; Dir Prof. Dr E. E. ERGOZHIN; publ. *Izvestya* (6 a year).

Chemical-Metallurgical Institute: 470032 Karaganda, Ul. Dzerhinskogo 63; tel. 51-36-12; attached to Kazakhstan Acad. of Sciences; Dir V. P. MALYSHEV.

Geological Surveying Oil Research Institute: 465002 Gurev, Ul. Ordzhonikidze 43; tel. 3-33-86; Dir S. U. UTGALIEV.

Institute of High Energy Physics: 480082 Almaty, Alatau; tel. 69-03-67; attached to Kazakhstan Acad. of Sciences; Dir E. G. BOOS.

Institute of Nuclear Physics: 480082 Almaty, Nauchnyi Gorodok; tel. 69-05-79; attached to Kazakhstan Acad. of Sciences; Dir A. K. ZHETBAEV.

Institute of Organic Catalysis and Electro-chemistry: 480100 Almaty, Ul. K. Marksa 142; tel. 61-58-08; attached to Kazakhstan Acad. of Sciences; Dir G. D. ZAKUMBAEVA.

Institute of Organic Synthesis and Carbon Chemistry: 470061 Karaganda, Ul.

40-let Kazakhstana; tel. 52-60-85; attached to Kazakhstan Acad. of Sciences; Dir S. M. MOLDAKHMETOV.

Institute of Petroleum Chemistry and Natural Salts: 465002 Atyrau, Ul. Lenina 2; tel. 2-26-74; attached to Kazakhstan Acad. of Sciences; Dir N. R. BUKEIKHANOV.

Institute of Seismology: 480060 Almaty, Pr. Al-Farabi 75; tel. 48-21-34; fax 49-44-17; e-mail adm@seism.academ.alma-ata.su; attached to Kazakhstan Acad. of Sciences; Dir A. K. KURSKEEV.

Institute of Space Research: 480034 Almaty, Akademgorodok; tel. 62-38-96; attached to Kazakhstan Acad. of Sciences; Dir U. M. SULTANGAZIN.

Institute of the Ionosphere: 480068 Almaty, Kamenskoe plato; tel. 65-14-74; attached to Kazakhstan Acad. of Sciences; Dir V. I. DROBZHEV.

Physical Technical Institute: 480082 Almaty, Alatau; tel. (3272) 69-05-66; fax (3272) 69-61-16; f. 1991; attached to Kazakhstan Acad. of Sciences; Dir Dr M. I. BITENBAEV; publ. *Annual Report*.

Satpaev, K. I., Institute of Geological Sciences: 480100 Almaty, Ul. Kalinina 69A; tel. 61-56-08; attached to Kazakhstan Acad. of Sciences; Dir A. A. ABDULLIN.

PHILOSOPHY AND PSYCHOLOGY

Institute of Philosophy: 480021 Almaty, Ul. Kurmangazy 29; tel. 69-59-11; attached to Kazakhstan Acad. of Sciences; Dir A. N. NYSANBAEV.

RELIGION, SOCIOLOGY AND ANTHROPOLOGY

Institute of Uigur Studies: 480100 Almaty, Ul. Pushkina 111/113; tel. 61-53-71; attached to Kazakhstan Acad. of Sciences; Dir K. T. TALIPOV.

TECHNOLOGY

Institute of Metallurgy and Ore Enrichment: 480100 Almaty, Ul. Shevchenko 29/33; tel. 61-57-81; telex 251263; attached to Kazakhstan Acad. of Sciences; Dir S. M. KOZHAKHMETOV.

Institute of Mining: 480046 Almaty, Pr. Abaya 191; tel. 40-97-13; attached to Kazakhstan Acad. of Sciences; Dir E. I. ROGOV.

Research Mining and Metallurgical Institute of Non-ferrous Metals: 492014 Ust-Kamenogorsk, Promyshlennaya 1; tel. (3232) 49-14-60; fax (3232) 47-37-71; f. 1950; library of 160,000 vols; Dir N. N. USHAKOV.

Virgin Lands Research Technological Institute for Repair and Use of Agricultural Machinery: Akmolinskya obl., Alekseeva.

Libraries and Archives

Almaty

Al-Farabi Kazakh State University Central Library: 480100 Almaty, Sovetskaya ul. 28; tel. 67-64-51; 1,500,000 vols; Dir E. Dz. ABULKAIROVA.

Central Library of the Kazakh Academy of Sciences: 480021 Almaty, Ul. Shevchenko 28; tel. 62-83-41; f. 1932; 6,186,000 vols, 2,041 MSS; Dir K. K. ABUGALIEVA.

National Library of Kazakhstan: 480013 Almaty, Pr. Abaya 14; f. 1931; 5,123,000 vols; Dir R. A. BERDIGALIEVA.

Scientific and Technical Library of Kazakhstan: 480096 Almaty, S. Mukanov 223B; tel. and fax 68-26-79; e-mail root@rntb.iatp.kz; f. 1960; library of 22,600,000 vols (including patents); Dir K. URMURZINA.

Karaganda

Karaganda State University Library: 471161 Karaganda, Ul. Kirova 16; 400,000 vols; Dir S. M. ZHERZHISOVA.

Museums and Art Galleries

Almaty

Botanical Garden: 480070 Almaty, Ul. Timiryazeva 46; tel. 47-66-92; attached to Kazakhstan Acad. of Sciences; Dir I. R. RAKHIMBAEV.

Central State Museum of Kazakhstan: Almaty, Park imeni 28 Panfilovtsev; history and natural history of Kazakhstan; Dir R. K. KOSHAMBEKOVA.

Kasteyev Kazakh State Art Museum: 480090 Almaty, Ul. Satpayeva 30A; tel. (3272) 47-82-49; f. 1976; Kazakh art, folk art, Soviet and European art; library of 50,000 vols; Dir BAYTURSUN E. UMORBEKOV.

Universities

KAZAKH AL-FARABI STATE NATIONAL UNIVERSITY

480078 Almaty, Al-Farabi ave 71
Telephone: 47-25-17
Fax: 2-47-26-09
Founded 1934 (fmrly Kazakh S.M. Kirov State University), present name and status 1994
State control
Languages of instruction: Kazakh, Russian
Academic year: September to July (two semesters)

Rector: Prof. K. N. NARIBAEV
Pro-Rectors: Prof. E. B. ZHATKANBAEV, Prof. Z. A. MANSUROV, M. K. ORUNKHANOV, K. M. BAIMURZAEV, Z. N. MURZABEKOV
Librarian: E. DZ. ABULKAIROVA

Library: see Libraries
Number of teachers: 1,530
Number of students: 14,000

Publication: *Vestnik KazGNU* (1 a year).

DEANS

Faculty of History, Archaeology and Ethnography: Prof. K. BURKHANOV
Faculty of International Relations: Prof. G. S. JAMBATIROVA.
Faculty of Philology: ZH. D. DADEBAEV
Faculty of Philosophy and Politics: Prof. N. A. LOGINOVA.
Faculty of Journalism: Prof. N. OMASHEV
Faculty of Mechanics and Mathematics: Prof. N. T. DANAEV
Faculty of Physics: Prof. F. B. BAIMBETOV.
Faculty of Chemistry: M. K. NAURYZBAEV
Faculty of Geography and Geosciences: Prof. V. M. BOLDIREV
Faculty of Biology: Prof. N. M. MUKHITDINOV
Faculty of Eastern Studies: N. A. ALDABEKOVA
Institute of Economics and Law: Prof. E. B. ZHATKANBAYEV (Dir)
Preparatory Faculty: ZH. S. SADYKOV

ATTACHED INSTITUTES

Institute of Experimental and Theoretical Physics Research: Dir I. L. TAZHIBAEVA.

Institute of New Chemical Technologies and Materials Research: Dir Prof. K. A. ZHUBANOV.

Institute of Problems in Biology and Biotechnology: Dir S. T. TULEKHANOV.

Institute of Ecological Problems: Dir Prof. A. B. BIGALIEV.

Institute of Mathematics and Mechanics Research: Dir Prof. SH. S. SMAGULOV.

Centre for Research and Education in Al-Farabi and Spiritual Culture: Dir Prof. A. H. KASIMZHANOV.

Centre for Physics and Chemistry Method Analysis: Dir Prof. B. YA. KOLESNIKOV.

KARAGANDA STATE UNIVERSITY

470074 Karaganda, Universitetskaya ul. 28
Telephone: 74-49-50
Founded 1972
Number of students: 8,436
Faculties of philology, economics, law, history, mathematics, physics, chemistry, biology.

KAZAKH NATIONAL TECHNICAL UNIVERSITY

Almaty 480013, Satbayev 22
Telephone: (3272) 67-69-01
Fax: (3272) 67-60-25
Founded 1934 as Kazakh Polytechnic Institute; present name and status *c.* 1996
Rector: Prof. E. M. SHAIKHUTDINOV
Library of 1,200,000 vols
Number of teachers: 1,081
Publication: *Vestnik KazNTU* (4 a year).

Faculties of Geological Prospecting, Mining, Metallurgy, Machine-Building, Oil and Gas, Automation and Control Systems, Information Science and Computer Science, Management and Economics, Chemical Engineering and Polygraphy.

Other Higher Educational Institutes

Akmola Agricultural Institute: 473032 Akmola, Pr. Pobedy 116; tel. 5-89-16; fax 5-31-94; eight faculties: 600 teachers; 10,000 students; library of 656,000 vols; br. in Kokchetav; Rector YAKOB MAUL; publ. *Proceedings* (annually).

Akmola Medical Institute: 473013 Akmola, Pr. Mira 51A; tel. 5-10-69.

Aktyubinsk State Medical Institute: 463000 Aktyubinsk, Ul. Lenina 52; tel. 4-39-04; library of 62,000 vols.

Almaty Animal Husbandry and Veterinary Institute: 480013 Almaty, Pr. Abaya 28; tel. 63-68-94; f. 1929; depts: animal husbandry, veterinary; 304 teachers; 5,670 students; library of 357,000 vols; Rector M. A. ERMAKOV; publ. *Veterinariya* (monthly).

Almaty Institute of Railway Engineers: 480012 Almaty, Ul. Shevchenko 97; tel. 68-55-07; f. 1976; faculties: railway construction, mechanical, traffic management, automation, telemechanics, communication; library of 60,000 vols; Rector Prof. I. S. KARABASOV; brs in Aktyubinsk and Akmola.

Almaty Kurman-gazy State Conservatoire: 480091 Almaty, Ablaikhan pr. 90; tel. 62-76-40; courses: piano, orchestral and folk instruments, academic and folk singing, choral and symphonic conducting, musicology, composition, cultural management; library of 266,060 vols.

Almaty Medical Institute: 480012 Almaty, Ul. Komsomolskaya 88; tel. 67-78-85; departments: general practice, paediatrics, stomatology, pharmacy; library of 221,000 vols; br. in Chimkent.

Almaty Institute of Power Engineering and Telecommunication: 480013 Almaty, Ul. Baytursynova 126; tel. 67-57-40; fax 67-50-57; e-mail aipet@online.ru; f. 1975; faculties: thermal engineering, radio engineering, power engineering; 2,800 students; library of 301,000 vols; Rector G. Zh. Daukeyev; publ. *Collections of Scientific Works* (2 a year).

Almaty State Theatrical and Cinema Institute: 480091 Almaty, Ul. Bogenbai Batyr 136; tel. 63-66-52; fax 50-62-84; f. 1992; acting and directing apprenticeship; 10 teachers; library of 400 vols.

East Kazakhstan Technical University: 492010 Ust-Kamenogorsk, Ul. Lugovaya 19, Studencheskii gorodok; tel. (3232) 44-24-81; fax (3232) 44-69-20; f. 1958; colleges: construction, power, mining-metallurgy, forest engineering, architecture; 390 teachers; 6,000 students; library of 566,000 vols; Rector Yu. V. Batalov.

Gumilev, L. N., Eurasion University: 473021 Astana, Tsiolkovsky 6; tel. 24-32-93; fax 24-30-90; f. 1964; faculties: mechanical engineering, civil engineering, economics, sanitary engineering; 265 teachers; 3,300 students; library of 1,000,000 vols; Rector Amangeldy Hussainovich Hussainov.

Karaganda Co-operative Institute: 470017 Karaganda, Ul. Akademicheskaya 9; tel. 57-29-58; economics, accountancy, trade; br. in Almaty; library of 150,000 vols.

Karaganda Metallurgical Institute: 472300 Temirtau, Pr. Lenina 34; tel. 3-56-26; f. 1963; faculties: mechanical engineering, metallurgy, chemical engineering, vocational; 240 teachers; 3,000 students; Rector Alexander Dyluk.

Karaganda Polytechnic Institute: 470075 Karaganda, Bulvar Mira 56; tel. 54-77-87; f. 1953; faculties: mining, electrical engineering, transport and road machine building, construction; brs in Dzhezkazgan and Petropavlovsk; Rector Prof. A. Lazutkin.

Karaganda State Medical Institute: 470061 Karaganda, Ul. Gogolya 40; tel. 54-62-91; fax 58-24-86; f. 1950; 702 teachers; 5,080 students; library of 377,000 vols; Rector Prof. M. T. Alyakparov.

Kazakh Agricultural Institute: 480021 Almaty, Pr. Abaya 8; tel. 64-05-68; depts: agronomy, plant protection, mechanization, electrification, forestry, economics and management, accounting; library of 167,000 vols; Rector Kh. A. Arystanbekov.

Kazakh State Academy of Architecture and Construction: 480043 Almaty, Ul. Ryskulbekova 28; tel. 29-46-11; fax 20-59-79; f. 1979; undergraduate and postgraduate courses and scientific research; faculties: technology, architecture, construction, engineering systems and constructions, water supply, sewerage and the environment, management in business and construction; Rector Pavel Atrushkevich; publ. *Collection of Scientific works* (1 a year).

Kazakh State Academy of Management: 480035 Almaty, Ul. Dzhandosova 55; tel. 20-28-45; faculties: management, marketing, finance and credit, accounting and economic cybernetics, international economic relations, humanitarian educational centre, international business school, marketing institute, banking and finance management research institute, economic research centre, marketing research centre, labour market research centre; Rector N. K. Mamyrov.

Kazakh State University of World Languages: 480072 Almaty 72, Ul. Muratbaeva 200; tel. 67-23-63; fax 67-44-73; f. 1941; faculties: English, German, French; 500 teachers; 2,350 students; library of 630,000 vols; Rector Dr A. Akmetov; publs scientific papers.

Kazakhstan Institute of Management, Economics and Strategic Research: 480100 Almaty, Ul. Abaya 4; tel. (3272) 64-26-15; telex 251303; fax (3272) 64-37-20; f. 1992; depts: business administration, economics, public administration; professional training centres in management, banking and natural resources; Exec. Dir Dr John Petroff.

Kustanai Agricultural Institute: Kustanai, Pr. Sverdlova 28; tel. 25-12-23; fax 25-34-76; f. 1966; library of 341,000 vols; Dirs L. M. Ovchinikova, V. S. Prokuratova.

Pavlodar State University: 637003 Pavlodar, Ul. Lomova 64; tel. (3182) 45-11-10; e-mail root@rector.scoutnet.iatp.kz; f. 1960; faculties: construction engineering, engineering, electrotechnical engineering, heating engineering, business and management, power, machine-building and metallurgy, information management, natural science, historical philology, physics and mathematics, Kazakh philology and foreign languages; 490 teachers; 5,400 students; library of 1,068,000 vols; Rector A. D. Frezorger; publ. *Scientific Transactions of Pavlodar State University* (4 a year).

Rudnyi Industrial Institute: 459120 Rudnyi, Ul. 50 let Oktyabrya 38; tel. 3-52-53; faculties: mining, automation of production processes, construction, economics; Rector Prof. I. M. Akhmetov.

Semipalatinsk Institute of Animal Husbandry and Veterinary Science: 490018 Semipalatinsk, Ul. Shugaeva 159; tel. 3-20-24; f. 1951; 180 teachers; 3,000 students; library of 100,000 vols; Rector U. S. Abdilmanov.

Semipalatinsk State Medical Institute: 490050 Semipalatinsk, Sovetskaya ul. 103; tel. 2-23-68.

Semipalatinsk Technological Institute of the Meat and Dairy Industry: 490047 Semipalatinsk, Ul. Glinki 20a; tel. 45-07-80; fax 45-36-72; faculties: mechanical engineering, technology, engineering economics; Rector N. Apsalyamov.

Shimkent State Institute of Culture: 486700 Shimkent, Ul. Vatutina 2; tel. 3-33-04; departments: library science, music and singing.

South Kazakh Technical University: 486050 Shimkent, Tauke-han 5; tel. 53-50-48; f. 1943; faculties: mechanical, chemical technology, economics; library of 524,000 vols; Rector T. Sh. Kalmenov; publ. *Science and Education in South Kazakhstan*†.

West Kazakhstan Agricultural Institute: 417025 Uralsk, gorodok SKhI; tel. 2-19-30; f. 1963; depts: agronomy, animal husbandry, mechanization, economics and management, accounting; 150 teachers; 2,700 students; Rector V. K. I. Konnikov.

Zhambul Institute of Irrigation, Land Reclamation and Construction: 484022 Zhambul, Ul. Acad. Satpayeva 28; tel. 4-36-51; depts: irrigation and land reclamation, economics, mechanical engineering, construction engineering; library.

Zhambul Technological Institute of Food and Light Industries: 484030 Zhambul, Ul. Tole be 58; tel. 4-36-64; telex 283130; fax 4-52-25; f. 1963; faculties: mechanization and automation, chemical technology, technology, economics, book-keeping, food production; 302 teachers; library of 359,000 vols; Rector Prof. U. Madiev.

KENYA

Learned Societies

GENERAL

African Network of Scientific and Technological Institutions (ANSTI): POB 30592, Nairobi; tel. 622620; fax 215991; f. 1980 under the auspices of UNESCO and UNDP, aided by the Fed. Repub. of Germany and based at the Unesco Regional Office for Science and Technology (*q.v.*); aims to bring about collaboration between African engineering, scientific and technological institutions involved in postgraduate training, and to undertake research and development in areas of developmental significance in the region; mems: 85 institutions in 32 countries; Project Co-ordinator Prof. J. G. Massaquoi; publs *ANSTI News, African Journal of Science and Technology, Directory of ANSTI Institutions.*

Kenya National Academy of Sciences: POB 47288, Nairobi; f. 1977; advancement of learning and research; 200 mems; Chair. Prof. T. R. Odhiambo; Sec. Prof. R. M. Munavu; publs *Proceedings of Symposia, Newsletter, Post Magazine, Kenya Journal of Science and Technology* (2 a year).

National Council for Science and Technology: POB 30623, Nairobi; tel. 336173; f. 1977; attached to Ministry of Regional Development, Science and Technology; advisory services to the Government; 35 council mems; library of 3,000 vols, collection of research reports; Sec. Prof. P. Gacii; publs *NCST Newsletter, Annual Report.*

Unesco Nairobi Office: POB 30592, Nairobi; tel. 621234; telex 22275; fax 215991; f. 1965 to promote and co-ordinate Unesco projects and activities in science, technology, education, culture, communication and social and human sciences in 44 sub-Saharan African member states in East, Central Southern and West Africa; library of 18,000 vols; Dir Dr Paul B. Vitta; publ. *Bulletin* (2 a year, English and French).

AGRICULTURE, FISHERIES AND VETERINARY SCIENCE

Agricultural Society of Kenya: POB 30176, Nairobi; tel. 566655; f. 1901; encourages and assists agriculture in Kenya; holds 12 shows a year and farming competitions; sponsors Young Farmers' Clubs of Kenya; 12,000 mems; Chair. R. W. Walukano; Chief Exec. W. E. Adero; publ. *The Kenya Farmer* (monthly).

BIBLIOGRAPHY, LIBRARY SCIENCE AND MUSEOLOGY

Kenya Library Association: POB 46031, Nairobi; fax (2) 336885; f. 1956 to organize, unite and represent the professions concerned with information work in Kenya, to promote professional integrity and to govern the members of the association in all matters of professional practice, etc.; *c.* 200 mems; Chair. Jacinta Were; Sec. Alice Bulogosi; publs *Maktaba—Official Journal* (2 a year), *Kelias News* (every 2 months).

ECONOMICS, LAW AND POLITICS

Law Society of Kenya: POB 72219, Nairobi; tel. 225558; fax 223997; f. 1949; 1,385 mems; Sec. P. M. Mwangi; publs *The Advocate, Law Journal* (quarterly).

HISTORY, GEOGRAPHY AND ARCHAEOLOGY

Historical Association of Kenya: c/o Prof. B. A. Ogot, History Department, Kenyatta University, POB 43844, Nairobi; f. 1966; Chair. Prof. Bethwell A. Ogot; Sec. Dr Karim K. Janmohamed; publs *Kenya Historical Review* (2 a year), *Hadith Series* (annually).

MEDICINE

Association of Surgeons of East Africa: POB 30726, Nairobi; tel. 340930; f. 1950 for the advancement of the science and art of surgery and the promotion of friendship and exchange of ideas among surgeons in East Africa; constituent countries: Kenya, Malawi, Mozambique, Tanzania, Uganda, Zambia and Zimbabwe; 500 mems; mem. of Int. Fed. of Surgical Colleges; annual conference; Chair. M. Y. D. Kodwavwala; Sec. K. C. Rankin; publ. *Proceedings.*

Kenya Medical Association: POB 48502, Nairobi; tel. 724617; f. 1962; 1,500 mems; Chair. Prof. W. Lore; Sec. Dr M. K. Adalja; publs *East African Medical Journal, Medicus* (monthly).

NATURAL SCIENCES

Biological Sciences

East Africa Natural History Society: POB 44486, Nairobi; tel. (2) 749957; fax (2) 741049; e-mail eanhs@africaonline.co.ke; f. 1909; 1,000 mems; library of 10,000 vols; Chair. Dr L. Bennun; publs *EANHS Bulletin, Journal of East African Natural History.*

East African Wildlife Society: POB 20110, Nairobi Hilton, Nairobi; tel. 748170; fax 746868; f. 1961; non-profit org.; safeguards and promotes the conservation and sustainable management of wildlife resources and their natural habitats in East Africa; 16,000 mems; Exec. Dir Nehemiah K. Arap Rotich; publs *Swara* (every 2 months), *African Journal of Ecology* (quarterly).

Physical Sciences

Kenya Astronomical Society: POB 59224, Nairobi.

RELIGION, SOCIOLOGY AND ANTHROPOLOGY

Theosophical Society: 55a Third Parklands Ave, POB 45928, Nairobi; tel. 745174.

TECHNOLOGY

Institution of Engineers of Kenya: POB 41346, Nairobi; tel. 721022; f. 1945, present name 1973; 1,500 mems; Hon. Sec. A. V. Otieno; publ. *Kenya Engineer* (every 2 months).

Research Institutes

AGRICULTURE, FISHERIES AND VETERINARY SCIENCE

Coffee Research Foundation: CRF Coffee Research Station, POB 4, Ruiru; tel. (151) 54027; fax (151) 54133; f. 1949; research on coffee cultivation, agronomy and management, marketing and economics of production; Dir W. R. Opile; publs *Annual Report, Kenya Coffee Bulletin.*

Grassland Research Station: POB 144, Molo; f. 1952; sub-station of the National Agricultural Research Station, Kitale; Officer-in-Charge I. J. Partridge.

Interafrican Bureau for Animal Resources: Maendeleo House, Monrovia St, POB 30786, Nairobi; f. 1953; veterinary and livestock health and production covering all mem. states of the OAU; library of over 5,000 vols; Dir Dr W. N. Masiga; publ. *Bulletin of Animal Health and Production in Africa* (quarterly).

Kenya Agricultural Research Institute: POB 57811, Nairobi; agricultural and veterinary sciences research; Dir C. G. Ndiritu.

Attached centre:

> **National Veterinary Research Centre (MUGUGA):** POB 32, Kikuyu; preparation and issue of biological products and research into animal health and animal diseases; Dir D. P. Kariuki; publs *Record of Research, Annual Report.*

Ministry of Agriculture, Livestock and Marketing, Veterinary Department: PO Kabete, Nairobi; f. 1903; control, diagnosis, veterinary research; vaccine production, advisory service to farmers; library of 27,500 vols; Dir Dr R. S. Kimanzi; publ. *Annual Report.*

National Agricultural Research Laboratories: POB 14733, Nairobi; tel. and fax (2) 444144; f. 1908; soil science research, crop protection research; library of 4,000 vols; Dir Dr F. N. Muchena; publs *Annual Report, Soil Survey Report.*

National Horticultural Research Centre: POB 220, Thika; tel. (151) 21281; f. 1955; research into crop protection, seed production, citriculture, viticulture, floriculture, temperate and tropical fruits, post-harvest physiology, vegetables; breeds for multiple disease resistance to common bean diseases; Dir D. O. Michieka.

Plant Breeding Station: Ministry of Agriculture, PO Njoro; f. 1927; 20 professional staff; Officer-in-Charge Dr R. C. McGinnis; improvement of wheat, barley and oats.

Pyrethrum Bureau: POB 420, Nakuru; tel. (37) 211567; fax (37) 45274; f. 1948; research and information on pyrethrum as a natural insecticide; Dir R. M. Kuria; publ. *Pyrethrum Post* (2 a year).

Tea Research Foundation of Kenya: POB 820, Kericho; tel. (361) 20598; fax (361) 20575; f. 1951; studies on the production and manufacture of tea, with special emphasis on agronomic, botanical, environmental, physical and chemical aspects and pests and diseases management; biochemistry and engineering of black tea processing, extension and training services; library of 5,000 vols; Dir J. K. Rutto; publs *Tea Journal* (2 a year), annual reports.

HISTORY, GEOGRAPHY AND ARCHAEOLOGY

British Institute in Eastern Africa: POB 30710, Nairobi; tel. 43330; fax (2) 43365; e-mail britinst@arcc.or.ke; f. 1960; library of 5,000 vols, 100 periodicals; research into the history and archaeology of Eastern Africa, for which occasional grants and studentships are offered; 350 mems; Dir J. E. G. SUTTON; publs *Azania* (annually), *Memoirs*.

MEDICINE

Alupe Leprosy and Skin Diseases Research Centre (The John Lowe Memorial): POB 3, Busia; tel. and fax (3362) 2410; f. 1952; part of KEMRI; Dir Dr P. A. OREGE; publ. *Annual Report*.

Institute for Medical Research and Training: National Public Health Laboratory Services, POB 20750, Nairobi; f. 1964 for research and medical training; see also College of Health Professions, Medical School, under Colleges.

Kenya Medical Research Institute (KEMRI): POB 54840, Nairobi; tel. 722541; telex 25696; fax 720030; e-mail kemrilib@ken.healthnet.org; f. 1979; under the Min. of Research and Technical Training; research in biomedical sciences, co-operates with other instns in training programmes and research, co-operates with the Min. of Health, the Nat. Ccl for Science and Technology and the Medical Science Advisory Research Cttee; nine centres: Alupe Leprosy and Skin Diseases Research Centre, Biomedical Sciences Research Centre, Clinical Research Centre, Vector Biology and Control Research Centre, Virus Research Centre, Centre for Microbiology Research, Medical Research Centre, Respiratory Diseases Research Centre, Traditional Medicines and Drugs Research Centre; 1,000 staff; health science library of 3,000 vols, collection of scientific reprints, theses and dissertations; conference theatre; Dir Dr DAVY KOECH; publs *African Journal of Health Sciences* (quarterly), *Annual Report, KEMRI Abstracts, KEMRI News*.

National Public Health Laboratory Services (Medical Department): POB 20750, Nairobi; tel. (2) 725601; fax (2) 729504; all branches of medicine; library; Dir Dr JACK NYAMONGO.

Respiratory Diseases Research Unit: POB 47855, Nairobi, Kenya; tel. 724262; fax 720030; f. 1960; part of KEMRI; research on all aspects of respiratory diseases, with special reference to (*a*) diagnostic and treatment procedures relevant to developing country situations and to (*b*) the epidemiology of the disease; Dir Dr J. A. ODHIAMBO; publ. *Annual Report*.

NATURAL SCIENCES

Biological Sciences

Institute of Primate Research: National Museums of Kenya, POB 24481, Nairobi; tel. 882571; telex 22892; fax 882546; research in primate medicine, virology, reproductive biology, infectious diseases, and ecology and conservation; Dir Dr CHARANJIT BAMBRA; publ. *IPR Report* (annually).

TECHNOLOGY

Kenya Industrial Research and Development Institute: POB 30650, Nairobi; tel. 557762; fax 540166; e-mail kirdi@arcc.or.ke; f. 1948; provides advice for established local industrial concerns and gives assistance in the establishment of new industries on the utilization of local materials; Dir Dr-Ing. H. L. KAANE; publs *Annual Report, Newsletter*, brochures.

Mines and Geological Department: Kencom House, City Hall Way/Moi Ave, POB 30009, Nairobi; tel. 229261; f. 1932; geological survey and research; mineral resources development; administers mineral and explosives laws; 96 scientific staff; library of 32,000 vols, 10,000 periodicals; Commr C. Y. O. OWAYO; publs *Annual Report, Mineral Statistics Data*, reports, maps, bulletins, statistics, etc.

National Fibre Research Centre, Kibos: POB 1490, Kisumu; Dir J. H. BRETTELL.

Libraries and Archives

Nairobi

Desai Memorial Library: POB 1253, Nairobi; f. 1942; public library and reading room; 31,800 vols; books in Swahili, Gujarati, Hindi, Urdu, Gurumukhi and English; reference, newspaper and periodic sections; 1,151 mems; Pres. A. M. SADARUDDIN; Sec. HARSHAD JOSHI.

High Court of Kenya Library: Law Courts, POB 30041, Nairobi; tel. 221221; e-mail hck.lib@nbnet.co.ke; f. 1935; comprises High Court Library and Court of Appeal Library in Nairobi and 10 major br. libraries at Mombasa, Kisumu, Eldoret, Kakamega, Nakuru, Nyeri, Kisumu, Bungoma, Machakos and Kisii; 100,000 vols, 65 periodicals on practitioner's law, with special emphasis on Kenyan and English law; Librarian R. G. OTWAL.

Ismail Rahimtulla Trust Library: POB 40333, Nairobi; tel. 212660; f. 1953; 7,200 vols; Librarian P. GITAU.

Kenya Agricultural Research Institute Library: POB 57811, Nairobi; f. 1928; extends current scientific awareness service to all research and academic centres and official depts within Kenya; acts as national centre for AGINLET; 150,000 vols; Research Librarian (vacant); publs *East African Agricultural and Forestry Journal* (quarterly), *Record of Research* (annual report).

Kenya National Archives and Documentation Service: POB 49210, Moi Ave, Nairobi; tel. (2) 228959; fax (2) 228020; e-mail k.n.a.archives@formnet.com; archival services f. 1946, National Archives f. 1965; preservation and custody of public records; assists government offices in the maintenance of records; over 1 million items, incl. reports; archival materials accessible to national and international researchers; library of 50,000 vols and periodicals, incl. over 9,000 government monographs; over 600 annual reports from government ministries and depts; Kenya Gazette, Laws of Kenya and parliamentary debates; 20,000 general and Africana vols; over 700 theses and dissertations; over 5,000 legal deposit collections; over 1,600 periodicals and journals, incl. 30 current titles; the library prepares accession lists for all collections, and alphabetical lists for annual reports and periodicals; Dir MUSILA MUSEMBI; publs indexes and guides to public records.

Kenya National Library Services: POB 30573, Ngong Rd, Nairobi; tel. 725550; f. 1967; 600,000 vols, 120 periodicals; public library services through Nat. Lending Library in Nairobi, 19 brs and 8 mobile units; Nat. Reference and Bibliographic Dept f. 1980; special collections: East Africana and Kenyana; Chair. Archbishop STEPHEN ONDIEKI; Dir S. K. NG'ANG'A; publs *Kenya National Bibliography* (annually), *Kenya Periodical Directory* (every 2 years), annual report, quarterly accessions list.

McMillan Memorial Library: POB 40791, Banda St, Nairobi; tel. 221844; f. 1931; two branch libraries at Kaloleni and Eastlands; comprises Nairobi City Library Services; Africana collection; 275,000 vols, 11,000 serial publs; Chief Librarian A. O. ESILABA.

University of Nairobi Libraries: POB 30197, Nairobi; f. 1959; 400,000 vols, 3,500 periodicals; 11 brs; acts as legal national depository and UN deposit library; Librarian Mrs M. E. KIMANI.

Museums and Art Galleries

Nairobi

National Museums of Kenya: POB 40658, Nairobi; tel. 742131; telex 22892; fax 741424; e-mail nmk@africaonline.co.ke; f. 1911; all branches of natural sciences, pre-history, and geology; joint library with East Africa Natural History Society, 30,000 vols; Dir Dr MOHAMED ISAHAKIA; Librarian A. H. K. OWANO; publ. *Journal of East Africa Natural History*.

Comprise:

National Museum, Nairobi: POB 40658; tel. 742161; Curator JAMES MAIKWEKI.

Fort Jesus Museum: POB 82412, Mombasa; tel. 312839; f. 1960; inside 16th-century Portuguese fortress overlooking Mombasa harbour; finds from various coastal Islamic sites, from Fort Jesus, and from a 17th-century Portuguese wreck show the history of the Kenya coast; library of 1,000 vols and numerous offprints; Curator ALI ABUBAKAR.

Kisumu Museum: POB 1779, Kisumu: tel. 40804; Curator ALI SALIM BAKAABE.

Kitale Museum: POB 1219, Kitale; tel. 20670; f. 1926; history and science, emphasis on education; library of *c.* 5,000 vols; Curator IBRAHIM MOHAMUD.

Lamu Museum: POB 48, Lamu; tel. 3073; Curator JOSEPH CHERUYOIT.

Meru Museum: POB 597, Meru; tel. 20482 Curator DENIS OKWARO.

Universities

EGERTON UNIVERSITY

POB 536, Njoro

Telephone: Nakuru 61620

Fax: 61527

E-mail: eu-vc@net2000ke.com

Founded 1939; university status 1987

State control

Language of instruction: English

Academic year: August to December, January to May

Vice-Chancellor: Prof. J. C. KIPTOON

Deputy Vice-Chancellors: Prof. W. K. KIPNG'ENO (Administration and Finance), Prof. A. M. MUTEMA (Academic Affairs), Prof. R. W. MWANGI (Research and Extension)

Principal of Laikipia Campus: Prof. P. L. SHALO

Principal of Kisii College Campus: Prof. I. SINDIGA

Registrars: Prof. N. J. K. KATHURI (Academic), P. K. METTO (Administration and Finance)

Librarian: S. C. OTENYA

Library of 150,000 vols

Number of teachers: 800

Number of students: 8,000

Publications: *Egertonian* (annually), *University Catalogue* (annually), *'Kumekucha'* (quarterly), *Annual Report, Newsflash* (2 a month), *Students Magazine* (2 a month), *Agricultural Bulletin* (2 a year), *Egerton Journal* (2 a year).

DEANS

Agriculture: Dr J. K. TUITOEK

Arts and Social Sciences: Dr KIMANI WA NJOROGE

Education and Human Resources: Dr A. M. SINDABI

Science: Prof. E. M. WATHUTA

Engineering: Dr G. NGUNJIRI

HEADS OF DEPARTMENTS

Agricultural Economic and Business Management: Dr B. K. Njihia
Agricultural Education and Extension: Prof. Dr G. Mwangi
Agricultural Engineering: Dr S. Owido
Agriculture and Home Economics: C. Munyua
Agronomy: Dr E. M. Njoka
Animal Health: Dr A. Chingi
Animal Science: Dr L. Musalia
Biochemistry and Molecular Biology: Prof. M. Limo.
Botany: Prof. J. N. M. Macharia
Chemistry: Dr S. Gakwahja
Computer Science: Dr W. Korir
Curriculum and Instruction: Dr H. Sambili
Dairy and Food Science and Technology: W. Lokuruka
Economics: Dr W. S. K. Wasike
Educational Administration and Planning: Dr M. N. Barasa
Educational Materials Centre: S. N. Siteti wa Ngero
Educational Psychology and Counselling: Dr B. E. E. Omulema
Geography: Dr R. Hayangah
History: Dr Mosonik arap Korir
Horticulture: Dr G. O. Tunya
Languages: Prof. R. Rocha Chimerah
Literature: Prof. C. L. Wanjala
Mathematics: Dr K. C. Sogomo
Natural Resources: Dr D. K. Too
Philosophy and Religious Studies: Prof. W. K. Lang'at
Physics: Prof. M. L. Muia
Sociology: Dr M. T. Kuria
Zoology: Dr J. Mathooko

JOMO KENYATTA UNIVERSITY OF AGRICULTURE AND TECHNOLOGY

POB 62000, Nairobi

Telephone: (151) 52181
Fax: (151) 52164
E-mail: dvcaca@nbnt.co.ke;

Founded 1981; university status 1994
State control
Language of Instruction: English
Academic year: April to December

Chancellor: The President of the Republic of Kenya
Vice-Chancellor: Prof. R. W. Michieka
Deputy Vice-Chancellors: Prof. H. M. Thairu (Academic Affairs), Prof. R. W. Mutua (Research, Production and Extension), Prof. F. N. Onyango (Administration, Planning and Development)
Registrar: J. M. Mberia
Librarian: L. M. Wanyama

Library of 42,000 vols
Number of teachers: 296
Number of students: 2,400

Publications: *Journal of Agriculture Science and Technology* (2 a year), *Journal of Civil Engineering* (1 a year), *Horizon DAT* (architecture, 1 a year).

DEANS

Faculty of Agriculture: Dr P. M. Kutima
Faculty of Engineering: Prof. S. M. Maranga
Faculty of Science: Prof. F. Kaberia

CHAIRMEN OF DEPARTMENT

Agricultural Engineering: Dr C. Nindo
Architecture: P. M. Maringa
Biochemistry: Prof. M. Imbuga
Botany: A. E. Muigai
Chemistry: Dr J. Keriko
Civil Engineering: Dr J. K. Z. Mwatelah
Electrical Engineering: Dr D. K. Murage
Food Science: Dr L. Wongo
Horticulture: Dr S. G. Agong
Mathematics and Computer Science: Prof. S. Uppal
Mechanical Engineering: Dr P. N. Kioni
Physics: Dr P. Karanja
Zoology: Dr E. C. Mwachiro

DIRECTORS OF INSTITUTES AND BOARDS

Institute of Human Resource Development: E. Mukulu
Institute for Biotechnology Research: Prof. E. M. Kahangi
Board of Postgraduate Studies: Dr J. S. Chacha
Regional Centre for Enterprise Development: G. S. Namusonge
Institute of Energy and Environmental Technology: Dr P. N. Oithira
Institute of Continuing Education: Prof. S. M. Kang'ethe

KENYATTA UNIVERSITY

POB 43844, Nairobi

Telephone: Kahawa 810901

Founded 1972 as constituent college of University of Nairobi, present status 1985
Language of instruction: English

Vice-Chancellor: Prof. P. M. Githinji
Deputy Vice-Chancellor: Prof. R. W. Murungi
University Secretary: Prof. E. K. Murhim
Registrar: Prof. S. N. Bogonko
Librarian: J. M. Ng'ang'a

Library of 166,000 vols, 1,500 periodicals
Number of teachers: 682
Number of students: 8,657

Publications: *Annual Report, Calendar, Directory of Research, BERC Bulletin, Newsletter.*

DEANS

Faculty of Education: Prof. H. O. Ayot
Faculty of Arts: Prof. O. J. E. Shiroya
Faculty of Science: Prof. H. M. Thairu
Faculty of Commerce: Dr G. Mwabu
Faculty of Environmental Education: Dr Korir-Koech

MOI UNIVERSITY

POB 3900, Eldoret

Telephone: (321) 43001
Fax: (321) 43047

Founded 1984
State control
Language of instruction: English
Academic year: September to June

Vice-Chancellor: Prof. Justin Irina
Chief Administrative Officer: Dr J. K. Sang
Chief Academic Officer: Prof. K. ole Karei
Principal of Maseno University College: Prof. W. R. Ochieng'
Principal of Chepkoilel Campus: Prof. M. J. Kamar
Librarian: T. arap Tanui

Library of 200,000 vols, 50,000 periodicals
Number of teachers: 709
Number of students: 5,266

DEANS

Faculty of Forest Resources and Wildlife Management: Dr B. C. C. Wangila
Faculty of Science: Prof. S. Rajab
Faculty of Education: Prof. E. M. Standa
Faculty of Technology: Prof. P. C. Egau
School of Social, Cultural and Development Studies: Prof. J. J. Akonga
Faculty of Information Sciences: Dr C. Odini
School of Environmental Studies: Dr W. K. Yabann
Faculty of Health Sciences: Prof. H. N. K. Mengech
Faculty of Agriculture: Prof. E. O. Auma
Faculty of Law: Prof. F. X. Njenga
Institute of Human Resources Development: Dr M. C. Mukhebi
Faculty of Arts and Social Sciences: (Maseno University College): Prof. Oluoch-Obura
Faculty of Education (Maseno University College): Prof. F. Q. Gravenir
Faculty of Science (Maseno University College): Prof. E. N. Waindi
Institute of Research and Postgraduate Studies: Prof. B. A. Ogot
School of Family Consumer Science and Technology: Prof. A. J. Sigot

HEADS OF DEPARTMENTS

Faculty of Forest Resources and Wildlife Management:

- Forestry: Dr J. K. Kiyiapi
- Wildlife Management: Dr J. M. Odanga
- Wood Science and Technology: Prof. J. G. Mwangi
- Fisheries: Dr M. Muchiri
- Tourism: B. M. Musyoki

Faculty of Science:

- Chemistry: Dr L. K. Cheruiyot
- Zoology: Dr F. M. F. Wanjala
- Physics: Prof. K. M. Khanna
- Mathematics: Prof. H. W. Makumi
- Botany: S. Gudu

Faculty of Education:

- Education, Communications and Technology: Dr Patrick Kafu
- Educational Foundations: Dr I. N. Kimengi
- Educational Psychology: S. O. Kebaya
- Educational Administration, Planning and Curriculum Development: Prof. S. A. Omulando
- Science Education: Dr Lois Konana
- Technology Education: C. W. Wosyanju
- Teaching Practice Unit: Dr A. M. Simiyu

Faculty of Technology:

- Production Engineering: Dr T. M. Ogada
- Electrical and Communications Engineering: Dr A. J. M. Chol
- Civil and Structural Engineering: Dr S. M. Shitote
- Chemical and Process Engineering: Dr K. Ofosu-Asiedu
- Textile Engineering: P. M. Wambua
- Computer Services and Instrumentation Centre: R. Onyancha

Faculty of Social, Cultural and Development Studies:

- Anthropology: Prof. J. Akong'a
- Economics: J. Obilo
- Government and Public Administration: L. L. Lole
- History: Dr Odhiambo-Ndege
- Kiswahili and Other African Languages: Dr N. Shitemi
- Linguistics and Foreign Languages: Dr H. Wario
- Literature: Prof. P. S. Amuka
- Philosophy: Fr Dr C. Munga
- Religion: Dr A. Chepkwony
- Sociology: Dr S. Chessa
- Technology and Management Studies: Dr A. Madut

Faculty of Information Sciences:

- Archives and Records Management: Dr J. Wamukoya
- Library and Information Studies: M. K. Majanja
- Information and Media Technology: G. Wanyembi
- Publishing and Book Trade: F. Mureithi
- Desktop Publishing Unit: T. Ouko

School of Environmental Studies:

- Environmental Economics and Human Ecology: Prof. M. P. Tole
- Environmental Planning and Management: Dr E. Ecakuwun
- Environmental Monitoring and Cartography: Dr E. Ucakuwun
- Environmental Law: Dr W. K. Yuban

Physical Sciences: Prof. T. C. SHARMA
Environmental Health: Prof. T. D. DAVIES
Biological Sciences: Prof. S. MANOHAR

Faculty of Health Sciences:
Microbiology and Parasitology: Dr K. K. KAMAR
Forensic Medicine and Toxicology: W. OCHIENG
Medicine: Dr P. AYUO
Medical Education: VINCENT NAWEYA
Health Management and Health Economics: Dr W. ODERO
Reproductive Health: Dr E. O. WERE
Dental Health: Dr C. KIBOSIA
Surgical Sciences and Traumatology: Prof. B. O. KHWA-OTSYULU
Aesthesiology and Critical Health: Dr J. O. WAMBANI
Pharmacology and Therapeutics: Dr A. MARITIM
Radiology and Imageing: G. D. E. ONDITI
Mental Health: Dr O. F. OMOLO
Human Anatomy: Dr M. NDIEMA
Child Health, Paediatrics and Adolescence: Dr F. ESAMAI
Medical Biochemistry: Dr J. WAKHISI
Medical Physiology: Prof. J. NSHAHO
Histopathology and Cytology: Prof. VLADIMIR KOZLOV
Immunology: Prof. A. K. CHEMATAI
Epidemiology and Preventive Medicine: Prof. P. R. KENYA
Behavioural Sciences: Dr D. NGARE
Nursing Sciences and Emergency Medicine: P. MANG'ERA
Haematology and Blood Transfusion: Dr N. BUZIBA
Environmental Health: G. RUKUNGA

Faculty of Agriculture:
Soil Science: Prof. C. O. OTHIENO
Crop Production and Seed Technology: Dr P. W. MATHENGE
Agricultural Marketing and Cooperatives: Prof. M. O. ODHIAMBO
Rural Engineering: J. K. KORIR

Institute for Human Resources Development:
Communication Studies: L. CHEMAI
Quantitative Skills: E. L. W. SIMIYU
Development Studies: E. G. CHAHENZA

UNIVERSITY OF NAIROBI

POB 30197, Nairobi
Telephone: (2) 334244
Fax: (2) 336885

Founded in 1956 as Royal Technical College of East Africa; present name 1970
State control
Language of instruction: English
Academic year: October to July

Chancellor: THE PRESIDENT OF THE REPUBLIC
Vice-Chancellor: Prof. F. J. GICHAGA
Deputy Vice-Chancellors:
Administration and Finance: Prof. R. M. MUNAVU
Academic: Prof. F. A. KARANI
Registrars: J. G. WACIIRA (Administration), M. M. GACHUHI (Academic) (acting), F. WAWERU (Planning)
Librarian: S. MATHANGANI (acting)

Number of teachers: 1,347
Number of students: 13,669

Publications: *University of Nairobi Varsity Focus, Annual Report, Calendar.*

PRINCIPALS

College of Agriculture and Veterinary Medicine: Prof. D. M. MUKUNYA
College of Health Sciences: Prof. S. K. SINEI
College of Architecture and Engineering: Prof. C. M. KIAMBA
College of Biological and Physical Sciences: Prof. A. G. TUMBO-OERI
College of Humanities and Social Sciences: Prof. F. N. KIBERA
College of Education and External Studies: Prof. L. OMONDI

DEANS

Agriculture: Prof. J. K. IMUNGI
Architecture, Design and Development: Prof. P. M. SYAGGA
Arts: Prof. E. H. O. AYIEMBA (acting)
Commerce: J. K. KENDUIWO
Engineering: Prof. F. W. O. ADUOL
Law: E. M. NDIRITU
Medicine: Prof. H. PAMBA
Science: Prof. W. OGANA
Veterinary Medicine: Prof. M. M. KAGIKO
External Studies: D. MACHARIA
Education: Dr P. O. DIGOLO
Social Sciences: Prof. C. M. ONIANG'O
Dental Sciences: Prof. W. R. LESAN
Pharmacy: Prof. A. N. GUANTAI

PROFESSORS

Faculty of Agriculture:
KARUE, C. N., Range Management
KEYA, S. O., Soil Science
MICHIEKA, R. W., Crop Science
MUKUNYA, D. M., Crop Science
WAITHAKA, K., Crop Science

Faculty of Veterinary Sciences:
GATHUMA, J. M., Public Health, Pharmacology and Toxicology
KIPTOON, J. C., Clinical Studies
MAINA, J. N., Veterinary Anatomy
MAITHO, T. E., Public Health, Pharmacology and Toxicology
MITEMA, S. E. O., Public Health, Pharmacology and Toxicology
MUGERA, G. M., Veterinary Pathology
MUTIGA, E. R., Clinical Studies
NYAGA, P. N., Veterinary Pathology
ODUOR-OKELLO, D., Veterinary Anatomy
WANDERA, J. G., Veterinary Pathology

Faculty of Engineering:
GICHAGA, F. J., Civil Engineering
LUTI, F. M., Mechanical Engineering
OTIENO, A. V., Electrical and Electronics Engineering

Faculty of Science:
GENGA, R., Physics
KHAMALA, C. P. M., Zoology
KOKWARO, J. O., Botany
MUNAVU, R. M., Chemistry
MWANGI, R. W., Zoology
NYAMBOK, I. O., Geology
OGALLO, L. T., Meteorology
OGANA, B. W., Mathematics
ONYANGO, F. N., Physics
OTIENO-MALO, J. B., Physics
PATEL, P. J., Physics
WANDIGA, S. O., Chemistry

Faculty of Medicine:
KIMANI, J. K., Human Anatomy
KUNGU, A., Human Pathology
KYAMBI, J. M., Surgery
MATI, J. K. G., Obstetrics and Gynaecology
MATTA, W. M., Human Anatomy
MEME, J. S., Paediatrics
MUNGAI, J. M., Human Anatomy
OKELLO, G. B. A., Medicine
OTIENO, L. S., Medicine
PAMBA, H. O., Medical Microbiology
WAMOLA, I. A., Medical Microbiology

Faculty of Dental Sciences:
OPINYA, G. N., Paediatric Dentistry, Orthodontics

Faculty of Pharmacy:
MAITAI, C. K., Pharmacology and Pharmacognosy

Faculty of Arts:
ABDULAZIZ, M. H., Linguistics and African Languages
ACHOLA AYAYO, A. B. C., Population Studies
MUGAMBI, J. N. K., Religious Studies
MUREITHI, L. P., Economics
MURIUKI, G., History
NYASANI, J., Philosophy
ODINGO, R. S., Geography
OJANY, F. F., Geography
OMONDI, L. N., Linguistics and African Languages
OYUGI, W. O., Government
SALIM, A. I., History

Faculty of Law:
MUTUNGI, O. K., Commercial Law
OJWANG, J. B., Private Law
OKOTH-OGENDO, H. W. O., Public Law

Faculty of Education:
KARANI, F. A., Educational Communication and Technology

Faculty of Social Sciences:
ONIANGO, C. M. P., Philosophy and Religious Studies

Institutes:
OCHOLLA-AYAYO, A. B. C., Population Studies and Research Institute
ODAK, O., Institute of African Studies
OUCHO, J. O., Population Studies and Research Institute
WANDIBBA, S. B. A., Institute of African Studies

ATTACHED INSTITUTES

Institute for Development Studies: Dir P. O. ALILA.

Institute of African Studies: Dir S. WANDIBBA.

School of Journalism: Dir J. MBINDYO.

Population Studies and Research Institute: Dir J. O. OUCHO.

Institute of Diplomacy and International Studies: Dir J. O. OLEWE-NYUNYA.

Institute of Computer Science: Dir T. M. WAEMA.

Housing and Building Research Institute: Dir J. O. ONDIEGE.

Institute of Nuclear Science: Dir A. M. KINYUA.

Colleges

Kenya Conservatoire of Music: POB 41343, Nairobi; tel. 222933; f. 1944; library of instrumental and vocal scores; Dir GILLIAN SPRAGG; publ. *Newsletter* (irregular).

Kenya Institute of Administration: POB 23030, PO Lower Kabete; tel. 582311; f. 1961; residential training for the Kenya Public Service in public administration, project development and management, population management, senior management seminars, research department, computer courses, effective management communication, management information systems, policy analysis, management of public enterprises, French courses; library of 40,000 vols, 200 current periodicals and a fully equipped audio-visual aids centre and language laboratory; 40 teachers, 280 students; Principal S. M. KARIGITHE; publs *Journal*, *Newsletter, K.I.A. Occasional Papers*.

Kenya Medical Training College: POB 30195, Nairobi; tel. 725711; f. 1924; library of 17,000 vols; 76 periodicals; 230 tutors, 2,000 students; Principal W. K. A. BOIT.

Kenya Polytechnic: POB 52428 Nairobi; f. 1961 with UNDP aid; depts of mechanical, electrical and electronic engineering, science, building, business studies, printing, institutional management, library and archive studies, general studies, mathematics, statistics, computing, media services; 271 teachers; 4,000 students; library of 40,000 vols, 150 periodicals; Principal P. O. OKAKA; Librarian S. K. NG'ANG'A.

Kenya School of Law: POB 30369, Nairobi; f. 1963; 300 students (postgraduate); library of 4,730 vols; Principal L. NJAGI; Librarian P. OKOTH.

Kiambu Institute of Science and Technology: POB 414, Kiambu; tel. (154) 22236; fax (154) 22319; f. 1973; library of 10,000 vols; depts of building, business education, electrical engineering, electronics, computer studies, bakery technology; 61 teachers; 600 students; Principal WILSON WANGOMBE MUCHEMI.

Kimathi Institute of Technology: POB 657, Nyeri; tel. 4005; f. 1974; library of 5,000 vols; 50 teachers; 401 students; Principal W. N. GICHUKI.

Mombasa Polytechnic: POB 90420, Mombasa; tel. 492222; f. 1948; full-time, sandwich, block-release and day-release courses; library of 20,000 vols; 170 teachers; 2,088 (1,912 full-time) students; Principal E. L. KISAME; Registrar D. M. MJOMBAH; Librarian R. KASINA.

HEADS OF DEPARTMENT

Business Studies: M. T. LEWA
Small Business Centre: J. M. WAMBUGU
Mechanical Engineering: E. C. OLILO
Electrical and Electronic Engineering: J. KIMANI
Building and Civil Engineering: N. K. NDUNGU
Applied Sciences: P. OCHOLA
Medical Engineering: C. KONOSI
Computing and Information Technology: B. A. OMOTO

Rift Valley Institute of Science and Technology: POB 7182, Nakuru; tel. (37) 211974; fax (37) 45656; f. 1972; library of 9,000 vols; 125 teachers; 1,200 students; Principal FRANCIS Z. K. MENJO.

Strathmore College: POB 59857, Nairobi; fax (2) 607498; e-mail strath@form-net.com; f. 1960; full-time, evening, distance learning and revision courses in accountancy, full-time and evening courses in data processing management, full-time courses in executive secretarialship (600 full-time, 1,100 evening students); library of 10,000 vols; Principal C. SOTZ.

Western College of Arts and Applied Sciences: POB 190, Kakamega; tel. 20724; f. 1977; library of 3,050 vols; 46 teachers, 250 students; Principal ALFRED F. O. MACHUKI; Librarian ALOYCE OMOLLO.

KIRIBATI

Libraries and Archives

Bairiki

National Library and Archives: POB 6, Bairiki, Tarawa; tel. 21337; f. 1979 (fmrly Gilbert Islands National Archives); lending section of 30,000 vols; reference library of 2,000 vols; 18,000 vols in small library units throughout Kiribati; National Collection (housed in Archives) of 3,500 published items; archives records of 70,000 items; special collections include 600 rolls of microfilm and 4,000 microfiches; small philatelic, photograph, and sound recording collections; Librarian/Archivist KUNEI ETEKIERA.

Museums and Art Galleries

Bairiki

National Museum: c/o Cultural Affairs Officer, POB 75, Bairiki, Tarawa; in process of formation; items stored in National Archives; Cultural Affairs Officer BWERE ERITAIA.

College

University of the South Pacific, Kiribati Extension Centre: POB 59, Bairiki, Tarawa; f. 1973; an external campus of the University of the South Pacific; part-time undergraduate and diploma courses; library of 5,000 vols; 5 staff; *c.* 300 students; Dir BETA TEWAREKA.

Atoll Research Programme: POB 206, Bikenibeu, Tarawa; research in all aspects of atoll life, including environmental, ecological, sociological and political fields; Programme Man. TEMAKEI TEBANO; publ. *Atoll Quarterly*.

DEMOCRATIC PEOPLE'S REPUBLIC OF KOREA

Learned Societies

GENERAL

Academy of Sciences: Ryonmot-dong, Jangsan St, Sosong District, Pyongyang; tel. 51956; f. 1952; brs of Biology (Chair. KIM SONG GUN), Construction and Building Materials (Chair. PYONG UNG HUI), Electronics and Automation (Chair. LI SON BONG), Light Industry (Chair. LI JU UNG), and brs in Pyongsong (Chair. HAN BYONG HUI) and Hamhung (Chair. (vacant)); attached research institutes: see Research Institutes; libraries: see Libraries and Archives; Pres. KIM KIL YON; publs *Bulletin* (6 a year), journals for Physics, Mathematics, Biology, Mechanical Engineering, Metals, Analysis (all quarterly) and for Chemistry and Chemical Engineering, Mining, Electronic and Automatic Engineering, Geology and Geography (all 6 a year).

Academy of Social Sciences: Central District, Pyongyang; f. 1952; attached research institutes: see Research Institutes; library: see Libraries and Archives; Pres. KIM SOK HYONG.

AGRICULTURE, FISHERIES AND VETERINARY SCIENCE

Academy of Agricultural Science: Ryongsong District, Pyongyang; f. 1948; attached research institutes: see Research Institutes; Pres. LI YONG GYUN.

Academy of Fisheries: Namgang-dong, Sung Ho District, Pyongyang; f. 1969; 6 attached research institutes; Chair SO GYONG HO.

Academy of Forestry: Samsin-dong, Taesong District, Pyongyang; f. 1948; 5 attached research institutes; Pres. IM ROK JAE.

MEDICINE

Academy of Medical Sciences: Saemauldong, Pyongchon District, POB 305, Pyongyang; tel. 46924; attached research institutes: see Research Institutes; Pres. (vacant).

TECHNOLOGY

Academy of Light Industry Science: Kangan 1-dong, Songyo District, Pyongyang; f. 1954; 7 attached research institutes; Chair. LI JU UNG.

Academy of Railway Sciences: Namgyodong, Hyongjaesan District, Pyongyang; 5 attached research institutes; Chair. AN BYONG HAK.

Research Institutes

AGRICULTURE, FISHERIES AND VETERINARY SCIENCE

Agricultural Chemical Research Institute: Ryongsong District, Pyongyang; attached to DPRK Acad. of Agricultural Science; Dir PAK JAE KUN.

Agricultural Irrigation Research Institute: Onchon County, South Pyongan Province; attached to DPRK Acad. of Agricultural Science; Dir HWANG CHANG HONG.

Agricultural Mechanization Research Institute: Sadong District, Pyongyang; attached to DPRK Acad. of Agricultural Science; Dir KANG SONG RYONG.

Crop Cultivation Research Institute: Ryongsong District, Pyongyang; attached to DPRK Acad. of Agricultural Science; Dir RYEM DOK SU.

Crop Science Research Institute: Sunchon City, South Pyongan Province; attached to DPRK Acad. of Agricultural Science; Dir PAK BYONG MUK.

Fruit Cultivation Research Institute: Sukchon County; South Pyongan Province; attached to DPRK Acad. of Agricultural Science; Dir JANG HY KUNG.

Poultry Science Research Institute: Hyongjaesan District, Pyongyang; attached to DPRK Acad. of Agricultural Science; Dir CHOI MAN SANG.

Reed Research Institute: Haeju City, South Hwanghae Province; attached to DPRK Acad. of Agricultural Science; Dir KIM IN SU.

Rice Research Institute: Ryongsong District, Pyongyang; attached to DPRK Acad. of Agricultural Science; Dir KIM SANG RYEN.

Sericulture Research Institute: Dongrim County, North Pyongan Province; attached to DPRK Acad. of Agricultural Science; Dir KIM SUN JONG.

Soil Science Research Institute: Ryongsong District, Pyongyang; attached to DPRK Acad. of Agricultural Science; Dir LI KUN HAENG.

Vegetable Science Research Institute: Sadong District, Pyongyang; attached to DPRK Acad. of Agricultural Science; Dir KIM HAK SON.

Veterinary Science Research Institute: Ryongsong District, Pyongyang; attached to DPRK Acad. of Agricultural Science; Dir PAK WON KUN.

Zoology Research Institute: Sariwon City, North Hwanghae Province; attached to DPRK Acad. of Agricultural Science; Dir KIM KYANG JUNG.

ARCHITECTURE AND TOWN PLANNING

Institute of Architecture and Building Engineering: C/o Academy of Sciences, Namgang-dong, Sung Ho District, Pyongyang; attached to DPRK Acad. of Science; Dir SIN DONG CHOL.

ECONOMICS, LAW AND POLITICS

Institute of International Affairs: C/o Academy of Social Sciences, Central District, Pyongyang; attached to DPRK Acad. of Social Sciences; Dir KIM HYONG U.

Institute of Law: C/o Academy of Social Sciences, Central District, Pyongyang; attached to DPRK Acad. of Social Sciences; Dir SIM HYONG IL.

Institute of Trade and Economics: C/o Academy of Social Sciences, Central District, Pyongyang; attached to DPRK Acad. of Social Sciences; Dir (vacant).

HISTORY, GEOGRAPHY AND ARCHAEOLOGY

Institute of Archaeology: C/o Academy of Social Sciences, Central District, Pyongyang; attached to DPRK Acad. of Social Sciences; Dir KIM MYONG NAM.

Institute of Geography: Ryonmot-dong, Jangsan St, Sosong District, Pyongyang; attached to DPRK Acad. of Sciences; Dir KIM JONG RAK.

Institute of History: C/o Academy of Social Sciences, Central District, Pyongyang; attached to DPRK Acad. of Social Sciences; Dir CHON YONG RYUL.

LANGUAGE AND LITERATURE

Institute of Ethnic Classics: C/o Academy of Social Sciences, Central District, Pyongyang; attached to DPRK Acad. of Social Sciences; Dir KIM SUNG PHIL.

Institute of Juche Literature: C/o Academy of Social Sciences, Central District, Pyongyang; attached to DPRK Acad. of Social Sciences; Dir KIM HA MYONG.

Institute of Linguistics: C/o Academy of Social Sciences, Central District, Pyongyang; attached to DPRK Acad. of Social Sciences; Dir JONG SUN GI.

MEDICINE

Industrial Medicine Institute: Sapo-dong, Sapo District, Hamhung City; tel. 2810; attached to DPRK Acad. of Medical Sciences; Dir JO UN HO.

Research Institute for the Cultivation of Medicinal Herbs: Wonju-dong, Sariwon City, North Hwanghae Province; attached to DPRK Acad. of Medical Sciences; Dir KIM KWANG SOP.

Research Institute of Antibiotics: Ryonpodong, Sunchon City, South Pyongan Province; attached to DPRK Acad. of Medical Sciences; Dir CHOE SUN JONG.

Research Institute of Biomedicine: Dongsan-dong, Rangnang District, Pyongyang; tel. 23545; attached to DPRK Acad. of Medical Sciences; Dir PAK YUI SUN.

Research Institute of Child Nutrition: Dangsan-dong, Mangyongdae District, Pyongyang, tel. 73430; attached to DPRK Acad. of Medical Sciences; Dir KIM YONG KWANG.

Research Institute of Endocrinology: Mirim-dong, Sadong District, Pyongyang; tel. 623828; attached to DPRK Acad. of Medical Sciences; Dir JANG HON CHOL.

Research Institute of Experimental Therapy: C/o Academy of Medical Sciences, Chonsong-dong, Haesang District, Hamhung City, South Hamgyong Province; attached to DPRK Acad. of Medical Sciences; Dir NAM ON GIL.

Research Institute of Hygiene: Dangsandong, Mangyongdse District, Pyongyang; tel. 44925; attached to DPRK Acad. of Medical Sciences; Dir JE HYONG DO.

Research Institute of Microbiology: Pyongsong City; South Pyongan Province; attached to DPRK Acad. of Medical Sciences; Dir KIM CHANG JIN.

Research Institute of Natural Drugs: Somun-dong, Donghumsan District, Hamhung City, South Hamgyong Province; tel. 53905; attached to DPRK Acad. of Medical Sciences; Dir LI HWAI SU.

Research Institute of Oncology: Saemaul-dong, Pyongchon District, Pyongyang; tel. 42208; attached to DPRK Acad. of Medical Sciences; Dir KIM CHUN WON.

Research Institute of Pharmacology: Daehung-dong, Songyo District, Pyongyang; tel. 623868; attached to DPRK Acad. of Medical Sciences; Dir RYU GYONG HUI.

Research Institute of Psychoneurology: Uiju County, North Pyongan Province; attached to DPRK Acad. of Medical Sciences; Dir LI GYUN.

Research Institute of Radiological Medicine: Saemaul-dong, Pyongchon District, Pyongyang; tel. 45347; attached to DPRK Acad. of Medical Sciences; Dir O SOK ROK.

Research Institute of Respiratory Ducts and Tuberculosis: C/o Academy of Medical Sciences, Chongsong-dong, Haesang District, Hamhung City, South Hamgyong Province; attached to DPRK Acad. of Medical Sciences; Dir LI CHU WAN.

Research Institute of Surgery: C/o Academy of Medical Sciences, Chongsong-dong, Haesang District, Hamhung City, South Hamgyong Province; attached to DPRK Acad. of Medical Sciences; Dir HAN BYONG GAP.

Research Institute of Synthetic Pharmacy: Sapo-dong, Sapo District, Hamhung City, South Hamgyong Province; attached to DPRK Acad. of Medical Sciences; Dir LI GI SOP.

NATURAL SCIENCES

General

Central Institute of Experimental Analysis: C/o Academy of Sciences, Doksan-dong, Pyongsong City, South Pyongan Province; attached to DPRK Acad. of Sciences; Dir KIM GUN ON.

Institute of Environmental Protection: Ryusong-dong, Central District, Pyongyang; attached to DPRK Acad. of Sciences; Dir KIM YONG CHAN.

Biological Sciences

Institute of Botany: Kosan-dong, Daesong District, Pyongyang; attached to DPRK Acad. of Sciences; Dir GUAK JONG SONG.

Institute of Genetics: C/o Academy of Sciences, Ryonmot-dong, Jangsan St, Sosong District, Pyongyang; attached to DPRK Acad. of Sciences; Dir BAEK MUN CHAN.

Institute of Molecular Biology: C/o Academy of Sciences, Ryonmot-dong, Jangsan St, Sosong District, Pyongyang; attached to DPRK Acad. of Sciences; Dir KO GWANG UNG.

Institute of Plant Physiology: C/o Academy of Sciences, Ryonmot-dong, Jangsan St, Sosong District, Pyongyang; attached to DPRK Acad. of Sciences; Dir KIM SONG OK.

Institute of Zoology: Daesong-dong, Daesong District, Pyongyang; attached to DPRK Acad. of Sciences; Dir BAEK JONG HWAN.

Mathematical Sciences

Institute of Mathematics: C/o Academy of Sciences, Doksan-dong, Pyongsong City, South Pyongan Province; attached to DPRK Acad. of Sciences; Dir HO GON.

Physical Sciences

Institute of Analytical Chemistry: C/o Academy of Sciences, Chongsong-dong, Hoesang District, Hamhung City, South Hamgyong Province; attached to DPRK Acad. of Sciences; Dir RIM CHUN RYOP.

Institute of Ferrous Metals: Sae Gori-dong, Chollima District, Nampo City; attached to DPRK Acad. of Sciences; Dir LI BANG GUN.

Institute of Geology: C/o Academy of Sciences, Doksan-dong, Pyongsong City, South Pyongan Province; attached to DPRK Acad. of Sciences; Dir KIM ZONG HUI.

Institute of Inorganic Chemistry: C/o Academy of Sciences, Chongsong-dong, Hoesang District, Hamhung City, South Hamgyong Province; attached to DPRK Acad. of Sciences; Dir CHU SUNG.

Institute of Macromolecular Chemistry: C/o Academy of Sciences, Chongsong-dong, Hoesang District, Hamhung City, South Hamgyong Province; attached to DPRK Acad. of Sciences; Dir LI JANG HYOK.

Institute of Non-Ferrous Metals: Jungdaedu-dong, Hangku District, Nampo City; attached to DPRK Acad. of Sciences; Dir KIM MYONG RIN.

Institute of Physical Chemistry: C/o Academy of Sciences, Chongsong-dong, Hoesang District, Hamhung City, South Hamgyong Province; attached to DPRK Acad. of Sciences; Dir KIM JUNG BAE.

Institute of Physics: C/o Academy of Sciences, Doksan-dong, Pyongsong City, South Pyongan Province; attached to DPRK Acad. of Sciences; Dir RYO IN KWANG.

Institute of Pure Metals: Kumbit-dong, Ryongsong District, Hamhung City, South Hamgyong Province; attached to DPRK Acad. of Sciences; Dir LI SANG BOM.

Pyongyang Astronomical Observatory: Daesong-dong, Daesong District, Pyongyang; attached to DPRK Acad. of Sciences; Dir KIM YONG HYOK.

Research Centre for Atomic Energy: Sosong District, Pyongyang; attached to State Cttee for Atomic Energy; Pres. PAK GWAN O.

PHILOSOPHY AND PSYCHOLOGY

Institute of Philosophy: C/o Academy of Social Sciences, Central District, Pyongyang; attached to DPRK Acad. of Social Sciences; Dir KIM CHANG WON.

TECHNOLOGY

Institute of Chemical Engineering: C/o Academy of Sciences, Chongsong-dong, Hoesang District, Hamhung City, South Hamgyong Province; attached to DPRK Acad. of Sciences; Dir LI JAE OP.

Institute of Constructional Mechanization: C/o Academy of Sciences, Namgang-dong, Sung Ho District, Pyongyang; attached to DPRK Acad. of Sciences; Dir PAK RYANG SOP.

Institute of Electricity: C/o Academy of Sciences, Doksan-dong, Pyongsong City, South Pyongan Province; attached to DPRK Acad. of Sciences; Dir CHOE WON GYONG.

Institute of Fuel: Dongsan-dong, Songrim City, North Hwanghe Province; attached to DPRK Acad. of Sciences; Dir KO YONG JIN.

Institute of Hydraulic Engineering: C/o Academy of Sciences, Namgang-dong, Sung Ho District, Pyongyang; attached to DPRK Acad. of Sciences; Dir KIM RYONG GYUN.

Institute of Industrial Biology: C/o Academy of Sciences, Doksan-dong, Pyongsong City, South Pyongan Province; attached to DPRK Acad. of Sciences; Dir LI CHUN HO.

Institute of Mechanical Engineering: C/o Academy of Sciences, Doksan-dong, Pyongsong City, South Pyongan Province; attached to DPRK Acad. of Sciences; Dir KIM UNG SAM.

Institute of Ore Dressing Engineering: C/o Academy of Sciences, Doksan-dong, Pyongsong City, South Pyongan Province; attached to DPRK Acad. of Sciences; Dir LI WON SOK.

Institute of Organic Building Materials: C/o Academy of Sciences, Namgang-dong, Sung Ho District, Pyongsong; attached to DPRK Acad. of Sciences; Dir PAK CHANG SUN.

Institute of Paper Engineering: Songdori, Anju City, South Pyongan Province; attached to DPRK Acad. of Sciences; Dir RYU SAM JIP.

Institute of Silicate Engineering: Sijong-gu, Taedong County, South Pyongan Province; attached to DPRK Acad. of Sciences; Dir KIM UNG SANG.

Institute of Thermal Engineering: C/o Academy of Sciences, Doksan-dong, Pyongsong City, South Pyongan Province; attached to DPRK Acad. of Sciences; Dir HAN DONG SIK.

Institute of Tideland Construction: C/o Academy of Sciences, Namgang-dong, Sung Ho District, Pyongyang; attached to DPRK Acad. of Sciences; Dir CHO SOK.

Institute of Welding: Ponghwa-dong, Chollima District, Nampo City; attached to DPRK Acad. of Sciences; Dir CHAE HON MUK.

Research Centre of Electronics and Automation: C/o Academy of Sciences, Doksan-dong, Pyongsong City, South Pyongan Province; attached to DPRK Acad. of Sciences; incorporates institutes of Electronics, of Computer Science, of Automation, of Technical Cybernetics, of Electronic Materials; Gen. Dir LI SON BONG.

Research Institute of Medical Instruments: Daesin-dong, Dongdaewon District, Pyongyang; tel. 623839; attached to DPRK Acad. of Medical Sciences; Dir JO MYONG SAM.

Libraries and Archives

Chongjin

Chongjin City Library: Chongjin; Librarian KANG CHAE GUM.

Chongjin Historical Library: Chongjin; Curator EU JAI GYONG.

North Hamgyong Provincial Library: Chongjin; Librarian CHOI MYONG OK.

Haeju

South Hwanghae Provincial Library: Haeju; Librarian CHOI CHI DO.

Hamhung

South Hamgyong Provincial Library: Hamhung; Librarian KIM SOOK JONG.

Hesan

Ryanggang Provincial Library: Hesan; Librarian KIM CHOL WOO.

Kaesong

Kaesong City Library: Kaesong; Librarian HAN IL.

Kaesong Historical Library: Kaesong; Curator CHOI SAE YONG.

Kangge

Chagang Provincial Library: Kangge; Librarian SONG AAI GUN.

Pyongsong

South Pyongan Provincial Library: Pyongsong; Librarian KIM DUK KWAN.

Pyongyang

Academy of Sciences Library: POB 330, Kwahakdong 1, Unjong District, Pyongyang; tel. 32353968; fax 814580; f. 1952; 3,200,000 vols; Dir Prof. KIM HYON OK; Chief Librarian Assoc. Prof. HONG SANG SU; publ. *Bulletin*.

Academy of Social Sciences Library: Central District, Pyongyang; Chief Librarian KIM SAE SONG.

Grand People's Study House: POB 200, Pyongyang; tel. (2) 321-5614; f. 1982; nat. library, in charge of nat. bibliography; also functions as correspondence univ.; 20,000,000 vols; Dir KIM JAE SUNG.

Pyongyang Scientific Library: Central District, POB 109, Pyongyang; tel. (2) 321-2314; f. 1978.

Sariwon

North Hwanghae Provincial Library: Sariwon; Librarian KIM HYO DAL.

Shinuiju

North Pyongan Provincial Library: Shinuiju; Librarian LI YONG SIK.

Wonsan

Kangwon Provincial Library: Wonsan; Librarian JI GYU HYOK.

Museums and Art Galleries

Haeju

Haeju Historical Museum: Haeju, South Hwanghae Province.

Hamhung

Hamhung Historical Museum: Hamhung, South Hamgyong Province; Curator KIM IK MYON.

Hyangsan county

Mt Myohyang-san Museum: Hyangsan County, North Pyongan Province; Curator CHOI HYONG MIN.

Pyongyang

Korean Art Gallery: Pyongyang; Curator KIM SANG CHOL.

Korean Central Historical Museum: Central District, Pyongyang; prehistory to early 20th century; Curator JANG JONG SIN.

Korean Ethnographic Museum: Central District, Pyongyang; Curator JON MOON JIN.

Korean Revolutionary Museum: Central District, Pyongyang; history from second half of 19th century to the present; Dir HWANG SUN HUI.

Memorial Museum of the War of Liberation: Moranbong District, Pyongyang; history from second half of the 19th century to the present; Dir THAE PYONG RYOL.

Shinchon county

Shinchon Museum: Shinchon County, South Hwanghae Province; Curator PAK IN CHAIK.

Shinuiju

Shinuiju Historical Museum: Shinuiju, North Pyongan Province; Curator PAK YONG GWAN.

Wonsan

Wonsan Historical Museum: Wonsan, Kangwon Province; Curator JO GANG BAIK.

Universities and Colleges

KIM IL SUNG UNIVERSITY

Daesong District, Pyongyang
Telephone: 54946
Founded 1946
State control
Academic year: September to August

President: PAK GWAN O
First Vice-President: O GIL BANG

Number of teachers: 2,000
Number of students: 12,000

Publications: natural science magazine, social science magazine.

Faculties of history, philosophy, economics, law, philosophy, foreign literature, geography, geology, physics and mathematics, chemistry, biology, atomic energy, computer science.

Kim Chaek University of Technology: Waesong District, Pyongyang; faculties of geology, mining, metallurgy, mechanical and electrical engineering, shipbuilding, electronics, nuclear technology; Pres. KIM GYONG WAN.

Kim Hyong-Jik University of Education: Pyongyang; f. 1946; faculties of revolutionary history, pedagogy, history and geography, language and literature, foreign languages, mathematics, physics, biology, music, fine arts, physical education; 2,500 students; 5-year degree course, short-term courses for teachers, correspondence and post-graduate courses; Pres. HONG IL CHON.

Pyongyang University of Agriculture: Pyongyang; f. 1981; depts of fruit and vegetable cultivation, stockbreeding, poultry; Pres. CHON SI GON.

Pyongyang University of Medicine: Woesong District, Pyongyang; Pres. CHU SONG UN.

There are colleges of higher and professional education (engineering, agriculture, fisheries, teacher training) situated in all the main towns; there are also Factory (Engineering) Colleges.

REPUBLIC OF KOREA

Learned Societies

GENERAL

Korea Foundation: POB 2147, 526, Namdaemunno 5-ga, Chung-gu, Seoul 100-095; tel. 753-3462; telex 27738; fax 757-2049; f. 1992 (fmrly Int. Cultural Soc. of Korea); promotes mutual understanding and friendship between Korea and the rest of the world; library of 6,000 vols; Pres. KIM JOUNGWAN; publs *Koreana* (quarterly, in English, Spanish, Japanese, Chinese and French), *Korea Focus* (6 a year, in English and Japanese), *Newsletter* (quarterly, in English and Korean).

National Academy of Sciences: San-94, Panpo-dong, Seocho-gu, Seoul; tel. 534-0737; fax 537-3183; f. 1954; divisions of Humanities and Social Sciences (Chair. KOH BYONG IK), Natural Sciences (Chair. KIM CHANG WHAN); 150 mems; library of 12,000 vols; Pres. KWON E.-HYOCK; Sec.-Gen. LO SOO-JUNG; publs *Bulletin, Journal.*

Royal Asiatic Society, Korea Branch: CPO Box 255, Seoul; tel. (2) 763-9483; fax (2) 766-3796; f. 1900 to stimulate interest in, and promote study and dissemination of knowledge about the arts, history, literature and customs of Korea and the neighbouring countries; 1,600 mems; reference library of 1,000 vols; Gen. Man. SUE J. BAE; *Transactions* (annually).

AGRICULTURE, FISHERIES AND VETERINARY SCIENCE

Korean Forestry Society: c/o Department of Forest Resources, Seoul National University, Suwon, Kyonggido 441-744; tel. (331) 290-2330; f. 1960 to foster the study of all aspects of forestry, to promote co-operation among members; 800 mems; Pres. Prof. JONG HWA YOUN; Sec. Assoc. Prof. JOO SANG CHUNG; publ. *Journal* (quarterly).

BIBLIOGRAPHY, LIBRARY SCIENCE AND MUSEOLOGY

Korean Library Association: 60-1, Panpo-dong, Seocho-ku, Seoul; tel. (2) 535-4868; fax (2) 535-5616; f. 1955; a social and academic institution comprising all the libraries and librarians in Korea; 1,000 institutional, 1,457 individual mems; Pres. CHUL SAKONG; Exec.-Dir WON-HO JO; publ. *KLA Bulletin* (6 a year).

Korean Research and Development Library Association: Room 0411, KIST Library, POB 131, Cheongryang, Seoul; tel. 967-3692; telex 27380; fax (82) 2963-4013 f. 1979; Pres. KE HONG PARK; Sec. KEON TAK OH.

ECONOMICS, LAW AND POLITICS

Korean Association of Sinology: c/o Asiatic Research Center, Korea University, Anam-dong, Seoul; f. 1955; 100 mems; Chair. JUN-YOP KIM; publ. *Journal of Chinese Studies.*

Korean Economic Association: 45, 4–ga, Namdae-mun-ro, Chung-gu, Seoul; f. 1952; theory, policy and history of economics and business administration; 2,800 mems; library of 3,000 vols; Pres. CHINKEUN PARK; Sec.-Gen. SUNGKEN HA; publ. *Korean Economic Review* (2 a year).

FINE AND PERFORMING ARTS

Music Association of Korea: Room No. 303, FACO Bldg, 81–6, Sejongro, Chongno-gu, Seoul; f. 1961; to develop Korean national music and to promote and protect Korean musicians; organizes concerts, encourages musical composition and nation-wide singing, is active in the international musical exchange and in music education; awards the Prize of Musical Culture; 700 mems; small library; Pres. Dr TAI JOON PARK; Sec. DAE YUP SOHN.

HISTORY, GEOGRAPHY AND ARCHAEOLOGY

Korean Geographical Society: Dept of Geography, College of Social Sciences, Seoul National University, Seoul 151-742; tel. (2) 880-6449; telex 29664; fax (2) 885-5272; f. 1945 to promote mutual co-operation in academic work and international understanding; 550 individual mems, 35 institutional mems; Pres. BO-WOONG CHANG; Sec.-Gen. SAM OCK PARK; publ. *Chirihak* (2 a year).

MEDICINE

Korean Medical Association: CPO Box 2062, Seoul; tel. (02) 794-2474; fax (02) 792-1296; e-mail kmabks@hitel.kol.co.kr; f. 1908; to develop the medical sciences and medical education by encouraging research and investigation; 59,292 mems; library of 10,000 vols; Pres. SUNG-HEE RYU; publ. *Journal* (monthly), *The KMA News* (2 a week).

PHILOSOPHY AND PSYCHOLOGY

Korean Psychological Association: Dept of Psychology, Seoul National University, Shinrim 2-dong, Kwanak-gu, Seoul; tel. 877-0101, ext. 2528; f. 1946; 420 mems; Pres. BONGYUN SUH; Sec. Gen. JUNGOH KIM; publs *Korean Journal of Psychology* (2 a year), *Korean Journal of Clinical Psychology* (2 a year), *Korean Journal of Social Psychology, Korean Journal of Industrial Psychology, Korean Journal of Developmental Psychology* (all annually).

Research Institutes

GENERAL

Academy of Korean Studies: 50 Unjung-dong, Songnam-si, Pundang-gu, Kyonggi-do 463-791; tel. (342) 709-8111; fax (342) 709-1531; f. 1978 to research and re-evaluate traditional Korean culture; library of 361,000 vols incl. 35,000 in Western languages; Pres. LEE YOUNG-DUG; publ. *Chongsin Munhwa / Academy News* (3–4 a year).

AGRICULTURE, FISHERIES AND VETERINARY SCIENCE

Rural Development Administration: Ministry of Agriculture, Forestry and Fisheries, Suwon; tel. 292-4370; telex 27361; fax 292-4163; f. 1906 to carry out agricultural research and rural community development; 13 subordinate research organizations, 9 provincial offices, 24 regional specialized crop stations; library of 98,720 vols; Administrator KWANG HEE KIM; publs *Annual Research Report* (Korean and English), *RDA Journal of Agricultural Science* (every 6 months), *Research and Extension* (quarterly), *Agricultural Technology* (monthly), *Rural Research and Extension Bulletin* (monthly).

ECONOMICS, LAW AND POLITICS

Korea Development Institute: POB 113, Cheongryang, Seoul 131-012; tel. 958-4114; fax 961-5092; f. 1971 to help determine the basic direction of the nation's development by formulating long-term goals and strategies based on accurate economic analysis; to conduct policy-oriented research relating to individual sectors of the economy that will help the country to maintain high economic growth with price stability; to provide consultation on policy issues relating to short-term economic management and planning; library of 100,000 vols, 39,000 research reports, govt documents, also data bank; Pres. DONG-SE CHA; publs *KDI Journal of Economic Policy* (quarterly, in Korean), *KDI Economic Outlook* (quarterly, in Korean).

Korea Institute for Industrial Economics and Trade (KIET): POB 205, Chongryang-ri, Seoul; tel. 962-6211-8; fax 963-8540; f. 1976; advises govt on industrial, trade and commercial policies; analyses Korean industry, int. economies, new technology and promotion of trade; library of 45,000 vols, 1,500 periodicals; Pres. KYU UCK LEE; publs *KIET Real Economy* (every 2 weeks), *Journal of Industrial Competitiveness* (annually), *KIET Economic Outlook* (2 a year).

Korean Research Center: 228 Pyong-dong, Chongno-gu, Seoul; f. 1956; research in social sciences; library; Pres. MUNAM CHON; publs *Journal of Social Sciences and Humanities, Korean Studies Series.*

EDUCATION

Korean Educational Development Institute: 92–6, Umyeon-dong, Seocho-gu, Seoul 137-791; tel. (2) 3460-0202; fax (2) 579-0746; f. 1972; independent, government-funded research and development centre; undertakes research and development activities on education; assists government in formulation of educational policies and in long-term development of education; produces educational television and radio programmes; library of 104,000 vols, 208 periodicals, 292,000 microfiches; Pres. Dr DON-HEE LEE; publs *Korean Education* (abstract in English, annually), *Educational Development* (Korean, 6 a year), *Annual Report* (English, Korean), *KEDI Newsletter* (Korean monthly, English annually), *Research Reports* (abstract in English, 70 vols annually), *Research Materials* (Korean, 10 units annually), *Educational Indicators in Korea* (Korean and English, annually).

National Institute for Training of Educational Administrators: 25 Samcheong-dong, Chongno-gu, Seoul 110–230; tel. (2) 733-2741; fax (2) 733-0149; f. 1970; government institute attached to Ministry of Education; library of 21,000 vols; Dir CHONG-TAEK CHANG.

NATURAL SCIENCES

Physical Sciences

Central Meteorological Office: 1 Songwol-dong, Chongro-gu, Seoul 110; under the control of the Ministry of Science and Technology;

Dir H. J. SON; publs Monthly and Annual Meteorological Reports.

PHILOSOPHY AND PSYCHOLOGY

Korean Institute for Research in the Behavioural Sciences: 1606-3 Socho-Dong, Kangnam-gu, Seoul 137-071; tel. 581-8611; f. 1968; basic and applied research in five areas: social, child, learning, organization, and psychological testing; 70 researchers; library of 5,000 vols; Dir SUNG JIN LEE; publs *Research Bulletin, Research Notes, Research Monograph*.

TECHNOLOGY

Electronics and Telecommunications Research Institute (ETRI): POB 8, Daedog Science Town, Daejeon City 302-350; tel. (860) 6114; telex 5532; fax (861) 1033; f. 1976; undertakes research and development in field of advanced information technology; library of 40,000 vols, 30,000 technical reports, and ETLARS databases; Pres. Dr SEUNG-TAIK YANG; publs include *Weekly Technology Trends* (weekly), *ETRI Journal* (quarterly), *Electronics and Telecommunications Trends* (quarterly), *Patent Announcement* (fortnightly), *Patent Information* (monthly).

Korea Atomic Energy Research Institute (KAERI): POB 105, Yu-Seong, Taejon 305-600; tel. 868-2000; fax 868-2702; f. 1959; reactor-related research and development, security and R&D of nuclear fuel, nuclear policy research, radiation application technology development and research and treatment of nuclear radiation, nuclear personnel training and other aspects of nuclear energy; library of 61,000 vols, 700,000 technical reports and 950 periodicals; Pres. SEONG-YUN KIM; publs *Won Woo* (6 a year), *Annual Report, KAERI Research Papers* (1 a year), *Journal*, etc.

Korea Institute of Energy and Research: POB 5, Taedok Science Town, Taejon 305-343; tel. (42) 861-9700; telex 45507; fax (42) 861-6224; f. 1977 to conduct research on energy and technology; supported by Ministry of Science and Technology; 500 mems; library of 30,000 vols; Pres. P. CHUNG MOO AUH; publs *Energy R&D, Technical Trends on NRSE, Annual Report.*

Korea Institute of Science and Technology (KIST): 39-1 Hawolkok-dong, Songbuk-ku, Seoul; tel. (2) 958-6114; telex 27380; fax (2) 958-5478; f. 1966; research in applied science, chemical engineering, polymer engineering, materials science and engineering, mechanical and control systems, electronics and information technology, environment and CFC alternatives technology, systems engineering, genetic engineering, science and technology policy; library of 50,000 vols, 15,000 technical reports; Pres. Dr WON HOON PARK; publs *Newsletter* (Korean, every 2 weeks), *KIST2000 Newsletter* (Korean, every 2 weeks), *Collection of Abstracts* (Korean and English, annually).

National Industrial Research Institute: 199 Dungsoong-dong, Chongno-gu, Seoul; f. 1883; Dir LEE BOM SOON.

Libraries and Archives

Pusan

Pusan National University Library: 30 Jangjeon-dong, Keumjeong-gu, Pusan 609-735; tel. (51) 510-1800; fax (51) 513-9787; f. 1946; 650,000 vols, 5,000 periodicals; Dir SAM-CHUL CHOI.

Seoul

Chung-Ang University Library: 221 Huksuk-dong, Dongjak-ku, Seoul; f. 1949; 442,667 vols; Dir DONG HUN SHON.

Dongguk University Library: 263-ga, Pil-dong, Seoul; f. 1906; Buddhist and Oriental studies; 350,000 vols, 1,100 periodicals; Dir Dr CHANG-WON CHUN.

Ewha Woman's University Library: 11–1, Daehyun-dong, Sudaemun-gu, Seoul 120-750; tel. 362-6075; e-mail libacq@mm.ewha.ac.kr; f. 1923; 1,125,000 vols; Dir BONG HEE KIM.

Government Archives and Records Service: 117 Chansong-dong, Chongno-gu, Seoul 110-034; tel. 720-4415; fax 739-8944; f. 1969; library of 336,275 vols, 1,188,226 diagrams, 1,539,666 cards, 181,311 rolls of microfilm; 740,463 audiovisual items; collection of records of the Yi dynasty; Archivist SUN-YOUNG KIM.

Korea University Library: 1 Anam-dong, Sungbuk-gu, Seoul 136-701; tel. (2) 3290-1472; fax (2) 924-0751; f. 1937; 400,132 vols; Dir HWA-YOUNG KIM.

National Assembly Library: 1 Yoido dong, Seoul; tel. 784-3565; telex 25849; fax 788-4193; f. 1952; library service for members of the National Assembly, the Executive, the Judiciary, and for scholars and legislative research activities and int. book exchange with 360 institutions worldwide; 900,000 vols, 12,101 current periodicals, 700 newspapers; Librarian CHONG-IL PARK; publs *National Assembly Library Review* (monthly), *Index to Korean-Language Periodicals* (every 2 months and annually), *Acquisitions List* (annually), *Index to National Assembly Debates* (irregular), *Index to Korean Laws and Statutes* (2 a year), *Issue Briefs* (irregular), *Legislative Information Analysis* (quarterly), *List of Theses for the Doctor's and Master's Degree in Korea* (annually).

National Library of Korea: 60–1, Panpo-Dong, Seocho-gu, Seoul 137-702; tel. (2) 535-4142; fax (2) 596-5749; e-mail nlkpc@sun.nl.or.kr; f. 1923; 2,900,000 vols; legal deposit library for Korean publications, ISBN, ISSN nat. centre, KOLIS-NET (Korean Library Information System Network) centre, international exchange, research in library and information science, training; Dir GI-YOUNG JEONG; publs *Korean National Bibliography* (annually), *Korean National Bibliography Monthly, Bibliographic Index of Korea* (annually), *Doseogwan* (4 a year), *Newsletter of Libraries* (monthly).

Seoul National University Library: San 56-1, Shillim-dong, Kwanak-gu, Seoul 151-742; tel. (2) 880-5284; fax (2) 871-2972; f. 1946; 2,077,000 vols, 13,000 periodicals, incl. Agricultural Library (121,000 vols), Medical Library (123,000 vols), Law Library (65,000 vols), Business Library (11,000 vols), Social Sciences Library (20,000 vols), Dental Library (9,000 vols) and Kyujang-gak Archives (special collection on Choseon Dynasty, 152,000 vols); collections on the arts, sciences, law, education, music, medicine, engineering, economics and commerce; Dir KYO-HUN CHIN; publs *Library Newsletter* (2 a year), *Kyujang-gak* (annually), *Ko-munseo* (annually).

Transport Library: 168, 2-ka, Bongnae-dong, Seoul; f. 1920; 32,000 vols; Dir CHO WOO HYUN; Chief Librarian KIM DOO HO; publ. *Korean National Railroad Bulletin* (monthly).

United Nations Depository Library: Korea University, 1 An-Am-dong, Sungbuk-gu, Seoul; tel. (2) 3290-1492; fax (2) 922-4633; e-mail mgc@kulib.korea.ac.kr; f. 1957; 38,000 vols; Dir HWA-YOUNG KIM; Librarian MI-GYOUNG CHO.

Yonsei University Library: Yonsei University, 134 Sinchon-dong, Sudaemoon-gu, Seoul; tel. 361-3308; f. 1915; 1,538,000 vols including Korean archives, 10,700 periodicals; Dir JONG CHUL HAN; publs *Dong Bang Hak Chi* (Journal of Korean Studies), *Inmun Kwahak* (Journal of Humanities), *International Journal of Korean Studies, Journal of East and West Studies, Kyo Yuk Non Jib* (Journal of Education), *Yonsei Non-Chong* (Journal of Graduate School), *Yonsei Social Science Review, Abstracts of Faculty Research Report, Yonsei Magazine.*

Taegu

Kyungpook National University Library: 1370, Sankyuk-dong, Puk-ku, Taegu 702-701; f. 1952; 680,000 vols; Dir CHOI DAL-HYUN.

Museums and Art Galleries

Pusan

Pusan National University Museum: Pusan; Korean archaeology with special collection of historical remains of Kyongsang-Namdo province, arts, ethnology, etc.; Dir Prof. SUK-HEE KIM; publ. *Research Reports* (irregularly).

Seoul

National Museum of Korea: 1 Sejong-ro, Chongno-gu, Seoul; tel. (2) 720-2714; fax (2) 734-7255; f. 1908; Korean archaeology, culture and folklore; *c.* 100,000 artefacts representing over 5,000 years of human endeavour on the Korean peninsula; education centre; library of *c.* 20,000 vols; brs in 8 other towns; Dir-Gen. YANG-MO CHUNG; publs *Report of Researches of Antiquities, Misul Charyo* (Materials in Art, 2 a year), *Bakmulkwan Sinmun* (Museum News, monthly).

National Museum of Modern Art: Dogsu Palace, Seoul; two-part national art exhibition held here annually; also special exhibitions; permanent collection occupies half of the museum.

National Science Museum: 2 Waryong-dong, Chongno-gu, Seoul 110; tel. 762-5209; f. 1926; holds National Science Fair, exhibitions, science classrooms, film service, etc.; library of 2,000 vols on science and technology; Dir CHI-EUN KIM; publ. *Bulletin*.

Seoul National University Museum: San 56–1, Sinlim-dong, Kwanak-gu, Seoul 151-742; tel. 874-5693; f. 1941; exhibition of Korean culture totalling 8,058 artefacts; library specializing in Korean archaeology, art history, anthropology and folklore; Dir Dr MONG-LYONG CHOI; publs *Bulletin* (annually), *Archaeological and Anthropological Papers of Seoul National University* (annually).

Yonsei University Museum: Shinchon-dong, Sudaemun-gu, Seoul; f. 1965; research; prehistory, history, fine arts, ethnic customs, medicine, geology, etc.; Dir Prof. WHANG WON-KOO; publs occasional papers, excavation reports.

Universities

AJOU UNIVERSITY

Suwon, Kyonggi-do 441-749

Telephone: (2) 231-7121

Founded 1973

President: HYO KYU KIM

Registrar: JOON YOP KIM

Librarian: JAE SUK LEE

Library of 230,000 vols

Number of teachers: 250

Number of students; 8,000

Colleges of engineering, business administration, natural sciences, medicine, social sciences, humanities; graduate school.

ANDONG NATIONAL UNIVERSITY

388 Song cheon dong, Angong, Kyung-buk 460-380

Telephone: (55) 1661

Founded 1979

President: KIM YUB
Registrar: KIM JONG-SIK
Librarian: KU SANG-MAN

Library of 55,000 vols
Number of teachers: 113
Number of students: 2,900

HEADS OF DEPARTMENTS

Korean: SIR BO-WOUL
Sino-Korean Literature: KIM SAR-HAN
History: KIM HO-JONG
Folklore: CHANG CHUL-SOO
Oriental Philosophy: OH SUK-WON
Law: KWON YEONG-JUN
Public Administration: LEE BYUNG-KAP
Business Administration: CHOI SUNG-KI
International Trade: RHEE SANG-CHOOL
Accounting: SIR YONG-SU
Physics: SOHN YEON-KYU
Chemistry: YEH JIN-HAE
Biology: LEE HEE-MOO
Computer Science and Statistics: CHA YOUNG-JOON
Home Economics: CHOI YONG-OK
Food Economics: YOON SUK-KYUNG
National Ethics Education: YI CHONG-KYUN
English: KIM YANG-SU
Mathematics: KIM SI-JOO
Music: CHO IN-CHAN
Fine Arts: SONG KI-SUK
Physical Education: KIM CHEONG-HAN
General Education: PAK CHAE-UK

CHONBUK NATIONAL UNIVERSITY

664-14 Deogjin-dong 1-ka, Chonju 561-756, Chonbuk

Telephone: 70-2114
Fax: 0652-70-2188

Founded 1947
State control
Academic year: March to February (two semesters)
President: Dr MYUNG SOO CHANG
Library Director: JIN KON OH

Library of 385,000 vols
Number of teachers: 800
Number of students: 24,000

Publications: *The Chonbuk University Newspaper, The Chonbuk University Herald* (weekly), *Chonbuk National University Bulletin* (annually), annual bulletins of research institutes.

VICE-PRESIDENTS

Academic Affairs: YEONG CHUL KIM
Student Affairs: EUNG KYO RYU
Research and Development: JEONG KEUN PARK
Graduate School: SUN YUNG CHO
Graduate School of Agricultural Development: SUNG YUN KANG
Graduate School of Business Administration: SUNG WOO HYUNG
Graduate School of Education: GWANG HYUN CHOI
Graduate School of Public Administration: YOUNG MIN HEO
Graduate School of Environmental Studies: JE BIN IM
Graduate School of Industrial Technology: SUK PYO HONG
College of Engineering: CHUL RO YU
College of Agriculture: JAI SIK HONG
College of Humanities: YOUNG CHUEL KIM
College of Law: KYU SUK SUH
College of Social Science: JAE YOUNG KIM
College of Education: SEUNG TAI PARK
College of Commerce: YEONG HEE CHEONG
College of Natural Science: CHOON HO LEE
Medical School: NO SUK KI
College of Dentistry: CHAN UN PARK
College of Arts: KYE IL SONG
College of Veterinary Medicine: JOO MOOK LEE
College of Home Economics: KEUM SODU CHI

DIRECTORS

Language Research Institute: KYU TAE CHO
Research Institute of Agricultural Development: SUN YOUNG CHOI
Institute of Local Government and Autonomy: CHEOL JONG RYU
Social Science Research Institute: SOON GOO CHO
Institute of Basic Science: KWANG HO SO
Institute of Science Education: SEUK BEUM KO
Institute of Social Education: DAE WOON CHANG
Research Institute of Engineering Technology: HAK SHIN KIM
Institute for Medical Science: HONG BAI EUN
Research Institute of Urban and Environmental Studies: EUNG KYO RYU
Laboratory of Electronics Industry and Development: SUNG JOONG KIM
Research Institute of Semiconductors: HYUNG JAE LEE
Research Institute of Sports Science: SANG JONG LEE
Institute of Rural Development: DONG HO LEE
Cholla Cultural Research Centre: HEE KWON LEE
Institute of Advanced Materials Development: CHONG KYO KIM
Biosafety Research Institute: BYUNG MOO LIM
Institute for Molecular Biology and Genetics: KWANG YEOP JANG
American Studies Research Institute: JANG RYUNG KIM
Research Institute of Law: KYU SUK SUH
Research Institute of Industry and Economy: SEUNG KI PARK
Electric and Electronic Circuit and Systems Research Institute: DONG YONG KIM
Research Institute of Communist Countries: WON HO YOON
Information Industry Research Institute: OK BAE CHANG
The Humanities Research Institute: KANG JE KWAK
Institute of Animal Research and Development: WON JIB SHIN
Institute of Dental Science: EUN CHUNG JHEE

HEADS OF DEPARTMENTS

College of Agriculture:

Agricultural Biology: HYUNG MOO KIM
Agricultural Chemistry: YOUNG HEE MOON
Agricultural Economics: DONG HO LEE
Agricultural Engineering: JAE YOUNG LEE
Engineering of Agricultural Machinery: CHUL SOO KIM
Agronomy: SUNG YOUNG CHOI
Animal Science: WON JIB SHIN
Food Science and Technology: DONG HWA SHIN
Forest Products and Technology: CHEOL SOO HAN
Forest Resources: KAE HWAN KIM
Horticulture: JAE CHEOL KIM
Landscape Architecture: SEI CHEON KIM

College of Arts:

Korean Music: HEOI CHUN CHUNG
Dance: WON KIM
Fine Arts: SEUNG TAEG LIM
Industrial Design: CHONG KI KIM
Music: HYUN JIN KIM

College of Commerce:

Accounting: JAE DUCK CHA
Business Administration: SANG MAN LEE
Economics: SEUNG KI PARK
International Trade: NAK PIL CHOI

College of Dentistry:

Dentistry: KWANG JOON KOH

College of Education:

Biology Education: MU YEOL KIM
Chemistry Education: SEUK BEUM KO
Earth Science Education: CHUL HEE KIM
Education: DONG HO SO
English Language Education: BYEONG HWA JEONG
Arts Education: IN HYUN PARK
German Language Education: MUN HI YI
Home Economics Education: HEE SOOK SOHN
Korean Language Education: BONG GEUN KANG
Mathematices Education: SANG CHEOL LEE
Music Education: JE HYUN PARK
National Ethics Education: CHANG SOON CHOI
Physical Education: KIL HWAN JUNG
Social Science Education: HEE HWAN LEE

College of Engineering:

Aerospace Engineering: SHIN JAE KANG
Architectural Engineering: YANG SEOB SOH
Chemical Engineering: KI JU KIM
Chemical Technology: DAI SOO LEE
Civil Engineering: JU SEONG BAE
Computer Engineering: YOUNG CHON KIM
Control Instrumentation Engineering: SUNG JOONG KIM
Electrical Engineering: DONG YONG KIM
Electronic Engineering: HEUNG KI BAIK
Environmental Engineering: CHAN HEE WON
Industrial Engineering: DONG WON KIM
Information and Telecommunications Engineering: MOON HO LEE
Mechanical Design: JAE KYOO LIM
Mechanical Engineering: YOUNG TAIG OH
Metallurgical Engineering: DONG KEON KIM
Materials Engineering: BOK HEE KIM
Mining and Mineral Resources Engineering: SEUNG GON KIM
Polymer Science and Technology: JOHNG MOON LEE
Precision Engineering: TAE YOUNG KIM
Textile Engineering: PYONG KI PARK

College of Humanities:

Korean Language and Literature: JEONG KU CHON
English Language and Literature: SOO GIL KIM
French Language and Literature: YOUNG KYUNG CHOU
Chinese Language and Literature: YOUNG JUN CHOI
German Language and Literature: CHO WANG JEONG
Japanese Language and Literature: CHANG KEE PARK
Spanish Language and Literature: NAK WON CHOI
Archaelogy and Anthropology: POOK KIM
History: GIL WON KANG
Philosophy: JEON KYU PARK

College of Law:

Civil Law: YOUNG MIN HEO
Private Law: JAI KIL CHUNG
Public Law: YANG KYUN SHIN

College of Natural Science

Biology: GOOK HYUN CHUNG
Chemistry: IN HO CHO
Computer Science: YUNG SUNG KIM
Statistics: KYUNG SOO HAN
Geology: JUNG HOO LEE
Mathematics: YANG KOHN KIM
Molecular Biology: CHUNG UNG PARK
Physics: CHAI HO RIM

Preliminary course in Medicine: WON KU LEE
Preliminary course in Dentistry: HWA SIN PARK

College of Social Science:

Journalism and Communication: JOON MANN KANG
Political Science and Diplomacy: CHEOL JONG RYU
Psychology: HYUCK CHEL KWON
Public Administration: IN JAE KANG
Social Welfare: WON KYU CHOI
Sociology: HARK SERB CHUNG

College of Veterinary Medicine:

Veterinary Medicine: IN HYUK CHOI

Medicine School:

Medicine: MOO SAM LEE
Nursing: MYUNG JA KIM

College of Home Economics:

Home Management: (vacant)
Clothing and Textiles: (vacant)

CHONNAM NATIONAL UNIVERSITY

300 Yongbong-dong, Puk-Gu, Kwangju 500-757

Telephone: (62) 530-0114
Fax: (62) 530-1015

Founded 1952
State control
Language of instruction: Korean
Academic year: March to February (two semesters)

President: Dr SUNG MAN ROWE
Dean of Academic Affairs: Dr JONG MOK LEE
Dean of Student Affairs: Dr JUNG MOOK YOON
Dean of Planning and Research: Dr SUNG SOO PARK
Librarian: Dr YOON JUNG HAN

Library of 600,000 vols, 6,000 periodicals
Number of teachers: 1,230 (420 part-time)
Number of students: 18,078

Publications: *Rural Development Review*, *The Journal of Research Institute for Catalysis*, *The Journal of Natural Science*, *Journal of Unification Studies*, *Research on Honam Culture*, *Journal of Humanities Studies*, *Language Teaching*, *Chonnam Review of American Studies*, *Social Science Review*, *The Journal of Regional Development*, *Industrial Relations Research*, *The Journal of Sports Science*, *Chonnam Medical Journal*, *Technological Review*, *Journal of Agricultural Science and Technology*, *Journal of Sciences for Better Living*, *Journal of Drug Development*, *Journal of Arts*, *Yongbong Review*.

DEANS

Graduate School: HA IL PARK
Graduate School of Education: KEUN HO CHUNG
Graduate School of Business Administration: SOUG SHIN CHOI
Graduate School of Public Administration: SEONG KIE KIM
Graduate School of Industry: KWAN SOO LEE
College of Education: KEUN HO CHUNG
College of Business Administration: SOUG SHIN CHOI
College of Engineering: KWAN SOO LEE
College of Agriculture: JAE HONG KIM
College of Law: SEONG KIE KIM
College of Medicine: YOUNG HONG PAIK
College of Dentistry: MONG SOOK VANG
College of Natural Sciences: JAE KEUN KIM
College of Pharmacy: BYUNG HO CHUNG
College of Arts: JONG IL KIM
College of Veterinary Medicine: NAM YONG PARK
College of Social Sciences: YOUNG KWAN CHOI
College of Home Economics: DUCK SOON HWANG

ATTACHED RESEARCH INSTITUTES

Management Research Centre: Dir JAE JEON KIM.
Educational Research Institute: Dir YONG NAM LEE.
American Studies Institute: Dir KIL HO SUNG.
Law and Administration Institute: Dir KYONG UN LEE.
Social Sciences Institute: Dir KEUN SIK CHUNG.
Arts Institute: Dir JONG IL KIM.
5.18 Institute: Dir SU SUNG OH.
Humanities Studies Institute: Dir DONG SOO KIM.
Culture and Religious Studies Institute: Dir JUNG HEE KIM.
Centre for Regional Development: Dir SUNG WOO HONG.
Research Institute for Asia and the Pacific Rim: Dir MOON JI BYUNG.
Honam Culture Research Centre: Dir KYU PARK MAN.
Science for Better Living Institute: Dir HYUN SOOK LIM.
Research Institute of Nursing Science: Dir HYE YOUNG KANG.
Engineering Research Institute: Dir NAM SOO SHIN.
Science Education Institute: Dir HEE KYUN OH.
Basic Sciences Institute: Dir WON KI CHOI.
Agricultural Science and Technology Institute: Dir YOUNG MAN LEE.
Veterinary Medicine Research Centre: Dir NAM YONG PARK.
Occupational Medicine Institute: Dir JAE DONG MUN.
Biotechnology Institute: Dir BAIK HO CHO.
Sports Science Centre: Dir DONG WON YANG.
Research Institute for Drug Development: Dir BYUNG HO CHUNG.
Research Institute for Medical Science: Dir SUNG SIK PARK.
Automobile Research Centre: Dir YOUNG KIL KIM.
Information and Research Communications Institute: Dir HYUN JAE KIM.
Research Institute for Catalysis: Dir CHANG SHIN SUNWOO.
Dental Science Institute: Dir BYUNG JOO PARK.
Environmental Research Institute: Dir CHONG BIN LEE.
Hormone Research Centre: Dir HYUK BANG KWON.
Advanced Materials Research Centre: Dir YONG HYUCK BAIK.
Polymer Science and Technology Research Centre: Dir KYU HO CHAE.
Research Centre for High Quality Electric Components and Systems: Dir YOUNG CHUL LIM.
Electronic Telecommunication Technology Research Centre: Dir YOUNG MIN KIM.
Construction-Environment-Cleaner Production Technology Research Centre: Dir CHONG JUN LEE.

CHOSUN UNIVERSITY

375, Seosuk-dong, Kwangju, Chollanam-do 500

Telephone: 232-8151

Founded 1946
Private control
Language of instruction: Korean
Academic year: March to February

Founder-President: CHYULL WOONG PARK
Dean of Academic Affairs: CHAI-KYUN PARK
Dean of Student Affairs: YANG-SOO SON
Dean of General Affairs: PYUNG-JOON PARK
Dean of Finance: JEI-WON KOH
Librarian: KI-SANG KIM

Library of 597,032 vols
Number of teachers: 556
Number of students: 26,164

Publications: various research journals.

DEANS

College of Humanities: JEONG-SEOK KANG
College of Natural Science: HAK-JIN JUNG
College of Law and Political Science: CHANG-HYEON KOH
College of Business Administration: BYUNG-KYU KIM
College of Engineering: WHAN-KYU PARK
College of Education: HONG-WON PARK
College of Foreign Languages: YONG-HERN LEE
College of Physical Education: DONG-YOON CHOE
College of Medicine: YO-HAN JUNG
College of Dentistry: CHANG-KEUN YOON
College of Pharmacy: YEONG-JONG YOO
College of Industry: HEUNG-KYU JOO
College of Arts: YONG-HYUN KUK
Evening College: JEONG-JOO CHOE
Graduate School: JOON-CHAE PARK
Graduate School of Education: SEOK-CHEOL PARK
Graduate School of Industry: SEONG-HYU JO

CHAIRMEN OF DEPARTMENTS

College of Humanities:

Korean Language and Literature: TAE-JIN JANG
English Language and Literature: HAK-HAENG JO
French Language and Literature: WOO-HYUN JO
History: OH-RYONG JUNG
Philosophy: MOON-JEONG PARK

College of Natural Science:

Mathematics: JONG-HO CHOE
Computer Science and Statistics: KYU-JUNG CHOE
Physics: SANG-YEOL LEE
Chemistry: IL-DOO KIM
Biology: HONG-SEOB KIM
Genetic Science: SEONG-JUN KIM

College of Law and Political Science:

Law: YEONG-KYU KIM
Public Administration: YEONG-KYU KIM
Political Science and Diplomacy: YANG-SOO SON

College of Business Administration:

Economics: IK-HYUN KIM
Management: BYUNG-KYU KIM
Accounting: OK-YOON PARK
Trade: MOON-SOO YOO

College of Engineering:

Civil Engineering: BYEONG-DAE LIM
Architectural Engineering: JEONG-SOO JANG
Mechanical Engineering: JONG-IL KIM
Precision Mechanical Engineering: SEON-JONG PARK
Mechanical Design Engineering: TAE-KWON JUNG
Electrical Engineering: BYEONG-SOO YOO
Electronics Engineering: JOON-HYUN KIM
Computer Systems Engineering: CHEOL SONG
Metallurgical Engineering: HWAN-JONG JO
Resource Engineeering: DONG-WOO SUH
Chemical Engineering: BYUNG-OOK JO
Industrial Management: HAK-YEONG BYUN
Environmental Engineering: SEONG-EUI SHIN
Aerospace Engineering: CHEOL-HYUNG JO
Nuclear Engineering: SEUNG-PYUNG CHOE
Naval Architecture Engineering: CHANG-EUN PARK

College of Education:
- Korean Language: OK-KEUN HAN
- Foreign Languages: KYU-EUL YUM
- English Major: KYU-EUL YUM
- German Major: JAE-MAN PARK
- Mathematics Education: SEOK-JOO PARK
- Sciences: HEE-NAM KIM
- Physics Major: KWAN-KYO LEE
- Chemistry Major: JAE-HEUNG JO
- Biology Major: SEONG-YONG KANG
- Earth Science Major: HEE-NAM KIM
- Home Economics: YEONG-SOOK KIM
- Music: KYU-YEOL CHAI

College of Foreign Languages:
- Spanish Language: KI-TAEK KIM
- German Language: YEONG-SOO JUNG
- Chinese Language: KIL-JANG PARK
- Japanese Language: SANG-IK PARK
- Arabic Language: HEE-MAN SAH
- Russian Language: SOO-HEE KIM

College of Physical Education:
- Physical Education: HYUNG-CHULL NO
- Dance: JOON-YEONG SONG

College of Medicine:
- Medicine: KWANG-SAM KOH
- Nursing: SONG-JA KIM

College of Pharmacy:
- Pharmacy: MYEONG-HYEON JUNG

College of Industry:
- Electronic Data Processing: HACK-JOO AHN
- Food and Nutrition: WHA-JOONG SUH
- Industrial Design: KIL-YONG SUH

College of Arts:
- Fine Arts: JONG-SOO KIM
- Applied Arts: JONG-HOON PARK
- Sculpture: JEONG-SOO KOH

Evening College:
- Law: YEONG-KON KIM
- Economics: KWANG-SOO JEE
- Management: KANG-OK LEE
- Accounting: KI-PYONG KIM
- Trade: SUNG-MIN LEE
- Civil Engineering: CHEOL-SOON KIM
- Architectural Engineering: MAN-TAEK LIM
- Mechanical Engineering: JIN-HEUNG KIM
- Mechanical Design Engineering: IN-YEONG YANG
- Precision Mechanical Engineering: JAE-KI SHIM
- Electrical Engineering: SANG-IL LEE
- Electronics Engineering: CHANG-KYOON PARK

ATTACHED INSTITUTES

Ja-yang Ultramodern Science and Technology Research Institute: CHYULL WOONG PARK.

Humanities Research Institute: Dir CHANG-WHAN KOO.

Social Science Research Institute: Dir CHANG-HYUN KOH.

Natural Science Research Institute: Dir HAK-JIN JUNG.

Production Technology Research Institute: Dir CHEOL-HYEONG JO.

National Development Research Institute: Dir BYEONG-DAE LIM.

Atomic Energy Research Institute: Dir BOK-NAM PARK.

Energy and Resources Research Institute: Dir JONG-IL KIM.

Korean History Research Institute: Dir HYUNG-KWAN PARK.

National Unification Research Institute: Dir JEONG-JOO CHOE.

Foreign Cultural Research Institute: Dir JEONG-SEOK KANG.

Educational Research Institute: Dir YONG-SUB CHOE.

Medical Research Institute: Dir YO-HAN JUNG.

Dental-Biology Research Institute: Dir CHANG-KEUN YOON.

Pharmaceutical Research Institute: Dir DON-IL LEE.

Management Research Institute: Dir OH-YOON PARK.

Environment and Pollution Research Institute: Dir JIN-WHAN LEE.

Agricultural Research Institute: Dir NAM-KI JO.

Saemaul Research Institute: Dir MOON-SOO YOO.

Student Guidance Research Institute: Dir IL-HOUN KIM.

Arts Research Institute: Dir YONG-HYUN KUK.

CHUNG-ANG UNIVERSITY

221 Huksuk-dong, Dongjak-ku, Seoul 156-756
Telephone: (2) 820-6124
Fax: (2) 813-8069

Founded 1918
Private control
Academic year: March to February (two semesters)

Chairman and Chancellor: HEE SU KIM
President: MIN HA KIM
Vice-Presidents: DUCK YOUNG CHOI (Seoul Campus), CHONG HOON LEE (Ansung Campus)
Provost of Medical Centre: SOON HYUN SHINN
Directors of Libraries: TOO YOUNG LEE (Seoul Campus), YANG HYUN LEE (Ansung Campus)

Number of teachers: 1,439 (618 full-time)
Number of students: 18,385 (undergraduate), 3,335 (graduate)

Publications: *Theses Collection, College Journals* (annually), *Korean Studies Journal* (quarterly), *Journal of Chung-Ang Pharmacy, Korean Journal of Comparative Law, Korean Education Index, Journal of Economic Development* (all annually), *Chung-Ang Press* (weekly), *Chung-Ang Herald* (monthly).

ACADEMIC DEANS

College of Construction: KI BONG KIM
College of Arts: SANG JUE SHIN
College of Education: YOUNG DUCK CHOI
College of Engineering: SUNG SUN KIM
College of Foreign Languages: SUNG MOO YANG
College of Home Economics: YANG HEE KIM
College of Industrial Studies: KWANG RO YOON
College of Law: YOUNG SOL KWON
College of Liberal Arts: NAM JOON CHANG
College of Medicine: IM WON CHANG
College of Music: LEE SUK CHEH
College of Pharmacy: IN HOI HUH
College of Political Science and Economics: IN KIE KIM
College of Sciences: SUK YONG LEE
College of Social Sciences: CHI SOON JANG
Graduate School: JO SUP CHUNG
Graduate School of Construction Engineering: SUNG SUN KIM
Graduate School of Education: JAE WOO LEE
Graduate School of the Information Industry: YOUNG CHAN KIM
Graduate School of International Management: HUN CHU
Graduate School of Mass Communication: SANG CHUL LEE
Graduate School of Public Administration: SANG YOON REE
Graduate School of Social Development: KYONG SUH PARK

DIRECTORS

Institute of Advertising and Public Relations: JUN IL RYEE
Institute of Arts: SEUNG KIL KOH
Institute of Basic Sciences: KYUNG HEE CHOI
Institute of Economic Research: YEN KYUN WANG
Institute of Environmental Science: SEI KWAN SOHN
Institute of Family Life: HYUN OK LEE
Institute of Food Resource: SOO SUNG LEE
Institute of Genetic Engineering: YUNG CHAI CHUNG
Institute of Humanities: JOONG SHIK HYUN
Institute of Industrial Construction Technology: YONG JU HWANG
Institute of Industrial Design: WON MO KWAK
Institute of Industrial Management: SEONG MU SUH
Institute of International Trade: JU SUP HAHN
Institute of International Women's Studies: JAE WOO LEE
Institute of Japanese Studies: KYUN IL KIM
Institute of Korean Education: SUNG YOON HONG
Institute of Korean Folklore: SEON POONG KIM
Institute of Legal Research: HYUK JU LEE
Institute of Management Research: DONG SUNG KWAK
Institute of Medical Science: DAE YONG UHM
Institute of North-East Asian Studies: JAE SUN CHOI
Institute of Overseas Korean Residents: SANG MAN LEE
Institute of Pharmaceutical Science: KI HO KIM
Institute of Production Engineering: SOO SAM KIM
Institute of Public Policy and Administration: SANG YOON RHEE
Institute of Social Sciences: HYUNG KOOK KIM
Institute of Sports Sciences Research: JIN YOO
Institute of Technology and Science: YOUNG CHAN KIM
Institute of Third World Studies: UJIN YI
Chung-Ang Music Institute: HAK WON YOON
Australian Studies Institute: HYUNG SHIK KIM

CHUNGBUK NATIONAL UNIVERSITY

48 Gaesin-dong, Heungdeok-gu, Cheongju, Chungbuk 310
Telephone: (431) 61-2884
Fax: (431) 273-2805
E-mail: jdoh@libl.chungbuk.ac.kr

Founded 1951 as Agricultural College, university status 1970
Academic year: March to July, September to December

President: JA MUN JU
Director of Administration: KEE UN CHUNG
Dean of Academic Affairs: YOUNG SOO JEONG
Dean of Student Affairs: SUNG HOO HONG
Dean of Planning and Research Affairs: SOON SEOP KWAK
Director of Library: SOON KEY JUNG

Library of 440,000 vols
Number of teachers: 700
Number of students: 17,000

Publications: *Journal of the Industrial Science and Technology Institute, Review of Industry and Management, Journal of the Institute of Construction Technology, Journal of Agricultural Science Research, Journal of Genetic Engineering Research, Law Journal, Journal of Humanities, Journal of Pharmaceutical Science, Journal of Social Science, Juris Forum, Jungwon Munhwa Nonchong, Journal of the Research Institute for Computer and Information Communication, Journal of Language and Literature.*

DEANS

College of Humanities: JANG SUNG JOONG
College of Social Science: HEE KYUNG KANG
College of Natural Science: BYUNG CHOON LEE
College of Engineering: LEE JAE KI
College of Commerce and Business Administration: DO WON SUH
College of Education: SHEON JOO CHIN
College of Pharmacy: HAN KUN

College of Medicine: YOUNG JIN SONG
College of Law: JUN HUR
College of Home Economics: KI NAM KIM
College of Veterinary Medicine: YOUNG WON YUN

ATTACHED INSTITUTES

Computer Center: Dir Y. S. KOO.

Student Guidance Institute: Dir D. J. PARK.

Health Center: Dir Y. J. OH.

Saemaul Research Institute: Dir S. W. KANG.

Natural Science Institute: Dir S. Y. HONG.

Institute of Unification Research of the Korean Peninsula: Dir H. K. AHN.

Institute of Construction Technology: Dir B. K. KOO.

Language Research Institute: Dir H. K. KIM.

CHUNGNAM NATIONAL UNIVERSITY

Taejon, Chungnam 302-764

Telephone: (42) 821-5114

Telex: 45571

Fax: (42) 823-1469

Founded 1952

Academic year: March to June, September to December

President: DUCK KYUN OH
Dean of Academic Affairs: CHUL KYU CHOI
Dean of Student Affairs: KUN MOOK CHOI
Registrar: MYUNG KYUN KIM
Librarian: JONG UP CHO

Number of teachers: 822
Number of students: 18,086

Publications: journals of 24 research institutes (annually).

DEANS

Graduate School: CHONG HOE PARK
Graduate School of Business Administration: KEAN SHIK LEE
Graduate School of Education: SANG CHUL KANG
Graduate School of Public Administration: JAE CHANG KA
Graduate School of Industry: GUNG SUCK NAM
Graduate School of Public Health: SAE JIN CHOI
College of Humanities: HAE KIL SUH
College of Social Sciences: TONG HOON KIM
College of Natural Sciences: JONG SUK CHOI
College of Economics and Management: CHUL HWAN CHUN
College of Engineering: SOO YOUNG CHUNG
College of Agriculture: JONG WOO KIM
College of Law: KANG YONG LEE
College of Pharmacy: BYUNG ZUN AHN
College of Home Economics: YOUNG JIN CHUNG
College of Medicine: JIN SUN BAI
College of Fine Arts and Music: CHEOL NAM
College of Veterinary Medicine: MOO HYUNG JUN

HEADS OF DEPARTMENTS

College of Humanities:

Korean Language and Literature: BYEONG WOOK KIM
English Language and Literature: JAE IK YU
German Language and Literature: SANG KUN CHUNG
French Language and Literature: MI YUN KIM
Chinese Language and Literature: JOON HO WOO
Japanese Language and Literature: MOON KI HUR
Sino-Korean Literature: JONG-UP CHO
History: SANG CHUL CHA
Korean History: SOO TAE KIM
Archaeology: KANG SEUNG LEE
Philosophy: MYEONG JIN NAM
Education: SAM HWAN JOO

College of Social Sciences:

Sociology: NO YOUNG PARK
Literary and Information Science: BOCK HEE HAHN
Psychology: KYO HEON KIM
Mass Communication: SEUNG MOCK YANG
Public Administration: KEUN BOK KANG
Local Government: DONG IL YOOK
Political Science and Diplomacy: KE HEE LEE

College of Natural Sciences:

Mathematics: KANG JOO MIN
Statistics: NAK YOUNG LEE
Computer Science: JI HOON KANG
Physics: JAE SHIK JUN
Chemistry: JUN GILL KANG
Biology: KWAN HEE YOU
Biochemistry: TAE IK KWON
Microbiology: PIL JAE MAENG
Geology: WON SA KIM
Oceanology: TAE WON LEE
Physical Education: DAE WOO CHOI
Pre-medicine: NAK YOUNG LEE
Socio-physical Education: CHOON-KI MIN
Astronomy and Space Science: KWANG TEA KIM

College of Economics and Management:

Economics: TECK SUNG KWON
Business Administration: TAE GYU YI
Accounting: SEH DO OH
International Management: JONG SOON KOO

College of Engineering:

Architectural Engineering Education: DEOG SEONG OH
Metallurgical Engineering Education: HONG RO LEE
Mechanical Engineering Education: JONG HO WON
Electrical Engineering Education: HEUNG HO LEE
Electronic Engineering Education: DAE YOUNG KIM
Civil Engineering Education: JAE CHUL SHIN
Industrial Technology Education: PAN WOOK KIM
Chemical Engineering Education: SEUNG KON RYU
Textile Engineering: KI SEA BAE
Naval Architecture and Ocean Engineering: CHANG SUP LEE
Material Engineering: GIL MOO KIM
Mechanical Design Engineering: SEONG YEON YOO
Computer Engineering: OH-SEOK KWON
Polymer Engineering: SUNG KWON
Environmental Engineering: CHOUNG KEUN WONG

College of Agriculture:

Agronomy: CHOONG SOO KIM
Horticulture: JONG-SUK LEE
Forestry: HO KYUNG SONG
Agricultural Biology: KWAN SAM CHOC
Animal Science: CHANG SIK PARK
Dairy Science: IN DUK LEE
Agricultural Engineering: TAI CHEOL KIM
Agricultural Machinery Engineering: MAN-SOO KIM
Agricultural Chemistry: KYU SEUNG LEE
Forest Products Technology: YANG JUN
Food Technology: NAM JIN OH

College of Veterinary Medicine:

Veterinary Medicine: DUCK KWAM KIM

College of Law:

Public Law: SANG OH BAC
Private Law: YOUNG WOO PARK

College of Pharmacy:

Pharmacy: KWANG IL KWON
Pharmaceutics: KYUNG LAE PARK

College of Home Economics:

Home Economics Education: JOON HO LEE
Clothing and Textiles: KYUNG HEE HONG
Food and Nutrition: MEE REE KIM

College of Medicine:

Medicine: JIN SUN BAI
Nursing: HEE YOUNG SO

College of Music and Arts:

Music: SANG LOCK PARK
Wind & Strings: BYUNG HOON
Painting: NYUNG BAC KIM
Sculpture: CHEOL NAM
Industrial Arts: BYUNG JIN CHOI

ATTACHED RESEARCH INSTITUTES

Student Guidance Centre: Dir CHAN WEON SEU.

Basic Science Research Institute: Dir SOCK YUN YUN.

Language Research Institute: Dir BONG JOO HWANG.

Educational Research and Development Institute: Dir CHOONG HOE KIM.

Canadian-American Studies Institute: Dir JAE SUK CHOI.

Unification Research Institute: Dir KI-DON CHUNG.

Institute of Environmental Science and Technology: Dir MOO YOUNG SONG.

Research Institute of Biological Engineering: Dir SANG GI PAIK.

Paekche Research Institute: Dir JOO TACK SEONG.

Industrial Education Research Centre: Dir TAE KYUN KIM.

Humanities Research Institute: Dir JAI YOUNG SONG.

Natural Sciences Research Institute: Dir YOUN DOO KIM.

Institute of Medicine Development: Dir GYE JU LEE.

Institute of Management and Economics: Dir SEUNG EUI PARK.

Industrial Technology Research Institute: Dir TAIK KEE KIM.

Institute of Law: KEUN RYUK CHOI.

Institute of Agricultural Science and Technology: Dir JAE CHANG LEE.

Institute of Community Medicine: Dir KIL CHUN KANG.

Research Institute of Physical Education and Sports Science: Dir Prof. SEONG-PYO HONG.

Research Institute of Home Economics: Dir JAE SOOK KIM.

Community Development Research Institute: BYANG GI AHN.

Co-operative Cancer Research Institute: KI SUB SON.

Institute of Social Science: YEONG SEONG KIM.

Art-Culture Research Institute: OUN MO SHIN.

DAN KOOK UNIVERSITY

San 8 Hannam-dong, Yongsan-gu, Seoul

Telephone: (797) 0581

Founded 1947, university status 1967
Private control
Language of instruction: Korean
Academic year: March to February

Chancellor: CHOONG-SIK CHANG
Vice-Chancellor: SUK-HA KIM
Registrar: YONG-WOO LEE

Library of 140,000 vols
Number of teachers: 321
Number of students: 13,557

Publications: Reviews, *Dan Won*.

DEANS

College of Liberal Arts and Science: MOON-SUP CHA
College of Law: YOO-HYUK KIM
College of Commerce and Economics: HAENG-XUH KIM
College of Engineering: MYUNG-WON KO
College of Education: SEUNG-KOOK KIM

HEADS OF DEPARTMENTS

Seoul Campus

College of Liberal Arts and Sciences:
Korean and Korean Literature: SUN-MOOK YIM
English and English Literature: TAE-JU LEE
Chinese and Chinese Literature: YOUNG-ZAI CHI
German and German Literature: SUNG-DAE KIM
Japanese and Japanese Literature: MUN-KI HUR
History: NAE-HYUN YOON
Counting and Statistics: GANG-SUP LEE
Chemistry: CHANG-BAE KIM
Food and Nutrition: SOON-JA CHUNG
Pottery Arts: BOO-WOONG LEE

College of Law and Political Science:
Law: DONG-SUB AHN
Administration: DONG-SHIM KEUM
Political Science: TAE-HOON KANG
Regional Development: KI-YONG HONG

College of Commerce and Economics:
Economics: DONG-UN PARK
Foreign Trade: SI-KYUNG KIM
Management: KWANG-JU LEE
Accounting: SEUNG-HIE KOH

College of Engineering:
Architectural Engineering: JUNG-SHIN KIM
Civil Engineering: KIL-CHOUM LEE
Mechanical Engineering: HIE-SONG KIM
Electrical Engineering: SEUK-YONG HWANG
Electronic Engineering: YEON-KANG JIN
Chemical Engineering: IL-HYUN JUNG
Textile Engineering: KANG JOO

College of Education:
Sino-Korean Education: CHUN-GUY PARK
Special Education: DO-SU KIM
Mathematics Education: YOUNG-SIK CHANG
Science Education: MOON-NAM LEE
Music Education: JOUNG-MON KOH
Physical Education: TAE-KYUN YOO

Cheonan Campus

College of Humanities and Science:
Korean and Korean Literature: MIN-YOUNG YOO
English and English Literature: YONG-HOON LEE
German and German Literature: CHA-SIK SHIN
French and French Literature: SUNG-GYU BOK
Chinese and Chinese Literature: TAE-HOON LEE
Spanish and Spanish Literature: HAE-SUN KOH
History: IL-BEOM SHIN
Industrial Arts: MYUNG-HYUNG CHO

College of Social Science:
Law: YONG-WOO KWOM
Administration: SOO-YOUNG KIM
Economics: BYUNG-SUP KWAK
Foreign Trade: BYUNG-JIN AHN
Management: DOO-HYU SHIN
Accounting: YONG-GI CHUN

College of Science and Engineering:
Applied Physics: SUNG-WON CHOI
Chemistry: IL KIM
Biology: KYEONG-SOOK LEE
Mathematics: SONG-KI CHUN
Agriculture: JAE-CHUN CHE
Agricultural Economics: DONG-HI KIM
Architectural Engineering: MOO-UNG CHUNG
Civil Engineering: YONG-KI CHA
Mineral and Petroleum Engineering: MYUNG-SUN GONG
Electronic Engineering: KUANG-JUN WOO
Industrial Chemistry: SEUNG-JAE CHOI
Physical Education: JONG-HAN OH

College of Dentistry:
Dentistry: KYEONG-UK KIM

ATTACHED INSTITUTES

Institute of Saemaul Studies: Dir Dr YOO-HYUK KIM.

Institute of Oriental Studies: Dir Dr PAE-KANG HWANG.

Industrial Research Institute: Dir Dr HE-CHEOL LIM.

Chinese Studies Institute: Dir Dr YOUNG-CHOON HAN.

Folk Arts Institute: Dir Dr JOO-SUN SUK.

Institute of Technological Research: Dir JEONG-RYEON HAN.

Statistics Studies Institute: Dir Dr HYUNG-BO KIM.

Institute of Anglo-American Studies: Dir Dr DAUK-RYONG KONG.

DONG-A UNIVERSITY

840, Hadan 2-dong, Saha-gu, Pusan 604-714
Telephone: (51) 200-6114

Founded 1946
Private control
Language of instruction: Korean
Academic year: March to February

President: TAE-IL LEE
Vice-President: BYUNG-TAE CHO
Head of Secretariat: YEONG-GI LEE
Dean of Academic Affairs: CHANG-OCK CHOI
Dean of Student Affairs: DAE-KYU LEE
Dean of Financial Affairs: YOON-SIK HWANG
Dean of Research: SOON-KYU CHOI
Dean of Administration: LI-KYOO KIM
Director of Library: KUN-BAE HAHN

Library of 582,134 vols
Number of professors: 513
Number of students: 17,217

Publications: faculty journals and bulletins, *General Culture Series* (2 a year).

DEANS

Graduate School: WOONG-DAL RYOO
Graduate School of Business Administration: YONG-DAE KIM
Graduate School of Education: CHONG-IL TCHOI
Graduate School of Industry: KUN-MO HAN
Graduate School of Mass Communication: MIN-NAM KIM
College of Humanities: SANG-BAK CHUNG
College of Natural Sciences: TAE-SEOP UHM
College of Law: MAN-HEE JEONG
College of Social Sciences: KWANG-SUK SUL
College of Business Administration: TAE-YOON JUN
College of Agriculture: DAE-SOO CHUNG
College of Engineering: CHUN-KEUN PARK
College of Physical Education: CHEOL-HO PARK
College of Arts: SOO-CHUL PARK
College of Human Ecology: SEOK-HWAN KIM
College of Medicine: DUCK-HWAN CHUNG

DIRECTORS

Agricultural Resources Research Institute: YOUNG-KIL KIM
Institute of Korean Resources Development: SUNG-GYO CHUNG
Environmental Problems Research Institute: JANG-HO KIM
Business Management Research Institute: SEONG-HWAN KIM
Sokdang Academic Research Institute of Korean Culture: HYENG-JU KIM
Social Science Research Institute: JAE-GYONG KIM
Population Research Centre: SOON CHOI
Language Research Institute: CHI-GUN HA
Research Institute of Sports Science: YOUNG-PIL AN
German Studies Institute: SANG-UG RHIE
Institute for the Study of Law: SANG-HO KIM
Basic Science Research Institute: WAN-SE KIM
Ocean Resources Research Institute: JIN-HOO KIM
Research Institute for Genetic Engineering: CHUNG-HAN CHUNG
MIS Research Institute: KAY-SEOB HAN
Research Institute for Humanities: YOUNG-DO CHUNG
Research Institute for Human Ecology: EUN-JOO PARK
Tourism and Leisure Research Institute: YUNG-MYUN AHN
Industrial Technology Research Centre: TAE-OK JUN
Institute of Data Communication: CHANG-HI HONG
Plastic Arts Rresearch Institute: SUNG-DO BACK
Life Science Research Institute: YONG-CHUN CHOI
Industrial Medicine Research Institute: JUNG-MAN KIM
Research Institute for Clinical Medicine: JEONG-MAN KIM

DONGDUCK WOMEN'S UNIVERSITY

23-1 Wolgok-dong, Sungbuk-ku, Seoul 136-714
Telephone: (2) 940-4000
Fax: (2) 940-4182

Founded 1950
Private control
Language of Instruction: Korean
Academic Year: March to February (2 semesters)

Chancellor: WON-YOUNG CHO
Vice-Chancellor: YOUNG-YON YOON
Registrar: DO-SEOK CHANG
Librarian: YOON-SIK KIM

Library of 232,000 vols
Number of teachers: 154
Number of students: 6,155

Publications: *Journal of Dongduck Women's University, Dongduk News Letter* (2 a year), Treatise (annually), *Dongduck Women's Newspaper* (weekly).

DEANS

College of Humanities: SANG-GI CHO
College of Social Sciences: SAE-YOUNG OH
College of Natural Sciences: SANG-SOON LEE
College of Computer and Information Sciences: YANG-HEE LEE
College of Pharmacy: IN-KOO CHUN
College of Arts: SUN-BAEK JANG
College of Design: DONG-JO KOO
College of Performing Arts: (vacant)
General Studies and Teaching Profession Division: HONG-TAE PARK

ATTACHED RESEARCH INSTITUTES

Research Institute for Humanities: Dir DOK-BONG LEE.

Industrial Research Institute: Dir YOON-SUNG LIM.

Research Institute for Life Sciences: Dir NAM-HEE WOO.

Central Pharmaceutical Research Institute: Dir HYO-JIN KIM.

Design Research Institute: Dir CHEOL-WOONG SIM.

DONGGUK UNIVERSITY

26 3-ga, Pil-dong, Chung-gu, Seoul
Telephone: 260-3114
Fax: 277-1274

Founded 1906, university status 1953
Private control

President: Dr BYUNG CHUN MINN
Librarian: Dr BO HWAN KIM

Library: see Libraries
Number of teachers: 500
Number of students: 16,050

Publications: *Dongguk Shinmun* (weekly), *Dongguk Post* (monthly), *Pulgyo Hakpo* (Journal of Buddhist Studies), *Dongguk Journal*, *Dongguk Sasang* (Dongguk Thought), and 20 others.

Colleges of Buddhism, liberal arts and sciences, law and political science, economics and commerce, agriculture and forestry, engineering, education, medical science; graduate school, graduate school of public administration, graduate school of business administration, graduate school of education, graduate school of information industry; colleges on Kyongju Campus.

Research Institutes: Buddhist culture, comparative literature, statistical science, law and political science, business management, agriculture and forestry, overseas development, national security, computer, Middle Eastern and East European affairs, Korean studies, Saemaul research, landscape art, industrial technology, translation of Buddhist scriptures.

DUKSUNG WOMEN'S UNIVERSITY

419 Ssangmoon-dong, Dobong-gu, Seoul 132–714
Telephone: 901-8114
Fax: 902-8125

Founded 1950
Private control
Language of instruction: Korean
Academic year: March to February

President: YONG-NAE KIM
Registrar: SOOK-JA LIM
Librarian: YOUNG-HWAN CHUNG

Library of 328,000 vols
Number of teachers: 148 full-time, 162 part-time
Number of students: 5,250

Publications: *Duksung Women's University Journal, Geunmack* (annually), *Duksung Women's University Newsletter* (24 a year), *Duksung Women's University Newsletter.*

DEANS

College of Humanities: JUNG-BOON YOON
College of Society Sciences: SUNG-CHUL KIM
College of Natural Science: SUK-IM YOON
College of Pharmacy: KI-HWA JUNG
College of Fine Arts: AIE-YUNG KIM

EWHA WOMAN'S UNIVERSITY

11–1 Daehyun-dong, Sodaemun-gu, Seoul 120-750
Telephone: (2) 360-2114
Fax: (2) 393-5903

Founded 1886
Languages of instruction: Korean and English
Academic year: March to February (two semesters)

Chancellor: Dr II-SOOK CHUNG
President: Dr SANG CHANG
Librarian: BONG-HEE KIM

Library: see Libraries
Number of teachers: 692
Number of students: 21,436

Publications: *Ewha Voice* (monthly, in English), *Edae Hakbo* (weekly, in Korean), *Ewha News* (monthly, in Korean).

DEANS

Graduate School: Dr KIHO LEE
Graduate School of Education: Dr SOON-JA KANG
Graduate School of Design: Dr KYUNG-JA LEE
Graduate School of Social Welfare: Dr CHUNG-SOOK LEE
Graduate School of Information Science: Dr SUK-JOON KIM
Graduate School of International Studies: JANG-HEE YOO
Graduate School of Translation and Interpretation: CHIE-SOU KIM
Graduate School of Theology: Dr SEUNG-HEE SOHN
Graduate School of Policy Sciences: Dr SOO-YOUNG AUH
College of Liberal Arts: Dr CHIE-SOU KIM
College of Social Sciences: Dr SOO-YOUNG UH
College of Natural Sciences: Dr SUNG-KU KIM
College of Engineering: Dr YOON-KYOO JHEE
College of Music: Prof. HAE-WON CHANG
College of Arts and Design: Prof. HEE-YOUNG RUE
College of Physical Education: Dr SOOK-JA KIM
College of Education: Dr YOUNG-SOO KIM
College of Law: Dr JAE-SANG LEE
College of Business Administration: Prof. BOO-GILL HONG
College of Medicine: Dr YOUNG-SOOK PAE
College of Nursing: Dr KYUNG-HYE LEE
College of Pharmacy: Dr KIL-SOO KIM
College of Home Science and Management: Dr SOOK-JAE MOON
Institute of Continuing Education: Prof. BOO-GILL HONG

ATTACHED RESEARCH INSTITUTES

Korean Cultural Research Institute: Dr HYONG-SIK SHIN
Korean Women's Institute: Dr SANG-WHA LEE
Asian Center for Women's Studies: Dr PILWHA CHANG
Asian Food and Nutrition Research Institute: Dr KWANG-OK KIM
Environmental Research Institute: Dr SEOK-SOON PARK
Research Institute of Life Sciences: Dr GIL-JA JHON
Research Institute for Basic Sciences: Dr JUNE-SEUNG LEE
Research Institute for Genetic Engineering: Dr GIL-JA JHON
Ewha Colour and Design Research Institute: Dr KYUNG-JA LEE
Institute of Information and Communication: Dr KIHO LEE
Institute of International Trade and Co-operation: Dr JANG-HEE YOO
Korean Language and Literature Research Institute: Dr HAI-SOON LEE
Ewha Historical Research Center: Dr BAE-YONG LEE
Institute for Semiotic Studies: Dr YONG-SOOK KIM
Ewha Institute for Women's Theological Studies: Dr KYUNG-SOOK LEE
Research Institute of Natural History: Dr KYU-HAN KIM
Institute of Mathematical Sciences: Dr DONG-SUN SHIN
Ewha Center of Engineering Research: Dr DONG-SUB CHO
Music Institute: Prof. HAE-WON CHANG
Ceramic Research Institute: Dr SUK-YOUNG KANG
Research Institute of Movement Science: Dr SOOK-JA KIM
Research Institute for Education Science: Dr YOUN-SOON CHO
Research Institute of Curriculum Instruction: Dr YOUNG-HA LEE
Management Research Center: Dr KUN-HEE LEE
Nursing Research Center: Dr SUSIE KIM
Research Institute of Pharmaceutical Science: Dr MYUNG-EUN SUH
Medical Research Center: Dr JANG-HYUN CHUNG
Human Ecology and Environmental Institute: Dr SOOK-JAE MOON
Ewha Legal Science Institute: Prof. BYONG-WOOK CHOI

HANKUK UNIVERSITY OF FOREIGN STUDIES

270 Imun-dong, Dongdaemun-gu, Seoul
Telephone: 965-7001

Founded 1954
Private control

President: Prof. BYUNG TAI HWANG
Dean of Academic Affairs: Prof. SUNG RAE PAK
Dean of Student Affairs: Prof. CHANG BOK LEE
Chief Administration Officer: SEOK JOO YOON
Librarian: Prof. KYU CHUL CHO

Library of 303,900 vols
Number of teachers: 292
Number of students: 12,838

Publications: *Oe-Dae Hakbo* (weekly, Korean), *Argus* (monthly, English and other foreign languages), *Journal* (annually).

DEANS

Graduate School: Prof. JOUNG YOLE REW
Graduate School of International Trade: Prof. HEE JOON LEE
Graduate School of Interpretation and Translation: Prof. I BAE KIM
Graduate School of Education: Prof. JIN KWON RHIM
Graduate School of Management Information Systems: Prof. JAE SEOK JUNG
College of Occidental Languages: Prof. YOUNG GUL LEE
College of Oriental Languages: Prof. KI IOB CHUNG
College of Law and Political Science: Prof. DEOK KIM
College of Trade and Economics: Prof. HEE JOON LEE
College of Education: Prof. HAN-JIN OH
College of Liberal Arts and Sciences: Prof. JIK HYUN KIM
Academic and Student Affairs (Evening Courses): Prof. DUCK YONG WOO
College of Foreign Languages: Prof. JONG SOO CHOI
College of Social Sciences: Prof. BYUNG HO PARK

DIRECTORS

Audio-Visual Education Institute: Prof. SOON-HAM PARK
Foreign Language Training and Research Centre: Prof. JAI MIN KIM
Institute for Research in Languages and Linguistics: Prof. SEONG JOON REW
Research Institute for Economics and Business Administration: Prof. BYUNG KWOON MIN
Chinese Studies Institute: Prof. KWAN-JANG CHOI
Russian and East European Institute: Prof. KYU WHA CHO
Institute of Latin-American Studies: Prof. MAN SHIK MIN
Institute of the Middle East: Prof. SOON NAM HONG
Institute of African Studies: Prof. WON TAK PARK
Institute of Korean Regional Studies: Prof. BYONG MAN AHN
Institute of International Communication: Prof. JONG KI KIM
Institute of History: Prof. SUNG RAE PAK

Institute of Foreign Language Studies: Prof. YOUNG JO KIM
Institute of Humanities: Prof. SUNG WI KANG
Student Guidance Center: Prof. JONG GEON YOON
Interpretation and Translation Center: Prof. I-BAE KIM

HANYANG UNIVERSITY

17 Haengdang-dong, Sungdong-gu, Seoul 133
Telephone: 292-2111, 292-3111
Founded 1939 as Hanyang Institute of Technology; present status 1959
Private control
Academic year: March to July, September to December

President: Dr PYUNG HEE LEE
Academic Dean: Dr HAINAM LEE
Library of 350,000 vols
Number of teachers: *c.* 950
Number of students: *c.* 27,000

Publications: *Hanyang Nonmun Dzip, Journal of Economic Studies, Sino-Soviet Affairs, Journal of Korean Studies, Journal of Student Guidance Research,* and numerous others.

Colleges of engineering (including architectural engineering), liberal arts and sciences (including journalism and cinema), commerce and economics, law and political science, music, physical education, education, medicine; evening engineering college; graduate school, graduate school of industrial management.

HONG-IK UNIVERSITY

72–1 Sangsu-dong, Mapo-gu, Seoul 121-791
Telephone: (2) 320-1114
Fax: (2) 320-1122
Founded 1946
Private control
Language of instruction: Korean
Academic year: March to June, September to December

President: Dr MYEON YOUNG LEE
Vice-President for Academic Affairs: SANG PIL SHIM
Vice-President for General Affairs: DO YOL KANG
Librarian: DONG SUK KIM
Library of 1,010,000 vols
Number of teachers: 423 full-time, 390 part-time
Number of students: 15,351

Publications: *Hong-Ik University Journal* (annually), *Hong-Ik Economic Review* (annually), *Journal of Student Life* (annually), *Management Review* (annually), *Papers on the Study of Education* (annually).

DEANS

College of Engineering: WON BOK LEE
College of Business Administration: KUN HO KIM
College of Fine Arts: SEUNG WON SUH
College of Education: HIE JUN BYUN
College of Liberal Arts: BYUNG GUI JANG
College of Law and Economics: YOON HYUNG JUNG
College of Business Management: IL CHOO CHUNG
College of Science and Technology: YOON HEE HAN
College of Visual Arts: KEUN JAE OH
Graduate School: DO KEUN YOON
Graduate School of Industrial Arts: HYUNG CHEOL PARK
Graduate School of Architecture and Urban Design: EON KON PARK
Graduate School of Education: SHIN UNG KANG
Graduate School of Industrial Technology: SEUNG EUI NAM
Graduate School of Information: YOO HUN WON
Graduate School of International Business Administration: CHAE KYU HAG
Graduate School of Tax Studies: BUM HO PARK
Graduate School of Industry: HEE GU KIM
Graduate School of Educational Management: CHUNG WHA SUH
Graduate School of Public Relations: MYUNG KWANG KWON

ATTACHED INSTITUTES

Environmental Development Institute.
Research Institute of Business Administration.
Institute of Economic Research.
Educational Research Institute.
Research Institute of Eastern and Western Cultures.
Research Center of Ceramic Art.
Research Institute for Science and Technology.
Research Institute of Modern Plastic Arts.
Research Institute of Industrial Design.
Research Institute of Law.
Research Institute of Industrial Technology.
Research Institute of Humanities.
Tribology Research Institute.
North-East Asia Research Institute.

INHA UNIVERSITY

253 Yonghyn-dong, Nam-gu, Inchon
Telephone: (32) 860-7114
Fax: (32) 863-1333
Founded 1954
Private control
Academic year: March to February

President: Dr SUNG-OK CHO
Vice-President: Dr BYUNG-HA CHOI
Registrar: Dr CHONG-BO KIM
Librarian: Dr MYUNG-KOO YUN
Library of 350,000 vols
Number of teachers: 471
Number of students: 21,233

Publications: bulletins of the research institutes.

DEANS

Graduate School: Dr JI-HOON CHOI
Graduate School of Business Administration: Dr YONG-HWI SHINN
Graduate School of Education: Dr KI-HO CHUNG
Graduate School of Engineering: Dr DONG-IL KIM
Graduate School of Public Administration: Dr YOUNG-SANG SHIN
Engineering: Dr BYUNG-HEE KANG
Natural Sciences: Dr DAE-YOON PARK
Business and Economics: Dr KI-MYUNG KIM
Education: Dr CHANG-GEOL KIM
Law and Political Science: Dr YOUNG-HEE LEE
Humanities: Dr WOO-JIN KIM
Home Economics: (vacant)
Medicine: Dr SEH-HWAN KIM

ATTACHED RESEARCH INSTITUTES

Aviation Management Research Institute: Dir Dr YOUNG-SIK HONG.
Basic Science Research Institute: Dir Dr SUH-YUNG YANG.
Center for International Studies: Dir Dr BYUNG-WON PARK.
Center for Korean Studies: Dir Dr PYONG-SUK YUN.
Environmental Research Institute: Dir Dr KWANG-MYEUNG CHO.
Humanities Research Institute: Dir Dr MOON-CHANG KIM.
Institute for Business and Economic Research: Dir Dr DAE-HWAN KIM.
Institute for Information and Electronics Research: Dir Dr SEUNG-HONG HONG.
Institute of Advanced Materials: Dir Dr WON-KOO PARK.
Institute of Computer Science and Applications: Dir Dr CHANG-JONG WANG.
Institute of Polymer Science and Engineering: Dir Dr DONG-CHOO LEE.
Management Research Institute: Dir Dr MYUNG-SUP CHUN.
Medicinal Toxicology Research Institute: Dir Dr YONG-NAM CHA.
Ocean Science and Technology Institute: Dir Dr YONG-CHUL LEE.
Science and Technology Research Institute: Dir Dr BONG-GOO WOO.
Social Science Research Institute: Dir Dr YONG-WOO KIM.
Sports Science Research Institute: Dir Dr YOUNG-JUN HA.
Student Life Research Institute: Dir Dr YOUNG-SOO JUNG.
Education Research Institute: Dir Dr HEUNG-KYU KIM.
Domestic Science Research Institute: Dir Dr CHAN-BOO PARK.

KANGWEON NATIONAL UNIVERSITY

192-1 Hyoja-dong, Chuncheon 200, Kangweon-do
Telephone: (361) 53-9000
Founded 1947

President: SANG-JOO LEE
Registrar: HYUNG-SIK LIM
Librarian: KYUNG-HO PARK
Library of 206,000 vols
Number of teachers: 378
Number of students: 16,000

DEANS

College of Business Administration: JONG-SEOP SHIM
College of Engineering: JE-SEON PARK
College of Agriculture: SANG-YOUNG LEE
College of Law: JEUNG-HU KIM
College of Education: KEUN-SEONG CHOI
College of Humanities and Social Science: HAN-SEOL PARK
College of Forestry: SU-CHANG KIM
College of Natural Sciences: CHONG-HYEOK LEE

KEIMYUNG UNIVERSITY

1000 Shindang-dong, Dalseo-Gu, Taegu, 704-701
Telephone: (53) 581-4142
Fax: (53) 580-5454
Founded 1954
Private control
Academic year: March to February

President: SYNN ILHI
Vice-President: PAEK SEUNG KYUN
Dean of Academic Affairs: NAM SEUK
Dean of Dongsan Library: CHUNG MAN DUK
Library of 1,000,000 vols
Number of teachers: 600 full-time, 500 part-time
Number of students: 22,848

Publications: *Journal of the Institute for Cross-Cultural Studies, Business Management Review, Journal of Educational Research, Bulletin of the Institute for Industrial Science, Proceedings of Mathematical Science, Journal of the Institute of Natural Sciences, Journal of Social Sciences, Journal of Art and Culture, Keimyung Theology, Journal of Communication Research, Keimyung Journal of Behavioral Sciences, Keimyung University Medical Journal, Journal of Language Stu-*

dies, Journal of International Studies, Keimyung Law Review, Keimyung Philosophy, Accounting Information Review.

DEANS

College of Fine Arts: KIM YOUNG TAE
College of Business Administration: KIM YOUNG KUN
College of Engineering: SHIN SUNG HEON
College of Environmental Science and Technology: LEE SUNG HO
College of Home Economics: EUN YOUNG JA
College of Humanities: KIM JONG SUN
College of International Studies and Commerce: YEU PARK DONG
College of Law: KIM HAE RYOUNG
College of Medicine: CHEUN JAE KYU
College of Music: KIM JEONG GIL
College of Natural Sciences: CHANG SUK HWAN
College of Nursing: PARK JEONG SOOK
College of Physical Education: LEE SOON CHEON
College of Social Sciences: PARK KYUNG KU
Teacher-Training College: PARK A. CHUNG
College for Evening Programs: KIM NAM SEUK

ATTACHED INSTITUTES

Research Institute for the Humanities: YOM SYNG SUP.

Institute for International Studies: HWANG CHIN.

Research Institute for Social Science: CHO YONG SANG.

Institute of Industrial Management Research: CHO BONG JIN.

Research Institute for Natural Sciences: UHM JAE KOOK.

Research Institute for Industrial Technology: SHIN SUNG HEON.

Research Institute for the Arts: LIM HAE JA.

Research Institute of Life Sciences: PARK HYE IN.

Research Institute for Medical Science: CHOE BYUNG KIL.

Research Institute for Medical Heredity: KANG CHIN MOO.

Research Institute for Nursing Science: PARK JEONG SOOK.

KON-KUK UNIVERSITY

93–1 Mojin-dong, Kwanjn-gu, Seoul 143-701
Telephone: (2) 450-3259
Fax: (2) 452-3257

Founded 1946, university status 1959
Private control
Academic year: March to February

President: HYOUNG-SUP YOON
Vice-Presidents: SUNG-WHA HONG (Seoul Campus), MYUNG-CHAN HWANG (Chungju Campus)
Registrar: HYEON-LYONG KIM
Librarian: YUNG-KWON KIM

Library of 558,000 vols
Number of teachers: 587 (full time)
Number of students: 17,177

Publications: *Newspaper* (weekly), *English Newspaper* (monthly).

ACADEMIC DEANS

Graduate School: JAE-UNG KO
Graduate School of Public Administration: WON-JOON LEE
Graduate School of Education: JEONG-KYU KIM
Graduate School of Engineering: TAE-JONG KWON
Graduate School of Business Administration: SHI-CHEON KOH
Graduate School of Agriculture and Animal Science: HWA-JEONG YOON
Graduate School of Social Sciences: JAE-WOO KIM
Graduate School of Architecture: KYUNG-JAE JOO
Graduate School of Mass Communication: BOK-RYONG SHN
College of Liberal Arts: YONG-NAM CHO
College of Sciences: HO JOON LEE
College of Engineering: SANG-YONG YI
College of Political Science: BOK-RYONG SHIN
College of Law: BYUNG HUI YANG
College of Commerce and Economics: YONG-DEUK CHO
College of Business Administration: SHI-CHEON KOH
College of Animal Husbandry: JO-CHANG RYOO
College of Agriculture: CHONG-CHON KIM
College of Arts and Home Economics: WON-JA LEE
College of Education: II HWANG
College of Humanities: DONG-SCON KIM
College of Social Sciences: NAM-KOO LEE
College of Natural Sciences: YOON SOO CHUNG
College of Art: KYE-SOO MYUNG
College of Medicine: YE-CHUL LEE

ATTACHED INSTITUTES

Humanities Research Institute
Basic Science Research Institute
Institute of Industrial Science and Technology
Social Science Research Institute
Public Administration Research Institute
Institute of Economics and Management
Animal Resources Research Center
Research Institute of Agricultural Resources Development
Institute of Life Culture
Education Research Institute
Joong Won Research Institute of Humanities
Institute for Social Development and Policy
Research Institute of Natural Science
Arts and Design Research Institute
Research Institute of Medical Sciences
Research Institute of Chinese Affairs
Research Institute of Korean Affairs
Institute of Korean Reunification Studies
Environmental Science Research Institute
Law Research Institute
Center for Real Estate Policy
Research Center for the Korean History of Technology
Research Institute of Korean Politics and Society
Research Institute of Livestock Management and Environmental Economics

KOOKMIN UNIVERSITY

861-1, Chongnung-dong, Songbuk-ku, Seoul 136

Telephone: (2) 914-3141

Founded 1946

President: IL YUNG CHUNG
Dean of Academic Affairs: Prof. KIM YOUNG-JEON
Dean of Student Affairs: Prof. LEE JONG-EUN
Dean of General Affairs: KIL YEONG-BAE
Dean of Planning and Development Affairs: Prof. KANG SIN-DON

Library of *c.* 200,000 vols
Number of teachers: 159 full-time, 211 part-time
Number of students: 7,626

Publications: *Kookmin University Press* (weekly), *Kookmin Tribune* (English, monthly), *Kookmin University Bulletin* (annually), *Theses* (annually), *Journal of Language and Literature, Papers in Chinese Studies, Theses of Korean Studies, Law and Political Review, Economic and Business Administration Review, Theses of Engineering, Design Review, Education Review, Journal of the Scientific Institute, Journal of Sports Science Research.*

DEANS

Graduate School: CHOI HWAN-YOL
Graduate School of Education: CHOI HWAN-YOL
Graduate School of Business Administration: CHOI HWAN-YOL
Graduate School of Public Administration: LEE YOUNG-SUN
College of Liberal Arts: Prof. LEE JUNG-KEE
College of Law and Political Science: LEE YONG-SUN
College of Economics and Business Administration: NAH OH-YOUN
College of Engineering: Prof. YOON TAI-YOON
College of Architecture and Design: Prof. KIM CHUL-SOO
College of Education: SHIN JOONG-SHIK
College of Forestry: KO YUNG-ZU

ATTACHED RESEARCH INSTITUTES

Economic Research Institute.
Institute for Saemaul Undong.
Institute for Korean Studies.
Institute of Language and Literature.
Legal Research Institute.
Institute of Industrial Technology.
Educational Research Institute.
Environmental Design Research Institute.
Myongwon Tea Ceremony Research Institute.
Sports Science Institute.
Basic Science Institute.
Institute for Chinese Studies.
Social Sciences Institute.

KOREA ADVANCED INSTITUTE OF SCIENCE AND TECHNOLOGY (KAIST)

373-1 Kusong-dong, Yusong-ku, Taejon 305-701

Telephone: (42) 869-2441
Fax: (42) 869-2260
E-mail: oir@sorak.kaist.ac.kr

Founded 1981 by merger of Korea Advanced Institute of Science (KAIS) and Korea Institute of Science and Technology (KIST); KIST separated from KAIST 1989; Korea Institute of Technology (KIT) merged with KAIST 1989
State control
Academic year: March to February

President: DUK YONG YOON

KOREA NATIONAL OPEN UNIVERSITY

169 Dongsung-dong, Chongro-ku, Seoul 110-791
Telephone: (2) 7404-114
Fax: (2) 744-5882

Founded 1972
State control
Academic year: March to February

President: Dr WAN-SANG HAN
Registrar: EUI-DONG KIM
Library Director: SUNG-KIH KIM

Library of 300,000 vols
Number of teachers: 112
Number of students: 215,788

Publications: *KNOU Journal*, *Distance Education*, *KNOU Newsletter, KNOU Weekly.*

DEANS

School of Liberal Arts: YONG-HAK LEE
School of Social Science: SOO-SIN KIM
School of Natural Science: HYE-SEON KIM
School of Education: CHONG-SOOK CHOI
School of General Education: YUNG-HO LEE

HEADS OF DEPARTMENTS

Korean: YONG-SHIK YOON
English: DONG-KOOK LEE
Chinese: SEONG-KON KIM
French: YONG-CHOL LEE
Law: NOHYUN KWAK
Public Administration: JI-WON KIM

Economics: KYWON KIM
Business Administration: DONG-HEE CHUNG
Trade: JONG-SUNG KIM
Media Arts and Science: CHUL-JU LEE
Agricultural Science: HYON-WON LEE
Home Economics: YOUNG-JA BAIK
Computer Science: EON-BAI LEE
Education: HWA-TAE CHO
Early Childhood Education: SUN-HEE PARK
Applied Statistics: TAE-RIM LEE
Health Hygienics: SOO-YOUL KWON

ATTACHED INSTITUTES

Institute of Distance Education: Dir SOON-JEONG HONG.

Educational Media Development Centre: Dir DUK-HUN KWAK.

KOREA UNIVERSITY

1, 5-ga, Anam-dong, Sungbuk-gu, Seoul
Telephone: Seoul 94-2641/9, 94-4381/9
Telex: 34138
Fax: 922 5820

Founded 1905, as Posung College
Private control: financed by the Korea-Choongang Educational Foundation
Language of instruction: Korean
Academic year: March to February (two semesters)

President: JIN WOONG KIM (acting)
Dean of Planning and Public Relations: MANN-JANG PARK
Dean of Academic Affairs: CHANG-YIL AHN
Dean of Students: SONG-BOK KIM
Dean of General Affairs: SA-SOON YOUN
Dean of Construction and Facility Management: YOUNG-HYUN PAIK
Librarian: IL-CHUL SHIN

Library: see Libraries
Number of teachers: 627 full-time, 781 part-time
Number of students: 21,685

Publications: *Kodai Shinmoon,* (Korean, weekly), *The Granite Tower* (English, fortnightly), *Gyongyong Shinmoon* (Korean, weekly), *Kodai Moonwha* (Korean, annually), *Phoenix* (bilingual, annually), *Korea University Bulletin* (English, annually), and many other periodicals.

DEANS

College of Agriculture: BEYOUNG-HWA KWACK
College of Business Administration: HIE-JIP KIM
College of Education: IN-JONG YOU
College of Engineering: JONG-HWI HONG
College of Law: HYUNG-BAE KIM
College of Liberal Arts: PONG-HEUM HAN
College of Medicine: SUNG-YONG PARK
College of Political Science and Economics: YONG-BUM CHO
College of Science: SI-JOONG KIM
Graduate School: BONG-WHAN LAU
Graduate School of Business Administration: DONG-KI KIM
Graduate School of Education: SUNG-TAI KIM
Graduate School of Food and Agriculture: HAN-CHUL YANG
Jochiwon Campus:
College of Liberal Arts and Science: JUNG-BAI KIM
College of Economics and Commerce: JUNG-BAI KIM

CHAIRMEN OF DEPARTMENTS

College of Agriculture:

Agricultural Chemistry: SE-YONG LEE
Agricultural Economics: YOUNG-SIK KIM
Agronomy: HYOK-JI KWON
Animal Science: YONG-SUK SON
Food Technology: CHUL-RHEE
Forestry: KI-HYON PAIK
Genetic Engineering: YONG-JIN CHOI
Horticulture: KUEN-WOO PARK
Plant Protection: BYUNG-KOOK HWANG

College of Business Administration:

Business Administration: PHIL-SANG LEE
International Trade: BYUNG-GUK HWANG

College of Education:

Education: KI-HANG WANG
English Language Education: CHONG-KEON KIM
Geography Education: YOUNG-JOON CHOE
History Education: HYUN-KOO KIM
Home Economics: OCK-BOON CHUNG
Korean Language Education: KWANG-SOO SUNG
Mathematics Education: JUNG-SOOK SAKONG
Physical Education: SANG-KYEM KIM

College of Engineering:

Architectural Engineering: DONG-YANG YANG
Chemical Engineering: SUK-IN HONG
Civil Engineering: EUI-SO CHOI
Electrical Engineering: GWI-TAE PARK
Electronic and Computer Engineering: KYUN-HYON TCHAH
Industrial Engineering: SUNG-SHICK KIM
Materials Science: DOK-YOL LEE
Mechanical Engineering: HYO-WHAN CHANG
Metallurgical Engineering: SOOK-IN KWON

College of Law:

Law: CHONG-BOK LEE

College of Liberal Arts:

Chinese Language and Literature: DONG-HYANG LEE
English Language and Literature: KYOUNG-JA PARK
French Language and Literature: SUNG-GI JON
German Language and Literature: SUNG-OCK KIM
History: IN-SUN YU
Japanese Language and Literature: HYUN-GI LEE
Korean Language and Literature: IN-HWAN KIM
Philosophy: CHO-SIK LEE
Psychology: MAHN-YOUNG LEE
Russian Language and Literature: HAK-SOO KIM
Spanish Language and Literature: HYOUNG-NAM NOH
Sociology: HY-SOP LIM

College of Medicine:

Premedical Course: YOUNG-MOO RO
Medicine: BOE-GWUN CHUN
Nursing: PYOUNG-SOOK LEE

College of Political Science and Economics:

Economics: CHANG-HO YOON
Mass Communications: KI-SUN HONG
Political Science and International Relations: HO-JEH LHEE
Statistics: MYUNG-HOE HUH
Public Administration: YOUNG-PYOUNG KIM

College of Science:

Biology: YUN-SHIK KIM
Chemistry: YOUNG-SANG CHOI
Computer Science: CHONG-SUN HWANG
Geology: KWANG-HO PAIK
Mathematics: IN-HO CHO
Physics: JOO-SANG KANG

Jochiwon Campus:

College of Economics and Commerce:

Applied Statistics: YOUNG-KYUN YOO
Business Administration: GYUN-HWA JUNG
International Trade: YOUNG-KYU KIM
Economics: WON-KYU KIM
Public Administration: SI-YUL PYO

College of Liberal Arts and Science:

Chemistry: SAM-ROK KEUM
Chinese Language and Literature: JAE-SOK KONG
English Language and Literature: YU-SONG SOHN
German Language and Literature: YONG-HO YUN
Korean Language and Literature: JONG-TAIK SEO
Mathematics: HI-CHUN EUN
Physics: SUN-UNG KIM
Sociology: TAE-HWAN JUNG

AFFILIATED RESEARCH INSTITUTES

Anglo-American Studies Institute: Dir Prof. CHONG-WHA CHUNG.

Asiatic Research Center: Dir Prof. SUNG-JOO HAN.

Behavioural Science Research Center: Dir Prof. SUNG-CHICK HONG.

Business Management Research Center: Dir Prof. CHUNG JEE.

German Studies Institute: Dir Prof. PONG-HEUM HAN.

Institute of Economic Development: Dir Prof. SANG-KYUNG KWAK.

Institute of Environmental Health: Dir Prof. CHUL-WHAN CHA.

Institute of Industrial Science and Technology: Dir Prof. BYUNG-HOON CHUN.

Institute of Law: Dir Prof. ZAI-WOO SHIM.

Institute of Medico-Legal Affairs: Dir Prof. KOOK-JIN MOON.

Institute of Plastic Reconstruction and Special Surgery: Dir Prof. SE-MIN BAEK.

Institute of Statistics: Dir Prof. JAE-CHANG LEE.

Institute of Tropical Endemic Diseases: Dir Prof. HAN-JONG RIM.

Institute of Viral Diseases: Dir Prof. HO-WANG LEE.

Korea Nutrition Research Institute: Dir Prof. WOO-IK HWANG.

Korean Cultural Research Center: Dir Prof. IL-SIK HONG.

Korean Entomological Institute: Dir Prof. HAK-RYUL KIM.

Labor Education and Research Institute: Dir Prof. TSCHONG-NAE SONG.

Mass Communications Research Institute: Dir Prof. YONG-YOON.

Research Institute of Basic Sciences: Dir Prof. TAE-HWAN CHANG.

Research Institute of Education: Dir Prof. SUK-KEE CHA.

Research Institute for Food Resources: Dir Prof. YONG-KYO KIM.

Research Institute for Sports Science: Dir Prof. BYUNG-KI SUN.

Russian Studies Institute: Dir Prof. HAK-SOON KIM.

Student Guidance Center: Dir Prof. CHANG-YIL AHN.

KYUNG HEE UNIVERSITY

1 Hoiki-dong, Dongdaemun-ku, Seoul 130-701
Telephone: (2) 961-0114
Fax: (2) 966-6452

Founded 1949; renamed 1952
Private control
Academic year: March to December (two terms)

Founder-Chancellor: Dr YOUNG SEEK CHOUE
President: Dr YONG-IL KONG
Vice-Presidents: CHUNG-WON CHOE (Seoul Campus), CHAN-HAN ZOH (Suwon Campus)
Registrars: SEUNG-HEE YOU (Seoul Campus), WON-KYUNG CHO (Suwon Campus)
Librarians: JUNG-IL DOH HWANG (Seoul Campus), JONG HUH (Suwon Campus)

Library of 600,000 vols, separate medical library of 12,000 vols

Number of teachers: 1,200
Number of students: 25,000

Publications: *The University Life* (English, monthly), *The University Weekly* (Korean), *Kohwang* (Korean, annually), *Peace Forum* (English, 2 a year), research bulletins for each college.

DEANS

Seoul Campus

College of Liberal Arts and Sciences: SANG-YUL NAM
College of Law: MYUNG-SUN YUN
College of Political Science and Economics: YUNG-HYON SHIN
College of Education: KYUNG-HEE LEE
College of Medicine: MOON-HO YANG
College of Dentistry: SANG-CHULL LEE
College of Oriental Medicine: BYUNG KEY SONG
College of Pharmacy: CHANG-SOO YOOK
College of Home Economics: YOUNG-JU YOO
College of Music: JEUNG HAUNG EUM
College of Physical Education: KEUN RIM RYOO
Graduate School: YOUNG-SHIK PAIK
Graduate School of Business Administration: KI-AN PARK
Graduate School of Public Administration: BYUNG-MOOK KIM
Graduate School of Education: KEE-SAW PARK
Graduate School of Peace Studies: JAE-SIK SOHN
Graduate School of Journalism and Mass Communication: KYUNG-JA LEE
Graduate School of Physical Science: YOUNG KEUN CHOI
Graduate School of International Judicial Affairs: MYUNG-SUN YUN

Suwon Campus

College of Foreign Languages and Literature: SOOK-JA LEE
College of Social Sciences: KEW-HONG PARK
College of Natural Sciences: JOOK-SIK YANG
College of Engineering: CHOO-HIE LEE
College of Industry: SANG-KEUN CHON
College of Physical Education and Sports: DOO-OK SON
Graduate School of Technology and Information Science: YONG-RAE KIM

CHAIRMEN OF DEPARTMENTS

College of Liberal Arts and Sciences:

Korean Language and Literature: YI-DO PARK
English Language and Literature: SANG-CHEOL AHN
Philosophy: SOO-JUNG KIM
History: SUK-WOO LEE
Biology: HO-KUN RHIE
Geography: SHI-HAK NOH
Physics: YAP KIM
Chemistry: MINSERK CHEONG
Mathematics: CHAN-HOON PARK

College of Law:

Law: KYUNG-SUNG PARK
Public Administration: BYUNG-CHIN KIM

College of Political Science and Economics:

Political Science: SUNG-HYUN BAEK
Mass Communication: DONG-SHIN RHEE
Economics: SEON LEE
Business Administration: KUN-WOO KIM
Trades: CHUL KIM
Accounting: KWON-JOUNG KIM

College of Education:

English Education: SUNG-MYUN HONG
Fine Arts Education: JONG-HAE PARK

College of Home Economics:

Housing, Child and Family Studies: HYE-KYUNG OH
Food and Nutrition: HYUN-SU PARK
Clothing and Textiles: CHOON-SUP HWANG

College of Medicine:

Medicine: TAE-SUNG KIM
Nursing: HYUN-SOOK KANG

College of Oriental Medicine:

Oriental Medicine: CHAN-KUK PARK

College of Dentistry:

Dentistry: KI SOO LEE

College of Pharmacy:

Pharmacy: SE-YOUNG CHOUNG

College of Engineering:

Mechanical Engineering: TAEL-YUL OH
Textile Engineering: YOU HUH
Electronic Engineering: YUN-HAE YEH
Chemical Engineering: CHANG HO PARK
Civil Engineering: ZU-OG AN
Architectural Engineering: SI-CHOON CHUNG
Industrial Engineering: JAI-RIP CHO
Nuclear Engineering: SANG-NYUNG KIM
Computer Engineering: DONG-HO CHO
Radio Science and Technology: IHN-SEOK KIM

College of Industry:

Agronomy: YEONG-DEOK RHO
Forestry: JONG-LAK LEE
Horticulture: GEUN-WON CHOI
Food Processing: UCK-HAN CHUN
Pottery Arts: HEON-GOOK LEE
Landscape Architecture: CHOO-HWAN SEO
Industrial Design: GYU-HYEON KIM

College of Music:

Composition : DONG-HEE WOO
Vocal Music: NAM OK PAIK
Musical Instruments: CHOON-SOO CHUNG

College of Physical Education:

Physical Education: JONG-HEE LEE
Dance: MUNGSOOK PARK

College of Foreign Languages and Literature:

English Language and Literature: SOO-YOUNG CHUN
French Language and Literature: HYE-DONG KIM
Chinese Language and Literature: KWANG-JIN JEON
Japanese Language and Literature: MI-SUN OH
Spanish Language and Literature: HYO-SANG LIM
Russian Language: SANG-YONG PYO

College of Social Sciences:

Public Administration: JONG-HO KIM
Business Administration: HAN-SOO HAN
International Trade: SANG-KYU LEE
Accounting: KWI-JIN HUH
Sociology: IL-SOON CHANG
International Politics: MANHAK KWON

College of Natural Sciences:

Mathematics: SUNG-NAM HA
Physics: HAEYANG CHUNG
Chemistry: HONG-DOO KIM
Environmental Science: TAE-HOE KOO
Genetic Engineering: KWANG-HEE BAEK
Astronomy and Space Science: DONG-HUN LEE

College of Physical Education and Sports:

Physical Education: HYOUNG-DON KIM
Taekwondo: YOUNG-RYAL CHOI

ATTACHED INSTITUTES

Centre for the Reconstruction of Human Society: Dir JONG-IL RA.
Institute of International Peace Studies: Dir JAE-SIK SOHN.
Institute for a Brighter Society: Dir BYUNG-KON HWANG.
Research Centre for Land Development: Dir YONG-HYUN KIL.
Research Institute of Educational Affairs: Dir MI-SOP SONG.
Kyung Hee Language Institute: Dir BYUNG-SOO PARK.
Research Institute of Social Science: Dir MYUNG-SIK LEE.
East-West Pharmaceutical Research Institute: Dir YOUNG SOO RHO.
Institute of Genetic Engineering: Dir TAE-RYONG HAHN.
Korean Institute of Ornithological Studies: Dir JEONCHIL YOO.
Research Institute of Physical Education: Dir YOUNG-KEUN CHOI.
Institute of Industrial Relations: Dir KI-AN PARK.
Kyung Hee Institute of Legal Studies: Dir BYUNG-MOOK KIM.
Research Centre for Student Life: Dir CHONG-KYU KIM.
Research Institute for Basic Science: Dir BOK-KEUN CHUNG.
Institute of Architecture and Urban Studies: Dir CHANG-HAN CHO.
Institute of Korean Classical Medicine: Dir WON-SEEK HONG.
Institute of Archaeology and Art History: Dir BYUNG-IK SOH.
Institute of Korean Political Studies: Dir BYUNG-KEY SONG.
Institute of Oral Biology: Dir HAN-GUK CHO.
Institute of Campus Development: Dir BYUNG-IK SO.
Institute of Landscape Architecture: Dir BONG-WON AHN.
Institute of Materials Science and Technology: Dir YOUNG-NAM PAIK.
Communication Research Institute: Dir KWANG-JAE LEE.
Institute of Korean Culture: Dir TAE-YEONG KIM.
Institute of Food Development: Dir JAE-SUN JO.
Solar Energy Research Institute: Dir HYUN-CHAE JUNG.
Institute for Laser Engineering: CHOO-HIE LEE.
Institute of Folklore: Dir MI-WON LEE.
Research Institute for East-West Medicine: Dir HWAN-JO SUH.
Kyung Hee Institute of Economic Research: Dir MYUNG-KWANG PARK.
Center for Asian Pacific Studies: Dir DAL-HYUN KIM.
Kyung Hee Research Institute of Public Affairs: YUN-HO PARK.
Institute of Hazardous Substances: Dir HYUNG-SUK KIM.
Research Institute for Endocrinology: Dir YOUNG-KIL CHOI.
Business Management Research Institute: Dir SUNG-SOO KIM.
Telematic Systems Engineering Research Institute: Dir YONG-WOOK JIN.
Research Institute for Taekwondo: Dir KYUNG-JI KIM.
Institute for Information Society Studies: Dir KYU-HONG PARK.

KYUNGNAM UNIVERSITY

449 Wolyoung-dong, Masan, Kyungnam 631-701

Telephone: (551) 45-5000
Fax: (551) 46-6184

Founded 1946
Private control

President: Dr JAE KYU PARK
Registrar: Dr JAE IN YANG
Librarian: Dr DOCK JOUNG YOUN
Library of 537,887 vols

Number of teachers: 674
Number of students: 13,070

DEANS

College of Arts: Dr JIN KI CHO
College of Science: Dr SUE DAE LEE
College of Education: Dr SEOK ZOO LEE
College of Engineering: Dr SOO HEUM LEE
College of Law and Political Science: Dr KYUNG SIK RA
College of Business Administration: Dr HYUN WOOK KOH
Graduate School: Dr CHOONG KYUN CHONG

KYUNGPOOK NATIONAL UNIVERSITY

1370 Sankyuk-dong, Puk-ku, Taegu 702–701
Telephone: (53) 950-6823
Fax: (53) 950-5099
E-mail: jhryu@bh.kyungpook.ac.kr

Founded 1952
State control
Academic year: March to February (two semesters)

President: CHAN-SUK PARK
Dean of Academic Affairs: WOO-CHURL PARK
Dean of Student Affairs: HAN-DONG BAE
Dean of Planning and Research Support: DUCK-KYU PARK
Dean of General Affairs: SUNG-DUCK KIM

Library: see Libraries
Number of teachers: 816
Number of students: 20,465

Publications: *Research Review* (1 a year), and various school and college publs.

DEANS

Graduate School: BYUNG-HYOO LEE
Graduate School of Agricultural Development: KIL-UNG KIM
Graduate School of Education: JAE-KUL KOH
Graduate School of Business Administration: YOUNG-HO KIM
Graduate School of Public Health: MIN-HAE YEH
Graduate School of Public Administration: JONG-HWA PARK
Graduate School of International Studies: JOOK-NAM EUN
College of Law: JONG-HWA PARK
College of Economics and Commerce: YOUNG-HO KIM
College of Social Sciences: YANG-CHOON PARK
College of Natural Sciences: YU-CHUL PARK
College of Engineering: SANG-CHUL SIM
College of Humanities: JOOK-NAM EUN
College of Agriculture: KIL-UNG KIM
Teachers' College: JAE-KUL KOH
School of Medicine: MIN-HAE YEH
School of Dentistry: KEANG-HUN JO
College of Music and Visual Arts: HAE-CHANG OH
College of Veterinary Medicine: IN-HO JANG
College of Human Ecology: HYE-SUNG LEE

PROFESSORS

College of Humanities:

CHEON, K.-S., Korean Syntax
CHO, M.-H., British and American Drama
CHOI, S.-S., German Literature, Classic Literature
CHOY, C.-H., Korean History
CHUNG, I.-S., Chinese Linguistics
CHUNG, J. S., English Linguistics, Syntax
EUN, J.-N., Modern Anglo-American Literature
HA, Y.-S., Western Philosophy
HAN, S.-Z., German Literature
HONG, S.-M., Korean Linguistics
HUH, Y., British and American Drama
HWANG, W.-Z., Korean Literature
JEONG, C., Korean Linguistics
JU, B.-D., Korean History
KIM, C.-G., Western History
KIM, C.-S., British Poetry
KIM, D.-M., Oriental Philosophy
KIM, H.-C., English Linguistics
KIM, I.-L., Korean Classical Literature
KIM, K.-C., English Linguistics
KIM, K.-S., Korean Classical Literature
KIM, S.-W., Korean Chinese Literature
KIM, Y.-K., Western Philosophy
KWON, G.-H., Modern Korean Literature
KWON, Y.-U., Korean History
LEE, C.-S., Chinese Literature
LEE, C.-S., Modern German Literature
LEE, D.-H., German Literature
LEE, H.-J., Chinese Literature
LEE, K.-J., German Idealism
LEE, M.-H., Western Philosophy
LEE, O.-B., Social Education
LEE, S.-G., Korean Dialectology
LEE, W.-K., English Literature
MOON, K. H., Korean History
PAEK, D.-H., Korean Philology
PAK, Y.-S., English Linguistics
PARK, C.-B., English Literature
PARK, J.-G., French Literature
PARK, S.-W., German Linguistics
SHIN, O.-H., Western Philosophy
YI, B.-K., Bronze Age Archaeology, Museology
YI, K.-S., Chinese History
YOO, K.-R., Modern Korean Literature
YOO, K.-S., Western History

College of Social Sciences:

CHIN, S.-M., Industrial Sociology
CHO, H.-C., Counselling Psychology
CHOE, D.-H., Library Materials Organization
CHOI, C.-M., Social Welfare Administration
HAN, N.-J., Sociology of Family
KIM, J.-H., Ethics and Legal Studies in Mass Communication
KIM, W.-G., Geomorphology and Applications
KIM, W.-H., International Relations
KIM, W.-T., Political Theory
KIM, Y.-H., Clinical Psychology
KWON, K.-S., Sociology of Religion
LEE, B.-G., Climatology, Environmental Science
LEE, Y.-J., Information Science
LEE, Y.-W., Comparative Politics
NOH, D.-I., Korean Politics
PARK, J.-S., Political Communication Theory
PARK, J.-W., Population Studies
PARK, Y.-C., Regional Development, Economic Geography
SHON, J.-P., Library Management
SON, Y.-O., Information Service
YOON, Y.-H., Comparative Politics

College of Natural Sciences:

BAE, Z.-U., Analytical Chemistry
CHAE, Y.-K., Topology
CHANG, K.-H., Stratigraphy, Historical Geology
CHANG, T.-W., Structural Geology
CHOI, J.-K., Probability, Stochastic Processes
CHOI, S.-D., Condensed Matter Theory
CHUNG, J.-J., Physical Chemistry
HA, J.-H., Microbial Genetics
HONG, S.-D., Biochemistry
JEE, J.-G., Physical Chemistry
JIN, I.-N., Enzymology
JUE, C.-K., High Energy Physics Theory
KANG, H.-D., Experimental Nuclear Physics
KANG, S.-S., Biochemistry and Animal Physiology
KIM, H.-S., Analysis
KIM, I.-S., Biochemistry
KIM, S.-W., Computer Languages
KIM, S.-W., Petrology
KIM, W., Ecology
KOH, I.-S., Sedimentology, Sedimentary Petrology
KWAK, Y.-W., Organic Chemistry
LEE, E.-W., Surface and Thin Films Experiments
LEE, H.-H., Analysis
LEE, H.-L., Analytical Chemistry
LEE, I.-S., Statistical Inference, Theoretical Statistics
LEE, J.-K., Organic Chemistry
LEE, J.-Y., Geochemistry, Environmental Geology
LEE, J.-Y., Virology
LEE, S.-H., Analysis
LEE, S.-Y., Thin Film and Electroluminescence Experiments
LEE, Y.-G., Palaeontology
LEE, Y.-H., Biochemical Engineering
MIN, K.-D., Atmospheric Energetics
MOON, B.-J., Biochemistry
PARK, B.-G., Reliability Analysis
PARK, H.-C., Animal Taxonomy
PARK, K.-S., Analytical Chemistry
PARK, T.-K., Developmental Biology
PARK, W., Molecular Biology
PARK, Y.-C., Inorganic Chemistry
PARK, Y.-S., Algebra
PARK, Y.-T., Organic Chemistry
SEO, B.-B., Genetics
SOHN, J.-K., Bayesian Decision Theory, Statistical Computing
SOHN, K.-S., Condensed Matter Theory
SOHN, U.-I., Molecular Biology
SON, D.-C., Experimental High Energy Physics
SONG, S.-D., Plant Physiology
SUH, Y.-J., Geometry

College of Economics and Commerce:

BAE, B.-H., Managerial Accounting
CHANG, H.-S., Marketing
CHO, J.-H., Managerial Accounting
CHOI, Y.-H., Korean Economy
HA, I.-B., Macroeconomics
HAN, D.-H., International Economics
JUNG, C.-Y., Operations Management
KANG, H.-Y., Managerial Accounting
KIM, H.-K., Labour Economics
KIM, J.-J., Marketing
KIM, S.-H., Monetary Economics, International Economics
KIM, Y.-H., Economic Development, Korean Economic History
KWON, C.-T., Financial Accounting
KWON, S.-C., Financial Accounting
LEE, D.-M., Management Information Systems
LEE, H.-W., Operations Management
LEE, J.-D., Financial Management
LEE, J.-K., International Commercial Law
LEE, J.-W., Income Distribution, Comparative Economics
LEE, S.-D., Personnel and Organization Management
LEE, S.-H., Marketing
LEE, Y.-S., International Transportation and Logistics
NAH, K.-S., Economic History
PARK, J.-H., Macroeconomics
PARK, U.-S., Personnel and Organization Management
SHIN, M.-S., Financial Management
SOHN, B.-H., International Economics

College of Law:

CHANG, J.-H., Civil Law
KIM, S.-Y., Public Personnel Administration
KIM, W.-J., Administrative Law
KIM, Y.-S., Land Policy
KWAK, D.-H., Civil Law
LEE, C.-W., Labour Law
LEE, Y.-J., Financial Administration
MOON, K.-S., Policy Sciences, Financial Management
PARK, J.-T., Commercial Law
RHEE, W.-W., Urban Administration

College of Engineering:

AHN, K.-S., Digital Engineering

Bae, K.-S., Digital Signal Processing, Speech Signal Processing, Digital Communication
Baek, Y.-S., Power Systems Analysis
Cho, H.-K., Phase Transformation
Cho, J.-H., Bioelectronics, Electronic Measurements
Cho, S.-H., Ceramics for Electronics
Cho, Y.-K., Antenna and Propagation, Ultrasonics
Choi, H.-M., Parallel Distributed Processing, Processors, Logic Design
Choi, M. H., Architectural Planning and Design
Choi, S.-J., Water Supply and Waste Water Treatment Engineering
Choi, S.-Y., Semiconductor Engineering
Chung, H.-S., Neural Networks, Fuzzy Logic
Chung, I.-S., Mechanical Metallurgy
Ha, J.-M., Urban Design and City Planning
Ha, Y.-H., Image Processing and Computer Vision Digital Signal Processing
Han, K.-Y., Water Resources Engineering
Hong, J.-K., Speech Signal Processing
Hwang, C.-S., Visual Communication
Jeon, G.-J., Intelligent Control, Systems Engineering
Kang, M.-M., Architectural Structure
Kim, C.-H., Applied Mechanics
Kim, C.-J., Architectural Design
Kim, C.-Y., Microwave Engineering
Kim, D.-G., Power Electronics
Kim, D.-H., Reaction Engineering
Kim, D.-R., Surface Science and Engineering
Kim, H.-G., Power Electronics
Kim, H.-J., Pattern Recognition
Kim, H.-S., Synthetic Organic Chemistry
Kim, K.-W., Thin Film Semiconductors
Kim, N.-C., Digital Communications, Image Communications
Kim, S.-J., Geometry, Numerical Analysis
Kim, S.-J., Optical Signal Processing, Circuits and Systems
Kim, S.-M., Automata Theory
Kim, S.-S., Tribology
Kim, T.-J., Inorganic and Organometallic Chemistry, Homogeneous Catalysis
Kim, W.-S., Polymer Synthesis
Kim, Y.-M., Computer Graphics, Image Processing
Kim, Y.-S., Geotechnical Engineering
Kwon, O.-J., Powder Metallurgy
Kwon, S.-B., Fluid Mechanics
Kwon, W.-H., Power Electronics
Kwon, Y.-D., Structural Analysis
Kwon, Y.-H., Architectural Structure
Lee, C.-W., Combustion
Lee, D.-D., Semiconductor Engineering
Lee, D.-H., Polymerization Catalysis
Lee, J.-H., Semiconductor Technology
Lee, J.-T., Process Control
Lee, K.-I., Audio and Video Engineering, Electronic Measurements
Lee, M.-H., Instrumental Analysis, NMR Spectroscopy
Lee, S.-J., Natural Language
Lee, T.-I., Process and Property Thermodynamics
Lee, Y.-H., Semiconductor Engineering
Lee, Y.-M., Precision Machining
Lim, Y.-J., Dyeing Chemistry
Min, K.-E., Physical Properties of Solid Polymers
Min, K.-S., Water Quality Engineering
Moon, J.-D., Applied Electrostatics and High Voltage Applications
Moon, S.-J., Telecommunications Engineering
Oh, C.-S., Computation, Analysis and Design of Electrical Machinery
Oh, T.-J., Polymer and Fibre Chemistry
Park, J.-K., Biochemical Engineering and Transport Phenomena
Park, J.-S., Instrumentation, CAD, VLSI Design
Park, K.-C., Joining and Metal Forming
Park, L.-S., Physical Properties of Polymer Solutions
Park, M.-H., Structural Engineering
Riu, K.-J., Heat Transfer
Shim, S.-C., Petroleum Chemistry, Organic and Organometallic Chemistry
Seo, B.-H., Automatic and Digital Control, Computer Applications
Sohn, B.-K., Semiconductor Engineering
Sohn, J.-R., Catalytic Chemistry, Inorganic Material
Sohng, K.-I., Video Engineering, Multiple Valued Logic Systems
Son, H., Satellite Communication
Song, J.-W., Optical Communication
Suh, C.-M., Materials and Mechanics
Yoon, B.-H., Physical Chemistry of Metals

College of Agriculture:

Chang, Y.-H., Animal Nutrition
Cho, R.-K., Food Chemistry
Cheong, S.-T., Fruit Science, Plant Propagation
Choi, J., Soil Science
Choi, J.-U., Food Preservation Engineering
Choi, K.-S., Animal Breeding
Choi, K.-S., Economic Statistics
Choi, S.-T., Floriculture, Protected Cultivation
Choi, Y.-E., Nematology
Choi, Y.-H., Food Engineering
Chung, J.-D., Plant Tissue Culture
Chung, M.-S., Tree Cultivation
Hong, S.-C., Forest Ecology
Jo, J.-K., Grass Physiology
Jung, S.-K., Landscape Construction
Kim, B.-S., Vegetable Cultivation, Pepper Cultivation
Kim, C.-S., Agricultural Policy
Kim, D.-S., Dairy Microbiology
Kim, D.-U., Plant Molecular Biology
Kim, J.-J., Crop Physiology
Kim, K.-R., Fruit Science, Apple Growing
Kim, K.-U., Weed Science
Kim, S.-G., Agricultural Marketing
Kim, S.-K., Maize Cultivation
Kim, Y.-S., Landscape Planning
Kwon, M.-N., Geotechnical and Foundation Engineering
Kwon, Y.-J., Systematic Entomology
Lee, H.-C., Agricultural Economic History
Lee, H.-T., Landscape Design
Lee, J.-T., Fungal Plant Pathology
Lee, J.-Y., Wood Chemistry
Lee, K.-C., Landscape Management
Lee, K.-M., Terramechanics, Greenhouse Controls
Lee, K.-W., Viral Plant Pathology
Lee, S.-G., Agricultural Buildings
Lee, W.-S., Vegetable Science
Park, K.-K., Post-Harvest Process, Systems Mechanics
Park, S.-J., Wood Anatomy
Park, W.-C., Plant Nutrition
Park, W.-G., Forest Genetics
Rhee, I.-J., Fibre Materials Science
Rhee, I.-K., Biochemistry
Ryu, J.-C., Agricultural Crops
Ryu, K.-S., Fibre Crops Science
Sohn, J.-K., Rice Cultivation
Sohn, H.-R., Sericulture
Son, D.-S., Forest Cultivation
Suh, S.-D., Hydrology, Land Engineering
Syn, Y.-B., Fruit Science, Plant Physiology
Uhm, J.-Y., Bacterial Plant Pathology
Yeo, Y.-K., Lipid Chemistry

College of Music and Visual Arts:

Byun, Y.-B., Sculpture
Chong, H.-I., Kayagum (12-Stringed Zither)
Chung, H.-C., Composition
Jung, W.-H., Piano
Kang, C.-S., Piano
Kim, G.-J., Voice (Soprano)
Kim, J.-W., Voice (Baritone)
Kim, K.-I., Piano
Kim, T.-H., Haegum (2-Stringed Fiddle)
Kim, W.-S., Korean Painting
Ku, Y.-K., Komungo (6-Stringed Zither)
Kwon, K.-D., Visual Design
Lee, D.-O., Oil Painting
Lim, H.-S., Clarinet
Oh, H.-C., Oil Painting
Park, N.-H., Art History
Shim, S.-H., Voice (Tenor)
Yoo, H., Korean Paining
Yi, T.-B., Theory of Korean Music and Taegum (Korean Transverse Flute)
Yoon, J.-R., Cello

Teachers' College:

Ahn, B.-H., Space Physics
An, T.-Y., Sociology of Education/Non-Formal Education
Bae, H.-D., Politics, Political Thought
Bae, J.-E., English Literature
Byun, C.-J., Evaluation of Education
Chae, H.-W., Training
Chang, D.-I., Medieval Korean History
Chin, W.-K., Teaching Theory and Educational Technology
Chong, S.-H., German Linguistics
Chung, D.-H., German Linguistics
Chung, H.-P., Philosophy of Education
Chung, H.-S., Cell Biology, Photosynthesis
Chung, S.-T., Sport Psychology
Hong, Y.-P., Politics, Political Thought
Hwang, J.-H., Shakespeare
Hwang, S.-G., Algebra
Hwangbo, S., French Linguistics
Im, J.-R., Korean Linguistics
Jo, P.-G., Clothing
Jo, W.-R., Geomorphology
Jun, B.-Q., English Linguistics
Kang, Y.-H., Astronomy
Ki, U.-H., Geometry
Kim, B.-K., Counselling
Kim, B.-S., Educational Psychology
Kim, H.-K., Economic Development
Kim, H.-S., Early Modern East Asian History
Kim, J.-J., Dance
Kim, J.-J., Philosophy, Asian Philosophy
Kim, J.-T., Korean Linguistics
Kim, J.-W., Contemporary Western History
Kim, K.-H., Measurement and Evaluation for Physical Education
Kim, M.-H., Educational Administration
Kim, M.-K., Korean Literature
Kim, M.-N., Philosophy of Education
Kim, Y.-H., Geometry
Kim, Y.-H., Principles of Physical Education
Koh, J.-K., Particle Physics, Physics Education
Lee, B.-H., Early Modern Korean History
Lee, J.-H., Korean Literature
Lee, J.-H., Politics, International Politics
Lee, J.-W., Population Geography, Geographical Education
Lee, K.-S., Curriculum and Teaching
Lee, M.-H., Biomechanics
Lee, M.-J., Educational Psychology
Lee, M.-S., Physical Chemistry
Lee, N.-G., Rural Sociology
Lee, S.-C., Sports Nutrition
Lee, S.-T., Korean Linguistics
Lee, Y.-J., Petrology
Lim, C.-K., German Literature
Oh, C.-H., Optics, Quantum Electronics
Oh, D.-S., History of Physical Education
Oh, Y.-S., Public Economics
Pak, J.-S., Geometry
Park, C.-Y., Educational Administration
Park, D.-K., Plasma Physics
Park, J.-Y., English Literature
Park, K.-S., Teaching English as a Second Language
Park, S.-H., Animal Systematics, Entomology
Park, T.-H., Urban Geography
Rim, S.-H., Algebra
Seo, J.-M., Korean Literature

SHIN, K.-J., French Literature
SHIN, Y.-E., Teaching of Physical Education
SONG, B.-H., Microbiology, Molecular Biology
SONG, W.-C., Politics, Political Thought
SUH, C.-K., Economic Geography
YANG, H.-J., Animal Morphology, Ecology
YANG, J.-S., Climatology
YANG, S.-H., Solid State Physics, Physics Education
YANG, S.-Y., Palaeobiology
YEO, H.-J., Inorganic Chemistry
YI, M.-S., French Linguistics
YOH, S.-D., Organic Chemistry
YOON, J.-L., Educational Psychology

School of Medicine:

BAEK, W.-Y., Intensive Care Therapy
BAIK, B.-S., Craniofacial Surgery, Cosmetic Surgery
CHANG, S.-I., Surgery, Paediatric Surgery
CHANG, S.-K., Transplantation, Tumours
CHO, D.-K., Nephrology
CHO, D.-T., Molecular Genetics
CHO, H.-J., Neuroanatomy
CHO, T.-H., Ontology
CHO, Y.-L., Gynaecological Oncology
CHOI, Y.-H., Gastroenterology
CHUN, S.-S., Reproductive Endrocrinology and Infertility
CHUNG, B.-Y., Adult Nursing, Cancer Nursing
CHUNG, S.-L., Dermatology, Leprosy
CHUNG, T.-H., Immunology
DOH, B.-N., Psychiatric and Mental Health Nursing
HAMM, I.-S., Cerebrovascular Disease, Neuro-Oncology
HONG, H.-S., Anatomy, Medical Genetics
HONG, J.-G., Pain Clinic
IHN, J.-C., Joint Reconstructive Surgery
JUN, J.-B., Dermatology, Mycology, Dermatopathology
JUN, J.-E., Cardiology
JUN, S.-H., Surgery, Colorectal Surgery
JUNG, M.-S., Women's Health Nursing
JUNG, T.-H., Pulmonology
KANG, B.-J., Psychiatry, Psychopharmacology
KANG, D.-S., Thoracic Radiology
KANG, S.-H., Psychiatry, Psychotherapy
KIM, B.-K., Cardiac Anaesthesia
KIM, B.-W., Endocrinology, Metabolism
KIM, B.-W., Tumours
KIM, C.-Y., Cardiovascular Pharmacology
KIM, H.-M., Paediatrics, Neonatology
KIM, J.-S., Diagnostic Immunology
KIM, K.-T., Paediatric Cardiovascular Surgery
KIM, M.-Y., Paediatric Nursing
KIM, N.-S., Allergology, Rheumatology
KIM, P.-T., Hand Surgery
KIM, S.-H., Vitreous Humour and Retina
KIM, S.-L., Cerebrovascular Disease
KIM, S.-S., Community Health Nursing
KIM, S.-Y., Vitreous Humour and Retina
KIM, Y.-J., Interventional Radiology
KOO, J.-H., Paediatrics, Nephrology
KWAK, J.-S., Forensic Pathology
KWON, J.-Y., Paediatric Ophthalmology
LEE, A.-H.
LEE, K.-S., Paediatrics, Haemato-Oncology and Genetics
LEE, S.-B., Paediatrics, Cardiology
LEE, S.-H., Otology, Neuro-Otology
LEE, S.-K., Biostatistics and Nutritional Epidemiology
LEE, W.-J., Renal Physiology
LEE, Y.-H., Surgery, Head and Neck Endocrine Surgery
LEE, Z.-N., Psychiatry, Psychotherapy
PARK, B.-C., Paediatric and Spinal Surgery
PARK, I.-K., Radiation Oncology, Radiation Biology
PARK, I.-S., Gynaecological Oncology
PARK, J.-H., Fundamentals of Nursing
PARK, J.-S., Cardiovascular Physiology
PARK, J.-S., Head and Neck Oncology
PARK, J.-W., Vascular Pharmacology and Anaesthesia
PARK, J.-Y., Health Care Administration and Health Policy
PARK, S.-Y., Adult Nursing
PARK, W.-H., Cardiology
PARK, Y.-K., Andrology
PARK, Y.-M., Spinal Neuro-Oncology, Neurotrauma
SEOL, S.-Y., Molecular Epidemiology
SEONG, C.-S., Rhinology Neuro-Otology
SUH, C.-K., Peripheral Neurology, Cerebrovascular Diseases
SUH, I.-S., Pathology of the Gastrointestinal Tract
SUH, S.-R., Adult Nursing
YEH, M.-H., Epidemiology and Population Dynamics
YU, W.-S., Surgery, Surgical Oncology
YUN, Y.-K., Surgery, Hepatobiliary Surgery

School of Dentistry:

CHO, S.-A., Prosthodontics
JO, K.-H., Prosthodontics
KIM, C.-S., Oral and Maxillofacial Surgery
KIM, Y.-J., Paediatric Dentistry
KWON, O.-W., Orthodontics
LEE, S.-H., Oral and Maxillofacial Surgery
SUNG, J.-H., Orthodontics

College of Veterinary Medicine:

BYUN, M.-D., Veterinary Obstetrics
CHOI, W.-P., Veterinary Microbiology
JANG, I.-H., Veterinary Surgery, Veterinary Obstetrics
KIM, B.-H., Veterinary Microbiology
KIM, Y.-H., Veterinary Obstetrics
KWUN, H.-B., Veterinary Surgery
LEE, C.-S., Veterinary Pathology
LEE, H.-B., Veterinary Medicine
LEE, H.-S., Veterinary Medicine
MOON, M.-H., Veterinary Parasitology
PARK, C.-K., Veterinary Microbiology
PARK, J.-H., Veterinary Pharmacology
TAK, R.-B., Veterinary Public Health
YU, C.-J., Veterinary Physiology

College of Human Ecology:

CHOI, B.-G., Child Development
LEE, H.-S., Nutrition
SUH, Y.-S., Textiles

ATTACHED INSTITUTES

Toigye Research Institute
Institute of Regional Development
Peace Research Institute
Research Institute for Economics and Business Administration
Institute of Humanities
Law Research Institute
Institute for Social Science
Institute of Pacific Rim Studies
Institute for Local Autonomy
Institute for City and Province Management
Institute of Secondary Education
Public Opinion and Public Relations Research Institute
Institute of Korean Residents in Foreign Countries
Institute of Geographic Information Systems
Institute of Basic Sciences
Research Institute for Genetic Engineering
Environmental Science Institute
Topology and Geometry Research Centre
Science Education Research Institute
Institute for Material Chemistry
Radiation Science Research Institute
Research Institute of Industrial Technology
Sensor Technology Research Centre
Institute of Electronic Technology
Research Institute of Engineering Design Technology
Engineering Tribology Research Institute
Advanced Materials Research Institute
Research Institute of Dyeing and Finishing
Information Institute of Dyeing and Finishing
Machinery Technology Institute
Institute of Agricultural Science and Technology
Institute of Veterinary Medical Sciences
Post-Harvest Technology Research Institute
International Agricultural Research Institute
Research Institute of the Environment and Open Spaces
Research Institute of Physical Education and Sports Science
Liver Research Institute
Cancer Research Institute
Cardiovascular Research Institute
Medical Imaging Research Institute
Institute of Biomaterials Research and Development
Medical Research Institute
Research Institute of Nursing Science
Language Institute

NATIONAL FISHERIES UNIVERSITY OF PUSAN

599–1 Daeyeon-dong Nam-gu, Pusan 608-737
Telephone: (51) 622-3951
Fax: (51) 625-9947

Founded 1941 as Pusan Fisheries College, attained university status 1990

President: SUN-DUCK CHANG
Dean of Academic Affairs: YONG RHIM YANG
Dean of Student Affairs: HYUN WOO CHUNG
Dean of Planning Research: YONG JOO KANG
Dean of General Affairs: SE WHA SONG
Librarian: JAI YUL KONG

Library of 130,000 vols
Number of teachers: 306
Number of students: 7,700

Publications: *Bulletin, Natural Sciences* (2 a year), *The Theses Collection of the Faculty Members, Social Sciences* (2 a year), *Publication of Institute of Marine Sciences* (annually).

DEANS

College of Fisheries Sciences: CHUL HYUN SOHN
College of Marine Sciences and Technology: YONG QUIN KANG
College of Natural Sciences: MAN DONG HUR
College of Engineering: CHUNG KIL PARK
College of Social Sciences: CHARLES KIM
College of Business Administration: CHUNG YUL YU

CHAIRMEN OF DEPARTMENTS

Fisheries Engineering: GAB DONG YOON
Aquaculture: DONG SOO KIM
Fisheries Education: KYUNG JUNE LEE
Biotechnology and Bioengineering: HYUNG HO LEE
Fish Pathology: JOON-KI CHUNG
Marine Production Management: JU HEE LEE
Ocean Engineering: CHEONG RO RYU
Oceanography: CHANG HO MOON
Applied Geology: YONG SUN SONG
Marine Biology: MYONG SUK YOO
Atmospheric Sciences: HEUI YONG BYUN
Applied Mathematics: YOUNG GILL BAIK
Nutrition and Food Science: DAE SEOK BYUN
Physics: JUNG HYUN JEONG
Chemistry: SEK WON KIM
Computer Science: JI HWAN PARK
Microbiology: HUN KU LEE
Food Science and Technology: YOUNG JE CHO

Environmental Engineering: SUK JUN YOA
Refrigeration Engineering: HOO KYU OH
Mechanical Engineering: DOO SUNG AHN
Naval Architecture: KWANG SEOK MOON
Materials Engineering: DONG JOON KIM
Telematics Engineering: KI WOO NAM
Electronic Engineering: YOON JONG PAK
Marine Engineering: JOO HO YANG
Electrical Engineering: CHUN DUCK KIM
Chemical Engineering: KWEN HACK SUH
Civil Engineering: DONG UK LEE
Resource Economics: SE HOON KANG
Korean Language and Literature: MYONG HEE SONG
English Language and Literature: KWANG WOONG UM
Law: JU SHIL SUH
Fisheries Business Administration: HYUNG CHAN JUNG
International Trade: MYONG SOP PAK
Business Administration: IL SEONG YU
Management Information Systems: YUNG YANG EU

ATTACHED INSTITUTES

Institute of Marine Sciences: 714, Woo-1 dong, Haeundaegu, Pusan 607-04; Dir JAE CHUL LEE.

Institute of Sea Food Science: 599-1, Daeyun-dong Namgu, Pusan 608-737; Dir EUNG HO LEE.

Institute of Fisheries Science: 599–1 Daeyun-dong Namgu, Pusan 608-737; Dir KI YUN KIM.

Institute of Fisheries Business: 599–1, Daeyundong Namgu, Pusan 608-737; Dir HYANG CHAN JUNG.

Institute of Student Guidance: Dir SEUNG RAI LEE.

Institute of Sea Culture: Dir MYONG HEE SONG.

Institute of Life Science and Biotechnology: Dir JAI YUL KONG.

Institute of Industrial Science and Technology: Dir UH JOH CIM.

Environmental Research Institute: Dir BYUNG HUN LEE.

Basic Sciences Institute: Dir KUM SHO HWANG.

Foreign Language Research Institute: Dir JAE DUCK BAE.

PUSAN NATIONAL UNIVERSITY

30 Jangjeon-dong, Kumjeong-ku, Pusan 609-735
Telephone: 510-1293
Fax: 512-9049

Founded 1946
Academic year: March to February
President: SOO-IN YUN
Dean of Academic Affairs: SANG-WOOK PARK
Dean of Student Affairs: IN-BO SIM
Dean of Planning and Research: JUNG-DUK LIM
Director of General Affairs: SANG-WOO HAN
Director of Library: DONG-HYUN JUNG

Library: see Libraries
Museum: see Museums
Number of teachers: 756
Number of students: 25,942

Publications: *University Academic Journal* (annual collection of theses), *PNU Weekly Newsletter, College Academic Journal.*

DEANS

Graduate School: JUNG-KEUN KIM
Graduate School of Management: TAE-GON SIN
Graduate School of Public Administration: SIN-HO AHN
Graduate School of Environment: JAE-CHANG KIM
Graduate School of Education: HONG-WOOK HUH
Graduate School of Industry: JAE-CHANG KIM
College of Humanities: DOO-SANG JO
College of Natural Sciences: CHUL-UN KIM
College of Engineering: JAE-CHANG KIM
College of Law: MYUNG-GIL KIM
College of Education: HONG-WOOK HUH
College of Social Sciences: SIN-HO AHN
College of Business: TAE -GON SIN
College of Arts: JUNG-MYUNG KIM
College of Pharmacy: YUNG-MI KIM
College of Medicine: IN-SE KIM
College of Dentistry: MYUNG-YUN KO
College of Home Economics: TAE-YUNG JUNG

ATTACHED INSTITUTES

Research Institute of Basic Sciences
Research Institute for Science Education
Research Institute of Mechanical Technology
Research Institute of Genetic Engineering
Research Institute of Information and Communication
Language Research and Education Institute
Research Institute of Korean National Unity
Industrial Technology Research Institute
Institute of Environmental Studies
Urban Affairs Research Institute
Institute of Law Studies
Social Welfare Research Institute
Institute for European and American Studies
Institute of Korean Cultural Studies
Research Institute of Physical Education and Sports Science
Local Government Research Institute
Educational Research Institute
Institute of Labour Problems
Research Institute for Oral Biotechnology
Research Institute of Medical Science
Research Institute for Drug Development
Social Survey Research Center
Research Center for Dielectric Advanced Matter Physics
Center for Women's Studies
Industrial Development Research Center
Asian Research Institute
Research Institute of Computer Engineering
Engineering Research Center for Net-Shape and Die Manufacturing
Center for Information and Communication Studies

SEOUL NATIONAL UNIVERSITY

Sinlim-dong, Kwanak-gu, Seoul 151
Telephone: 877-1601, 0101

Founded 1946
State control
Academic year: March to February

President: JUNG-HO SONU
Vice-President: SONG-HWA CHOI
Dean of Academic Affairs: SHIN-BOK KIM
Dean of Student Affairs: SUNG-HYUN PARK
Dean of Research Affairs: UN-CHUL LEE
Dean of Planning and Co-ordination: KWANG-HA KANG
Director-General of General Administration: BUM-SUK SUH
Director-General of Library: KYO-HUN CHIN

Library: see Libraries
Number of teachers: 1,598
Number of students: 32,115

Publication: *University Gazette* (weekly).

DEANS

College of Agriculture and Life Sciences: HO-TAK KIM
College of Humanities: PYUNG-KUN YU
College of Dentistry: KWANG-NAM KIM
College of Fine Arts: SU-AUN BOU
College of Engineering: JANG-MOO LEE
College of Law: YOO-SUNG KIM
College of Natural Sciences: HO-WAN CHANG
College of Music: SUNG-CHUN YI
College of Medicine: JUNG-SANG LEE
College of Pharmacy: MIN-HWA LEE
College of Education: JAE-KIE HWANG
College of Nursing: JUNG-HO PARK
College of Social Sciences: YONG-HA SHIN
College of Veterinary Medicine: SUN-JOONG KIM
College of Business Administration: SOO-IL KWAK
College of Human Ecology: KI-YOUNG LEE
Graduate School: SANG-OK LEE
Graduate School of Public Administration: WHA-JOON RHO
Graduate School of Public Health: MOON-HO CHUNG
Graduate School of Environmental Studies: BYOUNG-E YANG

ATTACHED RESEARCH INSTITUTES

Natural Products Research Institute: Dir KUK-HYUN SHIN.

Language Research Institute: Dir MYONG-YOL KIM.

Centre for Social Sciences: Dir TAI-HWAN KWON.

Institute of Economic Research: Dir YOUNG-IL CHUNG.

Law Research Institute: Dir SEUNG-KYU YANG.

Institute of Korean Studies: Dir SEUNG-HI CHOI.

Institute of American Studies: Dir YOUNG-SUN HA.

Research Institute for Basic Sciences: Dir KOOK-JOE SHIN.

Medical Research Centre: Dir CHAN-WOONG PARK.

Institute of Communication Research: KWANG-YUNG CHOO.

Centre for Educational Research: Dir NAM-KEE CHANG.

Institute of Environmental Science and Engineering: Dir WHA-YOUNG LEE.

Institute for Molecular Biology and Genetics: Dir JEONG-BIN YIM.

Inter-University Semiconductor Research Centre: Dir HYEONG-JOON KIM.

Research Institute of Engineering Science: Dir DONG-CHUL HAN.

Institute of Humanities: Dir IN-SOK OH.

Research Institute of Advanced Materials: Dir HU-CHUL LEE.

Automation and Systems Research Institute: Dir CHANG-KYU LEE.

Institute of Advanced Machinery and Design: Dir SUNG-TACK RO.

Research Institute of Advanced Computer Technology: Dir CHU-SHIK JHON.

Graduate Institute for International and Area Studies: Dir-Gen. WON-TACK HONG.

Institute of New Media and Communications: Dir KOENG-MO SUNG.

SEOUL WOMAN'S UNIVERSITY

126 Kongnung 2-dong, Nowon-gu, Seoul 139-744

Telephone: 972-2031

Founded 1961
Private control
Academic year: March to February

President: Dr KOO-YOUNG CHUNG
Dean of Academic Affairs: Dr NOON-HEE KANG
Director of General Affairs: Assoc. Prof. JONG-CHEOL LEE
Chief Librarian: Dr YOUNG-HYUN SIM

Number of teachers: 297
Number of students: 3,138

Publications: *Seoul Woman's University News* (every 2 weeks), *Journal, Rural Development Research Series, Journal of Women's Studies, Journal of Humanities and Social Science* (all annually).

DEANS

Faculty of Humanities: Dr CHONG-SUH PARK
Faculty of Social Science: Prof. JONG-JOO YOON
Faculty of Natural Science: Dr IN-DON LEE
Faculty of Fine Arts: Prof. KYOUNG-HAN CHOI

HEAD OF DEPARTMENTS

Faculty of Humanities:

Korean Language and Literature: KI-SUK PARK
English Language and Literature: CHONG-SIK PAIK
French Language and Literature: JEONG-SOP SIM
German Language and Literature: WON-UNG BONG
History: YOON-MO AHN

Faculty of Social Science:

Business Administration: DONG-YOUNG LEE
Economics: HAN-KYOUNG BAI
Social Work: YEA-SUN EUM
Library Science: BON YOUNG KOO
Child Development: YEAN-ZIP JANG
Education and Psychology: OK-JOO LEE

Faculty of Natural Science:

Rural Science: KYUNG-EUN YOON
Clothing Science: MOON SOOK KIM
Food Science: SUNG-OH PARK
Nutrition: HYE-BOCK NA
Chemistry: TAIK-SOO LEE
Biology: KYUNG AI CHO
Mathematics: KEH WHA KWON
Physical Education: JU-HAN PARK

Faculty of Fine Arts:

Arts and Crafts: JUNG-SOOK LEE
Visual and Industrial Design: BYUNG-KY SUH
Western Painting: SOO-HWAN OH

SOGANG UNIVERSITY

CPO 1142, Seoul 100-611
Telephone: (2) 715-8114
Fax: (2) 705-8204
E-mail: yongsuk@ccs.sogang.ac.kr

Founded 1960
Private control
Languages of instruction: Korean, with some English
Academic year: March to December (two semesters)

President: Rev. LEE SANG IL
Vice-President: PYUN CHONG SUH
Academic Dean: CHOI HYUNE MOO
Director of Library: KEEL HEE SUNG

Number of teachers: 267
Number of students: 9,699

Publications: *Sogang Herald* (monthly), *Sogang Hakbo* (monthly).

DEANS

Graduate School: SO HYUNSOO
Graduate School of Business: SUH SANG RYONG
Graduate School of Public Policy: OH BYUNG SUN
Graduate School of Education: SUNG HYUN KYUNG
Graduate School of Economics: KIM KWANG DOO
Graduate School of Mass Communication: CHOI CHANG SUP
Graduate School for Religion: SIM JONG HYEOK
Graduate School of International Studies: CHO YONG HYO
Graduate School of Information and Technology: CHANG JIK HYUN
College of Humanities: SUNG HYUN KYUNG
College of Social Science: CHOI CHANG SUP
College of Natural Science: CHUNG DONG MYUNG
College of Engineering: LEE JAE WOOK
School of Economics: KIM KWANG DOO
School of Business Administration: SUH SANG RYONG
General Education Division: KIM YOON TAE

PROFESSORS

College of Humanities:

AN, S. J., English Language
CHO, B. H., History
CHOI, H.-M., French Language
CHOI, R., German Language
CHUNG, D. H., History
CHUNG, I. C., Philosophy
CHUNG, Y. M., Theology
HAN, I. S., German Language
HONG, S. K., History
JEONG, Y. I., Korean Language
KEEL, H. S., Religious Studies
KIM, C. H., Theology
KIM, H. D., Korean Language
KIM, H. G., History
KIM, K. B., French Language
KIM, S. H., Religious Studies
KIM, W. D., English Language
KIM, W. S., Philosophy
KIM, Y. H., History
KIM, Y. S., English Language
KISTER, D. A., English Language
LEBRUN, H., French Language
LEE, D. H., German Language
LEE, H. B., English Language
LEE, J. D., German Language
LEE, J. S., Korean Language
LEE, J. W., History
LEE, T. D., English Language
PAK, C. T., Philosophy
PARK, C. H., Korean Language
PARK, H., Theology
SHIN, K. W., English Language
SHIN, S. W., English Language
SONG, H. S., Korean Language
SONG, W. Y., German Language
SPALATIN, C. A., Philosophy
SUH, J. M., Korean Language
SUNG, H. K., Korean Language
SYE, K. S., Theology
UM, J. S., Philosophy

College of Social Science:

CHANG, Y. H., Mass Communication
CHO, O. L., Sociology
CHOI, C. S., Mass Communication
KERSTEN, K. F., Mass Communication
KIM, H. S., Mass Communication
KIM, K., Mass Communication
LEE, K. Y., Political Science
OH, B. S., Law
OH, K. P., Political Science
PARK, H. S., Political Science
PARK, M. S., Sociology
PARK, S. T., Sociology
RHEE, S. W., Political Science
SUH, K. M., Law
YOON, Y. D., Sociology

College of Natural Science:

CHIN, C. S., Chemistry
CHO, T. G., Mathematics
CHUNG, D. M., Mathematics
HONG, S. S., Mathematics
KANG, J. H., Chemistry
KIM, W. S., Life Science
LEE, D. H., Chemistry
LEE, H. S., Chemistry
LEE, J. G., Mathematics
MAENG, J. S., Life Science
PAIK, W.-K., Chemistry
PARK, B. S., Physics
PARK, G. S., Physics
PARK, S. A., Mathematics
PARK, S. H., Mathematics
PARK, Y. J., Physics
PYUN, C. S., Chemistry
RHEE, B. K., Physics
SO, H. S., Chemistry
YANG, J. M., Life Science
YOON, B. H., Mathematics

College of Engineering:

AN, C., Electronic Engineering
CHANG, I. S., Electronic Engineering
CHANG, J. H., Computer Science
CHOI, C. S., Chemical Engineering
HWANG, S. Y., Electronic Engineering
KIM, S. C., Computer Science
LEE, J. W., Chemical Engineering
LEE, K. H., Electronic Engineering
LEE, K. S., Chemical Engineering
LEE, W. H., Chemical Engineering
OH, K. W., Computer Science
PARK, H. S., Chemical Engineering
PARK, R. H., Electronic Engineering
PARK, S., Computer Science
VILLARREAL, F. M., Computer Science
YOO, K. P., Chemical Engineering
YUN, S. W., Electronic Engineering

School of Economics:

JO, S. H., Economics
KIM, B. U., Economics
KIM, D. C., Economics
KIM, K. D., Economics
KIM, K. H., Economics
KIM, P. J., Economics
KIM, S. T., Economics
KIM, S. Y., Economics
KWACK, T. W., Economics
LEE, D. S., Economics
LEE, H. K., Economics
LEE, Y. G., Economics
NAHM, J. W., Economics
NAM, S. I., Economics
RHEE, T. W., Economics
SUH, J. H., Economics

School of Business Administration:

BAEK, J. H., Business Administration
CHEE, Y. H., Business Administration
CHOI, W. Y., Business Administration
CHUN, S. B., Business Administration
JON, J. S., Business Administration
KANG, H. S., Business Administration
KIM, S. K., Business Administration
KOOK, C. P., Business Administration
LEE, D. S., Economics
LEE, J. B., Business Administration
LEE, J. H., Business Administration
LEE, K. L., Business Administration
LEE, N. J., Business Administration
LEE, W. Y., Business Administration
PARK, K. K., Business Administration
PARK, N. H., Business Administration
PARK, T. W., Business Administration
PARK, Y. K., Business Administration
RHO, B. H., Business Administration
SUH, S. R., Business Administration
VAN, B. G., Business Administration

General Education Division:

CHO, G. H., General Education
CHOI, H. N., General Education
KIM, H. R., General Education
KIM, Y. T., General Education
KOH, I. C., General Education
MACE, J. D., General Education
RYU, J. S., General Education

Graduate School of International Studies:

BYUN, K. Y.
CHO, Y. H.
CHO, Y. J.

ATTACHED RESEARCH INSTITUTES

Institute for Economic Research: Dir C. O. CHO.

Institute for Business Research: Dir B. H. RHO.

Research Institute for Basic Science: Dir Y. J. PARK.

Applied Science Research Institute: Dir K. H. LEE.

Research Institute for Humanities: Dir J. W. LEE.

Institute for Religion: Dir H. S. KEEL.

Institute for Theology: Dir J. H. SIM.

Institute for the Study of Media and Culture: Dir C. H. KIM.

Research Institute for East Asian Studies: Dir I. C. CHUNG.

Technology Management Institute: Dir S. H. JEON.

Institute for Philosophical Studies: Dir C. T. PAK.

Institute for Social Science: Dir S. T. PARK.

Organic Chemistry Research Center: Dir N. M. YOON.

SOOKMYUNG WOMEN'S UNIVERSITY

53–12 Chungpa-dong 2-ga, Yongsan-gu, Seoul 140

Telephone: (713) 9391

Founded 1938, university status 1955
Private control
Language of instruction: Korean
Academic year: March to August, September to February

President: KYU-SUN CHUNG
Dean of Academic Affairs: JONG-KYU HAM
Dean of Student Affairs: SOOK-HI PARK
Dean of Administrative Affairs: JAE-NYUM PARK
Dean of Planning: KYUNG-SOOK LEE
Librarian: SOON-JA LEE

Library of *c.* 300,000 vols
Number of teachers: 158
Number of students: 6,303

Publications: *Theses Collection of Research Institute of Economy*, *Theses Collection of Sookmyung Women's University*, *Sookdae-Shinbo* (Sookmyung Women's Weekly), *Sookmyung Times*, *Theses Collection of the Research Center for Asian Women*, *Journal of the Sookmyung Pharmaceutical Association*, *Journal of the Graduate School Student Association*, *Language and Literature*, *Chinese Culture*, *Student Guidance Journal*, *Journal of Social Development*.

DEANS

Graduate School: CHAN-WOO SHIN
Graduate School of Education: EUN-SOOK CHO
Graduate School of Industry: EUN-SOOK CHO
College of Liberal Arts: KWI-KYUNG LEE
College of Natural Sciences: MYUNG-JA KIM
College of Home Economics: JUNG-WOO LEE
College of Political Science and Law: YO-SUP CHUNG
College of Economics and Commerce: MIN-SHIK PARK
College of Music: HEI-JUNG JOO
College of Pharmacy: SOOK-YEON LEE
College of Fine Arts: CHUNG-UN AHN

HEADS OF DEPARTMENTS

Korean Language and Literature: EUL-HWAN LEE
English Language and Literature: JIN-SOON CHA
French Language and Literature: HEA-GYUNG IM
Chinese Language and Literature: DUCK-JOU KWON
German Language and Literature: JOO-YOUN KIM
Education: YONG-IL KIM
Educational Psychology: IN-SUP SONG
History: EUN GYUN MOK
Korean History: MAN-YUL LEE
Library Science: HEE-JAE LEE
Physics: SUNG-DAHM OH
Chemistry: KWANG-HYUN NO
Biology: KYUNG-HEE MIN
Mathematics: YOUNG-HEE HONG
Computer Science: BONG-HEE MOON
Physical Education: CHUNG-MOO LEE
Dance: IN-JA PARK
Home Management: SUN-JA KYE
Clothing and Textiles: SUN-JAE LEE
Food and Nutrition: CHO-AE YUM
Child Study: KWANG-WOONG KIM
Political Science and Diplomacy: NAM-YOUNG LEE
Law: SANG-TAE LEE
Public Administration: DO-HOON KIM
Economics: SOON-HYUN OH
Business Administration: JONG-UI KIM
Foreign Trade: SEON-SIK KIM
Consumer Economics: JUNG-SOOK MOON
Piano: MYUNG-SUN KIM
Instrumental Music: UN-CHANG PAIK
Vocal Music: YUN-JA KIM
Composition: SEUNG-JOON CHOI
Pharmacy: EUN-HEE PARK
Manufacturing Pharmacy: OK-NAM KIM
Design: HAN-TAE YU
Crafts: CHUN-HAK OH
Painting: BONG-YUL LEE

ATTACHED INSTITUTES

Research Center for Asian Women: Dir IN-BOK LEE.

Research Institute of Pharmaceutical Science: Dir KYU-JA WHANG.

Institute of Economic Studies: Dir SEON-SIK KIM.

Research Institute of Life Science: Dir CHO-AE YUM.

Institute of Education: Dir YONG-IL KIM.

Language and Literature Research Institute: Dir JIN-SOON CHA.

Institute for Child Study: Dir JAE-YEON LEE.

Institute of Korean Studies: Dir HANG-RAE CHO.

Institute of Korean Linguistics and Literature: (vacant).

Centre d'études francophones: Dir YOUNG-HAI PARK.

East-West Music Research Center: Dir COOK-LOCK PARK.

Institute of China Studies: Dir DUCK-JOO KWON.

Korean Unification Institute: Dir OK-YUL KIM.

Institute of Industrial Design: Dir TUK-KYUM KIM.

Research Center of National Sciences: Dir YUN-KYUNG JANG.

Institut für Kulturforschung des Deutschen Sprachraums: Dir JOO-YOUN KIM.

Research Center for Social Development: Dir YO-SUP CHUNG.

SOONGSIL UNIVERSITY

1–1 Sangdo 5-dong, Dongjak-ku, Seoul 156-743

Telephone: (2) 820-0111
Fax: (2) 814-7362

Founded 1897
Private control
Academic year: March to June, September to December

Chancellor: SUN-HEE KWAK
President: YOON-BAE OUH
Vice-President for International Affairs: HAE-SEOK OH
Vice-President for Academic Affairs: BONG-CHUL SEO
Librarian: PYUNG-SYK RO

Library of 367,000 vols
Number of teachers: 252 full-time, 334 part-time
Number of students: 10,167

DEANS

College of Humanities: HONG-ZIN KIM
College of Natural Science: YOUNG-JA YUN
School of Basic Sciences: CHANG-BAE KIM (Head)
College of Law: SUNG-SOOK KIM
College of Social Sciences: KWANG-SEOB SHIN
College of Economics and Commerce: WON-WOO LEE
School of Economics and World Commerce: SUNG-SUP RHEE (Head)
School of Business Administration: (Head vacant)
College of Engineering: MUN-HEON KIM
School of Electronics, Electrics and Information Telecommunication: SOON-CHUL JO (Head)
College of Information Science: CHUL-HEE LEE
School of Computing: CHAE-WOO YOO (Head)
Evening Courses: YOUNG-JONG KIM
Graduate School (General): YOUNG-HOON KIM
Graduate School of Industry: HYEON-TAE CHO
Graduate School of Small Business: DONG-KIL YOO
Graduate School of Information Science: SUNG-YUL RHEW
Graduate School of Labour and Industrial Relations: WOO-HYEON CHO
Graduate School of Unification Policy: TUK-CHU CHUN
Graduate School of International and Regional Studies: LEE-SOO KANG
Graduate School of Education: JAE-HYEON HAN
Graduate School of Christian Studies: YOUNG-HAN KIM

DIRECTORS

Institute of Humanities: HONG-ZIN KIM
Institute of Social Science: SOO-EON MOON
Institute of Korean Christian Culture Research: YOUNG-HAN KIM
Institute of Law: DOO-HWAN KIM
Christian Institute of Social Studies: SAM-YEUL LEE
Institute of Industrial Technology: YOUNG-PIL KWON
Institute for Adult and Continuing Education: KWANG-MYUNG KIM
Institute of Business and Economic Strategies: DAE-YONG JEONG
Institute of Natural Sciences: CHONG-IN YU
Resource Recycling Research Centre: KAP-SOO DOH

HEADS OF DEPARTMENTS

College of Humanities:

Korean Language and Literature: CHONG-CHUL PARK
English Language and Literature: JUN-EON PARK
German Language and Literature: YONG-SAM PARK
French Language and Literature: SAI-LYONG LEE
Chinese Language and Literature: JONG-SEONG KIM
Philosophy: SAM-YEUL LEE
History: EUN-KOO PARK

College of Natural Sciences:

Mathematics: EUN-SOON PARK
Statistics: GUN-SEOG KANG

School of Basic Sciences

Physics: CHANG-BAE KIM
Chemistry: KUAN-SOO SHIN

College of Law:

Law: CHEOL-HONG YOON

College of Social Sciences:

Social Work: HE-LEN NOH
Public Administration: YOON-SHIK LEE

Political Science and Diplomacy: JANG-KWON KIM
Japanese Studies: JANG-CHUL SHIN

College of Economics and Commerce:

School of Economics and World Commerce
Economics: YOU-YOUNG PARK
World Commerce: HEON-DEOK YOON

School of Business Administration
Business Administration: JAE-KWAN LEE
Small Business: DAE-YONG CHUNG
Accounting: DAE-KEUN KIM

College of Engineering:
Chemical Engineering: YOUNG-WOO NAM
Textile Engineering: YONG-HO KIM
Mechanical Engineering: YOUNG-PIL KWON
Architectural Engineering: MOON-SANG CHO
Industrial Engineering: IN-SOO CHOI

School of Electronics, Electrics and Information Telecommunication
Electronics Engineering: SUN-TAE JEONG
Electrical Engineering: JAE-CHUL KIM
Information Telecommunication Engineering: CHUL-HUN SEO

SUNG KYUN KWAN UNIVERSITY

53, 3-Ga, Myongnyun-dong, Chongo-gu, Seoul 110-745 (Humanities and Social Sciences Campus); 300, Chunchun-dong, Jangan-gu, Suwon, Kyonggi-do 440-745 (Natural Sciences Campus)

Telephone: (2) 760-0114
Fax: (2) 744-2453

Founded 1398
University status 1953
Private control
Academic year: March to August, September to February

Chairman of the Board of Trustees: PAIK NAM-OK
President: CHUNG BUM-JIN
Vice-Presidents: YUN KUN-SHIK, JEON MONG-GAG
Academic Affairs Officer: SHIM YUN-CHONG
Librarian: CHOI SUNG-JIN

Library of 600,000 vols; additional college libraries
Number of teachers: 450
Number of students: 21,000

Publications: *Sung Kyun Newspaper* (weekly, in Korean), *Sung Kyun Times* (weekly, in English), *Journal of Eastern Culture, Journal of Humanities, Social Science Review, Korean Economic Review, Report of the Institute of Science and Technology* (annually), *Student Guidance, Sung Kyun Law Review, Sung Kyun Pharmaceutical Journal, Journal of Natural Sciences.*

DEANS

College of Life Science and Natural Resources: DONG-HYUK KEUM
College of Education: SHEON-CHONG KIM
College of Humanities: MIN-HONG LEE
College of Confucian Studies: JAI-HYUCK YANG
College of Law: HONGUIN RHIM
College of Social Science: KEE-SOON PARK
College of Economics and Business: DOUNG-WOONG HAHN
College of Sciences: BYUNG-LAE CHAE
College of Engineering: JAE-HWA CHOI
College of Pharmacy: OK-PYO ZEE
College of Human Life Sciences: KYOUNG-SOOK CHOI
College of Sports Science: TAE-YUL SON
College of Medicine: JUNG-DON SEO
College of Art: KUM-NAM BAIK
Graduate School: DAE-KYUNG SUNG
Graduate Evening School of Foreign Trade: WON-SUK OH
Graduate Evening School of Business Administration: JAY-YOUNG CHUNG
Graduate Evening School of Public Administration: BOM HUR
Graduate Evening School of Education: GIK-SOO SOHN
Graduate Evening School of Confucian Studies: JAI-HYUCK YANG
Graduate Evening School of International Co-operation: CHANG-HYUN CHOI
Graduate Evening School of Mass Communication and Journalism: YONG-SOON YIM
Graduate Evening School of Information and Communication: JUNG-BAE BANG
Graduate Evening School of Design: JIN-WOOK CHUNG

HEADS OF FACULTIES, SCHOOLS AND DEPARTMENTS

College of Confucian Studies:
School of Oriental Studies: JAI-HYUCK YANG

College of Humanities:
Faculty of Language and Literature: HAK-SONG KIM
Faculty of Humanities: JWA-YONG LEE

College of Law:
Department of Law: HYUNG-SUNG KIM

College of Social Sciences:
Faculty of Social Sciences: KEE-SOON PARK

College of Economics and Business:
School of Economics: YONG-HOON LEE
School of Business Administration: TAE-UNG KIM

College of Sciences:
Faculty of Natural Sciences: BYUNG-LAE CHAE

College of Engineering:
School of Electrical and Computer Engineering: KEUN-YOUNG LEE
School of Chemical, Polymer and Textile Engineering: DOO-SUNG LEE
School of Metallurgical and Materials Engineering: HYUN-KU CHANG
School of Mechanical Engineering: CHUL-JU KIM
School of Architecture, Landscape Architecture and Civil Engineering: DONG-GUEN LEE
Department of Industrial Engineering: DONG-WON CHOI

College of Life Science and Natural Resources:
Faculty of Life Science and Natural Resources: DONG-HYUK KEUM

College of Pharmacy:
Faculty of Pharmacy: OK-PYO ZEE

College of Human Life Sciences:
Faculty of Human Life Sciences: KYOUNG-SOOK CHOI

College of Education:
Department of Education: NAM-SUNG KIM
Department of Education in Classical Chinese: KYUNG-CHUN KIM
Department of Mathematics Education: OK-KI KANG
Department of Computer Education: JIN-WOOK CHUNG

College of Sports Science:
Department of Sports Science: SEUNG-HO YOON

College of Art:
School of Art: KUM-NAM BAIK

Graduate School:
Department of Confucian Studies: HANG-LYONG SONG
Department of Korean Philosophy: YOUNG-JIN CHOI
Department of Oriental Philosophy: SANG-HWAN BAK
Department of Philosophy: JWA-YONG LEE
Department of Korean Language and Literature: WOO-SIK KANG
Department of Korean Literature in Classical Chinese: KYUNG-CHUN KIM
Department of English Language and Literature: MAHN-GUNN YOUE
Department of French Language and Literature: BYUNG-DAE CHOI
Department of Chinese Language and Literature: IL-HO IM
Department of German Language and Literature: SUNG-KIE IM
Department of History: CHANG-HEE LEE
Department of Library and Information Science: YOUNG-MAN KO
Department of Education: NAM-SUNG KIM
Department of Psychology: YONG-WON SUH
Department of Law: HYUNG-SUNG KIM
Department of Public Administration: DONG-HYUN KIM
Department of Political Science: IN-SUB MAH
Department of Journalism and Mass Communication: JEONG-TAK KIM
Department of Sociology: YOON-CHANG SHIM
Department of Economics: KYUNG-HWAN BAIK
Department of Agricultural Economics: HO-SUNG OH
Department of Business Administration: TAE-UNG KIM
Department of Accounting: TAE-YOUNG PAIK
Department of Statistics: NAM-KUNG PYONG
Department of Foreign Trade: WON-SUK OH
Department of Home Management: KEE-OK KIM
Department of Fashion Design: JEE-HYE CHANG
Department of Art: IN-KIE WHANG
Department of Child Psychology and Education: YOUNG-SUK LEE
Department of Sports Science: SEUNG-HO YOON
Department of Biology: WOO-SUNG LEE
Department of Mathematics: WOO-SUNG LEE
Department of Physics: YOUNG-IL CHOI
Department of Chemistry: SEUNG-KYE KIM
Department of Electrical and Computer Engineering: KEUN-YOUNG LEE
Department of Chemical Engineering: JI-HEUNG KIM
Department of Advanced Materials: DONG-BOK LEE
Department of Mechanical Engineering: CHANG-SUNG SEOK
Department of Textile Engineering: BOONG-SOO JEON
Department of Civil Engineering: KYUNG-SOO JUN
Department of Architecture: CHANG-BOK YIM
Department of Mechanical Design: NAK-WON SUNG
Department of Industrial Engineering: DONG-WON CHOI
Department of Materials Engineering:-DEUNG-JOONG KIM
Department of Polymer Science and Engineering: JUNG-HO AHN
Department of Dairy Science: SOO-WON LEE
Department of Bio-Mechatronic Engineering: CHANG-HYUN CHOI
Department of Landscape Architecture: YOO-ILL KIM
Department of Genetic Engineering: SUNG-YOUL HONG
Department of Pharmacy: SUN-MEE LEE
Department of Pharmaceutics: YOUNG-HOON JUNG
Department of Industrial Design: JOONG-SOO LIM

UNIVERSITY OF SEOUL

90 Jeonnong-dong, Dongdaemun-ku, Seoul 130-743

Telephone: (2) 210-2114
Fax: (2) 210-2732

Founded 1918; Seoul City University until c. 1996
Maintained by Seoul Metropolitan Government
Language of instruction: Korean
Academic year: March to February

President: Dr JIN-HYUN KIM
Dean of Academic Affairs: Dr SANG-BURN LEE
Dean of Student Affairs: Dr JUNHO SONG
Dean of Planning and Development: Dr WON-YONG KWON
Director General of General Administration: KYUNG-TAE MIN
Director of Central Library: Dr SANG-SOON YIM

Library of 260,000 vols
Number of teachers: 237
Number of students: 9,492

Publication: *University Press* (weekly).

DEANS

College of Law and Public Administration: CHUL-WHA CHOI
College of Economics and Business Administration: CHAE-CHUL CHUNG
College of Engineering: SEUNG-YONG RHO
College of Liberal Arts and Natural Sciences: SANG-BAE KIM
College of Urban Sciences: KYU-MOK LEE
Liberal Arts Division: BOH-YOUNG CHIN
Graduate School: DONG-KYU KIM
Graduate School of Urban Administration: KYU-MOK LEE
Graduate School of Business Administration: CHAC-CHUL CHUNG
Graduate School of Engineering: SEUNG-YONG RHO

ATTACHED INSTITUTES

Institute of Metropolitan Development Studies: f. 1976; multidisciplinary research and other academic activities to solve problems arising in a rapidly expanding metropolis; Dir Dr CHANG-SEOK KIM.

Student Guidance Center: contributes to development of students through counselling and studying every phase of student activities; Dir Dr EU-YONG KIM.

Institute of Industrial Management: conducts various economic and business management research; promotes a close relationship between business corporations and the university; Dir Dr KYUN-SIK LEE.

Institute of Law and Administration: Dir Dr KI-BOUM KWON.

Institute for Humanities: Dir Dr MUN-KYU LEE.

Institute of Industrial Science and Technology: Dir Dr SANG-UK KIM.

Institute of Seoul Studes: aims to rediscover important values imbedded in the cultural and historical city of Seoul and to develop them academicaly and systematically; Dir Dr JON-HEE LEE.

Urban Anti-Disaster Research Center: Dir Dr HEE-IL RHO.

Center of Environmental Science and Technology: Dir Dr SHIN-DO KIM.

WON KWANG UNIVERSITY

344–2 Sinyong-Dong, Iri, Chollabuk-Do

Telephone: 50-5114

Founded 1946
Private control
Academic year: March to August, September to February

President: KIM SAM-RYONG
Vice-President (Academy): SONG CHON-EUN
Vice-President (Medicine): CHON PAL-KHN
Dean of Academic Affairs: GO GUN-IL
Dean of Planning Office: CHOI SEONG-SIK
Dean of Student Affairs: KIM JONG-SU
Dean of Financial and General Affairs: OH HAE-GEUM
Director of Library: LEE MAN-SANG

Number of teachers: 462
Number of students: 23,200

Publications: *Theses Collection,* departmental studies, etc.

DEANS

Graduate School: YU GI-SU
Graduate School of Education: YU JAE-YEONG
Graduate School of Industry: YUN YANG-WOONG
College of Won Buddhism: KIM HONG-CHULO
College of Liberal Arts and Sciences: OHM JEONG-OAK
College of Education: SHIN YO-YOUNG
College of Law: KIM DAE-KYOO
College of Agriculture: LEE KAP-SANG
College of Pharmacy: OCK CHI-WAN
College of Oriental Medicine: MAENG UNG-JAEO
College of Engineering: CHUNG SA-HEE
College of Social Sciences: KIM GUY-KON
College of Management: PARK JAE-ROK
College of Home Economics: MOON BUM-SOO
College of Dentistry: KIM SU-NAM
School of Medicine: CHUNG YEUN-TAI

HEADS OF DEPARTMENTS

College of Won Buddhism:

- Won Buddhism: KIM SEONG-JANG
- Won Buddhist Oriental Religion: RO KWON-YONG

College of Liberal Arts and Sciences:

- Korean Language and Literature: CHAE KYU-PAN
- English Language and Literature: YONG BYUNG-SEOK
- German Language and Literature: KIM CHANG-RYOL
- French Language and Literature: WON YOO-SANG
- Chinese Language and Literature: KANG TAE-KWON
- History: LEE JU-CHEON
- Dance: RHEE GIL-JU
- Philosophy: KIM SEONG-KWAM

College of Natural Science:

- Archaeology and Art History: SHIN SOON-CHUL
- Mathematics: LEE SEUNG-WOO
- Physics: LIM SUNG-WOO
- Statistics: KIM TAE-SUNG
- Chemistry: BAEK SEUNG-HWA
- Molecular Biology: KIM BYUNG-JIN
- Physical Education: KIM YONG-KYU

College of Law:

- Law: PEE JUNG-HYUN

College of Management:

- Management: CHUNG SOO-JIN
- International Trade: KIM JOONG-SHIK
- Accounting: SUL SUNG-JIN

College of Social Sciences:

- Public Administration: LIM KWANG-HYUN
- Mass Communication and Journalism: SONG HAE-RYONG
- Economics: JEONG GAB-WON
- Information Management: PARK RYUN
- Politics and Diplomacy: LEE WOO-JUNG
- Social Welfare: KIM SUNG-CHUN
- Health Policy and Management: KIM JONG-IN

College of Pharmacy

- Pharmacy: OK CHIN-WAN

College of Education:

- Korean Language Education: JEONG MYUNG-GI
- English Language Education: JUNG TAE-JIN
- Japanese Language Education: PARK JUNG-EUI
- Chinese Language Education: KIM DAE-HYUN
- History Education: YOON YONG-EE
- Education: KIM JUN-GI
- Commercial Education: KO YONG-BU
- Child Education: PARK HWA-YOUN
- Mathematical Education: CHOI KYU-HYUCK
- Physics Education: LEE HYUN-SOON
- Biology Education: PARK EUN-KYU
- Home Economics Education: PARK IL-ROCK
- Music Education: KIM YOUNG-SUN
- Physical Education: SHIN JONG-SOUN

College of Agriculture:

- Agriculture: LEE JOONG-HO
- Agricultural Chemistry: HAN SEONG-SOO
- Horticulture: YU SUNG-OH
- Forestry: RYU TAEK-KYU

College of Oriental Medicine:

- Pre-Oriental Medicine: YU HEUI-YOUNG
- Oriental Medicine: MAENG WOONG-JAE

College of Engineering:

- Construction Engineering: YANG KEEK-YOUNG
- Electric Engineering: JANG SUNG-HWAN
- Civil Engineering: LEE BYUNG-KOO
- Electronic Engineering: KANG YUNG-JIN
- Urban Planning Engineering: JUNG JUNG-KWEON
- Computer Engineering: HAN SUNG-KOOK
- Mechanical Engineering: KIM DONG-HYUN
- Control and Instrumentation Engineering: AHN TAE-CHON
- Materials Engineering: PARK HEE-SOON

College of Home Economics:

- Clothing: LEE SUN-HEUI
- Home Management: CHAE OCK-HI
- Food Nutrition: KIM IN-SOOK

College of Dentistry:

- Pre-Dentistry: KIM SANG-CHUL
- Dentistry: JIN TAI-HO

School of Medicine:

- Pre-Medicine: CHOI BONG-KYU
- Medicine: PARK SUK-DON

College of Fine Arts:

- Applied Fine Arts: NAM SANG-JAE
- Ceramic Crafts: KIM GI-CHUN
- Western Painting: LEE CHUNG-HEE
- Metal Crafts: OH YOUNG-KYUNG
- Korean Painting: KIM GUM-CHAUL
- Sculpture: YUN SEK-KU
- Calligraphy: KIM YANG-DONG

ATTACHED INSTITUTE

Won Kwang Medical Center: Dir JEON PAL-KEUN.

YEUNGNAM UNIVERSITY

Gyongsan 632

Telephone: Taegu 82-5111

Founded 1967 by amalgamation of Taegu College and Chunggu College
Private control
Academic year: March to February (two semesters)

President: Dr LEW JOON
Dean of Academic Affairs: Dr PARK BONG MOK
Dean of Student Affairs: Dr KIM JUNG YUEP
Dean of Business Affairs: Dr PARK SUNG KYU
Dean of Planning and Development: Dr YOON BYUNG TAE
Director of Library: Dr OH MYUNG-KUN

Library of 398,690 vols
Number of teachers: 549
Number of students: 22,506

Publications: *Yeungnam University Theses Collection, Library Guide, Yeungdae Munha* (Yeungnam University Culture), *Student Guide* (annually), and various faculty and institutional publs.

DEANS

College of Liberal Arts: KIM TAIK-KYOO
College of Science: KIM JONG DAE
College of Engineering: LEE DONG IN
College of Law and Political Sciences: RHEE CHANGWOO
College of Commerce and Economics: RYU CHANG OU
College of Medicine: KIM WON JOON
College of Pharmacy: SEO BYEONG CHEON
College of Agriculture and Animal Sciences: SYE YOUNG-SYEK
College of Home Economics: LEE KAP RANG
College of Education: SONG BYUNG SOON
College of Fine Arts: HONG SUNG MOON
College of Music: KIM SHIN WHAN
Evening College: BYUN JAE-OCK
Graduate School KIM HOGWON
Graduate School of Business Administration: KIM KIE-TAEK
Graduate School of Environmental Studies: JIN KAP DUCK
Graduate School of Education: CHUNG SOON MOK

PROFESSORS

College of Liberal Arts:

CHAE, S. H., Buddhist Philosophy
CHANG, H. K., Psychology
CHO, K.-S., Korean Language and Literature
CHUNG, Y. W., Archaeology
HU, J. W., Western Philosophy
HUH, C. Y., European History
HWANG, S.-M., English and Linguistics
KEWN, S.-H., English Drama
KIM, B. K., Western Philosophy
KIM, C. S., Korean Language and Literature
KIM, S. H., English Novel
KIM, S. J., Korean History
KIM, S. K., English Literature
KIM, S. M., English Poetry
KIM, T. K., Anthropology
KIM, W.-W., English Poetry
KWON, Y. G., English Language and Literature
LEE, B. J., Asian History
LEE, B. L., Korean Language and Literature
LEE, C. H., Western Philosophy
LEE, J. W., Chinese Prose, Phonology
LEE, S.-T., English Literature
LEE, S.-D., English Poetry
LEE, S. K., Korean History
LEE, Y. K., Philosophy of History, Social Philosophy
LEE, W. J., Philosophy
LIM, B.-J., French Language
MUN, C.-B., English Philosophy
O, S. C., Korean History
OH, M.-K., Sociology
SUH, I., American Literature
SUH, K. B., Chinese Poetry
YOH, K. K., English Language
YOUN, Y.-O., Korean Literature

College of Science:

CHANG, G. S., Physics
CHANG, K., Mathematics
CHO, H. S., Physics
CHO, Y., Mathematics
CHOE, O.-S., Physics
DOH, M. K., Inorganic Chemistry
KANG, S. G., Physics
KIM, D. S., Analytical Chemistry
KIM, J. D., Organic Chemistry
KIM, J.-C., Mathematics
KIM, M. M., Physics
KIM, Y. H., Physics
PAHK, G.-H., Mathematics
PARK, B. K., Physical Chemistry
PARK, H.-S., Mathematics
PARK, W. H., Biology
RO, H. K., Physics
WOO, J., Statistics

College of Engineering:

BAE, J. H., Electrical Engineering
BYUN, D. K., Civil Engineering
CHANG, D. H., Textile Engineering
CHO, B., Chemical Engineering
CHO, H., Textile Engineering
CHOI, S.-G., Electronic Engineering
CHOI, S.-H., Mechanical Design
CHUNG, K.-H., Eletronic Engineering
CHUNG, W.-G., Textile Engineering
HA, Z.-H., Mechanical Engineering
JOO, H., System Engineering
KANG, S. H., Chemical Engineering
KIM, D. O., Traffic Engineering
KIM, G.-C., Civil Engineering
KIM, H. S., Architectural Engineering
KIM, I.-J., Architectural Engineering
KIM, J. Y., Mechanical Engineering
KIM, K. S., Industrial Chemistry
KIM, S.-K., Textile Engineering
LEE, D. H., Control Engineering
LEE, D.-I., Electrical Engineering
LEE, J. H., Industrial Chemistry
LEE, K. S., Mechanical Engineering
LEE, M. H., Industrial Chemistry
LEE, M. Y., Electronic Communication
LEE, S. T., Civil Engineering
LEE, T.-S., Marine Engineering
PARK, J. Y., Civil Engineering
PARK, W.-K., Chemical Engineering
PARK, Y.-K., Industrial Chemistry
RO, C. K., Electrical Engineering
RO, H. J., Architectural Engineering
SOHN, Y. K., Computer Engineering
SONG, J. S., Textile Engineering
UM, W.-T., Urban Engineering
WU, M. J., Civil Engineering

College of Law and Political Science:

BYUN, J.-O., Constitutional and Administrative Law
CHANG, T.-O., Public Administration
CHO, C.-H., Civil Law
CHOI, J.-C., Public Administration
CHEUNG, W. J., International Law
KIM, J.-S., Public Administration
KIM, K.-D., Civil Law
KWON, H. K., Political Science and Diplomacy
LEE, W. S., Political Science and Diplomacy
PAIK, S. K., Public Administration
PARK, S.-W., Criminal Law
RHEE, C.-W., Political Science and Diplomacy
YOON, B. T., Public Administration

College of Commerce and Economics:

BAE, Y. S., Economics
HAR, C. D., Business Policy
KIM, J. H., Foreign Trade
KIM, K.-T., Economics
KIM, T. W., Business Administration
KWON, B. T., Economics
LEE, W.-D., Economics
PARK, S.-K., Business Administration
RYU, C. O., Foreign Trade
SANG, M. D., Business Administration
SHIN, H. J., International Theory and Policy
YI, Y. W., Economics
YOON, I. H., Economics
YU, H. K., Economics

College of Medicine:

CHUNG, J. H., Preventive Medicine
CHUNG, J. K., Microbiology
CHUNG, W. Y., Obstetrics and Gynaecology
HAH, Y. M., Dermatology
HAHN, D. K., Ophthalmology
HAM, D. S., Anatomy
IHIN, J. C., Orthopaedic Surgery
KIM, C. S., Internal Medicine
KIM, C. S., Pathology
KIM, S. H., General Surgery
KIM, W. J., Pharmacology
KWUN, K. B., General Surgery
LEE, S. K., Physiology
LEE, T. S., Pathology
LEE, Y. C., Anatomy
PARK, C. S., Neurology
SONG, K. W., Oto-rhino-laryngology

College of Pharmacy:

CHANG, U. K., Pharmacy
CHUNG, K. C., Pharmacy
CHUNG, S. R., Pharmacy
DO, J. C., Industrial Pharmacy
HAN, B. S., Industrial Pharmacy
HUH, K., Pharmacy
JIN, K. D., Pharmacy
KIM, J. Y., Industrial Pharmacy
LEE, M. K.,, Industrial Pharmacy
LEE, S. W., Pharmacology
SEOH, B. C., Industrial Pharmacy

College of Agriculture and Animal Science:

BYUN, J. K., Horticulture
CHOI, C., Food Technology and Science
CHUNG, H. D., Horticulture
CHUNG, Y. G., Food Science and Technology
JUNG, K. J., Animal Science
KIM, B. D., Community Development
KIM, J. K., Applied Microbiology
LEE, H. C., Animal Science
PARK, C. H., Agronomy
SON, J. Y., Animal Science
SYE, Y. S., Animal Science
YOON, W., Community Development

College of Home Economics:

CHO, S. Y., Food and Nutrition
HAN, J. S., Food Preparation
KIM, K. S., Food Science
LEE, J. O., Clothing Science
LEE, J. S., Home Management
LEE, K. R., Food and Nutrition
PARK, J. R., Food Science

College of Education:

AHN, Y. T., Business Education
BAEK, U. H., Developmental Psychology
CHO, D. B., Personality and Education
CHUN, B. K., Audio-Visual Method
CHUNG, S. M., History of Korean Education
CHUNG, Y. K., Linguistics
KIM, H., Evaluation
KIM, J. R., Physical Education
KWON, J. W., Educational Psychology
LEE, J. H., Physical Education
LEE, K. T., English Language Education
LEE, S. B., Mathematics Education
LIM, M. S., Physical Education
PARK, B. M., Philosophy of Education
PARK, Y. B., Curriculum and Instruction
SONG, B. S., Educational Psychology

College of Fine Arts:

HONG, S. M., Sculpture
KIM, Y. Z., Painting

College of Music:

KIM, S. W., Vocal Music

ATTACHED RESEARCH CENTRES

National Unification Research Center: Dir LEE WEON SUL.

Institute of Industrial Technology: Dir Prof. CHOI SUN-HO.

Institute of Social Science: Dir Prof. KIM KI-DONG.

Institute of Resources Development: Dir CHO SEO YEUL.

Saemaul and Regional Development Research Institute: Dir YOON WOOK.

Institute of Korean Culture: Dir Prof. O SEI CHANG.

Institute of Environmental Studies: Dir CHANG TAI-OK.

Institute of Natural Science: Dir KIM DONG SOO.

Institute of Humanities: Dir SHIN GUI HYUN.

Institute of Management and Economics Research: Dir HONG YOON-IL.

Marine Science Institute: Dir KIM KI TAE.

Institute of Basic Medicine: Dir HAM DOCK SANG.

Institute of Clinical Medicine: Dir HAHN DUK KEE.

YONSEI UNIVERSITY

134 Shinchon-dong, Sudaemoon-gu, Seoul 120-749

Telephone: 361-2114
Fax: 392-0618

Founded 1885
Private control
Languages of instruction: Korean and English
Academic year: March to February (two semesters)

President: BYUNG SOO KIM
Vice-President for Academic Affairs: JU HYUN YU
Vice-President for Medical Affairs: DONG GWAN HAN
Vice-President for Wonju Campus: JONG SOO KIM
Vice-President for University Development and Alumni: KEE YOUNG KIM
Dean of the University: YOUNG PIL PARK

Library: see Libraries
Number of teachers: 2,429
Number of students: 43,357

Publications: *Yonsei Chunchu, Yonsei Annals, Yonsei Non*-Chong, Abstracts of Faculty Research Reports, Journal of Humanities, Journal of Far Eastern Studies, Journal of East and West Studies, Social Science Review, Journal of Education Science, Engineering Review, Business Review, etc.

Faculties of: Liberal Arts, Business and Economics, Science, Engineering, Theology, Social Science, Medicine, Dentistry, Nursing, Law, Sciences in Education, Liberal Arts and Sciences, Commerce and Law, Health Science, Music, Human Ecology; Wonju Medical College.

Graduate School (Academic), United Graduate School of Theology, graduate schools of Business Administration, Education, Public Administration, Engineering, Health Science and Management, International Studies, Administrative Sciences, Mass Communication, Intellectual Property and Law.

AFFILIATED INSTITUTES

Institute of Korean Studies

Institute of East and West Studies

Lexicographical Center for the Korean Language

Bioproducts Research Center

Atomic-Scale Surface Science Research Center

Institute for Korean Unification Studies

Maeji Research Institute

Educational Research Institute

Research Institute for Community Development

Institute of Urban Studies and Development

Research Institute of ASIC Design

Center for Signal Processing Research

Research Center for Women's Concerns

Institute for the Humanities

Institute of Literary Translation

Institute for Social Development Studies

Research Institute for Human Behavior

Management Research Center

Yonsei Economic Institute

Institute of Natural Science

Institute for Mathematical Sciences

Institute of Life Science

Protein Research Institute

Global Environmental Laboratory

Research Institute for Software Application

Institute for Groundwater and Soil Environment

Engineering Research Institute

New Energy Systems Research Institute

Automation Technology Research Institute

Institute of Medical Instruments Technology

Institute of Automobile Technology

Information and Telecommunications Research Institute

Disaster Research Center

Radio Communication Research Center

Advanced Building Science and Technology Research Center

Urban and Transportation Science Research Center

Research Institute of Iron and Steel Technology

Yonsei Engineering Research Center

Institute of Christianity and Korean Culture

Center for Social Welfare Research

Social Science Research Institute

Institute for Communication Research

Legal Research Institute

Music Research Institute

Human Ecology Research Institute

Research Institute of Food and Nutritional Sciences

Research Institute of Clothing and Textile Sciences

Institute of Sports, Physical Education and Leisure Studies

Sports Science Institute

Institute of Health Services Research

Institute of Tropical Medicine

Institute of Environmental Research

Institute of Handicapped Children

Institute for Occupational Health

Institute for Cancer Research

Institute for Logopedics and Phoniatrics

Cardiovascular Research Institute

Institute of Genetic Science

Institute of Gastroenterology

Institute of Chest Diseases

Institute of Endocrinology

Institute for Transplantation Research

Yonsei Brain Research Institute

Institute of Vision Research

Rehabilitation Institute of Muscular Disease

Institute of Kidney Disease

Institute of Andrology

Research Institute of Traditional Medicine

Institute of Dental Research

Yonsei Dental Materials Institute

Institute of Craniofacial Deformity

Institute for Periodontal Tissue Regeneration

Nursing Policy Research Institute

Nursing Research Center for Injury Prevention

Research Institute of Home Health Care

Institute of Basic Science

Institute of Regional Studies and Development

Institute of Health Science Research

Medical Engineering Research Institute

Yonsei Institute of Environmental Science and Technology

Institute of Occupational Medicine

Institute of Basic Medical Science

Colleges

University of Korea, Songeui Campus: 505 Banpo-dong, Socho-gu, Seoul 137-701; tel. (2) 590-1141; fax (2) 590-1099; e-mail khmeng@cmc.cuk.ac.kr; f. 1954; library of 100,000 vols; 800 teachers; 900 students; Vice-President for Songeui Campus Prof. BOO-SUNG KIM; Dean of College of Medicine Prof. KWANG-HO MENG; Dean of College of Nursing Prof. JUNG-SOON MOON; publs *Journal* (quarterly), *Sungui Hakbo* (monthly), *Korean Journal of Occupational Health,* (quarterly), *Eui Mak* (annually), *Bulletin of Clinical Research Institute* (annually), *Catholic Medical Center Bulletin* (annually).

Catholic University of Taegu-Hyosung: 330 Kumnak 1-ri, Hayang-up, Kyongsan-shi, Kyongbuk 712-702; tel. (53) 850-3001; fax (53) 850-3600; e-mail presid@cuth.cataegu.ac.kr; f 1995; 4 graduate schools, 14 colleges (67 depts), 22 research institutes; 780 teachers, 11,132 students; library of 410,000 vols; Pres. Mgr KYUNG-HWAN KIM; publs *Research Bulletin* (1 a year), *University Bulletin* (1 a year).

KUWAIT

Learned Societies

GENERAL

National Council for Culture, Arts and Literature: POB 23996, 13100 Safat; tel. 4877085; fax 4873694; f. 1973; guidance and support in all fields of culture; sponsors art exhibitions, drama, publishes books and periodicals; Sec.-Gen. Dr FAROUQE AL-OMAR; publs *Al-Thagafa, Al-Alamiah, Alam Al-Ma'arifa.*

Research Institutes

ECONOMICS, LAW AND POLITICS

Arab Planning Institute, Kuwait: POB 5834, 13059 Safat; tel. 4843130; fax 4842935; f. 1966 with assistance from the UN Development Programme, and since 1972 financed by 17 Arab mem. states; trains personnel in economic and social devt planning; undertakes research and advisory work and organizes conferences and seminars on problems affecting economic and social devt in the Arab world; information centre consisting of 40,000 vols, 400 periodicals (in English and Arabic); special collection (institute publications) 103 titles; Dir Dr E. AL-SHAREEDAH.

EDUCATION

Gulf Arab States Educational Research Center: POB 12580, 71656 Shamia; tel. 4835203; fax 4830571; e-mail gaserc@kuwait.net; f. 1978 as part of Arab Bureau of Education for the Gulf States (see under Saudi Arabia); research on all educational topics; also provides training courses in developed curricula, educational statistics, educational evaluation, and educational research; Dir Dr RASHEED AL-HAMAD; Librarian MOHEI A. HAK.

MEDICINE

Arab Centre for Medical Literature: POB 5225, 13053 Safat; tel. 5338610; fax 5338618; f. 1983; part of Council of Arab Ministers of Health—Arab League; aims: the Arabization of medical literature and translation into Arabic of medical sciences, development of a current bibliographic data-base, issuing of Arabic medical directories, training of manpower in the field of medical information and library science; library of *c.* 1,000 vols; Sec.-Gen. Dr ABDEL RAHMAN AL-AWADI: publs *Arab Medical Doctors Directory, Directory of Hospitals and Clinics in Arab World, Directory of Health Education and Research Organizations in Arab Countries,* and other titles.

NATURAL SCIENCES

General

Kuwait Institute for Scientific Research: POB 24885, 13109 Safat; tel. 4816988; telex 22299; fax 4846891; f. 1967 to promote and conduct scientific research in the fields of food resources, water resources, oil sector support, environmental studies, infrastructure services and urban development, and economics and applied systems; scientific and technical information centre (see below); Dir-Gen. Prof. ADNAN H. AL-AQEEL; publs *Annual Research Report, Annual Report, Kuwait Bulletin of Marine Sciences.*

Libraries and Archives

Kuwait City

Kuwait University Libraries: POB 17140, Kuwait City; f. 1966; 253,000 vols, 3,690 periodicals, 2,941 MSS, 50 CD-ROM databases; Dir Dr HUSAIN AL-ANSARI; publs see University.

Safat

National Library of Kuwait: POB 26182, 13122 Safat; tel. 2415192; fax 2415195; f. 1936; 165,000 vols; 24 brs; Dir-Gen. WAFA'A AL-SANE.

National Scientific and Technical Information Centre: Kuwait Institute for Scientific Research, POB 24885, 13109 Safat; tel. 4818713; fax 4836097.

Museums and Art Galleries

Safat

Department of Antiquities and Museums: POB 23996, 13100 Safat; tel. 2426521; fax 2404862; Dir Dr FAHED AL-WOHAIBI.

Controls:

Kuwait National Museum: Arabian Gulf St, Kuwait City; f. 1957; antiquities dating from late Bronze Age to Hellenistic period, found at Failaka Island; ethnographic material.

Failaka Island Archaeological Museum: exhibits from excavations. (In 1997 the Museum was reported to be closed for reconstruction.)

Failaka Island Ethnographic Museum: collection of material from Failaka Island, housed in the old residence of the island's Sheikh. (Museum reported to be closed for reconstruction.)

Educational Science Museum: Ministry of Education, POB 7, 13001 Safat; tel. 2421268; fax 2446078; f. 1972; lectures, exhibitions, film shows, etc.; sections on natural history, science, space, oil, health; planetarium, meteorology; library of 2,000 vols; Dir KASSIM KHODAIR KASSIM.

University

KUWAIT UNIVERSITY

POB 5969, 13060 Safat, Kuwait

Telephone: 4811188

Founded 1962, inaugurated 1966

State control

Language of instruction: Arabic, except in faculties of science, engineering and petroleum, allied health science and nursing, medicine and department of English

Academic year: September to June (2 semesters)

Chancellor: HE The Minister of Higher Education Prof. ABDULLAH AL-GHUNAIM

President: Prof. FAIZA MOHAMMED AL-KHARAFI

Vice-President for Academic Affairs: Prof. HASSAN AL-ALAWI

Vice-President for Planning and Evaluation: Dr MOUDI AL-HUMOUD

Vice-President for Research and Graduate Studies: Dr ADEL AL-SABEEH

Vice-President for Academic Support Services: Prof. MALEK HUSSAIN

Dean of Admissions and Registration: Dr ABDULLA AL-FUHAID

Secretary-General: Prof. SA'AD AL-HASHIL

Library Director: Dr HUSEIN AL-ANSARI

Library: see Libraries

Number of teachers: 918

Number of students: 17,447

Publications: *The Journal in Science, The Journal of Social Sciences, Medical Principles and Practice, Islamic Studies Magazine, Journal of the Gulf and Arabian Peninsula, The Educational Journal, Arab Journal for Humanities, Annals of the Faculty of Arts, Journal of Law, Journal of Palestine Studies, The Arab Journal of Management Sciences, The Arab Journal of Linguistics.*

DEANS

College of Arts: Dr ABDULLAH AL-MOHANNA

College of Science: Prof. NOURIA AL-AWADI

College of Education: Dr ABDULAZIZ AL-GHANIM

College of Law: Dr AHMED AL-SAMDAN

College of Sharia and Islamic Studies: Dr MOHAMMED AL-SHAREEF

College of Commerce, Economics and Political Science: Dr SADIK AL-BASSAM

College of Engineering and Petroleum: Prof. HASAN AL-SANAD

College of Medicine: Dr ABDEL-LATIF AL BADR

College of Graduate Studies: Prof. NADER AL-JALLAL

College of Allied Health Sciences and Nursing: Dr HUSSEIN AL-MAHMOOD

College of Administrative Sciences: Dr YOUSUF AL-EBRAHEEM

College of Pharmacy: Dr DAVID BIGGS

College of Dentistry: Prof. JAN ROSENQUIST

Language Centre: Dr YAHYA ALI

(The College of Arts is in the process of being reorganized into two new Faculties. The Faculty of Humanities will consist of the departments of Arabic, English, History, Geography and Philosophy; the other faculty will include Information and Library Sciences, Mass Media, Sociology, Political Science and Psychology departments.)

HEADS OF DEPARTMENTS

College of Arts: POB 23448, Safat 13096.

- Arabic Language and Literature: Prof. MOHAMMED FATTOUH
- English Language and Literature: Prof. MOHAMED HELIEL
- History: Dr HUSSAIN AL-MISSRI
- Sociology and Social Work: Prof. FAROUK ZAKI YUNIS
- Philosophy: Prof. IMAM ABDEL FATTAH
- Geography: Dr FATEMA AL ABDUL-RAZZAK
- Psychology: Dr OWAIED AL-MASHAN
- Mass Communication: Dr JAMEL AL-MENAYES

College of Administrative Sciences: POB 5486, Safat 13055.

- Accounting: Prof. YOUSEF EL-ADLY
- Economics: Dr YOUSEF JAWAD
- Political Science: Dr AHMAD AL-BAGHDADI
- Quantitative Methods and Management Information Systems: Dr MOHAMMAD AL-AHMED

Management and Marketing: Dr HAMAD AL-DUAIJ
Finance and Financial Institutions: Dr NABEEL AL-LOUGHANI
Public Administration: Dr BADER AL-DAIHANI

College of Engineering and Petroleum: POB 5969, Safat 13060.

Chemical Engineering: Dr HABIB SHABAN
Civil Engineering: Dr OMAR AL-SALEH
Electrical and Computer Engineering: Prof. NASSER SHIHAB
Mechanical and Industrial Engineering: Dr NAJEM AL-NAJEM
Petroleum Engineering: Dr HABIB SHABAN

College of Law: POB 5476, Safat 13055.

International Law: Dr AHMED AL-SAMDAN
Private Law: Dr TAMAH AL-SHEMMARI
Public Law: Dr IBRAHIM AL-HAMOUD
Criminal Law: Dr MUBARAK A. AL-NUWAIBET

College of Education: POB 13281, Keifan 71953.

Educational Administration and Planning: Prof. ZEINAB AL-JABER
Educational Foundations: Dr JASEM AL-KANDARI
Educational Psychology: Dr BADR AL-OMAR
Curriculum and Methodology: Dr SALEH JASIM

College of Sharia and Islamic Studies: POB 17438, Keifan 74255.

Islamic Jurisprudence: Dr HASSANEIN MAHMOOD
Faith and Propagation: Prof. MUSSALEH BAYOUMI
Quranic Interpretation and Hadith: Dr ABDULAZEEZ SAQUR
Comparative Jurisprudence: Prof. MAHMOUD HASSAN

College of Medicine: POB 24932, Safat 13110.

Anatomy: Dr MOHAMMED ZAKI IBRAHIM
Biochemistry: Dr ARMS GRASSPIK
Community Medicine: Dr PHILIP MOODY
Medicine: Prof. K. V. JOHNY
Microbiology: Prof. T. D. CHUGH
Physiology: Prof. J. S. JUGGI
Pharmacology-Toxicology: Prof. CHARLES PILCHER
Psychiatry: Dr A. FIDO
Surgery: Dr A. BEHBEHANI
Organ Transplantation: Dr A. BEHBEHANI
Obstetrics and Gynaecology: Dr ALEXANDER OMO
Paediatrics: Prof. ALI MOOSA
Pathology: Dr NABEEN N. C. NAYAK
Radiology: Dr DAVID WATMOUGH
Nuclear Medicine: Dr A. OWUNWANNE

College of Allied Health Sciences and Nursing: POB 314704, Sulaibikhat 90805.

Medical Technology: Prof. MICHAEL MIKHIB
Health Sciences: Dr M. ALI SHAH
Radiology: Prof. DAVID NEWMAN
Nursing: Dr KATHLEEN SIMPSON
Physiotherapy: (vacant)

College of Science:

Mathematics and Computer Science: Dr BADER AL-SAQABI
Chemistry: Prof. MOHAMED ZAKI
Physics: Dr YACOUB MAKDESI
Zoology: Dr ABDUL MAJEED SAFAR
Botany and Microbiology: Dr AZZA MUSSALLAM
Geology: Dr OMAR SHERIF
Biochemistry: Prof. JASSIM AL-HASSAN
Statistical and Operational Research: Prof. ABDUL HAMED TAHA

Colleges

College of Technological Studies: POB 42325, 70654 Shuwaikh; tel. 4816122; fax 4813691; f. 1976; training-orientated engineering college; library of 6,510 vols, 180 periodicals; 322 teachers, 1,950 students; Dean Dr HAMED A. HAMADAH.

Telecommunications and Navigation Institute: POB 23778, 13098 Safat; tel. 4816677; telex 22269; fax 4834904; f. 1966; 1,500 students; Dir KHALEEL I. AL-ABDULLAH.

KYRGYZSTAN

Learned Societies

GENERAL

Kyrgyz Academy of Sciences: 720071 Bishkek, Chuy pr. 265A; tel. 26-45-41; f. 1954; depts of Physical-Engineering, Mathematical and Mining-Geological Sciences (Chair. ZH.ZH. ZHEENBAEV), Chemical-Technological, Medical-Biological, Agricultural and Biological Sciences (Chair. K. S. SULAIMANKULOV), Economics and Humanities (Chair. V. M. PLOSKIKH), Southern Region (Chair. ZH.T. TEKENOV); 31 mems, 53 corresp. mems; attached research institutes: see Research Institutes; library: see Libraries and Archives; Pres. T. KOLCHUEV; Chief Learned Sec. A. V. FROLOV; publ. *Izvestiya* (bulletin).

AGRICULTURE, FISHERIES AND VETERINARY SCIENCE

Kyrgyz Society of Soil Scientists: C/o Kyrgyz Academy of Sciences, 720071 Bishkek, Chuy pr. 265A; attached to Kyrgyz Acad. of Sciences; Chair. A. M. MAMYTOV.

HISTORY, GEOGRAPHY AND ARCHAEOLOGY

Kyrgyz Geographical Society: 720081 Bishkek, Bul. Erkindik 30; tel. 26-47-21; Chair. S. U. UMURZAKOV.

NATURAL SCIENCES

Biological Sciences

Kyrgyz Biochemical Society: C/o Kyrgyz Academy of Sciences, 720071 Bishkek, Chuy pr. 265A; attached to Kyrgyz Acad. of Sciences; Chair. P. P. VALUISKY.

Kyrgyz Genetics and Selection Society: 720071 Bishkek, Chuy pr. 265A; tel. 24-39-94; Chair. M. M. TOKOBAEV.

Kyrgyz Ornithological Society: C/o Kyrgyz Academy of Sciences, Chuy pr. 265, 720071 Bishkek, Chuy pr. 265A; attached to Kyrgyz Acad. of Sciences; Chair. ERKIN S. KASYBEKOV.

Kyrgyz Physiological Society: C/o Kyrgyz Academy of Sciences, 720071 Bishkek, Chuy pr. 265A; attached to Kyrgyz Acad. of Sciences; Chair. V. A. PECHENOV.

Kyrgyz Society of Helminthology: C/o Kyrgyz Academy of Sciences, 720071 Bishkek, Chuy pr. 265A; attached to Kyrgyz Acad. of Sciences; Chair. M. M. TOKOBAEV.

Physical Sciences

Kyrgyz Astronomic-Geodesy Society: C/o Kyrgyz Academy of Sciences, 720071 Bishkek, Chuy pr. 265A; attached to Kyrgyz Acad. of Sciences;Chair. I. B. BIYBOSUNOV.

Kyrgyz Mineralogical Society: C/o Kyrgyz Academy of Sciences, 720071 Bishkek, Chuy pr. 265A; attached to Kyrgyz Acad. of Sciences; Chair. A. B. BAKIROV.

PHILOSOPHY AND PSYCHOLOGY

Kyrgyz Philosophical Society: C/o Kyrgyz Academy of Sciences, 720071 Bishkek, Chuy pr. 265A; attached to Kyrgyz Acad. of Sciences; Chair. A. A. SALIEV.

Kyrgyz Psychological Society: C/o Kyrgyz Academy of Sciences, 720071 Bishkek, Chuy pr. 265A; attached to Kyrgyz Acad. of Sciences; Chair. A. A. BRUDNIY.

Research Institutes

AGRICULTURE, FISHERIES AND VETERINARY SCIENCE

Institute of Forest and Nut Studies: 720015 Bishkek, Karagachovaya rosha; tel. 27-90-82; attached to Kyrgyz Acad. of Sciences; Dir B. I. VANGLOVSKY.

Research Technological Institute of Pastures and Fodder: Sokuluksky raion, Pos. Komsomolsky; f. 1976.

Soil Science Research Institute: 720000 Bishkek, Ul. Orozbekova 44; tel. 22-16-11; f. 1964.

ECONOMICS, LAW AND POLITICS

Institute of Economics and Politics: 720071 Bishkek, Chuy pr. 265A; tel. 25-53-90; attached to Kyrgyz Acad. of Sciences; Dir D. S. LAILIEV.

Institute of Philosophy and Law: 720071 Bishkek, Chuy pr. 265A; tel. 25-53-54; attached to Kyrgyz Acad. of Sciences; Dir O. A. TOGUSAKOV.

EDUCATION

Pedagogical Research Institute: 720319 Bishkek, Pr. Dzerzhinskogo 25; tel. 22-03-13; f. 1951.

HISTORY, GEOGRAPHY AND ARCHAEOLOGY

Institute of History: 720071 Bishkek, Chuy pr. 265A; tel. 25-19-75; attached to Kyrgyz Acad. of Sciences; Dir S. S. DANIYAROV.

LANGUAGE AND LITERATURE

Institute of Linguistics and Literature: 720071 Bishkek, Chuy pr. 265A; tel. 24-34-95; fax 24-36-07; f. 1954; attached to Kyrgyz Acad. of Sciences; Dir Prof. DZH. SYDYKOV.

MEDICINE

Institute of Medical Problems: Osh; tel. 3-17-18; attached to Kyrgyz Acad. of Sciences; Dir R. T. TOLCHUEV.

Kyrgyz Institute of Cardiology: 720040 Bishkek, Togolok Moldo 3; tel. (3312) 26-12-95; fax (3312) 22-76-37; f. 1977; library of 5,000 vols; Dir ALEFTINA BIRUKOVA; publ. *Central Asian Medical Journal* (6 a year).

Kyrgyz Research Institute of Obstetrics and Paediatrics: 720040 Bishkek, Togolok Moldo 1; tel. (3312) 22-67-19; fax (3312) 26-42-75; e-mail oroz@uzakov.bishkek.su; f. 1961; library of 14,000 vols; Dir DUYSHA KUDAYAROV.

Research Institute of Prophylaxis and Medical Ecology: 720005 Bishkek, Sovetskaya 34; tel. 44-41-39; f. 1988; library of 22,000 vols; Dir Prof. R. O. KHAMZAMULIN.

NATURAL SCIENCES

Biological Sciences

Institute of Biochemistry and Physiology: 720071 Bishkek, Chuy pr. 265; tel. 52-47-32; attached to Kyrgyz Acad. of Sciences; Dir P. P. VALUISKY.

Institute of Biology and Soil: 720071 Bishkek, Chuy pr. 265A; tel. 25-53-70; attached to Kyrgyz Acad. of Sciences; Dir E. DZH. SHUKUROV.

Mathematical Sciences

Institute of Mathematics: 720071 Bishkek, Chuy pr. 265; tel. 24-38-50; attached to Kyrgyz Acad. of Sciences; Dir M. I. IMANALIEV.

Physical Sciences

Institute of Geology: 720481 Bishkek, Bul. Erkindik 30; tel. 26-48-60; attached to Kyrgyz Acad. of Sciences; Dir A. B. BAKIROV.

Institute of Mountain Physiology and Experimental Pathology of High Rocks: 720022 Bishkek, Ul. Gorkogo 1/5; tel. 23-94-00; attached to Kyrgyz Acad. of Sciences; Dir A. S. SHANAZAROV.

Institute of Physics: 720071 Bishkek, Chuy pr. 265A; tel. 25-52-59; attached to Kyrgyz Acad. of Sciences; Dir ZH. ZH. ZHEENBAEV.

Institute of Physics and Mechanics of Rocks: 720815 Bishkek, Ul. Mederova 98; tel. 44-38-01; f. 1960; attached to Kyrgyz Acad. of Sciences; library of 500,000 vols; Dir I. T. AITMATOV.

Institute of Seismology: 720060 Bishkek, Asanbay 52/1; tel. (3312) 46-29-42 fax (3312) 46-29-04; Dir A. T. TURDUKULOV.

Institute of the Biosphere: Dzhalal-Abad; tel. 3-40-54; attached to Kyrgyz Acad. of Sciences; Dir K. S. ASHYMOV.

RELIGION, SOCIOLOGY AND ANTHROPOLOGY

Centre for Social Research: 720071 Bishkek, Chuy pr. 265A; tel. 24-37-35; attached to Kyrgyz Acad. of Sciences; Dir N. A. OMURALEV.

Institute of Social Sciences: Osh; tel. 7-51-42; attached to Kyrgyz Acad. of Sciences; Dir P. K. KUPUEV.

TECHNOLOGY

Institute for the Complex Utilization of Natural Resources: 744017 Osh, Ul. Isanova 83; tel. 5-38-80; attached to Kyrgyz Acad. of Sciences; Dir ZH. T. TEKEPOV.

Institute of Automation: Bishkek, Chuy pr. 265; tel. 25-43-73; attached to Kyrgyz Acad. of Sciences; Dir ZH. SH. SHARSHENALIEV.

Institute of Chemistry and Chemical Technology: 720071 Bishkek, Chuy pr. 265; tel. 25-38-81; attached to Kyrgyz Acad. of Sciences; Dir SH. ZH. ZHOROBEKOVA.

Institute of Energetics and Microelectronics: Dzhalal-Abad; tel. 3-22-06; attached to Kyrgyz Acad. of Sciences; Dir T. B. BEKBOLOTOV.

Institute of Machinery Studies: 720055 Bishkek, Ul. Skryabina 23; tel. (3312) 24-27-29; fax (3312) 42-27-85; attached to Kyrgyz Acad. of Sciences; Dir S. ABDRALPSOV.

Institute of New Technologies: Osh; tel. 2-45-32; attached to Kyrgyz Acad. of Sciences; Dir A. M. MARIPOV.

Institute of Water Problems and Hydro-Power Engineering: 72003 Bishkek, Ul. Frunze 533; tel. 21-06-74; attached to Kyrgyz Acad. of Sciences; Dir D. M. MAMARKANOV.

Libraries and Archives

Bishkek

Central Library of the Kyrgyz Academy of Sciences: 720071 Bishkek, Chuy pr. 265A; tel. 24-27-59; f. 1943; 985,000 vols; Dir L. A. BONDAREVA.

Chernyshevskii, N. G., State Public Library of Kyrgyzstan: 720873 Bishkek, Ul. Ogonbaeva 242; tel. 6-25-70; 3,514,700 vols; Dir A. S. SAGIMBAEVA.

Kyrgyz State University Library: 720024 Bishkek, Ul. Frunze 547; tel. 9-98-26; 931,500 vols; Dir M. A. ASANBAEV.

Scientific and Technical Library of Kyrgyzstan: 720302 Bishkek, Chuy pr. 106; 5,817,000 vols (without patents); Dir S. I. MAKAROV.

Museums and Art Galleries

Bishkek

Botanical Garden: 720676 Bishkek, 50 Let. Oktyabrya 1A; tel. 43-53-55; f. 1938; attached to Kyrgyz Acad. of Sciences; library of 15,000 vols; Dir V. P. KRIVORUCHKO; publ. *Introduktsiya i Akklimatizatsiya Rastenii v Kyrgyzstane* (1 a year).

Kyrgyz State Museum of Fine Art: Bishkek, Pervomaiskaya ul. 90; modern art; Dir K. N. UZUBALIEVA.

State Historical Museum of Kyrgyzstan: Bishkek, Krasnooktyabrskaya ul. 236; Dir N. M. SEITKAZIEVA.

University

KYRGYZ STATE UNIVERSITY

720024 Bishkek, Ul. Frunze 537

Telephone: 26-26-34

Founded 1951

Rector: M. Z. ZAKIROV

Number of teachers: 600

Number of students: 13,000

Faculties of history, law, Russian philology, Kyrgyz philology and journalism, foreign languages, economics, geography, physics, mathematics, information science and applied mathematics, biology, chemistry; br. at Przhevalsk

Other Higher Educational Institutes

Kyrgyz Agricultural Academy: 720005 Bishkek, Ul. Mederova 68; tel. 44-19-34; fax 44-47-07; f. 1933; depts: agronomy, agricultural engineering, veterinary science, agricultural economics, zootechnics, irrigation and land reclamation, agricultural business; 289 teachers; 7,000 students; library of 1,043,000 vols; Pres. J. AKIMALIEV; publ. *Ayil Charba Adisi* (monthly).

Kyrgyz State Institute of Fine Art: 720460 Bishkek, Ul. Dzhantosheva 115; tel. 47-02-25; f. 1967; music, cultural studies, language and literature, theatre, ballet; 186 teachers; 765 students; library of 4,500 vols; Rector A. ASAKEEV.

Kyrgyz State Medical Institute: 720061 Bishkek, Ul. 50 let. Oktyabrya 92; tel. 4-50-51; library of 600,000 vols; Rector Prof. A. M. MURZALIEV.

Kyrgyz Technical University: 720044 Bishkek, Pr. Mira 66; tel. (3312) 44-09-70; fax (3312) 44-53-69; f. 1954; faculties: automated production management, mechanical engineering, technology, power engineering, fundamental sciences, distance education; 440 teachers; 4,569 students; library of 719,000 vols; Pres. Dr R. N. USUBAMATOV.

LAOS

Learned Societies

RELIGION, SOCIOLOGY AND ANTHROPOLOGY

Lao Buddhist Fellowship: Maha Kudy, That Luang, Vientiane; f. 1964; Pres. Rev. THONG KHOUNE ANANTASUNTHONE; Vice-Pres. Rev. PHONG SAMALEUX, Rev. PRECHA SOUTHAMAKOSANE; Sec.-Gen. Rev. SIHO SIHAVONG.

Libraries and Archives

Vientiane

Bibliothèque Nationale: BP 122, Ministry of Information and Culture, Vientiane; tel. 21-21-24-52; fax 21-21-30-29; e-mail pfd-mill@pan.laos.net.la; f. 1956; compiles nat. bibliography; 300,000 vols, 120 periodicals, 250 maps, 6,000 MSS; spec. collns include palm leaf MSS; Dir KONGDEUANE NETTAVONGS; publs magazine on preservation of Lao palm-leaf MSS (3 a year), *Vannasinh* (3 a year), *Siengkhene* (3 a year).

National University of Laos Central Library: Dongdok, Vientiane; f. 1995; 50,000 vols.

Museums and Art Galleries

Vientiane

Ho Phakeo: Setthathiraj Rd, Vientiane; built 1563 by King Setthathiraj, became national museum 1965.

That Luang: Saysettha District, Vientiane; built 1566 by King Saysetthathiraj, restored 1930.

Wat Sisaket: Lane Xang Ave, Vientiane; f. 1828 by King Anuvong.

University

NATIONAL UNIVERSITY OF LAOS

POB 7322, Vientiane
Telephone: 21-41-36-31
Fax: 21-41-23-81
E-mail: kongsy@pan-laos.net.la
Founded 1995
State control
Language of instruction: Lao
Academic year: September to June
Rector: Dr BOSENGKHAM VONGDARA
Vice-Rectors: SAYAMANG VONGSAK (Academic and Student Affairs), TUYEN DONGVAN (Administration and Finance)
Chief Administrative Officer: Dr KONGSY SENGMANY
Librarian: CHANSY PHUANGSOUKET
Library of 68,000 vols
Number of teachers: 506
Number of students: 9,889

DEANS

Faculty of Education: KHAM-ANE SAYASONE
Faculty of Sciences: BOUAKHAYKHONE SVENGSUKSA
Faculty of Social Sciences and Humanities: SOUPHAB KHUANGVICHITH
Faculty of Economics and Management: KHAMLUSA NOUANSAVANH (acting)
Faculty of Engineering and Architecture: SOMKOT MANGNOMEK
Faculty of Medical Science: BOUNSAY THOVISOUK
Faculty of Agriculture and Forestry: THONGPHANH KOUSONSAVATH
Faculty of Law and Administration: THONGDY KEOMANY

LATVIA

Learned Societies

GENERAL

Latvian Academy of Sciences 1524 Riga, laukums 1; tel. 722-53-61; fax 782-11-53; e-mail lza@ac.lza.lv; divisions of Physical and Technical Sciences (Chair. J. Ekmanis, Scientific Sec. E. L. Tjunina), Chemical and Biological Sciences (Chair. M. J. Līdaka, Scientific Sec. B. Ādamsone), Social Sciences and Humanities (Chair. V. V. Hausmanis, Scientific Sec. I. Tālberga); 79 mems, 59 corresp. mems, 76 foreign mems, 47 hon. mems; attached research institutes: see Research Institutes; library: see Libraries and Archives; President: T. Millers; Sec.-Gen. A. Siliņš; publs *Vestis* (Proceedings), *Latvijas Fizikas ur Tehnisko Zinātnu Žurnāls* (Latvian Journal of Physical and Technical Sciences), *Kompozītmateriālu Mehānika* (Mechanics of Composite Materials), *Magnitnaya Gidrodinamika* (Magnetic Hydrodynamics), *Heterociklisko Savienojumu Ķīmija* (Chemistry of Heterocyclic Compounds), *Latvijas Kīmijas Žurnāls* (Latvian Chemical Journal), *Automātika un Skaitlošanas Tehnika* (Automation and Computer Engineering).

Research Institutes

ECONOMICS, LAW AND POLITICS

Institute of Economics: 1050 Riga, Akadēmijas laukums 1; tel. 722-28-30; fax 782-06-08; e-mail raimara@ac.lza.lv; attached to Latvian Acad. of Sciences; Dir Raita Karnīte.

EDUCATION

Educator Training Support Centre: 1011 Riga, 72 Brivibas iela; tel. 731-20-81; fax 731-20-82; e-mail jvvpvd@acad.latnet.lv; f. 1995; provides information and technical support for govt policy in further training of educators and adult training; attached to Min. of Education and Science; Dir Dr Sarmis Mikuda; publ. *Skolotājs*.

HISTORY, GEOGRAPHY AND ARCHAEOLOGY

Institute of History of Latvia: 1050 Riga, Akadēmijas laukums 1; tel. 522-37-15; fax 722-50-44; f. 1936; library of 4,000 vols; Dir Ą. Caune; publ. *Latvijas Vēstures Institūta Žurnāls* (Journal).

LANGUAGE AND LITERATURE

Institute of Literature, Folklore and Art: 1524 Riga, Akadēmijas laukums 1; tel. 721-28-72; attached to Latvian Acad. of Sciences; Dir V. Hausmanis.

Latvian Language Institute: 1050 Riga, Akadēmijas laukums 1; tel. and fax 722-76-96; e-mail latv@ac.lza.lv; Dir J. Valdmanis; publ. *Linguistica Lettica* (2 a year).

MEDICINE

Research Institute of Experimental and Clinical Medicine: 1004 Riga, O. Vaciesa iela 4; tel. 61-20-38; f. 1946; physiology, oncology; Dir Dr Velta Bramberga.

NATURAL SCIENCES

Biological Sciences

Institute of Biology: 2169 Rīgas rajons, Salaspils, Miera iela 3; tel. 294-49-88; fax 294-49-86; attached to Latvian Acad. of Sciences; library of 22,000 vols; Dir G. P. Andrušaitis.

Institute of Organic Synthesis: 1006 Riga, Aizkraukles iela 21; tel. 755-18-22; fax 782-10-38; f. 1957; attached to Latvian Acad. of Sciences; Dir E. Lukēvics; publ. *Chemistry of Heterocyclic Compounds* (in Russian and English, monthly).

Institute of Wood Chemistry: 1006 Riga, Dzērbenes iela 27; tel. 755-30-63; fax 731-01-35; f. 1958; attached to Latvian Acad. of Sciences; library of 5,000 vols; Dir J. Dolacis

Kirchenstein Institute of Microbiology and Virology: 1067 Riga, Ratsupites iela 1; tel. 242-61-97; fax 242-80-36; e-mail mikrob@acad.latnet.lv; attached to Min. of Education and Science; Dir V. Saulīte.

Research Centre of Applied Biochemistry: 2114 Rīgas rajons, Olaine, Rupnicu iela; tel. 96-43-22; Dir E. Ārens.

Physical Sciences

Institute of Astronomy of the University of Latvia: 1586 Riga, Raiņa blvd 19; tel. 722-31-49; fax 782-01-80; e-mail astra@acad.latnet.lv; f. 1946; Dir A. Balklavs-Grīnhofs; publs *Astronomiskais kalendārs* (Astronomical Calendar, 1 a year), *Zvaigžņotā Debess* (The Starry Sky, 4 a year).

Institute of Inorganic Chemistry: 2169 Rīgas rajons, Salaspils, Miera iela 34; tel. 794-47-11; fax 790-12-57; e-mail director@iic.sal.lv; f. 1946; attached to Latvian Acad. of Sciences; Dir Dr Janis Grabis.

Institute of Physical Energetics: 1006 Riga, Aizkraukles iela 21; tel. 755-20-11; fax 782-03-39; e-mail fei@edi.lv; f. 1946; attached to Latvian Acad. of Sciences; Dir Prof. J. A. Ekmanis; publ. *Latvian Journal of Physics and Technical Sciences* (6 a year).

Institute of Physics: 2121 Rīgas rajons, Salaspils, Miera iela 32; tel. 94-47-00; fax 782-01-13; attached to Latvian Acad. of Sciences; Dir O. Lielausis.

Nuclear Research Centre: 2169 Rīgas rajons, Salaspils, Miera iela 31; tel. 790-12-10; fax 790-12-12; attached to Latvian Acad. of Sciences; Dir A. Lapenas.

PHILOSOPHY AND PSYCHOLOGY

Institute of Philosophy and Sociology: 1940 Riga, Akadēmijas laukums 1; tel. 722-92-08; fax 721-08-06; e-mail fsi@ac.lza.lv; Dir Maija Kūle.

TECHNOLOGY

Institute of Electronics and Computer Science: 1006 Riga, Dzērbenes iela 14; tel. 755-45-00; fax 782-82-11; e-mail bilinsk@edi.lv; f. 1960; library of 10,000 vols; Dir Ivars Bilinskis; publ. *Automatika i vychislitelnaya technika* (6 a year).

Institute of Polymer Mechanics: 1006 Riga, Aizkraukles iela 23; tel. 755-11-45; fax 782-04-67; e-mail polmech@edzi.lza.lv; f. 1963; Dir J. Jansons; publ. *Mechanics of Composite Materials* (6 a year).

Research Institute for the Use of Polymer Materials in Land Reclamation and Water Management: 3000 Jelgava, Dobeles iela 43; telex 161826.

Scientific Research Institute of Microdevices: 1063 Riga, Maskavas iela 240; tel. 25-16-19; fax 25-10-00; f. 1962; semi-conductor devices and integrated circuits; Dir Arnis Kundzins.

Libraries and Archives

Riga

Latvian National Library: 1423 Riga, Kr. Barona iela 14; tel. 728-98-74; fax 728-08-51; e-mail lnb@com.latnet.lv; f. 1919; 5,100,000 units; Dir Andris Vilks; publs *Bibliotēku zinātnes aspekti* (annually), *Latviešu Zinātne un Literatūra* (irregular).

Library of the Latvian Academy of Sciences: 1235 Riga, Rūpniecības iela 10; tel. 710-62-06; fax 710-62-02; f. 1524; 3,100,000 vols, incunabula, MSS; spec. collns incl. Latvian literature; Dir Dr E. Karnītis.

Patent and Technology Library of Latvia: 1974 Riga, Šķūņu iela 17; tel. 722-73-10; fax 721-07-67; f. 1949; 15,500,000 vols (13,900,000 patents, 251,000 standards); Dir Agnese Buholte.

University of Latvia Library: 1820 Riga, Kalpaka blvd 4; tel. 22-39-84; telex 161172; fax 22-50-39; f. 1862; 2,100,000 vols; Dir G. Mangulis.

Museums and Art Galleries

Bauska

Bauska Castle Museum: 3901 Bauska, Brīvības blvd 2A; tel. 2-37-93; f. 1990; Bauska Castle history; Dir M. Skanis.

Cēsis

Cēsis Association of Museums: 4101 Cēsis, Pils iela 9; tel. 2-26-15; f. 1925; 9 ind. museums; history, ethnography; library of 8,000 vols; Dir A. Vanadziņš.

Riga

History Museum of Latvia: 1050 Riga, Pils laukumā 3; tel. 722-30-04; fax 722-05-86; f. 1869; Dir I. Baumane.

Latvian Open-Air Ethnographical Museum: 1056 Riga, Brīvības iela 440; tel. 799-45-10; fax 799-41-78; f. 1924; wooden structures from all over Latvia; archive of 70,000 units; Dir Juris Indāns.

Museum of Foreign Art: 1050 Riga, Pils laukumā 3; tel. and fax 722-87-76; f. 1773; library of 15,300 vols; Dir D. Upeniece.

Museum of the History of Riga and Navigation: 1050 Riga, Palasta iela 4; tel. 721-13-58; fax 721-02-26; e-mail gems@acad.latnet.lv; f. 1773; library of 24,000 vols; Dir K. Radziņa.

Rainis Museum of the History of Literature and Arts: 1629 Riga, Smilšu iela 12; tel. 22-01-34; fax 33-19-20; f. 1925; Dir P. ZIRNITIS; publ. *Raksti* (annually in Latvian).

State Museum of Art: 1342 Riga, K. Valdemāra iela 10A; Dir M. LĀCE.

Stradin Museum of the History of Medicine: 1360 Riga, Antonijas iela 1; tel. 722-29-14; fax 721-13-23; f. 1957; library of 48,000 vols, 17,153 rare books; Dir K. E. ARONS; publ. *Acta medico-historica Rigensia*.

Salaspils

National Botanical Gardens: 2169 Salaspils, Miera iela 1; tel. 294-54-60; fax 790-12-50; e-mail nbd@nbd.ord.lv; f. 1956; attached to Latvian Acad. of Sciences; library of 24,000 vols; Dir Dr K. BUIVIDS; publ. *The Baltic Botanical Gardens: Index Seminum* (annually).

Universities

RIGA TECHNICAL UNIVERSITY

1658 Riga, Kalku str. 1

Telephone: 22-58-85, 22-59-18
Telex: 161172
Fax: 22-58-85

Founded 1990

Rector: Prof. E. LAVANDELIS

Number of teachers: 1,400
Number of students: 14,600

Publication: *Scientific Transactions.*

Faculties of electrical engineering, civil engineering, radio engineering and communications, automation and computing, mechanical engineering, instrumentation and automation, architecture and construction, engineering economics and chemical engineering; preparatory and extra-mural departments.

UNIVERSITY OF LATVIA

1586 Riga, Bulvar Raina 19
Telephone: 722-90-76
Fax: 782-01-13
Founded 1919
Language of instruction: Latvian
Academic year: September to June
Rector: Prof. Dr J. ZAKIS
Vice-Rectors: J. KRUMINSH, J. LACIS
Librarian: G. MANGULIS
Number of teachers: 885
Number of students: 9,670
Publications: *Latvian Mathematical Annual, Humanities and Social Sciences Latvia, Latvijas Vēsture.*

Faculties of history and philosophy, foreign languages, physics and mathematics, chemistry, biology, geography, law, philology, teacher training, theology, economics and management, medicine.

ATTACHED INSTITUTES

Biomedical Research and Study Centre
Institute of Astronomy
Institute of Atomic Physics and Spectroscopy
Institute of Biology
Institute of Chemical Physics
Institute of Education and Psychology
Institute of Electronics and Computer Science
Institute of Geology
Institute of History
Institute of History of Latvia
Institute of Hydroecology
Institute of International Affairs
Institute of Land-Surveying and Geoinformatics
Institute of Latvian Language
Institute of Mathematics
Institute of Mathematics and Informatics
Institute of Molecular Biology and Biotechnology
Institute of Physics
Institute of Polymer Mechanics
Institute of Solid State Physics

Other Higher Educational Institutions

Latvian Academy of Arts: 1867 Riga, Kalpaka blvd 13; tel. 733-22-02; fax 722-89-63; f. 1921; depts: painting, sculpture, graphic arts, industrial design, textiles, fashion design, art history and theory, interior design, environmental art, graphic design, metal design, ceramics, glass, art education; 100 teachers; 638 students; library of 32,000 vols; Rector Prof. JANIS ANDRIS OSIS.

Latvian Academy of Medicine: 1007 Riga, Dzirciema iela 16; tel. 45-97-52; telex 161172; fax 782-81-55; f. 1951; higher medical education (faculties of medicine, dentistry, pharmacy and nursing), research work; 2,460 students; library of 319,000 vols; Rector Dr JĀNIS VĒTRA.

Latvian Academy of Music: 1050 Riga, Krishyana Barona iela 1; tel. 722-86-84; fax 782-02-71; f. 1919; piano, orchestral instruments, singing, choral conducting, music education, composition, musicology; 246 teachers; 426 students; library of 195,000 vols; Rector JURIS KARLSONS.

Latvian University of Agriculture: 3001 Jelgava, Lielā iela 2; tel. 2-25-84; fax 2-72-38; f. 1939; 7 faculties, 44 depts; 412 teachers; 4,450 students; library of 488,955 vols; Rector Prof. Dr VOLDEMĀRS STRĪĶIS; publ. *Works* (annually).

Riga Aviation University: 1019 Riga, Lomonosova iela 1; tel. 724-10-83; fax 724-15-91; e-mail rau@rau.lv; f. 1919 (present status 1992); faculties: mechanical engineering, radio electronics and computer systems, economics; 254 teachers; 3,038 students; library of 450,000 vols; Rector BORISS HEIMANIS.

LEBANON

Learned Societies

BIBLIOGRAPHY, LIBRARY SCIENCE AND MUSEOLOGY

Lebanese Library Association: POB 113/5367 Beirut; or c/o American University of Beirut, University Library/Gifts and Exchange, Beirut; tel. 374374, ext. 2623; telex 20801; fax (1) 351706; f. 1960; Pres. AIDA NAAMAN; Sec. LINDA SADAKA.

ECONOMICS, LAW AND POLITICS

Association Libanaise des Sciences Juridiques: Faculté de Droit et des Sciences politiques, Université Saint Joseph, BP 293, Beirut; tel. 200629; f. 1963; represents the Lebanon in the International Association of Legal Science; study of legal problems in Lebanon, conferences etc; 40 mems; Pres. PIERRE GANNAGÉ; Sec.-Gen. MELINÉ TOPAKIAN; publs. *Proche-Orient, Etudes Juridiques*.

Research Institutes

GENERAL

Centre d'études et de recherches sur le Moyen-Orient contemporain, Beirut: c/o Ambassade de France au Liban, (valise diplomatique), 128 bis rue de l'Université, 75531 Paris 07 SP, France; tel. (1) 615895; fax (1) 615877; e-mail cermoca@lb.refer.org; f. 1977; study of the Middle East in all its aspects: history, sociology, economy, human geography, physical geography, towns; library of 13,000 vols; Dir ELIZABETH PICARD.

Orient-Institut der Deutschen Morgenländischen Gesellschaft Beirut (Orient Institute of the German Oriental Society, Beirut): 44 rue Hussein Beyhum, Zokak al-Blat, POB 2988, Beirut; tel. (1) 602390; fax (1) 602397; e-mail oib@netgate.com.lb; f. 1961; activities in the field of Oriental research (Islamic, Arabic, Persian, Turcological, Semitic), philology, and contemporary history, incl. field research, history of the eastern Churches; co-operates with universities in the Middle East and Germany; library of 100,000 vols; br. in Istanbul (Turkey); Dir Prof. Dr ANGELIKA NEUWIRTH; publs *Beiruter Texte und Studien*, *Bibliotheca Islamica*.

ECONOMICS, LAW AND POLITICS

Centre for Arab Unity Studies: Sadat Tower Bldg, 9th floor, Lyon St, Hamra POB 113-6001, Beirut; tel. (1) 801582; fax (1) 865548; e-mail info@caus.org.lb; f. 1975; an independent, non-political centre for scientific research on all aspects of Arab society and Arab unity, particularly in the fields of economics, politics, sociology and education; activities are governed and implemented by three bodies: Board of Trustees, Executive Committee and General Secretariat; 50 staff; library of 8,000 vols, 634 periodicals; Dir-Gen. Dr KHAIR EL-DIN HASEEB; publs *Al-Mustaqbal Al-Arabi* (monthly), *Studies*.

Institut de Recherches d'Economie Appliquée: Faculté de Sciences Economiques, Université Saint Joseph, BP 293, Beirut; f. 1980; economic studies of the Lebanon and other Middle Eastern countries; Pres. Prof. LOUIS HOBEIKA; publ. *Proche-Orient, études économiques* (quarterly).

Institute for Palestine Studies, Publishing and Research Organization: POB 11-7164, Anis Nsouli St (off Verdun St), Beirut; tel. and fax (1) 868387; e-mail ipsbrt@cyberia.net.lb; (or 3501 M St N.W., Washington, DC 20007, USA; tel. (202) 342-3990; fax (202) 342-3927; e-mail jps@cais.com; or 13 Hera St, POB 5658, Nicosia, Cyprus; tel. 456165; fax 456324); f. 1963; independent non-profit Arab research organization; promotes a better understanding of the Palestine problem and the Arab-Israeli conflict; library of 32,000 vols (Arabic, Hebrew, English, French, German, Spanish and Russian); microfilm collection, private papers and archives; Chair. Dr HISHAM NASHABE; Exec. Sec. Prof. WALID KHALIDI; publs *Journal of Palestine Studies* (English, quarterly), *Revue d'études palestiniennes* (French, quarterly), *Majallat al-Dirasat al-Filistiniyah* (Arabic, quarterly).

HISTORY, GEOGRAPHY AND ARCHAEOLOGY

Institut Français d'Archéologie du Proche Orient: Rue de Damas, POB 11-1424, Beirut; tel. (1) 615844; fax (1) 615866; e-mail ifapo@lb.refer.org; f. 1946; Dir JEAN-MARIE DENTZER; library of 45,000 vols; brs in Syria and Jordan; publs *Syria, Revue d'Art et d'Archéologie, Bibliothèque Archéologique et Historique*.

Libraries and Archives

Beirut

American University of Beirut Libraries: POB 11/0236, Beirut; tel. (1) 340460; fax (1) 351706; f. 1866; 474,000 vols, 1,414 MSS, 2,918 current periodicals, 951,000 audiovisual items, 1,739 maps; Librarian HELEN BIKHAZI.

Beirut Arab University Library: POB 11-5020, Beirut; tel. (1) 300110; fax (1) 818402; e-mail bau@inco.com.lb; f. 1960; important collections on Lebanese, Arabic and Islamic studies; 110,000 vols and 1,500 periodicals; Chief Librarian SAID TAYARA.

Bibliothèque de l'Ecole Supérieure des Lettres: Rue de Damas, Beirut; 22,000 vols; Librarian FADL KASSEM.

Bibliothèque Nationale du Liban: Place de l'Etoile, Beirut; tel. 486374; fax 374079; f. 1921; copyright library, depository for UN documents; 150,000 vols, 2,500 MSS; Dir-Gen. RAMEZ ESBER; Librarian MONA BATAL.

Bibliothèque Orientale: Rue de l'Université St Joseph, POB 166 775, Beirut; fax (1) 200297; e-mail bibor@cyberia.net.lb; f. 1875; 174,058 vols, 2,800 MSS, 700 periodicals; Dir Rev. MARTIN MCDERMOTT.

Bibliothèques de l'Université St Joseph: BP 175 208, Beirut; faculties of law, economics, politics, administration: 100,000 vols, 550 periodicals; medical sciences (POB 115076): 12,000 vols, 125 periodicals; engineering (POB 1514): 10,000 vols, 115 periodicals; arts: 65,000 vols, 300 periodicals.

Near East School of Theology Library: POB 13-5780, Chouran, Beirut; tel. 354194; telex 44246; fax (1) 374129; e-mail nest .adm@inco.com.lb; f. 1932; ATLA; 40,000 vols; collection of MSS, collection of The American Press; 135 religious periodicals; Librarian Dr G. SABRA; publ. *Theological Review* (2 a year).

Daroon-Harissa

Library of the Syrian Patriarchal Seminary: Seminary of Charfet, Daroon-Harissa; tel. (9) 903040; f. 1786; 36,000 vols and 3,100 Syriac and Arabic MSS; Librarian Fr JOSEPH MELKI; publ. *Trait d'Union*.

Khonchara

Library of the St John Monastery: Khonchara; f. 1696; Basilian Shweiriet Order; 12,000 vols, 372 MSS; the Order preserves the first printing press in the Middle East with Arabic and Greek letters (first book 1734); Abbot-General Rt Rev. Mgr ATHANASE HAGE.

Saïda

Library of the Monastery of Saint-Saviour: Saïda; f. 1711; Basilian Missionary Order of Saint-Saviour; 28,500 vols and 2,550 MSS; Librarians SLEIMAN ABOU-ZEID, MAKARIOS HAIDAMOUS; publs *Ar-Riçalat* (monthly), *Al-Wahdat* (quarterly), *L'Ordo Grec-Catholique*, *An-Nahlat* (quarterly), *Nafhat Al-Moukhalles* (quarterly).

Museums and Art Galleries

Beirut

American University Museum: Ras Beirut; tel. 340549; telex 20801; fax (1) 351706; e-mail badre@aub.edu.lb; f. 1868; Stone Age flint implements; bronze tools and implements from Early Bronze Age to Byzantine Period; pottery and other artefacts from the Bronze and Iron Ages, Classical, Hellenistic, Roman and Byzantine Periods; Arabic pottery from the 8th–16th centuries; Phoenician glassware; Egyptian artefacts from Neolithic to Dynastic Periods; pottery from the Neolithic Period of Mesopotamia and cylinder seals and cuneiform tablets from Sumer and Akkad; numismatics of the countries in the eastern basin of the Mediterranean; Dir Dr LEILA BADRE; publs *Newsletter* (2 a year), *Berytus* (annually).

Daheshite Museum and Library: POB 202, Beirut; contains aquarelles, gouaches, original paintings, engravings, sculptures in marble, bronze, ivory and wood carvings; library of 30,000 vols (20,000 Arabic, 10,000 English and French), on arts, philosophy, history, literature, religions, etc.; Dir Dr A. S. M. DAHESH.

Musée des Beaux-Arts: POB 3939, Beirut; Dir Dr DAHESH.

Musée National (National Museum of Lebanon): Rue de Damas, Beirut; f. 1920; exhibits: royal jewellery, arms and statues of the Phoenician epoch; sarcophagus of King Ahiram (13th century BC), with first known alphabetical inscriptions; the collection of Dr G. Ford of 25 sarcophagi of the Greek and Hellenistic epoch; large collection of terracotta statuettes of the Hellenistic period; Roman and Byzantine mosaics; Arabic woods and ceramics; Dir-Gen. Dr CAMILE ASMAR; publs *Bulletin* and monographs.

Sursock Museum: Beirut.

Besharre

Musée Khalil Gibran: Besharre; dedicated to the life and works of the author.

Universities

AMERICAN UNIVERSITY OF BEIRUT

Bliss St, Beirut
Telephone: 350000
Fax: (1) 351706
Founded 1866
Private control
Language of instruction: English
Academic year: October to June

President: JOHN WATERBURY
Deputy President: SAMIR MAKDISI
Vice-Presidents: MAKHLUF HADDADIN (Academic), GEORGE NAJJAR (Regional External Programmes), GEORGES TOMEY (Administration).
Registrar: WADAH NASR
Librarian: HELEN BIKHAZI
Number of teachers: 420
Number of students: 5,000

Publications: *Berytus Archaeological Studies* (English, annually), *Al-Abhath* (Arab Studies, English and Arabic, quarterly), *Annual Research Report, University Catalogue.*

DEANS

Faculty of Arts and Sciences: KHALIL BITAR
Faculty of Health Sciences: MAKHLUF HADDADIN (acting)
Faculty of Engineering and Architecture: NASSIR SABAH
Faculty of Agricultural and Food Sciences: NUHAD DAGHIR
Faculty of Medicine and Medical Center: SAMIR NAJJAR
Division of Education Programs: MUNIR BASHSHUR
Student Affairs: FAWZI HAJJ

BEIRUT ARAB UNIVERSITY

Tarik El-Jadidé, POB 115020, Beirut
Telephone: (1) 300110
Fax: (1) 818402
E-mail: bau@inco.comb.lb
Founded 1960
Private control, established by the Welfare Society; academically associated with the University of Alexandria
Languages of instruction: Arabic and English
Academic year: October to June

President: Prof. Dr FATHY MOHAMED ABOU-AYANA
Secretary General: ISSAM HOURY
Secretary-General Responsible for Students' Affairs: MOUSTAFA HINNO
Chief Librarian: SAID TAYARA

Library of 110,000 vols
Number of teachers: 463
Number of students: 13,000 (internal and external)

DEANS

Faculty of Arts: Prof. Dr KHALIL HILMI E. KHALIL ABDALLAH
Faculty of Law: Prof. Dr OKASHA M. ABD. EL-AAL M.
Faculty of Commerce: Prof. Dr EL-SAYED A. M. DEBIAN
Faculty of Architecture: Prof. Dr MOHAMED A. IBRAHIM
Faculty of Engineering: Prof. Dr HASSAN NADIR A. H. KHEIRALLAH
Faculty of Science: Prof. Dr MOHAMED FAWZY A. A. AMIRA
Faculty of Pharmacy: Prof. Dr ADEL M. M. MOTAWAA
Faculty of Medicine: Prof. Dr MAMDOUH KOREITEM
Faculty of Dentistry: Prof. Dr SHERIF S. M. MOSTAPHA

PROFESSORS

Faculty of Arts:
ABOURADY, F. A., Geography
GHAZI, O. M. M., Applied Linguistics
SELIM, A. A. M., Ancient History

Faculty of Architecture:
EL-REMALY, M. A., Architecture and Urban Planning

Faculty of Commerce:
ABD. EL-FATTAH H., W., Accounting

Faculty of Engineering:
EL-MONEM, T. M. A., Automatic Control
FAROUKH, O. O., Electromagnetics and Optics
MOHAMED, F. E. M., Mathematics and Physics for Engineering
MOSTAFA A., M. Z., Electrical Engineering

Faculty of Law:
AL-MAJZOUB, M. M., International Law
AWAD, N. I. S., Civil Law
AWAD ALLA I., Z. H., Economics and Public Finance
BASSIOUNI A., ABD. EL-GHANY, Public Law
OMAR, N. I. H., Procedural Law

Faculty of Medicine:
EL-SHAMY, E. A. M. A., Physiology
FARAG, M. M. S., Histochemistry and Electron Microscopy
HEIKAL, F. S. A. M., Neuroanatomy

Faculty of Pharmacy:
CHAABAN A. M., I., Pharmaceutical Chemistry
EL-SHIBINI, H. A. M., Pharmaceutical Technology
KORANY S., M. A., Pharmaceutical Analytical Chemistry

Faculty of Science:
ALY, A. E. A., Physics
DOMA, S. E. B. A., Mathematics
HAMZA, F. A., Applied Mathematics

LEBANESE AMERICAN UNIVERSITY

POB 13-5053, Beirut
Telephone: (1) 867618
Fax: (1) 867098
Founded 1924 by the United Presbyterian Church, USA
Private control
Language of instruction: English
Academic year: October to June

President: RIYAD F. NASSAR
Vice-Presidents: Dr NABEEL HAIDAR (Academic Affairs), ELIAS BAZ (Finance and Administration), Dr LAYLA NIMAH (Student Affairs), Dr JAMES PELOWSKI (Development and Relations)
Registrars: FOUAD SALIBI (Beirut campus), EDGAR RIZK (Byblos campus)
Librarians: AIDA NAAMAN (Beirut campus), FAWZ ABDALLAH (Byblos campus)

Libraries with 160,000 vols, 1,100 periodicals
Number of teachers: 130 full-time, 215 part-time
Number of students: 4,650

Publications: LAU magazine (4 a year), *Al-Raida* (4 a year)

DEANS

School of Arts and Sciences (Beirut campus): Dr HADIA HARB
School of Arts and Sciences (Byblos campus): Dr NUHAD AKL
School of Business (Beirut campus): Dr TAREQ MIKDASHI
School of Business (Byblos campus): Dr WASSIM SHAHINE
School of Engineering and Architecture: Dr ABDALLAH SFEIR
School of Pharmacy: Dr SHIHADEH NAYFEH
School of Graduate Studies: Dr SHIHADEH NAYFEH

ATTACHED INSTITUTES

Institute for Women's Studies in the Arab World: Dir MONA KHALAF.
Institute for International Banking and Finance: Dir Dr ELIAS RAAD.
Centre for Research and Development: Dir Dr GEORGE NICOLAS.

UNIVERSITÉ DE BALAMAND

Box 100, Tripoli; located at: Koura
Telephone: (3) 335683
Fax: (6) 400742
E-mail: pr@balamand.edu.lb
Founded 1988
Private control
Languages of instruction: Arabic, English, French
Academic year: October to June

Chancellor: GHASSAN TUENI
President: ELIE SALEM
Vice-President: GEORGES NAHAS
Dean of Admissions and Registration: WALID MOUBAYED
Librarian: SAMEERA BASHIR

Library of 50,000 vols
Number of teachers: 320
Number of students: 1,619

DEANS

Faculty of Arts and Social Sciences: ELIE SALEM (acting)
Faculty of Engineering: MICHEL NAJJAR
Faculty of Health Sciences: NADIM KARAM
Faculty of Sciences: ROBERT HANNA
St John of Damascus Institute of Theology: Arch. PAUL YAZIGI
Lebanese Academy of Fine Arts: GEORGES HADDAD

UNIVERSITÉ LIBANAISE

Place du Musée, Beirut
Telephone: (1) 426440
Fax: (1) 395501
Founded 1951
State control
Languages of instruction: Arabic, French and English
Academic year: October to June

Rector: Dr ASSAD DIAB
Secretary-General: LATIFÉE LAKIS
Librarian: CHAKIB ANDRAOS

Number of teachers: 3,438
Number of students: 44,549

DEANS

Faculty of Literature and Humanities: Dr NASSIF NASSAR
Faculty of Sciences: Dr MOHSEN JABER
Faculty of Law, Political and Administrative Sciences: Dr IBRAHIM KOBEISSI
Faculty of Pedagogy: Dr JOSEPH ABOU-NOHRA
Faculty of Economics and Business Administration: Dr MOHAMMAD MARAACHLI
Faculty of Information and Documentation: Dr ELIE ASSAF
Faculty of Engineering: Dr ATA JABBOUR
Faculty of Agronomy: Dr MOUIN HAMZÉ
Faculty of Public Health: Dr BERNADETTE ABI-SALEH
Faculty of Medical Sciences: Dr ASSAD DIAB (acting)

Faculty of Pharmacy: Dr FATHI OUAIDA

ATTACHED INSTITUTES

Institute of Social Sciences: Dr ASSAD ZEBIAN.

Institute of Fine Arts: Dr HANI ABDEL NOUR.

Institute of Legal Information: Dr IBRAHIM KOBEISSI.

UNIVERSITÉ SAINT-ESPRIT DE KASLIK

POB 446, Jounieh

Telephone: (9) 640664

Fax: (9) 642333

Founded 1950

Private control (Lebanese Maronite Order of Monks)

Languages of instruction: French, English and Arabic

Academic year: October to June

Chancellor: Abbot JEAN TABET

Rector: Fr ANTOINE KHALIFE

Vice-Rector: Fr BASILE BASILE

Secretary-General: Fr NEHEMTALLAH YOUNES

Librarian: Fr SIMON SALIBA

Library of 200,000 vols

Number of teachers: 620

Number of students: 3,910

Publications: *Parole de l'Orient* (2 a year), *Bibliothèque de l'Université Saint-Esprit, Les Conférences de l'Université Saint-Esprit, Le Bulletin de l'USEK* (3 a year), faculty and institute publs.

DEANS

Pontifical Faculty of Theology: Fr BOULOS SFEIR

Faculty of Philosophy and Human Sciences: Fr GEORGES HOBEIKA

Faculty of Business Administration and Commercial Sciences: Fr LOUIS FERKH

Faculty of Arts: Fr CHOUKRALLAH CHOUFANI

Faculty of Fine Arts: Prof. HENRI EID

Faculty of Law: Fr BASILE BASILE

Faculty of Agricultural Sciences: Dr ELIE MECHELANY

Faculty of Music: Fr JOSEPH MIKHAEL

DIRECTORS

Institute of Liturgy: Fr HANI MATAR

Institute of History: Fr KARAM RIZK

Institute of Sacred Art: Fr ABDO BADWI

Department of Education: FRANCIS IMBS

Department of Interpretation and Translation: Fr CHOUKRALLAH CHOUFANI

Section of Foreign Languages: Fr CHOUKRALLAH CHOUFANI

Department of Architecture: GEORGES GHORAYEB

Department of Interior Design: MIGUEL DEBAILY

Department of Graphic Arts and Publicity: ANTOINE MATAR

Department of Photography: PAUL ZGHEIB

Department of Audiovisual Arts: ELIE KHALIFÉ

Scientific Institute of Nursing: Sr MATHILDE ZGHEIB

UNIVERSITÉ SAINT JOSEPH

Rue de Damas, BP 175208, Beirut

Telephone: (1) 426456

Fax: (1) 423369

E-mail: rectorat@usj.edu.lb

Founded 1875

Private control (Jesuit)

Languages of instruction: French, Arabic and English

Academic year: October to June

Rector: Rev. Fr SÉLIM ABOU

Vice-Rector (Research): MOUNIR CHAMOUN

Vice-Rector (Administration): Rev. Fr BRUNO SION

Secretary-General: HENRI AWIT

Library: see Libraries

Number of teachers: 1,867

Number of students: 6,609

DEANS AND DIRECTORS

Institute of Islamic/Christian Studies: Rev. Fr LOUIS BOISSET

Higher Institute of Religious Studies: MARIE-CLAUDE ROQUES

Faculty of Medicine: Dr PIERE FARAH

Faculty of Nursing: RUTH AKATCHERIAN

Faculty of Pharmacy: HERMINÉ AYDENIAN

Faculty of Dentistry: Dr ANTOINE HOKAYEM

Faculty of Engineering: MAROUN ASMAR

Faculty of Law and Political Science: RICHARD CHEMALY

Faculty of Economics: ALEXANDRE CHAIBAN

Faculty of Administration and Management: GEORGES AOUN

Faculty of Arts and Humanities: Rev. Fr RENÉ CHAMUSSY

Faculty of Sciences: RAGI ABOU CHACRA

Institute of Languages and Translation: HENRI AWAISS

Lebanese Education Institute: LEILA DIRANI

Institute of Theatrical, Audiovisual and Cinema Studies: AIMÉE BOULOS

Institute of Oriental Art: AHIAF SINNO

Institute of Laboratory Technicians in Medical Analysis: MICHEL ABOU KHALED

Higher Institute of Speech Therapy: ROUBA EL-KHOURY

Institute of Physiotherapy: Rev. Mother MARIE-LÉON CHALFOUN

National Institute of Communication and Information: WILLIAM HABRE

University Institute of Technology: MIREILLE MOUNSEF ABBOUD

University Institute of Teacher Development: HENRI AWIT

School of Midwifery: NAYLA DOUGHANE

Lebanese School of Social Development: HYAM KAHI

Higher School of Mediterranean Agricultural Engineers: MICHEL AFRAM

Centre of Banking Studies: FERNAND SANAN

Centre of Insurance Studies: CHARLES DAHDAH

ATTACHED RESEARCH INSTITUTES

Centre for Modern Arab World Research: Dir Rev. Fr JOHN DONOHUE

University Ethics Centre: Dir Rev. Fr JEAN DUCRUET

Centre for Arab-Christian Research and Documentation: Dir Rev. Fr SAMIR KHALIL

Institute of Health and Social Security Management: Dir Dr TOBIE ZAKHIA

Laboratory of Molecular and Cytogenetic Biology: Dir Rev. Fr JACQUES LOISELOT

Centre for Water and the Environment: Dir WAJDI NAJEM

Centre for the Study of Law in the Arab World: Dir ERIC CANAL-FORGUES

Centre for the Study of Markets and Distribution in the Middle East: Dir CAMILLE ASSAF

Centre for Economic Research on the Near East: Dir JOSEPH GEMAYEL

Lebanese Centre of Building Studies and Research: Dir (vacant)

Colleges

Académie Libanaise des Beaux-Arts: POB 55251, Sin-El-Fil, Beirut; tel. 480056; f. 1937; schools of architecture, decorative arts, publicity, plastic arts; library of 4,300 vols; 180 teachers, 600 students; Chair. Mgr GEORGES KHODR; Dir-Gen. GEORGES HADDAD.

Haigazian University: POB 11-1748, Beirut; tel. (1) 349230; fax (1) 350926; e-mail wcholakian@haigazian.edu.lb; f. 1955; private control; academic year: October to June; BA and BS in Arabic Studies, Armenian Studies, Biology, Business Administration, Chemistry, Christian Education, Computer Science, Education, English Literature, History, Mathematics, Medical Laboratory Technology, Physics, Political Science, Psychology; M.A. programmes in Educational Administration and Supervision, General Psychology and Clinical Psychology, MBA from autumn 1999; libraries (Armenian, Arabic and English) of 59,000 vols; 20 full-time teachers, 24 part-time; 500 students; Pres. JOHN KHANJIAN; Deans WILMA CHOLAKIAN (Administration), ARDA EKMEKJI (Arts and Sciences), FADI ASRAWI (Business and Economics); Librarian ZEVART TANIELIAN; publs *Haigazian Herald* (monthly), *Armenological Review* (1 a year).

Imam Ouzai College of Islamic Studies: POB 14-5355, Beirut; tel. (1) 704452; fax (1) 704453; f. 1979; BA, MA, PhD in Islamic Studies; incorporates documentation centre for bibliographic information on Islam and the Muslim world (Dir Dr BASSAM ABDUL-HAMID); teaching and examination centre in many countries; library of 50,000 vols, 1,400 periodicals, 1,000 maps, 700 audiovisual items; 50 teachers; 1,000 students; Chair. TOUFIC HOURY; Dean Prof. Dr KAMEL MOUSA: Sec. BADR-EDDINE NAWAR.

Islamic College of Business Administration: POB 14-5355, Beirut; tel. (1) 704452; fax (1) 704453; f. 1988; library of 10,000 vols, 200 periodicals; 19 teachers; 407 students; BA, MA, PhD in Business Administration; incorporates Islamic Institute for the Supervision of Food Products (Dir Dr IBRAHIM ADHAM); Chair. TOUFIC HOURY; Dean Prof. MOHAMED ISKANDARANI; Sec. SALIM ABIAD.

Middle East College: POB 90481, Jdeidet El Matn, Beirut; tel. (1) 883065; fax (1) 883055; e-mail mecolleg@inco.com.lb; private control; language of instruction: English; academic year: October to June (two terms), and six-week summer session; library of 26,000 vols; offers degrees in business administration, computer science, education (elementary), religion; also diploma courses; Pres. S. MYKLEBUST; Registrar S. ISSA.

Near East School of Theology: POB 13–5780, Beirut; tel. 354194; fax 347129; f. 1932; a Protestant ecumenical institution of higher learning; offers theological education and pastoral training to qualified candidates for church ministries, as well as to lay candidates regardless of church affiliation, sex, race or nationality; library of 42,000 vols; 7 teachers; 36 students; Pres. Dr MARY MIKHAEL; publ. *NEST Theological Review*.

LESOTHO

Learned Societies

BIBLIOGRAPHY, LIBRARY SCIENCE AND MUSEOLOGY

Lesotho Library Association: Private Bag A26, Maseru; f. 1978; 53 individual mems, 22 institutions; Chair. E. M. Nthunya; Sec. M. M. Moshoeshoe-Chadzingwa; publ. *Journal* (annually).

Research Institutes

AGRICULTURE, FISHERIES AND VETERINARY SCIENCE

Research Station of the Ministry of Agriculture, Co-operatives and Marketing: POB 24, Maseru 100; tel. 22741; telex 330; research station at Maseru and field experimental stations.

NATURAL SCIENCES

Physical Sciences

Geological Survey Department: Dept of Mines and Geology, POB 750, Maseru 100; Commr. M. Mofilo.

Libraries and Archives

Maseru

Lesotho Government Archives: POB 52, Maseru; tel. 313034 ext. 45; telex 4228; fax 310194; f. 1958; undertakes research; records date from 1869; Senior Archivist M. Qhobosheane.

Lesotho National Library Service: POB 985, Maseru 100; tel. 323100; telex 4228; fax 327890; f. 1976; 30,000 vols; Senior Librarian M. Mabathoana (acting).

University

NATIONAL UNIVERSITY OF LESOTHO

PO Roma 180
Telephone: Roma 340601
Telex: 4303
Fax: 340000

Founded 1945 as Pius XII College, became campus of University of Botswana, Lesotho and Swaziland 1966; present name 1975

Language of instruction: English
Academic year: August to May

Chancellor: HM King Letsie III
Vice-Chancellor: Prof. R. I. M. Moletsane
Pro-Vice-Chancellor: Dr L. T. Jonathan
Registrar: A. M. Mphuthing
Librarian: A. M. Lebotsa

Number of teachers: 171
Number of students: 1,800

Publications: *Lesotho Law Journal, Mohlomi Journal* (History), *NUL News, Mophatlatsi, Light in the Night, Announcer, NUL Research Journal.*

DEANS

Faculty of Science: Prof. K. K. Gopinathan
Faculty of Humanities: Dr T. H. Mothibe
Faculty of Social Sciences: Prof. A. Ejigou
Faculty of Education: B. T. Mokhosi
Faculty of Law: Dr W. Kulundu-Bitonye
Faculty of Agriculture: Prof. A. C. Ebenebe
Faculty of Postgraduate Studies: Prof. T. A. Balogun

DIRECTORS

Institute of Extra-Mural Studies: Dr A. M. Setsabi, Prof. D. Braimoh, Prof. Y. D. Bwatwa
Institute of South African Studies: Prof. B. B. J. Nachobane
Institute of Education: P. Lefoka
Institute of Labour Studies: S. Santho

PROFESSORS

Faculty of Agriculture:

Braide, F. G.
Ebenene, A. C.
Okelw-Uma, I.
Sutton, P. M.

Faculty of Science:

Gopinathun, K. K., Physics
Malu, O.

Faculty of Social Sciences:

Ejigou, A., Statistics

Faculty of Law:

Kumar, U., Private Law

Faculty of Education:

Mats'ela, Z. A., Language and Social Education

Faculty of Postgraduate Studies:

Balogun, T. A.

Institute of Southern African Studies:

Prasad, G.

College

Lesotho Agricultural College: PB A4, Maseru; tel. 322484; fax 400022; f.1955; state control; language of instruction: English; academic year: August to May (two semesters); library of 6,0000 vols; Principal Dr S. L. Ralit-s'oele.

LIBERIA

Learned Societies

LANGUAGE AND LITERATURE

Society of Liberian Authors: POB 2468, Monrovia; f. 1959; aims to stimulate general interest in writing and encourage literature in local vernacular; publ. *Kaafa* (2 a year).

TECHNOLOGY

Geological, Mining and Metallurgical Society of Liberia: POB 902, Monrovia; f.1964; 78 mems; Pres. CLETUS S. WOTORSON; Sec. Dr MEDIE-HEMIE NEUFVILLE; publ. *Bulletin* (2 a year).

Liberia Arts and Crafts Association: POB 885, Monrovia; f. 1964; 14 mems; aims to encourage artists and craftsmen through exhibitions, sales, workshops; Pres. R. VANJAH RICHARDS.

Research Institutes

AGRICULTURE, FISHERIES AND VETERINARY SCIENCE

Central Agriculture Research Institute: Mailbag 3929, Suakoko; tel. 223443; telex 44265; f. 1946; under Ministry of Agriculture; research on crops, animal husbandry, horticulture, soil, and inland fisheries; bilateral and international agencies; service centre for supply of improved seeds, plant material and animals; library of 8,700 vols; Dir WALTER T. WILES; publ. *CARI News*.

MEDICINE

Liberian Institute for Biomedical Research: POB 10-1012, 1000 Monrovia-10; f. 1952, renamed 1975; administrative centre for biomedical research; conducts research and attracts research projects; Dir Dr ALOYSIUS P. HANSON.

NATURAL SCIENCES

Biological Sciences

Nimba Research Laboratory: c/o Lamco J. V. Operating Co., Grassland, Nimba, Robertsfield; (POB 69, Monrovia); f. 1962; under supervision of Nimba Research Committee of International Union for Conservation of Nature and Natural Resources in co-operation with UNESCO; biological and ecological exploration and field work in the Mount Nimba region and conservation; library of 100 vols and access to LAMCO library, Yekepa; Chair. KAI CURRY-LINDAHL, Bruce House, Standard St, Nairobi.

Libraries and Archives

Monrovia

Government Public Library: Ashmun St, Monrovia; f. 1959; 15,000 vols.

Liberian Information Service Library: POB 9021, Monrovia; reference.

UNESCO Mission Library: Ministry of Education, POB 1545, Monrovia.

University of Liberia Libraries: University of Liberia, POB 9020, Monrovia; f. 1862; general library and separate law library; 107,384 vols, 2,118 periodicals; Dir Mrs ANNABEL U. TINGBA (acting).

Museums and Art Galleries

Cape Mount

Tubman Centre of African Cultures: Cape Mount; local art, history and ethnology.

Monrovia

Africana Museum: Cuttington University College, c/o Episcopal Church Office, POB 277, Monrovia; f. 1960; items from Liberia and neighbouring countries; traditional arts and crafts, ethnographical material; 2 traditional houses representing Kpelle and Grebo architecture; depository for archaeological collections; serves as a teaching collection for the College and as a research facility for visiting scholars; specialized research library in the college; Dir EDWARD O. N'GELE.

National Museum: Broad and Buchanan Sts, POB 3223, Monrovia; f. 1962; Liberian history, art and ethnography; Dir Mrs BURDIE UREY-WEEKS.

University

UNIVERSITY OF LIBERIA

POB 9020, Monrovia
Telephone: 224671
Founded as Liberia College 1862; University 1951
State control
Language of instruction: English
Academic year: March to December (two semesters)
President: Dr PATRICK L. N. SEYON
Vice-President for Administration: Dr WINGROVE C. DWAMINA (acting)
Vice-President for Academic Affairs: Dr FREDERICK S. GREGBE
Dean of Admissions: MOORE T. WORRELL
Libraries: see Libraries
Number of teachers: 282
Number of students: 5,056

Publications: *University of Liberia Catalogue and Announcements, University of Liberia Journal, This Week on Campus, Liberian Law Journal, Varsity Pilot.*

DEANS

College of Social Sciences and Humanities (Liberia College): Dr BEN A. ROBERTS
College of Agriculture and Forestry: Dr BISMARCK REEVES
College of Science and Technology: Prof. FREDERICK D. HUNDER (acting)
Louis Arthur Grimes School of Law: Cllr LUVENIA ASH-THOMPSON
Dogliotti College of Medicine: Dr TAIWO DARAMOLA
College of Business and Public Administration: Prof. WILLIE BELLEH Jr
William V. S. Tubman Teachers College: Dr JOSHUA D. CLEON
Student Affairs: HARRISON MLE-SIE WOART

CO-ORDINATORS OF SCHOOLS

School of Pharmacy: Dr ARTHUR S. LEWIS
Graduate School of Regional Planning: Dr JAMES N. KOLLIE Sr
Graduate School of Education Administration: Dr HENRY KWEKWE

Colleges

Booker Washington Institute: Kakata; state control; agricultural and industrial courses; Principal T. KUDAR JARRY.

Cuttington University College: c/o Episcopal Church Building, POB 10-277, 1000 Monrovia 10; tel. 227413; f. 1889 (closed 1990 due to war; expected to re-open September 1998); maintained by int. donors incl. Episcopal Church in the USA, Episcopal Church of Liberia; subsidized by the Government, receives donated service from the Peace Corps, the Fulbright Program and others; language of instruction: English; academic year: September to June; library stock subjected to looting during war, 250 periodicals; 75 teachers; 960 students; Chair. of the Board of Trustees Bishop EDWARD W. NEUFVILLE II; Pres. Dr MELVIN J. MASON; Vice-Pres. (Administration) Dr HENRIQUE F. TOPKA; Vice-Pres. (Academic) Dr SAAIM MAAME; Registrar and Dir of Admissions THOMAS GAIE; Dean of Students (vacant); Librarian (vacant).

William V. S. Tubman College of Technology: POB 3570, Monrovia; f.1970; opened 1978; state control; language of instruction: English; academic year: March to December; 21 teachers; 200 students; three-year associate degree course in engineering technology; Pres. Dr THEOPHILUS N. SONPON; Dean/Admin. Dr SOLOMON S. B. RUSSELL.

LIBYA

Learned Societies

LANGUAGE AND LITERATURE

Union of Libyan Authors, Writers and Artists: POB 1017, Tripoli; f. 1980; all fields of culture, education and art; 800 mems; library of 4,000 vols; Pres. AMIN MAZEN.

Research Institutes

GENERAL

National Academy for Scientific Research: POB 8004, Tripoli; telex 20956; fax 39841; f. 1981 to conduct, finance and support scientific studies and research in all branches of knowledge; 330 mems; library of 19,000 vols; Dir-Gen. Dr TAHER H. JEHEMI; publs *Al-Fikr Al-Arabi, Al-Fikr Al Istratiji Al-Arabi, Al-Ilm Wa Atteknolojia*.

HISTORY, GEOGRAPHY AND ARCHAEOLOGY

Libyan Studies Centre: POB 5070, Sidi Munaider, Tripoli; tel. 3333996; telex 20424; fax 3331616; f. 1978; historical studies and documentation; 140 mems; library of 100,000 vols, 700 periodicals, 3,000 MSS, 60,000 photographs; Dir Dr MOHAMED T. JERARY; publs *Majallat al-Buhuth at-Tarikhia* (2 a year), *As-Shahid* (The Martyr) (annually), *Index of Libyan Periodicals* (annually), *Al-Wathaiq wa al-Makhtutat* (annually), *Al Insaf* (annually), *Al-Kunnasha* (The Scrap Book, 2 a year).

Libraries and Archives

Benghazi

National Library of Libya: POB 9127, Benghazi; tel. (61) 90509; fax (61) 96379; f. 1971; Head of Administration Dept. S. GUMAHA.

Public Library: Shar'a 'Umar al-Mukhtar, Benghazi; f. 1955; 11,000 vols; Librarian AHMAD GALLAL.

Qurinna Library: Mukhtar St, Benghazi; Arab, French and English books.

University of Garyounis Library: POB 1308, Benghazi; tel. 29021; f. 1955; 294,844 vols; 2,170 periodicals; 7 depts, including 2,360 MSS, 70,000 documents, 10,000 microfilms and rare books; Chief Librarian AHMED GALLAL; publs available for exchange.

Tripoli

Agricultural Research Centre Library: POB 2480, Tripoli; f. 1973; 6,000 vols, 220 periodicals; Librarian LAMIS AL-GABSI.

Government Library: 14 Shar'a al-Jazair, Tripoli; f. 1917; 35,500 vols; Librarian BASHIR AL-BADRI.

National Archives: Castello, Tripoli; tel. 40166; f. 1928; controlled by Department of Antiquities, General People's Committee for Education, Tripoli; extensive collection of documents relating to the history of Libya mostly in Turkish from the Ottoman period; 5 libraries, 55,000 vols; Curator ABDULAALI OWN; publ. *Libya Antiqua*.

Museums and Art Galleries

Shahat

Department of Antiquities, Shahat (Cyrene): responsible for archaeological sites from Shahat west to the frontiers of Tocra, east to Msa'd; Controller BRAYEK ATTIYA.

Tripoli

Department of Antiquities: Assarai al-Hamra, Tripoli; responsible for all museums and archaeological sites in Libya; Pres. Dr ABDULLAH SHAIBOUB.

Responsible for:

Archaeological, Natural History, Epigraphy, Prehistory and Ethnography Museums: Assarai al-Hamra, Tripoli.

Leptis Magna Museum: Leptis Magna.

Sabratha Museum of Antiquities: Sabratha.

Islamic Museum: Tripoli.

Gaigab Museum: Gaigab (near Cyrene).

Cyrene Museum: Cyrene (Shahat).

Ptolemais Museum: Tolmeitha.

Tauchira Museum: Tokra.

Apollonia Museum: Marsa Soussa.

Germa Museum: Germa (Fezean).

Benghazi Museum: Benghazi; mausoleum of Omar el Mukhtar.

Zanzur Museum: Zanzur (Tripoli).

Universities

AL-FATEH UNIVERSITY

POB 13482, Tripoli
Telephone: (22) 605441
Telex: 20629
Fax: 605460

Founded 1957
State control
Language of instruction: Arabic
Academic year: September to June

President: Dr YOUSEF MABSOUT
Vice-President: Dr GIUMA AL-MAHJUBI
Secretary-General: MOHAMED MAJDOUB
General Registrar: ABDULBASET AL-JABOU
Librarian: Dr MOHAMED ABDUL JALEEL

Number of teachers: 2,046
Number of students: 35,988

Publications: *Libyan Journal of Sciences, Libyan Journal of Agriculture, Bulletin of the Faculty of Education, Bulletin of the Faculty of Engineering.*

DEANS

Faculty of Science: Dr ABDULLA EL-MANSURY
Faculty of Engineering: Dr AHMED EL-WA'ER
Faculty of Agriculture: Dr ALI ABDULATI
Faculty of Education: Dr AGHEEL EL-BARBAR
Faculty of Veterinary Medicine: Dr MUJAHED BUSHWAYREB (acting)
Faculty of Languages: Dr RAWHIYA KARA
Faculty of Fine Arts: Dr MOHAMED SHARAFEDDEAN
Faculty of Social Sciences: Dr ABDULGADER EL-MISRATI
Faculty of Physical Education: Dr MUSA EL-GANDOOZ
Faculty of Economics and Political Science: Dr MASOUD BAROUNI (acting)
Faculty of Law: Dr MOHAMED EL-HARARI

AL-ARAB MEDICAL UNIVERSITY

POB 18251, Benghazi
Telephone: (61) 25007
Telex: 40204
Fax: (61) 20051

Founded 1984
State Control
Languages of instruction: Arabic and English
Academic year: September to May

President: Dr AMER RAHIL
Registrar: ABU-BAKER AMMARI
Librarian: MOHAMMED EL-SAID

Library of 30,000 vols, 600 periodicals
Number of teachers: 256
Number of students: 1,615

Publication: *Garyounis Medical Journal.*

DEANS

Faculty of Medicine: Dr ABDUL HADI MOUSSA
Faculty of Dentistry: Dr ABDULLA OMAR DOURDA
Faculty of Pharmacy: Dr ABDUSALAM A. AL-MAYHOUB

BRIGHT STAR UNIVERSITY OF TECHNOLOGY

POB 58158, Ajdabia
Telephone: (64) 23012
Fax: (54) 61870

Founded 1981
State control
Language of instruction: Arabic
Academic year: October to June

Chancellor: Engr ALI SALEH ELFAZZANI
Registrar: Engr MANSOOR MASOOD FARAJ
Chief of Administration: Engr ABD ELSALAM ELZAROUG
Librarian: IBRAHIM MOHAMED AMIR

Number of teachers: 67
Number of students: 1,160

HEADS OF DEPARTMENT

Basic Engineering Science: Dr SHAHADA ELASADI
Electrical and Electronic Engineering: Dr SAMI ESSA MOUSA
Mechanical and Production Engineering: Dr ABD ELATIF ELGIZAWI
Chemical Engineering: Dr MOHAMED ABD ELAZIZ
Petroleum Engineering: Dr MUSTAFA AWAD

UNIVERSITY OF GARYOUNIS

POB 1308, Benghazi
Telephone: 20148

Founded 1955 as University of Libya, renamed 1973, present name 1976
State control
Language of instruction: Arabic

Chancellor: Dr MUHAMID A. ALMAHDAWI
Registrar: MAHMUD M. FAKHRI

Library: see Libraries
Number of teachers: 610
Number of students: 15,000

Publications: various faculty bulletins.

DEANS

Faculty of Arts and Education: Dr FATHI AL-HARIM
Faculty of Economics: Dr ABDELGADIR AMIR
Faculty of Law: Dr SULMAN AL-GURISH
Faculty of Science: Dr MUHAMID EL-AWIME
Faculty of Engineering: Dr BELAID EIKWARI

SEBHA UNIVERSITY

POB 18758, Sebha

Telephone: (71) 21575
Telex: 30622
Fax: (71) 29201

Founded 1983 from the Faculty of Education of Al-Fateh University
State control
Languages of instruction: Arabic and English
Academic year: October to August

Chancellor: Dr ABU BAKR ABDULLAH OTMAN
Vice-Chancellor: SALEM ABDULLAH SAID
Registrar: MISBAH AL-GHAWIL
Librarian: ZIDAN AL-BREIKY

Number of teachers: 280
Number of students: 3,000

Publications: *Al-Shifa* (medicine, annually), *Physical Education Magazine* (every 6 months).

DEANS

Faculty of Agriculture: Dr MOHAMMAD ABDUL KARIM
Faculty of Arts and Education: HAMED MASHMOOR
Faculty of Dentistry: Dr HASAN AL-BUSAIFY
Faculty of Economics and Accountancy: Dr BASHIR ABU-QILA
Faculty of Engineering and Technology: MOHAMMAD ARAHOOMA
Faculty of Medicine: Dr OMAR IBRAHIM AL-SHAIBANI
Faculty of Physical Education: ABDUL RAHMAN AL-ANSARI
Faculty of Science: Dr MOHAMMAD BASHIR HASAN

Colleges

African Centre for Applied Research and Training in Social Development (ACARTSOD): POB 80606, Tripoli; tel. 833228; telex 20803; fax 832357; f. 1977 as an intergovernmental institution under the auspices of the UN Economic Comm. for Africa and the OAU; aims to promote and co-ordinate applied research and training in the field of social development at regional and sub-regional levels, organizes seminars, etc.; Officer-in-Charge LAMIS GABSI; publs *ACARTSOD Newsletter* (3 a year), *African Social Challenges* (annually).

Arts and Crafts School: Shar'a 24 December, Tripoli; Principal Mr SALIM ZEGALLAI.

Faculty of Engineering: POB 61160, Hoon; tel. (57) 602841; fax (57) 2842; f. 1976; BSc level studies; 650 students; library of 22,000 vols, 100 periodicals; Dean I. ELAGTAL.

Higher Institute of Electronics: POB 21, Bani Walid; first degree courses.

Higher Institute of Technology: POB 68, Brack; tel. 45300; telex 30621; fax 27600; f. 1976; first degree courses in general sciences, medical technology, food technology and environmental sciences; library of 10,000 vols; 60 teachers, 500 students; Dean Dr ABDUSSALAM M. ALMETHNANI.

National Institute of Administration: POB 3651, Tripoli; tel. (21) 462-34-20; fax (21) 462-34-23; f. 1953; offers higher diploma in administration and accounting; library of 10,000 vols; 30 teachers; publ. *National Magazine of Administration*.

Posts and Telecommunications Institute: POB 2428, Tripoli; f. 1963; library of 510 vols; Dir K. MARABUTACI.

LIECHTENSTEIN

Learned Societies

HISTORY, GEOGRAPHY AND ARCHAEOLOGY

Historischer Verein für das Fürstentum Liechtenstein (Historical Society for the Principality of Liechtenstein): 9495 Triesen; tel. (75) 392-17-47; fax (75) 392-19-61; f. 1901; 770 mems; small library; Pres. Dr RUPERT QUADERER; Sec. KLAUS BIEDERMANN; publ. *Jahrbuch*.

NATURAL SCIENCES

General

Liechtensteinische Gesellschaft für Umweltschutz (Environmental Protection): Im Bretscha 22, 9494 Schaan; tel. (75) 232-52-62; f. 1973; 750 mems; Pres. BARBARA RHEINBERGER; publs *Liechtensteiner Umweltbericht* (1 or 2 a year), *LGU-Mitteilungen* (quarterly), *LGU-Schriftenreihe*.

Research Institutes

ECONOMICS, LAW AND POLITICS

Liechtenstein-Institut: Auf dem Kirchhügel, Oberbendern 134, 9487 Bendern; tel. (75) 373-30-22; fax (75) 373-54-22; e-mail liechtenstein-institut@lie-net.li; f. 1986; research on topics related to Liechtenstein in the fields of law, political science, economics and social science, history; Exec. Cttee (6 mems), Scientific Ccl (6 mems); Pres. Dr GUIDO MEIER; Dir lic. iur. EVA HASENBACH; publ. *Annual Report* (in German).

Libraries and Archives

Vaduz

Liechtensteinische Landesbibliothek: 9490 Vaduz; tel. (75) 236-63-62; fax (75) 233-14-19; f. 1961; public, academic and national library; 180,000 vols; Librarian Dr ALOIS OSPELT; publ. *Liechtensteinische Bibliographie*.

Liechtensteinisches Landesarchiv: 9490 Vaduz; tel. (75) 236-61-11; fax (75) 236-63-59; e-mail alois.ospelt@la.llv.li; f. 1961; national archives; reference library of *c.* 3,000 m. documents; Archivist Dr ALOIS OSPELT.

Museums and Art Galleries

Vaduz

Liechtensteinisches Landesmuseum (Liechtenstein National Museum): Städtle 43, 9490 Vaduz; tel. (75) 236-75-50; fax (75) 236-75-52; f. 1954; includes items from the collections of the Prince, the State, and the Liechtenstein Historical Soc.; Dir Lic. phil. I. NORBERT W. HASLER. (In 1998, the museum was reported to be temporarily closed for renovation.)

Postmuseum des Fürstentums Liechtenstein: Städtle 37, 9490 Vaduz; tel. (75) 236-61-05; f. 1930; Liechtenstein stamps, historical postal documents, postal instruments.

College

Liechtensteinische Musikschule: St Florinsgasse 1, 9490 Vaduz; tel. (75) 232-46-20; fax (75) 232-46-42; e-mail emu@pingnet.li; f. 1963; 96 teachers; 2,450 students; library of *c.* 12,000 vols, special collection of works of composer Josef Gabriel Rheinberger; summer int. master classes; Dir JOSEF FROMMELT.

LITHUANIA

Learned Societies

GENERAL

Lithuanian Academy of Sciences: 2600 Vilnius, Gedimino pr. 3; tel. (2) 61-36-51; fax (2) 61-84-64; e-mail prezidium@ktl.mii.lt; f. 1941; divisions of Mathematics, Physics and Chemistry (Head Prof. H. PRAGARAUSKAS), Biology, Medicine and Geosciences (Head Prof. V. KONTRIMAVIČIUS), Technical Sciences (Head Prof. R. BANSEVIČIUS), Humanities and Social Sciences (Head Prof. A. GAIŽUTIS), Agriculture and Forestry (Head Prof. V. VASILIAUSKIENĖ); 37 mems, 55 corresp. mems, 50 expert mems, 19 foreign mems; attached research institutes: see Research Institutes; library: see Libraries and Archives; Pres. Prof. BENEDIKTAS JUODKA; Sec.-Gen. Prof. ALGIRDAS ŠILEIKA; publs journals of linguistics (4 a year), art studies (2 a year), ecology (4 a year), philosophy and sociology (4 a year), chemistry (4 a year), power engineering (4 a year), biology (4 a year), geology (2 a year), geography (2 a year), medicine (4 a year), agriculture (4 a year), physics (6 a year), mathematics (4 a year), building construction (4 a year), transport engineering (2 a year), Baltica (1 a year), informatics (4 a year).

LANGUAGE AND LITERATURE

PEN Centre of Lithuania: 2600 Vilnius, Sirvydo 6; tel. (2) 22-39-19; f. 1989; fights for freedom of expression, human rights and democratic causes; 34 mems; Pres. GALINA BAUŽYTĖ-ČEPINSKIENĖ; Sec. ANTANAS DANIELIUS.

Research Institutes

AGRICULTURE, FISHERIES AND VETERINARY SCIENCE

Lithuanian Forest Research Institute: 4312 Kauno rajonas, Girionys 1; tel. (7) 79-99-21; fax (7) 54-74-46; e-mail miskinst@mi.lt; f. 1950; library of 57,000 vols; Dir Dr habil. REMIGIJUS OZOLINČIUS; publs *Baltic Forestry* (2 a year), *Miškinikystė* (Forestry, 2 a year).

ECONOMICS, LAW AND POLITICS

Institute of Economics: 2600 Vilnius, Goštauto 12; tel. (2) 62-35-02; fax (2) 22-75-06; f. 1992; attached to Lithuanian Acad. of Sciences; library of 2,500 vols; Dir Prof. EDUARDAS VILKAS.

Lithuanian Institute of Philosophy and Sociology: 2600 Vilnius, Saltoniškių 58; tel. (2) 75-24-55; fax (2) 75-18-98; e-mail lfsi@ktl.mii.lt; f. 1977; attached to Lithuanian Acad. of Sciences; Dir Dr VACYS BAGDONAVIČIUS; publs *Philosophy and Sociology* (4 a year), *Revue Baltique* (4 a year).

FINE AND PERFORMING ARTS

Institute of Culture and Arts: 2001 Vilnius, Tilto 4; attached to Lithuanian Acad. of Sciences; Dir S. JUKNEVIČIUS.

HISTORY, GEOGRAPHY AND ARCHAEOLOGY

Institute of Geography: 2600 Vilnius, Akademijos 2; tel. and fax (2) 72-92-45; f. 1990; attached to Lithuanian Acad. of Sciences; Dir G. B. PAULIUKEVIČIUS; publs *Geografija* (Geography), *Geografijos metraštis* (Geographical Yearbook, 1 a year).

Institute of Lithuanian History: 2001 Vilnius, Kražių g. 5; tel. (2) 61-44-36; fax (2) 61-44-33; attached to Lithuanian Acad. of Sciences; library of 135,000 vols; Chair. Prof. Dr habil. VYTAUTAS MERKYS; publs *Lituanistica, Lietuvos archeologija* (Lithuanian Archaeology).

LANGUAGE AND LITERATURE

Institute of Lithuanian Language: 2055 Vilnius, Antakalnio 6; tel. (2) 22-61-26; fax (2) 22-65-73; e-mail lki@ktl.mii.lt; f. 1939; Dir A. SABALIAUSKAS; publs *Problems of Lithuanian Linguistics* (irregular), *Culture of Speech (2 a year), Terminology* (1 a year).

Institute of Lithuanian Literature and Folklore: 2055 Vilnius, Antakalnio 6; tel. (2) 62-19-43; fax (2) 61-62-54; e-mail llti@ktl.mii.lt; f. 1939; library of 260,000 vols; Dir LEONARDAS SAUKA; publs *Lituanistica* (4 a year), *Tautosakos darbai* (Folklore Studies, 1 a year), *Senoji Lietuvos literatura* (Old Lithuanian Literature, 1 a year).

MEDICINE

Institute of Hygiene: 2001 Vilnius, Didžioji 22; tel. (2) 62-45-83; fax (2) 62-46-63; e-mail vytjurk@ktl.mii.lt; f. 1808; library of 8,000 vols; Dir Dr V. JURKUVENAS; publ. *Public Health* (2 a year).

Institute of Immunology: 2600 Vilnius, Mokslininkų 12; tel. (2) 72-91-92; fax (2) 72-98-27; attached to Lithuanian Acad. of Sciences; Dir V. TAMOŠIŪNAS.

Lithuanian Oncology Centre: 2600 Vilnius, Santariškių 1; tel. (2) 72-01-35; fax (2) 72-01-64; e-mail aizenas@loc.elnet.lt; f. 1990; Dir Prof. Dr K. VALUCKAS.

Tuberculosis Research Institute: Vilnius, Gilioi 8.

NATURAL SCIENCES

Biological Sciences

Institute of Biochemistry: 2600 Vilnius, Mokslininkų 12; tel. (2) 72-91-44; fax (2) 72-91-96; Dir V. RAZUMAS.

Institute of Botany: 2021 Vilnius, Žaliųjų ežerų 49; tel. (2) 69-74-62; fax (2) 72-99-50; e-mail botanika@ktl.mii.lt; f. 1959; Dir Dr R. PAKALNIS; publ. *Botanica Lithuanica* (4 a year).

Institute of Ecology: 2600 Vilnius, Akademijos 2; tel. (2) 72-92-75; fax (2) 72-92-57; e-mail ekoi@ktl.mii.lt; f. 1945; library of 75,000 vols; Dir Prof. Dr habil. JUOZAS VIRBICKAS; publ. *Acta Zoologica Lituanica* (mainly in English, 4 a year).

Mathematical Sciences

Institute of Mathematics and Cybernetics: 2600 Vilnius, K. Poželos 54; tel. 35-92-09; telex 261131; attached to Lithuanian Acad. of Sciences; Dir V. A. STATULEVIČIUS.

Physical Sciences

Institute of Chemistry: 2600 Vilnius, A. Goštauto 9; tel. (2) 61-26-63; fax (2) 61-70-18; e-mail vaskelis@ktl.mii.lt; f. 1945; Dir A. VAŠKELIS.

Institute of Physics: 2600 Vilnius, K. Poželos 54; tel. 61-26-10; telex 261135; attached to Lithuanian Acad. of Sciences; Dir R. BALTRAMIEJUNAS.

Institute of Theoretical Physics and Astronomy: 2600 Vilnius, A. Goštauto 12; tel. (2) 62-09-47; fax (2) 22-53-61; e-mail atom@itpa.lt; f. 1990; attached to Lithuanian Acad. of Sciences; library of 112,000 vols; Dir Z. RUDZIKAS; publs *Lithuanian Journal of Physics* (6 a year), *Baltic Astronomy* (4 a year), *Sky of Lithuania* (1 a year).

TECHNOLOGY

Institute of Biotechnology: 2028 Vilnius, V. Graičiūno 8; tel. 64-10-22; fax 64-26-24; e-mail ziuk@ibt.lt; f. 1975; Dir A. PAULIUKONIS.

Institute of Semiconductor Physics: 2600 Vilnius, A. Goštauto 11; tel. (2) 61-97-59; fax (2) 62-71-23; e-mail spiadm@uj.pfi.lt; f. 1967; Dir S. AŠMONTAS; publ. *Annual Report*.

Lithuanian Energy Institute: 3035 Kaunas, Breslaujos 3; tel. (7) 75-24-03; fax (7) 75-12-71; e-mail mokslas@isag.lei.lt; f. 1956; attached to Lithuanian Acad. of Sciences; library of 40,000 vols; Dir J. VILEMAS; publ. *Energetika* (Power Engineering, 4 a year).

Libraries and Archives

Vilnius

Library of the Lithuanian Academy of Sciences: 2632 Vilnius, Žygimantu 1/8; tel. 62-95-37; fax 22-13-24; e-mail root@liblas .aiva.lt; f. 1941; 3,676,000 vols; Dir Dr J. MARCINKEVIČIUS.

Lithuanian Technical Library: 2600 Vilnius, Šv. Ignoto 6; tel. 61-87-18; fax 22-58-81; e-mail info@tb.lt; f. 1957; 23,844,000 vols; Dir K. MACKEVIČIUS.

Martynas Mažvydas National Library of Lithuania: 2635 Vilnius, Gedimino pr. 51; tel. 62-90-23; fax 62-71-29; f. 1919; 5,200,000 vols; Dir VLADAS BULAVAS; publ. *Tarp Knygų* (monthly).

Vilnius University Library: 2633 Vilnius, Universiteto 3; tel. (2) 61-06-16; fax (2) 61-38-09; e-mail mb@vu.lt; f. 1570; 5,225,000 vols, 226,000 MSS, 79,000 graphic art items, 387,000 UN publs; Dir BIRUTĖ BUTKEVIČIENĖ.

Museums and Art Galleries

Kaunas

Botanical Garden: 3018 Kaunas, Ž. E. Žilibero 6; tel. (7) 29-86-58; fax (7) 29-53-22; e-mail bs@fc.vdu.lt; f. 1923; attached to Vytautas Magnus University; library of 10,000 vols; Dir Dr A. R. BUDRIŪNAS.

M. K. Čiurlionis State Museum of Art: 3000 Kaunas, Vlado Putvinskio 55; tel. (7) 22-97-38; fax (7) 20-46-12; f. 1921; Lithuanian and European art, folk art, oriental and ancient Egyptian art, numismatics; library of 24,000 vols; Dir OSVALDAS DAUGELIS.

War Museum of Vytautas the Great: 3000 Kaunas, K. Donelaičio 64; tel. 22-96-06;

f. 1921; Lithuania's history and wars, archaeology, numismatics; Dir J. JUREVIČIUS.

Trakai

Trakai Historical Museum: Trakai, Kęstučio 4; tel. 5-12-74; f. 1948; local history; Dir VIRGILIJUS POVILIŪNAS.

Vilnius

Lithuanian Art Museum: 2001 Vilnius, Didžioji 4; tel. 62-80-30; fax 22-60-06; f. 1940; library of 20,040 vols; br. museums incl. National Art Gallery, Foreign Art Gallery, Museum of Applied Arts, Klaipėda Clock Museum; Dir ROMUALDAS BUDRYS.

National Museum of Lithuania: 2001 Vilnius, Arsenalo 1; tel. (2) 62-77-74; fax (2) 61-10-12; f. 1855; history, ethnography, numismatics, archaeology, iconography; library of 55,000 vols; Dir BIRUTĖ KULNYTĖ; publs *Numismatics, Archaeology, Ethnography* (annually), *Museum* (annually).

Universities

KAUNAS UNIVERSITY OF TECHNOLOGY

3006 Kaunas, K. Donelaičio 73

Telephone: (7) 22-70-44
Fax: (7) 20-26-40
E-mail rastine@cr.ktu.lt

Founded 1922
State control
Academic year: September to June

Rector: Prof. KĘSTUTIS KRIŠČIŪNAS
Vice-Rectors: Prof. ALEKSANDRAS TARGAMADZĖ (Academic Affairs), Prof. ARŪNAS LUKOŠEVIČIUS (Research), Dr PETRAS BARŠAUSKAS (Infrastructure)
Head of Administration: Dr ARVYDAS BARILA
Librarian: GENOVAITE DUOBINIENĖ

Library of 2,142,000 vols
Number of teachers: 974
Number of students: 11,629

Publications: *Chemical Technology* (annually), *Electronics and Electrical Engineering* (annually), *Information Technology and Control* (annually), *Measurements* (annually), *Mechanics* (annually), *Materials Science* (annually), *Social Science* (annually), *Environmental Research, Engineering and Management* (annually), *Ultrasound* (annually).

DEANS

Faculty of Chemical Technology: Dr RIMANTAS ŠIAUČIŪNAS
Faculty of Electrical Engineering and Control Systems: Dr ALGIMANTAS S. NAVICKAS
Faculty of Telecommunications and Electronics: Dr BRUNONAS DEKERIS
Faculty of Informatics: Dr BRONISLOVAS KILDA
Faculty of Design and Technology: Dr SIGITAS STANYS
Faculty of Mechanical Engineering: Dr PETRAS AMBROZA
Faculty of Civil Engineering and Architecture: Dr HENRIKAS ELZBUTAS
Faculty of Management: Dr BRONIUS NEVERAUSKAS
Faculty of Administration: Dr VIKTORIJA BARŠAUSKIENĖ
Faculty of Basic Sciences: Prof. VIDMANTAS P. PEKARSKAS
Panevėžys Polytechnic Faculty: Dr ALGIMANTAS ŽENKEVIČIUS

ATTACHED RESEARCH INSTITUTES

Innovation Centre: Dir Dr PRANAS MILIUS.

Construction Reliability Centre: Dir Prof. RIMANTAS BARAUSKAS.

'Vibrotechnika' Research Centre: Dir Prof. VALENTINAS SNITKA.

Packaging Research Centre: Dir Dr ANTANAS VOSYLIUS.

Institute of Environmental Engineering: Dir Prof. JURGIS STANIŠKIS.

Institute of Transport Problems: Dir Prof. ALGIRDAS JURKAUSKAS.

Physical Electronic Institute: Dir Dr JUOZAS MARGELEVIČIUS.

Meteorological Institute: Dir Prof. RIMVYDAS ŽILINSKAS.

Design Centre: Dir Dr SALVINIJA PETRULYTĖ.

Centre for Research and Wealth Assessment: Dir Dr PRANAS CHMIELIAUSKAS.

VILNIAUS GEDIMINO TECHNIKOS UNIVERSITETAS (Vilnius Gediminas Technical University)

2040 Vilnius, Saulėtekio alėja 11

Telephone: (2) 70-04-78
Fax: (2) 70-01-12
E-mail: urd@adm.vtu.lt

Founded 1956
State control
Languages of instruction: Lithuanian, English, French
Academic year: September to June

Rector: Prof. Dr habil. EDMUNDAS KAZIMIERAS ZAVADSKAS
Vice-Rectors: Assoc. Prof. ALFONSAS DANIŪNAS, Prof. Dr habil. RIMANTAS KAČIANAUSKAS, Assoc. Prof. Dr ARŪNAS KOMKA; Assoc. Prof. Dr habil. ALGIRDAS VALIULIS
Librarian: R. PŪGŽLIENĖ

Library of 676,000 vols
Number of teachers: 733
Number of students: 7,500

Publications: *Transport Engineering* (4 a year), *Town Planning and Architecture* (4 a year), *Environmental Engineering* (4 a year), *Geodesy and Cartography* (4 a year), *Civil Engineering* (4 a year), *Real Estate Valuation and Investment* (2 a year).

DEANS

Faculty of Architecture: Prof. V. DIČIUS
Faculty of Civil Engineering: Assoc. Prof. P. VAINIŪNAS
Faculty of Environmental Engineering: Assoc. Prof. K. SAKALAUSKAS
Faculty of Electronics: Assoc. Prof. K. MACEIKA
Faculty of Mechanical Engineering: Prof. M. MARIŪNAS
Faculty of Basic Sciences: Assoc. Prof. A. ČIUČELIS
Faculty of Business Management: Assoc. Prof. R. GINEVIČIUS
Faculty of Transport Engineering: Prof. L. LINGAITIS
Institute of Aviation: Prof. J. STANKŪNAS

PROFESSORS

Faculty of Architecture:

BUČIŪTĖ, N.
DIČIUS, V.
DINEIKA, A.
NASVYTIS, A.
PARASONIS, J.
ŠEŠELGIS, K.
VANAGAS, J.

Faculty of Civil Engineering:

ATKOČIŪNAS, J.
KAMINSKAS, A.
MAČIULAITIS, R.
MARČIUKAITIS, G.
ZAVADSKAS, E. K.

Faculty of Environmental Engineering:

BALTRĖNAS, P.
BAUBINAS, A.
JAKOVLEVAS-MATECKIS, K.
KAMAITIS, Z.
ŠIMAITIS, R.
SKEIVALAS, J.
SKRINSKA, A.
VAINAUSKAS, V.

Faculty of Electronics:

DAMBRAUSKAS, A.
JANKAUSKAS, Z.
KAJACKAS, A.
KIRVAITIS, R.
MARCINKEVIČIUS, A.
POŠKA, A.
ŠMILGEVIČIUS, A.
ŠTARAS, S.
TELKSNYS, L.
VAINORIS, Z.

Faculty of Mechanical Engineering:

AUGUSTAITIS, V.
KANAPĖNAS, R.
KASPARAITIS, A.
MARIŪNAS, M.
VALIULIS, A.
VEKTERIS, V.

Faculty of Basic Sciences:

ADOMĖNAS, P.
BELEVIČIUS, R.
BENTKUS, R.
BUMELIS, V.
BUTKUS, E.
ČESNYS, A.
ČIEGIS, R.
ČIŽAS, A.
DIENYS, G.
GALDIKAS, A.
GARILIAUSKAS, A.
JAKIMAVIČIUS, J.
KAČIANAUSKAS, R.
KAZRAGIS, A.
KUBILIUS, K.
KULVIETIS, G.
LAURINAVIČIUS, V.
MOCKUS, J.
PRAGARAUSKAS, H.
REKLAITIS, A.
RUDZKIS, R.
ŠAPAGOVAS, M.
ŠPILEVSKIS, A.
STYRA, D.
VASILJEVAS, P.

Faculty of Business Management:

BIVAINIS, J.
JANKAUSKAS, V.
MARČIUKAITIS, S.
MELNIKAS, B.
MUREIKA, J.
PALIULIS, N.
PUŠKORIUS, S.
RUTKAUSKAS, V.
ŠILEIKA, A.
SIMANAUSKAS, L.
STAŠKEVIČIUS, J.

Faculty of Transport Engineering:

ADOMĖNAS, P.
AMBRAZEVIČIUS, A.
BAUBLYS, A.
LINGAITIS, L.
LUKOŠEVIČIENE, O.
PALŠAITIS, R.
ŠPRUOGIS, B.
ŽEROMSKAS, R.
ŽVIRBLIS, A.

Institute of Aviation:

STANKŪNAS, J.

ATTACHED INSTITUTES

Centre for Continuing Education: Dir P. KUISYS.

International Studies Centre: Dir Prof. ZENONAS KAMAITIS.

VILNIUS UNIVERSITY

2734 Vilnius, Universiteto 3

Telephone: (2) 62-37-79
Fax: (2) 22-35-63

Founded 1579
State control
Language of instruction: Lithuanian
Academic year: September to July

Rector: Prof. ROLANDAS PAVILIONIS
Pro-Rectors: Prof. BENEDIKTAS JUODKA, Dr SAULIUS VENGRIS, ALEKSAS PIKTURNA
Chief Administrative Officer: SIGITAS SUNELAITIS
Director of the Library: BIRUTĖ BUTKEVIČIENĖ

Library: see Libraries and Archives
Number of teachers: 1,320
Number of students: 10,200

Publications: *Information Sciences, Baltistica, Problems of the History of Lithuania, Problems, Psychology, Economics, Biology, Geography, Geology, Law, Linguistics, Literature, Book Science, Bulletin of Vilnius Observatory* (all annually), *Universitas Vilnensis* (weekly), *Information Bulletin* (weekly).

DEANS

Faculty of Chemistry: Prof. ROLANDAS KAZLAUSKAS
Faculty of Communication: Dr RENALDAS GUDAUSKAS
Faculty of Economics: Prof. STANISLOVAS MARTIŠIUS
Faculty of History: Dr ALFREDAS BUMBLAUSKAS
Faculty of Humanities in Kaunas: Dr ALGIRDAS ŠALČIUS
Faculty of Law: Prof. VALENTINAS MIKELĖNAS
Faculty of Mathematics: Dr RIČARDAS KUDŽMA
Faculty of Medicine: Prof. GINTAUTAS ČESNYS
Faculty of Natural Sciences: Dr JONAS REMIGIJUS NAUJALIS
Faculty of Philology: Dr KĘSTUTIS URBA
Faculty of Philosophy: Dr BIRUTĖ POCIŪTĖ
Faculty of Physics: Dr GINTARAS DIKČIUS

PROFESSORS

Faculty of Chemistry:

BUTKUS, E.
DAUKŠAS, V.
DIENYS, G.
KAZLAUSKAS, R.
LEVINSKAS, A.
SURVILA, A.
VAINILAVIČIUS, P.

Faculty of Communication:

BRONIUKAITIS, R. K.
KAUNAS, D.
VOVERIENĖ, O.

Faculty of Economics:

BERŽINSKAS, G.
KAZILIŪNAS, A.
LAKIS, V.
MACKEVIČIUS, J.
MARČINSKAS, A.
MARTIŠIUS, S.
PAJUODIS, A.
POVILIŪNAS, A.
PRANULIS, V.
SAUSANAVIČIUS, A.
SIMANAUSKAS, L.
VENGRAUSKAS, P. V.
ŽEBRAUSKAS, A.

Faculty of History:

JUČAS, M.
LAZUTKA, S.
MICHELBERTAS, M.

Faculty of Humanities in Kaunas:

BURAČAS, A.
GENIUŠAS, A. T.
GRONSKAS, V.
JANKAUSKAS, V.

Faculty of Law:

MAKSIMAITIS, M.
MIKELĖNAS, V.
NEKROŠIUS, I.
VANSEVIČIUS, S.
VITKEVIČIUS, P.

Faculty of Mathematics:

BIKELIS, A.
GOLOKVOSČIUS, P.
IVANAUSKAS, F.
KUBILIUS, J.
LAURINČIKAS, A.
MACKEVIČIUS, V.
MANSTAVIČIUS, E.
PAULAUSKAS, V.
RAČKAUSKAS, A.

Faculty of Medicine:

AMBROZAITIS, A.
BALČIŪNIENĖ, I.
BALEVIČIENĖ, G.
BALTAITIS, V.
BARKAUSKAS, E. V.
BASYS, V.
BAUBINAS, A.
BUBNYS, A.
ČESNYS, G.
DAINYS, B.
DEMBINSKAS, A.
DUBAKIENĖ, R.
GAIDELIS, P.
GRYBAUSKAS, G.
IRNIUS, A.
IVAŠKEVIČIUS, J.
KALIBATAS, J.
KALIBATIENĖ, D.
KALTENIS, P.
KAVOLIŪNAS, D.
KIAULEIKIENĖ, M.
KUČINSKAS, V.
KUČINSKIENĖ, Z. A.
LAUCEVIČIUS, A.
MAČIŪNAS, L. L.
MARKIENĖ, Z. O.
MOTIEJŪNAS, L.
NOREIKA, L. A.
PARNARAUSKIENĖ, R.
PAULIUKAS, P.
PLEVOKAS, P.
PLIUŠKYS, J. A.
PRONCKUS, A.
PTAŠEKAS, R.
RAMANAUSKAS, J.
RAUGALĖ, A.
SIAURUSAITIS, B. J.
ŠIRVYDIS, V.
ŠATKAUSKAS, B.
TAMULEVIČIŪTĖ, D. S.
TRIPONIS,V. J.
USONIS, V.
UŽDAVINYS, G.
VAIČEKONIS, V.
VALIULIS, A.
VITKUS, K.
ŽVIRONAITĖ, V.

Faculty of Natural Sciences:

DVARECKAS, V.
GAIGALAS, A. J.
GLEMŽA, A.
JANKAUSKAS, T.
JUODKA, B.
JUODKAZIS, V.
JURGAITIS, A.
KABAILIENĖ, M.
KAVALIAUSKAS, P.
KILKUS, K.
KUBLICKIENĖ, O.
LAZUTKA, J. R.
LEKEVIČIUS, R. K.
NAUJALIS, J. R.
RANČELIS, V. P.
VALENTA, V. J.

Faculty of Philology:

ČEKMONAS, V.
DRAZDAUSKIENĖ, M. L.
GIRDENIS, A. S.
GIRDZIJAUSKAS, J.
IDZELIS, R.
JAKAITIENĖ, E. M.
JOVAIŠAS, A.
KOSTIN, E.
LABUTIS, V.
LASSAN, E.
NASTOPKA, K. V.
PAKERIENĖ-DAUJOTYTĖ, V.
PAULAUSKIENĖ, A.
STEPONAVIČIUS, A.
STUNDŽIA, B.
TEKORIENĖ, D.
VALEIKA, L. V.
ZABULIS, H.

Faculty of Philosophy:

ARAMAVIČIŪTĖ, V.
NEKRAŠAS, E.
PAVILIONIS, R.
PLEČKAITIS, R.
PŠIBILSKIS, V.
ŠETKAUSKIS, P.
ŠLIOGERIS, M. A.

Faculty of Physics:

BALEVIČIUS, V.
BANDZAITIS, A.
GARŠKA, E.
GAVRIUŠINAS, V.
GRIGAS, J.
IVAŠKA, V.
JARAŠIŪNAS, K.
JUŠKA, G.
KALADĖ, J.
KIMTYS, L.
MONTRIMAS, E.
ORLIUKAS, A. F.
PISKARSKAS, A.
RAKAUSKAS, R. J.
SAKALAUSKAS, S.
ŠTABINIS, A. P.
ŠUGUROV, V.
VAITKEVIČIUS, P. H.
VAITKUS, J. V.
ŽILINSKAS, P. J.
ŽUKAUSKAS, A.

Sports Centre:

JANKAUSKAS, J. P.
SAPLINSKAS, J.

Centre for Jewish Studies:

SUBAS, M.

ATTACHED INSTITUTES

Algirdas Greimas Centre for Semiotics: Head Dr SAULIUS ŽUKAS.

Centre for Environmental Studies: Head Dr STASYS SINKEVIČIUS.

Centre for Jewish Studies: Head Prof. MEJERIS ŠUBAS.

Centre for Oriental Studies: Head DALIA ŠVAMBARYTĖ.

Centre for Religious Studies and Research: Head Dr IRENA EGLĖ LAUMENSKAITĖ.

Centre for Women's Studies: Head Dr MARIJA AUŠRINĖ PAVILIONIENĖ.

Institute of International Relations and Political Sciences: Dir Dr EGIDIJUS KŪRIS.

Institute of Materials Science and Applied Research: Dir Prof. JUOZAS VIDMANTIS VAITKUS.

Sports Centre: Head Prof. JUOZAS SAPLINSKAS.

VYTAUTAS MAGNUS UNIVERSITY

3000 Kaunas, Daukanto 28
Telephone: (7) 22-27-39
Fax: (7) 20-38-58

Founded 1922, closed 1950, re-opened 1989
State-supported
Languages of instruction: Lithuanian, English
Rector: B. VAŠKELIS

Pro-Rectors: P. Zakarevičius (Undergraduate Studies), V. Kaminskas (Graduate Studies)
Registrar: J. Valantinienė
Librarian: J. Masalskienė

Library of 85,000 vols
Number of teachers: 265
Number of students: 2,600

Publications: *Darbai ir Dienos* (Works and Days), *Organizacijų Vadyba* (Management of Organizations), *Aplinkos tyrimai, inžinerija ir vadyba* (Environmental Research, Engineering and Management).

DEANS

Faculty of Business Administration: P. Zakarevičius
Faculty of Informatics: V. Kaminskas
Faculty of Environmental Sciences: M. Venslauskas
Faculty of Fine Arts: V. Stauskas
Faculty of Humanities: E. Aleksandravičius
Faculty of Catholic Theology: V. Vaičiūnas
Faculty of Social Sciences: J. Lapė

PROFESSORS

Aleksandravičius, E., History
Bentkus, R., Mathematics
Bumelis, V., Biochemistry
Buračas, A., Economics
Çonstable, R., Social Welfare
Černius, V., Education
Goštautas, A., Social Welfare
Gudaitis, L., Lithuanian Literature
Jasaltis, A., Biochemistry
Juknys, R., Environmental Sciences
Jūraitis, J., Theology
Kaminskas, V., Informatics
Kamuntavičius, G., Physics
Katilius, R., Physics
Kazlauskas, V., Theology
Kubilius, V., Lithuanian Literature
Lujanas, V., Physics
Maciejauskienė, V., Lithuanian Language
Matulis, A., Physics
Musteikis, A., Sociology
Pikunas, J., Psychology
Pranevičius, L., Physics
Raudys, S., Informatics
Sapagovas, M., Mathematics
Statulevičius, V., Mathematics
Ştauskas, V., Architecture
Šernas, V., Education
Telksnys, A., Informatics
Tyla, A., History
Vaškelis, B., Literature
Vėlius, N., Ethnology and Folklore
Żakarevičius, P., Business Administration
Žilinskas, A., Informatics

ATTACHED CENTRES

Computer Science Centre: Dir V. Kaminskas.

Management Centre: Dir P. Zakarevičius.

Centre for Social Welfare: Dir R. Constable.

Lithuanians in Exile Centre: Dir E. Aleksandravičius.

Letonics Centre: Dir A. Butkus.

Computer Linguistics Centre: Dir R. Marcinkevičienė.

Centre for Education: Dir V. Černius.

Other Higher Educational Institutes

Kaunas Medical Academy: 3000 Kaunas, Mickeviciaus 9; tel. (7) 22-61-10; telex 269268; fax (7) 22-07-33; f. 1922; faculties: medicine, public health, dentistry, pharmacy, nursing; 371 teachers; 2,127 students; library of 870,000 vols; Rector Prof. Dr Vilius Grabauskas; publ. *Medicina* (annually).

Lithuanian Academy of Music (Lietuvos Muzikos Akademija): 2600 Vilnius, Gedimino pr. 42; tel. (2) 61-26-91; fax (2) 22-00-93; e-mail muzakad@mafd.vno.osf.lt; f. 1933; subjects: musicology, piano, composition, singing, orchestral instruments, folk instruments; conducting, drama, television and film, musical education; libraries with 341,000 vols, record libraries with 32,000 records; institute of musicology with depts of history and theory of music, ethnomusicology (recorded collection of 85,000 items) and music teaching; 326 teachers; 923 students; Rector Prof. Dr Juozas Antanavičius; publ. *Menotyra* (Science of Art, annually).

Lithuanian University of Agriculture: 4324 Kaunas-Akademija; tel. (7) 29-82-55; fax (7) 29-65-00; e-mail laa@nora.lzua.lt; f. 1924; depts: agronomy, agricultural engineering, water and land management, economics, forestry; research station (70 ha) engaged in rape growing, forest monitoring, organic farming, pollution; 450 teachers; 4,400 students; library of 500,000 vols, 200 periodicals; Rector A. Kusta; publs *Agricultural Engineering, Silviculture, Water Management, Agriculture, Baltic Forestry.*

Lithuanian Veterinary Academy: 3022 Kaunas, Tilžės 18; tel. 26-03-83; fax 26-14-17; f. 1936; faculties: veterinary medicine and animal husbandry, technology; 138 teachers; 600 students; library of 320,000 vols; Rector V. Bižokas; publ. *Veterinary Science and Zootechnics* (annually).

Vilnius Academy of Arts: 2601 Vilnius, Maironio 6; tel. (2) 61-30-04; fax (2) 61-99-66; e-mail vda@vda.lt; f. 1793; depts: painting, sculpture, printmaking, ceramics, architecture, textiles, art theory and history, design, interior and furnishing, industrial art, fashion design, monumental and decorative arts; 264 teachers; 1,002 students; library; museum; Rector Prof. Arvydas Šaltenis.

LUXEMBOURG

Learned Societies

GENERAL

Institut Grand-Ducal: Luxembourg; includes six sections: (*a*) Historical (Pres. PAUL SPANG; Sec. JEAN SCHROEDER), (*b*) Medical (Pres. HENRI METZ; Sec. JEAN NEUEN), (*c*) Scientific (Pres. JACQUES BINTZ; Sec. PIERRE SECK), (*d*) Linguistic and Folklore (Pres. WILL REULAND; Sec. HENRI KLEES), (*e*) Arts and Literature (Pres. FERNAND HOFFMANN; Sec. HENRI BLAISE), (*f*) Moral and Political Sciences (Pres. EDMOND WAGNER; Sec. HENRI AHLBORN).

MEDICINE

Collège Médical: 57 blvd de la Pétrusse, Luxembourg; f. 1818; governmental consultative body; 11 mems; Pres. Dr GEORGES ARNOLD; Sec. PIERRE SCHROEDER.

NATURAL SCIENCES

Biological Sciences

Société des Naturalistes Luxembourgeois: BP 327, L-2013 Luxembourg; f. 1890; 575 mems; Pres. CLAUDE MEISCH; Sec. M. MOLITOR; Librarian M. MEYER; publ. *Bulletin* (annually).

Research Institutes

ECONOMICS, LAW AND POLITICS

Service central de la statistique et des études économiques: BP 304, 6 blvd Royal, 2013 Luxembourg; tel. 478-1; fax 464-289; e-mail stotec.post@stotec.etat.lu; f. 1962; attached to Min. of Economics; library of 9,000 vols, 500 periodicals; Dir ROBERT WEIDES; publs *Annuaire statistique du Luxembourg* (annually), *Statistiques Historiques*, *Le Luxembourg en Chiffres*, *Le Recueil de Statistiques par Commune*, *Répertoire des entreprises*, *Cahiers économiques* (irregular), *Le Bulletin du STATEC* (8 a year), *Note de conjoncture* (quarterly), *Indicateurs rapides* (13 series), *Recensements de la Population*.

EDUCATION

Commission grand-ducale d'Instruction: 29 rue Aldringen, 2926 Luxembourg; tel. 478-5119; fax 478-5123; e-mail klein.paul@ci.educ.lu; f. 1843; Pres. JEAN-PIERRE KRAEMER; Sec. PAUL KLEIN.

MEDICINE

Centre de Recherche Public de la Santé: 120 route d'Arlon, 1150 Luxembourg; tel. 453213; fax 453219; e-mail secretariat@crp-sante.lu; Pres. Dr DANIÈLE HANSEN-KOENIG; Dir Dr ROBERT KANZ.

TECHNOLOGY

Centre de Recherche Public Henri Tudor: 6 rue Richard Coudenhove-Kalergi, 1359 Luxembourg-Kirchberg; tel. 425991-1; fax 436523; f. 1988; applied science; Pres. JEAN DE LA HAMETTE; Dir CLAUDE WEHENKEL.

Libraries and Archives

Esch-sur-Alzette

Bibliothèque de la Ville: 26 rue Emile Mayrisch, Esch-sur-Alzette; tel. 547383; f. 1919; German, French, English and Italian literature; popular science books; library of 60,000 vols; special collection of Luxembourgensia; Record Library; Chief Librarian FERNAND ROELTGEN.

Luxembourg

Archives Nationales: Plateau du Saint-Esprit, BP 6, 2010 Luxembourg; tel. 478-6660; fax 474692; Dir CORNEL MEDER.

Bibliothèque Nationale: 37 blvd F. D. Roosevelt, 2450 Luxembourg; tel. 229755-1; fax 475672; f. 1798, re-organized 1897, 1945, 1958 and 1973; library of 650,000 vols, 800 MSS, 145 incunabula; special collection of 150,000 Luxemburgensia; Dir JEAN CLAUDE MULLER; publs *Bibliographie Luxembourgeoise*, *Bibliographie d'histoire luxembourgeoise* (annually), special bibliographies.

Museums and Art Galleries

Luxembourg

Musée National d'Histoire et d'Art (National Museum of History and Art): Marché-aux-Poissons, 2345 Luxembourg; tel. 479-330-1; fax 223760; f. 1845; archaeology, fine arts, industrial and popular arts, history of Luxembourg; library of 25,000 vols; Dir PAUL REILES.

University

CENTRE UNIVERSITAIRE DE LUXEMBOURG

162A ave de la Faïencerie, 1511 Luxembourg

Telephone: 466644-1
Fax: 466644-508

Founded 1969
State control

Languages of instruction: French, German, English
Academic year: October to June

President: PAUL DE BRUYNE
Director: JEAN-PAUL MOSSONG
Administrative Officer: MARIE-ANNE SOMMER SCHUMACHER
Librarians: GILBERT GRAFF, EMILE SCHOLTES

Library of 120,000 vols
Number of teachers: 200 (mostly part-time)
Number of students: 1,100

HEADS OF DEPARTMENTS

Letters and Human Sciences: JEAN-PAUL LEHNERS
Law and Economics: JEAN-MARIE JANS
Sciences: PIERRE SECK
Teacher Training: J.-P.-R.-STRAINCHAMPS
Legal Training: JACQUES DELVAUX

CONSTITUENT INSTITUTE

Institut Universitaire International de Luxembourg: f. 1974; postgraduate summer courses; 12 teachers; 90 students; Pres. ROMAIN SCHINTINGEN.

HEADS OF DEPARTMENTS

Centre international d'études juridiques et de droit comparé: NICOLAS DECKER
Centre international d'économie politique: MARC MULLER
Centre international d'études et de recherches européennes: ROMAIN SCHINTGEN

Colleges

Conservatoire de Musique d'Esch-sur-Alzette: 50 rue d'Audun, BP 145, 4002 Esch-sur-Alzette; tel. 549727; f. 1969 (formerly Ecole Municipale de Musique f. 1926); 60 teachers; 1,200 students; Principal Prof. FRED HARLES; Secs N. CRUCHTEN, J.-J. BLEY, M. TREINEN; publ. *Annuaire* (Year Book).

Conservatoire de Musique de la Ville de Luxembourg: 33 rue Charles Martel, 2134 Luxembourg; tel. 456555-1; fax 449686; f. 1906; 150 teachers; Dir FERNAND JUNG; Sec. PIERRE BERG; publ. *Compte rendu* (annually).

Ecole Professionnelle et Ménagère: 101 rue de Luxembourg, Esch-sur-Alzette; Dir M. MARIA-HILF.

Institut Supérieur de Technologie: Rue Richard Coudenhove-Kalergi, 1359 Luxembourg-Kirchberg; tel. 43-66-61; telex 3586; fax 432124; f. 1979; mechanical, electrical and civil engineering, industrial computing; 50 teachers; 400 students; library of 10,000 vols; Pres. PROSPER SCHROEDER; Dir ALBERT RETTER.

FORMER YUGOSLAV REPUBLIC OF MACEDONIA

(Note: at the time this chapter was compiled, a dispute over the use of the name 'Macedonia' was preventing the country's worldwide recognition under that name.)

Learned Societies

GENERAL

Društvo za nauka i umetnost (Association of Sciences and Arts): 97000 Bitola, POB 145; tel. (97) 22-683; f. 1960; main activities: scientific meetings, symposia, research; 154 mems, 25 assocs; sections of social sciences and law, natural and mathematical sciences, medical, technical and applied sciences, arts, linguistics and literature, history and geography; Pres. SOTIR PANOVSKI; Sec.-Gen. TRAJKO OGNENOVSKI; publs *Prilozi* (Contributions, 2 a year), *Scientific Thought*.

Makedonska Akademija na Naukite i Umetnostite (Macedonian Academy of Sciences and Arts): 91000 Skopje, Bulevar Krste Misirkov 2, POB 428; tel. (91) 114-200; fax (91) 115-903; f. 1967; sections of Linguistics and Literary Sciences (Sec. PETAR HR. ILIEVSKI), Social Sciences (Sec. NIKOLA UZUNOV), Biological and Medical Sciences (Sec. GEORGI FILIPOVSKI), Arts (Sec. TOME SERAFIMOVSKI), Mathematical and Technical Sciences (Sec. TOME BOŠEVSKI); 32 mems, 7 assoc. mems, 36 foreign mems; library of 100,000 vols; Pres. KSENTE BOGOEV; Chief Scientific Sec. TAŠKO GEORGIEVSKI; publs *Letopis* (annually), *Prilozi na Oddelenieto za opštestveni nauki* (Contributions of the Dept of Social Sciences), *Prilozi na Oddelenieto za lingvistika i literaturna nauka* (Contributions of the Dept of Linguistics and Literary Sciences), *Prilozi na Oddelenieto za biološki i medicinski nauki* (Contributions of the Dept of Biological and Medical Sciences), *Prilozi na Oddelenieto za matematičko-tehnički nauki* (Contributions of the Dept of Mathematical and Technical Sciences).

AGRICULTURE, FISHERIES AND VETERINARY SCIENCE

Sojuz na Društvata na Veterinarnite Lekari i Tehničari na Makedonija (Union of Associations of Veterinary Surgeons and Technicians of Macedonia): Veterinaren institut, 91000 Skopje, Lazar Pop-Trajkov 5, POB 95; f. 1950; 450 mems; Pres. SILJAN ZAHARIEVSKI; Sec. ADŽIEVSKI BLAŽE; publ. *Makedonski veterinaren pregled* (Macedonian Veterinary review).

Sojuz na Inženeri i Tehničari po Sumarstvo i Industrija za Prerabotka na Drvo na Makedonija (Union of Forestry Engineers and Technicians of Macedonia): Šumarski institut, 91000 Skopje, Engelsova 2; f. 1952; 500 mems; Pres. Dipl. Ing. ŽIVKO MINČEV; Sec. Dipl. Ing. MILE STAMENKOV; publ. *Sumarski pregled* (Forester's review).

Združenie na Zemjodelski Inženeri na Makedonija (Association of Agricultural Engineers of Macedonia): Zemjodelski fakultet, P. Fah. 297, 91000 Skopje; tel. (91) 115-277; fax (91) 238-218; f. 1994; 3,000 mems; publ. *Macedonian Agriculture Review* (annually).

BIBLIOGRAPHY, LIBRARY SCIENCE AND MUSEOLOGY

Društvo na Muzejskite Rabotnici na Makedonija (Museum Society of Macedonia): Muzej na grad Skopje, 91000 Skopje, Mito Hadži-Vasilev-Jasmin b.b.; f. 1951; 100 mems; Pres. KUZMAN GEOGRIEVSKI; Sec. GALENA KUCULOVSKA.

Sojuz na društvata na arhivskite rabotnici na Makedonija (Union of Societies of Archivists of Macedonia): 91001 Skopje, Gligor Prličev 3, POB 496; tel. (91) 237-211; fax (91) 234-461; f. 1954; 340 mems; publ. *Makedonski arhivist* (annually).

Sojuz na Društvata na Bibliotekarite na Makedonija (Union of Librarians' Associations of Macedonia): Narodna i univerzitetska biblioteka "Kliment Ohridski", 91000 Skopje Bul. Goce Delčev, br 6; f. 1949; 550 mems; Pres. TRAJČE PIKOV; Sec. POLIKSENA MATKOVSKA; publ. *Bibliotekarska iskra*.

ECONOMICS, LAW AND POLITICS

Društvo za Filozofija, Sociologija i Politikologija na Makedonija (Society for Philosophy, Sociology and Politics of Macedonia): Institut za sociološki i političko-pravni istražuvanja, 91000 Skopje, Bul. Partizanski odredi b.b.; f. 1960; 170 mems; Pres. Dr DRAGAN TAŠKOVSKI; Sec. SVETA ŠKARIĆ; publ. *Zbornik* (Collected Papers).

Sojuz na Ekonomistite na Makedonija (Union of Economists of Macedonia): 91000 Skopje, Ekonomiski Fakultet, K. Misirkov b.b.; tel;. 224-311; fax 224-973; f. 1950; 3,000 mems; Pres. Prof. Dr TAKI FITI; Sec. ACO SPASOVSKI; publ. *Stopanski pregled* (Economic review).

Sojuz na Združenijata na Pravnicite na Makedonija (Union of Associations of Jurists of Macedonia): Ustaven sud na Makedonija, 91000 Skopje, XII udarna brigada 2; f. 1946; 4,000 mems; Pres. BORO DOGANDŽISKI; Sec. PETAR GOLUBOVSKI; publ. *Pravna misla* (Legal opinion).

FINE AND PERFORMING ARTS

Društvo na Istoričarite na Umetnosta od Makedonija (Society of Art Historians of Macedonia): Arheološki muzej na Makedonija, 91000 Skopje, Curčiska b.b.; f. 1970; 130 mems; Pres. MILANKA BOŠKOVSKA; Sec. MATE BOŠKOVSKI; publ. *Likovna umetnost* (Plastic Arts).

Društvo na Likovnite Umetnici na Makedonija (Society of Plastic Arts of Macedonia): 91000 Skopje, 13 Noemvri b.b., PF 438; tel. (91) 211-533; f. 1944; 333 mems; Pres. GLIGOR ČEMERSKI; Sec. BRANISLAV MIRČEVSKI.

Sojuz na Kompozitorite na Makedonija (Society of Macedonian Composers): 91000 Skopje, Maksim Gorki 18; tel. (91) 220-567; fax (91) 235-854; f. 1950; 49 mems; Pres. VLASTIMIR NIKOLOVSKI; Sec. MARKO KOLOVSKI; publ. *Informer*.

HISTORY, GEOGRAPHY AND ARCHAEOLOGY

Geografsko Društvo na R. Makedonija (Geographical Society of Macedonia): Geografski institut pri Prirodnomatematički fakultet, 91000 Skopje, PF 146; f. 1949; 600 mems; Pres. Prof. VASIL GRAMATNIKOVSKI; Sec. Ass. NIKOLA PANOV; publs *Geografski razgledi* (Geographical surveys), *Geografski vidik* (Geographical outlook).

Sojuz na Društvata na Istoričarite na Republika Makedonija (Union of Societies of Historians of the Republic of Macedonia): Institut za nacionalna istorija, 91000 Skopje, ul. Grigor Prličev br.3, POB 591; tel. (91) 114-078; fax (91) 115-831; f. 1952; Pres. Dr TODOR CHEPREGANOV; Sec. GHORGHI CHAKARJANEVSKI; publ. *Istorija* (History).

Združenie na Arheolozite na Makedonija (Archaeological Society of Macedonia): Muzej na Makedonija, Ćurčiska b. b. 91000 Skopje (Kuršumlian); tel. (91) 116-044; fax (91) 116-439; f. 1970; 150 mems; Pres. VOISLAV SANEV; Sec. DRAGIŠA ZDRAVKOVSKI; publ. *Macedoniae acta archaeologica*.

LANGUAGE AND LITERATURE

Društvo na Literaturnite Preveduvači na Makedonija (Society of Literary Translators of Macedonia): 91000 Skopje, PF 3; f. 1955; 102 mems; Pres. Prof. Dr BOŽIDAR NASTEV; Sec. TAŠKO ŠIRILOV.

Društvo na Pisatelite na Makedonija (Society of Writers of Macedonia): 91000 Skopje, Maksim Gorki 18; tel. (91) 117-668; fax (91) 228-345; f. 1947; 269 mems; Pres. JOVAN PAVLOVSKI; Secs PASKAL GILOVSKI, SVETLANA HRISTOVA-JOCIĆ.

Sojuz na Društvata za Makedonski Jazik i Literatura (Union of Assens for Macedonian Language and Literature): Filološki fakultet, 91000 Skopje, Bul. Krste Misirkov b.b.; f. 1954; 700 mems; Pres. ELENA BENDEVSKA; Sec. LJUPČO MITREVSKI; publ. *Literaturen zbor* (Literary word).

Združenie na Folkloristite na Makedonija (Association of Folklorists of Macedonia): Institut za folklor, 91000 Skopje, Ruzveltova 3; tel. 233-876; fax 319; f. 1952; 60 mems; Pres. GORGI SMOKVARSKI; Sec. ERMIS LAFAZANOVSKY; publ. *Narodno Stvaralaštvo* (1 or 2 a year).

MEDICINE

Farmaceutsko Društvo na Makedonija (Pharmacological Society of Macedonia): 91000 Skopje, Ivo Ribar Lola MI/6; Pres. LAZAR TOLOV; Sec. GALABA SRBINOVSKA; publ. *Bilten* (Bulletin).

Makedonsko Lekarsko Društvo (Medical Society of Macedonia): 91000 Skopje, Gradski zid blok 11/6; f. 1946; 2,000 mems; publ. *Makedonski medicindki pregled* (Macedonian Medical Review).

NATURAL SCIENCES

Mathematical Sciences

Sojuz na Društvata na Matematičarite i Informatičarite na Makedonija (Society of Mathematicians and Computerists of Macedonia): 91000 Skopje, PF 162; tel. (91) 261-330; fax (91) 228-141; f. 1950; Chief Officers Prof. Dr NAUM CELAKOSKI, Prof. Dr DIMITRA KARČICKA: publ. *Matematički Bilten* (Mathematical Bulletin).

Physical Sciences

Društvo na Fizičarite na Makedonija (Society of Physicists of Macedonia): 91000 Skopje, POB 162; tel. (91) 118-706; fax (91) 228-141; f. 1949; 60 mems; Pres. Prof. VIKTOR URUMOV; Sec. Dr ZORICA MITREVSKA; publs *Bilten* (Bulletin), *Impuls*.

Makedonsko Geološko Društvo (Macedonian Geological Society): Geološki zavod, 91001 Skopje, POB 28; tel. 230-873; telex 51871; f. 1954; 300 mems; library of 20,000 vols; Pres. NIKOLA TUDŽAROV; Sec. ROZA PETROVSKA.

TECHNOLOGY

Sojuz na Inženeri i Tehničari na Makedonija (Society of Engineers and Technicians of Macedonia): 91000 Skopje, Nikola Vapcarov b.b.; f. 1945; 27,000 mems; Pres. Prof. Dr Ing. DIME LAZAROV; Sec. BORO RAVNJANSKI.

Research Institutes

AGRICULTURE, FISHERIES AND VETERINARY SCIENCE

Institut za Ovoštarstvo (Institute of Pomology): 91000 Skopje, Prvomajska 5; tel. 230-557; f. 1953; attached to Skopje University; fruit research; library of 3,670 vols; Dir Dr IVAN KUZMANOVSKI.

Institut za Pamuk (Cotton Institute): 92400 Strumica, Goce Delčev 27; f. 1956; Dir HRISTO HRISTOMANOV; publ. *Zbornik* (Collected Papers).

Institut za Stočarstvo (Institute of Animal Breeding): 91000 Skopje, Ile Ilievski 92A; tel. (91) 253-607; fax (91) 257-755; f. 1952; part of Faculty of Agriculture of Skopje University; Dir Prof. Dr KIRIL FILEV; Sec. TIMKO TRAJKOV.

Institut za Tutun (Tobacco Institute): 97500 Prilep, Kičevsko Džade; tel. 26-760; fax 26-763; f. 1924; library of over 5,000 vols; Dir Dr KIRIL FILIPOSKI; publ. *Tutun* (Tobacco, every 2 months).

Veterinaren Institut na Makedonija (Veterinary Institute of Macedonia): 91000 Skopje, Univerzitet Kiril i Metodij, Ul. Lazar Pop Trajkov 5-7; f. 1927; Dir CANE PEJKOVSKI; Sec. DIMITAR ANASTASOV.

Zavod za Unapreduvanje na Lozarstvoto i Vinarstvoto na Makedonija (Institute for the Advancement of Viticulture of Macedonia): 91000 Skopje, Naselba Butel 1; f. 1952; Dir Dr DIME PEMOVSKI; publs *Lozarstvo i vinarstvo* (Viticulture), *Godišen izveštaj* (Annual Report).

Zavod za Unapreduvanje na Stočarstvoto na Makedonija (Institute for the Advancement of Animal Husbandry of Macedonia): 91000 Skopje, Avtokomanda; f. 1952; Dir Prof. Dr BLAGOJ VASKOV.

ECONOMICS, LAW AND POLITICS

Ekonomski Institut na Univerzitetet 'Sveti Kiril i Metodij' (Institute of Economics of Sts Cyril and Methodius University): 91000 Skopje, Prolet 1, POB 250; tel. (91) 115-076; fax (91) 226-350; f. 1952; library of 18,540 vols; Dir Dr ALEKSANDAR PETROSKI: publ. *Annual*.

HISTORY, GEOGRAPHY AND ARCHAEOLOGY

Institut za Nacionalna Istorija (Institute of National History): 91000 Skopje, Ul. Gligor Prlicev br.3; fax 591; f. 1948; history of Macedonian peoples; 56 mems; library of 27,350 vols, 37,500 periodicals, 1,300 vols newspapers; Dir Dr VLADO IVANOVSKI; publ. *Glasnik* (Journal).

LANGUAGE AND LITERATURE

Institut za Folklor (Institute of Folklore): 91000 Skopje, Ruzveltova 3, PF 319; tel. (91) 233-876; f. 1950; Dir Dr BLAGOJ STOIČOVSKI; publ. *Makedonski folklor*.

Institut za Makedonski Jazik 'Krste Misirkov' (Krste Misirkov Institute of Macedonian Language): 91000 Skopje, Grigor Prličev 5; e-mail kvesna@ukim.edu.mk; f. 1953; Dir MARIJA KOROBAR-BELČEVA; publs *Makedonski jazik* (The Macedonian Language), *Stari tekstovi* (Ancient Texts), *Makedonistika* (Macedonian Studies).

TECHNOLOGY

Geološki Zavod (Geology Institute): 91001 Skopje, POB 28; f. 1944; geological mapping, exploration of mineral deposits, drilling, mining, grouting; *c.* 700 mems; library of *c.* 10,000 vols; Gen Dir DRAGAN ANGELESKY; publ. *Trudovi* (Transactions).

Zavod za vodostopanstvo na R. Makedonija (Water Development Institute of Macedonia): 91000 Skopje, Železnička 62, PF 310; tel. (91) 228-028; fax (91) 239-401; f. 1951; library of 1,800 vols; Dir Ing. METODI BOEV; publ. *Vodostopanski problemi* (Water Development Problems, every 5 years).

Libraries and Archives

Bitola

Istoriski arhiv na Bitola (Historical Archives of Bitola): 97000 Bitola, 1 May 171; f. 1954; conservation, collection and printing of archive materials; 3,946 vols; Dir JOVAN KOCHANKOVSKY.

Matična i Univerzitetska Biblioteka 'Kliment Ohridski' (Kliment Ohridski Municipal and University Library): 97000 Bitola, Laninova 39; tel (97) 33-208; f. 1945; Dir DOBRI PETREVSKI.

Ohrid

Arhiv na Makedonija: 97300 Ohrid; tel. (96) 32-104; f. 1957; 3,000 vols; special collections: Old Church Slavonic MSS, early Greek and Arabic books; Dir DIMITAR SMILESKI.

Skopje

Arhiv na Makedonija: 91001 Skopje, POB 496, Gligor Prličev 3; tel. (91) 116-571; fax (91) 115-827; f. 1951; over 10,000 vols, 872 periodicals; Dir Dr KIRO DOJČINOVSKI; publ. *Makedonski archivist*.

Arhiv na Skopje (Archives of Skopje): 91000 Skopje, Moskovska 1, reon 45; tel. (91) 259-420; f. 1952; 3,000 vols; *c.* 1.5 km of archive records, 333,152 units of published information; Dir Dr MILOŠ KONSTANTINOV; publ. *Dokumenti i materiali za istorijata na Skopje* (irregular).

Biblioteka 'Braka Miladinovci' (District of Skopje Public Library): 91000 Skopje, Partizanski odredi b.b.; tel. (91) 232-544; f. 1935; about 800,000 vols; 27 brs; Dir GOJKO IKONOMOV.

Narodna i univerzitetska biblioteka 'Sv. Kliment Ohridski' (National and University Library 'St Kliment Ohridski'): 91000 Skopje, Bul. Goce Delčev 6; tel. (91) 115-177; fax (91) 226-846; e-mail kliment@nubsk.edu.mk; f. 1944; State copyright, central and deposit library; 3,000,000 vols; special collections: Slav MSS, incunabula and rare books, oriental, music, maps and design, doctoral theses; Head VERA KALAJLIEVSKA; publs. *Makedonska bibliografija* (3 series, quarterly), *Bibliografija Makedonika* (annually).

Museums and Art Galleries

Bitola

Zavod, muzej i galeriya (Institute, Museum and Gallery): 97000 Bitola, Ul. Kliment Ohridski b.b.; tel. (97) 35-387; fax (97) 35-292; f. 1948; archaeology, history, ethnology, art; library of 10,000 vols; Dir NIKOLA IVANOVSKI.

Skopje

Muzej na Makedonija (Museum of Macedonia): 91000 Skopje, Ćurčiska b.b.; tel. (91) 116-044; fax (91) 116-439; f. 1924; archaeology, history, ethnology; library of 19,000 vols; Dir Dr ELEONORA PETROVA; publ. *Zbornik* (Collected Papers, annually).

Muzej na Grad Skopje (Museum of Skopje): 91000 Skopje, Mito Hadzivasilev b.b.; tel. (91) 115-367; f. 1949; Dir KLIME KOROBAR.

Muzej na Sovremena Umetnost (Museum of Contemporary Art): 91000 Skopje, Samoilova b.b., PF 482; tel. (91) 117-735; f. 1964; Dir ZORAN PETROVSKI.

Prirodonaučen muzej na Makedonija (Natural History Museum of Macedonia): 91000 Skopje, 55 Bulevar Ilinden 86; f. 1926; library of 44,000 vols; Dir BRANISLAVA MIHAJLOVA; publs *Acta*, *Fragmenta Balcanica*, *Fauna na Makedonija*.

Umetnička Galerija (Art Gallery): 91000 Skopje, Kruševska 1A, POB 278; tel. (91) 233-904; f. 1948; modern art; Dir DRAGAN BOŠNAKOSKI.

Universities

UNIVERZITET BITOLJ
(Bitola University)

97000 Bitola, Bulevar 1 Maj b.b.
Telephone: (38-97) 23788
Founded 1979
Rector: Prof. Dr DAME NESTOROVSKI
Administrative Officer: JORDAN MITREVSKI

UNIVERZITET 'SV. KIRIL I METODIJ'
(University of Skopje)

91000 Skopje, POB 576, Bulevar Krste Misirkov b.b.
Telephone: (91) 116-323
Fax: (91) 116-370
E-mail: postmaster@ukim.edu.mk

Founded 1949
State control
Language of instruction: Macedonian
Academic year: October to June

Rector: Prof. Dr RADMILA KIPRIJANOVA
Secretary-General: DUŠKO SEKOVSKI

Number of teachers: 1,300
Number of students: 25,967

Publications: *Univerzitetski bilten, Univerzitetski vesnik i Studentski zbor.*

DEANS

Faculty of Law: Prof. Dr MIODRAG MICAJKOV
Faculty of Economics: Prof. Dr BOBEK SUKLEV
Faculty of Philology: Prof. Dr TRAJAN GOCEVSKI
Faculty of Philosophy: Prof. Dr LILJANA TODOROVA
Faculty of Architecture: Prof. Dr ZIVKO POPOVSKI
Faculty of Civil Engineering: Prof. Dr DUŠAN ZLATKOVSKI
Faculty of Agriculture: Prof. Dr EFTIM ANCEV
Faculty of Veterinary Medicine: Prof. Dr METODIJA DODEVSKI
Faculty of Forestry: Prof. Dr JOSIF DIMEVSKI
Faculty of Medicine: Prof. Dr MILCO BOGOEV
Faculty of Pharmacy: Prof. Dr KIRIL DOREVSKI
Faculty of Electrotechnical Engineering: Prof. Dr LJUPČO PANOVSKI
Faculty of Mechanical Engineering: Prof. Dr DRAGI DANEV
Faculty of Technology and Metallurgy: Prof. Dr MARIJA LAZAREVIĆ
Faculty of Natural and Mathematical Sciences: Prof. Dr GLIGOR JOVANOVSKI
Faculty of Physical Education: Prof. Dr DIMITRIJA POPOVSKI
Faculty of Stomatology: Prof. Dr METODI SIMONOVSKI
Faculty of Geology and Mining: Prof. Dr BLAZO BOEV
Faculty of Drama: Prof. DANČO ČEVRESKI
Faculty of Music: Prof. Dr DIMITRIJE BUZAROVSKI
Faculty of Fine Arts: Prof. STEFAN MANEVSKI
Faculty of Education (Skopje): Prof. Dr NIKOLA PETROV
Faculty of Education (Stip): Prof. SPASKO SIMONOVSKI

MADAGASCAR

Learned Societies

GENERAL

Académie Malgache: BP 6217, Tsimbazaza, Antananarivo; tel. and fax 210-84; f. 1902; studies in human and natural sciences; four sections: language, literature and arts, moral and political sciences, basic sciences, applied sciences; 140 mems, 60 foreign mems in each section; library of 100,000 vols; Pres. Dr C. RABENORO; publs *Bulletin de l'Academie* (annually), *Mémoires*, *Bulletin d'Information et de Liaison*.

BIBLIOGRAPHY, LIBRARY SCIENCE AND MUSEOLOGY

Association des Bibliothécaires, Documentalistes, Archivistes et Muséographes de Madagascar: Bibliothèque Nationale, BP 257, Antananarivo; tel. 22-258-72; f. 1976; promotion, development, preservation and conservation of national collections; Pres CHRISTIANE ANDRIAMIRADO; Secs SAMOELA ANDRIANKOTONIRINA, FRANÇOISE RAMANANDRAISOA; publ. *Haren-tsaina* (2 a year).

Research Institutes

GENERAL

Institut Français de Recherche Scientifique pour le Développement en Coopération (ORSTOM): Mission ORSTOM, BP 434, Antananarivo 101; tel. and fax (2) 330-98; e-mail riviere@represent.orstom.mg; research into economics, statistics, fisheries, environment, health, deforestation, biodiversity and water; library of 200 vols; Rep. FRANÇOIS RIVIÈRE. (See main entry under France.)

AGRICULTURE, FISHERIES AND VETERINARY SCIENCE

Centre National de Recherche Appliquée au Développement Rural (CENRADERU): BP 1690, Antananarivo; tel. and fax 402-70; e-mail fofifa@bow.ats.mg; f. 1974; research into agriculture, forestry and fisheries, zoology, veterinary studies and rural economy; publ. *Rapport d'activité* (annually).

Attached institute:

CENRADERU—IRCT: BP 227, Mahajanga; research on cotton and other fibres; main research station at Toliary; regional station at Tanandava; sisal research at Mandrare.

Centre Technique Forestier Tropical: BP 745, Antananarivo; tel. 40623; fax 20999; f. 1961; silviculture, genetics, soil conservation; Dir J. P. BOUILLET. (See main entry under France.)

Département de Recherches Agronomiques de la République Malgache: BP 1444, Antananarivo; stations at Alaotra, Antalaha, Ambanja, Ambovombe, Ivoloina, Mahajanga, Fianarantsoa, Ilaka Est, Kianjavato, Kianjasoa, Tanandava; Dir CLAUDE RATSIMBAZAFY.

Institut d'Elevage et de Médecine Vétérinaire des Pays Tropicaux: Antananarivo; central laboratory, research stations at Kianjasoa and Miadana. (See main entry under France.)

Institut de Recherches Agronomiques Tropicales (IRAT): 4 rue Rapiera, Anjohy, BP853, Antananarivo; tel. 2271-82; telex 22591; part of *Centre de Cooperation Internationale en Recherche Agronomique pour le Développement (CIRAD)*.

FINE AND PERFORMING ARTS

Institut Malgache des Arts Dramatiques et Folkloriques (IMADEFOLK): Centre Culturel Albert Camus, Ave de l'Indépendance, Antananarivo; f. 1964; traditional songs and dances; Dir O. RAKOTO.

HISTORY, GEOGRAPHY AND ARCHAEOLOGY

Institut Geographique et Hydrographique National: Làlana Dama-Ntsoha R. JB, BP 323, Antananarivo 101; tel. (2) 229-35; fax (2) 252-64; f. 1945; Dir NAINA ANDRIAMPARANY AIMÉ.

NATURAL SCIENCES

Biological Sciences

Institut Pasteur: BP 1274, Antananarivo 101; tel. (20) 22-401-64; fax (20) 22-284-07; e-mail roux@pasteur.mg; f. 1898; biological research; library of 6,200 vols; Dir Prof. JEAN ROUX; publ. *Archives* (every 2 years).

Physical Sciences

Institute and Observatory of Geophysics at Antananarivo: University of Antananarivo (Rectorate), Antananarivo 101; tel. 253-53; f. 1889, affiliated to the University 1967; study of seismology, geomagnetism, applied geophysics, exploration geophysics, time service, meteorological and astronomical observation; library of 3,000 vols, 800 periodicals; Dir J. B. RATSIMBAZAFY; publs *Bulletin Magnetique* (monthly and annually), *Bulletin Sismique* (annually), *Bulletin Méteorologique* (monthly).

Service Géologique: BP 322, Antananarivo; f. 1926; library of 3,000 vols; Dir J. R. RATSIMBAZAFY; publs *Rapport annuel, Travaux du Bureau Géologique, Annales géologiques, Documentation du Service Géologique, Atlas des fossiles caractéristiques de Madagascar.*

TECHNOLOGY

Bureau de Recherches Géologiques et Minières (BRGM): BP 458, Antananarivo; Dir G. BOURNAT. (See main entry under France.)

Libraries and Archives

Antananarivo

Archives Nationales: BP 3384, Antananarivo; f. 1958; historical library of 30,000 vols; Dir Mme RAZOHARINORO; publ. *Tantara* (annually).

Bibliothèque du Centre Culturel 'Albert Camus': 14 ave de l'Indépendance, BP 488, Antananarivo; tel. 236-47; telex 22507; fax 213-38; f. 1962; 30,000 vols, 178 periodical titles; Librarian VERONIQUE SINGARÉ REINHARD.

Bibliothèque Municipale: Ave du 18 juin, Antananarivo; f. 1961; 22,600 vols.

Bibliothèque Nationale: Anosy, BP 257, Antananarivo; tel. 22-258-72; fax 294-48; f. 1961; 230,000 vols; also public library; special collections: History, Literature, the Arts, Applied Sciences, Information on Madagascar; Dir L. RALAISAHOLIMANANA; publ. *Bibliographie Nationale de Madagascar* (quarterly).

Bibliothèque Universitaire: Campus Universitaire d'Ankatso, BP 908, Antananarivo; tel. 232-28; f. 1960; 280,000 vols; special MSS collection: Madagascar and Indian Ocean; Dir JEAN-NOËL RANDRIANTSARA; publ. *Bibliographie Annuelle de Madagascar*.

Antsirabé

Bibliothèque Municipale: Antsirabé; tel. 484-57; f. 1952; 2,700 vols; Librarian ALBERT DENIS RAKOTO.

Museums and Art Galleries

Antananarivo

Musée d'Art et d'Archéologie de l'Université de Madagascar: BP 564, Antananarivo 101; tel. 210-47; f. 1970; art, archaeology and social sciences; library of 1,800 vols; Dir J.-A. RAKOTOARISOA; publs *Taloha* (annually), *Travaux et Documents* (irregular).

Musée Historique: Rue Pasteur Ravelojaona, Antananarivo; tel. 200-91; f. 1897; history and arts; Curator ALDINE RAVAONATOANDRO.

Universities

UNIVERSITÉ D'ANTANANARIVO

Campus Universitaire Ambohitsaina, BP 566, 101 Antananarivo

Telephone: 241-14

Founded 1961

Rector: EMILE RALAISOA RAKOTOMAHANINA
Administrative and Financial Director: GEORGES RAMANANTOANINA

Library: see Libraries
Number of teachers: 635
Number of students: 14,069

HEADS OF FACULTIES AND HIGHER SCHOOLS

Law, Economics, Business Studies, Sociology: RADO RAKOTOARISON
Sciences: DÉSIRÉ RAZAFY ANDRIAMAMPIANINA
Letters: RABEARIMANANA GABRIEL
Polytechnic: BENJAMIN RANDRIANOELINA
Agriculture: DANIEL RAZAKANINDRIANA
Health Sciences: PASCAL RAKOTOBE
Ecole Normale Supérieure: WILLIAM RATREMA (Dir)

UNIVERSITÉ NORD MADAGASCAR

BP 0, 201 Antsiranana

Telephone: 21137
Fax: 29409

Founded 1976
State control
Academic year: January to September

Rector: SAID MZE
Administrative Director: FRANCIS MANANJARA

Librarian: VIRGINIE MILISON
Number of teachers: 64 permanent, 33 temporary
Number of students: 826

DEANS

Faculty of Science: JEAN VICTOR RANDRIANOHAVY
Faculty of Letters: CÉCILE MANOROHANTA

DIRECTORS

Ecole Supérieur Polytechnique: MAX ANDRIANANTENAINA
Ecole Normale Supérieure pour l'Enseignement Technique: ANDRÉ TOTOHASINA

UNIVERSITÉ DE FIANARANTSOA

BP 1264, 301 Fianarantsoa

Telephone: 75-508-02
Fax: 75-506-19
E-mail: crasoama@syfed.refer.mg

Founded 1988
State control
Language of instruction: French
Academic year: November to July

Rector: MARIE DIEUDONNÉ MICHEL RAZAFINDRANDRIATSIMANIRY
Administrative and Financial Director: DOMINIQUE RAZAFIMANAMPY
Director of Studies and Research: VOAHANGINIRINA RANOROARIVONY
Librarian: BRUNO JEAN ROMUALD RANDRIAMORA
Number of teachers: 63
Number of students: 1,836

DEANS

Faculty of Sciences: TSILAVO MANDRESY RAZAFINDRAZAKA
Faculty of Law: PATRICE GOUSSOT
École Normale Supérieure: ROGER RATOVONJANAHARY
École Nationale d'Informatique: JOSVAH PAUL RAZFIMANDIMBY

UNIVERSITÉ DE MAHAJANGA

BP 652, 401 Mahajanga
Telephone: 227-24
Founded 1977
State control
Academic year: January to September
Rector: Prof. GABRIEL ZAFISAONA
Registrar: FRANCOIS HEVIDRAZANA
Librarian: JUSTINE RAZANAMANITRA
Number of teachers: 80 full-time
Number of students: 1,532
Publication: *IOSTM Bulletin* (quarterly).

DEANS

Faculty of Natural Sciences: MARTIAL ZOZIME RASOLONJATOVO
Faculty of Medicine: Prof. RANDRIANJAFISAMINDRAKOTROKA
Institute of Dentristry and Stomatology: Prof. GEORGETTE RALISON

UNIVERSITÉ DE TOAMASINA

BP 591, 501 Toamasina
Telephone: 324-54
Founded 1977 as Centre Universitaire Régional de Toamasina, present status 1988
State control
Language of instruction: French
Rector: EUGÈNE RÉGIS MANGALAZA
Secretary-General: ANDRÉ BIAS RAMILAMANANA
Librarian: ELIANE JOSÉPHINE RENÉ
Number of teachers: 54
Number of students: 3,391

DEANS

School of Economics and Management: SETH ARSÈNE RATOVOSON
School of Arts and Research: ABRAHAM LATSAKA

HEADS OF DEPARTMENT

Geography: JACQUES RANDRIANATOANDRO
History: SOLOFO RANDRIANJA
Philosophy: ETIENNE RAZAFINDEHIBE
French Literature: MONIQUE ANDRÉA DJISTERA
Economics: JEANNOT RAMIARAMANANA
Management: ARISTIDE RAMANANTSALAMA

Université de Toliary: BP 185, 601 Toliary; tel. (9) 410-33; Rector JEANNE DINA.

Colleges

Collège Rural d'Ambatobe: BP 1629, Antananarivo; Dir M. ROGER RAJOELISOLO.

Institut National des Sciences Comptables et de l'Administration d'Entreprises: Maison des Produits, 67 Ha, BP 946, Antananarivo 101; tel. 284-44; telex 22332; f. 1986; 4-year courses and in-service training in accountancy and management; library of 19,700 vols, 20 periodicals; 268 full-time students, 434 in-service students; Dir-Gen. FLAVIEN TODY.

Institut National des Télécommunications et des Postes: Antanetibe, 101 Antananarivo; tel. 442-61; f. 1968; *c.* 200 students.

MALAWI

Learned Societies

GENERAL

Society of Malawi: POB 125, Blantyre; f. 1948; study and records of history and natural sciences; 400 mems; library of 1,650 vols, 3,000 journals; Chair. A. SCHWARZ; Sec. Mrs P. ROYLE; publ. *Journal* (2 a year).

BIBLIOGRAPHY, LIBRARY SCIENCE AND MUSEOLOGY

Malawi Library Association: POB 429, Zomba; tel. 522222; fax 523225; f. 1976; 340 mems; trains library assistants, provides professional advice, holds seminars and workshops; Pres. RALPH MASANJIKA; Sec.-Gen. DICKSON B. VUWA PHIRI; publ. *MALA Bulletin*.

MEDICINE

Medical Association of Malawi: POB 30605, Chichiri, Blantyre 3; tel. 630333; fax 631353; f. 1967; 265 mems, 100 assoc. mems; Chair. Dr B. MWALE; Sec. Dr E. MTITIMILA; publ. *Malawi Medical Journal*.

Research Institutes

AGRICULTURE, FISHERIES AND VETERINARY SCIENCE

Baka Agricultural Research Station: POB 43, Karonga; f. 1974; attached to Min. of Agriculture; applied research on the general agronomy of the Karonga and Chitipa regions.

Bvumbwe Agricultural Research Station: POB 5748, Limbe; tel. 662206; f. 1950 attached to Min. of Agriculture; conducts applied research into tree and horticultural crops, especially tung, macadamia, cashew, vegetables, spices, coffee, mushrooms, roots and tubers, and the general agronomy of the Southern uplands; Head N. NSANJAMA.

Central Veterinary Laboratory: POB 517, Lilongwe; f. 1974; attached to Min. of Agriculture; research into endemic diseases.

Chitala Agricultural Research Station: Private Bag 13, Salima; f. 1978; attached to Min. of Agriculture; part of Lakeshore Rural Development Programme; conducts research on cereals, cotton, groundnuts, mango, cashew and livestock; provides citrus seedlings for sale.

Chitedze Agricultural Research Station: POB 158, Lilongwe; tel. 767222; f. 1948; attached to Min. of Agriculture; conducts applied research into cereals, grain legumes, oil seeds, pasture and the general agronomy of the Central Region and into livestock improvement, especially of local Zebu cattle; library of 10,000 vols, 300 periodicals; Head Dr P. SIBALE.

Fisheries Research Unit: POB 27, Monkey Bay; f. 1954; attached to Min. of Forestry and Natural Resources; researches into fisheries of Lake Malawi.

Forest Research Institute of Malawi: POB 270, Zomba; attached to Min. of Forestry and Natural Resources; research into silviculture, tree breeding, pathology, entomology, soils, mycorrhizae and wood products.

Kandiya Research Station: POB 418, Lilongwe; f. 1979; attached to Min. of Agriculture; applied research on improvement and production of burley and fire-cured tobaccos in Malawi.

Kasinthula Agricultural Research Station: POB 28, Chikwawa; f. 1976; attached to Min. of Agriculture; irrigation research.

Lifuwu Agricultural Research Station: POB 102, Salima; tel. 261401; fax 784184; f. 1973; attached to Dept of Agricultural Research and Technical Services; rice research; Officer in Charge T. R. MZENGEZA.

Lunyangwa Agricultural Research Station: POB 59, Mzuzu; tel. 332633; f. 1968; attached to Min. of Agriculture; conducts applied research into the general agronomy of the Northern Region, specializing in rice, coffee, tea, cassava, pasture work, and tropical fruits at its Mkondezi sub station; Head Dr A. GADABU.

Makoka Agricultural Research Station: Private Bag 3, Thondwe; tel. 534211; fax 534208; f. 1969; cotton entomology, armyworm cotton breeding, agronomy, biometrics; library of 1,300 vols; Head M. H. P. BANDA; publs *Makoka Agricultural Research Station Annual*, quarterly reports.

Mbawa Agricultural Research Station: POB 8, Embangweni; tel. 342362; f. 1952; attached to Min. of Agriculture; applied research on livestock and pastures, maize and grain legumes.

Mikolongwe Livestock Improvement Centre: POB 5193, Limbe; f. 1955; attached to Min. of Agriculture; seeks to improve productive capacity of local Zebu cattle and fat tailed sheep; the station also contains the Poultry Improvement Unit and the Veterinary Staff training school.

Mwimba Tobacco Research Station: POB 224, Kasungu; f. 1979; attached to Min. of Agriculture; applied research on improvement and production of flue cured and oriental tobacco in Malawi.

Ngabu Research Station: PMB Ngabu; f. 1972; attached to Min. of Agriculture; applied research on sorghum, millet, cotton, cowpeas, guar beans and the general agronomy of the Shire Valley.

Tea Research Foundation (Central Africa): POB 51, Mulanje; tel. 462277; fax 462209; f. 1966; promotes research into tea production in Central and Southern Africa, and other tea producing regions; Dir A. M. WHITTLE.

Veterinary Research Laboratory: POB 55, Blantyre; attached to Min. of Agriculture; diagnostic laboratory.

NATURAL SCIENCES

Physical Sciences

Geological Survey of Malawi: POB 27, Liwonde Rd, Zomba; tel. 522166; telex 44382; f. 1921; geological mapping and surveys; mineral investigation, engineering, geology, geophysics, drilling, seismology etc.; library of 5,000 vols; Chief Geologist F. R. PHIRI; publs *Bulletins, Records, Memoirs*.

Libraries and Archives

Lilongwe

Malawi National Library Service: POB 30314, Lilongwe 3; tel. 783-700; f. 1968; 185,000 general and reference works; nation-wide loan service; Dir R. S. MABOMBA; publs *Annual Report, Bulletin, Staff Newsletter*.

Zomba

National Archives of Malawi: POB 62, Zomba; tel. 522922; fax 522148; f. 1947, as branch of Central African Archives, became National Archives of Malawi 1964; public archives, records management, historical manuscripts, legal deposit library, films, tapes, microfilms, gramophone records, philatelic collection, maps, and plans; national ISBN agency; 30,000 vols, 240 periodicals; Dir CHARLES B. MALUNGA; Librarian OSWIN W. AMBALI; publ. *Malawi National Bibliography* (annually).

University of Malawi Libraries: POB 280, Zomba; tel. 522-222; fax 523-225; e-mail smwiyeriwa@unima.wn.apc.org; f. 1965; 375,000 vols; Librarian S. MWIYERIWA; publs *Library Bulletin, Report to Senate* (annually), *Nthambi Zisanu*.

Museums and Art Galleries

Blantyre

Museums of Malawi, The: POB 30360, Chichiri, Blantyre 3; tel. 630288; fax 632096; f. 1959; Dir of Museums M. G. KUMWENDA; publs *Ndiwula*, (newsletter, annually).

University

UNIVERSITY OF MALAWI

POB 278, Zomba

Telephone: Zomba 522-622
Telex: 45214
Fax: 522-760
E-mail: university.office@unima.wn.apc.org

Founded 1964
Language of instruction: English
Private control
Academic year: January to September

Chancellor: State Pres. BAKILI MULUZI
Vice-Chancellor: Prof. B. B. CHIMPHAMBA
Registrar: J. E. CHIPETA
Librarian: S. MWIYERIWA

Publications: *UNIMA Newsletter* (quarterly), *Research Report to Senate, Malawi Journal of Science and Technology, Journal of Social Science, Journal of Humanities*.

CONSTITUENT INSTITUTES

Bunda College of Agriculture: POB 219, Lilongwe; tel. 277-222; telex 43622; fax 277-364; library of 30,000 vols; 53 teachers; 519 students; Principal Dr Z. M. KASOMEKERA; Registrar J. A. KADZANJA.

DEAN

Faculty of Agriculture: Dr G. Y. KANYAMA-PHIRI

PROFESSORS

KAMWANJA, L. A., Animal Science
KASOMEKERA, Z. M.
SAKA, V. W.

Chancellor College: POB 280, Zomba; tel. 522-222; telex 44742; fax 522-046; library of 194,426 vols; 165 teachers; 1,544 students; Principal Dr E. FABIANO; Registrar R. M. MUSHANI.

DEANS

Faculty of Humanities: Dr H. F. CHIDAMMODZI
Faculty of Science: Dr J. D. SAKA
Faculty of Education: O. J. KATHAMALO
Faculty of Law: E. DOKALI
Faculty of Social Science: Dr ISAAC LAMBA

PROFESSORS

CHIMOMBO, M., Curriculum and Teaching Studies
CHIMOMBO, S., English
KADZAMIRA, Z. D., Government
KALUWA, B. M., Economics
KISHIMBO, P. A. K., Sociology
ROSS, Rev. K. R., Theology and Religious Studies

College of Medicine: PB 369, Chichiri, Blantyre 3; tel. 674-744; telex 43744; fax 674-700; library of 6,000 vols; 63 teachers; 66 students; Principal Prof. J. D. CHIMPHANGWI; Registrar B. W. MALUNGA.

DEAN

Faculty of Medicine: R. L. BLOADHEAD

PROFESSORS

ADELOYE, A., Surgery
BROADHEAD, R. L., Paediatrics
CHIMPHANGWI, J. D., Obstetrics and Gynaecology
DUGGAN, M. B., Community Health and Paediatrics
FAPARUSI, S. I., Biochemistry
MOLYNEUX, M. E., Medicine
MTIMAVALYE, L. A. R., Obstetrics and Gynaecology
MUKIBI, J. M., Haematology

Kamuzu College of Nursing: PB 1, Lilongwe; tel. 721-622; fax 721-647; library of 13,000 vols; 63 teachers; 262 students; Principal C. CHIHANA; Registrar S. L. MUSSA.

DEAN

Faculty of Nursing: L. J. CHIMANGO

Malawi Polytechnic: PB 303, Chichiri, Blantyre 3; tel. 670-411; telex 44613; fax 670-578; library of 51,000 vols; 85 teachers; 1,210 students; Principal H. CHIBWANA; Registrar J. K. LUWANI.

DEANS

Faculty of Applied Studies: FLOSIE GOMILE-CHIDYAONGA
Faculty of Commerce: Dr G. B. MTHINDI
Faculty of Engineering: W. A. B. KUNJE

PROFESSOR

MHANGO, L. G. M., Mathematics and Science

Malawi Institute of Education: POB 50, Domasi; tel. 531-261; telex 44527; fax 522-139; library of 36,500 vols; 23 teachers; Dir N. T. KAPEREMERA; Registrar S. M. MALIAKINI.

MALAYSIA

Learned Societies

ARCHITECTURE AND TOWN PLANNING

Malaysian Institute of Architects: 4–6 Jl. Tangsi, POB 19855, 50726 Kuala Lumpur; tel. 2928733; fax 2982878; e-mail info@pammy.org; f. 1967; 2,267 mems; library of 1,000 vols; Pres. P. KASI; publs *Berita Akitek* (monthly), *Majalah Akitek* (6 a year), *Panduan Akitek* (annually).

BIBLIOGRAPHY, LIBRARY SCIENCE AND MUSEOLOGY

Library Association of Malaysia: POB 12545, 50782 Kuala Lumpur; tel. (3) 273114; fax (3) 2731167; f. 1955; 600 mems; Pres. CHEW WING FOONG; Sec. RASLIM ABU BAKAR; publs *Berita PPM* (quarterly), *Majalah PPM* (annually).

HISTORY, GEOGRAPHY AND ARCHAEOLOGY

Malaysian Historical Society: 958 Jl. Hose, 50460 Kuala Lumpur; tel. (3) 2481469; fax (3) 2487281; f. 1953; activities include restoration and preservation of historical sites; 200 indiv. and institutional mems; Pres. Dato MUSA HITAM; publs *Malaysia in History, Malaysia Dari Segi Sejarah* (annually).

LANGUAGE AND LITERATURE

Dewan Bahasa dan Pustaka (National Language and Literary Agency): POB 10803, 50926 Kuala Lumpur; tel. 2481011; f. 1956 to develop and enrich the Malay language; to develop literary talent, to standardize spelling and pronunciation and devise technical terms, etc. in Malay, to print or assist in the production of publs in Malay and the translation of books into Malay; library: see Libraries; Dir-Gen. Haji JUMAAT MOHD NOOR.

Tamil Language Society: c/o Department of Indian Studies, University of Malaya, Kuala Lumpur; f. 1957; 350 mems; aims at the promotion and propagation of the Tamil language and Indian culture; Pres. M. JAYAKUMAR; Hon. Sec. L. KRISHNAN; publs *Tamil Oli* (Tamil, English and Bahasa Malaysia, annually).

MEDICINE

Academy of Family Physicians of Malaysia: Room 7, 5th Floor, MMA House, 124 Jalan Pahang, 53000 Kuala Lumpur; tel. (3) 4417735; fax 4425206; f. 1973; 800 mems; Pres. Dr RUBY ABDUL MAJEED: Chair. Dr ANIS AHMAD Haji ABDUL AZIZ; publ. *The Family Physician* (3 a year).

Malaysian Medical Association: 4th Floor, MMA House, 124 Jl. Pahang, 53,000 Kuala Lumpur; tel. (3) 4420617; fax (3) 4418187; f. 1959; 5,500 mems; Pres. Dato' Dr R. S. McCOY; Exec. Sec. MORGAN S. RAJAH; publs *Medical Journal of Malaysia* (quarterly), *MMA Newsletter* (monthly).

NATURAL SCIENCES

General

Malaysian Scientific Association: POB 10911, 50728 Kuala Lumpur; f. 1955; 356 mems, engaged in scientific and technological works; Pres. Dr SOON TING KUEH; Hon. Sec. Dr NG SWEE CHIN.

Biological Sciences

Malaysian Nature Society: POB 10750, 60724 Kuala Lumpur; tel. (3) 6329422; fax (3) 6358773; e-mail natsoc@po.jaring.my; f. 1940; an independent society to promote an interest in natural history in Malaysia and the surrounding region; 5,000 mems; small library; Pres. Dato Dr SALLEH MOHD NOR; CEO Dr RIZAL ROY SIRIMANNE; publs *The Malayan Nature Journal* (quarterly), *The Naturalist* (quarterly).

Malaysian Society for Biochemistry and Molecular Biology: c/o Biochemistry Dept, Faculty of Medicine, University of Malaya, 50603 Kuala Lumpur; f. 1973; lectures, workshops and seminars, annual conference; 120 mems; Pres. Prof. PERUMAL RAMASAMY; Sec. Dr SHEILA NATHAN; publs *Proceedings of Annual Conference, Malaysian Journal of Biochemistry and Molecular Biology.*

Malaysian Zoological Society: 301 Lee Yan Lian Bldg, Jl. Tun Perak, 50050 Kuala Lumpur; Pres. Y. B. Tan Sri Dato V. M. HUTSON; Sec.-Treas. YUEN TANG & CO.

RELIGION, SOCIOLOGY AND ANTHROPOLOGY

Royal Asiatic Society, Malaysian Branch: 130M Jl. Thamby Abdullah, off Jl. Tun Sambanthan, Brickfields, 50470 Kuala Lumpur; fax (3) 2743458; f. 1877; 1,079 mems; history, literature, sociology, anthropology; Pres. Datuk ABDULLAH BIN ALI; Sec. Haji BURHANUDDIN BIN AHMAD TAJUDIN; publs *Journal* (2 a year), monographs, reprints.

Research Institutes

AGRICULTURE, FISHERIES AND VETERINARY SCIENCE

Department of Agriculture: Ministry of Agriculture, Wisma Tani, Jl. Mahameru, 50624 Kuala Lumpur; f. 1905; undertakes all aspects of research and extension for improvement of crops; pest forecasting and surveillance; establishing Agricultural Information System; library of 15,000 vols; Dir ABU BAKAR BIN MAHMUD; publs *Malaysian Agricultural Journal, Technical Bulletins, Leaflets in Vernacular and English, Statistical Digest.*

Forest Research Institute Malaysia (FRIM): Kepong, 52109 Kuala Lumpur; tel. (3) 6342633; telex 27007; fax (603) 6367753; f. 1929; consists of 1,319 ha of experimental plantations, 5 arboreta, a nursery, a museum, a herbarium of 125,000 sheets of tree species, a wood collection of nearly 10,000 specimens, and a library (see Libraries); 3 substations; Rattan Information Centre est. 1982; Dir-Gen. Dato' Dr SALLEH BIN MOHD NOR; publs *Malayan Forest Records, Research Pamphlets, Research Programme, Annual Report, FRIM Technical Information, Urban Forestry Bulletin, Journal of Tropical Forest Science, Journal of Tropical Forest Products, RIC Bulletin, Bamboo Bulletin.*

Freshwater Fish Research Centre: Batu Berendam, 75350 Malacca; tel. (6) 8172485; fax (6) 3175705; e-mail pppat@po.jaring.my; f. 1957, under MARDI (see below) since 1972; research on freshwater fish and aquaculture; special emphasis on carp, study of fishes in lakes and reservoirs, breeding of indigenous freshwater fish; air-breathing fish, cichlid (Tilapia) and aquarium fish; library of 3,800 vols; Chief Officer HAMBAL HANAFI; publ. *Annual Report.*

Malaysian Agricultural Research and Development Institute (MARDI): POB 12301, GPO 50774, Kuala Lumpur; tel. (3) 943711; telex 37115; fax (3) 9483664; f. 1969; an autonomous organization which conducts scientific, technical, economic and sociological research in Malaysia with respect to the production, utilization and processing of all crops (except rubber and oil palm), and livestock; library of 50,000 vols; Dir-Gen. Dato' MD. SHARIF BIN AHMAD; Librarian Mrs JARIAH JAIS; publs *MARDI Research Journal, Technology Commodity Bulletin, Makalah Sesekala* (economics and social publication), *Berita Penyelikan* (research newsletter).

Malaysian Rubber Research and Development Board: 148 Jl. Ampang, POB 10508, 50716 Kuala Lumpur; tel. 2614422; fax (603) 2613139; f. 1959 to plan and determine policies and programmes for natural rubber research, technical development and promotion nationally and worldwide; to collate and interpret information pertaining to the rubber industry; to co-ordinate all research, development and publicity financed by the Board; dependent units are the Rubber Research Institute of Malaysia (see below), the Tun Abdul Razak Research Centre, UK, and Malaysian Rubber Bureaux located in major rubber consuming areas; Controller of Rubber Research and Chair. ENCIK HARON BIN SIRAJ; publs *Annual Report, Malaysian Rubber Review* (quarterly), *Rubber Developments* (2 a year).

Rubber Research Institute of Malaysia: POB 10150, 50908 Kuala Lumpur; tel. 4567033; telex 30369; fax 03-4573512; f. 1925, operates under the Rubber Research Institute of Malaysia (RRIM) Extension and Amendment Bill, 1972; consists of a Directorate, 4 depts (11 divisions), 3 sections, research laboratories, 3 experimental stations of over 10,000 acres; engaged in research, extension services, technical advisory service and information on all aspects of rubber production; library: see Libraries; Dir Datuk Dr ABDUL AZIZ BIN S. A. KADIR: Deputy Dir (Research) Dr WAN RAHMAN BIN WAN YACOB (acting); publs *Journal* (3 a year), *Jurnal Sains* (Malay, 2 a year), *Planters' Bulletin* (quarterly), *Chung Tze Jen Chee Kan* (Mandarin, quarterly), *Siaran Pekebun* (Malay, quarterly), *Natural Rubber Research* (quarterly), *Annual Report,* divisional reports.

ECONOMICS, LAW AND POLITICS

Asian and Pacific Development Centre: Pesiaran Duta, POB 12224, 50770 Kuala Lumpur; tel. 6511088; telex 30676; fax 6510316; e-mail info@apdc.po.my; f. 1980; promotes and undertakes research and training, acts as a clearing house for information on development, offers consultancy services; current programme: to overcome poverty, to assist development instns to manage national development and change, to increase the policy-making capacity of Asian-Pacific countries, to increase the capacity of the region to adjust to the changing world environment; 19 full mem. govts, 1 assoc. mem., 1 contributing non-mem.; library of 43,200 vols; Dir Dr MOHD. NOOR Hj HARUN; publs *APDC Annual Report, APDC Newsletter* (3 a year), *Issues in Gender and Development.*

MEDICINE

Institute for Medical Research (IMR): Jl. Pahang, 50588 Kuala Lumpur; tel. (3) 2986033; f. 1901; now research branch of Ministry of Health; researches into biomedical and social aspects of tropical diseases, provides specialised diagnostic, consultative and information services, trains medical and paramedical staff, also WHO Centre for Research and Training in Tropical Diseases for the Western Pacific Region, and SEAMEO-TROPMED National Centre, WHO Collaborating Centre for Taxonomy and Immunology of Filariasis and Screening and Clinical Trials of Drugs against Brugian Filariasis, and WHO Collaborating Centre for Ecology, Taxonomy and Control of Vectors of Malaria, Filariasis and Dengue; 598 staff; library of 20,000 vols; Dir Dr M. S. LYE (acting); publs *IMR Quarterly Bulletin, Bulletin of the Institute for Medical Research* (irregular), *Study of the Institute for Medical Research* (irregular), *Annual Report, International Medical Journal, IMR Handbook.*

NATURAL SCIENCES

Physical Sciences

Geological Survey of Malaysia: Scrivenor Rd, Ipoh, Perak; f. 1903; 792 mems; basic geological information on East and West Malaysia with special emphasis on mineral resources; library of 18,720 vols (East Malaysia), 34,000 vols (West Malaysia); Dir-Gen. E. H. YIN; publs *Annual Reports, Regional Memoirs, Reports* and *Bulletins* (East), *Map Report and Proceedings (W. Malaysia), Economic Bulletins, Annual Reports* and *Professional Papers* (West), *Geochemical Report.*

Geological Survey of Malaysia: Locked Bag 2042, 88999 Kota Kinabalu, Sabah; tel. (88) 260311; fax (88) 240150; e-mail jkbkk@po.jaring.my; f. 1949; 32 mems; geological mapping, mineral investigations, engineering geology, hydrogeology, geophysics, mineralology and petrology, lab. analysis; library of 3,500 vols; Dir YUNNUS ABD. RAZAK; publs *Annual Reports, Geological Papers, Memoirs, Geotechnical Reports.*

Geological Survey of Malaysia: POB 560, 93712 Kuching, Sarawak; tel. 240152; fax (82) 415390; f. 1949; 183 staff; geological mapping, mineral investigations, engineering geology, hydrogeology; library of 18,000 vols; Dir CHEN SHICK-PEI; publs *Annual Report,* Bulletins, Geological Papers, Technical Papers, Maps, Memoirs, Reports.

TECHNOLOGY

Malaysian Institute of Microelectronic Systems (MIMOS): Lot 7.2 and 7.3, 7th Floor, Exchange Square Bldg, off Jalan Semantan, Damansara Heights, 50490 Kuala Lumpur; tel. (3) 255-2700; telex 28145; fax (3) 255-2755; f. 1985; research and development in microelectronics, information technology and related areas; provides advisory and technical services to the govt and the private sector; encourages and supports the creation of new industries based on high technology and modern microelectronics; collaborates with other bodies in the fields; library of 6,200 vols, 202 periodicals; Dir-Gen. Dr TENGKU MOHD AZZMAN SHARIFFADEEN; publs *MOSMEDIA* (quarterly), *MIMOS IT Paper* (2 a year), *MIMOS Teknologi Buletin* (quarterly).

Standards and Industrial Research Institute of Malaysia (SIRIM): POB 35, 40700 Shah Alam, Selangor; tel. (3) 5591630, 5591601; telex 38672; fax (603) 5508095; f. 1975 by merger of National Institute of Scientific and Industrial Research and the Standards Institution of Malaysia; facilitates industrial development through research into existing and future problems relating to engineering and production of processed and fabricated industrial products; provides a range of technical services that include quality assurance, metrology, industry testing, technology modification and improvement, technology transfer, consultancy, industrial information and extension services; undertakes applied research and prototype production to adapt or modify known processes and technologies; finds new uses for locally available raw materials and by-products, and develops new products and processes based on indigenous raw materials; the drafting and publications of Malaysian standards and standards testing; library of 13,000 vols; 165,000 standards and specifications, 400 periodicals; Controller Dr AHMAD TAJUDDIN ALI; publs *Berita SIRIM* (SIRIM News, quarterly), *Annual Report, Malaysian Standards.*

Libraries and Archives

Alor Setar

Kedah State Public Library Corporation: Jalan Kolam Air, 05100 Alor Setar, Kedah Darul Aman; tel. 7333592; fax 7336232; f. 1974; includes Alor Setar Public Library, five branch libraries, six mobile libraries and seven village libraries; 684,776 vols; Dir Mrs MAZIZAH Bt. Hj. MD DARUS; publs *Annual Report, Bibliographies, Indexes, Guide to the Library.*

Ipoh

Tun Razak Library: Jl. Panglima Bukit Gantang Wahab, 30000 Ipoh, Perak Darul Ridzuan; tel. (5) 508073; f. 1931; special collections on Malaysia and Singapore; UNESCO depository; special language section; 245,816 vols in English, Chinese, Malay and Tamil; Asst Librarian NOOR AFITZA Hj. PAWAN CHIK; publs *Annual Reports, Malaysiana Collection.*

Jitra

Perpustakaan, Universiti Utara Malaysia: Sintok, 06010 Jitra, Kedah; tel. (4) 9241740; fax (4) 9241959; f. 1984; 183,000 vols, 6,000 periodicals; Chief Librarian PUAN JAMILAH MOHAMED.

Johor Baharu

Perpustakaan Sultan Ismail: Jl. Dato Onn, Johor Baharu; f. 1964; administered by the Town Council; 40,600 vols in Chinese, English, Malay and Tamil; Librarian (vacant); publ. *Lapuran Tahunan* (Annual Report).

Perpustakaan Sultanah Zanariah, Universiti Teknologi Malaysia: Karung Berkunci 791, 80990 Johor Baharu; tel. (7) 5576160; telex 60205; fax (7) 5572555; f. 1972; 344,000 vols, 9,300 periodicals; audio-visual collection; Chief Librarian ROSNA TAIB; publs *Bibliography series, Library Handbook, Berita Perpustakaan Sultanah Zanariah, Buletin MAKIN.*

Kota Baharu

Kelantan Public Library Corporation: Jl. Mahmood, 15200 Kota Baharu, Kelantan; tel. (9) 7444522; fax (9) 7487736; e-mail ppak@kel.lib.edu.my; f. 1938, present name 1974; 261,000 vols; special collection: Kelantan Collection; State Librarian NIK ARIFF BIN NIK MANSOR.

Kota Kinabalu

Sabah State Library/Perpustakaan Negeri Sabah: 88572 Kota Kinabalu, Sabah; tel. (88) 54333; fax (88) 233167; f. 1951; now a state department within the Ministry of Social Services (Sabah); public reference and lending library of 841,914 vols, mainly in Bahasa Malaysia, English and Chinese; special local history collection on Borneo; comprises 20 brs (in addition to main library), 10 mobile libraries for rural areas and 26 village libraries; Dir ADELINE LEONG.

Kuala Lumpur

Kuala Lumpur Public Library: Sam Mansion, Jl. Tuba, Kuala Lumpur; f. 1966; 45,000 vols; Librarian SOONG WAN YOONG.

Library, Forest Research Institute Malaysia: Kepong, 52109 Kuala Lumpur; tel. (3) 6342633; telex 27007; fax (603) 6367753; f. 1929; 50,000 vols on forestry and related subjects; collection consists of books, reports, standards, conference papers, gazettes, maps; services include SDI, RIC (Rattan Information Centre), Current Awareness Services, literature searches, etc.; Librarian Mrs KONG HOW KOOI; publs *Accessions List* (monthly), *RIC Bulletin* (every 6 months), *RIC Occasional Papers, Bibliographies, Bamboo Bulletin* (every 6 months), *FRIM Bulletin* (every 6 months).

Malaysian Rubber Board Library: Jl. Ampang, POB 10150, 50908 Kuala Lumpur; tel. 4567033; telex 30369; fax (3) 4573512; e-mail rabiah@lgm.gov.my; f. 1925; 150,000 vols, mainly science and technology, particular emphasis on subjects relating to rubber research; Librarian RABIAH BT. MOHD. YUSOF; publs *Bibliographies, Recent Additions to the Library, List of RRIM Translations, List of Journal Holdings, List of Forthcoming Conferences,* etc.

Ministry of Agriculture Library: Wisma Tani, Jl. Sultan Salahuddin, 50624 Kuala Lumpur; tel. (3) 2982011; telex 33045; fax 2913758; f. 1906; 80,000 vols; publs *Bulletin* (irregular), *Malaysian Agricultural Journal* (2 a year).

National Archives of Malaysia: Jl. Duta, 50568 Kuala Lumpur; tel. 2543244; f. 1957; public records, archives, audio-visual records, private and business records; Prime Minister's archives, Tun Abdul Razak Memorial Library, Declaration of Independence Memorial, P. Ramlee Memorial; reference library of 4,000 vols; Dir-Gen. Mrs ZAKIAH HANUM NOR; publs *Annual Report, Accessions List, Hervey Papers, National Archives of Malaysia, Swettenham Papers, Records Management Manual,* etc.

National Library of Malaysia: 232 Jalan Tun Razak, 50572 Kuala Lumpur; tel. (3) 2943488; telex 30092; fax (3) 2927899; e-mail pnmweb@www.pnm.my; f. 1966; national bibliographic centre, national depository, national centre for Malay MSS, national centre for ISBN and ISSN; depository for UN publs; 1,413,348 vols; Dir-Gen. Datin MARIAM ABDUL KADIR; publs *Jurnal Filologi Melayu* (annually), *Selitan Perpustakaen* (2 a year).

Pusat Dokumentasi Melayu (Malay Documentation Centre, Institute of Language and Literature): POB 10803, 50926 Kuala Lumpur; tel. (3) 2481011, ext. 201; telex 32683; fax (3) 2442081; e-mail rohani@dbp.gov.my; f. 1956; 120,000 vols, 3,000 periodicals, audiovisual materials; directory of Malaysian writers; Chief Librarian Mrs ROHANI RUSTAM; publs *Mutiara Pustaka* (annually), *Subject Bibliography* (occasional).

University of Malaya Library: Pantai Valley, 50603 Kuala Lumpur; tel. (3) 7575887; fax (3) 7573661; f. 1957; 1,239,749 vols, 8,040 periodicals; special collections include medical (124,339 vols), legal (99,382 vols), Malay language and culture (75,525 vols), Chinese (61,406 vols), Tamil (16,658 vols); Librarian ZAITON OSMAN; publs *Maklumat Semasa* (bulletin, monthly), *Kekal Abadi* (quarterly newsletter), bibliographies, indexes, etc.

Kuching

Sarawak State Library: Jl. P. Ramlee, 93572 Kuching; tel. (82) 242911; fax (82) 246552; f. 1950; administered by the Ministry of Environment; 1,232,780 vols in Bahasa Malaysia, English, Iban and Chinese; State Librarian JOHNNY K. S. KUEH.

Melaka

Malacca Public Library Corporation: 242-1 Jalan Bukit Baru, 75150 Melaka; tel. (6) 2824859; fax (6) 2824798; f. 1977; 250,000 vols; Librarian RIZA FEISAL BIN SHEIK SAID.

Penang

Penang Public Library Corporation: 2nd Floor, Dewan Sri Pinang, 10200 Penang; tel. (4) 2622255; fax (4) 2628820; e-mail ppapp@png.lib.edu.my; f. 1817; reorganized 1973; 415,000 vols; Chair. Y. B. Dr TOH KIN WOON; Dir ENCIK ONG CHAI LIN; publ. *Buletin Mutiara* (4 a year).

Perpustakaan Universiti Sains Malaysia: Minden, 11800 Penang; tel. (4) 6577888; telex 40254; fax (4) 6571526; f. 1969; main library: 644,000 vols, 5,500 periodicals; medical library: 87,000 vols, 1,370 periodicals; engineering library: 78,000 vols, 487 periodicals; media 121,000 items, 9,290 reels microfilm, 102,000 sheets microfiche; Chief Librarian RASHIDAH BEGUM FAZAL MOHAMED; publ. *MIDAS Bulletin* (every 2 months).

Serdang

Perpustakaan Universiti Pertanian Malaysia: 43400 UPM, Serdang, Selangor Darul Ehsan; tel. (3) 9486101; telex 37454; fax (3) 9483745; f. 1971; 368,332 vols in main library, 6,294 vols in branch libraries; 6,195 periodicals in main library, 74 in branch libraries; 59,450 units a/v material (420 in branch libraries); Chief Librarian KAMARIAH ABDUL HAMID; publs *TUNAS* (quarterly), *INFORMAN* (quarterly).

Shah Alam

Selangor Public Library: c/o Perpustakaan Raja Tun Uda, Persiaran Perdagangan, 40572 Shah Alam, Selangor; tel. (3) 5597667; f. 1971; 1,435,803 vols; 8 brs; 31 village libraries and 16 mobile units; Dir SHAHANEEM HANOUM; publs *Annual Report*, *Accession List*, *Perutusan RATU Darul Ehsan Newsletter*.

Tun Abdul Razak Library: MARA Institute of Technology, 40450 Shah Alam, Selangor; tel. (3) 5564041; fax (3) 5503648; f. 1957; two main libraries and 10 brs; 898,000 Chief Librarian RAHMAH MUHAMAD.

Museums and Art Galleries

Kota Kinabalu

Sabah Museum: Jl. Muzium, 88000 Kota Kinabalu, Sabah; tel. (88) 253199; fax (88) 240230; f. 1886 in Sandakan, closed 1905, officially reopened 1965, moved to present location 1983; anthropological, archaeological, natural history and historical collections, heritage village, ethno-botanical gardens, Islamic civilization museum, Agop Batu Tulug site museum; library of 5,000 vols; Dir NONI J. SAID; publs *Journal* (annually), etc.

Kuala Lumpur

National Museum of Malaysia/Muzium Negara: Jl. Damansara, 50566 Kuala Lumpur; tel. (3) 2826255; fax (3) 2827294; e-mail kbb@tm.net.my; f. 1963; houses collections of ethnographical, archaeological and zoological materials; comprehensive reference library on Malaysia and many Asian subjects, reference collections of archaeology, zoology and ethnography are also preserved in the Perak Museum, Taiping; Dir-Gen. Dr KAMARUL BAHARIN BIN BUYONG; publ. *Federation Museums Journal* (1 a year).

Kuching

Sarawak Museum: Jl. Tun Abang Haji Openg, 93566 Kuching, Sarawak; tel. (82) 258388; fax (82) 246680; f. 1886; ethnographic, archaeological, natural history and historical collections; reference library; State archives; Dir SANIB SAID; publ. *Sarawak Museum Journal*.

Penang

Penang Museum and Art Gallery: Farquhar St, Penang; tel. (4) 2613144; f. 1963; Chair., Penang State Museum Board NAZIR ARIFF; Curator Encik KHOO BOO CHIA; publ. *Annual Report*.

Taiping

Perak Museum: Taiping, Perak; f. 1883; antiquities, Perak archives, ethnography, zoology and a library; Dir-Gen. SHAHRUM BIN YUB.

Universities

INTERNATIONAL ISLAMIC UNIVERSITY MALAYSIA

POB 70, Jl. Sultan, 46700 Petaling Jaya, Selangor Darul Ehsan

Telephone: (3) 7555322
Telex: 37161
Fax (3) 7579598

Founded 1983
Ministry of Education control
Languages of instruction: Arabic and English
Academic year: September to April
Open to Muslims and non-Muslims from Malaysia and abroad

Chancellor: HRH THE SULTAN of PAHANG
President: Hon. Dato' Seri ANWAR BIN IBRAHIM
Rector: Dato' Dr ABDULHAMID AHMAD ABUSULAYMAN
Deputy Rector (Academic Affairs): Prof. Dr MOHD. KAMAL BIN HASSAN
Deputy Rector (Student Affairs and Discipline): Dr SIDEK BABA
Chief Librarian: Prof. Dr MUMTAZ ALI ANWAR

Library of 155,000 vols
Number of teachers: 802
Number of students: 10,393

Publications: *Newsletter, Newsbulletin, IIUM Law Journal, Intellectual Discourse, Development and Finance in Islam.*

DEANS OF KULLIYYAH

Kulliyyah of Economics and Management: Dr MOHD AZMI OMAR
Kulliyyah of Laws: Prof. Tan Sri Datuk AHMAD BIN MOHAMED IBRAHIM
Kulliyyah of Islamic Revealed Knowledge and Human Sciences: Prof. Dr JAMAL BARZINJI
Kulliyah of Engineering: Prof. Dr SYED IMTIAZ AHMAD
Kulliyah of Medicine: Prof. Dr MD. TAHIR AZHAR
Kulliyah of Architecture and Environmental Design: Assoc. Prof. Dr ISMAWI BIN Haji ZEN

ATTACHED INSTITUTE

International Institute of Islamic Thought and Civilization (ISTAC): POB 11961, 50762 Kuala Lumpur; tel. (3) 7576905; fax (3) 7577042; f. 1991; financed by Ministry of Education; postgraduate research and teaching in fields of Islamic thought and civilization; library of 40,000 vols; Dir Prof. Dr SYED MUHAMMAD NAQUIB AL-ATTAS.

UNIVERSITI KEBANGSAAN MALAYSIA (National University of Malaysia)

43600 Bangi, Selangor

Telephone: (3) 8250001
Telex: 31496
Fax: (3) 8256484

Founded 1970
State control
Language of instruction: Malay
Academic year: July to June

Chancellor: Tuanku JAAFAR Ibni AL-MARHUM Tuanku ABDUL RAHMAN
Vice-Chancellor: Prof. Datuk Dr ANNWAR ALI
Deputy Vice-Chancellors: Prof. Dr Dato' Dr WAN HASHIM WAN TEH, Prof. Dr MOHD SALLEH MOHD. YASIN, Prof. Dato' Dr ZAKRI ABDUL HAMID
Registrar: BASIR ELON
Librarian: NORSHAM MUSLIM

Library of 945,000 vols, 4,000 journals
Number of teachers: 1,634
Number of students: 11,022

Publications: *University Calendar, Jurnal Sari, Jurnal Islamiyyat, Jurnal Jebat, Jurnal Pendidikan, Jurnal Pengurusan, Jurnal Psikologi Malaysia, Jurnal Kejuruteraan, Jurnal Ekonomi Malaysia, Jurnal Perubatan UKM, Jurnal Akademika, Sains Malaysiana* (quarterly).

DEANS

Faculty of Allied Health Sciences: Prof. Dr MOHD AZMAN ABU BAKAR
Faculty of Economics: Dr MOHAMMAD Haji ALIAS
Faculty of Islamic Studies: Prof. Dato' Dr ABDUL SHUKOR Hj. HUSIN
Faculty of Medicine: Prof. Datin Dr NAFISAH ADEEB
Faculty of Social Sciences and Humanities: Prof. Dr SHAMSUL AMRI BAHARUDDIN
Faculty of Business Management: Assoc. Prof. Dr MUHAMAD MUDA
Faculty of Science and Natural Resources: Prof. Dr OTHMAN HAGI ROSS
Faculty of Physical and Applied Sciences: Prof. Dr SUKIMAN SARMANI
Faculty of Life Sciences: Prof. Dr NOR MUHAMMAD MAHADI
Faculty of Law: Assoc. Prof. SHAMSUDDIN SUHOR
Faculty of Engineering: Assoc. Prof. Dr ABDUL HALIM SHAMSUDDIN
Faculty of Development Sciences: Assoc. Prof. A. HALIM ALI
Faculty of Mathematical Science: Assoc. Prof. Dr ABDUL AZIZ JEMAIN
Faculty of Education: Assoc. Prof. Dr ZAHZAN MOHD JELAS
Faculty of Language Studies: Assoc. Prof. Dr FADILLAH MERICAN
Faculty of Science and Information Technology: Assoc. Prof. Dr ABDUL RAZAK HAMDAN
Centre for Graduate Studies: Prof. Dr ABDUL SAMAD HADI

Centre for General Studies: Dr ABDUL LATIF SAMIAN
Centre for Distance Learning: Assoc. Prof. Dr MOKHTAR BIDIN
Institute of Malay World and Civilization: Prof. Dr MUHAMMAD Hj. SALLEH
Institute of Environment and Development: Prof. Dr MOHD NORDIN Hj. HASSAN
Institute of Malaysian and International Studies: Prof. Dr ISHAK SHARI

PROFESSORS

ABDUL HAMID, Z., Genetics
ABDUL KADER, A. J., Microbiology
ABDUL KADIR, K., Medicine
ABDUL RAHMAN, R., Chemical and Process Engineering
ABDUL RAZAK, T., Pharmacology
ABDULLAH A., Food Science and Nutrition
ABDULLAH, A. H., Geography
ABDULLAH, A. R., Computer Industry
ABDULLAH, H., Anthropology and Sociology
ABDULLAH, I., Chemistry
ABDULLAH, M., Statistics
ABU BAKAR, M. A., Biomedical Sciences
ADEEB, N., Obstetrics and Gynaecology
AHMAD, H., Surgery
AHMAD, I., Microbiology
AHMAD, Z., Political Science
AIDID, S. B. S., Physics
ALATAS, S. H., Psychology
ALI, A., Economic Development and Planning
ALI, O., Community Health
AZHAR, M. T., Medicine
BABA, I., Chemistry
BABJI, A. S., Food Science and Nutrition
BAHARUDDIN, S. A., Anthropology and Sociology
BARDAI, B., Accounting
BARNES, I. E., Dentistry
BOO NEM YUN, Paediatrics
CHAND, H., Law
CHENG, L. S., Physics
CLYDE, M. M., Genetics
COLLINS, J. T., Malay Society and Culture
DARUS, Z. M., Electronics and Systems
DIN, L., Chemistry
EMBI, M. N., Biochemistry
FREDA MEAH, Surgery
GEORGE, E., Pathology
HADI, A. S., Geography
HAMDAN, A. R., Systems Management and Science
HAMID, A. A., Business Management
HARUN, Psychiatry
HASSAN, M. N., Zoology
HASSAN, O. R., Economic Development and Planning
HASSAN, Z. A. A., Zoology
HUSIN, A. S., Theology and Philosophy
IBRAHIM, A. F. H., Theology and Philosophy
IDID, S. A., Communication
IDZAM CHEONG KWANG SENG, Medicine
IMAM, M., Law
ISMAIL, H., Accounting
JAHI, J. M., Geography
JAMAL, F., Microbiology
JANGI, S., Microbiology
JASIN, B., Geology
KADRI, A., Zoology
KAMIS, A., Zoology
KASSIM, K., Psychiatry
KENG, C. S., Pathology
KOMOO, I., Geology
KONG CHIEW TONG, N., Medicine
KRISHNASWAMY, S., Psychiatry
KYAW MYINT, Anatomy
LAZAN, H., Botany
LIEW, C. G., Family Medicine
LIM, K. E. V., Microbiology
LING, W. L., Paediatrics
LUKE, D. A., Dentistry
MAHADI, N. M., Microbiology
MAT SALLEH, M., Physics
MEERAH, T. S. M., Education
MD. HASHIM MERICAN, Z. M., Pharmacy
MEAH, F., Surgery
MISIRAN, K., Anaesthesiology
MOHAMAD, A. L., Botany
MOHAMED YASIN, M. S., Allied Sciences
MOHAMMED ADEEB, N. N., Obstetrics and Gynaecology
MOHAMMED ONN, F., Linguistics
MOHD NOOR, M. I., Dietetics
MOHD NOOR, N., Botany
MOHD SALLEH, H., Anthropology and Sociology
MOHD ZAWAWI, M., Medicine
MOHAMAD, H., Geology
MOHAMMED SANI, M. S., Geography
MOHAMMED ZAIN, S. BIN, Mathematics
NGAH, W. Z. W., Biochemistry
NIK ABD. RAHMAN, N. H. S., History
NIK ISMAIL, N. M., Obstetrics and Gynaecology
NIK MUSTAPHA, N. H., Agricultural and Resource Economics
NORDIN, A. B., Education
OMAR, M., Microbiology
OMAR, O., Biochemistry
OOTHUMAN, P., Parasitology
OSMAN, S., History
OTHMAN, A. H., Chemistry
OTHMAN, M., Physics
OTHMAN, M. Y., Physics
ROSS, O., Science and Natural Resources
SAHID, I., Botany
SAID, M. I. M., Chemistry
SAIM, L., Otorhinolaryngology
SAKIJAN, A. S., Radiology
SALLEH, A. R., Mathematics
SALLEH, K. M., Physics
SALLEH, M. Haji, Literature
SALLEH, S. H., Malay Literature
SAMSUDIN, A. R., Geology
SANGAL, P. S., Law
SARMANI, S., Nuclear Science
SELLADURAI, B. M., Surgery
SELVARAJAH, S., Ophthalmology
SHAARI, I., Economic Statistics
SHAHABUDIN, S. H., Medical Education
SHAMSUDIN, M. W., Chemistry
SHERIF, I. H., Medicine
SIDIN, R., Education
SIWAR, C., Agricultural and Resource Economics
SULAIMAN, S., Biomedical Science
SYED HUSSAIN, S. N. A., Pathology
TAP, A. O. T., Mathematics
TENGKU SEMBOK, T. M., Computer Studies
TOON SOO HAR, Biochemistry
WALKER, R. T., Dentistry
YAHAYA, MAHAYUDIN, History
YAHAYA, MUHAMMAD, Physics
YAMIN, B. M., Chemistry
YATIM, B., Physics
YONG, O., Accounting
YUSOFF, K., Medicine
YUSUF, M. Hj, Psychology

UNIVERSITI MALAYA
(University of Malaya)

Lembah Pantai, 50603 Kuala Lumpur

Telephone: (3) 7560022
Telex: 39845
Fax: (3) 7564004

Founded 1962
Languages of instruction: Bahasa Malaysia and English
State control
Academic year: May to April (2 semesters)

Chancellor: Duli Yang Maha Mulia Paduka Seri Sultan Perak Darul Ridzuan Sultan AZLAN MUHIBBUDDIN SHAH
Pro-Chancellors: Duli Yang Teramat Mulia Raja Muda Perak Darul Ridzuan Raja NAZRIN SHAH, Yang Amat Berbahagia Orang Kaya Bendahara Seri Maharaja Tun Haji SYED ZAHIRUDDIN BIN SYED HASSAN
Vice-Chancellor: Tan Sri Dato' Dr ABDULLAH SANUSI AHMAD
Deputy Vice-Chancellors: Prof. Dato' Dr OSMAN BAKAR, Prof. Dr FIRDAUS Hj ABDULLAH, Assoc. Prof. Dr HAMZAH ABDUL RAHMAN
Registrar: YAACOB HUSSEIN
Librarian: Dr ZAITON OSMAN

Number of teachers: 1,641
Number of students: 21,726

Publications: *University of Malaya Calendar, Annual Report, University of Malaya Gazette* (all annually).

DEANS

Faculty of Arts and Social Sciences: Prof. Datuk Dr ZAINAL KLING
Faculty of Computer Science and Information Technology: Prof. Dr MASHKURI Hj. YAACOB
Faculty of Dentistry: Prof. Dato' Dr HASHIM YAACOB
Faculty of Economics and Administration: Prof. Dr JAHARA YAHAYA
Faculty of Education: Prof. Dr RAHIMAH BT. Hj. AHMAD
Faculty of Engineering: Prof. Dr WAN ABU BAKAR WAN ABAS
Faculty of Law: Prof. Dato' Dr N. S. SOTHI RACHAGAN
Faculty of Medicine: Prof. Dato' Dr ANUAR ZAINI MOHD. ZAIN
Faculty of Science: Prof. Dr MUHAMAD RASAT MUHAMAD
Faculty of Business and Accounting: Prof. Dr MANSOR MD ISA
Institute of Postgraduate Studies and Research: Prof. Dr ANSARY AHMED

DIRECTORS OF ACADEMY

Academy of Islamic Studies: Prof. Dato' Dr MAHMOOD ZUHDI Hj. ABDUL MAJID
Academy of Malay Studies: Prof. Dr WAN ABDUL KADIR WAN YUSOFF

PROFESSORS

Academy of Islamic Studies:

ABDULLAH ALWI, H.
ABDUL MOMEN, I. O. E.
MAHMOOD ZUHDI, A. M.
MAHFODZ, M.
LUTPI, I.

Academy of Malay Studies:

ABDUL WAHAB, A.
ABU HASSAN, M. S., Malay Literature
ASMAH, O., Malay Linguistics
HASHIM, M.
NIK SAFIAH, A. K., Malay Studies
RAHMAH, B.
WAN ABDUL KADIR, W. Y.
YAACOB, H.

Centre of Cultural Dialogue:

CHANDRA MUZAFFAR

Faculty of Arts and Social Sciences:

AZIZAH, K.
CHENG, G. N., Chinese Studies
FATIMAH HASNAH, D.
KHOO, K. K.
LEE, B. T.
LIM, C. S.
LOW, K. S.
MOHD FAUZI, Y.
MOHD YUSOFF, H.
NATHAN, K. S.
RANJIT SINGH, D. S.
ROKIAH, A. T.
SHAHARIL, T. R.
VOON, P. K., Land Use Studies
ZAINAL, K., Anthropology and Sociology

Faculty of Business and Accounting:

MANSOR, M. I.
SIEH, M. L., Business Administration
SIVALINGAM, G.

Faculty of Computer Science and Information Technology:

MASHKURI, Y., Computer Science

Faculty of Dentistry:
- HASHIM, Y., Oral Pathology and Oral Medicine
- ISHAK, A. R., Preventive Dentistry
- LIAN, C. B., Oral Surgery
- LING, B. C.
- LUI, J. L., Conservative Dentistry
- PRABU, S. R.
- RAHIMAH, A. K.
- SIAR, C. H.
- TOH, C. G.

Faculty of Economics and Administration:
- FIRDAUS, A.
- JAHARA, Y.
- JAMILAH, M. A.
- JOMO, K. S.
- KOK, K. L.
- LEE, H. L., Applied Economics
- LEE, K. H.
- NAGARAJ, S.
- RUGAYAH, M.
- SIVALINGAM, G.

Faculty of Education:
- CHEW, S. B., Sociology of Education
- CHIAM, H. K., Social Psychology of Education
- GAUDART, H. M.
- ISHAK, H.
- RAHIMAH, Hj. A.
- RAMIAH, A. L.
- SAFIAH, O.
- SURADI, S.
- YONG, M. S. LEONARD

Faculty of Engineering:
- ABDUL GHANI, K.
- EZRIN, A
- FAISAL, A., Civil Engineering
- GOH, S. Y.
- KHALID, M. N.
- LU, S. K. S., Electrical Engineering
- MASITAH, H.
- MOHD ALI, H., Chemical Engineering
- MOHD ZAKI, A. M.
- ONG, K. S.
- RAMACHANDRAN, K. B., Biochemical Engineering
- WAN ABU BAKAR, W. A.
- WOODS, P. C.

Faculty of Law:
- BALAN, P.
- JAIN, M. P., Comparative Law
- KHAW, L. T.
- MIMI KAMARIAH, A. M.
- SOTHI RACHAGAN, N. S.

Faculty of Medicine:
- ALJAFRI, A. M.
- AMIR, S. M. K.
- ANUAR ZAINI, M. Z.
- ASMA, O.
- BUSCO, J. J.
- CHANDRA, S. N.
- DELLIKAN, A. E., Anaesthesiology
- DEVA, M. P., Medical Psychology
- EL-SABBAN, Farouk M. F.
- GOH, K. L.
- KHAIRULL, A. A., Parasitology
- KHOR, H. T.
- KULENTHRAN, A.
- LAM, S. K., Medical Microbiology
- LANG, C. C.
- LIM, C. T.
- LIN, H. P., Paediatrics
- LOOI, L. M., Pathology
- MENGKA, N.
- NGEOW, Y. F.
- ONG, S. V. G.
- PARAMSOTHY, M.
- PATHMANATHAN, R.
- PERUMAL, R.
- PRASAD, U., Oto-rhino-laryngology
- PUTHUCHEARY, S. D.
- RAMAN, S.
- RAMANI, V. S.
- RAMANUJAM, T. M.
- ROKIAH, I.
- SENGUPTA, S.
- SIVANESARATNAM, V., Obstetrics and Gynaecology
- SUBRAMANIAM, K., Anatomy
- TAN, C. T.
- TAN, N. H.
- TEOH, S. T.
- YAP, S. F.

Faculty of Science:
- A. HAMID, A. H.
- ANSARY, A.
- CHIA, S. P.
- CHONG, K. M., Pure Mathematics
- DAS, K.
- FON, W. C.
- HARITH, A.
- HO, C. C.
- HO, C. C., Microbiology
- KOH, C. L.
- LIM, M. H.
- LOW, K. S.
- MAK, C.
- MOHAMED, A. M.
- MUHAMAD RASAT, M.
- MUHAMAD, Z.
- MUKHERJEE, T. K., Genetics
- NAIR, H., Plant Physiology
- OSMAN, B., Philosophy of Science
- RADHAKRISHNA, S.
- RAJ, J. K., Engineering Geology
- WONG, C. S.
- YEAP, E. B.
- YONG, H. S., Zoology

Institute of Postgraduate Studies and Research:
- PANG, T. E., Biomedical Sciences

UNIVERSITI PUTRA MALAYSIA
(Putra University, Malaysia)

43400 Serdang, Selangor Darul Ehsan
Telephone: (3) 9486101
Telex: 37454
Fax: (3) 9483244
E-mail: cans@admin.upm.edu.my

Founded 1971
State control
Languages of instruction: Malay and English
Academic year: May to November (two semesters)

Chancellor: The Governor of Penang
Vice-Chancellor: Prof. Dr SYED JALALUDIN BIN SYED SALIM
Deputy Vice-Chancellors: Prof. Dr KAMEL ARIFFIN BIN MOHD. ATAN (Academic), Prof. Dr RAHIM BIN MD. SAIL (Student Affairs), Prof. Dato' Dr MOHD. ZOHADIE BIN BARDAIE (Development)
Registrar: AHMAD ZEKRI BIN ABDUL KHALIL
Librarian: KAMARIAH BT. ABDUL HAMID

Total staff: 3,431
Number of students: 23,320

Publications: *Universiti Pertanian Handbook, Universiti Pertanian Calendar, Faculty Handbook, Newsletter, Annual Report, University Scientific Journal, University Gazette, Postgraduate Studies Brochure, University Prospectus.*

DEANS

Faculty of Agriculture: Prof. Dr MOHD. YUSOF HUSSEIN
Faculty of Forestry: Assoc. Prof. Dr RUSLI MOHD
Faculty of Design and Architecture: Dr MUSTAFA KAMAL BIN MOHD SHARIF
Faculty of Educational Studies: Prof. Dr ABDUL RAHMAN MD. AROFF
Faculty of Medicine and Health Sciences: Prof. Datuk Dr MOHD SHAM KASSIM
Faculty of Human Ecology: Assoc. Prof. Dr HALIMAH BINTI Hj. AHMAD
Faculty of Veterinary Medicine and Animal Science: Prof. Dato' Dr Sheik OMAR ABDUL RAHMAN
Faculty of Modern Language Studies: Prof. Dr Haji AMAT JUHARI MOAIN
Faculty of Science and Environmental Studies: Prof. Dr Haji MUHAMAD BIN AWANG
Faculty of Engineering: Prof. Ir. ABANG ABDULLAH BIN ABANG ALI
Faculty of Economics and Management: Assoc. Prof. Dr ZAINAL ABIDIN BIN KIDAM
Faculty of Food Science and Biotechnology: Prof. Dr GULAM RUSUL BIN RAHMAT ALI
School of Graduate Studies: Assoc. Prof. Dr KAMIS AWANG
Malaysian Graduate School of Management: Assoc. Prof. Dr MD. ZABID ABDUL RASHID
Institute for Distance Education and Learning: Assoc. Prof. Dr AZAHARI ISMAIL (Dir)
Computer Centre: Dr ABD. AZIM ABD. GHANI (Dir)
Islamic Centre: Assoc. Prof. Dr Haji SAIDIN TEH (Dir)

HEADS OF DEPARTMENTS

Faculty of Agriculture:
- Agronomy and Horticulture: Assoc. Prof. Dr MOHD RIDZWAN ABDUL HALIM
- Plant Protection: Assoc. Prof. Dr DZOLKHIFLI OMAR
- Soil Science: Assoc. Prof. Dr SHAMSUDDIN JUSOH

Faculty of Engineering:
- Civil Engineering: Dr MOHAMAD RAZALI ABDUL KADIR
- Electrical and Electronic Engineering: Dr BAMBANG SUNARYO BIN SUPARJO
- Aerospace Engineering: Assoc. Prof. Dr Ir. SHAHNOR BASRI
- Process and Food Engineering: Assoc. Prof. Dr MOHD NORDIN IBRAHIM
- Mechanical and Manufacturing Engineering: Dr SHAMSUDIN SULAIMAN
- Biological and Agricultural Engineering: Dr AZMI YAHYA
- Chemical and Environmental Engineering: Assoc. Prof. Ir. Dr TAN KA KHENG
- Computer and Communication Systems Engineering: Dr ABD. RAHMAN RAMLI

Faculty of Modern Language Studies:
- Malay Language: Tuan Hj. MOHD AMIN ARSHAD
- English Language: Dr ROSLI TALIF
- Foreign Languages: Dr Hjh. JAMALLEAH ISMAIL

Faculty of Forestry:
- Forest Management: Dr AWANG NOOR BIN ABD. GHANI
- Forest Production: Dr MOHD. HAMAMI BIN SAHRI

Faculty of Design and Architecture:
- Landscape Architecture: OSMAN MOHD TAHIR

Faculty of Educational Studies:
- Education: Tuan Sheikh KAMARUDDIN SHEIKH AHMAD
- Education and Extension Education: Assoc. Prof. Dr AMINAH AHMAD

Faculty of Medicine and Health Studies:
- Biomedical Science: Assoc. Prof. Dr KASSIM HAMID
- Medical Science: Assoc. Prof. Dr JAMMAL AHMAD ESSA
- Nutrition and Community Health: Dr MAZNAH ISMAIL

Faculty of Economics and Management:
- Accounting and Finance: Assoc. Prof. Dr ANUAR MD. NASIR
- Agricultural Economics: Assoc. Prof. Dr MAD. NASIR SHAMSUDIN

Economics: Assoc. Prof. Dr MOHAMD YUSOF
Management and Marketing: Assoc. Prof. Dr SAMSINAR MD. SIDIN
Natural Resource Economics: Assoc. Prof. Dr AHMAD SHUIB

Faculty of Science and Environmental Studies:

Biochemistry and Microbiology: Assoc. Prof. Dr NOR ARIFFIN BIN SHAMAAN
Biology: Prof. Dr TAN SOON GUAN
Chemistry: Assoc. Prof. Dr MAWARDI BIN RAHMANI
Environmental Sciences: Dr RAMDZANI ABDULLAH
Mathematics: Assoc. Prof. Dr Hj. HARUN BIN BUDIN
Physics: Assoc. Prof. Dr Hj. W. MAHMOOD MAT YUNUS
Computer Science: Dr MOHD YAZID MD. SAMAN

Faculty of Veterinary Medicine and Animal Science:

Animal Sciences: Dr ZAINAL AZNAM BIN MOHD. JELAN
Veterinary Clinical Studies: Assoc. Prof. Dr FATIMAH NACHIAR ISKANDAR
Veterinary Pathology and Microbiology: Assoc. Prof. Dr REHANA ABDULLAH SANI

Faculty of Food Science and Biotechnology:

Biotechnology: Prof. Dr MOHAMED ISMAIL BIN ABDUL KARIM
Food Sciences: Assoc. Prof. Dr JINAP SELAMAT
Food Technology: Dr RUSSLY ABDUL RAHMAN

Faculty of Human Ecology:

Communication Studies: Assoc. Prof. Dr Hj. MD. SALLEH Hj. HASSAN
Social Development Studies: Assoc. Prof. Dr JAYUM A. JAWAN
Resource Management and Consumer Studies: Assoc. Prof. Dr NURIZAN YAHAYA
Family Development Studies: Dr RUZUMAH BAHARUDDIN
Music: Dr MINNI ANG KIM HUAI

ATTACHED RESEARCH INSTITUTES

Institute of Bioscience: Dir Prof. Dr ABDUL RANI BAHAMAN.

Sultan Salahuddin Abdul Aziz Shah Cultural and Arts Centre: Dir Assoc. Prof. Dr ALI RAJION.

UNIVERSITI SAINS MALAYSIA
(University of Science, Malaysia)

Minden, 11800 Penang
Telephone: (4) 6577888
Fax: (4) 6575113
E-mail: sharifah@notes.usm.my

Founded 1969
Federal control
Languages of instruction: Bahasa Malaysia and English
Academic year: from July

Chancellor: HRH Tuanku Syed PUTRA IBNI AL-MARHUM SYED HASSAN JAMALULLAIL
Pro-Chancellors: Tun DAIM ZAINUDDIN, Tun Dr LIM CHONG EU
Vice-Chancellor: Hon. Dato' Prof. Haji ISHAK BIN TAMBI KECHIK
Deputy Vice-Chancellors: Hon. Dato' Prof. GHAZALI OTHMAN, Prof. JAMJAN RAJIKAN, Prof. HASSAN SAID
Registrar: Hon. Dato' SITI MAZENAH BT. SAAD

Library: see Libraries
Number of teachers: 1,138
Number of students: 13,317 full-time, 6,538 part-time

Publications: *Annual Report, Schools' Handbooks, Calendar, Prospectus, Library Handbook, University Gazette, Students' Handbook* (all annually), *MIDAS* (monthly industrial and scientific information), *Perantara* (newsletter, every 2 months).

DEANS

School of Biological Sciences: Assoc. Prof. AHYAUDDIN ALI
School of Chemical Engineering: Dr ABDUL RAHMAN MOHAMED
School of Chemical Sciences: Prof. MUHAMMAD IDIRIS SALEH
School of Civil Engineering: Assoc. Prof. SABARUDIN MOHD
School of Educational Studies: MUSTAPA KASSIM
School of Electrical and Electronics Engineering: Assoc. Prof. ALI YEON MOHD SHAKAFF
School of Housing, Building and Planning: Prof. IBRAHIM BIN WAHAB
School of Humanities: Prof. MOHD SALLEH YAAPAR
School of Communications: Prof. RAMLI B. MOHAMED
School of Industrial Technology: Prof. MOHD AZEMI BIN MOHD NOR
School of Management: Assoc. Prof. DAING NASIR IBRAHIM
School of Materials and Mineral Resources Engineering: Assoc. Prof. KAMARUDIN HUSIN
School of Mathematical Sciences: Assoc. Prof. ROSIHAN M. ALI
School of Computer Sciences: Prof. ZAHARIN B. YUSOFF
School of Mechanical Engineering: Assoc. Prof. AHMAD YUSOFF BIN HASSAN
School of Medical Sciences: Assoc. Prof. MAFAUZY MOHAMAD
School of Pharmaceutical Sciences: Assoc. Prof. AHMAD PAUZI MD YUSOF
School of Physics: Assoc. Prof. ABDUL AZIZ B. TAJUDDIN
School of Social Sciences: Prof. SYED AHMAD HUSSEIN
Institute of Postgraduate Studies: Prof. MAHINDAR SANTOKH SINGH

DIRECTORS

Centre for Policy Research: Assoc. Prof. MOHD ISA Haji BAKAR
School of Distance Education: Assoc. Prof. MD NOOR SALEH
Centre for Education Technology and Media: Prof. Haji ABDUL RAHIM BIN MOHD SAAD
Centre for Languages and Translation: TENGKU SEPORA TENGKU MAHADI
Matriculation Centre: Assoc. Prof. MOHD JAIN NORDIN MOHD KASSIM
Drug Research Centre: Prof. V. NAVARATNAM
Art Centre: Assoc. Prof. ISMAIL BIN ABDULLAH
Centre for Marine and Coastal Studies: Assoc. Prof. ZUBIR Haji DIN
Doping Centre: Assoc. Prof. AISHAH A. LATIFF
National Poison Centre: Prof. DZULKIFLI A. RAZAK
Centre for Archaeological Research Malaysia: Hon. Dato' Prof. SITI ZURAINA A. MAJID
Innovation and Consultancies Centre: Prof. GAN EE KIANG
Information Technology Centre: Dr SHUKRI SULAIMAN (acting)
Computer Centre: ALIAS YUSOF
Islamic Centre: Haj. ABDUL AZIZ AHMAD MOHD
University Hospital: Dr RAMLI SAAD

PROFESSORS

CHARTTERJEE, A., Physiology
CHUAH, C. C., Biotechnology
FARID, M. M., Separation Process Engineering
GAN, E. K., Pharmacology
GHOSH, B. N., Economics
HOE, Q. S., Quality Control and Experimental Design
HUSSEIN, S. A., Political Sciences
IBRAHIM WAHAB, Transport Planning
ILYAS, M., Geophysics
ISHAK BIN T. KECHIK, Zoology
JAMJAN BIN RAJIKAN, Physical Chemistry
JOHAN SARAVANAMUTHU, A., Political Science
KHANGAONKAR, P. R., Metallurgy
LEE, B. S., Theoretical Physics
LIEW, K. Y., Physical Chemistry
MAHINDAR SANTOK SINGH, Geography
MASHUDI, K., Linguistics
MAZNAH, I., Basic Education
MIRZA, S. S., Management
MOHAMED, R. B., Persuasive Communication
MOHD GHOUSE NASURUDDIN, Theatre and Dance
MUSTAFFA BIN EMBONG, Medicine
NAIR, N. K., Physical Chemistry
NASIR-UDDIN MAHMOOD QURAISHI, Film Direction and Production
NAVARATNAM, V., Clinical Pathology
NOH, L. M., Paediatrics (Clinical Immunology)
NOR, M. A. M., Food Technology
ONG, J. E., Aquatic Biology
ONG, L. K., Biophysics
OTHMAN, G. B., Education
POH, B. L., Organic Chemistry
RAMACHANDRAN, N., Polymer Technology
RANGGASAMY, K. A., Film and Television
RAZAK, D. A., Pharmacology
ROSLANI, A. M., Pathology
SAAD, Haji A. R. M., Instructional Systems, Motivation and Evaluation
SAID, H. B., Applied Mathematics
SALEH, M. I., Analytical Chemistry
SALLEH, B. B., Plant Pathology
SAM, T. W., Organic Chemistry
SENG, L. T., Applied Parasitology
SHAHNON BIN AHMAD, Literature
SHARMA, J. N., Pharmacology
SING, C. C., Biotechnology
SITI, Z. M., Anthropology and Sociology
SIVALINGAM, P. M., Environmental Biology
SUBRAMANIAM, R. K., Computer Systems
SULAIMAN, M., Strategic Management and Marketing
TAIB, Hj. M. K. B., Literature
TAN, K. H., Entomology
TENG, T. T., Chemical Process Technology
TEO, C. K. H., Botany
TEO, S. B., Inorganic Chemistry
TILLEY, D. R., Physics
VENKATACHALAM, P. A., Computer Electronics
WAZIR, J. A. K., Anthropology and Sociology
YAP, H. H., Entomology
YUSOFF, Z. B., Computational Linguistics and Algebraic Geometry
ZAMOULINE, A., Computer Science

UNIVERSITI TEKNOLOGI MALAYSIA
(Technological University of Malaysia)

Mail Bag 791, 80990 Johor Bahru
Telephone: (7) 5576160
Telex: 60205
Fax: (7) 5579376

Founded 1904; University status 1972
State control
Language of instruction: Bahasa Malaysia and English
Academic year: July to April

Chancellor: HM BAGINDA Sultanah ZANARIAH BTE ALMARHUM Tunku AHMAD, Sultanah of Johor
Vice-Chancellor: Dr AHMAD ZAHARUDIN BIN IDRUS
Deputy Vice-Chancellor (Development): Prof. Dr MOHAMMAD NOOR BIN SALLEH
Deputy Vice-Chancellor (Academic): Prof. Dr ABU AZAM BIN MD YASSIN
Deputy Vice-Chancellor (Student Affairs): Prof. Dr MD YUSOFF BIN ABU BAKAR
Registrar: ISMAIL BIN IBRAHIM
Librarian: ROSNA TAIB

Library: see Libraries
Number of teachers: 1,272
Number of students: 12,602

Publications: *Annual Report, Corporate Report, Academic Calendar, UTM in Brief* (annually), *Unitek* (weekly), *Satelit* (quarterly).

DEANS

Faculty of Civil Engineering: Prof. Dr MOHD ZULKIFLI BIN MOHD GHAZALI
Faculty of Mechanical Engineering: Prof. MOHD AFIFI BIN ABD. MUKTI
Faculty of Chemical and Natural Resources Engineering: Prof. Dr HAMDANI BIN SAIDI
Faculty of Electrical Engineering: Prof. Dr MOHD. RUDDIN AB GHANI
Faculty of Built Environment: Prof. PARID WARDI SUDIN
Faculty of Surveying and Real Estate: Assoc. Prof. Dr AYOB SHARIF
Faculty of Science: Assoc. Prof. Dr AZHARI BIN SALLEH
Faculty of Management and Human Resources Development: ABD. AZIZ BUANG
Faculty of Computer Science and Information Systems: Assoc. Prof. ZAMRI BIN MOHAMED
Faculty of Education: Assoc. Prof. Dr RAMLI BIN SALEH
Teacher Training Centre: Assoc. Prof. Dr ASARUDIN BIN Hj. ASHARI
School of Professional and Continuing Education: Assoc. Prof. OMAR MUNIR
School of Graduate Studies: Prof. Dr ZAINAI BIN MOHAMED
Research and Development Unit: Assoc. Prof. Dr MOHD. NOV BIN MUSA
Technology Design Centre: KAMAL AZAM BIN Hj. BANI HASHIM

HEADS OF DEPARTMENTS

Faculty of Civil Engineering:

Geotechnics and Transport: Assoc. Prof. Dr JUSOH. B. BESAR
Environmental Engineering: Dr MOHD. RAZMAN BIN SALIM
Structures and Materials: Dr SALIHUDDIN BIN RADIN SUMADI
Hydraulics and Hydrology: Dr AMIR HASHIM BIN MOHD KASSIM

Faculty of Chemical & Natural Resources Engineering:

Petroleum: Dr AHMAD KAMAL BIN IDRIS
Chemical Engineering: Dr BADHRULHISHAM BIN ABDUL AZIZ
Bioprocess: MOHD ROJI SARMIDI
Polymers and Gas: HANIZAM SULAIMAN

Faculty of Electrical Engineering:

Electrical Power: Assoc. Prof. Dr ABDULLAH ASUHAIMI BIN MOHD ZIN
Electrical Control: Dr JOHARI HALIM SHAH OSMAN
Electrical Communication: Dr KAMARUZZAMAN SEMAN
Electronics: Assoc. Prof. MOHD. HARUN BIN ISMAIL

Faculty of Mechanical Engineering:

Mechanics and Design: Assoc. Prof. Dr HISHAMUDDIN JAMALUDDIN
Thermofluids: Assoc. Prof. Dr ABAS ABDUL WAHAB
Industrial Production and Management: Assoc. Prof. ZAINAL ABIDIN AHMAD

Faculty of Built Environment:

Architectural Technology: MD. RAJEH BIN SALLEH
Construction Economics and Project Management: ABD. WAHID KAMARULZAMAN
Construction Technology: HASNAN BIN ABDULLAH
Design and Practice: MOHD SAROFIL BIN ABU BAKAR
Planning: ABD. RAHIM BIN MOHD YUNUS
Strategic Planning: Assoc. Prof. Dr NOOR SHARIFAH SUTAN SIDI

Faculty of Surveying and Real Estate:

Property Management and Valuation: Assoc. Prof. Hj. MOHD. HARITH ABD. HAMID
Geoinformatics: Assoc. Prof. GHAZALI DESA
Geodesy and Astronomy: MOHD SAUPI BIN CHE AWANG
Land Surveying: BAHAVIN AHMAD

Faculty of Science:

Chemistry: Assoc. Prof. Dr MOHD YUSOF BIN OTHMAN
Physics: Assoc. Prof. Dr BAKAR ISMAIL
Mathematics: Assoc. Prof. Dr MUKHETA ISA

Faculty of Management and Human Resources Development:

Language: KHAIRI IZWAN ABDULLAH
Islamic Education: AB. GHANI JALIL
Management: EBI SHAHRIN SULEIMAN
Human Management Resource: Dr NORFADZILLAH HITAM

Faculty of Computer Science and Information Systems:

Computer Systems: ALAWIDDIN KHAIRUDDIN
Management Information Systems: Dr MOHD. NOOR MD. SAP
Software Engineering: Dr ABD. HANAN ABDULLAH
Operational Research: MOHD YUNUS BIN MAJID

ATTACHED CENTRES AND INSTITUTES

Business Advanced Technology Centre: Dir Prof. ISHAK ISMAIL
Institute of Tall Buildings and Urban Habitat: Dir Prof. Dr AZMAN BIN AWANG
Institute of Noise and Vibration: Prof. Dr MOHD SALMAN LEONG
Institute of Coastal and Offshore Engineering: Prof. Dr ABD. AZIZ BIN IBRAHIM

UNIVERSITI UTARA MALAYSIA (Northern University of Malaysia)

Sintok, 06010 Jitra, Kedah Darul Aman

Telephone: (4) 9241801
Telex: 42052
Fax: (4) 7003046

Founded 1984
State control
Language of instruction: Malay
Academic year: July to June (two semesters)
Chancellor: HRH THE SULTAN OF KEDAH
Vice-Chancellor: Dr SHAMSUDDIN BIN KASSIM
Deputy Vice-Chancellor (Academic Affairs): Assoc. Prof. Dr MOHD SALLEH BIN Hj. DIN
Deputy Vice-Chancellor (Development): Assoc. Prof. Dr JAMALLUDIN BIN SULAIMAN
Deputy Vice-Chancellor (Student Affairs): Prof. Dr MOHD NAWI BIN ABDUL RAHMAN
Registrar: LATIFAH BT Hj. HASSAN (acting)
Librarian: JAMILAH BT MOHAMMED (acting)

Number of teachers: 278
Number of students: 9,692

Publications: *Annual Report, Calendar* (annually), *School/Centre Handbooks, Uniutama* (quarterly), *Mutakhir* (weekly).

DEANS/DIRECTORS

School of Languages and Scientific Thinking: Dean A. Z. BIN SHEIKH MAHMOOD
School of Economics: Dean Assoc. Prof. Dr R. BIN MATA ZIN
School of Social Development: Dean Assoc. Prof. Dr A. FAWZI BIN MOHD BASRI
School of Management: Dean Assoc. Prof. Dr M. HANAPI BIN MOHAMED
School of Accountancy: Dean A. H. BIN Hj. HASSAN
School of Information Technology: Dean Assoc. Prof. SHAHRUM BIN HASHIM
Centre for Research and Consultancy: Dir M. N. BIN MOHAMED
Matriculation Centre: Dir MOHD NOOR MOHD TAHIR
School of Graduate Studies: Dean Assoc. Prof. Dr I. BIN ABDUL HAMID
Institute for Entrepreneurship Development: Dir Assoc. Prof. M. S. BIN MOHD SOHOD
Institute for Quality Management: Dir Assoc. Prof. Dr R. BIN ZIEN YUSOF
Computer Centre: Dir ISHAK BIN ISMAIL

Colleges

Co-operative College of Malaysia: 103 Jl. Templer, 46700 Petaling Jaya, Selangor; tel. (3) 7574911; fax (3) 7570434; e-mail mkm@mkm.edu.my; f. 1956; provides in-service and pre-service training; Diploma and Certificate courses in co-operative management; specialized courses in business management, accounting, computer studies, co-operative management; library of 30,000 vols; 2,905 students; Dir ARMI Hj. ZAINUDIN.

Institut Bahasa Melayu Malaysia (Malaysian Institute of the Malay Language): Lembah Pantai, 59990 Kuala Lumpur; f. 1958; 1,000 students; offers a 3-year pre-service diploma course, a one-year in-service course, a 14-week in-service course in the teaching of the Malay language, to trained teachers; students are selected by the Ministry of Education; also offers short courses of Malay language as a foreign and second language.

Institut Teknologi MARA: 40450 Shah Alam, Selangor; tel. 5592950; fax 5500226; f. 1956; under the Ministry of Education; offers training in courses at three levels: sub-professional, professional and degree level; 2,595 teachers; 30,832 full-time students, 6,663 part-time; 9 br; Dir Dato' Ir Haji AHMAD ZAIDEE BIN LAIDIN.

Kolej Damansara Utama: Jl. SS 22/41, 47400 Petaling Jaya, Selangor; tel. (3) 7188123; fax (3) 7177096; e-mail info@kdu.edu.my; f. 1983; library of 22,560 vols; 250 teachers; 5,000 students; pre-university and foundation courses, diploma courses in business administration, computer science, engineering, hotels and tourism; degrees in business, accounting and finance, economics; Dir Dr Y. Y. CHUA; Deputy Registrar LEE KUP JIP.

Learning Resources Centre: Penang Branch Campus, 32 Jl. Anson, 10400 Penang; tel. (4) 2280053; fax (4) 2280362; e-mail beste@kdupg.edu.my; f. 1991; library of 7,800 vols; Principal Dr KOO WEE KOR; Registrar YEOH LOY CHENG.

Politeknik Kuching, Sarawak: Km. 22, Jl. Matang, Locked Bag 3094, 93050 Kuching, Sarawak; tel. (82) 428796; fax (82) 428023; f. 1989; library of 10,000 vols; 130 teachers; 1,200 students; diploma and certificate courses in civil, electrical and mechanical engineering and commerce/business, apprentice training in oil, gas and petroleum technology in co-operation with PETRONAS; Principal AYOB BIN Haji JOHARI (acting).

Tunku Abdul Rahman College: POB 10979, 50932 Kuala Lumpur; tel. (3) 4214977; fax (3) 4226336; f. 1969; 290 teachers, 8,123 students; library of 122,715 vols; Principal Dr LIM KHAIK LEANG; Registrar CHEE AH KIOW.

HEADS OF SCHOOLS

Arts and Science: Dr CHENG SU CHIAU (acting)
Business Studies: YOONG LAI THYE (acting)
Technology: HEW HIOEN ON
Pre-University Studies: TSEN WEI KONG (acting)

Ungku Omar Polytechnic: Dairy Rd, 31400 Ipoh, Perak; f. 1969 with Unesco aid; library of 33,300 vols, 60 periodicals; 305 teachers;

3,400 students; Principal Ir CHEONG SEE LEONG; Admin. Officer ROFBIAH BT KAMARUDDIN; Librarian PHANG TOO NAM.

HEADS OF DEPARTMENTS

Mechanical Engineering: MOHD HASHIM B. BUYONG
Civil Engineering: HASHIM B. MUSLIM
Electrical Engineering: DZULKIFLI B. ISMAIL
Marine Engineering: MOHD SOPIAN B. BAHAUDDIN
Commerce: CHOONG MEE LING
Language: KHALIPAH MASTURA BT. ABD. GHANI.

Yayasan Pengurusun Malaysia (Malaysian Institute of Management): 227 Jl. Ampang, 50450 Kuala Lumpur; tel. 2425255; fax 2643168; f. 1966; MBA, BA, diploma and certificate courses; Pres. Raja Tun MOHAR BIN RAJA BADIOZAMAN; CEO Dr TARCISIUS CHIN; publs *Malaysian Management Review* (2 a year), *Management Newsletter* (4 a year).

MALDIVES

Research Institutes

GENERAL

Institute of Islamic Studies: Male'; tel. 322718; f. 1980; attached to Min. of Education; aims to provide educational opportunities for the country's young people, to encourage the spread of the Arabic language, to provide training and refresher courses for imams, lawyers, judges, and teachers of the Quran and Islamic studies, to promote study of the Quran, to upgrade the Islamic curriculum in accordance with the needs of the country, to publish and translate books on all aspects of Islam; 40 staff; library of 19,000 vols; Dir-Gen. IBRAHIM RASHEED MOOSA; publ. *Al-Manhaj* (annually).

National Centre for Linguistic and Historical Research: Sunny Side, Male' 20-05; tel. 323206; fax 326796; f. 1982; research on history, culture and language of the Republic of Maldives; Dir IBRAHIM ZUHOOR; publ. *Faiythoora* (monthly).

Libraries and Archives

Male'

Islamic Library: Islamic Centre, Medhuziyaaraiy Magu, Male' 20-02; tel. 323623; f. 1985; Islamic Studies and literature; 4,500 vols; Dir Imaam AHMED SHATHIR.

National Library: 59 Majeedi Magu, Galolhu, Male' 20-04; tel. 323485; f. 1945; public library facilities; 14,000 vols; special collections: Dhivehi, English, Arabic, Urdu, FAO, UNESCO, Dir Mrs HABEEBA HUSSAIN HABEEB; publ. *Bibliography of Dhivehi Publications*.

Museums and Art Galleries

Male'

National Museum: National Centre for Linguistic and Historical Research, Male' 20–05; tel. 322-254; fax 326-796; f. 1952; conservation and display of historical items; Senior Curator ALI WAHEED.

MALI

Research Institutes

GENERAL

Centre National de la Recherche Scientifique et Technologique: BP 3052, Bamako; tel. 229-085; telex 2602; f. 1986; co-ordinates all research activity in Mali; 57 research instns, 443 staff; Dir-Gen. Dr MAMADOU DIALLO IAM; publs *Revue Malienne de Science et de Technologie* (annually), *Vie de la Recherche* (quarterly).

Institut Français de Recherche Scientifique pour le Développement en Coopération (ORSTOM): BP 84, Bamako; tel. 22-43-05; fax 22-75-88; environmental and social sciences for development; library of 4,000 books and journals; Dir Dr J. F. DUPON. (See main entry under France.)

AGRICULTURE, FISHERIES AND VETERINARY SCIENCE

Centre National de Recherches Fruitières: BP 30, Bamako; f. 1962; controls experimental plantations, phytopathological laboratory, technological laboratory and pilot schemes; Dir P. JEANTEUR.

Centre National de Recherches Zootechniques: BP 262, Bamako; f. 1927; experimental farm with sections on genetics (bovine, swine, poultry), nutrition and biochemistry, pasture, veterinary medicine; library of 1,000 vols; Dir Dr FERNAND TRAORE.

Centres de Recherche Rizicole: Two rice research centres, at Kankan and at Ibetemi.

Institut de Recherches Agronomiques Tropicales et des Cultures Vivrières (IRAT): BP 438, Bamako; f. 1962; controls stations at Bamako, Koulikoro, Kogoni par Nioro, Ibetemi (Mopti), and sub-stations at Kita and Koporokenie-Pe; general agronomy, land amelioration, cultivation techniques, fertilization needs, plant breeding (sorghum, pennisetum, short and floating rices, maize, wheat, groundnuts and formerly sugar cane); Dir M. THIBOUT. (See main entry under France.)

Institut du Sahel: BP 1530, Bamako; tel. 22-21-48; fax 22-23-37; f. 1977; a specialized institution of the Comité Interétats de Lutte contre la Sécheresse dans le Sahel (CILSS); aims to combat effects of drought and achieve food security in the Sahel (consisting of Burkina Faso, Cape Verde, Gambia, Guinea-Bissau, Mali, Mauritania, Niger, Senegal, Chad), through the promotion and coordination of research, circulating scientific and technical information; library of 12,000 vols, 240 periodicals; Dir Gen. MOMODOU SULTAN SOMPO-CEESAY; publs *Sahel PV Info* (quarterly), *RESINDEX* (2 a year), *Pop Sahel* (quarterly).

Office du Niger: BP 1660, Ségou; f. 1932, taken over by Mali govt 1958; research stations at Bougomi and Sahel (cotton), Kayo (rice), Soninkoura (fruit).

MEDICINE

Institut d'Ophtalmologie Tropicale de l'Afrique de l'Ouest Francophone: BP 248, Bamako; tel. 22-27-22; fax 22-51-86; e-mail iota@malinet.ml; f. 1953; research in tropical eye diseases and prevention of blindness, training courses for technicians and doctors specializing in ophthalmology; Dir Dr ALAIN AUZEMERY.

Institut Marchoux: BP 251, Bamako; tel. 22-51-31; fax 22-95-44; f. 1935; part of *Organisation de Coordination et de Coopération pour la Lutte contre les Grandes Endémies (q.v.)*; medical research, teaching, treatment and epidemiology, specializing in leprosy; Dir SOMITA KEITA.

NATURAL SCIENCES

Physical Sciences

Direction Nationale de la Météorologie: BP 237, Bamako; library of 1,265 vols; Dir K. KONARE; publs *Bulletin agrométéorologique*, *Bulletin climatologique* (monthly).

TECHNOLOGY

Société Nationale de Recherches et d'Exploitation des Ressources Minières de Mali (SONAREM), Service de Documentation: BP 2, Kati; f. 1961; geology, mining (gold mining in Kalana, phosphates in Bourem), hydrogeology; 5 staff; library of 5,000 vols; Dir DAOUDA DIAKITE.

Libraries and Archives

Bamako

Bibliothèque Municipale: Bamako.

Bibliothèque Nationale du Mali: BP 159, Ave Kassé Keïta, Bamako; tel. 22-49-63; f. 1913; *c.* 18,000 vols, 2,000 current periodicals; Dir MAMADOU KONOBA KEÏTA.

Attached institution:

Archives Nationales du Mali: Koulouba, Bamako; tel. 22-58-44; f. 1913; Archivist ALI ONGOÏBA.

Centre Culturel Français: BP 1547, Bamako; tel. 22-40-19; f. 1962; public library of 27,000 vols; Librarian JOSETTE MARIN.

Timbuktu

Centre d'Etudes, de Documentation et de Recherches Historiques 'Ahmed Baba' (CEDRAB): BP 14, Timbuktu; f. 1970; to preserve the historical heritage of the region; collects and conserves Arabic MSS; *c.* 5,000 archives; Dir MAHAMOUD A. ZOUBER.

Museums and Art Galleries

Bamako

Musée National du Mali: BP 159, Bamako; library of 1,900 vols; Dir ABDOULAYE SYLLA.

Colleges

Ecole des Hautes Etudes Pratiques: BP 242, Bamako; tel. 22-21-47; f. 1974, present name 1979; diploma courses in accountancy, business studies; 35 teachers, 471 students; Dir-Gen. SIDI MOHAMED TOURE.

Ecole Nationale d'Ingénieurs: BP 242, Bamako; tel. 22-21-47; Dir MAMADOU DIAKITE.

Ecole Normale Supérieure: BP 241, Bamako; tel. 22-21-89; f. 1962; 150 teachers; 1,754 students; Dir SÉKOU B. TRAORÉ; publ. *Cahiers de l'ENSup.*

Faculté de Médecine, de Pharmacie et d'Odonto-Stomatologie: BP 1805, Bamako; tel. 22-52-77; fax 22-96-58; f. 1969 (formerly Ecole Nationale de Médecine et de Pharmacie); 100 teachers, 1,800 students; library of 6,800 vols, 289 periodicals; Dir Prof. ISSA TRAORE; publ. *Mali Médical*.

Faculté des Sciences Juridiques et Economiques: 1185 Ave de la Liberté (Route de Koulouba), BP 276, Bamako; tel. 22-27-19; fax 23-18-95; e-mail sacko.@ena.ena.ml; f. 1958 (formerly École Nationale d'Administration); Dean DUSMANE O. SIDIBE; publ. *Cahier du CERES*.

Institut de Productivité et de Gestion Prévisionnelle: BP 1300, Bamako; tel. 22-55-11; f. 1971; library of 3,000 vols; in-service training, business advice; 15 staff; Dir-Gen. SIDIKI TRAORE.

Institut Polytechnique Rural de Katibougou: BP 6, Koulikoro; tel. 26-20-12; f. 1965; teaching and research in agronomy, agricultural economics, stockbreeding, forestry, veterinary science, rural technology; *c.* 300 teachers; *c.* 12,000 students; Dir-Gen. OUSMANE BELCO TOURE.

MALTA

Learned Societies

AGRICULTURE, FISHERIES AND VETERINARY SCIENCE

Agrarian Society: Palazzo de la Salle, Valletta; f. 1844; 200 mems; Pres. Prof. JOSEPH A. MICALLEF; Hon. Sec. JOSEPH BORG.

ARCHITECTURE AND TOWN PLANNING

Chamber of Architects and Civil Engineers: Malta Federation of Professional Bodies, Medisle Village, St Andrews STJ 14; tel. 338851; fax 376540.

BIBLIOGRAPHY, LIBRARY SCIENCE AND MUSEOLOGY

Ghaqda Bibljotekarji: c/o University Library, Msida MSD 06; f. 1969; professional association to safeguard the interests of librarians and promote legislation concerning libraries; holds courses in librarianship; 125 mems; Chair. LAURENCE V. ZERAFA; Sec. MARIAN BORG; publ. *Newsletter*.

ECONOMICS, LAW AND POLITICS

Malta Society of Arts, Manufactures & Commerce: 219 Kingsway, Valletta.

FINE AND PERFORMING ARTS

Malta Cultural Institute: 44C Flat 2, St Dominic St, Valletta; f. 1948; concerts, ballet; 800 mems; Dir Cmdr VINCENT CIANCIO; publ. *Bulletin* (monthly).

NATURAL SCIENCES

Biological Sciences

Malta Ecological Foundation (ECO): POB 322, Valletta CMR 01; premises at: Dar ECO, 10B St Andrew's St, Valletta VLT 12; tel. 611486; fax 640636; f. 1992; 4,010 mems; library of 5,000 vols; Dir DUNSTAN HAMILTON.

Libraries and Archives

Gozo

Gozo Public Library: Vajringa Street, Victoria, Gozo; tel. 556200; f. 1853, amalgamated with the Royal Malta (now National) Library 1948; national and reference library; copyright deposit library; library of 35,000 vols; Librarian GEORGE V. BORG.

Msida

University of Malta Library: Msida; tel. 310239; fax 314306; e-mail dis@lib.um.edu.mt; f. 1769; library of 600,000 vols, 1,500 current periodicals; Dir A. MANGION; publ. *Bibliography of Maltese Bibliographies*.

Valletta

National Library of Malta: Old Treasury St, Valletta; tel. 224338; fax 235992; e-mail joseph.boffa@magnet.mt; f. 1555; incorporates the archives of the Order of St John of Jerusalem; Librarian JOSEPH M. BOFFA; publ. *Bibljografija Nazzjonali Malta/Malta National Bibliography* (annually).

Museums and Art Galleries

Valletta

Museums Department: Valletta; f. 1903; Dir Dr T. C. GOUDER; Curator D. CUTAJAR.

University

UNIVERSITY OF MALTA

Msida
Telephone: 333903
Fax: 336450

Founded as Collegium Melitense 1592, reconstituted as university 1769
Language of instruction: English
Academic year: October to June

Chancellor: Prof. J. RIZZO NAUDI
Rector: Prof. R. ELLUL-MICALLEF
Pro-Rectors: Prof. C. J. FARRUGIA, Prof. J. LAURI
Registrar: A. GELLEL
Librarian: A. MANGION

Library: see Libraries
Number of teachers: 550
Number of students: 7,000

Publications: *Annual Report*, *University Gazette* (quarterly), *Journal of Anglo-Italian Studies*, *Journal of Maltese Studies*, *Journal of Mediterranean Studies*, *Centro* (environmental studies in the Mediterranean).

DEANS OF FACULTIES

Faculty of Architecture and Civil Engineering: D. DE LUCCA
Faculty of Arts: Prof. V. MALLIA-MILANES
Faculty of Dental Surgery: Prof. J. M. PORTELLI
Faculty of Economics, Management and Accountancy: Prof. D. DARMANIN
Faculty of Education: Dr R. G. SULTANA
Faculty of Laws: Prof. I. REFALO
Faculty of Engineering: Prof. P. P. FARRUGIA
Faculty of Medicine and Surgery: Prof. M. BRINCAT
Faculty of Science and Information Technology: Prof. A. VELLA
Faculty of Theology: Prof. G. GRIMA

HEADS OF DEPARTMENTS

Faculty of Architecture and Civil Engineering:
- Architecture and Urban Design: D. DE LUCCA
- Building and Civil Engineering: Dr A. TORPIANO

Faculty of Arts:
- Maltese: Prof. O. FRIGGIERI
- Classics and Archaeology: Dr A. J. FRENDO
- Arabic: Rev. Prof. E. FENECH
- English: Prof. P. VASSALLO
- Italian: Dr J. EYNAUD
- French: Dr L. SEYCHELL
- Philosophy: Prof. J. FRIGGIERI
- Sociology: Rev. Dr J. INGUANEZ
- History: Prof. V. MALLIA MILANES

Faculty of Dental Surgery:
- Dental Surgery: Prof. J. M. PORTELLI

Faculty of Economics, Management and Accountancy:
- Accountancy: Prof. D. DARMANIN
- Banking and Finance: Dr J. FALZON
- Economics: E. P. DELIA
- Management: C. FSADNI
- Marketing: Dr S. P. GAUCI
- Public Policy: Prof. E. L. ZAMMIT

Faculty of Education:
- Arts and Languages in Education: Dr A. CAMILLERI
- Foundations in Education: Dr R. SULTANA
- Primary Education: Dr J. MIFSUD
- Mathematics, Science and Technical Education: Dr P. PACE
- Communications and Instructional Technology: Rev. Prof. S. CHIRCOP
- Psychology: Dr M. G. BORG

Faculty of Laws:
- Civil Law: Dr T. MALLIA
- Commercial Law: Dr A. MUSCAT
- Criminal Law: Dr S. CAMILLERI
- Public Law: Prof. I. REFALO
- European and Comparative Law: Prof. P. G. XUEREB
- International Law: Prof. D. ATTARD

Faculty of Engineering:
- Communications and Computer Engineering: P. MICALLEF
- Electrical Power and Control Engineering: C. MUSCAT
- Manufacturing Engineering: F. E. FARRUGIA
- Metallurgy and Materials Engineering: Dr M. GRECH
- Microelectronics Engineering: Dr J. MICALLEF
- Mechanical Engineering: Prof. P. P. FARRUGIA

Faculty of Medicine and Surgery:
- Anatomy: Prof. M. T. CAMILLERI PODESTA
- Clinical Pharmacology and Therapeutics: Prof. R. ELLUL-MICALLEF
- Medicine: Dr J. AZZOPARDI
- Obstetrics and Gynaecology: Prof. M. BRINCAT
- Paediatrics: Dr P. VASSALLO AGIUS
- Pathology: Prof. M. CAUCHI
- Pharmacy: Prof. A. SERRACINO INGLOTT
- Physiology and Biochemistry: Prof. W. H. BANNISTER
- Psychiatry: Dr J. R. SALIBA
- Public Health: (vacant)
- Surgery: Prof. C. L. CUTAJAR

Faculty of Science and Information Technology:
- Biology: Prof. V. AXIAK
- Chemistry: Prof. A. J. VELLA
- Computer Information Systems: Prof. A. LEONE GANADO
- Computer Science and Artificial Intelligence: Prof. J. CAMILLERI
- Mathematics: Prof. S. FIORINI
- Physics: Dr C. V. SAMMUT
- Statistics and Operations Research: Dr L. SANT

Faculty of Theology:
- Church History, Patrology and Palaeochristian Archaeology: Rev. Dr J. BEZZINA
- Fundamental and Dogmatic Theology: Rev. Dr R. CAMILLERI
- Moral Theology: Rev. Prof. G. GRIMA

Pastoral Theology, Liturgy and Canon Law: Rev. Prof. J. A. Frendo
Philosophy: Prof. J. Friggieri
Sacred Scripture, Hebrew and Greek: Rev. Dr J. Calleja

ATTACHED CENTRES AND INSTITUTES

Centre for Communication Technology: Dir Prof. S. Chircop.

European Documentation and Research Centre: Chair. Prof. P. G. Xuereb.

Institute for Energy Technology: Chair. E. Scerri.

Institute of Anglo-Italian Studies: Dir Prof. P. Vassallo.

Institute of Health Care: Dir Prof. A. Serracino Inglott (acting).

Institute of Linguistics: Chair. Prof. A. Borg.

Mediterranean Institute: Chair. Prof. P. Serracino Inglott.

Institute of Agriculture: Dir Prof. A. Scicluna Spiteri.

Institute of Forensic Studies: Chair. Dr J. L. Grech.

Institute of Masonry and Construction Research: Dir Dr A. Torpiano.

Workers' Participation Development Centre: Dir Prof. E. Zammit.

Gozo Centre: Dir Prof. P. Briguglio (acting).

Mediterranean Academy of Diplomatic Studies: Dir Dr F. Meier.

Foundation for International Studies: Chief Exec. L. N. Agius.

Institute for Islands and Small States.

International Social Sciences Institute.

Institute of International Affairs.

International Environment Institute.

European Centre on Insular Coastal Dynamics.

MAURITANIA

Learned Societies

BIBLIOGRAPHY, LIBRARY SCIENCE AND MUSEOLOGY

Association Mauritanienne des Bibliothécaires, Archivistes et Documentalistes: c/o Bibliothèque Nationale, BP 20, Nouakchott; f. 1979; Pres. O. DIOUWARA; Sec. SID'AHMED FALL.

Research Institutes

AGRICULTURE, FISHERIES AND VETERINARY SCIENCE

Institut Supérieur des Sciences et Techniques Halieutiques: Nouadhibou-Cansado; tel. 49-047; telex 451; fax 49028; f. 1983; part of Economic Community of West Africa; research and training in the fisheries industry; Dir-Gen. D. SOGUI.

TECHNOLOGY

Direction des Mines et de la Géologie: BP 199, Nouakchott; f. 1968; 17 mems; library of 3,000 vols; Dir M. L. BENAHI.

Libraries and Archives

Boutilimit

Arab Library: Boutilimit; library of the late Grand Marabout, Abd Allah Ould Chelkh Sidya.

Chinguetti

Arab Library: Chinguetti; several private religious libraries; totalling 3,229 vols, including pre-Islamic MSS; Librarian MOHAMED ABDALLAHI OULD FALL.

Kaédi

Arab Library: Kaédi; ancient religious texts.

Nouakchott

Archives Nationales: BP 77, Nouakchott; tel. 52317, ext. 32; telex PRIM 580 MTN; f. 1955; library of 3,000 vols, 1,000 periodicals; documentation centre; Dir M. MOKTAR OULD HEMEINA; publ. *Chaab* (daily).

Bibliothèque Nationale: BP 20, Nouakchott; tel. 24–35; dependent on Ministry of Culture; f. 1965; depository for all the country's publications; documentation centre for western Africa; 10,000 vols, collection of over 4,000 old MSS; 8 mems; Head Librarian OUMAR DIOUAWARA; Historian Prof. MOKTAR OULD HAMIDOU.

Centre de Documentation Pédagogique: BP 171, Nouakchott; f. 1962; 1,000 vols; 58 periodicals; educational and general works; Librarian MOHAMMED SAID.

Oualata

Arab Library: Oualata.

Tidjikja

Arab Library: Tidjikja; Librarian AHMEDOU OULD MOHAMED MAHMOUD.

University

UNIVERSITÉ DE NOUAKCHOTT

BP 798, Nouakchott

Telephone: 53977

Telex: 710

Founded 1981

State control

Languages of instruction: Arabic, French, English

Academic year: October to June

Rector: MOHAMED EL-HACHEN OULD LEBATT

Librarian: SID 'AHMED FALL DIT DAH

Number of teachers: 72

Number of students: 2,850

DEANS

Faculty of Letters and Human Sciences: DIALLO IBRAHIMA MOUSSA

Faculty of Law and Economics: (vacant)

Colleges

Ecole Nationale d'Administration: BP 664, Nouakchott; f. 1966; library of 8,000 vols; a documentation and research centre for the study of administration and politics in Mauritania; first degree courses; 33 teachers, 266 students; Librarian YARBA FALL; Dir CHEIK MOHAMED SALEM OULD MOHAMED LEMINE; publs *Annales, Futurs Cadres* (3 a year).

Institut national des hautes études islamiques: Boutilimit; f. 1961; 300 students.

Institut Supérieur Scientifique: BP 5026, Nouakchott; tel. 51382; telex 598; fax 53997; f. 1986; mathematics, physics, chemistry, biology, geology, computer studies, natural resources, ecology; library of 30,000 vols; Dir AHMEDOU OULD HAMED.

MAURITIUS

Learned Societies

GENERAL

Royal Society of Arts and Sciences of Mauritius: Sugar Industry Research Institute, Réduit; tel. 4541061; telex 4899; fax 4541971; f. 1829; Royal title 1847; 3 hon., 190 ordinary mems; Pres. Dr J. C. AUTREY; Hon. Sec. ROSEMAY NG KEE KWONG; publ. *Proceedings*.

AGRICULTURE, FISHERIES AND VETERINARY SCIENCE

Société de Technologie Agricole et Sucrière de Maurice: Mauritius Sugar Industry Research Institute, Réduit; tel. 4541061; telex 4899; fax 4541971; f. 1910; 395 mems; Pres. JEAN CLAUDE DESVAUX DE MARIGNY; Hon. Sec. C. BARBE; publ. *Revue Agricole et Sucrière de l'Ile Maurice*.

HISTORY, GEOGRAPHY AND ARCHAEOLOGY

Société de l'Histoire de l'Ile Maurice: rue de Froberville, Curepipe Rd, Port Louis; f. 1938; 810 ordinary mems; Hon. Sec. G. RAMET; publs *Bulletin, Dictionary of Mauritian Biography.*

Research Institutes

AGRICULTURE, FISHERIES AND VETERINARY SCIENCE

Institut Français de Recherche Scientifique pour le Développement en Coopération (ORSTOM): Mission ORSTOM auprès du Ministère de l'Agriculture, des Pêches et des Ressources Naturelles, Mauritius; oceanography and fish biology; Dir B. STEQUERT. (See main entry under France.)

Sugar Industry Research Institute: Réduit; tel. 454-1061; telex 4899; fax 454-1971; e-mail ressourc@syfed.mu.refer.org; f. 1953; research on cane breeding, agronomy, soils, diseases, pests, weeds, botany, mechanization, biotechnology, sugar manufacture, by-products, also on food crops cultivated in association with sugar-cane and between cane cycles; library: see Libraries; Dir Dr J. C. AUTREY; publs *Annual Report*, *Occasional Papers*, Advisory Bulletins, Recommendation Sheets, *Interim Reports,* technical circulars, monographs.

NATURAL SCIENCES

Biological Sciences

Research Centre for Mauritius Flora and Fauna: C/o Mauritius Institute, POB 54, Port Louis; tel. 212-0639; fax 212-5717; attached to Mauritius Institute.

Libraries and Archives

Beau-Bassin

Mauritius Archives: Development Bank of Mauritius Complex, Coromandel, Beau-Bassin; f. 1815; contains records of the French Administration (1721–1815) and the British Administration (1810 to Independence); comprises Divisions of MS Records, Printed Records, Notarial Registry, Land Registry and Maps and Plans, and a Photographic Service; Chief Archivist Dr P. H. SOOPRAYEN; publs *Annual Reports*, *Memorandum of Books Printed in Mauritius* (quarterly), *Bulletin.*

Curepipe

Carnegie Library: Queen Elizabeth II Ave, Curepipe; tel. 674-2287; fax 676-5054; f. 1920; spec. colln on Indian Ocean islands; 90,000 vols; Senior Librarian T. K. HURRYNAG-RAMNAUTH.

Port Louis

City Library: City Hall, POB 422, Port Louis; tel. 212-0831 ext. 161; fax 212-4258; f. 1851; 110,000 vols; important collections on Mauritius and archives of Port Louis Municipal Council; music scores; depository for WHO publications; Head Librarian BENJAMIN SILARSAH; publs *Annual Report*, *Subject Index to Local Newspapers* (2 a year), *Subject Bibliography on Mauritius* (annually).

Mauritius Institute Public Library: POB 54, Port Louis; tel. 212-0639; f. 1902; legal deposit library and depository library for UNESCO; 60,000 vols, including an extensive collection of books, articles and reports on Mauritius; Head Librarian S. ANKIAH.

Réduit

Sugar Industry Research Institute Library: Réduit; tel. (230) 454-1061; telex 4899; fax (230) 4541971; e-mail rng@msiri .internet.mu; f. 1953; 28,000 vols; representative collection on all aspects of sugar cane cultivation and sugar manufacture, and expanding collection on food crops; wide coverage of technical periodical literature; collection of prints and drawings and early publications on sugar cane; botanical and agricultural archives; collection of Mauritiana on the natural sciences; Librarian Mrs ROSEMAY NG KEE KWONG.

University of Mauritius Library: Réduit; tel. 454-1041; fax 464-0905; e-mail goordyal@ dove.uom.ac.mu; f. 1965; important collections in fields of administration, social sciences, agriculture, science and technology, law, textile engineering, medical research and Mauritiana; partial depository for UN publications; depository for World Bank publs; liaison office for AGRIS, CARIS; 95,000 vols; Chief Librarian B. R. GOORDYAL.

Museums and Art Galleries

Mahebourg

Historical Museum: Mahebourg; tel. 631-9329; f. 1950; a branch of the Mauritius Institute; comprises collection of old maps, engravings, water-colours and naval relics of local interest, exhibited in an 18th-century French house; Dir R. GAJEELEE.

Port Louis

Port Louis Museum: Mauritius Institute, Port Louis; f. 1880; comprises a Natural History Museum, collections of fauna, flora and geology of Mauritius and of the other islands of the Mascarene region; Dir R. GAJEELEE.

Réduit

Mauritius Herbarium: Sugar Industry Research Institute, Réduit; f. 1960; public herbarium for education and research; specializes in flora of Mascarene Islands; Curator J. GUÉHO.

University

UNIVERSITY OF MAURITIUS

Réduit

Telephone: 454-1041
Fax: 454-9642

Founded 1965
Languages of instruction: English, French
Academic year: August to July

Chancellor: (vacant)
Vice-Chancellor: Prof. G. T. G. MOHAMEDBHAI
Pro Vice-Chancellors: Prof. J. BAGUANT, Prof. A. PEERALLY
Registrar: S. D. GOORDYAL
Chief Librarian: B. R. GOORDYAL

Library: see Libraries
Number of teachers: 161 full-time, 177 part-time
Number of students: 2,602

Publications: *Vice-Chancellor's Report*, *Calendar* (annually), *University Newsletter* (6 a year).

DEANS

Faculty of Agriculture: Assoc. Prof. A. M. OSMAN
Faculty of Engineering: Assoc. R. DUBOIS
Faculty of Law and Management: Prof. S. K. SASTRY
Faculty of Science: Prof. I. FAGOONEE
Faculty of Social Studies and Humanities: Assoc. Prof. V. Y. HOOKOOMSING

PROFESSORS

BAGUANT, J., Sugar Technology
FAGOONEE, I., Environmental Sciences
JAIN, M., Mathematics
JOYNATHSING, M., Social Studies
KASENALLY, A., Chemistry
LAMUSSE, R., Economics
NATH, P., Mathematics
NATH, S., Economics
PEERALLY, A., Botany
SASTRY, K. S., Accounting and Finance

Colleges

Mahatma Gandhi Institute: Moka; tel. 433-1277; fax 433-2235; e-mail asibmgi@ internet.mu; f. 1970; serves as a centre for the study of Indian culture and traditions, and the promotion of education and culture; courses in Indian Music and Dance, Fine Arts, Indian Languages, Mandarin; research in Indian and Immigration Studies, Culture and Civilization, Bhojpuri, Folklore and Oral Traditions and Mauritian History, Geography and Literature; 221 teachers, 3,000 students; library of 75,000 vols; special collections: Gandhi, Mauritius, archive relating to Indian immigration to Mauritius 1842–1912; Chair. S. VEERASAMY; Dir UTTAMA BISSOONDOYAL; publs *Journal of Mauritian Studies, Vasant* (Hindi, 4 a year), *Rimjhim* (Hindi, 6 a year).

Mauritius College of the Air: Réduit; tel. 464-7106; fax 464-8854; f. 1972; runs a distance education programme; provides the national broadcasting organization with programmes for schools; produces audio-visual material for use by children and adults in projects of formal and non-formal education; acquires pre-recorded media-based educational material from overseas and makes it available to schools in Mauritius; library of 4,000 vols; Dir MEENA SEETULSINGH; publs annual reports.

Robert Antoine Sugar Industry Training Centre: Réduit; tel.454-7024; fax 454-7026; f. 1980; courses in sugarcane agronomy, cane sugar manufacture and chemical control in sugar factories, mechanization of field operations, agricultural management skills; courses in English and French; Dir MONICA MAUREL.

MEXICO

Learned Societies

GENERAL

Colegio Nacional: Luis González Obregón 23, México 1, DF; f. 1943 by the Government for the dissemination of national culture; 36 mems; library of 25,000 vols, 380 periodicals, tapes; Sec./Administrator Lic. FAUSTO VEGA Y GÓMEZ; publ. *Memoria* (annually).

AGRICULTURE, FISHERIES AND VETERINARY SCIENCE

Sociedad Agronómica Mexicana (Mexican Agricultural Society): Mariano Azuela 121, 2° piso, Del. Cuauhtémoc, 06400 México, DF.

Sociedad Forestal Mexicana (Mexican Forestry Society): Calle de Jesús Terán 11, México 1, DF; f. 1921; 225 mems; Exec. Pres. Ing. RIGOBERTO VÁSQUEZ DE LA PARRA; Sec.-Gen. Lic. ADOLFO AGUILAR Y QUEVEDO; publ. *México Forestal* (every 2 months).

ARCHITECTURE AND TOWN PLANNING

Asociación de Ingenieros y Arquitectos de México (Association of Mexican Engineers and Architects): 3A Calle del Puente de Alvarado 58, México, DF; f. 1868; 560 mems; library of 7,565 vols; Pres. Ing. FEDERICO DOVALI RAMOS; Sec. Ing. JOSÉ ACOSTA SÁNCHEZ; publ. *Revista Mexicana de Ingeniería y Arquitectura* (quarterly).

BIBLIOGRAPHY, LIBRARY SCIENCE AND MUSEOLOGY

Asociación Mexicana de Bibliotecarios, AC (Mexican Library Asscn): Apdo 27-651, 06760 México, DF; tel. 575-1135; f. 1924; 1,061 mems; Pres. ELSA RAMIREZ LEYVA; Sec. Lic. JOSE L. ALMANZA MORALES; publs *Noticiero de la AMBAC* (quarterly), *Jornadas Mexicanas de Biblioteconomía Memorias* (annually).

Centro de Información Científica y Humanística: Universidad Nacional Autónoma de México, Ciudad Universitaria, Apdo 70–392, 04510 México, DF; tel. 622-39-60; telex 01774523; fax 616-25-57; f. 1971; documentation service, current awareness and SDI services, computerized bibliographical searches; online database Latinamerican Bibliography, also available on CD-ROM, includes subfiles BIBLAT CLASE and PERIODICA; regional centre for FAO-ASFIS, centralized serial subscriptions system for UNAM (10,000 titles distributed to 162 department libraries); library of 3,485 vols; special collection of 230 titles of abstracting and indexing periodicals; 2,845 Latin American periodicals; Dir JUAN VOUTSSAS MARQUEZ; Librarian JAVIER DOMÍNGUEZ GALICIA; publs *CLASE* (quarterly index of Latin American citation in social sciences and humanities), *PERIODICA* (quarterly index of Latin American science and technology journals), *BIBLAT 1* (papers published by Latin Americans in foreign journals, 2 a year), *BIBLAT 2* (papers on Latin America published in foreign journals, 2 a year), *PORTAL* (monthly content tables of library and information science periodicals, and register of library acquisitions).

ECONOMICS, LAW AND POLITICS

Barra Mexicana—Colegio de Abogados (Mexican Bar Association— College of Advocates): Varsovia No. 1, Esq. P. de la Reforma, 06600 México, DF; tel. (5) 24-85; fax 533-6775; f. 1922; 1,685 mems; library of 5,260 vols; Pres. Lic. OCTAVIO IGARTUA ARAIZA; Sec. Lic. FABIAN AGUINACO BRAVO; publ. *El Foro* (quarterly), *La Barra*.

Instituto Nacional de Estadística, Geografía e Informática (National Institute of Statistics, Geography and Informatics): Av. Héroe de Nacozari sur 2301, Fracc. Jardines del Parque, 20270 Aguascalientes; tel. (49) 18-14-77; fax (49) 18-07-39; f. 1983; integrates and develops the National System of Statistics and Geography; undertakes the National Census; library of 5,000 vols; Pres. Dr CARLOS M. JARQUE; publs *Anuario Estadístico de los Estados Unidos Mexicanos, Anuarios Estadísticos Estatales, Anuario Estadístico de Comercio Exterior, La Industria Química en México, La Industria Automotriz en México, La Industria Textil y del Vestido en México, La Minería en México, El Sector Alimentario en México, La Industria Petrolera, La Industria Maquiladora de Exportación, La Industria Siderúrgica en México, Serie de Estadísticas Económicas.*

EDUCATION

Asociación Nacional de Universidades e Instituciones de Educación Superior (ANUIES): Avda Insurgentes Sur 2133, 3° piso, 01000 México, DF; tel. 550-27-55; f. 1950; co-ordinates and represents institutions of higher education, studies academic and administrative problems of the national higher education system; promotes exchange of personnel, information and services between the affiliated institutions; 99 affiliated universities, centres and colleges; library of 11,500 vols; Exec. Sec.-Gen. CARLOS PALLÁN FIGUEROA; Library Dir Lic. MARÍA ISABEL ADER EGGEL; publs *Confluencia* (monthly), *Revista de la Educación Superior* (every 3 months).

Centro Nacional de Documentación e Información Pedagógica y Museo Pedagógico Nacional: Calle Presidente Masaryk 526, México 5, DF; f. 1971; library of 10,000 vols; Dir Prof. MARIANO CRUZ PÉREZ; publs *Sep-Forjadores* (monthly), *Documentación e Información* (monthly), *Lista de Canje* (2 a year).

Dirección General de Relaciones Educativas, Científicas y Culturales (Board of Educational, Scientific and Cultural Relations): Secretaría de Educación Pública, Brasil 31, 2° piso, México 1, DF; f. 1960; comprises Sections of Technical Assistance, International Relations in the fields of Education, Science and Culture and Exchange; serves as co-ordinating agency between the UN, UNESCO, the OAS and the Mexican Govt; Dir Dr ENRIQUE G. LEÓN LÓPEZ.

FINE AND PERFORMING ARTS

Asociación Musical Manuel M. Ponce, AC: Bucareli No. 12, Desp. 411, México 1, DF; tel. 5-21-72-60; f. 1949 to promote annual concert seasons of traditional, modern and contemporary Mexican and foreign music; library of musical scores, tapes, records and books; Pres. LUIS HERRERA DE LA FUENTE; Vice-Pres. JESÚS ALVARADO ORTÍZ; Musical Dir MARÍA DE LOS ANGELES CALCÁNEO; Secs VÍCTOR URBAN, EDELMIRA ZUÑIGA.

Ateneo Veracruzano (Veracruz Atheneum): Edif. Lonja Mercantil, Independencia 924, Vera Cruz; f. 1933; 68 mems (18 corresp.); Pres. C.P.T. FRANCISCO BROISSIN A.; Sec. Prof. ANTONIO SALAZAR PÁEZ; publ. *Boletín* (monthly).

Instituto Nacional de Bellas Artes (National Institute of Fine Arts): Paseo de la Reforma y Campo Marte, Atras del Auditorio Nacional, 2° piso, Bosque de Chapultepec, Miguel Hidalgo, México, DF 11560; tel. 5-280-54-74; f. 1947; consists of depts of music, visual arts, opera, literature, dance, theatrical production, architecture, artistic education and administration; responsible for cultural insts throughout Mexico; Dir GERARDO ESTRADA; publs *Revista Pauta* (every two months), *Revista Hetereofonía* (every four months), *Revista de Educación Artística* (quarterly), *Boletín de Literatura* (every two months).

Has affiliated:

Centro Nacional de Conservación y Registro del Patrimonio Artístico Mueble: San Ildefonso 60, Col. Centro, México 1, DF; tel. 5-702-21-43; f. 1963; restoration of works of art incl. buildings; Dir WALTHER BOELSTERLY.

HISTORY, GEOGRAPHY AND ARCHAEOLOGY

Academia de Ciencias Históricas de Monterrey (Academy of Historical Sciences of Monterrey): Apdo 389, Nuevo León, Monterrey; f. 1947; Pres. CARLOS PÉREZ-MALDONADO; Sec. JOSÉ P. SALDAÑA; publ. *Memorias.*

Academia Mexicana de la Historia (Mexican Academy of History): Plaza Carlos Pacheco 21, Cuauhtémoc, 06070 México, DF; tel. and fax 521-96-53; f. 1919; correspondent of Real Academia, Madrid; library of 10,000 vols; Dir Dr MIGUEL LEÓN-PORTILLA; Sec. Dr GISELA VON WOBESER; publ. *Memorias* (2 a year).

Academia Nacional de Historia y Geografía (National Academy of History and Geography): Londres 60, México 6, DF; f. 1925; 179 mems; Dir ANTONIO FERNÁNDEZ DEL CASTILLO; publ. *Revista*.

Departamento de Antropología e Historia de Nayarit: Avda México 91, Tepic, Nayarit; f. 1946; Dir EVERARDO PEÑA NAVARRO; Sec. MARÍA A. GONZÁLEZ A.

Sociedad Mexicana de Geografía y Estadística (Mexican Society of Geography and Statistics): Calle de Justo Sierra 19, Apdo 10739, Del. Cuauhtémoc, 06020 México, DF; tel. 542-73-40; f. 1833; 1,204 active mems; 640 corresponding mems; library of 450,000 vols; Pres. IRENE ALICIA SUÁREZ SARABIA; Sec.-Gen. LEOPOLDO CHAGOYA MORGAN; publs *Boletín* (3 a year), and special works.

Sociedad Mexicana de Historia de la Ciencia y la Tecnología (Mexican Society for History of Science and Technology): Apdo 21873, Coyoacán, 04000 México, DF; fax (5) 659-64-06; f. 1964; Pres. Dr JUAN JOSÉ SALDAÑA; publs *Anales, Memorias, Quipu, Actas*.

LANGUAGE AND LITERATURE

Academia Mexicana de la Lengua (Mexican Academy of Letters): Donceles 66, Centro, Delegación Cuauhtémoc, 06010 México, DF;

corresp. of the Real Academia Española (Madrid); 28 mems; Dir JOSÉ G. MORENO DE ALBA; Sec. MANUEL ALCALÁ ANAYA.

PEN Club de México: Medellín 162, 06700 México, DF; tel. 5-64-50-78; f. 1924; 62 mems; Pres. EDUARDO LIZALDE; Sec. ALEJANDRO OLMEDO; publ. *Directory of Writers* (annually).

MEDICINE

Academia Mexicana de Cirugía (Mexican Academy of Surgery): Brasil y Venezuela, México 1, DF; f. 1933; Pres. Dr MANUEL MATEOS FOURNIER; publ. *Revista* (monthly).

Academia Nacional de Medicina de México (Mexican National Academy of Medicine): Apdo 7–813, Bloque 'B' sotano de la Unidad de Congresos del Centro Médico Nacional, Avda Cuauhtémoc 330, 06741 México 7, DF; f. 1864; 14 sections; 340 mems; library of 20,000 vols; Editor LUIS BENÍTEZ; publ. *Gaceta Médica de México*.

Asociación de Médicas Mexicanas, AC (Mexican Association of Women Doctors): Oklahoma 151, México 18, DF; f. 1923; 3,000 mems; represents members' interests as doctors, citizens and women; Pres. Dra IRENE TALAMAS V.; publ. *Revista*.

Asociación Médica Franco-Mexicana (Franco-Mexican Medical Association): Dr Balmis 148, México 7, DF; f. 1928; 600 mems; library of 3,500 vols; Pres. Dr JORGE ESPINO VELA; Vice-Pres. Dr JESÚS KUMATE; Sec. Dr EMILIO STOOPEN; Librarian Dr SERGE BRACHET; publ. *Pasteur* (quarterly).

Asociación Mexicana de Facultades y Escuelas de Medicina: Avda V. Carranza No. 870, Desp. 15, Apdo 836, San Luis de Potosí; f. 1957; mems 30 medical schools; Pres. Dr RAMÓN ARRIZABALAGA; Sec.-Gen. Dr MIGUEL R. BARRIOS; publ. *Boletín*.

Consejo Mexicano de Dermatología, AC: Durango 324, Desp. 101, Col. Roma, 06700 México, DF; tel. 5534518; f. 1974; 349 mems; qualifies specialists as part of Nat. Academy of Medicine Comm. of Postgraduate Studies; Gen. Sec. Prof. ERNESTO MACOTELA RUÍZ; publ. *Roster*.

Federación Mexicana de Ginecología y Obstetricia: Nueva York No. 38, Col. Nápoles, Delg. Benito Juárez, 03810 México, DF; tel. (5) 682-48-23; fax (5) 682-01-60; f. 1946; 3,900 mems; Pres. CARLOS FERNÁNDEZ DEL CASTILLO; Sec. Dr JORGE DELGADO URDAPILLETA; publ. *Ginecología y Obstetricia de México* (monthly).

Sociedad Latinoamericana de Alergología: Calle Dr Márquez 162, México, DF; f. 1964; 485 mems; Pres. Dr LUIS GÓMEZ-ORAZCO; Sec. Dr LUIS VILLANUEVA; publ. *Alergia* (monthly).

Sociedad Mexicana de Cardiología: Juan Badiano 1, Tlalpan, 14080 México, DF; tel. and fax 573-21-11; f. 1935; 900 mems; Pres. Dr EULO LUPI-HERRERA; Sec. Dr CARLOS MARTÍNEZ-SÁNCHEZ; publ. *Arch. Inst. de Cardiología de México*.

Sociedad Mexicana de Eugenesia (Mexican Society of Eugenics): 3A Acapulco 44, México, DF; f. 1931; 150 mems; library of 2,800 vols; Pres. Dr EUGENIO ECHEVERRÍA ARNAUX; Sec. Dr ALFREDO M. SAAVEDRA.

Sociedad Mexicana de Nutrición y Endocrinología, AC: Vasco de Quiroga 15, Col. Sección XVI, Tlalpan, 14000 México, DF; tel. and fax 655-17-68; f. 1960; 519 mems; Pres. Dra MA. DEL CARMEN CRAVIOTO; Sec. Dra ELISA NISHIMURA MEGURO; publ. *Revista de Endocrinología y Nutrición*.

Sociedad Mexicana de Parasitología, AC: Nicolás de San Juan 1015, Apdo 12813, México 12, DF; f. 1960; 20 active mems and 31 hon. mems from 14 countries; Dir LUIS FLORES BARROETA.

Sociedad Mexicana de Pediatría (Mexican Paediatrics Society): Tehuantepec 86-503, Col. Roma Sur, Del. Cuauhtémoc, 06760 México, DF; tel. 564-83-71; f. 1930; 1,200 mems; Pres. Dr CARLOS J. ARNAIZ TOLEDO; publ. *Revista Mexicana de Pediatría* (monthly).

Sociedad Mexicana de Salud Pública (Mexican Public Health Society): Leibnitz 32, 1° piso, 11560 México, DF; f. 1944; 1,000 mems; small library; Pres. Dr JUAN ALBERTO HERRERA MORO GÓMEZ; Sec. Gen. Dr RICARDO LOEWE REISS; publ. *Higiene* (every 2 months).

NATURAL SCIENCES

General

Academia Nacional de Ciencias (National Academy of Science): Apdo M-77-98, México 1, DF; f. 1884; library of 420,000 vols; 24 mems; Pres. Dr MANUEL VELASCO SUÁREZ; Perm. Sec. Dr ANTONIO POMPA Y POMPA; publs *Revista*, *Memorias*.

Ateneo Nacional de Ciencias y Artes de México (National Athenaeum of Sciences and Arts): Bucareli 12, México, DF; f. 1920 as Ateneo Estudiantil de Ciencias y Artes, then Ateneo de Ciencias y Artes de México 1926, present name 1934; comprises sections of architecture, astronomy and mathematics, biology, broadcasting, cinematography, criminology and penal law, engineering, eugenics, geography, history, hygiene, law (civil, industrial, and international), literature, medicine, military studies, music, pedagogics, political economy, natural science, statistics; 7 corresp. centres: Monterrey, Mérida, Veracruz, Chiapas, Tijuana, Oaxaca, Tlaxcala; over 1,000 mems, including hon. and corresponding; library of 10,000 vols; Hon. Pres. Dr ALFONSO PRUNEDA; Pres. EMILIO PORTES GIL; Vice-Pres. LUIS GARRIDO and Arq. EDMUNDO ZAMUDIO; Sec.-Gen. JOSÉ L. COSSIO; publs *Boletín*, pamphlets.

Centro Científico y Técnico Francés en México (French Scientific and Technical Centre in Mexico): Liverpool 67, México 06600, DF; tel. (5) 25-01-80; fax (5) 25-01-83; f. 1960; a dependency of the French Embassy in Mexico; undertakes scientific and technical co-operation between France and Mexico; service of French scientific documentation and film library; Dir JEAN-PIERRE TIHAY; publ. *Interface* (3 a year).

Biological Sciences

Asociación Mexicana de Microbiología, AC: Ciprés 176, Mexico 4, DF; f. 1949; Pres. ARMANDO BAYONA; publ. *Revista Latinoamericana de Microbiología y Parasitología*.

Sociedad Botánica de México, AC (Mexican Botanical Society): Apdo 70–385, Ciudad Universitaria, 04510 México, DF; f. 1941; promotes the study, teaching and technology of botany; organizes 12 meetings a year, and the National Botanic Congress every 3 years; 1,000 mems; library of 850 vols, 312 periodicals; Pres. H. SANCHÉZ-MEJORADA; Exec. Sec. ARMANDO RODRÍGUEZ; publs *Boletín* (2 a year), *Macpalxochitl* (quarterly newsletter).

Sociedad Mexicana de Biología (Mexican Biological Society): Avda de Brasil, México 1, DF; f. 1921; Pres. FERNANDO OCARANZ; publ. *Revista Mexicana de Biología*.

Sociedad Mexicana de Entomología (Mexican Entomological Society): Apdo 63, 91000 Xalapa, Veracruz, México; f. 1952; 650 mems; Pres. JORGE LEYVA; publs *Folia Entomológica Mexicana* (3 a year), *Boletín*.

Sociedad Mexicana de Fitogenética (Mexican Society of Plant Genetics): Apdo 21, Chapingo, Edo de México, 56230 México; tel. (595) 4-22-00, ext. 5795; fax (595) 46652; f. 1965; 1,000 mems; Pres. PORFIRIO RAMIREZ VALLEJO; Sec. Dr FRANCISCO ZAVALA GARCIA; publs *Revista Fitotecnia Mexicana, Revista Germen, Recursos Fitogenéticos Disponibles en México, Memorias de Congresos*.

Sociedad Mexicana de Fitopatología, AC (Mexican Society of Phytopathology): Apdo postal 85, 56230 Chapingo, Edo de México; f. 1958; 400 mems; holds one national meeting per year; Pres. Dr GUSTAVO FRIAS; Sec. Dr FRANCISCO D. HERNANDEZ; publs *El Vector, Revista Mexicana de Fitopatología* (2 a year).

Sociedad Mexicana de Historia Natural (Mexican Natural History Society): Avda Dr Vertiz 724, México 12, DF; tel. (5) 519-45-05; fax (5) 538-45-20; e-mail raulg@mar.icmyl.unam.mx; f. 1868, refounded 1936; 400 mems; library of 5,000 vols; Pres. Dr RAUL GIO ARGAEZ; publ. *Revista*.

Sociedad Mexicana de Micología (Mexican Society of Mycology): Apdo 26–378, México 02860, DF; tel. 541-1333; f. 1965; 400 mems; library of *c.* 12,000 vols; Pres. JOAQUÍN CIFUENTES; publs *Boletín S.M.M., Revista de Micología* (annually).

Mathematical Sciences

Centro de Investigación en Computación: Unidad Profesional Zacatenco-IPN-Lindavista, 07738 México DF; tel. (5) 586-29-90; fax (5) 586-29-36; e-mail aguzman@pollux.cenac.ipn.mx; f. 1963; 250 mems; library of 4,000 vols; Dir Dr ADOLFO GUZMÁN; publs *Informes Técnicos, Computación y Sistemas*.

Sociedad Matemática Mexicana (Mexican Mathematical Society): Apdo 70–450, 04510 México, DF; tel. (473) 2-71-55; fax (473) 2-57-49; f. 1943; 1,100 mems, 20 institutional mems; promotes mathematics, sponsors National Congresses and Regional Assemblies of mathematicians, and The National Mathematical Olympics; Pres. Dr J. C. GÓMEZ LARRAÑAGA; Sec. Dr F. SABINA; publs *Boletín de la SMM* (2 a year), *Miscelánea Matemática* (2 a year), *Carta informativa* (quarterly), *Aportaciones Matemáticas*.

Physical Sciences

Asociación Mexicana de Geólogos Petroleros (Mexican Association of Petroleum Geologists): Torres Bodet 176, 06400 México, DF; f. 1949; 600 mems; Pres. Ing. JAVIER MENESES GYVES; Sec. ISRAEL HERNÁNDEZ ESTÉVEZ; publ. *Boletín* (quarterly).

Sociedad Astronómica de México, AC (Mexican Astronomical Society): Jardín Felipe Xicotencatl, Colonia Alamos, México 13, DF; tel. 519-47-30; f. 1902; library of 6,500 vols; 500 mems; Pres. MARTE TREJO SANDOVAL; Sec.-Gen. JORGE RUBÍ GARZA; publ. *El Universo* (quarterly).

Sociedad Geológica Mexicana, AC (Mexican Geological Society): Torres Bodet 176, C.P. 06400 México, DF; tel. 547-26-66; f. 1904; 1,000 mems; library of 4,500 vols; Pres. Ing. BERNARDO MARTELL ANDRADE; Vice-Pres. Ing. HERIBERTO PALACIOS; Sec. Ing. LUIS VELÁZQUEZ AGUIRRE; publ. *Boletín*.

Sociedad Química de México (Mexican Chemical Society): Mar del Norte No. 5, Col. San Alvaro, Deleg. Azcapotzalco, CP 02090, Apdo 4–875, México, DF; f. 1956; 2,300 mems; Pres. M. C. ARNULFO M. CANALES GAJÁ; Sec. (vacant); publ. *Revista de la SQM* (every 2 months).

PHILOSOPHY AND PSYCHOLOGY

Sociedad Mexicana de Estudios Psico-Pedagógicos (Mexican Society for Psycho-Pedagogical Studies): Nayarit 86, México, DF.

RELIGION, SOCIOLOGY AND ANTHROPOLOGY

Sociedad Mexicana de Antropología (Mexican Anthropological Society): Apdo 105-100, México DF 11581; tel. (5) 622-95-70; fax (5) 622-96-51; e-mail lmanza@servidor.unam.mx; f. 1937; 480 mems; Heads Dr LINDA MANZANILLA NAIM, Mtro JOSÉ ANTONIO POMPA; publ. *Revista Mexicana de Estudios Antropológicos* (1 a year).

TECHNOLOGY

Asociación Franco-Mexicana de Ingenieros y Técnicos, AC (Franco-Mexican Association of Engineers and Technicians): Liverpool 67, México 6, DF; association for the development of relations between Mexican and French engineers living in Mexico.

Sociedad Mexicana de Ingeniería Sísmica, AC (Mexican Society of Seismic Engineering): Apdo 70–227, 04510 Coyoacán, DF; tel. 606-23-23, ext. 49; f. 1962; 466 mems; Pres. Ing. NEFTALÍ RODRÍGUEZ C.; Sec. Ing. PABLO ENRÍQUEZ Y MEZA; publ. *Revista Ingeniería Sísmica*.

Research Institutes

AGRICULTURE, FISHERIES AND VETERINARY SCIENCE

Campo Agrícola Experimental Río Bravo: Apdo 172, Río Bravo, Tamps; f. 1965; research into regional problems and diversification; Dir Ing. Agr. MANUEL CARNERO HERNÁNDEZ.

Centro Internacional de Mejoramiento de Maíz y Trigo (International Maize and Wheat Improvement Center): see under International.

Instituto Mexicano del Café: Km 4.5 Carretera Jalapa-Veracruz, 91190 Jalapa, Ver; tel. 2505543; telex 15536; f. 1958; Dir-Gen. Lic. ANTONIO GAZOL SÁNCHEZ.

Instituto Nacional de Investigaciones Forestales y Agropecuarias (National Institute of Forestry, Agriculture and Livestock Research): Insurgentes Sur 694-10o, Piso 03100 México, DF; tel. 6-87-76-47; fax 5-36-38-42; f. 1985 through the integration of Instituto Nacional de Investigaciones Agrícolas, Instituto Nacional de Investigaciones Pecuarias and Instituto Nacional de Investigaciones Forestales; conducts research in all aspects of agricultural development and production; 2,000 staff; agronomy library, livestock library and forestry library; publs *Agricultura técnica en México* (2 a year), *Tecnica Pecuaria en México* (2 a year), *Ciencia Forestal* (2 a year), other irregular publs.

BIBLIOGRAPHY, LIBRARY SCIENCE AND MUSEOLOGY

Instituto de Investigaciones Bibliográficas: c/o Biblioteca Nacional de México and Hemeroteca Nacional de México, Insurgentes Sur s/n, Centro Cultural, Ciudad Universitaria, 04510 México, DF; tel. and fax 665-0951; f. 1867, present name 1967; compiles the national bibliographies and books on bibliographical subjects; Dir JOSÉ MORENO DE ALBA; publs *Boletín* (annually), *Bibliografía Mexicana* (annually).

ECONOMICS, LAW AND POLITICS

Centro de Estudios Demográficos y de Desarrollo Urbano: Camino al Ajusco 20, 01000 México, DF; tel. 5-645-59-55; fax 5-645-04-64; f. 1964; demography and urban development; library of 500,000 vols; Dir G. CABRERA; publ. *Revista de Estudios Demográficos y Urbanos*.

Centro de Relaciones Internacionales: Ciudad Universitaria, FCPS, UNAM, 04510 México, DF; tel. 6551344, exts. 7957, 7961; attached to the Faculty of Political and Social Sciences of the Universidad Nacional Autónoma de México; f. 1970; co-ordinates and promotes research in all aspects of international relations and Mexico's foreign policy, as well as the training of researchers in different fields: Disciplinary construction problems, Co-operation and International Law, Developing nations, Actual problems in world society, Africa, Asia, Peace Research; 30 full mems; library of 6,000 vols, 35 special collections, 16,000 journals, etc; Dir Lic. ILEANA CID CAPETILLO; publs *Relaciones Internacionales* (quarterly), *Cuadernos*, *Boletín Informativo del CRI*.

Institut Français de Recherche Scientifique pour le Développement en Coopération (ORSTOM): Mission auprès du CEDDU, Colegio de México, Apdo 20671, México 20, DF; demography; Dir M. LIVENAIS. (See main entry under France.)

Instituto Mexicano del Desarrollo, AC: M. Escobedo 510, 8° piso, México 5, DF; tel. 531-0823; telex 01763289; research on socio-economic development and planning; 470 staff; Dir-Gen. Lic. ERNESTO SÁNCHEZ AGUILAR.

EDUCATION

Centro de Cooperación Regional para la Educación de Adultos en América Latina y el Caribe (CREFAL)/Centre for Regional Co-operation for Adult Education in Latin America and the Caribbean: Quinta Eréndira s/n, 61600 Pátzcuaro, Mich.; tel. (434) 2-00-05; fax (434) 2-00-92; f. 1951 by UNESCO and OAS, now administered by a Board of Directors from mem. countries; regional technical assistance, specialist training, research; library of 70,000 vols; CEDEAL/CREFAL Adult Education documentation centre for Latin America: 10,000 vols, database of 13,000 entries; publs *Erájpani*, *Cuadernos del CREFAL*, *Revista Interamericana de Educación de Adultos* (quarterly), *Circular Informativa CREFAL/REDMEX* (quarterly), *Boletín de Resúmenes Analíticos CREFAL/REDUC* (every 6 months).

Centro de Estudios Educativos, AC: Avda Revolución 1291, Col. Tlacopac, San Angel, Del. Alvaro Obregón, 01040 México, DF; tel. (5) 5935719; fax (5) 6642728; f. 1963; scientific research into the problems of education in Mexico and Latin America; library of *c.* 25,000 vols and 400 periodicals; Dir-Gen. LUIS MORFIN LÓPEZ; publ. *Revista Latinoamericana de Estudios Educativos* (quarterly).

MEDICINE

Centro de Higiene y Estación de Adiestramiento en Enfermedades Tropicales (Hygiene Centre and Training Station for Tropical Diseases): Avda Veracruz, Boca del Río, Ver.; f. 1946; Dir Dr ARNOLDO LÓPEZ RICO.

Instituto Nacional de Cardiología 'Ignacio Chávez' (National Cardiological Institute): Juan Badiano 1, Tlalpan, Sección XVI, 14080 México, DF; tel. 573-29-11; fax 655-10-16; f. 1944; 390 medical mems; library of 7,050 medical vols and 625 periodical titles; Dir Dr IGNACIO CHÁVEZ RIVERA; Subdirs: Medical Attendance Dr FAUSE ATTIE; Research Division Dr EDMUNDO CHÁVEZ COSSIO; Medical Education Division Dr EDUARDO SALAZAR DÁVILA; Administrative Division Dr CARLOS MARTÍNEZ GUTIÉRREZ; Library Dir MARIO F. FUENTES INIESTRA; publ. *Archivos des Instituto de Cardiología de México* (6 nos, 1 vol. per year).

Instituto Nacional de Diagnóstico y Referencia Epidemiológicos (National Institute of Epidemiological Diagnosis and Reference): Calle de Carpio 470, 11340 México, D.F.; tel. (5) 341-43-89; fax (5) 341-32-64; f. 1938; performs epidemiological laboratory reference services nationwide; carries out technological development and research in laboratory for support of epidemiological surveillance; trains and supervises laboratory personnel and performs quality control procedures for the National Laboratory Network; library of 3,930 vols, 603 journals. MEDLINE terminal; Dir Dr ANA FLISSER.

Instituto Nacional de Higiene de la S.S.A. (National Institute of Hygiene): Gerencia General de Biológicas y Reactivos, Czda Mariano Escobedo 20, México 17, DF; tel. 5-27-73-68; telex 1764004; fax 5-27-66-93; f. 1895; 300 mems; library of 10,000 vols; Dir Dr MANUEL SERVÍN MASSIEU.

Instituto Nacional de Neurología y Neurocirugia (National Institute of Neurology and Neurosurgery): Insurgentes Sur 3877, Col. La Fama, 14269 México, DF; tel. 606-45-32; fax 606-32-45; e-mail arcnuro@liceaga.facmed.unam.mx; f. 1964; library of 2,600 vols; Dir-Gen. Dr JULIO SOTELO MORALES; publ. *Archivos de Neurociencias* (review, 3 a year).

NATURAL SCIENCES

General

Centro de Investigación y de Estudios Avanzados del Instituto Politécnico Nacional: Apdo 14-740, 07000 México, DF; tel. (5) 747-70-91; telex 017-72826; fax (5) 747-70-93; f. 1961; postgraduate research and training centre in sciences; integrates the work of the depts of biochemistry, physics, applied physics, physiology and biophysics, electrical engineering, mathematics, genetics, cellular biology, molecular biology, marine biology, plant biology, experimental pathology, chemistry, biotechnology, bio-engineering, neuroscience, epistemology, pharmacology, bio-electronics, educational mathematics, toxicology, metallurgy engineering, and educational sciences; 500 mems; library of 256,000 vols, 3,200 special collections; Dir Dr ADOLFO MARTÍNEZ PALOMO; publ. *Avance y Perspectiva* (every 2 months).

Consejo Nacional de Ciencia y Tecnología (CONACYT) (National Council for Science and Technology): Circuito Cultural, Centro Cultural Universitario, Ciudad Universitaria, 04515 México, DF; tel. 655-63-66; f. 1970; co-ordinates scientific research and development and formulates policy; Dir-Gen. Dr HÉCTOR MAYAGOITIA DOMÍNGUEZ; publs *Ciencia y Desarrollo* (every 2 months), *Información Científica y Tecnológica* (monthly).

Instituto Mexicano de Recursos Naturales Renovables, AC (Institute for the Conservation of Natural Resources): Dr Vertiz 724, 03020 Col. Narvarte: tel. 519-45-05; fax 538-45-20; e-mail imernar@laneta.apc.org; f. 1952; library of 7,000 vols and 200 regular periodicals; Dir Arq. ENRIQUE BELTRÁN G.

Biological Sciences

Institut Français de Recherche Scientifique pour le Développement en Coopération (ORSTOM): UAM – I, Dpto de Biotecnología, Apdo 55535, 09340 México, DF; microbiology, biotechnology; Dir M. RAIMBAULT. (See main entry under France.)

Institut Français de Recherche Scientifique pour le Développement en Coopération (ORSTOM): Proyecto CENID-RASPA y ORSTOM, AP 225-3, Zi, 35071 Gómez Palacio, Durango; pedology, ecology, hydrology. (See main entry under France.)

Instituto de Ecología, AC: Apdo 63, 91000 Xalapa, Veracruz; tel. (28) 42-18-00; fax (28) 18-78-09; f. 1974; plant and animal ecology and taxonomy, biogeography, dynamics and structure of ecosystems, conservation and management of natural resources, environmental biotechnology; postgraduate programmes in Ecology and Natural Resource Management, and in Wildlife Management and Systematics; library of 20,000 vols, 250 periodicals; Dir Dr SERGIO GUEVARA; publs *Acta Zoologica Mexicana*, *Acta Botanica Mexicana*, *Flora de Veracruz*, *Flora del Bajío y de Regiones Adyacentes*, *Madera y Bosques*.

Instituto Nacional de Pesca (National Fishery Institute): Alvaro Obregón 269, 10°, México 7, DF; f. 1962; research in marine biology; library of 3,000 vols; Dir Ing. JOSÉ ANTONIO CARRANZA; publs *Serie científica*, *Serie Técnica*, *Serie Informativa*, *Serie Divulgación*.

Instituto Tecnológico del Mar: 94290 Boca del Río, Veracruz; tel. 91-29-860189; f. 1975, renamed 1981; 150 mems; library of 4,500 vols; Dir ALMILCAR SUÁREZ ALLEN.

Mathematical Sciences

Instituto de Matemáticas (Institute of Mathematics): Area de la Investigación Científica, Circuito Exterior, Ciudad Universitaria, 04510 México, DF; tel. 622-45-23; telex 1760155; fax 550-13-42; f. 1942; research in mathematics; 59 mems; library of 20,000 vols; Dir Dr LUIS MONTEJANO PEIMBERT; publs *Anales* (annually), *Monografías* (irregular), *Aportaciones Matemáticas* (irregular), *Publicaciones Preliminares*.

Physical Sciences

Instituto de Astronomía (Institute of Astronomy): Apdo 70–264, 04510 México, DF; tel. 622-39-06; telex 017-060155; fax 616-06-53; f. 1878; an Institute of the National Autonomous University of Mexico; research in astronomy and astrophysics; library of 7,000 vols, 1,550 journals; Dir Dr GLORIA KOENIGSBERGER; publs *Revista Mexicana de Astronomía y Astrofísica* (quarterly), *Anuario del Observatorio Astronómico Nacional* (annually).

Instituto Nacional de Astrofísica, Optica y Electrónica: Apdos 216 y 51, 72000 Puebla, Pue.; tel. 47-20-11; f. 1971; formerly Observatorio Nacional de Astrofísica, f. 1942; 22 research mems; library of 7,000 vols, 144 periodicals; Gen. Dir Dr ALFONSO SERRANO PÉREZ-GROVAS; Gen. Academic Sec. Dr MANUEL G. CORONA GALINDO; publ. *Boletín del Instituto de Tonantzintla*.

Instituto Nacional de Investigaciones Nucleares (National Institute of Nuclear Research): Apdo 18-1027, 11800 México, DF; tel. 521-9402; telex 1773824; fax 521-3798; f. 1979 (previously part of *Instituto Nacional de Energía Nuclear*, f. 1955); planning, research and development of nuclear technology, including peaceful use of nuclear energy; library of 41,500 vols (incl. theses), 75,000 periodicals, 7,300 consulting works, 6,000 pamphlets, 1,000 official pubs, 125 video tapes, 835,000 reports on microfiche and 25,000 in printed form; Gen. Dir JULIAN SANCHEZ GUTIERREZ.

Servicio Meteorológico Nacional (National Meteorological Dept): Avda Observatorio 192, Col. Observatorio, Del. M. Hidalgo, 11860 México, DF; telex 1777331; fax 2710878; f. 1915; library of 80,000 vols, 90,180 pamphlets; Dir Ing. G. ENRIQUE ORTEGA GIL.

RELIGION, SOCIOLOGY AND ANTHROPOLOGY

Centro Coordinador y Difusor de Estudios Latinoamericanos: Primer Piso de la Torre I de Humanidades, Ciudad Universitaria, 04510 México, DF; tel. 622-10-09; fax 622-19-10; f. 1978; attached to Univ. Nacional de México; study of Latin America and the Caribbean in all disciplines (history, literature, philosophy, etc.); library of 11,898 monographs, 8,700 magazines, 3,000 pamphlets, 160 theses and 150 records; Dir Dr IGNACIO DÍAZ RUÍZ; publs *Anuario Estudios Latinoaméricanos*, *Serie Nuestra América* (3 a year).

Instituto Indigenista Interamericano: Avda de las Fuentes 106, Col Jardines de Pedregal, 01900 México, DF; tel. (5) 595-84-10; f. 1940; supplies technical assistance to member governments for the Indian population of the continent; library of 40,000 vols; Dir Dr JOSÉ MATOS MAR; publs *América Indígena* (quarterly), *Serie Ediciones Especiales*, *Serie Antropología Social*.

Instituto Nacional de Antropología e Historia (National Institute of Anthropology and History): Córdoba 45, Col. Roma, 06700 México, DF; tel. (5) 533-20-15; e-mail difusion@inah.gob.mx; f. 1939; controls Museo Nacional de Antropología, Museo Nacional de Historia, Museo Nacional del Virreinato, Museo Nacional de las Intervenciones, Museo Nacional de las Culturas, Museo del Templo Mayor, Galería de Historia, Escuela Nacional de Antropología e Historia and 95 regional museums; Dir-Gen. TERESA FRANCO GONZALEZ SALAS; publs *Boletín*, *Colección Científica*, *Colección Divulgación*, etc.

Instituto Nacional Indigenista: Avda Revolución 1279, Col Tlacopac, CP 01040 México, DF; tel. 651-85-76; fax 593-59-67; f. 1948; the integration of Indian communities into national life; in addition to the central office there are 84 Coordinating Centres in the interior; specialized library of 25,000 vols; Dir-Gen. CARLOS TELLO MACÍAS; publs *Boletín INI*, *Colección Presencias*, *Colec. Letras Mayas Contemporáneas*, *Colec. El Gran Nayart*, *Biblioteca 'Gonzalo Aguirre-Beltrán'*.

TECHNOLOGY

Instituto de Investigaciones Eléctricas: Apdo 1–475, 62001 Cuernavaca, Mor.; tel. (73) 18-38-11; fax (73) 18-25-21); e-mail postmaster@iie.org.mx; f. 1975 to promote and undertake research and experimental development in the electrical industry; consulting service; library of 60,000 vols; Exec. Dir Dr JULIÁN SÁNCHEZ; publs *Boletín IIE*, *Referencias*, technical reports.

Instituto Mexicano de Investigaciones Tecnológicas (IMIT, AC): Calz. Legaria 694, Col. Irrigación, Del. Miguel Hidalgo, 11500 Mexico DF; tel. 557-10-22; telex 1773264; fax 395-41-47; f. 1950; applied research on natural resources and development of industrial processes; pre-investment studies, reports process and conceptual engineering; specialized library in chemical technology of 12,000 vols, 250 periodicals; Dir Dr MARTÍNEZ FRÍAS.

Instituto Mexicano del Petróleo (Mexican Petroleum Institute): Eje Central L. Cardenas norte 152, POB 14–805, 07730 México, DF; tel. 567-66-00; telex 017-73-116; f. 1967; research on petroleum products and equipment, petroleum and petrochemical industries, economic studies, exploration, refining; training and specialist courses; 5,000 mems; library of 46,000 vols; Gen. Dir JOSÉ LUIS GARCÍA-LUNA H.; publ. *Revista* (quarterly).

Libraries and Archives

Chapingo

Biblioteca Central: Universidad Autónoma Chapingo, 56230 Chapingo; tel. and fax (595) 5-08-77; e-mail rsuarez@taurusl.chapingo.mx; f. 1870; 142,000 vols, 3,500 periodicals; spec. colln on the Mexican Agricultural Congress; Dir ROSA MARIA OJEDA TREJO; publs *Revista de Chapingo* (2 a year), *Ciencias Forestales*, *Horticultura*, *Zootecnia*, *Ingeniería Agrícola*, *Revista de Geografía Agrícola* (2 a year).

Guadalajara

Instituto de Bibliotecas, Universidad de Guadalajara: Guanajuato 1045, Col. Alcalde Barranquitas, Apdo 2-39, 44280 Guadalajara, Jal.; f. 1861; depository for UNESCO publs; 452,303 vols; Dir HELEN LADRÓN DE GUEVARA COX.

Mexico City

Archivo General de la Nación (National Archives): Apdo postal 1999, Eduardo Molina y Albañiles, Col. Penitenciaría, 15350 México, DF; f. 1795; documents relating to the vice-regal administration of New Spain, the Inquisition, independence 1821–40, the 19th century, the Mexican Revolution 1910, and the years up to 1976 (151,000 vols); 45,000 books; 1,050 prehispanic paintings; newspaper collection of 1,272,000 copies; microfilm service and library; Dir-Gen. Mtra PATRICIA GALEANA; publs *Boletín* (quarterly), *Serie* (technical reports).

Biblioteca Central de la Universidad Nacional Autónoma de México: Ciudad Universitaria, 04510 México, DF; tel. 622-16-03; fax 616-06-64; f. 1924; 350,000 vols; 10,000 periodicals; Dir Mtro ADOLFO RODRÍGUEZ GALLARDO.

Biblioteca de Derecho y Legislación de la Secretaría de Hacienda (Law Library, Finance Ministry): Correo Mayor 31, México, DF; f. 1925, present form 1928; 13,000 vols; specialized library relating to ancient and existing federal laws, tax laws from 1831, foreign and international laws; Librarian SOFÍA SILVA.

Biblioteca de Historia de la Secretaría de Hacienda (Historical Library, Finance Ministry): Palacio Nacional, 06066 México, DF; f. 1939 with the collections of the old library of the Finance Ministry and those of Genaro Estrada acquired by the Government; 8,750 vols, 14,000 pamphlets relating to Mexico.

Biblioteca de la Secretaría de Comercio y Industria: Avda Cuauhtémoc y Dr Liceaga, México 7, DF; f. 1918; economic material, statistical annuals, census returns for population, livestock, etc; trade statistics; 42,250 vols; Librarian Lic. MARÍA TERESA HERNÁNDEZ G.

Biblioteca de la Secretaría de Comunicaciones y Transportes (Library of the Ministry of Communications and Transport): Tacuba y Xicotecatl, México, DF; f. 1891; 10,000 vols; Dir RENATO MOLINE ENRÍQUEZ.

Biblioteca de la Secretaría de Gobernación (Library of the Ministry of the Interior): Bucareli 99, 06699 México, DF; f. 1917; 45,000 vols.

Biblioteca de la Secretaría de Relaciones Exteriores (Library of the Ministry of Foreign Affairs): R. Flores Magón 1, 06995 México, DF; f. 1922; 40,000 vols; specializes in history and social sciences; Dir Lic. JORGE ALVAREZ FUENTES.

Biblioteca de México: Plaza de la Ciudadela 4, 06040 México, DF; tel. (5) 709-11-13; fax (5) 709-11-73; e-mail bibmex@servidor.unam.mx; f. 1946; 230,000 vols, 15,000 children's books, 925 periodicals, 15 daily newspapers, special collections, hall for blind people; Dir Mtro EDUARDO LIZALDE; publ. *Biblioteca de México* (6 a year).

Biblioteca del Honorable Congreso de la Unión (Congress Library): Biblioteca Unidad Centro Histórico, Edif. de la ex-Iglesia de Santa Clara, Tacuba 29, 06000 México, DF; tel. 510-38-66; fax 512-10-85; Dir ENRIQUE MOLINA LEÓN.

Has attached:

Sistema Integral de Información y Documentación (SIID): Palacio Legislativo de

San Lázaro, Avda Congreso de la Unión s/n, 15969 México, DF; tel. 628-13-84; fax 522-43-40; f. 1936; collns of the old libraries of the Chamber of Deputies and the Chamber of Senators; 200,000 vols; Dir Lic. D. M. LIAHUT BALDOMAR.

Biblioteca del Instituto Nacional de Salud Pública (National Institute of Public Health Library): Insp-Biblioteca, Avda. Universidad 655, Col. Sta. Ma. Ahuacatitlán, 62508 Cuernavaca, CP; tel. 11-01-11, ext. 2465; fax 11-11-56; f. 1884; specialized collections in public health medical administration, hygiene, preventive medicine, epidemiology, statistics, mental hygiene, nutrition, rehabilitation, occupational safety, industrial hygiene and water, air, noise and waste pollution engineering; 32,000 vols, 404 periodical titles; Librarian ANDREE LERA BUCHDID; publ. *Salud Publica de Mexico* (every 2 months).

Biblioteca 'Miguel Lerdo de Tejada' de la Secretaría de Hacienda y Crédito Público (General Library, Finance Ministry): Avda República de El Salvador 49, México 1, DF; f. 1928; 250,000 vols; Dir ROMÁN BELTRÁN MARTÍNEZ.

Biblioteca Nacional de Antropología e Historia 'Dr Eusebio Dávalos Hurtado' (National Library of Anthropology and History): Paseo de la Reforma y Calzada Gandhi, 11560 México, DF; tel. 553-63-42; f. 1880 as Library of the Instituto Nacional de Antropología e Historia de México (see under Research Institutes); specializes in archaeology, linguistics, history, ethnography and anthropology; 500,000 vols; 11,000 periodicals; Dir Dra STELLA MA GONZALEZ CICERO; publs *Serie Archivo Histórico, Serie Bibliografía, Serie Códices, Serie Investigación, Serie Microfilm, Serie Procesos Técnicos, Información actualizada en antropología y ciencias sociales.*

Biblioteca Nacional de México (National Library): Centro Cultural, Ciudad Universitaria, Del. Coyoacán, 04510 México, DF; tel. 622-68-08; fax 665-09-51; f. 1867; run by Bibliographic Research Institute of the National University of Mexico; 3,000,000 vols, and other items relating to the political, social, artistic, literary and historical development of Mexico; Library Dir JOSE MORENO DE ALBA; publs *Bibliografía Mexicana, Boletín del Instituto de Investigaciones Bibliográficas* (2 a year).

Hemeroteca Nacional de México (National Library of Periodicals): Centro Cultural, Ciudad Universitaria, Del. Coyoacán, 04510 México, D.F.; tel. 622-68-08; fax 665-09-51; f. 1912; 250,000 vols; newspapers and periodicals; Mexican Gazette of 18th century; Dir JOSE MORENO DE ALBA.

Instituto Nacional de Bellas Artes (Dirección de Literatura): Lázaro Cárdenas 2, 3er Piso (Torre Latinoamericana), México 1, DF; tel. 521-19-54; incorporates several centres, each of which inherited specialist material from the former Biblioteca Ibero-Americana y de Bellas Artes.

Incorporated centres:

Centro de Documentación y Biblioteca: Eje Lázaro Cárdenas 2, 3er Piso (Torre Latinoamericana), Col. Centro, 06007 México, DF; f. 1984; specializes in Mexican literature; 3,500 vols; database LIME-INBA of the Mexican literature contained in the principal libraries of Mexico City; Dir Lic. JORGE PEREZ-GROVAS.

Centro Nacional de Investigación e Información Teatral Rodolfo Usigli: Chihuahua 216, Esquina Monterrey, Col. Roma, 06760 México, DF.

Centro Nacional de Investigación de Información y Documentación de la Danza: Campos Eliseos 480, Col. Polanco, 11560 México, DF.

Centro Nacional de Investigación, Documentación e Información Musical Carlos Chávez: Liverpool 16, Col. Juárez, 06600 México, DF.

Centro Nacional de Investigación, Documentación e Información de Artes Plásticas del INBA (CENIDIAP): Calle Nueva York 224, Col. Nápoles, 03810 México, DF.

Monterrey

Biblioteca del Instituto Tecnológico y de Estudios Superiores de Monterrey: Sucursal de Correos 'J', 64849 Monterrey (Nuevo León); tel. (83) 358-20-00; fax (83) 328-40-67; e-mail marreola@campus.mty.itesm.mx; f. 1943; 221,000 vols, 3,000 periodicals; Dir Ing. MIGUEL ARREOLA; publs *Transferencia* (quarterly), *Cursor* (quarterly), *Integratec* (every two months), *Calidad Ambiental* (quarterly).

Puebla

Biblioteca de la Universidad de las Américas: POB 100, Santa Catarina Mártir, 72820 Puebla, Pue.; tel. (22) 29-22-57; fax (22) 29-20-78; e-mail ename@udlapvms.pue.udlap.mx; f. 1940; humanities, science and technology; 400,000 vols, 2,200 periodicals; special collection; M. Covarrubias archives, R. Barlow archives, Herrera Carrillo archives, Porfirio Díaz archives; Dir ENIKO S. NAME.

Toluca

Biblioteca Pública Central del Estado de México: Centro Cultural Mexiquense, 50000 Toluca (Estado de México); f. 1827; 40,012 vols, 128 periodicals; Dir MARÍA CRISTINA PÉREZ GÓMEZ.

Tuxtla Gutiérrez

Biblioteca Pública del Estado de Chiapas: Blvd Angel Albino Corzo Km 1087, Tuxtla Gutiérrez (Chiapas); tel. 3-06-64; f. 1910; 45,000 vols; Dir JOSÉ LUIS CASTRO.

Zacatecas

Biblioteca Pública del Estado 'Elias Amador': Plaza Independencia 1, 98000 Zacatecas (Zacatecas); tel. 2-59-29; fax 2-59-29; f. 1832; history, religion, philosophy; 22,000 vols; Dirs MANUEL VILLAGRÁN REYES, JESÚS RODRÍGUEZ MARÍN.

Museums and Art Galleries

Actopán

Museo Regional de Actopán: Actopán, Hidalgo; f. 1933; collections relating to the Otomie Indians housed in the former convent of Actopán.

Campeche

Museo Regional de Campeche: Calle 59 entre 16 y 14, Campeche, Camp.; f. 1985; archaeology and history; Dir Arq. JOSÉ E. ORTÍZ LAN.

Guadalajara

Museo del Estado de Jalisco: Liceo 60, Centro Histórico, 44100 Guadalajara, Jalisco; tel. (3) 613-27-03; fax (3) 614-52-57; f. 1918; collections of early Mexican objects; folk art and costumes; archaeological discoveries; anthropological, archaeological and historical research; library of 6,000 vols; Dir CARLOS R. BELTRÁN BRISEÑO.

Museo Regional de Guadalajara: Liceo 60, S.H. 44100 Guadalajara, Jalisco; tel. 14-99-57; f. 1918; special collections of pre-Spanish and Colonial period art and paintings; Dir Lic. CRISTINA SANCHEZ DEL REAL.

Museo-Taller José Clemente Orozco: Calle Aurelio Aceves 27, Sector Juárez, 44100 Guadalajara; f. 1951; paintings and sketches by the artist; Dir MARGARITA V. DE OROZCO.

Guanajuato

Museos de la Universidad de Guanajuato (University Museums): Lascuraín de Retana 5, 36000 Guanajuato, Guan.; f. 1870; comprise: Natural History, Geology, Mineralogy, and include the natural history collection of Alfredo Duges with many rare specimens.

Jalapa

Museo de Antropología de Jalapa, Universidad Veracruzana: Avda Jalapa s/n, 91010 Jalapa, Veracruz; tel. and fax (281) 15-09-20; f. 1959; special regional archaeological collections of the Olmec, Totonac and Huastec cultures of ancient Mexico; Dir RUBÉN B. MORANTE LÓPEZ.

Madero

Museo de la Cultura Huasteca (Museum of Huastec Culture): POB 12, Avda 1° de Mayo y Sor J.I. de la Cruz, 89440 Madero, Tam.; tel. and fax (12) 10-22-17; f. 1960; attached to the Instituto Nacional de Antropología e Historia; library of 1,750 vols, 95 discs; Dir C.P. MA. ALEJANDRINA ELÍAS ORTIZ.

Mérida

Museo Regional de Antropología: Palacio Canton, Calle 43 por Paseo de Montejo, Mérida, Yucatán; f. 1920; attached to the Instituto Nacional de Antropología e Historia; collections of Pre-hispanic Mayan and Olmec culture, precious stones, ceramics, jade, objects in copper and gold; Dir AGUSTÍN PEÑA CASTILLO.

Mexico City

Museo de Arte Alvar y Carmen T. de Carrillo Gil: Avda Revolución 1608, Col. San Angel Inn, Del. Alvaro Obregón, 01000 México, DF; tel. 550-39-83; fax 550-42-32; f. 1974; contemporary Mexican art; library of 3,000 vols; Dir SYLVIA PANDOLFI; publ. *Gazeta del Museo* (monthly).

Museo de Arte Contemporáneo Internacional Rufino Tamayo: Paseo de la Reforma y Gandhi, Bosque de Chapultepec, Del. Miguel Hidalgo, 11580 México, DF; tel. 286-58-39; fax 286-65-39; f. 1981; permanent collection of contemporary art, permanent exhibition of Rufino Tamayo's work; temporary exhibits of international artists; library specializing in Rufino Tamayo, contemporary art and artists; Dir CRISTINA GÁLVEZ GUZZY.

Museo de Arte Moderno (Museum of Modern Art): Bosque de Chapultepec, Paseo de la Reforma y Gandhi, 11560 México, DF; tel. (5) 553-63-33; fax (5) 553-62-11; f. 1964; mainly Mexican collection of modern and contemporary art and temporary exhibitions of modern Mexican and foreign art; Dir Dra TERESA DEL CONDE.

Museo de Historia Natural de la Ciudad de México: 2° Sección del Bosque de Chapultepec, Apdo Postal 18–845, Del. Miguel Hidalgo, 11800 México, DF; tel. 515-63-04; fax 515-68-82; f. 1964; exhibitions on the universe, the earth, the origin of life, plant and animal taxonomy, evolution and adaptation of species, biology, man and bio-geographical areas; contains replicas of prehistoric creatures; library of 6,000 vols; Dir MARIA ELENA FERNANDEZ DE CAMINO.

Museo de las Culturas: Calle de Moneda 13, 06060 México, DF; tel. (5) 542-01-65; fax (5) 542-04-22; attached to the Instituto

Nacional de Antropología e Historia; f. 1965; collections of archaeology and ethnology from all over the world; public lectures, special courses for teachers, training in plastic arts; library of 18,205 vols; Dir Etnlga. JULIETA GIL ELORDUY.

Museo de San Carlos: Puente de Alvarado 50, 06030 México, DF; tel. (5) 592-37-21; fax (5) 535-12-56; e-mail mnsancarlos@compuserve.com.mx; f. 1783; part of Instituto Nacional de Bellas Artes (*q.v.*); exhibition of 14th–19th-century European paintings; library of 2,000 vols; Dir ROXANA VELÁSQUEZ; publs *Bulletin* (annually), *Guia Museo de San Carlos*, catalogues.

Museo del Palacio de Bellas Artes: Avda Juárez y Eje Central 'Lázaro Cardenas', Centro Historico, Del. Cuauhtémoc, 06050 México, DF; tel. and fax (5) 510-13-88; f. 1934; attached to the Instituto Nacional de Bellas Artes; permanent exhibition 'Los Grandes Muralistas'; Dir Arq. AGUSTÍN ARTEAGA.

Museo Don Benito Juárez (Juárez Museum): Palacio Nacional, Centro Histórico, 06000 México, DF; tel. and fax 521-53-66; f. 1957; historical relics related to the life and work of Benito Juárez; specialized library of 2,000 vols on history of reform in Mexico; Dir JUANA INÉS ABREU.

Museo Estudio Diego Rivera: Diego Rivera esq. Altavista, Col. San Angel Inn, Del. Alvaro Obregón, 01060 México, DF; tel. 550-11-89; fax 550-10-04; permanent exhibition 'Estudio Taller de Diego Rivera'.

Museo Etnográfico de Esculturas de Cera (Wax Sculpture Ethnographical Museum): Seminario No. 4 esquina con Guatemala, México, DF; f. 1964; sculptures of indigenous dancers, idols and figures from temples; Dir CARMEN DE ANTÚNEZ.

Museo Nacional de Antropología (National Museum of Anthropology): Paseo de la Reforma y Calz. Gandhi, 11560 México, DF; tel. (5) 553-19-02; fax (5) 286-17-91; f. 1964; attached to the Instituto Nacional de Antropología e Historia; anthropological, ethnological, and archaeological subjects relating to Mexico; 6,000 exhibits; library of 300,000 vols; Dir Dr MARI CARMEN SERRA PUCHE; publs *Cuadernos, Guides*, etc.

Museo Nacional de Arte: Tacuba 8, Centro Histórico, Del. Cuauhtémoc, 06010 México, DF; tel. (5) 512-16-84; fax (5) 521-73-20; f. 1982; permanent exhibitions of Mexican art from 16th century to 1950; library of 4,000 vols; Dir GRACIELA REYES RETANA; publ. *Revista Memoria*.

Museo Nacional de Artes e Industrias Populares del Instituto Nacional Indigenista: Avda Juárez 44, 06050 México, DF; f. 1951; examples of popular Mexican art of all periods, conservation and encouragement of traditional handicrafts; Dir MARÍA TERESA POMAR.

Museo Nacional de Historia (National Historical Museum): Castillo de Chapultepec, CP 11580 México, DF; f. 1825, moved to Chapultepec Castle 1941, opened 1944, attached to the Instituto Nacional de Antropología e Historia; history of Mexico from the Conquest in the 16th century to the Constitution of 1917; over 52,000 objects (historical paintings, flags, weapons, documents, jewellery, clothing and other objects of social and cultural history); Dir Dra MARGARITA LOERA CHÁVEZ.

Museo Nacional de la Estampa: Avda Hidalgo 39, Col. Centro, Delg. Cuauhtémoc, 06050 México, DF; tel. and fax (5) 521-22-44; permanent exhibition 'Proceso Histórico de la Estampa en México'.

Museo Nacional de las Intervenciones: General Anaya y 20 de agosto, Coyoacán, 04100 México, DF; tel. 604-06-99; fax 604-09-81; f. 1981; government-owned museum; exhibitions show history of invasions and Mexican independence; library of 800 vols; Dir Lic. MONICA CUEVAS Y LARA.

Pinacoteca Virreinal de San Diego (San Diego Viceregal Art Gallery): Dr Mora 7, Col. Centro Histórico, 06050 México, DF; tel. (5) 510-27-93; fax (5) 512-20-79; f. 1962; under auspices of Instituto Nacional de Bellas Artes; collection of paintings of the colonial era in Mexico; library of 5,000 vols; Dir VIRGINIA ARMELLA DE ASPE.

Monterrey

Museo Regional de Nuevo León: Rafael Jose Verger s/n, Col. Obispado, Apdo 291, 64010 Monterrey, Nuevo León; tel. 46-04-04; f. 1956; regional and Mexican history, archaeology and painting; Dir Arq. JAVIER SANCHEZ GARCIA.

Morelia

Museo Regional Michoacano (Michoacan Museum): Calle de Allende 305, 58000 Morelia, Michoacán; tel. 2-04-07; telex 91451; f. 1886; archaeological, ecological, ethnographical and prehistoric collections of the district; library of 10,000 vols; Dir Arq. PAUL DELGADO LAMAS; publ. *Anales*.

Oaxaca

Museo Regional de Oaxaca: Apdo 68000, Ex-Convento de Santo Domingo, Oaxaca, Oax.; tel. 62991; f. 1933; anthropology, archaeology, ethnography and religious art; contains the famous archaeological treasures found in Tomb No. 7, Monte Albán, jewellery, etc.; Dir JORGE EFREN ROJAS HERNANDEZ.

Patzcuaro

Museo Regional de Artes Populares (Regional Museum of Arts and Crafts): Enseñanza y Alcantarilla s/n, Patzcuaro, Michoacán; tel. 21029; f. 1935; ancient and modern ethnographical exhibits relating to the Tarascan Indians of Michoacán; colonial and contemporary native art; Dir RAFAELA LUFT DÁVALOS.

Puebla

Museo de Arte 'José Luis Bello y González': Avda 3 Poniente 302, Puebla, Pue.; tel. 32-94-75; f. 1938, opened to the public 1944; contains: ivories, porcelain, wrought iron, furniture, clocks, watches, musical instruments, etc., Mexican, Chinese and European paintings, sculptures, pottery, vestments, tapestries, ceramics, miniatures, etc.

Museo Regional de Santa Mónica: Avda Poniente 103, Puebla, Pue.; f. 1940; religious art; comprises the collections of various disbanded convents and now housed in that of Santa Mónica.

Museo Regional del Estado de Puebla: Casa del Alfeñique, 4 Oriente No. 416, Puebla, Pue.; f. 1931; notable historical collections; Dir JUAN ARMENTA CAMACHO.

Querétaro

Museo Regional de Querétaro (Querétaro Historical Museum): Calle Corregidora 3 Sur, 76000 Querétaro, Qro; tel. 12-20-31; fax 12-20-36; f. 1936; local history and art; Dir MANUEL OROPEZA SEGURA.

Tepotzolán

Museo Nacional del Virreinato (National Museum of the Vice-Royalty): Plaza Hidalgo 99, 54600 Tepotzotlán; tel. 876-02-45; fax 876-03-32; f. 1964; attached to the Instituto Nacional de Antropología e Historia; collections on the art and culture of the Colonial period; housed in 17th- and 18th-century building, formerly belonging to the Jesuits; library of 4,000 vols dating from 16th to 19th centuries; Dir MARÍA DEL CONSUELO MAQUÍVAR MAQUÍVAR.

Toluca

Museo de las Bellas Artes (Museum of Fine Arts): Calle de Santos Degollado 102, Toluca, México Estado; paintings, sculptures, Mexican colonial art; exhibitions, theatre, lectures, art courses; Dir Prof. JOSÉ M. CABALLERO-BARNARD.

Tuxtla Gutiérrez

Museo Regional de Chiapas: Calzada de los Hombres Ilustres s/n, Parque Madero, 29000 Tuxtla Gutiérrez, Chiapas; tel. 2-04-59; fax 3-45-54; f. 1939; archaeological and historical collections; Dir Arq. ELISEO LINARES VILLANUEVA.

Tzintzuntzan

Museo Etnográfico y Arqueológico: Tzintzuntzan, Michoacán; f. 1944; ethnographical and archaeological collections relating to the Tzinztuntzan and Tarascan zones of Lake Pátzcuaro.

Universities

UNIVERSIDAD NACIONAL AUTÓNOMA DE MÉXICO

Ciudad Universitaria, Del. Coyoacán, 04510 México, DF

Telephone: 622-07-75

Fax: 550-90-17

E-mail: dgia@condor.dgsca.unam.mx

Founded 1551

Language of instruction: Spanish

Academic year: August to May

Rector: Dr FRANCISCO JOSÉ BARNES DE CASTRO

Secretary-General: M. en Arq. XAVIER CORTES ROCHA

Secretary for Planning: Dr SALVADOR MALO ALVAREZ

Administrative Secretary: Dr LEOPOLDO HENRI PAASCH MARTÍNEZ

Secretary for Student Affairs: Dr FRANCISCO RAMOS GÓMEZ

Librarian: Mtro. ADOLFO RODRÍGUEZ GALLARDO

In addition to the National Library and Central Library (see under Libraries), there are 142 specialized libraries attached to the faculties, schools and research institutes

Number of teachers: 29,979

Number of students: 268,615

Publications: *Investigación Económica, Estudios de Cultura Náhuatl, Estudios de Cultura Maya, Crítica: Revista Hispanoamericana de Filosofía, Estudios de Historia Moderna y Contemporánea de México, Anales de Antropología, Revista Mexicana de Ciencias Políticas y Sociales, Problemas del Desarrollo: Revista Latinoamericana de Economía, Anuario Jurídico, Boletín del Instituto de Investigaciones Bibliográficas, Anales del Instituto de Biología: Serie Botánica, Revista Mexicana de Sociología, Boletín Mexicano de Derecho Comparado, Anuario de Letras, Estudios de Historia Novohispana, Anales del Instituto de Investigaciones Estéticas, Relaciones Internacionales, Estudios Políticos, Acta Sociológica, Anales del Instituto de Biología: Serie Zoología, Anuario de la Historia del Derecho Mexicano, Biblioteca Universitaria, Ciencias, Cuadernos de Arquitectura Mesoamericana, Demos: Carta Demográfica sobre México, Discurso: Cuadernos de Teoría y Análisis, Economía Informa, Mathesis, Momento Económico, Omnia, Perfiles Educativos, Revista de Derecho Privado, Revista Mexicana de Astronomía y Astrofísica, Revista de la Escuela Nacional de Artes Plásticas, Revista de la Facultad de Medicina, Universidad de México,*

UNAM Hoy, Los Universitarios, Voices of Mexico, Acta Poética, AM Arquitectura Mexicana, Anales del Instituto de Ciencias del Mar y Limnología, Anuario de Letras Modernas, Anuario Mexicano de la Historia del Derecho, Archivos Hispanoamericanos de Sexología, Armonía, Atmósfera, Bibliografía Latinoamericana, Boletín de Estudios Médicos y Biológicos, Boletín de Mineralogía, Carrizos, Chicomóztoc: Boletín del Seminario de Estudios para la Descolonización de México, Clase: Citas Latinoamericanas en Ciencias Sociales y Humanidades, Contaduría y Administración, Crítica Jurídica, Cuadernos Americanos, Cuadernos de Arquitectura Virreinal, Cuadernos de Urbanismo, Desde el Sur: Humanismo y Ciencia, Dianoia: Anuario de Filosofía, Diógenes, Educación Química, Emprendedores, Estudios de Antropología Biológica, Estudios de Lingüística Aplicada, Experiencia Literaria, Investigación Bibliotecológica, Intercambio Académico: Boletín Informativo, Investigaciones Geográficas, Latinoamérica: Anuario de Estudios Latinoaméricanos, Medievalia, Nova Tellus, Nuevo Consultorio Fiscal, Laboral y Contable-Financiero, Periódica: Indice de Revistas Latinoamericanas en Ciencias, Periódico de Poesía, Revista CIHMECH, Revista de Literatura Mexicana, Revista Mexicana de Ciencia Geológica, Revista de Zoología, Revista Veterinaria, Serie Varia, Sinopsis, Tempus, Theoría: Revista del Colegio de Filosofía, Trabajo Social, Vida en Zaragoza.

DIRECTORS OF FACULTIES AND SCHOOLS

Faculty of Accounting and Administration: M. F. ARTURO DÍAZ ALONSO
Faculty of Advanced Studies (Cuautitlán): Dr JUAN ANTONIO MONTARAZ CRESPO
Faculty of Advanced Studies (Zaragoza): Mtro ROSENDO ARTURO GONZÁLEZ PINEDA
Faculty of Architecture: Arq. FELIPE GERARDO LEAL FERNÁNDEZ
Faculty of Chemistry: Dr ENRIQUE RODOLFO BAZUA RUEDA
Faculty of Dentistry: Dr JOSÉ ANTONIO VELA CAPDEVILA
Faculty of Economics: Lic. GUILLERMO RAMÍREZ HERNÁNDEZ
Faculty of Engineering: Ing. JOSÉ MANUEL COVARRUBIAS SOLÍS
Faculty of Law: Dr MÁXIMO CARVAJAL CONTRERAS
Faculty of Medicine: Dr ALEJANDRO CRAVIOTO QUINTANA
Faculty of Philosophy and Letters: Mtro GONZALO CELORIO BLASCO
Faculty of Political and Social Sciences: Mtra CRISTINA PUGA ESPINOSA
Faculty of Psychology: Dr ARTURO BOUZAS RIANO
Faculty of Sciences: Dr RAFAEL PÉREZ PASCUAL
Faculty of Veterinary Medicine and Zootechnics: Dr LUIS ALBERTO ZARCO QUINTERO

National Schools:
- Music: Mtro LUIS ALFONSO ESTRADA RODRÍGUEZ
- Nursing and Obstetrics: Lic. SUSANA SALAS SEGURA
- Plastic Arts: Mtro EDUARDO ANTONIO CHÁVEZ SILVA
- Social Work: Lic. NELIA ELENA TELLO PEÓN
- *Escuela Nacional de Estudios Profesionales Acatlán:* Lic. JOSÉ NÚÑEZ CASTAÑEDA
- *Escuela Nacional de Estudios Profesionales Aragón:* Lic. CARLOS LEVY VÁZQUEZ
- Escuela Nacional de Estudios Profesionales Iztacala: Mtro FELIPE TIRADO SEGURA

ATTACHED RESEARCH INSTITUTES AND CENTRES

Sciences:

Instituto de Astronomía (Astronomical Institute): Dir Dra GLORIA SUZANNE KOENIGSBERGER HOROWITZ.

Instituto de Investigaciónes en Matemáticas Aplicadas y en Sistemas (Institute of Applied Mathematics and Systems Research): Dir Dr ISMAEL HERRERA REVILLA.

Instituto de Biología (Institute of Biology): Dir Dr HÉCTOR MANUEL HERNÁNDEZ MACÍAS.

Instituto de Investigaciones Biomédicas (Institute of Biomedical Research): Dir Dr CARLOS LARRALDE RANGEL.

Instituto de Química (Institute of Chemistry): Dir Dr FRANCISCO LARA OCHOA.

Instituto de Ingeniería (Institute of Engineering): Dir Dr JOSÉ LUIS FERNÁNDEZ ZAYAS.

Instituto de Geografía (Institute of Geography): Dir Dr JOSÉ LUIS PALACIO PRIETO.

Instituto de Geología (Institute of Geology): Dir Dr DANTE JAIME MORÁN ZENTENO.

Instituto de Geofísica (Institute of Geophysics): Dir Dr JAIME URRUTIA FUCUGAUCHI.

Instituto de Matemáticas (Institute of Mathematics): Dir Dr JOSÉ ANTONIO DE LA PEÑA MENA.

Instituto de Física (Institute of Physics): Dir Dr OCTAVIO NOVARO PEÑALOSA.

Centro de Ciencias de la Atmósfera (Centre of Atmospheric Sciences): Dir Dr FERNANDO GARCÍA GARCÍA.

Centro de Instrumentos (Instruments Centre): Dir Dr FELIPE LARA ROSANO.

Instituto de Ciencias del Mar y Limnología (Institute of Marine Sciences and Limnology): Dir Dr ANTONIO PEÑA DÍAZ.

Instituto de Investigaciones en Materiales (Institute of Materials Research): Dir Dr GUILLERMO AGUILAR SAHAGÚN.

Centro de Investigación sobre Fijación del Nitrógeno (Centre of Nitrogen Fixation Research): Dir Dra GEORGINA HERNÁNDEZ DELGADO.

Instituto de Ciencias Nucleares (Institute of Nuclear Sciences): Dir Dr OCTAVIO CASTAÑOS GARZA.

Instituto de Fisiología Celular (Institute of Cellular Physiology): Dir Dr GEORGES DREYFUS CORTÉS.

Instituto de Biotecnología (Biotechnology Institute): Dir Dr XAVIER SOBERÓN MAINERO.

Instituto de Ecología (Ecology Institute): Dir Dr DANIEL PIÑERO DALMAU.

Centro de Neurobiología (Neurobiology Centre): Dir Dr FLAVIO M. MENA JARA.

Centro de Investigación en Energía (Energy Research Centre): Dir Dr MANUEL MARTÍNEZ FERNÁNDEZ.

Humanities:

Instituto de Investigaciones Antropológicas (Institute of Anthropological Research): Dir Dra LINDA ROSA MANZANILLA NAIM.

Instituto de Investigaciones Estéticas (Institute of Aesthetics Research): Dir Dra RITA EDER ROZENCWAIG.

Instituto de Investigaciones Bibliográficas (Institute of Bibliographical Research): Dir Dr JOSÉ G. MORENO DE ALBA.

Instituto de Investigaciones Económicas (Institute of Economics Research): Dir Dra ALICIA ADELAIDA GIRÓN GONZÁLEZ.

Instituto de Investigaciones Históricas (Institute of Historical Research): Dir Dra VIRGINIA GUEDEA RINCÓN GALLARDO.

Instituto de Investigaciones Jurídicas (Institute of Juridical Research): Dir Dr JOSÉ LUIS SOBERANES FERNÁNDEZ.

Instituto de Investigaciones Filológicas (Institute of Philological Research): Dir Lic. FERNANDO CURIEL DEFOSSE.

Instituto de Investigaciones Filosóficas (Institute of Philosophical Research): Dir Dra OLGA E. HANSBERG TORRES.

Instituto de Investigaciones Sociales (Institute of Social Research): Dir Dr RENÉ MILLÁN VALENZUELA.

Centro de Estudios sobre la Universidad (Centre for Studies on the University): Dir Dr ANGEL ROGELIO DÍAZ BARRIGA.

Centro de Investigaciones Interdisciplinarias en Ciencias y Humanidades (Centre for Interdisciplinary Research in Science and Humanities): Dir Dr PABLO GONZÁLEZ CASANOVA.

Centro Regional de Investigaciones Multidisciplinarias (Regional Centre for Multidisciplinary Research): Dir Mtro HÉCTOR HIRÁM HERNÁNDEZ BRINGAS.

Centro Universitario de Investigaciones Bibliotecológicas (University Centre for Library Science Research): Dir Lic. ELSA MARGARITA RAMÍREZ LEYVA.

Centro de Investigaciones sobre América del Norte (Centre for Research on North America): Dir Mtra PAZ CONSUELO MÁRQUEZ-PADILLA.

Centro Coordinador y Difusor de Estudios Latinoamericanos (Centre for the Co-ordination and Promotion of Latin American Studies): Dir Dr IGNACIO DÍAZ RUIZ.

Programmes:

Programa de Investigaciones Multidisciplinarias sobre Mesoamérica y el Sureste (Programme of Multidisciplinary Research on Mesoamerica and the Southeast): Dir Dr PABLO GONZÁLEZ CASANOVA HENRÍQUEZ.

Programa Universitario de Alimentos (University Programme on Food): Dir Dr ALEJANDRO POLANCO JAIME.

Programa Universitario de Investigación en Salud (University Programme for Research on Health): Dir Dr HUGO ARÉCHIGA URTUZUÁSTEGUI.

Programa Universitario de Energía (University Programme on Energy): Dir Dr PABLO MULAS DEL POZO.

Programa Universitario de Medio Ambiente (University Programme on the Environment): Dir Dr FRANCISCO JAVIER GARFIAS Y AYALA.

Programa Universitario de Estudios de Género (University Programme on Gender Studies): Dir Dra GRACIELA HIERRO PÉREZ CASTRO.

Programa Universitario de Estudios sobre la Ciudad (University Programme on Studies of the City): Dir Arq. FRANCISCO COVARRUBIAS GAITÁN.

Proyecto Universitario de Ciencias Espaciales y Planetarias (University Project on Space and Planetary Sciences): Dir Dr GIANFRANCO BISIACCHI GIRALDI.

Proyecto Universitario de Conservación de la Biodiversidad (University Project on Biodiversity Conservation): Dir JESÚS ESTUDILLA LÓPEZ.

Extension and Cultural Centres:

Centro de Enseñanza de Lenguas Extranjeras (Centre for Foreign Language Teaching): Dir Mtra MA. AURORA MARRÓN OROZCO.

Centro de Enseñanza para Extranjeros (Educational Centre for Foreign Students): Dir Mtro RICARDO ANCIRA GONZÁLEZ.

Centro de Enseñanza para Extranjeros en Taxco (Educational Centre for Foreign Students in Taxco): Dir Lic. GUSTAVO PEÑA HERNÁNDEZ.

Centro Universitario de Estudios Cinematográficos (University Centre for Cinematographic Studies): Dir Mtro MITL VALDEZ SALAZAR.

Centro Universitario de Teatro (University Centre for Theatre): Dir Mtro JOSÉ RAMÓN ENRÍQUEZ.

Dirección General de Actividades Musicales (General Administration for Musical Activities): Dir Mtro RAÚL HERRERA MÁRQUEZ.

Dirección de Literatura (Administration for Literature): Dir Mtro IGNACIO SOLARES BERNAL.

Dirección de Teatro y Danza (Administration for Dramatic Arts and Dance): Dir Lic. ANTONIO CRESTANI.

Dirección General de Actividades Cinematográficas (General Administration for Cinematographic Activities): Dir Biol. SERGIO IVAN TRUJILLO.

Dirección General de Artes Plásticas (General Administration for Plastic Arts): Dir Mtra SYLVIA PANDOLFI ELLIMAN.

Escuela Permanente de Extensión en San Antonio, Texas (Permanent Extension School, San Antonio, Texas, USA): Dir Dr GUILLERMO PULIDO GONZÁLEZ.

Escuela de Extensión en Hull, Quebec, Canadá (Extension School, Hull, Quebec, Canada): Dir Mtra ESPERANZA GARRIDO REYES.

UNIVERSIDAD AUTÓNOMA DEL ESTADO DE MÉXICO

Av. Instituto Literario No. 100 OTE. Col. Centro, 50000 Toluca

Telephone: (721) 13-47-32
Fax: (721) 14-55-46
E-mail: webmaster@www.uamex.mx

Founded 1956
State control
Language of instruction: Spanish
Academic year: September to August

Rector: M. en A. URIEL GALICIA HERNANDEZ
Academic Secretary: M. en S.P. EZEQUIEL JAIMES FIGUEROA
Administrative Secretary: M.A.E. PEDRO LIZOLA MARGOLIS
Librarian: M. en E.L. RUPERTO RETANA RAMIREZ

Library of 292,000 vols
Number of teachers: 3,045
Number of students: 36,642

DIRECTORS

School of Anthropology: M. en E.L. RODRIGO MARCIAL JIMENEZ
School of Sciences: Biol. PEDRO DEL AGUILA JUAREZ
School of Nursing: L. en Enf. LUZ MARIA FRANCO BERNAL
School of Art and Architecture: M. en Pl. JESUS AGUILUZ LEON
School of Agricultural Sciences: Ing. ARTURO MAYA GOMEZ
School of Behavioural Sciences: Lic. én Psic. TERESA PONCE DAVALOS
School of Political Sciences and Public Administration: M. en C.P. JOSE MARTINEZ VILCHIS
School of Accountancy and Administration: M.A.E. IGNACIO MERCADO
School of Law: M. en D. JOAQUIN BERNAL SANCHEZ
School of Economics: M. en E. RICARDO RODRIGUEZ MARCIAL
School of Geography: L. en G. VICENTE PEÑA MANJARREZ
School of Humanities: L. en E.L. GERARDO MEZA GARCIA
School of Engineering: M. en I. ANGEL ALBITER RODRIGUEZ
School of Medicine: M.C. GABRIEL GERARDO HUITRON BRAVO
School of Veterinary Medicine: M. en C.E. EDUARDO GASCA PLIEGO
School of Dentistry: C.D. FRANCISCO MONTIEL CONZUELO
School of Urban and Regional Planning: M. en Pl. ALBERTO VILLAR CALVO
School of Chemistry: M. en C. JUAN CARLOS SANCHEZ MEZA
School of Tourism: L. en T. MARICRUZ MORENO ZAGAL

UNIVERSIDAD FEMENINA DE MÉXICO

Avda Constituyentes 151, 11850 México, DF
Telephone: 515-13-11, 515-93-18
Founded 1943
Private control
Language of instruction: Spanish
Academic year: September to June

Rector: Dra ELIZABETH BAQUEDANO
Secretary-General: Lic. LUIS SILVA GUERRERO
Registrar: Lic. PABLO TORRES MORÁN
Librarian: Srta AGUEDA CANEDO GUTIÉRREZ

Library of 12,000 vols
Number of teachers: 243
Number of students: 1,300

Publications: *Catálogo General Anual*, *Periódico Bimestral*.

DEANS

School of Law: Lic. ANTONIO ADOLFO LÓPEZ GARCÍA
School of Education: Lic. LUZ BEATRIZ UNNA DE TORRES
School of Pharmacobiological Chemistry: Q.F.B. ENRIQUE CALDERÓN GARCÍA
School of Interior Decoration: Arq. CARLOS CANTÚ BOLLAND
School of Pedagogy: Lic. MARÍA ELENA NAVARRETE TOLEDO
School of Social Work: Profa T.S. MARÍA DEL SOCORRO SUSANA CAMPOS GARCÍA
School of Psychology: Lic. LUZ ANTONIETA POLANCO DE GARZÓN
School of Tourist Business Administration: Lic. ARMANDO GONZÁLEZ FLORES
School of International Relations: Lic. EMILIA WITTE MONTES DE OCA
School of Clinical Laboratories: Q.B.P. VÍCTOR MANUEL SÁNCHEZ HIDALGO; Dr JOSÉ AGUILAR CASTILLO (daytime courses)
School of Museology: Lic. ROBERTO ALARCÓN
School of History of Art: ELIZABETH BAQUEDANO
School of Interpreting and Translating: Lic. MAUREEN ANNE IVENS MCCULLAGH

UNIVERSIDAD AUTÓNOMA DE AGUASCALIENTES

Avda Universidad 940, 20100 Aguascalientes, Ags
Telephone: (491) 12-33-45
Founded 1973
State control
Language of instruction: Spanish
Academic year: August to June (two semesters)

Rector: Lic. FELIPE MARTÍNEZ RIZO
Secretary-General: Lic. en Psic. ONÉSIMO RAMÍREZ JASSO
Librarian: C.P. IRMA DE LEON DE MUÑOZ

Library of 141,000 vols
Number of teachers: 1,305
Number of students: 10,393

Publications: *Gaceta Universitaria* (monthly), *Correo Universitario*, *Evaluación* (annually), *Caleidoscopio* (3 a year), *Scientiae Natural* (2 a year).

DEANS

Centre for Biomedical Sciences: Dr ARMANDO GONZALEZ PEREZ
Centre for Agricultural Sciences: M.V.Z. ENRIQUE HERNANDEZ AYALA
Centre for Arts and Humanities: Dr BONIFACIO BARBA CASILLAS
Centre for Secondary Education: Lic. ed. LETICIA VAZQUEZ MENDEZ
Centre for Economics and Administration: L.A.E. SANTIAGO CORTES CHAVEZ
Centre for Design and Construction Sciences: L.D.G. VICTOR MARTINEZ VIRAMONTES
Centre for Basic Sciences: Ing. HUGO LIZALDE VIRAMONTES

UNIVERSIDAD DE LAS AMÉRICAS – PUEBLA

Sta Catarina Mártir, Apdo Postal 100, 72820 Cholula, Puebla
Telephone: (22) 29-20-00

Founded 1940 as Mexico City College; became Universidad de las Américas in 1963
Private control
Languages of instruction: Spanish and English
Academic year: August to May

President: Dr ENRIQUE CÁRDENAS SÁNCHEZ
Academic Vice-President: Dr JORGE WELTI CHANES
Administrative Vice-President: Lic. JOSÉ MANUEL BLANCO ASPURU
Registrar: Lic. MIGUEL RODRÍGUEZ DURÁN
Librarian: ENIKO SINGER DE NAME

Library: see Libraries
Number of teachers: 241 full-time
Number of students: 6,000

Publications: *Notas Mesoamericanas, Perfiles Universitarios, La Pluma del Jaguar, Este Mes.*

DEANS

Faculty of Administration: Dr ROBERTO SOLANO
Faculty of Basic Sciences : Dr JORGE OJEDA CASTAÑEDA
Faculty of Engineering: Dr JOSÉ RAFAEL ESPINOSA VICTORIA
Faculty of Humanities: Dr BASILIO ROJO RUIZ
Faculty of Social Sciences: Dr ROBERT SHADOW
Research and Graduate Studies: Dr MARCO A. ROSALES MEDINA

HEADS OF DEPARTMENTS

Accounting and Finance: Dr JORGE DURÁN ENCALADA
Actuarial Sciences and Statistics: Mtro SERGIO VARGAS GALINDO
Anthropology: Mtra GABRIELA URUÑUELA
Applied Arts: Mtra MA. LUISA VILAR-PAYA
Architecture: Arq. EDUARDO GUTIÉRREZ REYES
Graphic Design: Mtro ROLF SEUL WEILAND
Business Administration: Dr JOSÉ LUIS RODAL ARCINIEGA
Chemical and Food Engineering: Mtro FIDEL VERGARA BALDERAS
Chemistry and Biology: Dr MARCO ANTONIO QUIRÓZ ALFARO
Civil Engineering: Mtro OCTAVIO CABEZUT
Communications: Mtro JOSÉ MANUEL RAMOS
Computer Systems Engineering: Dr ROGELIO DÁVILA PÉREZ
Economics: Dr GONZALO ALBERTO CASTAÑEDA RAMOS
Education: Dr LEÓN GARDUÑO
Electronics Engineering: Dr JUAN MANUEL RAMÍREZ CORTÉS
Hotel Management: Mtra PATRICIA DOMÍNGUEZ SILVA
International Relations: Dr ISIDRO MORALES
Languages: Mtra PATRICIA ANN MCCOY BABALLE
Law: Lic. MOISÉS ROMERO BERISTÁIN
Literature: Mtra ROBIN RICE DE MOLINA
Mechanical Engineering: Mtro CARLOS ENRIQUE JORGE ACOSTA MEJÍA
Physics and Mathematics: Dr GUILLERMO AURELIO ROMERO MELÉNDEZ
Psychology: Dr AGRIS GALVANOVSKIS KASPARANE

UNIVERSIDAD ANÁHUAC

Apdo 10-844, México 11000 DF; Avenida Lomas Anáhuac s/n, Lomas Anáhuac, 52760 Huixquilucan
Telephone: 627-02-10

Fax: 589-97-96

Founded 1963
Private control
Academic year: August to June (two terms)

Rector: Lic. RAYMUND COSGRAVE
Secretary-General: Dr ALFONSO LÓPEZ
General Academic Director: Mtro JAVIER VARGAS
Librarian: Mtro DANIEL MATTES

Library of 500,000 vols
Number of teachers: 1,100
Number of students: 7,300

DEANS

School of Actuarial Sciences: Act. OLIVA SÁNCHEZ
School of Architecture: Arq. FERNANDO PAZ Y PUENTE
School of Accounting and Business Administration: Dr RAMÓN LECUONA
School of Economics: Dr RAMÓN LECUONA
School of Engineering: Ing. JORGE GUTIÉRREZ VERA
School of Psychology: Mtro JOSÉ MARÍA LÓPEZ
School of Communication Sciences: Dr CARLOS GÓMEZ PALACIO
School of Education: Dra NIEVES PEREIRA RÚA
School of Law: Lic. BERNARDO PÉREZ FERNÁNDEZ DEL CASTILLO (acting)
School of Medicine: Dr JOSÉ KUTHY PORTER
School of Industrial and Graphic Design: Lic. LEONOR AMOZURRUTIA
School of Tourism Administration: Mtra LORIS ESTEFÁN

UNIVERSIDAD AUTÓNOMA AGRARIA 'ANTONIO NARRO'

Buenavista, Saltillo, 25315 Coahuila
Telephone: 17-31-84
Telex: 038-128
Fax: 17-36-64

Founded 1923, University status 1975
Academic year: January to December

Rector: Ing. EDUARDO FUENTES RODRIGUEZ
Vice-Rector: M. V. Z. JOSÉ L. BERLANGA FLORES
Registrar: Ing. GUSTAVO OLIVARES SALAZAR
Librarian: LUZ ELENA PEREZ MATA (acting)

Number of teachers: 430
Number of students: 2,583

CO-ORDINATORS OF FACULTIES

Animal Science: Dr EDUARDO AIZPURU GARCIA
Agronomy: Dr MARCO ANTONIO BUSTAMANTE G.
Engineering: M. C. LUIS M. LASSO MENDOZA
Social and Economics Science: Ing. FRANCISCO MARTINEZ GOMEZ

UNIVERSIDAD AUTÓNOMA DE BAJA CALIFORNIA

Apdo Postal 459, Avda Alvaro Obregón y Julian Carrillo s/n, 21100 Mexicali, Baja California

Telephone and fax: (65) 54-22-00

Founded 1957
Language of instruction: Spanish
Academic year: August to June

Rector: Lic. LUIS JAVIER GARAVITO ELÍAS
Vice-Rector: M. C. JUAN JOSÉ SEVILLA GARCÍA
Secretary-General: M. C. ROBERTO DE JESÚS VERDUGO DÍAZ
Librarian: Ing. JULIO CÉSAR VELARDE MEZA

Number of teachers: 3,099
Number of students: 21,548

Publications: *Caláfia, Cuadernos de Ciencias Sociales, Cuaderno de Taller Literario, Estudios Fronterizos, Revistas Universitarias, Divulgare, Semillero, Yubai, Paradigmas.*

PRINCIPALS

Mexicali Campus:

School of Accountancy and Administration: M. A. ROSA ELISA PÉREZ REYES
Faculty of Architecture: Arq. ANA MARÍA FERNÁNDEZ BUTCHART
Faculty of Odontology: C. D. MANUEL OSCAR LARA BETANCOURT
Faculty of Humanities: M. A. MARCO ANTONIO VILLA VARGAS
School of Engineering: Ing. VICTOR HUGO AMARO HERNÁNDEZ
Faculty of Law: Lic. DANIEL SOLORIO RAMÍREZ
School of Medicine: Dr JAIME E. HURTADO DE MENDOZA BATIZ
School of Nursing: Enf. MARÍA IRMA RUÍZ CHÁVEZ
School of Social Sciences: Lic. OSCAR ORTEGA VELEZ
School of Pedagogy: Prof. JESÚS ACEVES GUTIÉRREZ
School of Languages: Lic. KORA EVANGELINA BASICH PERALTA

Tijuana Campus:

Faculty of Accountancy and Administration: C.P. JOSÉ RAÚL ROBLES CORTEZ
Faculty of Chemistry: Dr JOSÉ MANUEL CORNEJO BRAVO
Faculty of Law: Lic. GUSTAVO ESPINOZA ULLOA
Faculty of Economics: Lic. RAMÓN DE JESÚS RAMÍREZ ACOSTA
Faculty of Medicine: Dr JOSÉ LORENZO ALVARADO GONZÁLEZ
Faculty of Odontology: Dr MIGUEL ANGEL CADENA ALCÁNTAR
School of Tourism: Lic. ONÉSIMO CUAMEA VELÁZQUEZ
School of Humanities: Lic. ROGELIO ARENAS MONREAL

Ensenada Campus:

School of Accountancy and Administration: L. A. E. GILDARDO TERRIQUEZ MARDUEÑO
Faculty of Marine Sciences: M. C. GUILLERMO TORRES MOYE
Faculty of Sciences: M. C. IRMA RIVERA GARIBALDI
School of Engineering: M. C. JOSÉ DE JESÚS ZAMARRIPA TOPETE

Tecate Campus:

DIRECTOR

School of Engineering: Quim. SERGIO VALE SÁNCHEZ

DIRECTORS OF RESEARCH INSTITUTES

Geography and History Institute (Mexicali Campus): Dr Ing. ADALBERTO WALTHER MEADE
Engineering Institute (Mexicali Campus): Dr MARGARITO QUINTERO NÚÑEZ
Social Research Institute (Mexicali Campus): M. C. ANA MARÍA AVILEZ NUÑEZ
Agriculture and Stockbreeding Research Institute: M. C. LUIS FERNANDO ESCOBOZA GARCÍA
Veterinary Science and Research Institute: M. C. ALEJANDRO PLASCENCIA JORQUERA
Educative Development and Research Institute: Mtro EDUARDO BACKHOFF ESCUDERO
Oceanology Research Institute (Ensenada Campus): M. C. EFRAÍN GUTIÉRREZ GALINDO
History Research Centre (Tijuana Campus): Lic. MARCO ANTONIO SAMANIEGO LÓPEZ

UNIVERSIDAD DEL BAJIO

Apdo Postal 1-444, 37000 Léon, Gto
Telephone: (47) 17-17-40
Fax: (47) 18-55-11

Founded 1968
Private Control
Academic year: August to December, February to June

Rector: Mtro RONALDO HENDERSON CALDERON
Vice-Rector: Mtro CESAR RANGEL BARRERA
Registrar: Lic. JOSE L. REGULES FAJARDO
Librarian: Lic. ALMA ROSA HERNÁNDEZ GARCÍA

Number of teachers: 730
Number of students: 6,450

Publications: *Espíritu Lasallista* (monthly), *Cuadernos* (2 a year).

DIRECTORS OF FACULTIES

Accountancy Administration and International Marketing: SARA BERTHA ROCHA VILLASEÑOR
Agronomy: Ing. PATRICIA MENA HERNANDEZ
Architecture: Arq. MIGUEL ANGEL GARCÍA GÓMEZ
Communication Sciences: Lic. GERARDO GONZALEZ DEL CASTILLO SILVA
Computing Engineering: Ing. EDEL ESPINO LEDESMA
Dentistry: Dr JOSÉ ALEJANDRO SEGOVIA GALLARDO
Engineering: Ing. RAFAEL BONILLA LIRA
Industrial, Environmental and Graphic Design: Lic. LUIS E. CERVANTES FERNANDEZ
Law: Lic. CARLOS V. MUÑOZ JIMÉNEZ
Telecommunications Engineering: Ing. JAIME PALACIOS CASTAÑÓN
Tourism and Hotel Studies: RODOLFO MUJICA SANTOYO
Veterinary Studies: M. V. Z. JESÚS ALVAREZ PEREZ
Preparatory School: Dr SALVADOR MUÑOZ SOLIS
Graduate School of Administration: Lic. GUSTAVO A. HERNANDEZ MORENO
Graduate School of Architecture: M. A. GREGORIO G. DE LA ROSA FALCON
Graduate School of Dentistry: Dr ENRIQUE NIEMBRO CAMPUZANO
Graduate School of Education: Lic. MANUEL CASTRO VILLICAÑA
Graduate School of Electronics and Computational Engineering: Ing. JAIME PALACIOS CASTAÑÓN

San Francisco del Rincón Campus: 550 students; Dir Ing. FELIPE AGUILERA MOTA.

Salamanca Campus: 750 students; Dir Lic. LUIS ERNESTO RIOS PEREZ.

UNIVERSIDAD AUTÓNOMA DEL CARMEN

Calle 31 × 56 s/n, 24176 Ciudad del Carmen, Camp.

Telephone: 2-11-33

Founded 1967

Rector: Ing. PEDRO OCAMPO CALDERÓN
Secretary-General: Lic. RAFAEL HUGO GARCÍA MORENO
Chief Administrative Officer: Lic. HILDA LÓPEZ LÓPEZ
Librarian: C. OLGA SÁNCHEZ PÉREZ

Number of teachers: 340
Number of students: 4,484

Publications: *Voz Universitaria, Senda Universitaria.*

Faculties of commerce and administration, law, chemistry, education.

UNIVERSIDAD AUTÓNOMA CHAPINGO

Domicilio Conocido, 56230 Chapingo, Edo de México

Telephone: 595-42200
Fax: 595-45006

Founded 1854 as Escuela Nacional de Agricultura; named changed 1978
Government control
Academic year: August to June

Rector: Dr IGNACIO MÉNDEZ RAMIREZ
Technical Secretary: Ing. SAID INFANTE GIL

Administrative Secretary: Dr JUAN A. LEOS RODRÍGUEZ
Librarian: ROSA MARÍA OJEDA TREJO

Library: see Libraries

Number of teachers: 932
Number of students: 5,163

Publications: *Revista Chapingo, Revista de Geografía Agrícola, Revista Textual.*

Depts of agricultural economics, agroecology, agricultural industries, irrigation, agricultural machinery, parasitology, phytotechnics, forestry, stock-breeding, soil science, rural sociology.

DIRECTORS OF GRADUATE COURSES

Rural Sociology: Ing. EMILIO LÓPEZ GÁMEZ
Agricultural Economics: M. C. ERNESTO ESCALANTE C.
Phytotechnics: Ing. JESÚS MA. GARZA LÓPEZ
Forestry: Ing. SAUL B. MONREAL RANGEL
Stockbreeding: M. C. JOSÉ SOLÍS RAMÍREZ

UNIVERSIDAD AUTÓNOMA DE CHIAPAS

Colina Universitaria, Carretera Panamericana Km. 1080, Blvd Belisario Domínguez, 29000 Tuxtla Gutiérrez, Chiapas

Telephone: 5-08-27
Fax: 5-06-64

Founded 1975
Private control
Academic year: September to July (two semesters)

Rector: Ing. PEDRO RENÉ BODEGAS VALERA
Secretary-General: LUIS MANUEL MARTÍNEZ ESTRADA
Academic Secretary: Ing. ROBERTO CRUZ DE LEÓN
Librarian: Lic. DOLORES SERRANO CANCINO

Number of teachers: 906
Number of students: 12,052

Publication: *Gaceta Universitaria*

DIRECTORS

Campus I (Tuxtla Gutiérrez):
Faculty of Accounting and Administration: C.P. CESAR MAZA GONZÁLEZ
School of Civil Engineering: Ing. ROBERTON Y CRUZ DIAZ
Faculty of Architecture: Arq. RICARDO GUILLÉN CASTAÑEDA

Campus II (Tuxtla Gutiérrez):
Faculty of Human Medicine: Dr JOSÉ LUIS AQUINO HERNÁNDEZ
School of Veterinary Medicine and Zootechnics: MVZ. ALBERTO YAMAZAKI MAZA

Campus III (San Cristóbal de las Casas):
Faculty of Law: Lic. ALFONSO RAMÍREZ MARTÍNEZ
Faculty of Social Sciences: JORGE ALBERTO LÓPEZ AREVALO

Campus IV (Tapachula):
Faculty of Accounting: C.P. JORGE FERNANDO ORDAZ RUÍZ
Faculty of Administration Sciences: KENY ORDAZ ESCOBAR
School of Chemical Sciences: JOSÉ RAMÓN PUIG COTA
Faculty of Agriculture: Ing. ALFONSO PÉREZ ROMERO

Campus V (Villaflores):
School of Agronomy: Dr ALFREDO MEDINA MELÉNDEZ

Campus VI (Tuxtla Gutiérrez):
Faculty of Humanities: CARLOS RINCÓN RAMÍREZ

UNIVERSIDAD AUTÓNOMA DE CHIHUAHUA

Escorza y Venustiano Carranza s/n, Apdo Postal 324, 31000 Chihuahua, Chih.

Telephone: (14) 15-24-27
Fax: (14) 15-93-85
E-mail: xvenegas@uachnet.mx

Founded 1954
Language of instruction: Spanish
Academic year: August to June

Rector: Dr JESÚS ENRIQUE GRAJEDA HERRERA
Secretary-General: Dr JESÚS XAVIER VENEGAS HOLGUÍN
Administrative Director: C.P. y L.A.E. GABRIELA RICO CABRERA
Librarian: C.P. FERNANDO SALOMÓN BEYER

Number of teachers: 1,428
Number of students: 12,429

Publications: various faculty journals.

DIRECTORS

Faculty of Accountancy and Administration: C.P. y M.A. FRANCISCO JAVIER LUJÁN DE LA GARZA
Faculty of Engineering: Ing. ARTURO LEAL BEJARANO
Faculty of Medicine: Dr CARLOS ENRIQUE MORALES ORTEGA
Faculty of Law: Lic. MARIO TREVISO SALAZAR
Faculty of Chemical Sciences: Ing. MANUEL RUIZ ESPARZA MEDINA
School of Nursing and Nutrition Science: M.E.M.I. ROSA MARÍA DOZAL MOLINA
Faculty of Stockbreeding: Dr GUILLERMO VILLALOBOS VILLALOBOS
Faculty of Agriculture and Forestry: M.S. ARTURO JAVIER OBANDO RODRÍGUEZ
Faculty of Agricultural Engineering: M.C. ALMA PATRICIA HERNÁNDEZ RODRÍGUEZ
Faculty of Physical Education and Sport Science: L.E.F. PRIMO ALBERTO GUNZÁLEZ ARZATE
Faculty of Philosophy and Literature: Lic. ISELA YOLANDA DE PABLO PORRAS
Faculty of Political and Social Sciences: Lic. SAMUEL GARCÍA SOTO
School of International Economics: Lic. MANUEL PARGA MUÑOZ
School of Dentistry: Dr JESÚS DUARTE MAYAGOITIA
Institute of Fine Arts: Lic. RUBEN TINAJERO MEDINA

ATTACHED INSTITUTES

Higher School of Graphic Communication: Dir Ing. JUAN RUÍZ TRUJILLO.

School of Architecture of Chihuahua: Dir Arq. EDUARDO GONZÁLEZ TEJEDA.

School of Psychology: Dir Lic. ROSARIO VALDÉZ CARAVEO.

Sigmund Freud School of Psychology and Pedagogy: Dir Lic. ELVA HERNÁNDEZ ALVÍDREZ.

Higher Institute of Architecture and Design: Dir Arq. CARLOS HÉCTOR CARRERA ROBLES.

School of Nursing of the Centro Médico de Especialidades, S.A., Ciudad Juárez: Dir Dr SERGIO ANTONIO ESPEJO POSADAS.

School of Nursing and Obstetrics of the General Hospital, Ciudad Juárez: Dir Dra ADRIANA SAUCEDO GARCÍA.

School of Nursing, Hidalgo del Parral: Dir Enf. LETICIA S. DE CHÁVEZ.

School of Nursing of the Hospital de Jesús: Dir Lic. NATALIA MORALES MONFIL.

School of Nursing of the Regional Hospital, Ciudad Cuauhtémoc: Dir Enf. CARMEN GUTIÉRREZ.

Nursing Educational Centre, El Parque: Dir Lic. Enf. TERESA DE JESÚS MENDOZA VIDAÑA.

School of Nursing and Obstetrics of the Sanatorio Palmore: Dir Enf. MARISELA PÉREZ DE LEÓN.

School of Nursing and Health Science Skills: Dir Enf. ARMIDA AVITIA DE RODRÍGUEZ.

School of Nursing, Ciudad Delicias: Dir Enf. FRANCISCO JAVIER LÓPEZ DÁVALOS.

UNIVERSIDAD AUTÓNOMA DE COAHUILA

Blvd Constitución y Durango, Apdo Postal 308, 25280 Saltillo, Coahuila

Telephone: 2-01-55

Founded 1867, refounded 1957
State control
Language of instruction: Spanish
Academic year: August to June (two terms)

Rector: L.Ab. OSCAR VILLEGAS RICO
Secretary-General: L.Ab.L. ALBERTO L. SALAZAR RODRÍGUEZ
Librarian: ANTONIO MALACARA

Number of teachers: *c.* 900
Number of students: 13,923

UNIVERSIDAD DE COLIMA

Avda Universidad 333, Apdo Postal 134, 28000 Colima, Col.

Telephone: 2-54-36
Telex: 62248
Fax: (331) 4-30-06

Founded 1940 as Universidad Popular de Colima, reorganized 1962
State control
Language of instruction: Spanish
Academic year: August to January, February to July

Rector: Lic. FERNANDO MORENO PEÑA
Secretary-General: Ing. LORENZO HERNANDEZ ARREGUIN
Librarian: Lic. LOURDES FERIA

Number of teachers: 1,204
Number of students: 10,517

Publications: *Estudios Sobre las Culturas Contemporaneas.*

DEANS AND DIRECTORS

School of Social and Political Sciences: Lic. ROBERTO PRECIADO CUEVAS
School of Economics: Lic. JOSE DE JESUS LOMELI PEÑA
School of Arts and Communications: Lic. MANUEL DELGADO CASTRO
School of Social Studies: Licda GABRIELA MARTINEZ GONZALEZ
Higher School of Educational Science: Prof. MARIO ENRIQUEZ CASILLAS
Higher School of Nursing: Licda GENOVENA AMADOR FIERROS
School of Languages: LUIS E. PIZA ESPINOSA
School of Chemical Science: Ing. JORGE DE JESUS ORDAZ MARTINEZ
School of Accountancy and Administration 1: C.P. LUCIANO GARCIA ROMERO
School of Accountancy and Administration 2: JOSE MARTIN TORRES RIOS
School of Medicine, Veterinary Studies and Zoology: HECTOR JAVIER LOPEZ PEREZ
School of Electro-mechanical Engineering: JAIME CRUZ ROSETE
Higher School of Marine Science: CARLOS CHAVEZ COMPARAN
Faculty of Accountancy and Administration: C.P. GUILLERMO TORRES GARCIA
Faculty of Law: Lic. JESUS FRANCISCO COELLO TORRES
Faculty of Medicine: Dr CHRISTIAN J. TORRES O.
Faculty of Education: SARA GRISELDA MARTINEZ COVARRUBIAS
Faculty of Architecture: Arq. LUIS GABRIEL GOMEZ AZPEITIA
Faculty of Civil Engineering: Ing. JUAN DE LA C. TEJEDA JACOME
Faculty of Biological Sciences and Agronomy: Ing. MARCELINO BAZAN TENE

UNIVERSIDAD JUÁREZ DEL ESTADO DE DURANGO

Constitución 404, Sur, 34000 Durango, Durango

Telephone: 2-00-44

Founded as a Civil College 1856, became University 1957
Private control
Language of instruction: Spanish
Academic year: January to June, August to December

Rector: Dr JORGE RAMÍREZ DÍAZ
Secretary-General: C.P. JUAN FRANCISCO SALAZAR BENÍTEZ
Chief Administrative Officer: T.S. ADRIANA AVELAR VILLEGAS
Librarian: A.B. JOSÉ LINO HERNÁNDEZ CAMPOS

Number of teachers: 1,116
Number of students: 20,160

DEANS

Faculty of Accountancy and Administration: C.P. MARÍA MAGDALENA MEDINA CÓRDOBA M.A.
Faculty of Law: Lic. VICENTE GUERRERO ITURBE
Faculty of Medicine: Dr JORGE RUIZ LEÓN
Faculty of Veterinary Medicine and Zootechnics: M.V.Z. RAÚL RANGEL ROMERO
School of Dentistry: C.D. MIGUEL ROJAS REGALADO
School of Social Work: T.S. MARÍA ANTONIA HERNÁNDEZ ESCAREÑO
School of Chemical Sciences: Ing. ENRIQUE TORRES CABRAL
School of Applied Mathematics: Ing. UBALDO ARENAS JUÁREZ
School of Forestry: Ing. ALFONSO HERRERA AYÓN
School of Nursing and Obstetrics: Lic. MARÍA ELENA VALDEZ DE REYES
School of Music: Prof. ABRAHAM E. VIGGERS ARREOLA
School of Painting, Sculpture and Crafts: Prof. FRANCISCO MONTOYA DE LA CRUZ

Gómez Palacio Campus:

School of Agriculture and Stockbreeding: Ing. JESÚS JOSÉ QUIÑONES VERA
School of Biology: BIOL. M.C. RAÚL DÍAZ MORENO
School of Medicine: Dr LUIS DE VILLA VÁZQUEZ
School of Civil Engineering: Ing. EVERARDO F. DELGADO SOLIS
School of Food Science and Technology: Ing. GERARDO FRANCISCO ALDANA RUIZ

ATTACHED INSTITUTES

Instituto de Investigación Científica (Institute of Scientific Research): Dir MARÍA DEL ROSARIO RUIZ A.

Instituto de Ciencias Sociales (Institute of Social Sciences): Dir Lic. MIGUEL PALACIOS MONCAYO.

Instituto de Investigaciones Históricas (Institute of Historical Research): Dir Lic. MARÍA GUADALUPE RODRIGUEZ LÓPEZ.

Instituto de Investigaciones Jurídicas (Institute of Legal Research): Dir Lic. ANGEL ISMAEL MEJORADO OLAGUEZ.

Museo de Antropología e Historia (Anthropology and History Museum): Dir Lic. ANGEL RODRÍGUEZ SOLÓRZANO.

UNIVERSIDAD DEL GOLFO

Obregón 203 Pte, Zona Centro, Tampico, Tam. 89000

Telephone: (12) 12-92-22
Fax: (12) 12-92-22
E-mail: unigolfo@tamps1.telmex.net.mx

Founded 1972
Private control
Languages of instruction: English, German, Spanish
Academic year: September to July

Rector: Dr HERIBERTO FLORENCIA MENÉNDEZ
Vice-Rector: Lic. HILARIO ZUÑIGA MENCHACA
Chief Administrative Officer: Lic. MARCO ANTONIO MALDONADO LUGO
Librarian: JUANA PIZAÑA MÁRQUEZ

Library of 25,000 vols
Number of teachers: 25 full-time, 123 part-time
Number of students: 2,300

DIRECTORS

Faculty of Accounting and Administration: Lic. IRMA DELIA ALEXANDRE RIVAS
Faculty of Law: Lic. PASCUAL MORA MORALES
Faculty of Economics and Computing: Ing. FRANCISCO DÍAZ FERNÁNDEZ
European Faculty for Foreign Students: Dr HERIBERTO FLORENCIA MENÉNDEZ (Dean)
Postgraduate Studies: Lic. PABLO JOSÉ JIMÉNEZ Y ALCORTA

UNIVERSIDAD DE GUADALAJARA

Avda Juárez 975, Sector Juárez, 44100 Guadalajara, Jal.

Telephone: (36) 825-88-88

Founded 1792, restructured 1925
State control
Academic year: September to August

Rector: Dr VICTOR MANUEL GONZALEZ ROMERO
Secretary-General: Lic. JOSE TRINIDAD PADILLA LOPEZ
Chief Administrative Officer: Ing. ADOLFO ESPINOZA DE LOS MONTEROS CARDENAS
Librarian: Mtra PASTORA RODRIGUEZ AVIÑOA

Library: see Libraries
Number of teachers: 10,269
Number of students: 214,986

Publications: *Revista Universidad de Guadalajara* (quarterly), *Gaceta*, *Jures*, and various faculty and departmental publs.

UNIVERSITY CENTRES

Art, Architecture and Design: Rector Arq. AGUSTIN PARODI UREÑA.

Health Sciences: Rector Dr JORGE ENRIQUE SEGURA ORTEGA.

Exact and Engineering Sciences: Rector Mtro HECTOR ENRIQUE SALGADO RODRIGUEZ.

Biological Sciences and Farming: Rector M. en C. SALVADOR MENA MUNGUIA.

Economic and Administrative Sciences: Rector Mtro IXCOATL TONATIUH BRAVO PADILLA.

Social Sciences and Humanities: Rector Lic. CARLOS FREGOSO GENNIS.

El Sur: Rector Lic. en Biol. JESUS ALBERTO ESPINOSA ARIAS.

La Cienega: Rector Mtro CARLOS JORGE BRISEÑO TORRES.

La Costa: Rector M. en C. JEFFRY STEVENS FERNANDEZ RODRIGUEZ.

La Costa Sur: Rector Mtro SALVADOR ACOSTA ROMERO.

Los Altos: Rectora Q. F. B. RUTH PADILLA MUÑOZ.

UNIVERSIDAD AUTÓNOMA DE GUADALAJARA

Apdo Postal 1-440, 44100 Guadalajara, Jalisco
Telephone: 641-50-51
Telex: 6822785
Fax: 642-54-27

Founded 1935
Private control
Language of instruction: Spanish
Academic year: August to June

Rector: Dr LUIS GARIBAY GUTIÉRREZ
Vice-Rector: Lic. ANTONIO LEAÑO ALVAREZ DEL CASTILLO
Chief Administrative Officer: Ing. JUAN JOSÉ LEAÑO ALVAREZ DEL CASTILLO
Librarian: Lic. ALBERTO OLIVARES DUARTE

Library of 178,000 vols, 3,760 maps, 3,400 periodicals
Number of teachers: 1,622
Number of students: 14,102

Publications: *Docencia* (3 a year), *Alma Mater* (monthly), *Nexo Universitario* (2 a month), *Actas de la Facultad de Medicina* (2 a year), *Boletín* (monthly), *Notiteco* (monthly), *Ocho Columnas* (daily).

DEANS AND DIRECTORS

Humanities and Social Sciences: Dir of Academic Affairs: Lic. ISMAEL ZAMORA TOVAR
School of Anthropology: Lic. CRISTINA RUÍZ DE HERNÁNDEZ
School of Architecture: Arq. RAÚL MENDOZA RIVERA
School of Graphic Design: Lic. CARLOS HERRERA PÉREZ
School of Law and Social Work: Lic. HUMBERTO LÓPEZ DELGADILLO
School of Business Administration: Ing. GUSTAVO GONZÁLEZ HERNÁNDEZ
School of Public Accountancy: C.P. RODRIGO CEDEÑO
School of Economics: Lic. JOSÉ LUIS SÁNCHEZ DE LA FUENTE
School of Tourism: Lic. CELINA GALLEGOS SATO
School of Linguistics: Prof. FERNANDO TORRES DE LA TORRE
School of Communication Sciences: Lic. EVA PATRICIA OROZCO DE GUERRERO
School of Psychology: Lic. GABRIEL HERNÁNDEZ MORALES
School of Pedagogy: Dra TERESITA CASTILLO DE SÁINZ
School of Industrial Design: Arq. FERNANDO GONZÁLEZ SUGASTI
School of Interior Design: SUSANA MAYTORENA MARTÍNEZ NEGRETE
School of Secretarial Science: Profa GUADALUPE CAMACHO CASILLAS

School of Nursing: Enf. MA GLORIA E. DE LA CERDA HERNÁNDEZ
Faculty of Medicine: Dr NÉSTOR VELASCO PÉREZ
School of Dentistry: Dr RAFAEL CHACÓN VARELA
Science and Technology: Dir of Academic Affairs Ing. ANTONIO E. PEIMBERTD VELARDE
Mechanical and Electrical Engineering: Ing. MANUEL URIARTE RAZO
School of Chemical Science: Ing. ANTONIO PEIMERTD VELARDE
School of Civil Engineering: Ing. MIGUEL ANGEL PARRA MENA
School of Mathematics: Ing. EDUARDO MANUEL OJEDA PEÑA
School of Information Management and Computer Systems: Ing. RAFAEL JAIME A.
School of Biology: Dr MAURICIO ALCOCER RUTHLING
Agricultural Engineering: Biol. MAURICIO ALCOCER RUTHLING
Computer Engineering: Ing. RAFAEL JAIME ALEJO

Postgraduate Studies: Lic. HUMBERTO LÓPEZ DELGADILLO
Continuing Education: Arq. JOSÉ MORALES GONZÁLEZ
University in the Community: Lic. RICARDO BELTRÁN ROJAS
Special Projects: Lic. JUAN JOSÉ LEAÑO ESPINOSA
International Programmes: Biol. JOSÉ LUIS ARREGUÍN ROMERO
Centre for Asian and Latin American Studies: Prof. FERNANDO TORRES DE LA TORRE

ATTACHED INSTITUTES

Institute of Biological Sciences: Dir Dr FRANCISCO RODRÍGUEZ GONZÁLEZ.

Institute of Exact and Earth Sciences: Dir Ing. ANTONIO PEIMBERTD VELARDE.

Institute of Humanities: Dir Lic. ISMAEL ZAMORA TOVAR.

Institute of Comparative International Higher Education: Dir Lic. RICARDO BELTRAN ROJAS.

Hospital 'Dr Angel Leaño': Dir Dr LEONEL SOLÍS MENA.

Hospital 'Dr Ramón Garibay': Dir JESÚS CASTILLO PACHECO.

Dental Clinic: Dir ROGELIO HINOJOSA TORRES.

UNIVERSIDAD DE GUANAJUATO

Lascuráin de Retana No. 5, 36000 Guanajuato

Telephone: 2-03-04
Fax: 2-71-48

Founded 1732 as Colegio de la Purísima Concepción; changed in 1928 to Colegio del Estado; present name 1945
State control

Rector: Lic. JUAN CARLOS ROMERO HICKS
Secretary: Dr SILVIA ALVAREZ BRUNELIERE
Librarian: Mtra ROSALIA MACIAS RODRIGUEZ

Library of 160,000 vols
Number of teachers: 1,809
Number of students: 18,400

Publications: *Colmena Universitaria* (quarterly), *Acta Universitaria*.

DIRECTORS

School of Law: Dr MANUEL VIDAURRI ARECHIQUE
Schools of Accountancy and Administration: BENITO ARTURO SILVA LULE, L.A.E. RENE MARTINEZ AVILA (Celaya)
School of Architecture: Arq. HÉCTOR BRAVO GALVÁN
School of Mining Engineering: ROBERTO DÍAZ FLORES
School of Civil Engineering: Ing. ELOY JUAREZ SANDOVAL
School of Hydraulic Engineering and Topography: Ing. MARTIN FERNANDEZ
School of Philosophy and Letters: Dr LUIS FERNANDO MACIAS GARCÍA
Schools of Nursing: Lic. VICTORIA MORAN AGUILAR (Guanajuato), Lic. ANA MARIA PADILLA (Celaya), Lic. (vacant) (Irapuato), Lic. PATRICIA CATALINA MARTÍNEZ (León)
School of Chemistry: Q. FERNANDO AMEZQUITA
School of Medicine: Dr JOSÉ ANGEL CÓRDOVA VILLALOBOS
School of Agronomy and Animal Husbandry: Dr JOSÉ LUIS BARRERA GUERRA
School of Industrial Relations: SEBASTIÁN SANBORRO LASTIRI
School of Design: EUGENIA TENORIO NÚÑEZ
Language Centre: Lic. CLAUDIA PATRICIA BEGNE RUIZ ESPAZRA
School of Mechanical and Electrical Engineering: Ing. RENE JAIME RIVAS
School of Music: Ing. ARMANDO LÓPEZ VALDIVIA
School of Plastic Arts: Arq. JOSÉ ESCALERA CHAGOYAN
School of Psychology: Dra MARÍA DEL CARMEN VARGAS VIVERO
Professional School of Accounting: C.P. PEDRO GONZALEZ
School of Mathematics: Dr ARTURO AGUSTÍN RAMÍREZ FLORES

ATTACHED INSTITUTES

Institute of Experimental Biological Research: Dir Dr FÉLIX GUTIÉRREZ CORONA.

Institute of Agricultural Sciences: Dir Dr JUAN MANUEL CABRERA SIXTO.

Institute of Humanistic Research: Dir Mtro LUIS RIONDA ARREGUÍN.

Inorganic Chemistry Research Institute: Dir Ing. SALVADOR AGUILAR BECERRA.

Department of Law Studies: Lic. NESTOR RAUL LUNA HERNANDEZ.

Department for Research: Dr SERGIO ARJAS NEGRETE.

Department of Library and Information Science: Mtra ROSALIA MACIAS RODRIGUEZ.

Medical Research Institute: Dir Dr JUAN MANUEL MALACARA HERNÁNDEZ.

Research Institute for Work Performance in Industry: Dir Dr FRANCISCO JOSÉ DÍAZ CISNEROS.

Institute of Scientific Research: Dir Dr PEDRO LUIS LÓPEZ DE ALBA.

Institute of Educational Research: Dir Mtra MARÍA DEL CARMEN SANDOVAL MENDOZA.

Astronomical and Meteorological Observatory: Dir Ing. J. JESÚS AVILA RANGEL.

Institute of Physics: Dir Dr OCTAVIO OBREGÓN DÍAZ.

Centre for Social and Administrative Research: MARÍA DEL CARMEN PAULA CEBADA CONTRERAS.

UNIVERSIDAD AUTÓNOMA DE GUERRERO

Abasolo 33, 03900 Chilpancingo, Guerrero

Telephone: 2-25-36

Founded 1869
Private control
Language of instruction: Spanish
Academic year: August to June

Rector: Ing. Agron. RAMÓN REYES CARRETO
General Secretary: M. C. CATALINO MACEDO VENCES
Librarian: Lic. ROBERT ALEXANDER ENDEAN GAMBOA

Number of teachers: 1,600
Number of students: 49,000

Publications: *Revista de la UAG, Gaceta Popular, Otatal.*

DIRECTORS

Higher School of Agriculture: Q.B. GILBERTO BIBIANO MORENO
School of Engineering: Ing. RODOLFO VÁZQUEZ ZEFERINO
School of Chemical-Biological Sciences: Q. B. P. MARCO ANTONIO LEYVA VÁZQUEZ
School of Marine Ecology: Biol. ARMANDO YOKOYAMA KANO
School of Medicine: Dr ASCENCIO VILLEGAS ARRIZON
School of Commerce and Administration: C.P. SALVADOR OLIVAR CAMPOS
Higher School of Tourism: Lic. ARMANDO BELLO RODRÍGUEZ
School of Economics: M. C. S. ANGEL CRESPO ACEVEDO
School of Law: Lic. ALEJANDRO BERNABE GONZÁLEZ
School of Philosophy: Lic. FAUSTO AVILA JUÁREZ
School of Veterinary Medicine and Animal Husbandry: M. V. Z. SALVADOR SÁNCHEZ PADILLA
School of Social Sciences: Lic. ANGEL ASCENCIO ROMERO
School of Architecture and Town Planning: Arq. CLAUDIO RIOS TORRES
Regional School of Earth Sciences: Geol. GERMÁN URBAN LAMADRID

UNIVERSIDAD AUTÓNOMA DE HIDALGO

Abasolo No. 600, Centro, 42000 Pachuca, Hidalgo

Telephone: 2-65-34

Founded 1869 as the Instituto Científico y Literario, present status 1961
Academic year: September to June

Rector: Lic. JUAN ALBERTO FLORES ÁLVAREZ
Secretary: Lic. JORGE HIRAM ROSSETTE PENAGOS
Registrar: L.A.E. JORGE DEL CASTILLO TOVAR
Librarian: Lic. EVARISTO LUVIAN TORRES

Number of teachers: *c.* 700
Number of students: *c.* 9,000

Publications: *Revista Técnica de Información, Boletín Informativo, Informe Anual de Rectoría.*

COURSE CO-ORDINATORS

Science and Technology: Ing. CARLOS HERRERA ORDOÑEZ
Professional Studies: Lic. YOLANDA MEJÍA VELASCO
Education: Quim. F.B. SILVIA PARGA MATEOS
Special Studies: Lic. FRANCISCO MURILLO BUTRON

DIRECTORS OF SCHOOLS AND INSTITUTES

Institute of Accountancy and Administration: C.P. HORACIO SOLIS LEYVA
Institute of Exact Sciences: Ing. JOSÉ CALDERÓN HERNÁNDEZ
Institute of Social Sciences: Lic. ALEJANDRO STRAFFON ARTEAGA
School of Medicine: Dr LUIS CORZO MONTAÑO
School of Odontology: Dr MIGUEL ANGEL ANTON DE LA C.
School of Nursing: Enf. LUZ MARÍA FLORES RAMÍREZ
School of Social Work: T.S. IMELDA MONROY DEL ANGEL
Preparatory School I: Ing. ERNESTO HERNÁNDEZ OCAÑA
Preparatory School II: Lic. LAURO PEREA MONTIEL
Preparatory School III: Lic. JUAN MANUEL CAMACHO BERTRAN

UNIVERSIDAD IBEROAMERICANA

Prolongación Paseo de la Reforma 880, Col. Lomas de Santa Fé, 01210 México, DF

Telephone: 292-3508
Fax: 292-3008

Founded 1943, University status 1954
Private control
Language of instruction: Spanish
Academic year: August to December, January to May, May to July

Rector: Mtro ENRIQUE GONZÁLEZ TORRES
Director-General (Academic): Mtro ENRIQUE BEASCOECHEA ARANDA
Director of Research and Graduate Programmes: Mtro. JESÚS L. GARCÍA
Librarian: Ing. PILAR VERDEJO

Library of 156,278 vols, 1,420 periodicals
Number of teachers: 279 full-time, 1,389 part-time
Number of students: 9,770 undergraduate, 738 postgraduate

Publications: *Boletín Bibliográfico* (monthly), *Boletín Bolsa de Trabajo* (monthly), *Caldero* (quarterly), *Didac* (2 a year), *Gallo* (5 a year), *Humanidades* (annually), *Idea Económica* (3 a year), *Intercambio Académico* (quarterly), *Jurídica* (annually), *El Ladrillo* (weekly), *Poesía y Poética* (3 a year), *Revista de Filosofía* (quarterly), *Revista del Departamento de Psicología* (3 a year), *Umbral XXI* (quarterly), *Prometeo* (3 a year), *Sociología y Política* (3 a year), *Historia y Grafía* (3 a year).

DIRECTORS OF DEPARTMENTS

Accounting: Mtro JOSÉ L. CHABAUD
Architecture and Urban Planning: Arq. MANUEL BUSTAMANTE ACUÑA
Art: Lic. ESTELA EGUIARTE
Business Administration: Lic. JOAQUÍN PEÓN ESCALANTE

Chemical Engineering: Dr Mario Bravo Medina
Civil Engineering: Ing. Santiago Martínez
Communication: Mtra Carmen Gómez-Mont
Computer Systems: Ing. Benjamín Casar
Economics: Mtro Javier Landa
History: Dra Valentina Torres-Septién
Human Development: Mtra A. M. González
Industrial and Graphic Design: D. I. Patricia Espinosa
Law: Lic. Francisco Borja Martínez
Literature: Dr José Ramón Alcantara Mejía
Mathematics: Fís. Cristóbal Cárdenas Oviedo
Mechanical and Electrical Engineering: Ing. Jorge Olavarrieta de la Torre
Nutrition and Food Sciences: Mtro Héctor E. Cejudo
Philosophy: Lic. Francisco Galán
Political and Social Sciences: Lic. Javier Torres
Psychology: Lic. Clementina Ramírez
Physics: Fís. Enrique Sánchez y Aguilera
Religious Sciences: Lic. Rubén Murillo

REGIONAL CAMPUSES

Universidad Iberoamericana, Plantel León

(León Campus)

Libramiento Norte Km 3, Apdo Postal 1-26, 37000 León, Guanajuato
Telephone: 11-38-60
Fax: 11-54-77
Founded 1978
Private control
Language of instruction: Spanish
Academic year: August to December, January to May, May to July
Rector: Arq. Carlos Velasco
Director-General (Academic): Ing. Miguel Ángel Arredondo
Director-General (University Educational Services): Ing. David Martinez
Registrar: Quím. Mario Alberto Arredondo
Librarian: Ing. José Manuel Córdoba
Library of 102,990 vols, 87 periodicals
Number of teachers: 44 full-time, 21 part-time
Number of students: 1,359 undergraduate, 35 postgraduate
Publication: *Presencia Universitaria* (monthly).

HEADS OF DEPARTMENTS

Art and Design: Arq. Ernesto Padilla
Economic and Administrative Sciences: M. A. Jesús Contreras
Human Sciences: Mtro Héctor Gómez
Law: Lic. Alfonso Fragoso
Engineering and Applied Sciences: Ing. Gonzalo Bayod
Basic Sciences: Ing. Juan Francisco Martínez

Universidad Iberoamericana, Plantel Laguna

(Laguna Campus)

Carretera a San Pedro Km 4 1/2, Apdo Postal 28D, Sucursal Abastos, 27000 Torreón, Coahuila
Telephone: 50-58-57
Fax: 50-55-39
Founded 1982
Private control
Academic year: August to December, January to May, May to July
Rector: Lic. Luis Narro
Director-General (Academic): Lic. Enrique Macías
Director-General (University Educational Services): Rosario Ramos
Registrar: Lic. Jaime Maravilia
Librarian: Lic. Luis Castañeda
Library of 22,000 vols, 205 periodicals
Number of teachers: 80 full-time, 309 part-time
Number of students: 1,700 undergraduate, 72 graduate

HEADS OF DEPARTMENTS

Human Sciences: Lic. Dora Gómez-Palacio
Economic and Administrative Sciences: Mtro Miguel Gamboa
Physics and Mathematics: Ing. Francisco Castro

Universidad Iberoamericana, Plantel Noroeste

(Northwest Campus)

Avda Centro Universitario Educativo s/n, Deleg. San Antonio de los Buenos y Playas de Tijuana, 22000 Tijuana, Baja California
Telephone: (66) 30-15-77
Fax: 30-15-91
Founded 1982
Language of instruction: Spanish
Academic year: August to December, January to May, May to July
Rector: Lic. Agustín Rozada
Director-General (Academic): Dr Victor Pérez
Registrar: Lic. Isabel Huerta
Librarian: Mtro Bernardo Torres
Library of 30,906 vols, 381 periodicals
Number of teachers: 34 full-time, 11 part-time
Number of students: 873 undergraduate, 50 postgraduate

HEADS OF DEPARTMENTS

Architecture: Arq. Manuel Rosen
Communication: Lic. Cecilia Castellanos
Electronics and Communications Engineering: Ing. Francisco J. Rodríguez
Foreign Trade and Customs: Lic. Adalberto Aceuez
Graphic Design: Lic. Raúl Olmos
Law: Lic. Luis Meza
Mechancial and Electrical Engineering: Ing. Vicente Reyes
Nursing: Dr Victor Manuel Caballero
Computer Systems: Ing. Francisco Rodríguez

Universidad Iberoamericana, Plantel Golfo Centro

(Golfo Centro Campus)

Km 3½ Carretera Federal Puebla Atlixco, Apdo Postal 1435, 72430 Puebla, Puebla
Telephone: 30-44-60
Fax: 31-08-86
Founded 1983
Private control
Academic year: August to December, January to May, May to July
Rector: Dr Armando Rugarcía
Director-General (Academic): Dr Alejandro Morales
Director-General (University Educational Services): Arq. Martín López
Registrar: Lic. Francisco J. Martínez
Librarian: Lic. María Eugenia Cabrera
Library of 26,000 vols, 327 periodicals
Number of teachers: 63 full-time, 7 part-time
Number of students: 2,751 undergraduate, 326 postgraduate

HEADS OF DEPARTMENTS

Economic and Administrative Sciences: Lic. Leandro Fernández
Art and Design: María Quijano
Human and Social Sciences: Mtro Diego García y Díaz
Architecture: Francisco Valverde
Engineering and Sciences: Ing. Alfonso Hernández

UNIVERSIDAD INTERCONTINENTAL

Insurgentes Sur 4303, Col. Santa Ursula Xitle, 14000 México, DF
Telephone: 573-87-57
Fax: 655-15-43
Founded 1976
Private control
Academic year: August to July
Rector: Juan José Corona López
General Secretary: José-Luis Vega Arce
Administrative Officer: C.P. José Luis Leon Zamudio
Librarian: Miguel Angel Sánchez Bedolla
Number of teachers: 773
Number of students: 4,500
Publication: *Extensiones, Voces, Psicología y Educación Turismo, Traduic, Intersticios, Boletín Jurídico.*

HEADS OF DEPARTMENTS

Architecture: Arq. Francisco Terrazas Urbina
Communication Sciences: Carlos Chávez López
Accountancy: Alberto González Carrera
Administration: Dr Sergio Chavarría y Aldana
Graphic Design: D. I. Marcela Castro Cantu
Informatics: Dra Victoria Raquel Bajar
International Commercial Relations: Valentina Perea Herrera
Law: Dr Carlos Casillas Velez
Philosophy: Alejandro Gutiérrez Robles
Languages: Lic. Luz Maria Vargas Escobedo
Odontology: Dr Alfredo Locht Miro
Pedagogy: Maria Elena Navarrete Toledo
Psychology: Dr Salvador Castro Aguilera
Theology: Sergio Espinosa González
Tourism: Omar Avendaño Reyes

UNIVERSIDAD AUTÓNOMA DE CIUDAD JUÁREZ

Avda López Mateos 20, 32310 Ciudad Juárez, Chihuahua
Telephone: (16) 16-57-78
Fax: (16) 13-23-34
Founded 1973
State control
Language of instruction: Spanish
Academic year: August to June
President: Rubén Lau Rojo
General Secretary: Carlos González Herrera
Chief Administrative Officer: Fernando Rovelo Camilo
Director of Academic Affairs: Ramón Mario López López
Librarian: Dr Jesús Lau Noriega
Number of teachers: 975
Number of students: 10,000
Publications: *Entorno*, Nóesis.

DEANS

Faculty of Social Sciences: Luis A. Mayorga
Faculty of Science and Engineering: Dr Ramon Parra
Faculty of Health Science: Dr Felipe Fornelli
Faculty of Architecture: Arq. Alfonso Luna
Institute of Engineering and Architecture: Arq. Dilia Prado de Estrada

UNIVERSIDAD DEL VALLE DE MÉXICO

Tehuantepec 250, Colonia Roma Sur, Del. Cuauhtémoc, 06760 México, DF
Telephone: 264-79-33
Fax: 574-04-22
E-mail: jnajera@uvmnet.edu
Founded 1960
Private control
Languages of instruction: Spanish, English and French
Academic year: August to June

President: C.P. Jesús M. Najera Martínez
Rectors: Lic. Luis Silva Guerrero (Region A), Ing. Jaime Pacheco Chávez (Region B), Lic. Patricia Puente H. (Region C), Lic. Silvia Rivera Damián (Region D)
Vice-Rector (Academic Affairs): Lic. Sergio Linares
Head of Administration: Lic. Jesús Carranza
Registrar: Lic. Edith Terán
Librarian: Lic. Salvador Cipres

Number of teachers: 2,300
Number of students: 25,500

Publications: *Adelante* (monthly), *Lince* (monthly), *Academias* (monthly).

DEANS OF CAMPUSES

San Rafael: Lic. María de la Luz Díaz Miranda
Roma: Lic. Guadalupe Zuñiga
San Angel: Lic. Griselda Vega Tato
Tlalpan: Lic. Luis Silva Guerrero
Xochimilco: Lic. Salvador Silva
Guadalupe Insurgentes: Lic. Martha Anides
Chapultepec: Lic. Elizabeth Manning
Lomas Verdes: Lic. Patricia Puente
Querétaro: Lic. Silvia Rivera
San Miguel de Allende: Dr Francisco Martínez
Lago Guadalupe: Lic. Gabriela Mota

UNIVERSIDAD LA SALLE DE MÉXICO

Benjamin Franklin 47, Col. Condesa, Del. Cuauhtémoc, 06140 México, DF; campuses at Cancun, Cuernavaca, Guadalajara, Morelia, Obregón and Pachuca

Telephone: 728-05-00
Fax: 271-85-85

Founded 1962
Private control
Language of instruction: Spanish
Academic year: August to June

Rector: Mtro Lucio Tazzer de Schrijver
Vice-Rector: Ing. Ambrosio Luna Salas
Registrar: Hortensia Negretti
Librarian: Alicia Grave de Vargas de Alba

Number of teachers: 1,100
Number of students: 10,311

Publications: *Gaceta*, *Diez Días*, *Boletín de Preparatoria*, *Boletín de Biblioteca*, *Revista Dirección*, *Revista Médica La Salle*, *Revista Logos*, *Humanitas*, *Reflexiones Universitarias*.

DIRECTORS

School of Preparatory Studies: Mtro Mario Ramírez Pérez
School of Administrative Sciences: Lic. Luis Porragas Ruiz
School of Architecture and Graphic Design: Arq. Oscar H. Castro Almeida
School of Chemistry: Quim. Maria Teresa Estrada de Gómez
Faculty of Law: Dr Luis Rodríguez Manzanera
Faculty of Medicine: Dr José Ramirez Degollado
School of Philosophy: Mtro José Antonio Dacal Alonso
School of Engineering: Ing. Edmundo Barrera Monsivais
School of Religious Sciences: Dr Manuel Alarcón Vázquez
Postgraduate Studies: Mtra María Elena Escalera Jiménez
School of Education: Mtro Carlos David Domínguez Trolle
Research Centre: Dra Aracelli Sánchez de Corral
Humanities: Lic. Rafael Ruiz Ramírez

UNIVERSIDAD AUTÓNOMA METROPOLITANA

Apdo Postal 325, Blvd Manuel Avila Camacho 90, Col. El Parque, Edo. de México, 53390 México, DF

Telephone: 723-56-44
Fax: 576-68-88
E-mail: riebeling@tonatiuh.uam.mx

Founded 1973
State control
Language of instruction: Spanish
Academic year: September to July

Rector-General: Julio Rubio Oca
Secretary-General: Magdalena Fresan Orozco
Librarian: Kamila Knap Roubal

Number of teachers: 3,700
Number of students: 45,000

Publication: *Semanario de la UAM* (weekly), *Casa del Tiempo* (monthly), *Revista Iztapalapa* (2 a year), *Revista A* (2 a year), *Diseño UAM* (3 a year), *Economía, Teoría y Práctica Sociológica, Pauta, Contactos* (6 a year), *Alegatos* (3 a year), El Cotidiano (6 a year), *Reencuentro* (irregular), *Topodrilo* (6 a year), *Universidad Futura* (irregular), *Argumentos* (3 a year).

Azcapotzalco Campus: Apdo postal 306, Av. San Pablo 180, Col. Reynosa-Tamaulipas, Del. Azcapotzalco, 02000 México, DF; tel. 382-41-32.

Rector: Edmundo Jacobo Molina
Secretary: Jordy Micheli Thirión
Librarian: Fernando Velázquez Merlo

DIRECTORS

Basic Sciences and Engineering: Ana Marisela Maubert Franco
Social Sciences and Humanities: Monica de la Garza Malo
Design, Arts and Sciences: Jorge Sánchez de Antuñano Barranco

HEADS OF DEPARTMENT

Basic Sciences: José Rubén Luevano Enríquez
Electronics: Rafael Quintero Torres
Energy: Silvye Turpin Morion
Materials: Antonio Martín Lunas Zarandieta
Systems: Angel Hernández Rodríguez
Business: Anahí Gallardo Velázquez
Law: Gerardo González Ascencio
Economics: Ernesto Turner Barragán
Humanities: Begoña Arteta Gamerdinger
Sociology: Paz Trigueros Legarreta
Evaluation and Design: Francisco José Santos Zertuche
Design Research and Information: Julia Vargas Rubio
Environment: Saúl Alcantara Onofre
Realization and Technique: Hector Schwabe Mayagoitia

Iztapalapa Campus: Apdo postal 55-535, Av. Michoacán y la Purísima, Col. Vicentina, Del. Iztapalapa, 09340 México, DF; tel. 612-46-65.

Rector: José Luis Gázquez Mateos
Secretary: Antonio Aguilar Aguilar
Librarian: Alfonso Romero Sánchez

DIRECTORS

Basic Sciences and Engineering: Luis Mier y Terán Casanueva
Biological and Health Sciences: José Luis Arredondo Figueroa
Social Sciences and Humanities: José Gregorio Vidal Bonifáz

HEADS OF DEPARTMENT

Physics: Salvador Cruz Jiménez
Electrical Engineering: Miguel Cadena Méndez
Hydraulics and Process Engineering: Alberto Soria López
Mathematics: Rodolfo Suárez Cortés
Chemistry: Fernando Rojas González
Biology: Carolina Müdespacher Ziehl
Biology of Reproduction: Jorge Hernando Haro Castellanos
Biotechnology: Jorge Soriano Santos
Health Sciences: Ernesto Rodríguez Aguilera
Hydrobiology: Margarita Gallegos Martínez
Anthropology: Rodrigo Díaz Cruz
Economics: Raúl Conde Hernández
Philosophy: José Lema Labadie
Sociology: Octavio Nateras Domínguez

Xochimilco Campus: Apdo postal 23-181, Calzada del Hueso 1100, Col. Villa Quietud, Del. Coyoacán, 04960 México, DF; tel. 594-66-56.

Rector: Jaime Kravzov Jinich
Secretary: Marina Altagracia Martínez
Librarian: Margarita Lugo Hubp

DIRECTORS

Biological and Health Sciences: Norberto Manjarréz Alvarez
Social Sciences and Humanities: Guillermo Villaseñor García
Art and Design: Emilio Pradilla Cobos

HEADS OF DEPARTMENT

Health Education: José Blanco Gil
Man and His Environment: José A. Viccon Pale
Agricultural and Animal Production: Salvador Vega y León
Biological Systems: Carlos Tomás Quirino Barreda
Education and Communication: Jorge Alsina Valdés y Capote
Politics and Culture: Ernesto Soto Reyes Garmendia
Economic Production: Cuauhtémoc Vladimir Pérez Llanas
Social Relations: Alberto Padilla Arias
Methods and Systems: Salvador Duarte Yuriar
Creative Synthesis: María Teresa del Pando Alonso
Technology and Production: Javier Santacruz Aceves
Theory and Analysis: Francisco Pérez Cortés

UNIVERSIDAD MICHOACANA DE SAN NICOLÁS DE HIDALGO

Edif. 'TR', Ciudad Universitaria, 58030 Morelia, Michoacán

Telephone: 16-70-20
Fax: 16-88-35

Founded 1539, University in 1917
State control
Language of instruction: Spanish
Academic year: September to June

Rector: Lic. Daniel Trujillo Mesina
Secretary-General: Dr Armando Roman Luna Escalante
Administrative Secretary: L.A.E. Domingo Bautista Farias
Director of Library: Lic. Adalberto Abrego Gutierrez

Library of 150,000 vols
Number of teachers: 2,158
Number of students: 31,769

Publications: *Boletín de Rectoría, Cuadernos de Derecho, Polemos, Cuadernos de Centro de Investigación de la Cultura Puehépecha.*

UNIVERSIDAD DE MONTEMORELOS

Apdo 16, Montemorelos, 67530 Nuevo León

Telephone: 3-30-80
Telex: 30104
Fax: 3-27-08

Founded 1973
Private control
Language of instruction: Spanish
Academic year: August to May

President: Dr Ismael Castillo Osuna
Vice-Presidents: Dr Emilio García (Academic), Ing. Filiberto Verduzco (Administrative), Abraham Murillo (Student Affairs)

Director of Admissions and Records: EKEL COLLINS
Librarian: ADÁN SURIANO

Number of teachers: 125
Number of students: 2,694

Publications: *Catálogo Universitario, Dinámica Universitaria, Vida Estudiantil, Manual del Estudiante, Catálogo Division de Postgrado.*

DEANS

Faculty of Administrative Sciences: C.P. JOEL SEBASTIÁN
Faculty of Biomedical Sciences: Dr NAIF CANO
Faculty of Engineering and Technology: Ing. RAMÓN MEZA
Faculty of Science, Art and Humanities: JULIAEMY DE FLORES
Faculty of Theology: Dr ELOY WADE

ATTACHED INSTITUTES

Institute of Modern Languages: Profa LENA CAESAR
Institute of Professional Development: OVIDIO MORALES

UNIVERSIDAD DE MONTERREY

Avda Ignacio Morones Prieto 4500 Pte, San Pedro, 66238 Garza García, Nuevo León
Telephone: (8) 338-50-50
Fax: (8) 338-56-19
E-mail: apuente@udem.edu.mx

Founded 1969
Private control
Language of instruction: Spanish
Academic year: August to May

President: Dr FRANCISCO AZCÚNAGA GUERRA
Vice-President (Graduate Programmes): JUAN SILLERO PÉREZ
Vice-President (High School and Integral Education): RAFAEL GARZA MENDOZA
Vice-President (Institutional Development): ADALBERTO VIESCA SADA
Registrar: MINERVA GARCÍA CESSARIO
Librarian: MARCELA GARZA

Library of 85,000 books, 1,100 electronic periodicals
Number of teachers: 802
Number of students: 7,708

ACADEMIC DIVISIONS

School of Technology and Business: Head JOSÉ M. AGUIAR LÓPEZ
School of Social Sciences and Health: Head ZETA MELVA TRIANA
Postgraduate Programmes and Research: Head SERGIO ROBLESGIL MAZA

HEADS OF UNDERGRADUATE PROGRAMMES

Architecture: JUAN FERNANDO SADA
Business Administration: MARGARITA GUTIÉRREZ
Chartered Accountancy and Auditing: GABRIELA GARZA
Computer Science: ELIZABETH GUTIÉRREZ
Economics: LAURA ZÚÑIGA
Education: LUIS FERNANDO MÁRQUEZ
Graphic Design: JOAQUÍN GARZAFOX
Human Relations: MARTHA TREVIÑO
Humanities and Social Studies: MARÍA GLORIA CARBAJAL
Industrial Design: JOAQUÍN GARZAFOX
Industrial Engineering: JOSÉ HERNÁNDEZ
Information Science and Communication: CECILIA QUINTANILLA
International Marketing: LAURA GARZA
International Studies: GERARDO GARZA
Law: MARIANA TÉLLEZ
Mechanical Engineering: JOSÉ HERNÁNDEZ
Medicine: CARLOS CANTÚ DÍAZ
Political Science and Public Administration: MARTHA TREVIÑO
Psychology: ALICIA VARELA
Visual Arts: FEDERICO LÓPEZ CASTRO

HEADS OF MASTER DEGREE PROGRAMMES

Master in Business Administration: ASENSIO CARRIÓN
Master in Education: (vacant)
Master in Humanities: GUADALUPE VIESCA
Master in International Business Administration: ASENSIO CARRIÓN
Master in Organizational Development: GUADALUPE MARTÍNEZ
Master in Total Quality Administration: MARTÍN IRETA

UNIVERSIDAD AUTÓNOMA DEL ESTADO DE MORELOS

Avda Universidad 1001, Col. Chamilpa, 62210 Cuernavaca, Morelos
Telephone: 29-70-01
Fax: 13-34-95

Founded 1953
State control
Language of instruction: Spanish
Academic year: September to July

Rector: M. en C. GERARDO AVILA GARCÍA
Secretary-General: Lic. JAVIER H. LÓPEZ BUENROSTRO
Academic Secretary: Psic. RENE SANTOVEÑA ARREDONDO
Librarian: Lic. ALMA ROSA CIENFUEGOS DOMÍNGUEZ

Number of teachers: 1,473
Number of students: 15,086

Publications: *Gaceta Universitaria, Perspectiva Universitaria, Universidad: Ciencia y Tecnología.*

DEANS AND DIRECTORS

Faculty of Accountancy, Administration and Informatics: M.A. RAUL TRUJILLO ESCOBAR
Faculty of Chemical and Industrial Sciences: Ing. MELCHOR ARAUJO MACEDO
Faculty of Architecture: M. en Arq. SERGIO MARTÍNEZ RAMÍREZ
Faculty of Stockbreeding: Ing. ALEJANDRO HULSZ PICCONE
School of Educational Sciences: M.I.E. MARTHA GEORGINA OCAMPO SAMANO
Faculty of Law and Social Sciences: Lic. JUAN MANUEL DÍAZ POPOCA
Faculty of Medicine: Dr JORGE MONTES ALVARADO
Faculty of Psychology: Psic. FERNANDO ITURBE ROBLEDO
School of Laboratory Technicians: Biol. ARTURO SANDOVAL CAMUÑAS
School of Nursing: Enf. CATALINA CARRILLO JAIME
Faculty of Human Communication: Lic. MA. LUISA PINEDA PINEDA
Institute of the Eastern Region: Dr JESÚS CUATHEMOC HERNÁNDEZ TOLEDANO
Institute of the South: Lic. ROBERTO TÉLLEZ

There are also 9 Preparatory Schools.

UNIVERSIDAD MOTOLINIA AC

Cerrado de Ameyalco 227, Col. del Valle, 03100 México, DF
Telephone: 523-48-13

Founded 1918
Private control
Language of instruction: Spanish
Academic year: August to July

Principal: LUZ MARÍA PORTILLO ARROYO
Chief Administrative Officer: MARÍA DEL REFUGIO HERRERA FLORES
Librarian: JUANA MARÍA CAMARGO MUÑOZ

Schools of law and chemistry.
There is also a campus at Pedregal.

UNIVERSIDAD AUTÓNOMA DE NAYARIT

Ciudad de la Cultura Amado Nervo, 63190 Tepic, Nayarit

Founded 1930 as Instituto de Ciencias y Letras de Nayarit, refounded as university 1969

Rector: Lic. RUBÉN HERNÁNDEZ DE LA TORRE
Secretary-General: Lic. FERMÍN FLETES A.

Number of teachers: *c.* 230
Number of students: *c.* 2,400

Schools of agriculture, dentistry, nursing, commerce and administration, law, economics, chemical engineering, medicine, zoology, veterinary medicine.

UNIVERSIDAD AUTÓNOMA DEL NORESTE

Monclova 1561, Col. República, 25280 Saltillo, Coahuila
Telephone: (84) 14-82-58
Fax: (84) 16-31-53

Founded 1974
Private control
Academic year: January to June, July to December

Rector: Lic. FRANCISCO AGUIRRE FUENTES
Vice-Rectors: Lic. MARÍA DEL CARMEN RUÍZ ESPARZA (Academic), C.P. GABRIEL DURÁN MALTOS (Administrative)
Librarian: Lic. NELLY BERMÚDEZ ARRAZATE

Number of teachers: 708
Number of students: 4,225

Courses in business administration, accountancy, education and psychology, law, tourism, architecture, computer studies, industrial and systems engineering, political science, graphic design.

UNIVERSIDAD AUTÓNOMA DE NUEVO LEÓN

Ciudad Universitaria, CP 66450, San Nicolás de los Garza, Nuevo León
Telephone: 329-40-00
Fax: 376-77-57

Founded 1933
Academic year: August to July

Rector: Dr REYES S. TAMEZ GUERRA
Vice-Rector: Dr JESÚS GALÁN WONG
Secretary for Administration and Finance: C.P. J. OVIDIO BUENTELLO GARZA

Number of teachers: 7,211
Number of students: 104,300 (incl. attached schools)

DEANS

Faculty of Agronomy: Dr JUAN F. VILLARREAL ARREDONDO
Faculty of Architecture: Arq. GUILLERMO ROBERTO WAH ROBLES
Faculty of Biological Sciences: M.C. JUAN M. ADAME RODRÍGUEZ
Faculty of Chemical Sciences: Ing. JOSÉ MANUEL MARTÍNEZ DELGADO
Faculty of Civil Engineering: Ing. FRANCISCO GÁMEZ TREVIÑO
Faculty of Communication Sciences: Lic. JUAN MARIO GÁMEZ CRUZ
Faculty of Earth Sciences: Dr COSME POLA SIMUTA
Faculty of Economics: Lic. JORGE MELÉNDEZ BARRÓN
Faculty of Forestry Sciences: Dr ALFONSO MARTÍNEZ MUÑOZ
Faculty of Law and Social Sciences: Lic. ALEJANDRO IZAGUIRRE GONZÁLEZ
Faculty of Mechanical and Electrical Engineering: Ing. CÁSTULO E. VELA VILLARREAL
Faculty of Medicine: Dr JESÚS Z. VILLARREAL PÉREZ

Faculty of Music: Lic. JUAN LUIS RODRÍGUEZ TRUJILLO
Faculty of Nursing: Lic. MARÍA GPE. MARTÍNEZ DE DÁVILA
Faculty of Odontology: Dr ROBERTO CARRILLO GONZÁLEZ
Faculty of Philosophy and the Arts: Lic. RICARDO C. VILLARREAL ARRAMBIDE
Faculty of Physical and Mathematical Sciences: Ing. JOSÉ OSCAR RECIO CANTÚ
Faculty of Political Science and Public Administration: Lic. RICARDO A. FUENTES CAVAZOS
Faculty of Psychology: Lic. GUILLERMO HERNÁNDEZ MARTÍNEZ
Faculty of Public Accounting and Administration: C.P. RAMIRO SOBERÓN PÉREZ
Faculty of Public Health: Lic. ELIZABETH SOLÍS DE SÁNCHEZ
Faculty of Social Work: Lic. MA. IRENE CANTÚ REYNA
Faculty of Sports Administration: Lic. RENÉ SALGADO MÉNDEZ
Faculty of Veterinary Medicine and Zootechnics: Dr JOSÉ ANTONIO SALINAS MELÉNDEZ
Faculty of the Visual Arts: Arq. MARIO ARMENDARIZ VELÁZQUEZ

UNIVERSIDAD AUTÓNOMA 'BENITO JUÁREZ' DE OAXACA

Apdo 76, Ciudad Universitaria, 68120 Oaxaca, Oax.

Telephone: 6-46-86

Founded 1827, university status 1955
Private control
Academic year: September to July

Rector: Dr CESAR MAYORAL FIGUEROA
General Secretary: Dr EDUARDO L. PEREZ CAMPOS
Librarian: Lic. DONAJI MENDOZA LUNA

Library of 77,237 vols
Number of teachers: 980
Number of students: 15,000

Publication: *Planeación.*

DEANS

School of Architecture: Arq. JORGE VARGAS GUZMÁN
School of Law and Social Sciences: Lic. ABEL GARCÍA RAMÍREZ
School of Medicine: Dr ALFONSO SANTOS ORTÍZ
Faculty of Commerce and Administration: L.A.E. SEVERINO ROJAS LÁZARO
School of Chemistry: Dr ARTURO SANTAELLA V.
School of Nursing and Obstetrics: Enf. NOEMI CÓRDOVA VARGAS
School of Fine Arts: Lic. EVELIO BAUTISTA TORRES
School of Odontology: C.D. AUSTREBERTO MARTÍNEZ MOLINA
School of Veterinary Studies: M.V.Z. CARLOS A. DE J. LEÓN LEDEZMA
Language Centre: Prof. ERIC O'CONNEL

UNIVERSIDAD DE OCCIDENTE

Apdo 81200, B. Juárez 435 pte, Los Mochis, Sinaloa

Telephone: (91-681) 5-10-61
Fax: 5-39-00

Founded 1978
Academic year: September to August

Chancellor: Dr FRANCISCO CUAUHTEMOC FRIAS CASTRO
Rector: RUBEN ELIAS GIL LEYVA
Secretary-General: M. S. P. JOSE GUILLERMO ALVAREZ GUERRERO
Chief Administrative Officer: Lic. FERNANDO ORPINELA LIZARRAGA
Librarian: DELPHA DELLA ROCCA KING

Number of teachers: 414
Number of students: 4,344

Publications: *Ciencia Jurídica, Un Sueño Del Paraíso, Los Mochis.*

CONSTITUENT INSTITUTIONS

Unidad Los Mochis: Carretera Internacional y Blvd Macario Gaxiola, Los Mochis; tel. (91-681) 5-60-60; Dir CILA MARIA HERNANDEZ ROJO.

HEADS OF DEPARTMENTS

Accountancy: Lic. R. RODRIGUEZ BELTRAN
Administration: Lic. J. R. CABRERAS GARCIA
Psychology: Lic. P. CEBALLOS RENDON
Communication: Lic. I. TORRES SANTINI
Biology: Ocean. F. G. CUPUL MAGAÑA
Mathematics: Ing. F. BARRERAS MANZANAREZ
Law: Lic. F. FRÍAS LOAIZA
Engineering: Ing. M. SOLER RIVERA

Unidad Culiacan: Blvd Madero 34 pte, Culiacan; tel. (91-671) 3-82-17; Dir Lic. GILBERTO HIGUERA BERNAL.

HEADS OF DEPARTMENTS

Administration: Lic. A. GONZÁLEZ LUNA
Economics: Lic. E. DAMKEN ALATORRE
Communication: Lic. M. L. ZAMBADA GALLARDO
Mathematics: Ing. M. MORÍN DEL RINCÓN
Law: Lic. R. RODRÍGUEZ LEAL
Sociology: Lic. C. HABERMANN GASTÉLUM
Engineering: Ing: L. CARLOS MEDINA AGUILAR

Unidad Guasave: Corregidora y Zaragoza, Guasave; tel. (91-687) 2-27-00; Dir Lic. JESUS TEODORO RAMIREZ JACOBO.

HEADS OF DEPARTMENTS

Administration: Lic. R. RIVERA MONTOYA
Accountancy: Lic. M. A. CAMACHO CRESPO
Communication: Lic. C. J. PEREZ DELAUMEAU
Mathematics: Ing. M. NARVAEZ FERNANDEZ
Law: Lic. P. HERNÁNDEZ BENÍTEZ
Sociology: Lic. Y. A. GUTIERREZ ALVAREZ

Unidad Mazatlan: Avda del Mar 1200, Mazatlan; tel. (91-687) 3-64-04; Dir Lic. LUIS O. MONTOYA HIGUERA.

HEADS OF DEPARTMENTS

Psychology: Lic. L.E. SÁNCHEZ LEYVA
Administration: Lic. F. ARELLANO ONTIVEROS
Mathematics: Ing. A. GUTTÉRREZ MÁRQUEZ
Language: Lic. A. G. RAMIREZ ZERTUCHE

Instituto de Antropología: Avda Benito Juárez 39, Mochicahui, El Fuerte; tel. 5-07-22; Dir Lic. G. ESCAMILLA HURTADO.

Unidad Guamuchil: Jose Maria Vigil y Blvd Lazaro Cardenas, Guamuchil, Sinaloa; tel. (91-673) 2-03-81; Dir Lic. BENITO GOMEZ URBALEJO.

Instituto de Investigaciones Tecnologicas Para el Desarrollo de la Acuacultura y la Pesca.

UNIVERSIDAD PANAMERICANA

Augusto Rodin 498, Col. Mixcoac, 03920 México, DF

Telephone: 563-26-55
Fax: 611-22-65

Founded 1966
Private control
Academic year: August to June

Rector: Dr RAMÓN IBARRA
Vice-Rectors: JESÚS MAGAÑA BRAVO, Lic. SERGIO RAIMOND-KEDILHAC NAVARRO
Administrative Director: Dr VÍCTOR MANUEL PIZÁ
Librarian: ELISA RIVA PALACIO

Library of 45,000 vols
Number of teachers: 450
Number of students: 5,000

Publications: *Boletín* (monthly), *Revista Istmo* (every 2 months), *Tópicos Journal of Philosophy* (2 a year), *Ars Juris* (2 a year).

Preparatory and first degree courses.

DIRECTORS

School of Administration: Ing. AMADEO VÁZQUEZ
School of Law: Dr ROBERTO IBÁÑEZ MARIEL
School of Economics: Lic. FLAVIA RODRÍGUEZ
School of Philosophy: Dr ROCIO MIER Y TERÁN
School of Education: Dra CARMEN RAMSO
School of Engineering: Ing. PEDRO CREUHERAS
School of Accounting: CLAUDIO M. RIVAS

AFFILIATED INSTITUTIONS

Instituto de Capacitación de Mandos Intermedios (Mid Management Institute): Mar Mediterráneo 183, Col. Popotla, 11400 México, DF; tel. 399-7272; f. 1966; 170 teachers; 2,400 students; library of 1,200 vols; business administration to supervisor and head of dept level; Dir CONRADO ANTONIO LARIOS.

Instituto de Desarrollo para Operarios: Norte 182, No. 477, Col. Peñón de los Baños, 15520 México, DF; tel. 760-3464; f. 1968; 45 teachers; 550 students; library of 500 vols; courses for worker-management; Dir ENRIQUE SIERRA.

Instituto Panamericano de Alta Dirección de Empresa (Pan-American Institute of Higher Business Studies): Floresta 20, Col. Clavería, 02080 México, DF; tel. 5270260; telex 017-72204; f. 1967; library of 8,000 vols; 40 teachers; 1,900 students; Dir SERGIO RAIMOND-KEDILHAC NAVARRO.

Instituto Panamericano de Ciencias de la Educación (Pan-American Institute of Education): Augusto Rodin 498, Col. Mixcoac, 03920 México, DF; Dir Dra MARCELA CHAVARRÍA.

BENEMÉRITA UNIVERSIDAD AUTÓNOMA DE PUEBLA

4 Sur No 104, 72000 Puebla, Pue.

Telephone: 41-32-69
Telex: 178350
Fax: 42-30-58

Founded 1937
State control
Academic year: January to December

Rector: M.C. SAMUEL MALPAICA URIBE
Secretary-General: Lic. ALEJANDRO SILVA ARIAS
Librarian: (vacant)

Number of teachers: 4,000
Number of students: 100,000

DIRECTORS

School of Public Administration: Lic. EDMUNDO PERRONI ROCHA
School of Architecture: Arq. BLANCA AMARO SÁNCHEZ
School of Public Accountancy: C.P. JORGE MALDONADO JIMÉNEZ
School of Chemical Sciences: Q. F. B. MARÍA EUGENIA DE LA CHAUSSÉE
School of Law: Lic. HUMBERTO SANCHEZ CASTILLO
School of Economics: Lic. MARÍA EUGENIA MARTINES
School of Philosophy and Letters: Psic. MARÍA TERESA ARRELLANO DIAZ
School of Physics and Mathematics: M. C. MIGUEL ANGEL SORIANO JIMÉNEZ
School of Chemical Engineering: Ing. JAVIER ENRÍQUEZ JIMÉNEZ
School of Civil Engineering: Ing. RAUL LÓPEZ BRETÓN
School of Medicine: Dr SALVADOR ROSALES DE GANTE
School of Dentistry: C.D. MANUEL REGUEIRA ROJAS
School of Veterinary Medicine and Animal Husbandry: M.V.Z. EDMUNDO PÉREZ DURÁN
School of Biology: Biol. ISMAEL LEDEEMA MATEOS, M. en C.
School of Nursing: Lic. Enf. JULIA HERNANDEZ ALVAREZ
Hospital: Dr EDUARDO VAZQUEZ VALDES

Science Institutes: M. C. JUVENCIO MONROY PONCE

UNIVERSIDAD POPULAR AUTÓNOMA DEL ESTADO DE PUEBLA

21 Sur 1103, 72000 Puebla, Pue.

Telephone: (22) 32-02-66
Fax: (22) 32-52-51

Founded 1973
Private control
Academic year: August to July

Chancellor: MANUEL RODRÍGUEZ CONCHA
President: MARIO IGLESIAS GARCÍA TERUEL
Vice-President: Ing. VICENTE PACHECO CEBALLOS
Registrar: Lic. MARÍA DE LOS ANGELES RONDERO CHEW
Public Relations Officer: Arq. JOSÉ M. ARGÜELLES REYES NIEVA
Librarian: Lic. LEOBARDO REYES JIMÉNEZ

Number of teachers: 652
Number of students: 5,084

Publication: *Vertebracíon* (6 a year).

HEADS OF DEPARTMENTS

Medicine: Dr JORGE BAUTISTA O'FARRILL
Dentistry: C.D. CARLOS PINEDA Y RÍOS
Nursing: Dra DULCE MA. PÉREZ SUÁREZ
Accountancy: C.P. GERMÁN GONZÁLEZ MARTIÑÓN
Agriculture and Animal Sciences: Ing. GERARDO VALLE FLORES
Architecture: Arq. FERNANDO RODRÍGUEZ CONCHA
Business Administration: Ing. TITO LIVIO DE LA TORRE
Civil Engineering: Ing. MARIO JIMÉNEZ SUÁREZ
Chemical Engineering: Ing. MA. JOSEFINA RIVERO VILLAR
Communication Sciences: Lic. VICTOR MANUEL SÁNCHEZ STEINPREIS
Industrial Engineering: Ing. JUAN ANTONIO ANAYA SANDOVAL
Political Sciences: Lic. JUAN DE DIOS ANDRADE MARTÍNEZ
Law: Lic. MATÍAS RIVERO AGUILAR
Psychology: Lic. MARTHA PATRICIA GUTIÉRREZ C.
Philosophy: Lic. JORGE LUIS NAVARRO CAMPOS
Education: Lic. PATRICIA CABALLERO CERVANTES
Computer Systems: Ing. JOSÉ MARÍA BEDOLLA CORDERO
International Business: Lic. JAVIER AGUAYO ORDÓÑEZ
Ecology: Mtro RUBEN P. RODRÍGUEZ TORRES
Institutional Administration: Lic. MARIA ELBA AMEZCUA DE N.
Economics: Lic. ALONSO IBÁÑEZ Y DURÁN
Advertising Design and Production: Arq. MIGUEL ANGEL BALANDRA JARA
Graduate Programmes and Continuous Education: Lic. GUADALUPE ESPINOSA ROMERO
English: Lic. HERLINDA CANTO VALENCIA
Social Studies: Arq. EDUARDO RAZO CISNEROS
Mathematics: Mtro ALEJANDRO NARVÁEZ H.
Physics: Ing. ROSARIO ACOSTA DE GALVÁN
Division of Art and Architecture: Arq. MIGUEL ANGEL BALANDRA JARA
Division of Basic Sciences: Ing. JOSÉ MARÍA BEDOLLA CORDERO
Division of Engineering: Ing. RAFAEL RANGÉL GONZÁLEZ
Division of Economics and Administration Sciences: Ing. TITO LIVIO DE LA TORRE
Division of Humanities: Lic. JOSÉ ANTONIO ARRUBARRENA ARAGÓN
Division of Health Sciences: Dr OCTAVIO CASTILLO Y LÓPEZ

UNIVERSIDAD AUTÓNOMA DE QUERÉTARO

Centro Universitario, Cerro de las Campanas, 76010 Querétaro, Qro

Telephone: 16-32-42
Fax: 16-85-15

Founded 1951
State control
Language of instruction: Spanish
Academic year: July to June

Rector: JOSÉ ALFREDO ZEPEDA GARRIDO
Academic Secretary: HUGO SANCHEZ VELEZ
Administrative Secretary: MIGUEL ANGEL ESCAMILLA SANTANA
Librarian: ARTURO HERNÁNDEZ SIERRA

Number of teachers: 1,428
Number of students: 18,000

Publications: *Revista de Egresados de Contabilidad, Revista Extensión Universitaria, Revista de Informática, Revista de Sociología, Revista de Medicina, Revista de Investigación, Revista Auriga, Revista Bellas Artes, Autonomía.*

DEANS

Faculty of Engineering: JESÚS HERNÁNDEZ ESPINO
Faculty of Chemistry: J. MERCED ESPARZA AGUILAR
Faculty of Psychology: ANDRES VELAZQUEZ ORTEGA
Faculty of Humanities: GABRIEL CORRAL BASURTO
Faculty of Law: ARSENIO DURAN BECERRA
Preparatory Faculty: DOLORES CABRERA MUÑOZ
School of Medicine: Dr SALVADOR GUERRERO SERVIN
School of Sociology: CARLOS DORANTES GONZALEZ
School of Veterinary Science and Zoology: M.V.Z. GUILLERMO DE LA ISLA HERRERA
School of Nursing: ALEJANDRINA FRANCO ESGUERRA
School of Journalism: LUIS ROBERTO AMIEBA PEREZ
School of Social Enterprise Management: FELIPE SAMAYOA
School of Computer Science: LUIS F. SAAVEDRA URIBE
School of Languages: AURORA IVETTE SILVA RODRIGUEZ
School of Fine Arts: JOSÉ ROBERTO GONZÁLEZ GARCÍA

UNIVERSIDAD REGIOMONTANA

Villagrán 238 Sur, Apdo Postal 243, CP 64000 Monterrey, NL

Telephone: (8) 344-76-04
Fax: (8) 340-04-02

Founded 1969
Private control
Language of instruction: Spanish
Academic year: September to August

Rector: Dr PABLO A. LONGORIA TREVIÑO
Administrative Director: Ing. GUILLERMO CHARLES LOBO
Registrar: Ing. GERARDO GONZÁLEZ
Librarian: Ing. JORGE MERCADO SALAS

Library of 42,952 vols
Number of teachers: 450
Number of students: 4,500

Publications: *Espresión* (weekly), *Veritas* (annually).

DEANS

Faculty of Engineering and Architecture: Dr RODOLFO SALINAS HERNÁNDEZ
Faculty of Economic and Administrative Sciences: Dr CARLOS OLIVARES LEAL
Faculty of Humanities and Social Sciences: Lic. DORA ANTINORI CARLETTI
Preparatory Division: Lic. NICOLÁS PALACIOS LOZANO

UNIVERSIDAD AUTÓNOMA DE SAN LUIS POTOSÍ

Alvaro Obregón 64, 78000 San Luis Potosí, S.L.P.

Telephone: 2-34-61
Fax: 4-03-72

Founded 1826 as Instituto Científico y Literario
Federal control
Language of instruction: Spanish
Academic year: August to June

Rector: Lic. ALFONSO LASTRAS RAMIREZ
Secretary-General: Ing. JAIME VALLE MÉNDEZ
Academic Secretary: Dr PEDRO MEDELLÍN MILÁN
Chief Administrative Officer: Dr ALDO TORRE FLORENZANO
Librarian: Lic. SOCORRO SILVA NIETO

Library of 68,000 vols
Number of teachers: 2,290
Number of students: 23,169

Publications: *Acta Cientifica Potosina* (2 a year), *Cuadrante* (3 a year), *Boletín Informativo Médico* (every 2 months), *Revista de Derecho* (quarterly), *Divulgación Económica* (quarterly).

DEANS

Faculty of Economics: Lic. HECTOR MONTOYA ESPINOZA
Faculty of Science: Fis. GUILLERMO MARX REYES
Faculty of Chemistry: Dr ROBERTO LEYVA RAMOS
Faculty of Accountancy and Administration: C.P. HECTOR A. DIAZ PEDROZA
Faculty of Law: Lic. HECTOR ALDASORO VELASCO
Faculty of Engineering: Ing. DAVID ATISHA CASTILLO
School of Agronomy: Ing. RODOLFO LOZAMARQUEZ LABASTIDA
School of Nursing: Lic. ISABEL VILLARREAL GUZMAN
School of Stomatology: Dr SERGIO LOPEZ MOCTEZUMA
School of Psychology: Fis. JUAN MANUEL TEJADA TAYABAS
School of Environmental Sciences: Arq. ALFREDO TELLES ARELLANO
Faculty of Medicine: Dr JOSE LUIS LEYVA GARZA

AFFILIATED INSTITUTES

Ciencias Educativas: Dir Dr ADRIAN PESINA ZAMARRIPA
Física: Dir Prof. JUAN FERNANDO CARDENAS RIVERO
Geología: Ing. GUILLERMO LABARTHE HERNANDEZ
Metalurgía: Dir M.C. JOSE DE JESUS NEGRETE SANCHEZ
Investigaciones Económicas: Lic. MARTHA MIRANDA DE TORRES
Zonas Desérticas: Biol. NICOLAS VAZQUEZ ROSILLO
Investigaciones Humanísticas: Lic. EUDORO FONSECA YERENA
Ciencias Jurídicas: Lic. FEDERICO CUADRA IPIÑA

UNIVERSIDAD AUTÓNOMA DE SINALOA

Apdo Postal 1919, Calle Angel Flores s/n, 80000 Culiacán, Sinaloa

Founded 1873
State control

Rector: Lic. DAVID MORENO LIZÁRRAGA
Secretary-General: Lic. ARTURO ZAMA ESCALANTE
Registrar: Lic. J.B. GAXIOLA COTA

Number of teachers: *c.* 400
Number of students: *c.* 6,000

Schools of law and social science, chemistry, physics and mathematics, accountancy, administration, economics, nursing, agriculture, social work.

Campuses in Mazatlán, Los Mochis, Guamúchil, Juan José Ríos.

UNIVERSIDAD DE SONORA

Apdo Postal 336 y 106, 83000 Hermosillo, Sonora

Telephone: 2-10-46

Charter granted 1938; opened and officially inaugurated 1942

Private control

Language of instruction: Spanish

Academic year: September to June

Rector: Ing. MANUEL RIVERA ZAMUDIO

Secretary-General: Ing. MANUEL BALCÁZAR MEZA

Librarian: Lic. ANA LILYA MOYA

Library of 45,000 vols

Number of teachers: 1,025

Number of students: 18,000

Publications: *Gaceta Universitaria* (monthly), *Revista de la Universidad* (quarterly), *Poemarios* (every 2 months), *Revista de Física* (2 a year), *Revista de Economía* (2 a year), *Sonora Agropecuario* (every 2 months).

CO-ORDINATORS

School of Social Work: T.S. AMELIA I. DE BLANCO

School of Nursing: Prof. ELVIRA COTA

School of Advanced Studies: Ing. IGNACIO AYALA ZAZUETA

School of Law and Social Sciences: Lic. MIGUEL CÁRDENAS

School of Chemical Sciences: Ing. OSVALDO LANDAVAZO

School of Engineering: Ing. MIGUEL A. MORENO N.

School of Accountancy and Administration: C.P. RAMÓN CÁRDENAS VALDÉS

School of Economics: Lic. RODOLFO DÍAZ CASTAÑEDA

School of Agriculture and Animal Husbandry: Ing. MARIO GUZMÁN

School of Psychology and Communication Sciences: Lic. DANIEL C. GUTIÉRREZ C.

Department of Biochemistry: HECTOR ESCÁRCEGA

Department of Mathematics: EDUARDO TELLECHEA ARMENTA

Department of Physics: ANTONIO JAUREGUI D.

Department of Humanities: JOSÉ SAPIEN DURÁN

Department of Geology: Ing. EFRÉN PÉREZ SEGURA

CAMPUS DIRECTORS

Unidad Sur: Lic. JOSÉ A. VALENZUELA

Unidad Norte: Ing. RODOLFO GUZMÁN

Unidad Santana: Ing. MARIO TARAZÓN H.

UNIVERSIDAD AUTÓNOMA DEL SUDESTE

Apdo Postal 204, Ciudad Universitaria, 24030 Campeche, Camp.

Telephone: (981) 6-22-44

Founded 1756, refounded 1965

State control

Academic year: September to June

Rector: Lic. TIRSO R. DE LA GALA

General Secretary: Lic. ALBAR J. COLONIA

Chief Administrative Officer: L.A.E. ROGER DEL C. ROMERO

Librarian: Lic. ADDA I. CRUZ

Number of teachers: 443

Number of students: 4,760

Publications: *Panorama*, *Pinceladas* (both every 2 months).

DEANS

Faculty of Law: Lic. HÉCTOR J. ORTIZ

School of Commerce: LUIS F. GUERRERO

Faculty of Engineering: Ing. LUIS A. GARCIA

School of Dentistry: Dr JUAN J. CASANOVA

School of Medicine: Dr ANTONIO E. GONZÁLEZ

School of Nursing and Obstetrics: ENNA E. MUÑOZ

School of Humanities: Prof. CARLOS FLORES

School of Chemical and Biological Sciences: Ing. JUAN M. CONDE

School of Political Sciences and Public Administration: Lic. RAMÓN RODRIGUEZ

School of Commerce: C.P. LUIS F. GUERRERO

UNIVERSIDAD JUÁREZ AUTÓNOMA DE TABASCO

Avda Universidad s/n. Zona de la Cultura, 86000 Villahermosa, Tabasco

Telephone: 12-29-93

Fax: 12-16-37

Founded 1958

State control

Academic year: September to August

Rector: Dr FERNANDO RABELO RUIZ DE LA PEÑA

Academic Secretary: Dr WALTER RAMÍREZ IZQUIERDO

Administrative Secretary: Ing. ARMANDO MORALES MURILLO

Secretary of the Rectorate: L.A. RICARDO SAIZ CALDERON

Librarian: Lic. TOMASA BARRUETA GARCÍA

Library of 174,608 vols

Number of teachers: 1,050

Number of students: 20,470

Publication: *Revista de la Universidad, Perspectivas Docentes, Universidad y Ciencias, Revista de la División de Ciencias Sociales y Humanidades, Revista Temas Biomédicos, Gaceta Juchiman, Revista Hitos de la División de Ciencias Economico-Administrativas/Centro, Revista Zenzontle de la División de Educación y Artes, Revista de la Unidad Chontalpa.*

DIRECTORS

Division of Health Sciences: Dr ESMELIN TRINIDAD VÁZQUEZ.

Division of Agricultural Sciences: M. V. Z. VICTOR DE JESUS PEREZPRIEGO COBIAN

Division of Humanities and Social Sciences: Lic. FREDDY PRIEGO PRIEGO

Division of Economic and Administrative Sciences: C.P. OLGA YERI GONZÁLEZ LÓPEZ (Centre Unit)

Division of Engineering and Technology: Ing. ARTURO ARIAS RODAS

Division of Biological Sciences: M. C. ANDRÉS ARTURO GRANADOS BERBER

Division of Arts and Education: Lic. EFRAIN PÉREZ CRUZ

Division of Basic Sciences: Fis. CARLOS GONZALEZ ARIAS

Chontalpa Unit: Dir-Gen. Ing. JUAN LUIS RAMIREZ MARROQUIN

UNIVERSIDAD AUTÓNOMA DE TAMAULIPAS

Apdo Postal 186, 87000 Ciudad Victoria, Tamaulipas

Telephone: 2-70-00

Founded 1950/51

Private control

Language of instruction: Spanish

Academic year: August to January, February to June

Rector: Lic. JOSÉ MANUEL ADAME MIER

Secretary-General: Ing. HUMBERTO FILIZOLA HACES

Academic Secretary: JORGE LUIS URIEGAS GARCIA

Administrative Secretary: FERNANDO ARIZPE GARCIA

Librarian: Lic. NATIVIDAD IBARRA

Library of 11,055 vols

Number of teachers: 1,646

Number of students: 22,161

Publication: *Boletín de Investigaciones* (monthly).

DIRECTORS

Tampico Campus:

Faculty of Medicine: Dr AMILCAR HUERTA PEREZ

Faculty of Dentistry: Dr FELIX ALVAREZ PEREZ

Faculty of Law and Social Sciences: Lic. OSCAR MORALES ELIZONDO

Faculty of Engineering: Ing. JOSÉ A. BOLAÑOS HERNÁNDEZ

Faculty of Architecture: Arq. LUIS RAMON SANDOVAL GUTIERREZ

Faculty of Commerce and Administration: C.P. URIEL DAVILA HERRERA

Faculty of Nursing and Obstetrics: Lic. GLORIA ACEVEDO PORRAS

Higher School of Music: Prof. MARIA DEL PILAR RAMOS DE C.

Victoria Campus:

Faculty of Veterinary Medicine: M.V.Z. JORGE L. ZERTUCHE RODRIGUEZ

Faculty of Agriculture: Ing. JUAN R. TREVIÑO HIGUERA

Faculty of Commerce and Administration: C.P. ENRIQUE C. ETIENNE

Faculty of Education: Lic. MATIAS TREVIÑO VILLASANA

Faculty of Law and Social Sciences: Lic. FELIPE FLORES GARCÍA

Faculty of Social Work: Lic. MARÍA CECILIA MONTEMAYOR MARIN

School of Nursing: Dr RIGOBERTO HINOJOSA CAMACHO

Mante Campus:

Faculty of Agriculture: Ing. GILBERTO MORALES BARRIOS

Matamoros Campus:

Faculty of Human Medicine: Dr VICTOR REYES ACOSTA

Faculty of Nursing: Lic. Enf. JOSEFINA CARRASCO ROBLEDO

Reynosa Campus:

Faculty of Chemical Sciences: Q. ZARAGOSA RODRIGUEZ FLORES

Faculty of Agro-industrial Sciences: Ing. JOSE SUAREZ FERNANDEZ

Nuevo Laredo Campus:

Faculty of Commerce and Administration: L.A.E. HOMERO AGUIRRE MILLING

Faculty of Nursing: Dr JAIME ALCORTA MALDONADO

UNIVERSIDAD AUTÓNOMA DE TLAXCALA

Apdo Postal 19, 90000 Tlaxcala, Tlax.

Telephone: 2-08-18

Founded 1976

Rector: MOISES BARCEINAS PAREDES

Administrative Director: GUILLERMO VIGUERAS GARCÍA

Librarian: JOSÉ R. RAMÍREZ LÓPEZ

Number of teachers: 400

Number of students: 7,500

Publications: *Comunidad* (monthly), *Enfoque* (univ. review, quarterly).

Depts of social sciences, biomedical sciences, education.

UNIVERSIDAD VERACRUZANA

Zona Universitaria, Lomas del Estadio s/n, 91090 Jalapa, Ver.

Telephone: (281) 17-34-27

Fax: (281) 17-63-70

E-mail: victora@speedy.coacade.uv.mx

Founded 1944

Academic year: September to August

Rector: Dr VÍCTOR A. ARREDONDO ALVAREZ

Academic Secretary: Dra SARA LADRÓN DE GUEVARA

Dean of Planning and Institutional Research: Dr RICARDO MERCADO DEL COLLADO
Librarian: Lic. DIANA GONZÁLEZ ORTEGA

Number of teachers: 4,173
Number of students: 47,067

Publications: *La Palabra y el Hombre*, *La Ciencia y el Hombre*.

HEADS OF DIVISIONS

Health Sciences: Dr RAFAEL GUERRERO GARCÍA
Humanities: Dr RICARDO CORZO RAMÍREZ
Agricultural and Biological Sciences: Dr JOSÉ SILICEO ROMERO
Technology: Mtro G. EVERARDO GARCÍA ALONSO
Economics: RAUL ARIAS LOVILLO
Arts: Mtro ENRIQUE VELASCO DEL VALLE

Jalapa Campus

DIRECTORS

Faculty of Architecture: Arq. DARIO HERNÁNDEZ REYNANTE
Faculty of Law: Lic. JOSÉ LORENZO ALVAREZ MONTERO
Faculty of Economics: Lic. MARCO ANTONIO MÉNDEZ GONZÁLEZ
Faculty of Psychology: Psic. CRISTÓBAL FELIPE RANGEL DELGADO
Faculty of Fine Arts: Mtro HÉCTOR VINICIO REYES CONTRERAS
Faculty of Dance: Mtra LILIA DEL CARMEN PALACIOS RAMÍREZ
Faculty of Music: Mtro ENRIQUE SALMERÓN CÓRDOBA
Faculty of Theatre: Mtro JUAN MANUEL ORTÍZ GARCÍA
Faculty of Medicine: Dr RAFAEL CANO ORTEGA
Faculty of Dentistry: C.D. JOSÉ LUIS ZUBIZARRETA RIOS
Faculty of Nutrition: Lic. en Nut. MA. CONCEPCIÓN SÁNCHEZ ROVELO
Faculty of Clinical Chemistry: Q. C. SANDRA LUZ GONZÁLEZ HERRERA
Faculty of Nursing: L.E. MARCIANA ROMÁN AGUILERA
Faculty of Accounting and Business Management: L.A.E. LUIS RICARDO OLIVARES MENDOZA
Faculty of Anthropology: Arq. SERGIO VÁZQUEZ ZÁRATE
Faculty of Philosophy: Mtra MA ANGÉLICA SALMERÓN JIMÉNEZ
Faculty of History: Mtro GERARDO ANTONIO GALINDO PELÁEZ
Faculty of Languages: Lic. MA DEL CARMEN HERNÁNDEZ JIMÉNEZ
Faculty of Spanish Language and Literature: Lic. MERCEDES LOZANO ORTEGA
Faculty of Education: Mtra MARTHA EVELINA CÓRDOVA RODRÍGUEZ
Faculty of Agriculture: Ing. ANDRÉS RIVERA FERNÁNDEZ
Faculty of Biology: Biol. SOLEDAD FLORES ROCHA
Faculty of Civil Engineering: Ing. DAVID HERNÁNDEZ SANTIAGO
Faculty of Mechanical and Electrical Engineering: Ing. JOSÉ ALBERTO VELÁSQUEZ PÉREZ
Faculty of Chemical Engineering: Ing. IGNACIO PAVÓN RIVERA
Faculty of Chemical Biological Pharmacy: Quim. ABRAHAM HERIBERTO SOTO CID
Faculty of Statistics and Computing: L.E. SERGIO HERNÁNDEZ GONZÁLEZ
Faculty of Administrative and Social Sciences: L.A.E. ADELAIDA RODRÍGUEZ ARCOS
Faculty of Sociology: Mtro ARTURO HINOJOSA LOYA
Faculty of Physics: Dr MANUEL MARTÍNEZ MORALES
Faculty of Electronics: M. I. IGNACIO MORA GONZÁLEZ
Faculty of Mathematics: Mtro LUIS FELIPE GONZÁLEZ GÁLVEZ

Veracruz Campus

Vice-Rector: M.V.Z. EMILIO ZILLI DEBERNARDI

DIRECTORS

Faculty of Communications Science: Lic. ARTURO E. GARCÍA NIÑO
Faculty of Medicine: Dr GUILLERMO BROISSIN RAMOS
Faculty of Dentistry: C.D. EMMA HERNÁNDEZ FIGUEROA
Faculty of Nutrition: Lic. en Nut. MA. DE LOURDES MALPICA CARLÍN
Faculty of Veterinary Medicine and Zootechnics: M.V.Z. MIGUEL A. RODRÍGUEZ CHESSANI
Faculty of Nursing: L.E. MARISELA SÁNCHEZ GÁNDARA
Faculty of Physical Education, Sports and Recreation: Prof. RUBÉN SALAS MENA
Faculty of Education: Mtra GUADALUPE HUERTA ARIZMENDI
Faculty of Clinical Chemistry: Dra MARINA TRUJILLO ORTÍZ
Faculty of Psychology: Psic. MA. EUGENIA PADILLA FARÍAS
Faculty of Accounting: C.P. CELIA DEL PILAR GARRIDO VARGAS
Faculty of Business Management: L.A.E. LILIANA BETANCOURT TRAVENDHAN
Faculty of Engineering: Ing. JOSÉ SALOMÉ BOBADILLA Y ALMEIDA

Orizaba-Córdoba Campus

Vice-Rector: Arq. ROBERTO OLAVARRIETA MARENCO

DIRECTORS

Faculty of Chemical Sciences: Ing. VÍCTOR KASHIGAMI NAKANISHI
Faculty of Nursing: Lic. Enf. INÉS HUERTA VÁSQUEZ
Faculty of Medicine: Dr GUSTAVO PIMENTEL SÁNCHEZ
Faculty of Mechanical and Electrical Engineering: Ing. CARLOS ROSALES VEGA
Faculty of Architecture: Arq. HONORIO ALFREDO HERRERA CABALLERO
Faculty of Dentistry: C.D. JOAQUÍN ROMERO RUÍZ ESPARZA
Faculty of Biological and Agricultural Sciences: Biol. ANTONIO PÉREZ PACHECO
Faculty of Dentistry: C.D. JOAQUÍN ROMERO RUÍZ ESPARZA
Faculty of Accountancy and Business Management: C.P. VÍCTOR I. MUÑOZ ROSAS

Poza Rica-Tuxpan Campus

Vice-Rector: Dra CLARA CELINA MEDINA SAGAHÓN

DIRECTORS

Faculty of Social Work: Mtra ROSALBA PERALTA SANTIAGO
Faculty of Education: Lic. ARIEL RIVERA TORRES
Faculty of Accountancy: C.P. PEDRO ERIK VEGA COBOS
Faculty of Medicine: Dr JORGE DURÁN CRUZ
Faculty of Dentistry: C.D. TERESA GRACIELA RIVERA LEÓN
Faculty of Psychology: Psic. CARLA IRENE REYES DE LA CONCHA
Faculty of Nursing: L.E. ALEJANDRA DINORAH MÁRQUEZ DOMÍNGUEZ
Faculty of Civil Engineering: Ing. MARCOS CASTILLO PONCE
Faculty of Chemical Sciences: Ing. GLORIA BOCARDI PÉREZ
Faculty of Architecture: Arq. ALVARO HERÁNDEZ SANTIAGO
Faculty of Biology, Agriculture and Animal Husbandry: Biol. JOSÉ LUIS ALANIS MÉNDEZ
Faculty of Electronic Engineering and Communications: Ing. LUIS DAVID RAMÍREZ GONZÁLEZ
Faculty of Mechanical and Electrical Engineering: Ing. JOSÉ LUIS JUÁREZ SUÁREZ

Coatzacoalcos-Minatitlán Campus

Vice-Rector: Arq. ANGEL LUIS HERNÁNDEZ JIMÉNEZ

DIRECTORS

Faculty of Accounting and Business Management: L.A.E. MIGUEL SÁNCHEZ LARA
Faculty of Medicine: Dr RODOLFO BARRIENTOS SANTIAGO
Faculty of Engineering: Ing. CIRO CASTILLO PÉREZ
Faculty of Dentistry: Dra CARMEN RÍOS GRACIA
Faculty of Social Work: Lic. en T.S. LUCINDA MIRANDA CHIÑAS
Faculty of Nursing: Enf. MANUELA TÉLLEZ ZÁRATE
Faculty of Agricultural Production Systems Engineering: Ing. ALBERTO HERNÁNDEZ QUIROZ
Faculty of Chemistry (Coatzacoalcos): Ing. ERUBIEL FLANDEZ ALEMÁN

UNIVERSIDAD AUTÓNOMA DE YUCATÁN

Apdo 1418-3, Calles 57 por 60, 97000 Mérida, Yucatán
Telephone: (99) 24-80-00
Fax: (99) 28-25-57

Founded 1624, refounded 1922
State control
Academic year: September to July

Rector: C.P. CARLOS M. PASOS NOVELO
General Director of Academic Affairs and Library Co-ordination: Dr VICTOR FERNÁNDEZ MEDINA

20 libraries with 126,000 vols, 8,000 periodical titles
Number of teachers: 1,485
Number of students: 13,469

Publication: *Revista*, faculty publs, etc.

DIRECTORS

Faculty of Medicine: Dr MARCO A. PALMA SOLÍS
Faculty of Nursing: Lic. ROSA O. GUEMEZ MEDINA
Faculty of Law: Abog. CARLOS TOLEDO CABRERA
Faculty of Chemistry: MIGUEL PACHECO ORTIZ
Faculty of Dentistry: C.D. ROLANDO G. PENICHE MARCÍN
Faculty of Engineering: Ing. MARIO I. GÓMEZ MEJÍA
Faculty of Accountancy and Administration: C.P. FRANCISCO J. ALVAREZ VALES
Faculty of Economics: Lic. JORGE L. CANCHÉ ESCAMILLA
Faculty of Veterinary Studies: M.V.Z. RAÚL GODOY MONTAÑEZ
Faculty of Architecture: Arq. ROBERTO ANCONA RIESTRA
Faculty of Anthropology: Dr R. DELFIN QUEZADA DOMÍNGUEZ
Faculty of Psychology: Lic. REYNALDO NOVELO HERRERA
Preparatory School 1: QFB Pastor SIERRA MENU
Preparatory School 2: C.P. FREDDY DUARTE ARANDA
Faculty of Education: Lic. SILVIA J. PECH CAMPOS
Faculty of Chemical Engineering: M.A. OCTAVIO GARCIA MADAHUAR
Faculty of Mathematics: Ing. RENÁN RUÍZ FLORES

ATTACHED INSTITUTE

Centro de Investigaciones Regionales 'Dr Hideyo Noguchi': Dir Dr FERNANDO I. PUERTO MANZANO.

UNIVERSIDAD AUTÓNOMA DE ZACATECAS

Jardin Juarez 147, 98000 Zacatecas, Zac.
Telephone: 2-29-24

Founded 1832
State control

Rector: FRANCISCO FLORES SANDOVAL

Secretary-General: Delfino García Hernández
Administrative Secretary: Salvador Santillán Hernández
Academic Secretary: Francisco Valerio Quintero
Librarian: Juan Ignacio Piña Marquina

Library of 35,265 vols
Number of teachers: 1,100
Number of students: 14,800

Publications: *Cuadernos de investigación, Diálogo, Gaceta universitaria, Azogue*.

DIRECTORS

School of Law: Lic. Virgilio Rivera Delgadillo
School of Engineering: Ing. Juan Francisco Rochín Salinas
School of Chemistry: Juana María Valadez Castrejón
School of Nursing: Ma Isabel Medina Hernández
School of Accounting and Administration: Jesús Limones Hernández
School of Economics: Lic. Rodolfo García Zamora
School of Animal Breeding and Veterinary Medicine: Antonio Mejía Haro
School of Dentistry: Dr Raúl Bermeo Padilla
School of Medicine: Dr Gerardo de Jesús Félix Domínguez
School of Agronomy: Ing. Pedro Zesati del Villar
School of Social Sciences: Pedro Gómez Sánchez
School of Mines and Metallurgy: Ing. Ruben de Jesús del Pozo Mendoza
School of Mathematics: Lic. Juan Antonio Pérez
School of Psychology: Lic. Ricardo Bermeo Padilla
School of Music: Lic. Esaul Arteaga Domínguez
School of Humanities: Lic. Veremundo Carrillo Trujillo
School of Physics: Lic. Humberto Vidales Roque
School of Education: Sergio Espinosa Proa

ATTACHED INSTITUTES

Centro de Investigaciones Agronómicas: Ing. Julio Lozano Gutiérrez.

Centro de Investigaciones en Ciencias Químicas: Dr Miguel Angel Juárez Pérez.

Centro de Investigaciones en Medicina Veterinaria y Zootecnia: Lic. Armando Talamantes Roque.

Centro de Investigaciones en Ingeniería Mecánica y Eléctrica: Ing. Manuel Reta Hernández.

Centro de Investigaciones Jurídicas: Lic. José Antonio Valenzuela Rios.

Centro de Investigaciones Históricas: Cuauhtemoc Esparza Sánchez.

Centro Regional de Estudios Nucleares: Leopoldo Quirino Torres.

Centro de Estudios Literarios: Lic. David Ojeda Alvarez.

Centro de Estudios en Ciencias Minerales y de la Tierra: Ing. Victor Manuel Navarro Hernández.

Centro Universitario de Investigación y Docencia: Dr Rafael Herrera Esparza.

Centro de Investigación y Análisis de la Economía Regional: Lic. Rigoberto Villa Vásquez.

Centro de Investigaciones Astronómicas: Ing. Manuel Rios Herrera.

Centro de Instrumentos: Ing. Alfonso Macías López.

Instituto de Investigaciones Odontológicas: Dr Oscar Saucedo Quintero.

Instituto de Investigaciones Economico-Sociales: Ing. Pedro Carrera Hernández.

Technical Universities

INSTITUTO POLITÉCNICO NACIONAL

Unidad Profesional Zacatenco, Col. Lindavista, 07738 México, DF

Telephone and fax: (905) 754-41-02

Founded 1936
State control
Language of instruction: Spanish
Academic year: September to July

Director-General: C.P. Oscar Joffre Velázquez
Secretary-General: Ing. Alfredo López Hernández
Administrative Director: Ing. Héctor Uriel Mayagoitia Prado
Librarian: Lic. Cesar Santomé Figueroa

Number of teachers: 12,356
Number of students: 107,200

Publications: *Gaceta Politécnica; Acta Politécnica, Acta Médica, Anales de la Escuela Nacional de Ciencias Biológicas, Economía Política.*

DIRECTORS

Higher School of Mechanical and Electrical Engineering: Ing. Arturo Zepeda Salinas
Higher School of Engineering and Architecture: Ing. Salvador Padilla Alonso
Higher School of Chemical Engineering and Mining Industries: Ing. Timoteo Pastrana Aponte
Higher School of Textile Engineering: Ing. Cassin Francisco Ale Guerrero
Higher School of Physics and Mathematics: M. en C. Olga Leticia Hernández Chávez
Higher School of Medicine: Dr Juan Ordorica Vargas
National School of Medicine and Homeopathy: Dr Jaime Ernesto Sánchez González
National School of Biological Sciences: Dra Thelma Lilia Villegas Garrido
Higher School of Commerce and Administration: C.P. José de Jesús Vázquez Bonilla
Higher School of Tourism: Lic. Víctor Chale Góngora
Higher School of Economics: Lic. Miguel Angel Correa Jasso
Interdisciplinary Professional Unit of Engineering and Social and Administrative Sciences: Ing. Ernesto Angeles Mejía
Interdisciplinary Centre for Health Sciences: Lic. Nut. Adrián Guillermo Quintero Gutiérrez
Interdisciplinary Centre for Marine Sciences: M. en C. Julian René Torres Villegas
Interdisciplinary Research Centre for Regional Development (Michoacán): M. en C. Víctor Manuel López López
Interdisciplinary Research Centre for Regional Development (Durango Centre): Dr Jóse Angel L. Ortega Herrera
Interdisciplinary Research Centre for Regional Development (Oaxaca Centre): Ing. Fernando Eli Ortíz Hernández
Centre for Research and Development in Digital Technology (in Tijuana): Dr José Mária Montoya Flores
Project for Technological and Scientific Social Studies: M. en C. Luis Fernando Castillo García
Interdisciplinary Project for the Environment and Integrated Development: Dr Juan Manuel Navarro Pineda

ATTACHED INSTITUTION

Centro de Investigación y de Estudios Avanzados: see under Research Institutes.

INSTITUTO TECNOLÓGICO Y DE ESTUDIOS SUPERIORES DE MONTERREY

Sucursal de Correos 'J', 64849 Monterrey, Nuevo León

Telephone: (8) 358-20-00
Fax: (8) 358-89-31

Founded 1943
Private control
Language of instruction: Spanish
Academic year: August to May

President: Dr Rafael Rangel Sostmann
Academic Vice-President: Dr Héctor Moreira
Financial Vice-President: Ing. Eliseo Vázquez Orozco
President of Monterrey Campus: Ing. Ramón de la Peña Manrique
President of Eugenio Garza Sada Campus: Dr José Treviño Abrego
Presidents for Out-of-State Campuses: Dr César Morales Hernández (Southern Zone); Ing. Luis Caraza (Central Zone); C. P. David Noel Ramírez (Northern Zone); Ing Juan Manuel Durán Gutiérrez (Pacific Zone), Ing. Carlos Cruz Limón (Virtual University)
Registrar: Lic. Sergio Sierra Cabada (Monterrey Campus), Ing. José Pantoja (State of Mexico Campus), Lic. Sergio Bravo (Pacific Zone), Lic. Marco Vinicio López (Querétaro Campus), Ing. Juan Manuel Ruiz (Northern Zone)
Librarian: Ing. Miguel Arreola

Library of 110,000 vols, 2,500 periodicals, 698,000 vols (Out-of-State Campuses)
Number of teachers: 5,148
Number of students: 68,947

DIRECTORS OF ACADEMIC DIVISIONS (Monterrey Campus)

Division of Administration and Social Sciences: C. P. Gerardo Luján
Division of Agricultural and Marine Sciences: Dr Juan D. Vega
Division of Sciences and Humanities: Ing. Patricio Lopez del Puerto
Division of Graduate Studies and Research: Dr Fernando Jaimes
Division of Engineering and Architecture: Dr Teófilo Ramos
Division of Health Sciences: Dr Carlos Díaz Montemayor

The Institute comprises 24 campuses in addition to the main Monterrey and Eugenio Garza Sada campuses.

Colleges

CENTRO DE ENSEÑANZA TÉCNICA Y SUPERIOR

Apdo Postal 3-797, Mexicali, Baja California Norte

Telephone: (65) 67-37-00
Fax: (65) 65-02-41

Founded 1961

Rector: Dr Enrique Carrillo-Barrios Gómez
Vice-Rector (Academic): Dr Fernando León García
Director-General of Mexicali Campus: Ing. Enrique C. Blancas de la Cruz
Director-General of Tijuana Campus: Lic. Rodrigo Gutiérrez
Director-General of Ensenada Campus: Ing. Rubén Magdaleno

Libraries with 51,000 vols
Number of students: 3,714

Courses in fields of engineering, accountancy, management, behavioural sciences.

COLEGIO DE LA FRONTERA SUR

Carretera Panamericana y Periférico Sur s/n, Apdo Postal 63, 29290 San Cristóbal de las Casas, Chiapas

Telephone: (967) 8-18-83
Fax: (967) 8-23-22

Founded 1994

Director-General: Dr PABLO FARÍAS CAMPERO

Divisions of Alternative Means of Production, of Agroecological Technology, of Health and Population, of the Conservation and Exploitation of Biodiversity.

COLEGIO DE MÉXICO

Camino al Ajusco 20, 10740 México, DF

Telephone: (5) 449-30-00
Fax: (5) 645-04-64

Founded 1940

President: ANDRÉS LIRA GONZÁLEZ
Secretary-General: DAVID PANTOJA MORÁN
Academic Co-ordinator: FERNANDO ESCALANTE GONZALBO
Library Director: ÁLVARO QUIJANO

Library of 710,000 vols
Number of teachers and researchers: 180
Number of students: 250

Publications: *Nueva Revista de Filología Hispánica* (2 a year), *Historia Mexicana*, *Foro Internacional*, *Estudios de Asia y África*, *Estudios Demográficos y Urbanos* (all quarterly), *Estudios Económicos* (2 a year), *Estudios Sociológicos* (3 a year).

DIRECTORS

Centre for Historical Studies: JAVIER GARCIADIEGO DANTAN
Centre for Sociological Studies: FRANCISCO ZAPATA
Centre for International Studies: CELIA TORO
Centre for Demographic and Urban Development Studies: MANUEL ORDORICA
Centre for Asian and African Studies: BENJAMÍN PRECIADO
Centre for Hispanic Linguistics and Hispanic Literary Studies: LUIS FERNANDO LARA
Centre for Studies in Economics: HORACIO SOBARZO

ESCUELA MILITAR DE INGENIEROS
(Military School of Engineers)

Batalla de Celaya No. 202, México 10, DF

Founded 1822

The school is dependent on the Secretaría de la Defensa Nacional

Director: Coronel I.C. JACOBO WITTMAN ROJANO

Library of 10,000 vols
Number of students: 142

Publications: *Apuntes*, *Conferencias*.

ESCUELA NACIONAL DE ANTROPOLOGÍA E HISTORIA PERIFERICO SUR Y ZAPOTE
(National School of Anthropology and History)

Col. Isidro Fabela, C.P. 14030, México, DF

Telephone: 6-06-17-58

Founded 1938

Director: GLORIA ARTÍS MERCADET
Librarian: REYNALDO FIGUEROA SERVÍN

Library of 30,000 vols
Number of teachers: 395
Number of students: 2,068

Publications: *Revista Cuicuilco*, *Folleto de Información Básica y Cuadernos de Trabajo.*

DEPARTMENT HEADS

GONZALEZ, N., Physical Anthropology
MELGAR, R., Social Anthropology
LOPEZ, J., Archaeology
MASFERRER, E., Ethnohistory
SANCHEZ, M., Ethnology
FLORES, R., Linguistics
VADILLO, C., History
SOBERANES, F., Social Anthropology (Oaxaca)
SARIEGO, J.L., Social Anthropology (Chihuahua)

ESCUELA NACIONAL DE BIBLIOTECONOMÍA Y ARCHIVONOMÍA
(National School of Librarianship and Archives)

Viaducto Miguel Aleman 155, México 13, DF

Founded 1945

Director: Mtro EDUARDO SALAS
Associate Director: Mtra CONCEPCION BARQUET TELLEZ
Secretary: Prof. GUILLERMO OROPEZA

Library of 5,000 vols
Number of teachers: 72
Number of students: 420

Publication: *Bibliotecas y Archivos*.

ESCUELA NACIONAL DE CONSERVACIÓN, RESTAURACIÓN Y MUSEOGRAFÍA 'MANUEL DEL CASTILLO NEGRETE'
(Manuel del Castillo Negrete National School of Conservation, Restoration and Museography)

Ex-Convento de Churubusco, Xicoténcatl y Gral Anaya, 04120 México, DF

Telephone: (5) 604-51-88
Fax: (5) 604-51-63

Founded 1968

Director: M. A. MERCEDES GOMEZ-URQUIZA

Library of 13,000 vols

INSTITUTO DE FILOLOGÍA HISPÁNICA

Pérez Treviño 844 Pte, Apdo 144, Saltillo, Coahuila

Telephone: 2-15-11

Founded 1968
Private control
Academic year: autumn and winter terms with extra sessions in January and summer
Director: RODOLFO VALDÉS
Academic Dean and Librarian: MARÍA BOEHM
Dean of Students and Registrar: ELIZABETH SÁNCHEZ
Secretary: MARÍA M. BARRÓN LÓPEZ

Courses in language, literature, history, sociology, folklore, art and native music.

INSTITUTO TECNOLÓGICO AUTÓNOMO DE MÉXICO

Río Hondo 1, Del. Alvaro Obregón, 01000 México, DF

Telephone: 550-93-00
Fax: 550-76-37

Founded 1946

President: ALBERTO BAILLERES
Rector: ARTURO FERNÁNDEZ PÉREZ

Library of 95,000 vols, 770 periodicals
Number of students: 3,500

Publication: *Revista Estudios* (quarterly).

Courses in business administration, economics, accounting, mathematics, law, computer sciences, public policy, literature, history, statistics and social sciences.

INSTITUTO TECNOLÓGICO Y DE ESTUDIOS SUPERIORES DE OCCIDENTE

Apdo P. 31175, 45051 Zapopan, Jal.; premises at Periférico Sur 8585, 45090 Tlaquepaque, Jal.

Telephone: (3) 669-34-34
Fax: (3) 669-34-35

Founded 1957

Rector: Lic. PABLO HUMBERTO POSADA VELÁZQUEZ
Secretary-General: CARLOS CORONA CARAVEO

Library of 76,810 vols
Number of teachers: 714
Number of students: 5,200

Publications: *Universidad ITESO* (monthly), *Revista RENGLONES* (3 a year), *Huella* (3 a year).

Undergraduate courses in architecture, business administration, communication, public accountancy, civil, industrial and electronic engineering, chemical processing and administration, computer systems, design, psychology, industrial relations, educational sciences, law, marketing. Postgraduate courses in business management, education, engineering, communication, human development, urban development, international business.

INSTITUTO TECNOLÓGICO DE CELAYA

Avda Tecnológico y Antonio Garcia Cubas, Apdo Postal 57, 38010 Celaya, Gto

Telephone: 2-20-23
Telex: 128857
Fax: 3-92-30

Founded 1958

Director: Dr JUAN SILLERO PEREZ
Academic Vice-Director: M.C. SAMUEL DOMINGUEZ TAMAYO
Administrative Vice-Director: M.C. RUBEN MARTINEZ BALDERAS
Librarian: Lic. TEODORO VILLALOBOS SALINAS

Library of 16,600 vols
Number of students: 2,623

Publications: *Apertura, Pistas Educativas*.

Courses in industrial engineering, mechanics, chemistry and biochemistry, production and business administration, computer systems, electronics.

INSTITUTO TECNOLÓGICO DE CHIHUAHUA

Apdo Postal 2-1549, Ave. Tecnológico No 2909, 31310 Chihuahua, Chih.

Telephone: (14) 13-74-74
Telex: 349682
Fax: 135187

Founded 1948

Director: Ing. MANUEL GALLARDO RODRÍGUEZ
Administrative Vice-Director: Ing. JUAN DE DIOS RUIZ
Academic Vice-Director: Ing. ANTONIO TREVIÑO RUIZ

Library of 29,000 vols
Number of teachers: 350
Number of students: 4,400

Publication: *Electro* (annually).

Degree courses in industrial, electrical, mechanical, chemical, electronic and materials engineering; postgraduate courses in electronics; degree and postgraduate courses in administration.

INSTITUTO TECNOLÓGICO DE DURANGO

Blvd F. Pescador 1830 Ote., Apdo Postal 465, 34080 Durango

Telephone: (181) 2-74-64
Telex: 066311

Founded 1948

Dependent on the Dirección General de Institutos Tecnológicos Regionales, SEP

Director: Ing. HECTOR ARREOLA SORIA
Librarian: JESÚS LAU

Library of 19,000 vols
Number of teachers: 267
Number of students: 2,677

First degree courses in industrial engineering in electronics, electricity, biochemistry, mechanics, information science, chemistry and civil engineering; Masters in industrial planning, biochemistry, civil engineering.

INSTITUTO TECNOLÓGICO DE CIUDAD JUÁREZ

Blvd. Tecnológico 1340, Apdo 2734, 32500 Ciudad Juárez, Chihuahua

Telephone: 17-38-94
Telex: 33888
Fax: (16) 17-35-12

Founded 1964

Director: ROBERTO ARANA MORAN
Vice-Directors: HUMBERTO C. MORALES MORENO (Administrative), ALFREDO ESTRADA GARCÍA (Academic), SALVADOR SÁNCHEZ CRUZ (Academic Support)

Library of 13,300 vols
Number of teachers: 268
Number of students: 4,468

INSTITUTO TECNOLÓGICO DE CIUDAD MADERO

Apdo Postal 20, 89440 Ciudad Madero, Tam.

Telephone: 15-63-39

Founded 1954

Director: Ing. JUAN MANEL TURRUBIATE MARTINEZ

Library of 17,781 vols
Number of students: 5,000

INSTITUTO TECNOLÓGICO DE MÉRIDA

Avda Tecnológico km. 5, Apdo Postal 9–11, 97118 Mérida, Yucatán

Telephone: (99) 44-81-22
Fax: (99) 44-81-81
E-mail: itm@uxmal.itmerida.mx

Founded 1961

Director: Ing. GELASIO LUNA CONZUELO
Vice-Director (Administration): Ing. ALFREDO DÍAZ MENDOZA
Vice-Director (Academic): Ing. RAÚL BARCELÓ PENICHE
Librarian: M.C. JUANA B. MEDINA Y UN

Library of 20,000 vols
Number of teachers: 369
Number of students: 4,146

Publications: *Revista del Centro de Graduados e Investigación* (quarterly), *La Quincena* (every 2 weeks).

HEADS OF DEPARTMENTS

Chemistry and Biochemistry: Ing. ANA ROSA CUEVAS SOSA
Earth Sciences: Ing. ISIDRO CALDERÓN ACOSTA
Electricity and Electronics: Ing. MARGARITA ALVAREZ CERVERA
Economics and Administration: Lic. NELLY MEJÍA VELASCO
Industrial Engineering: Ing. MANUEL MEDINA M.
Metal-Mechanics: Ing. JOSÉ D. BORGES PASOS
Systems and Computing: Ing. LUIS GANZO FIGUEROA
Graduate Studies and Research: Ing. EMANUEL CONDE ONTIVEROS

INSTITUTO TECNOLÓGICO DE MORELIA

Carretera Morelia Salvatierra, Apdo Postal 262, 58120 Morelia, Michoacán

Telephone: 2-15-70

Founded 1965

Director: Ing. JAIME ZORAGOZA BUENO

Library of 15,000 vols
Number of students: 3,500

Courses in industrial engineering and iron and steel industry.

INSTITUTO TECNOLÓGICO DE OAXACA

Calz. Tecnológico y Wilfrido-Massieu s/n, 68030 Oaxaca, Oax.

Telephone: 6-17-22, 6-44-13, 6-52-48

Founded 1968

Director: Ing. ARMANDO D. PALACIOS GARCÍA

Number of teachers: 280
Number of students: 3,000

Publication: *Itrosíntesis.*

Courses in mechanical, electrical, chemical and civil engineering, business management and industrial planning.

INSTITUTO TECNOLÓGICO DE ORIZABA

Avda Instituto Tecnológico 852, Col E. Zapata, Apdo Postal 324, 94320 Orizaba, Ver.

Telephone: 4-40-96
Telex: 15439
Fax: 5-17-28

Founded 1957

Director: Ing. ENRIQUE LEAL CRUZ
Administrative Assistant Director: Ing. BLAS REYES T.
Assistant Director (Planning): Ing. ROSENDO MARTÍNEZ
Academic Assistant Director: Ing. KIKEY GONZÁLEZ F.

Number of teachers: 308
Number of students: 2,994

Courses in chemical, industrial mechanical, electrical and electronic engineering, and computer science.

INSTITUTO TECNOLÓGICO DE QUERÉTARO

Apdo Postal 124, Avda Tecnológico y Gral Escobedo s/n, 76000 Querétaro, Qro

Telephone: 16-35-97
Fax: 16-99-31

Founded 1967

Director: Ing. JUAN VALDESPINO MARTÍNEZ
Academic Vice-Director: Ing. JORGE MARIO ELIAS MARTÍNEZ
Vice-Director (Planning and Extension): Ing. FERNANDO QUIROZ GATICA

Library of 28,000 vols
Number of teachers: 314
Number of students: 3,596

Courses in industrial and mechanical engineering, architecture, systems engineering, electrical and electronic engineering and industrial administration.

INSTITUTO TECNOLÓGICO DE SALTILLO

Apdo Postal 600, Venustiano Carranza 2400, 25280 Saltillo, Coahuila

Telephone: 5-55-11
Telex: 381165

Founded 1951

Director: Ing. JOSÉ C. TAMEZ SAENZ

Library of *c.* 15,100 vols
Number of students: 3,000

Publications: *Boletín de Seguridad Industrial, Boletín de Fundación, Boletín de Microenseñanza* faculty bulletins.

Courses in industrial, metallurgical and computer science engineering and technology.

INSTITUTO TECNOLÓGICO DE SONORA

5 de Febrero 818 Sur, 85000 Ciudad Obregón, Son.

Telephone: (64) 17-07-83
Fax: (64) 17-02-44
E-mail: orusso@itson.mx

Founded 1955 as Preparatory school, became University in 1973

Rector: Dr OSCAR RUSSO VOGEL
Vice-Rector for Academic Affairs: Lic. JAVIER VALES GARCÍA
Vice-Rector for Administrative Affairs: Lic. JORGE OROZCO PARRA

Library of 87,000 vols
Number of teachers: 914
Number of students: 16,355

Publications: *Revista de la Sociedad Académica* (2 a year), *ITSON-DIEP* (research reports, 2 a year).

Courses in biotechnological, electrical, electronic, systems and industrial, civil, chemical and agricultural engineering, chemistry, business administration, accounting, management information systems, education, psychology, veterinary medicine, natural resources and water resources management.

INSTITUTO DE ESTUDIOS SUPERIORES EN CIENCIA Y TECNOLOGÍA DEL MAR

Circunvalación Norte e Icazo, Veracruz, Ver.

Founded 1957

Dependent on the Dirección General de Enseñanzas Tecnológicas (Ministry of Education)

Director: Ing. JOSÉ LÓPEZ MEDINA

School of Music

Conservatorio Nacional de Música (National Conservatoire): Avda Presidente Masaryk 582, México 5, DF; tel. 280-63-47; fax 280-37-26; f. 1866; 170 teachers; Dir Maestro LEOPOLDO TELLEZ; library of 48,900 vols; publs *Heterofonía, Gaceta de la Biblioteca*.

MOLDOVA

Learned Societies

GENERAL

Academy of Sciences of Moldova: 2001 Chişinău, B-dul Ştefan cel Mare 1; tel. 26-14-78; fax 54-28-23; f. 1961; sections of Physico-Mathematical Sciences (Academician-Co-ordinator ALEXEI SIMAŞCHEVICI), Biological and Chemical Sciences (Academician-Co-ordinator ANDREI URSU), Humanities and Social Sciences (Academician-Co-ordinator HARALAMBIE CORBU), Technical Sciences (Academician-Co-ordinator NICOLAE ANDRONATI), Agricultural Sciences (Academician-Co-ordinator ILIE UNTILĂ), Medical Sciences (Academician-Co-ordinator GHEORGHE PALADI); 45 mems, 56 corresp. mems, 14 hon. mems; attached research institutes: see Research Institutes; library: see Libraries and Archives; Pres. ANDREI ANDRIEŞ; Chief Learned Sec. GHEORGHE ŞIŞCANU; publs *Izvestiya* (Bulletin-Series: Economics and Sociology, Mathematics, Physics and Engineering Sciences, every 4 months, Biological and Chemical Sciences, every 2 months), *Elektronnaya Obrabotka Materialov* (Electronic Processing of Materials, every 2 months), *Revista de Lingvistică şi Ştiinţă Literară* (Journal of Linguistics and Study of Literature, every 2 months), *Revista de Istorie a Moldovei* (Moldovan Historical Journal, quarterly), *Revista de filozofie şi drept* (Journal of Philosophy and Law, every 2 months).

HISTORY, GEOGRAPHY AND ARCHAEOLOGY

Geographical Society of Moldova: 277012 Chişinău, Bul. Ştefan cel Mare 43; tel. 22-72-48; Chair. A. M. CAPCELEA.

LANGUAGE AND LITERATURE

PEN Centre of Moldova: 277068 Chişinău, Bulevardul Miron Costin 21 (ap. 24); tel. 44-35-40; f. 1991; 25 mems; Pres. SPIRIDON VANGHELI; Sec. ANDREI BURAC.

NATURAL SCIENCES

Biological Sciences

Entomological Society of Moldova: 2028 Chişinău, Str. Academiei 1; tel.73-98-96; Chair B. V. VEREŞCIAGHIN.

Hydrobiological Society of Moldova: 2028 Chişinău, Str. Academiei 1; tel. (2) 73-12-55; f. 1968; 36 mems; Chair. ION TODERAŞ.

Microbiological Society of Moldova: 2028 Chişinău, Str. Academiei 1; tel. 73-98-78; Chair. V. RUDIC.

Ornithological Society of Moldova: 2028 Chişinău, Str. Academiei 1; tel. 73-75-09; Chair. (vacant).

Protozoological Society of Moldova: 2028 Chişinău, Str. Academiei 1; tel. 73-75-11; Chair. C. A. ANDRIUŢĂ.

Society of Botanists of Moldova: 277018 Chişinău, Str. Pădurilor 18; tel. 52-38-96; Chair. A. G. NEGRU.

Society of Geneticists of Moldova: 277049 Chişinău, Str. Gribova 44; tel. 43-23-08; Chair. V. D. SIMINEL.

Society of Plant Physiology and Biochemistry of Moldova: 2002 Chişinău, Str. Pădurilor 22; tel. 55-55-14; fax 55-00-26; f. 1988; 50 mems; Pres. Prof. SIMION I. TOMA.

Teriological Society of Moldova: 2028 Chişinău, Str. Academiei 1 (Room 220); tel. (2) 72-55-66; fax (2) 73-12-55; 19 mems; Chair. A. I. MUNTEANU.

Physical Sciences

Mendeleev Chemical Society: 277028 Chişinău, Str. Academiei 3; tel. 73-97-55; Chair K. I. TURTĂ.

Physical Society of Moldova: 277028 Chisinău, Str. Academiei 5; tel. 72-58-87; Chair. T. I. MALINOVSCHI.

RELIGION, SOCIOLOGY AND ANTHROPOLOGY

Moldovan Sociological Association: 279200 Beltsi, Str. Puşkin 38; tel. (231) 2-44-79; Chair. N. V. ŢURCANU.

Research Institutes

AGRICULTURE, FISHERIES AND VETERINARY SCIENCE

National Institute of Animal Husbandry and Veterinary Medicine: 6525 Regiune Anenii Noi, S-ul Maximovca; tel. and fax 38-43-50; f. 1956; library of 19,000 vols; Dir MIHAIL BAHCIVANJI; publ. *Scientific Transactions* (annually).

Research Institute of Maize and Sorghum: Regiune Criulan, S-ul Paşcani.

Research Institute of Viticulture and Wine-making: Reguine Kutuzov, S-ul Codru.

Tobacco Research Institute: Regiune Criulan, S-ul Gratieşti; tel. and fax 44-50-77; f. 1968.

ECONOMICS, LAW AND POLITICS

Centre for the Study of Marketing Problems: 2001 Chişinău, B-dul Ştefan cel Mare 1; tel. (2) 26-23-91; fax (2) 26-23-91; attached to Acad. of Sciences of Moldova; Dir P. V. COJUCARI.

Institute of Economic Research: 2001 Chişinău, B-dul Ştefan cel Mare 1; tel. (2) 26-24-01; attached to Acad. of Sciences of Moldova; Dir V. CIOBANU.

FINE AND PEFORMING ARTS

Institute of the History and Theory of Art: 2001 Chişinău, B-dul Ştefan cel Mare 1; tel. (2) 26-06-02; fax (2) 22-33-48; f. 1991; attached to Acad. of Sciences of Moldova; fine art, architecture, music, performing arts; Dir LEONID M. CEMORTAN; publ. *Arta* (2 series: fine arts and architecture, and music and the performing arts, each 1 a year).

HISTORY, GEOGRAPHY AND ARCHAEOLOGY

Institute of Archaeology and Ancient History: 2712 Chişinău, Str. Mitr. Banulescu-Bodoni 35; tel. and fax (2) 22-22-42; attached to Acad. of Sciences of Moldova; Dir VALENTIN DERGACEV.

Institute of Geography: 2028 Chişinău, Str. Academiei 1; tel. (2) 73-98-38; e-mail mjuc@c.c.acad.md; f. 1992; attached to Acad. of Sciences of Moldova; Dir T. S. CONSTANTINOV.

Institute of History: 2012 Chişinău, Str. 31 August 82; tel. (2) 23-33-10; attached to Acad. of Sciences of Moldova; Exec. Dir D. DRAGNEV.

LANGUAGE AND LITERATURE

Institute of Linguistics: 2012 Chişinău, Str. 31 August 1989 82; tel. (2) 23-33-05; fax (2) 23-77-52; f. 1991; attached to Acad. of Sciences of Moldova; library of 10,000 vols; Dir SILVIU BEREJAN; publ. *Revistă de Lingvistică şi Ştiinţă Literară* (6 a year).

Institute of Literary Theory and History: 2001 Chişinău, B-dul Ştefan cel Mare 1; tel. (2) 26-27-19; f. 1991; attached to Acad. of Sciences of Moldova; Exec. Dir VASILE CIOCANU; publ. *Revistă de Lingvistică şi Ştiinţă Literară* (6 a year).

MEDICINE

National Centre for Scientific and Applied Hygiene and Epidemiology: 2028 Chişinău, Str. Gh. Asachi 67A; Dir V. CHICU.

NATURAL SCIENCES

Biological Sciences

Centre for Pathology and Pathobiology: 277012 Chişinău, Str. 31 August 151; tel. (2) 22-75-19; attached to Acad. of Sciences of Moldova; Dir. V. ANESTIADE.

Institute of Biological Protection of Plants: 277072 Chişinău, B-dul Dăcii 58; tel. (2) 57-04-66; fax (2) 57-04-33; attached to Acad. of Sciences of Moldova; Dir I. S. POPUŞOI.

Institute of Botany: 2002 Chişinău, Str. Pădurilor 18; tel. (2) 55-04-43; fax (2) 52-38-98; f. 1950; attached to Acad. of Sciences of Moldova; library of 43,000 items; Dir A. A. CIUBOTARU; publ. *Botanical Research* (1 a year).

Institute of Genetics: 2002 Chişinău, Str. Pădurii 20; tel. (2) 77-04-47; fax (2) 55-61-80; e-mail kanc@insgen.as.md; attached to Acad. of Sciences of Moldova; Dir A. G. JACOTĂ.

Institute of Microbiology: 2028 Chişinău, Str. Academiei 1; tel. (2) 73-80-13; attached to Acad. of Sciences of Moldova; Dir V. F. RUDIC.

Institute of Physiology: 2028 Chişinău, Str. Academiei 1; tel. (2) 72-51-55; attached to Acad. of Sciences of Moldova; Dir I. I. FURDUI.

Institute of Plant Physiology: 277018 Chişinău, Str. Pădurilor 22; tel. (2) 53-84-05; fax (2) 55-00-26; f. 1961; attached to Acad. of Sciences of Moldova; library of 9,000 vols; Dir Prof. S. I. TOMA.

Institute of Zoology: 2028 Chişinău, Str. Academiei 1; tel. (2) 73-98-09; fax (2) 73-12-55; attached to Acad. of Sciences of Moldova; Dir ION TODERAŞ.

Mathematical Sciences

Institute of Mathematics: 2028 Chişinău, Str. Academiei 5; tel. (2) 72-59-82; fax (2) 73-80-27; e-mail imam@math.md; f. 1964; attached to Acad. of Sciences of Moldova; Dir CONSTANTIN V. GAINDRIC; Sec. MIHAIL POPA; publs *Buletinul Academiei de Ştiinţe a Republicii Moldova: Matematica* (3 a year), *Computer Science Journal of Moldova* (3 a year).

Physical Sciences

Institute of Applied Physics: 277028 Chişinău, Str. Academiei 5; tel. (2) 72-58-95; fax (2) 73-81-49; attached to Acad. of Sciences of Moldova; Dir M. C. BOLOGA.

Institute of Chemistry: 2028 Chişinău, Str. Academiei 3; tel. (2) 72-54-90; fax (2) 73-99-54; f. 1959; attached to Acad. of Sciences of Moldova; Dir N. GÂRBĂLĂU.

Institute of Geophysics and Geology: 277028 Chişinău, Str. Academiei 3; tel. (2) 73-90-27; fax (2) 73-97-20; attached to Acad. of Sciences of Moldova; Dir A. V. DRUMEA.

Institute of Power Engineering: 2028 Chişinău, Str. Academiei 5; tel. (2) 72-70-40; fax (2) 73-53-86; f. 1964; attached to Acad. of Sciences of Moldova; Dir Dr MIHAI V. CHIORSAC.

Seismic Station: 277028 Chişinău, Str. Academiei 3; tel. (2) 73-71-79; attached to Acad. of Sciences of Moldova; Dir I. ILIEŞ.

RELIGION, SOCIOLOGY AND ANTHROPOLOGY

Institute of Ethnography and Folklore: 2001 Chişinău, B-dul Ştefan cel Mare 1; tel. (2) 26-45-14; f. 1991; attached to Acad. of Sciences of Moldova; Dir N. A. DEMCENCO; publ. *Revista de Etnologie* (1 a year).

Institute of National Minorities Studies: 2001 Chişinău, B-dul Ştefan cel Mare 1; tel. (2) 26-44-91; attached to Acad. of Sciences of Moldova; Dir C. F. POPOVICI.

Institute of Philosophy, Sociology and Law: 2001 Chişinău, B-dul Ştefan cel Mare 1; tel. (2) 26-14-69; attached to Acad. of Sciences of Moldova; Dir A. N. ROŞCA.

Libraries and Archives

Chişinău

Central Scientific Library of the Moldovan Academy of Sciences: 2001 Chisinău, B-dul Ştefan cel Mare 1; tel. 26-27-91; f. 1947; 1,150,000 vols; Dir E. COROTENCO.

Centre for Scientific Information in the Social Sciences: 2001 Chişinău, B-dul Ştefan cel Mare 1; tel. (2) 23-23-39; attached to Acad. of Sciences of Moldova; Dir V. I. MOCREAC.

Moldovan State University Library: 2009 Chişinău, Str. A. Mateevici 60; tel. 24-07-77; f. 1946; 1,810,000 vols; Dir T. V. SPINEI.

National Library of the Republic of Moldova: 2012 Chişinău, Str. 31 August 1989 78A; tel. and fax (2) 22-14-75; e-mail bnrm@nlib.un.md; f. 1832; national library and principal depository of Moldova; 2,953,000 vols; Dir A. A. RAU.

Scientific and Technical Library of Moldova: Chişinău, Str. Creanga 45; tel. 62-87-42; telex 163268; fax 62-34-47; f. 1968; 560,000 vols, 11,000,000 patents, 750,000 standards; Dir P. T. RACU.

Museums and Art Galleries

Chişinău

Moldovan State Art Museum: Chişinău, Str. Lenin 115; Dir T. V. STAVILA.

Universities

MOLDOVA STATE UNIVERSITY

2009 Chişinău, Str. A. Mateevici 60
Telephone: (2) 24-00-41
Fax (2) 24-06-55

Founded 1946
Languages of instruction: Romanian, Russian
Academic year: September to June

Rector: GH. RUSNAC
Pro-Rectors: P. GAUGAŞ, T. PASECINIC, A. STAHI
Registrar: T. LUCHIAN
Librarian: T. SPINEI

Library: see Libraries
Number of teachers: 640
Number of students: 10,000

Publication: *Jurnalistul.*

DEANS

Faculty of Physics: P. GAŞIN
Faculty of Mathematics and Informatics: P. COJOCARU
Faculty of Chemistry: G. DRAGALINA
Faculty of Biology and Soil Science: V. CIOBANU
Faculty of Letters: M. PURICE
Faculty of Foreign Languages and Literature: E. AXENTI
Faculty of Philosophy and Psychology: P. VIZIR
Faculty of History: I. NICULIŢĂ
Faculty of Journalism and Communication: V. MORARU
Faculty of Law: I. SEDLEŢCHI
Faculty of Political Sciences: D. STRAH
Faculty of Foreign Citizens: I. LUPU

TECHNICAL UNIVERSITY OF MOLDOVA

2004 Chişinău, B-dul Ştefan cel Mare 168
Telephone: (2) 23-45-28
Fax: (2) 24-90-28
E-mail: amariei@mail.utm.md

Founded 1964
State control
Languages of instruction: Romanian, Russian
Academic year: September to June

Rector: Dr S. ION BOSTAN
Vice-Rectors: Prof. Dr PETRU TODOS, Prof. Dr VALENTIN AMARIEI, Prof. Dr DUMITRU UNGUREANU

Library of 1,040,000 vols
Number of teachers: 740
Number of students: 8,740

DEANS

Faculty of Power Engineering: Asst Prof. Dr NICOLAE MOHOREANU
Faculty of Engineering and Management in Machine-Building: Asst Prof. Dr VASILE JAVGUREANU
Faculty of Engineering and Management in Mechanics: Asst Prof. Dr GHEORGHE POPOVICI
Faculty of Computers, Informatics and Microelectronics: Asst Prof. Dr VICTOR SONTEA
Faculty of Radioelectronics: Asst Prof. Dr ION CORNEA
Faculty of Technology and Management in the Food Industry: Asst Prof. Dr GRIGORE MUSTEATA
Faculty of Industrial and Civil Engineering: Asst Prof. Dr ION CIUPAC
Faculty of Urban Planning and Architecture: Asst Prof. Dr NISTOR GROZAVU
Faculty of the Textile Industry: Asst Prof. Dr CONSTANTIN SPANU

Other Higher Educational Institutions

Chişinău State Medical Institute: 277017 Chişinău, Pr. Lenina 165; tel. 23-46-17; library of 232,000 vols; publ. *Transactions.*

State Agricultural University of Moldova: 277049 Chişinău, Str. Mirceşti 44; tel. (2) 24-64-22; fax (2) 24-63-26; f. 1932; faculties of agronomy, agricultural engineering, animal husbandry, economics, veterinary medicine, irrigation and drainage, horticulture; 480 teachers; 7,500 students; library of 1 m. vols; Rector GHEORGHE CIMPOIEŞ; publ. *Research Works.*

Moldovan G. Musicescu Academy of Music: 2009 Chişinău, Str. Mateevici 87; tel. (2) 22-43-44; fax (2) 24-20-36; f. 1919; 170 teachers; 500 students; library of 120,000 vols; Rector C. V. RUSNAC.

Moldovan State Institute of Fine Arts: 277014 Chişinău, Sadovaya ul. 85; tel. 22-23-44; musical comedy direction, graphic arts, decorative applied art, design for light and textile industries, interior design; extramural dept.

MONACO

Learned Societies

HISTORY, GEOGRAPHY AND ARCHAEOLOGY

Association monégasque de Préhistoire: Musée d'Anthropologie, Blvd du Jardin exotique, Monte Carlo; tel. 93-15-80-06; fax 93-30-02-46; f. 1984; 100 mems; Pres. SUZANNE SIMONE.

Research Institutes

NATURAL SCIENCES

General

Centre Scientifique de Monaco: Villa Girasole, 16 blvd de Suisse, Monte Carlo 98000; tel. 93-25-89-54; fax 93-25-70-90; f. 1960; pure and applied research in the fields of oceanography, marine biology and the protection and regeneration of the marine environment; laboratories in Musée Océanographique de Monaco *(q.v.)*; Pres. of Admin. Ccl ROGER PASSERON; Pres. of Progress Cttee (vacant); publ. *Bulletin* (in French and in English, annually).

Libraries and Archives

Monte Carlo

Archives du Palais Princier de Monaco: BP 518, Monaco 98015 Cedex; tel. 93-25-18-31; private archives of the princes of Monaco including documents from the 13th century. Curator RÉGIS LÉCUYER.

Bibliothèque Louis Notari: 8 rue Louis Notari, 98000 Monaco; tel. 93-30-95-09; fax 93-30-34-26; f. 1909; 290,000 vols, 18,000 phonograms; Librarian HERVÉ BARRAL; publ. *Bibliographie de Monaco* (data base).

Princess Grace Irish Library: 9 rue Princesse Marie de Lorraine, Monaco-Ville 98000; tel. 93-50-12-25; fax 93-50-66-65; e-mail pglib@monaco.mc; f. 1984; part of the Princess Grace Foundation; Irish and Celtic studies library; 10,000 books, 2,000 sheet items of Irish music and folk songs, 250 theses, 250 video cassettes; facsimile Book of Kells; paintings, prints, sculptures.

Museums and Art Galleries

Monte Carlo

Musée d'Anthropologie préhistorique: Blvd du Jardin exotique, Monte Carlo; tel. 93-15-80-06; fax 93-30-02-46; f. 1902; prehistory, quaternary geology; library of 3,000 vols, 200 periodicals; Curator SUZANNE SIMONE; publ. *Bulletin* (annually).

Musée National: 17 ave Princess Grace, 98000 Monaco; tel. 93-30-91-26; fax 92-16-73-21; f. 1972; Galéa collection: automatons, miniature furniture and antique dolls.

Musée Océanographique de Monaco: Ave Saint-Martin, Monaco-Ville, MC 98000; tel. 93-15-36-00; fax 93-50-52-97; inaugurated 1910 by Prince Albert I of Monaco; part of Institut Océanographique, Paris; as well as a museum, there is an aquarium which contains 3,000 fish of 450 species; library of 50,000 vols; Dir Prof. FRANÇOIS DOUMENGE.

College

Académie de Musique Prince Rainier III de Monaco: 1 Blvd Albert 1er, 98000 Monaco; tel. 93-15-28-91; f. 1933; 53 professors, 650 students; Dir JOËL RIGAL.

MONGOLIA

Learned Societies

GENERAL

Mongolian Academy of Sciences: Sühbaatar Square 3, Ulan Bator 11; tel. and fax (1) 321638; e-mail mas@magicnet.nm; f. 1921; depts of Agriculture (Dir N. ALTANSÜH), Geology and Geography (Dir (vacant)), Medicine and Biology (Dir P. NYAMDAVAA), Physics, Mathematics, Chemistry and Technology (Dir D. HAYSAMBUU), Social Sciences (Dir H. NAMSRAY); attached research institutes: see Research Institutes; Pres. BAATARYN CHADRAA; Scientific Sec. T. GALBAATAR; publs *News of the Mongolian Academy of Sciences* (6 a year), *Studia Mongolica, Studia Ethnographica, Studia Folclorica, Studia Historica, Studia Archaeologica, Studia Museologica.*

AGRICULTURE, FISHERIES AND VETERINARY SCIENCE

Academy of Agricultural Sciences: Ulan Bator; f. 1998; Pres. N. ALTANSÜH.

NATURAL SCIENCES

General

Academy of Natural Sciences: Ulan Bator; f. 1998; Pres. CH. TSEREN; Learned Sec. T. ERDENEJAV.

RELIGION, SOCIOLOGY AND ANTHROPOLOGY

Academy of Anthropology: Ulan Bator; f. 1998; Pres. L. DASHNYAM.

TECHNOLOGY

Association of Academies of Science and Technology: Ulan Bator; f. 1998; Pres. L. DASHNYAM.

National Academy of Engineering: Ulan Bator; f. 1998; Pres. N. SODNOM.

Research Institutes

AGRICULTURE, FISHERIES AND VETERINARY SCIENCE

Agricultural Economics Research Institute: C/o Academy of Sciences, Sühbaatar Square 3, Ulan Bator 11; attached to Mongolian Acad. of Sciences; Dir YU. ADYAA.

Agricultural Research Institute: Hovd; tel. 3720; f. 1994; library of 10,000 vols; Dir P. BAATARBILEG.

Institute of Forestry and Hunting: Ulan Bator; Dir D. ENHSAYHAN.

Institute of Pasture and Fodder: Darhan; Dir D. TSEDEV.

Institute of Veterinary Research: Zaysan 210153, Ulan Bator; tel. (1) 341553; f. 1960; attached to Mongolian Agricultural Univ.; library of 4,000 vols; Dir B. BYAMBAA; publ. *Proceedings of the Institute of Veterinary Research and Training*.

Research Institute of Animal Husbandry: Mongolian Agricultural University, 21053 Ulan Bator; tel. and fax (1) 341572; e-mail riah@magicnet.mn; f. 1961; attached to Mongolian Acad. of Sciences; library of 800 vols; Dir TS. BAT-ERDINE; publ. *Proceedings* (in Mongolian, with English summary).

Research Institute of Pastoral Animal Husbandry in the Gobi Region: Bulgan district, Ömnögov province; f. 1959; attached to Mongolian Acad. of Sciences; camel and goat husbandry; Dir N. BIYCHEE.

Research Institute of Plant Protection: C/o Academy of Sciences, Sühbaatar Square 3, Ulan Bator 11; attached to Mongolian Acad. of Sciences; Dir D. TSEDEV.

ARCHITECTURE AND TOWN PLANNING

Building Institute: C/o Academy of Sciences, Sühbaatar Square 3, Ulan Bator 11; attached to Mongolian Acad. of Sciences; Dir D. LHANAG.

Institute of Agricultural Architecture: Ulan Bator; Dir O. JADAMBA.

Institute of Architecture and Town Planning: C/o Academy of Sciences, Sühbaatar Square 3, Ulan Bator 11; attached to Mongolian Acad. of Sciences; Dir D. HAYSAMBUU.

Research Institute of Soils and Foundations Engineering: C/o Academy of Sciences, Sühbaatar Square 3, Ulan Bator 11; attached to Mongolian Acad. of Sciences; Dir Dr A. ANAND.

ECONOMICS, LAW AND POLITICS

Centre for North-East Asian Studies: Mongolian Technical University Bldg (2nd Floor), POB 4, Ulan Bator 51; tel. (1) 358317; fax (1) 321638; f. 1990; attached to Mongolian Acad. of Sciences; library of 2,000 vols; Dir CH. DALAY; publ. *North-East Asian Studies* (2 a year).

Centre of Strategic Studies: Ulan Bator; Dir S. ZORIG.

Institute of Economics: C/o Academy of Sciences, Sühbaatar Square 3, Ulan Bator 11; tel. (1) 320802; fax (1) 322216; f. 1962; attached to Mongolian Acad. of Sciences; library of 2,000 vols; Dir P. LUVSANDORJ.

Institute of Management Development: Ulan Bator; Dir D. TSERENDORJ.

Institute of Market Studies: Chamber of Commerce and Industry, Ulan Bator; Dir S. DEMBEREL.

Institute of Mongol Studies: C/o Academy of Sciences, Sühbaatar Square 3, Ulan Bator 11; attached to Mongolian Acad. of Sciences; Dir TS. SHAGDARSÜREN.

Institute of Oriental and International Studies: C/o Academy of Sciences, Sühbaatar Square 3, Ulan Bator 11; attached to Mongolian Acad. of Sciences; Dir A. OCHIR.

Institute of State Administration and Management Development: Ulan Bator 36; tel. 342175; fax 343037; f. 1994; Dir TS. GOMBOSÜREN.

Institute of Strategic Studies: Ministry of Defence, Ulan Bator; Dir Lt-Gen. L. MOLOMJAMTS.

Research Institute for Land Policy: Chingünjavyn gudamj 2, Ulan Bator 35; tel. (1) 60506; f. 1975; library of 1,100 vols; Dir Dr G. PÜREVSÜREN.

Research Institute of Economic Studies: Ulan Bator; f. 1991; microeconomics; Dir Prof. T. DORJ.

EDUCATION

Institute for Educational Research and Methodology: C/o Academy of Sciences, Sühbaatar Square 3, Ulan Bator 11; attached to Mongolian Acad. of Sciences; Dir N. JADAMBAA.

FINE AND PERFORMING ARTS

Research Institute of Culture and Arts: C/o Academy of Sciences, Sühbaatar Square 3, Ulan Bator 11; attached to Mongolian Acad. of Sciences; Dir S. TSERENDORJ.

HISTORY, GEOGRAPHY AND ARCHAEOLOGY

Institute of Geography: C/o Academy of Sciences, Sühbaatar Square 3, Ulan Bator 11; attached to Mongolian Acad. of Sciences; Dir Dr S. DORJGOTOV.

Institute of History: C/o Academy of Sciences, Sühbaatar Square 3, Ulan Bator 11; tel. and fax (1) 358305; f. 1921; attached to Mongolian Acad. of Sciences; Dir TS. BATBAYAR.

LANGUAGE AND LITERATURE

Institute of Mongolian Language and Literature: C/o Academy of Sciences, Sühbaatar Square 3, Ulan Bator 11; attached to Mongolian Acad. of Sciences; Dir H. SAMPILDENDEV.

MEDICINE

Institute of Hygiene, Epidemiology and Microbiology: C/o Academy of Sciences, Sühbaatar Square 3, Ulan Bator 11; attached to Mongolian Acad. of Sciences; Dir J. KUPUL.

Institute of Traditional Medicine: C/o Academy of Sciences, Sühbaatar Square 3, Ulan Bator 11; attached to Mongolian Acad. of Sciences; Dir D. DAGVATSEREN.

Medical Research Institute: C/o Academy of Sciences, Sühbaatar Square 3, Ulan Bator 11; attached to Mongolian Acad. of Sciences; Dir YO. BODHÜÜ.

National Institute of Medicine: C/o Academy of Sciences, Sühbaatar Square 3, Ulan Bator 11; attached to Mongolian Acad. of Sciences; Learned Sec. B. TSERENDASH.

National Research Centre for Health and Infections: Ulan Bator; Dir S. TSOODOL.

Research and Production Institute of Biological Preparations and Blood: Ulan Bator; Dir A. DANDIY.

State Research Centre of Mother and New-Born Child: C/o Academy of Sciences, Sühbaatar Square 3, Ulan Bator 11; tel. (1) 362633; attached to Mongolian Acad. of Sciences; Dir G. CHOYJAMTS.

NATURAL SCIENCES

General

Institute of Scientific and Technical Development: Ulan Bator; Dir D. NYAMAA.

Biological Sciences

Institute of Biology: C/o Academy of Sciences, Sühbaatar Square 3, Ulan Bator 11; attached to Mongolian Acad. of Sciences; Dir BÜ. DASHNYAM.

Institute of Biotechnology: C/o Academy of Sciences, Sühbaatar Square 3, Ulan Bator

11; attached to Mongolian Acad. of Sciences; Dir T. PUNTSAG.

Institute of Botany: C/o Academy of Sciences, Sühbaatar Square 3, Ulan Bator 11; attached to Mongolian Acad. of Sciences; Learned Sec. CH. DUGARJAV.

Institute of General and Experimental Biology: C/o Academy of Sciences, Sühbaatar Square 3, Ulan Bator 11; attached to Mongolian Acad. of Sciences; Dir Dr TS. JANCHIV.

Institute of Geoecology: C/o Academy of Sciences, Sühbaatar Square 3, Ulan Bator 11; attached to Mongolian Acad. of Sciences; Dir J. TSOGTBAATAR.

Palaeontology Centre: Enh Tayvny gudamj 63, 210351 Ulan Bator; fax (1) 358935; e-mail barsgeodin@magicnet.mn; attached to Mongolian Acad. of Sciences; Dir R. BARSBOLD.

Mathematical Sciences

Institute of Mathematics: C/o Academy of Sciences, Sühbaatar Square 3, Ulan Bator 11; attached to Mongolian Acad. of Sciences; Dir Dr S. BUDNYAM.

Physical Sciences

Astronomical Observatory: Hürel-Togoot (CPO Box 788), 210613 Ulan Bator; tel. 52929; f. 1961; attached to Mongolian Acad. of Sciences; library of 1,500 vols; Dir G. NOONOY.

Centre of Seismology and Geomagnetism: C/o Academy of Sciences, Sühbaatar Square 3, Ulan Bator 11; attached to Mongolian Acad. of Sciences; Dir U. SÜHBAATAR.

Hydrometeorological Research Institute: Hudaldaany gudamj 5, Ulan Bator 11; tel. (1) 326614; fax (1) 321401; f. 1966; library of 13,000 vols; Dir L. NATSAGDORJ; publ. *Environment*.

Institute of Chemistry: C/o Academy of Sciences, Sühbaatar Square 3, Ulan Bator 11; attached to Mongolian Acad. of Sciences; Dir D. BADGAA.

Institute of Geology: C/o Academy of Sciences, Sühbaatar Square 3, Ulan Bator 11; attached to Mongolian Acad. of Sciences; Dir R. BARSBOLD.

Institute of Geology and Mineral Enrichment: POB 110, Ulan Bator 37; tel. 332895; f. 1973; library of 1,000 vols; Dir O. TÖMÖRTOGOO; publ. *Hayguulchin* (quarterly).

Institute of Physics and Technology: Enh Tayvny gudamj 54B, 210651 Ulan Bator; tel. and fax 358397; e-mail instphys@magicnet.mn; f. 1961; attached to Mongolian Acad. of Sciences; library of 50,000 vols; Dir D. NYAMAA.

Research Centre for Astronomy and Geophysics: C/o Academy of Sciences, Sühbaatar Square 3, Ulan Bator 11; attached to Mongolian Acad. of Sciences; Dir B. BEHTÖR.

RELIGION, SOCIOLOGY AND ANTHROPOLOGY

Institute of Buddhist Studies: Ulan Bator; Dir G. LUVSANTSEREN.

Institute of Philosophy, Sociology and Law: Jukovyn gudamj 77, Ulan Bator; tel. 453493; attached to Mongolian Acad. of Sciences; Dir TS. BÜJINLHAM.

TECHNOLOGY

Centre of Informatics: C/o Academy of Sciences, Sühbaatar Square 3, Ulan Bator 11; attached to Mongolian Acad. of Sciences; Dir P. NERGÜY.

Experimental and Research Centre for Leather: C/o Academy of Sciences, Sühbaatar Square 3, Ulan Bator 11; attached to Mongolian Acad. of Sciences; Dir D. GANBOLD.

Experimental and Research Centre for Wool: C/o Academy of Sciences, Sühbaatar Square 3, Ulan Bator 11; attached to Mongolian Acad. of Sciences; Dir G. YONDONSAMBUU.

Institute of Geodesic and Geological Engineering: Ulan Bator; Dir TS. TSERENBAT.

Institute of Heat Technology and Industrial Ecology: Ih Surguuliyn gudamj 2A, Sühbaatar district, Ulan Bator; tel. 324959; attached to Mongolian Acad. of Sciences; Dir S. BATMÖNH.

Institute of Information Science: C/o Academy of Sciences, Sühbaatar Square 3, Ulan Bator 11; attached to Mongolian Acad. of Sciences; Dir M. GANZORIG.

Institute of the Forestry and Wood Processing Industry: C/o Academy of Sciences, Sühbaatar Square 3, Ulan Bator 11; attached to Mongolian Acad. of Sciences; Dir SAYNBAYAR.

Mining Institute: C/o Academy of Sciences, Sühbaatar Square 3, Ulan Bator 11; attached to Mongolian Acad. of Sciences; Dir S. MANGAL.

National Institute for Standardization and Metrology: Enh Tayvny gudamj 46A, Ulan Bator 51; tel. (1) 358349; fax (1) 358032; e-mail mncsm@magicnet.mn; f. 1992; library of 70,000 vols; Dir-Gen. N. BAYARMAGNAY; publ. *Standards and Metrology* (monthly).

Natural Freezing and Food Technology Institute: C/o Academy of Sciences, Sühbaatar Square 3, Ulan Bator 11; attached to Mongolian Acad. of Sciences; Dir N. LONJID.

Power Institute: C/o Academy of Sciences, Sühbaatar Square 3, Ulan Bator 11; attached to Mongolian Acad. of Sciences; Dir D. BUMAYUUSH.

Research and Experimental Institute of Light Industry: C/o Academy of Sciences, Sühbaatar Square 3, Ulan Bator 11; attached to Mongolian Acad. of Sciences; Dir B. DASHTSEREN.

Research and Production Corporation for Renewable Energy: C/o Academy of Sciences, Sühbaatar Square 3, Ulan Bator 11; attached to Mongolian Acad. of Sciences; Dir B. CHADRAA.

Research and Production Corporation for Roads: C/o Academy of Sciences, Sühbaatar Square 3, Ulan Bator 11; attached to Mongolian Acad. of Sciences; Dir B. HUNDGAA.

Research and Production Corporation for Transport: C/o Academy of Sciences, Sühbaatar Square 3, Ulan Bator 11; attached to Mongolian Acad. of Sciences; Dir L. TÜDEV.

Research and Production Institute of Communication: C/o Academy of Sciences, Sühbaatar Square 3, Ulan Bator 11; attached to Mongolian Acad. of Sciences; Dir D. LHAGVAA.

Research Centre for the Chemistry and Technology of Coal: Ministry of Fuel and Energy, POB 52/59, Ulan Bator; tel. 341493; f. 1990; Dir TSEYENGIYN TSEDEVSÜREN.

Research Centre of Petrochemical Technology: Ulan Bator; tel. 24779.

Research Institute of Military Science of the Ministry of Defence: Ulan Bator; Dir SH. PALAMDORJ.

Research Institute of Water Policy: Baruunselbe 13, 211238 Ulan Bator; tel. 325487; fax 321862; f. 1965; library of 3,500 vols; Dir N. CHULUUNHUYAG.

Libraries and Archives

Ulan Bator

D. Natsagdorj Central Public Library: Ulan Bator; Dir T. MIJIDDORJ.

Gandan Library: Gandantegchinlen Buddhist Monastery, Ulan Bator; f. 1838; Buddhist theology and philosophy, xylographs, secular works of science and literature.

National Archives of Mongolia: 210646 Ulan Bator; tel. and fax (1) 324533; e-mail jganbold@magicnet.mn; f. 1996; history, art, literature, science, technology, film, sound recordings; Dir-Gen. J. GERELBADRAH; publ. *Archives News* (2 a year).

State Central Library: Ulan Bator; f. 1921; 4,000,000 vols, incl. rare and ancient editions; Dir Dr J. SERJEE.

Museums and Art Galleries

Ulan Bator

Art Gallery: Ulan Bator; Dir D. URANCHIMEG.

Botanical Garden: Ulan Bator; attached to Mongolian Acad. of Sciences; Dir G. OCHIRBAT.

Military Museum: Ulan Bator; Dir Col P. BYAMBASÜREN.

National Museum of Mongolian History: POB 332, Ulan Bator 46; tel. and fax (1) 326802; f. 1924; Dir Dr S. IDSHINNOROV; publ. *Museologia* (1 a year).

Museum of Religious History: Ulan Bator; housed in Choyjin Lamyn Hüree, a former lamasery, and Bogd Khan's Winter Palace; Dir G. TÖVSAYHAN.

Natsagdorj Museum: Ulan Bator; life and works of the author and poet Dashdorjiyn Natsagdorj.

Natural History Museum: Ulan Bator; natural history, Gobi desert dinosaur eggs and skeletons; Dir P. ERDENEBAT.

Ulan Bator Museum: Ulan Bator; history of Ulan Bator.

Wildlife Museum: Baygaliyn Hishgiyn ordon, Gandangiyn denj, Ulan Bator; tel. (1) 360248; fax (1) 360067.

Zanabazar Fine Arts Museum: Ulan Bator; paintings, sculpture; Dir D. GUNGAA.

Zhukov, G. K., Museum: Ulan Bator; career of Soviet Marshal Zhukov.

Universities

MONGOLIAN AGRICULTURAL UNIVERSITY

Zaysan, 210153 Ulan Bator

Telephone: (1) 341630

Fax: (1) 341770

E-mail: haaint@magicnet.mn

Founded 1942 as veterinary dept of Mongolian State University; became Institute of Agriculture 1958; university status 1991; present name 1996

Director: Dr N. ALTANSÜH

Library of 200,000 vols

Number of teachers: 200

Number of students: 3,400

Faculties of Animal Husbandry, Veterinary Medicine (Dean B. LUVSANSHARAV), Agricultural Engineering, Agronomy, Basic Education, Agricultural Economics (Dean A. BAKEY).

ATTACHED RESEARCH INSTITUTES

Research Institute of Animal Husbandry

Research Institute of Agricultural Engineering

Darhan Research Institute of Plant Science and Agriculture

Eastern Region Agricultural Research Institute

Altai Region Agricultural Research Institute
Gobi Region Pastoral Livestock Research Institute
Research Institute of High-Mountain Agriculture
Ulaangom Crop Research Institute
Beekeeping Research Institute
Yak Research Centre
Camel Research Centre

NATIONAL UNIVERSITY OF MONGOLIA

POB 46/377, Ulan Bator
Telephone: (1) 320892
Fax: 320159
E-mail: numelect@magicnet.mn

Founded 1942
State control
Academic year: September to June

Rector: TSERENSODNOMYN GANTSOG
Pro-Rectors: TSAGAANY BOLDSÜH, SÜRENGIYN DAVAA

Library of 350,000 vols
Number of teachers: 500
Number of students: 6,500

Publication: *Proceedings.*

FACULTIES AND TRAINING AND RESEARCH INSTITUTES

School of Mathematics and Computing, incl. depts of algebra, geometry, mathematical analysis, probability theory and mathematical statistics, applied mathematics, and methods of teaching mathematics, computer programming.

Faculty of Natural Sciences, incl. depts of general chemistry (analytical and physical chemistry), organic chemistry (coal and petrochemistry), ferrous-metal and rare-element chemistry, chemistry and technology of new materials, geology, and geography.

School of Physics and Electronics, incl. depts of theoretical physics, nuclear physics, geophysics, optics, radiophysics, solid-state physics, hydrology, electronics, and meteorology; Dean H. TSOOHÜÜ.

Faculty of Social Sciences, incl. depts of philosophy, sociology, history, politics, and culture and art.

Faculty of Biology, incl. depts of zoology, botany, ecology, forestry, biochemistry and microbiology, biophysics, and genetics; Dir G. TSEDENDASH.

Higher School of Mongol Studies, incl. depts of linguistics, Mongolian language, literature, and journalism; Dir J. BAT-IREEDÜI.

Higher School of Law, incl. depts of constitutional law, civil law, state administration, international law, and criminal process law; Dir I. DASHNYAM.

Higher School of Economics, incl. depts of the theory of economics, management, accountancy, credit and finance, statistics, economic data processing, marketing, demography, mathematics, and foreign languages; Dir B. SUVD.

School of Foreign Service, incl. depts specializing in Russia, UK, Germany, France, China, Japan, Korea, Slav nations, and foreign relations; Dir J. BAYASAH.

MONGOLIAN TECHNICAL UNIVERSITY

POB 46/520, 210646 Ulan Bator
Telephone: (1) 324118
Fax: (1) 324121
E-mail: badarch@magicnet.mn

Founded 1969
State control
Language of instruction: Mongolian
Academic year: September to July

President: Dr DENDEVIYN BADARCH
Vice-Presidents: Dr TS. SARANTUYAA (Academic), L. BOLDBAATAR (Finance and Development), Dr S. BATMÖNH (Research and Student Affairs)
Chief Administrative Officer: Dr B. DOGSOM
Librarian: A. DOLOONTÖMÖR

Library of 230,000 vols
Number of teachers: 530
Number of students: 5,000

Publication: *Scientific Transactions.*

DEANS

School of Power Engineering: Dr B. MANDAH
School of Mechanical Engineering: Dr J. OSORHÜÜ
School of Civil Engineering: Dr Z. BINDERYAA
School of Geology: Dr D. CHULUUN
School of Mining: Dr S. GERELTUYAA
School of Telecommunication: Dr B. DAMDINSÜREN
School of Computer Science and Management: Dr D. ENHBOLD
School of Food Technology: Dr G. GOMBO
School of Light Industry Technology: Dr B. DAVAASÜREN
School of Foreign Languages: T. BATBAYAR
School of Engineering Education: Dr J. BAASANDORJ
School of Technology in Darhan: Dr YA. ZENEEMEDER
Graduate Study Centre: Dr H. TSAGAAN

MONGOLIAN UNIVERSITY OF ARTS AND CULTURE

Baga toiruu 22, 210646 Ulan Bator
Telephone: (1) 327335
Fax: (1) 325205

Founded 1990
State control
Academic year: September to June

Rector: TSERENNADMIDIYN TSEGMED
Vice-Rector: JAMBALYN ENEBISH
Registrar: ALTANGERELIYN GANBAATAR
Librarian: DAMBAJAVYN NYAMDULAM

Number of teachers: 230
Number of students: 1,900

DEANS

College of Music: CH. CHINBAT
College of Culture: L. BATCHULUN
College of Theatre Art: (vacant)
College of Radio and Television: B. BADARUGAN

MEDICAL UNIVERSITY OF MONGOLIA

Jamyan güni gudamj 4, P.O. 48, Box 111, Ulan Bator
Telephone: (1) 328670
Fax: (1) 321249
E-mail: nmumtlhs@magicnet.mn

Founded 1942
State control
Academic year: September to August

President: Prof. TS. LHAGVASÜREN
Vice-President: Prof. D. DUNGERDORJ
Chief Administrative Officer: N. BATHÜREL
Librarian: TSAGAACH

Number of teachers: 310
Number of students: 2,300

DEANS

Faculty of Medicine: (vacant)
Faculty of Dentistry: N. PÜREVJAV
Faculty of Hygiene and Health Management: CH. TSOLMON
Faculty of Traditional Medicine: N. TÖMÖRBAATAR
Faculty of Pharmacy: S. TSETSEGMAA

Higher Schools

Foreign Language Institute (Orhon): Chingisiyn örgön chölöö, POB 176, 210136 Ulan Bator; tel. (1) 342413; fax (1) 342696; f. 1992; library of 3,000 vols; 39 teachers; 650 students; Dir N. HAJIDSÜREN.

Higher School of Accountancy and Auditing: Ulan Bator; tel. 541650.

Higher School of Business: Ard Ayuushiyn gudamj 26, Bayangol district, POB 715, 210524 Ulan Bator; tel. (1) 367018; fax (1) 366995; degree courses in management, economics, finance, marketing; Dir B. ERDENESÜREN.

Higher School of Finance and Economics: Enh Tayvny gudamj 12A, Ulan Bator; tel. 457701.

Higher School of Foreign Languages: Ulan Bator; Dir B. CHULUUNDORJ.

Higher School of Information Technology: Ulan Bator; Dir G. TSOGBADRAH.

Higher School of Language and Civilization: Ulan Bator; promotes knowledge of classical Mongolian; Dir (vacant).

Higher School of Legal Studies: Ulan Bator; tel. 529798; Dir I. DASHNYAM.

Higher School of Oriental Literature: Ulan Bator; Dir S. BATMÖNH.

Private Higher School of Oriental Philosophy and History: Enh Tayvny gudamj 35, POB 283, Ulan Bator 44; tel. (1) 322628; fax (1) 320210; f. 1992; library of 5,000 vols; 150 students; Dir R. NANSAL.

Zanabazar Buddhist University: Ulan Bator; attached to Gandantegchinlen monastery; Dir T. BULGAN.

Colleges

College of Agriculture: Darhan; hydrology, land improvement, meteorology.

College of Agricultural Technology: Bayanchandman; training of tractor and combine harvester drivers and repair technicians, agricultural electricians.

College of Economics: Ulan Bator 49; tel. 50378; f. 1991; based on former Vocational School of Finance and Economics; taxation, accountancy, banking and finance, business management; 40 teachers, 700 students; library of 40,000 vols; Dir (vacant).

College of Law: Ulan Bator; f. 1991.

College of Visual Arts: Ulan Bator; Dir TS. TSEGMID.

Institute of Commerce and Business: Ulan Bator 48; tel. (1) 325724; fax (1) 326748; e-mail icbm@magicnet.mn; f. 1991; 1,200 students; two libraries with 22,000 books; business management, marketing, international trade, accountancy, etc; Rector Asst Prof. S. NYAMZAGD; publ. *Mercury* (3 a year).

MOROCCO

Learned Societies

GENERAL

Académie du Royaume du Maroc: Charia Imam Malik, BP 5062, Rabat; tel. 75-51-13; fax 75-51-01; f. 1977; 65 mems; promotes the development of research and reflection in the principal fields of intellectual activity; library of 14,000 vols; Permanent Sec. Dr ABDELLATIF BERBICH; publs *Academia*, various monographs.

AGRICULTURE, FISHERIES AND VETERINARY SCIENCE

Société d'Horticulture et d'Acclimatation du Maroc: BP 13.854, Casablanca 01; f. 1914; 260 mems; Pres. JOSETTE DUPLAT; Sec. RENÉ TRIPOTIN.

BIBLIOGRAPHY, LIBRARY SCIENCE AND MUSEOLOGY

Association Nationale des Informatistes: BP 616, Rabat-Chellah; tel. 749-07; f. 1982; information science, documentation, library economics, archives; *c.* 400 mems; Pres. LAYDIA BACHR; publ. *L'Informatiste* (2 a year).

ECONOMICS, LAW AND POLITICS

Société d'Etudes Economiques, Sociales et Statistiques du Maroc: BP 535, Rabat–Chellah; f. 1933; 20 mems; Dir NACER EL FASSI; publ. *Signes du Présent* (quarterly).

FINE AND PERFORMING ARTS

Association des Amateurs de la Musique Andalouse: c/o 133 ave Ziraoui, Casablanca; f. 1956 to preserve and catalogue traditional Moroccan (Andalusian) music; maintains a School of Andalusian music at Casablanca, directed and subsidized by the Ministry of Culture; Dir Hadj DRISS BENJELLOUN.

HISTORY, GEOGRAPHY AND ARCHAEOLOGY

Association Nationale des Géographes Marocains: Faculté des Lettres et des Sciences Humaines, Université Mohammed V, Rabat; tel. (7) 77-18-93; fax (7) 77-20-68; f. 1916; Sec.-Gen. TAOUFIK AGOUMY; publ. *Revue de Géographie du Maroc* (2 a year).

Research Institutes

GENERAL

Centre National de Coordination et de Planification de la Recherche Scientifique et Technique: 52 Omar Ibn Khattab, BP 8027, Rabat; tel. 77-42-15; fax 77-12-88; e-mail cnr@cnr.ac.ma; f. 1976; prepares the National Plan for Science and Technology, with the help of special commissions: food and agriculture, communication, environment, natural resources, energy, health, population; research activities include astronomy, geophysics, biotechnology, image processing, geology, computer science, mathematics, social sciences (international business), environment, energy and maintenance; library of 3,500 vols, 70 periodicals; Dir SAID BELCADI (acting); Gen. Sec. MOHAMED RAIMI; publ. *Lettre d'Information* (3 a year).

AGRICULTURE, FISHERIES AND VETERINARY SCIENCE

Centre d'Expérimentations d'Hydraulique Agricole: Rabat; f. 1953; Dir E. DAGNELIES.

Institut National de la Recherche Agronomique: BP 6512 R.I., Rabat; tel. 77-55-30; telex 21702; fax 77-40-03; f. 1930; research in agronomy; library of 40,000 vols, 300 periodicals; Dir A. ARIFI; publs *Al Awamia* (quarterly), *Les cahiers de la recherche agronomique* (irregular).

Institut Scientifique des Pêches Maritimes: 2 rue de Tiznit, Casablanca; tel. 22-20-90; telex 23-823; fax 26-69-67; f. 1947; applied fisheries oceanography, marine biology, evaluation of resources, aquaculture, environmental studies, fishing gear technology, fish processing technology, fisheries management; library of 1,100 vols, 50 periodicals; Dir ABDELATIF BERRAHO; publs *Bulletin, Travaux et Documents*, *Notes d'Information*.

Mission Pédologique: Ministère de la Réforme Agraire, BP 432, Rabat; pedology; Dir J. L. GEOFFROY.

ECONOMICS, LAW AND POLITICS

Centre d'Etudes, de Documentation et d'Informations Economiques et Sociales (CEDIES–Informations): Angle ave des Forces Armées Royales et angle rue Mohamed Errachid, Casablanca 20100; tel. (2) 25-26-96; fax (2) 25-38-39; Pres. ABDERRAHIM LAHJOUJI; publ. *CEDIES Informations.*

HISTORY, GEOGRAPHY AND ARCHAEOLOGY

Comité National de Géographie du Maroc: Institut Universitaire de la Recherche Scientifique, Rabat; f. 1959; Pres. The MINISTER OF EDUCATION; Sec.-Gen. A. LAOUINA; publs *Atlas du Maroc,* maps.

LANGUAGE AND LITERATURE

Instituto Muley El Hassan: PB 84, Tétouan; research on Hispano-Muslim works; library of 5,500 vols; Dirs MOHAMMED BEN TAUÍT, MARIANO ARRIBAS PALAU.

MEDICINE

Direction de l'Epidémiologie et de Lutte Contre les Maladies: Ministère de la Santé Publique, 14 rue Ibn Al Haïtam, Agdal, 10000 Rabat; tel. (7) 77-19-69; fax (7) 77-20-14; f. 1990; applied research in epidemiology and environmental hygiene; Dir Dr JAOUAD MAHJOUR; publs *Bulletin Epidémiologique* (quarterly).

Institut National d'Hygiène: POB 769, Rabat Agdal; tel. (7) 77-19-02; fax (7) 77-20-67; f. 1930; departments of microbiology, parasitology, physics and chemistry, toxicology, serology, immunology, molecular biology, genetics, entomology; National Poison Control Centre; 120 mems; Toxicological Documentation Centre of 400 vols; library of 3,000 vols; Dir LARBI IDRISSI.

Institut Pasteur: Place Charles Nicolles, Casablanca.

Institut Pasteur: BP 415, Tanger; f. 1912; Dir Dr M. MAILLOUX.

NATURAL SCIENCES

General

Institut Scientifique: Ave Ibn Battota, BP 703, Agdal, 10106 Rabat; tel. (7) 77-45-48; telex 36361; fax (7) 77-45-40; f. 1920, reorganized 1975; fundamental research on nature; departments of botany and plant ecology; zoology and animal ecology; geology; geomorphology and cartography; seismology and geomagnetism; teledetection; 30 researchers; attached to Univ. Mohammed V; Dir DRISS NAJID; publs *Travaux*, *Bulletin*, *Documents*.

Physical Sciences

Direction de la Géologie: c/o Ministry of Energy and Mines, BP 6208, Rabat-Instituts; tel. 77-28-24; fax 77-79-43; f. 1921; National Geological Survey; library of 25,000 vols; Dir Dr MOHAMMED BOUTALEB; publs *Notes et Mémoires du Service Géologique du Maroc*, *Mines, Géologie et Energie*.

TECHNOLOGY

Bureau de Recherches et de Participations Minières (BRPM): 5 Charia Moulay Hassan, BP 99, Rabat; tel. 76-30-35; telex 31066; fax 76-24-10; f. 1928; state agency to develop mining research and industry; Gen. Man. ASSOU LHA TOUTE; publ. *Rapport d'Activité* (annually).

Laboratoire Public d'Essais et d'Etudes: 25 rue d'Azilal, Casablanca; tel. 30-04-50; telex 278-53; fax 30-15-50; f. 1947; hydraulics, environment, roads, study of soil, materials and methods of construction; library of 7,000 vols; Dir-Gen. AHMED HAKIMI; publs *Revue Marocaine de Génie Civil* (quarterly), *Ingénierie* (monthly).

Libraries and Archives

Casablanca

Bibliothèque de la Communauté Urbaine de Casablanca: 142 ave des Forces Armées Royales, Casablanca; tel. 31-41-70; f. 1917; law, political economy, sciences, philosophy, history, literature, the arts, geography, medicine, sport, travel, fiction; 91,307 vols in Arab section, 267,149 vols in foreign section; 137 periodicals, several foreign daily newspapers; Dir HAJ MOHAMED BOUZID.

Fès

Bibliothèque de l'Université Quaraouyine: Place des Seffarines, Fès; 22,071 vols, 5,157 MSS, 38 archives.

Marrakesh

Bibliothèque Ben Youssef: Dar Glaoui, Rue Rmila, Marrakesh; 10,128 vols, 24,000 MSS; Dir SEDDIK BELLARBI.

Rabat

Bibliothèque de l'Institut Scientifique: Ave Ibn Battota, BP 703, Agdal, 10106 Rabat; tel. (7) 77-45-48; fax (7) 77-45-40; f. 1920; zoology, botany, geomorphology, cartography, ecology, earth sciences, geophysics, remote detection; 15,700 vols, 1,728 periodicals; Librarian ABDELLATIF BAYED; publs *Bulletin de l'Institute Scientifique, Travaux de l'Institut Scientifique.*

Bibliothèque Générale et Archives: BP 1003, Ave Ibn Battouta, Rabat; tel. (7) 77-18-90; fax (7) 77-60-62; f. 1920; 600,000 vols, 31,000 MSS and 2,000 linear metres of archives; Dir AHMED TOUFIQ; publ. *Bibliographie Nationale*† (2 a year).

Centre National de Documentation: BP 826, Rabat 10004; tel. (7) 77-49-44; fax (7) 77-31-34; f. 1966; documentation on the economic, social, scientific and technical development of the country; regional reps in Fès, Tangier, Casablanca, Agadir, Marrakech, Meknès, Oujda; mem. of FID and IFLA; library of 9,000 vols, 250,000 microfiche titles, 100 periodicals; Dir AHMED FASSI-FIHRI; publs *KATAB* (bibliography), *Retrospective indexes* (irregular), guides, catalogues, etc.

Tangier

Biblioteca Española: Instituto Cervantes, 99 ave Sidi Mohammed Ben Abdellah, 90000 Tangier; tel. (9) 93-23-99; fax (9) 94-76-30; e-mail ictanger@mail.sis.net.ma; f. 1941; the library is divided into Arabic and European sections; 60,000 vols; Dir and Librarian JAUME BOVER PUJOL; publ. *Miscelanea de la Biblioteca Española*.

Tétouan

Bibliothèque Générale et Archives: BP 692, Tétouan; tel. 96-32-58; f. 1939; general and public library; 45,000 vols, 200 MSS, 2,050 periodicals, 22,000 historical archive items, 670,000 administrative archive items, 40,000 photographs, 1,322 numismatic items; Dir M. M. RIAN.

Museums and Art Galleries

Fès

Musée Batha: Ksar et Batha, Fès-Ville; built as a royal residence in the 19th century; restored 1978; history of art; Curator HNIA CHIKHAOUI.

Musée d'Armes: Borj-Nord, Fès; Curator MOHAMED ZAIM.

Marrakesh

Musée Dar Si Saïd: Derb el Bahia Riad El Zaitoun El Jadid, Marrakesh; Dir HASSAN BEL ARBI.

Meknès

Musée Dar El Jamaï: Sahat El Hdim, Meknès; tel. 05-53-08-63; f. 1920; Moroccan art; Chief Curator HASSAN CHERRADI.

Moulay Driss Zerhoun

Site Archéologique de Volubilis: Conservation du Site de Volubilis, Moulay Idriss Zerhoun, Meknès; tel. 05-54-41-03; f. 1950; archaeological site; library of 250 vols; Archaeologist HASSAN LIMANE.

Rabat

Musée Archéologique: 23 rue Al-Brihi, Rabat; f. 1920; Curator ABDELWAHED BEN-NCER.

Musée de la Kasbah: 23 rue el Brihi, Rabat; archaeology and folklore; Curator MOHAMMED HABIBI.

Musée des Oudaïa: Kasba des Oudaïa, Rabat; f. 1915; Moroccan art; Curator HOUCEINE EL KASRI.

Safi

Musée National de la Céramique: Kachla, Safi; f. 1990; Curator NOUREDDINE ESSAFSAFI.

Tangier

Tangier American Legation Museum: 8 Zankat America, Tangier; tel. (9) 353-17; f. 1976; operated by the Tangier American Legation Museum Soc., Inc.; permanent collection of 16th–20th-century paintings, etchings, aquatints, prints and maps of Morocco; also documentation and artifacts concerning Moroccan-American relations; sponsors short-term exhibitions of contemporary artists; research library of 4,500 vols on North Africa and Morocco in English, French, Spanish, Arabic and Portuguese; Dir THOR H. KUNIHOLM.

Tétouan

Musée Archéologique: 2 rue Boukçein, Tétouan.

Musée des Arts Traditionnels: Tétouan; Curator AMRANI AHMED.

Universities

UNIVERSITÉ CADI AYYAD

Blvd Prince Moulay Abdellah, BP 511, Marrakech

Telephone: (4) 43-48-13
Telex: 74869
Fax: (4) 43-44-94

Founded 1978
State control
Languages of instruction: Arabic, French
Academic year: September to July

Rector: Prof. MOHAMED KNIDIRI
Secretary-General: SALAH EDDINE BERRAHOU

Number of teachers: 897
Number of students: 36,522

Publications: *Revue de la Faculté des Sciences, Revue de la Faculté de Droit, Revue de la Faculté des Lettres.*

DEANS

Faculty of Sciences: Prof. ABDELKADER MOUKHLISSE
Faculty of Science and Technology: MOHAMED ARSALANE
Faculty of Letters and Humanities (Marrakech): Prof. MOHAMED BOUGHALI
Faculty of Letters and Humanities (Beni Mellal): MOHAMED ESSAOURI
Faculty of Law, Economics and Social Sciences: Prof. AHMED TRACHEN
Institute of Technology: AHMED SOUISSI

UNIVERSITÉ HASSAN II AÏN CHOCK

BP 9167, 19 rue Tarik Bnou Ziad, Casablanca

Telephone: (2) 27-37-37
Fax: (2) 27-51-60

Founded 1975
Languages of instruction: Arabic and French
Academic year September to July

Rector: AZIZ HASBI
Chief Administrative Officer: NOREDDINE SIRAJ
Librarian: K. EL HAMZAOUI

Number of teachers: 1,190
Number of students 33,213

Publications: faculty reviews.

DEANS

Faculty of Law: BACHIR EL KOUHLANI
Faculty of Medicine and Pharmacy: NAJIB ZEROUALI OUARITI
Faculty of Arts and Human Sciences: AHMED BOUCHARB
Faculty of Dentistry: LATIFA TRICHA
Faculty of Sciences: DRISS EL KHYARI
National Higher School of Electronics and Mechanics: ABDELILAH SMILI (Director)
Technology High School: MOHAMMED BARKAOUI (Director)

HEADS OF DEPARTMENTS

Faculty of Law, Economics and Social Sciences:
- Judicial Science: MOHAMMED EL KACHBOUR
- Political Science: OMAR BOUZIANE
- Economics: BACHIR EL KOUHLANI

Faculty of Arts and Human Sciences:
- Islamic Studies: ZINELABIDINE BELAFREJ
- Arabic Language and Literature: MOHAMMED BALAJI
- History: (vacant)
- Geography: EL MOSTAFA CHOUIKI
- French Language and Literature: KACEM BASSFOU
- English Language and Literature: M'BAREK ROUANE
- Spanish Language and Literature: (vacant)
- German Language and Literature: FATHALLAH EL BADRI

Faculty of Sciences:
- Mathematics: MOHAMED KHALID BOUHAIA
- Chemistry: EL MAHJOUB LAKHDAR
- Biology: MOHAMMED LOTFI
- Physics: MOHAMMED SAGHIR EL AADI
- Geology: OMAR SEDDIKI

Faculty of Dentistry:
- Children's Dentistry: SOUÂD LAMSEFFER
- Prosthesis: AÏDA EL KASSLASSI
- Biology and Basic Sciences: NEZZA EL ALAMI
- Conservative Dentistry: HOUSSINE HIRCHE
- Dental Surgery: ISHAK BENYAHIA
- Paradontology: JAMILA EL KASSA
- Prosthesis: SAMIRA BELMKHNETH

Faculty of Medicine and Pharmacy:
- Surgery: ABDELMAJID BOUZIDI
- Medicine: AHMED FAROUQI
- Preclinic Biology: KHADIJA ZARROUCK
- Clinical Biology: NAIMA M'DAGHRI
- Oto-Neuro-Ophthalmology: MOSTAPHA TOUHAMI
- Paediatrics: ABDERRAHMAN ABID
- Respiratory Diseases: MOHAMMED BARTAL
- Medico-Surgical Emergency: RAJAE AGHZADI
- Cardio-Vascular Diseases: NACER CHRAIBI
- Social and Community Medicine: SAID LOUAHLIA

Technology High School:
- Management: MOUSSA YASSAFI
- Mechanical Engineering: ABDELHAK BOUAZIZ
- Electrical Engineering: BOUMHDI EL HANOUNI
- Process Engineering: ABELKRIM OMOUMOU

National Higher School of Electronics and Mechanics:
- Principles of Engineering: ALI ZAKI
- Electrical Engineering: HASSAN BAZI
- Mechanical Engineering: ABDELKHALEK LATRACH

UNIVERSITÉ IBNOU ZOHR

BP 3215, Agadir

Founded 1989

Rector: MUSTAPHA DKHISSI

Number of students: 9,724

Faculties of Letters and Humanities and of Sciences.

UNIVERSITÉ MOHAMMED I

BP 524, 60000 Oujda

Telephone: (6) 74-47-83
Fax: (6) 74-47-79

Founded 1978
State control
Languages of instruction: Arabic and French
Academic year: October to June

Rector: EL-MADANI BELKHADIR
Secretary-General: ABDERRAHMAN HOUTECH
Librarian: ZOUBIDA CHAHI

Number of teachers: 593
Number of students: 19,872

Publications: *Al Mayadine, Revue de la Faculté des Lettres, Cahiers du CEMM.*

DEANS

Faculty of Letters and Human Sciences: MOHAMMED LAAMIRI
Faculty of Law and Economics: EL-LARBI M'RABET
Faculty of Science: BENAÏSSA N'CIRI
Institute of Technology: Dir MOHAMMED BARBOUCHA

HEADS OF DEPARTMENT

Arabic Language and Literature: HASSAN LAMRANI
English Language and Literature: MOSTAFA SHOUL
French Language and Literature: MOHAMMED HAMMOUTI
History: MOHAMMED MENFAA
Geography: MOHAMMED BEN BRAHIM
Islamic Studies: RACHID BELAHBIB
Economics: HACHEMI BENTAHAR
Private Law: ABDERRAHMAN OUSSAMA
Public Law: (vacant)
Mathematics: OMAR ANANE
Physics: LARBI ROUBI
Chemistry: ASSOU ZAHIDI
Biology: MOHAMED SEGHROUCHNI
Geology: MIMOUN BOUGHRIBA
Electrical Engineering: MOHAMMED MOKHTARI
Management Techniques: YAHYA HOUAT

ATTACHED CENTRE

Centre d'Etudes sur les Mouvements Migratoires Maghrébins: f. 1990

UNIVERSITÉ MOHAMMED V

BP 554, 3 rue Michlifen, Agdal, Rabat
Telephone: 67-13-18
Fax: 14-01
Founded 1957
State control
Languages of instruction: Arabic and French
Academic year: October to June
Rector: ABDELLATIF BEN ABDELJALIL
Librarian: NADIA BELHAJ
Number of teachers: 1,960
Number of students: 38,229
Publications: various faculty periodicals.

DEANS

Faculty of Letters and Human Sciences: BP 1040, Ave Ibn Batouta; ABDELWAHED BENDAOUD
Faculty of Law and Economics: BP 721, Ave des Nations Unies; ABDELAZIZ BENJELLOUN
Faculty of Sciences: BP 1014, Ave Ibn Batouta; ABDERRAHMANE ESSAID
Faculty of Medicine and Pharmacy: BP 6203; MOULAY TAHAR ALAOUI
Faculty of Dental Medicine: BP 6212, Ave Maa El Aïnine; BOUCHAÏB JIDAL
Mohammadia School of Engineering: BP 756, Ave Ibn Sina; TAEB BENNANI
Faculty of Education: BP 1072, Haut Agdal; M'HAMED ZAIMI
National Higher School of Computer and Systems Analysis: ABDELFADEL BENNANI

HEADS OF DEPARTMENTS

Faculty of Letters and Human Sciences:

Arabic Language and Literature: AHMED EL-MAADAOUI
English Language and Literature: MOHAMMED DAHBI
French Language and Literature: NAIMA EL-HARIFI
Geography: ISMAIL EL-ALAOUI
German Language and Literature: OMAR BENAICH
History: ABDERRAHMANE EL-MOIDDEN
Philosophy, Psychology and Social Sciences: SALIN YAFOUT
Spanish Language and Literature: MOHAMMED SALHI

Faculty of Law and Economics:

Economics: LARBI HANNANE
Private Law: OMAR ABOU TAIB
Public Law: ABDELLAH SAAF

Faculty of Sciences:

Biology: W. BENJELLOUN
Chemistry: MOKTAR SASSI
Geology: NAJIB HATIMI
Mathematics and Computer Studies: ABDELHAMID BOURASS
Physics: OMAR KIFANI

Faculty of Medicine and Pharmacy:

Cardio-vascular System: M. BENOMAR
Clinical Biology: ABDELAZIZ AGOUMI
Digestive System: ABDELLAH BENNANI
Endocrinology: ABDELKARIM EL-KADIRI
Medicine: ABDELAZIZ EL-MAOUNI
Muscular System: MOHAMMED LAMNOUAR
Obstetrics and Gynaecology: OSSTOWAR
Oto-neuro-ophthalmology: MUSTAFA RAFAI
Paediatrics: AMINA EL MALKI
Pre-clinical Medicine: MOHAMMED BENSOUDA
Respiratory System: BOUZEKRI
Social Medicine: S. NEJMI
Surgery: ABDELKADER TOUNSI
Urology: ABDELLATIF BENCHEKROUN

Faculty of Dental Medicine:

Dental Conservation: BERNARD HANZEL, HOUSAINE HIRCH
Dental Orthopaedics: HIMMICH
Dental Prosthesis: BOMBAROUTTA

Mohammadia School of Engineering:

Civil Engineering: ABDELLAH AL-PAROUJI
Electrical Engineering: NOUREDDINE GHALMI
General and Technical Education: EL-GHALA BENAMROU
Mechanical Engineering: DRISS BOUAMI
Mining Engineering: NOUREDDINE BENALI
Industrial Engineering: ABDELHALIM SKALLI

Faculty of Education:

Basis and Sociology of Education: (vacant)
Psychology of Education: AHMED OUZI
Language Teaching: MILOUD HABIBI
Humanities Teaching: MOHAMED ZEKOUA
Exact Sciences Teaching: KHADIJA HAMDAN
Technology of Education: (vacant)

ATTACHED INSTITUTES

Institut d'Etude et de Recherche pour l'Arabisation (Institute of Study and Research for Arabization): BP 430, Ave Maa El Aïnine, Rabat; Dir AHMED LAKHDAR GHAZAL.

Institut Scientifique: see under Research Institutes.

Institut Universitaire de la Recherche Scientifique: BP 447, Ave Maa El Aïnine, Rabat; research in geographical linguistics, anthropology, national history and civilization; Dir ABDELHADI TAZI.

Institut des Etudes Africaines.

UNIVERSITÉ QUARAOUYINE

Dhar Mahraz, BP 2509, Fès
Telephone: (5) 64-10-06
Fax: (5) 64-10-13
Founded AD 859, enlarged in 11th century, reorganized 1963
State control
Language of instruction: Arabic
Academic year: September to July
Rector: Prof. ABDELOUAHHAB TAZI SAOUD
Secretary-General: MOHAMMED BENNANI ZOUBIR
Number of teachers: 115
Number of students: 6,000

CONSTITUENT INSTITUTES

Faculty of Sharia (Law): BP 60, Saïs, Fès; Dean Prof. MOHAMMED YESSEF.

Faculty of Arabic Studies: Ave Allal Al-Fassi, B.P. 1483, Marrakech; Dean Prof. HASSAN JELLAB.

Faculty of Theology: Blvd Abdelkhalek Torres, BP 95, Tétouan; Dean Prof. DRISS KHALIFA.

Faculty of Sharia: BP 52, Agadir; Dean Prof. MOHAMMED ATTAHIRI.

UNIVERSITÉ SIDI MOHAMED BEN ABDELLAH

BP 2626, Ave des Almohades, Fès
Telephone: (5) 62-55-85
Fax: (5) 62-24-01
Founded 1975
State control
Languages of instruction: Arabic, French
Academic year: September to July
Rector: AMAL JELLAL
Secretary-General: MOHAMED FERHANE
Libraries with 225,000 vols
Number of teachers: 1,010
Number of students: 35,088

DEANS

Faculty of Letters and Human Sciences (Dhar Mehrez): CHAD MOHAMED
Faculty of Science (Dhar Mehrez): SAGHI MOHAMED
Faculty of Law, Economics and Social Sciences: SKALI HOUSSAINI ALI
High School of Technology: OUAZZANI CHAHDI TAOUFIK (Dir)
Faculty of Letters and Human Sciences (Saiss): MOHAMED MEZZINE
Faculty of Science and Technology (Saiss): ABDELILAH HALLAOUI

HEADS OF DEPARTMENTS

Faculty of Letters and Human Sciences (Dhar Mehrez):

Arabic: ABDELMALEK CHAMI
English: KHALID EL-BERKAOUI (Co-ordinator)
French: ABDERRAHMANE TENKOUL
Geography: MOHAMED REHHOU (Co-ordinator)
German: MASLEK ABDERRAZAK
History: MOULAY HACHEM ALAOUI KACIMI
Islamic Studies: HAMID FETAH
Philosophy, Psychology and Sociology: ALI AFERFAR
Spanish: IMAMI ABDELLATIF

Faculty of Science (Dhar Mehrez):

Biology: BOUYA DRISS
Chemistry: KARBAL ABDELALI
Geology: ABDELLAH BOUSHABA
Mathematics: AMEZIANE HASSANI RACHID
Physics: FOUAD LAHLOU

Faculty of Law, Economics and Social Sciences:

Economics: IDRISSI HASSAN
Private Law: ABDELGHANI DHIMEN
Public Law: AHMED ELGOURARI

High School of Technology:

Electrical Engineering: BENSLIMANE RACHID
Industrial Maintenance: ABDELLATIF SAFOUAN
Management: ALI BEN GHAZI AKHLAKI
Mechanical and Production Engineering: KIHEL BACHIR
Process Engineering: BENTAMA JILALI

Faculty of Letters and Human Sciences (Saiss):

Arabic: MOHAMED BOUTAHER
English: ABDELJALIL NAOUI ELKHIR
French: FATOUMA MELOUK
Geography: IBRAHIM ACDIM

History: MOHAMED LABBAR
Islamic Studies: LAHSEN ZIN FILALI

Faculty of Science and Technology (Saiss):

Biology: YAMANI JAMAL
Chemistry: LHOUSINE EL-GHADRAOUI
Mathematics: OUAKILI HASSAN
Physics: CHARKANI EL-HASSANI MOHAMED

Colleges

Conservatoire de musique: Rue Souk, Hay Essenaï, Agadir; Dir NAFIL BOUZKARN.

Conservatoire de musique: Chefchaouen; Dir AL HACHMI ESSAFYANI.

Conservatoire de musique: Dar Adaîl, Fès; Dir ABDELKARIM RAÏSS.

Conservatoire de musique: Kasr El Kebir; Dir BAHMED ABDELGHANI.

Conservatoire de musique: Dar Al Makhzen, Larache; tel. (4) 322-92; f. 1948; teaches classical music and Moroccan and Arab heritage; Dir MOHAMED MAHSSINE.

Conservatoire de musique: Arsat El-Hamed-Bab-Doukkala, Marrakech; tel. (4) 44-00-66; f. 1948; teaches Western classical and modern music and classical Moroccan and Arab music; Dir MAHASSINE MOHAMED.

Conservatoire de musique: Ave Al Konsolia Al Faransia, Dar El Bacha Alkadima, Safi; Dir NAJIH MOHAMMED.

Conservatoire de musique: Place de l' Istiqulal, Taza; tel. (67) 38-01; f. 1972; study of musical theory, Arab instruments and Moroccan, Andalusian and Classical music; Dir ABDELLAH KHARRAZ.

Conservatoire de musique: Tétouan; Dir MED LARBI TEMSAMANI.

Conservatoire National de Musique et de Danse: 33 rue Tensift-Agdal, Rabat; tel. 77-37-94; trains students in Western and Arabic music and classical dance; the Conservatoire has an orchestra for modern Arab music, an orchestra for Andalusian and Moroccan music, two youth orchestras and a big band orchestra; Dir MOHAMMED EL BAHJA.

Conservatoire de Tanger: Ave Belgique, Tanger; Dir MOHAMED RAÏSSI.

Ecole des Métiers d'Art (School of Native Arts and Crafts): Bab Okla, BP 89, Tétouan; f. 1921; textiles, carpets, rugs, ceramics, engraving, plaster inlays, woodwork, precious metal work, leather and Arabic woodcarving; 350 mems; Dir ABDELLAH FEKHAR.

Ecole Hassania des Travaux Publics: Km 7, Route d'El Jadida, BP 8108, Oasis, Casablanca; tel. 23-07-90; fax 23-07-17; e-mail ehtpnet@mbox.azure.net; f. 1971; civil engineering, electrical engineering, meteorology, geographical sciences; 72 teachers, 330 students; library of 15,000 vols; Dir ABDESLAM MESSOUDI.

Ecole Nationale d'Administration: BP 165, 2 ave de la Victoire, Rabat; tel. 73-14-50; fax 73-09-29; f. 1948; library of 18,000 vols; 36 teachers, 646 students; Dir AMINE MZOURI; publ. *Administration et Société* (3 a year).

Ecole Nationale de l'Industrie Minérale: Rue Hadj Ahmed Cherkaoui, BP 753, Agdal, Rabat; tel. 77-13-60; fax 77-10-55; f. 1972; specializes in geology, material sciences, mining sciences, chemical process engineering, electro-mechanical engineering, energy sciences, computer science; 80 teachers; 296 students; library of 11,000 vols; Dir ABDERRAHMANE ALJ; publs *Report* (annually), research papers.

Ecole Nationale des Beaux-Arts: Ave Mohamed V, Cité Scolaire BP 89, Tétouan; f. 1946; drawing, painting, sculpture, decorative arts; Dir MOHAMMED M. SERGHINI.

Ecole Nationale de musique: 133 blvd Ziraoui, Casablanca 01; tel. 26-90-61; Dir NABYL EDDAHAR.

Ecole Nationale de musique: 22 rue Marrakchia, Kaa Ouarda, Meknès; Dir ABDELAZIZ BENABDELJALIL.

Ecole Nationale Forestière d'Ingénieurs: BP 511, Salé; tel. (7) 78-97-04; fax (7) 78-71-49; f. 1968; 20 teachers, 160 students; library of 5,000 vols; Dir MY. Y. ALAOUI.

Ecole des Sciences de l'Information: BP 6204, Rabat-Instituts; tel. 749-04; fax 77-02-32; f. 1974; 4-year undergraduate courses and 2-year postgraduate courses for archivists, librarians, documentalists; library of 13,000 vols, 342 periodicals, 415 audio-visual documents; UNESCO publications, research papers, courses, syllabuses etc.; 64 teachers, 512 students; Dir MOHAMED BENJELLOUN.

Institut Agronomique et Vétérinaire Hassan II: BP 6202-Instituts, Rabat; fax (7) 77-81-35; e-mail lemallem@syfed.ma.ma .refer; f. 1966; library of 34,000 documents, 1,200 periodicals; 350 teachers, 2,500 students; Dir Dr MOHAMED SEDRATI; Sec.-Gen. Dr FOUAD GUESSOUS; publs *Revue Scientifique et Technique Multidisciplinaire* (quarterly), *AgroVetMagazine* (monthly), *Les Actes de l'Institut.*

Institut National de musique et de danse: Ave Mohamed V (derrière le 2° arrondissement), Kénitra; Dir ABBÈS ALKHAYYATI.

Institut National de Statistique et d'Economie Appliquée: BP 6217, Rabat; tel. (7) 77-09-15; fax (7) 77-94-57; f. 1961; library of 15,000 vols; 398 students; Dir ABDELAZIZ EL GHAZALI; publ. *Revue*† (1 a year).

Instituto Politécnico Español 'Severo Ochoa' (Spanish Institute in Tangier): Plaza Kuwait 1, Tanger; tel. (212-9) 936338; f. 1949; 32 teachers, 280 students; library of 7,500 vols; Dir CONRADO PARRA MARTÍNEZ; publs *Revista Kasbah* (annually), *Revista Makada* (annually).

MOZAMBIQUE

Learned Societies

LANGUAGE AND LITERATURE

PEN Centre of Mozambique: C/o Associação dos Escritores Moçambicanos, Av. 24 de Julho 1420, Caixa Postal 4187, Maputo; Sec. PEDRO CHISSANO.

Research Institutes

AGRICULTURE, FISHERIES AND VETERINARY SCIENCE

Instituto de Algodão de Moçambique (Cotton Research Institute): Av. Eduardo Mondlane No. 2221, 1° andar, CP 806, Maputo; tel. 424264; telex 6547; f. 1962; departments of agronomy, botany, soils, economics, genetical cytology, entomology and phytopathology; 4 experimental stations; library of 2,500 vols, 210 journals and reviews; Dir Eng. Agr. ERASMO MUHATE; publ. *Somente Relatório Anual de Actividades*.

Instituto Nacional de Investigação Agronómica: CP 3658, Maputo 4; tel. 97-100; telex 6209; f. 1965; Dir LUIS XAVIER JUNIOR; publs *Comunicações / INIA*.

MEDICINE

Instituto Nacional de Saúde (National Health Institute): Av. Eduardo Mondlane 296, CP 264, Maputo; telex 6239; fax 423726; f. 1980; study, research and training in ecology, epidemiology, immunology, malaria, microbiology, parasitology, trypanosomiasis; traditional medicine; documentation and information depts; 32 staff; library of 6,500 vols; Dir Dr RUI GAMA VAZ; publs *Revista Médica de Moçambique*, newsletter.

NATURAL SCIENCES

Physical Sciences

Direcção Nacional de Geologia: CP 217, Maputo; tel. 424031; telex 6584; fax 429216; f. 1928; regional geology, geological mapping and mineral exploration; library of 30,000 vols, maps, technical material, etc; Dir JOÃO MANUEL P. R. MARQUES; publs *Boletim Geológico de Moçambique*, maps.

Instituto Nacional de Meteorologia: CP 256, Maputo; tel. 490148; fax 491150; f. 1907; library of 2,200 vols; Dir ERNESTO M. MUSSAGE; publs *Anuário de Observações* (2 vols): I *Observações Meteorológicas de Superficie*, II *Observações Meteorológicas de Altitude*, *Boletim Bibliográfico do INAM*, *Informações de Carácter Astronómico*, *Boletim Meteorológico para a Agricultura* (every 10 days).

Libraries and Archives

Maputo

Arquivo Histórico de Moçambique: CP 2033, Maputo; tel. 42-11-77; fax 42-34-28; f. 1934; attached to the University; 24,000 vols, 11,600 periodicals; special collections: written reports of administrative or governmental offices and business; cartography; iconography; Dir Prof. Dr INÊS NOGUEIRA; publs *Arquivo*, *Estudos* (series), *Documentos* (series), *Instrumentos de Pesquisa* (series).

Biblioteca Municipal: Maputo; 7,951 vols.

Biblioteca Nacional de Moçambique (National Library of Mozambique): CP 141, Maputo; tel. 425676; f. 1961; 110,000 vols; Dir ANTÓNIO M. B. COSTA E SILVA.

Centro Nacional de Documentação e Informação de Moçambique: CP 4116, Maputo; tel. 26666; telex 6399; f. 1977; part of Council of Ministers Secretariat; library of 12,000 vols; Dir RICARDO SANTOS; publ. *Documento Informativo*.

Direcção Nacional de Geologia, Centro de Documentação: CP 217, Maputo; tel. 424031-4; telex 6584; fax 429216; f. 1928; documentation centre for geology and mineral exploration; 10 special collections; Dir JOÃO MANUEL P. R. MARQUES; publs *Boletim Geológico, Notícias Explicativas da Geologia de Moçambique*, maps.

Museums and Art Galleries

Maputo

Museu de História Natural: CP 1780, Maputo; tel. 741145; f. 1911; natural history museum and ethnographic gallery; attached to the University; Dir AUGUSTO J. PEREIRA CABRAL.

University

UNIVERSIDADE EDUARDO MONDLANE

CP 257, Maputo

Telephone: (1) 425972
Fax: (1) 428128

Founded 1962
State control
Language of instruction: Portuguese
Academic year: August to July

Rector: Prof. Dr BRAZÃO MAZULA
Vice-Rector for Academic Affairs: Prof. Dr ANTÓNIO SARAIVA DE SOUSA
Vice-Rector for Administrative Affairs: Eng. VENÂNCIO MASSINGUE
International Relations Officer: Dra SANDRA LOPES
Director of Documentation Services: Prof. Dr ANTÓNIO SARAIVA DE SOUSA (acting)

Number of teachers: 712
Number of students: 5,762

DEANS

Faculty of Agriculture: Prof. Dr FIRMINO MUCAVELE
Faculty of Architecture: Prof. JOSÉ FORJAZ
Faculty of Arts: Dra JULIETA LANGA
Faculty of Economics: Dr ALBERTO BILA (acting)
Faculty of Engineering: Prof. Dr MANUEL CUMBI
Faculty of Law: Dr ARMANDO DIMANDE
Faculty of Medicine: Dr JOÃO SCHAWLBACH
Faculty of Veterinary Science: Dr GERALDO DIAS
Faculty of Science: Prof. Dr ISIDRO MANUEL
Unit for Teaching and Research in Social Science: Prof. Dr LUÍS DE BRITO

ATTACHED INSTITUTES

Centre for African Studies: Dir Prof. Dra TERESA CRUZ E SILVA.
Centre for Electronic Technology and Instrumentation: Dir Eng. VENÂNCIO MATUSSE.
Centre for Informatics: Dir Eng. VENÂNCIO MASSINGUE.

MYANMAR

Research Institutes

AGRICULTURE, FISHERIES AND VETERINARY SCIENCE

Forest Research Institute: Yezin, Pyinmana; tel. (67) 21101; f. 1978; 252 staff; library of 10,261 vols; Dir U SHWE KYAW.

ECONOMICS, LAW AND POLITICS

Department of Research and Management Studies: Institute of Economics, Hlaing Campus, Yangon; conducts research into various aspects of the Burmese economy; current activities include investigation of problems of modernization and development of agriculture, industrial development, planning and economic management, trade and development, etc.; also conducts courses for senior management personnel; Head (vacant); publs. occasional papers and research monographs.

MEDICINE

Department of Medical Research: 5 Ziwaka Rd, Yangon 11191; tel. (1) 251508; fax (1) 251514; formerly Burma Medical Research Institute; f. 1963; 24 divisions and 7 clinical research units: animal services, bacteriology, biochemistry, computer diagnostics and vaccine research, epidemiology, experimental medicine, finance and budget, health systems research, clinical research, immunology, instrumentation, library, medical entomology, medical research statistics, nuclear medicine, nutrition, parasitology, pathology, pharmacology, physiology, publications, radioisotope and virology; clinical research units: malaria (DSGH), malaria (2MH), cerebral and complicated malaria (DMR), snakebites, traditional medicine, HIV/AIDS, research unit (IM II); Dir-Gen. Dr THAN SWE; publs *DMR Bulletin*, *Myanmar Health Sciences Research Journal*, *DMR Special Report Series*, *DMR CBL Newsletter*.

National Health Laboratories: Yangon; f. 1968 by amalgamating the Harcourt-Butler Institute of Public Health, the Pasteur Institute, Office of the Chemical Examiner and Office of the Public Analyst; composed of five divisions: Administration, Public Health, Chemical, Food and Drugs and Clinical; Dir Dr MEHM SOE MYINT.

RELIGION, SOCIOLOGY AND ANTHROPOLOGY

Department of Religious Affairs: Kabaaye Pagoda compound, Yangon; a government-supported centre for research and studies in Buddhist and allied subjects; library of 17,000 vols, 7,000 periodicals, 7,650 palm-leaf MSS, etc; Dir-Gen. U ANT MAUNG.

TECHNOLOGY

Myanmar Scientific and Technological Research Department: Kanbe, Yankin Post Office, Yangon; tel. (1) 665695; fax (1) 665292; a dept of the Ministry of Science and Technology; composed of the Analysis Dept, Metallurgy Research Dept, Physics and Engineering Research Dept, Technical Information Centre, Fine Instruments Dept and Workshop, Applied Chemistry Research Dept, Ceramics Research Dept, Standards and Specifications Dept, Polymer Research Dept, Pharmaceutical Research Dept, Food Technology Research Dept; research in applied sciences; library of 17,000 vols, 1,200 periodicals; Dir-Gen. Col TIN HTUT.

Union of Myanmar Atomic Energy Centre: Central Research Organization, 6 Kaba Aye Pagoda Rd, Yangon; f. 1955; environmental radiation monitoring, nuclear instrumentation; Chair U ANG KOE.

Libraries and Archives

Bassein

Bassein Degree College Library: Bassein; f. 1958; 27,560 vols; Librarian NYAN HTUN.

State Library: Bassein; f. 1963; 1,453 vols.

Kyaukpyu

State Library: Kyaukpyu; f. 1955; 8,651 vols.

Magwe

Magwe Degree College Library: Magwe; f. 1958; 26,900 vols; Dir KHIN MYINT MYINT.

Mandalay

Institute of Medicine Library: Seiktaramahi Quarters, Mandalay; f. 1964; 28,362 vols, 47 periodicals; Librarian KAUNG NYUNT.

State Library: Mandalay; f. 1955; 7,004 vols.

University of Mandalay Library: University Estate, Mandalay; 146,000 vols; Librarian U NYAN TUN.

Mawlamyine

Mawlamyine University Library: Mawlamyine, Mon State; f. 1964; 60,916 vols, 35 periodicals; Librarian U THEIN LWIN; publ. *Newsletter* (every 2 months).

State Library: Mawlamyine; f. 1955; 13,265 vols; 1,262 MSS.

Myitkyina

Myitkyina Degree College Library: Myitkyina, Kachin State; Librarian (vacant).

Pyinmana

Institute of Agriculture Library: Yezin, Pyinmana; f. 1924, autonomous 1964; 26,000 vols, 130 periodicals; Chief Librarian U MYINT THEIN.

Institute of Animal Husbandry and Veterinary Science Library: Yezin, Pyinmana; f. 1964; 4,500 vols; Librarian HTAY HTAY KHIN.

Tyaunggyi

Taunggyi Degree College Library: Taunggyi, Shan State; Librarian (vacant).

Yangon

Central Biomedical Library: Department of Medical Research, 5 Ziwaka Rd, Yangon 11191; formerly Burma Medical Research Institute Library; f. 1963; 26,000 vols, 170 periodicals; Chief Librarian U MAUNG MAUNG WIN.

Institute of Computer Science and Technology Library: Yangon; Library Asst Daw YU YU TIN.

Institute of Economics Library: University Estate, POB 473, Yangon; tel. (1) 532433; f. 1964; 87,000 vols; Librarian Daw KHIN KYU.

Institute of Education Library: University Estate, Yangon; f. 1964; 36,166 vols; Librarian Daw GILDA TWE.

Institute of Medicine I Library: 245 Myoma Kyaung Rd, Lanmadaw P.O. 11131, Yangon; f. 1929; 30,000 vols; Librarian KHIN MAW MAW TUN.

Institute of Medicine II Library: N/okkalapa, Yangon 11031; f. 1964; 25,000 vols; Librarian U THI TAR.

Myanmar Education Research Bureau: 426 Pyay Rd, University PO 11041, Yangon; tel. 31860; f. 1965; a dept of the Ministry of Education; library of 56,000 vols; educational materials resource centre; Chair. Daw KHIN SWE HTUN; publs *The World of Education* (quarterly).

National Library: Strand Road, Yangon; tel. (1) 272058; f. 1952; incorporating the Bernard Free Library; 158,800 vols, 12,321 MSS, 411,426 periodicals; Chief Librarian U KHIN MAUNG TIN.

Sarpay Beikman Public Library: 529 Merchant St, Yangon; f. 1956; 74,404 vols (56,729 Burmese, 17,675 English); Librarian NU NU.

Universities' Central Library: University PO, Yangon; f. 1929; 350,000 vols; central library for all higher education institutes; specializes in Burmese books, palm-leaf MSS (over 11,000), and books on Burma and Asia; Chief Librarian THAW KAUNG.

University of Yangon Library: Yangon; tel. 533250; re-f. 1986; 100,000 vols; Head Librarian CI MYAT SOE.

Workers' College Library: Yangon; f. 1964; 19,500 vols; Librarian KHIN THIN KYU.

Yangon Institute of Technology Library: Insein PO, Gyogon, Yangon; f. 1964; 48,000 vols, 560 periodicals; Librarian U TIN MAUNG LWIN.

Museums and Art Galleries

Bagan

Bagan Archaeological Museum: opposite Gawdawpalin Temple, Bagan, Mandalay Division; f. 1904, new bldg opened 1975; site museum for ancient capital of 11th- to 14th-century; lithic inscriptions, Buddha images, statuary and artefacts; administered by Dept of Archaeology; Curator U KYAW NYEIN.

Mandalay

State Museum: Corner of 24th and 80th Sts, Mandalay; f. 1955; over 1,500 exhibits; also br. museum in fmr Mandalay Palace grounds; Curator U SOE THEIN.

Mawlamyine

Mon State Museum: Dawei Tada Rd, Mawlamyine; f. 1955; over 750 exhibits; Curator U MIN KHIN MAUNG.

Sitture

Rakhine State Museum: Chin Pyan Rd, Kyaung-gyi Quarter, Sitture, Rakhine State; f. 1955; over 500 exhibits (silver coins, costumes etc.); also site museum at Mrauk-U, ancient capital; Curator Daw NU MYA ZAN.

Taunggyi

Shan State Museum: Min Lan, Thittaw Quarter, Taunggyi, Shan State; f. 1957; over 600 exhibits; Curator U SAN MYA.

Yangon

Bogyoke Aung San Museum: 25 Bogyoke Museum Rd, Bahan PO, Yangon; tel. (1) 50600; f. 1959; 571 exhibits relating to the life and work of General Aung San.

National Museum of Art and Archaeology: 26/42 Pansodan, Yangon; tel. (1) 73706; f. 1952; 1,652 antiquities; 354 paintings; replica of King Mindon's Mandalay Palace; Dir-Gen. Dr YE TUT; Chief Curator U KYAW WIN.

Universities and University Institutes

UNIVERSITY OF MANDALAY

University Estate, Mandalay

Telephone: 02-21211

Founded 1925, granted autonomy 1958

Rector: U TIN MAUNG
Pro-Rector: U LU NI
Registrars: U WIN MYINT (Student Affairs and Hostels), Daw SEIN SEIN (Examination and Convocation)
Librarian: U NYAN TUN

Library of 175,000 vols
Number of teachers: 821
Number of students: 21,045

HEADS OF DEPARTMENTS

Botany: U NYUNT LWIN
Chemistry: U KHIN MG KYI
Economics: Daw KHIN SAN MAY
English: Daw WINNIE MURRAY
History: Daw SAN SAN AYE
Geography: Daw FAITH WILLIAM LAY
Psychology: U KHIN MAUNG THAN
Philosophy: Daw MYA KYAING
International Relations: Daw KHIN HTWE YI
Physics: U KYEE MYINT
Mathematics: Dr KYAW NYUNT
Geology: Dr MYINT THEIN
Zoology: Dr KHIN MG AYE
Oriental Studies: U BA SUN
Law: U KHIN MG THEIN
Myanmar: Daw HLA MYAT

There are 9 affiliated colleges.

MAWLAMYINE UNIVERSITY

Mawlamyine, Mon State

Telephone: (32) 21180

Founded 1953, university status 1986
State control
Academic year: November to September

Rector: HLA TUN AUNG
Pro-Rector: HLA PE
Librarian: THEIN LWIN

Number of teachers: 305
Number of students: 11,500, incl. 17,800 corresp. students

HEADS OF DEPARTMENTS AND PROFESSORS

Myanmar: Assoc. Prof. YIN YIN MYINT
English: Assoc. Prof. SEINE SEINE MYINT
Geography: Prof. THAN MYA
History: Assoc. Prof. MYINT MYINT THAN
Philosophy: Assoc. Prof. TIN HLA
Oriental Studies: TIN OO
Mathematics: Assoc. Prof. KHIN MAUNG LATT
Physics: Prof. SEIN HTOON
Chemistry: Prof. MAUNG MAUNG HTAY
Botany: Assoc. Prof. SANN TINT
Zoology: Assoc. Prof. MYA MYA NU
Geology: Prof. NYAN THIN
Marine Science: Assoc. Prof. KYI WINN

AFFILIATED COLLEGES

Bago College: Principal HLA MYINT.
Hpa-an College: Principal LAWRENCE THAW.
Dawei College: Principal THIN HLAING.

UNIVERSITY OF YANGON

Mein University Estate, Yangon, University PO

Telephone: (1) 31144

Founded 1920

Campuses in Hling Region, Kyimyindine Region, Botataung Region

Rector: TIN OO HLAING
Registrar: NYUNT NYUNT WIN

Number of teachers: 2,060
Number of students: 47,131

HEADS OF DEPARTMENT

Anthropology: SEIN TAN
Botany: Dr KYAW SOE
Burmese: SHWE THWIN
Chemistry: Dr NYUNT WIN
English: HAN TIN
Geography: TIN AYE
Geology: Dr MAUNG THEIN
History: TUN AUNG CHEIN
Industrial Chemistry: Dr MIN MYINT
International Relations: KHIN KHIN MA
Law: Dr TIN AUNG AYE
Library Studies: THAW KAUNG
Mathematics: SEIN MIN
Oriental Studies: LAY MYING
Philosophy: (vacant)
Physics: Dr ZIN AUNG
Psychology: AYE THAN
Zoology: KYI KYI

There are 3 affiliated degree-granting colleges in Pathein, Sittwe and Yangon, and 2 colleges in Hinthada and Pyay.

Institute of Agriculture: Yezin, Pyinmana; tel. (67) 21434; f. 1924, autonomous 1964.

Rector: Dr KYAW THAN
Pro-Rector: Dr AUNG THAN
Registrars: HLA TUN, SAW LWIN

Number of teachers: 105
Number of students: 1,161

Institute of Animal Husbandry and Veterinary Science: Yezin, Pyinmana; tel. (67) 21448; f. 1957, autonomous 1964.

Rector: U MAUNG MAUNG SA
Registrar: U MYA THEIN TUN
Librarian: Daw HTAY HTAY KHIN

Library of 13,204 vols, 53 periodicals

Number of teachers: 57
Number of students: 1,000

Institute of Computer Science and Technology: Hlaing Campus, Hlaing PO 11052, Yangon; tel. (1) 65686; f. 1988 (fmrly Universities Computer Centre).

Rector: Dr TIN MAUNG
Pro-Rector: Dr KYAW THEIN
Registrar: U KYIN HTWE
Librarian: Daw KHIN MAR AYE

Library of 8,333 vols

Number of teachers: 22
Number of students: 519

Institute of Dental Medicine: Shwedagon Pagoda Rd, Latha Po, Yangon; tel. (1) 83755; f. 1964.

Rector: Prof. Dr HTAY SAUNG.

Institute of Economics: University PO, 11041 Yangon; tel. (1) 532433; f. 1964; library of 87,000 vols.

Rector: U MAW THAN

Number of teachers: 237
Number of students: 5,096

Institute of Education: University Estate, University PO, 11041 Yangon; tel. (1) 31345; f. 1964.

Rector: U MYO NYUNT.

Institute of Foreign Languages: University PO, 11041 Yangon; tel. (1) 31985; f. 1984.

Principal: U MYO NYUNT (acting)
Librarian: Daw SANDAR TUN

Library of 26,000 vols

Number of teachers: 51
Number of students: 1,318

Language courses in Chinese, English, French, German, Japanese, Russian and Thai; Myanmar language courses for foreign students.

Institute of Medicine (I): 245 Myoma Kyaung Rd, Lanmadaw PO, 11131, Yangon; tel. (1) 74344; f. 1964.

Rector: Prof. MYA OO

Number of teachers: 57
Number of students: 4,015

Institute of Medicine (II): 13 Mile Pyay Rd, Mingaladon, Yangon; tel. (1) 45507; f. 1964.

Rector: Dr THA HLA SHWE

Institute of Medicine: Seiktaramahi Quarters, Mandalay; tel. (2) 22011; f. 1964.

Rector: Dr TUN THIN

Mandalay Institute of Technology: Patheingyi PO, Mandalay, f. 1991; 6-year first degree courses.

Pro-Rector: U THEIN TAN.

Yangon Technological University: Gyogon, Insein PO, Yangon; fax (1) 642410; f. 1964; 6-year first degree courses, 1-year postgraduate diploma and 2- and 3-year postgraduate degree courses.

Rector: Prof. U NYI HLA NGE

Colleges

Defence Services Academy: Maymyo; f. 1955; an independent degree college under the Ministry of Defence; degree courses for cadets training for service as regular commissioned officers in the Burma Army, Navy and Air Force; *c.* 120 staff, *c.* 400 students; Commanding Officer Col. AUNG WIN.

Magway Degree College: University Campus, Magway, Magway Division; tel. (63) 21030; 129 teachers; 3,555 students; Principal U SEIN WIN.

Myitkyina Degree College: University Campus, Myitkyina, Kachin State; tel. (101) 21053; 90 teachers, 1,752 students; Principal U SUM HLOT NAW.

Pathein Degree College: University Campus, Pathein, Ayeyarwady Division; tel. (42) 21135; 178 teachers; 5,158 students; Principal Dr MAUNG KYAW.

Sittwe Degree College: University Campus, Sittwe, Rakhine State; tel. (43) 21236; 97 teachers; 1,730 students; Principal U KWAW MYA THEIN.

State School of Fine Arts: Mandalay; f. 1953; Principal KAN NYUNT.

State School of Fine Arts: Kanbawza Yeiktha, Kaba Aye Pagoda Rd, Bahan PO, Yangon; tel. (1) 52176; f. 1952; courses in drawing, fine art, commercial art, sculpture and wood-carving; Principal U SOE TINT.

State School of Music and Drama: East Moat Road, Mandalay; tel. (2) 21176; f. 1953; courses in dancing, singing, Burmese harp and orchestra, xylophone, piano, oboe, stringed instruments and stave notation; Principal KAN NYUNT.

State School of Music and Drama: Kanbawza Yeiktha, Kaba Aye Pagoda Rd, Bahan PO, Yangon; tel. (1) 52176; f. 1952; courses in dancing, singing, Burmese harp and orchestra, piano, oboe, xylophone, stringed instruments, stave notation and Burmese verse; Principal U AUNG THWIN.

Taunggyi State College: Taunggyi Shan State; tel. (81) 21160; 125 teachers; 3,456 students; Principal U SAW HLINE.

Workers' College: 273/279 Konthe Lan, Botahtaung PO, Yangon; tel. (1) 92825; 47 teachers; 5,650 students; Principal U SAN MAUNG.

NAMIBIA

Learned Societies

GENERAL

Namibia Scientific Society: POB 67, Windhoek 9000; tel. 225372; f. 1925; ornithology, spelaeology, botany, archaeology, herpetology, astronomy, ethnology; 900 mems and 200 exchange mems; library of 8,000 vols; Pres. Dr J. BRANDMAYR; publs *Mitteilungen / Newsletter / Nuusbrief, Mitteilungen der Ornithologischen Arbeitsgruppe, Journal* (annually), and others irregularly.

ARCHITECTURE AND TOWN PLANNING

Namibia Institute of Architects: POB 1478, Windhoek; f. 1952; 98 mems; Pres. K. AFSHANI.

Research Institutes

NATURAL SCIENCES

Biological Sciences

Desert Ecological Research Unit of Namibia: POB 953, Walvis Bay; fax (64) 205197; e-mail gobabeb@iafrica.com.na; f. 1963; research in Namib Desert and semi-arid Namibia, emphasizing basic and applied research, conservation biology, community applications and environmental education; library of 1,600 vols, 15,000 documents; Dir M. K. SEELY; publ. *Namib Bulletin* (occasionally).

National Botanical Research Institute: C/o Ministry of Agriculture, Water and Rural Development, Private Bag 13184, Windhoek; tel. (61) 2022167; fax (61) 258153; e-mail nbri@namib.com; library of 1,700 books, 220 periodicals.

Libraries and Archives

Swakopmund

Sam Cohen Library: POB 361, Swakopmund; tel. (64) 402695; fax (64) 400763; f. 1977; 6,000 vols on SW Africa and Africana; attached to Swakopmund Museum (see below).

Windhoek

National Agricultural Information Centre: Private Bag 13184, Windhoek 9000; tel. (61) 224550 ext. 242; fax (61) 222974; f. 1974; 16,000 books, 988 periodical titles; depository for FAO publs; Librarian M. HOFFMANN.

National Archives of Namibia: Private Bag 13250, 4 Lüderitz Street, Windhoek 9000; tel. (61) 2934308; e-mail natarch@.natarch.mec.gov.na; f. 1939; houses government records, private collections, maps, photographs, microforms, films, sound recordings, posters, 1,000 periodical titles and 9,000 other publications; Chief J. KUTZNER.

National Library of Namibia: Cnr of Peter Müller and Rev. Michael Scott Sts, Private Bag 13349, Windhoek; tel. (61) 2934490; fax (61) 229808; e-mail johan@natlib.mec.gov.na; f. 1994; legal deposit and general reference library; deposit library for UN, GATT and World Bank publications; Head JOHAN LOUBSER.

Windhoek Public Library: Private Bag 13183, Windhoek 9000; tel. (61) 224899; f. 1924; 75,000 vols; Librarian L. HANSMANN.

Museums and Art Galleries

Lüderitz

Lüderitz Museum: POB 512, Lüderitz 9000; tel. 2346; fax 3267; f. 1966; incorporates finds of Friedrich Eberlanz of archaeological, herpetological, botanical and mineralogical interest, incl. Bushman Stone Age tools; Supervisor G. SCHEELE-SCHMIDT.

Swakopmund

Museum Swakopmund: POB 361, Strand St, Swakopmund; tel. (64) 402046; fax (64) 400763; f. 1951; natural history, mineralogy, marine life, history, archaeology, ethnology, technology; Chair. M. WEBER; publ. newsletter (trilingual).

Windhoek

National Art Gallery of Namibia: POB 994, Windhoek 9000; tel. (61) 231160; fax (61) 240930; f. 1947; exhibitions, lectures, educational programmes; Curator A. H. EINS; publs *Newsletter* (4 a year), catalogues.

National Museum: POB 1203, Windhoek; tel. (61) 2934360; fax (61) 228636; e-mail library@natmus.cul.na; 229808; f. 1907; natural and human sciences; library of 6,000 vols, 600 journal titles; Dir E. MOOMBOLAH; publs *Cimbebasia, Memoirs.*

University

UNIVERSITY OF NAMIBIA

Private Bag 13301, 340 Mandume Ndemufayo Ave, Pioneerspark, Windhoek

Telephone: (61) 206-3111

Fax: (61) 206-3866

Founded 1992 upon the dissolution of the Academy, Windhoek

State control

Language of instruction: English

Academic year: January to November

Chancellor: Dr SAM NUJOMA (President of Namibia)

Vice-Chancellor: Prof. PETER H. KATJAVIVI

Pro Vice-Chancellor (Academic Affairs and Research): Prof. K. E. MSHIGENI

Pro Vice-Chancellor (Administration and Finance): R. KIRBY-HARRIS

Registrar: MILKA MUNGUNDA (acting)

Librarian: K. E. AVAFIA

Library of 66,000 vols, 40,000 UNIN books and documents

Number of teachers: 250

Number of students: 4,500 f.t.e.

DEANS

Faculty of Agriculture and Natural Resources: Dr O. D. MWANDEMELE

Faculty of Economics and Management Science: Prof. A. DU PISAN

Faculty of Education: Dr J. KATZA

Faculty of Humanities and Social Science: Dr HARLECH JONES

Faculty of Law: Prof. WALTER J. KAMBA

Faculty of Medical and Health Sciences: Prof. AGNES S. B. VAN DYK

Faculty of Science: Prof. G. KIANGI

NEPAL

Learned Societies

GENERAL

National Council for Science and Technology: Kirtipur, Kathmandu; tel. 216348; f. 1976; advisory body to the govt; aims to formulate science and technology policy, and to promote scientific and technological research; Chair. Hon. PRITHVI RAJ LIGAL; Sec. D. D. SHAKYA.

Royal Nepal Academy: Kamaladi, Kathmandu; tel. 221283; f. 1957; 178 mems; library of 10,562 vols, 4,697 periodicals; Vice-Chancellor MADAN MANI DIXIT; Mem.-Sec. Dr DHANUSH CHANDRA GAUTAM; publs *Prajna* (quarterly), *Kabita* (on Nepalese poetry, quarterly).

Royal Nepal Academy of Science and Technology (RONAST): POB 3323, New Baneswor, Kathmandu; tel. 215316; fax 228690; f. 1982; 157 mems; library of 6,000 vols, 150 periodicals; Vice-Chancellor Prof. KEDAR LAL SHRESHTHA; Sec. RISHI SHAH; publs *Bulletin* (quarterly), *RONAST Communicator* (monthly).

Research Institutes

GENERAL

International Centre for Integrated Mountain Development (ICIMOD): 4/80 Jawalakhel, POB 3226, Kathmandu; tel. (1) 525313; fax (1) 524509; e-mail dits@icimod.org.np; f. 1983; sponsored by the govts of the Hindu Kush-Himalayan countries, Austria, Denmark, Finland, Germany, the Netherlands, Sweden and Switzerland, to help promote an economically and environmentally sound ecosystem, and to improve the living standards of the population in the Hindu Kush-Himalayan region; serves as a focal point for multi-disciplinary documentation training and applied research, and as a consultative centre; participating countries: Afghanistan, Bangladesh, Bhutan, China, India, Myanmar, Nepal, Pakistan; Dir-Gen. EGBERT PELINCK.

Libraries and Archives

Kathmandu

Bir Library: Ranipokhari, Kathmandu; f. 14th century; *c.* 15,000 MSS.

National Archives: Ramshah Path, Kathmandu; tel. 251315; f. 1967; 35,000 MSS, 60,000 microfilm copies of MSS in private collections, 16,000 historical documents, 10,000 vols; facilities for researchers; Archivist SANI MAIYA; publ. *Abhilekh*.

Nepal-India Cultural Centre and Library: RNAC Bldg, Tundikhel, Kathmandu; f. 1952; 43,000 vols; Librarian GURMAIL SINGH.

Singh Darbar: Secretariat Library, Kathmandu.

Tribhuvan University Central Library: Kirtipur, Kathmandu 2; tel. (1) 212834; fax (1) 226964; f. 1959; 200,000 vols; depository for UN; Librarian KRISHNA MANI BHANDARY (acting); publs *Journal of Tribhuvan University*, *Education Quarterly*, *Nepalese National Bibliography*, *Bulletin* (quarterly), journals, etc.

Lalitpur

Madan Puraskar Pustakalaya: Lalitpur; tel. 521014; fax 521013; f. 1941; books, periodicals and posters in Nepali language; 15,000 vols, 3,200 periodical titles; Librarian KAMAL MANI DIXIT.

National Library: Pulchowk, Lalitpur; tel. 521132; f. 1956; 70,000 vols; Librarian SHUSILA DWIVEDI.

Museums and Art Galleries

Kathmandu

National Museum of Nepal: Museum Rd, Chhauni, Kathmandu; tel. 211504; f. 1928; art, history, culture, ethnology, philately, natural history; reference library of 10,000 vols; art gallery; illustrates the art history of Nepal; Chief SANU NANI KANSAKAR; publ. *Nepal Museum*.

Universities

MAHENDRA SANSKRIT UNIVERSITY

POB 5003, Kathmandu

Telephone: 213245 (Kathmandu), 20019 (Beljhundi, Dang)

Founded 1986

State control

Languages of instruction: Sanskrit, Nepali and English

Chancellor: HM King BIRENDRA BIR BIKRAM SHAH DEV

Vice-Chancellor: Prof. SHREE KRISHNA ACHARYA

Rector: Dr TIKARAM PANTHI

Registrar: MADHAV RAJ GAUTAM

Librarian: KHEM RAJ GYNAWALI

Number of teachers: 189

Number of students: 1,304

There are 8 campuses under the University.

TRIBHUVAN UNIVERSITY

POB 8212, Kirtipur, Kathmandu

Telephone: 330433

Fax: (1) 331964

E-mail: v.c.-office@npl.healthnet.org

Founded 1959

Autonomous control

Languages of instruction: Nepali and English

There are 61 campuses under the University, and about 140 private campuses throughout the country affiliated to Tribhuvan University.

Chancellor: HM King BIRENDRA BIR BIKRAM SHAH DEV

Vice-Chancellor: Dr KAMAL KRISHNA JOSHI

Rector: Dr MADHAB PRASAD SHARMA

Registrar: BAL MUKUNDA KHAREL

Library: see Libraries

Number of teachers: 5,580

Number of students: 99,259

Publications: *TU Bulletin* (fortnightly), *TU Journal* (2 a year), *Contribution to Nepalese Studies* (CNAS, 4 a year), *Journal of Development and Administrative Studies* (CEDA, 1 a year); journals of the various institutes.

DEANS

Institute of Science and Technology: Dr KRISHNA MANUNDHAR

Institute of Medicine: Dr HARI GOVINDA SHRESTHA

Institute of Agriculture and Animal Science: Dr DURGA DUTTA DHAKAL

Institute of Forestry: ABHAYA KUMAR DAS

Institute of Engineering: Dr RAJENDRA DHOJ JOSHI

Faculty of Management: Dr KUNDAN DUTTA KOIRALE

Faculty of Education: Dr PRITHU CHARAN BAIDYA

Faculty of Humanities and Social Science: Dr TRI RATNA MANANDHAR

Faculty of Law: KANEK HIKRAM THAPA

ATTACHED RESEARCH INSTITUTES

Research Centre for Applied Science and Technology: Exec. Dir Dr TULSI PATHAK

Research Centre for Economic Development and Administration: Exec. Dir Dr PITAMBER RAWAL

Research Centre for Nepal and Asian Studies: Exec. Dir Dr PREM KUMAR KHATRI

Research Centre for Educational Innovation and Development: Exec. Dir Dr HRIDYA RATNA BAJRACHARYA

NETHERLANDS

Learned Societies

GENERAL

Hollandsche Maatschapij der Wetenschappen (Dutch Society of Sciences): Spaarne 17, POB 9698, 2003 LR Haarlem; f. 1752; furthering contact between scientists and laymen by arranging lectures on scientific subjects and awarding annual prizes and subsidies for research and publication of scientific work; 550 mems; Pres. M. C. VAN VEEN; Secs Prof. Dr A. A. VERRIJN STUART (Natural Sciences), Prof. Dr D. M. SCHENKEVELD (Humanities and Social Sciences).

Koninklijke Nederlandse Akademie van Wetenschappen (Royal Netherlands Academy of Arts and Sciences): Kloveniersburgwal 29, POB 19121, 1000 GC Amsterdam (Trippenhuis); tel. (20) 5510700; fax (20) 6204941; e-mail knaw@bureau.knaw.nl; f. 1808; sections of Mathematics and Natural Sciences (Pres. Prof. Dr R. S. RENEMAN, Sec. Prof. Dr K. VRIEZE), Philology, Literature, History and Philosophy (Pres. Prof. Dr W. P. GERRITSEN, Sec. Prof. Dr M. E. H. N. MOUT); 200 mems, 40 corresp. mems, 60 foreign mems; Pres. Prof. Dr Ir P. J. ZANBERGEN; Sec.-Gen. Prof. A. S. HARTKAMP; Dir-Gen. Drs C. H. MOEN; publs *Jaarboek*, *Akademienieuws*, *Proceedings of the Section of Sciences*, *Indagationes Mathematicae*, *Verslag van de Gewone Vergaderingen der Afdeling Natuurkunde*, *Verhandelingen Eerste en Tweede Reeks der Afdeling Natuurkunde*, *Mededelingen der Afdeling Letterkunde*, *Verhandelingen der Afdeling Letterkunde*.

Suid-Afrikaanse Instituut: Keizersgracht 141, 1015 CK Amsterdam; tel. (20) 624-9318; fax (20) 638-2596; f. 1939; study of Afrikaans language and literature, history and culture of South Africa; library of 30,000 vols.

AGRICULTURE, FISHERIES AND VETERINARY SCIENCE

Koninklijke Landbouwkundige Vereniging (Royal Society for Agricultural Science): POB 79, 6700 AB Wageningen; tel. (317) 484013; fax (317) 483976; f. 1886; agricultural and environmental research; 9,000 mems; Pres. W. M. GELUK; Sec. Ir L. KUPER-HENDRIKS; Dir Ir. H. J. VAN 'T KLOOSTER; Admin. S. VAN PROOIJEN; publs *LT Journal* (17 a year), *Netherlands Journal of Agricultural Science* (English, quarterly).

Koninklijke Maatschappij Tuinbouw en Plantkunde (Royal Dutch Horticultural Society): POB 87910, 2508 DH The Hague; tel. (70) 3514551; f. 1872; 60,000 mems; Pres. T. J. KOEK; publ. *Groei & Bloei* (monthly).

Koninklijke Nederlandse Bosbouw Vereniging (Royal Netherlands Forestry Society): Utrechtseweg 68, POB 139, 6800 AC Arnhem; f. 1910; 620 mems; Chair. Ir. W. H. J. DE BEAUFORT; Sec. Ir T. WINKELMAN; publ. *Nederlands Bosbouw Tijdschrift* (every 2 months).

Nederlandse Tuinbouwraad (Netherlands Horticultural Council): Schiefbaanstraat 29, 2596 RC The Hague; tel. (70) 3450 600; fax (70) 3453902; f. 1908; represents the common technical and economic interests of the mem. organizations; mems: 10 national organizations of co-operatives and producers of edible and non-edible horticultural products; Sec. Ir. J. M. GERRITSEN.

ARCHITECTURE AND TOWN PLANNING

Bond Heemschut (Assen for the safeguarding of the architectural heritage of the Netherlands): 'Korenmetershuis', NZ Kolk 28, 1012 PV Amsterdam; tel. (20) 6225292; fax (20) 6240571; f. 1911; mems: *c.* 10,000 societies and individuals; Chair. Ir E. H. Baron VAN TUYLL VAN SEROOSKERKEN; 11 Provincial subcttees; publ. *Heemschut* (illustrated magazine, 6 a year).

College van Toezicht (Architects' Supervisory Commission): Keizersgracht 321, 1016 EE, POB 19611, 1000 GP Amsterdam; f. 1988 to supervise Code of Conduct; 9 mems; Chair. H. B. A. VERHAGEN; Secs A. M. GUNCKEL, J. J. ROOS.

Genootschap Architectura et Amicitia (A. et A.): Waterlooplein 211, 1011 PG Amsterdam; tel. (20) 6220188; f. 1855; 225 mems; Chair. R. JANSMA; Sec. F. BROEHSMA; publ. *FORUM* (quarterly).

Koninklijke Maatschappij tot Bevordering der Bouwkunst Bond van Nederlandse Architekten (BNA) (Royal Institute of Dutch Architects): POB 19606, 1000 GP Amsterdam; premises at: Keizersgracht 321, 1016 EE Amsterdam; tel. (20) 5553666; fax (20) 5553699; f. 1842; 2,750 mems; publ. *BladNA* (monthly).

Netherlands Architecture Institute: Museum Park 25, 3015 CB Rotterdam; tel. (10) 4401200; fax (10) 4366975; e-mail info@nai.nl; f. 1988; museum, archives, collections; library of 40,000 vols; Dir K. FEIREISS; publ. *Archis* (monthly).

Raad voor Cultuur (Council for Culture): POB 61243, 2506 AE Den Haag; tel. (70) 3106686; fax (70) 3614727; f. 1995; 25 mems; Pres. J. JESSURUN; Sec. Drs A. NICOLAI; publs Annual Report, *Newsletter*.

Rijksdienst voor de Monumentenzorg (Department for Conservation): POB 1001, 3700 BA Zeist; premises at: Broederplein 41, 3703 CD Zeist; tel. (30) 6983211; fax (30) 6916189; f. 1918; re-formed 1947; library of 50,000 vols, 500 periodicals; publs *Annual Report*, *Newsletter*.

BIBLIOGRAPHY, LIBRARY SCIENCE AND MUSEOLOGY

Federatie van Organisaties van Bibliotheek-, Informatie-, Dokumentatiewezen (FOBID) (Federation of Library Information and Documentation Organizations): POB 43300, 2504 AH Den Haag; tel. (70) 3090107; fax (70) 3090200; e-mail fobid@nblc.nl; f. 1975; promotion of co-operation and integration among public, research and special libraries in the Netherlands; mems: Nederlandse Vereniging van Bibliothekarissen and Nederlands Bibliotheek en Lektuur Centrum; Chair. Drs R. VAN DER VELDE; Sec. G. KOERS.

Nederlandse Museumvereniging (Netherlands Museums Association): POB 74683, 1070 BR Amsterdam; premises at: Prins Hendriklaan 12–14, 1075 BB Amsterdam; tel. (20) 6701100; fax (20) 6701101; e-mail info@museumvereniging.nl; f. 1926; 380 museum mems; Chair. Drs R. H. C. VOS; Dir Drs A. VELS HEIJN; publs *Museumvisie* (quarterly), *Museumberichten* (monthly).

Nederlandse Vereniging van Bibliothecarissen, Documentalisten en Literatuur Onderzoekers (Netherlands Society of Librarians, Documentalists and Literary Researchers): NVB-Verenigingsbureau Plompetorengracht 11, 3512 CA Utrecht; tel. (30) 2311263; fax (30) 2311830; e-mail nubinfo@wxs.nl; f. 1912; 3,000 mems; maintenance of lawful regulation of library system, arrangement of meetings and international co-operation, professional education; Pres. Drs H. C. KOOYMAN-TIBBLES; Sec. R. TICHELAAR; publs *NVB—Nieuwsbrief*, *Informatie Professional*.

Vereniging NBLC (Dutch Centre for Public Libraries and Literature): POB 43300, 2504 AH The Hague, Platinaweg 10, 2544 EZ; tel. (70) 3090100; fax (70) 3090200; f. 1972; Sec.-Gen. L. POPMA; publ. *BibliotheekBlad*.

ECONOMICS, LAW AND POLITICS

Internationaal Juridisch Instituut (International Juridical Institute): Spui 186, 2511 BW The Hague; tel. (70) 3460974; fax (70) 3625235; e-mail iji@worldonline.nl; f. 1918; supplies legal opinions regarding private international law and foreign—also mostly private–law to the Netherlands judiciary, the Netherlands bar and to other mems of the legal profession, such as civil law notaries; also gives information to judges and lawyers outside the Netherlands; Pres. A. V. M. STRUYCKEN; Sec. F. J. A. VAN DER VELDEN; Dir A. L. G. A. STILLE.

Nederlandse Vereniging voor Internationaal Recht (Netherlands Branch of International Law Asscn): Hugo de Grootstraat 27 (Kamer 058), 2711 XK Leiden; tel. (71) 5277748; fax (71) 5277748; f. 1910; 560 mems; Pres. M. V. POLAK; Hon. Sec. E. N. FROHN; publ. *Mededelingen* (2 a year).

Vereniging voor Agrarisch Recht (Agrarian Law Society): 'de Leeuwenborch' Hollandseweg 1, 6706 KN Wageningen; tel. (317) 484486; Sec. H. C. A. WALDA.

Vereniging voor Arbeidsrecht (Labour Law Society): POB 132, 3440 AC Woerden; tel. (6) 51108682; fax (348) 434701; f. 1946; 940 mems; Sec. G. J. J. RENSINK; publs monographs.

Vereniging voor de Staathuishoudkunde (Royal Netherlands Economic Association): c/o De Nederlandsche Bank NV, POB 98, 1000 AB Amsterdam; tel. (20) 5242280; fax (20) 5242524; f. 1862; 3,200 mems; Chair. Prof. Dr F. A. G. DEN BUTTER; Sec. Drs J. KONING; publs *De Economist* (quarterly), *Proceedings of the Annual Meeting*.

Volkenrechtelijk Instituut (Institute of Public International Law): Utrecht University, Achter Sint Pieter 200, 3512 HT Utrecht; tel. (30) 2537060; fax (30) 2537073; f. 1955; library of 21,000 vols; publ. *Nova et Vetera Iuris Gentium*.

EDUCATION

Nederlandse organisatie voor internationale samenwerking in het hoger onderwijs (Netherlands Organization for International Co-operation in Higher Education—Nuffic): Kortenaerkade, POB 29777, 2502 LT The Hague; tel. (70) 4260260; telex 33565; fax (70) 4260399; e-mail nuffic@nufficcs.nl; f. 1952 by the Netherlands universities to promote international co-operation in the academic and scientific fields; provides information on postgraduate international courses; advises various educational and government bodies on matters of academic equivalence and the recognition of professional credentials; promotes international co-operation in several European and national exchange programmes; offers educational and scientific help to developing countries; Dir Drs P. J. C. VAN DIJK; publ. *International Courses in the Netherlands* (annually).

Nederlandse Vereniging van Pedagogen en Onderwijskundigen (Dutch Society of Educational Psychologists): Korte Elisabethstraat 11, 3511 JG Utrecht; tel. (30) 2322407; f. 1962; maintenance of standards in university education; 2,800 mems; publs *Nederlands Tijdschrift voor Opvoeding, Vorming en Onderwijs* (every 2 months).

Rectoren College (Netherlands Rectors' Conference): POB 19270, 3501 DG Utrecht; tel. (31) (30) 334441; fax (31) (30) 333540; Chair. Prof. Dr TH. J. M. VAN ELS; Sec. H. J. GRAAFLAND.

Vereniging van Samenwerkende Nederlandse Universiteiten (Asscn of Universities in the Netherlands): POB 19270, 3501 DG Utrecht; tel. (30) 2363888; fax (30) 2333540; e-mail post@vsnu.nl; f. 1985; Chair. Prof. Dr M. H. MEIJERINK; Dir Dr G. J. M. VAN DEN MAAGDENBERG.

FINE AND PERFORMING ARTS

Koninklijke Nederlandse Toonkunstenaars-vereniging (Royal Netherlands Asscn of Musicians): Keizersgracht 480, 1017 EG Amsterdam; tel. (20) 6238202; fax (20) 6200229; f. 1875; 3,400 mems; Chair. H. VAN DER HEIJDEN; Sec. DICK VISSER; publ. *KNTV-Magazine* (6 a year).

Maatschappij 'Arti et Amicitiae': Rokin 112, Amsterdam; tel. (20) 6233508; f. 1839; a national society of painters, sculptors and graphic artists; 440 artist mems, 1,000 mems; gallery for members' works; Pres. HENK RIJZINGA; Sec.-Gen. MARC VOLGER.

Maatschappij tot Bevordering der Toonkunst: (Society for Advancement of Music): 1e Jac. Van Campenstraat 59, 1072 BD Amsterdam; tel. (20) 6713091; f. 1829; 6,500 mems; library of 18,000 vols; Chair. Ms F. M. BOT-TIDDENS; publ. *Toonkunst-Nieuws*.

Nederlandse Toonkunstenaarsraad (Council of Organizations of Musicians in the Netherlands): Valeriusplein 20, Amsterdam; f. 1948 to protect professional interests; 3,000 mems; Chair. Dr N. J. C. M. KAPPEYNE VAN DE COPPELLO; Man. Dir Ir. R. C. BROEK; publ. *A Musical Guide for Holland* (every 2 years).

Rijksbureau voor Kunsthistorische Documentatie (Netherlands Institute for Art History): POB 90418, 2509 LK The Hague; premises at 5 Prins Willem Alexanderhof, 2595 BE The Hague; tel. (70) 3339777; fax (70) 3339789; e-mail bib@rkd.nl; f. 1932; library of 415,000 vols, periodicals and catalogues; press-cuttings, archives, 3,500,000 photos and reproductions; Dir RUDOLF E. O. EKKART; publ. *Oud-Holland* (quarterly).

Stichting Nederlands Filminstituut (Netherlands Film Institute): POB 515, Hilversum, Steynlaan 8; f. 1948; film and TV academy; lecture and information service, and a film and group media distribution service; Man. Dir Dr J. A. HES.

Theater Instituut Nederland (Netherlands Theatre Institute): Herengracht 168, 1016 BP Amsterdam; tel. (20) 5513300; fax (20) 5513303; e-mail info@tin.nl; f. 1993; service organization and research institute for the professional theatre; theatre museum; library of 50,000 vols and sound archives and videotapes of the Dutch theatre; Netherlands centre of the International Theatre Institute; Dir D. KLAIĆ; publ. *Carnet* (in French and Dutch).

Vereniging 'Sint Lucas' (St Luke Asscn): Zomerdijk-straat 20, Amsterdam; f. 1880; Chair. BART PEIZEL; Sec. THEO SWAGEMAKERS.

Wagnervereeniging (Wagner Society): Gabriël Metsustr. 32, Amsterdam; f. 1883; Chair. Mr W. TH. DOYER; Sec. EVERT CORNELIS.

HISTORY, GEOGRAPHY AND ARCHAEOLOGY

Centraal Bureau voor Genealogie (Central Bureau of Genealogy): Prins Willem Alexanderhof 22, POB 11755, 2502 AT The Hague; tel. (70) 3150500; fax (70) 3478394; f. 1945; large genealogical and heraldic collections; 12,800 mems; library of *c.* 100,000 vols; Dir Dr A. J. LEVER; publs *Genealogie, Kwartaalblad van het Centraal Bureau voor Genealogie* (quarterly), *Jaarboek Centraal Bureau voor Genealogie* (annually).

Fries Genootschap van Geschied-, Oudheid- en Taalkunde (Society of Frisian Archaeology, History and Philology): Turfmarkt 11, 8911 KT Leeuwarden; f. 1827; 1,700 mems; Pres. B. VAN HAERSMA BUMA; Sec. Drs O. D. J. ROEMELING; publs *De Vrije Fries* (annually), *Fryslân* (quarterly).

Internationaal Instituut voor Sociale Geschiedenis (International Institute of Social History): Cruquiusweg 31, 1019 AT Amsterdam; tel. (31-20) 6685866; fax (31-20) 6654181; e-mail inf.gen@iisg.nl; f. 1935; library of 500,000 vols, archives, especially on the labour movement, 60,000 periodicals; Dir J. KLOOSTERMAN; publs *Annual Report, International Review of Social History* (3 a year plus supplement).

Koninklijk Nederlands Aardrijkskundig Genootschap (Royal Dutch Geographical Society): POB 80123, 3508 TC Utrecht; tel. (30) 2534056; fax (30) 2535523; f. 1873; 4,000 mems; Sec. A. HARKINK; publs *Geografie* (6 a year), *Geografie-Educatief* (quarterly), *Journal of Economic and Social Geography* (5 a year), *KNAG-Nieuws* (10 a year), *Netherlands Geographical Studies* (irregular).

Koninklijk Nederlands Historisch Genootschap (Royal Historical Asscn): POB 90406, 2509 LK The Hague; e-mail info@knhg.nl; f. 1845; 1,800 mems; Pres. Prof. Dr J. C. H. BLOM; Dir Drs G. N. VAN DER PLAAT; publs *Bijdragen en Mededelingen betreffende de Geschiedenis der Nederlanden, HG-Nieuws, Nederlandse Historische Bronnen, Kroniek, Bibliografische Reeks*.

Koninklijk Oudheidkundig Genootschap (Royal Antiquarian Society): Rijksmuseum, Amsterdam; f. 1858; possesses a collection of applied art (furniture, silver, sculpture, etc.), paintings, objects of historical value, prints and drawings concerning the topography of Amsterdam, manners and customs of the Netherlands; coins, medals, books; *c.* 500 mems; library of 6,100 vols; Pres. Prof. Dr J. E. G. C. DIBBITS; Sec. Mrs Drs E. CALJÉ VAN DEN BERG; publ. *Jaarverslagen* (illustrated annual reports).

Vereniging Gelre: Markt 1, 6811 CG Arnhem; f. 1897; historical society of the province of Gelderland; publs *Bijdragen en Mededelingen, Werken*.

Vereniging 'Het Nederlandsch Economisch-Historisch Archief' (The Netherlands Economic-Historical Archives Society): Cruquiusweg 31, 1019 AT Amsterdam; tel. (20) 6685866; fax (20) 6654181; e-mail neha@iisg.nl; f. 1914; specializes in economic history and business studies; library of 70,000 vols on economic history; Librarian H. J. M. WINKELMAN; Dir J. KLOOSTERMAN; publs *NEHA-Jaarboek* (annually), *NEHA series* (irregular), *NEHA Bulletin* (2 a year).

LANGUAGE AND LITERATURE

Maatschappij der Nederlandse Letterkunde (Society of Netherlands Literature): POB 9501, Witte Singel 27, 2300 RA Leiden; tel. (71) 5144962; fax (71) 5272836; f. 1766; 1,300 mems; Chair. Dr E. K. GROOTES; Sec. Dr L. L. VAN MARIS; publs *Tijdschrift voor Nederlandse Taal- en Letterkunde, Jaarboek der Maatschappij* (annually).

Nederlandsche Vereeniging voor Drukken Boekkunst (Netherlands Society for the Art of Printing and Book-production): J. van Banning str. 2C, 2381 AV Zoeterwoude; f. 1938; 300 mems; Chair. Drs G. J. KEYSER; Sec. Drs K. THOMASSEN; publs *Mededelingen* (irregular), books.

Netherlands Centre of the International PEN: Rogneurdonk 17, 1218 HG Maastricht; f. 1923; 350 mems; Pres. HANS VAN DE WAARENBURG; Sec. MARIA VAN DAALEN; publ. *PEN Nieuwsbrief* (2 a year).

MEDICINE

Genootschap ter bevordering van Natuur-, Genees- en Heelkunde (Asscn for Advancement of Natural, Medical and Surgical Sciences): Plantage Muidergracht 12, Amsterdam; tel. (20) 525-5125; fax (20) 5255124; e-mail secr.ecsi@chem.uva.nl; f. 1790; Pres. Dr G. N. BOUMAN; Sec. Dr F. M. M. GRIFFOEN.

Koninklijke Nederlandsche Maatschappij tot bevordering der Geneeskunst (Royal Dutch Medical Association): Lomanlaan 103, 3526 XD Utrecht; tel. (30) 823911; fax (30) 823326; f. 1849; library on history of medicine in the Netherlands; 24,000 mems; Sec.-Gen. TH. VAN BERKESTIJN; publ. *Medisch Contact* (weekly).

Koninklijke Nederlandse Maatschappij ter Bevordering der Pharmacie (Royal Dutch Asscn for Advancement of Pharmacy): Alexanderstraat 11, 2514 JL The Hague; tel. (70) 3624111; fax (70) 3106530; f. 1842; *c.* 3,500 mems; Pres. Drs M. A. HAGENZIEKER; Sec. Drs L. H. A. J. ARTS; publ. *Pharmaceutisch Weekblad*.

Nederlandse Vereniging van Specialisten in de Dento-Maxillaire Orthopaedie: Weezenhof 14–16, Nijmegen; f. 1963; Pres. Prof. Dr H. S. DUTERLOO; Sec. Dr TH. P. M. VAN BLADEREN.

Nederlandse Vereniging voor Heelkunde (Asscn of Surgeons of the Netherlands): POB 20061, Lomanlaan 103, 3502 LB Utrecht; tel. (30) 2823327; fax (30) 2823329; f. 1902; 1,400 mems; Hon. Sec. Dr A. B. BIJNEN; publ. *The European Journal of Surgery* (monthly, in English).

Nederlandse Vereniging voor Microbiologie (Netherlands Society for Microbiology): C/o National Institute for Public Health and the Environment (RIVM), POB 1, 3720 BA Bilthoven; tel. (30) 2742040; fax (30) 2744413; e-mail michiel.rutger@rivm.nl; f. 1911; microbiology, bacteriology, virology; 1,300 mems; Pres. Prof. J. E. DEGENER; Sec. Dr M. RUTGERS; publ. *Bionieuws*.

Nederlandse Vereniging voor Neurologie: POB 20050, 3502 LB Utrecht; f. 1871, reorganized 1974; 800 mems; Pres. Prof. Dr M. DE VISSER; Sec. Prof. Dr C. H. POLMAN; publ. *Clinical Neurology and Neurosurgery*.

Nederlandse Vereniging voor Orthodontische Studie (Netherlands Orthodontics Society): Schelluinsevliet 5, 4203 NB Gorinchem; tel. (183) 635476; f. 1946; 700 mems; Sec. J. W. BOOIJ.

Nederlandse Vereniging voor Psychiatrie (Netherlands Assn for Psychiatry): POB 20062, 3502 LB, Utrecht; tel. (30) 2823303; fax (30) 2888400; f. 1871, reorganized 1973; 2,053 mems; Pres. Prof. Dr W. VAN TILBURG; Sec. D. E. R. VANDENBERGHE; publ. *Tijdschrift voor Psychiatrie*.

Nederlandse Vereniging voor Tropische Geneeskunde (Netherlands Society of Tropical Medicine): POB 244, 3970 AE Driebergen-Rijsenburg; tel. (343) 517126; fax (343) 517126; e-mail nadamo@wxs.nl; f. 1907; 950 mems; Chair. H. T. J. CHABOT; Sec. S. M. RYPKEMA.

Vereniging voor Volksgezondheid en Wetenschap (Netherlands Society of Public Health and Science): Admiraal Helfrichlaan 1, 3527 KV Utrecht; tel. (70) 3030045; fax (30) 2913242; e-mail euphavw@knoware.nl; f. 1985 (formerly Algemene Nederlandse Vereniging voor Sociale Gezondheidszorg); scientific approach to health and health care questions; 1,000 mems; Pres. Prof. Dr D. POST; Sec. Dr KARIEN STRONKS; publs *Tijdschrift voor Gezondheidswetenschappen*, *European Journal of Public Health*.

NATURAL SCIENCES

General

Koninklijke Nederlandse Natuurhistorische Vereniging (Royal Dutch Society for Natural History): Oudegracht 237, 3511 NK Utrecht; tel. (30) 2314797; fax (30) 2368907; f. 1901; 10,000 mems; Chair. Drs Ing. V. P. A. LUKKIEN; publ. *Natura* (6 a year).

Stichting Natuur en Milieu (Society for Nature and Environment): Donkerstraat 17, 3511 KB Utrecht; tel. (30) 2331328; fax (30) 2331311; f. 1972; nature conservation and environmental protection; Dir A. J. M. VAN DEN BIGGELAAR; publ. *Natuur en milieu* (monthly).

Thijmgenootschap (Society of Christian Scholars in the Netherlands): Huygensweg 14, 6522 HL Nijmegen; tel. (24) 3232122; f. 1904; 1,500 mems; Pres. Prof. Dr H. VAN DER PLAS; Sec. Dr G. A. M. BEEKELAAR; publ. *Annalen van het Thijmgenootschap* (quarterly).

Vereniging tot Behoud van Natuurmonumenten in Nederland (Society for the Preservation of Nature Reserves in the Netherlands): Noordereinde 60, 1243 JJ 's-Graveland; tel. (35) 6559933; fax (35) 6563174; f. 1905; 860,000 mems; the society controls 300 nature reserves; Pres. Dr P. WINSEMIUS; Dirs. C. N. DE BOER, F. W. R. EVERS; Ir. A. W. J. BOSMAN; publ. *Natuurbehoud* (quarterly).

Biological Sciences

Koninklijke Nederlandse Botanische Vereniging (Royal Dutch Botanical Society): c/o Dr A. M. Wagner, Biologisch Laboratorium, Vrije Universiteit, De Boelelaan 1087, 1081 HV Amsterdam; tel. (20) 5485538; f. 1845; 635 mems; Pres. Prof. Dr H. VAN DEN ENDE; 1st Sec. Dr A. M. WAGNER; publ. *Acta Botanica Neerlandica*.

Nederlandse Dierkundige Vereniging (Netherlands Zoological Society): Dept of Aquatic Ecology, University of Amsterdam, Kruislaan 320, 1098 SM Amsterdam; f. 1872; 610 mems; Pres. Prof. Dr J. W. M. OSSE; Sec. Dr P. J. ROOS; publ. *Netherlands Journal of Zoology*.

Nederlandse Entomologische Vereniging (Netherlands Entomological Society): Plantage Middenlaan 64, 1018 DH Amsterdam; tel. (20) 5256246; fax (20) 5256528; e-mail biblionev@bio.uva.nl; f. 1845; library of 80,000 vols; *c.* 650 mems; Pres. Drs J. VAN TOL; Sec. Drs P. KOOMEN; publs *Tijdschrift voor Entomologie*, *Entomologische Berichten*, *Proceedings sect. Experimental and Applied Entomology of the Netherlands Entomological Society*.

Nederlandse Mycologische Vereniging (Netherlands Mycological Society): Centraalbureau voor Schimmelcultures, POB 273, 3740 AG Baarn; tel. (35) 5481211; f. 1908; 600 mems; study of fungi; Pres. Dr TH. W. KUYPER; Sec.-Gen. Dr G. J. M. VERKLEY; publ. *Coolia* (quarterly).

Nederlandse Ornithologische Unie (Netherlands Ornithological Union): Couwenhoven 56-12, 3703 EW Amsterdam; f. 1901; study of ornithology; 1,067 mems; library of *c.* 120 periodicals; Pres. Dr R. H. DRENT; publs *Ardea* (2 a year), *Limosa* (quarterly).

Nederlandse Vereniging voor Parasitologie (Netherlands Society for Parasitology): Erasmus University Medical Centre, Department of Medical Microbiology and Infectious Diseases, Dijkzigt L327, Dr Molewaterplein 40, 3015 GD Rotterdam; f. 1961; 169 mems; Pres. Prof. Dr A. W. C. A. CORNELISSEN; Sec. Dr J. F. SLUITERS.

Nederlandse Zoötechnische Vereniging (Netherlands Association for Animal Production): Gaastmeerstraat 8, 8226 HV Lelystad; f. 1930; 850 mems; Pres. Prof. Dr Ir E. W. BRASCAMP; Sec. Dr G. C. M. BAKKER.

Stichting Koninklijk Zoölogisch Genootschap 'Natura Artis Magistra' (Royal Zoological Society): Plantage Kerklaan 40, 1018 CZ Amsterdam; tel. (20) 5233400; fax (20) 5233419; f. 1838; Dirs Dr M. T. FRANKENHUIS, Drs R. P. VAN DER POL; publs *Bijdragen tot de Dierkunde* (quarterly), *Artis* (every 2 months).

Mathematical Sciences

Vereniging voor Statistiek en Operations Research (Netherlands Society for Statistics and Operations Research): POB 2095, 2990 DB Barendrecht; tel. (180) 623796; fax (180) 623670; e-mail hwander@wxs.nl; f. 1945; 1,250 mems; Pres. Prof. Dr G. T. TIMMER; Sec. Dr A. J. KONING; publs *Statistica Neerlandica* (quarterly), *VVS-Bulletin* (10 a year), *Kwantitatieve Methoden* (3 a year).

Wiskundig Genootschap (Mathematical Society): Technical University Delft, POB 5031, 2600 GA Delft; tel. (15) 2787286; fax (15) 2787255; f. 1778; *c.* 1,270 mems; library of *c.* 16,400 vols and journals of mathematics and its applications; Pres. Prof. Dr M. HAZEWINKEL; Sec. Dr J. A. M. VAN DER WEIDE; publ. *Nieuw Archief voor Wiskunde* (3 a year).

Physical Sciences

Koninklijk Nederlands Geologisch Mijnbouwkundig Genootschap (Royal Geological and Mining Society of the Netherlands): POB 157, 2000 AD Haarlem; f. 1912; 1,500 mems; Pres. Dr E. C. KOSTERS; Sec. Ir J. A. BOSWINKEL; publs *Geologie en Mijnbouw* (quarterly), *Nieuwsbrief* (10 a year).

Koninklijk Nederlands Meteorologisch Instituut (Royal Netherlands Meteorological Institute): Wilhelminalaan 10, POB 201, 3730 AE De Bilt; tel. (30) 2206911; telex 47096; fax (30) 2210407; e-mail biblioth@knmi.nl; f. 1854; meteorology, climatology, oceanography, seismology; library of 140,000 vols; spec. collns incl. Polar expeditions; Dir-in-Chief Dr H. M. FIJNAUT; publs *Maandover zicht van het weer*, *North Sea* (monthly), *Seismological Bulletin*, scientific reports and technical reports, daily weather maps, rain observations.

Koninklijke Nederlandse Chemische Vereniging (Royal Netherlands Chemical Society): Burnierstraat 1, 2596 HV The Hague; tel. (70) 3469406; f. 1903; 15,000 mems; Sec. Ir. E. J. DE RYCK VAN DER GRACHT; publs *Chemisch Weekblad* (weekly), *European Journal of Inorganic Chemistry* (monthly), *European Journal of Organic Chemistry* (monthly), *Chemisch Jaarboek* (1 a year).

Nederlandse Natuurkundige Vereniging (Netherlands Physical Society): POB 302, 1170 AL Badhoevedorp; tel. (020) 658-0228; fax (20) 659-2477; f. 1921 to improve the study of physics in every way and safeguard the interests of physicists; 3,800 mems; Chair. Prof. Dr A. W. KLEYN; Sec. Dr E. W. A. LINGEMAN; publ. *Nederlands Tijdschrift voor Natuurkunde*.

Nederlandse Vereniging voor Weer- en Sterrenkunde (Netherlands Society for Meteorology and Astronomy): Stichting De Koepel, Sterrenwacht 'Sonnenborgh', Zonnenburg 2, 3512 NL Utrecht; tel. (30) 2311360; fax (30) 2342852; e-mail dekoepel@knoware.nl; f. 1901; 6,000 mems; publs *Zenit* (monthly), *De Sterrengids* (annually).

PHILOSOPHY AND PSYCHOLOGY

Algemene Nederlandse Vereniging voor Wijsbegeerte (General Netherlands Philosophical Society): C/o Faculteit Wijsbegeerte, K.U.B., POB 90153, 5000 LE Tilburg; f. 1933; 150 mems; Pres. Drs MARGA JAGER; Sec. R. GUDE; publ. *Algemeen Tijdschrift voor Wijsbegeerte*.

Affiliated societies:

Vereniging 'Het Spinozahuis': Paganinidreef 66, 2253 SK Voorschoten; Sec. TH. VAN DER WERF.

Vereniging voor Wijsbegeerte te 's-Gravenhage: Spreeuwenlaan 10, 2566 ZN 's-Gravenhage; Sec. M. ZUIDGEEST.

Internationale School voor Wijsbegeerte: (International School of Philosophy): Dodeweg 8, 3832 RD Leusden; tel. (33) 4650700; fax (33) 4650541; e-mail isvw@wxs.nl; f. 1916; courses and conferences in philosophy; 1,800 mems; library of 3,000 vols; Man. Dir PAUL WOUTERS; Pres. Prof. FRANS JACOBS; publ. *Filosofie Magazine* (monthly).

Wijsgerige Vereniging Thomas van Aquino: POB 37, 5260 AA Vught; tel. (73) 6579017; f. 1933; philosophical conferences; 160 mems; Pres. Prof. Dr H. H. BERGER; Sec. Prof. Dr W. DERKSE.

Vereniging voor Reformatische Wijsbegeerte: POB 2156, 3800 CD Amersfoort; tel. (33) 4657078; fax (33) 4657304; e-mail reform.philos@wxs.net; Sec. W. EIKELBOOM.

Nederlandse Vereniging voor Logica en Wijsbegeerte der Exacte Wetenschappen: POB 80103, 3508 TC Utrecht; f. 1947; organizes scientific symposia; 150 mems; Chair. J.-J. CH. MEYER; Sec. J. VAN EIJCK.

Stichting Internationaal Signifisch Genootschap: Beelslaan 20, 2012 PK Haarlem; Sec. P. H. ESSER.

Vereniging voor Filosofie-Onderwijs: D. van Polderveldweg 283, 6523 CW Nijmegen; tel. (80) 237711; f. 1995; 300 mems; Sec. JO MARTENS; publ. *Contactblad V.I.C.*

Nederlandse Vereniging voor Wetenschapsfilosofie (Netherlands Society for Philosophy of Science): Department of History and Foundations of Science, University of Utrecht, PO Box 80000, 3508 TA Utrecht; tel. (30) 2532841; telex 40048; fax (30) 2537468; e-mail h.w.deregt@fys.ruu.nl; f. 1979; organisation of conferences and lectures; 150 mems; Sec. Prof. H. VISSER.

Vereniging voor Filosofie en Geneeskunde: POB 616, 6200 MD Maastricht; tel. (43) 881144; f. 1981; Sec. G. A. M. WIDDERSHOVEN.

Bataafsch Genootschap der Proefondervindelijke Wijsbegeerte (Experimental Natural Philosophy Society): POB 597, 3000 AN Rotterdam; f. 1769; Pres. Prof. Dr A. J. MAN IN'T VELD; Sec. Dr J. R. TER MOLEN.

Nederlands Psychoanalytisch Genootschap (Netherlands Psychoanalytical Association): Maliestraat 1A, 3581 SH Utrecht; tel. (30) 2307080; fax (30) 2343883; f. 1947; 155 mems; Sec. Dr J. N. SCHREUDER.

RELIGION, SOCIOLOGY AND ANTHROPOLOGY

Fryske Akademy: POB 54, 8900 AB Ljouwert; premises at: Doelestrjitte 8, 8911 DX Ljouwert/Leeuwarden; tel. (58) 2131414; fax (58) 2131409; e-mail fa@fa.knaw.nl; f. 1938; devoted to the scientific study of Friesland, the Frisians and their language, history and culture; 490 mems; 3,000 donors; library of 20,000 vols; Man. Dir M. BOSMA; Scientific Dir Dr L. G. JANSMA; publs *It Beaken* (scientific), *Ut de Smidte fan de Fryske Akademy* (information), *De Vrije Fries* (history).

Koninklijk Instituut voor Taal-, Land- en Volkenkunde (Royal Institute of Linguistics and Anthropology): Reuvensplaats 2, POB 9515, 2300 RA Leiden; tel. (71) 5272295; fax (71) 5272638; e-mail kitlv@rullet.leidenuniv.nl; f. 1851; advances the study of the linguistics, anthropology and history of South-East Asia, the Pacific area and the Caribbean; 2,321 mems; library of 500,000 vols; Pres. Prof. Dr R. SCHEFOLD; Gen. Sec. Prof. Dr P. BOOMGAARD; publs *Bijdragen* (quarterly), *Verhandelingen*, *Nieuwe West-Indische Gids* (quarterly), *Bibliotheca Indonesica*, *European Newsletter of South-East Asian Studies*, *Excerpta Indonesica*.

TECHNOLOGY

Koninklijk Instituut van Ingenieurs (Royal Inst. of Engineers in the Netherlands): POB 30424, 2500 GK The Hague; tel. (70) 3919900; fax (70) 3919840; e-mail kivi@kivi.nl; f. 1847; 21,000 mems; Pres. Ir. B. VAN NEDERVEEN; Sec.-Gen. Ir. J. N. P. HAARSMA; publ. *De Ingenieur* (fortnightly).

Stichting Economisch Instituut voor de Bouwnijverheid (Economic Institute for the Building Industry): De Cuserstraat 89, 1081 CN Amsterdam; tel. (20) 6429342; f. 1956; Dir Prof. Drs A. P. BUUR; publ. *Bouw / Werk* (4 vols a year).

Technologiestichting STW (Technology Foundation): Van Vollenhovenlaan 661, POB 3021, 3502 GA Utrecht; tel. (30) 6001211; fax (30) 6014408; e-mail info@stw.nl; f. 1981; improves and stimulates applied sciences and engineering by sponsoring research at (technical) universities in the Netherlands and promotes co-operation between those institutes and industry; also assists in implementing special governmental research programmes; Dir Dr C. LE PAIR; publ. *Jaarverslag* (annual report).

Research Institutes

AGRICULTURE, FISHERIES AND VETERINARY SCIENCE

ATO-DLO (Agrotechnological Research Institute): POB 17, 6700 AA Wageningen; tel. (8370) 75000; fax (8370) 12260; f. 1989 by merger of Sprenger Inst. and Inst. for Storage and Processing of Agricultural Produce; 320 staff; research on post-harvest physiology and quality parameters, storage and container systems, processing and cell and molecular biology, product development, logistics expert systems and computer image analyses; Dir Dr Ir A. H. EENINK.

Centrum voor Plantenveredelings- en Reproduktieonderzoek (CPRO-DLO) (Centre for Plant Breeding and Reproduction Research): Droevendaalsesteeg 1, POB 16, 6700 AA Wageningen; tel. (317) 477001; fax (317) 418094; e-mail post@cpro.dlo.nl; f. 1991; 270 mems; library of 50,000 vols; Dir Dr N. G. HOGENBOOM; publs *Annual Report*, *Descriptive List of Varieties of Field Crops*, *Descriptive List of Varieties of Vegetable Crops* (annually), *Descriptive List of Fruit Varieties* (every 5 years), *Descriptive List of Ornamental Crops* (every 2 years), *Descriptive List of Trees* (every 5 years).

DLO-Instituut voor Agrobiologisch Onderzoek (Research Institute for Agrobiology and Soil Fertility): Bornsesteeg 65, POB 14, 6700 AA Wageningen; tel. (317) 475750; fax (317) 423110; e-mail j.h.j.spiertz@ab.dlo.nl; f. 1976; research in biochemistry, plant physiology and ecology, theoretical and experimental crop science, weed science, vegetation science and agrosystems research; Dir Dr J. H. J. SPIERTZ.

DLO-Rijksinstituut voor Visserijonderzoek (Netherlands Institute for Fisheries Research): POB 68, 1970 AB IJmuiden; tel. (255) 564646; fax (255) 564644; e-mail postmaster@rivo.dlo.nl; f. 1912; biological, chemical, hydrographical, technical and technological fisheries research; annexe of the Shellfish Department at Yerseke; Dir Dr JAN W. D. M. HENFLING.

DLO Winand Staring Centre for Integrated Land, Soil and Water Research: POB 125, 6700 AC Wageningen; premises at: Staring-building Marijkeweg 11; tel. (317) 474200; fax (317) 424812; f. 1989 as merger of four insts; Dir A. N. VAN DER ZANDE; publs *SC Reports*, *SCAN*.

Instituut voor Bos- en Natuuronderzoek (Institute for Forestry and Nature Research IBN-DLO): POB 23, 6700 AA Wageningen; tel. (317) 477700; fax (317) 424988; f. 1991; applied research into the natural resources of nature, woods and public parklands; Dir Dr A. B. J. SEPERS; numerous publs.

Internationaal Agrarisch Centrum/ International Agricultural Centre: Lawickse Allee 11, Wageningen; POB 88, 6700 AB Wageningen; tel. (317) 490111; telex 45888; fax (317) 418552; f. 1951 by the Ministry of Agriculture, Nature Management and Fisheries; advises Ministers of Agriculture and Fisheries and Development Co-operation on matters concerning Netherlands foreign aid in the field of agriculture in the broadest sense; postgraduate, in-service and mid-career courses mainly for citizens of developing countries; Dir J. J. HOOFT.

International Institute for Land Reclamation and Improvement (ILRI): Lawickse Allee 11, POB 45, 6700 AA Wageningen; tel. (317) 490967; telex 45888; fax (317) 417187; e-mail ilri@ilri.nl; f. 1955; collects and disseminates information on land reclamation and improvement and undertakes supplementary research work; postgraduate courses; 30 staff; Dir Ir M. J. H. P. PINKERS; publs series: *Publications, Bibliographies, Annual Report*.

Koninklijk Instituut voor de Tropen (KIT) (Royal Tropical Institute): Mauritskade 63, 1092 AD Amsterdam; tel. (20) 5688711; fax (20) 6684579; f. 1910; int. research and training org. that focuses on improving communication between the Western and non-Western world; collects and disseminates information on the developing world; 850 mems; library: see Libraries; Tropical Museum: see Museums and Art Galleries; Chair. Ir. J. M. H. VAN ENGELSHOVEN; Pres. N. H. VINK; publs *Survey of activities* (annual report), *KIT Newsletter* (2 a year), *Agriculture and Environment for Developing Regions*.

Landbouw-Economisch Instituut (Agricultural Economics Research Institute): POB 29703, 2502 LS The Hague; premises at: Burgemeester Patijnlaan 19, 2585 BE The Hague; tel. (70) 3308330; fax (70) 3615624; f. 1940 to further the knowledge of business and social economics and related problems concerning Dutch agriculture and fisheries in the widest sense; library of 16,000 vols; Dir Prof. Dr L. C. ZACHARIASSE; publs *Leidraad* (every 2 months), etc.

Nederlands Agronomisch-Historisch Instituut (Institute of Agricultural History): Oude Kijk in 't Jatstraat 26, Groningen; tel. (50) 3635949; f. 1949 to advance the study of and to facilitate scientific research in agricultural history by maintaining an Institute at Groningen University and an international library of 12,000 vols; Dir (vacant); publ. *Historia Agriculturae* (1 or 2 a year).

Plantenziektenkundige Dienst (Plant Protection Service): Geertjesweg 15, POB 9102, 6700 HC Wageningen; tel. (317) 496911; fax (317) 421701; f. 1899; activities include phytosanitary inspection of plants, issue of plant health certificates and design of laws for disease and pest prevention and control, diagnostics of diseases and pests, testing of pesticides; District Offices; Drs Ing. H. A. DURINGHOF; publ. *Verslagen en Mededelingen Plantenziektenkundige Dienst* (Reports and Communications Plant Protection Service).

Praktijkonderzoek Rundvee, Schapen en Paarden (PR) (Research Station for Cattle, Sheep and Horse Husbandry): Runderweg 6, 8219 PK Lelystad; tel. (320) 293211; fax (320) 241584; e-mail info@pr.agro.nl; f. 1970; grassland management, fodder harvesting and conservation, livestock improvement, livestock feeding, calf and foal rearing, milk and beef production, horse performance, animal health, housing systems, farm management, training advisory officers, etc.; 140 mems; library of 20,000 vols; Dir Dr Ir. A. KUIPERS; Deputy Dir Dr Ir. J. A. C. MEIJS; publs *Rapporten* (6 a year), *Publikaties* (10 a year), *Jaarverslag* (annually), *Periodiek* (6 a year).

BIBLIOGRAPHY, LIBRARY SCIENCE AND MUSEOLOGY

NBBI Projectbureau voor Informatiemanagement (NBBI Project Bureau for Information Management): Burg. Van Karnebeeklaan 19, 2585 The Hague; tel. (31-70) 3607833; fax (31-70) 3615011; f. 1987; promotes, stimulates and co-ordinates information handling activities for professional, entrepreneurial and administrative purposes and within the field of science and technology; consultancy and project management for innovation in the field of STI; Dir Dr J. DE VUYST; publ. *NBBI-Bericht* (4 a year).

ECONOMICS, LAW AND POLITICS

Centraal Bureau voor de Statistiek (Central Bureau of Statistics): Prinses Beatrixlaan 428, POB 4000, 2270 JM Voorburg; tel. (70) 3373800; fax (70) 3877429; f. 1899; Dir-Gen. Prof. Dr A. P. J. ABRAHAMSE; economic and social statistical research; library of 365,000 vols, 45,000 microfiche; publs *Statistical Yearbook of the Netherlands*, *Statistisch Bulletin* (weekly), *Historical Statistics of the Netherlands*, many others.

Centre for Peace and Conflict Research of the University of Groningen: Oude Kijk in 't Jatstraat 5/9, 9712 EA Groningen; tel. (50) 635655; fax (50) 635635; f. 1961 as Polemical Institute of the University of Groningen; peace research centre for multi-disciplinary research on war, conflict and security, and university teaching; library of 10,000 vols, 150 periodicals; Research Co-ordinator Prof. Dr HERMAN DE LANGE; publs *Transaktie*, *Peace and Security Yearbook* (in Dutch).

Institute of Social Studies: see under Colleges.

International Institute for Asian Studies: Nonnensteeg 1–3, 2311 VJ Leiden; tel. (71) 5272227; fax (71) 5274162; e-mail iias@rullet.leidenuniv.nl; f. 1993 by Royal Netherlands Acad. of Arts and Sciences and three Dutch univs; postdoctoral research in humanities and social sciences; Dir Prof. W. A. L. STOKHOF; publ. *Newsletter* (4 a year).

Nederlands Instituut voor Internationale Betrekkingen 'Clingendael' (Netherlands Institute of International Relations 'Clingendael'): 7 Clingendael, 2597 VH The Hague; tel. (70) 3245384; fax (70) 3282002; e-mail info@clingendael.nl; f. 1983; research on international issues; lectures; postgraduate courses, training in international negotiation; information and documentation; library of 22,000 vols, 300 periodicals; Dir Prof. Dr A. VAN STADEN; publ. *Internationale Spectator* (monthly).

Nederlands Interdisciplinair Demografisch Instituut (Netherlands Interdisciplinary Demographic Institute): POB 11650, 2502 AR The Hague; tel. (70) 3565200; fax (70) 3647187; f. 1970; research, training, information and documentation in the field of population studies; 40 mems; library of 2,500 vols, 2,500 reprints, 15,000 articles, etc.; Dir Prof. Dr J. GIERVELD; publs *Bevolking en Gezin* (Population and Family, 3 a year), *Demos* (10 a year), working papers, monographs, *NIDI Reports*, *Selected annotated bibliography of population studies in the Netherlands* (annually).

Netherlands Economic Institute (NEI): K. P. van der Mandelelaan 11, POB 4175, 3006 AD Rotterdam; tel. (10) 4538800; telex 25490; fax (10) 4530768; f. 1929; economic research, mainly on a quantitative basis, on behalf of public authorities and private companies at home and abroad; Chair. Prof. Dr W. T. M. MOLLE; Dirs Prof. Dr A. KUYVENHOVEN, Drs W. J. B. KUIJPERS; publ. *Economisch Statistische Berichten* (weekly).

EDUCATION

Centre for International Research and Advisory Networks (CIRAN): Kortenaerkade 11, POB 29777, 2502 LT The Hague; tel. (70) 4260321; telex 33565; fax (70) 4260329; e-mail civan@nuffic.nl; f. 1992 as a dept of Nuffic (Netherlands Organization for International Co-operation in Higher Education); promotes, facilitates and co-ordinates international networks of persons and institutions working on development-related research; Dir Drs G. W. VON LIEBENSTEIN; publ. *Indigenous Knowledge and Development Monitor* (3 a year).

MEDICINE

Nederlands Instituut voor Hersenonderzoek (Netherlands Institute for Brain Research): Meibergdreef 33, 1105 AZ Amsterdam Zuidoost; tel. (20) 5665500; fax (20) 6961006; f. 1909; research into maturation, adaptation and ageing of the nervous system; 90 mems; library of 5,000 vols; Dir Prof. D. F. SWAAB; publ. *Yearly Progress Report* with list of publications.

TNO Preventie en Gezondheid (TNO Prevention and Health): POB 2215, 2301 CE Leiden; tel. (71) 5181818; fax (71) 5181910; scientific research in the fields of public health and prevention of illness; postgraduate courses in occupational health; library of 20,000 vols; Dir Dr W. R. F. NOTTEN; publ. *Annual Report*.

Vereniging Het Nederlands Kanker Instituut (Netherlands Cancer Institute): Plesmanlaan 121, 1066 CX Amsterdam; tel. (20) 5129111; fax (20) 6172625; f. 1913; library of 14,600 vols; Patron HKH BEATRIX, Queen of the Netherlands; Pres. W. F. DUISENBERG; Sec J. VISSER; publ. *Scientific Report*.

NATURAL SCIENCES

General

Nederlandse Organisatie voor Toegepast - Natuurwetenschappelijk Onderzoek (TNO) (Netherlands Organization for Applied Scientific Research): Schoemakerstraat 97, POB 6000, 2600 JA Delft; tel. (15) 2696900; fax (15) 2612403; f. 1930; strategic policy and innovation consultancy; building, materials and information technology, mechanical and production engineering, product design and development, telecommunications, quality control, health and safety, nutrition, environment and energy; library of 16,000 vols; Pres. J. A. DEKKER; publs *TNO Magazine* (English), *Toegepaste Wetenschap* (Dutch), *Annual Report* (in Dutch and English).

Nederlandse Organisatie voor Wetenschappelijk Onderzoek (NWO) (Netherlands Organization for Scientific Research): POB 93138, Laan van Nieuw Oost Indië 131, 2509 AC The Hague; tel. (70) 3440640; fax (70) 3850971; f. 1988; stimulates and co-ordinates pure and applied research in all fields of learning; Pres. Dr J. BORGMAN; Dir Dr W. HUTTER; publs *Jaarboek* (Annual Report), *Newsletter* (research reports in the Netherlands).

Stichting voor Wetenschappelijk Onderzoek van de Tropen (WOTRO) (Netherlands Foundation for the Advancement of Tropical Research): POB 93138, Laan van Nieuw Oost Indië 131, 2509 AC The Hague; tel. (70) 3440735; fax (70) 3850971; f. 1964; advancement of tropical research both pure and applied by awarding grants; Pres. Prof. Dr A. W. C. A. CORNELISSEN; Sec. Dr R. R. VAN KESSEL-HAGESTEIJN; publ. *Annual Report*.

Biological Sciences

Afdeling Biologisch Rijksuniversiteit Groningen: (Department of Biology, University of Groningen): Kerklaan 30, POB 14, 9750 AA Haren; tel. (50) 3632021; fax (50) 3635205; f. 1969; ecology, genetics, microbiology, plant and animal physiology, biotechnology, marine biology, environmental biology; library of 50,000 vols; Dir Prof. Dr J. M. KOOLHAAS.

Hortus Haren: POB 179, 9750 AD Haren (Gr); tel. (50) 632010; f. 1642, renewed 1929; 8,000 species; Dir J. L. REINHARD.

Instituut voor Plantenziektenkundig Onderzoek (IPO-DLO) (DLO—Research Institute for Plant Protection): Binnenhaven 5, POB 9060, 6700 GW Wageningen; tel. (317) 476000; fax (317) 410113; e-mail info@ipo.dlo.nl; f. 1949; prevention, management and control of plant diseases and pests; library of 24,000 vols; Dir Dr Ir N. G. HOGENBOOM; publ. *Annual Report*.

Rijksherbarium en Hortus Botanicus (National Herbarium and Botanical Garden): POB 9514, Einsteinweg 2, Leiden; tel. (71) 273500; fax (71) 273511; f. 1829 (Botanical Garden in 1590); investigation of the flora (taxonomy, geography), particularly of the Netherlands and tropical Asia; library of 18,200 vols, over 1,000 periodicals; Dir Prof. Dr P. BAAS; publs *Blumea* (general), *Persoonia* (Mycology), *Gorteria* (Netherl. flora), *Flora Malesiana* (Phanerog., ferns), *Flora Malesiana Bulletin*, *Internat. Ass. Wood Anatomists Journal*.

Mathematical Sciences

Stichting Mathematisch Centrum (SMC) (Foundation Mathematical Centre): Kruislaan 413, 1098 SJ Amsterdam; f. 1946; carries out research through 9 research communities and its own institute, CWI.

Attached centre:

CWI (Centre for Mathematics and Computer Science): Kruislaan 413, 1098 SJ Amsterdam; tel. 5929333; fax 5924199; f. 1946; 120 mems; six sections: (1) Analysis, Algebra and Geometry (Prof. Dr M. HAZEWINKEL); (2) Operations Research, Statistics and System Theory (Prof. Dr O. J. BOXMA); (3) Numerical Mathematics (Prof. Dr P. J. VAN DER HOUWEN); (4) Algorithmics and Architecture (Dr M. L. KERSTEN); (5) Software Technology (Prof. Dr J. W. DE BAKKER); (6) Interactive Systems (Drs P. J. W. TEN HAGEN); library: see Libraries; Gen. Dir Dr Ir G. VAN OORTMERSSEN; publs *Report* (series), *CWI Tracts*, *CWI Syllabus*, *CWI Quarterly*, *Jaarverslag*, *Annual Report*.

Physical Sciences

Astronomical Institute: University of Utrecht, POB 80,000, 3508 TA Utrecht; tel. (30) 2535200; telex 40048; fax (30) 2535201; f. 1643 (formerly Sonnenborgh Observatory); studies in solar physics, stellar atmospheres, plasma and high energy astrophysics, space research; library of 30,000 vols; Scientific Dir Prof. Dr A. G. HEARN.

Nationaal Instituut voor Kernfysica en Hoge Energie Fysica (NIKHEF) (National Institute for Nuclear Physics and High Energy Physics): POB 41882, 1009 DB Amsterdam; tel. (20) 5922000; fax (20) 5925155; has a 900 MeV pulse stretcher and storage ring (AmPs) and auxiliary instrumentation for basic research in hadronic structure physics; Scientific Dir Prof. Dr G. VAN MIDDELKOOP; Man. Dir Dr J. LANGELAAR.

Nederlands Instituut voor Onderzoek der Zee (Netherlands Institute for Sea Research): 't Horntje, POB 59, 1790 AB Den Burg, Texel; tel. (222) 369300; fax (222) 319674; f. 1876; scientific marine research; ships; Dir Prof. Dr J. W. DE LEEUW; publ. *Journal of Sea Research* (quarterly).

Netherlands Institute of Applied Geoscience TNO–National Geological Survey: POB 157, 2000 AD Haarlem; tel. (23) 5300300; fax (23) 5351614; f. 1903; Dir Dr H. SPEELMAN; publs Annual Reports, Geological Maps, Memoir.

Stichting Ruimteonderzoek Nederland (SRON) (Space Research Organization Netherlands): Sorbonnelaan 2, 3584 CA Utrecht; tel. (30) 2535600; fax (30) 2540860; f. 1983 to continue the activities of the Cttee for Geophysics and Space Research; responsible for research at the Nat. Space Institute and co-ordinates space research in general; Chair. Dr F. BAEDE; Gen. Dir Prof. Dr J. A. M. BLEEKER.

Incorporates:

SRON—Utrecht (Laboratory for Space Research): Sorbonnelaan 2, 3584 CA Utrecht; tel. (30) 2535600; fax (30) 2540860; f. 1961; X-ray and infra-red astronomy.

SRON—Groningen (Laboratory for Space Research): POB 800, 9700 AV Groningen; tel. (50) 3634074; fax (50) 3634033.

Stichting voor Fundamenteel Onderzoek der Materie (FOM) (Foundation for Fundamental Research on Matter): POB 3021, 3502 GA Utrecht; tel. (30) 6001211; fax (30) 6014406; e-mail press@fom.nl; f. 1946; carries out physics research through 150 university teams and in 4 institutes of its own, and in 2 used in co-operation with universities; Man. Dir Dr K. H. CHANG.

Attached institutes:

FOM-Instituut voor Atoom- en Molecuulfysica (FOM Institute of Atomic and Molecular Physics): Kruislaan 407, POB 41883, 1009 DB Amsterdam; tel. (20) 6081234; fax (20) 6684106; f. 1953; 150 mems; facilities include mass-spectrometers, spectrographs, molecular beam apparatus, microwave interferometers, laser equipment, beam plasma experiments, and a PDP 11 computer; library of 2,200 vols; Gen. Dir Prof. Dr J. T. M. WALRAVEN; publs *Annual Report*, and articles, lectures, etc.

FOM-Instituut voor Plasmafysica (FOM Institute of Plasma Physics): Rijnhuizen, Edisonbaan 14, POB 1207, 3430 BE Nieuwegein; tel. (30) 6096999; fax (30) 6031204; f. 1959; research in plasma physics, plasma containment, heating; free electron laser; 120 mems; library of 7,000 vols, 13,000 reports; Dir (vacant).

KVI (Nuclear Accelerator Facility): Zernikelaan 25, 9747 AA Groningen; tel. (050) 3633600; fax (50) 3634003; f. 1975; AVF cyclotron; Dir Prof. Dr M. HARAKEH.

FOM-Instituut voor Subatomaire Fysica (FOM-Institute for Subatomic Physics): Kruislaan 409, POB 41882, 1009 DB Amsterdam; tel. (20) 5922000; fax (20) 5925155; f. 1981; 300 staff; 900 MeV linear electron accelerator; Dir Prof. Dr G. VAN MIDDELKOOP.

DIMES/S (Section for Submicron Physics and Technology in DIMES): Lorentzweg 1, POB 5046, 2600 GA Delft; tel. (15) 2782600; fax (15) 2618820; f. 1984; Dir Prof. Dr J. E. MOOIJ.

FOM-Instituut voor de Gecondenseerde Materie (FOM Institute for Condensed Matter Physics): C/o Van Vollenhovenlaan 659, POB 3021, 3502 GA Utrecht; tel. (30) 2923217; fax (30) 2946099; f. 1992; materials research, high magnetic fields, electron microscopy; Dir Prof. Dr Ir J. C. MAAN.

RELIGION, SOCIOLOGY AND ANTHROPOLOGY

Netherlands Institute for Advanced Study in the Humanities and Social Sciences (NIAS): Meijboomlaan 1, 2242 PR Wassenaar; tel. (70) 5122700; fax (70) 5117162; e-mail nias@nias.knaw.nl; f. 1970; maintained by the Royal Netherlands Academy of Arts and Sciences, aims to stimulate research in the humanities and social sciences; fellowships awarded annually (20 to foreign scholars, 20 to Dutch scholars); Rector Prof. Dr H. L. WESSELING; Exec. Dir W. R. HUGENHOLTZ; publ. *Annual Report*.

SISWO—Instituut voor Maatschappijwetenschappen (Netherlands Universities' Institute for Co-ordination of Research in Social Sciences): Plantage Muidergracht 4, 1018 TV Amsterdam; tel. (20) 5270600; fax (20) 6229430; e-mail siswo@siswo.uva.nl; f. 1960; Chair. Prof. Dr H. H. VAN DER WUSTEN; Dir Dr J. G. M. STERK; publ. *FACTA*.

TECHNOLOGY

Instituut voor Milieu en Agritechniek (IMAG-DLO) (Institute of Agricultural and Environmental Engineering): POB 43, 6700 AA Wageningen; tel. (8370) 76300; fax (8370) 25670; f. 1974; 220 mems; Dir Ir. A. A. JONGEBREUR.

Nationaal Lucht- en Ruimtevaartlaboratorium (NLR) (National Aerospace Laboratory): Anthony Fokkerweg 2, POB 90502, 1006 BM Amsterdam; tel. (20) 5113113; fax (20) 5113210; e-mail info@nlr.nl; f. 1919; fluid dynamics, flight mechanics, flight testing and operations, structures and materials, space technology, remote sensing, information technology, electronics and instrumentation; library of 7,000 vols, 4,800 conference proceedings, 2,500 theses, 112,000 reports, etc.; Chair. of Board J. VAN HOUWELINGEN; Dir Ir. B. M. SPEE; publs technical reports, miscellaneous.

Netherlands Energy Research Foundation (ECN): Westerduinweg 3, Petten (NH); POB 1, 1755 ZG Petten (NH); tel. (224) 564949; fax (224) 564480; f. 1955 as *Reactor Centrum Nederland —RCN*; name changed 1976, and scope broadened to research in the whole field of energy supply and end use; Chair. J. C. TERLOUW; Gen. Man. Dirs F. W. SARIS, W. SCHATBORN.

Libraries and Archives

Alkmaar

Regionaal Archief (Regional Record Office): Hertog Aalbrechtweg 5, POB 9232, 1800 GE Alkmaar; tel. (72) 5662626; fax (72) 5622227; municipal archives, books about Alkmaar and North Holland, etc.; also regional archives for the area; pictures, prints, maps, relating to Alkmaar and surroundings; library of 40,000 vols; Municipal Archivist C. STREEFKERK; publs *Annual Report*, *Inventories of Archives*.

Amersfoort

Bibliotheek van het Oud Katholiek Seminarie (Library of the Old Catholic Seminary): Koningin Wilhelminalaan 3, 3818 HN Amersfoort; tel. (33) 4617569; f. 1725; library of 25,000 vols; Librarian L. NIEUWENHUIZEN.

Openbare Leeszaal en Bibliotheek (Public Library): Zonnehof 12, 3811 ND Amersfoort; tel. (33) 631914; f. 1913; library of 190,000 vols; Librarian E. A. MURRIS.

Amsterdam

Bibliotheca Philosophica Hermetica: Bloemgracht 19, 1016 KB Amsterdam; tel. (20) 6258079; fax (20) 6200973; e-mail bph@ritmanlibrary.nl; f. 1957; private library, open to researchers by appt; library of 5,000 vols printed before 1800, 600 MSS, 15,000 modern titles; specialises in early printed books and MSS in the field of the Christian-hermetic tradition (alchemy, hermetism, mysticism and rosicrucianism); also modern biographical and bibliographical reference works, text-editions, scholarly works, books on the modern esoteric tradition; Dir Prof. Dr F. A. JANSSEN.

Bibliotheek CWI-Centrum voor Wiskunde en Informatica (Library of the Centre for Mathematics and Computer Science): Kruislaan 413, POB 94079, 1090 GB Amsterdam; f. 1946; special scientific library on non-elementary mathematics and its applications and computer science; library of 43,000 vols, 1,300 current periodicals, 123,000 reports; Librarian Drs F. A. ROOS; publs *Aanwinstenlijst* (list of acquisitions), *CWI Newsletter* (quarterly), *Indagationes Mathematicae* (quarterly), *Report* series.

Bibliotheek der Rijksakademie van Beeldende Kunsten (Library of State Academy of Fine Arts): Sarphatistraat 470, 1018 GW Amsterdam; tel. (20) 5270300; fax (20) 5270301.

Bibliotheek van de Vrije Universiteit (Library of the Free University): De Boelelaan 1103, 1081 HV Amsterdam; tel. (20) 4445140; fax (20) 4445259; f. 1880; library of 700,000 vols on sciences, medicine and social sciences, 11,000 periodicals, 50,000 maps; Librarian Dr J. H. DE SWART.

Bibliotheek van het Koninklijk Instituut voor de Tropen (Library of the Royal Tropical Institute): Mauritskade 63, 1092 AD Amsterdam; tel. (20) 5688246; telex 15080; fax (20) 6654423; e-mail library@kit.nl; f. 1910; library of 230,000 vols, 11,000 periodicals, 24,000 maps; Head of Information, Library and Documentation Drs J. H. W. VAN HARTEVELT.

Boekmanstichtings Bibliotheek (Library of the Boekman Foundation): Herengracht 415, 1017 BP Amsterdam; tel. (20) 6243739; fax (20) 6385239; e-mail secretariaat@boekman.nl; f. 1963; all fields of art and culture, and related policy; library of 24,500 vols, 150 current periodicals; Librarian M. LINDHOUT.

Economisch-Historische Bibliotheek Amsterdam: Cruquiusweg 31, 1019 AT Amsterdam; tel. (20) 6685866; fax (20) 6654181; f. 1932; a dept of Netherlands Economic-Historical Archives Society; library of 100,000 vols; special collection of 16–18th century books on commerce and book-keeping, and on Dutch business history and companies; Librarian H. J. M. WINKELMAN.

KB, Bureau Nederlands Centrum voor Rechtshistorische Documentatie en Rechtsiconografie (Netherlands Centre for Documentation of History of Law, National Library of the Netherlands): O. Z. Achterburgwal 217, 1012 DL Amsterdam; tel. (20) 5253412; f. 1967; documentation system of catchword data from 33,000 articles, brochures and books on the history of law in the Netherlands; juridical iconography (*c.* 5,000 pictures and 3,000 slides); Dir Mrs M.A. BECKER-MOELANDS; publ. *Rechtshistorisch Nieuws* (3 a year).

Nederlands Instituut voor Wetenschappelijke Informatiediensten (Netherlands Institute for Scientific Information Services): Joan Muyskenweg 25, POB 95110, 1090 HC Amsterdam; tel. (20) 4628628; fax (20) 6685079; e-mail info@niwi.knaw.nl; f. 1808; library of 520,000 vols, 26,000 (incl. 9,000 current) periodicals, mainly in the biomedical disciplines and chemistry, biology, mathematics and physics; social sciences library of 80,000 reports and 300 current periodicals; historical data archive, Steinmetz archive, Dutch literature database, environmental database, research database; Dir (vacant).

Rijksinstituut voor Oorlogsdocumentatie (Netherlands State Institute for War Documentation): Herengracht 380, 1016 CJ Amsterdam; tel. (20) 5233800; fax (20) 5233888; e-mail info@riod.nl; f. 1945; extensive Dutch, German and allied collections on the history of World War II; library of 50,000 vols; Dir Dr J. C. H. BLOM.

Stadhuis Bibliotheek: Stadhuis Amsterdam, kamer 1131, Amstel 1, 1011 PN Amsterdam; f. 1892; library of 75,000 vols on law, administration and statistics; Librarian N. E. MOKKUM.

Universiteitsbibliotheek Amsterdam (Amsterdam University Library): Singel 421–425, 1012 WP Amsterdam; POB 19185, 1000 GD Amsterdam; tel. (20) 5252301; fax (20) 5252311; f. 1578; library of 4,000,000 vols, 135,000 maps, 160 medieval and 70,000 modern MSS, 500,000 letters; includes Bibliotheca Rosenthaliana (f. 1880, 100,000 vols, 850 MSS), Réveil-Archives, Vondel, Frederik van Eeden and Albert Verwey collections; Tetterode collection; several historical Church collections; libraries of Royal Dutch Book Trade Assen, Royal Geographical Soc., Royal Netherlands Soc. of Medicine, etc.; Chief Librarian A. J. H. A. VERHAGEN; Chief Curator P. VISSER; publ. *Studia Rosenthaliana* (every 6 months).

Arnhem

Rijksarchief in Gelderland: Markt 1, 6811 CG Arnhem; tel. (26) 4420148; fax (26) 4459792; e-mail ragld@worldonline.nl; f. 1878; contains the archives of the Dukes of Guelders and succeeding provincial administrations, and of other regional and local authorities; and of private persons, families, enterprises, religious bodies, etc. (12th–20th century);

Archivist Dr F. KEVERLING BUISMAN; publ. *Gelderse Inventarissen-reeks* (series of archival repertories).

Stichting Arnhemse Openbare en Gelderse Wetenschappelijke Bibliotheek (Arnhem Public and Learned Library): Koningstraat 26, 6811 DG, POB 1168, 6801 ML Arnhem; tel. (26) 3543111; fax (26) 4458616; e-mail bibliotheekarnhem@biblioarnhem.nl; f. 1856; library of 700,000 vols, 130 MSS; Librarian A. J. HOVY.

Assen

Rijksarchief in Drenthe te Assen (State Archives of Drenthe): Brink 4, 9401 HS Assen; POB 595, 9400 AN Assen; tel. (592) 313523; f. 1879; public records of the Province of Drenthe; archives of private persons, institutions and enterprises; library of 7,500 vols; Dir Dr P. BROOD.

De Bilt

Bibliotheek van het Koninklijk Nederlands Meteorologisch Instituut (Library of the Royal Netherlands Meteorological Institute): Wilhelminalaan 10, POB 201, 3730 AE De Bilt; tel. (30) 2206855; telex 47096; fax (30) 2210407; e-mail jansenw@knmi.nl; f. 1854; library of 120,000 vols on meteorology, physical oceanography and geophysics (especially seismology); Librarian W. J. JANSEN.

Delft

Bibliotheek Gemeentelijke Archiefdienst (Library of the Municipal Archives of Delft): Oude Delft 169, 2611 HB Delft; tel. (15) 602350; fax (15) 602355; f. 1859; library of 30,000 vols mainly on history of Delft, genealogy and heraldry; special collections: Delft early printed books, House of Orange-Nassau, Naundorff; Librarian J. A. METER.

Bibliotheek Technische Universiteit Delft (Library of the Delft University of Technology): Prometheusplein 1, Postbus 98, 2600 MG Delft; tel. (15) 2785678; fax (15) 2572060; e-mail info@library.tudelft.nl; f. 1842; library of 980,000 vols, 10,500 current periodicals, 1,108,000 microfiches; University Librarian Dr L. J. M. WAAIJERS; publ. *Delft Informatie Aktuel*.

Deventer

Gemeente-Archief (Record Office): Klooster 3, 7411 NH Deventer; tel. (570) 693713; f. 1853; municipal archives 1241–1950, judicial archives 1423–1811, archives of chapter 1123–1591, church registers 1542–1811, notarial archives 1811–1905; library of 10,000 vols; Archivist Drs E. T. SUIR.

Stads- of Athenaeumbibliotheek (Municipal Library): POB 351, 7400 AJ Deventer; Klooster 12, 7411 NH Deventer; tel. (570) 693887; fax (570) 693747; e-mail info@sab.hsij.nl; f. 1560; library of 250,000 vols, 550 MSS, 380 incunabula, 400 post-incunabula; Librarian Dr H. PEETERS.

Dordrecht

Stadsarchief (Record Office): Stek 13, 3311 XS Dordrecht; tel. (78) 6492311; fax (78) 6492388; e-mail gad@worldonline.nl; f. 1885; archives of the City of Dordrecht; books and prints of Dordrecht and its environs; library of 35,000 vols; Archivist J. N. T. VAN ALBADA; Librarian J. ALLEBLAS.

Echt

Bibliotheca Lilboschensis (Lilbosch Abbey Library): Pepinusbrug 6, 6102 RJ Echt; f. 1885; library of 40,000 vols; theology, monastica, cisterciensia; Librarian (vacant).

Eindhoven

Bibliotheek der Technische Universiteit Eindhoven (Library of the Eindhoven University of Technology): POB 90159, 5600 RM Eindhoven; tel. (40) 2472360; fax (40) 2447015; e-mail secretariaat@libr.tue.nl; f. 1956; library of 600,000 vols, 5,100 current periodicals; Dir Drs C. T. J. KLIJS.

Openbare Bibliotheek Eindhoven (Common Public Library): Gebouw de Witte Dame Emmasingel 22, 5611 AZ Eindhoven; tel. (40) 2604260; fax (40) 2461225; e-mail info@obeindhoven.nl; f. 1916; library of 881,000 vols; Librarian H. T. DAS.

Enschede

Universiteitsbibliotheek Twente: POB 217, 7500 AE Enschede; tel. (53) 4892092; fax (53) 4351805; e-mail iub@ub.utwente.nl; library of 375,000 vols, 2,700 periodicals; Dir (vacant).

Groningen

Bibliotheek der Rijksuniversiteit te Groningen (Library of the State University): POB 559, 9700 AN Groningen; premises at: Broerstraat 4, 9712 CP Groningen; tel. (50) 3635002; fax (50) 3634996; f. 1615; library of 2,800,000 vols, 1,100 MSS, 210 incunabula; Librarian A. C. KLUGKIST.

Groninger Archieven (Archives of Groningen): Cascadeplein 4, Postbus 30040, 9712 JN Groningen; tel. (50) 5992000; fax (50) 5992050; e-mail gronarch@castel.nl; f. 1824; Archivist Dr P. BROOD.

Haarlem

Bibliotheek van Teylers Museum (Teyler Museum Library): Spaarne 16, 2011 CH Haarlem; tel. (23) 5319010; fax (23) 5342004; f. 1778; library of 125,000 vols (natural sciences); Librarian Drs M. A. M. VAN HOORN; publs *Verhandelingen Teylers Godgeleerd Genootschap*, *Verhandelingen Teylers Tweede Genootschap*, *Archives du Musée Teyler*, *Teylers Museum Magazijn*.

Rijksarchief in Noord-Holland te Haarlem (State Archives of North Holland): Kleine Houtweg 18, 2012 CH Haarlem; tel. (23) 5172700; fax (23) 5172720; Dir Drs R. C. HOL.

Stadsbibliotheek (Municipal and Public Library): Doelenplein 1, 2011 XR Haarlem; tel. (23) 5157600; fax (23) 5157669; e-mail sbhbeheer@multiweb.nl; f. 1596; library of 552,000 vols, 280 MSS, 192 incunabula; Dir A. F. SKOLNIK-KOOIMAN.

Kampen

Gemeente-Archief (Record Office): Molenstraat 28, 8261 JW Kampen; tel. (38) 331952; archives of the town 1251–1965; Archivist J. GROOTEN; publ. *De Archieven der gemeente Kampen, I, II* and *III*.

Leeuwarden

Archief der Gemeente Leeuwarden en Stedelijke Bibliotheek (Archives of the City of Leeuwarden, Municipal Library and Topographical Collection): Grote Kerkstraat 29, 8911 DZ Leeuwarden; tel. (58) 2338399; fax (58) 2332315; f. 1838; works (incl. MSS) about Leeuwarden; topographical collection, mainly historical; library of 18,000 vols; Archivist and Librarian (vacant).

Buma Bibliotheek (Buma Library): POB 464, 8904 BG Leeuwarden; located at: Boterhoek 1, 8911 DH Leeuwarden; f. 1876; books on Greek and Roman antiquities; library of 45,000 vols; Librarian Dr G. P. VAN DEN BROCK.

Provinsjale Bibliotheek fan Fryslân (Frisian Provincial Library): POB 464, Boterhoek 1, 8901 BG Leeuwarden; tel. (58) 2133285; fax (58) 2130884; f. 1852; library of 450,000 vols; Dir-Librarian Dr G. J. VAN DEN BROEK.

Rijksarchief in Friesland (State Archives of Friesland): POB 97, 8900 AB Leeuwarden, Boterhoek 3; tel. (58) 2127103; fax (58) 2136854; e-mail rijksarg@euronet.nl; Dir D. P. DE VRIES.

Leiden

Bibliotheek der Rijksuniversiteit Leiden (Library of the State University): Witte Singel 27, POB 9501, 2300 RA Leiden; tel. (71) 5272801; fax (71) 5272836; e-mail secrl@rulub.leidenuniv.nl; f. 1575; library of 2,200,000 vols, 19,000 MSS, 40,000 maps; Librarian Drs P. W. J. L. GERRETSEN.

Bibliotheek van de Maatschappij der Nederlandse Letterkunde (Library of the Society of Netherlands Literature): Witte Singel 27, POB 9501, Leiden; fax (71) 3272836; f. 1766; library of 107,000 vols, 2,100 MSS; Librarian Drs P. W. J. L. GERRETSEN.

Maastricht

Kunst, Cultuur en Onderwijs afdeling, Gemeentearchief Maastricht (Art, Culture and Education Department, Municipal Record Office of Maastricht): Grote Looiersstraat 17, Maastricht; tel. (43) 292222; f. 1849; municipal and family archives, church records, MSS, topographical collections relating to Maastricht and the Province of Limburg; Archivist Drs P. A. W. DINGEMANS.

Rijksarchief in Limburg (State Archives of Limburg): St Pieterstraat 5–7, 6211 JM Maastricht; Archivist TH. L. M. GERRITSEN (acting).

Stadsbibliotheek Maastricht (Municipal Library): Nieuwenhofstraat 1, 6211 KG Maastricht; tel. (43) 3505600; fax (43) 3505599; f. 1662; library of 500,000 vols, including 107 incunabula, 297 post-incunabula, 1,600 periodicals, special collections and documentation relating to the Province of Limburg, devotional material and chess literature; Librarian C. DE KOSTER; publs *Publicaties*, *Limburgensia*.

Middelburg

Rijksarchief in Zeeland (Zeeland State Archives): St Pieterstraat 38, 4331 EW Middelburg; tel. (118) 638920; fax (118) 628094; f. 1843; Archivist Drs R. L. KOOPS.

Zeeuwse Bibliotheek (Zeeland Library): Kousteensedijk 7, 4331 JE Middelburg; tel. (118) 654000; fax (118) 654001; e-mail zbsec@mail.zebi.nl; formed by amalgamation of Middelburg Public Library and Zeeland Provincial Library; library of 750,000 vols, 7,500 MSS, 4,000 periodicals; Dir G. E. HUISMAN.

Nijmegen

Bibliotheek Katholieke Universiteit (Library of the Catholic University): Erasmuslaan 36, POB 9100, 6500 HA Nijmegen; tel. (24) 3612440; fax (24) 3615944; f. 1923; library of 2,000,000 vols; Librarian Dr A. H. LAEVEN.

Rotterdam

Gemeentebibliotheek (Municipal Library): Hoogstraat 110, 3011 PV Rotterdam; tel. (10) 2816100; fax (10) 2816181; f. 1604; library of 1,550,000 vols, 200 MSS, Erasmus collection 5,000 vols; Dir Ir F. H. MEIJER.

Gemeentelijke Archiefdienst (Municipal Record Office): Hofdijk 651, POB 71, 3000 AB Rotterdam; tel. (10) 2434567; fax (10) 2434666; e-mail info@gemeentearchief.rotterdam.nl; f. 1857; city archives, church records, notarial archives, Chamber of Commerce records 1797–1922, family archives, topographical collection, sound archives, historical library; Archivist Drs E. A. G. VAN DEN BENT.

Rotterdamsch Leeskabinet (Rotterdam Library): Burg. Oudlaan 50, POB 1738, 3000 DR Rotterdam; f. 1859; philosophy, theology, social sciences, language and literature, history, art, art history, geography; library of 215,000 vols; Librarian Drs J. W. DE JONG; publs *Kwartaalbericht*, *Jaarverslag*.

Universiteitsbibliotheek Erasmus Universiteit Rotterdam (Library of the Erasmus University of Rotterdam): POB 1738, 3000 DR Rotterdam; tel. (10) 408-1201; fax (10) 4532311; f. 1913; library of 1,000,000 vols; economy, management, sociology, law, history, philosophy; medical library: POB 1738, 3000 DR Rotterdam; University Librarian Dr P. E. L. J. SOETAERT.

's-Hertogenbosch

Rijksarchief in de Provincie Noord-Brabant (State Archives of North Brabant): Zuid-Willemsvaart 2, 5211 NW 's-Hertogenbosch; tel. (73) 6818500; fax (73) 6146439; f. 1860; records from 13th–20th centuries; Record Office contains *c.* 200,000 vols; library of 30,000 vols, 8,000 charters, special collection of 5,000 vols on Vlaamse Beweging (Flemish Movement); Archivist Dr J. A. M. Y. BOS-ROPS; publ. *Inventarisreeks*.

Stadsbibliotheek 's-Hertogenbosch: Hinthamerstraat 72, 5211 MR 's-Hertogenbosch; tel. (73) 6123033; f. 1915; library of 270,000 vols, 22,000 compact discs; Librarian G. DE ROOIJ.

The Hague

Algemeen Rijksarchief te 's-Gravenhage (General State Archives): Prins Willem Alexanderhof 20, 2595 The Hague; tel. (70) 3315400; fax (70) 3315499; f. 1802; 80 km of archives; library of 80,000 vols, 700 journals; Dir Dr J. E. A. BOOMGAARD; publ. *Inventories of Archives*.

Bibliotheek van het Centraal Bureau voor de Statistiek (Library of Statistics Netherlands): Prinses Beatrixlaan 428, POB 4000, 2270 JM Voorburg; tel. (70) 3375151; fax (70) 3375984; e-mail bibliotheek@cbs.nl; f. 1899; library of 380,000 vols; Librarian M. WIJNGAARDEN.

Bibliotheek van het Vredespaleis (Peace Palace Library): 2 Carnegieplein, 2517 KJ The Hague; tel. (70) 3024242; fax (70) 3024166; f. 1913; int. public and municipal law, diplomatic history, int. relations; Grotius Collection; library of 700,000 vols; Dir and Chief Librarian J. C. SCHALEKAMP; publs acquisitions list (quarterly), *Bibliography for the Centre for Studies and Research of the Hague Academy of International Law* (annually).

Koninklijke Bibliotheek (Royal Library): POB 90407, Prins Willem-Alexanderhof 5, 2509 LK The Hague; tel. (70) 3140911; fax (70) 3140651; f. 1798; National Library, responsible for the development, documentation and management of the nat. cultural heritage; depository for all Dutch publs and the nat. bibliography; research library for the humanities and social sciences; centre of expertise in preservation and restoration; focal point of inter-library co-operation; 2,200,000 books, 15,000 current periodicals, newspapers, MSS; spec. collns incl. chess, cookery, children's books; Chief Exec. Dr W. VAN DRIMMELEN; publs *Jaarverslag*, *Nederlandse Bibliografie*, special bibliographies, exhibition catalogues.

Openbare Bibliotheek (Public Library): Spui 68, POB 12653, 2500 DP The Hague; tel. (70) 3534455; fax (70) 3534504; e-mail secr@dbadenhaag.nl; f. 1906; library of 1,042,284 vols, 131,559 children's books, music library of 52,854 vols and 57,512 compact discs, 7,599 audio-visual items, 18 branch libraries, 2 mobile libraries; Dir W. M. RENES.

Tweede Kamer der Staten-Generaal; Dienst Bibliotheek en Dienst Documentatie (Second Chamber of the States-General; Library Department and Documentation Department): Plein 2, POB 20018, 2500 EA The Hague; tel. (70) 3182315; fax (70) 3182307; e-mail bibliotheek@tk.parlement.nl; f. 1815; library of 100,000 vols; Librarian J. C. KEUKENS; Head of Documentation P. VAN RIJN.

Tilburg

Bibliotheek Katholieke Universiteit Brabant (Tilburg University Library): Warandelaan 2, POB 90153, 5000 LE Tilburg; tel. (13) 662124; telex 52426; fax (13) 662996; e-mail library@kub.nl; f. 1927; economics, applied computer sciences, social sciences, law, history, philosophy, linguistics; library of 750,000 vols; Librarian H. GELEIJNSE.

Centrale Bibliotheek Fraters: Gasthuisring 54, Tilburg; f. 1845; scientific and educational; library of 145,000 vols; Librarian H. G. SIEBELT.

Utrecht

Gemeentebibliotheek Utrecht (Municipal Library): Oude Gracht 167, POB 80, 3500 AB Utrecht; tel. (30) 2861800; fax (30) 2861990; f. 1892; library of 795,000 vols, 10 brs, music library; Dir A. G. J. VAN VLIMMEREN.

Rijksarchief in de Provincie Utrecht (State Archives of Utrecht): Alexander Numankade 199–201, 3572 KW Utrecht; tel. (30) 2866611; fax (30) 2866600; e-mail utrecht@ad.archief.nl; f. 1805; records of the City and Province of Utrecht; library of 50,000 vols; Archivist Drs J. T. J. JAMAR; publs *Inventories Series*, *Church Records*.

Universiteitsbibliotheek Utrecht (Library of Utrecht University): POB 16007, 3500 DA Utrecht; premises at: Wittevrouwenstraat 7–11, 3512 CS Utrecht; tel. (30) 2538002; fax (30) 2538398; f. 1584; library of 4,500,000 vols, 2,500 MSS, 900 incunabula, 110,000 vols printed before 1800, MSS and printed books of the medieval libraries of the Utrecht churches and religious houses, two 16th-century private libraries, special collections in the fields of literature, theology, history, botany, medicine, 18th- 19th-century science libraries, and on the province and city of Utrecht; Librarian Drs J. S. M. SAVENIJE.

Wageningen

Bibliotheek Landbouwuniversiteit Wageningen (Library of Wageningen Agricultural University): Gen. Foulkesweg 19, POB 9100, 6700 HA Wageningen; tel. (317) 484440; fax (317) 484761; f. 1873; library of 1,500,000 vols, 15,000 current periodicals; Chief Librarian Drs J. M. SCHIPPERS; publs *Wageningen Agricultural University Papers*, Theses.

Zwolle

Rijksarchief in Overijssel (State Archives of Overijssel): Eikenstraat 20, 8021 WX Zwolle; tel. (38) 4540722; fax (38) 4544506; e-mail rao@euronet.nl; f. 1838; provincial archives 1528–1948, judicial archives 1333–1939, notarial archives 1811–1915, old church registers and civil registers 1592–1932, archives of monasteries 1225–1811, industrial archives 1850–1980, etc.; historical library of 40,000 vols; 9,500 metres of archives, 9,500 charters; 12,220 maps and drawings; 100,000 photographs and negatives; Archivist H. BORDEWIJK.

Museums and Art Galleries

Alkmaar

Stedelijk Museum Alkmaar: Doelenstraat 5, 1811 KX Alkmaar; f. *c.* 1550; municipal museum; antiquarian and art collection from Alkmaar and its environs, paintings by van Heemskerck, van de Velde the Elder, Allart and Caesar B. van Everdingen, Honthorst; objects include old silver, glass, pottery, porcelain, tiles and modern art; collection of antique toys and dolls; Dir M. E. A. DE VRIES.

Amsterdam

Allard Pierson Museum Amsterdam: Oude Turfmarkt 127, 1012 GC Amsterdam; tel. (20) 5252556; fax (20) 5252561; e-mail apm@let.uva.nl; f. 1934; the archaeological museum of the University of Amsterdam; scientific research centre for students of archaeology and history of art, and public museum; archaeology of ancient Egypt, Near East, Greece, Etruria, Roman Empire; Dir Prof. Dr H. A. G. BRIJDER; publs *Mededelingenblad van de Vereniging van Vrienden*, Allard Pierson series.

Amstelkring Museum: (Our Lord in the Attic): Oudezijds Voorburgwal 40, Amsterdam; tel. (20) 6246604; fax (20) 6381822; f. 1888; merchant's house of 1661 with a clandestine Catholic church in the attic; exhibits of 16th–20th-century ecclesiastical art; library of 1,500 vols; concerts; Dir A. H. P. J. VAN DEN HOUT.

Amsterdams Historisch Museum (Amsterdam Historical Museum): Kalverstraat 92 (postal address: Nieuwezijds Voorburgwal 359, 1012 RM Amsterdam); tel. (20) 5231822; fax (20) 6207789; f. 1926; exhibits of the city's history over 700 years including archaeological finds, artefacts, paintings, prints and models; library of 22,000 vols on history of Amsterdam, Dutch art history and applied industrial arts; special collection: Jan and Casper Luyken collection.

Nederlands Scheepvaartmuseum (Netherlands Maritime Museum): Kattenburgerplein 1, 1018 KK Amsterdam; tel. (20) 5232222; fax (20) 5232213; f. 1916; models, paintings, charts, globes, technical drawings, nautical instruments, arms and relics, full-size replica East-Indiaman; library of 60,000 vols; special collections: early navigation textbooks, voyages and travel, navigation, Dutch sea atlases; Dir W. BIJLEVELD; publ. *Zee Magazijn* (quarterly).

Rembrandthuis Museum: Jodenbreestr. 4–6, 1011 NK Amsterdam; tel. (20) 6249486; fax (20) 6232246; f. 1907; Rembrandt etchings and drawings, and paintings by his teacher and pupils; the artist lived here 1639–58; Dir A. R. E. DE HEER; publs catalogues, *Bulletin* (2 a year).

Rijksmuseum (State Museum): Stadhouderskade 42, Amsterdam; tel. (20) 6732121; fax (20) 6798146; e-mail info@rijksmuseum.nl; f. 1808; paintings, sculpture, drawings, history, porcelain, glass, costumes, silver, furniture, Asiatic art; library of 80,000 vols; Dir-Gen. Prof. Drs R. DE LEEUW; Curators Drs W. TH. KLOEK (Paintings), Dr R. J. BAARSEN (Sculpture and Applied Art), Dr J. P. SIGMOND (National Historical Collection), Drs P. C. SCHATBORN (Print Room), Drs P. C. M. LUNSINGH SCHEURLEER (Asiatic Art); Librarian Drs G. J. M. KOOT; publs *Bulletin* (quarterly), annual reports.

Stedelijk Museum: Paulus Potterstraat 13, Amsterdam; tel. (20) 5732911; fax (20) 6752716; f. 1895; modern paintings and sculpture, especially American and European trends since 1950; graphics and drawings; applied arts and industrial design; temporary exhibitions on contemporary art; library of 23,000 vols, 95,000 catalogues; Dir RUDI FUCHS; publs *Bulletin* (in Dutch and English), Catalogues.

Tropenmuseum (Museum of the Royal Tropical Institute): Linnaeusstraat 2, Amsterdam; tel. (20) 5688215; fax (20) 5688331; f. 1916; presents a picture of life and work in the tropics and sub-tropics; children's museum;

library of 18,000 vols; Dir H. J. GORTZAK; publs occasional papers.

Van Gogh Museum: Paulus Potterstraat 7, POB 75366, 1070 AJ Amsterdam; tel. (20) 5705200; f. 1973 to house collections of the Vincent van Gogh Foundation; paintings and drawings by van Gogh and his contemporaries; his correspondence with his brother Theo, Theo's collection, his own collection including English and French prints and graphics, Japanese wood-cuts, documents; library of 12,500 vols; archives of the art historian M. E. TRALBAUT; special collection: 19th-century literature (mainly French) read by van Gogh; Dir JOHN LEIGHTON; publs *Van Gogh Bulletin* (quarterly), *Cahier Vincent* (Scientific research, annually).

Apeldoorn

Paleis Het Loo: Koninklijk Park 1, 7315 JA Apeldoorn; tel. (55) 5772400; fax (55) 5219983; f. 1971; collection of portraits, furniture, documents, etc., relating to the Dutch royal family, the House of Orange-Nassau; library of 10,000 vols; Dir Dr A. W. VLIEGENTHART.

Arnhem

Historisch Museum het Burgerweeshuis: Bovenbeekstraat 21, 6811 CV Arnhem; tel. (26) 4426900; fax (26) 4436315; f. 1995; pre-1900 applied art, history, archaeology, glass and silver, Delftware, topographic collection of Gelderland.

Museum voor Moderne Kunst (Museum for Modern Art): Utrechtseweg 87, 6812 AA Arnhem; tel. (26) 34512431; fax (26) 4435148; f. 1856; post-1900 sculpture, Dutch paintings, design; Dir Drs L. BRANDT CORSTIUS.

Nederlands Openluchtmuseum (Netherlands Open Air Museum): Postbus 649, 6800 AP Arnhem; premises at: Schelmseweg 89, 6816 SJ Arnhem; tel. (85) 3576111; f. 1912; history of daily life; information retrieval; library of 40,000 vols, 400 periodicals; Dir J. A. M. F. VAESSEN; publ. *Annual Report*.

Delft

Koninklijk Nederlands Leger- en Wapenmuseum 'Generaal Hoefer' (Royal Netherlands Army and Arms Museum 'General Hoefer'): Korte Geer 1, 2611 CA Delft; tel. (15) 2150500; fax (15) 2150544; f. 1913; exhibition covering 2,000 years of Netherlands' military history; weapons from prehistory to the present; uniforms, equipment, medals, paintings; library of 225,000 vols and collection of prints; Dir J. A. BUYSE; publs *Annual Report*, *Armamentaria* (annually).

Museum Lambert van Meerten: Oude Delft 199, 2611 HD Delft; tel. (15) 2602358; fax (15) 2138744; f. 1909; Dutch tiles, furniture, paintings, Delftware; Chief Curator Drs M. C. C. KERSTEN.

Stedelijk Museum 'Het Prinsenhof': St Agathaplein 1, 2611 HR Delft; tel. (15) 2602358; fax (15) 2138744; f. 1948; contains historical collection, paintings of the Delft School, Eighty Years' War, William the Silent; Dir Drs D. H. A. C. LOKIN.

Den Helder

Marinemuseum: Hoofdgracht, Den Helder; tel. (223) 657137; fax (223) 657282; e-mail marmus@havy.disp.mindef.nl; f. 1962; history of the Royal Netherlands Navy from 1813 to the present day, collections of models, navigational instruments, paintings, photographs, etc.; three-cylinder submarine 'Tonijn'; small specialized library; Dir Cmdr HARRY DE BLES.

Deventer

Gemeentemusea van Deventer (Municipal Museums of Deventer): POB 5000, 7400 GC Deventer; tel. (570) 693783; fax (570) 693788; f. 1915; Dir N. HERWEIJER.

Museums include:

Museum de Waag: Deventer; local history, paintings, drawings, applied arts.

Speelgoed- en Blikmuseum: Deventer; toys, mechanical toys, trains, historical cans.

Eindhoven

Municipal Van Abbemuseum in Eindhoven: Vonderweg 1, POB 235, 5600 AE Eindhoven; tel. (40) 2755275; fax (40) 2460680; e-mail vanabbe@wxs.nl; f. 1936; large collection of modern and contemporary art including Lissitzky collection and conceptual collection; library of 100,000 vols; Dir J. DEBBAUT; publ. exhibition catalogues (8 a year).

Enschede

Rijksmuseum Twenthe, Enschede: Lasondersingel 129, Enschede; tel. (53) 4358675; fax (53) 4359002; e-mail info@rijksmuseum-twenthe.nl; f. 1930; fine and applied art from Middle Ages to the present; library of 15,000 vols; Dir Drs D. A. S. CANNEGIETER; publ. *Bulletin* (quarterly).

Gouda

Stedelijk Museum 'de Moriaan' ('The Blackamoor' Municipal Museum): 29 Westhaven, Gouda; tel. (182) 588444; fax (182) 588671; Dutch Merchants' house containing authentic 18th-century tobacco shop; collection of Dutch clay pipes and Gouda pottery; Dir Dr N. C. SLUIJTER-SEIJFFERT.

Stedelijk Museum 'Het Catharina Gasthuis' (St Catherine Hospital, Municipal Museum): Oosthaven 9, Gouda; tel. (182) 588440; fax (182) 588671; 18th-century town dispensary; antique toys, surgeons' Guild Room, decorative art from late 16th to 20th century, Gasthuis kitchen and chapel, important collection of 15th- to 20th-century art; Dir Dr N. C. SLUIJTER-SEIJFFERT.

Groningen

Groninger Museum: Museumeiland 1, 9711 ME Groningen; tel. (50) 3666555; fax (50) 3120815; f. 1894; prehistory and history; paintings of local school; Dutch and Flemish of 16th and 17th centuries: Fabritius, Jordaens, Rubens, Sweerts, Teniers; drawings: Rembrandt, Averkamp, Van Goyen, Cuyp, Lievens; 19th- and 20th-century painting; extensive collection of Far-Eastern ceramics; collection of applied art; library of 38,000 vols incl. book collection on modern art and artists and collection of post-1979 modern art; Dir R. VAN DER LUGT.

Haarlem

Frans Halsmuseum: Groot Heiligland 62, POB 3363, 2001 DJ Haarlem; tel. (23) 5115775; fax (23) 5115776; f. 1913; pictures from 15th to 20th centuries, with a focus on the Haarlem school and Frans Hals; applied arts, contemporary art; Dir D. P. SNOEP.

Teylers Museum: Spaarne 16, 2011 CH Haarlem; tel. (23) 5319010; fax (23) 5342004; e-mail teyler@euronet.nl; f. 1778; paintings, drawings, palaeontology, geology, mineralogy, natural history, physics, numismatics; library of 125,000 vols (natural science); Dir E. EBBINGE; publs *Verhandelingen van Teylers Godgeleerd Genootschap*, *Verhandelingen van Teylers Tweede Genootschap*, *Archives du Mušee Teyler*, *Teylers Magazijn* (quarterly), exhibition and collection catalogues.

Heerlen

Thermenmuseum Heerlen: Coriovallumstraat 9, POB 1, 6400 AA Heerlen; tel. (45) 5605100; fax (45) 5603915; f. 1977; collection includes Roman bath house excavated in 1940–41 and other objects from Roman period; Dir Drs F. W. JANSEN.

Hoorn

Westfries Museum: Rode Steen 1, Hoorn; tel. (229) 280028; fax (229) 280029; the baroque building dates from 1632, museum f. 1879; 17th- and 18th-century painting, prints, oak panelling, glass, pottery, silver, furniture, costumes, interiors, objects of trade, navigation and business, folk art, historical objects from Hoorn and West Friesland, prehistoric finds; Dir R. J. SPRUIT; publs annual reports.

Leerdam

Stichting Nationaal Glasmuseum (National Glass Museum): Lingedijk 28, 4142 LD Leerdam; tel. (3451) 13662; fax (3451) 13662; f. 1953; art glass, industrial glass and bottles, contemporary Dutch collection and works from other European countries and America; small library; Curator Drs T. G. TE DHITS.

Leeuwarden

Fries Museum: Turfmarkt 11, POB 1239, 8900 CE Leeuwarden; tel. (58) 2123001; fax (58) 2132271; f. 1827; painting, local history, archaeology, decorative arts, prints and drawings, Second World War, Mata Hari gallery, modern art; Dir WIM VAN KRIMPEN; publs *Visitor's Guide* (English, French and German), exhibition catalogues.

Keramiekmuseum het Princessehof (Princessehof Museum of Ceramics): Grote Kerkstraat 11, 8911 DZ Leeuwarden; tel. (58) 2127438; fax (58) 2122281; Asian and European ceramics and tiles, contemporary ceramics; library of 30,000 vols; Dir W. VAN KRIMPEN; publ. *Keramika* (quarterly).

Leiden

Naturalis (National Museum of Natural History): Darwinweg 2, POB 9517, 2300 RA Leiden; tel. (71) 5687600; fax (71) 5687666; e-mail naturalis@naturalis.nnm.nl; f. 1820; zoology, geology and palaeontology; zoology library of 78,000 vols, 5,000 periodicals; geology library of 30,000 vols; 3,000 periodicals; Dir Drs W. G. VAN DER WEIDEN; publs *Zoölogische Mededelingen*, *Zoölogische Verhandelingen*, *Scripta Geologica*, *Jaarverslag* (Annual Report), *Zoölogische Monographieën*, *Zoölogische Bijdragen*.

Rijksmuseum Het Koninklijk Penningkabinet (Royal Coin Cabinet): Rapenburg 28, POB 11028, 2301 EA Leiden; tel. (71) 120748; e-mail museum@penningkabinet.nl; f. 1816; coins from Greek and Roman times to the present day, medals, paper money, engraved gems; library of 12,000 vols on numismatics and glyptics; Dir Drs M. SCHARLOO; Curators Drs H. W. JACOBI, Dr J. P. A. VAN DER VIN; Drs A. POL; publs *Jaarboek voor Munt- en Penningkunde*, *De Beeldenaar* (every 2 months).

Rijksmuseum van Oudheden (National Museum of Antiquities): Rapenburg 28, POB 11114, 2301 EC Leiden; tel. (71) 5163163; fax (71) 5149941; e-mail info@rmo.nl; f. 1818; prehistoric, Roman and Medieval periods in the Netherlands; Egyptian, Mesopotamian, Greco-Roman and ancient European collections; library of 60,000 vols, 400 periodicals; Dir Drs J. R. MAGENDANS; publ. *Oudheidkundige Mededelingen van het Rijksmuseum van Oudheden te Leiden* (annually).

Rijksmuseum voor de Geschiedenis van de Natuurwetenschappen en van de Geneeskunde 'Museum Boerhaave' (National Museum of the History of Science and Medicine): Lange St. Agnietenstraat 10, POB 11280, 2301 EG Leiden; tel. (71) 5214224; fax (71) 5120344; f. 1928; historical scientific instruments and documents, anatomical preparations, portraits; library of 25,000 vols, MSS; Dir Dr G. A. C. VEENEMAN; publ. *Communications Series* (irregular).

Rijksmuseum voor Volkenkunde (National Museum of Ethnology): Steenstraat 1, Postbus 212, 2300 AE Leiden; tel. (71) 5168800; fax (71) 5128437; f. 1837; collections from Africa, the Middle East, the Islamic and Indian cultural areas, the Far East, Pacific, South-East Asia, the Americas and the circumpolar regions; library of 50,000 vols; Dir Dr S. B. ENGELSMAN; publs *Annual Report*, *Mededelingen*.

Stedelijk Museum 'de Lakenhal' Leiden: Oude Singel 28–32, POB 2044, 2301 CA Leiden; tel. (71) 5165360; fax (71) 5134489; f. 1872; pictures of Leiden school; memorial table (triptych) and altar pieces by Lucas van Leyden and C. Engebrechtsz; Rembrandt, Jan Steen, Jan van Goyen, van Mieris, Dou, modern Leiden school: Verster, Kamerlingh Onnes and contemporary Dutch art; furniture, silver, glass, tapestry, etc.; period rooms; history of the town; library of 3,000 vols, 7,000 catalogues; Dir Drs H. BOLTEN-REMPT; publs various, incl. catalogue.

Maastricht

Bonnefantenmuseum — Provinciaal Museum Limburg (Limburg Provincial Museum): Postbus 1735, 6201 BS Maastricht; premises at: Avenue Céramique 250, Maastricht; tel. (43) 3290190; fax (43) 3290199; f. 1863, refounded 1968; prehistory, Roman archaeology, ecclesiastical art, ancient, modern and contemporary painting and sculpture; temporary exhibitions; library of 5,000 vols; Dir A. M. U. VAN GREVENSTEIN.

Natuurhistorisch Museum Maastricht (Maastricht Natural History Museum): Postbus 882, 6200 AW Maastricht; premises at: Bosquetplein 6, 6211 KJ Maastricht; tel. (43) 3505490; fax (43) 3505475; e-mail mail@nhmmaastricht.nl; f. 1912; flora, fauna and soils of the Limburg area, late Cretaceous fossils; library of 30,000 vols; Chief Officer Drs D. TH. DE GRAAF; publ. *Natuurhistorisch Maandblad* (monthly).

Muiden

Muiderslot: Muiden; tel. (294) 261325; fax (294) 261056; 13th-century castle furnished in early 17th-century style: paintings, tapestries, furniture and armoury; Dir W. 'T HOOFT; publs *Annual Report*, *Guides*, *Het Muiderslot*, *Bloemen*, *Constig Geschikt*.

Naarden

Comenius Museum: Kloosterstraat 33, 1411 RS Naarden; tel. (35) 6943045; fax (35) 6941949; f. 1924; J. A. Comenius mausoleum and exhibition; library of 2,500 vols; Dir Drs W. F. JANSEN.

Nijmegen

Museum Het Valkhof: Kelfkensbos 59, 6511 TB Nijmegen; tel. (24) 3608805; fax (24) 3608656; f. 1998; archaeology, cultural history and modern art, mainly related to Nijmegen; Dir Drs A. M. GERHARTL-WITTEVEEN; the museum was expected to open in May 1999.

Provinciaal Museum G. M. Kam te Nijmegen: Museum Kamstraat 45, Nijmegen; tel. (24) 3220619; fax (24) 3604799; f. 1922; contains Roman antiquities (pottery, glass, bronzes, etc.) found in Nijmegen and the province of Gelderland; also prehistoric and Frankish antiquities; collections include those of the town of Nijmegen and of the St Canisius College; Dir Drs A. M. GERHARTL-WITTEVEEN; publs *Annual Report* (in Dutch), various catalogues in Dutch, English and German.

Otterlo

Kröller-Müller Museum: Nationale Park de Hoge Veluwe, Houtkampweg 6, 6731 AW Otterlo; tel. (318) 591241; fax (318) 591515; f. 1938; large collection of paintings by Van Gogh, paintings and sculpture of the 19th and 20th centuries, old masters, open-air modern sculpture collection (Moore, Serra, Volten), ceramics, drawings, graphic art; library of 40,000 vols; Dir Dr E. J. VAN STRAATEN.

Tegelmuseum Otterlo (Netherlands Tile Museum): Eikenzoom 12, 6731 BH Otterlo; tel. (318) 591519; f. 1961; extensive collection of Netherlands tiles, dating from 1500 to the present day; library of 734 vols; Dir P. B. M. BOLWERK.

Roermond

Stedelijk Museum Roermond (Municipal Museum): Andersonweg 4, 6041 JE Roermond; tel. (475) 333496; fax (475) 336299; f. 1932; archaeology, historical and contemporary art and design, architecture and art of Dr P. J. H. CUYPERS (1827–1921); Curator H. PH. A. TILLIE.

Rotterdam

Historisch Museum der Stad Rotterdam: Korte Hoogstraat 31, 3011 GK Rotterdam; tel. (10) 2176767; fax (10) 4334499; history, archaeology, domestic life, technology, art; Dir C. O. A. Baron SCHIMMELPENNINCK VAN DER OIJE.

Maritiem Museum 'Prins Hendrik': Scheepvaart en Havenmuseum Rotterdam, Leuvehaven 1, POB 988, 3000 AZ Rotterdam; tel. (10) 4132680; fax (10) 4137342; f. 1873, new building 1986; models of ships dating back to 15th century, globes, atlases, 20,000 books; ironclad warship 'Buffel'; special children's exhibition; Dir C. O. A. Baron SCHIMMELPENNINCK VAN DER OIJE; publs *Plaatsbepaling* (quarterly), *Jaarverslag*.

Museum Boijmans–Van Benningen: Museumpark 18–20, 3015 CB Rotterdam; tel. (10) 4419400; fax (10) 4360500; f. 1847; Dutch School including paintings by Van Eyck, Bosch, Pieter Brueghel, Hals, Rembrandt, van Ruysdael, Hobbema, Jan Steen; Baroque School, French School, Impressionists; old, modern and contemporary paintings and sculpture; drawings from 15th–20th-century Dutch, Flemish, French, German, Italian and Spanish schools, old and modern prints; glass, Dutch silver, old pewter, laces and ceramics, among which an important collection of Persian, Spanish, Italian and Dutch pottery and tiles, furniture, industrial design; library of *c.* 125,000 vols and catalogues, *c.* 200 periodical titles; Dir CH. DERCON; publs catalogues.

Museum voor Volkenkunde (Museum of Ethnology): Willemskade 25, 3016 DM Rotterdam; tel. (10) 4111055; fax (10) 4118331; f. 1885; exhibitions on regional collections, festivities, music, coins, arts and crafts, modern non-western art; ethnological and archaeological collections from Indonesia, realm of Islam, Asia, Africa, America and Oceania; numismatic collection; Dir Drs H. REEDIJK; publ. *Jaarverslag*.

's-Hertogenbosch

Noordbrabants Museum: Verwersstraat 41, POB 1004, 5200 BA 's-Hertogenbosch; tel. (73) 6877877; f. 1837; North Brabant prehistorical, historical and folklore collections, paintings, sculpture, metalwork, prints, coins, etc.; Dir Drs M. M. A. VAN BOVEN; publ. *Noordbrabants Museum Nieuws* (quarterly).

The Hague

Haags Gemeentemuseum: Stadhouderslaan 41, 2517 HV The Hague; tel. (70) 3381111; fax (70) 3557360; f. 1862; Modern Art (19th- and 20th-century); Decorative Arts (ceramics, glass, silver, furniture) and 20th-century design; costumes and fashion from 1750 to the present; musical instruments from 15th century to the present; art and music library; Dir Dr J. L. LOCHER (acting).

Koninklijk Kabinet van Schilderijen Mauritshuis (Royal Picture Gallery): Korte Vijverberg 8, 2513 AB The Hague; tel. (70) 3023456; fax (70) 3653819; opened to public as museum 1822; 15th, 16th and 17th century Dutch and Flemish masters (Rembrandt, Vermeer, Hals, Rubens, Ruisdael, Ter Borch, Van Dyck, Holbein, R. v.d. Weyden); Dir F. J. DUPARC; publs catalogues, illustrated guide books, etc. and Annual Report.

Museon: Stadhouderslaan 41, 2517 HV The Hague; tel. (70) 3381338; fax (70) 3541820; f. 1904; astronomy and geology, biology and ecology, history and archaeology, geography and ethnology, science and technology; library; Dir B. MOLSBERGEN.

Museum Mesdag te 's-Gravenhage: Laan van Meerdervoort 7F, The Hague; tel. (70) 3621434; fax (70) 3614026; f. 1903; Dutch pictures 1860–1920; French pictures of the Barbizon school; Oriental objects; Dir J. LEIGHTON; publs *Annual Report*, *Museum Mesdag Nederlandse 19e eeuwse Schilderijen*, *Catalogue de l'école française XIX siècle*.

Museum van het Boek – Museum Meermanno-Westreenianum: Prinsessegracht 30, 2514 AP The Hague; tel. (70) 3462700; f. 1848; medieval MSS, incunabula; modern typography, book plates; Curator Dr J. A. BRANDENBARG.

Nederlandse PTT Museum (Netherlands Post and Telecommunications Museum): Zeestraat 82, The Hague; tel. (70) 330-7500; fax (70) 360-8926; f. 1929; objects and documents, etc., concerning the history and working of the services of posts, telegraphs and telephones in the Netherlands; international stamp gallery; library of 20,000 vols; Dir Drs B. KOEVOETS; publs annual reports, illustrated guide.

Utrecht

Centraal Museum Utrecht: Agnietenstraat 1, Utrecht; tel. (30) 2362362; fax (30) 2332006; f. 1921; paintings and sculpture of Utrecht School, Utrecht Caravaggisti; doll's house, 12th-century Utrecht ship, applied art and design; period rooms from the Middle Ages and 17th, 18th, 19th and 20th centuries; special exhibitions; Dir SJAREL EX; publs exhibition and collection catalogues.

Veere

Museum 'De Schotse Huizen': Kaai 25–27, 4351 AA Veere; tel. (1181) 1744; Chinese and Japanese ceramics; prints, national costumes, furniture, ships' models; sited in 16th-century merchants' houses; special exhibitions of plastic arts.

Museum 'De Vierschaar': Markt 5, POB 5, 4350 AA Veere; tel. (1181) 1951; f. 1881; tribunal, council-chamber and exhibition rooms; old standards and flags; pictures; golden cup of Maximilian from Burgundy (1546); memorabilia from the house of Oranje-Nassau; Dir P. BLOM.

Venlo

Limburgs Museum: Goltziusstraat 21, 5911 AS Venlo; tel. (77) 3522112; fax (77) 3548396; f. 1967; prehistory, Roman and medieval collection, history of Limburg, art and applied art; coins and medals; Dir J. M. W. C. SCHATORJÉ; the museum was expected to be closed to the public until June 2000.

Vlissingen

Stedelijk Museum te Vlissingen: Bellamypark 21, 4381 CG Vlissingen; f. 1890; maritime collection (pilotage, lighthouses, sea archaeology, fishery); local history (souvenirs of Admiral de Ruyter, paintings, ceramics, wood carvings, engravings, tiles, coins and medals); library of 700 vols; Curator W. WEBER.

Wageningen

Museum Historische Landbouwtechniek (Museum for the History of Agricultural Engineering): Droevendaalsesteeg 50, 6708 PB Wageningen; tel. (8370) 15774; f. 1980; library of 500,000 vols; Dir J. W. VAN BRAKEL.

Universities

UNIVERSITEIT VAN AMSTERDAM (University of Amsterdam)

Spui 21, 1012 WX Amsterdam
Telephone: (20) 525-9111
Telex: 16526
Fax: (20) 525-2136
Founded 1632
State university
Language of instruction: Dutch
Academic year: September to July
Chairman of the Board of Trustees: Drs C. G. G. SPAAN
President: Drs J. K. M. GEVERS
Vice-President: Dr S. J. NOORDA
Rector Magnificus: Prof. Dr J. J. M. FRANSE
Secretary General: Drs R. H. T. BLEIJERVELD
Librarian: Drs A. J. H. A. VERHAGEN
Library: see Libraries
Number of teachers: 550
Number of students: 24,000
Publications: *Gids van de Universiteit van Amsterdam* (1 a year), *Athenaeum Illustre* (4 a year).

DEANS

Faculty of Law: Prof. Dr J. W. ZWEMMER
Faculty of Medicine: Prof. Dr N. A. M. URBANUS
Faculty of Dentistry: Prof. Dr J. R. BAUSCH
Faculty of Mathematics, Computer Science, Physics and Astronomy: Prof. Dr K. J. F. GAEMERS
Faculty of Chemistry: Prof. Dr K. VRIEZE
Faculty of Biology: Prof. Dr A. W. SCHRAM
Faculty of Humanities: Prof. Dr K. VAN DER TOORN
Faculty of Economics and Econometrics: Prof. Dr J. VAN DER GAAG
Faculty of Social Sciences: (vacant)
Faculty of Psychology: Prof. Dr W. T. A. M. EVERAERD
Faculty of Educational Science: Prof. Dr J. DRONKERS
Faculty of Environmental Sciences: Prof. Dr S. MUSTERD

VRIJE UNIVERSITEIT, AMSTERDAM (Free University, Amsterdam)

De Boelelaan 1105, 1081 HV Amsterdam
Telephone: (20) 4447777
Fax: (20) 4445300
Founded 1880
Language of instruction: Dutch
Academic year: September to September
Rector Magnificus: Prof. Dr T. SMINIA
Co-Rectors: Prof. Dr F. K. DE GRAAF, Prof. A. SVETEMAN
Registrar: Drs D. M. SCHUT
Library: see Libraries
Number of teachers: 1,400
Number of students: 14,000

DEANS

Faculty of Theology: Prof. Dr H. M. VROOM
Faculty of Law: Prof. A. SOETEMAN
Faculty of Medicine: Prof. Dr E. A. VAN DER VEEN
Faculty of Dentistry: Prof. Dr J. R. BAUSCH
Faculty of Mathematics and Computer Sciences: Prof. Dr R. P. VAN DE RIET
Faculty of Physics and Astronomy: Prof. Dr D. LENSTRA
Faculty of Chemistry: Prof. Dr N. P. E. VERMEULEN
Faculty of Biology: Prof. Dr F. K. DE GRAAF
Faculty of Earth Sciences: Prof. Dr W. ROELEVELD
Faculty of Arts: Prof. Dr H. D. MEIJERING
Faculty of Cultural and Social Sciences: Prof. Dr D. T. H. KUIPER
Faculty of Economics, Business Administration and Econometrics: Prof. Dr L. F. VAN MUISWINKEL
Faculty of Psychology and Education: Prof. Dr A. F. SANDERS
Faculty of Philosophy: Prof. Dr W. R. DE JONG
Faculty of Human Movement Sciences: Prof. Dr A. P. HOLLANDER

ATTACHED INSTITUTES

Institute for Teaching and Educational Practice: Dir Drs C. DE RAADT.

Institute for Environmental Studies: Dir Dr Ir P. VELLINGA.

TECHNISCHE UNIVERSITEIT DELFT (Delft University of Technology)

Julianalaan 134, POB 5, 2600 AA Delft
Telephone: (15) 2789111
Fax: (15) 2786522
Founded 1842
State control
Language of instruction: Dutch
Academic year: September to July
President: Dr N. DE VOOGD
Rector Magnificus: Prof. Ir K. F. WAKKER
Vice-President (Research): Prof. Dr Ir A. J. BERKHOUT
Registrar: J. M. BRONNEMAN
Librarian: Dr L. J. M. WAAIJERS
Library of *c.* 550,000 vols
Number of teachers: 190 full-time professors
Number of students: 13,000
Publications: *Studiegids, Statistisch Jaarboek, Delta, Delft Integraal, Delft Outlook, Quarterly Progress Report, Jaarverslag, Wetenschappelijk Verslag.*

DEANS

Faculty of Aerospace Engineering: Prof. Dr Ir. TH. DE JONG
Faculty of Architecture: Prof. C. G. DAM
Faculty of Information Technology and Systems: Prof. Dr Ir E. BACKER
Faculty of Applied Sciences: Prof. Ir. K. C. A. M. LUYBEN
Faculty of Civil Engineering and Geosciences: Prof. Ir. H. J. OVERBEEK
Faculty of Design, Engineering and Production: Prof. Dr J. M. DIRKEN
Faculty of Technology, Policy and Management: Prof. Dr P. J. IDENBURG

TECHNISCHE UNIVERSITEIT EINDHOVEN (Eindhoven University of Technology)

Den Dolech 2, Postbus 513, 5600 MB Eindhoven
Telephone: (40) 2479111
Telex: 51163
Fax: (40) 2475187
Founded 1956
State control
Language of instruction: Dutch
Academic year: September to August
Chairman of the Executive Board: Dr Ir. H. G. J. DE WILT
Secretary of the University: Ir. H. P. J. M. ROUMEN
Rector Magnificus: Prof. Dr M. REM
Chairman of the University Council: Dr Ir. E. G. F. VAN WINKEL
Librarian: Drs C. T. J. KLIJS
Number of teachers: 225 professors
Number of students: 5,369
Publications: *Jaarverslag, Studiegids, Matrix.*

DEANS

Faculty of Mathematics and Computing Science: Prof. Dr Ir. J. C. M. BAETEN
Faculty of Technology Management: Prof. Dr W. J. M. VAN GELDER
Faculty of Applied Physics: Prof. Dr W. G. M. DE JONGE
Faculty of Mechanical Engineering: Prof. Dr Ir. M. J. W. SCHOUTEN
Faculty of Electrical Engineering: Prof. Dr Ir. W. M. G. VAN BOKHOVEN
Faculty of Chemical Engineering: Prof. Dr R. METSELAAR
Faculty of Architecture and Construction: Prof. Dr Ir. J. G. M. KERSTENS

ATTACHED INSTITUTES

IPO, Centre for Research on User–System Interaction: Dir Prof. Dr TH. M. A. BEMELMANS.

Stan Ackermans Institute, Centre for Technological Design: Dir Prof. Dr J. H. VAN LINT.

Euler Institute for Discrete Mathematics and its Applications: Man. Prof. Dr Ir. H. C. A. VAN TILBORG.

Netherlands Institute for Catalysis Research: Man. Prof. Dr R. A. VAN SANTEN.

Institute for Programming and Algorithmic Science: Man. Prof. Dr J. C. M. BAETEN.

Polymers PTN: Dir Prof. Dr P. J. LEMSTRA.

Communication Technology – Basic Research and its Applications (COBRA): Prof. Dr J. H. WOLTER.

Stevin Centre for Computational and Experimental Engineering: Dir Prof. Dr Ir. D. H. VAN CAMPEN.

Institute for Business Engineering and Technology Application: Dir Prof. Dr Ir. J. W. M. BERTRAND.

Centre for Plasma Physics and Radiation Technology: Dir Prof. Dr F. W. SLUYTER.

J. F. Schouten Institute for User–System Interaction Research: Dir Prof. Dr A. J. M. HOUTSMA.

Engineering Mechanics Institute: Dir Prof. Dr Ir. D. H. VAN CAMPEN.

UNIVERSITEIT TWENTE (University of Twente)

POB 217, Enschede
Telephone: 899111
Telex: 44200
Founded 1961
Rector: Prof. Dr TH. F. A. VAN VUGHT
Board of Governors: Prof. Dr Ir B. P. TH. VELTMAN, Dr Ir F. SCHUTTE
Librarian: Dr G. A. J. S. VAN MARLE
Number of students: 7,000

CHAIRMEN OF DEPARTMENTS

Mechanical Engineering: Prof. Ir H. GROOTENBOER
Electrical Engineering: Prof. Dr Ir J. VAN AMERONGEN
Chemical Technology: Prof. Dr W. E. VAN DER LINDEN
Technical Physics: Prof. Dr J. GREVE
Applied Mathematics: Prof. Dr A. BAGCHI

Social Sciences and Philosophy: Prof. Dr E. SEYDEL
Business Administration: Prof. Dr Ir J. J. KRABBENDAM
Public Administration: Prof. H. M. DE JONG
Applied Educational Science: Prof. Dr J. M. PIETERS
Informatics: Prof. Dr H. BRINKSMA

ATTACHED CENTRE

Center for Higher Education Policy Studies: POB 217, 7500 AE Enschede; tel. 893263; fax 356695; Man. Dir Dr P. MAASSEN.

RIJKSUNIVERSITEIT GRONINGEN (University of Groningen)

Broerstraat 5, POB 72, 9700 AB Groningen
Telephone: (50) 3639111
Fax: (50) 3635380

Founded 1614
State control
Language of instruction: Dutch
Academic year: September to September

President: Prof. Dr E. BLEUMINK
Secretary: H. J. D. BRUINS
Rector Magnificus: Prof. Dr D. F. J. BOSSCHER
Librarian: Dr A. C. KLUGKIST

Number of teachers: 2,200
Number of students: 18,500

Publications: *Jaarverslag*, *Universiteitskrant* (weekly), *Broerstraat 5* (3 a year), *Der Clerke Cronike*.

DEANS

Faculty of Theology: Prof. Dr J. N. BREMMER
Faculty of Law: Prof. L. TIMMERMAN
Faculty of Medicine: Prof. Dr H. J. HUISJES
Faculty of Science: Prof. Dr D. WIERSMA
Faculty of Arts: Prof. Dr H. HERMANS
Faculty of Economics: Prof. Dr J. L. BOUMA
Faculty of Social Sciences: Prof. Dr J. PESCHAR
Faculty of Philosophy: Prof. Dr J. W. DE BEUS
Faculty of Geography and Prehistory: Prof. Dr P. P. P. HUIGEN
Faculty of Organization and Management: Prof. Dr J. WYNGAARD

OPEN UNIVERSITEIT

Postbus 2960, 6401 DL Heerlen
Telephone: (45) 762222
Telex: 56559
Fax: 711486

Founded 1984; university level courses or higher vocational training in seven fields of study; distance education courses consist of one or two modules/units of 100 hours of study; 18 study centres

State control
Language of instruction: Dutch

Executive Board: Drs B. DE HAAN (Pres.), Drs C. W. VAN SEVENTER, Drs J. A. J. KROSSE
Rector: Prof. Dr Ir. W. H. DE JEU
Pro-Rector: Prof. Dr J. F. M. CLAESSEN
Registrar: (vacant)
Librarian: W. G. M. VERHOEVEN

Library of 20,000 vols
Number of teachers: 275
Number of students: 50,000

Publication: *Modulair*.

DEANS

Faculty of Business and Public Administration: Drs J. A. M. BAAK
Faculty of Cultural Studies: Prof. Dr R. ROLF
Faculty of Economics: Prof. Dr H. W. G. M. PEER
Faculty of Law: Prof. Mr J. M. REIJNTJES
Faculty of Physics: Prof. Dr Ir. W. H. DE JEU
Faculty of Social Science: Prof. Dr J. F. M. CLAESSEN
Faculty of Technology: Prof. Dr K. L. BOON

PROFESSORS

Faculty of Business Administration:
- KORSTEN, A. F. A.
- STORM, P. M.

Faculty of Cultural Studies:
- BERGH, H. VAN DEN
- DUSSEN, W. J. VAN DER
- ROLF, R.

Faculty of Economics:
- BEEK, A.
- GROOT, T. L. C. M.
- HERST, A. C. C.
- JEPMA, C. J.
- KEUS, J.
- PEER, H. W. G. M.
- VERHAEGEN, P. H. A. M.

Faculty of Law:
- BOON, P. J.
- DORRESTEIJN, A. F. M.
- NICOLAI, P.
- REIJNTJES, J. M.
- SLOOT, B.

Faculty of Physics:
- DAM, M. C. E. VAN
- GLASBERGEN, P.
- JEU, W. H. DE
- VRIES, J. DE

Faculty of Social Science:
- CLAESSEN, J. F. M.
- GRUMBKOW, J. VON
- HOOF, J. J. B. M. VAN
- KEMENADE, J. VAN

Faculty of Technology:
- BAKKERS, A. W. P.
- BOON, K. L.
- MULDER, F.
- STEELS, L. L. L.
- SWIERSTRA, S. D.
- TILBORG, H. C. A. VAN

Centre for Educational Technology:
- WOLF, H. C. DE

RIJKSUNIVERSITEIT LEIDEN (Leiden University)

Stationsweg 46, POB 9500, 2399 RA Leiden
Telephone: (71) 5272727
Fax: (71) 5273118

Founded 1575
State control
Language of instruction: Dutch
Academic year: September to July

President: Drs L. E. H. VREDEVOOGD
Secretary: Ir W. C. L. H. M. VAN DEN BERG
Rector: Prof. Dr W. A. WAGENAAR
Librarian: Drs P. W. J. L. GERRETSEN

Number of teachers: 1,625
Number of students: 15,262

DEANS

Faculty of Theology: Prof. Dr E. G. E. VAN DER WALL
Faculty of Law: Prof. H. FRANKEN
Faculty of Medicine: Prof. Dr B. J. VERMEER
Faculty of Science: Prof. Dr K. R. LIBBENGA
Faculty of Arts: Prof. Dr B. WESTERWEEL
Faculty of Social Science: Prof. Dr R. B. ANDEWEG
Faculty of Philosophy: Prof. Dr D. T. RUNIA
Faculty of Archaeology: Prof. Dr L. P. LOUWE KOOIJMANS

AFFILIATED INSTITUTE

Instituut voor Internationale Studien: POB 9555, 2333 AK Leiden; tel. 5273411; fax 5273619; f. 1970; promotes co-operation between university depts in teaching and research on contemporary int. affairs; Dir Dr PH. P. EVERTS.

RIJKSUNIVERSITEIT LIMBURG (University of Limburg)

POB 616, 6200 MD Maastricht
Telephone: (43) 3882222
Fax: (43) 3252195

Founded 1976
State control
Language of instruction: Dutch
Academic year: September to June

Chairman of Board of Trustees: Dr K. L. L. M. DITTRICH
Rector: Prof. Dr A. C. NIEUWENHUIJZEN KRUSEMAN
Chairman of the University Board: Dr A. DE GOEIJ
Administrative Director: Ir H. E. FEKKERS
Librarian: J. D. GILBERT

Library of 500,000 vols, 5,000 current periodicals
Number of students: 9,005

DEANS

Faculty of Medicine: Prof. Dr A. C. NIEUWENHUIJZEN KRUSEMAN
Faculty of Health Sciences: Prof Dr J. A. M. MAARSE
Faculty of Law: Prof. C. A. SCHWARZ, Prof. G. MOLS
Faculty of Economics: Prof. Dr A. VAN WITTELOOSTUIJN
Faculty of Cultural Studies: Prof. Dr Ir W. E. BIJKER
Faculty of General Sciences: Prof. Dr. K. L. BOON
Faculty of Psychology: Prof. Dr A. J. BOON, Prof. Dr H. PHILIPSEN

KATHOLIEKE UNIVERSITEIT NIJMEGEN (University of Nijmegen)

Comeniuslaan 4, POB 9102, 6500 HC Nijmegen
Telephone: (24) 3616161
Telex: 48211
Fax: (24) 3564646

Founded 1923
Private control
Languages of instruction: Dutch, English
Academic year: September to July

Trustees: STICHTING KATHOLIEKE UNIVERSITEIT
Chairman of the University Board: Dr TH. H. J. STOELINGA
Rector Magnificus: Prof Dr T. J. M. VAN ELS
Secretary-General: Dr M. KAEKEBEKE
Librarian: Dr A. H. LAEVEN

Number of teachers: 2,019
Number of students: 14,000

Publications: *K. U. Nieuws* (weekly), *K. U. Zien* (quarterly).

DEANS

Faculty of Theology: Prof. Dr J. A. VAN DER VEN
Faculty of Arts: Prof. Dr A. M. HAGEN
Faculty of Law: Prof. P. J. P. TAK
Faculty of Medical Sciences: Prof. Dr G. P. VOOIJS
Faculty of Natural Sciences: Prof. Dr Ir G. D. VOGELS
Faculty of Mathematics and Informatics: Prof. Dr J. H. M. STEENBRINK
Faculty of Social Sciences: Prof. Dr J. R. M. GERRIS
Faculty of Policy Sciences: Prof. Dr J. M. MASTOP
Faculty of Philosophy: Prof. Dr L. C. M. HEYDE

ATTACHED INSTITUTES

Dienst Instituut voor Toegepaste sociale wetenschappen: Toernooiveld 5, 6525 ED Nijmegen; applied social sciences; Dir Drs A. J. MENS.

Universitair Instituut voor de Lerarenopleiding: Erasmusplein 1, 6525 HT Nijmegen; university teacher training; Dir Dr E. V. SCHALKWIJK.

Titus Brandsma Institute: Erasmusplein 1, 6525 HT Nijmegen; bibliography and documentation of the study of religious experience and spiritual life; Dir Prof. Dr H. H. BLOMMESTIJN.

Katholiek Documentatiecentrum: Erasmuslaan 36, POB 9100, 6500 HA Nijmegen; documentation of Dutch catholicism; Dir Dr J. H. ROES.

Nijmeegs Instituut voor Cognitie en Informatie: Montessorilaan 3, POB 9104, 6500 HE Nijmegen; institute for cognition and information; Dir Prof. Dr E. E. C. I. ROSKAM.

Thomas More Academie: Thomas van Aquinostraat 5, POB 9044, 6500 KD Nijmegen; Dir Drs C. R. J. GOVAART.

Institute for Cellular Signalling: Toernooiveld 1, POB 9010, 6500 GL Nijmegen; Prof. Dr J. J. H. H. M. DE PONT.

Katholiek Studiecentrum: Erasmuslaan 36, POB 9100, 6500 HA Nijmegen; study of topics relating to the Christian inspiration; Dir Drs G. P. A. DIERICK.

Instituut voor Onderwijskundige Dienstverlening: Erasmusplein 1, 6525 HT Nijmegen; research and development in higher education; Dir Dr J. M. H. M. WILLEMS.

Max Planck Institut für Psycholinguistik: Wundtlaan 1, 6525 XD Nijmegen; Dir Prof. Dr W. J. M. LEVELT.

Research Instituut voor Materialen: Toernooiveld 1, POB 9010, 6500GL Nijmegen; materials research; Dir Dr TH. H. M. RASING.

Nijmegen SON Research Instituut: Toernooiveld 1, POB 9010, 6500 GL Nijmegen; Dir Prof. Dr C. W. HILBERS.

ERASMUS UNIVERSITEIT ROTTERDAM

Burgemeester Oudlaan 50, POB 1738, 3000 DR Rotterdam

Telephone: (10) 4081111

Founded 1973 by amalgamation of the Nederlandse Economische Hogeschool and the Medische Faculteit Rotterdam.

Academic year: September to July

President of Board of Governors: Dr H. J. VAN DER MOLEN

Rector: Prof. Dr P. W. C. AKKERMANS

Secretary: H. P. PATOIR

Librarian: Dr P. E. L. J. SOETAERT

Number of students: 15,000

Publications: *Calendar*, *Annual Report*, *Erasmus Magazine* (fortnightly).

DEANS

Faculty of Economics: Prof. Dr H. BART
Faculty of Law: Prof. H. DE DOELDER
Faculty of Medicine: Prof. Dr C. D. A. VERWOERD
Faculty of Philosophy: Prof. Dr J. DE MUL
Subfaculty of Social–Cultural Sciences: Prof. Dr P. B. LEHNING
Subfaculty of Social History: Prof. Dr A. M. BEVERS
Faculty of Business Administration: Prof. Dr P. H. A. M. VERHAEGEN

KATHOLIEKE UNIVERSITEIT BRABANT (Tilburg University)

Warandelaan 2, POB 90153, 5000 LE Tilburg
Telephone: (13) 4669111
Telex: 52426
Fax: (13) 4663019
Founded 1927
State control
Academic year: September to August
Chancellor and Rector: Prof. Dr L. F. W. DE KLERK
Chief Administrative Officer: Drs J. J. A. VAN DE RIET
Librarian: Mr H. GELEIJNSE
Number of teachers: 450
Number of students: 10,000
Publication: *UNIVERS* (weekly).

DEANS

Faculty of Economics and Business Administration: Prof. Dr P. A. NAERT
Faculty of Social and Behavioural Sciences: Prof. Dr G. L. VAN HECK
Faculty of Law: Prof. P. C. GILHUIS
Faculty of Philosophy: Prof. Dr P. G. COBBEN
Faculty of Theology: Prof. Dr B. H. VEDDER
Faculty of Arts: Prof. H. C. BUNT

RESEARCH CENTRES

CentER, Centre for Economic Research: Dir Prof. Dr Ir A. KAPTEYN.

IVA, Institute for Applied Social Research: Dir Prof. Dr P. ESTER.

EIT, Tilburg Economic Institute: Dir Prof. Dr Ir. A. KAPTEYN.

IVO, Development Research Institute: Dir Drs B. H. EVERS.

TIAS, Tilburg Institute of Advanced Studies: Dir Prof. Dr Ir. P. A. NAERT.

WORC, Work and Organization Research Centre: Dir Prof. Dr A. SORGE.

Schoordijk Institute: Comparative Law and Jurisprudence; Dir Prof. P. C. M. VAN SETERS.

CLS, Centre for Language Studies: Dir Prof. Dr R. VAN HOUT.

UNIVERSITEIT UTRECHT (Utrecht University)

Heidelberglaan 8, POB 80125, 3508 TC Utrecht
Telephone: (30) 2539111
Telex: 40087
Fax: (30) 2533388
Founded 1636
Academic year: September to July
President: Drs J. G. F. VELDHUIS
Rector Magnificus: Prof. Dr H. O. UOORMA
President of the University Council: C. T. M. KUYPERS-GROENSMIT
University Secretary: Drs W. KARDUX
University Librarian: Drs J. S. M. SAVENIJE (acting)
Number of teachers: 3,728
Number of students: 25,125
Publications: *Jaarverslag*, *Gids*, *Universiteitsblad* (weekly).

DEANS

Faculty of Theology: Prof. Dr H. J. TIELEMAN
Faculty of Law: Prof. Dr A. H. A. SOONS
Faculty of Medicine: Prof. Dr W. H. GISPEN
Faculty of Mathematics and Informatics: Prof. Dr J. VAN LEEUWEN
Faculty of Physics and Astronomy: Prof. Dr J. E. J. M. VAN HIMBERGEN
Faculty of Chemistry: Prof. Dr G. VAN KOTEN
Faculty of Earth Sciences: Prof. Dr R. K. SNIEDER
Faculty of Biology: (vacant)
Faculty of Pharmacy: Prof. Dr A. BULT
Faculty of Arts: Prof. Dr M. A. SCHENKEVELD-VAN DER DUSSEN
Faculty of Veterinary Medicine: Prof. Dr H. W. DE VRIES
Faculty of Social Sciences: Prof. Dr W. ZWANENBURG
Faculty of Philosophy: Prof. Dr J. MANSFELD
Faculty of Geographical Sciences: Prof. Dr E. A. KOSTER

PROFESSORS

Faculty of Theology:

ANDREE, T. G. I. M., Ideological Upbringing and Formation in a Multi-religious context
BECKING, B. E. H. J., Old Testament
BELZEN, J. A. VAN, Psychology of Religion
BOEFT, J. DEN, Religious History of Hellenism
BRÜMMER, V., Philosophy of Religion
HEEGER, F. R., Ethics
HORST, P. W. VAN DER, New Testament
HOUTEPEN, A. W. P., Ecumenics
IMMINK, F. G., Practical Theology
JONGENEEL, J. A. B., Missiology
KLOPPENBORG, M. A. G. T., History of Religions and Comparative Religious Studies
LEEUWEN, TH. M. VAN, Science of the Old Testament and History of Israelite Religion
MAAS, T. A., Relationships between Christianity and Modern Culture
MUIS, J., Dogmatics
OTTEN, W., Church History
REUVER, A. DE, Education in Calvinist Theology
SCHROTEN, E., Christian Ethics
TIELEMAN, H. J., Sociology of Religions
VRIES, O. H. DE, History and Dogmas of the Baptism

Faculty of Law:

ANDRIESSEN, F. H. J. J., European Integration
BACKES, CH. W., Environmental Law
BAEHR, P. R., Human Rights
BAHLMAN, J. P., Business Economics
BERGE, J. B. J. M. TEN, Administrative Law
BERGH, R. VAN DEN, Economics of Law
BOELE-WOELKI, K. S. R. D., International and Comparative Private Law
BOON, D., Animals and Law
BOVENKERK, F., Criminology
BOVENS, M. A. P., Philosophy of Law
BRANTS, C. H., Penal Law and Law of Criminal Procedure
BRINKHOFF, J. J., Industrial Property
BRUINSMA, J. F., Sociology of Law
BUUREN, P. J. J. VAN, Governmental Law
CURTIN, D. M., Law of International Organizations
DALHUISEN, J. H., International Commercial Law
GROSHEIDE, F. W., Private Law
HALL, A. VAN, Law of Public Water and Water Boards
HARTKAMP, A. S., Private Law, particularly Civil Law
HEYMAN, H. W., Notarial Law
HOL, A. M., Theory of Law
HONDIUS, E. H., Civil Law
HOOF, G. J. H. VAN, Social Economic Law
HUIZEN, P. H. J. G. VAN, Commercial Traffic Law
IDENBURG, PH. A., Management Sciences
IN 'T VELD, R. I., Management of Public Government
JASPERS, A. PH. C. M., Social Law
KABEL, J. J. C., Mass Media Law
KELK, C., Penitentiary Law
KOERS, A. W., International Law
KUMMELING, H. R. B. M., Constitutional and Administrative Law
KWIATKOWSKA, B., International Maritime Law

MEIJKNECHT, P. A. M., Civil Law
MENS, K. L. H. VAN, Fiscal Law
MOOIJ, A. W. M., Forensic Psychiatry
MORTELMANS, K. J. M., Social Economic Law
NIEUWENBURG, C. K. F., Political Economy
REENEN, P. VAN, Causes of Violations of Human Rights
ROSCAM ABBING, H. D. C., Health Law
SCHILFGAARDE, P., Business Law
SIEGERS, J. J., Economics
SOONS, A. H. A., International Law
SPRUIT, J. E., History of Roman Law
STILLE, A. L. G. A., Notarial Law
SWART, A. H. J., Penitentiary Law
VERVAELE, J. A. E., Maintenance of Law and Order
VREE, J. K. DE, International and Political Relations

Faculty of Medicine:

AKKERMANS, L. M. A., Gastrointestinal Physiology
BÄR, P. R., Experimental Neurology
BATTERMAN, J. J., Radiotherapy
BAX, N. M. A., Paediatric Surgery
BEEMER, F. A., Clinical Genetics
BEL, F. VAN, Neonatology
BERGE HENEGOUWEN, G. P. VAN, Gastroenterology
BERGER, R., Chemistry of Hereditary Metabolic Diseases
BERNARDS, R. A., Molecular Carcinogenesis
BIJLSMA, J. W. J., Rheumatology
BLIJHAM, G. H., Clinical Medicine
BORST, C., Experimental Cardiology
BOS, J. L., Physiological Chemistry
BOSMAN, F., Dental Physics
BOUMA, B. N., Biochemistry of Haemostasis
BREDEE, J. J., Cardio-pulmonic Surgery
BRONSWIJK, J. E. M. H. VAN, Biological Agents in Domestic Hygiene
BRUYNZEEL-KOOMEN, C. A. F. M., Dermatology-Allergology
BUITELAAR, I. K., Biopsychosocial Determinants in Human Behaviour
BURBACH, J. P. H., Molecular Biology of Neuropeptides
CAPEL, P. J. A., Experimental Immunology
CLEVERS, J. C., Clinical Immunology
COHEN-KETTENIS, P. T., Gender Development and Child and Youth Psychopathology
DEJONCKERE, P. H., Speech Therapy and Phoniatrics
DONK, J. A. W. M. VAN DER, Cell Biology
DUIJNSTEE, M. S. H., Innovations in Home Care
DUURSMA, S. A., Clinical Medicine
EIKELBOOM, B. C., Vascular and Transplant Surgery
ENGELAND, H. VAN, Psychiatry of Children
ERKELENS, D. W., Clinical Medicine
FELDBERG, M. A. M., Radiodiagnostics
GAST, G. C. DE, Haematology
GEUZE, J. J., Cytology
GIJN, J. VAN, Neurology
GISPEN, W. H., Molecular Pharmacology and Neuro-Pharmacology
GOOSZEN, H. G., Surgery
GROBBEE, D. E., Clinical Epidemiology
GRYPDONCLE, M. H. F., Nursing Science
HAUER, R. N. W., Clinical Electrophysiology
HEEREN, TH. J., Psychogeriatrics
HEINTZ, A. P. M., Oncological Gynaecology
HELDERS, P. J. M., Physiotherapy
HENGEVELD, M. W., Sexology
HILLEN, B., Functional Anatomy
HORDIJK, G. J., Oto-rhino-laryngology
HORN, G. H. M. M. TEN, Psychiatric Care-Management
HUFFELEN, A. C. VAN, Clinical Neurophysiology
HUIZING, E. H., Oto-rhino-laryngology
JONGSMA, H. J., Medical Physiology
KAHN, R. S., Clinical and Biological Psychiatry
KATER, L., Clinical Immunopathology
KNAPE, J. TH. A., Anaesthesiology
KOERSELMAN, G. F., Psychotherapy
KON, M., Plastic and Reconstructive Surgery
KOOMANS, H. A., Nephrology
LAMMERS, J. W. J., Pulmonary Diseases
LONDEN, J. VAN, General Health Care
MALI, W. P. TH. M., Radiodiagnostics
MARX, J. J. M., General Internal Medicine
MOSTERD, W. L., Clinical Sports Medicine
NIEUWENHUIZEN, O. VAN, Paediatric Neurology in relation to functional morphology
NORREN, D. VAN, Ophthalmological Physics
OKKEN, A., Paediatrics
PEARSON, P. L., Medical Molecular Genetics
PETERS, A. C. B., Paediatric Neurology
PETERS, P. W. J., Teratology
POLL-THE, B. E., Clinical Congenital Metabolic Diseases
PUTTER, C. DE, Special Dental Surgery
REE, J. M. VAN, Psychopharmacology
ROBLES DE MEDINA, E. O., Clinical Cardiology
SANGSTER, B., Health Protection
SAVELKOUL, T. J. F., Toxicology
SCHRIJVERS, A. J. P., General Health Care
SCHULPEN, T. W. J., Social Paediatrics
SITSEN, J. M. A., Clinical Pharmacology
SIXMA, J. J., Haematology
SLOOTWEG, P. J., Oral Pathology
SMOORENBURG, G. F., Experimental Audiology
SMOUT, A. J. P. M., Pathophysiology
STAAL, G. E. J., Enzymology
STILMA, J. S., Ophthalmology
STROUS, G. J. A. M., Cellular Biology
SUSSENBACH, J. S., Molecular Biology
THIJSSEN, J. J. H., Clinical Chemistry
TREFFERS, W. F., Ophthalmology
TULLEKEN, C. A. F., Neurosurgery
TWEEL, J. G. VAN DEN, Pathology
VEELEN, C. W. M. VAN, Functional Neurosurgery
VELDE, E. R. TE, Desirable Fertility
VELDMAN, J. E., Experimental Otology and Otoimmunology
VERBOUT, A. J., Orthopaedic Aspects of Spinal and Neuromuscular Disorders
VERHEIJ, T. J. M., Family Medicine
VERHOEF, J., Clinical Microbiology
VERSTEEG, D. H. G., Medical Pharmacology
VIERGEVER, M. A., Image-processing in Medicine
VISSER, G. H. A., Obstetrics
VLIET, P. C. VAN DER, Physical Chemistry
VLOTEN, W. A. VAN, Dermatology
VOORN, TH. B., General Practice
VROONHOVEN, TH. J. M. V. VAN, General Surgery
WAES, P. F. G. M. VAN, Röntgen Diagnostics
WAL, H. J. C. M. VAN DE, Cardiopulmonic Surgery of Infants and Children
WERKEN, CHR. VAN DER, Acute Surgery
WESTENBERG, H. G. M., Neurochemical Aspects of Psychiatry
WILDT, D. J. DE, Medical Pharmacology
WIMERSMA GREIDANUS, TJ. B. VAN, Neuroendocrinology
WINKEL, J. G. J. VAN DER, Immunotherapy
WINNUBST, J. A. M., Psychology of Health and Illness
WOKKE, J. H. J., Neurology focusing on Neuromuscular Diseases
WOLTERS, W. H. G., Paediatric Psychology
ZEGERS, B. J. M., Paediatric Immunology
ZONNEVELD, F. W., Medical Representation Techniques

Faculty of Mathematics and Informatics:

DALEN, D. VAN, Logic and Philosophy of Mathematics
DIEKMANN, O., Applied Mathematics
DUISTERMAAT, J. J., Pure and Applied Mathematics
GILL, R. D., Stochastics
HAZEWINKEL, M., Algebraic Chemistry
LANGE, J. DE, Didactics of Teaching Mathematics and Computer Science
LEEUWEN, J. VAN, Informatics
LOOIJENGA, E. J. N., Pure Mathematics
MARS, J. G. M., Mathematics
MEERTENS, L. T. G., Programming Technology
MEIJER, J. J. CH., Informatics
OORT, F., Mathematics
OVERMARS, M. H., Computer Science
SIERSMA, D., Mathematics
SWIERSTRA, S. D., Informatics
TREFFERS, A., Field-Specific Education
VERHULST, F., Quantitative Analysis of Dynamic Systems
VORST, H. A. VAN DER, Mathematics
ZAGIER, D. B., Pure Mathematics

Faculty of Physics and Astronomy:

ANDRIESSE, C. D., Electricity Supplies
BEIJEREN, H. VAN, Theoretical Physics
BEIJERINCK, H. C. W., Atomic and Interface Physics
BLEEKER, J. A. M., Space Research
BUIJS, A., Experimental Physics
BUILTJES, P. J. H., Chemistry of the Atmosphere
CROWE, A., Medical and Physiological Physics
DIEKS, D. G. B. J., Foundations and Philosophy of the Natural Sciences
DIJKHUIS, J. I., Semiconductor Laser Optics
DRONKERS, J., Physics of Coastal Systems
ERKELENS, C. J., Human Physics
ERNÉ, F. C., Current Issues in Physics
ERNST, M. H. J. J., Theoretical Physics
FEINER, L. F., Theory of Condensed Materials
HABRAKEN, F. H. P. M., Physics Education
HEARN, A. G., Astrophysics
HEIDEMAN, H. G. M., Experimental Physics
HIMBERGEN, J. E. J. M. VAN, Theoretical Physics
HOLTSLAG, A. A. M., Meteorology (Forecasting) Techniques
JANSSEN, G. 'T., Theoretical Physics
HOOFT, T. W. J. M., Theory of Solids
KAMERMANS, R., Experimental Physics and Experimental Nuclear Physics
KOENDERINK, J. J., Human Physics
KUPERUS, M., Astrophysics
LAMERS, H. J. G. L. M., Astronomy
LELIEVELD, J., Atmospheric Chemistry
LEVINE, Y. K., Biophysics
LIJNSE, P. L., Development of Physics Concepts and Methods in Education
LOURENS, W., Physics Informatics
NIEHAUS, A., Experimental Physics
OERLEMANS, J., Dynamics of the Climate
POLMAN, A., Advancement of Atomic and Interface Physics
RUIJGROK, TH. W., Theoretical Physics and Mechanics
RUIJTER, W. P. M. DE, Physical Oceanography
SARIS, F. W., Atomic and Molecular Physics
SCHÜLLER, F. C., Plasma Physics
SCHUURMANS, C. J. E., Meteorology
SINKE, W. C., Physical and Chemical Properties of Thin Layers
SMIT, J., Theoretical High-Energy Physics
TJON, J. A., Theoretical Physics
VERBUNT, F. W. M., High-Energy Astrophysics
VERLINDE, E. P., Theoretical Physics
WEG, W. F. VAN DER, Technical Physics
WIT, B. Q. P. J. DE, Theoretical Physics
WITT HUBERTS, P. K. A. DE, Reactor Physics
WIJN, H. W. DE, Solid State Physics
ZIMMERMAN, J. TH. F., Physical Oceanography

Faculty of Chemistry:

BOSCH, H. VAN DEN, Biochemistry
BRANDSMA, L., Organic Chemistry

DUIJNEVELDT, F. B. VAN, Theoretical Chemistry
EERDEN, J. P. J. M. VAN, Macroscopic Physical Chemistry
EGMOND, M. R., Applied Enzymology
EIJNDHOVEN, J. C. M. VAN, Technological Research of Aspect
FRENKEL, D., Physical Computer Simulation
GEUS, J. W., Inorganic Chemistry
HAAS, G. H. DE, Biophysics
HAVERKAMP, J., Analytical Chemistry
HOLLANDER, J. A., In vivo NMR Spectroscopy
JENNESKENS, L. W., Physical Organic Chemistry
KAMERLING, J. P., Organic Chemistry of Natural Substances
KAPTEIN, R., NMR Spectroscopy
KELLY, J. J., Electrochemistry
KONINGSBERGER, D. C., Inorganic Chemistry
KOTEN, G. VAN, Organic Chemistry
KROON, J., Chemistry
KRUIJF, H. A. M. DE, Toxicology and Society
KRUIJFF, B. DE, Molecular Biology of Biomembranes
LEKKERKERKER, H. N. W., Physical Chemistry
MAAS, J. H. VAN DER, Spectrochemical Analysis
MEIJERINK, A., Chemistry of Solids
PHILIPSE, A. P., Physical Chemistry
TURKENBURG, W. C., Science and Society
VELDINK, G. A., Organic Aspects of Bio-Catalysis
VEN, J. VAN DE, Materials Science
VERHEIJ, H. M., Biochemistry
VLIEGENTHART, J. F. G., Bio-Organic Chemistry
WIRTZ, K. W. A., Biochemistry

Faculty of Earth Sciences:

DAS, H. A., Radioanalysis in Geochemistry
EISMA, D., Marine Sedimentology
JONG, B. M. W. S. DE, Petrology and Experimental Petrology
LEEUW, J. W. DE, Organic Geochemistry
MEULENKAMP, J. E., Stratigraphy and Palaeontology
MONDT, J. C., Exploratory Geophysics
OONK, H. A. J., Thermodynamics
PRIEM, H. N. A., Isotope Geology
SNIEDER, R. K., Seismology
SPIERS, CH. J., Experimental Rock-Deformation
WEIJDEN, C. H. VAN DER, Marine Geochemistry and Hydrochemistry
WHITE, S. H., Structural Geology and Tectonics
WONG, TH. E., Sedimentary Geology of Subsoils in the Netherlands
WORTEL, M. J. R., Tectonophysics

Faculty of Biology:

BIGGELAAR, J. A. M. VAN DEN, Experimental Embryology
BOERSMA, K. TH., Didactics of Biology
DAMME, J. M. M. VAN, Ecological Population Genetics
DURSTON, A. J., Organismal Embryology
GOOS, H. J. TH., Comparative Endocrinology
GRIND, W. A. P. F. L. VAN DE, Comparative Physiology
HOEKSTRA, W. P. M., Microbiology
HOGEWEG, P., Theoretical Biology
HOOFF, J. A. R. A. M. VAN, Comparative Physiology
HORST, D. J. VAN DER, Metabolic Physiology
KOLLÖFFEL, CHR., Botany
LAAT, S. W. DE, Developmental Biology
LAMBERS, J. T., Ecophysiology
LEEUWEN, C. J. VAN, Biological Toxicology (Ecological Risk Assessment)
LOON, L. C. VAN, Phytopathology
MAAS, P. J. M. VAN DER, Plant Taxonomy
NOORDWIJK, A. J. VAN, Population Ecology of Animals
SAYER, J. A., International Aspects of Nature Protection
SEINEN, W., Biological Toxicology
VERKLEIJ, A. J., Electromicroscopy
VERRIPS, C. T., Applied Molecular Biology
VISSCHER, H., Palaeobotany
VOORMA, H. O., Molecular Biology
WEISBEEK, P. J., Molecular Genetics
WERGER, M. J. A., Botanical Ecology

Faculty of Pharmacy:

BAKKER, A., Pharmaceutical Practice
BEIJNEN, J. H., Bio-Analysis (Research in Clinical Medicine)
BULT, A., Pharmaceutical Analysis
CLERCK, F. F. P., Applied Pulmonary and Cardiovascular Pharmacology
CROMMELIN, D. J. A., Biopharmacy
DIJK, H. VAN, Immunology of Phytochemicals
GLERUM, J. H., Clinical Pharmacy
HENNINK, W. E., Pharmaceutical Technology
JANSSEN, L. H. M., Pharmaceutical Chemistry
JONG, J. G. A. M. DE, Management Aspects of Pharmaceutical Practice
LABADIE, R. P., Pharmacognosy
LISKAMP, R. M. J., Molecular Medicinal Chemistry
MAES, R. A. A., Toxicology
NIJKAMP, F. P., Molecular Pharmacology
OLIVIER, B., Applied Pharmacology of the Central Nervous System
PORSIUS, A. J., Pharmacotherapy
RUITER, A., Food Chemistry and Bromatology
THIJSSEN, J. H H., Clinical Chemistry
TOLLENAERE, J. P. A. E., Computational Medicinal Chemistry
VERBATEN, M. N., Human Psychophysiology and Psychopharmacology

Faculty of Arts:

AKKER, W. J. VAN DEN, Modern Dutch Literature
BERG, J. VAN DEN, Home Computerization
BERTENS, J. W., American Literature
BRAIDOTTI, R., Comparative Women's Studies
BUUREN, M. B. VAN, Modern Literature (French)
EDEL, D. R., Celtic Languages
EIJCK, D. J. N. VAN, Logical Aspects of Computational Linguistics
GERRITSEN, W. P., Dutch Medieval Literature
GROOT, R. DE, Music of the Low Countries after 1600
HART, P., Utrecht Studies
HECHT, P. A., History of Visual Arts in Renaissance and Modern Times
HERRLITZ, W., German Language
HOVEN, P. J. VAN DEN, Linguistics
JANSSEN, H. L., Studies of Medieval Castles
JONG, F. DE, Islam Languages and Cultures
JONG, Mrs M. B., Medieval History
KLAMT, J. C. J. A., History of Medieval Art
KLOEK, J. J., Social History of Litrature
LANDSBERGEN, S. P. J., Language and Speech Automation
LASARTE, F. J., Latin-American Studies
MEYER, B. W., Visual Arts during the Renaissance in Italy and the Netherlands and their Underlying Relationship
MIJNHARDT, W. W., Post-Middle Ages History
MOORTGAT, J., Linguistics, Language Informatics
NOOTEBOOM, S. G., Linguistics, in particular Phonetics
OP DE COUL, P. M., History of Music after 1600
ORBÁN, A. P., Vulgar and Medieval Latin
OTTENHEYM, K. A., History of Architecture
POLLMANN, M. M. W., Social Functions of Language Disciplines
PRAK, M. R., Post-Medieval History (Social Relationships)
REULAND, E. J., Linguistics, specifically Syntax
RIGHART, J. A., Post-Medieval History, in particular Internal Political Relations
SANCISI-WEERDENBURG, H. W. A. M., Ancient History and Culture
SCHENKEVELD VAN DER DUSSEN, M. A., Dutch Renaissance Literature
SCHOENMAKERS, H., Theatre Science
SCHWEGMAN, M. J., Women's History
SICCAMA, J. G., History of Security Issues
STUMPEL, J. F. H. J., Iconology and Art Theory
URICCHIO, W., History of Film and Television
VELLEKOOP, C., History of Music before 1600
VERKUIJL, H. J., Dutch Language
VOOGD, P. J. DE, Modern Literature
VOORT, C. M. M. VAN DER
WESTHOFF, G. J., Didactics of Modern Languages
ZANDEN, J. L. VAN, Post-Medieval History (Social Relationships)
ZONNEVELD, W., Linguistics, in particular Phonology, English Linguistics

Faculty of Veterinary Medicine:

BARNEVELD, A., General Surgery and Surgery of Large Domestic Animals
BEYNEN, A. C., Experimental Animals
BREUKINK, H. J., Clinical Veterinary Medicine
COLENBRANDER, B., Fertility
CORNELISSEN, A. W. C. A., Parasitology
DIK, K. J., Radiology
DIJK, J. E. VAN, Pathology of Rare Animals/ Spontaneous Laboratory Animal Pathology
EDEN, W. VAN, Veterinary Immunology
EVERTS, M. F., Veterinary Physiology
FERON, V. J., Biological Toxicology
FINK-GREMMELS-GEHRMANN, J., Pharmacology of Domestic Animals
GIELKENS, A. J. L., Veterinary Medicine for Poultry Farms
GOLDE, L. M. G. VAN, Veterinary Biochemistry
GROMMERS, F. J., Relationship between Man and Animal
GRUYS, E., Pathology of Domestic Animals
HELLEBREKERS, L. J., Anaesthesiology of Laboratory Animals
HORZINEK, M. C., Virology
HUIS IN 'T VELD, J. H. J., Microbiology of Food Products of Animal Origin
JANSSEN, J., Knowledge of Veterinary Law
KNAPEN, F. VAN, Hygiene of Food of Animal Origin
KROES, R., Biological Toxicology
MELOEN, R. H., Biomedical Identification
MIERT, A. S. J. P. A. M. VAN, Veterinary Pharmacology
MOUWEN, J. M. V. M., Pathology
OIRSCHOT, J. T. VAN, Veterinarian Vaccinology
OOST, B. A. VAN, Clinical and Molecular Genetics of Domestic Animals
OSTERHAUS, A. D. M. E., Environmental Virology
OTTER, W. DEN, Cell Biology and Histology
PIJPERS, A., Veterinary Medicine for Poultry Farms
ROTTIER, P. J. M., Molecular Virology
RUITENBERG, E. J., Veterinary Immunology
RIJNBERK, A., Medicine of Small Domestic Animals
SCHALKEN, J. A., Veterinary Oncology
SLUYS, F. J., Medicine of Domestic Animals, Reproduction and Surgery
SPRUIJT, B. M., Good Health of Animals
TIELEN, M. J. M., Lodging and Provision of Animals
VERHEIJDEN, J. H. M., Medicine of Pigs
VOS, J. G., Toxicological Pathology

VRIES, H. W. DE, Medicine of Small Domestic Animals
WEIJS, W. A., Veterinary Anatomy and Embryology
WEYDEN, G. C. VAN DER, Obstetrics
ZEIJST, B. A. M. VAN DER, Veterinary Bacteriology
ZUTPHEN, L. F. M. VAN, Animals and Experimental Application

Faculty of Social Sciences:
ADRIAANSENS, H. P. M., Social Sciences and Social Processes and Structures
BANCK, G. A., Anthropology of Brazil
BECKER, H. A., Sociology
BENSING, J. M., Clinical Psychology and Health Psychology
BIERMAN, D. J., Parapsychology
BOUT, J. VAN DEN, Bereavement Acceptance Process
BRINKGEVE, C. D. A., Primary forms of Cohabitation, Life-course and Identity
COENEN, Dr H. M. H., Labour Issues
DEEN, N., Theory and Practice of Pupil Accompaniment
DERCKSEN, W. J., Social Sciences (Socio-Economic Policy)
DUBBELDAM, L. F. B., Education in Developing Countries
ELBERS, E. P. J. M., Communication, Thought and Culture Issues
ENGBERSEN, G. B. M., Welfare State System
ENTZINGER, H. B., Studies of Multi-Ethnic Societies
GANZENBOOM, H. B. G., Sociology (Informatics in Science and Society)
GRIENSVEN, G. J. P., Social Epidemiology with respect to HIV/AIDS
GROEBEL, F. J., Social Sciences (Psychology of Mass Communication)
HAAN, E. H. F. DE, Applied Experimental Psychology
HAGENDOORN, A. J. M. W., Social Sciences
HART, H. 'T, Statistics and Methodology of Pedagogical Research
HEIJDEN, P. G. M. VAN DER, Statistics for Social Sciences
HEIJMANS, P. G., Life Psychology
HOKSBERGEN, R. A. C., Adoption
HOX, J. J., Survey Research
IDENBURG, PH. A., Management Sciences
IMELMAN, J. D., Principles of Pedagogics
INGLEBY, J. D., Life Psychology
KANSELAAR, G., Educational Sciences, in particular Educational Psychology
KNULST, W. P., Education in Arts and Cultural Participation
KRUIJT, D. A. N. M., Development Issues
LAAN, G. VAN DER, Foundations of Social Work
LAGERWEIJ, N. A. J., Pedagogics and Innovation in Teaching
LEEUW, F. L., Empirical Theoretical Analysis of the Social Effects of Government Policy
MANTE MEIJEE, E. A., Management and Renewal Processes in Large Organizations
OOSTINDIE, G. J., Anthropology of Comparative Sociology (Caribbean)
PILOT, A., Didactics
RAUB, W., Theoretical Sociology
RISPENS, J., Education of Problem Children
ROBBEN, A. C. G. M., Anthropology of Comparative Sociology (Latin America)
RUIJTER, A. DE, Social Anthropology
SCHAUFELI, W. B., Organizational Psychology
SCHETTKAT, R., Social and Institutional Economics
SCHNABEL, P., Mental Health Care
SCHOFFELEERS, J. H., Socio-Economic Changes and Forms of Meaning-Making
SEVENHUYSEN, S. L., Comparative Women's Studies
SON, M. J. M. VAN, Clinical and Health Care Psychology
STEVENS, L. M., Orthopedagogics
STROEBE, W., Social and Organizational Psychology
TAZELAAR, F., Sociology
THIJSSEN, J. G. L., Business and Professional Education
TIELMAN, R. A. P., Social and Cultural Aspects of Humanism
TREFFERS, A., Field-Specific Education
VEENHOVEN, R., Humanism
VERMEER, A., Remedial Education
VRIENS, L. J. A., Peace Studies
VROON, P., Theoretical Psychology
WAARDEN, B. F. VAN, Intervention, Organization and Policy Issues in Social Sciences
WERTHEIM, A. H., Cognitive Ergonomics
WIJNGAARDEN, P. J. VAN, Sociological Aspects of Social Security Issues
WILTERDINK, N. A., Study of Long-term Processes in Social Sciences
WINTER, M. DE, Innovations in Primary Parent and Child Care
WUBBELS, TH., Teacher Behaviour as a factor in the Learning Environment
WYNGAARDEN, P. J. VAN, Social Security Issues
ZANTWIJK, R. A. M. VAN, Anthropology and Ethno-History of the Indian Peoples of Latin America
ZWAN, A. VAN DER, Development of Views on the Adjustment of the Welfare State

Faculty of Philosophy:
BERGSTRA, J. A., Applied Logic
DALEN, D. VAN, Logic and Philosophy
GEERTSEMA, H. P., Calvinist Philosophy
MANSFELD, J., History of Philosophy in the Ancient World and the Middle Ages
MIDDELBURG, C. A., Applied Logic
REIJEN, W. L. VAN, Political and Social Philosophy
RUNIA, D. T., The Tradition of Platonism in Relation to Early Christianity
SCHUHMANN, K. J., History of Modern and Renaissance Philosophy
VERBEEK, TH. H. M., 17th-Century Ideology from the Dutch Perspective

Faculty of Geographical Sciences:
AKKER, C. VAN DEN, Ground and Surface Water Quality
BERG, M. VAN DEN, Urban and Regional Planning
BURROUGH, P. A., Physical Geography of Landscapes
DIELEMAN, F. M. J., Human Geography of Urban Industrialized Countries
GINKEL, J. A. VAN, Human Geography
GLASBERGEN, P., Environmental Policies
GROENEWEGEN, P. P., Environmental and Social Aspects of Health and Health Care
HAUER, J., Methods and Techniques in Geographical Research
HOEKVELD, G. A., Education and Regional Geography
HOOIMEIJER, P., Regional Aspects of Population Issues
KOSTER, E. A., Landscape Architecture
KREUKELS, A. M. J., Urban and Regional Planning
LAMBOOY, J. G., Geographical Economics
LUNING, H. A., Town and Country Planning in Developing Countries
NIEUWENHUIS, J. D., Soil Mechanics of Natural Systems
ORMELING, F. J., Cartography
OTTENS, H. F. L., Human Geography
RIJN, L. C. VAN, Mechanics of Fluids (Geographical Modelling)
SCHILDER, G. G., History of Cartography
TERWINDT, J. H. J., Physiogeographical Processes
VELLINGA, M. L., Human Geography (Developing Countries)
VONKEMAN, G. H., Environmental Studies
WEESEP, J. VAN, Human Geography
WEVER, E., Human Geography (Economic Geography and International Economics)

ATTACHED RESEARCH INSTITUTES

Netherlands School for Advanced Studies in Theology and Religion (NOSTER).

Research School for Human Rights.

Netherlands School for Social and Economic Policy Research (AWSB).

Dutch Postgraduate School for Art History.

Netherlands Research School for Women's Studies (NOV).

National Graduate School of Linguistics (LOT).

Mathematical Research Institute (MRI).

Dutch Research School of Theoretical Physics.

Debye Research School.

Research School for Atmospheric and Marine Studies (SAMO).

Helmholtz School for Autonomous Systems Research.

Bijvoet Research School for Biomolecular Chemistry.

Research School for Biomembranes.

Research School of Developmental Biology.

National Research School for the Pathophysiology of the Nervous System.

Graduate School for Infection and Immunity.

Centre for Resource Studies for Development (CERES).

Research School for Psychology and Health (SPH).

Netherlands Graduate School of Housing and Urban Research (NETHUR).

UNIVERSITEIT VOOR HUMANISTIEK
(University for Humanist Studies)

Postbus 797, 3500 AT Utrecht
Telephone: (30) 2390100
Fax: (30) 234738
E-mail: bureau.ieb@uvh.nl

Founded 1989
State control
Academic year: September to June

Vice-Chancellor: Prof. H. A. M. MANSCHOT
Librarian: Drs A. GASENBEEK

Library of 22,000 vols
Number of teachers: 31
Number of students: 260

PROFESSORS

COENEN, H. L. M., Sciences of Man, Society and Culture
ELDERS, A. D. M., Theories of World Views
HOUTEN, D. J. VAN, Social Policy, Planning and Organization
KUNNEMAN, H. P., Practical Humanist Studies
MANSCHOT, H. A. M., Philosophy and Ethics
MASO, I., Philosophy of Science, Methodology and the Theory of Research
VRIES, T. DE, Regional Health Care

ATTACHED INSTITUTE

Research Institute: Van Asch van Wijckskade 28, 3512 VS Utrecht; Dir Prof. H. P. KUNNEMAN.

LANDBOUWUNIVERSITEIT (Agricultural University)

Costerweg 50, POB 9101, 6700 HB Wageningen
Telephone: (317) 489111
Telex: 45854
Fax: (317) 484449
Founded 1918
State control
Languages of instruction: Dutch, English
Academic year: September to August
Rector Magnificus: Dr Ir M. P. M. VOS
Dean of the Faculty of Agriculture: Prof. Dr C. M. KARSSEN
Administrative Officer: H. M. VAN DEN HOOFDAKKER
Librarian: Drs J. M. SCHIPPERS
Information Officer: Ir T. THEIJSE
Number of teachers: 600, including 120 professors
Number of students: 6,000
Publication: *Wageningen Agricultural University Papers*.

DEANS

Faculty of Plant Sciences: F. A. H. M. SCHELBERGEN
Faculty of Animal Sciences: J. WIEN
Faculty of Biosciences and Product Technology: Drs P. WOLDENDORP
Faculty of Land Use and Environment: Ir A. G. OLDE DAALHUIS
Faculty of Agriculture and Society: Dr Ir P. DE VISSER

Institutes of University Standing

NIJENRODE, UNIVERSITEIT VOOR BEDRIJFSKUNDE (Nijenrode University, the Netherlands Business School)

Straatweg 25, 3621 BG Breukelen
Telephone: (346) 291211
Fax: (346) 264204
Founded 1946
Private control
Languages of instruction: English, Dutch
Academic year: September to July
President: Drs N. KROES
Dean: Prof. Dr A. VAN DER ZWAN
Registrar: R. GULJT
Librarian: A. B. M. TER WOERDS
Library of 25,000 vols
Number of teachers: 68
Number of students: 350
Publications: *Gids*, *Annual Report*.

PROFESSORS

BAHLMANN, T., Organizational Learning and Change
BLOMMAERT, A. M. M., Economics
BOMHOFF, E. J., Financial Economics
BROEKSTRA, G., Systems and Organizational Theory
DYK, G. VAN, Entrepreneurship
GORTEMAKER, J. C. A., Accountancy
KAMERLING, R. N. J.
LACHOTZKI, F. W. I., Business Policy
LANGENDYK, H. P. A. J.
LUIJK, H. J. L. VAN, Business Ethics
NIEUWKERK, M. VAN, International Monetary Environment
O'KEEFE, W. T., Management Accounting
PALM, J., Communication
ROBBEN, H., Marketing
ROOBEEK, , Economics and Technology
STORM, P. M., Business Law
THIBEAULT, A., Finance
TISSEN, R. J., Human Resources Management
WILT, H. G. J. DE, Distribution and Retailing
WISSIMA, J. G., Business Policy
ZANDEN, P. M. VAN DER, Financial Accounting
ZWAN, A. VAN DER

ATTACHED RESEARCH CENTRES

Nijenrode Executive and Management Development Centre: Dir K. HAZELWINKEL.

Centre for Finance: Dir A. THIBEAULT.

Centre for Supply Chain Management: Dir H. ROBBEN.

Centre for Entrepreneurship: Dir G. VAN DYK.

Centre for Human Resources and Organizational Management: Dir R. TISSEN.

European Institute for Business Ethics: Dir H. VAN LUYK.

Centre for Organizational Learning and Change: Dir T. BAHLMANN.

KATHOLIEKE THEOLOGISCHE UNIVERSITEIT TE UTRECHT

POB 80101, 3508 TC Utrecht
Telephone: (30) 2532149
Fax: (30) 2533665
Founded 1967
Academic year: September to September
Chairman of the Board: Prof. Dr J. H. G. I. GIESBERS
Rector and Chairman of University Council: Prof. Dr P. C. BEENTJIES
Registrar: E. TRIETSCH
Number of teachers: 53
Number of students: 390

PROFESSORS

BEENTJES, P. C., Old Testament
FRISHMAN, J., Rabbinic Literature and Judaism
HELLEMANS, G. A. F., Social Sciences
HONÉE, E. M. V. M., Church History
JONKERS, P. H. A. I., Philosophy and History of Philosophy
MENKEN, M. J. J., New Testament
RIKHOF, H. W. M., Systematic Theology and History of Theology
ROUWHORST, G. A. M., History of Liturgy

ATTACHED INSTITUTE

Franciskaans Studiecentrum: c/o K. T. U., POB 80101, 3508 TC Utrecht; tel. (30) 533875; research in Franciscan spirituality and the history of the movement in the Netherlands; Dir J. VAN DEN EIJNDEN.

THEOLOGISCHE UNIVERSITEIT VAN DE CHRISTELIJKE GEREFORMEERDE KERKEN IN NEDERLAND

Wilhelminapark 4, 7316 BT Apeldoorn
Telephone: (55) 5213156
Founded 1892
President: Prof. Dr H. J. SELDERHUIS
Librarian: Prof. Dr J. W. MARIS
Library of 30,000 vols
Number of teachers: 5 full-time, 8 part-time
Number of students: 84 full-time, 13 part-time

THEOLOGISCHE UNIVERSITEIT VAN DE GEREFORMEERDE KERKEN (Theological University of the Reformed Churches)

Broederweg 15, 8261 GS Kampen
Telephone: (38) 3312878
Fax: (38) 3330270
E-mail: tukampen@worldaccess.nl
Founded 1854
President of Curators: Rev. C. J. SMELIK
Rector: Prof. Dr C. J. DE RUIJTER
Secretary of the University: G. LUHOFF
Librarian: Drs G. D. HARMANNY

PROFESSORS

BRUGGEN, J. VAN, New Testament Exegesis
KAMPHUIS, B., Dogmatics
KWAKKEL, G., Old Testament Exegesis
MEIJER, J. A., Classical Languages
POL, F. VAN DER, Church History and History of Dogma
RUIJTER, C. J. DE, Pastoral Theology
VELDE, M. TE, Church History and Polity

THEOLOGISCHE UNIVERSITEIT VAN DE GEREFORMEERDE KERKEN IN NEDERLAND (Theological University of the Reformed Churches in The Netherlands)

Postbus 5021, 8260 GA Kampen
Telephone: (38) 3392666
Fax: (38) 3392613
Founded 1854
Languages of instruction: Dutch, English
Academic year: September to August
Rector: Prof. Dr C. HOUTMAN
Dean of Students: Drs G. DOUMA
Registrar: Drs H. C. VAN DER SAR
Librarian: D. M. KLUNDER-ROEPERS
Library of 150,000 vols
Number of teachers: 31
Number of students: 250
Publications: *Zeitschrift für Dialektische Theologie* (2 a year, in German), *Documentatieblad voor de geschiedenis van de Nederlandse zending en overzeese kerken* (2 a year, in Dutch).

PROFESSORS

HEYER, C. J., New Testament
HOLTROP, P. N., Missiology
HOUTMAN, C., Old Testament
JELSMA, A. J., Church History
KOFFEMAN, L. J., Church Polity
LAAN, J. H. VAN DER, Pastoral Theology
LANGE, F. DE, Ecumenical Theology
MANENSCHIJN, G., Ethics
MOOR, J. C. DE, Semitics
NEVEN, G. W., Dogmatics
SCHUMAN, N. A., Liturgics

Institutes of International Education

EUROPEAN INSTITUTE OF PUBLIC ADMINISTRATION

POB 1229, 6201 BE Maastricht
Telephone: (43) 3296222
Fax: (43) 3296296
Founded 1981
Supported by states of the European Union and the Commission of the EU
General Director: I. CORTE-REAL
Library of 19,000 vols, 300 current periodicals; European documentation centre; depositing library of the Council of Europe
Publication: *EIPASCOPE* (quarterly bulletin).
Personal and organizational developments and policy support in European policy-making and implementation; EU institutions and political integration, European public management, community policies and internal markets, legal systems of the EU.

HOGESCHOOL VOOR ECONOMISCHE STUDIES (International School of Economics Rotterdam)

Postbus 4030, 3006 AA Rotterdam

Telephone: (10) 4526663
Fax: (10) 4527051

Founded 1957
State control

President: Drs J. W. L. STUBBE
Director: Drs A. W. SIDDRÉ
Registrar: Drs I. J. D. BLAAUW
Librarian: CARIN KLOMPEN

Number of teachers: 300
Number of students: 4,000

INSTITUTE OF SOCIAL STUDIES

POB 29776, 2502 LT The Hague
Premises at: Kortenaerkade 12, 2518 AX The Hague

Telephone: (70) 4260460
Telex: 31491
Fax: (70) 4260799

Founded 1952
Language of instruction: English

Rector: Prof. G. LYCKLAMA À NIJEHOLT
External Relations Officer: Drs M. F. KLATTER

Library of 45,000 vols
Number of teachers: 82
Number of students: 250

Publications: *Development and Change* (quarterly), *Working Papers, Occasional Papers* (irregular).

Ph.D. and M.Phil. in development studies; MA in: agriculture and rural development, economics of development, labour and development, politics of alternative development strategies, public policy and administration, urban and regional development, women and development; diploma programmes in: development planning techniques, international relations and development, international law and organization for development, rural policy and project planning, development law and social justice.

INTERNATIONAL INSTITUTE FOR AEROSPACE SURVEY AND EARTH SCIENCES (ITC)

Hengelosestraat 99, POB 6, 7500 AA Enschede

Telephone: (53) 4874444
Fax: (53) 4874400

Founded 1950

Assists developing countries in human resources development in aerospace surveys, remote sensing applications, the establishment of geoinformation systems and the management of geographical data.

Rector: Prof. Dr Ir. K. HARMSEN
Vice-Rector: Dr N. RENGERS
Head, Educational Affairs: Ir. F. PAATS
Librarian: M. T. KOELEN

Library of 20,000 vols
Number of teachers: 100
Number of students: 400

Publications: *ITC Journal* (quarterly), *Annual Report*.

CHAIRMEN OF DEPARTMENTS

Land Resources and Urban Sciences: Prof. Dr Ir. G. W. W. ELBERSEN
Earth Resources Surveys: Prof. Dr C. V. REEVES
Geoinformatics: Prof. Ir. R. GROOT

INTERNATIONAL INSTITUTE FOR INFRASTRUCTURAL, HYDRAULIC AND ENVIRONMENTAL ENGINEERING (IHE)

Postbus 3015, 2601 DA Delft

Telephone: (15) 2151715
Fax: (15) 2122921

Founded 1957
Language of instruction: English

Rector: Prof. Ir W. A. SEGEREN

Library of 12,000 vols
Number of teachers: 70 full-time, 400 part-time
Number of students: 400

Postgraduate MEng, MSc and PhD programmes, and short courses, in Hydraulic Engineering, Hydrology and Water Resources Management, Sanitary Engineering, Water Quality Management, Environmental Science and Technology, Transportation and Road Engineering, Underground Space Technology.

LARENSTEIN INTERNATIONAL AGRICULTURAL COLLEGE DEVENTER

POB 7, 7400 AA Deventer

Telephone: (570) 684600
Fax: (570) 684608

Founded 1912; present name 1989

Director: (vacant)
Librarian: L. H. C. STOKMANS

Library of 12,000 vols
Number of teachers: 100
Number of students: 850

First degree courses.

MAASTRICHT SCHOOL OF MANAGEMENT (MSM)

Endepolsdomein 150, POB 1203, 6201 BE Maastricht

Telephone: (43) 3618318
Fax: (43) 3618330
E-mail: information@msm.nl

Founded 1952
Language of instruction: English

Chairman of the Board: Prof. B. L. TH. VELTMAN
Director: Dr M. S. S. EL-NAMAKI
Assoc. Dean: Dr R. SAMSON

Number of teachers: 40 resident, 100 visiting
Number of students: 600

Publication: *MSM Research Papers: Management & Development* (2 a year).

Management training and research; PhD and MBA degrees and executive management programmes.

Schools of Art, Architecture and Music

Academie van Beeldende Kunsten Rotterdam (Rotterdam Academy of Art): Blaak 10, 3011 TA Rotterdam; tel. (10) 2414750; fax (10) 2414751; f. 1773 to develop talent in art and design; 120 staff; library of 6,000 vols; Pres. RICHARD E. OUWERKERK.

Academie van Bouwkunst (Academy of Architecture): Waterlooplein 211, 1011 PG Amsterdam; tel. (20) 6220188; fax (20) 6232519; f. 1908; part of Amsterdam School of the Arts; architecture, urban design and landscape architecture; library of 30,000 vols; 200 students; Dir Drs A. OXENAAR.

Academie van Bouwkunst: Onderlangs 9, 6812 CE Arnhem; tel. (26) 3535635; fax (20) 3535678; Dir Ir. J. C. CARP.

Academie van Bouwkunst: Amsterdamse Hogeschool voor de Kunsten, Tongersestraat 49A, 6211 LM Maastricht; tel. (43) 3219645; fax (43) 3252493; e-mail acbwkmtr@wxs.nl.

Academie van Bouwkunst Rotterdam (Rotterdam Academy of Architecture): Overblaak 85, 3011 MH Rotterdam; tel. (10) 4130554; fax (10) 4331856; f. 1965; library of 10,000 vols; 225 students; Dir B. VAN MEGGELEN; Secs J. BOSMA-MENSINGA, I. DE JONGBOT.

Academie voor Architectuur en Stedebouw: Prof. Cobbenhagenlaan 205, 5037 DB Tilburg; tel. (13) 5355835; e-mail e.bolle@fontys.nl; f. 1936; architecture and town planning/design; library of *c.* 8,000 vols; 70 teachers; 80 students; Man. Dir Dr E. A. BOLLE.

Academie voor Beeldende Kunst en Vormgeving, HVG (School of Visual Arts and Architecture, Academie Minerva HVG): Gedempte Zuiderdiep 158, 9711 HN Groningen; tel. (50) 666700; fax (50) 139352; e-mail p.g.j.leijdekkers@pl.hanze.nl; courses in fine arts, graphic design, textile design, fashion, interior design, architecture, computer graphics, computer animation, illustration; postgraduate courses in computer graphics, computer animation, architecture; 100 teachers; 750 students; Dir Drs P. G. J. LEIJDEKKERS (postgraduate courses).

Akademie voor Beeldende Kunst Enschede (Academy of Fine Arts, Architecture and Design): Roessinghsbleekweg 155, 7522 AH Enschede; tel. (53) 4824400; f. 1949; fine arts, design, fashion, architecture; library of 8,000 vols; Dir Prof. S. HUISMANS.

Akademie voor Kunst en Vormgeving Hogeschool 's-Hertogenbosch (Academy of Art and Design): POB 732, 5201 AS 's-Hertogenbosch; premises at: Sportlaan 56, 5223 AZ 's-Hertogenbosch; tel. (73) 6295460; fax (73) 6214725; f. 1950; courses in painting, sculpture, graphic art, ceramics, environmental art, illustration, graphic design; library of 10,000 vols; 50 teachers; 350 students; Dir ALEX DE VRIES.

Conservatorium van Amsterdam: Van Baerlestraat 27, POB 78022, 1070 LP Amsterdam; tel. (20) 5277550; fax (20) 6761506; e-mail info@sca.ahk.nl; f. 1884; 200 teachers; 800 students; library of 30,000 vols; Dir L. VIS.

Design Academy: POB 2125, 5600 CC Eindhoven; located at: Emmasinger 14, Eindhoven; tel. (40) 2122425; fax (40) 2126015; f. 1950; 200 teachers; 700 students; Dir J. L. TH. A. LUCASSEN.

Hogeschool Brabant, Faculteit voor Beeldende Kunsten St Joost: POB 90116, 4800 RA Breda; tel. (76) 5250302; fax (76) 5250305; f. 1945; Dir H. J. H. M. VAN DE VIJVEN.

Hogeschool Maastricht, Faculteit Conservatorium voor Muziek: Bonnefanten 15, 6211 KL Maastricht; 110 teachers; 545 students; library of 30,000 vols; Dir HARRY CUSTERS (acting).

Hogeschool voor de Kunsten Arnhem: Onderlangs 9, 6812 CE Arnhem; tel. (26) 3535635; fax (26) 3535678; Dir W. S. HILLENIUS.

Hogeschool voor de Kunsten Utrecht (Utrecht School of the Arts): Lange Viestraat 2B, POB 1520, 3500 BM Utrecht; tel. (30) 2332256; fax (30) 2332096; e-mail biz@central.hku.nl; f. 1987 by amalgamation of Utrechts Conservatorium, Academie voor Beeldende Kunsten Utrecht and Academie voor Expressie en Gebaar; faculties of visual arts and design, art, media and technology, music, and theatre; 350 teachers; 2,900 students; library of 36,000 vols; Dir BERT GROENEMEIJER.

Institute for Housing and Urban Development Studies: POB 1935, 3000 BX Rotterdam; tel. (10) 4021523; fax (10) 4045671; e-mail ihs@ihs.nl; f. 1971; library of 10,000 vols; 25 teachers; 120 students; Dir Dr E. A. WEGELIN.

Koninklijk Conservatorium (Royal Conservatory of Music and Dance): Juliana van Stolberglaan 1, 2595 CA The Hague; tel. (70) 3814251; fax (70) 3853941; f. 1826; 215 teachers; 750 students; library of 28,500 vols; Dir FRANS DE RUITER.

Koninklijke Academie van Beeldende Kunsten (Royal Academy of Art): until June 1999: Wegastraat 60, 2516 AP The Hague; tel. (70) 3154777; fax (70) 3154778; e-mail post@kabk.nl; from June 1999: Prinsessegracht 4, 2514 AN The Hague; tel. (70) 3643835; fax (70) 3561124; f. 1682; departments of painting, sculpture, monumental and environmental design, graphic and typographic design, textile design, fashion design, interior and furniture design, industrial, photographic and video design; Dir Dr C. M. REHORST.

Rijksakademie van Beeldende Kunsten (State Academy of Fine Arts): Sarphatistraat 470, 1018 GM Amsterdam; tel. (20) 5270300; fax (20) 5270301; e-mail info@rijksakademie.nl; f. 1870; postgraduate, one- and two-year courses; Rector Prof. JW. SCHROFER.

Rotterdams Conservatorium (Rotterdam Conservatory of Music): Pieter de Hoochweg 222, 3024 BJ Rotterdam; tel. (10) 4767399; fax (10) 4768163; Dir L. VLEGGERT (acting).

ARUBA

Libraries and Archives

Oranjestad

Biblioteca Nacional Aruba: Madurostraat 13, Oranjestad, Aruba; tel. 821580; fax 825493; f. 1949; nat. library, with public library function; library of 200,000 vols; br. in San Nicolas.

Universities and Colleges

Aruba Public School of Music: Oranjestad, Aruba; Government support.

UNIVERSIDAT DI ARUBA

San Nicholas, Aruba

Telephone: 45287

Founded 1970
Private control
Language of instruction: English
Academic year: September to June

President: Dr CARLIN I. BROWNE
Registrar: HILTONIA PETER
Librarian: LISA WEBB

Library of 6,000 vols
Number of teachers: 20
Number of students: 300

DEANS

College of Liberal Arts: Rev. Fr WILLIAM LAKE
College of Business Administration: Dr CARLIN I. BROWNE
College of Languages: Dr JOSSY MANSUR
College of Education: Dr RACHEL JONES

UNIVERSITEIT VAN ARUBA

J. Irausquinplein 4, Postbus 5, Oranjestad

Telephone: 823901
Fax: 831770
E-mail: univaruba@setarnet.aw

Founded 1988
State control
Language of instruction: Dutch
Academic year: September to June

President: Dr A. L. NICOLAAS
Rector: Dr H. J. QUICK
Secretary: Dr P. PRONK
Librarian: F. CROES

Library of 10,000 vols
Number of teachers: 30
Number of students: 200

DEANS

Faculty of Law: (vacant)
Faculty of Economics: (vacant)

NETHERLANDS ANTILLES

Research Institutes

HISTORY, GEOGRAPHY AND ARCHAEOLOGY

Archeologisch-Antropologisch Instituut Netherlandse Antillen: Johan van Walbeeckplein 6B, Willemstad, Curaçao; tel. 616555; fax 611193; f. 1967; research into the archaeology, prehistory and anthropology of the Netherlands Antilles; conservation of cultural remains; study of social problems from an anthropological perspective; library of over 2,000 vols; Dir EDWIN N. AYUBI; publ. *Reports* (irregular).

NATURAL SCIENCES

Biological Sciences

CARMABI Foundation: Piscadera Baai, Curaçao; f. 1956; terrestrial and marine ecology; library of 3,000 vols; Pres. Dr M. A. HORSFORD; Dir Dr WALTER L. BAKHUIS.

Physical Sciences

Meteorologische Dienst van de Nederlandse Antillen (Meteorological Service of the Netherlands Antilles): Seru Mahuma z/n, Curaçao; tel. (9) 683933; fax (9) 683999; f. 1950; Dir A. J. DANIA; publ. *Statistics of Meteorological Observations in Netherlands Antilles* (annually).

Libraries and Archives

Willemstad

Biblioteka Públiko Kòrsou/Openbare Bibliotheek Curaçao (Public Library, Curaçao): Abr. M. Chumaceiro Blvd, Willemstad, Curaçao; tel. (9) 4617055; fax (9) 4656247; f. 1922; library of 180,000 vols and small collection of audio-visual material; Antillean and Caribbean collection; adult, children's, mobile and schools' library services, 1 branch library, 2 mobile libraries; Librarian Miss R. M. DE PAULA; publs *Monthly Acquisition List*, *Quarterly Antillean Caribbean Acquisition List*.

Centraal Historish Archief: Scharlooweg 77, Willemstad, Curaçao; tel. (9) 4614866; fax (9) 4616794; e-mail cha@cura.net; f. 1969; repository for all non-current government records; library of 10,000 vols; Dir N.C. ROMER-KENEPA; publ. *Lantèrnu*.

Museums and Art Galleries

Willemstad

Curaçao Museum: Van Leeuwenhoekstraat, Willemstad, Curaçao; tel. (9) 4623873; fax (9) 4623777; f. 1946; housed in an old Dutch quarantine station, built 1853; paintings by early 20th-century Dutch masters and contemporary Curaçao artists; 19th-century mahogany furniture; folklore collection; Indian artifacts; library of Antillean books;

regular exhibitions of local and international artists; botanical garden and music pavilion; Dir D. ENGELS; publ. *De Museumbode* (quarterly).

Universities and Colleges

Academy of Music: Koninginnelaan z/n, Emmastad, Curaçao; tel. 73510; f. 1960; run by the Cultural Centre; 534 students; Dir E. PROVENCE.

UNIVERSITY OF THE NETHERLANDS ANTILLES

POB 3059, Willemstad, Curaçao
Telephone: (9) 84422
Fax: 85465
Founded 1970 as Institute of Higher Studies, university status 1979
Language of instruction: Dutch
Academic year: September to June
President: Ir H. GEORGE
Rector: E. JOUBERT
Secretary: H. F. HOLLANDER
Chief Administrative Officer: R. RAVENSTEIN
Librarian: Drs S. R. CRIENS
Library of 100,000 vols
Number of teachers: 93
Number of students: 600

DEANS

Law: Dr G. LIEUW
Technical Sciences: Ir. R. M. LIBIER
Social and Economic Sciences: M. HASHAM

NEW ZEALAND

Learned Societies

GENERAL

Royal Society of New Zealand: POB 598, Wellington; tel. (4) 472-7421; fax (4) 473-1841; f. 1867; science, technology; 223 fellows, 60 constituent socs; Pres. Prof. Philippa Black; CEO V. R. Moore; publs: *New Zealand Journal of Agricultural Research, New Zealand Journal of Botany, New Zealand Journal of Crop and Horticultural Science, New Zealand Journal of Geology and Geophysics, New Zealand Journal of Marine and Freshwater Research, New Zealand Journal of Zoology, Journal of the Royal Society of New Zealand* (all quarterly).

AGRICULTURE, FISHERIES AND VETERINARY SCIENCE

Agronomy Society of New Zealand: c/o Plant and Ecological Sciences Division, Lincoln University, POB 84, Canterbury; e-mail mckenzie@lincoln.ac.nz; 200 mems; Sec. Dr B. A. McKenzie.

New Zealand Dairy Technology Society (Inc.): Dairy Science Section, c/o Anchor Products Ltd, Waitoa; tel. (7) 889-3989; 250 mems; Sec. H. Singh.

New Zealand Institute of Agricultural Science (Inc.): Secretariat, POB 121063, Henderson, Waitakere City; tel. (9) 8128-506; fax (9) 8128-503; f. 1954; 512 mems; Pres. Dr J. Caradus; Sec. Dr P. Williams; publ. *Agricultural Science* (4 a year).

New Zealand Institute of Forestry: POB 19-840, Christchurch; tel. and fax (3) 3842-432; e-mail sheppars@ihug.co.nz; f. 1926 to promote the best use of New Zealand's resources and to encourage wise use of forest lands; 850 mems; Pres. J. E. Galbraith; Sec. H. Chapman; publ. *New Zealand Forestry* (quarterly).

New Zealand Society for Horticultural Science: 3/11 Brothers St, New Windsor, Auckland 1007; tel. (9) 820-0397; fax (9) 815-4201; e-mail mplmjb@dslak.co.nz; f. 1981; 350 mems; Pres. Dr C. N. Hale; publ. *Horttalk* (every 2 months).

New Zealand Society of Animal Production (Inc.): C/o Crop and Food Research, Private Bag 4704, Christchurch; tel. (3) 3256400; fax (3) 3252074; e-mail fraserp@crop.cri.nz; Pres. P. Gregg; Sec. P. M. Fraser; publ. *Soil News* (6 a year).

New Zealand Society of Soil Science (Inc.): C/o Crop and Food Research, Private Bag 4704, Christchurch; tel. (3) 325-6400, fax (3) 325-2074; f. 1952; 400 mems; Pres. P. Gregg; Sec. P. Fraser; publ. *Soil News* (every 2 months).

New Zealand Veterinary Association (Inc.): POB 11-212 Manners Street, Wellington; tel. (4) 471-0484; fax (4) 471-0494; e-mail nzva@xtra.co.nz; f. 1923; 1,150 mems; Pres. R. Blanks; Exec. Dir Murray Gibb; publs *New Zealand Veterinary Journal* (quarterly), *New Zealand Vetscript* (monthly).

Royal Agricultural Society of New Zealand (Inc.): POB 3095, Wellington; tel. (4) 472-4190; fax (4) 471-2278; e-mail royal@shandwick.co.nz; f. 1924; co-ordination of agricultural associations, administers United Breeds Society which comprises all stud Breed Societies in NZ; library of 1,000 vols; Pres. Ken McKenzie; Sec. C. Mason; publ. *On Show* (2 a year).

ARCHITECTURE AND TOWN PLANNING

New Zealand Institute of Architects: POB 438, 13th Floor, Greenock House, 102–112 Lambton Quay, Wellington; tel. (4) 473-5346; fax (4) 472-0182; f. 1905; Pres. B. K. Elliott.

New Zealand Institute of Surveyors: POB 831, Wellington; tel. (4) 471-1774; fax (4) 471-1907; e-mail nzis@clear.net.nz; f. 1888; 1,300 mems; Pres. D. M. Stewart; publs *N.Z. Surveyor* (annually), *Survey Quarterly* (quarterly).

BIBLIOGRAPHY, LIBRARY SCIENCE AND MUSEOLOGY

Museums Association of Aotearoa New Zealand Te Ropu Hanga Kaupapa Taouga: c/o Museum of New Zealand, POB 467, Wellington; tel. (4) 385-9609; fax (4) 385-7157; f. 1947 to represent, promote and invigorate museums and the museum profession; 200 mems; Pres. Steve Lowndes; Sec. Lynda Wallace; publs *MAANZ News* (quarterly), *MAANZ Newsletter* (every 2 months), *New Zealand Museum Journal* (2 a year).

New Zealand Book Council: 1st floor, Old Wool House, 139–141 Featherston St, Wellington; tel. (4) 499-1569; fax (4) 499-1424; e-mail karenross.nzbookcouncil@xwg.co.nz; f. 1972; 1,600 mems (individuals, schools, libraries, booksellers, publishers); Pres. Sir Kenneth Keith; Dir Karen Ross.

New Zealand Library and Information Association: Level 6, Old Wool House, 139–141 Featherston St, Wellington 6038; tel. (4) 473-5834; fax (4) 499-1480; e-mail nzlia@netlink.co.nz; f. 1910; 1,500 mems; Pres. Sue Cooper; Office Man. Steve Williams; publs *New Zealand Libraries* (quarterly), *Library Life* (monthly, except January).

ECONOMICS, LAW AND POLITICS

New Zealand Institute of International Affairs: c/o Victoria University of Wellington, POB 600, Wellington; tel. (4) 471-5356; fax 473-1261; f. 1934; to promote understanding of international questions and problems, particularly those relating to New Zealand, the Pacific, Asia, and the Commonwealth; Pres. Sir Frank Holmes; Dir B. W. Harland; publ. *New Zealand International Review* (every 2 months).

New Zealand Law Society: POB 5041, Wellington; 26 Waring Taylor St, Wellington; tel. (4) 472-7837; fax (4) 473-7909; e-mail inquiries@nz-lawsoc.org.nz; f. 1869; 7,428 mems; Exec. Dir A. D. Ritchie; publ. *LawTalk* (fortnightly).

Population Association of New Zealand: POB 225, Wellington; tel. (4) 4716146; fax (4) 4714412; f. 1974; to promote population research, understanding and policy development; 132 mems; Sec. N. J. Pole; publs *New Zealand Population Review* (2 a year), *Technical Papers, Monographs* (occasional).

FINE AND PERFORMING ARTS

Creative New Zealand (Arts Council of New Zealand Toi Aotearoa): POB 3806, Wellington; tel. (4) 473-0880; fax (4) 471-2865; f. 1994; a statutory body formed to foster, encourage and promote the practice and appreciation of the arts; invests in a wide variety of artists and artistic organizations involved with all areas of the arts; awards grants for postgraduate study to professional arts practitioners; 7 mems; Chair. Brian Stevenson; Dir Peter Scott; various publs.

New Zealand Maori Arts and Crafts Institute: POB 334, Rotorua; tel. (73) 489-047; fax (73) 489-045; f. 1963; aims: the appreciation, promotion, preservation and perpetuation of Maori arts, crafts and culture; Chief Exec. B. Hughes; publ. *Whaka*.

HISTORY, GEOGRAPHY AND ARCHAEOLOGY

New Zealand Archaeological Association (Inc.): POB 6337, Dunedin North; tel. (3) 477-2372; fax (3) 477-5993; f. 1957; 500 mems; Pres. R. McGovern-Wilson; Sec. M. White; publs *Newsletter* (quarterly), *Journal* (annually), *Monographs* (irregular).

New Zealand Cartographic Society (Inc.): POB 12454, Thorndon; f. 1971; 220 mems; Pres. R. B. Phillips; Sec. D. Harvey; publs *New Zealand Cartography and Geographic Information Systems* (2 a year), *Cartogram Newsletter* (quarterly).

New Zealand Geographical Society Inc.: Department of Geography, University of Waikato, Private Bag 3105, Hamilton; f. 1944 to promote and stimulate the study of geography; brs in Auckland, Christchurch, Dunedin, Hamilton, Palmerston North and Wellington; 500 mems in New Zealand, 400 overseas mems; Pres. Dr G. Campbell; Sec. Dr Peter Unch; publs *New Zealand Geographer* (2 a year), *New Zealand Journal of Geography* (2 a year), *Proceedings of the New Zealand Geography Conference* (every 2 years).

New Zealand Historic Places Trust: POB 2629, Wellington 1; tel. (4) 472-4341; fax (4) 499-0669; e-mail nzhistoricplaces@xtra.co.nz; f. 1955; independent trust with statutory responsibilities; identifies, investigates, registers and preserves historic places, including archaeological sites, traditional sites and old European and Maori buildings; 32,000 national mems; Chair. Dame Catherine Tizard; Dir P. Atkinson; publ. *New Zealand Historic Places* (every 2 months).

New Zealand Historical Association: c/o Historical Branch, Department of Internal Affairs, POB 805, Wellington; tel. (4) 495-7200; fax (4) 495-7212; f. 1979; promotes historical study, teaching and research; holds regular national and regional conferences, gives financial or other assistance to the publication of historical research in NZ, expresses opinion on issues of public policy which concern historical study, teaching or research; 300 mems; Pres. Charlotte Macdonald; Sec. J. Martin; publ. *Newsletter* (2 a year).

LANGUAGE AND LITERATURE

New Zealand Society of Authors (PEN N.Z. Inc): POB 67013, Mt Eden, Auckland 3; f. 1934; promotes co-operation and support amongst writers; encourages writing in New Zealand and works to protect the interests of writers; awards annual and bi-annual prizes; reps on major bodies associated with writers;

800 mems; publ. *The New Zealand Author* (every 2 months).

MEDICINE

Australian Association of Clinical Biochemists (New Zealand Branch, Inc.): Registrar, Hamilton Medical Laboratory, P.O. Box 52, Hamilton; telex 8380594; f. 1967; routine diagnostic biochemistry; research and development in both hospital and private medical laboratories; 60 mems; Registrar G. SCHEURICH; publ. *Newsletter* (quarterly).

New Zealand Dietetic Association (Inc.): Box 5065, Wellington.

New Zealand Medical Association: POB 156, Wellington; tel. (4) 472-4741; fax (4) 471-0838; f. 1887; 4,500 mems; Chair. Dr A. WILES; Chief Exec. Officer C. MCIVER; publ. *New Zealand Medical Journal* (2 a month).

Physiological Society of New Zealand (Inc.): c/o Dept of Physiology, University of Otago, POB 913, Dunedin; tel. (3) 479-7334; fax (3) 479-7323; f. 1972; 156 mems; Sec. Dr P. A. CRAGG; publ. *Proceedings* (annually).

NATURAL SCIENCES

General

New Zealand Association of Scientists: Box 1874, Wellington; fax (4) 389-5095; f. 1940; Pres. BRION JARVIS; Sec. MICHAEL BERRIDGE; publ. *New Zealand Science Review* (quarterly).

Biological Sciences

Entomological Society of New Zealand (Inc.): 8 Maymorn Rd, Te Marua, Upper Hutt; 250 mems; Sec. Mrs S. MILLAR.

New Zealand Ecological Society (Inc.): POB 25178, Christchurch; tel. and fax (3) 384-2432; e-mail sheppars@ihug.co.nz; f. 1951; 481 mems; Sec. CAROLINE MASON; publ. *New Zealand Journal of Ecology* (2 a year).

New Zealand Genetics Society: Institute for Veterinary, Animal and Biomedical Sciences, Massey University, PB 11-222 Palmerston North; tel. (6) 350-5122; fax (6) 350-5699; f. 1949; 131 mems; Pres. Prof. H. T. BLAIR.

New Zealand Limnological (Freshwater Sciences) Society: POB 11-115 Hamilton; f. 1968; 320 mems; Sec. Dr K. COLLIER; publ. *Newsletter* (1 a year).

New Zealand Marine Sciences Society: POB 434, Cambridge; tel. (7) 856-7026; f. 1960; concerned with all aspects of marine science in New Zealand; 270 mems, 47 inst. mems; Sec. Dr J. HALL; publ. *Review* (annually).

New Zealand Microbiological Society (Inc.): Dept of Biochemistry, University of Otago, POB 56, Dunedin 9001; tel. (3) 479-7869; fax (3) 479-7866; f. 1956; 465 mems; Pres. Prof. G. W. TANNOCK; Sec. Dr I. L. LAMONT; publ. *Newsletter* (3 a year).

New Zealand Society for Parasitology: C/o Novartis New Zealand Ltd, Private Bag 19-980, Avondale, Auckland 7; tel. (9) 828-3149; fax (9) 828-6565; f. 1972; study of parasites of plants and animals; 120 mems; Pres. Dr P. C. MASON; Sec. B. C. HOSKING; publ. *Proceedings* (annually).

New Zealand Society of Plant Physiologists: c/o NZ Institute for Crop and Food Research, PB 11-600, Palmerston North; tel. (6) 356-8300; fax (6) 351-7050; f. 1976; 130 mems; Pres. Dr GAVIN ROSS; Sec./Treasurer Dr JULIAN HEYES.

Ornithological Society of New Zealand (Inc.): c/o POB 12397, Wellington; f. 1939; 1,150 mems; Pres. CHRISTOPHER J. ROBERTSON; Sec. RAEWYN A. EMPSON; publs *Notornis* and *OSNZ News* (quarterly).

Mathematical Sciences

New Zealand Mathematical Society: c/o Dept of Mathematics, University of Waikato, PMB 3105, Hamilton; tel. (7) 856-2889; fax (7) 838-4666; e-mail stephenj@math.waikato.ac.nz; f. 1974; 247 mems; Pres. Prof. R. I. GOLDBLATT; Sec. Dr S. JOE; publs *NZMS Newsletter* (3 a year), *NZ Journal of Mathematics*.

New Zealand Statistical Association (Inc.): POB 1731, Wellington; f. 1950; sponsors prizes for statistics, holds workshops and an annual conference; 390 mems; small library; publs *Statistician* (2 or 3 a year), *Newsletter* (quarterly).

Physical Sciences

Geological Society of New Zealand (Inc.): c/o Institute of Geological and Nuclear Sciences, POB 30-368, Lower Hutt; tel. (4) 570-1444; fax (4) 566-6168; f. 1955 to encourage the advancement of geological sciences in New Zealand; 7 branches; 820 mems; Pres. J. PETTINGA; Sec. G. BROWNE; publs *Newsletter* (quarterly), guidebooks, field guides, etc.

Meteorological Society of New Zealand: c/o POB 6523, Te Aro, Wellington; f. 1979; 330 mems; Pres. Dr B. MULLAN; Sec. Dr D. C. THOMPSON; publs *Weather and Climate* (2 a year), *Newsletter* (quarterly).

New Zealand Geophysical Society (Inc.): POB 30-368, Lower Hutt; tel. (4) 570-4815; fax (4) 570-4603; e-mail a.melhuish@gns.cri.nz; f. 1980; 140 mems; Pres. J. BEAVAN; Sec. A. MELHUISH; publ. *Newsletter* (3 a year).

New Zealand Institute of Chemistry (Inc.): POB 39-283, Howick, Auckland; tel. (9) 535-6495; fax (9) 535-3476; f. 1931; 1,500 mems; Pres. Dr A. K. H. MACGIBBON; Hon. Gen. Sec. G. D. BOSTON; publs *Chemistry in New Zealand* (6 a year), *Chem NZ* (quarterly).

New Zealand Institute of Physics: c/o Dept of Physics, University of Waikato, Hamilton; fax (7) 838-4219; 400 mems; Sec. A. STEYN-ROSS.

New Zealand Society for Biochemistry and Molecular Biology (Inc.): C/o New Zealand Pastoral Agricultural Research Institute Ltd (AgResearch), Ruakura Research Institute, Private Bag 3123, Hamilton; tel. (7) 838-5099; fax (7) 838-5628; 350 mems; Chair. Dr M. R. GRIGOR; Sec. Dr T. T. WHEELER; publ. *NZ BioScience* (4 a year).

Royal Astronomical Society of New Zealand (Inc.): POB 3181, Wellington; f. 1920; 373 mems; Pres. A. GILMORE; Exec. Sec. G. WITHEFORD; publs *Southern Stars* (2 a year), *Newsletter* (monthly).

Waikato Geological and Lapidary Society (Inc.): POB 62, Hamilton; f. 1966; Pres. G. T. MATTHEWS; Sec. R. RAY.

PHILOSOPHY AND PSYCHOLOGY

New Zealand Psychological Society (Inc.): POB 4092, Wellington; e-mail psychsoc@actrix.gen.nz; 800 mems; Exec. Sec. L. CROWTHER; publ. *NZ Journal of Psychology* (2 a year).

RELIGION, SOCIOLOGY AND ANTHROPOLOGY

Polynesian Society: f. 1892 to promote studies and publications about the Polynesians and other Pacific peoples past and present; library; 1,100 mems; Pres. Prof. Sir HUGH KAWHARU; Sec. Prof. J. HUNTSMAN, Anthropology Dept, Univ. of Auckland, Private Bag, Auckland; fax (9) 373-7441; publs *Memoirs, Journal* (quarterly), *Maori Monographs, Maori Texts*.

TECHNOLOGY

Institution of Professional Engineers New Zealand: POB 12241, 101 Molesworth St, Wellington; f. 1914; 7,500 mems; 15 brs; Pres. Dr FRANCIS SMALL; Chief Exec. A. T. MITCHELL; publ. *New Zealand Engineering* (monthly).

New Zealand Computer Society (Inc.): POB 10044, Wellington; tel. (4) 473-1043; fax (4) 473-1025; f. 1960; 1,650 mems; Dir R. A. HENRY.

New Zealand Electronics Institute (Inc.): POB 1868, Wellington; f. 1946; 420 mems; Exec. Officer L. HAWKINS; publs *NZ Electron, NZEI Ralph Slade Memorial Lecture* (annually), *Newelectronics Journal* (monthly).

New Zealand Hydrological Society: POB 12-300, Wellington North; tel. (3) 325-6700, fax (3) 325-2418; f. 1961; 500 mems; Pres. A. FENEMOR; Sec. B. FAHEY; publs newsletter, *Journal of Hydrology (New Zealand)* (2 a year).

New Zealand Institute of Food Science and Technology (Inc.): POB 1656, Whangarei; tel. and fax (9) 437-2235; e-mail coralie@nzifst.org.nz; f. 1964; 730 mems; Pres. DAVID BUISSON; publ. *Food Technologist* (5 a year).

New Zealand National Society for Earthquake Engineering: POB 48048, Silverstream, Upper Hutt; tel. (4) 528-4906; fax (4) 528-4907; e-mail quirke@ihuq.co.nz; f. 1968; membership open to engineers, architects, scientists and others concerned with earthquake phenomena; 800 mems; Pres. A. B. KING; Admin. Sec. G. M. QUIRKE; publ. *Bulletin* (quarterly).

Operational Research Society of New Zealand (Inc.): POB 904, Wellington; f. 1964; 170 mems; Sec. G. ENG; publ. *Asia Pacific Journal of Operational Research* (2 a year, jointly with Singapore Operational Research Society) for the Association of Asian Pacific Operational Research Societies.

Research Institutes

AGRICULTURE, FISHERIES AND VETERINARY SCIENCE

Horticulture and Food Research Institute of New Zealand Ltd: Private Bag 11030, Palmerston North; tel. (6) 356-8080; fax (6) 354-0075; library of 40,000 vols, 350 periodicals; Chief Exec. Dr IAN WARRINGTON.

New Zealand Dairy Research Institute: Private Bag 11029, Palmerston North; tel. (6) 3504649; fax (6) 3561476; established 1927 as a unit of the DSIR, inc. 1947; central research organization within New Zealand dairy industry; concerned with fundamental and applied research and development related to the composition and manufacture of dairy products; CEO Dr A. ANDERSON.

New Zealand Forest Research Institute: PMB 3020, Rotorua; tel. 347-5899; fax 347-9380; e-mail library@fri.cri.nz; f. 1947; a govt-owned company providing research and technology development for the forestry and wood products industries; library of 300,000 vols (incl. monographs and periodicals); Chief Exec. (vacant); publs *NZ Journal of Forestry Science* (3 a year), *Science Report, NZFRI Research Directions, FRI Bulletins, What's New in Forest Research* (irregular).

New Zealand Institute for Crop and Food Research Ltd: Private Bag 4704, Christchurch; tel. (3) 325-6400; fax (3) 325-2074; Chief Exec. Dr MIKE DUNBIER.

New Zealand Pastoral Agriculture Research Institute Ltd: Private Bag 3115,

Hamilton; tel. (7) 834-6600; fax (7) 834-6640; Chief Exec. Dr BILL KAIN.

ECONOMICS, LAW AND POLITICS

New Zealand Institute of Economic Research: POB 3479, Wellington; tel. (4) 472-1880; fax (4) 472-1211; f. 1958; research into New Zealand economic development; quarterly analysis and forecast of economic conditions; quarterly survey of business opinion; economic investigations; Dir JOHN YEABSLEY; Chair. KERRIN M. VAUTIER; Business Man. A. G. FROGGATT; publs *Quarterly Predictions, Quarterly Survey of Business Opinion*.

EDUCATION

New Zealand Council for Educational Research: POB 3237, Wellington; tel. 3847-939; fax 3847-933; f. 1934; research into educational issues; develops assessment resources for NZ schools, and acts as clearing-house for research and information on educational matters; library of 10,000 vols; Chair. Prof. TED GLYNN; Dir Dr ANNE MEADE; publs *Annual Report*, *Newsletter* (2 a year), *New Zealand Journal of Educational Studies* (2 a year), *set—Research Information for Teachers* (2 a year), and others.

MEDICINE

Auckland Medical Research Foundation: POB 7151, Auckland; tel. 307-2886; f. 1956; financed by public subscription to sponsor and encourage medical research; Pres. G. S. BLANCHARD; Sec. LESLIE CORKERY; publ. *Annual Report*.

Canterbury Medical Research Foundation: promotion and support of all aspects of medical research; privately financed; Sec. G. R. JOHNSON, POB 2682, Christchurch.

Hawke's Bay Medical Research Foundation (Inc.): POB 596, Napier.

Health Research Council of New Zealand: POB 5541, Wellesley St, Auckland; tel. 379-8227; fax 377-9988; e-mail info@hrc.govt.nz; f. 1990; initiates, funds and supports health research; advises the govt on issues of health research ethics; Chair. GAE GRIFFITHS; Dir Dr BRUCE SCOGGINS; publs *Annual Report, Newsletter* (quarterly), *Ethics Notes* (3 a year).

Palmerston North Medical Research Foundation: c/o POB 648, Palmerston North; f. 1959; privately financed; general medical research; Sec. BRIAN BOCKETT; publ. *Annual Report*.

Wellington Medical Research Foundation: c/o The Secretary, POB 51-211, Wellington; tel. (4) 232-5475; fax (4) 232-5475; privately financed; supports all forms of medical research.

NATURAL SCIENCES

Biological Sciences

Cawthron Institute: Private Bag 2, Nelson; tel. (3) 548-2319; fax (3) 546-9464; e-mail info@environment.cawthorn.org.nz; f. 1919; chemical and biological testing and consulting, research in marine biology, environmental studies, marine and freshwater consulting; library of 4,500 vols; Chief Exec. G. ROBERTSON; publ. *Cawthron Lectures*.

Institute of Environmental Science and Research Ltd: POB 12444, 15–17 Murphy St, Wellington; tel. (4) 499-0540; fax (4) 499-0541; f. 1992; provides scientific research, consulting and analytical services related to public health, environmental health and forensic science to public and private sectors in New Zealand and the Asia-Pacific region; Chief Exec. MARK TEMPLETON.

Landcare Research New Zealand Ltd: POB 40, Lincoln; tel. (3) 325-6700; fax (3) 325-2127; research to provide a scientific basis for managing New Zealand's land environment; Chief Exec. Dr ANDREW PEARCE.

Physical Sciences

Carter Observatory: POB 2909, Wellington; tel. (4) 472-8167; fax (4) 472-8230; f. 1938; the national observatory; astronomical research; binary stars, lunar occultations, galactic structure and evolution, star cluster dynamics, stellar evolution, variable star dynamics, astronomical optics, distribution of galaxies; co-operation with schools, colleges and universities for education in astronomy; national centre for receipt and distribution of astronomical information; library of 20,000 vols, 434 journals; Exec. Dir Dr W. ORCHISTON; publs *Annual Report, Newsletter*.

Institute of Geological and Nuclear Sciences Ltd: Gracefield Rd, POB 30-368, Lower Hutt, tel. (4) 570-1444; fax (4) 570-4600; f. 1865 as New Zealand Geological Survey (name changed to DSIR Geology & Geophysics in 1990, and to present form in 1992); a crown research institute; maintains collections of rocks, minerals and fossils of New Zealand and other countries, including Suter collection of New Zealand Mollusca; responsible for national geological mapping, geophysics and hazard studies, and all applied geology; library of 40,000 vols; CEO Dr ANDREW WEST; publ. *NZ Volcanological Record* (annually).

Mount John University Observatory: POB 56, Lake Tekapo 8770; tel. (3) 680-6000; fax (3) 680-6005; e-mail mjuo@csc.canterbury.ac.nz; f. 1963; operated by Univ. of Canterbury; research especially into variable stars and stellar spectroscopy; two 60 cm and one 1m telescopes; Dir Prof. J. B. HEARNSHAW.

National Institute of Water and Atmospheric Research Ltd: Private Bag 99940, Newmarket, Auckland; tel. (9) 375-2090; fax (9) 375-2091; Chief Exec. PAUL HARGREAVES.

New Plymouth Astronomical Society Observatory: POB 818, New Plymouth; f. 1920; 60 mems; Dir J. CALCOTT.

TECHNOLOGY

New Zealand Institute for Industrial Research and Development (Industrial Research Ltd): POB 2225, Auckland; tel. (9) 303-4116; fax (9) 307-0618; Chief Exec. Dr GEOFF PAGE.

Libraries and Archives

Auckland

Auckland City Libraries: POB 4138, Wellesley St, Auckland 1; tel. (9) 377-0209; fax (9) 307-7741; f. 1880; 16 community libraries, 2 mobile libraries, central library; 1,032,591 vols, 17,450 gramophone records, 24,714 music scores, 12,000 compact discs, 2,000 videos; special collections: Grey and Shaw Collections of MSS and incunabula, Grey Maori Collection, Lewis Eady Music Collection, Reed Dumas Collection; photographic collections; City Librarian BARBARA BIRKBECK.

University of Auckland Library: PMB 92019, Auckland; tel. (9) 373-7999; fax (9) 373-7565; f. 1884; 1,610,000 vols, 17,000 periodicals; consists of General Library and 14 divisional libraries; Librarian JANET COPSEY; publ. *Bibliographical Bulletin*.

Christchurch

Canterbury Public Library: POB 1466, cnr Gloucester St and Oxford Tce, Christchurch; tel. (3) 379-6914; fax (3) 365-1751; e-mail thelma.willett@govt.nz; f. 1859; 360,000 vols; 11 brs and 2 mobile libraries; Library Manager SUE SUTHERLAND; publs *Bookmark* (monthly), *Connect* (monthly).

Lincoln University Library: Lincoln University, POB 64, Canterbury; tel. (3) 325-2811; fax (3) 325-2944; e-mail library@lincoln.ac.nz; f. 1960; 154,000 vols; specializes in commerce and management, primary production and natural resources, science and engineering, social sciences; Librarian ISOBEL MOSELEY; publ. *Annual Report*.

University of Canterbury Library: Private Bag 4800, Christchurch; tel. (3) 366-7001; fax (3) 364-2055; f. 1873; 1,400,000 items; spec. collns incl. Macmillan Brown Collection of New Zealand and Pacific Materials; Librarian R. W. HLAVAC.

Dunedin

Dunedin Public Library: POB 5542, Moray Place, Dunedin; tel. (3) 4743-690; fax (3) 4743-660; e-mail library@dcc.govt.nz; f. 1908; 610,790 vols; collection of illuminated MSS, McNab New Zealand collection 70,000 vols, Reed/ Bible/ Dickens/Johnson/ Farjeon/ Hymnbook/ early printed MSS collection 8,000 vols; Librarian ALLISON DOBBIE.

Otago District Law Society Library: Private Bag 1901, Dunedin; tel. (3) 4770596; fax (3) 4741886; e-mail library@odls.org.nz; f. 1859; 13,500 vols; Librarian A. J. KELLY.

University of Otago Library: POB 56, Dunedin; tel. (3) 479-1100; fax (3) 479-8947; f. 1870; 1,285,000 vols; Librarian M. J. WOOLISCROFT.

Hamilton

University of Waikato Library: Private Bag 3105, Hamilton; tel. (7) 856-2889; fax (7) 838-4017; e-mail library@waikato.ac.nz; f. 1964; 784,000 vols, 5,985 current periodicals; incorporates Central, Education, Law and Map libraries, and New Zealand Collection; Librarian SUE PHARO.

Palmerston North

Palmerston North Public Library: POB 1948, Palmerston North; tel. (6) 358-3076; fax (6) 356-8869; f. 1876; 250,000 vols; lending, reference, children's, audiovisual, archives sections; 3 brs; one mobile library; Librarian ANTHONY LEWIS.

Ponsonby

Leys Institute Branch, Auckland Public Libraries: 20 St Mary's Rd, Ponsonby; f. 1905; early New Zealand history; general literature, basic vocabulary collection for children with literacy difficulties; Librarian Miss N. FOSTER.

Upper Hutt

AgResearch Library: POB 40771, Upper Hutt; tel. (4) 5286-089; fax (4) 528-1374; serves New Zealand Pastoral Agriculture Research Institute and Wallaceville Research Centre; agricultural and veterinary sciences; Library Man. CAROLE DEVINE.

Wellington

Museum of New Zealand, Te Papa Tongarewa, Hector Library: Cable St, Wellington; tel. (4) 381-7000; fax (4) 381-7370; f. 1990, incorporates National Museum Library, National Art Gallery Library and Royal Society of New Zealand Library; 150,000 vols; Librarian MANUELA C. ANGELO.

National Archives: 10 Mulgrave Street, Wellington (POB 12-050 Wellington); tel. (4) 499-5595; fax (4) 495-6210; f. 1926; 50,000 linear metres of archives; 200,000 photographs; 3,000 films; 600,000 maps and plans; legislative, executive and judicial records of New Zealand government (incl. provincial govts); ministerial papers; National War Art Collection; public reference services in Wellington and at regional offices in Auckland, Christchurch and Dunedin; records centres in Auckland and Wellington; Dir KATHRYN PATTERSON; publs Inventories, leaflets and microfilms.

National Library of New Zealand (Te Puna Matauranga o Aotearoa): POB 1467, Wellington 6000; tel. (4) 474-3000; fax (4) 474-3035; f. 1966; 750,000 vols, 8,500 periodical titles, 10 main microform collections, 13,000 audiobook titles, 28 online databases; provides nat. online bibliographic database to mem. libraries; National Librarian P. G. SCOTT.

Constituent library:

Alexander Turnbull Library: POB 12-349, Wellington 6000; tel. (4) 474-3000; fax (4) 474-3063; f. 1918; 260,000 vols, including 16,000 rare books, chiefly in English literature; special collections include New Zealand and Oceania, Milton, Katherine Mansfield, oral history; 5,000 linear metres of MSS; 50,000 drawings and prints; 846,000 photographs; 41,000 maps; Chief Librarian M. CALDER; publs *TLR* (annually), *Off the Record* (annually).

Parliamentary Library: Parliament House, Wellington; tel. (4) 471-9623; fax (4) 471-1250; f. 1858; 310,000 vols monographs, 186,000 vols periodicals; exchange repository; special collections: New Zealand, overseas official and parliamentary materials; Parliamentary Librarian D. I. MATHESON.

Victoria University Library: POB 3438, Wellington; tel. (4) 472-1000; fax (4) 471-2070; f. 1899; 936,000 vols; Librarian V. G. ELLIOTT.

Wellington Public Library: POB 1992, Wellington; tel. (4) 801-4040; fax (4) 801-4047; f. 1893; 686,145 vols, 51,328 audiovisual items, 100,000 periodicals; 11 br. libraries and mobile surburban service; Man. (Libraries) J. HILL.

Museums and Art Galleries

Auckland

Auckland Art Gallery Toi o Tāmaki: POB 5449, Auckland 1; tel. (9) 307-7700; fax (9) 302-1096; f. 1888; 12th–20th-century European paintings, sculpture, prints and drawings, Frances Hodgkins collection, Colin McCahon collection, Fuseli drawings, 19th- and 20th-century New Zealand painting, sculpture and prints; photographs and artists' books, audio- and video-tapes; John Weeks archive; research library of 33,000 vols; Dir CHRIS SAINES; publs *Auckland Art Gallery Toi O Tāmaki News*.

Auckland Museum: Private Bag 92018, Auckland 1; tel. (9) 309-0443; fax (9) 379-9956; f. 1852; natural history, ethnology (especially NZ Maori and Oceanic), applied arts (especially Asian, European and NZ ceramics, English furniture, textiles), social and war history; conservation laboratory; museum, scientific and historical library of 100,000 vols; Exec. Dir Dr T. L. R. WILSON; Librarian J. CHONG; publs *Annual Report*, *Records* (annually), *Bulletin* (occasional), handbooks and educational leaflets.

Museum of Transport and Technology (MOTAT): Great North Rd, Western Springs, Auckland; tel. (9) 846-0199; fax (9) 846-4242; f. 1960; vehicles, aircraft, machinery and equipment of historical and technical interest; includes Aviation Hangar and Victorian Village; operates electric tramway and steam locomotives; Walsh Memorial Library of 11,000 monographs, 850 serial titles, technical manuals, photographic plans, archives, special collections of Whites Aviation Photographic prints, archives of pioneer aviators Jean Batten and Richard Pearse; Man. GRANT KIRBY.

Christchurch

Canterbury Museum: Rolleston Ave, Christchurch 1; tel. (3) 366-5000; fax (3) 366-5622; e-mail postmaster@cantmus.govt.nz; f. 1867; cultural and natural history of Canterbury region in NZ and world perspective, Antarctic exploration; archaeology, ethnology, Canterbury history, geology, zoology, extinct bird studies; Asian and European arts; Canterbury archives; pictorial history; Dir ANTHONY E. WRIGHT; publs *Records*, *Bulletin* (occasional), *Annual Report*, pamphlets.

Robert McDougall Art Gallery and McDougall Contemporary Art Annex: Rolleston Ave, Christchurch; tel. (3) 3650-915; fax (3) 3653-942; f. 1932; New Zealand, European works; Dir P. ANTHONY PRESTON; publs *Bulletin* (4 a year), exhibition catalogues.

Dunedin

Dunedin Public Art Gallery: The Octagon, Dunedin; tel. (3) 4677-477; fax (3) 4677-466; f. 1884; maintains a conservation laboratory; holdings include: 14th–19th-century European paintings, New Zealand paintings from 1870, Australian paintings 1900–70, British watercolours, portraits and landscapes; 18th–20th-century Japanese prints, 19th- and 20th-century New Zealand prints; de Beer collection of old and modern masters, includes oils by Claude Lorrain and Monet; decorative arts collections of furniture, ceramics, glass, oriental rugs; Dir JOHN MCCORMACK; publs *Annual Report*, *Gallery* (quarterly newsletter), *Midwest* (3 a year).

Otago Museum: Great King St, Dunedin; tel. (3) 477-2372; fax (3) 477-5993; f. 1868; natural sciences, NZ and Pacific anthropology, classical archaeology, European and Asian ceramics, 'Discovery World' Science Centre, NZ crafts; Dir S. C. PAUL; publs *Annual Report*, *Newsletter*.

Theomin Gallery, Dunedin: 'Olveston', 42 Royal Terrace, Dunedin; tel. (3) 4773-320; fax (3) 4792-094; built 1904–06; Jacobean-style house designed by British architect Sir Ernest George for David Edward Theomin, bequeathed to the city by his daughter, Dorothy, 1966, opened to the public 1967; antique furniture, ceramics, crystal, bronzes, Persian rugs, silver, early English, European and NZ oils and watercolours; Man. G. D. BARRON.

Gisborne

Gisborne Museum & Arts Centre: POB 716, Gisborne; tel. (6) 867-3832; fax (6) 867-2728; f. 1954; art gallery and studios; local history, Maori studies, natural history; Dir GREG MCMANUS; publs *Gisborne Museum & Arts Centre Newsletter* (quarterly), *Gisborne Museum Occasional Papers* (1 or 2 a year).

Gore

Eastern Southland Gallery (Inc.): Cnr Main and Norfolk Sts, POB 305, Gore, Southland; tel. (20) 89-907; f. 1983; exhibitions: art works, craft work, historical displays; cultural centre for presentation of films, lectures, music, poetry, etc.; Dir JIM GEDDES; publ. *Activities Bulletin* (2 a year).

Hokitika

West Coast Historical Museum: Tancred St, POB 180, Hokitika, Westland; tel. and fax (3) 755-6898; social and natural history exhibits, working models, historical records; audio visual programme on 19th-century West Coast goldmining industry and colonial settlement; Poutini Maori and 19th-century immigrant histories; pounamu (NZ greenstone), gold, NZ flora and fauna; Dir CLAUDIA LANDIS.

Invercargill

Anderson Park Art Gallery (Inc.): POB 755, Invercargill; mainly New Zealand works; Pres. S. BRADSHAW.

Southland Museum and Art Gallery: POB 1012, Queen's Park, Invercargill; tel. (3) 2189-753; natural history, Maori and colonial history, 'Victoriana', art gallery, astronomical observatory; live Tuatara enclosure; Subantarctic centre; Dir RUSSELL J. BECK.

Napier

Hawke's Bay Cultural Trust: POB 248, Napier; tel. (6) 835-7781; fax (6) 835-3984; e-mail hbct@inhb.co.nz.

Operates:

Hawke's Bay Exhibition Centre: Eastbourne St, Hastings; tel. and fax (6) 876-2077; e-mail hbec@inhb.co.nz; regional venue for temporary touring exhibitions.

Hawke's Bay Museum: 9 Herschell St, Napier; tel. (6) 835-7781; fax (6) 835-3984; e-mail hbct@inhb.co.nz; Maori and NZ art and material culture, painting, pottery and sculpture, decorative arts, 1931 earthquake and dinosaur exhibitions; regional archives.

Faraday Centre: under development; Faraday St, Napier; science and technology.

Nelson

Nelson Provincial Museum: POB 645, Nelson; tel. and fax (3) 547-9740; f. 1841; Maori and European history; reference library, 1,200,000 photographs (from 1860s), archives (from 1840s); Man. M. H. KLAASSENS.

Suter Art Gallery: Queen's Gardens, Nelson; tel. (3) 548-4699; fax (3) 548-1236; f. 1895, rebuilt 1978; important collection of early NZ watercolours; programme of exhibitions, performances and films; Dir HELEN TELFORD; publ. *Newsletter* (quarterly).

Oamaru

Forrester Gallery: Waitaki District Council, Private Bag 50058, Oamaru; tel. (3) 434-1653; fax (3) 434-1654; f. 1983; works of art and architectural drawings related to North Otago and New Zealand; programme of exhibitions and cultural events; Dir WARWICK SMITH; publ. *Newsletter* (quarterly).

Paihia

Waitangi Treaty House: Waitangi National Reserve, Paihia, Bay of Islands; site of Treaty of Waitangi; carved Maori meeting house and war canoe; exhibits of New Zealand historical interest up to 1840; visitor centre complex and audio-visual programme on signing of treaty between Maori Chiefs and British Crown.

Timaru

Aigantighe Art Gallery: 49 Wai-iti Rd, Timaru; tel. (3) 688-4424; fax (3) 6848346; f. 1956; New Zealand and European paintings, prints, sculpture and ceramics; Dir FIONA CIARAN; publs *Members' Newsletters* (quarterly).

Wanganui

Sarjeant Gallery: Queen's Park, POB 998, Wanganui; f. 1919; 18th-, 19th- and 20th-century European and English watercolours, representative New Zealand collection, Gilfillan collection, Barraud collection, drawings after Bernardino Poccetti, collection of First World War cartoons.

Whanganui Regional Museum: POB 352, Wanganui; tel. (6) 345-7443; fax (6) 347-6512; e-mail sharon.dell@wrmuseum.org.nz; f. 1895; ethnology, natural history and colonial history; regional archival repository; Dir S. E. DELL.

Wellington

New Zealand Academy of Fine Arts: POB 467, National Museum Bldg, Buckle St, Wellington 1; tel. (4) 385-9267; fax (4) 385-9229; f. 1882; art gallery promoting NZ artists and the visual arts in NZ through 8 annual exhibitions; Pres. PHILIP MARKHAM; publ. *Academy Arts News* (4 a year).

Te Papa: Cable St, POB 467, Wellington; tel. (4) 381-7000; fax (4) 381-7070; f. 1992 by merger of the National Art Gallery and the National Museum; art, history, Maori culture, natural environment; collection of Maori taonga, incl. Te Hau-ki-Turanga (oldest extant Maori building in New Zealand); Polynesian, Micronesian and Melanesian art and culture; paintings, drawings, graphic art, photography and sculpture by New Zealand and foreign artists; collections of works by Natalia Gontcharova, Frances Hodgkins, Raymond McIntyre and Colin McCahon; maintains Hector Library (systematic biology, ethnology, early European South Pacific exploration and art reference material); Chief Exec. CHERYLL SOTHERAN.

Universities

UNIVERSITY OF AUCKLAND

Private Bag 92019, Auckland 1
Telephone: 3737999

Founded 1882 as Auckland University College; university status 1958

Chancellor: Hon. Justice Sir IAN BARKER
Pro-Chancellor: H. TITTER
Vice-Chancellor: Prof. A. MACCORMICK (acting)
Registrar: W. B. NICOLL

Library: see Libraries
Number of teachers: 1,117 (full-time)
Number of internal students: 23,926

Publications: *University Calendar, News.*

DEANS

Faculty of Arts: D. SUTTON
Faculty of Science: R. P. COONEY
Faculty of Commerce: B. SPICER
Faculty of Law: B. V. HARRIS
Faculty of Architecture, Property and Planning: M. H. PRITCHARD
Faculty of Engineering: P. BROTHERS
Faculty of Medicine and Health Science: P. D. GLUCKMAN

PROFESSORS AND HEADS OF DEPARTMENTS

(H = Head of Department)

AUSTIN, G. L., Physics (H)
BEAGLEHOLE, R., Community Health (H)
BELICH, J. C., History
BELLAMY, A. R., Biological Sciences (Dir)
BERGQUIST, P. L., Biological Sciences
BINNEY, J. M. C., History
BISHOP, J. C., Philosophy (H)
BLACK, P. M., Geology
BOURASSA, S. C., Property (H)
BOWMAN, M. J., Environmental and Marine Sciences (H)
BOWMAN, R. G., Accounting and Finance
BOYS, J. T., Electrical and Electronic Engineering (H)
BRADBURY, M. E., Accounting and Finance
BRODIE, R. J., Marketing (H)
BROOM, N. D., Engineering
BUCHANAN, I. B., Art History
BUTCHER, J. C., Mathematics and Statistics
CALUDE, C. S., Computer Science
CANNELL, M., Physiology (H)
CARTER, I. R., Sociology (H)
CARTWRIGHT, R. W., International Business
CHEN, J. J. J., Chemical and Materials Engineering (H)
CLARK, G. R., Chemistry
CLARK, P. J. A., Asian Languages and Literatures (H)
CLARK, R. G., Paediatrics
COLLINS, I. F., Engineering Science
CONDER, M. D. E., Mathematics (H)
COONEY, R. P., Chemistry
COOPER, G. J. S., Biological Sciences
CORBALLIS, M. C., Psychology
COSTER, G. D., General Practice (H)
CRAIG, J. L., Environmental Management
DALE, I. R., Education
DALZIEL, R. M., History (H)
DANAHER, P. J., Marketing
DAVISON, M. C., Psychology
DEEKS, J. S., Management and Employment Relations (H)
DEYO, F. C., Development Studies
DIAZ, J. A., Management Science and Information Systems (H)
DORAN, R. W., Computer Science
DUFFY, G. G., Chemical and Materials Engineering
DUNN, M. R., Fine Arts (H)
DURING, M. J., Molecular Medicine (H)
EAGLES, I. G., Commercial Law
ELLIOTT, R. B., Paediatrics
EMANUEL, D. M., Accounting and Finance (H)
EVANS, P. J., Law
FAULL, R. L. M., Anatomy (H)
FOOKES, T. W., Planning (H)
FORER, P. C., Geography
GARNER, L. F., Optometry and Vision Science (H)
GAULD, D. B., Mathematics
GAVIN, J. B., Pathology (H)
GIBBONS, P. B., Computer Science (H)
GILMOUR, R. S., Molecular Medicine
GLUCKMAN, P. D., Paediatrics
GRAY, V. J., Classics and Ancient History (H)
GREEN, R. C., Anthropology
GUSTAFSON, B. S., Political Studies
HAARHOF, E. J., Architecture (H)
HARDING, J. E., Paediatrics
HARRIS, B. V., Law (H)
HARVEY, J. D., Physics
HAWORTH, N. A. F., International Business (H)
HAY, J. E., Environmental and Marine Sciences
HAZLEDINE, T. J., Economics
HEAP, S. W., Anatomy
HILL, G. L., Surgery
HOHEPA, P. W., Maori Studies
HOOL, R. B., Economics (H)
HOSKING, P. L., Geography (H)
HUNT, J. G., Architecture (H)
HUNTER, P. J., Engineering Science
INKSON, J. H. K., Management and Employment Relations
IRWIN, G. J., Anthropology
IRWIN, R. J., Psychology
JACKSON, M. P., English
JACKSON, P. S., Mechanical Engineering (H)
KIRKNESS, A. C., Germanic Languages and Literature
KLETTE, R., Computer Science
KYDD, R. R., Psychiatry and Behaviour Science (H)
LEE, A. J., Statistics (H)
LE HERON, R. B., Geography
LEES, H., Music
LEIMS, T., Asian Languages and Literatures
LENNON, D. R., Paediatrics
LILLY, I. K., Russian (H)
LIPSKI, J., Physiology
LORIMER, P. J., Mathematics
LOVELL, P. H., Biological Sciences
LOWE, P. G., Civil and Resource Engineering
MCCARTHY, D. C., Medical Administration
MCNAUGHTON, S. S., Education (H)
MACPHERSON, R. J. S., Professional Development (Dir)
MANGAN, G. L., Psychology
MANTELL, C. D., Maori and Pacific Islands Health (H)
MARSHALL, J. D., Education
MARSHALL, R. N., Sport and Exercise Science (H)
MARTIN, G. J., Mathematics
MAXTON, J. K., Law
MITCHELL, M. D., Pharmacology and Clinical Pharmacology (H)
MOLLOY, M. A., Women's Studies
MORAN, W., Geography
MOSKO, M. S., Anthropology (H)
NEILL, M. A. F., English
O'CONNOR, C. J., Chemistry
OWENS, R. G., Psychology
PARRY, B. R., Surgery (H)
PAVLOV, B., Mathematics
PEDDIE, R. A., Continuing Education (Dir)
PENDER, M. J., Civil and Resource Engineering (H)
POLETTI, A. R., Physics
POWELL, M. J., Management and Employment Relations
RAMSAY, R. L., French (H)
REAY, B. G., History
REILLY, I. L., School of Mathematical and Information Sciences (Dir)
RICHARDS, G. E., Paediatrics (H)
RICHMOND, D. E., Medicine
RICKETT, C. E. F., Commercial Law, Law
RIDDELL, R. B., Planning
RIMMER, J. F., Music (H)
ROPER, W. R., Chemistry
RUSSELL, D. K., Chemistry
RYAN, D. M., Management Science and Information Systems, Engineering Science (H)
SALMOND, Dame M. A., Anthropology, Maori Studies
SCOTT, A. J., Statistics
SEBER, G. A. F., Statistics
SHARP, R. A., Political Studies (H)
SHARPE, D. N., Medicine (H)
SIMMONS, L. E., Italian (H)
SIMPSON, I. J., Medicine
SMITH, D. I. B., English
SPICER, B. H., Accounting and Finance
STURM, T. L., English (H)
SUTTON, D. G., Anthropology
SUTTON, M. J., German
TAGGART, M. B., Law
THOMAS, D. R., Community Health
THOMBORSON, C. D., Computer Science
TITTLER, J., Spanish (H)
TURNER, G. M., Obstetrics and Gynaecology (H)
VALE, B. A., Architecture
VAUGHAN, G. M., Psychology (H)
WAKE, G. C., Mathematics
WALLS, D. F., Physics
WELCH, B. J., Chemical and Materials Engineering
WELLS, R. M. G., Biological Sciences
WENDT, A., English
WILLIAMS, P. W., Geography
WILLIAMSON, A. G., Electrical and Electronic Engineering
WONG, J., Accounting and Finance

ATTACHED CENTRES

Centre for Pacific Studies: Dir MELENAITI TAUMOEFOLAU.
Geothermal Institute: Dir P. R. L. BROWNE.

UNIVERSITY OF CANTERBURY

Private Bag 4800, Christchurch
Telephone: 366-7001
Fax: 364-2999
Founded 1873
State control
Academic year: February to November

Chancellor: I. D. LEGGAT
Vice-Chancellor: A. D. BROWNLIE
Deputy Vice-Chancellor: R. PARK

Registrar: A. W. HAYWARD
Librarian: R. W. HLAVAC

Library: see Libraries
Number of teachers: 465, including 38 professors
Number of students: 11,771

Publications: *University Calendar*, *Student Guide, Enrolment Handbook, Chronicle* (fortnightly in term).

DEANS

Faculty of Arts: J. E. CAMERON
Faculty of Commerce: B. J. CLARKE
Faculty of Engineering: A. J. SUTHERLAND
Faculty of Forestry: R. O'REILLY
Faculty of Law: G. F. ORCHARD
Faculty of Music and Fine Arts: B. W. PRITCHARD
Faculty of Science: K. W. DUNCAN

PROFESSORS

ADSHEAD, S. A. M., History
ARRILLAGA, J., Electrical and Electronic Engineering
ASTLEY, R. J., Mechanical Engineering
BAGGALEY, W. J., Physics and Astronomy
BLANK, R. H., Political Science
BURROWS, J. F., Law
CAMPBELL, L., Linguistics
CEGRELL, U., Mathematics and Statistics
CLARKE, B. J., Accountancy Finance and Information Systems
COLE, J. W., Geological Sciences
COXON, J. M., Chemistry
DAELLENBACH, H. G., Management
ELMS, D. G., Civil Engineering
GUNBY, D. C., English
HAMILTON, R. T., Management
HEARNSHAW, J. B., Physics and Astronomy
HOUSE, D. A., Chemistry
KEEY, R. B., Chemical and Process Engineering
KIRK, R. M., Geography
MCINTYRE, W. D., History
NUTHALL, G. A., Education
ORCHARD, G. F., Law
PALLOT, J., Accountancy, Finance and Information Systems
PARK, R., Civil Engineering
PENNY, J. P., Computer Science
PHILLIPS, L. F., Chemistry
POWELL, H. K. J., Chemistry
ROBINSON, W. T., Chemistry
SANDS, R. M., Forestry
STEDMAN, G. E., Physics and Astronomy
STRONGMAN, K. T., Psychology
TAKAOKA, T., Computer Science
TAYLOR, D. P., Electrical and Electronic Engineering
THORNS, D. C., Sociology
TODD, S. M. D., Law
WILKINSON, D. L., Civil Engineering
WILLMOTT, W. E., Sociology
WINTERBOURN, M. J., Zoology

NON PROFESSORIAL HEADS OF DEPARTMENTS

ALLOTT, K., French and Russian
BELL, T. C., Computer Science
BRACEY, E. N., Fine Arts
BROWNE, D. E., Philosophy and Religious Studies
BUCKTON, R. M., Music
CHETWIN, M., Accountancy, Finance and Information Systems
COLE, A. L. J., Plant and Microbial Sciences
COOKE, N., Civil Engineering
COOKSON, J. E., History
DALRYMPLE-ALFORD, J. C., Psychology
DUKE, R. M., Electrical and Electronic Engineering
EARL, W. B., Chemical and Process Engineering
FISHER, R. W., German
FREEMAN, C. G., Chemistry
GEORGE, J. A., Management
HALL, R. R., Sociology
HARRISON, R., Economics
HEAD, L. F., Maori
HENDERSON, J., Political Science
KUIPER, K., Linguistics
MCDONALD, D. J., Social Work
MCGEORGE, C. M., Education
MAZER, S. L., Theatre and Film Studies
MONTGOMERY, M. E., American Studies
PEARMAN, G. R., Continuing Education
RENAUD, P. F., Mathematics and Statistics
ROWE, D. W., Law
SEELEY, C., Asian Languages
SPENCE, G. W., English
SYME, R. W. G., Physics and Astronomy
TULLY, J., Journalism
WEAVER, S. D., Geological Sciences
WITTMANN, L. K., Feminist Studies

LINCOLN UNIVERSITY

POB 94, Lincoln University, Canterbury
Telephone: (3) 325-2811
Fax: (3) 325-2965

Founded 1878; formerly the Canterbury Agricultural College and from 1961 to 1989 Lincoln College, a constituent college of the University of Canterbury; from 1990 an autonomous university
State control
Academic year: March to October

Chancellor: MALCOLM L. CAMERON
Vice-Chancellor: Dr FRANK WOOD
Registrar: A. J. SARGISON
Librarian: A. J. DEWE

Library: see Libraries
Number of teachers: 200, including 17 professors
Number of students: 4,000 including short-course students

Publications: *University Calendar, Technical Publications* (irregular), *Research Publications* (irregular), *Lincoln Outlook* (2 a year), *Infolinc* (fortnightly), *Alumni News* (1 a year).

PROFESSORS

BOYD, T., Real Estate, Valuation and Property Management
BYWATER, A. C., Farm Management
CAMERON, K. C., Soil Science
CORNFORTH, I. S., Soil Science
CUSHMAN, J. G., Parks, Recreation and Tourism
EARL, P. E., Economics
FIELD, R. J., Plant Science
GAUNT, R. E., Pathology
GOH, K. M., Soil Science
KISSLING, C. C., Transport Studies
LATTIMORE, R. G., Agricultural Economics
RICHARDS, L. R., Natural Resources Engineering
ROWE, R. N., Horticulture
SYKES, A. R., Animal Science
WOOD, E., Wool Science
WRATTEN, S. D., Ecology
ZWART, A. C., Marketing

ATTACHED RESEARCH INSTITUTES

Agribusiness Economics Research Unit: Dir A. C. ZWART.

Animal and Veterinary Sciences Blood Group Typing Unit: Dir Dr R. MCFARLANE.

Centre for Molecular Biology: Dir (vacant).

Centre for Mountain Studies: Dir Dr R. CULLEN.

Centre for Resource Management: Dir Dr I. SPELLERBERG.

Equine Research Unit: Dir Prof. C. H. G. IRVINE.

Lincoln Soil Quality Research Centre, Lincoln Ventures Ltd: Dir Prof. K. CAMERON.

Management Systems Research Unit: Dir Dr P. NUTHALL.

Plant Protection Research Unit, Lincoln Ventures Ltd: Manager Dr M. R. BUTCHER.

MASSEY UNIVERSITY

Palmerston North
Telephone: (6) 356-9099
Fax: (6) 350-5630

Founded 1926 as Massey Agricultural College and merged with the Palmerston North Branch of the Victoria University of Wellington 1963; full autonomy granted 1964
State control
Academic year: February to November

Chancellor: M. O. CROXSON
Vice-Chancellor: Dr J. A. MCWHA
Assistant Vice-Chancellor (Academic): G. S. FRASER
Assistant Vice-Chancellor (Research): S. N. MCCUTCHEON
Assistant Vice-Chancellor (Resources) and Registrar: W. J. TITHER
Assistant Vice-Chancellor (Support Services): M. C. THOMSON
Principal, Albany Campus: I. D. WATSON
Librarian: H. R. RENWICK

Number of teachers: 1,023
Number of students: 32,338

Publications: *Massey University Calendar, Massey Focus* (quarterly), *Massey Alumnus, Newsletter* (2 a year), *Massey University Research Report, Massey News* (weekly).

PRO VICE-CHANCELLORS

College of Business: Prof. R. D. CREMER
College of Education: Prof. L. MEYER
College of Humanities and Social Sciences: Prof. B. K. MACDONALD
College of Sciences: Prof. R. D. ANDERSON

PROFESSORS

BHAMIDIMARRI, R., Process and Environmental Technology
BAILEY, W. C., Agribusiness and Resource Management
BAKER, E. N., Chemistry and Biochemistry
BANKS, N. H., Plant Science
BARNES, D. J., Manufacturing and Quality Systems
BARRY, T., Animal Science
BLAIR, H. T., Animal Science
BODDY, J., Nursing Studies
BRODIE, A. M., Chemistry
BROOKS, R. R., Soil Science
BROWN, T. J., Microbiology and Genetics
CALLAGHAN, P. T., Physics
CHAPMAN, J. W., Educational Psychology
CHATTERJEE, S., Applied and International Economics
CLELAND, A. C., Food Engineering
CLELAND, D. J., Process and Environmental Technology
CODD, J. A., Policy Studies in Education
CORBALLIS, R. P., English
CROPP, G. M., Modern Languages
DEVLIN, M. H., Executive Development
DEWE, P. J., Human Resource Management
DURIE, M. H., Maori Studies
FIRTH, E. C., Veterinary Clinical Science
FLENLEY, J. R., Geography
GARRICK, D. J., Animal Science
GENDALL, P. J., Marketing
HARGREAVES, R. V., Property Studies
HENDY, M. D., Mathematics
HEWETT, E. W., Plant Science
HILL, M. J., Plant Science
HODGSON, J., Plant Science
HODGSON, R. M., Production Technology
HOWE, K. R., History
HUNT, G. J., School of Aviation
HUNTER, J. J., Statistics
JAMESON, P. E., Plant Biology
JESSHOPE, C. R., Computer Science
KINROSS, N. J., Management Systems

LAGROW, S. J., Rehabilitation Studies
LAMBERT, D., Ecology
LOCK, A. J., Psychology
LONG, N. R., Psychology
MCDERMOTT, P. J., Resource and Environmental Planning
MCGREGOR, J., Human Resource Management
MCKIBBIN, R., Applied Mathematics
MCLENNAN, G., Sociology
MATHEWS, M. R., Accountancy
MEISTER, A. D., Agricultural Economics and Business
MELLOR, D. J., Physiology and Anatomy
MILNE, K. S., Plant Science
MOORE, C. I., Banking
MORRIS, R. S., Veterinary Clinical Sciences
MOUGHAN, P. J., Monogastric Biology
ONO, K., East Asian Studies
OVERTON, J., Development Studies
PARKER, W. J., Agribusiness and Resource Management
PARRY, D. A., Physics
PENNY, E. D., Plant Biology
PERERA, H. M. B., Accounting
PORTER, B. A., Accountancy
PREBBLE, T. K., Extramural Studies
RAE, A. N., Applied and International Economics
ROSE, L. C., Finance
SCHOULS, P. A., Philosophy
SCOTT, D. B., Microbiology and Genetics
SHIRLEY, I. F., Social Policy and Social Work
SISSONS, J., Social Anthropology
SPOONLEY, P., Sociology
SPRINGETT, B. P., Zoology
SULLIVAN, P. A., Biochemistry
THOMAS, R. G., Plant Biology
TILLMAN, R. W., Soil Science
THOMSON, D. W., History
TRAWICK, M., Social Anthropology
VAN DER WALT, N., Management Systems
VITALIS, A., Management Systems
VOGEL, W., Mathematics
WALL, G. L., Agricultural Engineering
WILKS, C. R., Veterinary Pathology and Public Health
WILLIAMS, A., Executive Development
WILLIAMSON, N. B., Veterinary Clinical Sciences
WINGER, R. J., Food Technology

ATTACHED RESEARCH INSTITUTES

Animal Health Centre and Animal Research Services: Dir A. M. ALEXANDER.
Applied Psychology Centre: Dir Prof. N. R. LONG.
Applied Statistics Consultancy Centre: Dir S. J. HASLETT.
Centre for Applied Economics and Policy Studies: Dir Prof. A. N. RAE.
Centre for Veterinary Continuing Education: Dir Dr R. SQUIRES.
Education Research and Development Centre: Dir C. J. P. NOLAN.
Equine Blood Typing and Research Centre: Dir I. L. ANDERSON.
Fertilizer and Lime Research Centre: Dir R. W. TILLMAN.
Food Technology Research Centre: Dir Prof. R. J. WINGER.
Molecular Genetics Laboratory: Dir D. B. SCOTT.
Monogastric Research Unit: Dir P. J. MOUGHAN.
New Zealand Centre for Japanese Studies: Dir J. M. HUNDLEBY.
New Zealand Natural Heritage Foundation: Dir Prof. B. P. SPRINGETT.
New Zealand Social Research Data Archives: Dir H. G. BARNARD.
Social Policy Research Centre: Dir Prof. I. F. SHIRLEY.

UNIVERSITY OF OTAGO

POB 56, Dunedin
Telephone: (3) 479-1100
Fax: (3) 474-1607

Founded 1869

Academic year: March to November

Chancellor: J. O. MEDLICOTT
Pro-Chancellor: E. S. EDGAR
Vice-Chancellor: G. FOGELBERG
Deputy Vice-Chancellors: P. H. MEADE (Academic), I. O. SMITH (Research and International)
Assistant Vice-Chancellors: L. MCLEAN (Division of Commerce), R. D. H. STEWART (Division of Health Sciences), A. A. TROTTER (Division of Humanities), R. A. HEATH (Division of Sciences).
Registrar: K. N. HOUGHTON
Librarian: M. J. WOOLISCROFT

Library: see Libraries
Number of teachers (full-time): 834
Number of students: 15,200

Publications: *University Calendar,* university prospectuses – undergraduate and postgraduate.

DEANS

Faculty of Law: J. S. ANDERSON
Otago Medical School: J. G. MORTIMER
Christchurch School of Medicine: A. R. HORNBLOW
Wellington School of Medicine: L. J. HOLLOWAY
Faculty of Dentistry: P. INNES
School of Pharmacy: P. F. COVILLE
School of Physical Education: L. R. T. WILLIAMS

PROFESSORS

AICKIN, D. R., Obstetrics and Gynaecology
ANDERSON, J. S., Law
BAIRAM, E. I., Economics
BANNISTER, P., Botany
BARBEZAT, G. O., Medicine
BARSBY, J. A., Classics
BEASLEY, C. R. W., Medicine
BOYLE, G. W., Finance and Quantitative Analysis
BRAITHWAITE, A. W., Pathology
BUISSON, D. H., Marketing
BURNS, C. W., Zoology
CAMPBELL, A. J., Medicine
CHETWYND, S. J., Public Health and General Practice
COVILLE, P. F., Pharmacy
COX, B. G., Computer Science
DELAHUNT, B., Pathology
DONALD, R. A., Medicine
DOWDEN, R. L., Physics
DOWELL, A. C., General Practice
DOYLE, T. C. A., Medicine
DRUMMOND, J. D., Music
DUFOUR, J. P., Consumer Services
ELLIS, P. M., Psychological Medicine
ELWOOD, J. M., Preventive and Social Medicine
ESPINER, E. A., Medicine
FERGUSON, M. M., Oral Medicine and Oral Surgery
FOX, A. G., English
GEARE, A. J., Management
GIBSON, C. A., English
GIBSON, R. S., Human Nutrition
GILLETT, G. R., Biomedical Ethics
GIN, T., Anaesthesia
GRIMWOOD, K., Paediatrics and Child Health
HANNAH, J., Surveying
HARRIS, J. M., English
HART, D. N. J., Pathology
HIGHAM, C. F. W., Anthropology
HOLLAND, P. G., Geography
HOLLOWAY, L. J., Pathology
HOLTON, D. A., Mathematics and Statistics
HORNBLOW, A. R., Public Health and General Practice
HORNE, J. G., Surgery
HUNTER, K. A., Chemistry
INNES, P. B., Dentistry
ISICHEI, E., Theology and Religious Studies
JEFFERY, A. K., Orthopaedic Surgery
JONES, D. G., Anatomy and Structural Biology
JONES, D. T., Microbiology
JOYCE, P. R., Psychological Medicine
KA'AI, T., Maori Studies
KEARSLEY, G. W., Advanced Business Programme
KIESER, J. A., Oral Biology and Oral Pathology
KIRK, E. E. J., Restorative Dentistry
LAVERTY, R., Pharmacology
LAWSON, R. W., Marketing
LORIGAN, G. B., Advanced Business Programme
LOY, J. W., Physical Education
MACGREGOR, A. C., Accountancy
MCKERRACHER, D. W., Education
MACKNIGHT, A. D. C., Physiology
MCLEAN, L., Accountancy
MCLEOD, W. H., History
MANLY, B. J. F., Mathematics and Statistics
MANN, J. I., Human Nutrition
MARK, A. F., Botany
MELTON, L. D., Consumer Studies
MILLER, J. O., Psychology
MLADENOV, P. V., Marine Science
MONTEITH, B. D., Restorative Dentistry
MORTIMER, J. G., Paediatrics and Child Health
MUSGRAVE, A. E., Philosophy
NICHOLLS, M. G., Medicine
OLDS, R. J., Pathology
OLSSEN, E. N., History
OWEN, P. D., Economics
PETERSEN, G. B., Biochemistry
PILLAY, G. J., Theology and Religious Studies
RICHARDS, A. M., Medicine
ROBINSON, B. H., Chemistry
ROMANS, S. E., Psychological Medicine
ROTHWELL, A. G., Orthopaedic Surgery
RUSSELL, D. G., Physical Education
SAINSBURY, R., Medicine
SALLIS, P. J., Information Science
SANDLE, W. J., Physics
SIBSON, R. H., Geology
SIMPSON, J., Chemistry
SKEGG, D. C. G., Preventive and Social Medicine
SKEGG, P. D. G., Law
SMILLIE, J. A., Law
SQUIRE, V. A., Mathematics and Statistics
STEWART, R. D. H., Otago School of Medicine
STONE, P. R., Obstetrics and Gynaecology
SULLIVAN, P. A., Biochemistry
SULLIVAN, S. J., Physiotherapy
SUTTON, R. J., Law
TANNOCK, G. W., Microbiology
TATE, W. P., Biochemistry
TEELE, D. W., Paediatrics
TEELE, R. L., Radiology
TILYARD, M. W., General Practice
TOWNSEND, C. R., Zoology
TROTTER, A. A., History
TUCKER, I. G., Pharmacy
VAN RIJ, A. M., Surgery
WHITE, K. G., Psychology
WILLETT, R. J., Accountancy
WILLIAMS, L. R. T., Physical Education
WILSON, P. D., Obstetrics and Gynaecology
WILSON, P. J., Anthropology
WINTERBOURN, C. C., Pathology
WOODWARD, A. J., Public Health

VICTORIA UNIVERSITY OF WELLINGTON

POB 600, Wellington
Telephone: (4) 499-4601
Fax: (4) 495-5239
E-mail: postmaster@vuw.ac.nz

Founded 1899

Language of instruction: English
Academic year: March to February (three semesters)

Chancellor: D. J. WHITE

Pro-Chancellor: M. A. Hirschfeld
Vice-Chancellor: Prof. L. C. Holborow
Deputy Vice-Chancellor: Prof. R. M. Sharp
Assistant Vice-Chancellor (Academic): P. Fenwick
Librarian: V. G. Elliott

Library: see Libraries

Number of full-time teachers: 457, including 58 professors

Number of students: 13,400

Publications: *Victoria University of Wellington Calendar* (1 a year), *Victoria Quarterly*, *Research at Victoria* (1 a year), *Victorious* (1 a year).

DEANS

Faculty of Humanities and Social Sciences: Prof. D. Mackay
Faculty of Commerce and Administration: Prof. N. C. Quigley
Faculty of Law: Prof. B. T. Brooks
Faculty of Science: Prof. J. B. J. Wells

PROFESSORS

(H = Head of Department)

Faculty of Humanities and Social Sciences:
- Alton-Lee, A., Education
- Besnier, N., Anthropology
- Clark, M., Politics
- Cresswell, M. J., Philosophy
- Dearden, C. W., Classics
- Delbrück, H. H. F., European Languages
- Fulcher, L., Applied Social Sciences
- Hall, C. G. W., Education
- Hamer, D. A., History
- Hill, M., Sociology and Social Policy
- Holmes, J., Linguistics and Applied Language Studies
- Kennedy, G. D., Linguistics and Applied Language Studies
- Knight, P., European Languages
- May, H., Education
- Morris, A., Criminology
- Morris, P., Religious Studies
- O'Sullivan, V., English, Film and Drama
- Pettman, R., Politics
- Robinson, R., English, Film and Drama
- Te Awekotuku, N., Maori Studies
- Walls, P., Music

Faculty of Commerce and Administration:
- Ball, I., Accountancy and Commercial Law
- Brittain, M., Communications and Information Management
- Evans, L. T., Economics and Finance
- Hall, V. B., Economics and Finance
- Harbridge, R., Business and Government
- Hawke, G. R., Economics and Finance
- Hince, K. W., Business and Government
- Scott, C. D., Business and Government
- Thirkell, P. C., Business and Government
- Tiffin, J., Communications Studies
- Trow, D. G., Accountancy and Commercial Law
- van Zijl, T., Accountancy and Commercial Law
- Weiss, A., Economics and Finance
- Winiata, W., Accountancy and Commercial Law

Faculty of Law:
- Angelo, A. H.
- McLauchlan, D. W.
- Prebble, J.
- Young, W. A.

Faculty of Science:
- Aasen, C., Architecture
- Barrett, P. J., Geography, Geology, Geophysics
- Beaglehole, D., Chemical and Physical Sciences
- Burns, G., Chemical and Physical Sciences
- Downey, R., Mathematical and Computing Sciences
- Garnock-Jones, P., Biological Sciences
- Goldblatt, R. I., Mathematical and Computing Sciences
- Halton, B., Chemical and Physical Sciences
- Harper, J. F., Mathematical and Computing Sciences
- Hine, J., Mathematical and Computing Sciences
- Lekner, J., Chemical and Physical Sciences
- Ng, S.-H., Psychology
- Smith, E., Geography, Geology, Geophysics
- Spencer, J. L., Chemical and Physical Sciences
- Tippett, H., Architecture
- Trodahl, H. J., Chemical and Physical Sciences
- Vere-Jones, D., Statistics
- Vignaux, G. A., Operations Research
- Walcott, R., Geography, Geology, Geophysics

ATTACHED RESEARCH INSTITUTES

Antarctic Research Centre: Dir Prof. P. J. Barrett.

Centre for Building Performance Research: Dir Prof. H. Tippett.

Centre for Continuing Education: M. Chambers.

Coastal Marine Research Unit: Dir Dr J. Gardner.

Deaf Studies Research Unit: Dir Prof. G. D. Kennedy.

Industrial Relations Centre: Dir Prof. K. W. Hince.

Institute of Criminology: Dir Prof. A. Morris.

Institute of Geophysics: Chair. Prof. E. Smith.

Institute of Policy Studies: Dir G. R. Hawke.

Institute of Statistics and Operations Research: Chair. Assoc. Prof. P. Thomson.

Stout Research Centre for the Study of New Zealand Society, History and Culture: Dir Prof. V. G. O'Sullivan.

University Teaching Development Centre: Dir Dr M. Recker (acting).

Centre for Strategic Studies: Dir T. O'Brien.

Centre for Asia-Pacific Law and Business: Dir T. Beal.

Health Services Research Centre: Dir Prof. G. Salmond.

Centre for Mathematics and Science Education: Dir Assoc. Prof. M. Clark.

UNIVERSITY OF WAIKATO

Private Bag 3105, Hamilton
Telephone: 856-2889
Fax: 856-0135

Founded 1964

Academic year: February to November

Chancellor: Caroline Bennett
Vice-Chancellor: Bryan C. Gould
Assistant Vice-Chancellor (Registrar): J. J. Callaghan
Librarian: S. Pharo
Library: see Libraries

Number of teachers: 642
Number of students: 11,618

Publication: *University of Waikato Calendar.*

DEANS

School of Arts and Social Sciences: P. Koopman-Boyden
School of Computing and Mathematical Sciences: I. D. Graham
School of Education: N. Alcorn
School of Law: M. Bedggood
School of Management Studies: M. J. Pratt
School of Maori and Pacific Development: T. Reedy
School of Science and Technology: R. Price

PROFESSORS

- Alcorn, N., Education
- Apperley, M. D., Computer Science
- Barber, L. H., History
- Barratt, A. A. T., English
- Bedford, R. D., Geography
- Bedggood, M., Law
- Bing, D., Political Science and Public Policy
- Black, K. P., Earth Sciences
- Bridges, D. S., Mathematics and Statistics
- Cleary, J. G., Computer Sciences
- Daniel, R. M., Biological Sciences
- de Ras, M. E. P., Women's and Gender Studies
- Dixon, B. R., Management Studies
- Enderwick, I. P., Marketing and International Management
- Evans, W. J. M., Psychology
- Farrell, R. L., Biological Sciences
- Foulds, L. R., Management
- Gibbs, B. R., Philosophy
- Gilson, C. H. J., Strategic Management and Leadership
- Glynn, E. L., Professional Studies
- Graham, I. D., Computer Science
- Havemann, P. L., Law
- Healy, T. R., Earth Sciences
- John, J. A., Statistics
- Kalnins, E. G., Mathematics
- Koopman-Boyden, P. G., Arts and Social Sciences
- Mackay, K. M., Chemistry
- Mahuta, R. T., Raupatu Research
- McLaren, M. C., Management Communication
- Middleton, S. C., Education Studies
- Milroy, J. W., Maori
- Mitchell, D. R., Education Studies
- Morgan, H. W., Biological Sciences
- Nelson, C. S., Earth Sciences
- Nicholson, B. K., Chemistry
- Oettli, P. H., German
- Oxley, L. T., Economics
- Pool, D. I., Population Studies
- Pratt, M. J., Management Studies
- Price, R., Science and Technology
- Ramsay, P. D. K., Education Studies
- Reedy, T., Maori and Pacific Development
- Ritchie, J., Psychology
- Sammes, N. M., Technology
- Selby, M. J., Earth Sciences
- Silvester, W. B., Biological Sciences
- Smith, B. V., Finance
- Spiller, P. R., Law
- Stokes, E. M., Geography
- Walker, G. M., English
- Wilkins, A. L., Chemistry
- Wilson, M. A., Law
- Witten, I. H., Computer Science
- Zorn, T. E., Management Communication

Polytechnic Institutions

Auckland Institute of Technology: Wellesley St East, Private Bag 92006, Auckland 1020; tel. (9) 307-9999 (Wellesley Street and Akoranga Campus), fax (9) 307-9968; f. 1854, name changed in 1989 from Auckland Technical Institute; 692 teachers; 24,509 students; library of 75,000 vols; Pres. Dr John C. Hinchcliff; Academic Registrar J. Carlson; publs *Prospectus, Annual Report, Research Report.*

Central Institute of Technology: Private Box 40740, Upper Hutt; tel. (4) 527-6398; fax (4) 527-6359; f. 1960; full-time technician and professional education; 330 staff; 5,000 enrolments; library of 29,000 vols, 800 periodicals (570 current); CEO T. Boyle.

Christchurch Polytechnic/Te Whare Runanga o Otautahi: Coventry St, POB 22-095, Christchurch 8032; tel. (3) 379-8150; fax (3) 366-6544; f. 1965; courses at trade technician, professional and degree levels, recreational and community courses; 350 full-time and 830 part-time teachers, 17,600 students; library of 48,000 items; Dir JOHN W. SCOTT; publs *Prospectus* (annually), *Annual Report*.

Hutt Valley Polytechnic: Private Bag 39803, Te Puni Mail Centre, Petone, nr Wellington; tel. (4) 568-3419; fax (4) 568-6849; f. 1976; courses in trades, commercial and technical subjects; 180 staff, 10,000 enrolments; library of 20,000 items; Chief Exec. W. J. MATTHEW.

Manukau Institute of Technology: Private Bag 94006, Manukau City; tel. (9) 274-6009; fax (9) 273-0701; f. 1970; courses in trades, technical and professional subjects; 300 teachers, 22,000 students; library of 32,000 vols; CEO J. R. MACDONALD; Librarian A. M. M. HUANG.

Open Polytechnic of New Zealand: Wyndrum Ave, Private Bag 31914, Lower Hutt; tel. (4) 566-6189; fax (4) 566-5633; f. 1946; certificate- to degree-level courses by distance and open learning methods in business, professional, technical, agriculture/horticulture, trades and self improvement subjects; 30,000 students; Chief Exec. SHONA E. BUTTERFIELD.

Otago Polytechnic: Private Bag, Dunedin; tel. (3) 477-3014; fax 477-5185; e-mail jbarbour@tekotago.ac.nz; f. 1966; courses in fine arts, commercial, technical, professional and health science subjects; 180 teachers, 9,000 students; library of 30,000 vols; Dir Dr N. IDRUS.

UNITEC Institute of Technology: Private Bag 92025, Auckland; tel. (9) 849-4180; fax (9) 849-4375; f. 1976; faculties of applied skills, architecture and design, arts and social sciences, business, health, science and technology; 456 f.t.e. teachers, 17,242 students; library of 62,000 vols; Dir DOUGLAS K. ARMSTRONG: Registrar TERENCE J. FULLJAMES.

Waikato Polytechnic: Private Bag HN 3036, Hamilton 2020; tel. (7) 834-8888; fax (7) 838-0707; e-mail info@twp.ac.nz; f. 1968; courses at degree, professional technician and trades levels, also community and retraining courses; library of 54,000 vols; 360 teachers, 3,400 full-time, 11,300 part-time students; CEO D. RAWLENCE.

Wellington Polytechnic: Private Box 756, Wellington; tel. (4) 801-5799; fax (4) 801-2692; f. 1962; six schools; programmes at degree (undergraduate and postgraduate), diploma and certificate levels, in business and information systems, education, tourism, design, engineering and construction, languages and communication, Maori studies, nursing, health and environmental sciences; 258 lecturers, 5,500 students; library of 50,000 vols, 770 periodicals; Pres. B. C. PHILLIPPS (acting); Executive Registrar E. R. OLIVER.

Schools of Art and Music

Elam School of Fine Arts: Faculty of Fine Arts, University of Auckland, Private Bag 92019, Auckland; e-mail enquiries@elam.auckland.ac.nz; f. 1950; library of 35,000 vols; Dean Prof. MICHAEL DUNN; publs *Prospectus, Fine Arts Library Bulletin*.

School of Fine Arts: Faculty of Music and Fine Arts, University of Canterbury, Christchurch; tel. 364-2161; fax 364-2858; f. 1882; BA, BA(Hons), BFA, BFA(Hons), MA, MFA and PhD degrees; courses in art theory, art history, film, graphic design, painting, photography, printmaking and sculpture; library of 10,000 vols, including index of NZ historic buildings, 84,000 slides; 20 teachers, 785 students; Head TED BRACEY; publ. *Calendar* (annually).

NICARAGUA

Learned Societies

BIBLIOGRAPHY, LIBRARY SCIENCE AND MUSEOLOGY

Asociación Nicaragüense de Bibliotecarios y Profesionales afines: Apdo postal 3257, Calle F. Guzman Bolanos, Altamira del Est, Casa 120, Managua; f. 1983.

LANGUAGE AND LITERATURE

Academia Nicaragüense de la Lengua (Nicaraguan Academy of Letters): Apdo 2711, Managua; f. 1928; corresp. of the Real Academia Española (Madrid); 13 mems; Dir PABLO ANTONIO CUADRA; Sec. JULIO YCAZA TIGERINO.

MEDICINE

Sociedad de Oftalmología Nicaragüense: Clínica Especializada, Managua; f. 1949; Pres. R. LACAYO G.

Sociedad Nicaragüense de Psiquiatría y Psicología: Centro Médico, Managua; f. 1962; Pres. Dr R. GUTIÉRREZ.

Research Institutes

ECONOMICS, LAW AND POLITICS

Instituto Nicaragüense de Investigaciones Económicas y Sociales (INIES): Apdo postal C-16, Managua; tel. 662485; telex 2361; fax 668503; f. 1981 to inform and conduct research on developing alternatives for the more vulnerable sectors of the national population; 16 researchers; documentation centre of 8,000 items, 250 periodicals; Dir BLADIMIR VARELA HIDALGO; publs *Cuadernos de Investigación* (irregular), *Boletín Socioeconómico* (quarterly).

NATURAL SCIENCES

Physical Sciences

Observatorio Geofísico: Apdo postal 1761, Managua; tel. 51023; telex 1084; f. 1980; geophysics, geology, seismology, vulcanology; publ. *Boletín Sismológico* (annually).

Libraries and Archives

Bluefields

Biblioteca Municipal: Bluefields, Zelaya.

Chinandega

Biblioteca 'Eduardo Montealegre': Chinandega.

León

Biblioteca Rubén Dário de la Universidad Nacional Autónoma de Nicaragua: León; f. 1816; 36,000 vols; Dir SIDOR MARIN.

Managua

Archivo Nacional de Nicaragua: Apdo 2087, Palacio Nacional de la Cultura, Managua; tel. (2) 226290; fax (2) 22722; e-mail binanic@tmx.com.ni; f. 1882; 40,356 vols; Dir ALFREDO GONZÁLEZ VILCHEZ; publs *Boletín Técnico Informativo*, *Gaceta Oficial*.

Biblioteca del Instituto Centroamericano de Administración de Empresas: Apdo 2485, Managua; specialized library of 38,974 vols on business administration, economic development and Central American social and economic conditions; collection of 15,000 case materials for teaching of management; Dir Lic. ANTONIO ACEVEDO.

Biblioteca Económica y Financiera (Economic and Financial Library): Managua; tel. (2) 277-0421; fax (2) 277-2644; f. 1961; Dir ANA ILCE GÓMEZ; publ. *Informe Anual.*

Biblioteca Nacional 'Ruben Dario': Apdo Postal 101, Managua; fax 94387; f. 1882; 80,000 vols.

Centro Nacional de la Información y Documentación Agropecuaria (CENIDA): Apdo postal 1487, Managua; tel. 31968; f. 1984; part of Min. of Agriculture; supplies scientific and technical information for the agricultural sector.

Masaya

Biblioteca 'El Ateneo': Masaya; f. 1941; new collection of literature on philately and numismatics; Dir Dr SANTIAGO FAJARDO F.

Matagalpa

Biblioteca 'Morazan': Matagalpa.

Nagarote

Biblioteca Municipal: Nagarote, León.

Ocotal

Biblioteca 'Segovia': Ocotal, Nueva Segovia.

Museums and Art Galleries

Managua

Museo Nacional de Nicaragua: Apdo 416, Colonia Dambach, Managua; f. 1896; archaeology, ceramics, zoology, botany and geology; library of *c.* 500 vols; Dir LEONOR MARTÍNEZ DE ROCHA.

Masaya

Museo 'Tenderi': Villa Nindirí, Masaya.

Universities

UNIVERSIDAD CENTROAMERICANA

Pista de la Resistencia, Apdo 69, Managua

Telephone: (2) 773026
Fax: (2) 670106

Founded 1961
Private control
Academic year: March to December

Rector: P. EDUARDO VALDÉS B.
Vice-Rector General: Fr JOSÉ A. IDIÁZQUEZ
Vice-Rector (Administration): (vacant)
Vice-Rector (Academic): Dra MAYRA LUZ PÉREZ DÍAZ
Vice-Rector (Research and Postgraduates): Fr PETER MARCHETTI
Secretary-General: Lic. GLORIA MA. MORALES
Librarian: Licda CONCEPCIÓN MÉNDEZ ROJAS

Number of teachers: 63 full-time, 243 part-time

Number of students: 4,554

Publications: *Encuentro*, *Cuadernos de Sociología*, *Diakonía*, *Envío*.

DEANS

Faculty of Agriculture and Stockbreeding: Lic. ARLENE DE FRANCO
Faculty of Law: Dra CARLOS ARGÜELLO
Faculty of Administration: Dr ALVARO ARGÜELLO
Faculty of Humanities: Lic. LIGIA ARANA
Faculty of Foreign Languages: Licda JESSICA MORENO
Faculty of Communications: Dr GUILLERMO ROTHSCHUH
Faculty of General Studies: Lic. BALBINO SUAZO

ATTACHED INSTITUTES

Instituto de Investigación NITLAPAN.
Instituto Histórico Centroamericano (IHCA).
Instituto de Investigación y Documentación de la Costa Atlántica (CIDCA).
Instituto de Comercio Exterior y Gerencia Empresarial (INCEG).
Instituto de Historia de Nicaragua (IHN).
Instituto Nicaragüense de Investigación y Educación Popular (INIEP).
Centro de Estudios Internacionales (C.E.I.).

UNIVERSIDAD NACIONAL AGRARIA

Km. 12½ Carretera Norte, Managua

Telephone: 331619
Fax: 331950

Founded 1929; present name and status 1990

Rector: Ing. GUILLERMO CRUZ ESCOBAR
Vice-Rector General: Ing. ALBERTO SEDILES JAEN
Secretary-General: Lic. ESTER CARBALLO MADRIGAL

Library of 12,000 vols, 500 periodicals
Number of students: 2,217

DEANS

Faculty of Agronomy: Ing. NICOLAS VALLE GOMEZ
Faculty of Animal Sciences: Ing. NADIR REYES SANCHEZ
Faculty of Natural Resources and the Environment: Ing. GEORGINA OROZCO
Faculty of Distance Education and Rural Development: Ing. TELEMACO TALAVERA SILES

UNIVERSIDAD NACIONAL AUTÓNOMA DE NICARAGUA

Recinto Universitario 'Ruben Dario', Managua

Telephone: 26-12

Founded 1812
Academic year: June to March
State control

Rector: Dr HUMBERTO LÓPEZ
Administrative Vice-Rector: Lic. JULIÁN CORALES MUNGUÍA

Library: see Libraries
Number of teachers: *c.* 800
Number of students: 22,000

Publications: *Gaceta Universitaria* (every 2 months), *Cuadernos Universitarios* (quarterly), *Revista Médica* (2 a year).

Faculties of agriculture, education, humanities, economics, sciences.

Universidad Nacional Autónoma de Nicaragua, Sede León

León

Rector: Dr Octavio Martinez Ordóñez

Faculties of medicine, dentistry, law, chemistry, humanities.

ATTACHED INSTITUTES

Instituto de Investigaciones del Desarrollo (Development Research Institute): Faculty of Economics; Dir Francisco Láinez.

Instituto de Capacitación Sindical (Institute of Trade Union Training): Faculty of Law; Dir Dr Luis Felipe Pérez Caldera.

UNIVERSIDAD NACIONAL DE INGENIERÍA

Avda Universitaria Frente Escuela de Danza, Apdo postal 5595, Managua

Telephone: 2771650
Fax: 2673709
E-mail: rector@ns.uni.edu.ni

Founded 1983
State control
Academic year: April to February

Rector: Ing. Marlo José Caldera Alfaro
Vice-Rector (General): Ing. Marcia Vargas Hernández
Vice-Rector (Academic): (vacant)
Vice-Rector (Administrative): (vacant)
Secretary-General: Ing. Aldo Urbina Villalta
Librarian: Lic. Violeta Boniche Somarriba

Number of teachers: 409
Number of students: 7,518

Publications: *Nexo* (quarterly scientific review), *Gaceta* (monthly).

DEANS

Faculty of Sciences and Systems: Lic. Ronald Torres Mercado
Faculty of Construction Technology: Dr Ing. Nestor Lanzas Mejia
Faculty of Industrial Technology: Ing. Clementino Solares Castillo
Faculty of Chemical Engineering: Ing. Javier Ramirez Meza
Faculty of Electrotechnology and Computer Science: Ing. Manuel Arcia Salmerón
Faculty of Architecture: Arq. Manuel Salgado Salgado

HEADS OF DEPARTMENTS

Sciences and Systems:

Mathematics: Lic. Manuel Mercado Navas
Physics: Lic. Mauricio Aguirre Aragón
Foreign Languages: Lic. Juana Castillo Caldera
Social Sciences: Lic. Inés López Romero
Sciences and Systems: Lic. María Auxiliadora Cortedano Larios
Graduate Studies: Maribel Duriez González
Research and Development: Gonzálo Zúniga Morales

Construction Technology:

Hydraulic Engineering: (vacant)
Structural Engineering: (vacant)
Road Transport: (vacant)
Construction: (vacant)
Agricultural Machinery: (vacant)
Irrigation and Drainage: (vacant)
Design: (vacant)

Industrial Technology:

Mechanical Theory and Application: Ing. William Urbina Espinoza
Optimization: Ing. Marión Pérez Bustos
Production: Ing. Agustin Cáceres Anton
Research and Development: Ing. Ramón Morgan Espinoza
Energy: Ing. Hooshang Dakhien Harooni
Economic Engineering and Costing: Ing. Denis Chavarria González
Technology: Ing. Gil Rolando Benavidez Sánchez

Chemical Engineering:

Chemistry: Lic Martha Benavente Silva
Unitary Operation: Ing. Maria Esther Baltodano Pilarte

Electrotechnology and Computer Science:

Digital Systems and Telecommunications: Ing. Melania Solís Miranda
Mathematics Simulation and Programming: Ing. María García Bucardo
Electrical: Ing. Ariel Roldán Paredes
Electrotechnology: Ing. Jamie Alvarez Calero
Architecture of Systems and Applications: Ing. Flor de María Valle Izaguirre
Maintenance: Ing. Carlos Espinoza Moraga
Graduate Studies: Lic. Marisela Quintana (Dir)

Architecture:

Design and Expression: Arq. Eduardo Rodriguez Vásquez
Technology: Arq. Danilo Ramírez Silva
Theory and Planning: Arq. Samuel González Jirón
Research and Development: Arq. Francisco Mendoza Velásquez.

UNIVERSIDAD POLITÉCNICA DE NICARAGUA

Apdo 3595, Managua
Telephone: 97740
Fax: 97659

Founded 1967 as institute, university status 1977
Private control
Academic year: March to December

Rector: Lic. Sergio Denis García Velázquez
Vice-Rector: Ing. Emerson Pérez Sandoval
Administrative Director: Lic. José Miguel Reyes
Registrar: Mayra Rodriguez Garcia
Librarian: Aura Cela Cortez de Ocón

Number of teachers: 101
Number of students: 1,475

DEANS

School of Nursing: Lic. Lydia Ruth Zamora
School of Administration, Commerce and Finance: (vacant)
School of Design: D. I. Eduardo Vanegas
School of Statistics: Lic. Melba Castillo

ATTACHED INSTITUTES

Institute of Accounting: Dir Dra Nubia Garcia.
Academy of Homoeopathic Medicine: Dir Dr Alfredo Ruiz.
Martin Luther King Centre of Social Research: Dir Lic. Denis Torrez Perez.
Bautista Conservatoire of Music: Dir (vacant).

Colleges

Colegio de Médicos y Cirujanos de Nicaragua: Apdo Postal 1867, Managua; f. 1965; Pres. Dr José Antonio Cantón; Dir Dr Jorge García Esquivel; publ. *Voz Médica Informativa*.

Instituto Centroamericano de Administración de Empresas (INCAE): Apdo 2485, Managua; f. 1964 with technical assistance from Harvard Business School; one-year degree programme in business administration; executive training programmes; management research and consulting; 53 teachers; library: see Libraries; Rector Dr Brizio Biondi-Morra.

Instituto Nicaragüense de Cine: Apdo postal 4660, Managua; f. 1979; attached to the Ministry of Culture; centre for artistic creation and training for all aspects of cinematography: production, distribution, exhibition, mobile cinema, film criticism, national film library; Dir Ramiro Lacayo Deshón.

NIGER

Research Institutes

GENERAL

Institut de Recherches en Sciences Humaines (IRSH) de l'Université de Niamey: BP 318, Niamey; tel. 73-51-41; telex 5258; f. 1975 as successor to *Institut Français d'Afrique Noire* and *Centre Nigérien de Recherches en Sciences Humaines*; library of 21,000 vols; 6 sections: art and archaeology, history and popular traditions, linguistics and national languages, Arabic MSS, geography and environmental development, sociology of development, development economics; Dir ZAKARI MAIKOREMA; publs *Etudes Nigériennes* (irregular), *Mu Kara Sani* (2 a year).

Institut Français de Recherche Scientifique pour le Développement en Coopération (ORSTOM): BP 11416, Niamey; tel. 75-38-27; fax 75-20-54; medical entomology, hydrology, genetics, ecology, soil sciences, botany, agronomy, economics, linguistics, sociology; in co-operation with Organization for Co-ordination and Co-operation in the Fight against Endemic Diseases; documentation centre of 2,500 vols; Dir A. CASENAVE. (See main entry under France.)

AGRICULTURE, FISHERIES AND VETERINARY SCIENCE

Institut de Recherches sur les Fruits et Agrumes (IRFA): BP 886, Niamey; Dir C. LENORMAND. (See main entry under France.)

Institut National de Recherches Agronomiques au Niger (INRAN): BP 149, Niamey; soil science; stations at Tarna and Kolo; Dir J. NABOS.

Laboratoire vétérinaire de Niamey: Niamey.

Station Avicole et Centre d'Elevage Caprin: Maradi; f. 1961; Dir HASSANE BAZA; publ. *Report* (annually).

Station Sahélienne Expérimentale de Toukounous: Service d'Elevage du Niger, Toukounous/Filingué; f. 1931; selection and breeding of Zebu Azaouak cattle and distribution of selected bulls to improve the local heterogeneous breed; Dir Dr MANFRED LINDAU; publs *Berlin Münchner Tierärztliche Wochenschrift*, Annual Report.

HISTORY, GEOGRAPHY AND ARCHAEOLOGY

Centre d'Etudes Linguistiques et Historiques par Tradition Orale: BP 878, Niamey; tel. 73-54-14; telex 5422; fax 73-36-54; f. 1974; 25 mems; library of 1,250 vols; oral tradition, African languages and cultures; publishes works in African languages, French and English; publ. *Les Cahiers du CELHTO*.

TECHNOLOGY

Bureau de Recherches Géologiques et Minières (BRGM): BP 11458, Niamey; tel. 72-23-25; telex 5228; Dir G. BERNERT. (See main entry under France.)

Office National de l'Energie Solaire: BP 621, Niamey; tel. 73-45-05; telex 5295; f. 1965; 40 staff; research, post-university and technical courses; Dir Eng. ALBERT WRIGHT.

Libraries and Archives

Niamey

Archives de la République du Niger: BP 550, Niamey; f. 1913; documents to the end of the 19th century.

Centre d'Information et de Documentation Economique et Sociale (CIDES): Ministère des Finances et du Plan, BP 862, Niamey; telex 5463; fax 73-59-83; f. 1988; 6,600 vols; Dir MALIKI ABDOULAYE; publ. *CIDES-Flash* (every 2 months).

Museums and Art Galleries

Niamey

Musée National du Niger: BP 248, Niamey; tel. 73-43-21; f. 1959; representative collection of tribal costumes, crafts, tribal houses; includes park and zoo, geological and mineral exhibition, ethnographic museum, palaeontology and pre-history museums; also Handicrafts Centre and Cultural Activities Centre; Curator ALBERT FERRAL.

Universities

UNIVERSITÉ DE NIAMEY

BP 237, 10896 Niamey
Telephone: 73-27-13
Telex: 5258
Fax: 73-38-62

Founded 1971; university status 1973
State control
Language of instruction: French
Academic year: October to June

Rector: Prof. YENIKOYE ALHASSANE
Vice-Rector: DAOUDA HAMANI
Secretary-General: DJIBO MAIGA
Librarian: SAIDOU HAROUNA

Number of teachers: 239
Number of students: 5,138

CONSTITUENT INSTITUTES

Faculté des Sciences: Dean Prof. ALZOUMA INEZDANE
Faculté des Lettres et Sciences Humaines: Dean ISMAEL YENIKOYE
Ecole Normale Supérieure: Dir MAHAMAN MARICHETOU ABDOULAYE
Faculté d'Agronomie: Dean AMBOUTA KARIMOU
Faculté des Sciences de la Santé: Dir MOUSSA ABDOUA KABO
Faculté des Sciences Economiques et Juridiques: Dean ABDO HASSANE MAMAN
Institut de Recherches en Sciences Humaines: see under Research Institutes
Institut des Radio-Isotopes (IRI): Dir ABDELKARIM BEN MOHAMED.

UNIVERSITÉ ISLAMIQUE DU NIGER

Say

Founded 1987 by the Islamic Conference Organization; in process of formation

Rector: Dr MOHAMMED AL KHAYAT

A college of Islamic Studies and Arabic Language is already functioning. Faculties of science and technology, medicine, and economics are planned.

College

Ecole Nationale d'Administration du Niger: BP 542, Niamey; tel. 72-31-83; f. 1963 to train civil servants and other officials; library of 27,000 vols; number of teachers: 56 full-time, 60 part-time; number of students: 431; Dir DJIBO ISSAKA; publ. *Revue* (2 a year).

NIGERIA

Learned Societies

AGRICULTURE, FISHERIES AND VETERINARY SCIENCE

Fisheries Society of Nigeria: POB 71228, Victoria Island, Lagos; f. 1976; 500 mems; Pres. Dr S. O. TALABI; Gen. Sec. B. B. ADEKOYA; publs *Proceedings*, *Fishery Bulletin, Fish Network* (4 a year).

Forestry Association of Nigeria: POB 4185, Ibadan, Oyo State; f. 1970 to further interest in forests and forest resources management and utilization; 61 life mems, 1,000 ordinary mems, 17 corporate mems; Pres. C. A. MATAN; Sec. P. C. OBIAGA; publs *Nigerian Journal of Forestry, Proceedings of Annual Conference, FAN Newsletter.*

Nigerian Veterinary Medical Association: POB 38, Vom; f. 1963 to advance the science and art of veterinary medicine, including its relationship to public health and agriculture; 891 mems; Pres. Dr A. A. FABUNMI; Sec. Dr D. S. ADEGBOYE; publ. *Nigerian Veterinary Journal, Zariya Veterinarian, Tropical Veterinarian* (all every 6 months).

West African Association of Agricultural Economists: c/o Dept of Agricultural Economics, University of Ibadan, Ibadan, Oyo State; tel. (90) 404305; fax (2) 8103127; f. 1972; 250 mems from Benin Republic, Burkina Faso, Cameroon, Côte d'Ivoire, Ghana, Liberia, Mali, Nigeria, Senegal, Sierra Leone and Togo; Pres. Prof. Dr ANTHONY E. IKPI; Sec. Dr THOMAS EPONOU; publ. *West African Journal of Agricultural Economics*.

ARCHITECTURE AND TOWN PLANNING

Nigerian Institute of Architects: 2 Idowu Taylor St, Victoria Island, POB 178, Lagos; tel. 2617940; fax 2617947; f. 1960; 87 Fellows, 1,370 full mems, 874 graduate mems; Pres. Arc. O. C. MAJOROH; Hon. Gen. Sec. Arc. M. J. FAWORAJA; publs *Shelter for Nigerians, NIA Journals, NIA Yearbook and Diary, NIA Newsletter.*

BIBLIOGRAPHY, LIBRARY SCIENCE AND MUSEOLOGY

Nigerian Library Association: c/o National Library of Nigeria, 4 Wesley St, PMB 12626, Lagos; tel. (1) 2631716; f. 1962; 3,000 mems; Pres. A. O. BANJO; Sec. D. D. BWAYILI; publs *Nigerian Libraries* (2 a year), *NLA Newsletter* (2 a year), occasional papers; a bulletin is published by each of the 31 State Chapters.

ECONOMICS, LAW AND POLITICS

Nigerian Bar Association: 25 Odion Rd, POB 403, Warri; f. 1962; Nat. Pres. Dr MUDIAGA ODJE; Chair. Chief V. O. ESAN; Gen. Sec. DEBO AKANDE.

Nigerian Economic Society: Department of Economics, University of Ibadan, Ibadan; f. 1957; to advance social and economic knowledge, particularly about Nigeria; 2,000 mems; Pres. Prof. MIKE I. OBADAN; Sec. Dr JOHN C. ANYANWU; publs *Nigerian Journal of Economic and Social Studies* (3 a year), *Proceedings of Annual Conferences, Workshops, Seminars, Symposia.*

Nigerian Institute of International Affairs: Kofo Abayomi Rd, Victoria Island, POB 1727, Lagos; tel. 615606-10; telex 22638; f. 1961; a non-political and non-profit making organization for the study of international affairs, to disseminate and maintain information on int. questions through conferences, lectures and discussions; 1,782 mems; library of 59,000 vols, 18,769 pamphlets, 278,680 press clippings and 2,010 journals; Dir-Gen. Dr G. A. OBIOZOR; publs *Nigerian Journal of International Affairs* (quarterly), *Nigerian Forum* (monthly), *Nigeria: bulletin on Foreign Affairs* (2 a year).

Nigerian Institute of Management: Plot 22, Idowu Taylor St, Victoria Island, POB 255, Lagos; tel and fax (1) 614116; f. 1961; a professional body for managers and administrators and a training and consultancy institution for practising managers, from both private and public sectors (trains more than 2,000 annually); 20,000 mems; library of 2,000 vols; Dir-Gen. Prof. GABRIEL OLAKUNLE OLUSANYA; publs *Management in Nigeria* (quarterly), *Management News* (quarterly).

Nigerian Political Science Association (NPSA): c/o The Secretariat, School of Social Sciences, University of Port Harcourt, PMB 5323, Port Harcourt; f. 1973 to research in politics and government in Nigeria; 200 mems; Pres. Prof. CLAUDE AKE; Vice-Pres. Dr Y. R. BARONGO; National Sec. Dr CLIFF EDOGUN; publ. *Newsletter*.

EDUCATION

Committee of Vice-Chancellors of Nigerian Federal Universities: 3 Idowu Taylor St, Victoria Island, PMB 12022, Lagos; tel. and fax (1) 612425; telex 23555; f. 1962; mems: 24 Fed. Univs.; Sec.-Gen. Prof. F. O. ABOABA.

HISTORY, GEOGRAPHY AND ARCHAEOLOGY

Historical Society of Nigeria: c/o Dept. of History, University of Lagos, Lagos; f. 1955 to encourage interest and work in connection with the study of history, especially Nigerian history; Pres. Prof. OBARO IKHIME; Sec. Prof. A. I. ASIWAJU; publs *Journal, Tarikh* (2 a year), *Bulletin of News* (quarterly).

Nigerian Geographical Association: c/o Dept of Geography, University of Ibadan, Ibadan; f. 1955; to further interest in geography and its methods of teaching with special reference to Nigeria; 500 mems; Pres. Prof. R. K. UDO; Sec. Dr I. ADALEMO; publ. *Nigerian Geographical Journal*.

MEDICINE

Medical and Dental Council of Nigeria: Plot PC 13, 25 Ahmed Onibudo St, Victoria Island, PMB 12611, Lagos; tel. 613323; f. 1963; responsible for the registration, licensing and discipline of medical and dental practitioners, the regulation and supervision of medical and dental education, and regulating the operations of clinical laboratories, issuing a code of conduct for the practice of medicine, dentistry and alternative medicine (in Nigeria); 50 mems; Chair. (vacant); Registrar and CEO Dr C. OKWUDILI EZEANI.

Nigerian Society for Microbiology: c/o Dept of Medical Microbiology, University College Hospital, Ibadan, Oyo State; f. 1973 to promote the advancement of medical, veterinary, agricultural and industrial microbiology; holds annual conferences in the Nigerian universities; 130 mems; Pres. Prof. E. O. OGUNBA; Sec. Prof. K. O. ALAUSA; publ. *Nigerian Journal for Microbiology* (2 a year).

Nutrition Society of Nigeria: c/o Dept of Food Science and Technology, Obafemi Awolowo University, Ile-Ife, Oyo State; f. 1966; 350 mems; Pres. Prof. OLUMBE BASSIR; Sec. Dr J. B. FASHAKIN; publ. *Nigerian Nutrition Newsletter.*

NATURAL SCIENCES

General

Nigerian Academy of Science: PMB 1004, University of Lagos PO, Akoka, Yaba, Lagos; tel. and fax (1) 863874; f. 1977; sections of Physical Sciences (Academic Sec. Prof. A. O. E. ANIMALU), Biological Sciences (Academic Sec. Prof. P. O. OKONKWO); 45 foundation fellows, 85 fellows; Pres. Prof. A. MADUEMEZIA; Sec. Prof. C. O. ORANGUN; publs *Discourses* (2 a year), *Newsletter* (2 a year), *Nigerian Journal of Agricultural Sciences* (annually), *Nigerian Journal of Medical Sciences* (annually), *Nigerian Journal of Natural Sciences* (annually).

Biological Sciences

Ecological Society of Nigeria: c/o Federal College of Forestry, PMB 2019, Jos, Plateau State; tel. (73) 55056; f. 1973; 373 mems; Pres. Prof. J. K. EGUNJOBI; Sec. C. CHIKE OKAFO; publs *Newsletter, Proceedings.*

Entomological Society of Nigeria: c/o National Stored Products Research Institute, PMB 5063, Port Harcourt, Rivers State; f. 1965 to further the study of insects in Nigeria; 250 mems; Pres. Prof. S. N. OKIWELU; Sec. O. O. ADU; publs *Nigerian Journal of Entomology* (annually), *Nigerian Entomologists' Magazine* (annually).

Genetics Society of Nigeria: c/o International Institute of Tropical Agriculture, Oyo Rd, PMB 5320, Ibadan, Oyo State; f. 1972 to further interest in genetics for the benefit of mankind and in the various areas of crops, livestock and medicine; 75 mems; Pres. Dr O. A. OJOMO; Sec. Dr A. O. ABIFARIN; publ. *Proceedings*.

Physical Sciences

Geological Survey of Nigeria: PMB 2007, Kaduna South; tel. 212003; f. 1919; geological mapping; mineral exploration; geophysical and geochemical surveys and consultation on geological problems; library of 34,000 vols; Chief Officer J. I. NEHIKHARE; publs *Annual Report, Bulletins, Occasional Papers, Records*, geological maps.

TECHNOLOGY

Nigerian Society of Engineers: 1 Engineering Close, PMB 72667, Victoria Island, Lagos; tel. 2617349; fax 2617315; e-mail nsehq@infoweb.abs.net; f. 1958; 18,000 mems; library of 1,500 vols; Pres. Eng. C. A. MBANEFO; Exec. Sec. Z. O. AYITOGO; publs *Nigerian Engineer* (quarterly), *Newsletter* (quarterly), *Technical Transaction* (quarterly), *Annual Proceedings.*

Research Institutes

GENERAL

Lake Chad Research Institute (LCRI): Malamfatori, PMB 1293, Maiduguri, Borno State; tel. (76) 232106; f. 1975; research into the hydrological behaviour and characteristics of Lake Chad and the limnology of the associated surface and ground waters; the abundance, distribution and other biological characteristics of species of fish and other aquatic life in the lake and practical methods of their exploitation; the behaviour and characteristics of the wildlife associated with the lake and its conservation; ecology and methods of control of crop pests and diseases of economic importance; improvement of the methods of control of dry farming and livestock husbandry in the severe environmental condition around the lake; improvement of cultivation of wheat, barley, and other crops by irrigation; the socio-economic and public health effects of the introduction of large-scale irrigation schemes and improved methods of animal husbandry and fishing on the rural populations around the lake; library of 16,000 vols; Dir Dr B. K. KAIGAMA; publs *Annual Report, LCRI Newsletter* (quarterly).

AGRICULTURE, FISHERIES AND VETERINARY SCIENCE

Cocoa Research Institute of Nigeria: Onigambari, PMB 5244, Ibadan, Oyo State; tel. (22) 410040; f. 1964; research into cocoa, cola, coffee, cashew and tea; research aspects include entomology, plant-breeding, plant pathology, soil chemistry and biochemistry; library of 15,000 vols; Dir S. T. OLATOYE; publs *CRIN News* (monthly), *Annual Report, Progress Report* (quarterly), advisory leaflets, research report papers (both quarterly).

Forestry Research Institute of Nigeria (FRIN): PMB 5054, Ibadan, Oyo State; tel. (22) 413327; f. 1954; conducts intensive research into all aspects of forestry and forest products utilization; 2 Forestry Schools at Ibadan and Jos, School of Wildlife Management at New Bussa and School of Forestry Mechanization at Afaka in Kaduna State; library of 10,000 vols; Dir Prof. P. R. O. KIO; publs *Annual Report, FRIN Newsletter* (quarterly).

Institute for Agricultural Research (IAR): Ahmadu Bello University, PMB 1044, Samaru, Zaria; tel. (69) 50681; fax (69) 50563; f. 1924; improvement of production of sorghum, millet, wheat, groundnuts, cotton and fibres, cowpea, sesame, soyabean and vegetables; maintenance of soil fertility; land resources assessment; crop environment; cropping systems and intercropping; mechanization; soil and water management; socio-economic studies of small farm management, marketing, credit, supply systems and extension; sub-stations at: Kano in Kano State, Kadawa in Kano State and Bakura in Sokoto State; library of 16,000 vols; Dir Prof. J. P. VOH; publs *Samaru Research Bulletins* (quarterly), *Samaru Miscellaneous Papers* (2 a year), *Samaru Agricultural Newsletter* (every 2 months), *Samaru Journal of Agricultural Research, Noma Magazine, Samaru Conference Papers* (occasionally), *Soil Survey Reports, Annual Report.*

Institute of Agricultural Research and Training (IART): Obafemi Awolowo University, Moor Plantation, PMB 5029, Ibadan, Oyo State; tel. (22) 311728; f. 1969, university institute 1970; comprises former research division of the Western State Ministry of Agriculture and Natural Resources and the various training schools of the Ministry; collaborates with the Ministry on conducting research directly related to problems of agricultural development and training of middle-level extension workers; 2 schools of agriculture at Akure and Ibadan, and a school of animal health and husbandry at Ibadan; library of 8,000 vols; Dir Prof. B. O. ADELANA; publs *Annual Report, Newsletter* (quarterly).

National Agricultural Extension and Research Liaison Services: Ahmadu Bello University, PMB 1044, Samaru, Zaria; tel. (69) 51868; f. 1963; a link between Research and Extension; interpretation and dissemination of research findings and practices of long standing to State extension field staff and identification and feedback to research institutes of field problems; in-service training for States extension staff; advisory services in pest and disease control, organization of agricultural shows and establishment of agricultural audio-visual units; consultancy services; preparation of audio-visual materials; applied research: testing recommendations, conducting surveys and extension methods. Programme areas are: crop production, including mechanization and irrigation; animal production, including poultry and veterinary service; home economics; farm management, including co-operatives; and rural youth organization; library of 2,000 vols, 1,400 periodicals; Dir S. S. ABUBAKAR; publs *Extension Bulletins* (quarterly), *Guides* (monthly), *Recommended Practices* (quarterly), *Conference and Seminar Proceedings* (occasional), *Extension Newsletter* (monthly), *Annual Report, The Nigerian Journal of Agricultural Extension* (2 a year).

National Animal Production Research Institute (NAPRI): Ahmadu Bello University, Shika, POB 1096, Zaria; tel. (69) 32596; f. 1928; research staff of 25; research on dairy, beef and sheep production with emphasis on nutrition, management and breeding, range and pasture research and improvement, livestock economics and rural sociology of pastoral nomads; library of 15,000 vols; Dir Prof. E. O. OYEDIPE; publs (jointly with IAR above), *Annual Report.*

National Centre for Agricultural Mechanization: Federal Ministry of Agriculture, PMB 1525, Ilorin, Kwara State; tel. 220914; f. 1977; testing and developing of agricultural machinery; standardization, extension and training services in agricultural mechanization; 120 staff; Dir H. L. MUSA.

National Centre for Genetic Resources and Biotechnology (NACGRAB): Moor Plantation, PMB 5382, Ibadan, Oyo State; tel. (22) 312622; f. 1986; husbandry of plant and animal genetic resources, research in developmental genetics; library of 1,500 vols; Project Man. Mr SAMURI; publ. *Annual Report.*

National Cereals Research Institute (NCRI): PMB 8, Badeggi, Bida, Niger State; tel. (66) 461233; f. 1975, formerly Federal Department of Agricultural Research; research into the production and products of rice, maize and grain legumes of economic importance for improving the genetic potential of the crops; improving agronomic and husbandry practices; mechanization and improvement of methods of cultivating, harvesting, processing and storage of crops; improving the utilization of by-products; ecology of crop pests and diseases and improved methods of their control; integration of crop cultivation into farming systems in different ecological zones and its socio-economic effects on the rural population; library of 6,078 vols; includes a Plant Quarantine Training Centre; Dir Dr BAWARANA B. WUDIRI; publs *Annual Report, Memoranda* (occasionally), Research Bulletins (quarterly), Information Papers (monthly).

National Horticultural Research Institute (NIHORT): Idi-Ishin, PMB 5432, Ibadan, Oyo State; tel. (22) 412230; two sub-stations at Mbato, near Okigwe, Imo State and at Bagauda, near Tiga, Kano State; f. 1975; research into fruit and vegetable production and consumption; in particular improvement of the genetic potentials of the cultivated, semicultivated and wild crops; improvement of agronomic and husbandry practices; mechanization and improvement of methods of cultivating, harvesting, processing and storage; improvement of the utilization of by-products; ecology of crop pests and diseases and improved methods of their control; integration of crop cultivation into farming systems in different ecological zones and its socio-economic effects on the rural populations; library of 9,056 vols; Dir S. A. O. ADEYEMI; publs *Annual Report, NIHORT Newsletter* (quarterly), information papers (monthly).

National Institute for Freshwater Fisheries Research (NIFFR): PMB 6006, New Bussa, Kwara State; f. 1965; research into the limnoligical behaviour and characteristics of the Kainji and other man-made lakes and their effects on the fish and other aquatic life; the abundance, distribution and other biological characteristics of species of fish and practical methods of their exploitation; the behaviour and characteristics of wildlife and its conservation; range ecology; the development of irrigated crops; public health problems, and the socio-economic effects of the construction of the Kainji and other man-made lakes on rural populations; library of 13,000 vols; Dir Dr J. S. O. AYENI; publs *Newsletter* (quarterly), *Annual Report.*

National Root Crops Research Institute (NRCRI): Umudike, PMB 7600, Umuahia, Imo State; tel. (88) 220188; f. 1955; federal status 1972; experimental farms; research on yams, cocoyams, cassava, sweet potato and Irish potato; library of 5,000 vols; Dir Dr L. S. O. ENE; publs *Annual Report, Programmes of Work* (annually), *Advisory Bulletins* (monthly).

National Veterinary Research Institute (NVRI): Vom, near Jos, Plateau State; tel. (73) 80812; f. 1924; intensive research into all aspects of animal diseases and their treatment and control; all aspects of animal nutrition; production of vaccine and sera; introduction of exotic stock to improve meat, milk and egg production; standardization and quality control of manufactured animal feeds; training livestock superintendents, laboratory technicians and technologists; library of 14,000 vols, 4,000 reports, etc.; Dir ABUBAKAR G. LAMORDE; publs *Index of Veterinary Research* (annually), *Annual Report*, Research Papers (irregular), *Newsletter* (quarterly).

Nigerian Institute for Oil Palm Research (NIFOR): PMB 1030, Benin City, Edo State; tel. (52) 440150; fax (52) 250668; f. 1939; research into the production and products of oil palm and other palms of economic importance and recommendation of improved methods; library of 13,000 vols; Dir Dr D. O. ATAGA; publs *Journal* (quarterly), *Annual Report.*

Nigerian Stored Products Research Institute (NSPRI): Km. 3, Asa Dam Rd, PMB 1489, Ilorin, Kwara State; tel. (31) 222143; fax (31) 221639; f. 1960; research into stored-product pests and primary processing; training, analytical services and advisory work; library of 2,500 vols; Dir Prof. A. M. DARAMOLA; publs *Annual Report, Newsletter* (quarterly).

Rubber Research Institute of Nigeria (RRIN): Iyanomo, PMB 1049, Benin City, Bendel State; tel. (52) 244625; f. 1961; research on natural rubber (*Hevea Brasiliensis*) production; sub-station at Akwete near Aba in Anambra; library of 1,000 vols; Dir Dr

E. K. OKAISABOR; publs *Annual Report*, RRIN's advisory leaflets (monthly), information booklets (quarterly).

BIBLIOGRAPHY, LIBRARY SCIENCE AND MUSEOLOGY

Centre for Museum Studies: PMB 2031, Jos, Plateau State; tel. (73) 53516; f. 1963; Principal J. FAMUYIWA.

ECONOMICS, LAW AND POLITICS

Centre for Management Development: PMB 21578, Ikeja; tel. (1) 901120; fax (1) 961167; f. 1973 to promote and co-ordinate the activities of institutions engaged in the education and training of managerial manpower; advises government on policy, formulates policies and guidelines, monitors standards of management education, assesses training programmes, provides advisory and consultancy service to Nigerian businesses; Library of 25,747 vols, 4,525 periodicals, also general publs and serials, teaching materials library, and audio-visual unit (provides aids and software hire service), reprographic unit; Dir-Gen. Dr A. P. EDET; Chief Librarian U. R. EKPU; publs *Nigerian Management Review* (quarterly), *Directory of Management Development Programmes in Nigeria* (annually), *Proceedings of National Conference of Management Development* (every 3 years), *Management Forum Series* (2 a year), *CMD Calendar of Management Development Programmes* (annually), *Mandev News* (quarterly).

Nigerian Institute of Social and Economic Research: PMB 5, University Post Office, Ibadan; tel. (2) 8102904; telex 31119; fax (2) 8101194; e-mail dg@niser.ng; f. 1950 as WA Institute of Social and Economic Research, present name 1960; government-financed; applied research on problems of immediate and long-term relevance to Nigerian development: economic planning and development, agricultural and industrial development, business and technology, foreign and international trade, public finance and social, physical and manpower planning and development; political development, population studies; training for staff of planning organizations; consultancy service for federal and state governments, private organizations and international bodies; library of 36,500 vols; Dir-Gen. Prof. ADEDOTUN O. PHILLIPS; publs *Monograph Series*, *Annual Report*, *Research for Development*.

EDUCATION

Nigerian Educational Research Council: POB 8058, Lagos; f. 1965; curriculum development and general educational research; 30 mems; library of 12,000 vols; Chair. Prof. S. N. NWOSU; Sec. J. M. AKINTOLA; publs conference and workshop reports.

MEDICINE

National Institute for Medical Research (NIMR): Edmund Crescent, PMB 2013, Yaba, Lagos; tel. (1) 861732; f. 1973; to identify the major health problems of the country and their determinants; research into environmental hazards and their effect on the population's health; library of 8,000 vols; Dir Prof. E. M. ESSIEN; publs *Annual Report*, *Newsletter* (quarterly).

National Institute of Pharmaceutical Research and Development (NIPRD): PMB 21, Idu, Abuja; research into medical plants, herbs and drug development and formulary; drug information centre; national centre for drugs; regulates the standardization of pharmaceutical substances; library of 1,000 vols; Dir Prof. C. O. N. WAMBEBE; publ. *Annual Report*.

Nigerian Institute for Trypanosomiasis Research (NITR): PMB 2077, Kaduna, Kaduna State; tel. (62) 238074; fax (62) 238075; e-mail nitr@linkserve.co.ng; f. 1951; research into trypanosomiasis and onchocerciasis generally; the pathology, immunology and methods of treatment of the diseases; the ecology and life-cycle of the vectors and the mode of transmission of the disease; chemical, biological and other methods of vector control, the socio-economic effects of the disease on the rural populations; maintains 2 brs,1 field station and approximately 100 sub-units attached to general hospitals and health centres; library of 4,000 vols; Dir Dr I. HALID; publ. *Annual Report*.

NATURAL SCIENCES

General

Nigerian Institute for Oceanography and Marine Research (NIOMR): Victoria Island, PMB 12529, Lagos; tel. (1) 617385; f. 1975; research into the resources and physical characteristics of the Nigerian territorial waters and the high seas beyond; library of 10,000 vols; Dir J. G. TOBOR; publs *Newsletter* (quarterly), *Annual Report*.

TECHNOLOGY

Federal Institute of Industrial Research (FIIRO): PMB 21023, Ikeja, Lagos; tel. (1) 523205; fax (1) 4525880; e-mail fiiro@rcl.nig.com; f. 1956; food technology, industrial fermentation through biotechnology, pulp and paper research, domestic and industrial water treatment, environmental studies, ceramic and engineering materials research, machinery and equipment design and fabrication; consultancy, analytical services, technical services to industry; library of 5,000 vols; Dir Prof. S. A. ODUNFA; publs *Annual Report*, brochure (monthly).

National Centre for Energy Research and Development: University of Nigeria, Nsukka, Enugu State; tel. (42) 771853; fax (42) 771855; e-mail misunn@aol.com; f. 1982; federal government-funded centre for research and development of solar and other renewable and non-renewable energy such as photovoltaic, photothermal, wind energy, radiation measurement, biomass, coal, energy management, etc.; Dir Prof. O. ODUKWE.

National Research Institute for Chemical Technology (NARICT): Samaru, PMB 1052, Basawa, Zaria, Kaduna State; tel. (22) 412230; f. 1988; trains Hides and Skins Improvement Officers, leather craftsmen, boot and shoe technologists; research into indigenous tanning materials and techniques; serves as the Nigerian Standards Organisation's centre for leather goods; four sub-centres at Kano, Jos, Maiduguri and Sokoto for extension services; Dir A. S. MSHELBWALA; publs *NARICT Newsletter* (monthly), *Annual Report*.

Nigerian Building and Road Research Institute (NBRRI): 15 Awolowo Rd, PMB 12568, S.W. Ikoyi, Lagos; tel. 684273; f. 1978; conducts research on road and allied construction materials and methods, socio-economics of construction and environmental factors which affect road building performance; library of 12,000 vols; Dir Dr A. O. MADEDOR; publs *Annual Report*, *Research Reports* (occasional), Information Leaflets (quarterly), *Technical Digest* (2 a year).

Projects Development Institute (PRODA): 3 Independence Layout, POB 609, Enugu, Anambra State; tel. (42) 337691; f. 1970, as Project Development Agency, present status 1977; research into design and fabrication, semi-conductor electronics and coal utilization; library of 4,000 vols; Dir Ir E. O. KAINE; publs *Annual Report*, *PRODA Newsletter* (quarterly).

Raw Materials Research and Development Council (RMRDC): 28 Berkley St, Onikan, Lagos; tel. (1) 2635206; f. 1988; supports and expedites industrial development and self-sufficiency through maximum utilization of local materials; library of 3,000 vols; Chief Exec. Dr A. A. ALIYU; publs *Annual Report*, *Research Reports* (occasional), *RMRDC Newsletter* (quarterly).

Libraries and Archives

Abeokuta

Ogun State Library: PMB 2060, Abeokuta, Ogun State; f. 1976; 21,736 vols; special collection on Ogun State; Chief Librarian Alhaji BAYO YISA ODULAJA.

Akure

Ondo State Library Board: PMB 719, Akure; tel. 230561; f. 1976, renamed 1985; reading and reference services, mobile- and school-library services, training of library assistants; 62,546 vols; Dir Mrs T. A. AJUMOBI.

Bauchi

Bauchi State Library Board: Ministry of Education, Bauchi; tel. 42220; telex 83263; f. 1976; lending and reference services, special services to rehabilitation centres, training of library staff; 3,5000 vols, 3,475 periodicals; Dir MUSA M. DEDE; publ. *Annual Report*.

Benin

Edo State Library Board: 17 James Watt Rd, PMB 1127, Benin City; tel. (52) 200810; f. 1971; 272,398 vols; Central Reference Library with emphasis on the needs of the State Government; Technical Service Division; School Library Division; Public Library Division (13 branch libraries, 3 Rural Information Centres); Mobile Service to remote areas; hospital and prison services; Dir Dr J. O. U. ODIASE; publs *Newsletters* (monthly), *Edo Library Accessions List* (2 a year), *Leagl Deposit Bulletin* (2 a year), *Annual Reports*, *Index to The Observer* (2 a year).

Enugu

Enugu State Library Board: PMB 01026, Enugu; tel. (42) 334103; f. 1955; Dir of Library Services C. C. UDE.

Attached library:

State Central Library: Market Road, Enugu; f. 1956; lending and reference library activities; legal deposit and regional centre for bibliographical information and research; c. 83,000 vols; Nigeriana collection; one mobile library unit; divisional library at Onueke; zonal libraries at Abakaliki and Nsukka; publ. *Annual Report*.

Ibadan

Federal Ministry of Science and Technology, Library and Documentation Centre: Moor Plantation, PMB 5382, Ibadan, Oyo State; f. 1973; 2,000 vols, 700 current periodicals, 22 microfiches, 350 reprints; newspaper clippings; the Liaison Office in Nigeria for both AGRIS (International Information System for Agricultural Sciences and Technology) and CARIS (Current Agricultural Research Information Service); Librarian O. A. ADIGUM; publs *List of Serials* (annually), *List of Reprints*.

Forestry Research Institute of Nigeria Library: PMB 5054, Ibadan; tel. 414441; telex 31207; f. 1941; 35,000 vols, 400 periodicals; special collections: Nigerian silvicultural records and working plans, Nigerian theses collection, and Harold Young collection of rare materials on forest mensuration, biometrics, photogrammetry and technometrics; Head of Library E. N. ETTE; publs *Reader's Guide, Library Accession Lists* (quarterly), *Current Contents* (monthly), *List of Institute Publications, Current Awareness Service on Agricultural Research and Development Bulletin* (monthly), subject bibliographies and reprints.

Kenneth Dike Library: University of Ibadan, Ibadan; tel. (2) 810-1100; fax (2) 8103118; e-mail library@ibadan.ac.ng; f. 1948; 400,000 vols, 1,500 current periodicals; depository for OAU and UN specialized agencies publs; special collection of Africana, private papers of eminent Nigerians; Librarian OLUFUNMILAYO G. TAMUNO; publs *Annual Report, Library Record*.

National Archives: PMB 4, University of Ibadan Post Office, Ibadan; f. 1951, legally recognized 1957; charged with collection, rehabilitation, reproduction and preservation of all public records including private papers; library of 8,500 vols; branch offices at Enugu and Kaduna; Dir COMFORT AINA UKWU; publs *Annual Report, Special Lists*, etc.

Ife

Hezekiah Oluwasanmi Library, Obafemi Awolowo University: Ile-Ife; tel. (36) 230290; e-mail ul@libraryoauife.edu.ng; f. 1961; 401,000 vols, 6,905 periodicals; special collections of Africana, audio-visual materials and government documents; Librarian M. A. ADELABU; publs *Abstracts of Theses* (annually), *Research in Progress at the Obafemi Awolowo University* (annually).

Ikeja

Federal Institute of Industrial Research, Oshodi Industrial Information Centre and Extension Services: PMB 21023, Ikeja, Cappa Bus Stop, Agege Motor Rd, Lagos State; tel. 4522905; telex 26006; fax 4525880; f. 1956; scientific, technological and industrial information documentation and dissemination, current awareness, extension and publications services; 12,500 vols; special collections: UNIDO, NTIS and IDRI publs; Librarian I. DEKWE; publs *Industrial Abstracts* (quarterly), *Latest Technology Index* (quarterly), *Annual Report*.

Ilorin

Kwara State Library Board: Sulu Gambari Rd, PMB 1561, Ilorin, Kwara State; tel. 22038; f. 1968; library of 45,000 vols; Dir Deacon BENSON BABATUNDE ODEWALE; publ. *Annual Report*.

Jos

Plateau State Library Services: c/o Bureau for Information, POB 2053, Jos, Plateau State; tel. (73) 54030; f. 1976; 45,293 vols; brs at Akwanga, Keffi, Lafia, Pankshin, Shendam; Librarian TIMOTHY P. A. ANGBA (acting).

Kaduna

Kaduna State Library Board: PMB 2061, Kaduna; f. 1953, renamed 1976; 200,000 vols; Dir JOSEPH AHMADU MAIGARI; publs *Annual Reports, Public Enlightenment, Legal Deposit Collection, Current Awareness Bulletin*, Bibliographies, Readers' Guides.

Kano

Kano State Library Board: PMB 3094, Kano; tel. (64) 645614; f. 1968; includes mobile and school library services, cultural programmes, outreach services to government departments, reference and documentation services, audiovisual services; 300,000 vols; Exec. Dir Alhaji MUHAMMAD WALADO.

Lagos

Central Medical Library: Federal Ministry of Health, PMB 2003, Yaba, Lagos; tel. (1) 868145; f. 1946; serves the entire country; 27,177 vols, 471 journals; Librarian S. O. OYESOLA; publs *Catalogue of Serials, Bulletin*, list of acquisitions.

Lagos City Libraries: PMB 2025, Lagos; f. 1950; 229,150 vols; Librarian Mrs B. B. OGUNLANA; publ. *Annual Report*.

National Library of Nigeria: 4 Wesley St, PMB 12626, Lagos; tel. 2600220; telex 21746; fax (1) 631563; f. 1964; 12 brs; 140,000 vols in main library, 18,000 at branches; special collections of Nigerian and UK government publications, UN documents, Rhodes House Library Collection (private papers of past colonial civil servants), Ranfurly Library Collection; depository for UN, OAU and Canadian publs; Chair. FRANCIS Z. GANA; National Librarian Alhaji MU'AZU H. WALI.

University of Lagos Library: Lagos; tel. 821273; telex 26983; fax 822644; f. 1962; 375,000 vols, 4,500 periodicals; legal depository for Lagos State; depository for all publications of ECA, GATT, ICJ and ILO; collections on UNESCO, WHO and FAO; Librarian A. K. ADENIJI (acting); publs *Annual Report, Unilag: Quarterly News Bulletin, Reader's Guide, Library Notes.*

Maiduguri

Borno State Library Board: PMB 1443, Maiduguri, Borno State; tel. (76) 231389; f. 1968; became library board 1984; 86,535 vols; 11 branches; provides information for the public, trains library staff, organizes school libraries, annual book exhibition, etc.; Dir JOHN YADU MALGWI.

Nsukka

University of Nigeria Libraries: Nnamdi Azikiwe Library, Nsukka, Enugu State; tel. 771444; telex 51496; fax 277-0644; f. 1960; 717,000 vols at Nsukka and Enugu campuses; medical library at Enugu with 42,000 vols; Africana collection of 30,000 vols; Librarian C. C. UWECHIE (acting); publs *Nsukka Library Notes, UNLAN, Annual Report*.

Owerri

Imo State Library Board: PMB 1118, Owerri, Imo State; tel. (83) 230280; f. 1976; lending, reference, children's library and library for the handicapped, bibliographic and information consultancy services; 112,000 vols; Dir of Library Services AGATHA C. NWACHUKWU; publs *Newsletter, Accession List, The Light, Annual Report.*

Museums and Art Galleries

Benin

Benin Museum: Benin; Benin antiquities, bronzes.

Esie

Esie Museum: PMB 301, Kwara State; f. 1945; stone antiquities (*c.* 1,000 half life size human figures); Dir (vacant).

Ife

Natural History Museum, Obafemi Awolowo University: Ile-Ife; tel. (36) 230291, ext. 2451; f. 1948; research, outreach activities, teaching, exhibition and identification of animal and plant specimens; botanical, entomological, geological and zoological collections; archaeological artifacts; Dir Prof. A. E. AKINGBOHUNGBE.

Jos

National Museum, Jos: PMB 2031, Jos, Plateau State; f. 1982; ethnography, architecture and archaeology of Nigeria; terracotta Nok figurines, modern and traditional Nigerian pottery; zoological and botanical gardens; museum of traditional architecture; transport museum; craft village; open-air theatre; library of 10,000 vols and 2,000 Arabic MSS; Dir M. DANDAURA.

Kaduna

National Museum, Kaduna: PMB 2127, Kaduna; tel. (62) 211180; fax (1) 2633890; f. 1975; archaeology and ethnography; houses the 'Craft Village' where traditional hair-plaiting, weaving, pottery, calabash decoration, wood carving, leather work, brass casting and smithery are done; library of 1,500 vols; Dir Dr K. S. CHAFE; publ. *Tambari*.

Kano

Gidan Makama Museum: Kano; f. 1959; local art work.

Lagos

National Museum, Lagos: Onikan Rd, Lagos; f. 1957; ethnography, archaeology and traditional art; library of 7,264 vols; Dir-Gen. Dr Y. GELLA.

Oron

National Museum, Oron: PMB 1004, Oron, Akwa Ibom State; f. 1959; ethnography; Chief Curator ANIEFIOK UDO AKPAN.

Owo

Owo Museum: Federal Dept of Antiquities, POB 84, Owo, Ondo State; f. 1959; arts and crafts; some ethnographic relics mainly from the Eastern part of the Yoruba region; Curator E. OLA ABEJIDE.

Universities

ABIA STATE UNIVERSITY

PMB 2000, Uturu, Abia State

Telephone: (88) 220785

Founded 1981 as Imo State University; present name *c.* 1993

State control

Language of instruction: English

Academic year: October to August

Chancellor: Ambassador Dr Chief M. T. MBU

Vice-Chancellor: Prof. S. O. IGWE

Deputy Vice-Chancellor (Administration): Prof. M. A. MKPA

Deputy Vice-Chancellor (Academic): Prof. A. I. NWABUGHUOGU

Registrar: I. UKEGBU CHILE

Librarian: K. K. OYEOKU

Library of 25,000 vols

Number of teachers: 400

Number of students: 15,389

DEANS

College of Agriculture and Veterinary Medicine: Prof. C. T. UWAKA

College of Biological and Physical Sciences: Prof. E. N. MGBENU

College of Business Administration: Prof. OGWO O. OGWO

College of Engineering and Environmental Studies: Dr M. A. IJIOMA (acting)

College of Humanities and Social Sciences: Prof. G. I. NWAKA

College of Legal Studies: E. OJUKWU (acting)

College of Medicine and Health Sciences: A. C. AKPUAKA

College of Education: Dr V. NEACHUKWU (acting)

College of Postgraduate Studies: Prof. S. O. EMEJUAIWE

PROFESSORS

AKPUAKA, F. C., Medicine and Surgery
ALUGBUO, M. A., Management
DIAKU, I., Economics
EMEJUAIWE, S. O., Microbiology
EZE, O. C., Law
EZEJELUE, A. C., Accounting
IGWE, S. O., Education Management and Planning
MGBENU, E. N., Physics
MKPA, M. A., Curriculum Studies
NWAKA, G. I., History
NWOSU, E. J., Economics
OGWO, O. OGWO
ONOH, J. K., Finance

ABUBAKAR TAFAWA BALEWA UNIVERSITY

PMB 0248, Bauchi
Telephone: (77) 543500
Founded 1988
Federal government control
Language of instruction: English
Academic year: October to September
Chancellor: ALH DR ISA MUSTAPHA AGWAII
Vice-Chancellor: Prof. ABUBAKAR S. SAMBO
Deputy Vice-Chancellor (Academic): Prof. J. P. FABIYI
Deputy Vice-Chancellor (Administration): Dr A. B. MUHAMMED
Registrar: Dr MUSA SULEIMAN
Librarian: S. A. OGUNROMBI
Number of teachers: 260
Number of students: 4,000
Publications: *Annual Report*, *University Bulletin* (4 a year), *Prospectus*.

DEANS

Dean of Students: Dr G. A. BABAJI
School of Science and Scientific Education: Prof. S. O. ALE
School of Engineering and Engineering Technology: Dr M. I. ONUGU
School of Agriculture and Agricultural Technology: Prof. T. A. ADEGBOLA
School of Environment and Environmental Technology: I. I. ADAMINDA

PROFESSORS

ABUBAKAR, M. M., Animal Science
ADEGBOLA, T. A., Animal Science
ALE, S. O., Mathematics Education
ALIYU, U. O., Electrical Engineering
CHAUDHARY, J. P., Crop Protection
FABIYI, J. P., Microbiology
MSHELIA, E. D., Theoretical Physics
OLAGBEMIRO, T. O., Chemistry
OLARINOYE, R. D., Physics Education
RAM, P. C., Applied Mathematics
SAMBO, A. S., Energy Studies (Mechanical Engineering)
SHARMA, B. M., Botany
SINGH, L., Soil Science
SULEIMAN, S., Industrial Design

UNIVERSITY OF ABUJA

PMB 117, Abuja, Federal Capital City
Telephone: (9) 8821380
Fax: (9) 8821605
Founded 1988
Federal government control
Language of instruction: English
Academic year: October to September
Chancellor: (vacant)
Vice-Chancellor: Prof. ISA BABA MOHAMMED
Registrar: Mallam YAKUBU HASSAN HABI
Librarian: Dr FAB. A. J. AKHIDIME
Number of teachers: 150
Number of students: 5,400

DEANS

College of Arts and Education: Dr JOSEPH N. UKWEDEH
College of Law, Management and Social Sciences: Dr NANA M. TANKO
College of Science and Agriculture: Prof. SIMON I. OKWUTE
Postgraduate School: Dr MICHAEL A. ADEWALE

PROFESSORS

ADELABU, J. A., Physics
AMDII, I. E. S., Political Science
BIRAI, U. M., Political Science
IKEOTUONYE, A. I., Education
OKWUTE, S. I., Chemistry
UJO, A. A., Political Science

UNIVERSITY OF AGRICULTURE

PMB 2240, Abeokuta, Ogun State
Telephone: (39) 245170
Telex: 24676
Fax: (39) 243031
Founded 1988 (previously a college of University of Lagos)
Federal control
Language of instruction: English
Academic year: October to July
Chancellor: HRH Alhaji Dr MUHAMMADU KABIR UMAR, Emir of Katagum
Vice Chancellor: Prof. JULIUS A. OKOJIE
Deputy Vice-Chancellor: Prof. I. F. ADU
Registrar: CATHERINE ADEBISI SOBOYEJO
Librarian: Dr T. M. SALISU
Number of teachers: 158
Number of students: 3,235
Publications: *UNAAB News*, *UNAAB Special Lecture Series*, *UNAAB Conference Proceedings Series*.

DEANS

College of Agricultural Management, Rural Development and Consumer Studies: Prof. P. A. OKUNEYE
College of Animal Science and Livestock Production: Prof. B. E. OGUNTONA
College of Environmental Resources Management: Prof. B. A. OLA-ADAMS
College of Natural Sciences: Dr F. O. BAMIRO (acting)
College of Plant Science and Crop Production: Prof. T. O. TAYO
Postgraduate School: Prof. O. A. OSINOWO

PROFESSORS

ADAMSON, R. I., Nutritional Biochemistry
ADDO, A. A., Nutrition and Dietetics
ADEDIPE, N. O., Plant Physiology
ADETORO, S. A., Industrial Design
ADU, I. F., Ruminant Production and Management
EKUNDAYO, O., Chemistry
FAWUSI, M. O. A, Horticulture and Environmental Physiology
LADEINDE, T. A. O., Plant Breeding and Seed Technology
OGUNTONA, B. E., Animal Nutrition
OJANUGA, O. A., Soil Science
OKOJIE, J. A., Forest Management and Biometrics
OKUNEYE, P. A., Farm Management and Accounting
OLADOKUN, M. O. A., Horticulture (Plantation Crops)
OSINOWO, O. A., Reproductive Physiology
TAYO, T. O., Crop Physiology

AHMADU BELLO UNIVERSITY

Zaria
Telephone: (069) 50581
Telex: 75252
Founded 1962
Federal control
Language of instruction: English
Chancellor: HRH Alhaji ALIYU MUSTAPHA
Administrator: Maj.-Gen. MAMMAN TSOFO KOHTAGORA
Registrar: Alhaji ABDULLAHI MUSA
Librarian: Alhaji INUWA DIKKO
Number of teachers: 2,064
Number of students: 29,832
Publications: *Vice-Chancellor's Annual Report*, *University Bulletin*, *University Research Report*, *University Public Lectures*, *Student Handbook*, *University Gazette*, annual reports of directors of attached institutes.

DEANS

Faculty of Administration: D. U. OSAGIEDE (acting)
Faculty of Agriculture: Prof. I. I. UVA
Faculty of Arts and Social Sciences: Prof. U. EZENWE
Faculty of Education: Dr I. U. JAHUN
Faculty of Engineering: Prof. O. ADEBISI
Faculty of Environmental Design: Dr A. A. HUSSEINI
Faculty of Law: Mallam I. N. SADA
Faculty of Medicine: Prof. A. M. YAKUBU
Faculty of Pharmaceutical Sciences: Dr A. B. BANGUDU
Faculty of Science: Prof. S. B. OJO
Faculty of Veterinary Medicine: Prof. J. U. UMOH
Postgraduate School: Prof. DALHATU MOHAMMED

PROFESSORS

Faculty of Administration:

ADEWUMI, J. B., Public Administration
ABDULSALAMI, I., Public Administration
DAUDU, P. C. A., Public Administration
IKOIWAK, E. A., Business Administration
LONGE, J. B., Public Administration
NZE, F. C., Local Government Studies
OSAZE, B. O., Accounting

Faculty of Agriculture:

ABALI, G. O. I., Agricultural Economics and Rural Sociology
ADEOYE, K. B., Soil Science
AHMED, M. K., Agronomy
ARINZE, E. A., Agricultural Engineering
BRAIDE, F. G., Agricultural Engineering
DIM, N. I., Animal Science
EBENEBE, A. O., Crop Protection
EGA, L. A., Agricultural Economics
EMECHEBE, A. M., Crop Protection
ERINLE, I. D., Crop Protection
KUMAR, V., Agronomy
LAGOKE, S. T. O., Agronomy
LOMBIN, L. G., Soil Science
MAURYA, P. R., Soil Science
NWASIKE, C. C., Crop Protection
OGUNBILE, A. O., Agricultural Economics
OGUNLELA, V. B., Agronomy
OHIAGU, C. E., Crop Protection
OLUGBEMI, L. B., Plant Science
OWONUBI, J. J., Soil Science
UMUNNA, N. N., Animal Science
YAYOCK, J. Y., Agronomy

Faculty of Arts and Social Sciences:

BRITWUN, K., French
EZENWE, U. I., Economics
IGBOZURIKE, M., Sociology
KISEKKA, M. N., Sociology
MAHADI, A., History
MENSAH, E., Sociology
MOHAMMED, D., History
ODEKUNLE, F., Sociology

Faculty of Education:

ADDO, A. A., Vocational and Technical Education

ADEYANJU, J. B., Education
ADEYANJU, T. K., Education
BOZIMO, D. D., Library Science
MUSAAZI, J. C. S., Education
OKON, S. E., Education
OMORUAN, J. C., Physical and Health Education
ONADIRAN, G. T., Education
ROBINSON, A. N. I., Education
SHUAIBU, M. J., Education

Faculty of Engineering:
ABATAN, A. O., Civil Engineering
ADEBISI, C. O., Mechanical Engineering
ADEFILA, S. S., Chemical Engineering
AKU, S. Y., Mechanical Engineering
ARINZE, E. A., Agricultural Engineering
EBEWELE, R. D., Chemical Engineering
FOLOYAN, C. O., Mechanical Engineering
KAUL, R. N., Agricultural Engineering
OGUNROMBI, J. A., Water Resources and Environmental Engineering

Faculty of Environmental Design:
FATUYI, R. B., Fine Arts
MOSAKU, T. O., Building
OGUNTONA, T., Industrial Design
OLORUKOOBA, B. K., Fine Arts
SA'AD, H. T., Architecture
SCHWEDTFEGER, F. W., Architecture
SOLANKE, A. O., Architecture
SULEIMAN, S., Fine Arts

Faculty of Law:
IMAM, M., Public Law
YAKUBU, M. G., Islamic Law

Faculty of Medicine:
ABENGOWE, C. U., Medical Microbiology
ABIOSE, A., Ophthalmology
ADEKEYE, E. A., Dental Surgery
ADESANYA, C. O., Medicine
ALI, M. A., Human Physiology
EGLER, L. J., Medical Microbiology
GANGULY, R., Surgery
GUPTA, P. K., Anaesthesia
LAWANDE, L. V., Medical Microbiology
MOHAMMED, I., Medicine
OBINECHE, E. N., Medicine
ONYEMELUKWE, G. C., Medicine
VERMA, O. P., Community Medicine
VIMAL, L. K. G., Anaesthesia
YAKUBU, A. M., Paediatrics

Faculty of Pharmaceutical Sciences:
ILYAS, M., Pharmacy and Medicinal Chemistry
LEGE-OGUNTONA, L., Pharmacy and Clinical Pharmacy
OLORINOLA, P. F., Pharmaceutical Microbiology
RAI, P. P., Pharmacognosy and Drug Development

Faculty of Science:
ABAA, S. I., Geology
ADETUNJI, J., Physics
AJAYI, C. O., Physics
ELEGBA, S. B., Physics
IKEDIOBI, E. O., Biochemistry
IKOHA, A. I., Biochemistry
KOLAWOLE, E. G., Textile Science and Technology
MOHAMMED, I. B., Mathematics
OGBADU, G. H., Biochemistry
OJO, S. B., Physics
OLATUNDE, A. A., Biological Sciences
OLAYEMI, J. Y., Chemistry
RASHID, M. A., Mathematics
THOMAS, S. A., Chemistry
UGBADU, G. H., Biochemistry
VAJIME, C., Biological Sciences

Faculty of Veterinary Medicine:
ABDULLAHI, S. U., Veterinary Surgery and Medicine
ABDULKADIR, T., Surgery and Medicine
ADEKEYE, J. O., Veterinary Pathology and Microbiology
ADEYANJU, J. B., Veterinary Surgery and Medicine
AGBEDE, R. I. S., Parasitology and Entomology
AKEREJOLA, O. O., Surgery and Medicine
ALIU, Y. O., Physiology and Pharmacology
EMA, A. N., Anatomy
ESIEVE, K A. N., Veterinary Pathology and Medicine
GHAJI, A., Veterinary Anatomy
GYANG, E. O., Veterinary Surgery and Medicine
MOLOKWU, E. C., Physiology and Pharmacology
NJOKU, C. O., Pathology and Microbiology
NWUDE, N., Physiology and Pharmacology
OGWU, D., Veterinary Surgery and Medicine
OJO, S. A., Veterinary Surgery and Medicine
SAROR, D. I., Pathology and Microbiology
UMOH, J. U., Veterinary Public Health and Preventive Medicine

Centres:
AHMED, U. B., Centre for Nigerian Cultural Studies
AWOGBADE, M., Centre for Social and Economic Research
EDUVIE, L. V., National Animal Production Research Institute
FADAHUNSI, A., Centre for Social and Economic Research
KISEKKA, M. N., Centre for Social and Economic Research
OGUNDIPE, S. O., National Animal Production Research Institute
OKITA, S. I. O., Centre for Nigerian Cultural Studies
OSINOWO, O. A., National Animal Production Research Institute
OTCHERE, E. O., National Animal Production Research Institute
OTUKA, J. O. E., Institute of Education
OYEBANJI, P. K., Institute of Education
OYEDIPE, E. O., National Animal Production Research Institute
UDOH, E. N. E., Institute of Education

ATTACHED INSTITUTES

Institute of Administration: PMB 1013, Zaria; f. 1954 and attached to the University in 1962; Dir Prof. M. G. YAKUBU.

Institute for Agricultural Research: see under Research Institutes.

Institute of Education: Main Campus, Samaru, Zaria; f. 1965; Dir Dr A. MOHAMMED.

Institute of Health: Main Campus, Zaria; Dir (vacant).

OTHER ATTACHED UNITS

Division of Agricultural Colleges: PMB 1044, Zaria; f. 1971; incorporates schools of agriculture in Bakura, Kaduna, Kabba and Samaru; Provost O. C. ONAZI.

National Agricultural Extension and Liaison Services: Dir. Alhaji M. B. ZARIA (acting).

Adult Education and Extension Services Centre: Main Campus, Zaria; Dir Alhaji GIDADO BELLO.

National Animal Production Research Institute: see under Research Institutes.

School of General and Remedial Studies: Main Campus, Samaru, Zaria; f. 1970; Dir Dr MUSA SHOK.

Centre for Nigerian Cultural Studies: Zaria; Dir Dr J. F. JEMKUR.

Educational Technology Centre: Zaria; Dir J. B. AKOLO.

Centre for Islamic Studies: PMB 1013, Zaria; Dir Mallam IBRAHIM N. SADA.

Centre for Social and Economic Research: Main Campus, Zaria; Dir Amb. AHMED BEITA YUSUF.

University Health Services: Dir Dr J. U. FARSHORI.

Iya Abubakar Computer Centre: Dir H. K. FRED.

Centre for Energy Research and Training: Dir Prof. S. B. ELEGBA.

Centre for Automotive Design and Development: Exec. Dir Prof. C. O. FOLOYAN.

Arewa House (Research Centre): Dir Prof. ABDULLAHI MAHDI.

FEDERAL UNIVERSITY OF TECHNOLOGY, AKURE

PMB 704, Akure, Ondo State
Telephone: (34) 200090
Fax: (34) 230450

Founded 1981
State control
Language of instruction: English
Academic year: October to September

Chancellor: Dr Sir CHUCKWUMELA NNAM, Obi II, The Eze Ogba of Ogbaland
Vice-Chancellor: Prof. L. B. KOLAWOLE (acting)
Deputy Vice-Chancellor: (vacant)
Registrar: B. A. ADEBAYO
Librarian: F. A. AKINYOTU

Number of teachers: 250
Number of students: 4,225

DEANS

School of Agriculture and Agricultural Technology: Prof. S. O. OJENIYI
School of Engineering and Engineering Technology: Prof. O. C. ADEMOSUN
School of Environmental Technology: Prof. E. A. ADEYEMI
School of Sciences: Prof. A. A. OSHODI
School of Postgraduate Studies: Prof. T. A. AFOLAYAN

HEADS OF DEPARTMENTS

Agricultural Economics and Extension Services: Dr P. B. IMODU (acting)
Agricultural Engineering: Dr A. S. OGUNLOWO (acting)
Animal Production and Health: Dr V. A. ALETOR (acting)
Applied Geology: Dr J. A. ADEKOYA (acting)
Applied Geophysics: Dr J. S. OJO (acting)
Architecture: O. ARAYELA (Co-ordinator)
Biochemistry: Dr T. L. OLAWOYE (acting)
Biology: Dr F. C. A. ADETUYI (acting)
Chemistry: Dr C. E. ADEEYINWO (acting)
Civil Engineering: Dr A. O. OWOLABI (Co-ordinator)
Crop Production: Dr T. I. OFUYA (acting)
Electrical and Electronic Engineering: J. O. ONI (acting)
Fisheries and Wildlife: Dr O. A. FAGBENRO (acting)
Forestry and Wood Technology: Dr J. A. FUWAPE (acting)
Industrial Design: Dr S. R. OGUNDUYILE (acting)
Industrial Mathematics and Computer Sciences: Dr S. O. FALAKI (acting)
Mechanical Engineering: Dr C. O. ADEGOKE (acting)
Metallurgical and Materials Engineering: J. A. OMOTOYINBO (Co-ordinator)
Meteorology: Dr Z. D. ADEYEFA (Co-ordinator)
Mining Engineering: Dr O. OJO (Co-ordinator)
Physics: Dr I. A. FUWAPE (Co-ordinator)
Quantity Surveying: O. L. OMONIYI (Co-ordinator)
Urban and Regional Planning: Dr D. O. OLANREWAJU (acting)

ATTACHED INSTITUTES

University Teaching and Research Farm: Dir (vacant).

Computer Centre: Dir Dr O. C. AKINYOKUN (acting).

General Studies Unit: Dir G. T. FATUNLA (acting).

F.U.T.A. Ventures: Dir Eng. J. ENABUREKHAN.

BAYERO UNIVERSITY

PMB 3011, Kano

Telephone: (64) 666023
Telex: 77189
Fax: (64) 665904

Founded 1977
Federal control
Language of instruction: English
Academic year: October to July (2 semesters)

Chancellor: HRH OFALA OKECHUKWU OKAGBUE, Obi of Onitsha
Chairman of Council: Dr A. I. ATTAH
Vice-Chancellor: Prof. B. B. DAMBATTA
Deputy Vice-Chancellor (Academic): (vacant)
Deputy Vice-Chancellor (Administration): Dr S. B. KURAWA
Registrar: I. ABDULHAMID (acting)
Librarian: M. A. SADIQ (acting)

Library of 170,000 vols, 2,200 periodicals
Number of teachers: 454
Number of students: 15,560

Publications: *Official Bulletin* (weekly), *Prospectus* (every 2 years), *University Public Lectures* (annually), *Calendar* (every 2 years).

DEANS

Faculty of Arts and Islamic Studies: Dr USMAN FARUK MALUMF ASHI
Faculty of Education: Prof. G. D. AZARE
Faculty of Law: Mall. N. AHMAD
Faculty of Medicine: Dr M. KABIR
Faculty of Science: Dr M. Y. BELLO
Faculty of Social and Management Sciences: Mall. M. BADARA
Faculty of Technology: Dr J. KATENDE
School of General Studies: Prof. USMAN HASSAN (Dir)
Centre for the Study of Nigerian Languages: Dr ABBA RUFAI (Acting Dir)
Postgraduate School: Prof. MAIWADA D. ABUBAKAR

PROFESSORS

ABBA, I. A., History
ABDUKALDIR, D., Centre for the Study of Nigerian Languages
ABDULRAHEEM, S. O., English and European Languages
ADEDOJA, T., Physical and Health Education
AZARE, G. D., Education
BALARABE, A., Arabic
BELLO, B. D., Chemistry
DANGAMBO, A., Nigerian Languages
HASSAN, U., School of General Studies
JIBRIL, M. M., English Language
MAIWADA, D. A., Education
MOHAMMED, S. Z., Islamic Studies
NDEFRU, J. T., Physics
OLOFIN, E. A., Geography
SALIM, B. A., Nigerian Languages
SEN, K. K., Biochemistry
SHEA, P., History
SUWAID, A. N., Arabic
UMAR, I. H., Physics

UNIVERSITY OF BENIN

PMB 1154, Ugbowo Campus, Benin City

Telephone: (52) 600553
Telex: 41365
Fax: (52) 241156

Founded 1970
Federal control
Language of instruction: English
Academic year: October to June

Chancellor: HRH Alhaji MUHAMMADU KABIR USMAN, Emir of Katsina
Pro-Chancellor: Hon. KAYODE ESO
Vice-Chancellor: Prof. A. G. ONOKERHORAYE
Deputy Vice-Chancellor (Academic): Prof. F. E. OKIEIMEN
Deputy Vice-Chancellor (Administrative): Prof. B. A. OBIORAH
Registrar: M. N. N. IDEHEN
Librarian: SAIBU AGUNU YAMAH

Library of 260,917 vols
Number of teachers: 694
Number of students: 20,660

Publications: *Faculty of Education Journals* (2 a year), *Benin Journal of Educational Studies, Physical Health Education and Recreational Journal, Faculty of Arts Journal* (quarterly), *Journal of the Humanities, University of Benin Law Journal* (annually).

DEANS

Faculty of Agriculture: Prof. U. J. IKHATUA
Faculty of Arts: Prof. K. ECHENIM
Faculty of Engineering: Prof. E. N. OHWOVORIOLE
Faculty of Education: Prof. I. OWIE
Faculty of Law: Dr T. B. E. OGIAMIEN
Faculty of Medicine: Prof. L. I. OJOGWU
Faculty of Dentistry: Prof. D. UFOMATA
Faculty of Pharmacy: Prof. E. E. OBASEIKI-EBOR
Faculty of Science: Prof. E. A. C. NWANZE
Faculty of Social Sciences: Prof. S. E. N. OKOH
School of Postgraduate Studies: Prof. B. E. BAFOR

PROFESSORS

ADEGOKE, D. A. , Chemistry
ADELUSI, S. A., Pharmaceutical Chemistry
ADEMOROTI, C. M. A., Chemistry
AGBADUDU, A. B., Business Administration
AGBAKWURU, E. O. P., Pharmaceutical Chemistry
AGHENTA, J. A., Educational Planning and Administration
AHONKHAI, S. I., Chemistry
AJISAFE, M. O., Physical and Health Education
AKERELE, A., Business Administration
ALIKA, J. E., Crop Science
ANAO, A. R., Accounting
ASALOR, J. O., Mechanical Engineering
AUDU, T. O. K., Chemical Engineering
AWANBOR, D., Educational Psychology
AWARITEFE, A., Mental Health
AYANRU, D. K. G., Microbiology
BADMUS, G. A., Educational Psychology
BAFOR, B. E., Geology
DUVIE, S.O. A., Surgery
EBEIGBE, A. B., Physiology
EBEWELE, R. O., Chemical Engineering
ECHENIM, K., French
EFERAKEYA, A. E., Pharmacology and Toxicology
EGBORGE, A. B. M., Hydrobiology
EGHAREVBA, P., Crop Science
EGUDU, R. N., English and Literature
EHIAMETALOR, E. T., Educational Planning and Administration
EKUNDAYO, J. A., Microbiology
ELAHO, R. O., French
FAWOLE, J. O., Physical and Health Education
GBENEDIO, U. P., Institute of Education
HUGBO, P. G., Pharmaceutical Microbiology
IFEDILI, S. O., Physics
IGBAFE, P. A., History
IGENE, J. O., Animal Science
IKEDIUGWU, F. E., Microbiology
IKHATUA, U. J., Animal Science
IMEOKPARIA, E. G., Geology
IMOGIE, A. I., Educational Psychology
IWU, G. O., Industrial Chemistry
IYOHA, M. A., Economics and Statistics
KIO, P. I. O., Forestry and Wildlife
KUALE, P. A., Electrical and Electronics Engineering
LAOGUN, A. A., Physics
NWAGWU, N. A., Educational Administration
NWANZE, E. A. C., Biochemistry
NWOKOYE, D. N., Civil Engineering
NZEMEKE, A. D., History
OBADAN, M. I., Economics
OBASEIKI-EBOR, E. E., Pharmaceutical Microbiology
OBIKA, L. F. O., Physiology
OBIORAH, B. A., Pharmaceutics and Pharmaceutical Technology
OBUEKWE, C. O., Microbiology
ODEBUNMI, A., Educational Psychology
ODUARAN, A. B., Adult Education
OFOEGBU, R. O., Surgery
OFUANI, O. A. English and Literature
OGBIMI, A. O., Microbiology
OGONOR, J. I., Pharmaceutical Chemistry
OGUDE, S. E., English and Literature
OHWOVUORIOLE, E. N., Mechanical Engineering
OJOGWU, L. I., Medicine
OKAFOR, F. C., Geography and Regional Planning
OKEH, P. I., French
OKEKE, E. O., Mathematics and Computer Science
OKHAMAFE, A. O., Pharmaceutics and Pharmaceutical Technology
OKIEIMEN, F. E., Chemistry
OKOH, N., Educational Psychology
OKOH, S. E. N., Economics
OKOLO, A. A., Child Health
OKOLOKO, G. E., Botany
OKHUOYA, J. A., Botany
OKONFUA, F. E., Obstetrics and Gynaecology
OKOR, R. S., Pharmaceutics and Pharmaceutical Technology
OLA, R. F., Political Science and Public Administration
OLOMU, J. M., Agriculture
OMATSEYE, J. N., Educational Administration
OMIUNU, F. G. I., Geography and Regional Planning
OMO-OMORUYI, Political Science
OMU, F. I. A., History
OMUTA, G. E. D., Geography and Regional Planning
ONOKERHORAYE, A. G., Geography & Regional Planning
ONWUEJEOGWU, M. A., Sociology and Anthropology
OPUTE, F. I., Botany
ORHUE, A. A. E., Obstetrics and Gynaecology
ORIAIFO, S. O., Institute of Education
ORONSAYE, A. U., Obstetrics and Gynaecology
OSAGIE, A. U., Plant Biochemistry
OSAZE, B. E., Business Administration
OSHODIN, O. G., Physical and Health Education
OSIME, U., Surgery
OSUIDE, G. E., Pharmaceutical Technology
OWIE, I., Physical and Health Education
OYAIDE, W. J., Agricultural Economics and Extension Services
SADA, P. O., Geography and Regional Planning
SALAMI, L. A., Mechanical Engineering
SANNI, S. B., Chemistry
UCHE, C., Sociology and Anthropology
UFOMATA, D., Restorative Dentistry
UGOCHUKWU, E. N., Biochemistry
URAIH, N., Microbiology
UREVBU, A. O., Educational Psychology
WANGBOJE, S. I., Creative Arts
WEMAMBU, S. N. C., Medical Microbiology
YESUFU, T. M., Economics and Statistics

ATTACHED INSTITUTES

Institute of Child Health: centre for health research and training; Dir Dr G. I. AKENZUA.

Institute of Public Administration and Extension Services: runs non-degree and postgraduate courses; Dir Dr S. U. AKPOVI (acting).

Institute of Education: runs postgraduate diploma course and Associateship Certificate; Dir Dr A. O. ORUBU.

UNIVERSITY OF CALABAR

PMB 1115, Calabar, Cross River State

Telephone: 222855
Telex: 65103
Fax 224996

Founded 1975; previously a campus of the University of Nigeria
Federal control
Language of instruction: English
Academic year: September to June

Chancellor: HRH Alhaji ABALI IBN MUHAMMADU, Emir of Fika
Vice-Chancellor: Prof. KEVIN M. O. ETTA
Deputy Vice-Chancellor: Prof. R. A. O. SULE
Registrar: E. J. AKPAN
Librarian: N. O. ITA

Number of teachers: 527
Number of students: 16,800

DEANS

Faculty of Agriculture: Prof. E. J. UDO
Faculty of Arts: Prof. O. E. A. ESSIEN
Faculty of Education: Prof. L. E. AMADI
Faculty of Law: Prof. U. O. UMOZURIKE
College of Medical Sciences: Prof. D. BOLARIN
Faculty of Science: Prof. E. J. USUA
Faculty of Social Sciences: Prof. E. J. ETUK
Graduate School: Prof. R. A. O. SULE (acting)

PROFESSORS

Faculty of Agriculture:

UDO, E. J., Soil Science

Faculty of Arts:

ABASIATTAI, M. B., History
ESSIEN, O. E. A., Languages and Linguistics
IKONNE, C. U. E., English and Literary Studies
IWE, N. S. S., Religious Studies and Philosophy
JOHN, E. E., Languages and Linguistics
UKA, K., Theatre Arts
UNOH, S. O., English and Literary Studies
UYA, O. E., History

Faculty of Education:

AMADI, L. E., Curriculum and Teaching
DENGA, D. I., Educational Foundations and Administration

Faculty of Law:

UMOZURIKE, U. O., Public and International Law

College of Medical Sciences:

ANDY, J. J., Medicine
BOLARIN, D. M., Chemical Pathology
BRAIDE, V. B., Pharmacology
EJEZIE, G. C., Medical Microbiology and Parasitology
EKA, O. U., Biochemistry
OTU, A. A., Surgery
SINGH, S. P., Anatomy
UMOH, I. B., Biochemistry

Faculty of Science:

BRAIDE, E. I., Parasitology
MBIPOM, E. W., Physics
NYA, A. E., Chemistry
PETERS, S. W., Geology
USUA, E. J., Biological Sciences

Faculty of Social Sciences:

AKINSANYA, A., Political Science
ETUK, E. J., Management Studies
IWOK, E. R., Management Studies
OFFIONG, D. A., Sociology
SULE, R. A. O., Geography and Regional Planning
TOYO, E., Economics
USORO, E. J., Economics
USORO, E. J., Geography and Regional Planning

Institute of Oceanography:

ENYENIHI, U. K.

Institute of Public Policy and Administration:

UCHENDU, V. C.

Institute of Education:

OMOJUWA, R. A.

EDO STATE UNIVERSITY

PMB 14, Ekpoma, Edo State

Telephone: (55) 98446

Founded 1981
State control
Language of instruction: English
Academic year: September to August

Chancellor: HRH Alhaji Dr UMARU FARUQ BAHAGO, Emir of Minna
Sole Administrator and Chief Executive: Prof. M. I. ISOKUN
Registrar: G. T. OLAWOLE
Librarian: Dr S. E. IFIDON

Number of teachers: 437
Number of students: 16,000

Publications: *Iroro* (Journal of the Faculty of Arts and Social Sciences), *Edsu* (Journal of the Faculty of Education) (both annually).

DEANS

Faculty of Arts and Social Sciences: Prof. T. A. IMOBIGHE
Faculty of Engineering and Technology: Engr S. K. MOMOH (acting)
Faculty of Environmental Studies: Prof. A. A. SEGYNOLA (acting)
Faculty of Basic Medical Sciences: Prof. C. P. ALOAMAKA
Faculty of Natural Sciences: Dr I. O. EGUAVOEN (acting)
Faculty of Law: Dr K. A. APORI (acting)
Faculty of Agriculture: Dr J. O. OMUETI (acting)
Faculty of Education: Dr D. O. AIGBOMIAN
Faculty of Clinical Sciences: Dr F. ALUFOHAI
Graduate School: Prof. S. A. OKECHA (acting)

PROFESSORS

ADESINA, S. O. A., Architecture
AFE, J. O., Psychology Education
AGBONLAHOR, D. E., Microbiology
AISIKU, J. A., Curriculum Studies
AKINBODE, A., Geography
BELLO-IMAN, I. B., Political Science
ECHEKWUBE, A. O., Philosophy
EMIOLA, A., Law
IJOMAH, B. I. C., Sociology
IMOBIGHE, T. A., Political Science
IVOWI, U. M. O., Education
LONGE, J. B., Economics
MOMODU, A., Vocational and Technical Education
NDIOKWERE, C. L., Chemistry
OAIKHINAN, E. P., Engineering
OKECHA, S. A., Chemistry
REMISON, S. U., Agriculture

ATTACHED INSTITUTE

Institute of Education: Dir Prof. O. OBANEWA.

ENUGU STATE UNIVERSITY OF SCIENCE AND TECHNOLOGY

PMB 01660, Enugu

Telephone: (42) 451244
Telex: 51440
Fax: 335705

Founded 1980
Campuses at Abakaliki, Adada and Enugu
State control
Academic year: October to June (2 semesters)
Language of instruction: English

Chancellor: Cheif Dr ERNEST ADEGUNLE OLADEINDE SHONEKAN
Pro-Chancellor: Justice ANTHONY N. ANIAGOLU (Rtd)
Vice-Chancellor: Prof. JULIUS O. ONAH
Deputy Vice-Chancellor: Prof. T. C. NWODO
Registrar: F. C. EZE
Librarian: Dr N. ENE

Number of teachers: 287
Number of students: 9,267

Publications: *Information Bulletin* (monthly), *ESUTLIB Library Bulletin* (2 a year), *University Calendar* (annually), *Journal of Science and Technology*† (2 a year).

DEANS

Faculty of Applied Natural Sciences: Prof. E. D. N. UMEH
Faculty of Agriculture: Prof. C. J. C. AKUBUILO
Faculty of Basic Medical Sciences: Prof. M. U. K. MGBODILE
Faculty of Education: Prof. M. O. NDUANYA
Faculty of Engineering: Prof. L. E. ANEKE
Faculty of Environmental Sciences: Dr I. C. UGWU
Faculty of Law: Prof. M. C. OKANY
Faculty of Management Sciences: Prof. S. C. CHUKWU
Faculty of Social Sciences: Dr S. I. UDABAH
School of Postgraduate Studies: Prof. S. O. ALAKU
Mature Students' Programme: Prof. E. OKEREKE ARII

PROFESSORS

ADIBE, E. C., Environmental Sciences
AKUBUILO, C. J. C., Agricultural Economics and Extension
ANEKE, L. E., Chemical Engineering
ANICHE, G. N., Applied Microbiology and Brewing
ATTAH, C. A., College of Health Sciences
CHUKWU, S. C., Marketing
EDEANI, D. O., Postgraduate School
EGWUATU, R. I., Crop Science
ENE, J. C., Applied Natural Sciences
EZE, O. C., Law
MADUEWESI, J. N. C., Applied Natural Sciences
MGBODILE, M. U. K., College of Health Sciences
MORDI, O., Insurance
NDUANYA, M. O., Education
NWABUFO ENE, K., Geology and Mining
NWODO, T. C., School of Postgraduate Studies
OCHO, L. O., Mature Students Programme
OKAFOR, N., Applied Microbiology and Brewing
OKAFOR, R. C., General Studies
OKAKA, J. C., Faculty of Agriculture
OKANY, M. C., Law
OKEKE, C. N., Faculty of Law
OKORIE, B. A., Industrial Training
ONUAGULUCHI, G. O., College of Health Sciences
ONUIGBO, W. I. B., College of Health Sciences
ONUOHA, G. B. I., Health and Physical Education
ONYEHALU, A. S., Educational Foundation
UMEH, E. D. N., Biotechnology and Pest Management

ATTACHED INSTITUTES

ESUT Business School, Lagos: Dir Dr O. J. ONWE.
Industrial Development Centre: PMB 01660, Enugu; Dir Dr G. N. ONOH.
Institute of Education: PMB 01660, Enugu; Dir A. E. EZE.
Social Research Institute: Dir Dr D. N. NWATU.

UNIVERSITY OF IBADAN

Ibadan

Telephone: (2) 8101100

Founded 1962; previously established as University College, Ibadan, 1948
Federal control
Language of instruction: English
Academic year: September to July

Chancellor: HH ORCHIVIRIGH ALFRED AKAWE, TORKULA TOR TIV IV

Vice-Chancellor: Prof. O. ADEWOYE
Deputy Vice-Chancellors: Prof. B. ONIMODE (Academic)
Registrar: M. LADIPO
Librarian: O. G. TAMUNO

Library: see Libraries
Number of teaching staff: 1,077
Number of students: 20,434

Publications: *Calendar*, *Annual Report*, *Research Bulletin of the Centre for Arabic Documentation* (2 a year), *The Gazette*, *Official Bulletin*.

DEANS

College of Medicine: Prof. M. T. SHOKUNBI (Provost)
Faculty of Arts: Prof. S. O. ODUNUGA
Faculty of Science: Prof. I. IWEIBO
Faculty of Basic Medical Sciences: Prof. O. O. OLORUNSOGO
Faculty of Pharmacy: Prof. H. A. ODELOLA
Faculty of Clinical Sciences and Dentistry: Prof. V. A. NOTTIDGE
Faculty of Agriculture and Forestry: Prof. A. O. AKINSOYINU
Faculty of Social Sciences: Prof. J. A. A. AYOADE
Faculty of Education: Prof. J. A. AYALA
Faculty of Veterinary Medicine: Prof. R. O. A. AROWOLO
Faculty of Technology: Prof. O. OFI
Faculty of Law: Dr J. D. OJO
Postgraduate School: Prof. B. O. FAGBEMI

PROFESSORS

Faculty of Arts:
ABOGUNRIN, S. O. K., Religious Studies
ADE-AJAYI, J. F., History
ADELUGBA, D., Theatre Arts
ADENIRAN, A., Linguistics and African Languages
ADEWOYE, O., History
ASEIN, S. O., English
BAMGBOSE, T. A., Linguistics and Nigerian Languages
BANJO, L. A., English
ELUGBE, B. O., Linguistics and African Languages
ILEVBARE, J. A., Classics
IZEVBAYE, D. S., English
KENNY, J., Religious Studies
MALIK, S. H. A., Arabic and Islamic Studies
MUNOZ, L. J., Modern European Languages
ODEJIDE, A. I., Communication and Language Arts
ODUNUGA, O. O., Modern European Languages
OLATUNJI, O. O., Linguistics and Nigerian Languages
OMAMOR, A. P., Linguistics and African Languages
OSOFISAN, B. A., Theatre Arts
OSUNDARE, N., English
OWOLABI, D. K. O., Linguistics and African Languages
SOBOLO, R. S., Philosophy
TAMUNO, T. N., African Studies

Faculty of Science:
ADELEKE, B. B., Chemistry
ADESOGAN, E. K., Chemistry
ADESOMOJU, A. A., Chemistry
AJAYI, S. O., Chemistry
AKIN-OJO, A., Physics
AKINYELE, O., Mathematics
AWE, O., Physics
BABALOLA, I. A., Physics
BADEJOKO, A., Geology
EGUNYOMI, A., Botany
EKHAGUERE, G. O. S., Mathematics
EKUNDAYO, O., Chemistry
EKWEOZOR, L. M., Chemistry
ELUEZE, A. A., Geology
FAGADE, S. O., Zoology
FANIRAN, J. A., Chemistry
FASADI, I. O., Botany and Microbiology
GIWA, F. B. A., Physics
HUSSAIN, L. A., Physics
ILORI, S. A., Mathematics
IWEIBO, I., Chemistry
KOLAWOLE, G. A., Chemistry
KUKU, A. O., Mathematics
LONGE, O., Computer Science
MADUEMEZIA, A., Physics
NWAGWU, M., Zoology
ODERINDE, R. A., Chemistry
ODUNFA, A., Botany and Microbiology
OGUNMOLA, G. B., Chemistry
OJO, A., Physics
OKONJO, K. O., Chemistry
OKORIE, D. A., Chemistry
OKORIE, T. G., Zoology
OLADIRAN, E. O., Physics
ONI, C. E. A., Physics
OSIBANJO, O., Chemistry
OSO, B. A., Botany and Microbiology
OSONUBI, O., Botany and Microbiology
SOWUNMI, M. A., Archaeology
UKOLI, F. M. A., Zoology

Faculty of Basic Medical Sciences:
AGBEDANA, E. O., Chemical Pathology
AJAYI, O. A., Human Nutrition
AKINYELE, I. O., Human Nutrition
ATINMO, T., Human Nutrition
BOLABINWA, A. F., Physiology
DAVID-WEST, T. S., Virology
ELEGBE, R. A., Physiology
EMEROLE, G. O., Biochemistry
FATUNSO, M., Biochemistry
MADUAGWU, C. N., Biochemistry
ODUOLA, A. M. J., Pharmacology and Therapeutics
OLORUNSOGO, O. O., Biochemistry
OKPAKO, D. T., Pharmacology and Therapeutics
OSIFO, B. O. A., Chemical Pathology
OSOTIMEHIN, B. O., Chemical Pathology
OYEBOLA, D. D. O., Physiology
SALIMONU, S. L., Chemical Pathology
SHOKUNBI, M. T., Anatomy
TAYLOR, G. O. L., Chemical Pathology
UWAIFO, A. O., Biochemistry

Faculty of Pharmacy:
JAIYEOBA, K. T., Pharmaceutical and Industrial Pharmacy
ODELOLA, H. A., Pharmaceutical Microbiology and Clinical Pharmacy
OLANIYI, A. A., Pharmaceutical Chemistry

Faculty of Clinical Sciences and Dentistry:
ADEBO, O. A., Surgery
ADEKUNLE, O. O., Surgery
ADENIYI, J. D., Preventive and Social Medicine
ADEUJA, A. O. G., Medicine
AJAGBE, H. A., Oral and Maxillofacial Surgery
AJAYI, O. O., Surgery
AJAO, O. G., Surgery
AKINKUGBE, F. M., Child Health
AKINKUGBE, O. O., Medicine
ANTIA, A. U., Paediatrics
BAMGBOYE, E. A., Preventive and Social Medicine
COLE, T. O., Medicine
FALASE, A. O., Medicine
FAMILUSI, J. B., Paediatrics
IJADUOLA, G. T. A., Otorhinolaryngology
KALE, O. O., Preventive and Social Medicine
LAGUNDOYE, S. B., Radiology
LAWANI, J., Surgery
NOTTIDGE, V. A., Preventive and Social Medicine
ODEJIDE, A. O., Psychiatry
OHAERI, J. U., Psychiatry
OJENGBEDE, A. O., Obstetrics and Gynaecology
OLATAWURA, M. O., Psychiatry
OLUBUYIDE, I. O., Medicine
ONADEKO, B. O., Medicine
OSUNTOKUN, O., Ophthalmology
OTOLORIN, E. O., Obstetrics and Gynaecology
OYEDIRAN, A. B. O. O., Preventive and Social Medicine
OYEMADE, A., Preventive and Social Medicine
SOLANKE, T. F., Surgery
SRIDHAR, M. K. C., Preventive and Social Medicine

Faculty of Agriculture and Forestry:
ADEDIPE, N. O., Crop Protection and Environmental Biology
ADEGBOYE, R. O., Agricultural Economics
ADEGEYE, A. J., Agricultural Economics
ADEKANYE, T. O., Agricultural Economics
ADELEYE, I. O. A., Animal Science
ADENEYE, J. A., Animal Science
ADESIYAN, S. O., Crop Protection and Environmental Biology
ADEYOJU, S. K., Forest Resources Management
AGBOOLA, A. A., Agronomy
AJAYI, S. S., Wildlife and Fisheries Management
AKEN'OVA, M. E., Agronomy
AKINSOYINU, A. O., Animal Science
AKINWUMI, J. A., Agricultural Economics
BABALOLA, O., Agronomy
BABATUNDE, G. M., Animal Science
EGBUNIKE, G. N., Animal Science
EGUNJOBI, J. K., Agricultural Biology
EKPERE, J. A., Agricultural Extension Services
ENABOR, E. E., Forest Resources Management
FAGBAMI, A. A., Agronomy
FALUSI, A. O., Agricultural Economics
FASEHUN, F. F., Forest Resources Management
IDACHABA, F. S., Agricultural Economics
IKOTUN, B., Agricultural Biology
IVBIJARO, M. F., Crop Protection and Environmental Biology
LONGE, G. O., Animal Science
LUCAS, E. O., Agronomy
NGERE, L. O., Animal Science
NWOKO, S. G., Agricultural Economics
OBIGBESAN, G. O., Agronomy
ODEBIYI, J. A., Agricultural Biology
ODU, C. T. I., Agronomy
OGUNMODEDE, B. K., Animal Science
OKALI, D. U. U., Forestry
OKUBANJO, A. O., Animal Science
OLAYEMI, J. K., Agricultural Economics
OLOGHOBO, A. D., Animal Science
OLUYEMI, J. A., Animal Science
OMUETI, J. A. I., Agronomy
OYENUGA, V. A., Animal Science
TEWE, O. O., Animal Science
WILLIAMS, C. E., Agricultural Extension Services

Faculty of Social Sciences:
ABUMERE, S. I., Geography
ADEKANYE, J. A., Political Science
AJAYI, S. I., Economics
AREOLA, O. O., Geography
AYENI, M. O., Geography
AYOADE, J. A. A., Political Science
AYOADE, J. O., Geography
EGUNJOBI, T. O., Urban and Regional Planning
FANIRAN, A., Geography
FILANI, M. O., Geography
GBOYEGA, E. A., Political Science
IKPORUKPO, C. O., Geography
INANGA, E. L., Economics
KAYODE, M. O., Economics
MBANEFOH, G. F., Economics
OLOFIN, S. O., Economics
ONIMODE, B., Economics
OTITE, K. J. O., Sociology
OTUBANJO, D. A., Political Science
OYEJIDE, T. A., Economics
SOYIBO, A., Economics

Soyode, A., Economics
Ugwuegbu, D. C. E., Psychology

Faculty of Education:

Adedeji, J. A., Physical and Health Education
Aiyepeku, W. O., Library Studies
Ajala, J. A., Physical and Health Education
Akinboye, J. O., Guidance and Counselling
Anyanwu, C. N., Adult Education
Ayodele, S. O., Institute of Education
Bajah, S. T., Education
Dada, A., Teacher Education
Falayajo, A., Institute of Education
Fayose, O. P., Library and Archival Studies
Gesindi, S. A., Guidance and Counselling
Igbanugo, V. C., Physical and Health Education
Longe, R. S., Educational Management
Nzotta, B. C., Library, Archival and Information Studies
Obemeata, J. O., Institute of Education
Okedara, C. A., Teacher Education
Okedara, J. T., Adult Education
Omolewa, M. A., Adult Education
Onibokun, Y. M., Institute of Education
Onwu, G. O. M., Teacher Education
Ubahakwe, E. E., Teacher Education
Udoh, C. O., Physical and Health Education
Yoloye, E. A., Institute of Education

Faculty of Veterinary Medicine:

Adene, D. F., Veterinary Medicine
Adetosoye, A. I., Veterinary Microbiology and Parasitology
Aire, T. A., Veterinary Anatomy
Akinboade, A. O., Veterinary Microbiology and Parasitology
Akravie, S. O., Veterinary Pathology
Akusu, M. O., Veterinary Surgery and Reproduction
Alonge, D. O., Veterinary Public Health and Preventive Medicine
Anosa, V. O., Veterinary Pathology
Arowolo, R. O. A., Veterinary Physiology and Pharmacology
Ayanwale, F. O., Veterinary Public Health and Preventive Medicine
Esuruoso, G. O., Veterinary Public Health and Preventive Medicine
Fagbemi, B. O., Veterinary Microbiology and Parasitology
Joshua, P. A., Veterinary Medicine
Nottidge, H. O., Veterinary Medicine
Obi, T. U., Veterinary Medicine
Oduye, O. O., Veterinary Medicine
Ogunrinade, A. F., Veterinary Microbiology and Parasitology
Ojo, M. O., Veterinary Microbiology and Parasitology
Oladosu, L. A., Veterinary Medicine
Olowookorun, M. O., Veterinary Physiology and Pharmacology
Olufemi, B. E., Veterinary Medicine
Osuagwuh, A. I. A., Veterinary Surgery and Reproduction
Otesile, E. B., Veterinary Medicine

Faculty of Technology:

Akingbala, J. O., Food Technology
Alabi, B., Mechanical Engineering
Aworh, O. C., Food Technology
Bamiro, O. A., Mechanical Engineering
Fagbenle, B. O., Mechanical Engineering
Falade, G. K., Petroleum Engineering
Igbeka, J. C., Agricultural Engineering
Lucas, E. B., Agricultural Engineering
Ofi, O., Mechanical Engineering
Olorunda, A. O., Food Technology

Faculty of Law:

Anifalaje, J. O., Private and Business Law
Ojo, J. D., Public and International Law
Shyllon, F., Public and International Law

ATTACHED INSTITUTES

Institute of African Studies: Dir Prof. M. Omibiyi-Obidike.
Institute of Education: Dir Prof. S. T. Bajah.
Institute of Child Health: Dir Prof. F. M. Akinkugbe.
Postgraduate Institute for Medical Research and Training: Dir Prof. A. M. J. Oduola.
Africa Regional Centre for Information Science: Dir Prof. Enikhamenor.

UNIVERSITY OF ILORIN

PMB 1515, Ilorin, Kwara State
Telephone: (31) 221552
Telex: 33144

Founded 1975
Federal control
Language of instruction: English
Academic year: September to February, March to June

Chancellor: HH Shekarau Angyu Kuvyo II, Aku Uka of Wukari
Pro-Chancellor and Chairman of Council: Prof. C. O. Taiwo
Vice-Chancellor: Prof. John O. Oyinloye
Deputy Vice-Chancellor: Prof. I. E. Owolabi
Registrar: A. O. A. Alao
Librarian: R. A. Ukoh (acting)

Library of 70,495 vols
Number of teachers: 450
Number of students: 10,200

Publications: *University Calendar*, *News Bulletin* (monthly), *Annual Report, Students' Handbook,* faculty publs, etc.

DEANS

Faculty of Agriculture: Prof. O. O. Balogun
Faculty of Arts: Prof. O. O. Olajubu
Faculty of Business and Social Sciences: Prof. A. A. Ogunsanya
Faculty of Science: Prof. M. A. Mesubi
Faculty of Education: Prof. A. A. Adeyinka
Faculty of Health Sciences: Prof. O. F. Komolafe
Faculty of Engineering and Technology: Prof. J. S. O. Adeniyi
Post-Graduate School: Prof. M. A. Ibiejugba
Student Affairs: Prof. S. O. Oyewole

HEADS OF DEPARTMENT

Faculty of Agriculture:

Agricultural Economics and Farm Management: Prof. P. A. Okuneye
Agricultural Extension and Rural Development: M. D. Awolola
Animal Production: K. L. Ayorinde
Crop Production: Prof. J. O. Babatola

Faculty of Arts:

History: H. O. Danmole
Linguistics and Nigerian Languages: Y. Awoyale
Modern European Languages: Prof. Olu Obafemi
Performing Arts: Prof. Z. Sofola
Religions: P. A. Dopamu

Faculty of Business and Social Science:

Accounting and Finance: B. O. Ogundele
Business Administration: T. Adewoye
Economics: I. O. Taiwo
Geography: Prof. O. J. Olaniran
Sociology and Social Administration: F. P. A. Oyedipe

Faculty of Science:

Biochemistry: A. A. Odutuga
Biological Sciences: Prof. V. L. Yoloye
Chemistry: S. A. Lawani
Geology and Mineral Science: A. E. Annor
Mathematics: J. A. Gbadeyan
Physics: Prof. T. O. Aro
Statistics: Prof. O. S. Adegboye

Faculty of Education

Curriculum Studies and Educational Technology: Y. Ajayi-Dopemu
Educational Foundations: D. O. Kolawole
Educational Management: Segun Ogunsaju
Guidance and Counselling: J. O. Boyuwoye
Physical and Health Education: L. Emiola

Faculty of Health Sciences:

Anatomy: A. O. Odekunle
Behavioural Sciences: O. A. Abiodun
Chemical Pathology and Immunology: B. A. Aiyedun
Child Health: O. A. Ajayi
Clinical Pharmacology: Prof. A. Olatunde
Epidemiology and Community Health: Prof. E. O. Adekolu-John
Medicine: B. U. Bojuwoye
Microbiology and Parasitology: B. A. Onile
Obstetrics and Gynaecology: O. Ogunbode
Pathology and Haematology: P. O. Olatunji
Physiology and Biochemistry: A. O. Soladoye
Radiology: D. A. Nzeh
Surgery: Prof. S. K. Odaibo

Faculty of Engineering and Technology:

Agriculture Engineering: K. C. Oni
Civil Engineering: O. A. Adetifa
Electrical Engineering: T. S. Ibiyemi
Mechanical Engineering: Prof. M. B. Adeyemi

ATTACHED INSTITUTES

Institute of Education: Dir Prof. A. Abdullahi
Sugar Research Institute: Dir Dr R. O. Fadayomi

UNIVERSITY OF JOS

PMB 2084, Jos, Plateau State
Telephone and fax: (73) 610514

Founded 1975
Federal control
Language of instruction: English
Academic year: September to June (2 semesters)

Chancellor: HRH Oba Dr Festus Ibidapo Adedinsewo Adesanoye Osemawe of Ondoland
Pro-Chancellor: Ambassador Yahya Aliyu
Vice-Chancellor: Prof. N. E. Gomwalk
Deputy Vice-Chancellor (Administration): Prof. I. L. Bashir
Deputy Vice-Chancellor (Academic): Prof. P. Onumanyi
Registrar: A. Y. Goshi
Librarian: A. B. Ojoade

Number of teachers: 711
Number of students: 13,408

Publications: *University Calendar, Information Booklet, Student's Handbook, University Diary* (annually), *News Bulletin* (monthly), *News Flash* (weekly).

DEANS AND DIRECTORS

Faculty of Arts: Prof. I. James
Faculty of Education: Prof. S. U. Udoh
Faculty of Environmental Sciences: Arch. Dr S. A. Madaki (acting)
Faculty of Law: Dr Onje Gye-Wado (acting)
Faculty of Medical Sciences: Dr C. H. Ihezue (acting)
Faculty of Natural Sciences: Prof. P. Onumanyi
Faculty of Pharmaceutical Sciences: Prof. T. A. Iranloye
Faculty of Social Sciences: Prof. A. Nweze
School of Postgraduate Studies: Dr J. O. Kolawole (acting)
Institute of Education: Dr I. Bulus (Co-ordinator)
Centre for Continuing Education: Dr E. Best (Co-ordinator)
Centre for Development Studies: Dr V. A. Adetula (acting)

PROFESSORS

Faculty of Arts:

Amali, S. O. O., Theatre Studies
Bashir, I. L., History

JAMES, I., History
HAGHER, I. H., Theatre Studies
IKENGA-METUH, E., Religious Studies
ODUMUH, A. E., Languages and Linguistics
OJOADE, J., African Folklore
TASIE, G. O. M., Church History
UMEZINWA, W. A., Languages and Linguistics

Faculty of Education:

ABANG, T., Special Education
ADEWOLE, M.A., Philosophy of Education
ASUN, P., Zoology Education
LASSA, P. N., Mathematics Education
MALLUM, M. P., Guidance and Counselling
UDOH, S. U., Social Science Education

Faculty of Environmental Sciences:

OKECHUKWU, G. C., Hydrology and Water Resources

Faculty of Law:

IGWEIKE, K. I., Commercial, Public, International and Constitutional Law
OFORI-AMANKWAH, E. H., Juridical Law

Faculty of Medical Sciences:

ANAKWE, G. E., Biochemistry
BELLO, C. S. S., Medical Microbiology
GOMWALK, N. E., Medical Microbiology
IBU, J. O., Physiology
IDOKO, J. A., Medicine
ISICHEI, U. P., Chemical Pathology
OKOYE, Z. S. C., Biochemistry
OTUBU, J. A., Obstetrics and Gynaecology
UBOM, G. A., Enzymology and Molecular Biology

Faculty of Natural Sciences:

AJAYI, J., Zoology
AKUESHI, C. O., Plant Pathology
DUHLINSKA, D. D., Protozoology, Insect Pathology
EKPENYONG, K. I., Chemistry
HUSSAINI, S. W. H., Plant Taxonomy and Cytogenetics
LIVERPOOL, L. S. O., Mathematics
OGBONNA, C. I., Botany
ONUMANYI, P., Mathematics
ONWULIRI, C. O. E., Zoology
SHAMBE, T. S., Chemistry

Faculty of Social Sciences:

ELAIGWU, J. I., Political Sciences
NWEZE, A., Psychology
ONOGE, O. F., Sociology

Faculty of Pharmaceutical Sciences:

IRANLOYE, T. A., Pharmacology and Pharmaceutical Technology
OKWUASABA, F., Pharmacology and Clinical Pharmacy
SOKOMBA, E. N., Pharmacology

LAGOS STATE UNIVERSITY

PMB 1087, Apapa, Lagos State
Telephone: (1) 884168
Telex: 27899

Founded 1983
State control
Language of instruction: English
Academic year: October to July

Vice-Chancellor: Prof. FATIU AKESODE
Registrar: ADEOLA O. JOHNSON (acting)
Librarian: T. A. B. SERIKI

Library of 38,000 vols
Number of teachers: 278
Number of students: 7,800

Publications: *Educational Perspectives*, *Journal of Humanities* (2 a year), *LASU Jurist*, *ECOFLASH*.

DEANS

Arts: Prof. SOLA OKE
Education: Prof. I. O. OSAFEHINTI
Engineering: Prof. O. O. AJAJA
Law: M. A. IKHARIALE
Science: Prof. T. K. OBIDAIRO
Social Sciences: Dr H. A. EKIYOR
Postgraduate School: Prof. I. O. OGUNBIYI

UNIVERSITY OF LAGOS

Lagos
Telephone: 821111
Fax: 822644

Founded 1962
Federal control
Language of instruction: English
Academic year: October to June

Chancellor: HRH OBA OKUNADE SIJUADE, Ooni of Ife
Vice-Chancellor: Prof. N. O. ALAO
Registrar: Dr A. A. OMOTOSO

Library: see Libraries
Number of teachers: 675
Number of students: 23,309

Publications: *Calendar, Annual Report, News Bulletin, Information Flash, Campus News.*

DEANS

Faculty of Social Sciences: Prof. F. O. FAJANA
Faculty of Law: Prof. A. O. OBILADE
Faculty of Engineering: Prof. A. A. SUSU
Faculty of Arts: Prof. T. G. O. GBADAMOSI
Faculty of Science: Prof. K. KUSEMIJU
Faculty of Business Administration: Dr J. F. AKINGBADE
Faculty of Education: Prof. A. O. KALEJAIYE
Faculty of Environmental Sciences: Prof. S. O. OJO
School of Postgraduate Studies: Prof. F. A. FAJEMIROKUN
College of Medicine: Prof. O. A. SOFOLA

PROFESSORS

ABASS, O., Computer Science
ABDUL, N. A., Mechanical Engineering
ACHOLONU, A. D., Microbiology
ADALEMO, I. A., Geography
ADEBONOJO, S. A., Surgery
ADEFUYE, A. I., History
ADEGBOLA, O., Geography
ADEGITE, A., Chemistry
ADEGOKE, E. A., Chemistry
ADEKOLA, S. A., Electrical Engineering
ADENIYI, P. O., Geography and Planning
ADENUBI, J. O., Dentistry
ADEOGUN, A. A., Commercial and Industrial Law
ADEPEGBA, D., Civil Engineering
ADEROGBA, K., Engineering Analysis
ADESINA, S.
ADETUGBO, A., English
ADEYEMI, A. A., Law
AGBEDE, I. O., Law
AGBOOLA, A., Obstetrics and Gynaecology
AJOSE, S. O.
AKEJU, T. A., Civil Engineering
AKERE, J. F., English
AKINLA, O., Obstetrics and Gynaecology
AKINOSI, J. O., Oral Surgery
AKINRIMISI, E. O., Biochemistry
AKINSETE, I.
AKINYANJU, O. O., Medicine
AKPATA, E. S., Restorative Dentistry
ALAO, N. O., Geography
AMAKU, E. O., Surgery
ARADEON, D. O., Environmental Science
ASHIRU, O. A., Anatomy
ASIWAJU, A. I., History
ASUNI, T., Psychiatry
AYENI, O. O., Surveying
BALOGUN, S. A., Mechanical Engineering
BAMGBOSE, S. A., Pharmacology
DA ROCHA AFODU, J. T., Surgery
EDEBIRI, U., French
EKWUEME, L. E. N., Music
EMOKPAE, T. A., Chemistry
ESHO, J. O., Surgery
ESSIEN, E. E., Pharmaceutical Chemistry
FAGBAMIYE, E. O., Educational Administration
FAJANA, F. O., Economics
FAJEMIROKUN, F. A., Surveying
FASHOYIN, T., Industrial Relations and Personnel Management
FFOULKES-CRABBE, D. J. O., Anaesthesia
FOLARIN, S. A., Psychology
GBADAMOSI, T. G. O., History
GEORGE, B., Medicine
GIWA-OSAGIE, D. O. F., Obstetrics and Gynaecology
IBIDAPO-OBE, O., Engineering Analysis
IWUGO, K. O., Civil Engineering
JACKSON, J. O., Civil Engineering
JAJA, M. O. A., Surgery
JOHNSON, T. O., Medicine
KALEJAIYE, A. O.
KENKU, M. A., Mathematics
KUKOYI, A. A., French
KUSEMIJU, K., Biological Sciences
KWOFIE, E. N., French
LASI, G. N., Anatomy
MABADEJE, A. F B., Pharmacology
MAJEKODUNMI, A. A., Surgery
MOSADOMI, H. A., Oral Biology and Oral Pathology
NNATU, S. N. N.
NWANKWO, G. O., Finance
NWOKU, A. L., Oral and Maxillofacial Surgery
NWUNELI, O., Mass Communication
OBE, E. O.
OBILADE, A. O., Jurisprudence and International Law
ODEYEMI, S. O.
ODIETE, W. O., Biological Sciences
ODUGBEMI, T., Microbiology and Parasitology
ODUNJO, E. O., Morbid Anatomy
ODUSOTE, K.
OGUNMEKAN, D. A., Community Health
OGUNSANWO, A. C. A., Political Science
OGUNYE, A. F., Chemical Engineering
OJO, E. F., Economics
OJO, J. A. T., Finance
OJO, S. A., Modern European Languages and Literature
OJO, S. O., Geography
OKEOWO, P. A.
OKON, E. E., Engineering Analysis
OKOTORE, R. O., Biochemistry
OLALOKU, F. A., Economics
OLATUNJI, E. O., Physics
OLORUNTIMEHIN, B. O.
OLOWE, S. A., Paediatrics
OLUBOYEDE, O. A., Haematology and Blood Transfusion
OLUMIDE, F., Surgery
OLUNLOYO, V. O. S., Engineering Analysis
OLUSANYA, G. O., History
OLUSANYA, P. O., Sociology
OLUWAFEMI, C. O., Physics
OMO-DARE, P., Surgery
OMOTOLA, J. A., Private and Property Law
ONITIRI, A. C., Clinical Pathology
OREBAMJO, T. O., Botany
OSIYALE, A. O., Education
OSUNTOKUN, J. A., History
OYEBANDE, B. L., Geography
OYEDEJI, L., Adult Education
OYEDIRAN, M. A., Community Health
OYEDIRAN, O., Political Science
OYERINDE, J. P. O.
RANSOME-KUTI, O., Child Health and Primary Health Care
ROTIMI, V. O., Medical Microbiology and Parasitology
SALAWU, R. I., Electrical Engineering
SIMPSON, E. O., French
SOFOLA, O. A., Physiology
SOMORIN, A. O., Medicine
SOMORIN, O., Chemistry
SOWEMIMO, G. O. A., Surgery
SUSU, A. A., Chemical Engineering
TAIWO, O., English
TAYO, F., Biopharmacy and Clinical Pharmacy
TOMORI, S., Economics
UGBOROGBO, R. E., Biological Sciences

UGONNA, N., African Languages and Literatures
UMO, J. U., Economics
UVIEGHARA, E. E., Law
UZOKA, A. F., Psychology
VINCENT, T., English
WILLIAMS, G. A., Mathematics (Education)

UNIVERSITY OF MAIDUGURI

PMB 1069, Maiduguri, Borno State
Telephone: 232949
Telex: 82102

Founded 1975
Federal control
Language of instruction: English
Academic year: October to June

Chancellor: HRH Alhaji ADO BAYERO, Emir of Kano
Vice-Chancellor: Prof. N. M. GADZAMA
Deputy Vice-Chancellor (Academic Services): Prof. P. O. UGHERUGHE
Deputy Vice-Chancellor (Central Administration): Prof. M. B. AHMED
Registrar: Mallam UMARU IBRAHIM
Librarian: Dr AHMAD TAHIR

Number of teachers: 630
Number of students: 10,000

Publications: *Information Bulletin*, *Annual Report*, *University Calendar*, *Prospectus*, *Inaugural Lecture and Convocation Speeches*, *Annals of Borno*, *Students' Handbooks*.

DEANS

Faculty of Agriculture: Prof. A. J. RAYAR
Faculty of Arts: Prof. D. S. M. KOROMA
Faculty of Education: Prof. P. F. C. CAREW
Faculty of Law: I. ULLAH (acting)
Faculty of Science: Prof. M. Y. BALLA
Faculty of Social and Management Studies: Prof. S. O. OKAFOR
College of Medical Science: Prof. I. MOHAMMED (Provost)
Faculty of Veterinary Medicine: Prof. T. I. O. OSIYEMI
Faculty of Engineering: Prof. J. O. OHU
School of Postgraduate Studies: Prof. M. A. W. MIAN
Department of Student Affairs: Dr L. T. ZARIA

PROFESSORS

ABUBAKAR, A., Languages and Linguistics
ABUBAKAR, S., History
ADENIJI, F. A., Agricultural Engineering
AGUOLU, C. C., Library Science
ANASO, A. B., Crop Science
AYUB, M., Continuing Education and Extension Services
BADEJO, B. R., Languages and Linguistics
BRANN, C. M. B., Language and Linguistics
BWALA, S. A., Medicine
CHHANGANI, R. C., Common Law
CHIBUZO, G. A., Veterinary Anatomy
EL-DARS, M., Surgery
ENYIKWOLA, O., Human Physiology
FIAWOO, D. K., Sociology and Anthropology
FOLORUNSO, O. A., Soil Science
GOPAL, B. V., Biological Sciences
IGUN, U. A., Sociology and Anthropology
MSHELIA, E. D., Physics
MUSTAPHA, A., Sharia
OLOWOKURE, T. O., Accountancy
OMOTARA, B., Community Medicine
PADONU, M. K. O., Community Medicine
PRASAD, B., Human Anatomy
RICHARDS, W. S., Biological Sciences
SEIDENSTICKER, W., Creative Arts
SHEHU, U., Community Medicine
SHUKLA, U. C., Soil Science
SRIVASTAVA, G. C., Veterinary Microbiology and Parasitology
THAMBYAHPILLAY, G. G. R., Geography
TIJANI, K., Political Science and Administration
UBOSI, C. O., Animal Science
VERINUMBE, I., Biological Sciences

UNIVERSITY OF AGRICULTURE, MAKURDI

PMB 2373, Makurdi, Benue State
Telephone: (44) 33204
Telex: 85304

Founded 1988, previously campus of the University of Jos, now a fully independent university
Federal control
Language of instruction: English
Academic year: October to September

Chancellor: HRH Oba ADEYINKA OYEKAN II, Oba of Lagos
Vice-Chancellor: Prof. ERASTUS O. GYANG
Registrar: E. KUREVE (acting)
Librarian: J. A. ACHEMA

Number of teachers: 224
Number of students: 2,684

Publication: *Journal for Agriculture, Science and Technology*.

DEANS

College of Agronomy: Prof. B. A. KALU
College of Agricultural Economics and Extension: Dr E. P. EJEMBI
College of Agricultural Engineering and Engineering Technology: Dr E. I. KUCHA
College of Animal Science and Fisheries: Dr S. A. IKURIOR
College of Food Technology: Dr M. A. AKPAPUNAM
College of Science, Agricultural and Science Education: Prof. F. N. ONYEZILI
School of Postgraduate Studies: Prof. M. C. NJIKE

HEADS OF DEPARTMENT, AND CO-ORDINATORS

Agricultural Economics: Dr G. B. AYOOLA
Agricultural and Science Education: Dr O. N. AGBULU
Agricultural Engineering: Dr I. N. ITODO
Agricultural Extension and Communication: Dr E. EKPE
Animal Production: Dr D. V. UZA
Biological Sciences: Dr E. U. AMUTA
Chemistry: Dr J. O. IGOLE
Civil Engineering: I. O. AGBEDE
Crop Production: Prof. E. O. OGUNWOLU
Electrics and Electronics: Dr G. A. IGWUE
Fisheries: V. NGBEDE
Forestry: Prof. I. VERINUMBER
Home Economics: G. ADOLE
Mathematics, Statistics, and Computer Science: Dr R. A. KIMBIR
Mechanical Engineering: Dr L. T. TULEUN
Physics: Dr. A. ONOJA
Soil Science: Dr S. A. AYUBA
General and Remedial Studies: T. A. TOR-ANYIIN
Co-operative Extension Centre: Dr D. K. ADEZWA
Centre for Food and Agricultural Strategy: Dr G. B. AYOOLA
Centre for Agrochemical Technology: Prof. I. ONYIDO

FEDERAL UNIVERSITY OF TECHNOLOGY, MINNA

PMB 65, Minna, Niger State
Telephone: (66) 222887
Telex: 72216
Fax: (66) 224482

Founded 1983
Federal control
Language of instruction: English
Academic year: October to September (2 semesters)

Chancellor: HRH Alhaji Dr SHEHU IDRIS, CFR Emir of Zazzau
Pro-Chancellor: Dr HAMIDU ALKALI
Vice-Chancellor: Dr MOHAMMAD ABDULLAHI DANIYAN
Deputy Vice-Chancellor: Prof. S. A. GARBA
Registrar: Alhaji U. A. SADIQ (acting)
Librarian: Dr NASSIR BELLO

Number of teachers: 270
Number of students: 4,318

Publications: *University Information Booklet* (annually), *University at a Glance* (annually), *University News Bulletin* (fortnightly), *Information Flash*, *Campus News* (weekly), *Nigeria Journal of Technological Research* (annually).

DEANS

School of Agriculture and Agricultural Technology: Dr J. A. OLADIRAN
School of Engineering and Engineering Technology: Dr Engr E. B. OYETOLA
School of Environmental Technology: Mallam M. B. A. WUNA
School of Science and Science Education: Prof. J. M. BABA
School of Postgraduate Studies: Prof. D. O. ADEFOLALU

HEADS OF DEPARTMENTS

Agricultural Engineering: A. AJISEGIRI
Animal Production: O. O. FASANYA
Architecture: O. SOLANKE
Biological Sciences: T. A. GBODI
Building: M. B. A. WUNA
Chemical Engineering: K. R. ONIFADE
Chemistry: M. A. T. SULEIMAN
Civil Engineering: E. B. OYETOLA
Computer Centre: Y. O. SULE
Crop Production: J. A. OLADIRAN
Electrical, Electronic and Computer Engineering: O. AJOSE
Estate Management: S. O. OYEGBILE
Fisheries: S. L. LAMAI
General Studies: M. S. IBRAHIM
Geography: G. N. NSOFOR
Geology: M. I. OGUNBAJO
Industrial and Technical Education: G. D. MOMOH
Land Surveying: I. J. NWADIALOR
Mathematics/Computer Science: K. R. ADEBOYE
Mechanical Engineering: F. O. AKINBODE
Physics: J. O. ADENIYI
Quantity Surveying: S. BOLAJI
Science Education: V. I. EZENWA
Soil Science: M. I. S. EZENWA

NATIONAL OPEN UNIVERSITY

PMB 1, Abuja, Federal Capital Territory

Founded 1980
Courses for adults by correspondence and distance teaching; five-year degree courses are planned

Vice-Chancellor: Prof. AFOLABI OJO

UNIVERSITY OF NIGERIA

Nsukka, Enugu State
Telephone: Nsukka 771911
Telex: 51496

Founded 1960
Federal control
Language of instruction: English
Academic year: September to June
Campus in Enugu

Chancellor: HRH G. T. AYOMI-EGBESIMI EMIKO, OGIAME ATUWASE
Vice-Chancellor: Prof. G. F. MBANEFOH (acting)
Registrar: G. I. ADICHIE (acting)
Librarian: C. C. UWAECHIE (acting)

Library: see Libraries
Number of teachers: 1,051
Number of students: 22,328

Publications: *University of Nigeria Calendar* (annually), *Undergraduate Prospectus, Postgraduate Prospectus* (annually), *University Gazette* (annually), *The Record* (weekly), *Information Bulletin* (fortnightly), *Academic Regulations* (annually), *Annual Report*.

DEANS

Faculty of Agriculture: Prof. I. U. OBI
Faculty of Arts: Prof. S. A. EKWELIE
Faculty of Biological Sciences: Prof. O. C. NWANKITI
Faculty of Business Administration: Prof. U. MODUM
Faculty of Education: Prof. V. F. HARBOR-PETERS
Faculty of Engineering: Prof. D. C. ONYEJEKWE
Faculty of Environmental Studies: Prof. S. AGAJELU
Faculty of Health Sciences and Technology: Rev. Canon E. O. UKAEJIOFOR
Faculty of Law: Prof. D. I. O. EWELUKWA
Faculty of Medical Sciences and Dentistry: Prof. M. A. C. AGHAJI
Faculty of Pharmaceutical Sciences: Prof. C. N. AGUWA
Faculty of Physical Sciences: Prof. C. O. OKOGBUE
Faculty of Social Sciences: Prof. D. S. OBIKEZE
Faculty of Veterinary Medicine: Prof. S. N. CHIEJINA
School of General Studies: Prof. S. O. OLAITAN
School of Postgraduate Studies: Prof. T. A. UME
College of Medicine: Prof. UCHE MEGAFU (Provost)

PROFESSORS

ADICHIE, J. N., Statistics
AGAJELU, S. I., Surveying
AGHAJI, M. A. C., Surgery
AGU, L. A., Electrical Engineering
AGUWA, C. N., Pharmacology and Toxicology
AKPALA, A., Management
AKUBUE, Rev. Fr A. U., Education
AKUBUE, P. I., Pharmacology and Toxicology
ALI, A., Institute of Education
AMAZIGO, J. C., Mathematics
AMUCHEAZI, E. C., Political Science
AMUCHIE, F. A., Health and Physical Education
ANIMALU, A. O. E., Physics and Astronomy
ANYA, A. O., Zoology
ANYANWU, C. H., Surgery
ANYANWU, E. A., Institute for Development Studies
ARUA, E. O., Agricultural Economics
ASUZU, I. U., Veterinary Physiology and Pharmacology
AZUBUIKE, J. C., Paediatrics
BOB-DURU, R. C., Geography
CHIDUME, C. E., Mathematics
CHIEJINA, S. N., Veterinary Parasitology and Entomology
CHIKWENDU, V. E., Archaeology
CHINEME, C. N., Veterinary Pathology and Microbiology
CHUKWU, C. C., Veterinary Medicine
CHUKWUDEBELU, W. O., Obstetrics and Gynaecology
CHUKWUMA, G. C., Mathematics
EBIGBO, P. O., Psychological Medicine
EBOH, D. O., Botany
EGBUNIWE, N., Civil Engineering
EGONU, I. T. K., Languages
EGWIM, P. O., Medical Biochemistry
EJIOFOR, L. U., Political Science
EKE, E. I., Education
EKEJIUBA, F. I., Sociology and Anthropology
EKPECHI, O. L. V., Medicine
EKWELIE, S. A., Mass Communication
ELUWA, M. C., Zoology
ENEKWE, O., English
ENWEZOR, W. O., Soil Science
EWELUKWA, D. I. C., Public and Private Law
EYO, I. E., Psychology
EZE, I. M. O., Botany
EZEASOR, D. N., Veterinary Anatomy
EZEIKE, G. O. I., Agricultural Engineering
EZEILO, G. C., Physiology
EZEJIOFOR, G., Commercial and Property Law
EZEKWE, C. I., Mechanical Engineering
EZEOKE, A. C. J., Chemical Pathology
EZE-UZOMAKA, O. J., Civil Engineering
GUGNANI, H. C., Microbiology
IFESIE, E. I., Religion
IGBOELI, G., Animal Science
IHEMELANDU, E. C., Veterinary Anatomy
IHENACHO, H. N. C., Medicine
IHEZUE, U. H., Psychology
IKEJIANI-CLARK, M. I. O., Political Science
IKEME, M. M., Veterinary Parasitology and Entomology
IKPEZE, N. I., Economics
ILEGBUNE, C. U., Commercial and Property Law
ILOBA, C., Crop Science
ILOEJE, O. C., Mechanical Engineering
IMAGA, E. U. L., Management
KALU, O. U., Religion
MADUEWESI, E. J., Education
MADUEWESI, J. N. C., Botany
MODUM, E. P., Languages
NDUBIZU, T. O. C., Crop Science
NGODDY, P. O., Food Science and Technology
NNANYELUGO, D. O., Home Science and Nutrition
NWAFOR, D. C., Surgery
NWAFOR, J. C., Geography
NWAKO, F. A., Surgery
NWANA, O. C., Health and Physical Education
NWANKITI, O. C., Botany
NWOGUGU, E. I., International Law and Jurisprudence
NWOKE, F. I. O., Botany
NWOSU, C. C., Animal Science
NWOSU, H. N., Political Science
OBANU, Z. A., Food Science and Technology
OBI, I. U., Crop Science
OBI, S. K. C., Microbiology
OBIAKO, M. N., Otolaryngology
OBIDOA, O., Biochemistry
OBIKEZE, D. S., Sociology and Anthropology
OBINNA, O. E., Economics
OBIOHA, F. C., Animal Science
OBIZOBA, I. C., Home Science and Nutrition
OBOEGBULAM, S. I., Veterinary Pathology and Microbiology
ODIGBOH, E. U., Agricultural Engineering
ODUKWE, A. O., Mechanical Engineering
OFOMATA, G. E. K., Geography
OGBUJI, R. O., Crop Science
OGUAKWA, J. U., Chemistry
OHAEGBU, A. U., Languages
OHAEGBULAM, S. C., Neurosurgery
OKAFOR, B. C., Otolaryngology
OKAFOR, C. A., English
OKAFOR, C. O., Chemistry
OKAFOR, E. C., Chemistry
OKAFOR, F. C., Education
OKAFOR, F. C., Zoology
OKAFOR, F. O., Finance
OKEKE, C. E., Physics and Astronomy
OKEKE, E. A. C., Education
OKEKE, P. N., Physics and Astronomy
OKOGBUE, C. O., Geology
OKONKWO, C. O., Public and Private Law
OKONKWO, J. I., English
OKONKWO, P. O., Pharmacology and Therapeutics
OKORAFOR, A. E., Economics
OKORIE, A. U., Animal Science
OKORIE, J. U., Vocational Teacher Education
OKOYE, J. O. A., Veterinary Pathology and Microbiology
OKOYE, S. E., Physics and Astronomy
OKPALA, J. I. N., Education
OKPARA, E., Psychology
OLAITAN, S. O., Vocational Teacher-Training
OLI, J. M., Medicine
OLISA, M. S. O., Political Science
OLUIKPE, B. O., Linguistics and Nigerian Languages
ONAH, J. C., Marketing
ONONOGBU, I. C., Biochemistry
ONUAGULUCHI, G. O., Pharmacology and Therapeutics
ONUKOGU, I. B., Statistics
ONUOHA, K. M., Geology
ONUORA, G. I., Veterinary Physiology and Pharmacology
ONWU, Rev. N., Religion
ONYEGEGBU, S. O., Mechanical Engineering
ONYEKWELU, S. S. C., Botany
ONYEWUENYI, I. C., Philosophy
ONYIRIUKA, S., Chemistry
ORANU, R. N., Vocational Teacher Education
OSUALA, E. C., Vocational Teacher Education
OZIGBOH, I. R. A., History
PAL, S., Physics and Astronomy
UCHE, P. I., Statistics
UDE, F. N., Surgery
UDEALA, O. K., Pharmaceutical Technology and Industrial Pharmacy
UDEKWU, F. A. O., Surgery
UKWU, I. U., Institue for Development Studies
UME, T. A., Adult Education and Extra-Mural Studies
UMEH, J. A., Estate Management
UMEJI, A. C., Geology
UMERAH, B. C., Radiation Medicine
UNAMBA-OPARA, I., Soil Science
WOSU, L. O., Veterinary Medicine

ATTACHED INSTITUTES

Curriculum Development and Instructional Materials Centre: Nsukka; Dir Prof. T. A. UMEH.

Institute for Development Studies: University of Nigeria, Enugu Campus, Enugu, Enugu State; Dir Prof. E. U. L. IMAGA.

Institute of African Studies: Nsukka; Dir Prof. I. T. K. EGONU.

Institute of Education: Nsukka; Dir Prof. A. ALI.

Centre for Energy Research and Development: Dir Prof. A. O. ODUKWE.

Centre for Rural Development and Co-operatives: Dir Prof. F. C. OBIOHA.

Veterinary Teaching Hospital: Dir Prof. C. C. CHUKWU.

OBAFEMI AWOLOWO UNIVERSITY

Ile-Ife

Telephone: Ife (036) 230290

Founded 1961 as University of Ife, present name 1987
Federal control
Language of instruction: English
Academic year: September to July
Chancellor: Alhaji UMARU SANDA NDAYAKO
Pro-Chancellor: A. I. ATTA
Vice-Chancellor: 'WALE OMOLE
Deputy Vice-Chancellors: A. A. AFONJA (Academic), F. A. OGUNBONA (Administration)
Registrar: Dr D. E. OJUTIKU
University Librarian: M. A. ADELABU

Library: see Libraries
Number of teachers: 1,327
Number of students: 18,415

Publications: *Quarterly Journal of Administration, Odu, A Journal of West African Studies, University Bulletin, Handbook, Gazette, Calendar, Second Order* (2 a year).

PROVOSTS

College of Health Sciences: K. ADETUGBO
Postgraduate College: E. ODU

DEANS

Faculty of Administration: O. ABORISADE
Faculty of Agriculture: A. A. JIBOWO
Faculty of Arts: B. AJUWOM
Faculty of Basic Medical Sciences: V. C. B. NUSUGA

Faculty of Clinical Sciences: F. E. OKONOFUA
Faculty of Dentistry: S. A. ODUSANYA
Faculty of Education: J. I. AGUN
Faculty of Environmental Design and Management: J. R. O. OJO
Faculty of Law: M. D. ADEDIRAN (acting)
Faculty of Pharmacy: F. A. OGUNBONA
Faculty of Science: P. O. OLUTIOLA
Faculty of Social Sciences: A. A. OLOWU
Faculty of Technology: O. A. AJIBOLA

PROFESSORS

Faculty of Administration:

ABORISADE, O., Public Administration
OJO, M. O., International Relations
OLOWU, C. A. B., Local Government
OMOPARIOLA, O., Management and Accounting
SANDA, A. O., Public Administration

Faculty of Agriculture:

ADEBAYO, A. A., Soil Science
ADEPETU, J. A., Soil Science
ADESIMI, A. A., Agricultural Economics
ADUAYI, E. A., Soil Science
AINA, P. O., Soil Science
AKINGBOHUNGBE, A. E., Plant Science
AKINOKUN, J. O., Animal Science
ALAO, J. A., Agricultural Extension and Rural Sociology
FABIYI, Y. L., Agricultural Economics
FATUNLA, T., Plant Science
ILORI, J. O., Animal Science
JIBOWO, A. A., Agricultural Extension and Rural Sociology
LADIPO, J. L., Plant Science
OLALOKU, E. A., Soil Science
OLUFOKUNBI, B., Agricultural Economics
OMOLE, T. A., Animal Science
ONI, S. A., Agricultural Economics
SOBULO, R. A., Soil Science

Faculty of Arts:

AJUWON, B., African Languages and Literature
BESTMAN, M. T., Foreign Languages
EKUNDAYO, S. A., Linguistics
OGUNBA, O., Literature in English
OJO, J. R. O., Fine Arts
OLANIYAN, R. A., History
OMOSINI, O., History
SODIPO, J. O., Philosophy

Faculties of Basic Medical Sciences, Clinical Sciences and Dentistry:

ADETUGBO, H. K., Haematology and Immunology
ADEYEMO, A. O., Surgery
LADIPO, G. O. A., Medicine
MAKANJUOLA, O. I., Radiology
MAKANJUOLA, R. O. A., Mental Health
MORAKINYO, V. O., Mental Health
NWUGA, V. C. B., Medical Rehabilitation
ODESANMI, W. O., Morbid Anatomy and Forensic Medicine
ODUSANYA, S. A., Maxillosurgery
OJOFEITIMI, E. O., Community Health and Nutrition
OYEDEJI, G. A., Paediatrics and Child Health
SOYINKA, O., Dermatology and Venereology

Faculty of Education:

FASOKUN, T. O., Continuing Education
FAWOLE, J. O., Physical Education
OJERINDE, A., Educational Foundations and Counselling
TAIWO, A. A., Special Education and Curriculum Studies

Faculty of Environmental Design and Management:

OJO, J. R. O., Fine Arts
OLIVETO, G., Building Technology
WAHAB, K. A., Building Technology

Faculty of Law:

FABUNMI, J. O., Business Law
IJALAYE, D. A., International Law
ORETUYI, S. A., Business Law

Faculty of Pharmacy:

ADESINA, S. K., Drug Research
DIXON, P. A. F., Pharmacology
LAMIKANRA, A., Pharmaceutics
OGUNBONA, F. A., Pharmaceutical Chemistry
OJEWOLE, J. A. O., Pharmacology
SOFOWORA, E. A., Pharmacognosy

Faculty of Science:

ABODERIN, A., Biochemistry
ADEBONA, A. C., Botany
AFOLAYAN, A., Biochemistry
AFUWAPE, M. A., Mathematics
AKINRELERE, E. A., Mathematics
AKO, B. D., Geology
ALADEKOMO, J. B., Physics
AMUSA, A., Physics
BALOGUN, E. E., Physics
BALOGUN, R. A., Zoology
FOLAYAN, J. O., Biochemistry
IMEVBORE, A. M. A., Zoology
IMORU, C. O., Mathematics
LASEBIKAN, B. A., Zoology
LAWANSON, A. O., Botany
ODEYEMI, O., Microbiology
ODU, E. A., Botany
OGUNADE, S. O., Physics
OGUNKOYA, L. O., Chemistry
OJO, J. F., Chemistry
OKE, O. L., Chemistry
OKON, E. E., Zoology
OLORODE, O., Botany
OLUTIOLA, P. O., Microbiology
OLUWOLE, A. F., Physics
OSADEBE, F. A. N., Physics
OSHOBI, E. O., Mathematics
RAHAMAN, M. A., Geology
SALAMI, M. B., Geology
SEGUN, A. O., Zoology

Faculty of Social Sciences:

ABIODUN, J. O., Geography
ADEJUYIGBE, O., Geography
ADEOKUN, L. A., Demography and Social Statistics
ADEWUYI, A. A., Demography and Social Statistics
AFONJA, S., Sociology and Anthropology
DARE, L. O., Political Science
JEJE, L. K., Geography
ODETOLA, T. O., Sociology and Anthropology
OGUNBADEJO, F. O., Political Science
OLORUNTIMEHIN, O., Sociology and Anthropology
OLOWU, A. A., Psychology

Faculty of Technology:

AFONJA, A. A., Metallurgical and Materials Engineering
AJAYI, G. O., Electronic and Electrical Engineering
AJIBOLA, O. A., Agricultural Engineering
IGE, M. T., Agricultural Engineering
KEHINDE, L. O., Electronic and Electrical Engineering
LASISI, F., Agricultural Engineering
MAKANJUOLA, G. A., Agricultural Engineering
MOJOLA, O. O., Mechanical Engineering
OGEDENGBE, M. O., Civil Engineering
SANNI, S. A., Chemical Engineering
WILLIAMS, V. A., Electronic and Electrical Engineering

AFFILIATED INSTITUTES

Institute of Agricultural Research and Training Ibadan: see under Research Institutes.

Institute of Education: Ile-Ife; f. 1962; sponsored by the University, the Oyo State Ministry of Education and the Association of Principals of Teacher Training Colleges and Secondary Schools in the State; a mobile library equipped with books, audio-visual aids and film aids demonstration among colleges and secondary schools; Dir O. J. EHINDERO; publ. *News Bulletin* (quarterly).

Institute of Physical Education: Ile-Ife; f. 1970; trains physical education specialist teachers, runs academic programmes in physical education in collaboration with the Faculties of Art and Education and caters for recreational interests of all students; Dir J. T. OGUNDARI (acting).

OGUN STATE UNIVERSITY

PMB 2002, Ago-Iwoye, Ogun State
Telephone: (37) 390149

Founded 1982
State government control
Language of instruction: English
Academic year: October to July

Chancellor: Chief Dr MOSES ADEKOYEJO MAJEKODUNMI
Pro-Chancellor: Dr Chief SUNNY F. KUKU
Vice-Chancellor: Prof. OLATUNJI YINUSA OYENEYE
Deputy Vice-Chancellor: Prof. S. O. ONAKOMAIYA
Registrar: N. O. SOTOYINBO
Librarian: LAIDE SOYINKA

Library of 75,000 vols
Number of teachers: 269
Number of students: 5,800

Publications: *OSU Calendar* (every 2 years), *OSU Convocation Order of Proceedings* (annually), *OSU Faculty of Social and Management Sciences Prospectus* (annually), *OSU News Bulletin* (every 2 months), *OSU Journal of Educational Studies* (annually), *OYE Journal of Arts* (annually).

DEANS

College of Agricultural Sciences: Dr O. O. OWERU (acting Provost)
Obafemi Awolowo College of Health Sciences: (vacant)
Faculty of Arts: Prof. O. O. OGUNREMI
Faculty of Basic Medical Sciences: Prof. J. O. OLOWOOKERE
Faculty of Clinical Sciences: Prof. O. O. ADETORO
Faculty of Education: Prof. T. HASSAN
Faculty of Law: D. H. AFEJUKU (acting)
Faculty of Science: Prof. V. W. OGUNDERO
Faculty of Social and Management Sciences: (vacant)

PROFESSORS

ADETORO, O. O., Obstetrics and Gynaecology
AJAYI, E. O. A., Educational Management
ALAUSA, O. K., Community Medicine and Primary Health Care
AWODERU, V. A., Biological Science
DADA, O., Chemical Pathology and Haematology
EJIWUNMI, A. B., Anatomy
ERINOSHO, O. A., Sociology
GBILE, Z. O., Biological Science
KAYODE, A. A., Geology
OGUNBIYI, O. A., Radiology
OGUNDERO, V. W., Biology
OSOBA, A. M., Economics
OYENEYE, O. Y., Sociology
SALIMONU, L. S., Pathology and Haematology

ONDO STATE UNIVERSITY

PMB 5363, Ado-Ekiti, Ondo State
Telephone: (30) 240711

Founded 1982
State control
Language of instruction: English
Academic year: October to July

Chancellor: HRH F. I. ADESANOYE
Pro-Chancellor: Chief AUGUSTUS ADEBAYO
Vice-Chancellor: Prof. P. O. BODUNRIN

Registrar: Chief J. G. O. ADEGBITE
Librarian: J.A. ARINKENBI

Number of teachers: 226
Number of students: 4,686

Publications: *Annual Report*, *News Bulletin* (weekly), *Handbook*, *Calendar*.

DEANS

Faculty of Arts: Prof. D. O. OLAGOKE
Faculty of Education: Prof. D. O. OWUAMANAM
Faculty of Science: Prof. O. A. EGUNJOBI
Faculty of Social Sciences: Prof. F. S. EBISEMIJU
Faculty of Engineering: Prof S. I. O. OJO
Faculty of Law: Prof. A. B. OYEBODE

PROFESSORS

Faculty of Arts:
- ADELOWO, E. D., Religious Studies
- AGBI, S. O., History
- ASHAOLU, A. O., English
- NWEZE, E. C., French
- OLAGOKE, D. O., English
- OLUTOYE, O., Yoruba

Faculty of Education:
- MAKINDE, I. D.
- OWUAMANAM, D. O., Educational Foundations

Faculty of Science:
- ABE, O., Mathematical Science
- EGUNJOBI, O. A., Zoology
- ETTE, S. I., Biochemistry
- FATUNLA, T., Botany

Faculty of Social Sciences:
- ADEJUWON, J. O.
- EBISEMIJU, F. S., Geography
- ORUBULOYE, I. O., Sociology
- UGURU-OKORIE, D. C., Psychology

Faculty of Engineering:
- OJO, S. I. A., Civil Engineering
- WILLIAMS, V. A., Electrical and Electronic Engineering

Faculty of Law:
- OYEBODE, A. B., International Law and Jurisprudence

FEDERAL UNIVERSITY OF TECHNOLOGY, OWERRI

PMB 1526, Owerri, Imo State
Telephone: (83) 233546

Founded 1980
Federal control
Language of instruction: English
Academic year: October to July

Chancellor: HRH Justice A. E. ALLAGOA
Vice-Chancellor: Eng. Prof. C. O. G. OBAH
Deputy Vice-Chancellors: Prof. J. O. DURU (Academic), Prof. S. C. O. UGBOLUE (Administration)
Registrar: Dr T. I. IGWE
Librarian: J. C. ANAFULU

Library of 40,000 vols
Number of teachers: 235
Number of students: 4,050

Publications: *Students' Handbook* (every 2 years), *Newsletter* (monthly), *University Calendar, Digest of Statistics, Brochure of Academic Regulations* (every 2 years), *University Annual Report, Centre for Industrial Studies, Annual Review, Introduction to the General Studies Unit* (annually), *Library Bulletins and Accessions List* (irregular) *Report of the University Librarian* (annually), *Erosion News* (quarterly).

DEANS

School of Agriculture and Agricultural Technology: Prof J. C. OBIEFUNA
School of Science: Prof. A. I. UKOHA
School of Engineering and Engineering Technology: Prof. G. U. OJIAKOR
School of Management Technology: Prof. T. Y. OBAH
Postgraduate School: Dr S. E. ANANABA (acting)

PROFESSORS

- ACHI, P. B. U., Mechanical Engineering
- BANIGO, E. O. I., Food Processing Technology
- CHUKU, A. O., Power Systems
- DURU, O. J., Agricultural Engineering
- EJIKE, U. B. C. O., Applied Mathematics
- ENYIEGBULAAN, E. M., Polymer Science and Technology
- IJIOMA, C. I., Agricultural Engineering
- ILOEJE, M. U., Animal Production
- IWUALA, M. E. O., Biology
- MADUAKO, H. O., Crop Production
- NDUBUIZU, C. C., Mechanical Engineering
- NDUKA, A., Theoretical Physics and Applied Mathematics
- NJOKU, J. E., Agricultural Economics
- NWACHUKWU, B. A., Civil Engineering
- NWACHUKWU, M. A., Electrical and Electronics Engineering
- NWODO, C. T., Electronics
- NWOKO, V. O., Materials and Metallurgical Engineering
- NWUFO, M. I., Crop Production
- OBAH, C. O. G., Electrical and Electronics Engineering
- OBIEFUNA, J. C., Crop Production
- OJIAKO, G. U., Civil Engineering
- OKEKE, P.O., Geology
- ONUCHUKWU, A. I., Chemistry
- ONWUAGBA, B. N., Physics
- ONWUEME, I. C., Crop Physiology and Agronomy
- ONYENWEAKU, C. E., Agricultural Economics and Extension
- OSONDU, K. E., Pure Mathematics
- OSUJI, G. E., Soil Physics
- UDEDIBIA, A. B. I., Animal Production
- UGBOLUE, S. C. O., Polymer Science and Textile Technology
- UKOHA, A. I., Biochemistry
- UKPOMNWAN, J. O., Polymer and Textile Technology

UNIVERSITY OF PORT HARCOURT

PMB 5323, Port Harcourt, Rivers State
Telephone: 335218

Founded 1975
Federal control
Language of instruction: English
Academic year: October to July

Chancellor: HRH Alhaji MUSTAPHA UMAR EL-KANEMI, Shehu of Borno
Pro-Chancellor: Chief FOLARIN COKER
Vice-Chancellor: Prof. THEO VINCENT
Registrar: EMMAN N. ACHERU
Librarian: G. B. AFFIA

Library of 47,540 vols
Number of teachers: 493
Number of students: 11,294

Publications: *Kiabara* (2 a year), *Biologia Africana* (2 a year), *Library Waves* (2 a year), *Journal of Education in Developing Areas—JEDA* (annually), *Delta Series*.

DEANS

Faculty of Humanities: Prof. R. N. C. OKAFOR-NWANYA
Faculty of Science: Prof. L. C. AMAJOR
Faculty of Social Sciences: Prof. S. EKPENYONG
Faculty of Education: Prof. B. A. EHEAZU
Faculty of Management Sciences: Prof. C. C. NWACHUKWU
College of Health Sciences: Prof. N. D. BRIGGS
School of Graduate Studies: Prof. E. O. ANOSIKE

DIRECTORS

Institute of Education: Dr S. B. NWEEDEDUH
Institute of Agricultural Research and Development: Dr N. H. IGWILO (acting)
School of Basic Studies: Dr C. E. W. JENEWARI
General Studies Unit: Prof. A. C. I. ANUSIEM
College of Continuing Education: Prof. C. N. BARIKOR
Instructional Resources Centre: FRED ALASIA (acting)
Arts Theatre: I. OHENE (Co-ordinator)
University Counselling Centre: Prof. A. I. JOE
Computing Services Centre: Dr V. ASIBONG-IBE
Science and Engineering Workshop: Dr I. L. NWAOGAZIE

PROFESSORS

Faculty of Humanities:
- ALAGOA, E. J., History
- ANOZIE, S. O., Comparative Literature
- ASIEGBU, J. U. J., History
- CHUKWUMA, H. O., Oral Literature
- COOKEY, S. J. S., History
- EJITUWU, N. C., History
- EMENANJO, E. N., Linguistics and Igbo
- HORTON, W. R. G., Philosophy
- IKONNE, C., English
- MADUKA, C. T., Comparative Literature
- NNOLIM, C. E., Literature
- NWODO, C. S., Philosophy
- OKAFOR, R. N. C., French and Comparative Literature
- WILLIAMSON, K., Linguistics

Faculty of Social Sciences:
- ANIKPO, M. O. C., Sociology
- BELL-GAM, W. I., Geography
- EKPENYOUNG, S., Sociology
- OGIONWU, W., Sociology
- OJO, O. J. B., Political and Administrative Studies
- SALAU, A. T., Urban and Regional Planning

Faculty of Science:
- AKPOKODJE, E. A., Geology
- AMAJOR, L. C., Geology
- ANOSIKE, E. O., Enzymology and Protein Chemistry
- ANUSIEM, A. C. I., Thermochemistry and Biophysical Chemistry
- EKEKE, G. I., Biochemistry
- EVWARAYE, A. O., Semiconductor Physics and Devices
- KINAKO, P. D. S., Botany
- OKIWELU, S. N., Entomology
- OKOLI, B. S., Genetics
- ONOFEGHARA, F. A., Plant Physiology
- UDOUSI, J. K., Zoology

Faculty of Engineering:
- IKOKU, CHI U., Petroleum Engineering

Faculty of Education:
- BARIKOR, C. N., Adult Education
- DIENYE, N. E., Science Education
- EHEAZU, B. A., Adult and Non-Formal Education
- ENAOWHO, J. O., Educational Management and Planning
- EZEWU, E. E., Sociology of Education
- JOE, A. I., Psychology, Guidance and Counselling
- KOSEMAMI, J. M., Educational Foundations
- OKOH, J. D., History and Philosophy of Education

College of Health Sciences:
- ANAH, C. O., Cardiology
- BRIGGS, N. D., Obstetrics and Gynaecology
- HARRISON, K. A., Obstetrics and Gynaecology
- OBUOFORIBO, A. A., Anatomy
- ORUAMABO, R. S., Paediatrics

Faculty of Management Sciences:
- NWACHUKWU, C. C., Management

RIVERS STATE UNIVERSITY OF SCIENCE AND TECHNOLOGY

PMB 5080, Port Harcourt, Rivers State
Telephone: (84) 335808
Fax: (84) 230720
E-mail rsust@alpha.linkserve.com

Founded 1971, university status 1980
State control
Language of instruction: English
Academic year: October to July
Chancellor: Maj.-Gen. MUHAMMADU SANI SAMI (Rtd.)
Pro-Chancellor: Amb. LAWRENCE EKPEBU
Vice-Chancellor: Prof. STEVE ODI-OWEE
Deputy Vice-Chancellors: Prof. ALEX MUNSI (Main Campus), Prof. B. A. FUBARA (Onne Campus)
Registrar: M. B. MIEYEBO
Librarian: J. A. OMBU
Library of 121,700 vols
Number of teachers: 456
Number of students: 10,465
Publications: *Annual Report, News Bulletin* (monthly).

DEANS

Faculty of Agriculture: Prof. M. S. IGBEN
Faculty of Engineering: Prof. K. I. IDONIBOYE
Faculty of Environmental Sciences: Dr M. O. ORUWARI (acting)
Faculty of Law: J. F. FEKUMO (acting)
Faculty of Management Sciences: Dr D. W. MACLAYTON (acting)
Faculty of Science: Prof. T. J. T. PRINCEWILL
Faculty of Technical and Science Education: Prof. O. C. TAWARI
Post-Graduate School: Prof. N. O. ISIRIMAH

PROFESSORS

Faculty of Agriculture:
ACHINEWHU, S. C., Food Science
ADENIJI, M. O., Crop/Soil Science
AMAKIRI, M. A., Soil Science
IGBEN, M. S., Agricultural Economics/Extension
ISIRIMAH, N. O., Crop/Soil Science
WAHUA, T. A. T., Crop/Soil Science

Faculty of Engineering:
IDERIAH, F. J. K., Mechanical Engineering
IDONIBOYE, K. I., Chemical/Petrochemical Engineering
JOHNARRY, T., Civil Engineering
ODI-OWEI, S., Mechanical Engineering
ODUKWE, O., Mechanical Engineering
OGUARA, T. M., Civil Engineering

Faculty of Science:
BAMGBOYE, T., Chemistry
MGBENU, E. N., Physics
NWANKWO, S. I., Chemistry
OFOEGBU, C. O., Physics
OKEKE, P. N., Physics
ONUOHA, K. M., Geophysics
PRINCEWILL, T. J. T., Biological Sciences

Faculty of Environmental Sciences:
FUBARA, D. M. J., Geodesy
TEME, S. C., Engineering Geology

Faculty of Management Sciences:
AHIAUZU, A. I., Business Administration
FUBARA B. A., Business Administration

Faculty of Law:
EZE, O.C., Law

Faculty of Technical and Science Education:
TAWARI, O. C., Educational Administration

HEADS OF DEPARTMENTS

Faculty of Agriculture:
Agricultural Economics and Extension: Dr E. C. CHUKWUIGWE (acting)
Animal Science: Prof. N. A. BEREPUBO
Crop/Soil Science: Prof. T. A. T. WAHUA
Fisheries: Chief M. B. INKO-TARIAH (acting)
Food Science and Technology: Prof. S. C. ACHINEWHU

Faculty of Engineering:
Agricultural Engineering: Dr B. A. OZOGU (acting)
Chemical and Petrochemical Engineering: Dr S. S. OVURU (acting)
Civil Engineering: Prof. T. M. OGUARA
Electrical Engineering: Engr O. O. ORUYE (acting)
Marine Engineering: Dr K. D. H. BOB-MANUEL (acting)
Mechanical Engineering: Engr H. I. HART (acting)

Faculty of Environmental Sciences:
Architecture: Dr N. O. IMAAH (acting)
Estate Management: V. A. AKUJURU (acting)
Land Surveying: T. A. OPUAJI (acting)
Quantity Surveying: Arch. K. F. WOODE (acting)
Urban and Regional Planning: Dr C. OBINNA (acting)

Faculty of Law:
Commercial, Private and Property Law: N. S. OKOGBULE (acting)
Jurisprudence, Public and International Law: B. B. JACK (acting)

Faculty of Management Sciences:
Accountancy: Dr J. J. M. BRIADE (acting)
Banking and Finance: T. A. UDENWA (acting)
Business Administration: Dr P. B. JOHNNIE (acting)
Secretarial Administration: Dr O. O. ENI (acting)

Faculty of Science:
Biological Sciences: Dr T. G. SOKARI (acting)
Chemistry: Dr I. F. ORUAMBO (acting)
Mathematics: Dr V. O. T. OMUARU (acting)
Physics: Dr G. TAY (acting)

Faculty of Technical and Science Education:
Business Education: Dr W. A. AMAEWHULE (acting)
Educational Foundations: B. AMIRIZE (acting)
Science and Technical Education: Dr J. ALAMINA (acting)

ATTACHED INSTITUTES

Institute of Geoscience and Space Technology: Dir Prof. S. C. TEME.
Institute of Pollution Studies: Dir Dr S. S. BRAIDE (acting).
Institute of Foundation Studies: Dir Dr A. O. I. GABRIEL (acting).
Institute of Agricultural Research and Training: Dir Dr N. A. NDEGWE.
Institute of Education: Dir Dr J. C. BUSERI (acting).

USMANU DANFODIYO UNIVERSITY

PMB 2346, Sokoto
Telephone: (60) 234039
Fax: (60) 235519
E-mail: registrar@udusok.edu.ng

Founded 1975
Federal control
Language of instruction: English
Academic year: November to July
Chancellor: (vacant)
Vice-Chancellor: Prof. AMINU SALIHU MIKAILU (acting)
Deputy Vice-Chancellor: Dr T. M. BANDE (Academic)
Registrar: A. S. USMAN
Librarian: AHMED ABDU BALARABE (acting)
Number of teachers: 371
Number of students: 8,944
Publications: *Calendar, Report, Convocation Speeches, University Lecture Series, News Bulletin, Student Handbook* (annually).

DEANS

Faculty of Agriculture: Dr M. D. MAGAJI (acting)
Faculty of Arts and Islamic Studies: Dr A. M. AMFANI (acting)
Faculty of Education and Extension Services: Dr M. M. JAGABA (acting)
Faculty of Science: Dr A. A. ZURU
Faculty of Law: MAL. M. I. SAID (acting)
Faculty of Social Sciences and Administration: Dr N. O. YAQUB (acting)
College of Health Sciences: Dr W. E. K. OPARA (acting)
Postgraduate School: Dr MUHAMMAD JUNAID (acting)
Faculty of Veterinary Medicine: Dr A. I. DANEJI (acting)

PROFESSORS

ABDULKARIM, A., Paediatrics
ALEX, O. U., Pharmacology
BADEJO, O. A., Surgery
BAGARI, D. M., Nigerian Languages
BALOGUN, S. U., Islamic Studies
EZE, K., Pathology
GHATAK, D. P., Obstetrics and Gynaecology
GWANDU, A. A., Islamic Studies
KANI, A. M., History
KOMOLAFE, O. O., Pathology
MIKAILU, A. S., Management
MUKOSHY, I. A., Nigerian Languages (Hausa)
MUSTAPHA, I. E.
OKOH, A. E. J., Surgery
OKOLO, J. E., Political Science
ONYEMOLUKWE, G., Medicine
RAHMAN, M. M., Biochemistry
SINGH, B. R., Soil Science
SUWAID, A. N., Arabic

ATTACHED INSTITUTES

Centre for Hausa Studies: Dir Prof. I. A. MUKOSHY.
Centre for Islamic Studies: Dir Dr J. M. KAURA.
Energy Research Centre: Dir Dr A. A. TAMBUWAL.

UNIVERSITY OF UYO

Uyo, Akwa Ibom State
Telephone: (85) 200303
Fax: (85) 202694
E-mail: root@csu.uniuyo.ed.ng

Founded 1983 as University of Cross River State, then re-named University of Akwa Ibom State; present name 1991
Federal government control
Language of instruction: English
Academic year: October to July
Chancellor: HRM OBA OYEBADE LIPEDE
Vice-Chancellor: Prof. FOLA LASISI
Deputy Vice-Chancellor: Prof. I. I. UKPONG
Registrar: Sir J. S. ABORISADE
Librarian: Dr E.E. OTU AKPAN
Number of teachers: 522
Number of students: 15,882
Publications: *Journal of Research in Education and the Humanities, Journal of Humanities, Uyo Social Science Journal.*

DEANS

Faculty of Agriculture: Prof. J. E. UMOH
Faculty of Arts: Prof. M. B. ABASIATTAI
Faculty of Business Administration: Prof. E. R. IWOK
Faculty of Education: Prof. A. J. A. ESEN
Faculty of Law: Prof. P. U. UMOH
Faculty of Natural and Applied Sciences: Prof. E. D. OKON

Faculty of Pharmacy: Prof. E. E. ESSIEN
Faculty of Social Sciences: Prof. E. M. ABASIE-KONG
Postgraduate School: Prof. A. ABODERIN

PROFESSORS

ABASIATTAI, M. B., History
ABASIEKONG, E. M., Sociology
ABODERIN, A., Chemistry
AKPABOT, S. E., Music
BAMGBOYE, T., Chemistry
BISONG, J. O., Language Education
EKONG, E. E., Sociology
EKPO, A. H., Economics
EKPO, O. E., Curriculum Studies
ESEN, A. J. A., Guidance and Counselling
ESHIET, I. T., Chemistry and Education
ESSIEN, E. E., Pharmacy
EZE, O. C., Law
IBE-BASSEY, G. S., Educational Technology
IKKIDEH, I. S., English
IWOK, E. R., Accounting
LASISI, R. A., Engineering
UDOH, E. J., Agronomy
UMOH, I. B., Biochemistry
UMOH, J. E., Animal Science
USORO, E., Geography

FEDERAL UNIVERSITY OF TECHNOLOGY, YOLA

PMB 2076, Yola, Adamawa State
Telephone: (75) 25532
Founded 1981, present status 1988
Federal control
Language of instruction: English
Academic year: October to September

Chancellor: OBA SIKIRU KAYODE ADETONA
Vice-Chancellor: Prof. ALIYU A. AHMAD
Registrar: Mallam MUHAMMADU AMINU
Librarian: Dr V. W. UDOH

Number of teachers: 204
Number of students: 3,515

DEANS

School of Science and Technology Education: Dr I. G. EROMOSELE
School of Environmental Sciences: Dr J. UYANGA
School of Engineering and Engineering Technology: Prof. M. I. EIGER
School of Agriculture and Agricultural Technology: Dr U. H. BASHIR
Postgraduate Studies: Prof. J. C. ODODE

HEADS OF DEPARTMENT

School of Science and Technology Education:
- Biological Sciences: Dr M. A. MADUSOLUMUO
- Chemistry: Dr I. C. EROMOSELE
- Mathematics, Statistics and Operations Research: M. O. EGWURUBE
- Physics: Prof. J. C. ODODO
- Technology Education: D. K. DIRASO
- Geology: Dr N. AHMED

School of Environmental Sciences:
- Geography: Dr A. BASHIR
- Urban and Regional Planning: Dr BUKAR D. YERIMA
- Land Survey: R. NTIMOAH

School of Engineering and Engineering Technology:
- Chemical Engineering: T. CHIROMA
- Mechanical Engineering: Dr V. G. TOKAREV
- Civil Engineering: C. O. ANAMETEMFIOK
- Electrical Engineering: D. K. ROGERS
- Agricultural Engineering: Prof. M. I. EIGER
- Food Science and Technology: Mallam M. A. USMAN

School of Agriculture and Agricultural Technology:
- Animal Sciences, Fisheries and Wildlife: Dr A. ZAKARI
- Forestry and Range Management: Dr D. F. JATAU
- Crop Production and Horticulture: Dr M. SANI SAIDU
- Agricultural Economics: Dr U. BASHIR

Colleges

FEDERAL POLYTECHNIC, ADO-EKITI

PMB 5351, Ado-Ekiti, Ondo State
Founded 1977

Rector: Chief AMOS O. OJO
Registrar: D. O. OLUKOWADE
Librarian: Y. A. IZEVBEKHAI

Library of 12,000 vols, 300 periodicals
Number of teachers: 237
Number of students: 7,488

HEADS OF SCHOOLS

Business Studies: V. O FABUNMI
Engineering: Eng. D. L. ATANDARE
Environmental Studies: ADEWALE ODUNIAMI
Science and Computer Studies: Dr AKIN. FALODI

AKANU IBIAM FEDERAL POLYTECHNIC, UNWANA

PMB 1007, Afikpo, Abia State
Telephone: (88) 521574
Founded 1981

Rector: Prof. ZAK A. OBANU
Registrar: IHEANACHOR V. OBI
Librarian: J. A. EKEH (acting)

Library of 10,122 vols
Number of teachers: 117
Number of students: 2,137

Publications: *Annual Report*, *Information Bulletin* (quarterly), *Student Handbook*.

DIRECTORS

School of Science and General Studies: J. O. E. ONYIA
School of Business: G. N. EZEBUIRO
School of Engineering: G. C. OCHIAGHA

FEDERAL POLYTECHNIC, AUCHI

PMB 13, Auchi, Edo State
Telephone: (57) 200148
Founded 1973

Rector: Prof. A. K. YESUFU
Registrar: F. O. OGUNBOR
Librarian: J. O. AGHOJA

Library of 38,250 vols
Number of teachers: 228
Number of students: 5,647

HEADS OF SCHOOLS

Art and Design: A. MOYE
Business Studies: O. F. EBOREIME
Engineering: M.M. DUZE
Environmental Studies: G. O. AKHIGBE
Vocational, Technical Education: A. S. EDE-AGHE

FEDERAL POLYTECHNIC, BAUCHI

PMB 0231, Bauchi
Telephone: (77) 43630
Telex: 83272
Founded 1979

Rector: Dr M. L. AUDU
Registrar: Alhaji I. A. ABUBAKAR
Librarian: Mallam ZUBEIRU MOHAMMED

Library of 19,000 vols
Number of teachers: 188
Number of students: 2,316

DIRECTORS

School of Business Studies: J. S. OKE
School of Engineering Technology: A. O. AKANI
School of General Studies: C. I. OKOYE
School of Environmental Studies: Mallam I. S. JAHUN
School of Technology: T. A. OKE

BENUE STATE POLYTECHNIC, UGBOKOLO

PMB 2215, Otukpo, Benue State
Founded 1976
State control
Language of instruction: English
Academic year: October to September

Rector: Dr Y. W. AWODI
Deputy Rector: A. T. IKEREVE
Registrar: D. O. ONA
Librarian: M. A. SHINYI

Number of teachers: 115
Number of students: 1,505

Publication: *New Bulletin* (monthly).

DEANS

School of Technology: P. U. ANYOGO
School of Art and Design: B. Y. EBUTE (acting)
School of Business and Administrative Studies: E. A. ADEGBE
School of Engineering: P. E. AGBESE

FEDERAL POLYTECHNIC, BIDA

PMB 55, Bida, Niger State
Telephone: (66) 461707
Founded 1977

Rector: (vacant)
Registrar: S. F. IKO (acting)
Librarian: S. A. KASIMU

Library of 22,000 vols
Number of teachers: 278
Number of students: 9,602

DIRECTORS

School of Business and Management: E. N. EKPO
School of Engineering: P. C. MADUMELU
School of Applied Arts and Science: C. C. UMEH
School of Environmental Studies: M. A. KOLEOLA
School of Preliminary Studies: ABDULLAHI MANN

POLYTECHNIC, CALABAR

PMB 1110, Calabar, Cross River State
Telephone: 222303
Telex: 65155
Founded 1973
State control
Language of instruction: English
Academic year: October to June

Rector: Engr R. E. EKANEM
Deputy Rector: Dr R. A. ITAM
Registrar: G. F. A. ONUGBA
Librarian: J. S. UMOH

Library of 25,000 vols
Number of teachers: 213
Number of students: 5,000

DIRECTORS OF SCHOOLS AND CENTRES

School of Agriculture: Dr E. J. OROK
School of Applied Science: U. U. ASUQUO
School of Business and Management: P. O. N. ABANG
School of Communication Arts: Dr M. E. EKERE
School of Education: Dr JOE IBANGA
School of Engineering: Dr E. U. UYE
School of Environmental Studies: A. DIAWUO
Computer Centre: T. O. EYO (acting)
Continuing Education Centre: N. U. UMOH

Centre for General and Preliminary Studies: L. O. I. OGUEZE
Industrial Co-ordination and Public Relations Unit: M. J. MBONG (acting)
Polytechnic Industrial Consultancy Services Unit: Dr I. U. UGOT

INSTITUTE OF MANAGEMENT AND TECHNOLOGY

PMB 01079, Enugu, Enugu State
Telephone: (42) 250416
Founded 1973
Rector: Dr C. C. NJEZE
Deputy Rector: E. O. ASANYA
Registrar: C. E. ATTAH
Library of 49,000 vols
Number of teachers: 333
Number of students: 19,005
Publications: *Calendar*, *Information Booklet*, *Bulletin* (monthly), *MANTECH* (quarterly).

DIRECTORS OF SCHOOLS
Business Studies: W. A. NNAMANI
Financial Studies: J. C. ODIKE
Technology: P. UGWU
Engineering: Engr Dr L. C. ONUKWUBE
Communication Arts: C. AMAFILI
Distance Learning and Continuing Education: M. ELUKA
Science, Vocational and Technical Education: O. O. OKORIE
General Studies: Dr M. A. EZUGU

POLYTECHNIC, IBADAN

PMB 22, U.I. Post Office, Ibadan
Telephone: (22) 410451
Telex: 31222
Founded 1961, Polytechnic status 1970
Rector: Prof. E. O. OSHOBI
Registrar: R. G. OLAYIWOLA
Librarian: O. A. OBIKOYA
Library of 75,114 vols
Number of teachers: 342
Number of students: 4,982
Publications: *Calendar/Prospectus* (annually), *PolyNews* (irregular).
Ordinary and Higher Diploma courses in commerce and communication sciences, engineering, environmental studies, natural sciences and NCE teacher education.

FEDERAL POLYTECHNIC, IDAH

PMB 1037, Idah, Kogi State
Telephone: (58) 800128
Founded 1977
Rector: Dr Y. W. AWODI
Vice-Rector: S. U. OFFONRY
Registrar: S. A. OGUNLEYE
Librarian: J. I. ITANYI
Library of 19,489 vols
Number of teachers: 153
Number of students: 2,768
Publication: *News Bulletin* (monthly).

DIRECTORS
School of Business Studies: S. N. AKALABU
School of Engineering: Dr D. BELLO
School of General Studies: A. N. ONYECHEFUNA
School of Technology: Dr S. S. AROGBA
School of Metallurgy and Materials Technology: Dr L. O. ASUQUO

HEADS OF DEPARTMENT
Accountancy: I. U. NWAUBANI
Business Administration: I. R. ONOJA
Civil Engineering: C. ENWELU
Continuing Education: T. U. ONWUBIKO
Electrical Engineering: G. I. UCHEGBULEM
Food Technology: S. S. AROGBA
Foundry Technology: E. E. MUKORO
Hotel and Catering Management: E. O. N. SULEIMAN
Languages and Liberal Studies: A. N. ONYECHEFUNA
Marketing: S. N. AKALUBU
Mathematics and Statistics: S. O. ARO
Mechanical Engineering: Dr D. BELLO
Metallurgy: L. O. ASUQUO
Science Technology: O. K. ACHI
Secretarial Studies: K. OJUKWU
Social Science and Humanities: M. A. OKPANACHI
Surveying: P. IYAJI

FEDERAL POLYTECHNIC, ILARO

PMB 50, Ilaro, Ogun State
Telephone: (39) 440005
Founded 1979
Rector: Prince Dr S. A. OLATERU-OLAGBEGI
Vice-Rector: Dr K. O. JIBODU
Registrar: R. O. EGBEYEMI
Librarian: R. OLA BELLO
Library of 16,000 vols
Number of students: 3,000

DIRECTORS
School of Applied Science: Dr J. O. A. OMOLE
School of Business Studies: J. O. ABIBU
School of Engineering: F. O. AREGBE

KADUNA POLYTECHNIC

PMB 2021, Kaduna
Telephone: 211551
Founded 1968
Rector: Alhaji YUSUFU ABOKI
Secretary: ABDULLAHI AHMAN
Librarian: S. I. SHIKA
Library on three campuses of 56,000 vols
Number of teachers: 700
Number of students: 10,000

DIRECTORS
College of Environmental Studies: A. B. OJO
College of Administration and Business Studies: Dr U. ZAHRADEEN
College of Science and Technology: M. B. SALAMI (acting)

KANO STATE POLYTECHNIC

PMB 3401, Kano
Telephone: (64) 625658
Founded 1976
Rector: Alhaji TIJJANI IBRAHIM
Registrar: Alhaji YUNUSA YUSUF
Chief Librarian: Mal. M. T. OTHMAN
Library of 25,000 vols
Number of teachers: 382
Number of students: 3,786
Publication: *Monthly Bulletin*.

DIRECTORS
School of Social and Rural Development: Alhaji YAHAYA IBRAHIM
Aminu School of Islamic Legal Studies: Alhaji YAKUBU AHMED DAKAWA
School of Management Studies: Dr NASIRU IBRAHIM DANTIYE
School of Technology: Eng. SHEHU ABUBAKAR
Audo Bako School of Agriculture: Dr MOHAMMED AUDU

HASSAN USMAN KATSINA POLYTECHNIC

PMB 2052, Katsina
Telephone: (65) 32816
Founded 1983
Rector: Alhaji ABDU SANI FASKARI
Registrar: Alhaji YAHAYA L. RAFINDADI
Librarian: Alhaji ISAH MANIR BATAGAWARA
Library of 18,000 vols
Number of teachers: 501
Number of students: 3,506

DIRECTORS OF COLLEGES
College of Administration and Management Studies: Alhaji ABDULLAHI BAWA
College of Science and Technology: ALIYU ABUBAKAR BAKORI
College of Legal and General Studies: Alhaji MUSA SULE

HEADS OF DEPARTMENTS
College of Administration and Management Studies:
- Accounting: RAKIYA M. DAN'ALI (acting)
- Business Administration: HAJIYA AMINA SULEIMAN
- Public Administration: Mallam SABIRU U. DABO
- Secretarial Administration: Mallam BATURE ABDULLAHI

College of Science and Technology:
- Agriculture and Irrigation Engineering: MUHAMMAD BISHIR (acting)
- Civil Engineering: WADA BAWA (acting)
- Electrical Engineering: MAGAJI BILYA
- Mechanical Engineering: BALARABE DAUDA KATSINA
- Building and Quantity Surveying: ABDULKADIR ABU LAWAL (acting)
- Food Science, Catering and Hotel Management: ISAH ADO BINDAWA
- Mathematics and Computer Studies: ALI YARO KANKIA
- Basic and Applied Sciences: IBRAHIM UMAR SAULAWA

College of Legal and General Studies:
- Public and Private Law: MUHAMMAD SALE
- Sharia: LAWAL YAKUBU
- General Studies: ABDU ABUBAKAR CHARANCHI
- Languages: GIDE UMAR SALE (acting)

FEDERAL POLYTECHNIC, KAURA NAMODA

PMB 1012, Kaura-Namoda, Sokoto State
Founded 1983
Rector: Ir H. MOHAMMED
Vice-Rector: M. ENEJI
Registrar: Alhaji M. A. ANKA
Librarian: J. L. ISHAYA (acting)
Library of 7,450 vols
Number of teachers: 100
Number of students: 1,350
Publications: *The Polytechnic News Bulletin* (monthly), *Namoda Telescope* (every six months).

DIRECTORS
School of Business Management: C. APRAKU
School of Environmental Studies: A. G. FOSUHENE (acting)
School of Science and Technology: M. K. ABDULLAHI (acting)
School of General Studies: A. P. NSOLO (acting)

KWARA STATE POLYTECHNIC

PMB 1375, Ilorin
Telephone: 221441
Founded 1972
Rector: S. A. OLADUSU
Registrar: M. S. UMAR
Librarian: E. S. AFOLABI
Library of 50,155 vols
Number of teachers: 650
Number of students: 12,000
Publications: *Calendar* (annually), *Library Bulletin* (3 a year), *Kwarapoly News* (every

2 months), *Snappy Information* (annually), *Techforum* (2 a year).

DIRECTORS

Institute of Basic Studies: Dr M. O. ABOLARIN
Institute of Management and Vocation: G. O. OSUNBUNMI
Institute of Mines and Metallurgy: J. A. AJIBOLU
Institute of Technology: Dr ISMAILA ISA

LAGOS STATE POLYTECHNIC

PMB 21606, Ikeja, Lagos State

Telephone: 523528

Founded 1977

Rector: B. OLORO
Deputy Rector: J. B. AGUNBIADE
Registrar: OLUWOLE O. OJIKUTU
Chief Librarian: E. O. SOYINKA

Library of 29,558 vols, 1,880 in special collections
Number of teachers: 222
Number of students: 4,287

Publications: *Poly Handbook* (annually), *Laspotech News* (quarterly).

FEDERAL POLYTECHNIC, MUBI

PMB 35, Mubi, Adamawa State

Telephone: (75) 82771

Founded 1979

Rector: Engr F. C. UDEAGWU (acting)
Deputy Rector: IBRAHIM UMAR (acting)
Registrar: Mallam U. BELLO GIREI
Librarian: T. S. TARFA

Library of 14,000 vols
Number of teachers: 153
Number of students: 2,066

DIRECTORS

School of Engineering: A. D. DZARA
School of Science Technology: J. L. JALINGO
School of General Studies: S. U. JEN
School of Business Studies: L. S. EKPENE

FEDERAL POLYTECHNIC, NEKEDE

PMB 1036, Owerri, Imo State

Founded 1978

Rector: Dr C. I. OSUOJI (acting)
Registrar: I. C. KAFOR
Librarian: M. OJI

Library of 16,417 vols
Number of teachers: 166
Number of students: 4,763

DIRECTORS

School of Business and Public Administration: B. C. DURU
School of Engineering Technology: Engr J. I. ONWUJI
School of Environmental Design: Surv. Dr A. O. OHAKWEH
School of General Studies: G. U. ODUM
School of Industrial Sciences: N. OKPA-IROHA

OGUN STATE POLYTECHNIC, ABEOKUTA

PMB 2210, Abeokuta, Ogun State

Telephone: (39) 241274

Founded 1979

Rector: Chief (Dr) K. O. JIBODU
Deputy Rector: Alhaji W. A. KADIRI
Registrar: Chief 'W. ABIODUN
Librarian: C. O. OGUNSEHINDE

Library of 18,000 vols
Number of teachers: 124
Number of students: 7,899

HEADS OF DEPARTMENTS

Accountancy: M. O. AGBOOLA
Business Administration: Prince T. OLATUNJI
Marketing: A. L. ADEEKO
Secretarial Studies: Dr S. A. ONIFADE
Mass Communication: Dr M. A. OSO
Continuing Education: E. O. KOJEKU
Liberal Studies: Alhaji A. A. SALAAM
Architecture: Arch. O. A. FOWODE
Civil Engineering: Engr O. S. A. FAMUYIWA
Town and Regional Planning: O. A. SOILE
Electrical and Electronic Engineering: A. ASHIRU
Science Laboratory Technology: M. O. POPOOLA
Food Science and Technology: O. I. ONIGBOGI
Building and Quantity Surveying: Arch. A. A. AKANDE
Estate Management: O. O. ODERINDE
Engineering Service Courses Unit: S. A. SANYAOLU
Business Studies: O. SOBANDE
Financial Studies: S. I. ODUSEGUN

FEDERAL POLYTECHNIC, OKO

PMB 21, Aguata, Anambra State

Telephone: (46) 911144

Founded: 1979

Rector: Dr U. C. NZEWI
Registrar: O. C. A. OFOCHEBE
Librarian: U. C. U. UCHEDILI

Library of 65,000 books
Number of students: 7,500

Courses in Business Studies, Information Technology, Environmental Design and Technology.

ONDO STATE POLYTECHNIC

POB 1019, Owo, Ondo State

Telephone: (51) 41045

Founded 1980

Rector: Prof. A. S. ADEDIMILA
Deputy Rector: KEHINDE ALAO
Registrar: R. F. AKERELE
Librarian: M. O. POPOOLA

Library of 25,000 vols
Number of teachers: 173
Number of students: 9,710

DEANS

Business Studies: Chief A. O. OLALEYE
Food Technology: J. K. AJAYI
Engineering: Rev. S. A. ADEGBEMIRO
Environmental Studies: E. A. ARIGBEDE

PETROLEUM TRAINING INSTITUTE

PMB 20, Effurun, Delta State

Telephone: 200010
Telex: 43492

Founded 1972

Principal: Engr H. O. ONIPEDE
Registrar: E. C. AKPOBI
Librarian: E. M. A. DUDU

Library of 49,000 vols
Number of teachers: 87
Number of students: 1,672

Publications: *Annual Report, PTI News* (quarterly).

HEADS OF DEPARTMENTS

Petroleum Processing Technology: Eng. P. K. UDE
Electrical and Electronics Engineering: Eng. W. D. KOKORUWE
General Studies: H. O ERIVONA
Industrial Continuing Education: Eng. M. I. IRONKWE
Industrial Safety and Environmental Engineering: L. YOUDE-OWEI
Marketing and Business Studies: E. E. ERUKAYE
Mechanical Engineering: Eng. G. D. AKPERI
Petroleum Engineering and Geosciences: E. NWANOKWALE
Welding and Underwater Operations: M. C. EDDOH

PLATEAU STATE POLYTECHNIC, BARKIN LADI

PMB 02023, Bukuru, Plateau State

Founded 1978, present status 1980

Rector: Engr ALEXANDER A. T. KEBANG
Registrar: TIMOTHY A. ANJIDE
Director of Administration: LAMI A. ENATTO
Librarian: J. E. KOTSO

Library of 11,393 vols
Number of teachers: 121
Number of students: 2,260

Publications: *News Bulletins*, *Students' Handbook*.

DEANS

School of Administration and General Studies: Mrs. L. A. ENATTO
School of Engineering and Environmental Studies: Dr R. JATAU
School of Management Studies: ELIZABETH PAM
School of Science and Technology: K. D. DABER

DIRECTORS

Consultancy and Applied Research Division: Engr O. O. OLUSANYA
Centre for Continuing Education: ELIZABETH K. PAM

POLYTECHNIC OF SOKOTO STATE

PMB 1034, Birnin Kebbi, Sokoto State

Telephone: (60) 97

Founded 1976

Rector: Alhaji ABUBAKAR N. ABDULLAH
Registrar: Alhaji BALA M. SAKABA
Librarian: J. O. GBADAMOSI

Library of 7,475 vols
Number of teachers: 737
Number of students: 1,556

ND and HND courses

DEANS

School of General Studies: JACOB GEORGE
School of Education (Business and Technical): Dr E. A. OGUNWOLE
School of Engineering: JERRY OJEDIRAN
School of Land Surveying: Mallam Y. DANIAN
School of Environmental Design: Mallam MUSA MAIDAMA
School of Management Studies: Mallam IBRAHIM MORI BABA
School of Public Administration: Mallam FARUK A. KALBO

YABA COLLEGE OF TECHNOLOGY

PMB 2011, Yaba, Lagos

Telephone: (1) 800160

Founded 1948

Federal control
Academic year: October to July

Rector: Chief F. A. ODUGBESAN
Registrar: F. F. TAIWO (acting)
Librarian: M. A. AFOLAYAN

Library of 70,000 vols
Number of teaching staff: 391

Number of students: 5,697 full-time, 6,781 part-time

Publications: *Prospectus, Newsletter, YCT Academic Journal.*

DIRECTORS

School of Applied Sciences: Dr K. A. JOAQUIM
School of Art, Design and Printing: A. N. OWODUNNI
School of Engineering: J. A. ADEOTI
School of Environmental Studies: E. FAGBUYI
School of Management and Business Studies: G. T. OGUNSOLA

Federal College of Agriculture: Institute of Agricultural Research and Training, PMB 5029, Moor Plantation, Ibadan; tel. (22) 312070; f. 1921; 16 teachers, 150 students; Provost Dr D. S. DARAMOLA.

Federal College of Forestry: Forestry Research Institute of Nigeria, PMB 5054, Ibadan; tel. (22) 411035; telex 31207; f. 1941; technical forestry training, National and Higher National Diploma courses; vocational courses; library of 4,800 vols; 20 teachers, 520 students; Dir Dr ISAAC I. ERO.

Federal School of Dental Hygiene: 1 Broad St, PMB 12562, Lagos; f. 1957; Principal Dr S. JOHNSON.

Institute of Business Administration of Nigeria: 4 Oregun Rd, Ikeja, Surulere, Lagos; f. 1979; 50 teachers, 4,000 students; library of over 2,000 vols; Dir Dr A. E. EDEBE.

National Eye Centre: Off Mando Rd, PMB 2267, Kaduna; tel. (62) 235026; fax (62) 215642; f. 1979; provides postgraduate ophthalmic training (medical and surgical), ophthalmic nursing training, clinical services, Chair. Dr E. O. AKINSETE; Dir Prof. A. ABIOSE; publ. *Newsletter* (quarterly).

National Institute of Ophthalmology: Federal Government Secretariat, POB 51551, Ikoyi, Lagos; tel. 684875; f. 1979; incorporates postgraduate ophthalmic medical school, and teaching hospital; Dir Prof. H. C. KODILINYE.

School of Agriculture: PMB 623, Akure, Ondo State; f. 1957; 500 students; library of 2,100 vols; Principal S. A. OYENEYE; publ. *The Tractor*.

NORWAY

Learned Societies

GENERAL

Kongelige Norske Videnskabers Selskab (Royal Norwegian Society of Sciences and Letters): Erling Skakkesgt. 47C, 7034 Trondheim; tel. 73-59-21-57; fax 73-59-58-95; f. 1760; sections of Humanities, of Natural Sciences; 322 Norwegian mems, 93 foreign mems, 2 hon. mems, 8 assoc. mems; Pres. Prof. PEDER BORGEN; Sec.-Gen. HARALD NISSEN; publs *Skrifter*, *Fordhandlinger*.

Norske Videnskaps-Akademi (Norwegian Academy of Science and Letters): Drammensveien 78, 0271 Oslo; tel. 22-12-10-90; fax 22-12-10-99; e-mail dnva@online.no; f. 1857; sections of Mathematics and Natural Sciences, of Historical and Philosophical Sciences; 447 Norwegian mems, 336 foreign mems, 2 hon. mems; Pres. Prof. LARS WALLØE; Sec.-Gen. Prof. HANS M. BARSTAD; publs *Skrifter*, *Avhandlinger*, *Årbok*.

ARCHITECTURE AND TOWN PLANNING

Norske Arkitekters Landsforbund (National Association of Norwegian Architects): Josefinesgt. 34, 0351 Oslo 3; tel. 22-60-22-90; fax 22-69-59-48; f. 1911; 3,050 mems; Pres. Architect MNAL KETIL KIRAN; publs *Byggekunst*, *Arkitektnytt*, *Norske Arkitektkonkurranser*.

BIBLIOGRAPHY, LIBRARY SCIENCE AND MUSEOLOGY

Norsk Bibliotekforening (Norwegian Library Asscn): Malerhaugveien 20, 0661 Oslo; tel. 22-68-85-50; fax 22-67-23-68; f. 1913; 3,900 mems; Pres. FRODA BAKEN; Sec. B. AAKER; publ. *Bibliotekforum* (10 a year).

Norske Kunst- og Kulturhistoriske Museer (Association of Museums of Art and Cultural History): Ullevålsveien 11, 0165 Oslo; tel. 22-20-14-02; fax 22-11-23-37; f. 1918; 470 mems; library of 1,500 vols; Gen. Sec. SIRI S. VESTERKJAER; publ. *Museumsnytt* (Museum News).

ECONOMICS, LAW AND POLITICS

Norsk Forening for Internasjonal Rett (Norwegian Society for International Law): POB 400 Sentrum, 0103 Oslo; located at Kirkegt. 15, 0103 Oslo; tel. 22-40-06-00; f. 1925; 95 mems; Pres HANS WILHELM LONGVA; Sec. WEGGER CHR. STRÖMMEN.

Statsøkonomisk Forening (Economic Association of Norway): Dronningensgt. 16, Oslo; f. 1883; approx. 300 mems; Pres. SIGMUND KJOS; Sec. BJÖRN STENSETH.

EDUCATION

Norsk Fjernundervisning (Norwegian State Institution for Distance Education): Pilestredet 56, 0167 Oslo 1; tel. 22-56-43-10; fax 22-56-43-11; e-mail nfu@nfu.no; f. 1977; facilitates adult education and general education through projects at various educational levels, develops projects for groups with special needs; Dir ALF BAKKEN.

Norwegian Council of Universities: Harald Harfagresgt. 17, 5020 Bergen; tel. 55-58-98-30; fax 55-58-98-40; f. 1977; 10 member institutions; Sec.-Gen. PER NYBORG.

FINE AND PERFORMING ARTS

Norges Kunstnerråd (Norwegian Artists' Council): POB 643 Sentrum, 0106 Oslo; tel. 22-47-80-40; fax 22-42-40-40; e-mail kunstner@raadet.filmenshuss.no; Pres. BJORN KRISTENSEN.

Norsk Musikkinformasjon (Norwegian Music Information Centre): Tollbugt. 28, 0157 Oslo; tel. 22-42-90-90; fax 22-42-90-91; f. 1978; objects: to promote and offer information on Norwegian music and composers, music institutions, performing groups and soloists; to build up a representative collection of contemporary Norwegian music; to stimulate community interest in Norwegian music; manuscript library, orchestral materials, reference library, copying service; Man. JOSTEIN SIMBLE; publs *Newsletter*, *Listen to Norway* (3 a year).

Norske Billedkunstnere (Association of Norwegian Visual Arts): Kongensgt. 3, 0153 Oslo 1; f. 1889, reorganized 1979 and 1988; a national association of professional artists' organizations; the Norwegian Government's Advisory Board on questions relating to graphic arts; 5 mems elected every other year represent some 2,300 painters, sculptors and artists; Pres. SVEIN RØMMING; Sec. (vacant); publ. *Billedkunstneren* (10 a year).

Norwegian Council for Cultural Affairs: Grev Wedels plass 1, 0105 Oslo 1; tel. 22-47-83-30; fax 22-33-40-42; f. 1965 in connection with the Cultural Fund to stimulate artistic life and cultural activities in Norway and to distribute the resources of the Fund in grants and subsidies; nine mems appointed by the Cabinet and four by the Storting (Parliament) all for a period of four years; Chair. JON BING; Dir-Gen. OLE JACOB BULL.

HISTORY, GEOGRAPHY AND ARCHAEOLOGY

Foreningen til norske Fortidsminnesmerkers Bevaring (Society for the Preservation of Ancient Monuments in Norway): Dronningensgt. 11, 0152 Oslo; tel. 22-42-27-32; fax 22-42-18-94; e-mail hovedadm@fortidsminne-foreningen.no; f. 1844; 8,500 mems; Chair. JOHAN S. HELBERG; Sec.-Gen. KRISTEN GRIEG BJERKE; publs *Årbok for Foreningen til norske Fortidsminnesmerkers Bevaring* (annually), *Fortidsvern* (quarterly).

Kirkehistorisk Samfunn (Church History Society): Markalléen 7, 1320 Stabekk; f. 1956; 52 mems; Pres. Prof. JAN SCHUMACHER; Sec. Rev. PEDER A. EIDBERG; publ. *Norvegia Sacra* (incl. *Bibliotheca Norvegiae Sacrae*).

Landslaget for lokalhistorie: Historisk institutt, 7055 Dragvoll; tel. 73-59-64-33; fax 73-59-64-41; f. 1920; local history; national association of 350 local history societies; Pres. EGIL NYSAETER; publs *Heimen* (quarterly), *Lokalhistorisk Magasin* (quarterly).

Norsk Arkeologisk Selskap (Norwegian Archaeological Society): Huk Aveny 35, 0287 Oslo 2; tel. 22-43-87-92; fax 22-44-55-81; f. 1936; 900 mems; Pres. LISE TSCHUDI; Sec.-Gen. EGIL MIKKELSEN; publ. *Viking* (1 a year).

Norsk Lokalhistorisk Institutt: POB 4017 Ullevål Hageby, 0806 Oslo; tel. 22-02-26-06; fax 22-23-74-89; e-mail nli@riksarkivet.dep.telemax.no; f. 1955; guidance for local historians, research in local history including publication of sources, etc., valuable for research; Dir HARALD WINGE.

Norsk Slektshistorisk Forening (Norwegian Genealogical Society): POB 59, Sentrum, 0101 Oslo; tel. 22-42-22-04; fax 22-42-22-04; f. 1926; about 1,500 mems; Pres. TORE S. FALCH; Sec. JAN KRISTIANSEN; publ. *Norsk Slektshistorisk Tidsskrift*.

Norske Historiske Forening (Norwegian Historical Society): Avdeling for historie, POB 1008 Blindern, 0315 Oslo; tel. 22-85-67-59; fax 22-85-52-78; f. 1869; Pres. ELLEN SCHRUMPF; Sec.-Gen. NILS-IVAR AGØY; publs *Historisk Tidsskrift* (quarterly), *HIFO-nytt* (quarterly).

LANGUAGE AND LITERATURE

Norsk PEN (Norwegian Centre of International PEN): Urtegt 50, 0187 Oslo; tel. 22-57-12-20; fax 22-57-00-88; f. 1922; contact of Norwegian writers with rest of writing world; Pres. ANTON FREDRIK ANDRESEN.

Norske Akademi for Sprog og Litteratur (Norwegian Academy for Language and Literature): Inkognitogt. 24, 0256 Oslo 2; f. 1953; protects and authorizes dictionaries of the traditional 'Riksmaal'; Pres. LARS ROAR LANGSLET; Sec. Prof. SISSEL LANGE-NIELSEN.

Norske Forfatterforening, Den (Norwegian Authors' Union): Rådhusgt. 7, Oslo 1; tel. 22-42-40-77; fax 22-42-11-07; e-mail dnf@sn.no; f. 1893; 470 mems; Pres. INGER ELISABETH HANSEN.

MEDICINE

Norsk Farmaceutisk Selskap (Norwegian Pharmaceutical Society): c/o Kari Bremer, POB 5070, Majorstua, 0301 Oslo 3; tel. 22-69-60-40; fax 22-60-81-73; f. 1924; to further the scientific and practical development of pharmacy; 450 mems; Chair. ELSE-LYDIA TOVERUD; Sec. KARI BREMER.

Norsk Kirurgisk Forening (Norwegian College of Surgeons): POB 17, Kjelsås, 0411 Oslo; fax 22-15-33-30; f. 1911; 804 mems; Chair. KNUT KVERNEBO; Gen. Sec. LARS R. VASLI; Scientific Sec. HENRIK A. HASGAARD; publ. *Vitenskapelige forhandlinger* (annually).

Norske Laegeforening, Den (Norwegian Medical Asscn): Akersgt. 2, POB 1152 Sentrum, 0107 Oslo; tel. 23-10-90-00; fax 23-10-90-10; f. 1886; 14,800 mems; Pres. Dr Med. HANS PETTER AARSETH; Sec. Dr HARRY MARTIN SVABÖ; publ. *Tidsskrift for den norske lægeforening* (3 a month).

Norske Medicinske Selskab, Det (Medical Society): Drammensvn. 44, 0271 Oslo 2; tel. 22-44-06-44; f. 1833; 600 mems; Medical Dir ØIVIND LARSEN.

Norske Tannlegeforening, Den (Norwegian Dental Association): Postboks 3063 Ellsenberg, 0207 Oslo 1; tel. 22-54-74-00; fax 22-55-11-09; e-mail tannlegeforeningen@tannlegeforeningen.no; f. 1884; 4,540 mems; Pres. ARILD VAUGSTEIN; Sec.-Gen. EIVIND KARLSEN; publ. *Den norske tannlegeforenings Tidende* (monthly).

NATURAL SCIENCES

General

Polytekniske Forening, Den (Polytechnical Society): Rosenkrantzgt. 7, 0159 Oslo; tel. 22-42-68-70; fax 22-42-58-87; f. 1852; 7,000 mems; Sec. NILS CHR. TØMMERAAS; publ. *Teknisk Ukeblad*.

Selskapet til Vitenskapenes Fremme (Society for the Advancement of Science): Fysisk Institutt, Universitetet i Bergen, Allégt. 55, 5007 Bergen; f. 1927; 325 mems; objects: to promote and stimulate intellectual activities generally by regular series of lectures, excursions; Pres. Assoc. Prof. SOLVEIG AASHEIM; Gen. Sec. Assoc. Prof. ARVID ERDAL.

Biological Sciences

Norsk Botanisk Forening (Norwegian Botanical Association): Botanical Institute, University of Bergen, Allégt. 41, 5007 Bergen; f. 1935; 1,100 mems; Pres. ANDERS LUNDBERG; publ. *Blyttia* (quarterly).

Physical Sciences

Norsk Geologisk Forening (Geological Society of Norway): NGU, POB 3006, 7002 Trondheim; tel. 73-90-40-11; fax 73-92-16-20; f. 1905; 950 mems; Chair. INGER FLESLAND STRASS; Gen. Sec. ARNE SOLLI; publ. *Norsk Geologisk Tidsskrift* (quarterly).

Norsk Kjemisk Selskap (Norwegian Chemical Society): POB 1107-Blindern, 0317 Oslo 3; tel. 22-85-55-31; fax 22-85-54-41; f. 1893; 2,100 mems; Gen. Sec. Prof. TORE BENNECHE; Pres. Res. Prof. JO KLAVENESS; publs *Kjemi*, *Acta Chemica Scandinavica*, *Year Book*.

TECHNOLOGY

Norges Tekniske Vitenskapsakademi (Norwegian Academy of Technological Sciences): Lerchendal Gaard, 7034 Trondheim; tel. 73-59-54-63; fax 73-59-08-30; f. 1955; 392 mems; Pres. Prof. JOHANNES MOE; Sec.-Gen. HEIN JOHNSON.

Norske Sivilingeniørers Forening (Norwegian Society of Chartered Engineers): POB 2312, Solli, 0201 Oslo; tel. 22-94-75-00; fax 22-94-75-01; f. 1874; professional society; promotes research and development; represents engineering profession in its relations with other organizations and countries; 30,600 mems; Pres. EINAR E. MADSEN; Sec.-Gen. TRYGVE DAHL; publs *Teknisk Ukeblad* (weekly), *Våre veger* (10 a year), *Sivilingeniøren* (10 a year).

Research Institutes

GENERAL

Chr. Michelsens Institutt for Videnskap og Aandsfrihet (Institute of Science and Intellectual Freedom): 5036 Fantoft, Bergen; f. 1930; pure and applied scientific research and cultural work; library of 50,000 vols; Chair. KNUT HELLE; Man. Dir HENRIK J. LISAETH; Dir of Research Dr GUNNAR M. SØRBØ; publs Research reports (irregular), *Årsberetning* (annual report).

Forskningspolitisk råd (Science Policy Council of Norway): Nedre Vollgt. 11, Oslo 1; f. 1965; 12 mems; advisory board to the Government on all problems concerning research; Chair. FRANCIS SEJERSTED; Dir TORE OLSEN.

Research councils:

Norges almenvitenskapelige forskningsråd (Norwegian Research Council for Science and the Humanities): Munthesgt. 29, Oslo 2; f. 1949; 45 mems; attached to Ministry of Science and Culture, semi-independent; comprises four divisional councils, Humanities, Social Sciences, Medicine and Natural Sciences; awards research grants and fellowships; finances some of Norwegian scientific periodicals; Chair. EVA SIVERTSEN; Dir ANDERS OMHOLT.

Norges Fiskeriforskningsråd (Norwegian Fisheries Research Council): Nedre Bakklandet 60, Trondheim; f. 1971; 27 mems; attached to Ministry of Fisheries; awards research grants and fellowships, runs a research institute; Chair. VIGGO MOHR; Dir ROALD VAAGE.

Norges Landbruksvitenskapelige Forskningsråd (Agricultural Research Council of Norway): Økernveien 145 II, POB 8154 Dep., 0033 Oslo 1; f. 1949; 30 mems; attached to Ministry of Agriculture; awards research grants and Fellowships; runs its own service and research establishments; Chair. ODDBJØRN NORDSET; Dir O. JAMT.

Norges Forskningsråd (Research Council of Norway): Stensberggata 26, POB 2700, St Hanshaugen, 0131 Oslo; tel. 22-03-70-00; fax 22-03-70-01; f. 1946; 40 mems; attached to Ministry of Industry; awards research grants and fellowships and runs its own research establishments (see under Technology); Chair. KAARE MOE; Dir INGE JOHANSEN.

BIBLIOGRAPHY, LIBRARY SCIENCE AND MUSEOLOGY

RBT – Riksbibliotektjenesten (National Office for Research Documentation, Academic and Special Libraries): Bygdøy allé 21, POB 2439 Solli, 0201 Oslo; tel. 22-43-08-80; fax 22-56-09-81; e-mail rbt@rbt.no; f. 1969; Dir-Gen. KIRSTEN ENGELSTAD; publ. *Synopsis* (every 2 months).

ECONOMICS, LAW AND POLITICS

Institute of Industrial Economics: Breiviken 2A, 5035 Bergen-Sandviken; tel. 55-95-06-60; f. 1975; independent, non-profit research institution, carrying out research into economic and social conditions of importance for industrial development in Norway; *c.* 30 staff; Pres. ARNE SELVIK; publs reports, books, discussion papers.

International Peace Research Institute, Oslo (PRIO): Fuglehauggta 11, 0260 Oslo; tel. 22-54-77-00; fax 22-54-77-01; e-mail info@prio.no; f. 1959, independent instn 1966; library of 13,000 vols, 400 journals; Chair FRIDA NOKKEN; Dir DAN SMITH; publs *Journal of Peace Research* (6 a year), *Security Dialogue* (4 a year).

Norsk Utenrikspolitisk Institutt (Norwegian Institute of International Affairs): POB 8159, Dep., 0033 Oslo; tel. 22-05-65-00; fax 22-17-70-15; f. 1959; international economics, development studies, European integration, collective security; library of 20,000 vols; Pres. ÅGE DANIELSEN; Dir SVERRE LODGAARD; Dir of Administration GRETE THINGIELSTAD; publs *International Politikk* (quarterly), *NUPI Notat*, *NUPI Rapport* (Research reports), *Forum for Development Studies*, *Hvor Hender Det?*, *Norwegian Foreign Policy Studies*.

Norwegian Nobel Institute: Drammensveien 19, 0255 Oslo; tel. 22-44-36-80; fax 22-43-01-68; f. 1903; follows the development of int. relations (especially the work for the pacific settlement of them) in order to advise the Nobel Peace Prize Committee; library of 173,000 vols; Dir GEIR LUNDESTAD.

Statistisk sentralbyrå (Statistics Norway): POB 8131, Dep, Kongensgt. 6, 0033 Oslo; tel. 22-86-45-00; fax 22-86-49-73; e-mail ssb@ssb.no; f. 1876; library of 160,000 vols; Dir-Gen. SVEIN LONGVA; Librarian HILDE RØDLAND; publs *Norges offisielle statistikk* (series, Official Statistics of Norway, irregular), *Månedsstatistikk over utenrikshandelen* (Monthly Bulletin of External Trade), *Ukens statistikk* (Weekly Bulletin of Statistics), *Sosiale og Økonomiske Studier* (Social and Economic Studies), *Statistiske analyser*.

NATURAL SCIENCES

Biological Sciences

Havforskningsinstituttet (Institute of Marine Research): POB 1870 Nordnes, 5024 Bergen; tel. 55-23-85-00; telex 42297; fax 55-23-85-31; f. 1900; part of the Ministry of Fisheries; applied research related to fisheries; three divisions: marine environment, marine living research, aquaculture (with two experimental stations); library of 80,000 vols; Dir ROALD VAAGE; publs research reports, *Årsmelding* (annual report), *IMR News*.

Physical Sciences

Norges Geologiske Undersøkelse (Geological Survey of Norway): POB 3006, 7002 Trondheim; tel. 73-90-40-11; fax 73-92-16-20; f. 1858; Man. Dir ARNE BJØRLYKKE; library of 75,000 vols and 950 periodicals; publs *Bulletin*, *Gråsteinen*.

Norsk Polarinstitutt (Norwegian Polar Research Institute): Middelthunsgate 29, Postboks 5072, Majorstua, 0301 Oslo; tel. 22-95-95-00; fax 22-95-95-01; f. 1948 as a continuation and expansion of Norges Svalbard- og Ishavs-undersøkelser (Norwegian Explorations in Svalbard and the Polar Seas); f. 1928; objects: preparation and publication of maps of Norwegian territories in the polar regions; scientific investigations in the fields of geology, geophysics and biology; responsible for Norwegian Antarctic Research expeditions; Sec. for the Norwegian Nat. Cttee on Polar Research; establishment and maintenance of aids to navigation; administration and maintenance of an all-year scientific station Ny-Ålesund, Svalbard; library of 20,000 vols and 12,000 pamphlets and authors' MSS; Dir Dr NILS A. ØRITSLAND; publs *Polar Research*, *Meddelelser*, *Årbok*, *Skrifter*, *Rapporter*, *Research in Svalbard*, *Polarhåndbok*.

Norske Meteorologiske Institutt, Det (Norwegian Meteorological Institute): Blindern, Oslo 3; f. 1866; library of 30,000 vols; Dir Dr A. GRAMMELTVEDT; Librarian Miss GRETE KROGVOLD; publs *Årsberetning* (annual report), *Klimatologisk månedsoversikt* (monthly), *Technical Report* (irregular).

RELIGION, SOCIOLOGY AND ANTHROPOLOGY

Instituttet for sammenlignende kulturforskning (Institute for Comparative Research in Human Culture): POB 2832 Solli, 0204 Oslo; tel. 22-55-42-07; fax 22-55-42-07; e-mail kulturfo@online.no; f. 1922; concerned mainly with comparative study of languages, religions, folklore, law, ethnology, archaeology, and sociology, sponsoring research programmes, arranging lectures and publishing; Pres. P. KVÆRNE; Vice-Chair. A. SOMMERFELT; publs *Lectures*, *Writings*, *Reports*.

TECHNOLOGY

Energiforsyningens Forskningsinstitutt A/S (EFI) (Norwegian Electric Power Research Institute): 7034 Trondheim; tel. 73-59-72-00; fax 73-59-72-50; f. 1951; part of SINTEF group (see below); research and development in the field of energy, especially electricity generation, transmission, distribution and consumption; Man. Dir SVERRE AAM.

Institutt for energiteknikk (Institute for Energy Technology): POB 40, 2007 Kjeller; tel. 63-80-60-00; fax 63-81-63-56; f. 1948; national energy research establishment; the main research centre is located at Kjeller, where, among other facilities, one research reactor,

JEEP II, is in operation; the Institute's boiling water reactor at Halden is the subject of a joint international research project under the auspices of OECD; the Institute's main activities are: nuclear energy, petroleum technology, new energy technology/energy conservation, industrial process- and materials technology, isotope production and irradiation services, and basic research in physics; Man. Dir KJELL H. BENDIKSEN.

Norges byggforskningsinstitutt (Norwegian Building Research Institute): POB 123, Blindern, 0314 Oslo 3; tel. 22-96-55-00; f. 1953, reorganized 1985 as an independent institute; library of 25,000 vols, 250 periodicals; Dir Å. HALLQUIST; publs *Rapporter* (Reports, English summary, irregular), *Håndbøker* (Handbooks, English summary), *Anvisninger* (Design Manuals, irregular), *Byggdetaljblad* (Norwegian building detail sheets), *Saertrykk* (reprints), technical briefs.

Norges Geotekniske Institutt (NGI) (Norwegian Geotechnical Institute): Sognsveien 72, POB 3930, Ullevaal Hageby, 0806 Oslo; tel. 22-02-30-00; fax 22-23-04-48; e-mail ngi@ngi.no; f. 1953; soil, rock and snow mechanics, foundation engineering, dams, offshore structures, instrumentation, rock engineering; library of 22,500 vols, 300 periodicals, Terzaghi Library; Dir SUZANNE LACASSE; publ. *Publications* (irregular, series of monographs and reprints).

Norsk institutt for by- og regionforskning (Norwegian Institute for Urban and Regional Research): POB 44, Blindern, 0313 Oslo; tel. 22-95-88-00; fax 22-60-77-74; f. 1965; 90 mems; library of 18,000 vols, 200 periodicals; Dir JON NAVSTDALSLID; publs *NIBR prosjektrapport*, *NIBR notat*, *Regionale Trender* (every 6 months).

Norsk institutt for luftforskning (Norwegian Institute for Air Research): POB 100, 2007 Kjeller; tel. 63-89-80-00; telex 74854; fax 63-89-80-50; f. 1969; national and international research and consultation in air pollution, atmospheric dispersion and measurements, meteorological measurements and analysis, instrumentation and chemical analysis; library of 9,000 vols, 130 periodicals; Dir Dr ØYSTEIN HOV; publs *Annual Report*, scientific reports.

Norsk Institutt for vannforskning (Norwegian Institute for Water Research): POB 173, Kjelsås, 0411 Oslo; tel. 22-18-51-00; telex 74190; fax 22-18-52-00; f. 1958; research and contract projects on technical, economical and sanitary problems in connection with water supply, waste water and pollution in rivers and lakes/fjords; library of 34,000 vols, 800 periodicals; Dir-Gen. HAAKON THAULOW; publ. *Reports*.

Norsk Regnesentral (Norwegian Computing Centre): POB 114, Blindern, 0314 Oslo 3; tel. 22-85-25-00; fax 22-69-76-60; f. 1958; image analysis and pattern recognition, computer technology and communication, information technology in practice, statistical analysis of natural resource data, statistical data analysis, interactive media; library of 4,000 vols, 250 periodicals; Man. Dir OLE HENRIK ELLESTAD.

Norsk Undervannsteknologisk Senter A/S (Norwegian Underwater Technology Centre): POB 6, 5034 Ytre Laksevåg/Bergen; tel. 55-94-20-23; telex 42 892; fax 55-94-20-01; f. 1976, present name 1981; test and research centre for underwater technology, full-scale testing, diving, hyperbaric medicine and physiology, safety analysis, education and training; consulting services; library of 5,000 vols, 170 periodicals; Man. Dir THORVALD MELLINGEN; publ. *NUTEC Reports*.

Norwegian Marine Technology Research Institute (MARINTEK): POB 4125 Valentinlyst, 7002 Trondheim; tel. 73-59-55-00; fax 73-59-57-76; e-mail marintek@marintek.sintef.no; mem. of the SINTEF Group; research, development and commission work related to technical, organizational, social and economic problems of design, construction and operation of ships and offshore constructions; laboratories: ocean basin, ship model tank, machinery and strength laboratory, materials applications; library of 11,000 vols, 365 periodicals; Man. Dir ODDVAR AAM; publs *Technical Abstracts*, *Project reports*, *Marintek Review*.

Norwegian Seismic Array (NORSAR): POB 51, 2007 Kjeller; tel. 63-80-59-00; fax 63-81-87-19; f. 1968/69; research on problems in distinguishing between subterranean nuclear explosions and earthquakes; applied seismology research; Dir Å. DAHLE; publ. *Technical Summary* (2 a year).

Papirindustriens Forskningsinstitutt (PFI) (Norwegian Pulp and Paper Research Institute): POB 24, Blindern, 0313 Oslo; tel. 22-14-00-90; fax 22-46-80-14; f. 1923; library of 11,000 vols; Head JAN M. OEVERLI; publ. *Papirforskning* (Paper Research Journal).

Senter for Internasjonal Økonomi og Skipsfart (SIØS) (Centre for International Economics and Shipping): Norwegian School of Economics and Business Administration, Helleveien 30, 5035 Bergen-Sandviken; tel. 55-95-93-90; fax 55-95-93-50; f. 1958; research and publication of results, aims to provide a centre for research fellows in sea transport and shipping economics from Norway and abroad, to promote co-operation with similar institutions; and post-graduate education in shipping economics; library of 3,500 vols, 1,600 periodicals, reports, etc.; Dirs Prof. Dr JAN HAALAND, Prof. VICTOR D. NORMAN, Assoc. Prof. LINDA ORVEDAL, Assoc. Prof. SIRI PETTERSEN STRANDENES, Asst Prof. TOR H. WERGELAND; Sec. ANNE LIV SCRASE.

Stiftelsen for industriell og teknisk forskning ved Norges tekniske høgskole (SINTEF) (Foundation for Scientific and Industrial Research at the Norwegian Institute of Technology): 7034 Trondheim; tel. 73-59-30-00; fax 73-59-33-50; f. 1950; carries out research in science and technology on contract with industry and others; 3 affiliated research institutes; Pres. R. ARNTZEN.

Transportøkonomisk institutt (Institute of Transport Economics): POB 6110 Etterstad, 0602 Oslo; tel. 22-57-38-00; fax 22-57-02-90; f. 1964; Norwegian centre for transport research; library of 24,000 vols, 240 periodicals; Dir KNUT ØSTMOE; publ. *Samferdsel* (Communication, 10 a year).

Libraries and Archives

Arendal

Arendal Bibliotek (Municipal Library): 4801 Arendal; e-mail arendal@arendal.folkebibl.no; f. 1832; 1972 incorporated *Aust-Agder Fylkesbibliotek* (County Library); library of 229,000 vols; Head Libr. GURI ERLANDSEN.

Ås

Norges Landbrukshøgskole Biblioteket (Library of the Agricultural University of Norway): POB 5012, 1432 Ås; tel. 64-94-75-00; fax 64-94-76-70; f. 1859; literature concerning all branches of agricultural science and forestry, conservation of natural resources, biology, etc.; library of 493,000 vols; Head Librarian PAUL STRAY.

Bergen

Bergen offentlige Bibliotek (Municipal and County Library): 5015 Bergen; tel. 55-56-85-95; fax 55-56-85-55; e-mail trine@bergen.folkebib.no; f. 1874; library of 634,000 vols; Grieg collection of 150 MSS and 5,800 letters; City Librarian TRINE KOLDERUP FLATEN.

Universitetsbiblioteket i Bergen (Bergen University Library): Haakon Sheteligs plass 7, 5007 Bergen; tel. 55-58-25-00; fax 55-58-97-03; e-mail adm@ub.uib.no; f. 1825 as Bergens Museums Bibliotek; library of 1,450,000 vols; special divisions for newspapers, manuscripts, pictures and maps, Norwegian depository library; Dir Dr KARI GARNES; publs *Sarsia* (Marine Biology), *Norwegian Archaeological Review*.

Drammen

Drammen Folkebibliotek (Public Library of Drammen): Gamle Kirkepl. 7, POB 1136, 3001 Drammen; tel. 32-80-63-00; fax 32-80-64-53; f. 1916; municipal library of Drammen and county library of Buskerud; 3 branch libraries, 3 children's branches, 2 bookmobiles; library of 310,000 vols; Pres. TERJEVEGARD KOPPERUD; Chief Librarian MAGNE HAUGE.

Hamar

Statsarkivet i Hamar (Regional State Archives): Lille Strandgt. 3, 2300 Hamar; tel. 62-52-36-42; fax 62-52-94-48; f. 1917; public record office, archives; public reading-room open on weekdays; library of 13,000 vols; Chief Archivist PER-ØIVIND SANDBERG.

Kristiansand

Kristiansands Folkebibliotek (Municipal Library): 4600 Kristiansand; tel. 38-02-91-65; fax 38-02-91-63; f. 1909; library of 268,000 vols; Chief Librarian ELSE MARGRETHE BREDLAND.

Oslo

Deichmanske Bibliotek (Oslo Public Library): Henrik Ibsensgt. 1, 0179 Oslo 1; tel. 22-03-29-00; fax 22-11-33-89; f. 1785; library of 1,246,000 vols; Chief Librarian LIV SÆTEREN.

Riksarkivet (National Archives of Norway): Folke Bernadottes vei 21, 4013 Ullevål Hageby, 0806 Oslo; tel. 22-02-26-00; fax 22-23-74-89; f. 1817; takes charge of the archives of the ministries and other branches of the central administration; library of 60,000 vols; Dir JOHN HERSTAD; publ. *Arkivmagasinet* (3 a year).

Statens bibliotektilsyn (Directorate for Public Libraries): Munkedamsveien 62A, POB 8145 DEP, 0033 Oslo 8; tel. 22-83-25-85; fax 22-83-15-52; e-mail sb@bibtils.no; Dir ASBJØRN LANGELAND; publ. *Bok og Bibliotek* (8 a year).

Statistisk sentralbyrås Bibliotek og Informasjonssenter (Norway Statistics Library and Information Centre): Kongensgt. 6, Oslo; postal address: POB 8131 Dep., 0033 Oslo; tel. 22-86-45-00; fax 22-86-49-73; e-mail biblioteket@ssb.no; f. 1876; library of 166,000 vols mainly economic, demographic and statistical literature (official and international statistics included); open to the public; Chief Librarian HILDE RØDLAND; publ. *Biblioteksnytt* (monthly).

Stortingsbiblioteket (Library of the Norwegian Parliament): Stortinget, 0026 Oslo 1; tel. 22-31-36-90; telex 21512; fax 22-31-38-59; f. 1871; literature on political and social science, law, and economics; reports from official and semi-official institutions; library of 180,000 vols; reference library mainly for members of Parliament and govt officials; open to the public on application; Head Librarian BRIT FLØISTAD; publs *Årsberetning* (Annual Report), *Nytt fra Stortingsbiblioteket* (monthly).

Styret for det Industrielle Rettsvern. Informasjonsavdelingen (Norwegian Patent Office Information Department): POB 8160 Dep., 0033 Oslo; tel. 22-38-73-00; telex 19152; fax 22-38-73-01; f. 1888; library of 50,000 vols scientific and technical books and periodicals of reference for patent research; 27,000,000 patent specifications; Head of Department TORIL FOSS; publs *Norske Patentskrifter*, *Norsk Patenttidende*, *Norsk varemerketidende*, *Norske mønstertidende*.

Universitetsbiblioteket i Oslo (University of Oslo Library): Drammensveien 42, 0242 Oslo 7; tel. 22-85-50-50; telex 76078; fax 22-85-90-50; f. 1811; library of 2,075,000 vols (4,500,000 vols, including institute libraries); special collections of manuscripts, maps, prints and drawings, music, drama, incunabula, papyri and orientalia; the University Library receives by law copies of all Norwegian books, and edits the official Norwegian book catalogue; Librarian JAN ERIK RØED; publs *Norsk Bokfortegnelse* (The National Bibliography), *Norske Tidsskriftartikler* (The Norwegian Index to Periodicals).

Utenriksdepartementets Dokumentasjons Senter (Documentation Centre of the Ministry of Foreign Affairs): 7 Juni-Plassen 1, Oslo, POB 8114 Dep., 0032 Oslo 1; tel. 22-24-31-31; telex 71004; fax 22-24-31-61; e-mail doksenter@ud.dep.telemax.no; f. 1901, reorganized 1919–22; objects: foreign affairs, international law and international relations—political, social, economic and commercial; reference library for Min. of Foreign Affairs; library of 120,000 vols, including periodicals and pamphlets; Head Librarian AUD GULBRANSEN; publs *Tilvekst Utenriksdepartementets Bibliotek* (New Acquisitions, every 2 months), *Løpende tidsskrifter* (Current Periodicals, annually).

Rjukan

Rjukan Bibliotek (Public Library of Rjukan): 3660 Rjukan; f. 1914; library of 114,544 vols; 3 brs; Chief Librarian INGEBORG BOTNEN.

Stavanger

Stavanger Bibliotek (Stavanger Library): POB 310, 4001 Stavanger; tel. 51-50-70-90; fax 51-50-70-25; f. 1885; municipal library for the town of Stavanger, central library for the county of Rogaland; library of 450,432 vols; music and picture collection; Librarian KURT KRISTENSEN.

Tønsberg

Tønsberg Bibliotek (Tønsberg Public Library): 3100 Tønsberg; tel. 33-31-94-85; fax 33-31-64-75; f. 1909; library of 250,000 vols; Chief Librarian METTE HENRIKSEN AAS.

Trondheim

Universitetsbiblioteket i Trondheim (University library of Trondheim): Høgskolerringen 1, 7034 Trondheim; tel. 73-59-51-10; fax 73-59-51-03; e-mail ubit@ub.ntnu.no; f. 1768; merged with Norges Tekniske Universitets bibliotek 1996; receives deposit copies of all Norwegian books; arts, social sciences, science, technology, architecture, medicine; nat. resource library for architecture and technology; library of 2,400,000 vols, 16,000 periodicals; Dir VIGDIS MOE SKARSTEIN.

Ulefoss

Telemark fylkesbibliotek/Telemark landbruksbibliotek: 3730 Ulefoss; tel. (036) 84668; telex 19504; f. 1942; county and agricultural library; library of 81,853 vols; Librarian LILLIAN NILSSEN.

Museums and Art Galleries

Bergen

Bergen Museum, Universitetet i Bergen: H. Hårfagresgt. 1, 5020 Bergen; tel. 55-58-93-60; fax 55-58-93-64; e-mail einar.aadland@bmu.uib.no; f. 1825, part of University 1948; anthropology, archaeology, botany, geology, Norwegian culture and folk art, zoology; Dir KÅRE HESJEDAL; publs *Arkeo*, *Bergen Museums Skrifter*, *UNIMUS*, *Årbok for Bergen Museum*.

Vestlandske Kunstindustrimuseum (West Norway Museum of Decorative Art): Nordahl Brungt. 9, 5014 Bergen; tel. 55-32-51-08; fax 55-31-74-55; f. 1887; 20,000 objects including Norwegian and European furniture, glass, porcelain, silver and textiles from the renaissance to modern times; Gen. Munthe's collection of Chinese art; specialized library of fine and applied arts contains 20,000 vols; Dir JORUNN HAAKESTAD; Curators ANNE BRITT YLVISÅKER, TROND INDAHL.

Bodø

Nordlandsmuseet: Prinsens gt. 116, 8005 Bodø; tel. 75-52-16-40; fax 75-52-58-05; f. 1888; covers most aspects of life in the county of Nordland; 80,000 items, specialities: fisheries, boats, etc.; library of 6,000 vols; Dir HARRY ELLINGSEN.

Drammen

Drammens Museum—Fylkesmuseum for Buskerud: Konnerudgaten 7, 3045 Drammen; tel. 32-83-89-48; f. 1908; local history, applied art; folk art, and open air museum; library of 16,000 vols; Dir ANNE-BERIT SKAUG; publ. *Årbok*.

Fredrikstad

Fredrikstad Museum: Isegran, Krakercy, Fredrikstad; f. 1903; cultural and military history of the town and district; Curator TOVE THØGERSEN; publ. *Yearbook*.

Hamar

Hedmarksmuseet og Domkirkeodden: POB 1053, 2301 Hamar; tel. 62-54-27-00; fax 62-54-27-01; e-mail domkirkeodden@ha-nett.no; f. 1906; open-air museum and medieval collection; ruins of the medieval cathedral, bishop's palace (now housing a modern exhibition), and other medieval ruins; excavations in progress; farm buildings depicting local history and domestic life; library of 14,000 vols; Dir STEINAR BJERKESTRAND; Chief Curator RAGNAR PEDERSEN; publ. *Årbok Fra Kaupang og bygd*.

Lillehammer

Lillehammer Kunstmuseum (Lillehammer Art Museum): Stortorget, 2601 Lillehammer; tel. 61-26-94-44; fax 61-25-19-44; e-mail kunstmus@online.no; f. 1927; contains collections of Norwegian paintings, sculpture and graphic art, historical and contemporary art exhibitions; Dir SVEIN OLAV HOFF; publs catalogues, etc.

Sandvigske Samlinger (Sandvig Collections): Maihaugen, 2600 Lillehammer; tel. 61-28-89-00; fax 61-26-95-93; f. 1887; 160 old houses of historical interest and 30 old workshops in a new exhibition hall; exhbn of Norwegian history; library of 18,000 vols; Dir OLAV AARAAS; publs *Guides*, *De Sandvigske Samlingers Yearbook*.

Oslo

Botanisk Hage og Museum (Botanical Garden and Museum, University of Oslo): Trondheimsveien 23B, 0562 Oslo; tel. 22-85-16-00; fax 22-85-18-35; e-mail per.sunding@toyen.vio.no; f. 1814 (garden), 1863 (museum); taxonomy and plant ecology; library of 45,000 vols; Dir Prof. PER SUNDING; publ. *Sommerfeltia* (irregular).

Forsvarsmuseet (Armed Forces Museum): Akershus festning, Oslo Mil, 0015 Oslo; f. 1978; library of 175,000 vols; Dir ROLF SCHEEN; publs *Annual Report*, *Fosvarsmuseets Årbok*.

Kunstindustrimuseet i Oslo (Oslo Museum of Applied Art): St Olavsgate 1, 0165 Oslo; tel. 22-03-65-40; fax 22-11-39-71; f. 1876; ancient and modern Norwegian and foreign applied art (incl. Baldishol tapestry); Dir ANNIKEN THUE.

Nasjonalgalleriet: Universitetsgaten 13, Oslo 1; tel. 22-20-04-04; fax 22-36-11-32; e-mail nga@nasjonalgallenet.no; f. 1837; the principal art gallery in Norway, containing collections of Norwegian paintings and sculpture to *c.* 1945, old European paintings, icon collection, French impressionists and post-impressionists, a collection of prints and drawings, and a small collection of Greek and Roman sculpture; also a collection of casts; library of *c.* 30,000 vols in library; Dir TONE SKEDSMO; Keepers MARIT LANGE, ERNEST HAVERKAMP (Paintings and Sculpture), SIDSEL HELLIESEN (Prints and Drawings); Librarian ANNE LISE RABBEN.

Norsk Folkemuseum (Norwegian Folk Museum): Bygdøy, Museumsv. 10, 0287 Oslo; tel. 22-12-37-00; fax 22-12-37-77; f. 1894; consists of indoor and open-air sections comprising more than 230,000 objects; special exhibits in the indoor section include: rural culture (including display of folk dresses and folk art), urban culture, church history, toys, Lapp collection; open-air museum consists of: 153 old buildings (including 13th-century Gol stave church), examples of different farms, relics from all over Norway arranged as an old town quarter, museum shop, artisans; library of 45,000 vols; Dir ERIK RUDENG.

Norsk Sjøfartsmuseum (Norwegian Maritime Museum): Bygdøynesvn. 37, 0286 Oslo 2; f. 1914; museum opened 1974; illustrates Norwegian maritime history; collection of portraits, models, instruments, historic ships (Amundsen's 'Gjøa', traditional small craft); library of 29,607 vols, archives of photographs and plans, MSS, maps; lectures, excavations, expeditions for young people; Dir BÅRD KOLLTVEIT; Curators JOHAN KLOSTER, DAG NÆVESTAD, PÅL NYMOEN; publ. *Norsk Sjøfartsmuseums årsberetning* (annually).

Norsk Teknisk Museum (Norwegian Museum of Science and Technology): Kjelsåsveien 143, 0491 Oslo 4; tel. 22-79-60-00; fax 22-79-61-00; e-mail post@norsk-teknisk.museum.no; f. 1914; library of 40,000 vols; Dir GUNNAR NERHEIM; publ. *Yearbook*.

Oslo Kommunes Kunstsamlinger (City of Oslo Art Collections): Tøyengata 53, POB 2812, Tøyen, 0608 Oslo; tel. 22-67-37-74; fax 22-67-33-41; general collns, and spec. collns of works by Munch and Vigeland; Dir RUTH LILIAN BREKKE.

Riksantikvaren (Directorate for Cultural Heritage): Dronningensgt. 13, POB 8196 Dep., 0034 Oslo; tel. 22-94-04-00; fax 22-94-04-04; f. 1912; directorate responsible for national monuments and sites, medieval buildings; archives: *c.* 500,000 photos; library of 40,000 vols; Dir-Gen. NILS MARSTEIN; publs *Norske Minnesmerker*, *Norges Kirker*, *Riksantikvarens Rapporter*, *Riksantikvarens Skrifter* (Antiquarian Bulletin).

Universitetets Etnografiske Museum (Ethnographic Museum, Department and Museum of Anthropology, University of Oslo): Frederiksgt. 2, 0164 Oslo; tel. 22-85-99-64; fax 22-85-99-60; e-mail etnografisk@ima.uio.no; f.

1857; permanent and temporary exhibitions; library of 30,000 vols; Dir PER B. REKDAL.

Universitetets Mineralogisk-Geologiske Museum: Sarsgt. 1, 0562 Oslo 5; tel. 22-85-16-00; fax 22-85-18-00; f. 1915; collections of rocks and minerals; research laboratories in mineralogy, petrology, geochemistry; library together with Universitetets Paleontologiske Museum (*q.v.*) of 75,000 vols; Dir TOM ANDERSEN.

Universitetets Paleontologisk Museum: Sars gate 1, 0562 Oslo; tel. 22-85-16-00; fax 22-85-18-10; f. 1916; main collections consist of Cambrian-Devonian, Permian and Pleistocene fossils from Norway and Cambrian-Pleistocene fossils from Arctic regions, especially Svalbard; library together with Universitetets Mineralogisk-geologisk museum (*q.v.*) of 85,000 vols.

Universitetets Oldsaksamling (University Museum of National Antiquities): Frederiksgt. 2, 0164 Oslo; sub-dept of Institutt for Arkeologi, Kunsthistorie og Numismatikk (Frederiksgt. 3); exhibits from prehistoric and Viking times, including Viking ships (at Bygdøy), and the Middle Ages; approx. 70,000 exhibits; library of 40,000 vols; publs *Universitetets Oldsaksamlings Årbok*, *Universitetets Oldsaksamlings Skrifter*, *Norske Oldfunn*, *Guides* (in English, French, German, Italian, Spanish and Norwegian for the Viking Ship Museum), *Universitetets Oldsaksamlings Varia*.

Vigeland-museet: Nobelsgate 32, 0268 Oslo; tel. 22-54-25-30; fax 22-54-25-40; f. 1947; life and work of sculptor Gustav Vigeland; Curator NILS MESSEL.

Zoologisk Museum Universitetet i Oslo (Zoological Museum): Sarsgt. 1, 0562 Oslo; tel. 22-85-50-50; fax 22-85-18-37; f. *c.* 1813 (present building 1904–08); public exhibitions of Norwegian and world fauna; Norwegian vertebrates and invertebrates, Arctic, Antarctic and exotic, particularly Australian, research collections; library of approx. 28,000 vols, 53,000 pamphlets; Dir JAN T. LIFJELD.

Sandefjord

Kommandør Chr. Christensens Hvalfangstmuseum (Commdr Chr. Christensen's Whaling Museum): Museumsgt. 39, 3210 Sandefjord; tel. 33-48-46-50; fax 33-46-37-84; e-mail sfjmus@sandefjordnett.no; f. 1917; shows the development of whaling from primitive to modern times; geography, ethnology, zoology, maritime history, etc.; library of 15,000 vols; Dir THOR N. DEVIG.

Skien

Fylkesmuseet for Telemark og Grenland (Historical Museum): Övregt. 41, 3700 Skien; f. 1909; conservation and research on items of historical interest from the Telemark region; situated in Brekkeparken, with open air museum (log houses dating from the Middle Ages) and a manor house furnished in 17th-, 18th- and 19th-century styles; collections on folk art, handicrafts, navigation, church art, Ibsen Collection and Ibsen's childhood home, Venstøp Farm; library of *c.* 6,000 vols; Dir TOR GARDÅSEN.

Stavanger

Arkeologisk Museum i Stavanger (Museum of Archaeology, Stavanger): POB 478, 4001 Stavanger; tel. 51-84-60-00; fax 51-84-61-99; e-mail ams@ark.museum.no; own library; Dir BJØRN MYHRE; publs *AmS-skrifter*, *AmS-varia*, *AmS-Småtrykk*, *AmS-Rapport*, *Fra haug ok heidni* (4 a year).

Stavanger Museum: 4005 Stavanger; tel. 51-52-60-35; fax 51-52-93-80; e-mail firmapost@stavanger.museum.no; f. 1877; urban and rural culture, zoology, ornithology; a maritime museum, a canning museum and the mansions of Ledaal and Breidablikk are in the museum's care; library of 46,000 vols; Dir OVE MAGNUS BORE; publs *Årbok* (yearbook), *Skrifter* (irregular).

Tromsø

Tromsø Museum (Universitetet i Tromsø: Institutt for museumsvirksomhet): 9000 Tromsø; tel. (083) 86080; f. 1872; has seven depts; Botany, Geology, Zoology, Marine Biology, Archaeology, Folk Culture, Sami Ethnography; library of 180,000 vols; Dir of Board JACOB MØLLER; Man. Dir BEN SCHEI; publs *Acta Borealia* (*A* and *B*), *Skrifter*, *Astarte*, *Årsberetninger* (annual report), *Ottar*, *Antikvariske registreringer i Nord-Norge*, *Tromura* (scientific reports).

Trondheim

Nordenfjeldske Kunstindustrimuseum (National Museum of Decorative Arts): Munkegaten 5, 7013 Trondheim; tel. 73-52-13-11; fax 73-53-51-11; f. 1893; approx. 12,000 exhibits; depts of furniture, textiles, glass, ceramics, metalwork from the Renaissance period to modern times; Dir JAN-L. OPSTAD.

Vitenskapsmuseet, Norges Teknisk-naturvitenskapelige Universitet (Museum of Natural History and Archaeology, of the Norwegian University of Science and Technology): 7034 Trondheim; tel. 73-59-21-45; fax 73-59-22-23; f. 1760; graduate and research institution of the univ.; archaeological, botanical and zoological depts; mineralogical and numismatic collections; marine station; schools service; Dir Prof. ARNE B. JOHANSEN; publ. *Gunneria*.

Universities

NORGES TEKNISK-NATURVITENSKAPELIGE UNIVERSITET
(Norwegian University of Science and Technology)

7034 Trondheim

Telephone: 73-59-50-00

Fax: 73-59-53-10

Founded 1996 to replace the University of Trondheim (which included the Norwegian Institute of Technology, the College of Arts and Science and the Museum of Natural History and Archaeology)

Rector: EMIL SPJØTVOLL

Pro-Rector: RIGMOR AUSTGULEN

University Director: VIGDIS MOE SKARSTEIN

Assistant University Director: PETER LYKKE

Number of teachers: 1,154

Number of students: 18,500

DEANS

Faculty of Architecture, Planning and Fine Art: Prof. HARALD HØYEM

Faculty of Civil and Environmental Engineering: Prof. EIVIND BRATTELAND

Faculty of Electrical Engineering and Telecommunications: Prof. HANS FAANES

Faculty of Physics, Informatics and Mathematics: Prof. ELVIND HIIS HAUGE

Faculty of Applied Earth Sciences: Prof. EINAR BROCH

Faculty of Chemistry and Biology: Prof. O. YNGVE ESPMARK

Faculty of Marine Technology: Prof. ANDERS ENDAL

Faculty of Mechanical Engineering: Prof. ARNE M. BREDESEN

Faculty of Arts: Prof. HÅKON WITH ANDERSEN

Faculty of Medicine: Prof. GUNNAR BOVIM

Faculty of Social Sciences and Technology Management: PETTER ÅSEN

PROFESSORS

Faculty of Architecture, Planning and Fine Art:

ASCHEHOUG, Ø., Building Technology
BLEIKLI, S., Architecture
COLD, B., Architecture
CORNEIL, E., Architecture
HAUGEN, T., Building Technology
HESTNES, A. G., Building Technology
HIORTHØY, E., Architecture
HØYEM, H., Architecture
LARSEN, K., Architecture
LARSEN, K. E., Architectural History
LUNDSTRØM, B., Form and Colour Studies
MOE, T., Architecture
MOGSTAD, A., Trondheim Academy of Fine Art
NOACH, K. S. M. G., Architectural History
RØE, B., Town and Regional Planning
SINDING-LARSEN, S., Architectural History
SIVERTSEN, J., Building Technology
STEEN, O., Architecture
SVENDSEN, S. E., Architecture
WELSH, J., Architecture, Planning and Fine Art

Faculty of Civil and Environmental Engineering:

BELL, K., Statics
BJØRKE, J. T., Cartography
BRATTELAND, E., Marine Technology
GJØRV, O. E., Building Materials
GRANDE, L. O., Marine Geotechnical Engineering
HAAGENSEN, P. J., Materials Evaluation and Structural Testing
HAAVALDSEN, T., Building Technology
HJORTH-HANSEN, E., Structural Engineering
HORVLI, I., Operations and Maintenance
HOVD, A., Highway Engineering
HUGSTED, R., Construction Engineering
HÅDEM, I., Photogrammetry
JOHANNESEN, S., Transport Engineering
JOHANNESSEN, O., Construction Engineering
JOHANSEN, R. I., Technology
KILLINGTVEIT, Å., Applied Hydrology
LANGSETH, M., Aluminium Structures
LARSEN, P. K., Steel Structures
LENSCHOW, R. J, Concrete Structures
LYSNE, D. K., Hydraulic Constructions
LØSET, S., Arctic Technology
MATHISEN, K. M., Structural Engineering
MOE, G., Port and Ocean Engineering
NORDAL, S., Geotechnical Engineering
NÆSS, A., Port and Ocean Engineering
REMSETH, S. N., Statics
SAGER, T. O., Transport Engineering
SCHILLING, W., Environmental Hydraulic Engineering
SELLEVOLD, E. J., Concrete Structures
SENNESET, K. G., Geotechnical Engineering
SYVERTSEN, T. G., Structural Engineering
SØRENSEN, S. I., Concrete Structures
THUE, J. V., Building Technology
ØDEGAARD, H., Environmental Hydraulic Engineering

Faculty of Electrical Engineering and Telecommunications:

ANDERSEN, O. W., Electrical Machines and Power Electronics
ANDERSEN, S., Telematics
ANKER, M. U., Electric Power Engineering
BLØTEKJÆR, K., Physical Electronics
EGELAND, O., Engineering Cybernetics
EMSTAD, P. J., Telematics
ENGAN, H. E., Physical Electronics
FJELDLY, T. A., Physical Electronics (Semiconductor Technology)
FOSS, B. A., Engineering Cybernetics
FOSSEN, T. I., Engineering Cybernetics
FÅNES, H. H., Electrical Power Engineering (Power Systems)
GREPSTAD, J., Physical Electronics

HELVIK, B., Telematics
HENRIKSEN, R., Engineering Cybernetics
HOLEN, A. T., Electrical Power Engineering
HOLTE, N., Telecommunications (Transmission Systems)
HOVEM, J. M., Acoustics
ILSTAD, E., Electric Power Engineering
KRISTIANSEN, U., Acoustics
KROKSTAD, A., Telecommunications (Acoustics)
MALVIG, K. E., Engineering Cybernetics
MUKHERJEE, S. D., Physical Electronics
NILSEN, R., Electrical Power Engineering
NILSSEN, R. K., Electrical Power Engineering
NORUM, L. E., Electrical Power Engineering
ONSHUS, T. E., Engineering Cybernetics
PETTERSEN, O., Engineering Cybernetics
RAMSTAD, T. A., Telecommunications
REIN, A. T., Electrical Power Engineering
RØNNEKLEIV, A., Physical Electronics
SKARSTEIN, Ø., Power Systems Engineering
STETTE, G. R., Telecommunications
SVENDSEN, T., Telecommunications
SVÅSAND, L. O., Applied Electronics
UNDELAND, T. M., Electrical Power Engineering
VIGRAN, T. E., Acoustics
ÅGESEN, F. A., Telematics
ÅS, E. J., Electronic Design Methodology
ÅSERUD, O. W., Physical Electronics

Faculty of Physics, Informatics and Mathematics:

BLAKE, R., Computer Science and Telematics
BRATSBERGENGEN, K., Data Processing
BÅS, N. A., Mathematics
CHAO, K.-A., Physics
CONRADI, R., Data Processing
ELGSÆTER, A., Biophysics and Biomedical Technology
ENGEN, S., Mathematics
FALNES, J., Experimental Physics
FOSSHEIM, K. J., Technical Physics
HALÅS, A., Data Processing
HANSEN, A., Physics
HAUGE, E. H., Theoretical Physics
HEMMER, P. C. M., Theoretical Physics
HOLDEN, H., Mathematics
HUNDERI, O. D. R., General Physics
HØIER, R. K. O., Material Physics
HØYE, J. S., Theoretical Physics
JOHNSSON, A., Experimental Physics
KOLBENSTVEDT, H., Physics
KOMOROWSKI, H. J., Computer Science and Telematics
LANDSTAD, M., Mathematics
LINDMO, T., Physics
LINDQVIST, B. H., Mathematical Statistics
LINDQVIST, L. P., Mathematics
LORENTZEN, L., Mathematics
LYUBARSKII, Y., Mathematics
LØKBERG, O. J., General Physics
MELØ, T. B., Biophysics
MO, F., Physics, X-ray Crystallography
MORK, K., Physics
MYRHEIM, J., Physics
NAQVI, K. R., Physics
NJÅSTAD, O., Mathematics
NYGÅRD, M., Computer Science and Information Services
NØRSETT, S. P., Numerical Mathematics
OLAUSSEN, K., Theoretical Physics
OMRE, K. H., Mathematics
PEDERSEN, H. M., General Physics
REITAN, A., Physics
REITEN, I., Mathematics
RÅEN, S., Physics
SAMUELSEN, E. J., X-ray Physics
SEIP, K., Mathematics
SIGMOND, R. S., Physics
SKAGERSTAM, B.-S., Physics
SKAU, C. F., Mathematics
SKRAMSTAD, T., Computer Science
SKULLERUD, H. R., Ion and Molecular Physics
SMALØ, S., Mathematics
STRAUME, E., Mathematics
SUDBØ, A., Physics
SØLVBERG, A., Data Processing
SØLVBERG, I., Information Processing
VALBERG, A., Physics
ÅMODT, A., Informatics
ÅRNES, J. FR., Mathematics
ØSTGAARD, E., Physics

Faculty of Applied Earth Sciences:

ASHEIM, H. A., Petroleum Engineering (Production)
BRATTLI, B., Engineering Geology
BROCH, E., Engineering Geology
GOLAN, M., Petroleum Engineering (Production)
GUDMUNDSSON, J. S., Petroleum Engineering
HOLT, R. M., Petroleum Engineering
KLEPPE, J., Petroleum Engineering (Reservoir Technology)
KRILL, A. G., Geology
LIPPARD, S., Geology and Mineral Resources Engineering
MALVIK, T., Geology and Mineral Resources Engineering
MYRVANG, A., Mining Engineering
NIELSEN, K. O., Mining Engineering
NILSEN, B., Geology and Mineral Resources Engineering
PRESTVIK, T., Geology
ROALDSET, E., Petroleum Geology
ROKOENGEN, K., Geology and Mineral Resources Engineering
RØDLAND, A., Petroleum Engineering (Drilling Technology)
SANDVIK, K. L., Mineral Dressing
SINDING-LARSEN, R., Ore Geology
SUNDBLAD, K, Geology and Mineral Resources Engineering
TORSÆTER, O., Petroleum Engineering
TORSÆTER, O., Petroleum Engineering, Applied Geophysics
URSIN, B., Petroleum Engineering
WHITSON, C.-H., Petroleum Engineering

Faculty of Chemistry and Biology:

ANDERSEN, R. A., Zoology
ANTHONSEN, T. O., Chemistry
ARMBRUSTER, W. S., Botany
ARNBERG, L., Metallurgy
BAKKE, J. M., Organic Chemistry
BAKKEN, J. A., Metallurgy
BECH, C., Zoology
BERGE, A. T., Applied Chemistry
BONES, A., Botany
BRUNVOLL, J., Physical Chemistry
CARLSEN, P. H., Organic Chemistry
CYVIN, S. J., Theoretical Chemistry
ENGH, T. A., Metallurgy
ERGA, O., Chemical Engineering
ESPMARK, O. Y., Zoology
GRASDALEN, H., Biotechnology
GRONG, Ø., Metallurgy
HAFSKJOLD, B., Physical Chemistry
HAGEN, G. K., Industrial Electrochemistry
HAGEN, K. T., Chemistry
HELLE, T., Paper Technology
HERTZBERG, T., Chemical Engineering
HOLM, J. L., Silicate and High Temperature Chemistry
HOLMEN, A., Applied Chemistry, Petrochemistry
HYTTEBORN, U. H., Botany
IVERSEN, T.-H., Botany
JENSEN, S. L., Organic Chemistry
KJELSTRUP, S. H., Physical Chemistry, Thermodynamics
KRANE, J., Chemistry
LEVINE, D. W., Biochemical Engineering
LIEN, K. M., Chemical Engineering
LJONES, T., Chemistry
LØVLAND, J., Chemical Engineering
MUSTAPARTA, H., Zoology
MYKLESTAD, S., Marine Biochemistry
MØRK, P., Applied Chemistry
NES, E. Å., Physical Metallurgy
NESSE, N., Chemical Engineering
NICHOLSON, D. G., Zoology
NILSSEN, K. J., Zoology
NISANCIOGLU, K., Industrial Electrochemistry
OLSEN, S. E., Metallurgy
ONSAGER, O. T., Industrial Chemistry, Petrochemistry
PAINTER, T. J., Biotechnology
REINERTSEN, H., Freshwater Ecology
ROVEN, H. J., Metallurgy
RYUM, N., Physical Metallurgy
SCHRØDER, K., Chemistry
SKJÅK-BRÆK, G., Biochemistry
SKOGESTAD, S., Petrochemistry
SMIDSRØD, O. A., Biochemistry
SOLBERG, J. K., Physical Metallurgy
STEINNES, E., Environmental Technology
STERTEN, Å., Industrial Electrochemistry
STRØM, A. R., Biotechnology
STØLEVIK, E. R., Chemistry
SVENDSEN, H. F., Chemical Engineering
SÆTHER, B. E., Zoology
THONSTAD, J., Industrial Electrochemistry
THORSEN, G., Chemical Engineering
TRÆTTEBERG, M., Chemistry
TUNOLD, R., Industrial Electrochemistry
TUSET, J. K., Metallurgy
VALLA, S., Biotechnology
YSTENES, M., Inorganic Chemistry
ZACHARIASSEN, K. E., Zoology
ØSTGAARD, K., Biotechnology
ØSTVOLD, T., Inorganic Chemistry
ØYE, H. A., Inorganic Chemistry

Faculty of Marine Technology:

ALMÅS, T., Marine Engineering
AMDAHL, J., Marine Structures
BERGE, S., Marine Structures
ENDAL, A., Marine Systems Design
ENGJA, H., Marine Engineering
ERICHSEN, S., Marine Systems Design
FALTINSEN, O. M., Marine Hydrodynamics
KRISTIANSEN, S., Marine Systems Design
LARSEN, C. M., Marine Structures
MINSÅS, K. J., Marine Hydrodynamics
MOAN, T., Marine Structures
MYRHAUG, D., Marine Hydrodynamics
PETTERSEN, B., Marine Hydrodynamics
RASMUSSEN, M., Marine Structures
WESTBY, O., Marine Systems Design
WHITE, M. F., Marine Engineering

Faculty of Mechanical Engineering:

ANDERSSON, H. I., Mechanics
ASBJØRNSEN, O. A., Thermal Energy and Hydropower
AUNE, A., Production and Quality Engineering
BARDAL, E., Machine Design and Materials Technology
BOELSKIFTE, P., Product Design
BRATT, J. F., Machine Design
BREDESEN, A. M., Refrigeration Engineering
BREKKE, H., Fluid Dynamics
BREVIK, I. H., Mechanics
CHAPPLE, P. J., Thermal Energy and Hydropower
FJELDAAS, S., Machine Design
FØRDE, M. J., Fluid Dynamics
GUSTAFSON, C.-G., Materials and Processes
HALMØY, E., Materials and Processes
HANSSEN, S. O., Heating, Ventilation and Sanitary Engineering
HUSTAD, J. E., Thermal Energy
HÄRKEGÅRD, G., Machine Design and Materials Technology
KROGSTAD, P. Å., Engineering Fluid Mechanics
LAMVIK, M., Applied Mechanics, Thermodynamics and Fluid Dynamics
LIEN, T. K., Production Engineering
MAGNUSSEN, B. F., Thermal Engineering

MAGNUSSEN, O. M., Industrial Fish Processing
NOVAKOVIC, V., Heating, Ventilation and Sanitary Engineering
NØRSTERUD, H., Fluid Mechanics
RASCH, F.-O., Production Engineering
RAUSAND, M., Machine Design
ROALDSTADÅS, A., Production Engineering
SIVERTSEN, O. I., Machine Design
STRØMMEN, I., Refrigeration Engineering
STØREN, S., Materials and Processes (Materials Technology)
SØNJU, O. K., Applied Thermodynamics and Combustion
THAULOW, C., Materials and Processes, Materials Technology
TØNDER, K., Machine Design
VALBERG, H. S., Materials and Processes
WANG, K., Production Engineering
YTREHUS, T., Mechanics
ØVERLI, J. M., Thermal Energy and Hydropower

Faculty of Arts:
AHLBERG, N. L., Religious Studies
ANDERSEN, H. W., History
BEHNE, D. M., English Language
DAHL, S. L., History
DOMMELEN, W. A. VAN, Linguistics
DYBVIG, M., Philosophy
EVENSEN, L. S., Applied Linguistics
FAUSKEVÅG, S. E., Romance Literature
FEIGS, W. G., Germanic Languages
FOSS, G., General Literature
FRETHEIM, T., Literature
FÅRLUND, J. T., Scandinavian Studies
GIMNES, S., Scandinavian Literature
HAGLAND, J. R., Scandinavian Studies and Comparative Literature
HALVORSEN, A., Romance Studies
HAWTHORN, J., English Literature
HELLAN, L., Applied Linguistics
HERNÆS, P. O., History
HOGNESTAD, O., Religious Studies
HÅRD, M., History
HÅRSTAD, K., History
IMSEN, S., History
JOHANNESON, N.-L., English
LEDANG, O. K., Musicology
LIE, S., Literature
MAURSETH, P., History
MELBY, K., Women's Research, History
MOLANDER, B., Philosophy
MÆHLUM, B. K., Norwegian
NEUMANN, B. O., German Literature
NILSEN, H. N., Literature
NORDGÅRD, T., Linguistics
PETERI, G. G., History
PÜTZ, H. M., Germanic Languages
SALVESEN, H., History
SAWYER, B., History
SHERRY, R. G., English
SIMENSEN, J., History
SKRETTING, K., Art and Media Studies
SLETTAN, D., History
STENE-JOHANSEN, K., General Literature
SUPPHELLEN, S., History
SØRENSSEN, B., Film Studies
ULRICHSEN, J. H., Religious Studies
ÅFARLI, T. A., Scandinavian Studies and Comparative Literature
ÅRSET, H. E., Literature
ÅSLESTAD, P., Scandinavian Studies and Comparative Literature
ØFSTI, A., Philosophy
ØSTERUD, E., Philosophy

Faculty of Medicine:
ANGELSEN, B. A. J., Biomedical Engineering
BERGH, K., Microbiology, Immunology
BOVIM, G., Neurology
BRATLID, D., Paediatrics
BRUBAKK, A. O., Physiology
DALE, O., Anaesthesiological Pharmacology
ELLINGSEN, Ø., Physiology
ESPEVIK, T., Cell Biology
FALKNER, S. E., Morphology
FINSEN, V., Orthopaedic Surgery
GÖTESTAM, K. G., Psychiatry
HAUGEN, O. A., Morphology
IDLE, J., Molecular Biology
IVERSEN, O.-J. E., Microbiology
JACOBSEN, G., Community Medicine and General Practice
JOHANNESSEN, T., Community Medicine and General Practice
JOHNSEN, R., Community Medicine and General Practice
JYNGE, P., Pharmacology and Toxicology
KROKAN, H. E., Biochemistry
KÅSA, S., Palliative Medicine
LIE, N., Child Psychiatry
MIDELFART, A., Ophthalmology
MYRVOLD, H. E., Surgery
NILSEN, O. G., Toxicology
RØNNINGEN, H., Orthopaedic Surgery
SANDVIK, A. K., Physiology
SAUNTE, C., Otorhinolaryngology
SVEBAK, S., Behavioural Medicine
SYVERSEN, T., Pharmacology and Toxicology
UNSGÅRD, G., Neurosurgery
VATTEN, L., Epidemiology
VIKAN, A., Child Psychiatry
WALDUM, H. L., Gastroenterology
WESTIN, S., Community Medicine and General Practice
ÅSE, S. T., Pathology

Faculty of Social Sciences and Technology Management:
BERGE, E., Sociology and Political Science
BJØRGEN, I. A., Psychology
BRØGGER, J. C., Social Anthropology
DALE, B. E., Geography
ERRING, B. B., Social Anthropology
GAIVORONSKI, A. A., Industrial Economics
HOPMANN, S., Geography
HOVDEN, J., Organizational Studies
HVINDEN, B., Sociology and Political Science
IMSEN, G. M., Education
INGVALDSEN, R. P., Sports Sciences
JONES, M. R. H., Geography
KOLSTAD, A., Psychology
KREKLING, S., Psychology
LAUGLO, J., Sociology
LEVIN, M., Organizational Studies
LINDBEKK, T., Sociology
LISTHAUG, O., Sociology
LUND, R., Geography
MARTINSEN, H., Psychology
MARTINUSSEN, W. M., Sociology
MATSON, E., Economics
NYGREN, B., Economics
PETTERSEN, P. A., Political Science
RATTSØ, J. G., Economics
RINGDAL, K., Sociology
SCHIEFLOE, P. M., Sociology
SJØBERG, B.-M. D., Psychology
SKÅLVIK, E. M., Education
SLETTA, J. O., Education
SOLEM, K. E., Political Science
SOLEM, O., Organizational Studies
STILES, T. C., Psychology
STRØMNES, Å., Education
SØRENSEN, K. H., Sociology
SØVIK, N., Education
TØSSEBRO, J., Programme for Social Work
WALLACE, S., Economics
WEEL, F. VAN DER, Psychology
WESTGÅRD, R. H., Organizational Studies
WHITING, H., Sports Sciences
WICHSTRØM, L., Psychology
WIJST, D. VAN DER, Economics
WÅGØ, S., Social Sciences and Technology Management
ÅSE, A., Geography

Museum of Natural History and Archaeology:
FLATBERG, K. I., Botany
HOGSTAD, O., Zoology
HOLTHE, T., Zoology
JOHANSEN, A. B., Archaeology
MOEN, A., Botany
MORK, J., Marine Biology
OLSEN, Y., Marine Biology
SAKSHAUG, E., Marine Biology
SOGNNES, K., Archaeology
STRØMGREN, T., Zoology

Centres:
BRATTBØ, H., Technology and Society
DYBDAHL, A., Medieval Studies
LORENTZEN, S., Teacher Education and School Development

UNIVERSITETET I BERGEN
(University of Bergen)

5020 Bergen
Telephone: 55-58-00-00
Fax: 55-58-96-43
Founded 1948
State control
Academic year: August to June
Rector: Prof. Dr J. F. BERNT
Vice-Rector: Prof. K. K. CHRISTENSEN
Director: K. ROMMETVEIT
Librarian: K. GARNES
Library: see Libraries
Number of teachers: 1,014
Number of students: 17,686
Publications: *Årsmelding* (annual report), *Naturen* (a popular scientific review), *Skrifter*, *Småskrifter*, *Sarsia*, *UOB News*, *UiB magasinet* (University Magazine).

DEANS

Faculty of Arts: Prof. LEIV EGIL BREIVIK
Faculty of Natural Sciences: Prof. EIRIK SUNDVOR
Faculty of Medicine: Prof. JON LEKVEN
Faculty of Social Sciences: Prof. SIGMUND GRØNMO
Faculty of Dentistry: Prof. PER JOHAN WISTH
Faculty of Law: Prof. HENRY JOHAN MÆLAND
Faculty of Psychology: Prof. HÅKAN SUNDBERG

PROFESSORS

Faculty of Arts:
ALVER, B. G., Folklore
BAGGE, S., History
BELL, J. N., Arabic
BLOM, I., History of Woman
BLUCHER, K., Italian
BREIVIK, L., English Philology
BØRTNES, J., Russian Literature
CHRISTENSEN, K. K., General Linguistics
DANBOLT, G., History of Art
DYRVIK, S., History
DYVIK, H. J. J., General Linguistics
FINNESTAD, R., Religion
GILHUS, I., Religion
GRANNES, A., Russian Language
GRIPSRUD, J., Media Studies
GRØNLIE, T., History
HALMØY, O., French Language
HARTVEIT, L., English Literature
HÄGG, T., Classical Philology
HÅLAND, R., African Archaeology
KENNEDY, A. K., English Language
KITTANG, A., General Literature
KOLLER, W., German Language
KRISTOFFERSEN, G., Nordic Language
LARSEN, P., Media Studies
MEYER, J. C., History of Art
MJELDHEIM, L., History
MORTENSEN, L. B., Latin
NES, O., Philology
NORDENSTAM, T., Philosophy
NORDHAGEN, P. J., History of Art
O'FAHEY, R. S., History
PIERCE, R. M., Egyptology
SANDBERG, B., German Literature
SANDBERG, H.-J., German Literature
SKIRBEKK, G., Philosophy
SKÅNLAND, M. H., Linguistics
SOLBERG, B., Archaeology
STENSTRÖM, A. B., English Language

THOMASSEN, E., Religion
ØVERLAND, O., American Literature

Faculty of Natural Sciences:

ASPVALL, B., Computer Science
BERG, C. C., Botany
BERGE, G., Mathematics
BIRKS, H. J. B., Botany
BJØRSTAD, P. E., Computer Science
BÅMSTEDT, U., Marine Biology
CSERNAI, L., Physics
DYSTE BARSTAD, K., Applied Mathematics
ESPEDAL, M., Mathematics
FLOOD, P., Zoological Anatomy
FRANCIS, G. W., Organic Chemistry
FURNES, H., Petroleum Geology
FYHN, H.-J., Milieu Physiology
GABRIELSEN, R., Petroleum Geology
GADE, H. G., Physical Oceanography
GRAUE, A., Physics
GRØNÅS, S., Meteorology
HAMMER, E. A., Physics
HANYGA, A., Applied Geophysics
HELLESETH, T., Computer Science
HEUCH, I., Statistics
HOBÆK, H., Physics
HOLME, A., Mathematics
HOV, Ø., Meteorology
HUSEBYE, S., Chemistry
HØGSTEDT, G., Ecology
HØILAND, H., Physical Chemistry
JOHANNESEN, O. M., Physical Oceanography
JØRGENSEN, P. M., Botany
KALAND, P. E., Botany
KLØVE, T., Computer Science
KNUTSEN, G. H., Botany
KRISTOFFERSEN, Y., Seismology
KRYVI, H., Zoology
LARSSON, P., Zoology
LIE, U., Marine Biology
LIEN, T., Microbiology
LILLESTØL, E., Physics
LØVHØIDEN, G., Physics
LØVLIE, R., Geomagnetism
MAALØE, S. B., Geology
MANGERUD, J., Quaternary Geology
MANNE, R. E., Chemistry
MELDAL, S., Informatics
MILNES, A. G., Structure Geology
MØLLER, D., Fisheries Biology
MORK, M., Oceanography
NÆVDAL, G., Fisheries Biology
OSLAND, P., Physics
SCHRADER, H., Geology
SEJRUP, H. P., Geology
SJØBLOM, J., Physical Chemistry
SKOGEN, A., Botany
SLETTEN, J., Inorganic Chemistry
SONGSTAD, J., Inorganic Chemistry
STAMNES, J. J., Physics
STEIHAUG, T., Informatics
STORETVEDT, K., Geomagnetism
STRAY, A., Mathematics
SUNDVOR, E., Seismology
SÆTHER, O. A., Zoology
TALBOT, M. R., Petroleum Geology
THINGSTAD, T. F., Microbiology
TJØSTHEIM, D., Statistics
TVERBERG, H. A., Mathematics

Faculty of Medicine:

AKSNES, L., Biochemistry
ANDERSEN, K. J., Biochemistry
BERGE, R. K., Clinical Biochemistry
BERGSJØ, P., Gynaecology and Obstetrics
BJELKE, E., Hygiene
BJORVATN, B., Tropical Medicine
BOMAN, H., Genetics
BROCH, O. J., Pharmacology
DAHL, O., Oncology
DØSKELAND, S. O., Anatomy
FARSTAD, M. N., Clinical Biochemistry
FLATMARK, T., Biochemistry
HAGA, H. J., Rheumatology
HALSTENSEN, A., Internal Medicine
HARTVEIT, F., Pathology
HELLE, K., Physiology
HEYERAAS, K. J., Physiology
HOFSTADS, T., Medical Microbiology
HOLE, K., Physiology
HOLMSEN, H. A., Biochemistry
HOLSTEN, F., Psychiatry
HØVDING, G., Ophthalmology
HAAHEIM, L. R., Virology
HAARR, L., Virology
IRGENS, L. M., Preventive Medicine
KVINNSLAND, I., Oral Anatomy
KVINNSLAND, S., Anatomy
LARSEN, J. L., Radiology
LEKVEN, J., Surgery
LIEN, E. A., Pharmacology
LJUNGGREN, E. A., Physiotherapy
LUND, J., Anatomy
LUND, T., Anaesthesiology
LUND-JOHANSEN, P., Clinical Medicine
LÆRUM, O. D., Experimental Pathology and Oncology
MALTERUD, K., General Practice
MARKESTAD, T., Paediatrics
MATRE, R., Immunology
MORILD, I., Forensic Medicine
MØLSTER, A., Surgery, Orthopaedics
NYLAND, H. J., Clinical Neurology
OLOFSSON, J., Otorhinolaryngology
PRYME, I. F., Biochemistry
QVARNSTRØM, U., Nursing
REED, R. K., Physiology
REFSUM, H., Pharmacology
SCHELINE, R. R., Biochemical Pharmacology
SCHREINER, A., Internal Medicine
SELAND, J. H., Clinical Medicine
SKARSTEIN, A., Surgery, Gastroenterology
SKJÆRVEN, R., Medical Statistics and Informatics
SOLBERG, C. O., Infectious Diseases
SVANES, K., Surgery
SØVIK, O., Paediatrics
TAXT, T., Medical Informatics
THUNOLD, S., Pathology
TONNING, F. M., Otorhinolaryngology
TRIPPESTAD, A., Surgery
TYSSEBOTN, I., Hyperbaric Medicine
ULSTEIN, M. K., Gynaecology and Obstetrics
URSIN, R., Physiology
AAKVAAG, A., Biochemical Endocrinology
AARLI, J. A., Neurology
AARSKOG, D., Paediatrics
AASJØ, E. B., Virology

Faculty of Dentistry:

BERG, E., Prosthodontics
BERGE, M., Prosthodontics
BIRKELAND, J. M., Cariology
BJORVATN, K., Dental Research
ESPELID, I., Paedodontics
GJERDET, N. R., Dental Materials
GUSTAVSEN, F., Prosthodontics
HALSE, A., Oral Radiology
HAUGEJORDEN, O., Community Dentistry
HOLM-PEDERSEN, P., Geriatric Dentistry
JOHANNESSEN, A. C., Oral Pathology
LIE, T., Periodontology
MOLVEN, O., Endodontics
NILSEN, R., International Health
RASMUSSEN, P. A., Paedodontics
SELVIG, K. A., Dental Research
SKAUG, N., Oral Microbiology
TVEIT, A. B., Cariology
WISTH, P. J., Orthodontics

Faculty of Social Sciences:

AMUNDSEN, E. S., Economics
ARRESTAD, J., Economics
BAKKE, M., Media Studies
BALDERSHEIM, H., Administration and Organization Theory
BARTH, F., Social Anthropology
BJELLAND, A. K., Social Anthropology
BLOM, J. P., Social Anthropology
DAVIDSON, P., Information Science
ERIKSEN, E. O., Administration and Organization Theory
FLÅM, S. D., Economics
GRØNHAUG, E., Social Anthropology
GRØNMO, S., Sociology
GULBRANDSEN, Ø., Social Anthropology
HANSEN, J. C., Geography
HENRIKSEN, G., Social Anthropology
HOLT-JENSEN, A., Geography
HÅLAND, G., Social Anthropology
JANSEN, A.-I., Administration and Organization Theory
KARVONEN, L., Comparative Politics
KNUDSEN, J. C., Social Anthropology
KNUDSEN, K., Sociology
KONRAD, K., Economics
KUHNLE, S., Comparative Politics
LILLEHAUG, B., Information Science
LINDSTRØM, B., Information Science
LINDSTRØM, U., Comparative Politics
LÆGREID, P., Administration and Organization Theory
MANGER, L., Social Anthropology
MURDOCK, G., Media Studies
MÅSEIDE, P., Sociology
NORDBOTTEN, S., Information Science
OFFERDAHL, A., Administration and Organization Theory
OLSEN, J. P., Administration and Organization Theory
OLSEN, T., Economics
RAFFELHÜSCHEN, B., Economics
RISA, E., Economics
ROTHSTEIN, B., Administration and Organization Theory
RUESCHEMEYER, D., Administration and Organization Theory
SCOTT, J., Sociology
SELLE, P., Comparative Politics
SKAR, S. L., Social Anthropology
STRAND, T., Administration and Organization Theory
STRØM, K., Comparative Politics
SVÅSAND, L. G., Comparative Politics
SAETREN, H., Administration and Organization Theory
SØDER, M., Sociology
THOMPSON, M., Comparative Politics
UHDE, A., Economics
VE, H., Sociology
WAERNESS, K., Sociology
ØSTBYE, H., Media Studies
ØYEN, Ø., Sociology

Faculty of Law:

BERNT, J. F.
DOUBLET, D. R.
HOLGERSEN, G.
KRÜGER, K.
LILLEHOTT, K.
MÆLAND, H. J.
MATNINGSDAL, M.
NORDTVEIT, E.
NYGAARD, N.
RASMUSSEN, Ø.
STAVANG, P.

Faculty of Psychology:

EIDE, R., Psychology
EVANS, T. D., Cognitive Psychology
FORSLIN, J., Organizational Psychology
HAGTVET, K. A., Psychometrics
HAVIK, O. E., Clinical Psychology
HELSTRUP, T., Cognitive Psychology
HUGDAHL, K., Somatic Psychology
HUNDEIDE, K., Developmental Psychology
HAALAND, W., Clinical Psychology
KAUFMANN, G., Cognitive Psychology
KILE, S., Organizational Psychology
KLØVE, H., Clinical Psychology
MELLIN-OLSEN, S., Practical Education
NIELSEN, G., Clinical Psychology
OLWEUS, D., Personal Psychology
RAAHEIM, K., Cognitive Psychology
URSIN, H., Physiological Psychology
AARØ, L. E., Social Psychology

ATTACHED INSTITUTES

Bergen Foundation of Science: HIB, Thormøhlensgt. 55, 5028 Bergen; Dir JAN S. JOHANNESSEN.

Bergen High Technology Centre, Limited: HIB, Thormøhlensgt. 55, 5028 Bergen; Dir JAN S. JOHANNESSEN.

Biological Station: University of Bergen; open to research workers from all countries; 4 research vessels.

Milde Arboretum: 5067 Milde; f. 1971; plant research, laboratory for students; open to the public; Head Prof. Dr CORNELIS CHR. BERG.

Centre for Feminist Research in the Humanities: H. Fossgt. 12, 5007 Bergen.

Centre for Development Studies: Strømgt. 54, 5007 Bergen; Dir GUNNAR M. SØRBØ.

Centre for Social Research: Professor Keysersgt. 2, 5007 Bergen.

LOS Centre (Norwegian Centre for Research in Organization and Management): Rosenberggt. 39, 5015 Bergen; Dir TERJE STEEN EDVARDSEN.

Medical Birth Registry of Norway: Haukelandsveien 10, 5021 Bergen.

Multidisciplinary Group for the Study of Work and Society: Hermann Fossgt. 5, 5007 Bergen.

Nansen Environmental and Remote Sensing Centre: Edv. Griegsvei 3A, 5037 Solheimsvik; Dir OLA M. JOHANNESSEN.

National Centre for Research in Virology: HIB, Thormøhlensgt. 55, 5028 Bergen; Chair. LARS HAARR.

Research Centre for Health Promotion: Oistelinsgt. 3, 5007 Bergen; Chair. JOSTEIN RISE.

Norwegian Social Science Data Services: Hans Holmboesgt. 22, 5007 Bergen; Dir BJØRN HENRICHSEN.

Bergen Scientific Centre IBM: Høyteknologisenteret, Thormøhlensgt. 55, 5008 Bergen; Dir PATRICK GAFFNEY.

Centre for Middle Eastern and Islamic Studies: Parkv. 22A, 5007 Bergen.

Centre for International Health: Haukelandsv. 10, 5009 Bergen; Chair. RUNE NILSEN.

Centre for the Study of the Sciences and Humanities: Allegaten 32, 5007 Bergen.

Centre for Studies of Environment and Resources: Thormøhlensgt. 55, 5008 Bergen; Chair. ULF LIE.

University Media Centre: Verftsgt. 2C, 5011 Bergen; Dir KNUT OLAV ASLAKSEN.

Norwegian Computing Centre for the Humanities: Harald Hårfagresgt. 31, 5007 Bergen.

See also under Museums

UNIVERSITETET I OSLO
(University of Oslo)

POB 1072, Blindern, 0316 Oslo

Telephone: 22-85-50-50

Telex: 72425

Fax: 22-85-44-42

Founded 1811

State control

Academic year: August to June (two semesters)

Rector: Prof. Dr LUCY SMITH

Vice-Rector: Prof. Dr KNUT FÆGRI

Director: TOR SAGLIE

Librarian: JAN ERIK RØED

Library: see Libraries

Number of teachers: 1,700

Number of students: 38,000

Publications: *Annual Report*, *Uniforum* (20 a year), *Apollon* (4 a year), catalogue of courses, handbooks.

DEANS

Faculty of Theology: Prof. TROND SKARD DOKKA

Faculty of Law: Prof. FREDERIK ZIMMER

Faculty of Medicine: Prof. JON DALE

Faculty of Arts: Prof. EVEN HOVDHAUGEN

Faculty of Mathematics and Natural Sciences: Prof. JAN TRULSEN

Faculty of Dentistry: Prof. INGEBORG JACOBSEN

Faculty of Social Sciences: Prof. AANUND HYLLAND

Faculty of Education: Prof. LISE VISLIE

PROFESSORS

Faculty of Theology:

BARSTAD, H. M., Old Testament
CHRISTOFFERSEN, S. A., Systematic Theology
DOKKA, T. S., New Testament and Systematic Theology
FURRE, B., Church History and Systematic Theology
HAFSTAD, K., Systematic Theology
HAUGE, M. R., Old Testament
HELLEMO, G., History of the Church
HELLHOLM, D., New Testament
KVANVIG, H. S., Old Testament
LØNNING, I., Systematic Theology
MONTGOMERY, I., History of the Church
MOXNES, H., New Testament
RASMUSSEN, T., History of the Church
SEIM, T. K., New Testament
THELLE, N. R., Systematic Theology

Faculty of Law:

ANDENÆS, M. H., Law
BING, J., Law
BOE, E., Law
BULL, H. J., Law
EIDE, E., Economics and Statistics
ENG, S., Law
ERICSSON, K., Criminology
ESKELAND, S., Law
FALKANGER, T., Law
FLEISCHER, C. A., Law
GRAVER, H. P., Sociology of Law
HAGSTRØM, V., Law
HOV, J., Law
HØIGÅRD, I. C., Criminology
JAKHELLN, H., Law
JOHANSEN, P. O., Criminology
JOHNSEN, J. T., Law
KAASEN, K., Law
KJØNSTAD, A., Law
LØDRUP, P., Law
MATHIESEN, T., Sociology of Law
MICHALSEN, D., Law
RØSÆG, E., Law
SCHARTUM, D. W., Administrative Informatics
SELVIG, E. H. O., Law
SMITH, E., Law
SMITH, L., Law
SYSE, A., Law
TORVUND, O., Law
ULFSTEIN, G., Law
WILHELMSEN, T. L., Insurance Law
WOXHOLTH, G., Law
ZIMMER, F., Law

Faculty of Medicine:

BENESTAD, H. B., Physiology
BERG, K. I., Genetics
BERG, T., Physiology
BJERTNESS, E., Epidemiology
BJUNE, G. A., International Health
BJÅLIE, E. G., Anatomy
BJØRNDAL, A., General Practice and Preventive Medicine
BLOMHOFF, R., Nutrition Research
BOE, J., Respiratory Medicine
BOGEN, B., Virology
BOTTEN, G. S., Health Administration
BRANTZAEG, P., Pathology
BREIVIK, H., Anaesthesiology
BRODAL, P., Anatomy
BROSSTAD, F. R., Internal Medicine Research
BRUUSGAARD, D., Social Security Medicine
BUKHOLM, G., Bacteriology
BØVRE, K., Microbiology
CHRISTIANSEN, E., Nutrition
CHRISTOFFERSEN, T., Pharmacology
DAHL, A. A., Psychiatry
DALGARD, O. S., Psychiatry
DEGRE, M., Virology
DREBORG, S. K. G., Paediatrics, Allergology
DREVON, C., Nutrition Research
EVENSEN, S. A., Internal Medicine
FINSET, A., Medical Behavioural Research
FOSSUM, S., Anatomy
FUGELLI, P., Social Medicine
FYRAND, O. L., Dermatology
GAUTVIK, K. M., Medical Biochemistry
GEIRAN, O., Cardiovascular Surgery
GLOVER, J., Physiology
GORDELADZE, J. O., Medical Biochemistry
GRAN, F. CH., Biochemistry
GRAV, H. J., Biochemistry
GRÜNFELD, B., Medical Social Psychiatry
GRØTTUM, P., Medical Computer Science
GUNDERSEN, W. B., Microbiology
HALL, C., Surgery
HANSSON, V., Med. Biochemistry
HARBOE, M., Immunology
HAUG, F. M., Anatomy
HAUGE, A., Physiology
HEGGELUND, P., Neurophysiology
HEIBERG, A. N., Psychiatry
HENRIKSEN, T., Nutrition
HJORTDAHL, P., Medicine
HOLCK, P., Anatomy
HOLTE, A., Medical Behavioural Research
HORN, R., Medical Biochemistry
HUITFELDT, H., Pathology
HUSBY, G., Rheumatology
HØGLEND, P. A., Psychiatry
HØSTMARK, T. A., Preventive Medicine
ILEBEKK, A. B., Experimental Medicine
INGSTAD, B., Social Medicine
IVERSEN, J. G., Physiology
JAHNSEN, T., Biochemistry
JELLUM, E., Clinical Biochemistry
KASE, B. F., Paediatrics
KIERULF, P., Clinical Chemistry
KIRKEVOLD, M., Medicine
KJEKSHUS, J., Experimental Research
KLEPP, K. I., Nutrition Research
KOLBENSTVEDT, A. N., Radiology
KRINGLEN, E., Medical Behavioural Research
KVITTINGEN, E. A., Clinical Biochemistry
LANDMARK, K. H., Pharmacology
LARSEN, Ø., Medical History
LAVIK, N. J., Psychiatry
LIE, S. O., Paediatrics
LORENSEN, M., Nursing Science
LÆRUM, E., Experimental Radiology
LØMO, T., Physiology/Neurophysiology
LØVSTAD, R., Medical Biochemistry
LAAKE, K., Geriatric Medicine
LAAKE, P., Medical Statistics
MADSHUS, I. H., Molecular Biology
MATHESON, I., Pharmacotherapeutics
MOUM, T., Medical Behavioural Research
NATVIG, J. B., Immunology
NICOLAYSEN, G., Physiology
NJÅ, A., Neurophysiology
NOREIK, K., Social Medicine
NORUM, K. R., Nutrition Research
NYBERG-HANSEN, R., Neurology
NÆSS, O., Pathology
OSNES, J. B., Pharmacology
OTTERSEN, O. P., Anatomy
PEDERSEN, J. I., Nutrition Research
PRYDZ, H. P., Medicine
REINHOLT, F. P., Pathology
RINGVOLD, A., Ophthalmology
RINVIK, E., Anatomy
ROGNUM, T. O., Forensic Medicine
ROLLAG, H., Bacteriology
ROLSTAD, B., Anatomy

SAGVOLDEN, T., Neurophysiology
SANDNES, D. L., Pharmacology
SAUGSTAD, O. D., Paediatrics
SEJERSTED, O. M., Experimental Research
SKOMEDAL, T., Pharmacology
SOLBAKK, J. H., Medical Ethics
SOLLID, L. M., Transplantation Immunology
SOLUM, N. O., Internal Medical Research
SPYDEVOLD, Ø., Medical Biochemistry
STEEN, P. A., Anaesthesiology
STOKKE, O., Clinical Biochemistry
STORM, J., Physiology
STORM-MATHISEN, J., Anatomy
STRAY-PEDERSEN, B., Obstetrics and Gynaecology
SØREIDE, O., Surgery
SØRENSEN, T., Psychiatry
TELLNES, G., Social Security Medicine
THELLE, D. S., Epidemiology
VAGLUM, P., Psychiatry
VELLAR, O. D., Hygiene
VØLLESTAD, N. K., Health Science
WALLØE, L., Physiology
WALAAS, S. I., Neurochemistry
WINTHER, F. Ø., Oto-rhino-laryngology
ZWETNOW, N., Neurosurgery
ØYE, I., Pharmacology
AALEN, O. O., Statistics
AASEN, A., Surgery

Faculty of Arts:

AHNSTRØM, L., Geography
AMUNDSEN, A. B., Folklore
ANDERSEN, Ø., Classical Philology
ANDERSEN, P. T., Nordic Literature
ASHEIM, O., Philosophy
ASKEDAL, J. O., German Language
ASTRUP, E. E., Archaeological Conservation Chemistry
BAUNE, Ø., Philosophy
BENEDICTOW, O. J., History
BENESTAD, F., Musicology
BENUM, E., History
BENSKIN, M., English Language
BERG, N., Classical Philology
BJERKE, S., History and Religion
BJORVAND, H., German Linguistics
BJØRKUM, A., Norwegian Linguistics
BJØRKVOLD, J. R., Musicology
BJØRNFLATEN, J. J., Slavonic Languages
BLIKSRUD, L., Nordic Literature
BRAAVIG, J., History of Religion
BRANDT, J. R., Classical Archaeology
BROWN, K. C., English Literature
BRULAND, K., History
BØ-RYGG, A., General Aesthetics
CHRISTENSEN, A. E., Scandinavian Archaeology
DAHL, H. F., Media and Communication Research
EIFRING, H., Modern Chinese Languages
ELSNESS, J., English Language
EMILSSON, E. K., Ancient Philosophy
ENDRESEN, R. T., African Languages
ERIKSEN, A., Folklore
ERIKSEN, R. T., Literary Theory
ERIKSEN, T. B., History of Ideas
FAARLUND, J. T., Nordic Language and Literature
FARNER, G., Dutch
FRØLICH, J., French Literature
FUGLESANG, S., Fine Art History
FUGLESTAD, F., History
FØLLESDAL, D., Philosophy
GJELSVIK, O., Philosophy
GLAMBEK, I., Art History
GRIMNES, O. K., History
GUNDERSEN, K., French Literature
GUSTAFSSON, A., Ethnology
HAFF, M. H., French Language
HAGEBERG, O., Nordic Literature
HAGEMANN, G., History
HANSEN, C. F., German Language
HANSEN, J. E. E., History of Ideas
HARALDSSON, H., Russian
HARBSMEIER, C. H., East Asian Languages
HAREIDE, J., Nordic Literature
HEDEAGER, L., Nordic Archaeology
HELGHEIM, K., Theatre Research
HJELDE, S., History of Religions
HODNE, B., Folklore
HOEL, K., Fine Art History
HOHLER, E. B., Art History
HOLTER, K., French Literature
HOVDHAUGEN, E., General Linguistics
HØYER, S., Media and Communication
HVENEKILDE, A., Norwegian as a Second Language
IVERSEN, I., General Literary Science
JERVELL, H. R., Computer Science
JOHANSSON, A., Modern Economic History
JOHANSSON, S. K. A., English Language
JOHNSEN, B. H., Folklore
JONES, A., Philosophy
KELLER, J. C., Nordic Archaeology
KERESZTES, L., Finno-Ugrian Languages
KJELDSTADLI, K., Modern History
KJETSAA, G., Russian Literature
KLEM, L. G., Romance Philology
KLEPP, A., Ethnology
KNIRK, J. E.
KOLSTØ, P., Russian and East European Studies
KRAGGERUD, E., Classical Philology
KROG, T., History of Ideas
KROGSETH, O., History of Christianity
KVIFTE, T., Folk Music
KVÆRNE, P., History of Religions
LANGHOLM, S., History
LAUSUND, O., English Literature
LINDEMAN, F. O., Linguistics
LORENTZ, E., History
LOTHE, J., British Literature
LUNDBY, K., Media and Communication
LØDRUP, H., Linguistics
LØNNING, J. T., Computer Science
MALMANGER, M., Fine Art History
MARKUSSEN, I., History of Ideas
MATHIASSEN, T., Slavonic Languages
MELBERG, B. A. E., Literature
MIKKELSEN, E., Nordic Archaeology
MOEN, I., Linguistics
MONTGOMERY, H., Classical Philology
MØNNESLAND, S., Slavonic Languages
MYHRE, J., History
NAGUIB, S. N., Cultural History, Cultural Analysis
NEDKVITNE, A., History
NERGAARD, T., Fine Art History
NIKANNE, U., Finnish Language
OLSEN, S. H., British Civilization
OTTOSSON, K., Icelandic
PLAHTER, U., Art Conservation Chemistry
PRICE, P. G., History
PHARO, H., History
RASMUSSEN, T., Media and Communication
REINTON, R., Literary Theory
RIAN, Ø., History
RINDAL, M., Nordic Onomastics
ROGAN, B., Ethnology
ROLL-HANSEN, N., Philosophy
RUUD, E., Musicology
RØNNING, H., Media and Communication Research
SAGMO, I., German Literature
SANDE, S., Classical Archaeology
SCHREINER, J. H., Ancient History
SCHØNDORF, K. E., German Language
SEEBERG, A., Classical Archaeology and Fine Art History
SEIP, A.-L., History
SEJERSTED, F., Economic and Social History
SIMSON, G. VON, Indian Language and Literature
SKEI, H. H., Literary Theory
SKAUG, E., Art Conservation
SKAARE, K., Numismatics
SOGNER, S., History
STEINFELD, T., Nordic Language and Literature
STEINSLAND, G. S., History of Religions
STENE-JOHANSEN, K., Literary Theory
STENGAARD, B., Ibero-Romance Philology
SVENSEN, Å., Nordic Literature
SYVERTSEN, T., Media and Communication
SØRENSEN, P., Nordic Philology
SØRENSEN, Ø., Modern History
SÆBØ, K. J., German Language
TANASE, A., French Philology
THORDARSON, F., Classical Philology
THORSEN, L. E., Ethnology
TYSDAHL, B., English Literature
VANNEBO, K. I., Nordic Languages
VIKØR, L. S., Nordic Linguistics
VINJE, F. E., Modern Nordic Language
WALDAHL, R., Media and Communication Research
WERENSKIOLD, M., Fine Art History
WESSEL, E., German Literature
WETLESEN, J., Philosophy
WIKBERG, K. B., English Literature
WIKSHÅLAND, S., Musicology
WINTHER, P., American Literature
YSTAD, V., Nordic Literature
ØSTBØ, J. G., German Literature
ØSTMO, E., Nordic Archaeology

Faculty of Mathematics and Natural Sciences:

ABDULLAH, M. I., Chemical Oceanography
AKSNES, K., Astrophysics
ALBREGTSEN, F., Computer Science
AMUNDSEN, T., Physics
ANDERSEN, K. I., Zoology
ANDERSEN, T. H., Geochemistry
ANDERSSON, K. K., Biochemistry
ANDRESEN, A., Geology
BAKKE, O., Biology
BAKKE, T. A., Zoology
BENNECHE, T., Chemistry
BERG, T., Cell Biology
BERTELSEN, A., Mechanics
BJØRKLUND, K. R., Palaeontology
BJØRLYKKE, K. O., Geology
BORGAN, Ø., Statistics
BORGEN, L., Botany
BRATSETH, A. M., Geophysics
BRATTELI, O., Mathematics
BROCHMANN, C., Biology (Botany)
BRODERSEN, H., Mathematics
BRUTON, D. L., Palaeontology
BUGGE, L., Physics
BURAN, T., Physics
BYE, R., Chemistry
BØLVIKEN, E., Statistics
CARLSSON, M., Astrophysics
CHRISTENSEN, T. B., Biochemistry
CHRISTOPHERSEN, Informatics
DAHL, O.-J., Computer Science
DØVING, K., Zoophysiology
DÆHLEN, M., Mathematical Modelling
EEG, J. O., Physics
ELDHOLM, O., Marine Geophysics
ELIASSEN, F., Computer Science
ELLINGSRUD, G., Mathematics
ELVEN, R., Botany
ELVERHØI, A., Quaternary Geology
ENGELAND, T., Physics
ENGVOLD, O., Astrophysics
ESKILD, W., Biochemistry
FALEIDE, J. I., Geology
FEDER, J. G., Physics
FENSTAD, J. E., Mathematical Logic
FINSTAD, T., Physics
FJELLVÅG, H., Chemistry
FJÆRTOFT, B., Chemistry
FRØYLAND, J., Physics
FURUSETH, S., Chemistry
FÆGRI, K., Chemistry
GABRIELSEN, S., Biochemistry
GALPERINE, I., Physics
GELIUS, L.-J., Geophysics
GJESSING, S., Computer Science
GJEVIK, B., Hydrodynamics
GOTTSCHALK, L., Geophysics
GRAY, J. S., Marine Zoology
GREIBROKK, T., Analytical Chemistry
GRUE, J., Mechanics
GULLIKSEN, T. H., Mathematics

GUNDERSEN, G., Chemistry
GUNDERSEN, K., Biology (Physiology)
GUTTORMSEN, M., Physics
GØRBITZ, C. H., Chemistry
HAGEBØ, E., Chemistry
HAGEN, J. O. M., Geography
HALVORSEN, O., Zoology
HANSEN, F. K., Chemistry
HELGAKER, T., Chemistry
HELGELAND, L., Biochemistry
HELLAND, I., Statistics
HELLESLAND, J., Mechanics
HESSEN, D., Zoology
HJORT, N. L., Statistics
HOFF, P., Chemistry
HOLM, P., Mathematics
HOLM, S., Signal Processing
HOLTER, Ø., Physics
HOLTET, J. A., Physics
HØEG, K., Geology
HØGÅSEN, H., Theoretical Physics
HØILAND, K., Biology
HAALAND, A., Chemistry
IMS, R., Zoology
INGEBRETSEN, F., Physics
ISAKSEN, I., Meteorology
IVERSEN, T., Geophysics
JACOBSEN, T., Physics
JAHREN, B., Mathematics
JAKOBSEN, K. S., Biology
JAMTVEIT, B., Geology
JOHANSEN, H. T., Pharmacy
JØSSANG, T. F., Physics
KANESTRØM, I., Geophysics
KARLSEN, J., Pharmacy
KIRKERUD, B., Computer Science
KJEKSHUS, A., Chemistry
KJELDSETH-MOE, O., Astrophysics
KJENSMO, J., Limnology
KLAVENESS, D., Biology
KLAVENESS, J., Pharmacy
KOLBOE, S., Chemistry
KOLSAKER, P., Chemistry
KOLSTØ, A. B., Microbiology
KRISTENSEN, T. A., Biochemistry
KROGDAHL, S., Computer Science
KAARTVEDT, S., Marine Biology
LAANE, C. M. M., Biology
LAMBERTSSON, A., Genetics
LAUDAL, O. A., Mathematics
LEER, E., Astrophysics
LEINAAS, H. P., Zoology
LEINAAS, J. M., Physics
LIESTØL, K., Mathematical Modelling
LIFJELD, J. T., Biology (Zoology)
LILJE, P. V., Astrophysics
LILLERUD, K. P., Chemistry
LINDQVIST, B. H., Zoology
LINDSTRØM, T., Mathematics
LOTHE, J., Physics
LUND, W., Chemistry
LUTKEN, C. A., Physics
LYCHE, C., French Philology
LYCHE, T. J. W., Mathematical Modelling
LYSNE, O., Communication Systems
LØVHØIDEN, G., Physics
LØVLIE, A. M., Zoology
LAANE, C. M., Botany
MALTBY, P., Astrophysics
MALTERUD, K. E., Pharmacognosy
MAUPIN, V., Geophysics
MOSTAD, A., Chemistry
MYHRE, A. M., Geology
MØLLENDAL, H., Chemistry
MØRKEN, K., Numerical Analysis
MÅLØY, K. J., Physics
NAGY, J., Geology
NATVIG, B., Mathematical Statistics
NEUMANN, E. R., Mineralogy
NIELSEN, C. J., Chemistry
NILSSON, G. E., Biology (Physiology)
NISSEN-MEYER, J., Biochemistry
NORBY, T., Chemistry
NORDAL, I., Botany
NORMANN, D., Mathematical Logic
NYSTRØM, B., Organic Chemistry

NØST, B., Physics
OLSEN, A., Physics
ORMEROD, J. G., Botany
OSNES, E., Physics
OWE, O., Computer Science
PAULSEN, B. S., Pharmacognosy
PAULSEN, R. E., Pharmacy (Microbiology)
PECSELI, H., Physics
PEDERSEN, B., Chemistry
PEDERSEN, G. K., Mathematics
PIENE, R., Mathematics
PRYDZ, K., Biochemistry
PAASCHE, E. K. M., Marine Biology
RASMUSSEN, K. E., Pharmaceutical Analysis
RAVNDAL, F., Theoretical Physics
READ, A. L., Physics
REKSTAD, J. B., Physics
ROGNES, S. E., Botany
ROOS, N., Cell Biology
ROOTS, J., Chemistry
RUENESS, J., Marine Biology
RUSTAN, A., Pharmacy
RYVARDEN, L., Botany
SAGSTUEN, E., Physics
SAMDAL, S., Chemistry
SAND, O., Zoophysiology
SANDHOLT, P. E., Physics
SANDLIE, I., Biology
SCHUMACHER, T., Botany
SEIP, H. M., Chemistry
SIREVÅG, R., Microbiology
SKRAMSTAD, J., Chemistry
SKAALI, T. B., Physics
SLAGSVOLD, T., Zoology
SLETTEN, K., Biochemistry
SOLLID, J. L., Geography
SPILLING, P., Telematics and Telecommunications
STABELL, B., Geology
STABELL, R., Astrophysics
STAPNES, S., Physics
STEEN, J. B., Zoophysiology
STENERSEN, J. H. V., Biology
STENSETH, N. C., Zoology
STØLEN, S., Chemistry
STØRMER, E., Mathematics
SUDBØ, AA., Optoelectronics
SUNDING, P., Botany
SWENSEN, A. R., Mathematics (Statistics)
SØRÅSEN, O., Microelectronics
TAFTØ, J., Physics
TAXT, T., Computer Science
THRONDSEN, J., Marine Biology
TILSET, M., Chemistry
TJØM, P. O., Physics
TOMTER, P., Mathematics
TROLLDALEN, J., Geography
TRULSEN, J., Astrophysics
TVEITO, A., Informatics
TØNNESEN, H. H., Clinical Pharmacy
UGGERUD, E., Chemistry
UNDHEIM, K., Chemistry
VESETH, L., Physics
VØLLESTAD, A. L., Biology (Zoology)
WANG, A., Computer Science
WEBER, J. E., Geophysics
WIELGOLASKI, F., Biology
WIIG, Ø., Zoology, Mammalogy
WINTHER, R., Mathematical Modelling
WOLD, J. K., Pharmacognosy
ØKLAND, J., Limnology
ØKLAND, R. H., Botany
ØKSENDAL, B., Mathematics
ØSTBY, E., Biology (Zoology)
ØYEN, T. B., Biochemistry
AAGAARD, P., Geology
AARNES, H., Biology
AASEN, A. J., Pharmacy
AASHAMAR, K., Physics

Faculty of Dentistry:

ARNEBERG, P., Cariology
ATTRAMADAL, A., Pedodontics
AXELL, T., Gerodontics
BARKVOLL, P., Dental Surgery
BRODIN, P., Physiology
DAHL, B., Prosthetic Dentistry
ELLINGSEN, J. E., Prosthetic Dentistry
ERIKSEN, H. M., Cariology
FEHR, F. R. VON DER, Cariology
GJERMO, P. E., Periodontics
GRYTTEN, J. I., Community Dentistry, Health Economics
HANSEN, B., Periodontology
HAUGEN, E., Periodontics
HAUGEN, L. K., Dental Surgery
HELGELAND, K., Microbiology
HOLST, D. J., Social Dentistry
HAANÆS, H. R., Dental Surgery
HAAPASALO, M., Endodontics
JACOBSEN, I., Pedodontics
JACOBSEN, N. J., Material Sciences
KLINGE, R. F., General and Oral Pathology
KOPPANG, H. S., General and Oral Pathology
KOPPANG, R., Material Sciences
KROGSTAD, O., Orthodontics
LARHEIM, T. A., Dentistry
LØKKEN, P., Dental Pharmacy
NORDBØ, H., Cariology
OLSEN, I., Microbiology
OSMUNDSEN, H., Physiology
PREUS, H. R., Periodontology
RISNES, S., General and Oral Anatomy
RØED, A., Physiology
SCHEIE, A. AA, Microbiology
SKJØRLAND, K., Restorative Dentistry
SKJØRLAND, K. KR, Cariology
SKOGLUND, L. A., Dental Pharmacology
SOLHEIM, T., Oral Pathology
SØNJU, T., Cariology
THRANE, P. S., Oral Pathology
TRONSTAD, L., Endodontics
VASSEND, O., Behavioural Science
ØGAARD, B., Orthodontics
ØILO, G., Prosthetic Dentistry
ØRSTAVIK, J. S., Dentistry
AARS, H., Physiology

Faculty of Social Sciences:

ARCHETTI, E. P., Social Anthropology
ASHEIM, B. T., Social Geography
ASHEIM, G., Economics
BALDERSHEIM, H., Political Science
BERG, O. T., Health Administration
BERKAAK, O. A., Social Anthropology
BJERKHOLT, O., Economics
BIØRN, E., Economics
BLAKAR, R. M., Social Psychology
BRAMNESS, G., Economics
BRÅTEN, S. L., Sociology
CHRISTENSEN, T., Political Science
CHRISTIANSEN, V., Economics
DUCKERT, F., Psychology
EGEBERG, M., Political Science
ENERSTVEDT, R., Sociology
ERIKSEN, G. T. H., Social Anthropology
FAGERBERG, J., Socio-Economics
FØRSUND, F. R., Economics
GRENNESS, C. E., Psychology
GULLESTAD, S. E., Psychology
HAGTVET, B., Political Science
HANSEN, T., Political Science
HEIDAR, K., Political Science
HELLEVIK, O., Political Science
HELSTRUP, T., Psychology
HESSELBERG, J., Social Geography
HOEL, M. O., Economics
HOLDEN, S., Economics
HOVI, J., Political Science
HOWELL, S. L., Social Anthropology
HUNDEIDE, K., Psychology
HVEEM, H., Political Science
HYLLAND, AA., Economics
HAAVIND, H., Psychology
KALLAND, A., Social Anthropology
KNUTSEN, O., Political Science
KRAVDAL, Ø., Demographics
LAFFERTY, W. M., Political Science
LEIRA, A., Sociology
LIAN, A., Psychology
LIE, I. R., Psychology
LIPPE, A. L. VON DER, Psychology

LUND, S. E., Social Anthropology
MAGNUSSEN, S. J., Psychology
MALNES, R. S., Political Science
MASTEKAASA, A., Sociology
MEINICH, P., Economics
MELHUS, M., Social Anthropology
MIDGAARD, K. O., Political Science
MJØSET, L., Sociology
MOENE, K. O., Economics and Statistics
MYDSKE, P. K., Political Science
NORDBY, T., Political History
NYMOEN, R., Economics
OTNES, P., Sociology
PETERSEN, T., Sociology
RASCH, B. E., Political Science
REINVANG, I., Psychology
ROSE, L. E., Political Science
RUDIE, I., Social Anthropology
RUND, B. R., Psychology
RØDSETH, A., Economics
RØNNESTAD, H., Psychology
SCHIOLDBORG, P., Psychology
SCHWEDER, T., Statistics
SEIERSTAD, A., Mathematics
SKIRBEKK, S., Sociology
SKOG, O., Sociology
SMEDSLUND, J. E., Psychology
SMITH, L., Psychology
STARK, O., Economics
STEEN, A., Political Science
STIGUM, B. P., Economics and Statistics
STRAND, J., Economics
STRØM, S., Economics and Statistics
SUNDET, J. M., Psychology
SYDSÆTER, K., Mathematics
TALLE, A., Social Anthropology
TETZCHNER, S. V., Psychology
THONSTAD, T., Economics
TORGERSEN, S. O., Psychology
TSCHUDI, F., Psychology
TØRNQUIST, O., Political Science
UNDERDAL, A., Political Science
VISLIE, J., Economics
WIDERBERG, K., Sociology
WIKAN, U., Social Anthropology
WILLASSEN, Y., Economics
WOLD, A. H., Psychology
ØSTERUD, Ø., Conflict and Peace Research

Faculty of Education:

BEFRING, E., Special Education
BIRKEMO, A., Pedagogy
BRÅTEN, I.
BROCK-UTNE, B., Pedagogy
DALE, E. L., Pedagogy
DALEN, M., Special Education
ENGELSEN, B. U., General Didactics
GJESME, T., Pedagogy
GJONE, G., Pedagogy
HANDAL, G., Pedagogy
HAUGE, T. E., Pedagogy
HERTZBERG, F., Norwegian
HOËM, A., Pedagogy
JENSEN, K., Pedagogy
JORDELL, K. Ø., Pedagogy
LAUVÅS, P., Pedagogy
LIE, S., Pedagogy
LUND, T., Special Education
LØVLIE, L., Pedagogy
MARTINSEN, H., Psychology
NIELSEN, H. B., Pedagogy
NYGÅRD, R., Pedagogy
RUDBERG, M., Pedagogy
RYE, H., Special Education
SIMENSEN, A. M.
SJØBERG, S., Pedagogy
SKOGEN, K., Special Education
SÆTERSDAG, B., Special Education
TELLEVIK, J. M., Special Education
TJELDVOLL, A., Pedagogy
TVEIT, K., Pedagogy
ULVUND, S. E., Pedagogy
VEDELER, L., Special Education
VISLIE, L., Pedagogy
WIGGEN, G., Pedagogy
ØSTERUD, S., Pedagogy

UNIVERSITETET I TROMSØ
(University of Tromsø)

Breivika, 9037 Tromsø

Telephone: 776-44000
Fax: 776-44900

Founded 1968
State control
Academic year: August to June

Rector: Prof. TOVE BULL
University Director: HARALD OVERVAAG
Director of Studies: INGRID B. SALVESEN
Librarian: HELGE SALVESEN

Number of teachers: 854
Number of students: 6,277

DEANS

Faculty of Science: ODD GROPEN
School of Medicine: EGIL ARNESEN
Faculty of Social Sciences: GEORGES MIDRÉ
Faculty of Humanities: TORIL SWAN
Norwegian College of Fishery Science: BJØRN HERSOUG
Faculty of Law: (vacant)

Colleges of University Standing

ARKITEKTHØGSKOLEN I OSLO
(Oslo School of Architecture, Urbanism and Industrial Design)

POB 6768, St Olavs plass, 0130 Oslo

Telephone: 22-20-83-16
Fax: 22-11-19-70

Founded 1945
State control
Academic year: September to June

Rector: PER OLAF FJELD
Pro-Rector: HALINA DUNIN-WOYSETH
Chief Administrative Director: OLA STAVE
Librarian: SIDSEL MOUM

Library of 37,000 vols
Number of teachers: 53
Number of students: 337

PROFESSORS

APELAND, K., Building Technology
DAHLE, E., Architectural Design II
DIGERUD, J., Form and Technology
DUNIN-WOYSETH, H., Planning II
EGGEN, A., Building Technology
ELLEFSEN, K. O., Planning I
FARSTAD, P., Industrial Design
FJELD, P. O., Architectural Design III
KLEVEN, T., Architectural Design I
KNUTSEN, B. E., Architectural Design I
KYLLINGSTAD, R., Planning I
NORDIN, E., Planning II
SKJØNSBERG, T., Form and Design
THIIS-EVENSEN, T., Architectural Theory and History
TOSTRUP, E., Architectural Design I

HANDELSHØYSKOLEN BI
(Norwegian School of Management)

POB 580, 1301 Sandvika

Telephone: 67-57-05-00
Fax: 67-57-05-70

Founded 1943
Private control
Languages of instruction: Norwegian, English
Academic year: September to June

President: TORGE REVE
Provost: JAN GRUND
Vice-President for Graduate Programmes: OLAV DIGERNES
Librarian: BENTE R. ANDREASSEN

Number of teachers: 262
Number of students: 8,396 full-time, 6,727 part-time

Publications: *BI-forum* (quarterly), *Scandinavian Leadership* (annually).

HEADS OF DEPARTMENTS

Business Economics: Prof. PÅL E. KORSVOLD
Organization and Management: Prof. SVEIN S. ANDERSEN
Strategy, Business History and Foreign Languages: Dr ROLV-PEETER AMDAM
Marketing and Logistics: Assoc. Prof. CARL ARTHUR SOLBERG
Norwegian School of Marketing: FRED SELNES

PROFESSORS

ANDERSEN, E. S., Organization and Management
ANDERSEN, S. S., Organizational Management, Energy
BØHREN, Ø., Project and Decision Analysis
ELIASSEN, K., Public Management, European Studies
GJEMS-ONSTAD, O., Law
GRIPSRUD, G., Market Analysis, International Marketing
GRUND, J., Administration of Health Services, Public Policy
HØYER, R., Applied Information Technology
ISACHSEN, A. J., International Economy
JESSEN, S. A., Project Management
KAUFMANN, G., Organizational Psychology
KORSVOLD, P. E., Capital Markets, International Finance
KRIGER, M., Strategy
KRISTIANSLUND, I., Statistics and Quantitative Methods
LANGE, E., Business History
MOXNES, P., Organizational Psychology
NORENG, Ø., Petroleum Economics, Political Economics
OLAISEN, J., Service Management, Strategic Management of Information
PERSSON, K. G., Logistics
PRIESTLEY, R., Finance
RANDERS, J., Policy Analysis
RUUD, F., Accounting
SELNES, F., Marketing Strategy
SIREVÅG, T., Recent American Political History, Decision-Making
SKAAR, A. A., Law
SPILLING, O. R., Entrepreneurship
STABELL, C. B., Administrative and Cognitive Sciences
STI, A. D., Financial Management
SØRENSEN, R. J., Public Policy, Economy and Administration
WELCH, L., International Marketing
WENSTØP, F., Decision Analysis and Statistics

HØGSKOLEN I BODØ
(Bodø University College)

8002 Bodø

Telephone: 75-51-72-00
Fax: 75-51-74-57

Founded 1970
State control
Languages of instruction: Norwegian, English
Academic year: August to June

Rector: FRODE MELLEMVIK
Director: STIG FOSSUM
Registrar: MAGNE RASCH
Librarian: LARS BAUNA

Number of teachers: 270
Number of students: 3,600

DEANS

Bodø Graduate School of Business: SVENN ARE JENSSEN
Department of Education: ANNE GRETE SOLSTAD
Department of Nursing: HELGA FINSTAD
Department of Humanities: GJERT TØMMERÅS

Department of Social Sciences: ROLV LYNGSTAD
Department of Fisheries and Natural Sciences: MAGNE HAAKSTAD

ATTACHED INSTITUTE

Nordlandsforskning (Nordland Research Institute): Dir BENTE INGEBRIGTSEN.

HØGSKOLEN I STAVANGER
(Stavanger College)

POB 2557, Ullandhaug, 4004 Stavanger
Telephone: 51-83-10-00
Fax: 51-83-10-50
E-mail: postmottak@his.no

Founded 1994
State control
Academic year: August to June

Rector: ERIK LEIF ERIKSEN
Vice-Rector: ELISE KIPPERBERG
Director-General: INGER ØSTENSJØ
Librarian: (vacant)
Number of teachers: 400
Number of students: 6,100

DEANS

School of Science and Technology: OLE ANDREAS SONGE-MØLLER
School of Health and Social Work Education: ANNE NORHEIM
School of Humanities: INGE SÆRHEIM
School of Arts Education: PER DAHL
School of Teacher-Training: ODD ESKILDSEN
Norwegian School of Hotel Management: REIDAR J. MYKLETUN
School of Business Administration, Cultural and Social Studies: HELGE MAULAND

NORGES HANDELSHØYSKOLE
(Norwegian School of Economics and Business Administration)

Helleveien 30, 5035 Bergen-Sandviken
Telephone: 55-95-90-00
Fax: 55-95-91-00

Founded 1936
State control
Academic year: September to June

Rector: CARL J. NORSTRØM
Vice-Rector: ARNE KINSERDAL
Director: GEIR KJELL ANDERSLAND
Librarian: MAGNHILD B. AASE

Library of 244,000 vols, 2,500 periodicals
Number of teachers: 155
Number of students: 2,700

Publications: exchange list sent on request.

DEANS

Faculty of Business Administration: GUNNAR E. CHRISTENSEN
Faculty of Economics: JAN I. HAALAND
Faculty of Languages: EINAR HANSEN

PROFESSORS

Faculty of Business Administration:
BERGSTRAND, J., Economics
BJERKSUND, P., Finance
COLBJOERNSEN, T., Organization
ECKBO, E., Finance
EKERN, S., Finance
ELLING, J., Accounting
GJESDAL, F., Accounting
GJØLBERG, O., Finance
GOODERHAM, P. N., Organization
GRØNHAUG, K., Marketing
GRØNLAND, S., Data Processing
GUNDERSEN, F. F., Law
HANNESSON, R., Fishery Economics
HANSEN, T., Finance
JOHNSEN, A., Accounting
JOHNSEN, T., Finance
JØRESKOG, K. G., Marketing
JØRNSTEN, K., Finance
KIIL, B., Organization
KINSERDAL, A., Accounting
KNUDSEN, K., Organization
KOLLTVEIT, B., Organization
LANGHOLM, O., Accounting
LENSBERG, T., Finance
LILLESTØL, J., Mathematics
MATHIESEN, L., Economics
MCKEE, T. E., Accounting
MESSIER, W. T., Accounting
METHLIE, L., Data Processing
NORDHAUNG, O., Organization
NORSTRØM, C., Accounting
OLSON, O., Accounting
ROGNES, J. K., Organization
SCHILBRED, C., Finance
STENSLAND, G., Finance
SYVERSEN, J., Law
TROYE, S., Marketing
ÅSE, K., Finance
ØKSENDAL, B., Finance

Faculty of Economics:
BIVAND, R., Geography
BJORNDAL, T., Fishery Economics
GORDON, D., Economics
HAGEN, K. P., Economics
HODNE, F. F., Economic History
HOPE, E., Economics
HÅLAND, J. I., Economics
KLOVLAND, J. T., Economics
KYDLAND, F., Economics
MATHIESEN, L., Economics
NORDVIK, H. W., Economic History
NORMAN, V. D., Economics
SALVANES, K. G., Economics
SANDMO, A., Economics
SCHROTER, H. G., Economic History
SOLHAUG, T., Economic History
STEIGUM, E., Economics
VATNE, E., Geography
VENABLES, A., Economics

Faculty of Languages:
BREKKE, M., English
CHRISTENSEN, C., German
PICHT, H., Languages

ATTACHED INSTITUTES

Administrative Research Foundation: Dir PER I. STRAND.

Foundation for Research in Economics and Business Administration: Dir PER HEUM.

NORGES IDRETTSHØGSKOLE
(Norwegian University of Sport and Physical Education)

POB 4014, Ullevål Hageby, 0806 Oslo
Telephone: 22-18-56-00
Fax: 22-23-42-20

Founded 1968
State control
Academic year: August to June

Rector: PER WRIGHT
Director: THOR VOLLA
Librarian: ANNE-METTE VIBE

Library of 60,000 vols
Number of teachers: 60
Number of students: 520

HEADS OF INSTITUTES

Institute for Social Sciences and Sport (IFS): SIGMUND LOLAND.

Institute for Sport and Biology (IFIB): PER TVEIT.

NORGES LANDBRUKSHØGSKOLE
(Agricultural University of Norway)

POB 5003, 1432 Ås
Telephone: 64-94-75-00
Fax: 64-94-75-05

Founded 1859 as State College
Academic year: August to August

Rector: Prof. ROGER K. ABRAHAMSEN
Vice-Rector: Prof. JESSICA KATHLE
Managing Director: K. AKSNES
Registrar: TOVE BLYTT HOLMEN
Librarian: PAUL STRAY

Number of teachers: 250, including 80 full professors
Number of students: 2,050, plus 250 postgraduates

Publication: *NLH-nytt* (4 a year).

TEOLOGISKE MENIGHETSFAKULTET
(Norwegian Lutheran School of Theology)

Gydas Vei 4, POB 5144, Majorstua, 0302 Oslo
Telephone: 22-59-05-00
Fax: 22-69-18-90
E-mail: ekspedisjon@menfak.no

Founded 1907
Private control
Languages of instruction: Norwegian, English
Academic year: August to June

Principal Dean: TORLEIV AUSTAD
Director: FINN OLAV MYHRE
Librarian: ELNA STRANDHEIM

Number of teachers: 37
Number of students: 700

Publications: *Lys og Liv*, *Mellom Søsken*, *Ung Teologi*.

PROFESSORS

AUSTAD, T., Dogmatics and Moral Theology
ENGELSVIKEN, T., Missiology
HEIENE, G., Philosophy of Religion
HENRIKSEN, J. O., Ethics and Moral Theology
KVALBEIN, H., New Testament Exegesis
OFTESTAD, B. T., Church History
SANDNES, K. O., New Testament Exegesis
SKARSAUNE, O., Church History
SKJEVESLAND, O., Practical Theology
SÆBØ, M., Old Testament Exegesis
TÅNGBERG, A., Old Testament Exegesis
WIGEN, T., Philosophy of Religion
ØSTNOR, L., Ethics and Moral Theology

NORGES VETERINÄRHØGSKOLE
(Norwegian School of Veterinary Science)

POB 8146 Dep, 0033 Oslo
Telephone: 22-96-45-00
Fax: 22-56-57-04

Founded 1935
Academic year: August to December; January to June

Rector: HALLSTEIN GRØNSTØL
Director-General: KJELL GJAEVENES
Registrar: TOVE JENSSEN
Librarian: ANNE CATHRINE MUNTHE

Library of 77,000 vols
Number of teachers: 114
Number of students: 340

PROFESSORS

ALESTRØM, P., Biochemistry
ANDRESEN, Ø., Reproduction
AULIE, A., Physiology
AUNE, T., Food Hygiene
BERG, K. A., Reproduction
BJERKÅS, I., Anatomy
BORREBÆK, B., Biochemistry
FARSTAD, W., Reproduction
FRØSLIE, A., Forensic Medicine
GJERDE, B., Parasitology
GRANUM, P. E., Food Hygiene
GRØNDALEN, J., Small Animal Clinical Sciences
GRØNSTØL, H., Large Animal Clinical Sciences
HARBITZ, I., Biochemistry

INGEBRIGTSEN, K., Pharmacology and Toxicology
JONSSON, P., Bacteriology
KARLBERG, K., Reproduction
KROGDAHL, Å., Nutrition
LANDSVERK, T., Pathology
LARSEN, J. J., Microbiology
LØKEN, T., Large Animal Clinical Sciences
NAFSTAD, I., Pharmacology and Toxicology
PRESS, CH. MCL., Anatomy
REITE, O. B., Aquaculture and Fish Diseases
ROPSTAD, E., Reproduction
RØNNINGEN, K., Animal Genetics
SIMENSEN, E., Research Farm
SJAASTAD, Ø., Physiology
SMITH, A., Laboratory Animals
SØLI, N., Pharmacology and Toxicology
TEIGE, J., Pathology
TEVIK, A., Large Animal Clinical Sciences
ULVUND, M., Sheep and Goat Research
UNDERDAL, B., Food Hygiene
WALDELAND, H., Sheep and Goat Research
YNDESTAD, M., Food Hygiene
ØDEGAARD, S., Reproduction

Schools of Art and Music

Agder Musikkonservatorium (Agder Conservatory of Music): Kongensgt. 54, 4610 Kristiansand; tel. 38-14-19-00; fax 38-14-19-01.

Grieg Academy: University of Bergen, Lars Hillesgt. 3, 5015 Bergen; tel. 55-58-69-50; fax 55-58-69-60; f. 1905; education of musicians, music teachers and organists; 118 students.

Kunstakademiet i Trondheim: Innherredsveien 7, 7034 Trondheim; tel. 73-59-79-00; fax 73-59-79-20; f. 1946; 12 staff; 65 students; library of 5,500 vols; Pres. ERIK HØIEM; Registrar KARIN LØHRE NILSEN; publ. *Kitsch* (quarterly).

HEADS OF DEPARTMENTS

Drawing and Painting: JON ARNE MOGSTAD
Sculpture: DUBRAVKA SAMBOLEC
Graphics: OVE STOKSTAD
Intermedia: JEREMY WELSH
First Year: ANNE-KARIN FURUNES
Theory: HEGE FABER

Kunsthøgskolen i Bergen: Strømgaten 1, 5015 Bergen; tel. 55-55-06-00; fax 55-55-06-10; e-mail khib@khib.no; university-level courses in fine arts, photography, visual communication, interior and furniture design, ceramics and textiles; 40 teachers; 225 students; library of 12,000 vols, 195 periodicals; Rector KLAUS JUNG; Dir JOHAN A. HAARBERG; publ. *Uten tittel* (2 a year).

Musikkonservatoriet i Trondheim (Trondheim Conservatory of Music): 7034 Trondheim; tel. 73-59-73-00; fax 73-59-73-01.

Norges Musikkhøgskole (Norwegian State Academy of Music): POB 5190, Majorstua, 0302 Oslo; tel. 23-36-70-00; fax 23-36-70-01; e-mail mh@nmh.no; f. 1973, merged with Eastern Norway Conservatory of Music 1996; libraries with 70,000 books and items of sheet music, 24,000 sound recordings; 170 teachers; 465 students; Principal (vacant).

Statens Kunstakademi (National Academy of Fine Arts): St. Olavs gate 32, 0166 Oslo 1; tel. 22-20-01-50; fax 22-20-05-73; f. 1909; university-level courses in painting, sculpture and printmaking; 17 teachers; 105 students; library of 13,000 vols, 100 periodicals; Rector JAN ÅKE PETTERSSON.

Statens Håndverks- og Kunstindustriskole (National College of Art and Design): Ullevålsv. 5, 0165 Oslo; tel. 22-20-12-35; fax 22-11-14-96; f. 1818; includes departments of ceramics, fashion and costume design, interior architecture and furniture design, metal and jewelry, painting and textile design; library of 50,000 vols; 70 teachers; 400 students; Rector DAG HOFSETH.

Tromsø College Music Conservatory: Krognessvn. 33, 9005 Tromsø; tel. 77-66-03-04; fax 77-61-88-99; f. 1971; Dean NIELS ESKILD JOHANSEN; Dir KJETIL SOLVIK.

OMAN

Learned Societies

HISTORY, GEOGRAPHY AND ARCHAEOLOGY

Historical Association of Oman: POB 3941, 112 Ruwi; tel. 795826; fax 601270; f. 1971; study of history, monuments and natural history of Oman; organizes lectures and field trips to places of interest; library of 400 vols; 450 mems; Pres. KAMAL ABDULREDHA SULTAN.

Research Institutes

AGRICULTURE, FISHERIES AND VETERINARY SCIENCE

Directorate of Water Resources Research: c/o Ministry of Environment and Water Resources, POB 323, Muscat; activities include hydrological surveys, water conservation, etc.

Marine Sciences and Fisheries Centre: c/o Ministry of Agriculture and Fisheries, POB 467, Muscat; f. 1987; conservation, ecology, oceanography, biological research, food technology; includes a library and aquarium.

Libraries and Archives

Bowshar

Central Medical Library: Ministry of Health – Royal Hospital, POB 1331, Seeb, 111 Bowshar; tel 595971 ext. 454; telex 5465; fax 594247; 7,000 vols, 122 periodicals; special collections: Ministry of Health reports, health reports, WHO collections; Senior Librarian K. W. A. JAYAWARDANE.

Muscat

Archives of the Directorate General of Heritage: Ministry of National Heritage and Culture, POB 668, Muscat; f. 1976; 5,000 MSS, 50,000 archives; Dir-Gen. MOHAMMED SAID AL-WOHAIBI.

Museums and Art Galleries

Muscat

Oman Natural History Museum (ONHM): Ministry of National Heritage and Culture, POB 668, Muscat 113; tel. 605400; fax 602735; f. 1983; includes the National Herbarium of Oman and the National Shell and Coral Collection, and the Insect and Osteological Collections.

Qurm

Qurm Museum: c/o Ministry of National Heritage and Culture, POB 668, Muscat; historical.

Ruwi

National Museum at Ruwi: c/o Ministry of National Heritage and Culture, POB 668, Muscat; historical.

University

SULTAN QABOOS UNIVERSITY

POB 50, 123 Al-Khod
Telephone: 513333
Fax: 513254

Founded 1985; opened 1986
Academic Year: September to May

Vice-Chancellor: H. E. YAHYA BIN MAHFOUD AL-MANTHERY
Secretary-General: H. E. HAMED BIN SULAIMAN AL-GHARIBI
Library Director: MUHAMMAD HAMAD AL-AMRY

Library of 95,000 vols
Number of teachers: 425
Number of students: 5,000

DEANS

College of Science: Prof. ANTON MCLACHLAN
College of Education and Islamic Sciences: Prof. ROUSHDY AHMED AL-TOIEMAH
College of Medicine: Prof. GILBERT D. HESELTINE
College of Commerce and Economics: Prof. QUENTIN N. GERBER
College of Engineering: Prof. JOHN A. TURNER
College of Agriculture: Prof. CHRISTOPHER D. LU
College of Arts: Prof. GAD MOHAMED TAHA MAHMOUD

DIRECTORS

Language Centre: BILQUIO AL-KHABOURI
Centre of Educational Technology: ALLAN J. BURREL
Computer Centre: Dr HAIDER ALI RAMADAN

Colleges

Institute of Health Sciences: POB 3720, 112 Ruwi, Muscat; tel. 560085; telex 5465; fax 560384; f. 1982; under the Ministry of Health; library of 5,000 vols; 36 teachers; 244 students; Dean ALYA MOHAMMED MUSALLEM AL-RAWAHY, publ. *Quarterly Medical News Journal*.

Institute of Public Administration: POB 1994, Ruwi 112; tel. 600205; fax 602066; f. 1977; training, research and consultancy; library of 12,000 Arabic vols, 3,800 foreign; 70 Arabic periodicals, 5 foreign; 1,000 students per year attend courses; 57 staff; Dir-Gen. SULEIMAN BIN HILAL AL-ALAWI; publ. *Al-Edari* (4 a year).

Muscat Technical Industrial College: POB 3845, 112 Ruwi; tel. 698280; f. 1984; library of 10,000 vols; 50 teachers, 500 students; Dir Dr MUNEER BIN SULTAN AL-MASKERY.

HEADS OF DEPARTMENTS

Business Studies: Dr AHMED ABDULLAH EL OBEID
General Studies: Dr WALTER JAMES
Computing and Maths: RAJINDER VIRK (acting)
Electrical Engineering: JOHN MCKAIN
Construction Engineering: GWYNFOR WILLIAMS
Laboratory Science: DR FAZAL QURAISHI
Mechanical Engineering: NASSER AL-KHAROUSI (acting)
Management and Secretarial: WALEED RAMADHAN

Vocational Training Centre: POB 3123, Ruwi; f. 1968; attached to the Ministry of Labour and Vocational Training; technical and commercial diploma courses; 100 staff, 450 full-time, 400 part-time students; Principal HILAL BIN MOHAMMED AL-ADAWI.

PAKISTAN

Learned Societies

GENERAL

Quaid-i-Azam Academy: 297 M. A. Jinnah Rd, Karachi 74800; tel. (21) 7218184; fax (21) 7219175; f. 1976; research on Quaid-i-Azam Mohammad Ali Jinnah, on the historical background (including cultural, religious, literary, linguistic, social, economic and political aspects) of the Pakistan Movement, and various aspects of Pakistan; gives scholarships and professorships; awards Quaid-i-Azam Academic and Literary Prizes for scholarly works; library of 20,000 vols; photostat vols of Archives of Freedom Movement; photostat files of Quaid-i-Azam Papers; 52 photostat vols of Shamsul Hasan collections, Sadar Abdur Rab Nishtar collections, 2,000 microfilms of various pre-partition newspapers and other collections; publs bibliographies, research studies, biographies, monographs and documents (in English, Urdu and dialects); Dir Dr MUHAMMAD ALI SIDDIQUI.

ARCHITECTURE AND TOWN PLANNING

Pakistan Council of Architects and Town Planners: E-6 Fourth Gizri St, Defence Housing Authority, Karachi 46; tel. 537416; f. 1983; all architects and town planners in Pakistan are mems by law; Chair. Mrs YASMEEN LARI.

BIBLIOGRAPHY, LIBRARY SCIENCE AND MUSEOLOGY

Library Promotion Bureau: Karachi University Campus, POB 8421, Karachi 75270; f. 1965; aims to promote librarianship in Pakistan; co-ordinates with all the other organizations engaged in promotional activities; publs reference books, books on library and information science, text books on library science, bibliographies, directories, etc.; Pres. M. ADIL USMANI; Sec.-Gen. Dr NASIM FATIMA; publ. *Pakistan Library Bulletin*.

National Book Foundation: 6-Mauve Area, G-8/4, Taleemi Chowk, Islamabad; tel. (51) 256795; fax (51) 264283; e-mail nbf@paknet2.ptc.pk; f. 1972; aims to make books available at moderate prices, promotes writing, research and publication, promotes literacy, organizes book festivals and exhibitions, operates book promotion schemes, publishes Braille books; Man. Dir Dr AHMAD FARAZ; Sec. MUHAMMAD ASLAM RAO; publ. *Kitab* (in English and Urdu).

Pakistan Library Association: c/o Pakistan Institute of Development Economics, University Campus, POB 1091, Islamabad; to advance the cause of the library movement throughout Pakistan; 1,329 mems; Pres. AZMAT ULLAH BHATTI; Sec.-Gen. HAFIZ KHUBAIB AHMAD; publs *Journal* (2 a year), *Newsletter* (every 2 months), *Conference Proceedings* (annually).

Pakistan Museum Association: c/o National Museum, Burns Garden, Karachi; tel. 211341; f. 1949; objects: to advance and improve the work of museums in Pakistan; establish close contact with universities, educational and services institutions; open new museums in important towns in Pakistan; provide facilities for the training of curators; establish an archaeological laboratory; and to popularize museum movement in the country by the following means: (1) sending circulating exhibitions, (2) guided tours, (3) delivering popular lectures and publishing literature on Pakistan museums; Pres. Dr F. A. KHAN; Gen. Sec. MUHAMMAD ABDUL HALEEM; publs *Museums Journal of Pakistan* (2 a year), *Museum Studies*.

ECONOMICS, LAW AND POLITICS

Institute of Cost and Management Accountants of Pakistan: Soldier Bazaar, POB 7284, Karachi 3; tel. 719907; telex 2733; f. 1951; regulates Management Accountancy profession in Pakistan and arranges professional development programmes; 326 Fellows, 571 Assoc. Mems; library of 32,000 vols; Exec. Dir Z. H. SUBZWARI; publs *Students' Handbook* (annually), *Industrial Accountant* (quarterly), *ICMAP News Letter*, *Professional Information Bulletin* (every 2 months), *Shoaib Memorial Lecture* (every 2 years), *Management Accountants Conference Proceedings* (every 3 years).

Pakistan Institute of International Affairs: Aiwan-e-Sadar Rd, POB 1447, Karachi 74200; tel. 5682891; f. 1947 to study international affairs and to promote the scientific study of international politics, Pakistan foreign policy, economics and jurisprudence; library: see Libraries; 650 mems; Chair. FATEHYAB ALI KHAN; Sec. Dr SYED ADIL HUSAIN; publs *Pakistan Horizon* (quarterly), books and monographs.

EDUCATION

Punjab Bureau of Education: 15A Mahmud Ghaznavi Rd, Lahore 6; tel. 66685; f. 1958, clearing house for information on education of all aspects and levels, at home and abroad; Documentation Section, Statistical Section, Publication Section and Research Section; library of 10,000 vols and periodicals; Dir. SAJJAD HUSSAIN NAQVI; publs *Educational Statistics* (annually), bibliographies, directories.

University Grants Commission: Sector H/9, Islamabad; tel. (51) 448371; f. 1974 for the promotion and co-ordination of university education, the maintenance of standards of teaching, examinations and research in universities, and the orientation of university courses to national needs; library of 41,000 vols, 232 periodicals; Chair. Capt. U. A. G. ISANI; publs *Higher Education News* (4 a year), *Statistics on Higher Education in Pakistan, Who's Who in Universities of Pakistan, Handbook of Universities of Pakistan, Handbook of Centres of Excellence and Advanced Studies, A Guide to Equivalence of Qualification* (irregular), *Annual Reports*.

FINE AND PERFORMING ARTS

Arts Council of Pakistan: M. R. Kayani Rd, Karachi; tel. 2635108; f. 1956 to foster the development of fine arts and crafts, drama, music, and to promote the study and appreciation thereof by sponsoring exhibitions, lectures, etc.; 1,850 mems; Pres. ZIA-UL-ISLAM; Dir SHAMIM ALAM; Sec. Mrs QUDSIA AKBAR.

Lok Virsa (National Institute of Folk and Traditional Heritage): POB 1184, Islamabad; tel. 823883; telex 54468; fax 813756; f. 1974; museum, publishing house, media centre, sound archive, library of over 20,000 vols on Pakistan culture, ethnology, folklore; films, videotapes, cassettes and publications on folk heritage and culture; Exec. Dir UXI MUFTI.

Music Foundation of Pakistan: Buch Terrace, Preedy St, Karachi 74400; tel. 7722743; f. 1964 to serve the cause of classical music through academic instruction, promote it by means of concerts, and foster an international exchange of ideas; Dir FEROSE BUCHOME.

HISTORY, GEOGRAPHY AND ARCHAEOLOGY

Department of Archaeology & Museums: 27-A, Central Union Commercial, Shaheed-e-Millat Rd, Karachi; tel. 430638; f. 1947; to explore and scientifically conserve the archaeological, historical and cultural wealth of the country; to develop a documentary and published record; and exhibit material in the museums for the purpose of educational research and amusement; Dir-Gen. Dr MOHAMMAD RAFIQUE MUGHAL; publ. *Pakistan Archaeology* (annually).

Pakistan Historical Society: 30 New Karachi Co-operative Housing Society, Karachi 5; tel. 410847; f. 1951; historical studies and research, particularly history of Islam and the Sub-continent; library of 7,709 vols; Pres. HAKIM MOHAMMED SAID; Gen. Sec. ANSAR ZAHID KHAN; publs *Journal* (quarterly), monographs, research studies.

LANGUAGE AND LITERATURE

Anjuman Taraqqi-e-Urdu Pakistan: D-159, Block 7, Gulshan-e-Iqbal, Karachi 75300; tel. 7724023; f. 1903 in pre-partition India, 1948 in Pakistan; promotion of the Urdu language and literature; preparing a 6-volume bibliography of Urdu books, in collaboration with Unesco; lending library of 20,000 vols, research library of 26,000 vols and 4,000 MSS; Pres. AFTAB AHMED KHAN; Hon. Sec. JAMILUDDIN A'ALI; publs *Urdu* (quarterly), *Qaumi Zaban* (monthly).

Baluchi Academy: Mekran House, Sariab Rd, Quetta, Baluchistan; tel. 22248; f. 1961 to promote Baluchi language and literature; publishes books on Baluchi history, poetry, culture, folk stories, and a Baluchi/Urdu dictionary and encyclopaedia; library of 35,000 vols; 37 mems; Chair. BASHIR AHMED BALUCH; Gen. Sec. AYUB BALUCH.

Idarah-i-Yadgar-i-Ghalib: POB 2268, Nazimabad 2, Karachi 18; tel. 464591; f. 1968; holds literary meetings; helps with research and university studies; library of 28,000 vols, 60,000 periodicals in Urdu; Sec.-Gen. MUKHTAR ZAMAN; Sec. RAANA FAROOQI.

Institute of Islamic Culture: 2 Club Rd, Lahore 3; tel. 636127; f. 1950; publications on Islamic subjects in English and Urdu; Dir Dr RASHID AHMAD JULLUNDHRI; publ. *Al-Ma'arif* (quarterly, in Urdu).

Iqbal Academy: POB 1308, GPO, Lahore; tel. (42) 6314510; fax (42) 6314496; e-mail dhikr.@lhr.infolink.net.pk; f. 1951; publishes books and pamphlets on Dr Allama Iqbal and maintains a special Iqbal research library (30,000 vols); Pres. Federal Minister for Culture, Sports, Tourism and Youth Affairs; Dir MUHAMMAD SUHEYL UMAR; publs *Iqbal Review* (2 a year, in English), *Iqbaliat* (2 a year in Urdu, annually in Arabic, Turkish and Farsi).

National Language Authority: Pitras Bukhari Rd, H-8/4, Islamabad; tel. (51) 449463; fax (51) 446883; f. 1979; promotes Urdu as the national, official, judicial and instructional language of Pakistan; organizes seminars and conferences; offers courses; develops Urdu terminology in various disciplines; compiles dictionaries; library of 25,000 vols; Chair. Dr IFTIKHAR ARIF; publ. *Akhbar-e-Urdu* (monthly).

Pakistan Academy of Letters: H-8/1, Islamabad; tel. 254638; fax 251198; f. 1976; promotion of literary works; determination of research priorities in literature; evaluation of the performance of literary bodies; setting up of Bureau of Translation; introduction of Pakistani literature to foreign readers; organizes seminars on literary and academic issues; advises the Government on international literary gatherings; nominates recipients for various literary awards and distinctions; provides financial assistance to scholars; Chair. NAZIR NAJI; Dir-Gen. SALEEM KAYANI; publs *Adbiat* (quarterly), *Academy* (monthly), *Pakistani Literature* (2 a year).

Pakistan Writers Guild: 11 Abbok Rd, Anarkali, Lahore; f. 1959; 4 regional offices; promotes authorship, dispenses literary prizes, concerned with welfare of writers; Sec.-Gen. MOHAMED TUFAIL; publ. *Ham Qalam* (monthly).

Panjabi Adabi Academy: 13-G, Model Town, Lahore 14; tel. 850608; f. 1957; publishes literary, historical and scientific works concerned with Panjab; 18,000 vols; Chair. Dr MUHAMMAD BAQIR.

Pashto Academy: University of Peshawar, Peshawar; tel. 41009; f. 1955; research into Pashto language and literature, history, art and culture; a research cell for the study of the life and works of Khushal Khan Khattak and his contemporaries; research library; Dir Prof. Dr RAJ WALI SHAH KHATTAK.

Shah Waliullah Academy: Hyderabad; tel. 24154; f. 1963; to propagate the philosophy of Shah Waliullah; library of his works; Dir ALLAMA GHULAM MUSTAFA QASMI; publ. *Al-Rahim* (monthly in Sindhi), *Alwali* (monthly in Urdu).

Sindhi Adabi Board: POB 12, Hyderabad, Sindh; tel. 771276; f. 1951; autonomous literary and cultural institution set up by the government to foster the language, literature and culture of the Sindh region; publishes books in English, Sindhi, Urdu, Persian and Arabic; library of 7,500 vols in these 5 languages, and 324 rare MSS; Chair. MUHAMMAD IBRAHIM JOYO; Sec. GHULAM RABBANI AGRO; publs *Mehran* (quarterly in Sindhi), *Gul Phul* (children's monthly in Sindhi), *Sartyoon* (women's monthly in Sindhi).

Urdu Academy: 33C Model Town 'A', Bahawalpur; tel. 2381; f. 1959 to develop Urdu literature and language; publishes books in English and Urdu; Sec. MASUD HASSAN SHIHAB; publ. *Az-Zubair* (Urdu, quarterly).

Urdu Dictionary Board: ST-18/A, Block 5, Gulshan-e-Iqbal, Off Karachi University Rd, Karachi 47; f. 1958 by Government of Pakistan; projects include a comprehensive, 20-vol. Urdu Dictionary; Chair. Federal Minister for Education; Editor-in-Chief and Sec. Dr FARMAN FATEHPURI.

Urdu Science Board: 299 Upper Mall, Lahore; tel. 5758674; f. 1962; aims to remove deficiencies in Urdu in technologies, natural and social sciences so that it can be used as the medium of instruction in higher education, and to co-ordinate the work of the other organizations engaged in similar work; to prepare standard dictionaries of scientific and technical terms; library of 10,000 vols; Chair. Federal Minister of Education; Dir Gen. ZAFAR IQBAL.

MEDICINE

College of Physicians and Surgeons, Pakistan: 7th Central St, Defence Housing Authority, Karachi 75500; tel. 5892801; fax 5887513; f. 1962 by government ordinance; aims to promote specialist practice of medicine, surgery and gynaecology and allied disciplines by means of improvement in hospital teaching and methods; arranges postgraduate medical, surgical and other specialist training; provides for medical research and organizes scientific conferences for Pakistani and foreign medical experts; awards diplomas of MCPS and FCPS; 3,876 Members (MCPS), 1,768 Fellows (FCPS); library of 7,000 vols, 106 periodicals; Pres. Prof. IJAZ AHSAN; Registrar Prof. Z. K. KAZI; Sec. SAGHIR AHMED; publ. *JCPSP*.

Pakistan Academy of Medical Sciences: 238 Jinnah Colony, Faisalabad; tel. 411-31795; f. 1975 for the advancement of medical sciences and arts, for the recognition of merit and scholarly achievement, for co-operation among professionals and with other similar orgs; awards annual Gold Medal and holds annual PAMS Lecture; 56 Fellows; Pres. Prof. KHALID J. AWAN; Sec.-Gen. IFTIKHAR A. MALIK; publs *Bulletin* (2 a year), *Pakistan Journal of Ophthalmology* (quarterly).

Pakistan Medical Association: PMA House, Garden Rd, POB 7267, Karachi 3; tel. 714632; Pres. IFTIKHAR AHMAD: Sec.-Gen. Dr HAROON AHMED.

NATURAL SCIENCES

General

Pakistan Academy of Sciences: 3 Constitution Ave, G-5, Islamabad; f. 1953; to promote research in pure and applied sciences, establish and maintain libraries; awards grants and fellowships and gold medals; 60 fellows; Pres. Dr A. Q. KHAN; Sec.-Gen. Prof. IFTIKHAR AHMAD MALIK; publs *Proceedings* (quarterly), *Proceedings of Symposia* (irregular), *Monographs* (irregular).

Pakistan Association for the Advancement of Science: 273-N, Model Town, Lahore; f. 1947 for the promotion of science in all its branches, including its application to practical problems and research; organizes national and international conferences; 1,500 mems; Pres. Prof. Dr AHMAD NADEEM SHERI; Gen. Sec. Dr MUHAMMAD SALEEM CHAUDHRY; publs *Pakistan Journal of Science, Pakistan Journal of Scientific Research*.

Scientific Society of Pakistan: Karachi University Campus, Karachi 32; tel. 463144; f. 1954 to promote and popularise science through the national language (Urdu); 3,500 mems; Pres. Dr SYED IRTIFAQ ALI; Sec. Maj. (retd) AFTAB HASAN; publs *Jadeed Science* (every 2 months), *Science Bachchon Key Liye* (monthly), *Science Nama* (fortnightly), *Proceedings of Annual Science Conferences* (all in Urdu).

PHILOSOPHY AND PSYCHOLOGY

Pakistan Philosophical Congress: Dept of Philosophy, University of the Punjab, New Campus, Lahore 20; tel. 5863984; f. 1954 for the promotion of philosophical studies; Pres. Dr ABDUL KHALIQ; Sec. Dr NAEEM AHMAD; publs *Annual Proceedings, Pakistan Philosophical Journal* (1 a year).

RELIGION, SOCIOLOGY AND ANTHROPOLOGY

Hamdard Foundation: Hamdard Centre, Nazimabad, Karachi 74600; tel. 6616001; telex 29370; fax 6611755; e-mail hlpak@paknet3.ptc.pk; f. 1953; conferences, seminars on religion (Islam), medicine, scholarships, charities, etc.; library: see Libraries; Pres. HAKIM MOHAMMED SAID; publs *Akhbar-ur-Tib* (fortnightly), *Hamdard-i-Sehat, Hamdard Naunehal* (monthly), *Hamdard Islamicus, Hamdard Medicus* (quarterly).

Jamiyat-ul-Falah: Akbar Rd, Saddar, POB 7141, Karachi 74400; tel. 721394; f. 1950 to work for the exposition, propagation and implementation of Islam; Tamizuddin Khan Memorial Library (8,000 vols), Quran, Tafseer, Hadees, and Seerat collection; Falah Islamic Centre, Falah Social Service Centre, Falah Majlis-e-Adab (literary society), Falah Pakistan Studies Centre, Falah Muslim World Studies Centre, Falah Science Studies Centre; Sec.-Gen. SHAMSUDDIN KHALID AHMED; publ. *Voice of Islam* (English, monthly).

Karachi Theosophical Society: Jamshed Memorial Hall, M. A. Jinnah Rd, Karachi 1; tel. 721275; f. 1896; 124 mems; activities include study of comparative religion, philosophy and science; investigation of unexplained laws of nature; library of 20,000 vols and reading room; Pres. G. K. MINWALLA; Gen.-Sec. A. HOODBHOY; publ. *Theosophy in Karachi* (monthly).

Society for the Preservation of Muslim Heritage: E6 Fourth Gizri Street, Karachi 75500; tel. 537521; f. 1981; Sec. SUHAIL ZAHEER LARI.

TECHNOLOGY

Institution of Electrical and Electronics Engineers Pakistan: 4 Lawrence Rd, Lahore; tel. 6305289; f. 1969; lectures, seminars and publications on electrical and electronic telecommunication engineering; 2,300 corporate mems, 2,150, individual mems; library of 2,050 vols, 6,000 periodicals; Pres. BASHIR AHMAD ABBASI; publs *Quarterly Electrical Journal, Newsletter, The Electrical Engineer* (monthly).

Institution of Engineers (Pakistan): IEP HQ Bldg, Engineering Centre, IEP Roundabout, Gulberg III, Lahore; tel. (42) 5756974; fax (42) 5759449.

Pakistan Concrete Institute: 11 Bambino Chambers, Garden Rd, Karachi 0310; Pres. UMAR MUNSHI; Sec. REHMAN AKHTAR.

Research Institutes

AGRICULTURE, FISHERIES AND VETERINARY SCIENCE

Central Cotton Research Institute: Old Shujabad Rd, POB 572, Multan; tel. (61) 545361; fax (61) 75153; e-mail ccri@infolink.net.pk; f. 1970; divisions: agronomy, breeding and genetics, cytogenetics, physiology/chemistry, fibre technology, transfer of technology, plant pathology, statistics and agricultural engineering; research on cotton plant; processing of cotton varieties and their release for general cultivation in the country; disease and pest resistance to pesticides, nutrition, irrigation and environmental interactions; library of 8,000 vols; Dir Dr ZAHOOR AHMAD; publ. *The Pakistan Cottons*.

Central Cotton Research Institute: Sakrand 67210, Nawabshah, Sindh; tel. (2234) 356; fax (2234) 456; f. 1976; divisions: agronomy, breeding and genetics, cytogenetics, entomology, pathology, physiology, fibre technology, statistics, transfer of technology; research on cotton plant; processing of cotton varieties and their release for general cultivation in the province; library of 1,050 vols; Dir Dr BARKAT ALI SOOMRO.

Pakistan Agricultural Research Council: POB 1031, Islamabad; tel. 9203966; telex 5604; fax 9202968; f. 1978; organizes, co-ordinates and promotes scientific research in agricultural sciences; library of 21,000 vols, 1,166 periodicals; Dr MUHAMMAD AKBAR; publs *Pakistan Journal of Agricultural Research* (quarterly), *Progressive Farming* (every 2 months), *Annual Report, PARC News* (monthly), *Pakistan Journal of Agricultural Social Sciences* (2 a year).

Pakistan Forest Institute: Peshawar, NWFP; f. 1947; library: see Libraries; Forestry Museum; two training courses leading to BSc and MSc in Forestry; Dir-Gen. Dr K. M. SIDDIQUI; publ. *Pakistan Journal of Forestry.*

Punjab Veterinary Research Institute: Ghazi Rd, Lahore Cantt.; tel. 370006; f. 1963; objects: to promote and improve the development of the livestock industry and control diseases; production of vaccines, research on animal health problems; disease diagnosis and investigation; development of improved laboratory techniques.

Rice Research Institute: Dokri, Sindh; tel. 60877; f. 1938; research on various aspects of rice incl. varietal improvement, control of insect pests, diseases and weeds, grain quality; library of 2,500 vols, 900 periodicals.

Veterinary Research Institute: Charsadda Rd, POB 367, Peshawar; tel. 76296; f. 1949; Dir M. Y. ANSARI.

ECONOMICS, LAW AND POLITICS

Applied Economics Research Centre: University of Karachi, Karachi 75270; tel. 474749; fax 4969729; f. 1974; policy-orientated quantitative research on problems in applied economics; 190 mems; library of 35,000 vols; Dir SHAHIDI WIZARAT, publs *Discussion Paper Series, Research Report Series, Pakistan Journal of Applied Economics* (2 a year).

Centre for South Asian Studies: University of the Punjab, Quaid-i-Azam Campus, Lahore 54590; tel. (42) 5864014; fax (42) 5867206; f. 1973; interdisciplinary research on South Asia, including economics, politics, sociology, foreign affairs, and other social developments of the area; programme includes data collection and analysis; sponsors seminars; library of 12,000 vols; Dir Dr SARFARAZ HUSSAIN MIRZA publ. *South Asian Studies* (2 a year, English).

Federal Bureau of Statistics: Statistics Division, Government of Pakistan, SLIC Building No. 5, China Chowk, Islamabad; tel. 9208489; fax 9203233; f. 1950; studies prices, foreign trade, national accounts, industry, agriculture, labour, business and communication, social statistics, demography, data processing, rural development, etc.; library of 4,500 vols, 41,000 periodicals; Dir-Gen. Dr NOOR MUHAMMAD LARIK; publs *Catalogue of Publications, Monthly Statistical Bulletin, Pakistan Statistical Yearbook* (annually), *Statistical Pocket Book of Pakistan* (annually), *Newsletter* (monthly), *Research Review* (quarterly), *Macro Economic Indicators of Pakistan* (quarterly), *National Accounts* (annually), *Census of Manufacturing Industries* (annually).

Institute of Strategic Studies: Sector F-5/2, Islamabad; tel. (51) 9204423; fax (51) 9204658; e-mail strategy@paknet2.ptc.pk; f. 1973; provides a broad-based and informed public understanding of vital strategic and allied issues affecting Pakistan and the international community at large; library of 11,000 vols and 70 foreign periodicals; Dir-Gen. Ambassador (retd) MOHAMMED WALIULLA KHAN KHAISHGI; publs *Strategic Studies* (quarterly).

National Institute of Public Administration: NIPA, 190 Scotch-Corner, Upper Mall, Lahore; tel. 464408; f. 1962; administrative training for management; research in government administration; in-service training courses; library of 30,000 vols; Dir ASLAM IQBAL; publ. *Public Administration Review* (2 a year).

Pakistan Economic Research Institute (PERI): 24 Mianmir Rd, Upper Mall Scheme, Lahore 15; f. 1955 to undertake socio-economic investigations and co-ordinate research in economic problems of Pakistan; to collect, compile and interpret statistical data; to publish the results and findings of investigations; Dir AZIZ A. ANWAR; Sec. A. R. ARSHAD; publs Research Papers.

Pakistan Institute of Development Economics: POB 1091, Islamabad 44000; tel. (51) 9206610; fax (51) 9210886; e-mail arshad@pide.sdnpk.undp.org.pk; f. 1957 for fundamental research on development economics and Islamic economics in general, and on Pakistan's economic problems in particular; also provides in-service training in economic analysis, research methods and project evaluation; library of 31,000 vols, 290 current periodicals, 6,200 microfiches, 17,000 research papers and reports; Dir Dr SARFRAZ KHAN QURESHI; Sec. ABDUL HAMEED; publs *Pakistan Development Review* (quarterly), *PIDE Tidings* (3 a year).

HISTORY, GEOGRAPHY AND ARCHAEOLOGY

National Institute of Historical and Cultural Research: 102 Fazlul Haq Rd, POB 1230, Islamabad; tel. 251023; f. 1973, name changed 1983; promotes studies on the history and culture of South Asian Muslims, and the genesis and growth of the Muslim freedom movement; publishes research studies in history and culture, bibliographies, indices etc.; library of 17,000 vols, a collection of historical records, old newspapers, journals, photocopies of rare material, microfilms, microfiches; Dir Dr S. M. ZAMAN; publs *Pakistan Journal of History and Culture* (2 a year), *Majallah-i-Tarikh wa Thaqafat* (2 a year, in Urdu).

Research Society of Pakistan: University of the Punjab Library, Old Campus, Lahore; tel. 7322542; f. 1963 to organize research in national affairs, particularly in the national struggle that led to the establishment of Pakistan; research on cultural, political, literary, linguistic, economic, historical, topographical and archaeological features of Pakistan; reference library of 12,000 vols; publishes research results; Pres. Dr KHALID HAMEED SHEIKH; Dir Dr A. SHAKOOR AHSAN; publ. *Journal* (quarterly).

MEDICINE

Cancer Research Institute: Dept and Institute of Radiotherapy, Jinnah Post-graduate Medical Centre, Karachi 75510; f. 1954.

Pakistan Medical Research Council: 162/0/III, Minhas House, PECHS, Karachi 29; tel. 416522; f. 1953; reconstituted 1962; aims to promote research in fields of medicine and public health, to disseminate and arrange for utilization of this research, and to establish liaison with national and international organizations; 19 mems; Chair. Lt Gen. M. A. Z. MOHYDIN; Exec. Dir Dr MUHAMMAD AKRAM PERVAIZ; publs *Pakistan Journal of Medical Research* (quarterly), monographs.

NATURAL SCIENCES

General

Fazi-i-Omar Research Institute: Rabwah, District Jhang; tel. (4524) 612; f. 1946; objects: to promote the study of science and the development of industries in the country; library of 6,000 vols; Dir MUBARAK MUSLEH-UD-DIN AHMAD.

Pakistan Council for Science and Technology: Off Constitution Avenue, Bank Road, Sector G-5/2, Islamabad; tel. 814416; fax: 825171; f. 1961; advises the Govt on science policy, reviews the progress of scientific research in the country, maintains liaison between national scientific efforts and the overall planning process; maintains a data bank, carries out futuristic and scientometric studies; library of 1,200 vols; Chair. Dr SHAFIQ AHMAD KHAN; Sec. Dr S. T. K. NAIM; publs *Science, Technology and Development* (every 2 months), *Science and Technology in the Islamic World* (quarterly) and numerous reports.

Pakistan Council of Scientific and Industrial Research (PCSIR): Press Centre, Shahrah-e-Kamal Ataturk, Karachi 74200; tel. 2628763; telex 24725; fax 2636704; f. 1953; promotes scientific and industrial research and its applications to the development of the national industries and the utilization of the natural resources of the country; Scientific Information Centre: see Libraries and Archives; Chair. Dr A. Q. ANSARI; Sec. Dr R. B. QADRI; publs *Pakistan Journal of Scientific and Industrial Research* (monthly), *PCSIR News Bulletin* (monthly).

Attached research institutes:

PCSIR Laboratories Complex: off University Rd, Karachi; tel. 4967609; fax 4967608; fish technology, pharmaceuticals, applied physics, paints, plastics, building materials, chemical engineering; rural technology and water decontamination; library of 45,000 vols, 900 journals and periodicals; Dir-Gen. Dr A. H. K. YOUSUFZAI.

PCSIR Laboratories: Jamrud Rd, POB Peshawar University, Peshawar; tel. 41272; fax 41476; indigenous drugs, fruit technology, minerals evaluation, wool and rural technology, process design and fabrication divisions; Dir Dr M. YOUSUF.

PCSIR Laboratories Complex: Lahore 16; tel. 5757429; fax 5757433; metallurgical, industrial fermentation, oils and fats, glass and ceramics, food technology research divisions and solar energy and environmental research; Dir-Gen. Dr KHALID FAROOQ.

PCSIR Laboratories: 131-B/F Block 3, Kalat Road, Satellite Town, POB 387, Quetta; tel. 447840; fax 440880; mineral processing and fruit technology; Dir Dr M. AHMAD.

PCSIR Leather Research Centre: D/102, SITE, South Ave, Karachi 16; tel. 2578748; leather technology, with special reference to tanning and upgrading of leathers, training in leather technology; Dir Dr YASMEEN BADER.

Fuel Research Centre: PCSIR Campus, off University Rd, Karachi; tel. 4969761; fax 4969806; coal analysis, upranking of coal, making of briquettes, hydrogen and alternative fuels division, coal conversion and combustion; Dir Dr S. M. ABDUL HAI.

PCSIR National Physical and Standards Laboratory: 16 Sector H/9, Islamabad; tel. (51) 281105; fax (51) 252373; maintains primary standards of physical measurements; develops sets of secondary standards; supplies standard materials for industrial calibration and standardization; Dir Dr M. PARVEZ.

Solar Energy Centre: POB 356, G.P.O. Super Highway, Hyderabad; tel. 650823; telex 2271; product development and dissemination of solar energy technology, solar refrigeration and photovoltaic applications, solar water desalination, solar air-conditioning and solar architecture, solar energy storage and power generation, wind energy converters, development of tidal waves and geo-thermal energy; Officer in Charge Mr PANDHIANI.

Institute of Industrial Electronic Engineering: ST-22/C, Block 6, Gulshan-e-Iqbal, Karachi; tel. 4982353; general research and development work, quality control, design and development of electronic components; Principal JAMSHEDUR REHMAN KHAN.

Biological Sciences

Centre of Excellence in Marine Biology: University of Karachi, Karachi 75270; tel. 470572; f. 1975; 20 mems; library of 3,000 vols, 50 periodicals; Dir Dr MUZAMMIL AHMED; publ. *Marine Research CEMB*, *Newsbulletin* (every 6 months).

Department of Plant Protection: Jinnah Ave, Malir Halt, Karachi 27; tel. (21) 4592011; telex 24057; fax (21) 4574373; e-mail plant@khi.compol.com; f. 1947; survey and control of desert locust, control of crop pests by air; executes Plant Quarantine Act 1976 and Pakistan Agriculture Pesticide Ordinance 1971 and its rules 1973; advises Federal and Provincial Govt on plant protection matters; library of 22,000 vols, 23 current periodicals; Dir Dr MUHAMMAD SHAFI; publ. *Locust Situation Bulletin* (fortnightly).

Zoological Survey Department: Block 61, Pakistan Secretariat, Shahrah-e-Iraq, Karachi 74200; tel. (21) 5680842; f. 1948; research in ecology, biodiversity, marine biology, and wildlife of Pakistan; library of 40,000 vols, 155 periodicals; Dir MUHAMMAD FAROOQ AHMAD; publ. *Records/Zoological Survey of Pakistan* (annually).

Physical Sciences

Astronomical Observatory of the University of the Punjab: Cust Rd, Lahore; f. 1920; tel. (42) 65327; works within the University's Dept of Space Science located at Allama Iqbal Campus; undergraduate and postgraduate courses; Dir MUMTAZ ALI SHAUKAT.

Pakistan Atomic Energy Commission: POB 1114, Islamabad; tel. (51) 9204276; telex 5725; fax (51) 9204908; f. 1956; the Commission is directly responsible for peaceful uses of atomic energy in the field of power generation, industry, agriculture and medicine; Chair. Dr ISHFAQ AHMAD; publ. *The Nucleus* (quarterly).

Attached research institutes:

Pakistan Institute of Nuclear Science and Technology (PINSTECH): PO Nilore, Islamabad; tel. (51) 452350; fax (51) 429533; houses a 10-MW research reactor of swimming-pool type; Dir Dr HAMEED A. KHAN.

Atomic Energy Minerals Centre: POB 658, Lahore; tel. (42) 5757364; fax (42) 5757903; prospecting, exploration and mining of indigenous nuclear minerals resources; Dir M. YOUNUS MOGHAL.

Atomic Energy Agricultural Research Centre (AEARC): Tandojam; tel. (2233) 750; fax (2233) 5284; application of isotopes and radiation in the field of plant physiology, soil science, entomology and plant genetics (mutation breeding); Dir Dr S. SHAMSHAD MEHDI NAQVI.

Nuclear Institute for Agriculture and Biology (NIAB): Jhang Rd, POB 128, Faisalabad; tel. (411) 654210; fax (411) 654213; research on applied biology and agriculture using nuclear and other modern techniques; Dir Dr MUHAMMAD ISMAEL.

Nuclear Institute for Food and Agriculture (NIFA): POB 446, Peshawar; tel. (521) 261683; fax (521) 262733; Dir Dr M. MOHSIN IQBAL.

Institute of Radiotherapy and Nuclear Medicine (IRNUM): Peshawar; tel. (521) 841956; fax (521) 841957; Dir Dr SHER MUHAMMAD KHAN.

Institute of Nuclear Medicine and Oncology (INMOL): Wahdat Rd, POB 10068, Lahore; tel. (42) 5864199; fax (42) 5864758; Dir Dr SAEEDA ASGHAR.

Nuclear Medicine, Oncology and Radiotherapy Institute (NORI): POB 1590, Islamabad; tel. (51) 255500; fax (51) 253816; Dir Dr N. A. KIZILBASH.

National Institute for Biotechnology and Genetic Engineering (NIBGE): Jhang Rd, POB 577, Faisalabad; tel. (411) 651471; fax (411) 651472; Dir-Gen. Dr KAUSER A. MALIK.

Pakistan Meteorological Department: Meteorological complex, POB 8454, University Rd, Karachi 75270; f. 1947; tel. 8112223; fax 8112885; e-mail pmd@paknet3.ptc.pk; Dir-Gen. Dr QAMAR-UZ-ZAMAN CHAUDHRY; Camp Office, National Agromet Centre, Sector H-8, POB 1214, Islamabad; tel. (51) 256274; fax (51) 255316; publs climatic summary of Pakistan (monthly), *Agromet Bulletin of Pakistan* (monthly).

RELIGION, SOCIOLOGY AND ANTHROPOLOGY

Institute of Sindhology: University of Sindh, Jamshoro, Sindh; tel. 71125; f. 1962 as Sindhi Academy, name changed 1964; aims to interpret Sindh and its contribution to history and civilization, encourage translation and original work in the fields of social and natural sciences; to project Sindh on an international level by publishing relevant research material in foreign languages, to develop working tools (dictionaries, historical surveys, etc.) for scholars, to advance research in history, culture, literature and fine arts; includes a bureau of production, publication and translation, a documentation, information and research cell, a research library, a dept of preservation of documents and rare material, anthropological research centre with Sindh Art Gallery and Museum, a dept of performing arts, sound and film with ethnomusical gallery; photographic and microform sections; 84 staff; library: see Libraries; Dir Dr NAZIR AHMED MUGHOL; publs *Sindhi Adab* (in Sindhi), *Sindhological Studies* (in English) (2 a year).

Islamic Research Institute: POB 1035, Islamabad 44000; tel. 850751; telex 54068; f. 1960, now research arm of Islamic Int. University; aims to develop and disseminate methodology for research in various fields of Islamic learning, to interpret the teachings of Islam so as to bring out its dynamic character in the context of the intellectual and scientific progress of the modern world; to study contemporary problems of the world of Islam; contribute to the revival of Islamic heritage; organizes study groups, serves as a clearing-house on various aspects of Islam, organizes seminars, conferences, etc.; 24 research staff; library of 55,000 vols and periodicals, 550 microfilms, 140 MSS, 760 photostats, 150 cassettes; Dir-Gen. Z. I. ANSARI; publs *Islamic Studies* (quarterly, in English), *Al-Dirasat al-Islamiyyah* (quarterly), *Fikr-o-Nazar* (quarterly), also monographs, reports, etc.

TECHNOLOGY

Hydrocarbon Development Institute of Pakistan: 230 Nazimuddin Rd, F-7/4, POB 1308, Islamabad; tel. (51) 9203092; telex 5516; fax (51) 9204902; e-mail dg@hdip1.isb.erum.com.pk; f. 1975; research and services in petroleum geology and geo-chemistry, resource estimation, enhanced oil recovery, petroleum products testing and evaluation, petroleum processing technology, coal utilization technology, interfuel substitution, energy conservation, environmental control, compressed natural gas, oil and gas advisory and training services; 300 mems; library of 1,500 vols, 44 periodicals; Dir-Gen. HILAL A. RAZA; Operations Man. (Karachi) S. N. SARWAR, (Islamabad) WASIM AHMAD; publ. *Pakistan Journal of Hydrocarbon Research* (2 a year).

Irrigation Research Institute: Shahrah-e-Quaid-e-Azam, Lahore; f. 1925; deals with irrigation and allied engineering problems in Pakistan; 2 field model stations, 2 sub-stations and subsidiary laboratories for soils, foundation engineering, tube well experiments, etc.; library of 20,000 vols; Administrator SAAD HARROON; publs reports, records, memoirs.

Pakistan Council of Research in Water Resources: H. 3 & 5 St 17 F-6/2, Islamabad; tel. (51) 9218980; f. 1964; aims to promote research in the fields of hydraulics, irrigation, drainage, reclamation, tube wells and flood control; library of 7,500 vols; Chair. Dr BASHIR AHMAD CHANDIO; Sec. MAKHMOOR-E-AHMAD GOHEER; publs *Bulletin* (2 a year), *Newsletter* (quarterly).

Pakistan Institute of Cotton Research and Technology: Moulvi Tamizuddin Khan Rd, Karachi 1; tel. 524104; telex 25992; f. 1956; to carry out fundamental and applied research work on cotton fibres, yarns and fabrics; provides testing facilities and training to agriculture, trade and industry; library of 30,000 vols, 350 periodicals; Dir I. H. RESHAMWALA; publ. *The Pakistan Cottons* (quarterly).

Pakistan Institute of Management: Management House, Shahrah Iran, Clifton, Karachi 75600; tel. 531039; f. 1954; 900 institutional and 250 individual mems; dedicated to the management development programme in Pakistan; offers 140 short courses in functional and integrated aspects of management each year; library of 6,000 vols, 60 films, 60 periodicals; Dir ZARRAR R. ZUBAIR; publ. *Pakistan Management Review* (quarterly).

Pakistan Standards Institution: 39 Garden Rd, Saddar, Karachi 74400; tel. (21) 7729527; fax (21) 7728124; f. 1951; member of ISO, International Electrotechnical Commission (IEC), Organisation Internationale de Métrologie Légale (OIML); objects: to recommend national standards for the measurement of length, weight, volume and energy, to prepare and promote general adoption of standards on national and international basis relating to materials and commodities, and simplification in industry and commerce, enforcement of standards, etc.; library of 1,852 technical books, 148,955 national and international standards; Dir Dr M. ASAD HASAN; publs *PSI Yearbook, PSI Annual Report, Pakistan Standards Specification, Test Methods and Code of Practice.*

Libraries and Archives

Bahawalpur

Central Library: Bahawalpur; tel. 80658; f. 1948; 105,960 vols (36,070 Urdu, 61,730 English, 8,160 other languages); 175 MSS (120 Arabic, 55 Persian and Urdu); 34 microfilms, 70 films; mobile library; audio-visual and microfiche sections; language laboratory; collections: books, newspapers and periodicals since 1948; some 19th-century newspapers and periodicals; map gallery; children's library of 22,400 vols; Braille library of 1,100 vols; computer training centre; Chief Librarian MUHAMMAD ASHRAF JALAL.

Islamia University Library: Bahawalpur; tel. 5122; f. 1975; 92,000 vols, 50 MSS; Librarian ABDUL RASHEED.

Dera Ismail Khan

Gomal University Library: D. I. Khan, NWFP; tel. 3695; f. 1974; 60,000 vols; Librarian MURID KAZIM SHAH.

Faisalabad

University of Agriculture Library: Faisalabad; tel. 25911; 87,000 vols, 4,450 MSS, 1,000 microfilms; Librarian NAJAF ALI KHAN.

Hyderabad

Pakistan National Centre Library and Culture Centre: Hyderabad, Sindh; f. 1958; 19,000 vols; Dir M. R. SIDDIQI.

Shamsul Ulema Daudpota Sindh Government Library: Hyderabad; f. 1951; reference and general; 59,000 vols; Librarian KHAIR MOHAMMED MUGHAL.

Islamabad

Allama Iqbal Open University Library: Islamabad; tel. 854306; f. 1974; 53,500 vols, 280 current periodicals; 165 films; 1,161 audio cassettes, 195 video cassettes; 4 multi-media kits; maps, globes; 335 slides; Librarian MAHMUDUL HASAN.

International Islamic University Central Library: POB 1243, Islamabad; tel. 855127; telex 54068; fax 853360; f. 1980; teaching and research facilities; 111,000 vols; 108 periodicals and journals; Chief Librarian MUHAMMAD RIAZ.

Islamabad Public Library: Block 5-B, Super Market, F-6 Markaz, Islamabad; tel. 9221382; f. 1950; spec. collns incl. central and provincial govt publs; Senior Librarian ABDUL LATIF KHAN.

Ministry of Agriculture and Works Library: Ministry of Agriculture, Food and Under-developed Areas, Library, Government of Pakistan, Islamabad; f. 1947; 26,000 vols; 159 periodicals; Librarian S. S. FATIMI; publs *Economic Survey of the Muslim Countries, Food and Forestry*.

National Archives of Pakistan: Administrative Block Area, Block N, Pak Secretariat, Islamabad; tel. 9202044; f. 1951; acquisition, classification and preservation of public and private records of permanent and historical value; provides reference service and assistance to accredited scholars; promotes ideology of Pakistan by projecting the Muslim efforts in acquiring independence; library of 35,000 vols, 325 MSS, 400 oral archives (250 cassettes, 80 video cassettes), 800 titles of newspapers and periodicals, gazetteers of 80 districts, 20,000 govt publs, Quaid-i-Azam Papers, Muslim League Records; Dir-Gen. ATIQUE ZAFAR SHEIKH; publs *The Pakistan Archives* (2 a year), *The Archives News* (quarterly), *Archival Sources in South Asia, Annual Report*.

National Assembly Library: Islamabad; tel. 825626; f. 1947; 52,000 vols, 125 current periodicals; United Nations publications; Librarian NAIM UDDIN SIDDIQUI.

National Library of Pakistan: Constitution Ave, POB 1982, Islamabad 44000; tel. (51) 9214523; fax (51) 9221375; e-mail nlpiba@paknet2.ptc.pk; depository library for all publications; 130,000 vols, 600 MSS, 48,000 microfiches; Dir-Gen. A. H. AKHTAR.

Pakistan Scientific and Technological Information Centre (PASTIC): c/o PO Quaid-i-Azam University Campus, Islamabad; tel. 824161; fax 9201341; e-mail pnc.pastic@sdnpk.undp.org.pk; f. 1956 as PANSDOC under Pakistan Council of Scientific and Industrial Research, reorganized 1974 under Pakistan Science Foundation; sub-centres at Karachi, Lahore, Peshawar and Quetta; facilities include National Science Reference Library, documentation services, scientific and technical information services, scientific and technical publications and compilation of scientific bibliographies, union catalogues, environmental information service, reprographic and printing services; Dir-Gen. Dr MOHAMMAD AFZAL; publs *Pakistan Science Abstracts* (quarterly), *Technology Information* (monthly).

Quaid-i-Azam University Library: Islamabad; tel. 812563; f. 1966; 164,600 vols, 185 current periodicals; 29,000-vol. special collection on Indo-Pakistani history and Oriental literature; Librarian Sheikh M. HANIF.

UNESCO Regional Office Library: POB 2034, Islamabad 44000; tel. 813308; fax 825341; f. 1958; 9,500 vols in English; special collection on Book Development and Communication, including UNESCO publs on Education, Science, Social Science and Culture; Librarian SHOUKAT H. MUGHAL.

Jamshoro

Allama I. I. Kazi Library (University of Sindh): Allama I. I. Kazi Campus, Jamshoro, Sindh; tel. 671292 ext. 58; f. 1947; 218,000 vols, 123 current periodicals, 650 MSS; Librarian MUHAMMAD ISHAQUE LAGHARI.

Institute of Sindhology Library: University of Sindh, Allama I. I. Kazi Campus, Jamshoro 76070; tel. (221) 771291; f. 1962; 102,000 vols (Sindhi, Urdu, English, Pashito, Persian, Balochi, Arabic and other languages); 14,000 periodical bound vols, 32,000 rare books, 490 microfilms; 2,000 audio tapes, 3,000 slides, 1,700 MSS, 700 bound vols newspaper clippings, 3,400 bound vols of newspapers; Librarian GUL MOHD N. MUGHOL.

Mehran University of Engineering and Technology Library: Jamshoro, Sindh; tel. and fax (221) 771169; e-mail mumtaz@uunet.uu.net; f. 1977; 125,000 vols, including journals; Librarian MUMTAZ S. MEMON.

Karachi

All Pakistan Educational Conference Library: 1-J, 45/10 Altaf Brelvi Rd, Karachi 18-74600; tel. 621195; 35,000 vols on Aligarh and Pakistan Movement; Sec. SYED MUSTAFA ALI BRELVI.

Bait al-Hikmah, Hamdard University Library: Madinat al-Hikmah, Muhammad bin Qasim Avenue, off Sharae Madinat al-Hikmah, Karachi 74700; tel. 9600000; telex 24529; fax 6641766; e-mail huvc@cyber.net.pk; f. 1989; 420,000 vols, 26,000 periodicals, 2,255 current periodicals, 1,546 MSS, 1,083 rare books, 682 microfilms, 936 audiotapes, photographs, stamps, maps and charts; specializes in medicine, science, history, Indo-Pakistan history, Islamic studies, management sciences; 3,600,000 newspaper clippings covering 1,100 subjects; Dir L. A. D'SILVA; Librarian MUMTAZUL ISLAM.

Dr Mahmud Hussain Library, University of Karachi: Karachi 75270; tel. 474953; fax 4969277; f. 1952; 316,000 vols, 6,150 microfilms, 270 current periodicals, 28,000 vols in special collections, 20,000 documents and reports; 18,000 vols in seminar libraries; 4,000 research reports; Librarian MALAHAT KALEEM SHERWANI; publ. *Library Bulletin*.

Islamic Documentation and Information Centre (IDIC): Karachi University Campus, Karachi 75270; tel. 453560; f. 1983; 3,005 vols in English and Urdu; 58 current periodicals; Dir-Gen Dr MANZOOR AHMED; publs bibliographies, catalogues and other reference works.

Khalikdina Hall Library Association: M. A. Jinnah Rd, Karachi; tel. 225470; f. 1856; reading room, library (7,381 vols), language classes, social and cultural events; Pres. RAFIQ DAWOOD; Chief Librarian QARI HILAL AHMED RABBANI.

Liaquat Hall Library: Bagh-e-Jinnah, Abdullah Haroon Rd, Karachi 4; f. 1852 as Frere Hall Library; 42,000 vols; Asst Dir Mrs RAZIA ZAIDI.

Liaquat Memorial Library: Stadium Rd, Karachi 5; tel. 4942298; f. 1950; copyright depository for all Pakistani publications (26,764); main library (106,882) includes UNESCO and ILO publications; Children's Library collection (10,354 vols); total holding 144,000 vols (73,000 English and European languages, 40,000 Oriental languages; Principal Librarian I. A. S. BOKHARI.

National Bank of Pakistan, Head Office Library: I. I. Chundrigar Rd, Karachi 2; tel. 2414783; f. 1965; 60,000 vols (45,000 English, 15,000 Oriental); 1,600 old coins of world currencies; 100 MSS in Urdu, Arabic and Persian; central and provincial government publs; 125 current periodicals; UN publs; Librarian SALIHA MOIN; publs *Index of Economic Literature* (monthly), *List of Acquisitions* (quarterly).

NED University of Engineering and Technology Library: University Rd, Karachi 75270; tel. 479261; f. 1977; 79,000 vols, 38 current periodicals; Chief Librarian FEROZ AHMED.

Pakistan Institute of International Affairs Library: Aiwan-e-Sadar Rd, POB 1447, Karachi 74200; tel. 5682891; f. 1947; 28,800 vols, 42 microfilms, 126 tapes; newspaper clippings on international politics, economics and jurisprudence; Librarian AFSAR MEHDI.

Scientific Information Centre: 39 Garden Rd, Karachi; tel. 7725943; attached to Pakistan Council of Scientific and Industrial Research; Dir Dr SYED NAEEM MAHMOOD; publs *Scientific Journal, Monthly Bulletin*.

State Bank of Pakistan Library: POB 5714, I.I. Chundrigar Rd, Karachi; tel. 2417928; telex 21774; fax 2416608; f. 1949; 70,000 books, 37,000 periodicals; special collections: annual reports of major banks and financial instns worldwide, news clipping files since 1949; Chief Librarian SYED ABAD ALI; publ. *Economic Literature: a selected bibliography* (monthly).

Lahore

Atomic Energy Minerals Centre Library: POB 658, Lahore; f. 1961; nuclear minerals; Librarian M. YOONUS QURESHI.

Dr Baqir's Library: 13-G, Model Town, Lahore 54700; tel. 850608; f. 1933; specializes in Indo-Pakistan history and culture; 14,000 vols, incl. 2,500 reference; 1,200 rare books, 20 MSS, 1,800 periodicals, 24 microfilms; Dir Dr MUHAMMAD BAQIR.

Dyal Singh Trust Library: 25 Nisbet Rd, Lahore; tel. 7229483; fax 7233631; f. 1908; 146,000 vols; Senior Librarian NUSRAT ALI ATHEER; publs *Minhaj* (quarterly), *Bulletin*.

Ewing Memorial Library: Forman Christian College, Lahore 16; f. 1866; 69,490 vols; Librarian JACOB LAL DIN.

Faisal Shaheed Library, University of Engineering and Technology: Grand Trunk Rd, Lahore 31; tel. 339243; f. 1961; 120,000 vols; Librarian MUZAFFAR AHMED.

Government College Library: Civil Lines, Lahore; f. 1864; 83,939 vols; Librarian RANA JAMAAT ALI KHAN.

Islamia College Library: Civil Lines, Lahore; f. 1958 after split of Old Islamia College; 50,061 vols, 53 current periodicals; Librarian MUNIR AHMAD NAEEM; publs *Faran* (annually), *College Bulletin* (every 2 months).

Pakistan Administrative Staff College Library: Shahrah-e-Quaid-e-Azam, Lahore; tel. 306389; f. 1960; 37,000 vols, 150 periodicals, 1,500 audio tapes; Librarian TALAT ALI SHER.

Punjab Public Library: Lahore; tel. 325487; f. 1884; 259,000 vols, 1,100 MSS, 121 European language and 100 Oriental language periodicals; Bait-ul-Quran Section with Quranic MSS, rare material on the Quran and audio-visual units; ladies' and children's section; arranges seminars and lectures for the promotion of library activities; Chief Librarian HAFIZ KHUDA BAKHSH; publ *Bulletin* (quarterly), *Annual Report*.

Quaid-e-Azam Library, Lahore: Bagh-e-Jinnah, Lahore; tel. 6304920; f. 1984; research and reference facilities; 91,000 vols, 250 current periodicals; special collection: dissertations on Pakistan and Islam; Chief Librarian MALIK SHER AFGAN; publ. *Bulletin* (quarterly).

University of the Punjab Library: 1, Quaid-e-Azam Campus, Lahore 54590; tel. 868853; f. 1882; 335,000 vols, 800 current periodicals, 1,000 microfilms; Librarian NASEER AHMAD.

Multan

Bahauddin Zakariya University Library: Bosan Rd, Multan; tel. 33162, 40316; f. 1975; 75,000 vols, 20 current periodicals, 20 slides; Chair. Dr MUMTAZ HUSSAIN BOKHARI; publs *Journal of Research* (Humanities), *Journal of Research* (Sciences), *Law Research Journal*, *News Bulletin* (monthly).

Muzaffarabad

University of Azad Jammu and Kashmir Library: Muzaffarabad; tel. 2466; f. 1980; 100,000 vols; Librarian MUHAMMAD YAQBOOB KHAN.

Peshawar

Archival Museum: Directorate of Archives, Govt of NWFP, Peshawar; tel. 274831; f. 1950; library of 71,000 items; Dir TARIQ MANSOOR JALALI.

Pakistan Forest Institute Library: PO Forest Institute, Peshawar; tel. 40580; f. 1947; 60,000 vols, 3,900 bound periodicals, 2,635 MSS; Librarian SYED SHAMSHAD ALI; publs institutional reports.

Peshawar University Library: Peshawar; f. 1951; 150,000 vols, 200 current periodicals, 800 MSS, 39 microfilms; Librarian RIAZ AHMAD.

Quetta

Baluchistan University Library: Sariab Rd, Quetta; tel. 41770; f. 1971; 120,000 vols, 1,000 rare books, 4,000 microfiche cards, periodicals, depository library of World Bank, UNESCO and UNICEF; Librarian B. G. MURTAZA.

Taxila

Archaeological Library: Taxila Museum, Taxila; f. 1960; 1,450 vols on history and arts, especially the ancient history and archaeology of Pakistan; Custodian GULZAR MOHAMMAD KHAN.

Museums and Art Galleries

Harappa

Archaeological Museum: Harappa, Dist. Sahiwal, Punjab; tel. 12; f. 1967; antiquities from site of the prehistoric city; Curator MOHAMMAD BAHADAR KHAN.

Karachi

National Museum of Pakistan: Burns Garden, Karachi 74200; tel. 211341; f. 1950: collections comprise palaeolithic and later implements and antiquities, Buddhist and Hindu sculptures, collection of coins from 6th century BC to date, handicrafts, miniature painting, calligraphic and other MSS of the Muslim period, ethnological material from various regions of Pakistan, material on the freedom movement which achieved the creation of Pakistan; Supt PERVEN T. NASIR; publs *Pakistan Archaeology, Museum Journal*.

Quaid-i-Azam Birthplace, Reading Room, Museum and Library: Kharadar, Karachi; tel. (21) 2434904; f. 1953; library of 5,000 vols (incl. spec. colln on Indo-Pakistani history); Custodian TAHIR SAEED.

Lahore

Directorate of Archives and Archival Museum: Punjab Civil Secretariat, Lahore; tel. 7322381; telex 44868; fax (42) 212693; f. 1924; consists of Historical Record Office, Central Record Office and Museum; library of 150,000 vols; Dir SYED ISHRAT ALI SHAH; publ. *Urdu Nama* (monthly).

Industrial and Commercial Museum: Poonch House, Multan Rd, Lahore; tel. 66209; permanent up-to-date collection of the raw material resources, handicrafts, art-ware and manufactured products of Pakistan; industrial library, reading-room and auditorium attached; provides free economic intelligence to trade and industry; Curator MUSHTAQ AHMAD.

Lahore Fort Museum: Lahore 54000; tel. 56747; Mughal Gallery: Mughal paintings, coins, calligraphy, MSS, carving; Sikh Gallery: arms and armour, paintings of Sikh period; Sikh Painting Gallery: oil paintings from the Princess Bamba Collection; Dir SAEED-UR RAHMAN; Curator IRSHAD HUSSAIN.

Lahore Museum: Shahrah-i-Quaid-i-Azam, Lahore; tel. 7322835; f. 1864; collections of Graeco-Buddhist sculpture, Indo-Pakistan coins and miniature paintings of the Mughal, Rajput, Kangra and Pahari schools; Hindu, Buddhist and Jaina sculpture, local arts, Chinese porcelain, armoury, fabrics, Pakistan postage stamps, modern paintings, oriental MSS, Islamic calligraphy, archives and photographs on Pakistan Movement; library of 35,000 vols; Dir Dr SAIFUR RAHMAN DAR; publs *Guide Book, Catalogue of Coins, Catalogue of Miniatures, Guide to Manuscripts, Lahore Museum Bulletin* (2 a year), *Guide to Gandhara Gallery*.

Zoological Garden: Shahrah-i-Quaid-i-Azam, Lahore; tel. (42) 304683; Dir Dr ZAFAR AHMAD QURESHI.

Larkana

Archaeological Museum: Moenjodaro, Larkana, Sindh; tel. 3; f. 1924; a variety of antiquities unearthed from the 5,000-year-old prehistoric site of Moenjodaro; Curator SAEED JATOI.

Peshawar

Forest Museum: Pakistan Forest Institute, Peshawar; f. 1952; forestry and allied subjects.

Peshawar Museum: Peshawar; f. 1906; the collections of this museum are devoted mainly to the sculptures of the Gandhara School; they comprise an unrivalled collection of images of Buddha, the Bodhisattvas, Buddhist deities, reliefs illustrating the life of the Buddha and Jataka stories, architectural pieces and minor antiquities excavated at Charsadda, Sahri-Bahlol, Shahji-ki-Dheri, Takht-i-Bahi and Jamal Garhi; a Muslim gallery of Koranic MSS and MSS in Arabic and Persian languages; ethnological section; Dir AURANGZEB KHAN.

Taxila

Archaeological Museum: Taxila, Rawalpindi; f. 1928; Gandhara sculptures in stone and stucco; gold and silver ornaments; household utensils, pottery; antiquities of every description from the sites of Taxila and monastic area, covering the years from 6th century BC to 5th century AD; library: see Libraries; Custodian GULZAR MOHAMMAD KHAN.

Universities

AGA KHAN UNIVERSITY

Stadium Rd, POB 3500, Karachi 74800
Telephone: 4930051
Telex: 23667
Fax: 4934294

Founded 1983
Private control (Aga Khan Foundation, Geneva)
Language of instruction: English
Academic year: September to August

Chancellor: HH The AGA KHAN
Rector: Dr CAMER VELLANI
Dean (Faculty of Health Sciences): ROGER SUTTON (acting)
Associate Deans: CAMER VELLANI (Education), FARHAT MOAZZAM (Postgraduate Education), YOUSUF KAMAL MIRZA (Clinical Affairs), PAULA HERBERG (Nursing), ALMAS G. BANA (Management and Operations), ARIF ALIZAIDI (Student and Alumni Affairs)
Librarian: AZRA QURESHI

Library of 201,000 vols
Number of teachers: 249 full-time, 12 part-time
Number of students: 472

PROFESSORS

FAIZI, A., Psychiatry
JAFRI, H. M., Islamic Studies
KAMAL, R., Anaesthesia
KHAN, A., Medicine
KHAN, H., Medicine
KHURSHID, M., Pathology
LINDBLAD, A. S., Paediatrics
MCCROMICK, J. B., Community Health Sciences
MOAZZAM, F., Surgery
RIZVI, I., Radiology
ROBINSON, S. C., Obstetrics and Gynaecology
SAEED, S. A., Pharmacology
SHORO, A., Anatomy
STURM, A. W., Microbiology
SURIA, A., Pharmacology
VELLANI, C., Medicine
WAQAR, M. A., Biochemistry
ZAMAN, V., Microbiology

ATTACHED INSTITUTES

School of Nursing: f. 1980; offers registered nurse programme and B.Sc. Nursing programme; Dir R. N. programme: PAMELA MARSHALL; Dir BSc (N) programme: CAROL ORCHARD.

Institute of Educational Development: Dir KAZIM BACCUS.

UNIVERSITY OF AGRICULTURE, FAISALABAD

Faisalabad
Telephone: (41) 30281
Fax (41) 647846

Founded 1909 as Punjab Agricultural College, present name 1973
Language of instruction: English

Chancellor: THE GOVERNOR OF THE PUNJAB
Vice-Chancellor: Prof. Dr AHMAD NADEEM SHERI
Registrar: MUHAMMAD AKRAM
Library: see Libraries

Number of teachers: 439
Number of students: 4,443
Publications: *Calendar, Journal of Agricultural Sciences* (quarterly), *Research Studies, Journal of Veterinary Science, Pakistan Entomologist,* and various other publications.

DEANS

Faculty of Agriculture: Dr MUHAMMAD AMIN KHAN
Faculty of Veterinary Science: Dr SHAUKAT ALI
Faculty of Animal Husbandry: Dr MUNAWAR AHMAD SIAL
Faculty of Agricultural Economics and Rural Sociology: Dr MUHAMMAD ASLAM CH.
Faculty of Agricultural Engineering and Technology: Dr A. D. CHAUDHRY
Faculty of Sciences: Dr M. A. BEG
College of Veterinary Sciences, Lahore: RASHID AHMAD CHAUDHRY

DIRECTORS

Advanced Studies: Haji MUHAMMAD ASLAM CHAUDHRY
Research: Dr RIAZ HUSSAIN QURESHI
Education and Extension: Dr S. A. KHAN

PROFESSORS

Faculty of Agriculture:

Department of Soil Science
HUSSAIN, T.
QURESHI, R. H.

Department of Plant Breeding and Genetics
GILANI, M. M.
HUSSAIN, M. K.
KHAN, I. A.
KHAN, M. A.

Department of Agronomy
CHAUDHRY, F. M.
SHAH, S. H.

Department of Forestry Range Management
QUERESHI, M. A. A.

Department of Horticulture
KHAN, M. A.
MALIK, M. N.

Department of Agricultural Entomology
RANA, M. A.
SHAMSHAD, A.
WAHLA, M. A.
YOUSAF, M.

Department of Plant Pathology
ILYAS, M. B.
KHAN, S. M.

Department of Crop Physiology
AHMAD, N.

Faculty of Agricultural Economics and Rural Sociology:

Department of Agricultural Economics
CHAUDHRY, M. A.
HUSSAIN, Z.

Department of Farm Management
AHMAD, B.

Faculty of Agricultural Engineering and Technology:

Department of Structural and Environmental Engineering
ALI, M. A.
SIAL, J. K.

Department of Farm Machinery and Power
CHAUDHRY, A. D.
SABIR, M. S.

Department of Food Technology
ALI, A.

Faculty of Animal Husbandry:

Department of Animal Nutrition
BURQ, A. R.
SIAL, M. A.

Department of Animal Breeding and Genetics
AHMAD, Z.

Department of Livestock Management
GILL, R. A.

Faculty of Veterinary Science:

Department of Physiology and Pharmacology
AKHTAR, M. S.
CHAUDRY, SH. A.
NAWAZ, M.

Department of Parasitology:
HAYAT, S.

Faculty of Sciences:

Department of Botany
RASOOL, I.

Department of Zoology and Fisheries
BAIG, M. A.
KHAN, A. A.
QURESHI, J. I.
SHERI, N. A.

Department of Chemistry
AHMAD, R.
CHUGHTAI, F. A.
KHAN, K. M.
NAWAZ, R.
YAQUB, M.

Division of Education and Extension:

Department of Agricultural Education:
KHAN, S. A.

Department of Continuing Education
SIDDIQUI, M. Z.

College of Veterinary Science, Lahore:
AHMAD, N.
BHATTI, M. A.
CHAUDHRY, R. A.
JAFRY, S. A.
RIZVI, A. R.

ALLAMA IQBAL OPEN UNIVERSITY

Sector H-8, Islamabad
Telephone: (051) 264880
Fax: (051) 264319
Founded 1974 as People's Open University, renamed 1977
Autonomous control
Languages of instruction: Urdu and English
Academic year: April to September, October to March
Chancellor: THE PRESIDENT OF PAKISTAN
Pro-Chancellor: THE MINISTER OF EDUCATION
Vice-Chancellor: Prof. Dr ANWAR HUSSAIN SIDDIQUI
Registrar: SAEED AHMAD CHOUDHARY
Librarian: ZAMURAD MAHMUD
Library: see Libraries
Number of teachers: 105
Number of students: 208,461
Publications: *Pakistan Journal of Distance Education (PJDE)* (2 a year), *Journal of Social Sciences* (2 a year).

DEANS

Faculty of Social Sciences and Humanities: Prof. Dr MUHAMMAD TUFAIL HASHMI
Faculty of Basic and Applied Sciences: Prof. Dr PARVEEN LIAQAT
Faculty of Education: Prof. Dr MUHAMMAD RASHID

CHAIRS OF ACADEMIC DEPARTMENT

Faculty of Social Sciences and Humanities:
Arabic: Prof. Dr MUHAMMAD TUFAIL HASHMI
Commerce: MUHAMMAD AMIN
Economics: Asst Prof. RASHID NAEEM
English: Prof. Dr SHEMEEM ABBASS
Social Sciences: Assoc. Prof. M. FAROOQ SOLONGI
Iqbaliyat: Assoc. Prof. Dr RAHIM BUKSH SHAHEEN
Islamic Studies: Prof. Dr MUHAMMAD TUFAIL HASHMI
Management Sciences: NISAR AHMAD AZIZ (acting)
Mass Communication: Asst Prof. SYED ABDUL SIRAJ
Library and Information Sciences: Prof. NAIZ HUSSAIN BHATTI
Pakistani Studies: Asst Prof. AMANULLAH
Urdu: Assoc. Prof. Dr RAHIM BUKSH SHAHEEN
Population Studies: Asst Prof. Dr RUKHSANA MASOOD

Faculty of Basic and Applied Sciences:
Agricultural Sciences: Assoc. Prof. SHAIKH ABDUL LATIF
Basic Sciences: Assoc Prof. SHAHIDA NAEEM
Mathematics, Statistics and Computer Science: Asst Prof. ARSHAD MEHMOOD
Technical and Vocational Education: Prof. Dr PARVEEN LIAQAT
Women's Education: Prof. Dr PARVEEN LIAQAT
Continuing and Remedial Education: S. M. A. ZAIDI

Faculty of Education:
Distance, Non-Formal and Continuing Education: Prof. Dr MUHAMMAD RASHID
Educational Planning and Management: Assoc. Prof. Dr A. R. SAGHIR
Science Education: Assoc. Prof. Dr QUDSIA RIFFAT
Special Education: Asst. Prof. MAHMOOD AWAN
Teacher Education: Assoc. Prof. Dr MUSSARAT ANWAR

Faculty of Mass Education:
Open Schooling: RIFFAT HAQ (acting)
Non-formal and Basic Education: ZAHIDA QAZI (acting)
Community Education: NIGHAT FAROOQ (acting)

UNIVERSITY OF AZAD JAMMU AND KASHMIR, MUZAFFARABAD

Azad Jammu and Kashmir, Muzaffarabad
Telephone: 6018
Fax: 4717
Founded 1980
State control
Languages of instruction: English and Urdu
Academic year: September to October
Chancellor: SARDAR SIKANDAR HAYYAT KHAN
Vice-Chancellor: Dr MUHAMMAD SARWAR ABBASI
Registrar: RAJA MUHAMMAD AZAD KHAN
Librarian: MUHAMMAD YAQBOOB KHAN
Library: see Libraries
Number of teachers: 246
Number of students: 1,155
Publications: *Kashmir Journal of Geology, Kashmir Economics Review.*

CONSTITUENT INSTITUTES

University College, Muzaffarabad: Dean of Faculty of Arts and Sciences Dr ABDUL RAUF KHAN.
University College of Engineering and Technology, Mirpur: Dean ABDUL GHAFOOR MIRZA.
University College of Management Sciences, Kotli: Dean SAEED AHMAD SHAIKH.
University College of Agriculture and Food Technology, Rawalakot: Dean Dr Prof. SHEIKH MUHAMMAD SHABBIR.
University College of Textile and Design, Muzaffarabad: Dean SALEEMA ATTA.
University College of Home Economics, Mirpur: Dean SAEEDA JEHAN ARA SHAH.

BAHAUDDIN ZAKARIYA UNIVERSITY

University Campus, Bosan Road, Multan 60800
Telephone: (61) 224371
Fax: (61) 220091
E-mail: registrar@zakuniv.bzu.nahe.uunet

Founded 1975 as University of Multan; present name 1979
State control
Languages of instruction: Urdu and English
Academic year: October to September

Chancellor: SHAHID HAMID
Vice-Chancellor: Prof. Dr ASHIQ MUHAMMAD KHAN DURRANI
Registrar: ZAIN-A-MALIK
Librarian: MAQBOOL AHMAD CHAUDHRY

Library: see Libraries
Number of teachers: 216
Number of students: 4,212

Publications: science and arts research journals, research directory, news bulletin, *Zulal* (university magazine).

DEANS

Faculty of Arts and Social Science: Prof. Dr ASHIQ MUHAMMAD KHAN DURRANI
Faculty of Commerce, Law and Business Administration: Prof. Dr HAYAT MUHAMMAD AWAN
Faculty of Islamic Studies and Languages: Prof. Dr ASHIQ MUHAMMAD KHAN DURRANI
Faculty of Medicine and Dentistry: Prof. Dr SHABBIR AHMAD NASIR
Faculty of Science, Engineering and Agriculture: Prof. Dr M. ABDUL RAUF
Faculty of Pharmacy: Prof. Dr MUHAMMAD AFZAL KHAN

ATTACHED RESEARCH INSTITUTES

Centre for Advanced Studies in Pure and Applied Mathematics: Dir Prof. Dr BASHIR AHMAD.

Institute of Pure and Applied Biology: Dir Dr ABDUL SALAM.

CONSTITUENT COLLEGES

University Gillani Law College: Multan; f. 1971; Principal Prof. Dr ABDUL RASHID.

University College of Agriculture: Multan; f. 1990; Principal Prof. Dr ASGHAR ALI.

University College of Engineering and Technology: f. 1994; Principal Dr AKHTAR ALI MALIK (acting).

There are 73 affiliated colleges.

UNIVERSITY OF BALOCHISTAN

Sariab Rd, Quetta
Telephone: 440431
Fax: 440323

Founded 1970
State control
Languages of instruction: English and Urdu
Academic year: March to December

Chancellor: MIAN GUL AURANGZEB
Vice-Chancellor: Dr D. K. RIAZ BALUCH
Registrar: ABDUL KABIR KHAN BAZAI
Librarian: GHULAM MURTAZA SHAHWANI

Library: see Libraries
Number of teachers: 255
Number of students: 3,650

Publications: *Acta Mineralogica Pakistanica* (2 a year), *Middle East Journal of Area Studies Centre.*

DEANS

Faculty of Science: Dr NAEEM M. HASSAN
Faculty of Arts: Prof. GHULAM NABI ACHAKZAI

HEADS OF DEPARTMENT

Faculty of Science:

Physics: Dr S. MOHSIN RAZA
Chemistry: Dr NAEEM M. HASSAN
Geology: Prof. GHULAM NABI
Botany: Dr S. A. KAYANI
Zoology: Dr MOHAMMAD NAWAZ
Pharmacy: Dr IZHAR HUSSAIN
Geography: Dr QAZI SHAKEEL AHMED
Mathematics: Dr IMDAD HUSSAIN
Statistics: MOHAMMAD NAEEM SAJJAD

Faculty of Arts:

Economics: Dr M. JAMIL CHAUDARY
Urdu: Prof. FIRDOUS ANWAR QAZI
Education: Dr MOHAMMAD NASEEM
Sociology: GHULAM NABI ACHAKZAI
Social Work: MAQSOOD H. RIZVI
English: ABDULLAH KHAN MENGAL
Commerce: MUHAMMAD JAMEEL
Administrative Science: BARKAT ALI
Political Science: Prof. MANSOOR KUNDI
International Relations: Dr SALAH-UD-DIN AHMED
Fine Arts: AKRAM DOST
Library Science: MIR HASSAN JAMALI
Islamic Studies: MOLVI ABDUL REHMAN
History: Dr MUNIR AHMED BALOCH
Mass Communication: SEEMI NAGHMANA
Philosophy: HAMID HUSSAIN
Psychology: NEELAM FIRDOUS
English Language Centre: REHMATULLAH
Persian: Prof. SHARAFAT ABBAS
Pashto: Prof. SYAL KAKAR
Balochi: ZEENAT SANA
Brahvi: Dr ABDUL RAZAQ SABIR

ATTACHED INSTITUTES

University Law College: Principal MIR AURANGZEB (acting).

Pakistan Study Centre of Languages, Social Structure and Culture: Dir Prof. BAHADUR KHAN.

Centre of Excellence in Mineralogy and Postgraduate Studies: (vacant).

Area Studies Centre: to promote co-operation with the Middle Eastern and Arab countries: Dir Dr MUNIR AHMAD BALOCH.

Institute of Biochemistry Research and Postgraduate studies: Dir Prof. M. A. K. MALGANI.

UNIVERSITY OF ENGINEERING AND TECHNOLOGY, LAHORE

Grand Trunk Rd, Lahore 54820
Telephone: (42) 339205
Fax: (42) 6822566

Founded 1961
Language of instruction: English

Chancellor: THE GOVERNOR OF THE PUNJAB
Vice-Chancellor: Lt-Gen. R. MUHAMMAD AKRAM KHAN
Registrar: Z. A. SHAH

Library: see Libraries
Number of teachers: 250
Number of students: 5,500

Publications: *ECHO* (annually), *Research Bulletin* (quarterly), *Varsity News* (fortnightly).

DEANS

Faculty of Architecture and Planning: Prof. Dr SHAUKAT MAHMOOD
Faculty of Civil Engineering: Prof. AHMAD SAEED SHEIKH
Faculty of Electrical Engineering: Prof. Dr NOOR MUHAMMAD SHEIKH
Faculty of Mechanical Engineering: MUMTAZ-UL-HASSAN ZUBAIRI
Faculty of Chemical and Metallurgical Engineering: Prof. ABDUL GHAFFAR KHAN
Faculty of Natural Sciences, Humanities and Islamic Studies: Prof. Dr MUHAMMAD AMJAD

PROFESSORS

Department of Electrical Engineering:

BUKHARI, S H.
CHUGHTAI, M. A.
DURRANI, K. E.
HAMEED, A.
IQBAL, M. A.
SALEEM, M. M.
SHAH, A. H.
SHAMI, T. A.
SHEIKH, N. M.
ZUBAIR, A. KHAN

Department of Civil Engineering:

AKHTAR, S.
ALI, M.
ASHRAF, M.
CHAUDHRY, M. Y.
CHISHTY, F. A.
MIAN, Z.
QURESHI, M. S.
RAZWAN, S. A.
SHEIKH, A. S.

Department of Mechanical Engineering:

ALI, S.
HAMEEDULLAH, M.
HUSSAIN, D.
HUSSAIN , M. I.
KHAN, M. I.
MIRZA, M. R.
PIRACHA, J. L.
QURESHI, A. H.
SHEIKH, M. A. R.
TABASSUM, S. A.
ZUBERI, M. U. H.

Department of Chemical Engineering:

AHMAD, M. M.
HAKIM, J.
KHAN, J. R.
MAMOOR, G. M.
SALARYA, A. K.

Department of Metallurgical Engineering and Materials Science:

HASAN, F.
MANSHA, M.
SHUJA, M. S.
ZAIDI, S. Q. H.

Department of Mining Engineering:

AHMAD, B.
AKRAM, M.
BUTT, N. A.
CHATTAH, N. H.
HUSSAIN, S. A.
KHAN, A. G.
KHOKHAR, A. A.
KIRMANI, F. A.
RANA, M. T.

Department of Petroleum Engineering:

KHAN, A. S.

Institute of Environmental Engineering and Research:

AHMED, K.
ALI, W.
AZIZ, J. A.
HYAT, S.
ZIAI, K. H.

Department of Architecture:

GELANI, I. A. S.
HUSSAIN, M.
MAHMOOD, S.

Department of City and Regional Planning:

BAJWA, E. U.
MALIK, T. H.
QAMAR-UL-ISLAM
ZAIDI, S.-UL-H.

Department of Chemistry:

AMJAD, M.
IQBAL, Q.

Department of Physics:

KAYANI, S. A.
SHAFIQ, M.

Department of Mathematics:

NASIR, M.
SADIQ, M. B.
SHAH, N. A.

Department of Humanities and Social Sciences:

ZAIDI, M. H.

Department of Islamic Studies:
HAFIZ, M. A.

Department of Computer Science:
AKHTER, Y. A.
MALIK, A. A.
RAJA, A. K.

GOMAL UNIVERSITY

Dera Ismail Khan, North West Frontier Province

Telephone: (961) 750235
Telex: 52352
Fax: (961) 750266

Founded 1974
State control
Language of instruction: English
Academic year: September to June

Chancellor: THE GOVERNOR OF NWFP
Vice-Chancellor: Prof. Dr ABDUL WAHEED
Registrar: NAWALIZADA UMER DARAZ KHAN
Librarian: S. M. K. SHAH

Library: see Libraries
Number of teachers: 356
Number of students: 4,405

Publication: *Gomal University Journal of Research* (2 a year).

DEANS

Faculty of Sciences: Prof. Dr AHMAD SAEED
Faculty of Agriculture: Prof. Dr MUHAMMAD QASIM KHAN
Faculty of Arts: Prof. Dr ABDUR RASHID
Faculty of Pharmacy: Prof. Dr KARAMAT A. JAVAID

PROFESSORS

BALOCH, A. K., Agriculture
HAMEED, U. K. A., Agriculture
JAVAID, K. A., Pharmacy
KHAN, E. U., Physics
KHAN, F. M., Pharmacy
KHAN, M., Economics
KHAN, M. A., Physics
KHATTAK, M. I., Pharmacy
MIANA, G. A., Chemistry
RASHID, A., Law
SAEED, A., Chemistry
SAQIB, N. U. Q., Pharmacy
WAHEED, A., Physics

CONSTITUENT COLLEGES

Law College.
University Commerce College.
University WENSAM College.

ATTACHED INSTITUTES

Institute of Education and Research: Dir Prof. Dr SAEED ANWAR.
Computer Centre: Dir BASHIR AHMED.

There are 23 affiliated colleges.

INTERNATIONAL ISLAMIC UNIVERSITY

POB 1243, Islamabad

Telephone: (51) 850751
Telex: 54068
Fax: (51) 853360

Founded 1980, present name 1985

Chancellor: THE PRESIDENT OF PAKISTAN
Pro-Chancellor: Dr ABDULLAH MOHSIN AL-TURKI
Rector: MARAJ KHALID
President: Dr HUSSAIN HAMID HASSAN
Vice-Presidents: Dr AHMED AL-ASSAL (Resource Development), Dr MAHMOOD AHMED GHAZI (Academic)

Library: see Libraries
Number of teachers: 184
Number of students: 1,093

DEANS AND DIRECTORS

Faculty of Shariah and Law: Dr TAYIB Z. AL-ABDEEN
Faculty of Usuluddin: Dr MUHAMMAD ABDUL TAWWAB
Faculty of Arabic: Dr RAJAA JABR
School of Economics: Dr MUHAMMAD RAMAZAN AKHTAR
Institute of Languages: Dr KAMAL ABDUL AZIZ

ATTACHED INSTITUTES

International Institute of Islamic Economics: Dir Dr ANWAR HUSSAIN SIDDIQUI.

Islamic Research Institute: Dir Dr ZAFAR ISHAQ ANSARI.

Academy for Dawah & Training of Imams: Dir Dr ANIS AHMED.

Academy for Shariah: Dir Dr MEHMOOD AHMED GHAZI.

ISLAMIA UNIVERSITY BAHAWALPUR

Bahawalpur

Telephone: 80331
Fax: 80372
E-mail: vc%iub%nahe@uunet.uu.net

Founded 1975
State control
Languages of instruction: Urdu and English
Academic year: September to August

Chancellor: SHAHID HAMID
Vice-Chancellor: Prof. Dr MUHAMMAD SHAFIQUE KHAN
Registrar: RANA MUHAMMAD ARSHAD
Deputy Librarian: ABDUL RASHID

Library: see Libraries
Number of teachers: 185
Number of students: 3,082

Publications: *Journal of Pure and Applied Sciences* (2 a year, English).

DEANS

Faculty of Islamic Learning: Prof. Dr MUHAMMAD YOUSUF FAROOQI
Faculty of Science: (vacant)
Faculty of Arts: (vacant)

HEADS OF DEPARTMENTS

Physics: Prof. Dr BARKAT ALI SHAFIQ FARIDI
Chemistry: Prof. Dr MUHAMMAD MOAZZAM
Mathematics: Dr GHULAM QANBAR ABBASI
Statistics: Prof. Dr MUNIR AKHTAR
Pharmacy: Prof. Dr MUHAMMAD SHAFIQUE KHAN
Economics: Dr MUHAMMAD ASHRAF
Geography: Dr MUHAMMAD KHAN MALIK
History and Pakistan Studies: Prof. Dr MUHAMMAD SALEEM AHMAD
Islamic Studies: Prof. Dr ABDUL RASHID REHMAT
Political Science: Dr HINA QANBAR ABBASI
Arabic: Dr SURRIYA DAR
English: Prof. Dr ZAHIR JANG KHATTAK
Urdu: Dr SHAFIQ AHMAD
Law: ABDUL QADOOS SIAL
Library and Information Science: Dr MUHAMMAD FAZIL KHAN
Cholistan Institute of Desert Studies: Dr ALTAF-UR-REHMAN RAO
Education: Prof. Dr MUHAMMAD ASLAM ADEEB
Persian: MUNIR AHMAD
Mass Communication: Prof. Dr MUHAMMAD ASLAM ADEEB
Saraiki: JAVAID HASSAN CHANDIO
Computer Science: AHSAN TAQVEEM
Management Sciences: IMTIAZ HAIDER
Educational Training: LUBNA WAHEED

There are 29 affiliated colleges (including one medical college).

UNIVERSITY OF KARACHI

University Campus, Karachi 75270

Telephone: 479001
Fax: 473226

Founded 1951
State control
Languages of instruction: Urdu and English
Academic year: September to August

Chancellor: THE GOVERNOR OF SINDH
Vice-Chancellor: Dr HAFIZ A. PASHA
Pro-Vice-Chancellor: (vacant)
Registrar: YOUNUS AHMED KHAN

Library: see Libraries
Number of teachers: 582
Number of students: 9,985

Publications: *Jareeda* (Journal of the Bureau of Composition, Compilation and Translation, annually), *Science* (quarterly), *Pakistan Journal of Psychology* (quarterly), *Pakistan Journal of Botany* (2 a year), *Karachi University Gazette* (monthly), *Islamics* (quarterly), *University Code, Prospectus* (annually), *Courses of Studies.*

DEANS

Faculty of Arts: Prof. Dr A. IMAM
Faculty of Pharmacy: Prof. Dr S. I. AHMED
Faculty of Science: Prof. Dr V. AHMED
Faculty of Medicine: Dr A. G BILLOO
Faculty of Islamic Studies: Dr A. S. SIDDIQUI
Faculty of Law: U. F. KHAN
Faculty of Education: Prof. A. A. KHAN

PROFESSORS

Faculty of Arts:
AFTAB, T., General History
AHMED, I., Islamic Learning
AHMED, N., Islamic History
ALI, M., Political Science
BALOCH, N. A., Sindhi
FARID, A., Philosophy
HAIDER, J., Library and Information Science
HASANY, S. M. U., Urdu
HUMAYUN, S., Political Science
HUSSIN, F., Sindhi
IMAM, A., Psychology
JAFRI, S. K. H., Social Work
KARIM, A. S., Political Science
KHAN, J. A., Urdu
KIZILBASH, A. H., Sociology
MEHDI, S. S., International Relations
MEMON, M. S., Sindhi
MURAD, H. Q., Islamic History
MURTAZA, M. R., Mass Communication
QURESHI, N., Library and Information Science
RASHID, A., Islamic Learning
RIZVI, S. N. H., Political Science
SAJIDIN, M., Economics
SHAH, M. A., Social Work
SHAMSUDDIN, M., Mass Communication
SIDDIQUI, M. A. S., Islamic Learning
SIDDIQUI, T., Persian
TAFHIMI, S., Persian
WAJIDI, M. A., Political Science
WAZARAT, T., International Relations
ZUBAIRI, N. A., Mass Communication

Faculty of Science:
AHMED, A., Applied Chemistry
AHMED, F., Physics
AHMED, I., Zoology
AHMED, M., Botany
AHMED, N., Genetics
AHMED, S., Botany
ALI, R. B., Food Science and Technology
ANSARI, A. A., Applied Physics
ATHAR, H. S. A., Biochemistry
AZMATULLAH, Geology
FAHIMUDDIN, Chemistry
FAROOQ, M., Zoology
HALEEM, D. J., Biochemistry
HAQ, M., Statistics
HASHMI, M. H., Botany
HASHMI, R. A., Physics
HASNAIN, S. M., Geology
HASNAIN, S. N., Biochemistry
IFZAL, S. M., Chemistry
ISHAQ, M., Biochemistry

JAMIL, N., Microbiology
JAWAID, W., Zoology
KAZMI, M. A., Zoology
KAZMI, S. A., Chemistry
KAZMI, S. U., Microbiology
KHAN, A. F., Microbiology
KHAN, I., Botany
KHAN, J. A., Zoology
KHAN, K. A., Microbiology
KHAN, K. R., Physiology
KHAN, MOHSIN A., Chemistry
KHAN, MUHAMMAD A., Chemistry
KHAN, M. A., Microbiology
KHAN, M. I., Botany
KHANAM, A., Biochemistry
KHATOON, H., Microbiology
MAHMOOD, Z., Statistics
MALIK, K. F., Zoology
MALIK, S. A., Chemistry
MALLICK, K. A., Geology
MOHSIN, S. I., Geology
NAIM, A., Chemistry
NAIM, M. E., Chemistry
NAQVI, I. I., Chemistry
NAQVI, N. H., Zoology
NAQVI, S. M. M. R., Physics
NAQVI, S. R. R., Chemistry
NIAZ, G. R., Applied Chemistry
QADEER, A., Applied Physics
QADRI, M. S., Botany
QAISAR, M., Botany
QAMAR, J., Mathematics
QASIM, R., Biochemistry
QIDWAI, A. A., Physics
QURESHI, A. M., Chemistry
QURESHI, M. A., Physiology
QURESHI, N. M., Physiology
RAFI, F., Physiology
RASOOL, S. A., Microbiology
RAZZAKI, T., Microbiology
REHMAN, K., Physiology
RIZVI, S. N., Zoology
SAIFULLAH, S. M., Botany
SAMI, A., Chemistry
SHAHABUDDIN, M., Microbiology
SHAIKH, M. R., Microbiology
SHAMEEL, M., Botany
SHAMS, N. Applied Chemistry
SHAUKAT, S., Botany
SIDDIQUI, K. A., Physics
SIDDIQUI, N. Y., Zoology
SIDDIQI, P. A., Zoology
SIDDIQI, P. Q. R., Physiology
SYED, A., Mathematics
USMANI, A. A., Chemistry
VAHIDY, A. A., Genetics
YUSUF, H. M., Chemistry
ZAHID, P., Botany
ZAIDI, S. M. S., Geology
ZAIDI, S. S. H., Applied Physics
ZUBAIRI, S. A., Chemistry

Faculty of Pharmacy:

AHMAD, I., Pharmaceutical Chemistry
AHMAD, T., Pharmaceutical Chemistry
AHMED, S. I., Pharmacology
ALI, S. A., Pharmaceutics
BEG, A. E., Pharmaceutics
KHAN, U. G., Pharmacognosy
RASHID, S., Pharmacology
SAIFY, Z. S., Pharmaceutical Chemistry
SHAIKH, D., Pharmaceutics

Faculty of Islamic Studies:

AHMAD, I., Islamic Learning
SIDDIQI, M. A. S., Islamic Learning

ATTACHED INSTITUTES

Institute of Business Administration: Dir Dr HAFEEZ A. PASHA.

Centre of Excellence in Marine Biology: see under Research Institutes.

Centre for European Studies: Dir N. TAHIR.

Hussein Ibrahim Jamal Research Institute of Chemistry: Dir Prof. Dr A. REHMAN.

Pure and Applied Physics Research Centre: Dir Prof. Dr RIAZ AHMAD HASHMI.

Institute of Marine Science: Dir Dr M. S. QADRI.

Institute of Environmental Sciences: Dir Dr M. ALTAF KHAN.

Applied Economics Research Centre: see under Research Institutes.

Pakistan Studies Centre: Dir Dr H. M. JAFRI.

National Nematological Research Centre: Dir Dr M. A. MAQBOOL.

Institute of Clinical Psychology: Dr FARRUK Z. AHMAD.

Centre of Excellence in Women's Studies: Dir Dr T. AFTAB.

There are 64 affiliated colleges.

LAHORE UNIVERSITY OF MANAGEMENT SCIENCES

Opposite Sector U, LCCHS, Lahore Cantt, Lahore 54792
Telephone: (42) 5722670
Fax: (42) 5722591

Founded 1985
Private control
Language of instruction: English
Academic year: September to June

Chancellor: President of Pakistan (ex-officio)
Pro-Chancellor: SYED BABAR ALI
Rector: RAZAK S. DAWOOD
Senior Administrator: M. ASHRAF
Librarian: BUSHRA RIAZ

Library of 13,000 vols
Number of teachers: 25
Number of students: 230

Publication: *Plums.*

PROFESSORS

ALI, I., Agribusiness
AZHAR, W., Marketing
GHANI, J. A., Management Information Systems
HASSAN, S. Z., Management Information Systems
NASIM, A., Business-Government Relations
QURESHI, Z. I., Human Resource Management and Organizational Behaviour

MEHRAN UNIVERSITY OF ENGINEERING AND TECHNOLOGY

Jamshoro, Sindh
Telephone: (221) 71197
Fax: (221) 71633

Founded 1963 as constituent college of University of Sindh; present status 1977
State control
Language of instruction: English
Academic year: October to August

Chancellor: THE GOVERNOR OF SINDH
Vice-Chancellor: S. M. A. SHAH
Registrar: GHULAM SAWAR SHAH

Library: see Libraries
Number of teachers: 115
Number of students: 2,216

Publications: *Mehran Varsity News* (monthly), *Research Journal of Engineering and Technology* (quarterly).

DEANS

Faculty of Engineering: Dr Haji MAHMOOD MEMON
Faculty of Technology: Dr A. Q. K. RAJPUT
Faculty of Architecture: A. K. BHATTI

DIRECTORS

Postgraduate Studies: MOHD. RAMRAN SABAYO
Research and Publications: Dr A. Q. RAJPUT
Continuing Education: Dr MUMTAZUL IMAM
Industrial Liaison: Prof. MOHAMMED DAWOOD MAKHDOOM
Institute of Irrigation and Drainage Engineering: Dr HAJI MEHMOOD MEMON
Institute of Technology: Dr FAIZULLAH ABBASI
Computer Centre: SUJAAJUDIN SIDDIQUI

CONSTITUENT COLLEGE

Mehran University College of Engineering and Technology: Nawabshah; f. 1980; 39 teachers, 1,388 students; Principal Prof. JAN MUHAMMAD KEREO.

There are three affiliated colleges.

NED UNIVERSITY OF ENGINEERING AND TECHNOLOGY

University Rd, Karachi 75270
Telephone: 4969261
Fax: 4961934

Founded 1922 as NED Government Engineering College, university status 1977
Language of instruction: English

Chancellor: THE GOVERNOR OF SINDH
Vice-Chancellor: Engr ABUL KALAM
Pro-Vice Chancellor: Prof. Dr-Ing. JAMEEL AHMAD KHAN
Registrar: SYED GHULAM KADIR SHAH

Library: see Libraries
Number of teachers: 142
Number of students: 3,091

Publications: *Prospectus* (annually), *Versity News* (monthly), *Research Journal* (quarterly).

DEANS

Faculty of Engineering: Prof. P. FAHIM AHSON
Faculty of Science and Technology: Prof. M. A. QUIDWAI
Faculty of Architecture and Planning: Prof. KAUSER BASHIR AHMED

PROFESSORS

AHMAD, A., Mechanical Engineering
AHMED, S. F., Civil Engineering
AHMED, Z., Civil Engineering
AHSAN, P. F., Civil Engineering
ALTAF, T., Electrical Engineering
ALVI, A. Q., Civil Engineering
HAQUE, M. A., Mechanical Engineering
HAQUE, S., Mathematics and Sciences
KHAN, A. A., Mathematics and Sciences
KHAN, A. S., Civil Engineering
KHAN, J. A., Mechanical Engineering
MAHMOOD, M., Mechanical Engineering
MAKHDUMI, S. M., Civil Engineering
QAZI, A. Q., Electrical and Computer Engineering
QUIDWAI, M. A., Mathematics and Sciences
QURESHI, N., Mechanical Engineering

AFFILIATED COLLEGES

Dawood College of Engineering and Technology: see under Colleges.

Government College of Technology: SITE, Karachi; Principal Prof. RASHEED AHMAD KHAN.

ATTACHED INSTITUTES

Institute of Industrial Electronics Engineering: Principal Eng. S. A. RIZVI.

KANUPP Institute of Nuclear Power Engineering: Principal Dr ANSAR PERVAIZ.

Institute of Material Sciences and Research: Principal MOINUDDIN ALI KHAN.

Institute of Environmental Engineering and Research: Chair. SAEED AHMED KHAN.

NORTH WEST FRONTIER PROVINCE AGRICULTURAL UNIVERSITY

Peshawar
Telephone: 40230

Founded 1981
Language of instruction: English
Academic year: January to December

Chancellor: The Governor of NWFP
Vice-Chancellor: Prof. JEHANGIR KHAN KHATTACK
Registrar: FIDA MUHAMMAD KHAN
Librarian: ATTAULLAH

Library of 72,500 vols
Number of teachers: 160
Number of students: 1,270

Publications: *Sarhad Journal of Agriculture* (every 2 months), *Journal of Development Studies* (irregular).

DEANS

Faculty of Rural Social Sciences: Prof. MUHAMMAD NAWAB
Faculty of Crop Production Sciences: Prof. JEHANGIR KHAN KHATTAK
Faculty of Animal Husbandry: Prof. Dr S. IQBAL SHAH
Faculty of Crop Protection Sciences: Prof. Dr N. HUSSAIN
Faculty of Nutrition Sciences: Prof. Dr M. SAEED

CHAIRMEN

AMJAD, M., Animal Nutrition
ASRAR, M., Agricultural Mechanization
BAKHSH, R., Agricultural Chemistry and Human Nutrition
BAYAN, A., Islamic and Pakistan Studies
HASSAN, S., Plant Pathology
HATAM, M., Agronomy
HUSSAIN, Z., Physics, Mathematics, Statistics and Computer Science
IBRAHIM, M., English
KHALIL, S. K., Plant Protection
KHAN, J. M., Food Science and Technology
KHAN, M. N., Agricultural Economics and Rural Sociology
MIAN, M. A., Poultry Science
MUHAMMAD, T., Livestock Management
MUHAMMAD, W., Horticulture
RASHID, A., Soil Science
SHAHID, M., Entomology
TARIQ, M., Water Management

ATTACHED INSTITUTE

Institute of Development Studies: f. 1981; Dir J. B. KHAN.

NORTH WEST FRONTIER PROVINCE UNIVERSITY OF ENGINEERING AND TECHNOLOGY

POB 814, University Campus, Peshawar
Telephone: (521) 40573
Fax: (521) 841758

Founded 1980
Language of instruction: English

Chancellor: Major-Gen. (retd) M. ARIF BANGASH
Vice-Chancellor: Prof. HUMAYUN ZIA
Registrar: Prof. GHULAM RUHULLAH
Dean: Prof. S. MUSSARAT SHAH
Librarian: ABDUR RASHID

Library of 850,000 vols
Number of teachers: 145
Number of students: 1,598

HEADS OF TEACHING DEPARTMENTS

Agricultural Engineering: Prof. ARSHAD AZIZ
Basic Science and Islamiat: Prof. KHADIM-UL-FAQIR
Chemical Engineering: Prof. S. MUSSARAT SHAH
Civil Engineering: Prof. ABDUL JABBAR
Electrical and Electronics Engineering: Prof. ABDUL QAHAR KHALIL
Mechanical Engineering: Dr IRFAN ULLAH
Mining Engineering: Prof. Dr M. MANSOOR KHAN

UNIVERSITY OF PESHAWAR

Peshawar, NWFP
Telephone: (521) 41001
Fax: (521) 41479

Founded 1950
State control
Languages of instruction: Urdu, Pashto, English, Persian, Arabic
Academic year: September to June

Chancellor: THE GOVERNOR OF THE NORTH WEST FRONTIER PROVINCE
Vice-Chancellor: Prof. Dr FARZAND ALI DURRANI
Registrar: Dr SHAKEEL AHMAD
Librarian: RIAZ AHMAD

Library: see Libraries
Number of teachers: 460
Number of students: 28,000

Publications: *Peshawar University Review* (annually), and various college and faculty journals.

DEANS

Faculty of Arts: Prof. GHANI MUHAMMAD KHAN
Faculty of Science: Prof. Dr MUHAMMAD SAID
Faculty of Islamic Studies and Arabic: Prof. Dr QAZI MUHAMMAD MUBARAK
Faculty of Oriental Languages: Prof. Dr MUHAMMAD AZAM AZAM
Faculty of Law: Prof. ABDUL GHAFOOR

PROFESSORS

AHMAD, A., Psychology
AHMAD, N., Law
ALI, L. B., History
ALI, T., Archaeology
ARA, J., Chemistry
ATTAULLAH, M., Geology
AYAZ, Q., Islamiyat (Seerat Studies)
AZAM, M. A., Pashto
BANGASH, G. T., History
DIN, I., Geography
GHAFAR, A., Chemistry
GHUFRANULLAH, Economics
HABIB, N., Chemistry
HAQ, M. I., Philosophy
HAYAT, Mathematics
HIDAYATULLAH, Public Administration
ISLAM, S.
JAN, M. Q., Geology
KABIR, A., Mathematics
KHALIL, A. J., Pashto
KHAN, H., History
KHAN, T. A., Chemistry
MABOOD, F., Chemistry
MAJID, M., Geology
MEHMOOD, I., Botany
MUBARAK, Q. M., Arabic
MUHAMMAD, F., Physics
MUHAMMAD, G., Economics
NAEEM, K., Mathematics
NASIRUDDIN, Chemistry
QAYYUM, A., Pharmacy
QAZI, S., Islamiyat
RAHMAN, C., English
RAUF, M., Urdu
RIZWANA, K., Home Economics
SADIQ, A., Botany
SAID, M., Geography
SALEEM, P. M., Zoology
SAMAD, A., Economics
SHAFIQ, M., Islamiyat
SHAH, J., Botany
SHAH, S. S. H., Botany
YAQOOB, M., Geography

CONSTITUENT COLLEGES

Islamia College: Peshawar; f. 1913; Principal Prof. ARBAB SIKANDAR HAYAT.

Jinnah College for Women: Peshawar; f. 1964; Principal Dr J. ARA.

College of Home Economics: University of Peshawar; f. 1954; Principal Prof. RIZWANA SIDDIQUI.

Quaid-e-Azam College of Commerce: Peshawar; f. 1962; Principal Prof. ABDUL KAFEEL SIDDIQUI.

Institute of Education: Peshawar; f. 1980; Principal Prof. ABDUL KHAKIQ.

Centre of Excellence in Geology: Peshawar; Dir Prof. Dr MUHAMMAD QASIM.

Centre of Excellence in Physical Chemistry: Peshawar; Dir Dr LUTFULLAH KAKA KHEL.

Shaikh Zayed Islamic Centre: Peshawar; Dir Prof. Dr SAEEDULLAH QAZI.

ATTACHED INSTITUTES

Area Study Centre: Peshawar; f. 1976; Dir Dr HAZMAT HAYAT KHAN.
Pashto Academy: see under Learned Societies.
Pakistan Study Centre: Dir PERVAZ AHMAD KHAN TORU.

There are 88 affiliated colleges.

UNIVERSITY OF THE PUNJAB

1 Shahrah-e-al-Beruni, Lahore 2
Telephone: 354428

Founded 1882
State control
Languages of instruction: Urdu and English
Academic year begins September

Chancellor: THE GOVERNOR OF THE PUNJAB
Vice-Chancellor: Lt-Gen. (retd) M. SAFDAR
Pro-Vice-Chancellor: Prof. Dr KHAWAJA AMJAD SAEED
Registrar: MUHAMMAD SAAD-UD-DIN

Library: see Libraries
Number of teachers: 381
Number of students: 10,047

Publications: various faculty and institute bulletins.

DEANS

Faculty of Arts: Prof. Dr A. R. JAFERY
Faculty of Science: Prof. Dr M. AFZAAL BAIG
Faculty of Chemical Engineering and Technology: Prof. Dr FAZAL KARIM
Faculty of Islamic and Oriental Learning: Prof. Dr ZAHOOR AHMAD AZHAR
Faculty of Law: Prof. Dr C. M. HANIF
Faculty of Pharmacy: Prof. M. AFZAL SHEIKH
Faculty of Commerce: Prof. M. AZHAR IKRAM AHMAD
Faculty of Education: Dr MUNAWAR SULTANA MIRZA
Faculty of Medicine: Prof. Dr EJAZ AHSAN

PROFESSORS

Faculty of Arts:

ANWAR, M., Sociology
BUTT, A. R., Economics
BUTT, N. R., English
CHAUDHRY, Mrs A. R., Economics
CHAUDHRY, M. A., Social Work
HIJAZI, M. A., Mass Communication
IKRAM, M. A., Business Administration
JAFRI, S. A. R., Administrative Science
MAHMUD, M. K., Fine Arts
MALIK, I. A., History
RIZVI, H. A., Political Science
SAEED, K. A., Business Administration
ZAIDI, H. S., Fine Arts

Faculty of Science:

AHMAD, R., Centre for South Asian Studies
AHMAD, S., Geology
AKHTAR, M. S., Zoology
AKHTAR, M. W., Chemistry
ALAM, M. A., Physics
ALAM, M. A., Zoology
BEG, A., Centre for High-Energy Physics
BEG, M. A., Statistics
BUTT, A. A., Geology
CHAUDHRY, A. R., Space Science
HABIBULLAH, G. M., Mathematics
ILYAS, H. M., Botany

IQBAL, J., Botany
IQBAL, M. Z., Chemistry
IQBAL, S. H., Botany
KAMRAN, M., Physics
MAJEED, A., Mathematics
MALIK, N. A., Computer Science
MIR, K. L., Mathematics
MIAN, M. A., Geography
NAWAZ, M., Geology
NAZAR, F. M., Centre for Solid-State Physics
RAFIQUE, M., Mathematics
RIAZUDDIN, S., Advanced Molecular Biology
SHAKOORI, A. R., Zoology
SHAMSI, S. R. A., Botany
SHEIKH, K. H., Botany
YOUNAS, M., Chemistry

Faculty of Chemical Engineering and Technology:

BUTT, M. A.
BUTT, M. A. A.
DILAWARI, A. H.
KARIM, F.
NAWAZ, S.
QURESHI, M. M.
SHEIKH, Z. U.

Faculty of Islamic and Oriental Learning:

ALVI, M. S. K., Islamic Studies
AZHAR, Z. A., Arabic and Persian
KHAN, S. A., Urdu
MALIK, S., Punjabi
SHAUKAT, J., Islamic Studies

Faculty of Law:

HANIF, C. M.
MALIK, D. M.

Faculty of Pharmacy:

ALAM, M.
SHEIKH, M. A.

Faculty of Commerce:

IKRAM, M. A.

Faculty of Education:

IQBAL, M. Z.
KHALID, M. I.
KHAN, Z. A.
MIRZA, M. S.
SIDDIQUI, M.

Research Departments:

AHSAN, A. R. S., Research Society of Pakistan
AKRAM, S. M., Iqbaliyat
ANWAR, M., Social Sciences Research Centre
ARIF, M., Urdu Encyclopaedia of Islam

ATTACHED INSTITUTES AND CONSTITUENT COLLEGES

Institute of Chemistry: Lahore; f. 1923; Dir Prof. Dr M. Z. IQBAL.

Institute of Chemical Engineering and Technology: Lahore; f. 1917; Dir Prof. Dr ZAFAR ULLAH SHEIKH.

Institute of Statistics: Lahore; f. 1950; Dir Prof. Dr M. A. BEG.

University Law College: Lahore; f. 1968; Principal Prof. C. M. HANIF.

Hailey College of Commerce: Lahore; f. 1927; Principal Prof. A. R. JAFRI.

Institute of Education and Research: Lahore; f. 1960; Dir Prof. Dr E. U. KHAN.

Oriental College: Lahore; f. 1882; Principal Prof. Z. A. AZHAR.

Institute of Business Administration: Lahore; f. 1972; Dir Prof. Dr K. A. SAEED.

Institute of Geology: Lahore; f. 1951; Dir Prof. Dr S. AHMAD.

QUAID-I-AZAM UNIVERSITY

Islamabad
Telephone: (51) 827259
Founded 1965; incorporated 1967; name changed 1976
Postgraduate students only
State control
Language of instruction: English
Chancellor: THE PRESIDENT OF THE ISLAMIC REPUBLIC OF PAKISTAN
Vice-Chancellor: Dr MUHAMMAD ARSLAN
Registrar: ASLAM FAROOQ BUTT
Librarian: MUHAMMAD HANIF SHEIKH
Library: see Libraries
Number of teachers: 183
Number of students: 1,932

Publications: *Prospectus, Scrutiny* (2 a year), *Journal of Social Science, Journal of Science* (2 a year).

DEANS

Faculty of Natural Sciences: Dr M. AFZAL
Faculty of Social Sciences: Dr M. RAFIQUE AFZAL
Faculty of Medicine: Maj.-Gen. ZAHEER-UD-DIN

ATTACHED INSTITUTES

Area Study Centre (US Studies)
Centre for Nuclear Studies (PINSTECH)
Centre for Central Asian Studies
National Institute of Historical and Cultural Research
National Institute of Modern Languages
National Institute of Pakistan Studies
National Institute of Psychology
Pakistan Institute of Medical Sciences

SHAH ABDUL LATIF UNIVERSITY

Khairpur, Sindh
Telephone: 3091
Fax: (792) 3137
Founded 1975 as campus and 1987 as university
State control
Languages of instruction: English, Sindhi and Urdu
Academic year: September to June
Chancellor: THE GOVERNOR OF SINDH
Vice-Chancellor: Prof. ABDUL HAMEED MEMON
Registrar: NOORULLAH MALIK
Librarian: MUHAMMAD SALEH BHATTI
Library of 28,000 vols
Number of teachers: 125
Number of students: 2,082

DEANS

Faculty of Science: Dr A. R. MALIK
Faculty of Arts: Prof. R. B. SHAIKH
Faculty of Law: Prof. Q. B. MEMON

HEADS OF DEPARTMENTS

Microbiology: Dr MIANDAD ZARDARI
Chemistry: Prof. Dr A. S. PATHAN
Economics: Prof. Dr A. MANWANI
Archaeology: Prof. N. SHAIKH
International Relations: ABDULLAH PHULPOTO
Statistics: Prof. ABDUL GHANI MEMON
Computer Science: A. W. SHAIKH (acting)
Mathematics: Dr K. D. SOOMRO
Botany: Prof. N. M. BHATTI
Physics: Dr K. D. SOOMRO
Commerce: Dr AMANAT AL-JALBINI
English: S. FARZAND ALI SHAH (acting)
Sindhi: ABDUL RAZAK MALIK
Urdu: MARGHOOB RAHAT (acting)
Business Administration: S. M. LUHRANI

UNIVERSITY OF SINDH

Jamshoro, District Dadu
Telephone: (221) 771681
Fax: (221) 771372
Founded in 1947 in Karachi
Languages of instruction: English, Urdu and Sindhi
Chancellor: THE GOVERNOR OF SINDH
Vice-Chancellor: Dr NAZIR A. MUGHAL
Registrar: NAWAZ ALI G. BHUTTO
Library: see Libraries
Number of teachers: 387
Number of students: 13,349

Publications: *Sindh University Journal of Education, Sindhological Studies, Sindhi Arab, Sindh University (Science) Research Journal, Kinjhar, Ariel, Tahqiq* (all annually), *Grass Roots* (every 6 months), *SU Bulletin* (quarterly), *Sindh University Research Journal (Social Sciences)* (annually), *University of Sindh Arts Research Journal* (annually).

DEANS

Faculty of Arts: Dr K. M. LARIK
Faculty of Commerce and Business Administration: Dr MUHAMMAD YAQUB ANSARI
Faculty of Education: Dr QAMAR WAHID
Faculty of Law: Prof. MUHAMMAD JAMIL ZUBEDI
Faculty of Medical and Health Sciences: Dr HAIDER ALI G. KAZI
Faculty of Natural Sciences: Dr GUL HASSAN KAZI
Faculty of Social Sciences: Prof. NIZAMUDDIN HALEPOTA
Faculty of Islamic Studies: AZIZ CHANNA

DIRECTORS

Centre of Excellence in Analytical Chemistry: Dr IQBAL AHMED ANSARI
Far East and South East Asia Study Centre: Dr IQBAL AHMED QURESHI
Institute of Business Studies: Dr SYED ANWAR ALI SHAH
Institute of Physics and Technology: Dr ABDUL HUSSAIN SHAH BUKHARI
Institute of Chemistry: Dr MUNIR AHMED QURESHI
Institute of Languages: MIR KHADIM HUSSAIN TALPUR
Institute of Sindhology: Dr NAZIR A. MUGHAL
Pakistan Study Centre: Dr MUHAMMAD YAKOOB
Institute of Mathematics and Computer Science: Prof. ASIF ALI G. KAZI
Sindh Development Studies Centre: Dr ABIDA TAHIRANI
Centre for Health and Physical Education: YASMIN IQBAL QURESHI

SINDH AGRICULTURE UNIVERSITY, TANDOJAM

Tandojam, District Hyderabad
Telephone: (2233) 5869
Fax: (2233) 5300
Founded 1977
State control
Language of instruction: English
Academic year: October to March
Chancellor: Lt-Gen. (Rtd) MOINUDDIN HAIDER
Vice-Chancellor: Dr RAJAB ALI MEMON
Registrar: Dr MIR MUHAMMAD RAJPER
Librarian: MUHAMMAD IDRIS KHOKHAR
Number of teachers: 254
Number of students: 3,894

Publications: *Zarat Sindh* (quarterly), *Pakistan Journal of Agriculture, Agricultural Engineering and Veterinary Sciences* (in English, every 6 months), *Seerat Supplement* (in English, Sindhi and Urdu, annually), *SAUNI News* (in English, Sindhi and Urdu, quarterly), *Sarang Magazine* (in English, Sindhi and Urdu, annually).

DEANS

Faculty of Animal Husbandry and Veterinary Sciences: Dr GHOUS BUX ISANI
Faculty of Agricultural Engineering: Prof. IMAM BUX KOONDHAR
Faculty of Crop Production: Dr RAHIM BUX MIR-BAHAR
Faculty of Crop Protection: MUMTAZ ALI PATHAN

Faculty of Agricultural Social Sciences: Dr PIR BUX PHULPOTO

PROFESSORS

ABRO, H. K., Plant Breeding and Genetics
ANSARI, N. N., Poultry Husbandry
BALOCH, G. M., Plant Protection
BALOCH, G. M., Animal Nutrition
BHATTI, M. H. R., Plant Pathology
BUKHARI, S., Farm Power and Machinery
BURIRO, S. N., Parasitology
CHANG, M. A., Plant Breeding and Genetics
CHOUDHRY, N. A., Statistics
DEVERAJANI, B. T., Land and Water Management
DHANANI, J., Animal Reproduction
ISANI, G. B., Livestock Management
KALHORO, A. B., Surgery and Obstetrics
KALWAR, G. N., Agronomy
KOONDHAR, I. B., Irrigation and Drainage
KUMBHAR, M. I., Animal Breeding and Genetics
LARIK, A. S., Plant Breeding and Genetics
MEMON, K. S., Soil Science
MEMON, M. I., Plant Breeding and Genetics
MEMON, N. A., Land and Water Management
MIRBAHAR, K. B., Animal Reproduction
MIRBAHAR, R. B., Physiology and Biochemistry
NIZAMANI, S. M., Plant Protection
PARDEHI, M., Anatomy and Histology
PATHAN, M. A., Plant Pathology
PHULPOTO, P. B., Agricultural Economics
RAJPER, M. M., Plant Breeding and Genetics
RAJPUT, M. J., Agronomy
SIDDIQUI, L. A., Microbiology
SOOMRO, G. H., Livestock Management
SOOMRO, H., Veterinary Pharmacology
SOOMRO, M. S., Energy and Environment
SIYAL, N. B., Soil Science

Colleges

Dawood College of Engineering and Technology: M. A. Jinnah Rd, Karachi 74800; tel. 424253; f. 1964; library of 40,000 vols; 80 teachers, 1,800 students; Principal Prof. ABDUL RAZZAQUE MEMON.

CHAIRMEN OF DEPARTMENTS

Architecture: Prof. M. AMIN SHAIKH
Chemical Engineering: Dr HAROON JANGDA
Electronic Engineering: Prof. ABDUL RAZZAQUE MEMON
Metallurgical Engineering: Dr F. H. USMANI
Industrial Engineering: Prof. SALMAN BALOCH
Basic Sciences and Humanities: Prof. J. A. SETHI
Urban Design: MOHAMMAD A. NAWAZ (Dir)
Graduate Programme: Prof. KAUSAR BASHIR AHMAD

Government College of Technology: Rasul, Mandi Baha-ud-Din, Punjab; tel. (456) 2509; f. 1912; diploma and degree courses in technology and civil engineering; 90 teachers, 1,200 students; library of 21,676 vols; Principal GULZAR AHMAD KHALID.

Government Institute of Technology: Jhelum; three-year diploma courses in electrical, mechanical, refrigeration and air conditioning technology, radio electronics; library of 24,000 vols.

Government Polytechnic Institute: Sialkot; three-year diploma courses in electrical, mechanical, civil engineering, auto and diesel technologies; library of 12,999 vols.

Jinnah Postgraduate Medical Centre: Government of Pakistan, Karachi 35; tel. 520039; f. 1958; provides postgraduate training and education (including to doctorate) in the basic medical subjects, leading potentially to Membership of the College of Physicians and Surgeons (FCPS, MCPS) of Pakistan; also degrees in occupational therapy and physiotherapy, diplomas in general and postgraduate nursing, and other full-time certificate courses; library of 18,000 books, 20,000 periodicals; Dir Prof. HASSAN AZIZ; publ. *Annals* (quarterly).

Pakistan Administrative Staff College: Shahrah-i-Quaid-i-Azam, Lahore; tel. 306367; fax 306368; f. 1960; training in administrative management for senior executives from govt and public enterprises, private sector Commonwealth and third world countries; also research and publications on the subject; consultancy and advisory service in public administration; library: see Libraries; Principal MUHAMMAD PARVEZ MASUD; publ. *Pakistan Administration* (2 a year).

Pakistani Swedish Institute of Technology: Landhi, GPO Box 186, Karachi 22; tel. 330071; f. 1955; training in electrical, mechanical, woodworking, welding and clothing technology; 35 teachers; library of 20,000 vols; Dir IMAM ALI SOOMRO.

Rawalpindi Government College of Technology: Shahrah-e-Shershah, Rawalpindi; f. 1958; three-year diploma courses in various subjects, degree courses in electrical power technology, electronics and communication technology; 1,700 students; library of 22,000 vols; Principal Col MUHAMMAD AFSAR; publ. *Technician* (annually).

Swedish Pakistani Institute of Technology: Gujrat; tel. (4331) 524819; f. 1966; three-year diploma courses in electrical, mechanical, electronics, instrumentation, motor vehicle and diesel technology, foundry, pattern making, metallurgy and welding technology; one-year post-diploma course in biomedical technology; Principal MIR MUHAMMAD YUNUS.

PANAMA

Learned Societies

HISTORY, GEOGRAPHY AND ARCHAEOLOGY

Academia Panameña de la Historia (Panama Academy of History): Apdo 973, Zona 1, Panama City; f. 1921; Pres. MIGUEL A. MARTÍN; Sec. ROGELIO ALFARO; publ. *Boletín*.

LANGUAGE AND LITERATURE

Academia Panameña de la Lengua (Panama Academy of Letters): Apdo 1748, Panama City; corresp. of the Real Academia Española (Madrid); 4 mems, 12 elected mems; Dir ISMAEL GARCÍA S.; Sec. TOBÍAS DÍAZ BLAITRY; publ. *Boletín*.

Research Institutes

EDUCATION

Instituto para la Formación y Aprovechamiento de Recursos Humanos (Institute for the Formation and Development of Human Resources): Apdo 6337, Panamá 5; tel. 269-6666; f. 1965 for the development of technical training and the rational use of the country's human resources in order to improve its economic and social development; 9 regional agencies, 8 student centres and an Information and Documentation Centre (see below); Dir Gen. Lic. HECTOR ALEMAN.

MEDICINE

Instituto Conmemorativo Gorgas de Estudios en Salud (Gorgas Commemorative Institute of Health Research): Avda Justo Arosemena entre calle 35 y 36, Apdo 6991, Panamá 5; tel. 227-4111; fax 225-4366; e-mail igorgas@sin.fonet; f. 1997; library: see Libraries; Dir Dr GUILLERMO CASTRO H.

NATURAL SCIENCES

Biological Sciences

Smithsonian Tropical Research Institute: POB 2072, Balboa; tel. 227-6023; fax 232-6197; f. 1923; administered by the Smithsonian Institution (see under USA, Learned Societies); for the research and promotion of tropical biology, education and conservation; the institute has extensive marine and terrestrial research facilities; library of 65,000 vols, 850 periodicals; Dir IRA RUBINOFF.

Libraries and Archives

Panama City

Archivo Nacional: Apdo 6618, Panama City; tel. 25-0944; f. 1912; 3,400 vols; Dir Dr GIOVANNA BENEDETTI; publ. *Boletín Informativo* (2 a year).

Biblioteca Bio-Médica del Instituto Conmemorativo Gorgas de Estudios en Salud (Biomedical Library of the Gorgas Commemorative Institute of Health Research): Avda Justo Arosemena entre calle 35 y 36, Apdo 6991, Panamá 5; tel. 227-4111; fax 225-4366; e-mail igorgas@sin.fonet; f. 1929; 50,000 vols, mainly in tropical medicine and related fields, 303 periodicals; Librarian Lic. ILDA M. DE PAZ.

Biblioteca de la Dirección de Estadística y Censo: Apdo 5213, Panamá 5; tel. 264-0777, ext. 412; fax 269-7294; f. 1949; specializes in statistics, accounting, auditing and finance; 65,000 vols; Librarian PERFECTA DE WILBURN B.; publs *Panamá en Cifras* (annually), *Series de Estadística Panameña, Volúmenes de los Censos Nacionales de 1990*.

Biblioteca Interamericana Simón Bolívar: Estafeta Universitaria, Panama City; f. 1935 as Biblioteca de la Universidad de Panamá, name changed 1978; 285,855 vols, including 9,000 vols in medical library; maintains interchange with 200 institutions; Dir Lic. MAXIMO DE ICAZA; publ. *Boletín Bibliográfico* (2 a year).

Biblioteca Nacional (National Library): Apdo 2444, Panama City; f. 1892 as Biblioteca Colón, reorganized as Biblioteca Nacional 1942; a branch of the Ministry of Education's Public Libraries system, its special function is to provide a Government information service; 200,000 vols (including bound reviews and periodicals); Dir Prof. ALGIS BORRERO E; publ. *LOTERIA*.

Centro de Información, Documentación y Orientacioń Educativa: Apdo 6337, Panamá 5; tel. 262-2109; fax 262-1179; e-mail ifarhu@anconup; f. 1980; library of 5,000 vols; Dir Lic. INES PERALTA DE VARGAS; publs *Orientifrhu, Cidinforma, Alertas*.

Museums and Art Galleries

Panama City

Dirección Nacional del Patrimonio Histórico: Apdo 662, Panamá 1; tel. 228-4902; fax 228-1905; f. 1974; conservation and administration of Panama's historical heritage; library of 8,000 vols; Dir Arq. CARLA M. LÓPEZ ABELLO; publs *Revista Patrimonio Histórico, Rescate Arqueológico en Panamá, Arqueología Histórica de Panamá, Salvemos lo Nuestro, Portobelo.*

Instituto Panameño de Arte/Museo de Arte Contemporáneo: Apdo 4211, Panamá 5; tel 262-8012; telex 2661; fax 262-3376; f. 1962; art gallery, museum; library of 3,000 vols; Dir ELDA C. DE GARUZ; publs catalogues (every 2 months).

Museo de Arte Religioso Colonial: Apdo 662, Panamá 1; f. 1974; located in restored 17th-century Dominican chapel; varied collection of objects of religious art of the Colonial period; cultural programmes, lectures, etc.; Dir. JORGE HORNA.

Museo de Ciencias Naturales: Avda Cuba, Calle 29 y 30, Apdo 662, Panamá; tel. 25-0645; f. 1975; natural history; fauna of Panama and other countries; library of 300 vols; Dir Lic. NURIA ESQUIVEL DE BARILLAS.

Museo de Historia de Panamá: Palacio Municipal, Apdo 662, Panamá 1; f. 1977; Dirs Prof. OSCAR A. VELARDE B., Lic. JULIETA DE LA GUARDIA DE ARANGO; publs guide books.

Museo del Hombre Panameño: Plaza 5 de Mayo, Apdo 662, Panamá 1; tel. 628130; f. 1976; archaeology and ethnography; Dir MARCELA CAMARGO R.

Universities

UNIVERSIDAD DE PANAMÁ

Ciudad Universitaria 'Dr Octavio Méndez Pereira', El Cangrejo, Apdo Estafeta Universitaria, Panama City

Telephone: 263-6133

Founded 1935
State control
Language of instruction: Spanish
Academic year: May to August, September to December

Rector: Dr GUSTAVO GARCÍA DE PAREDES
Vice-Rector (Academic): Dr ROLANDO MURGAS TORRAZA
Vice-Rector (Administration): Prof. GLORIELA H. DE RENGIFO
Vice-Rector (Research and Graduate Studies): Prof. JULIO A. VALLARINO R.
Vice-Rector (Student Affairs): Dr OSMAN ROBLES DE SALAS
Vice-Rector (Extension): Dr JUSTO MEDRANO
General Secretary: Lic. EGBERT WETHERBORNE
Librarian: Dr OCTAVIO CASTILLO

Number of teachers: 2,656
Number of students: 50,371

Publications: *Campus, Hacia La Luz, Boletines Estadísticos, Revistas Jurídicas Panameñas, Scientia, EDU, ECO, Revista Universidad, Memoria.*

DEANS

Faculty of Agriculture: Ing. RODRIGO CAMBRA
Faculty of Architecture: Arq. ANIBAL FIGUEROA
Faculty of Economics: Dr EDUARDO HEART
Faculty of Law and Political Sciences: Dr JULIO LOMBARDO
Faculty of Medicine: Dr CARLOS BRANDARIS
Faculty of Sciences: Prof. ELVIA A. DE LOS RIOS
Faculty of Odontology: Dr NELSON NOVARRO
Faculty of Business Administration and Accountancy: Prof. MAYRA LEE
Faculty of Public Administration: Prof. RUFINO FERNÁNDEZ
Faculty of Humanities: Dr ARIOSTO ARDILA
Faculty of Social Communication: Prof. RAFAEL B. AYALA
Faculty of Education: Prof. TOMÁS GARIBALDI
Faculty of Nursing: Dra LYDIA DE ISAACS
Faculty of Pharmacy: Dra ANGELA DE AGUILAR
Faculty of Fine Arts: Prof. EFRAIN CASTRO

ATTACHED INSTITUTES

Institute of Food and Nutrition: Dir Dra MIRIAM FERNÁNDEZ.

Central American Institute for Educational Administration and Supervision: Dir Dr DIÓGENES CEDEÑO CENCI.

Institute of Environmental Sciences and Cryobiology: Dir Dr JUAN J. GUTIÉRREZ.

Institute of Criminology: Dir Dra MARCELA MÁRQUEZ.

Institute of the Panama Canal and International Affairs: Dir Prof. MIGUEL MONTIEL.

Institute of National Affairs: Dir Prof. JUÁN JOVANÉ.

Institute of Earth Sciences: Dir Prof. NIDIA CARDOZE.

Institute of Ethnic and Cultural Traditions (Chiriqui Province): Dir Prof. GONZALO BRENES.

Institute of Analysis: Dir Dr JERÓNIMO AVERZA.

UNIVERSIDAD SANTA MARÍA LA ANTIGUA

Apdo 6-1696, El Dorado, Panama 6

Telephone: 236-1311
E-mail: secretar@canaa.usma.ac.pa

Founded 1965
Private control
Language of instruction: Spanish
Academic year: April to December

Chancellor: Mons. JOSÉ DIMAS CEDEÑO
Rector: Dr. STANLEY MUSCHETT I.
Vice-Rector (Academic): Prof. CARLOS A. VOLOJ
Vice-Rector (Postgraduate and Research): Dra PAULINA FRANCESCHI
Vice-Rector (Administrative): Prof. Lic. ALCIDES CERRUD
Registrar: Prof. NARCISO ARENAS
Librarian: Lic. ONDINA HERNANDEZ

Number of teachers: 400
Number of students: 6,000

Publications: *Boletín Informativo* (annually), *Revista La Antigua* (2 a year).

DEANS

Law and Political Science: Prof. NARCISO ARELLANO
Administrative Sciences: Prof. LUIS PABÓN
Technology and Natural Science: Prof. MARÍA HELENA DE MARIÑAS
Humanities and Religious Studies: R. P. PABLO VARELA
Social Sciences: Prof. MARÍA EUGENIA DE ALEMÁN

UNIVERSIDAD TECNOLOGICA DE PANAMA

Ciudad Universitaria 'Dr Octavio Méndez Pereira', Apdo Postal 6-2894, El Dorado, Panamá

Telephone: 263-8000
Fax: 264-9149

Founded 1981
State control
Academic year: March to December

Rector: Ing. HÉCTOR MONTEMAYOR
Vice-Rector for Academic Affairs: Ing. MYRIAM GONZALEZ BOUTET
Vice-Rector for Administrative Affairs: Lic. VIERIA DE EPIFANIO
Vice-Rector for Research and Graduate Studies: Ing. ERNESTO REGALES
Librarian: Lic. EDILDA F. DE MORALES

Number of teachers: 1,100
Number of students: 11,300

Publications: *Boletín Informativo*, *Memorias*.

DEANS

Faculty of Civil Engineering: Ing. SALVADOR RODRIGUEZ
Faculty of Mechanical Engineering: Ing. BENIGNO VARGAS
Faculty of Industrial Engineering: Ing. DELIA DE BENITEZ
Faculty of Electrical Engineering: Ing. ROBERTO BARRAZA
Faculty of Computer Science Engineering: Ing. INMACULADA DE CASTILLO

ATTACHED RESEARCH CENTRES

Design and Planning Centre: Dir Dr DAVID WONG.
Computing Centre: Dir Ing. BORIS GÓMEZ.
Hydraulic Research Centre: Dir Ing. RICARDO GONZALEZ.
Engineering Experimental Centre: Dir Ing. AMADOR HASSELL.
Production and Agro-industrial Research Centre: Dir Ing. VICTOR GUILLEN.

Other Institutes

Escuela Nacional de Música: Apdo 1414, Panama 1; affiliated to Instituto Nacional de Cultura (*q.v.*); f. 1941; 41 teachers, 396 students; Dir MO. JORGE LEDEZMA BRADLEY.

Escuela Nacional de Artes Plásticas: Apdo 1004, Panama 1; f. 1913; affiliated to Instituto Nacional de Cultura (*q.v.*); 10 teachers, 128 students; Dir Prof. ADRIANO HERRERABARRÍA; publs *La Estrella de Panamá, El Matutino, El Panamá Americano*.

Escuela Nacional de Danzas: Apdo 662, Panama 1; affiliated to Instituto Nacional de Cultura (*q.v.*).

Escuela Nacional de Teatro: Apdo 662, Panama 1; f. 1974; attached to Instituto Nacional de Cultura (*q.v.*); 10 teachers, 40 students; Dir Prof. IVÁN R. GARCÍA.

Escuela Náutica de Panamá: Apdo 55-1988 Paitilla, Panamá; tel. 264-8737; fax 264-8625; f. 1959 for secondary studies, higher studies 1972; courses in nautical engineering, specializing in naval machinery and maritime navigation and transport; offers professional training and qualification; library of 4,900 vols, 1,500 periodicals; 32 higher level teachers; 250 higher level students; Pres. Capt. ANTONIO MOTTA D.; publs *Boletín Informativo, El Cadete*.

PAPUA NEW GUINEA

Learned Societies

BIBLIOGRAPHY, LIBRARY SCIENCE AND MUSEOLOGY

Papua New Guinea Library Association: POB 5368, Boroko; f. 1973; 200 mems; Pres. MARGARET J. OBI; Sec. JENNY WAL; publs *Toktok bilong haus buk* (Journal, quarterly), *Directory of Libraries in Papua New Guinea*, *PNGLA Nius* (2 a year), *PNG Librarians' Calendar* (monthly).

ECONOMICS, LAW AND POLITICS

Papua New Guinea Institute of Management: POB 1060, Port Moresby; tel. 21-3437; f. 1972; training in all aspects of management and development; 190 personal, 99 company mems; Pres. IAN SMITH; Exec. Officer WILLIAM KWARA; publ. *Management Newsletter*.

NATURAL SCIENCES

General

Papua New Guinea Scientific Society: c/o National Museum, POB 5560, Boroko; f. 1949 to promote the sciences, exchange scientific information, preserve scientific collections and establish museums; 203 mems; Pres. H. SAKULAS; publ. *Proceedings*.

Research Institutes

GENERAL

National Research Institute: POB 5854, Boroko; tel. 260300; fax 260213; f. 1989; promotion of research into social, political, economic, educational and cultural issues in Papua New Guinea; practical research opportunities for trainee research workers; library of 10,000 vols; Dir Dr BENO B. BOEHA; publs *Post Courier Index* (annually), *TaimLain: A Journal of Contemporary Melanesian Studies*, *Current Issues Sope Bikmaus* (cultural, quarterly).

AGRICULTURE, FISHERIES AND VETERINARY SCIENCE

Lowlands Agricultural Experiment Station: Kerevat, POB 204, Kokopo, East New Britain Province; tel. 9839145; fax 9839129; f.1928; of int. standing.

ECONOMICS, LAW AND POLITICS

Institute of National Affairs: POB 1530, Port Moresby; tel. 3211045; e-mail inapug@daltrow.com.pg; f. 1979; aims to foster the development of the national economy by encouraging discussion and research on issues which are important in the public and private sectors; undertakes research in matters of interest to management in both sectors, the findings of which are published; organizes seminars, public meetings, etc., on matters of importance to economic development; Pres. F. J. L. HAYNES; Treas./Sec. M. J. MANNING; publs discussion and working papers, speech series.

MEDICINE

Papua New Guinea Institute of Medical Research: POB 60, Goroka; tel. 7322800; fax 7321998; f. 1968; medical, human biological, nutritional and sociological research, all matters relating to research into human health and disease within Papua New Guinea; library of 5,000 vols; Dir Dr M. ALPERS; publs monographs (irregularly), *Annual Report*.

Libraries and Archives

Boroko

National Archives and Public Records Service: POB 1089, Boroko; tel. (675) 254754; telex 22234; fax 251331; f. 1957; branch of National Library Service, Division of the Department of Education; repository for the public archives and records of Papua New Guinea; Reference Service and Microfilm Unit, Records Management Service and Records Centre Service for government offices and statutory bodies; branch repository in Lae: *c.* 10,000 linear metres plus *c.* 1,000 maps and plans, and photographic archives; Chief Archivist GABRIEL GERRY; publs *Patrol Reports* (microfiche, irregular), *Guides to Groups of Records in the National Archives* (irregular).

Lae

Matheson Library, Papua New Guinea University of Technology: Private Mail Bag, Lae; telex 42428; fax 434355; f. 1965; 125,000 monograph vols, 2,190 serial titles, 4,000 a/v items; special collection: Papua New Guinea; microfilm unit produces microfiche edns of all major PNG serial publs; University Librarian D. TEMU.

Waigani

National Library Service: POB 734, Waigani; tel. 3256200; fax 3251331; e-mail ola@datec.com.pg; f. 1975; national reference library; legal deposit library; advisory services, lending and educational services; important holdings of New Guineana, particularly Government publications; Papua New Guinea collection; 45,000 vols, 4,000 films and video recordings; National Librarian DANIEL PARAIDE; publs *OLA Nius* (every 2 months), *Papua New Guinea National Bibliography* (annual), , *Annual Report*, film and video catalogues (irregular), *Papua New Guinea Directory of Information Sources in Science and Technology* (irregular), *Times Index* (annual), *Directory of Libraries in Papua New Guinea* (irregular).

University of Papua New Guinea Michael Somare Library: Box 319, University Post Office, Waigani; tel. 267280; telex 22366; fax 267187; f. 1965; 458,000 vols, 2,000 current periodicals; special collections: law, New Guinea; Librarian (vacant); publs *New Guinea Archives: A Listing* (microfiche), *New Guinea Photographic Index* (microfiche).

Subordinate library:

Medical Library: POB 5623, Boroko; f. 1976; 65,000 vols; Librarian L. WANGATAU; publ. *Papua New Guinea Medical Journal*.

Museums and Art Galleries

Boroko

Papua New Guinea National Museum and Art Gallery: POB 5560, Boroko; tel. 252405; telex 23472; fax 259447; f. 1954; field research in archaeology, cultural anthropology, natural history; educational tours, public programmes, broadcasts, etc.; aims to implement the National Cultural Property (Preservation) Act to protect Papua New Guinea's cultural heritage, and establish museums; library of 4,500 vols; Dir SOROI MAREPO EOE.

Universities

UNIVERSITY OF PAPUA NEW GUINEA

Box 320, University Post Office, Waigani

Telephone: 267201
Telex: 22366
Fax: 267187

Founded 1965
Language of instruction: English
State control
Academic year: February to November (two semesters)

Chancellor: Sir ALKAN TOLOLO
Pro-Chancellor: Dr ROSEMARY KEKEDO
Vice-Chancellor: Dr RODNEY C. HILLS
Deputy Vice-Chancellor: N. R. KUMAN
Registrar: T. IAMO

Library: see Libraries
Number of teachers: 700
Number of students: 4,416

Publications: *Calendar*, *Faculty Research Reports*, *Handbooks of Courses*, *PNG Law*, *South Pacific Journal of Psychology* (all annually), *Melanesian Law Journal* (2 a year), *Research in Melanesia* (2 a year),*Yagl-Ambu*, *Science in New Guinea* (quarterly).

DEANS

Faculty of Arts: Dr B. D. YEATES
Faculty of Creative Arts: Dr E. AMODCIC
Faculty of Education: A. MAHA
Faculty of Law: Prof. R. W. JAMES
Faculty of Medicine: Prof. J. D. IGO
Faculty of Science: Dr L. HILL

HEADS OF DEPARTMENTS

Faculty of Arts:

- Anthropology and Sociology: H. GAUDI
- Commerce: T. SENTHEYVAL
- Economics: J. KALINOE
- Geography: Dr G. SEM
- History: Prof. R. HUCH
- Language and Literature: J. DAVANI
- Library Information: Dr J. EVANS
- Political and Administrative Studies: Prof. Y. O. SAFFU
- Psychology and Philosophy: W. WANINARA

Faculty of Education:

- Education: W. KALEVA

Faculty of Law:

- Law: Dr. J. LULUAKI
- Legal Clinical Programme: Dr J. NONGGORR

Faculty of Medicine:
- Basic Medical Sciences: Dr B. AMEVO
- Clinical Sciences: Prof. J. D. VINCE
- Community Medicine: Dr A. SLEIGH
- Pathology: Dr S. K. SEN-GUPTA

Faculty of Science:
- Biology: Dr I. BURROWS
- Chemistry: Dr J. TAMATE
- Geology: Prof. H. DAVIES
- Mathematics: Dr C. S. NEMBOU
- Physics: Dr K. AGYEMAN

PROFESSORS

Faculty of Arts:
- SAFFU, Y. O., Political and Administrative Studies

Faculty of Education:
- AVALOS-BEVAN, B., Education

Faculty of Medicine:
- IGO, J. D., Pathology
- KLUFIO, C. A., Clinical Science
- NARAQI, S., Clinical Science
- VINCE, J. D., Clinical Science
- WATTERS, D., Clinical Science
- ZIVANOVIC, S., Basic Medical Sciences

Faculty of Sciences:
- DAVIES, H., Geology
- SINGH, K., Chemistry
- YEBOAH-AMANKWAH, D., Physics

PAPUA NEW GUINEA UNIVERSITY OF TECHNOLOGY

Private Mail Bag, Lae
Telephone: 43 4999
Telex: 42428
Fax: 45-7667

Founded 1965
Language of instruction: English
State control
Academic year: February to November (two semesters)

Chancellor: A. TOLOLO
Pro-Chancellor: R. KEKEDO
Vice-Chancellor: M. BALOILOI
Deputy Vice-Chancellor: (vacant)
Registrar: T. CHAN
Librarian: C. BAKER

Library: see Libraries
Number of teachers: 199
Number of students: 1,653

Publications: *Calendar, Reporter, Research Report, Course Handbook, Student Handbook, Vice-Chancellor's Report.*

HEADS OF DEPARTMENTS

- Business Studies: L. TORRES
- Agriculture: P. KOHUN (acting)
- Applied Physics: Prof. W. MCCUBBIN
- Applied Sciences: Prof. R. KHAN
- Civil Engineering: Prof. B. YOUNG
- Electrical and Communications Engineering: Prof. G. BRYANT
- Forestry: Dr P. SIAGURU
- Language and Communication Studies: Prof. J. MOODY
- Mathematics and Statistics: Prof. A. J. PYTHIAN
- Mechanical Engineering: Prof. M. A. SATTER
- Mining Engineering: Prof. S. BORDIA
- Surveying and Land Studies: Assoc. Prof. T. M. NACINO

College

Papua New Guinea Institute of Public Administration: POB 1216, Boroko; tel. 326-0433; fax 326-1654; f. 1963; 60 teachers, *c.* 700 students; library of 75,000 vols; diploma, certificate and short courses in public and land administration, public finance and accountancy, local government, management, law, social development, library studies, business development, communication skills, mathematics and statistics, rural development; Dir GEI ILAGI; publs *Handbook* (annually), *Administration for Development* (2 a year).

PARAGUAY

Learned Societies

GENERAL

Academia de la Lengua y Cultura Guaraní: (Academy of the Guaraní Language and Culture): Calle España y Mompox, Asunción; f. 1975; Pres. Dr RUFINO AREVALO PARIS; Sec. ANTONIO E. GONZÁLEZ; publ. *Revista*.

Academia Paraguaya (Paraguayan Academy): Avda España y Mompox, Asunción; f. 1927; corresp. of the Real Academia Española (Madrid); 34 mems; Pres. JULIO CÉSAR CHAVES; Sec. LUIS A. LEZCANO; publ. *Anales*.

HISTORY, GEOGRAPHY AND ARCHAEOLOGY

Instituto de Numismática y Antigüedades del Paraguay: Hernandarias 1313, Asunción; tel. 81855; f. 1943; Pres. CARLOS ALBERTO PUSINERI SCALA.

MEDICINE

Sociedad de Pediatría y Puericultura del Paraguay (Paediatrics and Child Welfare Society): 25 de Mayo y Tacuaí, Asunción; f. 1928; 28 mems; Pres. Dr GUIDO RODRÍGUEZ ALCALÁ; Sec. Dr GUSTAVO A. RIART; publ. *Revista Médica del Paraguay*.

RELIGION, SOCIOLOGY AND ANTHROPOLOGY

Asociación Indigenista del Paraguay: Calle España y Mompox, Casilla 1838, Asunción; f. 1942; anthropology, development of indigenous communities; 170 mems; library of 1,640 vols; Pres. Dr RAFAEL REYES PARGA; Exec. Sec. Lic. AMÉRICO PÉREZ PEÑA.

TECHNOLOGY

Unión Sudamericana de Asociaciones de Ingenieros (USAI) (South American Union of Engineers' Associations): Head Office: Casilla de Correos 336, Asunción; f. 1935; mem. countries: Argentina, Bolivia, Brazil, Chile, Colombia, Ecuador, Paraguay, Peru, Uruguay and Venezuela; Dir and Pres. Ing. CARLOS ESPINOZA MACIEL; Sec. Ing. HERMANN BAUMANN.

Research Institutes

ECONOMICS, LAW AND POLITICS

Centro Interdisciplinario de Derecho Social y Economía Política (CIDSEP): Independencia Nacional y Comuneros, Casilla de Correo 1718, Asunción; tel. (21) 97926; f. 1986; Dir CARLOS ALBERTO GONZÁLEZ.

Centro Paraguayo de Estudios de Desarrollo Económico y Social: Casilla 1189, Asunción.

HISTORY, GEOGRAPHY AND ARCHAEOLOGY

Instituto Geográfico Militar: Avda Perú y Artigas, Asunción; Dir Gral. Brig. RUBEN ORTIZ P.; Sec. E. LOPEZ MOREIRA.

MEDICINE

Instituto Nacional de Parasitología (National Institute of Parasitology): Instituto de Microbiología, Facultad de Medicina, Casilla Correo 1102, Asunción; f. 1963; 5 mems; library; Dir Dr ARQUIMEDES CANESE; publ. *Revista Paraguaya de Microbiología* (annually).

RELIGION, SOCIOLOGY AND ANTHROPOLOGY

Centro de Estudios Antropológicos de la Universidad Católica: Casilla de Correo 1718, Asunción; tel. 446251; fax 445245; f. 1950, affiliated to Universidad Católica 1971; 25 mems; Dir JOSÉ ZANARDINI; Sec. FELICIANO PEÑA PÁEZ; publs *Suplemento Antropológico, Universidad Católica* (2 a year).

Centro Paraguayo de Estudios Sociológicos: Eligio Ayala 973, Casilla 2157, Asunción; tel. 43734; f. 1964; research and development in social sciences: migration, bilingualism, population structure, rural development, role of women in the work-force, education, etc.; specialized library of 5,000 vols, 4,000 documents; 15 staff; Dir DOMINGO M. RIVAROLA; Sec. MIRTHA M. RIVAROLA; publ. *Revista Paraguaya de Sociología* (3 a year).

TECHNOLOGY

Centro Paraguayo de Ingenieros: Avda España 959, Casilla 336, Asunción; tel. 202424; fax 205019; f. 1939; 1,044 mems; Pres. Ing. HUMBERTO YALUK ORREGO; Sec. Ing. HUGO RAMON RUIZ FLEITAS.

Instituto Nacional de Tecnología y Normalización: Avda Artigas y Gral Roa, Asunción; tel. 290160; fax 290873; carries out research and technological studies, and lays down technical norms; publ. *Normas Técnicas Paraguayas*.

Libraries and Archives

Asunción

Biblioteca Americana (American Library): Mariscal Estigarribia e Iturbe, Asunción; attached to the Museo Nacional de Bellas Artes (*q.v.*).

Biblioteca de la Sociedad Científica del Paraguay (Library of Paraguayan Scientific Society): Avda España 505, Asunción; f. 1921; 29,300 vols on science.

Biblioteca Pública del Ministerio de Defensa Nacional (Public Library of Ministry of Defence): Avda Mariscal López 1040, Asunción; Dir Col MANUEL W. CHAVES.

Biblioteca y Archivo del Ministerio de Relaciones Exteriores (Library of the Ministry of Foreign Affairs): Palacio de Gobierno, Asunción.

Biblioteca y Archivo Nacionales: Mariscal Estigarriba 95, Asunción; f. 1869; 44,000 vols; Dir MANUEL MARÍA PÁEZ MONGES.

Museums and Art Galleries

Asunción

Casa de la Independencia: 14 de Mayo y Pte Franco, Asunción; tel. 493918; f. 1965; historical museum of colonial period; Pres. Dr GERARDO FOGEL; Dir Prof. CARLOS ALBERTO PUSINERI SCALA.

Colección Carlos Alberto Pusineri Scala: Hernandarias 1313, Asunción; tel. 81855; f. 1950; collections of Guaraní archaeology, trophies of Paraguyan wars, colonial objects; small library of Paraguayan history, numismatics and anthropology; Dir CARLOS ALBERTO PUSINERI SCALA.

Jardín Botánico y Museo de Historia Natural (Botanical Gardens and Natural History Museum): Residencia López, Trinidad, Asunción; f. 1914; Dir Ing. GILDO INSFRÁN GUERROS; herbarium, zoological garden and museum, bacteriological laboratory, agricultural experimental station; publ. *Revista*.

Museo de Cerámica y Bellas Artes 'Julián de la Herreria': Estados Unidos 1120, Asunción; f. 1938; ceramics by Herreria; other modern works by Paraguayan artists; Paraguayan folk art; library of 6,000 vols, 1,000 of which concerned with the arts, particularly ceramics; Founder and Dir JOSEFINA PLÁ.

Museo Etnográfico 'Andres Barbero': España 217, Asunción; tel. 441696; f. 1929; archaeology, ethnography, archives, manuscripts, books; Library of 5,000 vols; Dir Lic. ADELINA PUSINERI.

Museo Histórico Militar (Museum of Military History): Avda Mariscal López 140, Asunción; recent war collections; Dir MANUEL WENCESLAO CHAVES.

Museo Nacional de Bellas Artes: Mariscal Estigarribia e Iturbe, Asunción; f. 1887; the paintings and sculpture of Juan Silvano Godoy form the basis of the collection; Dir JOSÉ LATERZA PARODI.

Yaguarón

Museo Doctor Francia: Yaguarón; f. 1968; relics of Paraguay's first dictator, 'El Supremo'; Pres. Dr FABIO RIVAS; Dir Dr JULIO CÉSAR CHAVES.

Universities

UNIVERSIDAD CATÓLICA 'NUESTRA SEÑORA DE LA ASUNCIÓN'

CC 1718, Independencia Nacional y Comuneros, Asunción

Telephone: (21) 441-044
Fax: (21) 445-245

Private control
Language of instruction: Spanish
Academic year: March to December
Founded 1960

Chancellor: Most Rev. Mgr Dr FELIPE SANTIAGO BENÍTEZ, Archbishop of Asunción
Rector: Mons. Dr JUAN OSCAR USHER
Vice-Rector: Lic. MANUEL MARSÁ RUIZ
Secretary-General: Abog. SIXTO VOLPE RÍOS
Librarian: Lcda MARGARITA KALLSEN

Number of teachers: 1,419
Number of students: 15,028

Publications: *Suplemento Antropológico, Estudios Paraguayos*.

DEANS

Faculty of Philosophy and Human Sciences: Dr LUIS A. GALEANO

Faculty of Business Administration and Accounting: Lic. ENRIQUE CÁCERES ROJAS
Faculty of Law and Diplomatic Science: Dr ANTONIO TELLECHEA SOLÍS
Higher Institute of Theology: R. P. MÁSTER ENRIQUE LÓPEZ
Faculty of Science and Technology: Ing. GERÓNIMO JOSÉ BELLASSAI BAUDO
Foundation Course: Abog. JOSÉ ANTONIO GALEANO

PROVINCIAL FACULTIES

Villa Rica
Faculty of Arts and Sciences: Dean Dr RUBÉN ECHAURI

Concepción
Faculty of Arts and Sciences: Dean Lic. NERY ANÍBAL SANABRIA SANABRIA

Encarnación
Faculty of Arts and Sciences: Dean Dr JESUS RENE HAURON

Pedro Juan Caballero
Faculty of Arts and Sciences: Dir Lic. LEILA GUERREÑO DE MACIEL (acting)

Ciudad del Este
Faculty of Arts and Sciences: Dean Ing. GUSTAVO DUARTE

UNIVERSIDAD NACIONAL DE ASUNCIÓN

Casilla 910, 2064 Asunción
Telephone: 507-080
Fax: (021) 213734

Founded 1889
State control
Language of instruction: Spanish
Academic year: March to December

Rector: Prof. Dr L. H. BERGANZA
Vice-Rector: Prof. Arq. J. R. UGARRIZA
Secretary-General: Prof. Dr G. B. BARRIENTOS
Librarian: Lic. E. R. DE GONZÁLEZ-PETIT

Number of teachers: 1,789
Number of students: 19,898

Publications: *Guía de cursos y carreras, Mundo universitario, Revista de la Universidad Nacional de Asunción.*

DEANS

Faculty of Economics: Dr EPIFANIO SALCEDO
Faculty of Medicine: Dr LUIS ALBERTO REYES
Faculty of Dentistry: Dr RUBÉN AYALA ARELLANO
Faculty of Chemistry: Dr RAFAEL CAMPERCHIOLI
Faculty of Exact and Natural Sciences: Dr ELBIO ESQUIVEL
Faculty of Philosophy: Dra OLINDA M. DE KOSTIANOVSKY
Faculty of Physical Sciences and Mathematics: Ing. HÉCTOR A. ROJAS
Faculty of Veterinary Sciences: Dr RAMON E. A. PISTILLI
Faculty of Agricultural Engineering: Ing. PEDRO G. GONZÁLES
Faculty of Architecture: Arq. JUAN R. UGARRIZA
Faculty of Law and Social Sciences: Dr CARLOS A. MERSÁN
Polytechnic Faculty: Lic. OSCAR BENÍTEZ ROA

DIRECTORS

Andrés Barbero Institute: Lic. YRMA DE SARUBBI
Institute of Electronic Engineering: Ing. EDUARDO KISHI
Institute of Geographical Sciences: Arq. MARÍA A. GONZÁLEZ TORRES
School of Librarianship: YOSHIKO MORIYA DE FREUNDORFER

PERU

Learned Societies

GENERAL

Academia Peruana de la Lengua (Peruvian Academy of Letters): Jr Conde de Superunda 298, Lima 1; fax 457424; f. 1887; corresp. of the Real Academia Española (Madrid); 30 mems; Dir Dr LUIS JAIME CISNEROS; Sec. Dr MARTHA HILDEBRANDT; publ. *Boletín* (annually).

ARCHITECTURE AND TOWN PLANNING

Colegio de Arquitectos del Perú: Avda San Felipe 999, Lima 11; tel. (14) 713772; fax (14) 713641; f. 1962; 3,717 mems; library of 3,500 vols; Dean NICANOR A. OBANDO OLIVA; Man. MARIANELLA VEGA JERI.

BIBLIOGRAPHY, LIBRARY SCIENCE AND MUSEOLOGY

Asociación Peruana de Archiveros (Peruvian Association of Archivists): Archivo General de la Nación, Calle Manuel Cuadros s/n, Palacio de Justicia, Apdo 3124, Lima.

Asociación Peruana de Bibliotecarios (Peruvian Association of Librarians): Bellavista 561, Miraflores, Lima 18, Apdo 995; tel. 474869; f. 1945; 680 mems; Pres. MARTHA FERNANDEZ DE LÓPEZ; Sec. LUZMILA TELLO DE MEDINA; publ. *Boletín Informativo* (2 a year).

EDUCATION

Asamblea Nacional de Rectores (Rectors' National Assembly): Calle Aldabas 337, Urb. Las Gardenias, Surco, Lima 33; tel. 495716; fax 496711; f. 1988; 34 mems; library of 30,000 vols; Pres. Dr CÉSAR PAREDES CANTO; Exec. Dir Ing. EDGARDO TORRES VERA; publs *Universidad, Escuelas y/o Carreras Profesionales, Grados y Títulos* (statistical bulletin), *Desarrollo Universitario* (bulletin).

Asociación Nacional de Educadoras Sampedranas: Máximo Abril 695, Jesús María, Lima 11; tel. 310562; f. 1910; aims to contribute to the development and improvement of national education; educational research, 'Education for Peace', educational innovation, institutional development; 6,200 mems; library of 1,000 vols with special collection: 'Education for Peace'; Pres. PEREGRINA MORGAN DE GOÑI; Sec. NANETE PÉREZ DE PILCO.

FINE AND PERFORMING ARTS

Asociación de Artistas Aficionados: Ica 323, Lima; f. 1938; 254 mems; presentation of plays, classical ballet and varied music programmes.

Instituto de Arte Peruano 'José Sabogal' (José Sabogal Institute of Peruvian Art): Apdo 3048, Alfonso Ugarte 650, Lima; under the control of Museo Nacional de la Cultura Peruana.

Instituto Nacional de Cultura: Casilla 5247, Ancash 390, Lima; tel. 28-7990; f. 1971; official cultural institute; 14 brs; Dir Dr FERNANDO SILVA SANTISTEBAN; publs *Fénix, Revista de Historia y Cultura, Runa*.

Instituto Peruano de Cultura Hispánica (Peruvian Institute of Hispanic Culture): Calle de la Riva 426, Lima; f. 1947; 280 mems; publ. *Boletín*.

HISTORY, GEOGRAPHY AND ARCHAEOLOGY

Centro de Estudios Histórico-Militares del Perú (Centre of Historico-Military Studies of Peru): Paseo Colón 190, Lima 1; tel. 230415; f. 1944; 1,098 mems; library of 13,800 vols; publ. *Revista*.

Centro de Investigación y Restauración de Bienes Monumentales del Instituto Nacional de Cultura: Casilla 5247, Jr Ancash 769, Lima.

Instituto Geográfico Nacional (National Geographical Institute): Avda Aramburú 1190, Lima 34; tel. (1) 475-3085; fax (1) 475-3075; e-mail postmast@ignperu.gob.pe; f. 1921; 250 mems; library of 3,200 vols; Dir Brig.-Gen. JOSÉ HERRERA ROSAS; publs topographical, physical and political maps of Peru, *Boletín Informativo*.

Instituto Vizcardo de Estudios Históricos (Vizcardan Institute of Historical Studies): Porta 540, Miraflores, Lima; f. 1954; study of revolutionary movements for Spanish-American independence (1781–1820); publ. *Revista*.

Sociedad Geográfica de Lima (Lima Geographical Society): Jirón Puno 450, Apdo 1176, Lima 100; tel. (1) 427-3723; fax (1) 426-9930; e-mail soc-geo+@amaute.rep.net.pe; f. 1888; library of 7,500 vols, also archives and museum; 750 mems, including corresp. and hon.; Pres. Arq. ERNESTO PAREDES ARANA; Sec. RAUL PARRA MAZA; publs *Boletín, Anuario Geográfico del Perú, Diccionario Geográfico del Perú*.

LANGUAGE AND LITERATURE

Centro del PEN Internacional (International PEN Centre): Apdo 1161, Lima; f. 1940; 25 mems; Pres. Dr JOSÉ GÁLVEZ; Sec. FERNANDO ROMERO.

MEDICINE

Academia de Estomatología del Perú (Peruvian Academy of Stomatology): Apdo 2467, Jr Chota 760, Lima; tel. 424-0853; f. 1929; 230 mems; library of 600 vols; Pres. Dr JUAN MANUEL FARAH HAYN; Sec. Dra SONIA GELLER DE VAISMAN; publ. *Academia*.

Academia Nacional de Medicina (National Academy of Medicine): Apdo 1589, Malecón Armendáriz 791, Miraflores, Lima 18; f. 1884; 40 mems, 40 associate mems, 40 corresp. and hon. mems; Pres. Dr GINO COSTA ELICE; Perm. Sec. Dr JAVIER MARIATEGUI; publ. *Boletín de la Academia Nacional de Medicina*.

Academia Peruana de Cirugía: Camaná 773, Lima; f. 1940; activities relate to the development of surgery in Peru; national and foreign membership; 100 titular mems and unlimited number of associates; Pres. Dr LUIS GURMENDI; publ. *Revista*.

Asociación Médica Peruana 'Daniel A. Carrión' (Peruvian Medical Association): Jirón Ucayali 218, Lima; f. 1920; 1,499 mems; Dir Dr MAX ARNILLAS ARANA; Sec. Dr MANUEL PAREDES MANRIQUE; publ. *Revista Médica Peruana*.

Federación Médica Peruana (Peruvian Medical Association): Almte Guisse 2165, Lima; f. 1942; 1,230 mems; Pres. Dr VICENTE UBILLÚS; Sec. Dr ENRIQUE FERNÁNDEZ V.; publ. *Boletín de la Federación Médica Peruana*.

Sociedad Peruana de Tisiología y Enfermedades Respiratorias (Peruvian Phthisiological Society): Domingo Casanova 116, Lince, Lima; f. 1935; 280 mems; Pres. CARLOS MENDOZA EUWING; Sec. RUBEN PAZ ANSSUINI; publ. *Revista Peruana de Tuberculosis y Enfermedades Respiratorias* (2 a year).

NATURAL SCIENCES

General

Academia Nacional de Ciencias Exactas, Físicas y Naturales de Lima (Lima Academy of Exact, Physical and Natural Sciences): Casilla 1979, Lima; f. 1939; publ. *Actas*.

Biological Sciences

Sociedad Entomológica del Perú: Apdo 14-0413, Lima 14; f. 1956; 700 mems; library of 9,500 vols; Pres. PEDRO G. AGUILAR F.; Sec. JESÚS ALCÁZAR S.; publ. *Revista Peruana de Entomología* (annually).

Mathematical Sciences

Instituto Nacional de Estadística (National Institute of Statistics): Avda Gral Garzón 662, Jesús María, Lima 11; tel. 333104; fax 333159; f. 1975; involved in population, housing, socio-economic and agricultural censuses and surveys; plans statistical policy of country; library of 6,000 vols; Dir FELIX MURILLO ALFARO; publs *Indice de precios al consumidor* (monthly), *Compendio Económico Mensual* (monthly), *Informe Económico Mensual* (monthly), *Cuentas Nacionales – PBI Nacional* (annually).

Physical Sciences

Asociación Peruana de Astronomía: Enrique Palacios 374, Chorrillos, Lima 9; tel. 718737; f. 1946; 550 mems; library of 1,000 vols, 1,000 periodicals; Pres. ENRIQUE SABLICH L.; Sec. JOSÉ GRADOS; publ. *Boletín* (3 a year).

Sociedad Geológica del Perú (Peruvian Geological Society): Apdo 2559, Lima; f. 1924; library of 40,000 vols; 800 mems; Pres Ing. ROBERT O. PLENGE; publ. *Boletín* (annually).

Sociedad Peruana de Espeleología (Peruvian Speleological Society): Jr Puno 450, Lima; f. 1965; Pres. Ing. CARLOS MORALES-BERMÚDEZ LÁMPARO; publ. *Cavernas Peruanas*.

Sociedad Química del Perú (Peruvian Chemistry Society): Apdo 14-0576, Lima 14; f. 1933; 1,200 mems; library of 5,600 vols; Pres. OLGA LOCK DE UGAZ; Sec.-Gen. Dr JUAN DE DIOS GUEVARA R.; publ. *Boletín* (quarterly).

RELIGION, SOCIOLOGY AND ANTHROPOLOGY

Centro Amazónico de Antropología y Aplicación Práctica (CAAAP): Apartado 14-0166, Lima 14; tel: 625811; fax 638846; f. 1974; defends the cultural identity and the way of life of marginalized Amazonian people and seeks to protect the Amazon region's natural resources; library of 5,000 vols; Dir FABIOLA LUNA; publs. *Amazonía Peruana* (2 a year), *Nuestra Tierra–Nuestra Vida* (quarterly), *El Trueno* (quarterly).

Instituto de Estudios Etnológicos (Institute of Ethnological Studies): Alfonso Ugarte

650, Lima; under auspices of Museo Nacional de la Cultura Peruana.

Instituto de Estudios Islámicos: Calle Rey de Bahamonde 121, Vista Alegre, Surco, Lima 33; tel. 489720; f. 1959; sound archives, numismatic collection, etc.; interests include economics, sociology and politics of contemporary Muslim world, the Palestinian problem, the Iranian Islamic revolution, the al-Fateh (Jamahiriya) revolution, and the diffusion of Islamic religious values in South America; special interest in Islamic-America relations in 16th and 17th centuries and nowadays; Pres. Dr RAFAEL GUEVARA BAZÁN; Chief Officer Prof. ELVA ZEGARRA TORREBLANCA.

Instituto Indigenista Peruano (Peruvian Institute of Indian Affairs): Avda Salaverry, Cuadra 6 s/n, 4° piso, Of. 402, Ministerio de Trabajo y Promoción Social, Lima; tel. 33-2090; f. 1946; studies the specific problems of indigenous groups; 25 mems; library of 1,500 vols, 1,046 periodicals; Dir Ing. CARLOS EDUARDO MENDOZA SALDIVAR; publ. *Perú-Indígena* (annually).

TECHNOLOGY

Asociación de Ingenieros Civiles del Perú: Nicolás de Piérola 788, 4° piso, Casilla 1314, Lima.

Asociación Electrotécnica Peruana: Avda República de Chile 284, Oficina 201, Lima; f. 1943; Pres. Ing. LEONCIO BARBA ARANJO.

Instituto Peruano de Ingenieros Mecánicos: Avda República de Chile 284, Of. 201, Lima; Dir ROBERTO HEREDIA ZAVADA.

Sociedad de Ingenieros del Perú (Society of Peruvian Engineers): Avda N. de Piérola 788, Casilla 1314, Lima; library of 15,000 vols; Sec. Ing. ADOLFO BUSTAMANTE T.; publ. *Ingenería* (3 a year).

Research Institutes

GENERAL

Mission ORSTOM au Pérou, Coopération auprès Instituto Geofisico, Instituto de Investigaciones de la Amazonia Peruana, Universidad Nacional Agraria, Universidad Catolica: Apdo 18-1209, Lima 18; tel. 224719; fax 408773; f. 1967; research in geology, agronomy, botany, ecology, economy, archaeology, geography; 15 staff; library of 950 vols; natural history museum; Dir FRANCIS KAHN; publ. *Boletín Sistemas Agrarios*. (See main entry under France).

AGRICULTURE, FISHERIES AND VETERINARY SCIENCE

Estación Experimental Agropecuaria de Tulumayo (Tulumayo Agricultural Research Station): Apdo 78, Tingo María, Huánuco; f. 1942; part of Instituto Nacional de Investigación y Promoción Agropecuaria (see below); library of 500 vols; 24 technical staff; Dir Ing. ALBERTO SALDAÑA SANTILLAN; publs *Informe Anual, Boletín Técnico, Guía de Cultivo, Informes Especiales.*

Estación Experimental Vista Florida: Km 8 Carretera Chiclayo-Ferreñafe, Casilla 116, Chiclayo; f. 1970; crops research (plant protection, rice, corn, beans, sorghum); 26 staff; library of 5,000 vols; Dir JOSÉ HERNÁNDEZ L.

Instituto Nacional de Investigación y Promoción Agropecuaria (National Agricultural Research Institute): Avda Guzmán Blanco 390, Lima 5; tel. 317159; f. 1929; library of 50,000 vols; technical staff 350; Exec. Dir Dr JAVIER GAZZO FERNÁNDEZ DÁVILA; publs *Revista de Investigación Avances en Investigación, Serie de Boletín Investigación, Avances en Investigación, Serie de Boletín Técnico, Informes Especiales, Divulgaciones, Boletín Bibliográfico.*

ECONOMICS, LAW AND POLITICS

Instituto Peruano para la Investigación de la Estadística: Avda Benavides 190, Lima 18; tel. 46-40-64; f. 1974; study of statistics in general, and especially in relation to economics; library of 5,000 vols; organizes symposia, seminars, courses, etc.

EDUCATION

Instituto Experimental de Educación Primaria No. 1: Barranco Avda Miraflores 200, Lima; f. 1940; to study systems and methods for the development of learning and the means to evaluate and control the results; library of scholastic texts; Dir Prof. NARCISO GONZÁLEZ CH.; publ. *Boletín.*

MEDICINE

Instituto de Cultura Alimentaria Birchner-Benner: Diez Canseco 487, Miraflores, Lima; fax 444-4250; f. 1979; research into diet, especially of meat-substitutes and high-nutrition and low-cost food mixtures; warns about inadequate diet; promotes agriculture by biological methods; library of 500 vols and periodicals; film and sound archives; Pres. CÉSAR MORALES GARCÍA; Sec. MARCELA CÁRDENAS.

Instituto de Investigaciones Alérgicas 'Dr Luis E. Betetta' ('Dr Luis E. Betetta' Allergy Research Institute): Avda La Marina 2501, Maranga, San Miguel, Lima 32.

Institutos Nacionales de Salud (National Institute of Health): Apdo 451, Lima 1; tel. 713254; fax 717443; f. 1936; communicable diseases, occupational diseases, nutritional disorders, food and drug quality control, research, production of vaccines and reagents; Head OSCAR GRADOS BAZALAR; publ. *Informativo Epidemiológico.*

NATURAL SCIENCES

General

Instituto del Mar del Perú (IMARPE) (Peruvian Marine Institute): Esq. Gral. Valle y Gamarra, Apdo 22, Callao; tel. 299811; fax 656023; f. 1964; oceanography, marine biology, microbiology, etc.; library of 65,000 vols; Pres. Vice-Almirante DANIEL MARISCAL GALIANO; Exec. Dir Ing. CÉSAR CHÁVEZ NAVARRO; publs *Informes, Boletín.*

Biological Sciences

Instituto de Biología Andina (Institute of Andean Biology): Apdo 5073, Lima; f. 1930; affiliated to the Faculty of Medicine, San Marcos Univ.; laboratories in Lima, Morococha and Puno; mobile laboratory research on physiology of inhabitants of the Andes and their resistance to high altitudes, acclimatization and fertility of animals taken to high altitudes with a view to industrial use, methods of hygiene, adaptive faculties of men at great heights, chronic mountain sickness and remedies, ecology and sociological problems; library of 1,091 vols, 400 periodicals; Dir Dr TULIO VELÁSQUEZ; publ. *Archivos de Biología Andina* (quarterly).

Physical Sciences

Dirección General de Meteorología del Perú (National Meteorological Service): Avda Arequipa 5200, Apdo 1308, Miraflores, Lima; f. 1928; 79 primary stations; publ. *Boletín* (annually).

Instituto Geofísico del Perú (Geophysical Institute): Apdo 3747, Lima; tel. (014) 365640; fax (014) 370258; f. 1919 as Huancayo Magnetic Observatory of the Carnegie Institution of Washington, transferred to the Peruvian Government 1947; education sector; observatories in Huancayo, Jicamarca, Ancón, Arequipa and Lima; basic and mission-oriented research; international programmes in geomagnetism, seismology, atmospheric sciences, solar activity and natural hazards; Pres. Dr MANUEL CHANG.

TECHNOLOGY

Instituto Geológico, Minero y Metalúrgico (Institute of Geology, Mining and Metallurgy): Apdo 889, Avda Canadá 1470, San Borja, Lima; tel. (1) 224-2963; fax (1) 225-4540; e-mail ingemmet5@chavin.rcp.net.pe; f. 1978 as result of merging Instituto Científico Tecnológico Minero and Instituto de Geología y Minería; carries out and co-ordinates research and evaluates mineral resources; library of 10,000 vols; Pres. JUAN MENDOZA MARSANO; Dir HUGO RIVERA MANTILLA; publs *Boletín Serie A, Serie D, Informes Técnicos.*

Instituto Peruano de Energía Nuclear (Peruvian Nuclear Energy Institute): Avda Canadá 1470, San Borja Dist., Lima 41, Apdo 1687, Lima 100; tel. 224-8998; fax 224-8991; 716883; fax 728081; f. 1975; research into peaceful uses of nuclear energy in medicine, biology, agriculture and industry, prospecting, mining and processing of uranium ores; management of nuclear reactor and operation of a radioisotope production plant; nucleo-electricity planning; training and research; information and documentation centre of 75,000 vols, periodicals, monographs; Pres. Vice-Alm. AP(r) JORGE DU BOIS GERVASI; Exec. Dir Dr CONRADO SEMINARIO ARCE; publs *Boletín de Informaciones* (quarterly), *Informes.*

Affiliated institute:

Centro Superior de Estudios Nucleares: Avda Canadá 1470, San Borja, Lima 41; tel. 224-5090; Dir Ing. IGNACIO FRISANCHO PINEDA.

Libraries and Archives

Arequipa

Biblioteca de la Universidad Nacional de San Agustín: Apdo 23, Arequipa; f. 1900; 430,000 vols; 1,204 pamphlets and 535 periodicals; in addition the University has 12 specialized libraries; Dir Dr JORGE DÍAZ ENCINAS; publ. *Revista de Investigación de la Universidad.*

Biblioteca Pública Municipal de Arequipa: Ejercicios 310, Apdo 435, Arequipa; f. 1879; 28,000 vols; Librarian ENRIQUE ALZÁGARA BALLÓN; also houses *Casa de la Cultura.*

Callao

Biblioteca de la Escuela Naval del Perú (Naval School Library): La Punta, Callao; f. 1914; Librarian ABEL ULLOA FERNÁNDEZ-PRADA; specialized library of 6,500 vols.

Biblioteca Pública Municipal Piloto: Esq. Ruiz y Colón, Callao; f. 1936, reorganized 1957; 48,312 vols; 42 mems; Dir ROSA SÁNCHEZ DE WU.

Lima

Archivo General de la Nación (National Archives): Palacio de Justicia, Calle Manuel Cuadros s/n., Apdo 3124, Lima; tel. 275930; fax 426-7221; f. 1861; two sections, Administrative and Historical; Dir Dra AIDA MENDOZA NAVARRO; publs *Legislación Archivística Peruana, Revista del AGN.*

Archivo Histórico Municipal: Apdo 605, Lima 1; f. 1963; documents, certificates from the 19th century; Librarian LUIS E. WUFFARDEN.

Biblioteca Central de la Pontificia Universidad Católica del Perú: Apdo 1761, Lima; tel. (1) 460-2870 ext. 176; fax (1) 463-

3773; e-mail biblio@pucp.edu.pe; f. 1917; 400,000 vols, 30,000 audio-visual items; Dir Dr CARMEN VILLANUEVA.

Biblioteca Central de la Universidad Nacional Mayor de San Marcos (San Marcos National University General Library): Pasaje Simón Rodríguez 697, Lima 1; tel. and fax (14) 428-5210; f. 1551; the collection corresponding to the colonial period was incorporated in the *Biblioteca Pública*—now the *Biblioteca Nacional*—when the latter was founded in 1821; the Peruvian Section has valuable material on history, law, and literature; Dir Dr OSWALDO SALAVERRY GARCÍA; 450,000 vols; publs *Boletín Bibliográfico* (annually).

Biblioteca de la Municipalidad de Lima: Pza. de Armas s/n, Lima; tel. 4279241; fax 4332422; f. 1935; gen. reference about Lima and its municipal govt; 22,000 vols; Librarian LUZMILA TELLO.

Biblioteca de la Universidad Nacional de Ingeniería: Apdo 1301, Lima; 29,000 vols; Librarian JUANA PAREJA MARMANILLO.

Biblioteca del Ministerio de Relaciones Exteriores (Library of the Ministry of Foreign Affairs): Palacio Torre-Tagle, Lima; f. 1921; 12,351 vols; Dir MANUEL G. GALDO; publ. *Maris Aestus*.

Biblioteca Nacional del Perú (National Library): Avda Abancay 4ta Cdra s/n, Lima; tel. (1) 4287690; fax (1) 4277331; e-mail jefatura@binape.gob.pe; f. 1821 by José de San Martín; possesses copies of the first printed works in Peru and the Americas; 736,465 vols, 32,500 MSS, 12,499 maps, 11,000 photographs, 2,164,413 periodicals; Dir MARTHA FERNÁNDEZ DE LÓPEZ; publs *Fénix* (1 a year), *Bibliografía Peruana, Boletín de la Biblioteca Nacional* (irregular), Gaceta Bibliotecaria del Perú (irregular).

Museums and Art Galleries

Arequipa

Museo Arqueológico (Archaeological Museum): Ciudad Universitaria, Pabellón de la Cultura, Altos, Casilla 23, Arequipa; tel. 22-9719; f. 1933; ceramics, mummies; Dir Dr E. LINARES MÁLAGA.

Ayacucho

Museo Histórico Regional de Ayacucho (Regional Historical Museum of Ayacucho): Centro Cultural Simón Bolívar, Avda Los Libertadores s/n, Ayacucho; f. 1954; archaeology, anthropology, history and popular crafts; library of 4,724 vols (including bound periodicals, etc.); Dir CÉSAR O. PRADO; Curator FREDY LAGOS ARRIARÁN; publ. *Anuario*.

Callao

Museo del Ejército del Perú (Army Museum of Peru): Fortaleza del Real Felipe, Plaza Independencia, Callao; f. 1984; Dir LUIS LOAYZA MORALES.

Museo Naval del Perú J. J. Elias Murguía (Naval History Museum): Avda Jorge Chávez 123, Plaza Grau, Callao; tel. 294793; f. 1958; specialist library of 7,948 vols; Dir Capitán de Fragata (retd) ALFONSO AGÜERO MORAS; publ. *Fuentes para la Historia Naval*.

Cuzco

Museo Arqueológico: Calle Tigre 165, Cuzco; Dir Dr LUIS A. PARDO.

Museo Histórico Regional de Cuzco: Cuesta del Almirante s/n, Palacio del Almirante s/n, Cuzco; f. 1946; Peruvian colonial art, Cuzco schools of painting affiliated to Inst. Nacional de Cultura; Dir ANTONIA VEGA CENTENO B.; publ. *Revista del Museo Histórico Regional*.

Huancayo

Museo Arqueológico 'Federico Gálvez Durand' de la Gran Unidad Escolar 'Santa Isabel': Pichcus s/n, Huancayo; f. 1952; 1,654 archaeological specimens from Nazca and other Peruvian cultures; examples of weaving, gold and bronze ornaments, fossils.

Huánuco

Museo-Biblioteca 'Leoncio Prado': 2 de Mayo y Tarapacá, Huánuco; f. 1945; natural history; Curator RICARDO E. FLORES.

Huaráz

Museo Regional de Ancash: Centro Cívico, Plaza de Armes, Huaráz, Ancash; f. 1936; 4,600 exhibits including 900 ceramics, 800 stone carvings and megalithic statues from Chavín, Recuay, and Huaráz; Dir Dr ODÓN ROSALES HUATUCO; publs *Guía de Esculturas, Pumacayán*.

Ica

Museo Cabrera: Plaza de Armas, Bolívar 174, Ica; f. 1966; collection of ancient engraved stones and pottery; library of 100,000 vols; Dir Dr JAVIER CABRERA.

Lambayeque

Museo Regional Arqueológico 'Bruning' de Lambayeque ('Bruning' Archaeological Museum): Calle 2 de Mayo 48, Lambayeque; f. 1924; nearly 8,000 exhibits, of which 1,366 gold, 110 silver; textile, ceramic, wooden and stone pieces; two unique blue and black granite mortars incised with mythological figures in 'Chavin' style; Dir WALTER ALVA.

Lima

Museo Arqueológico 'Rafael Larco Herrera' (Archaeological Museum): Avda Bolívar 1515, Pueblo Libre, Lima 21; tel. (1) 461-1312; fax (1) 461-5640; e-mail museolarco@tsi.com.pe; 2642278; f. 1926; Peruvian Pre-Columbian artefacts, erotica; library of 10,000 vols; Exec. Dir ANDRÉS ALVAREZ-CALDERÓN LARCO.

Museo de Arte de Lima (Museum of Art): Paseo Colón 125, Lima; tel. (1) 423-4732; fax (1) 423-6332; e-mail artelima@tsi.com.pe; inaugurated in its present form in 1961; exhibits of Peruvian art from its origins to the present day; Pre-Colombian Department: ceramics, carvings, Paracas woven material dating from 400 BC; Colonial Department: furniture, sculpture, paintings, religious art, silver; Modern Department: furniture and paintings from the 19th century to the present day; an important film archive; studio art courses; library of 4,000 items; restoration and conservation laboratory; Dir PEDRO PABLO ALAYZA; publ. *Bulletin* (monthly).

Museo de Arte Italiano: Paseo de la República 250, Lima 1; tel. (1) 423-9932; f. 1923; permanent exhibition of the museum's collection of 1920 Italian art; temporary exhibitions, courses, conferences, etc.; Dir IRENE VELAOCHAGA REY.

Museo de Historia Natural de la Universidad Nacional Mayor de San Marcos (Natural History Museum of the National University of San Marcos): Avda Arenales 1256, Apdo 14-0434, Lima 14; tel. 471-0117; fax 265-6819; e-mail museohn@unmsm.edu.pe; f. 1918; includes Herbario San Marcos (USM), with 300,000 specimens largely of Peruvian flora and units of zoology, botany, ecology, and geosciences; zoological collections; library of 8,000 vols; Dir Prof. Dr NIELS VALENCIA; publs *Serie 'A' Zoología, Serie 'B' Botánica, Serie 'C' Geología, Memorias, Serie de Divulgación* (irregular), *Boletín del Museo de Historia Natural UNMSM, Nueva Serie* (irregular).

Museo del Virreinato (Museum of the Viceroys): Quinta de Presa, Lima; f. 1935; sited in an 18th-century mansion; exhibits relating to the period of the Spanish Viceroys; Dir JOSÉ FLORES ARAOS; publ. *Revista*.

Museo Geológico de la Universidad Nacional de Ingeniería del Perú (Geological Museum of the National University of Engineering): Avda Tupac Amaru, Lima; f. 1891 as Museo de Yacimentos Minerales y Metalíferos de la Escuela Nacional de Ingenieros, name changed 1955; incorporates the Raymondi collections; Chief of Dept. of Geology JULIO DAVILA V.; publs catalogues.

Museo Nacional de Arqueología, Antropología e Historia del Perú (National Museum of Archaeology, Anthropology and History): Plaza Bolívar s/n, Pueblo Libre, Lima 21; tel. (14) 635070; fax (14) 632009; f. 1945; library of 29,000 vols; collection contains pre-Inca and Inca remains; Dir FERNANDO ROSAS MOSCOSO; publs *Boletín, Arqueológicas, Historia y Cultura*.

Museo Nacional de la Cultura Peruana: Avda Alfonso Ugarte 650, Apdo 3048, Lima 100; tel. 4235892; f. 1946; responsible for Instituto de Estudios Etnológicos and the Instituto de Arte Peruano 'José Sabogal'; popular art and ethnography; also has an ethno-historical library and a photographic archive; Dir SARA ACEVEDO BASURTO; publ. *Revista del Museo Nacional*.

Museo Postal y Filatélico Correo Central de Lima (Postal and Philatelic Museum): Conde Superunda 170, Lima 1; f. 1931; library of 100 vols; Dir DORA IBERICO CASTRO.

Trujillo

Museo de Arqueología de la Universidad de Trujillo: Apdo 299, Calle Bolívar 466, Trujillo; f. 1946; Dir Dr JORGE ZEVALLOS QUIÑONES; publ. *Chimor*.

National Universities

UNIVERSIDAD NACIONAL AGRARIA LA MOLINA

Apdo 456, La Molina, Lima
Telephone: (14) 352035
Fax: (14) 352473

Founded 1902; formerly Escuela Nacional de Agricultura
Language of instruction: Spanish
Academic year: April to July, September to December (two semesters)

Rector: Ing. JOSÉ DANCÉ CABALLERO
Vice-Rector (Academic): Ing. FRANCISCO DELGADO DE LA FLOR BADARACCO
Vice-Rector (Administrative): Dr MANUEL MIRANDA ZUÑIGA
Secretary-General: Dr EDUARDO URDANIVA BERTARELLI
Librarian: WILLIAM HURTADO DE MENDOZA SANTANDER

Number of teachers: 495
Number of students: 4,100

Publication: *Anales Científicos* (3 a year).

DEANS

Agronomy: ABEL BASURTO LAVANDA
Sciences: Ing. CÉSAR GUERRERO FLORES
Food Science: Ing. LEYLA ESTRADA ORÉ
Fisheries: Ing. HUGO NAVA CUETO
Zootechnics: Ing. ANGEL MORENO ROJAS
Forestry: Ing. MANUEL RÍOS RODRIGUEZ
Agricultural Engineering: Ing. RODOLFO MUÑANTE SANGUINETTI

Economics and Planning: Ing. WALTER FEGAN ESCOBAR
Postgraduate School: Ing. LUIS MAEZONO YAMASHITA

ATTACHED INSTITUTES

Centro de Investigaciones en Zonas Aridas: Avda Camilo Carrillo 300, Lima.

Instituto Nacional de Desarrolla Agro-Alimentario: Avda La Universidad s/n, La Molina, Lima 12.

UNIVERSIDAD NACIONAL AGRARIA DE LA SELVA

Apdo 156, Tingo María, Huánuco
Telephone: (64) 562341
Fax: (64) 561156

Founded 1964
State control
Language of instruction: Spanish
Academic year: April to December

Rector: ALBERTO SILVA DEL AGUILA
Vice-Rector (Academic): TEODOLFO VALENCIA CHAMBA
Secretary-General: CLODOALDO CREDO VALDIVIA
Librarian: TULIO JURADO BAQUERIZO

Number of teachers: 190
Number of students: 1,533

Publication: *Tropicultura.*

DIRECTORS OF ACADEMIC PROGRAMMES

Agronomy: Ing. ROLANDO RIOS RUIZ
Animal Breeding: Ing. EBER CARDENAS RIVERA
Food Industries: Ing. GUILLERMO DE LA CRUZ CARBANZA
Resources: Dr CESAR AUGUSTO MAZABEL TORRES
Economics and Administration: Lic. JAIME PEÑA CAMARENA

HEADS OF ACADEMIC DEPARTMENTS

Resource Sciences: Lic. EVA DORIS FALCON TARAZONA
Food Sciences and Technology: Ing. WASHINGTON PAREDES PEREDA
Food Sciences (Physical and Material): Ing. WALTER BERNUY BLANCO
Agricultural Sciences: Ing. SEGUNDO RODRIGUEZ DELGADO
Cattle Sciences: Ing. MIGUEL PEREZ OLANO
Economics and Administration: Eco. JUAN SOLANO NONALAYA, C.P.C. FIDILBERTO VARGAS PAITA, Adm. INOCENTE SALAZAR ROJAS
Basic Sciences and Languages: CÉSAR MAZABEL TORRES

UNIVERSIDAD NACIONAL DEL ALTIPLANO

Avda Ejercito No 329, Apdo 291, Puno
Telephone: 352912
Telex: 54772

Founded 1856
Academic year: March to December

Rector: Dr VICTOR TORRES ESTEVES
Administrative Vice-Rector: Econ. FRANCISCO GUTIERREZ GUTIERREZ
Academic Vice-Rector: Prof. VICTOR GALLEGOS MONROY
Head of Personnel and General Services: HERMOGENES MENDOZA ANCCO
Librarian: Prof. SERAFÍN CALSIN MAMANI

Number of teachers: 623
Number of students: 10,202

Publications: *Revistas problematicas, Revista Universitaria, Revista Visión Agraria.*

DEANS

Agriculture: R. SERRUTO COLQUE
Veterinary Medicine and Stockbreeding: Prof. C. SANCHEZ VIVEROS
Economic Engineering: L. AVILA ROJAS
Accounting and Administration: E. PINEDA QUISPE
Statistics for Engineering: E. CALMET URIA
Social Sciences: M. CANO OJEDA
Mining Engineering: V. NAVARRO TORRES
Metallurgy and Geological Engineering: H. MANRIQUE MEZA
Civil Engineering, Architecture and Systems: P. ARROYO GONZALES
Agricultural Engineering: W. SALAS PALMA
Law and Political Science: J. VALDEZ PEÑARANDA
Chemical Engineering: N. VILLAFUERTE PRUDENCIO
Biological Sciences: S. ATENCIO LIMACHI
Education: J. L. CACERES MONROY
Health Sciences: R. LOPEZ VELASQUEZ
Nursing: N. CALSIN CHIRINOS
Social Work: G. PINTO SOTELO
Postgraduate School: F. CÁCEDA DÍAZ

UNIVERSIDAD NACIONAL DE LA AMAZONÍA PERUANA

Sargento Lores 385, Apdo 496, Iquitos, Loreto
Telephone: 2343657
Fax: 233657

Founded 1962
State control
Language of instruction: Spanish
Academic year: April to February (two terms)

Rector: JOSÉ ROJAS VÁSQUEZ
Academic Vice-Rector: Lic. PEDRO VÁSQUEZ PÉREZ
Librarian: MARGARITA FASANANDO VÁSQUEZ

Number of teachers: 400
Number of students: 3,200

Publication: *Conocimiento.*

DEANS

Faculty of Agronomy Science: Ing. JULIO VÁSQUEZ RAMÍREZ
Faculty of Biology: ANDRÉS URTEAGA CAVERO
Faculty of Education and Humanities: Prof. JOSÉ ZUMAETA TORRES
Faculty of Administration and Accountancy: Prof. HEDMER PASQUEL CHONG
Faculty of Nursing: Enf. PABLO CASTRO TRELLES
Faculty of Food Sciences: Ing. JORGE TORRES LUPERDI
Faculty of Forestry: Ing. JOSÉ TORRES VÁSQUEZ
Faculty of Chemistry: Ing. JESÚS LÓPEZ SANGAMA
Faculty of Human Medicine: Dr MARIO THEMME RUNCIMAN
Faculty of Zootechnics: Ing. FERNANDO ARAUJO PAREDES

UNIVERSIDAD NACIONAL DE ANCASH 'SANTIAGO ANTÚNEZ DE MAYOLO'

Apdo 70, Huáraz, Ancash
Telephone: 721452
Fax: 721393

Founded 1977
State control
Language of instruction: Spanish
Academic year: April to July, September to December (2 semesters)

Rector: Ing. JOSÉ NARVÁEZ SOTO
Vice-Rector (Academic): M. Env. Des. EDME LANDEO ALVAREZ
Vice-Rector (Administrative): Lic. BAILÓN SÁNCHEZ GUERRERO
Secretary: Lic. EVA ZARZOSA MÁRQUEZ
Librarian: Ing. PABLO ESPINOZA TUMIALÁN

Number of teachers: 350
Number of students: 4,076

Publication: *Informativo UNASAM.*

DEANS

Faculty of Agricultural Sciences: Ing. GUILLERMO CASTILLO ROMERO
Faculty of Civil Engineering: Ing. SAMUEL TAMARA RODRÍGUEZ
Faculty of Food Industry Engineering: Ing. ANGEL QUISPE TALLA
Faculty of Environmental Sciences: Ing. JUAN VILCHEZ CORNEJO
Faculty of Mining, Geological and Metallurgical Engineering: Ing. JESÚS VIZCARRA ARAÑA
Faculty of Law and Political Science: Dr NÉSTOR ESPINOZA HARO
Faculty of Economic and Administrative Sciences: Lic. JOSÉ LINARES CAZOLA
Faculty of Medicine: Dr LEONCIO SUSUKI LÓPEZ
Faculty of Education: Lic. FÉLIX GONZALES ILLANES
Faculty of Science: Lic. CARLOS REYES PAREJA

UNIVERSIDAD NACIONAL DE CAJAMARCA

Apdo 16, Jr Lima 549, Cajamarca
Telephone: 2796

Founded 1962
State control
Language of instruction: Spanish
Academic year: March to December (two semesters)

Rector: Prof. CÉSAR A. PAREDES CANTO
Vice-Rectors: Dr HOMERO BAZÁN ZURITA, Ing. AURELIO MARTOS DÍAZ
Librarian: LUIS RONCAL

Number of teachers: 387
Number of students: 5,700

Publications: *Gaceta Universitaria, Revista de la UNTC.*

DEANS

Agriculture: Dr ISIDORO SÁNCHEZ VEGA
Economics, Administration and Accountancy: Prof. SEGUNDO CIEZA YAÑEZ
Education: Dr JOSUÉ TEJADA ATALAYA
Engineering: Ing. JULIO GUZMÁN PERALTA
Health: Dr JORGE CÉSPEDES ABANTO
Social Sciences: Prof. ALIDOR LUNA TELLO
Veterinary Medicine: Dr ROBERTO ACOSTA GÁLVEZ
Animal Husbandry: Ing. TULIO MONDRAGÓN RONCAL

HEADS OF DEPARTMENT

Chemistry: OSCAR MENDOZA MENDIVES
Biology: JOSÉ MANUEL CABANILLAS SORIANO
Physics: Prof. SEGUNDO GALLARDO ZAMORA
Agronomy: Ing. MANUEL MALPICA RODRÍGUEZ
Economics, Administration and Accountancy: FRANCISCO CRUZADO CERDÁN
Education: Prof. MARÍA ABANTO FLORIDA
Language and Literature: Prof. IVÁN LEÓN CASTRO
Engineering: Ing. CARLOS ESPARZA DÍAZ
Animal Husbandry: Ing. MIGUEL DÍAZ CABANILLAS
Social Sciences: Prof. SEGUNDO ARRÉSTEGUI ANGASPILCO
Mathematics: Prof. ANIANO RODRÍGUEZ CUEVA
Veterinary Medicine: Dra JUANA CAMPOS CRUZADO
Cultural Affairs: Prof. WILSON ALCÁNTARA VIDAL

UNIVERSIDAD NACIONAL DEL CALLAO

Saenz Peña 1060, Apdo 138, Callao
Telephone: 429-1600
Fax: 429-6607
E-mail: rector@redunac.unac.edu.pe

Founded 1966
State control
Language of instruction: Spanish
Academic year: April to December (two terms)

Rector: Alberto Arroyo Viale
Vice-Rectors: Pedro Quispe Tasayco, José Zuta Rubio
Registrar: Pablo Arellano Ubilluz
Librarian: Carlos Quiñones Monteverde

Number of teachers: 550
Number of students: 10,500

DEANS

Chemical Engineering: José Alvarado Rivadeneyra
Fish and Food Engineering: Emilio Rengifo Ruiz
Mechanical Engineering: Gabriel Salcedo Escobedo
Environmental Engineering: César Soto Hipolito
Electrical and Electronic Engineering: Víctor Gutiérrez Tocas
Mathematics and Physics: Víctor Veliz Becerra
Health Sciences: Sisinio Morales Zapata
Administration: Marco Guerrero Caballero
Accounting: Víctor Merea Llanos
Economics: David Pavila Cajahuanca
Industrial and Systems Engineering: Leoncio Tito Ataurima
Postgraduate School: Teresa Valderrama

UNIVERSIDAD NACIONAL DEL CENTRO DEL PERÚ

Calle Real 160, Casilla Postal 138, Huancayo 570, Junín

Telephone: (64) 235531
Fax: (64) 235981

Founded 1959
State control
Language of instruction: Spanish
Academic year: April to December (two terms)

Rector: Ing. Esaú Tiberio Caro Meza
Academic Vice-Rector: Ing. Hugo Ayala Sínchez
Chief Administrative Officer: Prof. Krúger Sarapura Yupanqui
Librarian: Dr Fernando Arauco Villar

Number of teachers: 705
Number of students: 8,395

Publications: *Boletín Informativo* (monthly), *Proceso* (irregular), *Ciencias Agrarias.*

DEANS

Accountancy: CPC Hernando Payano Rojas
Administration: Lic. Andrés Ildefonso Suárez
Agronomy: Ing. Glicerio López Orihuela
Forestry: Ing. Pedro Arizapana Anccasi
Stockbreeding: Ing. Humberto Rodríguez Landeo
Economics: Econ. Manuel Larrauri Rojas
Anthropology: Ing. Julio Barrera Yupanqui
Architecture: Arq. Felipe Arias Matos
Nursing: Lic. Héctor Zapata Rivera
Medicine: Dr Rigoberto Zúñiga Mera
Food Engineering: Ing. Libia Gutiérrez Gonzales
Mechanical Engineering: Ing. Raúl Mayco Chávez
Mining Engineering: Ing. Órison Delzo Salomé
Electrical, Electronic and Systems Engineering: Ing. Héctor Torres Maraví
Metallurgical Engineering: Ing. Eugenio Mucha Benito
Education and Humanities: Lic. Carlos Gamboa del Carpio
Chemical Engineering: Ing. Antonio Cochachi Guadalupe
Social Work: Lic. Lidia Lagones Miranda
Postgraduate School: Dr Pablo Mosombite Pinedo

UNIVERSIDAD NACIONAL 'DANIEL ALCIDES CARRIÓN'

Edif. Estatal 4, Apdo 77, Cerro de Pasco, Pasco
Telephone: 2197
Founded 1965
Rector: Prof. Norberto Gonzales Peralta
Number of teachers: *c.* 90
Number of students: *c.* 1,000
Faculties of economics, education, mining and metallurgy.

UNIVERSIDAD NACIONAL DE EDUCACIÓN 'ENRIQUE GUZMÁN Y VALLE'

La Cantuta s/n, Chosica, Lima 15
Telephone: 910052
Founded 1967
State control
Language of instruction: Spanish
President: Dra Doraliza Tovar Torres
First Vice-President (Academic): Dra Luz Doris Sánchez Pinedo
Second Vice-President (Administrative): Vidal Bautista Carrasco
General Secretary: Dra Gladys Ramírez Adrianzén
Registrar: Prof. Mireia Solé Alabart
Librarian: Margarita López M.
Library of 16,500 vols
Number of teachers: 190
Number of students: 9,744
Publication: *Cantuta.*

DEANS

Faculty of Humanities: Humberto Vargas Salgado
Faculty of Sciences: Liliana Sumarriva Bustinza
Faculty of Technology: José Astolaza de la Cruz
Postgraduate School: Dr Jorge Jhoncon Kooyip (Dir)

UNIVERSIDAD NACIONAL 'FEDERICO VILLARREAL'

Calle Carlos González 285, Maranga, San Miguel, Lima 32
Telephone: (14) 4641301
Fax: (14) 4644370
Founded 1963
State control
Language of instruction: Spanish
Academic year: April to December
Rector: Arq. Santiago Agurto Calvo
Vice-Rector (Academic): Dr Ernesto Melgar Salmón
Vice-Rector (Administrative): Dr Oswaldo Alvarado Sánchez
General Secretary: Dr Luis E. Alcázar Uribe
Librarian: (vacant)
Number of teachers: 1,500
Number of students: 25,000
Publications: *Boletín Unavi, Noticiero Unavi, Revista Yachaywasi.*

DEANS

Education: Dr Ibico Rojas Rojas
Humanities: Dr Antonio Peña Cabrera
Law and Political Sciences: Dr Felipe García Escudero
Social Sciences: Lic. Rosario Giraldo Urueta
Public and Private Administration: Dr Jaysuño Abramovich Schwartzberg
Economics: Ec. Imelda Trancón Peña
Finance and Accountancy: C.P.C. Blanca Cardenas Cardenas
Architecture and Town Planning: Arq. Luis Velásquez Diaz
Odontology: Dr Plinio Torres de la Gala
Oceanography Fisheries and Food Sciences: Dr Néstor Teves Rivas
Medicine: Dr Jorge Santiago Vereau Moreno
Medical Technology: Dr Jorge Villena Pierola
Geographical Engineering: Ing. John Walter Gómez Lora
Electronic Engineering and Information Science: Ing. Dario Biella Bianchi Diamandescu
Psychology: Dr José Anicama Gómez
Civil Engineering: Ing. Enrique Gutiérrez Correa
Industrial and Systems Engineering: Ing. Oscar Benavides Cavero
Natural Sciences and Mathematics: Dr Carlos Santa Cruz Carpio

UNIVERSIDAD NACIONAL DE HUÁNUCO 'HERMILIO VALDIZÁN'

Jr Dos de Mayo 680, Apdo 278, Huánuco
Telephone: 512341
Fax: 513360
Founded 1964
State control
Language of instruction: Spanish
Academic year: April to July, August to December (2 semesters)
Rector: Edgardo Torres Vera
Vice-Rectors: Abner Chavez Leandro (Academic), Lic. Luis Sara Rato (Administrative)
Head of Administration: Esteban Medina Avila
Librarian: Lic. Aurora Ampudia Davila
Library of 25,967 vols
Number of teachers: 261
Number of students: 5,637
Publications: *Cuadernos de Investigación, Boletines Informativos, Visita de la Provincia de León de Huánuco en 1562—Iñigo Ortíz de Zúñiga, visitador—Vols I and II, Antología Huanuqueña Vol I* (prose), *Vol II* (poetry) and *Vol III* (essays).

DEANS

Agriculture: N. V. Marce Perez Saavedra
Business Management: CPC Arturo Rivera y Caldas
Education and Humanities: Lic. Jesus Alfonso Farfan Gutierrez
Health Sciences: Psic. Rosario Sanchez Infantas
Law and Political Science: Abog. Manuel Cornejo Huapalla
Engineering: Mg. Doris Alvarado Linares

UNIVERSIDAD NACIONAL DE INGENIERÍA

Casilla 1301, San Martín de Porres, Lima
Telephone: 811035
Founded 1896 as Escuela Nacional de Ingenieros del Perú, present name 1955
State control
Language of instruction: Spanish
Academic year: April to December
Rector: Dr José Ignacio Lopez Soria
Vice-Rectors: Ing. Miguel Angel Saenz Lizarzaburu, Dr Casio Ore Ore
Secretary-General: Dr Abelardo Ludeña Luque
Library: see Libraries
Number of teachers: 996
Number of students: 12,241
Publications: *Boletín 'Quilca', Revista Técnica 'Tecnia', Revista Artes y Ciencias 'Amaru'.*

DEANS OF FACULTIES

Architecture, Town Planning and Fine Arts: Arq. Javier Sota Nadal
Science: Dr Jaime Avalos Sanchez
Economics and Social Sciences: Lic. Jorge Abadie Linares
Civil Engineering: Ing. Genaro Humala Aybar

Geology, Mining and Metallurgical Engineering: Ing. PEDRO MAXIMO ANGELES BETETA
Industrial and Systems Engineering: Ing. LUIS FLORES FONSECA
Mechanical Engineering: Ing. JUAN HORI ASANO
Electrical and Electronic Engineering: Ing. JUBERT CHAVEZ SERRANO
Petroleum Engineering: Ing. ARTURO BURGA ACOSTA
Chemical and Manufacturing Engineering: Ing. LUCIO RAMOS BENAVENTE
Environmental Engineering: Ing. JORGE PFLUCKER

UNIVERSIDAD NACIONAL JORGE BASADRE GROHMANN

Casilla 316, Tacna
Telephone: (54) 727871
Fax: (54) 721985
E-mail: cote@principal.unjbg.edu.pe
Founded 1971 as Universidad Nacional de Tacna
State control
Language of instruction: Spanish
Academic year: April to December
Chancellor: Dr CARLOS VALENTE ROSSI
Rector: Mgr ALBERTO COAYLA VILCA
Vice-Rectors: Dr hab. VICENTE CASTAÑEDA CHÁVEZ, Mgr LEONCIO MOLINA VÁSQUEZ
Secretary-General: Lic. RAMÓN VERA ROALCABA
Librarian: OLGA PONCE CALDERÓN
Library of 29,000 vols
Number of teachers: 275
Number of students: 4,412
Publications: *Memoria de Gestión, Ciencia y Tecnología, Revista Materno Infantil, Revista Nueva Imagen.*

DEANS

Administration: Lic. DAVID CAJAHUANCA GIRALDEZ
Accounting: FERNANDO TENORIO VICENTE
Fishing Engineering: Ing. WILFREDO NOEL GUEVARA
Obstetrics: Obst. JUANA BARREDA GRADOS
Food Industry Engineering: Ing. ESTANISLAO SAAVEDRA V.
Agriculture: Dr OSCAR FERNÁNDEZ CUTIRE
Mining Engineering: Ing. DANTE MANZANARES CÁCERES
Metallurgical Engineering: Ing. FRANCISCO GAMARRA GÓMEZ
Education: Prof. OLIVER BALLÓN MONTESINOS
Science: Biól. VICTORINO DELGADO TELLO
Nursing: Enf. NORA VELA PAZ
Medicine: Mgr MIGUEL ARROYO PANCLAS
Postgraduate School: Mgr ABEL MIRANDA PERALTA (Dir)

ATTACHED RESEARCH INSTITUTE

Instituto de Investigación Sísmica.

UNIVERSIDAD NACIONAL 'JOSÉ FAUSTINO SÁNCHEZ CARRIÓN'

Avda Grau 592, Of. 301, Apdo 81, Huacho, Lima
Telephone: 324741
Founded 1968
Rector: Lic. SEVERO LLANOS BAYONA
Library of 5,000 vols
Number of teachers: *c.* 100
Number of students: *c.* 3,000
Departments of fisheries, administration, engineering, nutrition, sociology.

UNIVERSIDAD NACIONAL DE LA LIBERTAD

Independencia 431, Of. 203, Trujillo
Telephone: 24-3721
Fax: 25-6629
Founded 1824 by Simón Bolívar
State control
Language of instruction: Spanish
Academic year: April to December
Rector: Dr GUILLERMO GIL MALCA
Vice-Rector (Academic): Dr HUGO REQUEJO VALDIVIESO
Vice-Rector (Administrative): Dr WALTER ARRASCUE VARGAS
Librarian: Dr HUGO CASANOVA HERRERA
Library of 23,806 volumes, 36,001 periodicals and pamphlets
Number of teachers: 845
Number of students: 12,500
Publications: *Memoria Rectoral, Revista de Derecho, Lenguaje y Ciencia, Revista del Museo de Arqueología y Antropología, Amauta—Archivos de Oftalmología del Norte del Perú.*

DEANS

Law and Political Sciences: Dr RÓGER ZAVALETA CRUZADO
Education: Dr VÍCTOR BALTODANO AZABACHE
Economic Sciences: Dr EDUARDO UPSON LEÓN
Medical Sciences: Dr RICARDO ROMERO CANO
Engineering: Ing. MANUEL TAM REYES
Biological Sciences: Dr JULIO ARELLANO BARRAGÁN
Physical and Mathematical Sciences: Dr AUGUSTO CHAFLOQUE CHAFLOQUE
Pharmacy and Biochemistry: Dr JOSÉ SILVA LARA
Social Sciences: Dr WEYDER PORTOCARRERO CÁRDENAS
Nursing: Dr ELVIRA RODRÍGUEZ ANTINORI
Chemical Engineering: Dr MARIO ALVA ASTUDILLO

UNIVERSIDAD NACIONAL MAYOR DE SAN MARCOS DE LIMA

Avda República de Chile 295, Of. 506, Casilla 454, Lima
Telephone: 314629
Founded 1551
Rector: Dr ANTONIO CORNEJO POLAR
Vice-Rector: Dr GUSTAVO S. MIRÓ QUESADA
Administrative Director: Dr VÍCTOR HONMA SAITO
Number of teachers: 3,150
Number of students: 34,223
Publications: *Boletín Informativo, Boletín Bibliográfico, Revista de San Marcos,* etc.

DIRECTORS OF ACADEMIC PROGRAMMES

Mathematics and Physics: Dr R. MOSQUERA RAMÍREZ
Chemistry and Chemical Engineering: Ing D. SÁNCHEZ MANTILLA
Geology and Geography: Dr A. ALBERCA CEVALLOS
Biology: Dra B. LIZÁRRAGA DE OLARTE
Pharmacy and Biochemistry: Dr A. DEL CASTILLO ICAZA
Veterinary Science: Dr V. FERNÁNDEZ ANHUAMÁN
Medicine: Dr J. CAMPOS REY DE CASTRO
Dentistry: Dr B. PEREA RUIZ
Social Science: Dr W. REÁTEGUI CHÁVEZ
Law and Political Science: Dr R. LA HOZ TIRADO
Philosophy, Psychology and Art: Dr A. CASTRILLÓN VIZCARRA
Linguistics, Literature and Philology: Dr M. MARTOS CARRERA
Education: Dr C. BARRIGA HERNÁNDEZ
Accountancy: Dr J. C. TRUJILLO MEZA
Economics: Dr A. MENDOZA DIEZ
Engineering: Dr P. MATÍAS ATÚNCAR
Metallurgy: Ing. M. CHÁVEZ AGUILAR
Nutrition: Dr T. AGUILAR FAJARDO
Administration: Dr A. PAÚCAR CARBAJAL
Completion Studies: Dr M. VELASCO VERÁSTEGUI
National School of Librarianship and Information Science: M. BONILLA DE GAVIRIA

UNIVERSIDAD NACIONAL PEDRO RUIZ GALLO

8 de Octubre 637, Apdo 557, Lambayeque
Telephone: 2080
Founded 1970
State control
Language of instruction: Spanish
Rector: Ing. ANGEL DIAZ CELIS
Vice-Rector: Ing. PEDRO CASANOVA CHIRINOS
Librarian: Dr GUILLERMO BACA AGUINAGA
Number of teachers: 261
Number of students: 5,460
Publications: *Boletín Informativo* (monthly), *Universidad* (annually).

DIRECTORS OF ACADEMIC PROGRAMMES

Administration: Ing. M. MORENO MESTA
Agriculture: Ing. D. OJE DA PEÑA
Biology: Ing. A. DÍAZ CELIS
Accounting: Ing. A. GIRALDO ESPINOSA
Law: Ab. C. VELA MARQUILLO
Economics: Econ. G. NINAHUAMAN MUCHA
Mathematics and Statistics: Mat. N. LÓPEZ SEGURA
Nursing: Enf. C. ROMERO DE CARCELEN
Agricultural Engineering: Ing. O. VIVAR PÁRRAGA
Civil Engineering: Ing. J. SALAZAR CASTILLO
Mechanical and Electrical Engineering: Ing. J. SAENZ QUIROGA
Human Medicine: Dr A. BURGA HERMÁNDEZ
Veterinary Medicine: Vet J. GUTIÉRREZ REYES
Sociology: M. RAMOS BAZÁN
Animal Husbandry: Ing. F. VILLENA RODRÍGUEZ

UNIVERSIDAD NACIONAL DE PIURA

Cusco 323, Apdo 295, Piura
Telephone: 321931
Founded 1961
State control
Language of instruction: Spanish
Academic year: March to December
Rector: ARTURO DAVIES GUAYLUPO
Vice-Rector: FRANCISCO JUÁREZ TIMANÁ
Administrative Director: Lic. VICENTE SÁNCHEZ JUÁREZ
Librarian: MANUEL CEVALLOS FLORES
Number of teachers: 309
Number of students: 5,500
Publications: *Boletines.*

DEANS

Faculty of Agronomy: Dr MARTÍN DELGADO JUNCHAYA
Faculty of Administrative Sciences: Lic. JOSÉ CASTRO PALACIOS
Faculty of Accounting and Finance: LUIS GINOCCHIO
Faculty of Physical and Mathematical Sciences: SAUL CÉSPEDES LOMPARTE
Faculty of Social Sciences and Education: JANET LAMAS DE MANTILLA
Faculty of Economics: Ing. EFRAÍN CHUECAS VELÁSQUEZ
Faculty of Industrial Engineering: Ing. ANDRÉS ORUNA CISNEROS
Faculty of Mining Engineering: Ing. ALBERTO WINCHONLONG CORONADO
Faculty of Fishing Engineering: MANUEL MOGOLLÓN LÓPEZ
Faculty of Human Medicine: MANUEL PURIZACA BENITES
Faculty of Animal Husbandry: Ing. ENGELBERTO ZURITA PEÑA

UNIVERSIDAD NACIONAL DE SAN AGUSTÍN DE AREQUIPA

Santa Catalina 117, Cercado, Arequipa
Telephone and fax: (54) 237808

Founded 1828
State control
Language of instruction: Spanish
Academic year: April to December

Rector: Dr JUAN MANUEL GUILLÉN BENAVIDES
Academic Vice-Rector: ROLANDO CORNEJO CUERVO
Administrative Vice-Rector: ROBERTO KOSAKA MASUNO
General Secretary: LUIS ALBERTO VALDIVIA RODRÍGUEZ

Library: see Libraries
Number of teachers: 1,453
Number of students: 22,899

Publications: *Boletín Bibliográfico, Boletín Estadístico* (annually).

DEANS

Architecture and Town Planning: CÉSAR MÁRQUEZ MARES
Biological and Agricultural Sciences: VALDEMAR MEDINA HOYOS
Accounting and Administration: EDGAR RÍOS VILLENA
History and Social Sciences: VÍCTOR RAÚL SACCA ABUSABAL
Education: VÍCTOR HUGO LINARES HUACO
Natural and Formal Sciences: ANDRÉS REYNOSO ORTIZ
Law: RAYMUNDO NÚÑEZ LOZADA
Economics: EDGAR ACOSTA Y GUTIÉRREZ
Nursing: ESPERANZA VALDIVIA AMPUERO
Philosophy and Humanities: TERESA ARRIETA TRONCOSO DE GUZMÁN
Geology and Geophysics: MELECIO LAZO ANGULO
Civil Engineering: ENRIQUE CAMPOS MATTOS
Production and Services Engineering: JOSÉ HERNÁNDEZ VALLEJOS
Process Engineering: MARIO LOZADA REYNOSO
Medicine: BENJAMÍN PAZ ALIAGA
Psychology and Industrial and Public Relations: CÉSAR SALAS MORALES

UNIVERSIDAD NACIONAL DE SAN ANTONIO ABAD

Avda de la Cultura s/n, Apdo 367, Cusco
Telephone: 222271

Founded 1962; reorganized 1969

Rector: Ing. CARLOS CHACON GALINDO

Number of teachers: *c.* 450
Number of students: *c.* 16,000

Publication: *Revista Universitaria* (annually).

Departments of economics, accountancy, education, technology, geology and mining, animal husbandry.

UNIVERSIDAD NACIONAL DE SAN CRISTÓBAL DE HUAMANGA

Portal Independencia No. 57, Apdo 220, Ayacucho
Telephone: 912522
Fax: 912510

Founded 1677; reopened 1959
State control
Language of instruction: Spanish
Academic year: March to July, August to December

Rector: Ing. PEDRO VILLENA HIDALGO
Academic Vice-Rector: (vacant)
Administrative Vice-Rector: Ing. LUIS LI PONCE
Secretary-General: Ing. MAURO VARGAS CAMARENA
Librarian: MARIA ISABEL MATTA DURAN

Number of teachers: 450
Number of students: 6,000

Publications: *Boletín UNSCH, Guamangengis, Signos y Obras.*

DEANS

Agronomy: Ing. CÉSAR ROLANDO RUIZ CANALES
Social Sciences: TULA RUTH ALARCON ALARCON
Law and Political Sciences: Dr DANIEL QUISPE PEREZ
Education: Prof. HECTOR ELIAS VEGA LEON
Economics and Administration: AURELIO ELORRIETA ESPINOZA
Mining and Civil Engineering: Ing. CARLOS AUBERTO PRADO PRADO
Biological Sciences: VICTOR ALEGRIA VALERIANO
Chemical and Metallurgical Engineering: Ing. CLEMENTE LIMAYLLA AGUIRRE
Nursing: Prof. VICENTE VALVERDE BALTAZAR
Obstetrics: Dr SADOT TORRES RAMOS

RESEARCH INSTITUTES

Research Institute of Agriculture and Animal Husbandry: Dir Ing. FERNANDO BARRANTES DEL AGUILA.

Research Institute of Biological Sciences: Dir VÍCTOR CORNEJO ALARCÓN.

Research Institute of Economics at Huamanga: Dir Econ. MARIO BRAVO CHACÓN.

Research Institute of Historico-Social Sciences: Dir JUAN JOSÉ GARCÍA MIRANDA.

Research Institute of Chemical Engineering: Dir Ing. CÉSAR GRANADOS RAFAEL.

Educational Research Institute of the Andean Region: Dir Prof. RANULFO CAVERO CARRASCO.

Research Institute of Mathematics and Physics: Dir Prof. CESAR AUGUSTO ROJAS JURADO.

Research Institute of Health and Population Studies: Dir Dr JESÚS PALACIOS SOLANO.

Research Institute of Linguistics and Literature: Dir Prof. ELMAR ALIAGA APAESTEGUI.

Research Institute of Civil and Mining Engineering: Dir Ing. JULIO CHAVEZ CASTILLO.

Research Institute of Juridical Sciences: Dir Abog. RAÚL PALACIO GARCÍA.

UNIVERSIDAD NACIONAL 'SAN LUIS GONZAGA'

Cajamarca 194, Ica
Telephone: 233201

Founded 1961

Rector: Dr CESAR ANGELES CABALLERO
Secretary-General: Dr MIGUEL CALDERÓN REINA

Number of teachers: 459
Number of students: 6,295

Publications: *Letras y Educación, Educación Dental.*

Academic Programmes in agronomy, economic and social sciences, law, arts and education, pharmacy and biochemistry, dentistry, civil engineering, mechanical engineering and electricity, medicine, veterinary medicine, fisheries and biological sciences.

UNIVERSIDAD NACIONAL DE SAN MARTÍN

Martínez de Compagñón 527, Apdo 239, Tarapoto

Founded 1979

Rector: Prof. DALÍN ENCOMENDEROS DÁVALOS
Secretary-General: Ing. ALEJANDRO CRUZ RENGIFO
Librarian: JORGE YUNGBLUTH ZEGARRA

Number of teachers: 41
Number of students: 410

HEADS OF ACADEMIC DEPARTMENTS

Agriculture and Forestry: Ing. A. QINTEROS GARCÍA
Civil Engineering: Lic. P. BALLENA CHUMIOQUE
Agricultural Engineering: Ing. C. MALDONADO TITO
Basic Sciences and Humanities: Prof. A. LINAREZ BENSIMÓN
Mother and Child Health: Dr J. SANDOVAL ROJAS

UNIVERSIDAD NACIONAL DE UCAYALI

Apdo postal 90, Pucallpa
Telephone and fax: (64) 571044

Founded 1979
State control
Language of instruction: Spanish

Rector: Dr VICTOR CHÁVEZ VÁSQUEZ
Vice-Rectors: Ing. DANIEL BALAREZO INFANTE (Academic), Dr MIGUEL NOLTE MANZANARES (Administration)
Registrar: Ing. Admin. ROMEL PINEDO RÍOS
Librarian: RAUL JAVIER GUTIÉRREZ PINEDA

Number of teachers: 178
Number of students: 1,400

DEANS

Agronomy: OSCAR LLAPAPASCA PAUCAR
Forest Sciences: Ing. CARLOS FACHIN MATOS
Health: ISABEL ESTEBAN ROBLADILLO
Administration and Accountancy: Lic. Admin. PEDRO ORMEÑO CARMONA

HEADS OF DEPARTMENT

Animal Husbandry: ILDEFONSO AYALA ASCENSIO
Agrarian Sciences: Ing. JAVIER AMACIFUEN VIGO
Management: Ing. OSCAR BARRETO VÁSQUEZ
Forest Industries: Ing. DAVID LLUNCOR MENDOZA
Environmental Conservation: Ing. ROLI BALDOCEDA ASTETE
Integrated Health Systems: JAIME PASTOR SEGURA
Surgery, Maternal and Child Health: AURISTELA CHÁVEZ VÁSQUEZ
Administrative Sciences: ELIAS MORENO MORENO
Accounting and Finance: NESTOR GOYZUETA DREYFUS

Private Universities

PONTIFICIA UNIVERSIDAD CATÓLICA DEL PERÚ

POB 1761, Lima 1; premises at: Avda Universitaria, Cdra 18 s/n, San Miguel, Lima 32
Telephone: (1) 460-28-70
Fax: (1) 461-17-85
E-mail: promydes@pucp.edu.pe

Founded 1917
Private control
Language of instruction: Spanish
Academic year: March to July, August to December (two terms)

Rector: Dr SALOMÓN LERNER FEBRES
Vice-Rector (Academic): Ing. LUIS GUZMÁN BARRÓN SOBREVILLA
Vice-Rector: (Administrative): Dr MARCIAL RUBIO CORREA
Secretary-General: Dr RAÚL CANELO R.
Registrar: ANGELITA BASSO
Librarian: Dra CARMEN VILLANUEVA

Library: see Libraries
Number of teachers: 1,284
Number of students: 12,007

Publications: *Pro-Mathematica, Química, Anthropológica, Debates en Sociología, Derecho, Economía, Lexis* (linguistic and literary review), *Historia, Psicología, Espacio y Desarrollo, Areté, Boletín del Instituto Riva-Agüero, Sinopsis.*

DEANS

Graduate School: Dr José Tola Pasquel (Dir)
School of Science and Engineering: Ing. Manuel Olcese Franzero
School of Law: Dr Lorenzo Zolezzi Ibárcena
School of Business Administration and Accounting: Dr Luis Gómez Martens
School of Social Sciences: Dr Orlando Plaza Jibaja
School of Letters and Humanities: Dr Franklin Pease García-Yrigoyen
School of Social Work: Lic. Haydée Alor Luna
School of General Studies:
Sciences: Dr Luis Montestruque Zegarra
Letters: Dr Roberto Criado Alzamora
School of Fine Arts: Dra Anna Cotroneo de Maccagno
School of Education: Dra Elsa Tueros Way

DIRECTORS

Languages Centre: Dra Isabel García Ponce
Tele-education Centre: Dr Juan Carlos Crespo López de Castilla

ATTACHED RESEARCH INSTITUTES

Instituto Riva-Agüero: Dir Dr José Agustin de la Puente y Candamo.

Instituto de Idiomas: Dir Aldo Higashi G.

Instituto de Informática: Dir Ing. Juan Carlos Flores Molina.

Instituto de Estudios Internacionales: Dir Dr Francisco Tudela van Breugel-Douglas.

Centro de Estudios Pre-Universitarios (CEPREPUC): Dir Héctor Viale T.

Centro de Investigaciónes y Servicios Educativos de la Pontificia Universidad Católica del Peru (CISE-PUCP): Dir Dra Francisca Bartra Gros.

Centro de Investigaciones Sociológicas, Económicas, Politicas y Antropológicas de la Pontificia Universidad Católica del Perú (CISEPA–PUCP): Exec. Sec. Prof. Sandra Vallenas.

UNIVERSIDAD FEMENINA DEL SAGRADO CORAZÓN

Avda Los Frutales 954, Urb. Santa Sofía, La Molina, Apdo 0005, Lima 41
Telephone: (14) 4364641
Fax: (14) 4363247
Founded 1962
Private control
Language of instruction: Spanish
Academic year: April to December (two semesters)

Rector: Dra R. M. Elga García Aste
Vice-Rector (Administrative): Dra Carmen Cornejo Tavella
Vice-rector (Academic): Dr Agustín Campos Arenas
Librarian: Lic. María La Serna de Más

Library of 57,000 vols
Number of teachers: 349
Number of students: 2,345

Publications: *Revista de Educación, Cuaderno de Psicología, Revista de Psicología, Puente, Consensus, Avances en Psicología.*

DEANS

Psychology and Humanities: Lic. Rosa María Reusche Lari
Education: Jorge Silva Merino
Translation, Interpreting and Communications: Lic. Mercedes Apraiz de Barrenechea
Architecture: Fernando Pérez-Rosas Díaz
Law and Political Sciences: Gabriela Aranibar Fernández-Davila
Engineering: Gloria Valdivia Camacho
Postgraduate School: Gladys Buzzio Zamora

UNIVERSIDAD 'INCA GARCILASO DE LA VEGA'

Avda Arequipa 3610, San Isidro, Lima
Telephone: 711421
Founded 1964
Private control

Rector: (vacant)
Secretary-General: Dr Alfonso Carrizales Ulloa
Librarian: Nancy Harman de Alvarado

Number of teachers: *c.* 240
Number of students: *c.* 7,000

Publication: *Garcilaso.*

DIRECTORS

Education: A. Castro Urbina
Economics: M. Delgado Ulloque
Accountancy: T. Moya de Rojas
Administration: G. Suxe Montero
Social Sciences: A. Castro Urbina
Law: R. Castro Nestarez
Social Work: B. Cordova Suárez
Industrial Engineering: L. Tito Ataurima

UNIVERSIDAD DE LIMA

Apdo 852, Lima 100
Telephone: (14) 4376767
Fax: (14) 4378066
Founded 1962
Private control
Language of instruction: Spanish
Academic year: April to July, August to December

Rector: Dr Ilse Wisotzki Loli
Vice-Rector: Ing. Bernardo Fernández Velásquez
Director of Administration and General Services: Ing. Eduardo Graña Luza
Librarian: Nancy Lizárraga Cano

Number of teachers: 793
Number of students: 10,466

Publications: *Lienzo* (1 a year), *Ciencia Económica* (2 a year), *Ius et Praxis* (2 a year), *Administratio* (2 a year), *Entorno Económico* (2 a year), *Contratexto* (1 a year), *La Gran Ilusión* (2 a year), *Contabilidad y Finanzas* (2 a year), *Ingeniería Industrial* (2 a year), *Humanitas* (2 a year), *Plural* (2 a year), *Scientia et Praxis* (2 a year).

DEANS

Accountancy: Dr Manuel Luna Victoria
Administration: Carlos Freundt Ramírez
Communication Sciences: María Teresa Quiroz Velasco
Economics: Javier Zúñiga Quevedo
Educational Administration: Dra Gabriela Porto de Power
Humanities: Dr Raúl Palacios Rodríguez
General Studies: Lic. Teresa Mouchard de Hidalgo
Industrial Engineering: Eduardo Velásquez Mendoza
Law and Political Sciences: Dr Augusto Ferrero Costa
Metallurgical and Iron and Steel Engineering: Ing. José Patroni Olcese
Systems Engineering: Marco Aurelio Zevallos y Muñiz
Psychology: Manuel Fernández Arata
Postgraduate School: Dr Desiderio Blanco López

HEADS OF ACADEMIC DEPARTMENTS

Accountancy: Maria Gamarra de Burga
Administration: Rocío Winkelried Vargas
Communication Sciences: Oscar Quesada Macchiavello
Economics: Juan José Marthans León
Humanities: Dr David Jauregiti Camasca
Industrial Engineering: Bertha Haydee Díaz Garay
Law and Political Sciences: Oswaldo Hundskopf Exebio
Systems Engineering: (vacant)
Metallurgical and Iron and Steel Engineering: Ing. Juan José Ibarra Panizo
Psychology: Javier Diaz-Albertini Figueras

ATTACHED RESEARCH INSTITUTES

Centro de Investigaciones Económicas y Sociales (CIESUL): Dir Percy Correa Espinoza.

Centro de Investigaciones en Comunicación Social (CICOSUL): Dir Lic. José Perla Anaya.

Instituto de Investigaciones Filosóficas (IDIF): Dir (vacant).

Centro de Investigación Jurídica: Dir (vacant).

Centro de Investigación Primo César Canaletti Alvarez de la Facultad de Ciencias Contables: Dr Emilia Miano Pique.

Centro de Investigación de la Producción Industrial (CIPI): Dir Doris Maravi Gutarra.

Centro de Investigación de la Facultad de Ciencias Administrativas (CIFCA): Dir Alejandro Caballero Romero.

Instituto de Investigación de Ingeniería Metalúrgica y Siderúrgica: Ing. Venancio Astucuri Tinoco.

Instituto de Cooperativismo: Lic. Lily Chan Sánchez.

Instituto de Investigación en Ingeniería de Sistemas e Investigación Operativa: Dir Julio Padilla Solís.

UNIVERSIDAD DEL PACÍFICO

Avda Salaverry 2020, Jesús María, Apdo 4683, Lima 11
Telephone: (1) 471-2277
Fax: (1) 265-0958
E-mail: dri@up.edu.pe
Founded 1962
Private control
Academic year: April to July, September to December

Rector: José Javier Pérez Rodríguez
Vice-Rector: Jürgen Schuldt Lange
Secretary-General: Prof. Carlos Gatti Murriel
Registrar: Prof. José Espinoza Durán
Librarian: Dra María Bonilla de Gaviria

Number of teachers: 190
Number of students: 1,681 full-time, 1,700 part-time

Publications: *Apuntes, Punto de Equilibrio.*

DEANS

Administration and Accountancy: Prof. Matilde Schwalb
Economics: Prof. Carlos Amat y León
Post-Graduate School: Mag. Estuardo Marrou Loayza

HEADS OF DEPARTMENT

Accountancy: Prof. Pedro Franco Concha
Administation: Prof. Gina Pipoli de Butrón
Economics: Prof. Bruno Seminario de Marzi
Mathematics: Prof. Ricardo Siu Koochoy
Humanities: Prof. Jorge Wiesse Rebagliati
Social Sciences and Politics: Prof. Oswaldo Medina García
Research Centre: Prof. Jorge Fernández Baca Llamosas
Language Centre: Prof. Gina Pipoli de Butrón

UNIVERSIDAD PERUANA 'CAYETANO HEREDIA'

Apdo 4314, Lima 100
Telephone: 82-0252
Fax: 82-4541
Founded 1961
Private control
Language of instruction: Spanish
Academic year: April to February

Rector: Dr CARLOS VIDAL
Vice-Rector for Academic Affairs: Dr ALBERTO RAMIREZ
Vice-Rector for Administrative Affairs: Dr MILENKO ZLATAR
Secretary-General: Dr GENARO HERRERA
Librarian: Dr FERNANDO CALMET

Number of teachers: 608
Number of students: 2,488

Publications: *Acta Herediana, Revista Médica Herediana, Revista Estomatológica, Revista Acta Andina, Boletín UPCH.*

DEANS

Faculty of Medicine: Dr OSWALDO ZEGARRA
Faculty of Sciences and Philosophy: Dr AGUSTÍN MONTOYA
Faculty of Stomatology: Dr DAVID LOZA

HEADS OF DEPARTMENTS

Biology: R. ISHIYAMA
Chemistry: H. MALDONADO
Gynaecology and Obstetrics: L. JEFFERSON
Medicine: O. SITU
Microbiology: A. YI
Morphology and Pathology: J. PEREDA
Oral Medicine, Surgery and Pathology: W. DELGADO
Paediatrics: L. CARAVEDO
Physics and Mathematics: J. GARCÍA
Physiology: R. CASTRO
Psychiatry: E. GALLI
Public Health: D. GONZÁLES
Radiology: L. PINILLOS
Social Odontology: N. BALAREZO
Social Sciences and Humanities: E. ARCE
Statistics and Demography: M. ZLATAR
Stomatology Clinic: F. DONAYRE
Surgery: H. CARRERO

ATTACHED RESEARCH INSTITUTES

'Alexander von Humboldt' Tropical Medicine Institute: Dir Dr HUMBERTO ALVAREZ.

Population Studies Institute: Dir Dra MAGDALENA CHU.

Genetics Institute: Dir Dra TERESA P. GIANELLA

UNIVERSIDAD DE PIURA

Apdo 353, Piura
Telephone: (74) 328171
Fax: (74) 328645
E-mail: postmas@udep.edu.pe

Founded 1968
Private control
Language of instruction: Spanish
Academic year: March to December

Rector: Dr ANTONIO MABRES TORELLÓ
Vice-Rector: Dra ISABEL GÁLVEZ ARÉVALO
Secretary-General: Mgtr PAUL CORCUERA GARCÍA
Librarian: Dr ANTONIO ABRUÑA PUYOL

Number of teachers: 196
Number of students: 2,729

Publication: *Amigos.*

DEANS

Faculty of Engineering: Ing. RAFAEL ESTARTÚS TOBELLA
Faculty of Sciences and Humanities: Dra LUZ GONZÁLEZ UMERES
Faculty of Information Sciences: Dra ISABEL GÁLVEZ ARÉVALO
Faculty of Law: Dr ANTONIO ABRUÑA PUYOL
Faculty of Economics and Business Administration: Mgtr PAUL CORCUERA GARCÍA
Faculty of Education: Dr PABLO PÉREZ SÁNCHEZ

UNIVERSIDAD PRIVADA VÍCTOR ANDRÉS BELAUNDE

Jirón Pedro Barroso 260, 4° piso, Apdo 241, Huánuco
Telephone: 2496

Founded 1984

Rector: RAUL ISRAEL OLIVERA
Vice-Rector: RAFAEL ISRAEL OLIVERA
Administrative Officer: MANUEL MANRIQUE MARCOS
Librarian: MARY DIAZ PAIVA

Number of teachers: 55
Number of students: 1,700

DEANS

Faculty of Law and Politics: EMERICO ISRAEL OLIVERA
Faculty of Obstetrics: MANUEL ISRAEL OLIVERA
Faculty of Forestry Engineering: NILO LOPEZ TELLO

UNIVERSIDAD RICARDO PALMA

Avda Benavides 5440, Urb. Las Gardenias, Santiago de Surco, Apdo 18-0131, Lima
Telephone: (1) 275-0450
Fax: (1) 275-0459
E-mail: postmaster@li.urp.edu.pe

Founded 1969
Private control
Language of instruction: Spanish
Academic year: April to December

Rector: Dr IVÁN RODRÍGUEZ CHÁVEZ
Vice-Rectors: Lic. RICARDO LUNA VICTORIA MUÑOZ (Academic), Arq. ABEL HURTADO RAMPOLDI (Administrative)
Secretary-General: Lic. WILMER MARTOS ROJAS
Librarian: Mg. MÓNICA BARRUETO PÉREZ

Number of teachers: 650
Number of students: 9,000

Publications: *Revista, Tradición, Revista de la Facultad de Lenguas Modernas, Revista Arquitextos, Revista Perfiles de Ingeniería, Revista de la Facultad de Ciencias Económicas, Revista de la Facultad de Psicología, Revista Biotempus.*

DEANS

Faculty of Architecture and Town Planning: Arq. ROBERTO CHANG CHAO
Faculty of Biological Sciences: Dr TOMÁS AGURTO SÁENZ
Faculty of Economics: CPC JESÚS HIDALGO ORTEGA
Faculty of Engineering: Ing. JORGE ARROYO PRADO
Faculty of Modern Languages: Dr PEDRO DÍAZ ORTIZ
Faculty of Psychology: Dr HUGO SÁNCHEZ CARLESSI

HEADS OF DEPARTMENTS

Sciences: Dra REYNA ZÚÑIGA DE ACLETO
Engineering: Ing. GONZALO LUQUE CONDADO
Psychology: Dr ALBERTO CORDOVA CADILLO
Humanities: Lic. MABEL MUÑOZ DE DÍAZ
Architecture: Arq. JOSÉ C. ORTECHO JAUREGUI

UNIVERSIDAD SAN MARTÍN DE PORRES

Martín Dulanto 101, Lima
Telephone: 446-1537

Founded 1969

Rector: Dr RICARDO NUGENT

Departments of arts and education; institutes of philosophy and social sciences, history, geography.

Colleges

ESCUELA DE ADMINISTRACIÓN DE NEGOCIOS PARA GRADUADOS, ESAN

(Graduate School of Business Administration)
Apdo 1846, Lima 100
Telephone: (1) 345-1565
Fax: (1) 345-1328

Founded 1963, as a joint venture between the Peruvian Government and the US Department of State Agency for International Development to promote the socio-economic development of the region; training in management at graduate level and for executives

Dean: ALFREDO NOVOA PEÑA

Library of 50,000 vols
Number of teachers: 37
Number of students: 3,000

Publications: *INFORMESAN* (fortnightly institutional bulletin), *Cuadernos de Difusión* (2 a year).

Instituto Superior de Administración y Tecnología: Avda Arequipa 173, Lima; f. 1965; 67 teachers, 980 students; library of 6,200 vols; Dir ARISTIDES VEGA N.; Registrar Prof. ALBERTO LÓPEZ; publ. *ISAT en Marcha*.

Schools of Art and Music

Escuela Nacional de Música (National School of Music): Emancipación 180, Lima; f. 1908 as Academia Nacional de Música 'Alcedo', present name 1946, autonomous since 1966; performance, musicology, education, composition; 400 students; specialized library *c.* 8,000 vols, and record library; choir and orchestra; Dir Gen. ARMANDO SÁNCHEZ MÁLAGA; Dir ELENA ICHIKAWA KIMATA; publ. *Conservatorio* (annually).

AFFILIATED INSTITUTES

Escuela Regional de Música de Arequipa: Dir AURELIO DÍAZ.

Escuela Regional de Música de Ayacucho: Dir CÉSAR BEDOYA.

Escuela Regional de Música del Cuzco: Dir JORGE DELGADO.

Escuela Regional de Música de Huánuco: Dir JAIME DÍAZ.

Escuela Regional de Música de Piura: Dir ERNESTO LÓPEZ MINDREAU.

Escuela Regional de Música de Trujillo: Dir ULISES CALDERÓN.

Escuela Nacional Superior Autónoma de Bellas Artes (Autonomous National School of Fine Arts): Ancash 681, Lima; fax 4270799; f. 1918; to train artists and teachers; library of 5,000 vols; Dir PEDRO BENITO ROTTA BISSO; publ. *Anuario Académico*.

Escuela Regional de Bellas Artes 'Diego Quispe Tito': Cuzco.

Instituto Superior de Arte 'Carlos Baca Flor': Calle Sucre 111, Arequipa.

PHILIPPINES

Learned Societies

GENERAL

Academia Filipina (Philippine Academy): 47 Juan Luna St, San Lorenzo Village, 1223 Makati, Metro Manila; corresp. of the Real Academia Española (Madrid); 15 mems; Dir and Sec. JOSE RODRIGUEZ.

AGRICULTURE, FISHERIES AND VETERINARY SCIENCE

Crop Science Society of the Philippines: Farming Systems and Soil Resources Institute, UPLB, Laguna; f. 1970; 3,000 mems; Pres. ROMEO V. LABIOS; Vice-Pres. MANUEL M. LOGROÑO; publ. *Philippine Journal of Crop Science* (3 a year).

Philippine Association of Agriculturists: 692 San Andres, Malate, Manila; f. 1946; 178 mems; Pres. ANTONIO S. DIMALANTA; Vice-Pres. JESÚS M. BONDOC; Sec. PATERNO N. ALCUDAI.

Philippine Veterinary Medical Association: Unit 233, Union Square Condominium, 15th Ave, Cubao, Quezon City; tel. 721-78-79; f. 1907; 1,500 mems; Pres. Dr BERNARDO B. RESOSO; Sec. Dr JOHN GLENN F. AGBAYANI.

Society for the Advancement of Research: University of the Philippines, Los Baños College, Laguna; f. 1930; 632 mems; Pres. Dr FELIX LIBRERO; Sec. Dr BLANDA R. SUMAYAO.

Society for the Advancement of the Vegetable Industry (SAVI): University of the Philippines at Los Baños College, Laguna; f. 1967; Pres. EUFEMIO T. RASCO, Jr; Exec. Sec. MARIA MALIXI-PAJE; publ. *Proceedings of Annual Seminar-Workshop*.

ARCHITECTURE AND TOWN PLANNING

Philippine Institute of Architects: POB 350, Manila; f. 1933; 405 mems; Pres. MANUEL T. MAÑOSA, Jr; Vice-Pres. G. A. DE LEON; Sec. M. P. ANGELES, Jr.

BIBLIOGRAPHY, LIBRARY SCIENCE AND MUSEOLOGY

Association of Special Libraries of the Philippines (ASLP): Room 301, National Library Bldg, Kalaw St, Manila; tel. 590177; f. 1954; 556 mems; Pres. ZENAIDA F. LUCAS; Sec. SOCORRO G. ELEVERA; publs *ASLP Bulletin* (quarterly), *Directory of Special Libraries*, *ASLP Newsletter* (quarterly).

Philippine Librarians Association Inc.: c/o National Library, Room 301, T. M. Kalaw St, Manila; tel. and fax 59-01-77; f. 1923; 750 mems; Pres. Atty ANTONIO M. SANTOS; Sec. ROSEMARIE ROSALI; publs *Bulletin* (annually), *PLAI Newsletter* (quarterly).

EDUCATION

Association of Catholic Universities of the Philippines, Inc.: University of Santo Tomas (Room 111, Main Building), España, Manila; tel. 731-35-44; f. 1973 to serve the interests of the 21 Catholic univs in the Philippines; Pres. Rev. Fr ROLANDO V. DE LA ROSA; Sec. Gen. Prof. GIOVANNA V. FONTANILLA; publ. *ACUP Newsletter* (2 a year).

Philippine Association of State Universities and Colleges: Palacio del Gobernador, 8th Floor, Intramuros, 1008 Manila; tel. 49-17-75; f. 1967; independent but attached to Dept of Education, Culture and Sports; aims to foster excellence in higher education, to promote communication among its mem. institutions, to encourage studies on higher education, to secure adequate government support for education, to encourage inter-institutional assistance through fellowships, grants, teacher exchange, accreditation; 75 mem. institutions; library with special collections on education; Pres. Dr FREDERICK S. PADA; Exec. Sec. Mrs ALICIA O. ASUNCION; publ. *Baliham* (quarterly).

HISTORY, GEOGRAPHY AND ARCHAEOLOGY

Institute of History: c/o University of Santo Tomás, España St, Manila.

Philippine Historical Association: c/o Office of External Affairs, St Mary's College, 37 M. Ignacia Ave, 1103 Quezon City; tel. 928-85-63; fax 928-60-38; f. 1955; 500 mems; Pres. Prof. OSCAR EVANGELISTA; Exec. Dir GLORIA M. SANTOS; publs *Philippine Historical Bulletin* (annually), *PHA Balita* (2 a year).

LANGUAGE AND LITERATURE

Komisyon sa Wikang Filipino: Watson Bldg, 1610 J. P. Laurel St, San Miguel, Manila; tel. 734-55-46; fax 736-03-15; f. 1991 (fmrly Institute of Philippine Languages); aims to develop, promote and standardize Filipino and other Philippine languages; library of 5,000 vols; Chair. Dr PONCIANO B. P. PINEDA; publ. *Sangwika* (newsletter, quarterly).

MEDICINE

Manila Medical Society: 1201 Florida St, Manila; f. 1902; 1,249 mems; Pres. Dr EDGARDO T. CAMPARAS; Sec.-Treas. Dr ERLINDA T. NOVALES.

Philippine Medical Association: PMA Bldg, North Ave, Quezon City; f. 1903; 90 component societies, 50 affiliated speciality societies; Pres. Dr MODESTO O. LLAMAS; Sec. Dr GIL C. FERNANDEZ; publ. *Journal*.

Philippine Paediatric Society, Inc.: POB 3527, Manila; f. 1947; 620 mems; Pres. EUSTACIA M. RIGOR; Sec. MIGUEL NOCHE, Jr; publ. *Philippine Journal of Paediatrics* (every 2 months).

Philippine Pharmaceutical Association: 10th Floor, Stanisco Towers, 999 Pedro Gil cor., F. Agoncillo Paco, Manila; tel. and fax 586977; f. and incorporated 1920; 8,000 mems; Pres. Dr LOURDES TALAG ECHAUZ; Exec. Sec. Dr NORMA V. LERMA.

Philippine Society of Parasitology: College of Public Health, University of the Philippines, POB EA 460, 625 Pedro Gil St, Ermita, Manila; tel. 59-68-08; fax (2) 521-1394; f. 1930; 450 mems; Pres. Dr WILFRED U. TIU; Sec. Dr ROBERTO B. MONZÓN; publ. *Newsletter* (quarterly).

NATURAL SCIENCES

Physical Sciences

Philippine Council of Chemists: 2227 Severino Reyes St, Sta Cruz, POB 1202, Manila 2805; f. 1958; 200 mems; Nat. Pres. MIGUEL G. AMPIL; Gen. Sec. P. B. CARBONELL; publ. *Bulletin*.

TECHNOLOGY

Philippine Society of Civil Engineers: c/o Bureau of Public Works, Bonifacio Drive, Manila; f. 1918; assumed present title 1933; Pres. FLORENCIO MORENO; Sec.-Treas. TOMAS DE GUZMÁN; publ. *The Philippine Engineering Record* (quarterly).

Philippine Society of Mining, Metallurgical and Geological Engineers: POB 1595, Manila; f. 1940; 117 mems; Pres. JONES R. CASTRO; Sec.-Treas. LEOPOLDO F. ABAD.

Research Institutes

GENERAL

Advanced Science and Technology Institute: C/o Department of Science and Technology, Gen. Santos Ave, Bicutan, Taguig 1604, Metro Manila.

Institute of Philippine Culture: Ateneo de Manila University, Loyola Heights, Quezon City, POB 154, Manila 1099; tel. 924-4567; fax 924-4690; e-mail ipc@pusit.admu.edu.ph; f. 1960 as a university research organization; undertakes studies directed towards solving development problems, particularly in the areas of upland development, local governance, agrarian reform, community health, resources management, irrigation, forestry, women and sustainable agriculture; assists development agencies; trains agency personnel and local communities in the use of research methodologies; library of 3,058 books, 4,050 reprints and vertical file, data bank; Dir Dr GERMELINO M. BAUTISTA; publs *IPC Papers*, *IPC Monograph Series*, *IPC Reprints*, *IPC Final Reports* (all irregular).

National Research Council of the Philippines: Bicutan, Taguig, Metro Manila; tel. 822-04-09; f. 1934; supports basic research in a wide variety of fields; 1,760 mems; library of 1,000 vols; Pres. Dr RAUL P. DE GUZMAN; Corp. Sec. Dr MAGDALENA C. CANTORIA; publs *Science Research Journal of the Philippines* (quarterly), *Technical Bulletin (Proceedings)*, *Newsletter* (quarterly), *Annual Report*.

AGRICULTURE, FISHERIES AND VETERINARY SCIENCE

Bureau of Plant Industry: Ministry of Agriculture, Manila; f. 1930; research, regulation and crop protection; library of 10,000 vols; Dir NERIUS I. ROPEROS; publ. *Philippine Journal of Plant Industry*.

Forest Products Research and Development Institute (FPRDI): College, Laguna 4031; tel. 536-23-77; fax 943630; e-mail edb@narra.fprdi.dost.gov.ph; f. 1957; to conduct basic and applied research on forest products, undertake the transfer of completed researches and provide technical services and industrial manpower training; library of 7,000 books, 3,000 reports, 4,000 vols of periodicals; Dir EMMANUEL D. BELLO; publs *FPRDI Journal*, *Annual Report*, *Forest Products Technoflow*, *Coconut Wood Utilization Research and Development*, *FPRDI Mature Technologies*, *Phil. Timber Series*, *How To Series*.

EDUCATION

Science Education Institute: C/o Department of Science and Technology, Gen. Santos Ave, Bicutan, Taguig 1604, Metro Manila.

SEAMEO Regional Center for Educational Innovation and Technology: Commonwealth Ave, Diliman, Quezon City; tel. 924-76-81; fax 921-02-24; f. 1970; identifies basic educational problems common to the Southeast Asian region and assists the Southeast Asian Ministers of Education Organization member countries in the solution of these problems; conducts training, development, research programmes; library of 14,000 vols; Dir Dr MINDA C. SUTARIA; publs *INNOTECH Newsletter* (6 a year), *INNOTECH Journal* (2 a year).

MEDICINE

Food and Nutrition Research Institute: C/o Department of Science and Technology, Gen. Santos Ave, Bicutan, Taguig 1604, Metro Manila.

NATURAL SCIENCES

Physical Sciences

Philippine Institute of Volcanology and Seismology: C/o Department of Science and Technology, PHIVOLCS Bldg, C. P. Garcia Ave, U.P. Campus, Diliman, Quezon City; tel. (2) 412-14-68; fax (2) 929-83-66; e-mail phivolcs@x5.phivolcs.dost.gov.ph; f. 1952; library of 3,000 vols; Dir Dr RAYMUNDO S. PUNONGBAYAN.

TECHNOLOGY

Industrial Technology Development Institute: C/o Department of Science and Technology, Gen. Santos Ave, Bicutan, Taguig 1604, Metro Manila.

Metals Industry Research and Development Center: C/o Department of Science and Technology, Gen. Santos Ave, Bicutan, Taguig 1604, Metro Manila.

Mines and Geosciences Bureau: North Avenue, Diliman, Quezon City, Metro Manila; tel. (2) 920-91-20; fax (2) 920-16-35; e-mail totie@pacific.net.ph; f. 1898; administers the utilization and management of the country's mineral wealth; conducts geological, mining technology, metallurgical and environmental management research; evaluates mineral deposits; conducts mining investment promotion; formulates mining laws and policies and regulates the mining industry; library of 4,200 vols; Dir HORACIO C. RAMOS; publ. *Mineral Gazette*.

Philippine Nuclear Research Institute: Commonwealth Ave, Diliman, Quezon City; tel. (2) 9296011; fax (2) 9201646; e-mail amr@sun1.dost.gov.ph; f. 1958; peaceful applications of nuclear energy; library of 16,000 vols; Dir Dr ALUMANDA M. DELA ROSA; publs *Philippine Nuclear Journal, PNRI Annual Report, PNRI Technical Progress Report* (all annually).

Libraries and Archives

Cebu

University of San Carlos Library: P. del Rosario St, 6000 Cebu City; tel. 220432; fax 54341; f. 1947; 228,709 vols incl. 19,205 vols of Filipiniana; 2,564 vols of rare Filipiniana; 834 titles of periodicals; 2,185 titles of audiovisual materials; spec. colln for local studies held in Cebuano Studies Center at above address; Dir of Libraries Dr MARILOU P. TADLIP.

Dumaguete

Silliman University Library: 6200 Dumaguete City, Negros Oriental; tel. 2252516; f. 1906; 107,000 vols, incl. 9,000 vols Filipiniana; Librarian Mrs LORNA TUMULAK-YSO; publ. *Silliman Journal* (quarterly).

Manila

Ateneo de Manila University Library: POB 154, Manila; 160,000 vols, 32,000 vols bound periodicals, 325,000 microforms; spec. collns incl. American Historical Collection; assoc. libraries: geo- and solar physics, philosophy and theology, graduate business and law; Dir CARMELO V. LOPEZ.

Far Eastern University Library: POB 609, Quezon Blvd, Manila; 130,942 vols; Chief Librarian ZENAIDA M. GALANG.

Manila City Library: 3rd Floor, City Hall, Manila 10401; Chief Librarian FILEMON L. GECOLEA.

National Library of the Philippines: POB 2926, T. M. Kalaw, 1000 Ermita, Manila; tel. (2) 525-31-96; fax (2) 524-23-29; e-mail amb@max.ph.net; f. 1901; Filipiniana Division: 153,000 Filipiniana books, 40,000 rare books, 4,500 microfiche items, 3,198 serial titles, 13,556 items in special collections, 3,000 reels of microfilm, 2,000 slides; Reference Division: 74,000 vols, 1,000 serial titles; Government Publications Division: 180,000 items; Dir ADORACION MENDOZA-BOLOS; publs *Philippine National Bibliography* (annually), *TNL Newsletter* (irregular), *TNL Research Guide Series, TNL Annual Report*.

Philippine Women's University Library: Taft Ave, 1004 Manila; nine branch libraries; 87,620 vols; archive collection; Librarian Mrs ESPERANZA A. SANTA CRUZ.

Science and Technology Information Institute, Department of Science and Technology: Bicutan, Taguig, Metro Manila, POB 3596; tel. 822-09-54; f. 1974; acquisition of scientific documents, technical information processing, science information services, training in library and information science and computer applications; 28,000 bound vols, 3,047 periodicals, 4,000 microfilms; Chief Dr IRENE D. AMORES; publs *Philippine Science and Technology Abstracts* (quarterly), *Bulletin of Researches* (quarterly), *Philippine Men of Science* (annually), *R & D Philippines* (annually), *Philippine Scientific Bibliographies* (irregular), *SEA Abstracts* (quarterly), *Technical Tips* (every 2 weeks), *Philippine Inventions* (quarterly), *Philippine Technical Information Sheets* (irregular).

University of Manila Central Library: 546 Dr M. V. de los Santos St, Sampaloc, Manila; f. 1913; 28,600 vols; other libraries 23,000 vols; Chief Librarian CORAZON G. PAYTE.

University of Santo Tomás Library: España St, Manila; *c.* 306,590 vols; collections of Filipiniana and rare and ancient books; special libraries of Ecclesiastical Faculties, Medicine, Music, Engineering, Fine Arts and Commerce; High School and Elementary School libraries; microfilms and slides; Prefect of Libraries Fr ANGEL APARICIO; Chief Librarian Prof. JUANA L. ABELLO.

University of the East Library: Claro M. Recto Ave, Manila ZC 2806; 183,000 vols; Librarian SARAH DE JESUS.

Quezon

Loyola School of Theology Library: POB 240, U.P. Quezon City; tel. 426-5966; e-mail lhslstli@pusit.admu.edu.ph; f. 1965; 69,000 vols, 18,000 vols of periodicals; Librarian CRISANTA C. ROSALES; publ. *Landas* (The Way) (every 6 months).

University of the Philippines Diliman University Library: Gonzalez Hall, Diliman, Quezon City 1101; tel. 920-53-01; fax 928-28-63; f. 1922; 988,000 vols, 17,000 periodical titles; 26 brs; Dir BELEN B. ANGELES; publ. *Index to Philippine Periodicals* (quarterly).

Museums and Art Galleries

Manila

Lopez Memorial Museum: Ground Floor, Benpres Bldg, Exchange Rd, cnr Meralco Ave, 1600 Pasig City, Metro Manila; tel. (2) 910-10-09; fax (2) 631-24-17; e-mail pezseum@skyinet.net; f. 1960; paintings of the Filipino painters Juan Luna, Felix Resureccion Hidalgo and others; letters and MSS of Jose Rizal; library of 14,000 vols, including rare Filipiniana; Dir MARILES E. MATIAS.

Malacañang Palace Presidential Museum: J. P. Laurel St, San Miguel, Manila; tel. 521-2301; f. 1993; memorabilia of all former Philippine presidents; Dir MA. EDNA S. GAFFUD.

Metropolitan Museum of Manila: Bangko Sentral ng Pilipinas Complex, Roxas Blvd, Manila; tel. (2) 524-5271; fax (2) 523-6841; f. 1976; fine arts museum: painting, sculpture, graphic arts, decorative arts, prehistoric gold, pottery; Pres. RITA LEDESMA; Dir CORAZON S. ALVINA.

Museum of Arts and Sciences: Main Building, University of Santo Tomas, España, 2806 Manila; tel. and fax (2) 740-97-18; e-mail isidro.a@ustcc.ust.edu.ph; f. 1872; divisions of natural history, Philippine ethnography, history (including numismatics), archaeology (including Philippine and Chinese ceramics), art gallery and the Hall of Philippine Religious Images; Dir Rev. Fr ISIDRO C. ABAÑO; publ. *UST Museum* (4 a year).

National Museum of the Philippines: POB 2659, Padre Burgos St, 1000 Manila; tel. (2) 5271215; fax (2) 5270306; e-mail nmuseum@webquest.com; f. 1901; divisions of anthropology, archaeology, botany, geology, zoology, museum education, restoration and engineering, arts, cultural properties, planetarium, archaeological sites and museums; library of 5,000 vols; Dir GABRIEL S. CASAL; publs monographs, serials, guide books, etc.

San Agustín Museum: POB 3366, General Luna St, Intramuros, Manila; tel. (2) 5274060; fax (2) 5274058; f. 1972; located in 400-year-old San Agustín monastery; Hispano-Philippino religious art (paintings, sculptures, etc.); library of 3,000 vols; Curator Dr PEDRO G. GALENDE.

Tanauan Batangas

Jose P. Laurel Memorial Museum and Library: Tanauan Batangas; documents and personal possessions of the late Dr J. P. Laurel (1890–1960).

Universities

ADAMSON UNIVERSITY

900 San Marcelino St, Ermita, 1000 Manila

Telephone: (2) 50-20-11

Founded 1932

Language of instruction: English

Private (Roman Catholic) control

Academic year: June to March

President: Fr JIMMY A. BELITA

Executive Vice-President: Fr FRANCISCO VARGAS

Vice-President for Finance: Fr CONSTANCIO GAN

Vice-President for Academic Affairs: Dr Rosario Alberto
Vice-President for Administration: Gervasia Cabel
Vice-President for Pastoral Affairs: Fr Danilo Carolino
Registrar: Sr Magdalena Bebida
Librarian: Zoraida Bartolome

Number of teachers: 600
Number of students: 20,944

Publications: *Adamson Chronicle* (monthly), *Adamson Newsletter* (every 2 months), *Vincere* (every 3 months), *Sofia* (annually), *Sci-Tech* (annually), *Law Journal* (annually), *LIA COM* (annually).

DEANS

College of Law: Ponciano Subido
Graduate School: Rosario Alberto
College of Liberal Arts: Sr Milagros Magistrado
College of Sciences: Adria Jocano
College of Engineering: Peter Ureta
College of Education: Domingo A. Bendero
College of Commerce: Robert Co
College of Architecture: Victoriano Aviguetero
College of Pharmacy: Eleodora Lorenzo

HEADS OF DEPARTMENTS

Chemistry: Prof. Asteria Poblete (acting)
Computer Science: Prof. Ronaldo Tan
English: Prof. Lucesa Diano
Spanish: Prof. Beatriz Pabito
Mathematics: Prof. Elsa Gerardo
Chemical Engineering: Engr Leonardo Briones (acting)
Civil Engineering: Engr Marilou Dungca
Computer Engineering: Engr Dante Macasaet
Mechanical Engineering: Engr Ramon Maniago (acting)
Electrical Engineering: Engr Eduardo Lindo (acting)
Electronics and Communications Engineering: Engr May Rose Imperial
Industrial Engineering: Engr Venusmar Quevedo
Geology, Ceramics and Mining Engineering: Engr Aldrich Philip Dirige
Social Sciences: Fr Ruperto Guiritan
Physics: Prof. Catherine Leonida
Accountancy: Prof. Hermogena Dimapilis (acting)
Natural Science: Prof. Myrna Añes (acting)
Secretarial Studies: Prof. Lilia Panal (acting)
Physical Education: Prof. Ricardo Matibag
Filipino: Prof. Janet Flores
Management, Economics, Banking and Finance: Virginia Sheydaei
Institute of Continuing Education and Professional Development: Prof. Janet Flores
Institute of Religious Education: Emmanuel Concordia

ANGELES UNIVERSITY FOUNDATION

Angeles City

Telephone: (45) 6028882
Fax: (45) 8882725

Founded 1962
Private control
Languages of instruction: English, Filipino
Academic year: June to March

President: Dr Emmanuel Y. Angeles
Executive Vice-President: Dr Antonio Y. Angeles
Vice-President for Finance: Loreto A. Canlas
Vice-President for Academic Affairs: Dr Buenavida A. Pareja
Vice-President for Research and Development: Dr Teresita B. Ireneo
Vice-President for Administration: Laureano B. Santos
Registrar: Dr Archimedes T. David
Librarian: Teresita M. Manarang

Library of 38,569 vols
Number of teachers: 317
Number of students: 5,473

Publications: *AUF Journal, The Pioneer, AUF News, Alumnews, Datalink, Nurscene, MPA Perspective.*

DEANS

Graduate School: Dr Concesa Milan Baduel
College of Arts and Sciences: Dr Nunilon G. Ayuyao
College of Education: Lucena P. Samson
College of Business Administration: Leonida F. Cayanan
College of Engineering and Technology: Eng. José L. Macapagal, Jr
College of Nursing: Zenaida S. Fernandez
College of Medicine: Dr Reynaldo V. Lopez
College of Allied Medical Professions: Consuelo P. Macalalad
College of Criminology: Lucia M. Hipolito
College of Computer Science: Caesar R. Mañalac

AQUINAS UNIVERSITY

Rawis, Legazpi City 4500

Telephone: (5221) 221-23

Founded 1948; University 1968
Private (Roman Catholic) control
Languages of instruction: English and Filipino
Academic year: June to May

President: Very Rev. Fr Dr Virgilio A. Ojoy
Vice-President: Very Rev. Fr Tereso M. Campillo, Jr
Secretary-General: Edith Rebecca S. Regino
Registrar: Ceferino A. Magdaong
Librarian: Aniceta M. Goyena

Library of 54,000 vols
Number of teachers: 213
Number of students: 6,123

Publication: *Aquinas University Research Journal.*

DEANS

College of Law: Atty Romulo L. Ricafort
College of Engineering: Eng. Virgilio Perdigon, Jr
College of Architecture and Fine Arts: Arch. Ernesto Tianco
College of Arts and Sciences: Mutya Paulino (acting)
College of Business Administration: Dr Romulo L. Lindio
College of Education: Dr Guadalupe M. Carranza
College of Nursing: Dr Norma L. Morante
Graduate Studies and Research: Dr Maria Lourdes M. Sabater

ARAULLO UNIVERSITY

Bitas, Cabanatuan City 2301

Telephone: (963) 3369

Founded 1950
Private control

President: Rolan C. Esteban
Vice-President for Administration: Atty Ruperto T. Sampoleo
Vice-President for Academic Affairs: Dr Manuel R. Guerrero
Dean of Admissions and Registrar: Raoul S. Esteban
Dean of Student Affairs: Antonio C. Santiago
Librarian: Remedios Viloria

Library of 56,257 vols
Number of teachers: 167 full-time, 25 part-time
Number of students: 8,700

DEANS

Graduate School: Dr Irene Villareal
College of Law: Juan S. Esteban
College of Engineering and Architecture: Fernando Hernandez
College of Commerce: Lourdes B. de Guzman
College of Arts: Dr Lily Buencamino
College of Education: Dr Edisteo B. Bernardez
College of Criminology: Erlinda Dela Cruz

ARELLANO UNIVERSITY

2600 Legarda Street, Sampaloc, Manila

Telephone: 60-74-41

Founded 1938
Language of instruction: English
Private control

Chairman, Board of Trustees: Atty Florentine Cayce, Jr
President: Jose T. Enriquez
Executive Vice-President: Paulino F. Cayco
Registrar: Mrs Josefa V. Lebron
Librarian: Alfredo C. Valdez

Number of teachers: 335
Number of students: 10,326

Publications: *Arellano Standard, Philippine Education Quarterly.*

DEANS

Graduate School: Dr Amparo S. Lardizabal
Arellano Law College: Atty Mariano M. Magsalin
College of Arts and Sciences: Dr Sergia G. Esguerra
College of Education and Normal College: Dr Amparo S. Lardizabal
College of Commerce: Francisco P. Cayco
College of Nursing: Dr Praxedes S. M. Dela Rosa

ATENEO DE DAVAO UNIVERSITY

POB 80113, E. Jacinto St, 8000 Davao City

Telephone: 221-2411
Fax: (82) 6-41-16

Founded 1948
Language of instruction: English
Private control
Academic year: June to October, November to March (two semesters)

President: Rev. Edmundo M. Martinez
Registrar: Nemesio J. Pagpaguitan
Librarian: Leonila Sales

Library of 92,000 vols
Number of teachers: 157 full-time; 141 part-time
Number of students: 13,262

Publication: *Tambara.*

DEANS

Law School: Hildegardo F. Iñigo
College for Graduate Programs: Bernadette I. del Rosario (Asst Dean)
College of Arts and Sciences: Rev. Gorgonio S. Esguerra

HEADS OF DIVISIONS

Accountancy: Magdelena T. Solis (acting)
Business Administration: Danilo M. Te
Engineering: Nenita A. Malaluan
Humanities: Macario D. Tiu
Natural Science and Mathematics: Elizabeth D. Calio
Philosophy: Rex T. Rola
Social Science and Education: Lourdesita S. Chan
Theology: Rev. Felix D. Unson

ATTACHED INSTITUTES

Computer Science Center: Dir E. V. Marañon
Regional Science Teaching Center: Dir P. E. Funa

Resource Center for Local Governance: Dir L. J. MAMAED
Institute of Small Farms and Industries: Dir J. E. CABO
Ignatian Institute for Religious Education: Dir Rev. WILLIAM J. MALLEY

ATENEO DE MANILA UNIVERSITY

POB 154, Manila
Telephone: 924-4601
Founded 1859; University 1959
Languages of instruction: English, Filipino
Private control
Academic year: June to March (two terms) and summer term
President: Rev. BIENVENIDO F. NEBRES
Vice-President for Finance and Treasurer: JOSE M. SANTOS
Academic Vice-President: Dr PATRICIA B. LICUANAN
Librarian: ROGELIO B. MALLILLIN
Number of teachers: 741
Number of students: 12,518
Publications: *Philippine Studies* (quarterly), *Guidon, Alumni Guidon, Pantas* (2 a year), *Landas—Journal of Loyola School of Theology, IPC Reports.*

DEANS

School of Arts and Sciences: Dr LEOVINO MA. GARCIA
Graduate School of Business: ENRIQUE H. DAVILA (Assistant Dean)
College of Law: Atty CYNTHIA R. DEL CASTILLO

UNIVERSITY OF BAGUIO

Baguio City 2600
Telephone: (74) 4223071
Fax: (74) 4422357
Founded 1948 as a Technical College
Private control
Languages of instruction: English and Filipino
Academic year: June to March
President: VIRGILIO C. BAUTISTA
Vice-President for Academic Affairs: Dr CRISPIN PURUGANAN
Vice-President for Administration: CRISTETA LEUNG
Registrar: MERLITA NAVARRO
Librarian: ZENAIDA J. DOMINGO
Library of 75,223 vols
Number of teachers: 235
Number of students: 10,790
Publications: *University of Baguio Journal* (2 a year), *The UB Bulletin* (monthly).

DEANS

College of Arts and Sciences: Dr AGNES T. BAUTISTA
College of Commerce: LILY CRUZ
College of Education: AGNES BAUTISTA
Graduate School: Dr CRISPIN PURUGANAN
Engineering and Technical College: Engr REBECCA CAJILOG
College of Dentistry: Dr CRISPIN RAMOS
College of Criminology: MILLER PECKLEY

BENGUET STATE UNIVERSITY

La Trinidad, Benguet 2601
Telephone: (74) 422-24-01
Fax: (74) 442-22-81
E-mail: bsu@burgos.slu.edu.ph
Founded 1916, university status 1985
Language of instruction: English
President: Dr CIPRIANO C. CONSOLACION
Vice-President: Dr FRANCO T. BAWANG
Designated Vice-Presidents:
Academic Affairs: Dr MARCOS A. BULIYAT
Research and Extension: Dr ROGELIO D. COLTING
Director of Admissions: Dr CAROLINE B. DIMAS
Director of Student Affairs: Prof. WILFREDO B. MINA
Registrar: Mrs ESTELA U. AQUINO
Librarian: Dr NORA J. CLARAVALL
Library of 31,000 vols
Number of teachers: 279
Number of students: 5,000
Publications: *BSU Research Journal, BSU Extension, BSU Newsletter, Highland Express,* college publications.

DEANS

College of Agriculture: Dr SONWRIGHT B. MADDUL
College of Arts and Sciences: Dr ROSENDO S. GUALDO
College of Forestry: For. PAQUITO P. UNTALAN
College of Engineering and Applied Technology: Eng. GENARO W. MACASIEB Jr
College of Teacher Education: Dr DOMINADOR S. GARIN
College of Veterinary Medicine: Dr BASITO S. COTIW-AN
College of Home Economics and Technology: Dr JANE K. AVILA
College of Nursing: Dr FLORENCE C. CAWAON
Graduate School: Dr JULIA A. SOLIMEN

BICOL UNIVERSITY

Rizal St, Legazpi City 4500
Telephone: (5221) 449-13
Founded 1970
State control
Languages of instruction: English, Filipino
Academic year: June to May (2 semesters and a Summer Term)
President: LYLIA CORPORAL-SENA
Vice-President: EMILIANO A. ABERIN
Vice-President for Academic Affairs: NELIA S. CIOCSON
Registrar: CARMELINA O. BALLARES
Librarian: EXALTACION R. RESONTOC
Library of 35,380 vols
Number of teachers: 568
Number of students: 12,572
Publications: *The Bicol Universitarian* (quarterly), *Graduate Forum* (2 a year), *The Gearcast, The Net, R & D Journal, The Cassette, The Mentor, Research Monitor* (2 a year), *Outreach* (quarterly), *BU Bulletin* (6 a year).

DEANS

Graduate School: NELIA S. CIOCSON
Arts and Sciences: SUSANA C. CABREDO
Agriculture: JUSTINO R. ARBOLEDA
Fisheries: OFELIA S. VEGA
Engineering: EDUARDO M. LORIA
Education: OSCAR L. LANDAGAN
Nursing: PAZ G. MUÑOZ
School of Arts and Trades: EDGAR R. CAMBA
Institute of Communication and Cultural Studies: RAMONA B. RAÑESES

HEADS OF DEPARTMENTS

Graduate Education: GRACIANO B. BAÑAGA
Humanities: CARMELITA Z. LANDAGAN
Language and Literature: ODILIA C. ESPINAS
Natural Sciences: CORAZON O. REANTASO
Social Sciences: CARLOS B. GEGANTOCA
Engineering Technology: MEDEL E. ALIGAN
Industrial Technology: ROMEO B. ORLAIN
Health and Nursing: FE L. BINALINGBING
Fisheries: ZENAIDA L. BULLECER
Professional Education: ADELINA A. MILLENA
Public Administration: FEDERICO O. RAGUINDIN, Jr
Physical Education and Sports: EULALIO M. DEL AYRE
Mathematics and Statistics: JOSEFINA R. NARVAEZ
Agriculture: ILDEFONSO C. PEQUEÑA

CAGAYAN STATE UNIVERSITY

Tuguegarao, Cagayan, Northern Luzon 1101
Telephone: (78) 844-01-07
Fax: (78) 844-41-19
E-mail: abcortes@scan.com.ph
Founded 1978 by merger of Northern Luzon State College of Agriculture and Cagayan Valley College of Arts and Trades
Academic year: June to March
President: Dr ARMANDO B. CORTES
Vice-President for Academic Affairs: Fr Dr RANHILIO C. AQUINO
Number of teachers: 500
Number of students: 10,300
Publications: *Research Journal of the Graduate School, Faculty Journal* (1 a year).
Colleges of agriculture, arts and sciences, engineering, fisheries, industrial technology, medicine, teacher training, and Graduate School.

CENTRAL LUZON STATE UNIVERSITY

Muñoz, Nueva Ecija
Telephone: 107
Founded 1907, attained university status 1964
State control
Languages of instruction: English and Filipino
Academic year: June to March
President: Dr FORTUNATO A. BATTAD
Executive Vice-President: Dr MARCELO M. ROGUEL
Vice-Presidents: Prof. REYNALDO S. GUTIERREZ (Administration), Dr EDGAR M. RICAMONTE (Academic Affairs), Dr HONORATO L. ANGELES (Research, Extension and Training)
Registrar: Dr EDUARDO PARAY
Administrative Officer: Atty RICARDO C. BERNARDO
Librarian: Prof. CELIA D. DE LA CRUZ
Number of teachers: 373
Number of students: 6,489
Publications: *CLSU Collegian* (semestral), *CLSU Newsletter* (monthly), *CLSU Scientific Journal* (2 a year).

DEANS

Institute of Graduate Studies: Dr JOSUE A. IRABAGON
College of Agriculture: Dr DANILO T. ELIGIO
College of Home Science and Industry: Dr CEFERINA AGNES
College of Education: Dr VIVENCIO C. ESTEBAN
College of Engineering: Dr JOSELITO V. DELA CRUZ
College of Arts and Sciences: Dr ANNIE MELINDA P. ALBERTO
College of Inland Fisheries: Dr TERESO ABELLA
College of Veterinary Science and Medicine: Dr JESUS S. DELA ROSA
College of Business Administration and Accountancy: Prof. DANILO S. CASTRO

HEADS OF DEPARTMENTS

College of Agriculture:
Agribusiness Management: Prof. ROCELYN M. BARROGA
Animal Science: Dr ERNESTO A. MARTIN
Crop Protection: Dr ELSA PADERES
Crop Science: Dr JUSTO G. CANARE
Soil Science: Prof. FLORIDA C. GARCIA

College of Arts and Sciences:
Humanities and English: Prof. LEONIDES CAJUCOM
Chemistry: Prof. IMELDA V. VENTURINA

Social Sciences: Dr ANSELMO D. LUPDAG
Biological Sciences: Dr NESTOR L. ALVAREZ
Mathematics, Statistics and Physics: Dr EDILBERTO LINA
Spanish and Filipino: Prof. DANTE C. LIM

College of Engineering:
Agricultural Engineering: Dr ROMEO B. GAVINO
Mechanical and Electrical Engineering: Prof. POLICARPIO BULANAN
Civil Engineering: Prof. PEDRO O. GELILIO

College of Inland Fisheries:
Aquatic Biology: Dr APOLINARIO V. YAMBOT
Aquaculture: Prof. RHODORA M. BARTOLOME
Inland Fisheries Management: Prof. DANILO C. MONJE

College of Education:
Extension Education: Dr VIRGINIA V. AROCENA
Elementary Education: VILMA M. SALAS
Secondary Education: Dr MONICA F. QUILANTANG

College of Home Science and Industry:
Textile and Garment Technology: Dr FIRMA C. VIRAY
Food Science and Technology: Dr NESTOR M. CANDELARIA
Home Economics Education and Extension: Prof. LOURDES F. SAN JUAN

College of Veterinary Science and Medicine:
Anatomy, Physiology and Pathology, and Microbiology, Parasitology and Public Health: Dr LUCIA M. RIGOS
Pharmacology, Medicine, Surgery and Clinical Sciences: Dr TEODORO T. VILLAVER

College of Business Administration and Accountancy:
Business Administration: Prof. ELIZABETH R. BAJIT
Accountancy: Prof. NITA S. SIBAYAN

Institute of Graduate Studies:
Aquaculture: Prof. RHODORA M. BARTOLOME
Agricultural Business Management: Prof. ALMA M. DELA CRUZ
Animal Science: Dr ERNESTO P. GARILLO
Agricultural Engineering: Dr JOSE L. TABAGO
Crop Protection: Prof. ELSA P. PADERES
Crop Science: Dr ROLANDO L. ENCARNACION
Soil Science: Prof. FLORIDA C. GARCIA
Education and Related Studies: Dr ELISA L. CARLOS
Rural Development and Communication: Dr AURORA S. PADERES
Science Education: Prof. CECILIA T. GALVEZ
Agricultural Technology: Dr PAULITA G. BOADO

AFFILIATED INSTITUTES

Centre for Central Luzon Studies: Dir Prof. MARILOU G. ABON.

Central Luzon Agricultural Research Center, CLSU: Dir Dr JOSE C. ALONZO.

Freshwater Aquaculture Center, CLSU: Dir Dr TERESO ABELLA.

CENTRAL MINDANAO UNIVERSITY

University Town, Musuan, Bukidnon 8710
Fax: (88) 8442520

Founded 1952 as the Mindanao Agricultural College; University 1965
State control
Languages of instruction: English and Filipino
Academic year: June to March (two semesters and a summer school)

President: Dr JAIME M. GELLOR
Vice-Presidents:
Academic Affairs: Dr DEMOSTHENES C. MATEO
Administration: Dr MARDONIO M. LAO
Research and Extension: Dr JUAN A. NAGTALON
Registrar: Prof. CARMENCITA M. TORTOLA
Librarian: Prof. ESTHER E. DINAMPO

Library of 23,000 vols
Number of teachers: 311
Number of students: 4,870

Publications: *CMU Journal of Food, Agriculture and Nutrition* (quarterly), *Barangay Balita* (quarterly), *Newsletter* (quarterly).

DEANS

College of Arts and Sciences: Dr JOSE A. LOMONGO
College of Agriculture: Dr WENCESLAO T. TIANERO
College of Education: Dr FORTUNATA V. CATALON
College of Engineering: Prof. LUCIO L. LAURENTE
College of Home Economics: Dr NERISSA A. MACARAYAN
College of Forestry: Dr TOMAS P. AUSTRAL
College of Veterinary Medicine: Dr LUZVIMINDA T. SIMBORIO
Graduate School: Dr RIGOBERTA T. HEBRON

DEPARTMENT CHAIRMEN

College of Agriculture:
Agribusiness: Dr JOSEFINO M. MAGALLANES
Agricultural Economics: Prof. SEGUNDINA Z. GONZAGA
Agricultural Education: Prof. FELISA CARPENTERO
Agronomy: Prof. NENITA B. BALDO
Animal Science: Prof. VALENTINO UNGAB
Development Communication: Prof. NELIA T. ESCARLOS
Entomology: Prof. ESTELITO CATLI
Horticulture: Prof. LYDIA C. SISON
Plant Pathology: Prof. CECILIA V. BAUTISTA
Soil Science: Dr MANUEL L. MARQUEZ

College of Arts and Sciences:
Behavioural Sciences: Prof. EMMA A. JUANILLO
Biological Sciences: Prof. VICTORIA T. QUIMPANG
Chemistry: Prof LETECIA C. MENDOZA
Languages and Literature: Prof. SOCORRO H. ABBU
Mathematics: ROLITO EBALLE
Physics: JUSEMIE V. ORTELANO
Social Science: ELEUTERIO D. TANO

College of Education:
Educational Services: Prof. LOURDES BAGO
Business Education: Prof. MAGDALENA R. REDOBLE
Physical Education: Prof. MARYLOU C. VILORIA

College of Engineering:
Agricultural Engineering: Prof. RODOLFO S. YADAO
Civil Engineering: Eng. REINERIO V. SUPREMO
Electrical Engineering: Prof. BENJAMIN V. QUIJOTE
Mechanical Engineering: Prof. MANUEL P. VARIAS

College of Forestry:
Forest Biological Science: Prof. DEOLITO T. CLAVEJO
Forest Resources Management: Prof. ROBERT MONOY
Wood Science Technology: Prof. JAMES O. LACANDULA

College of Home Economics:
Education and Family Life: Prof. NORMA C. CULAS
Food Science and Nutrition: Prof. ANGELITA R. BOKINGO
Clothing and Applied Arts: Prof. AMELIA T. CABACUNGAN

College of Veterinary Medicine:
Anatomy, Physiology and Pharmacology: Dr HAZEL MARIE R. BOLORON
Medicine and Surgery: Dr JOSE TRINIPIL LAGAPA
Microbiology, Parasitology, Pathology and Public Health: Dr ROY V. VILLOREJO

CENTRAL PHILIPPINE UNIVERSITY

POB 231, Iloilo City 5000
Telephone: (33) 7-34-71
Fax: (33) 20-36-85

Founded 1905
Language of instruction: English
Private control
Academic year: June to March (two terms)

President: AGUSTIN A. PULIDO
Treasurer: ROSALENE J. MADERO
Vice-President for Academic Affairs: ELMA S. HERRADURA
Registrar: ESTHER S. BASIAO
Librarian: VICTORY D. GABAWA

Number of teachers: 280
Number of students: 9,280

Publications: *The Central Echo* (student paper), *Centralite* (student annual), *Link* (Alumni organ), *Southeast Asia Journal*.

DEANS

College of Agriculture: ENRIQUE S. ALTIS
College of Arts and Sciences: LYNN J. PAREJA
College of Commerce: MILAGROS V. DIGNADICE
College of Education: LORNA D. GELLADA
College of Engineering: WALDEN S. RIO
College of Law: JUANITO M. ACANTO
College of Nursing: BETTY T. POLIDO
College of Theology: JOHNNY V. GUMBAN
School of Graduate Studies: MIRIAM M. TRAVIÑA

CENTRO ESCOLAR UNIVERSITY

9 Mendiola St, San Miguel, Manila
Telephone and fax: (2) 735-59-91

Founded 1907
Languages of instruction: English and Filipino
Private control
Academic year: June to March

President: Dr LOURDES T. ECHAUZ
Vice-Presidents: Dr ROSITA L. NAVARRO (Academic Affairs), Dr MARIA L. AYUYAO (Executive), JUAN J. CARLOS (Finance), JOSE M. TIONGCO (Special Affairs), CARMELITA E. LA O' (Business Affairs), LUCILA C. TIONGCO (Alumni Affairs), Dr ROSITA G. SANTOS (Research), Dr CLAIRE Z. MANALO (Student Affairs).
Registrar: LUCIA D. GONZALES
Librarian: TERESITA G. HERNANDEZ

Number of teachers: 827
Number of students: 28,000

Publications: *Faculty and Graduate Studies* (annually), *Rose and the Leaf, Rosebud* (both annually), *Ciencia y Virtud* (quarterly), *The Clarion* (quarterly).

DEANS

College of Liberal Arts: Dr CECILIA G. VALMONTE
College of Accountancy, Commerce and Secretarial Administration: Dr CONRADO E. IÑIGO
College of Dentistry: Dr RENATO M. SISON
College of Education and Social Work: Dr PAZ I. LUCIDO
College of Medical Technology: Dr PRISCILLA A. PANLASIGUI
College of Science: Dr ZENAIDA M. AUSTRIA
Conservatory of Music: Dr ALFREDO S. BUENAVENTURA
College of Nursing: Prof. ANGELINA A. LIN
College of Nutrition, Home Economics and Tourism: Prof. CARMINA P. CATAPANG

College of Optometry: Dr MARIANO M. TAÑADA
College of Pharmacy: Prof. OLIVIA M. LIMUACO
Graduate School: Dr ROSITA L. NAVARRO

HEADS OF DEPARTMENTS

Behavioural Sciences: A. G. SOLIVEN
Biological Sciences: T. R. PEREZ
Computer Education: T. DE GUZMAN
Counselling and Testing: E. I. G. RAMOS
Educational Technology: P. I. LUCIDO
English: M. GO
Filipino: MA. L. R. BAELLO
Home Economics: C. P. CATAPANG
Library Science: T. G. HERNANDEZ
Mathematics: P. R. SORIANO
Physical Education: L. G. PANGANIBAN
Physical Science: B. M. LONTOC
Religion: E. B. SANTOS
Science Laboratory: L. CIÑO
Social Arts: T. AVENILLA
Social Sciences: L. R. REYES
Social Work: J. A. REYES

DE LA SALLE UNIVERSITY

2401 Taft Ave, Malate, Manila 1004
Telephone: (2) 526-14-02
Fax: (2) 526-14-03
E-mail: evpciq@dlsu.edu.ph

Founded 1911
Private control (sectarian)
Languages of instruction: English and Filipino
Academic year: June to May

President: Bro. ANDREW GONZALEZ
Executive Vice-President: Dr CARMELITA QUEBENGCO
Vice-President for Academics: Dr WYONA PATALINGHUG
Assistant Vice-President for Administrative Services: Engr AURELLANO DELA CRUZ, Jr
Assistant Vice-President for Academic Services: AGNES YUHICO
Assistant Vice-President for Research and Faculty Development: Dr YOLANDO BERONQUE
Registrar: Dr RICHARD GONZALES
Librarian: PERLA GARCIA

Number of teachers: 860
Number of students: 12,556

Publications: *Green and White Yearbook* (annually), *The La Sallian, Ang Pahayagang Plaridel* (monthly), *Alumnews, Computer Issues, Sophia, Malate Literary Journal* (quarterly), *Malay Journal, Agham,* (quarterly), *Dialogue* (annually), *Business and Economic Review, Engineering Journal* (2 a year), *DLSU Newsletter* (weekly), *Abut-tanaw* (fortnightly), *SC Bulletin.*

DEANS

College of Education: Dr ALLAN BERNARDO
Graduate School of Business: Dr LYDIA ECHAUZ
College of Liberal Arts: Dr ESTRELLITA GRUENBERG
College of Science: Dr FLORENCIA CLAVERIA
College of Engineering: Dr AIDA VELAZCO
College of Business and Economics: Dr TERESO TULLAO, Jr
College of Computer Studies: JONATHAN DAYAO

PROFESSORS

BALAJADIA, B., Religious Studies
BAUTISTA, C., Literature
BAUTISTA, M. L., English Language
CALUYO, F., ECE
CLAVERIA, F., Biology
CLEMEÑA, R. M., Education of Counsellors
CORPUZ, C., History
CRUZ, I., Filipino
DE CASTRO, L., Civil Engineering
DE JESUS, M. B., Educational Management
DEL MUNDO, C., Jr, Communication
DERY, L., History
DIAZ, V., Commercial Law
DIESTO, S., Mathematics
EDRALIN, D., Business Management
ESTAÑERO, R., Civil Engineering
FORMILLEZA, E., Economics
GALLARDO, S., Chemical Engineering
GASPILLO, P., Chemical Engineering
GERVACIO, S., Mathematics
GONZALEZ, A., Religious Education and English Language
MEDINA, B., Jr, Filipino
OLAÑO, S., Jr, Chemical Engineering
OSTERIA, T., Behavioural Sciences
PATALINGHUG, W., Chemistry
PUERTOLLANO, A., Chemical Engineering
RAGASA, C., Chemistry
SALAZAR, C., Chemical Engineering
SILAO, L., Chemical Engineering
TRANCE, A., Mathematics
TIMBREZA, F., Philosophy
TULLAO, T., Jr, Economics
VILLACORTA, W., Political Science
WRIGHT, G., History

DIVINE WORD UNIVERSITY OF TACLOBAN

Veteranos Ave, Tacloban City, Leyte
Telephone: 321-2307

Founded 1929, University status 1966
Private control
Language of instruction: English
Academic year: June to March

President: Fr CECILIO P. JAYME
Vice-Presidents: Bro. PAULINO BONGCARAS (Academic), Fr EDGARDO D. ABUNDO (Administration), Rev. Fr JOSÉ BAGADIONG (Finance)
Registrar: ANSELMO BUGAL
Librarian: REMEDIOS ABELLA

Number of teachers: 249
Number of students: 6,144

Publications: *Leyte-Samar Studies, Power* (2 a year)*, DWU Bulletin* (monthly)*, Pulong* (quarterly).

DEANS

College of Arts and Sciences: Fr ORLANDO G. GUZMAN
College of Commerce: CAROLINA P. CANIGA
College of Education: (vacant)
College of Engineering: Eng. JOVENIANO A. NERVES
College of Law: Atty SERGIO C. SUMAYOD
College of Medicine: Dr GIL A. ASOY
College of Nursing: SOCORRO S. GASCO
Graduate School: NENITA G. TAMAYO

HEADS OF DEPARTMENTS

College of Arts and Sciences:

English: AURORA J. CASIMPAN
Medical Technology: THELMA P. LIM
Natural Sciences: CLETA M. SALVATIERRA
Social Sciences: Fr. EDGARDO D. ABUNDO
Social Work: FELICITAS D. TABIONGAN
Theology: Fr SAMUEL CLARIN

College of Commerce:

Accounting: CAROLINA P. CANIGA
Business Management, Banking and Finance, Economics: FELMA FREDA LOPEZ
Secretarial: MARILU P. PEREZ

College of Engineering:

Civil Engineering: (vacant)
Mechanical, Electrical and Chemical Engineering: (vacant)

College of Law:

Criminology: NILO M. DE VEYRA

Graduate School:

MBA/MBEd Chairman: EDWARD Y. CHUA

College of Medicine:

Anatomy: ROLANDO B. OCHOA
Human Biochemistry and Nutrition: DENISA P. MORETO
Medicine: AVITO SALINAS
Microbiology-Parasitology, Family Preventive and Community Medicine: LYTHINDA P. PALOMINO
Pathology: EDUARDO C. GO
Paediatrics: LEONOR BARRION
Physiology: MA. LOURDES A. AQUITANIA
Obstetrics and Gynaecology: IDERLINA M. FRANCISCO
Surgery: CESAR A. AQUITANIA

UNIVERSITY OF THE EAST

2219 Claro M. Recto Ave, Manila
Telephone: 741-5471

Founded 1946 as the Philippine College of Commerce and Business Administration; University of the East 1951
Private control

President: Dr JOSEFINA R. CORTES (acting)
Senior Vice-President for Academic Affairs: Dr JOSEFINA R. CORTES
Senior Vice-President for Administrative Affairs: CARMELITA G. MATEO
Chancellor of UE Caloocan: DESIDERIA R. REX
Vice-President for Academic Affairs: Dr JESUSA J. DACUMOS
Vice-President for Administration: ANTONIO M. DE GUZMAN
Registrar: ROMEO Q. ARMADA
Librarian: SARAH DE JESUS

Library: see Libraries
Number of teachers: 783
Number of students: 34,200

Publications: *Dawn, Panorama, UE Today,* college journals: *EURDC Research Journal, Law, CAS, Engineering, Education, Business Administration.*

DEANS

Graduate School of Business: Dr ROSARIO E. MAMINTA
Graduate School of Education: Dr ROSARIO E. MAMINTA
College of Arts and Sciences (Manila campus): CARMELITA S. FLORES
College of Arts and Sciences (Caloocan campus): Dr TERESITA E. ERESTAIN
College of Business Administration: ESTER LEDESMA
College of Business Administration (Caloocan campus): Dr FELINO L. AMPIL Jr
College of Law: CARLOS M. ORTEGA
College of Dentistry: Dr DIAMPO J. LIM
College of Education: Dr LETICIA P. CORTES
College of Medicine: Dr ROMEO A. DIVINAGRACIA
College of Nursing: Dr CARMELITA DIVINAGRACIA
UERM Hospital: Dr ESPERANZA C. LANSANG
College of Computer Studies and Systems: PRESIDIO R. CALUMPIT Jr
College of Engineering: Dr GENARO T. MAZAN
College of Fine Arts: ALFREDO S. REBILLON Sr
Elementary and Secondary Laboratory Schools: ESMYRNA F. ESTACIO
Physical Education Department: LUZ R. SANTA ANA

UNIVERSITY OF EASTERN PHILIPPINES

University Town, Northern Samar 6400

Founded 1918
State control
Languages of instruction: English and Filipino

President: Dr PEDRO D. DESTURA
Vice-Presidents: Dr PEDRO A. BASILOY (Administration), Dr NILO E. COLINARES (Academic Affairs), Dr NESTOR L. RUBENECIA (External Affairs)
Registrar: ROGELIO L. NOBLE
Librarian: FE G. BAOY

Number of teachers: 339
Number of students: 7,511

Publications: *UEP Graduate Journal, The Pacific Journal of Science and Technology, The Pillar.*

DEANS

College of Agriculture: Prof. LEON A. GUEVARA
College of Arts and Communication: Dr LYDIA E. DE LA ROSA
College of Business Administration: Dr LOURDES O. MOSCARE
College of Education: Dr ZENAIDA S. LUCERO
College of Engineering: Engr ROMEO D. ATENCIO
College of Law: Atty Mar P. DE ASIS
College of Veterinary Medicine: Dr EDUARDO L. ALVAREZ
College of Nursing: Dr ELBIE Y. BALDO
College of Science: Dr NESTOR L. RUBENECIA
Graduate School: Dr MINDANILLA B. BROTO

FAR EASTERN UNIVERSITY

POB 609, Manila

Telephone: (2) 735-56-21
Fax: (2) 735-02-32

Founded 1928 as Institute of Accountancy, incorporated in 1934 as Far Eastern University
Private control
Language of instruction: English
Academic year: June to March

President: EDILBERTO C. DE JESUS
Vice-President on Academic Affairs: LYDIA A. PALAYPAY
Registrar: MARISSA A. FERNANDEZ
Chief Librarian: ZENAIDA M. GALANG

Library: see Libraries
Number of teachers: 684
Number of students: 24,080

Publications: *Far Eastern University Journal* (2 a year), *Transition* (annually), *Ambon* (annually), *Arts and Science Review* (2 a year), *Cultural Forum* (irregular), *FEU Newsletter* (4 a year), *Papers Etcetera* (2 a year).

DEANS

Institute of Accounts, Business and Finance: RAYMOND E. LOYOLA (Assoc. Dean)
Institute of Architecture and Fine Arts: VICTORIANO O. AVIGUETERO Jr (Assoc. Dean)
Institute of Arts and Sciences: ANGEL O. ABAYA
Institute of Education: JOVITO B. CASTILLO
Institute of Graduate Studies: JOVITO B. CASTILLO (Co-ordinator)
Institute of Law: OSCAR M. HERRERA, Sr
Institute of Nursing: NORMA M. DUMADAG

FEATI UNIVERSITY

Helios St, Santa Cruz, Manila

Telephone: 48-59-51

Founded 1946
Private control
Academic year: June to March (two semesters)

President: JOSE M. SEGOVIA
Executive Vice-President: AURELIO S. UGALDE
Vice-President and Treasurer: MA. LINA A. SANTIAGO
Vice-President for Legal Affairs: HOSPICIO B. BIÑAS
Registrar: DOLORES O. ROQUE
Librarian: SUELLEN S. TONGSON

Library of 42,000 vols
Number of teachers: 246
Number of students: 8,700

Courses in arts and education, fine arts, business administration, engineering.

FOUNDATION UNIVERSITY

Dumaguete City 6200

Telephone: (35) 225-06-18
Fax: (35) 225-06-20

Founded 1949
Language of instruction: English
Private control
Academic year: June to March (two semesters)

President: LEANDRO G. SINCO
Vice-President for Academic Affairs: Dr ESTER V. TAN
Vice-President for Student Life and External Affairs: DINNO WILLIE D. DEPOSITARIO
Registrar: Mrs NATIVIDAD P. DURAN
Librarian: NENA S. GUASA

Library of 55,000 vols
Number of teachers: 143
Number of students: 4,639

Publications: *Foundation Time,* (monthly), *Graduate Journal* (2 a year), *University Recorder* (2 a year), *Law Forum.*

DEANS

Graduate School: Dr GENARO B. DELORIA
College of Arts and Sciences: MARJORIE P. PILAS
College of Education: Dr THELMA E. FLORENDO
College of Business and Economics: Dr EVA C. MELON
College of Agriculture: CANDIDA S. BASUBAS
College of Law and Jurisprudence: ENRIQUE S. EMPLEO
School of Industrial Engineering: Engr JUANITO S. RENACIA

GREGORIO ARANETA UNIVERSITY FOUNDATION

Araneta University Post Office, Malabon, Metro Manila 1404

Telephone: 366-90-53
Fax: 361-90-54

Founded 1946; reorganized as a foundation 1965
Languages of instruction: English and Filipino
Private foundation
Academic year: June to March

President: Dr MANUEL D. PUNZAL
Executive Vice-President: Dr ROSENDA A. DE GRACIA
Director for Academic Affairs: Dr MA. CORAZON V. TADENA
Registrar: Prof. TERESITA R. GUTIERREZ
Librarian: FELISA W. DADOR

Number of teachers: 69 full-time, 87 part-time
Number of students: 3,012

Publications: *Araneta Research Journal* (quarterly), *Tinig* (monthly), *Harvest* (annually), *Compendium of Veterinary Research* (annually).

DEANS

College of Agriculture and Forestry: Dr ANASTACIO T. MERCADO
College of Arts and Sciences: Dr LILLIAN L. PENA
College of Business and Accountancy: Dr NELLIE A. ASUNCION
College of Education: Dr LYDIA S. JUSAY
College of Engineering and Technology: Dr LEOVIGILDO A. MANALO
College of Veterinary Medicine: Dr DANIEL C. VENTURA, Jr.
Graduate School: Dr MA. CORAZON V. TADENA

UNIVERSITY OF ILOILO

Iloilo City

Founded 1968

Schools of arts, science, commerce, civil and mechanical engineering, education and law

ISABELA STATE UNIVERSITY

San Fabian, Echague, Isabela 1318

Telephone: 22013

Founded 1978
State control
Language of instruction: English
Academic year: June to May

President: Dr RODOLFO C. NAYGA
Vice-President: Dr MARIANO P. BALUAG
Registrar: THELMA T. LANUZA
Librarian: ROMULA P. ROMERO

Library of 11,818 vols
Number of teachers: 477
Number of students: 4,340

Publications: *Research Journal*, *CVIARS Monitor*, *Forum*, *Mediator*, *Hexachord*, *Geyser*.

DEANS

College of Agriculture: Dr FRANCISCO M. BASUEL
School of Business Administration: Prof. RELLI C. PABLEO
School of Development Communication: Prof. LOLITA G. SARANGAY
School of Engineering: Eng. JOSE J. LORENZANA
College of Arts and Sciences: Dr JESUS B. GOLLAYAN
Polytechnic College: Dr ESPERANZA BUENO
Teachers' College: Dr SACRIFICIA T. CATABUI
College of Forestry: Dr ROBERTO R. ARAÑO
Graduate Studies: Dr NELSON T. BINAG

UNIVERSITY OF MANILA

546 Dr M. V. de los Santos St, Sampaloc, Manila 1008

Telephone: 7413637
Fax: 7413640

Founded 1913
Private, non-sectarian institution
Language of instruction: English
Academic year: June to May (three terms)

President: Dr VIRGILIO DE LOS SANTOS
Executive Vice-President: Atty ERNESTO LL. DE LOS SANTOS
Vice-President for Academic Affairs: Dr EMILY D. DE LEON
Registrar: Atty ERNESTO LL. DE LOS SANTOS
Chief Librarian: CORAZON G. PAYTE

Number of teachers: 250
Number of students: 7,500

Publications: *The University of Manila Graduate School Journal, The UM Law Gazette, The Gold Leaf.*

DEANS

College of Law: MICHAEL P. MORALDE
College of Education: EMILY D. DE LEON
College of Liberal Arts: ROSALIA V. MOLINA
College of Business Administration and Accountancy: NELSON S. ABELEDA
College of Engineering: ARSENIO A. RONQUILLO
College of Foreign Service: BENJAMIN D. QUINERI
College of Criminology: FORTUNATO S. RIVERA
Graduate Studies: EMILY D. DE LEON

MANILA CENTRAL UNIVERSITY

V. Fugoso St Cor. Oroquieta St, Sta Cruz, 1003 Manila

Telephone: 711-7341

Founded 1904
Private control
Language of instruction: English
Academic year: June to March

President: LUALHATI TANCHOCO-GONZALEZ
Vice-Presidents: Dr FELICIANA A. REYES (Academic Affairs), Dr ARISTOTLE T. MALABANAN (Administrative Affairs), LEZITA H. REYES (Finance)

Registrar: Braulia Musñgi
Librarian: Adalgesa Masangkay

Number of teachers: 240
Number of students: 9,028

Publications: *The Pharos, Research Journal, Gold and Purple.*

DEANS

College of Medicine: Dr Jesus Fotas
College of Pharmacy and Medical Technology: Luzviminda Ong
College of Dentistry: Dr Eliza Puzon
College of Arts and Sciences: Amanda Lorenzana
College of Business Administration: Percy Garcia
College of Nursing: Lina Salarda
College of Optometry: Dr Francisco Baetiong Jr
College of Physical Therapy: Dr José Redentor C. Bucu
School of Midwifery: Lina Salarda
Graduate School: Dr Felicidad C. Robles
High School Principal: Riorica Navarro
Head, Elementary Department: Remedios Batac

MARIANO MARCOS STATE UNIVERSITY

Batac, Ilocos Norte

Telephone: 792-31-91
Fax: (77) 792-31-31

Founded 1978
State control
Language of instruction: English
Academic year: June to March

President: Dr Elias L. Calacal
Vice-President for Administration: Dr Heraldo L. Layaoem
Vice-President for Academic Affairs: Dr Nancy B. Balantac
Vice-President for Research and Extension: Dr Rodolfo A. Natividad
Registrar: Dr Nenita P. Blanco
Administrative Officer: Manuel B. Corpuz
Librarian: Prof. Bucalen C. Saboy

Library of 55,511 vols
Number of teachers: 485
Number of students: 11,761

DEANS

Graduate School: Dr Lorenza S. Matias
College of Arts and Sciences: Dr Anabelle C. Felipe
College of Agriculture and Forestry: Dr Salud F. Barroga
College of Education: Dr Vicente A. Bondan
College of Business, Economics and Accountancy: Dr Marietta M. Bonoan
College of Engineering and Technology; Engr Carlos F. Ungson
Institute of Health Sciences: Prof. Violeta M. Glova
College of Technology: Prof. Nestor M. Agngaraygay
College of Aquatic Sciences and Technology: Prof. Rodolfe V. Laddaran

ATTACHED CENTRES:

Iloko Research and Information Center: Dir Dr Ernesto Ma. Cadiz

Regional Science Teaching Center: Dir Prof. Leo Ver Domingo

Fulbright American Studies Resource Center: Dir Prof. Bucalen C. Saboy

Business Resource Development Center: Head Prof. Lorna Fernandez

Center for Applied Research and Technology Transfer: Dir Prof. Felipe R. Esta

PAMANTASAN NG LUNGSOD NG MAYNILA
(University of the City of Manila)

Intramuros, Manila 1002
Telephone: (2) 527-35-51
Fax: (2) 527-35-52
E-mail: plm@mail.cnl.net

Founded 1967
City government control
Languages of instruction: English and Filipino
Academic year: June to March (2 semesters); summer term for graduate schools; trimestral for graduate programmes in management and engineering.

President: Dr Virsely M. dela Cruz
Vice-President for Academic Affairs: Dr Ma. Corazon T. Veridiano
Vice-President for Administration: Atty Fe P. Sumilong
Vice-President for Finance and Planning: Angelita G. Solis
Registrar: Ofelia D. Lazarte
Librarian: Rebecca M. Jocson

Library of 49,000 vols
Number of teachers: 613
Number of students: 9,684

Publications: *PLM Review, Ang Pamantasan.*

DEANS

Graduate School of Arts, Sciences, Education and Nursing: Dr Domingo B. Nuñez
Graduate School of Business and Government: Prof. J. Waldemar V. Valmores
Graduate School of Engineering: Eng. Felix F. Aspiras
College of Arts and Sciences: Dr Dolores B. Liwag
College of Business and Public Administration: Nonalyn L. Vengco
College of Education: Dr Daisy P. Hicarte
College of Engineering and Technology: Eng. Felix F. Aspiras
College of Law: Atty Angel P. Aguirre Jr
College of Medicine: Dr Victoria Edna G. Monzon
College of Nursing: Laura Evelyn P. Ciabal
College of Physical Therapy: Dr Caroline C. Ynion
College of Physical Education, Recreation and Sports: Alejandro L. Dagddag Jr

MINDANAO STATE UNIVERSITY

MSU Campus, Marawi City
Telephone: 50-82-22

Founded 1961
Language of instruction: English

President: Dr Ahmad E. Alonto, Jr
Executive Vice-President and Chancellor: Dr Datumanong A. Sarangani
Vice-President for Academic Affairs: Dr Corazon M. Batara
Vice-President for Planning and Development: Dr Milandre Rusgal
Vice-President for Administration and Finance: Atty Abdul S. Aguam
Registrar: Jessie Silang (acting)
Librarian: Lawansan Mangorac

Number of teachers: 659
Number of students: 6,944

Publications: *Mindanao Varsitarian, Pagsibol, Darangen, Piglas, Alumni Monitor, OVCRE Bulletin, Unirescent.*

DEANS

College of Agriculture: Prof. Mangompia U. Angod
College of Natural Sciences and Mathematics: Dr Emmanuel Lagare (acting)
College of Social Sciences and Humanities: Prof. Monaorai S. Aquino (acting)
College of Business Administration: Dr Perla Manzano (acting)
College of Community Development and Public Administration: Dr Nasrodin B. Guro
College of Education: Dr Erlinda Ola-Casan
College of Engineering: Prof. Mamalangkas K. Abdullah
College of Fisheries: Prof. Saidale S. Mohamad
College of Forestry: Prof. Gerardo Gavine
College of Health Sciences: Prof. Hannipha B. Derico (acting)
College of Hotel and Restaurant Management: Prof. Cecile B. Mambuay
College of Law: Atty Oga M. Mapupuno
College of Medicine: Dr Angelo L. Manalo
College of Sports, Physical Education and Recreation: Prof. Nessie Tingson
Graduate School: Dr Solomon U. Molina
King Faisal Center for Islamic and Arabic Studies: Prof. Mustapha L. Dimaro
Science Training Center: Dr Thelma Antonio

Iligan Institute of Technology of the Mindanao State University

POB 5644, Iligan City 9200
Telephone: (63) 221-40-50
Fax: (63) 221-40-56

Founded 1961, present status 1988
State control
Languages of instruction: English and Filipino
Academic year: June to April

President (MSU System): Dr Emily M. Marohombsar
Chancellor: Dr Camar A. Umpa
Vice-Chancellor (Academic Affairs): Prof. Marcelo P. Salazar
Vice-Chancellor (Research and Extension): Prof. Jimmy Y. Balacuit
Vice-Chancellor (Administration and Finance): Luzmindo V. Mamauag
Registrar: Gorgonio H. Loable
Librarian: Consejo M. Cariaga

Library of 48,000 vols
Number of teachers: 519
Number of students: 9,607

DEANS

College of Arts and Social Sciences: Prof. Evelyn M. Jamboy
College of Science and Mathematics: Dr Luis D. Carrillo
School of Graduate Studies: Dr Zenaida L. Ochotorena
School of Engineering Technology: Prof. Roberto E. Salarza
College of Engineering: Prof. Rosalinda C. Balacuit
College of Business Administration: Prof. Annie J. Orejana
College of Law: Arthur L. Abundiente
College of Education: Dr Remedios B. Grageda
Integrated Development School: Prof. Gloria Madulara

UNIVERSITY OF MINDANAO

Bolton St, Davao City, Mindanao
Telephone: (82) 227-54-56

Founded 1946
Private control
Language of instruction: English
Academic year: June to March

President: Dolores P. Torres
Executive Vice-President for Broadcasting: Guillermo P. Torres
Executive Vice-President for Education: Saturnino R. Petalcorin
Senior Vice-President for Academic Affairs: Dr Paquita D. Gavino

Vice-President for Treasury: SANDRA G. ANGELES
Vice-President for Accounting: GLORIA E. DETOYA
Vice-President for Administration: ANTONIO M. PILPIL
Vice-President for MIS/EDP: EDGARDO O. CASTILLO
Registrar: GLORIA E. DETOYA
Number of teachers: 455
Number of students: 22,569
Publications: *UM Faculty Journal*, *News Bulletin*.

DEANS
Post-Doctoral: Dr EFIGENIA C. OCCEÑA
Graduate School: Dr JULIAN RODRIGUEZ, Jr
College of Engineering: CARMENCITA E. VIDAMO
College of Architecture: ILUMINADO C. QUINTO
College of Commerce and Accountancy: VICENTE B. VALDEZ
College of Law: Atty JOSÉ C. ESTRADA
College of Arts and Sciences: Dr HERNANDO ZAMORA
Teachers' College: Dr NECITA I. JOYNO
College of Forestry: DAN D. MITCHAO
College of Criminology: GEOFFREY GIRADO (Asst Dean)

NATIONAL UNIVERSITY

551 Mariano F. Jhocson St, Sampaloc, Manila
Telephone: 61-34-31
Founded 1900
Language of instruction: English
Private control
Academic year: June to March
President: JESUS M. JHOCSON
Registrar: LETICIA J. PAGUIA
Head of Graduate Studies: ZENAIDA N. MAGIBA
Librarian: CONSUELO J. MIGUEL

DEANS
College of Commerce: LETICIA J. PAGUIA (acting)
College of Dentistry: Dr GREGORIO D. GABRIEL
College of Pharmacy: CELIA V. LANSANG
College of Education: DOMINGO L. DIAZ
College of Liberal Arts: ZENAIDA N. MAGIBA
College of Electrical, Industrial and Mechanical Engineering: ROMULO D. COLOMA
College of Civil, Chemical and Sanitary Engineering: ROMULO D. COLOMA
College of Architecture: FERNANDO ABAD

UNIVERSITY OF NEGROS OCCIDENTAL-RECOLETOS

Lizares Ave, POB 214, 6100 Bacolod City
Telephone: 433-1849
Fax: 433-1709
Founded 1941
Private control
Language of instruction: English
Academic year: June to March
President: Fr CONSTANTINO B. REAL
Comptroller: Fr LEOPOLDO V. ESTIOKO
Registrar: Eng. ISMAEL L. EXITO
Librarian: ARABELLA M. ANANORIA
Number of teachers: 280
Number of students: 12,000
Publications: *The Tolentine Star* (2 a semester), *UNO-R Journal of the Graduate School*.

DEANS
Graduate School: Dr JOSE B. FERRARIS
School of Agriculture: Dr EVANGELINE O. ABOYO
College of Arts and Sciences: MAGDALENA S. CLAUOR
College of Law: NELSON P. LO
Teachers' Formation Centre: Dr JOSE B. FERRARIS
College of Engineering: Eng. NICANOR P. NAVARRO
College of Criminology: JOSE MANUEL J. LOPEZ-VITO
College of Commerce: WILHELMINA R. GONZALES
High School Department: DEBORAH D. BORROMEO
Elementary Department: MARCELA D. YAP

UNIVERSITY OF NORTHERN PHILIPPINES

Vigan, Ilocos Sur
Telephone: 28-10, 28-11, 28-12
Founded 1965
State control
Languages of instruction: English and Filipino
Academic year of two semesters
President: Dr DOROTEA C. FILART
Executive Vice-President: Prof. LEO OANDASAN
Vice-President for Academic Affairs: Dr PACITA B. ANTIPORDA
University Secretary: Prof. RAMONA VEGA
Director of Admissions: Miss ELEUTERIA REMUCAL
Director of Research: Prof. NORMA I. CACHOLA
Librarian: Mrs PEROMA L. PACIS
Library of 28,369 vols
Number of teachers: 392
Number of students: 7,017
Publications: *Tandem* (every 2 months), *New Vision* (quarterly).

DEANS AND DEPARTMENT HEADS
Faculty of Arts and Sciences: Dr FRANCISCO C. MACANAS
Faculty of Business Administration: Dr LUMEN ALMACHAR
Institute of Criminology: Prof. PLACIDO UNCIANO
Institute of Engineering: Eng. ROGELIO ANINAG
Institute of Fine Arts: Prof. FLORO PERLAS
Institute of Nursing and Paramedical Services: Prof. LILIA SALVADOR
Faculty of Teacher Education: Dr CIRILO PARRA
Institute of Social Work and Community Development: DANIEL COLCOL
Institute of Technical Education and Cottage Industries Development: Prof. WILHELMINA VERGARA
Faculty of the Graduate School: SALVADOR S. EDER

NOTRE DAME UNIVERSITY

Notre Dame Ave, 9600 Cotabato City
Telephone: 21-43-12
Founded 1948; University status 1969
Private (Roman Catholic) control
Language of instruction: English
Academic year: June to March
President: Fr ELISEO R. MERCADO
Vice-President for Academic Affairs: Dr OFELIA L. DURANTE
Registrar: SONIA A. NAVARRA
Librarian: JOSEPHINE J. OCHIA
Library of 80,440 vols
Number of teachers: 230
Number of students: 6,077
Publications: *Notre Damer*, *Notre Dame Journal* (4 a year).

DEANS
Graduate School: Dr TEODORO M. CARRASCO
College of Engineering: Eng. FLORIANO M. ARANEZ
College of Arts and Sciences: RUFA C. GUIAM
College of Commerce: TERESA N. PIA
College of Law: Atty MAMA S. DALANDAG
Teachers' College: EVELINA E. AYSON
College of Nursing: ELSA C. TAMSE
Community College: ESSEX L. GIGUIENTO

UNIVERSITY OF NUEVA CACERES

Jaime Henandez Ave, Naga City 4400
Telephone: 21-21-84
Founded 1948
Private control
Languages of instruction: English and Filipino
Academic year: June to March (two semesters)
President: Dr DOLORES H. SISON
Executive Vice-President: PERFECTO O. PALMA
Vice-President for Administration: JAIME HERNÁNDEZ, Jr
Registrar: NELIA E. SAN JOSE
Librarian: Dr PERPETUA S. PORCALLA
Number of teachers: 327
Number of students: 8,061
Publications: *Nueva Caceres Review*, *Nueva Caceres Bulletin* (every 2 months), *Red and Gray* (annually), *The Trailblazer* (monthly).

DEANS
College of Arts and Sciences and Education: LOURDES S. ANONAS
College of Engineering: MAXIMINO O. PANELO, Jr
College of Law and Commerce: PERFECTO O. PALMA
School of Graduate Studies and Research: MILAGROS Z. REYES

ACADEMIC HEADS OF DEPARTMENT
Accounting: RODOLFO C. BORROMEO
Civil Engineering: LEON PALMIANO
Economics: NINFA Y. ALIPANTE
English: MARILOU L. FALCON
Finance: EUGENIO V. KILATES
Industrial Engineering: FLOR P. VILLAREY
Management: MELINDA S. B. GIMAL
Marketing: EVELYN I. PIMENTEL
Mathematics: ANITA AUTOR
Mechanical Engineering: MANUEL L. BALAQUIAO
Natural Science: CLARITA B. PADILLA
Secretarial: ADELINA VISTAL
Social Science: REMEDIOS S. MILANO

PROFESSORS
ANONAS, L. S., Methods of Research
ALMOITE, G. E. O., Public Administration
BARIAS, A. M.
CADAG, D., Engineering Management, Highway Engineering, Water Resources Engineering, Hydrology
CONDA, A., Development of the Novel
ENOJADO, V. F., Human Relations, Principles of Guidance
EVORA, M., Electrical Engineering, Refrigeration Engineering
FORTUNO, R. Z., Production, Planning Control
GROYON, S., Psychology
PALMA, M. B., Civil Procedure, Special Proceedings
PORCALLA, P., Library Science
REYES, M., Educational Planning, Personnel Administration, Inferential Statistics
SEPTIMO, C., Power Plant Design, Steam Power Engineering, Industrial Plant Design

PANGASINAN STATE UNIVERSITY

Lingayen, Pangasinan
Telephone: 2-5-2
Founded 1979
State control
Languages of instruction: English and Filipino
Academic year: June to May
President: Dr RUFINO O. ESLAO
Vice-President for Academic Affairs: Dr REYNALDO P. SEGUI
Vice-President for Research and Extension: Dr PORFERIO L. BASILIO

Vice-President for Administration: Dr ALFREDO F. AQUINO
Administrative Officer: EMERITO J. URBANO
Librarian (Lingayen): Miss ARACELI P. UNTALAN

Library of 50,000 vols
Number of teachers: 308
Number of students: 5,830

Publications: *PSU Graduate School Journal*, *PSU Annual Reports* (annually), *PSU Chronicle*, *The Technotrends*, *The Reflections*, *The Farm Breeze*, *The Golden Harvest*, *The Green Hills*, *The Technologist*, *The Aqua Sounds*, *The Ocean View*, *Banyuhay* (2 a year), *Research and Extension Bulletin* (quarterly).

DEANS

Graduate School (Urdaneta Center, Bayambang Center, Lingayen Center): Dr RODOLFO C. ASANION
College of Arts, Trades and Technology, PSU-Asingan: Prof. ESTER E. LOMBOY
College of Engineering and Technology, PSU-Urdaneta: Dr EUSEBIO E. MICLAT
College of Fisheries, PSU-Binmaley: Dr PORFERIO L. BASILIO
College of Agriculture, PSU-Santa Maria: Dr LYDIO E. CALONGE
College of Education, PSU-Bayambang: Dr APOLINARIO G. BAUTISTA
College of Agriculture, PSU-Infanta: Prof. ARTEMIO M. REBUGIO
College of Arts, Sciences and Technology, PSU-Lingayen: Dr VICTORIANO C. ESTIRA
College of Agriculture: PSU-San Carlos City: Dr LEONARDO E. MONGE

UNIVERSITY OF PANGASINAN

Dagupan City
Telephone: 38-50

Founded 1925; University status 1968
Private control
Languages of instruction: English and Filipino
Academic year: June to March

President: GEORGE O. RAYOS
Registrar: GERARDO Z. RAYOS
Librarian: MARCELINO C. RUIZ

Library of 45,238 vols
Number of teachers: 309
Number of students: 11,119

DEANS

School of Graduate Studies: Dr FELIX N. PAMINTUAN
College of Education, Home Economics, Industrial Education, and Nutrition: Mrs JULITA R. PAMINTUAN
College of Commerce and Secretarial Administration: MANUEL R. POCO
College of Liberal Arts: RUFINO F. FERNANDEZ
College of Engineering: Engr MANUEL F. FERNANDEZ
College of Law: Atty HERMOGENES S. DECANO
College of Architecture: Arch. BONIFACIO C. LANGIT
College of Nursing: Mrs ROSA C. RIMANDO
University High School: EULOGIO V. JIMENEZ (Principal)
University Elementary Laboratory School: Mrs TERESITA R. VISTRO

HEADS OF DEPARTMENT

English: Dr CRISTETA M. DUMARAN
Mathematics and Natural Science: FRANCISCO B. GAZMEN
Pilipino: Mrs MARIETTA A. ABAD
Physical Education: Mrs ELENITA G. TAEZA
Social Science: JOSE G. JACINTO
Spanish: RUFINO F. FERNANDEZ
Home Economics, Nutrition and Dietetics: Mrs REMEDIOS V. S. FABIA

PHILIPPINE WOMEN'S UNIVERSITY

Taft Ave, 1004 Manila
Telephone: (2) 526-69-34
Fax: (2) 536-81-69

Founded 1919
Private control
Language of instruction: English
Academic year: June to March

Chairman of the Board of Trustees: Hon. HELENA Z. BENITEZ
President: Dr JOSE CONRADO BENITEZ
Chancellor, Manila Campus, and Vice-President for Academic Affairs: Dr DOLORES LASAN
Chancellor, Quezon City Campus: Dr SYLVIA MONTES
Chancellor, Cavite Campus: Dr AMELIA REYES
Vice-Presidents: JULITA DADO (Administration and Finance), ENCARNACION RARALIO (Planning, Development and External Affairs)
Registrar: LILIA ROBOSA
Librarian: DIONISIA ANGELES

Library: see Libraries
Number of teachers: 479
Number of students: 10,675

Publications: *The Philwomenian* (monthly), *The Maroon and White* (annually), *PWU Research Journal* (2 a year) *Journal on Women's Health, Journal on the Environment and Habitat, PWU Bulletin* (quarterly), *Philippine Educational Forum* (2 a year).

DEANS

College of Arts and Sciences: Dr ELIZABETH DELA CRUZ
College of Education: Dr CECILIO DUKA
College of Music: MERCEDES DUGAN (Head)
College of Nursing: CONSTANCIA P. PITPITAN
College of Pharmacy: ZENAIDA SADIWA
Conrado Benitez Institute of Business Education: Dr CONSUELO ANG
Institute of Fine Arts and Design: LORNA SALUTAL (Head)
Institute of Medical Sciences and Technology: Dr NINI FESTIN LIM
Philippine Institute of Nutrition, Food Science and Technology: ROMUALDA GUIRRIEC
Philippine School of Social Work: Dr NENITA M. CURA (Dir)
College of Distance Education: LUMEN LARGOZA

UNIVERSITY OF THE PHILIPPINES

UP Diliman, Quezon City
Telephone and fax: (2) 928-01-10
E-mail: eqj@nicole.upd.edu.ph

Founded 1908
Languages of instruction: English and Filipino
State control
Academic year: June to March (two terms, one summer session)

President: EMIL Q. JAVIER
Vice-President for Academic Affairs: OLIVIA C. CAOILI
Vice-President for Finance and Administration: LEONOR M. BRIONES
Vice-President for Planning and Development: FORTUNATO T. DELA PEÑA
Vice-President for Public Affairs: MARIA LUISA C. DORONILA
Vice-President for Communication and Information Systems: EMANUEL VELASCO
Secretary: HELEN E. LOPEZ

Library: see Libraries
Number of teachers: 4,383
Number of students: 48,090

Publications: *Annual Report*, *Carillon* (3 a year), *UP Gazette* (quarterly), *UP Newsletter* (monthly), *UP Newsbriefs* (weekly), *Facts and Figures* (annually), *Pananaw* (quarterly), *Daluyan* (quarterly), *Pahinungod Newsletter* (quarterly), *UP-CIDS Chronicle* (quarterly).

UP at Diliman:

Chancellor: CLARO T. LLAGUNO
Registrar: ELENA L. SAMONTE
Librarian: BELEN ANGELES

DEANS AND DIRECTORS

College of Architecture: HONRADO FERNANDEZ
College of Arts and Letters: JOSEFINA A. AGRAVANTE
 Department of Art Studies: PATRICK D. FLORES
 Department of English and Comparative Literature: CORAZON D. VILLAREAL
 Department of European Languages: EDGARDO TIAMSON
 Department of Filipino and Philippine Literature: LIGAYA T. RUBIN
 Department of Speech Communication and Theatre Arts: AMIEL LEONARDIA
Asian Centre: ARMANDO MALAY
College of Business Administration: RAFAEL A. RODRIGUEZ
 Department of Accounting, Finance, Business Economics and Law: ERNESTO P. PINEDA
 Department of Business Administration: EMERLINDA R. ROMAN
School of Economics: FELIPE M. MEDALLA
College of Education: LILIA M. RABAGO
 Division of Curriculum and Instruction: JULIAN E. ABUSO
 Division of Educational Leadership and Professional Services: ELIZA PACQUEO ARRE
 UP Integrated School: MA. THERESA L. DE VILLA
College of Engineering: EDGARDO G. ATANACIO
 Department of Chemical Engineering: JOSE C. MUÑOZ
 Department of Civil Engineering: PETER PAUL M. CASTRO
 Department of Computer Science: MARK JAMES K. ENCARNACION
 Department of Electrical Engineering: ROWENA CRISTINA L. GUEVARRA
 Department of Engineering Sciences: MARK ALBERT H. ZARCO
 Department of Geodetic Engineering: ANSELMO D. ALMAZAN
 College of Industrial Engineering and Operational Research: EDGARDO G. ATANACIO
 Department of Mechanical Engineering: FERDINAND G. MANEGDEG
 Department of Metallurgical and Mining Engineering: MANOLO G. MENA
College of Fine Arts: NESTOR O. VINLUAN
 Department of Arts and Theory: VIRGINIA D. DANDAN
 Department of Studio Arts: BENJAMIN CABANGIS
 Department of Visual and Communication Arts: LEONARDO C. ROSETE
College of Home Economics: LYDIA B. ARRIBAS
 Department of Clothing, Textiles and Related Arts: RACQUEL B. FLORENDO
 Department of Family Life and Child Development: LILIAN L. JUADIONG
 Department of Food Science and Nutrition: FLOR CRISANTA F. GALVEZ
 Department of Home Economics Education: MARILOU R. LIM
College of Human Kinetics: LEILANI L. GONZALO
 Department of Professional Studies: GILDA L. UY
 Department of Service Physical Education: RONUALDO U. DIZER
 Department of Sports: NOEL K. RIVERA
Institute of Islamic Studies: WADJA K. ESMULA
School of Labour and Industrial Relations: MARAGTAS SOFRONIO V. AMANTE
College of Law: MERLIN M. MAGALLONA
Institute of Library Science: JOSEPHINE C. SISON

College of Mass Communication: LUIS V. TEODORO
Department of Broadcast Communication: ROSA MARIA T. FELICIANO
Communication Research Department: JOSE R. LACSON
Film and Audiovisual Communication Department: ELLEN J. PAGLINAUAN
Graduate Studies Department: REYNALDO V. GUIOGUIO
Journalism Department: CAROLINA MALAY OCAMPO
College of Music: REYNALDO T. PAGUIO
Department of Composition and Theory: JOSEFINO J. TOLEDO
Department of Conducting and Choral Ensemble: JOEL P. NAVARRO
Department of Music Education: FE C. NERA
Department of Music Research: FELICIDAD A. PRUDENTE
Department of Piano and Organ: IMELDA ONGSIAKO
Department of Strings and Chamber Music: ARTURO T. MOLINA
Department of Voice and Theatre Music: ELMO Q. MAKIL
Department of Wing and Percussion: ENRIQUE D. BARCELO
College of Public Administration: JOSE N. ENDRIGA
College of Science: DANILO M. YANGA
Department of Mathematics: VITTORIO D. ALMAZAR
Department of Meteorology and Oceanography: EMMANUEL C. ANGLO
College of Social Science and Philosophy: CONSUELO PAZ
Department of Anthropology: FRANCISCO A. DATAR
Department of Geography: DARLENE O. GUTIERREZ
Department of History: MA. LUISA T. CAMAGAY
Department of Linguistics: RICARDO MA. D. NOLASCO
Department of Philosophy: LEONARDO D. DE CASTRO
Department of Political Science: MALAYA C. RONAS
Department of Psychology: ANNADAISY J. CARLOTA
Department of Sociology: LUZVIMINDA C. VALENCIA
College of Social Work and Community Development: EVELINA A. PANGALANGAN
Department of Community Development: ROSARIO S. DEL ROSARIO
Department of Social Work: BENILDA B. TAYAG
Women and Development Program: SYLVIA ESTRADA-CLAUDIO
Statistical Centre: LISA GRACE S. BERSALES
School of Urban and Regional Planning: BENJAMIN V. CARIÑO
UP Extension Program in San Fernando/Olongapo: REYNALDO A. TABBADA

UP at Los Baños:

Chancellor: RUBEN L. VILLAREAL
Registrar: ERLINDA S. PATERNO
Librarian: LEONOR B. GREGORIO

DEANS AND DIRECTORS

College of Agriculture: CECILIO R. ARBOLEDA
Institute of Animal Science: DOMINGO B. ROXAS
Institute of Food Science and Technology: ERNESTO V. CARPIO
Institute of Development Communication: MA. CELESTE H. CADIZ
Department of Agricultural Education and Rural Studies: VIRGINIA R. CARDENAS
Rural High School: LEONIDO R. NARANJA
Department of Agronomy: ENRIQUE C. PALLER
Department of Entomology: ELISEO P. CADAPAN
Department of Horticulture: CALIXTO M. PROTASIO
Department of Plant Pathology: MARINA P. NATURAL
Department of Soil Science: IRENEO MANGUIAT
College of Forestry: LUCRECIO L. REBUGIO
Department of Forest Biological Sciences: MUTYA Q. MANALO
Department of Social Forestry: DAYLINDA B. CABANILLA
Department of Wood Science and Technology: ELVIRA C. FERNANDEZ
Department of Silviculture and Forest Influences: ARTURO SA. CASTILLO
Department of Forest Resources Management: SEVERO R. SAPLACO
College of Arts and Sciences: PACIFICO C. PAYAWAL
Institute of Biological Sciences: MACRINA T. ZAFARRALA
Institute of Chemistry: ERNESTO J. DEL ROSARIO
Institute of Environmental Science and Management: BEN S. MALAYANG III
Institute of Mathematical Sciences and Physics: ARTURO S. PACIFICADOR Jr
Institute of Computer Science: ELIEZER A. ALBACEA
Department of Humanities: REMEDIOS V. NARTEA
Department of Social Sciences: DWIGHT DAVID A. DIESTRO
Department of Human Kinetics: VENERANDA L. GENIO
College of Human Ecology: FLORENTINO L. LIBRERO
Institute of Human Nutrition and Food: CORAZON V. C. BARBA
Department of Social Development Services: EDUARDO A. DACANAY
Department of Community and Environmental Resources Planning: RAYMUNDO B. MENDOZA Jr
Department of Human and Family Development Studies: DELFINA M. TORRETA
College of Engineering and Agro-Industrial Technology: ERNESTO P. LOZADA
Department of Agricultural Machinery and Engineering Technology: CARLOS R. DEL ROSARIO
Department of Civil Engineering: SENEN M. MIRANDA
Department of Electrical Engineering: MAXIMO G. VILLANUEVA
College of Economics and Management: MARIO V. PERILLA
Agricultural Credit and Co-operative Institute: SEVERINO L. MEDINA
Institute of Agrarian Studies: RENATO L. TALATALA
Department of Development Management: RUFINO S. MANANGHAYA
Department of Agricultural Economics: EUSEBIO P. MARIANO
Department of Economics: ACHILLES C. COSTALES
Department of Agribusiness Management: HIPOLITO C. CUSTODIO Jr
College of Veterinary Medicine: MAURO F. MANUEL
Department of Veterinary Clinical Sciences: JEZZIE A. ACORDA
Department of Basic Veterinary Sciences: MA. AMELITA C. ESTACIO
Department of Paraclinical Sciences: LOINDA R. BALDRIAS
Graduate School: ANN INEZ N. GIRONELLA

UP at Manila:

Chancellor: PERLA D. SANTOS OCAMPO
Registrar: LEONOR C. LAGO
Librarian: ROSVIDA ROSAL

DEANS AND DIRECTORS

College of Arts and Sciences: JOSEFINA G. TAYAG
Department of Arts and Communication: RAFAEL A. VILLAR
Department of Biology: MA. OFELIA M. CUEVAS
Department of Physical Education: FLOZERFIDA L. LINSAO
Department of Physical Sciences and Mathematics: MARILOU G. NICOLAS
Department of Social Sciences: SABINO G. PADILLA
Field School: DENNIS N. MILLAN
College of Allied Medical Professions: POLICARPIA M. MAGPILI
Department of Physical Therapy: MA. ELIZA SD. RUIZ
Department of Occupational Therapy: MA. CONCEPCION C. CABATAN
Department of Speech Pathology: JOCELYN CHRISTINA B. MARZAN
College of Dentistry: LEONOR C. LAGO
Department of Basic Health Sciences: SUSAN S. BANZON
Department of Clinical Health Sciences: NANETTE V. VERGEL DE DIOS
Department of Community Dentistry: ELIZABETH G. DE CASTRO
Graduate Program in Orthodontics: SANDRA REGINA C. HERNANDO
College of Medicine: RAMON L. ARCADIO
Department of Anatomy: NOEL G. GUISON
Department of Anaesthesiology: VIRGILIO T. GENUINO
Department of Biochemistry: JASMYNE C. RONQUILLO
Department of Pharmacology: CLEOTILDE H. HOW
Department of Pathology: ARIEL M. VERGEL DE DIOS
Department of Physiology: XENIA T. TIGNO
College of Nursing: CECILIA M. LAURENTE
College of Pharmacy: LETICIA-BARBARA B. GUTIERREZ
Department of Pharmaceutical Chemistry: ILEANA R. F. CRUZ
Department of Pharmacy: MILDRED B. OLIVEROS
Department of Industrial Pharmacy: MARISSA L. PANGANIBAN
College of Public Health: BENJAMIN C. VITASA
Department of Environmental and Occupational Health: BENJAMIN C. VITASA
Department of Epidemiology and Biostatistics: JESUS N. SAROL Jr
Department of Health Promotion and Education: RAFAELITA A. ONG
Department of Medical Microbiology: ADALBERTO M. ALDAY
Department of Nutrition: EMILIE G. FLORES
Department of Parasitology: LILIAN A. DELAS LLAGAS
Department of Public Health Administration: IRMA L. PARALAJAS
Graduate School: LILIA A. REYES
National Teacher-Training Centre for the Health Professions: CRISTINA F. MENCIAS
National Institutes of Health: PERLA SANTOS OCAMPO

UP in the Visayas:

Chancellor: ARSENIO S. CAMACHO
Registrar: MARILYN Z. ALCARDE
Librarian: TERESITA LEDESMA

DEANS AND DIRECTORS

College of Fisheries: PEPITO M. FERNANDEZ
Institute of Aquaculture: ARNULFO A. MARASIGAN
Institute of Fish Processing: JOSE P. PERALTA
Institute of Fisheries Policy and Development Studies: CARLOS C. BAYLON
Institute of Marine Fisheries and Oceanology: RICARDO P. BABARAN
College of Arts and Sciences: MINDA J. FORMACION

College of Management: EVELYN T. BELLEZA
Department of Accounting: PERLA D. DE LOS SANTOS
Department of Management: EDUARDO T. CONCEPCION
School of Technology: JOSE ALI F. BEDAÑO
UP Cebu College: JESUS V. JUARIO
UP Tacloban College: VIOLA C. SIOZON

UP Open University:
Chancellor: MA. CRISTINA D. PADOLINA

UP on Mindanao:
Dean: ROGELIO V. CUYNO

POLYTECHNIC UNIVERSITY OF THE PHILIPPINES

Anonas St, Santa Mesa, Manila
Telephone: (2) 716-26-44
Fax: (2) 716-11-43
Founded 1904
State control
Languages of instruction: English and Filipino
Academic year: June to March
President: Dr ZENAIDA A. OLONAN
Executive Vice-President: Dr OFELIA M. CARAGUE
Vice-President for Academic Affairs: Dr SAMUEL M. SALVADOR
Vice-President for Administration and Finance: Dr DANTE GUEVARRA
Vice-President for Student Services: Dr MOISES S. GARCIA
Vice-President for Branches: Dr NORMITA A. VILLA
Registrar: Prof. MELBA D. ABALETA
Library Officer: Prof. MONALISA LEGUIAB
Library of 205,365 vols
Number of teachers: 1,381
Number of students: 42,988
Publications: *PUP Studies, Statistical Bulletin, PUP Monograph* (annually), *The Catalyst* (monthly), *Trends* (quarterly), *Journal of Economics and Politics* (quarterly), *BISIG* (Journal of Labour and Industrial Relations), *Graduate Forum, Campus Circular, CLMC Update.*

DEANS
Graduate School: Dr RODOLFO T. DE LARA
College of Accountancy: Dr RELLITA D. PAEZ
College of Arts: Dr AMALIA C. ROSALES
College of Business: ERLINDA C. GARCIA
College of Business Teacher Education and Office Administration: Prof. AVELINA C. BUCAO
College of Computer Management & Information Technology: Prof. MELY R. LUYA
College of Economics and Politics: Prof. JOSE RONAN
College of Engineering and Architecture: Eng. DANTE GEDARIA
College of Languages and Mass Communication: Prof. WILHELMINA N. CAYANAN
College of Physical Education and Sports: Prof. MARIPRES P. PASCUA

DEPARTMENT HEADS
Undergraduate Colleges:
Mass Communication: Prof. MA. LOURDES GARCÍA
Languages (English): Prof. WILHELMINA N. CAYANAN
Filipino: Dr CORAZON P. SAN JUAN
History: Dr CORAZON P. COLOMA
Mathematics: Prof. ROBERTO HERNANDEZ
Sociology: Prof. FE B. AGPAOA
Natural Science: Dr THERESITA V. ATIENZA
Psychology: Dr LORETO JAO
Humanities: Prof. SAMUEL FERNANDEZ
Accountancy (Basic): Prof. LIGAYA M. ESPINO
Accountancy (Higher): Prof. LILIAN M. LITONJUA
Law: Atty JESUS BIEN
Management: Prof. ROSE MARIE A. GUERZON
Advertising: Prof. ELIZABETH T. SANTOS
Tourism: Prof. MELAIDA ESTACIO
Business Teacher Education: Prof. MILAGRINA A. GOMEZ
Office Administration: Prof. CHARITO A. MONTEMAYOR
Computer Engineering: Eng. RAFAEL OQUINDO
Mechanical Engineering: Eng. JESUS D. CALLANTA
Civil Engineering: Eng. MANUEL M. MUHI
Electronics and Communication Engineering: Eng. ELENA A. NORIEGA
Architecture: Arch. VILMA M. PABELLO
Banking and Finance: Prof. DIOSDADO F. CRUZ
Economics and Politics: Prof. ALBERTO C. GUILLO
Political Science and Public Administration: Prof. HENRY V. PASCUA
Computer Technology and Computer Data Processing Management: Prof. GISELA MAY A. ALBANO
Co-operatives: Prof. FIRMO A. ESGUERRA
Hotel Restaurant Management: Prof. NORA AUSTRIA
Information Technology and Software Research: Prof. ROSICAR E. ESCOBER
Food Science and Technology: Prof. ADELA C. M. JAMORABO
Nutrition and Dietetics: Prof. ADELA JAMORABO
Sports: Prof. CEFERINO LANIPA
Physical Education Service: Prof. RENE L. LATORRE
Professional Program: Dr CAROLINA A. PANGANIBAN

Graduate School:
Business Administration: Dr RODOLFO DE LARA
Business Education: Prof. ISABELA CRISOSTOMO
Industrial Engineering and Management: Dr PABLO GABRIEL
Management: Dr RODOLFO DE LARA
Accounting: Dr FLORA GONZALEZ
Economics: Dr ELMER ABUEG
Public Administration: Dr MOISES S. GARCIA
Public/Business Administration: Dr PRISCILA PAGIRUIGAN
Applied Statistics: Prof. TOMAS P. AFRICA
Education Management: Dr FORTUNATA VILLAMAR

ATTACHED INSTITUTES
Research Institute for Politics and Economics: Dir Prof. DANILO CUETO
Institute of Labor and Industrial Relations: Dir Prof. ROGELIO ORDOÑEZ
Center for International Relations: Dir JOSE D. LAPUZ

MANUEL L. QUEZON UNIVERSITY

916 R. Hidalgo, Quiapo, Manila
Telephone: 742-42-01
Founded 1947
President: AMADO C. DIZON
Vice-President for Academic Affairs: MARTHA A. MOGOL
Executive Officer, Regent: MA. VICTORIA O. CHAN
Registrar: Prof. GREGORIO A. DEL VALLE, Jr
Treasurer, Regent: AMADOR P. ALVENDIA
Chief Librarian: Prof. FLORDELIZA M. TORRES
Number of teachers: 291
Number of students: 8,355
Publications: *MLQU Newsletter, Junior Quezonian, MLQU Graduate Journal, MLQU Law Quarterly.*

DEANS
Faculty of Law: NORBERTO S. GONZALES
Faculty of Arts and Science: LETICIA L. LAVA
Faculty of Accountancy and Business: ENRIQUE A. B. GABRIEL
Faculty of Education: VIRGINIA P. GANIR
Faculty of Graduate Studies: MARTHA A. MOGOL
Faculty of Engineering: ANTERO P. MANGUNDAYAO
Faculty of Architecture: CARLOS B. BANAAG
Faculty of Criminology: CLETO B. SENOREN
Faculty of Secretarial Education and Technology: PILAR E. SOTO
Faculty of the Institute of Computer Education: JUANITA M. UMAGAT

SAINT LOUIS UNIVERSITY

POB 71, 2600 Baguio City
Telephone: 442-2793
Fax: 442-2842
Founded 1911
Languages of instruction: English and Filipino
Private control (Roman Catholic)
Academic year: June to May (three terms)
President: Rev. Fr PAUL VAN PARIJS
Executive Assistant to the President: Rev. Bro. RAMON G. CORONEL
Vice-President for Academic Affairs: Dr CARLOS R. MEDINA
Vice-President for Administration: Atty EMETERIO MANANTAN
Vice-President for Finance: EVANGELINE O. TRINIDAD
Registrar: VIOLETA GARCIA
Director of Libraries (College-level): ILUMINADA ADAN
Library of 178,000 vols
Number of teachers: 543
Number of students: 21,304
Publications: *Saint Louis Chronicle* (quarterly), , *SLU Research Journal* (2 a year), *General Bulletin* (annually), *SLU Journal of Medicine* (quarterly), *SLU-EISSIF Newsletter* (quarterly), *Student Handbook* (annually), *Administrative Handbook* (annually), *Faculty Handbook* (annually).

DEANS
College of Engineering and Architecture: Engr PETRONILO BALLESCA
College of Accountancy and Commerce: MYRNA A. RAMOS
College of Human Sciences: Dr JOSEFINA N. DOMINGO
College of Education: Dr LUCITA JACALNE (acting)
College of Law: Atty GALO R. REYES
College of Natural Sciences: Dr GAUDELIA A. REYES
College of Medicine: Dr ROBERTO LEGASPI
College of Nursing: FATIMA F. FANGAYEN
College of Information and Computing Sciences: Engr JOSE MARIA PANGILINAN

DIRECTORS
Saint Louis University Extension Institute for Small-scale Industries: Dr ERLINDA T. MANOPOL
Institute of Philosophy and Religion: Rev. Fr LODE WOSTYN
SLU Hospital of the Sacred Heart: Dr ROBERTO LEGASPI
Institute of Physical Education: LAUREL C. BANGAOET

UNIVERSITY OF SAN AGUSTÍN

General Luna St, 5000 Iloilo City
Telephone: (33) 7-48-41
Fax: (33) 7-44-03
E-mail: usanag@iloilo.net
Founded 1904; University status 1953
Languages of instruction: English and Filipino
Private control
Academic year: June to March

President, and Vice-President for Academic Affairs: Rev. Dr MAMERTO A. ALFECHE
Vice-President for Administration: Rev. Fr BERNARDO B. COLECO
Vice-President for Student Affairs: Rev. Fr RAYMUNDO EDSEL T. ALCAYAGA
Registrar: MADELA O. DUERO
Librarian: REGINA MALIGAD

Number of teachers: 435
Number of students: 11,872

Publications: *The Augustinian, The Augustinian Mirror, Views, Communitas.*

DEANS

Graduate School: Dr REMEDIOS SOMCIO
School of Law: Atty JUANA JUDITA P. NAFARRETE
College of Pharmacy/Medical Technology: GILDA RIVERO
College of Technology: Eng. MAURA BASCO
College of Commerce: TERESITA BUENAFLOR
Teachers' College: Dr FELICISIMA CAMPOS
College of Nursing: SOFIA COSETTE MONTEBLANCO
Conservatory of Music: SALVACION S. JARDENIL
College of Liberal Arts: AMORITA RABUCO

DEPARTMENT CHAIRMEN AND CO-ORDINATORS

English: DULCE ADRIAS
Filipino: TERESITA HONTIVEROS
Mathematics and Physics: NENITA QUIÑON
Social Sciences: NORA LEGASPI
Humanities: GORGONIA SISCAR
Physical Education: AMBROSIA CIASICO (acting)
Chemistry: NOEMI PEÑEIRO
Biology and Natural Sciences: MA. DELSA GANGE
Nutrition: LILIA S. TEVES
Civil Engineering: MAKEV ERIC YTURRALDE
Mechanical Engineering: EDGAR ALLAN VARGAS
Chemical Engineering: MAURA BASCO
Architecture: ROLANDO M. SIENDO
Computer Science: Engr REYNALDO ASUNCION (acting)

UNIVERSITY OF SAN CARLOS

Cebu City 6000

Telephone: 253-10-00
Fax: 5-43-41

Founded 1595; University status 1948
Language of instruction: English
Private (Roman Catholic) control
Academic year: June to March (two terms)

President: Fr ERNESTO M. LAGURA
Vice-President for Academic Affairs: Fr HEINZ KULUEKE
Vice-President for Administration: Fr MAXIMO T. ABALOS
Vice-President for Finance: Fr ARTHUR Z. VILLANUEVA
Registrar: ROBERTO V. IRATAGOTIA
Director of Library System: Dr MARILOU P. TADLIP

Number of teachers: 594 full-time, 206 part-time
Number of students: 23,081

Publications: *The University Bulletin* (fortnightly), *Philippine Scientist* (annually), *Philippine Quarterly of Culture and Society* (quarterly), *University Journal* (2 a year).

DEANS

Graduate School: Fr FLORENCIO LAGURA
College of Law: Atty GABRIEL T. INGLES
College of Arts and Sciences: Fr FRANCISCO T. ESTEPA
College of Education: Dr MONTANA C. SANIEL
College of Commerce: Dr VICTORINA H. ZOSA
College of Engineering: Engr LUZ G. PACA
College of Pharmacy: MARILYN Y. TIU
College of Nursing: ANTONIA F. PASCUAL
College of Architecture and Fine Arts: Arch. ROBERTO T. RAFANAN

CHAIRMEN

Graduate Engineering: Eng. NESTOR SY
Graduate Science and Technology: Dr GUILLERMO O. LARGO, Jr
Graduate Education: Dr ELLEN C. BASILGO
Graduate Social Sciences: Dr ANDRES S. GERONG
Graduate Business Administration: MARIAN R. SIONZON
Graduate Humanities: Fr Dr MARK MATHIAS
Biology: Dr DANILO B. LARGO
Chemistry: Dr RAMON S. DEL FIERRO
Economics: OSCAR R. BUCOG
History: RENE E. ALBURO
Library Science: EVELYN A. SANSON
Philosophy: Dr VIRGINIA L. JAYME
Psychology: Dr FREDOLINA B. CALOPE
Languages and Literature: RAYMUNDA V. MONTAÑO
Teachers' Education: MILAGROS L. TABASA
Home Technology: PAZ B. REYES
Physical Education: DOLORES M. SUZARA
Accountancy: MARICHU S. FORNOLLES
Business Administration: GALO A. MONTAÑO
Secretarial Administration: VIOLETA NUÑEZ
Chemical Engineering: Eng. GEMMA V. CABANILLA
Civil Engineering: Eng. VICENTE B. SENO
Mechanical and Industrial Engineering: Dr NICANOR S. BUENCONSEJO
Computer Engineering: Eng. JOSEPHINE BORJA
Electrical, Electronics and Communications Engineering: Eng. ALBERTO S. BANACIA
Fine Arts: PAUL M. VEGA
Architecture: Arch. OMAR MAXWELL P. ESPINA
Political Science: JESSE T. PACARDO
Religious Education: Fr FRANCISCO T. ESTEPA
Mathematics and Computer Science: DORIS E. CASTAÑEDA
Physics: HELENA S. DE LOS REYES
Sociology and Anthropology: PISCALINA A. NOLASCO

ATTACHED INSTITUTES

Office of Population Studies: Dir Fr WILHELM FLIEGER.
Water Resources Centre: Dir Fr HERMAN VAN ENGELEN.
San Carlos Publications: Dir RESIL B. MOJARES (Editor).
Cebuano Studies Centre: Dir Dr ERLINDA K. ALBURO.
USC Museum: MARLENE SOCORRO R. SAMSON (Curator).
Community Extension Services: Dir Fr HEINZ KULUEKE.
Business Resource Centre: TERESITA C. ABARQUEZ (Project Officer).
Institute of Planning and Design: Dir Arch. ANTONIO G. VALENZOLA.

UNIVERSITY OF SAN JOSE-RECOLETOS

Corner Magallanes and P. Lopez Sts, 6000 Cebu City

Telephone: 7-22-71
Fax: 254-17-20

Founded 1947, university status 1984
Private (Roman Catholic) control
Language of instruction: English
Academic year: June to March

President: Rev. Fr EMETERIO D. BUÑAO
Vice-President for Administration and Academics: Rev. Fr WALTHRODE B. CONDE
Vice-President for Business and Finance: Rev. Fr EMILIO L. LARLAR
Vice-President for Student Welfare: Rev. Fr ANDRES R. S. GOTERA
Registrar: FELIX G. ETURMA
Librarian: REMEDIOS M. ESTELLA

Library of 150,000 vols
Number of teachers: 421
Number of students: 12,000

Publications: *Forward, USJ-R Journal of Research* (2 a year), *Josenian* OAR, *Synthesis.*

DEANS

College of Arts and Sciences: Dr MILAGROS C. ESPINA
College of Commerce: Dr MARIANO M. LERIN
College of Engineering: Eng. ERNESTO P. TABADA
College of Law: Atty ALICIA E. BATHAN
Graduate School: Dr MARIANO M. LERIN, Dr MILAGROS C. ESPINA
Teachers' College: Dr LUCILA S. BONILLA
Grade School: PURA S. WAGAS
High School: Dr MARIA A. REYES

ATTACHED INSTITUTES

Institute of Management: Dir Dr MARIANO M. LERIN
Research, Planning and Scholarship Center: Dir Dr CARMEN M. ETURMA
Institute of Non-formal Education and Community Outreach Projects (INFECOP): Consultant Dr VICTORIA D. GABISON

UNIVERSITY OF SANTO TOMÁS

España St, Manila

Telephone: 731-31-01
Fax: 732-74-86

Founded 1611
Private (Roman Catholic) control

Grand Chancellor: Very Rev. Fr TIMOTHY RADCLIFFE
Vice-Chancellor: Very Rev. Fr QUIRICO PEDREGOSA
Rector: Rev. Fr ROLANDO DE LA ROSA
Vice-Rector: Fr HONORATO CASTIGADOR
Secretary-General: Fr RODEL ALIGAN
Registrar: Prof. RODOLFO N. CLAVIO
Prefect of Libraries: Rev. Fr ANGEL APARICIO
Chief Librarian: Prof. ERLINDA FLORES

Number of teachers: 1,438
Number of students: 33,983

Publications: *Academia, Thomasian, Varsitarian, Journal of Medicine, Law Review, Unitas, Boletín Eclesiástico, Commerce Journal, Nursing Journal, Education Journal, Science Journal,* etc.

DEANS

Faculty of Sacred Theology: Rev. Fr TAMERLANE LANA
Faculty of Canon Law: Rev. Fr JOSE MA TINOKO
Faculty of Philosophy: Fr ERNIE ARCEO
Faculty of Civil Law: Dr AMADO DIMAYUGA
Faculty of Medicine and Surgery: Dr RAMON SIN
Faculty of Pharmacy: Dr NORMA LERMA
Faculty of Arts and Letters: Dr OPHELIA DIMALANTA
Faculty of Engineering: Eng. ALBERTO LAURITO
College of Education: Dr LOURDES CUSTODIO
College of Science: Dr GLORIA BERNAS
College of Commerce and Business Administration: Prof. AMELIA HALILI
College of Architecture and Fine Arts: Arch. YOLANDA REYES
College of Nursing: Prof. NATALIA MARALIT
Graduate School: Fr JOSE ANTONIO AUREADA
Religion: Fr TAMERLANE LANA
Conservatory of Music: Prof. ERLINDA FULE

SILLIMAN UNIVERSITY

Hibbard Ave, Dumaguete City 6200, Negros Oriental

Telephone: (35) 225-4766
Fax: (35) 225-4768

Founded 1901
Private control
Language of instruction: English
Academic year: June to March

President: Dr MERVYN J. MISAJON

Vice-President for Academic Affairs: Dr MA. TERESITA S. SINDA
Vice-President for Administration: CLEONICO Y. FONTELO
Vice-President for Development Planning and Enterprise Management: ROBERTO D. MONTEBON
Vice-President for Finance and Administration: Mrs NATIVIDAD C. ONGCOG
Registrar: REYNALDO Y. RIVERA
Librarian: LORNA TUMULAK-YSO

Library: see Libraries
Number of teachers: 253
Number of students: 8,077

Publications: *The Silliman Journal* (quarterly), *Sillimanian Magazine* (2 a year), *Sands and Corals* (annual literary magazine), *Portal* (yearbook), *Educator* (2 a year), *Engineering Network* (2 a year), *Engineering Newsletter* (2 a year), *Harvest* (2 a year), *Infoline* (monthly), *Insights* (2 a year), *Non-con Energizer* (quarterly), *Nurse* (2 a year), *Scoop* (annually), *Stones and Pebbles* (annually).

DEANS

College of Arts and Sciences: Dr GERARDO MAXINO
College of Education: Dr THELMA E. FLORENDO
College of Law: LEVI ESTOLLOSO
College of Engineering: ISAGANI LEPITEN
Divinity School: Dr EVERETT MENDOZA
College of Nursing and Allied Medical Sciences: MA. ARSENIA LOPEZ
College of Business Administration: NORMA CALUSCUSAN
School of Communication: ROSE BASELERES
School of Music and Fine Arts: ELIZABETH S. V. ZAMAR
College of Agriculture: Dr VICENTE JURLANO

ATTACHED INSTITUTES

Center for Tropical Conservation Studies: Dir Dr ELY ALCALA.
Silliman University Marine Laboratory: Dir Dr HILCONIDA CALUMPONG.

UNIVERSITY OF SOUTHERN MINDANAO

Kabacan 9407, North Cotabato

Founded 1954 as Institute of Technology, present name 1980
State control
Languages of instruction: English, Filipino
Academic year: June to October, November to December (2 semesters)

President: KUNDO E. PAHM
Vice-President: VIRGILIO OLIVA
Registrar: RASUL BUISAN
Librarian: PILAR A. BAUTISTA

Number of teachers: 393
Number of students: 6,000

Publications: *Usmaro Monitor, CA Research Journal, USM Research and Development Journal* (every 6 months).

Colleges of agriculture, agricultural engineering, arts and trades, home economics, education and humanities, art and sciences

UNIVERSITY OF SOUTHERN PHILIPPINES

Mabini Street, Cebu City

Telephone: 7-23-31, 7-29-26

Founded 1927; University status 1949
Private control

President: OSCAR JEREZA
Registrar: ERLINDA M. CAMPOS

Number of teachers: 197
Number of students: 7,439

DEANS

College of Arts and Sciences: INOCENTA GO
Graduate School of Law: RONALD DUTERTE
College of Engineering: ROMULO JEREZA
College of Commerce: GERONIMO S. ANA
College of Education: ISABELITA CONALES (acting)
Graduate School: Dr ROSETTA MANTE
School of Social Work: INOCENTA GO

SOUTHWESTERN UNIVERSITY

Villa Aznar, Urgello St, Cebu City 6000
Telephone: (32) 9-07-21
Fax: (32) 5-27-99

Founded 1946
Private control
Languages of instruction: English and Filipino
Academic year: June to March

President: Dr ALICIA P. CABATINGAN
Vice-President (Academic): Dr FRANCES F. LUMAIN
Vice-President (Administration): Dr ADELAIDA A. T. CASTILLO
Vice-President (Finance): LASSO MATTI A. HOLOPAINON
Registrar: FRANCISCO B. BACALLA
Librarian: SUSAN P. ALUNAN

Number of teachers: 436
Number of students: 10,768

DEANS

Graduate School: Dr ALICIA P. CABATINGAN
College of Law: Atty FROILAN V. QUIJANO
College of Arts and Sciences: Dr ADELAIDA A. T. CASTILLO
College of Dentistry: Dr DALISAY M. RODIS
College of Optometry: Dr ARLEN O. DORIO
College of Commerce: FLORDELIS R. RIVERA
College of Pharmacy: Dr GLORIA R. PANULAYA
College of Engineering: Eng. CARLOS S. SATIEMBRE
College of Medical Technology: ALMA A. HOLOPAINEN
College of Veterinary Medicine: Dr PILAR P. ROMERO
College of Medicine: Dr EMELIA D. DACALOS
College of Nursing: Dr CARMEN V. N. SAN LORENZO
Teachers' College: Dr FRANCES F. LUMAIN
Maritime College: Comm. CARMELO T. SIMOLDO
College of Physical Therapy: Dr VICENTE E. VILLAREAL
Institute of Computer Science: ROLAND D. GO
Institute of Physical Education and Sports: MELQUIADES B. GONZALEZ

TECHNOLOGICAL UNIVERSITY OF THE PHILIPPINES

POB 3171, Ayala Blvd, Ermita, Metro Manila

Telephone: 523-22-93
Fax: 523-60-15

Founded 1901
Languages of instruction: English and Filipino
State control
Academic year: June to March

President: FREDERICK SO. PADA
Vice-President (Academic Affairs): CARLOS Q. TRINIDAD
Vice-President (Administration and Finance): RADAMES M. DOCTOR
Vice-President (Planning and Development): PERLA S. ROXAS
Vice-President (Research and Extension): EMILIANA VR. TADEO
Registrar: ELISA L. GRANADA
Librarian: ESTHER T. GUTIERREZ

Library of 27,000 vols
Number of teachers: 537
Number of students: 15,000

Publications: *The Philippine Artisan, Lahok.*

DEANS

Graduate School: VAUGHN S. BUAQUIÑA
College of Sciences: JULIETA A. SALAMAT
College of Liberal Arts: MARCELO B. APAR
College of Architecture and Fine Arts: DIOSDADO C. NICDAO
College of Engineering: SONIA C. MANALASTAS
College of Industrial Education: ESTELITA B. CAMURUNGAN
College of Industrial Technology: JOSEFINO P. GASCON

PROFESSORS

AGBAYANI, J., Economics
ALMENIANA, Q., Industrial Education
ALTO, R., Science, Educational Administration
APAR, M., Filipino
ARRIETA, C., III, Industrial Education
ASINAS, E., Physical Education
BELGICA, A., Guidance and Counselling, Career Education
BERNAL, H., Industrial Technology
BONILLA, C., Administration of Higher Education, Educational Technology
BONILLA, L., Social Science, Teaching
BUAQUIÑA, V., Mathematics
CALO, R. M., Physical Education
CAMURUNGAN, E., Industrial Education Management
DELOS REYES, V., General Education, Industrial Education
DE PANO, E., Home Economics
DOMANTAY, D., Industrial Education Management, Guidance and Counselling, Home Economics, General Education
ESPINO, I., Industrial Education Management, Home Economics
GASCON, J., Industrial Technology
GOLLAYAN, R., Chemistry
GRANADA, E., Health Education
GRAZA, N., Chemical and Mechanical Engineering
HUANG, A., Mathematics
IGNACIO, M., Research and Evaluation
IMLAN, J., Public Administration and Management
JERESANO, L., Physics, Education
LABUGUEN, F., Industrial Education Management
LOMOTAN, M., Guidance and Counselling
MANALASTAS, J., Civil Engineering
MANALASTAS, S., Chemistry
MANGAO, F., Educational Curriculum and Supervision
MANGAOIL, E., Industrial Education
MATIC, V., Educational Administration, Chemistry
NICDAO, D., Industrial Technology
OBNAMIA, C., Education
PACIO, A., Mathematics
PANGAN, M., Educational Administration
PANGILINAN, M., Educational Management
PAPA, R. S., Psychology, Career Guidance
PEREDA, P., Industrial Educational Management
PILI, A., Chemistry
RIVERA, A., General Education, Industrial Education
ROLLUQUI, G., Computer Management
ROXAS, P., Chemical Engineering
SALAMAT, J., Chemistry
SEALTIEL, S., Industrial Technology
TABANERA, M. L., Physics
TADEO, E., School Administration, Mathematics, Science
TRINIDAD, C. Q., Educational Management, Educational Technology
VALDERRAMA, L., Public Administration
VELAS, F., Physical Education
VILLAMEJOR, S., English

UNIVERSITY OF THE VISAYAS

6000 Cebu City

Telephone: (32) 253-28-85

Founded 1919
Private control
Languages of instruction: English and Filipino
Academic year: June to May

President: EDUARDO R. GULLAS
Executive Vice-President: JOSE R. GULLAS
Registrar: JOSEFINA T. ARREZA
Librarian: EDNA CAGA

Number of teachers: 600
Number of students: 18,214

Publications: *The Visayanian*, *Spectrum* (Graduate Research Journal), *Strategies* (Education Journal), *Statistical Bulletin*, etc.

DEANS

College of Commerce: SOLEDAD CUMBRA
College of Criminology: EMMANUEL PEPITO
College of Engineering and Architecture: MARCIALITO VALENZONA
Graduate School: FE NECESARIO
College of Law: AMADEO SENO
College of Arts and Sciences: ERLINDA L. PEPITO
College of Medicine: RENATO ESPINOSA
Nautical School: GODOFREDO COSIDO
College of Nursing: LOURDES FERNAN
College of Pharmacy: CARMEN YAP
Teachers' College: AURORA A. ECONG

DIRECTORS

Research, Development and Planning Centre: NICERIO L. LEANZA
Instructional Media Centre: ALICE RABOR

WESTERN MINDANAO STATE UNIVERSITY

Normal Rd, Baliwasan, 7000 Zamboanga City

Telephone: 991-1040
Fax: 991-3065

Founded 1918
State control
Languages of instruction: English and Filipino
Academic year: June to October, October to March (two semesters)

President: Dr ELDIGARIO D. GONZALES
Vice-President for Academic Affairs: Dr MARLENE C. TILLAH
Vice-President for Research Extension and Training: (vacant)
Vice-President for Administration and Finance: Dr CLEMENCIO M. BASCAR
Registrar: JULIETA A. DEL ROSARIO
Librarian: SALUD C. LAQUIO

Library of 50,000 vols
Number of teachers: 436
Number of students: 12,397

Publication: *Bulletin*.

DEANS

College of Agriculture: ERIBERTO D. SALANG
College of Arts and Sciences: Dr RAIMUNDA J. BANICO
College of Education: Prof. FELICITAS F. FALCATAN
College of Engineering and Technology: Eng. MOHAMMAD NUR MOHAMMAD
College of Law: Atty EDUARDO F. SANSON
College of Home Economics: Prof. NOEMI S. ENRIQUEZ
College of Forestry: Prof. DINO A. SABELLINA
College of Nursing: Prof. TERESITA C. MARBELLA
College of Science and Mathematics: Dr ELBIA P. AQUINO
College of Social Work: Prof. BAGIAN ABDULKARIM
College of Criminology: Prof. EFFRENDY ESTIPONA
Institute of Asian and Islamic Studies: Prof. NURUDDIN I. UNGGANG
Institute of Physical Education, Sports and Cultural Affairs: Prof. ALICIA LOURDES SORIANO
Extension Services: Dr ABDULAJID A. IBBA
Graduate School: Prof. OFELIO R. MENDOZA
Research Center: Dr ALFREDO DUCANES
Admissions: Prof. RUTH N. JUNIO
Student Affairs: Eng. ARMANDO ARQUIZA

XAVIER UNIVERSITY

Ateneo de Cagayan, Corrales Ave, 9000 Cagayan de Oro City

Telephone: (8822) 72-27-25
Fax: (8822) 72-63-55
E-mail: pres@xu.edu.ph

Founded 1933
Private control
Language of instruction: English
Academic year: June to March (two terms)

President: Rev. ANTONIO S. SAMSON
Registrar: AURORA M. GAPUZ
Librarian: ANNABELLE P. ACEDERA

Number of teachers: 256
Number of students: 9,962

Publications: *Kinaadman* (Wisdom), *XU Development News* (quarterly), *Crusader* (annually).

DEANS

Faculty of Agriculture: Dr LILLIAN G. OCCEÑA
Faculty of Arts and Sciences: Dr IMELDA G. PAGTULON-AN
Faculty of Commerce: ALFONSO B. HORTELANO
Faculty of Education: Dr AMOR Q. DE TORRES
Faculty of Engineering: ANTONIO C. SEVILLANO, Jr
Faculty of Law: Atty ROMULO V. BORJA
Faculty of Medicine: Dr FRANCISCO L. OH
Faculty of Nursing: HEIDE C. PALAD
Graduate School: Dr ESTER L. RAAGAS

HEADS OF DEPARTMENTS

Faculty of Agriculture:
- Agricultural Engineering: Eng. ALEJANDRO S. VILLAMOR
- Agricultural Sciences: ALEX F. JOYA
- Development Communication: MA. THERESA M. RIVERA
- Food Technology: Dr LILLIAN G. OCCEÑA

Faculty of Arts and Sciences:
- Biology: JOSEPHINE C. ZARSUELO
- Chemistry: Dr LINA G. KWONG
- Economics: EDITHA G. LANGREO
- English: BERDITA G. BINONGO
- Filipino: MARGARITA R. HORTELANO
- History and Political Science: HERMINIA Q. YAPTENCO
- Mathematics: JULIETA S. OCLARIT
- Philosophy: CARLOS D. MAGTRAYO
- Physics: CARMELO B. ALBA
- Psychology and Guidance: MARITZA M. TALEON
- Religious Studies: LINO P. PANGDA
- Sociology and Anthropology: LITA P. SEALZA

Faculty of Commerce:
- Accountancy: VIRGINIA C. YACAPIN
- Business Administration: CORAZON S. MENDOZA
- Information Management: EDWIN BRIX T. PALMES

Faculty of Education:
- Physical Education: ANGELITA SAYOSAY

Faculty of Engineering:
- Chemical and Civil Engineering: MA. THERESA CABARABAN
- Electrical and Mechanical Engineering: ELISEO B. LINOG, Jr

Faculty of Medicine:
- Anatomy: Dr FE J. HERNANDEZ
- Biochemistry: Dr ELVIRA V. PILONES
- Eyes, Ears, Nose and Throat: Dr AUGUSTO V. DEJOS
- Medicine: Dr EDNA RICARTE
- Microbiology and Parasitology: Dr EVELYN LOMARDA
- Obstetrics and Gynaecology: Dr ZENAIDA A. FLOIRENDO
- Pathology: Dr EXEQUIEL PILONES
- Paediatrics: Dr ROSARIO CABRERA
- Physiology, Pharmacology and Therapeutics: Dr AGATHON T. PANOPIO
- Preventive and Community Medicine: Dr GINA ITCHON
- Surgery: Dr HERNANDO R. EMANO

DIRECTORS

Research Institute for Mindanao Culture: Dr ERLINDA BURTON
Southeast Asian Rural Social Leadership Institute: Dr ANSELMO B. MERCADO
Institute for the Development of Educational Administrators: ALFONSO B. HORTELANO
Philippine Folklife and Folklore Research and Archives: LORD OSTIGUE
Appropriate Technology for Small Farmers: RACQUEL POLESTICO
Legal Aid and Research Center for Human Rights: (vacant)
Mindanao Lumad Muslim Development Center: Rev. EMETERIO J. BARCELON
Center for Industrial Technology: ANTONIO C. SEVILLANO, Jr
Computer Center: ELVIRA B. YANZA

Colleges

AGRICULTURE

Don Severino Agricultural College: Indang, Cavite 4122; tel. 097378-3542; f. 1906; 155 teachers, 2,690 students; library of 26,000 vols; Pres. Dr RUPERTO S. SANGALANG; publs *The Cultivator* (2 a year), *DSAC Gazette* (2 a year), *Midland Forum* (quarterly), *Ugnayan* (quarterly), *DSAC Research Journal* (2 a year), *Student Chronicle* (monthly), *Sandiwaan* (2 a year).

GENERAL

San Beda College: Mendiola St, Manila; tel. 7410021; f. 1901; private control; constituent grade and high schools and colleges of law, arts and sciences; 248 staff, 6,156 students; libraries total 107,703 vols; Rector Rev. BERNARDO M. PEREZ; Librarian Rev. PAUL DE VERA.

St Paul College of Manila: 680 Pedro Gil St, Malate, Manila, POB 3062; f. 1912; private control; first degree courses in computer and information science, hotel and restaurant management, psychology, education, commerce, secretarial administration, nursing, communication arts, music; 144 staff, 2,954 students; library of 46,600 vols; Pres. Sister NATIVIDAD FERAREN .

St Scholastica's College: 2560 Leon Guinto Sr. St, Malate, Manila, POB 3153; tel. (2) 524-7686, fax (2) 521-2593; f. 1906; private control; schools of liberal arts, commerce, education, music, hotel and restaurant management, mathematics, nutrition and dietetics, psychology, women's studies, secretarial; small and medium enterprise management; fine arts; Pres. Sister MARY JOHN MANANZAN.

State Polytechnic College of Palawan: Aborlan, 5302 Palawan; tel. 433-4480; f. 1910; courses in agriculture, forestry, fisheries, environmental management, engineering and technology, education, arts, science; library of 40,000 vols; Pres. Dr TERESITA L. SALVA; publs *SPCP-IMS Research Journal* (2 a year), *SPCP Research Journal* (irregular), *SPCP Newsletter* (monthly).

EDUCATION

Philippine Normal University: Taft Ave, Metro Manila; tel. and fax (2) 527-03-72; f. 1901; graduate and postgraduate courses in education, linguistics, literature, values education and a wide range of subjects; operates Language Study Centre for Philippine languages, Health Education Centre, Child Study Centre, Special Education Centre, Media Centre and Early Childhood Education Centre; library of 141,000 vols; 350 teachers, 11,000 students; brs in Isabela (Northern Luzon), Quezon (Southern Luzon), Cadiz City (Visayas), Prosperidad, Agusan del Sur (Mindanao); Officer in charge Atty LILIA S. GARCIA; publs *Siyasik* (2 a year), *Research Bulletin* (4 a year), *Sangguni* (2 a year), *Graduate Theses Abstracts* (1 a year).

MEDICINE

Bicol Christian College of Medicine: AMEC-BCCM Postal Station, Rizal St, Legazpi City 4901; tel. (5221) 44433; fax (5221) 455058; f. 1980; 4-year undergraduate courses; library of 30,052 vols; Pres. EMMANUEL F. AGO; Dean, College of Medicine Dr ANGELITA F. AGO.

Cebu Doctors' College of Medicine: Osmeña Blvd, Cebu City; tel. 5-36-92; f. 1977; 26 staff, 512 students; library of 6,065 vols; Dean ENRICO B. GRUET; publ. *The Cebu Doctors' Proceedings* (2 a year).

TECHNOLOGY

Central Luzon Polytechnic College: Gen. Tinio St, Cabanatuan City; tel. 463-12-01; fax 463-02-26; f. 1964; library of 30,000 vols; Pres. Dr GEMILIANO C. CALLING; publs *Polytechnic Journal* (quarterly), *Research Journal* (2 a year).

Leyte Institute of Technology: Salazar St, Tacloban City; f. 1965; courses in engineering, science, industrial technology, education and vocational training; postgraduate courses; 309 staff; library of 17,000 vols; Pres. GREGORIO T. DE LA ROSA; Registrar FRANKLIN A. COLASITO; publs *Annual Report, Graduate School Bulletin, College Journal, Industrial Wheel.*

Lyceum of the Philippines: Real and Muralla Sts, Intramuros, POB 1264, Manila; f. 1952; private control; faculties of law, graduate studies, civil, electrical, electronic, industrial and mechanical engineering, computer education, mass communication, journalism, arts and sciences, foreign service, economics, business administration, education, office management, technical vocational, hotel and restaurant management, secretarial science; 15,000 students; library of 25,000 vols; Pres. Dr SOTERO H. LAUREL.

Mapùa Institute of Technology: Muralla St, Intramuros, Manila; tel. (832) 527-7916; fax (832) 527-5161; f. 1925; private control; faculties of architecture and planning, industrial design, industrial engineering, mining and metallurgical engineering, civil engineering, electrical engineering, electronics and communications engineering, mechanical engineering, geology, environmental and sanitary engineering, chemical engineering and chemistry, computer engineering; 13,000 students; Pres. OSCAR B. MAPÙA, Sr.

Namei Polytechnic Institute: 123 A Mabini St, Mandaluyong, Metro Manila; tel. 531-73-28; fax 815-63-37; f. 1947; private control; courses in Naval Architecture and Marine Engineering, B.S. Marine Transportation, Marine Engineering, Mechanical Engineering and Electrical Engineering; Pres. MARIA VICTORIA P. ESTRELLA; Registrar PERLA G. CRUZ..

Naval Institute of Technology: Naval, Biliran 6543; f. 1972; library of 10,000 vols; 83 teachers, 2,500 students; Pres. Dr JUANITO S. SISON.

Pablo Borbon Memorial Institute of Technology: Rizal Ave, Batangas City; tel. 725-3138; f. 1903; library of 21,774 vols; 185 teachers, 3,884 students; Pres. Dr ERNESTO M. DE CHAVEZ.

Palompon Institute of Technology: Palompon, Leyte; f. 1972; courses in marine transportation and engineering; engineering technology; technical and vocational education; customs administration; radio communication; domestic science; industrial technology; library of 7,339 vols; 112 teachers; 2,500 students; Pres. Dr JOSÉ SALTAN.

Tarlac College of Technology: Tarlac 2101; tel. 2905; f. 1965; courses in engineering, architecture, trade and technical education, teacher-training and business administration; also graduates courses; library of 10,000 vols; Pres. ERNESTO COSME; Registrar Prof. AURORA A. CASTAÑEDA.

POLAND

Learned Societies

GENERAL

Białostockie Towarzystwo Naukowe (Białystok Scientific Society): 15-565 Białystok, ul. Dojlidy Fabryczne 23; tel. and fax (85) 326-126; Pres. Dr JÓZEF MAROSZEK; Sec.-Gen. Dr WŁODZIMIERZ JARMOLIK.

Bydgoskie Towarzystwo Naukowe (Bydgoszcz Scientific Society): 85-102 Bydgoszcz, ul. Jezuicka 4; tel. 22-20-09; f. 1959; 531 mems; library of 35,000 vols; Pres. Prof. Dr hab. ROMAN MAZUR; Sec.-Gen. Prof. Dr hab. KRYSTYNA KWAŚNIEWSKA; publs *Bydgostiana* (annually), *Prace Wydziału Nauk Humanistycznych, Prace Wydziału Nauk Przyrodniczych, Prace Wydziału Nauk Technicznych, Źrodła do dziejów Bydgoszczy, Prace Popularno-Naukowe,* etc. (all occasional).

Częstochowskie Towarzystwo Naukowe (Częstochowa Scientific Society): 42-200 Częstochowa, II Aleja 22; tel. 424-49; Pres. Prof. Dr Lab. MARIAN GŁOWACKI; Sec.-Gen. Prof. Dr hab. ANDRZEJ ZAKRZEWSKI; publ. *Ziemia Częstochowska* (annually).

Gdańskie Towarzystwo Naukowe (Gdańsk Scientific Society): 80-841 Gdańsk, ul. Grodzka 12; tel. (58) 301-21-24; fax (58) 305-81-31; e-mail gtn@fs-samba.com.pl; f. 1922 as Gdańsk Society of Friends of Science and Art; sections of Social Sciences and Humanities, Biological and Medical Sciences, Mathematical, Physical and Chemical Sciences, Technical Sciences, Earth Sciences; 507 mems; Pres. Prof. Dr JAN DRWAL; Sec. Prof. Dr ROMAN KALISZAN.

Karkonoskie Towarzystwo Naukowe (Karkonosze Mountains Scientific Society): 58-500 Jelenia Góra, ul. Bartka Zwycięzcy 1; tel. 244-10; Pres. Dr TADEUSZ BUGAJ; Sec.-Gen. Dr MARIAN IWANEK; publ. *Prace Karkonoskiego Towarzystwa Naukowego* (irregular).

Kieleckie Towarzystwo Naukowe (Kielce Scientific Society): 25-009 Kielce, ul. Zamkowa 5; tel. 454-53; f. 1958; 546 mems; regional scientific research in history, philology, medicine, geology, geography and nature conservation, psychology, sociology and education, physics, mathematics, engineering; library of 3,670 vols; Pres. Prof. Dr hab. ADAM MASSALSKI; Sec. Prof. Dr hab. MARTA MEDUCKA; publs *Rocznik Świętokrzyski* (Yearbook), *Studia Kieleckie* (irregular).

Łódzkie Towarzystwo Naukowe (Łódź Scientific Society): 90-447 Łódź, Piotrkowska 179; tel. (42) 36-10-26; fax (42) 36-19-95; f. 1936; Pres. STANISŁAW LISZEWSKI; Sec. JULIAN ŁAWRYNOWICZ; publs *Rozprawy Komisji Językowej, Biuletyn Peryglacjalny, Bulletin de la Société des Sciences et des Lettres de Łódź, Sprawozdania z Czynności i Posiedzeń, Przegląd Socjologiczny, Zagadnienia Rodzajów Literackich, Prace Polonistyczne, Acta Archæologica Lodziensia, Acta Geographica Lodziensia, Studia Prawno-Ekonomiczne* and others.

Łomżyńskie Towarzystwo Naukowe im. Wagów (The Brothers Waga Łomża Scientific Society): 18-400 Łomża, ul. Długa 13; tel. 16-32-56; f. 1975; history, ethnology, linguistics, veterinary science, environmental protection, natural history, geography, agriculture, settlement of Northeast Poland; *c.* 250 mems; library of *c.* 20,000 vols; Pres. Prof. Dr hab. MICHAŁ GNATOWSKI; Dir Mgr inż. ELŻBIETA ŻEGALSKA; publ. *Studia Łomżyńskie*.

Lubelskie Towarzystwo Naukowe (Lublin Scientific Society): 20-080 Lublin, Pl. Litewski 2; tel. 213-00; f. 1957; 722 mems; five sections: humanities, biology, mathematics-physics-chemistry, technical science, mining and geography; Pres. Prof. Dr hab. EDMUND K. PROST; Sec.-Gen. Prof. Dr JAN MALARCZYK.

Opolskie Towarzystwo Przyjaciół Nauk (Opole Society of Friends of Science): 45-058 Opole, ul. Ozimska 46A; tel. 54-58-71; f. 1955; 378 mems; library of 9,060 vols; Pres. Prof. Dr hab. JERZY POŚPIECH; publs *Kwartalnik Opolski* (quarterly), *Sprawozdania* (2 series, annually), *Zeszyty Przyrodnicze* (annually), *Prace Medyczne* (annually).

Polska Akademia Nauk (PAN) (Polish Academy of Sciences): 00-901 Warsaw 134, POB 24, Palace of Culture and Science; tel. (22) 656-60-00; fax (22) 620-76-51; f. 1952; sections of Social Sciences (Chair. Prof. JANUSZ TAZBIR), Biological Sciences (Chair. Prof. TADEUSZ CHOJNACKI), Mathematical, Physical and Chemical Sciences (Chair. Prof. JERZY KOŁODZIEJCZAK), Technical Sciences (Chair. Prof. KAZIMIERZ THIEL), Agricultural and Forestry Sciences (Chair. Prof. SATURNIN ZAWADZKI), Medical Sciences (Chair. Prof. JANUSZ KOMENDER), Earth and Mining Sciences (Chair. Prof. JERZY JANKOWSKI); 184 mems, 133 corresp. mems, 228 foreign mems; attached research institutes: see Research Institutes; libraries: see Libraries and Archives; Pres. Prof. LESZEK KUŹNICKI; publs *Bulletin de l'Académie Polonaise des Sciences:* Series: *Biological Sciences* (4 a year), *Mathematical Sciences* (4 a year), , *Chemical Sciences* (4 a year), *Sciences of the Earth* (4 a year), *Technical Sciences* (4 a year); *Nauka* (4 a year), *Acta Arithmetica* (4 a year), *Acta Neurobiologicale Experimentalis* (4 a year), *Acta Physica Polonica* (4 a year), *Acta Protozoologica* (4 a year), *Acta Theriologica* (4 a year), Chemia Analityczna (4 a year), *Fundamenta Mathematicae* (4 a year), *Studia Mathematica* (4 a year).

Poznańskie Towarzystwo Przyjaciół Nauk (Poznań Society of Friends of Arts and Sciences): 61-725 Poznań, ul. Sew. Mielżyńskiego 27/29; tel. (61) 852-74-41; fax (61) 852-22-05; e-mail sekretariat@ptpn.poznan.pl; f. 1857; 1,023 mems; library of 294,000 vols; Pres. Prof. Dr hab. ALICJA KARŁOWSKA-KAMZOWA; Sec.-Gen. Dr STANISŁAW JAKÓBCZYK; publs scientific, historical, social, legal, philological and philosophical works, including *Roczniki Historyczne, Roczniki Dziejów Spolecznych i Gospodarczych, Lingua Posnaniensis, Slavia Antiqua, Slavia Occidentalis, Bulletin de la Société des Amis des Sciences et des Lettres de Poznań—Série D: Sciences Biologiques; Badania Fizjograficzne nad Polską Zachodnią,* Series A (Geography), Series B (Botany), Series C (Zoology), *Sprawozdania Poznańskiego Towarzystwa Przyjaciół Nauk.*

Radomskie Towarzystwo Naukowe (Radom Scientific Society): 26-600 Radom, Słowackiego 1; tel. 272-59; Pres. Dr KRZYSZTOF ORZECHOWSKI; Sec. Dr HELENA KISIEL; publ. *Biuletyn Kwartalny Radomskiego Towarzystwa Naukowego* (quarterly).

Szczecińskie Towarzystwo Naukowe (Szczecin Scientific Society): 70-481 Szczecin, ul. Wojska Polskiego 96; tel. 23-18-62; f. 1956; library of *c.* 16,130 vols; Pres. Prof. Dr hab. JÓZEF RUTKOWSKI; Sec.-Gen. Prof. Dr hab. JERZY STRASZKO; Sections (I) Social Sciences, (II) Agriculture and Natural Sciences, (III) Medicine, (IV) Technical Sciences and Mathematics, (V) Maritime Sciences; publs in each section *Series I, II, III, IV, V, Szczecińskie Roczniki Naukowe* (Szczecin Scientific Annuals).

Towarzystwo Naukowe Płockie (Płock Scientific Society): 09-402 Płock, plac Narutowicza 8; tel. 622-604; f. 1820; 472 mems; Zielińskich library of 255,000 vols; Pres. Dr inż. JAKUB CHOJNACKI; Sec.-Gen. Dr WIESŁAW KOŃSKI; publs *Notatki Płockie* (quarterly), *Sprawozdanie z działalności* (Yearbook).

Towarzystwo Naukowe w Toruniu (Scientific Society of Toruń): 87-100 Toruń, ul. Wysoka 16; tel. 239-41; f. 1875; 520 mems; concerned with historical, legal and social studies, philology and philosophy, mathematics, astronomy and natural sciences; library of 90,836 vols; Pres. Prof. MARIAN BISKUP; Gen. Sec. Prof. MARIAN KALLAS; publs include *Roczniki* (annually), *Fontes* (irregular), *Zapiski Historyczne* (quarterly, concerned chiefly with Pomeranian problems), *Prace Wydziału Filologiczno-Filozoficznego, Sprawozdania, Studia Iuridica, Studia Societatis Scientiarum Toruniensis, Prace Popularnonaukowe, Prace Archaeologiczne.*

Towarzystwo Naukowe Warszawskie (Warsaw Scientific Society): 00-330 Warsaw, ul. Nowy Świat 72; tel. (22) 657-28-26; f. 1907; 420 mems; Pres. Prof. Dr WITOLD RUDOWSKI; Sec.-Gen. Prof. EWA RZETELSKA-FELESZKO; publ. *Rocznik TNW* (annually).

Towarzystwo Przyjaciół Nauk w Legnicy (Society of Friends of Science in Legnica): 59-220 Legnica, ul. Zamkowa 2; tel. 226-34; f. 1959; 110 mems; library of over 8,000 vols; Pres. Dr inż. WOJCIECH MORAWIEC; Sec. Dr KRZYSZTOF KOSTRZANOWSKI; publ. *Szkice Legnickie* (annually).

Towarzystwo Przyjaciół Nauk w Międzyrzecu Podlaskim (Society of Friends of Science in Międzyrzec Podlaski): 21-350 Międzyrzec Podlaski, ul. Warszawska 37; tel. 714-126; Pres. Dr MARIAN KOWALSKI; Sec. Mgr LUCJAN BERNAT; publs *Rocznik Międzyrzecki, Biblioteka TPN.*

Towarzystwo Przyjaciół Nauk w Przemyślu (Society of Science and Letters of Przemyśl): 37-700 Przemyśl, Rynek 4; tel. (16) 678-56-01; f. 1909; 284 mems; library of 50,000 vols; Pres. Prof. Dr hab. ZDZISŁAW BUDZYŃSKI; Sec.-Gen. Mgr MACIEJ DALECKI; publs include *Rocznik Przemyski, Rocznik Nauk Medycznych, Biblioteka Przemyska.*

Towarzystwo Wiedzy Powszechnej (Society for Adult Education): 00-901 Warsaw, Pałac Kultury i Nauki, VI flor; tel. (22) 826-56-30; fax 620-33-06; f. 1950; general adult education; 6,000 mems; library of 2,000 vols; Pres. Prof. Dr hab. ALEKSANDER ŁUCZAK; Gen. Dir Dr STANISŁAW KARAS; publ. *Edukacja Dorosłych* (monthly).

Towarzystwo Wolnej Wszechnicy Polskiej (Society of the Polish Free University): 00-484 Warsaw, ul. Górnośląska 20; tel. (22) 621-73-55; fax (22) 625-38-34; f. 1957; permanent education, research and application services, specialized interests clubs; 1,000 mems; library of 10,000 vols; Pres. Dr Eng. MIKOŁAJ LIPOWSKI; Sec.-Gen. (vacant); publs *Kalendarz Samorzadowy, Człowiek w Społeczeństwie* (irregular), *Zeszyty Naukowe* (irregular).

Włocławskie Towarzystwo Naukowe (Włocławek Scientific Society): 87-800 Włocławek, Pl. Wolności 20; tel. (54) 32-28-08; f. 1979; popularization of science, research, publications; 450 mems; library of 13,000 vols; Pres. Prof. SZYMON KUBIAK; Sec. Dr STANISŁAW KUNIKOWSKI; publs *Zapiski Kujawsko-Dobrzyńskie* (annually), *Ziemia Dobrzyńska* (annually), *Przestrzeń* (6 a year).

Wrocławskie Towarzystwo Naukowe (Wrocław Scientific Society): 51-616 Wrocław, ul. Parkowa 13; tel. 48-40-61; f.1946 to study social and exact sciences; 482 mems; Pres. Prof. MARIAN PIEKARSKI; Sec. Prof. JAN ZARZYCKI; publs include *Prace Wrocławskiego Towarzystwa Naukowego* (Series A: Humanistic Sciences, Series B: Exact Sciences), *Śląskie Prace Bibliologiczne i Bibliotekoznawcze, Rozprawy Komisji Historii Sztuki, Rozprawy Komisji Językowej, Sprawozdania* (series A and B), *Annales Silesiae, Litteraria.*

Zamojskie Towarzystwo Przyjaciół Nauk (Zamość Society of Friends of Science): 22-400 Zamość, ul. Akademicka 8; tel. 22-06; Pres. Dr BOGDAN SZYSZKA; Sec. GERTRUDA SOWIŃSKA.

AGRICULTURE, FISHERIES AND VETERINARY SCIENCE

Polskie Towarzystwo Gleboznawcze (Polish Society of Soil Science): 02-520 Warsaw, ul. Wiśniowa 61; tel. (22) 49-48-16; f. 1937; 750 mems; Pres. Prof. Dr hab. PIOTR SKŁODOWSKI; Sec. Dr JÓZEF CHOJNICKI; publ. *Roczniki Gleboznawcze* (quarterly).

Polskie Towarzystwo Leśne (Polish Forest Society): 02-362 Warsaw, ul. Bitwy Warszawskiej 1920r. 3; tel. (22) 822-14-70; f. 1882; 3,360 mems; library of 1,700 vols; Pres. Prof. Dr ANDRZEJ GRZYWACZ; Sec. Dr GUSTAW MATUSZEWSKI; publ. *Sylwan.*

Polskie Towarzystwo Nauk Weterynaryjnych (Polish Society of Veterinary Sciences): 03-849 Warsaw, ul. Grochowska 272; tel. (22) 810-33-97; f. 1952; lectures and seminars in 17 divisions throughout Poland; congress every 4 years; 1,500 mems; library of 2,500 vols; Pres. Prof. Dr JERZY KITA; Sec. Dr JAROSŁAW KABA; publ. *Medycyna Weterynaryjna* (monthly).

Polskie Towarzystwo Zootechniczne (Polish Society of Animal Production): 02-316 Warsaw, Kaliska 9; tel. and fax (22) 22-17-23; f. 1922; 1,290 mems; library of 2,630 vols; Pres. Dr JÓZEF LUCHOWIEC; Dir Inż.ANNA ZABŁOCKA-IDCZAK; publs *Animal Production Review* (monthly), *Animal Production Review Applied Science Reports* (annually).

Towarzystwo Ogrodnicze (Horticultural Society): 31-425 Cracow, Al. 29 Listopada 54; tel. 22-79-46; Pres. Prof. WŁADYSŁAW PONIEDZIAŁEK; Sec. Eng. TADEUSZ LEŚNIAK; publs *Informator Ogrodniczy* (annually), *Hasło Ogrodnicze* (monthly).

ARCHITECTURE AND TOWN PLANNING

Stowarzyszenie Architektów Polskich (Association of Polish Architects): 00-950 Warsaw, ul. Foksal 2; tel. (22) 827-87-12; fax (22) 827-87-13; f. 1934; 6,040 mems; Sec.-Gen. JERZY GROCHULSKI; publ. *Komunikat SARP* (monthly).

Towarzystwo Urbanistów Polskich (Polish Town Planners' Society): 00-277 Warsaw, Pl. Zamkowy 10; tel. (22) 831-07-73; fax (22) 831-28-30; f. 1923; 1,400 mems; Pres. Dr STANISŁAW WYGANOWSKI; Sec.-Gen. Dr LILIANA SCHWARTZ; publ. *Biuletyn TUP* (quarterly).

BIBLIOGRAPHY, LIBRARY SCIENCE AND MUSEOLOGY

Stowarzyszenie Archiwistów Polskich (Polish Archivists' Association): 00-950 Warsaw, ul. Długa 6; tel. (22) 831-32-08; Pres. Dr WŁADYSŁAW STĘPNIAK; Sec.-Gen. (vacant); publ. *Archiwista* (quarterly).

Stowarzyszenie Bibliotekarzy Polskich (Polish Librarians Association): 02-103 Warsaw, ul. Hankiewicza 1; tel. (22) 823-02-70; fax (22) 822-51-33; f. 1917; 10,000 mems; Pres. STANISŁAW CZAJKA; Sec.-Gen. JANINA JAGIELSKA; publs *Bibliotekarz* (monthly), *Poradnik Bibliotekarza* (monthly), *Przegląd Biblioteczny* (quarterly).

ECONOMICS, LAW AND POLITICS

Polskie Towarzystwo Demograficzne (Polish Demographic Society): 02-554 Warsaw, al. Niepodległości 164, room 3; tel. (22) 49-12-51 ext. 690; f. 1982; 250 mems; Pres. ZBIGNIEW STRZELECKI; Sec. LUCYNA NOWAK; publ. *Polish Population Review* (2 a year).

Polskie Towarzystwo Ekonomiczne (Polish Economic Society): 00-042 Warsaw, Nowy Świat 49; tel. 27-99-04; fax 27-99-04; f. 1918; 55,000 mems; Pres. Prof. Dr hab. ZDZISŁAW SADOWSKI; Gen. Sec. Prof. Dr hab. URSZULA PŁOWIEC; publ. *Ekonomista* (every 2 months).

Polskie Towarzystwo Towaroznawcze (Polish Society for Commodity Science): 30-033 Cracow, ul. Sienkiewicza 4; tel. (012) 33-08-21; f. 1963; 500 mems; Pres. Prof. Dr WACŁAW ADAMCZYK; Sec. Dr ADRZEJ CHOCHÓŁ; publ. *Towaroznawstwo—Problemy Jakości* (annually).

EDUCATION

Polskie Towarzystwo Pedagogiczne (Polish Pedagogics Society): 00-389 Warsaw, ul. Smulikowskiego 6/8; tel. (22) 826-10-11, ext. 249; f. 1981; 800 mems; Pres. Prof. Dr hab. ZBIGNIEW KWIECIŃSKI; Sec.-Gen. Prof. Dr hab. MARIAN WALCZAK; publs *Forum Oświatowe* (Educational Forum, 2 a year), *Przegląd Historyczno-Oświatowy* (Historical-Educational Review, quarterly).

Poznańskie Towarzystwo Pedagogiczne (Poznań Pedagogics Society): 60-568 Poznań, ul. Szamarzewskiego 89; tel. 464-61, ext. 295; Pres. Dr DZIERŻYMIR JANKOWSKI; Sec. WANDA HEMMERLING.

FINE AND PERFORMING ARTS

Polskie Stowarzyszenie Filmu Naukowego (Polish Association of Scientific Film): 00-534 Warsaw, ul. Mokotowska 58 pok. 1; tel. (22) 629-08-32; Pres. GRZEGORZ KOWALEWSKI; Sec.-Gen. STANISŁAW ŚLEDŹ; publ. *Film Naukowy* (2 a year).

Stowarzyszenie Historyków Sztuki (Art Historians Association): 00-272 Warsaw, Rynek Starego Miasta 27; tel. 31-37-73; f. 1934; search and publication, popularization of art history; 1,481 mems; library of 26,000 vols; Pres. Prof. Dr hab. TADEUSZ CHRZANOWSKI; Sec.-Gen. Dr MARIAN SOŁTYSIAK; publs *Materiały Sesii SHS, Materiały do Dziejów Rezydencji w Polsce, Materiały Seminariów Metodologicznych, Materiały Sesji Oddziałowych.*

Towarzystwo im. Fryderyka Chopina (Frederic Chopin Society): 00-368 Warsaw, Ostrogski Castle, Okólnik 1; tel. 27-95-89; fax 27-95-99; f. 1934; 500 mems; permanent Secretariat of the Int. Chopin Piano Competitions and Int. Chopin Record Competitions "Grand Prix du Disque-Fryderyk Chopin"; central Chopin museum, library, phototheque and phonotheque for study of Chopin's life and preparation of complete edition of his works; organization of concerts; patronage of Chopin's birth-place in Zelazowa Wola; Gen. Dir ALBERT GRUDZIŃSKI; publs *Annales Chopin, Chopin Studies.*

Warszawskie Towarzystwo Muzyczne im. Stanisława Moniuszki (Stanisław Moniuszko Music Society in Warsaw): 02-511 Warsaw, ul. Morskie Oko 2; tel. 49-68-56; 300 mems; Pres. STEFANIA WOYTOWICZ; Sec. ALEKSANDER ROWIŃSKI.

HISTORY, GEOGRAPHY AND ARCHAEOLOGY

Polskie Towarzystwo Geograficzne (Polish Geographical Society): 00-325 Warsaw, Krakowskie Przedmieście 30; tel. (22) 826-17-94; f. 1918; 1,500 mems; library of 17,000 vols; Pres. Prof. Dr ANDRZEJ BONASEWICZ; Sec. Dr JERZY BAŃSKI; publs *Czasopismo Geograficzne* (quarterly), *Polski Przegląd Kartograficzny* (quarterly), *Fotointerpretacja w Geografii* (annually).

Polskie Towarzystwo Historyczne (Polish Historical Society): 00-272 Warsaw, Rynek Starego Miasta 29/31; tel. 31-63-41; f. 1886; 4,137 mems; Pres. Prof. Dr JACEK STASZEWSKI; Sec.-Gen. Mgr ZOFIA T. KOZŁOWSKA; 53 local branches, 4 research centres; publs *Przegląd Historyczny* (quarterly), *Sobótka-Śląski Kwartalnik Historyczny* (quarterly), *Studia i Materialy do dziejów Wielkopolski i Pomorza* (series), *Komunikaty Mazursko-Warmińskie* (quarterly), and several annuals.

Polskie Towarzystwo Numizmatyczne (Polish Numismatic Society): 00-958 Warsaw 40, skr. poczt. 2; tel. 31-39-28; f. 1991; 6,200 mems; library of *c.* 12,000 vols; Pres. LECH KOKOCIŃSKI; Sec. ADAM ZAJĄC; publ. *Biuletyn Numizmatyczny* (quarterly).

Polskie Towarzystwo Studiów Latynoamerykanistycznych (Polish Society for Latin American Studies): 00-272 Warsaw, Rynek Starego Miasta 29/31; tel. 310261, ext. 41; f. 1978; 112 mems; Pres. Dr ANDRZEJ KRZANOWSKI; Sec. ANNA GRUSZCZYNSKA-ZIOŁKOWSKA; publ. *Documentos de Trabajo.*

Stowarzyszenie Miłośników Dawnej Broni i Barwy (Historic Arms and Uniforms Association): 30-062 Cracow, al. 3 Maja 1; tel. (12) 634-33-77 ext. 430; fax (12) 633-97-67; Pres. Prof. Dr hab. JANUSZ BOGDANOWSKI; publ. *Studia do dziejów dawnego uzbrojenia i ubioru wojskowego.*

Towarzystwo Miłośników Historii i Zabytków Krakowa (Society of Friends of the History and Monuments of Cracow): 31-018 Cracow, Sw. Jana 12; tel. (12) 21-27-83; fax (12) 23-10-74; f. 1896; 650 mems; Pres. Prof. Dr JERZY WYROZUMSKI; Sec. OLGA DYBA; publs *Rocznik Krakowski, Biblioteka Krakowska, Kraków Dawniej i Dziś, Rola Krakowa w dziejach narodu.*

Towarzystwo Przyjaciół Pamiętnikarstwa (Memoirs Society): 00-373 Warsaw, ul. Nowy Świat 18/20; tel. 26-02-18; f. 1969; sociology; 300–400 mems; Pres. Prof. Dr hab. JAN SZCZEPAŃSKI; Sec.-Gen. Dr hab. FRANCISZEK JAKUBCZAK; publ. *Pamiętnikarstwo Polskie* (quarterly).

LANGUAGE AND LITERATURE

Polskie Towarzystwo Filologiczne (Polish Philological Society): 00-330 Warsaw, ul. Nowy Świat 72; tel. 26-52-31, ext. 256; f. 1893; aims to promote classical studies; 600 mems; library of 2,500 vols; Pres. Prof. Dr hab. JERZY AXER; Sec. Mgr ROBERT A. SUCHARSKI; publ. *Eos* (annually).

Polskie Towarzystwo Fonetyczne (Polish Phonetic Association): 61-704 Poznań, ul. Noskowskiego 10; tel. (61) 483-374; fax (61) 531-

984; f. 1980; linguistic phonetics, phonetics in medicine and technology; 112 mems; Pres. Prof. Dr hab. WIKTOR JASSEM; Sec.-Gen. MARIUSZ OWSIANNY.

Polskie Towarzystwo Językoznawcze (Polish Linguistic Society): 31-120 Cracow, al. A. Mickiewicza 9/11; tel. (12) 633-63-77; f. 1925; 807 mems; Pres. Prof. WIESŁAW BORYŚ; Sec. Dr ELŻBIETA KOSSAKOWSKA; publ. *Biuletyn Polskiego Towarzystwa Językoznawczego* (annually).

Polskie Towarzystwo Neofilologiczne (Modern Language Association of Poland): 61-725 Poznań, ul. Mielżyńskiego 27/29; tel. 53-26-82; f. 1931; 200 mems; Pres. Prof. Dr hab. TERESA SIEK-PISKOZUB; Sec. Dr ALEKSANDRA JANKOWSKA; publ. *Neofilolog* (2 a year).

Towarzystwo Kultury Języka (Society of Language Culture): 00-330 Warsaw, ul. Nowy Świat 72; tel. 26-52-31, ext. 90; Pres. Prof. Dr hab. STANISŁAW SKORUPKA; Sec. Prof. Dr MARIAN JURKOWSKI; publ. *Poradnik Językowy* (monthly).

Towarzystwo Literackie im. Adama Mickiewicza (Mickiewicz Literary Society): 00-330 Warsaw, Nowy Świat 72; tel. 26-52-31, ext. 279; f. 1886; 1,600 mems; arranges lectures on literature mainly in the provinces; Pres. Prof. Dr ZDZISŁAW LIBERA; Sec. Dr BARBARA KRYDA; publ. *Rocznik* (Yearbook).

Towarzystwo Miłośników Języka Polskiego (Society of Friends of the Polish Language): 31-113 Cracow, Straszewskiego 27; tel. 22-26-99; f. 1920; *c.* 1,000 mems; Pres. Prof. STANISŁAW URBAŃCZYK; Sec. Prof. MARIA MALEC; publ. *Język Polski*.

Związek Literatów Polskich (Union of Polish Writers): 00-079 Warsaw, Krakowskie Przedmieście 87/89; tel. (22) 826-57-85; f. 1920; 700 mems; library of 40,000 vols and cuttings; Chair. PIOTR KUNCEWICZ.

MEDICINE

Polskie Lekarskie Towarzystwo Radiologiczne (Polish Medical Society of Radiology): 00-576 Warsaw, Marszalkowska 24; tel. (22) 628-52-19; fax (22) 621-41-55; f. 1925; 1,700 mems; Pres. Prof. Dr hab. ANDRZEJ MARCIŃSKI; Sec.-Gen. Dr MICHAŁ BRZEWSKI; publ. *Polski Przegląd Radiologiczny* (quarterly).

Polskie Towarzystwo Anatomiczne (Polish Anatomical Society): 02-004 Warsaw, ul. Chałubińskiego 5; tel. (22) 629-52-83; fax (22) 629-52-82; f. 1923; 400 mems; Pres. WITOLD WOŹNIAK; Sec. Dr ELŻBIETA MAKOMASKA-SZAROSZYK; publs *Folia Morphologica, Postępy Biologii Komórki* (Advances in Cell Biology).

Polskie Towarzystwo Anestezjologii i Intensywnej Terapii (Polish Society of Anaesthesiology and Intensive Therapy): 40-752 Katowice, ul. Medyków 14; tel. (32) 252-56-65; fax (32) 202-21-15; e-mail anestzg@infomed.slam.katowice.pl; f. 1959; Pres. Prof. Dr hab. n. med. ANNA DYACZYŃSKA-HERMAN; Sec.-Gen. Dr EWA KARPEL; publ. *Anestezjologia, Intensywna Terapia* (every 2 months).

Polskie Towarzystwo Badań Radiacyjnych im. Marii Skłodowskiej-Curie (M. Skłodowska-Curie Polish Society for Radiation Research): 02-094 Warsaw, Choumska 12, P2H; tel. 49-77-74; f. 1967; 229 mems; Pres. Prof. Dr hab. ANTONI GAJEWSKI; Sec. Dr MAŁGORZATA ROCHALSKA.

Polskie Towarzystwo Chirurgów Dziecięcych (Polish Society of Paediatric Surgeons): 00-909 Warsaw, ul. Szaserów 128; tel. and fax (22) 10-45-11; f. 1965; 810 mems; Pres. Pers. Prof. Dr ZYGMUNT KALICIŃSKI; Sec.-Gen. Prof. Dr EUGENIA ZDEBSKA; publs *Problemy Chirurgii Dziecięcej* (annually), *Polski Przegląd Chirurgiczny* (monthly), *Surgery in Childhood* (quarterly).

Polskie Towarzystwo Dermatologiczne (Polish Dermatological Assn): 02-008 Warsaw, Koszykowa 82a; tel. 621-51-80; fax 622-67-81; f. 1921; research and post-graduate education in dermatology and venereology; 1,200 mems; Pres. Prof. WIESLAW GLINSKI; Sec. Dr. ANNA GORKIEWICZ-PETKOW; publs *Przegląd Dermatologiczny* (every 2 months).

Polskie Towarzystwo Diagnostyki Laboratoryjnej (Polish Laboratory Diagnostics Society): 02-097 Warsaw, ul. Banacha 1A; tel. and fax (22) 823-59-82; f. 1963; 3,500 mems; Pres. Prof. DAGNA BOBILEWICZ; publ. *Diagnostyka Laboratoryjna* (quarterly).

Polskie Towarzystwo Elektroencefalografii i Neurofizjologii Klinicznej (Polish Society of Electroencephalography and Clinical Neurophysiology): 04-073 Warsaw, ul. Grenadierów 51/59; tel. 10-18-79; Pres. Prof. Dr hab. WŁADYSŁAW Z. TRACZYK; Sec. Dr WALDEMAR SZELENBERGER.

Polskie Towarzystwo Endokrynologiczne (Polish Endocrinological Society): 02-015 Warsaw, pl. Starynkiewicza 3; tel. 628-12-40; f. 1951; 1,093 mems; Pres. Prof. Dr ANDRZEJ LEWIŃSKI; publ. *Endokrynologia Polska* (Polish Journal of Endocrinology, quarterly with English summary).

Polskie Towarzystwo Epidemiologów i Lekarzy Chorób Zakaźnych (Polish Society of Epidemiology and Infectious Diseases): 85-030 Bydgoszcz, ul. Św. Floriana 12; tel. and fax (52) 22-48-70; f. 1958; 1,200 mems; Pres. Prof. WALDEMAR HALOTA; Sec. Dr EWA TOPCZEWSKA-STAUBACH; publ. *Przegląd Epidemiologiczny* (quarterly).

Polskie Towarzystwo Farmaceutyczne (Polish Pharmaceutical Society): 00-238 Warsaw, ul. Długa 16; tel. (22) 831-15-42; fax (22) 831-02-43; f. 1947; 7,000 mems; Pres. Prof. Dr W. WIENIAWSKI; publs *Farmacja Polska* (fortnightly), *Acta Poloniae Pharmaceutica* (every 2 months), *Bromatologia i Chemia Toksykologiczna* (quarterly).

Polskie Towarzystwo Farmakologiczne (Polish Pharmacological Society): 15-230 Bialystok, Mickiewicza 2C, Dept. Pharmacodyn., Med. Acad.; tel. and fax 42-18-16; f. 1965; 545 mems; Pres. Prof. WŁODZIMIERZ BUCZKO; Sec. Assoc. Prof. BARBARA MALINOWSKA; publ. *Information Bulletin* (in Polish, 2 a year).

Polskie Towarzystwo Fizjologiczne (Polish Physiological Society): 31-531 Kraków, ul. Grzegórzecka 16; tel. 21-10-06; fax 21-15-78; f. 1936 to promote scientific activity in all fields of physiology; 300 mems; Pres. WIESŁAW W. PAWLIK; Sec. ARTUR DEMBIŃSKI; publ. *Journal of Physiology and Pharmacology*.

Polskie Towarzystwo Fizyki Medycznej (Polish Society of Medical Physics): 02-034 Warsaw, Wawelska 15; tel. 23-68-09; f. 1965; 280 mems; Pres. Prof. G. PAWLICKI; Sec. EWA ZALEWSKA; publ. *Polish Journal of Medical Physics and Engineering*.

Polskie Towarzystwo Ftizjopneumonologiczne (Polish Phthisiopneumonological Society): 01-138 Warsaw, ul. Płocka 26; tel. (22) 691-21-00; f. 1934; research into tuberculosis and chest diseases; Pres. Prof. MICHAŁ PIROŻYŃSKI; Sec. ANDRZEJ KAZIMIERCZAK; publ. *Pneumonologia i Alergologia Polska* (monthly).

Polskie Towarzystwo Gerontologiczne (Polish Gerontological Society): 15-230 Białystok, ul. Kilińskiego 1; tel. (85) 42-20-21, ext. 2188; fax (85) 42-49-07; f. 1973; 320 mems; Pres. Prof. WOJCIECH PĘDICH; Sec. Dr MAŁGORZATA HALICKA; publ. *Gerontologia Polska* (quarterly).

Polskie Towarzystwo Ginekologiczne (Polish Gynaecological Society): 71-252 Szczecin, ul. Unii Lubelskiej 1; tel. and fax (91) 487-37-55; e-mail ptgzg@r1.pam.szczecin.pl; br. in Wrocław; Pres. Prof. Dr hab. STANISŁAW RÓŻEWICKI; Sec. Dr ANDRZEJ PUCHALSKI; publ. *Ginekologia Polska* (monthly).

Polskie Towarzystwo Hematologów i Transfuzjologów (Polish Haematology and Transfusion Medicine Society): 02-097 Warsaw, ul. Banacha 1A; tel. and fax (22) 659-75-77; f. 1950; Pres. Prof. Dr WIESLAW WIKTOR-JEDRZEJCZAK; Sec. Prof. Dr BARBARA ZUPANSKA; publ. *Acta Haematologica Polonica* (quarterly).

Polskie Towarzystwo Higieniczne (Polish Hygiene Society): 00-324 Warsaw, ul. Karowa 31; tel. (22) 826-63-20; fax (22) 826-82-36; e-mail jsobotka@plearn.edu.pl; f. 1898; Pres. Assoc. Prof. CEZARY W. KORCZAK; Sec. Dr PAWEŁ GORYŃSKI; publs *Problemy Higieny*, *Problemy Higieny Pracy*, *Druk Bibliofilski 'Hygeia'* (all irregular).

Polskie Towarzystwo Higieny Psychicznej (Polish Mental Hygiene Society): 03-729 Warsaw, Targowa 59/16; tel. 18-65-99; safeguarding the mental and moral health of the individual; f. 1935; 1,250 mems; library of 2,500 vols; Pres. Prof. Dr hab. BRUNON HOŁYST; publ. *Zdrowie Psychiczne* (quarterly).

Polskie Towarzystwo Histochemików i Cytochemików (Polish Histochemical and Cytochemical Society): 50-368 Wrocław, ul. Chałubińskiego 6A; tel. (71) 20-95-61; fax (71) 22-90-61; email mazab@am.wroc.pl; f. 1961; histo- and cytochemistry, cell biology, electron microscopy, tissue and cell culture; 250 mems; Pres. Prof. Dr hab. MACIEJ ZABEL; Sec. Dr IZABELA LESISZ; publ. *Folia Histochemica et Cytobiologica* (quarterly).

Polskie Towarzystwo Historii Medycyny i Farmacji (Polish Society of History of Medicine and Pharmacy): 00-791 Warsaw, ul. Chocimska 22; f. 1957; 390 mems; Pres. Prof. Dr hab. JANUSZ KAPUŚCIK; Sec. Mgr HANNA BOJCZUK; publ. *Archiwum Historii i Filozofii Medycyny* (quarterly).

Polskie Towarzystwo Immunologii Doswiadczalnej i Klinicznej (Polish Society for Experimental and Clinical Immunology): 02-106 Warsaw, ul. Pawinskiego 5; tel. (22) 60-86-405; fax (22) 66-85-334; f. 1969; 500 mems; Pres. WALDEMAR L. OLSZEWSKI; Sec.-Gen. IRENA GRZELAK; publs *Central European Journal of Immunology* (quarterly, in English), *Integryna – Biuletyn PTI* (quarterly, in Polish).

Polskie Towarzystwo Kardiologiczne (Polish Cardiological Society): 04-073 Warsaw, ul. Grenadierów 51/59; tel. 10-17-38; fax (4822) 10-17-38; Pres. Prof. Dr LESZEK CEREMUŻYŃSKI; Sec. Dr JADWIGA KŁOŚ; publ. *Kardiologia Polska* (monthly).

Polskie Towarzystwo Lekarskie (Polish Medical Assn) 00-478 Warsaw, Al. Ujazdowskie 24; tel. and fax 628-86-99; f. 1951; 25,000 mems; Pres. Prof. Dr hab. med. JERZY WOY-WOJCIECHOWSKI; Secs Dr FELICJA ŁAPKIEWICZ, Dr ZBIGNIEW MILLER; publs *Polski Tygodnik Lekarski* (weekly), *Wiadomości Lekarskie* (fortnightly), *Przegląd Lekarski* (monthly).

Polskie Towarzystwo Logopedyczne (Polish Logopaedic Society): 20-031 Lublin, pl. Marii Curie-Sklodowskiej 1; tel. (81) 537-61-26; fax (81) 537-61-91; e-mail adamczyk@tytan.umcs.lublin.pl; f. 1963; 950 mems; Pres. Prof. Dr hab. BOGDAN ADAMCZYK; Sec. Dr ELZBIETA SMOŁKA; publ. *Logopedia* (annually).

Polskie Towarzystwo Medycyny Pracy (Polish Society of Occupational Medicine): 90-950 Łódź, ul. Teresy 8; tel. (42) 31-46-67; fax (42) 55-61-02; e-mail impx@krysia.uni.lodz.pl; f. 1969; Pres. Dr LECH T. DAWYDZIK; Sec. JERZY KOPIAS; publs *Medycyna Pracy* (every 2 months), *International Journal of Occupational Medicine and Environmental Health* (quarterly, in English).

Polskie Towarzystwo Medycyny Sądowej i Kryminologii (Polish Society of Forensic Medicine and Criminology): 85-094 Bydgoszcz, ul. M. Skłodowskiej-Curie 9; tel. and fax (52) 41-12-49; Pres. Prof. Dr hab KAROL ŚLIWKA; Sec. Prof. Dr hab. BARBARA ŚWIĄTEK; publ. *Archiwum Medycyny Sądowej i Kryminologii* (quarterly).

Polskie Towarzystwo Medycyny Społecznej (Polish Society of Social Medicine): 00-739 Warsaw, ul. Stępinska 19/25; tel. 41-13-13; Pres. Prof. Dr hab. CZESŁAW BARAN; Sec. Dr JANUSZ OPOLSKI; publ. *The Problems of Social Medicine* (2-3 a year).

Polskie Towarzystwo Medycyny Sportowej (Polish Society of Sports Medicine): 00-491 Warsaw, ul. Konopnickiej 6; tel. 21-82-52; f. 1937; Pres. Prof. ARTUR DZIAK; Sec. WOJCIECH DRYGAS; publ. *Medycyna Sportowa* (quarterly).

Polskie Towarzystwo Nauk Żywieniowych (Polish Society of Nutritional Sciences): 02-787 Warsaw, ul. Nowoursynowska 166; tel. (22) 843-83-15; f. 1980; 300 mems; Pres. Prof. Dr hab. ANNA GRONOWSKA-SENGER; Sec. Prof. Dr hab. HANNA KUNACHOWICZ..

Polskie Towarzystwo Neurochirurgów (Polish Neurosurgeons' Society): 20-954 Lublin, ul. Jaczewskiego 8; tel. (81) 742-59-81; fax (81) 747-08-73; f. 1964; 279 mems; Pres. Prof. TOMASZ TROJANOWSKI; Sec. Prof. EDWARD ZDERKIEWICZ; publ. *Neurologia i Neurochirurgia Polska* (every 2 months).

Polskie Towarzystwo Neurologiczne (Polish Neurological Society): 02-957 Warsaw, al. Sobieskiego 1/9; f. 1934; Pres. Prof. ANNA CZŁONKOWSKA; Sec. Asst Prof. U. FISZER; publ. *Neurologia i Neurochirurgia Polska* (every 2 months).

Polskie Towarzystwo Okulistyczne (Polish Ophthalmological Society): 02-007 Warsaw, ul. Lindleya 4; tel. 628-41-87; f. 1907; 1,750 mems; Pres. Prof. KRYSTYNA PECOLD; Sec.-Gen. Prof. ROMAN GOŚ; publ. *Klinika Oczna* (monthly).

Polskie Towarzystwo Onkologiczne (Polish Oncological Society): 31-115 Cracow, ul. Garncarska 11; tel. 22-87-60; telex 325437; f. 1921; 720 mems; Pres. Prof. Dr ANTONINA MARCZYŃSKA; Sec. Dr JAN KULPA; publ. *Nowotwory* (quarterly).

Polskie Towarzystwo Ortopedyczne i Traumatologiczne (Polish Orthopaedic and Traumatological Society): 80-206 Gdańsk, ul. Nowe Ogrody 4: tel. 32-18-64; Pres. Prof. Dr JÓZEF SZCZEKOT;Sec. Prof. STANISŁAW MAZURKIEWICZ; publ. *Chirurgia Narządów Ruchu i Ortopedia Polska* (every 2 months).

Polskie Towarzystwo Otolaryngologiczne (Polish Oto-rhino-laryngological Society): 71-344 Szczecin, ul. Unii Lubelskiej 1; tel. 706-91; fax 720-26; f. 1889; Pres. Prof. EUGENIUSZ ZIĘTEK; Sec. Dr hab CZESŁAWA TARNOWSKA; publ. *Otolaryngologia Polska* (every 2 months).

Polskie Towarzystwo Patologów (Polish Society of Pathologists): 90-549 Łódź, ul. Żeromskiego 113; tel. 32-51-45; f. 1958; 581 mems; Pres. Prof. Dr hab. ANDRZEJ KULIG; Sec. Doc. KRZYSZTOF W. ZIELIŃSKI; publ. *Patologia Polska* (quarterly, in English).

Polskie Towarzystwo Pediatryczne (Polish Paediatric Society): 01-211 Warsaw, ul. Kasprzaka 17A; tel. and fax (22) 632-62-24; f. 1908; 4,500 mems; Pres. Prof. Doc. Dr hab. WANDA KAWALEC; Sec. Doc. Dr hab. TADEUSZ MAZURCZAK; publs *Pediatria Polska* (monthly), *Przegląd Pediatryczny* (quarterly).

Polskie Towarzystwo Pielęgniarskie (Polish Nursing Asscn): 00-564 Warsaw, ul. Koszykowa 8; tel. 621-50-66; f. 1924, revived 1957; 6,500 mems; library of 3,000 vols; Pres. KRYSTYNA WOLSKA-LIPIEC; Sec. ELŻBIETA CHRÓŚCICKA; publ. *Biuletyn Polskiego Towarzystwa Pielęgniarskiego* (quarterly).

Polskie Towarzystwo Psychiatryczne (Polish Psychiatric Asscn): 02-957 Warsaw, Al. Sobieskiego 1/9; tel. 642-66-11; fax 642-53-75; 1,400 mems; Pres. Prof. Dr ADAM BILIKIEWICZ; Sec. Dr JOANNA MEDER; publs *Psychoterapia* (quarterly), *Psychiatria Polska* (every 2 months).

Polskie Towarzystwo Reumatologiczne (Polish Rheumatology Society): 02-637 Warsaw, ul. Spartańska 1; tel. (22) 44-87-57; fax (22) 44-95-22; f. 1933; 1,260 mems; Pres. Prof. Dr hab. ANNA FILIPOWICZ-SOSNOWSKA; Sec Dr med. ANNA ZUBRZYCKA-SIENKIEWICZ; publ. *Reumatologia* (quarterly).

Polskie Towarzystwo Stomatologiczne (Polish Dental Association): 02-005 Warsaw, Ul. Lindley'a 4; tel. and fax 621-24-02; f. 1951; 7,200 mems; Pres. Prof. Dr hab. JANUSZ PIEKARCZYK; Vice-Pres. Prof. Dr hab. EUGENIUSZ SPIECHOWICZ; publs *Czasopismo Stomatologiczne* (monthly), *Protetyka Stomatologiczna* (every 2 months).

Polskie Towarzystwo Synergetyczne (Polish Synergetics Society): 00-991 Warsaw, ul. Poligonowa 30, PIT, room 238; tel. 10-23-81; Pres. Prof. Dr hab. Eng. ARKADIUSZ GÓRAL; Sec. Dr hab. ZBIGNIEW CZYŻ; publ. *Topics in Fundamental Science* (irregular), *Synergetics*.

Polskie Towarzystwo Szpitalnictwa (Polish Hospital Society): 04-628 Warsaw, ul. Alpejska 42; tel. (22) 815-25-46; fax (22) 815-25-24; f. 1929; Pres. Dr MARIAN MIŚKIEWICZ; Sec. RYSZARD NIEPORĘCKI; publ. *Szpital Polski* (monthly).

Polskie Towarzystwo Toksykologiczne (Polish Toxicological Society): 31-062 Kraków, 19 Krakowska ul.; tel. (12) 56-28-99; fax (12) 22-38-50; f. 1978; 325 mems; Pres. Prof. Dr hab. ANDRZEJ STAREK; Sec. Dr MARIA KAŁA; publ. *Acta Poloniae Toxicologica.*

Polskie Towarzystwo Urologiczne (Polish Urological Society): 02-005 Warsaw, ul. Lindleya 4; tel. and fax (2) 628-18-96; f. 1949; 800 mems; Pres. Prof. Dr hab. ANDRZEJ BORKOWSKI; Vice-Pres. Prof. Dr hab. ADAM SZKODNY; publ. *Urologia Polska (quarterly).*

Polskie Towarzystwo Walki z Kalectwem (Polish Society for Rehabilitation of the Disabled): 00-629 Warsaw, ul. Oleandrów 4 m. 10; tel. and fax 25-70-50; f. 1960; popularizing progressive ideas in prophylaxis and changing social attitudes towards the disabled; Pres. Dr PIOTR JANASZEK; Sec. Dr ZBIGNIEW KAŹMIERAK; publs *Life of the Polish Society for Rehabilitation of the Disabled Information Bulletin*.

Stowarzyszenie Neuropatologów Polskich (Association of Polish Neuropathologists): 02-106 Warsaw, ul. Pawińskiego 5; tel. (22) 608-65-60; fax (22) 668-55-32; f 1964; 84 mems; Pres. Prof. Dr MIROSŁAW J. MOSSAKOWSKI; Sec. Dr HALINA WEINRAUDER; publ. *Folia Neuropathologica* (quarterly).

Towarzystwo Chirurgów Polskich (Society of Polish Surgeons): 50-368 Wrocław, M. Skłodowskiej-Curie 66; tel. 22-33-79; f. 1889; 3,150 mems; Pres. Prof. Dr B. ŁAZARKIEWICZ; Sec.-Gen. Prof. Dr W. NOSZCZYK; publ. *Polski Przegląd Chirurgiczny* (monthly).

Towarzystwo Internistów Polskich (Polish Society of Internal Medicine): 70-111 Szczecin, Al. Powstańców Wlkp. 72; tel. and fax (91) 82-03-63; e-mail psim@free.polbox.pl; f. 1909; 6,000 mems; Pres. Prof. Dr EUGENIUSZ SZMATŁOCH; Sec. Dr KRZYSZTOF KLIMEK; publ. *Polskie Archiwum Medycyny Wewnętrznej* (monthly).

Warszawskie Towarzystwo Lekarzy Medycyny Fizykalnej (Warsaw Physicians' Society of Physical Medicine): 02-097 Warsaw, ul. Banacha 1A, Dział Rehabilitacji CSK AM; tel. 23-64-11, ext. 563; 220 mems; Pres. WŁODZISŁAW KULIŃSKI; Sec. GRAŻYNA CISZKOWSKA.

Zrzeszenie Polskich Towarzystw Medycznych (Federation of Polish Medical Societies): 00-324 Warsaw, ul. Karowa 31; tel. (22) 826-63-20; fax (22) 826-82-36; e-mail jsobotka@p.learn.edu.pl; Pres. of Main Council Prof. Dr hab. BOLESŁAW GÓRNICKI; Sec. Prof. JERZY MAJKOWSKI; Pres. General Board Prof. Dr hab. REGINA OLĘDZKA; Sec. RYSZARD NIEPORĘCKI; Dir-Gen. Prof. Assoc. CEZARY W. KORCZAK; publs *Informator Zrzeszenie Polskich Towarzystw Medycznych* (irregular), *Problemy Medycyny i Farmacji* (irregular), *Druk Bibliofilski* (irregular).

NATURAL SCIENCES

Biological Sciences

Polskie Towarzystwo Biochemiczne (Polish Biochemical Society): 02-093 Warsaw, ul. Pasteura 3; tel. 658-20-99; fax 22-53-42; e-mail ptbioch@nencki.gov.pl; f. 1958; 1,285 mems; Pres. Prof. LILIANA KONARSKA; Sec. Dr EWA TURSKA; publ. *Postępy Biochemii* (Advances in Biochemistry, quarterly), *Acta Biochimica Polonica* (quarterly).

Polskie Towarzystwo Biofizyczne (Polish Biophysical Society): Dept of Biophysics, Institute of Biology, Maria Curie-Skłodowska University, ul. Akademicka 19, 20-033 Lublin; tel. (81) 537-50-80; f. 1972; 250 mems; Pres. Prof. Dr hab. TADEUSZ ZAWADZKI; Sec. Dr hab. JAN SIELEWIESIUK; publ. *Current Topics in Biophysics* (2 a year, in English; supplement in Polish).

Polskie Towarzystwo Biometryczne (Polish Biometrical Society): 51-151 Wrocław, ul. Przesmyckiego 20; tel. (71) 325-12-71; fax (71) 325-12-71; f. 1961; 230 mems; biometry, applied mathematical statistics in medicine, agriculture, biology, etc; Pres. Prof. Dr hab. STANISŁAW MEJZA; Sec. Dr DANUTA KACHLICKA; publ. *Listy Biometryczne – Biometrical Letters* (2 a year).

Polskie Towarzystwo Botaniczne (Polish Botanical Society): 00-478 Warsaw, Al. Ujazdowskie 4; tel. 621-36-69; f. 1922; 1,320 mems; library of 25,048 vols; Pres. Prof. STEFAN ZAJĄCZKOWSKI; Sec. Dr ZBIGNIEW MIREK; publs include *Acta Societatis Botanicorum Poloniae, Acta Agrobotanica, Monographiae Botanicae, Rocznik Sekcji Dendrologicznej Pol. Tow. Bot., Wiadomości Botaniczne, Acta Mycologica, Biuletyn Ogrodów Botanicznych Muzeów i Zbiorów.*

Polskie Towarzystwo Entomologiczne (Polish Entomological Society): 50-335 Wrocław, Sienkiewicza 21; tel. 22-50-41; f.1920; theoretical and applied entomology; 700 mems; library of 10,700 vols; Pres. Prof. JAROSŁAW BUSZKO; publs *Polskie Pismo Entomologiczne-Bulletin Entomologique de Pologne*, *Klucze do oznaczania owadów Polski* (Keys to Identification of Polish Insects), *Wiadomości Entomologiczne* (Entomological News).

Polskie Towarzystwo Fitopatologiczne (Polish Phytopathological Society): 60-625 Poznań, ul. Wojska Polskiego 71c; tel. (61) 848-77-13; fax (61) 848-71-45; f. 1971; 380 mems; Pres. Prof. Dr hab. MAŁGORZATA MAŃKA; Sec. Dr hab. MONIKA KOZŁOWSKA; publ. *Phytopathologia Polonica* (2 a year, in English).

Polskie Towarzystwo Genetyczne (Polish Genetics Society): 02-532 Warsaw, ul. Rakowiecka 36; tel. 48-09-75; f. 1963; 762 mems; Pres. Prof. HENRYK HÜBNER; Sec. Dr REGINA OSIECKA; publ. *Genetica Polonica* (quarterly).

Polskie Towarzystwo Hydrobiologiczne (Polish Hydrobiological Society): 02-097 Warsaw, ul. Stefana Banacha 2; tel. (22) 822-46-25; fax (22) 822-47-04; e-mail igor@hydro .biol.uw.edu.pl; 600 mems; Pres. Prof. Dr STANISŁAW RADWAN; Sec. Dr JAN IGOR RYBAK;

publs *Wiadomości Hydrobiologiczne* (in quarterly *Wiadomości Ekologiczne*), *Fauna Słodkowodna Polski.*

Polskie Towarzystwo Mikrobiologów (Polish Society of Microbiologists): 00-791 Warsaw, ul. Chocimska 24; fax (22) 49-74-84; f. 1927; 800 mems; Pres. Prof. DANUTA DZIERŻANOWSKA; Sec. Dr JOLANTA SZYCH; publs *Acta Microbiologica Polonica* (English, quarterly), *Medycyna Doświadczalna i Mikrobiologia* (Experimental Medicine and Microbiology, Polish, quarterly), *Postępy Mikrobiologii* (Advances in Microbiology, Polish, quarterly).

Polskie Towarzystwo Parazytologiczne (Polish Parasitological Society): 50-375 Wrocław, C. Norwida 29; tel. 21-66-61, ext. 245; f. 1948; 390 mems; library of 5,853 vols; Pres. Prof. Dr LESZEK GRZYWIŃSKI; publs *Wiadomości Parazytologiczne*, *Monografie Parazytologiczne.*

Polskie Towarzystwo Zoologiczne (Polish Zoological Society): 50-335 Wrocław, Sienkiewicza 21; tel. 22-50-41, ext. 16; f. 1935; 1,050 mems; library of 8,600 vols; Pres. JAN WOJTASZEK; Sec. ANDRZEJ JABŁOŃSKI; publs *Zoologica Poloniae*, *Przegląd Zoologiczny*, *The Ring* (quarterlies), *Notatki Ornitologiczne.*

Mathematical Sciences

Polskie Towarzystwo Matematyczne (Polish Mathematical Society): 00-950 Warsaw, ul. Śniadeckich 8; tel. 29-95-92; f. 1919; 2,080 mems; Pres. Prof. Dr KAZIMIERZ GOEBEL; publs *Annales Societatis Mathematicae Polonae: Series I Commentationes Mathematicae*, *Series II Wiadomości Matematyczne* (Mathematical News), *Series III Matematyka Stosowana* (Applied Mathematics), *Series IV Fundamenta Informaticae,* Series V Dydaktyka Matematyki (Didactics of Mathematics), *Popularny Miesięcznik Matematyczno-Fizyczno-Astronomiczny DELTA* (Mathematical and Physical popular monthly).

Polskie Towarzystwo Statystyczne (Polish Statistical Asscn): 00-925 Warsaw, Al. Niepodległości 208; tel. (22) 625-42-89; f. 1912; statistics, informatics, economics and econometrics; *c.* 1,000 mems; Pres. Prof. CZESŁAW DOMAŃSKI; Sec. JÓZEF GWOZDOWSKI; publs *Biuletyn Informacyjny* (Bulletin of Information, quarterly), *Wiadomości Statystyczne* (Statistics in Transition, journal, monthly).

Physical Sciences

Polskie Towarzystwo Astronomiczne (Polish Astronomical Society): 00-716 Warsaw, ul. Bartycka 18; tel. 41-00-41 ext. 146; f. 1923; 221 mems; Pres. Prof. JERZY KREINER; Sec. Dr MIROSŁAW GIERSZ; publs *Postępy Astronomii* (Progress in Astronomy), *Delta.*

Polskie Towarzystwo Chemiczne (Polish Chemical Society): 00-227 Warsaw, ul. Freta 16; tel. and fax (22) 831-13-04; f. 1919; 3,000 mems; library of 2,400 vols; Pres. Prof. T. M. KRYGOWSKI; Sec. Prof. R. BILEWICZ; publs *Wiadomości Chemiczne* (Chemical News), *Polish Journal of Chemistry*, *Orbital* (Society News, 6 a year).

Polskie Towarzystwo Fizyczne (Polish Physical Society): 00681 Warsaw, ul. Hoża 69; tel. and fax (22) 621-26-68; f. 1920; 1,800 mems; library of 1,300 vols; Pres. Prof. Dr I. STRZAŁKOWSKI; Gen. Sec. Prof. Dr MACIEJ KOLWAS; publs *Postępy Fizyki* (Advances in Physics, every 2 months), *Acta Physica Polonica A* and *B* (monthly, in English, French, German and Russian), *Reports on Mathematical Physics* (every 2 months, in English), *Delta* (monthly, in Polish).

Polskie Towarzystwo Geofizyczne (Polish Geophysical Society): 01-673 Warsaw, ul. Podleśna 61; tel. 34-16-51, ext. 494; f. 1947; development of geophysical sciences and their popularization; 450 mems; library of 5,000 vols; Pres. Dr ALFRED DUBICKI; Sec.-Gen. Dr WŁODZIMIERZ MEYER; publ. *Przegląd Geofizyczny* (Geophysical Review, quarterly).

Polskie Towarzystwo Geologiczne (Polish Geological Society): 30-063 Cracow, Oleandry 2a; tel. (12) 633-20-41; fax (48-12) 22-63-06; f. 1921; 1,200 mems; congresses, meetings, field conferences, etc; two prizes and a research grant are awarded annually; library of 23,000 journals and 9,000 books; Pres. Prof. Dr hab. ANDRZEJ ŚLĄCZKA; Sec. Dr inż. JANUSZ MAGIERA; publ. *Annales Societatis Geologorum Poloniae/ Rocznik Polskiego Towarzystwa Geologicznego/Annals of the Polish Geological Society* (quarterly).

Polskie Towarzystwo Miłośników Astronomii (Polish Amateur Astronomical Society): 31-027 Cracow, ul. św. Tomasza 30/8; tel. 22-38-92; f. 1919; 3,000 mems; amateur observations, instrument-making, popularization of astronomy; Pres. Prof. ZBIGNIEW KOWALSKI; Sec. Dr HENRYK BRANCEWICZ; publs *Urania* (monthly) and reports.

Polskie Towarzystwo Mineralogiczne (Mineralogical Society of Poland): 30-059 Cracow, Al. Mickiewicza 30; tel. (12) 633-43-30; f. 1969; 190 mems; Pres. Prof. Dr MARIAN BANAŚ; Sec. Dr MARZENA SCHEJBAL-CHWASTEK; publ. *Mineralogia Polonica* (2 a year).

Polskie Towarzystwo Nautologiczne (Polish Nautological Society): 81-374 Gdynia, ul. Sienkiewicza 3; tel. 20-49-75; f. 1958; history of human ties with the sea; 150 mems; library of 2,800 vols; Pres. Prof. Dr DANIEL DUDA; Sec. ELŻBIETA SKUPIŃSKA-DYBEK; publ. *Nautologia* (quarterly).

Polskie Towarzystwo Przyjaciół Nauk o Ziemi (Polish Society of Friends of Earth Sciences): 00-545 Warsaw, ul. Marszałkowska 62 m. 6; tel. and fax (22) 621-69-51; f. 1972; study and protection of the natural environment; makes inventory of Polish caves and speleological research; and non-professional collecting of minerals, rocks, fossils; *c.* 4,000 mems; library of 2,000 books and periodicals; Pres. Dr JERZY GRODZICKI; Sec. Mgr JERZY MIKUSZEWSKI.

Polskie Towarzystwo Przyrodników im. Kopernika (Polish 'Copernicus' Society of Naturalists): 02-532 Warsaw, ul. Rakowiecka 36; tel. 49-01-71; f. 1875; natural science; 1,007 mems; library of 4,635 vols; Pres. WIESŁAW RZĘDOWSKI; Sec. ANDRZEJ FAGASIŃSKI; publs *Wszechświat* (monthly), *Kosmos A* (quarterly).

PHILOSOPHY AND PSYCHOLOGY

Polskie Towarzystwo Filozoficzne (Polish Philosophical Society): Warsaw, Nowy Swiat 72, p.160; tel. 26-52-31, ext. 159; f. 1904; study of all traditional philosophical disciplines; 826 mems; library of 7,200 vols; Pres. Prof. Dr WŁADISŁAW STRÓŻEWSKI; Sec. Doc. Dr hab. BARBARA MARKIEWICZ; publ. *Ruch Filozoficzny* (Philosophical Movement, quarterly).

Polskie Towarzystwo Psychologiczne (Polish Psychological Association): 00-183 Warsaw, Stawki 5/7; tel. (22) 831-13-68; fax (22) 635-79-91; f. 1948; 2,000 mems; Pres. Dr MAŁGORZATA TOEPLITZ-WINIEWSKA; Sec. URSZULA BURYN; publs *Przegląd Psychologiczny* (Psychological Review, quarterly), *Nowiny Psychologiczne* (Psychological Newsletter, quarterly).

RELIGION, SOCIOLOGY AND ANTHROPOLOGY

Polskie Towarzystwo Antropologiczne (Polish Anthropological Society): Dept of Biology, 51-612 Wrocław, ul. Paderewskiego 35; tel. (71) 348-70-77; f. 1925; 300 mems; library of *c.* 10,000 vols; Pres. Prof. Dr PAWEL BERGMAN; Sec. Dr EWA NOWACKA-CHIARI; publ. *Przegląd Antropologiczny.*

Polskie Towarzystwo Kryminalistyczne (Polish Society of Criminologists): 02-520 Warsaw, ul. Wiśniowa 58; tel. (22) 48-49-28; fax (22) 48-54-28; f. 1973; forensic science; 350 mems; Pres. Prof. MARIUSZ KULICKI; Sec. Col. KAROL KWILMAN; publ. *Z Zagadnień Współczesnej Kryminalistyki* (irregular).

Polskie Towarzystwo Ludoznawcze (Polish Ethnographical Society): 50-139 Wrocław, ul. Szewska 36; tel. 44-38-32; f. 1895; cultural anthropology, folklore; 1,307 mems; library of 38,000 vols; Pres. Z. KŁODNICKI; Sec. M. ROSTWOROWSKA; publs *Lud* (annually), *Atlas Polskich Strojów Ludowych*, *Prace i Materiały Etnograficzne*, *Prace Etnologiczne*, *Literatura Ludowa* (every 2 months), *Archiwum Etnograficzne*, *Biblioteka Popularna*, *Dzieła Wszystkie O. Kolberga*, *Łódzkie Studia Etnograficzne* (annually), *Biblioteka Zesłańca*, *Komentarze do Polskiego Atlasu Etnograficznego*, *Dziedzictwo Kulturowe.*

Polskie Towarzystwo Orientalistyczne (Polish Oriental Society): 00-656 Warsaw, ul. Śniadeckich 8, Zarząd Główny; tel. 628-24-71 ext. 43; f. 1922; 200 mems; Pres STANISŁAW KAŁUŻYŃSKI, ALEKSANDER DUBIŃSKI, CZESŁAW ZWIERZ; Sec. MAREK DZIEKAN; publ. *Przegląd Orientalistyczny* (quarterly).

Polskie Towarzystwo Religioznawcze (Polish Society for the Science of Religions): 00-959 Warsaw, 30 skr. poczt. 151, Jaracza 1 Lok. 6; tel. (22) 625-26-42; f. 1958; history, theory, methodology, sociology, psychology of religions; 165 mems; Pres. Prof. Dr hab. ZBIGNIEW STACHOWSKI; Scientific Sec. Prof. Dr hab. ANDRZEJ WÓJTOWICZ; publ. *Przegląd Religioznawczy* (quarterly).

Polskie Towarzystwo Rusycystyczne (Polish Society for Russian Studies): 00-366 Warsaw, ul. Foksal 10; tel. (22) 826-48-43; Pres. Prof. Dr JANUSZ HENZEL; Sec.-Gen. Dr ARTUR KOWALCZYK; publ. *Przegląd Rusycystyczny* (quarterly).

Polskie Towarzystwo Semiotyczne (Polish Semiotics Society): 00-927 Warsaw, C/o Dept of Logical Semiotics, Warsaw University, ul. Krakowskie Przedmieście 3; tel. 26-43-88; telex 825439; fax 26-57-34; e-mail pelc%plearn.bitnet@plearn.edu.pl; f. 1968; all aspects of semiotics: signs, sign systems, information, communication, indirect cognition; applied semiotics; 140 mems; library of 1,500 vols; Pres. Prof. Dr JERZY PELC; publs *Studia Semiotyczne*, *Polski Biuletyn Semiotyczny* (annually), *Sygnały Semiotyczne.*

Polskie Towarzystwo Socjologiczne (Polish Sociological Association): 00-330 Warsaw, ul. Nowy Świat 72; tel. and fax (22) 826-77-37; f. 1957; Pres. Prof. ANDRZEJ KOJDER; Sec. Doc. Dr hab. MARIAN KEMPNY; publ. *Polish Sociological Review* (4 a year), *Informacja Bieżąca* (Current News, quarterly).

Polskie Towarzystwo Teologiczne w Krakowie (Polish Theological Society of Cracow): 31-002 Cracow, ul. Kanonicza 3; tel. (12) 422-56-90; f. 1924; Pres. Rev. Dr hab. KAZIMIERZ PANUŚ; Sec. Rev. Mgr KAZIMIERZ MOSKAŁA; publ. *Ruch Biblijny i Liturgiczny* (quarterly).

Towarzystwo Naukowe Organizacji i Kierownictwa (Scientific Society for Organization and Management): 00-564 Warsaw, ul. Koszykowa 6, Box C; tel. 29-99-73; telex 813649; fax 29-21-27; f. 1925; 32,000 individual mems, 5,000 collective mems; library of 15,000 vols; Pres. Prof. Dr HENRYK SADOWNIK; Dir JERZY MAJTERSKI; publs *Przegląd Organizacji* (monthly), *Problemy Organizacji* (quarterly).

TECHNOLOGY

Akademia Inżynierska w Polsce (Academy of Engineering in Poland): 00-950 Warsaw, Ul. Czackiego 3/5; tel. 27-36-07; telex 813225; fax 27-29-49; Pres. WOJCIECH GAWEDA; Sec.-Gen. KAZIMIERZ WAWRZYNIAK.

Federacja Stowarzyszeń Naukowo-Technicznych – Naczelna Organizacja Techniczna (FSNT-NOT) (Polish Federation of Engineering Associations): 00-950 Warsaw, ul. Czackiego 3/5; tel. (22) 827-16-86; fax (22) 827-29-49; e-mail fsntnot@medianet.com.pl; Pres. Prof. ANDRZEJ ZIELINSKI; Sec.-Gen. KAZIMIERZ WAWRZYNIAK; publ. *Przegląd Techniczny* (weekly).

Polskie Towarzystwo Akustyczne (Polish Acoustical Society): 60-769 Poznań, ul. Matejki 48/49; tel. 666-420; Pres. Prof. Dr hab. JERZY RANACHOWSKI; Sec.-Gen. Dr TADEUSZ PUSTELNY; publ. *Archives of Acoustics* (continuous).

Polskie Towarzystwo Astronautyczne (Polish Astronautical Society): 01-755 Warsaw, St. Krasińskiego 54; tel. 6852703; fax 403131; f. 1954; 386 mems; scientific, educational, and popular astronautics, planetology, bio-astronautics, space physics, CETI, and space law; brs in Warsaw, Cracow, Katowice, Włocławek, Olsztyn, Grudziądz; Pres. Dr MAREK BANASZKIEWICZ; Exec. Sec. MARIAN GOLA; publ. *Postępy Astronautyki* (Progress in Astronautics, yearbook).

Polskie Towarzystwo Elektrotechniki Teoretycznej i Stosowanej (Polish Society for Theoretical and Applied Electrical Engineering): 00-662 Warsaw, Ul. Koszykowa 75, Politechnika Warszawska, Wydz. Elektryczny, Gmach Fizyki p. 34; tel. and fax (22) 625-72-73; f. 1961; brs in 10 main towns; 750 mems; Pres. Prof. Dr hab. EUGENIUSZ KOZIEJ; Gen. Sec. Dr Eng. WŁODZIMIERZ KAŁAT.

Polskie Towarzystwo Ergonomiczne (Polish Ergonomics Society): 00-926 Warsaw, ul. Krucza 38/42; tel. (22) 661-93-94; fax (22) 625-47-70; Pres. Dr HALINA ĆWIRKO; Sec.-Gen. Dr EWA GÓRSKA; publ. *Ergonomia* (2 a year).

Polskie Towarzystwo Mechaniki Teoretycznej i Stosowanej (Polish Society of Theoretical and Applied Mechanics): 00-632 Warsaw, Dept of Civil Engineering, Warsaw University of Technology, Al. Armii Ludowej 16, p. 650; tel. (22) 825-71-80; f. 1958; brs in 17 other towns; 1,217 mems; Pres. Prof. Dr JERZY MARYNIAK; Gen. Sec. Prof. Dr JÓZEF KUBIK; publs *Mechanika Teoretyczna i Stosowana* (Theoretical and Applied Mechanics, quarterly).

Polskie Towarzystwo Metaloznawcze (Polish Society of Metallography): 30-059 Cracow, al Mickiewicza 30; tel. 33-38-23; f. 1970; 225 mems; Pres. Prof. Dr hab. STANISŁAW GORCZYCA; Sec. Dr Eng. ZBIGNIEW KĘDZIERSKI.

Research Institutes

GENERAL

Instytut Kultury (Institute of Culture): 00-075 Warsaw, ul. Senatorska 13/15; tel. and fax 26-24-77; f. 1974; library of 35,000 vols; Dir Doc. Dr hab. MACIEJ MROZOWSKI; publ. *Prace Instytutu Kultury.*

Instytut Podstaw Inżynierii Środowiska PAN (Institute of Environmental Engineering): 41-800 Zabrze, ul. M. Skłodowskiej-Curie 34; tel. 171-64-81; telex 036401; fax 171-74-70; f. 1961; attached to Polish Acad. of Sciences; air and water pollution control, land reclamation, energy conservation, influence of pollutants on plants; library of 14,000 vols; Dir Assoc. Prof. JAN KAPAŁA (acting); publs *Archiwum Ochrony Środowiska* (Archives of Environmental Protection, quarterly, with summaries in English and Russian), *Prace i Studia* (irregular).

Instytut Slawistyki PAN (Slavonic Institute): 00-478 Warsaw, Al. Ujazdowskie 18 m. 16; tel. 24-99-40; f. 1954; attached to Polish Acad. of Sciences; 88 mems; library of 115,000 vols; Dir Prof. EWA RZETELSKA-FELESZKO; publs *Acta Baltico-Slavica, Studia z Filologii Polskiej i Słowiańskiej, Slavia Meridionalis, Studia Literaria Polono-Slavica.*

Instytut Sportu (Institute of Sport): 01-892 Warsaw 45, ul. Trylogii 2, POB 30; tel. (22) 34-62-88; fax (22) 35-09-77; f. 1978; library of 6,130 vols; Dir Prof. RYSZARD GRUCZA; publ. *Biology of Sport* (quarterly).

Zakład Badań Narodowościowych PAN (Centre for the Study of Nationalities): 61-772 Poznań, Stary Rynek 78/79; tel. 52-09-50; f. 1973; attached to Polish Acad. of Sciences; library of 1,800 vols; Dir Prof. Dr hab. JERZY WISŁOCKI; publ. *Sprawy Narodowościowe* (Issues of Nationality, 2 a year).

Zakład Krajów Pozaeuropejskich PAN (Centre for Studies on Non-European Countries): 00-330 Warsaw, Nowy Świat 72; tel. (22) 826-63-56; f. 1978; attached to Polish Acad. of Sciences; library of 16,000 vols; Dir Dr JERZY ZDANOWSKI.

AGRICULTURE, FISHERIES AND VETERINARY SCIENCE

Instytut Agrofizyki im. Bohdana Dobrzańskiego PAN (Institute of Agrophysics): 20-236 Lublin, Doświaczalna 4; tel. (81) 744-50-61; fax (81) 744-50-67; e-mail agrof@demeter.ipan.lublin.pl; f. 1968; attached to Polish Acad. of Sciences; 132 staff; library of 3,000 vols; Dir Prof. Dr hab. JAN GLIŃSKI; publs. *Acta Agrophysica* (quarterly), *International Agrophysics* (quarterly).

Instytut Badawczy Leśnictwa (Forestry Research Institute): 00-973 Warsaw, ul. Bitwy Warszawskiej 1920 r. 3; tel. (22) 822-24-57; fax (22) 822-40-35; e-mail biblioteka@ibles.waw.pl; f. 1930; comprises 23 scientific sections covering all aspects of forestry, especially factors of environment, silviculture and selection, tree-planting, forest economics, management, forest work organization, protection, forest plant pathology, game management, water economy, logging mechanization and transport; main documentation and information centre of forestry; library of 60,000 vols; Dir Prof. Dr hab. eng. A. KLOCEK; publs *Folia Forestalia Polonica* (series, in English), *Prace IBL* (Works of the FRI) series A and series B, *Notatnik Naukowy* (Scientific Notes); brs at Cracow, Białowieża, Katowice, Sękocin near Warsaw, and Szklarska Poręba.

Instytut Biotechnologii Przemysłu Rolno-Spożywczego (Institute of Agricultural and Food Biotechnology): 02-532 Warsaw, ul. Rakowiecka 36; tel. 49-02-24; fax 49-04-26; e-mail ibprs@ibprs.waw.pl; f. 1954; biotechnology: improvement of microbial strains, fermentation processes (beer, wine, spirits, organic acids), malt, yeasts, enzymatic preparations, microbial preparations; technology of fruit and vegetable products, food analysis; maintains culture colln of industrial micro-organisms; library of 24,000 vols; Dir Prof. ROMAN GRZYBOWSKI; publ. *Prace Instytutów i Laboratoriów Badawczych Przemysłu Spożywczego* (irregular).

Instytut Budownictwa, Mechanizacji i Elektryfikacji Rolnictwa (Institute for Building, Mechanization and Electrification in Agriculture): 02-532 Warsaw, ul. Rakowiecka 32; tel. (22) 49-32-31; fax (22) 49-17-37; e-mail selian@ibmer.waw.pl; f. 1950; research into the mechanization of farming, economics and management, land reclamation, farm building and energy sources; library of 57,000 vols; Dir ALEKSANDER SZEPTYCKI; publs *Prace NaukowoBadawcze IBMER* (annually), *Przegląd Dokumentacyjny—Technika Rolnicza* (6 a year), *System Maszyn Rolniczych* (every 5 years), *Problemy Inżynierii Rolniczej* (quarterly), *Przegląd Dokumentacyjny—Ergonomia i Bezpieczeństwo Pracy w Technice Rolniczej* (1 a year), *Inżynieria Rolnicza* (irregular).

Instytut Celulozowo-Papierniczy (Pulp, Paper Research Institute): 90-950 Łódź, ul. Gdańska 121; tel. (42) 36-53-00; fax (42) 36-53-23; e-mail icpndi@ld.onet.pl; f. 1951; research in pulp, paper, analysis and testing, protection of the environment; library of 16,000 vols; Dir PIOTR STANISŁAWCZYK; publ. *Celuloza i Papier—Informacja Ekspresowa* (monthly).

Instytut Ekonomiki Rolnictwa i Gospodarki Żywnościowej (Institute of Agricultural and Food Economics): 00-002 Warsaw, ul. Świętokrzyska 20, POB 984; tel. (22) 826-61-17; fax (22) 827-19-60; e-mail ierigz@ierigz.waw.pl; f. 1983, fmrly Inst. of Agricultural Economics; library of 36,000 vols; Dir Prof. Dr WOJCIECH JÓZWIAK; publs *Zagadnienia Ekonomiki Rolnej* (Problems of Agricultural Economics, 6 a year), *Rynek Rolny* (Agricultural Market, monthly).

Instytut Fizjologii i Żywienia Zwierząt im. Jana Kielanowskiego PAN (Kielanowski Institute of Animal Physiology and Nutrition): 05-110 Jabłonna, Ul. Instytucka 3; tel. (22) 782-41-75; fax (22) 774-20-38; f. 1955; attached to Polish Acad. of Sciences; study of nutrition of ruminants, pigs and poultry, digestive processes, neuroendocrinology, endocrinology of reproduction; staff of 38 graduates; library of 5,000 vols; Dir Prof. Dr TERESA ŻEBROWSKA.

Instytut Genetyki i Hodowli Zwierząt PAN (Institute of Genetics and Animal Breeding): 05-551 Mroków, Jastrzębiec; tel. 756-17-11; fax 756-16-99; f. 1955; attached to Polish Acad. of Sciences; research work in animal genetics with special reference to farm animals; 147 mems; library of 6,000 vols, 5,640 journals; Dir Prof. Dr ZYGMUNT REKLEWSKI; publs *Prace i Materiały Zootechniczne* (irregular), *Animal Science Papers and Reports* (quarterly).

Instytut Genetyki Roślin PAN (Institute of Plant Genetics): 60-479 Poznań, ul. Strzeszyńska 34; tel. (61) 823-35-11; fax (61) 23-36-71; e-mail office@igr.poznan.pl; f. 1961; attached to Polish Acad. of Sciences; basic genetic research on cultivated plants and the development of new plant genotypes; Dir Prof. JERZY CHEŁKOWSKI; publ. *Journal of Applied Genetics* (quarterly).

Instytut Hodowli i Aklimatyzacji Roślin (Plant Breeding and Acclimatization Institute): 05-870 Błonie, Radzików; tel. (22) 725-36-11; fax (22) 725-47-14; f. 1951; 6 departments, 18 experimental stations for plant breeding, botanical garden in Bydgoszcz; research in plant breeding, genetics, physiology, biochemistry, phytopathology, seed testing of agricultural plants and agrotechnics of sugar beet and oil plants; library of 23,000 vols; Dir Prof. Dr H. J. CZEMBOR; publs *Biuletyn IHAR* (4 a year), *Index Seminum* (every 2 years), *Delectus Seminum* (every 2 years), *Plant Breeding and Seed Science* (2 a year), *Oil Plants* (1 a year), *Polish Potato* (4 a year).

Instytut Melioracji i Użytków Zielonych (Institute for Land Reclamation and Grassland Farming): Falenty, 05-090 Raszyn; tel. 628-37-63; f. 1953; grassland farming, water management in agriculture, rural sanitation; library of 47,200 vols and 8,900 vols special collections; Dir EDMUND KACA; publs *Wiadomości IMUZ* (2 a year), *Biblioteczka Wiado-*

mości IMUZ (series), *Materiały Informacyjne* (series), *Materiały Instruktażowe* (series).

Instytut Meteorologii i Gospodarki Wodnej (Institute of Meteorology and Water Management): 01-673 Warsaw, ul. Podleśna 61; tel. (22) 834-18-51; fax (22) 34-54-66; f. 1973 from former State Institute of Hydrology and Meteorology and the Institute of Water Management; collections of data from 61 meteorological stations, 159 meteorological posts, 818 hydrological posts, 1,009 pluviometric posts, 768 groundwater posts; library of 95,000 vols; Dir Prof. Dr eng. JAN ZIELIŃSKI; publs *Wiadomości Instytutu Meteorologii i Gospodarki Wodnej* (Reports, quarterly), *Materiały Badawcze* (Research Papers) and non-periodical series.

Instytut Nawozów Sztucznych (Fertilizers Research Institute): 24-110 Puławy; tel. (81) 887-64-44; fax (81) 887-65-66; f. 1948; technology of production, handling and application of chemical fertilizers, organic derivatives of methanol and urea; library of 35,000 vols; Dir BOLESŁAW SKOWROŃSKI; publ. *Przemysł Nawozowy* (monthly).

Instytut Ochrony Roślin (Institute of Plant Protection): 60-318 Poznań, ul. Miczurina 20; tel. (61) 864-90-00; fax (61) 867-63-01; e-mail tjk@ior.poznan.pl; f. 1951; library of 100,000 vols; Dir Prof. Dr STEFAN PRUSZYŃSKI; publs *Progress in Plant Protection* (1 a year), *Journal of Plant Protection Research* (1 a year), *Ochrona Roślin* (monthly).

Instytut Przemysłu Cukrowniczego (Institute of the Sugar Industry): 02-532 Warsaw, ul. Rakowiecka 36; tel. (22) 49-04-24; fax (22) 48-09-01; e-mail inspcukr@atos .warman.com.pl; f. 1898; research into all branches of the Sugar Industry; Raw Product, Sugar Beet, Technological, Analytical, Mechanical, Environmental Protection Depts; library of 1,500 vols; Dir ANTONI LAUDAŃSKI; publs *Informacja o wynikach produkcyjnych i danych techniczo-technologicznych przemysłu cukrowniczego* (1 a year), *Informacja dekadowa z przebiegu Kampanii* (9 a year).

Instytut Przemysłu Mięsnego i Tłuszczowego (Meat and Fat Research Institute): 04-190 Warsaw, ul. Jubilerska 4; tel. and fax (22) 610-63-68; f. 1949; chemical and technological research on meat and meat products, edible oils and fats; laboratories in Warsaw and Poznań; library of 5,000 vols; Dir Dr ANDRZEJ BORYS; publs *Roczniki Instytutu Przemysłu Mięsnego i Tłuszczowego* (annually), *Tłuszcze Jadalne* (quarterly).

Instytut Roślin i Przetworów Zielarskich (Research Institute of Medicinal Plants): 61-707 Poznań, ul. Libelta 27; tel. 52-56-16; fax 52-74-63; f. 1947; botany, plant breeding, agrotechnology, pest control, phytochemistry, pharmaceutical analysis, technology of plant drugs, pharmacology; library of 12,000 vols; Dir Prof. Dr hab. Dr h.c. JERZY LUTOMSKI; publs *Herba Polonica* (quarterly), *Index Seminum* (annually).

Instytut Rozwoju Wsi i Rolnictwa PAN (Institute of Rural and Agricultural Development): 00-330 Warsaw, Nowy Świat 72; tel. and fax (22) 826-63-71; e-mail irwir@irwirpan .waw.pl; f. 1971; attached to Polish Acad. of Sciences; research into the process of developing agriculture and rural society; 43 mems; library of 5,000 vols; Dir Prof. MAREK KŁODZIŃSKI; publs *Countryside and Agriculture* (quarterly in Polish, summaries in English), *Problems of Rural and Agricultural Development*.

Instytut Rybactwa Śródlądowego (Inland Fisheries Institute): 10-719 Olsztyn-Kortowo, ul. M. Oczapowskiego 10; tel. (89) 527-31-71; fax (89) 527-25-05; Dir Prof. JAN SZCZERBOWSKI.

Instytut Sadownictwa i Kwiaciarstwa (Institute of Pomology and Floriculture): 96-100 Skierniewice, ul. Pomologiczna 18; tel. (46) 833-20-21; fax (46) 833-32-28; f. 1951; three divisions; pomology, floriculture, bee-keeping, covering field of applied research; five interdivisional laboratories: chemical, botanical, physiological, biochemical and isotopes; experimental greenhouses, phytotrone, cold storage and freezing facilities; 6 field stations; library of 37,578 vols; Dir Dr D. GOSZCZYŃSKA; publs *Journal of Fruit and Ornamental Plant Research, Zeszyty Naukowe Instytutu Sadownictwa i Kwiaciarstwa, Pszczelnicze Zeszyty Naukowe,* (Bee Research Bulletin), *Sprawozdanie Roczne.*

Instytut Technologii Drewna (Institute of Wood Technology): 60-654 Poznań, ul. Winiarska 1; tel. (61) 822-40-81; fax (61) 822-43-72; f. 1952; responsible for solving problems of the wood processing industry and for developing new technical processes; library of 28,000 vols; 6,000 special exhibits; Dir Prof. E. URBANIK; publ. *Prace Instytutu Technologii Drewna* (quarterly).

Instytut Uprawy, Nawożenia i Gleboznawstwa (Institute of Soil Science and Plant Cultivation): 24-100 Puławy, Osada Pałacowa; tel. (81) 886-34-21; telex 0642410; fax (81) 886-45-47; f. 1917; pedology; utilization and protection of agricultural land; soil chemistry, plant physiology, biochemistry, microbiology, soil and crop management, production technology of cereals, forage crops, tobacco and hops, etc.; Dir Dr SEWERYN KUKUŁA; publs *Pamiętnik Puławski* (2 or 3 a year), *Zalecenia Agrotechniczne* (every 5 years).

Instytut Warzywnictwa (Research Institute of Vegetable Crops): 96-100 Skierniewice, ul. Konstytucji 3 Maja 1/3; tel. (46) 833-34-34; fax (46) 833-31-86; e-mail iwarz@ainwarz .skierniewice.pl; f. 1964; research into the development of practical guidelines for the rational and economic development of vegetable production; Dir STANISŁAW KANISZEWSKI; publs *Biuletyn Warzywniczy* (Vegetable Crops Research Bulletin, 2 a year), *Nowości Warzywnicze* (Vegetable News, 2 a year).

Państwowy Instytut Weterynaryjny (National Veterinary Research Institute): 24-100 Puławy, ul. Partyzantów 57; tel. (81) 886-30-51; fax (81) 886-25-95; e-mail ekozska@ esterka.piwet.pulawy.pl; f. 1945; veterinary microbiology, immunology, parasitology, toxicology, etc.; 19 scientific departments including those at Bydgoszcz, Zduńska Wola and Swarzędz, and 3 specialized laboratories; library of 19,080 vols; Dir Prof. Dr MARIAN TRUSZCZYŃSKI; publ. *Bulletin of the Veterinary Institute in Puławy* (every 6 months).

Instytut Ziemniaka (Institute for Potato Research): 76-009 Bonin, nr. Koszalin; tel. (94) 42-30-31; telex 0532219; fax (94) 42-70-28; f. 1966; study of the breeding, genetics, physiology, biochemistry, control, virology, production and storage of potatoes: 11 depts, 5 research stations; library of 20,000 vols; Dir Doc. Dr hab. M. KOSTIW; publs *Biuletyn Instytutu Ziemniaka* (2 a year), *Ziemniak Polski* (quarterly).

Instytut Zootechniki (Institute of Animal Husbandry): 32-083 Balice k. Krakowa; tel. (12) 285-67-77; fax (12) 285-67-33; e-mail izooinfo@izoo.krakow.pl; f. 1950; 10 Scientific Depts, 11 Experimental Stations; library of 125,000 vols; Dir Prof. J. KRUPIŃSKI; publs *Information Bulletin* (4 a year), *Annals of Animal Science* (4 a year), *D.Sc. Dissertations, Reports on Animal Performance Testing* (1 a year).

Morski Instytut Rybacki (Sea Fisheries Institute): 81-332 Gdynia, ul. Kołłątaja 1; tel. 20-28-25; telex 54348; fax (058) 20-28-31; f. 1923; departments of ichthyology, oceanography, fishing technique, technology of fish processing, sea-fishery economics, scientific information; two branches at Szczecin and Swinoujście; library of 24,000 vols; Dir Prof. Dr ZYGMUNT POLAŃSKI; publs Reports, Studies and Materials, *Bulletin of the Sea Fisheries Institute in Gdynia*

Zakład Badań Srodowiska Rolniczego i Leśnego PAN (Research Centre for Agricultural and Forest Environmental Studies): 60-809 Poznań, ul. Bukowska 19; tel. 47-56-01; fax 47-36-68; f. 1979; attached to Polish Acad. of Sciences; study of energy flow and cycling of matter, evaluation of ecological guidelines for landscape management, and strategy for nature conservancy; 47 staff; library of 35,000 vols; Dir Prof. Dr hab. LECH RYSZKOWSKI.

Zakład Fizjologii Roślin im. Franciszka Górskiego PAN (Department of Plant Physiology): 31-016 Cracow, Sławkowska 17; tel. (12) 422-79-44; fax (12) 421-79-01; f. 1956; attached to Polish Acad. of Sciences; laboratories; plant growth and development, photosynthesis, environmental research, biorhythms; myxomycetes; Dir Prof. Dr MARIAN CZARNOWSKI; publ. *Acta Physiologiae Plantarum* (quarterly).

ARCHITECTURE AND TOWN PLANNING

Instytut Gospodarki Mieszkaniowej (Housing Research Institute): 00-925 Warsaw, ul. Filtrowa 1; tel. (22) 825-09-53; fax (22) 825-06-83; e-mail 001@polbox.com; f. 1952; research and development in housing problems: dwelling construction and stock, investment process, construction market; library of 8,770 vols, 76 periodicals; Dir Dr RYSZARD UCHMAN; publs *Problemy Rozwoju Budownictwa* (quarterly), *Sprawy Mieszkaniowe* (quarterly).

Instytut Gospodarki Przestrzennej i Komunalnej (Institute of Physical Planning and Municipal Economy): 02-078 Warsaw, ul. Krzywickiego 9; tel. and fax (22) 825-09-37; f. 1986; physical planning, architecture, municipal economy; library of 100,000 vols, including several special collections; Dir Dr Ing. JACEK MALASEK; publs *Człowiek i Środowisko* (quarterly).

Instytut Techniki Budowlanej (Building Research Institue), 00-950 Warsaw, ul. Filtrowa 1; tel. (22) 825-04-71; fax (22) 825-52-86; f. 1945; research in the use of building materials and methods of construction library of 75,000 vols; Dir STANISŁAW WIERZBICKI; publs *Prace Instytutu Techniki Budowlanej* (quarterly), reports, monographs, papers.

BIBLIOGRAPHY, LIBRARY SCIENCE AND MUSEOLOGY

Instytut Informacji Naukowej, Technicznej i Ekonomicznej (Institute for Scientific, Technical and Economic Information): 00-503 Warsaw, ul. Zurawia 4A; tel. 629-56-24; fax 629-79-89; e-mail iinte@cc.cup.gov.pl; f. 1949; reorganized 1972; research, development activities in the field of scientific, technical and economic information; provides professional advice and other forms of methodological and organizational assistance; information software development, especially in CDS ISIS package, in co-operation with UNESCO; library of 8,000 vols; Dir Dr HELENA DRYZEK; publs *Informacja Naukowa* (Information Science, irregular), *UKD—Zmiany i Uzupełnienia* (Corrections and Extensions to the UDC, quarterly), *Tablice UKD* (Schedules of UDC, irregular).

ECONOMICS, LAW AND POLITICS

Centrum Badań Przedsiębiorczości i Zarządzania PAN (Institute of Management,

Polish Academy of Sciences): 00-901 Warsaw, Pałac Kultury i Nauki; tel. and fax 620-86-61; f. 1983; attached to Polish Acad. of Sciences; library of 8,500 vols; Dir Prof. STANISŁAW WALUKIEWICZ; publ. *Organizacja i Kierowanie* (quarterly).

Instytut Administracji i Zarządzania (Institute of Public Administration and Management): 02-067 Warsaw, ul. Wawelska 56; tel. 25-64-19; Dir Prof. Dr ADAM JAROSZYŃSKI; pubis *Organizacja – Metody – Technika* (monthly), *Doskonalenie Kadr Kierowniczych* (monthly).

Instytut Bałtycki (Baltic Institute): 80-958 Gdańsk, ul. Tkacka 11/13; tel. 31-47-86; f. 1925; research into the modern history of relations between Poland and Germany, Estonia, Latvia, Lithuania and Scandinavia; Dir Prof. Dr CZESŁAW CIESIELSKI; publ. *Komunikaty Instytutu Bałtyckiego* (annually).

Instytut Ekonomiki Przemysłu Chemicznego (Institute of Chemical Industry Economics): 01-793 Warsaw, ul. Rydygiera 8; tel. 633-93-32; fax 633-94-18; f. 1974; research into development and restructuring of industrial branches and individual enterprises; economic analyses and expert opinions, feasibility studies, market research; consulting in enterprise management and organization; management information systems; computerized databases with statistical information on business and manufacture in Polish chemical industry; library of 4,793 vols., 42,944 microcopies; Dir MARIAN SURDYK; publ. *Przemysł Chemiczny w Świecie* (Information Bulletin, fortnightly).

Instytut Ekspertyz Sądowych (Institute of Forensic Research): 31-033 Cracow, ul. Westerplatte 9; tel. (12) 422-87-55; fax (12) 422-38-50; e-mail ies@ies.krakow.pl; f. 1929; departments of: criminalistics, traffic accident investigation, forensic toxicology, forensic psychology, forensic serology, 47 mems; library of 9,000 vols; Dir ALEKSANDER GŁAZEK; publ. *Z Zagadnień Nauk Sądowych* (Problems of Forensic Sciences, 2 a year).

Instytut Finansów (Institute of Finance): 00-916 Warsaw, ul. Świętokrzyska 12; tel. (22) 826-33-18; e-mail instfin@if.gov.pl; Dir ANDRZEJ WERNIK.

Instytut Gospodarki Narodowej (Institute of National Economy): 00-507 Warsaw, ul. Żurawia 4A; tel. 21-10-87; Dir MARIAN OSTROWSKI; publs *Studia i Materiały* (5 a year), *Raporty* (7 a year), *Occasional Papers* (5 a year), *Izobrannyje Raboty* (5 a year).

Instytut Koniunktur i Cen Handlu Zagranicznego (Foreign Trade Research Institute): 00-483 Warsaw, ul. Frascati 2; tel. (22) 826-89-08; telex 814501; fax (22) 826-55-62; f. 1928; Polish and world economics, European studies, Polish foreign trade, int. trade; library of 24,000 vols; Dir Dr BARBARA DURKA.

Instytut Nauk Ekonomicznych PAN (Institute of Economics): 00-330 Warsaw, Pałac Staszica, ul. Nowy Świat 72; tel. 26-72-54; fax 26-05-57; f. 1981; attached to Polish Acad. of Sciences; library of 15,000 vols; Dir Prof. Dr hab. MAREK BELKA; publs *Studia Ekonomiczne* (quarterly), *Monografie, Opera Minora*.

Instytut Nauk Prawnych PAN (Institute of Law Studies): 00-330 Warsaw, Nowy Świat 72 (Pałac Staszica); tel. and fax 26-78-53; f. 1956; attached to Polish Acad. of Sciences; legal research; 92 mems; library of 43,000 vols; Dir Prof. ANDRZEJ WASILKOWSKI; periodical publs *Państwo i Prawo* (monthly), *Droit Polonais Contemporain* (quarterly, in French), *Studia Prawnicze* (quarterly), *Orzecznictwo sądów polskich* (monthly), *Prawo rolne* (quarterly), *Archiwum Kryminologii* (irregular), *Polish Yearbook of International Law* (in English), *Polska Bibliografia Prawnicza* (yearbook).

Instytut Organizacji i Zarządzania w Przemyśle 'ORGMASZ' (Institute of Organization and Management in Industry): 00-879 Warsaw, ul. Żelazna 87; tel. 24-92-65; telex 813747; fax 20-43-60; f. 1953; library of 10,000 vols, special collections; Dir Prof. WIESŁAW M. GRUDZEWSKI; publ. *Ekonomika i Organizacja Przedsiębiorstwa* (monthly).

Instytut Pracy i Spraw Socjalnych (Institute of Labour and Social Studies): 00-389 Warsaw, Smulikowskiego 4A; tel. (22) 827-77-97; fax (22) 828-52-87; f. 1963; research into labour, wages, income distribution, living standards, social security and social insurance, labour law; Dir STANISŁAWA BORKOWSKA; publs *Studia i Materiały* (continuous), *Materiały z Zagranicy* (irregular), *Polityka Społeczna* (Social Policy, monthly), *Raport IPiSS* (irregular).

Instytut Rynku Wewnętrznego i Konsumpcji (Institute of Home Market and Consumption): 00-950 Warsaw, Pl. Trzech Krzyży 16; tel. 28-77-22; telex 817643; f. 1950; 135 mems; library of *c.* 40,000 vols; Dir MARIAN STRUŻYCKI; publs *Monografie i Syntezy* (series), *Materiały Informacyjno-Szkolebiowe* (series), *Rocznik IRWIK* (series), *Przedsiębiorstwo i Rynek* (quarterly), *Biuletyn Informacyjny COINTE* (every 2 months), *Przegląd Dokumentacyjny* (quarterly), *Bieżąca informacja o publikacjach z zakresu rynku w kraju i na świecie* (monthly).

Instytut Studiow Politycznych PAN (Institute of Political Studies): 00-625 Warsaw, ul. Polna 18/20; tel. 25-52-21; fax 25-21-46; f. 1990 to develop theoretical work and empirical studies of post-communist societies; attached to Polish Acad. of Sciences; library of 9,000 vols; Dir Prof. WOJCIECH ROSZKOWSKI; publs. *Culture and Society, Political Studies, Polis* (all quarterly), *Archive of Political Thought* (annually), *Politicus* (newsletter), *Polish Archive of Sociological Research* (bulletin).

Instytut Turystyki (Institute of Tourism): 02-511 Warsaw, ul. Merliniego 9A; tel. (22) 844-63-47; fax (22) 844-12-63; f. 1972; social, economic and spatial aspects of tourism, professional training and provision of information; library of 19,300 vols, 2,880 periodicals, special collections of 8,800 vols; Dir Dr KRZYSZTOF ŁOPACIŃSKI; publs *Problems of Tourism* (annually), *Problemy Turystyki* (4 a year).

Instytut Wymiaru Sprawiedliwosci (Institute of Justice): 00-950 Warsaw, Krakowskie Przedmiescie 25; tel. (22) 826-03-63; fax (22) 826-24-01; f. 1974; re-organized 1990; research into social pathology phenomena, and into the functioning of the law, of the system of justice and of the prison system in Poland; civil and commercial law; library of 5,500 vols; Dir ANDRZEJ SIEMASZKO.

Instytut Zachodni (Institute for Western Affairs): 61-772 Poznań, Stary Rynek 78/79; tel. (61) 852-76-91; fax (61) 852-49-05; f. 1945; for the study of Polish–German relations up to the acquisition of Polish western territories, and from 1945 to present day, and of Western European economic, political, historical, juridical, social and cultural matters; library of 89,000 vols; Dir Prof. Dr ANNA WOLFF-POWĘSKA; publ. *Przegląd Zachodni* (quarterly).

Państwowy Instytut Naukowy – Instytut Śląski w Opolu (Government Research Institute – Silesian Institute in Opole): 45-082 Opole, ul. Piastowska 17; tel. and fax 53-60-32; f. 1957; departments: Historical and German–Polish Relationships Research, Regional Research; library of 72,000 vols (19th–20th-century history, contemporary history, social economics, Silesiana); Dir Prof. Dr WIESŁAW LESIUK; publs *Studia Śląskie* (annually), *Śląsk Opolski* (quarterly), *Zeszyty Odrzańskie* (annually), *Region and Regionalism* (in English, irregular).

Polski Instytut Spraw Międzynarodowych (Polish Institute of International Affairs): 00-950 Warsaw, ul. Warecka 1a; tel. 26-30-21; fax 27-24-54; f. 1947; international relations after World War II; library of 125,000 vols; Dir Prof. ANTONI Z. KAMIŃSKI; publs *Zbiór Dokumentów* (quarterly, in various languages), *Sprawy Międzynarodowe* (quarterly).

Śląski Instytut Naukowy w Katowicach (Silesian Scientific Institute): 40-956 Katowice, ul. Graniczna 32; tel. 156-5873; f. 1957; regional history, sociology, economics, culture and international relations in Central Europe; social politics; territorial self-government and civil service; Dir Prof. Dr hab. WOJCIECH ŚWIĄTKIEWICZ; publs *Zaranie Śląskie* (quarterly), series: *Studia i Materiały z dziejów Śląska, Studia nad ekonomiką regionu, Górnośląskie Studia Socjologiczne, Bibliografia Śląska, Śląski Słownik Biograficzny, Kwestie Społeczne regionu wysoko uprzemysłowionego.*

EDUCATION

Centrum Badań Polityki Naukowej i Szkolnictwa Wyższego (Centre for Science Policy and Higher Education): 00-046 Warsaw, ul. Nowy Świat 69; tel. and fax (22) 26-07-46; f. 1973; planning and forecasting development of higher education; modernization of instruction and organization of higher education; Dir IRENEUSZ BIAŁECKI; publ. *Nauka i Szkolnictwo Wyższe* (Science and Higher Education, 2 a year).

Instytut Badań Edukacyjnych (Institute for Educational Research): 01-180 Warsaw, ul. Górczewska 8; tel. 632-18-69; fax 632-18-95; f. 1950; library of 100,000 vols; depts of fundamental research, vocational education, educational information; Dir Prof. Dr STEFAN KWIATKOWSKI; publ. *Edukacja* (quarterly).

Instytut Kształcenia Zawodowego (Institute of Vocational Education): 00-561 Warsaw, ul. Mokotowska 16/20; tel. 285-661; f. 1972; 113 staff; library of 18,000 vols; Dir STANISŁAW KACZOR; publs *Pedagogika Pracy* (annually), *Biblioteka Kształcenia Zawodowego, Szkoła-Zawód-Praca* (annually).

FINE AND PERFORMING ARTS

Instytut Sztuki PAN (Institute of Art): 00-950 Warsaw, ul. Długa 28, POB 994; tel. (22) 831-31-49; f. 1949; attached to Polish Acad. of Sciences; fine arts, music, theatre, film; photographic archive of 450,000 negatives; 125 mems; library of 140,000 vols, phonograph archive of 16,000 tapes; Dir Prof. Dr STANISŁAW MOSSAKOWSKI; Joint Dir Doc. LECH SOKÓŁ; publs *Biuletyn Historii Sztuki, Konteksty. Polska Sztuka Ludowa, Pamiętnik Teatralny, Muzyka, Kwartalnik Filmowy* (all quarterly).

HISTORY, GEOGRAPHY AND ARCHAEOLOGY

Instytut Archeologii i Etnologii PAN (Institute of Archaeology and Ethnology): 00-140 Warsaw, Al. Solidarności 105; tel. (22) 620-28-81; fax (22) 624-01-00; e-mail director@iaepan.edu.pl; f. 1953, formerly Institute of History of Material Culture; attached to Polish Acad. of Sciences; prehistoric, classical, early medieval and industrial archaeology, medieval and contemporary history of material culture, ethnography, ethnology; 293 mems; library of 175,000 vols; Dir Prof. ROMUALD SCHILD; publs *Archaeologia Polona, Archaeology of Poland, Archaeology, Polish Archaeological Researches, Archaeological Reports, Archaeological Review, Inventaria Archaeolo-*

gica, Archaeologia Urbium, Polish Archaeological Abstracts, Ethnologia Polona, Bibliotheca Antiqua, Quarterly Journal of the History of Material Culture, Studies and Materials of the History of Material Culture, Library of Polish Ethnography, Polish Ethnographic Atlas, Polish Ethnography, Culture of Early Medieval Europe, Studia Ethnica.

Instytut Geodezji i Kartografii (Institute of Geodesy and Cartography): 00-950 Warsaw, ul. Jasna 2/4; tel. 27-03-28; Dir ADAM LINSENBARTH; publs *Prace IGIK* (2-3 a year), *Rocznik Astronomiczny* (annually), *Biuletyn IGIK* (every 2 months), *Biuletyn Informacyjny Branżowego Ośrodka Informacji Naukowej, Technicznej i Ekonomicznej Geodezji i Kartografii* (quarterly).

Instytut Geografii i Przestrzennego Zagospodarowania PAN (Institute of Geography and Spatial Organization): 00-818 Warsaw, ul. Twarda 51/55; tel. (22) 697-88-41; fax (22) 620-62-21; e-mail igipz@twarda.pan.pl; f. 1953; attached to Polish Acad. of Sciences; geomorphology, hydrology, climatology, geoecology, economic geography, urban and population studies, geography of agriculture and rural areas, global development, political geography, regional planning, environmental management, ecodevelopment, European studies, cartography, geographic information systems; library of 125,000 vols, 47,000 vols of periodicals, 4,000 atlases, 103,000 maps; Dir Prof. Dr PIOTR KORCELLI; publs *Przegląd Geograficzny* (quarterly), *Prace Geograficzne, Bibliografia Geografii Polskiej, Dokumentacja Geograficzna, Zeszyty IG i PZ PAN, Geographia Polonica.*

Instytut Historii im. Tadeusza Manteuffla PAN (Institute of History): 00-272 Warsaw, Rynek Starego Miasta 29/31; tel. and fax (22) 831-36-42; e-mail ihpandr@warman.com.pl; f. 1953; attached to Polish Acad. of Sciences; study of political and social history; specific fields of research: Poland and Central-Eastern Europe; origins and history of modern Poland, history of Polish culture; social changes in post-World War II Poland; library of 48,000 vols; Dir Prof. STANISLAW BYLINA; publs *Kwartalnik Historyczny* (quarterly), *Dzieje Najnowsze* (quarterly), *Odrodzenie i Reformacja w Polsce* (annually), *Studia Zródłoznawcze* (annually), *Acta Poloniae Historica* (2 a year in foreign languages), *Czasopismo Prawno-Historyczne* (2 a year), *Studia z Dziejów ZSRR i Europy Srodkowej* (annually).

Zakład Archeologii Śródziemnomorskiej PAN (Research Centre for Mediterranean Archaeology): 00-330 Warsaw, Nowy Swiat 72, Pałac Staszica (room 33); tel. and fax (22) 826-65-60; f. 1956; attached to Polish Acad. of Sciences; study, documentation and publication of results of Polish excavations in the Middle East, publication of ancient objects in Polish museums, Nubian studies; library of 8,000 vols; Dir Prof. Dr KAROL MYŚLIWIEC; publs Scientific Series: *Palmyre, Nubia, Corpus Signorum Imperii Romani, Corpus Vasorum Antiquorum, Deir el-Bahari, Travaux du Centre d'Archéologie Méditerranéenne, Alexandrie, Nea Paphos, Etudes et Travaux.*

LANGUAGE AND LITERATURE

Instytut Badań Literackich PAN (Institute of Literary Research): 00-330 Warsaw, Nowy Świat 72, Pałac Staszica; tel. (22) 826-99-45; f. 1948; attached to Polish Acad. of Sciences; 20 scientific departments, and sections in Poznań, Toruń and Wrocław; research in the theory of literature, history of Polish literature, and sociology of literature; library of 450,000 vols, special collections: 85,000; Dir Prof. ELŻBIETA SARNOWSKA-TEMERIUSZ; publs *Pamiętnik Literacki* (Literary Journal, quarterly), *Teksty Drugie* (Texts, every 2 months).

Instytut Języka Polskiego PAN (Polish Language Institute): 31-113 Cracow, ul. Straszewskiego 27; tel. and fax 22-59-29; f. 1973; attached to Polish Acad. of Sciences; library of 20,000 vols; Dir KAZIMIERZ RYMUT; publs *Polonica* (annually), *Prace* (series), *Słownik gwar polskich* (annually), *Słownik staropolski, Atlas gwar mazowieckich* (continuous), *Studia gramatyczne* (series), *Studia leksykograficzne* (series).

MEDICINE

Centrum Naukowe Medycyny Kolejowej (Centre of Science and Research in Railway Medicine): 00-973 Warsaw, POB 214, ul. Grójecka 17A; tel. and fax 22-53-97; f. 1960; research in railway and traffic medicine; library of 33,000 vols; Dir Dr JACEK A. PIĄTKIEWICZ; publ. *Lekarz Kolejowy* (2 a year).

Centrum Onkologii, Instytut im. Marii Skłodowskiej-Curie (Marie Sklodowska-Curie Memorial Cancer Centre and Institute of Oncology): 02-781 Warsaw, ul. W. K. Roentgena 5; tel. (22) 644-02-00; telex 812704; fax (22) 644-02-08; f. 1932; brs at Cracow and Gliwice; fundamental cancer research, clinical research, diagnosis and treatment, epidemiology; co-ordinates Nat. Cancer Programme; 247 scientific staff; library of 23,458 vols; Dir Prof. ANDRZEJ KUŁAKOWSKI; publ. *Nowotwory* (quarterly).

Instytut Biocybernetyki i Inżynierii Biomedycznej PAN (Institute of Biocybernetics and Biomedical Engineering): 02-109 Warsaw, ul. Trojdena 4; tel. 659-91-43; fax 659-70-30; f. 1975; attached to Polish Acad. of Sciences; library of 23,000 vols; collaborates with WHO; mem. of UNESCO Global Network for Molecular and Cell Biology; field of activities: biomeasurements, artificial internal organs, mathematical and physical modelling of physiological systems and processes, computerized image analysis; Dir Prof. ANDRZEJ WERYŃSKI; publs *Biocybernetics and Biomedical Engineering* (quarterly), *Prace IBiIB PAN.*

Attached centre:

Miedzynarodowe Centrum Biocybernetyki (International Biocybernetics Centre): 02-109 Warsaw, ul. Trojdena 4; tel. 6599143; fax 6582872; f. 1988; attached to Polish Acad. of Sciences; collaborating centre with WHO for research and training in biocybernetics and biomedical engineering; organizes five seminars a year; Dir Prof. MACIEJ NAŁECZ; publ. lecture notes.

Instytut-Centrum Medycyny Doświadczalnej i Klinicznej PAN (Medical Research Centre): 02-106 Warsaw, ul. Pawińskiego 5; fax (22) 668-55-32; e-mail ja@ibbrain.ibb.waw.pl; f. 1967; attached to Polish Acad. of Sciences; consisting of Departments of Neurosurgery, Surgical Research and Transplantology, Endocrinology, Neurophysiology, Neuropathology, Developmental Neuropathology, Neurochemistry, Applied Physiology, Neurotoxicology, Cellular Signalling, Neuromuscular Unit, Neuroimmunological Unit, Outpatient Cardiac Unit for Diagnosis and Therapy; Laboratories; Cardiovascular, Ultrastructure of the Nervous System, Neuropeptides, Renal and Body Fluids Physiology, Experimental Pharmacology, Scientific Instruments—MEDIPAN; library of 11,000 vols, 164 periodicals; Dir Prof. Dr MIROSŁAW J. MOSSAKOWSKI; publs *Report on Scientific Activities* (1 a year), *Folia Neuropathologica* (4 a year).

Instytut Farmaceutyczny (Pharmaceutical Research Institute): 01-793 Warsaw, ul. Rydygiera 8; tel. and fax 633-82-96; telex 825176; chemistry, analytical chemistry, pharmacology, technology; information, statistical and extension services, breeding of laboratory animals; library of 12,200 vols, 350 periodical titles; Dir Dr WIESŁAW SZELEJEWSKI.

Instytut Farmakologii PAN (Institute of Pharmacology): 31-343 Cracow, ul. Smętna 12; tel. (12) 637-40-22; fax (12) 637-45-00; e-mail wypchal@if-pan.krakow.pl; f. 1954; attached to Polish Acad. of Sciences; pharmacology, neuropsychopharmacology (behavioural, biochemical, electrophysiological, pharmacokinetic and histochemical research), synthesis of new drugs, pharmacology of steroid hormones, acclimatization of medicinal plants, their phytochemical and pharmacological investigation; library of 11,000 vols, 14,000 periodicals; Dir Prof. Dr hab. EDMUND PRZEGALIŃSKI; publ. *Polish Journal of Pharmacology* (every 2 months).

Instytut Gruźlicy i Chorób Płuc (Tuberculosis and Pulmonary Diseases Institute): 01-138 Warsaw, ul. Płocka 26; tel. (22) 691-21-00; f. 1948; chest diseases, including tuberculosis, lung cancer, heart disease, etc.; medical library of 33,000 vols; Dir Prof. Dr hab. med. KAZIMIERZ ROSZKOWSKI-ŚLIŻ; publ. *Pneumonologia i Alergologia Polska* (6 a year).

Instytut Hematologii i Transfuzjologii (Institute of Haematology and Blood Transfusion): 00-957 Warsaw, ul. Chocimska 5; tel. 49-85-07; telex 815463; fax 48-89-70; Dir Prof. ROMUALD SCHARF; publs *Acta Haematologica Polonica* (quarterly), *Sprawozdania Roczne z Działalności Instytutu* (annually).

Instytut Immunologii i Terapii Doświadczalnej im. Ludwika Hirszfelda PAN (L. Hirszfeld Institute of Immunology and Experimental Therapy): 53-114 Wrocław, ul. Rudolfa Weigla 12; tel. (71) 73-22-74; fax (71) 67-91-11; f. 1952; attached to Polish Acad. of Sciences; research work in basic and clinical immunology, microbiology, immunochemistry, immunogenetics, experimental and bacteriophage therapy; library of 24,000 vols; Dir Prof. Dr MARIAN MORDARSKI; publs *Archivum Immunologiae et Therapiae Experimentalis* (English, every 2 months), *Postępy Higieny i Medycyny Doświadczalnej* (Polish, every 2 months).

Instytut Kardiologii (National Institute of Cardiology): 04-628 Warsaw, ul. Alpejska 42; tel. (22) 815-30-11; fax (22) 815-25-24; f. 1980; library of 7,000 vols; Dir Prof. ZYGMUNT SADOWSKI.

Instytut Leków (Institute for Drug Research and Control): 00-725 Warsaw, ul. Chełmska 30/34; tel. 41-29-40; analytical, pharmacological and microbiological testing of drugs, including antibiotics, mutagenicity, detection of abuse-causing drugs, etc.; Dir Prof. ALEKSANDER P. MAZUREK; publs *Biuletyn Informacyjny Instytutu Leków* (irregular), *Biuletyn Leków* (quarterly).

Instytut Matki i Dziecka (Mother and Child Research Institute): 01-211 Warsaw, ul. Kasprzaka 17A; tel. (22) 632-34-51; fax (22) 632-68-58; f. 1948; research into the physiology and medicine of reproduction; Dir Prof. JANUSZ SZYMBORSKI; publ. *Development Period Medicine* (4 a year).

Instytut Medycyny Morskiej i Tropikalnej (Institute of Maritime and Tropical Medicine): 81-519 Gdynia, ul. Powstania Styczniowego 9B; tel. (58) 622-33-54; fax (58) 622-33-54; research in maritime occupational health, tropical medicine and epidemiology, toxicology, microbiology, travel medicine; clinic; postgraduate courses; 340 staff; Dir Dr W. RENKE ; publs *Bulletin of the Institute of Maritime and Tropical Medicine in Gdynia, Biuletyn Metodyczno-Organizacyjny IMMIT w Gdyni, Maritime Occupational Health Newsletter* (all quarterly).

Instytut Mędycyny Pracy i Zdrowia Środowiskowego (Institute of Occupational Medicine and Environmental Health): 41-200 Sosnowiec, ul. Kościelna 13; tel. (32) 66-08-85; fax (32) 66-11-24; f. 1950; occupational toxicology; Dir JERZY A. SOKAL.

Instytut Medycyny Pracy im. prof. dra med. Jerzego Nofera (Nofer Institute of Occupational Medicine): 90-950 Łódź, ul. Św. Teresy 8, POB 199; tel. (42) 55-25-05; telex 885360; fax (42) 34-83-31; f. 1952; research in occupational medicine and hygiene, physiology, psychology, toxicology, neurotoxicology, carcinogenesis, pathology and epidemiology, management of occupational health service, radiation protection and the diagnosis and treatment of occupational diseases and acute poisonings, scientific information; Dir Prof. JANUSZ A. INDULSKI; publs *Medycyna Pracy* (every 2 months), *International Journal of Occupational Medicine and Environmental Health* (in English, 6 a year), *Studia i Materiały Monograficzne* (irregular), *Przeglad Bibliograficzno-Dokumentacyjny, Medycyna Pracy* (2 a year), *Substancje Rakotwórcze w Srodowisku Pracy* (irregular), scripts, postgraduate teaching materials and information bulletins.

Instytut Medycyny Uzdrowiskowej (National Research Institute of Health Resort Medicine): 60-569 Poznań, ul. Szamarzewskiego 84; tel. 411-547; f. 1952; balneology, climatology, physical medicine and rehabilitation; Dir Prof. Dr med. hab. GERARD STRABURZYŃSKI; publ. *Balneologia Polska* (annually).

Instytut Medycyny Wsi im. Witolda Chodźki (W. Chodźko Institute of Agricultural Medicine): 20-950 Lublin, POB 185, ul. Jaczewskiego 2; tel. (81) 747-80-27; fax (81) 747-86-46; f. 1951; environmental and agricultural medicine, family doctor training, health service organization in rural areas; library of 14,000 vols; Dir JERZY ZAGÓRSKI; publs *Medycyna Ogólna* (quarterly), *Sprawozdania z działalności Instytutu* (annually), *Annals of Agricultural and Environmental Medicine* (2 a year).

Instytut Psychiatrii i Neurologii (Institute of Psychiatry and Neurology): 02-957 Warsaw, Al. Sobieskiego 1/9; tel. 42-68-02; fax 642-53-75; f. 1951; library of 24,500 vols; Dir Prof. STANISŁAW PUŻYŃSKI; publs *Postępy Psychiatrii i Neurologii* (quarterly), *Farmakoterapia w Psychiatrii i Neurologii* (quarterly) *Alkoholizm i Narkomania* (quarterly).

Instytut Żywności i Żywienia (National Food and Nutrition Institute): 02-903 Warsaw, ul. Powsińska 61/63; tel. 42-21-71; fax 42-11-03; f. 1963; multidisciplinary scientific research in the field of human nutrition; 15,000 vols; Dir LUCJAN SZPONAR; publs *Zywienie Człowieka i Metabolizm* (4 a year), *Zywność, Zywienie a Zdrowie*† (4 a year).

Państwowy Zakład Higieny (National Institute of Hygiene): 00-791 Warsaw, ul. Chocimska 24; tel. 49-40-51; telex 816712; fax 49-74-84; f. 1918; 15 departments covering all aspects of epidemiology, bacteriology, virology, parasitology, vaccines and sera control, medical statistics, radiologic control and radiobiology, immunopathology, communal hygiene, foodstuffs, environmental toxicology, school hygiene, health education, biological contamination control; courses in public health; library of 45,000 vols; Dir-Gen. Prof. Dr hab. JANUSZ JELJASZEWICZ; publs *Roczniki Państwowego Zakładu Higieny* (4 a year), *Medycyna Doświadczalna i Mikrobiologia* (4 a year), *Przegląd Epidemiologiczny* (4 a year).

Zakład Amin Biogennych PAN (Department of Biogenic Amines): Tylna 3, 90-950 Łódz, POB 225; tel. 81-70-07; fax 815283; f. 1958; attached to Polish Acad. of Sciences; research into metabolic and allergic diseases; role of biogenic amines, polyamines and respective enzymes in fast growing tissue; the visual system; mast cells development, differentiation and functions; library of 7,000 vols; Dir Prof. Dr JANINA WYCZÓŁKOWSKA.

Zakład Genetyki Człowieka PAN (Institute of Human Genetics): 60-479 Poznań, ul. Strzeszyńska 32; tel. (61) 823-30-11; fax (61) 823-32-35; f. 1974; attached to Polish Acad. of Sciences; Dir Prof. Dr JERZY NOWAK.

NATURAL SCIENCES

General

Instytut Historii Nauki PAN (Institute for the History of Science): 00-330 Warsaw, Pałac Staszica, Nowy Świat 72; tel. (22) 826-87-54; fax (22) 826-61-37; e-mail ihn@ihnpan.waw.pl; f. 1954; attached to Polish Acad. of Sciences; library of 20,000 vols; Dir Prof. ANDRZEJ ŚRÓDKA; publs *Kwartalnik Historii Nauki i Techniki* (quarterly), *Monografie z dziejów nauki i techniki, Źródła do dziejów nauki i techniki, Organon* (annually in French, English and Russian), *Monografie z Dziejów Oświaty, Archiwum Dziejów Oświaty, Analecta*.

Instytut Oceanologii PAN (Institute of Oceanology): 81-712 Sopot, ul. Powstańców Warszawy 55, POB 68; tel. (58) 551-72-81; fax (58) 551-21-30; e-mail office@iopan.gda.pl; f. 1976; attached to Polish Acad. of Sciences; marine physics, hydrodynamics, marine chemistry, marine ecology; library of 7,000 vols, 240 periodicals; Dir Prof. Dr hab. JERZY DERA; publ. *Oceanologia* (4 a year, in English).

Biological Sciences

Instytut Biochemii i Biofizyki PAN (Institute of Biochemistry and Biophysics): 02-106 Warsaw, ul. Pawińskiego 5A; tel. 658-47-24; fax 658-46-36; f. 1954; attached to Polish Acad. of Sciences; research work in the fields of nucleic acids (structure, function, metabolism, mutagenesis, repair), protein biosynthesis, regulation of gene function, structure of plant viruses and the structure of genes and chromosomes; 65 graduate students; library of 7,280 vols and 201 periodicals; Dir Prof. WŁODZIMIERZ ZAGÓRSKI-OSTOJA; publ. *Acta Biochim. Polon.*

Instytut Biologii Doświadczalnej im M. Nenckiego PAN (M. Nencki Institute of Experimental Biology): 02-093 Warsaw, ul. Pasteura 3; tel. 659-85-71; fax 22-53-42; e-mail sekr@nencki.gov.pl; f. 1918; attached to Polish Acad. of Sciences; scientific research work in the fields of biochemistry, cell biology, molecular biology, neurophysiology and experimental psychology; library of 65,000 vols; Dir Prof. MACIEJ NAŁĘCZ; publs *Acta Neurobiologiae Experimentalis* (quarterly), *Acta Protozoologica* (quarterly).

Instytut Botaniki im. Władysława Szafera PAN (W. Szafer Institute of Botany: 31-512 Cracow, Lubicz 46; tel. (12) 421-51-44; fax (12) 421-97-90; f. 1954; attached to Polish Acad. of Sciences; library of 164,000 vols; Dir Prof. Dr LEON STUCHLIK; publs *Fragmenta Floristica et Geobotanica, Fragmenta Floristica et Geobotanica (Series Polonica), Acta Palaeobotanica.*

Instytut Chemii Bioorganicznej PAN (Institute of Bio-organic Chemistry): 61-704 Poznań, ul. Noskowskiego 12/14; tel. 52-89-19; telex 413600; fax 52-05-32; f. 1980; attached to Polish Acad. of Sciences; bio-organic chemistry, crystallochemistry of nucleic acids, proteins and their components; molecular biology, genetics and genetic engineering of plants; applied phytochemistry; library of 2,167 vols; Dir Prof. ANDRZEJ B. LEGOCKI.

Instytut Dendrologii PAN (Institute of Dendrology): 62-035 Kórnik, nr. Poznan, ul. Parkowa 5; tel. (61) 817-00-33; fax (61) 817-01-66; e-mail idkornik@rose.man.poznan.pl; f. 1952; attached to Polish Acad. of Sciences; dendrology, acclimatization, systematics and geography of woody plants, tree genetics, tree physiology, seed physiology, tree resistance to pathogens, frost and pollution; *c.* 40 scientists; library of 40,000 vols; Dir Prof. Dr TADEUSZ PRZYBYLSKI; publs *Arboretum Kórnickie* (annually), *Chorology of Trees and Shrubs in South-West Asia and Adjacent Regions, Monographs on Forest Trees* (both irregular).

Instytut Ekologii PAN (Institute of Ecology): 05-092 Łomianki, Dziekanów Leśny, Ul. M. Konopnickiej 1; tel. (22) 751-30-46; fax (22) 751-31-00; e-mail ekolog@warman.com.pl; f. 1952; attached to Polish Acad. of Sciences; population and community studies, landscape ecology, ecological bioenergetics, biogeochemistry, agroecology, human ecology, polar research, hydrobiology, plant ecology, soil ecology, vertebrate ecology, modelling of ecological processes; library of 75,000 vols; Dir Prof. Dr LESZEK GRÜM; publs *Ekologia Polska* (Polish Journal of Ecology, original papers in English, quarterly), *Polish Ecological Studies* (monographs and syntheses in English, quarterly), *Wladomości Ekologiczne* (with English summary), *International Studies on Sparrows* (original papers, in English, 2 a year), *Studies in Human Ecology* (original papers in English, irregular).

Instytut Ekologii Terenów Uprzemysłowionych (Institute for the Ecology of Industrial Areas): 40-833 Katowice, Ul. Kossutha 6; tel. (32) 254-60-31; fax (32) 254-17-17; f. 1992; Dir Dr EWA MARCHWINSKA.

Instytut Ochrony Przyrody PAN (Institute of Nature Conservation): 31-512 Cracow, ul. Lubicz 46; tel. and fax 21-03-48; f. 1920; attached to Polish Acad. of Sciences; research work on all problems relating to nature conservation; library of 34,538 vols and 1,487 periodicals; Dir Prof. Dr ZYGMUNT DENISIUK; publs *Ochrona Przyrody* (Protection of Nature, 1 a year), *Studia Naturae, Chrońmy Przyrodą Ojczystą* (Let Us Protect the Nature of our Homeland, every 2 months).

Instytut Paleobiologii im. Romana Kozłowskiego PAN (Institute of Palaeobiology): 00-818 Warsaw, Twarda 51/55; tel. (22) 697-88-50; fax (22) 620-62-25; e-mail paleo@twarda.pan.pl; f. 1952; attached to Polish Acad. of Sciences; Dir Prof. HUBERT SZANIAWSKI; publs *Palaeontologia Polonica, Acta Palaeontologica Polonica.*

Instytut Parazytologii im Witolda Stefańskiego PAN (W. Stefański Institute of Parasitology): 00-818 Warsaw, ul. Twarda 51/55; f. 1952; attached to Polish Acad. of Sciences; scientific research work in parasitology, including animal parasitism, its origin, prevalence, manifestations and effects in natural and experimental parasite-host systems; departments of biodiversity, molecular biology, epizootiology and pathology, and deer farming; documentation centre and library of 27,600 vols; Dir Prof. Dr ANDRZEJ MALCZEWSKI; publs *Acta Parasitologica* (quarterly), *Polska Bibliografia Parazytologiczna* (Polish Bibliography of Parasitology, annually).

Instytut Systematyki i Ewolucji Zwierząt PAN (Institute of Systematics and Evolution of Animals): 31-016 Cracow, ul. Sławkowska 17; tel. 22-19-01; telex 0322414; fax 22-27-91; f. 1865; attached to Polish Acad. of Sciences; library of 85,000 vols; Dir Prof. JÓZEF RAZOWSKI; publs *Folia Biologica* (quarterly), *Acta Zoologica Cracoviensia* (annually), *Monografie Fauny Polski* (irregular).

Zakład Badania Ssaków PAN (Mammal Research Institute): 17-230 Białowieża, woj. Białystok, ul. Gen. Waszkiewicza 1; tel. 12-278; telex 853491; fax 12-289; f. 1954;

attached to Polish Acad. of Sciences; scientific research in biomorphology, ecology, ecophysiology, taxonomy and fauna of mammals; collection of 177,000 specimens; library of 31,000 vols; Dir Prof. ZDZISŁAW PUCEK; publ. *Acta Theriologica* (quarterly).

Zakład Biologii Wód im. Karola Starmacha PAN (Institute of Freshwater Biology): 31-016 Cracow, ul. Sławkowska 17; tel. (12) 421-50-82; fax (12) 422-21-15; e-mail office@zbw.pan.krakow.pl; f. 1952; attached to Polish Acad. of Sciences; study of the plant and animal communities in ponds, rivers and dam reservoirs and productivity of these ecosystems, hydrochemistry and fisheries; hydrobiological station at Goczałkowice; biological fisheries station at Brzączowice; library of 29,000 vols and 1,520 periodicals; Dir Prof. Dr JANUSZ STARMACH; publ. *Acta Hydrobiologica*.

Mathematical Sciences

Instytut Matematyczny PAN (Institute of Mathematics): 00-950 Warsaw, ul. Śniadeckich 8, POB 137; tel. (22) 629-66-92; fax (22) 629-39-97; f. 1948; attached to Polish Acad. of Sciences; promotion of mathematical knowledge and application; local brs in Cracow, Gdańsk, Katowice, Łódź, Poznań, Toruń and Wrocław; approx. 100 mems; library of 126,000 vols; Dir BOGDAN BOJARSKI; publs *Colloquium Mathematicum, Acta Arithmetica, Fundamenta Mathematicae, Studia Mathematica, Annales Polonici Mathematici, Dissertationes Mathematicae, Applicationes Mathematicae*.

Attached centre:

Międzynarodowe Centrum Matematyczne im. Stefana Banacha (Stefan Banach International Mathematical Centre): 00-950 Warsaw, ul. Mokotowska 25, POB 137; tel. (22) 629-52-21; branch of the Institute of Mathematics; f. 1972 by an agreement of Academies of East European countries; promotion of international co-operation in mathematics through organizing research-and-training semesters, workshops, conferences and symposia in different fields of maths; no permanent staff; Dir BOGDAN BOJARSKI; publ. *Banach Centre Publications*.

Physical Sciences

Centrum Astronomiczne im. Mikołaja Kopernika PAN (Copernicus Astronomical Centre): 00-716 Warsaw, ul. Bartycka 18; tel. 41-10-86; fax 41-00-46; telex 813978; f. 1957; attached to Polish Acad. of Sciences; 48 staff; library of 20,000 vols; Dir Prof. Dr JÓZEF SMAK; publ. *Acta Astronomica* (quarterly).

Centrum Badań Kosmicznych PAN (Space Research Centre): 00-716 Warsaw, ul. Bartycka 18A; tel. 40-37-66; telex 815670; fax 40-31-31; f. 1977; attached to Polish Acad. of Sciences; space physics, planetary geodesy, remote sensing; library of 9,000 vols; Dir Prof. ZBIGNIEW KŁOS; publ. *Artificial Satellites – Journal of Planetary Geodesy* (quarterly).

Centrum Badań Wysokociśnieniowych PAN (High Pressure Research Centre): 01-142 Warsaw, ul. Sokołowska 29/37; tel. (22) 632-50-10; fax (22) 632-42-18; f. 1972; attached to Polish Acad. of Sciences; effects of high pressure on metals and semiconductors, high pressure metal formation and crystal growth, cold isostatic pressing, hot isostatic pressing and sintering; manufacture of high pressure laboratory equipment; Dir Prof. SYLWESTER POROWSKI.

Centrum Chemii Polimerów PAN (Centre of Polymer Chemistry): 41-800 Zabrze, Marie Curie-Skłodowskiej 34; tel. (32) 271-60-77; fax (32) 271-29-69; e-mail polymer@usctoux1.cto.us.edu.pl; f. 1969; attached to Polish Acad. of Sciences; divisions of polymer chemistry (3 laboratories) and polymer physical chemistry (3 laboratories); library of 17,000 vols; Dir Dr DANUTA SĘK.

Centrum Fizyki Teoretycznej PAN (Centre for Theoretical Physics): 02-668 Warsaw, Al. Lotników 32/46; tel. (22) 847-09-20; fax (22) 843-13-69; f. 1980; attached to Polish Acad. of Sciences; classical and quantum field theory, general relativity, statistical physics, quantum optics; 12 staff; Dir Prof. IWO BIAŁYNICKI-BIRULA.

Instytut-Centrum Badań Molekularnych i Makromolekularnych PAN (Centre for Molecular and Macromolecular Studies): 90-363 Łódź, ul. Sienkiewicza 112; tel. 81-58-32; telex 886742; fax 847126; f. 1972; attached to Polish Acad. of Sciences; hetero-organic chemistry, organic chemistry of sulphur, bio-organic chemistry, polymer physics, polymer chemistry, hetero-organic polymers, instrumental and elemental analysis; library of over 10,000 vols; Dir Prof. Dr MARIAN MIKOŁAJCZYK.

Instytut Chemii Fizycznej PAN (Institute of Physical Chemistry): 01-224 Warsaw, Kasprzaka 44/52; tel. (22) 632-73-43; fax (22) 632-52-76; f. 1955; attached to Polish Acad. of Sciences; research work in physico-chemical fundamentals including chemical engineering and chemical technology as follows: physical chemistry of metal-hydrogen systems including surface science and heterogeneous catalysis, analytical physical chemistry and instrumentation, experimental thermodynamics of organic mixtures, spectroscopy, including special-purpose apparatus, calorimetry including special-purpose apparatus and instrumentation, theory of chemical kinetics, electrochemistry and corrosion, fuel cells, molten salts, process kinetics, statistical mechanics and thermodynamics of irreversible phenomena; library of 73,230 vols; Dir Prof. Dr JANUSZ LIPKOWSKI.

Instytut Chemii Organicznej PAN (Institute of Organic Chemistry): 01-224 Warsaw, Kasprzaka 44; tel. 632-05-78; fax 632-66-81; f. 1954 as Research Centre for Organic Synthesis; became Institute 1964; attached to Polish Acad. of Sciences; research in synthetic organic chemistry and natural products chemistry; library of 19,648 vols; Dir Prof. Dr MIECZYSŁAW MĄKOSZA.

Instytut Fizyki Jądrowej im. Henryka Niewodniczanskiego (H. Niewodniczanski Institute of Nuclear Physics): 31-342 Cracow, ul. Radzikowskiego 152; tel. 37-02-22; fax 37-54-41; f. 1955; library of 19,000 vols and 7,500 periodicals; Dir Prof. Dr hab. ANDRZEJ BUDZANOWSKI; publs Reports (irregular).

Instytut Fizyki Molekularnej PAN (Institute of Molecular Physics): 60-179 Poznań, ul. Smoluchowskiego 17; tel. (61) 861-23-00; fax (61) 868-45-24; f. 1975; attached to Polish Acad. of Sciences; physics of magnetics and dielectrics, radiospectroscopy; library of 19,000 vols; Dir Prof. Dr hab. NARCYZ PIŚLEWSKI; publ. *Molecular Physics Reports* (quarterly).

Instytut Fizyki PAN (Institute of Physics): 02-668 Warsaw, Al. Lotników 32/46; tel. (22) 843-68-71; fax (22) 843-09-26; f. 1953; attached to Polish Acad. of Sciences; research in experimental physics, semiconductors, magnetics, superconductors, atomic and molecular physics, quantum optics, spectroscopy, x-ray crystallography, crystal growth; over 400 mems; library of 28,000 vols; Dir Prof. Dr H. SZYMCZAK; publs *Acta Physica Polonica* (monthly), *Proceedings of Conferences in Physics* (irregular), *Monographs in Physics* (irregular).

Instytut Fizyki Plazmy i Laserowej Mikrosyntezy im. Sylwestra Kaliskiego (S. Kaliski Institute of Plasma Physics and Laser Microfusion): 00-908 Warsaw 49, POB 49, ul. Hery 23; tel. (22) 638-14-60; fax (22) 666-83-72; e-mail office@ifpilm.waw.pl; f. 1975; library of 1,000 vols; Dir Dr ZYGMUNT SKŁADANOWSKI; publ. *Raporty IFPiLM*.

Instytut Geofizyki PAN (Institute of Geophysics): 01-452 Warsaw, ul. Księcia Janusza 64; tel. 36-44-40; telex 81-75-82; fax 37-05-22; f. 1953; attached to Polish Acad. of Sciences; seismology and physics of the Earth's interior, geomagnetism, physics of the atmosphere, hydrology and polar research; library of 32,000 vols; Dir Prof. Dr JERZY JANKOWSKI; publs *Acta Geophysica Polonica* (quarterly), *Publications* (irregular).

Instytut Katalizy i Fizykochemii Powierzchni PAN (Institute of Catalysis and Surface Chemistry): 30-239 Cracow, ul. Niezapominajek; tel. (12) 425-28-14; fax (12) 425-19-23; e-mail ncczerwe@cyf-kr.edu.pl; f. 1968; attached to Polish Acad. of Sciences; kinetics and mechanism of heterogeneous, homogeneous and enzymatic catalytic reactions, solid state chemistry, properties and dynamics of colloids, inter-facial phenomena, electrochemistry of interfaces; library of 9,000 vols; Dir Prof. Dr JERZY HABER.

Instytut Mechaniki Górotworu PAN (Strata Mechanics Research Institute): 30-059 Cracow, ul. Reymonta 27; tel. 37-62-00; fax 37-28-84; f. 1954; attached to Polish Acad. of Sciences; mechanics of granular media, rock deformation, gas and rock-mass outbursts, low-speed flow of fluids, dynamics of air flow, flow through porous media, micromeritics; library of 23,000 vols; Dir Prof. Dr WACŁAW TRUTWIN; publ. *Archives of Mining Sciences* (quarterly).

Instytut Nauk Geologicznych PAN (Institute of Geological Sciences): 00-818 Warsaw, Twarda 51/55; tel. and fax (22) 620-62-23; e-mail ingpan@twarda.pan.pl; f. 1956; attached to Polish Acad. of Sciences; stratigraphy, sedimentology, tectonics, petrography, mineralogy and isotope geochemistry, Quaternary geology, hydrogeology; library (in Warsaw and Cracow) of 42,700 books, 100,700 periodicals 11,030 maps; Dir Prof. ANDRZEJ PSZCZÓŁKOWSKI; publs *Studia Geologica Polonica* (irregular), *Geologia Sudetica* (irregular).

Instytut Niskich Temperatur i Badań Strukturalnych PAN (Institute of Low Temperature and Structure Research): 50-950 Wrocław 2, POB 937; tel. (71) 343-50-21; fax (71) 44-10-29; f. 1966; attached to Polish Acad. of Sciences; physics and chemistry of solids: electronic and crystallographic structure, low temperature phenomena, magnetism, superconductivity; library of 22,000 vols; Dir Prof. Dr JÓZEF SZNAJD; publ. *Physics and Chemistry of Solids* (quarterly).

Instytut Problemów Jądrowych im. Andrzeja Sołtana (A. Sołtan Institute for Nuclear Studies): 05-400 Otwock-Świerk; tel. (22) 7798948; fax (22) 7793481; e-mail sins@ipj.gov.pl; f. 1983, fmrly part of Institute of Nuclear Research; library of 27,000 vols; nuclear physics, elementary particle physics, plasma physics, accelerator physics and technology, material research using nuclear technology, spectrometric technology and nuclear electronics; Dir Prof. ZIEMOWID SUJKOWSKI; publs Reports.

Państwowy Instytut Geologiczny (Polish Geological Institute): 00-975 Warsaw, ul. Rakowiecka 4; tel. 49-53-51; telex 825541; fax 49-53-42; f. 1919, name changed 1987; geological, geophysical, hydrogeological and environmental research; eight brs; library of 104,000 vols, 27,000 bound periodicals, 430,000 maps and atlases, 315,000 geological documents; Dir Prof. STANISŁAW SPECZIK; publs *Biuletyn* (irregular), *Prace* (irregular), *Bibliografia Geologiczna Polski* (annually), *Kwart-*

alnik Geologiczny (quarterly), maps and atlases, occasional books and monographs.

Zakład Fizyki Ciała Stałego PAN (Solid State Physics Laboratory): 41-800 Zabrze, ul. Wandy 3; tel. (32) 271-34-24; fax (32) 271-06-58; e-mail zfcs@zfcs-pan.zabrze.pl; f. 1968; attached to Polish Acad. of Sciences; physics of semiconductors and of thin films; library of 4,000 vols; Dir Prof. JAN CISOWSKI.

Zakład Karbochemii PAN (Institute of Coal Chemistry): 44-102 Gliwice, ul. Sowińskiego 5; tel. (32) 38-07-91; fax (32) 31-28-31; e-mail inbox@gepard.karboch.gliwice.pl; f. 1954; attached to Polish Acad. of Sciences; research on structure, properties and reactivity of coals and studies on coal conversion methods; thermodynamics data banks, membrane separation processes; library of 5,000 vols; Dir Dr ANDRZEJ DWORAK.

PHILOSOPHY AND PSYCHOLOGY

Instytut Filozofii i Socjologii PAN (Institute of Philosophy and Sociology): 00-330 Warsaw, Pałac Staszica, Nowy Świat 72; fax (22) 826-99-48; e-mail inform@ifispan.waw.pl; f. 1956; attached to Polish Acad. of Sciences; library of 145,846 vols; Dir Prof. ANDRZEJ RYCHARD; publs *Studia Logica* (quarterly, in English), *Archiwum Historii Filozofii i Myśli Spolecznej, Przegląd Filozoficzny, Studia Mediewistyczne, Studia Socjologiczne, Mediaevalia Philosophica Polonorum, Prakseologia, Sisyphus, Etyka, ASK—Spoleczenstwo. Badanie. Metody, Sociological Review.*

Instytut Psychologii PAN (Institute of Psychology): 01-673 Warsaw, ul. Podleśna 61; tel. and fax (22) 34-09-07; e-mail jreykow@atos .psychpan.waw.pl; f. 1980; attached to Polish Acad. of Sciences; social psychology, personality, general psychology, psycholinguistics, cognitive and decision processes; library of 8,000 vols; Dir Prof. Dr hab. JANUSZ REYKOWSKI; publ. *Studia Psychologiczne* (2 a year).

RELIGION, SOCIOLOGY AND ANTHROPOLOGY

Zakład Antropologii PAN (Institute of Anthropology): 50-951 Wrocław, ul. Kuźnicza 35; tel. (71) 343-86-75; fax (71) 343-81-50; e-mail panantro@pwr.wroc.pl; f. 1952; attached to Polish Acad. of Sciences; biological aspects of social stratification, genetics of growth, developmental norms, craniology, morphology; library of 16,000 vols; Dir Prof. Dr hab. TADEUSZ BIELICKI.

Żydowski Instytut Historyczny w Polsce (Jewish Historical Institute in Poland): 00-090 Warsaw, ul. Tłomackie 3/5; tel. (22) 827-92-21; fax (22) 827-83-72; f. 1947; includes a museum of Jewish art and martyrology, archives; library of 60,000 vols, 600 MSS; Dir Prof. Dr FELIKS TYCH; publ. *Biuletyn* (quarterly, summary in English).

TECHNOLOGY

Centralny Instytut Ochrony Pracy (Central Institute for Labour Protection): 00-701 Warsaw, ul. Czerniakowska 16; tel. (22) 623-46-01; fax (22) 623-36-95; f. 1950; research into work safety and ergonomics, testing protective equipment, consulting, training, certification, standardization; library of 35,000 vols; Dir DANUTA KORADECKA; publs *Bezpieczeństwo Pracy* (monthly), *International Journal of Occupational Safety and Ergonomics* (in English, quarterly), *Katalog-informator Ochrony Osobiste* (annually), *Karty Charakterystyk Substancji Niebezpiecznych, Podstawy i Metody Oceny Środowiska Pracy, Działalność Centralnego Instytutu Ochrony Pracy* (annual report).

Główny Instytut Górnictwa (Central Mining Institute): 40-166 Katowice, Plac Gwarków 1; tel. 58-16-31; telex 0312359; fax 59-65-33; f. 1945; research work in rock mechanics, mining systems, blasting technique, gas, dust, water and rock burst hazards, clean coal technologies utilization and recovery of waste water, material engineering, noise and vibration control, environmental protection; 980 mems; library of 180,000 vols; Gen. Dir Eng. A. GRACZYŃSKI; publs *Prace* (Transactions, irregular, about 20 papers a year), *Annual Report* (in English and Russian), *Biuletyn Informacyjny.*

Instytut Automatyki Systemów Energetycznych (Institute of Power Systems Automation): 51-618 Wrocław, ul. Wystawowa 1; tel. (71) 48-42-21; telex 0712773; fax (71) 48-21-83; f. 1949; automatic control systems, computer systems and networks, database systems, data communication for Electric Power System operation, expert systems, exploitation and management; library of 21,000 vols; 5,400 vols of reports; Dir JAN BUJKO; publs *Prace IASE* (annually), *Biuletyn IASE* (2 a year in monthly *Energetyka* journal), *Informator Patentowy Energetyki* (4 a year).

Instytut Badań Systemowych PAN (Systems Research Institute): 01-447 Warsaw, ul. Newelska 6; tel. 36-44-14; fax 37-27-72; f. 1977; attached to Polish Acad. of Sciences; control and optimization theory and applications, methods of systems analysis; library of 44,000 vols; Dir Prof. Dr ROMAN KULIKOWSKI; publs *Control and Cybernetics* (quarterly), *Working Papers IBS PAN* (continuous), *Badania Systemowe* (series of monographs).

Instytut Badawczy Dróg i Mostów (Road and Bridge Research Institute): 03-301 Warsaw, ul. Jagiellońska 80; tel. (22) 811-03-83; Dir LESZEK RAFALSKI; publs *Prace Instytutu Badawczego Dróg i Mostów* (quarterly), *Nowości Zagranicznej Techniki Drogowej* (3-4 a year), *Studia i Materiały* (irregular).

Instytut Budownictwa Wodnego PAN (Institute of Hydroengineering): 80-953 Gdańsk, ul. Kościerska 7; tel. (58) 552-39-03; fax (58) 552-42-11; e-mail sekr@ibwpan .gda.pl; f. 1953; attached to Polish Acad. of Sciences; river, estuary and reservoir hydraulics, maritime hydraulics, soil mechanics and foundation engineering, environmental engineering; 100 mems; library of 24,000 vols; Dir Prof. PIOTR WILDE; publs *Archives of Hydroengineering and Environmental Mechanics* (quarterly), *Hydrotechnical Transactions* (irregular).

Instytut Chemicznej Przeróbki Węgla (Institute for Chemical Processing of Coal): 41-803 Zabrze, ul. Zamkowa 1; tel. (3) 171-51-52; telex 316548; fax (3) 171-08-09; f. 1955; application of coal as an energy carrier and chemical feedstock, environmental protection; library of 16,000 vols; Dir Dr MAREK ŚCIĄŻKO; publ. *Karbo-Energochemia-Ekologia* (monthly).

Instytut Chemii i Techniki Jądrowej (Institute of Nuclear Chemistry and Technology): 03-195 Warsaw, ul. Dorodna 16; tel. (22) 811-06-56; fax (22) 811-15-32; e-mail sekdyrn@orange.ichtj.waw.pl; f. 1955; library of 35,000 vols; Dir Dr LECH WALIŚ; publ. *Nukleonika* (4 a year), Annual Report.

Instytut Chemii Nieorganicznej (Institute of Inorganic Chemistry): 44-101 Gliwice, ul. Sowińskiego 11; tel. 31-30-51; telex 36132; f. 1948; 229 staff; library of 15,772 vols; Chief Manager Dr Eng. S. FOLEK; publ. *Bieżąca Informacja Chemiczna seria—NIEORGANIKA* (Bibliography selected from current papers, monthly).

Instytut Chemii Przemysłowej (Industrial Chemistry Research Institute): 01-793 Warsaw, Rydygiera 8; tel. (22) 633-93-34; fax (22) 633-82-95; e-mail ichp@aquila .ichp.waw.pl; f. 1922; research into carbo- and petrochemistry, organic synthesis, polymer and plastics technology, industrial catalysis, household chemistry products and disinfectants, environmental impact technology, process safety, chemical process engineering, instrumental analysis, medical diagnostic tests, biotechnology; Bureau for Ozone Layer Protection; Nat. Centre for Ecological Management in the Chemical Industry; library of 101,730 vols, 1,637 periodicals; Dir WOJCIECH LUBIEWA-WIELEŻYŃSKI; publ. *Polimery* (monthly).

Instytut Ciężkiej Syntezy Organicznej (Institute of Heavy Organic Synthesis): 47-225 Kędzierzyn-Koźle, ul. Energetyków 9; tel. (77) 83-32-41; telex 39222; fax (77) 83-26-60; f.1952; research in adsorption, alcoxylation, alkylation, amination, chlorination, condensation, hydroformylation, hydrogenation, nitration, oxidation, polymerization, polyaddition; library of 29,000 vols, 67,000 copies (special collections); Dir Prof. Dr JERZY WASILEWSKI.

Instytut Elektrotechniki (Electrotechnical Institute): 04-703 Warsaw, ul. Pożaryskiego 28; tel. (22) 12-20-68; fax (22) 615-75-35; f. 1946; research and manufacture of electric machines, apparatus and appliances; library of 40,000 vols; Dir.-Gen. STEFAN PARADOWSKI; publs *Prace IEL* (continuous), *Przegląd Dokumentacyjny Elektrotechniki* (monthly), *Bieżąca Informacja Tematyczna* (fortnightly).

Instytut Energetyki (Institute of Power Engineering): 01-330 Warsaw, ul. Mory 8; tel. 36-75-51; fax 366363; e-mail energ4@warman .com.pl; f. 1953; library of 53,000 vols; Man. Dr JACEK WAŃKOWICZ; publs *Biuletyn Instytutu Energetyki* (every 2 months), *Prace Instytutu Energetyki* (irregular), *Nowa Technika w Energetyce Zagranicznej* (monthly).

Instytut Energii Atomowej (Institute of Atomic Energy): 05-400 Otwock-Świerk; tel. and fax (22) 779-38-88; f. 1983; fmrly Inst. of Nuclear Research; reactor technology, radiation protection and dosimetry, quality standards for nuclear reactors, condensed matter physics, nuclear power plants, radioactive waste management; library of 15,000 vols; Dir JACEK MILCZAREK.

Instytut Górnictwa Naftowego i Gazownictwa (Oil and Gas Institute): 31-503 Cracow, ul. Lubicz 25a; tel. (12) 421-00-33; fax (12) 421-00-50; e-mail office@igng.krakow.pl; f. 1945; oil and gas recovery industry, gas transport and storage, gas use, and related topics; library of 110,000 vols; Dir Prof. Dr JÓZEF RACZKOWSKI; publs *Prace, Nafta-Gaz* (monthly), *Przegląd Bibliograficzno-Faktograficzny 'Nafta-Gas'* (4 a year).

Instytut Informatyki Teoretycznej i Stosowanej PAN (Institute of Theoretical and Applied Informatics): 44-100 Gliwice, ul. Bałtycka 5; tel. 31-73-19; telex 036319; fax 31-70-26; f. 1969; attached to Polish Acad. of Sciences; 52 staff; library of 6,000 vols; Dir Prof. Dr STEFAN WĘGRZYN; publ. *Archiwum Informatyki Teoretycznej i Stosowanej* (quarterly).

Instytut Inżynierii Chemicznej PAN (Institute of Chemical Engineering): 44-100 Gliwice, ul. Bałtycka 5; tel. and fax (32) 31-03-18; e-mail secret@iich.gliwice.pl; f. 1958; attached to Polish Acad. of Sciences; chemical and process engineering; library of 6,000 vols; Dir Prof. Dr hab. inż. ANDRZEJ BURGHARDT; publ. *Inżynieria Chemiczna i Procesowa* (quarterly).

Instytut Komputerowych Systemów Automatyki i Pomiarów (Institute of Computer Systems for Automation and Measurement): 51-608 Wrocław, ul. L. Różyckiego 1C; tel. (071) 48-10-81; telex 0712555; fax (071) 48-15-69; f. 1977; automatics, computer electronics, measurement and control systems, instruments and systems for environmental protection; library of 1,800 vols; Dir JANUSZ FIUT.

Instytut Łączności (Institute of Telecommunications): 04-894 Warsaw, ul. Szachowa 1; tel. (22) 872-90-21; fax (22) 872-90-07; e-mail info@itl.waw.pl; f. 1934; telecommunications, data transmission, satellite telecommunications, optical transmission; library of 42,000 vols; Dir ANDRZEJ P. WIERZBICKI; publs *Prace Instytutu Łączności* (every 6 months), *Biuletyn Informacyjny* (monthly), *Przegląd Dokumentacyjny* (monthly).

Instytut Lotnictwa (Aviation Institute): 02-256 Warsaw, Al. Krakowska 110/114; tel. (22) 846-09-93; fax (22) 846-42-32; f. 1926; library of 72,000 vols; Dir Dr W. WIŚNIOWSKI; publs *Prace Instytutu Lotnictwa* (quarterly), *Informacja Ekspresowa Lotnicza i Silnikowa* (monthly), *Przegląd Dokumentacyjny* (monthly), *Tematy Prac Wykonawczych w Instytucie Lotnictwa* (annually), *Prace Przemysłu Lotniczego* (annually) *Opracowania Problemowe* (15–20 a year).

Instytut Maszyn Matematycznych (Institute of Mathematical Machines): 02-078 Warsaw, ul. Krzywickiego 34; tel. (22) 621-84-41; fax (22) 629-92-70; e-mail imasmat@imm.org.pl; f. 1957; computer science and technology, training and education; library of 28,000 vols; Dir ROMAN CZAJKOWSKI; publ. *Techniki Komputerowe—Biuletyn Informacyjny* (irregular).

Instytut Maszyn Przepływowych PAN (Institute of Fluid Flow Machinery): 80-952 Gdańsk-Wrzeszcz, ul. Gen. J. Fiszera 14; tel. (58) 41-60-71; telex 0512042; fax (58) 41-61-44; f. 1956; attached to Polish Acad. of Sciences; fundamental research, design methods, construction and development of machines and equipment for energy conversion in flow, measuring techniques and instrumentation in connection with fluid-flow machines, solid-state mechanics, machinery diagnostics, plasma physics; library of 23,000 vols; Dir Prof. Dr hab. JERZY KRZYŻANOWSKI; publs *Prace* (Transactions), *Zeszyty Naukowe* (Reports, in series), *Annual Report*, monographs.

Instytut Maszyn Spożywczych (Research Institute of Food Processing Machinery): 03-759 Warsaw, ul. Otwocka 1B; tel. 619-30-62; fax 619-87-94; f. 1954; research and application in all fields of food processing, marketing and catering machinery and equipment; automation; energy-saving techniques; library of 4,984 vols, 141 periodicals, 20,066 leaflets, etc.; Dir Dr WALDEMAR RACZKO; publs *Postępy Techniki* (Developments in Food Processing Technology, 3 a year), *Biuletyn Informacyjny* (Bulletin of Food Processing Machinery, irregular).

Instytut Materiałów Ogniotrwałych (Institute of Refractory Materials): 44-101 Gliwice, ul. Toszecka 99; tel. (32) 270-18-01; fax (32) 270-19-34; e-mail imo23@gateway.imo.gliwice.pl; f. 1953; raw materials, manufacture, application and testing of refractory materials; library of 60,000 vols; Dir Dr JÓZEF WOJSA; publ. *Przegląd Dokumentacyjny Materiałów Ogniotrwałych i Ceramiki Specjalnej* (monthly).

Instytut Mechaniki Precyzyjnej (Institute of Physical Metallurgy, Heat Treatment, Protective Coating): 00-967 Warsaw, ul. Duchnicka 3; tel. (22) 663-43-35; fax (22) 663-43-32; e-mail info@imp.edu.pl; Dir Prof. ALEKSANDER NAKONIECZNY; publ. *Inżynieria Powierzchni* (Surface Engineering, 4 a year).

Instytut Mechanizacji Budownictwa i Górnictwa Skalnego (Institute for Building Mechanization and Mineral Mining): 02-673 Warsaw, ul. Racjonalizacji 6/8; tel. (22) 843-02-01; fax (22) 843-59-81; e-mail imbigs@plearn.edu.pl; f. 1951; mechanization of building sites, mineral mining processing; earth-moving, construction and mining machinery for quarries, equipment research, development and state quality testing and certifying; training of machinery operators; library of 8,800 vols, 54 periodicals; Dir Assoc. Prof. EUGENIUSZ BUDNY; publs *Działalność Instytutu Mechanizacji Budownictwa* (annually), *Wiadomości IMB* (quarterly).

Instytut Metali Niezelaznych (Institute of Non-ferrous Metals): 44-101 Gliwice, ul. Sowińskiego 5; tel. 380-200; fax 316933; e-mail imnskldz@zeus.polsl.gliwice.pl; f. 1952; library of 35,000 vols, 270 current periodicals, 15,000 reports; Dir Prof. ZBIGNIEW ŚMIESZEK; publ. *Rynki Metali Nieżelaznych* (6 a year).

Instytut Metalurgii i Inżynierii Materiałowej im. Aleksandra Krupkowskiego PAN (A. Krupkowski Institute for Metals Research): 30-059 Cracow, ul. W. Reymonta 25; tel. 37-42-00; fax 37-21-92; f. 1953; attached to Polish Acad. of Sciences; metallurgical thermodynamics, physical metallurgy, metal working; library of 25,000 vols; Dir Prof. Dr hab. WOJCIECH TRUSZKOWSKI; publ. *Archives of Metallurgy*.

Instytut Metalurgii Żelaza (Institute of Ferrous Metallurgy): 44-100 Gliwice, ul. Miarki 12; tel. (32) 31-40-51; fax (32) 31-35-94; e-mail imz@imz.gliwice.pl; f. 1949; library of 37,000 books, 21,000 vols of periodicals; Dir EDWARD BARSZCZ; publ. *Prace Instytutu Metalurgii Żelaza* (quarterly).

Instytut Mineralnych Materiałow Budowlanych (Institute of Mineral Building Materials): 45-641 Opole, ul. Oświęcimska 21; tel. 56-32-01; telex 732309; fax 56-26-61; f. 1954; research in cement, lime and gypsum, energy saving, automation of industrial control systems, environmental engineering, use of industrial waste; library of 16,400 vols, 4,700 in special collections; Dir JERZY DUDA; publ. *Prace IMMB* (2 a year).

Instytut Morski (Maritime Institute): 80-830 Gdańsk, ul. Długi Targ 41/42; tel. 31-18-79; telex 0512830; f. 1950; economic and technical research in shipping, harbour and coastal engineering, corrosion, maritime law; 120 staff; library of 80,000 vols; Dir Asst Prof. Dr Eng. JAN CURZYTEK; Scientific Dir Prof. M. KRZYŻANOWSKI; publs *Prace Instytutu Morskiego, Zeszyty Problemowe Gospodarki Morskiej, Materiały Instytutu Morskiego*, *Przegląd Informacji, Informacja ekspresowa.*

Instytut Obróbki Plastycznej (Metal Forming Institute): 61-139 Poznań, ul. Jana Pawła 14; tel. (61) 877-10-81; fax (61) 879-16-82; e-mail inop@inop.poznan.pl; f. 1948; library of 18,000 vols; Dir ANDRZEJ PLEWIŃSKI; publ. *Obróbka Plastyczna Metali* (5 a year).

Instytut Obróbki Skrawaniem (Institute of Metal Cutting): 30-011 Cracow, ul. Wrocławska 37a; tel. (12) 633-93-33; fax (12) 633-94-90; e-mail int@ios.krakow.pl; f. 1949; library of 12,000 vols; Dir JAN BARCENTEWICZ; publs *Prace Instytutu Obróbki Skrawaniem* in series: *Zeszyty Naukowe, Referaty, Materiały Instruktażowe, Opracowania Analityczno-Syntetyczne, Przegląd Dokumentacyjny IOS* (2 a month), *Biuletyn IOS* in *Mechanik*.

Instytut Odlewnictwa (Foundry Research Institute): 30-418 Cracow, ul. Zakopiańska 73; tel. (12) 266-50-22; fax (12) 266-08-70; f. 1946; research into foundry materials, technological processes, alloys and additives; library of 10,000 vols, 45 periodicals; Pres. JERZY TYBULCZUK; publ. *Biuletyn Instytutu Odlewnictwa* (6 a year).

Instytut Podstaw Informatyki PAN (Institute of Computer Science): 01-237 Warsaw, ul. Ordona 21; tel. 36-28-41; fax 37-65-64; e-mail ipi@ipipan.waw.pl; f. 1961; attached to Polish Acad. of Sciences; library of 22,000 vols; Dir Prof. PIOTR DEMBIŃSKI; publs *Prace IPI PAN* (ICS PAS Reports, irregular), *Machine Graphics and Vision* (4 a year).

Instytut Podstawowych Problemów Techniki PAN (Institute of Fundamental Technological Research): 00-049 Warsaw, ul. Świętokrzyska 21; tel. (22) 826-12-81; fax (22) 826-98-15; f. 1953; attached to Polish Acad. of Sciences; applied mechanics, vibrations, ultrasonics, ultrasound in medicine, acoustics, electromagnetic fields, mechanical systems, energy problems, automatics and robotics, building structures; library of 80,000 vols; Dir Prof. MICHAŁ KLEIBER; publs *Archives of Acoustics*, *Archives of Mechanics* (every 2 months), *Archives of Civil Engineering*, *Engineering Transactions*, *Journal of Technical Physics* (quarterly), *Biblioteka Mechaniki Stosowanej* (Applied Mechanics Series), *Prace IPPT* (IFTR Reports), *CAMES–Computer Assisted Mechanics and Engineering Sciences*.

Instytut Przemysłu Gumowego 'Stomil' ('Stomil' Rubber Research Institute): 05-820 Piastów, ul. Harcerska 30; tel. (22) 723-60-25; fax (22) 723-71-96; e-mail ipgum@pol.pl; f. 1953; research in all brs of rubber technology and of its development; library of 7,800 vols; Dir R. CIEŚLAK; publs *Elastomery* (6 a year), *Guma–Elastomery–Przetwórstwo, Bieżąca Informacja* (Rubber–Elastomers–Processing Technology, Current Information, 9 a year).

Instytut Przemysłu Organicznego (Institute of Industrial Organic Chemistry): 03-236 Warsaw, ul. Annopol 6; tel. (22) 811-12-31; fax (22) 811-07-99; e-mail inorg@atos.warman.com.pl; f. 1952; research on plant pesticides and biocides, auxiliary chemical products, organic intermediate products, blasting materials, chemical safety, toxicology and ecotoxicology; library of 30,000 vols, 186 periodicals; Dir Dr W. MOSZCZYŃSKI; publs *Organika—Prace Naukowe Instytutu Przemysłu Organicznego, Pestycydy* (4 a year).

Instytut Przemysłu Skórzanego (Leather Research Institute): 90-960 Łódź, ul. Zgierska 73; tel. 57-62-10; telex 886423; fax 57-62-75; f. 1951; research into leather biotechnology, tanning, furriery and shoe industries, control of environmental pollution; library of 11,000 vols and special collections of 14,379 vols; Dir MACIEJ URBAWIAK.

Instytut Przemysłu Tworzyw i Farb (Institute of Plastics and Paint Industry): 44-101 Gliwice, ul. Chorzowska 50; tel. (32) 31-21-81; fax (32) 31-26-74; e-mail main@iptif.com.pl; f. 1953; research, developmental, technological and designing activities in the field of paint and varnish products and plastics processing; library of 19,000 vols; Dir PAWEL SZEWCZYK; publs *Farby i Lakiery* (Paints and Varnishes, monthly), *Przetwórstwo Tworzyw* (Processing of Plastics, monthly).

Instytut Spawalnictwa (Institute of Welding): 44-101 Gliwice, ul. Bł. Czesława 16/18; tel. 31-00-11; telex 316288; fax 31-46-52; f. 1945; fundamental and developmental research, acceptance tests, certification, consulting, training, safety of welders, standardization, manufacture; library of 12,000 vols, 36 periodicals; Dir Prof. JAN PILARCZYK; publs *Biuletyn Instytutu Spawalnictwa* (every 2 months), *Informacja Expressowa* (every 2 months).

Instytut Systemów Sterowania (Institute of Control Systems): 40-161 Katowice, Al. Korfantego 101; tel. 58-56-71; fax 58-87-23; f. 1977; Dir LESZEK E. ŻYCHOŃ; publs *Prace Naukowe Instytutu Systemów Sterowania* (irregular), *Komunikaty Naukowe ISS*.

Instytut Szkła i Ceramiki (Institute of Glass and Ceramics): 02-676 Warsaw, ul. Postępu 9; tel. 43-74-21; fax 43-17-89; e-mail home@ceram.isc.ifpan.edu.pl; f. 1952; basic research on all aspects of glass and ceramics technology; library of 15,000 vols and special collections of 5,000 vols; Dir ZBIGNIEW POLESIŃSKI; publ. *Szkło i Ceramika* (every 2 months).

Instytut Techniki Cieplnej (Institute of Heat Engineering): 93-208 Łódź, ul. Dąbrowskiego 113; tel. 43-26-50; telex 884143; fax 43-66-22; f. 1948; library of 20,110 vols, 85 periodical titles; Dir FRANCISZEK STRZELCZYK; publs *Informacja Ekspresowa* (every 2 months), *Przegląd Dokumentacyjny* (quarterly).

Instytut Technologii Elektronowej (Institute of Electron Technology): 02-668 Warsaw, Al. Lotników 32/46; tel. (22) 843-30-93; fax (22) 847-06-31; e-mail cambroz@ite.waw.pl; f. 1968; library of 11,000 vols; Dir Prof. Dr hab. inż. C. AMBROZIAK; publs *Electron Technology* (quarterly), *Biblioteka Elektroniki* (irregular), *Prace ITE* (monthly).

Instytut Technologii Materiałów Elektronicznych (Institute of Electronic Materials Technology): 01-919 Warsaw, ul. Wólczyńska 133; tel. and fax 34-90-03; e-mail itme@atos.warman.com.pl; f. 1970; library of 20,000 vols; Dir Dr ZYGMUNT ŁUCZYŃSKI; Sec. Prof. ANDRZEJ JELEŃSKI; publs *Materiały Elektroniczne* (quarterly), *MST News – Poland* (quarterly).

Instytut Technologii Nafty im. Prof. Stanisława Pilata (Institute of Petroleum Processing): 31-429 Cracow, ul. Łukasiewicza 1; tel. 11-44-62; telex 00325269; f. 1958; petroleum refining and petro-chemistry, standardization of products and testing methods, new methods of analysis and production; 410 mems; library of 20,000 vols; Dir K. KOLARZYK.

Instytut Tele- i Radiotechniczny (Electronics Research Institute): 03-450 Warsaw, ul. Ratuszowa 11; tel. 619-22-41; fax 619-27-66; f. 1956; library of *c.* 40,000 vols; Dir JÓZEF GROMEK; publ. *Prace ITR in Elektronika* (2 a year).

Instytut Transportu Samochodowego (Motor Transport Institute): 03-301 Warsaw, ul. Jagiellońska 80; tel. (22) 811-09-44; fax (22) 811-09-06; f. 1952; focuses on operation of motor transport in the market economy, road traffic organization, and environmental protection; library of 23,000 vols; Dir Prof. Dr CZESŁAW ŁEPKOWSKI; publs *Zeszyty Naukowe* (2-3 a year), *Biuletyn Informacyjny* (6 a year).

Instytut Włókien Chemicznych (Institute of Chemical Fibres): 90-570 Łódź, ul. M. Skłodowskiej-Curie 19–27; tel. (42) 637-65-10; fax (42) 637-62-14; f. 1952; chemistry, technology, application of chemical fibres, environmental protection, natural polymers, their modification, applied biotechnology, medical and agricultural applications of polymers and fibres; library of 11,000 vols; Dir A. URBANOWSKI; publ. *Fibres and Textiles in Eastern Europe*.

Instytut Włókien Naturalnych (Institute of Natural Fibres): 60-630 Poznań, ul. Wojska Polskiego 71B; tel. 22-48-15; telex 0413486; fax 417-830; f. 1930; production and processing of natural fibres; environmental protection; processing of waste products; 27,400 vols, 7,800 in special collections; Dir Prof. Dr RYSZARD KOZŁOWSKI; publs *Włókna Naturalne* (Natural Fibres, annually), *Biblioteczka dla Praktyków* (irregular), *Euroflax Newsletter* (2 a year).

Instytut Włókiennictwa (Textile Research Institute): 92-103 Łódź, ul. Brzezińska 5/15; tel. (42) 679-26-50; fax (42) 679-26-38; e-mail info@mail.iw.lodz.pl; f. 1948; textile raw materials, technology of yarn manufacturing, nonwoven fabrics, textile chemical processing; library of 17,559 vols and 12,879 in special collections; Dir Dr WITOLD RAKOWSKI; publ. *Prace Instytutu Włókiennictwa* (annually).

Instytut Wzornictwa Przemysłowego (Institute of Industrial Design): 00-236 Warsaw, ul. Świętojerska 5/7; tel. (22) 31-22-21; telex 816715; fax (22) 31-64-78; f. 1950; research into design and ergonomics of industrial products; ergonomic research and data selection; design for the disabled; standardization; technical information service; organization of national and foreign exhibitions, seminars, conferences etc.; library of 42,000 vols, 270 titles of periodicals, collection of special editions, etc.; Dir Prof. RAFAŁ KRAWCZYK; publs *Studies and Materials, Express News, Design Library Series*.

Naukowo-Produkcyjne Centrum Półprzewodników 'CEMI' (Scientific and Production Centre of Semiconductors): 02-675 Warsaw, Wołoska ul. 5; tel. 43-21-21; Dir WIKTOR LEDÓCHOWSKI; publ. *Biuletyn Informacyjny UNITRA-CEMI* (every 2 months). (Centre includes two institutes: Institute of Electron Technology and Industrial Institute of Electronics.)

PKP Centrum Naukowo-Techniczne Kolejnictwa (PKP Railway Scientific and Technical Centre): 04-275 Warsaw, ul. Chłopickiego 50; tel. (22) 610-08-68; telex 814791; fax (22) 610-75-97; f. 1951; research into transport management systems, track maintenance, rolling stock operation and maintenance, signalling and communications; library of 26,000 vols; Dir RADOSŁAW ZOŁNIERZAK; publs *Informacja Ekspresowa Bibliografia Piśmiennictwa Kolejowego* (Express Information Railway Literature Bibliography, monthly), *Prace CNTK* (CNTK Proceedings, 3–4 a year), *Problemy Kolejnictwa* (Problems Concerning Railways, 3–4 a year).

Polski Komitet Normalizacyjny (Polish Committee for Standardization): 00-139 Warsaw, ul. Elektoralna 2; tel. (22) 620-02-41; fax (22) 620-07-41; f. 1924; library has collections of Polish National Standards, ISO, IEC, EN and foreign standards; Pres. JANUSZ ROSZIJ; publ. *Normalizacja* (monthly).

Przemysłowy Instytut Automatyki i Pomiarów (Industrial Research Institute of Automation and Measurements): 02-486 Warsaw, Al. Jerozolimskie 202; tel. (22) 874-00-00; fax (22) 863-81-76; f. 1965; development of automation equipment, measuring instruments and industrial robots; library of 24,000 vols; Dir Prof. STANISŁAW KACZANOWSKI; publ. *Pomiary Automatyka Robotyka* (monthly).

Przemysłowy Instytut Elektroniki (Industrial Institute of Electronics): 00-241 Warsaw, ul. Długa 44/50; tel. (22) 831-38-39; fax (22) 831-30-14; e-mail pie@pie.edu.pl; automatic production lines and technical equipment, equipment for thermal and chemical processes, test and measuring systems; Dir KRZYSZTOF BADŹMIROWSKI; publ. *Prace PIE* (quarterly).

Przemysłowy Instytut Maszyn Budowlanych (Industrial Institute of Construction Machinery): 05-230 Kobyłka, ul. Napoleona 2; tel. (22) 786-23-26; fax (22) 786-18-30; e-mail pimb@warman.com.pl; library of 14,000 vols; Dir Dr ANDRZEJ MACHNIEWSKI.

Przemysłowy Instytut Maszyn Rolniczych (Industrial Institute of Agricultural Machinery): 60-963 Poznań, ul. Starołęcka 31; tel. (61) 876-55-17; fax (61) 879-32-62; e-mail office@pimr.poznan.pl; f. 1946; construction, testing and research on economical viability of agricultural machines and equipment; library of 11,000 vols; Dir KAZIMIERZ MIELEC; publs *Prace PIMR* (quarterly), *Katalog Maszyn i Urządzeń Rolniczych* (quarterly).

Przemysłowy Instytut Motoryzacji (Automotive Industry Institute): 03-301 Warsaw, ul. Jagiellońska 55; tel. 11-14-21; telex 813880; fax 11-09-75; f. 1972; Dir LECH SOKALSKI; publ. *Przegląd Dokumentacyjny* (monthly).

Przemysłowy Instytut Telekomunikacji (Telecommunications Research Institute): 04-051 Warsaw, ul. Poligonowa 30; tel. and fax (22) 810-23-81; e-mail dufrene@pit.edu.pl; f. 1934; radar technology, microwave technology and antennas, command control communication, intelligent systems (C3I); library of 22,000 vols; Dir ROMAN DUFRENE; publ. *Prace Przemysłowego Instytutu Telekomunikacji* (every 2 months).

Libraries and Archives

Białystok

Biblioteka Główna Politechniki Białostockiej (Central Library of Białystok Technical University): 15-351 Białystok, ul. Wiejska 45C; tel. and fax 42-85-77; e-mail bgpb@libra.pb.bialystok.pl; f. 1951; 297,000 vols, incl. 176,000 books, 36,000 periodicals, 84,000 special collections; Dir Mgr BARBARA KUBIAK; publs *Wykaz Wydawnictw Ciągłych* (List of Periodicals, annually), *Bibliografia Publikacji Pracowników* (Bibliography of Workers' Publications, irregular).

Bydgoszcz

Wojewódzka i Miejska Biblioteka Publiczna w Bydgoszczy (Bydgoszcz Voivodship and Public Municipal Library): 85–034 Bydgoszcz, ul. Długa 39; tel. (52) 345-77-62; fax (52) 28-73-90; e-mail staszek@mail.atr.bydgoszcz.pl; f. 1903; 1,119,000 vols, including 8,200 old books, 6,000 maps and atlases, 1,800 MSS; Dir EWA STELMACHOWSKA.

Cracow

Biblioteka Główna Akademii Górniczo-Hutniczej im. Stanisława Staszica w Krakowie (Central Library of the Stanisław Staszic University of Mining and Metallurgy): 30-059 Cracow, Al. Mickiewicza 30; tel. and fax (12) 634-14-04; e-mail bgagh@libnvl.biblio.agh.edu.pl; f. 1919; Central Library 1,268,000 units, Department Libraries 573,000 units; Dir ANNA KEGEL; publs *Wykaz Czasopism Bieżących Biblioteki Głównej i Bibliotek Sieci Akademii Górniczo-Hutniczej* (List of Current Periodicals, annually), *Bibliografia Publikacji Pracowników AGH* (Bibliography of Publications of Staff, annually).

Biblioteka Główna Akademii Sztuk Pięknych (Central Library of the Academy of Fine Arts): 31-108 Cracow, ul. Smoleńsk 9; tel. (12) 422-15-46; fax (12) 422-65-66; e-mail zewalcza@cyf-kr.edu.pl; f. 1868; 75,000 vols, 21,000 graphics, 7,000 posters, 8,231 old prints including special collection; Dir Mgr ELŻBIETA WARCHAŁOWSKA.

Biblioteka Główna Politechniki Krakowskiej (Central Library of Cracow University of Technology): 31–155 Cracow, ul. Warszawska 24; tel. and fax (12) 633-29-09; e-mail listy@biblos.pk.edu.pl; f. 1945; 745,000 vols, incl. 219,000 books, 76,000 periodicals, 405,000 standards, patents, etc.; Dir Mgr MAREK NAHOTKO; publs *Wykaz Ważniejszych Nabytków Zagranicznych* (Selected List of Recent Foreign Acquisitions), *Bibliografia Publikacji Pracowników Politechniki Krakowskiej* (Bibliography of Publications of the Staff of Cracow University of Technology).

Biblioteka Główna Wyższej Szkoły Pedagogicznej im. KEN (Central Library of Cracow Pedagogical University): 30–084 Cracow, ul. Podchorążych 2; tel. (12) 37–82-49; fax (12) 37-22-43; e-mail info@tessa.wsp.krakow.pl; f. 1946; 591,000 vols, 43,000 periodicals, 1,000 sound recordings, also audio-visual materials, CD-ROMs and microforms; 9,000 special collections; Dir TERESA WILDHARDT.

Biblioteka Jagiellońska (Jagiellonian Library): 30–059 Cracow, ul. Mickiewicza 22; tel. (12) 33-63-77; fax (12) 33-09-03; f. 1364; collection: national library for old books up to 1800, central library of general scientific, Polish affairs, humanities, Polish writing of the 15th–18th centuries; 3,346,000 vols and units, incl. 592,000 periodicals, 105,000 old prints (3,586 incunabula), 25,000 MSS, 35,000 music prints, 47,000 drawings and items of graphic art, 13,000 maps and atlases, and also fly-sheets and microforms; includes 46 university institute libraries: 1,537,000 units; Dir Dr KRZYSZTOF ZAMORSKI; publ. *Bulletin of the Jagiellonian Library* (annually).

Biblioteka PAN w Krakowie (Library of the Polish Academy of Sciences in Cracow): 31–016 Cracow, ul. Sławkowska 17; tel. and fax (12) 422-29-15; e-mail bibliote@biblioteka .pan.krakow.pl; f. 1856; 691,000 vols; 352,000 annual vols of periodicals relating to the social and biological sciences, 132,000 MSS, old prints, cartography, graphic arts; Dir KAROLINA GRODZISKA; publ. *Rocznik Biblioteki PAN w Krakowie* (Yearbook).

Wojewódzka Biblioteka Publiczna w Krakowie (Cracow County Public Library): 31–124 Cracow, ul. Rajska 1; tel. (12) 632-59-07; fax (12) 633-22-10; f. 1945; educational, scientific and belles-lettres collection; 550,000 items; Dir Prof. Dr hab. JACEK WOJCIECHOWSKI; publ. *Notes Biblioteczny* (2 a year).

Częstochowa

Biblioteka Główna Politechniki Częstochowskiej (Central Library of Częstochowa Technical University): 42-201 Częstochowa, Al. Armii Krajowej 36; tel. 61-44-73; fax 65-15-07; f. 1950; 409,000 vols, incl. 120,000 books, 70,000 periodicals, 219,000 standards, patents, etc.; Dir Mgr MAŁGORZATA HANKIEWICZ; publs *Wykaz Nabytków Zagranicznych* (List of Foreign Acquisitions, monthly), *Wykaz Zbiorów Czasopism i Innych Wydawnictw Ciągłych* (Collection of Periodicals and Serials, irregular).

Gdańsk

Biblioteka Gdańska PAN (Gdańsk Library of the Polish Academy of Sciences): 80–858 Gdańsk, Wałowa 15; tel. 31-22-51; fax 31-29-70; former City Library; f. 1596; collection: humanities, social sciences, maritime, Pomeranian and Gdańsk affairs; 732,000 vols, incl. 55,000 old books, 818 incunabula, 74,000 periodicals, 5,000 MSS, 8,000 maps, 8,000 graphics, etc; Dir Prof. Dr hab. ZBIGNIEW NOWAK; publ. *Libri Gedanenses* (annually).

Biblioteka Główna Politechniki Gdańskiej (Central Library of Gdańsk Technical University): 80-952 Gdańsk, ul. G. Narutowicza 11/12; tel. 47-25-75; fax 47-27-58; e-mail library@sunrise.pg.gda.pl; 1,096,000 vols incl. 494,000 books, 113,000 periodicals, 491,000 standards, patents; Librarian Mgr JANINA LIGMAN; publs *Bibliografia Publikacji Pracowników Naukowych Politechniki Gdańskiej* (Bibliography of Publications of Scientific Workers of the Technical University of Gdańsk, irregular), *Raport Politechniki Gdańskiej* (Report of the Technical University of Gdansk, 1 a year), *Wykaz Nabytków* (List of Acquisitions, monthly).

Gliwice

Biblioteka Główna Politechniki Śląskiej (Central Library of Silesian Technical University): 44-100 Gliwice, Ul. Kaszubska 23; tel. 37-12-69; fax 37-15-51; f. 1945; 876,000 vols; Dir HALINA BAŁUKA.

Katowice

Biblioteka Główna Śląskiej Akademii Medycznej (Central Library of the Silesian Medical Academy): 40–952 Katowice, ul. Poniatowskiego 15; tel. and fax 57-12-34; e-mail biblio@infomed.slam.katowice.pl; f. 1948; 191,000 vols; Dir Dr ALFRED PUZIO; publs *Bibliografia publikacji pracowników* (annually), *Wykaz czasopism prenumerowanych przez Bibliotekę Śląskiej Akad. Med.* (annually), *Wykaz nowych nabytków zagranicznych – druki zwarte* (quarterly), *Biuletyn Informacyjny SAM* (every 2 months).

Biblioteka Główna Uniwersytetu Śląskiego (Central Library of the Silesian University): 40–007 Katowice, ul. Bankowa 14; tel. and fax 58-29-01; e-mail bgsekr@lib.bg.us .edu.pl; f. 1969; 265,000 vols; Dir WANDA DZIADKIEWICZ.

Biblioteka Śląska (Silesian Library): 40–956 Katowice, ul. Damrota 30; tel. (32) 208-37-00; fax (32) 208-37-07; e-mail bs@libra.bs .katowice.pl; f. 1922; collection: social science, economics, literature relating to Silesia; 1,184,000 vols, incl. 1,005,000 books, 27,000 old vols, 152,000 vols of periodicals, 11,000 MSS, 11,000 maps and atlases, 7,000 drawings and prints, 23,000 postcards, 11,000 photographs; Dir Prof. Dr hab. JAN MALICKI; publs *Książnica Śląska* (irregular), *Bibliografia Śląska* (annually).

Kielce

Biblioteka Główna Politechniki Świętokrzyskiej (Central Library of Świętokrzyska Technical University): 25-314 Kielce, Al. Tysiąclecia Państwa Polskiego 7; tel. (41) 342-44-83; fax (41) 344-76-35; e-mail library@eden.tu.kielce.pl; f. 1966; 106,000 vols, 16,000 vols current periodicals, 68,000 standards, catalogues, CD-ROM; Dir Mgr DANUTA KAPINOS.

Łódź

Biblioteka Główna Politechniki Łódzkiej (Central Library of Łódź Technical University): 90-924 Łódź, Żwirki 36; tel. (42) 31-20-59; fax (42) 36-31-65; e-mail info@sunlib .p.lodz.pl; f. 1945; 247,000 vols, 113,000 periodicals, 192,000 patents, standards, etc.; Librarian Mgr CZESŁAWA GARNYSZ.

Biblioteka Uniwersytecka w Łodzi (Library of Łódź University): 90-950 Łódź, ul. Matejki 34/38; tel. and fax (42) 78-16-78; e-mail bulinf@krysia.uni.lodz.pl; f. 1945; scientific collection; 1,568,000 vols, incl. 28,000 old vols, 369,000 periodicals, 7,000 original MSS, 14,000 maps and atlases, 52,000 vols of music, 43,000 drawings and illustrations, and 2,907 microfilms, 27,000 microfiches, 801,000 vols in departmental libraries; Dir Dr JAN JANIAK.

Wojewódzka i Miejska Biblioteka Publiczna im. Marszałka Józefa Piłsudskiego (J. Piłsudski Scientific Public Regional Library of Łódź): 90–508 Łódź, ul. Gdańska 100/102; tel. (42) 37-30-90; fax (42) 37-21-02; e-mail informacja@bib.wimbp.lodz.pl; f. 1917; general; special subjects socio-economic science and the arts; 449,000 books, 98,000 periodicals, 48,000 vols of special collections; Dir ELŻBIETA PAWLICKA; publ. *Sprawozdanie z działalności WiMBP.*

Lublin

Biblioteka Główna Politechniki Lubelskiej (Library of Lublin Technical University): 20–950 Lublin, ul. Nowotki 11; tel. 37-58-77; f. 1953; 172,000 vols, 97,000 standards, technical catalogues, etc; Dir IRENA PAWELEC; publs *Bibliografia Publikacji Pracownikow, Prace Naukowe Politechniki Lubelskiej.*

Biblioteka Główna Uniwersytetu Marii Curie-Skłodowskiej w Lublinie (Library of the M. Curie-Skłodowska University): 20-950 Lublin, ul. Radziszewskiego 11; tel. (81) 537-58-35; fax (81) 537-58-47; f. 1944; general scientific collection of 2,251,000 vols, including 19,000 old books, 457,000 vols of periodicals, 780 MSS, 34,000 maps and atlases, 32,000 drawings and illustrations, 14,000 vols of music, 3,000 tapes and records, 6,000 microfilms, 363,000 patents; Dir Dr BOGUSŁAW KASPEREK.

Biblioteka Uniwersytecka Katolickiego Uniwersytetu Lubelskiego (Library of the Catholic University of Lublin): 20-950 Lublin, ul. Chopina 27; tel. (81) 743-75-33; fax (81) 743-77-83; f. 1918; general collection, with emphasis on theology, philosophy and humanities; 1,700,000 vols (including department libraries) of which 49,000 old vols, 336,000 vols periodicals, 4,600 MSS, 9,000 maps and atlases, 9,000 music scores; Dir ANDRZEJ PALUCHOWSKI; publs *Archiwa, Biblioteki i Muzea Kościelne* (2 a year), *Paginae Bibliothecae* (irregular).

Wojewódzka Biblioteka Publiczna im H. Łopacińskiego (H. Łopacińskiego Voivodship Public Library): 20-950 Lublin, ul. Narutowicza 4; tel. and fax (81) 532-39-47; f. 1907; scientific and educational collection; 745,000 vols, 16,000 old vols, 31,000 periodicals, 2,700 MSS, 3,000 maps and atlases, 20,000 drawings and illustrations, 2,400 microfilms; Dir ZDZISŁAWA PIOTROWSKA-JASIŃSKA; publs *Bibliotekarz Lubelski* (annually), *Dostrzegacz Biblioteczny* (irregular).

Poznań

Biblioteka Główna Politechniki Poznańskiej (Central Library of Poznań University of Technology): 60-965 Poznań, Pl. Skłodowskiej-Curie 5; tel. and fax (61) 831-33-68; e-mail office_ml@put.poznan.pl; f. 1945; 294,000 vols, 36,000 standards; Librarian Mgr HALINA GANIŃSKA.

Biblioteka Kórnicka PAN (Library of the Polish Academy of Sciences, Kórnik): 62-035 Kórnik, near Poznań; tel. (61) 817-00-81; fax (61) 817-19-30; e-mail bkpan@amu.edu.pl; f. 1828; collection: History, History of Polish Literature, Mathematics and Natural Sciences; 356,000 vols, incl. 30,055 old prints, 70,000 periodicals, 15,222 MSS, 14,000 graphics; museum with 8,869 exhibits; Dir Prof. Dr hab. JERZY WISŁOCKI; publ. *Pamiętnik Biblioteki Kórnickiej.*

Biblioteka Poznańskiego Towarzystwa Przyjaciół Nauk (Library of the Poznań Society of Friends of Arts and Sciences): 61–725 Poznań, Sew. Mielżyńskiego 27–29; tel. (61) 852-74-41; e-mail bibl.adm@ptpm.poznan.pl; f. 1857; collection: scientific humanities; 294,000 vols, incl. 17,000 old vols, 1,500 MSS, 4,000 photographs, 1,600 maps and atlases 60,000 periodicals, 715 microfilms; Dir Doc. Dr hab. RYSZARD MARCINIAK.

Biblioteka Raczyńskich (Raczyńscy Library): 60–967 Poznań, Plac Wolności 19; tel. (61) 852-94-42; fax (61) 852-98-68; f. 1829; scientific and educational collection; 1,323,000 vols, 18,000 old books, 34,000 periodicals, 9,000 MSS, 10,000 maps and atlases, 36,000 ex-libris, 18,000 photos, 1,500 drawings and illustrations, 430 microfilms, 73,000 audio and video items; Dir WOJCIECH SPALENIAK.

Biblioteka Uniwersytecka (Library of Adam Mickiewicz University): 60–967 Poznań, Skr. Poczt. 526, ul. Ratajczaka 38/40; tel. (61) 852-74-16; fax (61) 852-29-55; e-mail library@bu-uam.amu.edu.pl; f. 1919; 2,655,000 vols in central library, incl. 100,240 old vols, 5,600 MSS, 28,000 maps and atlases; 1,647,000 vols in departmental libraries; Dir Dr ARTUR JAZDON.

Rzeszów

Biblioteka Główna Politechniki Rzeszowskiej (Central Library of Rzeszów University of Technology): 35–959 Rzeszów, ul. Pola 2; tel. and fax (17) 854-25-33; e-mail bgprz@prz.rzeszow.pl; 140,000 vols; Dir Mgr ELŻBIETA KAŁUŻA.

Sopot

Biblioteka Główna Uniwersytetu Gdańskiego (Central Library of Gdansk University): 81-824 Sopot, ul. Armii Krajowej 110; tel. (58) 550-90-05; fax (58) 551-52-21; e-mail bib@bg.univ.gda.pl; f. 1970; 1,058,000 vols, incl. 108,000 in special collections; 244,000 vols of periodicals; Dir Mgr URSZULA SAWICKA.

Szczecin

Biblioteka Główna Politechniki Szczecińskiej (Central Library of Szczecin Technical University): 70-322 Szczecin, ul. Pułaskiego 10; tel. and fax (91) 433-65-04; e-mail alozps@mailbox.chemo.tuniv.szczecin.pl; f. 1946; 261,000 books, 930 current periodicals, 2,723,000 patents, standards, technical catalogues and audio-visual materials; Dir Mgr ANNA GRZELAK-ROZENBERG; publs *Prace Naukowe* (research, irregular), *Bibliografia Publikacji Pracowników Politechniki Szczecińskiej* (every 2 years).

Biblioteka Główna Uniwersytetu Szczecińskiego (Library of University of Szczecin): 70-384 Szczecin, ul. A. Mickiewicza 16; tel. (91) 845-338; telex 422719; fax (91) 845-338; f. 1985; 1,111,000 vols; Dir JOLANTA GOC; publs *Wykaz ważniejszych nabytków* (irregular), *Bibliografia publikacji pracowników Uniwersytetu Szczecińskiego*.

Książnica Pomorska im. Stanisława Staszica (Stanisław Staszic Pomeranian Library): 70–205 Szczecin, ul. Podgórna 15; tel. (91) 434-48-31; fax (91) 433-96-78; e-mail kp@aci.com.pl; f. 1905; 768,000 vols, 148,000 vols of periodicals, 2,500 MSS, 30,000 early books, 201,000 govt documents (incl. 62,000 standards), 5,000 maps and atlases, 19,000 records, 810 CDs, 900 microforms; Dir STANISŁAW KRZYWICKI; publs *Bibliografia Pomorza Zachodniego. Piśmiennictwo polskie i Piśmiennictwo zagraniczne* (Bibliography of Western Pomerania. Polish Literature and Foreign Literature), *Bibliotekarz Zachodniopomorski* (The West Pomeranian Librarian, quarterly).

Toruń

Biblioteka Uniwersytecka w Toruniu (Library of Nicholas Copernicus University in Toruń): 87–100 Toruń, Gagarina 13; tel. and fax (56) 654-29-52; e-mail umklibr@bu.uni .torun.pl; f. 1945; 2,412,000 units, incl. 831,000 books, 440,000 vols of periodicals, 63,000 old books, 4,500 MSS, 10,000 cartographic publications, 221,000 graphics, posters, etc., 84,000 musical scores, 9,000 records; 599,000 vols in departmental libraries; special collection (Pomeranica, Copernicana, Baltica); Dir STEFAN CZAJA; publs *Studia o bibliotekach i zbiorach polskich, Studia o działalności i zboriach Biblioteki Uniwersytetu Mikołaja Kopernika*.

Wojewódzka Biblioteka Publiczna i Książnica Miejska im. Kopernika w Toruniu (Copernicus District and Municipal Library): 87–100 Toruń, ul. Słowackiego 8; tel. (56) 661-65-44; fax (56) 661-65-43; e-mail biblio1@man .torun.pl; f. 1923; international exchange of information, bibliographic inquiries, archival researches, expositions of books and printed works on educational, cultural and political history of Pomerania; 898,000 vols, incl. 28,000 old vols; Dir Mgr TERESA E. SZYMOROWSKA; publs *Works of the Copernicus Municipal Library, Profiles of Distinguished Pomeranians*.

Warsaw

Archiwum Akt Nowych (Archive of Modern Records): 02–103 Warsaw, ul. Hankiewicza 1; tel. (22) 822-52-45; fax (22) 223-00-42; f. 1919; Dir Dr TADEUSZ KRAWCZAK.

Archiwum Dokumentacji Mechanicznej (Mechanical Documentation Archives): 00-202 Warsaw, ul. Świętojerska 24; tel. 31-17-36; f. 1955; Dir Dr JAN BONIECKI.

Archiwum Główne Akt Dawnych (Central Archives of Historical Records): 00–263 Warsaw, ul. Długa 7; tel. (22) 831-15-25; fax (22) 831-16-08; f. 1808; archives from 12th century to 1918; 412,704 vols; Dir Dr HUBERT WAJS.

Archiwum Polskiej Akademii Nauk (Archives of the Polish Academy of Sciences): 00-330 Warsaw, ul. Nowy Świat 72; tel. and fax (22) 826-81-30; f. 1953; 26,000 vols; brs in Cracow, Poznań, Katowice; Dir Dr HANNA KRAJEWSKA; publs *Biuletyn Archiwum PAN* (annually).

Biblioteka Główna Akademii Sztuk Pięknych w Warszawie (Central Library of the Academy of Fine Arts): 00–068 Warsaw, Krakowskie Przedmieście 5; tel. 26-62-51; f. 1904; 23,000 vols, 6,000 periodicals; Dir EWA WĘGŁOWSKA; publ. bulletin of references to new books (irregular).

Biblioteka Główna Politechniki Warszawskiej (Central Library of Warsaw Technical University): 00–661 Warsaw, Plac Politechniki 1; tel. (22) 621-13-70; fax (22) 628-71-84; e-mail bgpw@bg.pw.edu.pl; f. 1915; 1,478,000 vols, (975,000 books, 218,000 journals, 289,000 special collections); Dir Mgr E. DUDZIŃSKA; publs *Bibliografia (Adnotowana) Prac Doktorskich i Habilitacyjnych* (Annotated Bibliography of Doctors' and Professors' Theses, annually), *Bibliografia Publikacji Pracowników Politechniki Warszawskiej* (Bibliography of Publications of Workers at the Technical University of Warsaw, every 2 years), *Sylwetki Profesorów Politechniki Warszawskiej* (irregular), *Przegląd Nabytków Biblioteki Głównej Politechniki Warszawskiej* (List of Foreign Acquisitions, every 2 weeks).

Biblioteka Główna Szkoły Głównej Gospodarstwa Wiejskiego w Warszawie (Central Library of the Warsaw Agricultural University): 02-528 Warsaw, ul. Rakowiecka 26/30; tel. and fax (22) 49-67-96; e-mail jmw_bg@delta.sggw.waw.pl; f. 1911; collection: agriculture, horticulture, forestry, zootechnics, veterinary science, wood technology, land improvement, agricultural economics, food processing technology and human nutrition; 157,000 books, 108,000 periodicals; Dir Mgr J. LEWANDOWSKI; publs *Annals* (8 subject series, irregular), *Rozprawy i Monografie* (Treatises and Monographs, irregular).

Biblioteka Narodowa (National Library): 00-973 Warsaw 22, POB 36, Al. Niepodległości 213; tel. (22) 608-29-99; fax (22) 825-52-51; e-mail biblnar@bn.org.pl; f. 1928; State central library; collection of writings in Polish and relating to Poland; basic foreign publications in the social sciences and humanities; library science literature; 7,153,000 vols, including books and periodicals, MSS, old books, maps and atlases, drawings, photographs, illustrations, leaflets and posters, music and phonographic materials; The National Library houses the Bibliographical Institute, the Books and Readers Institute; Dir MICHAŁ JAGIEŁŁO; publs *Rocznik Biblioteki Narodowej* (National Library Year Book, scientific library science periodical, with English summaries), *Biuletyn Informacyjny Biblioteki Narodowej* (quarterly), *Przewodnik Bibliograficzny* (Bibliographical Guide, weekly), *Polska Bibliografia Bibliologiczna* (Polish Bibliography of Library Science, annually), *Bibliografia Bibliografii Polskich* (Bibliography of Polish Bibliographies, annually), *Bibliografia Zawartości Czasopism* (Index to Periodicals, monthly), *Ruch Wydawniczy w Liczbach* (Polish Publishing in Figures, annually), etc.

Biblioteka PAN w Warszawie (Library of the Polish Academy of Sciences in Warsaw): 00-901 Warsaw, Pałac Kultury i Nauki 6 p; tel. and fax (22) 620-33-02; e-mail biblpan@ warman.com.pl; f. 1908; collection: science of science and technology, future studies, praxiology, library and information science, bibliography; 415,000 vols; Dir Doc. Dr hab. BARBARA SORDYLOWA; publs *Polska Bibliografia Naukoznawstwa i Technoznawstwa* (Polish Bibliography of the Science of Science and of Technology, every 3 years), *Przegląd Biblioteczny* (Library Review, quarterly, with the Polish Librarians' Asscn).

Biblioteka Publiczna m. st. Warszawy — Biblioteka Główna (Public Library — Main Library): 00-950 Warsaw, ul. Koszykowa 26; tel. 621-78-52; fax 621-19-68; e-mail glowna@ bibl.publ.waw.pl; f. 1907; general collection; 1,177,000 vols, 13,000 old prints, 4,000 MSS, 15,000 maps and atlases, 65,000 standards, 4,000 drawings, 6,000 records; Dir Mrs JANINA JAGIELSKA; publ. *Bibliotekarz* (The Librarian, monthly).

Biblioteka Sejmowa (Sejm Library): 00-902 Warsaw, ul. Wiejska 4; tel. (22) 628-85-45; fax (22) 694-17-78; f. 1919; law, political and social sciences, modern history, economics; 247,000 vols, 109,000 vols of periodicals, 72,000 parliamentary, official and international publs, 22,000 microforms, 437 metres of archival documents, 18,000 sound and video recordings of Sejm meetings; Dir WOJCIECH KULISIEWICZ; publs *Wykaz ważniejszych nabytków* (quarterly), *Bliżej NATO* (Closer to NATO, 6 a year).

Biblioteka Szkoły Głównej Handlowej – Centralna Biblioteka Ekonomiczna (Library of Warsaw School of Economics – Central Economics Library): 02-521 Warsaw, ul. Rakowiecka 22B; tel. and fax (22) 49-50-98; e-mail infnauk@sgh.waw.pl; f. 1906; collection: social and economic science, geography and economic history, national economy, statistics and demography, accounting, finance, co-operative movement, law, labour problems and special economics; 858,000 vols, 196,000 periodicals, 55,000 special collections; Dir Mgr ALICJA KENSKA; publs *Przegląd Bibliograficzny Piśmiennictwa Ekonomicznego* (quarterly), *Bibliografia Opublikowanego Dorobka Pracowników Naukowo-Dydaktycznych SGH*.

Biblioteka Uniwersytecka w Warszawie (Library of the University of Warsaw): 00–927 Warsaw, Krakowskie Przedmieście 32; tel. and fax (22) 826-41-55; f. 1817; 2,380,000 vols, inc. 130,000 old vols, 597,000 periodicals, 4,000 MSS, 11,000 maps and atlases, 35,000 drawings and prints, 14,000 microforms; Dir Dr HENRYK HOLLENDER; publs *Acta Bibliothecae Universi-tatis Varsoviensis* (irregular), *Wykaz Nabytków Zagranicznych Bibliotek Uniwersytetu Warszawskiego* (35 series, irregular), *Wykaz Bieżących Czasopism Zagranicznych Bibliotek Uniwersytetu Warszawskiego* (irregular), *Skład Osobowy Uniwersytetu Warszawskiego* (annually), *Spis Zajęć Dydaktycznych w Proku Akademickim* (annually).

Centralna Biblioteka Geografii i Ochrony Środowiska (Library of the Institute of Geography and Spatial Organization of the Polish Academy of Sciences): 00–818 Warsaw, Twarda 51/55; tel. (22) 697-88-32; fax (22) 620-62-21; e-mail geoglib@twarda.pan.pl; f. 1954; 125,000 vols, 47,000 vols of periodicals, 4,000 atlases, 103,000 maps; Dir DOROTA GAZICKA; publs *Bibliografia geografii polskiej* (irregular), *Przegląd geograficzny, Prace geograficzne, Geographia Polonica, Dokumentacja geograficzna, Zeszyty IGiPZ PAN*.

Centralna Biblioteka Rolnicza (Central Agricultural Library): 00–950 Warsaw, POB 360; tel. (22) 826-60-41; fax (22) 826-01-57; e-mail cebibrol@atos.warman.com.pl; f. 1955; branches at Puławy and Bydgoszcz; mem. of

Agris-FAO; 417,000 vols on agriculture and related sciences; centre for information and documentation in agriculture and for exchange with scientific institutions abroad; Gen. Dir Dr KRYSTYNA KOCZNOROWSKA; publs *Bibliography of Polish Agricultural and Food Economy Literature, Modern Agriculture: Science, Advice and Practice.*

Centralna Biblioteka Statystyczna im. Stefana Szulca (Central Statistical Library): 00–925 Warsaw, Al. Niepodległości 208; tel. (22) 25-03-45; fax (22) 608-31-88; f. 1918; collection: scientific and specialized (economic and social subjects, with emphasis on statistics); 420,000 vols, 4,000 maps, 5,900 metres of archives; Dir JANINA PAWLIK; publs *Bibliografia Wydawnictw Głównego Urzędu Statystycznego* (irregular), *Bibliografia Polskiego Piśmiennictwa Statystycznego* (irregular), *Roczniki zagraniczne w zboriach Centralnej Biblioteki Statystycznej* (irregular), *Biuletyn Nabytków CBS* (4 a year).

Centralna Biblioteka Wojskowa (Central Military Library): 04-041 Warsaw, ul. Ostrobramska 109; tel. (22) 673-76-25; fax (22) 681-69-40; f. 1919; 254,000 vols, 137,000 periodicals; special collection: 135,000 vols; Dir Płk Dr KRZYSZTOF KOMOROWSKI; publs *Polska Bibliografia Wojskowa* (Polish Military Bibliography, quarterly), *Biuletyn Nabytków Piśmiennictwa Wojskowego Centralnej Biblioteki Wojskowej* (irregular).

Centralne Archiwum Wojskowe (Central Military Archives): 00-910 Warsaw 72; tel. and fax (2) 681-32-02; f. 1918; military history from 1914; 6,500 vols, archive of 1,418,000 items; Dir ANDRZEJ BARTNIK; publ. *Biuletyn Wojskowej Służby Archiwalnej* (1 a year).

Główna Biblioteka Lekarska (Central Medical Library): 00–791 Warsaw, Chocimska 22; tel. 49-78-51; fax 49-78-02; e-mail gbl@atos.warman.com.pl; f. 1945; mainly scientific collection; 472,000 vols, incl. 4,000 old vols, 16,000 MSS and 148,000 periodicals; collection of medical items, drawings and illustrations; Dir Prof. JANUSZ KAPUŚCIK; publs *Biuletyn Głównej Biblioteki Lekarskiej* (2 a year), *Polska Bibliografia Lekarska* (year book).

Główna Biblioteka Pracy i Zabezpieczenia Społecznego (Central Library of Labour and Social Security): 00-496 Warsaw, ul. Nowy Świat 11/13; tel. and fax 629-96-33; e-mail gbpizs@gbpizs.mpips.gov.pl; f. 1974; affiliated to Ministry of Labour and Social Policy; collection: labour, wages, social affairs and related problems; 50,000 vols, 13,000 vols of periodicals; Dir MAŁGORZATA KŁOSSOWSKA; publs *Bibliography of economic and social problems of labour* (annually), *Documentation Review* (monthly), special bibliographies (irregular).

Naczelna Dyrekcja Archiwów Państwowych (Main Directorate of the Polish State Archives): 00-950 Warsaw, ul. Długa 6; tel. (22) 831-32-06; fax (22) 831-75-63; f. 1945; library of 17,000 vols; Dir-Gen. Doc. Dr hab. DARIA NAŁĘCZ; publs *Archeion* (2 a year), *Teki archiwalne* (annually).

Ośrodek Informacji Naukowej Polskiej Akademii Nauk (Scientific Information Centre of the Polish Academy of Sciences): 00–330 Warsaw, Pałac Staszica, Nowy Świat 72; tel. 26-84-10; telex 82-5414; fax 26-98-21; f. 1953; library of 23,000 vols and microcopies of title pages of *c.* 900 scientific periodicals from all over the world on social science and other scientific disciplines; Dir Dr ANDRZEJ GROMEK; publs *Przegląd Informacji o Naukoznawstwie* (Review of Information on Science of Science, quarterly), *Zagadnienia Informacji Naukowej* (Problems of Information Science, 2 a year), *Przegląd Literatury Metodologicznej* (Review of Methodological Literature, 2 a year).

Ośrodek Przetwarzania Informacji (Information Processing Centre): 00-950 Warsaw, Al. Niepodległości 188B, POB 355; tel. (22) 825-61-78; fax (22) 825-33-19; e-mail opi@opi.org.pl; f. 1990; international co-operation, technology transfer, information services on research and development; database management; Dir Dr PAWEL GIERYCZ; publs *Science-Information-Business* (2 a year), *Informator Nauki Polskiej* (Polish Research Directory, every 2 years).

Wrocław

Biblioteka Główna i Ośrodek Informacji Naukowo-Technicznej Politechniki Wrocławskiej (Central Library and Scientific Information Centre of Wrocław University of Technology): 50–370 Wrocław, Wybrzeże S. Wyspiańskiego 27; tel. (71) 320-23-05; fax (71) 328-29-60; e-mail bg@bg.pwr.wroc.pl.; f. 1946; 903,900 books, 1,600 periodicals; Dir Dr inż. HENRYK SZARSKI; publs *Prace Naukowe Biblioteki Głównej i OINT Politechniki Wrocławskiej* (irregular), *Prace Bibliograficzne* (annually).

Biblioteka Uniwersytecka we Wrocławiu (Library of the University of Wrocław): 50-076 Wrocław, Szajnochy 10; tel. and fax (71) 44-34-32; e-mail infnauk@bu.uni.wroc.pl; f. 1945; collection: 3,230,000 vols, incl. 14,000 manuscripts, 310,000 old prints, 11,000 cartographic items, 45,000 vols of music, 45,000 items of graphic art; Silesiaca and Lusatica; bibliography, international relations Poland—Germany — the slavonic countries; Dir Dr ANDRZEJ ŁADOMIRSKI; publs *Bibliografia Publikacji Pracowników Uniwersytetu Wrocławskiego* (annually), *Bibliografia Piśmiennictwa o Uniwersytecie Wrocławskim* (irregular), *Bibliothecalia Wratislaviensia* (irregular).

Biblioteka Zakładu Narodowego im. Ossolińskich (Ossolinski National Institute Library): 50-139 Wrocław, ul. Szewska 37; tel. (71) 44-44-71; fax (71) 44-85-61; e-mail znio@win.oss.wroc.pl; f. 1817; 1,450,000 vols; also MSS, old prints, iconography and other special collections; Dir Dr ADOLF JUZWENKO; publ. *Czasopismo Zakładu Narodowego im. Ossolińskich.*

Wojewódzka i Miejska Biblioteka Publiczna im. Tadeusza Mikulskiego we Wrocławiu (T. Mikulski Voivodship and Municipal Public Library): 50-116 Wrocław, Rynek 58; tel. 44-40-01; fax 44-18-08; 245,000 vols, 125,000 special collections; Dir LEON KRZEMIENIECKI; publs *Książka i Czytelnik* (2 a year), *Kultura Wrocławia w Publikacjach* (Bibliography, annually).

Museums and Art Galleries

Bydgoszcz

Muzeum Okręgowe im. Leona Wyczółkowskiego (L. Wyczółkowski Museum): 85-006 Bydgoszcz, Gdańska 4; tel. and fax (52) 22-75-76; f. 1880; Polish art of 19th and 20th centuries; paintings and graphic art of Leon Wyczółkowski and gallery of contemporary Polish paintings; Archaeological and Local History brs and Coin Room; library of 41,000 vols; Dir Mgr MAŁGORZATA WINTER.

Bytom

Muzeum Górnośląskie w Bytomiu (Upper Silesian Museum): 41-902 Bytom, Pl. Jana III Sobieskiego 2; tel. (32) 281-82-94; fax (32) 281-34-01; e-mail mgbytom@us.edu.pl; f. 1927 in Katowice, transferred in 1945; history, archaeology, ethnography, natural history, Polish and foreign art; library of 46,000 vols; 2 branch museums (ul. W. Korfantego 34 and 38); Dir MIECZYSŁAW DOBKOWSKI; publs *Rocznik Muzeum Górnośląskiego w Bytomiu, Series: Archeologia, Historia, Sztuka, Etnografia, Przyroda, Entomology* (in English, annually).

Cracow

Muzeum Archeologiczne w Krakowie (Archaeological Museum in Cracow): 31-002 Cracow, ul. Senacka 3; tel. (12) 422-75-60; fax (12) 422-77-61; f. 1850; library of 11,753 vols, 16,726 periodicals; Dir JACEK RYDZEWSKI; publs *Materiały Archeologiczne* (annually), *Materiały Archeologiczne Nowej Huty* (annually).

Muzeum Etnograficzne im. S. Udzieli w Krakowie (Ethnographic Museum in Cracow); 31-060 Cracow, Pl. Wolnica 1; tel. (12) 656-56-01; fax (12) 656-36-12; f. 1910; history, folk art and folk culture of Poland; also foreign collections from Europe, Asia, Africa, S. America; library of 22,000 vols; archives; Dir MARIA ZACHOROWSKA; publ. *Rocznik Muzeum Etnograficznego w Krakowie* (annually).

Muzeum Historyczne m. Krakowa (History Museum of the City of Cracow): 31-011 Cracow, Krzysztofory, Rynek Główny 35; tel. 22-32-64; f. 1899; traditions, history and culture of the city of Cracow, arms and clocks, history of the theatre in Cracow, history and culture of the Jews in Cracow; library of 23,810 vols; special collection of 1,171 items; Dir ANDRZEJ SZCZYGIEŁ; publ. *Krzysztofory-Zeszyty Naukowe* (annually).

Muzeum Narodowe w Krakowie (National Museum in Cracow): 30-062 Cracow, 3 Maja ave 1; tel. (12) 634-33-77; fax (12) 633-97-67; f. 1879; history, fine art, costume and textiles, arms and armour, numismatics, house-museums of Matejko, Wyspiański, Mehoffer and Szymanowski, Japanese art and technology; library of 300,000 vols and Czartoryski Library; Dir TADEUSZ CHRUŚCICKI; publs, *Rozprawy i Sprawozdania Muzeum Narodowego w Krakowie* (Yearbook), *Notae Numismaticae Zapiski Numizmatyczne* (yearbook).

Zamek Królewski na Wawelu (Wawel Royal Castle): 31-001 Cracow, Wawel 5; tel. and fax (12) 422-19-50; e-mail zamek@wawel.krakow.pl; f. 1930; (*a*) Collections of art in the Royal Castle: Italian Renaissance furniture, King Sigismund August's 16th-century collection of Flemish tapestries, Italian and Dutch painting, Polish carpets; (*b*) Royal treasury, crown jewels, historical relics, banners, gold objects; (*c*) Armoury: Polish and West European weapons; (*d*) Oriental objects of art: Persian and Turkish weaponry and tents; oriental rugs, Chinese and Japanese pottery; (*e*) Collection relating to the history of Wawel Hill, other archaeological materials, Polish stove tiles from the 15th–18th centuries; (*f*) 18th-century Meissen porcelain; library of 12,000 vols, 370 periodicals; Dir Prof. JAN OSTROWSKI; publs *Studia Waweliana, Biblioteka Wawelska* (Library of the Wawel), *Acta Archaeologica Waweliana.*

Frombork

Muzeum Mikołaja Kopernika (Nicholas Kopernik Museum): 14–530 Frombork, ul. Katedralna 8; tel. (55) 243-72-18; e-mail frombork@softel.elblag.pl; f. 1948; biographical exhibits, history of astronomy, astronomical observatory, example of Foucault's pendulum, planetarium; modern art gallery; library of 20,000 vols; Dir Mgr HENRYK SZKOP; publ. *Komentarze Fromborskie* (annually).

Gdańsk

Centralne Muzeum Morskie (Polish Maritime Museum): 80–835 Gdańsk, ul. Szeroka 67/68; tel. and fax 31-84-53; f. 1960; depts of ports development, history of shipbuilding, history of maritime shipping and trade, marine fine arts, history of yachting, underwater archaeology, educational services; special vessel for underwater archaeological investigations; laboratory for conservation of artefacts recovered from sea; Lighthouse Museum in Rozewie; also br. in Hel (history of Polish fishery; open-air exhibition of types of fishing boats); br. in Tczew (history of Polish inland navigation); four historic ships (incl. sailing ship 'Dar Pomorza', fmr Polish schoolship); library of 34,000 vols, archives: plans, drawings, photos, documents; Dir Doc. Dr Hab. ANDRZEJ ZBIERSKI.

Muzeum Archeologiczne w Gdańsku (Archaeological Museum in Gdańsk): 80–958 Gdańsk, ul. Mariacka 25/26; tel. (58) 301-50-31; fax (58) 301-52-28; e-mail mag@gdansk.cnt.pl; f. 1953; library of 23,000 vols; Dir HENRYK PANER; publ. *Pomorania Antiqua*.

Muzeum Historii Miasta Gdańska (History Museum of the City of Gdańsk): 80–831 Gdańsk, Ratusz Głównego Miasta, ul. Długa 47; tel. and fax (58) 301-48-71; f. 1970; Dir ADAM KOPERKIEWICZ.

Muzeum Narodowe w Gdańsku (National Museum in Gdańsk): 80-822 Gdańsk, ul. Toruńska 1; tel. (58) 301-70-61; fax (58) 301-11-25; f. 1872; 12th- to 20th-century art, 15th- to 20th-century craftwork, photography, ethnography (collns held at various locations); library of 16,000 vols, 3,000 periodicals; Dir TADEUSZ PIASKOWSKI.

Kielce

Muzeum Narodowe w Kielcach (National Museum in Kielce): 25–010 Kielce, Pl. Zamkowy 1; tel. (41) 344-40-14; fax (41) 344-82-61; f. 1908; State Museum in 17th-century palace; Polish baroque interiors; Polish painting from the 17th to the 20th century; arms and armour; numismatic exhibits; museum showing history and culture of the Kielce province (25-303 Kielce, Rynek 3–5); library of 37,000 vols; brs: Museum of Stefan Żeromski's early years, Henryk Sienkiewicz Museum in Oblęgorek; Dir ALOJZY OBORNY; publ. *Rocznik Muzeum Świętokrzyskiego* (annual) from vol. 10 *Rocznik Muzeum Narodowego w Kielcach*.

Łódź

Centralne Muzeum Włókiennictwa (Central Museum of Textiles): 93–034 Łódź, ul. Piotrkowska 282; fax (42) 684-33-55; f. 1960; collections of textile tools and machines, documents of history of textile industry, Polish and foreign artistic textiles, industrial textiles, ancient and modern clothes; library of 12,000 vols; Dir NORBERT ZAWISZA; publ. *Bulletin*.

Muzeum Archeologiczne i Etnograficzne: 91-415 Łódź, Pl. Wolności 14; tel. (42) 632-84-40; fax (42) 632-97-14; f. 1956 as amalgamation of Archaeological and Ethnographical Museums (f. 1931); archaeology, ethnography, numismatics; radio-chemical laboratory; library of 43,000 vols; Dir Doc. Dr hab. RYSZARD GRYGIEL; publs *Guides and Reports, Prace i Materiały Muzeum Archeologicznego i Etnograficznego* (archaeology, ethnography, numismatics and conservation series).

Muzeum Sztuki w Łodzi (Art Museum): 90–734 Łódź, ul. Więckowskiego 36; tel. (42) 33-97-90; telex 884700; fax (42) 32-99-41; f. 1930; departments: Gothic art; foreign painting of the 15th–19th centuries; Polish painting of the 18th–20th centuries; international modern and contemporary art; Księży Młyn house with late-19th-century interior décor; Dir NAWOJKA CIEŚLIŃSKA.

Lublin

Muzeum Lubelskie w Lublinie (Lublin District Museum): 20–117 Lublin, The Castle (Zamek); tel. (81) 532-17-43; f. 1906; regional archaeological, historical and ethnographic collection, Polish and foreign paintings and decorative art; armoury; numismatics; conservation dept; library of 20,000 vols; Dir ZYGMUNT NASALSKI; publ. *Studia i Materiały Lubelskie*.

Państwowe Muzeum na Majdanku (State Museum in Majdanek): 20–325 Lublin, ul. Droga Męczenników Majdanka 67; tel. (81) 744-26-47; fax (81) 744-05-26; former Nazi concentration camp; Dir EDWARD BALAWEJDER; publ. *Zeszyty Majdanka* (annually).

Olsztynek

Muzeum Budownictwa Ludowego—Park Etnograficzny w Olsztynku (Museum of Building, Ethnographic Park in Olsztynek): 11-015 Olsztynek, ul. Sportowa 21; tel. 519-21-64; f. 1962; library of 6,000 vols; Dir TADEUSZ KUFEL.

Oświęcim

Państwowe Muzeum Oświęcim-Brzezinka: 32–603 Oświęcim 5, ul. Więźniów Oświęcimia 20; tel. (33) 43-20-22; telex 35198; fax (33) 43-19-34; f. 1947; in former Nazi concentration camp at Auschwitz-Birkenau, illustrating system of mass extermination; library of 23,000 vols and archives; Dir Mgr JERZY WRÓBLEWSKI; publs *Zeszyty Oświęcimskie* (in Polish and German).

Poznań

Muzeum Archeologiczne: 61-781 Poznań, ul. Wodna 27; tel. (61) 852-64-30; fax (61) 852-53-06; e-mail lechk@man.poznan.pl; f. 1857; archaeology of Great Poland and the Nile basin; library of 50,000 vols; Dir Prof. Dr LECH KRZYŻANIAK; publs *Fontes Archaeologici Posnanienses* (annually), *Biblioteka Fontes Archaeologici Posnanienses*, *Studies in African Archaeology*.

Muzeum Narodowe (National Museum): 61–745 Poznań, Al. Marcinkowskiego 9; tel. (61)) 852-80-11; fax (61) 851-58-98; f. 1857; Medieval Art, European paintings 14th–19th centuries, Polish paintings 15th–20th centuries, Prints and drawings, Sculpture, Numismatics, Modern art; library of 89,000 vols; br. museums specializing in ethnography, Poznań history, military history, musical instruments, applied arts; Dir Prof. Dr KONSTANTY KALINOWSKI; publs *Studia Muzealne* (annually), *Monographs*, catalogues, guides.

Sanok

Muzeum Budownictwa Ludowego w Sanoku (Museum of Folk Architecture in Sanok): 38–500 Sanok, ul. Traugutta 3; tel. (13) 463-09-04; fax (13) 463-53-81; f. 1958; traditional architecture, interiors, folk arts and crafts, icons; library of 17,000 vols, collection of Orthodox church books; Dir Doc. Dr hab. JERZY CZAJKOWSKI; publs *Materiały Muzeum Budownictwa Ludowego w Sanoku* (annually), *Acta Scansenologica* (annually).

Szczecin

Muzeum Narodowe w Szczecinie (National Museum in Szczecin): 70-561 Szczecin, ul. Staromłyńska 27; tel. 336-070; fax 347-894; f. 1945; archaeological, maritime, ethnographical and history of art collections, sociology, numismatics; special African collection and corresponding library; library of 72,000 vols; Dir WŁADYSŁAW FILIPOWIAK; publ. *Materiały Zachodniopomorskie* (annually).

Sztutowo

Państwowe Muzeum Stutthof w Sztutowie (State Museum in Sztutowo): 82–110 Sztutowo; tel. (55) 247-83-53; fax (55) 247-83-58; former Nazi concentration camp of Stutthof; f. 1962; Dir JANINA GRABOWSKA; publ. *Zeszyty Muzeum Stutthof* (annually).

Toruń

Muzeum Etnograficzne w Toruniu (Ethnographical Museum in Toruń): 87–100 Toruń, Wały gen. Sikorskiego 19; tel. 280-91; f. 1959; folk culture of northern Poland; library of 18,142 vols; Dir ROMAN TUBAJA; publ. *Rocznik Muzeum Etnograficznego w Toruniu* (annually).

Muzeum Okręgowe w Toruniu (District Museum in Toruń): 87–100 Toruń, Rynek Staromiejski 1, Ratusz; tel. 236-84; fax 24029; f. 1861; 14th–20th-century art (painting, graphics, sculpture, handicrafts), Far-Eastern art, history, archaeology, militaria, numismatics, Copernicus museum; library of 22,000 vols; Dir MICHAŁ WOŹNIAK; publs *Rocznik Muzeum w Toruniu* (irregular), *Biuletyn* (4 a year).

Warsaw

Muzeum Historyczne m. st. Warszawy (History Museum of the City of Warsaw): 00-272 Warsaw, Rynek Starego Miasta 28; tel. (22) 635-16-25; fax (22) 831-94-91; f. 1947; exhibits relating to the history of Warsaw from the 10th century; 42,000 vols; Dir Prof. Dr JANUSZ DURKO; publ. *Bibliography of Warsaw*.

Muzeum i Instytut Zoologii PAN (Institute of Zoology): 00-679 Warsaw, ul. Wilcza 64; tel. 628-73-04; fax 629-63-02; f. 1819; attached to Polish Acad. of Sciences; research in various fields of zoology; research station at Łomna near Warsaw; zoological collections of 4,500,000 specimens; archives and documents; library of some 220,000 vols, 1,500 current periodicals; Dir Prof. STANISŁAW A. SLIPIŃSKI; publs *Annales Zoologici*, *Fragmenta Faunistica*, *Acta Ornithologica*, *Memorabilia Zoologica*, *Catalogus Faunae Poloniae*, *Fauna Poloniae*, *Keys for the Identification of Polish Invertebrates*.

Muzeum Literatury im. Adama Mickiewicza (Adam Mickiewicz Museum of Literature): 00-272 Warsaw, Rynek Starego Miasta 20; tel. (22) 831-40-61; fax (22) 831-76-92; f. 1951; museum of literary history of Poland especially 19th and 20th centuries; 100,000 vols; Dir JANUSZ ODROWĄŻ-PIENIĄŻEK; publ. *Blok-Notes Muzeum Literatury*.

Muzeum Narodowe (National Museum): 00-495 Warsaw, Al. Jerozolimskie 3; tel. 621-10-31; fax 622-85-59; f. 1862; paintings and sculpture; prints and drawings; numismatics; decorative arts and crafts; photography; Egyptian, Greek, Roman and Byzantine (Nubian) art; medieval and modern Polish art from 12th century to present day; 14th–19th-century foreign painting; also administers the Ignacy Paderewski Museum, the Poster Museum at Wilanów, Królikarnia palace in Warsaw and, outside Warsaw, Nieborów Palace; library of 130,000 vols; Dir FERDYNAND RUSZCZYC; publs *Rocznik Muzeum Narodowego w Warszawie* (Yearbook), *Bulletin du Musée National de Varsovie* (quarterly).

Muzeum Niepodległości (Museum of Independence): 00-240 Warsaw, Al. Solidarności 62; tel. (22) 827-37-70; fax (22) 827-03-23; f. 1990; history of Polish independence movements; library of 21,000 vols, 1,500 periodicals; Dir Dr ANDRZEJ STAWARZ.

Muzeum Techniki w Warszawie (Museum of Technology): 00-901 Warsaw, Pałac Kultury i Nauki; tel. and fax 620-47-10; f. 1875; popularization of science and technology and their history, preservation of monuments of technology; planetarium; cinema, library of 15,000 vols; Dir JERZY JASIUK; local branches: Museum of Ancient Metallurgy in Nowa Słupia, Museum of the old Polish Basin in Sielpia, water-worked forges in Stara Kuźnica and Gdańsk, 19th-century blast furnace in Chlewiska, Museum of Industry in Old Rolling Mill, Warsaw.

Muzeum Wojska Polskiego (Museum of the Polish Army): Warsaw 43, Al. Jerozolimskie 3; tel. (22) 629-52-71; fax (22) 629-52-73; f. 1920; collection of 79,000 weapons, uniforms, banners, decorations, etc; permanent exhibition showing Polish military history from the 10th to the 20th centuries; militaria from Asia, Africa, Australia; collection of modern paintings, sculptures and graphics; iconographic collection; conservation workshops for metal, textile, wooden, leather and paper exhibits; library of 40,000 vols; Dir Colonel Zbigniew Święcicki; publ. *Muzealnictwo Wojskowe* (Military Museology, irregular).

Muzeum Ziemi PAN (Museum of the Earth): 00-488 Warsaw, al. Na Skarpie 20–26; tel. and fax (22) 629-74-97; f. 1932; attached to the Academy of Sciences; most important collections: Polish minerals, rocks, meteorites, fossil flora and fauna, Baltic amber; Dir Doc. Krzysztof Jakubowski; publ. *Prace Muzeum Ziemi PAN* (1 or 2 a year).

Ogród Botaniczny – Centrum Zachowania Różnorodności Biologicznej PAN (Botanical Garden) – Centre for the Conservation of Biological Diversity): 02-973 Warsaw 34, ul. Prawdziwka 2, POB 84; tel. (22) 648-38-56; fax (22) 757-66-45; e-mail obpan@ikp.atm.com.pl; f. 1974; attached to Polish Acad. of Sciences; conservation and evaluation of genetic resources of plants; library of 8,000 vols; Dir Jerzy Puchalski; publs *Biuletyn* (annually), *Prace* (reports, irregular).

Państwowe Muzeum Archeologiczne (State Archaeological Museum): 00-950 Warsaw 40, ul. Długa 52; tel. (22) 831-32-21; fax (22) 831-51-95; e-mail pma@ternet.pl; f. 1923; prehistoric and proto-historic exhibits; organizes regional and field exhibitions, and carries out archaeological excavations throughout Poland; br. at Biskupin (an Iron Age fortified settlement), archaeological stores at Rybno; library of 40,000 vols; Dir Dr Jan Jaskanis; publs *Wiadomości Archeologiczne, Materiały Starożytne i Wczesnośredniowieczne.*

Państwowe Muzeum Etnograficzne w Warszawie (State Ethnographic Museum in Warsaw): 00-056 Warsaw, ul. Kredytowa 1; tel. (22) 827-76-41; fax (22) 827-66-69; f. 1888; Polish and non-European ethnographical collection; library of 23,000 vols; Dir Dr Jan Witold Suliga; publ. *Zeszyty Państwowego Muzeum Etnograficznego w Warszawie* (Reports, annually).

Zamek Królewski w Warszawie—Pomnik Historii i Kultury Narodowej (Royal Castle in Warsaw, National History and Culture Memorial): 00-277 Warsaw, Pl. Zamkowy 4; tel. (22) 657-21-70; fax (22) 635-08-08; f. 1980; furniture, prints, paintings, sculptures, applied arts, drawings; library of 25,000 vols; Dir Andrzej Rottermund; publs *Kronika Zamkowa* (quarterly), books and guides.

Wieliczka

Muzeum Żup Krakowskich Wieliczka (Cracow Salt Works Museum in Wieliczka): 32-020 Wieliczka, Zamkowa 8; tel. 422-19-47; fax 278-30-28; f. 1951; history, archaeology, geology, history of art and ethnography, archives, metal conservation laboratory; library of 18,000 vols, special collections: photographs, mining maps; Dir Antoni Jodłowski; publ. *Studia i Materiały do Dziejów Żup Solnych w Polsce* (annually).

Wrocław

Muzeum Archeologiczne we Wrocławiu (Archaeological Museum in Wrocław): 50-077 Wrocław, ul. Kazimierza Wielkiego 35; tel. and fax (71) 44-28-29; Dir Doc. Dr Jerzy Lodowski; publ. *Silesia Antiqua* (annually).

Muzeum Architektury (Museum of Architecture): 50-156 Wrocław, ul. Bernardyńska 5; tel. (71) 343-36-75; fax (71) 44-65-77; f. 1965; Polish and other architecture; modern art; library of 6,400 vols; Dir Prof. Dr hab. Olgierd Czerner; publs catalogues.

Muzeum Historyczne we Wrocławiu (Historical Museum in Wrocław): 50-107 Wrocław, ul. Sukiennice 14/15; tel. 44-57-30; fax 44-47-85; f. 1970; Dir Maciej Łagiewski.

Muzeum Narodowe we Wrocławiu (National Museum in Wrocław): 50-153 Wrocław, Pl. Powstańców Warszawy 5; tel. 388-30; telex 071-2542; fax 356-43; f. 1948; collection of medieval art, 17th–20th-century Polish painting, 16th–20th-century European painting, decorative arts, prints, photographs, ethnography and history relating to Silesia, panoramic painting 'Battle of Racławice'; numismatics; library of 82,000 vols; Dir Mariusz Hermansdorfer; publ. *Roczniki Sztuki Śląskiej* (annually).

Muzeum Sztuki Medalierskiej (Museum of Medallic Art): 50-108 Wrocław, ul. Kielbaśnicza 5; tel. 44-39-83; f. 1965; medals, medallions, plaques, orders and decorations of all countries; special library: 6,000 vols, MSS, old books, posters; Dir Zdzisław Olszanowski; publ. *Biuletyn*.

Zakopane

Muzeum Tatrzańskie im. Tytusa Chałubińskiego (T. Chałubiński Tatra Museum): 34-500 Zakopane, ul. Krupówki 10; tel. (18) 201-52-05; fax 638-72; e-mail museum@zakopane.top.pl; f. 1888; geology, regional flora, fauna, history and ethnography; glass paintings, pottery, sculpture, wooden, metal and leather ware, costumes, musical instruments, etc.; collection of furniture, textiles, ceramics and jewellery made in the Zakopane style; collection of oriental carpets; contemporary pictures by St. Ignacy Witkiewicz and Marek Żuławsky; Wł. Hasior Art Gallery; library of 50,000 vols; Dir Mgr Teresa Jabłońska; publ. *Rocznik Podhalański*.

Universities

UNIWERSYTET GDAŃSKI
(University of Gdańsk)

80-952 Gdańsk, Ul. Bażyńskiego 1A
Telephone: 52-50-71
Fax: 52-22-12
Founded 1970
State control
Academic year: October to June
Rector: Prof. Dr hab. Marcin Pliński
Pro-Rectors: Prof. Dr hab. Jolanta Jabłońska-Bonca, Prof. Dr hab. Andrzej Ceynowa, Dr Mirosław Krajewski
Administrative Director: Dr Andrzej Friedrich
Librarian: Mgr Urszula Sawicka
Library: see Libraries
Number of teachers: 1,438
Number of students: 24,000
Publications: *Zeszyty Naukowe*, *Prace Habilitacyjne, Skrypty.*106

DEANS

Faculty of Biology, Geography and Oceanology: Dr hab. Halina Piekarek-Jankowska
Faculty of Chemistry: Prof. Dr hab. Bernard Lammek
Faculty of Business Management: Dr hab. Joanna Senyszyn
Faculty of Economics: Prof. Dr hab. Jan Burnewicz
Faculty of Languages and History: Prof. Dr hab. Jan Iluk
Faculty of Social Sciences: Prof. Dr hab. Bohdan Dziemidok
Faculty of Mathematics and Physics: Prof. Dr hab. Robert Alicki
Faculty of Law and Administration: Dr hab. Andrzej Szmyt
Faculty of Biotechnology: Prof. Dr hab. med. Wiesław Makarewicz

ATTACHED INSTITUTES

Biological Station: 80-680 Gdańsk-Górki Wschodnie; Dir Prof. Dr hab. Edward Skorkowski.

Limnological Station: 83-300 Borucino, województwo gdańskie; Dir Dr hab. Władysław Lange.

Maritime Field Laboratory: 84–150 Hel, ul. Morska 2; Dir Dr Krzysztof Skóra.

Bird Migration Station: Przebędowo, 84–210 Choczewo; Dir Prof. Dr hab. Przemysław Busse.

UNIWERSYTET JAGIELLOŃSKI
(Jagiellonian University)

31-007 Cracow, Gołębia 24
Telephone: (12) 422-10-33
Telex: 322297
Fax: (12) 422-63-06
E-mail: rektor@adm.uj.edu.pl
Founded 1364
Academic year: October to June
Rector: Prof. Dr hab. Aleksander Koj
Vice-Rectors: Prof. Dr hab. Franciszek Ziejka (General Affairs), Prof. Dr hab. med. Stanisław Konturek (School of Medicine), Prof. Dr hab. Marek Szymoński (International Relations), Prof. Dr hab. Stanisław Hodorowicz (Research), Prof. Dr hab. Tadeusz Marek (Education)
Administrator: Dr Tadeusz Skarbek
Librarian: Dr hab. Krzystof Zamorski
Library: see Libraries
Number of teachers: 3,200
Number of students: 27,000
Publications: *Zeszyty Naukowe Uniwersytetu Jagiellońskiego* (annually in 26 series), *Kronika Universytetu Jagiellońskiego* (annually), *Acta Universitatis Iagellonicae* (monthly), *Alma Mater* (4 a year).

DEANS

Faculty of Law and Administration: Prof. Dr hab. Sylwester Wójcik
Faculty of Management and Social Communication: Prof. Dr Emil Orzechowski
Faculty of Medicine: Prof. Dr med. Wiesław Pawlik
Faculty of Pharmacy: Dr hab. Maciej Pawłowski
Faculty of Health Care: Dr hab. Antoni Czupryna
Faculty of Philosophy: Prof. Dr hab. Zdzisław Mach
Faculty of History: Prof. Dr hab. Andrzej Chwalba
Faculty of Philology: Prof. Dr hab. Jan Michalik
Faculty of Mathematics and Physics: Prof. Dr hab. Krzysztof Fiałkowski
Faculty of Biology and Earth Sciences: Prof. Dr hab. Antoni Jackowski
Faculty of Chemistry: Prof. Dr hab. Maria Nowakowska

PROFESSORS

Faculty of Law and Administration:

Beksiak, J., Theory of Economics
Biernat, S., European Law
Brzeziński, B., Financial Law
Cziomer, E., International Relations

DODA, Z., Criminal Procedure
DROZD, E., Civil Law, Private International Law
FILIPEK, J., Administrative Law
GABERLE, A., Criminology
GAWLIK, B., Civil Law
GIZBERT-STUDNICKI, T., Theory and Philosophy of Law
GRODZISKI, S., History of State and Law
GRZYBOWSKI, M., Modern Political Systems
HANAUSEK, T., Forensic and Police Science
JASKÓLSKI, M., History of Political and Legal Thought
KOZUB-CIEMBRONIEWICZ, W., Modern Political Movements and Political Thought
LANKOSZ, K., International Public Law
LICHOROWICZ, A., Agricultural Law
LITEWSKI, W., Roman Law
MAJCHROWSKI, J. M., Recent Political History of Poland, History of Political and Legal Doctrines, Religion Policy
MANIA, A., Contemporary History
MĄCIOR, W., Criminal Law, Criminal Liability
MĄCZYŃSKI, A., Civil and International Private Law
PAŁECKI, K., Theory and Sociology of Law
PANKOWICZ, A., Self-Government
PISAREK, W., Press Research
PŁAZA, S., History of Polish State and Law
PREUSSNER-ZAMORSKA, J., Civil Law
PYZIOŁ, W., Private Business Law
SARNECKI, P., Constitutional Law
SONDEL, J., Roman Law
STELMACH, J., Theory and Philosophy of Law
SWIĄTKOWSKI, A., Labour Law and Social Policy
SZEWCZYK, M., Criminal Law
URUSZCZAK, W., History of Ecclesiastical Law, Human Rights.
WALASZEK-PYZIOŁ, A., Public Business Law
WALTOŚ, S., Criminal Procedures, History of Law
WASILEWSKI, A., Environmental Protection Law
WEISS, I., Business and Commercial Law
WÓJCIK, S., Civil and Agricultural Law
WOJCIKIEWICZ, J., Forensic and Police Science
WOŚ, T., Administration Law, Administration Procedures Law
ZAWADA, K., International Private Law
ZIMMERMAN, J., Administrative Procedures
ZOLL, A., Criminal Law
ZYBLIKIEWICZ, L., Political Science, International Relations

Faculty of Medicine:

ALEKSANDROWICZ, J., Psychotherapy, Psychiatry
ARMATA, J., Paediatrics, Haemato-oncology
BARCZYŃSKI, M., Surgery
BARTKOWSKI, S., Maxillofacial and Oral Surgery
BILSKI, R., Physiology, Biophysics
BOGDAŁ, J., Gastroenterology
BOGDASZEWSKA-CZABANOWSKA, J., Dermatology
BOMBA, J., Psychiatry
CABAN, J., Infectious Diseases
CICHOCKI, T., Histology
CHŁAP, Z., Physiopathology
DANILEWICZ, B., Neurology
DEMBIŃSKA-KIEĆ, A., Clinical Biochemistry
DEMBINSKI, A., Physiology
DOLEŻAL, M., Infectious Diseases
DUBIEL, J., Cardiology
DZIATKOWIAK, A., Cardiology
DZIATKOWIAK, H., Paediatrics and Adolescent Endocrinology
FRENDO, J., Biochemistry
GAJDA, Z., History of Medicine
GEDLICZKA, O., Surgery
GOŚCIŃSKI, I., Neurology
GROCHOWSKI, J., Paediatric Surgery
GRODZIŃSKA, L., Pharmacology
GRYGLEWSKI, R., Pharmacology
HECZKO, P., Microbiology
JANICKI, K., Internal Medicine
JĘDRYCHOWSKI, W., Epidemiology and Preventive Medicine
KACZMARCZYK-STACHOWSKA, A., Dentistry
KAŁUŻA, J., Neuropathology
KARCZ, D., Surgery
KAWECKA-JASZCZ, K., Cardiology
KIEĆ, A., Toxicology, Internal Medicine
KLIMEK, R., Gynaecology, Obstetrics
KOCEMBA, J., Geriatrics
KONIECZNY, L., Biochemistry
KONTUREK, S., Physiology
KORBUT, R., Pharmacology
KOSTKA-TRĄBKA, E., Clinical Pharmacology
KUŚMIDERSKI, J., Neurology, Neuroradiology
LITWIN, J., Histology
MAJEWSKI, S., Dental Prosthetics
MARCINKIEWICZ, J., Immunology
MIODOŃSKI, A., Laryngology
MIRECKA, J., Histology
MUSIAŁ, J., Internal Medicine
NASKALSKI, J., Clinical Biochemistry
NIŻANKOWSKA, E., Pulmonology
OLSZEWSKI, E., Otolaryngology
ORWID, M., Psychiatry
PACH, J., Toxicology
PAWLIK, W., Experimental Physiology
PIETRZYK, J., Paediatrics
PIWOWARSKA, W., Cardiology
POPCZYŃSKA-MAREK, M., Paediatric Cardiology
POPIELA, T., Gastroenterological Surgery
PTAK, W., Microbiology, Immunology
RYN, Z., Psychiatry
SĘDZIWY, L., Electrocardiology
SIERADZKI, J., Metabolic Diseases
SKOTNICKI, A., Haematology
SREBRO, Z., Medical Genetics
STACHURA, J., Pathomorphology
STARZYCKA, M., Ophthalmology
STOPYRA, J., Paediatrics
SUŁOWICZ, W., Nephrology
SZAFRAN, Z., Biochemistry
SZCZEKLIK, A., Internal Medicine
SZYBIŃSKI, Z., Internal Medicine, Endocrinology, Nuclear Medicine
SZYMUSIK, A., Psychiatry
THOR, P., Physiopathology
TOBIASZ-ADAMCZYK, B., Epidemiology and Preventive Medicine
TRACZ, W., Cardiology
TRĄBKA, J., Neurology
TUROWSKA, B., Forensic Medicine
TUROWSKI, G., Immunology
ZDEBSKA, E., Paediatric Cardiac Surgery
ZDEBSKI, Z., Gynaecology and Obstetrics
ZEMBALA, M., Microbiology, Immunology
ŻARNECKI, A., Genetics, Medical Statistics

Faculty of Pharmacy:

BOJARSKI, J., Organic Chemistry
BRANDYS, J., Toxicology
CZARNECKI, R., Pharmacodynamics
GUMINSKA, M., Biochemistry
KOHLMUNZER, S., Pharmaceutical Botany
RZESZUTKO, W., Inorganic Chemistry
STAREK, A., Biochemical Toxicology
ZACHWIEJA, Z., Food Chemistry, Nutrition
ZEJC, A., Pharmaceutical Chemistry

Faculty of Philosophy:

ADAMSKI, F., Sociology of Family and Religion
ALEKSANDER, T., Adult Education
DRABINA, J., History of Christianity
FRYSZTACKI, K., Sociology
GAŁDOWA, A., General Psychology
GALEWICZ, W., Philosophy
GROTT, B., Religious Studies
KOCIK, L., Sociology
KUBIAK, H., Sociology of Politics
ŁAGOWSKI, B., Philosophy
LIPIEC, J., Philosophy
MACH, Z., Anthropology
NĘCKA, E., Psychology
OCHMAN, J., Religious Studies
PACŁAWSKA, K., Pedagogy
PACZKOWSKA-ŁAGOWSKA, E.
NĘCKI, Z., Social Psychology
PALKA, S., Methodological Elements of Education
PALUCH, A., Sociology
PAWLICA, J., Philosophy
PAWLUCZUK, W., Comparative History of Religion
PERZANOWSKI, J., Philosophy
PIĄTEK, Z., Philosophy of Natural Sciences
RODCIŃSKI, S., Pedagogy
SAMEK, J., Education
SOSKĄPSKA, G., Sociology of Law
STRÓZEWSKI, W., Philosophy, Ontology
SUCHOŃ, W., Philosophy
SZMATKA, J., Group Processes
SZTOMPKA, P., Sociological Theory
SZYMAŃSKA, B., Philosophy
WASILEWSKI, J., Sociology
WIERCIŃSKI, A., Religious Studies
WŁODEK-CHRONOWSKA, J., Pedagogy
WOLEŃSKI, J., Philosophy, Epistemology
WROŃSKI, A., Logic
ZARNECHA-BIAŁY, E., Philosophy

Faculty of History:

BACZKOWSKI, K., General Medieval History
CHWALBA, A., Documentation of Polish Independence Movements
CZERSKA, D., East European History
DĄBROWA, E., Ancient History
DYBIEC, J., History of Science and Culture
DZIĘGIEL, L., Ethnology
DZIELSKA, M., Byzantine History
GADOMSKI, J., History of Medieval Art
GEDL, M., Archaeology
GINTER, B., Archaeology
GOĆKOWSKI, J., Ethnology
KOZŁOWSKI, J., Archaeology
KULCZYKOWSKI, M., Modern Polish History
MICHALEWICZ, J., Economic and Social History
OSTROWSKI, JAN, History of Art
OSTROWSKI, JANUSZ, Classical Archaeology
PARCZEWSKI, M., Polish and Modern Archaeology
PIROZYŃSKI, J., General Modern History
PURCHLA, J., Economic History and History of Art
RÓZYCKA-BRYZEK, A., History of Byzantine Art
SZWEYKOWSKI, Z., Musicology
ŚLIWA, J., Mediterranean Archaeology
WYROZUMSKI, J., Medieval History

Faculty of Philology:

BALBUS, S., Theory of Literature
BOCHENEK-FRANCZAKOWA, R., Romanian Philology
BOROWSKI, A., Polish Philology
BORYŚ, W., Comparative and Historical Slavic Linguistics, Slavic Etymology, Serbo-Croatian Linguistics
BŁOŃSKI, J., History of Polish Literature
BRZEZINA, M., Linguistics
BUBAK, J., Hungarian Philology
DĄMBSKA-PROKOP, U., Romance Philology
DRZEWICKA, A., French Literature
DUNAJ, B., Linguistics
FIUT, A., Polish Philology
GRZESZCZUK, S., History of Polish Literature
JAWORSKI, S., History of Polish Literature
KŁAŃSKA, M., German Philology
KORNHAUSER, J., Slavonic Philology
KORPANTY, J., Classical Philology
KORUS, K., Teaching of Classical Languages
KOWALIK, J., Linguistics
KUREK, H., Polish Philology
KURZOWA, Z., Modern Polish Language
LIPIŃSKI, K., German Philology
MAŃCZAK-WOHLFELD, E., English Philology
MAŚLANKA, J., History of Polish Literature
MELANOWICZ, M., Japanese Studies
MICHALIK, J., Theatre Studies
MIODOŃSKA-BROOKES, E., Polish Philology

MUSKAT-TABAKOWSKA, E., Linguistic Pragmatics and the Theory of Translation
NAGUCKA, R., English Linguistics
NAUMOW, A., Slavonic Philology
ORŁOŚ, T., Czech Philology
PISAREK, K., General Linguistics
POLAŃSKI, K., General and Indo-European Linguistics
RAĆNY, A., East Slavonic Philology
RUSEK, J., Bulgarian and Macedonian Philology
SMOCZYŃSKI, W., General and Indo-European Linguistics
STABRYŁA, S., Latin Literature
STACHOWSKI, S., Turkish and Slavonic Linguistics
STĘPIEŃ, M., History of Polish Literature
STRUTYŃSKI, J., Polish Philology
SUCHANEK, L., Russian and Soviet Literature
SZYMAŃSKI, W., History of Polish Literature
TURASIEWICZ, R., Greek Literature
WESOŁOWSKA, D., Polish Philology
WOŹNOWSKI, W., History of Polish Literature
WYKA, M., History of Polish Literature
ZABORSKI, A., Chamito-Semitic Linguistics
ZIEJKA, F., History of Polish Literature

Faculty of Mathematics and Physics:

ARODŹ, H., Field Theory
BAŁANDA, A., Nuclear Physics
BARA, J., Nuclear Physics
BIAŁAS, A., Theory of Elementary Particles, Astrophysics
BLICHARSKI, J. S., Radiospectroscopy, Biophysics
CZYŻ, W., Theory of Elementary Particles, Astrophysics
DENKOWSKI, S., Optimization and Control Theory
DOHNALIK, T., Experimental Physics
FIAŁKOWSKI, K., Theoretical Physics
FULIŃSKI, A., Statistical Physics
GABŁA, L., Surface Physics, Atomic Spectroscopy
GANCARZEWICZ, J., Geometry
GAWLIK, W., Experimental Physics
GROTOWSKI, K., Nuclear Physics
JAKUBOWSKI, R., Image Processing and Recognition
JARCZYK, L., Nuclear Physics
JARNICKI, M., Mathematics
JĘDRZEJEK, C., Theoretical Physics
JURKIEWICZ, J., Theoretical Physics
KAMYS, B., Nuclear Physics
KISIEL, A., Solid State Physics, Semiconductors
KLEINER, W., Mathematics in Natural Sciences
KOTAŃSKI, A., Computer Science, High Energy Physics
KRÓLAS, K., Nuclear Physics
KULESSA, R., Nuclear Physics
LASOTA, A., Mathematics
ŁOJASIEWICZ, S., Analysis, Biomathematics, Differential Equations
MACHALSKI, J., Radioastronomy and Extragalactic Astronomy
MAJKA, Z., Hot Matter
MASŁOWSKI, J., Radioastronomy and Cosmic Physics
MAZURKIEWICZ, A., Computer Science
MICEK, S., Experimental Computer Physics
MOŚCIKI, J., Soft Matter Physics
MUSIOŁ, K., Atomic Physics
OLEŚ, A., Theoretical Physics
PAWŁUCKI, W., Real Functions
PELCZAR, A., Analysis, Differential Equations
PLEŚNIAK, W., Analysis, Complex Functions, Theory of Approximations
RUDNICKI, K., Extragalactic Astronomy
SĘDZIWY, S., Numerical Methods
SICIAK, J., Analysis, Complex Functions
SOKALSKI, K., Soft Condensed Matter Physics
SPAŁEK, J., Condensed Matter Theory
ŚREDNIAWA, B., Theoretical Physics
STARUSZKIEWICZ, A., General Relativity, Electrodynamics, Astrophysics
STRZAŁKOWSKI, A., Nuclear Physics
SZAFIRSKI, B., Analysis, Differential Equations, Theory of Turbulence
SZAFRANIEC, F. H., Functional Analysis, Theory of Operators
SZWED, J., Applied Numerical Methods
SZYMOŃSKI, M., Experimental Physics
SZYTUŁA, A., Solid State Physics, Magnetism
TOMALA, K., Radiospectroscopy
URBAN, S., Molecular Physics
WALUŚ, W., Nuclear Physics
WINIARSKI, T., Analytic and Algebraic Geometry
WITAŁA, H., Nuclear Physics
WOSIEK, J., Theoretical Computer Physics
WRÓBEL, S., Solid State Physics
ZAKNEWSKI, J., Atomic Physics
ZALEWSKI, K., Particle Theory

Faculty of Biology and Earth Sciences:

BILIŃSKI, Sz., Cell Biology
BOBEK, B., Wildlife Research
CZAPIK, A., Protozoology
CZAPIK, R., Plant Cyto- and Embryology
DĄBROWSKI, Z., Animal Physiology
DZWONKO, Z., Plant Ecology
FRONCISZ, W., Biophysics
GÓRECKI, A., Ecology
HARAŃCZYK, C., Mineralogy and Petrography
HARMATA, W., Zoopsychology and Animal Ethology
JACKOWSKI, A., Geography of Religion
JAKUBOWSKI, M., Vertebrate Morphology
JELONEK, A., Human Population Geography
KACZANOWSKI, K., Anthropology
KILARSKI, W., Animal Cytology and Histology
KLAG, J., Zoology
KLEIN, A., Biochemistry
KOJ, A., Animal Biochemistry
KOROHODA, W., Cell Biology
KOZŁOWSKI, J., Hydrobiology
ŁOMNICKI, A., Population Ecology
ŁUKIEWICZ, S., Biophysics
MARCHLEWSKA-KOJ, A., Mammalian Reproduction
MORYCOWA, E., Palaeozoology
MYDEL, R., Geographical Studies on Japan
OBRĘBSKA-STARKEL, B., Climatology
OLECH, M., Plant Taxonomy
OSZCZYPKO, N., Geology
PŁYTYCZ, B., Evolutionary Immunology
PRYJMA, J., Microbiology and Immunology
RADOMSKI, A., Geology
RYCZKOWSKI, M., Plant Physiology and Biology of Development
SARNA, T., Biophysics
STRZAŁKA, K., Biochemistry
SUBCVZYŃSKI, W., Molecular Biology
SUROWIAK, J., Animal Physiology
SZCZEPANEK, K., Palaeobotany
ŚLĄCZKA, A., Tectonics and Stratigraphy
TRZCINSKA-TACIK, H., Botany
TURAŁA-SZYBOWSKA, K., Botany
WASYLEWSKI, Z., Animal Biochemistry
WEINER, J., Ecological Bioenergetics and Evolutionary Ecosystems
WIĘCKOWSKI, S., Plant Biochemistry and Physiology
WOJTUSIAK, J., Zoology
ZAJĄC, A., Plant Taxonomy and Phytogeography
ŻAK, Z., Animal Biochemistry

Faculty of Chemistry:

BARAŃSKI, A., Chemical Kinetics
BOGDANOWICZ-SZWED, K., Chemistry of Enamines
DATKA, J., Infrared Spectroscopy, Zeolites
DYREK, K., Physicochemistry of Oxide Catalysts
DZIEMBAJ, R., Catalysis and Solid State Chemistry
HODOROWICZ, S. A., Crystallography and Solid State Chemistry
NAJBAR, J., Physical Chemistry, Photophysics and Photochemistry
NALEWAJSKI, R. F., Theoretical Chemistry, Quantum Chemistry
NOWAKOWSKA, M., Photochemistry and Spectroscopy of Polymers
PARCZEWSKI, A., Chemometrics and Analytical Chemistry
PETELENZ, P., Organic Semiconductors
SAMOTUS, A., Photochemistry and Coordination Compounds
STASICKA, Z., Inorganic Chemistry
WITKOWSKI, A., Theoretical Molecular Physics
WÓJCIK, M., Molecular Spectroscopy and Macromolecular Research
ZIELIŃSKI, M., Nuclear Chemistry

Faculty of Management and Social Communication:

BARCZAK, A.
BARTA, J., Inventiveness and the Protection of Intellectual Property
BIEŃKOWSKI, W., Librarianship and Information Science
BORKOWSKI, T., Management
BRALCZYK, J., Journalism, Political Communication
GOBAN-KLAS, T., Social Communication
GODZIC, W., Audiovisual Arts
HELMAN, A., Audiovisual Arts
KOCÓJ, M., Librarianship
KRYSITOFEK, K.
MAREK, T., Management
MARKIEWICZ, R., Inventiveness and the Protection of Intellectual Property
MATCZEWSKI, A., Strategic Management
NĘCKI, Z., Psychology of Social Relations
NIEMCZYŃSKI, A., Psychology
OKONI-HARODYŃSKA, E.
PIEKAN, H., Management
PILECKA, B., Management
POCZTOWSKI, A., Human Resource Management
SOWA, K., Management
STABRYŁA, A., Management
SURDYKOWSKA, S., Management
SZROMNIK, A., Management
SZWAJA, J., Inventiveness and the Protection of Industrial Property
TECSKE, J., Management
WILK, E., Audiovisual Arts
WOJCIECHOWSKI, J., Librarianship

Faculty of Health Care:

HAŁUSZKA, J.
MIĘDZOBRODIKA, A.
PILC, A.
ROBAK, J.
SZAFRAN, Z.
SZMATKA, J.
WLODARCZYK, W.

Interfaculty Institutes:

BROŻEK, A., Social and Economic History
BUJNICKI, T., History of Polish Literature
JASIŃSKI, B., Economics
MIODUNKA, W., Applied Linguistics

UNIWERSYTET ŁÓDZKI
(University of Łódź)

90–131 Łódź, Narutowicza 65
Telephone: (42) 35-40-02
Fax: (42) 678-39-58
E-mail: rektorat@krysia.uni.lodz.pl

Founded 1945
State control
Language of instruction: Polish
Academic year: October to September
Rector: Prof. Dr hab. STANISŁAW LISZEWSKI
Pro-Rectors: Prof. Dr hab. WANDA KRAJEWSKA, Prof. Dr hab. WIESŁAW PUŚ, Prof. Dr hab. KRYSTYNA PIOTROWSKA-MARCZAK, Prof. Dr hab. MAREK ZIRK-SADOWSKI
Chief Administrative Officer: ALICJA KORYTKOWSKA

Librarian: Dr JAN JANIAK

Library: see Libraries

Number of professors: 385

Number of students: 30,782

Publications: *Acta Uniwersitatis Lodziensis* (Research Bulletin), *Kronika Uniwersitetu Łódzkiego.*

DEANS

Faculty of Philology: Prof. Dr hab. MAREK CYBULSKI

Faculty of Philosophy and History: Prof. Dr hab. JAN SZYMCZAK

Faculty of Educational Sciences: Prof. Dr hab. TADEUSZ JAŁMUŻNA

Faculty of Physics and Chemistry: Prof. Dr hab. WACŁAW TYBOR

Faculty of Mathematics: Prof. Dr hab. ANDRZEJ NOWAKOWSKI

Faculty of Biology and Earth Sciences: Prof. Dr hab. ANTONI RÓŻALSKI

Faculty of Law and Administration: Prof. Dr hab. WŁODZIMIERZ NYKIEL

Faculty of Economics and Sociology: Prof. Dr hab. WITOLD KASPERKIEWICZ

Faculty of Management: Prof. Dr hab. BOGDAN GREGOR

Institute of International Studies: Prof. Dr hab. WALDEMAR MICHOWICZ

PROFESSORS

Faculty of Philology:

ANDRZEJCZYK, K., American Literature and Culture
BAJOR, K., Russian Philology
BIEŃKOWSKA, D., Polish Language
BŁAŻEJEWSKI, T., Polish Literature
BOGOŁĘBSKA, B., Teaching of Language
BOLECKI, W., Romance Literature and Contemporary Literature
CIEŚLIKOWSKA, T., Theory of Literature
CYBULSKI , M., Polish and Slavonic Languages
CZARNIK, O., Library and Information Science
CZYZEWSKI, S., Theory of Film
DĄBEK-WIRGOWA, T., Slavonic Philology
DANKA, I., Classical Philology, Indo-European Linguistics
DEJNA K., Polish and Slavonic Languages
DUNIN-HORKAWICZ, J., Research on Books
EDELSON, M., English Literature
GAJOS, M., Teaching of Romance Languages
GALA, A., Polish Languages
GAZDA, G., Theory of Literature
GŁÓWKO, O., Literature and Russian Culture
GOGOLEWSKI, S., Slavonic and Romance Linguistics
GWÓŹDŹ, A., Theory of Literature, Theatre and Film
HABRAJSKA, G., History of the Polish Language, Slavonic Philology
HELMAN, A., Film
JABŁKOWSKA, J., German Literature
JANICKA-ŚWIDERSKA, I., English Philology
KAMIŃSKA, M., Polish and Slavonic Languages
KAPUŚCIK, J., Research on Books
KORYTKOWSKA, M., Slavonic Studies
KRUPSKA-PEREK, A., History of Polish and Slavonic Languages
KUCZYŃSKI, K. A., German Literature
KULIGOWSKA-KORZENIEWSKA, A., History of Theatre
LEWANDOWSKA-TOMASZCZYK, B., English Language
MAŁEK, E., Russian Literature
MAZAN, B., Polish Literature
MICHALEWSKI, K., Polish Languages
MUCHA, B., Russian Literature
NAŁĘCZ-WOJTCZAK, J., English Literature
NALIWAJEK, Z., Romance Languages
NOWIKOW, W., Spanish Language
NURCZYŃSKA-FIDELSKA, E., Theory of Literature
OKOŃ, J., Old Polish Literature
OSTROMĘCKA-FRĄCZAK, U., Polish Language
OSTROWSKI, M., German Literature
POKLEWSKA, K., Polish Literature
PORADECKI, J., Polish Literature
PUSZ, W., History of Polish Literature
RYTTER, G., Russian Literature
SADZIŃSKI, R., German Language
SALSKA, A., American Literature
STARNAWSKI, J., Old-Polish Literature
STROKOWSKA, A., Polish Language
ŚWIĘTOSŁAWSKA, B., Teaching of Language and Polish Literature
ŚWIONTEK, S., Theory of Drama and Theatre
SYPNICKI, J., French Language
TADEUSIEWICZ, H., Research on Books
TARANTOWICZ, A., German Philology
UMIŃSKA-TYTOŃ, E., Polish Language
WICHER, A., Drama and English Poetry
WIŚNIEWSKI, B., Classical Philology
WOLSKA, B., Polish Literature
WOŹNICZKO-PARVZEL, B., Library and Information Science
WRÓBLEWSKI, W., Classical Philology and Philosophy
ZALEWSKI, A., Film

Faculty of Philosophy and History:

BADZIAK, K., Recent Polish History
BANASIAK, S., Recent Polish History
BANIA, L., History of Art
BARANOWSKI, W., Russian Religions
BARNYCZ-GUPIENIEC, R., Medieval Archaeology
BARSZCZEWSKA-KRUPA, A., Modern Polish History
BLOMBERG, M., Archaeology
BRZEZIŃSKI, A., Recent History
CERAN, W., Byzantine Studies
DĄBROWSKA, M., History of Byzantium
DĄBROWSKI, J., Bronze and Iron Ages
DOMAŃSKA, L., Archaeology
GŁOSEK, M., Prehistory
GRABARCZYK, T., Bronze and Iron Ages
GRABSKI, A., History of Social Theory
GROBIS, J., Modern World History
GROMCZYŃSKI, W., History of 19th- and 20th-century Philosophy
GRYGOROWICZ, M., Philosophy
HARASIMOWICZ, A., Modern World History
HASSAN ALI JAMSHEER, Near East Studies
HUNGER, R., History of Art
JANCZAK, J., History, Historical Demography
KAJZER, L., Medieval History, Archaeology
KOZŁOWSKI, M., Philosophy
KOZŁOWSKI, W., Recent Polish History
KRAWCZYK-WASILEWSKA, V., Ethnology
LECH, A., Ethnology
LIPIŃSKA, J., History of Art
MALINOWSKI, G., Logic
MARKOWSKA, D., Ethnology
MARXEN-WOLSKA, E., History of Art
MATERSKI, W., Recent World History
MĄCZYŃSKA, M., Archaeology
NOWACZYK, A., Logic
NOWAKOWSKA, W., History of Art
NOWAKOWSKI, A., Prehistory
OLCZYK, S., Philosophy
PANASIUK, R., History of 19th Century Philosophy
PIÓRCZYŃSKI, J., Philosophy
POBOJEWSKA, A., Philosophy
POTĘPA, M., Philosophy
PUŚ, W., 19th- and 20th-century Economic History of Poland
PYTLAS, S., Socio-Economic History
SAMUŚ, P., Recent Polish History
SKUPIŃSKA-LØVSET, C., Archaeology
ŚMIAŁOWSKI, J., Modern Polish History
STEFAŃSKI, K., History of Art
STYCZYŃSKI, M., Philosophy
SZCZYGIELSKI, W., Modern Polish History
SZTABIŃSKI, G., Aesthetics
SZYMCZAK, J., Medieval History
SZYNKIEWICZ, S., Ethnology
TUCHAŃSKA, B., Philosophy of Science
WACHOWSKA, B., Recent Polish History
WEJLAND, A., Sociology
WIŚNIEWSKI, E., History of Russia
ZAJĄCZKOWSKI, S. M., Medieval Polish History

Faculty of Educational Sciences:

BITTNER, I., Philosophy
BŁASZCZYK, J., Physical Education
BŁASZCZYK, T., Science of Art
BUCZYŃSKI, A., Physical Education
CIEŚLAK, L., Music Education
CZERNIAWSKA, O., Social Pedagogy
DOWLASZ, B., Music Education
FALKOWSKI, A., Psychology
FLIS, F., Science of Fine Arts
FLORKOWSKI, A., Psychology
FUDALI, J., Didactics
GOLIŃSKA, L., Psychology
JAŁMUŻNA, T., Pedagogy
JUCZYŃSKI, Z., Psychology
KĘDZIORA, J., Biochemistry
KOSTRZEWSKI, J., Psychology
MARYNOWICZ-HETKA, E., Social Pedagogy
NIEBRZYDOWSKI, L., Psychology
ORKISZ, S., Physical Education and Health
PAŃCZYK, J., Pedagogy
PIEKARSKI, J., Pedagogy
ROSTOWSKI, J., Psychology
RUDENKO, L., Pedagogy
SIBIŃSKA, E., Physical Education, Health Education
ŚLIWERSKI, B., Pedagogy
SZAŁAŃSKI, J., Psychology
SZEWCZYK, T., Physical Education
WIĘCKOWSKI, R., Pedagogy, Didactics
WIERZBIŃSKI, A., Musical Education
ZAPĘDOWSKI, Z., Anatomy
ŻUKOWSKA, Z., Pedagogy, Physical Education

Faculty of Physics and Chemistry:

ANDRIJEWSKI, G., General and Inorganic Chemistry
BALCERZAK, T., Solid State Physics
BALD, A., Physical Chemistry
BALD, E., Organic Chemistry
BARTCZAK, W., Theoretical Physics
BARTNIK, R., Organic Chemistry
BRODA, B., Theoretical Chemistry
CIESIELSKI, W., Analytical Chemistry
CZERBNIAK, J., Solid State Physics
DZIEGIEĆ, J., Inorganic Chemistry
EPSZTAJN, J., Organic Chemistry
GILLER, M., Experimental Physics
GILLER, S., Theoretical Physics
GRABOWSKI, M., Crystallography
GRZEJDZIAK, A., General and Inorganic Chemistry
JANKOWSKI, J., Experimental Nuclear Physics
JĘDRZEJEWSKI, J., Theoretical Physics
JÓŹWIAK, A., Organic Chemistry
KEMPA, J., Nuclear Physics
KINART, C., Teaching of Chemistry
KINART, W., Organic Chemistry
KOSIŃSKI, P., Theoretical Physics
KOWALSKI, K., Theoretical Physics
KRYCZKA, B., Organic and Applied Chemistry
KUDZIN, Z., Organic Chemistry
ŁAWRYNOWICZ, J., Complex Analysis
LEŚNIAK, S., Organic and Applied Chemistry
MAJEWSKI, M., Theoretical Physics
MAŁECKI, H., Nuclear Physics
MAŚLANKA, P., Theoretical Physics
MLOSTOŃ, G., Organic Chemistry
NOWAK, B., Functional Analysis
PIEKARSKI, H., Physical Chemistry
PŁAZA, S., Inorganic Chemistry
PRZANOWSKI, M., Theoretical Physics
PRZYTUŁA, M., Low Energy Nuclear Physics
REMBIELIŃSKI, J., Theoretical Physics
ROMANOWSKI, S., Physical and Theorectical Chemistry
SCHOLL, H., Physical Chemistry

Skowroński, R., Organic Chemistry
Stepiński, M., Experimental Physics
Sukiennicki, A., Solid State Physics
Turowska, M., Inorganic Chemistry
Tybor, W., Theoretical Physics
Wojtczak, L., Solid State Physics
Zakrzewski, J., Organic Chemistry

Faculty of Mathematics:

Balcerzak, M., Real Analysis
Banaszczyk, W., Functional Analysis
Chądzyński, J., Complex Variables
Filipczak, M., Algebra
Goldstein, S., Functional Analysis
Hensz-Chądzyńska, E., Functional Analysis
Jajte, R., Probability Theory
Jakubowski, Z., Analytical Functions
Krasiński, T., Complex Variables
Łuczak, A., Probability Theory
Mikołajczyk, L., Analytical Functions
Nowakowski, A., Optimization Theory
Paszkiewicz, A., Functional Analysis
Pawlak, R., Functional Analysis
Przeradzki, B., Functional Analysis
Studniarski, M., Optimization Theory
Wagner-Bojakowska, E., Real Analysis
Walczak, P., Geometry
Walczak, S., Analytical Functions
Waliszewski, W., Geometry
Wilczyński, W., Real Analysis
Włodarczyk, K., Functional Analysis, Complex Analysis

Faculty of Biology and Earth Sciences:

Bańbura, J., Zoology, Ecology
Bartosz, G., Biophysics
Błasiak, J., Biochemistry
Bryszewska, M., Biophysics
Czyżewska, K., Botany
Długoński, J., Microbiology
Duda, W., Biochemistry
Dzieciuchowicz, J., Economic Geography
Dziegieć, E., Urban Geography and Tourism
Gabara, B., Cytology and Cytochemistry
Gabryelak, T., Biophysics
Galicka, W., Zoology, Ecology
Gaździcki, A., Geology
Godlewski, M., Cell Biology
Grzybkowska, M., Zoology, Ecology
Gwoździński, K., Molecular Biology
Heffner, K., Political Geography and Regional Studies
Hereźniak, J., Plant Geography
Jakubowska-Gabara, J., Plant Geography
Janas, K., Plant Physiology
Jaworski, A., Microbiology
Jażdżewski, K., Zoology
Jokiel, P., Physical Geography
Jóźwiak, Z., Biophysics
Kaca, W., Microbiology
Kapica, Z., Anthropology
Kiliańska, Z., Biochemistry
Kittel, W., Zoology of Invertebrates and Hydrobiology
Klajnert, Z., Physical Geography
Kłysik, K., Climatology and Meteorology
Knypl, S. J., Plant Physiology and Biochemistry
Konopacki, J., Neurophysiology
Koter, M., Economic Geography
Koter, M., Environmental Biophysics
Kożuchowski, K., Physical Geography
Krajewska, W., Biochemistry
Krajewski, T., Biochemistry
Krzemiński, T., Physical Geography, Geomorphology
Kukulska-Gościcka, T., Immunology
Kurowski, J., Biology, Plant Ecology
Kwiatkowska, M., Plant Cytology and Cytochemistry
Laskowski, S., Pedology
Ligowski, R., Biology, Ecology
Lipińska, A., Biochemistry
Liszewski, S., Economic Geography
Ławrynowicz, M., Botany, Mycology
Maksymiuk, Z., Physical Geography
Malinowski, A., Anthropology
Manikowska, B., Physical Geography
Marciniak, K., Plant Cytology and Cytochemistry
Markowski, J., Biology, Theriology
Marszał, T., Economic Geography
Maszewski, J., Cell Biology
Matczak, A., Economic Geography
Myszkiewicz-Niesiołowski, S., Zoology, Entomology
Olaczek, R. S., Plant Systems and Geography
Olszewska, M., Plant Cytology and Cytochemistry
Osiecka, R., Genetics, Cytogenetics
Penczak, T., Zoology, Fish Ecology
Piechocki, A., Zoology
Puchała, M., Molecular Biophysics
Romaniuk, A., Animal Physiology and Neurophysiology
Różalska, B., Infectious Biology
Różalski, A., Microbiology
Rudnicka, W., Immunology
Sedlaczek, L., Metabolism of Micro-organisms
Sidorczyk, Z., Microbiology
Sowa, R., Plant Systems and Geography
Stolarczyk, H., Anthropology
Szajnowska-Wysocka, A., Political Geography and Regional Studies
Szweda-Lewandowska, Z., Biophysics
Tomaszewski, C., Zoology
Turkowska, K., Geomorphology
Urbanek, H., Biochemistry
Wachowicz, B., Biochemistry
Walter, Z., Biochemistry
Warcholińska, A. U., Botany
Werwicki, A., Economic Geography
Zalewski, M., Biology
Zgirski, A., Biochemistry

Faculty of Law and Administration:

Bińczycka-Majewska, T., Labour Law
Borkowski, J., Administrative Law
Boruta, I., European Law
Broniewicz, W., Civil Procedure
Chróścielewski, W., Administrative Procedure
Daranowski, P., International Law
Dębowska-Romanowska, T., Financial Law
Dębski, R., Penal Law
Domagała, M., Constitutional Law
Góral, Z., Labour Law
Goździ-Roszkowski, K., History of State and Polish Law
Górecki, D., Constitutional Law
Górski, M., Administrative Law
Grzegorczyk, T., Penal Procedure
Hołyst, B., Criminology
Jankowski, J., Civil Law
Jaworska-Dębska, B., Administrative Law
Katner, W., Civil Law
Kmieciak, Z., Administrative Procedure
Kosikowski, C., Financial Law
Król, M., Theory and Philosophy of Law
Królikowska-Olczak, M., Economic Public Law
Kulesza, W., Penal Law
Lelental, S., Penal Law
Lewandowski, H., Labour Law
Lewaszkiewicz-Petrykowska, B., Civil Law
Marciniak, A., Civil Procedure
Matuszewski, J., Medieval History, History of Law
Matuszewski, J., History of State and Law
Nykiel, W., Law
Pajor, T., Civil Law and International Law
Promińska, U., Economic and Commercial Law
Pyziak-Szafnicka, M., Civil Law
Rau, Z., Roman Law
Rymaszewski, Z., History of State and the Law
Seweryński, M., Labour Law
Stahl, M., Administrative Law
Stefańska, K., Agricultural Law
Strzyczkowski, K., Financial Law
Szpunar, A., Civil Law
Szymczak, T., Constitutional Law
Tarno, J., Administrative Law
Tylman, J., Penal Procedure
Włodarczyk, W. C., Social Policy
Wójcicka, B., Penal Procedure
Wyrozumska, A., European Law
Zirk-Sadowski, M., Theory of State and Law

Faculty of Economics and Sociology:

Bednarek, W., Political Economy of Capitalism
Bilski, J., International Finance
Bokszański, Z., Cultural Sociology
Borkowska, S., Business Administration
Buchner-Jeziorska, A., Sociology
Caban, W., Economic Theory
Chudy, B., Environmental Planning
Dębski, W., Econometrics
Doktór, K., Industrial Sociology
Domański, C., Statistics
Dudek, B., Social Sciences
Duraj, J., Economics and Organization of Industry
Dzięcielska-Machnikowska, S., Labour Sociology
Fornalczyk, A., Economics
Gajda, J., Economics
Godłów-Legiędź, J., Economics
Gostkowski, Z., Methodology of Social Research
Jabłońska, A., History of Economic Theory
Janusz, T., Industrial Economics
Jewtuchowicz, A., Economics of Urban Development
Józefiak, C., Economics
Juszczak-Szumacher, G., Econometric Models and Forecasts
Kasperkiewicz, W., Economics
Kaźmierczak, Z., Planning and Economic Policy
Kietlińska, K., Finance
Konecki, K., Industrial Sociology
Kowaleski, J. T., Demography
Kowalewicz, K., Sociology of Culture
Krajewska, A., Economics
Krajewski, S., Economics
Kryńska, E., Planning and Economic Policy
Kucharska-Stasiak, E., Economics of Urban Development
Kulpińska, J., Industrial Sociology
Kwiatkowska, W., Economics
Kwiatkowski, E., Political Economy of Capitalism
Łapińska-Sobczak, N., Econometrics
Lewandowska, L., Economics
Lipiński, C., Theory and Analysis of Economic Systems
Mackiewicz-Golnik, L., Finance
Marszałek, A. G., Economics
Matuszak, G., Sociology
Mikołajczyk, B., Labour Economics
Mikosik, S., Economics
Milewski, R., Political Economy
Milo, W., Econometrics, statistics
Mortimer-Szymczak, H., Planning and Economic Policy
Niedźwiedziński, M., Informatics
Piasecki, R., Theory of Industrial Development
Piątkowski, W., History of Economic Theory
Piotrowska-Marczak, K., Finance
Pruska, K., Statistics
Rokicka, E., General Sociology
Rudolf, S., Political Economy of Capitalism
Rutkowski, J., Finance
Skodlarski, J., International Economic Relations
Spychalski, G., History of Economic Theory
Starosta, P., Sociology
Starzyńska, W., Econometrics, Statistics
Suchecka, J., Economics
Suchecki, B., Econometrics
Sułkowski, B., Cultural Sociology
Swierkocki, J., International Trade and Finance

SZTAUDYNGER, J., Econometrics
TOBERA, P., Sociology
TOMASZEWICZ, Ł., Econometrics
TRZASKALIK, T., Economics
WALCZAK-DURAJ, D., Sociology
WARZYWODA-KRUSZYŃSKA, W., Sociology
WELFE, A., Econometrics
WELFE, W., Econometrics and Statistics
WESOŁOWSKI, W., General Sociology
WIETESKA, S., Economics of Urban Development
WIĘCEK, J., Econometrics
WITKOWSKA, D., Econometrics
WITKOWSKA, J., Economics
WOJCIECHOWSKA-MISZALSKA, A., General Sociology
WOJCIECHOWSKI, E., Economics of Urban Development
WYPYCH, M., Industrial Economics
WYSOKIŃSKA, Z., Economics
ZABIELSKI, K., Economics of Foreign Trade
ZARZYCKA, Z., Social Statistics
ZIELIŃSKI, R., Economics
ŻÓŁTOWSKA, E., Econometrics

Faculty of Management:
BIELSKI, M., Organization and Management
BURY, P., Economics
DIETL, J., Commercial Economics
GAJEWSKI, S., Commercial Economics
GREGOR, B., Commercial Economics
GRZEGORCZYK, W., Marketing
JANOWSKA, Z., Organization and Management
JARUGA, A., Cost Accounting, Management Accountancy
JEŻAK, J. A., Business Policy and Strategic Management
LACHIEWICZ, S., Business Administration
LIWOWSKI, B., Business Administration
MARKOWSKI, T., Economics of Urban Development
MIKOŁAJCZYK, Z., Theory of Organization and Management
PIASECKI, B., Economics and Organization of Industry
SIKORSKI, C., Organization and Management
SOBAŃSKA, I., Accounting
SZYMCZAK, J., Management
WITKOWSKI, J., Marketing
ZIELIŃSKI, J. S., Computer Science

Institute of International Studies:
DE LAZARI, A., Eastern Studies
DOMAŃSKI, T., Marketing
DUBICKI, T., History
KMIECIŃSKI, J., Archaeology
KOZŁOWSKI, A., German Philology
KUCZYŃSKI, K., German Literature
KUJAWIŃSKA-COURTNEY, K., English Literature
MEISSNER, L., German Studies
MICHOWICZ, W., Institute of International Relations (Dir)
OLEKSY, E., American Literature
SKRZYPEK, A., Brazilian Studies
STĘPIEŃ, A., Eastern Studies
WILK, M., History of Russia

Polish Language Tuition Centre for Foreign Students:
RAKOWSKI, B., History

Liaison Centre for Foreign Graduates of Polish Universities:
GRZELAK, Z., Economic Policy

Translation Centre:
HARTZELL, J. F., Law

KATOLICKI UNIWERSYTET LUBELSKI
(Catholic University of Lublin)

20-950 Lublin, Al. Racławickie 14
Telephone: (81) 533-25-72
Fax: (81) 533-25-72
E-mail: kulzagr@zeus.kul.lublin.pl

Founded 1918
Private control
Academic year: October to June

Chancellor: Archbp Prof. Dr hab. JÓZEF ŻYCIŃSKI
Rector: Rev. Prof. Dr hab. ANDRZEJ SZOSTEK
Vice-Rectors: Rev. Prof. Dr hab. STANISŁAW WILK, Rev. Prof. Dr hab. FRANCISZEK KAMPKA, Dr hab. ANDRZEJ BUDZISZ
Librarian: Rev. Dr TADEUSZ STOLZ

Library: see Libraries
Number of professors: 820
Number of students: 16,600

Publications: *Zeszyty Naukowe KUL* (quarterly), *Roczniki Teologiczne* (annually), *Roczniki Filozoficzne* (annually), *Roczniki Humanistyczne* (annually), *Roczniki Nauk Społecznych* (annually), *Ethos* (quarterly), *Przegląd Uniwersytecki* (6 a year), *Roczniki Nauk Prawnych* (annually).

DEANS

Faculty of Theology: Rev. Prof. Dr hab. ANZELM WEISS
Faculty of Canon and Civil Law: Rev. Prof. Dr hab. MARIAN STASIAK
Faculty of Philosophy: Sr Prof. Dr hab. ZOFIA ZDYBICKA
Faculty of Humanities: Rev. Prof. Dr hab. REMIGIUSZ POPOWSKI
Faculty of Social Sciences: Prof. Dr hab. ADAM BIELA
Faculty of Mathematics and Natural Sciences: (vacant)

PROFESSORS

Faculty of Theology:
BARTNIK, C., Dogmatic Theology, Theology of History
BIELECKI, S., Pastoral Theology
CHWAŁEK, J., Musicology
DĄBEK, S., Musicology
DRĄCZKOWSKI, F., Patristics
DZIUBA, A., Moral Theology
GŁOWA, W., Pastoral Theology, Liturgy
GÓRSKI, K., Musicology
GÓŹDŹ, K., Dogmatic Theology
HRYNIEWICZ, W., Ecumenism, Orthodox Theology
JASKÓŁA, P., Ecumenism, Orthodox Theology
KAMIŃSKI, R., Pastoral Theology, Organization of Pastoral Care
KOPEĆ, J. J., Pastoral Theology, Liturgy
KULPACZYŃSKI, S., Pastoral Theology, Catechetics
LANGKAMMER, H., Biblical Studies
MAJEWSKI, M., Pastoral Theology, Catechetics
MISIUREK, J., Dogmatic Theology, History of Spirituality
MROCZKOWSKI, I., Moral Theology
NAGÓRNY, J., Moral Theology
NAPIÓRKOWSKI, S., Mariology, Ecumenism, Dogmatic Theology
NIKODEMOWICZ, A., Musicology
NOWAK, A., Spirituality
PACIOREK, A., Biblical Studies
PAŁUCKI, J., Patristics
PAWLAK, I., Musicology
RUBINKIEWICZ, R., Biblical Studies
RUSECKI, M., Fundamental Theology
RYCZAN, K., Pastoral Theology, Sociology of Religion
ŚCIBOR, J., Musicology
SŁOMKA, W., Theology of Catholic Spirituality
ŚRUTWA, J., Ancient Church History
SZYMIK, J., Dogmatic Theology
TRONINA, A., Biblical Studies
WEISS, A., Methodology of Church History
WILK, S., Church History
WIT, Z., History of Liturgy
WITASZEK, G., Biblical Studies
WOJTYSKA, H., History of Theology
ZAHAJKIEWICZ, M., Medieval Church History
ZASĘPA, T., Theology and Contemporary Media for Handing on the Faith; Mass Media
ZIELIŃSKI, Z., 19th- and 20th-century Church History
ZIMOŃ, H., Religious Studies

Faculty of Canon and Civil Law:
CHRZANOWSKI, W., Civil Law
CIOCH, H., Civil Law
DĘBIŃSKI, A., Canon Law
DZIĘGA, A., Canon Law of Procedures
GÓRSKI, G., History of Law
GOŹDZIEWICZ, G., Labour and Social Welfare Law
GRANAT, M., Constitutional Law
GRZEŚKOWIAK, A., Criminal Law
KARBOWNIK, H., History of the Polish State and Law
KRUKOWSKI, J., Canon Law
KURYŁOWICZ, M., Roman Law
ŁĄCZKOWSKI, W., Financial Law, Administrative Law
MISIUK-JODŁOWSKA, T., Civil Law
MISZTAL, H., Canon Law, Law and Religion
POŹNIAK-NIEDZIELSKA, M., Civil Law
SAFJAN, M., Civil Law
SKOCZYLAS, J., Civil Law
SKUBISZ, R., Business Law
STASIAK, M., Canon Law
STRZEMBOSZ, A., Criminal Law
ŚWITKA, J., Criminal Law
SZAJKOWSKI, A., Business Law
WIDACKI, J., Criminology, Criminal Justice
WÓJTOWICZ, W., Financial Law
ZDYB, M., Administrative Law
ZUBERT, B., Canon Law

Faculty of Philosophy:
BRONK, A., Philosophy of Science
CISZEWSKI, M., History of Philosophy
CZERKAWSKI, J., History of Philosophy
DYWAN, Z., Logic
GAŁKOWSKI, J., Ethics, Political Philosophy
HAJDUK, Z., Philosophy of Nature
HERBUT, J., Methodology of Philosophy
JAROSZYŃSKI, P., Philosophy of Culture, Aesthetics
JUDYCKI, S., Epistemology
KICZUK, S., Logic
KIEREŚ, H., Aesthetics
MARYNIARCZYK, A., Metaphysics
STĘPIEŃ, A., Epistemology, Aesthetics
STYCZEŃ, T., Ethics
SZOSTEK, A., Ethics
TUREK, J., Philosophy of Nature
WIELGUS, S., History of Philosophy, Medieval Philosophy
WNUK, M., Philosophy of Nature
ZDYBICKA, Z., Philosophy of Religion, Metaphysics
ZIELIŃSKI, E., History of Philosophy

Faculty of Humanities:
BARAŃSKA, E., Romance Languages and Literatures
BARSZCZEWSKI, A., Theory of Belorussian Literature
BENDER, R., 19th- and 20th-century History
BLOCH, C., 19th- and 20th-century History
BORKOWSKA, U., History of Medieval Culture
BUDZISZ, A., Classical Philology
CHODKOWSKI, R., Classical Linguistics, Greek Literature
CZYŻEWSKI, F., Slavic Languages
DEPTUŁA, C., History of Medieval Culture
DROB, J., History of the 16th to 18th Centuries
DYBCIAK, K., History of Contemporary Polish Literature
DYLĄG, H., Modern and Contemporary History of East-Central Europe
ECKMANN, A., Classical Linguistics, Ancient Christian Literature
FERT, J., History of Polish Literature

FITA, S., History of Polish Literature
GAPSKI, H., Modern History
GAWEŁKO, M., Romance Languages and Literatures
GUSSMANN, E., English Linguistics, Celtic Linguistics
IWASZKIEWICZ-WRONIKOWSKA, B., Art History
JABŁOŃSKA-DEPTUŁA, E., History of Modern Polish Culture
JASINSKA-WOJTKOWSKA, M., History of Contemporary Polish Literature
JESZKE, J., German Linguistics
KACZMARKOWSKI, M., General Linguistics, Latin Linguistics
KNAPIŃSKI, R., Art History
KOŁBUK, W., Modern History
KOLEK, L., History of English Literature
KOZAK, S., Ukrainian and Eastern Slavic Literature, Folklore and Social Thought
KUCZYŃSKA, J., History of Polish Medieval Art
ŁESIÓW, M., Slavic Languages and Literatures
LESZCZYŃSKI, Z., Linguistics
LILEYKO, J., History of Modern Art
MACIEJEWSKI, M., Literature of the Enlightenment and Romantic Periods in Polish Literature
MAKARSKI, W., Linguistics
MALICKA-KLEPARSKA, A., English Linguistics
MAREK, B., English Linguistics
MAZURCZAK, U., Art History
MÜLLER, W., History of the 16th–18th Centuries
OLCZAK, S., Modern History
OLDAKOWSKA-KUFEL, M., History of Polish Literature
OLSZEWSKI, A., Art History
ORŁOWSKI, J., History of Russian Literature
PALUCHOWSKA, D.,History of Polish Literature
PODBIELSKI, H., Classical Greek Philology
POPOWSKI, R., Classical Philology, Greek Linguistics
SAWECKA, H., Romance Languages and Literature
SAWICKI, S., Polish Literary Theory
STAWECKA, K., Classical Philology, Neo-Latin Studies
SZYMANEK, B., English Linguistics
WĄSONOWICZ, H., Historical Auxiliary Sciences
WIŚNIOWSKI, E., Medieval History
WITKOWSKA, A., History of Medieval Culture
WÓJTOWICZ, H., Classical Philology, Ancient Christian Literature
WOLICKA, E., Theory of Art and History of Artistic Theories
WOŹNIAK, A., Slavic Languages and Literatures
ZARZYCKA-STAŃCZAK, K., Classical Linguistics, Latin Literature
ZIÓŁEK, J., Modern History
ŻWIRKOWSKA, E., History of Polish Literature
ZWOLSKI, E., Ancient History

Faculty of Social Sciences:
ADAMCZYK, M., Modern History, History of Education
BIELA, A., Experimental Psychology, Industrial Psychology, Environmental Psychology
BRAUN-GAŁKOWSKA, M., Educational Psychology, Family Psychology
CEKIERA, C., Clinical Psychology, Psychology of Personality
CHLEWIŃSKI, Z., Experimental Psychology
CHUDY, W., History of Education, Philosophy and Epistemology
CIEŚLA, S., Sociology
CZUMA, Ł., History of Political and Economic Theories
DYCZEWSKI, L., Sociology of Culture, Sociology of Family
DZWONKOWSKI, R., Sociology of Migration
EBERHARDT, P., Geography of Settlement and Population
FALKOWSKI, A., Experimental Psychology
GILOWSKA, Z., Economics, Local Finance
GRUSZECKI, T., Economics, Management
HAŁAS, E., Sociology
IMBS, H., Socio-economic History
JAROSZ, A., Economics
JURGA, A.
KAMPKA, F., Catholic Social Thought
KAROLEWICZ, G., History
KAWCZYŃSKA-BUTRYM, Z., Sociology of Medicine
KŁOSIŃSKI, K., International Economic Relations
KOWALCZYK, S., Theoretical Philosophy, Social Philosophy
KRYCZKA, P., Urban Sociology, Sociology of the Family
KUKOŁOWICZ, T., Social Pedagogy, Sociology of Education
KUROWSKI, S., Political Economics
LITAK, S., Church History, History of Education
MARIAŃSKI, J., Sociology of Religion, Sociology of Morals
MASIAK, M., Psychology
MATULKA, Z., Pedagogy
MAZUREK, F., Catholic Social Thought
MAZURKIEWICZ, E., Social Pedagogy
OLEŚ, P., Experimental Psychology
OSTRIHANSKA, Z., Criminal Justice
PIWOWARSKI, W., Sociology of Religion, Pastoral Theology
POMORSKA, A., Financial Law
POPIELSKI, K., Psychotherapy, Logotherapy
PRĘZYNA, W., Social Psychology, Psychology of Religion
PRYMON, M., Market Function and Demand
REBETA, J., History of Social and Political Thought
RONEK, H., Economics, Accountancy
SĘKOWSKI, A., Rehabilitative Psychology
STEUDEN, S., Clinical Psychology
STYK, J., Rural Sociology
SZEWCZYK, L., Clinical Psychology, Paediatrics
UCHNAST, Z., General Psychology
WALESA, C., Developmental Psychology
WALEWANDER, E., History of Education, Theology
WĘCŁAWSKI, J., Political Economics
WILK, J., Family Pedagogy, Theology
WITKOWSKI, T., Rehabilitative Psychology
ZALESKI, Z., Experimental Psychology

Faculty of Mathematics and Natural Sciences:
ANDRZEJEWSKI, R., Ecology
JANECKI, J., Ecology, Landscape Architecture
KOZŁOWSKI, S., Geology of Rock Deposits, Environmental Protection
KRASINKIEWICZ, J., Mathematics
PARTYKA, D., Mathematics
PIERSA, H., Philosophy of Physics
PIKULSKI, S., Law
SMARZEWSKI, R., Numerical Analysis
STACHURA, A., Mathematics
STUDNICKA, M., Toxicology
SZAPIEL, W., Theory of Analytical Functions
TYBURCZYK, W., Biochemistry
WOJCIECHOWSKA, W., Ecology, Hydrobiology
WOJTOWICZ, R., Ergology
ZAJĄC, J., Mathematics
ZAPAŁA, A., Mathematics
ZIĘBA, S., Humanistic Ecology
ZYGMUNT, W., Theory of Real Functions

UNIWERSYTET MARII CURIE-SKŁODOWSKIEJ
(Marie Curie-Skłodowska University)

20-031 Lublin, Plac Marii Curie-Skłodowskiej 5
Telephone: (81) 537-51-07
Fax: (81) 537-51-02
Founded 1944
Rector: Prof. Dr hab. KAZIMIERZ GOEBEL
Pro-Rectors: Prof. Dr hab. MARIAN HARASIMIUK, Prof. Dr hab. WOJCIECH WITKOWSKI, Prof. Dr hab. MAREK KURYŁOWICZ, Prof. Dr hab. ZBIGNIEW KRUPA
Chief Administrative Officer: MACIEJ GRUDZIŃSKI
Librarian: B. KASPEREK
Library: see Libraries
Number of teachers: 1,760
Number of students: 23,592, including 10,225 extra-mural students
Publications: *Annales Universitatis Mariae Curie-Skłodowska.*

DEANS

Faculty of Law and Administration: Prof. Dr hab. TADEUSZ BOJARSKI
Faculty of Humanities: Prof. Dr hab. RYSZARD SZCZYGIEŁ
Faculty of Mathematics and Physics: WIESŁAW ZIĘBA
Faculty of Biology and Earth Sciences: Prof. Dr hab. JÓZEF WOJTANOWICZ
Faculty of Economics: Prof. Dr hab. JERZY WĘCŁAWSKI
Faculty of Psychology and Pedagogy: Prof. Dr hab. MARIAN OCHMAŃSKI
Faculty of Chemistry: Prof. Dr hab. TADEUSZ BOROWIECKI
Faculty of Politology: Prof. Dr hab. JAN JACHYMEK
Faculty of Philosophy and Sociology: Prof. Dr hab. ZDZISŁAW CZARNECKI
Faculty of Fine Arts: Prof. MAKSYMILIAN SNOCH

PROFESSORS

Faculty of Law and Administration:
ANTONOWICZ, L., International Public Law
BOJARSKI, T., Penal Law
CHORĄŻY, K., Administrative Law
CIĄGWA, J., History of State and Law
ĆWIĄKALSKI, Z., Penal Law
ĆWIK, W., History of State and Law and of Political Doctrines
DUBEL, L., History of Political Legal Doctrines
GDULEWICZ, E., Consitutional Law
GROSZYK, H., Theory of State and Law
KLEMENTOWSKI, M., History of State and Law
KMIECIK, R., Penal Law
KOROBOWICZ, A., History of State and Law
KORYBSKI, A., Theory of State and Law
KURYŁOWICZ, M., Roman Law
LESZCZYŃSKI, L., Theory of State and Law
LISZCZ, T., Labour Law
ŁĘTOWSKI, J., Administrative Law
ŁUKASIEWICZ, J., Administrative Law
MALARCZYK, J., History of State and Law and of Political and Law Doctrines
MARKOWSKI, D., Sociology
MOZGAWA, M., Penal Law
NAZAR, M., Civil Law
NIEWIADOMSKI, Z., Administrative Law
OLESZKO, B., Civil Law
OPAS, T., History of State and Law
PIENIĄŻEK, A., Theory of State and Law
POLICZKIEWICZ, Z., Civil Law
POŹNIAK-NIEDZIELSKA, M., Economic Law
SAWCZUK, M., Civil Procedure
SEIDLER, G., Theory of State and Law
SKRĘTOWICZ, E., Penal Law
SKRZYDŁO, W., Constitutional Law
SKUBISZ, R., Economic Law
SOBOLEWSKI, Z., Penal Procedure
STELMASIK, J., Administrative Law
SZRENIAWSKI, J., Administrative Law and Administrative Science
ŚWIEBODA, Z., Civil Procedure
TOKARCZYK, R., History of Political Thought
URA, E., Administrative Law
WĄSEK, A., Penal Law and Criminology
WIECZORSKA, B., Administrative Law
WITKOWSKI, W., History of State and Law

WÓJCIK, S., Civil Law
WÓJTOWICZ, W., Financial Law
WRATNY, J., Labour Law
WRÓBEL, A., Administrative Law
ZDYB, M., Administrative Law
ZIĘBA-ZAŁUCKA, H., State Law
ŻOŁNIERCZUK, M., Roman Law
ŻUKOWSKI, L., Administrative Law

Faculty of Economics:

GRABOWIEUCKI, J., Political Economy
GRZYBOWSKI, W., Political Economy and Economic Planning
KARPUS, P., Economics
KITOWSKI, J., Economic Geography
KUREK, W., Industrial Economy and Organization of Industries
LEWANDOWSKI, Z., Mathematics Applied to Economics
MAKARSKI, S., Marketing
MASŁYK-MUSIAŁ, E., Economics
MIDURA, S., Mathematics
MUCHA-LESZKO, B., Political Economy, Economic Planning
NOWAK, E., Economics
ORŁOWSKI, R., Economic History and Economic Thought
POMORSKA, A., Finances
RUDNICKI, M., Economics of Agriculture
SIKORSKI, C., Economics
SKOWRONEK, Cz., Industrial Ecomomics
SKRZYPEK, E., Economics
SOBCZYK, G., Economy
TOKARZEWSKI, T., Agricultural Economics
WĘCŁAWSKI, J., Economics
WICH, U., Urban Planning
WOŹNIAK, M., Microeconomics
WOŹNIAK, M. G., Economics
ZALEWA, J., Agricultural Economics
ZIOŁO, Z., Economic Geography
ZUKOWSKI, M., Economics

Faculty of Humanities:

ALEKSANDROWICZ, A., History of Polish Literature
BANIECKA, B., History of the Polish Language
BARTMIŃSKI, J., Polish Linguistics
BLAIM, A., English Literature
BORSUKIEWICZ, I., History of Russian Literature
BRYŁA, W., Linguistics
CYMBORSKA-LEBODA, M., History of Russian Literature
DURCZAK, J., American and English Literature
FALICKI, J., Romance Philology
GMITEREK, M., Modern History
GRABIAS, S., Applied and Sociolinguistics
HOROCH, E., Contemporary History
HYRDZIK, B., History of Polish Literature
KARDELA, H., English Philology
KĘSIK, M., French Linguistics
KŁOCZOWSKI, W., History
KMIECIŃSKI, J., Archaeology
KOLEK, L., English Literature
KOPRUKOWNIAK, A., Modern History
KORDELA, H., English Philology
KOSYL, Cz., Polish Philology
KOWALCZYK, W., Russian Literature
KRAJKA, W., Theory of Literature, History of English Literature
KRUK, S., History of Polish Theatre
KUTYŁOWSKA, J., Archaeology
ŁESIÓW, M., Slavonic Linguistics
LEWANDOWSKI, J., Modern History
LEWICKI, A., Linguistics
ŁOCH, E., Polish Literature
MADZIK, H., History of the USSR
MAŃKOWSKI, Z., Contemporary History
MAZUR, J., Polish Linguistics
MIKULEC, B., Modern History
MISIEWICZ, J., Theory of Literature
NIEZNANOWSKI, S., Old Polish Literature
NOWICKA-KOŹLUK, J., German Philology
ORŁOWSKI, J., History of Russian Literature
PELC, H., Linguistics
PIĄTKOWSKI, Z., Contemporary History
PLISIECKI, J., Film
POMORSKI, J., Methodology and History of Historiography
RADZIK, T., Contemporary History
RAWIŃSKI, M., Modern Polish Literature
ROJEK, B., Linguistics
RZEWUSKA, E., Modern Polish Literature, History of Polish Theatre
SAWECKA, H., Theory of Romance Literature
SKUBALANKA, T., Polish Linguistics
ŚOCHACKA, A., Medieval History
ŚLADKOWSKI, W., Modern History
ŚTĘPNIK, K., Polish Literature
ŚWIĘCH, J., Modern Polish Literature
SZALA, A., History of English Literature
SZCZYGIEŁ, R., Medieval History
SZYMAŃSKI, J., Auxiliary Sciences of History
SZYNDLER, B., Modern History of Poland
TOKARSKI, R., Polish Language
TRELIŃSKA, B., Auxiliary Sciences of History
WARCHOŁ, S., Polish and Slavonic Philology
WILLAUME, M., Modern History
WIŚNIEWSKA, J., Polish Linguistics
WOŹNIAKIEWICZ-DZIADOSZ, M., Theory of Literature
WRÓBEL-LIPAK, Modern History
ZAPOROWSKI, Z., Contemporary History

Faculty of Biology and Earth Sciences:

BEDNARA, J., Anatomy and Plant Cytology
BURACZYŃSKI, J., Geomorphology
BYSTREK, J., Plant Systematics
DERNAŁOWICZ-MALARCZYK, E., Biochemistry
DROŻAŃSKI, W., Microbiology
FIEDUREK, J., Microbiology
GAWRON, A., Biology
GŁOWACKA, M., Microbiology
GRANKOWSKI, N., Molecular Biology
HARASIMIUK, M., Geomorphology
HENKIEL, A., Geomorphology
ILCZUK, Z., Applied Microbiology
JAKUBOWICZ, T., Molecular Biology
JAROSZ, J., Microbiology, Invertebrate Immunology
KAŁKOWSKA, K., Animal Physiology
KANDEFER-SZERSZEŃ, M., Microbiology
KARCZMARZ, K., Plant Systems
KASZEWSKI, B. M., Geography and Climatology
KLIMOWICZ, Z., Geography and Soil Science
KOWALSKI, M., Microbiology
KRUPA, Z., Plant Physiology
KUREK, E., Environmental Microbiology
LEONOWICZ, A., Biochemistry
LORKIEWICZ, Z., Microbiology
ŁĘTOWSKI, J., Zoology
ŁOBARZEWSKI, J., Biochemistry
MAŁEK, W., Microbiology
MICHALCZYK, Z., Hydrography
MODRZEJEWSKI, E., Animal Physiology
PĘKALA, K., Physical Geography and Geomorphology
PUSZKAR, T., Nature Preservation
ROGALSKI, J., Molecular Biology
RUSSA, R., Microbiology
SAŁATA, B., General Botany
SIRKO, M., Cartography
SKORUPSKA, A., Microbiology
ŚNIEZKO, R., Botany
ŚWIĘS, F., Botany
SZCZODRAK, J., Microbiology
TRĘBACZ, K., Biology and Biophysics
TUKIENDORF, A., Plant Physiology
WARAKOMSKI, W., Meteorology
WOJCIECHOWSKI, K., Hydrography
WOJTANOWICZ, J., Physical Geography and Geomorphology
ZAWADZKI, T., Plant Physiology

Faculty of Mathematics and Physics:

ADAMCZYK, B., Experimental Physics
BUDZYŃSKI, M., Experimental Physics
GLADYSZEWSKI, L., Theoretical Physics
GOEBEL, K., Differential Equations
GOWOREK, T., Nuclear Physics
GÓŹDŹ, A., Theoretical Physics
GRUSZECKI, W., Biophysics
HAŁAS, ST., Experimental Physics
JAŁOCHOWSKI, M., Experimental Physics
KAMIŃSKI, W., Nuclear Physics
KORCZAK, Z., Solid Body Physics
KOZICKI, J., Analytical Functions
KRAWCZYK, W., Biophysics
KRZYŻ, J., Analytic Functions
KUCZUMOW, T., Differential Equations
KUREK, J., Differential Geometry
MĄCZKA, D., Experimental Physics
MICHALAK, L., Experimental Physics
MIKOŁAJCZAK, P., Solid Body Physics
POMORSKA, B., Theoretical Physics
POMORSKI, K., Theoretical Physics
PRUS, S., Functional Analysis
ROZMEJ, P., Theoretical Physics
RYCHLIK, Z., Probability Theory
RZYMOWSKI, W., Differential Equations
SIELANKO, J., Nuclear Physics
SIELEWIESIUK, J., Physics and Biophysics
SZPIKOWSKI, S., Theoretical Physics
SZYNAL, D., Probability Theory
SZYNAL, J., Analytical Functions
TARANKO, R., Theoretical Physics
WANIURSKI, J., Analytical Functions
WYSOKIŃSKI, K., Theoretical Physics
ZĄBEK, S., Numerical Methods
ZAŁUŻNY, M., Theoretical Physics
ZIĘBA, W., Probability Theory
ZŁOTKIEWICZ, E., Analytic Functions

Faculty of Psychology and Pedagogy:

CACKOWSKA, M., Didactics
CHODKOWSKA, M., Sociology
GAJDA, M., Pedagogy
GAŚ, Z., Psychopathology
GUZ, S., Pedagogy
HERZYK, A., Neuropsychology
KACZMAREK, B., Psychology
KĘPSKI, Cz., Pedagogy
KUCHA, R., History of Learning and Education
ŁOBOCKI, M., Theory of Education
OCHMAŃSKI, M., High School Pedagogy
PILECKA, B., Clinical Psychology
POPEK, S., Psychology
POSPISZYL, K., Psychology
SARAN, J.

Faculty of Chemistry:

BARCICKI, J., Chemical Technology
BOROWIECKI, T., Chemical Technology
BORÓWKO, M., Physical Chemistry
BRZYSKA, W., General and Inorganic Chemistry
CHARMAS, W., Organic Chemistry
CHIBOWSKI, E., Physical Chemistry
CHIBOWSKI, S., Physical Chemistry
DAWIDOWICZ, A., Physical Chemistry
DĄBROWSKI, A., Theoretical Chemistry
DUMKIEWICZ, R., Analytical Chemistry
FERENC, W., Inorganic Chemistry
GAWDZIK, B., Physical Chemistry
GOWOREK, J., Physical Chemistry
HUBICKA, H., Inorganic Chemistry
HUBICKI, Z., Inorganic Chemistry
JAŃCZUK, B., Physical Chemistry
JURKIEWICZ, K., Theoretical Chemistry
KOZIOŁ, A., Chemistry, X-ray Crystallography
LEBODA, R., Physical Chemistry of Surfaces and Chromatography
MAJDAN, M., Inorganic Chemistry
MATYNIA, T., Organic Chemistry
MATYSIK, J., Analytical Chemistry and Instrumental Analysis
NASUTO, R., Physical Chemistry of Surfaces
NAZIMEK, D., Physical Chemistry
OŚCIK, J., Physical Chemistry of Surfaces
OŚCIK-MENDYK, B., Physical Chemistry
PATRYKIEJEW, A., Chemical Physics
PILUS, S., Chemistry
PODKOŚCIELNY, W., Organic Synthesis
RAYSS, J., Physical Chemistry
RÓŻYŁŁO, J., Physical Chemistry
RUDZINSKI, W., Theoretical Chemistry

RZĘCZYŃSKA, Z., Inorganic Chemistry
SOKOŁOWSKI, S., Theoretical Chemistry
STASZCZUK, P., Physical Chemistry
SUPRYNOWICZ, Z., Physical Chemistry
SYKUT, K., Analytical Chemistry and Instrumental Analysis
SZCZYPA, J., Radiochemistry
WAKSMUNDZKI, A., Physical Chemistry
WÓJCIK, W., Physical Chemistry

Faculty of Fine Arts:

GÓRSKI, K., Conducting
HERMAN, M., Painting
JAWORSKA, A., Conducting
JAWORSKI, L., Conducting
KŁECZEK, J., Applied Fine Arts
KOŁWZAN-NOWICKA, D., Fine Arts
LECH, P., Graphics
MAZUREK, G., Graphics
MIELESZKO, S., Teaching of Sculpture
NALEPKA, J., Music Education
NIEDŹWIEDŹ, Z., Graphics
ORDYK-CZYŻEWSKA, E., Conducting
PRZYCHODZIŃSKA-KACICZAK, M., Music Education
ŚNOCH, M., Graphics
ŚWIECA, C., Music Education
ZAGAJEWSKI, B., Sculpture

Faculty of Philosophy and Sociology:

BOROWIECKA, E., Ethics and Aesthetics
CACKOWSKI, Z., Theory of Recognition
CZARNECKI, Z., History of Philosophy
FILIPIAK, M., Sociology, Culture and Education
JEDYNAK, S., Ethics
KOSIŃSKI, S., Sociology
KWIATKOWSKI, T., History of Logic and Philosophy
LIBISZEWSKA-ŻÓŁTKOWSKA, M., Sociology
MIZIŃSKA, J., Epistemology
OGRYZKO-WIEWIÓROWSKA, M., Sociology
PAŚNICZEK, J., Logic
STYK, J., Sociology
SYMOTIUK, S., Philosophy of Culture
TANALSKI, D., Political Science
TOKARSKI, S., Sociology of Medicine
ZACHARIASZ, A., History of Philosophy

Faculty of Politology:

CHAŁUPCZAK, H., Contemporary History
CZARNOCKI, A., Political Science
GRZEGORZ, J., Contemporary History
HOŁDA, Z., Human Law
JACHYMEK, J., 19th- and 20th-century Political Thought
JELENKOWSKI, M., Political Doctrines
KUCHARSKI, W., Study of the Polish People in Other Countries
LUDOROWSKI, L., Polish Literature
MAY, C., Political Science
MICH, W., Contemporary History
MICHAŁOWSKI, S., Contemporary History
MIECZKOWSKI, A., 19th- and 20th-century Political Thought
OLSZEWSKI, E., Movements and Political Doctrines
PIETRAŚ, J. Z., International Relations
SZELIGA, Z., Constitutional Law
WÓJCIK, A., Contemporary History
ŻMIGRODZKI, M., Political Systems

UNIWERSYTET IM. ADAMA MICKIEWICZA W POZNANIU (Adam Mickiewicz University in Poznań)

61-712 Poznań, ul. H. Wieniawskiego 1

Telephone: (61) 852-64-25
Telex: 0413260
Fax: (61) 853-65-36

Founded 1919

Rector: Prof. Dr hab. STEFAN JURGA
Pro-Rectors: Prof. Dr hab. JOACHIM CIEŚLIK, Prof. Dr hab. PRZEMYSŁAW HAUSER, Prof. Dr hab. MAREK KRĘGLEWSKI, Prof. Dr hab. SYLWESTER DWORACKI, Prof. Dr hab. STANISŁAW LORENC
Registrar: Mgr STANISŁAW WACHOWIAK
Librarian: Dr ARTUR JAZDON

Library: see Libraries
Number of teachers: 2,209
Number of students: 31,226

Publications: various faculty publs.

DEANS

Faculty of Law and Administration: ANDRZEJ ZIELIŃSKI
Faculty of History: TOMASZ JASIŃSKI
Faculty of Modern Languages and Literature: Prof. Dr hab. STANISŁAW PUPPEL
Faculty of Polish and Classical Philologies: Prof. Dr hab. BOGDAN WALCZAK
Faculty of Mathematics and Computer Science: Prof. Dr hab. MICHAŁ KAROŃSKI
Faculty of Chemistry: Prof. Dr hab. HENRYK KORONIAK
Faculty of Biology: Prof. Dr hab. KAZIMIERZ ZIEMNICKI
Faculty of Physics: Prof. Dr hab. WOJCIECH NAWROCIK
Faculty of Geography and Geology: Prof. Dr hab. ANDRZEJ KOSTRZEWSKI
Faculty of Social Sciences: Prof. Dr hab. ANNA MICHALSKA
Faculty of Educational Studies: Prof. Dr hab. ZBIGNIEW KWIECIŃSKI

PROFESSORS

Faculty of Law and Administration:

DASZKIEWICZ, K., Criminal Law
DASZKIEWICZ, W., Criminal Procedure
GULCZ, M., Economics
JANOWICZ, Z., Administrative Procedure
KIJOWSKI, A., Labour Law
KOMAR, A., Financial Law
LEOŃSKI, Z., Administrative Law
LESIŃSKI, B., Roman Law and History of Judicial Law
ŁĄCZKOWSKI, W., Financial Law
MICHALSKA, A., International Law
NIEDBAŁA, Z., Labour Law
NOWAK, T., Criminal Procedure
OLSZEWSKI, H., Political Law
OWOC, M., Criminal Law
PATRYAS, W., Theory of State and Law
PIOTROWSKI, W., Labour Law
RABSKA, T., Public Economic Law
RATAJCZAK, A., Criminal Law
ROZWADOWSKI, W., Roman Law and History of Judicial Law
SMYCZYŃSKI, T., Civil Law
SOŁTYSIŃSKI, S., Civil Law
STACHOWIAK, S., Criminal Procedure
SZWARC, A. J., Criminal Law
TOBIS, A., Criminal Law
TYRANOWSKI, J., International Law
WALACHOWICZ, J., History of State Political Systems
WĄSIEWICZ, A., Civil Law
WRONKOWSKA-JAŚKIEWICZ, S., Theory of State and Law
ZEDLER, F., Civil Procedure
ZIELIŃSKI, M., Theory of State and Law

Faculty of History:

BŁASZCZYK, G., East European History
BORAS, Z., Modern History prior to the 18th Century
BRENCZ, A., Ethnology of Poland and the Balkan Countries
BUCHOWSKI, M., European Ethnology, Theory of Anthropology
BURSZTA, W., Ethnology of Ethnicity, Theory of Anthropology
COFTA-BRONIEWSKA, A., Prehistory of Poland
CZAMAŃSKA, I., Balkan Studies
CZUBIŃSKI, A., 19th- and 20th-century History
DROZDOWSKI, M., Modern Polish History
DWORECKI, Z., Contemporary Polish History
DWORZACZKOWA, J., Modern Polish History
FOGEL, J., Bronze and Early Iron Age Prehistory
HAUSER, P., Contemporary History
JANKOWSKA, D., Stone Age Prehistory
JASIEWICZ, Z., Ethnology of Poland and Central Asia
JASIŃSKA, D., Musicology
JASIŃSKI, T., Medieval History
JURKIEWICZ, J., East European History
KALINOWSKI, K., History of Modern Art
KARŁOWSKA-KAMZA, A., History of Medieval Art
KIJAS, A., East European History
KÓĆKA-KRENZ, H., Medieval Archaeology
KOŚKO, A., Prehistory of Poland
KOTŁOWSKI, T., Contemporary History
KOWAL, S., Economic History
KRZYŻANIAK, J., Medieval History
KUBCZAK, J., History of Ancient Art
KUJAWSKA, M., Didactics of History
KÜRBIS, B., Medieval History
LABUDA, A., History of Art
LABUDA, G., Medieval History
LAPIS, B., History of Culture
ŁAZUGA, W., Modern History
ŁUCZAK, C., Economic History
ŁYSIAK, W., Folklore
MAKIEWICZ, T., Roman Iron Age Prehistory
MAKOWSKI, E., Contemporary History of Poland
MINTA-TWORZOWSKA, D., Methodology and History of Prehistory
MIŚKIEWICZ, B., Military History
MOLIK, W., Modern Polish History
MROZEWICZ, L., Ancient History
NAWROCKI, S., Modern and Contemporary Polish History
OLEJNIK, K., Military History
OLSZEWSKI, W., Modern and Contemporary History
PAJEWSKI, J., 19th- and 20th-century History
PIETKIEWICZ, K., Medieval East European History
PILARCZYK, Z., Military History
PIOTROWSKI, P., History of Contemporary Art
POPIOŁ-SZYMAŃSKA, A., Economic History
POSERN-ZIELIŃSKI, A., Ethnology of the Americas, Anthropology of Ethnicity
SCHRAMM, T., Modern History
SERWAŃSKI, M., Modern History
SIERPOWSKI, S., Contemporary History
SKIBIŃSKI, S., History of Medieval Art
SKURATOWICZ, J., History of Modern Art
STĘSZEWSKI, J., Musicology
STRZELCZYK, J., Medieval History
SUCHOCKI, W., History of Modern Art
SZULC, W., Balkan Studies
SZYFER, A., Polish Ethnology
TOPOLSKI, J., Methodology of History, Modern History
TRZECIAKOWSKI, L., 19th- and 20th-century Polish History
VORBRICZ, R., African Ethnology
WIELGOSZ, Z., Medieval History
WOJTKOWIAK, Z., Modern East European History
WRONIAK, Z., Contemporary History
WROSEK, W., Methodology of History
WUJEWSKI, T., History of Ancient Art
WYRWA, A., Medieval History
ZAWADZKI, S., Ancient History

Faculty of Modern Languages and Literature:

ADAMSKA-SAŁACIAK, A., English Linguistics
ANDRUSZKO, Cz., Russian Literature
AWEDYK, S., Scandinavian Linguistics
AWEDYK, W., English Linguistics
BAŃCZEROWSKI, J., General Linguistics
BARTOSZEWICZ, A., Russian Linguistics
BIALIK, W., German Literature
BZDĘGA, A., German Linguistics
CHAŁACIŃSKA-WIERTELAK, H., Russian Literature
DARSKI, J., German Linguistics
DROŹDZIAŁ-SZELEST, K., English Linguistics

Dziubalska-Kołaczyk, K., English Linguistics
Filipowska, I., Romance Literature
Fisiak, J., English Linguistics
Gaca, A., German Linguistics
Hasiuk, M., Baltic Linguistics
Jackiewicz, M., Comparative Linguistics
Jankowski, H., Oriental Linguistics
Kaliszan, J., Russian Linguistics
Karolak, Cz., German Literature
Kaszyński, S., Austrian Literature and Culture
Kątny, A., German Linguistics
Koniuszaniec, G., German Linguistics
Kopcewicz, A., American Literature
Kopczyński, A., English Linguistics
Kopytko, R., English Linguistics
Krygier, M., English Linguistics
Kryk-Kastovsky, B., English Linguistics
Krysztofiak-Kaszyńska, M., Danish Literature
Krzemińska, W., Romance Linguistics
Lipoński, W., Anglo-Saxon Studies
Lis, J., Romance Literature
Litwinow, J., Russian Literature
Łobacz, P., General Linguistics
Maciejewski, W., General Linguistics
Majewicz, A., Oriental Linguistics
Malinowski, W., Romance Literature
Markunas, A., Methodology of Russian Language Teaching
Marton, W., English Linguistics
Misterski, H., Romance Languages
Myczko, K., Applied Linguistics
Nowikow, W., Spanish Linguistics
Orłowski, H., German Literature
Papiór, J., German Literature and Culture
Pfeiffer, W., Applied Linguistics
Piotrowski, B., History of Scandinavia
Pisarska, A., English Linguistics
Pogonowski, J., Mathematical Linguistics
Połczyńska, E., German Literature
Prokop, I., German Linguistics
Puppel, S., English Linguistics
Rajnik, E., Danish Linguistics
Schatte, Ch., German Linguistics
Schatte, Cz., German Linguistics
Salwa, P., Italian Literature
Siek-Piskozub, T., Applied Linguistics
Sikorska, L., English Literature
Skowronek, B., Applied Linguistics
Sobkowiak, W., English Linguistics
Stefański, W., English Linguistics
Steffen-Batogowa, M., General Linguistics
Sypnicki, J., Romance Linguistics
Tomaszkiewicz, T., Romance Linguistics
Wąsik, Z., General Linguistics
Wilczyńska, W., Applied Linguistics
Wójtowicz, M., Russian Linguistics
Woźniewicz, W., Methodology of Russian Language Teaching
Zabrocki, T., English Linguistics
Zgółka, T., General Linguistics

Faculty of Polish and Classical Philologies:

Abramowska, J., Polish Literature, Historical Poetics
Adamczyk, M., Old Polish Literature
Bąba, S., Idioms and Culture of Polish Language
Bakuła, B., 20th-century Literature
Balcerzan, E., Polish Literature, Theory of Literature and 20th-century Literature
Bartol, K., Hellenistic Philology
Borejszo, M., Polish Linguistics
Chrząstowska, B., New Teaching Methods, History of Polish Literature
Danielewicz, J., Hellenistic Philology
Dworacki, S., Hellenistic Philology
Hendrykowska, M., Film History and Theory
Hendrykowski, M., Film History and Theory
Kasprzakowa, B., Teaching of Polish Language and Literature
Kornaszewski, M., Teaching of Polish Linguistics
Krajewska-Stasiak, A., Theory of Literature, History of Literature
Krążyńska, Z., Polish Linguistics
Legeżyńska, A., Theory of Literature
Lewandowski, I., Latin Philology
Lewandowski, T., Polish Literature
Liman, K., Latin Philology
Marciniak, R., Bibliology
Mikołajczak, S., Polish Grammar and Lexicology
Naumow, A., Slavic Literatures
Nowak, H., Polish Dialectology
Pieścikowski, E., Polish Literature
Pokrzywniak, J. T., Old Polish Literature
Przybylski, R. K., Theory of Literature, History of Literature
Ratajczak, D., Polish Drama
Rzepka, W., Polish Linguistics
Sajkowski, A., History of Polish Literature and Culture
Sarnowska-Giefing, I., Polish as a Foreign Language
Słowiński, L., History of the Teaching of Polish Literature
Smuszkiewicz, A., Teaching of Polish Language and Literature
Sobierajski, Z., Polish Dialectology
Świdziński, J., Comparative Studies on Slavic Literatures
Trojanowicz, Z., 19th-century Polish Literature
Walczak, B., Polish Linguistics
Wiegandt, E., History of Contemporary Literature
Witczak, T., Old Polish Literature
Wójcik, A., Latin Philology
Wydra, W., Editorial and Bibliography
Wysłouch, S., Polish Literature, Theory of Literature and 20th-Century Literature
Zagórski, Z., Polish Dialectology
Zdancewicz, T., Slavonic Philology
Zgółkowa, H., Polish Linguistics
Zierhoffer, K., Polish Linguistics

Faculty of Mathematics and Information Sciences:

Banaszak, G., Algebraic K-theory, Algebraic Number Theory
Bartz, K., Number Theory
Batóg, T., Mathematical Logic, Mathematical Linguistics
Błażewicz, J., Computer Science
Bobrowski, D., Differential Equations, Probability
Buszkowski, W., Logic, Linguistics, Computation Theory
Domański, P., Functional Analysis
Drewnowski, L., Functional Analysis
Hudzik, H., Functional Analysis
Jaroszewska, M., Functional Analysis, Teaching of Mathematics
Kaczorowski, J., Number Theory
Kąkol, J., Functional Analysis, Topology
Karoński, M., Discrete Mathematics and Probability
Katulska, K., Mathematical Statistics
Korcz, M., Teaching of Mathematics
Krzyśko, M., Mathematical Statistics
Kubiaczyk, I., Differential Equations
Kubiak, T., Topology of Fuzzy Sets
Łuczak, T., Discrete Mathematics and Probability
Marzantowicz, W., Nonlinear Analysis
Mastyło, M., Functional Analysis
Murawski, R., Mathematical Logic, Philosophy of Mathematics
Musielak, J., Mathematical Analysis, Functional Analysis
Nawrocki, M., Functional Analysis
Nowak, W., Teaching of Mathematics
Palka, Z., Discrete Mathematics and Probability
Pych-Taberska, P., Approximation Theory
Ruciński, A., Discrete Mathematics and Probability
Sołtysiak, A., Functional Analysis
Staś, W., Number Theory
Stoiński, S., Functional Analysis, Fourier Series
Świrydowicz, K., Logic
Szufla, St. , Differential Equations
Szulc, T., Numerical Linear Algebra
Taberski, R., Approximation Theory
Urbanski, R., Optimization Theory
Vetulani, Z., Computer Linguistics and Artificial Intelligence
Waszak, A., Functional Analysis
Wiertelak, K., Number Theory
Wisła, M., Functional Analysis
Wnuk, W., Functional Analysis
Wygralak, M., Fuzzy Sets and Systems

Faculty of Chemistry:

Antkowiak, W., Organic Spectrochemistry
Augustyniak, W., Photochemistry
Bełtowska-Brzezińska, M., Electrochemistry
Boczoń, W., Organic and Natural Products Chemistry
Borowiak, T., Organic Crystal Chemistry and X-ray Crystallography
Brycki, B., Organic Chemistry
Brzeziński, B., Bio-organic Physical Chemistry
Burewicz, A., Teaching of Chemistry
Dega-Szafran, Z., Physical Organic Chemistry
Domka, F., Kinetics and Catalysis, Environmental Biotechnology
Domka, L., Technology of Inorganic Chemistry, Physics and Chemistry of Solid-state Surfaces
Duczmal, W., Organometallic and Co-ordination Chemistry
Dutkiewicz, E., Electrochemistry
Elbanowski, M., Rare Earths
Fiedorow, R., Catalysis
Gawroński, J., Organic Chemistry, Stereochemistry
Gdaniec, M., Crystallography
Golankiewicz, K., Synthesis and Structure of Organic Compounds
Guliński, J., Organometallic Chemistry
Jarczewski, A., Physical Organic Chemistry
Jaskólski, M., Crystallography and Biological Chemistry
Jaworska-Augustyniak, A., Photochemistry
Juskowiak, B., Analytical Chemistry
Kania, W., Chemical Technology
Katrusiak, A., Crystallography
Kiełczewski, M., Organic Chemistry, Stereochemistry, Pheromones
Kirszensztejn, P., Environmental Chemistry, Heterogeneous Catalysis
Konarski, J., Theoretical Chemistry
Koput, J., Molecular Spectroscopy
Koroniak, H., Synthesis and Structure of Organic Compounds
Kosturkiewicz, Z., Crystallography
Kowalak, S., Heterogeneous Catalysis
Kręglewski, M., High Resolution Rotational-Vibrational Spectroscopy
Langer, J., Physical Organic Chemistry
Laniecki, M., Heterogeneous Catalysis
Lis, S., Rare Earths
Łomozic, L., Co-ordination Chemistry, Bioinorganic Chemistry
Maciejewski, A., Photochemistry and Photophysics
Makarewicz, J., Theoretical Chemistry
Marciniak, B., Photochemistry
Marciniec, B., Organometallic Chemistry, Molecular Catalysis
Molski, A., Theoretical Chemistry
Nawrocki, J., Water Treatment Technology
Nowińska, K., Heterogeneous Catalysis
Paryzek, Z., Organic and Natural Products Chemistry
Paszyc, S., Chemical Physics
Płaziak, A., Analytical Chemistry

Radecka-Paryzek, W., Co-ordination and Macrocyclic Chemistry, Bioinorganic Chemistry
Rozwadowska, M., Asymmetric Synthesis, Alkaloid Chemistry
Rychlewska, U., Crystallography and X-ray Structure Analysis
Rychlewski, J., Theoretical Chemistry
Sarbak, Z., Adsorption and Catalysis, Environmental Protection
Schroeder, G., Organic Chemistry
Siepak, J., Water and Soil Analysis
Skalski, B., Bio-organic Photochemistry
Szafran, M., Physical Organic Chemistry
Szczepaniak, W., Instrumental Analysis, Analytical Chemistry
Wachowska, H., Chemistry of Coal
Wachowski, L., Inorganic Chemistry, Catalysis
Wasiak, W., Instrumental Analysis
Wenska, G., Bio-organic Photochemistry
Wiewiórowski, M., Natural Products and Bio-organic Chemistry
Wojciechowska, M., Heterogeneous Catalysis
Wolska, E., Solid-state Chemistry and Magnetochemistry
Wolski, W., Solid-state Chemistry and Magnetochemistry
Wyrzykiewicz, E., Mass Spectrometry of Organic Compounds
Wysocka, W., Natural Products Chemistry
Zasępa, W., Colloid Chemistry
Zieliński, S., Inorganic Chemistry
Ziołek, M., Heterogeneous Catalysis

Faculty of Biology:

Augustyniak, H., Biochemistry
Augustyniak, J., Biochemistry
Balcerkiewicz, S., Plant Ecology
Bartkowska, K., Animal Taxonomy
Bednorz, J., Animal Ecology
Bielawski, J., Animal Cytology
Błaszak, Cz., Animal Ecology
Bobowicz, M., Plant Genetics
Borysiak, J., Plant Ecology
Bujakiewicz, A., Mycology
Burchardt, L., Hydrobiology
Cieślik, J., Anthropology
Czosnowski, E., Plant Cytology and Histology
Drozdowska, M., Anthropology
Dziabaszewski, A., Zoology
Goździcka-Józefiak, A., Biochemistry
Gwóźdź, E., Plant Ecophysiology
Hryniewiecka, L., Biochemistry
Jackiewicz, M., Zoology
Jackowski, G., Plant Physiology
Kaczmarek, M., Anthropology
Klimko, M., Plant Taxonomy
Kraska, M., Hydrobiology
Krzak, M., Plant Genetics
Latowski, K., Plant Taxonomy
Legocka, J., Plant Physiology
Lesicki, A., Animal Physiology
Lisiewska, M., Mycology
Lisowski, S., Tropical Botany
Mazur, H., Biochemistry
Michalska, Z., Zoology
Michejda, J., Biochemistry
Mossor-Pietraszewska, T., Biochemistry
Niedbała, W., Animal Ecology
Piontek, J., Anthropology
Prus-Głowacki, W., Plant Genetics
Ratajczak, L., Plant Physiology
Ratajczak, W., Plant Physiology
Rosiński, G., Animal Physiology
Schneider, J., Plant Physiology
Stępczak, K., Zoology
Strzałko, J., Anthropology
Szweykowska, A., Plant Physiology
Szweykowska-Kulińska, Z., Biochemistry
Szweykowski, J., Plant Genetics
Szyfter, Z., Animal Cytology and Histology
Tomaszewska, B., Biochemistry
Winiecki, A., Animal Ecology
Włodarczak, K., Microbiology
Woźny, A., Plant Cytology
Zenkteler, M., Plant Embryology
Ziemnicki, K., Animal Physiology
Żukowski, W., Plant Taxonomy

Faculty of Physics:

Alexiewicz, W., Nonlinear Optics
Bancewicz, T., Molecular Optics
Barnas, J., Solid-state Physics
Błaszak, M., Mathematical Physics
Błaszczak, Z., Molecular Optics
Bochyński, Z., Condensed Matter Physics
Dobek, A., Biophysics
Dutkiewicz, M., Dielectric Physics
Fechner, B., Solid-state Physics
Ferchmin, I., Dielectric Physics
Hilczer, T., Physics of Dielectrics
Hojan, E., Electroacoustics
Hołderna-Natkaniek, K., Molecular Crystals
Jacyna-Onyszkiewicz, Z., Statistical Physics
Jurga, K., Radiospectroscopy
Jurga, S., Radiospectroscopy and Molecular Physics
Kaczmarek, F., Laser Physics
Kamieniarz, G., Computer Physics
Kowalewski, L., Solid-state Physics
Kozierowski, M., Nonlinear Optics
Krzyminiewski, R., Medical Physics
Kurzyńska, K., Astrometry
Kurzyński, M., Statistical Physics
Łabowski, M., Molecular Acoustics
Lulek, T., Mathematical Physics
Makarewicz, R., Environmental Acoustics
Micnas, R., Solid-state Physics
Mróz, B., Ferroelectrics
Nawrocik, W., Molecular Physics
Nogaj, B., Radiospectroscopy
Ożgo, Z., Nonlinear Optics
Ozimek, E., Psychoacoustics
Pająk, Z., Solid-state Spectroscopy
Parzyński, R., Quantum Electronics
Patkowski, A., Molecular Biophysics
Pietrzak, J., Solid-matter Spectroscopy
Puszkarski, H., Solid-state Physics
Robaszkiewicz, S., Solid-state Physics
Schwarzenberg-Czerny, A., Astrophysics
Śliwińska-Bartkowiak, M., Liquid Physics
Stankowska, J., Molecular Physics
Surma, M., Optics
Szcześniak, E., Radiospectroscopy
Szlachetka, P., Mathematical Physics
Szweykowska, A., Condensed-matter Theory
Szydłowski, H., Teaching of Physics
Szymański, M., Molecular Protophysics
Tanaś, R., Nonlinear Optics
Tylczyński, Z., Ferroelectric Physics
Wąsicki, J., Radiospectroscopy
Wnuk, E., Celestian Mechanics
Wojciechowski, R., Condensed-matter Theory
Woźniak, S., Molecular Nonlinear Optics

Faculty of Geography and Geology:

Biderman, E., Socioeconomic Geography
Choiński, J., Hydrology
Chojnicki, Z., Socioeconomic Geography, Methodology
Cierniewski, J., Remote Sensing
Czyż, T., Economic Geography
Fedorowski, J., Palaeozoology
Głazek, J., Dynamic Geology
Głębocki, B., Economic Geography
Górski, J., Hydrogeology
Kaniecki, A., Hydrology and Water Management
Karczewski, A., Glacial Geomorphology
Kłysz, P., Glacial Geomorphology
Kostrzewski, A., Dynamic Geomorphology and Geoecology
Kozacki, L., Integrated Physical Geography
Liszkowski, J., Engineering Geology, Dynamic Geology
Lorenc, S., Geology, Petrography
Muszyński, A., Geology, Petrography
Nowaczyk, B., Geomorphology
Parysek, J., Socioeconomic Geography
Przybyłek, J., Hydrogeology
Rogacki, H., Socioeconomic Geography
Rotnicka, J., Geography, Hydrology
Rotnicki, K., Geomorphology, Palaeogeography
Skoczylas, J., Archaelogy
Solowiej, D., Geoecology of Recreation, Integrated Physical Geography
Stankowska, A., Physical Geography, Geochemistry
Stankowski, W., Pleistocene Sedimentology, Cenozoic Geology
Tamulewicz, J., Geography, Climatology
Tobolski, K., Palaeobotany
Woś, A., Climatology
Żynda, S., Integrated Physical Geography

Faculty of Social Sciences:

Andrzejewski, B., History of German Philosophy
Babiak, J., Economics and Social Science
Baniak, J., Philosophy and Sociology of Religion
Bańka, A., Environmental Psychology
Blok, Z., Political Science
Brzezińska, A., Development
Brzeziński, J., Methodology of Psychology
Buczkowski, P., Local Community and Self-government Studies
Buksiński, T., Social Philosophy, Philosophy of History
Chmara, M., Sociology of International Relations
Chyta, W., Theory of Cinema
Domachowski, W., Social Psychology
Drozdowicz, Z., Philosophy of Religion
Dziamski, G., Contemporary Culture
Dziamski, S., Social Philosophy
Gałganek, A., Political Science
Golka, M., Sociology of Culture, Social Anthropology
Grzegorczyk, A., Philosophy of Culture
Harwas-Napierała, B., Family and Developmental Psychology
Jamroziakowa, A., Aesthetics
Jeliński, E., History of Philosophy
Kaczmarek, U., Forms of Culture, Local and Regional Culture, Animation
Klawiter, A., Cognitive Sciences
Kmita, J., Philosophy of Science
Kocikowski, A., Computer Ethics
Kosman, M., History
Kostyrko, T., Aesthetics
Koszel, B., History and Political Science
Kotowa, B., Phenomenology, Philosophy of Humanities
Kowalik, S., Social Psychology
Kozłowski, R., History of Polish Philosophy
Kozyr-Kowalski, S., Economics and Society
Kubicki, R., Aesthetics
Kwaśniewski, K., Sociological Theory
Łastowski, K., Philosophy of Natural Science
Ławniczak, W., Aesthetics
Liberkowski, R., History of Philosophy
Lisiecki, S., Sociology of the Transborder Area
Malendowski, W., Political Science
Maruszewski, T., Psychology of Cognition and Emotion
Michalska, A., Sociology of Family
Miluska, J., Social and Political Psychology, Development
Mojsiewicz, Cz., Political Science
Nowak, L., Philosophy of Science, Political Philosophy
Nowakowa, I., Philosophy of Science
Orczyk, J., Economics and History
Pałubicka, A., Theory of Culture
Piotrowska, E., Philosophy of Mathematics
Poznaniak, W., Clinical Psychology
Przyłębski, A., History of Philosophy
Puślecki, Z., International Economic Relations
Rewers, E., Philosophy of Culture

ROBAKOWSKI, K., History
SAKSON, A., Sociology of Ethnic Minorities, Sociology of Youth
SĘK, H., Health and Clinical Psychology
SOBCZAK, J., Law
SOBCZYŃSKA, D., Philosophy of Science
SÓJKA, J., Philosophy of Culture, Business Ethics
STACHOWSKI, R., History of Psychological Thought
STRYKOWSKA, M., Organizational Psychology
SUCH, J., Philosophy of Science
SZYMAŃSKI, J., Philosophy of Technology
TITTENBRUN, J., Theory and Practice of Privatization
TYSZKA, Z., Sociology of Family
WALKOWIAK, J., Methodology of Sociological Research
WĘCŁOWSKI, T., Theology
WESOŁY, M., History of Ancient Philosophy
WIŚNIEWSKI, J., Philosophy of Mathematics
WŁODAREK, J., Sociology of Education, History of Sociology
WOŹNIAK, Z., Sociology of Medicine
ZAMIARA, T., Philosophy of Science
ZEIDLER, P., Philosophy of Science
ZEIDLER-JANISZEWSKA, A., Philosophy of Culture
ZIÓŁKOWSKI, M., Sociological Theory
ŻYROMSKI, M., Historical Sociology

Faculty of Educational Studies:

AMBROZIK, W., Resocialization
BROMBEREK, B., Higher Education
DENEK, K., Didactics
DOMKA, L., Ecological Education
DUDZIKOWA, M., School Education
DYKCIK, W., Special Education
FRĄCKOWIAK, T., Social Education
GAPIK, L., Psychology, Psychotherapy
GNITECKI, J., Methodology of Education
HELLWIG, J., History of Education
KUJAWIŃSKI, J., Primary Education
KWIECIŃSKI, Z., Sociology of Education
MELOSIK, Z., Comparative Education
MODRZEWSKI, J., Social Education
MUSZYŃSKI, H., Theory of Education
OBUCHOWSKA, I., Clinical Psychology
PIOTROWSKI, E., Didactics
POTULICKA, E., Comparative Education
PRZYSZCZYPKOWSKI, K., Adult Education
SKRZYPCZAK, J., Adult Education
SOLARCZYK-AMBROZIK, E., Adult Education
SOWIŃSKA, H., Theory of Education
STRYKOWSKI, W., Educational Technology
ZANDECKI, A., Youth Educational Problems

UNIWERSYTET MIKOŁAJA KOPERNIKA W TORUNIU (Nicholas Copernicus University of Toruń)

87-100 Toruń, ul. Gagarina 11
Telephone: (56) 654-29-51
Fax: (56) 654-29-44

Founded 1945
State control
Language of instruction: Polish
Academic year: October to September (two terms)

Rector: Prof. Dr hab. ANDRZEJ JAMIOŁKOWSKI
Vice-Rectors: Prof. Dr hab. STANISŁAW CHWIROT, Prof. Dr hab. CZESŁAW ŁAPICZ, Prof. Dr hab. RYSZARD ŁASZEWSKI, Prof. Dr hab. MAREK J. STANKIEWICZ, Prof. Dr hab. WOJCIECH POPŁAWSKI
Registrar: Dr STEFAN NIELEK
Librarian: STEFAN CZAJA

Library: see Libraries
Number of teachers: 1,117
Number of students: 20,300

Publications: *Acta Universitatis Nicolai Copernici, Reports on Mathematical Physics, Open Systems and Information Dynamics, Comparative Law Review, Topological Methods in Non-Linear Analysis, Eastern European Countryside, Logic and Logical Philosophy, Theoria et Historia Scientiarum.*

DEANS

Faculty of Biology and Earth Sciences: Prof. Dr hab. JAN KOPCEWICZ
Faculty of Chemistry: Prof. Dr hab. MAREK ZAIDLEWICZ
Faculty of Economics and Management: Prof. Dr hab. JERZY WIŚNIEWSKI
Faculty of Fine Arts: Prof. Dr hab. ROMUALD DRZEWIECKI
Faculty of History: Prof. Dr hab. JANUSZ MAŁŁEK
Faculty of Humanities: Prof. Dr hab. RYSZARD BOROWICZ
Faculty of Law and Administration: Prof. Dr hab. GRZEGORZ GOŹDZIEWICZ
Faculty of Mathematics and Computer Science: Prof. Dr hab. DANIEL SIMSON
Faculty of Physics and Astronomy: Prof. Dr hab. FRANCISZEK ROZPŁOCH

PROFESSORS

Faculty of Biology and Earth Sciences:

ANDRZEJEWSKI, L., Physical Geography
BARGIEL, Z., Animal Physiology
BEDNAREK, R., Soil Sciences
BEDNARSKA, E., Plant Cytology
BUSZKO, J., Entomology, Zoography
CAPUTA, M., Animal Physiology
CEYNOWA, M., Plant Taxonomy, Geobotany
CHURSKI, Z., Hydrology, Water Management
CHWIROT, B., Plant Cytology
CZARNECKI, A., Animal Ecology
DONDERSKI, W., Microbiology
FALKOWSKI, J., Economic Geography
GIZIŃSKI, A., Hydrobiology
GNIOT-SZULŻYCKA, J., Biochemistry
GÓRSKA-BRYLASS, A., Plant Cytology
GRZEŚ, M., Hydrology and Water Management
JACUŃSKI, L., Arachnology
KĄDZIELA, W., Biophysics
KOPCEWICZ, J., Plant Physiology
KOWALCZYK, S., Biochemistry
KRIESEL, G., Anthropology
MAIK, W., Social Geography and Tourism
PAWLIKOWSKI, T., Ecology
PLICHTA, W., Soil Science
PRZYSTALSKI, A., Vertebrate Zoology
REJEWSKI, M., Plant Ecology
ROCHNOWSKI, H., Economic Geography
SADURSKI, A., Geology
STRZELCZYK, E., Microbiology
SZYMAŃSKA, D., Social Geography
TĘGOWSKA, E., Animal Physiology
TRETYN, A., Plant Physiology
WIŚNIEWSKI, E., Geomorphology
WÓJCIK, G., Climatology

Faculty of Chemistry:

BUSZEWSKI, B., Environmental Chemistry
CEYNOWA, J., Physical Chemistry
DEMBIŃSKI, B., Analytical Chemistry
GRODZICKI, A., Inorganic Chemistry
KAMIŃSKA, A., Physical Chemistry
KITA, P., Inorganic Chemistry
KREJA, L., Physical Chemistry
MALINOWSKI, P., Theoretical Chemistry
NARĘBSKA, A., Physical Chemistry
ROZWADOWSKI, M., Physical Chemistry
RYCHLICKI, G., Physical Chemistry
SADLEJ, A., Quantum Chemistry
SIEDLEWSKI, J., Physical Chemistry
SZYMAŃSKI, W., Radiation Chemistry
TRYPUĆ, M., Chemical Technology
UZAREWICZ, A., Organic Chemistry
ZAIDLEWICZ, M., Physical Chemistry

Faculty of Economics and Management:

BOGDANIENKO, J., Investment Economics
CIEŚLIŃSKI, Z., Food Production Economics
DREWIŃSKI, M., Management
GŁUCHOWSKI, J., Finance Management
JAWOROWSKI, P., Agricultural Economics
KACZMARCZYK, S., Marketing
KOSIEDOWSKI, T., Economy
MELLER, J., Human Resources Management
NIEŻURAWSKI, L., Business Management
POLSZAKIEWICZ, B., Economics
POPŁAWSKI, W., Business Management
RADZIKOWSKI, W., Management
RZECZKOWSKI, R., Building Economics
SKAWIŃSKA, E., Agricultural Economics
SOBKÓW, C., Marketing and Management
SOJAK, S., Financial Management
STANKIEWICZ, M. J., Management
STAWICKI, J., Econometrics and Statistics
SUDOŁ, S., Industrial Management
TOMALA, J., Economics
WIŚNIEWSKI, J. W., Econometrics and Statistics
WIŚNIEWSKI, Z., Employment Policy
ZIELIŃSKI, Z., Econometrics

Faculty of Fine Arts:

ARSZYŃSKI, M., History of Art, Protection of Monuments
BRZUSZKIEWICZ, H., Sculpture
CANDER, K., Painting
DOMASŁOWSKI, W., Restoration of Stone Monuments
DRZEWIECKI, R., Painting
FLIK, J., Technology and Painting Techniques
GUTTFELD, A., Art Education
JANIAK, S., Graphics
KRUSZELNICKI, Z., History of Art
MALINOWSKI, J., History of Art
PIETRUSZKIEWICZ, B., Visual Art
PIOTROWSKI, M., Graphics
POKLEWSKI, J., History of Art
PRZYBYLIŃSKI, B., Graphics
ROUBA, B., Restoration of Painting
ROZNERSKA, M., Restoration of Paintings
SKIBIŃSKI, S., History of Art
SŁOBOSZ, J., Graphics
STRZELCZYK, A., Restoration of Paper and Leather Objects
SZAŃKOWSKI, M., Sculpture
SZCZEPKOWSKA-NALIWAJEK, K., History of Art
SZCZYPKA, J., Sculpture
TAJCHMAN, J., Preservation of Historical Monuments
WIŚNIEWSKI, M., Painting
ZIOMEK, M., Painting

Faculty of History:

ALEXANDROWICZ, S., Medieval History
BIENIAK, J., Medieval History
CACKOWSKI, S., Economic History
CHUDZIAK, J., Archaeology of Buildings
CZACHAROWSKI, A., Medieval History
DUNIN-KARWICKA, T., Ethnography
DYGDAŁA, J., Modern History
GRÜNBERG, K., Russian History
JACZYNOWSKA, M., History of Ancient Rome
KALEMBKA, S., Polish and General History
KOLA, A., Subaquatic Archaeology
KOZŁOWSKI, R., Modern History
KWIATKOWSKI, S. F., Medieval History
MALISZEWSKI, K., General and Polish History
MAŁŁEK, K., Polish and General History
MIELCZAREK, M., Archaeology
NOWAK, Z. H., Medieval History
NOWAKOWSKI, A., History of Arms and Armour
OLCZAK, J., History of Glass
PAKULSKI, J., History
PRZEWOŹNA-ARMON, K., Prehistory
RADZIMIŃSKI, A., Social History of the Middle Ages
REZMER, W., Military History
RYSZEWSKI, B., Archival Studies
SERCZYK, J., Methodology of History Education
STASZEWSKI, J., Polish and General History
SZILING, J., Modern History
TANDECKI, J., Medieval History
TOMCZAK, A., Archival Studies
TONDEL, J., Library Science

WAJDA, K., Polish and General History
WAŹBIŃSKI, Z., History of Art
WENTA, J., History
WOJCIECHOWSKI, M., Military History
WOŹNICZKA-PARUZEL, B., Library Science
ZAJĄC, J., Ancient History

Faculty of Humanities:

APPEL, W., Greek Poetry, Lexicography
BAGROWICZ, J., Christian Education
BEZWIŃSKI, A., Russian Literature
BOROWICZ, R., Sociology
BRZOZA, H., Russian Literature
BYBLUK, M., Glottodidactics
DEPTA, H., Education
FRIEDEL, T., Slavonic and Polish Linguistics
GRABOWSKI, M., Philosophy
GROCHOWSKI, M., General Linguistics, Semiotics
GRUENBERG, K., Slavonic Languages
GRZYBOWSKI, S., Russian Linguistics
GUMAŃSKI, L., Logic
GUTOWSKI, W., Polish Literature
HUEBNER, P., Sociology
HUTNIKIEWICZ, A., Polish Literature
JAKOWSKA, K., 20th-century Prose
JAKUBOWSKI, M., Philosophy
JAWORSKA, W., German Literature
KALETA, A., Rural Sociology
KALINOWSKA, M., Polish Romantic Literature and Theatre
KALLAS, K., Polish Linguistics
KASJAN, J. M., Literary Folklore
KOWALIK, S., Special Education
KRUPIANKA, A., History of the Polish Language
KRYSZAK, J., Contemporary Polish Poetry
KRZEWIŃSKA, A., History of Polish Literature
KWIECIŃSKI, Z., Education, Cultural Studies
ŁAPICZ, C., Slavonic Linguistics
LIMONT, W., Education of Children
LAZARI, A., Slavonic Languages
MIKOŁAJCZYK, I., Classics
MOCARSKA-TYC, Z., Polish Philology
MUCHA, J., Sociology, Social Anthropology
NALASKOWSKI, S., General Education
NIEDZIELSKI, C., 20th-century Prose
OLUBIŃSKI, A., Social Education
PAWLAK, J., History of Philosophy and Social Thought
PERZANOWSKI, J., Logic
PIĄTEK, K., Education
PÓŁTURZYCKI, J., General Education
SAUERLAND, K., German Literature
SAWICKA, I., Slavonic Languages
SAWRYCKI, W., Teaching of the Polish Language
SCHULZ, R., General Education
SIEMIENIECKI, B., Technology in Education
SKUCZYŃSKI, J., History of Polish Drama and Theatre
SMULSKI, J., Contemporary Polish Prose
SPEINA, J., 20th-century Polish Novel
STEFAŃSKI, W., Romance Philology
STOFF, A., Polish Literature
STRZELECKI, A., Psychology
SZAHAJ, A., Contemporary Philosophy
SZARMACH, M., Classics
SZUPRYCZYŃSKA, M., Polish Linguistics
SZWEDEK, A., English Linguistics
TYBURSKI, W., Ethics
TYSZKA, T., Psychology
URCHS, M., Logic
WESOŁOWSKA, E., Sociology of Education
WINCLAWSKI, W., Sociology
WIŚNIEWSKI, R., Ethics
WISZNIOWSKA-MAJCHRZYK, M., English Literature
WITKOWSKI, L., Contemporary Philosophy
WOJCIECHOWSKI, A., Special Education
WOJCISZKE, B., Psychology
WRÓBLEWSKI, W., Greek Literature, Sophistry
ŻEGLEŃ, U., Epistemology
ZELAZNY, M., History of Modern Philosophy and Ethics

Faculty of Law and Administration:

BĄCZYK, M., Civil Law
BOJARSKI, W., Canon Law, Roman Law
BORODO, A., Financial Law
BRZEZIŃSKI, B., Public Finance Law
BULSIEWICZ, A., Criminal Law
FILAR, M., Penal Law
GALSTER, J., Constitutional Law
GILAS, J., International Law
GOŹDZIEWICZ, G., International Law
JASUDOWICZ, T., Human Rights
JĘDRZEJEWSKI, S., Economic Administration
JUSTYŃSKI, J., Political and Legal Doctrines
KALLAS, M., History of the Polish State
KAMIŃSKA, K., History of State and Law
KOLASIŃSKI, K., Labour Law
KOWALEWSKI, E., Civil Law
KULICKI, M., Criminal Law
KWAŚNIEWSKI, Z., Commercial Law
LANG, W., Theory of Law and State
ŁASZEWSKI, R., History of Law
LUBIŃSKI, K., Civil Law
MAREK, A., Criminal Law
MIK, C., European Law, Human Rights
MORAWSKI, L., Theory of Law and State
NESTEROWICZ, M., Civil Law
OCHENDOWSKI, E., Administrative Law
SALMONOWICZ, S., German Law
STECKI, L., Civil Law
SZWAJDLER, W., Administrative Law
WIERZBOWSKI, B., Agricultural Law
WITKOWSKI, Z., Constitutional Law

Faculty of Mathematics and Computer Science:

BALCERZYK, S., Algebra
GÓRNIEWICZ, L., Nonlinear Analysis
JAKUBOWSKI, A., Theory of Probability
JARZEMBSKI, G., Informatics
KAMIŃSKI, B., Ergodic Theory
KOTAS, J., Mathematical Logic
KWIATKOWSKI, J., Ergodic Theory
LEMAŃCZYK, M., Ergodic Theory
NAGAEV, A., Theory of Probability, Statistics
SIMSON, D., Algebra
SKOWROŃSKI, A., Algebra
SŁOMIŃSKI, J., Universal Algebra
SŁOMIŃSKI, L., Probability and Statistics
TYC, A., Algebra

Faculty of Physics and Astronomy:

BĄCZYNSKI, A., Molecular Spectroscopy, Optoelectronics
BALTER, A., Molecular Spectroscopy, Optoelectronics
BALTER, A., Molecular Biophysics
BIELSKI, A., Atomic and Molecular Physics
CHWIROT, S., Atomic Physics
DEMBIŃSKI, S., Quantum Optics
DROŻYNER, A., Celestial Mechanics, Astrodynamics
DUCH, W., Computer Sciences
DYGDAŁA, R., Spectroscopy, Microelectronics
GORGOLEWSKI, S., Radio Astronomy
INGARDEN, R. S., Statistical Physics
IWANOWSKA, W., Astrophysics, Stellar Astronomy
JAMIOŁKOWSKI, A., Statistical Physics, Dynamic Systems
JANKOWSKI, K., Quantum Chemistry, Atomic and Molecular Physics
KARWOWSKI, J., Atomic and Molecular Physics
KOSSAKOWSKI, A., Theoretical Physics
KREŁOWSKI, J., Observational Physics
KUS, A., Radio Astronomy
KWIATKOWSKI, J. S., Molecular Biophysics
ŁĘGOWSKI, S., Atomic and Molecular Physics
MARSZAŁEK, T., Molecular Spectroscopy, Quantum Electronics
MĘCZYŃSKA, H., Solid State Physics
MRUGAŁA, R., Mathematical Physics
ROZPŁOCH, F., Solid State Physics
SZUDY, J., Atomic and Molecular Physics
WASILEWSKI, J., Computer Sciences
WOJTOWICZ, A., Optoelectronics
WOLNIEWICZ, L., Theoretical and Computational Physics
WOLSZCZAN, A., Radio Astronomy
WOSZCZYK, A., Astrophysics, Spectroscopy of Stars and Comets
WYBOURNE, B., Molecular Physics
ZAREMBA, J., Atomic and Molecular Physics

UNIWERSYTET SZCZECIŃSKI (Szczecin University)

70-453 Szczecin, Al. Jedności Narodowej 22A
Telephone: (91) 434-25-36
Fax: (91) 434-29-92
E-mail: rektorat@univ.szczecin.pl

Founded 1985
State control
Language of instruction: Polish
Academic year: October to September

Rector: Prof. zw. Dr hab. HUBERT BRONK
Vice-Rectors: Prof. zw. Dr hab. JAN PURCZYŃSKI (Academic Affairs), Prof. Dr hab. ZDZISŁAW CHMIELEWSKI (Education Affairs), Prof. Dr hab. STANISŁAW MUSIELAK (Development and International Relations)
Administrative Officer: EUGENIUSZ KISIEL
Library: see Libraries
Number of teachers: 1,001
Number of students: 24,716

DEANS

Faculty of Arts: Prof. Dr hab. EDWARD WŁODARCZYK
Faculty of Economics and Management: Prof. Dr hab. TERESA LUBIŃSKA
Faculty of Mathematics and Physics: Prof. Dr hab. RYSZARD LEŚNIEWICZ
Faculty of Natural Sciences: Prof. Dr hab. LUCJAN AGAPOW
Faculty of Law and Administration: Prof. Dr hab. WŁADYSŁAW ROZWADOWSKI
Faculty of Management and Economics of Services: Prof. Dr hab. ADAM SZEWCZUK

PROFESSORS

ALEKSIEJENKO, M., Arts
BĄKOWSKI, W., Economics
BIAŁECKI, T., Arts
BRONK, H., Economics
CHMIELEWSKI, Z., Arts
CHWESIUK, K., Economics
CZAPLEWSKI, R., Economics
CZERNIATIN, W., Mathematics
DEPTUŁA, W., Natural Sciences
DOROZIK, L., Economics
DUDZIŃSKI, J., Economics
DZIEDZICZAK, I., Economics
FALKIEWICZ, R., Economics
FARYŚ, J., Arts
GIZA, A., Arts
GŁODEK, Z., Economics
GŁOWACKI, A., Arts
GÓRBIEL, A., Law
GRANOWSKI, J., Physics
GRZYWACZ, W., Economics
HADACZEK, B., Arts
HŁYŃCZAK, A. J., Natural Sciences
HOZER, J., Economics
JANASZ, W., Economics
JASKOT, K., Arts
JASZCZANIN, J., Natural Sciences
KARWOWSKI, J., Economics
KIZIUKIEWICZ, T., Economics
KOPYCIŃSKA, D., Economics
KOROBOW, W., Mathematics
KOŹMIAN, D., Arts
KUCHARSKA, E., Arts
LUKS, K., Economics
MADEJ, T., Economics
MEJBAUM, W., Arts
NOWAKOWSKI, A., Economics
PERENC, J., Economics
PRUSAK, F., Law
ROGALSKA, S., Natural Sciences
ROGALSKI, M., Natural Sciences

SIERGIEJEW, N., Physics
ŚLAWIK, K., Law
ŚLIAŻAS, J., Natural Sciences
STANIELEWICZ, J., Arts
SULIKOWSKI, A., Arts
SUŁKOWSKI, C., Economics
SYGIT, M., Medical Sciences
SZAŁEK, B., Economics, Arts
SZLAUER, L., Natural Sciences
WAŚNIEWSKI, T., Economics
WIERZBICKI, T., Economics
WOŹNIAK, R., Arts
ZALEWSKI, P., Economics
ZAWADZKI, J., Economics

UNIWERSYTET ŚLĄSKI (University of Silesia)

40-007 Katowice, Bankowa 12
Telephone: (32) 599-601
Fax: (32) 599-605
E-mail: dwz@usl.adm.us.edu.pl

Founded 1968

State control
Language of instruction: Polish
Academic year: October to June

Rector: Prof. Dr hab. TADEUSZ SŁAWEK
Pro-Rectors: Prof. Dr hab. JACEK JANIA, Prof. Dr hab. KRYSTIAN ROLEDER, Prof. Dr hab. ZOFIA RATAJCZAK, Prof. Dr hab. ALOJZY KOPOCZEK
Registrar: Dr JAN JELONEK
Librarian: Mgr WANDA DZIADKIEWICZ
Library: see Libraries
Number of teachers: 1,619
Number of students: 36,418
Publication: *Zeszyty Naukowe Wydziałów.*

DEANS

Faculty of Philology: Prof. Dr hab. WIESŁAW BANYŚ
Faculty of Mathematics, Physics and Chemistry: Prof. Dr hab. JERZY ZIOŁO
Faculty of Law and Administration: Prof. Dr hab. GENOWEFA GRABOWSKA
Faculty of Technology: Dr hab. MARIAN SUROWIEC
Faculty of Biology and Environmental Protection: Prof. Dr hab. IWONA SZAREJKO
Faculty of Earth Sciences: Prof. Dr hab. ANDRZEJ JANKOWSKI
Faculty of Social Sciences: Prof. Dr hab. JAN IWANEK
Faculty of Education and Psychology: Dr hab. WŁADYSŁAWA ŁUSZCZUK
Faculty of Radio and Television: Dr KRYSTYNA DOKTOROWICZ
Faculty of Pedagogic and Artistic Education: Prof. Dr hab. ANDRZEJ WÓJTOWICZ

PROFESSORS

Faculty of Mathematics, Physics and Chemistry:
BARON, K., Mathematics
BŁASZCZYK, A., Mathematics
BUHL, F., Chemistry
CHEŁKOWSKI, A., Physics
DŁOTKO, TADEUSZ, Mathematics
DZIĘGIELEWSKI, J., Chemistry
ERNST, S., Chemistry
GER, R., Mathematics
HAŃDEREK, J., Physics
JEŻABEK, M., Physics
JURCZYK, J., Chemistry
KULPA, W., Mathematics
LASOTA, A., Mathematics
ŁUCZKA, J., Physics
MAŃKA, R., Physics
MATKOWSKI, J., Mathematics
MIODUSZEWSKI, J., Mathematics
OKOŃSKA-KOZŁOWSKA, I., Chemistry
RATAJCZAK, A., Chemistry
SZYMICZEK, K., Mathematics
ŚLEBARSKI, A., Physics
ŚLIWIOK, J., Chemistry
UJMA, Z., Physics
WARCZEWSKI, J., Physics
WESTWAŃSKI, B., Physics
ZAREK, W., Physics
ZIELIŃSKI, J., Physics
ZIOŁO, J., Physics
ZIPPER, E., Physics
ZIPPER, W., Physics
ZRAŁEK, M., Physics

Faculty of Biology and Environmental Protection:
BADURA, L., Natural Sciences
CHMIELOWSKI, J., Natural Sciences
CZECHOWICZ, K., Zoology
HEJNOWICZ, Z., Biophysics
KLAG, J., Zoology
KLIMASZEWSKI, S., Biology
MAŁUSZYŃSKA, J., Biology
MAŁUSZYŃSKI, M., Biology
MIGULA, P., Biology
ROSTAŃSKI, K., Botany
STOLAREK, J., Botany
WIKA, S., Botany
WOJCIECHOWSKI, W., Zoology

Faculty of Law and Administration:
AGOPSZOWICZ, A.
CHEŁMICKI-TYSZKIEWICZ, L.
CIĄGWA, J.
GÓRNIOK, O.
GOSTYŃSKI, Z.
GRABOWSKA, G.
GRABOWSKI, J.
KORZAN, K.
KUDEJ, M.
LIPIŃSKI, A.
LITYŃSKI, A.
MAŁAJNY, R.
MARSZAŁ, K.
NOWACKI, J.
PAZDAN, M.
SOBAŃSKI, R.
STRZĘPKA, J.
SZYMOSZEK, E.
ZWIERZCHOWSKI, E.

Faculty of Earth Sciences:
BUKOWY, S., Geology
DZIADEK, S., Geography
JACHOWICZ, S., Geology
JANIA, J., Geography
KLIMEK, K., Geology
KONSTANTYNOWICZ, E., Geology
KOZŁOWSKI, K., Geology
KRUSZEWSKA, K., Geology
NIEDŹWIEDŹ, J., Climatology, Meteorology
PULINA, M., Geography
RÓŻKOWSKI, A., Geology
TREMBACZOWSKI, J., Geography
ZUBEREK, W., Geophysics

Faculty of Education and Psychology:
HESZEN-NIEJODEK, I., Psychology
KOWALIK, J., Pedagogy
POPLUCZ, J., Education
RADZIEWICZ-WINNICKI, A., Education
RATAJCZAK, Z., Psychology
STRELAU, J., Psychology
ŻECHOWSKA, B., Education

Faculty of Social Sciences:
BAŃKA, J., Philosophy
CHOJECKA, E., History
DOBROWOLSKI, P., Political Science
FRĄCKIEWICZ, L., Political Science
GŁOMBIK, C., Philosophy
JACHER, W., Sociology
KANTYKA, J., History
KOCÓJ, H., History
KOMASZYŃSKI, M., History
KUNISZ, A., History
KWAK, J., History
MIKUŁOWSKI-POMORSKI, J., Political Science
PROMIEŃSKA, H., Philosophy
PRZEWŁOCKI, J., History
SERAFIN, F., History
SKAWIŃSKA, E., Economics
SZCZEPAŃSKI, M., Sociology
SZTUMSKI, J., Sociology
WANATOWICZ, M., History
WÓDZ, J., Sociology
WÓDZ, K., Sociology
ŻECHOWSKI, Z., Sociology

Centre of Democracy and European Studies:
KRAKOWSKI, J., Economics, Finance

Faculty of Philology:
ABŁAMOWICZ, A., French Philology
ARABSKI, J., English Philology
BASAJ, M., Slavonic Philology
CZAJKA, H., Slavonic Philology
CZAPIK-LITYŃSKA, B., Slavonic Philology
CZERWIŃSKI, P., Russian Philology
DZIĘGIEL, L., Ethnography
FAST, P., Russian Philology
GRZESZCZUK, S., History of Literature
HESKA-KWAŚNIEWICZ, K., Polish Philology
HUCZEK, M., Economics
JANASZEK-IVANIĆKOVA, H., Slavonic Philology
KŁAK, T., Polish Philology
KOWALSKA, A., Polish Philology
MALICKI, J., Polish Philology
MICZKA, T., Polish Philology
OCIECZEK, R., Polish Philology
OPACKI, I., Polish Philology
PASZEK, J., Polish Philology
POLAŃSKI, E., Polish Philology
POLAŃSKI, K., English Philology
PORĘBA, S., Russian Philology
RATAJEWSKI, J., Polish Philology
SŁAWEK, T., English Philology
STYKA, J., Classical Philology
TOKARZ, M., Logic
TURASIEWICZ, R., Classical Philology
UDALSKA, E., Philology
WILKOŃ, A., Philology
WÓJCIK, W., Polish Philology
ZABŁOCKI, S., Classical Philology
ZIENIUK, J., Polish Philology
ŻMIGRODZKI, Z., Polish Philology

Faculty of Technology:
BOJARSKI, Z., Chemistry
CZECH, Z., Computer Science
GĄSIOR, E., Chemistry
ŁĄGIEWKA, E., Physics
MORAWIEC, H., Materials Science
PIECHA, J., Computer Science
SUROWIAK, Z., Materials Science

Faculty of Radio and Television:
BIENIOK, H., Economics
DUDEK, W., Political Science
MORSKI, K., Musical Education
NOWICKI, M., Film Arts
SZCZECHURA, D., Film Arts
ZACHER, L., Sociology
ZAJICEK, E., Economics
ZANUSSI, K., Film Arts

Faculty of Pedagogic and Artistic Education:
DELEKTA, E., Graphics
GŁADYSZ, A., Sociology
KADŁUBIEC, D., Polish Philology
KANTOR, R., Ethnology
KOJS, W., Pedagogy
KOPOCZEK, A., Music
LEWOWICKI, T., Pedagogy
LIS, Z., Graphics
OBER, J., Information Engineering
STARCZEWSKI, A., Graphics
ŚWIDER, J., Music
WITEK, N., Graphics

UNIWERSYTET WARSZAWSKI (University of Warsaw)

00-927 Warsaw, Krakowskie Przedmieście 26-28
Telephone: (22) 620-03-81
Fax: (22) 826-32-62

Founded 1818
Academic year: October to June

Rector: Prof. Dr hab. WŁODZIMIERZ SIWIŃSKI
Vice-Rectors: Prof. Dr hab. MAREK WĄSOWICZ, Prof. Dr hab. JANUSZ GRZELAK, Prof. Dr hab. JAN MADEY, Prof. Dr hab. MICHAŁ NAWROCKI.
Administrative Director: JERZY PIESZCZIELRYKOW
Librarian: Dr HENRYK HOLLENDER

Library: see Libraries
Number of professors: 762
Number of students: 48,154
Publications: *Acta Philologica, American Studies, Biuletyn Geologiczny, Biuletyn Instytutu Języka i Kultury Polskiej dla Cudzoziemców, Ekonomia, Fasciculi Historici, Phytocoenosis, Prace Filologiczne, Quaestiones Medii Aevi, Roczniki Uniwersytetu Warszawskiego, Studia i Materiały Instytutu Archeologii, Studia Palmyreńskie, Światowit, Zeszyty Naukowe Instytutu Nauk Politycznych* (irregular), *Analiza i Synteza Informacji, Africana Bulletin, Przegląd Informacji o Afryce.*

DEANS

Faculty of Biology: Prof. Dr hab. EWA SYMONIDES
Faculty of Chemistry: Prof. Dr hab. STANISŁAW GŁĄB
Faculty of Journalism and Political Science: Prof. Dr hab. TADEUSZ MOŁDAWA
Faculty of Physics: Prof. Dr hab. KATARZYNA CHAŁASIŃSKA-MACUKOW
Faculty of Geography and Regional Studies: Prof. Dr hab. ANDRZEJ RICHLING
Faculty of Geology: Prof. Dr hab. MICHAŁ SZULCZEWSKI
Faculty of History: Prof. Dr hab. ANDRZEJ GARLICKI
Faculty of Mathematics, Informatics and Mechanics: Prof. Dr hab. WŁADYSŁAW MAREK TURSKI
Faculty of Economic Science: Prof. Dr hab. JERZY WILKIN
Faculty of Philosophy and Sociology: Prof. Dr hab. MICHAŁ POHOSKI
Faculty of Modern Languages and Oriental Studies: Prof. Dr hab. JACEK WIŚNIEWSKI
Faculty of Polish Philology: Prof. Dr hab. STANISŁAW DUBISZ
Faculty of Law and Administration: Prof. Dr hab. JÓZEF OKOLSKI
Faculty of Pedagogy: Prof. Dr hab. ALICJA SIEMAK-TYLIKOWSKA
Faculty of Applied Linguistics and East Slavonic Languages: Prof. Dr hab. ANNA DUSZAK
Faculty of Psychology: Prof. Dr hab. JAN MATYSIAK
Faculty of Management: Prof. Dr hab. KRYSTYNA BOLESTA-KUKUŁKA
Faculty of Applied Social Sciences and Resocialization: Prof. Dr hab. MARCIN KRÓL

PROFESSORS

Faculty of Biology:

BARTNIK, E., Botany
BRYŁA, J., Biochemistry—Metabolism
CHRÓST, R., Botany
CYMBOROWSKI, B., Physiology
DOBROWOLSKI, K., Zoology
DOBRZAŃSKA-KACZOROWSKA, J., Zoology
FALIŃSKI, J., Botany
GLIWICZ, M., Zoology
HREBENDA, J., Microbiology
IZDEBSKA-SZYMONA, K., Microbiology
JANISZOWSKA, W., Plant Biochemistry
JERZMANOWSKI, A., Biochemistry
KACPERSKA-LEWAK, A., Botany
KACZANOWSKA, J., Zoology
KACZANOWSKI, A., Zoology
LEWAK, S., Plant Physiology
MARKIEWICZ, Z., Microbiology
MATUSZEWSKI, B., Cytology
MORACZEWSKI, J., Zoology
MYCIELSKI, R., Microbiology
PIECZYŃSKA, E., Zoology
PIEKAROWICZ, A., Microbiology
POSKUTA, J., Plant Physiology
SIŃSKI, E., Zoology
SYMONIDES, E., Botany
TARKOWSKI, A., Embryology
TOMASZEWICZ, H., Botany
WĘGLEŃSKI, P., Botany
WOJCIECHOWSKI, Z., Biochemistry

Faculty of Chemistry:

BILEMICZ, R., Analytical Chemistry
BUKOWSKA, J., Physical Chemistry and Molecular Spectroscopy
FIGASZEWSKI, Z., Physical Chemistry
GALUS, Z., Mineral Chemistry
GŁĄB, B., Analytical Chemistry
GOLIMOWSKI, J., Analytical Chemistry
HULANICKI, A., Mineral Chemistry
IZDEBSKI, J., Organic Chemistry
JASTRZĘBSKA, J., Chemistry
JAWORSKI, J., Chemistry and Food Technology
JEZIORSKI, B., Analytical Chemistry
JURCZAK, J., Organic Chemistry
KALINOWSKI, M., Physical Chemistry
KASPRZYCKA-GUTTMAN, T., Chemical Technology
KOCZOROWSKI, Z., Electrochemistry
KOLIŃSKI, A., Theoretical and Physical Chemistry
KOŁOS, W., Theoretical Chemistry
KRYGOWSKI, T., Physical Chemistry
NIEDZIELSKI, J., Organic Chemistry
OSZCZAPOWICZ, J., Organic Chemistry
PIELA, L., Theoretical Chemistry
PYŻUK, W., Physio-chemistry
SADLEJ, J., Physical Chemistry
SAMOCHOCKA, K., Radiochemistry
SOBKOWSKI, J., Physical Chemistry
STOJEK, Z., Electrochemistry
SZCZEPEK, W., Organic Chemistry
SZYCHOWSKI, J., Organic Chemistry
SZYDŁOWSKI, J., Radiochemistry
TEMERIUSZ, A., Organic Chemistry
TROJANOWICZ, M., Analytical Chemistry
WERBLAN, L., Physical Chemistry

Faculty of Geography and Regional Studies:

BOGACKI, M., Geomorphology
BONASEWICZ, A., Regional Geography
BORYCZKA, J., Climatology
CIOŁKOSZ, A., Cartography
DEMBICZ, A., Economic Geography
DUMANOWSKI, B., Regional Geography
EBERHARDT, P., Regional Geography
GORZELAK, G., Economy
GRYGORENKO, W., Cartography
GUDOWSKI, J., Economic Geography
GUTRY-KORYCKA, M., Hydrogeology
JAŁOWIECKI, B., Sociology of Towns
KACPRZYŃSKI, B., Electronics
KANTOWICZ, E., Economic Geography
KENIG-WITKOWSKA, M., International Public Law
KOSTROWICKA, A., Economic Geography
KOSTROWICKI, A., Physical Geography
KUBIAK, W., Regional Geography
KUKLIŃSKI, A., Economic Geography
LUBBE, A., International Economic Relations
MAKOWSKI, J., Physical Geography
MIKULSKI, Z., Hydrogeography
MILEWSKI, J., History of Economics
MYCIELSKA-DOWGIAŁŁO, E., Geomorphology
OLĘDZKI, J., Geomorphology
OTOK, S., Economic Geography
PARZYMIES, A., Economic Geography
PASŁAWSKI, J., Regional Geography
PASZYNSKI, J., Physical Geography
PLIT, F., Regional Geography of Africa
RICHLING, A., Physical Geography
SKOCZEK, M., Regional Geography
SOCZYŃSKA, U., Hydrology
STOPA-BORYCZKA, M., Climatics
URBANIAK-BIERNACKA, U., Physical Geography
WIELOŃSKI, A., Economic Geography
WORONIECKI, J., Economy, International Economic Relations

Faculty of Philosophy and Sociology:

AUGUSTYNEK, Z., Philosophy
BEDNARCZYK, A., Philosophy
BOCZAR, M., Philosophy
CHAŁUBIŃSKI, M., Sociology
CIUPAK, E., Sociology
FRIESKE, K., Sociology
GADACZ, T., Philosophy
GÓRNICKA-KALINOWSKA, J., Philosophy
HOŁÓWKA, J., Philosophy
HOŁOWKA. T., Moral Philosophy
JADACKI, J., Philosophy
JANKOWSKI, H., Sociology
JASIŃSKA-KANIA, A., Sociology
KABIA, A., Philosophy
KAMIŃSKI, A., Sociology
KRZENIŃSKI, I., Sociology
KUCZYŃSKA, A., Philosophy
KUCZYŃSKI, J., Philosophy
LISSOWSKI, G., Sociology
MACKIEWICZ, W., Philosophy
MAJEWSKI, Z., Logic
MARODY, M., Sociology
MARKIEWICZ, B., Philosophy
MIŚ, A., Philosophy
MODZELEWSKI, W., Sociology
MORAWSKI, W., Sociology
MUSIAŁ, Z., Philosophy
NOWICKA-RUSEK, E., Sociology
OCHOCKI, A., Philosophy
OMYŁA, M., Logic Philosophy
PAZURA, ST., Aesthetics
PELC, J., Logic
PIERÓG, ST., Philosophy
PIETRUSKA-MADEJ, E., Philosophy
POHOSKI, M., Sociology
ROSIŃSKA, Z., Aesthetics
SIEMEK, M. J., Philosophy
SIEMIEŃSKA-ZOCHOWSKA, R., Sociology
SIKORA, A., Philosophy
SIURY, D., Ancient and Medieval Philosophy
SŁOMCZYŃSKI, K., Sociology
STANISZKIS, J., Sociology
STUCHLIŃSKI, J., Philosophy
SUŁEK, A., Sociology
SZACKA, B., Sociology
SZACKI, J., History of Social Thought
SZAWARSKI, Z., Moral Philosophy
TYSZKA, A., Sociology of Culture
WĘGLEŃSKI, J., Sociology of Towns
WIATR, J., Sociology
WOLNIEWICZ, B., Philosophy

Faculty of Journalism and Political Science:

ANIOŁ, W., Political Science
AULEYTNER, J., Economy
BASZKIEWICZ, J., Political Science
BODIO, T., Political Science
BRALCZYK, J., Specialization in Journalism
DANECKI, J., Political Economy
DOBRZYCKI, W., Law and International Relations
FILIPIAK, T., Political Science
FILIPOWICZ, S., History of Social-Political Thought
GEBETHNER, S., Political Science
GOLKA, B., Journalism
GOŁĘBIOWSKI, B., Political Science
GOŁEMBSKI, F., Political Science
GÓRALSKI, W., Political Science
HALIŻAK, M., Political Science, International Relations
KASPRZYK, L., International Relations
KIEŁMIŃSKI, Z., Modern Political Systems
KSIĘŻOPOLSKI, M., Political Science
KUKUŁKA, J., Political Science
KUŹNIAR, R., Political Science
LATO, S., Journalism
ŁUCZAK, A., Political Science
ŁUKASZUK, L., International Law
MAGIERSKA, A., Modern Polish History
MICHAŁOWSKA, G., International Relations
MICHALSKI, B., Journalism
MOŁDAWA, T., Political Science

MROZEK, A. B., Political Science
OLĘDZKI, J., Theory of Propaganda
OSUCHOWSKI, J., Law of Denomination
PARZYMIES, S., International Relations
PAWLAK, S., International Relations
PIEKARA, A., Social Politics
PRZYBYSZ, K., Political Science
SATKIEWICZ, A. H., Theory of Style, Polish Language
SUPIŃSKA-MODZELEWSKA, J., Political Science
SZULCZEWSKI, M., Journalism
SZYLKO-SKOCZNY, M., Political Science
ULICKA, G., Political Science
WŁADYKA, W., Political History
WOJTASZCZYK, K., Political Science
ZIELIŃSKI, E., Modern Political Systems

Faculty of Polish Philology:

AXER, J., Classical Philology
BARTNICKA, B., Polish Philology
BOROWSKA, M., Classical Philology
CICHOCKA, H., Classical Philology
CYTOWSKA, M., Classical Philology
CZAPLEJEWICZ, E., Polish Literature
DĄBEK-WIRGOWA, T., Bulgarian Philology
DĄBROWSKI, M., Polish Literature
DREWNOWSKI, T., History of Polish Literature
DUBISZ, S., Polish Philology
FELESZKO, K., Linguistics
FRYBES, S., Polish Literature
GRONCZEWSKI, A., Polish Literature
GRZEGORCZYKOWA, R., Polish Philology
HANDKE, R., Theory of Literature
JADACKA, H., Polish Philology
JANION, M., History of Literature
JUREWICZ, O., Classical Philology
KARWACKA, H., Polish Literature
KLEBANOWSKA, B., Linguistics
KUPISZEWSKI, W. M., Polish Philology
LAM, A., Polish Philology
ŁOSSOWSKA, I., History of Literature
MACIEJEWSKI, J., History of Polish Literature
MAKOWIECKI, A., History of Literature
MARKOWSKI, A., Polish Philology
MINDAK, J., Philology
MITOSEK, Z., Theory of Literature
MAKOWSKI, S., Polish Literature
NAGÓRKO, A., History of Literature
NOWICKA-JEŻOWA, A., Literature, History of Polish Literature
OSIŃSKI, Z., Polish Culture
OWCZAREK, B., Theory of Literature
PĄKCIŃSKA, M., Greek Literature
PELC, J., History of Literature
PODRACKI, J., Linguistics
PORAYSKI-POMSTA, J., Polish Philology
PUZYNINA, J., Polish Philology
RAPACKA, J., History of Slavonic Literature
ROHOZIŃSKI, J., Polish Literature
ROWIŃSKI, C., History of Literature
RYTEL, J., Polish Literature
RYTEL-KUC, D., Slavonic Philology
SAMBOR, J., Linguistics
SARNOWSKA-TEMERIUSZ, E., History and Theory of Literature
SAWICKA, J., History of Polish Literature
SĘKOWSKA, E., Polish Philology
SIATKOWSKA, E., Slavonic Philology
SIATKOWSKI, J., Linguistics
SIEKIERSKI, S., Polish Culture
SINIELNIKOFF-SKUP, R., Linguistics
SLASKI, J., History of Polish Literature
SMOCZYŃSKI, W., Indo-European Studies
SMUŁKOWA, E., Ukrainian Philology
STAROWIEYSKI, M., Classical Philology
SUDOLSKI, Z., Polish Philology
ŚULIMA, R., History of Literature
ŚWIDZIŃSKI, M., Polish Literature
TABORSKI, R., Polish Literature
WASZAKOWA, K., Polish Philology
WIERZBICKI, J., Slavonic Philology
WOJTCZAK, J., Classical Philology
WROCŁAWSKI, K., Slavonic Philology
ZIĘTARSKA, J., Polish Literature

Faculty of Applied Linguistics and East Slavonic Languages:

BARSZOZEWSKI, A., Belarus Philology
BARTOSZEWICZ, A., Russian Philology
CZYKWIN, J., Russian Literature
DUSZAK, A., Linguistics
FIGARSKI, W., Russian Philology
GRUCZA, F., Linguistics
JANCEWICZ, Z., Slavonic Linguistics
KIELAR, B., Linguistics
KOPCZYŃSKI, A., Linguistics
KOZAK, S., Ukrainian Philology
KRZESZOWSKI, T., Linguistics
LEWANDOWSKI, J., Slavonic Linguistics
LUKSZYN, J., Russian Philology
NAMOWICZ, T., German Philology
NIEUWAŻNY, F., Russian Philology
SEMCZUK, A., Russian Philology
SIATKOWSKI, S., Russian Linguistics
ŚKRUNDA, W., Russian Literature
ŚLIWOWSKI, R., Russian Philology
SZYSZKO, T., Russian Philology
ZMARZER, W., Linguistics
ŻMIJEWSKA, H., Romance Philology

Faculty of Modern Languages and Oriental Studies:

ASZYK, U., Spanish Studies
BOGACKI, B. K., Italian Philology
BOGUSŁAWSKI, A., Russian Philology
BOJAR, B., Formal Linguistics
BRAUN, J., Oriental Philology
BYRSKI, M. K., Oriental Philology
BYSTYDZIEŃSKA, G., English Studies
CHUDAK, H., Romance Philology
CZARNECKI, T., German Philology
DANECKI, J., Oriental Philology
FORYCKI, R., French Literature
GIERMAK-ZIELIŃSKA, T., French Philology
GODZIŃSKI, S., Oriental Philology
GOŁĘBIOWSKI, M., English Studies
GRUDZIŃSKA, G., Latin American Studies
HARRIS, E., English Studies
KAŁUŻYŃSKI, S., Oriental Philology
KLAWE, J., Portuguese Philology
KLIMASZEWSKA, Z., German Studies
KOLAGO, L., German Studies
KOMOROWSKA-JANOWSKA, H., Linguistics
KOTAŃSKI, W., Japanology
KÜNSTLER, M., Sinology
LEWICKI, A., English Philology
ŁYCZKOWSKA, K., Oriental Philology
MAJDA, T., Oriental Philology
MAŁCUŻYŃSKI, P., Spanish Literature
MANTEL-NIEĆKO, J., Ethiopian Philology
MELANOWICZ, M., Oriental Philology
MIODUSZEWSKA-CRAWFORD, E., English Studies
PIEŃKOS, J., Romance Philology
PIŁASZEWICZ, S., African Philology
POPKO, M., Oriental Philology
RUBACH, J., English Philology
SALWA, P., Italian Literature
SAUERLAND, K. K., German Philology
SEMENIUK-POLKOWSKA, M., Formal Linguistics
SIEROSZEWSKI, A., Hungarian Philology
SKŁADANEK, B., Iranian Philology
SKARŻYŃSKA-BOCHEŃSKA, K., Oriental Philology
SKŁADANEK-ŻOŁNA, M., Oriental Philology
SŁUPSKI, Z., Oriental Philology
SUROWSKA-SAUERLAND, B., German Studies
TUBIELEWICZ, J., Oriental Philology
UGNIEWSKA-DOBRZAŃSKA, J., Italian Philology
WEŁNA, J., English Linguistics
WESELIŃSKI, A., English Literature
WIKTOROWICZ, J., German Philology
WIŚNIEWSKI, J., English Literature
ŻABOKLICKI, K., French Philology
ZAWADZKA, E., German Philology

Faculty of Geology:

BAŁUK, A. W., Geology
BARCZYK, W., Geology
BIAŁOWOLSKA, A., Geochemistry
CHLEBOWSKI, R., Petrography
DRĄGOWSKI, A., Engineering Geology
GÓRKA, H., Geology
GRABOWSKA-OLSZEWSKA, B., Engineering Geology
JAROSZEWSKI, W., Geology
KACZYŃSKI, R., Engineering Geology
KOCISZEWSKA-MUSIAŁ, G., Geology
KRAJEWSKI, S., Hydrogeology
KRYNICKI, T., Hydrogeology
KUTEK, J., Geology
LINDNER, L., Geology
ŁYDKA, K., Petrography
MACIOSZCZYK, A., Hydrogeology
MACIOSZCZYK, T., Hydrogeology
MAŁECKA, D., Hydrogeology
MARCINOWSKI, R., Geology
MARKS, L., Geology
MASTELLA, L., Dynamic Geology
MATYJA, B., Geology
MATYSIAK, S., Geology
MYŚLIŃSKA, E., Engineering Geology
ORŁOWSKI, S., Geology
PININSKA, J., Hydrogeology
RADWAŃSKI, A., Geology
RONIEWICZ, P., Geology
SPECZIK, S., Geology
STUPNICKA, E., Geology
SZPILA, K., Mineralogy
SZULCZEWSKI, M., Geology
SZYMANKO, J., Hydrogeology
TRAMMER, J., Geology
WIERZBOWSKI, A., Geology
WIERZCHOŁOWSKI, B., Petrography
WYRWICKI, R., Geology
WYSOKIŃSKI, L., Engineering Geology

Faculty of History:

AUGUSTYNIAK, U., Modern History
BANASZKIEWICZ, J., Medieval History
BARTNICKI, A., Modern History
BIELIŃSKI, P., Archaeology
BORODZIEJ, W., Modern History
BRAVO, B., Ancient History
BUCHWALD-PELCOWA, P., Library Science
BUKO, A., Archaeology
BUKOWSKI, Z., Archaeology
CHMIELEWSKI, W., Archaeology
CHODKOWSKI, A., Musicology
CHOJNOWSKI, A., History
CHROŚCICKI, J., History of Art
CYBULSKI, R., Library Science
CZEKANOWSKA-KUKLIŃSKA, A., Musicology
DASZEWSKI, W., Archaeology
DOBROWOLSKI, W., Archaeology
DRZEWIECKI, N., Library Science
FIAŁKOWSKI, K., Library Science
GARLICKI, A., History
GĄSSOWSKI, J., Archaeology
GAWLIKOWSKI, M., Archaeology
GIEYSZTOR, A., Medieval History
GODLEWSKI, W., Archaeology
GOŁĄB, M., Musicology
GROCHULSKA, B., History
GRZYBKOWSKI, A., History of Art, Geography
HELMAN-BEDNARCZYK, Z., Musicology
HOLZER, J., History
IHNATOWICZ, I., History
JAROSZEWSKI, T. S., History of Art
JAŚKIEWICZ, D., History of the USSR
JASTRZĘBOWSKA, E., Archaeology
JUSZCZAK, W., History of Art
KARPOWICZ, M., History of Art
KEMPISTY, A., Archaeology
KIENIEWICZ, J., History
KIZWALTER, T., 19th-century History
KOCZERSKA, J., Medieval History
KOLENDO, J., Archaeology
KOWALCZYK, E., Archaeology
KOZŁOWSKI, S., Archaeology
KRUPPE, J., Medieval History of Poland
KUBIŃSKA, J., Archaeology
KUCZYŃSKA-IRACKA, A., History of Art
KULA, M., General History
LANGAUER, W., History
ŁUKASIEWICZ, J., History

Maciszewski, J., History
Mączak, A., Modern History
Maternicki, J., History
Mazurowski, R., Archaeology
Michałek, K., History
Michałowski, R., Medieval History
Mikocki, T., History of Art
Miłobędski, J. A., History of Art
Miśkiewicz, M., Archaeology
Modrzewska-Pianetti, I., Archaeology
Modzelewski, K., Medieval History
Mróz, L., Ethnology
Muraszkiewicz, M., Library Science
Nałęcz, T., Polish History
Nietyksza, M., 19th- and 20th-century Polish History
Niwiński, M., Archaeology
Nowak, B., History
Nyśliwiec, K., Archaeology
Okulicz, Ł., Archaeology
Okulicz-Kozaryn, J., Archaeology
Perz, M., Musicology
Piekarczyk, S., Pre-18th Century Polish History
Podgórski, W., Library Science
Pokropek, M., Ethnography
Pomorski, J., Teaching of History
Poniatowska, I., History of Music
Poppe, A., Medieval History
Poprzęcka, M., History of Art
Potkowski, E., History
Press, L., Archaeology
Rakowski, A., Musical Acoustics
Rudnicki, S., 19th- and 20th-century Polish History
Rusin, I., History
Sadurska, A., Archaeology
Samsonowicz, H., Medieval History
Sarnowski, T., Archaeology
Skowronek, J., 19th-Century History
Skubiszewski, P., Medieval History of Art
Sochacki, Z., Archaeology
Sokolewicz, Z., Ethnography
Şuchodolski, S. J., Archaeology
Świderek, A., Papyrology
Szaflik, J., History
Sztetyłło, Z., Mediterranean Archaeology
Szwarc, A., 19th-century History
Tanty, M., History of Slavonic Countries
Tomaszewski, J., Political Science
Tymowski, M., Modern History
Tyszkiewicz, J., Medieval History
Wasilewski, T., Medieval History
Wawrykowa, M., Modern History
Wawrzynczak, J., Library Science
Wierciński, A., Archaeology
Winnicki, J., Ancient History
Wipszycka-Bravo, E., Ancient History
Witych, T., Modern History
Wojakowski, J., Library Management
Wojciechowski, M., Modern History
Wyrobisz, A., Medieval History
Zadrożyńska-Barącz, A., Ethnography
Zahorski, A., Modern History
Żarnowska, A., Modern Polish History
Żerańska-Kominek, S., Musicology
Zielińska, Z., Modern History
Ziołkowski, A., Ancient History
Zybert, E., Library Science

Faculty of Mathematics, Informatics and Mechanics:

Adamowicz, Z., Mathematics
Bessaga, C., Mathematical Analysis
Betley, S., Mathematics
Białynicki-Birula, A., Mathematics
Bojarski, B., Mathematical Analysis
Bojdecki, T., Theory of Elasticity
Browkin, J., Mathematics
Burnat, M., Mathematics
Chaber, J., Mathematics, Topology
Chlebus, B., Informatics
Czaja, L., Mathematics
Dryja, M., Informatics
Engelking, R., Mathematics
Grabowski, J., Mathematics
Guzicki, W., Mathematics
Jackowski, S., Mechanics
Jaworski, P., Mathematics
Jurkiewicz, J., Algebraic Geometry
Kacewicz, B., Mathematics
Kiełbasiński, A., Mathematics
Kołakowski, J. H., Mathematics
Kordos, M., Geometry
Kowalski, M., Mechanics
Krempa, J., Mathematics
Krzyżewski, K., Mathematics
Kubik, L., Mathematics
Kwapień, S., Mathematics
Lachowicz, M., Mechanics
Ligocka, E., Mathematics
Łukaszewicz, W., Mechanics
Madey, J., Informatics
Mirkowska, M., Mathematical Logic
Mostowski, T., Mathematics
Moszyńska, M., Mathematics
Moszyński, K., Mathematical Analysis
Niezgódka, M., Applied Mathematics
Nowak, S., Mathematics
Nowicki, T., Mathematics
Okniński, J., Mathematics
Olesiak, Z., Mechanics
Palczewski, A., Mathematics
Patkowska, H., Mathematics
Piskorek, A., Mathematics
Pol, R., Mathematics
Puczyłowski, E., Mathematics
Rytter, W., Informatics
Semadeni, Z., Mathematics
Sieklucki, K., Mathematics
Skowron, A., Mathematics
Szakas, A., Informatics
Tarlecki, A., Informatics
Tiuryn, J., Mathematics
Turski, W., Informatics
Urzyczyn, P., Informatics
Waligórski, S., Informatics
Wiśniewski, J., Mathematics
Wojtaszczyk, P., Mathematics and Functional Analysis
Wojtyński, W., Mathematics
Woźniakowski, H., Informatics
Zakrzewski, P., Mechanics
Zawadowski, W., Mathematics
Zbierski, P., Mathematics
Żołądek, H., Mathematics

Faculty of Physics:

Badełek, B., Experimental Physics
Baj, M., Solid Body Physics
Baranowski,J., Experimental Physics
Bardyszewski, W., Theoretical Physics
Bartelski, J., Theoretical Physics
Bartnik, E., Theoretical Physics
Bażański, S., Theoretical Physics
Białynicki-Birula, I., Optics and Mechanics
Blinowski, J., Solid Body Physics
Chałasińska-Macukow, K., Optics
Cichocki, B., Theoretical Physics
Cieślak-Blinowska, K., Medical Physics
Czochralska, B., Biophysics
Demiański, M., Theoretical Physics
Droste, C., Nuclear Theory
Ernst, K., Atomic Physics
Gaj, J., Solid Body Physics
Ginter, J., Experimental Physics
Grad, M., Geophysics
Grynberg, M., Solid Body Physics
Haman, K., Geophysics
Hennel, A., Solid Body Physics
Hofmokl, T., Experimental Physics
Kalinowski, J., Molecule Elementary Physics
Kamińska, M., Solid Body Physics
Kijowski, J., Theoretical Physics
Kopczynski, W., High Energy Physics
Kownacki, J., Atomic Physics
Kozłowski, M., Atomic Physics
Krolikowski, J., High Energy Physics
Królikowski, W., Atomic Physics
Kruszewski, A., Astronomy
Kubiak, M., Astrophysics
Lefeld-Sosnowska, M., Experimental Physics
Leliwa-Kopystyńska, A., Atomic Physics
Leliwa-Kopystyński, J., Geophysics
Lesyng, B., Biophysics
Maurin, K., Mathematical Analysis
Mielnik, B., Theoretical Physics
Namysłowski, J., Theoretical Physics
Napiórkowski, K., Mathematical Methods in Physics
Napiórkowski, M., Statistics Physics
Nazarewicz, W., Experimental Physics
Nazarewicz, W., Solid Body Physics
Piasecki, J., Theoretical Physics
Plebański, J., Mathematical Methods in Physics
Pniewski, T., Particle Elementary Physics
Pokorski, S., Theoretical Physics
Rohoziński, St., Atomic Physics
Różyczka, M., Physics
Skrzypczak, E., High Energy Physics
Sosnowska, I., Experimental Physics
Spałek, J., Solid Body Physics
Stępień, K., Astronomy
Sym, A., Physics
Szoplik, T., Optics
Szymacha, A., Atomic Physics
Szymański, Z., Nuclear Theory
Trautman, A., Electrodynamics and Theory of Relativity
Urbański, P., Mathematical Analysis
Werle, J., Thermodynamics
Wilhelmi, Z., Atomic Physics
Woronowicz, S., Mathematical Methods in Physics
Wódkiewicz, K., Optics
Wróblewski, A., Experimental Physics
Zakrzewski, J., High Energy Physics
Żylicz, J., Experimental Physics

Faculty of Pedagogy:

Bartnicka, K., Education History
Depta, H., Aesthetics Education
Hulek, A., Pedagogy
Izdebska, H., Pedagogy
Jaczewski, A., Pedagogy
Konarzewski, K., Theory of Education
Kruszewski, K., Pedagogy
Kupisiewicz, C., Didactics
Kwiatkowska, H., Pedagogy
Lewowicki, T., Adult Pedagogy
Mazur, B., Pedagogy
Mońka-Stanikova, A., Comparative Pedagogy
Połturzycki, J., Pedagogics
Przecławska, A., Pedagogy
Siemak-Tylkowska, A., Pedagogy
Szybiak, I., Pedagogy
Turos, L., Adult Pedagogy
Wilgocka-Okoń, B., Pedagogy
Wojnar, I., Pedagogy
Zaczyński, W., Didactics

Faculty of Psychology:

Bokus-Rauch, B.
Ciarkowska, W.
Czapiński, J.
Gałkowski, T.
Grzelak, J.
Grzesiuk, L.
Jagodzinska, M.
Jarymowicz, M.
Jurkowski, A.
Kądzielawa, D.
Kofta, M.
Kościelska, M.
Kozielecki, J.
Kurcz-Piesowicz, I.
Lis, S.
Matczak, A.
Materska, M.
Matysiak, J.
Mika, S.
Sędek, G.
Shugar, G. E.
Sosnowski, T.
Strelau, J.

TRZEBIŃSKI, J.
WRZEŚNIEWSKI, K.
ZALEWSKA, M.

Faculty of Law and Administration:
BAŁTRUSZAJTYS-PIOTROWSKA, G., History of Law
BŁESZYŃSKI, J., Civil Law
BRZOZOWSKI, A., Civil Law
CHOJNA-DUCH, E., Administrative Law
CIEŚLAK, Z., Administrative Law
CZACHÓRSKI, W., Civil Law
CZECHOWSKI, P., Administrative Law
DĄBROWSKA, M., Civil Law
DOMAŃSKI, G., Civil Law
DYBOWSKI, T., Civil Law
ERECIŃSKI, T., Civil Law
FALANDYSZ, L., Penal Law
FLOREK, L., Labour Law
GALICKI, Z., International Law
GARDOCKI, L., Penal Law
GARLICKI, L., History of Law
GIARO, T., Roman Law
GINTOWT-JANKOWICZ, M., Administrative Law
GÓRALCZYK, W., Administrative Law
GRONKIEWICZ-WALTZ, H., Administrative Law
IZDEBSKI, H., History of Law
JAGIELSKI, J., Administrative Law
JAROSZ, Z., Civil Law
JĘDRASIK-JANKOWSKA, I., Administrative Law
JĘDRZEJEWSKA, M., Civil Law
KORZYCKA-IWANOW, M., Agricultural Law
KRÓL-BOGONILSKA, M., Penal Law
KRUSZYŃSKI, P., Penal Law
KULESZA, M., Administrative Law
KUPISZEWSKI, H., Roman Law
LAMENTOWICZ, W., Theory State and Law
LANG, J., Administrative Law
LITWIŃCZUK, H., Administrative Law
MALINOWSKI, A., State Law
MISIUK, T., Civil Law
MODZELEWSKI, W., Administrative Law
OKOLSKI, J., Civil Law
PIEŃKOS, J., International Law
PIETRZAK, M., History of Law
PIETRZYKOWSKI, K., Civil Law
PIONTEK, E., International Law
RAJSKI, J., Civil Law
RUSSOCKI, S., History of Law
SAFJAN, N., Civil Law
SAWICKI, S., International Law
SENKOWSKI, J., History of Law
SKOWROŃSKA-BOCIAN, E., History of Law
SŁUŻEWSKI, J., Administrative Law
SÓJKA-ZIELIŃSKA, K., History of Law
SZACHUKOWICZ, J., Agricultural Law
SZYSZKOWSKA, N., Administrative Law
TOMASZEWSKI, T., Penal Law
TURSKA, A., State Law
WĄSOWICZ, M., History of Law
WIERZBOWSKI, M., Administrative Law
WINCZOREK, P., Theory State and Law
WOŁODKIEWICZ, W., Roman Law
WYRZYKOWSKI, M., Administrative Law
ZABŁOCKA, M., History of Law
ZIELIŃSKA, E., Penal Law
ZIELIŃSKI, A., Civil Law

Faculty of Economic Sciences:
BAKA, W., Political Economy
BEDNARSKI, M., Political Economy
CHRUPEK, Z., Political Economy
DANILUK, M., Industry and Defence Economy
DOBROCZYŃSKI, M., Political Economy
DZIEWULSKI, J., Political Economy
GMYTRASIEWICZ, M., Economics of Teaching
GÓRECKI, B., Economics
JEZIERSKI, A., Economic History
KASPRZAK, T., Political Economy
KLEER, J., Theory of Economics
KLUCZYŃSKI, J., Political Economy
KOCHANOWICZ, J., Economic History
KOZIŃSKI, W., International Economic Relations
KRENCIK, W., Political Economy
KUDŁA, W., Political Economy
KUDLIŃSKI, R., Political Economy
LUBBE, A., International Economic Relations
ŁUKASZEWICZ, A., Political Economy
MACIEJEWSKI, W., Economic Cybernetics
MICHAŁEK, J., International Economic Relations
MORECKA, Z., Political Economy
OKÓLSKI, M., Statistics
OPOLSKI, K., Banking and Finance
RUTKOWSKI, J., Political Economy
SADOWSKI, Z., Political Economy
SIWIŃSKI, W., Political Economy
SZEWORSKI, A., Political Economy
SZTYBER, W., Political Economy
TIMOFIEJUK, I., Statistics
WELLISE, S., Microeconomics
WIECZORKIEWICZ, A., Political Economy
WILKIN, J., Political Economy
WIŚNIEWSKI, M., Statistics
WISZNIEWSKI, Z., Economics
WŁODARSKI, W., Political Economy

Faculty of Management:
BUCZOWSKI, L., Techniques of Management
DOBRZYŃSKI, M., Sociology and Psychology of Organization
DOMAŃSKI, G., Management
GŁOWACKI, R., Marketing
GÓRSKI, M., Organisation and Management
GOŚCIŃSKI, J., Management and Informatics
JAROSZYŃSKI, A., Administrative Law
JĘDRZEJCZAK, G., Organization and Management
JEŁOWICKI, M., Organization and Management
KISIELNICKI, J., Industrial Economy and Informatics
KOS, C., Economics
KOŹMIŃSKI, A., Systems Analysis
KRZYŻEWSKI, R., Social Economics
KWIATKOWSKI, S., Economic Trade
LIPIEC-ZAJCHOWSKA, M., Economics
MAJCHRZYCKA-GUZOWSKA, A., Finance
MATUSZEWICZ, J., Management
MUSZALSKI, L., Employment
NOWAK, A., Organization and Management
OBŁÓJ, K., Organization and Management
PATULSKI, A., Employment
PIĄTEK, S., Science Administration
RADZIKOWSKI, W., Techniques of Management
RYĆ, K., Economic Theory
SKOCZNY, T., Organization and Management
ŚLIWA, J., Planning
SLIWIŃSKI, A., Economic Cybernetics
SOBCZAK, K., Administrative Law
SOPOĆKO, A., Theory of Organization
SZPRINGER, W., Administrative Law
ZAWIŚLAK, A., Theory of Management

Institute of Social Prevention and Resocialization:
BAŁANDYNOWICZ, A., Resocialization
JAWŁOWSKA, A., Sociology
KACZYNSKA, E., History of Social Economics
KICIŃSKI, KRZ., Sociology
KOSEWSKI, M., Psychology
KURCZEWSKI, J., Sociology
KWAŚNIEWSKI, J., Labour Law, Deviation Sociology
OSTROWSKA, K., Social Psychology
PILCH, T., Social Pedagogy
PODGÓRECKI, A., Ethics
PRZECŁAWSKI, K., Sociology
PYTKA, L., Resocialization Pedagogy
RZEPLIŃSKI, A., Criminology
SIEMASZKO, A., Law
ŚWIDA-ZIEMBA, H., Sociology
SZYMANOWSKI, T., Penal Law
TYMOWSKI, A., Social Politics
WOJCIK, P., Political Science, Social Politics
ZABOROWSKI, Z., Psychology
ZIEMBA, Z., Philosophy
ZIEMSKA, M., Social Psychology

UNIWERSYTET WROCŁAWSKI
(University of Wrocław)

50-137 Wrocław, Plac Uniwersytecki 1
Telephone: (71) 402-212
Telex: 0712791
Fax: (71) 402-232

Founded 1702, rebuilt 1945
State control
Language of instruction: Polish
Academic year: October to June (two terms)

Rector: Prof. Dr hab. ROMAN DUDA
Vice-Rectors: Dr hab. ZDZISŁAW LATAJKA (Academic Affairs and Foreign Relations), Dr hab. WŁADYSŁAW DYNAK (General Affairs), Prof. Dr hab. ANDRZEJ WITKOWSKI (Education), Dr hab. JERZY KRAKOWSKI (Student Affairs)
Administrative Officer: Mgr MAREK KORNATOWSKI
Librarian: Dr ANDRZEJ ŁADOMIRSKI

Library: see Libraries
Number of teachers: 1,758
Number of students: 20,101

Publications: *Acta Universitatis Wratislaviensis,* and departmental publications.

DEANS

Faculty of Philology: Dr hab. KRYSTYNA GABRYJELSKA
Faculty of Social Sciences: Prof. Dr hab. ROMUALD GELLES
Faculty of Historical and Pedagogical Sciences: Prof. Dr hab. KRZYSZTOF WACHOWSKI
Faculty of Law and Administration: Prof. Dr hab. ZDZISŁAW KEGEL
Faculty of Natural Sciences: Dr hab. TERESA OBERC-DZIEDZIC
Faculty of Chemistry: Prof. Dr hab. JÓZEF ZIÓŁKOWSKI
Faculty of Physics and Astronomy: Prof. Dr hab. STEFAN MRÓZ
Faculty of Mathematics and Computer Science: Prof. Dr hab. WŁADYSŁAW NARKIEWICZ

PROFESSORS

Faculty of Philology:
CIEŃSKI, A., Library Science
CYGAN, J., English Language
DEGLER, J., Theory of Culture
FURDAL, A., Linguistics
GAJEK, K., German Literature
HERNAS, C., Polish Literature
HONSZA, N., German Literature
INGLOT, M., Methodology of Language Teaching
JANIKOWSKI, K., Germanic Languages
JASTRZĘBSKI, J., Theory of Culture
KLIMOWICZ, T., Slavonic Literatures
KOLBUSZEWSKI, J., Polish Literature
KOSIŃSKI, J., Library Science
ŁAWIŃSKA-TYSZKOWSKA, J., Classical Languages and Literature
MALECZYŃSKA, K., Library Science
MIGOŃ, K., Library Science
MIODEK, J., Polish Language
MORCINIEC, N., Germanic Languages
PETELENZ-ŁUKASIEWICZ, J., Polish Literature
POŹNIAK, T., Slavonic Literatures
PRĘDOTA, S., Netherlands Philology
SAWICKI, P., Spanish Philology
SZASTYŃSKA-SIEMION, A., Classical Languages and Literature
SZCZEPANIEC, J., Library Science
SLĘK, L., Polish Literature
WIECZOREK, D., Slavonic Languages
ŻABSKI, T., Polish Literature

Faculty of Social Sciences:
ALBIN, J., Political Sciences
ANTOSZEWSKI, A., Political Sciences
BAL, K., Philosophy
BŁACHUT, K., Contemporary History
DABROWSKI, S., Political Sciences
FIEDOR, K., Contemporary History

Gajda-Krynicka, J., Philosophy
Gelles, R., Contemporary History
Jabłoński, A., Political Sciences
Kowalski, T., Sociology
Łoziński, R., Philosophy
Łukaszewicz, R., Special Education
Pisarek, H., Philosophy
Siemianowski, A., Sociology
Surmaczyński, M., Sociology
Wolański, M., Contemporary History

Faculty of Historical and Pedagogical Sciences:

Bagniewski, Z., Archaeology
Banaś, P., History of Art
Bazielich, B., Ethnology
Bobowski, K., Medieval History
Czapliński, M., Modern History
Gediga, B., History of Art
Kargul, J., Pedagogy
Kwaśny, Z., History
Łukaszewski, W., Psychology of Personality
Matwijowski, K., Modern History
Nosal, C., Psychology
Ochmann-Staniszewska, S., Modern History
Ostrowska-Kębłowska, Z., History of Art
Pater, M., Modern History
Pazda, S., Archaeology
Pietraszek, E., Ethnology
Pietraszko, S., Theory of Culture
Skorny, Z., Psychology
Tyszkiewicz, L., Medieval History
Wachowski, K., Archaeology
Wiatrowski, L., History
Wojciechowski, W., Archaeology
Wrzesiński, W., Contemporary History
Zawadzka, A., Leisure Studies
Zlat, M., History of Art

Faculty of Law and Administration:

Boć, J., Administrative Law
Bojarski, M., Criminal Law
Chełmoński, A., Administrative Law
Działocha, K., Constitutional Law
Jonca, K., Political and Legal Doctrines
Jończyk, J., Labour Law
Kaozmarek, T., Criminal Law
Kaźmierczyk, S., Theory of State and Law
Kegel, Z., Criminal Law
Kolasa, J., International Law
Konieczny, A., History of Law
Mastalski, R., Fiscal Law
Połomski, F., History of Law
Szurgacz, H., Labour Law
Swida, Z., Criminal Law
Trzciński, J., Constitutional Law

Faculty of Natural Sciences:

Baraniecki, L., Regional Geography
Bocheńska, T., Hydrogeology
Borowiec, L., Animal Systematics and Zoogeography
Buczek, J., Plant Physiology
Don, J., Geological Cartography
Dumicz, M., Structural Geology
Dyrcz, A., Avian Ecology
Dziedzic, K., Structural Geology
Gunia, T., Stratigraphic Geology
Jerzmańska, A., Comparative Anatomy
Krupiński, T., Anthropology
Kubicz, A., Molecular Biology
Łoboda, J., Social and Economic Geography
Morawiecka, B., Molecular Biochemistry
Morawiecki, A., Microbiology
Niśkiewicz, J., Geology
Ogorzałek, A., Zoology
Otlewski, J., Biotechnology
Pawlak, W., Cartography
Polanowski, A., Biotechnology
Sachanbiński, M., Mineralogy
Sadowska, A., Palaeobotany
Sarosiek, J., Ecology and Environmental Protection
Sikorski, A., Genetic Biochemistry
Szopa-Skórkowski, J., Genetic Biochemistry
Tomiałojć, L., Avian Ecology
Warchałowski, A., Animal Systematics and Zoogeography
Wiktor, A., Zoology
Wilusz, T., Biotechnology
Witkowski, A., Ecology of Fishes
Wojciechowska, I., Geology
Wyrzykowski, J., Geography of Tourism
Złotorzycka-Kalisz, J., Parasitology

Faculty of Chemistry:

Głowiak, T., Crystallography
Hawranek, J., Physical Chemistry
Jezierski, A., Inorganic Chemistry
Kisza, A., Physical Chemistry
Koll, A., Physical Chemistry
Konopińska, D., Organic Chemistry
Kozłowski, H., Bioinorganic Chemistry
Latos-Grażyński, L., Co-ordination Chemistry
Legendziewicz, J., Analytical Chemistry
Lis, T., Crystallography
Malarski, Z., Physical Chemistry
Mroziński,. J., Inorganic Chemistry
Pruchnik, F., Inorganic Chemistry
Ratajczak, H., Physical Chemistry
Siemion, I., Organic Chemistry
Sobczyk, L., Physical Chemistry
Sobota, P., Inorganic Chemistry and Catalysis
Ziółkowski, J., Inorganic Chemistry and Catalysis

Faculty of Physics and Astronomy:

Galasiewicz, Z., Theoretical Physics
Haba, Z., Theoretical Physics
Jadczyk, A., Theoretical Physics
Jakimiec, J., Astronomy
Jerzykiewicz, M., Astronomy
Karwowski, W., Theoretical Physics
Lukierski, J., Theoretical Physics
Męclewski, R., Solid State Physics
Mozrzymas, J., Theoretical Physics
Mróz, S., Solid State Physics
Paszkiewicz, T., Theoretical Physics
Pękalski, A., Theoretical Physics
Rompolt, B., Astronomy
Stęślicka, M., Solid State Physics
Szuszkiewicz, M., Solid State Physics
Świątkowski, W., Solid State Physics
Wojciechowski, K., Solid State Physics

Faculty of Mathematics and Computer Science:

Biler, P., Mathematics, Differential Equations
Bożejko, M., Mathematics, Functional Analysis
Charatonik, J., Mathematics, Topology
Duda, R., History and Methodolgy of Mathematics
Głowacki, P., Mathematics, Functional Analysis
Hulanicki, A., Mathematics, Functional Analysis
Kopocińska, I., Applied Mathematics
Kopociński, B., Applied Mathematics
Łukaszewicz, J., Applied Mathematics
Marcinkowska, H., Mathematics, Differential Equations
Narkiewicz, W., Mathematics, Algebra and Theory of Numbers
Pacholski, L., Computer Science
Pytlik, T., Mathematics, Functional Analysis
Rolski, T., Applied Mathematics
Roter, W., Mathematics, Geometry
Rybarski, A., Mathematical Analysis
Sysło, M., Computer Science
Urbanik, K., Mathematics, Theory of Probability
Węglorz, B., Logic and Fundamentals of Mathematics

Technical Universities

AKADEMIA GÓRNICZO-HUTNICZA IM. STANISŁAWA STASZICA W KRAKOWIE
(Stanisław Staszic University of Mining and Metallurgy)

30-059 Cracow, al. Mickiewicza 30
Telephone: (12) 633-49-98
Fax: (12) 633-10-14

Founded 1919
State control
Languages of instruction: Polish and English
Academic year: October to September

Rector: Prof. Dr hab. Inż. Ryszard Tadeusiewicz
Vice-Rectors: Prof. Dr hab. Inż. Andrzej Gołaś (General Affairs), Prof. Dr hab. Inż. Bronisław Barchański (Student Affairs), Prof. Dr hab. Inż. Andrzej Korbel (Science)
Chief Administrative Officer: Mgr Inż. Henryk Zioło
Librarian: Mgr Anna Kegel

Library: see Libraries
Number of teachers: 1,808
Number of students: 20,118

Publications: *Elektrotechnika* (Electrical Engineering), *Geologia* (Geology), *Górnictwo* (Mining), *Mechanika* (Mechanics), *Folia Malacologia*, *Opuscula Mathematica* (all irregular).

DEANS

Faculty of Mining: Prof. Dr hab. Inż. Antoni Tajduś
Faculty of Drilling, Oil and Gas: Prof. Dr hab. Inż. Andrzej Gonet
Faculty of Mining Surveying and Environmental Engineering: Prof. Dr hab. Inż. Józef Beluch
Faculty of Geology, Geophysics and Environmental Protection: Doc. Dr hab. Inż. Marek Lemberger
Faculty of Materials Science and Ceramics: Prof. Dr hab. Stanisław Komornicki
Faculty of Metallurgy and Materials Science: Prof. Dr hab. Inż. Janusz Łuksza
Faculty of Non-Ferrous Metals: Prof. Dr hab. Inż. Józef Zasadziński
Faculty of Foundry Engineering: Prof. Dr hab. Inż. Wojciech Kapturkiewicz
Faculty of Electrical Engineering, Automatics, Informatics and Electronics: Prof. Dr hab. Lidia Maksymowicz
Faculty of Mechanical Engineering and Robotics: Prof. Dr hab. Inż. Janusz Kowal
Faculty of Fuels and Energy: Prof. Dr hab. Inż. Aleksander Długosz
Faculty of Management: Prof. Dr hab. Zdzisław Cięciwa
Faculty of Physics and Nuclear Engineering: Prof. Dr hab. Danuta Kisielewska
Faculty of Applied Mathematics: Prof. Dr hab. Stanisław Białas

POLITECHNIKA BIAŁOSTOCKA
(Białystok Technical University)

15-351 Białystok, ul. Wiejska 45A
Telephone: 223-93
Telex: 852424

Founded 1949
State control
Language of instruction: Polish
Academic year: October to June

Rector: Prof. Dr hab. Inż. Tadeusz Citko
Vice-Rectors: Prof. Dr hab. Inż. Michał Bołtryk, Dr Inż. Franciszek Siemieniako
Registrar: Eng. Mirosław Milewski
Librarian: Mgr Barbara Kubiak

Library: see Libraries
Number of teachers: 440
Number of students: 2,600

Publications: *Zeszyty Naukowe,* series: *Nauki Techniczne, Matematyka, Fizyka i Chemia, Nauki Społeczno-Polityczne* (irregular).

DEANS

Faculty of Architecture: Dr Inż. arch. JERZY M. ULLMAN

Faculty of Civil Engineering and Environmental Engineering: Prof. ANDRZEJ KRÓLIKOWSKI

Faculty of Electrical Engineering: Prof. Dr hab. Inż. MIKOŁAJ BUSŁOWICZ

Faculty of Mechanical Engineering: Prof. Dr hab. Inż. JAN ŁACH

Institute of Computer Science: Prof. Dr hab. WIKTOR DAŃKO

Institute of Mathematics and Physics: Doc. JAN AMBROSIEWICZ

Department of Social Science: Prof. Dr hab. KAZIMIERZ TRZĘSICKI

PROFESSORS

Faculty of Architecture:

CHMIELEWSKI, J. B., Sculpture
CZARNECKI, W., Town Planning, Industrial Architecture
DEBIS, J., Painting
GUTOWSKI, M., History of Art and Architecture
RYCHTER, Z., Theory of Building
RYMASZEWSKI, B., Preservation of Monuments
SAWCZUK, H., Town Planning and Environmental Engineering
WŁODARCZYK, J., Architecture
ZANIEWSKA, H., Spatial Planning of Agricultural Areas

Faculty of Civil Engineering and Environmental Engineering:

BANASZUK, H., Environmental Protection
BARSZCZAK, T., Agricultural Engineering, Agricultural Chemistry
BOŁTRYK, M., Civil Engineering
BRAMSKI, Cz., Building and Metal Constructions
BRONAKOWSKI, H., Economics
CZERWIŃSKI, A., Forest Botany, Phytosociology
GRABOWSKI, R., Engineering and Industrial Geodesy
HOLNICKI-SZULC, J., Technical Mechanics
KAMIŃSKI, S., Technology, Mechanization and Organization of Building
KOWALCZYK, R., Building Constructions
ŁAPKO, A., Civil Engineering
PIEŃKOWSKI, K., Fluid Mechanics, Thermal Mechanics
RÓG, Z., Environmental Protection
SASINOWSKI, H., Economics
SERWIN, M., Environmental Protection
SIKORSKA-TOMICKA, H., Inorganic Chemistry, Analytical Chemistry
SIKORSKI, J., Economics
STACHURSKI, W., Civil Engineering
SYCZEWSKI, M., Civil Engineering
SZYMAŃSKI, E., Civil Engineering
TRIBIŁŁO, R., Theory of Building Structures
WIERZBICKI, T., Environmental Engineering, Water and Waste Technology

Faculty of Electrical Engineering

BADURSKI, J. , Medicine
BORKOWSKI, A., Automatic Control and Robotics
BUSŁOWICZ, M., Control Theory, Automatics
CITKO, T., Electrical Engineering, Automatics
CYWIŃSKI, K., Electrotechnology
DMOCHOWSKI, Z., Electrical Engineering, Machines and Electrical Metrology
DYBCZYŃSKI, W., Lighting
GOŁĘBIOWSKI, J., Electrotechnology
JORDAN, A., Electrical Engineering, Electrical Metrology
ŁUKASZEWICZ, T., Physics
MASŁOWSKI, A., Dynamics of Physical Systems
NAZARKO, J., Electrical Power Engineering
NIEBRZYDOWSKI, J., Electrical Engineering
RAFAŁOWSKI, M., Mechanics
ROSŁONIEC, S., Electronics
SOWA, A., Electrotechnology
TWARDY, L., Electro-energetics
VOGT, R., Automatic Control and Robotics

Faculty of Mechanics:

CELMEROWSKI, Cz., Agricultural Machines
DĄBROWSKI, J. R., Mechanics
GAWRYSIAK, M., Mechanical Engineering, Design
HEJFT, R., Mechanics
IGNATIUK, S., Agricultural Engineering
JAKOWLUK, A., Technical Mechanics, Rheology
JUREWICZ, S., Economics, Mechanics
KUREK, J., Automatic Control and Robotics
ŁACH, J., Mechanics
NADOLSKI, W., Mechanics
PEŁCZYŃSKI, T., Plastic Working
PUCIŁOWSKI, K., Mechanics
PIWNIK, J., Mechanics, Plastics
SKALSKI, K., Mechanics
STOLARSKI, M., Computer Science
ZIENCIK, H., Metallography, Röntgenography

Institute of Computer Science:

BOBROWSKI, L., Biocybernetics
DAŃKO, W., Mathematical Logic
KOSTKA, M., Economics, Environmental Economics
OSTANIN, A., Computer Science
SZODA, Z., Mathematics

Institute of Mathematics and Physics:

BARTOSIEWICZ, Z., Mathematical Theory of Control
KULASZEWICZ, S., Experimental Physics
KWAŚNIEWSKI, A., Mathematical Physics
PUCZYŁOWSKI, E., Mathematics
ROTKIEWICZ, A., Mathematics
SULINSKI, A., Mining and Engineering Geology

Department of Social Sciences:

CZUMA, Ł., Economics
NOWAKOWSKI, A., History of Law
TRZĘSICKI, K., Logic

POLITECHNIKA CZĘSTOCHOWSKA (Częstochowa Technical University)

42-201 Częstochowa, ul. Dąbrowskiego 69

Telephone: (34) 325-52-11
Fax: (34) 61-23-85
E-mail: dn@matinf.pcz.czest.pl

Founded 1949
State control
Academic year: October to June

Rector: Prof. Dr hab. JANUSZ SZOPA

Pro-Rectors: Prof. Dr hab. Inż. JANUARY BIEŃ, Prof. Dr hab. Inż. ROMAN JANICZEK, Prof. Dr hab. Inż. IRENEUSZ DURLIK

Chief Administrative Officer: Mgr ALICJA ROMAN

Librarian: Mgr MAŁGORZATA HANKIEWICZ

Library: see Libraries
Number of teachers: 635
Number of students: 12,391

Publication: *Turbulence* (annually).

DEANS

Faculty of Mechanical Engineering: Prof. Dr hab. Inż. JÓZEF KOSZKUL

Faculty of Metallurgy and Materials Engineering: Prof. Dr hab. Inż. HENRYK DYJA

Faculty of Electrical Engineering: Prof. Dr hab. Inż. ANDRZEJ RUSEK

Faculty of Civil Engineering: Prof. Dr hab. Inż. ZBIGNIEW KOWAL

Faculty of Management: Prof. Dr hab. MARIA NOWICKA-SKOWRON (Dir)

Faculty of Environmental Engineering: Prof. Dr hab. Inż. JÓZEF DZIOPAK

PROFESSORS

Faculty of Mechanical Engineering:

CUPIAŁ, K., Machines and Internal Combustion Engines
DROBNIAK, S., Fluid Mechanics, Fluid Flow Machines
DZIUBDZIELA, W., Mathematics
GAJEWSKI, W., Thermodynamics
GIERZYŃSKA-DOLNA, M., Mechanical Engineering, Plastic Working Machines and Technology
GORECKI, W., Mechanical Engineering, Plastic Working Machines
JARŻA, A., Fluid Mechanics
JEZIERSKI, J., Machine Building Technology
KATKOW, A., Informatics
KENSIK, R., Welding
KOMPANEC, L., Informatics
KOSZKUL, J., Plastic Materials
KUBARSKI, J., Mathematics
LECHOWSKI, T., Machine Building Technology
MAJCHRZAK, E., Mathematics
MAZANEK, E., Machine Design
MELECHOW, R., Machine Building Technology
MOCHNACKI, B., Mathematics
PARKITNY, R., Applied Mechanics and Foundry Technology
PIECH, H., Computer Engineering
RUTKOWSKI, L., Informatics, Cybernetics
SKALMIERSKI, B., Theoretical Mechanics
SZOPA, J., Theoretical and Applied Mechanics, Applied Mathematics, Computers
TOMSKI, L., Machine Design, Applied Mechanics
TUBIELEWICZ, K., Machine Building Technology
WOLAŃSKI, R., Thermodynamics, Thermal Processes in Welding
WOŹNIAK, C., Mathematics, Mechanics
WYRZYKOWSKI, R., Informatics

Faculty of Metallurgy and Materials Engineering:

BALA, H., Corrosion of Metals
BENESCH, R., Metallurgy
BOCHENEK, A., Metallurgy, Meterials Science
BRASZCZYŃSKI, J., Metallurgy, Foundry Technology
BUDZIK, R., Metallurgy of Ferrous Metals
DYJA, H., Plastic Working of Metals
GOLIS, B., Plastic Working of Metals
JEZIORSKI, L., Metallurgy, Metals Science
KNAP, F., Plastic Working of Metals
KULESZA, P., Electrochemistry, Organic Chemistry, Physical Chemistry
KUSIAK, J., Plastic Working of Metals
MIELCZAREK, E., Thermodynamics in Power Engineering, Heat Engineering
MOREL, S., Heat Engineering
NITKIEWICZ, Z., Metallurgy, Materials Engineering
PIETRZYK, M., Metallurgy
PIŁKOWSKI, Z., Foundry, Steelmaking
SŁUPEK, S., Metallurgy, Heat Engineering
STACHURA, S., Metals Science
SVJAZIN, A., Metals Science
SZYMURA, S., Physics of Magnetic Materials
WALKOWIAK, W., Metallurgy, Organic Chemistry, Hydrometallurgy
WARCHALA, T., Pig-iron Casting
WASZKIELEWICZ, W., Organization and Management, Metallurgy
WIERZBICKA, B., Metallurgy, Casting of Nonferrous Metals
WOLKENBERG, A., Metals Science
WYSŁOCKI, B., Physics of Magnetic Materials

WYSŁOCKI, J., Physics, Physics of Magnetic Materials
ZAPART, W., Physics of Magnetic Materials

Faculty of Electrical Engineering:
BIERNACKI, Z., Electrotechnics, Measurements, Design of Measuring Equipment
BRZOZOWSKI, W., Electrical Engineering, Power Stations
DOBRZAŃSKA, I., Electrical Engineering, Electrical Power Management
JANICZEK, R., Electrotechnology
KRUCZININ, A. M., Electrotechnology
KURYTNYK, I., Electronics, Computer Engineering
MINKINA, W., Electronics
ROJEK, R., Electrical Engineering
ROLICZ, P., Electrotechnics
ROMAN, A., Electronics, Magnetic Materials
RUSEK, A., Electric Motors
SOIŃSKI, M., Magnetic Materials, Material Engineering
TOPÓR-KAMIŃSKI, L., Electrotechnology
WYSOCKI, J., Electronics, Computer Engineering
ZĄBKOWSKA-WACŁAWEK, M., Electrotechnics

Faculty of Civil Engineering:
BOBKO, T., Technology, Organization of Building
CZECH, L., Geometrical Construction, Civil Engineering
DREWNOWSKI, S., Materials Engineering, Structural Engineering
KLEIBER, M., Mechanics, Computational Methods in Mechanics
KOSIŃSKI, S., Structural Mechanics
KOWAL, Z., Civil Engineering, Steel Constructions
KWIATEK, J., Civil Engineering
LINCZOWSKI, C., Technology and Organization of Building
ŁUKSZA, L., Civil Engineering
PABIAN, A., Organization of Building
PRYKIN, B., Civil Engineering
PRZYBYŁO, W., Structural Mechanics, Civil Engineering
PUSHKARYNOWA, E., Building Materials
SŁUŻALEC, A., Mathematics, Mechanics
SYGUŁA, S., Bridge Construction, Civil Engineering
ZIMNY, J., Thermal Processes in Building, Ecopower Engineering

Faculty of Management:
BORKOWSKI, S., Organization and Management, Metallurgy
BRZEZIN, W., Economics, Organization and Methods
DURLIK, I., Marketing
FIEDOROWICZ, K., Economics
GORCZYCKA, E., Economics, Organization and Management
GRYCNER, S., Law
GRZESZCZYK, T., Economics, Law
KIEŁTYKA, L., Automatics in Management
KLISIŃSKI, J., Economics, Marketing
KONODYBA-SZYMAŃSKI, B., Metallurgy
KROSZEL, J., Economics
LEWANDOWSKI, J., Organization and Management, Machine Building Technology
MILIAN, L., Sociology, Organization and Management
NOWAK, C., Agricultural Technology
NOWICKA-SKOWRON, M., Economics, Organization and Management
PAJĄCZKOWSKI, S., History
PARTYKA, M., Mathematics, Informatics
PRZYBYLSKI, H., Management Administration, Economics
SOBOLAK, L., Organization and Management
SUCHECKA, J., Economics
SZTUKA, J., Marketing
TOKARZ, M., Philosophy, Logic
VARKOLY, L., Materials Engineering, Computer Engineering
WOŹNIAK-SOBCZAK, B., Economics, Organization and Management
ZACHOROWSKA, A., Economics
ŻÓŁTOWSKI, B., Process Engineering and Organization

Faculty of Environmental Engineering:
BIEŃ, J., Geology, Hydrogeology
BOHDZIEWICZ, J., Environmental Engineering
BURACZEWSKI, G., Environmental Engineering, Water Supply and Sewage Disposal
DEWIATOW, W., Mechanics, Structural Engineering
DĘBOWSKI, Z., Sanitary Engineering
DZIOPAK, J., Sanitary Engineering
GIRCZYS, J., Sanitary Engineering
GOSTOMCZYK, M., Environmental Engineering, Atmosphere Protection
GUMNITSKY, J., Biochemistry, Biotechnology
JANOSZ-RAJCZYK, M., Environmental Engineering
JASKÓLSKI, J., Environmental Engineering
NOWAK, W., Sanitary Engineering
SUŁKOWSKI, W., Sanitary Engineering
SYBIRNY, A., Environmental Engineering

POLITECHNIKA GDAŃSKA (Technical University of Gdańsk)

80-952 Gdańsk, ul. G. Narutowicza 11/12
Telephone: (58) 341-57-91
Fax: (58) 341-58-21

Founded 1945

Rector: Prof. ALEKSANDER KOŁODZIEJCZYK
Vice-Rectors: JAN GODLEWSKI, WŁODZIMIERZ PRZYBYLSKI, ALICJA KONCZAKOWSKA
Chief Administrative Officer: Mgr E. MAZUR
Librarian: Mgr JANINA LIGMAN

Library: see Libraries
Number of teachers: 1,203
Number of students: 14,800

Publications: *Zeszyty Naukowe Politechniki Gdańskiej* (Scientific Papers of the Technical University of Gdańsk—irregular), *Wykazy Nowych Nabytków Biblioteki* (Library Acquisitions Lists—quarterly).

DEANS

Faculty of Civil Engineering: Z. CYWIŃSKI
Faculty of Mechanical Engineering: A. BALAWENDER
Faculty of Chemistry: J. NAMIEŚNIK
Faculty of Electrical and Control Engineering: P. PAZDRO
Faculty of Electronics, Telecommunications and Informatics: J. WOŹNIAK
Faculty of Architecture: W. ANDERS
Faculty of Environmental Engineering: R. SZYMKIEWICZ
Faculty of Ocean Engineering and Ship Technology: K. ROSOCHOWICZ
Faculty of Applied Physics and Mathematics: H. SODOLSKI
Faculty of Management and Economics: P. DOMINIAK

PROFESSORS

Faculty of Mechanical Engineering:
BALAWENDER, A., Hydrostatic Transmission
BALCERSKI, A., Marine Diesel Engines and Ship Power Plants
BARYLSKI, A., Abrasive Machining
CICHY, M., Piston Steam Engines
EJSMONT, J., Construction and Maintenance of Machines
KNYSZEWSKI, J., Food Processing
KRUSZEWSKI-MAJEWSKI, J., Applied Mechanics
KUCHARSKI, T., Mechanics and Machine Dynamics, Applied Mechanics
LESIŃSKI, K., Welding
NEYMAN, A., Tribology, Principles of Machine Design
NIESPODZIŃSKI, S., Thermodynamics
OLSZEWSKI, O., Machine Construction
OSIECKI, A., Hydrostatic Transmission
PRZYBYLSKI, W., Machine Technology
PUDLIK, W., Thermodynamics
PUZYREWSKI, R., Hydraulic Engineering
STASIEK, J., Thermodynamics and Heat Transfer
STOLARSKI, T., Tribology and Surface Mechanics
WALCZAK, W., Welding
WALCZYK, Z., Mechanics and Machine Dynamics
WITTBRODT, E., Mechanics and Machine Dynamics, Applied Mechanics
ZIELIŃSKI, A., Materials Engineering

Faculty of Chemistry:
ANDRUSZKIEWICZ, R., Organic Chemistry, Medicinal Chemistry
BALAS, A., General Chemistry
BECKER, B., Organometallic Chemistry
BIAŁŁOZÓR, S., Electrochemistry
BIERNAT, J., General Chemistry
BIZIUK, M., Environmental Analytical Chemistry, Elemental Analysis, Spectrophotometric Analysis
BOROWSKI, E., Biochemistry
CHIMIAK, A., Organic Chemistry
DAROWICKI, K., Electrochemistry, Corrosion and Corrosion Protection
DROZDOWSKI, B., Fat Technology
GRZYBKOWSKI, W., Solution Chemistry, Aquatic Chemistry
HERMAN, A., Inorganic Chemistry
HUPKA, J., Chemical Technology
JUCHNIEWICZ, R., Corrosion Protection Technology
KAMIŃSKI, M., Separation Methods and Petroleum Products Analysis
KASTERKA, B., Analytical Chemistry, Trace Analysis
KAWALEC-PIETRENKO, B., Chemical Engineering
KOŁODZIEJCZYK, A., Organic Chemistry
KONOPA, J., Organic Chemistry
KUR, J., Molecular Biology
LEWANDOWSKI, W., Heat Technology, Chemical Engineering
LIBUŚ, Z., Physical Chemistry
MASIULANIS, B., Chemistry and Technology of Polymers
MAZERSKI, J., Computational Chemistry, Chemometrics
MĘDRZYCKA, K., Environmental Technology, Colloid Chemistry
MILEWSKI, S., Biochemistry
NAMIEŚNIK, J., Analytical Chemistry
PASTUSZAK, R., Inorganic Chemistry
PAWLAK, J., Bio-organic Chemistry, Chemistry of Natural Products
PIKIES, J., Organosilicon Chemistry
PILARCZYK, M., Physical Chemistry
POŁOŃSKI, T., Organic Chemistry, Stereochemistry, Molecular Modelling, Chiroptical Spectroscopy
RACHOŃ, J., Organic Chemistry
SADOWSKA, M., Food Technology
SIKORSKI, Z., Food and Fish Technology
STOŁYHWO, A., Analytical Chemistry, Food Analysis
SYNOWIECKI, J., Chemical Technology
URUSKA, I., Physical Chemistry
WARDENCKI, Z., Analytical Chemistry
WILCZEWSKI, T., Numerical Heat Transfer and Fluid Flow
WOJNOWSKI, W., Inorganic Chemistry
ZIELKIEWICZ, J., Physical Chemistry of Solutions, Thermodynamics of Solutions
ZWIERZYKOWSKI, W., Fat Technology
ZYGMUNT, B., Analytical Chemistry

Faculty of Electrical and Control Engineering:
GRONO, A., Electrotechnics, Automatic Control
HRYŃCZUK, J., Principles of Electrical Engineering

IWICKI, M., Industrial Electrical Engineering
JAKUBIUK, K., Principles of Electrotechnics, Electrical Apparatus
KARWOWSKI, K., Electric Traction
KOWALSKI, Z., Industrial Automation
KRZEMIŃSKI, Z., Electrical Drives and Power Electronics
MARECKI, J., Electrical Power Engineering
MATULEWICZ, Electrical Machines
MILKIEWICZ, F., Industrial Automation
PAZDRO, P., Electrical Apparatus and Traction
RONKOWSKI, M., Electrical Machines and Power Electronic Systems, Modelling and Simulation
ROSKOSZ, R., Electrical Measurement and Instrumentation
SZCZERBA, Z., Electrical Power Engineering
SZCZĘSNY, R., Power Electronics
WASEK, K., Control Engineering
WOLNY, A., High-Voltage Current Switching
ZAJCZYK, R., Electrical Power Systems and Systems Control
ZIMNY, P., Theoretical Electromagnetic Field
ŻYBORSKI, J., Electrical Apparatus and Traction

Faculty of Electronics, Telecommunications and Informatics:
CHRAMIEC, J., Microwave Circuits
CZARNUL, Z., Electronic Circuits
CZYŻEWSKI, A., Sound Engineering
DYKA, A., Signal Analysis, Digital Signal Processing
GÓRSKI, J. K., Software Engineering, Informatics
GRABOWSKI, K., Microwave Technique
HERMANOWICZ, E., Discrete Time Signals and Systems
KACZMAREK, J., Electronic Components
KACZMAREK, S., Telecommunications Switching
KITLIŃSKI, M., Microwave Technique
KONCZAKOWSKA, A., Electronic Components
KOSMOWSKI, B., Optoelectronics
KOWALCZUK, Z., Automation and Computer Control
KRAWCZYK, H., Computer Science, Parallel, Architectures and Fault-Tolerance
KUBALE, M., Discreet Optimization
LASOTA, H., Communications Acoustics
MALINA, W., Cybernetics
MAZUR, J., Microwave Techniques
MAZUREK, S., Control Engineering
MROZOWSKI, M., Electromagnetic Field Theory, Microwaves
NIEDŹWIECKI, MACIEJ, Automatic Control
NOWAKOWSKI, A., Electronics Technology
NOWAKOWSKI, J., Electronic Equipment Technology
PIWAKOWSKI, B., Acoustics
POLOWCZYK, M., Telecommunications Technology
PORĘBSKI, W., Automation
RUTKOWSKI, D., Principles of Telecommunications
RYKACZEWSKI, R., Computer Communication Systems
SALAMON, R., Underwater Acoustics
SOBCZAK, W., Cybernetics
SPIRALSKI, L., Electronic Equipment
STEPNOWSKI, A., Marine Acoustics, Telecommunications
STEPOWICZ, W., Cybernetics
WILAMOWSKI, B., Telecommunications Technology
WOŹNIAK, J., Telecommunications, Computer Communication Systems
ZIELONKO, R., Electronic Equipment Technology
ZIENTALSKI, M., Electronic Equipment Technology

Faculty of Architecture:
ANDERS, W., Town Planning
BAUM, SZ., Public Buildings
CHMIEL, J., Public Buildings
GÓRA, J., Painting
KITA, A., Painting
KOCHANOWSKI, M., Town Planning
KOHNKE, A., Office Building Architecture
KOŁODZIEJSKI, J., Regional Planning
KULOWSKI, A., Architectural Acoustics
PRZEWOŹNIAK, M., Landscape Ecology and Planning
STAWICKA-WAŁKOWSKA, M., Architecture and Building, Urban Acoustics
TARASZKIEWICZ, L., Architecture of Housing

Faculty of Civil Engineering:
BIELEWICZ, E., Structural Mechanics
BOGDANIUK, B., Traffic Engineering
CHRÓŚCIELEWSKI, J., Structural Mechanics
CYWIŃSKI, Z., Structural Mechanics
GODYCKI-ĆWIRKO, T., Reinforced and Prestressed Concrete Constructions Theory
GOSŁAWSKI, J., Technology and Construction Management
JUDYCKI, J., Road Construction
KOC, W., Railways
KOWALCZYK, Z., Economics and Organization of Buildings
KRYSTEK, R., Traffic Engineering
MAŁASIEWICZ, A., Building Materials
SZYMCZAK, CZ., Structural Mechanics
TEJCHMAN-KONARZEWSKI, J., Mechanics of Granular Materials
WALUKIEWICZ, H., Structural Mechanics
ZIÓŁKO, J., Steel Structures

Faculty of Environmental Engineering:
BEDNARCZYK, S., Hydraulic Construction
DEMBICKI, E., Soil Mechanics and Foundation Engineering
GWIZDAŁA, K., Geotechnology and Foundation Engineering
KOWALIK, P., Geodesy
KOZERSKI, B., Hydraulic Engineering
KULIK-KUZIEMSKA, J., Hydrobiology
MAJEWSKI, W., Hydraulic Structures and Water Management
MAZURKIEWICZ, B., Offshore Structures
OBARSKA-PEMPKOWIAK, H., Water, Sanitary and Ecological Engineering
ODROBIŃSKI, W., Ground Mechanics and Foundation
OLAŃCZUK-NEYMAN, K., Environmental Microbiology
SAWICKI, J., Hydromechanics
SIKORA, Z., Theoretical Soil Mechanics
SUBOTOWICZ, W., Ground Mechanics
SULIGOWSKI, Z., Water Supply
SZYMKIEWICZ, R., Hydrology
TEJCHMAN, A., Ground Mechanics
TOPOLNICKI, M., Marine Engineering, Soil Mechanics
ZADROGA, B., Soil Mechanics and Foundation Engineering
ŻUROWSKI, A., Geodesy

Faculty of Ocean Engineering and Ship Technology:
BRANDOWSKI, A., Engineering Safety and Reliability, Ship Technology
CUDNY, K., Ship Materials, Principles of Ship Machine Construction
CYULIN, W., Construction and Operation of Machines, Ship Power Plants
CZAJGUCKI, J., Construction and Operation of Machines, Ship Power Plants
DOERFFER, J., Naval Ship Technology
DOMACHOWSKI, Z., Automatic Control of Power Engineering Plants
KOLENDA, J., Mechanics of Ship Structures
KOLAGO, M., Technology of Ships
KOSOWSKI, K., Mechanics, Construction and Operation of Machines, Steam and Gas Turbines
KRĘPA, J., Marine Fisheries Technology, Fishing Vessel and Fishing Gear
KRĘŻELEWSKI, M., Theory of Shipbuilding
KURSKI, W., Mechanics of Ship Structures
LENART, A., Navigation, Ship Automation
METSCHKOW, B., Mechanics, Shipbuilding
PASZOTA, Z., Applied Hydraulics, Hydrostatic Drive
PRÓCHNICKI, W., Steam and Gas Turbine, Power Plant Automation
ROSOCHOWICZ, K., Ship Technology
ROWINSKI, L., Construction and Operation of Machines, Automation of Design Processes
SPERSKI, M., Construction and Operation of Machines, Mechanics of Ship Construction
SZALA, J., Mechanics, Construction and Operation of Machines
SZANTYR, J., Mechanics, Ship Hydrodynamics

Faculty of Applied Physics and Mathematics:
CHYBICKI, M., Physics
GŁAZUNOW, J., Mathematical Analysis, Applied Mathematics
GODLEWSKI, J., Physics
JANKOWSKI, T., Differential Equations and Numerical Analysis
KALINOWSKI, J., Physics
KUŚBA, J., Physics, Molecular Physics
LEBLE, S., Theoretical and Mathematical Physics
MURAWSKI, L., Solid State Physics
ROMANOWSKI, A., Algebra
SADOWSKI, W., Solid State Physics
SIENKIEWICZ, J., Theoretical Physics
SODOLSKI, H., Physics
SZMYTKOWSKI, CZ., Atomic and Molecular Physics
TOPP, J., Combinatorics, Graph Theory
TURO, J., Differential Equations
ZUBEK, M., Molecular Physics

Faculty of Management and Economics:
BŁAWAT, F., Economics
DOMINIAK, P., Economics
DURLIK, J., Engineering Management, Production Systems and Operational Management
GARBACIK, B., Political Science
GOMÓŁKA, K., Political Science
KUBKA, J., Social Philosophy
OSSOWSKI, J., Microeconomics, Econometrics
RÓŻAŃSKA, H., Economics
SYNOWIECKI, A., Philosophy
SZCZERBICKI, E., Industrial Engineering
SZPAKOWSKA, M., Commodities Science
TUBIELEWICZ, A., Economics
ZALEWSKI, H., Finance
ZAWADZKA, L., Quantitative Methods in Organization and Management

POLITECHNIKA KRĄKOWSKA IM. TADEUSZA KOŚCIUSZKI (Cracow University of Technology)

31-155 Cracow, Warszawska 24
Telephone: (12) 633-03-00
Fax: (12) 633-57-73

Founded 1945
State control
Language of instruction: Polish
Academic year: October to June (two semesters)

Rector: Prof. Dr hab. Inż. K. FLAGA
Pro-Rectors: Prof. Dr hab. Inż. M. CHRZANOWSKI
Assoc. Prof. Dr hab. Inż. E. NACHLIK, Prof. Dr hab. Inż. R. KOZŁOWSKI
Chief Administrative Officer: Mgr Inż. Z. SKAWICKI
Librarian: Mgr M. NAHOTKO

Library: see Libraries
Teaching staff: 1,131
Number of students: 11,033

Publications: *Czasopismo Techniczne* (Technical Bulletin, irregular; series on Architecture, Civil Engineering, Chemistry, Mechanical Engineering, Electrotechnology, the Environment), *Zeszyty Naukowe Politechniki Krakowskiej* (Scientific Sheets, irregular; series on

Architecture, Civil Engineering, Hydraulic and Sanitary Engineering, Mechanics, Electrical Engineering, Economics, Chemical Engineering and Technology, Basic Technical Sciences).

DEANS

Faculty of Architecture: Prof. Dr hab. Inż. arch. A. KADŁUCZKA

Faculty of Civil Engineering: Assoc. Prof. Dr hab. Inż. K. FURTAK

Faculty of Chemical Engineering and Technology: Prof. Dr hab. R. KIJKOWSKA

Faculty of Environmental Engineering: Assoc. Prof. Dr hab. Inż. T. LUBOWIECKA

Faculty of Mechanical Engineering: Prof. Dr hab. Inż. J. CYKLIS

Faculty of Electrical and Computer Engineering: Prof. Dr hab. Inż. T. SOBCZYK

PROFESSORS

Faculty of Architecture:

- BARTKOWICZ, T., Urban Design and Spatial Planning
- BOGDANOWSKI, J., Landscape Architecture, Military Architecture, Art of Gardening
- BRUZDA, J., Interior Design
- BULIŃSKI, W., Architectural Design
- GAWŁOWSKI, J. T., Design and Theory of Architecture
- KADŁUCZKA, A., History of Architecture and Monument Preservation
- MAŃKOWSKI, T., Architectural Design
- SKOCZEK, A., Architectural Design of Public Buildings

Faculty of Civil Engineering:

- CHRZANOWSKI, M., Fracture Mechanics and Rheology
- CYUNEL, B., Technology and Organization of Construction
- DYDUCH, K., Reinforced and Prestressed Concrete Structures, Industrial Buildings, Modernization
- FLAGA, K., Bridges, Tunnels, Concrete Structures, Technology of Concrete, Nondestructive Testing
- JAMROŻY, Z., Technology of Concrete
- KAWECKI, J., Structural Mechanics
- MACIĄG, E., Structural Mechanics Dynamics of Structure
- MENDERA, Z., Metal Structures, Theory of Structure
- MURZEWSKI, J., Steel Structures, Theory of Reliability, Structural Mechanics
- OLSZOWSKI, B., Theory of Structure, Numerical Analysis, Modelling
- ORKISZ, J., Theory of Structure, Structural Mechanics
- PIECHNIK, S., Solid Mechanics, Rheology
- PIWOWARSKI, K., Concrete Structures
- STACHOWICZ, A., Structural Mechanics, General and Industrial Building, Concrete Structures
- SZEFER, G., Solid and Structural Mechanics
- TRACZ, M., Traffic and Highway Engineering
- WASZCZYSZYN, Z., Structural Mechanics, Strength of Materials
- ZIOBROŃ, W., Concrete Structures

Faculty of Chemical Engineering and Technology:

- BULEWICZ, E., Combustion Processes
- KIJKOWSKA, R., Solid State Chemistry
- PIELICHOWSKI, J., Chemistry and Technology of Polymers, Organic Synthesis
- STOKŁOSA, A., Physical Chemistry, Solid State Physical Chemistry
- TABIS, B., Chemical and Process Engineering
- WĘGIEL, J., Chemical Technology of Coal
- WOŹNIAK, M., Organic Chemistry, Heterocyclic Chemistry

Faculty of Environmental Engineering:

- BRYŚ, H., Surveying in Engineering
- KORDECKI, Z., Structural Mechanics
- KURBIEL, J., Water and Waste Water Treatment
- PIETRZYK, K., Soil Mechanics and Foundation Engineering
- PLEWA, M., Geology, Petrography, Petrophysics
- WIECZYSTY, A., Water Supply and Waste Water Disposal, Engineering Hydrogeology

Faculty of Mechanical Engineering:

- BOGACZ, R., Transporation, Stability
- CYKLIS, J., Production Engineering
- DYLĄG, M., Chemical Engineering, Chemical Industry Equipment, Environmental Engineering
- GOLEC, K., Internal Combustion Engines, Engine Starting, Feed Systems, Turbocharging
- KNAPCZYK, J., Theory of Mechanisms, Motor Cars and Tractors, Robotics
- KOZŁOWSKI, R., Physical Metallurgy and Heat Treatment, Power Engineering Materials Science
- MAZURKIEWICZ, S., Experimental Mechanics, Experimental Stress Analysis
- NAWARA, L., Machine Technology, Metrology of Geometrical Quantities, Ergonomics
- NIZIOŁ, J., Theoretical and Applied Mechanics, Machine Dynamics
- OPRZĘDKIEWICZ, J., Reliability of Mechanical Devices
- OSYCZKA, A., Machine Tools, Robotics, Computer-Aided Design
- POLAŃSKI, Z., Machine Technology and Metal Working
- RYŚ, J., Machinery Construction, Gears
- SENDYKA, B., Internal Combustion Engines
- SKRZYPEK, J., Theory of Plasticity, Rheology
- STOLARSKI, B., Motor Car Technology and Reliability
- SZEWCZYK, K., Heavy Duty Machines, Cranes, Hydraulic Drives and Control
- TALER, J., Power Machines and Engineering, Heat Transfer
- WOŁKOW, J., Hydraulic and Pneumatic Control and Drives
- ŻYCZKOWSKI, M., Theory of Plasticity, Rheology

Faculty of Electrical and Computer Engineering:

- HEJMO, W., Optimal Control, Process Automation
- SAPIECHA, K., Computer Architecture and Programming
- SOBCZYK, T., Electrical Machines
- SZARANIEC, E., Mathematical Geophysics

Institute of Economics, Sociology and Philosophy:

- DACH, Z., Microeconomics, Social Policy
- KULWICKI, E., Management, History of Economic Theory
- ZIN, W., History of Architecture, Preservation of Monuments

Institute of Mathematics:

- BOCHENEK, J., Differential Equations, Functional Analysis

Institute of Physics:

- KOZARZEWSKI, B., Theoretical Physics of Solids, Magnetic Materials
- OSTOJA-GAJEWSKI, A., Applied Mechanics

POLITECHNIKA ŁÓDZKA
(Technical University of Łódź)

90-924 Łódź, Ks. I. Skorupki 6/8

Telephone: 31-20-01

Telex: 886136

Fax: 36-85-22

Founded 1945

Academic year: September to June (2 semesters)

Rector: Prof. Dr hab. JÓZEF MAYER

Pro-Rectors: Prof. Dr hab. KRZYSZTOF KUŹMIŃSKI, Prof. Dr hab. EDWARD RYBICKI, Prof. Dr hab. ANDRZEJ JOPKIEWICZ, Prof. Dr hab. ANDRZEJ WŁOCHOWICZ

Administrative Director: Dr JERZY PRYWER

Librarian: Mgr CZESŁAWA GARNYSZ

Library: see Libraries

Number of teachers: 1,600

Number of students: 14,000

Publication: *Zeszyty Naukowe Politechniki Łódzkiej, Bulletin.*

DEANS

Faculty of Mechanical Engineering: Prof. Dr hab. M. KRÓLAK

Faculty of Electrical and Electronic Engineering: Prof. Dr J. LESZCZYŃSKI

Faculty of Chemistry: Prof. Dr. hab. T. PARYJCZAK

Faculty of Textile Engineering: Prof. Dr hab. W. KOBZA

Faculty of Food Chemistry and Biotechnology: Prof. Dr hab. S. BIELECKI

Faculty of Civil Engineering, Architecture and Environmental Engineering: Prof. Dr hab. S. KONIECZNY

Faculty of Process and Environmental Engineering: Prof. Dr hab. C. STRUMIŁŁO

Faculty of Technical Physics, Informatics and Applied Mathematics: Prof. Dr hab. W. NAKWASKI

Faculty of Organization and Management: Prof. Dr hab. C. SZMIDT

Faculty of Machine Design (Branch in Bielsko-Biała): Prof. Dr hab. M. SOBIESZCZAŃSKI

Faculty of Textile Engineering and Environmental Protection (Branch in Bielsko-Biała): Prof. Dr hab. W. GĄDOR

Institute of Papermaking and Paper Machines: Prof. Dr hab. W. KAWKA

PROFESSORS

Faculty of Mechanical Engineering:

- AWREJCEWICZ, J., Dynamics, Control, Biomechanics
- DAJNIAK, H., Theory and Design of Land Vehicles
- GAŁKIEWICZ, T., Strength and Stability of Structures
- GUNDLACH, W., Fluid Flow Machinery
- HAŚ, Z., Surface Engineering
- JAROSIŃSKI, J., Thermodynamics, Combustion, Combustion Engines
- KANIEWSKI, W., Mechanics, Machine Design
- KAPITANIAK, T., Mechanics
- KAZIMIERSKI, Z., Applied Fluid Mechanics
- KOZIARSKI, A., Machine Tools
- KRÓLAK, M., Applied Mechanics
- KRYSIŃSKI, J., Fluid-Flow Machinery
- KWAPISZ, L., Machine Mechanics
- NIEZGODZIŃSKI, M. E., Strength of Materials
- NOWACKI, J., Materials Science, Surface Engineering
- ORZECHOWSKI, Z., Fluid Mechanics
- RAFAŁOWICZ, J., Machine Tools
- SZCZEPANIAK, C., Theory and Design of Land Vehicles

Faculty of Electrical and Electronic Engineering:

- BOLANOWSKI, B., Electrical Apparatus
- JABŁOŃSKI, M., Electric Machines and Transformers
- KARBOWIAK, H., Electric Traction
- KOŁACIŃSKI, Z., Electrical Apparatus
- KORZEC, Z., Electronics
- KOSTRUBIEC, F., Electrical Engineering, Materials Science
- KOSZMIDER, A., Instrument Transformers, Electromagnetic Compatibility
- KOWALSKI, Z., Electrical Power Engineering
- KOZŁOWSKI, M., Electrical Machines
- KRYNKE, M., Automatic Control and Electrical Drives
- KUŚMIEREK, Z., Electrical Metrology

KUŹMIŃSKI, K., Automatic Control
LESZCZYŃSKI, J., Electrical Engineering, Materials Science
LUCIŃSKI, J., Semiconductor Power Electronics
MATERKA, A., Electronics
MICHALSKI, L., Electroheat Temperature Measurement and Control
NAPIERALSKI, A., Electronics
NOWACKI, Z., Control of Electrical Drives, Power Electronics
PAWLIK, M., Power Plant
PEŁCZEWSKI, W., Automatic Control and Electrical Drives
PIOTROWSKI, Z., Instrument Transformers
TADEUSIEWICZ, M., Circuit Theory
TUROWSKI, J., Electric Machines and Transformers
WALCZUK, E., Electrical Apparatus
ZAKRZEWSKI, K., Electric Machines and Transformers

Faculty of Chemistry:

BARTCZAK, W., Radiation Chemistry
BODALSKI, R., Organic Chemistry
BUKOWSKA-STRZYŻEWSKA, M., X-ray Structure Analysis
CYGAŃSKI, A., Analytical Chemistry
CZAKIS-SULIKOWSKA, D., Co-ordination Chemistry
GAŁDECKI, Z., Crystallography
GĘBICKI, J. M., Organic Physical Chemistry, Photochemistry, Spectroscopy, Radiation Chemistry, Biocrystallography
GŁÓWKA, M., Biocrystallography
KAROLAK-WOJCIECHOWSKA, J., Physical Chemistry
KRASKA, J., Chemistry and Technology of Dyes
KROH, J., Physical Chemistry, Radiation Chemistry
KRYSZEWSKI, M., Physical Chemistry, Physics of Polymers
LEPLAWY, M., Organic Chemistry
MAYER, J., Physical Chemistry, Radiation Chemistry
PAKUŁA, T., Physics of Polymers
PANETH, P., Physical and Theoretical Chemistry
PARYJCZAK, T., Chemical Catalysis
PŁONKA, A., Physical Chemistry, Radiation Chemistry
REIMSCHÜSSEL, W., Organic Physical Chemistry, Radiation Chemistry
SZADOWSKI, J., Chemistry and Technology of Dyes
ŚLUSARSKI, L., Rubber Chemistry and Technology
ULAŃSKI, J., Physics and Physical Chemistry of Polymers
WŁODARCZYK, M., Chemistry and Polymer Technology
ZWIERZAK, A., Organic Chemistry

Faculty of Textile Technology:

DEMS, K., Structural Mechanics
JACKOWSKI, T., Mechanical Technology of Textiles, Spinning
KOPIAS, K., Knitting Technology
KORLIŃSKI, W., Mechanical Technology of Textiles, Knitting
ŁASZKIEWICZ, B., Chemistry of Polymers and Technology of Man-made Fibres
MALINOWSKI, M., Mechanical Technology of Textiles, Spinning
POŁOWIŃSKI, S., Physical Chemistry of Polymers
SKWARSKI, T., Physico-chemistry of Polymers and Technology Man-made Fibres
STASIAK, M., Mechanical Technology of Textiles, Spinning
SZMELTER, W., Textile Metrology
SZOSLAND, J., Mechanical Technology of Textiles, Weaving
URBAŃCZYK, G., Fibre Science and Fibre Physics
WIĘŹLAK, W., Structure and Manufacture of Clothing
ŻUREK, W., Structure of Textiles, Textile Engineering

Faculty of Food Chemistry:

GALAS, E., Technical Biochemistry, Biotechnology
GÓRA, J., Organic Chemistry, Chemistry of Natural Products
MASŁOWSKA, J., Analytical Chemistry, Food Chemistry
MICHAŁOWSKI, S., Chemical Food Technology
OBERMAN, H., Microbiology
SUGIER, H., Physical Chemistry
SZOPA, J., Technical Microbiology
TWARDOWSKI, T., Technical Biochemistry
WIECZOREK, M., X-ray Crystallography
WILSKA-JESZKA, J., Food Chemistry

Faculty of Civil Engineering, Architecture and Environmental Engineering:

KARDASZEWSKI, B., Architecture of Public Buildings
KLEMM, P., Building Physics and Building Materials
KRYGIER, S., Town Planning, Sculpture and Painting
PRZEWŁOCKI, S., Engineering Geodesy and Building Metrology
RADWAN-DĘBSKI, R., Village and District Planning
SUCHAR, M., Theoretical and Applied Mechanics
ŚWIECHOWSKI, Z., Preservation of Monuments and History of Architecture
WOŹNIAK, C., Mechanics of Solids

Faculty of Process and Environmental Engineering:

HEIM, A., Mechanical Processes in Chemical Engineering
KAMIŃSKI, W., Heat Transfer, Simultaneous Heat and Mass Transfer
KEMBŁOWSKI, Z., Engineering Rheology, Multiphase Flow
LEDAKOWICZ, S., Chemical Engineering and Bioprocess Engineering
SERWIŃSKI, M., Liquid–Liquid Systems Separation, Thermodynamics of Multicomponent Mixtures
STRUMIŁŁO, Cz., Simultaneous Heat and Mass Transfer, Bioprocess Engineering
ZARZYCKI, R., Diffusional Processes in Environmental Engineering

Faculty of Technical Physics, Informatics and Applied Mathematics:

DZIUBIŃSKI, I., Differential Equations, Analytical Functions
KĄCKI, E., Computer Science
KARNIEWICZ, J., Solid State Physics
MIKA, J., Applied Mathematics
NAKWASKI, N., Computer Physics
WILCZYŃSKI, W., Real Functions

Faculty of Organization and Management:

GRZELAK, Z., International Economic Relations

Faculty of Machine Design (Branch in Bielsko-Biała):

GDULA, S. J. Thermodynamics, Heat Transfer
MATKOWSKI, J., Functional Equations, Interactive and Fixed-points Theory
SZADKOWSKI, J., Machine Technology, Machining
TROMBSKI, M., Applied Mechanics
WAJAND, J., Internal Combustion Engines
WOJNAROWSKI, J., Machine Dynamics, Graph Theory

Faculty of Textile Engineering and Environmental Protection (Branch in Bielsko-Biała):

BRZEZIŃSKI, S., Chemical Treatment of Fibres
WŁOCHOWICZ, A., Fibre Science and Fibre Physics

Faculty of Organization and Management (Branch in Bielsko-Biała):

GROS, U., Management
GRZYWAK, A., Automation

Institute of Papermaking and Paper Machines:

PRZYBYSZ, K., Paper Technology
RUTKOWSKI, J., Pulp and Paper Technology
SUREWICZ, W., Pulp and Paper Technology

POLITECHNIKA LUBELSKA
(Technical University of Lublin)

20-950 Lublin, ul. Bernardyńska 13
Telephone: (81) 532-22-01
Fax: (81) 532-73-64
E-mail: tul@rekt.pol.lublin.pl
Founded 1953
State Control
Language of Instruction: Polish
Academic year: October to June (two semesters)

Rector: Prof. Dr Inż. KAZIMIERZ SZABELSKI
Pro-Rectors: Prof. Dr hab. EDWARD ŚPIEWLA, Prof. Dr hab. Inż. TADEUSZ JANOWSKI
Chief Administrative Officer: MAREK MAZUŚ
Librarian: RYSZARD BANIA

Library: see Libraries
Number of teachers: 520
Number of students: 7,500

DEANS

Faculty of Mechanical Engineering: Prof. Dr hab. Inż. ANDRZEJ WEROŃSKI
Faculty of Electrical Engineering: Prof. Dr hab. Inż. WIKTOR PIETRZYK
Faculty of Civil and Sanitary Engineering: Prof. Dr hab. Inż. JAN KUKIEŁKA
Faculty of Management Sciences and Principles of Technology: Prof. Dr hab. Inż. KLAUDIUSZ LENIK

PROFESSORS

Faculty of Mechanical Engineering:

KOCZAN, L., Mathematics, Analytical Functions
KUCZMASZEWSKI, J., Machining, Adhesive Joints
LIPSKI, J., Automation
LUTEK, K., Machining
NIEWCZAS, A., IC Engines
OPIELAK, M., Food Processing Engineering
PEŁCZYŃSKI, T., Machine Technology
PŁASKA, S., Automatic Control
POPKO, H., Food Processing Machinery
SIKORA, R., Mechanics, Polymer Processing
STAROŃ, T., Deposit Deep Working
SZABELSKI, K., Applied Mechanics
TARKOWSKI, P., Tribology, Motor Vehicles and Internal Combustion Engines
WEROŃSKI, A., Physical Metallurgy, Heat Treatment
WEROŃSKI, W., Metal Forming
WIATR, I., Hydrogeology, Ecoengineering
WITUSZYŃSKI, K., IC Engines

Faculty of Electrical Engineering:

GRZEGÓRSKI, S., Informatics
HORODECKI, A., Electrical Driving
JANOWSKI, T., Electrical Engineering, Applied Superconducting
JAWORSKI, J., Electrical Engineering, Metrology
KISYŃSKI, J., Mathematics, Functional Analysis
KOSMULSKI, M., Colloid Chemistry, Adsorption
KOZŁOWSKI, A., Electrical Traction
KROLOPP, W., Electrical Engineering, Electrical Metrology
LATOCHA, T., Electrical Engineering, Energoelectronics
MAJKA, K., Power Engineering

NAFALSKI, A., Computer Science and Electrical Engineering
PAWELSKI, W., Energoelectronics
PIETRZYK, W., Industrial Electrotechnics
PILAT, B., Mathematics
RATAJEWICZ, Z., Chemistry, Electrochemistry
RUTKA, Z., Electrical Engineering
STABROWSKI, M., Computer Science, Electrical Engineering
ŻUKOWSKI, P., Physics of Semiconductors

Faculty of Civil and Sanitary Engineering:

BUREK, R., Physics, Environmental Protection
CIEŚLAK, W., Mathematics, Geometry
CIĘŻAK, T., Reinforced Concrete Structures
FLAGA, A., High Building Aerodynamics
GRYCZ, J., Civil Engineering
HNIDEC, B., Building Construction
KOZAK, Z., Chemistry in Environmental Protection
KRÓL, M., Prefabrication Technology, Reinforced Concrete Structures
KRZOWSKI, Z., Geotechnics
KUKIEŁKA, J., Highway Engineering
KWIATKOWSKI, J., Heating and Ventilation
LITWINOWICZ, L., Soil Mechanics, Geotechnics of Mining Areas
MURAWSKI, K., Physics, Environmental Protection
OLSZTA, W., Land Reclamation and Improvement
PAWŁOWSKI, L., Environmental Protection
POLLO, I., Chemical Engineering and Technology
STĘPNIEWSKA, Z., Chemistry of Soil
STĘPNIEWSKI, W., Agricultural Engineering
SYZMAŃSKI, A., Chemistry of Materials
ZARĘBSKI, W., General Building, Building Technology

Faculty of Management and Principles of Technology:

BAŁTOWSKI, M., Production Management
BANEK, T., Applied Mathematics
BAUM, T., Human-factor Engineering
BOJAR, E., Economics
BOROWSKI, H., Philosophy of Culture
CHALAS, K., Pedogogics
CZERNIEC, M., Solid State Mechanics
GŁADYSZEWSKI, G., Physics
GRODZKI, Z., Mathematics, Computer Science
GUDOWSKI, J., Economics
KOWALCZEWSKI, W., Organization and Management
KRAWCZYK, R., Economics, Public Finance
LENIK, K., Machine Technology
LIS, F., Sociology and Pedagogics
OLCHOWIK, J., Physics of Semiconductors
PAWLAK, M., Organization and Management
SANGWAL, K., Physics, Solid State Physics
ŚITKO, W., Organization and Management
ŚPIEWLA, E., Physics, Biophysics
ŚWIĆ, A., Machine Technology
ZINOWICZ, Z., Materials Technology
ŻUKOWSKI, M., Economics, Banking System Management
ŻUKOWSKI, P., Economics, Management in Industry

POLITECHNIKA POZNAŃSKA
(Poznań University of Technology)

60-965 Poznań, Pl. Marii Skłodowskiej-Curie 5
Telephone: (61) 831-32-37
Fax: (61) 833-02-17

Founded 1919
State control
Academic year: October to September

Rector: Prof. EUGENIUSZ MITKOWSKI
Vice-Rectors: Prof. JERZY RAKOWSKI (Scientific and International Affairs), Prof. ANTONI ISKRA (Educational Affairs), Prof. ANDRZEJ OLSZANOWSKI (General Affairs)
Chief Administrative Officer: Dr MIROSŁAW STROIŃSKI
Registrar: Mgr KRYSTYNA DŁUGOSZ
Librarian: Mgr HALINA GANIŃSKA

Library: see Libraries
Number of teachers: 1,068
Number of students: 11,038

Publications: *Zeszyty Naukowe Politechniki Poznańskiej* (Faculty Bulletins, in Polish and English), *Foundations of Computing and Decision Sciences* (in English, quarterly), *Fasciculi Mathematici* (in English).

DEANS

Faculty of Chemical Technology: Prof. JULIUSZ PERNAK
Faculty of Civil and Environmental Engineering and Architecture: Prof. HALINA KOCZYK
Faculty of Electrical Engineering: Prof. BOLESŁAW ZAPOROWSKI
Faculty of Mechanical Engineering and Management: Prof. CZESŁAW CEMPEL
Faculty of Technical Physics: Prof. JERZY DEMBCZYŃSKI
Faculty of Working Machines and Vehicles: Prof. JANUSZ WALCZAK

ATTACHED INSTITUTES

Institute of Structural Engineering: Dir Prof. OLEG KAPLIŃSKI.

Institute of Civil Engineering: Dir Prof. WITOLD WOŁOWICKI.

Institute of Environmental Engineering: Dir Prof. EDWARD SZCZECHOWIAK.

Institute of Architecture and Spatial Planning: Dir Prof. ROBERT AST.

Institute of Applied Mechanics: Dir Prof. STEFAN JONIAK.

Institute of Management Engineering: Dir Prof. LESZEK PACHOLSKI.

Institute of Mechanical Technology: Dir Prof. ANDRZEJ ŁAWNICZAK.

Institute of Materials Technology: Dir Dr ANDRZEJ MODRZYŃSKI.

Institute of Materials Science and Engineering: Dir Prof. ANDRZEJ BARBACKI.

Institute of Electric Power Engineering: Dir Dr JÓZEF LORENC.

Institute of Computing Science: Dir Prof. JAN WĘGLARZ.

Institute of Industrial Electrical Engineering: Dir Prof. RYSZARD NAWROWSKI.

Institute of Electronics and Telecommunications: Dir Prof. ANDRZEJ DOBROGOWSKI.

Institute of Machines and Motor Vehicles: Dir Prof. KAROL NADOLNY.

Institute of Internal Combustion Engines and Basics of Machine Design: Dir Prof. JERZY MERKISZ.

Institute of Chemistry and Technical Electrochemistry: Dir Prof. JAN KURZAWA.

Institute of Technology and Chemical Engineering: Dir Prof. JAN SZYMANOWSKI.

Institute of Mathematics: Dir Prof. JAROSŁAW WERBOWSKI.

Institute of Physics: Dir Prof. MIROSŁAW DROZDOWSKI.

POLITECHNIKA RZESZOWSKA
(Rzeszów University of Technology)

35-959 Rzeszów, POB 85, ul. W. Pola 2

Telephone: (17) 62-54-06
Fax: (17) 854-12-60

Founded 1963 as High School of Engineering; University status 1974
Academic year: October to September

Rector: Prof. STANISŁAW KUŚ
Vice-Rectors: Prof. ROMANA ŚLIWA, Prof. JERZY BAJOREK, Prof. JAN KALEMBKIEWICZ
Administrative Director: Mgr JANUSZ BURY
Library Director: Mgr ELŻBIETA KAŁUŻA

Library: see Libraries
Number of teachers: 601
Number of students: 9,189

Publications: *Zeszyty Naukowe, Folia Scientiarum Universitatis Technicae Resoviensis.*

DEANS

Faculty of Civil and Environmental Engineering: Prof. ZBYSZKO STOJEK
Faculty of Chemistry: Prof. MIECZYSŁAW KUCHARSKI
Faculty of Electrical Engineering: Prof. KAZIMIERZ BUCZEK
Faculty of Management and Marketing: Prof. WŁADYSŁAW FILAR
Faculty of Mechanical Engineering and Aeronautics: Prof. TADEUSZ MARKOWSKI

HEADS OF DEPARTMENT

Faculty of Civil and Environmental Engineering:

Building Structures: Assoc. Prof. S. WOLIŃSKI
Physics: Assoc. Prof. A. DRZYMAŁA
Structural Mechanics: Prof. Z. STOJEK
Descriptive Geometry: Assoc. Prof. B. JANUSZEWSKI
Geodesy: Dr M. GAŁDA
Town Planning and Architecture: Assoc. Prof. N. NOWAKOWSKI
Building Engineering: Assoc. Prof. L. FARYNIAK
Geotechnic and Hydraulic Engineering: Assoc. Prof. A. ZIELIŃSKI
Water Supply and Sewer System: Assoc. Prof. J. RAK
Materials Engineering and Building Technology: Assoc. Prof. G. PROKOPSKI
Environmental and Chemical Engineering: Assoc. Prof. J. TOMASZEK
Water Purification and Protection: Assoc. Prof. M. GRANOPS

Faculty of Chemistry:

Inorganic and Analytical Chemistry: Assoc. Prof. S. KOPACZ
Computer Chemistry: Prof. Z. HIPPE
General Chemistry: Prof. B. FLESZAR
Organic Chemistry: Assoc. Prof. M. KUCHARSKI
Chemical Engineering and Process Control: Assoc. Prof. R. PETRUS
Polymer Technology: Dr M. HENECZKOWSKI
Industrial and Materials Chemistry: Assoc. Prof. H. GALINA

Faculty of Electrical Engineering:

Control and Computer Engineering: Prof. L. TRYBUS
Digital Systems: Assoc. Prof. F. GRABOWSKI
Principles of Electrical Engineering: Assoc. Prof. J. BAJOREK
Electrodynamics and Electrical Machinery: Assoc. Prof. S. APANASEWICZ
Electronic Systems: Assoc. Prof. W. KALITA
Principles of Electronics: Prof. A. KUSY
Metrology and Measurement Systems: Asst Prof. A. KOWALCZYK
Power Electronics and Power Engineering: Asst Prof. K. BUCZEK

Faculty of Management and Marketing:

Organization and Management: Assoc. Prof. K. JAREMCZUK
Marketing: Assoc. Prof. S. ŚLUSARCZYK
Economics: Prof. A. JAROSZ
Social Sciences: Assoc. Prof. A. DASZKIEWICZ
Mathematical Methods in Economics: Assoc. Prof. M. KRÓL
Law and Administration: Assoc. Prof. K. RAJCHEL

Finance and Banking: Assoc. Prof. WŁ. FILAR

Faculty of Mechanical Engineering and Aeronautics:

Manufacturing Techniques and Automation: Prof. K. E. OCZOŚ
Mathematics: Assoc. Prof. J. BANAŚ
Materials Engineering: Assoc. Prof. T. POMIANEK
Machine Design: Assoc. Prof. T. MARKOWSKI
Manufacturing Processes and Production Organization: Prof. J. ŁUNARSKI
Motor Vehicles and Internal Combustion Engines: Assoc. Prof. K. LEJDA
Plastics: Assoc. Prof. F. STACHOWICZ
Computer Science: Assoc. Prof. S. WOŁEK
Mechanics: Prof. H. KOPECKI
Control Systems: Assoc. Prof. J. GRUSZECKI
Thermodynamics: Assoc. Prof. B. BIENIASZ
Aircraft: Dr Z. KLEPACKI
Fluid Mechanics and Aerodynamics: Assoc. Prof. Ł. WĘSIERSKI
Aircraft Engines: Dr P. WYGONIK
Materials Science: Prof. J. SIENIAWSKI

POLITECHNIKA ŚLĄSKA
(Silesian Technical University)

44-100 Gliwice, ul. Akademicka 2

Telephone: (32) 31-23-49
Fax: (32) 37-16-55
E-mail: rek.sekr@polsl.gliwice.pl

Founded 1945
State control
Academic year: October to June

Rector: Prof. BOLESŁAW POCHOPIEŃ
Pro-Rectors: Prof. JAN CHOJCAN, Prof. REMIGIUSZ SOSNOWSKI, Prof. WOJCIECH ZIELIŃSKI
Chief Administrative Officer: Mgr Inż. WOJCIECH WYDRYCHIEWICZ

Library: see Libraries
Number of teachers: 1,600
Number of students: 23,000

Publications: *Zeszyty Naukowe Politechniki Śląskiej* (Research Review—various titles).

DEANS

Faculty of Architecture: Prof. ANDRZEJ NIEZABITOWSKI
Faculty of Automation, Electronics and Computer Science: Prof. STANISŁAW KOZIELSKI
Faculty of Civil Engineering: Prof. MACIEJ GRYCZMAŃSKI
Faculty of Chemistry: Prof. JAN ZAWADIAK
Faculty of Electricity: Prof. TADEUSZ RODACKI
Faculty of Environmental and Mechanical Engineering: Prof. RYSZARD WILK
Faculty of Mining and Geology: Prof. MARIAN DOLIPSKI
Faculty of Mechanical Technology: Prof. WOJCIECH CHOLEWA
Faculty of Physics and Mathematics: Prof. RADOSŁAW GRZYMKOWSKI
Faculty of Materials Science, Metallurgy and Transport: Prof. CZESŁAW SAJDAK
Faculty of Organization and Management: Prof. JÓZEF BENDKOWSKI

POLITECHNIKA ŚWIĘTOKRZYSKA
(Kielce University of Technology)

25-314 Kielce, Al. Tysiąclecia Państwa Polskiego 7

Telephone: 24-100
Telex: 612331
Fax: 42997

Founded 1965
State control
Academic year: October to June

Rector: Prof. Dr ANDRZEJ NEIMITZ
Vice-Rectors: Prof. Dr KRZYSZTOF GRYSA (Teaching), Prof. Dr MIECZYSŁAW PONIEWSKI (Research and Co-operation with National Economy), Prof Dr ROMAN NADOLSKI (General Affairs)
Administrative Officer: WITOLD ZIĘBA

Library: see Libraries
Number of teachers: 347
Number of students: 2,445

DEANS

Faculty of Civil Engineering: Prof. Dr JANUSZ WIŚNIEWSKI
Faculty of Mechanical Engineering: Prof. Dr JACEK CHAŁUPCZAK
Faculty of Electrical Engineering, Automation and Computer Science: Prof. Dr ANDRZEJ DZIECH

PROFESSORS

Faculty of Civil Engineering:

BOROWICZ, T., Structural Mechanics
DZIURLA, M., Bridge Engineering and Underground Structures
FARYNIAK, L., General Building Engineering
GOSZCZYŃSKI, S., Reinforced Concrete Structures and Industrial Building
KOWAL, Z., Metal Building and Structure Theory
KULICZKOWSKI, A., Waterworks and Sewage Systems
KURBIEL, J., Water and Water Waste Technology
LEWINOWSKI, CZ., Road Making and Traffic Engineering
PIASTA, J., Concrete Technology and Prefabrication
PIETRZYK, K., Geotechnology
POLAK, T., Architecture and Protection of Monuments
RUDZINSKI, L., Mechanization of Repair and Construction Work
RUSIN, Z., Special Materials
SZPLIT, A., Economics and Marketing
WIŚNIEWSKI, J., Structures Maintenance
WOJTAS, R., Technical Chemistry

Faculty of Mechanical Engineering:

AMBROZIK, A., Automotive Vehicles and Internal Combustion Engines
BODASZEWSKI, W., Strength of Materials
CHAŁUPCZAK, J., Machine Technology
DURMAŁA, Z., Metal Technology
DZIUBDZIELA, W., Probability Mathematics
GRYSA, K., Devices for Automatics and Robotics
LUBUŚKA, A., Metal Sciences and Heat Treatment
NEIMITZ, A., Basis of Machine Construction
OKNIŃSKI, A., Physics
OSIECKI, J., Mechanical Equipment
OTMIANOWSKI, T., Agricultural Technique
PŁOSKI, A., Mathematics
PONIEWSKI, M., Thermodynamics and Fluid Mechanics
RADOWICZ, A., Mechanics

Faculty of Electrical Engineering and Automation:

BOBROWSKI, C., Power Engineering
DZIECH, A., Electronics and Teletransmission
NADOLSKI, R., Electrical Machines
POPŁAWSKI, E., Power Engineering Electronics and Electrical Drive
PRAZEWSKA, M., Exploitation of Electrical Equipment
PRZYGODZKI, J., Theoretical Electrotechnics and Metrology
SAPIECHA, K., Informatics
STEFAŃSKI, T., Methods and Systems of Control
ZABOROWSKI, M., Operations Research

Interfaculty Unit:

NAUMIAK, J., History of Science and Technology

POLITECHNIKA SZCZECIŃSKA
(Szczecin Technical University)

70-310 Szczecin, al. Piastów 17

Telephone: 34-67-51

Founded 1946

Rector: Prof. Dr hab. Inż. STEFAN BERCZYŃSKI
Pro-Rectors: Prof. Dr hab. Inż. ANDRZEJ BRYKALSKI, Prof. Dr hab. Inż. TADEUSZ SPYCHAJ, Dr hab. Inż. RYSZARD GETKA
Registrar: Mgr Inż. FRANCISZEK KAMOLA
Librarian: Mgr ANNA GRZELAK-ROZENBERG

Library: see Libraries
Number of teachers: 742
Number of students: 8,380

Publications: *Prace Naukowe Politechniki Szczecińskiej* (Scientific Papers—a series for each faculty and also a monographic series and a Town and Country Planning Research series).

DEANS

Faculty of Civil Engineering and Architecture: Prof. Dr hab. Inż. WŁODZIMIERZ KIERNOŻYCKI
Faculty of Mechanical Engineering: Prof. Dr hab. Inż. MIECZYSŁAW WYSIECKI
Faculty of Chemical Engineering: Prof. Dr hab. Inż. KAZIMIERZ KAŁUCKI
Faculty of Electrical Engineering: Prof. Dr hab. Inż. STANISŁAW BAŃKA
Faculty of Maritime Technology: Prof. Dr hab. Inż. STEFAN ŻMUDZKI

PROFESSORS

Faculty of Civil Engineering and Architecture:

BUCHHOLZ, W., Hydro-engineering
BOCZAR, J., Applied Hydraulics
CIEŚLUKOWSKI, R., Heating and Heat Engineering
JARZYNKA, W., Architectural Design
KIERNOŻYCKI, W., Reinforced Concrete Structures, Building Materials
LATOUR, S., Theory and History of Architecture, Conservation and Restoration of Architectural and Urban Monuments
MATYSZEWSKI, T., Construction Materials
MEYER, Z., Hydro-engineering, Applied Hydraulics, Hydromechanics
MIELCZAREK, Z., Timber Building Constructions
RACINOWSKI, R., Geology
STEFAŃCZYK, B., Technology of Road and Building Materials
SZAFLIK, W., Central Heating and Ventilation, Heat Exchange
SZYMSKI, A., Theory of Architecture, Systems and Town-planning Design
TOKARCZYK, R., Painting
WASILIEW, A., Diagnostics and Assessment of Road Conditions
WILK, R., Sculpting

Faculty of Mechanical Engineering:

BERCZYŃSKI, S., Machine Technology
BES, T., Heat Technology
GRONOWICZ, J., Vehicle Maintenance
GRUDZIŃSKI, K., Mechanics, Mechanics of Contact
HONCZARENKO, J., Bases of Constructing Machine Tools
IGLANTOWICZ, T., Tool Engineering, Machine Dynamics
MARCHELEK, K., Machining Processes
MYSŁOWSKI, J., Construction and Operating Machines
NOWAK, W., Thermodynamics
OLSZAK, W., Machining Processes
PIECH, T., Construction and Operating Machines
SOBAŃSKI, R., Thermodynamics
SZWENGIER, G., Machine Construction, Engineering Machines
WIERZCHOLSKI, K., Dynamics of Machine Tools, Applied Mechanics, Theory of Compression and Fluid Mechanics

WITEK, A., Vibration Insulation of Machines
WYSIECKI, M., Material Engineering, Copper Alloys
ŻMIJEWSKI, W., Cutting Tools

Faculty of Chemical Engineering:

ANTOSZCZYSZYN, M., Organic Technology
ARABCZYK, W., Inorganic Technology, Technology of Catalysts and Catalytic Processes
BŁĘDZKI, A., Polymer Technology
CHUDZIKIEWICZ, R., Foundry Engineering
GRECH, E., Physical Organic Chemistry
JAGODZIŃSKI, T., Organic Chemistry
KAŁUCKI, K., Inorganic Technology and Catalysis
KARCZ, J., Mixing of Liquids in Single and Multiphase Systems
KRÓLIKOWSKI, W., Polymer Technology and Engineering
MACHOY, Z., Biochemistry
MASIUK, S., Chemical Engineering
MILCHERT, E., Organic Technology
MORAWSKI, A., Technology of Water and Atmosphere Protection, Catalytic Processes
MYSZKOWSKI, J., Organic Technology
PADEREWSKI, M., Chemical Engineering
SPYCHAJ, T., Chemistry and Polymer Technology
STRASZKO, J., Physical-chemical Bases of Reactor Processes
STRĘK, F., Chemical Engineering
SZAFKO, J., Physical Chemistry of Polymers
TRZESZCZYŃSKI, J., Environmental Protection, Organic Technology
WALCZAK, J., Inorganic Chemistry
WASĄG, T., Inorganic Chemistry, Analytical Chemistry
WOJCIKIEWICZ, H., Chemical Fibres Engineering

Faculty of Electrical Engineering:

AFONIN, A., Electric Machines
BAŃKA, ST., Automation
BRYKALSKI, A., Electrical Engineering
DACA, W., Industrial Automation, Systems of Digital Temperature Control
EMIRSAJŁOW, Z., Control and Systems Theory
GAMAJUNOW, A., Electronics
GAWRYLCZYK, K., Electromagnetic Field Theory
KUBISA, S., Electrical Metrology and Electrotechnology
LIPIŃSKI, W., Theoretical Electrical Engineering
MIKOSZA, H., Electronics
PAŁKA, R., Methods of Analysis and Synthesis of Electromagnetic Fields
PURCZYŃSKI, J., Theoretical Electrotechnics
SIDIELNIKOW, B., Electric Machines
SIKORA, R., Theoretical Electrotechnics
SKOCZOWSKI, S., Automatics
WOŁOŻIN, A., Macromolecular Chemistry
ŻUCHOWSKI, A., Automatics

Faculty of Maritime Technology:

BILECKI, W., Parallel Computing and Distributed Systems
BINIEK, Z., Informatics, Cybernetics
BUDZIŃSKI, R., Computer Systems for Executives
DZIEWANOWSKI, H., Marine Engineering
FOMICZEW, W., Computer Programming
HANN, M., Mechanics, Construction and Operating Machines
HIEN, T. D., Computational Mechanics
JASTRZĘBSKI, T., Ship Construction and Design
KRAWIEC, B., Information Science in Local Administration and Agriculture
KUCHARIEW, G., Computer Engineering
METSCHKOW, B., Ship Design
MOISIEJEW, W., Optimization
MURSAJEW, A., Architecture of Computer Systems
NIEBYLSKI, W., Naval Metrology
PASZOTA, Z., Mechanical Hydrostatic Power Transmission
PIEGAT, A., Artificial Intelligence, Fuzzy and Neuro-Fuzzy Systems in Modelling and Control
POPOW, O., Real Time Systems, Control Theory
SIEMIONOW, J., Shipbuilding and Ship Design, Systems Engineering
SKRZYMOWSKI, E., Shipbuilding Technology
SOŁDEK, J., Ship Automation Systems
SZMERKO, W., Computers, Computer Systems and Networks
WEYNA, S., Vibro-acoustic Analysis, Sound Intensity Techniques, Noise and Vibration, Noise Control
WILIŃSKI, A., Real Time Systems, Underwater Robotics
ŻMUDZKI, S., Engines

Interfaculty Institutes:

Economics and Management:

SUCH, J., Philosophy, Philosophy of Science
SUŁKOWSKI, C., Investment

Mathematics

WĘGRZYNOWSKI, S., Differential Geometry

Musical Education Section:

SZYROCKI, J., Music, Choir Conducting

Physics:

GOUSKOS, N., Solid-State Physics
KRUK, I., Biophysics
KURIATA, J., Microwave and Radio Frequency Spectroscopy of Solids
MALINOWSKI, L., Thermodynamics and Heat Transfer
REWAJ, T., Solid State Physics
WABIA, M., Opto-electronics

POLITECHNIKA WARSZAWSKA
(Warsaw University of Technology)

00-661 Warsaw, Pl. Politechniki 1
Telephone: (22) 660-72-11
Fax: (22) 621-68-92

Founded 1826
State control
Academic year: October to June

Rector: Prof. Dr hab. Inż. JERZY WOŹNICKI
Vice-Rectors: Prof. Dr Inż. STANISŁAW BOLKOWSKI, Prof. Dr hab. Inż. JACEK KUBISSA, Prof. Dr hab. Inż. KRZYSZTOF KURZYDŁOWSKI, Prof. Dr hab. Inż. MIROSŁAW MOJSKI, Prof. Dr hab. Inż. WŁADYSŁAW WŁOSIŃSKI
Registrar: Mgr Inż. MAREK LEPA
Librarian: Mgr ELŻBIETA DUDZIŃSKA

Library: see Libraries
Number of teachers: 2,653
Number of students: 19,213

Publication: *Prace naukowe — Politechnika Warszawska* (Scientific Works — Warsaw University of Technology).

DEANS

Faculty of Architecture: Prof. Dr hab. STEFAN WRONA
Faculty of Chemistry: Prof. Dr hab. ZBIGNIEW FLORJAŃCZYK
Faculty of Civil Engineering: Prof. Dr hab. TADEUSZ ŻÓŁTOWSKI
Faculty of Electrical Engineering: Prof. Dr hab. JACEK CZAJEWSKI
Faculty of Electronics and Information Technology: Prof. Dr hab. KRZYSZTOF MALINOWSKI
Faculty of Mechatronics: Prof. Dr hab. EUGENIUSZ RATAJCZYK
Faculty of Geodesy and Cartography: Prof. Dr hab. PIOTR SKŁODOWSKI
Faculty of Production Engineering: Prof. Dr hab. BOGDAN NOWICKI
Faculty of Applied Physics and Mathematics: Prof. Dr hab. STANISŁAW JANECZKO
Faculty of Power and Aeronautical Engineering: Prof. Dr hab. TADEUSZ RYCHTER
Faculty of Environmental Engineering: Prof. Dr hab. STANISŁAW MAŃKOWSKI
Faculty of Automobiles and Heavy Machinery Engineering: Prof. Dr hab. WŁODZIMIERZ KURNIK
Faculty of Chemical and Process Engineering: Doc. Dr hab. ROMAN GAWROŃSKI
Faculty of Materials Science and Engineering: Prof. Dr hab. TADEUSZ WIERZCHOŃ
Faculty of Transport: Prof. Dr hab. JERZY LESZCZYŃSKI
Faculty of Civil Engineering and Agricultural Machines: Prof. Dr hab. WOJCIECH WŁODARCZYK
Centre for Social Sciences: Dr TADEUSZ ZEMBRZUSKI

PROFESSORS

Faculty of Architecture:

BENEDEK, W., Housing Design and Public Utilities
CHMIELEWSKI, J. M., Urban Design and Town Planning
DĄBROWSKI, H., Hand Drawing and Fine Arts
GINTOWT, M., Industrial and Sport Buildings
GRUSZECKI, A., Conservation of Monuments, History of Architecture
HANDZELEWICZ-WACŁAWEK, M., Public Utilities
HRYNIAK, Z., Urban Design and Town Planning
KŁOSIEWICZ, L., Contemporary Architecture
PAWŁOWSKI, Z., Building Structures
SKIBNIEWSKA, H., Housing Design
SZPARKOWSKI, Z., Industrial Buildings
TOBOLCZYK, S., Public Utilities
TOMASZEWSKI, A., Conservation of Monuments, History of Architecture
WRONA, S., Computer-Aided Architectural Design
ZARĘBSKA, T., History of Towns and Architecture

Faculty of Chemistry:

FLORJAŃCZYK, Z., Organic Chemistry, Polymer Science
GRZYWA, E., General Chemistry
JASIOBĘDZKI, W., Organic Chemistry
JOŃCZYK, A., Organic Chemistry and Technology
KASIURA, K., Inorganic and Analytical Chemistry
KIJEŃSKI, J., Organic Chemistry, Catalysis
KURAN, W., Chemistry and Organic Technology
MAKARUK, L., Organic Chemistry, Polymer Science
MĄKOSZA, M., Organic Chemistry and Technology
PASYNKIEWICZ, S., Organometallic Chemistry, Catalysis
PROŃ, A., Polymer Science, Solid State Technology
PRZYŁUSKI, J., Solid State Technology
RUDNICKI, R., Inorganic Chemistry
STAROWIEYSKI, K., Organometallic Chemistry
SZYMAŃSKI, A., Mineralogy, Ceramics

Faculty of Civil Engineering:

ABRAMOWICZ, M., Reinforced Concrete Structures
CHRABCZYŃSKI, G., Building Production and Prefabrication
CIESZYŃSKI, K., Technology and Organization of the Production of Prefabricated Materials
CZERSKI, Z., Precast and Prestressed Structures
CZUDEK, H., Construction of Bridges
GOMULIŃSKI, A., Structural Mechanics
GRABOWSKI, Z. T., Soil Mechanics and Foundation Engineering
KARCZEWSKI, J., Metal Constructions, Spatial Structures

NAGÓRSKI, R., Structural Mechanics
OBRĘBSKI, J., Structural Mechanics
RADOMSKI, W., Bridge Engineering
RAKOWSKI, G., Structural Mechanics
REIPERT, Z., Structural Mechanics
SIECZKOWSKI, J., General Building
STACHURSKI, W., Building Construction
SUCHORZEWSKI, W., Construction of Roads, Streets and Bridges
SZYMAŃSKI, E., Technology of Building Materials
WOJEWÓDZKI, W., Theory of Elasticity and Plasticity

Faculty of Electrical Engineering:

BĄK, J., Lighting Technology
BEŁDOWSKI, T., Power Systems and Electrical Networks
BOLKOWSKI, S., Circuit Theory and Electromagnetic Fields
CELIŃSKI, Z., Nuclear Technology
CIOK, Z., High-voltage Technology
DMOWSKI, A., Industrial Electronics
FLISOWSKI, Z., High-voltage Technology
HERING, M., Electro-heating Technology
JAWORSKI, J., Electrical Measurements
KACZOREK, T., System Control
KAŹMIERKOWSKI, M., Industrial Electronics
KŁOS, A., Electrical Networks and Power Systems
KOCZARA, N., Electrical Drives
KOZIEJ, E., Electrical Machines
KUJSZCZYK, S., Power Systems and Electrical Networks
KWIATKOWSKI, W., Electrical Measurements
MACHOWSKI, J., Power Systems and Electrical Networks
MAKSYMIUK, J., Electrical Apparatus
MATUSIAK, T., Electric Traction
MIKOŁAJUK, K., Circuit Theory and Electromagnetic Fields
OSOWSKI, S., Neural Methods
ROGUSKI, A., High-voltage Technology
SOCHOCKI, R., Automated Electrical Micromachines
STABROWSKI, M., Applied Computer Science, Electrical Measurements
TRZASKA, Z., Circuit Theory and Electromagnetic Fields
TUNIA, H. J., Power Electronics and Electric Drives
WASILUK, W., Industrial Power Systems

Faculty of Electronics and Information Technology:

BARANOWSKI, J., Fast-pulse Electronics Circuitry
BRDYŚ, M., Control Science and Robotics
DĄBROWSKI, M., Digital Communication Networks and Systems
DOBROWOLSKI, J., Computer-aided Design of Microwave Circuits
EBERT, J., High-power Radiotechnology
FILIPKOWSKI, A., Analogue Integrated Circuits
FINDEISEN, W., Automatic Control
FIOK, A., Radioelectronic Measurements
GALWAS, B., Microwave Electronics
GOSIEWSKI, A., Control Theory
HELSZTYŃSKI, J., Electronic and Optoelectronic Measurements
HOLEJKO, K., Telecommunications and Optoelectronics
JACHOWICZ, R., Measurement Systems and Sensors
JAKUBOWSKI, A., Microelectronics, Metal-oxide-semiconductor Devices
KUDREWICZ, J., Theory of Electronic Systems
ŁADZIŃSKI, R., Theory of Dynamic Systems
ŁUBA, T., Digital Systems Design
LUBACZ, J., Network Management
MAJEWSKI, A., Optical Fibre Technology
MAJEWSKI, W., Teletransmission, Theory of Logical Systems
MALINOWSKI, K., Automatic Control and Robotics
MODELSKI, J., Microwaves, Satellite and Cable Television
MORAWSKI, T., Microwave Technology
OSIOWSKI, J., Circuit Theory
PAWLAK, Z., Computer Science
PAWŁOWSKI, Z., Medical and Nuclear Electronics
PIĄTKOWSKI, A., Nuclear Electronics
RUSZCZYŃSKI, A., Optimization Methods
RYDEL, M., Telecommunications, Digital Signal Transmission, Line Codes and Theory of Coded Signals
ŚWIT, A., Semiconductor Devices Theory, Measurements and Technology
TRACZYK, W., Digital Automata
WIERZBICKI, A., Optimization and Decision Theory
WOLIŃSKI, W., Quantum Electronics
ZABRODZKI, J., Computer Science, Computer Graphics

Faculty of Mechatronics:

JANKOWSKI, J., Industrial Measurement
JÓŹWICKI, R., Applied Optics, Optical Instruments Engineering
KACPERSKI, T., Fundamentals of Machine Construction
LEŚKIEWICZ, H., Automatic Control
MRUGALSKI, Z., Precision Instrument Design
OLEKSIUK, T., Precision Instrument Design
PAŁKO, T., Biomedical Engineering
PATORSKI, K., Applied Optics, Design of Optical Instruments
RATAJCZYK, E., Measuring Apparatus

Faculty of Geodesy and Cartography:

ADAMCZEWSKI, Z., Theory of Adjustment, Geodetic Computation
BARLIK, M., Dynamic Geodesy, Gravimetry
BIAŁOUSZ, S., Soil Mapping and Remote Sensing, Geographical Information Systems
CZARNECKI, K., Geodesy
CZICHON, H., Technology of Printing
MAKOWSKI, A., Cartography
MARTUSEWICZ, J., Surveying for Tunnelling
PRÓSZYŃSKI, W., Engineering Surveying
ROGOWSKI, J., Geodetic Astronomy, Satellite Geodesy
SKŁODOWSKI, P., Soil Science
SKÓRCZYŃSKI, A., Surveying, Theory of Adjustment
ŚLEDZIŃSKI, J., Satellite Geodesy
WILKOWSKI, W., Rural Land Management
ZĄBEK, Z., Dynamic Geodesy, Gravimetry

Faculty of Production Engineering:

BEDNARSKI, T., Metal-forming Processes
BOSSAK, M., Computational Mechanics, Computer-aided Design
DWORCZYK, M., Engineering Development Management
ERBEL, S., Metal-forming Equipment and Processes
GASPARSKI, W., Methodology Design
GRUDZEWSKI, W., Organization and Management
HEJDUK, J., Organization and Management
KOCAŃDA, A., Metal-forming
KOZAK, J., Production Engineering
LIS, S., Organization and Management in Machine Industry
ŁĄCZYŃSKI, B., Plastic Processing
NOWICKI, B., Production Engineering
SZAFARCZYK, M., Machine Tools Control and Drive
SZENAJCH, W., Mechanical Engineering, Automatic Control of Industrial Processes
WILCZYŃSKI, A., Mechanical Engineering
WŁOSIŃSKI, W., Materials Technology
WROTNY, L. T., Fundamentals of Machine Tool Design

Faculty of Applied Physics and Mathematics:

BORZYMOWSKI, A., Mathematics
JAKUBOWSKI, W., Solid-state Physics
KOCIŃSKI, J., Ferromagnetism
KUJAWSKI, A., Optics
MĄCZYŃSKI, M., Mathematics
MUSZYŃSKI, J., Mathematics
PLUCIŃSKA, A., Probability
PRZEDMOJSKI, J., Solid-state Physics
ROMANOWSKA, A., Mathematics
SŁOWIŃSKI, B., Nuclear Physics
STRUGALSKI, Z., Nuclear Physics
SUKIENNICKI, A., Physics of Magnetism
TRACZYK, T., Mathematics
TRYKOZKO, R., Solid-state Physics
WIŚNIEWSKI, R., High-pressure Physics
WOLSKA-BOCHENEK, J., Mathematics
ZEKANOWSKI, Z., Mathematics

Faculty of Power and Aeronautical Engineering:

BORKOWSKI, A., Automation, Artificial Intelligence
BRODOWICZ, K., Chemical Engineering
DIETRICH, M., Mechanical Engineering, Biomedical Engineering
DOMAŃSKI, R., Heat Transfer, Thermodynamics
GOGÓŁ, W., Heat Transfer
GUTOWSKI, R., Theoretical Mechanics and Applied Mathematics
JACKOWSKI, K., Hydraulic Machines and Pumps
JAWORSKI, Strength of Materials
KĘDZIOR, K., Modelling of Human Movement, Systems Dynamics, Robotics and Biomechanics
LEWITOWICZ, J., Aircraft Maintenance, Aerospace Engineering
MARYNIAK, J., Flight Mechanics
MILLER, A., Gas and Steam Turbines
MORECKI, A., Automation and Robotics
OLĘDZKI, A., Theory of Machines and Mechanisms
RYCHTER, T., Internal Combustion Engines, Combustion
STUPNICKI, J., Fundamentals of Machine Construction
STYCZEK, A., Mathematical Methods of Fluid Mechanics
SZUMOWSKI, A., Fluid Mechanics, Gas Dynamics, Aerodynamic Noise Control
WOLAŃSKI, P., Combustion, Aero Engines
ŻOCHOWSKI, M., Strength of Materials

Faculty of Environmental Engineering:

JĘDRZEJEWSKA-ŚCIBAK, T., Indoor Air Quality, Ventilation and Air Conditioning
KAŃSKA, Z., Environmental Engineering, Environmental Biology
MAŃKOWSKI, S., Heat Engineering
NAWALANY, M., Environmental Engineering, Groundwater Protection
OSIADACZ, A., Gas Engineering
OZGA-ZIELIŃSKA, M., Hydrology
PISARCZYK, S., Environmental Engineering, Building Engineering, Geotechnology
ROMAN, M., Water Supply and Sewerage Systems, Sanitary and Environmental Engineering

Faculty of Automobiles and Heavy Machinery Engineering:

BERNHARDT, M., Internal Combustion Engines
BIAŁAS, S., Geometrical Accuracy in Machinery Design, Tolerance Technology
JAŚKIEWICZ, Z., Theory and Design of Automotive Vehicles
MADEJ, J., Mechanics of Rail Vehicles
OSIŃSKI, J., Dynamics of Mechanical Systems
OSIŃSKI, Z., Applied Mechanics
SOBOCIŃSKI, R., Applied Thermodynamics, Car Engines
SZUMANOWSKI, A., Electromechanical Propulsion Systems, Energy Storage, Hybrid and Electric Vehicles
TYLIKOWSKI, A., Dynamics of Mechanical Systems, Mechatronics
TYRO, G., Earth-moving Machines
WICHER, J., Mechanics, Dynamics of Mechanical Systems

Wójcik, Z., Manfacturing of Gears
Wróbel, J., Theory of Machine Design

Faculty of Chemical and Process Engineering:

Biń, A. K., Process Kinetics, Environmental Protection Processes
Gradoń, L., Chemical Engineering, Aerosol Mechanics
Marcinkowski, R., Process Dynamics, Systems Engineering
Pohorecki, R., Chemical Reactor Engineering, Bioprocess Engineering
Sieniutycz, S., Process Thermodynamics, Nonequilibrium Thermodynamics
Urbanek, A., Chemical Engineering
Wolny, A., Chemical Engineering
Wroński, S., Process Kinetics, Separation Processes

Faculty of Materials Science and Engineering:

Grabski, M. W., Physics of Plastic Strain, Processes in Metal Alloys
Karpiński, T., Materials Engineering
Kurzydłowski, K. J., Materials Characterization and Modelling
Matyja, H., Materials Science
Sokołowska, A., Physical Chemistry, Nonmetallic Materials
Szummer, A., Materials Engineering
Wierzchoń, T., Surface Engineering
Wojciechowski, S., Materials Science and Engineering
Wyrzykowski, J. W., Materials Science and Engineering

Faculty of Transport:

Bajon, W., Investigation and Optimization of the Technical Means of Transport
Basiewicz, T., Infrastructure of Transport
Borgoń, J., Traffic Control
Chodkowski, A., Maintenance and Operation of Vehicles
Dąbrowa-Bajon, M., Traffic Control
Kisilowski, J., Dynamics and Diagnostics of Mechanical Systems
Leszczyński, J., Organization and Technology of Transport
Smalko, Z., Maintenance and Operation of Vehicles

Faculty of Civil Engineering and Agricultural Machines:

Bukowski, A., Technology of Plastics
Dwiliński, L., Construction and Reliability of Agricultural Machinery
Kajdas, Cz., Technology and Processing of Petroleum and its Products, Tribopolymerization
Pysiak, J., Physical Solid-state Chemistry
Różycki, C., Trace Analysis, Chemometrics
Urbaniec, K., Food Industry Machinery
Włodarczyk, W., Building Constructions
Wolski, L., Physics of Buildings, Sanitary Systems

Centre for Social Sciences:

Białoń-Soczińska, L., Economics of Industry, Economics of Science
Marciniak, S., Economics of Innovation, Macroeconomics
Müller, A., Macroeconomics
Obrębski, T., Economics, Labour Economics, Industrial Relations

POLITECHNIKA WROCŁAWSKA
(Wrocław University of Technology)

50-370 Wrocław, Wybrzeże Wyspiańskiego 27
Telephone: (71) 320-22-77
Fax: (71) 22-36-64

Founded 1945
State control
Language of instruction: Polish
Academic year: October to June

Rector: Prof. Andrzej Mulak
Vice-Rectors: Prof. Jerzy Zdanowski, Prof. Lucjan Jacak, Dr Ludomir Jankowski
Chief Administrative Officer: Mgr Inż. Andrzej Kaczkowski
Librarian: Dr Henryk Szarski

Library: see Libraries
Number of teachers: 2,051
Number of students: 20,176

Publications: *Environmental Protection Engineering* (4 a year), *Optica Applicata* (4 a year), *Studia Geotechnica et Mechanica* (4 a year), *Systems Science* (4 a year), *Badania Operacyjne i Decyzje* (4 a year), *Fizykochem. Problemy Mineralurgii* (1 a year), *Architectus* (2 a year), *Systems* (2 a year), *Pryzmat* (fortnightly), *Semestr* (monthly), *Geometria Wykreślne i Grafika Inżynierska* (4 a year).

DEANS

Faculty of Architecture: Prof. Stanisław Medeksza
Faculty of Basic Problems of Technology: Prof. Ryszard Grząślewicz
Faculty of Civil Engineering: Prof. Ernest Kubica
Faculty of Chemistry: Prof. Henryk Górecki
Faculty of Computer Science and Management: Prof. Jerzy Świątek
Faculty of Electronics: Prof. Romuald Nowicki
Faculty of Electrical Engineering: Prof. Zbigniew Wróblewski
Faculty of Environmental Engineering: Prof. Jerzy Zwoździak
Faculty of Mechanical Engineering: Prof. Jan Koch
Faculty of Mechanical and Power Engineering: Prof. Mieczysław Lech
Faculty of Mining Engineering: Prof. Monika Hardygóra

Higher Institutes

AGRICULTURE

SZKOŁA GŁÓWNA GOSPODARSTWA WIEJSKIEGO W WARSZAWIE
(Warsaw Agricultural University)

02-787 Warsaw, ul. Nowoursynowska 166
Telephone and fax: (22) 843-85-88
E-mail: rector@sggw.waw.pl

Founded 1816
Academic year: October to June

Rector: Prof. hab. Dr W. Kluciński
Pro-Rectors: Prof. Dr hab. Elżbieta Biernacka, Prof. Dr hab. Andrzej Pisula, Prof. Dr hab. Tomasz Borecki
Chief Administration Officer: Dr Władysław Skarżyński
Librarians: Mgr Jerzy Lewandowski, Mgr Krystyna Zdzieszyńska

Library: see Libraries
Teaching staff: 1,070
Number of students: 11,000

Publications: *Annals* (in 8 series), treatises, monographs, dissertations, etc.

DEANS

Faculty of Agriculture: Dr hab. Sławomir Podlaski
Faculty of Veterinary Medicine: Prof. Dr hab. Jerzy Kita
Faculty of Forestry: Prof. Dr hab. Heronim Olenderek
Faculty of Horticulture (and Division of Landscape Architecture): Prof. Dr hab. Stefan Malepszy
Faculty of Land Reclamation and Environmental Engineering: Dr hab. Tomasz Brandyk
Faculty of Wood Technology: Prof. Dr hab. Witold Dzbeński
Faculty of Animal Science: Prof. Dr hab. Tadeusz Żarski
Faculty of Agricultural Economics: Prof. Dr hab. Bogdan Klepacki
Faculty of Food Technology: Prof. Dr hab. Tadeusz Haber
Faculty of Human Nutrition and Home Economics: Prof. Dr hab. Anna Gronowska-Senger
Faculty of Agriculture and Forestry Engineering: Prof. Dr hab. Alojzy Skrobacki

PROFESSORS

Faculty of Agriculture:

Barszczak, T., Agricultural Chemistry
Czerwiński, Z., Soil Science
Gawrońska-Kulesza, A., Soil and Plant Management
Golinowski, W., Botany
Kalinowska-Zdun, M., Crop Production
Kołpak, R., Crop Production
Mercik, S., Agricultural Chemistry
Muszyński, S., Genetics and Plant Breeding, Mutagenesis
Nalborczyk, E., Plant Physiology
Radecki, A., Soil and Land Management
Starck, Z., Plant Physiology

Faculty of Veterinary Medicine:

Barej, W., Animal Physiology
Boryczko, Z., Animal Gynaecology, Animal Reproduction
Borzemska, W., Poultry Diseases
Empel, W., Surgery and Radiology
Frymus, T., Epizootiology
Hartwig, A., Bee Pathology
Kita, J., Infectious Diseases and Epizootiology
Kluciński, W., Physiopathology, Internal Medicine
Kobryńczuk, F., Animal Anatomy
Kulasek, G., Animal Physiology
Malicki, K., Microbiology, Virology, Immunology
Malinowska, A., Animal Biochemistry
Motyl, T., Animal Physiology
Roskosz, T., Animal Anatomy
Sitarska, E., Pathophysiology, Veterinary Laboratory Diagnostics
Szczawiński, J., Hygiene of Food of Animal Origin
Tropiło, J., Hygiene of Food of Animal Origin
Wiechetek, M., Veterinary Pharmacology and Toxicology, Environmental Protection

Faculty of Forestry:

Bernadzki, E., Silviculture
Bruchwald, A., Forest Mensuration and Productivity
Dzięciołowski, R., Ecology, Game Management
Dudzińska, T., Forest Mensuration and Productivity
Gliwicz, J., Ecology, Forest Zoology
Goszczyński, J., Ecology, Game Management
Grzywacz, A., Forest Phytopathology
Klocek, A., Forest Ecology, Forest Economics
Laurow, Z., Logging
Mazur, S., Entomology and Forest Protection
Olenderek, H., GIS in Forestry
Paschalis, P., Forest Resources Utilisation
Szujecki, A., Forest Entomology and Insect Ecology
Wodzicki, T. J., Botany, Tree Physiology
Zajączkowski, S., Tree Physiology

Faculty of Horticulture (and Division of Landscape Architecture):

Bartman, E., Landscape Planning and Design
Chmiel, H., Ornamental Plants
Cichocka, E., Applied Entomology, Aphidology
Dąbrowski, Z. T., Applied Entomology, Resistance of Plants to Pests

GOSIEWSKI, W., Vegetable Crops, Greenhouse Production
IGNATOWICZ, S., Applied Entomology
KARWOWSKA, K., Horticulture, Food Chemistry, Herbs, Flavour and Spice Plants
KROPCZYŃSKA-LINKIEWICZ, D., Applied Entomology
KRYCZYŃSKI, S., Phytopathology
MAJEWSKI, T., Phytopathology, Mycology, Taxonomy
MALEPSZY, S., Plant Genetics, Biotechnology
NIEMIROWICZ-SZCZYTT, K., Plant Genetics and Breeding, Biotechnology
SADOWSKA, A., Medical and Anticancer Plants, Plant Propagation, Environmental Protection
SADOWSKI, A., Pomology
SKĄPSKI, H., Vegetable Crops
SUCHORSKA, K., Medicinal and Spice Plants
ZIMNY, H., Environmental Protection

Faculty of Land Reclamation and Environmental Engineering:

BIERNACKA, E., Soil Science, Environmental Protection
BRUNARSKI, L., Structural Mechanics, Reinforced Concrete Constructions, Non-Destructive Testing
BYCZKOWSKI, A., Hydrological Engineering
DĄBKOWSKI, S., Hydraulics
GRABARCZYK, C., Fluid Mechanics, Hydraulics of Rural Plant Water Supply
MADANY, R., Meteorology and Climatology
PAWŁAT, H., Natural Bases of Environmental Engineering
SKWARCZYŃSKI, M., Mathematical Analysis
SOKOŁOWSKI, J., Technology of Land Reclamation
SOMOROWSKI, C., Land Reclamation
WOLSKI, W., Soil Mechanics and Foundation Engineering, Hydraulic Structures

Faculty of Wood Technology:

DZBEŃSKI, W., Wood Materials Engineering, Sawmilling
GOS, B., Wood Materials Engineering
KOCOŃ, J., Physics
MATEJAK, M., Drying of Wood
ONIŚKO, W., Technology of Wood Composites
SZUKALSKI, J., Automation in the Wood Industry
WAŻNY, J., Wood Protection

Faculty of Animal Science:

CHACHUŁOWA, J., Non-Ruminant Nutrition
KOŚLA, T. Z., Animal Hygiene
KRYŃSKI, A., Animal Hygiene
KULISIEWICZ, J., Animal Breeding
NIŻNIKOWSKI, R., Animal Breeding
ROKICKI, E., Animal Hygiene
SULGOSTOWSKA, T., Parasitology
SWIERCZEWSKA, E., Animal Breeding
WOJDA, R., Ichthyobiology and Fishery
ŻARSKI, T., Animal Hygiene

Faculty of Agricultural Economics:

ADAMOWICZ, M., Agricultural Economics
ADAMOWSKI, Z., Agricultural Economics
BUD-GUSAIM, J., Agricultural Economics
FARKOWSKI, C., Agricultural Economics and Marketing
GÓRECKI, J., Worldwide Agriculture
KLEPACKI, B., Farm Economics and Organization
KOSICKI, J. M., Farm Economics and Organization
LEWANDOWSKI, J., Farm Economics and Organization
MANIECKI, F., Farm Economics and Organization
PRZYCHODZEŃ, Z., Agricultural Pedagogics
RUNOWSKI, H., Farm Economics and Organization
WIATRAK, A., Agricultural Economics
WIECZOREK, T., Agricultural Pedagogics, History of Education
WOJTASZEK, Z., Farm Economics and Organization
ZIĘTARA, W., Farm Economics and Organization

Faculty of Food Technology:

DRZAZGA, B., Fruit and Vegetable Technology and Food Analysis
HABER, T. A., Technology of Cereals
JARCZYK, A., Fruit and Vegetable Technology and Freezing of Foods
KLEPACKA, M., Food Chemistry
LENART, A., Food Technology
LEWICKI, P., Food Technology
MOLSKA, L., Microbiology of Dairy Products
MROCZEK, J., Poultry and Meat Technology
PISULA, A., Meat Technology
SOBCZAK, E., Technology of Industrial Fermentation and Technical Microbiology
WZOREK, W., Wine, Juice and Beer Technology
ZMARLICKI, S., Milk Technology

Faculty of Human Nutrition and Home Economics:

GRONOWSKA-ŞENGER, A., Human Nutrition
GRZESZCZAK-ŚWIETLIKOWSKA, U., Animal Nutrition
KELLER, J. S., Physiology of Nutrition
NERYNG, A., Human Nutrition
PAŁASZEWSKA-REINDL, T., Home Economics
ROSZKOWSKI, W., Human Nutrition
ŚWIDERSKI, F., Human Nutrition
ZALEWSKI, S., Human Nutrition

Faculty of Agricultural and Forestry Engineering:

PABIS, J., Drying of Agricultural Products. Horticultural Mechanization
SKROBACKI, A., Farm Machinery and Equipment
WASZKIEWICZ, CZ., Farm Machinery
WIĘSIK, J., Forestry Engineering
ZDUN, K., Mechanization of Animal Production

Akademia Rolnicza im. Augusta Cieszkowskiego (August Cieszkowski Agricultural University): 60-637 Poznań, ul. Wojska Polskiego 28; tel. (61) 847-03-34; fax (61) 848-71-46; f. 1951; faculties of horticulture, agronomy, animal breeding and biology, forestry, wood technology, food technology, land reclamation and environmental engineering; 782 teachers, 9,016 students; library of 641,000 vols; Rector Prof. Dr JERZY PUDEŁKO; publs *Annals* and other irregular works.

Akademia Rolnicza im. Hugona Kołłątaja w Krakowie (Hugo Kołłątaj Agricultural University in Cracow): 31-121 Cracow, al. Mickiewicza 21; tel. (12) 633-13-36; fax (12) 633-62-45; e-mail rector@ar.krakow.pl; f. 1890; faculties of agriculture, food technology, animal breeding and biology, environmental engineering and geodesy, forestry, horticulture, engineering and energetics in agriculture, economics; 907 teachers, inc. 74 professors; 9,900 students; library of 569,000 vols; Rector Prof. Dr KAZIMIERZ KOSINIAK-KAMYSZ; publs *Zeszyty Naukowe* (Scientific Papers—series), *World Agriculture*.

Akademia Rolnicza w Lublinie (University of Agriculture in Lublin): 20-033 Lublin, ul. Akademicka 13; tel. and fax (81) 533-35-49; telex 064 3176; f. 1955; faculties of veterinary science, agriculture, animal husbandry, agricultural engineering, horticulture; 640 staff, 6,000 students; library of 336,000 vols; Rector Prof. Dr hab. MARIAN WESOŁOWSKI; publs *Annales UMCS, Sectio DD Medicina Veterinaria, Sectio E Agricultura, Sectio EE Zootechnica, Sectio EEE Horticulture, Excerpta Veterinaria Lublin* (in English).

Akademia Rolniczo-Techniczna w Olsztynie im. Michała Oczapowskiego (University of Agriculture and Technology in Olsztyn): 10-957 Olsztyn, Kortowo; tel. (89) 527-33-10; fax (89) 527-39-08; e-mail stesmo@moskit.art.olsztyn.pl; f. 1950; faculties of agriculture, animal husbandry, food technology, veterinary medicine, geodesy and regional planning, mechanics, civil engineering, water protection and inland fisheries, management, biology; 8,340 students; library of 500,000 vols, 969 current periodicals; Rector Prof. Dr STEFAN SMOCZYŃSKI; publs *Acta* (irregular, in Polish, with Russian and English summaries).

Akademia Rolnicza w Szczecinie (Szczecin Agricultural University): 71-424 Szczecin, ul. Janosika 8; tel. 22-35-15; fax 423-24-17; f. 1954; faculties of agriculture, animal science, marine fisheries and food technology, economics and organization of food economy; 385 teachers, 6,257 students; library of 264,000 vols; Rector Prof. Dr ARKADIUSZ KAWĘCKI; publs *Acta Ichthyologica et Piscatoria* (in English), *Advances in Agricultural Sciences* (in English), *Zeszyty Naukowe* (Scientific Papers, in Polish, with English summary), *Rozprawy* (Treatises, in Polish, with English summary).

Akademia Rolnicza we Wrocławiu (Academy of Agriculture in Wrocław): 50-375 Wrocław, Norwida 25; tel. 20-51-01; f. 1951; faculties of agriculture, veterinary science, animal husbandry, land reclamation and improvement, food technology; divisions of agricultural mechanization, agricultural building, land surveying; 700 staff, 2,770 resident students, 430 non-resident; library of 180,000 vols; Rector Prof. Dr JERZY KOWALSKI; publ. *Zeszyty Naukowe*.

Akademia Techniczno-Rolnicza im. J. J. Śniadeckich w Bydgoszczy (University of Technology and Agriculture in Bydgoszcz): 85-225 Bydgoszcz, ul. Kordeckiego 20; tel. (52) 73-14-50; telex 562292; fax (52) 73-03-70; f. 1951; agriculture, animal husbandry, civil engineering, electronics and telecommunication, chemical technology and engineering, environmental engineering, management and marketing, mechanics and machine construction, technical physics; library of 146,000 vols, 455 periodicals; 582 teachers, 6,837 students; Rector Prof. JANUSZ SEMPRUCH; publ. *Zeszyty Naukowe* (irregular, Polish, with Russian and English summaries).

ECONOMICS, SOCIAL SCIENCES

Akademia Ekonomiczna w Krakowie (University of Economics in Cracow): 31-510 Cracow, Rakowicka 27; tel. (12) 616-74-20; fax (12) 421-05-36; e-mail akademia@ae.krakow.pl; f. 1925; faculties of economics, management and commodity science; library of 430,000 vols, 1,577 periodicals; 750 teachers; 17,681 students; Rector Prof. Dr hab. TADEUSZ GRABIŃSKI; publ. *Zeszyty Naukowe* (Scientific Papers).

Akademia Ekonomiczna im. Karola Adamieckiego w Katowicach (Karol Adamiecki University of Economics in Katowice): 40-287 Katowice, 1 Maja 50; tel. and fax (32) 59-99-72; e-mail wojtyla@ae.katowice.pl; f. 1937; faculties of management and economics; 446 teachers, 9,784 students; library of 330,000 vols; Rector Prof. JAN WOJTYŁA; publ. *Studia Ekonomiczne* (Economic Studies, irregular).

Akademia Ekonomiczna w Poznaniu (University of Economics in Poznań): 60-967 Poznań, al. Niepodległości 10; tel. (61) 869-92-61; fax (61) 866-89-24; f. 1926; faculties of management, economics and commodity science; 496 teachers; 13,600 students; library of 373,000 vols; Rector Prof. Dr EMIL PANEK; publs *Zeszyty Naukowe Seria I, Zeszyty Naukowe Seria II–Prace habilitacyjne, Podręczniki*.

Akademia Ekonomiczna im. Oskara Langego we Wrocławiu (O. Lange University of Economics in Wrocław): 53-345 Wrocław, Komandorska 118/120; tel. (71) 68-01-00; fax (71) 67-27-78; f. 1947; faculties: industrial engineering and economics, national economy, computer science and management, regional economy and tourism; branch in Jelenia Góra; 5,974 full-time students, 7,273 external and postgraduate students; library of 350,000 vols; Rector Prof. Dr hab. ANDRZEJ BABORSKI; publ. *Prace Naukowe Akademii Ekonomicznej im O. Langego we Wrocławiu*.

Szkoła Główna Handlowa (Warsaw School of Economics): 02-554 Warsaw, Al. Niepodległości 162; tel. (22) 48-50-61; telex 816031; fax (22) 49-53-12; f. 1906; faculties of economics, public administration, quantitative methods and information systems, finance and banking, international economics and political relations, management and marketing; 800 staff, 13,200 (internal and external) students; library: see Libraries; Rector Prof. JANINA JÓŹWIAK; publ. *Poland: International Economic Report* (1 a year).

MEDICINE

Akademia Medyczna w Białymstoku (Medical Academy of Białystok): 15-230 Białystok, Ul. Kilińskiego 1; tel. (85) 42-17-05; fax (85) 42-49-07; f. 1950; medical faculty and division of stomatology; faculty of pharmacy; 653 staff, 2,200 students; library of 200,000 vols; Rector Prof. Dr hab. JAN GÓRSKI; publ. *Roczniki Akademii Medycznej w Białymstoku* (Annals, in English).

Akademia Medyczna im. Ludwika Rydygiera w Bydgoszczy (Ludwik Rydygier Medical University in Bydgoszcz): 85-067 Bydgoszcz, ul. Jagiellońska 13; tel. (52) 22-98-48; fax (52) 22-62-29; f. 1984; 400 teachers; 1,140 students; library of 64,000 vols, 16,000 periodicals; Rector Prof. Dr JAN DOMANIEWSKI; publ. *Annales*.

Akademia Medyczna w Gdańsku (Medical University of Gdańsk): 80-210 Gdańsk, ul. Marii Skłodowskiej-Curie 3a; tel. (58) 341-92-69; telex 0512997; fax (58) 301-61-15; f. 1945; faculties of medicine, stomatology and pharmacy; 912 staff, 2,407 students; library of 551,000 vols; Rector Prof. Dr ZDZISŁAW WAJDA; publ. *Annales Academiae Medicae Gedanensis* (annually).

Akademia Medyczna w Lublinie (Medical University in Lublin): 20-059 Lublin, ul. Aleje Racławickie 1; tel. (81) 532-00-61; fax (81) 532-89-03; e-mail eskulap@am.lublin.pl; f. 1950; faculties of medicine, pharmacy and nursing; 1,180 teachers; 3,535 students; library of 250,000 vols; Rector Prof. Dr hab. ZDZISŁAW KLEINROK.

Akademia Medyczna w Łodzi (Medical University of Łódź): 90-419 Łódź, Al. Kościuszki 4; tel. 32-21-13; fax 32-23-47; f. 1945; faculty of medicine (Dean Prof. ANDRZEJ JOSS) with sub-faculty of stomatology, and faculty of pharmaceutics (Dean Prof. Dr RYSZARD WIERZBICKI) with sub-faculty of medical analysis; library of 277,000 vols; 989 staff, 2,544 students; Rector Prof. HENRYK STĘPIEŃ; publ. *Annales Academiae Medicae Lodziensis* (irregular).

Akademia Medyczna im. Karola Marcinkowskiego w Poznaniu (K. Marcinkowski University of Medical Sciences in Poznań): 61-701 Poznań, ul. Fredry 10; tel. (61) 852-11-61; fax (61) 852-04-55; f. as University faculty 1920, as Academy 1950; faculties of medicine, pharmacy, health sciences (with nursing, physiotherapy, public health); sections of stomatology, clinical analysis; library of 287,000 vols; 3,630 students; Rector Prof. Dr JANUSZ GADZINOWSKI; publs *Annual* (with supplements), *Annual Medical News*.

Akademia Medyczna w Warszawie (Medical University of Warsaw): 02-032 Warsaw, Filtrowa 30; tel. (22) 825-19-04; fax (22) 825-73-00; f. 1789; faculties of medicine, dentistry and pharmacy; 1,185 teachers, 3,200 students; library of 400,000 vols; Rector Prof. Dr ANDRZEJ GÓRSKI; publ. *Medycyna-dydaktyka-wychowanie* (Medicine-Didactics-Education, quarterly).

Akademia Medyczna we Wrocławiu (Medical Academy in Wrocław): 50-367 Wrocław, ul. Pasteura 1; tel. (71) 22-18-91; fax (71) 21-57-29; f. 1950; faculties of medicine, dentistry, nursing and pharmacy, postgraduate training; 1,644 staff, 2,657 students; library of 130,000 books, 61,000 papers; Rector Prof. Dr hab. med. JERZY CZERNIK; publ. *Postępy medycyny klinicznej i doświadczalnej* (quarterly).

Centrum Medyczne Kształcenia Podyplomowego (Medical Centre for Postgraduate Education): 01-813 Warsaw, ul. Marymoncka 99; tel. (22) 834-68-47; fax (22) 834-04-70; f. 1970; faculties of basic sciences, clinical medicine, stomatology, pharmacy, family medicine; school of public health and social medicine; library of 46,000 vols; Dir Prof. Dr hab. med. JAN DOROSZEWSKI..

Collegium Medicum Uniwersytetu Jagiellońskiego (Jagiellonian University, Medical College): 31-008 Cracow, ul. Św. Anny 12; tel. (12) 422-04-11; fax (12) 422-25-78; e-mail mabertma@cyf-kr.edu.pl; f. 1364; faculties of medicine (with dental sub-faculty), pharmacy (with medical analysis), health care; Deputy Rector Prof. Dr STANISŁAW KONTUREK; 1,962 staff, 2,599 students; library of 210,000 vols; publs *Annales Collegii Medici Universitatis Jagiellonicae Cracoviensis* (annually), *The Methodical Review* (annually).

Pomorska Akademia Medyczna w Szczecinie (Pomeranian Medical Academy in Szczecin): 70-204 Szczecin, ul. Rybacka 1; tel. 336-303; f. 1948; 551 staff, 1,375 students; Rector Prof. Dr hab. KRZYSTOF MARLICZ; publ. *Annales Academiae Medicae Stetinensis*.

Śląska Akademia Medyczna w Katowicach (Silesian Medical University in Katowice): 40-952 Katowice, ul. Poniatowskiego 15; tel. 51-20-01; fax 51-50-46; e-mail rektor@infomed.slam.katowice.pl; f. 1948; medical, dental, pharmaceutical and nursing faculties; research in medicine and medical analysis, with special interest in cardiology, cardiac surgery, nephrology, gastroenterology, pulmonary diseases, environmental and occupational medicine; 3,666 students; library: see Libraries; Rector Prof. Dr hab. ZBIGNIEW RELIGA; publs *Annales* (annually), *Annales Societatis Doctrinae Studentium* (irregular).

TECHNOLOGY AND ENGINEERING

Politechnika Koszalińska (Technical University of Koszalin): 75-620 Koszalin, ul. Racławicka 15–17; tel. (94) 342-78-81; fax (94) 42-59-63; f. 1968; faculties of mechanical engineering, civil and environmental engineering, electronics, and management and marketing; English college; library of 95,000 vols; 446 teachers, 10,100 students; Rector Prof. Dr hab. WOJCIECH KACALAK; publs *Zeszyty Naukowe* (Research Review), *Monografie*, *Skrypty*.

Politechnika Opolska (Technical University of Opole): 45-233 Opole, ul. Stanisława Mikołajczyka 5; tel. (77) 556-041; telex 733876; fax (77) 556-080; f. 1966; faculties of civil engineering, electrical engineering and automatic control, mechanical engineering, computer engineering, environmental engineering, management and business administration, physical education and sport; 350 teachers; 5,000 students; library of 370,000 vols; Rector JÓZEF SUCHY; publs *Zeszyty Naukowe*, *Studia i Monografie*, *Skrypty*.

Politechnika Radomska im. Kazimierza Pułaskiego (K. Pułaski Technical University in Radom): 26-600 Radom, ul. Malczewskiego 29; tel. and fax (48) 362-63-33; f. 1950; faculties of mechanical engineering, transport, materials science and footwear production technology, economics, teacher training; 556 teachers; library of 135,000 vols, 63,000 in special collections; Rector Prof. Dr hab. WIESŁAW WASILEWSKI; publ. *Prace Naukowe* (5 series, 3 or 4 of each a year).

Politechnika Zielonogórska (Technical University of Zielona Góra): 65-246 Zielona Góra, ul. Podgórna 50; tel. (68) 325-48-31; telex 0432215; fax (68) 324-55-97; f. 1965; building, mechanical, electrical and environmental engineering departments; 7,510 students; library of 110,000 vols; Rector Prof. Dr hab. MICHAŁ KISIELEWICZ; publs *Zeszyty Naukowe, Discussiones Mathematicae, Applied Mathematics and Computer Science, Manufacturing Management, Applied Mechanics and Engineering*.

Wyższa Szkoła Morska w Gdyni (Gdynia Maritime Academy): 81-225 Gdynia, ul. Morska 83; tel. (58) 620-75-12; fax (58) 620-67-01; f. 1920; mechanics, navigation, management and marketing, electrical engineering; library of 84,000 vols, 7,000 in special collections; Rector Prof. PIOTR PRZYBYŁOWSKI; publs *Zeszyty Naukowe, Scientific Journal, Joint Proceedings*.

Wyższa Szkoła Morska w Szczecinie (Maritime University Szczecin): 70-500 Szczecin, Wały Chrobrego 1; tel. (91) 34-42-26; telex 0422585; fax (91) 33-81-23; f. 1969; faculties of navigation and marine engineering; 200 staff, 1,871 students; library of 93,000 vols; Rector Prof. Dr Capt. STANISŁAW GUCMA; publ. *Zeszyty Naukowe* (quarterly).

THEOLOGY

Akademia Teologii Katolickiej (Catholic Theological Academy): 01-815 Warsaw, ul. Dewajtis 5; tel. 395221; fax 395245; f. 1954; 330 staff, 7,000 students; library of 123,000 vols; Rector Prof. Dr ROMAN BARTNICKI; Dean of Theology Prof. Dr R. MURAWSKI, of Philosophy Prof. Dr A. STRZAŁECKI, of Canon Law Prof. Dr W. GÓRALSKI, of History and Social Sciences Prof. Dr H. SKOROWSKI; publs *Studia Theologica Varsoviensia* (2 a year), *Studia Philosophiae Christianae* (2 a year), *Jus Matrimoniale* (2 a year), *Kroniki ATK* (2 a year), *Maqom* (2 a year), *Saeculum Christianum* (2 a year), *Studia o Rodzinie* (2 a year), *Prawo Kanoniczne* (quarterly), *Collectanea Theologica* (quarterly).

Chrześcijańska Akademia Teologiczna (Christian Theological Academy): 00-246 Warsaw, ul. Miodowa 21; tel. and fax 31-95-97; f. 1954; 49 teachers, 550 students; library of 55,000 vols; Rector Bishop Prof. Dr hab. JEREMIASZ JAN ANCHIMIUK; publ. *Rocznik Teologiczny* (2 a year).

Schools of Art and Music

Akademia Muzyczna im. Feliksa Nowowiejskiego w Bydgoszczy (F. Nowowiejski Academy of Music in Bydgoszcz): 85-008 Bydgoszcz, ul. Słowackiego 7; tel. 21-11-42; fax 21-17-54; f. 1979; Rector Doc. FRANCISZEK WOŹNIAK.

Akademia Muzyczna im. Stanisława Moniuszki w Gdańsku (Stanisław Moniuszko Academy of Music in Gdańsk): 80-847 Gdańsk, ul. Łagiewniki 3; tel. 301-77-15; fax 301-43-65; f. 1947; faculties of composition and theory, music performance, music education; 164 teachers, 444 students; library of 77,000 vols; Rector Prof. WALDEMAR WOJTAL; publs *Rocznik Informacyjny, Zeszyty Naukowe, Prace Specjalne, Kultura Muzyczna Północynch Ziem Polski, Muzyka Pomorza*.

Akademia Muzyczna im. Karola Szymanowskiego w Katowicach (Academy of Music in Katowice): 40-025 Katowice, ul. Zacisze 3; tel. (32) 255-40-17; fax (32) 256-44-85; f. 1929; faculties of composition, theory and conducting, instrumental music, vocal music and theatrical art, music teaching, jazz and popular music; 116 teaching staff, 465 students; library of 100,000 vols; special collection: music in Silesia; Rector Prof. JULIAN GEMBALSKI.

Akademia Muzyczna w Krakowie (Academy of Music in Cracow): 31-038 Cracow, ul. Starowiślna 3; tel. (12) 422-32-50; fax (12) 422-23-43; f. 1888; faculties of composition, theory and conducting; instrumental performance; vocal technique; teacher training and choir conducting; also postgraduate studies; library of 35,000 vols; Principal Prof. MAREK STACHOWSKI.

Akademia Muzyczna w Łodzi (Academy of Music in Łódź): 90-716 Łódź, Gdańska 32; tel. (42) 33-92-39; fax (42) 33-79-36; e-mail rektorat@sp.amuz.lodz.pl; f. 1945; composition, theory, eurhythmics, music education; instrumental and vocal technique, performance; 208 teachers, 444 students; library of 32,000 scores, 8,000 vols, 6,000 records and CDs, 300 periodicals; Rector Prof. BOGDAN DOWLASZ.

Akademia Muzyczna im. Ignacego Jana Paderewskiego w Poznaniu (Academy of Music in Poznań): 61-808 Poznań, ul. Sw. Marcin 87; tel. 53-67-55; fax 53-66-76; f. 1920; faculties of composition, theory, conducting, instrumental technique, vocal technique, music teaching; Rector Prof. MIECZYSŁAW KOCZOROWSKI.

Akademia Muzyczna im. Fryderyka Chopina w Warszawie (Frederick Chopin Academy of Music in Warsaw): 00-368 Warsaw, ul. Okólnik 2; tel. (22) 827-72-41; fax (22) 827-83-10; f. 1810; 7 faculties: composition, conducting and theory of music, keyboard instruments, orchestral instruments, vocal performance, general music education, sound engineering; teacher training; 257 teachers; library of 20,000 books and 71,000 scores; Rector Prof. ANDRZEJ CHOROSIŃSKI; publs *Zeszyty Naukowe*, *Prace Biblioteki Głównej*.

Akademia Muzyczna im. Karola Lipińskiego we Wrocławiu (Academy of Music in Wrocław): 50-043 Wrocław, pl. 1-go Maja 2; tel. 55-55-43; fax 55-91-05; f. 1948; departments of composition, conducting, music theory and music therapy, instrumental music, vocal music, music education; 136 teachers, 426 students; library of 52,000 vols; Rector Prof. JERZY MROZIK; publ. *Zeszyty Naukowe* (papers, 2 or 3 a year).

Akademia Sztuk Pięknych im. Jana Matejki w Krakowie (Academy of Fine Arts in Cracow): 31-157 Cracow, pl. Matejki 13; tel. (12) 422-24-50; fax (12) 422-65-66; f. 1818; faculties of painting, sculpture, conservation and restoration of works of art, graphic arts, industrial design, interior design; postgraduate studies in theatre, film and TV stage design; br. in Katowice: graphic arts and industrial design; European poster collection up to 1939; library: see Libraries; 265 teachers, 806 students; Rector Prof. STANISŁAW RODZIŃSKI; publ. *Studia i materiały konserwatorskie*† (1 a year).

Akademia Sztuk Pięknych w Poznaniu (Academy of Fine Arts in Poznan): 60-967 Poznań, Al. Marcinkowskiego 29; tel. (61) 855-25-21; fax (61) 852-23-09; e-mail office@adm.asp.poznan.pl; f. 1919, state-controlled from 1921; faculties of painting, graphics and sculpture, interior architecture and design, art education, multimedia communication; 123 full-time teachers; 560 full-time students; library of 60,000 vols; Rector Prof. WŁODZIMIERZ DRESZER.

Akademia Sztuk Pięknych w Warszawie (Academy of Fine Arts in Warsaw): 00-068 Warsaw, Krakowskie Przedmieście 5; tel. (22) 26-19-72; fax (22) 26-21-14; f. 1904 as Szkoła Sztuk Pięknych (School of Fine Arts), renamed 1927; departments of painting, sculpture, interior design, graphics, industrial design, conservation of works of art; special studies: tapestry, scenography; 850 students; library: see Libraries; Rector Prof. WOJCIECH KURPIK; publs *Rocznik* (annually, in English and Russian), *Zeszyty Naukowe ASP* (Scientific Copy Books ASP).

Akademia Sztuk Pięknych we Wrocławiu (Academy of Fine Arts in Wrocław): 50-156 Wrocław, Plac Polski 3/4; tel. and fax (71) 343-15-58; f. 1946; faculties of painting, sculpture, graphic arts, glass and ceramics design, interior architecture, industrial design; library of 14,000 vols; Rector KONRAD JARODZKI.

Akademia Teatralna im. Al. Zelwerowicza w Warszawie (A. Zelwerowicz Academy of Theatre in Warsaw): 00-246 Warsaw, ul. Miodowa 22/24; tel. (22) 831-02-16; fax 635-74-14; f. 1946; faculties of acting and directing, puppet acting and theatre studies; library of 39,000 vols; Rector Prof. JAN ENGLERT.

Państwowa Wyższa Szkoła Filmowa, Telewizyjna i Teatralna im. Leona Schillera w Łodzi (National School of Film, Television and Theatre in Łódź): 90-323 Łódź, Targowa 61/63; tel. (42) 674-39-43; fax (42) 674-81-39; f. 1948; faculties of film and TV direction, film and TV camera work, acting, production; courses in screen-writing, TV realization; library of 40,000 vols; 120 teachers, 260 students (including 60 extra-mural); Rector Prof. HENRYK KLUBA.

Państwowa Wyższa Szkoła Sztuk Plastycznych w Gdańsku (State Higher School of Fine Arts in Gdańsk): 80-836 Gdańsk, Targ Węglowy 6 (Zbrojownia); tel. 31-28-01; telex 51-22-89; fax 31-22-00; f. 1945; faculties of painting and graphics, sculpture, architecture and industrial design; 130 teachers, 387 students; library of 10,450 vols; Rector Prof. STANISŁAW RADWAŃSKI.

Państwowa Wyższa Szkoła Sztuk Plastycznych w Łodzi (Strzemiński Academy of Fine Arts and Design): 91-726 Łódź, Ul. Wojska Polskiego 121; tel. (42) 56-10-56; f. 1945; textile faculty (depts of textile, fashion, hosiery, painting, sculpture, drawing and composition); faculty of graphic art and painting (depts of graphic design, workshop, painting, etc., visual problems); faculty of art education; dept of industrial forms; 232 teachers, 500 students; library of 24,000 vols; Rector Prof. JERZY TRELIŃSKI; Librarian KRYSTYNA LOREK.

Państwowa Wyższa Szkoła Teatralna im. Ludwika Solskiego w Krakowie (State Theatre Academy in Cracow): 31-109 Cracow, ul. Strasewskiego 21–22; tel. (12) 422-81-96; fax (12) 422-02-09; e-mail rektor@pwst.krakow.pl; f. 1945; faculties of acting and stage craft; puppet theatre section (Wrocław); Rector Prof. Dr hab. JACEK POPIEL.

PORTUGAL

Learned Societies

GENERAL

Academia das Ciências de Lisboa (Lisbon Academy of Sciences): Rua da Academia das Ciências 19, 1200 Lisbon; tel. (1) 321-97-30; fax (1) 342-03-95; f. 1779; divisions of Sciences (Sec. Prof. A. J. L. POMBEIRO), Arts (Sec. Prof. JUSTINO MENDES DE ALMEIDA); 60 mems; attached research institutes: see Research Institutes; library: see Libraries and Archives; Pres. Prof. JOSÉ V. DE PINA MARTINS; Sec.-Gen. Prof. JUSTINO MENDES DE ALMEIDA; publs *Memórias*, *Ciências e Letras*.

Sociedade Científica da Universidade Católica Portuguesa (Scientific Society of the Portuguese Catholic University): Universidade Católica Portuguesa, Palma de Cima, 1600 Lisbon; tel. 726-58-17; f. 1980 to further the intellectual, artistic, moral and spiritual forms of a Christian-inspired culture as a means to the fulfilment of man, and to promote research in a perspective of inter-disciplinarity aiming at a synthesis of knowledge; seven sections: philosophy, theology, law, history, social sciences, literature and arts, natural sciences and technology; 200 mems; Pres. Prof. M. J. DE ALMEIDA COSTA; Dir Prof. JOSÉ DA CRUZ POLICARPO.

AGRICULTURE, FISHERIES AND VETERINARY SCIENCE

Sociedade Portuguesa de Ciências Veterinárias (Portuguese Society of Veterinary Science): Rua de D. Dinis 2-A, 1250 Lisbon; tel. 388-01-88; f. 1902; 580 mems; library of 2,860 vols and 43,000 periodicals; Pres. Prof. JOSÉ ROBALO SILVA; Gen. Sec. Prof. CARLOS LOPES VIEIRA MARTINS; publ. *Revista Portuguesa de Ciências Veterinárias* (quarterly).

Affiliated societies:

Sociedade Portuguesa Veterinária de Anatomia Comparativa (Portuguese Veterinary Society of Comparative Anatomy): Av. E.U.A. 96-RC-D, 1700 Lisbon; f. 1974; 47 mems; Pres. Prof. Dr PAULO MARQUES.

Sociedade Portuguesa Veterinária de Estudos Sociológicos (Portuguese Society of Sociological Veterinary Studies): Rua Abel Botelho 24, 3°-Dir., 1500 Lisbon; f. 1965; 39 mems; Pres. Prof. Dr MARIA-ANA MARQUES.

Sociedade Portuguesa de Patologia Animal (Portuguese Society of Animal Pathology): Lisbon; Pres. Prof. MARIA DA CONCEIÇÃO PELETEIRO.

Sociedade Portuguesa de Reprodução Animal (Portuguese Society of Animal Reproduction): Lisbon; Pres. Dr RAMIRO DOUTEL DE MASCARENHAS.

BIBLIOGRAPHY, LIBRARY SCIENCE AND MUSEOLOGY

Associação Portuguesa de Bibliotecários, Arquivistas e Documentalistas (Portuguese Association of Librarians, Archivists and Documentalists): Rua Morais Soares, 43C-1° Dto, 1900 Lisbon; tel. 8154479; fax 8154508; e-mail badbn@mail.telepac.pt; f. 1973; 1,200 mems; Pres. ANTÓNIO PINA FALCÃO; Secs E. A. DOS SANTOS CORDEIRO RODRIGUES, M. F. LEAL CONCEIÇÃO; publs *Cadernos de Biblioteconomia, Arquivística e Documentação, Notícia BAD*.

ECONOMICS, LAW AND POLITICS

Associação Portuguesa de Economistas: Rua da Estrela 8, 1200 Lisbon; tel. 66-15-84; f. 1976; 3,500 mems; Pres. JOSÉ DE ALMEIDA SERRA; Sec.-Gen. GUILHERME VAZ; publs *Economy Directory* (quarterly), *The Economist* (annually).

EDUCATION

Conselho de Reitores das Universidades Portuguesas (Council of Rectors of the Portuguese Universities): Rua Florbela Espanca, 1700 Lisbon; tel. (351-1) 549170; telex 44733; Pres. Prof. ESPERANÇA PINA; Sec. Dr MÁRIO MARCHANTE.

Instituto Açoriano de Cultura (Azorean Institute of Culture): Apdo 67, 9701 Angra do Heroísmo-Codex, Terceira, The Azores; f. 1956; Pres. Dr JORGE A. PAULUS BRUNO; Sec. Dr JOSÉ MENDONÇA BRASIL ÁVILA; publs *Atlântida*, *Atlântida-Médica* (annually), *Insula* (annually).

Instituto Camões (Camões Institute): Cp. Grande 56-6°, 1700 Lisbon; f. 1929 as Junta de Educação Nacional, present name 1992; attached to the Ministry of Foreign Affairs; promotes teaching of Portuguese language and culture abroad; awards grants to foreign students in Portugal; publs works on Portuguese language and culture; 250 mems; library of 4,500 vols; Pres. Prof. Dr LUÍS ADÃO DA FONSECA; publ. *Boletim do Instituto Camões* (monthly in Portuguese, French and English).

Instituto de Coimbra (Coimbra Institute): Rua da Ilha, Coimbra; f. 1851; 150 mems; 13 hon., 156 correspondents in Portugal, 280 foreign corresponding; library of 21,000 vols; Pres. Prof. LUIS GUILHERME MENDONÇA DE ALBUQUERQUE; Sec. ARMANDO CARNEIDA SILVA; publ. *O Instituto* (scientific and literary).

FINE AND PERFORMING ARTS

Academia Nacional de Belas Artes (National Academy of Fine Arts): Largo da Academia Nacional de Belas Artes, Lisbon; f. 1932; library of 25,000 vols, including some 16th-century work; 20 mems; Pres Prof. Arq. AUGUSTO PEREIRA BRANDÃO; Sec. Investigador JOÃO LOUREIRO DE FIGUEIREDO; publs *Inventário Artístico de Portugal*, *Revista-Boletim de Belas Artes*.

Instituto Gregoriano de Lisboa (Lisbon Institute of Gregorian Studies): Av. 5 de Outubro 258, 1600 Lisbon; tel. 7930004; fax 7950415; e-mail igl@mail.telepac.pt; Dir (vacant); publs *Modus*, *Musica Lusitaniae Sacra*.

Sociedade Nacional de Belas Artes (National Society of Fine Arts): Palacio das Belas Artes, Rua Barata Salgueiro 36, 1250 Lisbon; tel. (1) 3138510; fax (1) 3138519; f. 1901; exhibitions of painting, sculpture, drawing, etc.; organises courses in design, painting, drawing, visual education, sociology and history of art; 1,350 associates; library of 5,000 vols; Pres FERNANDO DE AZEVEDO.

HISTORY, GEOGRAPHY AND ARCHAEOLOGY

Academia Portuguesa da História (Portuguese Academy of History): Palácio da Rosa, Largo da Rosa 5, Lisbon; f. 1720; 40 mems, 190 corresp. mems; library of 70,000 vols; Pres. Prof. JOAQUIM VERÍSSIMO SERRÃO; Sec.-Gen. Col HENRIQUE REMA; publs *Anais*, *Boletim*, *Documentos Medievais Portugueses*, *Subsídios para a História Portuguesa*, *Fontes Narrativas da História Portuguesa*, *Itinerários Régios*.

Associação dos Arqueólogos Portugueses (Association of Portuguese Archaeologists): Largo do Carmo, Lisbon; tel. 3460473; f. 1863; 640 mems; library of 10,500 vols; Pres. Dr JOSÉ MORAIS ARNAUD; Sec. Dr JACINTA BUGALHÃO; publ. *Arqueologia e História* (annually).

Centro de Estudos de História e Cartografia Antiga: Rua da Junqueira 30 r/c, 1300 Lisbon; tel. (1) 3622621; fax (1) 3622626; f. 1958; history of Portuguese expansion overseas, African history; library of 9,000 vols, 430 periodicals; Dir MARIA EMÍLIA MADEIRA SANTOS; publs *Studia* (2 a year), *Boletim da Filmoteca Ultramarina Portuguesa* (irregular), *Separatas*, *Memórias* (irregular).

Instituto Histórico da Ilha Terceira (Terceira Historical Institute): Edifício de São Francisco, 9700 Angra do Heroísmo, The Azores; f. 1942; 20 mems; Chair. Dr ÁLVARO MONJARDINO; Sec. Dr FRANCISCO MADURO-DIAS; publ. *Boletim* (annually).

Instituto Português de Arqueologia, História e Etnografia (Portuguese Archaeological, Historical and Ethnographical Institute): Edificio dos Jerónimos, Praça do Imperio, Belém, Lisbon; Pres. (vacant); Sec. Dr JOÃO L. SAAVEDRA MACHADO; publ. *Ethnos*.

Real Instituto Arqueológico de Portugal (Royal Archaeological Institute of Portugal): Praça Rainha D. Filipa 4, 6°, Dto, 1600 Lisbon; tel. 7591109; f. 1868; Pres. Dr JOÃO PAULO CAXARIA; Sec.-Gen. Dr JOSÉ ANTÓNIO FALCÃO; publs *Actas*, *Trabalhos*.

Real Sociedade Arqueológica Lusitana (Royal Lusitanian Archaeological Society): Hospital do Espírito Santo, Praça Conde do Bracial 3, 7540 Santiago do Cacém; tel. 826380; f. 1849; archaeological, historical and ethnological studies; has own museum, archives and library; 50 fellows, 150 mems, 97 corresp. mems; Pres. Dr JOSÉ ANTÓNIO FALCÃO; Gen.-Sec. Dr LÍLIA RIBEIRO DA SILVA TAVARES; publs *Anais*, *Memórias*, *Trabalhos*, *Boletim*, *Repertorium Fontium Studium Artis Historiae Portugaliae Instaurandum*.

Sociedade de Geografia de Lisboa (Lisbon Geographical Society): Rua das Portas de Santo Antão 100, 1150 Lisbon; tel. 342-5401; fax 346-45-53; f. 1875; library of 200,000 vols, 6,000 maps; 1,600 mems; Pres. Adm. ANTONIO EGIDIO SOUSA LEITÃO; Sec.-Gen. NUNO PEDRO DA SILVA; publs *Relatório*, *Boletim* (scientific and literary journal, 2 a year).

Sociedade Martins Sarmento: Rua Paio Galvão, 4810 Guimarães; tel. (53) 415969; fax (53) 415969; f. 1881; archaeology and culture; 542 mems; library of 80,000 vols; publs *Revista de Guimarães* (annually), *Boletim* (quarterly).

LANGUAGE AND LITERATURE

Associação Portuguesa de Escritores: Rua de S. Domingos à Lapa 17, 1200 Lisbon;

f. 1973; protects the interests of Portuguese writers, promotes Portuguese literature abroad, supports cultural activities, conferences, debates, confers several literary prizes, etc; over 600 mems; library of 7,500 vols; Pres. JOSÉ MANUEL MENDES.

Sociedade Portuguesa de Autores: Av. Duque de Loulé 31, 1069 Lisbon Codex; tel. 3578320; fax 3530257; f. 1925; copyright protection and authors' rights; cultural activities; 500 full, 18,000 assoc. mems; library of 20,000 vols; Pres. Dr LUIZ FRANCISCO REBELLO; publ. *Autores* (quarterly).

MEDICINE

Ordem dos Médicos (Medical Association): Av. Almirante Reis 242, 2° Esq., 1000 Lisbon; tel. 80-54-92; telex 42904; f. 1938; 24,851 mems; Pres. MANUEL MACHADO MACEDO; publ. *Revista* (monthly).

Sociedade Anatómica Luso-Hispano-Americana (Portuguese-Spanish-Latin American Anatomical Society): Instituto de Anatomia Humana Normal, Faculdade de Medicina de Lisboa, Av. Egas Moniz, Lisbon 4; f. 1935; Pres. Prof. Dr ARMANDO DOS SANTOS FERREIRA (acting); publ. *Arquivo de Anatomia e Antropologia*.

Sociedade Anatómica Portuguesa (Portuguese Anatomical Society): Lab. de Anatomia Normal, Faculdade de Medicina de Coimbra, 3049 Coimbra Codex; f. 1930; 184 mems; Pres. Prof. Dr ANTÓNIO CARLOS MIGUÉIS.

Sociedade Farmacêutica Lusitana (Portuguese Pharmaceutical Society): Rua Sociedade Farmacêutica 18, Lisbon; tel. 3141424; fax 3524480; f. 1835; 6,600 mems; library of 4,800 vols on botany, medicine, natural history, pharmacy, etc; famous collection of Portuguese pharmacopoeias; unique MS *Historia Pharmaceutica das Plantas Exóticas* by Frei João de Jesus Maria, with permit to print from the Holy Office; Pres. Prof. JOÃO SILVEIRA; publ. *Revista Portuguesa de Farmacia*; affiliated to Fédération Internationale Pharmaceutique; mem. of Associação Portuguesa para o Progresso das Ciências.

NATURAL SCIENCES

General

Serviço de Informação e Documentação (Information and Documentation Service): Av. Prof. Gama Pinto 2, 1699 Lisbon Codex; tel. (1) 7972886; telex 62593; fax 7965622; f. 1936; national centre of scientific and technical information; attached to Fundação para a Ciência e a Tecnologia; 3,000 Portuguese, 5,000 foreign books, 350 periodicals; Dir GABRIELA LOPES DA SILVA.

Biological Sciences

Sociedade Broteriana (Botanical Society): Instituto Botânico, Coimbra Univ., 3049 Coimbra; tel. (39) 22897; fax (39) 20780; e-mail socbrot@ci.uc.pt; f. 1880; 300 mems; library of 122,000 vols; Chair. Prof. JOSÉ F. M. MESQUITA; publs *Anuário, Boletim, Memórias*.

Sociedade Portuguesa de Ciências Naturais (Portuguese Natural Science Society): Faculdade de Ciências, Rua da Escola Politécnica, 1294 Lisbon Codex; f. 1907; 938 mems; library destroyed by fire 1978; publs *Boletim, Naturalia, Natura*.

Mathematical Sciences

Instituto Nacional de Estatística (National Statistical Institute): Ministério do Equipamento, Planeamento e Administração do Território, Av. António José de Almeida, 1000 Lisbon; tel. 842-61-00; fax 842-63-65; f. 1935; 800 mems; library of 14,000 vols, 3,950 periodicals; Pres. Eng. CORREA GAGO; publs numerous statistical works, including *Estatísticas Demográficas, Anuário Estatístico, Boletim Mensal de Estatística, Comércio Internacional, Estatísticas Agricolas, Estatísticas da Produção Industrial Indice de Preços no Consumidor* (monthly), *Estatísticas do Emprego* (4 a year), etc.

Physical Sciences

Sociedade Geológica de Portugal (Geological Soc.): Faculty of Science, Lisbon Univ., Rua Escola Politécnica, 1294 Lisbon Codex; tel. (1) 605850; fax (1) 2957668; f. 1940; 600 mems; library of *c*. 1,000 vols; Pres. Prof. ROGÉRIO ROCHA; Sec. Dra FILOMENA DINIZ; publs *Boletim, Maleo*.

Sociedade Portuguesa de Química (Portuguese Chemical Society): Av. da República 37-4°, 1050 Lisbon; 2,800 mems; Pres. S. FORMOSINHO; publs *Revista Portuguesa de Química* (annually), *Química* (quarterly).

RELIGION, SOCIOLOGY AND ANTHROPOLOGY

Academia Internacional da Cultura Portuguesa (International Academy of Portuguese Culture): Rua das Portas de Santo Antão 110, 1150 Lisbon; f. 1965; seeks to promote research into the culture of Portuguese communities living outside the national territory; 50 mems; Pres. Pe. Dr JOAQUIM A. DE AGUIAR; Sec.-Gen. Prof. Dr ADELINO MALTEZ; publ. *Boletim*.

Sociedade Portuguesa de Antropologia e Etnologia (Portuguese Anthropological and Ethnological Soc.): Faculdade de Ciências, Univ. do Porto, Praça Gomes Teixeira, 4050 Porto; tel. 2084656; f. 1918; 400 mems; library of 10,000 vols; Pres. Prof. VÍTOR OLIVEIRA JORGE; Sec. HENRIQUE G. ARAÚJO; publ. *Trabalhos de Antropologia e Etnologia* (1 vol. annually).

TECHNOLOGY

Ordem dos Engenheiros (Portuguese Association of Engineers): Av. de António Augusto de Aguiar 3-D, 1069 Lisbon Codex; tel. 3562438; fax 352-46-32; e-mail ordeng@mail.telepac.pt; f. 1936; 28,000 mems; library of 23,000 vols, 500 periodical titles; Pres. FRANCISCO SOUSA SOARES; Gen. Sec. JOÃO VAZ LOPES; publ. *Ingenium* (review, monthly).

Sociedade de Estudos Técnicos SARL-SETEC: Rua Joaquin António de Aguiar 73, Lisbon 1; 10,000 mems; Pres. Eng. ARMANDO LENCASTRE; Sec. Eng. JORGE RAMIRO; publ. *Boletim Informativo Nacional* (monthly).

Research Institutes

GENERAL

Instituto de Altos Estudos (Institute of Higher Research): C/o Academia das Ciências de Lisboa, Rua da Academia das Ciências 19, 1200 Lisbon; f. 1931; attached to Lisbon Acad. of Sciences; Pres. Prof. MANUEL JACINTO NUNES.

Instituto de Investigação Científica Tropical (Institute for Tropical Scientific Research): Ministério da Ciência e da Tecnologia, Rua da Junqueira 86, 1300 Lisbon; tel. (1) 364-50-71; telex 66932; fax (1) 363-14-60; f. 1883; documentation and information centre (Rua Jau 47, 1300 Lisbon), and Overseas Historical Archives (Calçada da Boa Hora 30, 1300 Lisbon); garden and museum of tropical agriculture: see Museums and Art Galleries; Pres. Prof. Dr J. A. CRUZ E SILVA; publs *Boletim da Filmoteca Ultramarina Portuguesa, Comunicações do IICT* (series: Agrarian Sciences; Biological Sciences; Ethnological and Ethnomuseological Sciences; Geographical Sciences; Historical, Economic and Sociological Sciences; Earth Sciences), *Estudos de Antropologia Cultural e Social, Estudos de História e Cartografia Antiga, Estudos Ensaios e Documentos, Index Seminum, Leba* (Quaternary, prehistory, archaeology), *Memorias, Revista Internacional de Estudos Africanos, Separatas do Centro de Estudos de História e Cartografia Antiga, Studia*.

Research centres:

Centro de Antropobiologia do Instituto de Investigação Científica Tropical (Anthropobiological Centre): Av. Óscar Monteiro Torres 34–1°, Esqdo, 1000 Lisbon; tel. (1) 7966670; e-mail cantp@.iict.pt; f. 1954; Dir Dra M. E. CASTRO E ALMEIDA.

Centro de Antropologia Cultural e Social do Instituto de Investigação Científica Tropical (Centre for Cultural and Social Anthropology): Av. Ilha da Madeira, a norte do Restelo, 1400 Lisbon; tel. (1) 3012118; e-mail cacst@.iict.pt; f. 1962; Dir Prof. Dr JOÃO PEREIRA NETO.

Centro de Botânica do Instituto de Investigação Científica Tropical (Botanical Centre): Trav. Conde da Ribeira 7–9, 1300 Lisbon; tel. (1) 3645071; fax (1) 3631460; e-mail cbotu@.iict.pt; f. 1948; Dir Prof. Dr I. SANTOS MOREIRA.

Centro de Cartografia do Instituto de Investigação Científica Tropical (Cartographic Centre): Trav. Conde da Ribeira 7–9, 1300 Lisbon; tel. (1) 3645071; fax (1) 3631460; e-mail ccart@.iict.pt; f. 1946; Dir Prof. Eng. ARMANDO SEPÚLVEDA.

Centro de Cristalografia e Mineralogia do Instituto de Investigação Científica Tropical (Centre of Crystallography and Mineralogy): Al. Afonso Henriques 41–4°, Esq., 1000 Lisbon; tel. (1) 8476596; e-mail ccris@.iict.pt; f. 1957; Dir Prof. Dra M. ONDINA FIGUEIREDO.

Centro de Estudos Africanos e Asiáticos do Instituto de Investigação Científica Tropical (Centre for African and Asiatic Studies): Rua da Junqueira 30, 1300 Lisbon; tel. (1) 3622621; fax (1) 3622626; e-mail cestaa@.iict.pt; f. 1983; Dir Prof. Dra JILL R. DIAS.

Centro de Estudos de Fitossanidade do Armazenamento do Instituto de Investigação Científica Tropical (Agricultural Stored Products Research Centre): Trav. Conde da Ribeira 7–9, 1300 Lisbon; tel. (1) 3645071; e-mail cesta@.iict.pt; f. 1955; Dir Prof. Dr ANTÓNIO H. MARQUES MEXIA.

Centro de Estudos de História e Cartografia Antiga do Instituto de Investigação Científica Tropical (History and Early Cartography Research Centre): Rua da Junqueira 30, 1300 Lisbon; tel. (1) 3622621; fax (1) 3622626; e-mail cesth@.iict.pt; f. 1961; Dir Dra M. E. MADEIRA SANTOS.

Centro de Estudos de Pedologia do Instituto de Investigação Científica Tropical (Centre of Pedological Studies): Tapada da Ajuda, 1300 Lisbon; tel. (1) 3638161; e-mail cestp@.iict.pt; f. 1960; Dir Prof. Eng. R. PINTO RICARDO.

Centro de Estudos de Produção e Tecnologia Agrícolas do Instituto de Investigação Científica Tropical (Centre for Agricultural Production and Technology Studies): Sitio do Carrascal, Calçada da Tapada, 1300 Lisbon; tel. (1) 3631072; e-mail cestt@.iict.pt; f. 1960; Dir Prof. Dr R. BRUNO DE SOUSA.

Centro de Estudos de Tecnologia Florestal do Instituto de Investigação Científica Tropical (Centre for Forest Technology Studies): Instituto Superior de Agronomia, Calçada da Tapada, 1300 Lisbon; tel. (1) 3634662; fax (1) 3645000;

e-mail cestf@.iict.pt; f. 1948; Dir Prof. Dra HELENA PEREIRA.

Centro de Fotogrametria do Instituto de Investigação Científica Tropical (Photogrammetric Centre): Rua João de Barros 27, 1300 Lisbon; tel. (1) 3642732; e-mail cfotg@.iict.pt; f. 1983; Dir Prof. ARMANDO SEPÚLVEDA.

Centro de Geodesia do Instituto de Investigação Científica Tropical (Geodetic Centre): Rua da Junqueira 534, 1300 Lisbon; tel. (1) 3631862; fax (1) 3641947; e-mail cgeod@.iict.pt; f. 1983; Dir Eng. J. FRIAS DE BARROS.

Centro de Geografia do Instituto de Investigação Científica Tropical (Geographical Centre): Rua Ricardo Espírito Santo 7, c/v Esq., 1200 Lisbon; tel. (1) 601978; e-mail cgeog@.iict.pt; f. 1983; Dir Prof. Dr ILÍDIO DO AMARAL.

Centro de Geologia do Instituto de Investigação Científica Tropical (Geological Centre): Al. Afonso Henriques 41–4° Dto, 1000 Lisbon; tel. (1) 8476405; e-mail cgeol@.iict.pt; f. 1958; Dir Prof. Dr R. A. QUADRADO.

Centro de Pré-História e Arqueologia do Instituto de Investigação Científica Tropical (Prehistory and Archaeology Centre): Trav. Conde da Ribeira 7–9, 1300 Lisbon; tel. (1) 3645071; fax (1) 3631460; e-mail cphst@.iict.pt; f. 1954; Dir Prof. Dr A. TEODORO DE MATOS.

Centro de Socioeconomia do Instituto de Investigação Científica Tropical (Socio-Economics Centre): Trav. Conde da Ponte 9-1°, 1300 Lisbon; tel. (1) 3635071; fax (1) 3639603; e-mail csocc@.iict.pt; f. 1956; Dir Prof. Dr J. BRAGA DE MACEDO.

Centro de Investigação das Ferrugens do Cafeeiro do Instituto de Investigação Científica Tropical (Coffee Rust Research Centre): Estação Agronómica Nacional, 2780 Oeiras; tel. (1) 4423323; fax (1) 4423023; e-mail cferc@.iict.pt; f. 1955; Dir Dr C. RODRIGUES JÚNIOR.

Centro de Veterinária e Zootecnia do Instituto de Investigação Científica Tropical (Veterinary and Zootechnic Centre): Faculdade de Medicina Veterinária, Rua Gomes Freire, 1199 Lisbon Codex; tel. (1) 3531071; fax (1) 3533088; e-mail cvetz@.iict.pt; f. 1983; Dir Prof. Dr A. MARTINS MENDES.

Centro de Zoologia do Instituto de Investigação Científica Tropical (Zoological Centre): Rua da Junqueira 14, 1300 Lisbon; tel. (1) 3637055; e-mail czool@.iict .pt; f. 1948; Dir Dr J. CRAWFORD-CABRAL.

Centro de Etnologia Ultramarina do Instituto de Investigação Científica Tropical (Centre for Foreign Ethnology): Av. Ilha da Madeira (a norte do Restelo), 1400 Lisbon; tel. (1) 3012118; e-mail ctnolu@ .iict.pt; f. 1962; Dir Prof. Dr JOÃO PEREIRA NETO.

Junta Nacional de Investigação Científica e Tecnológica (National Board for Scientific and Technological Research): Av. D. Carlos I 126-2°, 1200 Lisbon; tel. 397-90-21; telex 12290; fax 60-74-81; f. 1967; attached to the Ministry of Science and Technology; national body responsible for funding, co-ordination and liaison with international organizations in the fields of science and technology; library of 13,584 vols; Pres. Prof. F. RAMÔA RIBEIRO; publs *Agenda de Ciência e Tecnologia* (annually), *ID: Investigação e Desenvolvimento* (monthly), *Relatório de Actividades* (annually), *Informação Bibliográfica* (about science and technology policies, 2 a year).

AGRICULTURE, FISHERIES AND VETERINARY SCIENCE

Estação Agronómica Nacional (National Agronomical Research Station): 2780 Oeiras; tel. 4416855; telex 63698; f. 1937; comprises departments of agronomy, chemistry, entomology, experimental statistics, genetics and plant breeding, pedology, phytopathology, plant physiology, microbiology, systematic botany and plant sociology; library of 172,000 vols; 120 research staff; Dir LUIS C. CARNEIRO; Librarian NAIR SÁ; publs *Agronomia Lusitana*, *Index Seminum*.

Estação Florestal Nacional (Forestry Research Station): Tapada das Necessidades, 1300 Lisbon; tel. 601661; fax (1) 3973163; f. 1919; forestry research unit of the Instituto Nacional de Investigação Agrária; 5 research departments; 178 staff; library of 3,000 vols; Dir Prof. Dr FRANCISCO CASTRO REGO; publ. *Silva Lusitana*.

EDUCATION

Instituto de Inovação Educacional: Travessa Terras de Sant'Ana 15, 1250 Lisbon; tel. 3895100; fax 3895299; f. 1987; educational research, innovation in teaching practice, curriculum development and evaluation, and special education; library of 23,000 vols, 1,500 periodicals; Pres. MARIA EMÍLIA BREDEROLE SANTOS; publs *Inovação* (3 a year), *Noesis* (quarterly).

HISTORY, GEOGRAPHY AND ARCHAEOLOGY

Centro de Estudos do Baixo Alentejo (Centre for Lower Alentejo Studies): c/o Real Sociedade Arqueológica Lusitana, Hospital do Espírito Santo, Praça Conde do Bracial 3, 7540 Santiago do Cacém; tel. 826380; f. 1944; Dir The Pres. of the Royal Lusitanian Archaeological Soc. (*q.v.*); Sec.-Gen. The Gen.-Sec. of the Royal Lusitanian Archaeological Society (*q.v.*).

Centro de Estudos Históricos e Etnológicos (Centre for Historical and Ethnological Studies): Serra do Balas, Areias, 2240 Ferreira do Zêzere; tel. (49) 391408; f. 1983; Pres. Dr JORGE M. RODRIGUES FERREIRA; Sec. ANABELA BENTO; publs *Boletim*, *Série Arqueológica*.

LANGUAGE AND LITERATURE

Instituto de Lexicologia e Lexicografia da Língua Portuguesa: C/o Academia das Ciências de Lisboa, Rua da Academia das Ciências 19, 1200 Lisbon; f. 1987; attached to Lisbon Acad. of Sciences; Pres. Prof. JOÃO MALACA CASTELEIRO.

Instituto Português da Sociedade Científica de Goerres (Portuguese Institute of the Goerres Research Society): C/o Universidade Catolica Portuguesa, Palma de Cima, 1600 Lisbon; tel. 7265554; f. 1962; research in the language and literature of the 16th and 17th centuries in Portugal and Brazil; library of 8,000 vols; publ. *Portugiesische Forschungen*.

MEDICINE

Centro de Estudos de Vectores e Doenças Infecciosas do Instituto Nacional de Saúde (Centre for Research into Vectors and Infectious Diseases of the National Institute of Health): 2965 Águas de Moura; tel. (65) 912222; fax (65) 912155; e-mail cevdi@mail .telepac.pt; f. 1938; study of arboviruses Lyme disease, rickettsias and rickettsioses, rodent-borne diseases and haemorrhagic fevers; library of 3,400 vols; Dir Prof. ARMINDO R. FILIPE.

Serviço de Medicina Nuclear, do Centro de Lisboa do Instituto Português de Oncologia de Francisco Gentil (Nuclear Medicine Department of the Francisco Gentil Portuguese Institute of Oncology): 1093 Lisbon Codex; tel. (1) 7269763; fax (1) 7269763; e-mail mrvnuclear@mail.telepac.pt; f. 1953, reorganized 1983; Dir MARIA DO ROSÁRIO VIEIRA.

NATURAL SCIENCES

General

Instituto de Investigação Científica 'Bento da Rocha Cabral' (Institute of Scientific Research): Calçada de Bento da Rocha Cabral 14, Lisbon; f. 1922; biochemical research, pathology, bacteriology, animal and plant physiology; Dir J. MIRABEAU CRUZ; publs *Travaux de Laboratoire*, *Relatórios*.

Sociedade Afonso Chaves: Rua de Santo André, Apdo 258, 9503 Ponta Delgada (Codex), The Azores; f. 1932; 15 Fellows, 290 mems; main interests of the Society are ethnography, natural history and geology of the Azores; Pres. Prof. A. M. FRIAS MARTINS; Sec. Dr CARLOS MEDEIROS; publ. *Açoreana* (annually).

Biological Sciences

Instituto de Investigação das Pescas e do Mar (Institute of Fisheries and Maritime Research): Av. de Brasília, 1400 Lisbon; tel. (1) 302700; fax (1) 3015948; f. 1978; marine biology, fisheries, aquaculture, marine environment, aquatic products technology; library of 9,500 vols, 900 periodicals; Pres. Dra CARMEN LIMA; publs *Boletim*, *Relatórios Técnicos e Científicos*, *Publicações Avulsas*.

Museu, Laboratório e Jardim Botânico (Museum, Laboratory and Botanical Gardens): Rua da Escola Politécnica, 58-1294 Lisbon Codex; f. 1878; attached to University of Lisbon; vegetation ecology and systematics; library of 18,000 vols; Dir Prof. F. M. CATARINO; publs *Portugaliae Acta Biologica Series A and B*, *Delectus Sporarum et Seminum*, *Revista de Biologia*.

Physical Sciences

Instituto de Meteorologia (Institute of Meteorology): Rua C do Aeroporto, 1700 Lisbon; f. 1946; library of 34,000 vols; Dir JORGE SIMÕES CRISTINA; publs *Anuário Climatológico de Portugal*, *Anuário Sismológico de Portugal* (annually), *Boletim Meteorológico para a Agricultura* (3 a month), *Boletim Geomagnético Prelimar* (monthly), *Projecto 12 do PIDDAC* (monthly), *Observações magnéticas de S. Miguel, Açores* (annually), *Revista do Instituto Nacional de Meteorologia e Geofísica* (quarterly), *Resumos Meteorológicos para a Aeronáutica* (monthly), *Boletim Actinométrico de Portugal* (monthly), *Boletim Informativo* (monthly), *Boletim Meteorológico* (daily), *Boletim do Centro de Física da Atmósfera de Lisboa / Gago Coutinho* (monthly), *Boletim da Estação de Aeronomia de Lisboa* (monthly).

Instituto Geológico e Mineiro (Geological and Mining Institute): Estrada da Portela, Apdo 7586, Zambujal, 2720 Alfragide; tel. (1) 4718922; fax (1) 4719018; f. 1848; library of 100,000 vols; Vice-Pres. MIGUEL MARQUES DE MAGALHÃES RAMALHO; publs *Comunicações*, *Memórias*, *Notícias*, geological maps.

Observatório Astronómico da Faculdade de Ciências de Lisboa (Astronomical Observatory of Faculty of Sciences): Cidade Universitaria, Lisbon; f. 1875 by Escola Politécnica; Repsold meridian, etc.; Dir Prof. Dr ANTONIO GIÃO.

Observatório Astronómico da Universidade de Coimbra (Coimbra Univ. Astronomical Observatory): Almas de Freire, Santa Clara, 3000 Coimbra; tel. (39) 814947; fax (39) 814935; f. 1772; library of 3,500 vols; publs *Efemérides Astronómicas* (annually), *Comunicações*, *Longitudinal Position of Sunspots and Chromospheric Filaments* (monthly).

Observatório Astronómico de Lisboa (Lisbon Astronomical Observatory): Tapada da Ajuda; tel. 3637351; fax 3621722; e-mail mmarques@ola.cc.fc.ul.pt; f. 1861; astrometry, meridian astronomy, time and latitude; Dir MANUEL N. MARQUES; publs *Boletim*, *Dados Astronómicos*.

RELIGION, SOCIOLOGY AND ANTHROPOLOGY

Comissão Nacional de Arte Sacra e do Património Cultural da Igreja (National Committee for Sacred Art and the Cultural Heritage of the Church): Santuário de Fátima, Apdo 31, 2496 Fátima Codex; tel. (49) 533347; fax (49) 533343; f. 1989; research centre; Pres. ANTÓNIO FRANCISCO MARQUES; Gen. Sec. Dr JOSÉ ANTÓNIO FALCÃO.

Instituto de Antropologia (Anthropological Institute): Departamento de Antropologia, Universidade de Coimbra, 3000 Coimbra; tel. (39) 829051; fax (39) 823491; f. 1885; cultural and physical anthropology; library of 42,000 vols, 300 periodicals; Pres. Prof. Dr AUGUSTO ABADE; publ. *Antropologia Portuguesa*.

Instituto Português de Artes e Tradições Populares (Portuguese Institute of Folk Arts and Traditions): Travessa do Passadiço 1, 7540 Santiago do Cacém; tel. 826380; f. 1979; Dir Prof. Dr PERE FERRÉ; Gen. Sec. Dr JOSÉ ANTÓNIO FALCÃO; publs *Biblioteca de Artes e Tradições Populares*, *Novos Inquéritos*.

TECHNOLOGY

Centro Aquicola do Rio Ave (Inland Fisheries Station): 4481 Vila do Conde Codex; tel. (52) 631241; f. 1886; fresh water fisheries and aquaculture; 15 staff; library of 1,000 vols; Dir EUARDO LENCASTRE.

Instituto Geológico e Mineiro (Geological and Mining Institute): Ministério da Economia, Rua Almirante Barroso 38, 1000 Lisbon; tel. 3537596; fax 3537709; f. 1918; mines, quarries, mineral waters, geology, archaeology; Pres. Eng. LUÍS RODRIGUES DA COSTA; publs *Boletim de Minas* (4 a year), *Comunicações do Instituto Geológico e Mineiro*, *Memórias do Instituto Geológico e Mineiro*, *Estudos, Notas e Trabalhos do Instituto Geológico e Mineiro*, maps.

Instituto Geológico e Mineiro: Rua da Amieira, 4465 S. Mamede de Infesta; tel. (2) 951-19-15; fax (2) 951-40-40; f. 1939; mining prospecting and research; 400 mems; library of 74,000 vols; Dir Eng. M. R. MACHADO LEITE; publs *Relatórios, Estudos, Notas e Trabalhos*.

Instituto Hidrográfico (Hydrographic Institute): Rua das Trinas 49, 1296 Lisbon Codex; tel. (1) 395-51-19; telex 65990; fax (1) 396-05-15; f. 1960; hydrographic surveys, physical oceanography, magnetic compass adjustments, laboratory; library of 10,000 vols; Dir-Gen. Vice-Admiral SARMENTO GOUVEIA; publ. *Anais*.

Instituto Nacional de Engenharia e Tecnologia Industrial: Azinhaga dos Lameiros à Estrada do Paço do Lumiar, 1699 Lisbon Codex; tel. (1) 7165181; telex 42486; fax (1) 7160901; f. 1977; attached to Min. of Industry and Energy; research and development in information technology and equipment, advanced materials, biotechnology, chemistry, environmental science and technology, food and feed processing, timber and cork technology, energy (solar, biomass, coal, etc.); technical assistance to industry; centre of technical information for industry; technical training centre; library of 38,000 vols; Pres. Prof. Dr MANUEL BARATA MARQUES; publs Technical Reports, *Revista da Corrosão e Protecção de Materiais* (quarterly).

Laboratório Nacional de Engenharia Civil, Ministério do Equipamento, do Planeamento e da Administração do Território (National Civil Engineering Laboratory, Ministry of Public Works, Planning and Territorial Administration): Av. do Brasil 101, 1799 Lisbon Codex; tel. (1) 848-21-31; telex 16-760; fax (1) 849-76-60; f. 1947; library of 120,000 vols; Dir Prof. E. R. DE ARANTES E OLIVEIRA; publs *Memórias* (technical papers), *Especificações* (standards), etc.

Libraries and Archives

Angra do Heroísmo

Biblioteca Pública e Arquivo de Angra do Heroísmo (Public Library and Archives): Palácio Bettencourt, Rua da Rosa 49, 9700 Angra do Heroísmo, The Azores; tel. 22697; f. 1957; library of 147,000 vols, *c.* 3,500,000 MSS; Dir Lic. MARIANA F. P. J. M. MESQUITA; publs *Boletim da Biblioteca Pública*, *Arquivo Distrital de Angra do Heroísmo*.

Bragança

Arquivo Distrital, Biblioteca e Museu Regional Abade de Baçal (District Archives, Library and Museum of Baçal Abbey): Bragança.

Cascais

Biblioteca 'Condes de Castro Guimarães': Av. Rei Humberto II, 2750 Cascais; tel. 4825402; fax 4836970; f. 1930; library of 35,000 vols; history, art, philosophy, literature, archaeology, local history; Librarian ANTÓNIO MANUEL GONÇALVES DE CARVALHO; publ. *Arquivo de Cascais—Boletim Cultural do Município* (annually).

Coimbra

Arquivo da Universidade de Coimbra (Archives of Coimbra Univ.): The University, Rua de S. Pedro 2, 3000 Coimbra; tel. 859855; fax 820987; f. 1290; Dir Prof. Dr MANUEL AUGUSTO RODRIGUES; publ. *Boletim* (annually).

Biblioteca Municipal (Municipal Library): Coimbra; f. 1922; library of 84,101 vols; Dir PINTO LOUREIRO; Librarian J. BRANQUINHO DE CARVALHO; publ. *Arquivo Coimbrão*.

Universidade de Coimbra: Bibliotecas: General Library: Largo da Porta Férrea, 3049 Coimbra Codex; tel. (39) 4109800; fax (39) 27135; e-mail bguc@ci.uc.pt; f. 1291; library of 800,000 vols, 27,300 periodicals; 7 faculty br. libraries; Dir Prof. ANÍBAL PINTO DE CASTRO; publs *Acta Univ. Conimbrigensis*, *Boletim da Biblioteca da Universidade de Coimbra*, *Revista da Universidade de Coimbra*, *Sumários de Publicações Periódicas Portuguesas*.

Évora

Biblioteca Pública e Arquivo Distrital de Évora (Public Library and District Archives): Évora; tel. 22369; f. 1805; library of 482,429 vols; Dir ISABEL CID.

Funchal

Arquivo Regional da Madeira (Madeira Regional Archives): Palácio de São Pedro, Rua da Mouraria, 9000 Funchal, Madeira; tel. (91) 220961; fax (91) 234272; f. 1931; library of 8,500vols on specialized history; 300,000 MSS; Dir Dr LUIS DE SOUSA MELLO; publ. *Arquivo Histórico da Madeira*.

Biblioteca Municipal do Funchal (Municipal Library): Palácio de São Pedro, Rua da Mouraria, Funchal, Madeira; f. 1838; library of 35,318 vols; Librarian RUI DE ORNELAS GONÇALVES.

Horta

Biblioteca Pública e Arquivo da Horta (Town Library): Rua D. Pedro IV 25, 9900 Horta; tel. 23341; f. 1886; library of 15,000 vols; Librarian JOSÉ E. TEIXEIRA DA ROCHA.

Leiria

Arquivo Distrital de Leiria (District Archives): Rua Marcos Portugal 4, Apdo 1145-2400, Leiria; tel. (44) 820050; fax (44) 820059; f. 1916; 30,000 books, 496 microfilms; Dir ACÁCIO FERNANDO DOS SANTOS LOPES DE SOUSA.

Lisbon

Arquivo Histórico Militar (Military Historical Archives): Largo dos Caminhos de Ferro, 1196 Lisbon Codex; tel. 8882131 ext. 23348; fax 8869080; f. 1921; Dir Tenente-Coronel ANICETO AFONSO; publ. *Boletim*.

Arquivo Histórico Parlamentar (Parliamentary Historical Archives): Palácio de S. Bento, 1296 Lisbon; tel. 660141; telex 13041; Dir Mrs MARIA TERESA LOPES.

Biblioteca Central da Marinha (Naval Library): Praça do Império, 1400 Lisbon; tel. 3620028; fax 3620031; f. 1835; valuable editions; library of 123,000 vols; Dir C/Alm. LUÍS JOEL ALVES DE AZEVEDO PASCOAL.

Biblioteca-Centro de Documentação dos Hospitais Civis de Lisboa (Library and Documentation Service of Lisbon Civic Hospitals): Rua José António Serrano, 1198 Lisbon Codex; tel. 886-01-31; fax 886-46-16; f. 1937; library of 6,000 vols, 1,260 periodicals; Dir TERESA MATIAS.

Biblioteca da Academia das Ciências de Lisboa (Library of the Academy of Sciences): Rua da Academia das Ciências 19, 1200 Lisbon; f. 1779; library of 360,000 vols, 3,000 MSS, 63 incunabula; Dir Prof. Dr JOSÉ V. DE PINA MARTINS.

Biblioteca da Assembleia da República (Library of the Assembly of the Republic): Palácio de S. Bento, 1296 Lisbon Codex; tel. (1) 396-01-41; telex 13041; fax (1) 395-59-45; f. 1836; library of 200,000 vols; special collections: national legislation and old books from the libraries of religious orders; Dir JOSÉ LUÍS M. TOMÉ; publs *Informação Especializada* (monthly), *Informação Europeia* (monthly), *Cadernos de Informação*.

Biblioteca de Ajuda (Ajuda Library): Palácio da Ajuda, Lisbon 3; f. 1756; library of 100,000 vols, 30,000 MSS, 5,000 music MSS, 213 incunabula; Dir Dr MARIANA AMÉLIA MACHADO SANTOS.

Biblioteca do Exército (Army Library): Rua Artilharia 1, Lisbon 2; f. 1837; library of 100,000 vols; Dir Col FRANCISCO DIAS COSTA.

Biblioteca e Arquivo Histórico do Ministério do Equipamento, do Planeamento e da Administração do Território (Library and Historical Archive of the Ministry of Equipment, Planning and Territorial Administration): Avda da Liberdade 193, 1250 Lisbon; tel. (1) 3573719; fax (1) 3573597; f. 1852; library of 13,000 vols, documents dating from the 16th century; 200,000 textual documents on industry, agriculture, forestry, trade, public works, etc.; 1,100 periodicals; Dir Dra MARIA TERESA AZEVEDO MENEZES.

Biblioteca Geral de Arte da Fundação Calouste Gulbenkian: Av. de Berna 45-A, 1067 Lisbon Codex; tel. 7935131; fax 7936015; e-mail artlib@gulbenkian.puug.pt; library of 171,000 vols specializing in art; Dir Dr JOSÉ AFONSO FURTADO.

Biblioteca Municipal Central (Central Municipal Library): Palácio Galveias, Largo do Campo Pequeno, 1000 Lisbon; tel. 7951823; fax 7970689; f. 1931; library of 332,673 vols; Dir MANUELA RÊGO.

Biblioteca Nacional (National Library): Campo Grande 83, 1751 Lisbon Codex; tel. 7950130; fax 7933607; f. 1796; library of 2,040,000 vols, 12,000 MSS; Dir MARIA LEONOR MACHADO DE SOUSA; publs *Boletim de Bibliografia Portuguesa*, *Porbase*, *Revista da Biblioteca Nacional*.

Biblioteca Popular de Lisboa: Rua Ivens 35, and Rua de Academia das Ciências 19, Lisbon; f. 1918; library of 97,774 vols, 835 periodicals; Librarian DURVAL PIRES DE LIMA; Principal Officers CARLOS ALBERTO DE MESQUITA, MARIA TERESA PIRES DE LIMA, JOSÉ PAULO RIBEIRO.

Instituto dos Arquivos Nacionais, Torre do Tombo (National Archives, Torre do Tombo): Alameda da Universidade, 1600 Lisbon; tel. 793-72-12; fax 793-772-30; f. *c.* 1378; collection dates from 9th century; library of 14,458 vols and 40km. of shelves of MSS; Dir Prof. Dr JOSÉ MATTOSO; publs *Inventários das Portarias do Reino e das Moradias da Casa Real*, etc.

Serviço de Biblioteca e Documentação Diplomática (Library and Diplomatic Documentation Service): Palácio das Necessidades, Lisbon; f. 1736; library of 80,000 vols; Dir MARIA HELENA LOPES DE NEVES PINTO.

Mafra

Biblioteca do Palácio Nacional de Mafra (Mafra National Palace Library): Terreiro de D. João V, Mafra; tel. 811888; f. 18th century; library of 40,000 vols; notable collection of rare books; Dir MARIA MARGARIDA MONTENEGRO.

Ponta Delgada

Biblioteca Pública e Arquivo de Ponta Delgada (Public Library and Archives): Rua Ernesto do Canto, 9500 Ponta Delgada, Azores; tel. (96) 22085; fax (96) 281216; e-mail bpapd@mail.telepac.pt; f. 1845; library of 120,000 vols in special collections, 40,000 monographs, 5,000 serials; 3,000 metres of archive material; Dir VALTER M. DE MELO REBELO.

Porto

Arquivo Distrital do Porto (District Archives): Praça da República 38, 4,050 Porto; tel. (2) 2004022; fax (2) 2006436; f. 1931; library of 150,000 vols; Dir HUMBERTO BAQUERO MORENO; publ. *Boletim do Arquivo Distrital do Porto*.

Biblioteca Pública Municipal do Porto (Municipal Library): Jardim de São Lázaro, 4099 Porto Codex; f. 1833; library of 1,325,000 vols, 9,411 MSS, 246 incunabula; Dir LUIS CABRAL; publ. *Bibliotheca Portucalensis*.

Santarém

Biblioteca Municipal de Santarém (Santarém Municipal Library): Santarém; f. 1880; library of 82,000 vols; Librarian Dr LUIS NAZARÉ FERREIRA.

Tôrres Novas

Biblioteca Gustavo Pinto Lopes: Tôrres Novas; f. 1937; library of 31,200 vols; Dir Dr JOÃO CARLOS LOPES.

Vila Real

Biblioteca Pública (Public Library): Vila Real; f. 1834; library of 11,000 vols; Dir AGOSTINHO CELESTINO DA SILVA.

Viseu

Arquivo Distrital (District Archives): Largo Alves Martins, 3500 Viseu; tel. (32) 430380; fax (32) 421800; f. 1932; 450,000 documents; Dir Dr MARIA DULCINEIA CABRAL SENA.

Museums and Art Galleries

Alenquer

Museu Municipal 'Hipólito Cabaço' (Municipal Museum): Rua Milne Carmo, 2580 Alenquer; tel. 73190; f. 1945; archaeological, historical and ethnographical collections; 34,600 exhibits; Dir JOÃO JOSÉ FERNANDES GOMES.

Alpiarça

Casa-Museu dos Patudos: Quinta dos Patudos, 2090 Alpiarça; tel. (43) 559100; fax (43) 55339; f. 1904; fine and applied arts, archaeology, ethnology; library of 40,000 vols incl. historical archive; Curator Dr NUNO SALDANHA; publ. *Boletim*.

Angra do Heroísmo

Museu de Angra do Heroísmo (Regional Museum): Edifício de São Francisco, 9700 Angra do Heroísmo, Ilha Terceira, The Azores; tel. (95) 23147; f. 1949 in a 17th-century Franciscan monastery; paintings, ceramics, furniture, sculpture, ethnography, arms, guns, carriages, etc; Dir Dr JOSÉ OLÍVIO MENDES DA ROCHA.

Bragança

Museu Regional Abade de Baçal (Baçal Abbey Museum): Bragança; Dir Dr MARIA DE LOURDES BARTHOLO.

Cascais

Museu 'Condes de Castro Guimarães': Av. Rei Humberto II de Itália, Cascais; tel. 483-08-56; telex 44996; fax 484-46-64; f. 1930; *Crónica* about the kings of the first dynasty of Duarte Galvão, 16th-century illuminated *Codex* on parchment, 17th-century Indo-Portuguese counting frames, prehistoric ceramics; furniture, silverware; library of 2,826 vols; Curator MARIA JOSÉ REGO DE SOUSA.

Castelo Branco

Museu de Francisco Tavares Proença Júnior: 6000 Castelo Branco; tel. (72) 344277; fax (72) 347880; f. 1910; important archaeological collection of objects found in megalithic tombs at Beira Baixa; Bronze-Age weapons and objects from a complete workshop found at Castelo Novo; illustrations of rupestral art in the Tagus sanctuary; Roman epigraphy; art gallery (16th-century Portuguese School, 16th-century Brussels tapestries); Bishop's Gallery (18th- and 19th-century paintings); ethnographic collections; ceramic collections; regional embroidery workshop; textiles, and oriental and Indo-Portuguese embroidered bedcovers; Dir Dr CLARA VAZ PINTO.

Coimbra

Museu Nacional de 'Machado de Castro' (Machado de Castro National Museum): Largo Dr José Rodrigues, 3000 Coimbra; tel. (39) 823727; fax (39) 822706; f. 1911; established in the old Bishop's Palace built over Roman galleries, renewed in the 16th century and recently adapted; antiquities, sculpture, paintings, silver-work, priests' vestments, tapestries, ceramics, glass, furniture; Dir Dra MARIA JOSE SAMPAIO.

Évora

Museu de Évora: Largo do Conde de Vila Flor, Évora; tel. (66) 22604; fax (66) 28094; f. 1915; paintings: large collections of 16th-century Flemish and Portuguese works; 17th-century works; local prehistoric tools and Roman art and archaeology; sculpture from middle ages to the 19th century; 18th-century Portuguese furniture and silver; Dir ARTUR GOULART.

Faro

Museu Arqueológico Infante D. Henrique (Infante D. Henrique Archaeological Museum): Convento de N.S. da Assuncão, Praça Afonso III, Faro; tel. 22042; f. 1894; historical, archaeological, ethnographical; Dir Prof. PINHEIRO E ROSA; publ. *Anais do Municipio do Faro*.

Museu Marítimo 'Almirante Ramalho Ortigão' (Maritime Museum): Departamento Marítimo do Sul, Faro; f. 1931; formerly Museu Industrial Marítimo; f. 1889; regional methods of fishing, instruments, models of ships and equipments, paintings of marine fauna, sailors' handicrafts; Curator Capt. CARLOS SARAIVA DA COSTA PECORELLI.

Museu S. Antonio (Museum of St Anthony): Ermida de Santo António do Alto, Faro; f. 1933; collections relating to the cult of St Anthony of Lisbon; Founder Dr MARIO LYSTER FRANCO; Dir Prof. PINHEIRO E ROSA.

Figueira da Foz

Museu Municipal 'Dr Santos Rocha' (Municipal Museum): Rua Calouste Gulbenkian, Figueira da Foz; tel. (33) 24509; f. 1894, reopened 1945; art, archaeology, ethnology; library of 14,300 vols; Man. MARIA ISABEL SOUSA PEREIRA.

Funchal

Museu de Arte Sacra (Museum of Sacred Art): Rua do Bispo 21, Funchal, Madeira; diocesan museum.

Museu da Quinta das Cruzes: 9000 Funchal, Madeira; tel. (91) 741382; fax (91) 741384; f. 1946; decorative arts; Dir A. M. ABREU SOUSA.

Museu Municipal do Funchal (Funchal Municipal Museum): 9000 Funchal, Madeira; tel. (91) 229761; fax (91) 225180; e-mail mmf@mail.telepac.pt; f. 1929; Natural History Museum and Marine Aquarium; large collection of marine animals, especially deep-sea fish and crustaceans; library on marine biology; Curator Dr MANUEL JOSÉ BISCOITO; publs *Boletim*, *Bocagiana*.

Guimarães

Museu de Martins Sarmento (Martins Sarmento Museum): Rua de Paio Galvão, Guimarães; f. 1885; archaeological; numerous exhibits relating to Portuguese Celtic, Roman and Visigothic periods; Dir MARIA JOSÉ MEIRELES.

Museu de Alberto Sampaio: Rua Alfredo Guimarães, 4800 Guimarães; tel. (53) 412465; fax (53) 517814; f. 1928; religious painting and sculpture, silversmith's art, priestly garments, ceramics; temporary exhibitions, conservation, cultural activities with schools, local organizations, research on industrial archaeology and anthropology; Dir MANUELA ALCÂNTARA.

Lamego

Museu de Lamego: Lamego; tel. (54) 62008; f. 1917; important collection of 16th-century Brussels tapestries, Portuguese painting of 16th and 18th centuries, sculpture, religious ornaments; Dir Dr AGOSTINHO RIBEIRO.

Lisbon

Centro de Arte Moderna José de Azeredo Perdigão, Fundação Calouste Gulbenkian: Rua Dr Nicolau de Bettencourt, 1093 Lisbon Codex; tel. 7935131; telex 12345; fax 7939294; f. 1979; Portuguese and foreign modern art; documentation and research depts, workshops, outdoor amphitheatre; Dir Dr JORGE MOLDER.

Colecção de Instrumentos Musicais (National Collection of Musical Instruments): Edifício da Biblioteca Nacional, Rua Oc. ao

Campo Grande 83, Lisbon Codex (temporary address); European wind, key and percussion instruments of the 16th to 19th centuries, Portuguese clavichords, harpsichords and 19th-century string instruments, also Asian and Portuguese folk instruments.

Jardim e Museu Agrícola Tropical do Instituto de Investigação Científica Tropical (Garden-Museum of Tropical Agriculture): Calçada do Galvão, 1300 Lisbon; tel. (1) 3620210; e-mail jmust@.iict.pt; f. 1906; Dir Eng. C. M. BUGALHO SEMEDO.

Museu Arqueológico (Archaeological Museum): Largo do Carmo, Lisbon; f. 1863; directed by Associação dos Arqueólogos Portugueses; prehistoric, Roman, Visigothic and medieval collections; sarcophagi, religious sculpture, coins, etc.; Curator (vacant).

Museu Calouste Gulbenkian: Av. Berna, 45A, 1067 Lisbon Codex; tel. (1) 7935131; fax (1) 7955249; f. 1969; Gulbenkian art collection covering the period 2800 BC to 20th century; antique classical and oriental art, Egyptian, Assyrian, Greek, Roman, Islamic and Far Eastern art; European painting, sculpture, illuminated MSS, tapestries and fabrics, furniture, silverware, jewellery, glass, medals; Dir Dr JOÃO CASTEL-BRANCO PEREIRA.

Museu da Cidade (City Museum): Palácio Pimenta, Campo Grande 245, 1700 Lisbon; f. 1942; history of development of Lisbon shown by archaeological, historical, artistic and ethnological documents and exhibits; an 'ensemble' of the 18th-century period and a large model of Lisbon before the earthquake of 1755; Dir ANA CRISTINA LEITE.

Museu de Arte Popular (Museum of Popular Art): Av. Brasília, 1400 Lisbon; tel. (1) 3011282; fax (1) 3011128; f. 1948; folk art, ethnology; Dir ELISABETH CABRAL.

Museu de Artes Decorativas (Museum of Decorative Arts): Fundação Ricardo do Espírito Santo Silva, Largo das Portas do Sol 2, 1100 Lisbon; tel. 886-21-83; fax 887-49-30; f. 1953; includes Ricardo do Espírito Santo Silva's private collection of Portuguese furniture, silver, china, paintings, rugs, tapestries etc., and workshops in which craftsmen are trained in all aspects of traditional interior arts.

Museu de São Roque: Largo Trindade Coelho, 1200 Lisbon; tel. 3235380; fax 3235060; f. 1905; collections of religious paintings, Church vessels in precious metals, embroidered vestments by Italian artists of the 18th century; works from the chapel of St John the Baptist in the adjacent 16th-century Church of St Roque; Curator Dr NUNO VASSALLO E SILVA.

Museu do Chiado (Chiado Museum): Rua Serpa Pinto 4, 1200 Lisbon; tel. (1) 3432148; fax (1) 3432151; f. 1911; painting and sculpture from 1850 to 1960; modern art; library of 5,000 vols; Dir PEDRO LAPA.

Museu Etnográfico da Sociedade de Geografia de Lisboa (Ethnographical Museum): Rua das Portas de Santo Antão 100, 1150 Lisbon; tel. 325401; f. 1875; native arts, arms, clothing, musical instruments from Africa, India, China, Indonesia and Timor, statues of navigators and historians, relics of voyages of discovery, scientific instruments; Dir Prof. Dr JOÃO BAPTISTA PEREIRA NETO.

Museu Militar (Military Museum): Largo do Museu de Artilharia, 1100 Lisbon; f. 1851; exhibits of Portuguese military history, light arms, ancient artillery and other equipment, paintings from the 18th to 20th centuries; Dir Brig. RUI ERNESTO FREIRE LOBO DA COSTA.

Museu Mineralógico e Geológico (Museum of Mineralogy and Geology): Rua da Escola Politécnica 58, 1294 Lisbon Codex; f. 1837; attached to the Universidade de Lisboa; geology, petrology, mineralogy, palaeontology and museology; Curators Prof. GALOPIM DE CARVALHO, Dra FILOMENA DINIZ, Dra LILIANA PÓVOAS, Dr CÉSAR LOPES; publ. *Revista de Geociências*.

Museu Nacional de Arqueologia do Dr Leite de Vasconcelos (National Museum of Archaeology): Praça do Império, 1400 Lisbon; tel. 362-00-00; fax 362-00-16; f. 1893; attached to Inst. Portugues de Museus; library of 25,000 vols; Dir Dr LUÍS RAPOSO; publ. *O Arqueólogo Português*.

Museu Nacional de Arte Antiga (National Museum of Ancient Art): Rua das Janelas Verdes, 1293 Lisbon Codex; tel. 397-27-25; fax 397-37-03; f. 1884; Portuguese and foreign plastic and ornamental art from the 12th to the 19th centuries; library of 36,000 vols; Dir Dr JOSÉ LUÍS PORFÍRIO.

Museu Nacional de História Natural (National Museum of Natural History): Universidade de Lisboa, Rua da Escola Politécnica 56, 1294 Lisbon Codex; tel. (1) 605850; fax (1) 605850; f. 1859; library of 27,000 vols; Dirs Prof. A. M. GALOPIM DE CARVALHO (Mineralogy and Geology), Prof. F. P. M. CATARINO (Botany), Prof. C. S. ALMAÇA (Zoology and Anthropology); publs *Arquivos do Museu Bocage, Portugaliae Acta Biologica, Boletim, Gaia–Revista de Geociências*.

Museu Nacional dos Côches (National Coach Museum): Praça de Afonso Albuquerque, Belém, Lisbon; tel. 3610850; fax 3637246; f. 1905 by Queen Amélia in the Riding School of the Royal Palace; National Museum 1908, enlarged 1944; comprehensive collection of carriages and coaches many by famous craftsmen, dating from 1619 and including those of the Portuguese ex-Royal Family; sedan chairs, harness and equipment, royal liveries, etc., silver trumpets; section of portraits, paintings and engravings; Dir Dra SILVANA BESSONE; publs catalogues.

Museu Numismático Português (Portuguese Numismatic Museum): Imprensa Nacional-Casa da Moeda, Av. Dr A. J. de Almeida, Lisbon; f. 1933; important collections of Portuguese and Colonial, Iberian, Roman and Visigothic coins; also Portuguese and foreign medals; temporarily closed to the public.

Museu Rafael Bordalo Pinheiro: Campo Grande 382, 1700 Lisbon; f. 1916 as a biographical museum; originals and reproductions of famous caricatures, ceramics, satirical documents; Chief Man. ANA CRISTINA LEITE.

Porto

Museu Nacional de Soares dos Reis (National Museum): Palacio dos Carrancas, Rua D. Manuel II, 4000 Porto; tel. 2081956; fax 2082851; f. 1833; paintings, sculpture, jewellery, furniture, pottery, glass; Dir Dra MÓNICA BALDAQUE.

Museu de Etnologia do Porto: Palácio de S. João Novo, 4000 Porto; ethnology, archaeology and history; Dir Arq. FERNANDO LANHAS.

Tôrres Novas

Museu Carlos Reis: Tôrres Novas; f. 1937; archaeological, historical, fine arts, ethnographical, religious art, numismatics; Dir Dr JOÃO CARLOS LOPES.

Vila Viçosa

Museu-Biblioteca da Casa de Bragança (Museum and Library of House of Braganza): Paço Ducal, Vila Viçosa; tel. (68) 98659; f. 1933; tapestry, furniture, tiles, European and Chinese ceramics, portraits of the Royal Family, arms, photographs, coaches and carriages; rare 16th-century printed books, Italian 16th-century majolica, and 17th- and 18th-century musical archives; library of 76,000 vols; Curator MARIA DE JESUS MONGE; Librarian Dr JOÃO LUÍS DA COSTA RUAS.

Viseu

Museu de 'Grão Vasco': Paço dos Tres Escalões, Viseu; tel. (32) 422049; f. 1916; furniture, tapestry, plate, ceramics and glassware, prints and Portuguese paintings; Dir ALBERTO CORREIA.

Universities

UNIVERSIDADE DOS AÇORES

Rua da Mãe de Deus, 9502 Ponta Delgada (Açores) Codex
Telephone: (96) 653029
Telex: 82115
Fax: (96) 653070

Founded 1976, university status 1980
State control
Academic year: October to July

Rector: Prof. Dr ANTÓNIO M. BETTENCOURT MACHADO PIRES
Academic Vice-Rector: Prof. Dr ERMELINDO M. B. PEIXOTO
Vice-Rector: Prof. Dr JOSÉ GUILHERME CAMPOS FERNANDES
Pro-Rectors: Prof. Dr DUARTE JOSÉ BOTELHO DA PONTE (Science and Development), Prof. Dra ROSA MARIA BATISTA GOULART (Cultural Extensions and Publications), Prof. Dra MÁRIA LEONOR PAVÃO S. DE MEDEIROS (Research and Services)
President of Scientific Committee: Prof. Dr MÁRIO JOSÉ AMARAL FORTUNA
Administrator: Dr LUIS SIMAS SOUSA ROCHA
Librarian: Dra MARIA DA GRAÇA CORREIA

Library of 205,000 vols
Number of teachers: 290
Number of students: 1,903

Publications: *Archipélago* (series: human sciences, natural sciences).

DIRECTORS

Department of Agriculture: Prof. Dr JOSÉ GABRIEL ÁLAMO DE MENESES
Department of Biology: Dr JOÃO ANTÓNIO CÂNDIDO TAVARES
Department of Economics and Administration: Prof. Dr FERNANDO R. R. LOPES
Department of Education: Prof. Dr MARIANO TEIXEIRA ALVES
Department of Earth Sciences: Dr VICTOR HUGO LECOR DE LACERDA FORGAZ
Department of History, Philosophy and Social Sciences: Prof. Dr AVELINO DE FREITAS DE MENESES
Department of Literature and Modern Languages: Dr CARLOS MANUEL CRAVO VENTURA
Department of Mathematics: Dra MARIA ISABEL MARQUES RIBEIRO
Department of Oceanography and Fisheries: Dr JOÃO GIL PEREIRA
Department of Technological Sciences: Prof. Dr MÁRIO ALEXANDRE POUSÃO DA COSTA GATA

UNIVERSIDADE DO ALGARVE

Quinta da Penha, 8000 Faro
Telephone: (89) 800100
Fax: (89) 801575

Founded 1979
State control
Language of instruction: Portuguese
Academic year: September to July

Rector: Prof. Dr EUGÉNIO MARIA ALTE DA VEIGA
Administrator: Dra MARIA CÂNDIDA RICO SOARES BARROSO
Librarian: Dra MARGARIDA VARGUES

Number of teachers: 575
Number of students: 7,971

DEANS

Faculty of Agricultural Science and Technology: Prof. Dra MARIA EMILIA LIMA COSTA
Faculty of Aquatic Science and Technology: Prof. Dra MARIA JOÃO BEBIANO
Faculty of Economics and Administration: Prof. Dr JOÃO ALBINO DE MATOS SILVA
Faculty of Exact Sciences and Humanities: Prof. Dr ANTÓNIO EDUARDO DE BARROS RUANO
Higher School of Education: Profa Adjunta MARIA ISABEL SANTANA DA CRUZ
Higher School of Management and Tourism: Prof. LUDGERO SEQUEIRA
Higher School of Technology: Prof. JOSÉ ANTÓNIO SILVESTRE

UNIVERSIDADE AUTÓNOMA DE LISBOA

Rua de Santa Marta 56, 1150 Lisbon
Telephone: (1) 3177600

Founded 1985
Private control

Rector: Prof. Dr JUSTINO MENDES DE ALMEIDA
Registrar: Prof. Dr JORGE TRACANA DE CARVALHO
Librarian: Prof. Dr MIGUEL FARIA

Library of 20,000 vols
Number of teachers: 500
Number of students: 8,700

HEADS OF DEPARTMENTS

History: Prof. Dr A. CARVALHO HOMEM
Law: Prof. Dr F. LUCAS PIRES
Modern Languages and Literature: Prof. Dr ÁLVARO MANUEL MACHADO
Economics: Prof. Dr ARLINDO DONÁRIO
Business Studies: Prof. Dr J. A. ALMAÇA
Applied Mathematics: Profa Dra FERNANDA LENCASTRE BERNARDO
Sociology: Prof. Dr POLICARPO LOPES
Engineering: Prof. Dr JOÃO TRAVASSOS
International Relations: Prof. Dr R. LADEIRO MONTEIRO
Information Sciences: Prof. Dr ANTÓNIO LENCASTRE BERNARDO
Informatics: Prof. CARLOS BILELO GONÇALVES

UNIVERSIDADE DE AVEIRO

3810 Aveiro
Telephone: (34) 370200
Fax: (34) 28600
E-mail: sre@adm.ua.pt

Founded 1973
State control
Academic year: October to July

Rector: Prof. Dr JÚLIO DOMINGOS PEDROSA DA LUZ DE JESUS
Vice-Rectors: Prof. Dr CARLOS ALBERTO DIOGO SOARES BORREGO, Profa Dra MARIA ISABEL LOBO DE ALARCÃO E SILVA TAVARES, Prof. Dr MANUEL ANTÓNIO COTÃO DE ASSUNÇÃO, Prof. Dr JORGE CARVALHO ALVES
Chief Administrative Officer: Dr JORGE BAPTISTA LOPES
Librarian: Dra MARIA EMÍLIA M. FERREIRA ARAÚJO

Number of teachers: 569
Number of students: 8,271

Publications: *Revista* (Series: *Geociências* (2 a year), *Letras, Electrónica e Telecomunicações*), *Net Surfer* (4 a year), *Folha Informativa* (monthly), *Antiguinho* (2 a year).

HEADS OF DEPARTMENTS

Biology: Prof. Dr V. M. DOS SANTOS QUINTINO
Ceramics and Glass Engineering: Prof. Dr J. A. L. BAPTISTA
Chemistry: Prof. Dr F. M. DOMINGUES
Didactics and Educational Technology: Profa Dra I. DA S. C. SÁCHAVES
Educational Sciences: Prof. Dr A. R. DA COSTA
Electronics and Telecommunications: Prof. Dr F. M. S. RAMOS
Environment and Planning: Prof. Dr E. A. CASTRO
Geosciences: Prof. Dr F. T. ROCHA
Languages and Cultures: Prof. Dr J. M. N. TORRÃO
Mathematics: Prof. Dr H. R. MALONEK
Physics: Prof. Dr J. L. PINTO
Management and Industrial Engineering Section: Prof. Dr R. A. G. SANTIAGO
Mechanics Section: Prof. Dr J. J. DE A. GRÁCIO
Civil Engineering Section: Prof. Dr J. C. CARDOSO

UNIVERSIDADE DA BEIRA INTERIOR

Rua Marquês de Ávila e Bolama, 6200 Covilhã
Telephone: (75) 25141
Telex: 53733
Fax: (75) 26198

Founded 1986

Rector: Prof. Dr C.M. PASSOS MORGADO
Administrative Officer: Dr JOSÉ ESTEVES CORREIA PINHEIRO
Librarian: Dr CRISTINA MARIA SEABRA DIAS

Library of 30,100 vols
Number of teachers: 245
Number of students: 3,000

Publication: *Boletim Informativo*.

HEADS OF DEPARTMENTS

Department of Mathematics and Computer Science: Prof. VITOR MANUEL CARVALHO DAS NEVES
Department of Physics: Prof. AVELINO HERMENIGILDO PASSOS MORGADO
Department of Chemistry: Profa MARIA ISABEL ALMEIDA FERRA
Department of Textile Science and Technology: Prof. JOSÉ MENDES LUCAS
Department of Business Administration: Prof. LUIS ANTÓNIO NUNES LOURENÇO
Department of Paper Science and Technology: Prof. MANUEL JOSE DOS SANTOS SILVA
Department of Electromechanical Engineering: Prof. LUIS CARLOS CARRILHO GONÇALVES
Department of Civil Engineering: Prof. GIL ERNESTO S. VASCONCELOS
Department of Sociology and Information and Social Sciences: Prof. JOSÉ CARLOS GASPAR VENÂNCIO
Department of Education: Profa ALICE ROSA FONTINHA FERNANDES DA SILVA

UNIVERSIDADE CATÓLICA PORTUGUESA

Palma de Cima, 1600 Lisbon
Telephone: (1) 7214000
Fax: (1) 7270256

Founded 1968
Private control
Language of instruction: Portuguese
Academic year: September to February; February to July

Chancellor: Patriarch JOSÉ POLICARPO
Rector: Rev. Prof. MANUEL ISIDRO ALVES
Vice-Rectors: Prof. V. XAVIER PINTADO, Prof. P. A. DE SOUSA, Prof. J. E. BORGES DE PINHO
Librarian: (vacant)

Number of teachers: 850
Number of students: 11,000

Publications: *Revista Portuguesa de Filosofia* (4 a year), *Didaskalia* (2 a year), *Theologica* (4 a year), *Economia* (3 a year), *Direito e Justiça* (3 a year), *Máthesis, Gestão e Desenvolvimento, Humanística e Teológica, Lusitania Sacra, Povos e Culturas, Revista Portuguesa de Humanidades*.

DIRECTORS

Faculty of Philosophy: Prof. ALFREDO DINIS
Faculty of Theology: Prof. M. SATURINO GOMES
Faculty of Human Sciences: Prof. J. M. TOSCANO RICO
Faculty of Law: Prof. G. MARQUES DA SILVA
Faculty of Economic and Managerial Sciences: Prof. J. L. BORGES DE ASSUNÇÃO
Faculty of Arts: Prof. MANUEL PULQUÉRIO
College of Biotechnology: FRANCISCO XAVIER MALCATA
College of Science and Technology: SEBASTIÃO F. S. SIMÕES
University Institute for Development and Social Progress: Prof. J. RIBEIRO GOMES
School of Fine Arts: (vacant)
European Studies Institute: ERNÂNI LOPES
Political Studies Institute: JOÃO CARLOS ESPADA
Education Institute: BÁRTOLO PAIVA CAMPOS
Institute for Development, Co-operation and Lifelong Learning: LUÍS VALADARES TAVARES

ATTACHED RESEARCH INSTITUTES

Centre for Applied Studies: Dir JOÃO BORGES DE ASSUNÇÃO.

Centre for Applied Economic and Managerial Studies: Dir ALBERTO CORACEIRO DE CASTRO.

Cardinal Hoeffner Centre for Social and Pastoral Studies: Dir LUÍS MARINHO ANTUNES.

Centre for Religious History: Dir CARLOS MOREIRA DE AZEVEDO.

Centre for Canon Law: Dir MANUEL SATURINO GOMES.

Information Problems Centre: Dir LUÍS VALADARES TAVARES.

Centre for Portuguese-speaking Peoples and Cultures: Dir ROBERTO CARNEIRO.

Centre for Portuguese and Brazilian Literature and Culture: Dir MANUEL DA COSTA FEITAS.

Human Rights Institute: Dir JORGE MIRANDA.

Centre for Opinion Polls: Dir MÁRIO LAGES.

Centre for Studies on Portuguese Thought: Dir ÂNGELO ALVES.

Bio-ethics Centre: Dir WALTER OSSWALD.

International Studies Centre: Exec. Dir NUNO PINHEIRO TORRES.

Centre for Studies on Ethical, Political and Religious Philosophy: Dir MENDO DE CASTRO HENRIQUES.

UNIVERSIDADE DE COIMBRA

Paço das Escolas, 3000 Coimbra
Telephone: (39) 859900
Fax: (39) 825841

Founded 1290 (in Lisbon)
State control
Language of instruction: Portuguese
Academic year: September to July

Rector: Prof. Dr FERNANDO MANUEL DA SILVA REBELO
Vice-Rectors: Prof. Dr JORGE VEIGA, Prof. Dr IRENE NORONHA DA SILVEIRA, Prof. Dr FERNANDO JORGE SEABRA SANTOS
Pro-Rectors: Prof. Dr MA. DE FATIMA SOUSA E SILVA, Prof. Dr LUSITANO MOREIRA MARTINS, Prof. Dr JOSE MANUEL NASCIMENTO COSTA
Registrar: Dr CARLOS JOSÉ LUZIO VAZ
General Library Director: Prof. Dr ANÍBAL PINTO CASTRO
Director of University Archives: Prof. Dr MANUEL AUGUSTO RODRIGUES
Library: see Libraries

Number of teachers: 1,472, including 494 professors
Number of students: 21,165

Publications: *Revista da Universidade*, *Anuário da Universidade*, *Biblos*, *Revista Portuguesa de História*, *Brasilia*, *Humanitas*, *Revista Portuguesa de Filologia*, *Acta Universitatis Conimbrigensis*, *Boletim da Faculdade de Direito*, *Revista de História Literária de Portugal*, *Boletim do Centro de Estudos Geográficos*, *Conimbriga*, *Boletim do Laboratório de Fonética Experimental*, *Revista Portuguesa de Pedagogia*, *Boletim das Ciências Económicas*, *Revista Ciência Biológica*, *Boletim do Arquivo da Universidade*, *Boletim da Biblioteca da Universidade de Coimbra*.

DEANS

Faculty of Arts: Prof. Dr FRANCISCO SÃO JOSÉ OLIVEIRA
Faculty of Law: Prof. Dr ANTÓNIO JOSÉ AVELÃS NUNES
Faculty of Medicine: Prof. Dr FREDERICO JOSÉ TEIXEIRA
Faculty of Science and Technology: Prof. Dr ANTÓNIO MARTIM PORTUGAL
Faculty of Pharmacy: Prof. Dr ADRIANO BARBOSA DE SOUSA
Faculty of Economics: Prof. Dr JOÃO LISBOA
Faculty of Psychology: Prof. Dr ADELINO DUARTE GOMES
Faculty of Sports Science and Physical Education: Prof. Dr FRANCISCO JOSÉ SOBRAL LEAL

ATTACHED INSTITUTES

Instituto Botânico 'Dr Júlio Henriques' (Botanical Institute): Arcos do Jardim, 3049 Coimbra Codex; tel. (39) 22897; f. 1775; library of 114,000 vols; Dir Prof. Dr J. FIRMINO MOREIRA MESQUITA; publs *Index Seminum*, *Boletim*, *Memórias* and *Anuário* of Sociedade Broteriana.

Instituto de Climatologia e Hidrologia (Climatological and Hydrological Institute): Faculdade de Medicina, Universidade de Coimbra, 3000 Coimbra; f. 1930; Pres. Prof. Dr FREDERICO TEIXEIRA; publ. *Publicações do Instituto de Climatologia e Hidrologia*.

Instituto de Estudos Clássicos (Classical Studies Institute): Faculdade de Letras, Universidade de Coimbra, 3049 Coimbra Codex; tel. (39) 4109900; f. 1947; library of 15,000 vols, 500 periodicals; Dir Prof. Dr JOSÉ RIBEIRO FERREIRA.

Instituto Geofísico (Geophysical Institute): Av. Dias da Silva, 3030 Coimbra; f. 1864; library of 16,000 vols; meteorological, magnetic and seismological observatory; Dir Prof. Dr ANTÓNIO FERREIRA SOARES; publs *Observações Meteorológicas, Magnéticas e Sismológicas* (annually).

Instituto de Medicina Legal (Legal Medicine Institute): Largo da Sé Nova, 3000 Coimbra; tel. (39) 23560; f. 1919; library of 5,000 vols, 45 periodicals; Dir Prof. Dr DUARTE NUNO PESSOA VIEIRA.

Centro de Estudos Sociais da Faculdade de Economia da Universidade de Coimbra (Social Studies Centre): Colégio de São Domingos, Largo de Dom Dinis, Apdo 3087, 3000 Coimbra; tel. (39) 26459; Dir Prof. Dr BOAVENTURA SOUSA SANTOS; publ. *Revista Crítica de Ciências Sociais* (quarterly).

Museums: see under Museums.

UNIVERSIDADE DE ÉVORA

Largo dos Colegiais, Apdo 94, 7001 Évora Codex
Telephone: (66) 740800
Telex: 18772
Fax: (66) 744969

Founded 1973, university status 1979
State control
Language of instruction: Portuguese
Academic year: September to September, including summer courses

Rector: JORGE QUINA RIBEIRO DE ARAÚJO
Vice-Rectors: EDUARDO ÁLVARO DO CARMO FIGUEIRA, JOSÉ ANTUNES AFONSO DE ALMEIDA, RUI MANUEL VASSALO NAMORADO ROSA

Number of teachers: 440
Number of students: 6,000

PROFESSORS

ALBUQUERQUE, J. C. D., Farm Mechanization
ALMEIDA, J. A. A., Animal Husbandry
AMARO, J. P. P., Plant Protection
ANDRADE, I. J. E. R., Sociology
ARAÚJO, J. A., Viticulture
ARAÚJO, J. Q. R., Entomology
AZEVEDO, A. L., General Agronomy
BARBOSA, J. M. M. G., Classical Languages
BARRADAS, M. J. T., Plant Breeding
BARRETO, M. S., Linguistics
BELIZ, J. V. M., Ecology
BRAUMANN, C. A. DOS S., Mathematics
BRISON, O. J., Mathematics
CAEIRO, V. M. P., Parasitology
CALAZANS, J., Biochemistry
CARMELO, J. M. P., Physics
DA COSTA, J. S. P., Animal Husbandry
DA SILVA, A., Sociology
DE CARVALHO, E. A. C., Ecology
DE MIRANDA, C. A. F., Chemistry
DE SEQUEIRA, F. M. B. M. L., Mathematics
DE VASCONCELOS, L. DA E. A. R. T., Microbiology
DOS SANTOS, A. G., JR, Hydraulics
FERNANDES, A. M. S., Plant Pathology
FERREIRA, A. A. C. G., Hydraulics
GONÇALVES, F. A., Geology
GUERREIRO, J. C. S., Mathematics
HENRIQUES, F. M. S. F., Botany
HENRIQUES, M. I. E. DA C., Plant Pathology
ÍNDIAS, M. A. C., Physics
JORGE, V. F., Landscape Architecture
LESSA, A. V., Human Ecology
LOPES, R. M. E. J., Economy
LOURENÇO, M. E. V., Crop Science
MORAL, A. S. DO C., Mathematics
MOREIRA, T. J. S., Plant Physiology
MOTA, M. E. G. M., Genetics
NEVES, F. C., Commercial Law
NUNES, A. E. R. F., Animal Husbandry
NUNES, J. F. L. DO R., Apiculture
PATRÍCIO, M. F., Pedagogy
PEÇA, J. M. N. DE O., Applied Mechanics
PINHEIRO, A. C. A., Management Sciences
PORTUGAL, L. A. M. S., Economy
POTES, N. M. V. B., Animal Husbandry
ROSA, R. M. V. N., Physics
SERRANO, J. M. E., Crop Science
SIDARUS, A. Y., Arabic Studies
TELES, G. P. R., Landscape Architecture
VIANA, C. A. N., Chemistry

UNIVERSIDADE DE LISBOA

Alameda da Universidade, 1699 Lisbon Codex
Telephone: 7967624

Founded 1288, restored 1911
State control
Academic year: October to July

Rector: Prof. JOSÉ BARATA-MOURA
Vice-Rectors: Prof. JOSÉ DAVID FERREIRA, Prof. EDUARDO DUCLA SOARES, Prof. MANUEL VILLAVERDE CABRAL
Administrator: Dr MARIA JOSÉ DE FREITAS
Librarian: Dr MARIA LEAL RAMOS VIEIRA

Number of teachers: 1,853
Number of students: 19,917

Publications: *Anuário*, *Guia da Universidade*, etc.

PRESIDENTS OF DIRECTIVE COUNCILS

Faculty of Arts: Prof. MANUEL DO CARMO FERREIRA
Faculty of Law: Prof. Dr JORGE MIRANDA
Faculty of Medicine: Prof. J. MARTINS E SILVA
Faculty of Science: Prof. JOSÉ MANUEL PINTO PAIXÃO
Faculty of Pharmacy: Prof. JOSÉ MORAIS
Faculty of Psychology and Educational Science: Prof. ALBANO ESTRELA
Faculty of Fine Arts: Prof. MARIA JOÃO GAMITO

HEADS OF DEPARTMENTS

Faculty of Arts:

Classical Languages and Literatures: Prof. Dr VICTOR JABOUILLE
Anglo-American Studies: Prof. Dr JOÃO FLOR
German Studies: Prof. Dr RITA R. IRIARTE
Literatures: Prof. CRISTINA ALMEIDA RIBEIRO
Linguistics: Prof. ISABEL HUB FARIA
History: Prof. ANTÓNIO DIAS FARINHA
Geography: Prof. Dr ANA RAMOS PEREIRA
Philosophy: Prof. ADRIANA SERRÃO
Portuguese Language and Culture for Foreign Students: Prof. Dr MALACA CASTELEIRO
Postgraduate Course of Librarianship and Information Sciences: Prof. AIRES DO NASCIMENTO

Faculty of Medicine:

Institutes:

Anatomy: Prof. J. DAVID FERREIRA
Biochemistry: Prof. Dr J. MARTINS E SILVA
Biomathematics: Prof. Dr GALVÃO DE MELO
Histology: Prof. Dr DAVID FERREIRA
Physiology: Prof. Dr SILVA CARVALHO
Physiological Chemistry: Prof. J. MARTINS E SILVA
Pharmacology: Prof. Dr TOSCANO RICO
Nuclear Medicine: Prof. FERNANDO GODINHO
Pathological Anatomy: Prof. MARIA JOSÉ FORJAZ LACERDA
Microbiology: Prof. GUSTAVO NOBRE
Medical Psychology: Prof. Dr SIMÕES DA FONSECA
Immunology: Prof. Dr A. PALMA CARLOS
Genetics: Prof. MANUEL PIRES BICHO
Preventive Medicine and Public Health: Prof. J. PEREIRA MIGUEL
Legal Medicine: Prof. JOÃO LOBO ANTUNES
Medical Deontology: Prof. LESSEPS DOS REYS
Museum (History of Medicine): Prof. GOMES PEDRO

University Clinics:

Medicine I: Prof. Dr A. G. PALMA CARLOS
Medicine II: Prof. Dr M. CARNEIRO DE MOURA
Medicine III: Prof. LUCIANO RAVARA
Dermatology: Prof. Dr GUERRA RODRIGO
Pneumology: Prof. ANTÓNIO RODRIGUES COUTO
Infectious Diseases: Prof. FRANCISCO ANTUNES
Cardiology: Prof. MARIA CELESTE VAGUEIRO
Vascular Surgery: Prof. Dr A. DINIS DA GAMA
Surgery I: Prof. Dr VEIGA FERNANDES
Surgery II: Prof. H. BICHA CASTELO
Surgery III: Prof. FERNANDO PAREDES
Cardio-Thoracic Surgery: Prof. RUI DE LIMA
Plastic Surgery: Prof. A. CORDEIRO FERREIRA
Orthopaedics: Prof. A. RODRIGUES GOMES
Urology: Prof. J. CARNEIRO DE MOURA
Ophthalmology: Prof. Dr RIBEIRO DA SILVA
Otorhinolaryngology: Prof. Dr MÁRIO ANDREA
Neurology: Prof. Dr CASTRO CALDAS
Neurosurgery: Prof. Dr LOBO ANTUNES
Gynaecology: Prof. MADALENA BOTELHO
Paediatrics: Prof. JOÃO GOMES PEDRO

Psychiatry: Prof. J. SIMÕES DA FONSECA
Radiology: Prof. JORGE CABRAL CAMPOS

Faculty of Science:
Mathematics: Prof. MÁRIO RODRIGUES FIGUEIRA
Statistics, Operational Research and Computation: Prof. KAMIL TURKMAN
Informatics and Computer Sciences: Prof. FÉLIX COSTA
Physics: Prof. JOÃO SOUSA LOPES
Chemistry: Prof. CARLOS ALBERTO NIETO DE CASTRO
Geology: Prof. FERNANDO BARRIGA
Plant Biology: Prof. FERNANDO CATARINO
Zoology: Prof. CARLOS ALMAÇA
Education: Prof. JOÃO PEDRO DA PONTE

Faculty of Law:
Historical and Juridical Sciences: Prof. Dr RUI DE ALBUQUERQUE
Juridical and Economic Sciences: Prof. PITTA E CUNHA
Juridical and Political Sciences: Prof. JORGE MIRANDA
Juridical Sciences: Prof. OLIVEIRA ASCENÇÃO

UNIVERSIDADE LUSÍADA

Rua da Junqueira 190/198, 1300 Lisbon
Campuses in Lisbon, Oporto and Vila Nova de Famalicão
Telephone: (1) 3639944
Fax: (1) 3638307
Founded 1986 by Cooperativa de Ensino Universidade Lusíada
Private control
Academic year: October to June
Rector: Prof. Dr ANTÓNIO JORGE MARTINS DA MOTTA VEIGA
Vice-Rector: Prof. Dr JOSÉ J. GONÇALVES DE PROENÇA
Librarian: Dr MADALENA FERNANDES
Library of 15,000 vols
Number of teachers: 986
Number of students: 17,041
Publications: *Boletim Informativo*, *Revista Lusíada de Ciência e Cultura*, *CDE Bulletin*.

HEADS OF DEPARTMENTS

Architecture: Prof. Dr Arqto AUGUSTO PEREIRA BRANDÃO (Lisbon), Prof. Dr Arqto MANUEL DIOGO (Oporto), Prof. Arqto CARLOS SANTOS (Famalicão)
Law: Prof. Dr A. PENHA GONÇALVES (Lisbon), Prof. Dr ROGÉRIO SOARES (Oporto)
Economics: Prof. Dr E. RAPOSO DE MEDEIROS (Lisbon), Prof. Dr LUÍS MARIA TEIXEIRA PINTO (Oporto)
Management: Prof. Dr C. CRUZ VIDAL (Lisbon), Profa Dra ISABEL SOARES (Oporto)
History: Prof. Dr JOÃO CASTRO NUNES
Mathematics: Prof. Dr A. PEREIRA GOMES (Lisbon), Profa Dra MARGARIDA BARROS (Oporto)
International Relations: Prof. Dr CARLOS CÉSAR LIMA MOTTA (Lisbon), Prof. Dr FERNANDO ROBOREDO SEARA (Oporto)
Advanced Management Accounting: Prof. Dr MANUEL TEIXEIRA (Famalicão)
Textile Engineering: Prof. Dr GUSTAVO DA COSTA PEREIRA (Famalicão)
Industrial Management and Engineering: Prof. Dr J. SANTOS CRUZ (Famalicão)
Industrial Design: Prof. Dr Arqto CARLOS SANTOS (Famalicão)
Electronic and Computer Engineering: Prof. Dr J. CAMPOS NEVES (Famalicão)

ATTACHED INSTITUTES

Cultural Institute.

Mathematics Research Centre: Dir Prof. Dr NUNO DA COSTA PEREIRA.

Archaeology and History of Art Centre: Dir Prof. Dr LUÍS RAPOSO.

Business Institute: Dir Prof. Dr P. REBELO DE SOUSA.

Management Research Centre: Dir Prof. Dr CAETANO LÉGLISE DA CRUZ VIDAL.

Historical Research Centre: Dir Prof. Dr FERNANDO CASTELO BRANCO CHAVES.

International Relationships Research Centre: Dir Prof. Dr JOAQUIM DE CARVALHO.

European Studies Institute: Dir Prof. Dr FERNANDO ROBOREDO SEARA.

Centre for the Study and Research of Drug Addiction: Dir Prof. Dr ANTÓNIO MARTINS DA CRUZ.

Consumer Law Institute: Dir Prof. Dr MÁRIO FROTA.

Environmental Law Institute: Dir Prof Dr B. MARTINS DA CRUZ.

Law and Mental Health Institute.

Law Research Centre.

Language Institute: Dir Prof. Dr MANUEL BREDA SIMÕES.

Information, Communication and Computer Research Centre: Dir Prof. Eng. COSTA MARTINS.

Institute of Water Quality: Dir Prof. Dr VÍTOR MATOS LOBO.

Environment Research Centre: Dir Prof. Dr G. COSTA PEREIRA.

Housing Research Centre: Dir Prof. Arqto. JOSÉ CALLADO.

Architecture Technologies Research Centre: Dir Prof. Arqto. N. SANTOS PINHEIRO.

UNIVERSIDADE DA MADEIRA

Edificio da Penteade (3° Andar), Penteade, 9000 Funchal, Madeira
Telephone: (91) 705070
Fax: (91) 105089
E-mail: cdi@dragoeiro.uma.pt
Founded 1988
State control
Academic year: September to August
President: Prof. Dr JOSÉ MANUEL CASTANHEIRA
Vice-Rectors: Profa Dra ALEXANDRA BRANCO, Profa Dra JESUS DE SOUSA, Profa Dra PAULA CASTILHO
Administrator: Dra ANA PAULA OLIVEIRA
Librarian: Dra MARIA YOLANDA PEREIRA DA SILVA
Library of 35,000 vols
Number of teachers: 167
Number of students: 2,127

PRESIDENTS AND DIRECTORS

Department of Biology: Prof. Dr RUBEN ANTUNES CAPELA (Pres.)
Department of Education: Profa Dra MARIA DO CARMO ROCHA (Pres.)
Department of Physics: Prof. Dr MIKHAIL BENILOV (Pres.)
Department of Modern Languages and Literature: Profa Dra ELISETE ALMEIDA (Pres.)
Department of Mathematics: Profa Dra RITA VASCONCELOS (Pres.)
Department of Chemistry: Prof. Dr JOSÉ CARLOS MARQUES (Pres.)
Section of Physical Education: Dr JOÃO MATEUS (Dir)
Section of Systems Engineering and Computers: Eng. ALBERTO VELEZ GRILO (Dir)
Section of Classical Languages and Literature: Dr JOSÉ SÍLVIO MOREIRA FERNANDES (Dir)
Section of Management: Dr SÍLVIO SANTOS (Dir)

UNIVERSIDADE DO MINHO

Largo do Paço, 4709 Braga Codex
Telephone: 612234
Telex: 32135
Fax: 616936
Founded 1973
State control
Language of instruction: Portuguese
Academic year: October to July
Rector: Prof. SÉRGIO MACHADO DOS SANTOS
Vice-Rectors: Prof. LICÍNIO CHAÍNHO PEREIRA, Prof. CARLOS A. A. BERNARDO, Prof. VITOR MANUEL AGUIAR E SILVA
Chief Administrative Officer: Eng. JOSÉ F. AGUILAR MONTEIRO
Librarian: ARMINDO RODRIGUES CARDOSO
Number of teachers: 967
Number of students: 14,800
Publications: *Factos e Ideias*, *UM Boletim*.

DEANS

Engineering: G. RODRIGUES
Science: C. LEÃO
Arts: A. S. ESTANQUEIRO ROCHA
Education and Psychology: A. P. MESQUITA
Social Sciences: M. MARTINS
Management: C. RIBEIRO

PROFESSORS

ALMEIDA, J. M. B., Electronics and Applied Physics
ALMEIDA, L. M. G., Textile Engineering
ALMEIDA, L. S., Psychology
ALMEIDA, M. P., Economics
ALVES, A., Sciences of Communication
ALVES, H. D., English and North American Studies
AMORIM, M. N., History
ANDRITSCHKY, M., Physics
ARAÚJO, M. D., Textile Engineering
BERNARDO, C. A. A., Polymer Engineering
CAPELA, J. V., History
CARVALHO, A. L. DE, Social Sciences
COUTO, C. A., Electronics Engineering
COVAS, A., Polymer Engineering
DIAS, J. R., Educational Sciences
FARHANGMEHR, M., Management
FERNANDES, A. J., Political Science
FERREIRA, M. I. C., Physics
GONÇALVES, O. F., Psychology
LEÃO, M. C., Biology
MACHADO, A. B., Information Science
MAIA, H. L. S., Chemistry
MARTINS, J. B., Civil Engineering
MARTINS, M. N., History
MELO, L. M. F., Biological Engineering
MESQUITA, A. P., Psychology
MIRANDA, A. A. S., Mechanical Engineering
MONTENEGRO, M. I. M., Chemistry
MOTA, M. J. G., Biological Engineering
NUNES, J. E. L., Earth Sciences
PEREIRA, L. C., Physics
PINHEIRO, J. D. R. S., Chemical Engineering
PINTO, J. J. C., Polymer Engineering
RIBEIRO, J. A. C., Economics
ROCHA, A. S. E., Philosophy
ROCHA, J. A., Management and Public Administration
RODRIGUES, A. J. M. G., Production and Systems Engineering
RODRIGUES, R. N. C., Economics
ROMERO, J. J. B. R., Chemical Engineering
SANTOS, M. P., Physics
SANTOS, S. M. DOS, Computer Sciences
SEQUEIRA, M. J. C., Education
SILVA, A. A. C., Textile Engineering
SILVA, L. C., Philosophy
SILVA, V. M. A. E, Linguistics
SOARES, L. J. S., Chemical Engineering
TORRES, A. R., Linguistics
VALENÇA, J. M. E., Control Theory
VALENÇA, M. R. DA G. P., Mathematics
VASCONCELOS, A. S. C. V., Economics

VAZ, E., Mathematics
VIEIRA, J. M., Civil Engineering

ATTACHED INSTITUTES

Archaeology Unit: Dir M. MARTINS.

Public Library: Dir H. B. NUNES.

Adult Education Unit: Dir L. V. LIMA.

Public Archives: Dir A. VASCONCELOS.

Nogueira da Silva Museum: Dir C. A. VALENÇA.

UNIVERSIDADE NOVA DE LISBOA
(New University of Lisbon)

Praça do Principe Real 26, 1250 Lisbon
Telephone: (1) 346-7972
Telex: 44733
Fax: (1) 346-1924

Founded 1973
State control
Academic year: October to July

Rector: Prof. Dr LUÍS SOUSA LOBO
Vice-Rectors: Prof. Dr JOSÉ ESTEVES PEREIRA, Prof. Dr MARIA DA GRAÇA MORAIS
Pro-Rectors: Prof. Dr ANTÓNIO J. C. MINEIRO, Prof. Dr RUEFF TAVARES, Prof. Dr JOSÉ TELHADO PEREIRA

Number of teachers: 1,234
Number of students: 10,306

Publications: *Guia*, *Anuário*, *Boletim da UNL*, *Boletim Informativo da Faculdade de Ciências Médicas*, *Comunicação e Linguagem – Revista da Faculdade de Ciências Sociais e Humanas*.

DEANS

Faculty of Sciences and Technology: Prof. Dr L. J. MARTINHO GUIMARÃES
Faculty of Social and Human Sciences: Prof. Dr J. F. DE OLIVEIRA CRESDO
Faculty of Economics: Prof. Dr FERNANDO DE BRITO SOARES
Faculty of Medical Sciences: Prof. Dr NUNO T. CORDEIRO FERREIRA
Institute of Hygiene and Tropical Medicine: Profa Dra WANDA CANAS FERREIRA
Institute of Chemical and Biological Technology: Prof. Dr ANTÓNIO V. XAVIER
Institute of Statistics and Information Management: Prof. Dr MANUEL VILLARES
School of Public National Health: Prof. Dr J. CALDEIRA DA SILVA

HEADS OF DEPARTMENTS

Faculty of Sciences and Technology:
Mathematics: ELVIRA MARTINS COIMBRA
Physics: MANUEL FERNANDES LARANGEIRA
Chemistry: MANUEL L. NUNES DA PONTE
Sciences and Environmental Engineering: FERNANDO J. SANTANA
Computer Science: LUÍS SANCHO MONIZ PEREIRA
Materials Sciences: RODRIGO P. MARTINS
Applied Social Sciences: ANTÓNIO NUNES DOS SANTOS
Biotechnology: LUÍS ARCHER
Earth Sciences: MIGUEL FERREIRA TELLES ANTUNES
Mechanical Engineering: ANTÓNIO RAFAEL JANEIRO BORGES
Physics (Autonomous Section): JOSÉ N. MARAT MENDES
Electronic Engineering: AMADEU LEÃO RODRIGUES
Industrial Engineering: VIRGÍLIO A. PÁSCOA MACHADO
Plant Biology: FERNANDO M. S. FERREIRA HENRIQUES

Faculty of Social and Human Sciences:
History: MARIA HELENA TRINDADE LOPES
Romance Languages and Literatures: NUNO JÚDICE
Anthropology: JILL DIAS
Sociology: MARIA LUÍS ROCHA PINTO
Philosophy: MARIA ISABEL S. C. R. RENAUD
Art History: JOSÉ C. VIEIRA DA SILVA
Geography and Regional Planning: MARIA JOSÉ ROXO FREITAS RODRIGUES
Portuguese Studies: MARIA SILVINA LOPES
Anglo-Portuguese Studies: MARIA LEONOR M. SOUSA
German Studies: KARL OBITZ
Communication Science: JOÃO MÁRIO GRILO
Musical Sciences: SALWA CASTELO BRANCO
Linguistics: MARIA DE LOURDES CRISPIM
History and Theory of Ideas: ZÍLIA B. OSÓRIO DE CASTRO
Education Sciences: FERNANDA ALEGRIA

Faculty of Economics:
Economics: P. PITA BARROS
Business Economics: J. AMARO DE MATOS
Management: L. ALMEIDA E COST

Faculty of Medical Sciences:
Anatomy: JOSÉ ANTÓNIO R. ESPERANÇA PINA
Pathological Anatomy: JORGE M. DE OLIVEIRA SOARES
Biochemistry: MARIA DA GRAÇA MORAIS
Surgery I: CARLOS M. ALVES PEREIRA
Surgery II: ALBERTO MATOS FERREIRA
Surgery III: JORGE DE QUEIRÓS MEDEIROS
Physiology: PEDRO M. FREIRE DA COSTA
Physiopathology: A. M. BENSABAT RENDAS
Genetics: JOSÉ RUEFF TAVARES
Histology and Embryology: JOSÉ A. R. ESPERANÇA PINA
Immunology: JOAQUIM MACHADO CAETANO
Internal Medicine I: ARMANDO SALLES LUÍS
Internal Medicine II: FRANCISCO MARTINS CORREIA
Internal Medicine III: MÁRIO GENTIL QUINA
Laboratory Medicine: JULIETA ESPERANÇA PINA
Neurology: ORLANDO COELHO LEITÃO
Obstetrics and Gynaecology: JORGE DA CUNHA BRANCO
Ophthalmology: LUÍS N. C. FERRAZ DE OLIVEIRA
Orthopaedics: ALBERTO DE SOUSA SALIS AMARAL
Otorhinolaryngology: RUI DA SILVA SANTOS PENHA
Paediatrics: NUNO T. CORDEIRO FERREIRA
Pneumophthisiology: RAMIRO V. GOULART DE ÁVILA
Medical Psychology: CAMILO DIAS CARDOSO
Mental Health and Psychiatry: JOSÉ M. B. CALDAS DE ALMEIDA
Radiology: LUÍS AIRES B. M. DE SOUSA
Public Health: NUNO T. CORDEIRO FERREIRA
Biomathematics and Computer Science: CARLOS M. MORAIS SARMENTO
Physical and Rehabilitation Medicine: MÁRIO DA SILVA MOURA
Biophysics: JOAQUIM M. GOMES DA SILVA
Cellular Biology: JOSÉ A. R. ESPERANÇA PINA
General Therapeutics: JOSÉ J. DE SOUSA G. SIMÕES
History of Medicine: LUÍS N. C. FERRAZ DE OLIVEIRA
Pharmacology: MANUEL A. SILVA E SOUSA
Medical Deontology: JOSÉ A. R. ESPERANÇA PINA
Maternal and Child Health: NUNO T. CORDEIRO FERREIRA
Legal Medicine: JOSÉ A. R. ESPERANÇA PINA
Dermatology and Venereal Diseases: ANTÓNIO CABRAL DE ASCENSÃO
Infectious Diseases: NUNO T. CORDEIRO FERREIRA
Oncology: MÁRIO O. DE MATOS BERNARDO
Urology: ALBERTO R. DE MATOS FERREIRA
Physical and Rehabilitation Medicine: MARIO DA SILVA MOURA

UNIVERSIDADE DO PORTO

Rua D. Manuel II, 4003 Oporto Codex
Telephone: (2) 6099519
Telex: 23121
Fax: (2) 6098736

Founded 1911
State control
Academic year: October to February; March to July

Rector: Prof. Dr ALBERTO M. S. C. AMARAL
Vice-Rectors: Prof. Dr CÂNDIDO A. DIAS DOS SANTOS, Prof. Dr MIRANDA MAGALHÃES, Prof. Dr NOVAIS BARBOSA

Number of teachers: 1,834
Number of students: 19,906

DEANS

Faculty of Science: Prof. Dr RIBEIRO DA SILVA
Faculty of Medicine: Prof. Dr JOAQUIM MACHADO DA SILVA
Faculty of Engineering: Prof. Dr J. MARQUES DOS SANTOS
Faculty of Humanities: Prof. Dr RIBEIRO DA SILVA
Faculty of Pharmacy: Prof. Dr F. MORAIS S. ESTEVES
Faculty of Economics: Prof. Dr RUI A. F. ALVES
Faculty of Psychology and Educational Science: Prof. Dr H. COSTA G. ARAÚJO
Faculty of Architecture: Prof. Arq. MANUEL CORREIA FERNANDES
Institute of Biomedical Sciences: Prof. Dr CORÁLIA VICENTE
Faculty of Sports and Physical Education: Prof. Dr J. A. PINTO SILVA MOTA
College of Nutrition: NORBERTO TEIXEIRA DOS SANTOS
Faculty of Dental Medicine: Prof. Dr FERNANDO PERES
Faculty of Fine Arts: Prof. PINTOR D. AUGUSTO ALVES
Faculty of Law: Prof. Dr CANDIDO DA AGRA
Postgraduate Institute of Business Studies: Prof. Dr RUI GUIMARÃES

ATTACHED INSTITUTES

Centre for Northern Portugal-Aquitaine Studies: Dir Prof. Dr OLIVEIRA RAMOS.

Centre for Population and Family Studies: Dir Prof. FERNANDO SOUSA.

Dr Gonçalo Sampaio Botanical Institute: Dir Prof. Dr ROBERTO SALEMA RIBEIRO.

Dr Mendes Correira Institute of Anthropology: Dir Prof. Dr MACHADO CRUZ.

Geophysics Institute: Dir Prof. Dr JOÃO MONTENEGRO.

Prof. Abel Salazar Institute of Histology: Dir Prof. Dr ANTÓNIO COIMBRA.

Prof. Pires de Lima Institute of Anatomy: Dir Prof. Dr MANUEL PAULA BARBOSA.

Zoology Institute and Dr Augusto Nobre Marine Zoology Station: Dir Prof. Dr JORGE EIRAS.

UNIVERSIDADE PORTUCALENSE INFANTE D. HENRIQUE

Rua Dr António Bernardino de Almeida 541-619, 4200 Oporto
Telephone: (2) 5570200
Fax: (2) 5570280

Founded 1986
Private control
Language of instruction: Portuguese
Academic year: October to July

Rector: Prof. Dr FRANCISCO DA COSTA DURÃO
Vice-Rectors: Prof. Dr HUMBERTO BAQUERO MORENO, Prof. Dr CAMILO CIMOURDAIN DE OLIVEIRA
General Secretary: Prof. Dr FERNANDO PACHECO DE AMORIM

Chief Administrative Officer: António Alves Monteiro
Librarian: Prof. Dr Machado e Moura
Library of 40,000 vols
Number of teachers: 266
Number of students: 4,652
Publications: *Revista de Ciências Históricas, Africana*.

HEADS OF DEPARTMENTS

Law: Prof. Dr Melo e Silva
Economics: Prof. Dr Almeida Garrett
Management: Prof. Dr Cimourdain de Oliveira
History: Prof. Dr Baquero Moreno
Mathematics: Prof. Dr Costa Durão
Computer Studies: Prof. Dr Reis Lima
Cultural Activities: Prof. Dr Silva Cunha

ATTACHED INSTITUTES

Information Technology Centre: Dir Prof. Dr Reis Lima.

Institute of Archaeology: Dir Dr Lopes da Silva.

Institute of Art History: Dir Dr José Manuel Tedim.

Research Centre for Applied Economics: Dir Prof. Dr Almeida Garrett.

Institute of Historical Sciences: Dir Prof. Dr Luis Oliveira Ramos.

Institute of Laws: Dir Dr Melo e Silva.

Centre for African and Eastern Studies: Prof. Dr Silva Cunha.

Institute for the Conservation and Restoration of the National Heritage: Dir Dr Albérico Mendonça Tavares.

Institute of Finance: Dir Prof. Dr Rui Conceição Nunes.

Institute of Information Development: Dir Dra Maria Helena Figueiroa Rego.

Research Centre for Pure and Applied Mathematics: Dir Prof. Dr Francisco da Costa Durão.

Institute of Ibero-American Studies: Prof. Dr Baquero Moreno.

UNIVERSIDADE TÉCNICA DE LISBOA

Alameda de Santo António dos Capuchos 1, 1150 Lisbon
Telephone: 8852434
Fax: 8852795
Founded 1930
State control
Academic year: September to July
Rector: Prof. Dr António Simões Lopes
Vice-Rectors: Prof. Dr António Alberto Monteiro Alves, Prof. Dr José Dias Lopes da Silva
Pro-Rectors: Prof. Dr Miguel M. J. de Azevedo Coutinho, Prof. Dr João Bettencourt da Câmara, Prof. Dra Maria da Conceição de Cunha e Vasconcelos Peleteiro
Administrator: Dr Pedro A. C. R. Vieira de Meireles
Librarian: Prof. Dr Antonio Monteiro Alves
Number of teachers: 1,917
Number of students: 20,338
Publications: *SDP/RUTL—Jornal da UTL, FMV—Anais da Faculdade de Medicina Veterinária, ISA—Anais do Instituto Superior de Agronomia, ISEG—Estudes de Economia, ISCSP—Estudes Politicos e Sociais, FMH—Anais da Faculdade de Motricidade Humana, Motricidade Humana, Ludens*.

PRESIDENTS OF THE DIRECTIVE COUNCILS

Faculty of Veterinary Medicine: Prof. Dr Tito Horácio Fernandes
Higher Institute of Agronomy: Prof. Dr J. M. Fernandes de Abreu
Higher Institute of Economics and Business Administration: Prof. Dr A. F. Espinho Romão
Higher Institute of Engineering: Prof. Dr D. de Freitas Gomes Durão
Higher Institute of Social and Political Sciences: Prof. Dr Óscar Soares Barata
Faculty of Human Kinetics: Prof. Dr Francisco Alberto Arruda Carreiro da Costa
Faculty of Architecture: Prof. Dr Carlos Antero Lopes Ferreira

UNIVERSIDADE DE TRÁS-OS-MONTES E ALTO DOURO

POB 202, 5001 Vila Real Codex
Telephone: (59) 321631
Telex: 24436
Fax: (59) 74480
Founded 1973, university status 1986
State control
Language of instruction: Portuguese
Academic year: October to July
Rector: Prof. Dr José Torres Pereira
Registrar: Dr Francisco Joaquim Pires
Administrative Director: Francisco Miguel Rodrigues
Academic Director: Lucinda Machado Rodrigues
Librarian: Dr Margarida Carvalho
Number of teachers: 361
Number of students: 4,479
Publications: *Boletim Informativo da UTAD, Annals of UTAD, Yearbook of UTAD*.

HEADS OF DEPARTMENTS

Animal Health: Prof. Dr Jorge Rodrigues
Animal Science: Prof. Dr Arnaldo Dias da Silva
Arts and Workmanship: Dr Manuel de Alcino Freitas
Biology: Prof Dr José M. G. Torres Pereira
Chemistry: Prof. Dr José I. Féria Seita
Crop Science and Rural Engineering: Prof. Dr Nuno M. V. Tavares Moreira
Economics and Sociology: Prof. Dr Artur Aréde Cristóvão
Educational Sciences: Prof. Dra Maria Adelaide Gregório Pires
Engineering: Prof. Dr Carlos Monteiro Couto
Food Technology: Profa Dra Maria Arlete Faia
Forestry: Prof. Dr. Aloísio Loureiro
Geology: Prof. Dr Vilela de Matos
Literature: Prof. Dr Armando Mascarenhas Ferreira
Mathematics: Prof. Dr José Fernandes Carvalho
Physics: Prof. Dr Luís Vaz de Sampayo
Plant Protection: Profa Dra Ana Maria Nazaré Pereira
Soils: Prof. Dr Ana Luísa Pires
Sports: Prof. Dr Carlos Alberto Sequeira
Veterinary Pathology and Clinics: Prof. Dr José Potes

Colleges

Instituto Nacional de Administração: Palácio dos Marqueses de Pombal, 2780 Oeiras; tel. (1) 4412846; fax (1) 4418609; f. 1979; training and research in public administration, legislative science, European affairs; documentation centre of 12,000 vols; European Documentation Centre; Pres. A. Correia de Campos; publs *Legislação, Cadernos de Ciência de Legislação*.

Instituto Politécnico de Beja: Rua de Santo António 1A, 7800 Beja; tel. (84) 329327; fax (84) 325771; f. 1985; 163 teachers; 2,136 students; library of 23,000 vols; Dir Profa Dra Rosa Maria Cabral Salgado da Cunha Fernandes.

DIRECTORS

Higher School of Agriculture: Eng. António Manuel da Costa Nunes Ribeiro
Higher School of Education: Dr José Luis Ildefonso Ramalho

Instituto Politécnico de Bragança: Apdo 172, 5300 Bragança; tel. 25570; telex 27750; fax 25405; f. 1983; 149 teachers; 1,460 students; Dir Prof. Dionísio A. Gonçalves.

HEADS OF DEPARTMENTS

Agroclimatology: Prof. Dionísio A. Gonçalves
Economy: Prof. Francisco J. T. Cepeda
Stockbreeding: Prof. Alfredo J. C. Teixeira

Instituto Politécnico de Castelo Branco, Escola Superior Agrária: Quinta de N. Sra. de Mércules, 6000 Castelo Branco; tel. (72) 327535; fax (72) 328881; e-mail sdbi@mail.telepac.pt; f. 1983; higher courses in agriculture (vegetable production, animal production, forestry production, natural resources management, edible oil production); 56 teachers; 862 students; library of 19,000 vols; Dir J. P. Várzea Rodrigues; publs *Boletim Bibliográfico, AGROforum, Bibliografia Temática, Folha Bibliográfica Mensal*.

Instituto Politécnico da Guarda: Av. Dr Francisco Sá Carneiro 50, 6300 Guarda; tel. (71) 220111; fax (71) 222690; f. 1980; 3,300 students; courses in education, public relations, computer science, civil engineering, mechanical engineering, and business management; Pres. Prof. Dr Álvaro Bento Leal; publ. *Educação e Tecnologia*.

Instituto Politécnico de Lisboa: Rua Professor Reinaldo dos Santos 5A, 1500 Lisbon; tel. (1) 7786441; fax (1) 7786448; e-mail iplsc@mail.esoterica.pt; f. 1985; state control; Pres. Dr Alberto A. Antas de Barros Júnior; Administrator Dr António José Carvalho Marques.

CONSTITUENT INSTITUTES:

Escola Superior de Communicação Social: Rua Carolina Michaelis de Vasconcelos, 1500 Lisbon; tel. (1) 7119000; fax (1) 7164877; f. 1987; academic year September to July; 62 teachers; 866 students; library of 3,919 vols, 8,799 periodicals; Pres. Dr Alberto A. Antas de Barros.

Escola Superior de Educação: Av. Carolina Michaelis de Vasconcelos (Junto à Est. de Benfica), 1500 Lisbon; tel. (1) 7115500; fax (1) 7166147; f. 1985; academic year September to July; 96 teachers; 1,065 students; library of 28,000 vols, 8,500 periodicals; Pres. Dra Amália Garrido Bárrios.

Escola Superior de Dança: Rua do Século 89–93, 1200 Lisbon; tel. (1) 3425355; fax (1) 3420271; f. 1983; academic year September to July; 17 teachers; 83 students; library of 1,270 vols; Dir Prof. Wanda Ribeiro da Silva; publ. *Dança*.

Escola Superior de Música: Rua do Ataíde 7, 1200 Lisbon; tel. (1) 3224940; fax (1) 3471489; f. 1983; academic year October to June; 43 teachers; 140 students; library of 1,500 vols and 5,000 music scores; Dir Prof. Christopher Consitt Bochmann.

Escola Superior de Teatro e Cinema: Rua dos Caetanos 29, 1200 Lisbon; tel. (1) 3461794; fax (1) 3470273; f. 1983; academic year September to July; 43 teachers; 208 students; library of 10,000 vols, 2,000 periodicals; Pres. Prof. João M. Mota Rodrigues.

Instituto Superior de Engenharia de Lisboa (ISEL): Rua Conselheiro Emídio Navarro, 1900 Lisbon; tel. (1) 8317000; fax (1) 8597046; f. 1852 as Instituto Industrial de Lisboa, present name 1974; academic year Sept. to July; 551 teachers; 5,495 students; library of 9,388 vols, 312 periodicals; Pres. Enga MARIA DA GRAÇA PAES DE FARIA.

Instituto Superior de Contabilidade e Administração de Lisboa (ISCAL): Av. Miguel Bombarda 20, 1050 Lisbon; tel. (1) 7984551; fax 7977079; f. 1754 as Aula de Comércio, present name 1976; academic year September to July; 202 teachers; 3,334 students; library of 6,566 vols, 211 periodicals; Administrator Dr VICTOR MACIEIRA.

Instituto Politécnico de Portalegre: Apdo 84, 7301 Portalegre Codex; tel. (45) 330034; fax (45) 330353; f. 1980; state control; Pres. Prof. Dr F. A. FORTUNATO QUEIRÓS.

CONSTITUENT SCHOOLS:

Escola Superior de Educação (ESE): Apdo 125, 7301 Portalegre Codex; 72 teachers; 671 students; Pres. Dr ABÍLIO JOSÉ M. AMIGUINHO; Librarian Dr DOMINGOS BUCHO; publ. *Aprender*.

Escola Superior de Tecnologia e Gestão (ESTG): Apdo 148, 7301 Portalegre Codex; 45 teachers; 695 students; Pres. Dr FRANCISCO J. C. TOMATAS; Librarian Bac. CATARINA ELIAS BARRADAS.

Escola Superior Agrária de Elvas (ESAE): Apdo 254, 7350 Elvas; 5 teachers; 25 students; Dir Eng. GONÇALO J. P. ANTUNES BARRADAS.

Instituto Politécnico de Santarém: Complexo Andaluz, Apdo 279, 2000 Santarém; tel. (43) 27521; fax (43) 332384; f. 1979; 189 teachers; 2,567 students; library of 24,000 vols; Dir Prof. J. A. GUERRA JUSTINO.

HEADS OF SCHOOLS

Agriculture: Prof. JOÃO GOMES MENDES
Education: Prof. ANTÓNIO MANIQUE
Administration: Prof. MANUEL RAMOS

Instituto Politécnico de Setúbal: Largo dos Defensores da República 1, 2900 Setúbal; tel. (65) 35301; fax (65) 31110; f. 1987; courses in education, management and technology; Pres. Prof. Eng. JOÃO DUARTE SILVA.

Instituto Politécnico de Viana do Castelo: Apdo 51, 4901 Viana do Castelo Codex; tel. 829063; telex 32941; fax 829065; f. 1980; first degree courses; Pres. Prof. A. LIMA DE CARVALHO.

HEADS OF SCHOOLS

Education: JOSÉ MELO DE CARVALHO
Technology: PAULO FERNANDES
Agriculture: MIGUEL BRITO

Instituto Superior de Línguas e Administração (ISLA): Rua do Sacramento à Lapa 14–16, 1200 Lisbon; tel. (1) 3955104; telex 63501; fax (1) 3966736; f. 1962; private control; business management, marketing, human resources, computer science for management, applied mathematics, translation, tourism, secretarial studies; 260 teachers; 3,000 students; library of 13,300 vols; Sec.-Gen. MIGUEL P. G. RODRIGUES.

Instituto Superior Politécnico de Viseu: Rua Maximiano Aragão, 3500 Viseu; tel. (32) 422028; fax (32) 425760; e-mail ispv@mail.telepac.pt; f. 1979; 260 teachers; 3,200 students; Dir Prof. JOÃO P. DE BARROS; publ. *Millenium*.

HEADS OF DEPARTMENTS

Higher School of Education: Dr FERNANDO ANDRADE AMARO
Higher School of Technology: Eng. FERNANDO LOPES R. SEBASTIÃO
Higher School of Agriculture: Dr ANTÓNIO FERNANDES P. MORAIS

Instituto Superior Politécnico Portucalense: Rua do Paço 3, 4560 Penafiel; tel. (55) 711054; fax (55) 711053; f. 1990; courses in local govt administration, accounting, management, computer studies; 73 teachers; 620 students; library of 5,000 vols; Dir Dr JOAQUIM M. SILVA CUNHA.

School of Art

Escola Superior de Belas-Artes (Higher School of Fine Arts): Av. Rodrigues de Freitas, Oporto; f. 1836; Dir Arch. CARLOS RAMOS.

MACAU

Learned Societies

ECONOMICS, LAW AND POLITICS

Associação de Ciências Sociais de Macau (Macau Society of Social Sciences): Estrada Adolfo Loureiro 3A, Edificio Tak On, 3rd Floor A, POB 957, Macau; tel. 319880; fax 319880; f. 1985 to study society and serve Macau; 40 mems; Pres. HUANG WEI-WEN; Sec. CHEONG CHOK FU; publ. *Huo Keng* (mirror of Macau, 2 a year).

FINE AND PERFORMING ARTS

Circulo de Cultura Musical (Circle of Musical Culture): Largo do Sto. Agostinho 3–2°, Macau; f. 1952; 68 mems; library of 876 vols; Artistic Dir FRANCISCO XAVIER FREIRE GARCIA.

Instituto Cultural de Macau: Praceta Miramar 87-U r/c, Macau; tel. 700391; fax 700405; f. 1984; cultural studies, classes for music, drama and ballet; Chair. Dra GABRIELA RAMILO POMBAS CABELO; publ. *Revista de Cultura* ((quarterly) in English Chinese and Portuguese).

Libraries and Archives

Macau

Arquivo Histórico de Macau: Av. Conselheiro Ferreira de Almeida 91–93, Macau; tel. 592919; fax 561495; e-mail icmctm04@macau.ctm.net; f. 1952; library of 7,000 vols; Dir MARIA HELENA ÉVORA; publ. *Boletim do Arquivo Histórico de Macau*.

Biblioteca Nacional (Central Library of Macau): Av. Conselheiro F. de Almeida 89 A–B, Macau; tel. 371623; fax 318756; f. 1895; library of 200,000 vols; special collections; Macau, Ancient Books, Chinese Books (Sir Robert Ho Tung); Librarian Dr JORGE MANUEL DE ABREU ARRIMAR; publs *Boletim Bibliográfico de Macau*, *Boletim de Literatura Infantil*, *Boletim Bibliográfico de Literatura Portuguesa*.

Biblioteca Sir Robert Ho Tung (Sir Robert Ho Tung's Chinese Library): Largo do Sto. Agostinho 3, Macau; tel. 377117; fax 314456; f. 1958; library of 17,592 vols; Librarian SAM CHAN FAI; publ. *Boletim Bibliográfico de Macau*.

Museums and Art Galleries

Macau

Galeria do Leal Senado: Macau; f. 1986 and sited in old municipal council building; temporary exhibitions of Portuguese and other artists.

Museu Luís de Camões (Luís de Camões Museum): Praça Luís de Camões, Macau; house built 18th century; f. 1960; Chinese pottery, paintings, sculpture; European emigré paintings; 17th–18th century furnishings, etc.; Curator ANTONIO CONCEIÇÃO JUNIOR; publ. *Catalogue of Chinese Paintings* (in English and Chinese).

University

UNIVERSIDADE DE MACAU
(University of Macau)

University Hill, Taipa, POB 3001, Macau
Telephone: 831622
Fax: 831694
E-mail: webmaster@umac.mo
Founded 1991
State control
Languages of instruction: Chinese, Portuguese, English
Academic year: September to July
Chancellor: H.E. THE GOVERNOR OF MACAU
Rector: Prof. LI-GAO ZHOU
Vice-Rector: Prof. RUI MARTINS
Administrator: Dr RUFINO RAMOS
Librarian: Dr JOAQUIM CORREIA
Library of 130,000 vols
Number of teachers: 300 full-time, 19 part-time
Number of students: 3,281

DEANS

Faculty of Social Sciences and Humanities: Assoc. Prof. BO-LONG LIU
Faculty of Business Administration: Prof. NELSON ANTÓNIO
Faculty of Science and Technology: Assoc. Prof. VAI-PAN IU
Faculty of Education: Assoc. Prof. KWOK-CHEUNG CHEUNG
Faculty of Law: Prof. JOÃO RUIZ DE ALMEIDA GARRETT

ATTACHED INSTITUTES

Institute of Chinese Studies: Dir Prof. CHEUNG-FAI CHING.

Institute of Portuguese Studies: Dir Profa MARIA ANTÓNIA E. SOARES.

PUERTO RICO

Learned Societies

GENERAL

Ateneo de Ponce: Apdo de Correos 1923, Ponce; f. 1956; Pres. Lic. HILDA CHAVIER; Sec. VICENTE RUIZ.

Ateneo Puertorriqueño: Apdo 902118, San Juan, PR 00902-1180; tel. 721-3877; fax 725-3873; e-mail atencopr@caribe.net; f. 1876; literature, theatre, arts and sciences; 600 mems; library of 17,000 vols; art gallery; Pres. Lic. EDUARDO MORALES COLL; Dir Prof. ROBERTO RAMOS PEREA.

BIBLIOGRAPHY, LIBRARY SCIENCE AND MUSEOLOGY

Sociedad de Bibliotecarios de Puerto Rico: Apdo 22898, San Juan 00931-2898; tel. (787) 764-0000 ext. 5204; fax (787) 763-5685; e-mail vtorres@upracd.upr.clu.edu; f. 1961; 275 mems; Pres. VÍCTOR F. TORRES (acting); Sec. DORIS RIVERA; publ. *Informa* (irregular).

FINE AND PERFORMING ARTS

Sociedad Mayagüezana Pro Bellas Artes: POB 5004, Mayagüez 00709; f. 1977; 300 mems; ballet, opera, concerts, lectures, symphonies, art and sculpture exhibitions; Pres. Dr LUIS E. BACÓ RODRÍGUEZ.

HISTORY, GEOGRAPHY AND ARCHAEOLOGY

Academia Puertorriqueña de la Historia: Apdo 1447, San Juan; f. 1932; 40 mems; Pres. LUIS E. GONZÁLEZ VALES; publ. *Boletín*.

LANGUAGE AND LITERATURE

Academia Puertorriqueña de la Lengua Española (Puerto Rican Academy): Apdo 4008G, San Juan 00936; f. 1955; corresp. of the Real Academia Española (Madrid); 33 mems; Dir Dr JOSÉ TRÍAS MONGE; Sec. MARÍA VAQUERO DE RAMÍREZ; publ. *Boletin* (quarterly).

PEN Club de Puerto Rico: Calle San Sebastián 270, San Juan 00901; f. 1966; 40 mems; Sec. ERNESTO JUAN FONFRÍAS.

Research Institutes

GENERAL

Instituto de Cultura Puertorriqueña: Apdo 4184, San Juan, PR 00902; f. 1955; studies and preserves Puerto Rican historical and cultural patrimony and promotes study of Puerto Rican culture; Dir Dr LUIS E. DÍAZ HERNÁNDEZ.

AGRICULTURE, FISHERIES AND VETERINARY SCIENCE

Institute of Tropical Forestry: USDA Forest Service, Southern Forest Experiment Station, Call Box 25000, Rio Piedras, PR 00928-2500; f. 1939; research in timber management, tropical ecosystem, plantation forestry, wildlife management, watershed management and global change research; co-operative assistance to State and private forest landowners, timber processors; co-operative research with universities and US and foreign governmental agencies; trains foreign forestry students in co-operation with FAO and USAID; library of 15,000 vols; Dir Dr ARIEL E. LUGO.

Tropical Agriculture Research Station: POB 70, Mayagüez, PR 00681; tel. 831-3435; fax 831-3386; attached to Agricultural Research Service of United States Department of Agriculture; Dir Dr ANTONIO SOTOMAYOR-RÍOS.

LANGUAGE AND LITERATURE

Instituto de Lexicografía Hispanoamericana Augusto Malaret: Apdo 3828, San Juan; f. 1969; study and conservation of indigenous languages, of native toponymy and of the lexicon of fauna and flora; study of the influence of the African languages in America, and of the origin of proverbs; determination of the appropriate use of technical terms; Dir (vacant).

NATURAL SCIENCES

Biological Sciences

Institute for Tropical Ecosystem Studies: GPO Box 363682, San Juan 00936; tel. 767-0350; fax 758-0815; f. 1957 as PR Nuclear Center; operated by the University of Puerto Rico; research, and development of tropical terrestrial ecological studies; graduate-level research and training centre in basic ecological principals primarily for minorities; Dir Dr JESS K. ZIMMERMAN; publ. *Long-Term Ecological Research Newsletter*.

Physical Sciences

Arecibo Observatory: POB 995 Arecibo, PR 00613; tel. (787) 878-2612; fax (787) 878-1861; f. 1960; world's largest radio/radar telescope, for use by scientists from all over the world; 1,000-ft diameter fixed spherical reflector with movable feeds; for use in the radar study of planets and the properties of the earth's upper atmosphere and reception of natural radio emissions from celestial objects including pulsars and quasars; reflector surface upgraded to work at higher frequencies; library of 4,100 vols, 85 periodicals; National Astronomy and Ionosphere Centre is operated by Cornell University under a co-operative agreement with the National Science Foundation; Dir of operations Dr DANIEL R. ALTSCHULER.

Libraries and Archives

Mayagüez

University of Puerto Rico, Mayagüez Campus, General Library: Mayagüez 00708; f. 1911; 360,013 vols; Dir MIGUEL ANGEL ORTIZ-GUERRA; publs *Conoce Tu Biblioteca* (annually), *Lista de Tesis y Tesinas* (annually), *Lista de libros catalogados* (monthly), *List of Publications on Agriculture and Related Sciences* (monthly), *Serials Holdings in the Mayagüez Library* (every 2 years).

Ponce

Ponce Public Library: Apdo Postal 7477, Ponce 00732; premises at: Calle Reina, Esquina Fogos, Ponce, 00731; f. 1942; 9,516 mems; 20,000 vols; Librarian M. MADERA.

Pontifical Catholic University of Puerto Rico, Encarnación Valdes Library: Ponce 00731; tel. (787) 841-2000, ext. 300; fax (787) 284-0235; f. 1948; 269,000 vols; special collections: Puerto Rican materials, Murga Collection; Dir ESTHER IRIZARRY VÁZQUEZ (acting).

Pontifical Catholic University of Puerto Rico Law Library: 2250 Avda Las Américas, Suite 544, Ponce 00731-6382; tel. (787) 841-2000, ext. 336; fax (787) 841-5354; f. 1961; 176,000 vols; special collections: US and United Nations documents, Puerto Rico; Dir NOELIA PADUA; publ. *Revista de Derecho Puertorriqueño* (quarterly).

San Juan

Archivo General de Puerto Rico: Instituto de Cultura Puertorriqueña, Apdo 9024184, San Juan, PR 00902-4184; tel. 722-2113; fax 722-9097; f. 1955; 55,000 cubic ft of records; Dir NELLY V. CRUZ RODRÍGUEZ.

Biblioteca Madre María Teresa Guevara (Universidad del Sagrado Corazón): Apdo 12383, San Juan, PR 00914-12383; tel. 728-1515 ext. 4353; fax 728-1515, ext. 4368; f. 1935; 191,000 vols, 1,000 periodicals; Librarian MARIA GARIN; publs *Delfilinea* (Library News, 3 a year), *Lista de Publicaciones Periódicas* (annually).

Caribbean and Latin American Studies Library: POB 21927, University Station, Rio Piedras, PR 00931; tel. 764-0000, ext. 3319; fax 763-5685; e-mail vtorres@upracd.upr.clu.edu; f. 1946 in Trinidad; moved to Puerto Rico 1961; specializes in humanities and social sciences in Latin America and the Caribbean; 120,000 vols; special collection of Caribbean Commission documents; Librarian VICTOR F. TORRES-ORTIZ.

Carnegie Public Library: 7 Avda Ponce de León, San Juan, PR 00901-2010; tel. (787) 722-4753; fax (787) 725-0261; f. 1916; 44,000 vols; Dir JOSEFINA GÓMEZ DE HILLYER.

Commonwealth of Puerto Rico, Department of Justice Library: Box 192, San Juan, PR 00902; f. 1950; law library of 75,000 vols; Librarian CARMEN M. CRUZ; publs *Opiniones del Secretario de Justicia de Puerto Rico, Informe Anual del Secretario de Justicia de Puerto Rico, Anuario Estadístico.*

Attached library:

Supreme Court of Puerto Rico Library: Ponce de León Ave, Stop 8, Apdo 2392, San Juan, PR 00903; tel. (787) 723-3863; f. 1953; law library with special collections of Puerto Rican law, common law, Spanish and French civil law; 75,243 vols; Librarian (vacant); publ. *Nuevas Adquisiciones* (monthly).

Public Library Services, Department of Education: POB 759, San Juan 00919; 1,500,000 vols; Dir MARIA LUGO.

University of Puerto Rico Law Library: POB 23310, University Station, San Juan 00931-3310; tel. (787) 763-7199; fax (787) 764-2660; f. 1913; 310,000 vols; Caribbean Basin legal collection, judicial archives; Dir Prof. MICHAEL WHIPPLE; publs *Boletín, Guía para Usarios.*

University of Puerto Rico Library System, Río Piedras Campus: Box 23302, San Juan, PR 00931-3302; tel. (787) 764-0000, ext. 3296; fax (787) 763-5685; f. 1903; main library and eleven departmental libraries; 4,092,000 vols; Librarian JORGE ENCARNACÍON

TORRES; publs *Lumbre* (every 2 months), *Perspectiva* (2 a year), *Boletines de Divulgación* (irregular), *Biblionotas* (monthly), *Servicio de Alerta* (irregular), *Entorno* (2 a year), *Al Día* (4 a year)

Museums and Art Galleries

Ponce

Museo de Arte de Ponce: c/o The Luis A. Ferré Foundation, Inc, Apdo 9027, Ponce 00732; tel. (787) 840-1510; fax (787) 841-7309; f. 1956; European, American and Hispanic American paintings and sculptures; library of 4,000 vols; Dir CARMEN T. RUIZ-FISCHLER; publs exhibition catalogues.

San Germán

Museo de Arte Religioso: Apdo 1160, San Germán 00683; located at: Iglesia Porta Coeli, Calle Ramas Esq. Dr Veves, San Germán; tel. 892-5845; 17th-century church of Porta Coeli, constructed as a chapel for convent of Dominican Friars in San Germán; restored and converted into museum of religious art; Administrator GUIDO BARLETTA.

San Juan

Casa del Libro: Calle del Cristo 255, POB S-2265, San Juan; tel. (787) 723-0354; f. 1955; library-museum devoted to the art of the book; library of 5,000 vols; Dir MARIA TERESA ARRARÁS DE COLÓN.

Museo de Bellas Artes: Calle Cristo 253, Old San Juan; f. 1967 by the Institute of Culture; exhibition of paintings and sculptures by Puerto Rican artists from 18th century.

Museo de Historia Militar y Naval: Fuerte San Jerónimo, Puerta de Tierra, San Juan; historical castle converted into museum of military history; collection of weapons, flags and uniforms; run by the Museums and Parks dept of Inst. de Cultura Puertorriqueña (see above).

Universities

BAYAMÓN CENTRAL UNIVERSITY

POB 1725, Bayamón, PR 00960

Telephone: 786-3030
Fax: 740-2200

Founded 1970
Private control
Language of instruction: Spanish
Academic year: August to May, and summer courses

President: JOSÉ GANDÍA CARO
Academic Dean: MODESTO FERNÁNDEZ
Registrar: VICTOR COLÓN-RODRÍGUEZ
Librarian: Prof. CARLOS ALTAMIRANO

Library of 50,000 vols
Number of teachers: 140
Number of students: 3,135

Publications: *President's Letter* (quarterly), *Cruz Ansata* (annually)

DEANS

Business Administration: NYDIA COLÓN
Natural Sciences: LYDIA VILLAMIL
Education: NÉLIDA MELÉNDEZ
Humanities: Dr ANGEL SANZ MARCO

INTER-AMERICAN UNIVERSITY OF PUERTO RICO

POB 363255, San Juan, PR 00936-3255

Telephone: (787) 766-1912

Founded 1912
Private control
Languages of instruction: Spanish and English
Academic year: August to May (two semesters)

President: Dr JOSÉ R. GONZÁLEZ
Executive Vice-President: Prof. ANGEL A. RIVERA
Vice-President for Academic Affairs and Planning: Dr ALEJANDRO RUIZ
Vice-President for Financial Affairs, Administration and Services: MANUELITA MUÑOZ

Number of teachers: 2,548
Number of students: 44,265

Publication: *Interamericana Newspaper.*

CONSTITUENT CAMPUSES

Aguadilla Campus: PO Box 20000, Aguadilla, PR 00605-2000; tel. (787) 891-0925; Chancellor HILDA BACÓ; Dean of Studies SYLVIA ALDEBOL; Registrar MYRIAM MARCIAL.

Arecibo Campus: PO Box 4050, Arecibo, PR 00614-4050; tel. (787) 878-5475; Chancellor Zaida Vega; Dean of Studies (vacant); Registrar CARMEN RODRÍGUEZ; Librarian SARA ABREU.

Barranquitas Campus: PO Box 517, Barranquitas, PR 00794; tel. (787) 857-3600; Chancellor IRENE FERNÁNDEZ; Dean of Studies CARLOS CINTRÓN; Registrar CARMEN COLÓN.

Bayamón Campus: PO Box 6657, Santa Rosa Unit, Bayamón, PR 00960-9006; tel. (787) 780-4040; Chancellor FÉLIX TORRES; Dean of Studies OMAR CUETO; Registrar EDDIE AYALA; Librarian CARMEN ORTEGA.

DEANS OF DIVISIONS

Professional and Technical Programs: REINALDO CINTRÓN
Arts and Sciences: LUZ D. TALAVERA

Fajardo Campus: PO Box 70003, Fajardo, PR 00738-7003; tel. (787) 863-2390; Chancellor YOLANDA ROBLES; Dean of Studies ISMAEL SUÁREZ; Registrar MARGARITA JIMÉNEZ.

Guayama Campus: PO Box 10004, Guayama, PR 00785; tel. (787) 864-2222; Chancellor SAMUEL FEBRES; Dean of Studies CARLOS E. COLÓN; Registrar LUIS SOTO.

Metropolitan Campus: PO Box 191293, San Juan, PR 00936-1293; tel. (787) 250-1912; Chancellor MANUEL FERNÓS; Dean of Studies GENEROSA VÁZQUEZ; Registrar MARÍA CARLOS; Librarian LUIS FLORES.

DEANS OF DIVISIONS

Science and Technology: MIGDALIA TEXIDOR
Behavioural Sciences: MIGUEL POUPART
Economic and Administrative Sciences: ANGEL RUIZ
Humanistic Studies: DALIA RODRÍGUEZ
Education: (vacant)
Nursing: GLORIA ORTIZ

Ponce Campus: Carr. 1 Bo. Sabanetas, Mercedita, Ponce, PR 00715; tel. (787) 284-1912; Chancellor MARILINA WAYLAND; Dean of Studies VILMA COLÓN; Registrar RAFAEL SANTIAGO.

San Germán Campus: PO Box 5100, San Germán, PR 00683; tel. (787) 264-1912; Chancellor AGNES MOJICA; Dean of Studies JUAN APONTE; Registrar CARMEN JUAN; Librarian MARÍA ORTIZ.

DEANS OF DIVISIONS

Arts and Sciences: RAQUEL VARGAS
Professional Programmes: ZULMA QUIÑONES

School of Law: PO Box 70351, San Juan, PR 00936-8351; tel. (787) 571-1912; DEAN CARLOS RAMOS; Dean of Studies LUIS SÁNCHEZ; Registrar LAURA TARRIDO; Librarian CARMEN CRUZ.

School of Optometry: PO Box 191049, San Juan, PR 00919-1049; tel. (787) 765-1915; Dean ARTHUR AFANADOR; Dean of Studies ANDRÉS PAGÁN; Librarian AMARILIS NORIEGA.

PONTIFICAL CATHOLIC UNIVERSITY OF PUERTO RICO

Ponce, PR 00731-6382

Telephone: (787) 841-2000
Fax: (787) 840-0029

Founded 1948
Languages of instruction: Spanish and English
Private control
Academic year: August to May (two semesters and two summer sessions)
Campuses at Arecibo, Guayama and Mayagüez

Chancellor: Most Rev. FREMIOT TORRES OLIVER
Vice-Chancellor: Most Rev. RICARDO SURIÑACH
President: Lcdo JOSÉ ALBERTO MORALES
Vice-Presidents: FERNANDO L. ROSADO (Finance), CARL B. SAUDER (Student Affairs)
Registrar: Prof. IVÁN DÁVILA
Librarian: ESTHER IRIZARRY

Number of teachers: 643
Number of students: 10,819

Publications: *Horizontes, Revista de Derecho Puertorriqueño.*

DEANS

College of Arts and Humanities: Dra ENID MIRANDA
College of Science: Prof. JULIO RIVERA
School of Law: Lcdo CHARLES CUPRILL
College of Education: Dr LILLIAN NEGRÓN
College of Business Administration: Prof. JAIME SANTIAGO CANET

HEADS OF DEPARTMENTS

College of Arts and Humanities:
- English: Profa SHIRLEY SANTIAGO
- Hispanic Studies: Dr JOSÉ JUAN BÁEZ
- History and Fine Arts: A. SANTIAGO
- Philosophy and Theology: P. JOSÉ L. ALONSO
- Political Sciences and Sociology: Prof. MARICELY TIRADO
- Social Work: NILSA VÁZQUEZ

College of Business Administration:
- Accounting, Economics and Finance: Profa MARLA LLORENS
- Graduate Studies in Business Administration: Prof. KENYA CARRASQUILLO
- Management, Marketing and General Business: LOURDES DE LEÓN
- Secretarial Sciences: Prof. ANA BAEZ

College of Education:
- Educational Technology: JOSÉ LUCAS RODRÍGUEZ
- Elementary Education: Prof. MARÍA DE LOS A. TORRES
- Graduate Studies in Education: Dr GILBERT TORO
- Physical Education: CARLOS RIVERA
- Secondary Education: Sr LYDIA PÉREZ
- Sports: Prof. CARLOS M. RIVERA

College of Sciences:
- Biology: Prof. HAYDEE MALTES
- Chemistry: Prof. CARMEN VELÁZQUEZ
- General Sciences: Prof. CARMEN PERELES
- Graduate Programme in Nursing: Dr LOURDES MALDONADO
- Home Economics: Dr EVANGELINA RIVERA
- Mathematics: Prof. LUCINDA PÉREZ
- Nursing: Dr CARMEN MADERA
- Physics: Prof. LUCINDA PÉREZ
- Psychology: Dr CLARA COLÓN
- School of Medical Technology: Profa MARIBEL FIGUEROA

UNIVERSITY OF PUERTO RICO

POB 364984, San Juan, PR 00936-4984

Telephone: (787) 250-0000
Fax: (787) 759-6917

Founded 1903
State control

Languages of instruction: Spanish and English
Academic year: August to May

President: NORMAN I. MALDONADO
Director, Academic Affairs: JORGE A. CRUZ EMERIC (acting)
Director, Planning and Development: JOSÉ A. VALENTÍN (acting)
Director, Budget: BRUNILDA PEREIRA
Director, Finance: LUIS ESQUILÍN
Director, Public Relations: (vacant)
Director, Financial Aid: HERNÁN VAZQUEZTELL
Director, Information Systems: BELINDA JUNQUERA

Number of teachers: 4,475
Number of students: 67,135

Publications: *RIE* (quarterly), *La Torre*.

CONSTITUENT CAMPUSES

Río Piedras Campus: POB 23300, UPR Station, San Juan, PR 00931-3300; tel. (787) 764-0000; fax (787) 764-8799; f. 1903; 1,450 teachers; 20,515 students; Chancellor EFRAÍN GONZÁLEZ TEJERA; Registrar JUAN M. APONTE; Librarian JOSÉ ENCARNACIÓN TORRES.

DEANS

Business Administration: SONIA BALET
Humanities: FRANCES SCHWARTZ
Law: ANTONIO GARCÍA PADILLA
Education: SYLVIA RODRÍGUEZ
Natural Sciences: GLADYS ESCALONA
Architecture: ESTEBAN SENNYEY (acting)
Social Sciences: JOSÉ L. MÉNDEZ
General Studies: VANESSA PASCUAL

Mayagüez Campus: POB 5000, College Station, Mayagüez, PR 00709-5000; tel. (787) 832-4040; fax (787) 834-3031; f. 1911; 762 teachers; 12,594 students; Chancellor STUART RAMOS; Registrar BRISEIDA MARRERO; Librarian IRAIDA OLIVER DE PADOVANI.

DEANS

Arts and Sciences: HALLEY SÁNCHEZ
Agricultural Sciences: JOHN FERNÁNDEZ VAN CLEVE
Engineering: JACK ALLISON

Ciencias Médicas Campus: POB 365067, San Juan, PR 00936-5067; tel. (787) 758-2525; fax (787) 767-0755; f. 1926; 760 teachers; 3,120 students; Chancellor ADOLFO FIRPO (acting); Registrar MYRIAM Z. RIVERA; Librarian FRANCISCA CORRADA DEL RÍO

DEANS

Biosocial Sciences and Graduate School of Public Health: ORLANDO NIEVES
Health Related Professions: ESTELA ESTAPÉ
Medicine: ANGEL ROMÁN FRANCO
Pharmacy: ILIA OQUENDO JIMÉNEZ
Dentistry: LUIS A. MARINI
Nursing: MYRTHA DÍAZ

CONSTITUENT COLLEGES

Cayey University College: Antonio R. Barceló Ave, Cayey, PR 00736; tel. (787) 738-2161; fax (787) 738-8039; f. 1967; 192 teachers; 3,758 students; Chancellor JOSÉ L. MONSERRATE; Registrar LUIS T. DE LA CRUZ.

Humacao University College: CUH Station, Humacao, PR 00792; tel. (787) 850-0000; fax (787) 852-4638; f. 1962; 296 teachers; 4,294 students; Chancellor ROBERTO MARRERO CORLETTO; Registrar OLGA GONZÁLEZ.

REGIONAL COLLEGES

Regional Colleges Administration: POB 21876, UPR Station, San Juan, PR 00931-1876; tel. (787) 758-3454; fax (787) 753-3081; f. 1970; Chancellor TOMÁS FLORES (acting); Registrar LUIS C. RODRÍGUEZ.

Arecibo Technological University College: POB 4010, Arecibo, PR 00613-4010; tel. (787) 878-2830; fax (787) 880-4972; f. 1967; 256 teachers; 4,715 students; Dean Dir JOSEFA GARCÍA FIRPI; Registrar DAVID ACEVEDO.

Ponce Technological University College: POB 7186, Ponce, PR 00732; tel. (787) 844-8181; fax (787) 840-8108; f. 1970; 179 teachers; 4,126 students; Dean Dir RAFAEL CAPÓ; Registrar JOEL QUIJANO.

Bayamón Technological University College: Bayamón, PR 00959-1919; tel. (787) 786-2885; fax (787) 798-1595; f. 1971; 204 teachers; 5,827 students; Dean Dir CARMEN A. RIVERA; Registrar GEORGINA BATISTA.

Aguadilla Regional College: POB 250160, Ramey, Aguadilla, PR 00604-0160; tel. (787) 890-2681; fax (787) 890-4543; f. 1972; 133 teachers; 2,730 students; Dean Dir JUANA SEGARRA DE JARAMILLO; Registrar ROBERTO ORTIZ.

Carolina Regional College: POB 4800, Carolina, PR 00984-4800; tel. (787) 257-0000; fax (787) 750-7940; f. 1974; 176 teachers; 3,851 students; Dean Dir MYRNA MAYOL; Registrar GLORIA ROSARIO.

La Montaña Regional College: POB 2500, Utuado, PR 00761; tel. (787) 894-2828; fax (787) 894-2891; f. 1979; 67 teachers; 1,217 students; Dean Dir RAMÓN COLÓN MURPHY; Registrar ADOLFO GARCÍA MORELL.

UNIVERSITY OF THE SACRED HEART

POB 12383, San Juan, PR 00914-0383

Telephone: (787) 728-1515
Fax: (787) 728-1692

Founded 1935
Private control
Language of instruction: Spanish

President: Dr JOSÉ JAIME RIVERA
Dean of Academic and Student Affairs: Dr CÉSAR REY
Dean of Administration: LOURDES BERTRÁN
Librarian: MARÍA DE LOS A. GARÍN

Number of teachers: 151 (full-time), 225 (part-time)
Number of students: 4,943

DIRECTORS

Department of Business Administration: Prof. YEZMIN HERNÁNDEZ
Department of Humanities: Prof. IRMA HERNÁNDEZ
Department of Natural Sciences: Dr CARMEN PADIAL
Department of Communications: Prof. MARÍA T. MARTÍNEZ
Department of Education: Prof. FERNANDO PIERAS
Department of Social Sciences: Lic. ROSA RAQUEL RUIZ
Department of Continuing Education: ELVIA AGOSTO
Evening Programs: NOEMÍ TORRES

College

Conservatory of Music of Puerto Rico: 350 Calle Rafael Lamar, San Juan 00918; f. 1959; library of 32,000 items; Chancellor Dr RAYMOND TORRES-SANTOS.

QATAR

Research Institutes

AGRICULTURE, FISHERIES AND VETERINARY SCIENCE

Soil Research Station: Rodet al-Farassa.

HISTORY, GEOGRAPHY AND ARCHAEOLOGY

Gulf Cooperation Council Folklore Centre: POB 7996, Doha; tel. 861999; fax 867170; f. 1982 to collect, study, disseminate and protect indigenous local folklore mainly in the fields of literature, customs and traditions, music and dance, arts and crafts; mem. states: Bahrain, Kuwait, Oman, Qatar, Saudi Arabia, UAE; archives: 4,853 books, 110 journals, also video cassettes, cassette recordings, audio tapes, slides, negatives, proofs, contact sheets; Dir ABDALRAHMAN AL-MANNAI; publ. *Al Ma'thurat Al Sha'biyyah* (folklore).

Libraries and Archives

Doha

National Library: POB 205, Doha; tel. 429955; fax 429976; f. 1962; 198,000 vols in Arabic, 31,000 vols in English, 1,300 vols Arabic MSS, 454 on microfilm, 1,079 periodicals on microfilm and 10,248 on microfiche, bibliographic services on subjects of local interest; 5 brs; Dir M. H. AL NASSER.

Research and Documents Section: POB 923, Amir's Office, Doha; tel. 321385; fax 427132; f. 1975; Dir MUHAMMAD KHALIFA AL-ATTIYAH.

Museums and Art Galleries

Doha

Qatar National Museum: Doha; opened 1975; consists of five major sections: the old Amiri Palace (11 1901 style buildings), the new palace, aquarium, lagoon, botanical garden; collections: ethnography, archaeo-history, geology, botany, zoology, jewellery, numismatics, perfumery; Dir IBRAHIM JABER AL-JABER.

University

UNIVERSITY OF QATAR

POB 2713, Doha
Telephone: 83-2222
Telex: 4630
Fax: 83-5111

Founded 1973 as Faculties of Education, University status 1977
State control
Language of instruction: Arabic
Academic year: September to June

Supreme Head: HH Sheikh HAMAD BIN KHALIFA AL THANI, Amir of Qatar
President: Dr IBRAHIM SALEH AL-NAOMI
Vice-President for Academic Affairs: Dr ABDUL RAHMAN HASSAN AL-IBRAHIM
Vice-President for Research and Social Services: Dr MOHAMED ABDULRAHIM QAFFOUD
Vice-President for Administrative Affairs: Dr SAIF SAYED AL-SOWADI
Library Director: AHMED M. AL-QATTAN
Library of 334,000 vols
Number of teachers: 637
Number of students: 7,794
Publications: Faculty bulletins (annually), *Fruits of Knowledge* (annually).

DEANS

Faculty of Education: Dr ABDUL AZIZ ABDULQADER AL-MOUGHASEEB
Faculty of Humanities and Social Sciences: Dr DARWISH AL-EMADI
Faculty of Science: Dr ABDULLA HOUSIN RASHED AL-KOBAISI
Faculty of Islamic Studies: Dr ALI YOUSIF AL-MOHAMADI
Faculty of Engineering: Prof. Dr ISMAEL A. TAG
Faculty of Administration and Economics: Dr YOUSEF MOHAMED OBIDAN

HEADS OF DEPARTMENTS

Faculty of Education:

- Foundations of Education: Dr SHAIKHA ABDULLA AL-MISNAD
- Administration and Educational Planning and Curriculum and Methods of Teaching: Prof. Dr MEDHAT AHMED AL-NIMER
- Educational Technology: Dr ABDULLAH ESSA. AL-MANNAI
- Art Education: Prof. Dr LAILA AHMED ALLEM
- Mental Health: Prof. Dr ALAA-ELDIN A. KAFAFI
- Educational Psychology: Prof. Dr ANWAR REYAD ABDUL RAHIM
- Home Economics: Dr FATIMA AL-BAKER
- Physical Education: Prof. Dr ESSAM AL-HILALI

Faculty of Humanities and Social Sciences:

- Arabic Language and Journalism: Prof. Dr OMMER MOHAMED AL-DAQAQ
- Geography: Prof. Dr AHMAD ABDULLAH ABU-BAKER
- History: Prof. Dr AHMAD BADR
- Social Work: Prof. Dr ABDULSABOOR IBRAHIM SAADAN
- Sociology: Prof. Dr ALI ABDUL RAZEK JALABI
- English and Modern European Languages: Dr MOHAMED JALEEM MUNLA
- English Language Teaching Unit: MUNEERA HAMAD AL-THANI
- Philosophy: Prof. Dr AMMAR JUMA AL-THALIBY

Faculty of Science:

- Chemistry: Dr ABDUL BASIT AL-ASSAR
- Physics: Prof. Dr LATIFA AL-HOUTY
- Botany: Dr AHMAD MOHAMED ALI
- Zoology: Prof. Dr MOHAMAD FATHI SOOD
- Marine Sciences: Prof. Dr ABDUL FATAH ALI GHOBASH
- Computer Science: Dr MOHAMED NAZIH AL-DOURINI
- Mathematics: Prof. Dr MOHAMED AL-AMIN AHMAD AL-TOM
- Geology: Prof. Dr MOHAMED ALI MOHAMED
- Environmental Studies Unit: Prof. Dr SAID EL-HAFFAR

Faculty of Islamic Studies:

- Philosophy of Religion: Prof. Dr MOHAMED AL-SAIED AL-DOSOQI
- Law: Dr YOUSEF IBRAHIM YOUSEF
- Islamic Culture, Theology and Comparative Religion: Dr MOHAMED ABDULSATAR NASSAR
- Koranic Interpretation and *Hadith*: Dr ADNAN MOHAMED ZARZOR

Faculty of Engineering:

- Mechanical Engineering: Prof. Dr MOHAMED MOUNIER SHAHEEN
- Electrical Engineering: Prof. Dr SAFWAT MAHROOS MAHMOOD
- Civil Engineering: Prof. Dr SHAMIM AHMAD MOHAMED
- Chemical Engineering: Prof. Dr SALAHAL-DEEN MURSHEDE HAMAM

Faculty of Administration and Economics:

- Accountancy: Prof. Dr SAMIR AHMAD ABUGHABA
- Business Administration: Prof. Dr MOHAMED MOHAMED ARISHA
- Economics: Prof. Dr MOHAMED KHALID AL-HARIRI
- General Administration: Prof. Dr NASIF ABDUL AL-KHALEQ
- College of Technology: Prof. Dr AHMED AL-MARAKSHI

ATTACHED INSTITUTES

Educational Research Centre: educational research and studies which contribute to the development of education in the State of Qatar, oriented among other things toward improvement of the educational process, curricula and textbooks; Dir Prof. Dr ABDUL AZIZ ABDUL REHMAN KAMAL.

Documentation and Humanities Research Centre: collection, classification and preparation of documents pertaining to the field of humanities as a basic source of research, and the issuing of documented research papers; specialized research on the heritage of the Gulf area in all its aspects: social, cultural, linguistic and literary; Dir Prof. Dr MUSTAFA AL-KHATEEB.

Scientific and Applied Research Centre: to develop experience in scientific, industrial and agricultural fields with special reference to industries, natural resources, agriculture and animal resources of Qatar; and to contribute to the transfer of technology and adapt it for application in Qatar; Dir HIMEAD AL-MIDFA.

Research Centre for *Sirra* and *Sunna Studies*: research related to the *Sirra* of the Prophet Mohamed, i.e. his preaching, moral and spiritual values, and his life, and the *Sunna* of the Prophet Mohamed, i.e. his sayings and acts which are the second source of guidance for the practice of Islam after the holy Koran; Dir Prof. Dr YOUSEF ABDULLAH AL-QARDHAWI.

Colleges

Language Teaching Institute: POB 3224, Doha; tel. 321690; f. 1972; library of 6,000 vols; 29 teachers, 504 students; part-time courses in Arabic, English, French, for mature students already in employment; Dir IBRAHIM AL-DIRBASTI.

Regional Training Centre: POB 1300, Doha; tel. 870000; f. 1970 with UNDP technical aid; library of 2,500 vols; 700 students; Dir F. KADDOURA.

ROMANIA

Learned Societies

GENERAL

Academia Română (Romanian Academy): 71102 Bucharest, Calea Victoriei 125; tel. (1) 650-76-80; telex 11470; fax (1) 312-02-09; f. 1866; sections of Philology and Literature (Chair. ZOE DUMITRESCU-BUŞULENGA), Historical Sciences and Archaeology (Chair. DAN BERINDEI), Mathematical Sciences (Chair. ROMULUS CRISTESCU), Physical Sciences (Chair. HORIA SCUTARU-UNGUREANU), Chemical Sciences (Chair. MARIA BREZEANU), Biological Sciences (Chair. GHEORGHE ZARNEA), Geonomical Sciences (Chair. MIRCEA SĂNDULESCU), Technical Sciences (Chair. GHEORGHE BUZDUGAN), Agricultural Sciences and Forestry (Chair. VALERIU COTEA), Medical Sciences (Chair. NICOLAE CAJAL), Economics, Legal Sciences and Sociology (Chair. NICOLAE N. CONSTANTINESCU), Philosophical, Theological and Psychological Sciences and Education (Chair. ALEXANDRU SURDU), Arts, Architecture and Audiovisual (Chair. MIHNEA GHEORGHIU), Science and Technology of Information (Chair. DAN DASCĂLU); 77 mems, 97 corresp. mems; attached research institutes: see Research Institutes; library: see Libraries and Archives; Pres. EUGEN SIMION; Sec.-Gen. MARIUS SABIN PECULEA; publs *Studii şi cercetări matematice* (Studies and Research in Mathematics); *Revue Roumaine de mathématiques pures et appliquées*; *Mathematica; Revue d'analyse numérique et de théorie de l'approximation*; *Romanian Astronomical Journal*; *Romanian Reports of Physics*; *Revue Roumaine de chimie*; *Romanian Chemical Quarterly Review*; *Cellulose Chemistry and Technology*; *Studii şi cercetări de mecanică aplicată* (Studies and Research in Applied Mechanics); *Revue Roumaine des sciences techniques: Série de mécanique appliquée; Revue Roumaine des sciences techniques: Série électrotechnique et énergétique*; *Functional and Architectural Electronics*; *Studii şi cercetări de biochimie* (Studies and Research in Biochemistry); *Revue Roumaine de biochimie*; *Studii şi cercetări de biologie: Seria biologie vegetală* (Studies and Research in Biology: Series of Plant Biology); *Revue Roumaine de biologie: Série de biologie végétale*; *Studii şi cercetări de biologie: Seria biologie animală* (Studies and Research in Biology: Series of Animal Biology); *Revue Roumaine de biologie: Série de biologie animale*; *Romanian Neurosurgery*; *Romanian Journal of Biophysics*; *Revue Roumaine des sciences économiques*; *Studii şi cercetări de antropologie* (Studies and Research in Anthropology); *Annuaire Roumain d'Anthropologie*; *Ocrotirea naturii şi a mediului înconjurător* (The Protection of Nature and of the Environment); *Travaux de l'Institut de spéléologie 'Emile Racovitza'*; *Studii şi cercetări de geologie, geofizică şi geografie* (Studies and Research in Geology, Geophysics and Geography, 3 series); *Revue Roumaine de géologie, géophysique et géographie* (3 series); *Studii şi cercetări lingvistice* (Studies and Research in Linguistics); *Revue Roumaine de Linguistique*; *Cahiers de linguistique théorique et appliquée*; *Cercetări de lingvistică* (Linguistic Researches); *Limba română* (The Romanian Language); *Nyelv- és Irodalomtudományi Közlemények*; *Fonetică şi dialectologie* (Phonetics and Dialectology); *Anuar de lingvistică şi istorie literară* (Yearbook of Linguistics and Literary History); *Synthesis - Bulletin du Comité National de Littérature comparée*; *Revista de etnografie şi folclor* (Journal of Ethnography and Folklore); *Revue des études sud-est européennes*; *Historia Urbana*; *Revue Roumaine des sciences juridiques*; *Romanian Journal of Sociology*; *Revista română de demografie* (Romanian Journal of Demography); *Calitatea vieţii* (Quality of Life); *Revue Roumaine de philosophie*; *Revista de psihologie* (Journal of Psychology); *Revue Roumaine de psychologie*.

Asociaţia Culturală 'Pro Basarabia şi Bucovina' (Bessarabia and Bucovina Cultural Association): 70601 Bucharest, B-dul Mihail Kogălniceanu 19; tel. 614-03-59; f. 1990; 60,000 mems; Exec. Pres. NICOLAE RADU HALIPPA.

Centrul European de Cultură (European Cultural Centre): 71297 Bucharest, B-dul Primăverii 50; tel. and fax (1) 223-26-19; f. 1990; promotes cultural tourism; library of 3,000 vols, 40 periodicals; Pres. Acad. DAN BERINDEI; Exec. Dir GARIA POPESCU.

Fundaţia Culturală Română (Romanian Cultural Foundation): 71273 Bucharest, Aleea Alexandru 38; tel. (1) 230-13-73; fax (1) 230-75-59; f. 1990; promotes Romanian culture abroad; Pres. AUGUSTIN BUZURA; publs *Curierul românesc* (Romanian Courier, monthly), *Dilema* (weekly), *Lettres internationales* (quarterly), *Transylvanian Review* (quarterly), *Romanian Civilisation* (quarterly), *Contrafort* (monthly), *Destin Românesc* (quarterly).

Societatea Cultural-Ştiinţifică 'Getica' (Getica Cultural Scientific Society): 70060 Bucharest 37, POB 37-149; premises at: 70308 Bucharest, Str. Plantelor 8–10 (provisional); tel. (1) 321-45-12; f. 1990; 87 mems; library of 4,000 vols; Pres. GABRIEL GHEORGHE; publ. *Getica*.

AGRICULTURE, FISHERIES AND VETERINARY SCIENCE

Academia de Ştiinţe Agricole şi Silvice 'Gheorghe Ionescu-Şişeşti' (Gheorghe Ionescu-Şişeşti Academy of Agricultural and Forestry Sciences): Bucharest, B-dul Mărăşti 61; tel. (1) 618-06-99; fax (1) 167-01-55; f. 1969; sections of Soil Science, Land Reclamation and Environmental Protection in Agriculture, Mechanization, Field Crops, Horticulture, Animal Husbandry, Veterinary Medicine, Forestry Science, Agricultural Economics, Food Industry; 80 mems, 85 corresp. mems; attached research institutes: see Research Institutes; library: see Libraries and Archives; Pres. ALEX. VIOREL VRÂNCEANU; Scientific Sec. ADRIAN PETRE; publs *Buletinul informativ al Academiei de Ştiinţe Agricole şi Silvice* (annually), *Bulletin de l'Académie des Sciences Agricoles et Forestières* (annually).

Asociaţia Economiştilor Agrarieni din România (Agrarian Economists' Association of Romania): 75114 Bucharest, B-dul Mărăşti 61; tel. 617-21-80; f. 1990; 42 mems; library of 4,000 vols; Pres. Prof. N. N. CONSTANTINESCU; Gen. Sec. RADU COTIANU.

Societatea Inginerilor Agronomi (Agronomists' Society): 71331 Bucharest, B-dul Mărăşti 59; tel. 618-22-30/241; f. 1990; 3,500 mems; Pres. Prof. Dr GHEORGHE BÎLTEANU; Gen. Sec. Dr RUXANDRA CIOFU.

Societatea Naţională Română pentru Ştiinţa Solului (Romanian National Soil Science Society): 71331 Bucharest, B-dul Mărăşti 61; tel. 222-76-20; fax 222-59-79; f. 1962; 644 mems; library of 3,000 vols; Pres. Dr RADU LĂCĂTUŞU; Gen. Sec. CONSTANTIN CRĂCIUN; publ. *Ştiinţa solului* (2 a year).

Societatea Română de Zootehnie (Romanian Society of Animal Production): 71331 Bucharest, B-dul Mărăşti 59; tel. (1) 618-22-30/262; fax (1) 312-56-93; f. 1990; 4,500 mems; Pres. Prof. STEFAN POPESCU-VIFOR; Senior Sec. Dr AGATHA POPESCU.

ARCHITECTURE AND TOWN PLANNING

Uniunea Arhitecţilor din România (Architects' Union of Romania): 79182 Bucharest, Str. Academiei 18–20; tel. (1) 614-07-43; fax (1) 312-09-56; f. 1891; 1,720 mems; library of 13,000 vols; Pres. Arch. ALEXANDRU BELDIMAN; publs *Architectura* (quarterly), *Buletin Informativ* (monthly).

ECONOMICS, LAW AND POLITICS

Asociaţia de Drept Internaţional şi Relaţii Internaţionale (Association of International Law and International Relations): 71268 Bucharest, Şos. Kiseleff 47; tel. (1) 222-44-22; fax (1) 222-74-62; f. 1965; 500 mems; library of 8,000 vols; Pres. CORNELIU MĂNESCU; Sec.-Gen. MIRCEA MALIŢA.

Asociaţia Română de Drept Umanitar (Romanian Association of Humanitarian Law): 75269 Bucharest, Calea Rahovei 147–151, Sector 5; fax (1) 335-41-75; f. 1990; 200 mems; library of 5,000 vols; Pres. Dr IONEL CLOŞCĂ; Gen. Sec. GHEORGHE BĂDESCU; publ. *Revista română de drept umanitar*.

FINE AND PERFORMING ARTS

Asociaţia Artiştilor Fotografi (Art Photographers' Association): 70700 Bucharest, POB 1–223; f. 1956; 1,500 mems; library of 12,000 photographic magazines; publ. *Fotografia şi Video* (every 2 months).

Asociaţia Artiştilor Plastici – Bucureşti (Artists' Association of Bucharest): 70036 Bucharest, Piaţa Rosetti 2; tel. 613-38-60; f. 1973; 1,800 mems; Pres. Dr Eng. IOAN CEZAR CORÂCI; Gen. Sec. DAN SEGĂRCEANU.

Uniunea Artiştilor Plastici din România (Romanian Union of Fine Arts): 71117 Bucharest, Str. Nicolae Iorga 21; tel. (1) 650-49-20; fax (1) 311-35-72; f. 1950; 4,170 mems; library of 12,000 vols; Pres. AUREL NICOLAE ALEXI.

Uniunea Compozitorilor şi Muzicologilor din România (Composers' and Musicologists' Union of Romania): 71102 Bucharest, Calea Victoriei 141; tel. 650-28-38; fax 650-28-25; f. 1920; 432 mems; library of 50,000 vols incl. spec. colln of Romanian music (printed scores and MSS); Pres. ADRIAN IORGULESCU; publs *Muzica* (quarterly), *Actualitatea Muzicală* (every 2 weeks).

Uniunea Cineaştilor din România (Romanian Film Makers' Union): 70169 Bucharest, Str. Mendeleev 28–30; tel. (1) 650-57-41; fax (1) 311-12-46; f. 1963; 830 mems; Pres. MIHNEA GHEORGHIU; Dir CONSTANTIN PIVNICIERU.

Uniunea Teatrală din România (Theatre Union of Romania): 70141 Bucharest 22, Str. George Enescu 2–4; tel. 615-36-36; fax 312-

09-13; e-mail uniter@buc.soros.ro; f. 1990; 860 mems; library of 1,700 vols; Pres. Ion Caramitru; publs *Bulletin informativ* (4 a year), *Semnal teatral* (Theatre Signal, 6 a year).

HISTORY, GEOGRAPHY AND ARCHAEOLOGY

Comitetul Naţional al Istoricilor (National Committee for Historical Sciences): 71102 Bucharest, Calea Victoriei 125; tel. (1) 650-76-80; f. 1955; Pres. Acad. Ştefan Pascu; Gen. Sec. Dan Berindei; publ. *Nouvelles d'études d'histoire* (irregular).

Federaţia Filatelică Română (Romanian Philatelic Federation): 70119 Bucharest, Str. Boteanu 6; tel. 613-89-21; f. 1958; 35,000 mems; library of 3,000 vols; Pres. Mircea Stănculescu; publ. *Filatelia* (monthly).

Societatea de Ştiinţe Geografice din România (Society of Geographical Sciences of Romania): 70111 Bucharest, B-dul Bălcescu 1; tel. 614-93-50; f. 1875; 5,000 mems; library of 4,000 vols; Exec. Pres. Posea Grigore; publs *Terra, Bulletin*.

Societatea de Ştiinţe Istorice din România (Society of Historical Sciences of Romania): 70032 Bucharest, B-dul Republicii 13; tel. (1) 613-13-29; fax (1) 321-05-35; f. 1949; 5,000 mems; Chair. N. Adăniloaie; Sec.-Gen. B. Teodorescu; publ. *Studii şi articole de istorie* (annually).

Societatea Numismatică Română (Romanian Numismatic Society): 70772 Bucharest, Str. Popa Tatu 20; tel. 642-26-02; f. 1903; 1,810 mems; library of 3,800 vols; Pres. Dr Constantin Preda; Sec.-Gen. Aurică Smaranda; publ. *Buletinul* (annually).

LANGUAGE AND LITERATURE

PEN Club: Bucharest, Calea Victoriei 113; 27 mems; Pres. Ana Blandiana; Sec. Mircea Martin.

Societatea de Ştiinţe Filologice din România (Society of Philological Sciences of Romania): 79664 Bucharest, B-dul Schitul Măgureanu 1; tel. (1) 615-17-92; f. 1949; 12,000 mems; Pres. Acad. Ion Coteanu; Gen. Sec. Prof. Dr Mircea Frânculescu; publs *Limbă şi literatură* (quarterly, summaries in foreign languages), *Limbă şi literatură română* (quarterly), *Buletinul SŞF* (annually).

Societatea Română de Lingvistică (Romanian Society of Linguistics): 76100 Bucharest, Calea 13 Septembrie 13; tel. (1) 641-27-57; f. 1941; Pres. Prof. Emanuel Vasiliu; Sec. Laurenţiu Theban.

Societatea Română de Lingvistică Romanică (Romanian Society of Romance Linguistics): 70106 Bucharest, Str. Edgar Quinet 7; f. 1962; 250 mems; library of 2,000 vols; Pres. Dr Marius Sala; Gen. Sec. Sanda Reinheimer Rîpeanu; publ. *Bulletin* (irregular).

Uniunea Scriitorilor din România (Romanian Writers' Union): Bucharest, Calea Victoriei 115 tel. 650-72-45; telex 11796; fax 312-96-34; f. 1949; Pres. Laurentiu Ulici; publs *România Literară, Luceafărul, Viaţa Românească, Secolul 20, Contrapunct, Caiete Critice, Memoria, Apostrof, Ramîuri, Helikon, Lato.*

MEDICINE

Academia de Stiinţe Medicale (Academy of Medical Sciences): 79173 Bucharest, B-dul 1 Mai 11; f. 1969; sections of Biomedical Research (Sec. Dr C. Taşcă), Clinical Medicine (Sec. Prof. Dr L. Gherasim), Prophylactic Medicine and Public Health (Sec. Dr Tr. Ionescu), Pharmaceutical Research (Sec. Prof. Dr Emanoil I. Manolescu); 82 mems, 14 corresp. mems; attached research institutes: see Research Institutes; Pres. Prof. Dr Ştefan M. Milcu; Gen. Sec. Dr Mihai Zamfirescu.

Asociaţia Medicală Română (Romanian Medical Association): 70754 Bucharest 1, Str. Ionel Perlea 10; tel. (1) 314-10-71; fax (1) 312-13-57; f. 1873; 38 affiliated socs; Pres. Prof. Dr Valeriu Popescu; Sec.-Gen. Prof. Dr Emanoil Popescu; publ. *Buletin A.M.R.* (quarterly).

Societatea de Medici şi Naturalişti Iaşi (Society of Physicians and Naturalists in Iaşi): 6600 Iaşi, B-dul Independenţei 16, POB 25; tel. (32) 14-29-80; f. 1830; medicine, pharmacy, dentistry; 1,640 mems; Chair. Prof. Ion Hăulică; publ. *Revista Medico-Chirurgicală* (quarterly, multi-lingual, English abstracts).

Societatea Română de Stomatologie (Romanian Society of Stomatology): 70754 Bucharest, Str. Progresului 12; tel. 613-93-12; f. 1938; Pres. Prof. Dr Lucian Ene; Sec. Prof. Dr Corneliu Burlibaşa; publ. *Stomatologia* (quarterly).

NATURAL SCIENCES

General

Asociaţia Oamenilor de Ştiinţă din România (Scientists' Association of Romania): 78101 Bucharest, Calea Griviţei 21 (Et. 5); tel. and fax (1) 613-62-34; f. 1956; Pres. Prof. Dr Vasile Cândea; Scientific Sec.-Gen. Prof. Dr Ing. Ion Hohan.

Biological Sciences

Societatea de Ştiinţe Biologice din România (Society of Biological Sciences of Romania): 77206 Bucharest, Intrarea Portocalelor 1-3; f. 1949; 9,000 mems; library of 6,100 vols; Chair. Prof. Dr Ion Anghel; Sec.-Gen. Dr Constantin Voica; publ. *Natura* (quarterly).

Mathematical Sciences

Societatea de Ştiinţe Matematice din România (Society of Mathematical Sciences of Romania): 70109 Bucharest, Str. Academiei 14; tel. (1) 314-46-53; fax (1) 312-40-72; f. 1895; 8,000 mems; Pres. P. Mocanu; Sec.-Gen. Florin Diac; publs *Bulletin Mathématique* (quarterly), *Gazeta Matematică* (monthly), *Gazeta Matematică – Perfecţionare Didactică şi Informare Ştiinţifică* (quarterly).

Physical Sciences

Societatea de Ştiinţe Fizice şi Chimice din România (Society of Physical and Chemical Sciences of Romania): 70626 Bucharest, B-dul Schitu Măgureanu 1; tel. and fax (1) 314-75-08; f. 1890; 20,000 mems; Pres. Prof. Dr Victor Emanuel Sahini; Gen. Sec. Prof. N. Martalogu; publ. *Revista de Fizică şi Chimie* (monthly).

Societatea Geologică a României (Geological Society of Romania): 78344 Bucharest, Str. Caransebeş 1; f. 1930; 500 mems; Pres. Prof. Dan Rădulescu; Gen. Sec. Titus Brustur; publ. *Buletinul* (annually).

RELIGION, SOCIOLOGY AND ANTHROPOLOGY

Asociaţia Slaviştilor din România (Slav Studies Association of Romania): 70151 Bucharest, Str. Pitar Moş 7-13; f. 1956; 150 mems; Pres. Prof. Dr Dorin Gămulescu; Gen. Sec. Dr Mariana Mangiulea; publ. *Romanoslavica* (annually).

Institutul Biblic şi de Misiune al Bisericii Ortodoxe Române (Biblical and Missionary Institute of the Romanian Orthodox Church): 70526 Bucharest, Intrarea Patriarhiei 7–9; tel. 336-45-49; f. 1990; Dir. Aurelian Marinescu; Sec. Fr Valentin Bogdan.

Societatea de Etnologie din România (Ethnology Society of Romania): 70714 Bucharest, Str. Zalomit 12; tel. (1) 311-03-23; f. 1990; 200 mems; library; Pres. Dr. Romulus Vulcănescu; Sec. Ion Moanţa; publ. *Etnologie românească* (quarterly).

TECHNOLOGY

Asociaţia Generală a Inginerilor din România (General Association of Engineers of Romania): 70179 Bucharest, Calea Victoriei 118; tel. (1) 659-41-60; fax (1) 312-55-31; e-mail agin@pcnet.pcnet.ro; f. 1881; 15,600 mems; library of 32,000 vols; Pres. Prof. Dr Eur. Ing. Mihai Mihăiţă; Gen. Sec. Luminita Scurei; publs *Univers Ingineresc* (2 a month), *Buletinul Tehnic AGIR* (quarterly), *Anuarul AGIR* (annually).

Research Institutes

AGRICULTURE, FISHERIES AND VETERINARY SCIENCE

Aquaproject, SA: 77703 Bucharest, Spl. Independenţei 294; tel. (1) 637-30-60; telex 10672; fax (1) 637-79-65; f. 1953; design institute for water resources engineering; library of 10,000 vols; Gen. Dir Eng. Dr Dan Marinovici.

Centrul de Cercetare şi Producţie pentru Piscicultură, Pescuit şi Industrializarea Pestelui (Research and Production Centre for Fish Culture, Fisheries and the Fish Industry): 6200 Galaţi, Str. Portului 2–4; tel. (934) 16914; telex 51296; attached to Acad. of Agricultural and Forestry Sciences; Dir Constantin Pecheanu.

Centrul de Cercetări pentru Protecţia Plantelor (Research Centre for Plant Protection): 71592 Bucharest, B-dul Ion Ionescu de la Brad 8; tel. 633-58-50; f. 1967; attached to Acad. of Agricultural and Forestry Sciences; library of 8,000 vols; Dir Dr Horia Iliescu; publs *Analele* (annually), *Pesticide Tests*, *Plant Protection Bulletin* (quarterly).

Institutul de Biologie şi Nutriţie Animală (Institute of Biology and Animal Nutrition): 8113 Baloteşti, Sect. Agricol Ilfov; tel. (179) 52001; fax (1) 222-44-10; f. 1970; attached to Acad. of Agricultural and Forestry Sciences; library of 5,000 vols; Dir Ioan Moldovan; publs *Anale*, *Archiva Zootechnica* (in English) (both annually).

Institutul de Cercetare şi Dezvoltare pentru Valorificarea Produselor Horticole (Institute of Research and Development for Marketing Horticultural Products): 75614 Bucharest, Intrarea Binelui 1A, POB 1-93; tel. (1) 312-90-37; fax (1) 330-36-85; f. 1967; attached to Acad. of Agricultural and Forestry Sciences; library of 3,575 vols; Dir Doc. Dr Eng. Andrei Gherghi; publ. *Lucrări ştiinţifice* (annually), *Horticultura* (monthly).

Institutul de Cercetare şi Inginerie Tehnologică pentru Irigaţii şi Drenaje (Research and Technological Engineering Institute for Irrigation and Drainage): 8384 Băneasa, Jud. Giurgiu; tel. (46) 28-50-23; telex 15762; fax (46) 28-50-24; f. 1977; attached to Acad. of Agricultural and Forestry Sciences; library of 5,700 vols, 763 periodicals; Dir Gheorghe Crutu; publ. *Scientific Papers on Irrigation and Drainage* (annually).

Institutul de Cercetare şi Producţie a Cartofului (Potato Research and Production Institute): 2200 Braşov, Str. Fundăturii 2; tel. (68) 15-06-47; fax (68) 15-15-08; f. 1977; attached to Acad. of Agricultural and Forestry Sciences; library of 7,800 vols; Dir Dr Constantin Draica; publs *Anale (Lucrări ştiinţifice), Cartoful în România.*

Institutul de Cercetare şi Dezvoltare pentru Apicultură (Research and Development Institute for Beekeeping): Bucharest, B-dul Ficusului 42, S1; tel. (1) 679-55-60; fax (1) 232-02-87; f. 1974; attached to Acad. of Agricultural and Forestry Sciences; library of 10,000 vols, 3,450 periodicals; Dir Dipl. Eng.

AUREL MĂLAIU; publ. *România apicolă* (monthly).

Institutul de Cercetare şi Producţie pentru Creşterea Bovinelor (Research and Production Institute for Bovine Breeding): 8113 Baloteşti, Sect. Agricol Ilfov; tel. (1) 795-12-07; f. 1970; attached to Acad. of Agricultural and Forestry Sciences; library of 11,000 vols; Dir Dr Ing. MIRCEA PĂTRAŞCU; publ. *Taurine—Scientific Works* (annually).

Institutul de Cercetare şi Producţie pentru Creşterea Ovinelor şi a Caprinelor (Research and Production Institute for Sheep and Goat Breeding): Constanţa Palas, Jud. Constanţa; f. 1897; attached to Acad. of Agricultural and Forestry Sciences; Dir Dr A. PIVOTA.

Institutul de Cercetare şi Producţie pentru Creşterea Păsărilor şi Animalelor Mici (Research and Production Institute for Poultry and Small Animal Breeding): Baloteşti, Sect. Agricol Ilfov; f. 1970; attached to Acad. of Agricultural and Forestry Sciences; Dir Dr GRIGORE MUSCALU.

Institutul de Cercetare şi Producţie pentru Creşterea Porcinelor (Research and Production Institute for Pig Breeding): 8111 Periş, Sect. Agricol Ilfov; tel. 614-15-63; f. 1970; attached to Acad. of Agricultural and Forestry Sciences; library of 8,000 vols; Dir Dr CONSTANTIN AURELIU; publ. *Lucrări ştiinţifice* (annually).

Institutul de Cercetare şi Producţie pentru Cultura Pajiştilor (Grassland Research and Production Institute): 2200 Braşov-Măgurele, Str. Cucului 5; tel. and fax (68) 15-06-50; f. 1969; attached to Acad. of Agricultural and Forestry Sciences; library of 7,000 vols; Dir Dr MIRCEA NEAGU; publ. *Lucrări ştiinţifice* (annually).

Institutul de Cercetare şi Producţie Pomicolă (Research Institute for Fruit Growing): 0312 Piteşti-Mărăcineni, Jud. Argeş; tel. (48) 63-20-66; telex 18294; fax (48) 63-42-92; f. 1967; attached to Acad. of Agricultural and Forestry Sciences; library of 20,000 vols; Dir Dr Ing. PARNIA PÂRVAN.

Institutul de Cercetare-Dezvoltare pentru Cultura şi Industrializarea Sfeclei de Zahăr şi Substanţelor Dulci (Research and Development Institute for the Cultivation and Processing of Sugar Beet and Sweet substances): 8264 Fundulea, Jud. Călarasi; tel. and fax (1) 312-16-28; f. 1981; attached to Acad. of Agricultural and Forestry Sciences; Dir Dr Ing. ALEXANDRU TIANU; publ. *Scientific Works – Beet and Sugar* (annually).

Institutul de Cercetări pentru Cereale şi Plante Tehnice (Research Institute for Cereals and Industrial Crops): 8264 Fundulea, Jud. Călăraşi; tel. and fax (1) 311-07-22; f. 1957; attached to Acad. of Agricultural and Forestry Sciences; library of 12,000 vols; Dir GHEORGHE SIN; publs *Analele* (annually), *Probleme de genetică teoretică şi aplicată, Probleme de agrofitotehnie teoretică şi aplicată, Probleme de protecţia plantelor* (quarterly), *Romanian Agricultural Research* (every 2 years).

Institutul de Cercetări pentru Ingineria Mediului (Research Institute for Environmental Engineering): Bucharest, Spl Independenţei 294; f. 1990; library of 5,000 vols; Dir IOAN JELEV.

Institutul de Cercetări pentru Legumicultură şi Floricultură (Research Institute for Vegetable and Flower Growing): 8268 Vidra, Judeţul Ilfov; tel. (1) 613-63-95; fax (1) 613-92-82; f. 1967; attached to Acad. of Agricultural and Forestry Sciences; library of 29,000 vols; Dir. Dr Eng. ION SCURTU; publ. *Annals*.

Institutul de Cercetări pentru Pedologie şi Agrochimie (Research Institute for Soil Science and Agrochemistry): 71331 Bucharest, B-dul Mărăşti 61; tel. (1) 222-94-42; fax (1) 222-59-79; e-mail icpa@icpa.ro; f. 1969; attached to Acad. of Agricultural and Forestry Sciences; library of 9,000 vols; Dir Dr Eng. MIHAIL DUMITRU; publ. *Anale* (annually).

Institutul de Cercetări pentru Viticultură şi Vinificaţie (Research Institute for Vine Growing and Wine Making): 2040 Valea Călugărească, Jud. Prahova; tel. (44) 12-02-00; fax (44) 11-52-89; f. 1967; attached to Acad. of Agricultural and Forestry Sciences; library of 14,000 vols; Man. Dr Eng. VIOREL STOIAN; publ. *Anale*.

Institutul de Cercetări şi Amenajări Silvice (Forest Research and Management Institute): 72904 Bucharest 2, Şoseaua Stefăneşti 128; tel. (1) 240-68-45; e-mail icas@com.pcnet.ro; f. 1933; attached to Acad. of Agricultural and Forestry Sciences; library of 32,000 vols; Dir Dr ROMICA TOMESCU; publs *Anale, Revista pădurilor* (quarterly).

Institutul de Chimie Alimentară (Research Institute for Food Chemistry): 71576 Bucharest, Str. Gârlei 1; tel. (1) 679-20-40; fax (1) 212-03-05; f. 1950; attached to Acad. of Agricultural and Forestry Sciences; library of 25,000 vols; Dir Prof. Dr GHEORGHE MENCINICOPSCHI; publ. *Ştiinţe şi Tehnologii Alimentare* (Food Sciences and Technology, 4 a year).

Institutul de Economie Agrară (Institute of Agrarian Economics): Bucharest, B-dul Mărăşti 61; tel. (1) 222-91-30; f. 1928; attached to Acad. of Agricultural and Forestry Sciences; library of 42,000 vols; Dir Dr TRAIAN LAZĂR; publs *Problems of Agrarian Economy–Annals, Economy and Organization of the Agricultural Units, Ex Terra Aurum*.

Institutul de Economie Agrară (Institute of Agricultural Economy): 70711 Bucharest, Piaţa Valter Mărăcineanu 1; tel. 614-84-04; attached to Romanian Acad.; Dir DUMITRU DUMITRU.

Institutul de Geodezie, Fotogrammetrie, Cartografie şi Organizarea Teritoriului (Institute for Geodesy, Photogrammetry, Cartography and Land Management): 79662 Bucharest, B-dul Expoziţiei 1 A, Sector 1; fax (1) 222-90-75; f. 1958; library of 6,000 vols; Dir Eng. ION BĂDESCU; publ. *Analele IGFCOT* (annually).

Institutul Naţional de Medicină Veterinară Pasteur (Pasteur National Institute of Veterinary Medicine): 77826 Bucharest 6, Şos. Giuleşti 333; tel. (1) 220-64-86; fax (1) 220-69-15; f. 1909; attached to Acad. of Agricultural and Forestry Sciences; library of 30,000 vols; Dir Dr C. ŞTIRBU; publ. *Studies and Research in Veterinary Medicine* (annually).

Institutul Român de Cercetări Marine (Romanian Institute of Marine Research): Constanţa, B-dul Mamaia 300, POB 3; tel. (916) 43288; f. 1970; attached to Acad. of Agricultural and Forestry Sciences; library of 30,000 vols and periodicals; Dir Eng. S. NICOLAEV; publ. *Cercetări Marine* (annually).

Staţiunea Centrală de Cercetări pentru Ameliorarea Solurilor Sărăturate (Central Research Station for Saline Soils Improvement): Brăila, Jud. Brăila; attached to Acad. of Agricultural and Forestry Sciences; Dir Eng. REMUS COŞOVEANU.

Staţiunea Centrală de Cercetări pentru Combaterea Eroziunii Solului (Central Research Station for Soil Erosion Control): Perieni, Jud. Vaslui; attached to Acad. of Agricultural and Forestry Sciences; Dir Eng. D. NISTOR.

Staţiunea Centrală de Cercetări pentru Cultura Plantelor pe Nisipuri (Central Research Station for Plant Cultivation on Sand): 1185 Dăbuleni, Jud. Dolj; tel. (51) 27-03-00; fax (51) 27-03-47; f. 1959; attached to Acad. of Agricultural and Forestry Sciences; library of 14,300 vols; Dir Dr Eng. DUMITRU GHEORGHE; publ. *Anales* (every 2 years).

Staţiunea Centrală de Cercetări pentru Cultura şi Industrializarea Tutunului (Central Research Station for Tobacco Growing and Industrialization): 71576 Bucharest, Str. Gîrlei 1; tel. (1) 230-45-75; fax (1) 230-51-58; f. 1929; attached to Acad. of Agricultural and Forestry Sciences; Dir MARIANA TIGĂU; publ. *Buletinul tutunului* (annually).

Staţiunea Centrală de Producţie şi Cercetări pentru Sericicultură (Central Production and Research Station for Sericulture): Bucharest, Şos. Bucureşti-Ploieşti 69, Sector 1; tel. 633-42-20; f. 1906; attached to Acad. of Agricultural and Forestry Sciences; library of 16,000 vols; Dir Eng. ION DOGARU; publ. *Sericulture* (quarterly).

ARCHITECTURE AND TOWN PLANNING

Centrul pentru Noi Arhitecturei Electronice (Centre for New Electronic Architecture): 70007 Bucharest, B-dul Armata Poporului 1–3, Sector 6; tel. 631-78-00; attached to Romanian Acad.; Dir ŞTEFAN GHEORGHE.

Prodomus SA – Institut de Studii şi Proiectare pentru Construcţii Civile (Institute of Research and Design for Civil Engineering Works): 70136 Bucharest, Str. Nicolae Filipescu 53–55, Sector 2; tel. 211-78-40; f. 1949; housing, social buildings; Dir Eng. CORNELIU VELICU; publ. *Prodomus – SA, 'bdi'* (bulletin of documentation and information).

Proed SA – Institut de Studii şi Proiectare pentru Lucrări Tehnico-Edilitare (Studies and Design Institute for Public Works): 70132 Bucharest, Str. Tudor Arghezi 21, Sector 2; tel. (1) 211-55-10; fax (1) 210-18-01; f. 1949; water, sewerage and other public facilities, traffic organization and public transport; Man. Dir Eng. VICTOR MOLDOVEANU; publ. 'bdi' (bulletin of documentation and information, four a year).

ECONOMICS, LAW AND POLITICS

Institutul de Cercetări Economice 'Gheorghe Zane' (Gheorghe Zane Institute for Economic Research): 6600 Iaşi, Str. Theodor Codrescu 2; tel. (32) 11-59-84; f. 1992; attached to Romanian Acad.; library of 34,000 vols; Dir Prof. Dr ALECSANDRU TACU; publ. *Anuarul*.

Institutul de Cercetări Juridice (Institute of Juridical Research): 76117 Bucharest, Calea 13 Septembrie 13, Sector 5; tel. 410-40-59; f. 1954; attached to Romanian Acad.; domestic, comparative and int. law; library of 7,120 vols, 2,210 periodicals; Dir Prof. PAUL COSMOVICI; publs *Studii de drept românesc* (quarterly), *Revue Roumaine des Sciences Sociales—Série de Sciences juridiques* (2 a year).

Institutul de Economie a Industriei (Institute of Industrial Economics): 70159 Bucharest, B-dul Gen. Magheru 28–30; tel. 659-75-50; attached to Romanian Acad.; Dir CORNELIU RUSSU.

Institutul de Economie Mondială (Institute of World Economics): 70348 Bucharest, B-dul Regina Elisabeta 7, CP 1-158; tel. (1) 311-07-60; fax (1) 311-07-59; e-mail iecmond@sunu.rnc.ro; f. 1967; attached to Romanian Acad.; library of 20,000 vols, 210 periodicals, World Bank depositary library; Dir Prof. Dr MUGUR ISĂRESCU; publs *Conjunctura economiei mondiale* (annually), *Evoluţia preţurilor internaţionale* (2 a year), *Piaţa internaţională* (3 a week), *Sinteza conjuncturală* (daily), *Biblioteca de Economie Mondială* (quarterly).

Institutul de Economie Națională (Institute of National Economy): 76117 Bucharest, Calea 13 Septembrie 13, Sector 5; tel. (1) 411-97-32; fax (1) 411-97-33; attached to Romanian Acad.; Dir GHEORGHE ZAMAN.

Institutul de Finanțe, Prețuri și Probleme Valutare 'Victor Slavescu' (Victor Slavescu Institute of Finance, Prices and Foreign Exchange Issues): 76117 Bucharest, Calea 13 Septembrie 13 (Etaj 5), Sector 5; tel. (1) 410-55-99; f. 1953; attached to Romanian Acad.; library of 40,000 vols; Dir Prof. Dr GHEORGHE MANOLESCU; publs *Revista Română de Științe Economice* (Romanian Economic Review), *Buletin Financiar* (Financial Survey, 4 a year).

Institutul de Prognoză Economică (Institute of Economic Forecasting): 70169 Bucharest, Str. Mendeleev 34–36; tel. 659-42-65; attached to Romanian Acad.; Dir MARIN COMȘA.

Institutul Național de Cercetări Economice (National Institute of Economic Research): 76117 Bucharest, Calea 13 Septembrie 13, Sector 5; tel. (1) 410-33-55; fax (1) 411-49-16; attached to Romanian Acad.; Dir CONSTANTIN IONETE.

EDUCATION

Centrul de Cercetări Avansate în Învătarea Automată, Prelucrarea Limbajului Natural și Modelarea Conceptuală (Centre for Advanced Research on Automatic Learning, Natural Language Processing and Conceptual Modelling): 74311 Bucharest, Calea 13 Septembrie 13, Sector 5; tel. (1) 410-41-13; fax (1) 411-39-16; attached to Romanian Acad.; Dir GHEORGHE TECUCI.

FINE AND PERFORMING ARTS

Institutul de Arheologie și Istoria Artei (Institute of Archaeology and History of Art): 3400 Cluj-Napoca 1, Str. C. Daicoviciu 2; tel. (64) 19-11-25; f. 1990; attached to Romanian Acad.; library of 20,000 vols; Dir Dr MARIUS PORUMB; publs *Ephemeris Napocensis* (annually), *Ars Transilvaniae* (annually).

Institutul de Istoria Artei 'George Oprescu' (George Oprescu Institute of the History of Art): 41104 Bucharest, Calea Victoriei 196; tel. 650-56-80; f. 1949; attached to Romanian Acad.; Romanian and European architecture, painting, sculpture, Romanian theatre, music, cinematography; library of 57,000 vols, 81,000 negatives, 80,000 photographs; Dir REMUS NICULESCU; publs *Studii și cercetări de istoria artei, Revue Roumaine d'Histoire de l'Art* (annually, with 2 series, on fine arts and on theatre, music and cinema).

HISTORY, GEOGRAPHY AND ARCHAEOLOGY

Centrul de Istorie și Civilizație Europeană (Centre for History and European Civilization): 6600 Iași, Str. Cuza Vodă 41; tel. (32) 21-24-41; fax (32) 21-11-50; attached to Romanian Acad.; Dir GHEORGHE BUZATU.

Centrul pentru Studiul Istoriei Evreilor din România (Centre for the Study of the History of Jews in Romania): 70468 Bucharest 4, Str. Mămulari 4 (Etaj 1, Ap. 1, Sectorul 3); tel. and fax (1) 336-10-51; f. 1977; attached to the Federation of Jewish Communities in Romania; Dir Dr EUGEN PREDA; publ. *Gazette* (2 a year).

Institutul de Arheologie (Institute of Archaeology): 71113 Bucharest, Str. Henri Coandă 11; tel. 650-34-10; f. 1956; attached to Romanian Acad.; Dir Prof. Dr PETRE ALEXANDRESCU; publs *Dacia—Revue d'Archéologie et d'Histoire Ancienne* (annually), *Studii și cercetări de istorie veche* (quarterly), *Studii și cercetări de numismatică* (annually), *Materiale și cercetări arheologice* (annually).

Institutul de Arheologie (Institute of Archaeology): 6600 Iași, Str. Lascăr Catargi 18; tel. (32) 21-19-10; attached to Romanian Acad.; Dir DAN GH. TEODOR; Sec. VASILE CHIRICA; publs *Arheologia Moldovei* (with supplement), *Bibliotheca Archaeologica Iassiensis.*

Institutul de Geografie (Institute of Geography): 70307 Bucharest, Str. Dimitrie Racoviță 12; tel. (1) 613-59-90; fax (1) 311-12-42; e-mail geoinst@fx.ro; f. 1944; attached to Romanian Acad.; library of 50,000 vols, 200 periodicals, 1,900 atlases and maps; Dir ION ZĂVOIANU; publ. Revista Geografică (1 a year).

Institutul de Istorie 'A. D. Xenopol' (A.D. Xenopol Institute of History): 6600 Iași, Str. Lascăr Catargi 15; tel. and fax (32) 21-26-14; e-mail xeno@mail.cccis.ro; f. 1941; attached to Romanian Acad.; Romanian and world history; library of 110,000 vols; Dir Dr ALEXANDRU ZUB; Sec. Dr GHEORGHE ONIȘORU; publ. *Anuarul* (with supplement).

Institutul de Istorie 'Nicolae Iorga' (Nicolae Iorga Institute of History): 71261 Bucharest, B-dul Aviatorilor 1; tel. (1) 650-90-45; fax (1) 311-03-71; f. 1936; attached to Romanian Acad.; library of 140,000 vols; Dir Prof. Dr ȘERBAN PAPACOSTEA; publs *Studii și materiale de istorie medie* (annually), *Studii și materiale de istorie contemporană* (annually), *Studii și materiale de istorie modernă* (annually), *Revista istorică* (6 a year) *Revue roumaine d'histoire* (4 a year).

LANGUAGE AND LITERATURE

Institutul de Filologie Română 'Al. Philippide' (Al. Philippide Institute of Romanian Philology): 6600 Iași, Str. Theodor Codrescu 2; tel. (32) 14-56-17; fax (32) 21-11-50; f. 1927; attached to Romanian Acad.; library of 45,000 vols; Dir DAN MĂNUCĂ; publ. *Anuar de Lingvistică și Istorie Literară* (Series A and B).

Institutul de Fonetică și Dialectologie 'Al. Rosetti' (Al. Rosetti Institute of Phonetics and Dialectology): 76117 Bucharest, Calea 13 Septembrie 13, Sector 5; tel. 641-27-57; attached to Romanian Acad.; Dir EMANUEL KANT VASILIU.

Institutul de Istorie și Teorie Literară 'George Călinescu' (George Călinescu Institute of Literary History and Theory): 76117 Bucharest, Calea 13 Septembrie 13, Sector 5; tel. (1) 410-32-00 ext. 2023; f. 1949; attached to Romanian Acad.; library of 11,000 vols; Dir Prof. Dr DAN GRIGORESCU; publs *Revista de Istorie și Teorie Literară* (quarterly), *Synthesis* (annually).

Institutul de Lingvistică (Institute of Linguistics): 76117 Bucharest, Calea 13 Septembrie 13, Sector 5; tel. (1) 411-36-98; attached to Romanian Acad.; Dir MARIUS SALA.

MEDICINE

Centrul de Sănătate Publică (Public Health Centre): 4300 Tîrgu-Mureș, Str. Gh. Marinescu 40; f. 1956; attached to Acad. of Medical Sciences; library of 12,000 vols; Dir Dr FRANCISC JESZENSZKY.

Centrul Metodologic de Parodontologie (Paradontology Methodological Centre): 70532 Bucharest, Str. 11 Iunie 10, Sector 4; tel. (1) 641-20-79; f. 1968; library of 326 vols; Dir Dr THEODORA GUȚU.

Centrul Național de Fono-Audiologie și Chirurgie Funcțională ORL (National Centre for Phono-Audiology and ENT Surgery): 76231 Bucharest, Mihai Cioranu 21; tel. 31-59-80; f. 1972; attached to Acad. of Medical Sciences; library of 2,000 vols; Dir Dr ROMEO CĂLĂRAȘU.

Institutul de Endocrinologie 'C.I. Parhon' (C.I. Parhon Institute of Endocrinology): 79660 Bucharest, B-dul Aviatorilor 34–36; tel. 33-40-10; f. 1946; attached to Acad. of Medical Sciences; library of 65,800 vols; Dir Dr CONSTANTIN DUMITRACHE; publ. *Romanian Journal of Endocrinology* (quarterly).

Institutul de Fiziologie Normală și Patologică 'D. Danielopolu' (D. Danielopolu Institute of Normal and Pathological Physiology): 79173 Bucharest 1, B-dul Ion Mihalache 11A; tel. (1) 312-89-38; fax (1) 312-59-37; f. 1949; attached to Acad. of Medical Sciences; library of 49,000 vols; Dir Dr MARCEL ULUITU; publ. *Romanian Journal of Physiology* (4 a year).

Institutul de Medicină Internă 'Nicolae Gh. Lupu' (Nicolae Gh. Lupu Institute of Internal Medicine): 72202 Bucharest, Șos. Ștefan cel Mare 19–21; tel. 611-13-70; f. 1949; attached to Acad. of Medical Sciences; library of 72,000 vols; Dir Prof. S. PURICE; publ. *Revue Roumaine de Médecine Interne* (quarterly).

Institutul de Neurologie și Psihiatrie (Institute of Neurology and Psychiatry): 75622 Bucharest, Șos. Berceni 10–12; tel. 683-78-31; f. 1950; attached to Acad. of Medical Sciences; library of 7,957 vols; Dir Prof. V. VOICULESCU; publ. *Neurologie et Psychiatrie* (series of *Revue Roumaine de Médecine,* quarterly).

Institutul de Sănătate Publică (Institute of Public Health): 3400 Cluj-Napoca, Str. Pasteur 4–6; tel. (64) 19-42-52; fax (64) 19-98-91; e-mail isbocsan@jeffmcm.soroscj.ro; f. 1930; library of 30,150 vols; Dir Prof. Dr IOAN STELIAN BOCȘAN.

Institutul de Sănătate Publică (Institute of Public Health): 6600 Iași, Str. Dr V. Babeș 14; tel. (32) 14-15-20; fax (32) 21-03-99; f. 1930; attached to Acad. of Medical Sciences; library of 15,000 vols; Dir R. DUDA.

Institutul de Sănătate Publică, București (Institute of Public Health, Bucharest): 75256 Bucharest, Str. Dr Leonte 1–3; tel. (1) 638-39-70; fax (1) 312-34-26; e-mail iphbuc@com.pcnet.ro; f. 1927; library of 36,000 books and separate medical history library of 41,000 vols; Dir Dr OCTAVIAN LUCHIAN.

Institutul de Sănătate Publică și Cercetări Medicale (Institute of Public Health and Medical Research): 1900 Timișoara, B-dul V. Babeș 16; tel. (961) 15021; f. 1946; attached to Acad. of Medical Sciences; library of 21,700 vols; Dir Prof. F. SCHNEIDER; publs. *Morphologie et Embryologie* (series of *Revue Roumaine de Morphologie, d'Embryologie et de Physiologie,* quarterly), *Documentary booklet* (annually).

Institutul de Virusologie 'Ștefan S. Nicolau' (Ștefan S. Nicolau Institute of Virology): 79650 Bucharest 77, Șos. Mihai Bravu 285; tel. and fax (1) 324-25-90; e-mail cernescu@valhalla.racai.ro; f. 1949; attached to Acad. of Medical Sciences; WHO Virus Collaborating Centre; library of 6,000 vols, 200 periodicals; Dir Prof. COSTIN CERNESCU; publs *Romanian Journal of Virology* (in English, 2 a year), *Studii și Cercetări de Virusologie* (in Romanian, 2 a year).

Institutul Național de Cercetare-Dezvoltare 'Dr I. Cantacuzino' (Dr I. Cantacuzino National Research and Development Institute): 70100 Bucharest 1, Spl Independenței 103, CP 1-525; tel. (1) 638-38-00; telex 11808; fax (1) 321-27-20; f. 1921; attached to Acad. of Medical Sciences; microbiology, immunology and epidemiology of communicable diseases; library of 109,000 vols; Dir Dr ANDREI AUBERT-COMBIESCU; publ. *Romanian Archives of Microbiology and Immunology* (quarterly).

Institutul Național de Medicină Legală 'Mina Minovici' (Mina Minovici National Institute for Forensic Medicine): 75669 Bucharest, Șos. Vitan-Bîrzești 9, Sector 4; tel. (1) 634-38-90; fax (1) 321-02-60; f. 1892; library of 21,000 vols; Dir Prof. Dr VLADIMIR BELIS;

publ. *Romanian Journal of Legal Medicine* (quarterly).

Institutul Oncologic (Institute of Oncology): 72435 Bucharest, Şos. Fundeni 252, Sector 2; f. 1949; attached to Acad. of Medical Sciences; library of 41,144 vols; Dir Prof. ION PANĂ; publ. *Oncologia* (quarterly).

Institutul pentru Controlul de Stat al Medicamentului şi Cercetări Farmaceutice 'Petre Ionescu-Stoian' (Petre Ionescu-Stoian State Institute for Drug Control and Pharmaceutical Research): 71324 Bucharest, Str. Aviator Sănătescu 48; tel. (1) 224-10-79; fax (1) 230-50-83; e-mail dd@ns.icsmcf.ro; f. 1929; Dir Prof. Dr DUMITRU DOBRESCU; publ. *Farmaco-vigilenţa* (Drug Monitoring) (quarterly).

Institutul 'V. Babeş' (V. Babeş Institute): 76201 Bucharest, Spl Independenţei 99–101; tel. (1) 638-51-60; fax (1) 638-51-05; f. 1887; attached to Acad. of Medical Sciences; genetics, immunology, pathology and ultra-structure; library of 20,000 vols; Dir Prof. Dr L. M. POPESCU; publ. *Romanian Journal of Morphology and Embryology* (quarterly).

NATURAL SCIENCES

Biological Sciences

Institutul de Biochimie (Institute of Biochemistry): 77700 Bucharest 17, Splaiul Independenţei 296; tel. (1) 673-28-60; fax (1) 223-24-70; e-mail stefana@linux.biochim.ro; f. 1990; attached to Romanian Acad.; Dir Dr STEFANA PETRESCU.

Institutul de Biologie (Institute of Biology): 79651 Bucharest, Splaiul Independenţei 296; tel. (1) 637-34-70; fax (1) 310-24-10; attached to Romanian Acad.; Dir MIRCEA OCTEAN.

Institutul de Biologie şi Patologie Celulară 'Nicolae Simionescu' (Nicolae Simionescu Institute of Cellular Biology and Pathology): 79691 Bucharest, Str. Bogdan Petriceicu Haşdeu 8, Sector 5, POB 3514; tel. (1) 311-08-60; fax (1) 312-11-43; f. 1979; attached to Romanian Acad.; Dir MAYA SIMIONESCU.

Institutul de Cercetare şi Proiectare Delta Dunării (Danube Delta Research and Design Institute): 8800 Tulcea, Str. Babadag 165; tel. 524242; fax 524547; e-mail icpdd@rlx.ssitl.ro; f. 1970; oversees ecological conservation and maintains biodiversity inventory for the Danube Delta area; library of 40,000 vols; Dir Eng. ROMULUS STIUCA; publs *Annals, Review of Ecological Restoration in the Danube Delta Biosphere Reserve*.

Institutul de Cercetări Biologice Cluj-Napoca (Biological Research Institute of Cluj-Napoca): 3400 Cluj-Napoca, Str. Republicii 48; tel. (64) 19-80-84; fax (64) 19-12-38; e-mail icb@mail.soroscj.ro; f. 1958; biology, biotechnology; library of 9,000 vols, 24,000 periodicals; Dir Dr GHEORGHE COLDEA; publ. *Contribuţii Botanice*.

Institutul de Cercetări Biologice Iaşi (Iaşi Biological Research Institute): 6600 Iaşi, B-dul Copou 20A; tel. and fax (32) 14-72-02; f. 1970; National library of 35,000 vols; Dir Dr ALEXANDRU MANOLIU.

Institutul de Cercetări Eco-Muzeale Tulcea (Tulcea Institute of Museum Research): 8800 Tulcea, Str. 14 Noiembrie 3; tel. (40) 51-29-82; fax (40) 51-53-75; f. 1950; archaeology, natural history, history, ethnography, art; library of 92,000 vols; Dir GAVRILĂ SIMION; publ. *Peuce*.

Mathematical Sciences

Centrul de Statistică Matematică (Centre for Mathematical Statistics): 76100 Bucharest, Calea 13 Septembrie 13, Casa Academiei Române; tel. and fax (1) 411-49-00; f. 1964; attached to Romanian Acad.; Dir MARIUS IOSIFESCU.

Institutul de Matematică (Institute of Mathematics): 78101 Bucharest, Calea Griviţei 21; tel. 650-05-92; attached to Romanian Acad.; Dir GHEORGHE GUSSI.

Institutul de Matematică (Institute of Mathematics): 6600 Iaşi, Str. Copou 8; tel. (51) 14-75-70; attached to Romanian Acad.; Dir VIOREL BARBU.

Institutul de Matematică Aplicată 'Caius Iacob' (Caius Iacob Institute of Applied Mathematics): 76117 Bucharest, Calea 13 Septembrie 13, Sector 5; tel. (1) 410-40-82; fax (1) 411-43-05; e-mail homent@ns.ima.ro; attached to Romanian Acad.; Dir Prof. Dr DOREL HOMENTCOVSCHI.

Physical Sciences

Institutul Astronomic (Institute of Astronomy): 75212 Bucharest, Str. Cuţitul de Argint 5; tel. (1) 335-68-92; fax (1) 337-33-89; e-mail magda@roastro.astro.ro; attached to Romanian Acad.; Dir MAGDALENA STAVINSCHI.

Institutul de Cercetări Chimice (Institute of Chemical Research): 77208 Bucharest 15, Splaiul Independenţei 202; tel. (1) 315-32-99; fax (1) 312-34-93; f. 1950; natural compounds and bioactive products, technological engineering; Gen. Man. SEVER ŞERBAN.

Institutul de Chimie (Institute of Chemistry): 1900 Timişoara, B-dul Mihai Viteazul 24; tel. (56) 19-18-18; fax (56) 19-18-24; e-mail manager@icht.sorostm.ro; f. 1967; attached to Romanian Acad.; library of 5,000 vols; Dir WALTER SCHMIDT.

Institutul de Chimie Fizică (Institute of Physical Chemistry): 77208 Bucharest, Splaiul Independenţei 202, Sector 6; tel. 638-53-70; attached to Romanian Acad.; Dir MIHAI VASILE POPA.

Institutul de Chimie Macromoleculară 'Petru Poni' (Petru Poni Institute of Macromolecular Chemistry): 6600 Iaşi, Aleea Grigore Ghica Vodă 41A; tel. (32) 21-74-54; fax (32) 21-12-99; f. 1949; attached to Romanian Acad.; research in polymer chemistry and physics; library of 89,000 vols; Dir CRISTOFOR SIMIONESCU.

Institutul de Chimie Organică 'Costin D. Neniţescu' (Costin D. Neniţescu Institute of Organic Chemistry): 77208 Bucharest, Splaiul Independenţei 202B Sector 6; tel. 637-59-48; attached to Romanian Acad.; Dir PETRE FILIP.

Institutul de Fizică Atomică (Institute of Atomic Physics): Bucharest-Măgurele 76900, Sector 5, POB MG-6; tel. and fax (1) 423-16-47; f. 1949; library of 385,000 vols; Dir-Gen. Prof. Dr V. LUPEI; publs *Romanian Journal of Physics* (monthly), *Romanian Reports in Physics* (monthly), *IFA-Preprints*, Conference Proceedings.

Institutul de Fizică Tehnică Iaşi (Iaşi Institute of Technical Physics): 6600 Iaşi 3, B-dul Mangeron 47; tel. (32) 13-06-80; fax (32) 23-11-32; e-mail hchiriac@phys-iasi.ro; f. 1951; library of 60,000 vols; Dir Prof. Dr HORIA CHIRIAC; publ. *Proceedings* (every 4 years).

Institutul de Geodinamică (Institute of Geodynamics): 70201 Bucharest, Str. Jean Louis Calderon 19–21; tel. 210-06-04; attached to Romanian Acad.; Dir DOREL ZUGRĂVESCU.

Institutul de Speologie 'Emil Racoviţă' (Emil Racoviţă Institute of Speleology): 78114 Bucharest, Str. Frumoasă 11; tel. (1) 650-38-76; fax (1) 211-38-74; attached to Romanian Acad.; Dir CONSTANTIN RĂDULESCU.

Institutul Geologic al României (Romanian Geological Institute): Bucharest, Str. Caransebeş 1; tel. (1) 224-20-93; fax (1) 224-04-04; e-mail geol@ns.igr.ro; f. 1906; library of 270,000 vols; museum; Dir Dr GHEORGHE UDUBAŞA; publs Romanian journals of mineralogy, petrology, mineral deposits and environmental geochemistry, stratigraphy, palaeontology, tectonics and regional geology, geophysics (all annually), *Anuarul, Studii tehnice şi economice* (Technical and Economic Papers, irregular), *Memorii* (irregular).

Institutul Naţional de Meteorologie şi Hidrologie (National Institute of Meteorology and Hydrology): Bucharest, Şos. Bucureşti-Ploieşti 97; f. 1884; Dir M. IOANA; publs daily weather reports, *Studii şi Cercetări* (2 parts: Meteorology, Hydrology, 1 vol. annually), *Meteorology Journal* (2 a year), *Hydrology Journal* (2 a year), *Bibliografia hidrologică* (annually), *Bibliografia meteorologică* (annually).

Institutul Naţional de Metrologie (National Institute of Metrology): 75669 Bucharest, Şos. Vitan-Bîrzeşti 11; tel. 634-35-20; telex 11871; fax 330-15-33; f. 1951; library of 15,000 vols; Dir A. MILLEA; publ. *Metrologie* (quarterly).

PHILOSOPHY AND PSYCHOLOGY

Institutul de Filosofie (Institute of Philosophy): 76117 Bucharest, POB 1-137, Calea 13 Septembrie 13; tel. and fax (1) 410-56-59; f. 1948; attached to Romanian Acad.; Dir ALEXANDRU SURDU; publs *Revista de Filosofie* (every 2 months), *Revue roumaine de Philosophie* (4 a year).

Institutul de Psihologie (Institute of Psychology): 76117 Bucharest, Calea 13 Septembrie 13, Sector 5, O.P. 5, C.P. 5–8; tel. (1) 410-30-99; attached to Romanian Acad.; Dir Dr CONSTANTIN VOICU; publs *Revista de Psihologie* (4 a year), *Revue Roumaine de Psychologie* (2 a year).

RELIGION, SOCIOLOGY AND ANTHROPOLOGY

Centrul de Cercetări Antropologice Francisc Rainer (Francisc Rainer Centre for Anthropological Research): 76241 Bucharest, B-dul Eroilor Sanitari 8, P. P. Box 35/13; tel. and fax (1) 638-28-55; e-mail rainer@sunu.rnc.ro; f. 1937; attached to Romanian Acad.; library of 7,000 vols, 25 periodicals; Dir Dr CRISTIANA GLAVCE; publs *Annuaire d'Etudes Anthropologiques* (1 a year), *Studii şi Cercetări de Antropologii* (1 a year).

Institutul de Cercetare a Calităţii Vieţii (Institute of Research on the Quality of Life): 76117 Bucharest, Calea 13 Septembrie nr 13, Sector 5; tel. (1) 411-48-05; fax (1) 411-48-00; attached to Romanian Acad.; Dir CĂTĂLIN ZAMFIR.

Institutul de Cercetări Socio-Umane (Institute for Research in Social and Human Sciences): 1100 Craiova, Str. Unirii 102; tel. (51) 12-33-30; f. 1965; attached to Romanian Acad.; library of 300,000 vols; Dir GHEORGHE POPILIAN; publ. *Arhivele Olteniei* (annually).

Institutul de Cercetări Socio-Umane (Institute for Research in Social and Human Sciences): 2400 Sibiu, Str. Lucian Blaga 13; tel. (69) 21-26-04; fax (69) 21-66-05; f. 1956; attached to Romanian Acad.; library of 6,000 vols, 300 periodicals; Dir Dr PAUL NIEDERMAIER; publs *Forschungen zur Volks- und Landeskunde* (2 a year), *Historia Urbana* (2 a year), *Anuarul* (1 a year), *Studii şi Comunicări de Etnologie* (1 a year).

Institutul de Cercetări Socio-Umane (Institute for Research in Social and Human Sciences): 1900 Timişoara, Str. Mihai Viteazu 24; tel. (56) 19-40-68; f. 1970; attached to Romanian Acad.; library of 8,000 vols; Dir EUGEN TODORAN; publs *Caietul Cercului de Studii* (2 a year), *Poetică, Dialectologie, Studii de istorie* *a Banatului, Toponimie, Limbăliterară* (all annually).

Institutul de Cercetări Socio-Umane (Institute for Research in Social and Human Sciences): 4300 Tîrgu Mureş, Str. Bolyai 17; tel. (65) 42-01-38; f. 1957; attached to Romanian Acad.; history, history of literature, folklore, sociology; library of 338,290 vols; Dir Dr IOAN CHIOREAN.

Institutul de Etnografie şi Folclor 'Constantin Brăiloiu' (Constantin Brăiloiu Institute of Ethnography and Folklore): 70166 Bucharest, Str. Take Ionescu 25; tel. 659-37-48; e-mail etnograf@sunu.rnc.ro; f. 1949; library of 44,000 vols; National Folk Archives of sound, image and manuscripts; Dir Dr SABINA ISPAS; publs *Revista de etnografie şi folclor* (6 a year), *Anuarul*.

Institutul de Sociologie (Institute of Sociology): 76117 Bucharest, Calea 13 Septembrie 13, Sector 5; tel. 312-41-88; f. 1965; attached to Romanian Acad.; Man. Dir Prof. Dr ION DRAGAN: publs *Revue Roumaine des Sciences Sociales — série de Sociologie* (quarterly, English version every 6 months), *Sociologie Românească* (every 2 months).

Institutul de Ştiinţe Socio-Umane (Institute of Social and Human Sciences): 6600 Iaşi, Str. T. Codrescu 2; tel. (32) 11-59-87; f. 1969; attached to Romanian Acad.; library of 35,000 vols; Dir TUDOREL DIMA; publ. *Anuar de Ştiinţe Socio-Umane*.

Institutul de Studii Sud-Est Europene (Institute for South-East European Studies): 70346 Bucharest, B-dul Republicii 13, CP 22-159; tel. 614-49-96; f. 1963; attached to Romanian Acad.; social sciences; library of 40,000 vols; Dir Prof. Dr ALEXANDRU N. DUŢU; publ. *Revue des études sud-est européennes* (quarterly).

Institutul de Teorie Socială (Institute of Social Theory): 70007 Bucharest, B-dul Armata Poporului 1–3, Sector 6; tel. 666-67-70; attached to Romanian Acad.; Dir FLORIAN HENRI RADU.

TECHNOLOGY

Institutul de Cercetări Stiinţifice pentru Protecţia Muncii (Scientific Research Institute for Occupational Safety): 70744 Bucharest, Str. Gral. Budişteanu 15, Sector 1; tel. 615-05-31; f. 1951; library of 20,000 books and journals; Dir Dr Ing. ALEXANDRU DARABONT; publ. *Risc şi Securitate în Muncă* (Occupational Risk and Safety).

Institutul de Informatică Teoretică (Institute of Theoretical Informatics): 6600 Iaşi, B-dul Copou 11; tel. (32) 14-65-34; attached to Romanian Acad.; Dir DAN GÂLEA.

Institutul de Mecanica Solidelor (Institute of Solids Mechanics): 70701 Bucharest, Str. Constantin Mille 15; tel. 614-40-36; attached to Romanian Acad.; Dir TUDOR SIRETEANU.

Institutul Naţional de Informare şi Documentare (National Institute for Information and Documentation): 70074 Bucharest, Str. George Enescu 27–29, Sector 1; tel. (1) 613-40-10; fax (1) 312-67-34; f. 1949; promotes the use of modern equipment for automatic data processing in the area of documentary information; library: see Libraries and Archives; Gen. Dir C. SULTANOVICI; publs *Abstracts of Romanian Scientific and Technical Literature* (in English, French and Romanian, 2 a year), *Probleme de informare şi documentare* (Information and Documentation Problems, in English and Romanian, quarterly).

Libraries and Archives

Alba Iulia

Biblioteca Batthyaneum (Batthyaneum Library): 2500 Alba Iulia, Str. Bibliotecii 1; tel. (58) 81-19-39; f. 1798; attached to Biblioteca Naţională; 69,061 vols; spec. collns of MSS dating from the 9th century, 609 incunabula, documents, rare books; mineralogical and numismatic colln; 18th-century astronomy observatory; Dir Prof. ILEANA DÂRJA.

Biblioteca Judeţeană 'Lucian Blaga' Alba (Alba 'Lucian Blaga' District Library): 2500 Alba Iulia, Trandafirilor 22; tel. (58) 81-14-43; f. 1943; 159,509 vols; Dir MIOARA POP.

Alexandria

Biblioteca Judeţeană 'Marin Preda' Teleorman: (Teleorman 'Marin Preda' District Library): 0700 Alexandria, Str. Mitiţă Filipescu 9; tel. (47) 32-28-94; f. 1949; 119,304 vols; Dir MARIA NEDELEA.

Arad

Biblioteca Judeţeană 'A. D. Xenopol' Arad (Arad District A. D. Xenopol Library): 2900 Arad, Str. Gh. Popa 2–4; tel. (57) 25-65-10; f. 1913; 507,450 books; Dir LIANA DRIG.

Bacău

Biblioteca Judeţeană 'C. Sturdza' Bacău (Bacău 'C. Sturdza' District Library): 5500 Bacău, B-dul Ioniţă Sturdza 1; tel. (34) 11-31-26; f. 1893; 375,087 vols and periodicals; Dir ECĂTERINA ŢURCANU.

Baia Mare

Biblioteca Judeţeană 'Petre Dulfu' Maramureş (Maramureş 'Petre Dulfu' District Library): 4800 Baia Mare, Str. Victoriei 76; tel. (62) 41-35-83; f. 1951; 317,872 vols; Dir LAURA TEMIAN.

Bistriţa

Biblioteca Judeţeană Bistriţa-Năsăud (Bistriţa-Năsăud District Library): 4400 Bistriţa, Str. Gării 2; tel. and fax (63) 22-29-30; f. 1951; 169,000 vols; Dir OLIMPIA POP.

Blaj

Biblioteca Documentară 'Timotei Cipariu' ('Timotei Cipariu' Documentary Library): 3175 Blaj, Str. Armata Roşie 2; f. 1754; attached to Cluj-Napoca br. library of Romanian Academy; 30,000 vols in humanities and sciences; spec. colln of rare and ancient books about history of the Romanian people.

Botoşani

Biblioteca Judeţeană 'Mihai Eminescu' Botoşani (Botoşani 'Mihai Eminescu' District Library): 6800 Botoşani, Str. Calea Naţională 148; tel. (31) 51-46-86; f. 1882; 321,549 vols; Dir CORNELIA VIZITEU.

Brăila

Biblioteca Judeţeană 'Panait Istrati' Brăila (Brăila 'Panait Istrati' District Library): 6100 Brăila, Calea Călăraşilor 52; tel. (39) 61-95-90; fax (39) 61-95-88; f. 1881; 400,000 vols; Dir RODICA DRĂGHICI; publs *Ex-libris* (1 a year), *Bibliography of Brăila* (1 a year).

Braşov

Biblioteca Centrală a Universităţii 'Transilvania' din Braşov (Transylvania University of Braşov Central Library): 2200 Braşov, B-dul Eroilor 9; tel. (68) 15-07-86; e-mail libr@vega.unitbv.ro; f. 1948; 650,000 vols; Dir Prof. Dr Ing. AUREL NEGRUŢIU.

Biblioteca Judeţeană 'George Bariţiu' Braşov (Braşov 'George Bariţiu' District Library): 2200 Braşov, B-dul Eroilor 35; tel. (68) 41-93-38; fax (68) 41-50-79; e-mail biblgb@deuroconsult.ro; f. 1835; 631,000 vols; Dir SILVIA TODEA.

Bucharest

Arhivele Naţionale (National Archives): Bucharest, B-dul Regina Elisabeta 49; tel. (1) 315-25-03; fax (1) 312-58-41; f. 1831; 1,221,500 medieval documents, 22,000 seals, 12,820 MSS, 816,929 ft modern documents, 735,680 vols of plans and maps; documentary libraries; Dir-Gen. Prof. Dr COSTIN FENEŞAN; publ. *Revista Arhivelor* (2 a year).

Attached library:

Biblioteca Documentară a Arhivelor Naţionale (Documentary Library of the National Archives): Bucharest, B-dul Regina Elisabeta 49; tel. (1) 315-25-03; f. 1862; 158,000 vols; Dir MARIN RADU MOCANU.

Biblioteca Academiei de Artă Bucureşti (Library of the Bucharest Academy of Fine Arts): 71104 Bucharest, CP 22-275, Cal. Victoriei 196; tel. (1) 659-54-95; f. 1864; 58,000 books, 261,262 slides and photographs; spec. colln: 19th- and 20th-century European fine-art periodicals; Dir GABRIELA BAJENARU.

Biblioteca Academiei de Muzică Bucureşti (Library of the Bucharest Academy of Music): Bucharest, Str. Ştirbei Vodă 33; f. 1864; 30,440 books, 144,498 scores, 14,702 recordings, 7,138 tapes, 17,561 periodicals, 1,677 rarities, scores and MSS, 2,921 theses; Dir IENCIU VERONA.

Biblioteca Academiei Române (Library of the Romanian Academy): 71102 Bucharest, Calea Victoriei 125; tel. (1) 650-30-43; fax (1) 650-79-78; e-mail: root@bar.acad.ro; f. 1867; legal nat. deposit for Romanian and UN publs; produces Romanian nat. bibliography of books and serials; 9,965,000 vols, 500,000 historical documents, 350,000 photographs; spec. collns incl. Romanian, Greek, Slavonic, Oriental and Latin MSS; numismatic colln; Dir Prof. GABRIEL STREMPEL; publs *Cărţi Străine intrate in Bibliotecile din România* (4 series, monthly), *Cărţi recente intrate in bibliotecă* (monthly), *Bibliografia Retrospectivă a Cărţii*.

Biblioteca Centrală a Academiei de Ştiinţe Agricole şi Silvice 'Gheorghe Ionescu-Şişeşti' (Central Library of the Gheorghe Ionescu-Sişeşti Academy of Agricultural and Forestry Sciences): Bucharest, B-dul Mărăşti 61; f. 1928; 136,000 vols; Chief Librarian N. FLORESCU; publs *Bibliografia agricolă curentă română* (quarterly), *Noutăţi documentare FAO* (monthly), *Cărţi străine intrate in bibliotecile din România—seria Agricultură* (monthly).

Biblioteca Centrală a Academiei de Studii Economice (Central Library of the Academy of Economic Sciences): 70167 Bucharest, Piaţa Romană 6, Sector 1; f. 1913; 1,200,000 vols; Chief Librarian VASILE CIUBOTARU.

Biblioteca Centrală Pedagogică (Central Education Library): 70714 Bucharest, Str. Zalomit 12; tel. and fax 311-03-23; f. 1880; methodological centre for the nat. network of school libraries; 450,000 educational books and periodicals; Dir-Gen. GEORGE ANCA; publs *L'enseignement et la pédagogie en Roumanie* (every 2 years), *Modernizarea invăţămîntului* (quarterly), *Informare tematică* (every 2 years), *Bibliografia pedagogică* (irregular).

Biblioteca Centrală Universitară (Central University Library): 70119 Bucharest 1, Str. Boteanu 1, tel. (1) 312-01-08; fax (1) 312-08-44; e-mail stoica@bcub.ro; f. 1891; 2,128,000 vols; Dir-Gen. Dr ION STOICA; publ. *Surse pentru Dvîn colecţiile bibliotecilor universitare din Bucureşti* (Sources in the Collections of the University Libraries of Bucharest, irregular).

Biblioteca Documentară de Istorie a Medicinei (Documentary Library of the History of Medicine): Bucharest, Str. Dr Leonte 1–3; f. 1953; 36,000 books, 1,100 periodicals, 3,500 MSS and documents, 5,200 museum pieces; Dir Prof. MARIOARA GEORGESCU; publs *Iconografia medicală românească, Studii şi cercetări de istoria medicinei.*

Biblioteca Institutului Naţional de Informare şi Documentare (Library of the National Institute for Information and Documentation): 70141 Bucharest, Str. George Enescu 27–29, Sector 1; tel. 613-40-10; telex 11247; fax 312-67-34; f. 1949; 700,000 vols incl. 100,000 periodicals; Chief Librarian CLAUDIA CERKEZ.

Biblioteca Centrala a Universităţii 'Politechnica' din Bucureşti (Central Library of Bucharest Polytechnic University): Bucharest, Spl. Independenţei 313; tel. (1) 312-70-44; fax (1) 312-53-65; f. 1868; 1,394,000 books and periodicals; Dir DAN-RADU POPESCU; publ. *Scientific Bulletin* (4 series: mechanical engineering, electrical engineering, chemistry and materials science, applied mathematics and physics).

Biblioteca Municipală 'Mihail Sadoveanu' (Mihail Sadoveanu Municipal Library): 79711 Bucharest 1, Str. Take Ionescu 4; tel. and fax (1) 211-36-25; f. 1935; 1,416,000 books, periodicals, newspapers, musical scores; Dir FLORIN ROTARU; publs *Bibliografia oraşului Bucureşti* (1 a year), *Biblioteca Bucureştilor* (monthly).

Biblioteca Naţională (National Library): 79708 Bucharest, Str. Ion Ghica 4; tel. (1) 615-70-63; fax (1) 312-33-81; e-mail bnr@lnx .bibnat.ro; f. 1836; acts as copyright deposit library and nat. bibliographic agency; incorporates research centre for librarianship and book pathology and restoration; 8,824,000 books and periodicals; spec. collns of MSS, old and rare books, musical scores, photographs, maps, prints and drawings; Dir ION-DAN ERCEANU; publs *Bibliografia Naţională Româna* (6 series), *Catalogul colectiv al cărtilor străine intrate în bibliotecile din România* (4 a year), *Repertoriul periodicelor străine intrate în bibliotecile din România* (annually), *ABSI – Abstracte în bibliologie şi ştiinţa informării* (monthly), *Biblioteconomie – Culegere de traduceri prelucrate* (quarterly), *Cultura în România* (every 2 months), *Aniversări culturale* (every 6 months), *Probleme de patologie a cărţii* (annually).

Biblioteca Universităţii de Ştiinţe Agronomice (Library of the University of Agronomic Sciences): 71331 Bucharest, B-dul Mărăşti 59, Sector 1; tel. (1) 222-37-00; fax (1) 223-26-93; f. 1948; 530,000 vols; Dir RODICA COVERCA; publs *Agronomie, Horticulture, Zootechnie, Médicine Vétérinaire.*

Centrul de Documentare Medicală 'Dr Dimitrie Nanu' (Dr Dimitrie Nanu Medical Documentation Centre): 70151 Bucharest, Str. Pitar Moş 15, Sect. 1; tel. 10-78-85; f. 1951; 310,556 vols; Dir Dr GABRIEL TINTĂRESCU; publ. *Revista de actualităţi medicale* (quarterly).

Centrul de Documentare pentru Construcţii, Arhitectură, Urbanism şi Amenajarea Teritoriului (Documentation Centre for Building, Architecture, Urban Studies and Town Planning): Bucharest, Şos. Pantelimon 266, C.P. 1-139; tel. (1) 624-16-49; f. 1957; library of 320,000 vols, 200 current periodicals; Dir AURELIA DOBRESCU.

Centrul de Informare şi Documentare Economică (Centre of Economic Information and Documentation): 76117 Bucharest, Calea 13 Septembrie 13, Sector 5; tel. (1) 411-60-75; fax (1) 411-54-86; f. 1990; attached to Romanian Acad.; Dir IOAN FRANC VALERIU; publs *Probleme Economice* (weekly), *Studii şi Cercetări Economice* (monthly), *Romanian Economic Research Observer* (monthly), *Analele INCE* (4 a year), *Marketing Management* (4 a year).

Chiminform Data SA: 77131 Bucharest, Calea Plevnei 139; tel. (1) 637-22-01; fax (1) 222-91-65; e-mail: root@cdn-gw.pub.ro; f. 1956; provides access to nat. and foreign scientific and technical literature; library of 48,000 vols, 140,000 vols of periodicals; Gen. Man. Prof. Dr IOSIF TRIPSA; publs *Revista de Chimie* (monthly), *Materiale Plastice* (4 a year), *Performanţe în Chimie* (weekly).

Serviciul de Documentare al Ministerului Învăţământului (Documentation Service of the Ministry of Education): 70738 Bucharest, Str. Spiru Haret 12; tel. 614-26-80; fax 312-47-53; f. 1971; information and documentation on teaching and educational management abroad; Romanian legislation on education; Head EUGENIU TOMA; publs include: *Educaţie-Învăţământ* (every 6 months), *Buletinul Ministerului Invăţământului* (quarterly).

Serviciul de Informare-Documentare-Informatizare al Academiei de Ştiinţe Agricole şi Silvice 'Gheorghe Ionescu-Şişeşti' (Information, Documentation and Electronic Information Service of the Gheorghe Ionescu-Şişteşti Academy of Agricultural and Forestry Sciences): Bucharest, B-dul Mărăşti 61; tel. (1) 618-25-54; fax (1) 617-01-55; f. 1965; attached to Acad. of Agricultural and Forestry Sciences; library of 146,000 vols and CD-ROMs; Head Prof. Dr VASILE JURUBESCU; publ. *Curierul ASAS* (4 a year).

Buzău

Biblioteca Judeţeană Buzău (Bazău District Library): 5100 Buzău, Str. Unirii 140; tel. (38) 79-15-09; f. 1873; 230,000 vols; Dir ALEXANDRU OPROIESCU.

Călăraşi

Biblioteca Judeţeană 'Al. Odobescu' Călăraşi (Călăraşi 'Al. Odobescu' District Library): 8500 Călăraşi, Str. Bucureşti 102; tel. and fax (42) 31-67-57; f. 1884; 150,000 vols; Dir GHIŢĂ DUMITRU.

Cluj-Napoca

Biblioteca Centrală Universitară 'Lucian Blaga' (University 'Lucian Blaga' Central Library): 3400 Cluj-Napoca, Str. Clinicilor 2; tel. (64) 11-70-92; fax (64) 11-76-33; f. 1872; 3,553,596 vols; Dir DORU RADOSLAV; publs *Bibliographical Indexes.*

Biblioteca Filialei Cluj-Napoca a Academiei Române (Library of the Cluj-Napoca Branch of the Romanian Academy): 3400 Cluj-Napoca, Str. M. Kogălniceanu 12–14; f. 1950; 700,000 books and periodicals on the humanities and science, 179 incunabula, 2,000,000 documents; spec. collns incl. Romanian, Latin, Hungarian, Slavonic MSS; Dir Acad. Prof. ŞTEFAN PASCU.

Biblioteca Judeţeană 'Octavian Goga' Cluj (Cluj 'Octavian Goga' District Library): 3400 Cluj-Napoca, Piaţa Ştefan cel Mare 1; tel. (64) 43-03-23; fax (64) 19-54-28; e-mail traian@bibl.jud.edu.sorosci.ro; f. 1950; 565,000 books and periodicals; Dir TRAIAN BRAD; publ. *Lectura*.

Biblioteca Universitaţii de Medicină şi Farmacie (Library of the University of Medicine and Pharmacy): 3400 Cluj-Napoca, Avram Iancu 31; tel. (64) 11-10-01; f. 1775; 321,000 books and periodicals; Dir I. ROBU; publ. *Clujul Medical* (quarterly).

Biblioteca Universităţii Technice din Cluj-Napoca (Libralry of Cluj-Napoca Technical University): 3400 Cluj-Napoca, Str. Constantin Daicoviciu 15; tel. (64) 19-48-34; fax (64) 19-20-55; f. 1884; 650,000 books and periodicals; Dir Ing. CĂLIN CÂMPEAN: publ. *Acta Technica Napocaensis* (in English, annually).

Constanţa

Biblioteca Judeţeană Constanţa (Constanţa District Library): 8700 Constanţa, Str. Arhiepiscopiei 23; tel. (41) 61-44-82; f. 1931; 563,000 vols; Dir D. CONSTANTIN-ZAMFIR; publ. *Bibliografia Dobrogei* (annually).

Craiova

Biblioteca Judeţeană 'Al. şi Aristia Aman' Dolj (Dolj 'Al. and Aristia Aman' District Library): 1100 Craiova, Str. M. Kogălniceanu 9; tel. (51) 13-22-67; f. 1908; 466,000 vols; Dir MARIANA LEFERMAN.

Biblioteca Universităţii Craiova (University of Craiova Library): 1100 Craiova, Str. Al. I. Cuza 13; f. 1966; 600,000 vols; Dir OCTAVIAN LOHON.

Deva

Biblioteca Judeţeană 'O. Densusianu' Hunedoara (Hunedoara 'O. Densusianu' District Library): 2700 Deva, Str. 1 Decembrie 28; tel. (54) 61-94-40; f. 1949; 260,853 books and periodicals; Dir VALERIA STOIAN.

Drobeta-Turnu Severin

Biblioteca Judeţeană 'I. G. Bibicescu' Mehedinţi (Mehedinţi 'I.G. Bibicescu' District Library): 1500 Drobeta-Turnu Severin, Str. Traian 115; tel. (52) 31-56-82; f. 1921; 264,300 vols; Dir ELENA ROMAN.

Focşani

Biblioteca Judeţeană 'Duiliu Zamfirescu' Focşani (Focşani 'Duiliu Zamfirescu' District Library): 5300 Focşani, Str. M. Kogălniceanu 12; tel. (37) 61-54-68; f. 1910; 168,000 vols; Dir Prof. VICTOR RENEA.

Galaţi

Biblioteca Judeţeană 'V. A. Urechia' Galaţi (Galaţi 'V. A. Urechia' District Library): 6200 Galaţi, Str. Mihai Bravu 16; tel. (36) 41-10-37; f. 1890; 599,000 vols; Dir EUGEN IORDACHE; publ. *Buletinul Fundaţiei 'V. A. Urechia'.*

Biblioteca Universităţii Galaţi (University of Galaţi Library): 6200 Galaţi, Str. Domnească 47; f. 1951; 475,000 vols mainly on technology, shipbuilding, chemistry, food industry, fishing; Dir (vacant); publ. *Annals*.

Giurgiu

Biblioteca Judeţeană 'J. A. Bassarabescu' Giurgiu (Giurgiu District 'J. A. Bassarabescu' Library): 8375 Giurgiu, Str. Mircea cel Bătrîn 23; tel. (46) 21-23-46; f. 1951; 182,000 books and periodicals; Dir ION MIHAI.

Iaşi

Biblioteca Centrală a Universităţii de Medicină şi Farmacie 'Gr. T. Popa' Iaşi (Central Library of the Gr. T. Popa University of Medicine and Pharmacy in Iaşi): 6600 Iaşi, Str. Vasile Alecsandri 7; tel. (32) 14-21-81; f. 1879; central library with 88 brs; 350,000 vols; Dir VIORICA SCUTARU; publ. *Buletin Bibliografic* (4 a year).

Biblioteca Centrală Universitară 'Mihai Eminescu' (University 'Mihai Eminescu' Central Library): 6600 Iaşi, Str. Păcurari 4; tel. (32) 14-07-09; f. 1640; 2,900,000 vols; Dir CORNELIU ŞTEFANACHE; publs *Buletinul cărţilor străine—seria Iaşi, Buletin bibliografic.*

Biblioteca Universităţii Tehnice 'Gheorghe Asachi' Iaşi (Library of the Iaşi Gheorghe Asachi Technical University): 6600 Iaşi, B-dul Copou 11; tel. (32) 14-07-72; fax (32) 21-17-73; e-mail library@tuiasi.ro; f. 1937; 531,000 books, 7,000 periodicals; Dir ALEXANDRINA FLOREA; publs *Bulletin of the Polytechnic Institute of Iaşi, Iaşi Polytechnic Magazine*.

Biblioteca Judeţeană 'Gh. Asachi' Iaşi (Iaşi 'Gh. Asachi' District Library): 6600 Iaşi,

Str. Palatului 1; tel. (32) 11-51-59; fax (32) 21-21-70; e-mail icpopa@tuiasi.ro; f. 1920; 550,000 vols, 12,000 records; Dir Prof. NICOLAE BUSUIOC; publ. *Bibliographical Annual of the Iaşi District*.

Miercurea-Ciuc

Biblioteca Judeţeană Harghita (Harghita District Library): 4100 Miercurea-Ciuc, Piaţa Libertăţii 1; tel. (66) 17-19-88; f. 1950; 209,289 books and periodicals; Dir KATALIN KOPACZ.

Năsăud

Biblioteca Documentară Năsăud (Năsăud Documentary Library): 1500 Năsăud, Str. Grănicerilor 41; f. 1931; attached to Cluj-Napoca br. library of Romanian Academy; 53,323 vols; Dir MARIA ŞUTEU.

Oradea

Biblioteca Judeţeană 'Gheorghe Şincai' Bihor (Bihor 'Gheorghe Sincai' District Library): 3700 Oradea, Piaţa Unirii 3; tel. (59) 13-12-57; f. 1912; 605,000 books and periodicals; Dir CONSTANTIN MĂLINAŞ.

Piatra-Neamţ

Biblioteca Judeţeană 'G. T. Kirileanu' Neamţ (Neamţ 'G.T. Kirileanu' District Library): 5600 Piatra-Neamţ, Str. Republicii 15; tel. (33) 21-15-24; fax (33) 21-03-79; f. 1956; 269,000 books and periodicals; Dir CONSTANTIN BOSTAN.

Piteşti

Biblioteca Judeţeană Argeş (Argeş District Library): 0300 Piteşti, Str. Victoriei 22; tel. (48) 62-29-93; f. 1880; 345,438 books and periodicals; Dir SILVESTRU VOINESCU.

Ploieşti

Biblioteca Judeţeană 'N. Iorga' Prahova (Prahova 'N. Iorga' District Library): 2200 Ploieşti, Str. Sublocotenent Erou Călin Cătălin 1; tel. (44) 12-24-92; f. 1921; 355,450 books and periodicals; Dir NICOLAE BOARU.

Biblioteca Universităţii 'Petrol-Gaze': 2000 Ploieşti, B-dul Bucureşti 39, POB 22; tel. (44) 17-31-71; fax (44) 11-98-47; f. 1948; 349,000 books and periodicals; Dir Assoc. Prof. Dr Eng. LAZAR AVRAM; publ. *Catalogul lucrărilor colaboratorilor UPG*.

Reşiţa

Biblioteca Judeţeană 'Paul Iorgovici' Caraş-Severin (Caraş-Severin 'Paul Iorgovici' District Library): 1700 Reşiţa, Str. Paul Iorgovici 50; tel. (55) 21-16-87; f. 1952; 287,000 vols; Dir NICOLAE SÂRBU; publ. *Revista Noastră*.

Rîmnicu Vîlcea

Biblioteca Judeţeană 'Antim Ivireanu' Vîlcea (Vîlcea 'Antim Ivireanu' District Library): 1000 Rîmnicu Vîlcea, Str. Ana Ipătescu 1; tel. (50) 73-92-21; f. 1950; 400,000 vols; Dir Prof. DUMITRU LAZĂR.

Satu Mare

Biblioteca Judeţeană Satu Mare (Satu Mare District Library): 3900 Satu Mare, Str. Decebal 2; tel. (61) 72-11-90; f. 1951; 294,488 books and periodicals; Dir GHEORGHE TODUŢ.

Sf. Gheorghe

Biblioteca Judeţeană Covasna (Covasna District Library): 4000 Sf. Gheorghe, Gabor Aron 14; tel. (67) 31-36-09; fax (67) 31-48-39; e-mail biblio@libcv1.sbnet.ro; f. 1927; 194,000 vols; Dir JENŐ KISS.

Sibiu

Biblioteca Judeţeană 'Astra' Sibiu (Sibiu 'Astra' District Library): 2400 Sibiu, Str. Gh. Bariţiu 5; tel. (69) 21-05-51; telex 215775; fax (69) 21-57-75; f. 1861; 736,000 books and periodicals, 34,966 documents and MSS, 12,325 iconographies; 10 brs; Dir Prof. ION MARIS.

Biblioteca Muzeului Brukenthal (Library of Brukenthal Museum): 2400 Sibiu, Piaţa Mare 4; tel. (69) 41-76-91; fax (69) 41-15-45; f. 1817; 280,000 vols; Chief Librarian AL. LUNGU.

Slatina

Biblioteca Judeţeană 'Ion Minulescu' Olt (Olt 'Ion Minulescu' District Library): 0500 Slatina, B-dul Al. I. Cuza 38; tel. (49) 43-28-36; f. 1950; 154,504 books and periodicals; Dir PAUL MATIU.

Slobozia

Biblioteca Judeţeană Ialomiţa (Ialomiţa District Library): 8400 Slobozia, B-dul Matei Basarab 26; tel. (43) 23-00-55; f. 1951; 132,242 books and periodicals; Dir DENCĂ ŞERBAN.

Suceava

Biblioteca Judeţeană 'I.G. Sbierea' Suceava (Suceava 'I.G. Sbierea' District Library): 5800 Suceava, Str. Mitropoliei 4; tel. (30) 21-33-26; f. 1923; 290,000 books and periodicals; Dir ION PÎNZAR.

Timişoara

Biblioteca Judeţeană Timiş (Timiş District Library): 1900 Timişoara, Piata Libertăţii 3; tel. (56) 13-07-46; f. 1904; 668,254 books, periodicals and MSS; Dir PAUL-EUGEN BANCIU.

Biblioteca Universităţii Timişoara (University of Timişoara Library): 1900 Timişoara, B-dul V. Pârvan 4; tel. (56) 19-03-53; fax (56) 19-40-04; f. 1948; 780,000 books and periodicals; Dir V. ŢÂRA.

Tîrgovişte

Biblioteca Judeţeană 'Ion Heliade Rădulescu' Dîmboviţa (Dîmboviţa 'Ion Heliade Rădulescu' District Library): 0200 Tîrgovişte, Str. Stelea 2; tel. (45) 61-23-16; f. 1944; 272,844 books and periodicals; Dir VICTOR PETRESCU.

Tîrgu Jiu

Biblioteca Judeţeană 'Christian Tell' Gorj (Gorj 'Christian Tell' District Library): 1400 Tîrgu Jiu, Str. Eroilor 23; tel. (53) 21-49-04; f. 1934; 222,000 books and periodicals; Dir ALEXANDRA ANDREI.

Tîrgu Mureş

Biblioteca Documentară Teleki-Bolyai ('Teleki-Bolyai' Documentary Library): 4300 Tîrgu Mureş, Str. Bolyai 17; tel. (65) 16-18-57; f. 1802; pre-19th-century books in the natural and social sciences, and maps, incunabula and MSS; Dir DIMITRIE POPTĂMAŞ.

Biblioteca Judeţeană Mureş (Mureş District Library): 4300 Tîrgu Mureş, Str. Georges Enescu 2; tel. (65) 16-26-31; f. 1913; 809,644 vols, 5,200 periodicals; Dir DIMITRIE POPTĂMAŞ.

Tulcea

Biblioteca Judeţeană 'Panait Cerna' Tulcea (Tulcea 'Panait Cerna' District Library): 8800 Tulcea, Str. Isaccea 20; tel. (40) 51-38-33; f. 1900; 228,887 books and periodicals; Dir DOINA POSTOLACHE.

Vaslui

Biblioteca Judeţeană 'Nicolae Milescu Spătarul' Vaslui (Vaslui 'Nicolae Milescu Spătarul' District Library): 6500 Vaslui, Hagi Chiriac 2; tel. (35) 31-37-67; f. 1951; 158,788 books and periodicals; Dir ELENA POAMA.

Zalău

Biblioteca Judeţeană 'Ioniţă Scipione Bădescu' Sălaj (Sălaj 'Ioniţă Scipione Bădescu' District Library): 4700 Zalău, Str. Iuliu Maniu 13; tel. (60) 63-20-07; f. 1954; 150,000 vols; Dir SILVIA COSMA.

Museums and Art Galleries

Aiud

Muzeul de Istorie Aiud (Aiud Museum of History): 3325 Aiud, Piaţa Republicii 24; tel. (58) 86-18-49; f. 1880; archaeology of the primitive commune, the Dacian-Roman period and the pre-feudal period; library of 1,800 vols; Dir MATILDA TAKACS.

Muzeul de Ştiinţele Naturii Aiud (Aiud Natural History Museum): 3325 Aiud, Str. Bethlen Gabor 1; tel. (58) 86-17-48; f. 1796; library of 500 vols; Dir ANA HERTA.

Alba Iulia

Muzeul Naţional al Unirii (National Museum of Union): 2500 Alba Iulia, Str. Mihai Viteazul 12–14; tel. (58) 81-33-00; fax 81-18-53; f. 1887; exhibits relating to prehistoric and Roman archaeology, and to Romanian Union; library of 55,000 vols; Dir Dr HORIA CIUGUDEAN; publs *Apulum—Acta Musei Apulensis* (1 a year), *Bibliotheca Musei Apulensis* (1 a year).

Alexandria

Muzeul Judeţean de Istorie Teleorman (Teleorman District Museum of History): 0700 Alexandria, Str. Dunării 137; tel. (47) 32-21-41; f. 1951; history, numismatics, ethnography; Dir ECATERINA ŢÂNŢĂREANU.

Arad

Muzeul Judeţean Arad (Arad District Museum): 2900 Arad, Piaţa Enescu 1; tel. (57) 21-64-99; f. 1893; history, ethnology, natural sciences, fine and applied art; Dir GEORGE PASCU HUREZEANU; publ. *Ziridava* (irregular).

Bacău

Muzeul Judeţean de Istorie 'Iulian Antonescu' Bacău (Bacău 'Iulian Antonescu' District Museum of History): 5500 Bacău, Str. Nicolae Titulescu 23; tel. (34) 11-24-44; f. 1957; history, art, ethnography, literature; library of 9,000 vols; Dir Dr VIOREL CĂPITANU; publ. *Carpica* (annually).

Muzeul Judeţean de Ştiintele Naturii Bacău (Bacău District Natural History Museum): 5500 Bacău, Str. Gheorghe Vrânceanu 44; tel. and fax (34) 11-20-06; f. 1964; library of 17,000 vols; Dir Dr NECULAI BARABAŞ; publ. *Studii şi Comunicări*.

Baia Mare

Muzeul Judeţean Maramureş (Maramureş District Museum): 4800 Baia Mare, B-dul Traian 8; tel. (62) 41-19-27; f. 1899; history, Romanian art; library of 20,000 vols; Dir IOAN IGNA; publ. *Marmaţia* (annually).

Associated museum:

Muzeul de Mineralogie Baia Mare (Baia Mare Mineralogical Museum): 4800 Baia Mare, B-dul Traian 8; tel. and fax (62) 43-76-51; f. 1989; Dir VICTOR GORDUZA.

Bistriţa

Muzeul Judeţean de Istorie Bistriţa (Bistriţa District History Museum): 4400 Bistriţa, Str. Gen. Grigore Bălan 53; tel. (63) 11063; f. 1950; Dir GHEORGHE MARINESCU; publ. *Studii şi Comunicări*.

Botoşani

Muzeul Judeţean Botoşani (Botoşani District Museum): 6800 Botoşani, Str. Unirii 13; tel. (31) 51-34-46; f. 1955; history, ethnography, fine arts; incl. 'Nicolae Iorga' and 'George Enescu' memorial houses; library of

10,000 vols; Dir GABRIELA ZIZI COROLIUC; publ. *Hierasus*.

Brad

Muzeul de Istorie şi Etnografie Brad (Brad History and Ethnography Museum): 2775 Brad; f. 1987; Curator MIHAI DAVID.

Brăila

Muzeul Brăilei: (Braila Museum): 6100 Brăila, Piaţa Traian 3; tel. and fax (39) 61-47-25; f. 1881; history, fine arts, ethnography, natural sciences; library of 20,000 books and periodicals; Dir IONEL CÂNDEA; publs *ISTROS* (every 2 years), *Analele Brailei* (every 2 years).

Bran

Muzeul Bran (Bran Museum): 2229 Bran, Str. Principală 460, Jud. Braşov; tel. (68) 23-65-38; f. 1957; history, ethnography, feudal art; Dir RAUL MIHAI.

Braşov

Muzeul, Biblioteca şi Arhiva Istorică a Primei Şcoli Româneşti din Şcheii Braşovului (Museum, Library and Historical Archive of First Romanian School of Braşov): 2200 Braşov, Piaţa Unirii 1; tel. (68) 14-38-79; f. 1933; historical museum in building of first Romanian school (15th century); Dir Dr VASILE OLTEANU.

Muzeul de Artă (Art Museum): 2200 Braşov, B-dul Eroilor 21; tel. (68) 14-01-38; f. 1950; Romanian fine arts and universal decorative arts; Dir TITUS HAŞDEU.

Muzeul de Etnografie (Ethnographical Museum): 2200 Braşov, B-dul Eroilor 21A; tel. (68) 15-22-52; Dir LIGIA FULGA.

Muzeul Judeţean de Istorie Braşov (Braşov District History Museum): 2200 Braşov, Piaţa Sfatului 30; tel. (68) 14-36-85; f. 1908; library of 15,500 vols, archives; Dir Dr FLOREA COSTEA; publ. *Cumidava* (Yearbook).

Bucharest

Muzeul Căilor Ferate Române (Romanian Railway Museum): 78216 Bucharest, Calea Griviţei 193A; tel. 618-01-40.

Muzeul Comunităţilor Evreieşti din România (Museum of the Jewish Communities in Romania): 70468 Bucharest, Str. Mămulari 3, Sector 3; tel. (1) 615-08-37; fax (1) 312-08-69; f. 1978; Dir BEATRICE STAMBLER.

Muzeul de Istorie şi Artă al Municipiului Bucureşti (Bucharest Museum of History and Art): 70058 Bucharest, B-dul I. C. Brătianu 2, Sector 3; tel. (1) 315-68-58; fax (1) 613-85-15; f. 1921; library of 50,000 vols; Dir IONEL IONIŢĂ.

Muzeul Literaturii Române (Museum of Romanian Literature): 71116 Bucharest, B-dul Dacia 12; tel. and fax (1) 650-33-95; f. 1957; library of 80,000 books and periodicals and 46,000 MSS and photographs; Dir ALEXANDRU DAN CONDEESCU; publ. *Manuscriptum* (quarterly review).

Muzeul Militar Naţional (National Military Museum): 77116 Bucharest, Str. Mircea Vulcănescu 125–127, Sector 1; tel. (1) 637-38-30; fax (1) 638-76-30; f. 1914; Dir Col ILIE SCHIPOR; publ. *Revista Muzeului Militar Naţional* (Review of the National Military Museum).

Muzeul Muzicii Române (Romanian Music Museum): 70179 Bucharest, Calea Victoriei 141; tel. 659-75-96; Dir ILINCA DUMITRESCU.

Muzeul Naţional de Artă al României (Romanian National Museum of Art): 70101 Bucharest, Calea Victoriei 49–53; tel. (1) 315-51-93; fax (1) 312-43-27; e-mail theodorescu@art.museum.ro; f. 1950; library of 40,000 vols; Dir ROXANA THEODORESCU; publ. *Buletinul*. (Partly open for temporary exhibitions.)

Muzeul Naţional Cotroceni (Cotroceni National Museum): 76238 Bucharest, B-dul Geniului 1; tel. (1) 63-74-11; fax (1) 312-16-18; f. 1991; Romanian art, medieval architecture, decorative art; Dir Dr ELEONORA COFAS.

Muzeul Naţional de Istorie a României (National History Museum of Romania): 70012 Bucharest, Calea Victoriei 12; tel. (1) 315-70-55; fax (1) 311-33-56; f. 1968; library of 45,000 vols; Dir Dr CRIŞAN MUŞEŢEANU; publs *Muzeul Naţional*, *Cercetări arheologice*, *Cercetări numismatice*, *Cercetări istorice* (annually), *Cercetări de conservare şi restaurare a patrimoniului muzeal* (annually).

Muzeul Naţional de Istorie Naturală 'Grigore Antipa' ('Grigore Antipa' National Natural History Museum): 79744 Bucharest, Şos. Kiseleff 1; tel. (1) 312-88-26; fax (1) 312-88-86; e-mail antipa@opensys.ro; f. 1834; library of 30,200 vols, 20,000 periodicals; Dir Dr DUMITRU MURARIU; publ. *Travaux* (annually).

Muzeul Satului (Village Museum): 71321 Bucharest, Şos. Kiseleff 28–30; tel. (1) 222-91-10; fax (1) 222-90-68; f. 1936; open-air nat. museum of village life from 17th to 20th centuries; library of 30,000 vols, 130,000 photographs; Dirs Dr ROMULUS ANTONESCU, Dr DOINA IŞFANONI; publ. *Caietele Muzeului Satului*.

Muzeul Ţăranlui Român (Romanian Peasants' Museum): 71268 Bucharest, Şos. Kiseleff 3; tel. (1) 650-53-60; fax (1) 312-98-75; e-mail muztar@sunu.rnc.ro; Dir HORIA BERNEA.

Muzeul Tehnic 'Prof. Ing. Dimitrie Leonida' (Prof. Eng. Dimitrie Leonida Museum of Technology): 75206 Bucharest, Str. Candiano Popescu 2; tel. 623-77-77; f. 1909; library of 25,000 vols; Dir Dipl. Eng. NICOLAE DIACONESCU; publ. *Yearbook*.

Buzău

Muzeul Judeţean Buzău (Buzău District Museum): 5500 Buzău, Str. Nicolae Bălcescu 50; tel. (38) 43-51-27; f. 1951; history, folk art, contemporary decorative arts; Dir VALERIU NICOLESCU; publ. *Musaios* (annually).

Călăraşi

Muzeul Dunării de Jos (Lower Danube Museum): 8500 Călăraşi, Str. Progresului 84; tel. (42) 11-31-61; f. 1951; history, ethnography, modern Romanian arts; Dir NEAGU MARIAN.

Caracal

Muzeul Romanaţiului Caracal (Caracal Museum of the Romanaţi): 0800 Caracal, Str. Libertăţii 26; tel. (49) 51-13-44; f. 1951; history, ethnography, art, lapidarium; Dir PAUL LICĂ.

Caransebeş

Muzeul Judeţean de Etnografie şi a Regimentului de Graniţă-Caransebeş (Caransebeş Border District Ethnographic and Regimental Museum): 1650 Caransebeş, Str. Gen. Ion Dragalina 2; tel. (55) 51-21-93; f. 1929; history, ethnography, folk-art; Dir Dr PETRE BONA; publ. *Tibiscum, Studii şi Comunicări de Etnografie şi Istorie*.

Cîmpulung

Muzeul Zonal Cîmpulung (Cîmpulung Zonal Museum): 0425 Cîmpulung, Str. Negru Vodă 119; tel. (48) 11737; f. 1880; history, arts, natural science, ethnography, folk art; Dir ŞTEFAN TRĂMBACIU; publ. *Studii şi comunicări, Istoria Cîmpulungului şi a zonei Muscel*.

Cîmpulung Moldovenesc

Muzeul Artei Lemnului (Wooden Art Museum): 5950 Cîmpulung Moldovenesc, Calea Transilvaniei 10; tel. (30) 31-13-78; f. 1936; ethnography, history, arts, folk art; Dir MARCEL ZAHANCIUC.

Cluj-Napoca

Grădina Botanică a Universităţii Babeş-Bolyai (Botanical Garden of Babeş-Bolyai University): 3400 Cluj-Napoca, Str. Republicii 42; tel. (64) 19-21-52; e-mail sasuteu@bioge.ubbcluj.ro; f. 1920; library of 25,000 vols; Dir Dr FELICIAN MICLE; publs *Contribuţii botanice, Flora Romaniae Exsiccata, Delectus seminum*.

Muzeul Etnografic al Transilvaniei (Transylvanian Museum of Ethnography): 3400 Cluj-Napoca, Str. Memorandumului 21; tel. (64) 19-23-44; fax (64) 19-21-48; e-mail metnog@hera.ubbcluj.ro; f. 1922; incl. open-air ethnographic nat. park; Dir TIBERIU GRAUR; publ. *Anuarul Muzeului etnografic al Transilvaniei*.

Muzeul Naţional de Artă Cluj: 3400 Cluj-Napoca, Piaţa Unirii 30; tel. (64) 11-69-52; f. 1951; Romanian and foreign art from 16th to 20th centuries; library of 9,000 vols; Dir Dr LIVIA DRĂGOI.

Muzeul Naţional de Istorie a Transilvaniei (National History Museum of Transylvania): 3400 Cluj-Napoca, Str. Constantin Daicoviciu 2; tel. (64) 19-86-77; fax (64) 19-17-18; f. 1859; library of 28,000 vols; Dir IOAN PISO; publs *Acta Musei Napocensis* (annually).

Muzeul Zoologic al Universităţii 'Babeş Bolyai' Cluj-Napoca (Zoological Museum of the Cluj-Napoca 'Babeş Bolyai' University): 3400 Cluj-Napoca, Str. Clinicilor 5–7; tel. (64) 11-61-01; f. 1859; Dir Dr GHERGHEL PANTE; publ. *Studia* (annually).

Constanţa

Complexul Muzeal de Ştiinţele ale Naturii (Natural History Museum Complex): 8700 Constanţa, B-dul Mamaia 255; tel. (41) 64-70-55; fax (41) 83-15-53; f. 1958; aquarium, dolphinarium, planetarium, astronomical observatory; Dir GABRIELA PLOTOAGĂ; publ. *Pontus Euxinus*.

Muzeul de Artă (Art Museum): 8700 Constanţa, B-dul Tomis 84; tel. (41) 61-70-12; f. 1961; Romanian paintings and other works of art; Dir DOINA PAULEANU.

Muzeul de Artă Populară (Folk Art Museum): 8700 Constanţa, B-dul Tomis 32; tel. (41) 61-61-33; Dir MARIA MAGIRU.

Muzeul de Istorie Naţională şi Arheologie din Constanţa (Constanţa National History and Archaeology Museum): 8700 Constanţa, Piaţa Ovidiu 12; tel. (41) 61-39-25; f. 1879; affiliated archaeological museums of Histria, Tropaeum Traiani, Capidava and Mangalia; library of 30,000 vols; Dir Dr A. RADULESCU; publ. *Pontica* (annually).

Muzeul Marinei Române (Romanian Maritime Museum): 8700 Constanţa, Str. Traian 53; tel. (41) 61-39-42; f. 1969; history of Romanian navy and merchant fleet; Dir Capt. RI CLONARU GHEORGHE.

Corabia

Muzeul de Arheologie şi Etnografie Corabia (Corabia Archaeological and Ethnographical Museum): 0875 Corabia, Str. Cuza Vodă 65; tel. (49) 56-13-64; Dir FLOREA BÂCIU.

Craiova

Muzeul Olteniei (Oltenia Museum): 1100 Craiova, Str. Popa Şapcă 4; tel. (51) 11-86-31; f. 1951; incorporates museums of art, ethnography, natural history, and archaeology and history; library of 12,000 vols; Dir ADRIAN NĂSTASE; publs *Oltenia—Studii şi cercetări*.

Curtea de Argeş

Muzeul de Istorie şi Etnografie (History and Ethnography Museum): 0450 Curtea de Argeş, Str. Negru Vodă 2; tel. (48) 1-14-46; Dir N. MOISESCU.

Deva

Muzeul Civilizaţiei Dacice şi Romane Deva (Deva Museum of Dacian and Roman Civilization): 2700 Deva, Str. 1 Decembrie 39; tel. (54) 21-54-09; fax (54) 21-22-00; f. 1882; archaeology, history, natural sciences, numismatics, art, ethnography; incorporates museum of Roman archaeology at Sarmizegetusa; library of 47,000 vols; Dir ADRIANA RUSU-PESCARU; publ. *Sargeţia*.

Drobeta-Turnu Severin

Muzeul Regiunii 'Porţile de Fier' ('Iron Gates' Regional Museum): 1500 Drobeta-Turnu Severin, Str. Independenţei 2; tel. (62) 81-21-77; f. 1882; natural history, ethnography, archaeology and Roman ruins; aquarium; Dir ION STÎNGĂ; publ. *Drobeta* (annually).

Focşani

Complexul Muzeal Judeţean Vrancea (Vrancea District Museum Complex): 5300 Focşani, B-dul Gării 5; tel. (37) 62-28-90; f. 1951; incorporates museums of ethnography (open-air), natural history, and history and archaeology; Dir HORIA DUMITRESCU.

Galaţi

Muzeul Judeţean de Istorie (District Museum of History): 6200 Galaţi, Str. Maior Iancu Fotea 2; tel. (36) 41-42-28; f. 1939; library of 8,000 vols; Dir ŞTEFAN STANCIU; publ. *Danubius*.

Attached museums:

Complexul Muzeal de Ştiinţele Naturii (Natural Science Museum Complex): 6200 Galaţi, Str. Domnească 91; tel. (36) 41-18-98; f. 1956; flora and fauna of the region, botanical and zoological gardens, aquarium; Curator AURORA MARCU.

Muzeul de Arte Vizuale (Visual Arts Museum): 6200 Galaţi, Str. Domnească 141; tel. (36) 41-34-52; f. 1956; Curator ION SIMION MĂRCULESCU.

Gherla

Muzeul de Istorie Gherla: 3475 Gherla, Str. Mihai Viteazul 6, Jud. Cluj; tel. (64) 24-19-47; f. 1881; library of 6,500 vols; Dir RODICA PINTEA.

Giurgiu

Muzeul Judeţean Giurgiu (Giurgiu District Museum): 8375 Giurgiu, Str. Constantin Dobrogeanu Gherea 3; tel. (46) 21-68-01; f. 1950; history, ethnography; Dir VASILE BARBU; publ. *File de istorie*.

Goleşti

Complexul Muzeal Goleşti (Goleşti Museum Complex): 0343 Goleşti, Ştefăneşti Commune, Jud. Argeş; tel. and fax (48) 26-63-64; f. 1939; history of fruit and vine growing; library of 9,100 vols; Dir CONSTANTIN ILIESCU; publ. *Museum*.

Gura Humorului

Muzeul Etnografic Gura Humorului (Gura Humorului Ethnographical Museum): 5900 Gura Humorului, B-dul Bucovinei 21; tel. (30) 23-11-08; f. 1956; library of 1,673 vols; Dir ELVIRA ROMANIUC.

Iaşi

Complexul Naţional Muzeal 'Moldova' Iaşi (Iaşi 'Moldova' National Museum Complex): 6600 Iaşi, Piaţa Ştefan cel Mare şi Sfânt 1; tel. and fax (32) 14-74-02; Dir Dr VASILE CHIRICA; publs *Cercetări istorice, Buletinul Ioan Neculce*.

Selected constituent museums:

Muzeul de Artă din Iaşi (Iaşi Art Museum): 6600 Iaşi, Piaţa Ştefan cel Mare şi Sfânt 1; tel. and fax (32) 14-74-02; f. 1860; Curator GEORGETA PODOLEANU.

Muzeul Etnografic al Moldovei (Ethnographic Museum of Moldavia): 6600 Iaşi, Piaţa Ştefan cel Mare şi Sfânt 1; tel. and fax (32) 14-74-02; f. 1943; Curator RODICA ROPOT.

Muzeul de Istorie a Moldovei (Moldavian History Museum): 6600 Iaşi, Piaţa Ştefan cel Mare şi Sfânt 1; tel. and fax (32) 14-74-02; f. 1916; incl. Al. I. Cuza Memorial Museum, in Ruginoasa, Mihail Kogalniceanu Memorial Museum, Museum of the Union (dedicated to the period of creating and maintaining the union of the Romanian lands), History Museum in Hârlău, and archaeological site at Cucuteni; Curator RODICA RADU.

Muzeul Ştiinţei şi Tehnicii 'Ştefan Procopiu' (Stefan Procopiu Museum of Science and Technology): 6600 Iaşi, Piaţa Ştefan cel Mare şi Sfânt 1; tel. and fax (32) 14-74-02; f. 1955; incl. Iaşi Chemistry Museum; Curator ELENA SCUTARIU.

Muzeul de Istorie Naturală Iaşi (Iaşi Natural History Museum): 6600 Iaşi, Str. Română 40; f. 1834; attached to Iaşi University; geology, palaeontology, zoology; Dir Dr C. MÂNDRU.

Mangalia

Muzeul de Arheologie 'Callatis' (Callatis Archaeological Museum): 8727 Mangalia, Şos. Constanţei 23; tel. (41) 75-35-80; f. 1928; prehistory, Greek and Roman periods, ancient Greek colony of Callatis; library of 500 vols; Dir Prof. NICOLAE GEORGESCU-CHELUŢĂ.

Mediaş

Muzeul Municipal Mediaş (Mediaş Municipal Museum): 3125 Mediaş, Str. M. Viteazu 46; tel. (69) 81-12-99; history, natural history, ethnography.

Miercurea Ciuc

Muzeul Secuiesc al Ciucului (Csiki Székely Múzeum, Ciuc Szekler Museum): 4100 Miercurea Ciuc, Piaţa Cetăţii 2; tel. (66) 81-17-27; f. 1950; history, ethnography; library of 9,000 vols; Dir SZABÓ ANDRÁS; publ. *A Csiki Székely Múzeum Közleményei*.

Mogoşoaia

Muzeul de Artă Brâncovenească Mogoşoaia (Mogoşoaia Museum of Brâncovan Art): Com. Mogoşoaia, Ilfov Agricultural Sector, Str. Donca Simo 18; tel. 667-02-40; f. 1702; medieval Romanian art. (Closed for reorganization.)

Năsăud

Muzeul Năsăudean: (Năsăud Museum): 4500 Năsăud, Str. Grănicerilor 19; tel. (63) 36-29-67; history, ethnography; Dir IOAN RADU NISTOR.

Oradea

Muzeul Ţării Crişurilor: (Criş County Museum): 3700 Oradea, B-dul Dacia 1–3; tel. (59) 47-99-17; fax (59) 47-99-18; f. 1971; history, art, ethnography and natural history; library of 30,000 vols; Dir AUREL CHIRIAC; publs *Biharea* (ethnography), *Crisia* (history) *Nymphaea* (natural sciences) (all annually).

Orăştie

Muzeul de Etnografie şi Artă Populară (Ethnography and Folk Art Museum): 8600 Orăştie, Str. Aurel Vlaicu 17; f. 1952; Curator COSMA AURELIAN.

Petroşani

Muzeul Mineritului (Mining Museum): 2675 Petroşani, Str. N. Bălcescu 21; tel. (54) 54-17-44; f. 1961; history of mining in the Jiu Valley; Dir DUMITRU PELIGRAD.

Piatra Neamţ

Complexul Muzeal Judeţean Neamţ (Neamţ District Museums Complex): 5600 Piatra Neamţ, B-dul Mihai Eminescu 10; tel. (33) 21-74-96; fax (33) 23-32-85; Dir GHEORGHE DUMITROAIA.

Selected affiliated museums:

Muzeul de Artă Piatra-Neamţ (Piatra-Neamţ Art Museum): 5600 Piatra-Neamţ, Piaţa Libertăţii 1; tel. (33) 21-68-08; f. 1980; Romanian art; Curator VIOLETA ŞERBAN.

Muzeul de Etnografie Piatra-Neamţ (Piatra-Neamţ Ethnography Museum): 5600 Piatra-Neamţ, Piaţa Libertăţii 1; tel. (33) 21-68-08; Curator TAMARA PLOSCARU.

Muzeul de Istorie şi Arheologie Piatra-Neamţ (Piatra-Neamţ History and Archaeology Museum): 5600 Piatra-Neamţ, B-dul Mihai Eminescu 10; tel. (33) 21-81-08; f. 1934; Curator GHEORGHE DUMITROAIA; publ. *Memoria Antiquitatis* (annually).

Muzeul de Ştiinţele Naturii Piatra-Neamţ (Piatra Neamţ Natural History Museum): 5600 Piatra-Neamţ, Str. Petru Rareş 26; tel. (33) 22-42-11; f. 1960; Curator MARIA APETREI; publ. *Studii şi comunicări* (1 a year).

Piteşti

Muzeul Judeţean Argeş (Argeş District Museum): 0300 Piteşti, Str. Armand Călinescu 44; tel. (48) 63-35-43; f. 1928; history, art, natural history; library of 18,000 vols; Dir Dr RADU STANCU; publ. *Studii şi comunicări* (Studies and Reports).

Ploieşti

Muzeul de Artă Ploieşti: 2200 Ploieşti, B-dul Independenţei 1; tel. (44) 12-57-75; f. 1929; Dir RUXANDRA IONESCU.

Muzeul de Biologie Umană (Human Biology Museum): 2200 Ploieşti, Str. Călin Cătălin 1; tel. (44) 12-19-00; f. 1956; Dir Prof. EMILIA IANCU; publ. *Comunicări şi referate*.

Muzeul Judeţean de Istorie şi Arheologie Prahova (Prahova District Museum of History and Archaeology): 2200 Ploieşti, Str. Toma Caragiu 10; tel. and fax (44) 11-44-37; f. 1953; library of 23,000 vols; Dir MARIA DULGHERU; publ. *Studii şi comunicări* (annually).

Muzeul Naţional al Petrolului (National Oil Museum): 2000 Ploieşti, Str. Dr Bagdasar 8; tel. (44) 12-35-64; fax (44) 11-95-42; f. 1961; history of the Romanian oil industry; library of 3,000 vols; Dir GABRIELA TĂNĂSESCU.

Rădăuţi

Muzeul Etnografic Rădăuţi (Rădăuţi Ethnographic Museum): 5875 Rădăuţi, Piaţa Unirii 63; tel. (30) 76-25-65; f. 1920; Dir DRAGOŞ CUSEAC.

Reghin

Muzeul Etnografic Reghin (Reghin Ethnographic Museum): 4225 Reghin, Str. Vînătorilor 51, Jud. Mureş; tel. (65) 52-14-48; f. 1960; library of 4,600 vols, 2,500 slides, 50 ethnological films; Dir MARIA BORZAN.

Reşiţa

Muzeul de Istorie al Judeţului Caraş-Severin (Caraş-Severin District History Museum): 1700 Reşiţa, B-dul Republicii 10; tel. (55) 43-73-82; f. 1950; Dir TEICU DUMITRU; publ. *Banatica*.

Rîmnicu Vîlcea

Muzeul Judeţean Rîmnicu Vîlcea (Rîmnicu Vîlcea District Museum): 1000 Rîmnicu Vîlcea, Calea Traian 159; tel. (50) 71-81-21; f. 1950; history, art, ethnography; Dir PETRE BARDASU.

Roman

Muzeul de Istorie Roman (Roman Museum of History): 5500 Roman, Str. Cuza Vodă 33; tel. (33) 62-42-11; f. 1957; Curator Dr VASILE URSACHI.

Satu Mare

Muzeul Judeţean Satu Mare (Satu Mare District Museum): 3900 Satu Mare, B-dul Vasile Lucaciu 21; tel. (61) 73-75-26; f. 1891; history, ethnography, paintings by Aurel Popp; library of 50,000 vols; Dir VIOREL CIUBOTA; publ. *Studii şi comunicări*.

Sf. Gheorghe

Muzeul Naţional Secuiesc (National Szekler Museum): 4000 Sfîntu Gheorghe, Str. Kos Karoly 10; tel. (67) 31-24-42; f. 1879; history, ethnography, natural history, icons, modern Romanian art; library of 70,000 vols; Dir KONYA ADAM; publ. *Aluta*.

Sibiu

Muzeul Civilizaţiei Populare Tradiţionale 'Astra' ('Astra' Folk Museum): 2400 Sibiu, Piaţa Mică 11; tel. (69) 42-02-15; fax (69) 21-80-60; f. 1963; library of 5,000 vols; publs *Studii şi comunicări de istorie a civilizaţiei populare din România*.

Muzeul Naţional Brukenthal (Brukenthal National Museum): 2400 Sibiu, Piaţa Revoluţiei 4; tel. (69) 41-76-91; f. 1817; history, ethnography, 15th- to 18th-century European painting; library: see Libraries and Archives; Dir AL. LUNGU; publs *Cibinium, Studii şi Comunicări*.

Affiliated museum:

- **Muzeul de Istorie Naturală din Sibiu** (Sibiu Natural History Museum): 2400 Sibiu, Str. Cetăţii 1; tel. (69) 43-68-68; f. 1849; library of 65,000 vols; Curator GH. BAN; publ. *Studii şi Comunicări de Ştiinţe Naturale*.

Sighetu Marmaţiei

Muzeul Maramureşan Sighetu Marmaţiei (Sighetu Marmaţiei Museum of Maramureş): 4925 Sighetu Marmaţiei, Str. Libertăţii 16; tel. (62) 51-15-21; f. 1873; history, ethnography, natural history, open-air museum; Dir MIHAI DĂNCUŞ.

Sighişoara

Muzeul de Istorie Sighişoara (Sighişoara History Museum): 3050 Sighişoara, Piaţa Muzeului 1; tel. (65) 57-11-08; f. 1899; Dir MIRCEA ALEXANDRU.

Slatina

Muzeul Judeţean de Istorie şi Etnografie Slatina (Slatina District History and Ethnography Museum): 0500 Slatina, Str. Ionaşcu 75; tel. (49) 42-22-59; f. 1953; Dir AURELIA GROŞU.

Slobozia

Muzeul Judeţean Ialomiţa (Ialomiţa District Museum): 8400 Slobozia, Str. Matei Basarab 30; tel. (43) 11-56-60; history, ethnography; Dir GHEORGHE MATEI; publ. *Ialomiţa, Studii şi comunicări*.

Suceava

Muzeul Naţional al Bucovinei (Bucovina National Museum): 5800 Suceava, Str. Ştefan cel Mare 33; tel. (30) 71-64-39; f. 1900; folk art, history, natural history, astronomical observatory, planetarium, Romanian fine arts; library of 91,000 vols; Dir PAVEL BLAJ; publs *Suceava—Anuarul Muzeului judeţean* (History and Natural Sciences sections).

Timişoara

Muzeul Banatului Timişoara (Timiş Museum of the Banat): 1900 Timişoara, Piaţa Huniade 1; tel. (56) 19-13-39; fax (56) 20-13-21; f. 1872; archaeology, natural history, ethnography, art; Dir Dr FLORIN DRAŞOVEAN; publ. *Analele Banatului* (annually).

Tîrgovişte

Complexul Muzeal Judeţean Dîmboviţa (Dîmboviţa District Museum Complex): 0200 Tîrgovişte, Str. Justiţiei 3–5; tel. (45) 61-28-77; f. 1940; archaeology, ethnography, fine arts, history of books and printing in Romania; Dir GH. BULEI; publ. *Vallachica*.

Tîrgu Jiu

Muzeul Judeţean Gorj (Gorj District Museum): C/o Muzeul de Istorie şi Arheologie, 1400 Tîrgu Jiu, Str. Geneva 8; tel. and fax (53) 21-20-44; Dir Prof. VASILE MARINOIU.

Constituent museums:

- **Muzeul Arhitecturii Populare din Gorj** (Gorj Museum of Folk Architecture): 1435 Bumbeşti-Jiu, open-air Curtişoara village; f. 1968; Curator Prof. VASILE PETRE.
- **Muzeul de Artă** (Art Museum): 1400 Tîrgu Jiu, Parcul Central; tel. (53) 21-85-50; f. 1982; Romanian contemporary art; sculptures by Brâncuşi; Curator CARMEN SILVIA ŞOCU.
- **Muzeul de Istorie şi Arheologie** (History and Archaeology Museum): 1400 Tîrgu Jiu, Str. Geneva 8, Jud. Gorj; tel. (53) 21-20-44; f. 1894; library of 10,000 vols.

Tîrgu Mureş

Muzeul Judeţean Mureş (Mureş District Museum): 4300 Tîrgu Mureş, Str. Horea 24; tel. (65) 42-56-34; Dir VALER POP; publ. *Marisia* (annually).

Attached museums:

- **Muzeul de Arheologie şi Istorie** (Archaeology and History Museum): 4300 Tîrgu Mureş, Str. George Enescu 2; tel. (65) 43-25-12.
- **Muzeul de Artă** (Art Museum): 4300 Tîrgu Mureş, Str. George Enescu 2; tel. (65) 43-21-79; f. 1913; art of the 19th and 20th centuries.

Vaslui

Muzeul Judeţean 'Ştefan cel Mare' Vaslui (Vaslui District 'Stephen the Great' Museum): 6500 Vaslui, Piaţa Independenţei 1; tel. (35) 31-16-26; f. 1975; history, ethnography, modern art; library of 4,000 vols; Dir CONSTANTIN POPESCU; publ. *Acta Moldaviae Meridionalis*.

Zalău

Muzeul Judeţean de Istorie şi Artă Sălaj (Sălaj District Museum of History and Art): 4700 Zalău, Str. Unirii 9; tel. (60) 61-22-23; fax (60) 66-17-06; f. 1951; library of 13,000 vols; Dir ALEXANDRU MATEI; publ. *Acta Musei Porolissensis* (annually).

Universities

UNIVERSITATEA DIN BUCUREŞTI

70609 Bucharest, B-dul M. Kogălniceanu 34–46

Telephone: (1) 312-04-19

Fax: (1) 613-17-60

Founded 1694

State control

Academic year: October to July

Rector: Prof. Dr IOAN MIHĂILESCU

Pro-Rectors: Prof. Dr CONSTANTIN BUŞE, Prof. Dr DANA MARINESCU, Prof. Dr ION MUNTEANU, Prof. Dr CORNELIU ZIDĂROIU

Registrar: MARIA PRUNĂ

Librarian: Prof. Dr ION STOICA

Library: see Libraries

Number of teachers: 1,209

Number of students: 29,568 (8,605 postgraduates)

Publications: *Analele Universităţii din Bucureşti, Acta horti botanicae bucurestiensis.*

DEANS

Faculty of Biology: Prof. Dr C. TESIO

Faculty of Chemistry: Prof. Dr V. MAGEARU

Faculty of Foreign Languages and Literature: Prof. Dr S. RAPEANU

Faculty of Geography: Prof. Dr M. IELENICZ

Faculty of Geology and Geophysics: Prof. Dr C. DINU

Faculty of History: Prof. Dr A. BARNEA

Faculty of Political Sciences and Administration: Prof. Dr D. BARBU

Faculty of Journalism and Human Communication Sciences: Prof. Dr M. COMAN

Faculty of Law: Prof. Dr C. BÎRSAN

Faculty of Letters: Prof. Dr D. H. MAZILU

Faculty of Mathematics: Prof. Dr V. PREDA

Faculty of Philosophy: Prof. Dr V. MUREŞAN

Faculty of Physics: Prof. Dr V. GRECU

Faculty of Sociology, Psychology and Education: Prof. Dr D. POTOLEA

Faculty of Orthodox Theology: Prof. Dr C. CORNIŢESCU

Faculty of Baptist Theology: Prof. Dr V. TALPOŞ

Faculty of Roman Catholic Theology and Social Work: Prof. Dr I. MĂRTINCĂ

PROFESSORS

Faculty of Biology:

- ATANASIU, L., Physiology
- CRISTUREAN, I., Botany
- DUMITRU, I., Biochemistry
- FLONTA, M.L., Animal Physiology and Biophysics
- GAVRILĂ, L., Plant Genetics
- IORDĂCHESCU, D., Biochemistry
- MAILAT, E., Anatomy
- MANOLACHE, V., Animal Biology
- MARIN, A., Botany
- MEŞTER, L. E., Animal Biology
- MEŞTER, R., Animal Biology
- MIHĂESCU, G., Plant Physiology
- MIŞCALENCU, D., Anatomy
- NĂSTĂSESCU, G., Animal Physiology and Biophysics
- NĂSTĂSESCU, M., Animal Biology
- STRUNGARU, G., Plant Genetics
- TEODORESCU, I., Ecology
- TOMA, N., Botany
- VĂDINEANU, A., Ecology
- VOICA, C., Plant Physiology

Faculty of Chemistry:

- ALBU, C., Inorganic Chemistry
- ANGELESCU, E., Chemical Technology and Catalysis
- ANTONIU, A. C., Inorganic Chemistry
- BACIU, I., Organic Chemistry
- BAIULESCU, G.-E., Analytical Chemistry
- CENUŞE ZOICA, A., Physical Chemistry
- CERCASOV, C., Organic Chemistry
- CIOBANU, A., Organic Chemistry
- CRISTUREANU, E., Inorganic Chemistry
- DĂNET, A. F., Analytical Chemistry
- DUMITRESCU, V., Analytical Chemistry
- FĂTU, D., Physical Chemistry
- HILLEBRAND, M., Physical Chemistry
- IVAN, L., Organic Chemistry
- KRIZA, A., Inorganic Chemistry
- LECA, M., Physical Chemistry
- MAGEARU, V., Analytical Chemistry
- MAIOR, O. C., Organic Chemistry
- MANDRAVEL, L. C., Analytical Chemistry
- MÜLLER, L., Physics
- NEGOIŬ, M., Inorganic Chemistry
- NICOLAE, A. R., Organic Chemistry
- OANCEA, D., Physical Chemistry
- OLTEANU, M.V., Physical Chemistry
- PATROESCU, C., Analytical Chemistry
- PODINA, C., Physical Chemistry

SAHINI, V., Physical Chemistry
SĂNDULESCU, I., Chemical Technology and Catalysis
SEGAL, E., Physical Chemistry
SZABÓ, A., Chemical Technology and Catalysis
UDREA, I., Chemical Technology and Catalysis
VÎLCU, R., Physical Chemistry
VLĂDESCU, L., Analytical Chemistry
ZĂVOIANU, D., Organic Chemistry

Faculty of Foreign Languages and Literature:
ANGHELESCU, N., Oriental Languages
BARBĂ, G., Russian
BARBORICĂ, C., Slovak Language
CHIORȚORAN, D., English
CIZEK, E. A., Classical Languages
CORNILESCU, A., English
COSĂCEANU, A., French
CUNIȚĂ, A., French
DERER, D., Italian
DOBREA, A., Russian Language and Literature
DOBRISAN, N., Oriental Languages
DUMITRIU, G., English
FISCHER, I., Classical Languages
GĂMULESCU, D., Serbo-Croat Language
GRUIA, S., Slavic Languages
GUȚU, G., German
IONESCU, A.-I., Slavic Languages
MICLĂU, P., French
MIHĂILĂ, GH., Slavonic Languages
MIHĂILĂ, R., American Literature
MIROIU, M., English
MOLNAR, S., Hungarian
MORNAI, O., Hungarian
MURĂREȚ, I., French
NICOLESCU, A., English
PETRICĂ, I., Slavic Languages
PREDA, G., English
REBAȘAPCĂ, I., Slavic Languages
RÎPEANU, S., Romance Languages
ROȘIANU, N., Russian
SANDU, D., German
SLUȘANSCHI, D. M., Classical Languages
ȘOPTEREANU, V., Russian
STĂNESCU, G., German
TOMA, D., French
TUȚESCU, M., French

Faculty of Geography:
CIULACHE, S., Meteorology and Hydrology
GRIGORE, M., Geomorphology and Pedology
IELENICZ, M., Geomorphology and Pedology
IONAȘ, I., Human and Economic Geography
MARIN, I., Regional Geography
NĂSTASE, A., Geomorphology and Pedology
POPESCU, N., Geomorphology and Pedology
POSEA, GR., Geomorphology and Pedology
TRUFAȘ, V., Meteorology and Hydrology
VELCEA, I., Economic Geography

Faculty of Geology and Geophysics:
ANASTASIU, N., Mineralogy
CALOTĂ, C., Geophysics
CONSTANTINESCU, E., Mineralogy
DINU, C., Geology and Palaeontology
DRAGASTAN, O., Geology
GEORGESCU, P., Geophysics
GRIGORESCU, D., Geology
NEAGU, TH., Geology and Palaeontology
NEGUȚ, A., Geophysics
POPESCU, G., Geophysics
RĂDULESCU, D., Mineralogy
ȘECLĂMAN, M., Mineralogy
ŽAMFIRESCU, F., Geological Engineering

Faculty of History:
BOIA, I., World History
BULEI, I., Modern Romanian History
BUȘE, C., World History
GIURESCU, D., Romanian History
IONIȚĂ, GH., Romanian History
ISAR, N., Romanian History
MAXIM, M., World History
MURGESCU, B., World History
PETRE, Z., World History
PIPPIDI, A. N., World History
SCURTU, I., Romanian History
ȘTEFĂNESCU, ST., Romanian History

Faculty of Law:
BÎRSAN, C., Civil Law
BULAI, C., Criminal Law
CĂRPENARU, ST., Civil Law
CIOBANU, V., Civil Law
CORNESCU, V., Economic Sciences
CREȚOIU, GH., Economic Sciences
DEAK, FR., Civil Law
DINCU, I., Criminal Law
FILIPESCU, I., Civil Law
MARINESCU, D., Civil Law
MELEȘCANU, T., International Public Law
MITRACHE, C., Criminal Law
MOLCUȚ, G., Public Law
MURARU, I., Public Law
NEAGU, I., Public Law
POPA, N., Public Law
SITARU DRAGOȘ, A., Private Law
STANCU, E., Criminal Law
VOLONCIU, N. D., Criminal Law

Faculty of Mathematics:
ALBU, T., Algebra
BOBOC, N., Analysis
BUCUR, GH., Analysis
CALUDE, C., Computer Science
CĂZĂNESCU, V., Computer Science
COLOJOARĂ, I., Analysis
CRISTESCU, N., Mechanics and Equations
CRISTESCU, R., Analysis
CUCULESCU, I., Probabilities
DINCĂ, GH. I., Mechanics and Equations
DRAGOȘ, L., Mechanics and Equations
GEORGESCU, GH., Computer Science
IANUȘ, S., Geometry
IFTIMIE, V., Mechanics and Equations
ION, D. I., Algebra
IONESCU, P., Algebra
JURCHESCU, M., Analysis
MIHĂILĂ, I., Mechanics and Equations
MIRICĂ, S., Mechanics and Equations
NĂSTĂSESCU, C., Algebra
NIȚA, C., Algebra
POPA, N., Analysis
POPESCU, D., Algebra
POPOVICI, C., Computer Science
PREDA, V., Statistics and Probability
RADU, N., Algebra
RUDEANU, S. A., Computer Science
SANDRU, N., Mechanics
STRĂTILĂ ȘERBAN, V., Analysis
TOMESCU, I., Computer Science
TUDOR, C., Probabilities
VĂDUVA, I., Computer Science
VAIDA, D., Computer Science

Faculty of Letters:
ANGELESCU, S., Folklore
ANGHELESCU, ST. M., Romanian Literature
BĂLAN, I. D., Romanian Literature
BANCIU, D., Library Science and Information Science
BERCIU, D.-A., Administrative and Secretarial College
BRÎNCUȘI, GR., Romanian Literature
CAZIMIR, Ș., Romanian Literature
CONSTANTINESCU, N., Folklore
CORNEA, L. P., Romanian Literature
DINDELEGAN, G., Romanian Language
FILIPAȘ, E., Romanian Literature
GANĂ, G., Romanian Literature
GRIGORESCU, D., Comparative Literature
HANȚĂ, A., Romanian Literature
HRISTEA, T., Romanian Language
MANOLESCU, N. A., Romanian Literature
MARTIN, M. A., Theory of Literature
MAZILU, D. H., Romanian Literature
MICU, D., Romanian Literature
NEGRICI, E., Romanian Literature
REGNEALĂ, M., Library Science and Information Science
SIMION, I. E., Romanian Literature
VASILIU, E., Romanian Language
ZAMFIR, M., Romanian Language
ZAMFIR, M., Romanian Literature

Faculty of Philosophy:
BOBOC, A., History of Philosophy
CAZAN, GH., History of Philosophy
ENESCU, GH., Logic
IANOȘI, I., Ethics and Aesthetics
MIROIU, A. F., Logic
MORAR, V., Ethics and Aesthetics
PÎRVU, I., Philosophy
PLEȘU, A., History of Philosophy
POPESCU, I., Philosophy
SURDU, A., Modern Philosophy
TONOIU, V., Philosophy
TUDOSESCU, I., Philosophy
ȚURLEA, M., Theoretical Philosophy and Logic
VALENTIN, A., Philosophy
VLĂDUȚESCU, GH., History of Philosophy

Faculty of Physics:
ANGELESCU, T., Atomic and Nuclear Physics
BEȘLIU, R. C., Atomic and Nuclear Physics
BORȘAN, D., Mechanics, Molecular Physics, Polymers
CIOBANU, GH., Quantum Mechanics
CONSTANTINESCU, A., Atomic Physics
CONSTANTINESCU, L. M., Physics of Polymers
COSTESCU, A., Theoretical Physics
DOLOCAN, V., Solid State Physics, Electrophysics
FLORESCU, V., Quantum Mechanics
GEORGESCU, L., Mechanics, Molecular Physics, Polymers
GHEORGHE, V., Electricity and Biophysics
GRECU, V.-VL., Atomic and Nuclear Physics
ION, R. M., Atomic and Nuclear Physics
IOVA, I., Optics, Spectroscopy, Plasma
JIPA, A., Atomic Physics
LICEA, I., Solid State Physics and Electrophysics
MIHUL, A., Atomic and Nuclear Physics
PĂTRASCU, A. ST., Mechanics, Molecular Physics, Polymers
PLĂVIȚU, C., Mechanics, Molecular Physics, Polymers
POPESCU, I., Mathematical Physics
RUXANDRA, V., Electricity and Biophysics
SPÎNULESCU, I., Electricity and Biophysics
TOADER, E., Optics, Spectroscopy, Plasma
TRUȚIA, A., Optics, Spectroscopy, Plasma
TUDOR, Ș. T., Optics, Spectroscopy, Plasma
TURBATU, ST., Mathematical Physics
TURCU, GR., Biophysics
VLĂDUCA, GH., Atomic and Nuclear Physics
VREJOIU, C., Theoretical Physics

Faculty of Sociology, Psychology and Education:
BĂDESCU, I., Sociology
CERGHIT, I., Education
DRĂGAN, I., Sociology
FĂTU, S., Education
GOLU, P., Psychology
LUCEANU, A., Political Psychology
MIHĂILESCU, I., Sociology
MITROFAN, I., Psychology
MITROFAN, N., Psychology
PĂUN, E., Education
POTOLEA, D., Education
RADU, I., Education
SANDU, D., Sociology
STANCIU, I., Education
VERZA, E., Rehabilitation
ZAMFIR, C., Sociology
ZAMFIR, E., Social Assistance
ZLATE, M., Psychology

Faculty of Journalism and Communication Sciences:
COMAN, M., Cultural Anthropology

Faculty of Orthodox Theology:
CORNIȚESCU, C., New Testament
CORNIȚESCU, E., Old Testament
DAVID, P., Missionary Studies

IONIȚĂ, V., Church History
MOLDOVEANU, N., Church Music
NECULA, N., Liturgy and Christian Art
POPESCU, D., Dogmatics
POPESCU, E., Byzantine Studies
RADU, D., Christian Ethics
RUS, R., History and Philosophy of Religions

Faculty of Baptist Theology:
BUNACIU, I., New Testament
TALPOȘ, V., Old Testament

Faculty of Roman Catholic Theology and Social Work:
MĂRTINCĂ, I., Dogmatic Theology, Law
SPORSCHILL, G., Training in Social Work

Faculty of Political Sciences and Administration:
BARBU, D., Political Sciences

UNIVERSITATEA 'TRANSILVANIA' DIN BRAȘOV

2200 Brașov, B-dul Eroilor 29
Telephone: (68) 14-25-76
Fax: (68) 15-02-74
E-mail: users@unitbv.ro
Founded 1971 by merger of Polytechnical and Pedagogical Institutes of Brașov
State control
Language of instruction: Romanian
Academic year: October to July
Rector: Prof. Dr Eng. SERGIU CHIRIACESCU
Vice-Rectors: Prof. Dr Eng. SIMION POPESCU, Prof. Dr Eng. RADU IOVĂNAS, Prof. Dr Math. ELEONOR CIUREA
Registrar: Mat. FLOAREA CERNAT
Library Director: Prof. Dr Eng. AUREL NEGRUȚIU
Library: see Libraries
Number of teachers: 617
Number of students: 11,112
Publication: *Buletinul Universității 'Transilvania' din Brașov.*

DEANS

Faculty of Mechanics: Prof. Dr Eng. GHEORGHE RADU
Faculty of Technical Engineering: Prof. Dr Eng. NICOLAE-VALENTIN IVAN
Faculty of Forestry and Forest Exploitation: Prof. Dr Eng. GHEORGHIȚĂ IONAȘCU
Faculty of Wood Technology: Prof. Dr Eng. VICTOR DOGARU
Faculty of Electrical Engineering: Prof. Dr Eng. WILIBALD SZABÓ
Faculty of Materials Science and Engineering: Prof. Dr Eng. IOAN GIACOMELLI
Faculty of Sciences: Prof. Dr Mat. NICOLAE PASCU
Faculty of Economic Sciences: Prof. Dr Ec. IOAN OPREI
Faculty of Music: Prof. STELA DRĂGULIN
Faculty of Medicine: Prof. Dr TEODOR LEAȘU

PROFESSORS

Faculty of Technical Engineering:
ALEXANDRU, P., Mechanisms
APETREI, GH., Mechanisms and Machine Components
BOBANCU, S., Mechanisms
BODEA, M., Physics
BONCOI, G., Automatic Machine Tools
BRANA, M., Descriptive Geometry and Technical Drawing
BUZATU, C., Automation of Technological Processes
CHIȘU, E., Machine Components
CIOBOTA, M., Precision Mechanics
CRUCIAT, P., Technical Measurements
DIACONESCU, D., Mechanisms
DUDIȚĂ, F., Mechanisms
DUMITRU, S., Physics
GOGU, G., Machine Elements and Mechanisms
ILIESCU, C., Technology of Cold-pressing
INȚA, I., Physics
IVAN, M., Machine Tools and Dimensional Control
IVAN, N., Machine Engineeering Technology
JULA, A., Machine Elements
MĂRĂSCU KLEIN, V., Unconventional Materials, Computer Aided Production Systems Design
MARTINESCU, I., Technology of Cold-pressing
MOLDOVEANU, GH., Machine Elements
OBACIU, G., Electric Drive and Machine Tools
POPESCU, I., Technical Measurement and Tolerance
ROSCA, D., Metal-cutting Theory
SECARĂ, C., Metal Cutting, Tool Design
SEITABLA, D., Physics
SOFONEA, L., Physics
TĂNĂSESCU, I., Machine Elements and Mechanisms
TUREAC, I., Machines for Processing by Deformation
VASII-ROȘCULEȚ, S., Design of Devices
VELICU, D., Descriptive Geometry and Technical Drawing
VISA, I., Mechanisms

Faculty of Mechanics:
ABĂITĂNCEI, D., Automobile Engines
BALCU, I., Vibrations in Mechanical Engineering
BENCHE, V., Fluid Mechanics
BOBESCU, GH., Auto-vehicle engines
BRĂTUCU, GH., Agricultural Mechanics
CHIRIACESCU, S., Vibrations in Mechanical Engineering, Strength of Materials
CHIRU, A., Autovehicle Engines
CÎMPEAN, V., Automobiles
CÎNDEA, I., Theoretical Mechanics
CIOFAIA, V., Strength of Materials
COFARU, C., Automobile Dynamics
CONSTANTIN, F., Mechanics
CURTU, I., Strength of Materials
DELIU, GH., Theoretical Mechanics
DUMITRIU, A. Data Processing
GOIA, I., Strength of Materials
IONESCU, E., Hydraulic Equipment
IONESCU, E., Tractors and Automobiles
MUNTEANU, M., Strength of Materials
MUREȘAN, M., Heat Engineering and Thermal Machines
NAGY, T., Transport
NASTASOIU, S., Turbomachines and Hydraulic Drives for Automobiles
OLTEANU, C., Devices for Mechanical Measurement
PEREȘ, GH., Service Road Theory and Traffic Safety
POPESCU, S., Agricultural Equipment
RADU, GH., Automobile Engines
RADU, GH., Strength of Materials
SĂLĂJAN, C., Transport
SEITZ, N., Electrical Equipment
ȘERBĂNOIU, N., Heat Engineering and Thermal Machines
SOARE, I., Automobile Repair
SOVA, V., Heat Engineering
SPERCHEZ, F., Strength of Materials
TĂNASE, F., Automobile Repair
TOFAN, M., Mechanics
VEȘTEMEANU, N., Heat Engineering and Equipment
VLASE, S., Mechanics

Faculty of Forestry and Forest Exploitation:
ALEXANDRU, V., Forest Roads
BELDEANU, E., Forestry Products
CHIȚEA, GH., Biostatistics
CIORTUZ, I., Forest Improvement
CIUBOTARU, A., Forest Exploitation
CLINCIU, I., Flood Control
DANCIU, M., Silviculture
FLORESCU, I., Silviculture
IONAȘCU, GH., Forest Equipment
KISS, A., Topography
LEAHU, I., Dendrometry
MARCU, M., Forest Meteorology and Climatology
MARCU, O., Forest Phytopathology, Entomology
NEGRUȚIU, A., Hunting and Pisciculture
OLTEANU, N., Forest Roads
OPREA, I., Design and Planning of Forest Sites
POPESCU, I., Mechanization in Silviculture
STĂNESCU, V., Dendrology, Forestry Genetics
TALPOSI, A., Metal Constructions
TAMAS, S., Operations Research
TÎRZIU, D., Pedology

Faculty of Wood Technology:
BUDĂU, G., Wood Processing Machinery
BULARCA, M., Hydraulic and Pneumatic Equipment
CISMARU, I., Furniture Technology
DOGARU, V., Basics of Mechanical Wood Processing
LAZĂRESCU, C., Forestry Equipment Production
MIHAI, D., Technological Materials
MITIȘOR, A., Multilayer Wood Products Technology
NĂSTASE, V., Furniture Production and Design
PETROVICI, V., Wood Chemical Processing
ȚĂRAN, N., Forestry Equipment Use
TUDOR, E., Machinery for Transport and Lifting
ZLATE, GH., Silviculture and Wood Exploitation

Faculty of Materials Science and Engineering:
ANDREESCU, F., Welding Equipment
BEJAN, V., Technology of Fabrication and Maintenance of Equipment
BOT, D., Heating Equipment, Foundry Technology
CIOBANU, I., Fundamentals of Foundry
CONSTANTINESCU, A., Foundry Equipment
ENE, V., Special Proceedings for Foundry
FĂTU, S., Study of Metals
GIACOMELLI, I., Equipment and Technologies for Thermal Treatments
IOVANĂS, R., Technology of Welding by Pressing
LUCA, V., Study of Metals
MACHEDON PISU, T., Welding Equipment, Non-Destructive Testing, Hydraulic and Pneumatic Engines
MUNTEANU, A., Thermal Treatments and Heat Processing
NOVAC, GH., Welding Equipment
POPA, A., Technology of Plastic Deformation
SAMOILĂ, G., Furnaces and Equipment for Heating
SCOROBETIU, L., Fundamentals of Welding Processes
ȘERBAN, C., Study of Metals
ȚICA, R., Chemistry
TRIF, R., Mechanization, Automation and Robots for Welding Processing
TUDORAN, P., Study of Metals

Faculty of Sciences:
ATANASIU, G., Linear Algebra, Analytical Geometry and Programming
CIUREA, E., Mathematical Analysis
LUPU, M., Special Mathematics
MARCU, GH., Physical Training and Sports
MARINESCU, C., Differential Equations
ORMAN, G., Measurement Theory
PASCU, N., Special Mathematics
PITIȘ, GH., Linear Algebra, Geometry
TITA, N., Mathematical Analysis

Faculty of Electrical Engineering:
ANDONIE, R., Computers and Electrotechnics
BIDIAN, D. S., Electrotechnics and Electrical Machines
CERNAT, M., Theoretical and Industrial Electrotechnics
DAN, ST., Electrical Drive
GOGIOIU, A., Electrical Machines
HELEREA, E., Electrotechnical Materials

MATLAC, I., Electrical Devices and Convertors
MĂRGINEANU, I., Process Control
NICOLAIDE, A., Electrical Machines
PESTEANU, O., Electrical Engineering
SCUTARU, GH., Electrical Engineering
SISAK, F., Electric Drives
STOIA, D., Electric Machines
SZABO, W., Electrical and Electronic Measurements
SZEKELY, I., Electronics
TATA, M., Electric Machines
TOACSE, GH., Electronics
TOPA, I., Electrical Machines

Faculty of Economic Sciences:

BUJDOIU, N., Philosophy
LEFTER, C., Economics, Marketing
OPREI, I., Organization and Management
PĂCURAR, D., Education
PANȚURU, S., Education, Psychology
POENARU, E., Jurisprudence
POPA, GH., Political Systems
POPA, M., Organization and Management
TARTAGA, I., Economics
TATU, C., Psychology

Faculty of Music:

BICA, N., Choir Conducting
DIMULESCU, M., Piano accompaniment
DRĂGULIN, S., Piano
DUCARU, S., Piano accompaniment
HAMZEA, R., Violin
ORBAN, C., Piano
SOREANU, C., Singing
ȚURCANU, N., Choir Conducting

UNIVERSITATEA 'BABEŞ-BOLYAI' CLUJ-NAPOCA

3400 Cluj-Napoca, Str. M. Kogălniceanu 1

Telephone: (64) 19-43-15
Fax: (64) 19-19-06

Founded 1919
Languages of instruction: Romanian, Hungarian, German
Academic year: October to July (two semesters)

Rector: Prof. Dr ANDREI MARGA
Pro-Rectors: Prof. Dr N. BOCŞAN, Prof. Dr W. W. BRECKNER, Prof. Dr M. MUTHU, Prof. Dr N. PAINA, Prof. Dr S. ŞIMON, Prof. Dr. P. SZILÁGYI
Secretary-General: MARIA BOIAN
Librarian: Prof. Dr DORU RADOSAV

Library: see Libraries
Number of teachers: 1,083
Number of students: 20,183

Publications: *Studia Universitatis Babeş-Bolyai, Judaic Library Collection, Colloquia: Journal of Central European History, Studi Italo-Romeni, Brain and Cognition and Behaviour, Botanical Contributions, Papers of Transition.*

DEANS

Faculty of Mathematics and Computer Science: L. ȚAMBULEA
Faculty of Physics: E. BURZO
Faculty of Chemistry and Chemical Engineering: S. MAGER
Faculty of Biology and Geology: V. CRISTEA
Faculty of Geography: I. MAC
Faculty of History and Philosophy: M. BĂRBULESCU
Faculty of Letters: I. POP
Faculty of Law: L. POP
Faculty of Psychology and Education: M. IONESCU
Faculty of Economics: D. RACOVIȚAN
Faculty of Orthodox Theology: I. ICĂ
Faculty of Greek Catholic Theology: A. GOȚIA
Faculty of Protestant Theology: Z. GÁLFI
Faculty of Roman Catholic Theology: J. MARTON
Faculty of Physical Education and Sports: M. ALEXEI
Faculty of European Studies: N. PĂUN
Faculty of Political Science and Public Administration: V. BOARI
Faculty of Business: I. A. GIURGIU

PROFESSORS

Faculty of Mathematics and Computer Science:

ANDRICA, D., Geometry
BLAGA, P., Numerical Analysis
BOIAN, F. M., Informatics
BOTH, N., Algebra
BRECKNER, W. W., Functional Analysis and Optimization
CĂLUGĂREANU, G., Algebra
COBZAŞ, Ş., Functional Analysis
COMAN, G., Numerical Analysis
DUCA, D., Mathematical Analysis
DUMITRESCU, D., Informatics
FRENȚIU, M., Informatics
KOLUMBÁN, I., Mathematical Analysis
MICULA, G., Differential Equations
MIHOC, I., Probability Theory
MOCANU, P., Mathematical Analysis
MOLDOVAN, G., Informatics
MUNTEAN, E., Informatics
MUREŞAN, A., Applied Mathematics
NÉMETH, A., Mathematical Analysis
PÂRV, B., Informatics
PETRILA, T., Fluid Mechanics
POP, M. I., Fluid Mechanics
POP, V., Astronomy
PURDEA, I., Algebra
RUS, A. I., Differential Equations
SĂLĂGEAN, G. Ş., Mathematical Analysis
SZILÁGYI, P., Differential Equations
TÂMBULEA, L., Informatics
TRIF, D., Differential Equations
URECHE, V., Astronomy
VASIU, A., Geometry

Faculty of Physics:

ARDELEAN, I., Materials Science
BARBUR, I., Solid State Physics
BURZO, E., Solid State Physics
COLDEA, M., Solid State Physics
COSMA, C., Physics of Radiation
COZAR, O., Atomic and Molecular Physics
CRIŞAN, M., Theoretical Physics
CRIŞAN, V., Solid State Physics
CRISTEA, G., Solid State Physics
ILIESCU, T., Optics and Spectroscopy
ILONCA, G., Solid State Physics
POP, I., Solid State Physics
SIMON, S., Solid State Physics
TĂTARU, E., Electronics
ZNAMIROVSCHI, V., Atomic and Nuclear Physics

Faculty of Chemistry and Chemical Engineering:

AGACHI, P. Ş., Chemical Engineering
BÂLDEA, I., Physical Chemistry
CORDOŞ, E., Analytical Chemistry
DIUDEA, M., Organic Chemistry
GROSU, I., Organic Chemistry
HOROVITZ, O., Physical Chemistry
MAGER, S., Organic Chemistry
POPESCU, C., Physical Chemistry
SILAGHI-DUMITRESCU, I., Inorganic Chemistry
SILBERG, I. A., Organic Chemistry
SILVESTRU, C., Inorganic Chemistry
VLASSA, M., Organic Chemistry

Faculty of Biology and Geology:

BALINTONI, I. C., Geotectonics
BEDELEAN, I., Mineralogy
BUCUR, I., Palaeontology
COMAN, N., Genetics
CRISTEA, V., Botany
DRĂGAN BULARDA, M., Microbiology
MUREŞAN, I., Mineralogy
PÉTERFI, L. S., Botany
PETRESCU, I., Palaeobotany
POPESCU, O., Cell Biology
TARBA, C., Biophysics
TOMESCU, N., Zoology
TRIFU, M., Plant Physiology
TUDORANCEA, C., Ecology
VLAD, Ş. N., Petrology

Faculty of Geography:

CIANGĂ, N., Human Geography
COCEAN, P., Regional Geography
GÂRBACEA, V., Regional Geography
MAC, I., Physical Geography
POP, G., Human Geography
RABOCA, N., Economic Geography
SOROCOVSCHI, V. E., Hydrology
SURD, V., Rural Geography

Faculty of History and Philosophy:

BĂRBULESCU, M., Ancient History and Archaeology
BOCŞAN, N., Modern History
CIPĂIANU, G. A., Contemporary History
CODOBAN, A. T., Philosophy
CSUCSUJA, Ş., Contemporary History
EDROIU, N., Medieval History of Romania
GLODARIU, I., Ancient History
ILUȚ, P., Sociology
MAGYARI, A., Modern History
MUSCĂ, V., History of Philosophy
PAVEL, T., Modern History
PISO, I., Ancient History and Archaeology
POP, I. A., Medieval History
PUŞCAŞ, V., Contemporary History
ROTARIU, T., Sociology
TEODOR, P., Medieval History of Romania
ȚOCA, M., History of Art
VESE, V., Contemporary History

Faculty of Letters:

BACIU, I., French Language
BORCILĂ, M., General Linguistics
CĂPUŞAN, M., French Literature
CSEKE, É., Hungarian Literature and Society
DRAGOŞ, E., History of the Romanian Language
FANACHE, V., History of Romanian Literature
GRUIȚĂ, G., Contemporary Romanian Language
KOZMA, D., Hungarian Literature
MUTHU, M., Theory of Literature and Aesthetics
OLTEAN, Ş, History of the English Language
PAPAHAGI, M. D., Italian Literature
PÉNTEK, J., General Linguistics
PETRESCU, L., History of Romanian Literature
POP, I., History of Romanian Literature
POP, R., French Literature
ŞEULEAN, I., Folklore and Cultural Anthropology
STANCIU, V., English Literature
VARTIC, I., Comparative Literature and Theory of Drama
ZDRENGHEA, M., Contemporary English Literature

Faculty of Law:

COSTIN, M. N., Commercial Law
POP, L., Civil Law
URSA, V., Criminal Law
ZĂPÎRȚAN, L., Political Science

Faculty of Psychology and Education:

GOIA, V., Methodology
IONESCU, M., Education
LĂSCUŞ, V., Education
MICLEA, M., Psychology
PITARIU, H., Psychology
PREDA, V., Psychology for Teaching

Faculty of Economics:

AVORNICULUI, C., Data Processing in Economics
AVRAM-NIȚCHI, R., Data Processing in Economics
BĂTRÎNCEA, I., Economic Analysis

Beju, V., Finance
Căinap, I., Economic Analysis
Cistelecan, L., Finance
Diţu, G., Political Economy
Drăgoescu, A., Political Economy
Drăgoescu, E., Finance
Dumbravă, P., Accountancy
Florea, I., Statistics
Frăţilă, R., Manufacture and Marketing of Products
Ghişoiu, N., Data Processing in Economics
Goron, S., Data Processing in Economics
Ilieş, L., Transport Management
Ionescu, T., Political Economy
Lazăr, D., Marketing
Lazăr, I., Agricultural Management
Mihuţ, I., Management
Naghi, M., Management
Nistor, I., Finance
Nistor, L. I., Macroeconomic Forecasting
Niţchi, I. Ş., Data Processing in Economics
Oprean, D., Data Processing in Economics
Oprean, I., Accountancy
Oprean, V., Data Processing in Economics
Paina, N., Marketing
Pântea, P., Accountancy
Plăiaş, I., Marketing
Pop, S. I., Management
Popescu, G., Political Economy
Postelnicu, G., Political Economy
Purdea, D., Management
Racoviţan, D., Data Processing in Economics
Roşca, T., Finance
Stăneanu, G., Finance
Temeş I., Accountancy
Tulai, C., Finance
Vincze, M., Agricultural Economics
Vorzsák, A., Marketing

Faculty of Orthodox Theology:

Ică, I., Fundamental Theology
Moraru, A., History of the Orthodox Church

Faculty of Greek Catholic Theology:

Goţia, A., Catechetical Theology
Gudea, N., History of the Greek Catholic Church

Faculty of Roman Catholic Theology:

Marton, J., Ecclesiastical History

Faculty of Physical Education and Sport:

Bengeanu, C., Volleyball
Brătucu, L. S., Anatomy and Physiology
Marolicaru, M., Methodology of Scientific Research
Neta, G., Football

Faculty of European Studies:

Bîrsan, M., Management of European Institutions
Gyemant, L., European Studies
Marga, A., Philosophy
Păun, N., Management of European Institutions

Faculty of Political Science and Public Administration:

Boari, V., Political Ideology
Stegăroiu, D. C., Management of Human Resources

Faculty of Business:

Giurgiu, A., Finance
Vorzsák, M., Micro- and Macroeconomics

ATTACHED INSTITUTES

Computer Science Research Institute: Dir Prof. M. Frenţiu.

Institute of Physics: Dir Prof. I. Ardelean.

Centre for Electrochemical Research: Dir Prof. L. Oniciu.

Institute of Gemology: Dir Prof. I. Mârza.

Institute of Geography: Dir Prof. I. Mac.

Institute of Central European History: Dir Prof. P. Teodor.

Institute of Oral History: Dir Prof. D. Radosav.

Institute of Anthropology: Dir I. Cuceu.

Institute of Classical Studies: Dir Prof. M. Bărbulescu.

Centre for Documentation and Comparative Studies of Universities: Dir Prof. M. Miclea.

Dr. Moshe Carmilly Institute of Jewish Studies and History: Dir Prof. L. Gyemant.

Institute for Modernity Research: Dir I. Copoeru.

Centre for Interethnic Relationship Studies: Dir Asst Prof. M. Lazăr.

Social Research Centre: Dir Prof. V. Boari.

Centre of Post-Totalitarian Society Studies: Dir Asst Prof. O. Pecican.

CONCORD-ERCIR Centre of Text Analysis: Dir Prof. M. Papahagi.

UNIVERSITATEA DIN CRAIOVA

1100 Craiova, Str. A. I. Cuza 13
Telephone: (51) 11-45-48
Fax: (51) 11-16-88
Founded 1966
State control
Academic year: October to July

Rector: Prof. Dr Mircea Ivănescu
Vice-Rectors: Marin Beşteliu, Maria Homeag, Tudor Hobeanu
Scientific Secretary: Ion Vladimirescu
General Secretary: Mircea Zăvăleanu
Librarian: Octavian Lohon

Library: see Libraries
Number of teachers: 975
Number of students: 15,000

Publication: *University Bulletin* (annually, in 10 series according to subject).

DEANS

Faculty of Mathematics and Computer Science: A. Dincă
Faculty of Sciences: Ecaterina Marinescu
Faculty of Letters and History: Emil Dumitrascu
Faculty of Law: Ion Dogaru
Faculty of Economics: Dumitru Constantinescu
Faculty of Medicine: Petre Georgescu
Faculty of Electrotechnics: Dumitru Topan
Faculty of Automatics, Computers and Electronics: Vladimir Rasvan
Faculty of Electromechanics: Aurel Campeanu
Faculty of Mechanics: George Petrescu
Faculty of Horticulture: Ion Olteanu
Faculty of Agriculture: Nicolae Voica
Faculty of Theology: Coravu Damaschin

PROFESSORS

Faculty of Mathematics and Computer Science:

Avramescu, C., Differential Equations
Badea, J., Special Mathematics
Bălan, T., Special Mathematics
Boju, V., Geometry
Dincă, Al., Algebra
Drăghicescu, D., Mechanics, Astronomy
Ionescu, V., Mathematics Applied to Economics
Kessler, P., Mathematical Analysis
Leonte, A., Theory of Probability
Murărescu, G., Geometry
Niculescu, C., Mathematical Analysis
Stavre, P., Mathematics Applied to Economics
Tandareanu, N., Systems, Informatics
Vraciu, G., Algebra

Faculty of Sciences:

Brad, I., Biochemistry
Burnea, I., Chemistry
Gănescu, I., Chemistry
Gherman, O., Physics
Mureşan, N., Chemistry
Mureşan, V., Inorganic Chemistry
Popescu, A., Analytical Chemistry
Preda, M., Chemistry
Scondac, I., Industrial Technology
Uliu, F., Physics

Faculty of Letters and History:

Beşteliu, M., Romanian Literature
Bolocan, G., Russian Language
Ceapraz, I., Logic
Mavrodin, I., French Literature
Nicola, T., Philosophy
Patroi, I., History
Popescu, R., Romanian Language
Sorescu, G., Romanian Literature
Stoica, M., Education
Toropu, O., History
Trăistaru, I., Romanian Literature

Faculty of Law:

Dogaru, I., Law

Faculty of Economics:

Băbeanu, M., Political Economics
Bărbăcioru, C., Political Economics
Bărbăcioru, V., Financial Accountancy
Bica, F., Languages for Computer Programmes
Buse, L., Economic and Financial Analysis
Ciobanu, V., Foreign Currency Relations
Constantinescu, D., Industrial Management and Organization
Fota, C., International Economic Relations
Georgescu, P., Statistics
Hobeanu, T., Management
Marin, E., Political Economics
Nicolae, A., Investment Efficiency
Nistorescu, T., Management
Opritescu, M., Currency and Credits
Pana, I., Agricultural Macro-economic Analysis
Pirvu, G., Political Economics
Radu, F., Economic Activities of Industrial Units
Ricu, L., Informatics
Roşca, C., Economics and Ergonomics
Roşu-Hamzescu, I., International Economic Relations
Sbora, T., Building and Transport Organization
Schiopoiu, A., Economic Geography
Staicu, C., Accountancy
Stefan, V., History of Economics
Stefanescu, I., Informatics
Toba, A., International Economic Relations
Topală, S., Management
Trăistaru, I., Political Economics
Trandafir, D., Accountancy
Vancea, I., Statistics
Vasilescu, N., Statistics

Faculty of Medicine:

Berilă, I., Hygiene
Bogdan, F., Histology
Bondari, A., Radiology
Bulucea, D., Paediatrics
Cernea, M., Obstetrics and Gynaecology
Cernea, P., Ophthalmology
Chita, O., Genetic Biology
Drăgoi, G., Anatomy
Georgescu, M., Medical Semiology
Georgescu, P., Surgical Semiology, Urology
Ghelase, F., Surgical Pathology
Ionescu, D., Paediatrics
Nedelcu, C., Biophysics
Neştianu, V., Physiology
Radu, C., Orthopaedics
Rica, N., Obstetrics and Gynaecology
Tănăsescu, D., Biochemistry
Traila, A., Physiopathology
Voiculescu, C.. Immunology, Virology

Faculty of Electrotechnics:

Badea, M., Basic Electrical Engineering
Cividjan, G., Electrical Apparatus

PUŞCAŞU, S., Basic Electrical Engineering
TOPAN, D., Basic Electrical Engineering

Faculty of Automatics, Computers and Electronics:

AMBROZIE, C., Electric and Electronic Measurement
IVĂNESCU, M., Discrete Industrial Automatics
MARIN, C., Automatic Regulators
RĂSVAN, V., Theory of Automatic Systems

Faculty of Electromechanics:

CAMPEANU, A., Electrical Machinery
CIOC, I., Design and Building of Electrical Machinery
DEGERATU, P., Automatization of Electrical Machinery
DRAGANESCU, O., Electrical Machinery
FLORIGANȚĂ, G., Design and Building of Electrical Machinery
MANOLEA, G., Electromechanics
SAVIUC, V., Special Machinery
VINTILĂ, N., Electrical Machinery

Faculty of Mechanics:

BUCULEI, I. M., Mechanics
CARAMAVRU, N., Thermotechnics and Thermic Machinery
CERNĂIANU, E., Resistance of Materials
ENE, AL., Descriptive Geometry and Drawing
PETRESCU, G., Theory of Elasticity and Material Resistance
POPESCU, I., Mechanisms
ŞONTEA, S., Technology
TÎRPE, GH., Technology of Machine Building

Faculty of Horticulture:

ANTON, D., Floriculture
BALASA, M., Vegetable Garden
BOBIRNAC, B., Plant Protection
COSTESCU, C., Entomology
GHEORGHIȚĂ, M., Oenology
GLODEANU, C., Phytopathology
GODEANU, I., General Pomiculture
MILITIU, I., Tropical Horticulture
OLTEANU, I., General Viticulture
POPA, A., Microbiology
POPESCU, M., Pomiculture
ROSU, L., Horticultural Technology
SORESCU, C., Anatomy of Vertebrates
TUȚĂ, V., Viticulture
ZĂVOI, A., Plant Improvement

Faculty of Agriculture:

BADEA, E., Animal Husbandry
MARIN, N., Agrochemistry
MATEI, I., Agrotechnics
NEAGU, I., Soil Improvement
PAVEL, C., Pasture Production and Conservation
POP, L., Agrotechnics
ŞOROP, G., Pedology
ŞTOICA, G., Zootechnics
VASILE, D., Pedology
VOICA, N., Genetics

Faculty of Theology:

DAMASCHIN, C., History of the Romanian Orthodox Church

UNIVERSITATEA 'DUNAREA DE JOS' DIN GALAȚI

6200 Galați, Str. Domnească 47
Telephone: (36) 46-19-04
Fax: (36) 46-13-53

Founded 1948, University status 1974
State control
Academic year: October to July

Rector: EMIL CONSTANTIN
Pro-Rectors: NICUŞOR VELICAN, EMIL ROŞU, MIRCEA BULANCEA
Secretary: BEATRICE BIANCA DRAŞOVEAN
Librarian: CALIOPI CATANĂ

Number of teachers: 548
Number of students: 7,133

Publication: *Annals.*

DEANS

Faculty of Food Technology, Aquaculture and Fisheries: BANU CONSTANTIN
Faculty of Mechanics: ALEXANDRU EPUREANU
Faculty of Naval and Electrical Engineering: ADRIAN FILIPESCU
Faculty of Metallurgy and Materials Science: ELENA DRUGESCU
Faculty of Engineering (in Brăila): AXINTE GAVRIL
Faculty of Economic and Juridical Sciences: EMIL GAVRILĂ
Faculty of Letters and Science: TURLAN VALENTIN

PROFESSORS

Faculty of Food Technology, Aquaculture and Fisheries:

ADAM, A., Fishing Materials, Mechanization in Pisciculture
BANU, C., Meat Technology
BORDEI, D., Baking Technology and Equipment
BULANCEA, M., Oenology
COSTIN, G. M., Milk Technology
CULACHE, D., Technology of Sugar Production
DAN, V., Microbiology
HOPULELE, T., Fermentation Technology and Equipment
MORARU, C., Mill Bread Processing
RĂUȚĂ, M., Hydrology and Oceanography
ROTARU, G., Milk Technology and Equipment
TOFAN, I., Cereals and Flour Preservation
VASILESCU, G., Hydrobiology, Aquatic Exploitation, Biological Non-piscatorial Resources

Faculty of Naval and Electrical Engineering:

BUMBARU, S., Computer Programming and Artificial Intelligence
CĂLUEANU, D., Electrical Engineering and Electrical Machines
CEANGĂ, E., Electronics and Automation
CEANGĂ, V., Shipboard Installations
MODIGA, M., Ship Structure
POPOVICI, O., Shipbuilding
VASILESCU, A., Hydromechanics

Faculty of Mechanics:

ANDREI, V., Mechanics of Fluids and Hydraulic Machines
ARADAU, D., Compressors, Engineering Thermodynamics
BEŞCHEA, R., Elements of Mechanical Engineering
CONSTANTIN, E., Machine Tool Design, Equipment and Welded Constructions
CONSTANTIN, V., Machine Parts and Mechanisms
CRUDU, I., Machine Design, Tribology
DUMITRU, G., Internal Combustion Engines
EPUREANU, A., Machine Building Technology
FĂLTICEANU, C., Mechanics, Strength, Machine Parts
GEORGESCU, V., Pressure Welding Technology
GHEORGHIU, C., Design and Structure of Internal Combustion Engines
IONIȚĂ, I., Steam Boilers and Thermal Equipment
IOSIFESCU, C., Refrigeration Techniques
JÂSCANU, M., Machine Parts
MATULEA, I., Mechanics and Vibrations
MUŞAT, S., Mechanics
OANCEA, N., Cutting and Surface Generation
ORĂNESCU, A., Theory of Mechanism and Machines
PORNEALĂ, S., Heat Pumps
STEFANESCU, I., Machine Parts
STOICESCU, L., Strength of Materials
TEODORESCU, M., Cold Deformation Technology
TÂRU, E., Tool-cutting Design

Faculty of Metallurgy and Materials Science:

DRUGESCU, E., Physical Metallurgy and Heat Treatments
GROŞU, V., Metallurgical Implements
MITOSERIU, O., Crystallography and Mineralogy

Faculty of Economics and Juridical Sciences:

COSTESCU, C., Management
GEORGESCU, T., World Economy
OLARU, A., Marketing and Economic Analysis
PANȚÎRU, P., Political Economy
PĂTRAŞC, A., Management in Industry
STOICA, A., Political Economy
VRABIE, D., Psychology and Education

Faculty of Letters and Science:

BEŞCHEA, M., Organic Chemistry and Biochemistry
BRUDIU, M., Romanian History
GEORGESCU, M., Chemistry
HERINEAN, I., Chemistry
LEONTE, M., Organic Chemistry
OLARU, E., Mathematics
SÂRBU, D., Physical Education
TIUTIUCA, D., Comparative Literature
TUDOSE, C., Physics
ȚURLAN, V., Linguistics
VELICAN, N., Physics

Faculty of Engineering (in Brăila):

BRATU, P., Engineering Mechanics and Vibration
CONSTANTINESCU, F., Building Materials; Civilian, Industrial and Agricultural Buildings

UNIVERSITATEA 'AL. I. CUZA' IAŞI

6600 Iaşi, B-dul Copou 11
Telephone: (32) 14-47-60
Fax: (32) 21-33-30
E-mail: rectorat@uaic.ro
Founded 1860
State control
Academic year: October to July

Rector: Prof. Dr GHEORGHE POPA
Vice-Rectors: Prof. Dr ION TODERAŞCU, Prof. Dr STEFAN AVĂDANEI, Prof. Dr ADRIAN NECULAU, Prof. Dr PANAITE NICA
Registrar: RODICA STEGARU
Librarian: Dr CORNELIU ŞTEFANACHE

Library: see Libraries
Number of teachers: 852
Number of students: 13,975

Publication: *Analele Universității 'Al. I. Cuza' din Iaşi.*

DEANS

Faculty of Biology: Prof. Dr CONSTANTIN TOMA
Faculty of Chemistry: Prof. Dr CONSTANTIN GHIRVY
Faculty of Computer Science: Prof. Dr TOADER JUCAN
Faculty of Economics: Prof. Dr DUMITRU OPREA
Faculty of Geography and Geology: Prof. Dr GHEORGHE POPA
Faculty of History: Prof. Dr IOAN CIUPERCĂ
Faculty of Law: Prof. Dr IOAN MACOVEI
Faculty of Letters: Prof. Dr IULIAN POPESCU
Faculty of Mathematics: Prof. Dr T. PRECUPANU
Faculty of Philosophy: Prof. Dr TEODOR DIMA
Faculty of Physics: Prof. Dr MIHAI TOMA
Faculty of Orthodox Theology: Rev. Assoc. Prof. PETRE SEMEN
Faculty of Physical Education and Sport: Prof. GHEORGHE LUCA
Faculty of Psychology and Education: Prof. Dr TEODOR COZMA

PROFESSORS

Faculty of Mathematics:

ANASTASIEI, M., Geometry

BANTAŞ, G., Mathematical Analysis
BARBU, V., Differential Equations
BRÂNZEI, D., Geometry
CRUCEANU, V., Geometry
DIACONIŢA, V., Mechanics
GHEORGHIU, N., Mathematical Analysis
IEŞAN, D., Continuum Mechanics
ILIOI, C., Numerical Analysis
LUCA, N., Differential Equations
MANOLACHI, A., Mechanics
MINUŢ, P., Probability Theory
MIRON, R., Differential Geometry
MOROŞANU, G., Differential Equations
MOTREANU, D., Equations
OPROIU, V., Differential Geometry
POP, I., Geometry
POPA, E., Mathematical Analysis
PRECUPANU, A., Mathematical Analysis
PRECUPANU, T., Mathematical Analysis
RADU, A., Theoretical Mechanics
RADU, GH., Algebra
SPULBER, D., Algebra
TAMAS, V., Algebra
VRABIE, I., Differential Equations
ZĂLINESCU, C., Mathematical Analysis

Faculty of Physics:

ALEXANDROAEI, D., Plasma Physics
BIBOROSCH, L., Plasma Physics
BLANARIU, D., Astrophysics
BURSUC, I., Solid State Physics
DELIBAS, M., Optics and Spectroscopy
DOROHOI, D., Optics and Spectroscopy
GEORGESCU, V., Magnetic Properties and Materials
GOTTLIEB, I., Theoretical Physics
GROSU, I., Nonlinear Physics
IGNAT, M., Theoretical Physics
LOZNEANU, E., Nuclear Physics
MAFTEI, G., Theoretical Physics
MANDRECI, A., Electricity and Magnetism
MERCHEŞ, I., Theoretical Physics
MIRON, V., Electricity and Magnetism
NICOLAESCU, I., Solid State Physics
PAPUSOI, C., Electricity and Magnetism
POP, V., Optics and Spectroscopy
POPA, G., Plasma Physics
RUSU, G., Semiconductor Physics
RUSU, M., Semiconductor Physics
SANDU, D., Electronic Devices and Circuits, Microwaves
SANDULOVICIU, M., Plasma Physics
SCUTARU, V., Physics
SINGUREL, G., Spectroscopy and Quantum Optics
SINGUREL, L., Optics and Spectroscopy
SOROHAN, M., Solid State Physics
STRAT, M., Optics and Spectroscopy
SULIŢANU, N., Magnetism
TOMA, M., Plasma Physics
VLAHOVICI, A., Molecular Spectroscopy

Faculty of Biology:

ACATRINEI, G., Plant Physiology
AILIESESEI, O., Microbiology, Immunology
ANDRIESCU, I., Entomology
ARTENIE, V., Biochemistry
BÂRA, I., Genetics
CHIFU, T., Ecology
COJOCARU, D., Enzymology
COMANESCU, G., Cytology, Histoembryology
HAIMOVICI, S., Anthropology, Anatomy
HEFCO, V., Animal Physiology
ION, I., Vertebrate Zoology
MIRON, I., Hydrobiology
MITITELU, D., Systematic Botany
MITITIUC, M., Phytopathology, Biogeography
MUSTATA, GH., Hydrobiology, Evolution
NEACŞU, I., Cellular Biology
NIMITAN, E., Microbiology, Biotechnology
PISICĂ, C., Invertebrate Zoology
TANASE, E., Chemistry
TOMA, C., Plant Anatomy
TUDOSE, I., Genetics
VALENCIUC, N., Vertebrate Zoology
VARVARA, M., Ecology

Faculty of Geography and Geology:

APĂVĂLOAIE, M., Human Geography
DONISĂ, I., Geomorphology, Theoretical Geography
ERHAN, E., Climatology
ERHAN, V., Mineralogy and Petrography
GANDRABURA, E., Geochemistry
GRASU, C., Geology of Romania
HĂRJOABĂ, I., Regional Geography
ICHIM, I., Geomorphology
IORGA, N., Mineralogy
MURARIU, T., Geology and Geochemistry of Ore Deposits
NIMIGEANU, V., Human Geography
OLARU, L., Palaentology
PETREUŞ, I., Crystallography and Mineralogy
POPA, GH., Geochemistry
SARAIMAN, A., Stratigraphy
TURCULET, I., Palaeontology
UNGUREANU, A., Human Geography
UNGUREANU, I., Environmental Science

Faculty of Letters:

ADĂSCĂLIŢEI, V., Romanian Folklore
AGRIGOROAIEI, V., French Language
ANDRIESCU, A., Romanian Language
ARVINTE, V., Romanian Language
AVADANEI, ST., English and American Literature
BĂLĂNESCU, S., Russian Literature
BLUMENFELD, O., English Language and Literature
CĂLINESCU, A., French Literature
CANTEMIR, N., Russian Literature
CARPOV, M., French Language
CONSTANTINESCU, I., Comparative Literature
COTORCEA, L., Russian Literature
DIACONESCU, T., Latin Literature
DIMITRIU, C., Romanian Language
DRĂGAN, M., Romanian Literature
FRÎNCU, C., Romanian Language
HOIŞIE, A., German Literature
HULBAN, H., English Language
ILIE, D., Romanian Language
IRIMIA, D., Romanian Language
LEONTE, L., Romanian Literature
MACARIE, G., Comparative Literature
MĂNUCĂ, D., Romanian Literature
MUREŞANU, M., French Literature
PARFENE, C., Romanian Literature
POPESCU, I., Romanian for Foreign Students
SÂRBU, I., Romanian Literature
SOROHAN, E., Romanian Literature
ŢUGUI, G., Romanian Literature
URSACHE, P., Aesthetics and Literary Theory
ZUGUN-ELOAE, P., Romanian Linguistics

Faculty of History:

AGRIGOROAIEI, I., Romanian Contemporary History
BOLD, E., Romanian Contemporary History
CAPROŞU, I., Medieval History
CIUPERCA, I., Contemporary World History
CLIVEŢI, G., World History
CRISTIAN, V., Modern World History
FILIMON, A., Modern World History
GOROVEI, S., Medieval History
LÁSZLÓ, A., Ancient World History
PLATON, G., Romanian Modern History
RUSU, D., Romanian Modern and Contemporary History
RUSSU, V., Romanian Modern History
SOLCANU, I., History of Art
SPINEI, V., Medieval History
TANASA, G., Romanian Contemporary History
TODERAŞCU, I., Medieval Romanian History
URSULESCU, N., Romanian Ancient History
VASILESCU, M., Ancient World History
ZUB, A., Romanian Modern History

Faculty of Philosophy:

AFLOROAEI, S., Ontology, Hermeneutics, Metaphysics
CARPINSCHI, A., Political Science
CELMARE, Ş., Systematic Philosophy
CERCEL, P., Physical Education
DIMA, T., Logic and Epistemology
DUMITRESCU, P., History of Philosophy
GHIDEANU, T., History of Philosophy
IOAN, P., Logic
MARIN, C., History of Philosophy
MIFTODE, V., Sociology, Social Anthropology
PUHA, E., Philosophy
RAVEICA, T., History of Philosophy

Faculty of Law:

ANDRONOVICI, C., Public International Law
CIOPRAGA, A., Criminology
FILIP, G., Labour Law, Transport Law
LOGHIN, O., Penal Law
MACOVEI, D., Civil Law
MACOVEI, I., Private International Law, International Commercial Law
RADU, D., Civil Law
RĂUSCHI, S., Civil Law
VRABIE, G., Constitutional Law

Faculty of Economics:

BELEI, I., Accounting
BRINZA, A., Marketing
CLIPA, N., Economics
COCRIŞ, V., Finance and Banking
COSTE, V., Management
DUMITREAN, E., Financial and Managerial Accounting
FĂTU, T., Principles of Computers
FILIP, G., Finance
FILIP, M., Computer Programming
FLOREA, I., Accounting and Financial Control
GEORGESCU, P., Political Economy
GHERASIM, T., Industrial Economy
GRĂDINARIU, M., Economic Analysis
IGNAT, I., Economics
JABA, E., Statistics
JABA, O., Management
MANDACHE, R., Agricultural Economy
NEAGOE, I., Finance
NEAGU, T., Computer Programming
NECHITA, V., Political Economy
NICA, P., Management
NICULICIOIU, C., Political Economy
OPREA, D., Business Information Systems
PARASCHIVESCU, M., Financial Accounting
PĂVĂLOAIA, W., Economic Analysis
PEKAR, V., Agricultural Economics
PETRESCU, S., Economic Analysis
PETRIS, R., Accounting
POHOAŢĂ, I., Contemporary Economic Thought
PRALEA, S., International Economic Relations
ROTARU, A., Ergonomic Organization of Labour
RUSU, D., Accounting
SECRIERU, C., Agricultural Economy and Politics
STOICA, N., Political Economy
TACU, A., Economic Statistics and Demography
ŢARCĂ, M., Economic Statistics and Demography
TATARU, A., Finance
TOFAN, A., Management
TURLIUC, V., Money and Banking
VOINEA, G., Finance
ZAIŢ, D., Econometry

Faculty of Chemistry:

BERDAN, I., Inorganic and Co-ordination Chemistry
BÎLBA, N., Material Sciences
BOURCEANU, G., Physical Chemistry
CAPROSU, M., Organic Chemistry
CASCAVAL, A., Organic Chemistry
CECAL, A., Inorganic and Nuclear Chemistry
CIOCOIU, I., Organic Chemistry
CIUGUREANU, C., General Chemistry
DULMAN, V., Analytical Chemistry
DRUTA, I., Organic Chemistry and Structural Analysis

GHIRVU, C., Quantum Chemistry and Physical Chemistry
HURDUC, N., Physical Chemistry
LEONTE, C., Organic and Macromolecular Chemistry
MIHAILA, G., Chemical Technology
MOCANU, R., Analytical Chemistry
NAUM, N., Chemical Technology and Catalysis
NICOLAESCU, T., Organic Chemistry
ODOCHIAN, L., Physical Chemistry
OFENBERG, H., Organic and Photo-organic Chemistry
ONOFREI, T., Analytical Chemistry
ONU, A., Physical Chemistry
PALAMARU, M., Inorganic Chemistry
POPOVICI, E., Material Sciences
SANDU, I., Inorganic Chemistry
SIMION, C., Analytical Chemistry
SUNEL, V., Organic Chemistry
SURPATEANU, G., Organic and Computational Chemistry

Faculty of Psychology and Education:

COSMOVICI, A., Psychology
COZMA, T., General Education
GRIGORAŞ, I., Ethics
MOISE, C., Education
NECULAU, A., Social Psychology
PRUNĂ, T., Social Psychology
RUDICĂ, T., Psychology
VĂIDEANU, G., Education

Faculty of Computer Science:

CAZACU, C., Theory of Algorithms, Computability, Logic, Proof Theory
CROITORU, C., Combinatorial Optimization Graph Theory
FELEA, V., Theory of Data Bases, Operating Systems
GRIGORAS, G., Formal Languages Complexities Theory
IGNAT, C., Numerical Analysis, Software Engineering
JUCAN, T., Formal Languages

Faculty of Orthodox Theology:

CIOBOTEA, D., Pastoral Theology
POPESCU, E., Byzantinism
SEMEN, P., Theology

Faculty of Physical Education and Sport:

CERCEL, P., History of Physical Education and Sport
FIEDLER, P., Methodology of Physical Education
LUCA, A., Acrobatic Gymnastics
LUCA, G., Theory of Physical Education and Sport

ATTACHED INSTITUTES

Astronomical Observatory: 6600 Iaşi, Aleea M. Sadoveanu 5.

Botanical Garden: 6600 Iaşi, Str. Dumbrava Roşie 7–9; Dir Prof. Dr M. MITITIUC.

Computing Centre: 6600 Iaşi, Str. Berthelot 16; Dir Prof. C. FILIPESCU.

Natural History Museum: see under Museums.

'Ion Borcea' Black Sea Biological Marine Research Station at Agigea; Dir Prof. Dr G. MUSTAŢĂ.

Biological Research Station at Potoci-Bicaz; Dir Prof. Dr I. MIRON.

UNIVERSITATEA 'PETROL-GAZE' DIN PLOIEŞTI

2000 Ploieşti, B-dul Bucareşti 39
Telephone: (44) 17-31-71
Fax: (44) 11-98-47

Founded 1948 as Institutul de Petrol şi Gaze; present name 1994
State control
Academic year: October to July
President: Prof. Dr N. N. ANTONESCU
Vice-Presidents: Prof. Dr V. ULMANU, Prof. Dr I. CREŢU
Librarian: Assoc. Prof. L. AVRAM

Number of teachers: 473
Number of students: 4,045

Publication: *Buletinul*.

DEANS

Faculty of Well-Drilling and Petroleum Reservoir Engineering: Assoc. Prof. Dr M. P. COLOJA
Faculty of Petroleum Technology and Petrochemistry: Assoc. Prof. Dr I. OPRIS
Faculty of Mechanical and Electrical Engineering: Prof. Dr GH. ZECHERU
Faculty of Letters and Sciences: Prof. Dr I. ANGHELACHE

HEADS OF DEPARTMENT

Drilling and Production: Prof. Dr G. IORDACHE
Hydraulics, Heat Energy and Reservoir Engineering: Prof. Dr AL. SOARE
Geophysics and Geology: Assoc. Prof. Dr I. MĂLUREANU
Physics: Assoc. Prof. Dr N. MOŞESCU
Petroleum and Petrochemical Equipment: Prof. Dr I. VLAD
Automation and Computers: Prof. Dr ST. DUMITRESCU
Management and Marketing: Assoc. Prof. Dr C. COROIAN-STOIESCU
Social and Legal Sciences: Assoc. Prof. Dr I. BAICU
Engineering in Petroleum Processing and Petrochemistry: Prof. Dr C. IONESCU
General Mechanical Disciplines: Prof. Dr N. POSEA
Electrotechnics and Electronics: Prof. Dr I. DUMITRESCU
Chemistry: Prof. Dr A. SCHIOPESCU
Chemical and Petrochemical Engineering: Prof. Dr C. STRĂTULĂ
Technology of Petroleum Equipment Manufacture: Assoc. Prof. Dr M. J. SĂVULESCU
Philology and Pedagogy: M.-J. WOJCICKI
Mathematics: Prof. Dr AL. PETCU
Economics, Accounting and Finance: I. DONE
Informatics: Prof. L. DUMITRAŞCU
Physical Education: Assoc. Prof. E. STĂNESCU

UNIVERSITATEA DE VEST DIN TIMIŞOARA

1900 Timişoara, V. Pârvan 4
Telephone: (56) 19-40-68
Fax: (56) 19-00-09
E-mail: rector@rectorat.uvt.ro

Founded 1944
State control
Academic year: September to June

Rector: Prof. DUMITRU GAŞPAR
Pro-Rectors: Prof. NICOLAE AVRAM (Academic Affairs), Prof. ADRIAN CHIRIAC (Student Affairs and Scientific Research), Prof. HORIA CRISTEA (Financial Affairs)
Scientific Secretary: Prof. ŞTEFAN BALINT
Secretary-General: VIRGIL DEBREŢIN
Librarian: Prof. VASILE ŢARA

Library: see Libraries
Number of teachers: 672
Number of students: 9,251

Publications: *Analele Universităţii din Timişoara—ştiinţe matematice, ştiinţe fizice, ştiinţe filologice, ştiinţe sociale şi economice.*

DEANS

Faculty of Mathematics: Prof. MIHAIL MEGAN
Faculty of Physics: Prof. IRINA NICOARĂ
Faculty of Chemistry, Biology and Geography: Assoc. Prof. AUREL FAUR
Faculty of Letters, Philosophy and History: Prof. ILEANA OANCEA
Faculty of Economics: Assoc. Prof. EMIL CAZAN
Faculty of Sociology and Psychology: Assoc. Prof. ŞTEFAN BUZĂRNESCU
Faculty of Law: Prof. RADU MOTICA
Faculty of Arts: Prof. CONSTANTIN FLONDOR
Faculty of Music: Prof. DAMIAN VULPE
Faculty of Physical Education and Sports: Prof. MARIA GÖNCZI-RAICU

PROFESSORS

Faculty of Mathematics:

ALBU, A., Differential Geometry
BALINT, Ş., Mathematical Analysis
BOCŞAN, GH., Numerical Analysis
BOROŞ, E., Algebra
CONSTANTIN, GH., Probability Theory
CRAIOVEANU, M., Spectral Geometry
GAŞPAR, D., Functional Analysis, Spectral Theory
IVAN, GH., Algebra
JEBELEAN, T., Parallel Computing
MĂRUŞTER, Ş., Non-Linear Optimization and Computer Science
MEGAN, M., Mathematical Analysis
OBĂDEANU, V., Theoretical Mechanics and Differential Geometry, Operational Research
OPRIŞ, D., Operational Research
PAPUC, D. I., Differential Geometry
PREDA, P., Mathematical Analysis
PUTA, M., Differential Equations in Geometry
RADU, V., Stochastic Analysis and Probability Theory
REGHIŞ, M., Differential Equations
SCHWAB, E., Homological Algebra
STRĂTILĂ, Ş., Mathematical Analysis and Operator Algebras
SUCIU, N., Complex Analysis

Faculty of Physics:

AVRAM, N., Atomic and Molecular Physics and Spectroscopy
BIRĂU, O., Thermodynamics and Molecular Physics
HRIANCA, I., Electricity and Magnetism
MUSCUTARIU, I., Electricity and Magnetism, Solid State and Semiconductor Physics
NICOARĂ, I., Laser Crystals
SCHLETT, Z., Plasma Physics, Semiconductor Materials and Devices

Faculty of Chemistry, Biology and Geography:

CHIRIAC, A., Physical Chemistry
DOCA, N., Chemical Engineering
MRACEC, M., Physical Chemistry
NUŢIU, R., Organic Chemistry
TRUŢI, S., Geography

Faculty of Letters, Philosophy and History:

BENEA, D., Ancient History
BIRIŞ, I., History of Culture and Civilization
BUCA, M., Russian Language
CHEIE, I., Romanian Literature
CIOCÂRLIE, L., French Literature
EVSEEV, I., Russian Language
FRĂŢILĂ, V., Dialectology
GRECU, C., Philosophy of Logic
GYURCSIK, M., French Literature
HARANGUŞ, C., Ontology
MIOC, S., Romanian Literature
MUNTEANU, I., Modern Romanian History
OANCEA, I., Romance Philology
PÂRLOG, H., English Linguistics
SÂRBU, R., Russian Language
ŢARA, V., History of the Romanian Language
VINTILESCU, V., Romanian Literature

Faculty of Economics:

BĂBĂIŢĂ, I., Political Economy
BĂBĂIŢĂ, V., Accounting
BĂILEŞTEANU, GH., Business Economics
BURTICĂ, M., Macroeconomic Forecasting
CĂTINIANU, FL., Prices and Tariffs
CERNA, S., Currency and Credits
CRĂCIUNESCU, V., Management
CRISTEA, H., Business Finance
DĂNĂIAŢĂ, I., Management

EPURAN, M., Accounting
FALNIŢĂ, E., Science of Commodities
GOIAN, M., Management
IONESCU, GH., Marketing
IVAN, ŞT., Informatics
LĂDAR, L., Marketing
LUPULESCU, M., Computer Programming
MARTIN, I., Microeconomic Analysis
MIHAI, I., Financial Analysis
NEGRUT, C., Agrarian Economics and Policy
OPRIŞ, L., Agrarian Policies in the World
POPOVICI, AL., Programming of Production
PUTZ, E., Transport in Tourism
ROTARIU, I., Management of Foreign Trade
SILAŞI, GR., Regional and World Economy
ŞOŞDEANU, A., Accounting
ŢALPOŞ, I. Public Finance
TRANDAFIR, N., Political Economy
VÂRLAN, GH., Economic Forecasting

Faculty of Sociology and Psychology:

DABU, R., Sociology
POENARU, R., Pedagogy, Deontology
VINTILESCU, D., Educational Theory

Faculty of Law:

DRESSLER, M., Forensic Medicine
MIHAI, GH., Philosophy of Law
MOTICA, R. I., Law
POPA, V., Roman Law, Labour Law

Faculty of Arts:

BREILEAN, A., Painting
FÂNTÂNARIU, S., Graphic Arts
FLONDOR, C., Painting
JECZA, P., Sculpture
NUŢIU, R., Painting
SULEA, I., Painting
ZIMAN, M., Textile Arts

Faculty of Music:

STANCOVICI, F., Piano
VULPE, D., Choral Conducting

Faculty of Physical Education and Sport:

GÖNCZI-RAICU, M., Gymnastics
IONESCU, I., Football

Technological Universities

UNIVERSITATEA 'POLITEHNICA' DIN BUCUREŞTI

77206 Bucharest, Splaiul Independenţei 313
Telephone: (1) 410-03-91
Fax: (1) 312-53-65

Founded 1819
State control
Academic year: October to July (two semesters)

Rector: Prof. Dr GHEORGHE ZGURĂ
Vice-Rectors: Prof. Dr DORIN CRISTESCU, Prof. Dr EMIL FLORIAN, Prof. Dr IOAN CONSTANTIN, Prof. Dr CORNELIU BERBENTE, Prof. Dr IOAN PĂUNESCU
Scientific Secretary: Prof. Dr MIRCEA COVRIG
Chief Administrative Officer: Prof. Dr DUMITRU CATRINA
Librarian: D. R. POPESCU

Library: see Libraries
Number of teachers: 1,830
Number of students: 20,300
Publication: *Scientific Bulletin*.

DEANS

Faculty of Electrical Engineering: Prof. Dr MIHAI OCTAVIAN POPESCU
Faculty of Power Engineering: Assoc. Prof. Dr CEZAR IONESCU
Faculty of Mechanical Engineering: Prof. Dr MIRCEA MARINESCU
Faculty of Automatic Control and Computer Science: Prof. Dr NICOLAE CUPCEA
Faculty of Electronics and Telecommunications: Prof. Dr MARIN DRĂGULINESCU
Faculty of Engineering and Management of Technological Systems: Prof. Dr CONSTANTIN ISPAS
Faculty of Transport Engineering: Prof. Dr ŞERBAN RAICU
Faculty of Aircraft Engineering: Prof. Dr STELIAN GĂLETUŞE
Faculty of Materials Science and Engineering: Prof. Dr PETRU MOLDOVAN
Faculty of Industrial Chemistry: Prof. Dr ECATERINA ANDRONESCU
Faculty of Biotechnical Systems Engineering: Prof. Dr LADISLAU DAVID

DIRECTORS

Technical College No. 1 (Mechanical College): Prof. Dr GHEORGHE AMZA
Technical College No. 2 (Electrical College): Dr ISTVAN SZTOJANOV
Department of Engineering Sciences (training in English, French and German): Prof. Dr ANDREI ŢUGULEA

PROFESSORS

Basic Training:

ACHIM, I., Psychology
ANGHEL, P., Modern Foreign Languages
ARDELEA, D., Industrial Management
ATANASIU, M., Mechanics
BACIU, A., Political Science
BĂDILĂ, N., Political Economy
CICU, V., Physical Exercise and Sport
COJOCARU, G., Industrial Management
CONSTANTINESCU, I., Strength of Materials
CRAIU, M., Special Mathematics
CREŢU, T., Physics
DECIU, E., Mechanics
ENESCU, N., Mechanics
HOMENTCOVSCHI, D., Mathematics
IORDACHE, D., Physics
IORDACHE, S., Economics
PANDREA, N., Mechanics
POPESCU, I., Physics
POPESCU, V., Education Science
STAN, A., Mechanics
STĂNĂŞILĂ, O., Algebra, Mathematical Analysis
STĂNCIOIU, I., Industrial Management
STANCIU, GH., Physics
STERIAN, P., Physics
UDRIŞTE, C., Special Mathematics
VASILESCU, E., Descriptive Geometry and Engineering Drawing
VOICULESCU, D., Mechanics
VOINEA, R., Mechanics

Specialized Training:

A. Electrical Engineering:

Faculty of Electrical Engineering:

APETREI, C., Electrical Machines
BĂLĂ, C., Electrical Machines
COVRIG, M., Electrical Machines
CRĂCIUNESCU, A., Drive Systems
CRISTEA, P., Basic Electrical Engineering
FIREŢEANU, V., Electrical Engineering
FLUERAŞU, C., Basic Electrical Engineering
FRANSUA, A., Electrical Machines and Drive Systems
GALAN, N., Electrical Machines
GAVRILĂ, H., Basic Electrical Engineering
GOLOVANOV, C., Theory and Design of Electrical Apparatus
HĂNŢILĂ, F., Basic Electrical Engineering
HORTOPAN, G., Theory and Design of Electrical Apparatus
IFRIM, A., Electrical Machines
ILIESCU, C., Theory and Design of Electrical Apparatus
IOAN, C. D., Basic Electrical Engineering
IONESCU, F., Theory and Design of Electrical Apparatus
LEON, M., Basic Electrical Engineering
MĂGUREANU, R., Micromachines and Drive Systems
MANEA, F., Basic Electrical Engineering
MARINOV, C., Basic Electrical Engineering
MORARU, A., Basic Electrical Engineering
NEMOIANU, C., Basic Electrical Engineering
NOŢINGHER, P., Electrical Materials
PANAITE, V., Reliability
POPESCU, M. O., Theory and Design of Electrical Apparatus
RADUŢI, C., Electrical Machines
SONEA, P., Basic Electrical Engineering
SPINEI, F., Basic Electrical Engineering
TĂNĂSESCU, F., Electrical Engineering
TOMEŞCU, F., Basic Electrical Engineering
TRUŞCĂ, V., Theory and Design of Electrical Apparatus
ŢUGULEA, A., Basic Electrical Engineering

Faculty of Automatic Control and Computer Science:

ATHANASIU, I., Computers
BORANGIU, T., Control Engineering
CRISTEA, V., Computers
CUPCEA, N., Control Engineering
DOBRESCU, R., Control Engineering
DUMITRACHE, I., Control Engineering
GIUMALE, C., Computers
ILIESCU, Ş., Control Engineering
IONESCU, G., Control Engineering
IONESCU, T., Control Engineering
IONESCU, V., Control Engineering
MIHOC, D., Control Engineering
MOISA, T., Computers
NIŢU, C., Control Engineering
PETRESCU, A., Computers
PETRESCU, M., Computers
POPEIA, C., Control Engineering
POPESCU, D., Control Engineering
ŞERBANAŢI, L. D., Computers
TĂPUŞ, N., Computers
TERTISCO, M., Control Engineering

Faculty of Electronics and Telecommunications:

BĂNICĂ, I., Telecommunications
BREZEANU, GH., Electronic Devices and Circuits
BUZULOIU, V., Information Theory
CĂTUNEANU, V., Electronic Devices and Circuits
CONSTANTIN, I., Telecommunications
CROITORU, V., Telecommunications
DASCĂLU, D., Electronic Devices and Circuits
DRĂGĂNESCU, M., Electronic Devices and Circuits
DRĂGULINESCU, M., Optoelectronics
IANCU, O., Optoelectronics
MANOLESCU, A., Electronic Devices and Circuits
MANOLESCU, A. M., Electronic Devices and Circuits
MATEESCU, A., Telecommunications
MURGAN, A., Information Theory
NEAGOE, V., Information Theory
NICOLAU, E., Telecommunications
PREDA, A., Telecommunications
PROFIRESCU, M., Electronic Devices and Circuits
RULEA, G., Telecommunications
RUSU, A., Electronic Devices and Circuits
SPĂTARU, A., Information Theory
STANOMIR, D., Telecommunications
STRUNGARU, R., Information Theory
ZACIU, R., Information Theory

Faculty of Power Engineering:

ARIE, A., Electric Networks
ATHANASOVICI, V., Electric Power Plants
BADEA, A., Electric Power Plants
BUHUS, P., Electric Power Plants
CAZACU, M., Hydraulics
CRISTESCU, D., High Voltage Technology
DĂNILĂ, N., Electric Power Plants
DIACON, A., Hydraulics
DRĂGAN, G., Electric Power Plants
EREMIA, M., High Voltage Technology
IACOBESCU, G., Electric Power Plants
IONESCU, D., Hydraulics

IONESCU, D. C., Reliability
IORDĂNESCU, I., Electric Power Plants
LECA, A., Electric Power Plants
MICULESCU, T., High Voltage Technology
MOȚOIU, S., Electric Power Plants
NISTREANU, V., Hydraulics
POTOLEA, E., High Voltage Technology
ROMAN, P., Hydraulics
VASILIU, N., Hydraulics

B. Mechanical Engineering:

Faculty of Mechanical Engineering:

ALEXANDRESCU, N., Fine Mechanics
APOSTOLESCU, N., Internal Combustion Engines
ARAMA, C., Internal Combustion Engines
BRĂTIANU, C., Thermomechanical Equipment
IATAN, R., Thermomechanical Equipment
IORDACHE, GH., Thermomechanical Equipment
IORDACHE, I., Thermomechanical Equipment
JINESCU, V., Thermomechanical Equipment
MARINESCU, M., Thermodynamics
MICU, C., Machine Elements
MIHĂESCU, L., Classical and Nuclear Thermomechanical Equipment
NEAGA, C., Thermomechanical Equipment
PĂNOIU, N., Internal Combustion Engines
PASCOVICI, D., Machine Elements
PASCU, A., Machine Elements
PAVELESCU, D., Machine Elements
PETRESCU, S., Thermodynamics
POSTELNICESCU, M., Internal Combustion Engines
RADCENCO, V., Thermodynamics
RĂDULESCU, GH., Machine Elements
TARAZA, D., Internal Combustion Engines
TUDOR, A., Machine Elements

Faculty of Engineering and Management of Technological Systems:

AMZA, GH., Technology of Materials
ANTONESCU, P., Mechanism Theory
ATANASIU, C., Strength of Materials
AURITE, T., Machine Tools
BLUMENFELD, N., Strength of Materials
BOGDAN, R., Mechanism Theory
BRAGARU, AL., Machine Building Technology
BUZDUGAN, GH., Strength of Materials
CALEA, GH., Technology of Materials
CATRINA, D., Machine Tools
CONSTANTINESCU, I., Strength of Materials
DORIN, A., Machine Tools
DRĂGĂNESCU, F., Machine Building Technology
GHEGHEA, I., Machine Tools
GHEORGHE, M., Machine Building Technology
ILIESCU, N., Strength of Materials
ISPAS, C., Machine Tools
MICLOȘI, V., Technology of Materials
MINCIU, C., Machine Tools
OPREAN, A., Machine Tools
RADEȘ, M., Strength of Materials
SIMIONESCU, I., Mechanism Theory
STURZU, A., Machine Building Technology
TACHE, V., Machine Building Technology
TEMPEA, I., Mechanism and Rotor Technology
VLASE, A., Machine Building Technology
ZGURĂ, GH., Technology of Materials

Faculty of Transport Engineering:

ALEXANDRESCU, C., Remote Controls and Electronics
FRĂȚILĂ, GH., Automotive Engineering
NEGRUȘ, E., Automotive Engineering
RAICU, Ș., Transport Engineering
SEBEȘAN, I., Railway Vehicles
TĂNĂSUICĂ, I., Transport Engineering

Faculty of Biotechnical Systems Engineering:

BABICIU, P., Agricultural Machines
NICU, M., Biotechnology
PĂUNESCU, I., Tractors
SCRIPNIC, V., Agricultural Machines
SEGĂRCEANU, M., Agricultural Machines
STROE, M., Mechanical Theory

Faculty of Aircraft Engineering:

BERBENTE, C., Aircraft Engineering
CONSTANTINESCU, V. N., Aircraft Engineering
GĂLETUȘE, S., Aircraft Engineering
NIȚĂ, M., Aircraft Engineering
PATRAULEA, N., Aircraft Engineering
PETRE, A., Aircraft Engineering
STANCIU, V., Aircraft Engineering

C. Metallurgical Engineering:

Faculty of Materials Science and Engineering:

BRABIE, V., Forge-Foundry
BRATU, C., Forge-Foundry
CAZIMIROVICI, E., Iron and Steel Metallurgy
COJOCARU, M., Metallurgy of Non-Ferrous Metals
DRAGOMIR, I., Iron and Steel Metallurgy
DULĂMIȚĂ, T., Metallurgy of Non-Ferrous Metals
DUMITRESCU, C., Metallurgy of Non-Ferrous Metals
FLORIAN, E., Metallurgy of Non-Ferrous Metals
MOLDOVAN, P., Metallurgy of Non-Ferrous Metals
MURGULEȚ, N., Metallurgical Aggregates
NICOLAE, A., Metallurgical Aggregates
NICOLAE, M., Iron and Steel Metallurgy
OPRESCU, I., Metallurgical Aggregates
PANAIT, N., Metallurgy of Non-Ferrous Metals
PETRESCU, M., Metallurgy of Non-Ferrous Metals
PETRESCU, N., Metallurgy of Non-Ferrous Metals
POPESCU, V., Metallurgy of Non-Ferrous Metals
RIPOȘAN, I., Forge-Foundry
SEGĂRCEANU, T., Metallurgy of Non-Ferrous Metals
SOFRONI, L., Forge-Foundry
TALOI, D., Metallurgy of Non-Ferrous Metals
TRIPȘA, I., Iron and Steel Metallurgy
VARCOLACU, I., Metallurgical Aggregates
ZAMFIR, S., Metallurgy of Non-Ferrous Metals

D. Chemical Technology:

Faculty of Industrial Chemistry:

ANDRONESCU, E., Silicate and Oxide Compound Chemistry
BADEA, D. F., Chemistry and Organic Technology
BALABAN, AL., Chemistry and Organic Technology
BALTA, P., Silicate and Oxide Compound Chemistry
BANCIU, M., Chemistry and Organic Technology
BOZGA, G., Chemical Engineering
CONSTANTINESCU, I., Inorganic Chemical Technology
DANCIU, E., Chemical Engineering
DIMONIE, M., Polymer Technology
FILIPESCU, L., Inorganic Chemical Technology
FLOREA, O., Chemical Engineering
FLORU, L., Polymer Technology
FRUMUZACHE, B., Polymer Technology
GEANĂ, D., Physical Chemistry and Electrochemical Technology
GEORGESCU, I., Radiochemistry
GEORGESCU, M., Silicate and Oxide Compound Chemistry
GHEORGHIU, M. D., Chemistry and Organic Technology
HUBCA, GH., Polymer Technology
JINESCU, GH., Chemical Engineering
JITARU, I., Inorganic Chemistry
LANDAUER, O., Theoretical Chemistry
LUCA, C., Analytical Chemistry
MEGHEA, A., Physical Chemistry and Electrochemical Technology
MUNTEAN, M., Silicate and Oxide Compound Chemistry
MUNTEAN, O., Chemical Engineering
PANAITESCU, C., Polymer Technology
PĂRĂUȘANU, V., Organic Chemistry
PINCOVSCHI, E., Inorganic Chemical Technology
POGANY, I., Organic Chemistry
RADOVICI, O., Theoretical Chemistry
RADU, D., Silicate and Oxide Compound Chemistry
ROȘCA, S., Chemistry and Organic Technology
STOICA, L., Inorganic Chemistry
TARABAȘANU, M., Polymer Technology
TEOREANU, I., Silicate and Oxide Compound Chemistry
VASILESCU, S., Polymer Technology
VIȘAN, T., Physical Chemistry and Electrochemical Technology

UNESCO Department:

LECA, A., Environment

UNIVERSITATEA TEHNICA DIN CLUJ-NAPOCA

3400 Cluj-Napoca, Str. Constantin Daicoviciu 15
Telephone: (64) 19-56-99
Fax: (64) 19-20-55

Founded 1948

Academic year: October to July

Rector: Dr Eng. GHEORGHE LAZEA
Pro-Rectors: Dr Eng. VASILE IANCU, Dr Eng. PETRU BERCE, Dr Eng. MIHAI ILIESCU
Registrar: T. NILAȘ

Library: see Libraries
Number of teachers: 628
Number of students: 7,504

Publications: *Scientific Bulletin of the Cluj-Napoca Technical University* (annually), *Acta Technica Napocensis, ACAM–Automation and Computers and Applied Mathematics, Electromotion.*

DEANS

Faculty of Civil Engineering: Dr Eng. ION POP
Faculty of Control and Computer Engineering: Dr Eng. KALMAN PUSZTAI
Faculty of Electrical Engineering: Dr Eng. RADU MUNTEANU
Faculty of Electronics and Telecommunications: Dr Eng. SERBAN LUNGU
Faculty of Machine Building: Dr Eng. GHEORGHE ACHIMAS
Faculty of Materials Science Engineering: Dr Eng. VICTOR CONSTANTINESCU
Faculty of Mechanical Engineering: Dr Eng. TEODOR MADARASAN

PROFESSORS

Faculty of Civil Engineering:

ALEXA, P., Theoretical Mechanics, Structural Dynamics, Structural Stability
ANDREICA, H., Timber Structures
BADEA, G., Water Supplies and Sewerage
BĂRSAN, G., Theoretical Mechanics, Structural Dynamics, Structural Stability
BIA, C., Strength of Materials, Theory of Elasticity
BORS, I., Theoretical Mechanics, Numerical Methods
BRUMARU, M., Buildings
BUCUR, I., Reinforced Concrete Structures
CĂTĂRIG, A., Structural Analysis
CHIOREAN, T., Economics of the Construction Industry, Management and Organization
CHISĂLIȚĂ, A., Theoretical Mechanics, Numerical Methods, Cable and Hinged Structures, Non-Linear Analysis
COMȘA, E., Buildings
CORDOS, GH., Sociology
DOMȘA, J., Construction Technology
DUMITRAS, M., Buildings

HOSSU, T., Management in Civil Engineering
ILIESCU, M., Road Engineering
IOANI, A., Strength of Materials, Theory of Elasticity
IONESCU, A., Reinforced Concrete Structures
JURCAU, N., Psychology
KOPENETZ, L., Computer-Aided Engineering and Design, Structural Analysis, Lightweight Structures
MAGUREANU, C., Reinforced and Prestressed Concrete
MARIAN, L., Hydraulics, Hydraulic Machines
MARȚIAN, I., Strength of Materials, Theory of Elasticity
MATEI, A., Architectural Composition
MOGA, A., Construction Technology
MOLDOVAN, M., History of World Architecture
MURADIN, C., Styles of Furniture
NISTOR, I., History of Culture and Civilization
OLARIU, I., Structural Analysis
ONEȚ, TR., Reinforced and Prestressed Concrete
OPRITOIU, A., Heat Engineering
PACURAR, V., Steel Structures
PANTEL, E., Strength of Materials, Theory of Elasticity, Numerical Methods
PETRINA, M., Structural Analysis, Computer Programming
POP, F., Electric Installation
POP, I., Seismic Engineering
POPA, A., Soil Mechanics and Foundations
POPA, P., Civil Engineering Technology
POPOVICI, T., Air Conditioning and Ventilation Plants
ROMAN, F., Soil Mechanics and Foundations
VERDES, D., Agricultural Buildings, Physics of Construction
VIOREL, G., Concrete Bridges
ZETEA, E., Descriptive Geometry, Drawing

Faculty of Control and Computer Engineering:

CAMPEANU, V., Mathematical Analysis
COLOSI, T., Theory of Systems, Automation
COROVEI, I., Algebra, Special Mathematics
CRIVEI, I., Algebra, Mathematical Analysis
FESTILA, C., Control Structures and Algorithms
GANSCA, I., Mathematical Analysis
GAVREA, I., Calculus
GORGAN, D., Fundamentals of Computer Graphics
IGNAT, I., Operating Systems
IVAN, D. M., Numerical Analysis, Mathematical Analysis
LAZEA, GH., Theory of Robot Control
LETIA, I. A., Real Time Control
LUNGU, N., Special Mathematics
NEDEVSCHI, S., Design with Microchips
OPRIS, GH., Special Mathematics, Differential Equations
PUSZTAI, K., Networks, Computers
RASA, I., Numerical Mathematics
SALOMIE, I., Design Techniques
TOADER, GH., Mathematical Analysis
VORNICESCU, N., Differential Equations, Mathematical Analysis

Faculty of Electrical Engineering:

BALAN, H., Electrical Equipment
BIRO, K., Electrical Machines
CATANA, GH., Marketing
CHINDRIS, M., Technological Design of Management Systems
CIUPA, R., Basis of Electrotechnics
DARIE, S., Electrical Power Stations, Electrical Apparatus
DRAGOMIR, N., Electrical Measuring
IANCU, V., Electrical Machines
IMECS, M., Theory of Automatic Control Systems
IUGA, A., Electrotechnical Engineering
MAIER, V., Electrothermics
MAN, E., Elements of Electrotechnics
MARSCHALKO, R., Electronics
MICU, D., Electrical Engineering
MUNTEANU, R., Data Acquisition, Sensors and Control
RADULESCU, M., Electrical Drives
SIMION, E., Non-linear Circuits, Basic Electrical Engineering
TODORAN, GH., Electrical Measurements
TRIFA, V., Applied Informatics and Microprocessor Systems
VIOREL, A., Electrical Machines

Faculty of Electronics and Telecommunications:

ALMASANU, D.
BORDA, M., Information Theory
CIRLIGELU, V.
FESTILA, L., Analogical Integrated Circuits
LUNGU, S., Electronics
MIRON, C., Electronics
TODOREAN, G., Communication Techniques

Faculty of Machine Building:

ABRUDAN, GL., Cutting Tools
ABRUDAN, I., Production Systems
ACHIMAS, GH., Metal Forming
ANTAL, A., Machine Components
BALAN, B., Mechanics
BANABIC, D., Manufacturing Technologies
BERCE, P., Manufacturing Technologies
BLEBEA, I., Industrial Robots
CANDEA, D., Industrial Management
CĂZILĂ, A., Machine Components
CRETU, M., Machine Tools and Industrial Robots
DEACU, L., Hydraulics
GALIS, M., Design of Machine Tools
GYENGE, CS., Manufacturing Technologies
IANCĂU, H., Plastics
ISPAS, V., Mechanics, Robotics
ITU, T., Technical Measurements
KEREKES, L., Manufacturing Technologies
LAȘONȚI, A., Accounting
MARCU, V., Computer Programming
MORAR, L., Numerical Control
OLTEANU, R., Manufacturing Technology
PLITEA, N., Mechanics
POP, D., Machine Components
POP, I., Hydraulics
POPA, M., Unconventional Technologies
POPESCU, S., Mechanics
PRUNEA, P., Economics
ROȘ, O., Manufacturing Technologies
SUCALĂ, F., Machine Components
URSU, N., Computer Programming
URSU-FISCHER, N., Computer Programming

Faculty of Materials Science Engineering:

ARGHIR, G., Crystallography
BICSAK, E., Science of Materials, Welded Constructions Technology
BIRIS, I., Heat Processes in Metallurgical Furnaces
CÂNDEA, V., Materials Science
CANTA, TR., Plastic Deformation Theory
COMAN, S., Notions of Mechanical Engineering, Mechanical Technology
CONSTANTINESCU, V., Materials Science and Technology
COSMA, I., Physics
DEMCO, D., Physics
DEMCO, I., Physics
DOMSA, S., Materials Technology
IANCU, D., Heat and Thermochemical Treatment Technologies
LUPSA, I., Physics
MATEI, GH., Structural Theory of Metal Properties, Machine Tools and Technical Control
MILEA, I., Physics
MILITARU, V., Physics
ORBAN, R., Materials Technology
POP, O., Physics
SOPORAN, V., Technology for Casting Alloys
SPĂRGHEZ, Z., Composite Materials, Metallurgical Physics
VERMESAN, G., Heat and Thermochemical Treatment Technologies
VIDA, S., Materials Manufacturing Technology
ZIRBO, GH., Foundry and Moulding

Faculty of Mechanical Engineering:

APAHIDEAN, B., Thermodynamics
BATAGA, N., Heat Machines
BEJAN, M., Strength of Materials
BRANZAS, P., Management and Marketing
CORDOS, N., Vehicle Dynamics
CRETU, A., Strength of Materials
HANDRA-LUCA, V., Mechanisms, Robotics
HARDAU, M., Strength of Materials
ILEA, H., Strength of Materials
MADARASAN, T., Thermodynamics and Thermal Machines
MATIES, V., Mechanics
ROS, V., Forming Machines

UNIVERSITATEA DE MEDICINĂ ȘI FARMACIE 'IULIU HAȚIEGANU' CLUJ-NAPOCA

3400 Cluj-Napoca, Str. Emil Isac 13
Telephone: (64) 19-55-24
Fax: (64) 19-72-57

Founded 1872
Language of instruction: Romanian
Academic year: October to July (two semesters)

Rector: Prof. Dr OLIVIU PASCU
Pro-Rectors: Prof. Dr MARIUS BOJITĂ, Prof. Dr MIRCEA GRIGORESCU, Prof. Dr IOAN STELIAN BOCSAN
Registrar: IOAN CHIRA
Librarian: IOANA ROBU

Library: see Libraries
Number of teachers: 590
Number of students: 3,500

Publications: *Clujul Medical, Anuarul Universității, Romanian Journal of Gastroenterology, Applied Medical Informatics, Minimally Invasive Surgery, Acta Neurologica Transilvanicae, The Heart, Radiology and Medical Oncology, Diabetes Management, Quo Vadis.*

DEANS

Faculty of Medicine: Assoc. Prof. Dr PETRU ADRIAN MIRCEA
Faculty of Stomatology: Prof. Dr DORIN BORZEA
Faculty of Pharmacy: Prof. Dr CORNELIA TĂRMURE

PROFESSORS AND HEADS OF DEPARTMENT

Faculty of Medicine:

ACALOVSCHI, I., Anaesthesiology and Intensive Care
ANDERCOU A., Surgery
ANGHEL, I., Physiology
BÂRSAN, M., Cardiology
BENGA, G., Cellular and Molecular Biology
BENGA, I., Paediatric Neurology
BOCȘAN, I., Epidemiology
BOLOSIU, H., Internal Medicine
CARDAN, E., Anaesthesiology and Intensive Care
CÂRSTINA, D., Infectious Diseases
CONDOR, M., Paediatrics
DUCA, S., Surgery
DUNCEA, C., Internal Medicine
FLORESCU, P., Morphopathology
FUNARIU, GH., Surgery
GHERGULESCU, N., Orthopaedics, Traumatology
GHILEZAN, N., Oncology
GHIRAN, V., Paediatric Psychiatry
GRIGORESCU-SIDO, F., Anatomy
GRIGORESCU-SIDO, P., Paediatrics
HANCU, N., Nutrition and Metabolic Diseases
HURGOIU, V., Paediatrics
HUTANU, I., Paediatric Surgery
IONUȚ, C., Hygiene

Jebeleanu, Gh., Biochemistry
Kory, S., Neurology
Lazar, L., Oncology
Lucan, M., Urology
Lupea, I., Neonatology
Macrea, R., Paediatric Psychiatry
Maier, N., Dermatology
Miu, N., Paediatrics
Motocu, M., Internal Medicine
Nanulescu, L., Epidemiology
Nanulescu, M., Paediatrics
Olinic, A., Histology
Olinic, N., Internal Medicine
Olinici, C., Morphopathology
Pascu, O., Gastroenterology
Plesca, L., Physiopathology
Pop, R., Ophthalmology
Protase, A., Genetics
Rândasu, S., Psychiatry
Salagean, V., Gynaecology
Sasca, C., Microbiology
Stamatiu, C., Public Health
Surcel, I. V., Gynaecology
Ţigan, S., Medical Informatics
Ţomescu, E., Otorhinolaryngology
Turdeanu, N., Surgery
Zdrenghea, D., Cardiology

Faculty of Stomatology:

Borzea, D., Stomatological Propaedeutics
Cocârlă, E., Orthodontics, Pedodontics
Dociu, I., Stomatological Propaedeutics
Negucioiu, M., Dental Propaedeutics
Popa, S., Dental Propaedeutics
Rotaru, A., Oral and Maxillofacial Surgery

Faculty of Pharmacy:

Bojită, M., Drug Control
Coman, M., Drug Industry
Ghiran, D., Pharmaceutical Chemistry
Leucuta, S., Pharmaceutical Technology
Neamţu, M., Inorganic Chemistry
Policinencu, C., Pharmaceutical Legislation, Marketing and Management
Popescu, H., Pharmacognosy
Prodan, A., Informatics
Roman, L., Analytical Chemistry
Suciu, Gh., Dermatopharmacy and Cosmeticology
Tămaş, M., Pharmaceutical Botany
Tărmure, C., Biochemistry
Vancea, D., Biochemistry

UNIVERSITATEA TEHNICĂ 'GHEORGHE ASACHI'

6600 Iaşi, B-dul Copou 22
Telephone: (32) 21-23-22
Fax: (32) 21-16-67
E-mail: rectorat@staff.tuiasi.ro

Founded 1912
State control
Languages of instruction: Romanian, English, French
Academic year: October to October

Rector: Prof. Dr Ing. Mihai Gafiţanu
Pro-Rectors: Prof. Dr Ing. Victor Bulacovschi, Prof. Dr Ing. Liviu Groll, Prof. Dr Ing. Nicolae Badea, Prof. Dr Ing. Liviu Goraş
Registrar: Gabriela Iurcan
Librarian: Alexandrina Florea

Library: see Libraries
Number of teachers: 1,124
Number of students: 10,204

Publication: *Scientific Bulletin* (2 a year), *Review Magazine* (2 a year).

DEANS

Faculty of Chemical Engineering: Ioan Balasanian
Faculty of Civil Engineering and Architecture: Paulică Răileanu
Faculty of Electrical Engineering: Mihai Creţu
Faculty of Mechanical Engineering: Dorel Leon
Faculty of Automatic Control and Computer Engineering: Mihail Voicu
Faculty of Electronics and Telecommunications: Dimitrie Alexa
Faculty of Hydrotechnical Engineering: Ion Giurma
Faculty of Materials Science and Engineering: Adrian Dima
Faculty of Mechanical Equipment Design and Manufacture: Mircea Cozmîncă
Faculty of Textiles and Leather Technology: Constantin Preda
Technical College No. 1: Gheorghe Georgescu
Technical College No. 2: Ion Şerbănoiu

PROFESSORS

Faculty of Chemical Engineering:

Aelenei, N., Physical Chemistry
Apostolescu, M., Mineralogy
Asandei, N., Macromolecular Chemistry and Man-made Fibres
Băcăouanu, A., Chemical Engineering
Balasanian, I., Technology of Inorganic Substances
Bandrabur, F., Technology of Inorganic Substances
Bejan, D., Analytical Chemistry
Bezdadea, M., General Chemistry
Bîlbă, D., Analytical Chemistry
Bobu, E., Equipment in the Pulp and Paper Industry
Bontaş, I., Biochemistry
Bulacovschi, V., Macromolecular Chemistry
Ciovică, S., Paper Technology
Cristian, Gh., Equipment for Organic Industry
David, G., Physical Chemistry of Polymers
Dărângă, M., Physical Chemistry of Polymers
Dumitriu, E., Organic Technology
Foca, N., Inorganic Chemistry
Gavrilescu, D., Pulp and Paper Technology
Gorduza, V., Technology of Dyes
Grigoriu, I., Equipment for Inorganic Technology
Grunghievici, E., General Technology
Hagiu, C., Technology of Inorganic Substances
Horoba, E., Biotechnology
Hulea, V., Biochemistry
Hurduc, N., Physicochemistry of Polymers
Ifrim, S., General Chemistry
Ionescu, Gh., Physical Chemistry
Ivănoiu, M., Physical Chemistry of Polymers
Lazăr, D., Electrochemistry
Luca, C., General Chemistry
Lungu, M., Rheology of Polymers
Macoveanu, M., General Technology
Matei, F., Analytical Chemistry
Mazilu, I., Organic Chemistry
Merică, E., Technology of Dyes
Mihăilescu, C., Physicochemistry of Polymers
Nacu, Al., Analytical Chemistry
Nicu, M., Technology of Polymers
Nicu, V., General Technology
Obrocea, P., Pulp and Paper Technology
Oniscu, C., Technology of Synthetic and Biosynthetic Drugs
Onu, P., General Chemistry
Oprea, Cl., Mechanochemistry of Polymers, Monomers and Polymer Technology
Oprea, Sp., Chemical Organic Technology
Petrescu, S., Materials Science
Popa, I. M., Physical Chemistry
Popa, M., Polymer Technology
Popa, V., Wood Chemistry
Roşca, I., Inorganic Chemistry
Rusu, M., Rubber and Plastic Materials Processing
Savin, Al., Organic Technology
Scutaru, D., Organic Chemistry
Siminiceanu, I., Technology of Inorganic Substances
Simionescu, B., Physical Chemistry of Polymers
Simionescu, C., Macromolecular Chemistry
Sîrghie, I., Analytical Chemistry
Şoldea, C., Biochemistry
Stancu, A., Transport Phenomena in the Chemical Industry
Ştefancu, E., Inorganic Chemistry
Şzep, A., Technology of Inorganic Substances
Tătaru, L., Organic Chemistry
Tudose, R., Transport Phenomena in the Chemical Industry
Ungureanu, Şt., Automation in the Chemical Industry
Vâţă, M., Organic Chemistry

Faculty of Civil Engineering and Architecture:

Amariei, C., Structural Mechanics, Plastic Design
Atanasiu, M. G., Structural Mechanics, Computer-Aided Design, Earthquake Engineering
Axinte, E., Steel Structures
Bliuc, I., Building Elements
Bobică, N., History of Philosophy
Boboc, V., Road Engineering
Boţi, N., Tunnels and Tunnelling
Boţu, N., Geotechnics
Broşteanu, M., Buildings
Broşteanu, T., Railways
Budescu, M., Structural Mechanics, Computer-Aided Design, Earthquake Engineering
Ciongradi, C., Computer Programming, Structural Mechanics
Ciongradi, I., Structural Mechanics, Computer-Aided Design, Earthquake Engineering
Ciornei, Al., Buildings
Cloşca, C., Cultural History
Corobceanu, S., Concrete and Reinforced Concrete Construction
Cososchi, B., Road Engineering
Cuciureanu, A., Reinforced and Prestressed Concrete
Dobrescu-Balahur, D., Sociology
Dumitraş, A., Structural Mechanics
Florea, N., Hydrotechnical Buildings
Gavrilaş, I., Construction
Giuşcă, N., Construction Technology
Gorbănescu, D., Strength of Materials, Theory of Elasticity and Plasticity
Gorincioiu, A., Building Materials
Grecu, V., Soil Mechanics and Foundations
Groll, L., Building Materials
Gugiuman, G., Road Engineering
Hîrhui, I., Building Materials
Humă, D., Philosophy
Ignat, J., Electrical Installations
Ionescu, C., Structural Mechanics, Earthquake Engineering
Isopescu, D., Design and Composite Structures
Jantea, C., Bridge Engineering
Jerca, St., Structural Mechanics, Numerical Methods
Jerghiuţă, V., Agricultural Buildings
Jofa, C., Cultural History
Leonte, C., Concrete and Concrete Structures
Mateescu, Th., Water Supply and Sewerage Installations, Installations for Buildings
Mihalache, N., Strength of Materials, Theory of Elasticity and Plasticity, Numerical Methods
Muşat, V., Soil Mechanics and Foundation
Nicuţă, A., Soil Mechanics and Foundations
Nour, S., Concrete and Reinforced Concrete Constructions
Pamfil, E., Construction Works Technology
Păstrăguş, M., Philosophy, Aesthetics
Pescaru, V., Steel Structures
Pichiu, D., Philosophy
Plătică, D., Soil Mechanics and Foundations
Popa, C., Descriptive Geometry

Popovici, D., Highways, Road Engineering
Precupanu, D., Strength of Materials, Theory of Elasticity and Plasticity
Radu, A., Building Sciences
Răileanu, P., Soil Mechanics and Foundations
Rujanu, M., Building Materials
Sârbu, T., Philosophy
Secu, Al., Industrial and Agricultural Constructions
Stanciu, A., Soil Mechanics and Foundations
Ştefănescu, D., Buildings
Strat, L., Structural Mechanics, Earthquake Engineering
Szolontay, C., Reinforced Concrete
Tănase, E., Philosophy
Ţăranu, N., Industrial Buildings and Composite Structures
Tompea, D., Philosophy
Ungureanu, N., Strength of Materials, Theory of Elasticity and Plasticity, Numerical Methods
Varlam, F., Concrete Bridge Engineering
Vasilescu, A., Technology of Civil Engineering
Velicu, C., Building Sciences
Vereş, Al., Buildings and Architectural Acoustics
Vlad, I., Strength of Materials, Theory of Elasticity and Plasticity, Numerical Methods
Vlad, N., Road Technology Engineering
Vulpe, A., Structural Mechanics
Zarojanu, H., Highways, Traffic, Airports

Faculty of Electrical Engineering:

Adam, M., Electrical Equipment, Power Electronics
Alexandrescu, V., Power Systems
Androne, C., Fundamentals of Electrical Engineering
Asaftei, C., Power Plants
Asandei, D., Power Plants
Balan, D., Fundamentals of Electrical Engineering
Balan, T., Electrical Materials
Băluţă, Gh., Electrical Drives, Power Electronics
Baraboi, A., Electrical Equipment, EMC, Power Electronics
Bârlădeanu, E., Industrial Electronic Networks
Caba, S., Electrical Drives, Optimal Control, Reliability
Căileanu, C., Systems Identification, Modelling, Electrical Drives, Systems Theory, Intelligent Control
Cantemir, L., Electric Traction, Uses of Electrical Energy
Cârţînă, Gh., Optimal Control and Computer Applications in Energetics
Ciobanu, L., Electrical Drives of Robots, Reliability
Ciobanu, R. C., Electrical Materials
Cleju, M., Electronic Engineering, Automatic Control
Cosma, V., Electrical Engineering
Creţu, A., Electrical Engineering
Creţu, E., Electrical Engineering
Creţu, M., Electrical Measurements and Transducers
Diaconescu, M., Electrical Drives, Electronics and Power Electronics
Gavrilaş, M., Power Plants
Gavrilaş, N., High-Voltage Technology
Georgescu, Gh., Power Networks
Graur, I., Power Electronics, Vector Control of AC Drives
Guşă, M., High-Voltage Engineering
Haba, P., Electrical Engineering
Hnatiuc, E., Electrical Apparatus Design, Environmental Protection
Istrate, M., High-Voltage Engineering
Ivas, D., Power Systems Reliability
Leonte, P., Electrical Equipment
Livinţ, Gh., Systems Theory, Automatic Control
Mitrea, S., Fundamentals of Electrical Engineering
Munteanu, F., Quality of Supply, Power Systems Reliability
Nemescu, M., Systems Theory and Industrial Automation
Olah, R., Overvoltages and Insulation Engineering
Olaru, R., Industrial Automation
Petrescu, C., Numerical Analysis of Electromagnetic Fields, High Dielectric Heating Frequency
Popescu, I., Fundamentals of Electrical Engineering
Preda, L., Electrical Equipment of Power Plants
Simion, A., Electrical Machines
Suchar, I., Electrical Engineering and Electronics
Teodoru, E., Electrical Machines and Drives

Faculty of Mechanical Equipment Design and Manufacture:

Acker, C., Theoretical Mechanics
Agop, M., Physics
Alexandrescu, A., Hydraulics
Axinte, E., Machine Repair and Manufacturing Technology
Belousov, V., Cutting Tools
Bohosievici, C., Technology of Machine Building
Braha, V., Mechanical Engineering
Braier, Al., Theoretical Mechanics and Vibrations
Budei, R. Gh., Theoretical Mechanics and Vibrations
Buzescu, F., Theoretical Mechanics
Călugăru, Gh., Physics
Carata, E., Cutting Tools
Chirilă, V., Technology of Machine Building
Ciocan, L., Fluid Mechanics and Hydraulic Machines
Ciubotariu, C., Physics
Ciumaşu, G., Theoretical Mechanics
Condurache, D., Theoretical Mechanics
Constantinescu, C., Cutting Tools
Cotae, C., Physics
Cozmîncă, M., Metal Cutting
Crăciunaş, A., Theoretical Mechanics and Vibrations
Druţu, C., Machine Tools
Duşa, P., Technology of Machine Building
Fetecău, C., Theoretical Mechanics
Gherghel, N., Design of Mechanical Devices
Gojineţchi, N., Devices
Grămescu, Tr., Technology of Machine Building
Ibănescu, I., Theoretical Mechanics
Ibănescu, R., Theoretical Mechanics
Istrate, M., Physics
Istrate, S., Physics
Jeflea, A., Physics
Lungu, Gh., Machine Tools
Melinte, S., Physics
Muscă, G., Computer-Aided Manufacturing
Neagu, E., Physics
Neagu, R., Physics
Panait, S., Metal Cutting
Paraschiv, Dr., Machine Repairing Technology
Pasnicu, C., Physics
Plăhteanu, B., Machine Tools
Popescu, D. E., Structural Mechanics
Poteraşu, V. F., Structural Mechanics
Pruteanu, O., Machine Building Technology
Rusu, E., Theoretical Mechanics
Rusu, I., Hydraulics
Salomeia, L., Theoretical Mechanics and Vibrations
Severincu, M., Cutting Tools
Slătineanu, L., Machine Building Technology
Strat, G., Physics
Ţura, L., Machine Tools
Ungureanu, Gh., Computer-Aided Design
Ursu, D., Physics
Zet, Gh., Physics
Zetu, D., Design of Automatic Machine Tools

Faculty of Materials Science and Engineering:

Alexandru, I., Technology of Materials
Andrei, E., Technology of Materials
Bulancea, V., Rolling
Carcea, I., Composites
Cojocaru Filipiuc, V., Metallurgy
Dima, A., Technology and Applied Metallurgy
Găluşcă, D. G., Technology of Thermal Treatment
Hopulele, I., Technology of Thermal Treatments
Mălureanu, I., Technology of Metals
Munteanu, C., Technology of Thermal Treatments
Petruş, O., Computational Metallurgy
Zaharia, L., Plastic Deformation

Faculty of Hydrotechnical Engineering:

Alexandrescu, O., Water Supply in Agriculture
Axinte, S., Ameliorative Agriculture
Bârsan, E., Water Supply
Bartha, I., Hydraulics
Blăgoi, O., Hydrology
Cismaru, C., Irrigation and Drainage
Cojocaru, I., Irrigation and Drainage
Daian, N., Physical Education
Damian, C., Physical Education
Dima, M., Hydrology
Gavrilov, Gh., Surveying
Giurma, I., Hydrology and Water Economy
Hobjilă, V., Construction Technology
Leu, D., Water Supply in Agriculture
Luca, M., Hydraulics
Manolovici, M., Hydrotechnical Constructions
Marica, I., Physical Education
Miroş, M., Physical Education
Morariu, A., Physical Education
Nicolau, A., Hydrology and Hydrogeology
Nistor, Gh., Surveying
Niţescu, E., Work Technology and Mechanization in Land Reclamation
Patraş, M., Reinforced Concrete
Popescu, C., Ameliorative Agriculture
Popescu, St., Pumping Plants, Numerical Methods
Popia, A., Surveying
Popovici, N., Soil Conservation, River Flow Regulation
Prepeliţă, D., Maintenance of Land Reclamation Projects, Automation
Stătescu, F., Physics of Soil, Pedology
Tobolcea, V., Waste Water Treatment, Sewerage Engineering
Zavati, V., Hydraulics

Faculty of Electronics and Telecommunications:

Alexa, D., Microwave Engineering, Power Electronics
Alexandru, D. N., Telecommunications
Andricioaie, Gh., Mathematics
Bârsan, T., Mathematics
Bejancu, A., Mathematics
Bogdan, I., Mobile Communications
Borş, D., Mathematics
Cărăuşu, Al., Mathematics
Casian, B. I., Microwave Engineering
Cehan, V., Radio Transmitters
Chiorescu, Gh., Mathematics
Chiper, F. L.
Chiriţă, S., Mathematics
Ciobanu, Gh., Mathematics
Cleju, I., Information Theory, Digital Circuits
Corduneanu, A., Mathematics
Costovici, Gh., Mathematics
Cotae, P., Digital Communication

CRĂCIUN, I., Mathematics
CRĂCIUNAŞ, P., Mathematics
DAVIDEANU, C., Mathematics
DIMITRIU, L., Electronic Measuring and Control Apparatus, Automation Electronics
FETECĂU, C., Mathematics
FLOREA, M., Electronic Devices and Circuits
GHEORGHIŢĂ, V., Mathematics
GORAS, L., Signals, Circuits and Systems
GRĂDINARU, N., Mathematics
GRIGORAŞ, V., Signals, Circuits and Systems
HRIŢCU, A., Architecture of Microprocessor Systems, Programmable Automata, Switched Mode Power Supplies
LUCANU, M., Industrial Electronics
MAXIM, G., Electronic Devices and Circuits
MUNTEANU, V., Information Theory
NEAGU, AL., Mathematics
NEGOESCU, N., Mathematics
NISTOR, I., Mathematics
NIŢESCU, C., Mathematics
ONCIULESCU, I., Mathematics
PAPAGHIUC, N., Mathematics
POPA, L., Mathematics
PROCOPIUC, GH., Mathematics
PUŞCAŞU, E., Mathematics
RADU, S., Electromagnetic Compatibility
REUS, N., Electronic Devices and Circuits
SABADÂŞ, AL., Mathematics
SAVA, V., Mathematics
SIMIRAD, C., Mathematics
SÎRBU, A., Computer Aided Design
ŞTIURCĂ, D., Analogue Integrated Circuits
TALPALARU, P., Mathematics
TEODORESCU, H., Medical Electronics, Image Processing, Neural Networks and Fuzzy Systems
TEODORU, G., Mathematics
TEŞU, I., Computer-aided Design
TURIC, L., Analogue Integrated Circuits, Electronic Devices and Circuits

Faculty of Automatic Control and Computer Engineering:

BALABAN, E., Digital Control Systems, Control of Electrical Drives
BOŢAN, C., Optimization Techniques, Optimal Control
BOTEZ, C., Databases and Computer Programming, Software Engineering
GÂLEA, D., Artificial Intelligence
GANCIU, T., Systems Identification, Data Processing
GRIGORAŞ, D., Parallel Computing
HOZA, F., Digital Computers, Microcontrollers
HUŢANU, C., Multiprocessor Systems, Microprocessor Systems
ILINCA, M., Computer Programming
LAZĂR, C., Control Engineering, Data Transmission
MARCU, T., Reliability and Fault Diagnosis
NEACŞU, D. O., Power Electronics
OLAH, I., Electrical and Electronic Control Equipment, Servomechanisms
OLARU, D., Advanced Techniques in Digital Logic Design
PAL, C., Robot Control Systems
PĂNESCU, A. D., Robot Control, Knowledge-Based Systems
PANTELIMONESCU, F., Man-Machine Interaction, Microprocessor-Based Design
PĂSTRĂVANU, O. C., Discrete Event Systems, Neural Networks in Control Engineering
POLI, E., Real-Time Programming
VALACHI, A., Digital Logic Design, Digital Systems Design
VOICU, M., Systems Theory, Fundamentals of Feedback Control

Faculty of Textiles and Leather Technology:

ANTONIU, GH., Textile Raw Materials
AVRAM, D., Weaving
AVRAM, M., Yarn Structure and Design
BADEA, N., Leather and Furs Chemistry and Technology
BERTEA, A., Rheology of Polymers for Textiles
BLAŞCU, V., Textile Fibres
BOIER, R., Marketing
BORDEIANU, D. L., Textile Raw Materials
BRUDARU, O., Fuzzy Systems
BUCEVSCHI, D., Technology of Leather Substitutes
BUDULAN, C., Equipment and Automation in the Knitwear Industry
BUTNARU, R., Chemistry and Technology of Textile Materials
CHINCIU, D., Woven Structure and Design, Computer-Aided Design
CIOCOIU, M., Weaving Process and Machinery, Statistical Methods in Textiles
CONDURACHE, GH., Quality Control and Analysis
CROITORU, D., Equipment and Automation in the Leather Manufacturing Industry
CUZIC-ZVONARU, C., Bast Fibre Spinning, Spinning Machine Design and Automation
DRĂGOI, L., Weaving Machinery Design and Automation
DUMITRIU, C., Management
GRIBINCEA, V., Textile Raw Materials
GRIGORIU, A., Special Technologies of Textile Products Finishing
HAGIU, V., Management
ILIESCU, E., Basics of Chemical Technology
IRIMIA, M., Economics and Accountancy
LIUŢE, D., Preparatory Weaving Processes, Weaving Technology
LUCA, P. G., Management
MĂLUREANU, G., Footwear Design
MATEESCU, M., Knitwear Technology
MIHAI, I., Organization and Systematization
MIHAI, I., Industrial Engineering Management in the Textile Industry
MITU, S., Clothing
MUNTEANU, A., Marketing and Economics
MUNTEANU, V., Marketing
MUREŞAN, R., Dyestuffs and Surfactants in Textile Chemistry
MUSTAŢĂ, A., Bast Fibre Spinning
NĂNESCU, V., Equipment in Leather Chemical Industry
NECULĂIASA, M., Textile Metrology, Textile Quality Control
NICULAE, M., Management in Industrial Engineering
NICULESCU, E., Marketing
NICULESCU, N., Economics and Finance
NIŢĂ, I., Economics
PAPAGHIUC, V., Technology and Equipment in the Clothing Industry
PETRESCU, GH., Marketing
PÎCA, A., Industrial Engineering Management in the Textile Industry
PINTILIE, E., Equipment and Automation in the Clothing Industry
PONŢA, M., Economics
PREDA, C., Nonwoven Textile Materials Technology
RUSU, C., Total Quality Management, Human Resources Management
SAMSON, N., French
ŞERBĂNOIU, I., Industrial Engineering Management in the Textile Industry
VÎLCU, M., Theoretical Bases of Spinning
VITAN, F., Transfer Phenomena and Equipment
VOICU, M., Interpersonal Communication
ZAMFIR, M., Structure and Properties of Materials for Knitwear and Clothing

Faculty of Mechanical Engineering:

ATANASIU, V., Mechanical Transmissions
BÂRJOIANU, A., Gas and Steam Turbines
BÂRSĂNESCU, P., Strength of Materials
BENDESCU, I., Thermotechnics and Heat Engines
BERCEA, M., Machine Design, Tribology and Vibration
COSTIN, D., Thermotechnics and Heat Engines
COZMA, D., Agricultural Machines
CRĂCIUN, V., Agricultural Machines
CREŢU, SP., Machine Design, Tribology and Vibration
DĂSCĂLESCU, D., Internal Combustion Engines
DRĂGAN, B., Machine Vibrations
DUCA, C., Applied Mechanics
DUMITRAŞCU, GH., Thermotechnics and Heat Engines
GAFIŢANU, M., Machine Design, Tribology and Vibration
GAIGINSCHI, R., Internal Combustion Engines
GIURCĂ, V., Gas and Steam Turbines
GOLGOŢIU, E., Internal Combustion Engines
GRIGORAŞ, Ş., Machine Design and Reliability
HAGIU, GH., Machine Design and Vibration
HANGANU, L., Machine Design
HORBANIUC, B., Thermotechnology and Heat Transfer
HOSTIUC, L., Machine Design
JUGUREANU, E., Gas and Steam Turbines
LEON, D., Strength of Materials
LOZONSCHI, GH., Thermotechnics and Heat Engines
MACRI, VAL., Thermotechnics and Heat Engines
MERTICARU, V., Machine Dynamics, Robotics
MIROŞ, I., Strength of Materials
NEAGU, C., Agricultural Machines
NECULĂIASA, V., Agricultural Machines
OLARU, D., Machine Design and Tribology
OPRIŞAN, C., Synthesis of Mechanisms
PALIHOVICI, VAL., Strength of Materials
POPOVICI, A., Mechanisms and Machine Design
RACOCEA, C., Machine Design
RECEANU, D., Mechanisms
TENU, I., Agricultural Machines
ZUBCU, V., Gas and Steam Turbines
ZUGRĂVEL, M., Internal Combustion Engines

UNIVERSITATEA DE MEDICINĂ ŞI FARMACIE 'GR. T. POPA' IAŞI

6600 Iaşi, Str. Universităţii 16
Telephone: (32) 11-61-04
Fax (32) 21-18-20

Founded 1879
State control
Languages of instruction: Romanian, English
Academic year: October to July

President: Prof. Dr CAROL STANCIU
Vice-Presidents: Prof. Dr EUSEBIE ZBRANCA, Prof. Dr CONSTANTIN COTRUTZ, Prof. Dr CRISTIAN DRAGOMIR, Prof. Dr GEORGE I. M. GEORGESCU
Registrar: Eng. DANA BUGEAC
Librarian: Prof. VIORICA SCUTARU

Library of 470,000 vols
Number of teachers: 598
Number of students: 5,257

DEANS

School of Medicine: Prof. Dr VALERIU RUSU
School of Stomatology: Prof. Dr VASILE BURLUI
School of Pharmacy: Prof. Dr URSULA HELENA STĂNESCU
School of Medical Bioengineering: Prof. Dr FLORIN TOPOLICEANU

PROFESSORS

School of Medicine:

ANTOHE, D. S., Anatomy
BĂDESCU, A., Histology
BRĂNIŞTEANU, D., Physiology
BRUMARU, O., Paediatrics
BUIUC, D., Microbiology
CARASIEVICI, E., Immunology

CHIRIAC, M., Anatomy
CHIRIAC, R. M., Rheumatology and Balneophysiotherapy
CHIRIȚA, V., Psychiatry
CHISĂLIȚA, D., Ophthalmology
CIORNIA, T., Forensic Medicine
COLEV, V., Physiopathology
COSOVANU, A., Internal Medicine
COSTĂCHESCU, GH., Obstetrics and Gynaecology
COSTINESCU, V., Otorhinolaryngology
COTRUTZ, C., Cell Biology
COTUȚIU, C., Histology
COVIC, M., Genetics
COVIC, M., Internal Medicine
DANIL, C., Radiology
DATCU, G., Internal Medicine
DIMITRIU, A. G., Paediatrics
DRAGOMIR, C., Infant Care
DRAGOMIR, C., Surgery
DRAGOMIR, D., Obstetrics and Gynaecology
DUDA, R. C., Social Medicine
FILIPESCU, D., Physical Education
GĂLEȘANU, M. R., Radiology
GAVĂT, V., Hygiene
GEORGESCU, G., Internal Medicine
GEORGESCU, N. M., Orthopaedics and Traumatology
GHEORGHIȚĂ, N., Biochemistry
GOȚIA, D. G., Paediatric Surgery
GOȚIA, S., Paediatrics
IANOVICI, N., Neurosurgery
IVAN, A., Epidemiology
LUCA, M., Parasitology and Mycoses
LUCA, V., Infectious Diseases
MĂTĂSARU, S., Paediatrics
MIHĂESCU, T., Pneumology
MIHĂESCU, V., Medical Psychology
MIHAILOVICI, M. S., Pathological Anatomy
MIHALACHE, C., Occupational Medicine
MIHALACHE, GR., Anatomy
MIHALACHE, ST., Surgery
MORARU, D., Paediatrics
MUNGIU, C. O., Pharmacology
NEAMȚU, C., Physiology
PANDELE, G. I., Internal Medicine
PETRESCU, GH., Physiology
PETRESCU, Z., Dermatology
PLESA, C., Surgery
PRICOP, F., Obstetrics and Gynaecology
PRICOP, M., Obstetrics and Gynaecology
RUSU, V., Biophysics
ȘELARU, M., Psychiatry
ȘTANCIU, C., Internal Medicine
ȘTEFANACHE, F., Neurology
ȘTOIAN, M., Surgery
STRATONE, A., Exploration Physiology
STRATONE, N., History of Philosophy and Sciences
TANSANU, I., Paediatrics
TOPOLICEANU, F., Exploring Physiology
ZAMFIR, M., Anatomy
ZBRANCA, E., Endocrinology

School of Stomatology:

BARNA, M., Dental Surgery
BURLUI, V., Prosthetics
DIACONESCU, M. R., Surgery
DOROBĂȚ, V., Infant Stomatology
FĂTU, C., Anatomy
GOGĂLNICEANU, D., Dental Surgery
HURJUI, J., Internal Medicine
LABA, E., Pathological Anatomy
MARIN, G., Community Dentistry
MÎRȚU, D. V., Otorhinolaryngology
NECHIFOR, M., Pharmacology
NIȚĂ, M., Histology
PATRAȘ, E., Endodontics
PAVEL, M., Biochemistry
SLĂTINEANU, S., Physiology
TURCU, T., Microbiology
VATAMAN, R., Odontology
VORONEANU, M., Anaesthesiology

School of Pharmacy:

CARAMAN, C., Inorganic Chemistry
CUCIUREANU, R., Environmental Chemistry
DANILĂ, GH., Pharmaceutical Chemistry
DIMA, F., Physical Chemistry
DORNEANU, V., Analytical Chemistry
FILIP, M., Biochemistry
GAFIȚEANU, E., Pharmaceutical Technology
LAZAR, M., Drug Control
MIFTODE, M., General and Inorganic Chemistry
PAVELESCU, M. D. G., Pharmacology
PROCA, M., Toxicology
STĂNESCU, U. H., Pharmacognosy
ȘTEFĂNESCU, E., Organic Chemistry

UNIVERSITATEA 'POLITEHNICA' TIMIȘOARA

1900 Timișoara, Piața Victoriei 2
Telephone: 22-03-76
Telex: 71347
Fax: 19-03-21

Founded 1920
State control
Academic year: October to July

Rector: Prof. Dr Ing. IOAN GHEORGHE CARTIS
Pro-Rectors: V. POPESCU, T. E. MAN, N. ROBU
Librarian: E. OTESTEANU

Number of teachers: 865
Number of students: 8,364

Publication: *Buletinul Științific și Tehnic* (Scientific and Technical Bulletin, annually).

DEANS

Faculty of Mechanical Engineering: G. URDEA
Faculty of Electrotechnical Engineering: M. NEMEȘ
Faculty of Computers and Automatization: ST. HOLBAN
Faculty of Electronics and Telecommunications: A. IGHEA
Faculty of Civil Engineering: I. COSTESCU
Faculty of Hydrotechnics and Environmental Engineering: GH. POPA
Faculty of Chemical Engineering: O. DAVIDESCU
Faculty of Management in Production and Transport: M. IZVERCIAN

PROFESSORS

Faculty of Mechanical Engineering:

ANCUSA, V., Fluid Mechanics, Transport Phenomena, Air and Water Pollution
BABEU, T., Theory of Elasticity and Strength of Materials
BACRIA, V., Mechanics
BAGIU, L., Electromechanical Engineering
BALEKICS, M., Machine Elements, Tribology
BĂRGLĂZAN, M., Hydraulic Turbines
BERINDEAN, V., Internal Combustion Engines
BRESTIN, A., Technology of Materials
BRÎNDEU, L., Mechanics and Vibration
CARTIS, I., Heat Treatment
CHIRIAC, A., Robotics and Automation in the Textile Industry
CRISTUINEA, C., Theory of Elasticity and Strength of Materials
CRUDU, M., Mechanisms
DAVID, I., Tolerances
DOBRE, I., Theory of Elasticity and Strength of Materials
DRĂGHICI, G., Manufacturing Engineering
DRĂGULESCU, D., Mechanical Engineering
GLIGOR, O., Components for Precision Mechanics Devices
GLIGOR, T., Mechanics
HEGEDUS, A., Mechanics
HOANCĂ, V., Thermal Engines
ICLĂNZAN, T., Plastics Manufacturing
IORGA, D., Internal Combustion Engines
KOVACS, F., Mechanisms
LĂNCRĂNGEAN, Z., Technology of Materials
MĂDĂRAS, L., Machine Elements
MICSA, I., Manufacturing Engineering
MILOȘ, L., Welding
MITELEA, I., Materials Science
NANU, A., Technology of Materials
NEGREA, V. D., Internal Combustion Engines
NICA, C. M., Basic Experimental Research
NICHICI, A., Technology of Materials
NICOARĂ, I., Optical Devices
PERJU, D., Mechanisms
POCINOG, G., Management of Production Systems
POPA, H., Management and Industrial Engineering
POPA, O., Mechanics of Fluids and Hydraulic Machines
POPOVICI, I., Technology of Materials
POPOVICI, V., Welding Equipment
POPOVICI, V., Technology of Fine Mechanics
POPOVICIU, M., Technology of Hydraulic Machines, Fluid Mechanics
PREDA, I., Hydroelectric Power Stations and Pumping Services
PUGNA, I., Production Systems Engineering
RADOSLAV, I., Civil Engineering
RAICA, T., Dynamics of Internal Combustion Engines
SAFTA, V., Welding Control and Welded Constructions
SANTĂU, I., Pumping Services
SAVII, G., Computer Aided Design
SMICALĂ, I., Mechanics
TOADER, M., Mechanics
TRUȘCULESCU, M., Materials Science
UNGUREANU, C., Steam Boilers
URDEA, G., Machine Tools

Faculty of Electrotechnical Engineering:

ATANASIU, G., Special Electrical Machines
BABESCU, M., Electrical Machines
BANZARU, T., Mathematics
BARTZER, S., Technology of Electrical Products
BOGOEVICI, N., Basics of Electrotechnics
BOJA, N., Mathematics
BOLDEA, I., Electrical Machines
BUTA, A., Power Delivery
CONSTANTIN, I., Mathematics
CRĂCIUN, P., Physics
DABA, D., Theoretical Electrotechnics
DE SABATA, I., Basics of Electrotechnics
DOBRE, S., Electrotechnics
DORDEA, T., Electrical Machines
HEINRICH, I., Stations and Transformation Posts
IVASCU, C., Automatics and Power Systems Protection
LIPOVAN, O., Mathematics
MARCU, C., Physics
MIHALCA, I., Physics
NEAGU, M., Mathematics
NEGRU, V., High-Voltage Engineering
NEMEȘ, M., Electrical Power Systems
NOVAC, I., Electrical Machines
SERACIN, E., Electrical Drives
SORA, C., Basics of Electrotechnics
SORA, I., Electroheat, Electrotechnology, Electrical Lighting
SUCIU, I., Electrical Equipment
VASILIEVICI, A., Electrical Equipment
VETRES, I., Basis of Electrotechnics

Faculty of Computers and Automatization:

CRETU, V., Advanced Data Structures and Programming Techniques
DRAGOMIR, T.-L., Systems Theory
GROZA, V., Numeric Seminals
HOLBAN, S., Basis of Artificial Intelligence
JURCĂ, I., Operating Systems Design
MUREȘAN, I., Knowledge Engineering
PREITL, S., Automatic Adjustment Engineering
STRUGARU, C., Peripheral Devices and Data Transmission
VLĂDUTIU, M., Computer Reliability

Faculty of Electronics and Telecommunications:

CIUGUDEAN, M., Integrated Circuits and Electronics

CRISAN, S., Electronic Measurements
MUREŞAN, T., Integrated Circuits and Electronics
NAFORNITĂ, I., Signals Processing
POLICEC, A., Communications Systems and Techniques
POP, E., Electric and Electronic Measurements
POPESCU, V., Power Electronics
STOICA, V., Information Transmission Theory
TĂNASE, E., Electronics
TIPONUT, V., Electronic Devices
TOMA, C., Television

Faculty of Civil Engineering:

BĂNCILĂ, R., Steel Structures
BOB, C., Chemistry and Construction Materials
BOTA, V., Concrete Bridges
CADAR, I., Reinforced Concrete Structures
CARABA, I., Steel Structures
CLIPII, T., Reinforced Concrete Structures
COSTESCU, I., Road Design and Construction
CUTEANU, E., Strength of Materials
DIMOIU, I., Earthquake Engineering
DUBINA, D., Construction
FURDUI, C., Civil Construction, Agricultural Construction
GĂDEANU, L., Steel Structures
GAVRA, S., History of Architecture
GIONCU, V., Structures
GRUIA, A., Soil Mechanics and Foundation Engineering
HAIDA, V., Soil Mechanics and Foundation Engineering
IVAN, M., Statics, Stability and Dynamics of Construction
MARIN, M., Soil Mechanics and Foundation Engineering
MATEESCU, D., Steel Structures
MERCEA, GH., Steel Structures
MIRSU, O., Reinforced Concrete Structures
PATCAS, I., Steel Structures
REGEP, Z., Steel Structures
SCHEIN, T., Soil Mechanics and Foundation Engineering
STOIAN, V., Civil Construction
TUDOR, D., Civil Construction

Faculty of Hydrotechnics and Environmental Engineering:

CIOMOCOS, F., Strength of Materials
CRETU, G., Hydrology, Water Resources Policy
DANILESCU, A., Statics, Stability and Dynamics of Construction
DAVID, I., Hydraulics, Transport, Groundwater Pollution Modelling
GUTESCU, D., Topography
ION, M., Hydrotechnical Construction
IONESCU, N., Machines for Construction, Technology of Irrigation and Drainage
MAN, E., Irrigation and Drainage
MIREL, I., Water Supply and Town Drainage
NEAMTU, M., Topography
NICOARĂ, T., Hydraulics
POPA, GH., Hydrotechnical Construction
ROGOBETE, GH., Soil Science
WEHRY, A., Irrigation and Drainage

Faculty of Chemical Engineering:

BECHERESCU, D., Furnaces and Drying Plants for the Silicate Industry
CSUNDERLIK, C., Organic Chemistry
DAESCU, C., Pharmaceutical Products
DRĂGOI, I., Cement Chemistry
IOVI, A., Technology of Mineral Fertilizers
JULEAN, I., Analytical Chemistry
KOHN, D., Chemical Engineering
LUPEA, A. X., Pharmaceutical Products
MANOVICIU, I., Macromolecular Components and Physical Chemistry
MENESSY, I., Crystallography and Mineralogy
NUŢIU, M., Organic Chemistry
PERJU, D., Process Modelling, Chemical Industry
PETCA, GH., Technology of General Chemistry; Water and Waste Water Technology
PUGNA, I., Chemical Industry
RĂDOI, I., Electrochemistry and Corrosion

Faculty of Agricultural Equipment and Transport:

DĂNILĂ, I., Harvesting Machines
GLĂVAN, ST., Agrobiological Basis of Agricultural Mechanics
IZVERCIAN, M., Management
NICA, C., Zootechnical Machines
POP, T., Philosophy
POPA, GH., Physical Training
SANDRU, A., Use of Agricultural Machinery
ŞTEFAN, C., Agricultural Engineering
TECUŞAN, N., Tractors and Automobiles

ATTACHED INSTITUTE

Institute of Engineers: Hunedoara, Str. Karl Marx 5; tel. (957) 1-19-19.

PROFESSORS

ILCA, I., Technology of Plastic Deformation
SAIMAC, A., Electrotechnics

UNIVERSITATEA DE ŞTIINŢE AGRICOLE A BANATULUI TIMIŞOARA

1900 Timişoara, Calea Aradului 119
Telephone: (56) 19-40-23
Telex: 71386
Fax: (56) 20-02-96

Founded 1945
State control
Academic year: October to September

Rector: Prof. Dr PAUN ION OTIMAN
Vice-Rectors: Prof. Dr GAVRILĂ STANCIU, Prof. Dr EUGEN CRĂINICEANU
Registrar: TIBERIU DEAN
Scientific Secretary: Prof. Dr IOAN BORCEAN
Librarian: Conf. GHEORGHE NISTOR

Library of 300,000 vols
Number of teachers: 422
Number of students: 2,015

Publication: *Lucrări Ştiinţifice* (series Agronomy, Veterinary Medicine and Animal Sciences, Food Technology, Horticulture, annually).

DEANS

Faculty of Agronomy: Prof. Dr ALEXANDRU MOISUC
Faculty of Animal Husbandry: Prof. Dr IOAN VINTILĂ
Faculty of Veterinary Medicine: Prof. Dr HORIA CERNESCU
Faculty of Horticulture: Prof. Dr GABRIEL NEDELEA
Faculty of Food Technology: Prof. Dr IONEL JIANU
College of Agriculture and Veterinary Medicine: Conf. Dr TRIF RADU (Dir)

PROFESSORS

Faculty of Agronomy:

ALBERT, F., Sociology
ANDERCA, C., Agrarian Economy
AUNGURENCE, N., Mechanization
BORCEAN, I., Plant Technology
COSTE, I., Botany
FRUJA, I., Agrarian Economy
GOIAN, M., Agrochemistry
LAUER, K. F., Agrochemistry
LAZUREANU, A., Agricultural Technology
MOISUC, A., Fodder Plants
ONU, N., Land Improvement
OTIMAN, P. I., Management
PĂLĂGEŞIU, I., Entomology
POP, A., Physiology
POPESCU, GH., Phytopathology
RUSU, I., Pedology
SÂMBOTIN, L., Management

Faculty of Animal Husbandry:

BURA, M., Breeding of Fur-bearing Animals
DRINCEANU, D., Animal Nutrition
GRIGOROIU, E., Management
LUNGULESCU, G., Horse Breeding
NĂFORNIŢĂ, M., Biology of Animal Reproduction
PLEŞCA, T., Zootechnical Construction
STANCIU, G., Technology of Cattle Breeding
VINTILĂ, C., Processing Technology for Animal Products
VINTILĂ, I., Animal Improvement

Faculty of Veterinary Medicine:

BOLTE, S., Surgery
CERNESCU, H., Animal Reproduction
COSOROABA, I., Parasitology
DECUN, M., Hygiene and Environmental Protection
FALCA, C., Semiology
MOGA-MANZAT, R., Infectious Diseases
POP, P., Medical Pathology
SINCAI, M., Histology
STUPARIU, M., Physiopathology
TRIF, AL., Pharmacology

Faculty of Horticulture:

BUTNARU, G., Genetics
BUTNARU, H., Vegetable Growing
DRĂGĂNESCU, E., Fruit Growing
NEDELEA, G., Plant Improvement
POP, A., Physiology

Faculty of Food Technology:

GĂRBĂU, Z., Biochemistry
JIANU, I., Food Technology

UNIVERSITATEA DE MEDICINĂ ŞI FARMACIE

4300 Tîrgu Mureş, Str. Gheorghe Marinescu 38
Telephone: (65) 21-31-27
Fax: (65) 21-04-07

Founded 1948
State control
Languages of instruction: Romanian, Hungarian
Academic year: October to September

Rector: Prof. Dr ION PASCU
Vice-Rectors: Prof. Dr LUDOVIC SERES-STURM, Prof. Dr SIMION COTOI
Chief Secretary: ELENA NISTOR
Scientific Secretary: Prof. Dr GEORGE SIMU
Librarian: FLORIN DAMIAN

Library of 281,000 vols
Number of teachers: 333
Number of students: 2,084

Publication: *Revista de Medicină şi Farmacie / Orvosi és Gyógyszerészeti Szemle* (2 a year).

DEANS

Faculty of Medicine: Prof. Dr MARIUS SABĂU
Faculty of Stomatology: Prof. Dr ALEXANDRU MONEA
Faculty of Pharmacy: Prof. Dr BÉLA TŐKÉS

PROFESSORS

Faculty of Medicine:

ANDREICUŢ, S., Cellular and Molecular Biology
BRASSAI, Z., Internal Medicine
BRATU, D., Internal Medicine
BUKARESTI, L., Biochemistry
BUŢIU, O., Dermatology
CHIOREAN, L., Genetics
CHIOREAN, M., Anaesthesiology and Intensive Care
COTOI, S., Internal Medicine
DEAC, R., Cardiac Surgery
DRAŞOVEANU, C., Otorhinolaryngology
DUDEA, C., Internal Medicine
GEORGESCU, C., Internal Medicine
GEORGESCU, T., General Surgery

GRECU, G., Psychiatry
MÓDY, E., Immunopathology
MUNTEAN, I., Paediatrics
NICOLAESCU, I., Biophysics
NICOLESCU, D., Urology
OLARIU, S. P., Obstetrics and Gynaecology
PAP, Z., Paediatrics
PASCU, I., Neurology
PASCU, R., Infectious Diseases
PÉTER, M., Microbiology
RĂDULESCU, C., Obstetrics and Gynaecology
ROŞCA, G., Histology
RUSNAC, C., Paediatrics
SABĂU, M., Physiology
SABĂU, M., Epidemiology
SERES-STURM, L., Anatomy and Embryology
STANCIU, G., Radiology
URECHE, R., Hygiene
VASILESCU, G., Endocrinology

Faculty of Stomatology:

BOCSKAY, S., Odontology
IEREMIA, L., Dental Prosthetics
MONEA, A., Odontology

Faculty of Pharmacy:

CSEDŐ, C., Pharmacognosy
POPOVICI, A., Pharmaceutical Technology

Other Institutes of Higher Education

Academia de Artă Bucureşti: 70744 Bucharest, Str. Gl. Budişteanu 19; tel. and fax 312-54-29; f. 1864; faculties of Fine Arts, Decorative Arts and Design, Art History, Theory of Art; 112 teachers, 747 students; library: see Libraries; Rector Prof. MIRCEA SPĂTARU.

Academia de Arte 'George Enescu': Iaşi, Str. Horia 7–9; tel. (32) 21-25-49; fax (32) 21-25-51; e-mail uarteis@ac.tuiosi.ro; f. 1860, renamed 1960; three faculties: composition, musicology and music pedagogy, theatre; plastic arts, decorative arts and design; musical interpretation; 216 teachers, 704 students; library of 135,000 vols, 7,000 records, 1,500 cassette tapes; Rector Prof. NICOLAE GĂSCĂ; Librarian IOAN BĂDULEŢ.

Academia de Arte Vizuale 'Ioan Andreescu' (Academy of Visual Arts 'Ioan Andreescu'): 3400 Cluj-Napoca, Piaţa Unirii 31; tel. (64) 19-15-77; fax (64) 19-28-90; f. 1950; faculties of fine arts and of decorative arts and design; 75 teachers, 553 students; library of 52,000 vols; Rector IOACHIM NICA; publ. termly bibliographical bulletin.

Academia Naţională de Educaţie Fizică şi Sport (National Academy of Physical Education and Sport): 77221 Bucharest, Str. Stefan Furtună 140, sector 6; tel. (1) 638-53-15; fax (1) 312-04-00; e-mail anefs@kappa.ro; f. 1922 (fmrly Institutul de Educatie Fizica şi Sport, renamed *c.* 1992); teacher training and army officer training, coaches and physiotherapists; 193 teachers, 2,500 students; library of 150,000 vols; Rector Prof. Dr IOAN SABAU; publ. *Discobolul*.

Academia de Muzică: 79551 Bucharest, Str. Stirbei Vodă 33; tel. 614-63-41; fax 615-83-96; f. 1864; faculties of performance and composition, musicology and musical pedagogy; 186 teachers, 800 students; library: see Libraries; Rector Prof. PETRE LEFTERESCU.

Academia de Muzică 'Gheorghe Dima': 3400 Cluj-Napoca, Str. I.C. Brătianu 25; tel. and fax (64) 19-38-79; e-mail amgd@amgd.edu.soroscj.ro; f. 1819, reorganized 1919; faculties of musical interpretation, composition, musicology and music education; 140 teachers, 628 students; library of 134,000 vols; Rector Prof. ALEXANDRU FĂRCAŞ; publ. *Lucrări de Muzicologie* (Musicological Works, annually).

Academia de Studii Economice: 70167 Bucharest, Piaţa Romană 6; tel. (1) 211-26-50; f. 1913; faculties of management, economics, agricultural and food production, economy and administration, finance and banking, administration and accounting, cybernetics, statistics and computer science for economics, trade, international economic relations, economic studies in foreign languages; college of economics at Buzău; 700 teachers; 22,000 students; library: see Libraries; Rector Prof. Dr PAUL BRAN; publs *Economic Computation and Economic Cybernetics Studies and Research* (quarterly, in Romanian and English), *Economics* (quarterly).

Institutul de Arhitectură 'Ion Mincu': 70109 Bucharest, Str. Academiei 18–20; tel. 613-80-80; fax 312-39-54; e-mail florin@gw.iaim.unibuc.ro; f. 1897; architecture and town planning; 140 teachers; 1,500 students; library of 203,000 vols; Rector Prof. Dr arch. ALEXANDRU M. SANDU; publ. *Simetria*.

Universitatea Agronomică şi de Medicină Veterinară 'Ion Ionescu de la Brad': 6600 Iaşi, Aleea M. Sadoveanu 3; tel. (32) 14-08-20; fax (32) 14-16-01; f. 1908; faculties of agriculture, horticulture, animal breeding and veterinary medicine; 325 teachers; 1,860 students; 185,000 vols in library; Rector Prof. Dr IOAN AVARVAREI; publ. *Lucrări Ştiinţifice* (3 a year).

Universitatea de Artă Teatrală şi Cinematografică 'J. L. Caragiale' (J. L. Caragiale University of Drama and Cinematography): 73224 Bucharest, Str. Matei Voievod 75–77; tel. (1) 252-80-20; fax (1) 252-58-81; f. 1954; 315 teachers, 437 students; library of 85,000 vols (including English theatre library of 5,000 vols); Rector Prof. FLORIN MIHĂILESCU.

Universitatea de Artă Teatrală Tîrgu-Mureş: (University of Dramatic Art of Tîrgu-Mureş): 4300 Tîrgu Mureş, Str. Köteles Sámuel 6; tel. (65) 16-62-81; fax (65) 16-27-49; f. 1948 (fmrly Institutul de Teatru 'Szentgyörgyi István'); depts of acting, stage direction, theatre studies, in both Romanian and Hungarian; 81 teachers, 130 students; library of 40,000 vols; Rector Prof. CĂLIN FLORIAN.

Universitatea de Medicină şi Farmacie: 1900 Timişoara, Str. Eftimie Murgu 2; tel. (56) 13-40-96; f. 1945 (fmrly Institutul de Medicină, renamed *c.* 1992); faculties of general medicine, paediatrics, stomatology; 294 teachers, 3,250 students; library of 195,000 vols; Rector Prof. Dr STEFAN DRĂGULESCU; publ. *Timişoara Medicală* (quarterly).

Universitatea de Medicină şi Farmacie 'Carol Davila': Bucharest, Str. Dionisie Lupu 37; tel. (1) 211-40-86; fax (1) 211-02-76; f. 1857 (fmrly Institutul de Medicina şi Farmacie, renamed 1990); faculties of general medicine, stomatology, pharmacy; postgraduate medical school; 1,189 teachers, 7,039 students; library: see Libraries; Rector Prof. Dr LAURENŢIU M. POPESCU.

Universitatea de Ştiinţe Agricole şi Medicină Veterinară Cluj-Napoca: 3400 Cluj-Napoca, Str. Mănăştur 3; tel. (64) 19-63-84; fax (64) 19-37-92; f. 1869 (fmrly Institutul Agronomic, renamed 1992); faculties of agriculture, horticulture, veterinary medicine and animal breeding; 208 teachers; 1,903 students; library of 207,000 vols; Rector Prof. Dr LEON MUNTEANU; publ. *Buletinul* (agricultural-horticultural series, animal husbandry-veterinary medicine series).

Universitatea de Ştiinţe Agronomice şi Medicină Veterinară Bucureşti: 71331 Bucharest, B-dul Mărăşti 59; tel. (1) 222-37-00; fax (1) 223-26-93; f. 1852 (fmrly Institutul Agronomic 'N. Bălcescu', renamed *c.* 1992); faculties of agriculture, horticulture, biotechnology, animal husbandry, veterinary medicine, and land reclamation and environmental engineering; 495 teachers, 3,797 undergraduate students, 275 postgraduates; library: see Libraries; Rector NICOLAI POMOHACI; publ. *Lucrări Ştiinţifice* (annually).

Universitatea Tehnică de Construcţii Bucureşti (Bucharest Technical University of Civil Engineering): 72302 Bucharest, Bd. Lacul Tei 124; tel. 242-12-08; f. 1864; faculties of civil, industrial and agricultural buildings, bridges, roads and railways, hydraulic engineering, building services, construction machines, geodesy and department of civil engineering and building services; 530 teachers, 6,964 students; library of 560,000 vols; Rector Prof. Dr Eng. PETRE PĂTRUŢ; publ. *Buletin Ştiinţific* (Scientific Bulletin, 4 a year).

RUSSIA

Learned Societies

GENERAL

Russian Academy of Sciences: 117901 Moscow, Leninsky pr. 14; tel. (095) 954-29-05; fax (095) 237-91-07; f. 1725; depts of Mathematics (Academician-Sec. L. D. Fadeyev), General Physics and Astronomy (Academician-Sec. A. A. Boyarchuk), Nuclear Physics (Academician-Sec. A. N. Skrinsky), Physical-Technical Problems of Power Engineering (Academician-Sec. O. N. Favorsky), Problems of Engineering, Mechanics and Control Processes (Academician-Sec. D. M. Klimov), Information Science, Computer Technology and Automation (Academician-Sec. S. V. Emelyanov), General and Technical Chemistry (Academician-Sec. V. A. Kabanov), Physical Chemistry and Technology of Inorganic Materials (Academician-Sec. Yu. A. Buslaev), Biochemistry and Biophysics (Academician-Sec. V. T. Ivanov), Physiology (Academician-Sec. Yu. V. Nitochkin), General Biology (Academician-Sec. V. E. Sokolov), Geology, Geophysics, Geochemistry and Mining Science (Academician-Sec. D. V. Rundkvist), Oceanology, Atmospheric Physics and Geography (Academician-Sec. Yu. A. Izrael, History (Academician-Sec. A. A. Fursenko), Philosophy, Sociology, Psychology and Law (Academician-Sec. B. N. Topornin), Economics (Academician-Sec. D. S. Lvov), Problems of the World Economy and International Relations (Academician-Sec. V. V. Zhurkin, Literature and Language (Academician-Sec. E. P. Chelyshev); Siberian division (630090 Novosibirsk, Pr. Akademika Lavrenteva 17; tel. 35-05-67; Chair. N. L. Dobretsov), incl. centres in Ulan-Ude and Yakutsk; Far Eastern division (690600 Vladivostok, Leninskaya 50; tel. 2-25-28; Chair. G. B. Elyakov); Urals division (620219 Ekaterinburg, Pervomaiskaya 91; tel. 44-02-23; Chair. G. A. Mesyats), incl. centres in Perm, Ufa and Komi; additional centres in Makhachkala, Petrozavodsk, Kazan and Apatity; 475 academicians, 694 corresp. mems, 177 foreign mems; attached research institutes: see Research Institutes; libraries and archive: see Libraries and Archives; Pres. Yu. S. Osipov; Chief Learned Sec. N. A. Platté; publs *Izvestiya Rossiiskoi Akademii Nauk* (Bulletin of the Russian Academy of Sciences, in 16 series: Biology, Geography, Literature and Language, Mathematics, Metals, Economics and Society, Mechanics of Liquids and Gases, Solid State Mechanics, Technical Cybernetics, Energy and Transport (6 a year); Geology, Inorganic Materials, Physics of Atmosphere and Ocean, Earth Physics, Physics, Chemistry (monthly)), *Doklady Rossiiskoi Akademii Nauk* (Proceedings of the Academy, 3 a month), *Izvestiya Sibirskogo otdeleniya Rossiiskoi Akademii Nauk* (Bulletin of the Siberian Branch of the Russian Academy of Sciences, in five series: Biological and Medical Sciences, History, Philology and Philosophy, Economics and Applied Sociology (4 a year); Technical Sciences, Chemical Sciences (6 a year)), *Nauka v Rossii* (Science in Russia, in Russian and English, 6 a year), *Vestnik Rossiiskoi Akademii Nauk* (Journal of the Russian Academy of Sciences, monthly), *Vestnik Dalnevostochnogo otdeleniya RAN* (Journal of the Far Eastern Division of the Russian Academy of Sciences).

Union of Scientific and Engineering Associations: 119034 Moscow, Kursovoi per. 17; tel. 290-62-86; fax 291-85-06; e-mail sitsev@mail.sitek.ru; Pres. Acad. I. Guliaev; Learned Sec. S. V. Pryanishnikov; Sec.-Gen. V. Sitsev.

AGRICULTURE, FISHERIES AND VETERINARY SCIENCE

Russian Academy of Agricultural Sciences: 107814 Moscow, Bolshoi Kharitonevsky per. 21; tel. (095) 207-39-42; f. 1992; depts of Plant Breeding and Genetics (Academician-Sec. V. S. Shevelukha), Arable Farming and the Use of Agricultural Chemicals (Academician-Sec. I. P. Makarov), Feed and Fodder Crops Production (Academician-Sec. (vacant)), Plant Protection (Academician-Sec. N. M. Golytsin), Livestock Production (Academician-Sec. (vacant)), Veterinary Science (Academician-Sec. V. P. Shishkov), Mechanization, Electrification and Automation in Farming (Academician-Sec. G. E. Listopad), Forestry (Academician-Sec. V. N. Vinogradov), the Economics and Management of Agricultural Production (Academician-Sec. (vacant)), Land Reform and the Organization of Land Use (Academician-Sec. (vacant)), Land Reclamation and Water Resources (Academician-Sec. B. B. Shumakov), the Storage and Processing of Agricultural Products (Academician-Sec. (vacant)); regional depts in St Petersburg (Non Black Soil Zone), Novosibirsk (Siberia), Khabarovsk (Far East); 150 mems, 128 corresp. mems, 73 foreign corresp. mems; attached research institutes: see Research Institutes; library: see Libraries and Archives; Pres. A. A. Nikonov; Chief Learned Sec. V. P. Shishkov; publs *Vestnik selskokhozyaistvennoi nauki* (Agricultural Science Journal), *Doklady* (Proceedings), *Mekhanizatsiya i elektrificatsiya selskogo khozyaistva* (Mechanization and Electrification of Agriculture), *Selskokhozyaistvennaya biologiya* (Agricultural Biology), *Selektsiya i Semenovodstvo* (Selection and Seed Science), *Sibirskii vestnik selskokhozyaistvennoi nauki* (Siberian Agricultural Science Journal).

Society of the Timber and Forestry Industry: 103062 Moscow, Ul. Chernyshevskogo 29; tel. 923-95-70; Chair. Yu. A. Yagodnikov.

Soil Science Society: 109017 Moscow, Pyzhevskii per. 7; tel. 231-43-59; attached to Russian Acad. of Sciences; Pres. G. V. Dobrovolsky.

ARCHITECTURE AND TOWN PLANNING

Union of Russian Architects: 103001 Moscow, Granatni per. 22; tel. 291-55-78; fax 202-81-01; f. 1932; 12,000 mems; First Sec. Yu. P. Gnedovsky.

ECONOMICS, LAW AND POLITICS

Association of International Law: 119841 Moscow, Ul. Frunze 10; attached to Russian Acad. of Sciences; Chair. Prof. G. I. Tunkin.

Association of Orientalists: 103753 Moscow, Ul. Rozhdestvenka 12; tel. 928-57-64; attached to Russian Acad. of Sciences; Chair. M. S. Kapitsa.

Association of Political Sciences: 118941 Moscow, Ul. Znamenka 10; attached to Russian Acad. of Sciences; Pres. Dr G. K. Shakhnazarov.

Association of Sinologists: 117218 Moscow, Nakhimovsky pr. 32; attached to Russian Acad. of Sciences; Pres. M. L. Titarenko.

Economics Society: 117259 Moscow, B. Cheremushkinskaya ul. 34; tel. 120-13-21; Chair. V. S. Pavlov.

Municipal Economy and Services Society: 103001 Moscow, Trekhprudny per. 11/13; tel. 299-83-00; Chair. A. F. Poryadin.

Society for Trade and Commerce: 121019 Moscow, Ul. Prechistenka 35, Stroenie 3; tel. 203-22-46; Chair. Yu. K. Tvildiani.

EDUCATION

Russian Academy of Education: 119905 Moscow, Pogodinskaya ul. 8; tel. (095) 245-16-41; fax (095) 248-51-70; e-mail oorao@tit-bit.msk.su; f. 1943; attached research institutes: see Research Institutes; library: see Libraries and Archives; Pres. Prof. A. V. Petrovsky; Chief Learned Sec. Prof. N. N. Nechaev; publs *Pedagogika* (Pedagogics, monthly), *Voprosy Psikhologii* (Problems of Psychology, monthly), *Defektologiya* (Defectology, every 2 months).

'Znanie': 101814 Moscow, Novaya pl. 3/4; tel. (095) 921-90-58; fax (095) 925-42-49; f. 1947; adult education; 500,000 mems; Chair Acad. I. F. Obraztsov.

FINE AND PERFORMING ARTS

International Confederation of Theatre Unions: 103009 Moscow, Tverskaya ul. 12, Stroenie 7, app. 228; tel. 209-24-36; fax 209-52-49; f. 1992; Pres. K. Yu. Lavrov.

Russian Academy of Arts: 119034 Moscow, Ul. Prechistenka 21; tel. and fax (095) 290-20-88; f. 1757; depts of Painting (Academician-Sec. T. T. Salakhov), Sculpture (Academician-Sec. Y. G. Orekhov), Graphic Art (Academician-Sec. M. P. Miturich-Khlebnikov), Decorative Arts (Academician-Sec. L. A. Sokolova), Architecture and Monumental Art (Academician-Sec. E. G. Rozanov); 66 mems, 81 corresp. mems; attached research institutes: see Research Institutes; library: see Libraries and Archives; Pres. Z. K. Tseretely; Chief Learned Sec. M. M. Kurilko-Ryumin.

Russian Union of Composers: Moscow, K-9, Bryusovsky per. 8/10; tel. and fax (095) 229-52-18; f. 1960; 1,336 mems; Chair. Vladislav Kazenin; publs *Muzikalnaya Akademia, Musical Life, Musical Review.*

Theatre Union of the Russian Federation: 103009 Moscow, Ul. Gorkogo 16/2; tel. 229-91-52; telex 411030; 30,124 mems; library of 300,000 vols; Chair. M. A. Ulyanov; publs *Information from the Secretariat* (quarterly), *Problems of Contemporary Theatre.*

Union of Arts of the Russian Federation: 103062 Moscow, Ul. Pokrovka 37.

Union of Russian Filmmakers: 123825 Moscow, Vasilevskaya 13; tel. 251-53-70.

HISTORY, GEOGRAPHY AND ARCHAEOLOGY

Russian Geographical Society: 190000 St Petersburg, tsentr, per. Grivtsova 10; tel. (812) 315-85-35; fax (812) 315-63-12; f. 1845; attached to Russian Acad. of Sciences; 20,000 mems; library of 470,000 vols, archive of 600,000 units; Pres. Prof. SERGEI B. LAVROV; publ. *Izvestiya RGS* (6 a year).

LANGUAGE AND LITERATURE

International Community of Writers' Unions: 121825 Moscow, Povarskaya ul. 52; tel. 291-63-07; f. 1992; 7,000 mems; Chair. G. M. MARKOV; First Sec. TIMUR PULATOV; publs *Literaturnaya Gazeta* (weekly), *Novyi Mir* (monthly), *Inostrannaya Literatura* (monthly).

Press Society: 103051 Moscow, Petrovka 26; tel. 921-82-98; Chair. B. A. KUZMIN.

Russian Association for Comparative Literature: 121069 Moscow, Ul. Vorovskogo 25A; tel. 290-17-09; attached to Russian Acad. of Sciences; Chair. Acad. YU. B. VIPPER.

Russian Linguistics Society: 103009 Moscow, Ul. Semashko 1/12; attached to Russian Acad. of Sciences; Chair. Acad. T. V. GAMKRELIDZE.

Russian PEN Centre: 103031 Moscow, Ul. Neglinnaya 18/1, Bldg 2; tel. 209-45-89; fax 200-02-93; e-mail 7416.g23@g23.relcom.ru; f. 1989; protection of freedom of expression, international exchange; writers in prison committee; 160 mems; Pres. ANDREI BITOV; Gen. Dir ALEXANDR TKACHENKO; publ. newsletter.

Union of Writers of the Russian Federation: 119087 Moscow, Komsomolsky pr. 13; tel. 246-43-50.

MEDICINE

Council of Scientific Medical Societies: 101431 Moscow, Rakhmanovskii per. 3; Chair. G. N. SERDYUKOVSKAYA; Learned Sec. S. S. YARMONENKO.

Federation of Anaesthesiologists and Reanimatologists: 125101 Moscow, Botkin Hospital K. 14; tel. 945-97-25; fax 945-97-25; e-mail damir@orc.ru; f. 1991 (fmrly All-Union Society, f. 1959); 600 mems; Chair. E. A. DAMIR; Sec. I. MOLCHANOV.

International Society for Pathophysiology: 125315 Moscow, Ul. Baltiiskaya 8; tel. 152-86-55; fax 151-95-40; 1,200 mems; Pres. Prof. GEORGY N. KRYZHANOVSKY; Sec.-Gen. VLADIMIR SHINKARENKO; publ. *International Journal of Pathophysiology* (every 2 months).

National Immunological Society: 115478 Moscow, Kashirskoe shosse 24/2; tel. 111-83-33; fax 117-10-27; f. 1983; 500 mems; Chair. R. V. PETROV; Gen. Sec. S. YU. SIDOROVICH; publ. *Immunologiya* (every 2 months).

National Medical and Technical Scientific Society: 129301 Moscow, Ul. Kasatkina 3; tel. 283-97-84; telex 412209; fax 187-37-34; f. 1968; 55,000 mems and 512 organizations; Central State Scientific Medical Library of 3,000,000 vols; Pres. B. I. LEONOV; Chief Learned Sec. B. E. BELOUSOV; publ. *Biomedical Engineering* (bi-monthly).

National Ophthalmological Society: 103064 Moscow, Ul. Sadovo-Chernogryazskaya 14/19; Chair. E. S. AVETISOV; Chief Learned Sec. T. I. FOROFONOFA; publ. *Vestnik oftalmologii* (every 2 months).

National Pharmaceutical Society: 117418 Moscow, Ul. Krasikova 34; Chair. M. T. ALYUSHIN; Chief Learned Sec. R. S. SKULKOVA.

National Scientific Medical Society of Anatomists, Histologists and Embryologists: 117869 Moscow, Ul. Ostrovityanova 1; Chair. V. V. KUPRIYANOV; Chief Learned Sec. V. V. KOROLEV.

National Scientific Medical Society of Endocrinologists: 117036 Moscow, Ul. Dm. Ulyanova 11; Chair. V. G. BARANOV; Chief Learned Sec. N. T. STARKOVA.

National Scientific Medical Society of Forensic Medical Officers: 123242 Moscow, Ul. Sadovaya-Kudrinskaya 32; Chair. A. B. KAPUSTIN; Chief Learned Sec. G. N. NAZAROV.

National Scientific Medical Society of Haemotologists and Transfusiologists: 125167 Moscow, Novozykovskii pr. 4-a; Chair. V. N. SHABALIN; Chief Learned Sec. M. P. KHOKHLOVA.

National Scientific Medical Society of Hygienists: 103064 Moscow, Mechnikova per. 5; Chair. G. N. SERDYUKOVSKAYA; Chief Learned Sec. A. G. SUKHAREV.

National Scientific Medical Society of Infectionists: 125284 Moscow, 1 Botkinskii pr. 3; Chair. V. N. NIKIFOROV; Chief Learned Sec. N. M. BELYAEVA.

National Scientific Medical Society of Nephrologists: 119021 Moscow, Ul. Rossolimo 11-A; tel. 248-53-33; f. 1969; holding of conferences, congresses, symposia; 1,200 mems; Chair. N. A. MUKHIN; Chief Learned Sec. S. O. ANDROSOVA.

National Scientific Medical Society of Neuropathologists and Psychiatrists: 119034 Moscow, Ul. Kropotkinskii per. 23; Chair. G. V. MOROZOV; Chief Learned Sec. G. Y. LUKACHER.

National Scientific Medical Society of Obstetricians and Gynaecologists: 113163 Moscow, Ul. Shabolovka 57; Chair. G. M. SAVELEVA; Chief Learned Sec. T. V. CHERVAKOVA.

National Scientific Medical Society of Oncologists: 188646 St Petersburg, pos. Pesochnyi-2, Ul. St. Petersbergskaya 68; Chair. N. P. NAPALKOV; Chief Learned Sec. E. S. KISELEVA.

National Scientific Medical Society of Oto-Rhino-Laryngologists: 119435 Moscow, Bolshaya Pirogovskaya 6; Chair. N. A. PREOBRAZHENSKII; Chief Learned Sec. N. P. KONSTANTINOVA.

National Scientific Medical Society of Paediatricians: 117963 Moscow, Lomonosovskii pr. 2/62; Chair M. YU. STUDENIKIN; Chief Learned Sec. G. V. YATSYK.

National Scientific Medical Society of Phthisiologists: 107564 Moscow, platforma Yauza, Ul. 6 kilometr Severnoi Zheleznoi Dorogi; Chair. A. G. KHOMENKO; Chief Learned Sec. V. V. EROKHIN.

National Scientific Medical Society of Physical Therapists and Health-Resort Physicians: 121099 Moscow, Kalinina pr. 50; Chair. A. N. OBROSOV; Chief Learned Sec. V. D. GRIGOREVA.

National Scientific Medical Society of Physicians in Curative Physical Culture and Sports Medicine: 117963 Moscow, Lomonosovskii pr. 2/62; Chair. S. V. KRUZSHEV; Chief Learned Sec. A. V. SOKOVA.

National Scientific Medical Society of Physicians-Analysts: 123242 Moscow, Ul. Sadovaya-Kudrinskaya 3; Chair. B. F. KOROVKIN; Chief Learned Sec. R. L. MARTSISHEVSKAYA.

National Scientific Medical Society of Roentgenologists and Radiologists: 117837 Moscow, Ul. Profsoyuznaya 86; Chair. A. S. PAVLOV; Chief Learned Sec. V. Z. AGRANAT.

National Scientific Medical Society of Stomatologists: 119435 Moscow, Ul. Pogodinskaya 5; Chair. N. N. BAZHANOV; Chief Learned Sec. V. M. BEZRUKOV.

National Scientific Medical Society of Surgeons: 119874 Moscow, Abrikosovskii per. 2; Chair. B. V. PETROVSKII; Chief Learned Sec. M. I. PERELMAN.

National Scientific Medical Society of the History of Medicine: 101838 Moscow, Petrovirigskii per. 6/8; Chair. YU. P. LISITSYN; Chief Learned Sec. I. V. VENGROVA.

National Scientific Medical Society of Therapists: 121500 Moscow, 3 Cherepkovskaya 15; Chair. A. S. SMETNEV; Chief Learned Sec. B. A. SIDORENKO.

National Scientific Medical Society of Toxicologists: 193019 St Petersburg, Ul. Bekhtereva 1; Chair. S. N. GOLIKOV; Chief Learned Sec. L. A. TIMOFEEVSKAYA.

National Scientific Medical Society of Traumatic Surgeons and Orthopaedists: 125299 Moscow, Ul. Priorova 10; Chair. YU. G. SHAPOSHNIKOV; Chief Learned Sec. S. M. ZHURAVLEV.

National Scientific Medical Society of Urological Surgeons: 105483 Moscow, Ul. 3-ya Parkovaya 51; tel. 164-96-52; f. 1925; 5,506 mems; Chair. N. A. LOPATKIN; Chief Learned Sec. A. F. DARENKOV; publ. *Urology and Nephrology* (every 2 months).

National Scientific Medical Society of Venereologists and Dermatologists: 107076 Moscow, Ul. Korolenko 3; Chair. O. K. SHAPOSHNIKOV; Chief Learned Sec. V. N. MORDOVTSEV.

Russian Academy of Medical Sciences: 109801 Moscow, Ul. Solyanka 14; tel. (095) 917-05-04; fax (095) 923-70-52; f. 1944; depts of Preventive Medicine (Academician-Sec. N. F. IZMEROV), Clinical Medicine (Academician-Sec. E. I. GUSEV), Medical and Biological Sciences (Academician-Sec. G. N. KRYZHANOVSKY); Siberian dept Academician-Sec. V. A. TRUFAKIN); 162 mems, 218 corresp. mems, 39 foreign mems; 60 specialist research ccls; attached research institutes: see Research Institutes; library: see Libraries and Archives; Pres. V. I. POKROVSKY; Gen. Sec. D. S. SARKISOV; publs *Vesti Meditsyny* (Medical News), *Vestnik Rossiiskoi Akademii Meditsinskikh Nauk* (Journal of the Russian Academy of Medical Sciences), *Arkhiv Patologii* (Pathology Archive), *Byulleten Eksperimentalnoi Biologii i Meditsiny* (Bulletin of Experimental Biology and Medicine), *Voprosy Virusologii* (Problems of Virology), *Voprosy Meditsinskoi Khimii* (Problems of Medical Chemistry), *Immunologiya* (Immunology), *Meditsinskaya Radiologiya* (Medical Radiology and Radiation Safety), *Morfologia* (Morphology), *Patologicheskaya Fiziologiya i Eksperimentalnaya Terapiya* (Pathological Physiology and Experimental Therapy), *Eksperimentalnaya i Klinicheskaya Pharmakologiya* (Experimental and Clinical Pharmacology), *Byulleten Sibirskogo Otdeleniya Rossiiskoi AMN* (Bulletin of the Siberian Division of the Russian Academy of Medical Sciences).

Russian Gastroenterological Association: 119881 Moscow, Ul. Pogodinskaya 5; tel. (095) 248-35-91; (095) 248-36-10; f. 1995; 2,500 mems; Pres. Prof. Dr. V. T. IVASHKIN; Sec. Dr A. S. TRUKHMANOV; publ. *Journal of Gastroenterology, Hepatology and Coloproctology* (6 a year).

Russian Neurosurgical Association: 603600 Nizhny Novgorod, Verkhne-Volskaya nab. 18; tel. (8312) 46-36-48; fax (8312) 36-05-95; Pres. A. P. FRAERMAN; Sec. S. N. KOLESOV.

Russian Pharmacological Society: 125315 Moscow, Ul. Baltiiskaya 8; tel. 151-18-81; fax 151-12-61; f. 1958 (fmrly All-Union Scientific Medical Soc. of Pharmacologists); 295 mems; library of 10,000 vols; Chair. D. A. KHARKEVICH; Chief Learned Sec. S. A. BORISENKO; publ. *Russian Journal of Experimental and Clinical Pharmacology.*

Russian Rheumatological Association: 115522 Moscow, Kashirskoye Shosse 34A; tel. 114-44-90; f. 1928; 1,418 mems; library of 82,872 vols; Chair. V. A. NASSONOVA; Gen. Sec. V. V. BADOKIN; publ. *Revmatologhia* (4 a year).

Russian Society of Medical Genetics: 115478 Moscow, Ul. Moskvoreche 1; tel. 111-85-94; fax 324-07-02; f. 1993; human genome project, human genetics, cytogenetics, clinical genetics, genetic counselling, experimental genetics, ecogenetics; 350 mems; Chair. E. K. GINTER; Chief Learned Sec. N. P. KULESHOV; publ. *Bulletin* (2 a year).

Scientific Medical Society of Anatomists-Pathologists: 109801 Moscow, Ul. Bolshaya Serpuhovskaya 27; Chair. D. S. SARKISOV.

Society of Cardiology: 101953 Moscow, Petroverigskii ul. 10; tel. 923-86-36; f. 1958; cardiology, diagnosis, treatment and prevention of cardiovascular disease; training courses; 10,000 mems; Pres. Dr RAPHAEL OGANOV; Sec. Dr NATALIA PEROVA; publ. *Kardiologiya* (monthly).

NATURAL SCIENCES

General

Moscow House of Scientists: 119821 Moscow, Kropotkinskaya ul. 16; tel. 201-45-55; attached to Russian Acad. of Sciences; Dir A. I. DERGACHEV.

St Petersburg M. Gorky House of Scientists: 191065 St Petersburg, Dvortsovaya nab. 26; tel. 315-88-14; attached to Russian Acad. of Sciences; Dir L. M. ANISIMOVA.

Biological Sciences

Biochemical Society: 117991 Moscow, Ul. Vavilova 34; tel. 135-97-79; attached to Russian Acad. of Sciences; Pres. Acad. S. E. SEVERIN.

Biotechnology Society: 109044 Moscow, B. Kommunisticheskaya ul. 27; tel. 272-67-49; Chair. V. E. MATVEYEV.

Hydrobiological Society: 103050 Moscow, Tverskaya ul. 27; tel. 299-65-04; attached to Russian Acad. of Sciences; Pres. L. M. SUSHCHENYA.

Microbiological Society: 117811 Moscow, Pr. 60-letiya Oktyabrya 7, Korp. 2; tel. 939-27-63; attached to Russian Acad. of Sciences; Pres. E. N. KONDRATEVA.

Moscow Society of Naturalists: 103009 Moscow, Ul. Gertsena 6; tel. 203-67-04; f. 1805; sections for zoology, botany, geology, hydrobiology, geography, biophysics, palaeontology, histology, experimental morphology, genetics, etc.; 2,700 mems; library of 500,000 vols; Chair A. L. YANSHIN; publ. *Byulleten Moskovskogo Obshchestva Ispytatelei prirody* (every 2 months).

Palaeontological Society: 199106 St Petersburg, Srednii Pr. 74; tel. (812) 218-91-56; attached to Russian Acad. of Sciences; Pres. Acad. B. S. SOKOLOV.

Russian Botanical Society: 197376 St Petersburg, Ul. Prof. Popova 2; tel. (812) 234-96-02; fax (812) 234-45-12; attached to Russian Acad. of Sciences; Pres. R. V. KAMELIN.

Russian Entomological Society: 199034 St Petersburg, Universitetskaya Nab. 1; tel. (812) 218-12-12; fax (812) 114-04-14; f. 1859; attached to Russian Acad. of Sciences; 2,000 mems; library of 80,000 vols; Pres. G. S. MEDVEDEV; publ. *Entomologicheskoe obozrenie* (4 a year).

Russian Society of Geneticists and Breeders: 117312 Moscow, Ul. Fersmana 11, Korp. 2; tel. 124-59-52; attached to Russian Acad. of Sciences; Pres. Acad. V. A. STRUNNIKOV.

Society of Helminthologists: 117259 Moscow, B. Cheremushkinskaya 28; attached to Russian Acad. of Sciences; Pres. A. S. BESSONOV.

Society of Ornithologists: 109240 Moscow, I-y Kotelnichesky per. 10; tel. 297-70-46; attached to Russian Acad. of Sciences; Pres. V. D. ILICHEV.

Society of Protozoologists: 194064 St Petersburg, Tikhoretsky pr. 4; tel. (812) 247-44-96; fax (812) 247-03-41; e-mail beyer@cit.ras.spb.ru; f. 1968; attached to Russian Acad. of Sciences; 200 mems; Pres. Prof. Dr IGOR B. RAIKOV; Sec.-Gen. Prof. Dr TAMARA V. BEYER.

Physical Sciences

Astronomical and Geodesical Society: 103001 Moscow, Sadovo-Kudrinskaya ul. 24; attached to Russian Acad. of Sciences; Pres. YU. D. BULANZHE.

Ferrous Metallurgy Society: 129812 Moscow, Pr. Mira 101; tel. 287-83-80; Chair. N. I. DROZDOV.

Geological Society: 113191 Moscow, 2-Roshinskaya ul. 10; tel. 237-33-33; Chair. V. F. ROGOV.

Gubkin, Acad. I. M., Petroleum and Gas Society: 117876 Moscow, 12-ya Parkovaya ul. 5; tel. 463-93-72; Chair. S. T. TOPLOV.

Mendeleev, D. I., Chemical Society: 101907 Moscow, Krivokolennyi per. 12; tel. 925-72-85; Chair. A. V. FOKIN.

Russian Mineralogical Society: 199026 St Petersburg, V. O., 21 liniya 2; tel. 218-86-40; attached to Russian Acad. of Sciences; Pres. Acad. D. V. RUNDKVIST; publ. *Zapiski*.

Society of Non-Ferrous Metallurgy: 103001 Moscow, Sadovaya-Kudrinskaya ul. 18; tel. 291-29-87; Chair. V. S. LOBANOV.

PHILOSOPHY AND PSYCHOLOGY

Philosophy Society: 121002 Moscow, Smolensky bul. 20; tel. 201-24-02; f. 1972; attached to Russian Acad. of Sciences; 1,750 mems; Pres. I. T. FROLOV.

Society of Psychologists: 129366 Moscow, Yaroslavskaya ul. 13; tel. 282-45-03; attached to Russian Acad. of Sciences; Chair. E. V. SHOROKHOVA.

RELIGION, SOCIOLOGY AND ANTHROPOLOGY

Russian Society of Sociologists: 117259 Moscow, Ul. Krzhizhanovskogo 24/35 b. 5; tel. (095) 719-09-71; fax (095) 719-07-40; e-mail valman@socio.msk.su; f. 1989; attached to Russian Acad. of Sciences; Chair. T. I. ZASLAVSKAYA.

TECHNOLOGY

Aircraft Building Society: 125040 Moscow, Leningradskii pr. 24a; tel. 214-22-88; Chair. A. M. BATKOV.

Civil Engineering Society: 103062 Moscow, Podsosensky per. 25; tel. 297-07-29; Chair. I. I. ISHENKO.

Computers and Informatics Society: 127486 Moscow, Deguninskaya ul. 1, Korp. 4; tel. 487-31-61; Chair. I. N. BUKREYEV.

Mapping and Prospecting Engineering Society: 117801 Moscow, Ul. Krzhizhanovskogo 14, Kor. 2; tel. 124-35-60; Chair. A. A. DRAZHNYUK.

Mechanical Engineering Society: 109004 Moscow, Ul. Zemlyanoi Val 64, Kor. 1; tel. 297-93-00; Chair. B. N. SOKOLOV.

Mining Engineers' Society: 103006 Moscow, Karetnyi ryad 10/18; tel. 299-88-15; Chair. A. P. FISUN.

Paper and Wood-Working Society: 103012 Moscow, Nikolskaya ul. 8/1, Kv. 12; tel. 924-47-28; Chair. YU. A. GUSKOV.

Popov, A. S., Radio Engineering, Electronics and Telecommunications Society: 103897 Moscow, Kuznetskii Most 20/6; tel. 921-71-08; Chair. YU. V. GULYAEV.

Power and Electrical Power Engineering Society: 191025 St Petersburg, Stremyannaya ul. 10; tel. 311-32-77; Chair. N. N. TIKHODEYEV.

Scientific-Technical Association: 198103 St Petersburg, Pr. Ogorodnikova 26; tel. 251-28-50; attached to Russian Acad. of Sciences; General Dir M. L. ALEKSANDROV.

Shipbuilding Engineering Society: 191011 St Petersburg, Nevskii pr. 44; tel. 315-50-27; Chair. I. V. GORYNIN.

Society for Railway Transport: 107262 Moscow, Staraya Basmannaya ul. 11; tel. 262-61-80; Chair. G. M. KORENKO.

Society of Light Industry: 117846 Moscow, Ul. Vavilova 69; tel. 134-90-01; Chair. R. A. CHAYANOV.

Society of the Food Industry: 103031 Moscow, Kuznetskii most 19, Podezd 2; tel. 924-49-30; Chair. A. N. BOGATYREV.

Society of the Instrument Manufacturing Industry and Metrologists: 103009 Moscow, Tverskaya ul. 12, Stroenie 2; tel. 209-47-98; Chair. G. I. KAVALEROV.

Vavilov, S. I., Society of Instrument Manufacturers: 121019 Moscow, Mokhovaya ul. 17, Stroenie 2; tel. 203-34-65.

Water Transport Society: 103012 Moscow, Staropansky per. 3; tel. 921-18-12; Chair. (vacant).

Research Institutes

AGRICULTURE, FISHERIES AND VETERINARY SCIENCE

Adygea Agricultural Research Institute: 352764 Krasnodar krai, Maikop, Podgornoe; attached to Russian Acad. of Agricultural Sciences.

Afanasev, V. A., Research Institute for the Breeding and Production of Rabbits and Fur-Bearing Animals: 140143 Moscow oblast, Ramensky raion, p/o Rodniki; tel. 558-72-83; attached to Russian Acad. of Agricultural Sciences; Dir V. N. POMYTKO.

Agrarian Institute: 103064 Moscow, B. Kharitonevskaya per. 21, Korp. 2, POB 34; tel. (095) 207-70-75; fax (095) 928-22-90; e-mail agrin@glas.apc.org; f. 1990; attached to Russian Acad. of Agricultural Sciences; Dir Dr A. V. PETRIKOV.

Agricultural Research Institute for the Central Areas of the Non-Black Soil (Nechernozem) Zone: 143104 Moscow oblast, Odintsovsky raion, Nemchinovka, Ul. Agrokhimikov 6; tel. 591-83-91; attached to Russian Acad. of Agricultural Sciences.

Agrophysical Research Institute: 195220 St Petersburg, Grazhdanskii Pr.14; tel. 543-46-30; attached to Russian Acad. of Agricultural Sciences; Dir I. B. USKOV.

All-Russia Legumes and Pulse Crops Research Institute: 303112 Orel, P/O Streletskoe; attached to Russian Acad. of Agricultural Sciences; Dir F. K. CHAPURIN.

All-Russia Maize Research Institute: 860022 Nalchik, Ul. Mechnikova 130A; tel. 5-03-16; attached to Russian Acad. of Agricultural Sciences.

All-Russia Meat Research Institute: 109316 Moscow, Ul. Talilikhina 26; tel. (095) 276-95-11; fax (095) 276-95-51; e-mail vniimp@glasnet.ru; f. 1930; attached to Russian Acad. of Agricultural Sciences; Dir L. A. BORISOVICH; publ. *Proceedings* (1 a year).

All-Russia Potato Research Institute: 140052 Moscow oblast, Lyuberetsky raion, pos. Korenevo, Ul. Lorkha; tel. and fax (095) 557-10-11; f. 1930; attached to Russian Acad.

of Agricultural Sciences; library of 500,000 vols; Dir Prof. A. V. KORSHUNOV; publ. *Proceedings* (1 a year).

All-Russia Poultry Research and Technology Institute: Moscow oblast, Sergiev Posad; attached to Russian Acad. of Agricultural Sciences.

All-Russia Rapeseed Research and Technological Institute: 398037 Lipetsk, Boevoi pr. 26, Kod 074; tel. 26-08-64; attached to Russian Acad. of Agricultural Sciences.

All-Russia Research and Technological Institute for Chemical Land Reclamation: 189520 St Petersburg, Pushkin, Ul. Lermontova 9; tel. 465-58-75; attached to Russian Acad. of Agricultural Sciences.

All-Russia Research and Technological Institute for Chemicalization in Agriculture: 143013 Moscow oblast, Odinstsovsky raion, Nemchinovka, Ul. Agrokhimikov 6; tel. 591-91-73; attached to Russian Acad. of Agricultural Sciences.

All-Russia Research and Technological Institute for Mechanization in Livestock Raising: 142004 Moscow oblast, Podolsky raion, p/o Znamya Oktyabrya; 31; tel. 119-74-97; fax 119-75-17; f. 1969; attached to Russian Acad. of Agricultural Sciences; Dir N. M. MOROZOV; publ. *Scientific Research Problems of Mechanization and Automation of Livestock Farming*.

All-Russia Research and Technological Institute for Organic Fertilizers: 601242 Vladimir oblast, Vyatkino; attached to Russian Acad. of Agricultural Sciences.

All-Russia Research Institute for Agricultural Biotechnology: 127550 Moscow, Timiryazevskaya ul. 42; tel. 976-65-44; fax 977-09-47; attached to Russian Acad. of Agricultural Sciences; Dir G. S. MUROMSTSEV.

All-Russia Research Institute for Agricultural Economics and Standards and Norms: 344006 Rostov on Don, Pr. Sokolova 52; tel. and fax (8632) 65-31-81; f. 1980; attached to Russian Acad. of Agricultural Sciences.

All-Russia Research Institute for Beef Cattle Breeding and Production: Orenburg, Yanvarskaya ul. 29; attached to Russian Acad. of Agricultural Sciences.

All-Russia Research Institute for Biological Control: 350039 Krasnodar, a/ya 39; tel. 50-81-91; attached to Russian Acad. of Agricultural Sciences.

All-Russia Research Institute for Cybernetics in the Agro-industrial Complex: 117218 Moscow, Ul. Krzhizhanovskogo 14/1; tel. 124-76-02; attached to Russian Acad. of Agricultural Sciences.

All-Russia Research Institute for Economics, Labour and Management in Agriculture: 111621 Moscow, Orenburgskaya ul. 15; tel. 550-06-71; attached to Russian Acad. of Agricultural Sciences.

All-Russia Research Institute for Electrification in Agriculture: 109456 Moscow, 1-i Veshnyakovskii pr. 2; tel.(095) 171-19-20; fax (095) 170-51-01; e-mail energy@viesh.msk.su; f. 1930; attached to Russian Acad. of Agricultural Sciences; library of 135,000 vols; Dir Acad. D. S. STREBKOV.

All-Russia Research Institute for Flowers and Tropical Crops: 354002 Sochi, Ul. Fabrikiusa 2/28; tel. 92-73-61; attached to Russian Acad. of Agricultural Sciences.

All-Russia Research Institute for Horse Breeding: 391128 Ryazan oblast, Rybnovsky raion; tel. 32-216; fax (096) 904-74-88; f. 1930; attached to Russian Acad. of Agricultural Sciences; library of 47,000 vols; publs *Stud Book* (every 4 years, with annual supplement), *Scientific Works* (annually).

All-Russia Research Institute for Irrigated Arable Farming: 400002 Volgograd, Timiryazevskaya ul. 9; tel. (8442) 43-49-79; fax (8442) 43-34-75; f. 1967; attached to Russian Acad. of Agricultural Sciences; library of 138,000 vols; Dir Dr I. P. KRUZHILIN.

All-Russia Research Institute for Irrigated Horticulture and Vegetable Crops Production: 416300 Astrakhan oblast, Kamyziak, Ul. Lubicha 13; attached to Russian Acad. of Agricultural Sciences.

All-Russia Research Institute for Mechanization in Agriculture: 109389 Moscow, 1-i Institutskii Pr. 5; tel. 171-19-33; attached to Russian Acad. of Agricultural Sciences; Dir Acad. V. A. KUIBYSHEV.

All-Russia Research Institute for Sheep and Goat Breeding: 355014 Stavropol, Zootekhnichesky per. 15; tel. 4-76-88; attached to Russian Acad. of Agricultural Sciences.

All-Russia Research Institute for the Agricultural Use of Reclaimed and Improved Land: 171330 Tver oblast, Emmaus; tel. (0822) 37-15-46; fax (0822) 36-07-63; f. 1977; attached to Russian Acad. of Agricultural Sciences; library of 20,000 vols; Dir Dr N. KOVALEV; publ. *Proceedings*.

All-Russia Research Institute for the Biosynthesis of Protein Substances: 109004 Moscow, B. Kommunisticheskaya ul. 27; tel. 272-70-09; attached to Russian Acad. of Agricultural Sciences.

All-Russia Research Institute for Vegetable Breeding and Seed Production: 143000 Moscow oblast, Odintsovsky raion, Lesnoi gorodok; tel. 593-52-26; attached to Russian Acad. of Agricultural Sciences.

All-Russia Research Institute for Veterinary Sanitation, Hygiene and Ecology: 123022 Moscow, Zvenigorodskoe shosse 5; tel. 256-35-81; attached to Russian Acad. of Agricultural Sciences.

All-Russia Research Institute of Agricultural Microbiology: 189620 St Petersburg-Pushkin 8, Shosse Podbelskogo 3; tel. (812) 470-51-00; fax (812) 470-43-62; f. 1930; attached to Russian Acad. of Agricultural Sciences; Dir Prof. I. A. TIKHONOVICH.

All-Russia Research Institute of Animal Husbandry: 142023 Moskovskaya oblast, Podolskii raion, Pos. Dubrovitsy; tel. 546-63-35; attached to Russian Acad. of Agricultural Sciences; Dir Acad. A. P. KALASHNIKOV.

All-Russia Research Institute of Arable Farming and Soil Erosion Protection: 305021 Kursk, Ul. Karla Marksa 70B; tel. (071) 33-42-56; fax (071) 33-67-29; f. 1970; attached to Russian Acad. of Agricultural Sciences; library of 20,000 vols, 40 periodicals; Dir V. M. VOLODIN.

All-Russia Research Institute of Economics in Agriculture: 123007 Moscow, Khoroshevskoe shosse 35, korp 3; tel. 195-60-16; attached to Russian Acad. of Agricultural Sciences; Dir I. G. USHCHACHEV.

All-Russia Research Institute of Information, Technological and Economic Research on the Agro-Industrial Complex: 107139 Moscow, Orlikov per. 3, Korp. A; tel. 204-43-60; attached to Russian Acad. of Agricultural Sciences; Dir Acad. V. I. NAZARENKO.

All-Russia Research Institute of Marine Fisheries and Oceanography: 107140 Moscow, Verkhnyaya Krasnoselskaya 17; tel. 264-93-87; Dir A. S. BOGDANOV.

All-Russia Research Institute of Medicinal and Aromatic Plants: 113628 Moscow, Ul. Grina 7; tel. 382-83-18; attached to Russian Acad. of Agricultural Sciences.

All-Russia Research Institute of Phytopathology: 143050 Moscow oblast, Vyazemy; tel. 592-92-87; attached to Russian Acad. of Agricultural Sciences.

All-Russia Research Institute of Plant Protection: 188620 St Petersburg, Pushkin, Shosse Podbelskogo 3; tel. 470-51-10; attached to Russian Acad. of Agricultural Sciences; Dir K. V. NOVOZHILOV.

All-Russia Research Institute of Plant Quarantine: 140150 Moscow oblast, Ramensky raion, pos. Bykovo, Pogranichnaya 32; tel. 556-23-29; f. 1979; library of 10,000 vols; Dir Dr ANATOLIY I. SMETNIK; Scientific Sec. Dr ELENA V. TERESHKOVA; publ *Problems of Plant Quarantine*.

All-Russia Research Institute of Pond Fishery: 141821 Moscow oblast, Dmitrovsky raion, p/o Rubnoe; tel. 587-21-98; attached to Russian Acad. of Agricultural Sciences.

All-Russia Research Institute of Tobacco, Makhorka and Tobacco Products: Krasnodar, A/Ya 55; attached to Russian Acad. of Agricultural Sciences.

All-Russia Rice Research Institute: 353204 Krasnodarskii krai, Dinskoi raion, Pos. Belozernoe; tel. (8612) 56-65-96; telex 279117; fax (8612) 50-91-24; attached to Russian Min. of Agriculture; Dir Prof. E. P. ALESHIN.

All-Russia Vegetable Production Research Institute: 141018 Moscow oblast, Mytishchi, Novomytishchinsky pr. 82; tel. 582-00-15; attached to Russian Acad. of Agricultural Sciences.

All-Russia Veterinary Research Institute for Poultry Diseases: St Petersburg, Moskovsky pr. 99; attached to Russian Acad. of Agricultural Sciences.

Altai Experimental Farm: 659739 Altaisky krai, Gorno-Altaisky avt. obl., Shebalinsky raion, selo Cherga; tel. 3-80; attached to Russian Acad. of Sciences; Dir YU. S. ZEMIROV.

Bashkir Research and Technological Institute for Animal Husbandry and Feed Production: 450025 Ufa, Pushkinskaya ul. 86, Kod 347; tel. 22-17-23; attached to Russian Acad. of Agricultural Sciences.

Bashkir Research Institute for Arable Farming and Field Crops Breeding: 450059 Ufa, Ul. Zorge 19; tel. 24-07-08; attached to Russian Acad. of Agricultural Sciences.

Caspian Research Institute for Arid Arable Farming: 431213 Astrakhan, Solenoe zaimishche; tel. (851) 24-38-36; fax (851) 192-17-00; f. 1991; attached to Russian Acad. of Agricultural Sciences; library of 30,000 vols.

Chelyabinsk Agricultural Research Institute: 436404 Chelyabinsk oblast, Chebarkulsky raion, Timiryazevsky; tel. 33-23-16; attached to Russian Acad. of Agricultural Sciences.

Daghestan Agricultural Research Institute: 367014 Makhachkala, Pr. K. Marksa, Nauchnyi park; tel. 3-66-60; attached to Russian Acad. of Agricultural Sciences.

Dokuchaev, V. V., Central Black Soil (Chernozem) Agricultural Research Institute: 397463 Voronezh oblast, Talov raion; attached to Russian Acad. of Agricultural Sciences.

Dokuchaev, V. V., Institute of Soil Science: 109017 Moscow, Pyzhevsky per. 7; tel. 231-50-37; attached to Russian Acad. of Agricultural Sciences; Dir Acad. V. V. YEGOROV.

Don Zone Agricultural Research Institute: 346714 Rostov oblast, Aksai raion, Rassvet; attached to Russian Acad. of Agricultural Sciences.

Flax Research Institute: 172060 Tverskii raion, Torzhok, Ul. Lunacharskogo 35; tel. 5-

16-45; fax 5-44-58; f. 1930; library of 50,000 vols; Dir ANATOLI N. MARCHENKOV; publ. *Trudy VNIL* (annually).

Horticulture Zonal Research Institute for the Non-Black Soil (Nechernozem) Zone: 115598 Moscow, Birulevo, Zagorie; tel. 329-31-44; attached to Russian Acad. of Agricultural Sciences.

Institute of Forestry: 620134 Ekaterinburg, Bilimbaevskaya ul. 32A; tel. 52-08-80; attached to Russian Acad. of Sciences; Dir. S. A. MAMAEV.

Institute of Forestry: 185610 Petrozavodsk, Pushkinskaya ul. 11; tel. and fax (8142) 77-81-60; e-mail krutov@post.krc.karelia.ru; f. 1957; attached to Russian Acad. of Sciences; Dir Dr VITALY KRUTOV.

Institute of Forestry: 143030 Moscow oblast, Odintsovsky raion, p/o Uspenskoe; tel. and fax 561-65-90; f. 1958; attached to Russian Acad. of Sciences; library of 51,000 vols; Dir S. E. VOMPERSKY; publ. *Lesovedenie* (Russian Forest Science, 6 a year).

Institute of Soil Science and Agrochemistry: 630099 Novosibirsk, Sovetskaya 18; tel. 22-53-58; attached to Russian Acad. of Sciences; Dir I. M. GADZHIEV.

Kovalenko, Ya. R., All-Russia Institute of Experimental Veterinary Science: 109472 Moscow, Kuzminki; tel. 377-29-79; attached to Russian Acad. of Agricultural Sciences; Dir G. F. KOROMYSLOV.

Krasnodar Research Institute for Soil Science and Agrochemistry: 350011 Krasnodar, Starokubanskaya ul. 2; tel. 33-82-49; attached to Russian Acad. of Agricultural Sciences.

Krasnodar Vegetable and Potato Production Research Institute: 353204 Krasnodar, Belozerny; tel. 50-92-04; attached to Russian Acad. of Agricultural Sciences.

Kursk Research Institute of the Agroindustrial Complex: 307026 Kursk oblast, Cheremushki; attached to Russian Acad. of Agricultural Sciences.

Lukianenko, P. P., Krasnodar Agricultural Research Institute: 350012 Krasnodar; tel. 56-28-15; attached to Russian Acad. of Agricultural Sciences.

Michurin, I. V., All-Russia Research Institute for Genetics and Breeding in Horticulture: 393740 Michurinsk oblast, Tambovskaya 10; tel. 4-23-52; attached to Russian Acad. of Agricultural Sciences; Dir G. A. KURSAKOV.

Michurin, I. V., All-Russia Research Institute for Horticulture: 393740 Tambov oblast, Michurinsk, Ul. Michurina 30; tel. 4-21-32; attached to Russian Acad. of Agricultural Sciences.

Nizhne-Volzhsky Agricultural Research Institute: 404013 Volgograd oblast, Nizheznensky; attached to Russian Acad. of Agricultural Sciences.

North Caucasus Mountains and Foothills Agricultural Research Institute: 363110 North Ossetia, Prigorny raion, Mikhailovskoe; attached to Russian Acad. of Agricultural Sciences.

North Caucasus Research Institute for Horticulture and Viticulture: 350029 Krasnodar, Ul. 40-letiya Pobedy 9; tel. 54-06-74; attached to Russian Acad. of Agricultural Sciences.

Orenburg Agricultural Research Institute: 460051 Orenburg, Ul. Gagarina 27/1; tel. 3-86-94; attached to Russian Acad. of Agricultural Sciences.

Pacific Scientific Research Institute of Fisheries and Oceanography (TINRO): 690600 Vladivostok, Ul. Shevchenko 4; tel. and fax (4232) 257783; f. 1925; ichthyology, oceanography, commercial invertebrates, commercial marine algae, parasitology of marine animals, commercial fisheries, mechanization of fish processing, technology of fish and marine production, aquaculture (marine and freshwater), study of marine pollution; brs at Kamchatka, Sakhalin, Amur (Khabarovsk), Magadan; library of 100,000 vols, 11,000 MSS; Dir Dr V. N. AKULIN; publ. *Izvestiya TINRO* (1–3 a year).

Potapenko, I. I., All-Russia Research Institute for Viticulture: 346421 Novocherkassk, Rostov, Pr. Platova 166; tel. 2-20-88; attached to Russian Acad. of Agricultural Sciences.

Povolzhsky Research Institute for the Economics and Development of the Agroindustrial Complex: 410020 Saratov, Ul. Shekhurdina 12; tel. 64-06-47; attached to Russian Acad. of Agricultural Sciences.

Pryanishnikov, D. N., All-Russia Research Institute of Fertilizers and Agropedology: 127550 Moscow, Ul. Pryanishnikova 31; tel. 976-01-75; attached to Russian Acad. of Agricultural Sciences; Dir N. Z. MILASHENKO.

Pustovoit, V. S., All-Russia Oil-Bearing Crops Research Institute: 350038 Krasnodar, Ul. Filatova 17; tel. 55-59-33; f. 1912; attached to Russian Acad. of Agricultural Sciences; library of 130,000 vols; Dir-Gen. V. P. BRAZHNIK; publ. *Bulletin of Scientific Information on Oil Crops* (1 a year).

Research and Technological Institute for Agricultural Biotechnology: 410020 Saratov, Ul. Tulaikova 7; tel. 64-04-31; attached to Russian Acad. of Agricultural Sciences.

Research Institute for Animal Nutrition: Moscow oblast, Dmitrovsky raion, pos. Ermolovo.

Research Institute for Breeding and Diversity in Horticulture: 303130 Orel, Zhilina; attached to Russian Acad. of Agricultural Sciences.

Research Institute of Agricultural Forest Reclamation: 400062 Volgograd, Krasnopresnenskaya ul. 39; tel. 43-40-02; fax 43-34-72; f. 1931; attached to Russian Acad. of Agricultural Sciences; library of 93,700 vols; Dir K. N. KULIK; publ. *Scientific Papers* (2 a year).

Research Institute of Chemical Means of Plant Protection: 109088 Moscow, Ugreshskaya 31; tel. 279-55-40; Dir N. N. YUKHTIN.

Research Institute of Farm Animal Physiology, Biochemistry and Nutrition: 249010 Kaluzhskaya oblast, Borovsk; attached to Russian Acad. of Agricultural Sciences; Dir Acad. V. I. GEORGIEVSKII.

Research Institute of Livestock Breeding and Genetics: 189620 St Petersburg, Pushkin, Moskovskoe shosse 55A; tel. 465-02-62; attached to Russian Acad. of Agricultural Sciences; Dir Acad. N. G. DMITRIEV.

Research Institute of Non-infectious Animal Diseases: Moscow oblast, Istrinsky raion.

Research Institute of Technological Studies in Agricultural Cybernetics: 107139 Moscow, Orlikov per. 1/11, korp 3A; attached to Russian Acad. of Agricultural Sciences.

Research Institute of the Economics and Development of the Agro-industrial Complex in the Central Black Soil (Chernozem) Zone: 394042 Voronezh, Ul. Sarafimovicha 23A; tel. 23-44-68; attached to Russian Acad. of Agricultural Sciences.

Research Institute of Veterinary Entomology and Arachnology: 625010 Tyumen, Institutskaya ul. 2; attached to Russian Acad. of Agricultural Sciences; Dir V. Z. YAMOV.

Russian Research Institute of Agricultural Radiology and Agroecology: 249020 Kaluga oblast, Obninsk; tel. (08439) 6-48-02; fax (095) 255-22-25; e-mail acr@wdc.meteo.ru; f. 1971; attached to Russian Acad. of Agricultural Sciences; library of 45,000 vols; Dir R. M. ALEXAKHIN.

St Petersburg Forestry Research Institute: 194021 St Petersburg, Institutsky pr. 21; tel. (812) 552-80-21; fax (812) 552-80-42; e-mail serg@forest.spb.su; f. 1929; library of 90,000 vols; Dir A. F. CHMYR; publ. *Proceedings*.

Samoilov, Ya. V., Research Institute of Fertilizers and Insectofungicides: 117333 Moscow, Leninskii Pr. 55; tel. 135-20-32; Dir V. M. BORISOV.

Skryabin, K. I., All-Russia Institute of Helminthology: 117259 Moscow, Bolshaya Cheremushkinskaya, 28; tel. 124-56-55; attached to Russian Acad. of Agricultural Sciences; Dir Acad. V. S. ERSHOV.

South Urals Agricultural Research Institute: 454002 Chelyabinsk, Shershni; tel. 42-42-01; attached to Russian Acad. of Agricultural Sciences.

South-East Agricultural Research Institute: 410020 Saratov, Ul. Tulaykova 7; tel. and fax (8452) 64-76-88; e-mail ariser@mail.saratov.ru; f. 1910; attached to Russian Acad. of Agricultural Sciences; library of 350,000 vols; Dir NIKOLAI I. KOMAROV.

Stavropol Agricultural Research Institute: 356200 Stavropol krai, Shpakovskoe; attached to Russian Acad. of Agricultural Sciences.

Sukachev, V. N., Institute of Forestry: 660036 Krasnoyarsk, Akademgorodok; tel. and fax (3912) 43-36-86; e-mail dndr@ifor.krasnoyarsk.su; f. 1944; attached to Russian Acad. of Sciences; library of 200,000 vols; Dir E. A. VAGANOV.

Tula Agricultural Research Institute: 301053 Tula oblast, Molochnye dvory; tel. (08752) 5-23-41; fax (08752) 2-30-15; f. 1956; attached to Russian Acad. of Agricultural Sciences; Dir Prof. V. I. SEVEROV.

Tulaikov, M. M., Samara Agricultural Research Institute: 446080 Samara oblast, Bezenchuk, Ul. K. Marksa 41; attached to Russian Acad. of Agricultural Sciences.

Ulyanovsk Agricultural Research Institute: 433115 Ulyanovsk oblast, Timiryazevskoe; tel. 31-78-58; attached to Russian Acad. of Agricultural Sciences.

Vavilov, N. I., Research Institute of Plant Breeding: 190000 St Petersburg, Ul. Gertsena 44; tel. 314-22-34; attached to Russian Acad. of Agricultural Sciences; Dir (vacant).

Vilyams, V. R., All-Russia Fodder Research Institute: 141740 Moscow oblast, Mytishchi raion, Lugovaya stantsiya; tel. 578-76-51; attached to Russian Acad. of Agricultural Sciences.

ARCHITECTURE AND TOWN PLANNING

Central Research and Design Institute of Dwellings: 127434 Moscow, Dmitrovskoe shosse 9, Korp. 8; tel. 976-28-19; telex 411357; fax 976-37-82; f. 1962; Dir STANISLAV V. NIKOLAEV.

Central Research and Design Institute of Town Planning: 117944 Moscow, Pr. Vernadskogo 29; tel. (095) 138-28-06; fax (095) 133-11-29; f. 1963; library of 25,000 vols; Dir YU. N. MAXIMOV.

Kucherenko, V. A., State Central Research and Experimental Design Institute for Complex Problems of Civil Engineering and Building Structures: 109428 Moscow, 2-ya Institutskaya 6; tel. 171-

26-50; fax 171-28-58; f. 1927; VASIL GORPINCHENKO; publs *Strength and Reliability of Structures, Numerical Methods of Analysis and Optimization of Building Structures, Investigations into Structural Earthquake Resistance, Timber Structures, Structural Dynamics* (all every 2 years), *New Forms and Strength of Metal Structures, Large-Panel and Masonry Structures* (both every 3 years), *Phosphate Materials, Investigation into Building Structures* (both annually), *Earthquake Engineering* (6 a year).

Panfilov, K. D., Academy of Municipal Economics: 123371 Moscow, Volokolamskoe shosse 116; tel. 490-31-66; telex 411088; fax 490-36-00; f. 1931; depts of scientific-technical co-ordination, municipal electrical supply, urban electric transport, anti-corrosion protection of underground metal structures, urban roads maintenance, municipal sanitation, urban landscaping, housing and municipal buildings, information, automation of technological processes, ecology; 6 research institutes (Moscow, St Petersburg, Rostov on Don, Tomsk, Ekaterinburg); 2 experimental factories (Moscow, St Petersburg); library of 740,000 vols; Dir V. F. PIVOVAROV; Scientific Sec. A. N. PROKHOROV.

Research Institute of Foundations and Underground Structures: 109428 Moscow, 2-ya Institutskaya 6; tel. (095) 171-22-40; fax (095) 171-37-01; f. 1931; Dir Prof. V. A. ILYICHEV; publ. *Soil Mechanics and Foundation Engineering* (every 2 months).

Scientific and Research Institute for Architecture and Town Planning Theory: 121019 Moscow, Pr. Vozdvizhenka 5; tel. and fax (095) 290-36-80.

BIBLIOGRAPHY, LIBRARY SCIENCE AND MUSEOLOGY

All-Russia Research Institute of Restoration: 109172 Moscow, Krestyanskaya ul. 10; tel. 276-99-90.

Book Research Institute: 103473 Moscow, 2-i Volkonsky per. 10; tel. 281-72-58; Dir. A. I. SOLOVEV.

ECONOMICS, LAW AND POLITICS

Africa Institute: 103001 Moscow, Ul. Spiridonovka 30/1; tel. (095) 290-63-85; fax (095) 202-07-86; e-mail dir@inafr.msk.su; attached to Russian Acad. of Sciences; Dir A. M. VASILIEV.

All-Russia Research and Design Institute of the Statistical Information System: 127486 Moscow, Deguninskaya ul. 1/3; tel. 488-14-04.

All-Russia Research Institute of Economic Problems in Development of Science and Technology: 111024 Moscow, Aviamotornaya ul. 26/5; tel. 273-52-31; f. 1986; library of 15,000 vols.

All-Russia Research Institute of the Consumer Market and Marketing: 101000 Moscow, Kolpachny per. 7; tel. 923-42-41.

Bank Credit and Finance Research Institute: 103016 Moscow, Ul. Alekseya Tolstogo 30/1; tel. 925-61-18.

Central Economics Research Institute: 119898 Moscow, Smolensky bul. 3/5; tel. 246-84-63.

Central Laboratory of Socio-Economic Measurements: C/o Russian Academy of Sciences, 117418 Moscow, Ul. Krasikova 32; attached to Russian Acad. of Sciences; Dir A. YU. SHEVYAKOV.

Central Mathematical Economics Institute: 117418 Moscow, Ul. Krasikova 32; tel. 129-16-44; attached to Russian Acad. of Sciences; Dir V. L. MAKAROV.

Centre for the Study of Nationality Problems: 117036 Moscow, Ul. Dm. Ulyanova 19; tel. 123-90-61; attached to Russian Acad. of Sciences; Head M. N. GUBOGLO.

Far East Institute: 117218 Moscow, Ul. Krasikova 27; tel. 124-02-17; attached to Russian Acad. of Sciences; Dir M. L. TITARENKO.

Financial Research Institute: 103006 Moscow, Nastasinsky per. 3 kor. 2; tel. (095) 299-74-14; fax (095) 299-31-69; f. 1937.

Institute for Comparative Political Studies: 101831 Moscow, Kolpachnyi per. 9a; tel. (095) 916-37-03; fax (095) 916-03-01; f. 1966; attached to Russian Acad. of Sciences; library of 50,000 vols; Dir T. T. TIMOFEEV; publs *Forum* (1 a year), *Polis* (6 a year).

Institute for Legislation and Comparative Law: 103728 Moscow, Vozdvizhenka 4/22; tel. 291-02-07; fax 290-58-56; f. 1925 (fmrly All-Union Research Institute of Soviet Legislation); controlled by Supreme Soviet of Russian Federation; library of 180,000 vols; Dir LEV A. OKUNKOV; publs *Problems of Perfecting Legislation* (3 a year), *Commentary on New Russian Legislation* (annually), *Materials of Foreign Legislation and International Private Law* (annually), *Legislation of Foreign Countries* (6 or 7 a year).

Institute for Socio-Economic Studies of Population: 117218 Moscow, Nakhimovsky pr. 32; tel. (095) 129-04-00; fax (095) 129-08-01; f. 1988; attached to Russian Acad. of Sciences; Dir N. M. RIMASHEVSKAYA; publs *Sociology and Demography* (4 a year), *Population*.

Institute of Economic and Social Problems of the North: 167610 Syktyvkar, Kommunisticheskaya ul. 26; tel. and fax (8212) 42-42-67; e-mail iespn@ksc.komi.ru; attached to Russian Acad. of Sciences; Dir V. N. LAZHENTSEV.

Institute of Economic Problems: 184200 Murmansk obl., Apatity, Ul. Fersmana 14; tel. (81555) 3-06-72; fax (81555) 3-48-44; e-mail luzin@ksc-iep.murmansk.su; f. 1984; attached to Russian Acad. of Sciences; Dir Prof. GENNADY P. LUZIN.

Institute of Economic Research: 680042 Khabarovsk, Tikhookeanskaya ul. 153; tel. 33-31-45; attached to Russian Acad. of Sciences; Dir Prof. P. A. MINAKIR.

Institute of Economics: 620219 Ekaterinburg, Moskovskaya ul. 29; tel. 51-07-26; attached to Russian Acad. of Sciences; Dir A. I. TATARKIN.

Institute of Economics: 117218 Moscow, Ul. Krasikova 27; tel. 129-02-54; attached to Russian Acad. of Sciences; Dir Acad. L. I. ABALKIN.

Institute of Employment Problems: 101000 Moscow, Malaya Lubyanka 16; tel. 921-61-11; fax 420-22-08; attached to Russian Acad. of Sciences; Dir A. SHOKHIN.

Institute of Europe: 103873 Moscow, Mokhovaya 8–3; tel. (095) 203-73-43; fax (095) 200-42-98; f. 1988; attached to Russian Acad. of Sciences; library of 3,000 vols; Dir VITALY V. ZHURKIN; publ. *Reports*† (6 a year).

Institute of Foreign Economic Research: C/o Russian Academy of Sciences, 117418 Moscow, Ul. Krasikova 32; attached to Russian Acad. of Sciences; Dir S. A. SITARYAN.

Institute of International Economic and Political Studies: 117418 Moscow, Novocheremushkinskaya 46; tel. 128-91-35; attached to Russian Acad. of Sciences; Dir Acad. O. T. BOGOMOLOV.

Institute of National Economic Forecasting: 117418 Moscow, Ul. Krasikova 32; tel. 129-39-44; fax 310-70-71; f. 1986; attached to Russian Acad. of Sciences; Dir Prof. YU. V. YARMENKO; publ. *Studies on Russian Economic Development* (6 a year).

Institute of Peace: 117859 Moscow, Ul. Profsoyuznaya 23; tel. 128-93-89; attached to Russian Acad. of Sciences; Dir A. K. KISLOV.

Institute of Philosophy and Law: 620144 Ekaterinburg, Ul. 8 Marta 68; tel. 22-23-46; attached to Russian Acad. of Sciences; Dir S. S. ALEKSEEV.

Institute of Problems of Assimilation of the North: 625003 Tyumen, a/ya 2774; tel. 7-82-76; attached to Russian Acad. of Sciences; Dir V. P. MELNIKOV.

Institute of Problems of the Marketplace: 117418 Moscow, Nakhimovsky pr. 47; tel. 129-10-00; attached to Russian Acad. of Sciences; Dir N. YA. PETRAKOV.

Institute of Social Sciences: 670042 Ulan-Ude, Ul. Marii Sakhyanovoi 6; tel. 3-66-25; attached to Russian Acad. of Sciences; Dir V. T. NAIDAKOV.

Institute of Socio-Economic Problems: 193015 St Petersburg, Ul. Voinova 50a; tel. 273-06-46; fax 315-17-01; attached to Russian Acad. of Sciences; Dir A. E. KOGUT.

Institute of Socio-Economic Problems of the Development of the Agroindustrial Complex: 401600 Saratov, pr. Lenina 94; tel. 24-25-38; attached to Russian Acad. of Sciences; Dir V. B. OSTROVSKY.

Institute of Socio-Political Research: 117334 Moscow, Leninsky pr. 32A; tel. 938-19-10; attached to Russian Acad. of Sciences; Dir G. V. OSIPOV.

Institute of State and Law: 119841 Moscow, Ul. Znamenka 10; tel. 291-33-81; attached to Russian Acad. of Sciences; Dir B. N. TOPORNIN.

Institute of the Economics of the Comprehensive Assimilation of the Natural Resources of the North: 677891 Yakutsk, Ul. Petrovskogo 2; tel. 3-52-46; attached to Russian Acad. of Sciences; Dir N. V. IGOSHIN.

Institute of USA and Canada Studies: 121814 Moscow, Khlebnyi per. 2/3; tel. (095) 291-20-52; fax (095) 200-12-07; e-mail iskran@glasnet.ru; attached to Russian Acad. of Sciences; Dir SERGEI ROGOV; publ. *US: Economy, Policy, Ideology* (monthly).

Institute of World Economics and International Relations: 117859 Moscow, Profsoyuznaya 23; tel. (095) 120-43-32; fax (095) 310-70-27; e-mail imemoran@glasnet.ru; attached to Russian Acad. of Sciences; Dir V. A. MARTYNOV (acting).

International Research Institute for Management Sciences: 117312 Moscow, Pr. 60-letiya Oktyabrya 9; tel. 137-28-57.

Latin America Institute: 113035 Moscow, B. Ordynka 21; tel. 231-53-23; attached to Russian Acad. of Sciences; Dir Dr V. V. VOLSKY.

Pricing Research Institute: 107078 Moscow, Kirovsky proezd 4/3; tel. 925-50-56.

Research Centre 'Management of the Development of Recreational Areas and Tourism': 354000 Sochi, Teatral'naya 8a; tel. 92-37-71; attached to Russian Acad. of Sciences; Dir M. M. AMIRKHANOV.

Research Institute for the Strengthening of the Legal System and Law and Order: 123805 Moscow, GSP 2-ya Zvenigorodskaya ul. 15; tel. 256-54-63.

Research Institute of Planning and Normatives: 125319 Moscow, Kochnovsky pr. 3; tel. 152-45-91; attached to Russian Acad. of Sciences; Dir B. V. GUBIN (acting).

Russian State Committee on Statistical Research: 123000 Moscow, Bolshoy Cherkassky per. 2/10; tel. and fax (095) 923-58-67; f. 1963; Dir M. G. NAZAROV.

St Petersburg Mathematical Economics Institute: St Petersburg; attached to Russian Acad. of Sciences; Dir B. L. OVSIEVICH.

Survey Technique and Applied Research (STAR) Centre of the Institute of Sociology: 117259 Moscow, Ul. Krzhizhanovskogo 24/35 (b.5); tel. (095) 719-09-71; fax (095) 719-07-40; e-mail valman@socio.msk.su; f. 1983; attached to Russian Acad. of Sciences; opinion survey design, data collection; Dir Prof. V. MANSUROV.

EDUCATION

Central Sports Research Institute: 107005 Moscow, Elizavetinsky per. 10; tel. 261-50-76.

Centre for Pre-School Education: 113035 Moscow, Ul. Osipenko 21; tel. 231-49-28; attached to Russian Acad. of Education; Dir A. S. SPIVAKOVSKAYA.

Centre for Social Pedagogics: 119905 Moscow, Pogodinskaya ul. 8; tel. 246-44-58; attached to Russian Acad. of Education; Dir V. G. BOCHAROVA.

Institute for Advanced Training: 109180 Moscow, Ul. B. Polyanka 58; tel. 237-31-51; attached to Russian Acad. of Education; Dir Y. A. ROODIE.

Institute for Educational Innovation: 117449 Moscow, Ul. Vinokurova 3-B; tel. 126-26-30; attached to Russian Acad. of Education; Dir V. I. SLOBODCHIKOV.

Institute for School Development in Siberia, the Far East and the North: 634050 Tomsk, Ul. Gertsena 68; tel. (3822) 21-28-21; attached to Russian Acad. of Education; Dir G. V. ZALEVSKY.

Institute for the Occupational Training of Youth: 119903 Moscow, Pogodinskaya ul. 8; tel. 245-05-13; attached to Russian Acad. of Education; Dir V. A. POLYAKOV.

Institute of Adult Education: 191187 St Petersburg, Nab. Kutuzova 8; tel. (812) 272-52-61; fax (812) 273-37-13; f. 1946; attached to Russian Acad. of Education; library of 200,000 vols; Dir V. G. ONUSHKIN; publs *Information Bulletin, Adult Education*.

Institute of Developmental Physiology: 119869 Moscow, Ul. Pogodinskaya 8, K. 2; tel. 245-04-33; attached to Russian Acad. of Education; Dir Dr M. M. BEZRUKIKH.

Institute of Higher Education: 103062 Moscow, Podsosensky per. 20; tel. 297-36-77; attached to Russian Acad. of Education; Dir A. Y. SAVELIEV.

Institute of National Problems of Education: 105077 Moscow, Pervomayskaya 101; tel. 461-92-45; fax 461-92-45; f. 1991; (fmrly Research Institute of National Schools, f. 1949); Dir Prof. M. N. KOUZMIN; publ. *Uchenye Zapiski* (annually).

Institute of Personality Development: 119906 Moscow, Ul. Pogodinskaya 8; tel. 247-06-06; attached to Russian Acad. of Education; Dir V. S. MUKHINA.

Institute of Secondary Education: 119906 Moscow, Ul. Pogodinskaya 8; tel. 245-37-33; attached to Russian Acad. of Education; Dir. V. S. LEDNEV.

Institute of Secondary Specialized Education: Tatarstan, 420039 Kazan, Ul. Isayeva 12; tel. (8432) 42-63-24; attached to Russian Acad. of Education; Dir G. V. MUKHAMETZYANOVA.

Institute of Teaching and Learning Resources: 119903 Moscow, Ul. Pogodinskaya 8; tel. 246-35-90; attached to Russian Acad. of Education; Dir T. S. NAZAROVA.

Institute of Theoretical Pedagogics and International Research in Education: 129278 Moscow, Ul. Pavla Korchagina 7; tel. 283-09-55; attached to Russian Acad. of Education; Dir B. S. GERSHUNSKY.

Institute of Vocational Education: 119186 St Petersburg, Nab. r. Moiki 48; tel. (812) 311-60-88; attached to Russian Acad. of Education; Dir A. P. BELYAEVA.

Psychological Institute: 103009 Moscow, Mokhovaya ul. 9, K. B; tel. 202-88-76; attached to Russian Acad. of Education; Dir V. V. RUBTSOV.

Research Centre for Aesthetic Education: 119034 Moscow, Kropotkinskaya nab. 15; tel. 202-25-97; attached to Russian Acad. of Education; Dir B. P. YUSOV.

Research Centre for the Teaching of Russian: 119903 Moscow, Pogodinskaya ul. 8; tel. 246-05-59; attached to Russian Acad. of Education; Dir E. A. BYSTROVA.

Research Institute of Remedial Education: 119869 Moscow, Ul. Pogodinskaya 8, Korp. 1; tel. 245-04-52; attached to Russian Acad. of Education; Dir N. N. MALOFEEV.

Siberian Institute of Educational Technologies: 630098 Novosibirsk, Primorskaya ul. 22; tel. (3832) 45-18-32; fax (3832) 45-87-51; f. 1985; attached to Russian Acad. of Education; Dir I. M. BOBKO; publ. *Information Technologies in Education* (2 a year).

FINE AND PERFORMING ARTS

Art Research Museum: St Petersburg, Universitetskaya nab. 17; attached to Russian Acad. of Arts; laboratories and bronze-casting studios; 3 brs; Dir E. V. GRISHINA.

Film Research Institute: 103050 Moscow, Degtyarny per. 8; tel. and fax (095) 299-56-79; f. 1974; library of 60,000 vols; Dir LUDMILA BUDIAK; publs *Kinovedcheskie Zapisky* (Film Notebooks, 4 a year), *Kinograph* (almanac).

Research Institute of the Theory and History of Fine Arts: 119034 Moscow, Ul. Prechistenka 21; tel. 201-42-91; attached to Russian Acad. of Arts; Dir V. V. VANSLOV.

State Institute for Art Studies: 103009 Moscow, Kozitsky per. 5; tel. (095) 200-03-71; fax (095) 229-57-24; e-mail rubin@riar.msk.su; f. 1944; research in fine art, theatre, music, architecture, folklore, mass media; library of 70,000 vols; Dir Dr A. I. KOMECH; publs *Questions of Art Research* (4 a year), *Theory of Culture* (1 a year).

HISTORY, GEOGRAPHY AND ARCHAEOLOGY

Institute of Archaeology: 117036 Moscow, Ul. Dm. Ulyanova 19; tel. 126-94-43; attached to Russian Acad. of Sciences; Dir V. P. ALEKSEEV.

Institute of Geography: 664033 Irkutsk, Ulanbatorskaya 1; tel. 46-43-20; attached to Russian Acad. of Sciences; Dir V. V. VOROBEV.

Institute of Geography: 109017 Moscow, Staromonetnii per. 29; tel. 238-82-77; telex 411781; fax 230-20-29; attached to Russian Acad. of Sciences; Dir Acad. V. M. KOTLYAKOV.

Institute of History and Archaeology: 620219 Ekaterinburg, Ul. R. Lyuksemburg 56; tel. (3432) 22-14-02; fax (3432) 22-42-30; attached to Russian Acad. of Sciences; Dir Prof. V. V. ALEKSEEV.

Institute of History, Language and Literature: 450054 Ufa, Pr. Oktyabrya 71; tel. 34-22-43; attached to Russian Acad. of Sciences; Dir Z. G. URAKSIN.

Institute of History, Philology and Philosophy: 630090 Novosibirsk, Pr. akademika Lavrenteva 17; tel. 35-05-37; fax 35-77-91; attached to Russian Acad. of Sciences; Dir Acad. A. P. DEREVYANKO.

Institute of Language, Literature and Arts: 367030 Makhachkala 3, Ul. 26 Bakinskikh Komissarov 75; tel. 62-93-95; f. 1924; attached to Russian Acad. of Sciences; library of 160,000 vols; Dir G. G. GAMZATOV.

Institute of Language, Literature and History: 167610 Syktyvkar, Kommunisticheskaya ul. 26; tel. (8212) 42-55-64; fax (8212) 42-52-66; f. 1970; attached to Russian Acad. of Sciences; Dir ALEXANDR F. SMETANIN.

Institute of Linguistics, Literature and History: 185610 Petrozavodsk, Pushkinskaya ul. 11; tel. 77-44-96; e-mail nikitina@post.krc.karelia.ru; attached to Russian Acad. of Sciences; Dir YU. A. SAVVATEEV.

Institute of Military History: 117330 Moscow, Universitetskii Pr. 14; tel. 147-45-65; attached to Russian Acad. of Sciences; Dir A. N. BAZHENOV.

Institute of Oriental Studies: 103777 Moscow, Rozhdestvenka 12; tel. 925-64-61; telex 412157; attached to Russian Acad. of Sciences; Dir M. S. KAPITSA; br. in St Petersburg: 192041 St Petersburg, Dvortsovaya nab. 18; tel. 315-87-19; Head YU. A. PETROSYAN.

Institute of Research in the Humanities: 677007 Sakha Republic, Yakutsk, Petrovskaya ul. 1; tel. and fax (41122) 5-49-96; f. 1935; attached to Acad. of Sciences of the Sakha Republic; history, language and culture of the peoples of the Sakha Republic; Dir VASILY N. IVANOV.

Institute of Russian History: 117036 Moscow, Ul. Dm. Ulyanova 19; tel. 126-94-49; fax 126-39-55; attached to Russian Acad. of Sciences; Dir A. N. SAKHAROV; br. at St Petersburg: 197110 St Petersburg, Petrozavodskaya 7; tel. 235-41-98; fax 235-64-85.

Institute of Slavonic and Balkan Studies: 125040 Moscow, Leninskii pr. 32A; tel. 938-17-80; fax 938-22-88; attached to Russian Acad. of Sciences; Dir V. K. VOLKOV.

Institute of the History, Archaeology and Ethnography of the Peoples of the Far East: 690600 Vladivostok, Ul. Pushkinskaya 89; tel. 2-05-07; attached to Russian Acad. of Sciences; Dir Acad. A. I. KRUSHANOV.

Institute of the History of Material Culture: 191065 St Petersburg, Dvortsovaya nab. 18; tel. 312-14-84; attached to Russian Acad. of Sciences.

Institute of World History: 117036 Moscow, Ul. Dm. Ulyanova 19; tel. 126-94-21; attached to Russian Acad. of Sciences; Dir A. O. CHUBARYAN.

Krasovsky, F. N., Central Research Institute for Geodesy, Aerial Photography, and Cartography: 125413 Moscow, Onezhskaya 26; tel. 456-95-31.

Oceanography Research Institute: St Petersburg, Naberezhnaya reki Moiki 120; Dir I. S. GRAMBERG.

Pacific Institute of Geography: 690041 Vladivostok, Ul. Radio 7; tel. (4232) 32-06-72; fax (4232) 31-21-59; f. 1971; attached to Russian Acad. of Sciences; library of 28,000 vols; Dir Prof. P. YA. BAKLANOV; publ. *Zov Taigi*.

State Oceanography Institute: 119838 Moscow, Kropotkinskii per. 6; tel. 246-72-88; Dir F. S. TERZIEV; br. 199026 St. Petersburg, V.O., 23-ya liniya 2-a; tel. 218-81-23.

Udmurt Institute of History, Language and Literature: 426004 Izhevsk, Ul. Lomonosova 4; tel. (3412) 75-53-21; fax (3412) 75-39-94; f. 1931; attached to Russian Acad. of Sciences; library of 60,000 vols; Dir KUZMA I. KULIKOV.

LANGUAGE AND LITERATURE

Gorkii, A. M., Institute of World Literature: 121069 Moscow, Ul. Vorovskogo 25a; tel. 290-50-30; attached to Russian Acad. of Sciences; Dir F. F. KUZNETSOV.

Ibragimov, G., Institute of Language, Literature and Art: 420503 Kazan, Ul. Lobachevskogo 2/31; tel. (8432) 38-70-59; fax (8432)

38-74-79; attached to Acad. of Sciences of the Republic of Tatarstan; Dir M. Z. Zakiev.

Institute of Linguistic Research: 199053 St Petersburg, Tuchkov per. 9; tel. 218-16-11; attached to Russian Acad. of Sciences.

Institute of Linguistic Studies: 103009 Moscow, Ul. Semashko 1/12; tel. 290-39-06; attached to Russian Acad. of Sciences; Dir V. M. Solntsev.

Institute of Russian Literature (Pushkin House): 199034 St Petersburg, Nab. Makarova 4; tel. 218-54-22; attached to Russian Acad. of Sciences; Dir N. N. Skatov.

Russian Institute for Cultural Research: 109072 Moscow, Bersenevskaya nab. 20; tel. (095) 230-01-77; fax (095) 230-08-82; f. 1932; attached to Russian Acad. of Sciences; library of 67,000 books and periodicals; Dir Prof. Kirill E. Razlogov.

Vinogradov Institute of the Russian Language: 121019 Moscow, Volkhonka 18/2; tel. (095) 202-65-40; fax (095) 291-23-17; e-mail irlras@irl.msk.su; f. 1944; attached to Russian Acad. of Sciences; library of 110,000 vols; Dir Dr A. M. Moldovan; publs *Rusistics Today* (4 a year), *Russian Speech* (6 a year).

MEDICINE

All-Russia Antibiotics Research Institute: 113105 Moscow, Nagatinskaya ul. 3a; tel. 111-42-38; telex 411878; fax 118-93-66; f. 1947; library of 65,000 vols; br. in Penza; Dir Prof. S. M. Navashin; publ. *Antibiotics and Chemotherapy*.

All-Russia Research Institute of Eye Diseases: 119021 Moscow, Ul. Rossolimo 11; tel. 248-01-25; f. 1973; micro-surgery of the eye, therapeutic ophthalmology, laser ophthalmology, new technical equipment in ophthalmology; 550 mems, 150 scientific staff; Chief officers Alekseev, Krasnov, Kuznetsova, Mustaev; publ. *Vestnik Oftalmologii* (bi-monthly).

All-Russia Research Institute of Pharmaceutical Plants: 113628 Moscow, Ul. Grina 7; tel. 382-83-18; Dir P. T. Kondratenko.

All-Russia Research Institute of the Technology of Blood Substitutes and Hormonal Preparations: 109044 Moscow, Per. Lavrov 6; tel. 276-43-60.

Allergen State Unitary Enterprise: 355004 Stavropol, Biologicheskaya Ul. 20; tel. (8652) 24-40-84; fax (8652) 25-31-46; f. 1918; vaccines and sera; library of 40,000 vols and periodicals; Dir-Gen. V. V. Ermolov.

Anokhin, P. K., Institute of Normal Physiology: 103009 Moscow, Ul. Bolshaya Nikitskaya 6; tel. (095) 203-66-70; fax (095) 203-54-32; attached to Russian Acad. of Medical Sciences; Dir K. V. Sudakov.

Arkhangelsk Institute of Epidemiology, Microbiology and Hygiene: Arkhangelsk, Pr. Ch.-Luchinskogo 32.

Bakulev Research Centre for Cardiovascular Surgery: 117049 Moscow, Leninskii pr. 8; tel. (095) 236-13-61; fax (095) 237-21-72; f. 1956; attached to Russian Acad. of Medical Sciences; Head L. A. Bokeriya; publs *Journal of Thoracic and Cardiovascular Surgery* (in Russian, 6 a year), *Annals of Surgery* (in Russian, 6 a year).

Blokhin, N. N., Oncology Research Centre: 115478 Moscow, Kashirskoe shosse 24; tel. (095) 324-11-14; fax (095) 230-24-50; attached to Russian Acad. of Medical Sciences; Dir N. N. Trapeznikov.

Incorporates:

Institute of Clinical Oncology: 115478 Moscow, Kashirskoe shosse 24; tel. 324-44-16; attached to Russian Acad. of Medical Sciences; Dir M. I. Davydov.

Institute of Carcinogenesis: 115478 Moscow, Kashirskoe shosse 24; tel. 324-14-70; attached to Russian Acad. of Medical Sciences; Dir D. G. Zaridze.

Institute of Children's Oncology: 115478 Moscow, Kashirskoe shosse 24; tel. 324-43-09; attached to Russian Acad. of Medical Sciences; Dir L. A. Durnov.

Institute of Experimental Diagnosis and Tumour Therapy: 115478 Moscow, Kashirskoe shosse 24; tel. 324-22-74; attached to Russian Acad. of Medical Sciences; Dir A. B. Syrkin.

Blood Transfusion Research Institute: 125167 Moscow, Novozykovsky proezd 4a; tel. (095) 212-45-51; fax (095) 212-42-52.

Burdenko Neurosurgical Institute: 125047 Moscow, Ul. Fadeeva 5; tel. (095) 251-65-26; fax (095) 250-93-51; attached to Russian Acad. of Medical Sciences; Dir A. N. Konovalov.

Cardiological Research Centre: 121552 Moscow, 3°, Cherepkovskaya ul. 15; tel. (095) 415-13-47; fax (095) 415-29-62; attached to Russian Acad. of Medical Sciences; Dir E. I. Chazov.

Incorporates:

Institute of Experimental Cardiology: 121552 Moscow, 3 Cherepkovskaya ul. 15A; tel. 415-00-35; attached to Russian Acad. of Medical Sciences; Dir V. N. Smirnov.

Myasnikov, A. L., Institute of Cardiology: 121552 Moscow, 3°, Cherepkovskaya ul. 15; tel. 415-52-05; attached to Russian Acad. of Medical Sciences; Dir Yu. N. Belenkov.

Central Institute of Traumatology and Orthopaedics: 125299 Moscow, Ul. Priorova 10; tel. 154-97-23; fax 154-31-39; f. 1921; eleven clinics; library of over 40,000 vols; Dir Prof. Yu. G. Shaposhnikov; publ. *Urgent Problems on Traumatology and Orthopaedics* (3–4 a year).

Central Research Institute for the Evaluation of Working Capacity and Vocational Assistance to Disabled Persons: 127486 Moscow, Ul. Susanina 3; tel. 906-18-31; fax 906-18-32; f. 1930; library of 50,000 vols; Dir D. I. Lavrova.

Central Research Institute of Dermatology and Venereal Diseases: 107076 Moscow, Ul. Korolenko 3; tel. 964-43-22.

Central Research Institute of Epidemiology: 111123 Moscow, Novogireevskaya 3-a; tel. 176-02-19; Dir A. Sumarokov.

Central Research Institute of Gastroenterology: 111123 Moscow, Shosse Entuziastov 86; tel. 304-30-43; Dir V. K. Vasilenko.

Central Research Institute of Prosthetics and Prosthesis Design: 127486 Moscow, Ul. Ivana Susanina 3; tel. 488-40-70; f. 1943; library of 30,000 vols; Dir A. M. Ivanov; publ. *Protezirovaniye i protezostroenie* (Prosthetics and Prosthesis Design, 3–4 a year).

Central Research Institute of Roentgenology and Radiology: 188646 St Petersburg, Pesochniy-2, Ul. Leningradskaya 70/4; tel. 237-84-62; f. 1918; Dir Prof. Dr Med. K. B. Tikhonov.

Central Research Institute of Tuberculosis: 107564 Moscow,Yauzskaya alleya 2; tel. (095) 268-49-60; fax (095) 268-49-40; attached to Russian Acad. of Medical Sciences; Dir A. G. Khomenko.

Centre for the Chemistry of Drugs—All-Russia Chemical and Pharmaceutical Research Institute: 119815 Moscow, Ul. Zubovskaya 7; tel. 246-97-68; fax 246-78-05; f. 1920; research on drugs; library of 150,000 items; Dir R. G. Glushkov; publ. *Collection of Proceedings* (annually).

Chumakov, M. P., Institute of Poliomyelitis and Virus Encephalitis: 142782 Moscow oblast, Kievskoe shosse, 27 Kilometr; tel. 439-90-07; attached to Russian Acad. of Medical Sciences; Dir S. G. Drozdov.

Chuvash Eye Diseases Research Institute: 428028 Cheboksary, Traktorostroitelei 10; tel. (8350) 26-05-75; fax (8350) 26-52-13; f. 1987; Dir Dr Nikolai Pashtaev.

Dagestan Medical Research Centre: 367020 Makhachkala, Ul. Gorikogo 53; tel. (87200) 7-49-97; attached to Russian Acad. of Medical Sciences; Dir S.-M. A. Omarov.

Eastern Siberian Research Centre: 664003 Irkutsk, Ul. Timiryazeva 16; fax (3952) 27-48-13; attached to Russian Acad. of Medical Sciences; Chair. of Presidium S. I. Kolesnikov.

Incorporates:

Institute of Epidemiology and Microbiology: 664000 Irkutsk, Ul. Karla Marksa 3; tel. (3952) 33-34-23; attached to Russian Acad. of Medical Sciences; Dir V. I. Zlobin.

Institute of Industrial Medicine and Human Ecology: 665827 Irkutskaya oblast, Angarsk 27, a/ya 1170; attached to Russian Acad. of Medical Sciences; Dir V. S. Rukavishnikov.

Institute of Paediatrics and Human Reproduction: 664003 Irkutsk, Ul. Gagarina 4; tel. (3952) 34-74-05; attached to Russian Acad. of Medical Sciences; Dir S. I. Kolesnikov.

Institute of Surgery: 664047 Irkutsk, Yubileiny mikroraion 100; fax (3952) 46-65-29; attached to Russian Acad. of Medical Sciences; Dir E. G. Grigorev.

Institute of Traumatology and Orthopaedics: 664003 Irkutsk, Ul. Bortsov Revolyutsii 1; tel. (3952) 27-54-30; attached to Russian Acad. of Medical Sciences; Dir A. P. Barabash.

Ekaterinburg Institute of Restorative Surgery, Traumatology and Orthopaedics: Ekaterinburg, Bankovsky per. 7.

Ekaterinburg Region Institute of Dermatology and Venereal Diseases: Ekaterinburg, Ul. K. Libknekhta 9.

Ekaterinburg Viral Infections Research Institute: 620030 Ekaterinburg, Letnyaya ul. 23; tel. (3432) 61-99-60; f. 1920; Dir Prof. Nina P. Glinskikh; publ. *Viral Infections: Urgent Problems* (annually).

Endocrinology Research Centre: 117036 Moscow, Ul. D. Ulyanova 11; tel. (095) 124-43-00; fax (095) 310-70-00; attached to Russian Acad. of Medical Sciences; Dir I. I. Dedov.

Incorporates:

Institute of Clinical Endocrinology: Institute of Clinical Endocrinology:Moscow; tel. 124-41-01; attached to Russian Acad. of Medical Sciences; Dir E. I. Marova.

Institute of Experimental Endocrinology: 112255 Moscow, Ul. Moskvorechie 1; tel. 111-85-00; attached to Russian Acad. of Medical Sciences; Dir I. G. Akmaev.

Institute of Diabetes: Moscow; tel. 124-45-00; attached to Russian Acad. of Medical Sciences; Dir M. I. Balabolkin.

Ersman Hygiene Research Institute: 141000 Mytishchi, Ul. Semashko 2; tel. 583-82-14.

Federal Research Institute for Health Education and Health Promotion: 103001 Moscow, Ul. A. Mitskevicha 3, tel. (095) 202-18-13; fax (095) 202-54-08; f. 1927; library of 10,000 vols; Dir Dr V. A Polesky.

Gamalei, N. F., Institute of Epidemiology and Microbiology: 123098 Moscow, Ul. Gamalei 18; tel. (095) 193-30-01; fax (095) 305-67-38; attached to Russian Acad. of Medical Sciences; Dir S. V. Prozorovskii.

Haematological Research Centre: 125167 Moscow, Novozykovsky proezd 4A; tel. (095) 212-21-23; fax (095) 212-42-52; attached to Russian Acad. of Medical Sciences; Dir A. I. VOROBIEV.

Herzen, P. A., Moscow Cancer Research Institute: 125284 Moscow, Vtoroy Botkinsky proezd 3; tel. 945-19-35; f. 1903; library of 19,336 vols; Dir Prof. V. I. CHISSOV.

Institute for the Protection of the Mother and Baby: 680028 Khabarovsk, Ul. Istomina 85, korp 13; tel. (4212) 35-71-37; fax (4212) 34-08-88; attached to Russian Acad. of Medical Sciences; Dir V. K. KOZLOV.

Institute of Biochemistry: 630117 Novosibirsk, Ul. Acad. Timakova 2; tel. (3832) 32-27-35; f. 1989; attached to Russian Acad. of Medical Sciences; Dir L. E. PANIN.

Institute of Biomedical Chemistry: 119832 Moscow, Pogodinskaya 10; tel. (095) 246-69-80; fax (095) 245-08-57; f. 1944; attached to Russian Acad. of Medical Sciences; library of 136,000 vols; Dir A. I. ARCHAKOV; publ. *Voprosy meditsinskoy khimii* (6 a year).

Institute of Biomedical Problems: 123007 Moscow, Khoroshevskoe sh. 76A; tel. (095) 195-23-63; telex 411048; fax (095) 195-22-53; f. 1963; environmental effects on the human body, with emphasis on the effect of space flights; library of 80,000 vols; Dir A. I. GRIGORIEV; publ. *Aerospatial and Environmental Medicine* (every 2 months).

Institute of Biomedical Research and Therapy: 113149 Moscow, Simferopolsky bul. 8; tel. 113-23-51; Dir A. V. KARAULOV.

Institute of Clinical and Experimental Lymphology: 630117 Novosibirsk, Ul. Acad. Timakova 2; tel. (3832) 32-56-53; fax (3832) 32-95-31; f. 1991; attached to Russian Acad. of Medical Sciences; library of 1,000 vols; Dir YU. I. BORODIN; publ. *Bulletin* (3 or 4 a year).

Institute of Clinical and Preventive Cardiology: 625026 Tyumen, Ul. Melnikaite 111; fax (3452) 22-53-49; attached to Russian Acad. of Medical Sciences; Dir V. A. KUZNETSOV.

Institute of Clinical Immunology: 630091 Novosibirsk, Ul. Yadrintsovskaya 14; fax (3832) 22-70-28; attached to Russian Acad. of Medical Sciences; Dir V. A. KOZLOV.

Institute of Complex Problems of Hygiene and Occupational Diseases: 654035 Novokuznetsk, Ul. Kutuzova 23; fax (3843) 47-48-84; f. 1976; attached to Russian Acad. of Medical Sciences; Dir V. D. SURZHIKOV.

Institute of Epidemiology and Microbiology: 690028 Vladivostok, Ul. Selskaya 1; tel. (4232) 29-43-03; attached to Russian Acad. of Medical Sciences; Dir N. N. BESEDNOVA.

Institute of Experimental Medicine: 197376 St Petersburg, Ul. Akad. Pavlova 12; tel. (812) 234-54-01; fax (812) 234-94-89; attached to Russian Acad. of Medical Sciences; Dir B. I. TKACHENKO.

Institute of Eye Diseases: 119021 Moscow, Ul. Rossolimo 11; tel. (095) 248-78-92; fax (095) 248-01-25; attached to Russian Acad. of Medical Sciences; Dir M. M. KRASNOV.

Institute of General Pathology and Human Ecology: 630117 Novosibirsk, Ul. Acad. Timakova 2; fax (3832) 32-55-56; attached to Russian Acad. of Medical Sciences; Dir V. P. KAZNACHEEV.

Institute of General Pathology and Pathological Physiology: 125315 Moscow, Ul. Baltiiskaya 8; tel. (095) 151-17-56; fax (095) 151-95-40; attached to Russian Acad. of Medical Sciences; Dir G. N. KRYZHANOVSKII.

Institute of Human Morphology: 117418 Moscow, Ul. Tsyuryupy 3; tel. (095) 120-80-65; fax (095) 120-14-56; attached to Russian Acad. of Medical Sciences; Dir N. K. PERMYAKOV.

Institute of Immunology: 142380 Moscow oblast, Chekhovsky raion, Lyubuchany; tel. and fax (095) 546-15-55; f. 1980; library of 2,800 vols; Dir V. P. ZAVYALOV.

Institute of Immunology: 115478 Moscow, Kashirskoe shosse 24, Korp. 2; tel. 111-83-01; Dir R. M. KHAITOV.

Institute of Influenza: 197022 St Petersburg, Ul. Prof. Popova 15/17; tel. (812) 234-58-75; fax (812) 234-01-50; attached to Russian Acad. of Medical Sciences; Dir O. I. KISELEV.

Institute of Medical and Biological Cybernetics: 630117 Novosibirsk, Ul. Acad. Timakova 2; tel. (3832) 32-12-56; fax (3832) 32-55-58; f. 1992; attached to Russian Acad. of Medical Sciences; Dir M. B. SHTARK; publ *Biofeedback* (every 3 years).

Institute of Medical Climatology and Rehabilitation: 690025 Vladivostok, Sadgorod 25; tel. (4232) 33-05-22; fax (4232) 25-11-83; f. 1984; attached to Russian Acad. of Medical Sciences; library of 20,000 vols; Dir Prof. Dr E. M. IVANOV.

Institute of Medical Primatology: 354385 Sochi-Adler, Veseloye 1; tel. (8622) 91-92-50; fax (095) 956-17-11; e-mail lapin@iprim.sochi.su; f. 1927; attached to Russian Acad. of Medical Sciences; Dir Prof. B. A. LAPIN.

Institute of Medical Problems of the Extreme North: 626711 Tumenskaya oblast, Nadym, Km 107; fax (34595) 4-03-22; attached to Russian Acad. of Medical Sciences; Dir A. A. BUGANOV.

Institute of Medical Problems of the North: 660022 Krasnoyarsk, Ul. Partizana Zheleznyaka 1B; fax (3912) 23-16-79; attached to Russian Acad. of Medical Sciences; Dir K. R. SEDOV.

Institute of Neurology: 123367 Moscow, Volokolamskoe shosse 80; tel. (095) 490-21-11; fax (095) 490-22-10; attached to Russian Acad. of Medical Sciences; Dir N. V. VERESHCHAGIN.

Institute of Nutrition: 109240 Moscow, Ustinskii proezd 2/14; tel. (095) 917-44-85; attached to Russian Acad. of Medical Sciences; Dir M. N. VOLGAREV.

Institute of Occupational Health: 105275 Moscow, Pr. Budennogo 31; tel. (095) 365-02-09; fax (095) 366-05-83; attached to Russian Acad. of Medical Sciences; Dir Prof. N. F. IZMEROV.

Institute of Paediatrics: 117296 Moscow, Lomonosovskii pr. 2/62; tel. (095) 134-03-61; fax (095) 134-13-08; attached to Russian Acad. of Medical Sciences; Dir M. YA. STUDENIKIN.

Institute of Paediatrics and Child Surgery of the Ministry of Public Health of the Russian Federation: 127412 Moscow, Taldomskaya ul. 2; tel. 484-02-92; fax (095) 438-62-32; Dir Prof. YURI E. VELTISCHEV; publ. *Vestnik* (Annals of Perinatology and Paediatrics).

Institute of Pharmacology: 125315 Moscow, Ul. Baltiiskaya 8; tel. (095) 151-18-41; fax (095) 151-12-61; attached to Russian Acad. of Medical Sciences; Dir S. B. SEREDENIN.

Institute of Physiology: 630117 Novosibirsk, Ul. Acad. Timakova 4; fax (3832) 32-42-54; attached to Russian Acad. of Medical Sciences; Dir V. A. TRUFAKIN.

Institute of Regional Pathology and Pathological Morphology: 630117 Novosibirsk, Ul. Acad. Timakova 2; tel. (3832) 32-31-56; attached to Russian Acad. of Medical Sciences; Dir L. M. NEPOMNYASHCHIKH.

Institute of Rheumatology: 115552 Moscow, Kashirskoe shosse 34-a; tel. (095) 114-44-90; fax (095) 114-44-68; attached to Russian Acad. of Medical Sciences; br. at Volgograd; Dir V. A. NASONOVA.

Institute of Roentgenology and Radiology: 117437 Moscow, Profsoyuznaya 86; tel. 333-91-20; f. 1924; laser diagnosis and treatment of malignant tumours; library of 51,700 vols; Dir Prof. V. P. KHARCHENKO.

Institute of the Brain: 107120 Moscow, Per. Obukha 5; tel. (095) 917-80-07; fax (095) 916-05-95; attached to Russian Acad. of Medical Sciences; Dir N. N. BOGOLEPOV.

Institute of the Molecular Pathology and Biochemistry of Ecology: 630117 Novosibirsk, Ul. Acad. Timakova 2; fax (3832) 32-31-47; attached to Russian Acad. of Medical Sciences; Dir V. V. LYAKHOVICH.

Institute of the Physiology and Pathology of Breathing: 675000 Blagoveshchensk, Ul. Kalinina 22; tel. (4162) 42-32-33; fax (4162) 42-12-28; f. 1981; attached to Russian Acad. of Medical Sciences; Dir M. T. LUTSENKO; publ. *Bulletin* (4 a year).

Institute of Therapy: 630003 Novosibirsk, Ul. Vladimirskii spusk 2a; tel. (3832) 22-55-11; fax (3832) 22-28-21; e-mail zima@fd.iim.nsk.su; attached to Russian Acad. of Medical Sciences; Dir Y. P. NIKITIN.

Institute of Viral Preparations: 109088 Moscow, 1 Dubrovskaya ul. 15; tel. (095) 274-81-45; fax (095) 274-57-10; attached to Russian Acad. of Medical Sciences; Dir O. G. ANDZHAPARIDZE.

Irkutsk Antiplague Research Institute of Siberia and the Far East: 664047 Irkutsk, Ul. Trilissera 78; tel. (3952) 23-00-60; fax (3952) 23-03-92; f. 1934; library of 55,000 vols; Dir Prof. E. P. GOLUBINSKY.

Irkutsk Institute of Orthopaedics and Traumatology: 664003 Irkutsk, Ul. Bortzov Revoliutsii 1; tel. 27-54-30; f. 1946; diseases of the skeleton and bone tissue regeneration; library of 32,000 vols; Dir Prof. A. P. BARABASH.

Irkutsk Research Institute of Epidemiology and Microbiology: 664000 Irkutsk, Ul. Karla Marksa 3; tel. 24-42-30; Dir V. I. ZLOBIN.

Ivanovskii, D. I., Institute of Virology: 123098 Moscow, Ul. Gamalei 16; tel. (095) 190-28-74; fax (095) 190-28-67; attached to Russian Acad. of Medical Sciences; Dir D. K. LVOV.

Kazan Institute of Epidemiology, Microbiology and Hygiene: 420015 Kazan, B. Krasnaya ul. 67; tel. 32-25-80; Dir F. Z. KAMALOV.

Kazan State Institute of Orthopaedics and Traumatology: 420015 Kazan, Ul. Gorkogo 3; tel. 38-59-05; f. 1945; library of 13,500 units; publ. *Transactions* (annually).

Khabarovsk Institute of Epidemiology and Microbiology: Khabarovsk, Ul. Shevchenko 2; tel. 33-52-28; Dir T. P. VLADIMIROVA.

Laboratory of Experimental Biological Models: 143412 Moscow oblast, PO Otradnoe, Pos. Svetlye Gory; tel. 561-53-70; attached to Russian Acad. of Medical Sciences; Dir T. I. ZAITSEV.

Laboratory of Polar Medicine: 663310 Norilsk 10, Ul. Talnakhskaya 7A, p/ya 625; fax (3919) 34-47-19; attached to Russian Acad. of Medical Sciences; Dir L. A. NADTOCHII.

Martsinovsky, I. E., Institute of Medical Parasitology and Tropical Medicine: 119435 Moscow, Malaya Pirogovskaya ul. 20; tel. (095) 246-80-49; fax (095) 246-90-47; f. 1920; library of 70,000 vols; Dir Prof. V. P. SERGIEV; publ. *Medical Parasitology and Parasitic Diseases* (quarterly).

Mechnikov I. I., Institute of Vaccines and Sera: 103064 Moscow, Maly Kazenny per. 5A; tel. (095) 917-49-00; fax (095) 917-54-60; f. 1919; attached to Russian Acad. of Medical Sciences; Dir B. F. SEMENOV.

Medical Research Centre for Preventive Medicine and the Protection of the Health of Industrial Workers: 620014 Ekaterinburg, Ul. Popova 30; tel. 51-18-32; Dir S. G. Dominin.

Moscow G. N. Gabrichevskii Institute of Epidemiology and Microbiology: 125212 Moscow, Ul. Admirala Makharova 10; tel. (095) 452-18-16; fax (095) 452-18-30; f. 1895; library of 8,922 vols; Dir Prof. Boris A. Shenderov; publ. *Medical Aspects of Microecology* (annually).

Moscow Helmholtz Research Institute of Eye Diseases: 103064 Moscow, Ul. Sadovaya-Chernogryazskaya 14/19; tel. 207-23-19; fax 975-24-00; f. 1900; library of 69,445 vols; Dir Alexander M. Yuzhakov.

Moscow Municipal Research First Aid Institute: 129010 Moscow, Sukharevskaya pl. 3; f. 1923; library of 30,000 vols; tel. 925-38-97; Dir Prof. B. D. Komarov.

Moscow Oblast Gynaecological Obstetrics and Research Institute: 101000 Moscow, Ul. Chernyshevskogo 22a; tel. 924-50-12.

Moscow Research Institute of Psychiatry: 107076 Moscow, Poteshnaya ul. 3; tel. (095) 963-76-26; fax (095) 162-10-03; f. 1920; social and biological psychiatry; treats alcohol and drug addiction; Dir Prof. V. N. Krasnov.

Nizhnii Novgorod Institute for Skin and Venereal Diseases: Nizhnii Novgorod, Ul. Kovalikhinskaya 49; f. 1930; library of 10,000 vols; Dir Prof. T. A. Glavinskaya.

Nizhnii Novgorod Institute of Industrial Hygiene and Occupational Diseases: Nizhnii Novgorod, Ul. Semashko 20.

Nizhnii Novgorod Region Institute of Mother and Child Care: Nizhnii Novgorod, Ul. Semashko 22.

Nizhnii Novgorod Research Institute of Traumatology and Orthopaedics: 603155 Nizhnii Novgorod, V. Volzhskaya nab. 18; tel. 36-01-60; f. 1945; 130 mems; library of 33,000 vols; Dir Prof. V. Azolov.

Novosibirsk Institute of Orthopaedics and Restorative Surgery: Novosibirsk, Ul. Frunze 33; tel. (3832) 24-54-74; telex 133287; fax (3832) 24-55-70; f. 1946; library of 33,000 vols.

Novosibirsk Institute of Tuberculosis: Novosibirsk, Ul. Chaplygina 75.

Omsk Institute of Infectious Diseases: Omsk, Internatsionalnaya ul. 25.

Omsk Research Institute of Naturally Occurring Infections: 644080 Omsk, Pr. Mira 7; tel. 65-06-33; Dir A. A. Matushenko.

Otto, D. O., Research Institute of Obstetrics and Gynaecology: 199034 St Petersburg, Liniya Mendeleeva 3; tel. (812) 218-14-02; fax (812) 218-23-61; attached to Russian Acad. of Medical Sciences; Dir E. K. Ailamazyan.

Pharmacy Research Institute: 117418 Moscow, Ul. Krasikova 34; tel. 128-57-88; Dir A. I. Tentsova.

Plague Prevention Research Institute for the Caucasus and Transcaucasia: 355106 Stavropol, Sovetskaya ul. 13; tel. 3-13-12; Dir V. I. Efremenko.

Research Centre for Medical Genetics: 115478 Moscow, Ul. Moskvorechye 1; tel. (095) 111-85-80; fax (095) 324-07-02; e-mail viimgnc@corbina.ru; attached to Russian Acad. of Medical Sciences; Dir V. I. Ivanov.

Incorporates:

Institute of Clinical Genetics: Moscow; tel. 111-85-94; attached to Russian Acad. of Medical Sciences; Dir E. K. Ginter.

Institute of Human Genetics: Moscow; tel. 111-85-87; attached to Russian Acad. of Medical Sciences; Dir S. S. Shishkin.

Research Centre for Molecular Diagnostics and Therapy: 113149 Moscow, Simferopolsky bul. 8; tel. (095) 113-23-65; fax (095) 113-26-33; e-mail svesh@aha.ru; f. 1985; Dir E. S. Severin.

Research Centre of Medical Radiology: 249020 Kaluga oblast, Obninsk, Ul. Koroleva 4; tel. (095) 956-14-39; fax (095) 956-14-40; f. 1958; attached to Russian Acad. of Medical Sciences; library of 121,000 vols; Dir A. F. Tsyb; publ. *Radiation and Risk* (2 a year).

Research Centre of Mental Health: 115552 Moscow, Kashirskoe shosse 34; tel. (095) 117-61-83; fax (095) 952-89-40; attached to Russian Acad. of Medical Sciences; Dir A. S. Tiganov.

Research Centre of Obstetrics, Gynaecology and Perinatology: 117815 Moscow, Ul. Akad. Oparina 4; tel. and fax 438-18-00; attached to Russian Acad. of Medical Sciences; Dir Vladimir Kulakov.

Research Centre of Surgery: 119874 Moscow, Abrikosovski per. 2; tel. and fax (095) 246-95-63; attached to Russian Acad. of Medical Sciences; Dir B. A. Konstantinov.

Research Institute of Children's Infections: 197022 St Petersburg, Ul. Prof. Popova 9; tel. 234-18-62; f. 1927; library of 25,000 vols; Dir V. V. Ivanova; publ. *Infectious Diseases of Childhood* (1 or 2 a year).

Research Institute of Epidemiology and Microbiology: 603600 Nizhnii Novgorod, Gruzinskaya ul. 44; tel. (8312) 33-40-07; fax (8312) 35-64-80; f. 1929; library of 10,000 vols; Dir I. N. Blokhina; publ. *Annual Collection of Research Articles*.

Research Institute of Forensic Medicine: 123242 Moscow, Ul. Sadovaya-Kudrinskaya 3, Korp. 2; tel. 254-32-49; Dir Prof. V. I. Prozorovsky.

Research Institute of Haematology and Intensive Therapy: 125167 Moscow, Novozykovsky proezd 4a; tel. (095) 212-45-51; fax (095) 212-42-52; f. 1926; library of 50,000 vols; publ. *Sovremennye Problemy Gematologii i Perelivaniya Krovi* (monthly).

Research Institute of Laser Medicine: 121165 Moscow, Studencheskaya ul. 40; tel. 249-39-05.

Research Institute of Occupational Safety under the auspices of the Independent Russian Trade Unions: 191187 St Petersburg, Ul. Furmanova 3; tel. 279-08-13; fax 315-48-56; f. 1927; electrical safety, noise control, respiratory protection, air conditioning, ventilation, air pollution analysis, hygiene and VDUs; library of 63,000 vols; Dir E. A. Kolodin.

Research Institute of Radiation Hygiene: 197101 St Petersburg, Ul. Mira 8; tel. (812) 233-26-12; fax (812) 232-43-29; e-mail frc@ekorant.spb.su; f. 1956; Dir Prof. P. V. Ramzaev.

Research Institute of the Technology and Safety of Medicines: 142450 Moscow oblast, Noginsky raion, pos. Staraya Kupavna, Ul. Kirova 23; tel. 524-09-36; attached to Russian Acad. of Sciences; Dir Yu. V. Burov.

Research Institute of Traditional Methods of Treatment: 103051 Moscow, Petrovsky bul. 8; tel. 200-27-91.

Research Institute of Transplants and Artificial Organs: 123436 Moscow, Shchukinskaya ul. 1; tel. 190-29-71.

Research Institute of Vaccines and Sera: 614089 Perm, GSP, NIIVS.

Research Institute of Vaccines and Sera: 634004 Tomsk, Ul. Lenina 32; tel. 22-45-12; Dir N. B. Cherny.

Rostov Institute of Radiology and Oncology: Rostov-on-Don, Voroshilovsky pr. 119; affiliated to the Chelyabinsk Radiation Hygiene Institute.

Rostov Region Paediatric Research Institute: Rostov-on-Don, Dolomanovsky per. 142.

Rostov Research Institute for Plague Control: 344007 Rostov on Don, Ul. M. Gorkogo 117; tel. 66-57-03; fax 34-13-76; f. 1934; library of 52,300 vols; Dir Prof. Yu. M. Lomov.

Russian Antiplague Research Institute 'Microbe': 410005 Saratov, Ul. Universitetskaya 46; tel. (8452) 24-21-31; fax (8452) 51-52-12; f. 1918; library of 95,000 vols; Dir Prof. A. V. Naumov; publ. *Problems of Particularly Dangerous Infections* (3 a year).

Russian Institute of Medical Parasitology: Rostov-on-Don, Moskovskaya 67.

Russian Polenov, A. L., Neurosurgical Institute: 191104 St Petersburg, Ul. Mayakovskogo 12; tel. (812) 272-98-79; fax (812) 275-56-03; e-mail igor@rnsi.spb.su; f. 1926; library of 36,000 vols; Dir V. P. Bersnev; publ. *Neurosurgery* (annually).

Russian Research Centre of Rehabilitation and Physiotherapy: 121099 Moscow, Novy Arbat 32; tel. 252-18-83; fax 292-65-11; f. 1920; library of 73,500 vols; Dir Dr V. M. Bogolyubov; publs *Problems of Health Resorts, Physiotherapy and Exercise Therapy* (every 2 months).

Russian Research Institute of Haematology and Transfusiology: 193024 St Petersburg, 2-a Sovetskaya ul. 16; tel. (812) 274-56-50; fax (812) 274-92-27; f. 1932; Dir Dr E. A. Selivanov.

Russian Research Institute of Phthisiopulmonology: 103030 Moscow, Ul. Dostoievskogo 4; tel. (095) 281-84-22; fax (095) 281-45-37; e-mail logosoev@glasnet.ru; f. 1918; library of 55,019 vols; Dir Prof. A. A. Prymak; publ. *Tuberculosis and Ecology* (6 a year).

Russian Vreden, R. R., Research Institute of Traumatology and Orthopaedics: 197046 St Petersburg, Park Lenina 5; tel. 556-08-28; fax 556-79-01; f. 1906; library of 57,000 vols; Dir N. V. Kornilov; publ. *Travmatologia i Ortopedia Rossii* (6 a year).

St Petersburg Artificial Limb Research Institute: St Petersburg, Pr. K. Marxa 9/12.

St Petersburg Institute of Ear, Throat, Nose and Speech: St Petersburg, Bronnitskaya 9; tel. 292-54-29; f. 1930; library of 45,000 vols; Dir A. A. Lantsov.

St Petersburg Institute of Eye Diseases: St Petersburg, Mokhovaya 38.

St Petersburg Institute of Phthisiopulmonology: 193036 St Petersburg, Ligovsky pr. 2–4; tel. (812) 279-25-54; fax (812) 279-25-73; f. 1923; library of 26,000 vols; Dir Prof. Alexandr V. Vasilev.

St Petersburg Institute of Tuberculosis: 193130 St Petersburg, Ligovsky pr. 2/4.

St Petersburg Institute of Vaccines and Sera: 198320 Krasnoe Selo, Ul. Svobody 52; tel. 132-19-78; Dir R. N. Rodionova.

St Petersburg Pasteur Institute of Epidemiology and Microbiology: 197101 St Petersburg, Ul. Mira 14; tel. 233-20-92; fax 232-92-17; f. 1923; library of 60,000 vols; Dir Anatoly Zhebrun; publ. *Proceedings* (1–2 a year).

St Petersburg Petrov, N. N., Research Institute of Oncology: 188646 St Petersburg, Pesochny 2, St Petersburgskaya ul. 68; tel. 237-89-94.

St Petersburg Research Institute of Industrial Hygiene and Occupational Diseases: 193036 St Petersburg, 2-a Sovetskaya ul. 4; tel. 279-40-11; f. 1924.

Samara Institute of Epidemiology, Microbiology and Hygiene: Samara, Chapaevskaya 87.

Saratov Institute of Restorative Surgery, Traumatology and Orthopaedics: Saratov, Ul. Chernyshevskogo 148.

Scientific Research Institute for General Reanimatology: 103031 Moscow, Ul. Petrovka 25; tel. (095) 200-27-08; fax (095) 209-96-77; f. 1936; attached to Russian Acad. of Medical Sciences; Dir Prof. V. V. MOROZ; br. at Novokuznetsk.

Scientific Research Institute for the Investigation of New Antibiotics: 119867 Moscow, B. Pirogovskaya 11; tel. (095) 246-99-80; fax (095) 245-02-95; attached to Russian Acad. of Medical Sciences; Dir YU. V. DUDNIK.

Semashko, N. A., Research Institute of Social Hygiene, Health Service Economics and Management: 103064 Moscow, Ul. Vorontsovo Pole 12; tel. 917-48-86; fax 916-03-98; f. 1944; attached to Russian Acad. of Medical Sciences; Dir O. P. SHCHEPIN; publs *Bulletin, Journal of Social Hygiene and the History of Medicine*.

Serbsky National Research Centre for Social and Forensic Psychiatry: 119034 Moscow, Kropotkinsky per. 23; tel. 201-52-62; fax 201-49-31; f. 1921; forensic psychiatry, social and clinical issues of psychiatry; library of 48,700 vols; Dir T. B. DMITRIEVA.

Sochi Health Research Institute: Sochi, Kurortny pr. 110.

State Institute of Natural Curative Factors: 357500 Pyatigorsk, Pr. Kirova 30; tel. 50-050; fax 55-618; f. 1920; neurology, rheumatology, pain assessment and management, behavioural therapy; library of 120,000 vols; Dir Prof. KRIVOBOROV.

State Research Institute for the Standardization and Control of Drugs: 117246 Moscow, Nauchni proezd 14A; tel. 128-26-32; Dir Prof. YU. F. KRYLOV.

State Scientific Research Institute of Medical Polymers: 117246 Moscow, Nauchni proezd 10; tel. (095) 120-21-62; fax (095) 120-05-61; f. 1966; library of 15,000 vols; Dir Prof. G. A. MATJUSHIN.

Sysin, A. N., Institute of Human Ecology and Environmental Hygiene: 119833 Moscow, Ul. Pogodinskaya 10; tel. (095) 246-58-24; fax (095) 247-04-28; f. 1931; attached to Russian Acad. of Medical Sciences; Dir G. I. SIDORENKO.

Tarasevich, L. A., State Research Institute for the Standardization and Control of Medical Biological Preparations: 121002 Moscow, Sivtsev-vrazhek 41; tel. and fax 241-39-22; f. 1919; library of 20,000 vols; Dir Prof. N. V. MEDUNTSIN.

Technological Research Institute for Antibiotics and Medical Enzymes: 198020 St Petersburg, Ogorodnikov pr. 41; tel. 251-19-44; telex 2516823; fax 121361; f. 1956; antifungal antibiotics, enzymes for medical use, nucleoside preparation of cardiovascular action; library of 55,000 vols; Dir Dr B. V. MOSKVICHEV.

Tomsk Institute of Physiotherapy and Spa Treatment: Tomsk, Ul. Rosa Luxembourg 1.

Tomsk Research Centre: 634012 Tomsk, Kievskaya ul. 111/2; fax (3822) 44-50-57; attached to Russian Acad. of Medical Sciences; Chairman of the Presidium R. S. KARPOV.

Incorporates:

Institute of Cardiology: 634012 Tomsk, Kievskaya ul. 111/2; tel. (3822) 44-33-97; attached to Russian Acad. of Medical Sciences; Dir R. S. KARPOV.

Institute of Oncology: 634001 Tomsk, Kooperativnyi per 5; tel. (3822) 23-04-86; attached to Russian Acad. of Medical Sciences; Dir B. N. ZYRYANOV.

Institute of Mental Health: 634014 Tomsk, Pos. Sosnovyi Bor; fax (3822) 77-84-25; attached to Russian Acad. of Medical Sciences; Dir V. YA. SEMKE.

Institute of Medical Genetics: 634050 Tomsk, Pos. Sputnik, Nab. Ushaika 10; tel. (3822) 22-22-28; attached to Russian Acad. of Medical Sciences; Dir V. P. PUZYREV.

Institute of Pharmacology: 634028 Tomsk, Pr. Lenina 3; fax (3822) 41-83-79; attached to Russian Acad. of Medical Sciences; Dir E. D. GOLDBERG.

Laboratory of Experimental Biomedical Models: 634009 Tomsk, Kooperativny per. 7B; tel. (3822) 22-36-26; attached to Russian Acad. of Medical Sciences; Dir S. A. KUSMARTSEV.

Toxicological Institute: 193019 St Petersburg, Ul. Bekhtereva 1; tel. 265-06-80; Dir S. N. GOLIKOV.

Turner Scientific Research Institute of Child Orthopaedics and Traumatology: 189620 St Petersburg, Ul. Parkovaya 64–68; tel. 465-28-57; f. 1932; library of 33,600 vols; Dir Prof. V. L. ANDRIANOV; publs scientific papers (2–3 a year).

Ufa Eye Research Institute: 450025 Ufa, Ul. Pushkinskaya 90; tel. 22-37-75; fax 22-08-52; e-mail eye@academy.bashnet.ru; f. 1926; Dir Prof. M. T. AZNABAYEV; publ. *Collected Articles* (annually).

Ufa Research Institute of Occupational Health and Human Ecology: 450106 Ufa, Ul. Kuvykina 94; tel. (3472) 28-53-19; fax (3472) 28-49-16; f. 1955; complex development of scientific fundamentals of labour hygiene and physiology, industrial toxicology, occupational pathology, environmental hygiene and aspects of hygiene in juvenile vocational training and the workplace in the oil, petrochemical, gas and microbiological industries; library of 63,000 vols; Dir A. B. BAKIROV; publ. *Production and Environmental Hygiene: Workers' Health Care in Oil and Gas Extracting and Petrochemical Industries* (annually).

Ufa Skin and Venereal Diseases Institute: Ufa, Ul. Frunze 43.

Urals Research Institute of Maternity and Childhood Care: 620028 Ekaterinburg, Ul. Repina 1; tel. (3432) 51-42-02; fax (3432) 51-22-12; f. 1877; library of 30,000 vols; Dir Dr G. A. CHERDANTSEVA.

Urals Research Institute of Phthisiopulmonology: 620039 Ekaterinburg, Ul. 22 partsezda 50; tel. 32-72-20; fax 32-77-52; f. 1931; library of 8,000 vols; Dir V. A. SOKOLOV.

Urology Research Institute: 105425 Moscow, 3-ya Parkovaya ul. 51; tel. 367-62-62.

Vishnevsky, A. V., Institute of Surgery: 113811 Moscow, Bolshaya Serpukhovskaya 27; tel. (095) 236-72-90; fax (095) 237-08-14; attached to Russian Acad. of Medical Sciences; Dir V. D. FEDOROV.

Volgograd Plague Prevention Research Institute: 400087 Volgograd, Golubinskaya ul. 7; tel. 37-37-74; fax 32-33-36; f. 1970; library of 13,320 vols; Dir N. G. TIKHONOV.

Voronezh Region Radiological and Oncological Institute: Voronezh, Ul. Kalyaeva 2.

NATURAL SCIENCES

General

Arctic and Antarctic Research Institute: 199397 St Petersburg, Ul. Beringa 38; tel. (812) 352-00-96; telex 121432; fax (812) 352-26-88; Dir I. YE. FROLOV.

Institute of Economic and International Problems of the Assimilation of the Ocean: 690600 Vladivostok, Ul. Sukhanova 5-a; tel: 5-77-31; attached to Russian Acad. of Sciences; Dir. R. SH.-A. ALIEV.

Institute of Global Climate and Ecology: 107258 Moscow, Glebovskaya 20B; tel. 169-01-43; attached to Russian Acad. of Sciences; Dir YU. A. IZRAEL.

Institute of Limnology: 664033 Irkutsk, Ulan-Batorskaya ul. 3; fax (3952) 46-04-05; e-mail root@lin.irkutsk.su; attached to Russian Acad. of Sciences; Dir M. A. GRACHEV.

Institute of Limnology: 196199 St Petersburg, Ul. Sevastyanova 9; tel. 297-22-97; attached to Russian Acad. of Sciences; Dir V. A. RUMYANTSEV.

Institute of Natural Sciences: 670042 Ulan-Ude, Ul. M. Sakhyanovoi 6; tel. 3-01-62; attached to Russian Acad. of Sciences; Dir K. A. NIKIFOROV.

Institute of the History of Natural Science and Technology: 103012 Moscow, Staropanskii per. 1/5; tel. (095) 921-80-61; fax (095) 925-99-11; e-mail postmaster@history.ihst.ru; f. 1953; attached to Russian Acad. of Sciences; library of 70,000 vols; Dir Dr VLADIMIR M. OREL; publ. *Voprosy istorii estestvoznaniya i tekhniki* (4 a year); br. in St Petersburg: 119034 St Petersburg, Universitetskaya nab. 5; tel. (812) 218-47-12.

Mountain Taiga Station: 692533 Primorskii krai, Ussuriisky raion, pos. Gornotaezhnoe; tel. 9-11-10; attached to Russian Acad. of Sciences; Dir B. S. PETROPAVLOVSKY.

North-Eastern Complex Scientific Research Institute: 685010 Magadan, Portovaya 16; tel. 3-06-11; fax 3-00-51; e-mail root@neisri.magadan.su; f. 1960; attached to Russian Acad. of Sciences; geology, geophysics, metallogeny, history, archaeology, economics; library of 450,000 vols; Dir Dr V. I. GONCHAROV.

P.P. Shirshov Institute of Oceanology: 117218 Moscow, Ul. Krasikova 23; tel. (095) 124-59-96; fax (095) 124-59-83; attached to Russian Acad. of Sciences; brs in Kaliningrad, Gelendzhik, St Petersburg; Dir Prof. S. S. LAPPO.

Pacific Oceanological Institute: 690041 Vladivostok, Baltiiskaya ul. 43; tel. (4232) 31-14-00; fax (4232) 31-25-73; attached to Russian Acad. of Sciences; Dir Prof. V. A. AKULICHEV.

Biological Sciences

All-Russia Research Institute for Nature Conservation: 113628 Moscow, Znamenskoe-Sadki, VNII Priroda; tel. (095) 423-03-22; fax (095) 423-23-22; f. 1981; research, general methodology, environmental protection strategy and co-ordination at home and internationally; five departments: animal protection, plant protection, ecosystem protection and recovery (including aquatic ecosystems), utilization of natural resources and nature reserves; library (books, journals, theses); Dir Prof. V. A. KRASILOV.

All-Russia Research Institute of Applied Microbiology: 142279 Moscow oblast, Serpukhovsky raion, Obolensk; tel. Serpukhov 2-77-61; Dir N. N. URAKOV.

All-Russia Research Institute of Especially Pure Biopreparations: 197110 St Petersburg, Pudozhskaya ul. 7; Dir E. N. SVENTITSKY.

Bakh, A. N., Institute of Biochemistry: 117071 Moscow, Leninskii Pr. 33; tel. 954-52-83; attached to Russian Acad. of Sciences; Dir B. F. POGLAZOV.

Bioengineering Research Centre: 117984 Moscow, Ul. Vavilova 34/5; tel. 135-73-19; telex

411755; fax 135-05-71; attached to Russian Acad. of Sciences; Dir K. G. SKRYABIN.

Biotechnical Research Institute: 119034 Moscow, Ul. Prechistenka 38; tel. 246-16-56; Dir A. M. KARPOV.

Biotechnologia JSC: 117246 Moscow, Nauchny proezd 8; tel. (095) 332-34-20; fax (095) 331-01-01; f. 1993 as private company (fmrly state enterprise, f. 1986); biotechnology, pharmaceuticals; Gen. Dir RAIF G. VASILOV.

Engelhardt Institute of Molecular Biology: 117984 Moscow, Ul. Vavilova 32; tel. (095) 135-23-11; fax (095) 135-14-05; attached to Russian Acad. of Sciences; Dir Acad. A. D. MIRZABEKOV.

Institute of Applied Molecular Biology: 113149 Moscow, Simferopolsky bul. 8; tel. 113-23-51; fax 13-26-33; Dir E. S. SEVERIN.

Institute of Biological Problems of the North: 685000 Magadan, Pr. K. Marksa 24; tel. (41322) 2-47-30; fax (41322) 2-01-66; e-mail ibpn@ibpn.magadan.su; f. 1972; attached to Russian Acad. of Sciences; Dir Prof. F. B. CHERNYAVSKY.

Institute of Biology: 630091 Novosibirsk, Ul. Frunze 11; tel. 20-96-14; attached to Russian Acad. of Sciences; Dir V. I. EVSIKOV.

Institute of Biology: 185610 Petrozavodsk, Pushkinskaya ul. 11; tel. 7-36-15; attached to Russian Acad. of Sciences; Dir S. N. DROZDOV.

Institute of Biology: 167610 Syktyvkar, Kommunisticheskaya ul. 28; tel. (8212) 42-52-02; fax (8212) 42-01-63; e-mail taskaev@biology.komitex.ru; f. 1962; attached to Russian Acad. of Sciences; Dir Dr A. I. TASKAEV.

Institute of Biology: 450054 Ufa, 25, Pr. Oktyabrya 69; tel. 34-34-01; attached to Russian Acad. of Sciences; Dir V. M. KORSUNOV.

Institute of Biology: 670042 Ulan-Ude, Ul. M. Sakhyanovoi 6; tel. 3-36-75; attached to Russian Acad. of Sciences; Dir V. M. KORSUNOV.

Institute of Biology: 677891 Yakutsk, Pr. Lenina 41; tel. 2-77-81; attached to Russian Acad. of Sciences; Dir. N. G. SOLOMONOV.

Institute of Biology and Soil Science: 690022 Vladivostok, Pr. Stoletiya Vladivostoka 159; tel. (4232) 31-13-85; fax (4232) 31-01-93; f. 1962; attached to Russian Acad. of Sciences; library of 80,000 vols; Dir Prof. YU. N. ZHURAVLEV; publ. *Proceedings* (in Russian, 1 a year).

Institute of Bio-organic Chemistry: 630090 Novosibirsk, Pr. Akademika Lavrenteva 8; tel. 35-64-41; fax 35-16-65; e-mail vlasov@modul.bioch.nsk.su; attached to Russian Acad. of Sciences; Dir Prof. V. V. VLASOV.

Institute of Biophysics: 660036 Krasnoyarsk, Akademgorodok; tel. (3912) 43-15-79; telex 288139; fax (3912) 43-34-00; attached to Russian Acad. of Sciences; Dir Dr A. G. DEGERMENDZHY.

Institute of Biophysics: 123182 Moscow, Zhivopisnaya ul. 46; tel. (095) 190-56-51; fax (095) 190-35-90; e-mail ibphgen@rcibph.dol.ru; f. 1946; radiobiology, radiation protection, health physics, medical radiology, non-ionizing radiation; Dir L. A. ILYIN.

Institute of Cell Biophysics: 142292 Moscow oblast, Serpukhovskii raion, Pushchino; tel. 925-59-84; fax 779-05-09; e-mail admin@ibfk.nifhi.ac.ru; attached to Russian Acad. of Sciences; Dir Prof. E. E. FESENKO.

Institute of Cytology: 194064 St Petersburg, Tikhoretskii, pr. 4; tel. 247-18-29; fax 247-03-41; attached to Russian Acad. of Sciences; Dir N. N. NIKOLSKY.

Institute of Cytology and Genetics: 630090 Novosibirsk, Pr. akademika Lavrenteva 10; tel. 35-12-65; fax 35-65-68; attached to Russian Acad. of Sciences; Dir V. K. SHUMNY.

Institute of Food Substances: C/o Russian Academy of Sciences, 117901 Moscow, Leninsky pr. 14; attached to Russian Acad. of Sciences; Dir M. N. MANAKOV.

Institute of General Biophysics: 142292 Moscow oblast, Serpukhovsky raion, Pushchino; attached to Russian Acad. of Sciences; Dir L. M. CHAILKHYAN.

Institute of Higher Nervous Activity and Neurophysiology: 117865 Moscow, Ul. Butlerova 5a; tel. 334-70-00; attached to Russian Acad. of Sciences; Dir Acad. P. V. SIMONOV.

Institute of Marine Biology: Petropavlovsk-Kamchatskii; attached to Russian Acad. of Sciences; Dir (vacant).

Institute of Marine Biology: 690041 Vladivostok, Ul. Palchevskogo 17; tel. (4232) 31-09-05; fax (4232) 31-09-00; e-mail aisa@vld.global-one.ru; f. 1970; attached to Russian Acad. of Sciences; library of 37,000 vols; Dir Prof. VLADIMIR L. KASYANOV; publ. *Biologiya morya* (6 a year).

Institute of Microbiology: 117811 Moscow, Pr 60-letiya Oktyabrya 7, Korp. 2; tel. 135-45-66; telex 411634; attached to Russian Acad. of Sciences; Dir Acad. M. V. IVANOV.

Institute of Molecular Biology of the Gene: 117333 Moscow, Ul. Vavilova 34/5; tel. 135-60-89; attached to Russian Acad. of Sciences; Dir Acad. G. P. GEORGIEV.

Institute of Molecular Genetics: 123182 Moscow, Pl. Kurchatova 46; tel. (095) 196-00-00; fax (095) 196-02-21; f. 1978; attached to Russian Acad. of Sciences; Dir E. D. SVERDLOV.

Institute of Parasitology: 117071 Moscow, Leninskii Pr. 33; tel. 952-57-46; attached to Russian Acad. of Sciences; Dir M. D. SONIN.

Institute of Physiologically Active Substances: 142432 Moscow oblast, Noginskii raion, p/o Chernogolovka; tel. 524-50-62; attached to Russian Acad. of Sciences; Dir Acad. N. S. ZEFIROV.

Institute of Physiology: C/o Russian Academy of Sciences, 117901 Moscow, Leninsky pr. 14; attached to Russian Acad. of Sciences; Dir O. G. GAZENKO.

Institute of Physiology: 167610 Syktyvkar, Kommunisticheskaya ul. 24; tel. (8212) 42-16-08; fax (8212) 42-22-64; f. 1988; attached to Russian Acad. of Sciences; Dir Prof. Dr M. P. ROSHCHEVSKY.

Institute of Plant and Animal Ecology: 620008 Ekaterinburg, Ul. 8 Marta 202; tel. 22-05-70; attached to Russian Acad. of Sciences; Dir Acad. V. N. BOLSHAKOV.

Institute of Problems of the Industrial Ecology of the North: 184200 Murmansk oblast, Apatity, Ul. Fersmana 14; tel. (81555) 3-00-83; fax (via Norway) 78-91-41-17; e-mail kalabin@inep.ksc.ru; f. 1989; attached to Russian Acad. of Sciences; library of 400,000 vols; Dir Prof. G. V. KALABIN.

Institute of Protein Research: 142292 Moscow oblast, Serpukhovskii raion, Pushchino; tel. and fax (095) 924-04-93; e-mail protres@sun.ipr.serpukhov.su; attached to Russian Acad. of Sciences; Dir Prof. A. S. SPIRIN.

Institute of Soil Science and Photosynthesis: 142292 Moscow oblast, Serpukhovskii raion, Pushchino; tel. 923-35-58; telex 205128; fax (0967) 79-05-32; attached to Russian Acad. of Sciences; Dir V. I. KEFELYA.

Institute of the Biochemistry and Physiology of Micro-organisms: 142292 Moscow oblast, Serpukhovskii raion, Pushchino; tel. 3-05-26; telex 412609; attached to Russian Acad. of Sciences; Dir A. M. BORONIN.

Institute of the Biochemistry and Physiology of Plants and Micro-organisms: 410015 Saratov, Pr. Entuziastov 13; tel. (8452) 44-38-28; fax (8452) 44-73-03; e-mail root@ibppm.saratov.su; f. 1980; attached to Russian Acad. of Sciences; library of 30,000 vols; Dir V. V. IGNATOV.

Institute of the Biology of Inland Waters: 152742 Yaroslavskaya oblast, Nekouzsky raion, p/o Borok; tel. and fax (0852) 25-38-45; telex 412583; attached to Russian Acad. of Sciences; Dir Dr A. I. KOPYLOV.

Institute of the Ecology and Genetics of Micro-organisms: 614081 Perm, Ul. Goleva 13; tel. (3422) 64-67-12; fax (3422) 64-67-11; e-mail mike@iegm.perm.su; f. 1988; attached to Russian Acad. of Sciences; library of 3,000 vols; Dir V. A. CHERESHNEV; publ. *Proceedings of Scientific Research* (1 a year).

Institute of the Ecology of Natural Complexes: Tomsk; attached to Russian Acad. of Sciences; Dir V. N. VOROBEV.

Institute of the Ecology of the Volga Basin: 445003 Tolyatti; tel. (8469) 23-54-78; fax (8469) 48-95-04; attached to Russian Acad. of Sciences; Dir G. S. ROZENBERG.

Institute of Water and Environmental Problems: 656099 Barnaul, Ul. Papanintsev 105; tel. (3852) 36-78-56; fax (3852) 24-03-96; e-mail iwep@iwep.altai.su; f. 1987; attached to Russian Acad. of Sciences; library of 30,000 vols; Dir Prof. YURI VINOKUROV.

Institute of Water and Ecological Problems: 680063 Khabarovsk, Ul. Kim Yu Chena 65; tel. (4212) 22-75-73; fax (4212) 22-70-85; attached to Russian Acad. of Sciences; Dir B. A. VORONOV.

Kazan Institute of Biology: 420111 Kazan, Ul. Lobachevskogo 2/31; tel. 32-64-91; attached to Russian Acad. of Sciences; Dir Dr A. I. TARCHEVSKY.

Koltsov, A. N., Institute of Developmental Biology: 117808 Moscow, Ul. Vavilova 26; tel. 135-64-83; attached to Russian Acad. of Sciences; Dir N. G. KHRUSHCHOV.

Komarov, V. L., Botanical Institute: 197376 St Petersburg, Ul. Prof. Popova 2; tel. (812) 234-12-37; fax (812) 234-45-12; attached to Russian Acad. of Sciences; Dir L. YU. BUDANTSEV.

Murmansk Marine Biological Institute: 183010 Murmansk, Vladimirskaya ul. 17; tel. (8152) 56-52-32; fax (512) 951-02-88; e-mail mmbi@online.ru; f. 1935; attached to Russian Acad. of Sciences; library of 70,000 vols; Dir Acad. G. G. MATISHOV.

Pacific Institute of Bio-organic Chemistry: 690022 Vladivostok, Pr. 100-letiya Vladivostoka 159; tel. (4232) 31-14-30; fax (4232) 31-40-50; f.1964; attached to Russian Acad. of Sciences; Dir Prof. G. B. ELYAKOV.

Palaeontological Institute: 117647 Moscow, Profsoyuznaya 123; tel. (095) 339-05-77; fax (095) 339-12-66; f. 1930; attached to Russian Acad. of Sciences; library of 20,000 vols; Dir Prof. A. YU. ROZANOV; publs *Journal* (quarterly), *Transactions* (3 or 4 a year).

Pavlov, I. P., Institute of Physiology: 199034 St Petersburg, Nab. Makarova 6; tel. 218-07-01; attached to Russian Acad. of Sciences; Dir Acad. V. A. GOVYRIN.

Pushchino Research Centre for Biological Research: 142292 Moscow Oblast, Pushchino; tel. Serpukhov 3-27-11; attached to Russian Acad. of Sciences; Dir E. L. GOLOVLEV.

Research Institute for Monitoring Land and Ecosystems: 101000 Moscow, Bolshevistaky per. 11; tel. 924-55-52.

Research Institute for the Biological Testing of Chemical Compounds: Moscow oblast, Kupavna, Ul. Kirova 23; Dir L. A. PIRUZYAN.

Research Institute for the Biosynthesis of Protein Substances: 109004 Moscow,

Bolshaya Kommunisticheskaya 27; tel. 912-70-09; Dir A. P. ZAKHARYUCHEV.

Research Institute for the Genetics and Selection of Industrial Micro-organisms: 113545 Moscow, 1-i Dorozhnyi per. 1; tel. 315-37-47; telex 411718; Dir V. G. DEBABOV.

Research Institute of Food Biotechnology: 109033 Moscow, Samokatnaya 4B; tel. 362-44-95.

Scientific Centre of Biological Research: Moscow oblast, Serpukhovskii raion, Pushchino; attached to Russian Acad. of Sciences; Dir E. L. GOLOVLEV.

Sechenov, I. M., Institute of Evolutionary Physiology and Biochemistry: 194223 St Petersburg, Pr. M. Toreza 44; tel. 552-79-01; attached to Russian Acad. of Sciences; Dir Acad. V. L. SVIDERSKY.

Severtsov, A. N., Institute of Evolutionary Morphology and Animal Ecology: 117071 Moscow, Leninskii Pr. 33; tel. 954-75-53; attached to Russian Acad. of Sciences; Dir Acad. V. E. SOKOLOV.

Shemyakin-Ovchinnikov Institute of Bio-organic Chemistry: 117871 Moscow, Ul. Miklukho-Maklaya 16/10; tel. (095) 335-01-00; fax (095) 310-70-07; e-mail ivavt@ibch.siobc.ras.ru; f. 1959; attached to Russian Acad. of Sciences; library of 250,000 vols; br. at Pushchino; Dir Prof. V. T. IVANOV; publ. *Journal of Bio-organic Chemistry* (in Russian and English, monthly).

Siberian Institute of Plant Physiology and Biochemistry: 664033 Irkutsk 33, a/ya 1243; tel. 46-07-21; attached to Russian Acad. of Sciences; Dir R. K. SALYAEV.

State Research Centre of Virology and Biotechnology: 633159 Novosibirsk oblast, pos. Koltsovo; tel. (3832) 64-01-40; fax (3832) 32-88-31; e-mail vector@vector.nsk.su; f. 1974; library of 90,000 vols; Dir Acad. LEV S. SANDAKHCHIEV.

Timiryazev, K. A., Institute of Plant Physiology: 127276 Moscow, Botanicheskaya 35; tel. 482-32-58; fax 482-16-85; e-mail vladimir@ad.plantphys.msk.ru; f. 1890; attached to Russian Acad. of Sciences; library of 83,000 vols; Dir Prof. VL. V. KUZNETSOV; publ. *Russian Journal of Plant Physiology* (6 a year).

Vavilov, N. I., Institute of General Genetics: 117809 Moscow, Ul. Gubkina 3; tel. (095) 135-62-13; fax (095) 135-12-89; e-mail postmaster@iogen.msk.su; attached to Russian Acad. of Sciences; library of 5,000 vols; Dir Prof. YU. P. ALTUKHOV.

Zoological Institute: 199034 St. Petersburg, Universitetskaya Nab. 1; tel. 218-02-11; attached to Russian Acad. of Sciences; Dir O. A. SKARLATO.

Mathematical Sciences

Euler, L., International Institute of Mathematics: St Petersburg; attached to Russian Acad. of Sciences; Dir Acad. L. D. FADDEEV.

Institute of Mathematics: 630090 Novosibirsk, Pr. Akad. Koptyuga 4; tel. (3832) 33-28-92; fax (3832) 33-25-98; e-mail gelios@math.nsc.ru; f. 1957; attached to Russian Acad. of Sciences; library of 120,000 vols; Dir Acad. M. M. LAVRENTEV; publs *Sibirsky Matematichesky Zhurnal* (6 a year), *Diskretny Analiz i Issledovanie Operatsii* (series 1, 4 a year; series 2, 2 a year), *Matematicheskie Trudy* (2 a year), *Sibirsky Zhurnal Industrialnoy Matematiki* (4 a year).

Institute of Mathematics: 450057 Ufa, Ul. Tukaeva 50; tel. 22-59-36; attached to Russian Acad. of Sciences; Dir V. V. NAPALKOV.

Steklov, V. A., Institute of Mathematics: 117966 Moscow, Ul. Gubkina 8; tel. 135-22-91; attached to Russian Acad. of Sciences; Dir Acad. YU. S. OSIPOV.

Steklov, V. A., Institute of Mathematics, St Petersburg Branch: 191011 St Petersburg, Nab. Fontanki 25–27; tel. 312-40-58; attached to Russian Acad. of Sciences; Dir Acad. L. D. FADDEEV.

Physical Sciences

All-Russia Geological Oil Research Institute (VNIGNI): 105819 Moscow, Shosse Entuziastov 36; tel. 273-26-51; fax 273-55-38; f. 1953; library of 80,000 vols; Dir Dr K. A. KLESCHEV; publs *Geology of Oil and Gas* (annually), *Proceedings* (6 a year).

All-Russia Research Institute for the Geology and Mineral Resources of the World's Oceans: 190121 St Petersburg, Angliisky 1; tel. (812) 113-83-79; fax (812) 114-14-70; f. 1948; library of 60,500 vols; Dir Prof. I. S. GRAMBERG.

All-Russia Research Institute of Chemical Technology: 115409 Moscow, Kashirskoe shosse 33; tel. 324-61-55.

All-Russia Research Institute of Hydrolysis: 198099 St Petersburg, Ul. Kalinina 13; tel. 186-29-22; Dir O. I. SHAPOVALOV.

All-Russia Research Institute of Natural Gases and Gas Technology: 142717 Moscow oblast, Leninsky raion, Pos. Razvilka; tel. (095) 355-92-06; fax (095) 399-16-77; e-mail samsr@gazprom.ru; f. 1948; library of 100,000 vols.

All-Russia Research Institute of Optical and Physical Measurements: 103031 Moscow, Ul. Rozhdestvenka 27; tel. 208-41-83; attached to Russian Acad. of Sciences; Gen. Dir I. G. BARANNIK.

All-Russia Research Institute of Physical-Technical and Radiotechnical Measurements: 147570 Moscow oblast, Solnechnogorsky raion, p/o Mendeleevo; tel. 535-92-78; attached to Russian Acad. of Sciences; Dir B. I. ALSKIN.

All-Russia Scientific Research Institute of Geological, Geophysical and Geochemical Systems: 113015 Moscow, Varshavskoe shosse 8; tel. (095) 954-53-50; fax (095) 958-37-11; f. 1961; library of 38,000 vols; Dir O. L. KUZNETSOV; publ. *Geoinformatika* (6 a year).

All-Russia Scientific Research Institute of Mineral Resources: 109017 Moscow, Staromonetni per. 31; tel. (095) 231-50-43; telex 911614; fax (095) 238-19-21; f. 1918; prospecting for and estimating ore deposits, research in processing; library of 345,000 vols; Dir Prof. A. N. EREMEEV.

Amur Complex Research Institute: 675000 Amur oblast, Blagoveshchensk, per. Relochnyi 1; tel. (4162) 42-72-32; fax (4162) 42-59-31; e-mail root@intpmr.amur.su; f. 1980; attached to Russian Acad. of Sciences; geology, minerals; library of 26,000 vols; Dir V. G. MOISEENKO.

Andreev, N. N., Acoustics Institute: 117036 Moscow, Ul. Shvernika 4; tel. 126-74-01; attached to Russian Acad. of Sciences; Dir N. A. DUBROVSKY.

Arbuzov, A. E., Institute of Organic and Physical Chemistry: 420083 Kazan, Ul. Ak. Arbuzova 8; tel. 76-82-54; attached to Russian Acad. of Sciences; Dir A. N. VERESHCHAGIN.

Baikov, A. A., Institute of Metallurgy: 117911 Moscow, Leninskii Pr. 49; tel. 135-86-11; telex 411577; attached to Russian Acad. of Sciences; Dir Acad. N. P. LYAKISHEV.

Bardin, I. P., Central Research Institute of Ferrous Metallurgy: 107005 Moscow, 2-ya Baumanskaya 9/23; tel. (095) 265-72-04; fax (095) 267-48-27; e-mail ferrum.sc.@online.ru; f. 1944; library of 65,000 vols; Dir-Gen. VLADIMIR I. MATORIN.

Bochvar, A. A., All-Russia Research Institute of Inorganic Materials: 123060 Moscow, Ul. Rogova 5A; tel. 190-82-97.

Boreskov Institute of Catalysis: 630090 Novosibirsk, Pr. akademika Lavrenteva 5; tel. 35-22-69; telex 133122; fax 35-57-66; attached to Russian Acad. of Sciences; Dir V. N. PARMON.

Central Aerological Observatory: 141700 Moscow, Dolgoprudny, Pervomayskaya St 3; tel. 408-61-48; telex 911577; fax 576-33-27; f. 1941; atmospheric physics and chemistry up to 100km, study and monitoring of ozone layer, cloud physics, applied meteorology, weather modification; use of aircraft, rocket, satellite, radar and other facilities; library of 61,000 vols; Dir A. CHERNIKOV; publ. *CAO Proceedings*.

Central Seismological Observatory: Obninsk; telex 412639; attached to Russian Acad. of Sciences.

Chita Institute of Natural Resources: 672014 Chita, Ul. Nedorezova 16; tel. and fax (302) 221-25-82; f. 1981; attached to Russian Acad. of Sciences; library of 6,000 vols; Dir V. V. MAZALOV; publ. *Report on Environmental Conditions in Zabailkalye* (1 a year).

Far Eastern Institute of Geology: 690022 Vladivostok, Pr. 100-letiya Vladivostoka 159; tel. (4232) 31-87-50; fax (4232) 31-78-47; e-mail fegi@online.marine.su; f. 1959; attached to Russian Acad. of Sciences; Dir A. I. KHANCHUK.

Frumkin, A. N., Institute of Electro-Chemistry: 117071 Moscow, Leninskii Pr. 31; tel. 952-04-28; attached to Russian Acad. of Sciences; Dir V. E. KAZARINOV.

Geological Institute: 670047 Ulan-Ude, Ul. Sakhyanova 6; tel. (3012) 33-09-55; fax (3012) 33-60-24; e-mail burgin@eastsib.ru; f. 1973; attached to Russian Acad. of Sciences; Dir A. G. MIRONOV.

Graphite Research Institute: 111524 Moscow, Elektrodnaya 2; tel. (095) 176-13-06; fax (095) 176-12-63; Dir V. I. KOSTIKOV.

Grebenshchikov, I. V., Institute of Silicates Chemistry: 199155 St Petersburg, Ul. Odoevskogo 24, Korp. 2; tel. 350-65-16; telex 121447; attached to Russian Acad. of Sciences; Dir Acad. M. M. SHULTS.

Institute for Superplasticity Problems in Metals: 450001 Ufa, Ul. St Khalturina 39; tel. (3472) 24-64-07; fax (3472) 25-37-59; e-mail nail@ipsm.bashkiria.su; f. 1985; attached to Russian Acad. of Sciences; library of 7,000 vols; Dir Prof. O. A. KAIBYSHEV.

Institute of Applied Astronomy: 197042 St Petersburg, Ul. Zhdanovskaya 8; tel. 230-74-14; telex 121391; fax 230-74-13; attached to Russian Acad. of Sciences; Dir A. M. FINKELSTEIN.

Institute of Applied Physics: 603600 Nizhnii Novgorod, Ul. Ulyanova 46; tel. 38-90-91; telex 151129; attached to Russian Acad. of Sciences; Dir Acad. A. V. GAPONOV-GREKHOV.

Institute of Astronomy: 109017 Moscow, Pyatnitskaya ul. 48; tel. (095) 951-54-61; attached to Russian Acad. of Sciences; Dir Acad. A. A. BOYARCHUK.

Institute of Atmospheric Physics: 109017 Moscow, Pyzhevskii per. 3; tel. (095) 951-55-65; fax (095) 953-16-52; e-mail adm@omega.ifaran.ru; f. 1956; attached to Russian Acad. of Sciences; library of 4,000 vols, 40 periodicals; Dir Acad. G. S. GOLITSYN; publ. *Izvestiya – Atmospheric and Oceanic Physics* (6 a year).

Institute of Chemical Kinetics and Combustion: 630090 Novosibirsk, Institutskaya 3; tel. (3832) 34-41-50; fax (3832) 34-23-50; e-mail root@kinetics.nsk.su; f. 1957; attached to Russian Acad. of Sciences; library of 88,000 vols; Dir Prof. YU. D. TSVETKOV.

Institute of Chemical Physics: Chernogolovka; attached to Russian Acad. of Sciences; Dir S. M. BATURIN.

Institute of Chemistry: 690022 Vladivostok, Pr. 100-letiya Vladivostoka 159; tel. (4232) 31-25-90; fax (4232) 31-18-89; f. 1971; attached to Russian Acad. of Sciences; library of 5,000 vols; Dir Prof. Dr V. YU. GLUSHCHENKO.

Institute of Coal: 650025 Kemerovo, Ul. Rukavishnikova 21; tel. (3842) 28-14-33; telex 215113; fax (3842) 21-18-38; f. 1983; attached to Russian Acad. of Sciences; library of 40,000 vols; Dir G. I. GRITSKO; publ. *Coalbed Methane* (4 a year).

Institute of Coal and Coal Chemistry: 650099 Kemerovo, Sovetsky pr. 18; tel. (3842) 28-14-33; fax (3842) 36-57-69; e-mail chem@sib1.kuzbass.net; f. 1998; attached to Russian Acad. of Sciences; Dir Prof. G. I. GRITSKO.

Institute of Electrophysics: 620219 Ekaterinburg, Komsomolskaya ul. 34; tel. 44-18-53; attached to Russian Acad. of Sciences; Dir Acad. G. A. MESYATS.

Institute of Energy Problems of Chemical Physics: 117829 Moscow, Leninskii pr. 38, Korp. 2; tel. 137-34-79; attached to Russian Acad. of Sciences; Dir V. L. TALROZE.

Institute of Experimental Meteorology: Obninsk; Dir M. A. PETROSYANTS.

Institute of Experimental Mineralogy: 142432 Moscow oblast, Noginskii raion, Chernogolovka; tel. (095) 524-50-39; fax (095) 913-21-12; e-mail fedkin@iem.ac.ru; f. 1969; attached to Russian Acad. of Sciences; Dir V. A. ZHARIKOV; publ. *Experiments in Geosciences* (4 a year).

Institute of General Physics: 117942 Moscow, Ul. Vavilova 38; tel. 135-23-66; telex 411074; attached to Russian Acad. of Sciences; br. in Tarusa; Dir Acad. A. M. PROKHOROV.

Institute of Geochemistry: 664033 Irkutsk, Ul. Favorskogo 1a; tel. 46-05-00; attached to Russian Acad. of Sciences; Dir M. I. KUZMIN.

Institute of Geology: Murmansk oblast, Apatity, Ul. Fersmana 14; fax (via Norway) 78-91-41-53; e-mail root@ksc-gi.murmansk.su; attached to Russian Acad. of Sciences; Dir F. P. MITROFANOV.

Institute of Geology: 367025 Makhachkala, Ul. Gadzhieva 45; attached to Russian Acad. of Sciences; Dir V. V. SUETNOV.

Institute of Geology: 109017 Moscow, Pyzhevskii per. 7; tel. (095) 230-80-29; fax (095) 231-04-43; f. 1930; attached to Russian Acad. of Sciences; Dir Y. G. LEONOV.

Institute of Geology: 185610 Petrozavodsk, Pushkinskaya ul. 11; tel. 7-27-53; attached to Russian Acad. of Sciences; Dir S. I. RYBAKOV.

Institute of Geology: 167610 Syktyvkar, Pervomaiskaya ul. 54; tel. (8212) 42-00-37; fax (8212) 42-53-46; e-mail institute@geo.komi.ru; f. 1958; attached to Russian Acad. of Sciences; Dir N. P. YUSHKIN; publ. *Vestnik* (monthly).

Institute of Geology: 450000 Ufa 25, Ul. K. Marxa 16/2; tel. 22-82-56; fax 23-03-68; attached to Russian Acad. of Sciences; Dir V. N. PUCHKOV.

Institute of Geology: 677891 Yakutsk, Pr. Lenina 39; tel. 3-53-81; attached to Russian Acad. of Sciences; Dir B. V. OLEINIKOV.

Institute of Geology and Precambrian Geochronology: 199034 St Petersburg, Nab. Makarova 2; tel. 218-47-01; attached to Russian Acad. of Sciences; Dir V. A. GLEBOVITSKY.

Institute of Geomechanics: C/o Russian Academy of Sciences, 117333 Moscow, Ul. Vavilova 44 (Korp. 2, Komn. 86); attached to Russian Acad. of Sciences.

Institute of Geophysics: 620219 Ekaterinburg, Ul. Amundsena 100; tel. 28-57-03; attached to Russian Acad. of Sciences; Dir B. P. RYZHII

Institute of Geothermal Problems: 367003 Makhachkala, Pr. Shamila 39-A; tel. and fax (8722) 62-93-57; f. 1980; attached to Russian Acad. of Sciences; Dir M.-K. M. MAGOMEDOV.

Institute of High-Pressure Physics: 142092 Moscow oblast, Troitsk; tel. (095) 334-00-10; fax (095) 334-00-12; attached to Russian Acad. of Sciences; Dir Prof. S. M. STISHOV.

Institute of High-Temperature Electrochemistry: 620219 Ekaterinburg, S. Kovalevskaya 20; tel. (3432) 74-50-89; fax (3432) 74-59-92; e-mail head@ihte.intec.ru; f. 1958; attached to Russian Acad. of Sciences; Head Dr V. A. KHOKHLOV; publ. *Rasplavy* (6 a year).

Institute of High Temperatures: 127412 Moscow, Izhorskaya 13/19; tel. 485-83-45; telex 411959; attached to Russian Acad. of Sciences; Dir V. M. BATENIN.

Institute of High-Energy Physics: 142284 Moscow oblast, Protvino; tel. (095) 924-67-52; telex 412657; fax (095) 230-23-37; f. 1963; library of 300,000 vols; Dir A. A. LOGUNOV.

Institute of High-Mountain Geophysics: 360030 Nalchik, Pr. Lenina 2; tel. (866) 222-75-44; fax (866) 227-00-24.

Institute of Hydrodynamics: 630090 Novosibirsk, Pr. akademika Lavrenteva 15; tel. and fax (3832) 33-16-12; e-mail root@hydro.nsk.ru; f. 1957; attached to Russian Acad. of Sciences; library of 85,000 vols; Dir V. M. TITOV; publs *Combustion Explosions and Shock Waves* (6 a year), *Journal of Applied Mechanics and Technical Physics* (6 a year).

Institute of Inorganic Chemistry: 630090 Novosibirsk, Pr. akademika Lavrenteva 3; tel. 35-59-50; attached to Russian Acad. of Sciences; Dir Acad. F. A. KUZNETSOV.

Institute of Macro-Molecular Compounds: 199004 St Petersburg, Bolshoi Pr. 31; tel. (812) 213-10-70; fax (812) 218-68-69; attached to Russian Acad. of Sciences; Dir E. F. PANARIN.

Institute of Marine Geology and Geophysics: 693002 Yuzhno-Sakhalinsk; Ul. Nauki 5; tel. 2-21-28; attached to Russian Acad. of Sciences; Dir K. F. SERGEEV.

Institute of Metal Physics: 620219 Ekaterinburg, GSP-170, Ul. S. Kovalevskoi 18; tel. (3432) 74-02-30; fax (3432) 74-52-44; e-mail phisica@ifm.e-burg.su; f. 1932; attached to Russian Acad. of Sciences; library of 18,000 vols, 92,000 periodicals; Dir V. V. USTINOV; publs *Fizika metallov i metallovedenie* (Physics of Metals and Metallography), *Defectoscopiya* (Journal of Non-Destructive Testing, monthly).

Institute of Metallo-organic Chemistry: 603600 Nizhnii Novgorod, Ul. Tropinina 49; tel. (8312) 66-27-09; fax (8312) 66-14-97; f. 1989; attached to Russian Acad. of Sciences; library of 50,000 vols; Dir G. A. ABAKUMOV.

Institute of Metallurgy: 620219 Ekaterinburg, Ul. Amundsena 101; tel. 28-53-00; attached to Russian Acad. of Sciences; Dir Acad. N. A. VATOLIN.

Institute of Mineralogy: 456301 Chelyabinsk obl., Miass; tel. 5-35-62; attached to Russian Acad. of Sciences; Dir V. N. ANFILOGOV.

Institute of New Chemical Problems: 142432 Moscow oblast, Noginsky raion, Chernogolovka; tel. 524-50-24; attached to Russian Acad. of Sciences; Dir V. N. TROITSKII.

Institute of Nuclear Physics: 630090 Novosibirsk, Pr. akademika Lavrenteva 11; tel. 35-97-77; telex 133116; fax 35-21-63; attached to Russian Acad. of Sciences; branch in Protvin; Dir Acad. A. N. SKRINSKY.

Institute of Nuclear Research: 117312 Moscow, Pr. 60-letiya Oktyabrya 7A; tel. 135-77-60; telex 411051; attached to Russian Acad. of Sciences; Dir Dr V. A. MATVEEV.

Institute of Oil Chemistry: 634055 Tomsk, Akademicheskii Pr. 3; tel. 1-86-23; attached to Russian Acad. of Sciences; Dir E. E. SIROTKINA.

Institute of Optics of the Atmosphere: 634055 Tomsk, Akademicheskii Pr. 1; tel. 1-82-26; telex 133190; attached to Russian Acad. of Sciences; Dir Acad. V. E. ZUEV.

Institute of Organic Chemistry: 630090 Novosibirsk, Akademgorodok, Pr. akademika Lavrenteva 9; tel. 35-16-52; attached to Russian Acad. of Sciences; Dir Acad. G. A. TOLSTIKOV.

Institute of Organic Chemistry: 450054 Ufa, Pr. Oktyabrya 71; tel. and fax (3472) 35-60-66; attached to Russian Acad. of Sciences; Dir M. S. YUNUSOV.

Institute of Organic Synthesis: 620219 Ekaterinburg, Ul. S. Kovalevskoi 20; tel. and fax (3432); 74-11-89; e-mail chupakhin@ios.uran.ru; f. 1993; attached to Russian Acad. of Sciences; Dir Prof. OLEG N. CHUPAKHIN.

Institute of Permafrost: 677010 Yakutsk, Merzlotovedenie; tel. and fax (41122) 44-44-76; e-mail lans@imzran.yacc.yakutia.su; f. 1961; attached to Russian Acad. of Sciences; library of 40,000 vols; Dir R. M. KAMENSKY.

Institute of Physical Chemistry: 117915 Moscow, Leninskii Pr. 31; tel. 955-46-36; telex 411029; attached to Russian Acad. of Sciences; Dir YU. M. POLUKAROV.

Institute of Physics: 367003 Makhachkala 3, Ul. 26 Bakinskikh Komissarov 94; tel. 2-51-60; attached to Russian Acad. of Sciences; Dir I. K. KAMILOV.

Institute of Problems of the Geology and Extraction of Oil and Gas: 117917 Moscow, Leninskii pr. 65; tel. 135-75-66; attached to Russian Acad. of Sciences; Dir V. N. VINOGRADOV.

Institute of Radiophysical Research: 603600 Nizhny Novgorod, Bolshaya Pecherskaya ul. 25; tel. (8312) 36-72-94; fax (8312) 36-99-02; e-mail spol@nirfi.sci-nnov.ru; f. 1956; library of 250,000 vols; Dir Dr S. V. POLYAKOV; publ. *Izvestiya vysshikh uchebnykh zavedenii – Radiofizika* (monthly).

Institute of Semiconductor Physics: 630090 Novosibirsk, Pr. akademika Lavrenteva 13; tel. (3832) 35-42-50; fax (3832) 35-17-71; f. 1962; attached to Russian Acad. of Sciences; Dir Prof. K. K. SVITASHEV.

Institute of Solid State Chemistry: 620219 Ekaterinburg, Ul. Pervomaiskaya 91; tel. (3432) 74-52-19; fax (3432) 74-44-95; e-mail gps@ihim.ural.ru; attached to Russian Acad. of Sciences; Dir Acad. G. P. SHVEIKIN.

Institute of Solid State Physics: 142432 Moscow oblast, Chernogolovka; tel. 524-50-22; telex 412654; attached to Russian Acad. of Sciences; Dir Acad. YU. A. OSIPYAN.

Institute of Solution Chemistry: 153045 Ivanovo, Akademicheskaya ul. 1; tel. (0932) 37-85-21; fax (0932) 37-85-09; e-mail adm@ihnr.polytech.ivanovo.su; f. 1981; attached to Russian Acad. of Sciences; library of 70,000 vols; Dir Acad. ALEXEI M. KUTEPOV; publs *Problems of Solution Chemistry* (4 a year), *Proceedings* (1 a year), *Textile Chemistry* (2 a year), *Chemical Thermodynamics and Thermochemistry* (2 a year).

Institute of Space Physics Research and Aeronomy: 677891 Yakutsk, Pr. Lenina 31; tel. (4112) 44-50-26; fax (4112) 44-55-51; e-mail ikfia@yacc.yacutia.su; f. 1962; attached to Russian Acad. of Sciences; library of 40,000 vols; Dir Dr E. G. BEREZHKO.

Institute of Space Physics Research and the Diffusion of Radio Waves: 684034

Kamchatka obl., Elizovsky raion, Paratunka, Mirnaya ul. 7; tel. 9-31-93; attached to Russian Acad. of Sciences; Dir I. N. AMIANTOV.

Institute of Space Research: 117810 Moscow, Profsoyuznaya 84/32; tel. 333-20-88; telex 411498; fax 310-70-23; attached to Russian Acad. of Sciences; Dir A. A. GALEEV.

Institute of Spectroscopy: 142092 Moscow oblast, Troitsk; tel. 334-05-79; fax 334-08-86; attached to Russian Acad. of Sciences; Dir E. A. VINOGRADOV.

Institute of Strength Physics and Materials Science: 634021 Tomsk, Akademicheskii pr. 2/1; tel. (3822) 25-94-81; fax (3822) 25-95-76; e-mail ispms@ispms.tomsk.su; f. 1984; attached to Russian Acad. of Sciences; Dir Acad. V. E. PANIN; publ. *Physical Mesomechanics* (2 a year).

Institute of Structural Macrokinetics: 142342 Moscow oblast, Noginsky raion, Chernogolovka; tel. (095) 962-80-00; attached to Russian Acad. of Sciences; Dir A. G. MERZHANOV.

Institute of Tectonics and Geophysics: 680063 Khabarovsk, Ul. Kim Yu Chena 65; tel. 33-06-35; attached to Russian Acad. of Sciences; Dir CH. B. BORUKAEV.

Institute of Terrestrial Magnetism, the Ionosphere and Radio Wave Propagation: 142092 Moscow oblast, Troitsk; tel. (095) 334-01-20; fax (095) 334-01-24; f. 1940; attached to Russian Acad. of Sciences; library of 100,000 vols; br. in St Petersburg; Dir Prof. VICTOR N. ORAEVSKY.

Institute of the Chemistry and Technology of Rare Elements and Mineral Raw Materials: 184200 Apatity, Ul. Fersmana 14; tel. 3-14-45; attached to Russian Acad. of Sciences; Dir V. T. KALINNIKOV.

Institute of the Chemistry of High-Purity Substances: 603600 Nizhny Novgorod, Ul. Tropinina 49, GSP-75; tel. (8312) 66-91-62; fax (8312) 66-86-66; e-mail sen@hp.nnov.su; f. 1988; attached to Russian Acad. of Sciences; Dir Prof. M. F. CHURBANOV.

Institute of the Earth's Crust: 664033 Irkutsk, Ul. Lermontova 128; tel. (3952) 46-40-00; fax (3952) 46-29-00; e-mail log@crust.irkutsk.su; f. 1949; attached to Russian Acad. of Sciences; library of 311,000 vols; Dir Acad. N. A. LOGACHEV.

Institute of the Geology of Ore Deposits, Petrography, Mineralogy and Geochemistry: 109017 Moscow, Staromonetnyi per. 35; tel. 231-45-79; attached to Russian Acad. of Sciences; Dir F. V. CHUKHROV.

Institute of the Mineralogy, Geochemistry and Crystallochemistry of Rare Elements: 121357 Moscow, Ul. Veresaeva 15; tel. 443-84-28; attached to Russian Acad. of Sciences; Dir E. K. BURENKOV.

Institute of Theoretical and Experimental Physics: 117259 Moscow, Bolshaya Cheremushkinskaya ul. 25; tel. 125-02-92; telex 411059; Dir E. P. CHUVAILO.

Institute of Theoretical Astronomy: 191187 St Petersburg, Nab. Kutuzova 10; tel. 279-06-67; e-mail ita@ita.spb.su; attached to Russian Acad. of Sciences; Dir A. G. SOKOLSKII.

Institute of Thermal Physics: 620219 Ekaterinburg, Pervomaiskaya 91; tel. (3432) 74-54-42; fax (3432) 74-54-50; e-mail iva@itp.e-burg.su; attached to Russian Acad. of Sciences; Dir V. P. SKRIPOV.

Institute of Thermophysics: 630090 Novosibirsk, Pr. akademika Lavrenteva 1; tel. (3832) 34-20-50; fax (3832) 34-34-80; e-mail aleks@itp.nsc.ru; f. 1957; attached to Russian Acad. of Sciences; library of 100,000 vols; Dir Dr S. V. ALEKSEENKO; publ. *Thermophysics and Aeromechanics* (4 a year).

Institute of Vulcanology: 683006 Petropavlovsk-Kamchatskii, Bul. Piipa 9; tel. 5-06-03; attached to Russian Acad. of Sciences; Dir S. A. FEDOTOV.

Institute of Water Problems: 107078 Moscow, Novaya Basmannaya ul. 10, POB 231; tel. (095) 265-97-57; fax (095) 265-18-87; e-mail iwapr@iwapr.msk.su; f. 1968; attached to Russian Acad. of Sciences; library of 35,000 vols; Dir M. G. KHUBLARYAN; publ. *Water Resources* (6 a year).

Institute of Water Problems of the North: Petrozavodsk, Pr. Uritskogo 50; tel. 5-34-71; attached to Russian Acad. of Sciences; Head N. N. FILATOV (acting).

International Institute of Earthquake Prediction Theory and Mathematical Geophysics: 113556 Moscow, Varshavskoe shosse 79, Korp. 2; tel. (095) 110-77-95; fax (095) 310-70-32; e-mail mitpan@mitp.ru; attached to Russian Acad. of Sciences; Dir A. A. SOLOVIEV.

Irkutsk Institute of Organic Chemistry: 664033 Irkutsk, Ul. Favorskogo 1; tel. (3952) 46-14-11; f. 1957; attached to Russian Acad. of Sciences; library of 9,000 vols, 52,000 periodicals; Dir BORIS A. TROFIMOV; publs. *Zhurnal obshchei khimii, Zhurnal organicheskoi khimii, Zhurnal prikladnoi khimii, Doklady Rossiiskoi Akademii Nauk, Izvestia Rossiiskoi Akademii Nauk, Khimiko-farmatsevtichesky zhurnal, Khimiya heterotsyklicheskikh soedinenii, Sulphur Letters, Journal of Organometallic Chemistry.*

Joint Institute for Nuclear Research: Moscow oblast, 141980 Dubna; tel. (09621) 65059; fax (09621) 65599; e-mail post@office.jinr.dubna.su; f. 1956; conducts studies on the structure of matter, high- and low-energy physics, condensed matter, heavy ion and neutron physics; 18 mem. states; library of 408,000 vols; Dir V. G. KADYSHEVSKY; publs *Journal of Elementary Particles and Atomic Nucleus* (every 2 months), *JINR Rapid Communications* (every 2 months), *JINR News* (quarterly), *JINR Annual Report.*

Kapitza, P. L., Institute of Physical Problems: 117973 Moscow, GSP-1, Ul. A. N. Kosygina 2; tel. 137-32-48; fax 938-20-30; e-mail andreev@kapitza.ras.ru; attached to Russian Acad. of Sciences; Dir Acad. A. F. ANDREEV.

Karpinskii, A. P., Geological Research Institute: 19026 St Petersburg, Vasilevsky ostrov, Sredny Pr. 74; tel. 218-92-55; Dir A. D. SHCHEGLOV.

Karpov Institute of Physical Chemistry: 103064 Moscow, Ul. Vorontsovo Pole 10; tel. (095) 917-32-57; fax (095) 975-24-50; f. 1918; library of 38,000 vols; Exec. Dir Prof. A. P. SIMONOV.

Khlopin, V. G., Radium Institute: 194021 St Petersburg, 2nd Murinskiy Ave 28; tel. (812) 247-56-41; fax (812) 247-57-81; e-mail moshkov@atom.nw.ru; f. 1922; radiochemistry, nuclear physics; library of 170,000 vols; Dir Dr ALEXANDER A. RIMSKY-KORSAKOV; publ. *Radiochemistry* (in Russian, 6 a year).

Kirensky, L. V., Institute of Physics: 660036 Krasnoyarsk; tel. (3912) 43-26-35; fax (3912) 43-89-23; f. 1956; attached to Russian Acad. of Sciences; Dir Acad. K. S. ALEKSANDROV.

Konstantinov, B. P., St Petersburg Institute of Nuclear Physics: 188350 St Petersburg oblast, Gatchina; tel. 297-91-25; fax (812) 713-71-96; attached to Russian Acad. of Sciences; Dir ANSELM.

Krylov, A. P., All-Russia Oil and Gas Research Institute: 125422 Moscow, Dmitrovsky pr. 10; tel. 976-83-01.

Kurchatov, I. V., Institute of Atomic Energy: 123182 Moscow, Ul. Kurchatova 46; tel. 196-61-07; telex 411594; fax 943-00-74; Dir Acad. EVGENII P. VELIKHOV.

Kurnakov, N. S., Institute of General and Inorganic Chemistry: 117907 Moscow, Leninskii Pr. 31; tel. 952-07-87; attached to Russian Acad. of Sciences; Dir. Acad. YU. A. ZOLOTOV.

Landau, L. D., Institute of Theoretical Physics: 117940 Moscow V-234, Ul. A. N. Kosygina 2; tel. 137-32-44; fax 938-20-77; attached to Russian Acad. of Sciences; Dir Acad. I. M. KHALATNIKOV.

Lebedev, P. N., Physics Institute: 117924 Moscow, Leninskii Pr. 53; tel. 135-14-29; telex 411479; fax 135-85-33; attached to Russian Acad. of Sciences; br. in Kuibyshev; Dir Acad. L. V. KELDYSH.

Lithosphere Institute: 109180 Moscow, Staromonetnyi per. 22; tel. 233-55-88; telex 411484; attached to Russian Acad. of Sciences; Dir N. A. BOGDANOV.

Main Astronomical Observatory: 196140 St Petersburg, Pulkovo; tel. 297-98-41; telex 12351; attached to Russian Acad. of Sciences; br. in Nikolaev oblast; Dir V. K. ABALAKIN.

Mendeleev, D. I., Research Institute of Metrology: 198005 St Petersburg, Moskovskii Pr. 19; tel. (812) 251-76-01; fax (812) 113-01-14; e-mail hal@onti.vniim.spb.su; f. 1842; attached to Russian Acad. of Sciences; library of 80,000 vols; Dir N. I. KHANOV.

Moscow Radiotechnical Institute: 113519 Moscow, Varshavskoe shosse 132; tel. 315-29-50; attached to Russian Acad. of Sciences; Dir G. I. BATSKIKH.

Nesmeyanov, A. N., Institute of Elementary Organic Compounds: 117813 Moscow V-334, GSP 1, Ul. Vavilova 28; tel. (095) 135-92-02; fax (095) 135-50-85; e-mail dir@ineos.ac.ru; f. 1954; attached to Russian Acad. of Sciences; Dir Prof. YU. N. BUBNOV.

Noginsk Research Centre: 142342 Moscow Oblast, Chernogolovka, Institutsky Pr. 8; tel. 524-50-70; attached to Russian Acad. of Sciences; Chair. Acad. YU. A. OSIPYAN.

Polar Geospace Physics Observatory 'Tiksi': 678400 Bulunsky raion, Tiksi, Leninskaya ul. 25; tel. 2-17-89; attached to Russian Acad. of Sciences; Head I. S. SAMSONOV.

Polar Institute of Geophysics: 183023 Murmansk, Ul. Khalturina 15; tel. 6-58-29; telex 126118; attached to Russian Acad. of Sciences; br. in Apatity; Dir V. G. PIVOVAROV.

Research Centre for the Study of Properties of Surfaces and Vacuums: 117334 Moscow, Andreevskaya nab. 2; tel. 133-14-79; attached to Russian Acad. of Sciences; Dir L. E. LAPIDUS.

Research Institute of Experimental Physics: 607200 Nizhegorodskaya oblast, Arzamas 16, Pr. Mira 37; tel. 5-46-38; Dir V. A. BELUGIN.

Research Institute of Geophysical Research on Exploration Wells: Bashkortostan, 452620 Oktyabrsky, Ul. Gorkogo 1; tel. 5-87-03; telex 662014; fax 5-50-16; f. 1956; geophysical well logging; library of 40,000 vols; Dir V. A. OPROKIDNEV.

Research Institute of Geophysical Shock Waves: Moscow oblast, Ramenskoe, Pryamolineinaya ul. 26.

Research Institute of Gold and Rare Metals: Magadan, Ul. Gagarina 2.

Research Institute of Oilfield Geophysics: 450005 Bashkortostan, Ufa, Ul. 8 Marta; tel. 28-81-73; Dir V. V. LAPTEV.

Research Institute of the Geochemistry of the Biosphere: 353918 Novorossiisk, Leninsky prospekt 54; tel. (8617) 23-03-03; fax (8617) 24-02-41; f. 1992; Dir V. A. ALEKSEENKO; publs *Geochemistry of the Biosphere* (annually), *Ecology: Experience, Problems, Research* (irregular).

Russian Research Institute of the Multipurpose Utilization and Protection of Water Resources: 620049 Ekaterinburg, Ul. Mira 23; tel. and fax (3432) 74-26-79; e-mail vhroot@water.uran.ru; f. 1969; library of 30,000 vols; Dir Prof. Dr A. M. CHERNYAEV; publs *Waters of Russia* (monthly), *Water Problems Journal* (2 a year).

Semenov, N. N., Institute of Chemical Physics: 117977 Moscow, Ul. A. N. Kosygina 4; tel. 137-29-51; fax (095) 938-21-56; attached to Russian Acad. of Sciences; Dir V. I. GOLDANSKY.

Shmidt, O. Yu., Institute of Earth Physics: 123810 Moscow, B. Gruzinskaya Ul. 10; tel. 254-27-10; telex 411196; fax 253-92-83; attached to Russian Acad. of Sciences; Dir M. S. ZHDANOV.

Shubnikov, A. V., Institute of Crystallography: 117333 Moscow, Leninskii pr. 59; tel. 135-63-11; fax 135-10-11; attached to Russian Acad. of Sciences; br. in Kaluga; Dir V. I. SIMONOV (acting).

Siberian Institute of Terrestrial Magnetism, the Ionosphere, and Radio Wave Propagation: 664033 Irkutsk, Ul. Lermontova 126; tel. 46-08-65; telex 133163; attached to Russian Acad. of Sciences; Dir G. A. ZHEREBTSOV.

Siberian Research Institute of Geology, Geophysics and Mineral Raw Materials: 630104 Novosibirsk, Krasny pr. 67; tel. 22-45-03.

Special Astrophysical Observatory: 357147 Karachai-Cherkessian Republic, pos. Nizhny Arkhyz; tel. and fax (901) 498-29-31; attached to Russian Acad. of Sciences; Dir YU. YU. BALEGA.

State Hydrological Institute: 199053 St Petersburg, V.O., 2-ya liniya 23; tel. 213-89-16; Dir I. A. SHIKLOMANOV.

State Research Institute of Non-ferrous Metals: 129515 Moscow, Ul. Akademika Koroleva 13; tel. (095) 215-61-73; fax (095) 215-34-53; e-mail gin@gintsvet.msk.ru; f. 1918; library of 500,000 vols; Dir ANDREI TARASOV; publ. *Gintsvetmet Proceedings* (annually).

Titanium Research Institute: 117393 Moscow, Ul. Obrucheva 52; tel. 332-95-55.

Troitsk Research Centre: 142092 Moscow Oblast, Troitsk, Yubileinaya 3; tel. (095) 334-06-35; fax (095) 334-06-32; e-mail gevorkov@a120.inr.troitsk.ru; attached to Russian Acad. of Sciences; Chair. Acad. VICTOR A. MATVEEV.

United Institute of Geology, Geophysics and Mineralogy: 630090 Novosibirsk, Pr. Academika Koptyuga 3; tel. (3832) 33-26-00; fax (3832) 33-27-92; attached to Russian Acad. of Sciences; Dir-Gen. Acad. N. L. DOBRETSOV.

Vernadsky, V. I., Institute of Geochemistry and Analytical Chemistry: 117975 Moscow, Ul. A.N. Kosygina 19; tel. (095) 137-41-27; fax (095) 938-20-54; e-mail galimov@geokhi.msk.su; f. 1947; attached to Russian Acad. of Sciences; library of 33,000 vols, 230 periodicals; Dir Prof. ERIC M. GALIMOV; publs *Geochemical International* (monthly), *Journal of Analytical Chemistry* (monthly).

Voeikov, A. I., Main Geophysical Observatory: 194018 St Petersburg, Ul. Karbysheva 7; tel. 247-01-03; fax 247-86-61; f. 1849; climatology, atmospheric physics, air pollution; library of 380,000 vols; Dir Dr V. P. MELESHKO; publ. *Trudy GGO*.

Zavaritsii, Acad. A. N., Institute of Geology and Geochemistry: 620219 Ekaterinburg, Pochtovy per. 7; tel. 51-80-40; attached to Russian Acad. of Sciences; Dir V. A. KOROTEEV.

Zelinskii, N. D., Institute of Organic Chemistry: 117913 Moscow, Leninskii Pr. 47; tel. 137-62-05; attached to Russian Acad. of Sciences; br. in Volgograd; Dir V. A. TARTAKOVSKY.

PHILOSOPHY AND PSYCHOLOGY

Institute of Philosophy: 119842 Moscow, Volkhonka 14; tel. (095) 203-95-69; fax (095) 200-32-50; e-mail iph@iphras.irex.ru; f. 1929; attached to Russian Acad. of Sciences; Dir V. S. STEPIN.

Institute of Psychology: 129366 Moscow, Yaroslavskaya ul. 13; tel. 282-51-49; attached to Russian Acad. of Sciences; Dir A. V. BRUSHLINSKY.

RELIGION, SOCIOLOGY AND ANTHROPOLOGY

Institute of Sociology: 117259 Moscow, Ul. Krzhizhanovskogo 24/35, Korp. 5; tel. 128-91-09; attached to Russian Acad. of Sciences; Dir V. A. YADOV; br. in St Petersburg: 198147 St Petersburg, Ul. Serpukhovskaya 38; tel. 292-27-65; fax 292-29-29.

Miklukho-Maklai, N. N., Institute of Ethnology and Anthropology: 117334 Moscow, Leninsky pr. 32A; tel. (095) 938-17-47; fax (095) 938-06-00; e-mail anthplib@jea.msk.su; f. 1934; attached to Russian Acad. of Sciences; library of 10,000 vols; Dir V. A. TISHKOV.

Research and Training Centre for Problems of Human Activity: 117279 Moscow, Ul. Profsoyuznaya 83B; tel. 333-01-02; attached to Russian Acad. of Sciences; Gen. Dir V. A. SHESTAKOV.

TECHNOLOGY

Accounting Machine Building Research Institute: 115230 Moscow, Varshavskoe Shosse 42; tel. 111-51-61.

All-Russia Electrotechnical Institute (VEI): 111250 Moscow, Krasnokazarmennaya 12; tel. (095) 362-55-08; fax (095) 362-56-17; e-mail vkozlov@online.ru.

All-Russia Institute of Aviation Materials (VIAM): 107005 Moscow, Ul. Radio 17; tel. (095) 267-62-81; fax (095) 267-86-09; Dir R. E. SHALIN.

All-Russia Logachev Scientific Research Institute of Exploration Geophysics: 193019 St Petersburg, Fayansovaya ul. 20; tel. 567-68-03; fax 567-87-41; e-mail virg@geoph.spb.su; f. 1945; development of instruments and technology for predicting, exploring, evaluating and mining ores and diamonds, drilling for oil and gas; solving environmental problems; provision of services in these areas; library of 54,000 vols; Dir G. N. MIKHAILOV; publs *Geophysical Instruments*, *Russian Journal of Geophysics* (both every 6 months).

All-Russia Oil Geological Prospecting Institute: 191104 St Petersburg, Liteinyi Pr. 39; tel. 273-43-83; telex 121345; fax 273-73-87.

All-Russia Research and Design Institute for Atomic Power Station Equipment: 125171 Moscow, Ul. Volkova Kosmonavta 6A; tel. 150-83-55.

All-Russia Research and Design Institute for Problems of the Development of Oil and Gas Resources on the Continental Shelf: 107078 Moscow, Ul. Kalanchevskaya ul. 11; tel. 971-51-03; telex 411866; fax 280-23-57; Dir I. B. DUBIN.

All-Russia Research and Design Institute of Electroceramics: 111024 Moscow, Shosse Entuziastov 17; tel. 273-13-34.

All-Russia Research and Design Institute of Metallurgical Engineering: 109428 Moscow, Ryazansky pr. 8A; tel. 174-37-00; attached to Russian Acad. of Sciences; Gen. Dir V. M. SINITSKY.

All-Russia Research and Design Institute of the Oil-Refining and Petrochemical Industry: 107005 Moscow, Ul. Fridrikha Engelsa 32; tel. 261-96-26; fax 261-66-44; Dir V. M. NIKITIN.

All-Russia Research, Design and Technological Institute of Lighting Technology: 129626 Moscow, Pr. Mira 106; tel. (095) 287-13-52; fax (095) 287-08-91; e-mail vnisi@com2com.ru; f. 1953.

All-Russia Research Institute for Nuclear Power Plant Operation: 109507 Moscow, Ferganskaya 25; tel. 376-15-43; telex 411026; fax 376-83-33; f. 1979; Dir-Gen. Prof. A. A. ABAGYAN.

All-Russia Research Institute for Oil Refining: 111116 Moscow, Aviamotornaya ul. 6; tel. 261-52-02; Dir E. D. RADCHENKO.

All-Russia Research Institute for the Canned and Vegetable Dry Products Industry: 142703 Moscow oblast, Vidnoe, Shkolnaya 78; tel. 541-08-72; attached to Russian Acad. of Agricultural Sciences.

All-Russia Research Institute for the Dairy Industry: 113093 Moscow, Lyusinovskaya 35; tel. 236-31-64; telex 411463; attached to Russian Acad. of Agricultural Sciences.

All-Russia Research Institute for the Protection of Metals from Corrosion: 125209 Moscow, Baltiiskaya ul. 14; tel. 151-55-01.

All-Russia Research Institute for the Refrigeration Industry: 125422 Moscow, Ul. Kostyakova 12; tel. 216-00-04; attached to Russian Acad. of Agricultural Sciences; Dir V. F. LEBEDEV.

All-Russia Research Institute of Electrical Insulating Materials and Foiled Dielectrics: 111250 Moscow, Krasnokazarmennaya ul. 12; tel. 273-24-78.

All-Russia Research Institute of Electromechanics (VNIIEM): 101000 Moscow, Glavpochtamt Ab/Box 496 VNIIEM, Khoromny Tupik 4; tel. 208-84-67; telex 411390; fax 207-49-62; f. 1941; research and development in space technology, monitoring and control systems for nuclear reactors, electromechanical systems, devices and materials; library of 200,000 vols; Dir Dr S. A. STOMA; publ. *Trudy VNIIEM* (proceedings, 3 a year).

All-Russia Research Institute of Exploration Geophysics: 101000 Moscow, Ul. Pokrovka 22; tel. (095) 925-45-13; fax (095) 956-39-38; f. 1944; library of 50,000 vols; Dir A. V. MIKHALTSEV; publs *Prikladnaya Geofizika* (2 a year), *Razvedochnaya Geofizika*.

All-Russia Research Institute of Fats: 191119 St Petersburg, Ul. Chernyakovskogo 10; tel. 112-01-15; attached to Russian Acad. of Agricultural Sciences.

All-Russia Research Institute of Fibre-Optic Systems of Communication and Data Processing: 107066 Moscow, Khiznyaya Krasnoselskaya ul. 13, Korp. 1; tel. 267-20-31.

All-Russia Research Institute of Food Biotechnology: 109033 Moscow, Samokatnaya ul. 4B; tel. 362-44-95; attached to Russian Acad. of Agricultural Sciences.

All-Russia Research Institute of Fuel and Energy Problems (VNIIKTEP): 117259 Moscow, Bolshaya Cheremushkinskaya 34; tel. 128-90-14; fax 128-85-91; f. 1975; library of 63,000 vols; Dir N. K. PRAVEDNIKOV; publ. *The Fuel and Energy Complex of Russia* (annually).

All-Russia Research Institute of Helium Technology: 119270 Moscow, Luzhnetskaya nab. 10A; tel. (095) 242-50-77; fax (095) 234-91-11.

All-Russia Research Institute of Organic Synthesis: 107055 Moscow, Ul. Radio 12; tel. 261-96-88; fax 261-66-44; Dir V. M. NITIKIN.

All-Russia Research Institute of Problems of Computer Technology and Information Science: 113114 Moscow, 2-i Kozhevnichesky per. 4/6; tel. 235-58-09; Dir V. ZAKHAROV.

All-Russia Research Institute of Radiotechnology: 107055 Moscow, B. Pochtovaya ul. 55–59; tel. 267-66-04.

All-Russia Research Institute of Refractory Metals and Hard Alloys: 115430 Moscow, Varshavskoe shosse 56; tel. 113-55-72.

All-Russia Research Institute of Starch Products: 140052 Moscow oblast, Pos. Korenevo, Ul. Nekrasova; tel. 557-15-00; attached to Russian Acad. of Agricultural Sciences.

All-Russia Research Institute of Systems Research: 117312 Moscow, Pr. 60-Letiya Oktyabrya 9; tel. 135-24-38; telex 411237; fax 135-70-86; attached to Russian Acad. of Sciences; Dir D. M. GVISHIANI.

All-Russia Research Institute of Technical Aesthetics: 129223 Moscow, Pr. Mira VVTs, Korp. 115; tel. 216-90-10.

All-Russia Research Institute of Television and Radio Broadcasting: 123298 Moscow, 3-ya Khoroshevskaya ul. 12; tel. 192-90-01.

All-Russia Research Institute of the Cable Industry: 111112 Moscow, Shosse Entuziastov 5; tel. 278-02-16.

All-Russia Research Institute of the Economics of Mineral Raw Materials and Geological Prospecting: 123853 Moscow, 3-ya Magistralnaya 38; tel. 259-69-88; attached to Russian Acad. of Sciences; Dir M. A. KOMAROV.

All-Russia Research Institute of Trunk Pipeline Construction: 105058 Moscow, Okruzhnoi proezd 19; tel. 366-68-39.

All-Russia Scientific Research Institute for Exploration Methods and Engineering: 199106 St Petersburg, Veselnaya ul. 6; tel. 217-11-62; fax 217-05-17; f. 1955; drilling equipment and techniques for minerals and water; library of 30,000 vols, patents; Dir IVAN S. AFANASYEV; publ. *Collection of Scientific Works* (4–6 a year).

All-Russia Scientific Research Institute of Natural and Synthetic Diamonds and Tools: 129110 Moscow, Ul. Giliarovskogo 65; tel. (095) 281-59-07; fax (095) 288-99-42; f. 1948; library of 25,000 vols; Dir N. A. KOLCHEMANOV; publ. *Works of VNIIALMAZ* (annually).

Blagonravov, A. A., Institute of Machine Science: 101830 Moscow, Ul. Griboedova 4; tel. 924-98-00; attached to Russian Acad. of Sciences; brs in St Petersburg, Samara, Saratov, Nizhnii Novgorod; Dir Acad. K. V. FROLOV.

Budnikov, P. P., All-Russia Research Institute of Construction Materials and Structures: 140080 Moscow, pos. Kraskovo, Ul. Karla Marksa 117; tel. 557-30-66; telex 411700; fax 557-30-09; f. 1931; library of 180,000 vols; Dir YU. GUDKOV; publs *Ceramic Materials, Gypsum binders and products, Autoclaved Materials* (all annually).

Burenie Scientific and Production Co.: 350624 Krasnodar, Ul. Mira 34; tel. and fax (8612) 62-23-34; f. 1970; drilling and maintenance of wells; library of 100,000 vols; Gen. Dir Dr SERGEI A. RYABOKON.

Central Automobile and Automobile Engine Scientific Research Institute: 125438 Moscow, Avtomotornaya ul. 2; tel. 456-36-91; fax 943-00-30; e-mail root@gnc.nami.extech.msk.su; f. 1918; library of 106,000 vols, special collections 93,600 vols; Dir Prof. V. KUTENEV; publs various journals.

Central Design and Research Institute of the Standard and Experimental Design of Livestock Units for the Production of Milk, Beef and Pork: 121002 Moscow, Maly Mogiltsevsky per. 3; tel. 241-36-82.

Central Design Bureau of Unique Instrument Manufacture: 117342 Moscow, Ul. Butlerova 15; tel. 333-61-42; attached to Russian Acad. of Sciences; Head I. N. SISAKYAN; Samara br. Dir V. A. SOIFER.

Central Diesels Research and Development Institute: 196158 St Petersburg, Moskovskoe shosse 25 korp. 1; tel. (812) 291-65-81; fax (812) 291-22-73; f. 1924; library of 62,000 vols; Dir V. BORDUKOV; publ. *Dvigatelestroynie* (4 a year).

Central Electronics Research Institute: 117415 Moscow, Pr. Vernadskogo 39; tel. (095) 432-93-30; fax (095) 431-58-86; f. 1964; Dir B. N. AVDONIN.

Central Institute of Aviation Engines: 111250 Moscow, Aviamotornaya ul. 2; tel. (095) 200-22-15; fax (095) 267-13-54; f. 1930; Dir Prof. D. A. OGORODNIKOV.

Central Marine Research and Design Institute Ltd (CNIIMF): 193015 St Petersburg, Kavalergardskaya ul. 6; tel. 271-12-83; telex 121458; fax 274-38-64; f. 1929; shipbuilding, marine equipment, navigation, transport technology, library of 312,000 vols; Dir VSEVOLOD I. PERESYPKIN; publ. *Transactions*.

Central Paper Research Institute: 141290 Moscow oblast, Pushkinsky raion, pos. Pravdinsky, Ul. Lenina 15/1; tel. 584-36-23; telex 911605; fax 292-65-11; f. 1918; library of 90,000 vols; Dir B. V. OREKHOV; publs *Research Papers of ZNIIB* (annually), *Pulp, Paper, Board* (monthly).

Central Research and Design Institute of Fuel Apparatus and Vehicle and Tractor Engines and Stationary Engines: 192102 St Petersburg, Volkovskii proezd 102; tel. 166-91-11.

Central Research Institute of Coating Materials and Artificial Leathers: 113184 Moscow, Ul. Bakhrushina 11; tel. 233-23-55.

Central Research Institute of Engineering Technology: 109088 Moscow, Sharikopodshipnikovskaya 4; tel. 275-83-00.

Central Research Institute of Geological Prospecting for Base and Precious Metals: 113545 Moscow, Varshavskoe shosse 129B; tel. 313-18-18; fax 315-27-01; f. 1935; Dir Dr IGOR MIGACHEV; publs *Otechestvennaya Geologia* (monthly), *Rudi i Metalli* (in Russian with English abstracts, 6 a year).

Central Research Institute of Papermaking Machinery: St Petersburg, Dvortsovaya ploshchad 6/8.

Central Research Institute of Telecommunications: 111141 Moscow, 1-i proezd Perova polya 8; tel. (095) 304-57-97; fax (095) 274-00-67.

Central Research Institute of the Ministry of Defence: 141090 Moscow oblast, Bolshevo, V/Ch 25840; tel. 472-92-12; Dir L. I. VOLKOV.

Central Research Institute of Transport Construction: 129329 Moscow, Kolskaya 1; tel. 180-20-42.

Central Research Laboratory for the Introduction of Personal Computers: 103706 Moscow K-12, Pl. Kuibysheva 1; tel. 298-88-97; attached to Russian Acad. of Sciences; Dir A. N. ILIN.

Central Scientific Research and Design Institute of the Wood Chemical Industry: 603603 Nizhny Novgorod, Moskovskoe shosse 85, GSP 703; tel. 41-36-98; fax 41-36-90; f. 1932; library of 146,000 vols; Dir VICTOR YA. BONDAREV; publ. *Scientific Works* (annually).

Central Scientific Research Institute for Machine Building: 141070 Moscow oblast, Korolev, Pionyerskaya ul. 4; tel. (095) 513-50-01; fax (095) 274-00-25; e-mail anfimov@mcc.rsa.ru; f. 1946; spacecraft and rocket engineering, aero and gas dynamics, heat and mass exchange, strength of materials, reliability, mission control for spacecraft and space stations; library of 100,000 vols; Dir VLADIMIR F. UTKIN; publs *Astronautics and Rocket Engineering* (irregularly), *Rocketry and Space Technology* (weekly).

Concrete and Reinforced Concrete Research Design and Technological Institute: 109428 Moscow, Vtoraya Institutskaya ul. 6; tel. 171-26-69; fax 170-60-13; f. 1927; library of 200,000 vols; publ. *Proceedings of NIIZLB* (3–4 a year).

Design and Research Institute of the Synthetic Rubber Industry: 105318 Moscow, Ul. Ibragimova 15; tel. 366-43-44; telex 111501; fax 369-52-55; Dir S. I. KARTASHOV.

Design and Technological Institute of Monocrystals: 630058 Novosibirsk, Russkaya ul. 43; tel. (3832) 33-22-39; fax (3832) 33-22-59; e-mail chepurov@crystal.nsk.su; f. 1978; attached to Russian Acad. of Sciences; Head ANATOLY I. CHEPUROV.

Efremov, D. V., Research Institute of Electrophysical Apparatus: 188631 St Petersburg, Kantemerovskaya ul. 8; tel. 265-53-33; Dir V. A. GLUKIKH.

Electronic Control Machines Research Institute: 117812 Moscow, Ul. Vavilova 24; tel. 135-32-21; Dir N. L. PROKHOROV.

Ershov, A. P., Institute of Informatics Systems: 630090 Novosibirsk, Pr. akademika Lavrenteva 6; tel. (3832) 35-56-52; fax (3832) 32-34-94; f. 1990; attached to Russian Acad. of Sciences; library of 100,000 vols; Dir Prof. ALEXANDER G. MARCHUK; publ. *Systems Informatics* (1 a year).

Experimental Factory for Analytical Instrumentation: 198510 St Petersburg, Lomonosov, Ul. Fedyuninskogo 3; tel. 473-06-48; attached to Russian Acad. of Sciences; Dir V. I. STEPANOV.

Experimental Factory for Scientific Instrumentation: 142342 Moscow Oblast, Noginsk raion, p/o Chernogolovka; tel. 524-50-05; attached to Russian Acad. of Sciences; Dir L. P. KOKURIN.

Experimental Research Institute of Metal-Cutting Machine Tools: 117419 Moscow, 5-i Donskoi proezd 21B; tel. 952-39-63; Dir V. S. BELOV.

Far Eastern Research Institute of Mineral Raw Materials: 680005 Khabarovsk, Ul. Gerasimova 31; tel. 34-28-43; Dir YU. I. BAKULIN.

Fedorov, E. K., Institute of Applied Geophysics: 129128 Moscow, Rostokinskaya ul. 9; tel. 181-37-14; Dir S. I. AVDYUSHIN.

Gubkin, I. M., Institute of the Petrochemical and Gas Industry: 117917 Moscow, Leninsky pr. 65; tel. 234-22-92.

High-Technology Ceramics Research Centre: 119361 Moscow, Ozernaya ul. 48; tel. (095) 430-77-70; fax (095) 437-98-93; attached to Russian Acad. of Sciences; Dir V. YA. SHEVCHENKO.

Hydrochemical Institute: 344104 Rostov on Don, Pr. Stachki 198; tel. (8632) 22-44-70; fax (8632) 28-04-85; f. 1920; library of 40,000 vols; Dir A. M. NIKANOROV; publ. *Gidrokhimicheskiye Materialy* (3 a year).

Institute of Analytical Instrumentation: 198103 St Petersburg, Rizhsky pr. 26; tel. (812) 251-86-00; fax (812) 251-70-38; attached to Russian Acad. of Sciences; Dir N. I. KOMYAK.

Institute of Applied Mathematics: 690041 Vladivostok, Ul. Radio 7; tel. (4232) 31-33-30; fax (4232) 31-18-56; f. 1988; attached to Russian Acad. of Sciences; library of 21,000 vols; Dir Prof. N. V. KUZNETSOV.

Institute of Applied Mechanics: Izhevsk; attached to Russian Acad. of Sciences; Dir A. M. LIPANOV (acting).

Institute of Applied Mechanics: C/o Russian Academy of Sciences, 117901 Moscow, Leninsky pr. 14; attached to Russian Acad. of Sciences; Dir I. F. OBRAZTSOV.

Institute of Automation and Control Processes: 690041 Vladivostok, Ul. Radio 5; tel. (4232) 31-04-39; fax (4232) 31-04-52; f. 1971; attached to Russian Acad. of Sciences; Dir V. P. MYASNIKOV.

Institute of Automation and Electrometry: 630090 Novosibirsk, Universitetskii Pr. 1; tel. (3832) 35-10-52; fax (3832) 35-48-51; e-mail malinovsky@iae.nsk.su; attached to Russian Acad. of Sciences; Dir Prof. S. T. VASKOV.

Institute of Biological Instrumentation: 123373 Moscow, Volokalamskoe shosse 91; tel. 491-73-72; Dir V. N. ZLOBIN.

Institute of Chemistry and Chemical Technology: 660049 Krasnoyarsk, Ul. K. Marksa 42; tel. (3912) 27-38-31; fax (3912) 23-86-58; e-mail root@metall.krasnoyarsk.su; f. 1981; attached to Russian Acad. of Sciences; Dir Prof. G. L. PASHKOV.

Institute of Continuum Mechanics: 614061 Perm, Ul. Ak. Koroleva 1; tel. 39-13-16; attached to Russian Acad. of Sciences; Dir V. V. MOSHEV.

Institute of Control Sciences, Automation and Telemechanics: 117806 Moscow, Ul. Profsoyuznaya 65; tel. (095) 334-89-10; fax (095) 334-93-40; e-mail vasmac@ipu.rssi.ru; attached to Russian Acad. of Sciences; Dir Acad. I. V. PRANGISHVILI.

Institute of Electronic Measurement 'Kvarts': 603009 Nizhny Novgorod, Pr. Gagarina 176; tel. (8312) 66-70-93; fax (8312) 66-55-62; e-mail kvarz@kis.ru; f. 1949.

Institute of Energy Research: 117333 Moscow, Ul. Vavilova 44, Korp. 2; tel. 127-48-34; attached to Russian Acad. of Sciences; Dir A. A. MAKAROV.

Institute of Engineering Science: 620219 Ekaterinburg, Pervomaiskaya ul. 91, GSP-207; tel. (3432) 44-13-25; fax (3432) 74-53-30; e-mail ges@inmach.intech.ru; attached to Russian Acad. of Sciences; Dir Prof. E. S. GORKUNOV.

Institute of Geothermal Problems: Makhachkala; attached to Russian Acad. of Sciences; Dir M.-K. M. MAGOMEDOV.

Institute of High Current Electronics: 634055 Tomsk, Akademicheskii Pr. 4; tel. (3822) 25-85-44; fax (3822) 25-94-10; attached to Russian Acad. of Sciences; Dir Prof. S. P. BUGAEV.

Institute of Information Science and Automation: 199178 St Petersburg, 14 liniya 39; tel. 218-03-82; attached to Russian Acad. of Sciences; Dir V. M. PONOMAREV.

Institute of Information Transmission Problems: 101447 Moscow, B. Karetny per. 19; tel. (095) 209-42-25; fax (095) 209-05-79; e-mail director@ippi.ac.msk.su; f. 1961; attached to Russian Acad. of Sciences; Dir N. A. KUZNETSOV.

Institute of Mathematics and Mechanics: 620219 Ekaterinburg, Ul. S. Kovalevskoi 16; tel. and fax (3432) 744-25-18; e-mail afsid@dir.imm.intec.ru; attached to Russian Acad. of Sciences; Dir Acad. A. F. SIDOROV.

Institute of Medical Instrument Making: 125422 Moscow, Timiryazevskaya ul. 1; tel. (095) 211-09-65; fax (095) 200-22-13; attached to Russian Acad. of Medical Sciences; Dir V. A. VIKTOROV.

Institute of Mining: 680000 Khabarovsk, Ul. Turgeneva 51; tel. 33-79-27; attached to Russian Acad. of Sciences; Dir G. V. SEKISOV.

Institute of Mining: 630091 Novosibirsk, Krasny pr. 54; tel. (3832) 17-03-37; fax (3832) 17-06-78; e-mail adm@misd.nsk.su; f. 1944; attached to Russian Acad. of Sciences; library of 40,000 vols; Dir Acad. M. V. KURLENYA; publ. *Journal of Mining Science* (6 a year).

Institute of Mining: 614007 Perm, Sibirskaya ul. 78A; tel. (3422) 16-75-02; fax (3422) 16-09-69; e-mail arc@mine.perm.su; f. 1988; attached to Russian Acad. of Sciences; library of 3,000 vols; Dir Prof. ARKADI E. KRASNOSHTEIN; publs *Mining Echo* (4 a year), *Collection of Scientific and Research Works* (1 a year), *Proceedings* (irregular).

Institute of Mining of the North: 677018 Yakutsk, Ul. Lenina 43; tel. (4112) 26-29-69; fax (41122) 26-27-23; f. 1980; attached to Russian Acad. of Sciences; Dir Dr M. D. NOVOPASHIN.

Institute of Petrochemistry and Catalysis: 450075 Bashkortostan, Ufa, Pr. Oktyabrya 141; tel. 31-27-50; Dir U. M. DZHEMILEV.

Institute of Petroleum Refining and Petrochemistry Problems: 450065 Bashkortostan, Ufa, Initsiativnaya ul. 12; tel. (347) 43-31-17; fax (347) 43-31-33; e-mail petoil@ufanet.ru; f. 1956; Dir E. G. TELIASHEV.

Institute of Physical and Technical Problems of the North: 677891 Yakutsk, Oktyabrskaya ul. 1; e-mail fteh@yacc.yakutia.su; attached to Russian Acad. of Sciences; Dir Acad. V. P. LARIONOV.

Institute of Physics and Power Engineering: 249020 Kaluga oblast, Obninsk, Pl. Bondarenko 1; tel. (08439) 98250; telex 911509; fax (095) 230-23-26; f. 1946; physics of metal cooled fast neutron reactors, medium- and low-power thermal neutron reactors, nuclear energy sources for space research; library of 320,000 vols; Dir V. M. MUROGOV.

Institute of Problems in Cybernetics: 117312 Moscow, Ul. Vavilova 37; tel. 124-77-67; attached to Russian Acad. of Sciences; Dir (vacant).

Institute of Problems in Information Science: 117900 Moscow, Ul. Vavilova 30/6; tel. 135-98-14; attached to Russian Acad. of Sciences; Dir I. A. MIZIN.

Institute of Problems in the Complex Utilization of Mineral Resources: 111020 Moscow, Kryukovskii tupik 4; tel. 360-89-60; attached to Russian Acad. of Sciences; Dir K. N. TRUBETSKOI.

Institute of Problems in the Safe Development of Nuclear Energy: 113191 Moscow, Bolshaya Tulskaya ul. 52; tel. 955-26-47; attached to Russian Acad. of Sciences; Dir L. A. BOLSHOV.

Institute of Problems of Marine Technology: 690600 Vladivostok, Ul. Sukhanova 5A; tel. (4232) 22-64-16; fax (4232) 22-64-51; e-mail ageev@eastnet.marine.su; f. 1988; attached to Russian Acad. of Sciences; Dir M. D. AGEEV.

Institute of Problems of Mechanics: 117526 Moscow, Pr. Vernadskogo 101; tel. (095) 434-32-38; fax (095) 938-20-48; f. 1965; attached to Russian Acad. of Sciences; library of 150,000 vols; Dir Prof. D. M. KLIMOV.

Institute of Programmable Systems: 152140 Pereslavl-Zalesskii; mestechko 'Botik'; tel. 2-05-93; telex 412531; attached to Russian Acad. of Sciences; Dir A. K. AILAMAZYAN.

Institute of Radio Engineering and Electronics: 103907 Moscow, Mokhovaya ul. 8; Pr. K. Marksa 18; tel. 203-52-93; telex 411429; fax 200-52-58; attached to Russian Acad. of Sciences; br. in Saratov; Dir Acad. YU. V. GULYAEV.

Institute of Regional Systems Research: Birobidzhan; attached to Russian Acad. of Sciences; (in process of formation).

Institute of Remote Sensing Methods for Geology (VNIIKAM): 199034 St Petersburg, Birzhevoi proezd 6; tel. (812) 218-28-01; fax (812) 218-39-16; Dir ALEXEI V. PERTSOV.

Institute of Solid State Chemistry and Mineral Raw Materials Processing: 630128 Novosibirsk, Ul. Kutateladze 18; tel. (3832) 32-96-00; fax (3832) 32-28-47; f. 1944; attached to Russian Acad. of Sciences; library of 50,000 vols; Dir Prof. N. Z. LYAKHOV.

Institute of Synthetic Polymer Materials: 117393 Moscow, Profsoyuznaya 70; tel. 335-91-00; attached to Russian Acad. of Sciences; Dir (vacant).

Institute of Technical Chemistry: 614000 Perm, Ul. Lenina 13; tel. (3422) 92-60-08; fax (3422) 92-43-75; f. 1985; attached to Russian Acad. of Sciences; Dir YU. S. KLYACHKIN.

Institute of the Automation of Design: 123056 Moscow, 2-ya Brestskaya; tel. 250-02-62; attached to Russian Acad. of Sciences; Dir O. M. BELOTSERKOVSKY.

Institute of the Chemistry and Technology of Rare Elements and Minerals: 184200 Murmansk oblast, Apatity, Ul. Fersmana 14; tel. 3-14-15; attached to Russian Acad. of Sciences; Dir V. T. KALINNIKOV.

Institute of the Economics and Organization of Industrial Production: 630090 Novosibirsk, Pr. akademika Lavrenteva 17; tel: 35-05-36; telex 133128; fax 35-55-80; attached to Russian Acad. of Sciences; Dir (vacant).

Institute of the Geology and Exploitation of Fossil Fuels: 117312 Moscow, Ul. Fersmana 50; tel. 124-91-55; attached to Russian Acad. of Sciences; Dir N. KRYLOV.

Institute of the Informatics and Mathematical Modelling of Technological Processes: 184200 Murmansk oblast, Apatity, Ul. Fersmana 14; tel. (81555) 3-40-50; fax (81555) 3-16-26; e-mail putilov@ksc-iimm.murmansk.su; f. 1989; attached to Russian Acad. of Sciences; Dir Dr V. A. PUTILOV; publ. *Computer-Aided Simulation*.

Institute of Theoretical and Applied Mechanics: 630090 Novosibirsk, Institutskaya 4/1; tel. (3832) 35-35-33; telex 133128; fax (3832) 35-22-68; f. 1957; attached to Russian Acad. of Sciences; library of 87,000 vols; Dir V. M. FOMIN.

Ioffe, Acad. A. F., Physical-Technical Institute: 194021 St Petersburg, Politeckhnicheskaya Ul. 26; tel. 247-21-45; telex 121453; fax 247-10-17; attached to Russian Acad. of Sciences; br. in Shuvalovo; Dir Acad. ZH. I. ALFEROV.

Joint Russian-Vietnamese Tropical Research and Testing Centre: 117071 Moscow, Leninsky Pr. 33; tel. 954-12-19; f. 1987; attached to Russian Acad. of Sciences; long-term health consequences of Agent Orange, ecology, tropical resistance of materials and equipment; Head Acad. V. E. SOKOLOV.

Kargin, V. A., Polymer Research Institute: 606006 Nizhegorodskaya oblast, Dzerzhinsk; tel. (8313) 25-50-00; fax (8313) 33-13-18; e-mail niip@kis.ru; f. 1949; library of 142,000 vols; Gen. Dir Prof. V. V. GUZEEV.

Kazan Physical-Technical Institute: 420029 Kazan, Ul. Sibirskii trakt 10/7; tel. 76-50-44; attached to Russian Acad. of Sciences; Dir K. M. SALIKHOV.

Keldysh, M.V., Institute of Applied Mathematics: 125047 Moscow, Miusskaya Pl. 4; tel. 972-37-14; attached to Russian Acad. of Sciences; Dir S. P. KURDYUMOV.

Kostyakov, A. N., All-Russian Research Institute of Hydraulic Engineering and Land Reclamation: 127550 Moscow, Bolshaya Akademicheskaya 44; tel. 153-72-70; fax 153-73-70; library of 8,000 vols; Dir Prof. Dr B. M. KIZYAEV; publ. *Transactions* (1 or 2 a year).

Krylov Shipbuilding Research Institute: 196158 St Petersburg, Moskovskoe shosse 44; tel. 127-93-48; telex 121467; fax 127-93-49; Dir V. M. PASHIN.

Krzhizhanovsky, G. M., State Energy Research Institute: 117927 Moscow, Leninsky pr. 19; tel. 954-37-32; attached to Russian Acad. of Sciences; Dir E. P. VOLKOV.

Laser Research Centre: 140700 Moscow oblast, Shatura, Svyatoozerskaya ul. 1; tel. (09645) 2-59-95; fax (09645) 2-25-32; f. 1979; attached to Russian Acad. of Sciences; library of 35,000 vols; Dir Prof. V. YA. PANCHENKO.

Lebedev, S. A., Institute of Precision Mechanics and Computing Technology: 117333 Moscow, Leninsky Pr. 51; tel. 137-15-67; attached to Russian Acad. of Sciences; Dir G. G. RYABOV.

Lebedev, S. V., All-Russia Synthetic Rubber Research Institute: 198035 St Petersburg, Gapsalskaya ul. 1; tel. (812) 251-40-28; fax (812) 251-48-13; f. 1928; synthetic elastomeric materials, production processes, applications; Dir Prof. VITALY A. KORMER.

Mining Institute: 184200 Murmansk oblast, Apatity, Ul. Fersmana 24; tel. 3-75-20; attached to Russian Acad. of Sciences; Dir N. N. MELNIKOV.

Mints, Acad. A. L., Institute of Radio Technology JSC: 125083 Moscow, Ul. 8 Marta 10; tel. (095) 212-42-83; fax (095) 212-10-81; e-mail vladi@rian.msk.su; Dir S. F. BOEV.

Moscow Scientific-Industrial Association 'Spektr': 119048 Moscow, Ul. Usacheva 35; tel. (095) 245-56-56; fax (095) 246-88-88; f. 1964; attached to Russian Acad. of Sciences; research, development and manufacture of non-destructive-testing equipment and instruments; Gen. Dir V. V. KLYUEV.

National Institute of Aviation Technology: 103051 Moscow, Petrovka 24; tel. (095) 200-76-01; fax (095) 292-65-11; f. 1920; Dir. O. S. SIROTKIN; publ. *Aviation Industry* (in Russian and English).

Paper Research Institute: 194018 St Petersburg, Pr. Shvernika 49; tel. 247-17-03; Dir A. IVANOV.

Pechora Research and Design Institute for the Oil Industry; 169400 Komi, Ukhta, Oktyabrskaya ul. 11; tel. 6-16-63; fax 6-03-36; Dir A. N. ILIN.

Physics-Technical Institute: 426001 Izhevsk, Ul. Kirova 12; tel. 23-00-32; attached to Russian Acad. of Sciences; Dir A. M. LIPANOV.

Plastics Research Institute: 111112 Moscow, Perovskii Pr. 35; tel. 361-64-21; Dir V. I. ILICH.

Polymer Plastics Research Institute: St Petersburg, Polyustrovskii Pr. 32; Dir Z. N. POLYAKOV.

Polzunov, I. I., Central Boiler and Turbine Institute: St Petersburg, Doroga v Sosnovku 16.

Polzunov, I. I., Scientific and Development Association for Research and Design of Power Equipment JSC: 194021 St. Petersburg, Politekhnicheskaya ul. 24; tel. (812) 277-95-64; fax (812) 277-40-95; f. 1927; attached to Russian Acad. of Sciences; Dir V. K. RYZHKOV; publ. *Proceedings*.

Railway Transport Research Institute: 129851 Moscow, 3-ya Mytishchinskaya 10; tel. 287-00-10.

Republic Engineering-Technical Centre for the Restoration and Strengthening of Components of Machines and Mechanisms: 634067 Tomsk, Khim ploshchadka; tel. 1-45-04; attached to Russian Acad. of Sciences; Dir V. F. PINKIN; br. at Novosibirsk: 63055 Novosibirsk, Ul. Musy Dzhalilya 9; tel. 32-12-49; Dir V. M. NEZAMUTDINOV.

Research and Design Institute for the Mechanical Processing of Minerals: 199026 St Petersburg, V. O., 21-ya liniya 8a; tel. 213-66-98; attached to Russian Acad. of Sciences; Dir (vacant).

Research and Design Institute of Artificial Fibres: 141009 Moscow oblast, Mytishchi, Ul. Kolontsova 5; tel. 284-44-78; Dir V. SMIRNOV.

Research and Design Institute of Autogenous Engineering: 109004 Moscow, Shelaputinsky per. 1; tel. (095) 915-09-60; fax (095) 915-08-41; f. 1944; equipment for thermal cutting and spraying; Dir NIKOLAI I. NIKIFOROV.

Research and Design Institute of Chemical Engineering: 125015 Moscow, Bolshaya Novodmitrovskaya 14; tel. 285-29-23; Dir N. SAMSONOV.

Research and Design Institute of Construction and Assembly Tools: 141400 Moscow oblast, Khimki, Leningradskoe shosse 1; tel. 571-25-38.

Research and Design Institute of Management Information Technology: 125083 Moscow, Ul. Yunnatov 18; tel. 212-60-60.

Research and Design Institute of Metallurgical Engineering: 109428 Moscow, Ryazanskii pr. 8A; tel. 174-37-00.

Research and Design Institute of Oil Engineering: 113191 Moscow, 4-i Roshchinsky proezd 19/21; tel. 952-16-63.

Research and Design Institute of Polymer Construction Materials: 117419 Moscow, 2-i Verkhny Mikhailovsky pr. 9; tel. 952-30-68; fax 954-40-91; attached to Polymerstroymateriali joint-stock company; Dir ALEXANDER V. POGORELOV.

Research and Design Institute of the Bearings Industry: 109088 Moscow, 2-ya ul. Mashinostroeniya 27; tel. 275-11-59.

Research and Design Institute of Woodworking Machinery: 107082 Moscow, Rubtsovskaya naberezhnaya 3; tel. (095) 261-16-73; telex 412229; f. 1948; library of 50,000 vols; publ. *Catalogue of Woodworking Machines* (annually).

Research and Design Technological Institute of Heavy Engineering: Ekaterinburg, Pl. 1-i Pyatiletki.

Research and Development Institute of Power Engineering: 101000 Moscow, POB 788; tel. (095) 264-46-10; telex 421278; fax (095) 975-20-19; f. 1953; nuclear power, thermal hydraulics, materials science; library of 200,000 vols; Dir E. O. ADAMOV.

Research and Experimental Design Institute of Machinery for the Food Industry: 123308 Moscow, Pr. Marshala Zhukova 1.

Research and Experimental Design Institute of Trade Machinery: 127521 Moscow, Staromarinskoe shosse 57; tel. 246-98-46.

Research Centre for Fundamental Problems of Computer Technology and Control Systems: 117218 Moscow, Ul. Krasikova 25A; tel. (095) 125-77-09; attached to Russian Acad. of Sciences; Chair. of Presidium: K. A. VALIEV.

Includes:

Institute for Problems in Microelectronics Technology and Ultra-pure Materials: 142432 Moscow oblast, Chernogolovka; tel. 962-80-47; fax 292-65-11; attached to Russian Acad. of Sciences; Dir V. V. ARISTOV.

Microelectronics Institute: 150007 Yaroslavl, Universitetskaya 21; tel. 11-65-52; attached to Russian Acad. of Sciences; Dir V. A. KURCHIDIS.

Institute of Computer Technology Problems: 150007 Yaroslavl, Universitetskaya 21; tel. 35-52-83; attached to Russian Acad. of Sciences; Dir YU. A. MAMATOV.

Research Institute of Systems of Automated Designing of Radioelectronic Apparatus and Very Large Scale Integrated Circuits: 103681 Moscow, Zelenograd, Ul. Sovetskaya 3; tel. 531-56-45; attached to Russian Acad. of Sciences; Dir A. L. STEMPKOVSKY.

Special Design Bureau for Microelectronics and Computer Technology: 15007 Yaroslavl, Universitetskaya 21; tel. 11-81-73; attached to Russian Acad. of Sciences; Dir A. M. GLUSHKOV.

Physical Technological Institute: 117218 Moscow, Ul. Krasikova 25-a; tel. 125-77-09; attached to Russian Acad. of Sciences; Dir K. A. VALIEV.

Research Centre for Space Probes: 117810 Moscow, Profsoyuznaya ul. 84/32; attached to Russian Acad. of Sciences; Head N. A. DOLGIKH (acting).

Research, Design and Technological Institute of Electrothermic Equipment: 109052 Moscow, Nizhegorodskaya 29; tel. 278-75-09.

Research Design-Technological Institute for Coal Machinery: 109193 Moscow, Ul. Petra Romanova 7; tel. 279-47-66.

Research Institute for Food Concentrates and Special Food Technology: 117279 Moscow, Miklukho-Maklaya ul. 32; tel. and fax (095) 429-04-11; f. 1981; attached to Russian Acad. of Agricultural Sciences; library of 7,000 vols; Dir VICTOR F. DOBROVOLSKY; publ. *Tea and Coffee in Russia* (4 a year).

Research Institute for Instrumentation: 125124 Moscow, Ul. Raskovoi 20; tel. 214-55-88.

Research Institute for Systems Research: 109280 Moscow, Avtozavodskaya 23; tel. 277-87-31; attached to Russian Acad. of Sciences; Dir V. B. BETELIN.

Research Institute for the Bakery and Confectionery Industry: 107553 Moscow, B. Cherkizovskaya ul. 26A; tel. 161-41-44; attached to Russian Acad. of Agricultural Sciences.

Research Institute for the Beer, Soft Drinks and Wine Industry: 119021 Moscow, Ul. Rossolimo 12; tel. 246-67-69; attached to Russian Acad. of Agricultural Sciences.

Research Institute for the Organization, Management and Economics of the Oil and Gas Industry: 117420 Moscow, Ul. Nametkina 14; tel. 332-00-22.

Research Institute for the Processing of Casing Head Gas: 350550 Krasnodar, Krasnaya ul. 118; tel. 55-85-52; telex 211130; Dir N. I. KORSAKOV.

Research Institute of Abrasives and Grinding: 197342 St Petersburg, Beloostrovskaya ul. 17; tel. (812) 245-33-05; fax (812)

245-47-90; f. 1931; library of 62,000 vols; Dir S. Molchanov.

Research Institute of Agricultural Engineering: 127427 Moscow, Dmitrovskoe shosse 107; tel. 485-55-81.

Research Institute of Applied Automated Systems: 103009 Moscow, Ul. Nezhdanovoi 2a; tel. 229-78-46; attached to Russian Acad. of Sciences; Dir O. L. Smirnov.

Research Institute of Atomic Reactors: Ulyanovsk oblast, 433510 Dimitrovgrad, Gvardeiskaya ul. 10; tel. (84235) 3-20-21; fax (84235) 3-56-48; e-mail gns@niiar .simbirsk.su; f. 1956; library of 96,000 vols; Dir Prof. V. B. Ivanov.

Research Institute of Automobile Electronics and Electrical Equipment: 105187 Moscow, Kirpichnaya 39–41; tel. 365-25-66.

Research Institute of Automobile Industry Technology: 115333 Moscow, Pr. Andropova 22/30; tel. 118-20-00; Dir S. V. Podoblyaev.

Research Institute of Building Ceramics: 143980 Moscow obl., Zheleznodorozhnyi-1; tel. 527-73-73.

Research Institute of Chemical Fibres and Composite Materials: 195030 St Petersburg, Ul. Khimikov 28; tel. 227-61-48; telex 121855; Dir P. E. Mikhailov.

Research Institute of Chemical Reagents and Ultrapure Chemical Substances: 107258 Moscow, Bogorodskii val 3; tel. 963-70-70; Dir E. A. Ryabenko.

Research Institute of Chemicals for Polymer Materials: 392680 Tambov, Ul. Montazhnikov 3; tel. 29-51-52; telex 226116; attached to Syntez joint-stock company; Dir B. N. Gorbunov.

Research Institute of Construction and Road Machinery: 123424 Moscow, Volokolamskoe shosse 73; tel. 491-10-33.

Research Institute of Construction Physics: 127238 Moscow, Lokomotivny pr. 21; tel. (095) 482-40-76; fax (095) 482-40-60; f. 1956; library of 2,000 vols; Dir G. L. Osipov.

Research Institute of Current Sources: 129626 Moscow; tel. 287-97-42; attached to Russian Acad. of Sciences; Dir Yu. V. Skokov.

Research Institute of Drilling Technology: 117957 Moscow, Leninsky pr. 6; tel. 236-01-70; Dir A. V. Mnashchakov.

Research Institute of Earthmoving Machinery: 198005 St Petersburg, 1-ya Krasnoarmeiskaya ul. 11; tel. (812) 316-49-11; fax (812) 316-74-69; attached to VNIIZEMMASH; Dir V. P. Korneev.

Research Institute of Elastic Materials and Products: 119048 Moscow, Malaya Trubetskaya ul. 28; tel. 242-53-42; fax 245-62-10; Dir S. V. Reznichenko.

Research Institute of Electrical Engineering: 191065 St Petersburg, Dvortsovaya nab. 18; tel. 315-01-97; attached to Russian Acad. of Sciences; Dir Acad. I. A. Glebov.

Research Institute of Electromeasuring Equipment: 195267 St Petersburg, Pr. Prosveshcheniya 85; tel. 559-51-41.

Research Institute of Electro-welding Technology: 194100 St Petersburg, Litovskaya ul. 10; tel. 245-40-95; Dir V. V. Smirnov.

Research Institute of Foundry Machinery and the Technology and Automation of Foundry Production: 123557 Moscow, Presnenskii val 14; tel. 252-27-25; Dir E. Krakovskii.

Research Institute of Gas Use in the Economy and Underground Storage of Oil, Oil Products and Liquefied Gases: 123298 Moscow, Ul. Berzarina 12; tel. 946-89-11.

Research Institute of Hydrogeology and Engineering Geology: 142452 Moscow oblast, Noginskii raion, p/o Kupavna, poselok Zelenyi; tel. (095) 521-20-00; telex 346418; fax (095) 913-51-26; f. 1939; Dir Acad. G. S. Vartanyan.

Research Institute of Instrumentation Technology: 113191 Moscow, Gamsonovskii per. 9; tel. 232-10-41.

Research Institute of Light Alloys: Moscow, Ul. Gorbanova 20; Dir N. I. Koryagina.

Research Institute of Light and Textile Machinery: 113105 Moscow, Varshavskoe shosse 33; tel. 111-00-30; fax 111-14-48; f. 1932; library of 95,000 vols; Dir R. M. Malafeyev.

Research Institute of Multiprocessor Computer Systems of the Taganrog Radio Technical University: 347928 Taganrog, Ul. Chekhova 2; tel. (86344) 6-44-88; fax (86344) 6-27-94; f. 1972; attached to Russian Acad. of Sciences; Dir V. I. Bozhich.

Research Institute of Organizational Technology: 119146 Moscow, Komsomolskii pr. 9a; tel. 246-41-21.

Research Institute of Radiation Technology: Moscow, Varshavskoe shosse; Dir A. S. Shtan.

Research Institute of Railway Car Building: 103848 Moscow, Bolshaya Dmitrovka 11; tel. 292-02-47.

Research Institute of Road Traffic Safety: 109389 Moscow, Malaya Lubyanka 16/4.

Research Institute of Rubber and Latex Products: 107564 Moscow, Krasnobogatyrskaya ul. 42; tel. 161-02-92; fax 963-49-11; Dir V. A. Berestenev.

Research Institute of Rubber Technical Products: 141300 Moscow oblast, Sergievsky Posad; tel. (09654) 4-57-59; fax (09654) 4-10-52; f. 1960; library of 15,000 vols; Dir V. V. Shvarts.

Research Institute of Special Engineering: 107082 Moscow, Cheshikhinsky proezd 18/20; tel. 261-50-76.

Research Institute of Synthetic Fibres: 170613 Tver, Ul. Pashi Savelevoi 45; tel. 5-36-10; Dir V. F. Loskutov.

Research Institute of Technical Physics: 454070 Chelyabinsk oblast, Chelyabinsk 70; Dir V. Z. Nechai.

Research Institute of the Chemistry and Technology of Elementary Organic Compounds: 111123 Moscow, Shosse Entuziastov 38; tel. 273-72-50; fax 273-13-23; Dir E. A. Chernyshev.

Research Institute of the Clock and Watch Industry: 125315 Moscow, Chasovaya 24/1; tel. 151-15-01.

Research Institute of the Factory Technology of Prefabricated Reinforced Concrete Structures and Items: 111524 Moscow, Ul. Plekhanova 7; tel. 176-27-04.

Research Institute of the Gas Industry: 142700 Moscow oblast, Vidnoe.

Research Institute of the Metrology Service: 117334 Moscow, Andreevskaya nab. 2; tel. 135-82-92; attached to Russian Acad. of Sciences; Dir V. V. Sazhin.

Research Institute of the Tyre Industry: 105118 Moscow, Ul. Burakova 27; tel. 273-69-01; telex 114771; fax 176-37-42; Dir A. A. Volnov.

Research Institute of Tooling: 105023 Moscow, Bolshaya Semenovskaya 49; tel. 366-94-11.

Research Institute of Tractor and Agricultural Engineering: 109404 Moscow, Marksistskaya ul. 22; tel. 272-04-84; telex 411946.

Research Institute of Vehicle and Tractor Materials: 113184 Moscow, Ozerkovskaya nal. 22/24; tel. 230-94-59.

Research-Training Centre 'Robototekhnika': 105037 Moscow, Izmailovskaya pl. 7; tel. (095) 165-17-01; fax (095) 367-06-36; e-mail yustch@rk10.bmstu.ru; f. 1983; attached to Russian Acad. of Sciences; Head Prof. A. S. Yuschenko.

Russian Research, Design and Technological Institute for Crane and Traction Electrical Equipment: 109280 Moscow, Ul. Masterkova 4; tel. 275-61-66; fax 275-49-03; f. 1960; library of 160,000 vols; Dir Anatoly D. Mashikhin.

Russian Research Institute of Information Technology and Automated Design Systems: 129090 Moscow, Ul. Shchepkina 22; tel. 288-19-24.

Russian Scientific Centre of Applied Chemistry: 197198 St Petersburg, Pr. Dobrolyubova 14; tel. (812) 325-66-45; fax (812) 325-66-48; f. 1919; library of 500,000 vols; Gen. Dir Prof. G. F. Tereshchenko; publ. *Annual Proceedings*.

Science Production Association 'Orgstankinprom': 105264 Moscow, 5-ya Parkovaya 37 kor. 2; tel. 164-56-53.

Scientific and Engineering Centre 'SNIIP': 123060 Moscow, Ul. Raspletina 5; tel. (095) 943-00-62; fax (095) 943-00-63; f. 1954; systems and instrumentation connected with nuclear power production, electronics and space research; Dir Dr S. B. Chebyshov; publ. *Proceedings* (annually).

Scientific and Research Institute for Standardization and Certification in the Engineering Industry: 123007 Moscow, Ul. Shenogina 4; tel. 256-04-49; telex 411378; fax 943-00-78; f. 1957; standardization, certification of products.

Scientific and Technical Complex 'Progress': 119034 Moscow, Kropotkinskaya ul. 13/7; tel. 301-23-25; attached to Russian Acad. of Sciences; General Dir L. N. Lupichev.

Scientific and Technical Complex 'Scientific Instruments': 198103 St Petersburg, Pr. Ogorodnikova 26; tel. 251-28-50; attached to Russian Acad. of Sciences; Gen. Dir M. L. Aleksandrov.

Includes:

Institute of Analytical Instrumentation: St Petersburg; tel. 251-28-50; attached to Russian Acad. of Sciences; Gen. Dir M. L. Aleksandrov.

Special Design Bureau for Analytical Instrument Manufacture: St Petersburg; tel. 251-71-32; attached to Russian Acad. of Sciences; Head A. I. Ivanov.

Scientific Centre of Complex Transportation Problems: 113035 Moscow, Sofiiskaya nab. 34 (k. V); tel. (095) 233-89-13; fax (095) 231-14-54; f. 1955; Dir V. Arsenov.

Scientific Research Institute of Comprehensive Engineering Problems in Animal Husbandry and Fodder Production (VNIIKOMZH): 101509 Moscow, Lesnaya 43; tel. (095) 250-37-90; fax (095) 978-91-38; f. 1974; library of 40,000 vols; Dir-Gen. I. V. Ilin; publ. *Scientific Research Works of VNIIKOMZH* (annually).

Scientific Research Institute of Cybernetics: 117218 Moscow, Ul. Krizhizhanovskogo 14, Korp. 1; tel. 124-76-02; attached to Russian Acad. of Sciences; Dir V. Pelizarov.

Scientific-Experimental Centre for the Automation of Air Traffic Control: 123182 Moscow, Volokolamskoe shosse 26; tel. 190-

42-18; attached to Russian Acad. of Sciences; Head T. G. ANODINA.

Scientific-Technical Co-operative 'Problems of Mechanics and Technology': 109180 Moscow, Ul. Bolshaya Polyanka 2/10; tel. 251-52-08; attached to Russian Acad. of Sciences; Chair. Acad. V. V. STRUMINSKY.

Siberian Power Institute: 664033 Irkutsk, Ul. Lermontova 130; tel. 46-46-53; attached to Russian Acad. of Sciences; Dir A. P. MERENKOV.

Siberian Research Institute of the Oil Industry: 625016 Tyumen, Ul. 50-let Oktyabrya 118; tel. 21-19-16; Dir R. I. KUZOVATKIN.

Skochinsky Institute of Mining: 140004 Moscow, Lyubertsy 4; tel. (095) 558-81-54; telex 206113; fax (095) 554-52-47; f. 1927; attached to Russian Acad. of Sciences; technology of open-cast and underground coal mining; library of 40,000 vols; Dir YU. L. KHOUDIN.

Special Design Bureau for Applied Geophysics: 630058 Novosibirsk, Russkaya ul. 35; tel. 32-36-45; attached to Russian Acad. of Sciences; Head N. P. RASHENTSEV.

Special Design Bureau for Automatic Systems of Marine Research: 693000 Yuzhno-Sakhalinsk, Ul. Gorkogo 25 A/ya 91; tel. 3-28-72; attached to Russian Acad. of Sciences; Head YU. S. BELYAVIN.

Special Design Bureau for Computer Technology: 630090 Novosibirsk, Pr. akademika Lavrenteva 6; tel. 35-33-61; attached to Russian Acad. of Sciences; Head S. T. VASKOV.

Special Design Bureau for High Capacity Electronics: 634055 Tomsk, Akademicheskii Pr. 4; tel. 1-84-59; attached to Russian Acad. of Sciences; Head A. P. KHUZEEV.

Special Design Bureau for Hydroimpulse Technology: 630090 Novosibirsk, Ul. Tereshkovoi 29; tel. 35-72-91; attached to Russian Acad. of Sciences; Head A. A. DERIBAS.

Special Design Bureau for Scientific Instruments: 630058 Novosibirsk, Russkaya ul. 41; tel. 35-30-41; attached to Russian Acad. of Sciences; Head YU. V. CHUGUI.

Special Design Bureau for Scientific Instruments 'Optika': 634055 Tomsk, Akademicheskii Pr. 2/3; tel. 1-97-58; attached to Russian Acad. of Sciences; Head A. F. KUTELEV.

Special Design-Technological Bureau for Special Electronics and Analytical Instrumentation: 630090 Novosibirsk, Ul. ak. Nikolaeva 8; tel. 32-24-40; attached to Russian Acad. of Sciences; Head K. K. SVITASHCHEV.

Special Design-Technological Bureau 'Nauka': 66049 Krasnoyarsk, Pr. Mira 53; tel. 27-29-12; attached to Russian Acad. of Sciences; Head V. F. SHABANOV.

State Design and Research Institute for the Design of Research Institutes, Laboratories and Research Centres of the Academy of Sciences: 117971 Moscow, Ul. Gubkina 3; tel. (095) 135-73-01; fax (095) 135-02-20; e-mail gp@gpran.msk.ru; f. 1938; attached to Russian Acad. of Sciences; Dir A. S. PANFIL.

State Design and Research Institute of Power Systems and Electricity Networks: 107884 Moscow, 2-ya Baumanskaya 7; tel. 261-98-21.

State Institute of Mined Chemical Raw Materials: 140000 Moscow oblast, Lyubertsy, Oktyabrsky pr. 259; tel. 554-42-46.

State Research and Project Development Institute of Maritime Transport: 125319 Moscow, Bolshoi Koptevsky proezd 6; tel. 152-36-51; telex 411197; fax 152-09-16; f. 1939; design of port structures and ship repair yards; economic problems of maritime transport; maritime law; Dir FELIX G. ARAKELOV.

State Research Institute for the Nitrogen Industry and the Products of Organic Synthesis: 109815 Moscow, Zemlyanoi val 50; tel. 227-00-04; Dir N. D. ZAICHKO.

State Research Institute for the Operation and Repair of Civil Aviation Equipment: Moscow, Ul. Krzhizhanovskogo 7.

State Research Institute of Automobile Transport: 123514 Moscow, Ul. Geroev-Panfilovtsev 24; tel. 496-57-22.

State Research Institute of Civil Aviation: 103340 Moscow Oblast, Sheremetevo Airport; tel. 578-48-01.

State Research Institute of the Cement Industry: 107014 Moscow, 3-i Luchevoi prosek 12; tel. 268-27-21.

State Research Institute of the Rare Metals Industry: 109017 Moscow, Bolshoi Tolmachevsky per. 5; tel. 239-90-66.

'Submicron' Research Institute: 103482 Moscow, Zelenograd, Korp. 331A; tel. 536-26-17.

Topchiev, A. V., Institute of Petro-Chemical Synthesis: 117912 Moscow, Leninskii Pr. 29; tel. 954-22-92; attached to Russian Acad. of Sciences; Dir Acad. N. A. PLATE.

Tractor Research Institute: 125040 Moscow, Verkhnyaya 34; tel. 257-01-10; Dir V. KARGOPOLOV.

Vavilov State Optical Institute: 199034 St Petersburg, Birzhevaya Liniya 12; tel. (812) 218-48-92; fax (812) 350-64-73; e-mail leader@soi.spb.su; f. 1918; library of 600,000 vols; Dir Dr G. PETROVSKY; publ. *Journal of Optical Technology* (monthly).

'VNIPIenergoprom' Association JSC: 105094 Moscow, Semenovskaya nab. 2/1; tel. (095) 360-76-40; fax (095) 360-65-77; f. 1942; design, research and development of energy transmission systems, combined heating and power plants, project management, export patents and licences.

Vologdin, V. P., Research Institute of High-Frequency Currents: 194902 St Petersburg, Shuvalskii park; tel. 594-81-23; Dir F. V. BEZMENOV.

Zhukovsky, N. E., Central Aero- and Hydro-dynamics Institute: 140160 Moscow oblast, Zhukovsky 3; tel. 556-41-79; Dir G. P. SVISHCHEV.

Libraries and Archives

Barnaul

Altai State University Library: 656099 Barnaul, Sotsialisticheskii pr. 68; 159,000 vols; Dir GALINA TRUSHNIKOVA.

Cheboksary

Chuvash State University Library: 428015 Cheboksary, Moskovskii pr. 15; tel. 248320; 1,138,241 vols; Dir L. V. PETROVA.

Ekaterinburg

Urals A. M. Gorkii State University Library: 620083 Ekaterinburg, Pr. Lenina 51; tel. 55-75-65; f. 1920; 1,200,000 vols; Dir K. P. KUZNETSOVA.

Elista

Kalmyk State University Library: Elista, Ul. R. Lyuksemburg 4; *c.* 350,000 vols; Dir P. A. DOLINA.

Grozny

Checheno-Ingush State University Library: 364907 Grozny, Ul. N. Buachidze 34/96; tel. 24548; 460,000 vols; Dir R. M. NAZARETYANI.

Irkutsk

Irkutsk State University Library: 664695 Irkutsk, Bulvar Gagarina 24; 3,200,000 vols; Dir R. V. PODGAICHENKO.

Ivanovo

Ivanovo State University Library: 153377 Ivanovo, Ul. Ermaka 37; 410,000 vols; Dir A. N. KRUPPA.

Izhevsk

Udmurt State University Library: 426034 Izhevsk, Krasnogeroiskaya ul. 71; 402,000 vols; Librarian L. P. BESKLINSKAYA.

Kaliningrad

Kaliningrad State University Library: 236040 Kaliningrad, Universitetskaya ul. 2; tel. 43-31-29; 458,660 vols; Dir A. D. SHKITSKAYA.

Kazan

Kazan State University N. I. Lobachevsky Library: 420008 Kazan, Ul. Lenina 18; tel. 32-07-78; f. 1804; 4,779,403 vols; Dir ZH. V. SHCHELYVANOVA; publs *Opisaniya rukopisei*, *Retrospektivnye bibliograficheskie ukazately*.

Kemerovo

Kemerovo State University Library: 650043 Kemerovo, Krasnaya ul. 6; tel. (3842) 23-14-26; e-mail nb@kemgu.kemerovo.su; f. 1928; 350,000 vols; Librarian N. P. KONOVALOVA.

Krasnodar

Kuban State University Library: 350040 Krasnodar, Stavropolskaya ul. 149; tel. 33-69-36; telex 211519; fax 33-98-87; f. 1920; 780,000 vols; Dir G. V. SOLOVEVA.

Krasnoyarsk

Krasnoyarsk State University Library: 660049 Krasnoyarsk, Ul. Maerchaka 6; tel. 90414; 166,000 vols; Librarian E. G. KRIVONOSOVA.

Makhachkala

Dagestan State University Library: Makhachkala, Sovetskaya ul. 8; tel. 7213; 780,000 vols; Dir A. M. SHAKHSHAEVA.

Moscow

All-Russia Patent Technical Library: 121857 Moscow, Berezhkovskaya nab. 24; tel. 240-64-25; telex 411774; fax 240-44-37; f. 1896; the only Russian library which receives Russian and all foreign patents; copies of 100,000,000 patent descriptions; Dir V. I. AMELKINA.

All-Russia Scientific and Research Institute of Patent Information (VNIIPI): 113035 Moscow, Raushskaya nab. 4; tel. (095) 959-33-13; fax (095) 959-33-04; f. 1964; Dir V. D. ZINOVIEV; publs *Inventions* (36 a year), *Utility Models. Industrial Designs* (monthly), *Trademarks, Service Marks. Appellations of Origin of Goods* (monthly).

Archives of the Russian Academy of Sciences: 117218 Moscow, Novocheremushkinskaya ul. 34; tel. 129-19-10; fax 129-19-66; f. 1728; 90 mems; library of 9,000 vols; Dir B. V. LEVSHIN; publs *Proceedings*, *Scientific Heritage*.

Central Library for the Blind: 129010 Moscow, Bezbozhnyi per. 9; tel. 280-26-14; f. 1954; 630,000 vols; acts as loan centre for special libraries throughout Russia; Dir A. D. MAKEEVA; publ. *Life of the Blind in Russia and Abroad* (monthly).

Central Library of the Academy of Medical Sciences: 125874 Moscow, Baltiiskaya ul. 8; tel. 155-47-93; f. 1935; 640,000 vols; acts as an enquiry, loan, research and guide centre for 42 libraries in the institutes and laboratories of the Academy of Medical Sciences; Dir G. I. BAKHEREVA.

Central Scientific Agricultural Library of the Russian Academy of Agricultural Sciences: 107139 Moscow, Orlikov per. 3 Korpus V; tel. (095) 207-54-48; fax (095) 207-89-72; e-mail dir@cnshb.msk.ru; f. 1930; centre for bibliographical information on national and foreign agricultural literature, and for scientific and methodological work of agricultural libraries in Russia; 3,000,000 vols, 3,300 periodicals; Dir V. POZDNYAKOV; publs *Selskokhozyaistvennaya literatura* (monthly), *Selskoe khozyaistvo* (monthly), *Subject Bibliographic Lists* (15 titles annually), *Bibliographic Information* (weekly).

Central State Archives: 125212 Moscow, Vyborgskaya 3; tel. 159-73-83; Dir A. PROKOPENKO.

Centre for the Preservation of Contemporary Documentation: Moscow, Ul. Ilinka 12; tel. (095) 206-50-06; fax (095) 206-23-21; based on the Archive of the General Department of the Communist Party of the former Soviet Union; Dir N. G. TOMILINA.

Centre for the Preservation of Documents of Youth Organizations: Moscow, B. Cherkassky per. 5; tel. 921-22-64; based on the Central Archive of Komsomol.

Centre for the Preservation of Historical Documentary Collections: Moscow, Vyborgskaya ul. 3; tel. 159-74-71; Dir V. BONDAREV; formerly Central State Archive of the USSR (TsGA SSSR) Special Archive.

Federal Archival Service of Russia: 103132 Moscow, Ilyinka 12; tel. (095) 206-35-31; fax (095) 206-55-87; f. 1996; Head V. P. KOZLOV; publ. *Otechestvenniye archivy* (6 a year).

Gorkii, A. M., Archives: 121069 Moscow, Ul. Vorovskogo 25A. tel. 291-19-23; telex 412418; fax 200-32-16; f. 1937; Dir VLADIMIR S. BARAKHOV.

Institute for Scientific Information on the Social Sciences of the Russian Academy of Sciences: 117418 Moscow, Ul. Krasikova 28/21; tel. 128-88-81; fax 420-22-61; f. 1969; sections on philosophy, history, economics, sociology, politology, culturology, global problems and international relations, law, science of sciences, linguistics, theory of literature; 13,500,000 vols; Dir V. A. VINOGRADOV; publs *The Human Being: Image and Essence* (annually), *Theory and Practice of Information in Social Sciences* (annually), various periodicals on social sciences and other subjects.

Institute of Scientific and Technical Information: 125219 Moscow, Ul. Usievicha 20A; tel. 155-43-96; attached to Russian Acad. of Sciences; Dir P. V. NESTEROV.

International Centre for Scientific and Technical Information: 125252 Moscow, Ul. Kuusinena 21B; tel. 198-72-41; telex 411925; fax 943-00-89; f. 1969; Dir Prof. ALEXANDER V. BUTRIMENKO.

Library for Natural Sciences of the Russian Academy of Sciences: 119890 Moscow, Ul. Znamenka 11; tel. (095) 291-22-89; fax (095) 291-24-03; e-mail rapoport@ben.irex.ru; f. 1973; 15.5m. items in main and associated libraries; covers all fields of natural sciences of interest to the Academy's institutions; Dir A. G. ZAKHAROV; publ. *Libraries of Academies of Sciences* (in Russian, 1 a year).

Library of the Museum of the Revolution: 103050 Moscow, Tverskaya ul. 21; tel. (095) 299-52-17; fax (095) 299-85-15; f. 1917; 360,000 vols, 825,000 periodicals; Dir IRINA V. ORLOVA.

Library of the State A. S. Pushkin Museum of Fine Arts: 121019 Moscow, Ul. Volkhonka 12; tel. (095) 203-97-28; fax (095) 203-46-74; f. 1898; 200,000 vols, 100,000 reproductions on paper and canvas, 120,000 negatives and photographs, 70,000 slides; Dir O. B. MALINKOVSKAYA.

Library of the State Literature Museum: Moscow, Rozhdestvenskii Bulvar 16; f. 1926; collection of 180,000 books, 27,644 periodicals; Russian and foreign works from 16th-20th centuries; letters and autographed works; folklore works; periodical collection; Dir ANNA IVANOVNA NIKULINA.

Library of the State Museum of Oriental Arts: 103064 Moscow, Vorontsovo pole 16; tel. (095) 916-34-29; fax (095) 202-48-46; f. 1918; 60,000 vols; Dir LUDMILA VOLKOVA; publs *Scientific reports* (annually).

Library of the State Theatrical A. Bakhrushin Museum: 113054 Moscow, Ul. Bakhrushina 31/12; tel. 233-44-18; fax 233-54-48; f. 1894; 120,000 vols on theatrical art; Dir T. B. BONILYA.

Library of the Tolstoy State Museum: 119034 Moscow, Ul. Prechistenka 11; tel. 202-78-51; f. 1911; 71,000 vols, 75,000 newspaper cuttings; Dir L. M. LUBIMOVA.

M. I. Rudomino State Library for Foreign Literature: 109189 Moscow, Nikolo-Yamskaya 1; tel. (095) 915-36-21; fax (095) 915-36-37; e-mail genieva@libfl.msk.su; f. 1922; 4,600,000 vols in 140 foreign languages; exchange arrangements with 1,300 libraries, publishing houses and universities in 92 countries; Dir E. YU. GENIEVA; publs *Diapazon, Suflor, Biblioteki za rubezhom*.

Moscow State University Scientific Library: 103009 Moscow, Mokhovaya 10.

Russian Centre for the Preservation and Study of Documents of Modern History: 103009 Moscow, Bolshaya Dmitrovka 15; tel. 229-97-26; fax 292-90-17; f. 1920s; library of 10,000 vols; Dir K. M. ANDERSON; publ. *Scientific Information Bulletin* (annually).

Russian National Public Library for Science and Technology: 103031 Moscow, Kuznetskii most 12; tel. 925-92-88; fax 921-98-62; e-mail root@gpntb.msk.su; f. 1958; 8,000,000 books, periodicals and documents on natural sciences, technology, agriculture and medicine; special collection of domestic literature of limited distribution; 24 original databases; permanent contacts with 7,000 enterprises in Russia and other republics of the former USSR; Dir Dr A. I. ZEMSKOV; publs *Proceedings, Russian Libraries of Scientific and Technical Literature*.

Russian Peoples' Friendship University Library: 117198 Moscow, Miklukho-Maklaia 6; f. 1960; 1,350,000 vols; Dir A. N. SHUMILOV.

Russian State Archives of Ancient Acts: 119817 Moscow, Bolshaya Pirogovskaya ul. 17; tel. 245-83-23; annals, charts of grand dukes and independent princes, legal documents of Early Russia (11th-15th centures), documents of central and local Russian institutions (16th-18th centuries), personal and patrimonial archives of nobility and gentry, archives of church establishments and the largest monasteries of Russia; Dir M. I. AVTOKRATOVA.

Russian State Archives of Sound Recording: 107005 Moscow, 2-ya Baumanskaya ul. 3; tel. 261-13-00; f. 1932; sound recordings from 1902 of artistic and documentary nature; Dir V. A. KOLIADA.

Russian State Archives of the National Economy: 119435 Moscow, Bolshaya Pirogovskaya ul. 17; tel. 245-26-64; documents of the state bodies in charge of management of industries, agriculture, transportation, communication, construction and of central bodies of financing, planning and statistics (1917–); Dir E. A. TYURINA.

Russian State Army Archives: 125212 Moscow, Ul. Admirala Makarova 29; tel. 159-80-91; documents of military authorities of the RSFSR and the USSR, of the military areas, detachments, units and establishments of the Soviet Army and Frontier Guards (1918–40); Dir V. D. ZAPOROZHNICHENKO.

Russian State Art Library: 103031 Moscow, B. Dmitrovka 8/1; tel. and fax (095) 292-06-53; e-mail silina@artlib.msk.ru; f. 1922; 1,701,000 items (books, periodicals, press cuttings, etc.); Dir T. I. SILINA; publ. *Yearbook* (annually).

Russian State Library: 101000 Moscow, Pr. Vozdvizhenka 3; tel. (095) 290-60-62; fax (095) 200-22-55; e-mail irgb@glas.apc.org; f. 1862 as the Rumyantsev Library, reorganized in 1925; 40,200,000 books, periodicals and serials; complete files of newspapers in all the 91 languages of the former Soviet Union and 156 foreign languages; 450,000 MSS; 860 archival collections; Department of Rare Books includes incunabula, Aldines, palaeotypes, Elzevirs, specimens of earliest Slavonic printing, rare editions of Russian secular works, etc.; acts as enquiry, loan and reference centre throughout Russia, as international book exchange centre and state national book depository, as information centre on culture and arts, as leading research institution in library science, bibliography and history of printing, and as methodological library centre; Dir VLADIMIR K. EGOROV; publs *Trudy* (Proceedings), *Zapiski otdela rukopisei* (Memoirs of the Manuscript Divison), *Bibliotekovedenie* (Library Science), *Bibliotekovedenie i bibliografiya za rubezhom* (Library Science and Bibliography Abroad), etc.

Russian State Literature and Art Archives: 125212 Moscow, Vyborgskaya 3, kor. 2; tel. (095) 150-78-10; fax (095) 159-73-81; f. 1941; documents of prominent Russian and Soviet writers, composers, artists, theatrical and cinema workers; documents of state and public organizations concerned with the arts (mid-18th century–present day); library of 1,154,000 vols; Dir N. B. VOLKOVA; publ. *Vstrechi s proshlym* (irregular).

Russian State Military Historical Archives: 107005 Moscow, Ul. 2-ya Baumanskaya 3; tel. (095) 261-20-70; fax (095) 267-18-66; f. 1797; documents of central and district military administrations and establishments of the Russian Army, private collections of prominent generals, military leaders and historians (end 17th century–1918); Dir I. O. GARKUSHA.

Scientific Library of the State Tretyakov Gallery: 113035 Moscow, 1-i Kadashevskii per. 14; tel. 231-41-85; f. 1899; 350,000 vols; Dir A. I. BOLOTOVA.

Scientific S. I. Taneev Library of the Moscow P. I. Tchaikovsky State Conservatoire: 103871 Moscow, Ul. Gertsena 13; f. 1866; Russian and foreign music and books on music; complete files of many Russian and foreign musical periodicals; 1,250,941 vols; Dir A. F. CHERKASOVA.

State Archives of the Russian Federation: 119817 Moscow, Bolshaya Pirogovskaya ul. 17; tel. (095) 245-81-41; fax (095) 245-12-87; 5,149,000 items; Dir SERGEY V. MIRONENKO; publ. *Archive of Contemporary Russian History* (3 series: catalogues, documents, research).

State Central Polytechnic Library: 101000 Moscow, Politekhnicheskii proezd 2; tel. 928-64-65; f. 1964; 3,000,000 vols, including periodicals; Dir N. G. REINBERG.

State Medical Library of Russia: 117418 Moscow, Nakhimovskaya ul. 49; tel. 128-33-46; fax 128-87-39; e-mail loginov@

server.scsml.rssi.ru; f. 1919; 3,000,000 vols; Dir Dr B. R. LOGINOV; publs *Medicine and Public Health* (bibliographical index), *New Medical Books*.

State Public Historical Library of Russia: 101000 Moscow, Starosadskii per. 9; tel. 925-65-14; fax 928-43-32; e-mail maf@shpl.ru; f. 1938; 3,229,696 vols, including 74,695 in the Department of Rare Books, 1,107,604 items in the Serials Department; special collection of 10,119 unofficial publications; Dir Dr MIKHAIL AFANASIEV.

Ushinsky, K. D., State Scientific Library of the Academy of Education: 109017 Moscow, Bolshoi Tolmachevskii per. 3; tel. (095) 231-05-85; fax (095) 231-73-56; f. 1925; 2 million units; covers all fields of education and pedagogics; Dir M. N. MIKHAILOVA (acting); publ. *Literatura po pedagogicheskim naukam i narodnomu obrazovaniyu* (annually).

Nalchik

Kabardino-Balkar State University Library: 360004 Nalchik, Ul. Chernyshevskogo 173; tel. 5254; 738,000 vols; Dir E. D. MIGUCHKINA.

Nizhny Novgorod

Nizhny Novgorod N. I. Lobachevskii State University Central Library: 603091 Nizhny Novgorod, Pr. Gagarina 23; tel. 311154; 1,210,470 vols; Dir A. I. SAVENKOV.

Novosibirsk

Novosibirsk State University Library: 630090 Novosibirsk, Akademgorodok; tel. 656260; 450,000 vols; Dir L. G. TORSHENOVA.

Scientific-Technical Centre for Chemical Information: 630090 Novosibirsk, Pr. akademika Lavrenteva 9; tel. 35-64-40; attached to Russian Acad. of Sciences; Head Acad. V. A. KOPTYUG.

State Public Scientific and Technical Library of the Siberian Department of the Russian Academy of Sciences: 630200 Novosibirsk, Voskhod 15; tel. (3832) 66-18-60; telex 133220; fax (3832) 66-33-65; f. 1918; 13,000,000 vols; acts as reference, loan, research and co-ordinating centre for 64 Academy institutes located in Siberia and the Far East; Dir Prof. B. S. ELEPOV.

Omsk

Omsk State University Library: 644077 Omsk, Pr. Mira 55a; 182,000 vols; Dir L. A. BALAKINA.

Perm

Perm A. M. Gorky State University Scientific Library: 614600 Perm, Ul. Bukireva 15; tel. 39-64-80; e-mail library@mail.psu.ru; f. 1916; 1,377,000 vols; Dir R. N. ROGALNIKOVA.

Petrozavodsk

Petrozavodsk State University Library: 185640 Petrozavodsk, Pr. Lenina 33; tel. 75131; fax 71021; 850,000 vols; Dir MARINA P. OTLIVANCHIK.

Rostov on Don

Rostov State University Library: 344049 Rostov on Don, Pushkinskaya 148; Librarian S. V. BEREZOVSKAYA.

St Petersburg

Central Music Library attached to the S. M. Kirov State Academic Theatre of Opera and Ballet: St Petersburg, Ul. Zodchego Rossi 2; contains one of the largest collections in the world of Russian music in MSS, single copies, first editions, etc, 1,500 copies of Russian vaudeville scores, 200 MSS of ballet scores, and a large collection of opera scores including 1,000 foreign operas; Dir S. O. BROG.

Department of the Art and Museum Book Collections of the State Russian Museum: 191011 St Petersburg, Inzhenernaya ul. 4; tel. 219-16-12; telex 121364; fax 314-14-53; f. 1898; 160,000 vols on fine arts, history, philosophy; Dir I. F. SOKOLOVA.

Library of the Pushkin Museum: 191186 St Petersburg, Nab. Moiki 12; tel. 311-06-19; f. 1954; collections of works by Pushkin and V. A. Krylov; 70,000 vols; Dir M. I. DUBROVINA.

Library of the Russian Academy of Sciences: 199034 St Petersburg, Birzhevaya liniya 1; tel. 218-35-92; fax 218-74-36; f. 1714; 20 million vols; collection of 19,000 MSS, 270,000 rare books, including 826 incunabula; acts as inter-library loan and reference service, exchange centre and book publisher; conducts research in library science, palaeography and conservation; co-ordinates network of 32 specialized libraries in the Academy's research institutes; Dir Prof. V. P. LEONOV; publs *Bibliography of Publications of the Russian Academy of Sciences* (annually), quarterly bibliographies.

Library of the State Hermitage Museum: St Petersburg, Dvortsovaya nab. 34; f. 1762; over 500,000 vols. on painting, sculpture and all branches of graphic arts throughout the centuries; Dir MAKAROVA.

Music Library of the St Petersburg Conservatoire: St Petersburg, Teatralnaya pl. 3; telex 121174; fax (812) 311-62-78; f. 1862; 500,000 vols, including 120,000 Russian and foreign works on music, 306,000 scores, 7,600 MSS, 490 incunabula; Dir E. NEKRASOVA.

Music Library of the St Petersburg Dmitri Shostakovich State Philharmonic Society: 191011 St Petersburg, Mikhailovskaya ul. 2; f. 1882; 200,000 scores and books on music, 40,000 engravings, lithographs and paintings of musicians, composers, etc; 1,000,000 newspaper cuttings; Dir G. L. RETROVSKAYA.

National Geological Library: 199026 St Petersburg, Srednii pr. 74; f. 1882; scientific and technical literature; over 1,000,000 books, monographs, periodicals and special maps; Dir I. G. DURNOVA; publ. *Geologicheskaya literatura* (Geological Literature, annually).

National Library of Russia: 191069 St Petersburg, Sadovaya ul. 18; f. 1795; tel. (812) 310-98-50; fax (812) 310-61-48; 32,064,000 items, including a large collection of incunabula and MSS; Dir VLADIMIR N. ZAITSEV; publ. *PNB-Informazia* (monthly).

Russian State Historical Archives: 190000 St Petersburg, Angliiskaya nab. 4; tel. (812) 311-09-26; fax (812) 311-22-52; f. 1918; documents of central state bodies of the Russian Empire, state and private banks, railways, industrial, trade and other companies; private collections of prominent political and public figures, etc. (18th century–1917); library of 350,000 vols; Dir A. R. SOKOLOV; publ. *Herald* (irregular).

Russian State Naval Archives: St Petersburg, Millionnaya ul. 36; tel. 315-90-54; f. 1724; documents of central institutions of the Russian pre-revolutionary and Soviet Navy and prominent naval officers (17th century–1940); library of 1,219,454 vols; Dir V. G. MISHANOV.

St Petersburg State University M. Gorky Library: 199034 St Petersburg, Universitetskaya nab. 7/9; tel. (812) 218-27-41; fax (812) 218-27-41; f. 1783; 7,000,000 vols; Dir N. A. SHESHINA; publs *Pravovedenie* (every 2 months), *Vestnik* (fortnightly).

St Petersburg Theatrical Library: St Petersburg, Ul. Zodchego Rossi 2; f. 1756; 800,000 vols of plays and works on theatrical subjects, department of French works with first editions of Corneille; MSS and letters by Chekhov, Turgenev, Diaghilev, Fokine; department of stage designs by Bakst, Benoit, etc; department of classical and contemporary fiction; Dir R. A. MIKHALIOVA.

Scientific Library attached to the Russian Institute for the History of Arts: 190000 St Petersburg, Isaakievskaya pl. 5; tel. (812) 315-55-87; fax (812) 315-72-02; f. 1912; 300,000 books and periodicals on theatre, music, cinematography, history of literature and art, fiction, philosophy, aesthetics, folklore; 13 brs; Chief Librarian I. V. KYMANOVA.

Scientific Library of the Russian Academy of Arts: 199034 St Petersburg, Universitetskaya nab. 17; f. 1757; 509,600 vols on art, architecture, applied and folk arts, including rare 16th- and 17th-century volumes and a notable collection of 18th-century works on architecture; Dir K. N. ODAR-BOYARSKAYA; Moscow Branch: 119034 Moscow, Ul. Prechistenka 21; 62,700 vols; Dir J. A. VAHRANEVA.

Samara

Russian State Scientific and Technical Archives: 443096 Samara, Ul. Michurina 58; tel. (8462) 36-17-81; fax (8462) 36-17-85; also: Moscow, Profsoyuznaya ul. 82; tel. 335-00-95; f. 1964; documentation of research and development projects in industry, construction, transport and communications; invention applications; Dir YURI A. SHASHARIN.

Samara State University Library: 443086 Samara, Ul. Potapova 64/163; tel. 42260; 245,000 vols; Dir N. I. PARANINA.

Saransk

Mordovian N. P. Ogarev State University Library: 430000 Saransk, Bolshevistskaya ul. 68; tel. 4-49-91; f. 1931; 1,954,861 vols; Dir Doc. A. V. SMOLYANOV.

Saratov

Saratov N. G. Chernyshevsky State University Library: 410601 Saratov, Universitetskaya ul. 42; tel. (8452) 24-54-14; fax (8452) 24-04-46; f. 1909; 2,903,000 vols; Dir V. A. ARTISEVICH.

Syktyvkar

Syktyvkar State University Library: 167001 Syktyvkar, Oktyabrskii pr. 55; tel. 3-65-68; fax 3-18-88; f. 1972; 514,416 vols; 739 MSS and books published in Russia before the 18th century; 17 personal archives of scientists; Dir NONNA F. AKOPOVA; publ. *Rubezh* (quarterly).

Tomsk

Russian State Historical Archive of the Far East: Tomsk, Ul. K. Marksa 26; tel. 2-29-15; formerly Central State Archive of the RSFSR of the Far East (TsGA RSFSR DV).

Tomsk State University Library: 634010 Tomsk, Leninskii pr. 34-a; tel. 24469; 3,320,000 vols; Dir E. SYNTIN.

Tver

Tver Medical Academy Library: 170000 Tver, Ul. Sovetskaya 4; tel. 03-27-26; f. 1954; 446,000 vols; Dir O. V. TULTSEVA.

Tyumen

Tyumen State University Library: 625036 Tyumen, Ul. Volodarskogo 38, 382,000 vols; Dir L. P. KRYUKOVA.

Ufa

Bashkir State University Library: 450074 Ufa, Ul. Frunze 32; tel. 33808; 780,000 vols; Dir E. G. GUIVANOVSKAYA.

Vladikavkaz

North-Ossetian K. L. Khetagurov State University Library: 362000 Vladikavkaz,

Ul. Vatutina 46; tel. 4952; 76,000 vols; Dir K. L. KOCHISOV.

Vladimir

Central State Archives of the Nation's Documentary Films and Photographs: Vladimir, Letneperevozinskaya ul. 9; tel. 2-79-95; also: Moscow oblast, Krasnogorsk, Rechnaya ul. 1; tel. 563-08-45; topical films, newsreels and historical material which was not included in finished films, negatives of documentary photographs (1854-); Dir L. P. ZAPRYAGAEVA.

Vladivostok

Far Eastern State University Central Library: 690652 Vladivostok, Okeanskii pr. 37/41; 700,000 vols; Dir A. G. TRETYAKOVA.

Voronezh

Scientific Library of the Voronezh State University: 394000 Voronezh, Pr. Revolyutsii 24; tel. 553559; e-mail root@lib.vsu.ru; f. 1918; 2,700,000 vols; Dir S. V. YANTS.

Yakutsk

Yakutsk State University Library: 677891 Yakutsk, Leninskii pr. 33; tel. 28749; 429,000 vols; Dir A. P. SEMENOV.

Yalutorovsk

Centre for the Preservation of the Reserve Collection: Tyumen oblast, Yalutorovsk, Ishimskaya ul. 136; tel. 2-29-87; formed from Central State Archive Reserve Collection of Documents of the State Archive Collection of the USSR (TsGA SF SSSR).

Yaroslavl

Yaroslavl State University Library: 150000 Yaroslavl, Ul. Kirova 8/10; tel. 28229; 263,000 vols; Dir V. A. DOKTOROVA.

Museums and Art Galleries

Arkhangelsk

Arkhangelsk State Museum: 163061 Arkhangelsk, Pl. V. I. Lenina 2; tel. 3-66-79; telex 02242518; f. 1737; contains 150,000 items featuring the history of the North coast area of Russia, dating back to ancient times; large collection of archaeology, ethnography, documents and photographs, library of 30,000 vols; Dir YU. P. PROKOPEV.

Arkhangelsk State Museum of Fine Arts: Arkhangelsk, Nab. Lenina 79; contains over 25,000 items of ancient North and Western European art; library of 20,000 vols; Dir M. V. MITKEVICH.

Ashaga-stal

Stalsky Memorial Museum: Dagestan Autonomous Republic, Kasumkentskii raion, Ashaga-stal; exhibits on the history of Dagestan literature; library of 20,000 vols.

Astrakhan

Astrakhan State B. M. Kustodiev Gallery: Astrakhan, Ul. Sverdlova 81; tel. and fax 22-66-65; f. 1918; fine arts; library of 15,000 vols; Dir L. J. ILINA.

Barnaul

Altai State Museum of Applied Arts: Barnaul, Ul. Sovetskaya 28; tel. 22-89-23; f. 1959; large collection, from 18th century onward, of wood carvings, ceramics, national costumes, etc.; library of 17,000 vols; Dir L. N. SHAMINA.

Belinsky

Belinsky, V. G., State Museum: Penza oblast, Belinsky, Ul. Belinskogo 11; f. 1938; 31,280 exhibits on the life and work of the literary critic V. G. Belinskii; Curator I. A. GERASEKIN.

Borodino

Borodino State War and History Museum: 143240 Moskovskaya oblast, Mozhaisk, village of Borodino; tel. and fax (09638) 5-10-57; f. 1839; research into 1812 campaign, the Battle of Borodino and the 1941–45 war; 60,000 exhibits include material on the Battle of Borodino; library of 9,000 vols; Dir ALICE D. KACHALOVA; Curator GALINA N. NEVSKAYA.

Bryansk

Bryansk State Museum of Soviet Fine Arts: Bryansk, Ul. Gagarina 19; Dir B. F. FAENKOV.

Cheboksary

Chuvash Art Museum: 428008 Cheboksary, Kalinin St 60; tel. 22-07-04; f. 1939; 12,000 exhibits, mainly modern Russian, Soviet and Chuvash artists and traditional Chuvash decorative art; library of 15,000 vols; Dir N. SADYUKOV.

Chelyabinsk

Chelyabinsk State Picture Gallery: Chelyabinsk, Ul. Truda 92-a; 5,000 items; Dir I. F. TKACHENKO.

Ekaterinburg

Ekaterinburg Picture Gallery: Ekaterinburg, Ul. Vainera 11; f. 1746; Western European, Russian and Soviet artists and objects from the Kishisk foundries; Dir E. V. KHAMTSOV.

State Amalgamated Museum of the Writers of the Urals: 620151 Ekaterinburg, Tolmacheva ul. 41; tel. 51-72-81; f. 1940 (amalgamated 1980); study and popularization of the heritage of the writers of the Urals, collections include the personal belongings and archives of Mamin-Sibiryak, Bazhov and other Ural writers, illustrations to editions of their works and various other artwork, 34,723 items in all; incorporates the House of D. N. Mamin-Sibiryak in Ekaterinburg, the House of P. P. Bazhov, the House of F. M. Reshetnikov; library of 37,700 vols; Dir L. A. KHUDYAKOVA.

Ural Geological Museum: 620120 Ekaterinburg, Ul. Kuibysheva 30; tel. (3432) 22-31-09; telex 221558; fax (3432) 29-48-38; f. 1937; Dir YURI A. POLENOV.

Gagarin

Yurii Gagarin Memorial Museum: Gagarin, Ul. Gagarina; tel. 4-19-26; f. 1970; exhibits depicting the life and career of Yurii Alekseevich Gagarin, the first man in space; Dir MARIA ANTONENKOVA.

Grozny

Checheno-Ingush Museum of Fine Arts: Grozny, Pr. Revolyutsii 26/36; 5,600 exhibits; Dir S. S. BRODSKII.

Ivanovo

Ivanovo Museum of Art: 153002 Ivanovo, Pr. Lenina 33; tel. 2-65-04; f. 1960; Greek, Roman and Ancient Egyptian art, icons, 18th–20th-century Russian art; library of 7,500 vols; Dir L. W. WOLOWENSKAYA.

Kaluga

Kaluga Museum of Art Kaluga, Ul. Lenina 104; 2,700 exhibits; Dir. A. V. KAZAK.

Tsiolkovsky, K. E., State Museum of the History of Cosmonautics: Kaluga, Ul. Koroleva 2; f. 1967; contains K. E. Tsiolkovsky's scientific works, history of rocket technique and cosmonautics, large collection of objects relating to astronautics and rocket techniques, including the first experimental rocket launched in 1933, the *Sputniks* and *Luniks*, models of orbital stations; library of 32,000 vols; Dir E. KOUZIN.

Kazan

Kazan State A. M. Gorky Memorial Museum: Kazan, Ul. Gorkogo 10; exhibits illustrating Gorky's life in the flat where he lived and wrote.

State United Museum: Tatarstan, 420111 Kazan, Kremlevskaya ul. 2; tel. and fax (8432) 32-14-84; f. 1894; 557,000 exhibits on the history, archaeology, ethnography, natural resources and decorative applied art of Tatarstan; library of 12,000 vols; 54 brs; Gen. Man. G. S. MYKHANOV.

Tatar Historical Museum (House of V. I. Lenin): Tatarstan, Kazan, Ul. Ulyanova 58; 10,000 exhibits including documents, photographs, works of art and other exhibits relating to Lenin's life.

Tatar State Museum of Fine Arts: 420015 Kazan, Ul. K. Marksa 64; tel. 36-69-21; f. 1959; large collections of Russian, West European and Soviet paintings; 10,000 exhibits.

Kirov

Kirov Victor and Apollinaris Vasnetsov Museum: 610000 Kirov, Ul. K. Marksa 70; tel. 62-26-46; f. 1910; Russian and West European sculpture, paintings, engravings and decorative arts; library of 14,000 vols; Dir ALLA A. NOSKOVA.

Kirovsk

Polar Alpine Botanical Garden Institute: 184230 Murmansk, obl. Kirovsk; tel. 2-13-51; attached to Russian Acad. of Sciences; Dir G. N. ANDREEV.

Klin

Tchaikovsky House-Museum: Klin; f. 1894; composer's last residence and first Russian musical museum; contains 149,000 documents and museum treasures associated with the life and work of Tchaikovsky and other Russian musicians; 42,000 vols; Dir G. I. BELONOVICH.

Komsomolsk on Amur

Komsomolsk-on-Amur Museum of Soviet Fine Arts: Komsomolsk-na-Amure, Pr. Mira 50; 5,000 exhibits; Dir E. Y. TURCHINSKAYA.

Konchanskoe-Suvorovskoe

Suvorov Museum: Novogorodskaya raion, Borovianskii raion, selo Konchanskoe-Suvorovskoe; the museum features the main periods in the life of A. V. Suvorov; Dir V. P. MALYSHEVA.

Kostroma

Kostroma Museum of Fine Arts: Kostroma, Pr. Mira 5; f. 1913; 5,700 items; collecting, exhibitions, sales, scientific and historical Russian art research, art restoration; library of 6,410 vols; special collections of Ancient Russian religious books and the work of Y. Chestnyakov; Dir V. Y. IGNATEV.

Krasnoyarsk

Krasnoyarsk Arts Museum: 660097 Krasnoyarsk, Parizhskoi Kommuny ul. 20; tel. 27-25-58; f. 1958; Russian art (including icons), Russian pre-revolutionary applied art, Siberian folk art and Soviet art; painting, sculpture, graphic art, applied arts; library of 7,700 vols; Dir A. F. EFIMOVSKII; publ. *Surikov Readings* (2 a year).

Kursk

Kursk Art Gallery: 305016 Kursk, Ul. Sovetskaya 3; tel. (071) 222-39-36; f. 1935; Russian, Soviet and European painting and sculpture; 7,000 exhibits; library of 50,000 vols; Dir I. A. PRIPACHKIN.

Lermontovo

Lermontov State Museum 'Tarkhany': Penza oblast, Belinskii raion, Lermontovo; tel. 2-12-03; f. 1939; life and work of M. YU. Lermontov; library of 14,000 books; Dir T. M. MELNIKOVA; publ. *Tarkhansky vestnik* (2 a year).

Makhachkala

Dagestan Museum of Fine Arts: Makhachkala, Ul. Markova 45; 7,000 exhibits.

Maloyaroslavets

Maloyaroslavets Museum of Military History of 1812: 249050 Maloyaroslavets, Moskovskaya ul. 27; tel. 2-27-11; f. 1939; collection and study of exhibits of the 1812 war; library of 1,100 vols; Dir N. V. KOTLYAKOVA; publ. *Nashe Nasledie* (Our Heritage, every 2 months).

Melikhovo

Chekhov, A. P., Memorial Museum: 142326 Moscow oblast, Chekhovskii raion, Melikhovo; tel. (272) 2-36-10; f. 1941; the house where the writer lived and worked; library of 11,000 vols and documents; Dir Y. A. BICHKOV.

Miass

Natural Science Museum of the Ilmen State Reserve: 456301 Chelyabinsk oblast, Miass 1; tel. (35135) 5-48-90; fax (35135) 5-02-86; e-mail founds@imin.urc.ac.ru; f. 1930; the museum shows the mineralogical resources of the Ilmen State Reserve, the grounds of which contain more than 250 minerals; library of 17,000 vols; Dir Dr S. N. NIKANDROV; publs *Trudy Ilmenskogo Zapovednika, Uralsky mineralogichesky Sbornik.*

Moscow

Anuchin, D. N., Anthropological Institute and Museum: 103009 Moscow, Institute of Anthropology, Moscow State University, Mokhovaya ul. 18; tel. 203-66-09; f. 1879; about 470,000 items; anthropology and archaeology of the Stone Age; collections from outstanding Russian explorers; Mousterien Man from Teshik-Tash and Staroselyie; Mesolithic burials from the Dnieper Region in the Ukraine; library of 30,000 vols; Dir Prof. Dr V. P. CHTETSOV.

Central A. A. Bakhrushin State Theatrical Museum: 113054 Moscow, Ul. Bakhrushina 31/12; tel. (095) 233-48-48; fax (095) 233-54-48; f. 1894; to collect, house, study and exhibit varied materials on history and theory of theatre; approx. 1,300,000 exhibits; library of 120,000 vols; archives of original MSS of Ostrovsky, Lensky, Stanislavsky, etc.; Dir V. V. GUBIN.

Central Museum of Aviation and Cosmonautics: 125167 Moscow, Krasnoarmeiskaya 4; tel. 212-73-01; f. 1924; to record the national development of aeronautics and astronautics; contains original full-size aircraft, spacecraft, recovered space exploration vehicles, instruments, flight clothing, accessories of technical, historical and biographical interest; library of 15,800 vols; Dir P. F. VYALIKOV.

Central Museum of the Armed Forces: 129110 Moscow I-110, Ul. Sovetskoi Armii 2, A/Ya 125; tel. 281-18-80; fax 281-77-35; f. 1919; military exhibits; library of 90,000 vols; Dir A. K. NIKONOV.

Chekhov, A. P., House-Museum: 103001 Moscow, Sadovaya-Kudrinskaya 6; tel. 291-61-54; f. 1954; flat where the writer lived from 1886–1890; branch of the State Literature Museum.

Dostoevsky, F. M., Museum: 103030 Moscow, Ul. Dostoyevskogo 2; tel. 281-10-85; f. 1928; affiliated to the State Literature Museum; exhibits illustrating Dostoyevsky's life, organized in the flat where he lived until sixteen years old; Dir GALINA B. PONOMAREVA.

Fersman Mineralogical Museum of the Academy of Sciences: 117071 Moscow, Leninskii pr. 18, Kor. 2; tel. 954-39-00; f. 1716; 130,000 mineral samples from throughout the world; library of 10,000 vols; Dir Prof. M. J. NOVGORODOVA.

Folk-Art Museum: 103009 Moscow, Ul. Stanislavskogo 7; tel. 290-52-22; f. 1885; three sections devoted to (*a*) handicrafts connected with peasant daily life; (*b*) applied arts both ancient and contemporary; (*c*) experimental decorative applied art; about 50,000 exhibits; under the jurisdiction of the Russian Council of Local Industries; Dir G. A. YAKOVLEVA.

'Glinka, M. I.', State Central Museum of Musical Culture: 125047 Moscow, Ul. Fadeeva 4; tel. (095) 972-32-37; fax (095) 251-13-68; f. 1943; based on the Museum of the Moscow Conservatoire; collects archives, MSS and memorabilia; musical instruments; musical iconography; records and tape recordings; music, books, posters, programmes—in all, 800,000 items; exhibits: musical instruments of the world; Russian musical culture; Dir-Gen. A. D. PANIUSHKIN.

Gogol, N. V., House Museum: 12109 Moscow, Suvorovskii Bul. 7; tel. 291-15-50; f. 1974; exhibits illustrating life and work of Gogol; library of 200,000 vols, Gogol special collection of 600 vols and manuscript room; Dir M. P. STATSEVICH.

Gorky, A. M., Memorial Museum: Moscow 121069, Malaya Nikitskaya ul. 6/2; tel. 290-05-35; f. 1965 in the house where the author lived; contains Gorky's private library of 10,000 vols, and his collection of Oriental arts (ivory); Dir L. P. BYKOVTSEVA.

Gorky, A. M., Museum: 121069 Moscow, Ul. Povarskaya 25A; tel. 291-51-30; f. 1937; 44,500 items, including literary and photographic documents, works of art, memorabilia; Dir L. P. BYKOVTSEVA.

Kremlin Museums: 103073 Moscow, Kreml; tel. 928-44-56; Dir I. A. RODIMTSEVA.

Include:

Armoury: 103073 Moscow, Kreml; f. 1857; 100,000 items: weapons, arms and jewels from the 12th century to the Revolution.

Kremlin Cathedrals: 103073 Moscow, Kreml; The cathedrals around the Cathedral Square (Sobornaya ploshchad) include, among others, the following: Cathedral of the Assumption (f. 1479); icons of the 14th–17th centuries; throne of Ivan the Terrible. Cathedral of the Annunciation (f. 1489); iconostasis by leading artists of the 15th century. Archangel Cathedral (1508); tombs of Ivan Kalita and other Russian Grand Dukes and Czars. Rizpolozhenskii Cathedral (f. 1485). Cathedral of the Twelve Apostles and Patriarch's Palace; 17th-century items of applied decorative art.

Main Botanical Garden: 127276 Moscow, Botanicheskaya Ul. 4; tel. 482-11-81; attached to Russian Acad. of Sciences; br. in Cheboksary; Dir L. N. ANDREEV.

Marx-Engels Museum: 121019 Moscow, Ul. Marksa-Engelsa 5 (reported in January 1992 to be about to move premises); f. 1962; 2,000 exhibits descriptive of the lives of Marx and Engels; Dir V. N. KUZNETSOV.

Moscow Arts Theatre Museum: 103009 Moscow, Proezd Khudozhestvennogo teatra 3A; tel. 229-00-80; f. 1923; Dir V. S. DAVIDOV.

Has attached:

Stanislavsky, K. S., House-Museum: 103009 Moscow, Ul. Stanislavskogo 6; tel. 229-28-55; affiliated to Theatre Museum; f. 1948; deals with Stanislavsky's work and the theatrical career of People's Artist, M. P. Lilina.

Nemirovich-Danchenko, V., Flat-Museum: 103009 Moscow, Ul. Nemirovicha-Danchenko 5/7, kv. 52; tel. 209-53-91; f. 1944; illustrating career of Nemirovich-Danchenko.

Moscow State University Museum of Zoology: 103009 Moscow, Ul. Gertsena 6; tel. 203-89-23; f. 1791; systematics, speciation, zoogeography, faunistic investigations, phylogenetics, museology; library of 100,000 vols; Dir Dr OLGA L. ROSSOLIMO; publ. *Proceedings of the Zoological Museum* (annually).

Museum of Earth Science of the Moscow State M. V. Lomonosov University: 119899 Moscow, Universitetskaya pl. 1, MGU; tel. (095) 939-14-15; fax (095) 939-15-94; f. 1955; includes material on the origin of the face of the earth, its geospheres, surface landscape sphere, earth crust, climates, waters, soils, plants, animals, economic resources; on the conservation, utilization and reconstruction of nature; complex geological and geographical characteristics of Russia and of the earth; science-teaching, geological-geographical museum for students of the Geological, Geographical, Biological and Pedological departments of Moscow University; 10,000 vols in library; Dir Prof. S. A. USHAKOV; publ. *Zhizn Zemli* (The Life of the Earth, 1 vol. every 1–2 years).

Museum of Frontier Guards: Moscow, Ul. B. Bronnaya 23; 110,000 exhibits featuring the history of Soviet frontier guards.

Museum of the History of the City of Moscow: 103012 Moscow, Novaya pl. 12; tel. and fax (095) 924-31-45; f. 1896; Dir G. I. VEDEZNIKOVA.

Museum of the Palaeontological Institute: 117647 Moscow, Profsoyuznaya ul. 123; tel. 339-05-77; fax (095) 339-12-66; f. 1930; about 6,000 exhibits; Dir A. YU. ROZANOV.

Museum of the Revolution: 103050 Moscow, Tverskaya ul. 21; tel. (095) 299-52-17; fax (095) 299-85-15; f. 1917; social and political history of Russia from 1850 to the present day; library of 360,000 vols and 825,000 periodicals; Dir Dr T. G. SHUMNAYA; publ. *Trudy* (Proceedings).

Museum of the State Academic Malyi Theatre: 103009 Moscow, Malyi teatr, Teatralnaya pl. 1/6; tel. 921-85-48; f. 1932, being developed out of 1927 exhibition; illustrates and studies history of the Theatre; Dir YU. M. STRUTINSKAYA.

Novodevichii Monastery Museum: 119435 Moscow, Novodevichii pr. 1; tel. 246-85-26; Smolensky Cathedral (1524) and other monuments of Russian architecture form the architectural ensemble of the monastery; Russian fine and decorative art (16th-17th centuries); Dir V. G. VERZHBITSKII.

Obraztsov's Central State Puppet Theatre Museum: Moscow, Sadovo Samotechnaya ul. 3; f. 1937; over 2,600 dolls from 50 countries; puppet theatres of the fmr Soviet Union and many other countries and the Central Puppet Theatre itself; library of over 5,300 books; Dir N. KOSTROVA.

Permanent Tchaikovsky Exhibition in the Tchaikovsky Concert Hall: Moscow, Pl.

Mayakovskogo 20; exhibits of the composer's life and works.

Petrographic Museum: 109017 Moscow, Staromonetnyi per. 35; tel. (095) 230-82-92; fax (095) 230-21-79; f. 1934; Dir V. A. PAVLOV.

Pharmaceutical Museum of the Central Drug Research Institute: 117418 Moscow, Ul. Krasikova 34; tel. 120-91-51; unique collection of about 6,000 items on the history of pharmacy in Russia and the fmr USSR; Dir B. M. SALO.

Polytechnical Museum: 101000 Moscow, Novaya pl. 3/4; tel. 925-06-14; fax 925-12-90; f. 1872; over 100,000 exhibits; features history and latest developments in science and technology; belongs to the Ministry of Culture; library of 3m. vols; Dir Prof. G. G. GRIGORIAN.

Rublev, Andrei, Central Museum of Ancient Russian Culture and Art: 107120 Moscow, Andronevskaya pl. 10; tel. (095) 278-14-89; fax (095) 278-50-55; f. 1947; Russian art, icons, applied art, manuscripts, old printed books; library of 23,000 vols; Dir Dr G. V. POPOV.

Shchukin, B. V., Museum-Room: Moscow, Flat 11, Ul. Shchukina 8; contains material he had about him during his lifetime as a great actor at the Vakhtangov Theatre.

Shchusev, A. V., State Research Architectural Museum: 121019 Moscow, Pr. Vozdvizhenka 5; tel. 291-21-09; fax 291-19-78; f. 1934; objects: study, collection, care and popularization of historical architecture, outstanding contemporary work, monumental sculpture and painting; collection and care of documents on architecture and town planning; over 70,000 sheets of architectural drawings; over 300,000 negatives and 400,000 photographs of architectural monuments throughout the world; library of 50,000 vols; Dir I. A. KASUS; Curator M. EVSTRATOVA.

Skryabin, A. N., Museum: 121002 Moscow, Ul. Vakhtangova 11; tel. 241-19-01; f. 1919, opened in 1922 in flat where the composer lived and died; MSS, letters, Skryabin's personal library and magnetic-tape archive of Skryabin's compositions performed by the composer and famous artists; excursions, lectures and concerts; 287 vols in Skryabin's personal library, 2,149 vols in scientific library; Dir RYBAKOVA.

State Academic Bolshoi Theatre Museum: 103009 Moscow, Bolshoi teatr, Okhotnyi Ryad 8/2; tel. 292-00-25; f. 1920; objects: documentation of the work of the Bolshoi Theatre, collection of materials and documents on its history and work, study of history of the theatre; Dir V. I. ZARUBIN.

State Collection of Antique Stringed Instruments: Moscow, Ul. Gertsena 13; f. 1919.

State Darwin Museum: 117292 Moscow, Vavilova 57; tel. (095) 135-33-76; fax (095) 135-33-84; e-mail darwin@museum.ru; f. 1907; illustrates Darwinism and the theory of evolution; library of 27,000 vols; Dir A. I. KLUKINA.

State Historical Museum: 103012 Moscow, Krasnaya pl. 1/2; tel. (095) 924-45-29; fax (095) 925-95-27; f. 1872; 4,500,000 exhibits covering Russian history from pre-history to the present; library of 229,000 vols, 29,000 MSS, 25,000 rare books; collection of birch-bark writings; Dir-Gen. ALEXANDER SHKURKO; publs *Trudy GIM*, *Ezhegodnik GIM*, *Numizmaticheskii sbornik* (irregular).

State Literature Museum: 103051 Moscow, Petrovka ul. 28; tel. (095) 921-38-57; fax (095) 923-30-22; f. 1934; the museum is a research and educational centre which collects, studies and publishes material on the history of Russian and Soviet literature; 10 brs (museums of Lermontov, Herzen, Dostoevsky, Chekhov, Pasternak, Prishvin, Aksakov and Bryusov, Gogol exhibition at the house of Aksakov, The Museum of Soviet Literature); library of 250,000 vols; Gen. Dir NATALYA V. SHAKHALOVA.

State Museum of Ceramics (country-seat Kuskovo): 111402 Moscow, Stantsiya Kuskovo, Yunosti ul. 2; tel. 370-01-60; large collection of Russian art: paintings, furniture, porcelain, pottery; collection of West European art, tapestries, furniture, paintings, porcelain, pottery, etc.; Dir E. S. ERITSAN.

State Museum of Oriental Art: 107120 Moscow, Suvorovskii bul. 12a; tel. 291-96-14; f. 1918; large collection of Middle and Far Eastern art, art of the fmr Soviet Central Asian Republics and Transcaucasia, carpets, fabrics, ceramics, etc.; Dir V. A. NABACHIKOV.

State Pushkin Museum: 119034 Moscow, Ul. Prechistenka 12/2; tel. and fax (095) 202-43-54; f. 1958; 200,000 exhibits; library of 51,000 vols; maintains br. in Pushkin's former home (Arbat 53); Dir E. BOGATYREV.

State Pushkin Museum of Fine Arts: 121019 Moscow, Volkhonka 12; tel. 203-69-74; fax 203-46-74; f. 1912; about 558,000 items of ancient Eastern, Graeco-Roman, Byzantine, European and American art; numismatic colln of 200,000 items; library of 200,000 vols; Dir I. A. ANTONOVA; publs *Soobshcheniya* (Information), *Lectures*.

State Tretyakov Gallery: 117049 Moscow, Krymskii val. 10-14; tel. 230-77-88; f. 1856; contains a rich collection of 40,000 Russian icons and works of Russian and Soviet painters, sculptors and graphic artists from the 11th century to modern times; Dir P. I. LEBEDEV.

State V. V. Mayakovsky Museum: 101000 Moscow, Pr. Serova 3/6; tel. 921-93-87; f. 1974 in the building where Mayakovsky lived 1919–30; manuscripts, documentary material, notebooks, memorial items; library and reading room with *c.* 200,000 vols, including periodicals; Dir S. E. STRIZHNIKOVA.

Timiryazev, K. A., Apartment Museum: 103009 Moscow, Ul. Romanova 2, kv. 29; tel. 202-80-64; f. 1942; cultural and historical memorial to K. A. Timiryazev; 7,545 exhibits and archives on his life and work; personal library of 4,871 vols; Dir T. A. KUZNETSOVA.

Timiryazev State Museum of Biology: 123242 Moscow, Malaya Gruzinskaya 15; tel. 252-55-42; f. 1922; about 56,000 exhibits trace the origin and evolution of life on earth; library of 11,500 vols; Dir I. V. POLIKARPOVA.

Tolstoy Residence Museum: 119021 Moscow, Ul. Lva Tolstogo 21; tel. 246-94-44; rooms arranged as they were when the author lived there; 4,200 exhibits; Dir A. V. SALOMATIN.

Tolstoy State Museum: 119034 Moscow, Ul. Prechistenka 11; tel. 201-58-11; f. 1911; MSS section contains 170,000 sheets of Tolstoy's writings and nearly 600,000 MSS and archive material on Tolstoy and his circle; library of 71,000 works by or about Tolstoy; nearly 75,000 newspaper cuttings, and over 42,000 exhibits in the form of painting, sculpture, photographs, etc.; Dir L. M. LUBIMOVA.

Vakhtangov Museum-Room: Moscow; houses relics connected with life and work of Vakhtangov in his former home.

Vakhtangov Theatre Museum: Moscow; history of the Vakhtangov Theatre; Dir I. L. SERGEEVA.

Vernadsky State Geological Museum: 103009 Moscow, Mokhovaya ul. 11, Korp. 2; tel. (095) 203-52-87; fax (095) 203-47-98; e-mail info@sgm.ru; f. 1755; Dir Prof. D. V. RUNDQVIST.

Zhukovskii, N. E., Memorial Museum: 107005 Moscow, Ul. Radio 17; tel. 267-50-54; 25,000 items feature the work of N. E. Zhukovskii, and Soviet contributions to aviation and astronautics; Dir V. I. MASLOV.

Nalchik

Kabarda-Balkar Art Museum: Nalchik, Pr. V. I. Lenina 35; 3,500 exhibits; Dir I. Z. BATASHOV.

Nizhny Novgorod

Nizhny Novgorod Historical Museum: Nizhny Novgorod, Nab. Zhdanova 7; 160,000 exhibits including collections of archaeology, featuring the history of the Central Volga area dating back to ancient times.

Nizhny Novgorod State Art Museum: Nizhny Novgorod, Nab. im. Zhdanova 3; 6,500 works of Soviet and Western European artists; Dir B. P. BATURO.

State A. M. Gorky Museum of Literature: Nizhny Novgorod, Ul. Minina 26; tel. 36-15-29; f. 1928; 102,000 exhibits, illustrating the life and work of the writer; library of 40,000 vols; Dir T. A. RYZHOVA.

Novocherkassk

Novocherkassk Museum of the History of the Don Cossacks: Novocherkassk, Sovetskaya ul. 38; tel. 2-41-14; f. 1899; deals with the traditions and exploits of the Don Cossacks; collections of porcelain and painting; library of 17,000 vols; Dir L. A. GUROV.

Novosibirsk

Central Siberian Botanical Garden: 630090 Novosibirsk, Zolotodolinskaya Ul. 101; tel. 35-41-01; attached to Russian Acad. of Sciences; Dir I. YU. KOROPACHINSKY.

Omsk

Omsk Fine Art Museum: Omsk, Ul. Lenina 23; 3,780 exhibits; Dir A. A. GERZON.

Orel

Turgenev, I. S., State Literary Museum: 302000 Orel, Ul. Turgeneva 11; tel. 62-7-37; f. 1918; library of 60,000 vols; Dir V. V. SAFRONOVA.

Branch museums:

T. N. Granovsky Museum: Orel, 7 Noyabrya ul. 24; tel. 63-4-65; f. 1985; devoted to public figures born in Orel; Man. E. A. IVUSHKINA.

Literary Museum: 302000 Orel, Turgenev ul. 11; tel. 63-5-28; f. 1957; devoted to writers born in Orel; Man. L. E. URAKOVA.

N. S. Leskov House Museum: 301028 Orel, Ul. Oktyabrskaya 9; tel. 63-3-04; f. 1974; Man. L. S. KAMYSHALOVA.

Bunin Museum: 302000 Orel, Oktyabrsky pr. 1; tel. 60-7-74; f. 1991; Man. I. A. KOSTOMAROVA.

N. Andreev House Museum: Orel, Pushkarnaya 41; tel. 64-8-24; f. 1991; Man. O. Y. VOLOGINA.

Orenburg

Orenburg Fine Art Museum: Orenburg, Ul. Pravdy 6; 3,500 items; Dir L. B. POPOVA.

Palekh

State Museum of Palekh Art: Ivanovskaya oblast, selo Palekh, Ul. Bakanova 50; 2,500 items of Palekh art; Dir G. M. MELNIKOV.

Pavlovsk

Museum Palaces and Parks in Pavlovsk: 189623 St Petersburg oblast, Pavlovsk, Ul. Revolyutsii 20; tel. 470-21-55; fax 465-11-04; f. 1918; many examples of Russian garden architecture, sculpture by 18th-century Italian and French masters; European paintings of the 16th to 19th centuries, Russian portraits of the 18th century, Russian decorative art of the 18th and 19th centuries; furniture, porcelain, bronzes and textiles; library of 17,000 vols; Dir N. S. TRETYAKOV.

Penza

Penza Picture Gallery: 660026 Penza, Sovetskaya ul. 3; tel. 66-64-00; f. 1892; library of 3,200 vols; 7,700 exhibits; also 3 memorial museums; Dir VALERYI SAZONOV.

Perm

Perm State Art Gallery: 614600 Perm, Komsomolskii pr. 4; tel. (3422) 12-23-95; fax (3422) 12-22-50; f. 1922; library of 27,000 vols; Dir NADEZHDA V. BELYAEVA.

Petrodvorets

Peterhof State Museum Reserve: St Petersburg, Petrodvorets, Ul. Rasvodnaya 2; tel. 427-74-25; fax 427-93-30; f. 1918; 18th–20th century architecture, painting and landscape gardening; library of 21,000 books, special collection of 2,000 rare books, 7,000 Russian book-plates, 1,300 printed graphics; Dir V. V. ZNAMENOV.

Petrozavodsk

Karelian Museum of Fine Arts: Republic of Karelia, 185035 Petrozavodsk, Pr. K. Marksa 8; tel. (8142) 77-98-60; f. 1960; Russian art, local folk art; library of 21,000 vols; Dir N. I. VAVILOVA.

Karelian State Regional Museum: Republic of Karelia, 185035 Petrozavodsk, Pl. Lenina 1; tel. 7-02-40; fax 7-35-40; f. 1871; history, economy, science, culture, and natural history of the area; three branches; library of 25,500 vols; Dir O. A. SOKOLOVA; publ. *Museum Herald* (annually).

Kizhi State Open-Air Museum of History, Architecture and Ethnography: 185610 Petrozavodsk, Dzerzhinsky ul. 39; tel. 7-00-87; f. 1961; wooden architecture, history, ethnography, early Russian and Karelian painting and folklore; library of 8,500 vols; Dir O. A. NABOKOVA.

Pushkin

State Park and Palace of Tsarskoe Selo: 189690 St Petersburg-Pushkin, Sadovaya ul. 7; tel. 466-66-69; fax 465-21-96; f. 1918; many examples of Russian garden architecture, sculpture by Italian and French masters of the 18th and 19th centuries, Catherine Palace, collection of the costumes of the Imperial Family, coach museum; library of 6,794 vols including collection of rare books of 2,278 vols; Dir I. P. SAUTOV.

Pushkinskie Gory

Pushkin State Preserve: Pskovskaya oblast, Pushkinskie Gory, Tsentr muzeya dlya issledovaniya i kultury; tel. 2-34-90; f. 1922; 28,000 exhibits on the life in exile of the poet; the preserve includes the family lands at Mikhailovskoe, Trigorskoe and Petrovskoe, the ancient towns of Voronich and Savkina Gorka, the grave of Pushkin; library of 11,000 vols; Dir G. N. VASILEVICH.

Pyatigorsk

State Lermontov Literary Memorial Museum: Pyatigorsk, Lermontovskaya ul. 4; tel. 5-27-10; f. 1912; exhibits feature the life and work of M. Yu. Lermontov in the Caucasus; library of 14,000 vols; Dir L. MOROZOVA.

Roslavl

Roslavl Historical Museum: Roslavl, Ul. Proletarskaya 63; tel. 3-18-49; f. 1920; collection tracing the history, economy and culture of Russian people from the earliest times; library of 1,300 vols; Dir M. I. IVANOVA.

Rostov on Don

Rostov Museum of Fine Art: 344007 Rostov-on-Don, Ul. Pushkinskaya 115; tel. 66-59-07; f. 1938; old Russian, Soviet and foreign descriptive art; library of 14,507 vols; Dir G. S. ALIMURZAEVA; publ. *Khudozhnik*.

Ryazan

Ryazan Historico-architectural Museum Reservation: Ryazan, Kreml. 118; over 108,000 items describing the history, culture and art of the peoples of Russia.

Ryazan Regional Art Museum: Ryazan, Svoboda ul. 57; tel. 77-95-00; f. 1913; old Russian (15th–20th centuries), European (16th–19th centuries) and Soviet art; library of 17,000 vols; Dir V. A. IVANOV.

St Petersburg

Acad. F. N. Chernyshev Central Scientific Geological and Prospecting Museum: 199026 St Petersburg, Vasilevskii ostrov, Srednii pr. 74; fax (812) 321-53-99; f. 1882, opened 1930; about 1,000,000 geological specimens including examples of mineral deposits from all over the fmr Soviet Union; monographic and palaeontological collections; popularization of geological knowledge; Dir A. M. KARPUNIN.

Academy of Sciences Museum of Zoology: 199164 St Petersburg, Universitetskaya nab. 1; tel. 218-01-12; f. 1832; over 40,000 items describe the origin and evolution of the animal world on earth; Chief R. L. POTAPOV.

Botanical Museum: 197022 St Petersburg, Ul. Prof. Popova 2; tel. 234-84-39; f. 1823; over 60,000 specimens; br. of V. L. Komarov Botanical Institute of Academy of Sciences; Dir L. YU. BUDANTSEV.

Central Museum of Railway Transport of Russia: St Petersburg, Sadovaya ul. 50; fax 315-10-84; f. 1813; traces the history of railway transport in Russia; includes unique collection of miniature models of engines and carriages; Dir G. ZAKREVSKAYA.

Central Naval Museum: 199034 St Petersburg, Birzhevaya pl. 4; tel. (812) 218-27-02; fax (812) 218-27-01; e-mail museum@mail.admiral.ru; f. 1709; relics and other materials from the Russian and Soviet Navies; departments of history of the Russian Navy, history of the Soviet Navy, history of the Navy in the 1941–45 period, history of the Navy in the post-war period; responsible for Kronstadt Fortress, cruiser Aurora and submarine Narodovolets; library of 15,000 vols; Dir E. N. KORCHAGIN.

Dokuchaev Central Soil Museum: St Petersburg, Birzhevoi proezd 6; tel. 218-56-02; f. 1904; about 5,000 specimens of soil from nearly every soil zone in the world; library of 14,000 vols (Dokuchaev personal library); Dir Dr B. F. APARIN.

Dostoevsky Memorial Museum: 191002 St Petersburg, Kuznechnyi per. 5/2; tel. 311-40-31; e-mail ashimbaeva@md.spb.ru; f. 1971; the house where the author lived 1878–81; manuscripts, documentary material, memorial items, library of 23,000 vols; Dir N. ASHIMBAEVA.

Literary Museum of the Institute of Russian Literature: 199034 St Petersburg, Pushkinskii dom, Nab. Makarova 4; tel. 218-05-02; based on the material of the Pushkin Anniversary Exhibition of 1899; contains 95,000 exhibits and over 120,000 items of reference material; seven halls containing permanent exhibitions devoted to Radishchev, Lermontov, Gogol, Dostoevsky, I. S. Turgenev, and other Russian writers; Dir T. A. KOMAROVA.

M. V. Lomonosov Museum: 199164 St Petersburg, Universitetskaya nab. 3; tel. 218-12-11; f. 1947; 3,000 exhibits; Dir E. P. KARPEEV.

Mining Museum of the St Petersburg Mining Institute: 199026 St Petersburg, 21-ya liniya, 2; tel. (812) 218-84-29; fax (812) 327-73-59; e-mail spml@mail.wplus.net; f. 1773; over 201,000 items on the history of the mining industry in the 19th and early 20th century; collection of precious and imitation stones; Dir J. POLYARNYA.

Museum of Artillery, Engineers and Signal Corps: 197046 St Petersburg, Aleksandrovsky park 7; tel. and fax (812) 238-47-04; f. 1756; library of 74,000 vols; Dir Col V. M. KRYLOV.

Museum of Sculpture: St Petersburg, Pl. A. Nevskogo 1; largest collection of Russian sculpture, collection and care of documents on architecture and town planning; over 150,000 sheets of architectural drawings; Dir N. H. BELOVA.

Museum of the Academic Maly Theatre of Opera and Ballet: St Petersburg, Pl. Iskusstv 1; f. 1935; collection of materials (sketches, posters, etc.) depicting the history of the theatre and its work; Dir V. LIPHART

Museum of the Gorky Bolshoi Drama Theatre: St Petersburg, Ul. Fontanka 65.

Museum of the History of Religion: 191186 St Petersburg, Kazanskaya pl. 2; fax 311-94-83; f. 1932; 186,000 exhibits on Russian Orthodox Church, Roman Catholic and other Christian churches, Judaism, Islam and Buddhism; library of 170,000 vols; Dir S. A. KUCHINSKY; publ. *Theses* (annually).

Museum of the Mariinsky State Academic Theatre of Opera and Ballet: 190000 St Petersburg, Teatralnaya pl. 1; tel. (812) 114-13-31; fax (812) 314-17-44.

Museum of the Medical Corps: 191180 St Petersburg, Lazaretnyi per. 2; tel. 315-67-29; e-mail kvc@vmm.medport.ru; f. 1942; 210,000 exhibits trace the history of Russian and Soviet military medicine; research library of 50,000 vols, collections of rare books; Dir Col A. A. BUDKO; publs *Military Medicine Abroad* (every 2 months), *Memorial Dates of Military Medicine* (annually), *Review of the History of Military Medicine* (annually).

National Pushkin Museum: 191186 St Petersburg, Nab. Moiki 12; tel. 311-38-01; f. 1938 in Moscow; under supervision of Ministry of Culture; 50,000 exhibits illustrating the life and work of the poet and his epoch; Dir S. M. NEKRASSOV.

Annexes:

Lyceum Museum: Pushkin, Komsomolskaya ul. 1.

Country-House Museum: Pushkin, Pushkinskaya ul. 2.

A. Pushkin Museum Flat: St Petersburg, Nab. Moiki 12; tel. 314-00-06.

N. A. Nekrassov Flat: St Petersburg, Liteyny pr. 36, tel. 272-01-65.

Permanent Exhibition of Musical Instruments: St Petersburg, 5 Isaakievskaya pl.; about 3,000 exhibits, including a large collection of instruments made by the outstanding Russian and foreign craftsmen: Batov, Leman, Nalimov, Krasnoshchekov, Fedorov, Amati, Villaume, Tilke and Denner.

Peter the Great Museum of Anthropology and Ethnography: 119034 St Petersburg, Universitetskaya nab. 3; tel. 218-14-12; fax 218-08-11; e-mail info@kunstkamera.ru; attached to Russian Acad. of Sciences; ethnographical, archaeological, and anthropological material on the native peoples of Africa, North and South America, Australia and Oceania, the Near East, Central and Eastern Asia, Russia and Europe; Dir Prof. CHUNER M. TAKSAMI; publs *Etnograficheskiye tetradi* (1 a year), *Kuryer* (newsletter, 2 a year).

Popov, A. S., Central Museum of Communications: St Petersburg, Pochtamtskaya ul. 7; f. 1872; over 7 million items representing the development of all types of communication used in Russia and the former USSR; includes the state postage stamp collection; Dir N. KURITSYNA.

Russian State Museum of the Arctic and the Antarctic: 191040 St Petersburg, Ul. Marata 24A; tel. (812) 113-19-98; fax (812) 164-68-18; f. 1937; 65,456 exhibits incl. documents, pictures and original equipment of Soviet Polar Expeditions; under State Cttee for the Protection of the Natural Environment; library of 4,900 vols; Dir V. I. BOYARSKY.

State Circus Museum: 191011 St Petersburg, Ul. Fontanka 3; tel. 210-44-13; telex 121285; f. 1928; 80,000 exhibits of plans, sketches, paintings; library of Russian and foreign works; section on 18th and 19th century circus in Western Europe and on Russian and fmr Soviet circus; library of 4,000 items; Dir NATALYA KUZNETSOVA.

State Hermitage Museum: St Petersburg, Dvortsovaya nab. 34; f. 1764 as a court museum; opened to public 1852; richest collection in fmr Soviet Union of the art of prehistoric, ancient Eastern, Graeco-Roman and mediaeval times; preserves 2,800,000 *objets d'art*, including 600,000 drawings and engravings; works by Leonardo da Vinci, Raphael, Titian, Rubens and Rembrandt; collection of coins, weapons and applied art; Dir MIKHAIL PETROVSKY.

State Museum of the Great October Socialist Revolution: St Petersburg, Ul. Kuibysheva 4; f. 1919; the 430,000 items, and 280,000 books, show the history of Russia and the USSR in the 19th and 20th centuries, cover the Civil War and the Second World War and the development of Soviet society; Dir M. P. POTIFOROVA.

State Museum of the History of St Petersburg: 197046 St Petersburg, Petropavlovskaya Krepost 3; tel. (812) 238-45-11; fax (812) 238-42-43; e-mail direct@ppk.spb.su; f. 1918; more than 1m. exhibits; the museum shows the history and architectural development of St Petersburg; brs at Oreshek fortress, memorial flat of A. Blok, Museum of Printing, S. M. Kirov Museum, Monument and Memorial Hall to the Heroic Defenders of Leningrad, Rumyantsevsky Palace, Museum of the Gas Dynamics Laboratory; Dir B. S. ARAKCHEEV.

State Museum of Theatrical and Musical Arts: 191011 St Petersburg, Pl. Ostrovskogo 6; tel. 315-52-43; fax 314-77-46; f. 1918; over 440,000 exhibits depicting the history of Russian, Soviet and foreign theatre; 31,000 stage designs, 7,000 prints, 900 sculptures, 268,000 photographs, 24,000 MSS and documents, 62,000 posters and programmes; library of 5,000 vols; museum branches: *Rimsky-Korsakov Museum:* f. 1971; memorial museum in house where the composer lived; *F. I. Chaliapin Museum:* f. 1975; museum of history of Russian opera, in former house of Chaliapin; *Musical Instruments Museum:* f. 1900; 3,000 instruments; *Sheremetev Palace:* f. 1990; museum of music, and international music centre; *Samoilov Family Museum:* f. 1994; museum of a dynasty of Russian actors; Dir of State Museum of Theatrical and Musical Arts I. V. EVSTIGNEEVA; publs *Peterburgskii Annual, Monography of M. Petipa* (annually).

State National Ethnographical Museum: St Petersburg, Inzhenernaya ul. 4/1; fax 315-85-02; f. 1902; 300,000 exhibits; 150,000 photographs; library of 105,000 vols; Dir Prof. I. V. DUBOV; publ. *Collected Articles* (every 6 months).

State Russian Museum: St Petersburg, Inzhenernaya 4; opened as an Art Museum in 1898; 360,000 exhibits of Russian and Soviet art; largest collection of Russian icons, painting, sculpture, drawings of the 11th to 19th centuries, and Soviet art; Dir V. A. GUSEV.

Summer Garden and Museum Palace of Peter the Great: 191186 St Petersburg, Letny Sad; tel. and fax (812) 312-96-66; e- mail letnisad@infopro.spb.su; f. 1934; 18th-century architecture and sculpture; Dir T. D. KOZLOVA.

Samara

Samara A. M. Gorky Memorial Museum: Samara, Ul. S. Razina 126; literary museum devoted to the life and work of Gorky; exhibits in the house and furniture which belonged to him.

Samara Art Museum: 443001 Samara 10, Pl. Kuibysheva, Palace of Culture; f. 1897; fine arts museum with 11,000 exhibits; library of 7,000 vols; Dir ANNETA YU. BASS.

Saransk

Mordovian Museum of Fine Arts: Saransk, Kommunisticheskaya ul. 61; tel. 17-56-38; f. 1960; painting, sculpture, prints, decorative arts; library of 10,000 vols; Dir M. N. BARANOVA.

Saratov

Chernyshevsky Memorial Museum: 41002 Saratov, Ul. Chernyshevskogo 142; tel. 26-35-83; f. 1920; study of the life and work of the writer and his time; library of 14,232 vols; Dir G. P. MURENINA; publ. *Propagandist Velikovo Naslediya* (Publicist of the Great Inheritance, once every five years).

Saratov A. N. Radishchev State Art Museum: 410600 Saratov, Ul. Radishcheva 39; tel. 24-19-18; f. 1885; 20,000 exhibits; library of 34,000 vols; Dir G. M. KORMAKULINA.

Sergievsky Posad

Sergievsky Posad State History and Art Museum: Moscow oblast, Sergievsky Posad, Lavra; tel. 4-13-58; f. 1920; items dealing with the development of Russian art from the 14th century to the present; icons, embroidery, jewellery, porcelain, glass, vestments; also secular applied arts; library of 17,000 vols; Dir K. V. BOBKOV.

Starki

Far Eastern State Marine Reserve: 690601 Vladivostok, o. Popova, pos. Starki, Olkhovaya 11; tel. 9-66-82; attached to Russian Acad. of Sciences; Head V. V. GORLACH.

Stavropol

Stavropol Museum of Fine Art: Stavropol, Ul. Dzerzhinskogo 115; tel. 3-00-05; f. 1962; 4,270 exhibits; Dir Z. A. BELAYA.

Syktyvkar

Komi Art Museum: Komi Republic, Syktyvkar, Ul. Kommunisticheskaya 6; tel. 2-60-66; 5,000 exhibits; Dir S. K. SVETLICHNAYA.

Taganrog

Chekhov, A. P., Museum: Taganrog, Ul. Oktyabrskaya 9; tel. 6-27-45; rooms arranged as they were when Chekhov lived there in his childhood.

Tambov

Tambov Picture Gallery: 392000 Tambov, Sovetskaya ul. 97; tel. 02-36-95; f. 1960; 3,500 exhibits; 7,000 vols; Dir T. N. SHESTAKOVA.

Tikhvin

Rimsky-Korsakov House-Museum: St Petersburg oblast, Tikhvin; tel. 11509; telex 187500; f. 1944 in house where composer was born; main exhibition devoted to composer's childhood; also material on his later life; special collections: original scores, etc.

Tobolsk

Tobolsk Picture Gallery: Tobolsk, Pl. Krasnaya 2; 1,800 items.

Tula

Tula Art Museum: 300012 Tula, Ul. Engelsa 144; tel. 25-42-72; f. 1919; specialist art library of 15,000 vols; Dir M. N. KUSINA.

Tula Museum of Regional Studies: Tula, Ul. Sovetskaya 68; tel. (0872) 36-22-08; f. 1919; natural sciences, archaeology, history of Tula region; library of 10,806 vols; Dir N. B. NEMOVA.

Tver

Tver Art Gallery: 170640 Tver, Ul. Sovetskaya 3; tel. 33-25-61; f. 1937; 17,000 exhibits; library of 33,000 vols; Dir TATYANA S. KUYUKINA.

Tyumen

Tyumen Picture Gallery: Tyumen, Ul. Republiki 29; 9,000 exhibits; Dir I. S. TERENTEV.

Uglich

Uglich Historical Museum: Uglich, Kreml. 3; exhibits on the history of the Russian people.

Vladikavkaz

North-Ossetian K. L. Khetagurov Memorial Museum: Vladikavkaz, Butirina 19; tel. (86722) 3-62-22; f. 1979; collection of materials on Caucasian poetry and literature; Dir E. A. KESAYEVA.

Vladivostok

Botanical Garden: 690038 Vladivostok, Ul. Mayakovskogo 142; tel. 2-94-57; attached to Russian Acad. of Sciences; Dir A. F. ZHURAVKOV

Oceanarium of the Pacific Scientific Fisheries Centre: 690600 Vladivostok, Batareinaya ul. 4; tel. (4232) 25-59-65; marine and freshwater aquarium; 11,000 exhibits of flora and fauna of the Pacific Ocean; Dir G. N. KURGANSKY.

Voeikovo

Meteorological Museum of the Central Geophysical Observatory: St. Petersburg oblast, Vsevolozhskii raion, Voeikovo; Dir A. A. VASILIEV

Volgograd

Volgograd Historical Museum: 400053 Volgograd, Ul. Marshal Chuykov 47; tel. 34-72-72; f. 1937; the 120,000 exhibits feature the defence of the city during the Civil War (1918–20) and the Battle of Stalingrad (1942–43); library of 14,450 vols; Dir V. V. PODZOROV.

Vologda

Vologda Historical, Architectural and Artistic Museum Reserve: 160035 Vologda, Orlov 15; tel. 72-22-83; f. 1885; history, archaeology, ethnography, nature, literature, handicrafts, folk art, decorative and applied art, old Russian painting, modern art of the Vologda region, architecture; library of 40,000 vols; Dir L. D. KOROTAYEVA; publs catalogues.

Vologda Picture Gallery: Vologda, Kremlevskaya pl.; 6,500 exhibits; Dir S. G. IVENSKII.

Voronezh

Voronezh Art Museum: Voronezh, Pr. Revolyutsii 18; tel. 55-28-43; f. 1933; 22,065 exhibits; library of 18,800 vols; Dir VLADIMIR Y. USTINOV.

Yakutsk

Yakutsk Museum of Fine Arts: 677000 Yakutsk, Ul. Khabarova 27; tel. 2-77-98; f. 1928; folk art, Western European, Russian and Soviet art of 17th to 20th centuries; Dir N. M. VASILEVA.

Yaroslavl

Yaroslavl State Historical Museum: 150000 Yaroslavl, Pl. Podbelskogo 25; tel. 22-02-72; f. 1865; over 370,000 exhibits on the history of the Russian people from ancient times to the present; library of 35,000 vols; Dir V. I. LEBEDEV; publ. *Kraevedcheskiye Zapiski* (irregular).

Yasnaya Polyana

Tolstoy Museum Estate: Tulskaya oblast, Shchekinskii raion, Yasnaya Polyana; tel. (0872) 33-98-32; fax (0872) 38-67-10; e-mail root@yaspol.tula.su; f. 1921; 40,000 exhibits in the house and estate belonging to L. N. Tolstoy; literary museum devoted to his life and work; estate with park grounds and forest; Dir VLADIMIR I. TOLSTOY; publ. *Yasnaya Polyana* (4 a year).

Universities

ALTAI STATE UNIVERSITY

656099 Barnaul, Ul. Dimitrova 66

Telephone: 22-18-07

Founded 1973
State control
Language of instruction: Russian
Academic year: September to June

Chancellor: VALERY MIRONOV
Vice-Chancellor: SERGEI SCHEGLOV
Chief Administrative Officer: NATALIA SEROVA
Librarian: GALINA TRUSHNIKOVA

Number of teachers: 447
Number of students: 6,000

DEANS

Faculty of Law: V. MUZYUKIN
Faculty of Economics: V. KOKOREV
Faculty of History: V. VLADIMIROV
Faculty of Philology: A. CHUVAKIN
Faculty of Mathematics: A. KAMYSHNIKOV
Faculty of Physics: D. RUDER
Faculty of Chemistry: V. NOVOZHENOV
Faculty of Biology: Y. KOCHETKOV
Faculty of Geography: V. RUDSKY
Department of Sociology: S. GRIGORYEV
Part-time Education Faculty: G. SHUPIK

PROFESSORS

BOBROV, M., Philosophy
BORODAVKIN, A., History
BUDKIN, A., Algebra and Theory of Numbers
BUKATY, V., General Physics
CHERNISHOV, Y., History
CHERVYAKOV, V., Geography
GAVLO, V., Criminology
GOLEV, N., Russian Language
GRIGORYEV, S., Sociology
KIRUSHIN, Y., Archaeology
KISELEV, V., Human and Animal Physiology
KOKOREV, V., Management
KUPRIYANOV, A., Biology
MALTSEV, Y., Algebra and Theory of Numbers
MEDVEDEV, N., Algebra and Theory of Numbers
MELNIKOV, A., Philosophy
MIRONOV, V., Algebra and Theory of Numbers
MISCHENKO, V., Economics
MOISEEV, V., History
MOROSOV, V., Philology
NEVEROV, V., History
OSCORBIN, N., Mathematics and Cybernetics
PERSHINA, L., Chemistry
PETRIN, V., History
PETROV, B., Analytical Chemistry
RASTOV, Y., Philosophy
RODIONOV, Y., Mathematics
SAGALAKOV, A., Theoretical Physics
SENKO, Y., Education
SKUBNEVSKY, V., Prerevolutionary Native History
STARSEV, O., Physics
VASILYEV, V., Biochemistry
VOROBYEVA, I., Philology
YELCHANINOV, V., Philosophy

ATTACHED INSTITUTES

Ecological Monitoring Research Institute: Dir N. OSCORBIN

Humanistic Research Institute: Dir A. SHAMSHIN

Thermoplastic Materials Research Institute: Dir M. CHEMERIS

AMUR STATE UNIVERSITY

675027 Amurskaya oblast, Blagoveshchensk, Ignatevskoe shosse 21

Telephone: (4162) 45-49-95
Fax: (4162) 45-45-97
E-mail: indep@amgu.amur.su

Founded 1975
State control
Language of instruction: Russian
Academic year: September to July

Rector: Prof. BORIS A. VINOGRADOV
First Prorector: Prof. VICTOR V. SADOVSKY
Chief Administrative Officer: TATYANA V. ASTAFUROVA
Librarian: NATALYA P. UDALOVA

Library of 205,000 vols
Number of teachers: 350
Number of students: 5,000

Depts of electric power networks and systems, automated management and data processing systems, world economics, law, linguistics, sociology, social work, journalism, finance, state and local government, commerce, design, applied mathematics.

BASHKIR STATE UNIVERSITY

450074 Bashkortostan, Ufa, Ul. Frunze 32

Telephone: (3472) 22-63-70
Telex: 6505894253
Fax: (3472) 22-61-05

Founded 1957
Language of instruction: Russian
Academic year: September to June

Rector: RAGHIB N. GUIMAYEV
Pro-Rectors: Prof. BAYAZIT GALIMOV, Prof. ALEXANDR CHUVYROV, Dr MICHEL MINEYEV
Chief Administrative Officer: N. S. AFANASYEV
University Librarian: E. G. GUIVANOVSKAYA

Number of teachers: 525
Number of students: 8,300

DEANS

Faculty of History: Dr I. D. CHIGRIN
Faculty of Philology: Dr V. I. KHRULEV
Faculty of Physics: Prof. M. KH. KHARISOV
Faculty of Mathematics: Prof. YA. SULTANAYEV
Faculty of Biology: Dr I. P. DZHYACHENKO
Faculty of Geography: Dr P. I. SHVETSOV
Faculty of Economics: Prof. M. N. SULEIMANOV
Faculty of Law: Prof. Z. D. ENIKEEV
Faculty of Chemistry: Dr YU. A. PROCHUKHAN
Faculty of Foreign Languages: Prof. R. Z. MURYASOV

CHECHENO-INGUSH STATE UNIVERSITY

364907 Checheno-Ingush Autonomous Republic, Groznyi, Ul. Sheripova 32

Telephone: 23-40-89

Founded 1972

Rector: (vacant)

Number of students: 5,600

Faculties of philology, romance and Germanic philology, history, mathematics, physics, chemistry and biology, economics, geography.

CHELYABINSK STATE TECHNICAL UNIVERSITY

454080 Chelyabinsk, Pr. Lenina 76

Telephone: (3512) 33-58-82
Fax: (3512) 34-74-08

Founded 1943
State control
Academic year: September to June

Rector: Prof. GERMAN P. VYATKIN
First Vice-Rector (Academic): Prof. GENNADY G. MIKHAILOV
Vice-Rector (Academic): Prof. YURI V. MAXIMOV
Vice-Rector (Scientific Work): Prof. VLADIMIR G. DUKMASOV
Registrar: VLADIMIR V. PASESHNIK
Director of Library: YULIA V. LEVANDOVSKAYA

Number of teachers: 1,500
Number of students: 12,000

Publication: *Technopolis* (weekly).

DEANS

Faculty of Aerospace Engineering: YURI S. PAVLYUK
Faculty of Automation and Mechanical Engineering: SERGEI GUREVICH
Faculty of Architecture and Civil Engineering: VLADIMIR V. SPASIBOZHKO
Faculty of Tractor Engineering: GENNADY D. DRAGUNOV
Faculty of Metallurgy: VASILY E. ROSHCHIN
Faculty of Mechanical Engineering Technology: PIOTR MAZEIN
Faculty of Instrumentation Technology: NIKOLAI T. VINICHENKO
Faculty of Power Engineering: EVGENY V. TOROPOV
Faculty of Economics and Management: ALEXANDER K. TASHCHEV
Faculty of Humanities: MAYA N. EVLANOVA
Faculty of Economics and Business: VALENTINA A. KISELEVA
Faculty of Commerce: VALENTINA Y. LOPATINA
Faculty of Applied Mathematics and Physics: YURI IZMAILOV
Faculty of the Service and Light Industries: TATYANA TRETYAKOVA

ATTACHED RESEARCH INSTITUTES

Institute of Digital Systems: Dir Prof. YURI T. KARMANOV.

Institute of Industrial Ecology: Dir Prof. ALEXANDER I. SIDOROV.

Institute of the Chemical Problems of Industrial Ecology: Dir Prof. YURI I. SUKHAREV.

CHELYABINSK STATE UNIVERSITY

454136 Chelyabinsk, Ul. Br. Kashirinykh 129

Telephone: (3512) 42-12-02
Fax: (3512) 42-08-59

Founded 1976
Academic year: September to July

Rector: Prof. V. D. BATUKHTIN
Registrar: YU. M. KOVALEV
Librarian: N. F. GROSHEVA

Number of teachers: 251 full-time, 25 part-time
Number of students: 2,900 full-time, 1,200 correspondence

Publication: *Vestnik*.

DEANS

Faculties of Mathematics: Dr V. I. UKHOBOTOV
Faculty of Physics and Engineering: A. P. YALOVETS
Faculty of Chemistry: A. V. BELIK
Faculty of History: Dr V. V. RABTSEVICH
Faculty of Philology: T. J. SHISHMARENKOVA

Faculty of Economics: A. Yu. Shumakov
Faculty of Law: Dr G. V. Khashimov
Faculty of Humanities: K. N. Sukhanov
Faculty of Social Work: V. F. Mamonov

PROFESSORS

Abramovsky, A. P., History
Alferova, T. V., Biology
Batukhtin, V. D., Mathematical Theory of Optimization and Control
Belkin, N. V., Political Economy
Buchelnikov, V. D., Physics
Chaptsov, R. P., Theory of Systems
Cherkasov, V. A., Pedagogics
Chernetsov, P. I., Pedagogics
Dudorov, A. Y., Physics and Mathematics
Duranov, M. E., Pedagogical Studies
Golikov, A. A., Economics
Kleiman, V. L., Theoretical Mechanics
Kornev, N. I., Economics
Matushkin, S. I., Didactics
Matveev, S. V., Topology
Pershin, V. K., Liquid Crystals
Popov, A. N. , Economics
Rabtsevich, V. V., History
Sedov, V. V., Political Economy
Sekerin, A. I., History
Shchennikov, G. K., Russian Language
Shkatova, L. A., Russian Language
Sukhanov, K. N., Philosophy
Sveshnikov, M. A., Astrophysics
Tampovtsev, V. I., Radiophysics
Tanana, V. P., Mathematics
Vasiliev, V. S., Economics
Yartsev, V. M., Quasi-one-dimensional Semiconductors
Zeldovich, B. I., Optics

CHUVASH I. N. ULYANOV STATE UNIVERSITY

428015 Chuvash Autonomous Republic, Cheboksary, Moskovskii pr. 15
Telephone: 24-03-79
Telex: 658127
Fax: 42-80-90

Founded 1967
State control
Languages of instruction: Chuvash, Russian
Academic year: September to July

Rector: Prof. Dr L. P. Kurakov
Vice-Rectors: M. S. Alatyrev (Instruction), L. G. Yefremov (Chief Administrative Officer), L. N. Tolstov (Finance)
Librarian: L. V. Petrova

Library: see Libraries
Number of teachers: 940
Number of students: 10,600

Publication: *Ulyanovets* (weekly).

DEANS

Faculty of Chemistry: O. Y. Nosakin
Faculty of Chuvash Philology and Culture: V. I. Sergeev
Faculty of Construction: Y. V. Chernov
Faculty of Economics: V. G. Khirby
Faculty of Electrical and Power Engineering: G. A. Belov
Faculty of History: A. V. Arsenteva
Faculty of Law: V. G. Timofeev
Faculty of Mathematics: V. G. Agakov
Faculty of Mechanical Engineering: Y. P. Kuznetsov
Faculty of Medicine: V. Y. Volkov
Faculty of Philology: Z. F. Myshkin
Faculty of Physics: A. I. Korotkov
Higher Business School: L. P. Kurakov (Dir)
Higher School for Training Engineers: V. A. Chedrin (Dir)

DAGESTAN STATE UNIVERSITY

Dagestan, 367025 Makhachkala, Sovetskaya ul. 8
Telephone: (87200) 7-29-50
Telex: 412062, box 51117
Fax: (87200) 7-81-21

Founded 1931
State control
Language of instruction: Russian
Academic year: September to July

Rector: Prof. O. A. Omarov
Vice-Rector: Prof. E. Z. Emirbekov
Registrar: Prof. M. I. Abakarov
Librarian: L. I. Alieva

Number of teachers: 628
Number of students: 9,000

Publication: *Transactions*.

DEANS

Faculty of Physics: Dr Kh. A. Magomedov
Faculty of Mathematics: Dr M. G. Mekhtiev
Faculty of Chemistry: Dr K. M. Yunusov
Faculty of Biology: Dr Kh. M. Ramazanov
Faculty of Law: Dr A. R. Omarov
Faculty of Management in Economics: Dr M. M. Magomaev
Faculty of Finance and Economics: Dr R. K. Kadiev
Faculty of History: Dr B. B. Bulatov
Faculty of Russian Language and Literature: Dr Sh. A. Mazanaev
Faculty of Dagestan Philology: Dr Z. A. Magomedov
Faculty of Romance and Germanic Philology: Dr M. M. Abdulsalamov
Faculty of Culture: Dr M. A. Israfilov

DUBNA INTERNATIONAL UNIVERSITY OF NATURE, SOCIETY AND MAN

141980 Moscow oblast, Dubna, Universitetskaya ul. 19
Telephone: (09621) 2-20-71
Fax: (09621) 2-24-64
E-mail: rector@uni-dubna.ru

Founded 1994
State control

President: V. G. Kadyshevsky
Rector: O. L. Kuznetsov
Vice-Rectors: M. S. Khozyainov (Scientific Work), Yu. S. Sakharov (Academic), E. N. Cheremisina (Computer Education and Information Systems)

Postgraduate programmes in fields of Linguistics, Systems Analysis and Management, Social Work, Ecology and the Use of Natural Resources, Economics, Law.

FAR EASTERN STATE UNIVERSITY

690600 Vladivostok, Primorskogo Kraya, Ul. Sukhanova 8
Telephone: (4232) 26-12-80
Telex: 213218
Fax: (4232) 25-72-00
E-mail: idp@online.ru

Founded 1899
State control
Language of instruction: Russian
Academic year: September to June

Rector: V. I. Kurilov
Pro-Rectors: R. P. Shepeleva, R. M. Samigulin, B. L. Reznik, V. P. Dikarev, N. M. Pestereva, G. V. Voropayev, T. I. Gorodnova
Librarian: N. N. Gaidarenko

Library: see Libraries
Number of teachers: 870
Number of students: 11,000

Publications: *Transactions, Far Eastern University* (monthly).

DEANS

Biology, Ecology and Soils: V. A. Kudryashov
Chemistry and Chemical Ecology: N. P. Kapustina
Chinese Studies: O. V. Kuchuk
Economics: R. V. Sabitova
English Philology: L. P. Bondarenko
Entrepreneurship Law: A. S. Shevchenko
Extramural Faculty: L. I. Romanova
Geophysics: Yu. B. Zonov
History and Philosophy: O. V. Sidorenko
Information Technology: I. V. Soppa
International Economic Relations and Management: A. A. Khamatova
International Law: V. V. Gavrilov
International Relations: A. V. Shkuropat
Institute of International Relations: M. Y. Shinkovsky (Dir)
Investigation and Public Prosecution: A. F. Rekhovsky
Japanese Studies: S. N. Ilyin
Journalism: V. V. Bakshin
Jurisprudence: A. G. Korchagin
Higher College of Korean Studies: V. V. Verkholyak
Law (in Petropavlovsk-Kamchatsky): L. A. Zakhozhy
Law (in Yuzhno-Sakhalinsk): V. F. Evstratov
Institute of Law: V. I. Kurilov (Dir)
Management and Business: S. B. Golovachev
Institute of Management and Business: A. A. Belusov (Dir)
Mathematics and Computer Science: V. B. Osipov
Physical Technology: V. G. Lifshits
Institute of Oriental Studies: V. I. Kurilov (Dir)
Physics: P. N. Kornyushin
Institute of Physics and Information Technology: V. I. Belokon (Dir)
Political Science and Social Control: O. P. Yelantseva
Institute of Preliminary Studies: N. A. Smal (Dir)
Institute of Professional Development and Staff Professional Enhancement: E. M. Chukhrayev (Dir)
Psychology and Social Work: A. V. Stetsiv
Russian Philology: K. A. Medvedeva
Basic Aspects of State and Law: V. P. Fedorov
FESU branch in Artem: Kharitonsky (Dir)
FESU branch in Nakhodka: A. I. Razgonov (Dir)

PROFESSORS

Abramova, L. A., Foreign Languages
Aleksandrov, A. V., Chinese Studies
Anikinov, D. S., Mathematics
Anisimov, A. P., Biology
Apakov, A. A., Law
Ashchepkov, L. T., Mathematics
Bagrina, N. P., Chemistry
Bakshim, V. V., Journalism
Basenko, V. L., Economics
Bazhanov, A. V., Mathematics
Belokon, V. I., Physics
Bereznikov, K. P., Geophysics
Binevsky, A. A., Philosophy
Bogolepova, T. G., History of Foreign Literature
Boiko, I. V., Economics
Bondarenko, L. P., English
Botnar, A. P., History and Philosophy
Brovko, P. F., Geography
Chizhov, L. N., Economics
Daricheva, L. V., Geophysics
Dashko, N. A., Geophysics
Elyakov, G. B., Chemistry
Ermakova, E. V., History
Feshchenko, L. A., Law
Galkina, I. A., Political Science
Galkina, L. V., Korean Studies
Gavrilov, V. V., Law
Gramm-Osipova, V. N., Chemistry
Ilyushin, I. A., Journalism
Ivankov, V. N., Water Ecology
Ivlev, A. M., Biology
Kharchenko, N. P., Russian Philology
Khristoforova, N. K., Ecology
Kleshchev, A. S., Mathematics

KNYAZEV, S. D., Law
KOCHETKOV, V. P., English
KOLBINA, L. M., Japanese Studies
KOLESOVA, M. V., Political Science
KOLOBOV, A. G., Mathematics
KONDRIKOV, N. B., Chemistry
KOROBEYEV, A. I., Law
KORYABINA, R. M., Chinese Studies
KOSTETSKY, E. Y., Biology
KRIVSHENKO, S. F., Russian Philology
KUDRYASHOV, V. A., Biology
KULEBYAKIN, Psychology and Social Work
KULESHOV, E. L., Computer Systems
KULIKOV, G. P., Culture Studies
KURKOVICH, E. P., Foreign Languages
LIFSHITS, V. G., Physics
LYKOV, K. F., History
MEDVEDEVA, K. A., Russian Philology
MIKHAILOVA, N. K., Journalism
MIKHINA, G. B., Education and Psychology
MIRONETS, Y. A., English Philology
MOLODYKH, V. I., Chinese Studies
OSTANIN, V. A., Economics
OVRAKH, G. P., Political Science
PAK, G. K., Mathematics
PESHCHERITSA, V. F., History
PESHEKHODKO, V. M., Biology
PESTEREVA, N. M., Geophysics
PLOKHIKH, S. V., History
POLISHCHUK, V. E., Physics
PROSHINA, Z. G., Translation
PRUDNIKOV, V. S., Mathematics
RADAYEV, E. F., Chemistry
RAGULIN, P. G., Economics
REKHOVSKY, A. F., Law
SABITOVA, R. G., Economics
SAMUSENKO, T. M., Law
SANACHEV, I. D., Political Science
SEMYONOV, V. G., Psychology
SHAKHOV, V. N., Economics
SHAPKIN, N. P., Chemistry
SHAVKUNOV, E. V., History
SHESTOPALOVA, V. I., Russian Philology
SHEVCHENKO, A. S., Law
SHINKOVSKY, M. Y., International Relations
SHKUROPAT, A. V., International Economic Relations
SHLYK, V. A., Mathematics
SHNYRKO, A. A., Japanese Studies
SHTANKO, G. V., Physics
SNEZHKOVA, S. A., Biology
SOKOLOVSKY, A. Y., Philology of Asian Pacific Countries
SOPPA, I. V., Electronics
STARODUMOVA, E. A., Russian Philology
STOLYAROVA, N. S., English Philology
SYROYED, N. S., Psychology and Social Work
TEREKHOVA, E. V., Foreign Languages
TKACHEV, V. A., Journalism
TRISHCHENKO, E. K., Mathematics
VASILIEVA, L. A., Journalism
VERESHCHAGINA, A. V., Political Science
VERISOVSKAYA, E. V., Japanese Studies
VYSOTSKY, V. I., Chemistry
YAKUNIN, L. P., Geography
YUDIN, V. V., Physics
YURKOVA, English Language
ZAITSEVA, G. D., Russian Philology
ZONOV, Y. B., Geophysics

IRKUTSK STATE UNIVERSITY

664003 Irkutsk, 3, Ul. K. Marksa 1

Telephone: (3952) 24-34-53
Fax: (3952) 24-22-38

Founded 1918
State control
Language of instruction: Russian
Academic year: September to May

Rector: Prof. ALEXANDER I. SMIRNOV
Vice-Rectors: I. GUTNIK, V. SAUNIN, V. GLEBETS
Librarian: R. V. PODGAICHENKO

Number of professors and lecturers: 650
Number of students: 7,579

Publications: *Transactions, Proceedings of the Biological Research Institute, Proceedings of the Applied Physics Research Institute, Proceedings of the Oil and Coal Products Research Institute, Collected Short Scientific Papers.*

DEANS

Faculty of History: Asst Prof. YU. S. PARKHOMENKO
Faculty of Geography: Prof. V. YA. MANGAZEEV
Faculty of Law: Assoc. Prof. O. P. LICHICHAN
Faculty of Philology: Asst Prof. V. P. DANILENKO
Faculty of Biology and Soil Sciences: Assoc. Prof. N. I. GRANINA
International Faculty: Asst Prof. V. YA. ANDRUKHOVA
Siberian-American Joint Faculty of Management: Asst Prof. A. V. DIOGENOV
Faculty of Geology: Prof. A. I. SIZYKH
Faculty of Chemistry: Prof. Dr A. YU. SAFRONOV
Faculty of Physics: Prof. YU. V. PARFENOV
Faculty of Psychology: Assoc. Prof. I. A. KONOPAK
Faculty of Social Sciences: Prof. V. A. RESHETNIKOV
Faculty of Service Industries and Advertising: Assoc. Prof. V. K. KARNAUKHOVA

ATTACHED RESEARCH INSTITUTIONS

Biological Research Institute: Dir Prof. O. M. KOZHOVA

Applied Physics Research Institute: Dir Prof. YU. V. PARFENOV

Oil and Coal Products Research Institute: Dir Asst Prof. V. P. LATYSHEV

Computing Centre: Dir Asst Prof. V. B. MANCYVODA

Astronomical Observatory: Dir Assoc. Prof. S. A. YAZEV

Botanical Garden: Dir Assoc. Prof. V. YA. KUZEVANOV

Lake Baikal Biological Station

IVANOVO STATE UNIVERSITY

153377 Ivanovo, Ul. Ermaka 39

Telephone: 4-02-16

Founded 1974

Number of students: *c.* 5,000

Faculties of biology and chemistry, economics, history, law, mathematics, philology, romance and Germanic philology, physics.

KABARDINO-BALKAR STATE UNIVERSITY

360004 Kabardino-Balkar Republic, Nalchik, Ul. Chernyshevskogo 173

Telephone: (095) 337-99-55
Fax: (095) 337-99-55
E-mail: bsk@kbgu-1.nalchik.su

Founded 1932
State control
Language of instruction: Russian
Academic year: September to June

Rector: BARASBI S. KARAMURZOV
Vice-Rectors: KARNYSH (Extramural Studies), SVETLANA K. BASHIEVA (Postgraduate and Scientific Studies), HAZESHA T. TAOV (Foreign Affairs)
Registrar: I. SHOMAKHOVA
Librarian: ROSA N. UNACHEVA

Library: see Libraries
Number of teachers: 790
Number of students: 8,500

DEANS

Faculty of Chemistry and Biology: S. H. SHKHAGAPSOEV
Faculty of Physics: B. I. KUNIEV
Faculty of Mathematics: M. H. KHAUPSHEV
Faculty of Economics: V. Z. SHEVLOKOV
Faculty of Law: H. P. KULTERBAEV
Faculty of Physical Education and Sport: M. ABREKOV
Faculty of Mechanical Engineering: V. D. BATYROV
Faculty of Medicine: ZAKHOKHOV
Faculty of Philology: H. T. TAOV
Faculty of Education: B. T. SOZAEV
Faculty of History and Social Work: M. Z. SOBLIROV
Faculty of Microelectronics: R. SH. TESHEV
Faculty of Computer Science and Systems Control: M. S. ALEINIKOV

KALININGRAD STATE UNIVERSITY

236041 Kaliningrad, Ul. A. Nevskogo 14

Telephone: 46-59-17
Telex: 262116
Fax: 46-58-13

Founded 1967

Rector: Prof. N. A. MEDVEDEV
Pro-Rector: V. V. BELYAKOV
Librarian: A. D. SHKITSKAYA

Library: see Libraries
Number of teachers: 380
Number of students: 6,000

Publication: *Proceedings.*

Faculties of physics, mathematics, history, philology, chemistry, biology, geography, economics and law, teacher training

KALMYK STATE UNIVERSITY

358000 Elista, Ul. Pushkina 11

Telephone: 2-50-60

Founded 1970

Number of students: 5,000

Rector: N. P. KRASAVCHENKO
Pro-Rector: S. B. BADMAEV

Faculties of general engineering, philology, biology, physics, mathematics, oriental studies, agriculture

KAZAN STATE UNIVERSITY

420008 Tatarstan, Kazan, Ul. Lenina 18

Telephone: 32-15-49
Telex: 224881
Fax: 38-73-21

Founded 1804
State control
Languages of instruction: Russian, Tatar
Academic year: September to June

Rector: YURI G. KONOPLEV
Librarian: ZHANA V. SHCHELYVANOVA

Number of teachers: 980
Number of students: 7,470

Publication: *Mathematics.*

DEANS

Department of Biology: A. I. GOLUBEV
Department of Geography: O. P. PEREVEDENTSEV
Department of Geology: R. K. TUKHVATULLIN
Department of History: I. R. TAGIROV
Department of Philology: YA. G. SAFIULLIN
Department of Mathematics: V. V. VISHNEVSKII
Department of Computer Sciences: YA. I. ZABOTIN
Department of Physics: A. V. AGANOV
Department of Chemistry: N. A. ULAKHOVICH
Department of Law: I. A. TARKHANOV
Department of Tatar Studies: T. N. GALIULLIN
Department of Ecology: YU. S. KOTOV
Department of Journalism: F. I. AGZAMOV

PROFESSORS

AGANOV, A. V., Physics
AKHMADULLIN, A. G., Philology
ALATYREV, V. I., Physiology

ANDRAMONOVA, N. A., Russian Philology
ANDREEV, V. I., Education
ARSLANOV, M. M. , Mathematics
BAKHTIN, A. I., Mineralogy
BALALYKINA, E. A., Philology
BARABANSHIKOV, B. I.., Genetics
BASHKIROV, SH. SH., Physics
BUDNIKOV, G. K., Chemistry
BUKHARAEV, R. G., Cybernetics
BUROV, B. V., Lithology
BUSYGIN, E. P., History
BUTAKOV, G. P., Geomorphology
CHERKASOV, R. A., Chemistry
ERMOLAEV, I. P., History
FARUKSHIN, M. H., Sociology
GABDULKHAEV, B. G., Mathematics
GALIULLIN, T. N., Philology
GOLUBEV, A. I., Zoology
KAIGORODOV, V. R., Physics
KHAIRUTDINOV, R. G., History
KHAKOV, V. H., Turkic Languages
KHALYMBADYA, V. G., Palaeontology
KHOKHLOVA, L. P., Plant Physiology
KOCHELAEV, B. I., Physics
KONOPLEV, YU. G., Mechanics
KOPOSOV, G. F., Soil Studies
KURDYUKOV, G. I., Law
KUZNETSOV, V. A., Ichthyology
LESHCHINSKAYA, I. B., Microbiology
LIASHKO, A. D., Computing Mathematics
LITVIN, A. L., History
LYUBARSKI, E. L., Botany
MAKLAKOV, A. I., Physics
MALKOV, V. P., Law
NAFIGOV, R. I., History
NEPRIMEROV, N. N., Electronics
NIKOLAEV, G. A., Philology
PEREVEDENTSEV, YU. P., Meteorology
RAKHMATULLIN, E. S., Sociology
RESHETOV, YU. S., Law
RYABOV, A. A., Law
SADYKOV, M. B., Philosophy
SAKHIBULLIN, N. A., Astrophysics
SALNIKOV, YU. I., Chemistry
SEMENOV, V. F., Political Economy
SHARIFYANOV, I. I., History
SHERSTNEV, A. N., Mathematics
SHIROKOV, A. P., Geometry
SIDOROV, V. V., Radiophysics
TAGIROV, I. R., History
TEPLOV, M. A., Physics
TEPTIN, G. M., Meteorology
TORSUEV, N. P., Geomorphology
TROFIMOV, A. M., Geomorphology
TUMASHEVA, D. G., Turkic Languages
USMANOV, M. A., History
YEGALOV, V. I., Differential Equations
YIGUNIN, V. D., History
ZABOTIN, YA. I., Computing Mathematics

ATTACHED RESEARCH INSTITUTIONS

N. G. Chebotarev Research Institute of Mathematics and Mechanics: Dir A. V. KOSTERIN

A. M. Butlerov Research Institute of Chemistry: Dir V. D. KISELEV

KEMEROVO STATE UNIVERSITY

650043 Kemerovo, Krasnaya ul. 6
Telephone: (3842) 23-12-26
Telex: 215350
Fax: (3842) 23-30-34
E-mail: rector@kemgu.kemerovo.su

Founded 1974
State control
Language of instruction: Russian
Academic year: September to July

Rector: YU. A. ZAKHAROV
Pro-Rectors: B. P. NEVZOROV, V. G. KRIGER, V. A. VOLCHEK, K. E. AFANASIEV
Librarian: N. P. KONOVALOVA

Number of teachers: 780
Number of students: 8,834

Faculties of biology, chemistry, economics, law, history, mathematics, philology, foreign languages, physics, social sciences, sport

KRASNOYARSK STATE UNIVERSITY

660041 Krasnoyarsk, Pr. Svobodnyi 79
Telephone: (3912) 44-82-13
Telex: 288155
Fax: (3912) 44-86-25
E-mail: root@krasgu.krasnoyarsk.su

Founded 1969
State control
Language of instruction: Russian
Academic year: September to July

Rector: A. S. PROVOROV
Pro-Rectors: B. K. RZHEBKO, V. A. SAPOZHNIKOV, A. PH. MITZKEVICH, V. I. PETRISHCHEV
Librarian: E. G. KRIVONOSOVA

Number of teachers: 876
Number of students: 8,358
Publication: *University Life* (fortnightly).

Faculties of philology, economics, law, physics, mathematics, chemistry, biology, modern foreign languages, psychology and education, physical training, philology, journalism

KUBAN STATE UNIVERSITY

350040 Krasnodar, Stavropolskaya ul. 149
Telephone: (8612) 33-75-02
Fax: (8612) 33-98-87
E-mail: bva@ksu.kuban.su

Founded 1920
State control
Language of instuction: Russian
Academic year: September to July

Rector: V. A. BABESHKO
Pro-Rectors: V. I. CHERNY, V. I. ZABOLOTSKY, V. A. DERBENIEV, A. V. SMIRNOVA, V. I. CHISTYAKOV
Registrar: I. K. MISENKO
Librarian: G. V. SOLOVIEVA

Number of teachers: 900
Number of students: 20,000

Publications: *Priroda, Obshchestvo i Chelovek* (4 a year), *Filologiya* (2 a year), *Golos Minuvshego* (4 a year), *Ekonomika, Upravleniya, Pravdy* (4 a year).

DEANS

Faculty of History: G. M. ACHAGU
Faculty of Economics: I. V. SHEVCHENKO
Faculty of Physics: N. A. YAKOVENKO
Faculty of Philology: L. P. LIPSKAYA
Faculty of Graphic Art: V. P. KUZMENKO
Faculty of Chemistry: V. D. BUYKLISKY
Faculty of Biology: V. YA. NAGALEVSKY
Faculty of Applied Mathematics: YU. V. KOLTSOV
Faculty of Mathematics: G. F. SOKOL
Faculty of Romance and Germanic Philology: V. I. TKHORIK
Faculty of Geography: M. YU. BELIKOV
Faculty of Law: I. A. NIKOLAYCHUK
Faculty of Management: A. M. ZHDANOVSKY

ATTACHED INSTITUTES

College of Economics, Law and Science.

Kuban department of Rostov Research Institute of Mechanics and Applied Mathematics.

Socio-Pedagogical College.

MARI STATE UNIVERSITY

424001 Mari Republic, Ioshkar-Ola, Pl. Lenina 1
Telephone: (83625) 12-59-20
Fax: (83625) 5-45-81

Founded 1972
State control
Academic year: September to July

Rector: V. P. IVSHIN
Vice-Rector: A. A. KOSOV
Chief Administrative Officer: L. N. STRELNIKOVA

Number of teachers: 384
Number of students: 3,900

Publication: *Arkheografichesky vestnik* (Archaeological News, 2 a year).

DEANS

Faculty of History and Philology: A. N. CHEMAEV
Faculty of Physics and Mathematics: V. P. YAGODAROV
Faculty of Biology and Chemistry: M. G. GRIGORIEV
Faculty of Agriculture: V. B. SMOLENTSEV
Faculty of Economics: K. V. SHAKIROV
Faculty of Law: A. M. LOMONOSOV
Faculty of Electric Power Technology: L. M. RIBAKOV

MORDOVIAN N. P. OGAREV STATE UNIVERSITY

Mordovian Republic, 430000 Saransk, Bolshevistskaya ul. 68
Telephone: (83422) 4-17-77
Fax: (8342) 17-57-91

Founded 1957
State control
Academic year: September to June

Rector: Prof. NIKOLAI P. MAKARKIN
Vice-Rectors: Prof. VIKTOR A. BALASHOV, Prof. VLADIMIR P. SELYAEV, Prof. YURI V. SAZHIN
Registrar: (vacant)
Librarian: A. V. SMOLIYANOV

Number of teachers: 1,400
Number of students: 18,500

Publications: *Vestnik Mordovskogo Universiteta* (quarterly), *Regionologiya* (quarterly).

DEANS

Faculty of Geography: S. P. EVDOKIMOV
Faculty of Philology: M. V. MOSIN
Faculty of National Culture: B. S. BRYZHINSKY
Faculty of Law: YU. A. KALINKIN
Faculty of Economics: N. D. GUSKOVA
Faculty of Biology: V. W. REVIN
Faculty of Mathematics: B. I. GRISHANOV
Faculty of Medicine: L. K. FEDOTKINA
Faculty of Industrial and Civil Construction: N. M. KUZNETSOV
Faculty of Mechanization and Electrification of Agriculture: P. V. SENIN

ATTACHED INSTITUTES

Institute of Physics and Chemistry: Dir N. E. FOMIN.

Institute of Electronics and Light Technology: Dir V. A. NECHAEV.

Institute of Agriculture: Dir S. I. AKHMETOV.

Institute of History and Sociology: Dir N. M. ARSENTEV.

Institute of Regional Studies: Dir A. I. SUKHAREV.

MOSCOW M. V. LOMONOSOV STATE UNIVERSITY

117234 Moscow, Leninskie gory
Telephone: 939-53-40, 939-13-89, 939-54-41

Founded 1755

Rector: VIKTOR SADOVNICHY
Pro-Rectors: Prof. E. M. SERGEEV, Prof. I. A. KHLYABICH, Prof. I. M. TERNOV, V. I. TROPIN, F. M. VOLKOV
Librarian: NINA AVALOVA

Number of teachers: 8,000
Number of students: 28,000

Publications: *Vestnik* (10 series), *Byulleten Moskovskogo Obshchestva Ispytatelei Prirody* (2 series), *Russkii Yazyk za Rubezhom.*

DEANS

Faculty of Mechanics and Mathematics: O. P. LUPANOV
Faculty of Computing Mathematics and Cybernetics: D. P. KOSTOMAROV
Faculty of Physics: Prof. V. I. TRUKHIN
Faculty of Chemistry: V. V. LUNIN
Faculty of Biology and Soil Science: Prof. M. V. GUSEV
Faculty of Basic Medicine: Prof. O. S. MEDVEDEV
Faculty of Geography: Prof. N. S. KASIMOV
Faculty of Geology: Prof. B. A. SOKOLOV
Faculty of History: Prof. YU. S. KUKUSHKIN
Faculty of Philosophy: A. B. PANIN
Faculty of Philology: M. L. REMNEVA
Faculty of Soil Science: Prof. A. D. VORONIN
Faculty of Law: Prof. E. A. SUKHANOV
Faculty of Psychology: Prof. E. A. KLIMOV
Faculty of Economics: Prof. V. P. KOLESOV
Faculty of Journalism: Prof. YA. N. ZASURSKII
Faculty of Sociology: Prof. V. I. DOBRENKOV
Institute of Oriental Languages: Prof. A. A. KOVALEV (Rector)
Faculty of Foreign Languages: Prof. SV. G. TER-MINASOVA
Institute of Countries of Asia and Africa: Dir A. B. MELIKSETOV
Faculty for Teachers in Higher Education Institutions: Doc. I. B. RAKOBOLSKAYA
Preparatory Faculty for Foreign Students: Doc. I. I. POTAPOVA
Br. in Ulyanovsk

ATTACHED INSTITUTES

Institute of Astronomy: 117234 Moscow, Universitetsky pr. 13; tel. 939-20-46; Dir P. K. SHTERNBERG.

Institute of Mechanics: 117234 Moscow, Michurinsky pr. 1; tel. 939-31-21.

Institute of Nuclear Physics: 119899 Moscow, GSP Leninskie gory; tel. 939-18-18; Dir M. I. PANYASUK.

Institute of Anthropological Studies.

NIZHNII NOVGOROD N. I. LOBACHEVSKII STATE UNIVERSITY

603600 Nizhnii Novgorod, Pr. Gagarina 23

Telephone: 65-84-90
Telex: 224846

Founded 1918
State control
Language of instruction: Russian
Academic year: September to June

Rector: Prof. A. F. KHOKLOV
Vice-Rectors: Prof. ROMAN G. STRONGIN, Prof. ANATOLY V. OLEYNIK, Assoc. Prof. VLADIMIR V. LEBEDEV
Librarian: A. I. SAVENKOV

Number of teachers: 800
Number of students: 9,500

DEANS

Faculty of Biology: A. P. VESELOV
Faculty of Chemistry: N. G. CHERNORUKOV
Faculty of History: O. A. KOLOBOV
Faculty of Radiophysics: S.. N. GURBATOV
Faculty of Physics: E. V. CHUPRUNOV
Faculty of Computer Science and Cybernetics: V. P. SAVELYEV
Faculty of Economics: YU. V. TRIFONOV
Faculty of Finance: V. N. YASENEV
Faculty of Business and Management: A. O. GRUDZINSKY
Faculty of Law: A. V. PETROV
Faculty of Philology: G. S. ZAITSEVA
Faculty of Mechanics and Mathematics: I. S. POSTNIKOV

ATTACHED RESEARCH INSTITUTES

Research Institute for Chemistry: Dir D. F. GRISHIN
Research Institute for Applied Mathematics and Cybernetics: Dir YU. G. VASIN
Research Institute for Mechanics: Dir V. G. BAZHENOV
Physico-Technical Research Institute: Dir O. N. GORSHKOV
Research Laboratory for Nitrogen Metabolism: Dir S. V. RUNKOV
Botanical Garden: Dir S. A. BUBLIKOV

NORTH-OSSETIAN K. L. KHETAGUROV STATE UNIVERSITY

Republic of North Ossetia, 362025 Vladikavkaz, Ul. Vatutina 46

Telephone: (8672) 74-31-91
Telex: 265277
Fax: (8672) 74-31-91
E-mail: indep@nosu.ru

Founded 1969
Language of instruction: Russian
Academic year: September to June

Chancellor: AKHURBEK M. MAGOMETOV
Vice-Chancellor: ANATOLI V. RAITSEV
Vice-Chancellor for International Affairs: OLEG S. KHATSAYEV
Vice-Chancellor for Scientific Research: VALERY G. SOZANOV
Chief Administrative Officer: VLADIMIR G. MAGKAYEV
Librarian: KLARA K. KOKAYEVA

Number of teachers: 700
Number of students: 10,500

DEANS

Faculty of Arts and Design: V. N. TSALAGOV
Faculty of Biology and Soil Studies: R. G. ZANGIONOVA
Faculty of Chemistry and Technology: N. I. KALOYEV
Faculty of Economics: Z. G. TEDEEV
Faculty of Foreign Languages: T. T. KAMBOLOV
Faculty of Geography: B. M. BEROYEV
Faculty of History: A. I. ABAYEV
Faculty of Law: E. G. PLIYEV
Faculty of Management: V. G. TSOGOYEV
Faculty of Mathematics: A. A. AZIYEV
Faculty of Ossetian Philology: R. Z. KOMAYEVA
Faculty of Education and Elementary Education: V. K. KOCHISOV
Faculty of Philology: L. M. BESOLOV
Faculty of Physical Education and Sports: F. G. KHAMIKOYEV
Faculty of Physics: A. P. BLIYEV

NOVGOROD STATE UNIVERSITY

173003 Novgorod, St Petersburgskaya ul. 41

Telephone: (816) 222-37-07
Fax: (816) 222-41-10

Founded 1974

Rector: VLADIMIR V. SOROKA

Number of teachers: 640

Faculties of physics and technology; mathematics and informatics; natural sciences; architecture, arts and construction; economics, management and law; history; philology; foreign languages; philosophy; technological engineering; medicine; education and psychology.

NOVOSIBIRSK STATE UNIVERSITY

630090 Novosibirsk, Ul. Pirogova 2

Telephone: (3832) 35-62-44
Telex: 133146
Fax: (3832) 35-52-37

Founded 1959
State control
Language of instruction: Russian
Academic year: September to June

Rector: Prof. VLADIMIR N. VRAGOV
Pro-Rector for Research: Prof. ANATOLY M. TUMAIKIN
Pro-Rectors for Studies: Prof. ALEXANDER A. NIKITIN, Prof. IVAN A. MOLETOTOV
Registrar: L. D. KRIVOGUZOVA
Librarian: L. G. TORSHENOVA

Number of teachers: 700
Number of students: 3,700

DEANS

Faculty of Geology and Geophysics: Prof. V. A. SOLOVEV
Faculty of Economics: Prof. G. M. MKRTCHAN
Faculty of Mechanics and Mathematics: Prof. A. I. SAKHANENKO
Faculty of Physics: Prof. V. G. FADIN
Faculty of Natural Sciences: Prof. V. A. SOBYANIN
Faculty of Humanities: Prof. L. G. PANIN

OMSK STATE UNIVERSITY

644077 Omsk 77, Pr. Mira 55A

Telephone: 64-25-87
Fax: 64-44-47

Founded 1974
State control
Language of instruction: Russian
Academic year: September to June

Rector: G. I. GERING
Deputy Rectors: A. V. REMNEV (Scientific), V. V. TCHUKHLOMIN (International Affairs), V. V. DUBITSKY (Academic)
Chief Administrative Officer: L. A. NASAROVA
Librarian: L. A. BALAKINA

Number of teachers: 354
Number of students: 4,765

DEANS

Faculty of Business: Y. P. DOVS
Faculty of Chemistry: A. S. FISYUK
Faculty of Economics: A. M. POPOVICH
Faculty of History: A. V. YAKUB
Faculty of Law: V. B. KODGINEVSKY
Faculty of Mathematics: V. B. NIKOLAEV
Faculty of Philology: N. N. MISYUROV
Faculty of Physics: V. I. STRUNIN
Faculty of Postgraduate Education: T. M. LARIONOVA

PROFESSORS

ADEEV, G. D., Theoretical Nuclear Physics
BORBAT, V. F., Chemistry and Technology of Non-ferrous and Noble Metals
ELOVIKOV, L. A., Methodology of Local Labour Management
GOOTS, A. K., Geometry
GRINBERG, M. S., Criminal Law
GRISHKOV, A. V., Algebra
KASANNIK, A. I., Ecological Law
KUKIN, G. P., Algebra
LAVROV, E. I. , Political Economy
MATYUSCHENKO, V. I., Archaeology
MYASNIKOV, A. G., Algebra
OSIPOV, B. I., Linguistics
REMESLENNIKOV, V. N., Algebra
SAGITULLIN, R. S., Chemistry of Heterocyclic Compounds
SKOBELKIN, V. V., Labour Law
SLESAREV, V. L., Civil Law
TCHUKHLOMIN, V. V., Innovation and Business Studies
TIKHOMIROV, V. V., Physics and Chemistry of Plasma
TIPUKHIN, V. N., Philosophy
TOLOCHKO, A. P., Pre-Revolutionary Native History
TOMILOV, N. A., Ethnography
VERSHININ, V. I., Analytical Chemistry
VETOSHKIN, A. P., Philosophy

PERM A. M. GORKII STATE UNIVERSITY

614600 Perm, GSP, Ul. Bukireva 15
Telephone: 33-61-83
Telex: 134249
Fax: 33-80-14

Founded 1916
State control
Language of instruction: Russian
Academic year: September to June

Rector: V. V. MALANIN
Vice-Rectors: Prof. V. I. KOSTYTSIN, Prof. B. M. OSOVETSKY, Prof. V. I. KACHEVROVSKY
Librarian: R. N. ROGALNIKOVA

Number of teachers: 683
Number of students: 9,167

Publications: *Uchenye Zapiski* (Transactions), *Mechanics of Controlled Movement Problems, Statistical Methods of Verifying and Estimating Hypotheses, Computer Systems and Processes Modelling, Radiospectroscopy, Caves Research Problems, Geophysical Methods of Oil and Gas Exploration* (all annually).

Faculties of history, philology, law, economics, mechanics and mathematics, physics, chemistry, biology, geology, geography

ATTACHED RESEARCH INSTITUTIONS

Computing Centre
Institute of Natural Sciences
Institute of Karstology and Speleology
Laboratory of Radiospectroscopy

PETROZAVODSK STATE UNIVERSITY

185640 Republic of Karelia, Petrozavodsk, Pr. Lenina 33
Telephone: (8142) 77-51-40
Fax: (8142) 77-10-21
E-mail: postmaster@mainpgu.karelia.ru

Founded 1940
State control
Language of instruction: Russian
Academic year: September to June

Rector: VICTOR VASILYEV
Pro-Rector: ANATOLY VORONIN
Librarian: MARINA OTLIVANCHIK

Number of teachers: 694
Number of students: 7,300

Publications: *Uchenye Zapiski* (annually), *Trudy* (Works, annually), *Petrozavodsk University* (weekly).

DEANS

Faculty of History: SERGEI VERIGIN
Faculty of Philology: VLADIMIR ZAKHAROV
Faculty of Physics: VALEREI SYSUN
Faculty of Mathematics: VLADIMIR SHESTAKOV
Faculty of Biology: ERNEST IVANTER
Faculty of Medicine: YURI LUPANDIN
Faculty of Forest Engineering: ALEXANDER PITUKHIN
Faculty of Industrial and Civil Engineering: ANATOLY SHISHKIN
Faculty of Agriculture: NIKITA ONISCHENKO
Faculty of Economics: VLADIMIR AKULOV
Faculty of Law: ROSTISLAV DUSAEV
Faculty of Baltic and Finnish Philology and Culture: TAMARA STARSHOVA

ROSTOV STATE UNIVERSITY

344711 Rostov-on-Don, Bolshaya Sadovaya ul. 105
Telephone: (8632) 64-84-66
Fax: (8632) 64-52-55
E-mail: rektorat@asu.rnd.runnet.ru

Founded 1915
State control
Language of instruction: Russian
Academic year: September to June

Rector: Prof. Dr A. V. BELOKON
Pro-Rectors: Assoc. Prof. Dr A. I. NAREZHNY (Finance), Assoc. Prof. Dr N. V. PELIKHOV (International Affairs), Prof. Dr O. G. CHORAYAN (Research), Prof. Dr A. M. YURKOV (Academic), Assoc. Prof. Dr N. V. IZOTOVA (Part-time and Distance Education) Prof. Dr YU. G. VOLKOV (Director of Institute for Retraining and the Improvement of Teachers' Proficiency in the Humanities and Social Sciences), A. A. KOVALEV (Administration and Facilities Maintenance), M. V. MOSHKOV (Facilities Development and Construction)
Library Director: S. V. BEREZOVSKAYA

Library of 2,312,000 vols

Number of teachers: 1,090
Number of students: 11,212

Publication: *Izvestiya SKNZ VS* (4 a year).

DEANS

Faculty of Biology and Soil Science: Prof. Dr V. N. DUMBAY
Faculty of Geology and Geography: Assoc. Prof. Dr S. G. PARADA
Faculty of Mechanics and Mathematics: Assoc. Prof. Dr YA. M. YERUSALIMSKY
Faculty of Physics: Prof. Dr. L. M. RABKIN
Faculty of Chemistry: Assoc. Prof. Dr YE. B. TSUPAK
Faculty of History: Prof. Dr I. M. UZNARODOV
Faculty of Psychology: Prof. Dr P. N. ERMAKOV
Faculty of Philology and Journalism: Prof. Dr YE. A. KORNILOV
Faculty of Philosophy: Prof. Dr V. I. KURBATOV
Faculty of Economics: Assoc. Prof. Dr A. A. ZAICHENKO
Faculty of Law: Assoc. Prof. Dr V. T. GAIKOV

ATTACHED INSTITUTES

Biological Research Institute: 344090 Rostov-on-Don, Stachki 194/1; Dir Prof. Y. P. GUSKOV.

North Caucasus Research Institute of Economic and Social Problems: 344006 Rostov-on-Don, Pushkinskaya 160; Dir Prof. V. N. OVCHINNIKOV.

Research Institute for Mechanics and Applied Mathematics: 344090 Rostov-on-Don, Stachki 200/1; Dir V. G. SAFRONENKO.

A. B. Kogan Research Institute for Neurocybernetics: 344090 Rostov-on-Don, Stachki 194/1; Dir Prof. B. M. VLADIMIRSKY.

Research Institute for Physics: 344090 Rostov-on-Don, Stachki 194; Dir Prof. V. P. SAKHNENKO.

Research Institute for Physical and Organic Chemistry: 344090 Rostov-on-Don, Stachki 194/2; Dir Prof. V. I. MINKIN.

Piezopriber Scientific and Technological Design Office: 344104 Rostov-on-Don, Ul. Milchakova 10; Dir A. Y. PANICH.

RUSSIAN PEOPLES' FRIENDSHIP UNIVERSITY

117198 Moscow, Ul. Miklukho-Maklaya 6
Telephone: (095) 434-66-41
Fax: (095) 433-15-11

Founded 1960 to train African, Asian and Latin-American students
Self-governing
Language of instruction: Russian
Academic year: September to July

Rector: Prof. V. M. FILIPPOV
Pro-Rectors: N. N. TROFIMOV, A. D. TARSIS, G. A. BALYKHIN, D. P. BILIBIN, E. A. UCHIN, E. L. SHESNYAK
Librarian: A. N. SHUMILOV

Number of teachers: 1,500
Number of students: 6,300

Publication: *Druzhba* (weekly university newspaper).

DEANS

Faculty of History and Philology: L. A. NOVIKOV
Faculty of Physico-Mathematical and Natural Sciences: A. N. GORDEEV
Faculty of Medicine: V. A. FROLOV
Faculty of Engineering: N. K. PONOMAREV
Faculty of Economics and Law: O. A. ZHYDKOV
Preparatory Faculty: V. L. VASILEVSKY
Faculty of Agriculture: V. V. GORCHAKOV
Faculty of Ecology: J. P. KOZLOV

ST PETERSBURG STATE UNIVERSITY

199034 St Petersburg, Universitetskaya nab. 7/9
Telephone: (812) 218-20-00
Fax: (812) 218-13-46
E-mail: office@inform.pu.ru

Founded 1724
State control
Academic year: September to June (two terms)

Rector: Dr L. A. VERBITSKAYA
Vice-Rector: Dr R. A. EVARESTOV
Head of Administration: V. D. SHEVTSOV
Librarian: N. A. SHESHINA

Library: see Libraries and Archives

Number of teachers: 2,770
Number of students: 22,017

Publications: *Vestnik* (Journal, in seven series), *Jurisprudence*, monographs.

DEANS

Faculty of Applied Mathematics: L. A. PETROSIAN
Faculty of Biology and Soil Science: I. A. GORLINSKY
Faculty of Chemistry: D. V. KOROLKOV
Faculty of Economics: G. G. BOGOMAZOV
Faculty of Geography and Geo-Ecology: P. P. ARAPOV
Faculty of Geology: I. V. BULDAKOV
Faculty of History: I. YA. FROYANOV
Faculty of International Relations: K. K. KHUDOLEI
Faculty of Journalism: M. E. SHISHKINA
Faculty of Law: V. S. PROKHOROV
Faculty of Management: V. S. KATKALO
Faculty of Mathematics and Mechanics: G. A. LEONOV
Faculty of Medicine: YU. V. NATOCHIN
Faculty of Oriental Studies: I. M. STEBLIN-KAMENSKY
Faculty of Philology: S. I. BOGDANOV
Faculty of Philosophy: Y. N. SOLONIN
Faculty of Physics: S. N. MANIDA
Faculty of Psychology: A. A. KRILOV
Faculty of Sociology: A. O. BORONOEV

ATTACHED INSTITUTES

Institute of Astronomy: Dir V. V. VITYAZEV.

Botanical Gardens: Dir V. N. NIKITINA.

Institute of Applied Mathematics: Dir D. A. OVSIANNIKOV.

Institute of Biology: Dir D. V. OSIPOV.

Institute of Chemistry: Dir A. B. VALIOTTI.

Institute of Complex Social Research: Dir V. T. LISOVSKY.

Institute of Geography: Dir A. I. CHISTOBAEV.

Institute of the Earth's Crust: Dir V. V. KURILENKO.

Institute of Mathematics and Mechanics: Dir M. K. CHIRKOV.

Institute of Physics: Dir E. I. RYUMTSEV.

Institute of Physiology: Dir V. P. GALANTSEV.

Institute of Radiophysics: Dir V. V. ZHEVELEV.

ST PETERSBURG STATE TECHNICAL UNIVERSITY

195251 St Petersburg, Politekhnicheskaya ul. 29

Telephone: (812) 247-20-88
Telex: 121187
Fax: (812) 552-60-86

Founded 1899
State control
Languages of instruction: Russian and English
Academic year: September to July

President: Prof. YU. S. VASILIEV

Library of 2,500,000 vols
Number of teachers: 2,000
Number of students: 16,000

Publications: *Transactions*, *Scientific and Engineering News*.

Faculties of hydraulic engineering, electrical engineering, power engineering, mechanical engineering, physics and mechanical sciences, technology and materials science, economics and management, computer science and engineering, radiophysical science and engineering, physical science and engineering, industrial engineering, biomedical engineering, humanities; brs at Pskov, Cherboksary and Orsk

SAMARA STATE UNIVERSITY

443011 Samara, Ul. Akademika Pavlova 1

Telephone: (8462) 34-54-03
Fax: (8462) 34-54-17
E-mail: avn@ssu.samara.ru

Founded 1969
State control
Academic year: September to June

Rector: G. P. YAROVOY
Vice-Rectors: P. S. KABYTOV, V. I. ASTAFEV
Chief Administrative Officer: G. A. AGAFONOVA
Chief Librarian: G. A. BARSUKOVA

Number of teachers 375
Number of students: 5,000

DEANS

Faculty of Mathematics and Mechanics: V. M. KLIMKIN
Faculty of Physics: V. V. IVAKHNIK
Faculty of Chemistry: S. V. KURBATOVA
Faculty of Biology: G. L. RYTOV
Faculty of Languages and Literature: A. A. BEZRUKOVA
Faculty of History: G. A. SHIROKOV
Faculty of Law: A. A. NAPROENKO
Faculty of Sociology: V. YA. MACHNEV

PROFESSORS

ASTAFIEV, V. I., Mechanics
BORISOV, V. N., Philosophy of Natural Sciences Faculties
DOBRYAKIN, A. V., Economics and Management
FILATOV, O. P., Equations of Mathematical Physics
KABYTOV, P. S., History of Russia
KHRAMKOV, I. V., History of Russia
KLIMKIN, V. M., Functional Analysis
KOMOV, A. N., Electronics
KONEV, V. A., Philosophy of the Humanities Faculties
KOZENKO, B. D., World History
MAGOMEDOV, N. M., Education and Psychology
MATVEEV, N. M., Ecology, Botany and Environmental Protection
MERKULOVA, N. A., Human and Animal Physiology
MOLEVICH, E. F., Sociology and Political Science
PURYGIN, P. P., Organic Chemistry
SARAEV, L. A., Mathematics and Computers
SEREZHKIN, V. N., Inorganic Chemistry
SHEIFER, S. A., Criminal Court Proceedings and Investigation
SOBOLEV, V. A., Differential Equations
VOSKRESENSKY, V. E., Algebra and Geometry
YAROVOY, G. P., Radiophysics and Computers
ZAGUZOV, I. S., Mechanics

ATTACHED RESEARCH INSTITUTES

Institute of the History and Archaeology of the Volga Region: Dir I. B. VASILIEV.

Institute of Applied Ecology: Dir P. P. PURYGIN.

Institute of Sociological Research: Dir E. G. MOLEVICH.

SARATOV N. G. CHERNYSHEVSKY STATE UNIVERSITY

410026 Saratov, Astrakhanskaya ul. 83

Telephone: 24-16-46
Telex: 241125
Fax: 24-04-46

Founded 1909
State control
Academic year: September to June

Rector: DMITRY TRUBETSKOV
Vice-Rectors: DMITRY USANOV (Science), LUDMILLA STRAKHOVA (International Exchanges)
Registrars: YURI SKLYAROV, SVETLANA MUSHTAKOVA
Librarian: VERA A. ARTISEVICH

Number of teachers: 808
Number of students: 9,800

Publication: *Applied Nonlinear Dynamics.*

DEANS

Faculty of History: Dr I. PARFENOV
Faculty of Philology: Dr V. PROZOROV
Faculty of Physics: Dr V. BEREZIN
Faculty of Chemistry: Dr I. KAZARINOV
Faculty of Geology: Dr KONCHENEBIN
Faculty of Geography: Dr T. POLYANSKAYA
Faculty of Biology: Dr G. SHLYAKHTIN
Faculty of Mechanics and Mathematics: Dr L. KOSOVICH
College of Applied Sciences: Dr U. LEVIN
Preparatory Department: Dr V. MASHNIKOV

SYKTYVKAR STATE UNIVERSITY

167001 Syktyvkar, Oktyabrskii Pr. 55

Telephone: (8212) 43-68-20
Fax: (8212) 43-18-88
E-mail: postmaster@ssu.komitex.ru

Founded 1972
State control
Language of instruction: Russian
Academic year: September to July

Rector: VASILY N. ZADOROZHNY
Vice-Rector: NIKOLAI A. TIKHONOV
Chief Administrative Officer: LUBOV S. SHABALOVA
Librarian: NONNA F. AKOPOVA

Number of teachers: 352
Number of students: 4,500

Publications: *Rubezh* (quarterly), *Verbum.*

DEANS

Faculty of Physics: YU. BELYAEV
Faculty of Mathematics: I. I. BAZHENOV
Faculty of Chemistry and Biology: M. M. DOLGIN
Faculty of Philology: A. N. VLASOV
Faculty of Law: M. NAIMUSHIN
Faculty of Finno-Ugric Studies: N. SERGIEVA
Faculty of History: V. N. KHUDYAEV
Faculty of Social Work: A. SOKOLOVA
Faculty of Physical Education: YE. SHOMYSOVA

PROFESSORS

ANDROSOV, G. K., Microbiology
GRINFIELD, T. J., Russian Literature
IGUSHEV, Y. A., Komi Language
IRZHAK, L. I., Physiology
KHUDYAEV, S. I., Mathematical Physics
MIKHAILOVSKY, Y. I., Computer Science
MIKUSHEV, A. K., Komi Language
NAGAEV, V. V., Psychology
POROSHKIN, A. G., Mathematical Analysis
PORTYANKO, M. L., General Theory of Economics
RAPOPORT, J. M., Political Science and Sociology
ROSHEVSKAYA, L. P., History
ROZHNEVA, L. S., Economics
VITYAZEVA, V. A., Geography
ZADOROZHNY, V. N., Economics

TOMSK STATE UNIVERSITY

634050 Tomsk, Pr. Lenina 36

Telephone: 23-44-65
Telex: 128258
Fax: 22-24-66

Founded 1880
State control

Rector: Prof. M. SVIRIDOV
Senior Vice-Rector: Dr M. BABANSKY
Vice-Rectors: Prof. A. REVUSHKIN (Academic Affairs), Dr G. MAYER (Research and Postgraduate Studies), Dr A. TIMOSHENKO (International Programmes)
Registrar: N. BUROVA
Librarian: E. SYNTIN

Library: see Libraries
Number of teachers and researchers: 3,000
Number of students: 6,500 full-time, 3,500 part-time

Faculties of biology and soil science, geology and geography, chemistry, history and international relations, philology and journalism, economics, law, philosophy, sociology and political science, mechanics and mathematics, applied mathematics and cybernetics, computer science, physics, radio-physics, technical physics

ATTACHED INSTITUTES

Siberian Physical Technical Institute

Institute of Applied Mathematics and Mechanics

Istitute of Biology and Biophysics

Institute of Socio-Economic Problems of Siberia

TVER STATE UNIVERSITY

170000 Tver, Ul. Zhelyabova 33

Telephone: 33-15-50
Fax: 33-12-74

Founded 1971

Rector: A. N. KUDINOV
Pro-Rector: V. P. GAVRIKOV
Librarian: E. I. BEREZKINA

Number of teachers: 720
Number of students: 10,000

Faculties of mathematics, cybernetics, physics, chemistry and biology and geography, philology, modern languages, pedagogics, economics, history, law, physical training

TYUMEN STATE UNIVERSITY

625610 Tyumen 3, Ul. Semakova 10

Telephone: 6-19-30

Number of students: 6,000

Faculties of history, philology, romance and Germanic philology, physics and mathematics, chemistry and biology, economics, geography

UDMURT STATE UNIVERSITY

Udmurt Republic, 426034 Izhevsk, Universitetskaya ul. 1

Telephone: (3412) 75-16-10
Fax: (3412) 75-58-66

Founded 1972

State control
Language of instruction: Russian
Academic year: September to June
Rector: Prof. VITALY A. ZHURAVLEV
Vice-Rector: VLADIMIR A. BAIMETOV
Vice-Rector for Research: Prof. VICTOR E. SHUDEGOV
Chief Administrative Officer: GALINA V. PARSHUKOVA
Librarian: LYUDMILA P. BESKLINSKAYA
Number of teachers: 750
Number of students: 12,000
Publications: *Herald* (monthly), *Collected Scientific Articles on the Professional Training of Experts* (quarterly).

DEANS

Faculty of History: M. Y. MALYSHEV
Faculty of Russian Philology: S. G. SHEYDANOVA
Faculty of Udmurt and Finno-Ugric Philology: A. V. ISHMURATOV
Faculty of Foreign Languages and Foreign Literature: T. I. ZELENINA
Faculty of Biology and Chemistry: N. E. ZUBTSOVSKY
Faculty of Geography: A. G. ILLARIONOV
Faculty of Physics: V. P. BOVIN
Faculty of Mathematics: Prof. A. P. BELTYUKOV
Faculty of Law: S. D. BUNTOV
Faculty of Economics: V. A. IVANOV
Faculty of Physical Training: A. E. ALABUZHEV
Faculty of Art and Design: V. B. KOSHAEV
Faculty of Psychology and Pedagogics: N. I. LEONOV
Faculty of Oil and Gas: A. YA. VOLKOV
Faculty of Philosophy and Sociology: Prof. N. S. LADYZHETS
Faculty of Medical Biotechnology: A. K. BARSUKOV
Faculty of New Technology in Training: Prof. V. A. ZHURAVLEV
Research Centre: M. A. PLETNEV

ATTACHED INSTITUTES

Institute of the History and Culture of the Finno-Ugric Peoples of the Urals: Dir Prof. R. D. GOLDINA.
Institute of Mathematical Modelling: Dir Prof. E. L. TONKOV.
Institute of Economics and Management: Dir Prof. R. A. GALIAKHMETOV.
Institute of Ecology and Bioresources: Dir N. E. ZUBTSOVSKY.
Institute of Thermophysics: Dir V. I. LADYANOV.
Institute of Mankind: Dir A. A. RASIN.
Institute of Geoecology: Dir Prof. V. I. STURMAN.
Institute of Natural Disasters: Dir V. M. KOLODKIN.
Institute of Experimental Natural Sciences: Dir Prof. V. V. SOBOLEV.
Institute of Regional Studies: Dir Prof. V. E. SHUDEGOV.

URALS A. M. GORKII STATE UNIVERSITY

620083 Ekaterinburg, Pr. Lenina 51
Telephone: (3432) 55-74-20
Fax: (3432) 55-59-64
Founded 1920
State control
Language of instruction: Russian
Academic year: September to July
Rector: Prof. VLADIMIR E. TRETYAKOV
Vice-Rectors: VITALY P. PROKOPEV (Academic), EVGENY A. PAMYATNYKH (International Cooperation)
Chief Administrative Officer: (vacant)
Librarian: KLAVDIYA P. KUZNETSOVA
Number of teachers: 2,200
Number of students: 7,000
Publications: *Uchenye Zapiski* (Scientific Reports, several series), *Matematicheskie Zapiski* (Mathematical Reports, annually in four parts).

DEANS

Faculty of Physics: Prof. A. N. BABUSHKIN
Faculty of Mathematics and Mechanics: Assoc. Prof. M. O. ASANOV
Faculty of Philology: Prof. V. V. BLAZHES
Faculty of Economics: Assoc. Prof. D. V. NESTEROVA
Faculty of Chemistry: Assoc. Prof. A. A. VSHIVKOV
Faculty of Journalism: Asst Prof. B. N. LOZOVSKY
Faculty of Biology: Prof. V. A. SHCHEPETKIN
Faculty of Philosophy: Prof. A. V. PERTSEV
Faculty of History: Asst Prof. D. V. BUGROV
Faculty of Psychology: Asst Prof. G. A. GLOTOVA
Faculty of Sociology and Politics: Asst Prof. B. B. BAGIROV
Faculty of Art Criticism and Culture: Asst Prof. T. A. RUNEVA

PROFESSORS

Faculty of Physics:
- BABUSHKIN, A. N., Low-Temperature Physics
- BARANOV, N. V., Condensed Matter
- BORISOV, S. F., General and Molecular Physics
- GULYAEV, S. A., Astronomy and Geodesy
- IVANOV, O. A., Magnetic Phenomena
- MOSKVIN, A. S., Theoretical Physics
- ZVEREV, L. P., Semiconductor Physics, Radiospectroscopy

Faculty of Mathematics and Mechanics:
- ALBREKHT, E. G., Applied Mathematics
- ARESTOV, V. V., Mathematical Analysis and Theory of Functions
- EREMIN, I. I., Mathematics for Economics
- IVANOV, A. O., Mathematical Physics
- PROKOPIEV, V. P., Theoretical Mechanics
- RYASHKO, L. V., Computational Mathematics
- SHEVRIN, L. N., Algebra and Geometry
- TRETYAKOV, V. E., Computer Information Science

Faculty of Philology:
- BABENKO, L. G., Modern Russian Language
- BAKLANOVA, A. G., Romance and Germanic Philology
- BLAZHES, V. V., Folklore
- BIKOV, L. P., Criticism of 20th-century Literary Theory
- KUPINA, N. A., Russian Language
- MATVEEV, A. V., General Linguistics
- PAVERMAN, V. M., Foreign Literature

Faculty of Economics:
- AKBERDINA, R. A., Economics
- GREBENKIN, A. V., Management of Socio-Economic Processes
- IVANTSOV, G. B., Theory of Economics
- MAZUROV, V. D., Economic Models and Information
- NESTEROVA, D. V., Economic History and World Economics
- SEMYAKIN, M. N., Economics and Law

Faculty of Chemistry:
- NEUCHADINA, L. N., Analytical Chemistry
- NEYMAN, A. YA., Inorganic Chemistry
- PETROV, A. N., Physical Chemistry
- SUVOROVA, A. I., Higher Molecular Compounds
- VSHIVKOV, A. A., Organic Chemistry

Faculty of Journalism:
- BRODSKY, I. S., Television, Radio and Technical Methods of Journalism
- KOVALEVA, M. M., History of the Press
- LAZAREVA, E. H., Stylistics and Russian Language
- MAROV, V. N., Periodical Press

Faculty of Biology:
- MUKHIN, V. A., Botany
- NOVOZHENOV, Y. I., Zoology
- PYANKOV, V. I., Plant Physiology
- RIBIN, I. A., Physiology

Faculty of Philosophy:
- BRYANIK, N. V., Ontology and Theory of Cognition
- EREMEEV, A. P., Aesthetics
- KEMEROV, V. E., Social Philosophy
- LYUBUTIN, K. N., History of Philosophy

Faculty of History:
- CHERNOUKHOV, A. V., Archives
- CHEVTAEV, A. G., Modern History
- MIKHAILENKO, V. I., Theory and History of Foreign Affairs
- MINENKO, N. A., Ethnology and Special Historical Sciences
- POLYAKOVSKAYA, M. A., Ancient and Medieval History
- ROMANCHUK, A. I., Archaeology
- SHASHKOV, A. G., Russian History

Faculty of Psychology:
- GLOTOVA, G. A., Social Psychology
- LUPANDIN, V. I., Psychophysiology

Faculty of Sociology and Politics:
- BAGIROV, B. B., Social Politics
- BARAZGOVA, E. S., Theory and History of Sociology
- MERENKOV, A. V., Sociology
- MIRONOV, D. A., History of Politics

Faculty of Art Criticism and Culture:
- GOLINETS, S. V., History of Art
- MEDVEDEV, A. V., Culture
- PIVOVAROV, D. V., History and Philosophy of Religion
- TROSHINA, T. M., Museology

RESEARCH INSTITUTES

Research Institute of Physics and Applied Mathematics: Dir L. P. ZVEREV.
Institute for Advanced Education in Social Sciences: Dir N. N. TSELISHEV.
Institute of Russian Culture: Dir Prof. B. V. EMELYANOV.
Institute of Economics and Law: Rector D. V. NESTEROVA.

VOLGOGRAD STATE UNIVERSITY

400062 Volgograd, 2-ya Prodolnaya ul. 30
Telephone: (8442) 43-81-24
Fax: (8442) 43-81-24
E-mail: root@ic.vgu.tsaritsyn.su
Founded 1978
State control
Languages of instruction: Russian, English, German, French
Academic year: September to June
Rector: OLEG V. INSHAKOV
First Vice-Rector: BORIS N. SIPLIVY
Chief Administrative Officer: SERGEI G. SIDOROV
Librarian: LARISA E. YAKOVLEVA
Library of 522,000 vols
Number of teachers: 490
Number of students: 8,331
Publication: *Vestnik VolGU* (4 a year).

DEANS

Faculty of Modern Languages: ALFIYA I. SMIRNOVA
Faculty of History and Philosophy: NIKOLAI V. OMELCHENKO
Faculty of Mathematics: VLADIMIR G. TKACHEV
Faculty of Physics: YURI M. TORGASHIN
Faculty of Economics: ELENA G. RUSSKOVA
Faculty of Law: FELIX V. GLAZYRIN

ATTACHED RESEARCH INSTITUTE

Problems of the Economic History of 20th-Century Russia: Dir ZAGORULKO M. MATVEEVICH.

VORONEZH STATE UNIVERSITY

394693 Voronezh, Universitetskaya pl. 1
Telephone (0732) 55-29-83
Telex: 153153
Fax: (0732) 55-28-36

Founded 1918
State control
Academic year: September to July

Rector: Prof. VLADIMIR V. GUSEV
Vice-Rectors: IVAN I. BORISOV, GENNADY A. CHIKIN, IGOR S. SUROVTSEV, EDUARD A. ALGAZINOV
Chief Administrative Officer: VLADIMIR S. LISTENGARTEN
Librarian: SVETLANA V. YANTS

Number of teachers: 1,000
Number of students: 12,000 (including 6,625 full-time)

Publication: *Vestnik Voronezhskogo Universiteta.*

DEANS

Faculty of History: A. Z. VINNIKOV
Faculty of Journalism: V. V. TULUPOV
Faculty of Philology: V. M. AKATKIN
Faculty of Romance and Germanic Philology: V. T. TITOV
Faculty of Economics: V. N. EITINGON
Faculty of Law: V. A. PANYUSHKIN
Faculty of Mathematics: S. A. SKLADNEV
Faculty of Applied Mathematics and Mechanics: V. V. YURGELAS
Faculty of Physics: A. M. VOROBEV
Faculty of Chemistry: J. P. AFINOGENOV
Faculty of Biology and Soil Science: V. G. ARTYUKHOV
Faculty of Geology: A. D. SAVKO
Faculty of Geography: V. I. FEDOTOV

YAKUTSK STATE UNIVERSITY

Republic of Sakha (Yakutia), 677000 Yakutsk, Ul. Belinskogo 58
Telephone: (4112) 26-33-44
Fax: (4112) 26-14-53
E-mail: oip@uni.sakha.ru

Founded 1956
State control
Languages of Instruction: Russian and Yakut
Academic year: September to July

Chancellor: ANATOLY N. ALEXEEV
Vice-Chancellor: EGOR E. PETROV
Librarian: ANATOLY P. SEMENOV

Number of teachers: 950
Number of students: 10,000

Publication: *Nauka i obrazovaniye* (4 a year).

DEANS

Faculty of Biology and Geography: BORIS M. PESTRYAKOV
Faculty of Engineering Technology: ANATOLY T. KOPYLOV
Faculty of Foreign Languages: LUDMILA S. ZAMORSHIKOVA
Faculty of Geology: IGOR I. KOLODEZNIKOV
Faculty of History and Law: YEGOR M. MAKHAROV
Faculty of Mathematics: VASILY I. VASILEV
Faculty of Philology: VLADIMIR M. PEREVERZIN
Faculty of Physics: GEORGY N. ROMANOV
Faculty of Yakut Philology and Native Culture: GAVRIL G. FILIPPOV
Institute of Economics: ANATOLY A. POPOV
Institute of Education: INNOKENTY A. GOLIKOV
Institute of Medicine: PALMIRA G. PETROVA
Teacher-Training Institute: RAISA E. TIMOFEEVA

PROFESSORS

ALEXEEV, A. N., History
ANISIMOV, V. M., Education
ANTONOV, N. K., Philosophy
BASHARIN, K. G., Medicine
BEGIEV, V. G., Medicine
BLOKHIN, I. P., Biology
BURTSEV, A. A., Philology
BURYANINA, N. S., Geology
BUSHKOV, P. N., Surgery
CHEMEZOV, E. N., Geology
DANILOV, D. A., Pedagogics
DIACHKOVSKY, N. D., Yakut Language and Literature
DOBROVOLSKY, G. N., Engineering
EGOROV, I. E., Mathematics
FEDOROV, M. M., Law
FOMIN, M. M., Pedagogics
GOGOLEV, A. I., General History
GOGOLEV, M. P., Medicine
IVANOV, A. I., Medicine
IZAKSON, V. Y., Mathematics
KALYTOKHANOV, A. P., Engineering
KERSHENGOLTS, B. M., Biology
KHATYLAEV, M. M., History
KOCHNEV, V. P., Education
KOLODEZNIKOV, I. I., Geology and Mineralology
KYCHKIN, I. S., Theoretical Physics
LUKOVTSEV, V. S., Philosophy
MAKHAROV, Y. M., Philosophy
MIKHAILOV, V. D., Philosophy
NEUSTROEV, N. D., Education
NIKOLAEV, N. S., Engineering
NOVIKOV, A. G., Philosophy
OKONESHNIKOVA, A. P., Psychology
PETROV, E. E., Mathematics
PETROV, N. E., Philology
PETROVA, P. G., Medicine
POPOV, B. N., Philosophy
PROKOPIEVA, S. M., Philology
SAMOKHIN, A. V., Mining
SHAMAEV, N. R., Education
SHEPELEV, V. S., Geology
SLASTENA, YU. L., Geology
SMIRNOV, V. P., Engineering
SOLOMONOV, N. G., Biology
STOGNY, V. V., Geology
TAZLOVA, R. S., Psychiatry
TIKHONOV, D. G., Medicine
TOBUROKOV, N. N., Linguistics
TOLSTIKHIN, O. N., Permafrost
TOMSKY, I. E., Economics
TYRLYGIN, M. A., Medicine
VASILIEV, E. P., Medicine
VASILIEVA-KRALINA, I. I., Biology
VIKULOV, M. A., Engineering
VINOGRADOV, A. V., Chemistry
YAKIMOV, O. D., Journalism
ZAROVNYAEV, B. N., Geology

YAROSLAVL STATE UNIVERSITY

150000 Yaroslavl, Sovetskaya ul. 14
Telephone: (0852) 30-23-54
Fax: (0852) 22-52-32

Founded 1970
Academic Year: September to July

Rector: Prof. G. S. MIRONOV
Vice-Rectors: Dr J. A. BRIUKHANOV, Dr V. A. SOKOLOV, Dr V. D. KUKUSHKIN
Registrar: V. P. ISAYEVA
Librarian: V. A. DOCTOROVA

Number of teachers: 332 full-time, 200 part-time
Number of students: 4,035 undergraduates, 137 postgraduates

Publication: *Yaroslavsky Universitet.*

DEANS

Faculty of Law: Dr N. N. TARUSINA
Faculty of History: Prof. M. Y. YERIN
Faculty of Economics: Dr I. M. LOKHANINA
Faculty of Psychology: Dr V. E. ORJOL
Faculty of Biology: Dr A. V. EREMEISHVILI
Faculty of Information Science and Computing Techniques: Dr A. V. ZAFIEVSKY
Faculty of Mathematics: Dr V. G. DURNEV
Faculty of Physics: Dr V. P. ALEKSEEV
Faculty of Social Sciences: Dr G. M. NAIMUDINOV

HEADS OF DEPARTMENT

Faculty of Law:

Civil Law and Civil Legal Proceedings: Dr V. D. BUTNEV
Criminal Law and Criminal Legal Proceedings: Dr L. P. KRUGLIKOV
History and Theory of State and Law: Prof. V. N. KARTASHOV

Faculty of History:

Contemporary Russian History: Prof. Y. Y. YERUSALIMSKY
Medieval and Modern Russian History: Prof. V. P. FEDYUK
Museum Management Studies: Dr A. M. SELIVANOV
World History: Prof. M. Y. YERIN

Faculty of Economics:

Accounting and Finance: Dr I. G. KUZMIN
Free Market Economy and Statistics: Prof. F. N. ZAVYALOV
Economic Analysis and Informatics: Dr T. V PLATOVA
Management and Free Enterprise: Prof. O. K. PLATOV

Faculty of Psychology:

Education and Educational Psychology: Dr S. N. BATRAKOVA
General Psychology: Prof. Y. K. KORNILOV
Psychology of Labour and Industrial Psychology: Dr A. V. KARPOV
Social and Political Psychology: Prof. V. V. NOVIKOV

Faculty of Biology:

Botany: Dr O. G. VERKHOVTSEVA
General and Bio-organic Chemistry: Prof. V. N. KOPEIKIN
Human and Animal Physiology: Dr A. I. DAVYDOV
Zoology and Cytology: Dr V. P. SEMERNOY

Faculty of Information Sciences and Computing Techniques:

Applied Informatics and Computer Architecture: Prof. Y. A. MAMATOV
Data Processing Systems: Prof. V. A. KURCHIDIS
Discrete Analysis: Dr V. A. BONDARENKO
Optimization and Information Technologies: Dr A. V. ZAFIEVSKY
Theoretical Informatics: Dr V. A. SOKOLOV

Faculty of Mathematics:

Algebra and Mathematical Logic: Prof. L. S. KAZARIN
Differential Equations: Dr Y. S. KOLESOV
General Mathematics: Dr V. A. KUZNETSOVA
Mathematical Analysis: Dr V. A. KRASNOV

Faculty of Physics:

General and Experimental Physics: Dr V. A. ALEXEYEV
Microelectronics: Dr L. V. BOCHKAREVA
Radiophysics: Dr I. A WINTER
Theoretical Physics: Prof. N. V. MIKHEYEV

Faculty of Social Sciences:

Economic Concepts: Prof. V. M. MELIKHOVSKY
Philosophy and Cultural Studies: Prof. G. M. NAZHMUDINOV
Social and Political Concepts: Prof. P. F. YANKEVICH
Social Technologies: Dr I. F. ALBEGOVA

Unaffiliated Departments:

Foreign Languages: Dr T. V. SHULDESHOVA
Physical Education: Prof. V. V. NASOLODIN

Polytechnics and Technical Universities

Altai State Technical University: 656099 Barnaul, Pr. Lenina 46; tel. (3852) 26-09-17; fax (3852) 26-16-09; e-mail nmn@oasis.secna.ru; f. 1942; faculties: mechanical technology, civil engineering, power engineering, motor car and tractor engineering, food technology, automated manufacturing, engineering pedagogics and informatics, chemical technology, information technology and business, humanities, engineering and economics; academy of law and economics; brs in Rubtsovsk and Biisk; 1,646 students; library of 1,250,000 vols; Rector Prof. V. V. YEVSTIGNEYEV.

Astrakhan State Technical University: 414025 Astrakhan, Ul. Tatishcheva 16; tel. (8512) 25-09-23; fax (8512) 25-64-27; e-mail inform@astu.astranet.ru; f. 1930; faculties: finance and credit, accountancy and auditing, economics and business management, naval engineering, marine power plants, low-temperature engineering and cryogenics, food processing machinery and equipment, electrical equipment and automated systems in ships, machinery for loading and unloading; 550 teachers; 3,500 students; library of 450,000 vols; Rector Y. N. KAGAKOV; publ. *Proceedings*.

Chita State Technical University: 672039 Chita, Ul. Aleksandro-Zavodskaya 30; tel. 6-43-93; f. 1974; faculties: motor transport, mining, power, civil engineering, mechanical engineering, regional studies; 2,500 students; library of 400,000 vols; Rector: Prof. YU. N. REZNIK.

Dagestan Polytechnic Institute: 367024 Makhachkala, Pr. Kalinina 70; tel. 5-74-77; faculties: mechanical, instrumentation, technological, construction, water supply and land reclamation.

Don State Technical University: 344010 Rostov-on-Don, Pl. Gagarina 1; tel. 38-15-25; fax 32-79-53; e-mail root@sintez.rud.su; f. 1930 (fmrly Rostov Institute of Agricultural Engineering, present name 1992); faculties: engineering, technology, design, automation and information, management; 520 teachers; 4,500 students; library of 837,000 vols; Rector Prof. Dr A. A. RYZHKIN.

Far Eastern State Technical University: 690600 Vladivostok, Pushkinskaya ul. 10; tel. (4232) 26-16-89; fax (4232) 26-69-88; e-mail root@dpicnit.marine.su; f. 1899; institutes: civil engineering, economics and management, maritime engineering, mining engineering, mechanics, automatics and advanced technologies; departments: architecture and design, information science, radioelectronics and electrical engineering, natural sciences, politics and law, humanities, continuing and distance education; 10,000 students; library of 1,150,000 vols; brs in Nakhodka, Arseniev, Petropavlovsk-Kamchatsky, Dalnegorsk, Dalnerechensk, Bolshoi Kamen, Artyom and Lesozavodsk; Rector GENNADY P. TURMOV; publ. *Proceedings* (annually).

Irkutsk State Technical University: 664074 Irkutsk, Ul. Lermontova 83; tel. (3952) 43-16-12; fax (3952) 43-05-83; e-mail oms@istu.irk.ru; faculties: civil engineering and municipal economics, architecture, geology, geological data processing and geological environment protection, mining, cybernetics, mechanical engineering, chemical engineering and metallurgy, power engineering, transportation systems, evening education and distance learning; 13,000 students; library of 1,215,000 vols; Rector Prof. S. B. LEONOV; publs *Ore Dressing, Dynamics of Vibroactive Systems.*

Kama Polytechnic Institute: 423810 Naberezhnye Chelny, Pr. Mira 68/19; tel. 53-73-96; fax 53-73-11; f. 1980; faculties: machine-building, automechanics, mechanics and technology, construction engineering, motor vehicles and tractors; library of 203,200 vols; Rector I. H. SADYKOV.

Kazan State Technical University: Tatarstan, 420111 Kazan, Ul. K. Marksa 10; tel. (8432) 38-50-44; fax (8432) 36-60-32; e-mail agishev@ikar.kcn.ru; f. 1932; faculties: aircraft engineering, aircraft engines, automation and electronic engineering, technical cybernetics and information science, radioengineering, management and business studies, humanities; 700 teachers; 7,500 students; library of 1,400,000 vols; Rector Prof. GENNADY L. DEGTYAREV; publs *Aviatsionaya Tekchnika* (Russian Aeronautics, in Russian and English, 4 a year), *Radioelectronnye Ustroistva* (in Russian, 2 a year), *Problemy Nelineinogo Analiza v Inzhenernykh Sistemakh* (Non-Linear Analysis Problems in Engineering Systems, in Russian and English, 2 a year), *Vestnik KGTU* (in Russian, 4 a year).

Khabarovsk State Technical University: 660035 Khabarovsk, Ul. Tikhookeanskaya 136; tel. and fax 72-07-12; f. 1958; faculties: mechanical, vehicle, forestry engineering, timber technology, architecture and construction, juridical, engineering economics and management software, computer sciences; library of 1,000,000 vols; Pres. VICTOR K. BULGAKOV.

Komsomolsk-on-Amur State Technical University: 681013 Komsomolsk-on-Amur, Pr. Lenina 27; tel. (42172) 3-23-04; f. 1955; faculties: automation and computer engineering, applied mathematics and informatics, power engineering, automated mechanical engineering, automated electromechanical systems, aircraft and helicopter construction, business studies, humanities; 3,500 students; Rector YURI G. KABALDIN.

Krasnoyarsk State Technical University: 660074 Krasnoyarsk, Ul. Kirenskogo 26; tel. (3912) 49-75-81; fax (3912) 43-06-92; e-mail root@kgtu.runnet.ru; f. 1956 as Krasnoyarsk Polytechnic Institute, present name 1993; faculties: electrical engineering, mechanical engineering, automation and computer technology, thermal power engineering, motor vehicle engineering, informatics and computer science, radio engineering, economics and management, engineering, physics, humanities; library of 2m. vols; Rector S. A. PODLESNY; publs *Bulletin, Polytechnic* (newspaper, fortnightly).

Kuban State University of Technology: 350072 Krasnodar, Moskovskaya ul. 2; tel. 55-84-01; telex 211548; fax 57-65-92; f. 1930; faculties: oil, gas and power engineering, mechanical engineering, food industry equipment and automation, chemical engineering, technology of grain products, food technology, civil engineering, highway engineering, economics; institute of mechanical engineering in Armavir, br. in Novorossiisk; 800 teachers; 10,000 students; library of 720,000 vols; Rector Prof. A. A. PETRIK; publ. *Izvestiya Vuzov, Pishevaya Teckhnologiya* (Food Technology) (6 a year).

Kursk State Technical University: 305040 Kursk, Ul. 50-letiya Oktyabrya 94; tel. (071) 222-57-43; fax (071) 256-18-85; e-mail rector@kstu.kursk.ru; f. 1964; faculties: machine-building, textile technology, civil and industrial construction engineering, computer engineering and automation systems, law, management, economics, finance and auditing; library of 536,000 vols; Rector Prof. F. N. RYZHKOV; publ. *Izvestia* (2 a year).

Kuzbass State Technical University: 650026 Kemerovo, Vesennyaya ul. 28; tel. (3842) 23-33-80; fax (3842) 23-08-08; f. 1950; faculties: mine construction, mechanical engineering, electrical and mechanical, mining engineering, construction, economics, chemical engineering, biotechnology; 688 teachers; 7,343 students; library of 600,000 vols; Rector V. V. KUREKHIN.

Lipetsk State Technical University: 398055 Lipetsk, Moskovskaya ul. 30; tel. 25-00-61; fax 25-69-86; depts: metallurgy, applied physics and technology, CAD/CAM, transport engineering, civil engineering, automated production, business and law; 500 teachers; Rector Prof. S. L. KOTSAR.

Mari State Technical University: 424024 Yoshkar-Ola, Pl. Lenina 3; tel. (83625) 9-68-62; fax (8362) 11-08-72; e-mail root@marstu.mari.su; f. 1932; faculties: radio engineering, radio-electronic systems, forestry, forestry engineering, civil engineering, machine construction, highway engineering, economics; biological garden; 548 teachers; 5,228 students; library of 1,000,000 vols; Rector G. S. OSHEPKOV.

Moscow Power Engineering Institute (Technical University): 111250 Moscow, E-250, Krasnokazarmennaya ul. 14; tel. 362-56-45; fax 361-16-20; e-mail sms@srv-g.mpei.ac.ru; f. 1930; faculties: power engineering industry, thermal power engineering, industrial heat engineering, electromechanical systems, electrical equipment and automation of industry and transport, electrical power engineering, automation and computers, electronic engineering, radio engineering, power physics; 2,200 teachers; 15,500 students; library of 2.1 m. vols; brs in Kazan, Smolensk, Volzgsky; Rector E. V. AMETISTOV; publ. *Vestnik MPEI* (6 a year).

Moscow State Automobile and Road Technical University: 125829 Moscow A-319, Leningradskii pr. 64; tel. (095) 151-05-81; fax (095) 151-03-31; e-mail info@madi.ru; f. 1930; faculties: motor vehicle transport, road and airport construction, bridge and tunnel construction, motor vehicle internal-combustion engines, traffic safety, hydraulics and control systems in construction and transport, traffic engineering and transport economics, transport management, financial analysis, road-building machinery, machinery design; library of 1,500,000 vols; 1,100 teachers; 12,000 students; Rector Prof. Dr V. N. LUKANIN; publ. *Proceedings* (with scientific papers) (irregular).

Moscow State Open University: 129805 Moscow, Ul. Pavla Korchagina 22; tel. 283-42-96; fax 283-80-71; f. 1992 (previously Extra-Mural Polytechnic Institute, f. 1932); faculties: economics and law, engineering, mining, construction, energy, chemical and technological studies, automation and electronics; 840 teachers; 22,000 students; library of 1 million vols; Rector Prof. V. I. BEILIN.

Moscow Technical University of Communication and Informatics: 111024 Moscow, Aviamotornaya ul. 8A; tel. (095) 273-27-62; fax (095) 274-00-32; f. 1921 (fmrly Moscow Telecommunications Institute, renamed *c.* 1992); faculties: radio communication and radio and television broadcasting, multi-channel communications, postal services automation, automatic telecommunications, engineering and economics; 850 teachers; 14,000 students; library of 1.3 m. vols; brs in Rostov-on-Don, Nizhnii Novgorod; Rector Prof. VAGAN V. SHAKGUILDIAN.

Murmansk State Technical University: 183010 Murmansk, Sportivnaya ul. 13; tel. (8152) 23-24-92; fax via Norway 78-91-05-48; e-mail msma@infotel.ru; f. 1950; faculties: navigation, electrical engineering, marine engineering, radio engineering, natural sciences, management, economics and law; 290

teachers; 3,700 students; library of 350,000 vols; Rector Prof. A. P. GALYANOV.

Nizhny Novgorod State Technical University: 603600 Nizhny Novgorod, Ul. K. Minina 24; tel. 36-23-25; fax 36-94-75; f. 1917 (fmrly Nizhny Novgorod A. A. Zhdanov Polytechnic Institute, present name *c.* 1992); faculties: motor transport, motor car engineering, automation and electrical engineering, metallurgy, physical chemistry, applied physics, radio-electronics and engineering cybernetics, shipbuilding, economics and machine-building; 1,166 teachers; 12,310 students; brs in Arzamas and Dzerzhinsk; Rector K. N. TISHKOV.

North Caucasian State University of Technology: 362021 North-Ossetian Republic, Vladikavkaz, Ul. Kosmonavta Nikolaeva 44; tel. (86722) 4-93-79; fax (86722) 4-99-45; f. 1931; faculties: mining, electromechanical, metallurgical, electronic engineering, building, management; library of 520,000 vols; Rector Prof. Z. M. KHADONOV; publ. *Izvestiya Vuzov*; *Tsvetnaya Metallurgia* (6 a year).

North-West Polytechnic Institute: 191186 St Petersburg, Millionnaya ul. 5; tel. (812) 110-62-59; fax (812) 311-60-16; e-mail fedorov@id.nwtu.spb.ru; f. 1930; faculties: power engineering and automation, radio electronics, instrumentation and engineering, machine technology, chemical technology and metallurgy, information and control systems, automobile engineering; library of 1,544,698 vols; Rector V. V. GURETSKY; publ. *Proceedings* (3-4 issues a year).

Novocherkassk State Technical University: 346428 Novocherkassk, Ul. Prosveshcheniya 132; tel. (86352) 5-54-48; fax (86352) 2-84-63; f. 1907; faculties: mining and geology prospecting, manufacturing machines and robots, mechanics, power, electrical engineering, chemical technology, construction, computer systems and robotics, humanities and social economic education; 12,229 students; library of 3,100,000 vols; Rector Prof. VITALY A. TARANUSHICH; publs *Elektromekhanika* (monthly), *Izvestiya SK NC Visshey Shkoly*.

Novosibirsk State Technical University: 630092 Novosibirsk, Pr. Karla Marksa 20; tel. (3832) 46-50-01; telex 133237; fax (3832) 46-02-09; e-mail rector@nstu.nsk.su; f. 1953; faculties: radio engineering, power engineering, aeronautics, electromechanics, applied mathematics and computer science, physical engineering, automated machine building, business studies, automation and computer engineering, general engineering, electronics and physics, humanities; 1,105 teachers; 9,354 students; library of 1,300,000 vols with 200 special collections; Rector Prof. A. S. VOSTRIKOV; publ. *Bulletin* (2 a year).

Omsk State Technical University: 644050 Omsk, Pr. Mira 11; tel. 65-33-43; fax 65-26-98; f. 1942; faculties: machine building, machine technology, electrical engineering, automation, radio engineering, aerospace, economics, humanities; library of 1,186,000 vols; 540 teachers; 6,200 students; Rector Prof. N. S. ZHILIN; publ. *Proceedings*.

Orenburg Polytechnic Institute: 460352 Orenburg, Pr. Pobedy 13; tel. 7-67-70; faculties: mechanics, electrical engineering technology, industrial and civil construction, building technology, road transport; br. in Orsk.

Penza Polytechnic Institute: 440017 Penza, Krasnaya ul. 40; tel. 66-37-44; telex 344652; f. 1943; faculties: instrument making, mechanical technology, engineering automation and information measuring technology, computer technology, radio electronics; 2,500 mems; library of 450,000 vols; Rector Prof. E. A. LOMTEV.

Perm State Technical University: 614600 Perm, Komsomolsky Pr. 29A; tel. (3422) 12-87-53; telex 134525; fax (3422) 12-11-47; e-mail mva@extrel.pstu.ac.ru; f. 1953; faculties: mining, electrical engineering, mechanical technology, applied mathematics and mechanics, road transport, aerospace technology, chemical technology, construction, humanities; 932 teachers, 12,500 students; library of 1,400,000 vols; Pres. A. A. BARTOLOMEI.

St Petersburg State Mining Institute (Technical University): 199026 St Petersburg, Vasilevskii ostrov, 21-ya Liniya 2; tel. (812) 213-60-78; fax (812) 327-73-59; f. 1773; faculties: prospecting, mining, mining electromechanics, economics, mine surveying, metallurgy; 8,000 students; library of 1,300,000 vols; br. in Vorkuta; Rector V. S. LITVINENKO.

Samara State Technical University: 443010 Samara, Galaktionovskaya ul. 141; tel. (8462) 32-00-43; fax (8462) 32-42-35; e-mail postman@star.sstu.samara.ru; f. 1914; faculties: machine building, oil technology, engineering technology, thermal power, electrotechnology, automation and information technology, physical technology, chemical technology, economics, humanities; 10,000 students; br. in Syzran; Rector Y. P. SAMARIN.

Saratov State Technical University: 410054 Saratov, Politekhnicheskaya ul. 77; tel. (8452) 25-73-01; fax (8452) 50-75-40; f. 1930; faculties: electronics and instrument-making, power engineering, motor vehicles, architecture and construction, mechanical engineering, highways and transport construction, social work, business; 1,100 teachers; 13,000 students; library of 2 m. vols; brs in Balakovo and Engels; Rector V. V. PETROV.

Stavropol Polytechnic Institute: 355038 Stavropol, Pr. Kulakova 2; tel. 6-32-86; f. 1971; faculties: food technology, automobile and mechanical engineering, power engineering and electronics, civil engineering, economics and management systems; 565 teachers; 8,610 students; library of 500,000 vols; Rector Prof. B. M. SINELNIKOV.

Tambov State Technical University: 392629 Tambov, Sovetskaya ul. 106; tel. (0752) 22-10-19; fax (0752) 21-02-16; e-mail postmaster@admin.tgtu.tambov.su; f. 1958; faculties: chemical engineering, agricultural production, mechanical engineering, design and technology, architecture and civil engineering, economics, law; 418 teachers; 5,137 students; library of 540,000 vols; Rector S. V. MISCHENKO; publ. *Vestnik* (4 a year).

Tolyatti Polytechnic Institute: 445002 Tolyatti, Belorusskaya Ul. 14; tel. 23-41-25; telex 290121; f. 1967; faculties: mechanical technology, motor vehicle construction, engineering, electronic computing centre; 3,500 students; library of 543,000 vols; Rector Prof. Dr V. I. STOLBOV.

Tomsk Polytechnic University: 634004 Tomsk, Pr. Lenina 30; tel. (3822) 224422; telex 128184; fax (3822) 224607; f. 1896; faculties: chemical-technological, electrophysical, physico-technical, geological and oil prospecting, automation and computer technology, automation and electromechanics; research institutes in nuclear physics, introscopy, high voltages; 1,500 teachers; 12,000 students; library of 2.5 m. vols; Rector YU. P. POKHOLKOV.

Tula State University: 300600 Tula, Pr. Lenina 92; tel. (0872) 25-21-55; fax (0872) 33-13-05; e-mail root@tsu.tula.ru; f. 1930; faculties: mechanical engineering, mechanics and mathematics, applied physics, engineering manufacturing, precision engineering, transport engineering, technical cybernetics, automation control systems, mining, economics, construction, medicine, humanities; 1,036 teachers; library of 1m. vols; Rector E. M. SOKOLOV; publ. *Izvestiya*.

Tver State Technical University: 170026 Tver, Nab. A. Nikitina 22; tel. (0822) 31-15-13; fax (0822) 31-43-07; e-mail sourinski@tstu.tver.ru; f. 1922; faculties: machine building, automatic control systems, civil and industrial engineering, environmental engineering, humanities, postgraduate, evening and distance education; library of 2,000,000 vols; Rector Prof. A. I. MATVEEV.

Ufa State Aviation Technical University: 450025 Ufa, Ul. K. Marksa 12; tel. (3472) 22-63-07; telex 214238; fax (3472) 22-99-09; f. 1932; faculties: aircraft engines, machine building, instrumentation, control systems, electronics, automation, informatics and robotics, economics, management, sociology; library of 1,000,000 vols; Rector S. T. KUSIMOV; publs *Higher School Collections on Research* (irregular), newspaper (weekly).

Ulyanovsk State Technical University: 432700 Ulyanovsk, Ul. Sev. Venets 32; tel. (8422) 34-77-34; telex 263010; fax (8422) 34-80-85; f. 1957; faculties: information systems and technology, natural sciences, radio engineering, power engineering, civil engineering, mechanical engineering, aircraft engineering, humanities; br. at Dimitrovgrad; 500 teachers; 7,000 students; library of 1,047,000 vols; Rector Prof. V. V. EFIMOV; publs scientific papers.

Urals State Technical University: 620002 Ekaterinburg, Ul. Mira 19; tel. (3432) 74-54-34; fax (3432) 74-38-84; e-mail inter@inter.ustu.ru; f. 1920; faculties: metallurgy, mechanical engineering, heat and power engineering, radio engineering, chemical technology, construction materials, civil engineering, economics and management, physical engineering, social work, physical training and sport; 2,300 teachers; library of 2,000,000 vols; Rector S. S. NABOICHENKO.

Vladimir State Technical University: 600026 Vladimir, Ul. Gorkogo 87; tel. (09222) 3-25-75; fax (09222) 3-33-58; f. 1958; faculties: chemistry, robot systems, machine technology, vehicle and tractor, technical cybernetics, computers, civil engineering, radio engineering, management, law, Russian language; brs in Kovrov and Murom; Rector A. G. SERGEEV.

Volgograd State Technical University: 400066 Volgograd, Pr. Lenina 28; tel. (8442) 34-00-76; fax (8442) 34-41-21; e-mail rector@vstu.ru; f. 1930; faculties: technology of engineering materials, road transport, motor vehicles and tractors, mechanical engineering, chemical engineering, electronics and computer science, economics and management; 745 teachers; 9,705 students; library of 900,000 vols; Rector Prof. I. NOVAKOV; publ. *Polytekhnika* (fortnightly).

Vologda Polytechnic Institute: 160000 Vologda, Ul. Lenina 15; tel. (817) 272-47-71; fax (817) 272-45-62; f. 1975; faculties: electric power engineering, mechanical engineering and technology, civil engineering and architecture, technical ecology of water systems, economics and management; 377 teachers; 2,855 students; library of 390,000 vols; Rector GENNADY TRUSOV.

Voronezh Polytechnic Institute: 394026 Voronezh, Moskovskii pr. 14; tel. 16-40-67; faculties: automation and mechanization of engineering, aviation, radio engineering, automation and electrical engineering, physical engineering, engineering economics; Rector Prof. V. S. POSTNIKOV.

Vyatka State Technical University: 610601 Kirov, GSP (Centre), Moskovskaya 36; tel. and fax (8332) 62-65-71; e-mail root@kpicnit.vyatka.su; f. 1963; faculties: electrical engineering, automation and computer technology, chemical technology, construction engineering, socio-economics, machine engineering; library of 1,000,000 vols; Pres. KONDRATOV V. MIKHAILOVICH; publ. *Transactions*.

Yaroslavl Polytechnic Institute: 150053 Yaroslavl, Moskovskii pr. 88; tel. 44-17-39; faculties: engineering, automative, technology of electrochemical coverings and paint and varnish, technology, construction.

Other Higher Educational Institutes

ENGINEERING AND INDUSTRY

MECHANICAL ENGINEERING

Baltic D. F. Ustinov Technical University: 198005 St Petersburg, 1-ya Krasnoarmeiskaya ul. 1/21; tel. (812) 259-11-22; fax (812) 316-24-09; f. 1930; departments: rocketry and aircraft, applied mechanics and automation, international industrial management, humanities, aerospace, guidance systems, natural sciences; 600 teachers; 5,300 students; library of 1,100,000 vols; Rector YURI P. SAVELEV.

Bauman Moscow State Technical University: 107005 Moscow, 2-ya Baumanskaya ul. 5; tel. 261-40-55; fax 267-98-93; e-mail irina@interd.bmstu.ru; f. 1830; faculties: informatics and control systems, electronics and laser technology, robotics and complex automation, power engineering, materials and technology, special machinery, basic sciences, engineering business and management, humanities; 2,500 teachers; 18,000 students; library of 3m. vols; br. in Kaluga; Rector I. B. FEDOROV; publs *Vestnik MGTU* (issues each on Instrumental Engineering and Mechanical Engineering), *Izvestiya Vuzov* (Mechanical Engineering).

Bryansk State Technical University: 241035 Bryansk 35, Bul. 50-let. Oktyabrya 7; tel. (0832) 56-09-05; fax (0832) 56-24-08; e-mail postmaster@bitmcnit.bryansk.su; f. 1929; faculties: transport engineering, power engineering, engineering technology; 4,000 students; library of 554,700 vols; Rector V. T. BUGLAEV.

Izhevsk State Technical University: 426069 Izhevsk, Studencheskaya ul. 7; tel. (3412) 58-38-75; fax (3412) 59-04-01; e-mail root@imi.udmurtia.su; f. 1952; faculties: machine design, computer science, instrument design, structural engineering, management and marketing, robotics, education, humanities; 769 teachers; 8,900 students; library of 4,700,000 vols; brs in Votkinsk, Glazov, Tchaikovsky and Sarapul; Rector Prof. I. V. ABRAMOV.

Kurgan State University: 640669 Kurgan, Ul. Gogolya 25; tel. 2-26-52; fax 2-20-51; f. 1959; depts: physics and mathematics, natural sciences, history and law, philology, foreign languages, mechanical engineering, design and technology, economics; 700 teachers; 8,000 students; library of 1,000,000 vols; Rector Prof. A. S. TEREKHOV.

Moscow Instrumentation Institute: 107076 Moscow, Ul. Stromynka 20; tel. 268-01-01; faculties: engineering, automation in instrument making, transport and power machine building; library of 250,000 vols; br. in Orel; Rector N. N. SHEVYAKOV.

Moscow State Academy of Automobile and Tractor Engineering: 105839 Moscow, B. Semenovskaya ul. 38; tel. (095) 369-28-32; fax (095) 369-01-49; e-mail decinter@mami.ru; f. 1939; faculties: motor vehicles and tractors, power engineering, automation and control, mechanical engineering, design and technology, machine-building, economics, engineering economics; 815 teachers; 7,500 students; library of 1,000,000 vols; Rector A. L. KARUNIN.

Moscow State Institute of Electronics and Mathematics – Technical University: 109028 Moscow, Bolshoi Trekhsvyatitelsky per. 3/12; tel. (095) 917-90-89; fax (095) 916-28-07; f. 1962; faculties: electronics, applied mathematics, computer science, informatics and telecommunications, mathematical economics; 5,000 students; library of 600,000 vols; Rector Dr DMITRI V. BYKOV.

Moscow State Technical University: 101472 Moscow, Vadkovskii per. 3-a; tel. (095) 973-30-66; fax (095) 973-31-67; f. 1930 (fmrly Moscow Machine Tool and Tooling Institute); faculties: technology, information technology, mechanics and control, physical engineering, economics and innovation technology, management; 5,483 students; library of 1,112,000 vols; Pres. Prof. YU. M. SOLOMENTSEV.

St Petersburg State Institute of Fine Mechanics and Optics: 197101 St Petersburg, Sablinskaya ul. 14; tel. (812) 238-87-13; fax (812) 232-97-04; f. 1930; faculties: fine mechanics and technology, computer technology and control, physical engineering, optics, natural sciences, humanities; 500 teachers; 4,000 students; library of 900,000 vols; Rector V. N. VASILEV; publ. *Izvestiya Vuzov (Priborostroenie)* (4 a year).

RADIO AND ELECTRICAL ENGINEERING

Ivanovo State Energy University: 153548 Ivanovo, Rabfakovskaya ul. 34; tel. 48-97-10; faculties: heat and power engineering, industrial heat and power engineering, power engineering, electrical engineering; libraries of 128,000 vols; Rector A. P. BAZHENOV.

Moscow Institute of Physics and Technology: 141700 Moscow oblast, Dolgoprudny, Institutskii per. 9; tel. (095) 408-57-00; fax (095) 408-68-69; f. 1951; faculties: radio engineering and cybernetics, general and applied physics, problems of physics and energy, molecular and chemical physics, aerodynamics and space research, aeromechanics and flight technology, management and applied mathematics, physical and quantum electronics, physical and chemical biology; 450 teachers (and 1,000 part-time); 3,900 students; library of 712,000 vols; Rector Prof. NIKOLAI V. KARLOV.

Moscow State Institute of Electronic Technology: 103498 Moscow, Zelenograd; tel. 534-55-53; fax 530-22-33; f. 1965; faculties: microtechnology, micro-devices and technical cybernetics, electronics and computer technology, automation and electronic engineering, economics and humanities; 530 teachers; 4,350 students; library of 680,000 vols; Rector V. D. VERNER; publ. *Collection of Research Work* (monthly).

Moscow State Institute of Engineering Physics: 115409 Moscow, Kashirskoe shosse 31; tel. (095) 324-89-35; fax (095) 324-85-20; faculties: experimental and theoretical physics, technical physics, automation and electronics, cybernetics, information security; 880 teachers; 6,000 students; library of 1,000,000 vols; Rector Prof. A. V. SHALNOV.

Moscow State Institute of Radio Engineering, Electronics and Automation: 117454 Moscow, Pr. Vernadskogo 78; tel. 433-00-66; fax 434-86-65; f. 1967; faculties: cybernetics, electronics and optical electronics technology, radio engineering systems and devices, automation and computer technology; 1,200 teachers; 14,500 students; library of 1,000,000 vols; br. at Dubna; Rector N. N. EVTIKHIEV; publ. *Proceedings of MIREA* (irregular).

Novosibirsk Telecommunications Institute: 630102 Novosibirsk, Ul. Kirova 86; tel. 66-10-38; fax 66-80-30; f. 1953; faculties: radio communication and broadcasting, automatic electrical communication, multi-channel electrical communication, engineering economics; library of 575,629 vols; br. in Khabarovsk; Rector V. P. BAKALOV.

Obninsk Institute of Nuclear Power Engineering: 249020 Obninsk, Studgorodok 1; tel. (08439) 3-69-31; fax (08439) 3-65-31; e-mail iate@storm.iasnet.com; f. 1985; physics and power engineering faculty with specialities: operation of nuclear power stations, nuclear reactor research and design, control and measuring devices, technical diagnostics, ecology, construction and commissioning of nuclear power plants; medical physics, applied psychology; cybernetics faculty with specialities: automatic control systems, applied mathematics, computers, economics; 340 teachers; 2,100 students; library of 140,000 vols; Pres. Prof. YU. A. KAZANSKY.

Ryazan State Radio Engineering Academy: 390005 Ryazan, Ul. Gagarina 59/1; tel. 72-18-44; fax 72-22-15; f. 1951; faculties: radio equipment design, radio engineering, electronics, automation and telemechanics, computer technology, engineering economics, humanities; library of 720,000 vols; Rector V. K. ZLOBIN.

St Petersburg Electrotechnical University: 197376 St Petersburg, Ul. Prof. Popova 5; tel. (812) 234-46-51; fax (812) 234-54-05; f. 1886; faculties: radio engineering, electronics, automation and computer science, industrial automation and electrical engineering, electrophysics, marine automation, electrical engineering, humanities, management; 10,000 students; library of 1,063,000 vols; Rector O. V. ALEKSEEV; publ. *Proceedings* (16 a year).

St Petersburg State University of Telecommunications: 191065 St Petersburg, Nab. reki Moiki 61; tel. (812) 315-01-18; telex 122781; fax (812) 315-76-10; f. 1930; faculties: telecommunication networks, switching systems and computer technology; multichannel telecommunication systems; radio communication, radio broadcasting and television; telecommunication technologies and biomedical electronics; economics and management; library of 90,000 vols; Rector Prof. MSTISLAV SIVERS.

Siberian Aerospace Academy: 660014 Krasnoyarsk, POB 486; tel. (3912) 33-00-14; fax (3912) 33-47-09; e-mail saa@stu.krasnoyarsk.su; f. 1959; 380 teachers, 3,000 students; library of 253,000 vols; Rector GENNADY P. BELYAKOV.

Taganrog State University of Radio Engineering: Rostov Region, 347928 Taganrog, GSP-17A, Ul. Nekrasova 44; tel. (86344) 6-50-67; fax (86344) 4-18-76; e-mail rector@trtu.rnd.su; f. 1952; faculties: general engineering, radio engineering, electronics and manufacturing engineering, automation and computer engineering, economics, management, law; 553 teachers; 5,400 students; library of 976,000 vols; Rector VLADISLAV G. ZAKHAREVICH; publs *Radiosignal* (weekly), *Perspectiva* (quarterly).

Tomsk State University of Control Systems and Radioelectronics: 634050 Tomsk, Pr. Lenina 40; tel. 22-32-27; fax 22-32-62; e-mail office@tasur.edu.ru; f. 1962; faculties: design technology, radio engineering, computer systems, control systems, electronic equipment; library of 620,000 vols; Dir I. N. PUSTYNSKY.

Volga Region State Academy of Telecommunication and Informatics: 443010 Samara, Ul. Lva Tolstogo 23; tel. (8462) 33-58-56; telex 214194; fax (8462) 32-48-64; faculties: radio engineering, radio communication and television, economics, telecommunication and informatics, electrical communication; library of 500,000 vols; Rector V. B. VITEVSKY.

CINEMA AND TELEVISION ENGINEERING

St Petersburg Institute of Cinema and Television: 191126 St Petersburg, Ul. Pravdy 13; tel. 315-72-85; fax 315-01-72; f. 1918; faculties: film equipment, electrical engineering, film and photographic materials, economics, art of cinema and television; 3,200 students; library of 500,000 vols; Rector A. N. DYAKONOV; publ. *Proceedings*.

CHEMISTRY, CHEMICAL ENGINEERING AND TECHNOLOGY

D. Mendeleev University of Chemical Technology of Russia: 125190 Moscow, Miusskaya pl. 9; tel. (095) 978-87-33; telex 411744; fax (095) 200-42-04; f. 1920; faculties: chemical technology of organic substances, chemical technology of inorganic substances, chemical technology of polymers, chemical technology engineering, physical chemistry engineering, ecological engineering, cybernetics of chemical technological processes, general engineering, economics; 1,003 teachers; 8,416 students; library of 1,700,000 vols; br in Novomoskovsk; Rector P. D. SARKISOV; publ. *Trudy* (every 2 months).

Ivanovo Institute of Chemical Technology: 153460 Ivanovo, Pr. F. Engelsa 7; tel. 2-92-41; faculties: inorganic chemistry, inorganic chemistry technology, silicates, engineering; Rector K. BELONOGOV.

Kazan State Technological University: 420015 Kazan, Ul. K. Marksa 68; tel. (8432) 36-75-42; fax (8432) 36-57-68; e-mail oms@chit.ksu.ras.ru; f. 1919; faculties: light industry engineering, mechanics, chemical engineering, oil and oil refining, polymers, chemical technology, energy engineering and technological engineering, power machinery construction and process equipment, management and automation, humanities, food technology; library of 1,600,000 vols; 850 teachers; 8,000 students; br. at Nizhnekamsk; Rector S. G. DJAKONOV; publs *Economy of Industrial Production, Heat and Mass Transfer in Chemical Engineering,* etc.

Moscow M. V. Lomonosov State Academy of Fine Chemical Technology: 117571 Moscow, Pr. Vernadskogo 86; tel. (095) 434-71-55; fax (095) 434-80-26; f. 1930; staff of 1,000; library of 220,000 vols; Rector Prof. V. S. TIMOFEEV.

DEANS

Faculty of Chemistry and Technology of Rare Elements and Materials for Electronic Technology: Prof. D. V. DROBOT
Faculty of Biotechnology and Organic Synthesis: Prof. A. F. MIRONOV
Faculty of Chemistry and Technology Polymer Processing: Prof. E. E. POTAPOV
Faculty of Natural Sciences: Prof. E. M. KARTASHOV
Faculty of Management, Ecology and Economics: Doc. I. H. ROZDIN
Faculty of Engineering: Prof. G. I. LAPSHENKOV
Preparatory Faculty: V. B. MARGULIS
Evening Classes: Doc. A. P. PETRUSENKO

Moscow State Academy of Chemical Engineering: 107884 Moscow, Ul. Staraya Basmannaya 21/4; tel. 267-07-01; fax 261-49-61; f. 1920; faculties: chemical machine building, cryogenic technology, chemical apparatus manufacture, technical cybernetics and automation of technological processes, chemical and biological engineering, economics; 400 teachers; 3,000 students; library of 650,000 vols; Rector Prof. M. B. GENERALOV.

St Petersburg State Institute of Technology: 198013 St Petersburg, Zagorodny pr. 49; tel. (812) 316-95-37; fax (812) 110-62-85; f. 1828; faculties: chemical technology of organic substances and microbiological synthesis, technology of organic synthesis and polymeric materials, high technologies and modern materials, environmental protection, economics and management, cybernetic engineering; library of 1,000,000 vols; 740 teachers; 5,500 students; Rector A. S. DUDYREV.

St Petersburg State Technological University of Plant Polymers: 198095 St Petersburg, Ul. Ivana Chernykh 4; tel. (812) 186-57-44; fax (812) 186-86-00; e-mail tupp@infopro.spb.su; f. 1931; faculties: chemical technology, heat and power engineering, mechanical, automatic control systems for technological processes, economics, correspondence, evening; 3,000 students; library of 740,000 vols; Rector O. A. TERENTYEV.

Voronezh Technological Institute: 394000 Voronezh, Pr. Revolyutsii 19; tel. and fax 55-42-67; f. 1930; faculties: mechanical, automation, chemical, technological, technology of meat and dairy products; 491 teachers; 4,800 students; library of 850,000 vols; Rector V. K. BYTYUKOV.

MINING AND METALLURGY

Krasnoyarsk State Academy of Non-Ferrous Metals and Gold: 660025 Krasnoyarsk, Krasnoyarsky rabochy 95; tel. (3912) 34-78-82; fax (3912) 34-63-11; e-mail postmaster@color.krasnoyarsk.su; f. 1958; institutes: mining, metallurgy, technology, economics and economic systems management; faculties: basic and social sciences, humanities; library of 500,000 vols; Rector Prof. V. V. KRAVTSOV.

Magnitogorsk G. I. Nosov Academy of Ore Mining and Metallurgy: 455000 Magnitogorsk, Pr. Lenina 38; tel. 32-12-87; fax 32-28-86; f. 1932; faculties: mining, metallurgy, mechanical, power engineering, technological, construction, humanities; library of 846,656 vols; Rector Dr B. A. NIKIFOROV.

Moscow Mining Institute: 117049 Moscow, Leninskii pr. 6; tel. 236-94-78; f. 1918; faculties: coal mining and underground construction, mining of mineral and non-mineral deposits, mining electrification and mechanization, mining automation and control, applied physics; 540 teachers; 5,270 students; library of 800,000 vols; Rector Prof. Dr L. A. PUCHKOV; publs *Gornyatskaya Smena* (weekly), *Scientific Papers* (2 a year).

Moscow State Evening Institute of Metallurgy: 111250 Moscow, Lefortovskii Val 26; tel. and fax (095) 361-14-46; f. 1931; faculties: metallurgy, technology, mechanization, automation, economics; 170 teachers; 2,700 students; library of 54,000 vols; 11 depts in factories and other organizations; Rector H. N. ELANSKY.

Moscow State Institute of Steel and Alloys: 117936 Moscow, Leninskii pr. 4; tel. 237-22-22; fax 237-80-07; f. 1918; faculties: semiconductor materials and instruments; metallurgical technologies, resource management and ecology; non-ferrous and precious metals; technology; properties of metals; informatics and economics; power and ecology; physics and chemistry; 830 teachers; 10,000 students; library of 1,300,000 vols; brs in Staryi Oskol and Elektrostal; Rector YURI S. KARABASOV; publs *Izvestiya Vysshikh Uchebnykh Zavedenii* (series for ferrous and non-ferrous metallurgy, both monthly).

Siberian State Academy of Mining and Metallurgy: 654007 Kemerovo oblast, Novokuznetsk, Pr. Kirova 42; tel. (3843) 46-35-02; fax (3843) 46-57-92; faculties: mining, metallurgy, electrometallurgy, foundry work, mechanical, technology, construction; 620 teachers; 6,000 students; library of 1,010,000 vols; Rector N. M. KULAGIN.

Urals State Academy of Mining and Geology: 620219 Ekaterinburg, Ul. Kuibysheva 30; tel. (3432) 22-25-47; telex 221558; fax (3432) 29-48-38; e-mail postmaster@ugi.rcupi.e-burg.su; f. 1917; faculties: geology, geophysics, mining technology, mining engineering, economics, environmental engineering; 1,500 teachers; 6,000 students; library of 800,000 vols; Rector Prof. I. V. DEMENTIEV; publs *Mining Journal* (monthly), *Urals Mining Review* (quarterly), *Transactions of the Academy* (3 a year).

PETROLEUM AND GAS

Groznyi Petroleum Institute: 364902 Groznyi, GSP-2, Pr. Revolyutsii 21; tel. 22-21-65; telex 247110; f. 1929; faculties: prospecting, geology, petroleum production, petroleum technology, mechanical engineering, construction engineering, electrification and automation of production processes; 301 teachers; 3,269 students; library of 700,000 vols; Rector R. M. MURDAEV.

Moscow Academician I. M. Gubkin Academy of Oil and Gas: 117917 Moscow, Leninskii pr. 65; tel. 930-92-25; telex 411637; fax 135-88-95; f. 1930; faculties: geology, geophysics and geochemistry of oil and gas deposits, mechanical engineering, oil and gas exploitation, pipeline design, construction and exploitation, automation and computer technology, chemical technology, engineering economics; brs in Almetevsk, Leninogorsk; 900 teachers; 8,000 students; library of 1,000,000 vols; Rector V. N. VINOGRADOV.

Ufa Oil Institute: 450062 Ufa, Ul. Kosmonavtov 1; tel. 25-24-00; faculties: oil and mining, pipeline transport, petrochemical, oil equipment, construction; library of 126,000 vols; brs in Oktyabrskii, Salavat, Sterlitamak; Rector V. A. BEREZIN.

CIVIL ENGINEERING

Belgorod State Technological Academy of Building Materials: 308012 Belgorod, Ul. Kostyukova 46; tel. (0722) 25-04-68; fax (0722) 25-71-39; e-mail rect@bgtasm.belgorod.ru; f. 1970; faculties: chemical technology of building materials, building technology, mechanical equipment, production automation and information technologies, humanities, economics and management; 1,300 teachers; 4,417 students; library of 600,000 vols; Pres. Prof. V. A. IVAKHNUK; publ. *Diapazon* (newspaper, 2 a week).

Ivanovo Academy of Civil Engineering and Architecture: 153002 Ivanovo, ul. Vosmoye Marta 20; tel. (0932) 32-85-40; fax (0932) 30-00-74; e-mail post@iisi.asinet.ivanovo.su; f. 1981; facilities: construction technology, economics, architecture; library of 250,000 vols; Rector Prof. Dr S. V. FEDOSOV.

Kazan State Academy of Architecture and Building: 420043 Kazan, Zelenaya ul. 1; tel. 36-25-32; f. 1946; faculties: construction, constructional technology, architecture, engineering systems and ecology, highway construction; 387 teachers; 3,500 students; library of 557,000 vols; Rector V. KUPRIYANOV.

Krasnoyarsk State Academy of Civil Engineering and Architecture: 660041 Krasnoyarsk, Pr. Svobodnyi 82; tel. 44-69-40; fax 44-58-60; f. 1982; faculties: construction, economics, highway engineering, architecture, engineering services; library of 429,000 vols; Rector V. D. NADELYAEV.

Moscow Architectural Institute: 103754 Moscow Centre GSP, Ul. Rozhdestvenka 11; tel. 924-79-90; fax 921-12-40; f. 1866; 400 teachers, 2,000 students; library of 400,000 vols; Rector ALEKSANDR P. KUDRYAVTSEV.

Moscow Institute of Municipal Economy and Construction: 109807 Moscow, Srednyaya Kalitnikovskaya ul. 30; tel. (095) 278-32-05; fax (095) 278-15-10; f. 1944; faculties: construction, technology, mechanical engineering, urban construction, ecology and sanitary engineering, engineering, management and economic, commerce; 500 teachers;

13,000 students; library of 600,000 vols; Rector N. V. KOLKUNOV.

Moscow State University of Civil Engineering: 129337 Moscow, Yaroslavskoe shosse 26; tel. (095) 183-44-38; fax (095) 183-53-10; e-mail noavtel@minas.rosmail.com; f. 1921; faculties: construction, hydraulic engineering, heat and ventilation, water and sewerage, constructional technology, mechanisation and automation of construction, economics organization and management of construction, industrial and civil construction, designs for industrial and civil construction, heat and power construction, urban construction and services; 1,300 teachers; 11,000 students; library of 1,600,000 vols; Rector Prof. V. YA. KARELIN; publ. *Proceedings of MSUCE* (4 a year).

Nizhny Novgorod State University of Architecture and Civil Engineering: 603600 Nizhny Novgorod, Ilyinskaya ul. 65; tel. (8312) 33-82-47; fax (8312) 33-73-66; e-mail rector@saace.nnov.su; f. 1930; programmes: architecture, design, urban development, environmental engineering, economics, law, industrial management, environmental management, occupational safety; 478 teachers; 5,000 students; library of 800,000 vols; Rector V. V. NAIDENKO; publ. *Collected Papers and Proceedings of Scientific Conferences* (2 a year).

Novosibirsk Architectural Institute: 630008 Novosibirsk, Belinskogo 151; tel. and fax 66-42-64; f. 1989; architecture, design; library of 50,000 vols.

Novosibirsk Civil Engineering Institute: 630008 Novosibirsk, Leningradskaya ul. 113; tel. 66-42-95, 66-07-39; faculties: hydraulic engineering, construction, construction economics; library of 278,000 vols; Rector K. L. PROVOROV.

Penza State Academy of Architecture and Construction: 440028 Penza, Ul. Titova 28; tel. (8412) 62-02-77; fax (8412) 62-05-01; faculties: architecture, construction, technology, engineering ecology, economics and management; library of 370,000 vols; Rector A. E. YEROMKIN.

Rostov State Institute of Architecture: 344082 Rostov-on-Don, Budennovsky pr. 39; tel. 39-09-43; fax 66-51-78; f. 1988; architecture, environmental design, arts and crafts, history of art, fashion design, management in architecture; library of 300,000 vols; Rector V. A. KOLESNIK; publ. *Problems of Architectural Education* (annually).

Rostov State University of Civil Engineering: 344022 Rostov-on-Don, Sotsialisticheskaya ul. 162; tel. (8632) 65-01-75; fax (8632) 65-57-31; e-mail rgsu@jeo.ru; f. 1943; institutes: industrial and civil engineering, civil engineering technology and materials, environmental engineering, highways and transport, economics and management; library of 710,000 vols; Rector V. I. SHUMEIKO; publ. *Izvestiya* (4 a year).

St Petersburg State University of Architecture and Civil Engineering: 198005 St Petersburg, 2-ya, Krasnoarmeiskaya ul. 4; tel. (812) 316-99-65; fax (812) 316-58-72; e-mail rector@spice.spb.ru; f. 1832; faculties: construction, architecture, motor vehicle engineering and road building, engineering, ecological systems; library of 850,000 vols; 5,000 students; Rector Prof. YURI PANIBRATOV; publ. *University Scientific Work* (10 a year).

Samara Institute of Architecture and Civil Engineering: 443644 Samara, Molodogvardeiskaya ul. 194; tel. (8462) 33-87-87; fax (8462) 32-19-65; f. 1930; faculties: civil engineering, architecture, construction technology, hydro-sanitary engineering; 400 teachers; 4,500 students; library of 640,000 vols; Rector V. A. SHABANOV.

Tomsk State Academy of Civil Engineering: 634003 Tomsk, Solyanaya pl. 2; tel. 75-39-30; fax 75-33-58; f. 1952; faculties: architecture, civil and industrial construction engineering, road building, mechanical engineering, technology; 458 teachers; 5,086 students; library of 638,000 vols; Rector G. M. ROGOV.

Tyumen Civil Engineering Institute: 625001 Tyumen, Ul. Lunacharskogo 2; tel. 3-45-31; faculties: construction, engineering networks and systems, road building.

Ural State Academy of Architecture and Arts: 620219 Ekaterinburg, GSP-1089, Ul. Karla Libknekhta 23; tel. (3432) 51-33-69; fax (3432) 51-95-32; e-mail vgafurov@mail.usaaa.ru; f. 1972 (fmrly Sverdlovsk Architectural Institute); depts of architecture, design, fashion design, monumental decorative art, applied decorative art; 1,100 students; library of 80,000 vols; Rector A. A. STARIKOV; publ. *Architecton* (4 a year).

Volgograd State Academy of Architecture and Engineering: 400074 Volgograd, Akademicheskaya ul. 1; tel. 44-13-72; telex 117342; fax 44-25-09; f. 1952; faculties: civil, sanitary engineering, roads, architecture, economics and management; 520 teachers; 6,425 students; library of 833,400 vols; br. in Volzhskii; Rector V. A. IGNATYEV.

Voronezh State Academy of Architecture and Civil Engineering: 394006 Voronezh, Ul. 20-Letiya Oktyabrya 84; tel. (0732) 71-52-68; fax (0732) 71-59-05; e-mail acher@vgasa.voronezh.su; f. 1930; faculties: arts, mechanical engineering and highway construction, engineering systems and buildings, architecture, construction, construction technology, engineering economics; library of 500,000 vols; Rector ALEXANDER M. BOLDYREV; publ. *Collection of Scientific Articles* (1 a year).

TEXTILE AND LIGHT INDUSTRIES

Ivanovo Textile Institute: 153475 Ivanovo, Pr. F. Engelsa 21; tel. 4-90-46; f. 1930; faculties: mechanical, spinning machinery, weaving machinery, sewn goods; 260 teachers; 4,200 students; library of 207,000 vols; Rector A. YU. UZMESTEVA.

Kostroma State University of Technology: 156005 Kostroma, Ul. Dzerzhinskogo 17; tel. (0942) 57-48-14; fax (0942) 57-83-98; e-mail inter@kti.kostroma.su; f. 1932; faculties: mechanical engineering, industrial economics, mechanical technology, forestry engineering, textile technology, arts; library of 500,000 vols; Rector YEVGENY A. SMIRNOV.

Moscow State Academy of Light Industry: 113127 Moscow, Ul. Osipenko 33; tel. 231-58-01; faculties: chemical technology, sewn goods technology, mechanical, leather goods technology, engineering economics; library of 392,000 vols; br. in Novosibirsk; Rector V. A. FUKIN.

Moscow State Textile Academy: 117918 Moscow, Malaya Kaluzhskaya ul. 1; tel. 954-70-73; fax 952-14-40; e-mail postmast@mgta.msk.su; f. 1919; faculties: mechanical technology, textile machinery, chemical technology, applied arts, economics and management, information, automation and energetics; 550 teachers; 5,000 students; library of 650,000 vols; Rector I. A. MARTYNOV; publs *Vestnik MTA* (newspaper, 4 a year), *Vestnik MGTA* (journal, 2 a year).

Moscow Technological Institute: 141220 Moscow oblast, Pushkinskii raion, pos. Cherkizovo 1, Glavnaya ul. 99; tel. 584-30-86; faculties: mechanical and radio engineering, chemical technology, engineering economics, art and technology; brs in St Petersburg, Ufa and Tolyatti.

Omsk Technological Institute for Service Industries: 644099 Omsk, Krasnogvardeiskaya 9; tel. 24-16-93; faculties: art and technology, engineering economics.

Russian Extra-Mural Institute of the Textile and Light Industries: 123298 Moscow, Ul. Narodnogo Opolcheniya 38, Korp. 2; tel. 943-63-59; f. 1932; faculties: textile industry technology, light industry technology, chemical technology, electrical engineering, engineering economics; 350 teachers; 13,000 students; library of 780,000 vols; brs in Barnaul, Ufa, Kemerovo and Omsk; Rector V. S. STRELYAEV.

St Petersburg State University of Technology and Design: 191186 St Petersburg, Bolshaja Morskaya ul. 18; tel. (812) 315-75-25; fax (812) 315-12-74; f. 1930 (fmrly St Petersburg Institute of Textile and Light Industry); six faculties; 490 teachers; 5,000 students (of whom 2,700 full-time); library of 700,000 vols; Rector Prof. V. E. ROMANOV.

Shakhty Technological Institute for Service Industries: Rostov oblast, 346500 Shakhty, Ul. Shevchenko 147; tel. 2-20-37; telex 8836; f. 1969; courses in fields of service industries, municipal finance and planning, light industry; 300 teachers; 2,000 full-time students; library of 370,000 vols, 250,000 patent documents; Rector Prof. VICTOR ROMANOV; publ. *Sbornik rabot instituta* (collected works, annually).

FOOD INDUSTRY

East Siberian Institute of Technology: 670042 Ulan-Ude, Klyuchevskaya ul. 40; tel. 7-56-00; fax 7-32-74; f. 1962; faculties: electrical engineering, food products technology, machine-building, economics and accounting, construction, computer science, leather and fur processing; 568 teachers; 7,000 students; library of 696,029 vols; Rector Prof. VLADIMIR N. BILTRIKOV.

Far Eastern Institute of Fish Industry and Economy: 690600 Vladivostok, Lugovaya ul. 52b; tel. 9-52-16; faculties: technology, economics, seamanship engineering, commercial fishery; full-time in-service courses; library of 100,000 vols; management school; Rector E. N. MALYAVIN.

Kaliningrad State Technical University: 236000 Kaliningrad, Sovetskii pr. 1; tel. (0112) 21-62-91; telex 262133; fax (0112) 273604; f. 1930; water bioresources and aquaculture, commercial fishing, fish food production technology, food production machinery, machine building, shipbuilding, electrical and automatic equipment for vessels, operation of shipboard machinery, automation of processing and production, computer systems and networks, computer-aided data processing and control systems, electrical power plants, heat and electricity generation plants, industrial and civil engineering, heating and ventilation engineering, accounting and auditing, business economics and management; 370 teachers; 4,000 students; library of 507,000 vols; Rector V. I. IVANOV; publ. scientific papers (3–4 a year).

Kemerovo Technological Institute of the Food Industry: 650060 Kemerovo, Bul. Stroitelei 21; tel. 51-13-43; faculties: mechanics, refrigeration machines, food products technology, meat and dairy products, technology and organisation of public catering.

Moscow State Academy of Applied Biotechnology: 109029 Moscow, Ul. Talalikhina 33; tel. (095) 276-19-10; fax (095) 276-14-23; f. 1931; faculties: dairy industry technology, meat industry technology, food production, automation, plastics processing, low-temperature technology, veterinary sanitation, book-keeping, management; library of 611,000 vols; Rector IOSIF A. ROGOV.

Moscow State Academy of Food Industry: 125080 Moscow, Volokolamskoe shosse 11; tel. and fax (095) 158-03-71; f. 1931; food technology, chemical engineering and biotechnology, information systems in economics, management and marketing, machinery, informatics, power engineering, agricultural engineering; 500 teaching staff; 6,000 students; library of 1m. vols; Pres. Prof. V. I. TUZHILKIN.

Moscow State Food Institute: 109803 Moscow, Zemlynoi Val 73; tel. (095) 915-03-40; fax (095) 915-08-77; f. 1953; faculties: fish breeding and biotechnology, mechanical engineering, bread products, industrial economics; 211 teachers; library of 380,000 vols; brs in Krasnoyarsk, Vyazma and Rostov; Rector O. K. FILATOV.

St Petersburg State Academy of Refrigeration and Food Technology: 191002 St Petersburg, Ul. Lomonosova 9; tel. 315-36-17; fax 315-05-35; depts of refrigeration engineering, equipment for food manufacturing and commerce, cryogenics and conditioning systems; faculties: refrigeration equipment, equipment for food industry, trade and public catering, cryogenic technology and conditioning; library of 850,000 vols; Rector A. V. BARANENKO.

TIMBER INDUSTRY

Arkhangelsk State Engineering University: 163007 Arkhangelsk, Severnaya Dvina Nab. 17; tel. and fax 44-11-46; e-mail agtu@online.ru; f. 1929; faculties: forestry engineering, forestry, forestry machinery, industrial power, timber processing technology, chemical technology of timber, industrial and civil construction, law, Institute of Economics, Finance and Business; 450 teachers; 4,500 students; library of 629,023 vols; Rector O. M. SOKOLOV; publ. *Lesnoi zhurnal* (Forestry Journal, every 2 months).

Bryansk Technological Institute: 241037 Bryansk, Ul. Stanke Dimitrova 3; tel. 119-12; faculties: forestry engineering, forestry machinery, timber technology, forestry management.

Moscow Forestry Technical Institute: 141001 Moscow oblast, Mytishchi, Pervaya Institutskaya ul. 1; tel. 583-64-90; faculties: electronics and computing equipment, automation and mechanization of wood working, automation and mechanization of production of wood boards, forestry and tree planting in towns; library of 400,000 vols; Rector A. KH. OBLIVIN.

St Petersburg Forest Technical Academy: 194018 St Petersburg, Institutsky per. 5; tel. 550-07-00; fax 550-08-15; f. 1803; faculties: forestry, forestry engineering, forest machinery, mechanical technology of timber, chemical technology, engineering economics; 613 teachers; 9,000 students; library of 1,400,000 vols; br. in Syktyvkar; Rector Prof. V. I. ONEGIN; publ. *Nauchnye trudy* (annually).

Siberian Institute of Technology: 660049 Krasnoyarsk, Pr. Mira 82; tel. (3912) 276382; fax (3912) 274440; f. 1930; faculties: forestry, automation and robot technology, timber technology and equipment, engineering for chemical technology, engineering economics, woodworking technology, chemical technology, humanities; library of 243,000 vols; br. in Lesosibirsk; Rector Prof. Dr E. BUKA.

Urals State Forestry Engineering Academy: 620032 Ekaterinburg, Sibirskii Trakt 37; tel. 24-23-73; f. 1930; faculties: forestry engineering, forestry economics, forestry machinery, timber technology, chemical technology, economics and management; 6,350 students; library of 690,000 vols; Rector V. N. STARZHINSKII.

Voronezh State Academy of Forestry Engineering: 394613 Voronezh, Ul. Timiryazeva 8; tel. and fax (0732) 52-86-10; f. 1918; faculties: forest engineering, forestry, wood-processing technology, motor-vehicle engineering, management; 315 teachers; 3,500 students; library of 434,000 vols; Rector Prof. V. K. POPOV.

PRINTING

Moscow Institute of Printing: 127550 Moscow, Ul. Pryanishnikova 2A; tel. 216-07-46; faculties: printing equipment, printing technology, engineering economics, book trade, layout; br. in St Petersburg.

INDUSTRIAL INSTITUTES

Bratsk Industrial Institute: 665709 Bratsk, Ul. Makarenko 40; tel. 7-22-14; faculties: power, mechanics, forestry engineering, construction.

Norilsk Industrial Institute: 663310 Norilsk, Ul. 50-let Oktyabrya 7; tel. (3919) 42-16-31; telex 288786; fax (3919) 42-17-41; f. 1961; faculties: mining, metallurgy, economics, mechanical technology, civil and electrical engineering; 500 teachers; 3,500 students; library of 300,000 vols; Rector A. A. KOLEGOV.

Rubtsovsk Industrial Institute: 658207 Rubtsovsk, Traktornaya ul. 2/6; tel. (38557) 3-26-29; fax (38557) 3-27-44; f. 1946; br. of Altai State Technical University; machine technology, motor car and tractor construction, motor vehicles and vehicle equipment, foundry machinery and technology, applied mathematics, management, industrial and civil engineering; 119 teachers; 1,458 students; library of 90,000 vols; Rector V. L. ZHIKAREV.

Tyumen State Oil and Gas University: 625000 Tyumen, Ul. Volodarskogo 38; tel. (3452) 25-08-61; fax (3452) 25-07-75; f. 1963; faculties: geology and geoinformatics, oil and gas fields, pipeline engineering, transport, technical cybernetics, oil and gas refining, management, drilling, mechanical engineering; library of 677,000 vols; Rector NIKOLAI N. KARNAUKHOV.

Ukhta Industrial Institute: 169400 Komi Autonomous Republic, Ukhta, Pervomaiskaya ul.13; tel. 6-06-10.

Urals State Vocational Pedagogical University: 620012 Ekaterinburg, Ul. Mashinostroitelei 11; tel. and fax (3432) 31-94-63; f. 1978; machine-building, power engineering, human sciences; 333 teachers; 4,164 students; library of 343,000 vols; Rector GENNADY M. ROMANTSEV; publs *Integrational Processes in Pedagogical Theory and Practice* (annually), *Improvement of Educational Processes in Vocational Schools* (annually), *Bulletin of Teaching Research* (2 a year), *Vocational Education Innovation Forms and Technologies* (annually), *Vocational Pedagogical Education* (annually).

Factory based Higher Technical Educational Establishments

Higher Technical Educational Establishment at Production Association 'Angarsknefteorgsintez': 665830 Angarsk, Ul. Charkovskogo 60; tel. 6-88-45; br. of Irkutsk Polytechnic Institute.

Moscow Vehicle Building Institute: 109068 Moscow, Avtozavodskaya ul. 16; tel. 275-52-37; faculties: mechanical technology, automotive.

Penza Technological Institute: 440600 Penza, Pr. Baidukova 1A; tel. 55-60-86; e-mail rector@vmis.pti.ac.ru; faculties: mechanical engineering, computer science, economics; library of 140,000 vols; Rector Prof. V. B. MOISEEV.

Rostov on Don Automation and Mechanical Engineering Institute: 344023 Rostov-na-Donu, Pl. Strany Sovetov 2; tel. 52-93-51; fax 54-84-11; f. 1960; faculties: agricultural engineering, mechanical engineering, automation and robotics; 565 teachers; 1,730 students; library of 237,424 vols; Rector N. G. CHEREDNICHENKO; publ. *Economics and Industrial Management*.

St Petersburg Institute of Machine Building (VTUZ-LMZ) 195108 St Petersburg, Polyustrovskii pr. 14; tel. 540-01-54; telex 121425; fax 540-03-02; f. 1930; faculties: mechanical engineering, nuclear power engineering, turbine manufacture; 3,000 students; library of 185,000 vols; Rector Prof. M. A. MARTYNOV.

GEOLOGY, HYDROLOGY AND METEOROLOGY

Moscow State Geological Prospecting Academy: 117873 Moscow, Ul. Miklukho-Maklaya 23; tel. (095) 433-62-56; fax (095) 433-56-33; faculties: geology, geophysics, hydrogeology, prospecting engineering and mining, economics; 439 teachers; 3,964 students; library of 410,335 vols; Rector L. G. GRABCHAK; publ. *Geology and Prospecting* (6 a year).

Russian State Hydrometeorological University: 195196 St Petersburg, Malookhtinskii pr. 98; tel. (812) 444-41-63; fax (812) 444-60-90; e-mail karlin@rgmi.spb.su; f. 1930; faculties: hydrology, oceanology, meteorology, ecology; library of 300,000 vols; Rector Prof. L. N. KARLIN; publ. *Proceedings* (quarterly).

LAND SURVEYING AND CARTOGRAPHY

Moscow State University of Geodesy and Cartography: 103064 Moscow, Gorokhovskii per. 4; tel. 261-31-52; fax 267-46-81; e-mail root@msugc.msk.ru; f. 1779; faculties: geodesy, photogrammetry, cartography, applied cosmonautics, land management, design of optical instruments, humanities; library of 800,000 vols; 400 teachers, 5,000 students; Rector V. P. SAVINYKH; publ. *Geodeziya i Aerofotosiomka* (6 a year).

Novosibirsk Institute of Engineers for Geodesy, Aerial Photography and Cartography: 630108 Novosibirsk, Ul. Plakhotnogo 10; tel. 43-37-01; faculties: geodesy, aerial photography and geodesy, optics; library of 100,000 vols; Rector K. L. PROVOROV.

TRANSPORT AND COMMUNICATIONS

RAILWAYS

All-Russian Correspondence Institute of Railway Engineers: 125808 Moscow, Chasovaya ul. 22/2; tel. 151-14-51; faculties: engineering, electrical engineering, electrification of railways, traffic management, construction, engineering economics; library of 500,000 vols; brs in Nizhnii Novgorod, Voronezh, Yaroslavl; Rector A. T. DENCHENKO.

Irkutsk Institute of Railway Engineers: 664074 Irkutsk, Ul. Chernyshevskogo 15; tel. 28-27-12; faculties: electromechanical, construction, traffic management; 497 teachers; library of 116,000 vols; Rector L. P. SURKOV.

Khabarovsk Institute of Railway Engineers: 680056 Khabarovsk, Ul. Serysheva 47; tel. 34-30-76; f. 1939; faculties: mechanical engineering, traffic management, electrification of railways, automation, telemechanics and telecommunications, railway construction, industrial and civil construction; 520 teachers; 7,000 students; library of 521,000 vols; br. in Chita; Rector V. G. GRIGORENKO.

Moscow State University of Railway Engineering (MIIT): 103055 Moscow, Ul. Obraztsova 15; tel. 284-21-41; telex 411798; fax 284-54-91; f. 1896; faculties: mechanical engineering, mechanical engineering technology, railway automation, telemechanics and communication, technical cybernetics, industrial and civil construction, traffic management, electrification of railways, railway construction, bridges and tunnels engineering, economics; 1,300 teachers, 12,000 students; library of 2m. vols; Rector V. G. INOZEMTSEV; publs *Inzhener Transporta*, *MREI* (Collection of Works).

Omsk State Transport University: 644046 Omsk, Pr. Karla Marksa 35; tel. 31-42-19; f. 1930; faculties: engineering, electrical transport, automation and telemechanics, electrical engineering, machine-building technology, heat and power engineering, international economic relations; 250 teachers; 4,200 students; library of 700,000 vols; Rector V. A. CHETVERGOV.

Rostov-on-Don University of Transport Communication: 344038 Rostov-on-Don, Pl. Narodnogo Opolcheniya 2; tel. and fax (8632) 31-36-83; e-mail root@rgups.rnd.ru; faculties: automation and telemechanics, power engineering, electromechanical engineering, railway construction, traffic and transport management, road building machinery, humanities; institute of management and law; library of 770,000 vols; Rector V. I. KOLESNIKOV.

St Petersburg State University of Means of Communication: 190031 St Petersburg, Moskovskii pr. 9; tel. 310-25-21; f. 1809; library of 1,500,000 vols; 700 teachers; faculties: construction, electrification, traffic management, mechanics, electrical engineering, bridge and tunnel construction; br. in Velikie Luki; Rector Prof. V. Y. PAVLOV; publ. *Proceedings* (annually).

Samara Institute of Railway Engineers: 443066 Samara 9, Pervyi Bezymyannyi per. 18; tel. 51-75-09; fax 51-77-90; faculties: construction, electromechanical, electrotechnical, operating; 6,000 students; library of 260,000 vols; Rector Prof. V. V. IVANOVICH.

Siberian State Academy of Transport: 630023 Novosibirsk, Ul. Dusi Kovalchuk 191; tel. 28-74-70; fax 26-79-78; f. 1932 (fmrly Novosibirsk Institute of Railway Engineers); faculties: railway traffic management, railway construction, construction and track machinery, civil engineering, water supply and sewerage, bridges and tunnels, economics and transport management, economics and building management, accounting and auditing, management, world economics; 473 teachers, 157 researchers; library of 773,000 vols; Rector K. L. KOMAROV; publ. *Proceedings* (5 or 6 a year).

Urals State Academy of Railway Transport: 620034 Ekaterinburg, Ul. Kolmogorova 66; tel. (3432) 58-30-36; fax (3432) 51-86-47; f. 1956; faculties: mechanics, electrical engineering, electrification, construction, traffic management; 401 teachers; 5,175 students; library of 600,000 vols; Rector Prof. A. V. EFIMOV; publs *Research Reviews* (every 2 years), *Annual Report*.

RIVER AND SEA TRANSPORT

Admiral Makarov State Maritime Academy: 199026 St Petersburg, Vasilevskii ostrov, Kosaya Liniya 15A; tel. 217-19-34; fax 217-07-82; f. 1876; faculties: arctic, navigation, radio engineering, international transport management, electrical engineering, marine engineering; 380 teachers, 4,400 students; library of 762,000 vols; brs in Arkhangelsk, Murmansk; Pres. IVAN I. KOSTYLEV.

Baltic Fishing Fleet State Academy: 236029 Kaliningrad oblastnoi, Molodezhnaya ul. 6; tel. 21-72-04; telex 262313; fax 27-58-00; f. 1966; faculties: navigation, marine engineering, radio engineering, library of 165,426 vols; Dir A. PIMOSHENKO; publ. *Research Work* (annually).

Far-Eastern State Maritime Academy: Vladivostok, Verkhneportovaya ul. 50A; tel. 22-49-58; fmrly Far Eastern Higher School of Marine Engineering; faculties: navigation, ship engineering, management of marine transport, electrical engineering, practical psychology; library of 360,000 vols; Rector V. I. SEDYKH.

Moscow State Academy of Water Transport: 115407 Moscow, Ul. Sudostroitelnaya 46; tel. 116-30-88; fax 118-31-11; f. 1980; faculties: marine engineering, operations, navigation, mechanization and automation of ports, hydrotechnical construction, engineering economics, legislation, international economic management for water transport; library of 106,000 vols; 5,000 students; Rector Prof. N. P. GARANIN.

Novorossiisk State Maritime Academy: 353918 Novorossiisk, Pr. Lenina 93; tel. (8617) 3-03-93; fax (8617) 23-22-95; f. 1975; trains specialists in navigation, ship power plant operation, ship electrical and automated equipment operation, ship radio equipment operation, economics and management for the merchant marine; library of 267,000 vols; Dir VASILY GUTSULYAK.

Novosibirsk Academy of Water Transport: 630099 Novosibirsk, Ul. Shchetinkina 33; tel. 22-64-68; f. 1951; faculties: waterways and ports, navigation and operation of water transport, ship engineers, electrical engineering; 253 teachers; 6,350 students; library of 400,000 vols; Dir O. N. LEBEDEV.

Petropavlovsk-Kamchatskii Maritime University: 683003 Petropavlovsk-Kamchatskii, Klyuchevskaya ul. 35; tel. and fax 22-45-38; f. 1987; trains specialists for fishing industry, navigators, marine engineers, electrical engineers, radio engineers, technologists and refrigeration engineers; 250 teachers; 2,000 students; library of 70,000 vols; Rector B. I. OLEINIKOV; publ. *Conference Papers* (annually).

St Petersburg State Marine Technical University: 190008 St Petersburg, Lotsmanskaya ul. 3; tel. (812) 114-07-61, fax (812) 113-81-09; f. 1902; faculties: naval architecture and ocean engineering, electronics and control systems, marine engineering, business and management; library of 862,380 vols; Rector Prof. D. M. ROSTOVTSEV.

St Petersburg State University for Water Communication: 198035 St Petersburg, Dvinskaya ul. 5/7; tel. (812) 259-68-68; fax (812) 251-01-14; e-mail nik@spguwc.spb.su; f. 1930; faculties: waterways and ports, marine engineering, electrical engineering, port handling and transport facilities, navigation, engineering, economics; 350 teachers; 2,500 students; library of 855,000 vols; Rector A. S. BUTOV.

Volga State Academy of Water Transport: 603600 Nizhny Novgorod, Ul. Nesterova 5; tel. (8312) 36-37-80; fax (8312) 32-17-91; courses in: transport operation and navigation, shipbuilding and ocean technology, land transport systems, electromechanics, electrical engineering, hydrotechnical construction, economics, business management, law; library of 500,000 vols.

ROAD TRANSPORT

Siberian Motor and Highway Institute: 644080 Omsk, Pr. Mira 5; tel. 65-03-02; f. 1930; faculties: road-building machinery, highway and airport building, bridges and tunnels, industrial and civil engineering, vehicles and vehicle services, traffic organization and services management, road transport economics and management; 500 teachers; 5,000 students; library of 747,000 vols; Rector V. F. AMELCHENKO.

AVIATION

Moscow Institute of Aviation Technology: 103767 Moscow, Petrovka 27; tel. (095) 141-18-40; fax (095) 141-19-50; e-mail intdep@intedu.mati.msk.ru; f. 1932; faculties: aerospace engineering and technology, materials science and technology, avionics, computer science, economics and business, ecology; library of 700,000 vols; Rector B. S. MITIN.

Moscow State Technical University of Civil Aviation: 125838 Moscow, Kronshtadtskii bul. 20; tel. (095) 459-07-07; fax (095) 457-12-01; f. 1971 (fmrly Moscow Institute of Civil Aviation Engineers, present name *c.* 1992); faculties: radio electronics and computer technology, aviation equipment, mechanical, economics; library of 650,000 vols; Rector Prof. VLADIMIR VOROBEV; publ. *Proceedings* (annually).

Moscow S. Ordzhonikidze Aviation Institute: 125871 Moscow, Volokolamskoe shosse 4; tel. 158-00-02; faculties: aircraft and helicopter building, aircraft engines, automatic control of aircraft, aircraft equipment, economics and organization of aircraft production, applied mathematics, aircraft radio-electronics, aircraft, applied mechanics; library of 909,000 vols; Rector YU. A. RYZHOV.

Rybinsk State Academy of Aviation Technology: 152934 Rybinsk, Ul. Pushkina 53; tel. (0855) 52-09-90; fax (0855) 52-86-88; f. 1955; faculties: aviation engineering, aviation and rocket building, radio engineering electronics and informatics; 2,000 students; library of *c.* 500,000 vols; Rector Prof. V. F. BEZYAZICHNY; publ. *Scientific Notes* (annually).

St Petersburg Academy of Civil Aviation: 196210 St Petersburg, Ul. Pilotov 38; tel. 291-28-43; faculty: air traffic control; Rector P. V. KARTAMYSHEV.

St Petersburg State Academy of Aerospace Instrumentation: 190000 St Petersburg, Bolshaya Morskaya 67; tel. (812) 110-65-00; fax (812) 315-77-70; e-mail sidorenko@aanet.ru; fields covered: instrumentation, informatics and computer systems, automation, information systems in economics, management, law, radio engineering; library of 1,000,000 vols; Rector L. A. PETROVICH; publ. *V polet* (monthly).

Samara State Aerospace University: 443086 Samara, Moskovskoje Shosse 34; tel. (8462) 35-18-26; telex 214181; fax (8462) 35-18-36; e-mail prokhorov@ssau.ru; f. 1942; faculties: aircraft construction, radio engineering, aircraft engines, aircraft transport engineering, plastic working of metals, information science, economics and management; 720 teachers; 6,500 students; library of 1,000,000 vols; Rector V. A. SOIFER.

MEDICINE

GENERAL MEDICINE

Altai Medical University: 656099 Barnaul, Pr. V. I. Lenina 40; tel. (3852) 36-88-48; fax (3852) 22-14-21; e-mail rector@unimed-gw.secna.ru; library of 121,000 vols.

Arkhangelsk State Medical Academy: 163061 Arkhangelsk, 51 Troitsky pr. 51; tel. (8182) 43-21-60; fax (8182) 26-32-26; f. 1932; faculties: general practice, paediatrics, stomatology, social work, medical management, medical psychology, prophylactic medicine, improvement of medical education; 330 teachers; 2,500 students; library of 400,000 vols; Rector P. I. SIDOROV; publs *Medik Severa* (monthly), *Human Ecology* (quarterly), *Diagnostics and Treatment* (quarterly).

Astrakhan Medical Institute: 414000 Astrakhan, Ul. Mechnikova 20; tel. 2-70-16; f. 1918; 3,000 students; library of 570,000 vols; Rector Prof. I. N. POLUNIN.

Bashkir Medical Institute: 450025 Bashkir Autonomous Republic, Ufa, Ul. Frunze 47; tel. 22-41-73; library of 216,000 vols.

Blagoveshchensk State Medical Institute: 675006 Blagoveshchensk-on-Amur, Ul. Gorkogo 95; tel. 2-27-13, 2-28-68.

Chelyabinsk State Medical Institute: 454092 Chelyabinsk, Ul. Vorovskogo 64; tel. 34-16-86; library of 500,000 vols; Rector D. A. GLUBOKOV.

Chita State Medical Institute: 672090 Chita, Ul. Gorkogo 39A; tel. 3-41-63; fax 23-54-59; f. 1953; library of 387,000 vols; Rector V. N. IVANOV.

Dagestan State Medical Institute: 367025 Dagestan Autonomous Republic, Makhachkala, Pl. Lenina 6; tel. 7-33-35.

Irkutsk State Medical Institute: 664003 Irkutsk, Ul. Krasnogo Vosstaniya 1; tel. 24-41-80; f. 1919; Rector Prof. A. K. MAKAZOV.

Ivanovo State Medical Institute: 153462 Ivanovo, Pr. F. Engelsa 8; tel. 4-15-75; library of 141,000 vols.

Izhevsk State Medical Academy: Udmurt Republic, 426034 Izhevsk, Revolyutsionnaya ul. 199; tel. (3412) 78-57-46; fax (3412) 75-72-91; e-mail rector@igma.udm.ru; f. 1933; library of 402,000 vols; Pres. Prof. N. S STRELKOV.

Kazan State Medical University: 420012 Kazan, Ul. Butlerova 49; tel. (8432) 36-06-52; fax (8432) 36-03-93; e-mail office@intdept.kcn.ru; f. 1814; faculties: medicine, paediatrics, dentistry, pharmacy, nursing, social work; 500 teachers; 4,500 students; library of 10,000 vols; Rector Prof. N. K. AMIROV; publ. *Kazan Medical Journal* (6 a year).

Kemerovo State Medical Institute: 650029 Kemerovo oblastnoi, ul. Voroshilova 22A; tel. 55-78-89; f. 1956; library of 170,000 vols; Rector A. D. TKACHEV.

Khabarovsk State Medical Institute: 680000 Khabarovsk, Ul. K. Marksa 35; tel. 33-20-49; f. 1930; 460 mems; library of 536,815 vols; Rector A. G. ROSLYAKOV.

Krasnoyarsk State Medical Academy: 660022 Krasnoyarsk, Ul. Partizana Zheleznyaka 1; tel. and fax (3912) 23-78-35; e-mail root@onmpi.krasnoyarsk.su; f. 1942; 634 teachers; 4,835 students; library of 472,000 vols; Rector Prof. VICTOR I. PROKHORENKOV; publ. *Medical Man* (monthly).

Kuban Medical Institute: 350003 Krasnodar, Ul. Sedina 4; tel. 52-85-95; library of 350,000 vols; Rector V. A. LATYSHEV.

Kursk State Medical Institute: 305033 Kursk, Ul. Karla Marksa 3; tel. 2-77-93; f. 1935; training of physicians and pharmacists; 434 mems; library of 320,214 vols; Rector Prof. A. V. ZAVYALOV.

Moscow I. I. Sechenov Medical Academy: 119435 Moscow, B. Pirogovskaya ul. 2/6; tel. 248-05-53; library of 600,000 vols.

Nizhny Novgorod State Medical Academy: 603005 Nizhny Novgorod, Pl. Minina i Pozharskogo 10/1; tel. and fax 39-09-43; f. 1920; library of 440,000 vols; Rector VIACHESLAV V. SHKARIN; publ. *Zhurnal* (quarterly).

North-Ossetian State Medical Academy: 362019 North Ossetia, Vladikavkaz, Pushkinskaya ul. 40; tel. (8672) 53-42-21; fax (8672) 53-03-97; e-mail nosma@dol.ru; f. 1796; 278 teachers; library of 265,000 vols; Rector Prof. K. D. SALBIEV.

Novosibirsk Medical Institute: 630091 Novosibirsk, Krasnyi pr. 52; library of 360,000 vols; tel. 21-45-44; Rector Prof. V. P. KAZNACHEEV.

Omsk State Medical Academy: 644099 Omsk, Ul. Lenina 12; tel. 23-32-89; fax 23-14-57; f. 1921; faculties: therapeutic and preventive medicine, paediatrics, stomatology; library of 573,199 vols; Rector L. V. POLUEKTOV.

Orenburg State Medical Institute: 460014 Orenburg, Sovetskaya ul. 6; tel. 7-61-03; library of 160,000 vols.

Perm State Medical Academy: 614600 Perm, GSP, Kuybyshevskaya ul. 39; tel. (3422) 33-75-27; fax (3422) 33-88-70; e-mail medic@pstu.ac.ru; library of 541,000 vols; Rector Prof. V. A. CHERKASSOV.

Rostov Medical Institute: 344718 Rostov-on-Don, Nakhichevanskii per. 29; tel. 65-33-38; f. 1931; library of 340,000 vols; Rector Prof. U. D. RYZHKOV.

Russian State Medical University: 117869 Moscow, Ul. Ostrovityanova 1; tel. 434-03-29; fax 434-47-87; f. 1906; faculties: general practice, paediatrics, medical biology; 1,200 teachers; 6,300 students; library of 900,000 vols; Rector Prof. Dr V. N. YARYGIN; publ. *Vestnik* (4 a year)

Ryazan Medical Institute: 390000 Ryazan, Ul. Mayakovskogo 105; tel. 77-68-95; library of 213,000 vols.

St Petersburg Institute of Sanitation and Hygiene: 195067 St. Petersberg, Piskarevskii pr. 47; tel. 543-24-23; library of 350,000 vols; Rector Prof. A. YA. IVANOV.

St Petersburg Pavlov State Medical University: 197022 St Petersburg, Ul. L. Tolstogo 6/8; tel. (812) 238-71-53; fax (812) 234-01-25; e-mail rector@spmu.rssi.ru; f. 1897; fields covered: medicine, dentistry, sports medicine, basic sciences; library of 953,000 vols; Rector Prof. N. YAITSKY; publs *Arterial Hypertension* (4 a year), *Nephrology* (4 a year), *Scientific Items* (4 a year), *St Petersburg Medical News* (6 a year).

St Petersburg State Academy of Medical Paediatrics: 194100 St Petersburg, Litovskaya ul. 2; tel. (812) 245-06-46; fax (812) 245-40-85; f. 1925; library of 600,000 vols; Rector Prof. M. V. NEZHENTSEV.

Samara State Medical University: 443099 Samara, Chapaevskaya ul. 89; tel. (8462) 32-16-34; fax (8462) 33-29-76; e-mail root@samsmu.samara.su; f. 1919; fields covered: general medicine, paediatrics, dentistry, pharmaceutics, psychology, medical management, nursing, military medicine; library of 300,000 vols; Rector A. F. KRASNOV; publ. *Annals of Traumatology* (6 a year).

Saratov State Medical Institute: 410710 Saratov, Ul. 20-let VLKSM 112; tel. 24-12-84; f. 1909; library of 950,000 vols; Rector Prof. N. R. IVANOV.

Siberian State Medical University: 634050 Tomsk, Moskovsky Trakt 2; tel. (3822) 23-04-23; fax (3822) 23-33-09; f. 1888; faculties: medicine, paediatrics, pharmaceutics, military medicine, nursing, biological medicine, postgraduate education, preparatory education; 3,600 students; library of 500,000 vols; Pres. Prof. V. V. NOVITSKY; publ. *Ecogen* (quarterly).

Smolensk State Medical Institute: 214000 Smolensk, Ul. Glinki 3; tel. 5-02-75; library of 207,000 vols.

Stavropol State Medical Institute: 355024 Stavropol kraevoi, Ul. Mira 310; tel. 5-55-90; f. 1937; library of 175,000 vols; Rector Prof. V. YU. PERVUSHIN.

Tver Medical Academy: 170642 Tver, Sovetskaya ul. 4; tel. 3-34-60; library of 446,000 vols; Rector B. N. DAVYDOV.

Tyumen Medical Academy: 625023 Tyumen, Odesskaya ul. 54; tel. (3452) 22-62-00; fax (3452) 25-23-19; f. 1963; 349 teachers; 3,000 students.

Urals State Medical Academy: 620219 Ekaterinburg, Ul. Repina 3; tel. (3432) 51-14-90; fax (3432) 51-64-00; e-mail urgma@urgma.mplik.ru; f. 1931; fields covered: therapeutics, surgery paediatrics, paediatric surgery, anaesthesiology, obstetrics, gynaecology, pathology, otolaryngology, ophthalmology, epidemiology, dentistry; library of 600,000 vols; Rector Prof. A. P. YASTREBOV; publ. *Herald* (monthly).

Vladivostok Medical Institute: 690600 Vladivostok, Pr. Ostryakova 2; tel. 5-16-24.

Volgograd Academy of Medical Sciences: 400066 Volgograd, Pr. Lenina 13; tel. 33-99-32; fax 33-68-00; e-mail vma@minas.rosmail.com; f. 1935; fields covered: general medicine, stomatology, paediatrics, pharmaceutics; library of 800,500 vols; Rector Prof. V. PETROV.

Voronezh State Medical Institute: 394622 Voronezh, Studencheskaya ul. 10; tel. 52-49-60; library of 170,000 vols.

Yaroslavl State Medical Institute: 150013 Yaroslavl, Ul. Chkalova 5; tel. 23-88-23; library of 137,000 vols.

PHARMACEUTICS

Khabarovsk State Pharmaceutical Institute: 680000 Khabarovsk, Ul. K. Marksa 30; tel. 34-68-26.

Perm Pharmaceutical Institute: 614600 Perm, GSP-277, Ul. Lenina 48; tel. 34-04-45; library of 80,000 vols.

Pyatigorsk Pharmaceutical Institute: 357533 Pyatigorsk, Pr. Kalinina 11; tel. 9-44-74; f. 1943; 308 teachers; 2,300 students; library of 370,000 vols; Rector V. G. BELIKOV.

St Petersburg State Chemical-Pharmaceutical Academy: 197376 St Petersburg, Ul. Professora Popova 14; tel. 234-57-29; fax 234-60-44; f. 1919; faculties: drug industry technology, pharmacy, further education; library of 334,200 vols; Rector G. P. YAKOVLEV.

STOMATOLOGY

Moscow Medical Stomatological Institute: 103473 Moscow, Delegatskaya ul. 20; tel. 281-65-13; f. 1935; library of 113,000 vols.

AGRICULTURE

GENERAL AGRICULTURE

All-Russian Extra-Mural Agricultural Institute: 143900 Moscow oblast, Balashikha 8; tel. 521-24-64; fax 521-24-56; f. 1930; depts: agriculture, zoological engineering, mechanization, economics and management, electrification, information technology in economics and law; library of 517,000 vols; Rector L. Y. KISELEV; publs collections of scientific works of the institute (annually).

Altai State Agricultural University: 656099 Barnaul, Krasnoarmeiskii pr. 98; tel. 25-45-35; f. 1943; depts: agronomy, animal production, veterinary, zoology, irrigation and land reclamation, mechanization, economics and management, accounting; 390 teachers; 4,000 students; library of 300,000 vols; research centre; Rector Prof. N. M. BONDARCHUK.

Bashkir Agricultural Institute: 450089 Bashkir Autonomous Republic, Ufa, Ul. 50-letiya Oktyabrya; tel. 22-90-40; depts: agronomy, animal husbandry, economics, mechanics; 260 teachers; 5,300 students; library of 150,000 vols; Rector N. R. BAKHTSIN; publ. *Works*.

Belgorod Agricultural Institute: 309103 Belgorod oblast, Belgorod raion, poselok Maiskii, Ul. Vavilova 24; tel. 2-04-15.

Blagoveshchensk Agricultural Institute: Amur oblast, 675005 Blagoveshchensk, Politekhnicheskaya ul. 86; tel. 2-32-06; f. 1950; depts: agronomy, animal husbandry, veterinary, accounting, mechanization; library of 160,000 vols; Rector E. V. BLINNIKOV; publ. *Works*.

Bryansk State Agricultural Academy: 243365 Bryansk oblast, Vygonicheskii raion, poselok Kokino; tel. (8341) 2-43-21; e-mail bgsha@bitmcnit.bryansk.su; f. 1980; library of 385,000 vols, 150 periodicals; Rector EGOR VASHCHEKIN; publ. *Collection of Scientific Papers* (1 a year).

Buryat State Agricultural Academy: 670024 Republic of Buryatia, Ulan-Ude, Ul. Pushkina 8; tel. (3012) 34-26-11; fax (3012) 34-22-54; e-mail bgsha@eastsib.ru; f. 1932; depts: animal husbandry, agronomy, veterinary medicine, economics, farm mechanization, land tenure regulations, accounting, management; 325 teachers; 4,800 students; library of 582,000 vols; Rector Prof. ALEXANDER P. POPOV.

Chuvash Agricultural Institute: 428000 Chuvash Autonomous Republic, Cheboksary, Ul. K. Marksa 29; tel. 22-41-16; depts: agronomy, mechanization, animal husbandry; library of 83,000 vols; extra-mural faculty.

Dagestan Agricultural Institute: 367032 Dagestan Autonomous Republic, Makhachkala, Ul. M. Gadzhieva 180; tel. 7-25-25; f. 1932; depts: zoo-technics, veterinary, fruit and vegetable growing, accounting; library of 200,000 vols; Rector M. M. ZHAMBULATOV; publ. *Works*.

Don Agricultural Institute: 346493 Rostov oblast, Station Persianovka; tel. 9-36-25; f. 1916; faculties: agronomy, animal husbandry, veterinary; 272 teachers; 4,500 students; library of 400,000 vols; Rector V. I. STEPANOV.

Gorsky State Agricultural University: 362040 North Ossetian Republic, Vladikavkaz, Ul. Kirova 37; tel. 3-23-04; depts: agronomy, animal husbandry, mechanization, economics and management, accounting; library of 208,000 vols; extra-mural faculty.

Irkutsk Agricultural Institute: 664038 Irkutsk, Poselok Molodezhnyi; tel. 23-18-39; f. 1934; depts: agronomy, plant protection, animal husbandry, mechanization, accounting; 290 teachers; 4,800 students; library of 280,000 vols; br. in Chita; Rector A. N. UGAROV.

Ivanovo Agricultural Institute: 153467 Ivanovo, Sovetskaya ul. 45; tel. 2-81-44; f. 1918; depts: agronomy, zootechnics; library of 112,000 vols; Rector N. I. BELONOSOV.

Izhevsk State Agricultural Academy: Udmurt Republic, 426069 Izhevsk, Studencheskaya ul. 11; tel. (3412) 58-99-48; e-mail root@izhsa.udm.ru; f. 1954; depts: agronomy, animal husbandry, veterinary, forestry, mechanization, bookkeeping and agricultural analysis, economics; 295 teachers; 4,300 students; library of 420,000 vols; extra-mural faculty; Pres. Prof. V. V. FOKIN.

Kazan Agricultural Institute: 420015 Kazan, Ul. Karla Marksa 65; tel. 36-65-22; depts: agronomy, mechanization, economics and management, accounting, library of 135,000 vols; Rector S. A. ILYIN.

Kostroma State Agricultural Academy: 157930 Kostroma, P/O Karavaevo; tel. (0942) 54-12-63; fax (0942) 54-34-23; e-mail mobot@ksaa.kostroma.su; f. 1949; depts: agronomy, zootechnics, veterinary science, farm mechanization, automobiles and automobile facilities, service and operation of vehicles and machines, electrification and automation of agricultural production, application of computers, architecture, industrial and civil engineering, economics and management, accountancy and auditing, finance and credit, fundamentals of law in agriculture, agricultural management; library of 510,000 vols; Rector V. I. VOROBEV.

Krasnoyarsk State Agrarian University: 660049 Krasnoyarsk, Pr. Mira 88; tel. and fax (3912) 27-03-86; e-mail adm@kgau.kgtu.krasnoyarsk.su; f. 1953; depts: agroecology, agronomy, animal husbandry, economics, electroenergetics, land exploitation, law, management, mechanization, technology, veterinary medicine; 408 teachers; 6,800 students; library of 318,000 vols; Rector N. V. TSUGLENOK.

Kuban Agricultural University: 350044 Krasnodar, Ul. Kalinina 13; tel. 56-49-42; f. 1991 (fmrly Kuban Agricultural Institute, f. 1922); depts: agrochemistry and soil science, agronomy, tropical and sub-tropical agriculture, veterinary, horticulture and viticulture, animal husbandry, mechanization, plant protection, electrification, construction, law, economics and management, accounting; library of 635,000 vols; Rector I. T. TRUBILIN.

Kurgan Agricultural Institute: 641311 Kurgan obl., Ketovskii raion, selo Lesnikovo; tel. 9-41-40; f. 1944; depts: agronomy, zootechnics, economics, mechanization, industrial and civil construction; library of 358,600 vols; Rector V. D. PAVLOV.

Kursk Prof. I. I. Ivanov Agricultural Academy: 305034 Kursk, Ul. Karla Marksa 70; tel. 3-13-30; f. 1956; depts: agronomy, plant protection, zootechnics, mechanization, economics and management, accounting, agroecology, veterinary medicine, seed processing and storage; library of 130,000 vols; Rector V. D. MOUKHA.

Michurinsk State Agricultural Academy: 393740 Tambov oblast, Michurinsk, Internatsionalnaya ul. 101; tel. (07545) 5-31-37; fax (07545) 5-26-35; e-mail root@mgsxa.mich.fpd.tambov.ru; f. 1931; fruit and vegetable production, viticulture, agronomy, selection and genetics of crops, storing and processing of produce, agroecology, commodity research, gardening, economics and management of agricultural production, livestock production, commerce, book-keeping and auditing, finance and credit; 350 teachers; 4,000 students; library of 300,000 vols; Rector A. I. ZAVRAZHNOV.

Moscow Timiryazev Academy of Agriculture: 127550 Moscow, Timiryazevskaya ul. 49; tel. 976-04-80; fax 976-29-10; f. 1865; seven faculties: agronomy, agricultural chemistry, soil science and ecology, zootechnics, economics, horticulture, agropedagogy; 480 teachers; 2,800 students. Thirty-three research stations and five experimental and instructional farms are attached to the Academy; br. in Kaluga; library of 1,500,000 vols; Rector Prof A. I. PUPONIN; publs *Proceedings of TSHA* (6 a year), *Papers of TSHA* (annually).

Nizhnii Novgorod Agricultural Institute: 603078 Nizhnii Novgorod Pr. Gagarina 97; tel. 66-34-60; telex 151104; fax 66-06-84; f. 1930; depts: agrochemistry, agronomy, animal husbandry, mechanization, accounting, veterinary medicine; 5,000 students; library of 500,000 vols; Rector A. W. GALKIN; publ. *Scientific Works* (annually).

Novgorod Agricultural Institute: 173015 Novgorod, Pskovskaya ul. 3; tel. 7-03-82.

Novosibirsk Agricultural Institute: 630039 Novosibirsk, Ul. Dobrolyubova 160; tel. 67-39-22; depts: agronomy, plant protection, mechanization, economics and management, accounting; library of 252,000 vols; br. in Kemerovo; Rector I. I. GUDILIN.

Omsk State Agricultural University: 644008 Omsk, Institutskaya pl. 2; tel. (3812) 65-17-35; fax (3812) 65-10-72; e-mail genetics@omgau.omsk.su; f. 1918; depts: agrochemistry, agronomy, animal sciences, agricultural engineering, food processing, geodesy, hydrology, veterinary medicine; library of 622,000 vols; Rector N. M. KOLYCHEV; publs *Vestnik OmGAU* (4 a year), *Kirovets* (monthly).

Orel Agricultural Institute: 302040 Orel, Krasnoarmeiskaya ul. 4; tel. 9-40-35.

Orenburg Agricultural Academy: 460795 Orenburg, Ul. Chelyuskintsev 18; tel. (3532) 47-52-30; fax (3532) 47-23-50; f. 1930; depts: agronomy, animal husbandry, veterinary, mechanization, economics and management, accounting, law; 500 teachers; 6,000 students; library of 580,600 vols; Rector N. I. VOSTRIKOV; publ. *Works*.

Penza State Agricultural Academy: 440014 Penza, Botanicheskaya ul. 30; tel. and fax (8412) 69-63-54; e-mail psaca@penza.sura.oom.ru; f. 1951; depts: agronomy, agroecology, animal husbandry, mechanization of agriculture, machine repairing, book-keeping and auditing, economics, administration; 264 teachers; 3,300 students; library of 250,000 vols; Rector Prof. A. F. BYNOKITVATOV.

Perm Academician D. N. Pryanishnikov Agricultural Institute: 614600 Perm, Kommunisticheskaya ul. 23; tel. 32-93-93; f. 1918; depts: agrochemistry and soil science, agronomy, animal husbandry, mechanization, economics and management, accounting; 260 teachers; 4,600 students; library of 320,000 vols; Rector A. A. EROFEEV.

Primorskii Agricultural Institute: 692510 Ussuriisk, Pr. Blyukhera 44; tel. 2-93-90; depts: agronomy, animal husbandry, mechanization, irrigation and land reclamation, forestry, economics and management, accounting; library of 72,000 vols; Rector P. K. SIDORENKO.

Ryazan Professor P. A. Kostychev Agricultural Institute: 390044 Ryazan, Ul. Kostycheva 1; tel. 55-35-01; depts: agronomy, animal husbandry, mechanization, economics and management, accounting; library of 94,000 vols; Rector M. I. SALIKOV.

St Petersburg State Agrarian University: 189620 St Petersburg, Pushkin, Peterburgskoye shosse 2; tel. 470-04-22; fax 465-05-05; f. 1904; depts: agroecology and soil science, agronomy, vegetable growing, plant protection, animal husbandry, farm electrification, economics, engineering, law; 571 teachers; 7,000 students; library of 782,700 vols; br. in Polessk; Rector V. S. SHKRABAK; publ. *Collection of Scientific Research Works* (8 a year).

Samara Agricultural Institute: 446400 Kinel, Poselok Ust-Kinelskii; tel. 4-68-72; f. 1919; depts: agronomy, animal husbandry, mechanization; 210 teachers; 3,500 students; library of 215,000 vols; Rector N. S. SHIBRAEV.

Saratov Agricultural Institute: 410601 Saratov, Pl. Revolyutsii 1; tel. 24-16-28; depts: agronomy, plant protection, forestry, economics and management, accounting; library of 314,000 vols; Rector E. D. MILOVANOV.

Stavropol State Agricultural Academy: 355014 Stavropol, Zootekhnicheskii per. 10; tel. (86522) 22-24-81; fax (86522) 24-65-88; f. 1930; depts: agronomy, animal husbandry, veterinary medicine, mechanization, electrification, economics and management, accounting, plant protection; 450 teachers; 6,500 students; library of 550,000 vols; Rector V. Y. NIKITIN; publ. *Collection of Research Works* (annually).

Tver Agricultural Institute: 171314 Tver, P/o Sakharovo; tel. 39-92-32.

Tyumen Agricultural Institute: 625003 Tyumen, Ul. Respubliki 7; tel. 6-16-43; depts: agronomy, animal husbandry; library.

Ulyanovsk Agricultural Institute: 432601 Ulyanovsk, Bul. Novyi Venets 1; tel. 31-42-72; depts: agronomy, animal husbandry, mechanization, veterinary; library of 80,000 vols; Rector V. A. BELOV.

Urals State Agricultural Academy: 620219 Ekaterinburg, Ul. K. Libknekhta 42; tel. 51-33-63; e-mail root@usaca.ru; depts: agronomy, animal husbandry, veterinary, mechanization; library of 450,000 vols; Rector A. N. SYOMIN.

Velikie Luki State Agricultural Academy: 182100 Pskov oblast, Velikie Luki, pl. V. I. Lenina 1; tel. 3-77-28; f. 1958; depts: agronomy, economics, zoological engineering, mechanization; 245 teachers; 3,200 students; library of 390,000 vols; Rector Prof. V. P. SPASOV; publ. *Works*.

Volgograd State Agricultural Academy: 400041 Volgograd, Institutskaya ul. 8; tel. 43-08-45; fax 43-18-07; f. 1944; depts: agronomy, animal husbandry, farm mechanization, farm electrification, ecology and land reclamation, accounting; 4,000 students; library of 568,000 vols; Rector Acad. A. M. GAVRILOV; publ. *Scientific Information* (2 a year).

Voronezh State Agricultural University: 394087 Voronezh, Ul. Michurina 1; tel. (0732) 52-80-83; telex 153210; fax (0732) 52-81-39; f. 1913; depts: agrochemistry and soil science, agronomy, land surveying, agricultural engineering, agricultural economics, veterinary science, animal sciences, agribusiness, food processing technology; 525 teachers; 7,085 students; library of 870,000 vols; Rector VLADIMIR E. SHEVCHENKO; publ. *Zapiski* (Notes).

Vyatka State Agricultural Academy: 610017 Kirov, Oktyabrsky pr. 133; tel. (8332) 62-97-19; fax (8332) 62-23-17; e-mail vsaa@vit.kirov.ru; f. 1930; depts: agronomy, biology, economics, veterinary medicine, mechanization; library of 407,000 vols; Rector A. K. BOLOTOV.

Yakutsk Agricultural Institute: 677891 Yakutsk, Ul. P. Morozova 2; tel. 2-23-20.

AGRICULTURAL ENGINEERING AND ELECTRIFICATION

Azov-Black Sea Institute of Agricultural Mechanization: 347720 Rostov oblast, Zernograd, Ul. Lenina 21; tel. 3-18-31; library of 192,000 vols; Rector B. M. TITOV.

Chelyabinsk State Agro-engineering University: 454080 Chelyabinsk, Pr. Lenina 75; tel. and fax (3512) 66-65-30; e-mail rec@agroun.chel.su; f. 1930; trains engineers, economists, agronomists, teachers and agro-ecologists for state and private farms and businesses; 400 teachers; 4,000 students; library of 400,000 vols; Rector V. V. BLEDNYKH; publs *Trudy Chimeskh, Vestnik Universiteta*.

Moscow V. P. Goryachkin State University of Agricultural Engineers: 127550 Moscow, Timiryazevskaya ul. 58; tel. 976-36-40; fax 976-78-74; e-mail mgau@mgau.msk.ru; f. 1930; faculties: agricultural mechanization, farm electrification, agricultural technical services, engineering, economics; library of 1,000,000 vols; 380 teachers; 3,000 students; Rector MIKHAIL N. EROCHIN.

Saratov Institute of Agricultural Engineering: 410740 Saratov, Sovetskaya ul. 60; tel. 24-37-66; f. 1932; 320 teachers; 3,500 students; library of 550,000 vols; Rector A. G. RYBALKO.

LAND IMPROVEMENT

Kabardino-Balkar Land Improvement Institute: 360004 Nalchik, Ul. L. Tolstogo 185; tel. 5-69-43.

Moscow Institute of Irrigation and Land Reclamation: 127550 Moscow, Ul. Pryanishnikova 19; tel. 976-29-62; f. 1930; depts: irrigation and land reclamation, mechanization of irrigation and land reclamation; Rector N. A. KHABAROVA.

Moscow Land Exploitation University: 103064 Moscow, Ul. Kazakova 15; tel. 261-31-46; f. 1779; depts: land use planning, applied geodesy, rural architecture, land law; library of 220,000 vols; Rector YU. K. NEUMIVAKIN; publs *Land Boundary Register* (annually), *Rural Architecture* (annually).

Novocherkassk Institute of Engineering Amelioration: 346409 Novocherkassk, Pushkinskaya 111; tel. 5-57-56; f. 1907; depts: irrigation and land reclamation, forestry; 250 teachers; 5,100 students; library of 170,000 vols.

ANIMAL HUSBANDRY AND VETERINARY SCIENCE

Kazan N. E. Bauman State Academy of Veterinary Medicine: Tatarstan, 420074 Kazan, Ul. Sibirskii trakt; tel. 76-15-05; f. 1873; advanced training of veterinary and animal husbandry specialists; 230 teachers; 3,700 students; library of 410,000 vols; Rector Acad. G. Z. IDRISOV; publ. *Nauchnye Trudy* (4–5 a year).

Moscow K. I. Skryabin State Academy of Veterinary Medicine and Biotechnology: 100472 Moscow, Ul. Akad. K. I. Skryabina 23; tel. 377-91-17; f. 1919; faculties: veterinary biological science, animal husbandry, pedagogical, animal products; 360 teachers; 3,500 students; library of 500,000 vols; Rector Acad. A. D. BELOV.

Omsk Veterinary Institute: 664007 Omsk, Oktyabrskaya ul 92; tel. 24-15-35; f. 1918; 130 teachers; 3,000 students; library of 184,000 vols; Rector N. F. BELKOV.

St Petersburg Veterinary Institute: 196006 St Petersburg, Moskovskii pr. 112; tel. 298-36-31; f. 1919; 140 teachers; 1,340 students; library of 194,000 vols; Rector G. S. KUZNETSOV; publ. *Trudy* (Works).

Saratov Animal Husbandry and Veterinary Institute: 410071 Saratov, B. Sadovaya 220; tel. 24-45-32; f. 1918; 213 teachers; 4,500 students; library of 376,500 vols; Rector V. I. VOROBJEV.

Urals State Academy of Veterinary Medicine: 457100 Chelyabinsk oblast, Troitsk, Ul. Gagarina 13; tel. (35163) 2-00-10; fax (35163) 2-04-72; f. 1929; 180 teachers; 1,434 students; library of 200,000 vols; Rector Prof. V. LAZARENKO.

Vologda N. V. Vereshchagin State Dairy Academy: 160901 Vologda oblast, Pos. Molochnoe, Ul. Shmidta 2; tel. 76-17-30; fax 76-10-69; e-mail moloko@vcom.ru; f. 1911; depts: dairy technology, zootechnics, mechanization of agriculture, agronomy, economics, veterinary science; 270 teachers; 4,000 students; library of 420,000 vols; Rector Dr V. N. OSTRETZOV; publ. *Works*.

SOCIAL SCIENCE

Academy of Social Sciences: 117606 Moscow, Pr. Vernadskogo 84; tel. 436-93-30; f. 1946; library of 2,000,000 vols; Rector R. G. YUNOVSKII.

ECONOMICS

GENERAL ECONOMICS

Irkutsk State Academy of Economics: 664015 Irkutsk, Ul. Lenina 11; tel. (3952) 24-10-55; fax (3952) 24-28-38; e-mail kvm@cc.isea.baikal.ru; f. 1930; faculties: law, world economics, finance, economics of mining industry and construction, economics of engineering and road transport, accounting, information systems, labour economics, public administration, management, economics of using natural resources; library of 530,000 vols; Rector M. A. VINOKUROV.

Khabarovsk State Academy of Economics and Law: 680042 Khabarovsk, Tikhookeanskaya ul. 134; tel. (4212) 35-87-37; fax (4212) 72-79-14; auditing and accounting, finance, management, commerce, law, foreign economic relations; 220 teachers; 7,000 students; library of 400,000 vols; Rector Prof. V. A. LIKHOBABIN.

Moscow Institute of Economics and Statistics: 119501 Moscow, Nezhinskaya ul. 7; tel. 442-65-77; faculties: statistics, mechanized processing of economic information, economic cybernetics; library of 150,000 vols; Rector M. A. KOROLEV.

Novosibirsk Institute of National Economy: 630070 Novosibirsk, Kamennaya ul. 56; tel. 24-27-22; f. 1968; faculties of industrial economics, economics and planning of supply, financial economics, accounting and statistics; 4,800 students; library of 250,000 vols; Rector V. N. SHCHUKIN.

Rostov-on-Don Academy of Economics: 344007 Rostov-on-Don, Ul. B. Sadovaya 69; tel. and fax (8632) 65-45-21; e-mail racadem@rosnet.rosmail.com; f. 1931; faculties: international economic relations and marketing, management and information systems, finance and economics, accounting and auditing, economics and business, law; 370 teachers; 7,500 students; library of 500,000 vols; Rector V. S. ZOLOTAREV; publ. *Bulletin* (4 a year).

Russian G. V. Plekhanov Economic Academy: 113815 Moscow M-54, Stremyannyi per. 28; tel. 236-40-94; f. 1907; faculties: general economics, industrial economics, trade economics, finance, economics and planning of supply, trade in industrial goods, trade in foodstuffs, accounting, economic cybernetics, technology, mechanics; 650 teachers; 15,000 students; library of 815,000 vols; Rector V. P. GROSHEV.

Samara State Academy of Economics: 443090 Samara, Ul. Sovetskoi Armii 141; tel. 22-15-42; fax 22-09-53; f. 1931; faculties: finance, industrial economics, commerce and marketing, agribusiness, law, management, accounting; library of 596,000 vols; Rector Prof. A. I. NOSKOV.

Saratov Institute of Economics: 410760 Saratov, Ul. Radishcheva 89; tel. 26-38-50; f. 1918; faculties: industry, agriculture, credit and economics, accounting; 160 teachers; 4,000 students; library of 255,000 vols; Rector K. I. BABAYTSEV.

Urals State University of Economics: 620001 Ekaterinburg, Ul. 8 Marta 62; tel. 22-02-46; f. 1967; faculties: economics, management and international economic relations, commerce, finance, engineering; 427 teachers; 5,422 students; library of 600,000 vols; Rector V. M. KAMYSHOV.

Vladivostok State University of Economics: 690600 Vladivostok, Ul. Gogolya 41; tel. (4232) 25-08-53; fax (4232) 25-09-54; e-mail international@vvsu.ru; f. 1967; schools: economics and law, business administration, fashion and design, information technology and electronic systems; 386 teachers, 3,401 students; library of 250,000 vols; Rector GENNADY I. LAZAREV; publ. *Student's Day* (monthly).

COMMERCE

Belgorod Co-operative Institute: 308023 Belgorod, Sadovaya ul. 116a; tel. 6-73-39; faculties: economics, trade management; br. in Stavropol.

Far Eastern Institute of Trade: 690600 Vladivostok, Okeanskii pr. 19; tel. 2-50-89; f. 1964; faculties: economics, accounting, foodstuffs and non-foodstuffs sciences, technology, organization of public catering; 572 teachers; 2,760 students; library of 220,000 vols; Rector Prof. L. S. PUZYREVSKY.

Institute of Business Studies: 117571 Moscow, Pr. Vernadskogo 82; tel. (095) 434-92-53; fax (095) 434-11-48; f. 1989; independent; library of 10,500 vols; 32 full-time and 150 part-time teachers, 1,500 students; Pres. Dr SERGEI MIASOEDOV.

Krasnoyarsk Institute of Commerce: 660049 Krasnoyarsk, Ul. L. Prushinskoi 14; tel. 21-93-33; f. 1989; 135 mems; library of

205,835 vols; chief officers Y. L. ALEXANDROV, B. K. GUSEV.

Moscow University of Commerce: 125817 Moscow, Smolnaya ul. 36; tel. 458-51-17; telex 412291; f. 1938; faculties: trade economics, trade in industrial goods, trade in foodstuffs, economics and accounting; 700 teachers; 30,000 students; library of 1,000,000 vols; faculties in 19 cities, six brs; Rector I. N. PUZIN.

Moscow University of Consumer Cooperatives: Moscow oblast, 141014 Mytischi, Ul. Very Voloshinoi 12; tel. (095) 582-97-37; fax (095) 582-93-10; f. 1913; fields covered: world economics, jurisprudence, finance and credit, management, marketing, accounting and auditing, economics, commodity science, commerce, economic information systems; 500 teachers; 12,000 students; Rector Prof. A. DANILOV.

Novosibirsk Institute of Commerce: 630087 Novosibirsk, Pr. K. Marksa 26; tel. 46-58-52; f. 1956; faculties: trade economics, trade, accounting, technology; 240 teachers; 7,500 students; library of 197,000 vols; br. in Chita; Rector N. N. PROTOPOPOV.

St Petersburg Institute of Trade and Economics: 194018 St Petersburg, Novorossiiskaya 50; tel. 247-78-06; f. 1930; faculties: trade economics, accounting, trade in industrial goods, trade in foodstuffs, technology; library of 595,300 vols; br. in Krasnoyarsk; Rector V. A. GULIAEV.

FINANCE

All-Russian Distance Institute of Finance and Economics: 121807 Moscow, Ul. Oleko Dundicha 23; tel. (095) 144-85-19; fax (095) 144-86-19; faculties: finance and credit, accounting, management, marketing; library of 1,500,000 vols; depts and brs in 21 Russian cities.

Finance Academy under the Government of the Russian Federation: 125468 Moscow, Leningradsky pr. 49; tel. 943-98-55; fax 157-18-62; f. 1918; depts: finance, credit, insurance, taxation, accounting and audit, international economic relations; 450 teachers; 7,000 students; Rector A. G. GRYAZNOVA.

Kazan Finance and Economics Institute: 420012 Tatarstan, Kazan, Ul. Butlerova 4; tel. 32-66-96; fax 38-30-54; f. 1932; faculties: general economics, business economics, finance and credit; 240 teachers; 5,000 students; library of 330,000 vols; Rector N. G. KHAIRULLIN.

St Petersburg University of Economics and Finance: 191023 St Petersburg, Kanal Griboedova 30/32; tel. 310-38-23; fax 110-56-74; f. 1930 (fmrly Leningrad N. A. Voznesensky Finance and Economics Institute); faculties: economic theory, industrial economics, finance, accounting, statistics, international economic relations, marketing, management, banking; 2,000 teachers; 12,000 students; library of 1m. vols; Rector L. S. TARASEVICH.

ENGINEERING ECONOMICS

St Petersburg State Academy of Engineering and Economics: 191002 St Petersburg, Ul. Marata 27; tel. 112-06-33; telex 121345; fax 112-06-07; f. 1930; faculties: engineering, construction and municipal economy, chemistry, road transport, automation of production management; dept of international business; 244 teachers; 2,944 students; library of 370,000 vols; Rector: A. I. MIKHAILUSHKIN; Scientific Proceedings of the Institute (annually).

State Academy of Management: 109542 Moscow, Ryazanskii pr. 99; tel. (095) 371-13-22; fax (095) 174-62-81; f. 1919 (fmrly Moscow Institute of Management); trains managers in machine-building, metallurgy, power engineering, chemical engineering, transport, construction and urban economy, and in economics and business; 700 teachers; 10,000 students; library of 280,000 vols; Rector A. G. PORSHNEV.

ARTS

Krasnoyarsk State Arts Institute: 660049 Krasnoyarsk, Ul. Lenina 22; tel. 23-35-02.

Moscow Higher School of Industrial Art: 125080 Moscow A-80, Volokolamskoe shosse 9; tel. 158-01-33; f. 1825; refounded 1945; faculties: industrial arts, decorative and applied art, interior design, monumental art; 1,300 students; library of 50,000 vols; Rector A. S. KVASOV.

Moscow V. I. Surikov State Art Institute: 109004 Moscow, Tovarishcheskii per. 30; tel. (095) 912-39-32; fax (095) 912-18-75; depts: painting, graphic arts, sculpture; library of 154,000 vols; Dir L. V. SHEPELEV.

St Petersburg Academy of Art and Design: 191028 St Petersburg, Solyanoi per. 13; tel. 273-38-04; fax 272-84-46; f. 1876 (fmrly St Petersburg V. I. Mukhina Higher Industrial Art School, present name *c.* 1992); faculties: decorative and applied art, monumental arts, design; 230 teachers; 1,100 students; library of 140,000 vols; Rector Prof. A. Y. TALASCHUK.

St Petersburg Repin Institute of Painting, Sculpture and Architecture: 199034 St Petersburg, Universitetskaya nab. 17; tel. 213-61-89; fax 213-65-48; f. 1757; attached to the Academy of Arts of Russia; departments: painting, sculpture, graphic art, architecture, theory and history of art; 160 teachers; 1,370 students; library of 500,000 vols; Rector Prof. O. A. YEREMEYEV.

HUMANITIES

Russian State University for the Humanities: 125267 Moscow, Miusskaya pl. 6; tel. (095) 250-61-18; fax (095) 250-51-09; e-mail afn@rggu.msk.su; library of 1,000,000 vols; Rector Acad. YURI N. AFANASEV.

INTERNATIONAL RELATIONS

Moscow State Institute of International Relations: 117454 Moscow, Pr. Vernadskogo 76; tel. 434-91-74; telex 412172; fax 434-90-66; f. 1944; faculties: international relations, international economic relations, international law, international information, international business and business administration; 844 teachers; 2,700 students; library of 718,000 vols; Rector A. V. TORKUNOV.

LANGUAGES

Irkutsk State Pedagogical Institute of Foreign Languages: 654670 Irkutsk, Ul. Lenina 8; tel. 24-41-20, 29-05-80.

Moscow State Linguistics University: 119837 Moscow, Ul. Ostozhenka 38; tel. 246-86-03; fax 246-83-66; f. 1930; depts of humanities and applied science, English and French teaching, interpretation and translation; in-service training for foreign-language teachers and advanced training for interpreters; Interdisciplinary In-Service Training Institute; Foreign Language Methodology Centre for Non-Philological Universities; Russian language programmes; library of 1,000,000 vols; 1,500 teachers; 10,000 students.

Nizhny Novgorod University of Linguistics: 603155 Nizhny Novgorod, Ul. K. Minina 31A; tel. (8312) 36-15-75; fax (8312) 36-20-49; e-mail ryabov@lunn.sci-nnov.ru; f. 1937; faculties: pedagogical, philological, translation and interpretation, business administration; library of 400,000 vols; Rector Prof. GENNADY P. RYABOV.

Pyatigorsk State Linguistic University: 357533 Pyatigorsk, Pr. Kalinina 9; tel. (86533) 9-35-29; fax (86533) 9-98-23; f. 1939; depts: English, French, German, Spanish, interpreting, state and municipal management; 500 teachers; 3,300 students; library of 700,000 vols; Rector YURI S. DAVIDOV; publs *Problems of Linguistics, Scientific Notes* (annually).

LAW

Extra-Mural Law Institute: 107005 Moscow, Starokirochnyi per. 13; tel. 267-33-62; library of 210,000 vols; five brs; Rector O. G. KUTAFIN.

Saratov State Academy of Law: 410720 Saratov, GSP, Ul. Chernyshevskogo 104; tel. (8452) 25-04-86; fax (8452) 25-32-78; f. 1931; 300 teachers; 3,000 students; library of 500,000 vols; Rector F. A. GRIGORIEV; publ. *Vestnik Saratovskoi gosudarstvennoi academii prava*.

Urals Law Academy: 620066 Ekaterinburg, Komsomolskaya ul. 21; tel. 44-43-63; fax 44-50-34; f. 1931; 310 teachers; 5,300 students; library of 731,688 vols; Rector M. I. KUKUSHKIN; publ. *Russian Law Journal* (quarterly).

LIBRARIANSHIP AND ARCHIVES

Altai State Institute of Culture: 656055 Barnaul, Ul. Yurina 277; tel. 44-57-09, 44-54-57; librarianship, cultural and educational work; br. in Omsk.

Chelyabinsk State Institute of Art and Culture: 454091 Chelyabinsk, Ul. Ordzhonikidze 36A; tel. 33-89-32; f. 1968; training in theatre direction, choreography, ballet, conducting, library science; 508 teachers; 2,700 students; library of 301,000 vols; Rector A. P. GRAI.

Eastern Siberian State Institute of Culture: 670005 Buryat Autonomous Republic, Ulan-Ude, Ul. Tereshkovoi 1; tel. 3-33-22; f. 1960; faculties: library science, bibliography; library of 420,000 vols.

Kazan State Institute of Culture: 420059 Kazan, Orenburgskii trakt 3a; tel. 37-31-27; librarianship, cultural and educational work.

Kemerovo State Institute of Culture: 650012 Kemerovo, Ul. Voroshilova 17; tel. 98-27-97; librarianship, educational and cultural work.

Khabarovsk State Institute of Culture: 680045 Khabarovsk, Krasnorechenskaya ul. 112; tel. 36-30-39; department: library science.

Krasnodar State Institute of Culture and Art: 350072 Krasnodar, Ul. 40-letiya, Pobedy 33; tel. 55-30-63; f. 1967; departments: library science, folk culture; 267 teachers; 2,800 students; library of 152,500 vols; Dir IRINA I. GORLOVA.

Moscow State Institute of Culture: 141400 Moscow oblast, Khimki 6, Bibliotechnaya ul. 7; tel. 570-31-33; f. 1930; librarianship, bibliography, information science, cultural studies, museum studies; 6,000 students; library of 786,814 vols; Rector L. P. BOGDANOV.

Perm State Institute of Culture: 614000 Perm, Ul. Gazety 'Zvezda' 18; tel. 32-45-93; telex 134911; f. 1975; educational and cultural work; 162 teachers; 1,819 students; library of 165,000 vols; Rector Prof. Z. E. VOROBIEVA.

St Petersburg State Institute of Culture: 191065 St Petersburg, Dvortsovaya nab. 4; tel. 314-11-21; f. 1918; librarianship, cultural, musical and theatrical studies, cinema and television; 492 teachers; 5,000 students; library of 600,000 vols; Rector Prof. P. A. PODBOLOTOV; publ. *Trudy Instituta* (Proceedings).

Samara State Institute of Culture: 443010 Samara, Ul. Frunze 167; tel. 32-76-54; f. 1971; librarianship, educational and cultural work; 200 teachers; library of 239,100 vols; Dir Prof.

I. M. KUZMIN; publs *Culture, Creative Activity, Humanity*.

LITERATURE

Moscow Gorkii Literary Institute of the Union of Writers: 103104 Moscow, Tverskoi bul. 25; tel. 291-22-66; library of 106,000 vols.

MUSIC

Astrakhan State Conservatoire: 414000 Astrakhan, Sovetskaya ul. 23; tel. 2-93-11; f. 1969; courses: choral conducting, orchestral instruments, piano, folk instruments, singing, musicology; 450 students; Rector GEORGI I. SLAVNIKOV.

Far-Eastern State Institute of Arts: 690600 Vladivostok, Petr Veliky 3; tel. (4232) 26-49-22; fax (4232) 26-44-88; f. 1962; piano, orchestral instruments, folk instruments, singing, choral conducting, musicology, drama, painting, directing; library of 102,000 vols; Rector I. I. ZASLAVSKY.

Kazan State Conservatoire: 420015 Tatarstan, Kazan, B. Krasnaya ul. 38; tel. 36-55-33; fax 36-56-41; f. 1945; piano, orchestral and folk instruments, composition, singing, choral conducting, musicology; 147 teachers; 614 students; library of 174,600 vols; Rector R. K. ABDULLIN.

Krasnoyarsk State Institute of Fine Arts: 660049 Krasnoyarsk, Ul. Lenina 22; tel. 23-35-02; courses: piano, orchestral instruments, folk instruments, singing, choral conducting, musicology, theatre and cinema acting.

Moscow P. I. Tchaikovsky State Conservatoire: 103009 Moscow K-9, Ul. Gertsena 13; tel. 229-06-41; fax 229-96-59; f. 1866; faculties: piano, orchestral instruments, singing, operatic and symphonic conducting, choral conducting, composition, musicology; 386 teachers; 865 students; library of 1,244,412 vols; Rector M. A. OVCHINNIKOV (acting).

Nizhnii Novgorod M. I. Glinka State Conservatoire: 603600 Nizhnii Novgorod GSP-30, Ul. Piskunova 40; tel. 36-45-27; fax 36-42-37; f. 1946; piano, orchestral and folk instruments, singing, choral conducting, opera and symphony conducting, composition, musicology; 170 teachers; 700 students; library of 130,000 vols; Rector E. B. FERTELMEISTER.

Novosibirsk M. I. Glinka State Conservatoire: 630099 Novosibirsk, Sovetskaya ul. 31; tel. (3832) 22-25-22; fax (3832) 23-95-37; f. 1956; piano, orchestral and folk instruments, singing, symphony and choral conducting, composition, musicology; library of 104,000 vols; Rector Prof. Dr E. G. GURENKO.

Rostov Rakhmaninov State Conservatoire: 344008 Rostov-on-Don, Budennovskii pr. 23; tel. (8632) 62-36-14; fax (8632) 62-35-84; f. 1967 (fmrly Rostov Musical Pedagogical Institute, present name *c.* 1992); courses: piano, orchestral instruments, folk instruments, singing, choral conducting, orchestral conducting, composition, musicology, jazz; 125 teachers; 460 students; library of 200,000 vols; Principal Prof. A. S. DANILOV.

Russian Gnesin Academy of Music: 121069 Moscow, Povarskaya ul. 30–36; tel. (095) 291-15-54; fax (095) 232-69-96; f. 1944; 472 teachers; 1,200 students; Principal S. M KOLOBKOV.

St Petersburg N. A. Rimsky-Korsakov State Conservatoire: 190000 St Petersburg, Teatralnaya pl. 3; tel. (812) 312-21-29; fax (812) 311-82-88; f. 1862; piano, orchestral instruments, singing, operatic, symphonic and choral conducting, composition, musicology, opera and ballet direction, musical comedy; br. in Petrozavodsk; 266 teachers; library of 462,000 vols, 2,431 incunabula, 7,000 MSS of Russian and European composers; Rector V. A. CHERNUSHENKO; publ. *Muzykalnye Kadry* (weekly).

Saratov L. V. Sobinov State Conservatoire: 410600 Saratov, Pr. Kirova 1; tel. (8452) 26-06-38; fax (095) 975-09-33; piano, orchestral and folk instruments, choral conducting, singing, composition, musicology, theatre and cinema acting, musical comedy acting; library of 54,065 vols; Rector Prof. VALERY P. LOMAKO.

Ufa State Institute of Fine Arts: 450025 Bashkir Autonomous Republic, Ufa, Ul. Lenina 14; tel. 23-49-56; departments: piano, orchestral instruments, folk instruments, choral conducting, singing, composition, musicology, theatre and cinema acting, folk theatre, painting; Rector Prof. Z. A. NURGALIN.

Urals M. P. Mussorgskii State Conservatoire: 620014 Ekaterinburg, Pr. Lenina 26; tel. (3432) 51-71-80; fax (3432) 51-73-69; f. 1934; piano, orchestral and folk instruments, singing, choral conducting, composition, musicology, sound production; library of 130,000 vols; Rector Prof. MIKHAIL V. ANDRIANOV; publs *Computers in Musicology, Computers in Education* (every 2–3 years).

Voronezh State Institute of Fine Arts: 394088 Voronezh, Ul. Lizyukova 42; tel. 13-14-81, 13-08-90; piano, orchestral instruments, folk instruments, singing, choral conducting.

THEATRE AND CINEMATOGRAPHY

Ekaterinburg State Theatrical Institute: 620151 Ekaterinburg, Ul. K. Libknechta 38; tel. 51-36-90; f. 1985; 350 students; Rector Prof. V. BABENKO.

Moscow Choreographic Institute: 119146 Moscow, 2-ya Frunzenskaya ul. 5; tel. 247-37-80.

Nemirovich-Danchenko, V. I., Studio-School attached to the Moscow Art Theatre: 103009 Moscow, Tverskaya ul. 6, stroenie 7; tel. 229-39-36; fax 200-42-41; f. 1943; drama and cinema acting, theatre directing, theatre technology, set and costume design, theatre management; 80 teachers; 230 students; library of 20,000 vols; Rector Prof. O. P. TABAKOV.

St Petersburg State Theatre Arts Academy: 192028 St Petersburg, Ul. Mokhovaya 34; tel. 273-15-81; f. 1918; drama and cinema acting, rock opera acting, puppet theatre, stage directing, theatre planning and organization, theatrical equipment and stage planning; 150 teachers; 1,160 students; research dept; library of 350,000 vols; Rector L. G. SOUNDSTREM.

Shchepkin, M. S., Drama School attached to the Malyi Theatre: 103012 Moscow, Pushechnaya ul. 2/6; tel. 923-18-80, 924-38-89; theatre and cinema acting.

Shchukin, B. V., Drama School attached to the E. B. Vakhtangov State Theatre: 121002 Moscow, Ul. Vakhtangova 12a; tel. 241-56-44; theatre and cinema acting.

State Institute of Cinematography: 129226 Moscow, Ul. Vilgelma Pika 3; tel. 181-38-68; f. 1919; direction, shooting, screen play and script writing, cinema studies, economics of cinematography, arts; library of 300,000 vols; 200 teachers; 1,550 students; Rector ALEXANDER NOVIKOV; publs *Tvorchestvo Molodykh* (Creations of Young Artists), etc.

State Institute of Dramatic Art: 103009 Moscow, Sobinovskii per. 6; tel. 290-31-53; drama and cinema acting, musical comedy, ballet direction, general stage management; library of 111,000 vols.

Yaroslavl State Theatre Institute: 150000 Yaroslavl, Pervomaiskaya ul. 43; tel. and fax (0852) 22-23-11; f. 1980; theatrical art; 300 students; library of 25,300 vols; Rector Prof. STANISLAV KLITIN.

RWANDA

Research Institutes

GENERAL

Institut de Recherche Scientifique et Technologique: BP 192, Butare; tel. 30395; telex 22605; fax 30939; f. 1989; pharmacology, energy, social sciences; library of 9,500 vols; Dir-Gen. Dr FRANÇOIS GASENGAYIRE; Dir of Pharmacology Centre ETIENNE HAKIZAMUNGU; Dir of Energy Centre Dr EUGÈNE UWIMANA; Dir of Centre for Rwanda Studies JEAN DE DIEU KAMUHANDA.

AGRICULTURE, FISHERIES AND VETERINARY SCIENCE

Institut des Sciences Agronomiques du Rwanda (ISAR): BP 138, Butare; f. 1962; attached to Min. of Agriculture; 1,000 personnel; library of 2,500 vols; Dir-Gen. Prof. BIKORO MUNYANGANIZI; publs *Annual Report*, *Technical Letters*.

Attached research stations:

Station Rubona: BP 138, Butare; laboratories (chemistry, technology, phytopathology), environmental studies, phytotechnics (living plants, cash crops: coffee, tobacco), zootechnics.

Centre de Sélection Bovine de Songa: BP 138, Butare; stockbreeding (cattle, sheep, poultry); Dir (vacant).

Station Rwerere: BP 73, Ruhengeri; high altitude cultures (wheat, peas, potato); Dir C. SEHENE.

Station Karama: BP 121, Kigali; plant breeding (living plants, irrigation), stockbreeding (cattle, goats); Dir Ir LAMBERT MAYALA.

Arboretum de Ruhande: BP 617, Butare; forestry; Dir Ir ATHANASE MUKURARINDA.

Station Tamira: BP 69, Gisenyi; high altitude cultures (pyrethrum); Dir C. NTAMBABAZI.

Station ISAR/PNAP: BP 73, Ruhengeri; Dir GERVAIS NGERERO.

TECHNOLOGY

Direction des Recherches Géologiques et Minières: Ministère de l'Artisanat, des Mines et du Tourisme, BP 2378, Kigali; tel. 77857; fax 77454; f. 1962; geological services to the Government and private industry; to prepare a geological map of Rwanda; prospecting; library of 6,000 vols; Dir A. NDACYAYISENGA; publ. *Bulletin du Service Géologique* (annually).

Libraries and Archives

Butare

Bibliothèque Universitaire: Campus Universitaire de Butare, Université Nationale du Rwanda, BP 117, Butare; tel. 30272; telex 22605; fax 30870; 138,700 vols; br. in Ruhengeri; Dir EMMANUEL SERUGENDO.

Kigali

Bibliothèque Nationale du Rwanda: BP 624, Kigali; tel. 72730; f. 1989; 6,000 vols; Dir. MICHEL NIYIBIZI.

Service de l'Information et des Archives Nationales: Présidence de la République, BP 15, Kigali; tel. 75432; telex 22517; f. 1979; 7 staff; library of 600 vols; Dir CHARLES UYISENGA; publ. *Presidential Speeches* (annually).

University

UNIVERSITÉ NATIONALE DU RWANDA

BP 56, Butare
Telephone: 30302
Fax: 30121

Founded 1963
Language of instruction: French, English
State control
Academic year: October to June (three terms)
Rector: Dr CHARLES MURIGANDE
Vice-Rectors: Dr JEAN-BOSCO BUTERA (Academic), Dr JEAN-DAMASCÈNE NTAWUKURIRYAYO (Administration and Finance)

Library: see Libraries
Number of teachers: 169
Number of students: 4,057

Publications: *Etudes Rwandaises* (termly), *Annuaire*, *Revue Juridique*.

DEANS

Faculty of Medicine: ANDRÉ MUSEMAKWELI (acting)
Faculty of Sciences: MAREMBO KAREMERA
Faculty of Social and Economic Sciences, and Management: Dr GÉRARD RUTAZIBWA
Faculty of Law: ALOYS MUBERANZIZA
Faculty of Agriculture: JEAN-BOSCO GASHAGAZA (acting)
Faculty of Applied Sciences: Dr PROSPER NKANIKA
Faculty of Education: Dr JEAN-DAMASCÈNE NDAYAMBAJE
Faculty of Letters: Dr KAREGA WA JYONI
Teacher-Training College: Dr FERDINAND KAYOBOKE
School of Journalism: Dr LAURENT NKUSI
School of Modern Languages: LAURENT SINTUKAMAZINA

Colleges

Institut Africain et Mauricien de Statistique et d'Economie Appliquée: BP 1109, Kigali; tel. 8-4989; f. 1975 by the OCAM states; 3-year diploma course; 7 staff, 38 students; library of 9,184 vols; Dir SÉRIGNE T. DIASSE; publ. *Rapport d'enquête* (annually).

Institut Supérieur des Finances Publiques (ISFP): BP 1514, Kigali; tel. 74302; f. 1987; attached to the Ministry of Finance; offers 2-year courses in the financial aspects of public administration; library; Dir JEAN-BAPTISTE BYILINGIRO.

SAINT LUCIA

Libraries and Archives

Castries

Central Library of St Lucia: POB 103, Castries; tel. (809-45) 22875; f. 1847; part of Min. of Education and Culture; government public library; 146,000 vols; Dir of Library Services NAULA WILLIAMS.

St Lucia National Archives: POB 3060, La Clery, Castries; tel. 452-1654; 3,000 vols; unselected government records; specialized historical collections; Archivist MARGOT THOMAS.

Museums and Art Galleries

Castries

St Lucia National Trust: POB 595, Castries; tel. 452-5005; fax 453-2791; e-mail natrust@candw.lc; f. 1975; responsible for Pigeon Island (history, geology, natural history), Fregate Islands (Amerindian history, wildlife), Maria Islands Nature Reserve; documentation centre; Exec. Dir PATRICIA CHARLES; publ. *Conservation News* (quarterly).

College

University of the West Indies, School of Continuing Studies: University Centre, POB 306, The Morne, Castries; tel. 452-3866; fax 452-4080; f. 1948; continuing education; houses the University's Distance Teaching Experiment (UWIDITE) linking the university campuses with eight university centres; Resident Rep. MATTHEW VERNON ROBERTS.

SAMOA

Learned Societies

GENERAL

Unesco Office for the Pacific States: Box 5766, Mata'utu-Uta, Apia; tel. 24276; telex 209; fax (685) 22253; f. 1984; integrated field office of Unesco; co-operation with the Pacific States to promote education, science, culture, communications, social and human sciences, information management, youth, etc.; Dir EDNA TAIT.

Libraries and Archives

Apia

Avele College Library: POB 45, Apia; 5,000 vols serving 520 students.

Nelson Memorial Public Library: POB 598, Apia; f. 1959; 90,000 vols; 1 branch library on Savaii island; 1 bookmobile; special collections: R. L. Stevenson, Samoa and Pacific; Senior Librarian Miss MATAINA TUATAGALOA TE'O.

Museums and Art Galleries

Vailima

Robert Louis Stevenson Museum: Vailima; Stevenson's house and estate.

University

IUNIVESITE AOAO O SAMOA (National University of Samoa)

POB 5768, Apia
Telephone: 21911
Founded 1988
Vice-Chancellor: TAU'ILI'ILI UILI
Registrar: P.C. PHILIP
Librarian: IOANE LAFOA'I
Number of teachers: 28
Number of students: 328

HEADS OF FACULTIES

Faculty of Arts: Mrs LUFI TAULE'ALO
Faculty of Science : SAPA SAIFALE'UPOLU

Colleges

Avele College: POB 45, Apia; f. 1924, under Education Department from 1966; five-year courses; 520 students, including students from the Tokelau Islands; Principal L. A. SANERIVI.

University of the South Pacific, School of Agriculture: Private Bag, Apia; tel. 21-671; telex 64251; fax 22-933; e-mail fuatai_l@samoa.net; f. 1977; academic year: February to December; library of 22,000 vols; diploma, degree and higher degree courses; 19 teachers; 130 (full-time) students; Pro Vice-Chancellor Dr LAFI FUATAI (acting); publs *Journal of South Pacific Agriculture* (quarterly), *IRETA South Pacific Agriculture News* (monthly), *The South Pacific Agricultural Teacher* (quarterly). (See also under Fiji.)

SAN MARINO

Libraries and Archives

San Marino

Biblioteca di Stato: Contrada Omerelli, 47031 San Marino; tel. 991918; over 10,000 vols, from 15th century to the present.

Museums and Art Galleries

San Marino

Museo di Stato – Galleria d'Arte Moderna e Contemporanea: Scala Bonetti 2, 47031 San Marino; tel. 882670; fax 882679.

University

UNIVERSITÀ DEGLI STUDI

Contrada del Collegio, 47890 San Marino

Telephone: 882541
Fax: 882545
E-mail: grazia@unirsm.sm

Founded 1987
State control

Rector: Prof. ATTILIO ATTO
Administrative Secretary: PAOLA PALMUCCI
Librarian: Dr ALESSIA GHIRONZI

Library of 30,000 vols
Number of students: 423

DEANS

Preparatory Department: Prof. RENZO CANESTRARI

Department of Semiotic and Cognitive Studies: PATRIZIA VIDI

Department of History: Prof. RENATO ZANGHERI

Department of Technology: GIORGIA PETRONI

SÃO TOMÉ E PRÍNCIPE

Libraries and Archives

São Tomé

Arquivo Histórico de São Tomé e Príncipe: CP 87, São Tomé; 5,000 boxes of documents; 2,000 vols of bibliography; Dir MARIA NAZARÉ DE CEITA.

Biblioteca do Ministério de Agricultura e Pesca: CP 47, São Tomé; tel. 22126; telex 230; f. 1973; 1,750 vols; Librarian TOMÉ DE SOUSA DA COSTA.

Biblioteca Municipal: São Tomé.

Centro de Documentação Técnica e Científica: São Tomé; tel. 22585; 45,000 vols of specialized documents on agriculture, fisheries, economics; 2,000 periodicals; Dir MARIA ROSÁRIO ASSUNÇÃO.

Museums and Art Galleries

São Tomé

Museu Nacional: CP 87, São Tomé; tel. 21874; history, ethnography, religious art.

SAUDI ARABIA

Learned Societies

BIBLIOGRAPHY, LIBRARY SCIENCE AND MUSEOLOGY

Arab Regional Branch of the International Council on Archives (ARBICA): Institute of Public Administration, POB 205, Riyadh 11141; tel. 476-1600, ext. 462; telex 201160; close collaboration with ICA, UNESCO and other international organizations; mems: 20 Arab countries; Pres. A. TAMINI (Tunisia); Sec.-Gen. FAHD AL-ASKAR (Saudi Arabia); publ. *Arab Archives Journal* (annually).

EDUCATION

Arab Bureau of Education for the Gulf States: POB 3908, Riyadh 11481; tel. (1) 4774644; telex 401441; fax (1) 4783165; f. 1975 to co-ordinate and integrate the efforts of the mem. states (Bahrain, Kuwait, Oman, Qatar, Saudi Arabia and the United Arab Emirates) in the fields of education, science and culture; aims to unify the educational system for all the mem. states; Gulf Arab States Educational Research Center: see Kuwait chapter; established Arabian Gulf University in Bahrain; Dir-Gen. Dr ALI M. AL-TOWAGRY.

NATURAL SCIENCES

Biological Sciences

Saudi Biological Society: King Saud University, POB 2455, Riyadh 11451; tel. 4675835; fax 4675833; f. 1975; 350 mems; Pres. Dr I. A. IRIF; Sec.-Gen. Dr F. AL-MANA; publs *Proceedings, Abstract and Programme of Annual Conference, Journal of the Saudi Biological Society, Special Publications*.

Research Institutes

GENERAL

King Faisal Centre for Research and Islamic Studies: POB 51049, Riyadh 11543; tel. 4652255; telex 405470; fax 4659993; f. 1983; part of King Faisal Foundation; research in various fields of Islamic civilization; library of over 80,000 books, 2,100 periodicals, 20,000 original MSS; 13,000 microfilmed MSS; audio-visual library of 10,000 items; children's library of 17,000 vols; Chair. HRH Prince TURKI AL-FAISAL; Sec.-Gen. Dr ZAID ABDULMOHSIN AL-HUSAIN; publ. *Al-Faisal* (monthly).

EDUCATION

Centre for Research in Islamic Education: POB 1034, Mecca; tel. (2) 5565677; telex 540295; fax (2) 5586707; f. 1980 by the Organization of the Islamic Conference, affiliated 1982 to Umm Al-Qura University; aims to promote Islamic values in education through research, development and training; Dir Dr ABDURRAZZAK AHMED ZAFAR; publ. books and monographs.

HISTORY, GEOGRAPHY AND ARCHAEOLOGY

King Abdul Aziz Research Centre: POB 2945, Riyadh 11461; fax (1) 441-7020; f. 1972 in memory of the late king; historical, geographical, literary and cultural material; library of 28,000 vols, 200 periodicals; also the private library of the late king (2,000 vols); historical archive including documents in various languages, especially Turkish and English, and Arabic MSS; King Abdul Aziz Memorial Hall shows events in the late king's life, especially his military battles; Sec.-Gen. Dr FAHD AL-SEMMARI; publ. quarterly cultural magazine.

TECHNOLOGY

Bureau de Recherches Géologiques et Minières (BRGM): POB 1492, Jeddah. (See main entry under France.)

Libraries and Archives

Jeddah

Educational Library: General Directorate of Broadcasting, Press and Publications, Jeddah.

Mecca

Abbas Kattan Library: Mecca; 7,800 vols, 200 MSS.

Library of Alharam: Mecca; 6,000 vols.

Madrasat Ahl Al Hadith Library: Mecca.

Medina

Islamic University Library: POB 170, Medina; tel. 8474080; telex 570022; fax 8474560; f. 1961; consists of a central library and eleven brs; 143,000 vols, 27,772 MSS, 8,761 microfilms, 3,247 theses.

King Abdul Aziz Library: Medina; tel. 8232134; fax 8232126; f. 1983; 120,000 vols and MSS; Dir D. ABDULRAHMAN BIN SULIMAN ALMUZINY.

Riyadh

Institute of Public Administration Library: POB 205, Riyadh 11141; tel. 4768888; telex 404360; fax 4792136; e-mail library@ipa.edu.sa; f. 1961; 227,800 vols in Arabic, English and French, 1,173 periodical titles, 53,585 Saudi public records, 4,586 official publications, 32,237 microforms, 764 CD-ROMs; Dir-Gen. EN MOSTAFA SADHAN.

King Abdulaziz Public Library: POB 86486, Riyadh 11622; tel. 491-1300; telex 406444; fax 491-1949; f. 1985; 275,000 vols (Arabic and non-Arabic), 1,100 current periodicals, 2,500 MSS, 53,000 historic documents on microform, 5,000 audiovisual items, doctoral dissertations; equestrian information; Supervisor-Gen. FAISAL A. AL-MUAAMMAR.

King Saud University Libraries: POB 22480, Riyadh 11495; tel. 4676148; fax 4676162; e-mail f10L001@ksu.edu.sa; f. 1957; central library and 7 branches; 1.1 million vols, 3,000 periodicals, 20,000 MSS, 90,000 government publications, 22,000 microfilm items, 4,000 microfiche items, 16,000 audiovisual items; Dean Dr SULAIMAN AL-OGLA; publs journals.

Library of the King Abdul Aziz City for Science and Technology: POB 6086, Riyadh 11442; tel. 488-3444; fax 488-3756; 50,000 vols, 75,000 technical reports.

National Library: King Faisal St, Riyadh; f. 1968; *c.* 37,000 vols in Arabic, English, French; 150 MSS; Dir ABDUR RAHMAN AL SARRA.

Saudi Arabian Standards Organization Information Centre: POB 3437, Riyadh 11471; tel. (1) 452-0000; telex 401610; fax (1) 452-0193; f. 1972; library of 10,000 vols, 650,000 nat., int. and foreign standards; Dir MOHAMMAD ALMESHARI.

Museums and Art Galleries

Riyadh

Museum of Archaeology and Ethnography: Riyadh; f. 1978; exhibits from Stone Age, the 'Age of Trade', and 'After the Revelation' (rise and spread of Islam).

Universities

ISLAMIC UNIVERSITY OF IMAM MUHAMMAD IBN SAUD

POB 5701, Riyadh 11432

Telephone: 2580812
Telex: 407956
Fax: 2590271

Founded 1953, University status 1974
State control
Language of instruction: Arabic
Academic year: August to June

President: Dr ABDULLAH IBN YOUSUF AL-SHIBL
Vice-Presidents: Dr MOHAMMAD IBN ABDULRAHMAN AL-RUBAYE, Dr SULAIMAN IBN ABDULLAH ABA AL-KHALIL
Vice-Rector for the Islamic Institutes: Dr SALEH IBN MOHAMMAD AL-HASSAN
Dean of Institutes Abroad: Dr BANDAR IBN FAHAD AL-SEWILEM
Dean of Students: Sheikh ALI IBN SULAIMAN AL-SALHI
Dean of Postgraduate Studies: Dr ABDUL AZIZ IBN MUHAMMED AL-FAISAL
Dean of Academic Research: Dr ABDULLAH IBN ABDULLRAHMAN AL-RABEE
Dean of Admission and Registration: Dr ABDULAZIZ IBN RASHID AL-OBAIDI
Dean of Libraries: Dr KHALID IBN ABDULATIF AL-ARFAJ
Dean of University Centre for Community Service and Continuing Education: Dr ALI IBN ABDULLAH AL-ZIBEN
Dean of Admission and Students' Affairs in Qassim: Dr MEZAYAD IBN IBRAHIM AL-MEZAYAD
Dean of Admission and Students' Affairs in the South: Dr SAAD IBN HUSAIN OTHMAN

Number of teachers: 1,648
Number of students: 39,938

Publications: *The Statistical Book, University Bulletin,* college magazines and guides.

DEANS AND DIRECTORS

College of Islamic Law (Sharia): Dr ABDULRAHMAN IBN MOHAMMAD AL-SADHAN
College of Arabic Language: Dr AHMED IBN HAFEZ AL-HAKAMI
College of Fundamentals of Religion: Dr MOHAMMAD IBN ABDULLAH AL-FEHAID

College of Social Sciences: Dr ASSAF IBN ALI AL-HAWASS
College of Islamic Call and Mass Communication: Dr ABDULAZIZ IBN IBRAHIM AL-ASKAR
College of Islamic Law and Fundamentals of Religion (Al-Qassim): Dr ABDUL RAHMAN AL-MEZAINI (acting)
Higher Judiciary Institute: Dr IBRAHIM IBN ABDULLAH AL-BARAHIM
College of Islamic Call Dawa (Medina): Dr MOSTAFA IBN OMAR HALABI
College of Arabic and Social Sciences (Qassim): Dr MOHAMMAD IBN SULAIMAN-RAJHI
College of Islamic Law and Fundamentals of Religion (in the South): Dr ABDULAZIZ IBN ALI AL-GHAMDI
College of Arabic and Social Sciences (in the South): Dr ALI IBN MUHAMMAD ARISH
College of Islamic Law and Islamic Studies (Ahsaa): Dr MOHAMMAD IBN ALI AL-MULHIM
Institute for Teaching Arabic to Non-Arabs (Riyadh): Dr MOHAMMAD IBN IBRAHIM AL-UHAIDIB
Female University Study Centre: Dr ABDUL-KARIM IBN MOHAMMAD ABDUL KARIM AL-HEMEDI

ISLAMIC UNIVERSITY AT MEDINA

POB 170, Medina
Telephone: 847-4080
Telex: 570022
Fax: 8274560

Founded 1961
State control
Language of instruction: Arabic

Chancellor: Dr ABDULLAH BIN SALAH AL-ABID
Vice-Rector: ABDUL MUHSIN BEN HAMAD AL-ABBAD

Number of teachers: 620
Number of students: 3,140

COLLEGES

College of Islamic Law (Sharia)
College of Dawa and Usul-Al-Din
College of the Holy Koran and Islamic Studies
College of the Arabic Language
College of Prophet Sayings (Hadeith) and Islamic Studies

KING ABDULAZIZ UNIVERSITY

POB 1026, Jeddah 21441
Telephone: (2) 952011
Fax: (2) 6405974

Founded 1967
State control
Languages of instruction: Arabic and English
Academic year: September to June

President: Prof. GHAZIO O. MADANI
Vice-President: Prof. OSAMA S. TAYEB
Vice-President for Graduate Studies and Academic Research: Prof. FOUAD M. GHAZALI
Supervisor-General for Administration and Financial Affairs: Dr SAMIR A. MURSHID
Librarian: Dr MOFAKHAR H. KHAN

Library of 500,000 vols
Number of teachers: 1,145
Number of students: 30,773

Publications: research publications, bulletins.

DEANS

Faculty of Arts and Humanities: Dr M. A. ABOZEID
Faculty of Economics and Administration: Prof. A. A. SOFI
Faculty of Science: Prof. M. A. ALHARBI
Faculty of Marine Science: Dr O. A. HASHIM
Faculty of Earth Sciences: Dr M. O. NASSIEF
Faculty of Engineering: Dr M. S. AL-JIFFRI
Faculty of Medicine and Allied Sciences: Dr S. A. MIRA
Faculty of Meteorology, Environment and Arid Land Agriculture: Dr R.A. KABLI
Faculty of Education: Dr A. I. HAFIZ
Faculty of Dentistry: Prof. H. H. FATANI

PROFESSORS

Faculty of Arts and Humanities:
AL-BAGHDADI, M. M., Arabic Literature
AL-DIGS, K. S., Islamic Literature
AL-JERASH, M. A., Climatology and Quantitative Methods
AL-KHERIJI, A. M., Social Development
AL-ZEID, I. M., History
ANQAWI, A. A., Medieval Islamic History
BAGADER, A. A., Social Changes
OMER, M. Z., Modern History
TASHKANDI, A. S., Arabic Manuscripts

Faculty of Economics and Administration:
AL-AMRI, B. O., Civil Law
AL-SOBIANI, A. A., Administration and Management Planning
ALAKI, M. A., Administration and Management Relations
AL-JEFRI, Y. A., Business Administration
ALSABBAB, A. A., Administration and Management Relations
BAIOUMI, A. M., Cost and Management Accounting
BAMOKHRAMA, A. S., Economics
FADEL, S. Y., International Relations
HASANAIN, O. S., Cost Accounting
MADANI, G. O., Finance and Investment
OMRAN, O. A., Law
SOFI, A. A., Financial Administration
ZA'ED, M. E., Cost Accounting
ZOBAIR, M. O., Monetary Theory

Faculty of Science:
ABOU-ZAID, A. A., Fermentation
AHMAD, I., Theoretical Nuclear Physics
AL-DESSOUKI, T. A., Laser Optics
ALHARBI, M. A., Theoretical Nuclear Physics
AL-SAYAD, G. M., Statistics
BAESHIN, N. A., Genetics
BANAGAH, A. A., Parasitology
BAGHLAF, A. O., Chemistry
BASAHEL, S. N., Chemistry
ELDIN, H. M., Environmental Microbiology
EL-MASHAK, E. M., Biophysics
EZMIRLI, T. S., Chemistry
FARAG, A. A., Vertebrate Zoology
GHANEM, K. M., Biotechnology
KHOJA, S. M., Enzymes and Metabolic Regulation
MAGHRABI, Y. M., Plant Physiology
MELIBARI, A. A., Biology
RAFI, M., Experimental Molecular Physics
SABBAK, O. A., Chemistry
SAHAB, S. M., Mathematics
SEJININ, M. J., Plant Pathology
SHAHAB, F., Theoretical Particle Physics
SOLEIMAN, A. H., Chemistry
TAHER, M. O., Entomology (Bionomics)
TAWFIK, K. A., Plant Pathology

Faculty of Engineering:
ABD. EL-LATIF, A. K., Mechanical Design and Stress Analysis
ABDEL RAHMAN, M. M., Aerodynamics
ABDIN, M. F., Metrology and Advanced Manufacturing Technology
ABDUL-MAJID, S., Nuclear Instrumentation
ABOKHASHABA, A., Metal Cutting and Spare Parts
ABOLANIN, G. M., Heat and Energy Transfer
ABOLFARAJ, W. H., Industrial Engineering
ABORAZIZAH, O. S., Civil Engineering
AHMED, K. M., Structure and Construction
AKYURT, M., Mechanisms and Robotics
AL-IDRISI, M. M., Operational Research
AL-NOURY, S. I., Structure
ALP, T. Y., Physical Metallurgy
ALY, S. E., Desalination Technology and Two-Phase Flow
AWAD, A. E., Biotechnology, Floriculture
DARWISH, M. A., Rock Blasting
ELGILLANI, D. A., Mineral Processing and Metallurgy
EL-NAGGAR, M. M., Extractive Metallurgy
FATHALAH, K., Heat and Mass Transfer
FATTAH, A. A., Nuclear Reactor Safety and Nuclear Desalination
FOUAD, A. A., Nuclear Desalination
GHAZALI, F. M., Geotechnics
HAQUE, M. Z., Mine Management and Mining Law
KUTBI, I. I., Nuclear Desalination
MOHAMED, S. E., Electrical Power Engineering
NAHHAS, M. N., Aviation Engineering
MOUSSA, H. A., Electrical Power Engineering
NAHHAS, M. N., Aviation Engineering
NAJJAR, Y., Gas Turbines, Engines and Energy Systems
NAWAIR, M. H., Human Factors
RAIH, M. A., Aviation Engineering
RUSHDI, A. M., Computer Engineering and Electrical Communication
SABBAGH, J. A., Heat and Energy Transfer
WAFA, F. F., Structural Engineering
WANAS, M. A., Electronics
YORULMAZ, Y. K., Petroleum Refining and Petrochemicals

Faculty of Medicine and Allied Sciences:
ABDULMONAM, N. A., Community Medicine
AHMAD, A. O., Haematology
AJABNOOR, M. A., Biochemistry
AL-ARDAWI, M. S., Biochemistry
AL-AWWAD, A. M., Chemistry
AL-BADWI, A. A., Surgery
AL-JOHARI, K. M., Anatomy
AL-KHATEEB, A. M., Physics
AL-MATRAWI, U. M., Parasitology
AL-QADASI, A. A., Biochemistry
AL-SHAIKH, S. A., Paediatrics
ALI, F. M., Medical Technology
ATTALLAH, A. A., Physiology
BASALAMAH, A. H., Obstetrics and Gynaecology
FATANI, H. H., Medicine
ISLAM, S. I., Pharmacology
KHAN, N. M., Anatomy
MATIX, F. A., Microbiology
MUKHTAR, A. M., Surgery
OSMAN, O. O., Pharmacology
RAFFAH, H. M., Surgery
RAZIK, S. M., Surgery
SAJINEE, S. A., Haematology
SALAMA, H. S., Biology
SALMAN, KH. M., Surgery
SHARIF, M. A., Radiology
SHARIF, M. T., Anatomy
SHOBOKSHI, O. A., Medicine
SIRAJ, A. A., E.N.T.
SOLIMAN, S. A., Chemistry
SUKKAR, M. Y., Physiology
SULAIMAN, N. K., Community Medicine
TAYEB, O. S., Pharmacology
TILMISANY, A. M., Pharmacology
YOUSIF, K. M., Surgery
ZAFAR, M. N., Radiology
ZAHRAN, F. M., E.N.T.

Faculty of Earth Sciences:
ALLOUSH, M. A., Building Materials
AL-MAHDI, O. R., Mineral Resources
AL-NASSER, H. S., Geophysics
AL-SHANTI, A. M., Mineralogy
BASAHEL, A. N., Structural Geology
MARZOUKI, M. H., Petrology and Mineralogy
NASSIEF, A. O., Petrology and Mineralogy
RADEEN, A. A., Petrology and Mineralogy
SHAREEF, F. A., Petroleum and Stratigraphy
SHEHATA, W. M., Engineering Geology

Faculty of Marine Sciences:
AHMAD, F., Residual and Tidal Currents
BEHAIRY, A. K. A., Modern Marine Sediments
EL-NAKKADI, A. N., Biochemistry
KHAFAJI, A. K., Marine Plant Physiology
NIAZ, G. R., Marine Biochemistry

Faculty of Meteorology, Environment and Arid Land Agriculture:

ABDURAZZAK, M. G., Water Resources
ABOHASSAN, A. A., Forest Management
AL-HASHIM, G. M., Environmental Toxicology and Health
AL-HIFNY, A. M., Entomology (Bees)
ARAFA, A. S., Environmental Health
EL-AGAMY, S. A., Horticulture
GOKNIL, M. H., Air Pollution
SAMARRAI, S. M., Genetics and Plant Breeding
SHAHEEN, M. A., Genetics and Fruit Breeding

Faculty of Education:

ABDULRADHI, H. M., Physics and Theory
AL-MOJADDADI, M. H. M., Shariah and Legal System
AL-OQABI, A. H., Modern History
AL-SHATAIRI, B. A., Chemistry
BADAWI, A. A., History
BADAWI, F. A., Ancient History
BAMASHMOOS, S. M., Educational Planning
BEDAIR, A. H. M., Biochemistry
HAMID, M. A. I., Weaving
HASSAN, N. M. A., Psychology
JALLOON, A. D., Archery
KHALIL, M. S. M., Fish Anatomy
KHATIR, K. I. M., Tradition of the Prophet
KHOGALI, M. M., Human Geography
MADBROOK, N. A., Principles of Language
REDWAN, M. N., Wrestling
SHAIKH, A. A., English Language Teaching Methods
SHEHATAH, M. N., Entomology

Faculty of Dentistry:

ABDULRAHMAN, A., Paediatric Dentistry
AL-JEYAR, I. L., Operative
AL-KHATEB, M. M., Fixed Prosthodontics
AL-SABBAGH, A. M., Oral Surgery
FARGHALY, M. M., Dental Public Health
KAMAR, A. A., Dental Biomaterials
KATALDO, A., Oral Pathology
MASOUD, A. J., Endodontics
MOHAMED, M. A., Operative
MOUSTAFA, M. A., Removable Prosthodontics, Partial Dentures
NADA, A. M., Removable Prosthodontics, Partial Dentures
OMAR, T. A., Oral Pathology
SAMAH, A., Paediatric Dentistry
SHARQAWI, M. M., Operative
SHOUKRY, M. M. S., Periodontics

ATTACHED RESEARCH INSTITUTES

Islamic Economics Research Centre: Dir Dr M. A. ELGARI.

King Fahad Medical Research Centre: Dir Dr Z. M. BANJAR.

KING FAHAD UNIVERSITY OF PETROLEUM AND MINERALS

Dhahran 31261

Telephone: (3) 860-0000
Fax: (3) 860-3306

Founded 1963, University status 1975
State control with semi-autonomous operation under a Board of the University
Languages of instruction: English (for science and engineering) and Arabic
Academic year: September to June (summer semester: June to August)

Chair. of Board of Trustees: HE The Minister of Higher Education Dr KHALID M. AL-ANGARY
Rector: Dr ABDULAZIZ A. AL-DUKHAYYIL
Vice-Rectors: Dr ABDULLAH H. AL-ABDUL-GADER (Research and Graduate Studies), Dr SALEH A. BAKHREBAH (Applied Research), Dr KHEDAIR S. AL-KHEDAIR
Dean, Admissions and Registration: Dr MAMDOUH M. NAJJAR
Dean of Library Affairs: Dr ABDUL-RAHIM A. AL-MEER

Library of 333,000 vols
Number of teachers: 806
Number of students: 7,602

Publications: *Arabian Journal for Science and Engineering* (4 a year), *Research Newsletter* (2 a year), *Science Newsletter* (2 a year), *Engineering Newsletter* (2 a year), *CED Newsletter* (2 a year), *CIM Trends* (2 a year), Library Newsletter (2 a year), *Graduate Bulletin* (every 2 years), *Undergraduate Bulletin* (every 2 years).

DEANS

Sciences: Dr ABDULAZIZ S. AL-HARTHI
Engineering Sciences and Applied Engineering: Dr HABIB I. ABUALHAMAYEL
Industrial Management: Dr MOHAMMED A. AL-SAHLAWI
Environmental Design: Dr ABDUL-MOHSEN AL-HAMMAD
Computer Science and Engineering: Dr KHALED S. AL-SULTAN
Graduate Studies: Dr ABDULLAH M. AL-SHEHRI

DEPARTMENTAL CHAIRMEN

College of Sciences:

Chemistry: Dr ABDUL-RAHMAN A. AL-ARFAJ
Earth Sciences: Dr ZAKI Y. AL-HARARI
Islamic and Arabic Studies: Dr ADNAN A. AKKAD
Mathematical Sciences: Dr WALID S. AL-SABAH
Physics: Dr MOHAMMAD A. GARWAN

College of Computer Science and Engineering:

Computer Engineering: Dr KHALID M. AL-TAWIL
Information & Computer Science: Dr TALAL H. MAGHRABI
Systems Engineering: Dr ABDULBASIT A. ANDIJANI

College of Engineering Sciences:

Chemical Engineering: Dr ABDULLAH A. SHAIKH
Civil Engineering: Dr SAHEL N. ABDUL-JAUWAD
Electrical Engineering: Dr SAMIR A. AL-BAIYAT
Mechanical Engineering: Dr MOHAMMAD O. BUDAIR
Petroleum Engineering: Dr ABDULAZIZ A. AL-MAJED

College of Industrial Management:

Management and Marketing: Dr SALEM M. S. AL-GHAMDI
Accounting and Management Information Systems: Dr MOHAMMAD A. AL-KHALDI
Finance and Economics: Dr SULAIMAN A. AL-SAKRAN

College of Environmental Design:

Architectural Engineering: Dir Dr ISMAIL M. BUDAIWI
Architecture: Dr THAMER A. AL-RUQAIB
City and Regional Planning: Dir Dr ADEL S. AL-DOSARY
Construction Engineering and Management: Dir Dr MOHAMMED O. JENNADI

Research Institute:

Petroleum and Gas Technology: Dr ALI G. MA'ADHAH (Man.)
Energy Resources: Dr FIDA F. AL-ADEL (Man.)
Geology, Minerals and Remote Sensing: Dr ALKHATTAB G. AL-HINAI (Man.)
Water Resources and Environment: Dr MOHAMMAD B. AMIN (Man.)
Metrology, Standards and Materials: Dr NUREDDIN M. ABBAS (Man.)
Economic and Industrial Research: Dr KHALID A. BUBSHAIT (Man.)
Development and Manufacturing: Dr TALAL O. HALAWANI (Man.)
Programme Development and Technology Transfer: Dr G. PARRY JONES (Man.)

KING FAISAL UNIVERSITY

POB 1982, Dammam 31441; *and* POB 380, Al-Hassa 31982

Telephone: (Dammam) (3) 8577000; (Al-Hassa) (3) 5800000
Telex: (Dammam) 870020; (Al-Hassa) 861028
Fax: (Dammam) (3) 8576748; (Al-Hassa) (3) 5801243

Founded 1975
State control
Languages of instruction: Arabic and English
Academic year: September to January, February to June

President: Prof. Dr YUSSUF M. AL-GINDAN
Vice-President: Dr ABDULAZIZ ABDULLATIF AL-QURAIN (Dammam)
Vice-President for Academic Affairs: Dr SAAD M. AL-HAREKY (Al-Hassa)
Vice-President for Graduate Studies and Scientific Research: Dr SAAD A. AL-BARRAK (Al-Hassa)
Secretary-General: Dr SAAD MUHAMMAD AL-HAREKY
Librarian: Dr ADEL A. AL-HAZAB (Al-Hassa)

Number of teachers: 790
Number of students: 10,972

DEANS

College of Agricultural and Food Sciences (Al-Hassa): Dr ABDULREHMAN I. AL-MAGEL
College of Architecture and Planning (Dammam): MOHAMMED SULAIMAN AL-MANSOUR
College of Education (Al-Hassa): Dr DAKHEL D. AL-HARTHI
College of Management Sciences and Planning (Al-Hassa): Dr SAUD FAYAD AL-FAYAD
College of Medicine and Medical Sciences (Dammam): Dr FAHD ABDULAZIZ AL-MOHANNA
College of Veterinary Medicine and Animal Resources (Al-Hassa): Dr ADEL I. AL-AFALAQ
Graduate Studies (Al-Hassa): Dr MOHAMMED A. AL-ABDULSALAM

KING SAUD UNIVERSITY

POB 2454, Riyadh 11451

Telephone: (1) 467-0000
Telex: 401019
Fax: (1) 467-8301

Founded 1957 as Riyadh University, name changed 1982
State control
Language of instruction: Arabic (English in Medicine and Engineering)
Academic year: October to June

President: Dr AHMED MOHAMMAD AL-DHOBAIB
Vice-President: Dr IBRAHIM ABDULRAHMAN AL-MISHAEL
Vice-President: Dr KHALED BIN ABDULRAHMAN FAHAD AL-HAMOUDI
Vice-President, Abha and Qasim Branches: Dr KHALED BIN ABDULRAHMAN FAHAD AL-HAMOUDI (acting)
Registrars and Deans of Admissions:
Riyadh Branch: Dr ABDULHALIM ABDULAZIZ MAZI
Abha Branch: Dr ALI BIN ESA AL-SHABI
Qasim Branch: Dr AHMED BIN SALEH AL-TAMI
Dean of Student Affairs: Dr ABDULELAH BIN SAAD BIN SAIED (acting)
Dean of Library Affairs: Dr SAAD ABDULLAH AL-DHOBYAN

Library: see Libraries
Number of teachers: 2,768
Number of students: 37,324

Publications: *Annual Report, Statistical Yearbook, University Bulletin, Journal of King Saud University.*

DEANS

College of Arts: POB 2456; Dr MOHAMMED BIN MANSHET AL-SHAFY
College of Science: POB 2455; Dr ABDULRAHMAN BIN MOHAMMED ABU EMMA
College of Administrative Sciences: POB 2459; Dr ABDULLAH BIN MOHAMMED AL-FAISAL
College of Pharmacy: POB 2457; Dr KHALED ABDUL MUHSAN EL-RUSHUD
College of Agriculture: POB 2460; Dr SALEH ABDULRAHMAN AL-SEHIBANI
College of Education: POB 2458; Dr MOHAMMAD BIN SHAT HUSSEIN AL-KHATIB
College of Engineering: POB 800; Dr ABDULAZIZ SALEM AL-ROWEIS
College of Medicine: POB 2925; Dr ABDULRAHMAN BIN SALEH AL-FERAIH
College of Dentistry: POB 5967; Dr ABDULLAH BIN MOHAMMED AL-DOUSARY
College of Applied Medical Sciences: POB 10219; Dr FAHD IBN JABER EL-SHAMMARI
College of Computer and Information Sciences: POB 51178; Dr ABDULLAH IBRAHIM AL-SALAMAH
College of Architecture and Planning: POB 57448; Dr SULEMAN BIN TURKI AL-SEDAIRY
College of Graduate Studies: POB 1241: Dr ALI BIN ABDULLAH FAWAZ AL-FERAIH
College of Education in Abha: POB 157, Abha; Dr ABDUL WAHHAB IBN SALEH BABEER
College of Medicine in Abha: POB 641; Dr MOHAMMAD YEHIA AL-SHEHRI
College of Economics and Administration (Al-Qasim Campus): POB 1482, Onaizah; Dr HAMED BIN SULAIMAN AL-BAZAE
College of Agriculture and Veterinary Medicine: POB 505, Boraidah; Dr AHMED BIN ALI AL-RUGEIBAH
Centre of Women's University Studies: POB 7695; Dr KHAIRIEH IBRAHIM EL-SAGGAF
Arabic Language Institute: POB 4274; Dr MOHAMMAD IBN YASIN ULFI
College of Languages and Translation: Dr JASER BIN ABDULRAHMAN AL-JASER
Centre of Continuing Education and Community Services: Dr ABDULRAHMAN BIN IBRAHIM AL-SHARE

UMM AL-QURA UNIVERSITY

POB 407/715, Mecca

Telephone: (2) 5564770
Telex: 440026

Founded 1979 from existing faculties of King Abdulaziz University

Rector: Dr RASHID BIN RAJIH
Vice-Rector: Dr MUHAMMAD ABDULLAH HAJAR AL-GHAMDI
Secretary-General: Dr MAHMOOD ASADULLAH
Library of 370,250 vols

DEANS

Faculty of Sharia and Islamic Studies: Dr ALI ABBAS AL-HAKMI
Faculty of Education: Dr SUHAIL HASSAN QADI
Faculty of Applied Sciences and Engineering: Dr ABDUL AZIZ MUSTAFA UQQAB
Arabic Language Institute: Dr ABDULLAH SULAIMAN AL-JARBOO
Faculty of Dawa and Usul al-Din: Dr ABDUL AZIZ AL-HAMEEDI
Faculty of English: Dr ULIAN MUHAMMAD EL-HAZMY
Faculty of Social Sciences: Dr SAUD AL SOBAIE

Umm Al-Qura University, Taif Campus

Al-Saddad Rd, Shihar, Taif

Telephone: 749-1917
Fax: 746-3008

Founded 1981

President: Dr RASHID BIN RAJIH
Vice-Presidents: Dr MUHAMMAD IBRAHIM AHMED ALI (Higher Studies and Research), Dr SAAD AL-SOBAI (Finance and Administration)
Registrar: ALI F. AL-FAER
Librarian: MOHD ADIL USMANI
Library of 50,000 vols
Number of teachers: 90
Number of students: 2,000

DEANS

Faculty of Education: Dr ABDULLAH ABDUL KARIM AL-ABBADI
Faculty of Library Studies: Dr HAMMAD MUHAMMAD AL-SOMALI

Institutes of Higher Education

English Language Teaching Institute: POB 58012, Al Mousa Bldg, Olaya Main Road, Riyadh 11594; tel. (1) 462-1818; fax (1) 462-0663; f. 1969 by Ministry of Education and directed by the British Council; brs in Jeddah and Dammam; Direct Teaching Operations Man. KEVIN SMITH.

Institute of Public Administration: POB 205, Riyadh 11141; tel. 4768888; telex 401160; fax 4792136; f. 1961; conducts training courses for govt and private-sector employees; researches into and offers advice on administrative problems; Dir-Gen. HAMAD I. AL-SALLOOM; publ. *PA Journal* (quarterly, in Arabic).

Islamic Research and Training Institute: POB 9201, Jeddah 21413; tel. 636-1400; telex 601137; fax 6378927; f. 1982; e-mail archive@isdb.org.sa; part of Islamic Development Bank; research to enable the economic and financial activities of the IDB's mem. countries to conform to the Islamic Sharia; research into all aspects of mem. countries' economic and financial systems; training of personnel; library of 9,000 vols; Dir Prof. Dr MABID ALI AL-JARHI.

Jeddah Health Institute: Jeddah; provides basic medical training; similar Institutes at Riyadh and Hofouf.

King Abdulaziz Military Academy: POB 5969, Riyadh; tel. 465-4244; f. 1955; courses given in modern languages, including English, French and Hebrew, science and military subjects; library of *c.* 20,000 vols; *c.* 1,300 students; publ. *Journal*.

Madrasat Ahl Al Hadith: Mecca; f. 1933; the College provides instruction in the Hadith, Koran, Fiqh, Tawheed and other Islamic religious studies; Principal Sheikh MUHAMMAD ABDUL RAZZAQ; Sec. MUHAMMAD OMAR ABDULHADI.

School of Applied Arts: Medina; f. 1955; *c.* 300 students.

Technical Institute: Riyadh; f. 1964; 1,000 students.

Yanbu Industrial College: POB 30436, Yanbu al-Sinaiyah; tel. (4) 394-6111; fax (4) 392-0213; f. 1989; engineering technology; 93 teachers, 638 students; library of 6,000 vols; Man. Dir BASSAM ABDULLAH YAMANI; Registrar HAMZA ATIK.

SENEGAL

Learned Societies

BIBLIOGRAPHY, LIBRARY SCIENCE AND MUSEOLOGY

Association Sénégalaise de Bibliothécaires, Archivistes et Documentalistes: ASBAD, BP 3252, Dakar; tel. 824-69-81; fax 824-23-79; f. 1988; 150 mems; Pres. MARIETOU DIONGUE DIOP; Sec. EMMANUEL KABOU.

EDUCATION

Bureau Régional de l'Unesco pour l'Education en Afrique/Unesco Regional Office for Education in Africa: BP 3311, 12 ave Roume, Dakar; f. 1970; 43 member states; 3 sections: educational planning and administration; educational content and programming; literacy, adult education and rural development; also a Multi Media Centre (13,000 vols and documents, 270 periodicals, 350 microfiches, 305 microfilms) and Co-ordinating Unit of the Network of Educational Innovations for Development in Africa (NEIDA); activities also in the field of natural sciences, social sciences, culture and communication; Dir PIUS A. I. OBANYA; publs *Liste trimestrielle des nouvelles acquisitions, Rapports trimestrielles d'activités, EducAfrica* (2 a year), studies, reports, etc.

Research Institutes

GENERAL

Institut Fondamental d'Afrique Noire Cheikh Anta Diop: BP 206, Université Cheikh Anta Diop de Dakar, Dakar; tel. 825-00-90; telex 51262; f. 1936, reconstituted 1959; scientific and humanistic studies on Black Africa; library and museums (see below); Dir DJIBRIL SAMB; publs *Bulletin de l'IFAN, Série A—Sciences Naturelles, Série B—Sciences Humaines, Notes Africaines* (quarterly), *Mémoires de l'IFAN, Initiations et Etudes Africaines, Instructions Sommaires, Catalogues et Documents,* etc.

Institut Français de Recherche Scientifique pour le Développement en Coopération (ORSTOM) Centre de Dakar: BP 1386, Route des Pères Maristes, Dakar; tel. 832-34-80; fax 832-43-07; e-mail durand@orstom.sn; soil biology, pedology, medical entomology, hydrology, geology, nematology, demography, economics, zoology, botany, agronomy, geography, sociology, nutrition; library of 10,000 vols; Dir J. R. DURAND. (See main entry under France.)

Institut Français de Recherche Scientifique pour le Développement en Coopération (ORSTOM) Station de M'Bour: BP 50, M'Bour; tel. 957-10-44; fax 957-15-00; e-mail ndiath@orstom.sn; geophysics, ecology, ornithology; Dir ABDOU SELAM NDIATH. (See main entry under France.)

AGRICULTURE, FISHERIES AND VETERINARY SCIENCE

Institut Sénégalais de Recherches Agricoles (ISRA): BP 3120, Route des Hydrocarbures, Bel-Air, Dakar; tel. 832-24-31; fax 832-24-27; e-mail bakhayok@isra.refer.sn; f. 1974; research in all fields of agriculture, forestry and pisciculture; Dir Dr MOUSSA BAKHAYOKHU; publ. *Rapport Annuel.*

Controls the following:

Centre National de Recherches Agronomiques (CNRA): BP 53, Bambey; tel. 973-60-50; fax 973-60-52; e-mail isracnra@telecomplus.sn; f. 1921; applied agricultural research; 45 research mems; library of 6,700 vols; stations at Louga and Thilmakha; Dir Dr DOGO SECK; publs *Rapport de synthèse, Annuaire analytique des travaux de l'IRAT au Sénégal.*

Centre de Recherches Océanographiques de Dakar-Thiaroye (CRODT): BP 2241, Dakar; tel. 834-05-36; f. 1956; for the study of oceanographic physics and biology; 67 scientists; library of 450 vols and 74 periodicals; Dir DIAFARA TOURE.

Centre de Recherches Zootechniques de Dahra-Djoloff: BP 01, Dahra-Djoloff; tel. 968-61-11; fax 968-62-71; f. 1950; amelioration of local bovine and ovine breeds, rearing and cross-breeding; Dir TAMSIR DIOP.

Centre de Recherches Zootechniques de Kolda: BP 53, Kolda; tel. and fax 996-11-52; f. 1972; amelioration of local bovine and ovine breeds; fodder cultivation; Dir Dr DEMBA FARBA MBAYE.

Centre de Recherche Agronomique de Djibélor: BP 34, Ziguinchor; tel. 991-12-05; fax 991-12-93; Dir SAMBA SALL.

Centre de Recherche Agronomique de Saint-Louis: BP 240, Richard-Toll; tel. 961-17-51; fax 961-18-91; Dir Dr SIDY SECK.

Direction des Recherches sur les Productions Forestières: BP 2313, Route des Pères Maristes, Dakar-Hann; tel. 832-32-19; fax 832-96-17; Dir Dr PAPE NDIENGOU SALL.

Centre de Recherche Agronomique de Kaolack: BP 199, Kaolack; tel. 941-29-16; fax 941-29-02; Dir Dr MODOU SENE.

Centre pour le Développement de l'Horticulture (CDH): BP 2619, Dakar; tel. 835-06-10; fax 835-10-75; f. 1972; market garden research; Dir Dr ALAIN MBAYE.

ECONOMICS, LAW AND POLITICS

Institut Africain de Développement Economique et de Planification (African Institute for Economic Development and Planning): BP 3186, Dakar; tel. 823-10-20; fax 822-29-64; e-mail idep@sonatel.senet.net; f. 1962 under the aegis of the Economic Comm. for Africa; financed jointly by African states and the UNDP; provides training through the organization of courses, seminars, etc., and undertakes research; library of 25,000 vols, 1,400 periodicals; Dir Dr JEGGAN C. SENGHOR; publs *IDEP Newsletter* (in English), *Bulletin d'Information* (in French).

MEDICINE

Institut d'Hygiène Sociale: Ave Blaise-Diagne, Dakar.

Institut Pasteur: BP 220, Dakar; tel. 839-92-00; fax 839-92-10; f. 1896; medical research; 19 scientists; library of 2,030 vols, 88 periodicals; Dir Dr J. P. MOREAU; publ. *Annual Report.*

Organisme de Recherches sur l'Alimentation et la Nutrition Africaines (ORANA): BP 2089, 39 ave Pasteur, Dakar; tel. 822-58-92; f. 1956; research of African foods and nutritional values, investigations, documentation, teaching; 30 mems; Dir Dr AMADOU MAKHTAR NDIAYE.

TECHNOLOGY

African Regional Centre for Technology/Centre Régional Africain de Technologie: BP 2435, Dakar; tel. 823-77-12; telex 61282; fax 823-77-13; f. 1977 as an intergovernmental institution under the auspices of the OAU and UNECA; aims to promote the use of technology to improve the socio-economic development of Africa; advises and sets up national institutions, holds training seminars and workshops; activities include food science and technology, energy technology, technological consulting and advisory services, training and information and documentation; 31 mem. states; library of 6,000 vols, patents, microfiches, video cassettes; Exec. Dir Dr OUSMANE KANE; publs *African Technodevelopment Bulletin* (English and French, 2 a year), *Alert Africa Newsletter* (quarterly), *Infonet* (irregular).

Bureau de Recherches Géologiques et Minières (BRGM): BP 268, Dakar; tel. 822-72-19; telex 275; mining, hydrogeology, irrigation; also directs research in Mali and Mauritania; Dir D. FOHLEN.

Libraries and Archives

Dakar

Archives du Sénégal: Immeuble administratif, Ave Léopold Sedar Senghor, Dakar; tel. 823-50-72; fax 822-51-26; f. 1913; 10 km of documents dealing with colonial and post-independence Senegal; library of 26,000 vols, 1,500 periodicals, 8,000 official publs, 12 km. of documents; Dir SALIOU MBAYE; publs *Bibliographie du Sénégal* (2 a year), *Rapport Annuel.*

Bibliothèque Centrale, Université Cheikh Anta Diop de Dakar: BP 2006, Dakar; tel. 824-69-81; telex 51262; fax 824-23-79; e-mail biblicad@ucad.sn; f. 1952; higher education, human and social sciences, law and economics, medicine and pharmacy; 347,000 vols, 5,000 periodicals (of which 1,000 are current); Dir H. SENE.

Bibliothèque de l'Alliance Française: BP 1777, 2 rue Assane Ndoye, Dakar; tel. 821-08-22; f. 1948; 12,000 vols; Dir PATRICK MANDRILLY.

Bibliothèque de l'Institut Fondamental d'Afrique Noire: BP 206, Dakar; tel. 825-00-90; e-mail bibifan@ifan.refer.sn; f. 1936; research in humanities and natural sciences; 70,000 vols, 8,200 brochures, 4,036 collections of periodicals, 1,600 microfilms, 2,566 maps, 32,000 photographs, 2,100 slides, 12,200 files of documents; Librarian GORA DIA.

Centre National de Documentation Scientifique et Technique (CNDST): Ministère chargé de la Modernisation de l'Etat et de la Technologie (MMET), 61 Blvd Djily Mbaye, BP 218, Dakar; tel. 822-96-19; f. 1976; bibliographical data base with 9,000 references; current index of economic, scientific and technical documentation; Dir MOHAMED FADHEL DIAGNE; publs *Répertoire des sources d'information au Sénégal, Répertoire des Recherches agricoles en cours (Programmes, Institutions, chercheurs)*, lists and indexes.

Centre Régional de Recherche et de Documentation pour le Développement Culturel (CREDEC) (Regional Research and Documentation Centre for Cultural Development): 13 ave du Pdt Bourguiba, Dakar; tel. 827-80-59; telex 61334; fax 821-75-15; e-mail fdiallo@infomie.fr; f. 1976; mems: 20 African states; part of African Cultural Institute (see under International); library of *c.* 3,200 vols, special collections on African crafts; Co-ordinator FALILOU DIALLO; publ. *ICA-Information* (quarterly).

Museums and Art Galleries

Dakar

Musée d'Art Africain de Dakar: BP 6167, Dakar-Étoile; f. 1936; administered by Institut Fondamental d'Afrique Noire; ethnography and African art; Curator Dr TAHIROU DIAW.

Gorée

Musée de la Mer: Gorée; f. 1959; administered by Institut Fondamental d'Afrique Noire; sea sciences, oceanography, fishing; Curator Dr SECK.

Musée Historique: Gorée; administered by Institut Fondamental d'Afrique Noire; Curator Dr ABDOULAYE CAMARA.

Universities

UNIVERSITÉ CHEIKH ANTA DIOP DE DAKAR

BP 5005, Dakar-Fann

Telephone: 825-05-30
Fax: 825-52-19

Founded 1949, University 1957
State control
Language of instruction: French
Academic year: October to July

Rector and President: SOULEYMANE NIANG
Vice-President: MOUSTAPHA SOURANG
Secretary-General: ALIOUNE BADARA DIAGNE
Librarian: HENRI SENE

Library: see Libraries
Number of teachers: 874
Number of students: 20,000

Publications (periodical): *Annuaire, Revue de la Faculté des Lettres, Notes Africaines, Bulletin de l'IFAN* (3 a year), *Dakar médical* (3 a year), *Journal de la Faculté des Sciences et Techniques* (2 a year), *Revue de l'Ecole Normale Supérieure* (2 a year).

DEANS

Faculty of Law and Political Science: MOUSTAPHA SOURANG
Faculty of Medicine, Pharmacy and Odonto-Stomatology: RENÉ NDOYE
Faculty of Science and Technology: LIBASSE DIOP
Faculty of Arts and Humanities: MAMADOU MOUSTAPHA SALL
Faculty of Economics and Management: MOUSTAPHA KASSE

DIRECTORS

Institut Fondamental d'Afrique Noire Cheikh Anta Diop: see under Research Institutes
Ecole Supérieure Polytechnique: OUMAR SOCK
Ecole Normale Supérieure: SEGA SECK FALL

ATTACHED RESEARCH INSTITUTES

Centre de Linguistique Appliquée de Dakar (CLAD): Dir CHERIF MBODJ.

Centre de Recherches, d'Etudes et de Documentation sur les Institutions et la Législation Africaines (CREDILA): Dakar; Dir AMSATOU SOW SIDIBE.

Centre de Recherches Biologiques sur la Lèpre: Dakar; Dir YVETTE PARES.

Centre de Recherches Economiques Appliquées (CREA): Dakar; Dir MOUSTAPHA KASSE.

Centre de Recherches psychopathologiques: Dakar; Dir BABACAR DIOP.

Centre d'Etudes des Sciences et Techniques de l'Information: Dakar; f. 1965; offers diploma courses in journalism; Dir BIRAHIM MOUSSA GUEYE.

Centre d'Etudes et de Recherches sur les Energies renouvelables 'Henri Masson': Dakar f. 1955; Dir MANSOUR KANE.

Centre des Hautes Etudes Afro-Ibéro-Américaines: Dakar; concerned with all matters relating to Africa and Latin America in the fields of law, science and the arts.

Ecole des Bibliothécaires, Archivistes et Documentalistes: Faculty of Arts and Social Sciences, BP 3252, Dakar; tel. 825-76-60; f. 1963, attained present status as university institute 1967; provides a two-year librarianship course, giving priority to students from French-speaking countries in Africa; 12 teachers; 195 students; Dir OUSMANE SANE.

Institut de Français pour les Etudiants étrangers: Dakar; Dir AMADOU LY.

Institut de Mathématiques appliquées 'Souleymane Fall': Dakar; Dir D. S. THIAM.

Institut de Médecine Tropicale Appliquée: Dakar; Dir OUMAR BAO.

Institut de Pédiatrie Sociale: Dakar; Dir MOUHAMADOU FALL.

Institut de Recherches sur l'Enseignement de la Mathématique, de la Physique et de la Technologie: Dakar; Dir MAMADOU SANGHARE.

Institut de Santé et Développement: Dakar; Dir IBRAHIMA WONE.

Institut des Sciences de l'Environnement: Dakar; Dir AMADOU TIDIANE BA.

Institut d'Odontologie et de Stomatologie: Dakar; Dir NDIORO NDIAYE.

Institut de Technologie nucléaire appliquée: Dakar; Dir CHRISTIAN SINA DIATTA.

Institut des Droits de l'Homme et de la Paix: Dakar; Dir El Hadj MOBODJ.

Institut des Sciences de la Terre: ABDOULAYE DIA.

Institut National Supérieur d'Education Physique et Sportive: GÉRARD DIAME.

UNIVERSITÉ DE SAINT-LOUIS (Université Gaston-Berger)

BP 234, Saint-Louis

Telephone: 961-19-06
Fax: 961-18-84

Founded 1990
State control
Language of instruction: French
Academic year: October to July

Rector: Prof. AHMADOU LAMINE NDIAYE
Secretary-General: ABDOULAYE DIAGNE
Librarian: MAMADOU LAMINE NDOYE

Number of teachers: 89
Number of students: 2,157

HEADS OF TEACHING AND RESEARCH UNITS

Arts and Social Sciences: NDIAWAR SARR
Law: BABACAR KANTÉ
Economics and Management: FRANÇOIS BOYE
Applied Mathematics and Computer Science: MARY TEW NIANE

Colleges

Ecole Inter-Etats des Sciences et Médecine Vétérinaires (EISMV): BP 5077, Dakar; tel. 823-05-45; telex 51403; fax 825-42-83; representing 13 French-speaking African countries.

Ecole Nationale d'Administration du Sénégal: BP 5209, Dakar; f. 1959; Dir A. N'DENE N'DIAYE.

Ecole Nationale d'Economie Appliquée: BP 5084, Dakar/Fann; tel. 824-79-28; f. 1963; library of 4,500 vols; 147 students; Dir SAMBA DIONE; publ. *Bulletin de Recherche Appliquée*.

Ecole Polytechnique de Thiès: BP 10, Thiès; tel. 51-13-84; telex 77108; fax 511476; f. 1973; attached to the Ministry of the Armed Forces; 5-year diploma courses in engineering; library of 20,000 vols; 23 full-time, 21 part-time teachers; 147 students; Commandant Col MAMADOU SECK; Registrar ARONA DIOP; Dean ROGER GOULET; Librarian Mrs PHILOMÈNE FAYE.

HEADS OF DEPARTMENTS

Common Stream: P. M. NDIAYE
Civil Engineering: MASSAMBA DIÈNE
Mechanical Engineering: NGOR SARR

Institut de Technologie Alimentaire: BP 2765, Hann, Dakar; Dir OUSMANE KANE.

Institut National de Développement Rural: BP 296 RP, Thiès; tel. 51-12-57; f. 1980; 5-year courses for agricultural engineers; 21 full-time teachers; library of 3,000 vols; Dir MOUSSA FALL.

SEYCHELLES

Research Institutes

GENERAL

National Heritage: La Bastille, Pointe Conan; tel. 224777; telex 2240; fax 322113; f. 1987; controlled by Culture Division of the Ministry of Education and Culture; carries out research into the cultural heritage of Seychelles; Asst Dir MARCEL BARRY ROSALIE.

Libraries and Archives

Victoria

National Archives: POB 720, 5th June Ave, Victoria, Mahé; tel. 321333; fax 322113.

National Library: POB 45, Francis Rachel St, Victoria, Mahé; tel. 321333; fax 322113; f. 1909 as Carnegie Library; 47,700 vols; 4 brs; special collection: documents on the Indian Ocean region; Asst Dir L. ERNESTA.

Museums and Art Galleries

Victoria

National Museum: POB 720, 5th June Avenue, Victoria, Mahé; tel. 321333; fax 322113; f. 1964; Curator STELLA DOWAY.

Polytechnic

SEYCHELLES POLYTECHNIC

POB 77, Victoria

Telephone: 371188
Fax: 371545

Founded 1983
State control
Language of instruction: English
Academic year: January to December

Director: ANNE LAFORTUNE
Assistant Director (Administration): (vacant)
Assistant Director (Studies): S. DE ZOYSA
Senior Librarian: DOROTHY LODOISKA

Library of 37,000 vols
Number of teachers: 157
Number of students: 1,402

HEADS OF SCHOOL

Adult and Continuing Education: J. BENOITON
Agriculture: J. ALCINDOR
Business Studies: L. DOMINGUE
Construction: R. WOODCOCK
Education and Community Studies: C. CAFRINE
Engineering: J. RASSOOL
Foundation Studies: J. LESPERANCE
Health Studies: M. SERVINA
Humanities and Science: J.-M. DOMINGUE
Maritime Studies: (vacant)

School of Music

National College of the Arts: Ministry of Youth and Culture, POB 1383, Mahé; tel. 224777; fax 322113; e-mail acollart@seychells.net; f. 1997; depts of music, dance, visual arts; Dir VIVIEN CLEMENT.

SIERRA LEONE

Learned Societies

BIBLIOGRAPHY, LIBRARY SCIENCE AND MUSEOLOGY

Sierra Leone Association of Archivists, Librarians and Information Scientists: 7 Percival St, Freetown; f. 1970; 90 mems; Pres. OLATUNGIE CAMPBELL; Sec. AGNES MOROVIA; publ. *SLAALIS Bulletin* (quarterly).

HISTORY, GEOGRAPHY AND ARCHAEOLOGY

Historical Society of Sierra Leone: c/o Dept of History, Fourah Bay College, University of Sierra Leone, Freetown; f. 1975; 30 mems; Pres. G. S. ANTHONY; Sec. Dr A. J. G. WYSE; publ. *Journal* (2 a year).

MEDICINE

Sierra Leone Medical and Dental Association: POB 850, Freetown; f. 1961; 220 mems; library of 3,000 vols (shared with main hospital); Pres. Dr S. U. M. JAH; Sec. Dr DESMOND WRIGHT; publs *Journal* (annually), *SLMDA Information Newsletter* (quarterly).

NATURAL SCIENCES

General

Sierra Leone Science Association: c/o Dept of Chemistry, Fourah Bay College, University of Sierra Leone, Freetown; tel. (22) 231617; telex 3210; fax (22) 224439; f. 1960; Hon. Pres. Prof. Dr ERNEST H. WRIGHT; Hon. Sec. (vacant).

Research Institutes

GENERAL

Institute of African Studies: c/o University of Sierra Leone, Fourah Bay College, Freetown; f. 1962; undertakes research in sociology, history and culture of Sierra Leone; offers undergraduate and postgraduate courses in cultural studies; Dir Dr ARTHUR ABRAHAM; publ. *Africana Research Bulletin* (2 a year).

NATURAL SCIENCES

Biological Sciences

Institute of Marine Biology and Oceanography: Fourah Bay College, University of Sierra Leone, Freetown; tel. 250775; f. 1966; 4-year degree programme in marine science, undergraduate diploma in aquatic biology and fisheries; research and training in oceanography, marine algae and ecology, fishery biology and management, aquaculture, marine pollution, estuarine dynamics, and coastal processes; Dir Dr I. W. O. FINDLAY; publ. *Annual Bulletin*.

Physical Sciences

Geological Survey Division: Ministry of Mines, Youyi Bldg, Brookfields, Freetown; f. 1918; to locate mineral deposits and to advise on all matters relating to the earth; library of 16,000 vols including periodicals; Dir A. H. GABISI; publs *Annual Report, Bulletin, Short Papers* (all annually).

Libraries and Archives

Freetown

Fourah Bay College Library: University of Sierra Leone, Freetown; tel. 22-94-71; f. 1827; 200,000 vols, 330 current periodicals; Librarian D. E. THOMAS.

Public Archives of Sierra Leone: c/o Fourah Bay College, Freetown; f. 1965; 63,000 linear ft of records; Hon. Govt Archivist Prof. AKINTOLA J. G. WYSE.

Sierra Leone Library Board: POB 326, Freetown; tel. 223848; f. 1959; nationwide public library service; also acts as a national library (legal deposit); 80,000 vols; 3 regional libraries, 10 brs; Chief Librarian IRENE O'BRIEN-COKER; publs *Annual Report, Sierra Leone Publications* (annually).

Museums and Art Galleries

Freetown

Sierra Leone National Museum: Cotton Tree Building, POB 908, Freetown; historical, ethnographical and archaeological collection; Curator DOROTHY A. VAN AMSTERDAM-CUMMINGS.

University

UNIVERSITY OF SIERRA LEONE

Private Mail Bag, Freetown

Telephone: 224921

Founded 1967

State control

Language of instruction: English

Academic year: October to June

Chancellor: The President of the Republic of Sierra Leone

Pro-Chancellor: Dr ARTHUR PORTER

Vice-Chancellor: Prof. DANIEL E. B. CHAYTOR

Pro-Vice-Chancellor: Prof. A. M. TAQI

Secretary and Registrar: J. A. G. THOMAS

Librarian: GLADYS JUSU-SHERIFF

Number of teachers: 301

Number of students: 4,310 (full-time)

Publications: *Varsity Update* (monthly), *Vice-Chancellor's Annual Report, Calendar and Prospectus* (annually), *African Research Bulletin* (2 a year).

CONSTITUENT COLLEGES

Fourah Bay College

Founded by the Church Missionary Society in 1827, it was affiliated to the University of Durham in 1876 and became a constituent college of the University in 1966

Principal: Prof. V. E. H. STRASSER-KING

Vice-Principal: Prof. A. J. G. WYSE

DEANS

Faculty of Economic and Social Sciences: Prof. A. ABRAHAM

Faculty of Arts: Rev. Dr L. E. T. SHYLLON

Faculty of Pure and Applied Science: Prof. V. E. GODWIN

Faculty of Engineering: Prof. O. R. DAVIDSON

Faculty of Law: Prof. H. M. JOKO-SMART

Postgraduate Studies: Prof. A. J. G. WYSE

PROFESSORS

Faculty of Arts:

WYSE, A. J. G., History

Faculty of Pure and Applied Science:

AWUNOR-RENNER, E. R. T., Physics
COLE, N. H. A., Botany
STRASSER-KING, V. E. H., Geology
WILLIAMS, M. O., Zoology
WRIGHT, E. H., Chemistry

Faculty of Law:

JOKO-SMART, H. M.

Faculty of Engineering:

DAVIDSON, O. R., Mechanical Engineering

Faculty of Economic and Social Sciences:

ABRAHAM, A., Institute of African Studies

DIRECTORS

Institute of Adult Education and Extra-Mural Studies: E. D. A. TURAY

Institute of African Studies: Prof. A. ABRAHAM

Institute of Marine Biology and Oceanography: Dr I. W. O. FINDLAY

Institute of Population Studies: Dr A. C. THOMAS

Njala University College

Founded 1964

Principal: Prof. HARRY M. TURAY

Vice-Principal: Assoc. Prof. N. G. KUYEMBEH

DEANS

Faculty of Agriculture: Assoc. Prof. A. M. ALGHALI

Faculty of Education: P. K. SAIDU

Faculty of Environmental Sciences: Dr B. J. TUCKER

PROFESSORS

Faculty of Agriculture:

DAHNIYA, M. T., Crop Science
GEORGE, J. B., Crop Science
RHODES, E. R., Soil Science

Faculty of Education:

TURAY, H. M., Geography

College of Medicine and Allied Health Sciences

Founded 1987

Principal: Prof. A. M. TAQI

Vice-Principal: Assoc. Prof. F. D. R. LISK

DEANS

Faculty of Basic Medical Sciences: Dr J. K. GEORGE

Faculty of Clinical Sciences: Dr. L. GORDON-HARRIS

Faculty of Pharmaceutical Sciences: Prof. E. AYITEY-SMITH

PROFESSORS

Faculty of Clinical Sciences:

TAQI, A. M., Paediatrics

Faculty of Pharmaceutical Sciences:

AYITEY-SMITH, E., Pharmacology

OFF-CAMPUS INSTITUTES

Institute of Education: Private Mail Bag, Tower Hill, Freetown; Dir MELISSA F. JONAH (acting).

Institute of Library Studies: Mount Aureol, Freetown; Dir GLADYS JUSU-SHERIFF.

Institute of Public Administration and Management: Private Mail Bag, Tower Hill, Freetown; Dir I. I. MAY-PARKER.

Colleges

Milton Margai Teachers College: Goderich, nr Freetown; f. 1960; trains secondary school teachers; library of 23,000 vols; 55 teachers; 624 students; Principal USMAN S. A. KAGBO; Registrar J. U. WRIGHT (acting).

Paramedical School: POB 50, Bo; f. 1979 with funds from the Government and the EEC; trains primary health workers; Principal Dr V. O. COLE.

Technical Institute: Congo Cross, Freetown; City and Guilds Craft and Technical Courses and Commercial Education; Principal A. JALLOH.

Technical Institute: Kenema; vocational courses.

SINGAPORE

Learned Societies

GENERAL

Singapore National Academy of Science: 1st Floor, Singapore Science Centre Building, off Jurong Town Hall Rd, Singapore 2260; established to promote the advancement of science and technology and to represent the mem. societies, institutes and other founder/affiliate mems of the Academy; Pres. Prof. LEO TAN WEE HIN; Sec. Dr CHIA WOON KIM.

Singapore Society of Asian Studies: Kent Ridge, POB 1076, Singapore 9111; f. 1982 to promote the study of Asian culture and heritage, with special emphasis on the Southeast Asian region; 130 mems; Pres. LIM GUAN HOCK; Sec. Dr YEO MANG THONG; publ. *Asian Culture* (annually).

ARCHITECTURE AND TOWN PLANNING

Singapore Institute of Architects: 72B Tras St, Singapore; f. 1923; 1,000 mems; Pres. EDWARD D'SILVA; Hon. Sec. JOHNNY TAN; publs *Singapore Architect* (quarterly), *SIA Year Book*.

BIBLIOGRAPHY, LIBRARY SCIENCE AND MUSEOLOGY

Library Association of Singapore: c/o Branch Library, Bukit Merah Central, POB 0693, Singapore 9115; f. 1955; 328 mems; Pres. CHOY FATT CHEONG; Hon. Sec. SITI HANIFAH; publs *Singapore Libraries* (2 a year), *Singapore Libraries Bulletin* (quarterly).

ECONOMICS, LAW AND POLITICS

Singapore Institute of International Affairs: 6 Nassim Rd, Singapore 1025; tel. 7349600; fax 7336217; f. 1961; organizes talks, conferences etc.; provides secretariat of Singapore National Cttee of Council for Security Co-operation in the Asia-Pacific Region; Chair. Dr LAU TEIK SOON; Dir M. RAJARETNAM.

FINE AND PERFORMING ARTS

Singapore Art Society: 6001 Beach Rd, No 18–08, Golden Mile Tower, Singapore 0719; tel. 2924244; f. 1949 to foster the practice and appreciation of art in Singapore; 325 mems; Pres. HO KOK HOE; Hon. Sec. QUEK KIAN GUAN.

MEDICINE

Academy of Medicine, Singapore: College of Medicine Bldg, Level 1, Left Wing, 16 College Rd, Singapore 0316; tel. 2238968; telex 40173; fax 2255155; f. 1957; professional corporate body of medical and dental specialists; also involved in the postgraduate training of doctors; Master Dr N. C. TAN; Chief Administrator Miss Y. L. LAM; publ. *Annals* (quarterly).

Singapore Medical Association: 2 College Rd, Alumni Medical Centre, Singapore 169850; tel. 223-1264; fax 224-7827; f. 1959; 2,600 mems; Pres. Dr P. Y. CHEONG; Hon. Sec. Dr C. Y. WONG; publs *Singapore Medical Journal* (every 2 months), *SMA Newsletter* (monthly).

NATURAL SCIENCES

General

Singapore Association for the Advancement of Science: 1st Floor, Singapore Science Centre Bldg, off Jurong Town Hall Rd, Singapore 2260; f. 1976 for the dissemination of science and technology; Pres. Prof. ANG KOK PENG; Sec. Dr LEO TAN WEE HIN.

Mathematical Sciences

Singapore Mathematical Society: Mathematics Dept, National University of Singapore, Kent Ridge, Singapore 119260; e-mail smsuser@math.nus.edu.sg; f. 1952; aims to maintain the status and advance the interests of the profession of mathematics, to improve the teaching of mathematics, and to provide means of intercourse between students, teachers and others interested in mathematics; 620 mems; Pres. Prof. LEE SENG LUAN; Sec. Dr LING SAN; publ. *Mathematical Medley* (2 a year).

Physical Sciences

Institute of Physics, Singapore: c/o Dept of Physics, National University of Singapore, Kent Ridge, Singapore 0511; tel. 7722604; fax 7776126; f. 1973 to promote study of and research in physics in Singapore; organizes conferences, talks, seminars, exhibitions, visits to industrial and commercial establishments and educational tours abroad; 180 mems; Pres. Prof. TANG SEUNG MUN; Sec. Dr KUOK MENG HAU; publs *Singapore Journal of Physics* (2 a year), *Physics Update* (2 a year).

Research Institutes

ECONOMICS, LAW AND POLITICS

Asian Mass Communication Research and Information Centre: 39 Newton Rd, Singapore 1130; tel. 2515106; telex 55524; fax 2534535; f. 1971; non-profit regional documentation centre; works in co-operation with UNESCO and other int. orgs to promote the understanding and development of communication and its application in the Asia-Pacific region with regard to economic, social and cultural progress; organizes seminars, workshops, refresher courses; convenes conferences; conducts communication research; library of 35,000 records in databases, 350 journals; regional centre for Japan Prize Circulating Library; Sec.-Gen. VIJAY MENON; publs *Media Asia* (quarterly), *AMCB* (every 2 months), *Mass Communication Periodical Literature Index* (every 6 months), *Asian Journal of Communication* (every 6 months).

Institute of Southeast Asian Studies: Heng Mui Keng Terrace, Pasir Panjang, Singapore 119614; f. 1968 to undertake research on South-East Asia, especially problems of development, modernization, political and social change; library of 400,000 vols; Dir Prof. CHIA SIOW YUE; Head of Administration Y. L. LEE; Librarian CH'NG KIM SEE; publs *Contemporary Southeast Asia* (3 a year), *Regional Outlook, Southeast Asian Affairs* (annually), *SOJOURN, Social Issues in Southeast Asia* (2 a year), *ASEAN Economic Bulletin* (3 a year).

EDUCATION

Institute of Technical Education (ITE): 10 Dover Drive, Singapore 0513; Chair. ERIC GWEE TECK HAI; Dir Dr LAW SONG SENG; publs *The Quality Workforce* (6 a year), *ITE News* (6 a year).

Libraries and Archives

Singapore

National Archives of Singapore: 140 Hill St Bldg, Hill St, Singapore 0617; f. 1968; custody of Singapore's public records; oral history and documentation units; 3,993 vols, 346 serials, 6,325 metres of govt files and publications, 153,833 photographs, 128,200 building plans, 6,386 maps, 1,882 film reels, records of clan associations, religious organizations, etc., 13,200 tapes of recorded interviews; Dir Mrs LILY TAN; publ. *Annual Report*.

National Library Board: 1 Temasek Ave, 06-00, Singapore 039192; tel. 3377355; fax 3309611; f. 1823; provides reference and lending library facilities; 3,134,049 vols, 65% of the collection in English, 22% in Chinese, 10% in Malay, 3% in Tamil; 32,872 serial titles; 69,906 audio-visual and other special materials; special collections: Southeast Asia Collection, Asian Collection of Children's Books; official repository for publications received under the National Library Board Act, United Nations publications and selected publications of its specialized agencies; 10 full-time branch libraries; national centre of bibliographical information and national exchange centre; Chief Exec. CHRISTOPHER CHIA; publs *Annual Report, Singapore Periodicals Index* (annually), *Books about Singapore* (every 3 years), *Singapore National Bibliography* (quarterly), other occasional bibliographies.

National University of Singapore Library: 10 Kent Ridge Crescent, Singapore 119260; fax 7771272; central library 1,016,000 vols, medical library 180,000 vols, science library 213,000 vols, law library 177,000 vols, Chinese library 411,000 vols, Japanese Resources Section 35,000 vols; Hon Sui Sen Memorial Library 90,000 vols; 20,000 current periodical titles; also microfilms, microfiches, AV collection, CD-ROM databases; Univ. Librarian JILL QUAH; publs bulletins, monthly accessions list.

Museums and Art Galleries

Singapore

National Heritage Board: 93 Stamford Rd, Singapore 78897; tel. (65) 3361460; fax (65) 3323568; f. 1849; consists of Asian Civilizations Museum, Singapore History Museum, Singapore Art Museum, Children's Discovery Gallery; library of 25,000 vols; history and oral history archives; CEO LIM SIAM KIM.

Singapore Botanic Gardens: National Parks Board, Cluny Rd, Singapore 259569; tel. 4719921; fax 4754295; f. 1859; botanical and horticultural research with particular reference to South-East Asia and the tropics; library of 20,000 vols; CEO Dr TAN WEE KIAT; Dir of Gardens Dr CHIN SEE CHUNG; Keeper of

Herbarium and Library Dr RUTH KIEW; publs *The Gardens Bulletin Singapore* (2 a year), and horticultural works.

Universities

NANYANG TECHNOLOGICAL UNIVERSITY

Nanyang Ave, Singapore 639798
Telephone: 7911744
Fax: 7911604

Founded 1981 as Nanyang Technological Institute; present name and status 1991
Chancellor: ONG TENG CHEONG
President: Dr CHAM TAO SOON
Deputy Presidents: Prof. CHEN CHARNG NING, Prof. LIM MONG KING, Prof. ER MENG HWA
Registrar: TEO HWEE CHOO
Librarian: FOO KOK PHEOW
Number of teachers: 1,013
Number of students: 16,690
Publication: *NTU News* (quarterly).

DEANS

School of Accountancy and Business: Assoc. Prof. NEO BOON SIONG
School of Applied Science: Prof. HARCHARAN SINGH
School of Civil and Structural Engineering: Assoc. Prof. CHEONG HEE KIAT
School of Electrical and Electronic Engineering: Prof. ER MENG HWA
School of Mechanical and Production Engineering: Prof. LIM MONG KING
School of Communication Studies: Prof. EDDIE KUO CHEN-YU
School of Arts: Assoc. Prof. KOH TAI ANN
School of Science: Prof. LEO TAN WEE HIN
School of Education: Assoc. Prof. SARAVANAN GOPINATHAN
School of Physical Education: Dr QUEK JIN JONG

DIRECTOR

National Institute of Education: Prof. LEO TAN WEE HIN

PROFESSORS

School of Accountancy and Business:
- LIM, C. Y., Applied Economics

School of Applied Science:
- FONG, H. S., Materials Engineering
- SINGH H., Computing Systems

School of Civil and Structural Engineering:
- CHEN, C. N., Water Resources and Transport
- CHOA, V. C. E., Geotechnics and Surveying
- FAN, H. S. L., Water Resources and Transport
- TAY, J. H., Water Resources and Transport

School of Electrical and Electronic Engineering:
- CHOO, S. C., Microelectronics
- ER, M. H., Information Engineering
- TAN, H. S., Microelectronics

School of Mechanical and Production Engineering:
- LIM, L. E. N., Manufacturing Engineering
- LIM, M. K.
- LIU, C. Y., Thermal and Fluids Engineering

School of Communication Studies:
- KUO, E. C. Y., Communications Research

School of Science:
- LEE, S., Physics
- TAN, L. W. H.

ATTACHED RESEARCH CENTRES

Gintic Institute of Manufacturing Technology: Dir Dr FRANS M. A. CARPAY.
Advanced Materials Research Centre: Dir Assoc. Prof. PETER HING.
Biomedical Engineering Research Centre: Dir Dr S. M. KRISHNAN.
NIE Centre for Educational Research: Head Assoc. Prof. SARAVANAN GOPINATHAN.
Centre for Advanced Construction Studies: Dir Assoc. Prof. Dr YIP WOON KWONG.
Centre for Graphics and Imaging Technology: Dir Dr WONG KOK CHEONG.
Centre for Signal Processing: Dir Assoc. Prof. SER WEE.
Centre for Transportation Studies: Dir Prof. HENRY FAN SHING LEUNG.
Entrepreneurship Development Centre: Dir TAN WEE LIANG.
Enviromental Technology Institute: Dir (vacant).
NTU-PWD Geotechnical Research Centre: Dir Dr HARIANTO RAHARDJO.
Information Communication Institute of Singapore: Dir DAVID SIEW CHEE KHEONG.
Innovation Centre: Dir Assoc. Prof. YEONG HIN YUEN.
Network Technology Research Centre: Dir Dr CHENG TEE HIANG.
Robotics Research Centre: Dir Dr GERALD SEET GIM LEE.
NTU-MINDEF Protective Research Centre: Dir Assoc. Prof. PAN TSO CHIEN.

NATIONAL UNIVERSITY OF SINGAPORE

10 Kent Ridge Crescent, Singapore 119260
Telephone: Singapore 7756666

Founded 1980 by merger of former University of Singapore and Nanyang University. (The University of Singapore had its origins in the King Edward VII College of Medicine, Raffles College and the University of Malaya in Singapore.)
State control
Language of instruction: English
Academic year: July to June (two semesters and a special term)
Chancellor: President ONG TENG CHEONG
Pro-Chancellors: Dr M. BAKER, Dr LIEN YING CHOW, RIDZWAN BIN Haji DZAFIR, S. R. NATHAN, Dr ANDREW CHEW GUAN KHUAN
Vice-Chancellor: Prof. LIM PIN
Deputy Vice-Chancellors: Prof. CHONG CHI TAT, Prof. HANG CHANG CHIEH
Registrar: JOANNA WONG
Librarian: JILL QUAH
Number of teachers: 1,600
Number of students: 26,909
Publications: *Campus News* (every 2 months), *Annual Report* (annually).

DEANS

Faculty of Architecture and Building: LAM KHEE POH
Faculty of Arts and Social Sciences: TONG CHEE KIONG
Faculty of Business Administration: WEE CHOW HOU
Faculty of Dentistry: CHEW CHONG LIN
Faculty of Engineering: ANDREW NEE
Faculty of Law: CHIN TET YUNG
Faculty of Medicine: TAN CHORH CHUAN
Faculty of Science: LEE SOO YING
School of Computing: CHUA TAT SENG

DIRECTORS

School of Postgraduate Dental Studies: CHEW CHONG LIN
School of Postgraduate Medical Studies: S. S. RATNAM
Graduate School of Business: WEE CHOW HOU
School of Postgraduate Engineering: POO AUN NEOW
Graduate School of Arts and Social Sciences: TONG CHEE KIONG

PROFESSORS

Faculty of Arts and Social Sciences:
- CHAN, H. C., Political Science
- KAPUR, B., Economics
- QUAH, S. T. J., Political Science
- SINGH, R., Social Work and Psychology
- WONG KAN, L. C. A., Sociology

Faculty of Business Administration:
- PANG, E. F., Business Policy
- TAN, C. H., Organizational Behaviour
- WEE, C. H., Business Policy
- WONG, K. A., Finance and Accounting

Faculty of Dentistry:
- CHEW, C. L., Restorative Dentistry
- LOH, H. S., Oral and Maxillofacial Surgery

Faculty of Engineering:
- CHAN, S. H. D., Electrical Engineering
- CHEONG, H. F., Civil Engineering
- CHEW, Y. T., Mechanical and Production Engineering
- CHUA, S. J., Electrical Engineering
- GOH, T. N., Industrial and Systems Engineering
- HANG, C. C., Electrical Engineering
- KOOI, P. S., Electrical Engineering
- LEONG, M. S., Electrical Engineering
- LI, M. F., Electrical Engineering
- LIEW, A. C., Electrical Engineering
- LING, C. H., Electrical Engineering
- LOW, T. S., Electrical Engineering
- NEE, Y. C. A., Mechanical and Production Engineering
- NUXALA, V., Mechanical and Production Engineering
- PARAMASIVAM, P., Civil Engineering
- PHANG, C. H. J., Electrical Engineering
- SHANG, H. M., Mechanical and Production Engineering
- SHANKAR, N. J., Civil Engineering
- TJHUNG, T. T., Electrical Engineering

Faculty of Law:
- JAYAKUMAR, S.
- KOH, T. B. T.
- SORNARAJAH, M.

Faculty of Medicine:
- BONGSO, A., Obstetrics and Gynaecology
- BOSE, K., Orthopaedic Surgery
- CHAN, H. L., Medicine
- CHAN, S. H., Microbiology
- CHEAH, J. S., Medicine
- CHIA, B. L., Medicine
- HWANG, L. H. P., Physiology
- KUA, E. H., Psychological Medicine
- LEE, E. H., Orthopaedic Surgery
- LEE, H. P., Community, Occupational and Family Medicine
- LEE, Y. S., Pathology
- LEONG, S. K., Anatomy
- LIM, P., Medicine
- LING, E. A., Anatomy
- NG, S. C., Obstetrics and Gynaecology
- OH, M. S. V., Medicine
- ONG, C. N., Community, Occupational and Family Medicine
- PHO, W. H. R., Orthopaedic Surgery
- PRASAD, R. N. V., Obstetrics and Gynaecology
- SINNIAH, R., Pathology
- SIT, K. H., Anatomy
- SIT, K. P., Biochemistry
- TAN, K. A. L., Diagnostic Radiology
- TAN, W. C., Medicine
- TI, T. K., Surgery
- TOCK, P. C. E., Pathology
- YEO, P. B. P., Medicine

Faculty of Science:
BERRICK, A. J., Mathematics
CHAN, S. O., Chemistry
CHEN, H. Y. L., Mathematics
CHONG, C. T., Mathematics
CHOW, S. N., Mathematics
GOH, C. J., Biological Sciences
GOH, S. H., Chemistry
KOH, K. M., Mathematics
LAM, T. J., Biological Sciences
LEE, C. K., Chemistry
LEE, S. L., Mathematics
LEE, S. Y., Chemistry
LIM, C. S., Mathematics
OH, C. H., Physics
ONG, C. K., Physics
ONG, P. P. P., Physics
PHILPOTT, M. R., Chemistry
SY, H. K., Physics
TANG, S. H., Physics
TANG, S. M., Physics
WILSON, S. J., Mathematics
WONG, M. K., Chemistry

School of Computing:
JAAFAR, J., Computer Science
PNG, P. L. I., Information Systems
YUEN, C. K., Computer Science

ATTACHED RESEARCH INSTITUTES

Data Storage Institute: Dir Prof. LOW TECK SENG

East Asian Institute: Dir Prof. WANG GUNGWU.

Institute of Microelectronics: Dir Dr BILL CHEN.

Institute of Molecular Agrobiology: Dir Prof. VENKETASAN SUNDARESAN.

Institute of Molecular and Cell Biology: Dir Dr CHRIS TAN YIM HWEE.

Institute of Systems Science: Dir LIM SWEE CHEANG.

National University Medical Institutes: Dir Prof. PETER HWANG.

Institute of High Performance Computing: Assoc. Prof. LAM KHIN YONG.

Bioprocessing Technology Centre: Dir Assoc. Prof. MIRANDA YAP.

Bioscience Centre: Dir Dr LIM TITMENG.

Chinese Language Proficiency Centre: Dir Assoc. Prof. CHEN CHUNG YU.

Centre for Advanced Studies: Dir Dr BRENDA YEOH.

Centre for Building Performance and Construction: Dir Dr TEO HO PIN.

Centre for Business Research and Development: Dir CHOW KIT BOEY.

Centre for Integrated Circuit Failure Analysis and Reliability: Dir Dr CHIN WAI KIN.

Centre for Management of Technology: Dir Assoc. Prof. WONG POH KAM.

Centre for Natural Product Research: Dir Assoc. Prof. MIRANDA YAP.

Centre for Optoelectronics: Dir Assoc. Prof. CHUA SOO JIN.

Centre for Real Estate Studies: Dir Dr LAWRENCE CHIN KEIN HOONG.

Centre for Remote Imaging, Sensing and Processing: Dir Assoc. Prof. LIM HOCK.

Centre for Research in Osteoporosis: Dirs Prof. KAMAL BOSE, Dr LEE SOON TAI.

Centre for Bone Banking Research: Dir Assoc. Prof. AZIZ NATHER.

Orthopaedic Implant Research Centre: Dir Prof. KAMAL BOSE.

Centre for Orthopaedic Bioengineering Research: Dir Dr JAMES GOH.

Centre for Transportation Research: Dir Assoc. Prof. FWA TIEN FANG.

Centre for Wireless Communications: Dir Assoc. Prof. LYE KIN MUN.

Productivity and Quality Research Centre: Dir Dr CHONG CHEE LEONG.

Surface Science Centre: Dir Prof. TAN KUANG LEE.

World Health Organization Collaborating Centre for Research and Training in Immunology: Dir Prof. CHAN SOH HA.

World Health Organization Collaborating Centre for Maternal and Child Health/Family Planning Services, Research and Training: Dir Prof. S. S. RATNAM.

World Health Organization Collaborating Centre for Clinincal Research in Human Reproduction: Dir Prof. S. S. RATNAM.

World Health Organization Collaborating Centre for Occupational Health: Dir Assoc. Prof. J. JEYARATNAM.

World Health Organization Collaborating Centre for Dementia Research: Dir Assoc. Prof. KUA EE HEOK.

Colleges

NGEE ANN POLYTECHNIC

535 Clementi Rd, Singapore 599489
Telephone: 4666555
Fax: 4687326
E-mail: dept-cc@np.ac.sg

Founded 1963
State control
Language of instruction: English
Academic year: July to May

Chairman: CHOO CHIAU BENG
Principal: KHOO CHIN HEAN
Deputy Principal (Academic): F. A. VASENWALA
Deputy Principal (Planning): KENNETH WONG
Chief Librarian: LOCK THI XUAN

Library of 160,000 vols, 1,500 periodicals
Number of teachers: 831
Number of students: 14,249 full-time, 844 part-time

Publications: *Prospectus* (annually), *Annual Report, Handbook on Short Courses* (2 a year), *Journal of Ngee Ann Polytechnic* (every 6 months), *NP Newsletter* (every 2 months).

HEADS OF DEPARTMENTS

Accountancy: PEE-KOH SEE HUA
Biotechnology: Dr SUSHILA CHANG
Building: LAURENCE LOON CHEE HOW
Business Studies: CHUA CHAP JEE
Centre for Computer Studies: DAVID CHAN FATT CHOW
Centre for Continuing Education: WANG FOOT TI
Electrical Engineering: GOH ENG KEE
Electronic and Computer Engineering: LEE TUCK SENG
Language and Communication Skills Centre: KATH WALSH
Film and Media Studies: Dr VICTOR VALBUENA
Mathematics and Science Centre: POK YANG MING
Mechanical Engineering: TAN AH SWAY
Shipbuilding and Offshore Engineering: TAN KIM PONG

SINGAPORE POLYTECHNIC

500 Dover Rd, Singapore 139651
Telephone: 7751133
Fax: 7721971

Founded 1954
Language of instruction: English
Academic year: July to May (four terms)

Offers diploma courses in accountancy, architectural technology, banking and financial services, biotechnology, building and property management, business administration, chemical process technology, chemical engineering, civil and structural engineering, computer information systems, electrical engineering, electronics, computer and communications engineering, instrumentation and control engineering, manufacturing engineering, marine engineering, maritime transportation, marketing, materials engineering, mechatronics, mechanical engineering, nautical studies, optometry; dual training diploma courses in architectural technology, business administration, civil and structural engineering, electronics, computer and communications engineering, and mechanical/manufacturing engineering; advanced diploma courses in analytical science and laboratory management, electronics and telecommunications engineering, strategic marketing, building automation and services, business information systems, civil and construction engineering, food technology, industrial engineering and management, information systems technology, marine engineering, maritime transport, mechatronics, plastics technology, power electronics and industrial applications, power systems engineering, process control and instrumentation, project coordination and construction management; certificate courses in engineering mathematics, occupational safety and health; short courses in a variety of technological disciplines.

Chairman: LIM YONG WAH
Principal: LOW WONG FOOK
Deputy Principal (Academic): EDWARD QUAH KOK WAH
Deputy Principal (Administration): YEOW KIAN PENG
Registrar: TAN PENG ANN
Librarian: Mrs TEO KOON NEO

Library of 207,000 vols, 5,200 multi-media titles
Number of teachers: 880
Number of students: 13,980 full-time, 5,790 part-time

Publications: *Prospectus, Singapore Polytechnic Guide to Courses and Careers, Annual Report, Polylife, Continuing Education Handbook, e.s.p. Magazine, Technical Journal* (all annually), *Polylink* (monthly), *Polynews* (every 2 months).

Southeast Asian Ministers of Education Organization (SEAMEO) Regional Language Centre (RELC): 30 Orange Grove Rd, Singapore 258352; tel. 7379044; telex 55598; fax 7342753; f. 1968; aims to improve the teaching of languages in the SEAMEO countries; conducts 6 courses, including MA in applied linguistics; research, regional conferences; provides technical services to national programmes; library of 50,000 vols; 45 staff and 500 students; Dir EDWIN GOH; publ. *RELC Journal*.

TEMASEK POLYTECHNIC

21 Tampines Ave 1, Singapore 529757
Telephone: 7878000
Fax: 7898164

Founded 1990

Principal: Dr N. VARAPRASAD
Registrar: MOSES WONG
Librarian: ESTHER ONG WOOI-CHEEN

Library of 104,300 vols

Number of teachers: 634
Number of students: 11,560
Publications: *Prospectus* (1 a year), *Annual Report, In Tempo* (4 a year), *Temasek Journal, T's* (2 a year).

DIRECTORS

School of Business: WONG LOKE JACK
School of Design: KHOO KENG GIE EDMOND
School of Engineering: LAY-TAN SIOK LIE
School of Information Technology and Applied Science: TAN DEK YAM

SLOVAKIA

Learned Societies

GENERAL

Slovenská Akadémia Vied (Slovak Academy of Sciences): 814 38 Bratislava, Štefánikova 49; tel. (7) 39-61-31; fax (7) 39-43-91; f. 1953; depts of Exact and Technical Sciences, of Natural Sciences and Chemistry, of Social Sciences; attached research institutes: see Research Institutes; library: see Libraries and Archives; Pres. ŠTEFAN LUBY; publs *Acta Physica Slovaca* (6 a year), *Acta Virologica* (6 a year), *Architektúra a urbanizmus* (quarterly), *ARS* (3 a year), *Asian and African Studies* (2 a year), *Biologia* (6 a year), *Building Research Journal* (quarterly), *Computers and Artificial Intelligence* (6 a year), *Ekológia* (quarterly), *Ekonomický časopis* (monthly), *Endocrine Regulations* (quarterly), *Entomological Problems* (2 a year), *Filozofia* (monthly), *General Physiology and Biophysics* (6 a year), *Geografický časopis* (quarterly), *Geographia Slovaca* (3 a year), *Geologica Carpathica* (6 a year), *Geologica Carpatica Clays* (2 a year), *Helminthologia* (quarterly), *Historický časopis* (quarterly), *Human Affairs* (2 a year), *Chemical Papers* (6 a year), *Jazykovedný časopis* (2 a year), *Journal of Electrical Engineering* (monthly), *Journal of Hydrology and Hydromechanics* (6 a year), *Kovové materiály* (6 a year), *Kultúra slova* (6 a year), *Mathematica Slovaca* (5 a year), *Neoplasma* (6 a year), *Organon F* (quarterly), *Právny obzor* (6 a year), *Slavica Slovaca* (2 a year), *Slovak Review* (2 a year), *Slovenská archeológia* (2 a year), *Slovenská literatúra* (6 a year), *Slovenská reč* (6 a year), *Slovenské divadlo* (quarterly), *Slovenské štúdie* (2 a year), *Slovenský národopis* (quarterly), *Sociológia* (6 a year), *Strojnícky časopis* (6 a year), *Studia Psychologica* (5 a year), *Sytematische Musikwissenschaften* (2 a year), *Tatra Mountains—Mathematical Publications* (3 a year), *Životné prostredie* (6 a year).

AGRICULTURE, FISHERIES AND VETERINARY SCIENCE

Slovenská spoločnosť pre polnohospodárske, lesnícke a potravinárske vedy (Slovak Society for Agriculture, Forestry and Food): 812 37 Bratislava, Radlinskeho 9; tel. 32-60-55; fax 39-31-98; e-mail dandar@checdek.chtf.stuba.sk; f. 1968; 564 mems; Pres. Prof. Dr A. DANDAR; Sec. Assoc. Prof. Dr M. TAKÁCSOVA.

ARCHITECTURE AND TOWN PLANNING

Spolok architektov Slovenska (Slovak Architects' Society): 811 01 Bratislava, Panská 5; tel. (7) 533-10-78; fax (7) 533-57-44; 1,900 mems; library of 2,500 vols; Pres. Arch. MARTIN KUSÝ; Dir FRANTIŠEK KYSELICA; publs *Projekt* (6 a year), *Fórum architektúry* (monthly).

ECONOMICS, LAW AND POLITICS

Slovenská spoločnosť pre medzinárodné právo (Slovak Society for International Law): 813 64 Bratislava, Klemensova 19; tel. 32-63-21; f. 1969; 63 mems; Pres. Prof. Dr JÁN AZUD; Sec. Dr CECILIA KANDRÁČOVÁ.

EDUCATION

Slovenská pedagogická spoločnosť (Slovak Education Society): 080 01 Prešov, Filozofická fakulta UPJŠ; tel. (791) 328-69; f. 1965; 365 mems; Pres. Prof. PhDr J. RÍČALKA; Sec. Doc. PhDr J. GALLO.

FINE AND PERFORMING ARTS

Slovenská výtvarná únia (Slovak Union for the Visual Arts): 813 51 Bratislava, Partizánská 21; tel. (7) 531-36-23; fax (7) 533-31-54; f. 1990; 1,800 mems; Pres. VIKTOR HULÍK; publs *Profil*, *Výtvarný život*.

HISTORY, GEOGRAPHY AND ARCHAEOLOGY

Slovenská archeologická spoločnosť (Slovak Archaeological Society): 949 21 Nitra, Akademická 2; tel. (87) 356-37; fax (87) 356-18; f. 1956; 350 mems; library of 860 vols; Pres. Dr DUŠAN ČAPLOVIČ; Sec. Dr KLÁRA KUZMOVÁ; publs *Informator* (2 a year), *Supplement* (annually).

Slovenská geografická spoločnosť (Slovak Geographical Society): 814 73 Bratislava, Štefánikova 49; tel. (7) 39-27-57; fax (7) 49-13-40; f. 1945; 500 mems; Pres. Prof. MICHAL ZAŤKO; Sec. Dr JÁN LACIKA.

Slovenská historická spoločnosť (Slovak Historical Society): 813 64 Bratislava, Klemensova 19; tel. 32-63-21; fax 36-16-45; 400 mems; Pres. PhDr VILIAM ČIČAJ; Sec. PhDr JÁN LUKAČKA.

LANGUAGE AND LITERATURE

Krúžok moderných filológov (Union for Modern Philology): 818 01 Bratislava, Gondova 2; tel. (7) 32-63-39; f. 1956; 205 mems; Pres. Prof. Dr J. OLEXA; Sec. Dr A. BÖHMEROVÁ.

Slovenská jazykovedná spoločnosť (Slovak Linguistics Society): 813 64 Bratislava, Panská 26; tel. (7) 533-17-61; fax (7) 533-17-56; e-mail slavoo@savba.sk; f. 1957; 266 mems; Pres. Prof. PhDr SLAMOMÍR ONDREJOVIČ; Sec. Dr MIRA NÁBĚLKOVÁ; publs *Recueil Linguistique de Bratislava*, *Zápisník slovenského jazykovedca*, *Varia*.

Slovenská jednota klassických filológov (Slovak Association of Classical Philologists): 818 01 Bratislava, Gondova 2; tel. 580-41; f. 1969; Pres. PhDr P. KUKLICA; Sec PhDr D. ŠKOVIERA.

Slovenská literárnovedná spoločnosť (Slovak Literary Society): 813 64 Bratislava, Konventná 13; tel. 531-33-91; fax 531-60-25; f. 1958; 320 mems; Pres. PhDr JÁN KOŠKA; Secs PhDr MÁRIA KUSÁ, Mgr MARIAN GAZDÍK.

Spolok slovenských spisovateľov (Society of Slovak Writers): 815 08 Bratislava, Štefánikova 14; tel. 436-15; f. 1949; 350 mems; Pres. JAROSLAV REZNÍK; Sec. PETER ANDRUŠKA; publs *Slovenské pohľady* (Slovak Review), *Literárny týždenník* (Literary Weekly), *Meridians* (bulletin of Slovak literature).

MEDICINE

Slovenská parazitologická spoločnosť (Slovak Society for Parasitology): 040 01 Košice, Hlinkova 3; tel. (95) 633-44-55; fax (95) 633-14-14; e-mail pausav@saske.sk; f. 1993; 92 mems; Pres. Assoc. Prof. Dr P. DUBINSKÝ; Sec. Prof. Dr V. LETKOVÁ; publ. *Správy slovenskej parazitologickej spoločnosti* (irregular).

NATURAL SCIENCES

General

Rada vedeckých spoločností (Council of Scientific Societies): 814 38 Bratislava, Štefánikova 49; tel. and fax (7) 39-61-48; f. 1990; 45 Slovak mem. socs; Pres. Prof. Dr Ing. JOZEF BRILLA.

Slovenská spoločnosť pre dejiny vied a techniky (Slovak Society for History of Science and Technology): 813 64 Bratislava, Klemensova 19; tel. (7) 32-63-21; fax (7) 36-16-45; f. 1965; 215 mems; Pres. Dr O. PÖSS; Sec. Dr M. MOROVICS.

Biological Sciences

Slovenská bioklimatologická spoločnosť (Slovak Bioclimatology Society): 812 54 Bratislava, Mickiewiczova 13; tel. 544-30; f. 1966; 180 mems; Pres. D. ZACHAR; Sec. RNDr Z. CABOJOVÁ; publs *Bulletin* (2 a year), papers, reports, etc.

Slovenská biologická spoločnosť (Slovak Biological Society): 811 08 Bratislava, Sasinkova 4; tel. 68-54-15; f. 1967; 180 mems; Pres. Prof. MUDr G. ČATÁR; Sec. Doc. RNDr I. TOMO; publ. magazine (2 a year).

Slovenská botanická spoločnosť pri SAV (Slovak Botanical Society): 842 23 Bratislava, Dúbravská cesta 14; tel. (7) 378-26-80; fax (7) 37-19-48; e-mail botuhsip@savba.savba.sk; f. 1955; 410 mems; Pres. RNDr O. ERDELSKÁ; Sec. RNDr H. ŠÍPOŠOVÁ; publ. *Bulletin* (annually).

Slovenská ekologická spoločnosť (Slovak Ecological Society): 949 01 Nitra, Akademická 2, POB 23B; tel. (87) 41-47-48; fax (87) 41-49-87; e-mail sekos@savba.sk; f. 1992; 150 mems; Pres. Assoc. Prof. Dr PAVOL ELIÁŠ; Sec. RNDr LUBOŠ HALADA; publ. *SEKOS Bulletin* (2 a year).

Slovenská entomologická spoločnosť (Slovak Entomology Society): C/o Dept of Zoology, Univerzita Komenského, 842 15 Bratislava, Mlynská dolina, tel. (7) 79-63-33; fax (7) 72-90-64; f. 1957; 235 mems; Pres. Dr L. JEDLIČKA; Sec. Dr Z. BIANCHI; publs *Entomofauna carpathica* (quarterly), *Entomological Problems* (every 6 months).

Slovenská spoločnosť pre biochémiu a molekulárnu biológiu (Slovak Society for Biochemistry and Molecular Biology): Faculty of Natural Sciences, Comenius University, 842 14 Bratislava, Mlynská dolina 1; tel. (7) 72-55-20; f. 1959; 220 mems; Pres. Dr J. KNOPP; Sec. Dr M. KOLLÁROVÁ; publ. *Bulletin* (quarterly).

Slovenská zoologická spoločnosť (Slovak Zoological Society): 814 34 Bratislava, Obrancov mieru 3; tel. 33-54-35; f. 1956; 300 mems; Pres. L. WEISMANN; Sec. RNDr E. KALIVODOVÁ.

Mathematical Sciences

Jednota slovenských matematikov a fyzikov (Association of Slovak Mathematicians and Physicists): 842 15 Bratislava, MFF UK, Mlynská dolina F1; tel. (7) 72-40-00; fax (7) 72-58-82; f. 1969; 2,860 mems; Pres. Prof. Dr B. REČIAN; Sec. Dr M. ŠABO; publ. *Obzory matematiky, fyziky a informatiky*.

Physical Sciences

Slovenská astronomická spoločnosť (Slovak Astronomical Society): 059 60 Tatranská Lomnica; tel. (969) 46-78-66; fax (969) 46-76-56; e-mail sas@ta3.sk; f. 1959; 311 mems; Pres. RNDr V. RUŠIN; Sec. RNDr R. KOMŽÍK.

Slovenská chemická spoločnosť (Slovak Chemical Society): 812 37 Bratislava, Radlinského 9; tel. and fax (7) 39-52-05; f. 1929; 1,100 mems; Pres. Dr D. BEREK; Sec. Assoc. Dr D. GYEPESOVÁ; publs *Bulletin* (2 a year), *Chemical Papers* (every 2 months).

Slovenská geologická spoločnosť (Slovak Geological Society): 817 04 Bratislava, Mlynská dolina 1; tel. (7) 59-37-52-25; fax (7) 37-19-40; f. 1965; 559 mems; Pres. RNDr P. REICHWALDER; Sec. RNDr M. ELEČKO; publ. *Mineralia slovaca* (quarterly).

Slovenská meteorologická spoločnosť (Slovak Meteorological Society): 833 15 Bratislava, Jeséniova 17; tel. (7) 37-39-25; fax (7) 37-56-70; f. 1960; 175 mems; Pres. Dr D. ZÁVODSKÝ; Sec. Dr F. HESEK.

PHILOSOPHY AND PSYCHOLOGY

Slovenské filozofické združenie (Slovak Philosophical Association): 813 64 Bratislava, Klemensova 19; tel. and fax (7) 32-12-15; e-mail ksbkemvi@savba.sk; f. 1990; 292 mems; Pres. PhDr EMIL VIŠŇOVSKÝ; Sec. PhDr DUŠAN GÁLIK.

RELIGION, SOCIOLOGY AND ANTHROPOLOGY

Slovenská antropologická spoločnosť (Slovak Anthropological Society): 842 15 Bratislava, Mlynská dolina B2; tel. (7) 79-64-72; f. 1965; 137 mems; Pres. Prof. RNDr M. POSPÍŠIL; Sec. RNDr EVA NEŠČÁKOVÁ.

Slovenská národopisná spoločnosť (Slovak Ethnography Society): 813 64 Bratislava, Jakubovo nám. 12; tel. (7) 33-49-25; f. 1958; 460 mems; Chair. MAGDALÉNA PARÍKOVÁ; Scientific Sec. VIERA FEGLOVÁ; publ. *Etnologické rozpravy* (Ethnological Review, 2 a year).

Slovenská orientalistická spoločnosť (Slovak Society for Oriental Studies): 813 64 Bratislava, Klemensova 19; tel. and fax (7) 32-63-26; e-mail kohollа@klemens.savba.sk; f. 1960; 42 mems; Pres. PhDr VIERA VILHANOVÁ-PAWLIKOVÁ; Sec. HENRIETA HATALOVÁ.

Slovenská sociologická spoločnosť (Slovak Sociological Society): 813 64 Bratislava, Klemensova 19; tel. (7) 32-63-21; fax (7) 36-13-12; f. 1964; 170 mems; Pres. Doc. DILBAR ALIJEVOVÁ; Scientific Sec. Dr BOHUMIL BÚZIK; publ. *Bulletin* (quarterly).

TECHNOLOGY

Slovenská spoločnosť pre mechaniku (Slovak Society for Mechanics): 842 20 Bratislava, Dúbravská cesta 9; tel. 378-25-30; fax 37-24-94; f. 1967; 252 mems; Pres. Prof. Dr Ing. J. BRILLA; Sec. RNDr V. SLÁDEK.

Research Institutes

ARCHITECTURE AND TOWN PLANNING

Institute of Construction and Architecture: 842 20 Bratislava, Dúbravská cesta 9; tel. (7) 37-35-48; fax (7) 37-24-94; attached to Slovak Acad. of Sciences; Dir Ing. ŠTEFAN HANEČKA; publ. *Architektura a urbanizmus* (4 a year).

ECONOMICS, LAW AND POLITICS

Institute of Economics: 811 05 Bratislava, Šancova 56; tel. (7) 39-54-80; fax (7) 39-51-06; attached to Slovak Acad. of Sciences; Dir Doc. Ing. EDUARD MIKELKA; publ. *Journal of Economics* (monthly).

Institute of Forecasting: 811 05 Bratislava, Šancova 56; tel. (7) 39-51-14; fax (7) 39-50-29; attached to Slovak Acad. of Sciences; Dir Ing. ŠTEFAN ZAJAC.

Institute of Political Science: 813 64 Bratislava, Dúbravská cesta 9; tel. (7) 378-97-27; fax (7) 378-97-26; attached to Slovak Acad. of Sciences; Dir PhDr JOZEF JABLONICKÝ.

Institute of State and Law: 813 64 Bratislava, Klemensova 19; tel. (7) 36-18-33; fax (7) 36-23-25; attached to Slovak Acad. of Sciences; Dir JUDr EDUARD BARÁNY; publ. *Právny odbor* (6 a year).

FINE AND PERFORMING ARTS

Institute of Art History: 842 34 Bratislava, Dúbravská cesta 9; tel. and fax (7) 37-34-28; attached to Slovak Acad. of Sciences; Dir Doc. PhDr JÁN BAKOŠ; publ. *ARS* (3 a year).

Institute of Musicology: 841 05 Bratislava, Dúbravská cesta 9; tel. and fax (7) 54-77-35-89; attached to Slovak Acad. of Sciences; Dir Doc. PhDr JURAJ LEXMANN; publ. *Ethnomusicologicum* (1 a year), *Musicologica Slovaca et Europaea* (1 a year).

Institute of Theatre and Film: 813 64 Bratislava, Dúbravská cesta 9; tel. (7) 54-77-71-93; fax (7) 54-77-35-67; e-mail kadfsekr@savba.savba.sk; f. 1990; attached to Slovak Acad. of Sciences; Dir PhDr MILOŠ MISTRÍK; publ. *Slovenské divadlo* (4 a year).

HISTORY, GEOGRAPHY AND ARCHAEOLOGY

Institute of Archaeology: 949 21 Nitra, Akademická 2; tel. (87) 356-17; fax (87) 356-18; attached to Slovak Acad. of Sciences; Dir Doc. PhDr ALEXANDER RUTTKAY; publs *AVANS* (1 a year), *Slovenská archeológia* (2 a year).

Institute of Geography: 814 73 Bratislava, Ul. Štefánikova 49; tel. (7) 39-55-87; fax (7) 39-13-40; attached to Slovak Acad. of Sciences; Dir Doc. RNDr ANTON BEZÁK; publs *Geografický časopis* (4 a year), *Geographia Slovaca* (1 a year).

Institute of Historical Studies: 813 64 Bratislava, Klemensova 19; tel. (7) 32-57-53; fax (7) 36-16-45; f. 1942; attached to Slovak Acad. of Sciences; library of 75,000 vols; Dir PhDr DUŠAN KOVÁČ; publs *Historický časopis* (Journal of History, 4 a year), *Historické štúdie* (Historical Studies, 1 a year), *Studia Historica Slovaca* (1 a year), *Slovanské štúdie* (Slavonic Studies, 2 a year), *Z dejín vied a techniky* (Studies in the History of Science and Technology, 1 a year), *Human Affairs* (2 a year).

LANGUAGE AND LITERATURE

Institute of Slovak Literature: 813 64 Bratislava, Konventná 13; tel. and fax (7) 531-60-25; f. 1943; attached to Slovak Acad. of Sciences; library of 50,000 vols; Dir Doc. PhDr PETER ZAJAC; publ. *Slovenská literatúra* (6 a year).

Institute of World Literature: 813 64 Bratislava, Konventná 13; tel. (7) 531-27-01; fax (7) 531-60-25; e-mail postmaster@usvl.savba.sk; attached to Slovak Acad. of Sciences; Dir PhDr JÁN KOŠKA; publ. *Slovak Review* (2 a year).

Ľudovít Štúr Institute of Linguistics: 813 64 Bratislava, Panská 26; tel. and fax (7) 533-17-56; f. 1943; attached to Slovak Acad. of Sciences; library of 22,000 vols; Dir PhDr IVAN RIPKA; publs *Jazykovedný časopis Slovenská reč*, *Kultúra slova*.

MEDICINE

Cancer Research Institute: 833 91 Bratislava, Vlárska 7; tel. (7) 532-72-60; fax (7) 532-72-50; e-mail exonalt@savba.sk; attached to Slovak Acad. of Sciences; Dir Doc. Ing. ČESTMÍR ALTANER; publ. *Neoplazma* (6 a year).

Institute for Heart Research: 842 33 Bratislava, Dúbravská cesta 9; tel. (7) 37-44-05; fax (7) 37-66-37; attached to Slovak Acad. of Sciences; Dir Doc. MUDr JÁN SLEZÁK.

Institute of Experimental Endocrinology: 833 06 Bratislava, Vlárska 3; tel. (7) 37-41-01; fax (7) 37-42-47; attached to Slovak Acad. of Sciences; Dir RNDr RICHARD KVETŇANSKÝ; publ. *Endocrine Regulations* (4 a year).

Institute of Experimental Pharmacology: 842 16 Bratislava, Dúbravská cesta 9; tel. (7) 37-35-86; fax (7) 37-59-28; e-mail exfabauv@savba.sk; attached to Slovak Acad. of Sciences; Dir Prof. MUDr VIKTOR BAUER.

Institute of Neurobiology: 040 01 Košice, Šoltésovej 4–6; tel. (95) 76-50-64; fax (95) 76-50-74; attached to Slovak Acad. of Sciences; Dir Prof. MUDr JOZEF MARŠALA.

Institute of Normal and Pathological Physiology: 813 71 Bratislava, Sienkiewiczova 1; tel. (7) 32-66-18; fax (7) 36-85-16; f. 1953; attached to Slovak Acad. of Sciences; Dir MUDr VLADIMÍR SMIEŠKO.

Institute of Parasitology: 040 01 Košice, Hlinkova 3; tel. (95) 633-44-55; fax (95) 633-14-14; e-mail pausav@saske.sk; f. 1953; attached to Slovak Acad. of Sciences; library of 8,000 vols; Dir Prof. Dr P. DUBINSKÝ; publ. *Helminthologia* (4 a year).

Institute of Virology: 842 46 Bratislava, Dúbravská cesta 9; tel. (7) 37-42-68; fax (7) 37-42-84; attached to Slovak Acad. of Sciences; Dir Doc. MUDr FEDOR ČIAMPOR; publ. *Acta Virologia* (6 a year).

NATURAL SCIENCES

Biological Sciences

Institute of Animal Biochemistry and Genetics: 900 28 Ivanka pri Dunaji; tel. (7) 594-30-52; fax (7) 594-39-32; attached to Slovak Acad. of Sciences; Dir Doc. RNDr MILOSLAV GREKSÁK.

Institute of Animal Physiology: 040 01 Košice, Šoltésovej 4; tel. (95) 76-31-21; fax (95) 76-21-62; attached to Slovak Acad. of Sciences; Dir MVDr JURAJ KOPPEL.

Institute of Botany: 842 23 Bratislava, Dúbravská cesta 14; tel. (7) 37-35-07; fax (7) 37-19-48; e-mail botuinst@savba.savba.sk; f. 1953; attached to Slovak Acad. of Sciences; library of 21,000 vols; Dir OTÍLIA GAŠPARÍKOVÁ; publ. *Biologica* (2 a year).

Institute of Experimental Phytopathology and Entomology: 900 28 Ivanka pri Dunaji, Nádražná 52; tel. (7) 594-32-51; fax (7) 594-34-31; attached to Slovak Acad. of Sciences; Dir RNDr HELENA BAUMGARTNEROVÁ; publ. *Entomological Problems* (2 a year).

Institute of Forest Ecology: 960 53 Zvolen, Štúrova 2; tel. (855) 209-14; fax (855) 274-85; attached to Slovak Acad. of Sciences; Dir Prof. Ing. EDUARD BUBLINEC.

Institute of Landscape Ecology: 814 99 Bratislava, Štefánikova 3; tel. (7) 39-38-82; fax (7) 39-45-08; attached to Slovak Acad. of Sciences; Dir Ing. JÚLIUS OSZLÁNYI; publs *Životné postredie* (6 a year), *Ecology* (4 a year).

Institute of Microbiology: 814 34 Bratislava, Štefánikova 3; tel. (7) 39-48-45; fax (7) 39-38-24; e-mail dt@ue.savba.sk; f. 1997; attached to Slovak Acad. of Sciences; library of 3,000 vols; Dir Dr DEZIDER TOTH; publ. *Biologia* (6 a year).

Institute of Molecular Biology: 842 51 Bratislava, Dúbravská cesta 9; tel. (7) 37-37-02; fax (7) 37-23-16; attached to Slovak Acad. of Sciences; Dir JOZEF TIMKO.

Institute of Molecular Physiology and Genetics: 833 34 Bratislava, Vlárska 5; tel. (7) 37-52-66; fax (7) 37-36-66; e-mail usrdtylo@savba.savba.sk; f. 1990; attached to Slovak Acad. of Sciences; library of 1,000 vols; Dir Dr ALBERT BREIER; publ. *General Physiology and Biophysics* (4 a year).

Institute of Plant Genetics and Biotechnology: 950 07 Nitra, Akademická 2, POB 39A; tel. (87) 366-59; fax (87) 366-60; e-mail pretova@savba.savba.sk; attached to Slovak Acad. of Sciences; Dir RNDr ANNA PRETOVÁ.

Institute of Zoology and Ecosociology: 842 06 Bratislava, Dúbravská cesta 9; tel. (7) 378-32-48; fax (7) 378-97-57; attached to Slovak Acad. of Sciences; Dir RNDr MILAN LABUDA; publs *Biologia* (6 a year), *Entomological Problems* (2 a year).

Mathematical Sciences

Institute of Mathematics: 814 73 Bratislava, Ul. Štefánikova 49; tel. and fax (7) 39-73-16; attached to Slovak Acad. of Sciences; Dir Prof. RNDr BELOSLAV RIEČAN; publ. *Mathematica Slovaca* (5 a year).

Physical Sciences

Institute of Astronomy: 059 60 Tatranská Lomnica; tel. (969) 46-78-66; fax (969) 46-76-56; e-mail zve@ta3.sk; f. 1943; attached to Slovak Acad. of Sciences; library of 9,000 vols, 6,000 vols of periodicals; Dir RNDr JURAJ ZVERKO; Scientific Sec. Dr A. KUČERA; publ. *Contributions of the Astronomical Observatory Skalnaté Pleso* (2 a year).

Institute of Chemistry: 842 38 Bratislava, Dúbravská cesta 9; tel. (7) 37-20-80; fax (7) 37-55-65; e-mail chemsekr@savba.sk; f. 1953; attached to Slovak Acad. of Sciences; Dir Dr JÁN HIRSCH; publ. *Chemical Papers* (6 a year).

Institute of Experimental Physics: 043 53 Košice, Watsonova 47; tel. and fax (95) 363-20; attached to Slovak Acad. of Sciences; Dir RNDr PETER KOPČANSKÝ.

Institute of Geology: 842 26 Bratislava, Dúbravská cesta 9; tel. (7) 378-20-12; attached to Slovak Acad. of Sciences; Dir RNDr JOZEF MICHALÍK; publs *Geologica Carpathica* (6 a year), *Geologica Carpathica Clays* (2 a year).

Institute of Geophysics: 842 28 Bratislava, Dúbravská cesta 9; tel. (7) 37-33-68; fax (7) 37-52-78; e-mail geoflabi@savba.sk; f. 1953; attached to Slovak Acad. of Sciences; Dir Dr IGOR TUNYI; publ. *Contributions to Geophysics and Geodesy* (4 a year).

Institute of Geotechnics: 043 53 Košice, Watsonova 45; tel. (95) 633-27-40; fax (95) 632-34-02; attached to Slovak Acad. of Sciences; Dir Prof. Ing. FÉLIX SEKULA.

Institute of Hydrology: 830 08 Bratislava, Račianská 75; tel. (7) 25-30-21; fax (7) 25-94-04; attached to Slovak Acad. of Sciences; Dir RNDr JÚLIUS ŠÚTOR; publ. *Journal of Hydrology and Hydromechanics* (6 a year).

Institute of Inorganic Chemistry: 842 36 Bratislava, Dúbravská cesta 9; tel. (7) 37-51-70; fax (7) 37-35-41; attached to Slovak Acad. of Sciences; Dir RNDr JOZEF NOGA.

Institute of Materials Research: 043 53 Košice, Watsonova 47; tel. (95) 633-71-07; fax (95) 633-71-08; e-mail imrsas@imrnow.saske.sk; f. 1955; attached to Slovak Acad. of Sciences; Dir ĽUDOVÍT PARILÁK; publ. *Kovové materiály* (6 a year).

Institute of Measurement Science: 842 19 Bratislava, Dúbravská cesta 9; tel. (7) 54-77-40-33; fax (7) 54-77-59-43; e-mail umersekr@savba.sk; f. 1953; attached to Slovak Acad. of Sciences; library of 8,000 vols; Dir Prof. Dr Ing. IVAN FROLLO.

Institute of Physics: 842 28 Bratislava, Dúbravská cesta 9; tel. (7) 37-24-79; fax (7) 37-60-85; attached to Slovak Acad. of Sciences; Dir RNDr PETER MRAFKO; publ. *Acta Physica Slovaca* (6 a year).

Institute of Polymer Research: 842 36 Bratislava, Dúbravská cesta 9; tel. (7) 37-34-48; fax (7) 37-59-23; attached to Slovak Acad. of Sciences; Dir RNDr PAVOL HRDLOVIČ.

PHILOSOPHY AND PSYCHOLOGY

Institute of Experimental Psychology: 842 34 Bratislava, Dúbravska cesta 9; tel. (7) 54-77-56-25; fax (7) 54-77-55-84; e-mail expspro@savba.sk; attached to Slovak Acad. of Sciences; Dir PhDr MICHAL STRÍŽENEC; publ. *Studia Psychologica* (4 a year).

Institute of Philosophy: 813 64 Bratislava, Klemensova 19; tel. (7) 36-15-27; fax (7) 32-12-15; attached to Slovak Acad. of Sciences; Dir PhDr TIBOR PICHLER; publ. *Filozofia* (monthly).

RELIGION, SOCIOLOGY AND ANTHROPOLOGY

Institute of Ethnology: 813 64 Bratislava, Jakubovo nám. 12; tel. and fax (7) 536-15-21; attached to Slovak Acad. of Sciences; Dir Mgr DUŠAN RATICA; publ. *Slovenský národopis* (4 a year).

Institute of Oriental and African Studies: 813 64 Bratislava, Klemensova 19; tel. and fax (7) 32-63-26; e-mail kohollа@klemens.savba.sk; attached to Slovak Acad. of Sciences; Dir VIKTOR KRUPA; publs *Asian and African Studies* (2 a year), *Human Affairs* (2 a year).

Institute of Social and Biological Communication: 813 64 Bratislava, Klemensova 19; tel. (7) 37-56-83; fax (7) 37-34-42; e-mail kvsbk@savba.sk; f. 1990; attached to Slovak Acad. of Sciences; Dir PhDr GABRIEL BIANCHI; publ. *Human Affairs* (2 a year).

Institute of Social Sciences: 040 00 Košice, Karpatská 5; tel. and fax (95) 625-58-56; e-mail sutaj@saske.sk; f. 1975; attached to Slovak Acad. of Sciences; library of 7,000 vols; Dir Dr ŠTEFAN ŠUTAJ; publ. *International Journal of Transdisciplinary Studies* (4 a year).

Institute of Sociology: 813 64 Bratislava, Klemensova 19; tel. (7) 36-43-55; fax (7) 36-13-12; attached to Slovak Acad. of Sciences; Dir Mgr ĽUBOMÍR FALŤAN; publ. *Sociológia* (6 a year).

TECHNOLOGY

Institute of Computer Systems: 842 37 Bratislava, Dúbravská cesta 9; tel. and fax (7) 37-10-04; attached to Slovak Acad. of Sciences; Dir Ing. LADISLAV HLUCHÝ; publ. *Computers and Artificial Intelligence* (6 a year).

Institute of Control Theory and Robotics: 842 37 Bratislava, Dúbravská cesta 9; tel. (7) 37-32-71; fax (7) 37-60-45; attached to Slovak Acad. of Sciences; Dir Doc. Ing. KAROL DOBROVODSKÝ.

Institute of Electrical Engineering: 842 39 Bratislava, Dúbravská cesta 9; tel. (7) 37-58-06; fax (7) 35-78-16; attached to Slovak Acad. of Sciences; Dir Ing. JOZEF NOVÁK; publ. *Journal of Electrical Engineering* (monthly).

Institute of Materials and Machine Mechanics: 830 08 Bratislava 38, Račianska 75, POB 95; tel. (7) 25-30-00; fax (7) 25-33-01; e-mail postmast@umms.savba.sk; f. 1980; attached to Slovak Acad. of Sciences; library of 10,000 vols; Dir Dr VLADIMÍR GIBA; publs *Kovové materiály* (Metallic Materials, 6 a year), *Strojnícky časopis* (Journal of Mechanical Engineering, 6 a year).

Research Institute for Nuclear Power Plants: 918 64 Trnava, Okružná 5; tel. (805) 60-51-11; fax (805) 50-25-74; f. 1977; library of 18,000 items; Dirs JÁN KOREC, MARIÁN ŠTUBŇA; publ. *Spravodajca VÚJE* (quarterly).

Transport Research Institute: 011 39 Žilina, Veľký Diel 3323, PP B-49; tel. (89) 65-28-19; fax (89) 65-28-83; e-mail management@vud.sk; f. 1954; library of 45,000 standards and reports; Dir Ing. PAVOL LAŠ; publ. *Horizonty dopravy* (quarterly).

Libraries and Archives

Banská Bystrica

Štátna vedecká knižnica (State Scientific Library): 975 58 Banská Bystrica, Lazovná 9; tel. (88) 542-13; fax (88) 546-21; e-mail bibliotheca@svk.bb.sanet.sk; f. 1924; 2,000,000 vols; Dir Mgr OĽGA KALISKÁ.

Bratislava

Archív hlavného mesta SR Bratislavy, Regionálna knižnica (Bratislava Regional Library): 814 71 Bratislava, Primaciálne nám. 2; tel. (7) 533-32-48; f. 1923; 90,000 vols; Dir PhDr JÁN ŠULAVÍK.

Centrum vedecko-technických informácií Slovenskej republiky (Slovak Centre for Scientific and Technical Information): 812 23 Bratislava, Nám. Slobody 19; tel. (7) 36-24-19; fax (7) 32-35-27; e-mail cvti@tbbl.sltk.stuba.sk; f. 1938; 362,000 books, 144,000 vols of periodicals, 28,000 trade publs, 239,000 patents, 90,000 standards; Dir ULRICH KOLOMAN; publs *Bulletin Centra VTI SR* (4 a year), *Signálne informácie* (monthly), *Euro-Info* (10 a year), *Infotrend* (4 a year).

Mestská knižnica Bratislava (Bratislava Municipal Library): 814 79 Bratislava, Klariská 16; tel. and fax (7) 533-51-48; f. 1900; 290,000 vols; Dir PhDr ELENA VEĽASOVÁ.

Slovenská ekonomická knižnica (Slovak Economic Library): 852 35 Bratislava, Dolnozemská cesta 1; tel. (7) 581-22-93; fax (7) 581-23-02; e-mail ka@sek.euba.sk; f. 1948; 333,000 vols, 434 periodicals; Dir Dr D. KRAUSOVÁ.

Univerzitná knižnica v Bratislave (University Library of Bratislava): 814 17 Bratislava, Michalská 1; tel. 533-32-47; fax 533-42-46; f. 1919; 2,230,000 vols; Dir PhDr JOZEF GERBÓC.

Ústav informácií a prognóz školstva (Institute of Information and Forecasting on Education): 842 44 Bratislava, Staré grunty 52; tel. (7) 65-42-51-66; fax (7) 65-42-10-48; f. 1954; 320,000 vols; Dir Mgr. MICHAL PRIDALA; publs *Academia*, *Mládež a spoločnosť* (Youth), *Informatika v škole* (Informatics in Education), *Expresná informácia* (Express Information), *Referátové listy* (Abstract Sheets).

Ústredná knižnica Slovenskej akadémie vied (Central Library of the Slovak Academy of Sciences): 814 67 Bratislava, Klemensova 19; tel. and fax (7) 32-17-33; e-mail knizhorv@klemens.savba.sk; f. 1953; 600,000 vols; Dir Dr MARCELA HORVÁTHOVÁ.

Košice

Štátna vedecká knižnica (State Scientific Library): 042 30 Košice, Hlavná 10; tel. 622-67-24; fax 622-23-31; e-mail svkk@ke.sanet.sk; f. 1657; 3,354,000 vols; Dir Mgr DANIELA DŽUGANOVÁ; publs *Zoznam zahraničných časopisov objednaných na východné Slovensko* (annually), *Súpis bibliografií a rešerší vypracovaných v ŠVK Košice* (annually).

Verejná knižnica Jána Bocatia (Ján Bocatius Public Library): 042 61 Košice, Hlavná 48; tel. (95) 622-32-91; fax (95) 622-32-92; f. 1924; 476,000 vols; Dir Dr KLÁRA KERNEROVÁ.

Martin

Matica slovenská (Slovak National Library): 036 52 Martin, L. Novomeského 32; tel. (842) 313-71; fax (842) 331-88; e-mail snk@matica.sk; f. 1863; 5,500,000 vols; literary archives and museum documents, and complete Slovak printed production; Dir DANIELA SLÍŽOVÁ; publs *Slovenská národná bibliografia—Knihy, Články, Slovenske pohľady, Knižnice a informácie* (all monthly), *Slovensko* (quarterly), *Slovenské národné noviny*, (weekly), *Bibliografický zborník, Knižničný zborník, Kniha, Literárny archív, Literárnomúzejný letopis, Biografické štúdie* (yearbooks), *Slováci v zahraničí, Inventar rukopisov ALU MS*.

Nitra

Slovenská poľnohospodárska knižnica (Slovak Agricultural Library): 949 59 Nitra, Štúrova 51, POB 20B; tel. and fax (87) 51-77-43; f. 1946; 525,000 vols; Dir Ing. DANKA JELA PETRÁŠOVÁ; publs *Agrobibliografia* (every 6 months), *Vybrané poľnohospodárske informácie* (Selected Agricultural Information, 3 a year).

Prešov

Krajská štátna knižnica (Regional State Library): 081 37 Prešov, Hlavná ul. 99; tel. and fax (91) 72-49-60; e-mail svkpo1@po.sanet.sk; f. 1952; 421,000 vols; Dir Dr O. STRAKOVÁ.

Zvolen

Slovenská lesnícka a drevárska knižnica (Slovak Library for Forestry and Wood Technology): 961 02 Zvolen, T. G. Masaryka 20; tel. (855) 235-36; f. 1952; attached to the Technical Univ. in Zvolen; 360,000 vols; Dir Ing. LUDVIGHOVÁ ĽUBICA; publs *Bibliography of the Technical University in Zvolen* (1 a year), *Forestry Bulletin* (monthly), *Wood Sciences Bulletin* (monthly), *Ecology Bulletin* (6 a year).

Museums and Art Galleries

Banská Bystrica

Múzeum Slovenského národného povstania (Slovak National Uprising Museum): 974 00 Banská Bystrica, Kapitulská č. 23; tel. 525-29; f. 1955; anti-fascist struggle of the Slovak people during the Second World War; library of 17,000 vols; PaedDr JÁN STANISLAV; publ. *Zborník musea SNP*.

Stredoslovenské múzeum (Central Slovakia Museum): 974 00 Banská Bystrica, Slovenského národného povstánia 4; tel. 249-38; f. 1889; natural sciences, history, ethnography; library of 12,000 vols; Dir MILAN ŠOKA; publ. *Stredné Slovensko* (annually).

Banská Štiavnica

Slovenské banské múzeum (Slovak Mining Museum): 969 00 Banská Štiavnica; tel. (859) 215-41; fax (859) 227-64; f. 1900; library of 21,000 vols; Dir Ing. IVAN HERČKO; publ. *Zborník SBM* (bulletin).

Bratislava

Galéria mesta Bratislavy (Municipal Gallery of Bratislava): 815 35 Bratislava, Mirbachov palác, Františkánske nám. 11; tel. (7) 533-51-02; fax (7) 533-26-11; e-mail gmb@netlab.sk; Slovak and Central European art; library of 12,000 vols; Dir Dr IVAN JANČÁR.

Mestské muzeum v Bratislave (Bratislava Municipal Museum): 815 18 Bratislava, Primaciálne nám. 3; tel. (7) 533-47-42; fax (7) 533-46-31; f. 1868; archaeology, history, art history, applied arts, numismatics, history of pharmacy, ethnography; library of 21,000 vols; Dir PETER HYROSS.

Slovenská národná galéria (Slovak National Gallery): 815 13 Bratislava, Riečna 1; tel. 33-07-46; f. 1948; art, applied art; library of 65,000 vols, 80,000 documents; Dir JURAJ ŽÁRY; publ. *Galéria* (quarterly).

Slovenské národné múzeum (Slovak National Museum): 814 36 Bratislava, Vajanského nábrežie 2; tel. (7) 36-68-67; fax (7) 36-66-53; f. 1893; history, natural history, art, archaeology; Dir PhDr PETER MARÁKY; publs *História, Prírodné vedy, Etnografia, Archeológia* (annually), *Fontes* (various publs on history, archaeology, ethnography), *Annotationes Zoologicae et Botanicae, Pamiatky a múzeá* (quarterly), *Múzeum* (quarterly), *Annual Reports of Slovak Museums*.

Košice

Východoslovenské múzeum (Museum of Eastern Slovakiá): 041 36 Košice, Hviezdoslavová 3; tel. (95) 622-03-09; fax (95) 622-86-96; f. 1872; history, natural sciences, art, ethnography; library of 49,000 vols; Dir JOZEF DUCHOŇ; publs *Historica Carpatica* (1 a year), *Natura Carpatica* (1 a year).

Kremnica

NBS—Múzeum mincí a medailí (National Bank of Slovakia—Museum of Coins and Medals): 967 01 Kremnica, Štefánikovo nám. 10; tel. and fax (857) 74-21-21; f. 1890; Dir MARIANA NOVOTNÁ.

Piešťany

Balneologické múzeum (Museum of Balneology): 921 01 Piešťany, Beethovenova 5; f. 1928; history of Slovak spas; Dir V. KRUPA.

Svidník

Dukelské múzeum (Dukal Museum): 089 01 Svidník; tel. (937) 213-98; f. 1965; battle of Dukla Pass and Second World War; library of 3,225 vols; Dir Dr JOZEF RODÁK.

Štátne múzeum ukrajinsko-rusínskej kultúry (State Museum of Ukrainian-Ruthenian Culture): 089 01 Svidník, Centrálna 258; tel. 213-65; fax 215-69; f. 1956; history and culture of the Ukrainians and Ruthenians in Slovakia; library of 42,000 vols; Dir PhDr MIRÓSLAV SOPÓLIGA.

Tatranská Lomnica

Múzeum Tatranského národného parku (Tatras National Park Museum): 059 60 Tatranská Lomnica; tel. (0969) 46-79-51; fax (0969) 46-79-58; f. 1957; mineralogy, natural history; ethnography, history; library of 31,000 vols; Dir MIKULÁŠ MICHELČÍK.

Universities

UNIVERZITA KOMENSKÉHO V BRATISLAVE (Comenius University of Bratislava)

818 06 Bratislava, Šafárikovo nám. 6

Telephone: (7) 32-15-94

Fax: (7) 36-38-36

E-mail: kr@rec.uniba.sk

Founded 1465 as Academia Istropolitana; re-opened with present name 1919

State control

Languages of instruction: Slovak, English

Academic year: September to January, February to June

Rector: Prof. Ing. FERDINAND DEVÍNSKY

Vice-Rectors: Assoc. Prof. RNDr PAVEL SŮRA, Assoc. Prof. JUDr PETER KRESÁK, Prof. MUDr PETER MRÁZ, Assoc. Prof. RNDr IVAN OSTROVSKÝ

Bursar: Ing. ZORA DOBRÍKOVÁ

Number of teachers: 1,884

Number of students: 24,528

Publications: numerous faculty publications.

DEANS

Faculty of Law: Assoc. Prof. JUDr MOJMÍR MAMOJKA

Faculty of Mathematics and Physics: Assoc. Prof. RNDr ĽUDOVIT FISCHER

Faculty of Medicine at Bratislava: Prof. MUDr IVAN ĎURIŠ

Jessenius Faculty of Medicine at Martin: Prof. MUDr ANDREJ HAJTMAN

Faculty of Philosophy: Assoc. Prof. PhDr LADISLAV KICZKO

Faculty of Natural Sciences: Assoc. Prof. RNDr VLADIMÍR FERÁK

Faculty of Pharmacy: Prof. MUDr PAVEL ŠVEC

Faculty of Physical Education and Sport: Assoc. Prof. PhDr VLADIMÍR HELLEBRANDT

Faculty of Education: Prof. PhDr MIRON ZELINA

Faculty of Roman Catholic Theology: Prof. ThDr JOZEF KUTARŇA

Faculty of Protestant Theology: Prof. ThDr KAROL GÁBRIŠ

Faculty of Management: Assoc. Prof. Ing. JÁN RUDY

PROFESSORS

Faculty of Law:

BAJCURA, A., Civil Law
BARANCOVÁ, E., Labour Law
BLAHO, P., History of Law
HUSÁR, E., Penal Law
LAZAR, J., Civil Law
MATHERN, V., Penal Law
MERTANOVÁ, Š., History of Law
POSLUCH, M., State Law
PRUSÁK, J., Theory of Law
ŠKULTÉTY, P., Administrative Law

Faculty of Mathematics and Physics:

BEZÁK, V., Solid State Physics
BRUNOVSKÝ, P., Mathematics
HIANIK, T., Biophysics
HUBAČ, I., Biophysics
CHORVÁT, D., Biophysics
KAČUR, J., Mathematics
KATRIŇÁK, T., Mathematics
KOSTYRKO, P., Mathematics
LICHARD, P., Theoretical Physics
LUKÁČ, P., Physics of Plasma
NOGA, M., Theoretical Physics
PÁZMÁN, A., Mathematics
PIŠÚT, J., Theoretical Physics
PLESNÍK, J., Mathematics
POVINEC, P., Nuclear Physics
ŠIRÁŇ, G., Geophysics
ŠÁRO, Š., Nuclear Physics
SITÁR, B., Physics
ŠKALNÝ, D., Physics
ŠTRBA, A., Experimental Physics

Faculty of Medicine in Bratislava:

ÁGHOVÁ, Š., Public Health
BADA, V., Internal Medicine
BAKOSS, P., Epidemiology
BALAŽOVJECH, I., Internal Medicine
BÁLINT, O., Infectious Diseases
BENIAK, M., Public Health
BERGENDI, Š., Biochemistry
BREZA, J., Urology
BUC, M., Immunology
BUCHVALD, J., Dermatovenereology
ČÁRSKY, J., Medical Chemistry and Biochemistry
DANIHEL, Š., Pathological Anatomy and Forensic Medicine
ĎURIŠ, I., Internal Medicine
FERENČÍK, M., Immunology
GERINEC, A., Ophthalmology
HOLOMÁŇ, K., Gynaecology and Obstetrics
HORŇAK, M., Surgery
HULÍN, I., Normal and Pathological Physiology
JAKUBOVSKÝ, J., Pathological Anatomy and Forensic Medicine
KAPELLEROVÁ, A., Paediatrics
KOTULOVÁ, D., Microbiology
KOVÁCS, L., Paediatrics

Kriška, M., Pharmacology
Makai, F., Surgery
Mikeš, Z., Internal Medicine
Mráz, P., Anatomy
Oláh, Z., Ophthalmology
Redhammer, R., Internal Medicine
Satko, I., Stomatology
Šiman, J., Surgery
Šuška, P., Gynaecology and Obstetrics
Švec, J., Oncology
Traubner, P., Neurology
Turčáni, P., Neurology
Traubner, P., Neurology
Vaško, J., Stomatology
Zaviačič, M., Pathological Anatomy and Forensic Medicine
Zlatoš, J., Normal Anatomy, Histology and Embryology
Zlatoš, L., Normal and Pathological Physiology
Žucha, I., Psychiatry

Jessenius Faculty of Medicine in Martin:

Buchancová, J., Internal Medicine
Buchanec, J., Paediatrics
Danko, J., Gynaecology and Obstetrics
Drobný, M., Neurology
Hajtman, A., Otorhinolaryngology
Hanáček, J., Physiology and Pathophysiology
Javorka, K., Physiology and Pathophysiology
Jurko, A., Paediatrics
Kliment, J., Urology
Kubisz, P., Internal Medicine
Mokáň, M., Internal Medicine
Nosáľová, G., Pharmacology
Novomesky, F., Foreign Illnesses
Plank, L., Pathological Anatomy
Straka, Š., Epidemiology
Stránsky, A., Physiology and Pathophysiology

Faculty of Philosophy:

Bajzíková, E., Slovak Language
Dolník, J., General Linguistics
Hvišč, J., Slavonic Philology
Kimlička, Š., Librarianship and Information Science
Kollárik, T., Psychology
Konopka, J., Psychology
Marcelli, M., Philosophy
Michálek, J., Ethnology
Mikula, V., Slovak Literature
Mlacek, J., Slovak Language
Novák, J., Allied Historical Sciences
Pauliny, J., Modern Non-Slavonic Philology
Perhács, J., Pedagogy
Povchanič, Š., Modern Non-Slavonic Philology
Pšenák, J., Pedagogy
Schenk, J., Sociology
Štefanovičová, T., Archaeology
Štúr, I., Psychology
Švec, Š., Pedagogy
Tandlichová, E., Theory of English Language Teaching
Trup, L., Modern Non-Slavonic Philology
Tušer, A., Journalism
Vojtek, J., General History
Zigo, M., Philosophy

Faculty of Natural Sciences:

Adamčíková, S., Physical Chemistry and Chemical Physics
Hensel, K., Zoology
Holba, V., Physical Chemistry
Hovorka, D., Petrology
Hudák, J., Plant Physiology
Kandráč, J., Analytical Chemistry
Kellö, V., Physical Chemistry and Chemical Physics
Kettner, M., Microbiology
Kolarov, J., Biochemistry
Kováč, L., Biochemistry
Kraus, I., Applied Geophysics
Krcho, J., Cartography
Macášek, F., Nuclear Chemistry
Masarovičová, E., Plant Physiology
Melioris, L., Hydrogeology
Mládek, J., Human and Regional Geography
Murín, M., Botany
Ondrášik, R., Hydrology and Geology
Schwendt, P., Inorganic Chemistry
Šefara, J., Geology
Ševčík, P., Physical Chemistry
Šoják, L., Analytical Chemistry
Šomšák, L., Botany
Šubík, J., Biochemistry
Toma, Š., Organic Chemistry
Urban, M., Chemical Physics
Zaťko, M., Geography

Faculty of Pharmacy:

Chalabala, M., Galenic Pharmacy
Čižmárik, J., Pharmaceutical Chemistry
Devínsky, F., Pharmaceutical Chemistry
Havránek, E., Pharmaceutical Chemistry
Kovács, P., Biochemistry
Mlynarčík, D., Biochemistry
Pšenák, M., Biochemistry
Rak, J., Galenic Pharmacy
Švec, P., Pharmacology and Toxicology

Faculty of Physical Education and Sport:

Grexa, J., History
Kasa, J.
Štulrajter, V., Physiology

Faculty of Education:

Kačala, J., Slovak Language
Lechta, V., Special Education
Marcinger, S., Music
Marčok, V., Theory and History of Slovak Literature
Ondreička, K., Fine Arts
Štraus, F., Theory and History of Slovak Literature
Šulka, R., Mathematics
Vašek, Š., Special Education
Zelina, M., Education

Faculty of Roman Catholic Theology:

Kutarňa, J., Theology
Tondra, F., Catholic Theology
Vragaš, S., Catholic Theology

Faculty of Protestant Theology:

Gábriš, K., New Testament Theology
Kišš, I., Protestant Theology
Ondrejovič, D., Protestant Theology

Faculty of Management:

Hlavatá, I., Economics
Komorník, J., Probability and Mathematical Statistics
Luknič, A., Economics
van Gemerden, J., Economics
Zapletal, V., Economics

UNIVERZITA PAVLA JOZEFA ŠAFÁRIKA V KOŠICIACH
(Šafárik University of Košice)

041 80 Košice, Šrobárova 2
Telephone: (95) 622-26-08
Fax: (95) 76-69-59
E-mail: zahrodd@kosice.upjs.sk

Founded 1959
State control
Languages of instruction: Slovak, English
Academic year: September to July

Rector: Prof. Dr Dušan Podhradský
Pro-Rectors: Prof. Igor Palúš, Assoc. Prof. Dr Oliver Rácz, Prof. Dr Július Vajó
Registrar: PhDr Ing. Jozef Lokša
Librarian: PhDr Darina Kožuchová

Number of teachers: 400
Number of students: 4,100

Publications: *Folia Facultatis Medicae Universitatis Šafarikianae Cassoviensia, Acta iuridica Cassoviensia, Thaiszia.*

DEANS

Faculty of Natural Sciences: Assoc. Prof. Alexander Feher
Faculty of Law: Assoc. Prof. Peter Mosný
Faculty of Medicine: Assoc. Prof. Ladislav Mirossav
Institute of Public Administration: Assoc. Prof. Juraj Špirko

PROFESSORS

Faculty of Law:

Gašpar, M., Administrative Law
Palúš, I., Administrative Law

Faculty of Medicine:

Jurkovič, I., Pathology
Kafka, J., Psychiatry
Kalina, I., General Biology
Kohút, A., Pharmacology
Mydlík, M., Internal Medicine
Pačin, J., Gynaecology and Obstetrics
Šašinka, A., Paediatrics
Tomori, Z., Physiology
Vajó, J., Surgery

Faculty of Natural Sciences:

Ahlers, I., General Biology
Ahlersová, E., Animal Physiology
Bukovský, L., Mathematics
Chalupka, S., Theoretical Physics
Gálová, M., Analytical Chemistry
Hončariv, R., Genetics
Jendroľ, S., Mathematics
Kristián, F., Organic Chemistry
Podhradský, D., Biochemistry
Síleš, E., Physics

Department of Languages:

Rybák, J., Slavonic Languages

ATTACHED INSTITUTES

Botanic Garden: Košice, Mánesova 23; Dir RNDr Sergej Mochacký.
Computer Centre: Košice, Park Angelinum 9; Dir Ing. Jozef Hugec.
Christian Academy: Košice, Šrobárova 2; Dir Ing. Jozef Palaščák.

UNIVERZITA VETERINÁRSKEHO LEKÁRSTVA V KOŠICIACH
(University of Veterinary Medicine in Košice)

041 81 Košice, Komenského 73
Telephone: (95) 622-99-24
Telex: 177322
Fax: (95) 632-36-66

Founded 1949
State control
Languages of instruction: Slovak and English
Academic year: September to June

Rector: Prof. Dušan Magic
Vice-Rectors: Assoc. Prof. Valent Ledecký, Assoc. Prof. Jozef Bíreš, Assoc. Prof. Jaroslav Legáth
Chief Administrative Officer: Ing. Rudolf Lukáč
Librarian: Dr Soňa Lemáková

Number of teachers: 153
Number of students: 659

Publication: *Folia veterinaria* (4 a year).

PROFESSORS

Bláhovec, J., Chemistry
Cabadaj, R., Food Hygiene and Food Technology
Kačmár, P., Ecology (Toxicology)
Kačmárik, J., Obstetrics and Gynaecology
Kováč, G., Internal Medicine
Lešník, F., Biology
Levkut, M., Pathological Anatomy
Magic, D., Nutrition and Veterinary Dietetics
Maretta, M., Anatomy and Histology
Michna, A., Internal Diseases of Ruminants and Pigs

MIKULA, I., Microbiology and Immunology
RAJTOVÁ, V., Anatomy and Histology
ROSIVAL, L., Biochemistry
ŠVRČEK, Š., Infectious Diseases
VÁRADY, J., Physiology
VRZGULOVÁ, M., Anatomy and Histology
ZIBRÍN, M., Anatomy and Histology

SLOVENSKÁ TECHNICKÁ UNIVERZITA
(Slovak University of Technology)

812 43 Bratislava, Vazovova 5
Telephone: (7) 39-71-96
Fax: (7) 359-43-33

Founded 1938
State control
Languages of instruction: Slovak, English
Academic year: September to July

Rector: Assoc. Prof. IGOR HUDOBA
Vice-Rectors: DUŠAN BUSTIN, JÁN KALUŽBÝ, MARIAN VESELÝ, PETER VIEST
Bursar: HELENA ŽIDEKOVÁ
Librarian: VIERA POLČÍKOVÁ

Number of teachers: 1,500
Number of students: 15,700

Publications: *Spektrum* (in Slovak, 10 a year), *Slovak Journal of Civil Engineering* (in English, 4 a year), *Journal of Electrical Engineering* (in English, monthly), *AT & P Journal* (in Slovak with summary in English, 6 a year), *EE – Journal for Electrical and Power Engineering* (in Slovak with summary in English, 6 a year), *Architektonické listy FA STU* (in Slovak with summary in English, 4 a year), *IB–Informačný bulletin FA STU* (in Slovak, monthly), *Vlákna a textil–Fibres and Textiles* (in co-operation with the Slovak Academy of Sciences, in Slovak and English, 4 a year), *Strojnícky časopis* (in Slovak, monthly), *Kovové materiály* (in Slovak, monthly).

DEANS

Faculty of Electrical Engineering and Information Technology: Prof. VIKTOR SMIEŠKO
Faculty of Architecture: Prof. RÓBERT SPAČEK
Faculty of Chemical Engineering: Prof. MILAN HRONEC
Faculty of Civil Engineering: Assoc. Prof. ĽUDOVÍT FILLO
Faculty of Mechanical Engineering: Assoc. Prof. KAROL JELEMENSKÝ
Faculty of Materials Science and Technology: Prof. MILAN TURŇA

PROFESSORS

Faculty of Electrical Engineering and Information Technology:

ANDRÁŠIK, L., Economics
BAJCSY, J., Measurement Engineering
BALÁŽ, I., Electronics
BARTA, Š., Solid State Physics
BÍZIK, J., Technical Cybernetics
CSABAY, O., Microelectronics
DONOVAL, D., Electronics
DURNÝ, R., Solid State Physics
FECKO, Š., Energy
FRIŠTACKÝ, N., Technical Cybernetics
GATIAĽ, J., Mathematics
GROŠEK, O., Applied Information Science
HARMAN, R., Electronics and Vacuum Technology
HORŇÁK, P., Energy
HORVÁTH, P., Applied Information Science
JURIŠICA, L., Technical Cybernetics
KALAŠ, V., Technical Cybernetics
KLUG, L., Electrical Energy and Electrical Engineering
KREMPASKÝ, J., Experimental Physics
LIPKA, J., Condensed Matter Physics and Acoustics
MAKÁŇ, F., Telecommunications Engineering
MIGLIERINI, M., Solid State Physics
MOLNÁR, Ľ., Computer Engineering
MURGAŠ, J., Automation and Control
NÁVRAT, P., Applied Information Science
RÁČEK, V., Electronic Drives
RIEČANOVÁ, Z., Mathematical Analysis
SEILER, V., History of Philosophy
SITEK, J., Condensed Matter Physics and Acoustics
SLÁMA, J., Theoretical Electrical Engineering
SMIEŠKO, V., Measurement Engineering
ŠAFAŘÍK, J., Applied Information Science
ULIČNÝ, J., Technical Cybernetics
VESELÝ, V., Technical Cybernetics

Faculty of Architecture:

ALEXY, T., Town Planning
ANTAL, E., Art Design
ANTAL, J., Architecture, Civic Buildings
BAŠO, M., Civic Buildings
HAVAŠ, P., Civic Buildings
KAVAN, J., Town Planning
KOTÚČ, J., Technical Cybernetics
LÝSEK, L., Building Structures
PETRÁNSKÝ, Ľ., Theory and History of Art Design
ŠARAFÍN, M., Housing Design
TRNKUS, F., Town Planning
TUŽINSKÝ, I., Building Structures

Faculty of Chemical Engineering:

ALEXY, J., Economics and Management in the Chemical Industry
AUGUSTÍN, J., Fermentation Chemistry and Technology
BAJUS, M., Fuel Technology
BAKOŠ, D., Macromolecular Chemistry and Engineering
BALÁŽ, S., Biochemistry and Molecular Biology
BÁLEŠ, V., Chemical Engineering and Process Control
BAXA, J., Chemical Processing of Fuels
BETINA, V., Microbiology
BISKUPIČ, S., Physical Chemistry and Chemical Physics
BOČA, R., Inorganic Chemistry
BORSIG, E., Macromolecular Chemistry and Engineering
BUSTIN, D., Analytical Chemistry
FELLNER, P., Technology of Inorganic Chemistry
FIŠERA, Ľ., Organic Chemistry
HORÁKOVÁ, K., Biology
HRONEC, M., Organic Technology
JESENÁK, V., Technology of Inorganic Chemistry
JÓNA, E., Inorganic Chemistry
KOHOUT, J., Inorganic Chemistry
KOMAN, V., Chemistry and Technology of Foodstuffs
KOPRDA, V., Environmental Chemistry and Engineering
KRUPČÍK, J., Analytical Chemistry
KRUTOŠÍKOVÁ, A., Organic Chemistry
KVASNIČKA, V., Chemical Physics
MACHO, V., Organic Technology and Petrochemistry
MELNÍK, M., Inorganic Chemistry
MIKLEŠ, J., Technical Cybernetics
MIKO, M., Biochemistry
MOCÁK, J., Analytical Chemistry
ONDREJOVIČ, G., Inorganic Chemistry
PELIKÁN, P., Physical Chemistry
PRÍBELA, A., Chemistry and Technology of Foodstuffs
ŠIMKOVIČ, J., Mathematics in Economics
STAŠKO, A., Physical Chemistry
TÖLGYESSY, J., Nuclear Chemistry and Environmental Engineering
VALACH, F., Physical Chemistry and Chemical Physics
VALKO, L., Physical Chemistry

Faculty of Civil Engineering:

AGÓCS, Z., Steel and Timber Structures
BAJZA, A., Non-Metallic Materials and Construction Materials
BALÁŽ, I., Construction Engineering
BARTOŠ, P., Geodesy and Cartography
BIELEK, M., Building Construction
BILČÍK, J., Construction Engineering
BÚCI, B., Concrete Structures and Bridges
DUDA, E., Humanities
FILLO, Ľ., Construction Engineering
GSCHWENDT, I., Transport Engineering
HULLA, J., Geotechnology
HYKŠ, P., Building Construction
IVANIČKA, I., Economics and Management in the Building Industry
KAISER, J., Structural Mechanics
KLEPSATEL, F., Building Construction
KUCBEL, J., Building Construction
LUKÁČ, M., Hydraulic Engineering
MAJDÚCH, D., Concrete Structures and Bridges
MARTOŇ, J., Sanitary Engineering Structures
OBOŇA, J., Economics and Building Industry Management
OHRABLO, F., Building Construction
OLÁH, J., Building Construction
PUŠKÁŠ, J., Building Construction
ŠIRÁŇ, J., Applied Mathematics
STAŇEK, V., Geodesy and Cartography
SUMEC, J., Building Construction
TRÁVNIK, I., Economics and Management in the Building Industry
TURČEK, P., Building Construction
VALÁŠEK, J., Building Construction
ZAJAC, J., Building Construction
ZÁMEČNÍK, J., Building Construction
ZAPLETAL, I., Technology and Materials Engineering

Faculty of Mechanical Engineering:

BENKO, B., Machine Technology
BUKOVECZKÝ, J., Machine Parts
DÚBRAVEC, B., Electrical Engines and Equipment
HAVALDA, A., Physical Metallurgy and Material Structures
HULKÓ, G., Automatic Control
CHUDÝ, V., Automatic Control
JAŠŠO, I., Machines for Chemical and Food Industry
JAVORČÍK, L., Machines for Engineering Production
KOVÁČ, A., Machine Tool Design
KRÁL, Š., Machine Parts
KRSEK, A., Production Systems
MOLNÁR, V., Thermal and Nuclear Machines
NOHEL, J., Thermal and Nuclear Machines
RUŽIČKA, K., Machines for Engineering Production
SKÁKALA, J., Automatic Control
SLAVKOVSKÝ, J., Materials and Technologies
STAREK, L., Applied Mechanics
STRÝČEK, O., Hydraulic Machines and Equipment
TICHÝ, J., Transport and Manipulation Technology
URBAN, J., Transport and Manipulation Technology
VALČUHA, Š., Machines for Engineering Production
VAVRO, K., Machines and Equipment for the Food Industry
ZÁHOREC, O., Applied Mechanics

Faculty of Materials Science and Technology in Trnava:

BAČA, J., Mechanical Engineering Technology
BÉKES, J., Machinery and Machine Tools
BLAŠKOVITŠ, P., Mechanical Engineering Technology
DRIENSKY, D., Engineering Education
ELIÁŠ, J., Mathematical Analysis
GARAJ, J., Applied Physics
GLESK, P., Teaching of Physical Training
HOLATA, L., Philosophy

HRIVŇÁK, I., Physical Metallurgy and Materials Engineering
HRIVŇÁKOVÁ, D., Physical Metallurgy
HRUBEC, J., Machinery
JANAČ, A., Machinery
KOVÁČ, J., Physics
KUSIN, V., Humanities
LINCZÉNYI, A., Economics and Management in the Building Industry
MORAVČÍK, O., Applied Information Science and Automation in Industry
MURGAŠ, M., Mechanical Production Engineering
POLÁK, K., Mechanical Engineering Technology
ŠÍMA, R., Humanities
TURŇA, M., Welding and Welding Machines
VRBAN, A., Applied Information Science and Automation
ŽITŇANSKÝ, M., Materials Science and Heat Processing

TECHNICKÁ UNIVERZITA V KOŠICIACH
(Technical University of Košice)

042 00 Košice, Letná 9
Telephone: (95) 632-24-60
Telex: 77410
Fax: (95) 633-27-48

Founded 1952
State control
Languages of instruction: Slovak, English
Academic year: October to June

Rector: Assoc. Prof. Dr MILOŠ SOMORA
Vice-Rectors: Assoc. Prof. Dr ANTON LAVRIN, Assoc. Prof. Dr DUŠAN ŠIMŠÍK, Assoc. Prof. Dr LUDMILA KOMOROVÁ, Assoc. Prof. Dr ĽUBOMIR CAIS
Questor: Dr MARIÁN TICHÝ
Librarian: Dr VALÉRIA KROKAVCOVÁ

Number of teachers: 748
Number of students: 9,695

Publication: *Transactions of the Technical University of Košice.*

DEANS

Faculty of Mining, Ecology, Control and Geotechnology: Prof. Dr DUŠAN MALINDŽÁK
Faculty of Metallurgy: Prof. Dr ĽUBOMÍR MIHOK
Faculty of Mechanical Engineering: Prof. Dr FRANTIŠEK TREBUŇA
Faculty of Electrical Engineering and Informatics: Assoc. Prof. Dr ANTON ČIŽMÁR
Faculty of Civil Engineering: Prof. Dr PAVOL JUHÁS
Faculty of Economics: Prof. Dr VINCENT ŠOLTÉS
Faculty of Production Technology: Prof. Dr KAROL VASILKO

PROFESSORS

Faculty of Mining, Ecology, Control and Geotechnology:
BOROŠKA, J., Mining Mechanization and Automation
DOJČÁR, O., Rock Disintegration
FABIÁN, J., Mining Mechanization and Automation
HATALA, J., Rock Disintegration
JACKO, S., Regional and Structural Geology
KMEŤ, S., Mineral Processing
KOŠTIAL, I., Technological Management
KUNÁK, L., Engineering Geodesy
MALINDŽÁK, D., Technological Management
ŠEKULA, F., Rock Disintegration
ŠIŠKA, F., Environmental Technologies
ŠTROFFEK, E., Power Machines and Mechanization
ŠÜTTI, J., Three-Dimensional Geodesy
VODZINSKÝ, V., Engineering Management
ZÁBRANSKÝ, F., Petrology

Faculty of Metallurgy:
BURŠÁK, M., Physical Metallurgy and Materials Science
FLÓRIÁN, K., Analytical Chemistry
HAVLÍK, T., Non-Ferrous Metallurgy
IMRIŠ, I., Non-Ferrous Metallurgy
KOCICH, J., Corrosion and Protection of Metals
KRAKOVSKÁ, E., Analytical Chemistry
LUKÁČ, I., Physical Metallurgy and Materials Science
MAJERČÁK, Š., Ferrous Metallurgy
MICHEĽ, J., Materials Science
MIHOK, Ľ., Ferrous Metallurgy
SCHMIEDL, J., Non-Ferrous Metallurgy
TOMÁŠEK, K., Non-Ferrous Metallurgy
VIRČÍKOVA, E., Non-Ferrous Metallurgy
ZÁBAVNÍK, V., Heat Treatment of Metals
ZRNÍK, J., Physical Metallurgy and Materials Science

Faculty of Mechanical Engineering:
BIGOŠ, P., Construction of Transport Machinery
GÓTS, I., Robots and Manipulators
HOSSZÚRÉTY, Z., Power Engineering
HRIVŇÁK, A., Technology of Mechanical Engineering
KAŽIMÍR, I., Technology of Mechanical Engineering
KLIMO, V., Machine Parts
KNIEWALD, D., Technology of Mechanical Engineering
KOVÁČ, M., Robots and Manipulation Devices
LACHVÁČ, J., Production Machines and Equipment
MURÁNSKY, J., Technology of Mechanical Engineering
POLLÁK, L., Technology of Mechanical Engineering
RITÓK, Z., Machine Parts
SALANCI, J., Transport Technology (Agricultural Machinery)
ŠIMŠÍK, D., Automation and Management
SINAY, J., Transport and Manipulation
SLIMÁK, I., Instrumentation and Regulation Technology
TAKÁČ, K., Technology of Mechanical Engineering
TREBUŇA, F., Mechanics

Faculty of Electrical Engineering and Informatics:
BANSKÝ, J., Radio Electronics
JELŠINA, M., Electronic Computers
KROKAVEC, M., Computers and Informatics
LEVICKÝ, D., Radio Electronics
MADARÁSZ, L., Technical Cybernetics
MARTON, K., Electroenergetics
MICHAELI, L., Radio Engineering
ŠARNOVSKÝ, J., Technical Cybernetics
ŠPÁNY, V., Radio Electronics
TIMKO, J., Electric Drives
TURÁN, J., Radio Electronics
ZBORAY, L., Electric Drives

Faculty of Civil Engineering:
HORNIAKOVÁ, L., Overground Building
JAVOR, T., Diagnostics of Concrete Structures and Bridges
JUHÁS, P., Metal and Timber Structures
TKÁČOVÁ, K., Environmental Studies

Faculty of Production Technology:
EGGENBERGER, G., Mechanics
FECKO, L., Building Engineering
GALAJDA, P., Mathematics
JENKUT, M., Production Machines and Equipment
MATHERNY, M., Analytical Chemistry
VASILKO, K., Mechanical Technology

Faculty of Economics
ŠAMSON, Š., Economic Theory
ŠOLTÉS, V., Mathematics

ATTACHED CENTRE

Computer Centre: Dir Prof. Dr J. SARNOVSKÝ

ŽILINSKÁ UNIVERZITA
(University of Žilina)

010 26 Žilina, Moyzesova 20
Telephone: (89) 62-17-81
Fax: (89) 62-69-61

Founded 1953 as Vysoká Škola Dopravy a Spojov; current title 1996
State control
Language of instruction: Slovak
Academic year: September to June

Rector: Prof. PhDr MILAN DADO
Vice-Rectors: Assoc. Prof. PhDr IVO ČÁP, Prof. PhDr JÁN ČOREJ, Prof. PhDr MARIÁN DZIMKO
Registrar: MSc. LADISLAV CIMERÁK
Librarian: PhDr MARTA SAKALOVÁ

Library of 177,000 vols
Number of teachers: 680
Number of students: 7,978

Publications: *Práce a štúdie ŽU* (Works and Studies, annually), *Zborník z vedeckých konferencií ŽU* (Proceedings of the Scientific Conferences, every 5 years), *Materiálové inžinierstvo* (Materials Engineering, annually), *Zborník z konferencie TRANSCOM* (Proceedings of the TRANSCOM Conference, every 2 years).

DEANS

Faculty of Operation and Economics of Transport and Communications: Prof. PhDr Ing. KAROL ACHIMSKÝ
Faculty of Civil Engineering: Prof. PhDr JÁN BENČAT
Faculty of Management and Informatics: Assoc. Prof. PhDr VLADIMÍR JAMRICH
Faculty of Mechanical Engineering: Assoc. Prof. PhDr PETER ZVOLENSKÝ
Faculty of Electrical Engineering: Assoc. Prof. PhDr FEDOR HRNČIAR
St Andrew's Catechetical and Pedagogical Faculty: Prof. PhDr JOZEF ĎURČEK
Faculty of Special Engineering: Col Assoc. Prof. PhDr LADISLAV ŠIMÁK

PROFESSORS

Faculty of Operation and Economics of Transport and Communications:
HOLLAREK, T., Transport Engineering
KAZDA, A., Transport and Communications Technology
KEVICKÝ, D., Transport and Communications Technology
KRÁLOVENSKÝ, J., Transport Economics
KŘÍŽ, J., Transport and Communications Technology
KULČÁK, L., Transport Engineering and Technology
MOKOŠOVÁ, G., Economics of Communications

Faculty of Civil Engineering:
BENČAT, J., Structural Mechanics
BITTERER, L., Theory and Construction of Engineering Structures
BUJŇÁK, J., Theory and Construction of Engineering Structures
ČOREJ, J., Theory and Construction of Engineering Structures
FERANEC, V., Structural Mechanics
MALÍČEK, I., Theory and Construction of Engineering Structures
MORAVČÍK, M., Applied Mechanics
TOMICA, V., Theory and Construction of Engineering Structures

Faculty of Management and Informatics:
ALEXÍK, M., Information and Control Engineering
KODNÁR, R., Applied Mathematics
SKÝVA, L., Technical Cybernetics

Faculty of Mechanical Engineering:
BARYSZ, I., Machine Elements and Mechanisms
BECHNÝ, L., Mechanical Technology
BOKUVKA, O., Materials Engineering

Dzimko, M., Machine Elements and Mechanisms
Gregor, M., Industrial Engineering and Management
Hlavňa, V., Transportation and Handling Technologies
Honner, K., Workplace Arrangement
Kompiš, V., Applied Mechanics
Košturiak, J., Industrial Engineering and Management
Kukuča, P., Transportation and Handling Technologies
Málik, L., Machine Elements and Mechanisms
Marušiak, P., Mathematics
Moravčík, P., Mathematics
Palček, P., Materials Engineering
Puškár, A., Physical Metallurgy and Threshold States of Materials
Skočovský, P., Materials Engineering
Štefánik, J., Industrial Management

Faculty of Electrical Engineering:
Blunár, K., Communications Engineering
Dado, M., Telecommunications
Dobrucký, B., Electric Traction and Electric Drives
Kejzlar, M., Electrotechnology
Neveselý, M., Theoretical Electrical Engineering
Tomašov, P., Information and Safety Systems
Trstenský, D., Communications Engineering
Vittek, J., Electric Traction and Electric Drives

St Andrew's Catechetical and Pedagogical Faculty:
Ďurček, J., Physics
Kluvánek, P., Organization and Management of Communication Systems
Novotná, M., History

Faculty of Special Engineering:
Maca, J., Mechanical Technology
Mikolaj, J., Transport Economics
Petro, V., Transport Technology
Poledňák, P., Construction Engineering
Szúttor, N., Applied Mechanics

ATTACHED INSTITUTES

Institute of Computer Technology: Dir MSc. Jozef Mužík.

Institute of Forensic Engineering: Dir Assoc. Prof. PhDr Gustáv Kasanický.

EKONOMICKÁ UNIVERZITA V BRATISLAVE
(University of Economics in Bratislava)

852 35 Bratislava, ul. Dolnozemská cesta 1/B
Telephone: (7) 581-14-78
Fax: (7) 84-73-48
E-mail: stern@euba.sk

Founded 1940, became State School 1945
State control
Languages of instruction: Slovak, English, French, German
Academic year: September to January, February to June

Rector: Prof. Dr Dr h.c. Juraj Stern
Vice-Rectors: Assoc. Prof. Dr Vojtech Kollár, Assoc. Prof. Dr Elena Beňová, Prof. Dr Štefan Majtán, Assoc. Prof. Dr Zlatica Ivaničová
Registrar: Dr Mária Dziurová
Librarian: Dr Darina Krausová

Number of teachers: 425
Number of students: 11,733

Publications: *Central European Journal of Operation Research and Economics* (quarterly), *Economic Review* (quarterly)

DEANS

Faculty of Business Economics (in Košice): Prof. Dr Jan Korčmároš
Faculty of Business Management: Prof. Dr Karol Zalai
Faculty of Commerce: Prof. Dr Ľudovít Tóth
Faculty of Economic Informatics: Assoc. Prof. Dr František Peller
Faculty of National Economy: Prof. Dr Juraj Trnovský

HEADS OF DEPARTMENT

Faculty of the National Economy:
General Economic Theory and Economic History: Assoc. Prof. Dr J. Lisý
Economic Policy: Prof. Dr P. Vincúr
Public Finance: Prof. Dr J. Trnovský
Monetary Science: Assoc. Prof. Dr A. Jankovská
Regional Economy, Geography and Environmental Economics: Prof. Dr M. Buček
Social Development and Labour: Assoc. Prof. Dr I. Laluha
Pedagogy: Assoc. Prof. Dr R. Šlosár

Faculty of Commerce:
Marketing: Assoc. Prof. Dr V. Vávra
International Business: Prof. Dr Ľ. Michník
Tourism and Services: Prof. Dr V. Sničšák
Commodities Science: Dr A. Lacková (acting)
Law: Assoc. Prof. Dr M. Sabo

Faculty of Economic Informatics:
Applied Informatics: Prof. Dr J. Kelemen
Mathematics: Assoc. Prof. Dr J. Eliaš
Operations Research and Econometrics: Assoc. Prof. Dr M. Fendek
Statistics: Assoc. Prof. Dr E. Sodomová
Accounting: Assoc. Prof. Dr B. Soukupová

Faculty of Business Management:
Business Economics: Prof. Dr M. Kupkovič
Management: Assoc. Prof. Dr Š. Slávik
Corporate Finance: Assoc. Prof. Dr J. Královič
Production Management and Logistics: Assoc. Prof. Dr A. Dupaľ

Faculty of Business Economics (in Košice):
Economics: Assoc. Prof. Dr M. Tušan
Management: Dr A. Daňkova
Finance and Accounting: Assoc. Prof. Dr Ľ. Lacová
Applied Informatics and Mathematics: Dr R. Jurga
Marketing: Assoc. Prof. Dr F. Gurský
Foreign Languages: Assoc. Prof. Dr E. Dzuriková

ATTACHED INSTITUTES

Centre for Advanced Education: Dir Assoc. Prof. Dr Ján Porvazník.
Institute of Languages: Dir Assoc. Prof. Dr Jana Lenghardtová.
Research Institute of National Economy: Dir Dr Eva Staneková.
Institute for Computing Facilities: Dir Dr Anton Zdarílek.

SLOVENSKÁ POĽNOHOSPODÁRSKA UNIVERZITA
(Slovak Agricultural University)

949 76 Nitra, Tr. A. Hlinku 2
Telephone: (87) 601
Fax: (87) 51-15-93
E-mail: postmaster@uniag.sk

Founded 1946 as Vysoká Škola Poľnohospodárska; new name *c.* 1996
State control
Languages of instruction: Slovak, English
Academic year: September to January, February to June

Rector: Assoc. Prof. Miroslav Zima
Vice-Rectors: Prof. Jozef Balla, Prof. Alojz Podolák, Assoc. Prof. Ján Tomáš, Assoc. Prof. Ján Brindza
Senior Administrative Officer: Ing. Jozef Beľa
Library: see 'Slovenská poľnohospodárska knižnica', under Libraries
Number of teachers: 461
Number of students: 6,141

Publications: *Acta Fytotechnica, Acta Zootechnica, Acta Operativo-Oeconomica, Acta Technologica Agriculturae* (all annually), *Acta Horticulturae et Regio Tecturae.*

DEANS

Faculty of Agronomy: Prof. Ivan Michalík
Faculty of Economics and Management: Assoc. Prof. Imrich Okenka
Faculty of Agricultural Engineering: Prof. Jozef Lobotka
Faculty of Gardening and Landscape Engineering: Prof. Dušan Húska

PROFESSORS

Faculty of Agronomy:
Bulla, J., Fundamental Zootechnics
Fecenko, J., Special Plant Production
Gálik, R., Fundamental Zootechnics
Halaj, M., Special Zootechnics
Hanes, J., Pedology
Holúbek, R., Special Plant Production
Kostrej, A., Plant Production
Kováč, M., Fundamental Zootechnics
Kúbek, A., Fundamental Zootechnics
Kulich, J., Plant Production
Michalík, I., Plant Production
Michalíková, A., Plant Protection
Paška, I., Special Zootechnics
Poláček, Š., Plant Production
Praslička, J., Plant Protection
Šťastný, P., Fundamental Zootechnics

Faculty of Economics and Management:
Podolák, A., Economics
Řepka, I., Economics
Simo, D., Economics
Višňovský, J., Economics
Zalabai, Z., Mathematics
Zoborský, I. M., Economics

Faculty of Agricultural Engineering:
Balla, J., Agricultural Engineering
Bátora, J., Agricultural Engineering
Jech, J., Technology and Mechanization of Agriculture
Lobotka, J., Technology and Mechanization of Agriculture
Páltik, J., Technology and Mechanization of Agriculture
Petranský, I., Technology and Mechanization of Agriculture
Šesták, J., Technology and Mechanization of Agriculture
Tolnai, R., Agricultural Engineering

Faculty of Gardening and Landscape Engineering:
Antal, J., Land Improvement
Demo, M., Plant Production
Hricovský, I., Plant Production
Huska, D., Land Improvement
Kabina, P., Land Improvement
Streďanský, J., Land Improvement

TECHNICKÁ UNIVERZITA VO ZVOLENE
(Technical University in Zvolen)

960 53 Zvolen, T.G. Masaryka 24
Telephone: (855) 33-51-11
Telex: 72267
Fax: (855) 33-00-27

Founded 1807, reorganized 1952 as University of Forestry and Wood Technology, renamed 1991
State control
Languages of instruction: Slovak, Czech; for graduate studies, also English, German and Russian
Academic year: September to June
Rector: Prof. Dr Milan Marčok

Vice-Rectors: Prof. ŠTEFAN ŽÍHLAVNÍK, Assoc. Prof. JURAJ MAHÚT, Assoc. Prof. JÁN ŠIMKO
Questor: Dr MÁRIA BÍZIKOVÁ
Librarian: Dr ĽUBICA LUDVIGHOVÁ

Library of 359,000 vols
Number of teachers: 243
Number of students: 2,200

Publications: *Acta Facultatis Forestalis* (annually), *Acta Facultatis Xylologiae* (annually), *Proceedings of Research Works of the Faculty of Ecology and Environmental Sciences* (annually), *Scientific and Pedagogical News* (annually).

DEANS

Faculty of Forestry: Assoc. Prof. MILAN HLADÍK
Faculty of Wood Sciences and Technology: Assoc. Prof. MIKULÁŠ ŠUPÍN
Faculty of Ecology and Environmental Science: Assoc. Prof. Dr IMRICH BESEDA
Faculty of Environmental and Manufacturing Technology: Assoc. Prof. JÁN ZELENÝ

PROFESSORS

Faculty of Forestry:

BUBLINEC, E., Nature and Environment
GARAJ, P., Forest Protection and Game Management
HLADÍK, M., Forest Management
KODRÍK, J., Forest Protection and Game Management
KOLENKA, I., Forest Economics
PAGAN, J., Silviculture
PAULE, L., Forest Genetics
ŠANIGA, M., Silviculture
ŠMELKO, Š., Biometry and Forest Management
VALTÝNI, J., Forest Hydrology – Torrent Control
ŽÍHLAVNÍK, S., Geodesy and Photogrammetry

Faculty of Wood Sciences and Technology:

BOROTA, J., Management of Tropical Forests
BUČKO, J., Chemistry and Chemical Technology
DEKRÉT, A., Mathematics
DUBOVSKÁ, R., Metal Processing Technology
HORSKÝ, D., Mechanical Technology of Wood
KURJATKO, S., Wood Science
LIPTÁKOVÁ, E., Wood Products Manufacturing
MARČOK, M., Physics and Applied Mechanics
OSVALD, A., Fire Protection
PETRANSKY, L., Design
RAJČAN, E., Physics and Applied Mechanics
REINPRECHT, L., Wood Technology Engineering
ŠUPÍN, M., Forestry Policy, Trade, Marketing
TREBULA, P., Technology of Wood
VINCÚR, P., Economics

Faculty of Ecology and Environmental Science:

CHRAPAN, J., Radioecology
KOŠTÁLIK, J., Physical Geography
MIDRIAK, R., Landscape Ecology
MIKLOS, L., Landscape Ecology
SUPUKA, J., Landscape Ecology

Faculty of Environmental and Manufacturing Technology:

DANKO, M., Processes and Technology of Forest Production
MIKLEŠ, M., Processes and Technology of Forest Production

Faculties of Theology

PRAVOSLÁVNA BOHOSLOVECKÁ FAKULTA PREŠOVSKEJ UNIVERZITY V PREŠOVE
(Orthodox Faculty of Theology of Prešov University)

080 80 Prešov, Masarykova 15

Telephone: (91) 72-47-29
Fax: (91) 73-26-77

Founded 1950

Dean: Prof. ThDr ŠTEFAN PRUŽINSKÝ
Pro-Deans: Doc. ThDr PETER KORMANÍK, Mgr JÁN JACOŠ

Number of teachers: 14
Number of students: 190

RÍMSKOKATOLICKÁ CYRILOMETODSKÁ BOHOSLOVECKÁ FAKULTA UNIVERZITY KOMENSKÉHO
(Cyril and Methodius Roman Catholic Faculty of Theology of the Comenius University)

814 58 Bratislava, Kapitulská 26

Telephone: (7) 533-51-09
Fax: (7) 533-02-66
E-mail: sd@frcth.uniba.sk

Founded 1935

Dean: J. KUTARŇA
Pro-Dean: Š. VRAGAŠ

Number of teachers: 160
Number of students: 2,500

EVANJELICKÁ BOHOSLOVECKÁ FAKULTA UNIVERZITY KOMENSKÉHO
(Evangelical Faculty of Theology of the Comenius University)

811 03 Bratislava, Svoradova 1

Telephone: (7) 531-63-75
Fax: (7) 531-11-40
E-mail: sd@ebfuk.sk

Founded 1933

Dean: Prof. Dr IGOR KIŠŠ
Pro-Deans: Doc. Dr JURAJ BÁNDY, Doc. Dr JÁN GREŠO

Number of teachers: 18
Number of students: 230

College

City University Bratislava: Mišíkova 21, 811 06 Bratislava; tel. and fax (07) 31-44-66; f. 1990; distance education in management, leading to Professional Certificate in Management, Professional Diploma in Management or MBA; languages of instruction: English and Slovak; 42 teachers; 1,200 students; library of 1,000 vols; Dir Dr JÁN MOROVIČ; Registrar Ing. BENEDIKT FRONC.

Schools of Art and Music

VYSOKÁ ŠKOLA MÚZICKÝCH UMENÍ
(Academy of Music and Dramatic Art)

813 01 Bratislava, Ventúrska 3

Telephone: (7) 533-23-06
Fax: (7) 533-01-25

Founded 1949

Rector: Prof. MILAN ČORBA

Library of 65,000 vols

DEANS

Faculty of Drama and Puppetry: Assoc. Prof. JURAJ SLEZÁČEK
Faculty of Music and Dance: Prof. STANISLAV ZAMBORSKÝ
Faculty of Film and Television: Assoc. Prof. ONDREJ ŠULAJ

VYSOKÁ ŠKOLA VÝTVARNÝCH UMENÍ
(Academy of Fine Arts and Design)

814 37 Bratislava, Hviezdoslavovo nám. 18

Telephone: (7) 533-24-31
Fax: (7) 533-23-40

Founded 1949

Rector: Prof. ŠTEFAN ŠLACHTA
Pro-Rectors: Doc. JÁN HOFFSTÄDTER, Doc. IMRICH VAŠKO, Doc. FRANTIŠEK BURIAN
Registrar: Ing. JANA TÓTHOVÁ
Library of 30,000 vols

Number of teachers: 65
Number of students: 500

HEADS OF DEPARTMENTS:

Architecture: Doc. MILOSLAV MUDRONČÍK
Painting: Doc. IVAN CSUDAI
Sculpture: Prof. JURAJ BARTUSZ
Graphic Arts: Assoc. Prof. RÓBERT JANČOVIČ
Applied Art I: Doc. JURAJ GAVULA
Applied Art II (Ružomberok): PAVOL RUSKO
Textiles: Doc. JOZEF BAJUS
Design: Doc. ŠTEFAN KLEIN
Restoration: Doc. VLADIMÍR PLEKANEC
History and Theory of Art: Doc. IVAN RUSINA
Visual Media: Doc. JÁN KŘÍŽIK
Gallery Medium: Dr SIMONA HUDECOVÁ

Konzervatórium: 042 03 Košice, Hlavná 89; tel. (95) 622-19-67; fax (95) 622-20-92; f. 1951; 99 teachers, 270 students; library of 20,185 vols and 3,079 records; Dir Mgr BARTOLOMEJ BURÁŠ.

SLOVENIA

Learned Societies

GENERAL

Slavistično društvo Slovenije (The Society for Slavic Studies of Slovenia): 1000 Ljubljana, Aškerčeva 2/II; f. 1935; a forum for professional Slavists, to provide a link between research and professional practice, to nurture cultural values regarding Slovene language and literature and awareness of Slovene history; to organize support for and publish Slavic research in academic and popular books and periodicals; *c.* 1,500 mems; Chair. Zoltan Jan; publs *Slavistična revija* (Slavonic Review; quarterly), *Jezik in slovstvo* (Language and Literature; 8 a year).

Slovenska Akademija Znanosti in Umetnosti (Slovenian Academy of Sciences and Arts): 1000 Ljubljana, Novi trg 3; tel. (61) 125-60-68; fax (61) 125-34-23; f. 1938; 96 mems; attached research institutes: see Research Institutes; library: see Libraries and Archives; Pres. France Bernik; Sec.-Gen. Matija Drovenik; publs *Annual Report*, *Opera*, *Acta Archaeologica*, *Acta Geographica*, *Acta Carsologica*, *Traditiones*.

BIBLIOGRAPHY, LIBRARY SCIENCE AND MUSEOLOGY

Zveza bibliotekarskih društev Slovenije (Union of Associations of Slovene Librarians): 1000 Ljubljana, Turjaška 1; tel. (61) 125-50-14; fax (61) 125-92-57; f. 1947; 1,000 mems; Pres. Stanislav Bahor ; Sec. Liljana Hubej; publ. *Knjižnica* (quarterly).

ECONOMICS, LAW AND POLITICS

Society of Jurists of Slovenia: Ljubljana, Dalmati-nova 4; f. 1947; 1,073 mems; Pres. Jože Pavličič; publ. *Jurist*.

EDUCATION

Pedagogical Society of Slovenia: 1000 Ljubljana, Gosposka ulica 3; tel. and fax (61) 221-832; f. 1920; active participation in social roles of education, organization of discussions of educators, continuing education of teachers; 2,100 mems; Pres. Dr Metod Resman; publ. *Sodobna pedagogika* (monthly).

FINE AND PERFORMING ARTS

Društvo slovenskih skladateljev (Society of Slovene Composers): Ljubljana, Trg francoske revolucije 6; tel. and fax (61) 213-487; f. 1945; 106 mems; Pres. Janez Gregorc; Sec. Maks Strmčnik; publs *Edicije DSS* (printed scores, etc., of its mems).

Slovensko umetnostno zgodovinsko društvo (Slovenian Society of Historians of Art): Ljubljana, Aškerčeva 12/III; tel. (61) 150-001, ext. 247; fax (61) 159-337; f. 1921; excursions, symposia, congresses; 299 mems; library of 15,100 vols; Chair. Nace Šumi; publs *Archives d'Histoire de l'Art, Zbornik za umetnostno zgodovino* (annually).

HISTORY, GEOGRAPHY AND ARCHAEOLOGY

Zveza geografskih društev Slovenije (Association of the Geographical Societies of Slovenia): Ljubljana, Univerza v Ljubljani, Filozofska fakulteta, Aškerčeva 2; tel. (61) 176-93-15; fax (61) 125-93-37; f. 1922; 700 mems; Pres. Prof. Dr Andrej Černe; Secs Marko Krevs, Dejan Rebernik; publs *Geografski vestnik* (annually), *Geografski obzornik* (quarterly).

Zveza zgodovinskih društev Slovenije (Slovenian Historical Association): 1000 Ljubljana, Aškerčeva 2; tel. (61) 176-92-10; fax (61) 159-337; f. 1839, reorganized 1946 and 1980; 1,649 mems; library of 5,215 vols; Pres. Dr Stane Granda; publs *Zgodovinski časopis* (Historical Review, quarterly), *Kronika* (3 a year), *Časopis za zgodovino in narodopisje* (2 a year).

LANGUAGE AND LITERATURE

Slovenska Matica (Slovenian Society): 1000 Ljubljana, Kongresni trg 8; tel. (61) 214-200; e-mail drago.jancar@guest.arnes.si; f. 1864; literary and publishing society; 2,800 mems; library of 10,000 vols; Pres. Prof. Dr Joža Mahnič; Sec. Drago Jančar.

NATURAL SCIENCES

General

Društvo matematikov, fizikov in astronomov Slovenije (Association of Mathematicians, Physicists and Astronomers of Slovenia): 1001 Ljubljana, POB 2964; tel. (61) 176-65-00; e-mail predsednik@dmfa.si; f. 1949; 1,100 mems; Chair. Prof. Dr Andrej Čadež; publs *Obzornik mat. fiz.* (every 2 months), *Presek* (every 2 months), *Presekova knjižnica, Knjižnica Sigma.*

Society for Natural Sciences of Slovenia: 1001 Ljubljana, Novi trg 2, p.p. 238; tel. and fax (61) 221-914; e-mail prirodoslovno .drustvo@guest.arnes.si; f. 1934; 3,000 mems; Pres. Andrej Seliškar; Sec. Gen. Marjana Peterlin; publ. *Proteus* (10 a year).

Physical Sciences

Jamarska zveza Slovenije (Speleological Asscn of Slovenia): 61109 Ljubljana, POB 44; tel. (61) 315-666; f. 1889; 43 caving societies and research groups with a total of *c.* 1,000 mems; Pres. Bogdan Urbar; Sec. Miran Erič; publ. *Naše jame* (2 a year).

Research Institutes

FINE AND PERFORMING ARTS

Muzikološki inštitut (Institute of Musicology): 1000 Ljubljana, Gosposka 13; tel. 125-60-68; fax 125-52-53; e-mail glasba@zrc-sazu.si; f. 1972; Slovenian musical history from the Middle Ages to the beginning of World War II; library of 15,000 vols; attached to Slovenian Acad. of Sciences and Arts; Head Dr Ivan Klemenčič; publ. *Monumenta Artis Musicae Sloveniae* (2 a year).

Umetnostnozgodovinski inštitut Franceta Steleta (France Stele Institute of Art History): 1000 Ljubljana, Novi trg 4; e-mail umzg@alpha.zrc-sazu.si; attached to Slovenian Acad. of Sciences and Arts.

HISTORY, GEOGRAPHY AND ARCHAEOLOGY

Geografski inštitut (Institute of Geography): 1000 Ljubljana, Gosposka 13; tel. (61) 125-60-68; fax (61) 125-77-93; e-mail gi@zrc-sazu.si; f. 1948; attached to Slovenian Acad. of Sciences and Arts; library of 34,000 books and periodicals; Head Dr Drago Perko; publ. *Geografski zbornik* (Acta Geographica, in English, 1 a year).

Inštitut za arheologijo (Institute of Archaeology): 1000 Ljubljana, Gosposka 13; tel. (61) 125-60-68; fax (61) 125-77-57; f. 1947; attached to Slovenian Acad. of Sciences and Arts; library of 35,000 vols; Dir Dr Janez Dular; publs *Opera Instituti archaeologici Sloveniae, Arheloški vestnik* (1 a year).

Uprava Republike Slovenije za kulturno dediščino (Cultural Heritage Office of the Republic of Slovenia): 1000 Ljubljana, Plečnikov trg 2; tel. (61) 125-94-67; fax (61) 213-012; f. 1913, to preserve and study historical and archaeological monuments, and sites of historical, artistic, scientific, ethnological and sociological interest; a complete register of historical monuments in Slovenia; library of 13,500 books; Dir Stane Mrvič; publs *Varstvo spomenikov* (Preservation of Monuments, annually), *Vestnik* (Bulletin), Series *Kulturni in naravni spomeniki Slovenije* (guides to the historical and natural monuments of Slovenia, 10 a year).

Zgodovinski inštitut Milka Kosa (Milko Kos Institute of History): 1000 Ljubljana, Novi trg 4; tel. (61) 125-60-68; fax (61) 125-52-53; e-mail zimk@zrc-sazu.si; attached to Slovenian Acad. of Sciences and Arts.

LANGUAGE AND LITERATURE

Inštitut za slovenski jezik Frana Ramovša (Fran Ramovš Institute of Slovene Language): 1000 Ljubljana, Novi trg 4; tel. (61) 125-60-68; fax (61) 125-52-53; e-mail isj@zrc-sazu.si; attached to Slovenian Acad. of Sciences and Arts; Head Dr Varja Cvetko Orešnik.

Inštitut za slovensko literaturo in literarne vede (Institute of Slovene Literature and Literary Sciences): 1000 Ljubljana, Novi trg 5; tel. (61) 125-60-68; fax (61) 125-52-53; attached to Slovenian Acad. of Sciences and Arts; library of 40,000 vols.

MEDICINE

Inštitut za medicinske vede (Institute of Medical Sciences): C/o Slovenian Academy of Sciences and Arts, 1000 Ljubljana, Novi trg 3; attached to Slovenian Acad. of Sciences and Arts.

NATURAL SCIENCES

Biological Sciences

Biološki inštitut Jovana Hadžija (Jovan Hadži Institute of Biology): 1000 Ljubljana, Novi trg 5; tel. (61) 125-60-68; fax (61) 125-52-53; attached to Slovenian Acad. of Sciences and Arts.

Paleontološki inštitut Ivana Rakovca (Ivan Rakovec Institute of Palaeontology): Scientific Research Centre, Slovenian Academy of Sciences and Arts, 1000 Ljubljana, Gosposka 13; attached to Slovenian Acad. of Sciences and Arts; tel. (61) 125-60-68; fax (61) 125-52-53; e-mail pi@alpha.zrc-sazu.si; f. 1949.

Physical Sciences

Geološki Zavod Ljubljana (Ljubljana Geological Institute): 61009 Ljubljana, Dimičeva 14; tel. (61) 181-542; telex 31448; fax (61) 182-557; f. 1946; geology, geotechnology, geophysics, mining, soil and rock mechanics, drilling and blasting, manufacturing and maintenance of drilling equipment; 1,300 mems; library of 14,000 vols, 300 periodicals; Dir TINE LAJEVEC; publ. *Geologija razprave in poročila* (annually).

Inštitut za raziskovanje krasa (Institute for Karst Research): 66230 Postojna, Titov trg 2; tel. (67) 24-781; fax (67) 23-965; e-mail izrk@zrc-sazu.si; f. 1947; karstology and speleology; library of 30,000 vols; Dir Dr TADEJ SLABE; publ. *Acta carsologica* (annually).

PHILOSOPHY AND PSYCHOLOGY

Filozofski inštitut (Institute of Philosophy): 1000 Ljubljana, Gosposka 13; tel. (61) 125-60-68; fax (61) 125-52-53; e-mail fi@zrc-sazu.si; f. 1977; attached to Slovenian Acad. of Sciences and Arts; Head Dr RADO RIHA; publ. *Filozofski vestnik* (2 a year).

RELIGION, SOCIOLOGY AND ANTHROPOLOGY

Inštitut za narodnostna vprašanja (Institute for Ethnic Studies): 1000 Ljubljana, Erjavčeva 26; tel. (61) 210-823; fax (61) 210-964; f. 1926; study of interethnic relations in Slovenia and abroad and of Slovene ethnic minorities in neighbouring countries; library of 30,000 vols; Pres. Dr VERA KRŽIŠNIK BUKIĆ; Dir Dr MITJA ŽAGAR; publ. *Razprave in gradivo* (Treatises and Documents, annually).

Inštitut za slovensko izseljenstvo (Institute for Slovene Emigration Studies): C/o Slovenian Academy of Sciences and Arts, 1000 Ljubljana, Novi trg 3; attached to Slovenian Acad. of Sciences and Arts.

Inštitut za slovensko narodopisje (Institute of Slovene Ethnology): C/o Slovenian Academy of Sciences and Arts, 1000 Ljubljana, Novi trg 3; attached to Slovenian Acad. of Sciences and Arts.

Libraries and Archives

Celje

Osrednja knjižnica Celje (Public Library of Celje): 63000 Celje, Muzejski trg 1a; tel. (63) 442-625; fax (63) 443-350; f. 1946; 365,000 vols; Librarian JANKO GERMADNIK.

Koper

Osrednja knjižnica Srečka Vilharja (Srečko Vilhar Public Library): 6000 Koper, Capodistria, Trg Brolo 1; tel. 272-408; fax 23-866; f. 1951; 250,000 vols; Librarian Prof. EVGEN KOŠTIAL.

Ljubljana

Arhiv Republike Slovenije (Archives of the Republic of Slovenia): 1127 Ljubljana, Zvezdarska 1, p.p. 21; tel. (61) 1251-222; fax (61) 216-551; f. 1945; collection of important archives, especially those connected with the territory populated by Slovenes from the 12th century onwards; archive of Slovene film production since 1905; Chief VLADIMIR ŽUMER.

Biblioteka Slovenske akademije znanosti in umetnosti (Library of the Slovenian Academy of Sciences and Arts): 1001 Ljubljana, Novi trg 3–5, POB 323; tel. and fax (61) 125-34-62; e-mail infosazu@zrc-sazu.si; f. 1938; 421,800 vols; Librarian MARIJA FABJANČIČ; publs *Seznam prejetih knjig* (monthly), *Poročilo o delu biblioteke* (annually), *Objave* (irregular).

Centralna ekonomska knjižnica (Central Economic Library): 1000 Ljubljana, Kardeljeva ploščad 17; tel. (61) 189-24-00; fax (61) 189-26-98; e-mail knjigecek@uni-lj.si; f. 1948; information centre for economic and related sciences and European documentation centre; 220,000 vols and periodicals, 475 current periodicals; Dir Prof. Dr VEKOSLAV POTOČNIK; publ. *Mesečni pregled novih knjig* (monthly).

Centralna medicinska knjižnica, Medicinska fakulteta (Central Medical Library, Faculty of Medicine): 1105 Ljubljana, Vrazov trg 2; tel. (61) 317-492; fax (61) 13-36-139; e-mail infocmk@animus.mf.uni-lj.si; f. 1945; central library for the Faculty of Medicine, Slovene health-care organizations and biomedical research institutions; literature of biomedicine; 196,000 books and periodicals, 970 current periodicals; Dir Dr ANAMARIJA ROŽIĆ-HRISTOVSKI.

Centralna tehniška knjižnica Univerze v Ljubljani (Central Technical Library of the University of Ljubljana): 1000 Ljubljana, Trg republike 3; tel. (61) 214-072; fax (61) 125-66-67; e-mail post@ctk.uni-lj.si; f. 1949; central technical library for the university and industry; specialized information centre for engineering, civil engineering and standards; consulting service for special and university libraries in science and technology; information and referral centre for science and technology; inter-library loan centre; 185,053 vols; research papers, standards, regulations; Chief Librarian Dr MATJAŽ ŽAUCER; publs *New Books Accession List* (quarterly), *Annual Report*.

Knjižnica Narodnega Muzeja (National Museum Library): 1000 Ljubljana, Prešernova 20, POB 529; tel. (61) 21-88-86; fax (61) 22-18-82; e-mail anja-dular@narmuz-lj.si; f. 1821; 150,000 vols; special collection of Slovene prints from 16th century; Librarian ANJA DULAR.

Knjižnica Pravne fakultete (Library of the Faculty of Law): Ljubljana, Trg revolucije 11; f. 1920; 84,000 vols; Librarian DANICA LOVREČIČ.

Narodna in univerzitetna knjižnica (National and University Library): 1000 Ljubljana, Turjaška 1; tel. (61) 150-141; telex 32285; fax (61) 150-134; f. 1774; incorporates state copyright and deposit library, National Slovene library, Univ. of Ljubljana library, library promotion and consultancy centre and library research centre; 2,000,000 vols; 4,000 MSS including 78 parchments and 508 incunabula; music collection of 78,000 vols; 23,000 maps; Dir IVAN KANIČ; publs *Slovenska bibliografija* (quarterly), *Catalogue of manuscript collection*, *Knjižničarske novice* (monthly), *Signalne informacije* (monthly).

Slovanska knjižnica (Slavic Library): Ljubljana, Gosposka 15/I; tel. 222-914; fax 126-40-47; f. 1901; language, literature and history of the Slavs; 120,000 vols; Dir Prof. MATEJA KOMEL SNOJ.

Maribor

Univerzitetna knjižnica Maribor (University of Maribor Library): 2000 Maribor, Gospejna 10; tel. (62) 215-851; telex 33328; fax (62) 227-558; f. 1903; 714,000 vols; Dir Mag. IRENA SAPAČ; publs *Časopis za zgodovino in narodopisje*, *Slavistična revija*.

Novo Mesto

Knjižnica Mirana Jarca ('Milan Jarc' Regional Library): Novo Mesto, Rozmanova ul. 26/28; tel. (68) 324-505; fax (68) 325-772; e-mail web@gea.nm.sik.si; f. 1945; 287,500 vols; Librarian ANDREJA PLENIČAR.

Museums and Art Galleries

Brežice

Posavski muzej (Regional Museum): 8250 Brežice, Cesta prvih borcev 1; tel. and fax (608) 61-271; f. 1949; collection of archaeological exhibits from Neolithic times to the early Middle Ages; also ethnographical collection; historical section: from Slovene-Croat peasants' revolt 1573 to the present; Baroque festival hall with frescoes (1703) and Baroque gallery; memorial room of painter Franjo Stiplovšek; library of 7,350 vols, 35 periodicals; Dir TOMAŽ TEROPŠIČ.

Celje

Pokrajinski muzej (Regional Museum): 3000 Celje, Muzejski trg 1; tel. (63) 442-633; fax (63) 443-384; f. 1882; collections of archaeology, art and cultural history, ethnography and history; library of 8,456 vols; Dir DARJA PIRKMAJER.

Ljubljana

Mednarodni Grafični Likovni Center (MGLC) (International Graphics and Art Centre): 1000 Ljubljana, Pod turnom 3; tel. (61) 1265-240; fax (61) 219-752; f. 1986; permanent collection of contemporary international graphics; organizes the International Biennial of Graphics; exhibitions of prints, drawings; print workshop; Dir Dr ZORAN KRŽIŠNIK; publs monographs, catalogues, prints, etc.

Mestni muzej (Municipal Museum): 1000 Ljubljana, Gosposka 15; tel. (61) 222-930; fax (61) 222-946; e-mail tajnistvoa@mm.lj.si; f. 1935; cultural history museum of Ljubljana; collections include archaeological dept, containing articles from lake dwellings of the chalcolithic period, cemeteries of the Illyrian-Celtic period and of Roman domination (Emona), and from the Old Slavic period; cultural historical collection; modern history; also fine arts exhibitions; information centre about the cultural and natural heritage in the Ljubljana area; library of 9,324 vols; Dir TAJA ČEPIČ; publs various guides.

Moderna galerija (Museum of Modern Art): 1000 Ljubljana, Tomšičeva 14; tel. (61) 214-106; fax (61) 214-120; f. 1947; permanent collection of contemporary Slovene art from the Impressionists to the present day and worldwide modern art; organizes regular art exhibitions; photographic archive; art library of 39,000 vols; Dir ZDENKA BADOVINAC; publ. *M'ARS* (quarterly).

Muzej novejše zgodovine (Museum of Modern History): 1000 Ljubljana, Celovška c. 23; tel. (61) 323-968; fax (61) 133-82-44; f. 1944 to collect all important archives, museum objects and library material from the War of Liberation, 1941–45; also includes museum objects of Slovene history from 1914 to the present day; Dir Dr IZTOK DURJAVA.

Narodna galerija (National Gallery): 1000 Ljubljana, Puharjeva 9; tel. (61) 126-31-09; fax (61) 126-31-38; e-mail info@grohar.ng-slo.si; f. 1918; collection of Gothic sculptural arts, mediaeval frescoes and copies of Gothic frescoes from Slovenia; collection of Slovenian Renaissance, Baroque and 19th-century paintings and sculptures; paintings by Slovenian impressionists; 14th–20th-century European painters; collection of Slovenian graphic arts from the 18th to the beginning of the 20th century; photo-documentation of works of art from Slovenia; library of 25,000 vols; Dir Dr ANDREJ SMREKAR; publs manuals, catalogues.

Narodni muzej Slovenije (National Museum of Slovenia): 1000 Ljubljana, Prešernova ul. 20, POB 529-X; tel. (61) 218-886; fax

(61) 221-882; f. 1821; departments of archaeology; history; history of applied arts; coins and medals; graphic arts; library of 150,000 vols; branch: Museum of Bled (medieval castle, and in Ljutomer the Exhibition of Tabori in Slovenia); Dir Dr PETER KOS; publs *Situla*, *Catalogi et Monographiae*, *Argo*, *Viri*.

Prirodoslovni muzej Slovenije (Slovenian Natural History Museum): 1001 Ljubljana, Prešernova 20, POB 290; tel. (61) 218-886; fax (61) 218-846; f. 1821; zoology, botany, geology; library of 12,000 books and periodicals; Dir Prof. MATIJA GOGALA; publs *Scopolia* (3 a year), *Acta Entomologica Slovenica* (2 a year).

Slovenski etnografski muzej (Ethnographical Museum): 1000 Ljubljana, Metelkova 2; tel. (61) 134-32-35; fax (61) 132-53-77; e-mail bojana.rogelj@guest.arnes.si; f. 1923; Slovene and non-European ethnographic collections; library of 30,000 vols; Dir INJA SMERDEL; publs *Etnolog* (annually), *Knjižnica Slovenskega etnografskega muzeja*.

Slovenski šolski muzej (Slovenian School Museum): 1000 Ljubljana, Plečnikov trg 1; tel. and fax (61) 213-024; f. 1898 to collect school documents and educational books from the 12th century onwards; 40,123 exhibits; library of 52,000 vols; 542 fascicules; 17,084 documents for all schools in Slovenia; permanent exhibition of development of schools in Slovenia; Dir Dr ANDREJ VOVKO; publ. *Collected Papers* (annually).

Zemljepisni muzej Slovenije (Geographical Museum of Slovenia): 1000 Ljubljana, Trg francoske revolucije 7; tel. (61) 213-458; f. 1946; attached to the Geography Institute of Ljubljana University; maps of Slovenia, geographical collections, and exhibitions; library; Dir RADO GENORIO.

Maribor

Pokrajinski muzej (Regional Museum): 62000 Maribor, Grajska ul. 2; tel. (62) 211-851; fax (62) 227-777; f. 1903 from collections of the Maribor Museum, the historical societies and the Episcopal Museum; archaeological, ethnological, historical, fine and applied art, costume collection exhibits; library of 12,000 vols; Dir VILI VUK.

Ptuj

Pokrajinski muzej (Regional Museum): 62250 Ptuj, Muzejski trg 1; tel. (62) 771-618; f. 1893; archaeological, art, historical and ethnographic departments covering prehistoric, Roman, Old Slavic and Feudal periods; ecclesiastical art, folklore, three temples of Mithras; local history; numismatic collection of Celtic and Roman coins; collection of minerals.

Škofja Loka

Loški Muzej: 64220 Škofja Loka, p.p. 9; tel. (64) 622-262; fax (64) 622-261; f. 1939 by the Museum Association of Škofja Loka; special collection of exhibits relating to the Freising dominion (973–1803); ethnographic, topographic, natural history and historical exhibits; records of altars from 17th century, exhibits of medieval guilds; relics of the struggle for national liberation; art gallery; open-air museum; library of 18,000 vols; Pres. FRANC PODNAR; publ. *Loški razgledi*.

Universities

UNIVERZA V LJUBLJANI (University of Ljubljana)

1000 Ljubljana, Kongresni trg 12

Telephone: (61) 125-40-55

Fax: (61) 125-40-53

Founded 1595, reconstituted 1809, reopened 1919

State control

Academic year: October to September (two terms)

Language of instruction: Slovene

Rector: Prof. Dr JOŽE MENCINGER

Vice-Rectors: Prof. Dr KATJA BRESKVAR, Prof. Dr JOŽE VIŽINTIN, Prof. Dr PETER FISTER

Secretary-General: MARJETA VILFAN

Librarians: LENART ŠETINC (National and University Library), Dr MATJAŽ ŽAUCER (Central and Technical Library)

Number of teachers: 1,800

Number of students: 35,000

Publications: *Objave, Vestnik, Seznam predavanj, Biografije in bibliografije univerzitetnih učiteljev in sodelavcev.*

DEANS

Faculty of Arts: Prof. Dr LUDVIK HORVAT
Faculty of Law: Prof. Dr JANEZ KRANJC
Faculty of Economics: Prof. Dr FERDINAND TROŠT
Faculty of Natural Science and Technology: Prof. Dr JAKOB LAMUT
Faculty of Architecture: Prof. Dr FEDJA KOŠIR
Faculty of Electrical Engineering: Prof. Dr FRANC BRATKOVIČ
Faculty of Mechanical Engineering: Prof. Dr FRANC KOSEL
Faculty of Medicine: Prof. Dr MIHA ŽARGI
Faculty of Veterinary Medicine: Prof. Dr MILAN POGAČNIK
Faculty of Pharmacy: Prof. Dr SLAVKO PEČAR
Faculty of Civil Engineering and Geodesy: Prof. Dr JURIJ BANOVEC
Faculty of Chemistry and Chemical Technology: Prof. Dr TINE KOLOINI
Faculty of Mathematics and Physics: Prof. Dr PETER PRELOVŠEK
Faculty of Computer and Information Science: Prof. Dr DUŠAN KODEK
Faculty of Biotechnical Engineering: Prof. Dr FRANC LOBNIK
Faculty of Social Sciences: Prof. Dr MARJAN SVETLIČIČ
Faculty of Sport: Doc. Dr KREŠIMIR PETROVIĆ
Faculty of Education: Prof. Dr MIRAN ČUK
Faculty of Theology: Prof. Dr JANEZ JUHANT
Faculty of Maritime Studies and Transport: Prof. Dr MARIJA BOGATAJ
Academy of Music: Prof. Dr DEJAN BRAVNIČAR
Academy of Theatre, Radio, Film and Television: Prof. Dr ANDREJ INKRET
Academy of Fine Arts: Prof. BOGOSLAV KALAŠ
University College of Social Work: Doc. Dr BLAŽ MESEC
University College of Health Care: Prof. Dr BOŽO KRALJ
University College of Public Administration: Prof. Dr MIHA BREJC

HEADS OF DEPARTMENT

Faculty of Arts:

- Philosophy: Prof. Dr TINE HRIBAR
- Sociology: Doc. Dr AVGUST LEŠNIK
- Pedagogy: Prof. Dr ANA KRAJNC
- Psychology: Prof. Dr KLAS BRENK
- History: Doc. Dr JANEZ CVIRN
- Archaeology: Prof. Dr BOŽIDAR SLAPŠAK
- Ethnology: Prof. Dr JANEZ BOGATAJ
- Geography: Prof. Dr MIRKO PAK
- Slavic Languages and Literature: Prof. Dr MIRAN HLADNIK
- Romance Languages and Literature: Prof. Dr MIHA PINTARIČ
- Germanic Languages and Literature: Prof. Dr META GROSMAN
- Classical Philology: Prof. Dr PRIMOŽ SIMONITI
- Comparative Literature and Literary Theory: Prof. Dr EVALD KOREN
- Comparative and General Philology: Prof. Dr JANEZ OREŠNIK
- Musicology: Prof. Dr KATARINA BEDINA
- Bibliography: Prof. Dr MARTIN ŽNIDERŠIČ
- African and Asian Studies: Prof. Dr ANDREJ BEKEŠ
- Translation and Interpreting: Doc. Dr IRENA KOVAČIČ

Faculty of Social Sciences:

- Sociology: Prof. Dr IVAN BERNIK
- Political Sciences: Prof. Dr BOGOMIL FERFILA
- Communication Studies: Prof. Dr TOMO KOROŠEC
- Cultural Studies: Doc. Dr FRANE ADAM

Faculty of Civil Engineering and Geodesy:

- Civil Engineering: Prof. Dr BOJAN MAJES
- Geodesy: Doc. Dr DUŠAN KOGOJ

Faculty of Chemistry and Chemical Technology:

- Chemistry and Biochemistry: (vacant)
- Chemical Technology: (vacant)
- Technical Safety: Prof. Dr VLADIMIR DRUSANY

Faculty of Mathematics and Physics:

- Mathematics and Mechanics: Prof. Dr JERNEJ KOZAK
- Physics: Prof. Dr SLOBODAN ŽUMER

Faculty of Medicine:

- Microbiology and Immunology: Prof. Dr MARIJA GUBINA
- Pathology: Prof. Dr ANDREJ MAŠERA
- Hygienics, Social Medicine and Medicine of Work: Doc. Dr MARJAN PREMIK
- Forensic Medicine: Doc. Dr JOŽE LOVŠIN
- Infectious Diseases and Epidemiology: Prof. Dr FRANJO PIKELJ
- Internal Medicine: Prof. Dr ANDREJA KOCIJANČIČ
- Surgery: Prof. Dr VLADIMIR SMRKOLJ
- Neurology: Prof. Dr. MARTIN JANKO
- Psychiatry: Prof. Dr MARTINA ŽMUS-TOMORI
- Dermatovenerology: Mag. TOMAŽ LUNDER
- Orthopaedics and Physical Therapy: Prof. Dr SREČKO HERMAN
- Radiology: Prof. Dr VLADIMIR JEVTIĆ
- Paediatrics: Prof. Dr CIRIL KRŽIŠNIK
- Gynaecology and Obstetrics: Prof. Dr BOŽO KRALJ
- Otolaryngology: Prof. Dr MIHA ŽARGI
- Ophthalmology: Prof. Dr GORAZD KOLAR
- Oncology and Radiotherapy: Prof. Dr ZVONIMIR RUDOLF
- Stomatological Prosthetics: Prof. Dr NENAD FUNDUK
- Dental Diseases: Prof. Dr VITO VRBIČ
- Maxillofacial and Oral Surgery: Prof. Dr VESNA KOŽELJ
- Child Dental Health: Prof. Dr MITJA BARTENJEV
- Dental and Jaw Orthopaedics: Prof. Dr FRANC FARČNIK
- Oral Dentistry: Prof. Dr UROŠ SKALERIČ
- Social Sciences: (vacant)
- Anaesthesiology and Reanimatology: Prof. Dr MARIJA PEČAN
- Family Medicine: Doc. Dr IGOR ŠVAB

Faculty of Biotechnical Engineering:

- Agronomy: Prof. Dr FRANC BATIČ
- Biology: (vacant)
- Forestry: Prof. Dr MIHA ADAMIČ
- Wood Engineering: Prof. Dr JOŽE RESNIK
- Zootechnology: Prof. Dr FRANC HABE
- Food Science and Technology: Prof. Dr VERONIKA ABRAM
- Landscape Architecture: Prof. Dr IVAN MARUŠIČ

Faculty of Natural Sciences and Technology:

- Materials and Metallurgy: Prof. Dr RADOMIR TURK
- Geotechnology and Mining Engineering: Prof. Dr RANKO TODOROVIĆ
- Geology: Prof. Dr STANKO BUSER

Textiles: Doc. Dr FRANC SLUGA
Chemical Education and Informatics: Prof. Dr METKA VRTAČNIK

Faculty of Education:

Special Education: Doc. Dr STANE KOŠIR
Social Work: Doc. Dr ALENKA KOBOLT
Basic Educational Studies: Doc. Dr MOJCA PEČEK-ČUK
Primary School Education: Doc. Dr MIRKO SLOSAR
Educators-Defectologists: (vacant)
Fine Arts: Prof. BOJAN KOVAČIČ
Biology, Chemistry and Home Economics: Prof. Dr BARBARA BAJD
Mathematics: Prof. Dr MARKO RAZPET
Physics and Technical Education: Doc. Dr TOMAŽ KRANJC
Pre-school Education: Doc. EDVARD MAJARON

Academy of Music:

Composition and Music Theory: Doc. MARKO MIHEVC
Conducting: Prof. ANTON NANUT
Singing: Prof. EVA NOVŠAK-HOUŠKA
String and Keyboard Instruments: Doc. HINKO HAAS
Wind and Brass Instruments: Prof. ROK KLOPČIČ
Music Pedagogy: Prof. Dr BREDA OBLAK
Religious Music: Prof. Dr MIRKO CUDERMAN

Academy of Theatre, Radio, Film and Television:

Theatre and Radio: Doc. MATJAŽ ZUPANČIČ
Film and Television Directing: Prof. FRANCI SLAK
Dramaturgy: Prof. Dr DENIS PONIŽ

Academy of Fine Arts:

Painting: Prof. GUSTAV GNAMUŠ
Sculpture: Prof. DUŠAN TRŠAR
Design: Prof. VLADIMIR PEZDIRC
Restoration: Prof. FRANC KOKALJ

University College of Health Care:

Health Care: VERA ŠTEBE
Physiotherapy: MIROLJUB JAKOVLJEVIĆ
Radiology: VERONIKA LIPOVEC
Occupational Therapy: TAMARA OŠNJAK-KUŠEJ
Sanitary Engineering: Mag. MARTIN BAUER
Orthopaedic Technology: MOJCA DIVJAK
Obstetrics and Gynaeecology: MIHAELA SKOBERNE

UNIVERZA V MARIBORU (University of Maribor)

62000 Maribor, Krekova Ulica 2

Telephone: (62) 223-611
Telex: 33334
Fax: (62) 23-541

Founded 1975
State control
Language of instruction: Slovene
Academic year: September to August

Rector: Prof. Dr LUDVIK TOPLAK
Vice-Rectors: Dr MAKS OBLAK, Dr ANDREJ UMEK, Dr RASTO OVIN, IGOR JURIŠIČ
Secretary-General: VALTER RATNER
Librarian: Mag. IRENA SAPAČ

Number of teachers: 442 full-time, 282 part-time
Number of students: 8,754 full-time, 3,479 external

Publications: *Naše gospodarstvo* (published by the School of Economics and Commerce, every 2 months), *Organizacija in Kadri* (published by the School of Management, 10 a year), *Časopis za zgodovino in narodopisje, Znanstvena revija, Univerzitetna revija.*

DEANS

Faculty of Business and Economics: Dr LEO GUSEL
Faculty of Electrical Engineering and Computer Science: Prof. Dr DALI DJONLAGIĆ
Faculty of Civil Engineering: Prof. Dr LUDVIK TRAUNER
Faculty of Chemistry and Chemical Engineering: Prof. Dr PETER SENČAR
Faculty of Mechanical Engineering: Prof. Dr ADOLF SOSTAR
Faculty of Organizational Sciences: Dr JOŽE FLORJANČIČ
Faculty of Education: Dr JOŽE POGAČNIK
Faculty of Law: Dr FRANC PERNEK
College of Agriculture: Dr BOŽIDAR KRAJNČIČ
College of Nursing Studies: Dr VILJEM BRUMEC

PROFESSORS

Faculty of Business and Economics:

BOBEK, D., Business Administration in Banking
GUSEL, L., Yugoslav Import-Export System
HAUC, A., Project Management
INDIHAR, S., Mathematics
KAJZER, Š., Cybernetics
KENDA, V., International Trade
LORBEK, F., Marketing Communication
MEŠKO, I., Quantitative Planning Methods
MULEJ, M., Dialectical Theory of Systems
PAUKO, F., Tourism
RADONJIČ, D., Market Research
REPOVŽ, L., Complex Analysis of Management
SAVIN, D., Political Economy
SRUK, V., Sociology, Philosophy and Political Science

Faculty of Mechanical Engineering:

ALUJEVIĆ, A., Mechanics, Thermodynamics
ANDREJČIC, R., Statistics
ČERNEJ, A., Motor Vehicles
ČREPINŠEK, L., Physics
DOBOVIŠEK, Ž., Internal Combustion Engines
JELER, S., Textile Processing
JEZERNIK, A., CAD/CAM
KRIŽMAN, A., Industrial Engineering, Metal Heat Processing
LEŠ, P., Transformation Techniques
OBLAK, M., Mechanics and Hydrodynamics
POLAJNAR, A., Work Study and Manufacturing Systems Planning
RAK, I., Welding Science and Technology, Production Measuring Technology and Science
ŠOSTAR, A., Technological Measurements
VERHOVNIK, V., Environment Protection

Faculty of Civil Engineering:

CVIKL, B., Physics
LEP, J., Mathematics
PŠUNDER, M., Building Economics
TRAUNER, L., Soil Mechanics, Geotechnics
UMEK, A., Earthquake Engineering

Faculty of Electrical Engineering and Computer Science:

BREŠAR, F., Mathematics
DONLAGIĆ, D., Remote Control Systems
HORVAT, B., Computing and Microcomputer Systems
HRIBERNIK, B., Electric Equipment and Plants
JEZERNIK, K., Robotics
KUMPERŠČAK, V., Physics
NOVAK, I., Electric Power Systems
PAULIN, A., Electromagnetic Fields
ŠTIGLIC, B., Databases
ZORIČ, M., Networks and Systems

Faculty of Chemistry and Chemical Engineering:

DOBČNIK, D., Analytical Chemistry
DOLEČEK, V., Physical Chemistry
GLAVIČ, P., Inorganic Technology
PREGL, G., Physics
VOLAVŠEK, B., Inorganic Chemistry

Faculty of Organizational Sciences:

ANDREJČIČ, R., Statistics
FLORJANČIČ, J., Personnel Administration
GRIČAR, J., Analysis and Design of Organizational Systems
HUDOKLIN, A., Reliability
KALTNEKAR, A., Production Process Organization
KLJAJIČ, M., Systems Theory
RANT, M., Production Planning and Control
VILA, A., Production Process Management
VRŠEC, E., Production Systems

Faculty of Education:

BELEC, B., Geography
BOŽIČ, D., Music
GOLIJA, B., Graphic Design
JUTRONIĆ-TIHOMIROVIĆ, D., English Linguistics
KRIŽMAN, M., German Language
MIŠČEVIĆ, N., History of Philosophy
MLINARIČ, J., History of Middle Ages
POGAČNIK, J., Slovene Literature
ROZMAN, F., History of Southeast Europe
ŠIMUNDIĆ, M., Serbo-Croatian Language
VUKMAN, J., Mathematics

Faculty of Law:

FLERE, S., Sociology
GEČ-KOROŠEC, M., Family Law
PERNEK, F., Financial Law
RUPNIK, J., Constitutional Law
TOPLAK, L., International Business Law

ATTACHED CENTRES

Centre for Applied Mathematics and Theoretical Physics: 62000 Maribor, Krekova 2; Dir Dr MARKO ROBNIK.

Computer Centre: 62000 Maribor, Gospejna ul. 10; Dir TOMAŽ KLOJČNIK.

European Centre for Ethnic and Regional Studies: 62000 Maribor, Mladinska 9; Dir Dr SILVO DEVETAK.

FACULTY OF THEOLOGY IN LJUBLJANA

1000 Ljubljana, Poljanska 4

Telephone: (61) 132-91-97
E-mail: teof-dekanat@uni-lj.si

Founded 1919

Dean: Dr JANEZ JUHANT
Pro-Deans: Dr ANTON STRES, Dr VINKO POTOČNIK

Library of 62,000 vols
Number of professors: 31
Number of students: 626

Publications: *Bogoslovni Vestnik* (quarterly), *Acta Ecclesiastica Sloveniae.*

SOLOMON ISLANDS

Libraries and Archives

Honiara

Solomon Islands National Archives: Ministry of Education and Training, POB 781, Honiara; tel. 21426; telex 66311; f. 1979; British Solomon Islands Protectorate records 1900–78, Solomon Islands Government records 1978–; collections of records, microfilm, film and sound recordings on Solomon Islands and Western Pacific; Government Archivist JOSEPH P. WALE.

Solomon Islands National Library: POB 165, Ministry of Education and Training, Honiara; tel. 21601; fax 25366; f. 1974; 120,000 vols; Solomon Islands collection and central reference collection; Dir WALTER HUBERTS-RHEIN; publ. *Solomon Islands National Library Newsletter*.

Museums and Art Galleries

Honiara

Solomon Islands National Museum and Cultural Centre: POB 313, Honiara; tel. 23351; part of Min. of Culture, Tourism and Aviation; collection began in 1950s, permanent site 1969; research into all aspects of Solomons culture (pre-history, language, oral tradition, music, dance, architecture, etc.); promotes traditional crafts, music and dance; Dir LAWRENCE FOANAOTA; publs *Journal, Custom Stories, Taem bifo Newsletter*.

Colleges

Solomon Islands College of Higher Education: POB G23, Honiara; tel. 30111; fax 30390; f. 1984; 135 teachers; 1,200 students; library of 2,500 vols; Dir G. TALOIKWAI; Registrar B. G. TEKULU.

HEADS OF SCHOOLS

Finance and Administration: JOHN IPO
Education: JOASH MANEIPURI
Nursing: WILLIAM MANEPOLO
Natural Resources: TITUS SURA (acting)
Marine and Fisheries Studies: Capt. STARLING DAEFA
Industrial Development: DONALD DUNA
Humanities and Science: ROSE WHALE (acting)

University of the South Pacific Solomon Islands Centre: POB 460, Honiara; tel. 21307; fax 21287; f. 1971; responsible for providing USP courses through extension; developing national continuing education courses; promoting research on subjects of national interest; library of 9,000 vols; Dir GLYNN GALO; publ. *Solomon Islands Research Register* (annually).

SOMALIA

Research Institutes

HISTORY, GEOGRAPHY AND ARCHAEOLOGY

Survey and Mapping Department: Ministry of Public Works, POB 24, Mogadishu; f. 1966; the official surveying and mapping department; Dir MUSA ADAN WADADID.

MEDICINE

Institute for the Preparation of Serums and Vaccines: Mogadishu.

Laboratory of Hygiene and Prophylaxy: Mogadishu; sections in medicine and chemistry.

NATURAL SCIENCES

Physical Sciences

Geological Survey Department: Ministry of Water Development and Mineral Resources, POB 744, Mogadishu; library of 500 vols; Dir V. N. KOZERENKO.

Libraries and Archives

Mogadishu

National Library of Somalia: POB 1754, Mogadishu; tel. 22758; f. 1970; research, legal deposit; 30,000 vols, 75 periodicals; training in library science; Dir HASSAN NOOR FARAH.

Somali Institute of Public Administration Library: Mogadishu.

Museums and Art Galleries

Mogadishu

Somali National Museum: Mogadishu; tel. 21041; f. 1934; ethnographical, historical and natural science collections; library of 3,000 vols; Dir AHMED FARAH.

University

SOMALI NATIONAL UNIVERSITY

POB 15, Mogadishu
Telephone: 80404
Founded 1954, University status 1969
Languages of instruction: Somali, Arabic, Italian, English
Rector: MOHAMED GANNI MOHAMED
Vice-Rector for Academic Affairs: MOHAMED ELMI BULLALE
Registrar: NUREYN SHEIKH ABRAR
Librarian: Mrs SIRAD YUSUF ISMAIL
Number of teachers: 549
Number of students: 4,640

DEANS

Faculty of Medicine: ABDI AHMED FARAH
Faculty of Agriculture: MOHAMED ALI MOHAMED
Faculty of Veterinary Medicine: ABDULHAMID Haji MOHAMED
Faculty of Engineering: ABDULLAHI JIMALE MOHAMED
Faculty of Geology: MOHAMMOUD ABDI ARUSH
Faculty of Industrial Chemistry: AHMED MAYE ABDURAHMAN
Faculty of Education: HUSSEIN MUSA ALI
Faculty of Law: ABUD MUSAD ABUD
Faculty of Economics: MOHAMED ISMAIL SHEIKH
Faculty of Languages: (vacant)
Faculty of Journalism: MOHAMOUD ISMAIL ABDI-RAHMAN
Faculty of Islamic and Arabic Studies: SHARIF MOHAMED ALI ISAAK
Faculty of Technical Teacher Education: ABDULLAHI MOHAMUD WARSAMME
Faculty of Political Science: ADEN ABDULLAHI NUR
Somali Institute of Development Administration and Management: IBRAHIM MOHAMUD ABYAN

Colleges

School of Industrial Studies: Mogadishu; departments of radio, carpentry, mechanics, electricity, building construction.

School of Islamic Disciplines: Mogadishu; includes a faculty of law.

School of Public Health: Mogadishu.

School of Seamanship and Fishing: Mogadishu; 170 students.

Technical College: Burgo; f. 1965; 4-year courses.

Veterinary College: Mogadishu; 30 students; 10 teachers; Projects Dir Dr J. NEILSEN.

SOUTH AFRICA

Learned Societies

GENERAL

Royal Society of South Africa: P.D. Hahn Bldg, POB 594, Cape Town 8000; tel. (21) 650-2543; fax (21) 650-3726; e-mail Roysoc@psipsy.uct.ac.za; f. 1877; 140 fellows, 5 hon. fellows, 31 foreign assocs, 325 mems; Pres. O. W. PROZESKY; Gen. Sec. D. E. RAWLINGS; Foreign Sec. B. WARNER; publ. *Transactions*.

South African Academy of Science and Arts/Suid-Afrikaanse Akademie vir Wetenskap en Kuns: POB 538, Pretoria 0001; tel. (12) 328-5082; fax (12) 328-5091; f. 1909; for the promotion of science, technology, arts and the Afrikaans language; 1,700 mems; Chair. Prof. F. P. RETIEF; Sec. Dr D. J. C. GELDENHUYS; publs *Tydskrif vir Geesteswetenskappe, SA Tydskrif vir Natuurwetenskappe en Tegnologie, Nuusbrief.*

AGRICULTURE, FISHERIES AND VETERINARY SCIENCE

South African Society of Animal Science/Suid-Afrikaanse Vereniging vir Veekunde: POB 102100, Moreleta Plaza, Pretoria 0167; tel. (12) 420-3268; fax (12) 420-3290; e-mail ryssen@scientia.up.ac.za; f. 1961; to promote the advancement of animal production and the interests of animal scientists, to encourage research, to exchange and disseminate information in this field; *c.* 700 mems; Pres. Prof. N. H. CASEY; publ. *South African Journal of Animal Science* (quarterly).

South African Society of Dairy Technology: POB 72300, Lynnwood Ridge 0040; tel. (12) 348-5345; fax (12) 348-6284; e-mail dairy-foundation@pixie.co.za; f. 1967; 400 mems; Pres. P. J. JOOSTE; Sec. Prof. B. H. BESTER.

Southern African Institute of Forestry/Suider-Afrikaanse Instituut van Boswese: POB 1022, Pretoria 0001; tel. and fax (12) 348-1745; f. 1937; aims to collect and publish information on all aspects of forestry, to conserve the forest estate, to encourage the practice of scientific forestry, to create a forum for discussion of topics related to forestry; 560 mems, 250 foreign subscribers; Chair. W. S. OLIVIER; Sec.-Treas. C. VILJOEN; publs *Southern African Forestry Journal* (3 a year), *South African Forestry Handbook*.

ARCHITECTURE AND TOWN PLANNING

Simon van der Stel Foundation: POB 12293 Centrahil 6006, Port Elizabeth; fax (41) 562849; f. 1959; SA National Trust; architectural conservation; 4,000 mems; Nat. Chair. G. COETZEE; publ. *Restorica* (annually).

South African Institute of Architects: Private Bag X10063, Randburg 2125; tel. (11) 886-9308; fax (11) 886-9362; f. 1927; 2,380 mems; Exec. Officer S. LINNING; publ. *Architecture SA*.

BIBLIOGRAPHY, LIBRARY SCIENCE AND MUSEOLOGY

South African Institute for Librarianship and Information Science/Suid-Afrikaanse Instituut vir Biblioteek- en Inligtingwese: POB 36575, Menlo Park, Pretoria 0102; f. 1930; 2,851 mems; Pres. C. M. WALKER; Hon. Sec. N. M. FERREIRA; publs *South African Journal for Library and Information Science / Suid-Afrikaanse Tydskrif vir Biblioteek- en Inligtingkunde* (quarterly), *Newsletter / Nuusbrief* (monthly) and a few irregular publications.

Southern African Museums Association: POB 29294, Sunnyside 0132; tel. (12) 341-6531; fax (12) 341-6146; f. 1936; 660 mems; Hon. Sec. GLYN BALKWILL; publ. *SAMAB* (2 a year).

ECONOMICS, LAW AND POLITICS

Economic Society of South Africa: POB 929, Pretoria 0001; tel. (11) 3133300; f. 1925 to promote the thorough discussion of, and research into economic questions, in particular those affecting South Africa; 700 mems; brs in Bloemfontein, Cape Town, Eastern Province, Johannesburg, Natal, Pretoria, Stellenbosch and Western Transvaal; Pres. P. D. F. STRYDOM; Sec. ELSE KRÜGER-CLOETE; publ. *The South African Journal of Economics* (quarterly).

Institute of Bankers in South Africa: POB 61420, Marshalltown 2107; tel. (11) 832-1371; fax (11) 834-6592; e-mail iobinfo@iob-co.za; f. 1904; 20,000 mems; Chief Exec. J. HODGES; publ. *South African Banker* (quarterly).

South African Institute of International Affairs: Jan Smuts House, POB 31596, Braamfontein, Johannesburg 2017; tel. (11) 339-2021; fax (11) 339-2154; e-mail saiiagen@global.co.za; f. 1934 to facilitate the scientific study of international questions, particularly those affecting Southern Africa; 3,000 mems; library of 30,000 books, 7,000 journals; spec. collns incl. UN colln (20,000 vols); Chair. Dr C. B. STRAUSS; Nat. Dir Dr GREG MILLS; publ. *South African Journal of International Affairs* (2 a year).

EDUCATION

National Association of Distance Education Organizations of South Africa (NADEOSA): POB 31822, Braamfontein 2017; tel. (11) 403-2813; fax (11) 403-2814; e-mail info@saide.org.za; 62 mem. orgs; Pres. JENNIFER GLENNIE; Sec. THAKUME MBATHA.

South African Universities' Vice-Chancellors' Association: POB 27392, Sunnyside 0132; tel. (12) 429-3161; fax (12) 429-3071; f. 1955 as Committee of University Principals, present name 1998; 21 mems; Chief Exec. P. KOTECHA; publ. *Newsletter* (2 a year).

FINE AND PERFORMING ARTS

Federasie van Afrikaanse Kultuurvereniginge (Association of Afrikaans Cultural Societies): POB 91050, Auckland Park 2006; tel. (11) 726-7134; fax (11) 726-2073; f. 1929; 2,300 affiliated Afrikaans cultural societies; Chair. C. SWANEPOEL HANDHAAF; CEO H. C. DE WUT; publs *Lectures, Handhaaf Newsletter* (every 4 months).

South African Association of Arts: POB 6188, Pretoria 0001; tel. (12) 28-7109; fax (12) 323-1275; f. 1945 as successor to South Africa Fine Arts Association (f. 1850) to encourage visual arts nationally and internationally; 31 autonomous brs with individual galleries, management committees; 5,500 mems; National Pres. CONRAD THEYS; National Vice-Pres EUNICE BASSON, ORIE KUTTA; publ. *South African Arts Calendar* (quarterly).

HISTORY, GEOGRAPHY AND ARCHAEOLOGY

Genealogical Society of South Africa: POB 2119, Houghton 2146; f. 1963; 1,150 mems; Pres. C. MERCER; Sec. N. DA SILVA; publ. *Familia* (quarterly).

Nederlands Cultuurhistorisch Instituut: University of Pretoria, Pretoria 0002; tel. (12) 420-3007; fax (12) 342-2453; f. 1931; offers books and information on Dutch culture, history and art: 250 mems; library of 32,000 vols; Dir Prof. E. D. GERRYTS.

Society of South African Geographers: POB 128, Wits 2050; f. 1917; 500 mems; Pres. Prof. U. J. FAIRHURST; Sec. Prof. L. ZIETSMAN; publs *South African Geographical Journal* (2 a year), *South African Geographical Society Newsletter* (irregular), *Geogram* (irregular).

South African Archaeological Society: POB 15700, Vlaeberg 8018; tel. (21) 24-3330; f. 1945; 1,200 mems; library of 1,000 vols, 5,000 periodicals; Hon. Sec. M. LESLIE; publs *South African Archaeological Bulletin* (2 a year), *Goodwin Series* (irregular), *The Digging Stick* (3 a year).

Van Riebeeck Society: c/o South African Library, POB 496, Cape Town 8000; tel. (21) 423-2824; fax (21) 24-48-48; f. 1918; 1,350 mems; publishes South African Historical Documents; Chair. Dr F. R. BRADLOW; Sec. A. ADEMA; publ. 1 volume annually.

LANGUAGE AND LITERATURE

Classical Association of South Africa: C/o Academia Latina, University of Pretoria, Pretoria 0002; tel. (12) 420-2368; fax (12) 420-4008; f. 1965; 350 mems; Chair. E. A. MACKAY; Sec. D. WARDLE; publs *Acta Classica* (annually), *Akroterion* (quarterly).

English Academy of Southern Africa: Box 124, WITS, Johannesburg 2050; tel. (11) 716-3683; f. 1961; to stimulate interest in the English language and its literature including the literature of Southern Africa; to promote literacy and maintain standards of English in schools and universities, especially in black education; to ensure the full and free use of English as an official language and defend the rights to free speech and publication; awards the English Academy Medal, the Oliver Schreiner Prize and the Thomas Pringle Awards; 500 full, 85 assoc. mems; Pres. MARCIA LEVESON; publ. *The English Academy Review* (annually).

Federasie van Rapportryerskopse: POB 91001, Aucklandpark 2006; f. 1961; 400 brs; 11,500 mems; Chair. Dr C. STANDER; Sec. C. DE JAGER.

South African PEN Centre (Cape): Apartment C, 2 Scott Rd, Claremont, Cape Town; f. 1960; 70 full and 30 associate mems; Pres. (vacant); Sec. ADÈLE NAUDÉ; publ. *Newsletter*.

MEDICINE

Association of Surgeons of South Africa/Chirurgiese Vereniging van Suid-Africa: POB 52027, Saxonwold, Johannesburg 2132; tel. (11) 837-1011; f. 1945; 250 mems; Chair. P. PERDIKIS; Sec. V. E. SOROUR; publ. *South African Journal of Surgery*.

College of Medicine of South Africa, The: 17 Milner Rd, Rondebosch 7700; tel. (21) 6899533; fax (21) 6853766; e-mail cmsa-adm@iafrica.com; f. 1956; provides postgraduate examinations in all branches of medicine for all doctors and dentists in South Africa; 9,000 mems; small archive and reference library; Sec. Mrs B. Bothma; publ. *Transactions* (2 a year).

Medical Association of South Africa: POB 20272, Alkantrant 0005; tel. 47–6101; f. 1927; 13,000 mems; professional organization for medical doctors in South Africa; Chair. of Council Dr B. B. Mandell; Sec.-Gen. Dr H. A. Hanekom; publs *South African Medical Journal* (monthly), *South Africa's Continuing Medical Education Monthly* (monthly), *South African Journal of Surgery* (quarterly).

Nutrition Society of Southern Africa: POB 1697, Brits 0250; f. 1955; 304 mems; Pres. Prof. H. H. Vorster; Chair. Dr M. McLachlan; Sec. P. M. N. Kuzwayo; publ. *The South African Journal of Food Science and Nutrition*.

South African Pharmacology Society: C/o Prof. Wimpie du Plooy, Dept of Pharmacology, Box 225, PO Medunsa 0204; tel. (12) 521-4123; fax (12) 521-4118; e-mail wdplooy@mcd4330.medunsa.ac.za; Pres. Prof. Jacques Snyman; Sec. Prof. Wimpie du Plooy.

South African Society of Obstetricians and Gynaecologists: Dept of Obstetrics and Gynaecology, POB 339, Bloemfontein 9300; tel. (51) 405-3444; fax (51) 447-8004; f. 1940; subgroup of the Medical Asscn of SA; 571 mems; Pres. Dr F. Hayward; Hon. Sec. Prof. H. S. Cronjé.

NATURAL SCIENCES

General

Associated Scientific and Technical Societies of South Africa: POB 93480, Yeoville 2143; 18a Gill St, Observatory 2198; tel. (11) 487-1512; fax (11) 648-1876; e-mail asts@global.co.sa; f. 1920; to promote the interests of scientific, professional and technical societies; to advance the knowledge of scientific and technical subjects; to assist in raising the standard of mathematics and science for underprivileged scholars; to raise awareness of career prospects in technology; and to provide secretarial, liaison, and meeting facilities, etc., for its member societies; 60,000 mems in 51 mem. socs; Pres. A. S. Meyer; Man. Errol H. van Rooy; publs *Annual Proceedings*.

Southern Africa Association for the Advancement of Science: POB 366, Irene 0062; tel. (12) 667-2544; f. 1902; 101 mems; Pres. Dr I. Raper; Sec. S. A. Korsman.

Biological Sciences

BirdLife South Africa: POB 84394, Greenside 2034; tel. (11) 888-4147; fax (11) 782-7013; e-mail info@birdlife.org.za; f. 1930; 6,000 mems; Pres. Dr W. R. Tarboton; Dir Dr A. Berruti; publs *Ostrich* (quarterly), *Africa Birds and Birding* (6 a year).

Botanical Society of South Africa: Private Bag X10, Newlands 7725; tel. (21) 797-2090; fax (21) 7972376; e-mail botsocsa@gem.co.za; f. 1913; 25,000 mems; aims to promote the conservation, cultivation, wise use and study of the indigenous flora of southern Africa; Pres. Prof. O. A. M. Lewis; Dir Dr Bruce McKenzie; publ. *Veld & Flora* (quarterly).

Herpetological Association of Africa: Port Elizabeth Museum, POB 13147, Humewood 6013; Sec. W. R. Branch; publ. *Journal*.

National Botanical Institute: Head Office: Private Bag X7, Claremont, Cape Province 7735; tel. (21) 7621166; fax (21) 7623229; National Botanical Gardens at Kirstenbosch (Cape Town), Worcester, Betty's Bay, Bloemfontein, Pietermaritzburg, Pretoria, Nelspruit, Roodepoort; f. 1913 for scientific and educational purposes; to promote knowledge and appreciation of southern African flora and to undertake the *ex situ* conservation of threatened plants; libraries of 5,000 vols (Cape Town), 8,500 vols (Pretoria); National Herbarium (Pretoria) 500,000 sheets, Compton Herbarium 30,000 sheets; Chief Dir B. J. Huntley; publs *Bothalia* (2 a year), *South African Journal of Botany* (6 a year), *Strelitzia* (irregular), *Flora of South Africa* (irregular), *Flowering Plants of Africa* (vols in two parts, one part a year).

South African Biological Society/Suid-Afrikaanse Biologiese Vereniging: POB 820, Pretoria; f. 1907; 144 mems; Pres. Dr N. van Rooyen; Hon. Sec. Mrs E. A. Boomker; publ. *Journal* (annually).

South African Society of Biochemistry and Molecular Biology: c/o Dr G. Bradley, Experimental Biology Programme, Medical Research Council, POB 19070, Tygerberg 7505; tel. (21) 938-0304; fax (21) 938-0456; e-mail gbradley@eagle.mrc.ac.za; f. 1973; 450 mems; Pres. A. I. Louw; Hon. Sec. Dr G. Bradley; publ. *SASBMB Newsletter* (3 a year).

Southern African Society of Aquatic Scientists: C/o POB 9, Pietermaritzburg 3200; tel. (331) 341-1111; fax (331) 341-1349; e-mail mark.graham@umgeni.co.za; f. 1963; holds annual congresses and general meetings; 250 mems; Pres. Dr C. Dickens; Hon. Sec. M. Graham; publ. *Journal* (2 a year).

Wildlife Management Association of South Africa: POB 3051, Pietermaritzburg; f. 1971; publishes original papers and reviews relating to research and management in the broad field of renewable natural resources; 900 mems; publs *South African Journal of Wildlife Research* (quarterly), *Scientific Journal*.

Wildlife Society of Southern Africa: POB 44189, Linden 2104; tel. 486-32-94; fax 486-33-69; f. 1926; conservation of fauna and flora; promotes environmental education; 28,000 mems; Pres. D. Hatton; CEO M. Powell; publs *African Wildlife* (English and Afrikaans, every 2 months), books, regional magazines, *Toktokkie* (children's magazine, English and Afrikaans, every 2 months), *The Naturalist* (3 a year).

Physical Sciences

Astronomical Society of Southern Africa: POB 9, Observatory 7935; f. 1922; 450 mems; Pres. M. D. Overbeek; Hon. Sec. B. Skinner; publs *Notes* (6 a year), *Handbook* (annually); local centres at Cape Town, Johannesburg, Bloemfontein, Durban, Pietermaritzburg, Harare, Somerset West and Pretoria.

Geological Society of South Africa: POB 44283, 2104 Linden; tel. (11) 888-2288; fax (11) 888-1632; f. 1895; 1,956 mems; publs include *Geobulletin, South African Journal of Geology*.

South African Chemical Institute: POB 93480, Yeoville 2143; 18a Gill St, Observatory, Johannesburg 2198; tel. and fax (11) 487-1543; f. 1912; 1,750 mems; Pres. Prof. Elj Breet; publs *South African Journal of Chemistry* (quarterly) and *Chemical Processing SA* (monthly).

South African Institute of Physics: C/o University of Zululand, Kwa Dlangezwa 3886; tel. (351) 93911; fax (351) 93571; f. 1955; has specialist groups in astrophysics, education, lasers, photonics and spectroscopy, nuclear-particle and radiation physics, solid-state and theoretical physics; 400 mems; Pres. Prof. M. A. Hellberg; Hon. Sec. Prof. B. Spoelstra.

RELIGION, SOCIOLOGY AND ANTHROPOLOGY

South African Bureau of Racial Affairs (SABRA): POB 2768, Pretoria; f. 1948; research on race relations; annual congress; Dir Prof. A. D. Pont; publ. *Journal of Racial Affairs* (quarterly).

South African Institute of Race Relations: POB 31044, Braamfontein 2017; Johannesburg; tel. 403-3600; fax 403-3671; f. 1929; research, publishing, bursary administration; library; Pres. H. Giliomee; Dir J. Kane-Berman; publs *South Africa Survey* (1 a year), *Spotlight* (occasionally), *Fast Facts* (monthly), *Frontiers of Freedom* (4 a year).

TECHNOLOGY

Aeronautical Society of South Africa: POB 130774, Bryanston 2021; tel. (11) 706-3763; f. 1911 to give a stronger impulse to the growth and scientific study of aeronautics; theoretical and practical research; offers advice, instruction and facilities for those studying the subject; organizes meetings, lectures, etc; affiliated with Royal Aeronautical Society; 621 mems; membership of the Soc. is a prerequisite for membership of the SA Inst. of Aeronautical Engineers (*q.v.*); Pres. G. Eckermann; Hon. Sec. D. P. du Plooy; publ. *Journal* (annually, in conjunction with SAIAeE).

Chartered Institute of Transport in Southern Africa: POB 95327, Grant Park 2051; tel. (11) 888-1813; fax (11) 782-8265; e-mail citsa@global.co.za; f. 1993; 700 mems; Pres. Malcolm F. Mitchell; Exec. Man. C. Larkin; publs *CITSA Handbook* (annually), *Pegasus* (quarterly).

Institution of Certificated Mechanical and Electrical Engineers, South Africa: POB 93480, Yeoville 2143; tel. 487-1683; f. 1911; 1,654 mems; Sec. G. N. Burgess.

Royal Aeronautical Society, Southern Africa Division: POB 69251 Bryanston 2021; tel. (11) 463-3100; fax (11) 463-3133; f. 1945; 130 mems; Pres. Noel Potter; Sec. L. Stokoe.

South African Institute of Aerospace Engineering: POB 14717, Sinoville 0129; tel. (12) 808-1359; fax (12) 808-1425; e-mail strydomi@iafrica.com; f. 1977; mem. of ICAS and ISOABE; aims to facilitate the exchange of aeronautical information and ideas, to establish links with kindred organizations, to provide facilities for the country's legislative bodies to confer with members on research and development in aeronautical engineering; 260 mems; Pres. Noel Potter; publ. *Aeronautica Meridiana* (annually).

South African Institute of Agricultural Engineers/Suid-Afrikaanse Instituut van Landbou-Ingenieurs: POB 912-719, Silverton 0127; tel. (12) 804-1540; telex 322108; fax (12) 804-0753; f. 1964; 500 mems; meetings, lectures, symposia, etc.; awards study bursaries; Pres. Prof. P. W. L. Lyne; Sec. F. B. Reinders; publs *Newsletter* (quarterly), *Agricultural Engineering in South Africa* (annually).

South African Institute of Assayers and Analysts: Kelvin House, 2 Hollard St, POB 61019, Marshalltown 2107, Transvaal; f. 1919 to uphold the status and interests of the profession of assaying in all its branches; 181 mems; Pres. J. W. Barnett; publ. *Bulletin* (quarterly).

South African Institute of Electrical Engineers: POB 93541, Yeoville 2143; f. 1909; 3,900 mems; publs *Transactions* (3 or 4 a year), *Elektron* (monthly), *Energize* (6 a year).

South African Institute of Mining and Metallurgy: Cape Towers, 11 – 13 MacLaren St., POB 61019, Marshalltown 2107,

Transvaal; tel. (11) 834-1273; fax (11) 838-5923; f. 1884; 3,000 mems; Pres. J. A. Cruise; Sec. Celeste Mackintosh; publs *Journal* (monthly), *SAIMM Monograph Series, Symposium*, special publications series.

South African Institution of Civil Engineering: POB 93495, Yeoville 2143; tel. (11) 487-3813; fax (11) 487-3817; e-mail saice@cis.co.za; f. 1903; 7,753 mems; Exec. Dir D. B. Botha; publs *Civil Engineering* (monthly), *Journal* (quarterly).

South African Institution of Mechanical Engineers (including Nuclear and Tribology Engineers): POB 31548, Braamfontein 2017; tel. 339-6678; f. 1892; 4,500 mems; publ. *Journal* (monthly).

Research Institutes

GENERAL

Africa Institute of South Africa: 2nd Floor, Bestmed Bldg, Cnr Hamilton and Belvedere Streets, Arcadia, POB 630, Pretoria 0001; tel. (12) 328-69-70; fax (12) 323-81-53; e-mail africain@iafrica.com; f. 1960; applied research and the collection of information in the fields of politics, socio-economics, development and international relations on the African continent, especially southern Africa; Exec. Dir Dr Denis Venter; publ. *Africa Insight* (4 a year).

CSIR (Council for Scientific and Industrial Research): Scientia, POB 395, Pretoria 0001; tel. (12) 841-2911; fax (12) 349-1153; f. 1945; operating divisions of Manufacturing and Aeronautical Systems Technology (Dir J. Ahlers), Building Technology (Dir G. Magomola), Earth, Marine and Atmospheric Science and Technology (Dir Dr D. H. Swart), Food Science and Technology (Dir Dr P. Terblanche), Forest Science and Technology (Dir Dr F. J. Kruger), Information and Communications Technology (Dir M. Madhi), Materials Science and Technology (Dir Dr N. Comins), Microelectronics and Communications Technology (Dir J. R. Ahlers), Mining Technology (Dir Dr G. Gürtünca), Roads and Transport Technology (Dir Dr H. Maree), Textile Technology (Dir Dr N. Trollip (acting)), Water, Environment and Forestry Technology (Dir A. Yannakou); library: see Libraries and Archives; Pres. Dr G. Garrett; Exec. Vice-Pres. (Finance and Marketing): A. Jordaan; Exec. Vice-Pres. (Human Resources) Dr N. Magau; Exec. Vice-Pres. (Technology and Policy) Dr A. Paterson; Exec. Vice-Pres. (Technology for Development) N. Moikonga; publs *Annual Report*, *Technobrief* (monthly), divisional newsletters, research reports.

AGRICULTURE, FISHERIES AND VETERINARY SCIENCE

Agricultural Research Council: POB 8783, Pretoria 0001; tel. (12) 436210; fax (12) 435814; e-mail tiksue@lnrl.agric.za; f. 1992; Pres. Dr Jons Terblanche.

Attached research institutes:

Agrimetrics Institute: Private Bag X640, Pretoria 0001; tel. (12) 342-9968; fax (12) 342-9969; interdisciplinary service of biometrical and datametrical input to all institutes of the Agricultural Research Council; planning of scientific experiments, analysis and interpretation of research results; datametric service for development and application of scientific data and management of computer systems; Dir Dr Piet Jooste.

Animal Improvement Institute, Irene: Private Bag X2, Irene 1675; tel. (12) 672-9111; fax (12) 665-1609; genetic and physiological methods are used to improve the quality and efficiency of national herd; library of 9,000 vols; Dir Dr Michiel Scholtz.

Animal Nutrition and Animal Products Institute, Irene: Private Bag X2, Irene 1675; tel. (12) 672-9111; fax (12) 665-1609; research and development in animal nutrition, meat and dairy products; Dir Dr Heinz Meissner.

Grain Crops Institute: Private Bag X1251, Potchefstroom 2520; tel. (148) 299-6100; fax (148) 294-7146; research on grain crops and oil and protein seeds; Dir Dr Jan Dreyer.

Infruitec: Private Bag X5013, Stellenbosch 7599; tel. (21) 883-9090; fax (21) 883-8669; research on the cultivation and post-harvest technology of deciduous fruit and other allotted crops; Dir Dr Leopoldt van Huyssteen.

Institute for Agricultural Engineering: Private Bag X519, Silverton 0127; tel. (12) 842-4000; fax (12) 804-0753; research on agricultural mechanization, farm structures, irrigation, resource conservation, energy, aquaculture and product processing; Dir Adriaan Louw.

Institute for Soil, Climate and Water: Private Bag X79, Pretoria 0001; tel. (12) 326-4205; fax (12) 323-1157; soil science, agrometeorology, water utilization, remote sensing, analytical services; library of 6,700 vols; Dir Dr Dries van der Merwe.

Institute of Tropical and Subtropical Crops: Private Bag X11208, Nelspruit 1200; tel. (13) 753-2071; fax (13) 752-3854; f. 1926; research on fruit, cocoa, and exotic crops; Dir Dr Johann van Zyl.

Nietvoorbij Institute for Viticulture and Oenology: Private Bag X5206, Stellenbosch 7599; tel. (21) 889-5500; fax (21) 889-5508; f. 1955; research on all aspects of cultivation of table, raisin and wine grapes, and on production of wine and brandy; library of 2,000 vols; Dir Dr Leopoldt van Huyssteen.

Onderstepoort Institute for Exotic Diseases: Private Bag X6, Onderstepoort 0110; tel. (12) 529-9501; fax (12) 529-9543; diagnostic service and research on infectious diseases and production of foot-and-mouth vaccine; Dir Dr Gavin Thompson.

Onderstepoort Veterinary Institute: Private Bag X5, Onderstepoort 0110, Pretoria; tel. (12) 529-9111; fax (12) 565-6573; f. 1908; research on animal diseases; production of vaccines; diagnostic service; library of 96,000 vols; Dir Dr Daan Verwoerd; publ. *Onderstepoort Journal of Veterinary Research* (quarterly).

Plant Protection Research Institute: Private Bag X134, Pretoria 0001; tel. (12) 808-0952; fax (12) 808-1489; promotes economically and environmentally acceptable pest control and sustainable farming; research on invertebrates, fungi, bacteria and viruses; advisory service on aspects of biological control; library of 9,000 vols; Dir Mike. Walters.

Range and Forage Institute: Private Bag X05, Lynn East, Pretoria 0039; tel. (12) 841-9611; fax (12) 808-2155; research on sustainable livestock and rangeland management systems; Head Dr Aimie Aucamp.

Roodeplaat Vegetable and Ornamental Plant Institute: Private Bag X293, Pretoria 0001; tel. (12) 841-9611; fax (12) 808-0844; f. 1949; research on vegetables, and on cut flowers, pot plants and other ornamental plants; Dir Dr Hennie van Zyl; publ. *Roodeplaat Bulletin*.

Small Grain Institute: Private Bag X29, Bethlehem 9700; tel. (58) 303-5686; fax (58) 303-3952; research on improvement and cultivation of small grain crops; Dir Cobus le Roux.

Tobacco and Cotton Research Institute: Private Bag X82075, Rustenburg 0300; tel. (142) 993150; fax (142) 993113; basic and applied research on tobacco and cotton; Dir Deon Joubert.

Attached unit:

Plant Genetic Resources Unit: C/o The Division Manager, Private Bag X05, Lynn East 0039; tel. (12) 841-9716; fax (12) 808-1001; centralizes and co-ordinates plant genetic resources activities within the plant science institutes and liaises with regional and international agencies; responsible for documenting Agricultural Research Council germplasm and for arranging safety base collection facilities; Man. Dr Roger Ellis.

MEDICINE

Natal Institute of Immunology: Private Bag X9044, Pinetown 3600; tel. (31) 719-6500; fax (31) 784988; f. 1968; division of the Natal Blood Transfusion Service; a research institute of the University of Natal; 3 research divisions with interests in HL-A typing, recombinant DNA, synthetic peptides, hybridomas, immuno-assay and human genetics; 41 staff; library of 2,000 vols; Dir Dr J. D. Conradie.

South African Brain Research Institute: 6 Campbell St, Waverley, Johannesburg 2192; tel. (11) 786-2912; fax (11) 786-1766; e-mail mag@africa.com; f. 1981; all aspects of pure and applied brain research; 12 mems; library of 10,000 vols; Exec. Dir M. A. Gillman.

South African Institute for Medical Research (SAIMR): Hospital St, Johannesburg; tel. 489-9000; telex 422211; fax 489-9001; f. 1912; medical research into the causes, treatment and methods of prevention of human diseases, with emphasis on those of particular relevance to Southern Africa; diagnostic pathology services in 85 regional laboratories situated in all provinces (except KwaZulu-Natal); training of laboratory technologists; teaching of under- and post-graduate students is provided by the School of Pathology, the staff being joint members of SAIMR and the University of the Witwatersrand; organized in four divisions: Research, Diagnostic, Production of Vaccines and Sera, Education; library of 15,000 vols, 520 serial titles, 4,000 reprint titles of staff papers; Chair. of Board of Management A. J. du Plessis; Dir Prof. K. Klugman; Head of Dept of Chemical Pathology Prof. P. Gray; Head of Dept of Haematology Prof. B. V. Mendelow; Head of Dept of Anatomical Pathology Prof. K. Cooper; Head of Dept of Microbiology Prof. H. Koornhof; Head of Dept of Human Genetics Prof. T. Jenkins; Head of Dept of Immunology Prof. A. A. Wadee; Head of Serum and Vaccine Division Dr J. Southern; Head of Dept. of Medical Entomology Dr R. Hunt; publ. *Annual Report*.

South African Medical Research Council: POB 19070, Tygerberg 7505; tel. (21) 938-0911; fax (21) 938-0395; e-mail gething@eagle.mrc.ac.za; f. 1969; maintains in-house programmes and research establishments; Pres. Dr O. W. Prozesky.

NATURAL SCIENCES

Biological Sciences

Municipal Botanic Gardens: 70 St Thomas Rd, Durban, KwaZulu-Natal; tel. (31) 211303; fax (31) 217382; f. 1849, for the propagation, display and landscape of ornamental, exotic and southern African indigenous flora,and as a place for the study of and instruction in botany and horticulture; extensive collections of orchids, cycads, palms and bromeliads; herb garden; garden for the blind; water lily pond, fern garden; Dir Parks Dept E. D. Scarr; Curator, Durban Botanic Gardens C. G. M. Dalzell.

National Zoological Gardens of South Africa: POB 754, Pretoria 0001; tel. (12) 3283265; fax (12) 3234540; e-mail zoologic@cis.co.za; f. 1899; library of 4,000 vols, 40 periodicals; Dir W. Labuschagne; publ. *Zoön*.

Physical Sciences

Atomic Energy Corporation of South Africa Ltd (AEC): POB 582, Pretoria 0001; tel. (12) 316-4911; fax (12) 316-5111; f. 1982; 10 mems; operates UF6 conversion, fuel fabrication facilities, isotope production centre, hot cell facility and food radurization plant; enrichment research; operates 20 MW ORR type research reactor (SAFARI-1); 3.75 MV Van der Graaff accelerator.

Council for Geoscience: Private Bag X112, Pretoria 0001; tel. (12) 841-1911; telex 350286; fax (12) 841-1203; f. 1912; applied and fundamental geological research, mapping; library of 200,000 books, 10,000 maps; Dir C. Frick; publs annual reports, bulletins, bibliographies, *Memoirs*, handbooks, *Seismological Series*, *Contributions to Engineering Geology*.

Hartebeesthoek Radio Astronomy Observatory: POB 443, Krugersdorp 1740; tel. (11) 642-4692; telex 3-21006; fax (12) 642-2424; f. 1961, since 1988 a national facility under Foundation for Research Development; radio telescope 26m in diameter used for observations of Local Galaxy, spectroscopy of interstellar and circumstellar atoms and molecules, masers, pulsars, quasars and active galaxies; collaborates in global VLBI Networks; library of 1,000 vols, 102 periodicals; Dir Dr G. N. Nicolson.

Leiden Southern Station: POB 13, Broederstroom 0240; astronomy; Superintendent D. F. Stevenson.

Satellite Applications Centre: Division of Microelectronics and Communications Technology, CSIR, POB 395, Pretoria 0001; tel. (11) 642-4692; telex 3-21005; fax (11) 642-2446; f. 1961 as part of US Satellite Tracking and Data Network; since 1975 part of CSIR; receives, archives and processes METEOSAT, LANDSAT, NOAA and SPOT data; on-line LANDSAT data catalogue; 45 staff; library of *c.* 500 vols, 30 periodicals; Man. W. J. Botha; publ. *Remote Sensing Newsletter for South Africa*.

South African Astronomical Observatory: POB 9, Observatory 7935; outstation: Sutherland, Northern Cape; tel. (21) 447-0025; fax (21) 447-3639; e-mail director@saao.ac.za; f. 1972 by a merger of the Royal Observatory Cape of Good Hope and the Republic Observatory, Johannesburg; equipment includes 1,900-, 1,000-, 750- and 500-mm reflectors; library of 30,000 vols; Dir Dr R. S. Stobie; publs *Annual Report*, *Newsletter* (2 a year).

RELIGION, SOCIOLOGY AND ANTHROPOLOGY

Human Sciences Research Council (HSRC): 134 Pretorius St, Private Bag X41, Pretoria 0001; tel. (12) 202-9111; telex 321710; fax (12) 326-5362; est. 1969 as a corporate body controlled by a council, consisting of a full-time President and ten other members; 70%-financed by South Africa Parliament; undertakes, promotes, co-ordinates and finances (by means of the SA Plan for Research in the Human Sciences) research in the field of human sciences, including the humanities and social sciences; liaises between South Africa and persons and authorities in other countries; awards bursaries and grants for research, publishes research findings or financially supports the publication thereof, fosters the training of persons for research work; incorporates research groups in broad fields of education, human resources, social dynamics and science development; Pres. Dr R. H. Stumpf; publs *HSRC Annual Report*, *Research Bulletin* (10 a year), *Africa 2001*, specialized newsletters.

Institute for the Study of Man in Africa: Room 2B17, University of the Witwatersrand Medical School, York Rd, Parktown, Johannesburg 2193; tel. (11) 647-2203; fax (11) 643-4318; f. 1960 to perpetuate the work of Prof. Raymond A. Dart on the study of man in Africa, past and present, in health and disease; serves as a centre of anthropological and medical field work; it functions partly through the auspices of the University of the Witwatersrand.

TECHNOLOGY

MINTEK: Private Bag X3015, Randburg 2125; tel. (11) 709-4111; telex 4-24867; fax (011) 793-2413; e-mail info@mintek.ac.za; f. 1934; library of 30,000 vols; research, development and technology transfer to promote mineral technology and to foster the establishment and expansion of industries in the fields of minerals and mineral products; investigates all aspects of mineral beneficiation, especially areas such as new alloys and chemical products; divisions specializing in mineralogy, minerals engineering, hydrometallurgy, pyrometallurgy, measurement and control, analytical science, physical metallurgy, analytical and process chemistry; sponsors university research groups; CEO Dr A. M. Edwards; publs *Research Reports* (irregular), *Annual Review*, *Mintek Bulletin* (monthly).

South African Bureau of Standards: Private Bag X191, 1 Dr Lategan Rd, Groenkloof, Pretoria 0001; tel. 428-7911; fax 344-1568; f. 1945; 1,300 staff; draws up national standards, specifications, codes of practice, administers the SABS mark and listing schemes; Pres. M. G. Kellermann (acting); publ. *SABS-Bulletin*.

Libraries and Archives

Alice

University of Fort Hare Library: Private Bag X1322, Alice 5700; tel. (404) 22011, ext. 2019; telex 250863; fax (404) 31423; f. 1916; 163,000 vols; contains the Howard Pim Library of Rare Books; University Librarian C. N. Tau.

Bloemfontein

Bloemfontein Regional Library/Bloemfonteinse Streekbiblioteek: Private Bag X20606, Bloemfontein 9300; tel. (51) 71993; telex 5/267056 SA; f. 1950; public library services to rural areas with 38 libraries and depots; school library services to southern region of province with 91 schools; *c.* 500,000 vols; Senior Librarian L. Orffer.

Free State Provincial Library Service: Private Bag X20606, Bloemfontein; tel. (51) 405-4680; fax (51) 403-3567; e-mail lubbe@majuba.ofs.gov.za; f. 1948; 4,000,000 books; serves 130 public libraries and 5 spec. libraries; Dir T. A. Lubbe; publ. *Free State Libraries* (quarterly).

Public Library: POB 1029, Bloemfontein; tel. (51) 405-8241; fax (51) 405-8604; f. 1875; Legal Deposit, National Drama Library, and Public library; 405,000 vols, 62,000 plays; Librarian P. J. van der Walt; publs *Catalogue of the National Drama Library* and supplement.

University of the Orange Free State Library and Information Services: POB 301, Blomfontein 9300; tel. (51) 401-2227; fax (51) 448-2879; f. 1906; the collection includes rare pamphlets and other early South African publications of the Dreyer-Africana Collection and items on the South Africa War; 576,000 vols (3,000 magazines); Dir A. M. Dippenaar.

Cape Town

Cape Provincial Library Service: POB 2108, Cape Town 8000; tel. (21) 410-9111; fax (21) 419-7541; f. 1945; 24 regional libraries, 472 affiliated libraries; collections of art prints, phonographic records, CDs, audio cassettes, 16mm films, videos; 7,000,000 vols; Central Information Service; Dir N. F. van der Merwe; publ. *The Cape Librarian/ Kaapse Bibliotekaris* (10 a year).

Cape Town City Libraries: POB 4728, Cape Town 8000; tel. (21) 462-4400; fax (21) 461-5981; e-mail hheymann@ctcc.gov.za; f. 1952; free municipal public library service; central library and 32 suburban brs, travelling, hospital, old age homes, homebound library services; 1,500,000 vols; special art, music and business collections; Librarian H. C. F. Heymann; publ. *Annual Report*.

Library of Parliament: Houses of Parliament, Parliament St, POB 18, Cape Town 8000; tel. (21) 403-2140; fax (21) 461-4331; f. 1857; provides general and legislative reference services and a press-cutting service to members and officers of Parliament; legal deposit library and depository for UN publs; 350,000 items, including the Mendelssohn Africana Collection; 2,700 current periodicals; local and foreign government and parliamentary publs; Librarian A. Ntunja.

Royal Society of South Africa Library: c/o University of Cape Town, Rondebosch 7700; f. 1877, Royal Charter 1908; 33,000 vols of scientific periodicals; Hon. Librarian Prof. J. R. E. Lutjeharms; publ. *Transactions of the Royal Society of South Africa* (irregular).

South African Library: Queen Victoria St, POB 496, Cape Town 8000; tel. (21) 246320; fax (21) 244848; f. 1818; national reference and preservation library with legal deposit privileges; 750,000 books and official publs, 200,000 bound periodicals, 8,000 current periodicals, 45,000 bound newspapers, 300 current newspapers, 20,000 maps, 100,000 iconographic items; MS collections of Cape and early SA; comprehensive Africana collection pertaining to South Africa, with materials on neighbouring Southern African countries; UN and World Bank depositary library; special collections incl. Grey Collection 115 medieval MSS, 5,000 vols incl. incunabula and early South African imprints; Dessinian (17th- and 18th-century); Nourse Cromwelliana (17th century); Fairbridge (19th-century); reference room for research; regular exhibitions of library material; microfilming, photographic and copying services; Dir P. E. Westra; publs *Quarterly Bulletin*, *Grey Bibliographies*.

University of Cape Town Libraries: Private Bag, Rondebosch, Cape 7700; tel. (21) 650-3097; fax (21) 689-7568; f. 1829; 1,013,000 vols, 8,000 current periodicals; J. W. Jagger Linear Library and branches: African Studies (Southern Africa), Architecture, Botany (Bolus), Education, Fine Arts and Drama (Hiddingh Hall), Institute of Child Health, Jewish Studies, Law, Medical, Music; special collections incl. rare books (incl. fore-edge paintings), Kipling, pre-1925 Africana, Bolus (antiquarian botanical), history of medicine, Van Zyl (antiquarian legal works), material relating to the history of Cape Province (incl. archives of the Black Sash (Cape Western Region), the Cape Chamber of Industries,

Syfrets and various trade unions), the papers of C. Louis Leipoldt, Pauline Smith and Olive Schreiner, and Bleek/Lloyd and G. P. Lestrade African language collections; Librarian (vacant).

Western Cape Education Library and Information Services: 9 Dorp St, Private Bag X9099, Cape Town 8000; tel. (21) 483-5265; fax (21) 483-5747; f. 1970; 130,000 vols, 162 current periodicals; Head L. METCALFE.

Chuenespoort

Lebowa National Library: Department of Education, Private Bag X03, Chuenespoort 0745; tel. 37137; fax 37149; f. 1980; 15,000 vols; special collection of official publs of the Lebowa Govt; Chief Librarians E. M. TLADI, R. M. PHAAHLA; publ. *Annual Report*.

Durban

Durban Metropolitan Libraries: City Hall, Smith St, POB 917, Durban; tel. (31) 300-6911; fax 300-6301; f. 1853; 1,371,600 vols; special collections of Africana and Shakespeareana; 38 brs.; Librarian R. JAYARAM.

University of Natal Library, Durban Campus: King George V Ave, Durban 4001; tel. (31) 2602317; fax (31) 2602051; University Librarian G. H. HAFFAJEE.

East London

East London Municipal Library Service: Gladstone St, POB 652, East London; tel. (431) 24991; fax (431) 431729; f. 1876; 30,000 mems; 225,000 vols; Librarian Mrs M. M. DAVIDSON.

Giyani

Gazankulu Library Services: Post Bag X9668, Giyani 0826; tel. (158) 23157; fax (158) 21941; f. 1979, for both academic and public use; attached to Dept of Education; 15,000 vols; Chief Librarian I. P. E. NDHAMBI.

Grahamstown

Grahamstown Public Library: POB 180, Grahamstown; f. 1842; 71,849 vols; Librarian Miss M. J. HARTZENBERG.

National English Literary Museum: P. Bag 1019, Grahamstown 6140; tel. (46) 622-7042; fax (46) 622-2582; e-mail nemh@hippo.ru.ac.za; f. 1972; 14,000 vols; research collections of literary manuscripts, photographs, journal articles and press clippings; Dir M. M. HACKSLEY.

Rhodes University Library: Rhodes University, POB 184, Grahamstown 6140; tel. (46) 603-8436; fax (46) 622-3487; e-mail library@ru.ac.za; f. 1904; 320,000 vols; Librarian FELIX N. UBOGU.

Johannesburg

Johannesburg Public Library: Cnr of Market and Fraser Sts, Johannesburg 2001; tel. (11) 836-3787; fax (11) 836-6607; e-mail library@mj.org.za; f. 1890; 1,877,000 vols; Librarian E. J. BEVAN; publs *Annual Report*, *Local Government Library Bulletin* (monthly).

Library of the South African Institute of Race Relations: POB 97, Johannesburg 2000; tel. (11) 403-3600; fax (11) 403-3671; f. 1929; 7,030 vols; valuable archival and documentary material; newspaper clippings from 1930 on race relations, politics, labour and economics; bibliographies on race relations; Librarian E. S. POTTER.

University of the Witwatersrand Library: Private Bag XI, PO Wits, 2050; tel. (11) 716-2330; telex 420765; fax (11) 403-1421; e-mail 056heath@libris.wwl.wits.ac.za; f. 1922; 1,069,000 vols; two central libraries (undergraduate and research), also br.libraries: architecture, biological and physical sciences, management, geological and mathematical sciences, education and commerce, engineering, law, health sciences, nuclear sciences; spec. collns incl. Africana, Hebraica and Judaica, Portuguese, Archaeology and Egyptology, Historical and Literary Papers (incl. Church of the Province of South Africa), Early Printed Books; Librarian HEATHER M. EDWARDS.

Kimberley

Kimberley Public Library: POB 627, Kimberley 8300; f. 1882; *c.* 127,000 vols; Africana Library (f. 1886) of 20,000 vols, 545 MSS 1,145 photographs (N. Cape and Diamond Fields); Judy Scott Library (f. 1966) of 40,000 vols; Librarian F. VAN DYK.

Mmabatho

North West Library Service: Private Bag X2044, Mmabatho 8681; tel. (140) 292374; fax (140) 22063; f. 1978; under Dept of Education; 15 public libraries, 7 college libraries, 400 high school libraries, 7 govt dept libraries; 1,446,000 vols; Dir N. B. NOMNGA.

Pietermaritzburg

KwaZulu-Natal Provincial Library Service: Private Bag X9016, Pietermaritzburg; tel. (331) 940241; fax 942237; e-mail bawar@kzntl.gov.za; f. 1952; consists of central organization and reference library at Pietermaritzburg; four regional offices for Coast, South Coast, Midlands and Northern areas, serving 171 public libraries, 54 departmental libraries; 2,800,000 vols; film lending service with 1,889 films; compact disc lending service with 9,000 compact discs; video cassette lending service with 29,050 video cassettes; Deputy Dir Dr ROOKAYA BAWA; Ref. Librarian SUE DAVIES (acting); publ. *KZN Librarian* (4 a year).

Natal Society Library: POB 415, Pietermaritzburg 3200, Natal; tel. (331) 452383; fax 940095; e-mail nsl@alphafuturenet.co.za; f. 1851; lending, children's, reference, legal deposit, school assignments, music, special collections, map collections, Africana collection; 6 brs, hospital, housebound and travelling library services; 600,000 vols; 6,332 current legal deposit periodicals and newspapers, 122 current overseas periodicals, numerous bound legal deposit and overseas periodicals and newspapers; Dir Mrs S. S. WALLIS; publs *Annual Report*, *Natalia* (annually), *AIDS Bibliography*.

University of Natal Library, Pietermaritzburg Campus: Private Bag X014, Scottsville 3209; tel. (331) 260-5911; fax (331) 260-5260; f. 1909; 375,000 vols; Librarian CHRISTOPHER MERRETT.

Port Elizabeth

Port Elizabeth City Libraries: POB 66, Port Elizabeth 6000; f. 1965; 500,000 vols; City Librarian A. LENNOX.

University of Port Elizabeth Library: Private Bag X6058, Port Elizabeth 6000; tel. (41) 504-2281; fax (41) 504-2280; e-mail libref@upe.ac.za; f. 1964; 350,000 vols, 1,543 current periodicals; L. C. Steyn Collection of Roman Dutch Law; Librarian D. W. FOKKER; publs *UPE Publications Series* (irregular).

Potchefstroom

Potchefstroom University for Christian Higher Education Libraries: Private Bag X05, Noordbrug 2522; tel. (18) 2992000; fax (18) 2992999; e-mail fpbcjhl@puknet.puk.ac.za; f. 1869; 651,000 vols, 2,092 current periodicals; Main Library (Ferdinand Postma Library), Library of the Theological School of the Reformed Churches in South Africa, Music Library, Natural Sciences Library, Vaal Triangle Campus Library at Vanderbijlpark; special collections: Carney Africana Collection, Hertzog Law Collection, Collection of the Institute for Research in Children's Literature; Dir Prof. C. J. H. LESSING; publs *Union Catalogue of Theses and Dissertations of South African Universities, 1918–*.

Pretoria

Council for Scientific and Industrial Research (CSIR) Central Library Services: POB 395, Pretoria 0001; tel. (12) 841-2911; fax (12) 349-1154; e-mail mlodder@csir.co.za; f. 1945; provides scientific, technical and business management information services to industry; *c.* 110,000 bound vols, 5,000 serial titles and 22,000 pamphlets; 12 brs; Man. MARGARET LODDER; publs *CSIR Annual Report, Impact, Technobrief*.

Department of Arts, Culture, Science and Technology Library: Private Bag X894, Pretoria 0001; tel. (12) 314-6033; fax (12) 323-2720; special collections: library science, science planning, state language services, national terminology services; 42,000 vols; 153 current periodicals; Librarian D.E. MOHLAKWANA.

Department of Education Library: Private Bag X895, Pretoria 0001; tel. (12) 312-5265; fax (12) 325-1475.

Department of Sport and Recreation Library: Private Bag X896, Pretoria 0001; tel. 312-3100; fax 21-6187; f. 1994; 300 vols, 15 current periodicals; Librarian N.P. RAMPEDI.

Gauteng Library and Information Services: Private Bag X098, Marshalltown 2107; tel. (11) 355-2567; fax (11) 355-2565; e-mail reference@gpg.gov.za; f. 1995; consists of Head Office in Johannesburg, Pretoria Regional Office and 4 Regional Libraries; provides library and information service to 324 public and community libraries and depots in Gauteng Province; 3,476,000 vols; Dir B. S. HANSEN.

Human Sciences Research Council, Centre for Library and Information Services: 134 Pretorius St, Private Bag X41, Pretoria 0001; tel. (12) 302-2968; fax (12) 302-2933; e-mail library@ludwig.hsrc.ac.za; f. 1969; 71,000 vols; 900 current periodical titles.

Mary Gunn Library, National Botanical Institute: Private Bag X101, Pretoria 0001; tel. (12) 804-3200; fax (12) 804-3211; 8,942 vols; Chief Exec. Prof. B. J. HUNTLEY.

National Archives and Heraldic Services: Private Bag X236, Pretoria 0001; tel. (12) 323-5300; fax (12) 323-5287; e-mail arg02@acts4.pwv.gov.za; provides a comprehensive archives service to all government offices and local authorities; processes and stores archive material; makes archives and facilities available to researchers; National Archivist for the Republic of South Africa M. E. OLIVIER.

National Department of Agriculture, Division of Library and Documentation Services: Private Bag X388, Pretoria 0001; tel. (12) 319-7060; telex 322149; fax (12) 319-6889; f. 1910; 54,000 vols, 520 current periodicals, 140,000 pamphlets; Librarian M. M. KOEN; publ. *Agrolibri* (latest accessions).

State Library: POB 397, Pretoria 0001; tel. (12) 21-8931; fax (12) 325-5984; f. 1887; national and legal depository library, and depository library for US Government and UN publications; 684,000 vols, 9,600 current serials; responsible for compiling the national bibliography and the joint catalogues of monographs and periodicals in South African libraries; international and national interlending centre; Southern African Book Exchange Centre; ISBN and ISSN centre for South Africa; Dir Dr PETER J. LOR; publs *South African National Bibliography* (quarterly and annual cumulations, paper and machine-readable format), *SA Joint Catalogue of Monographs* (microfiche, 2 a year), *Periodicals in Southern African Libraries* (microfiche, 2 a year), *Index to South African Periodicals* (CD-ROM and machine-readable format), *RSA Government Gazette* (microfiche, quarterly), *Directory of Southern African Libraries, South African Newspapers on Microfilm, Bibliography of the Xhosa Language, Northern Sotho Bibliography, Directory of South African Publishers, Official Publications of Southern African States* (microfiche), *Annual Report, Informat.*

Transvaal Education Department, Education Media Service: 328 Van der Walt St, Private Bag X290, Pretoria 0001; tel. (12) 322-7685; fax (12) 322-7699; f. 1951; 385,000 vols, 600 periodicals, 3,000 videos; Dir J. A. BIERMAN.

University of Pretoria Libraries: Academic Information Service, University of Pretoria, Pretoria 0002; tel. (12) 420-2235; fax 362-5100; e-mail gerryts@acinfo.up.ac.za; f. 1908; 989,000 vols, pamphlets, Govt. publs, periodicals, etc, 8,000 gramophone records, 24,000 sheet-music, 15,000 audiovisual material, 2,000 CDs; Academic Information Centre, Central Medical Library, Basic Medical Science Library, Music Library, Veterinary Science Library, Agricultural Sciences Library, Electronic Information Retrieval, Strategic Management; Special Collections: Africana, South African Sheet Music; Dir E. D. GERRYTS.

University of South Africa Library: POB 392, Pretoria 0003; tel. (12) 429-3131; fax (12) 429-2925; e-mail willej@alpha.unisa.ac.za; f. 1947; 1,435,000 vols, 215,000 bound serials, 205,000 microfiche items, 114,000 audiovisual materials, 7,300 current periodicals; science library and law collection specializing in foreign and comparative law; brs in Cape Town, Durban, East London, Johannesburg and Pietersburg; Exec. Dir. Prof. J. WILLEMSE; publ. *Mousaion* (irregular).

Stellenbosch

University of Stellenbosch Library: University of Stellenbosch, Private Bag 5036, Stellenbosch 7599; tel. (21) 808-4880; telex 520383; fax (21) 808-4336; e-mail jhvi@maties.sun.ac.za; f. 1900; 810,000 vols, 6,900 current periodicals; 6 brs; Librarian Prof. Dr J. H. VILJOEN.

Ulundi

Ulundi Community Library: Private Bag X17, Ulundi 3838; fax (358) 700836; 18,334 vols; Librarian T. R. KHUMALO.

Umtata

Transkei Library: Private Bag X5095, Umtata; tel. (471) 22524; fax (471) 22524; f. 1978; attached to Dept of Education; legal deposit library; compiles national bibliography; specializes in reference and research work; 23,661 vols, 65 periodical titles; special collections: Moffat Collection of 406 vols, mainly on law, sociology and history of Africa; Africana collection of 600 vols; Dir N. NGENDANE; publ. *Annual Report*.

Museums and Art Galleries

Bloemfontein

National Museum: POB 266, Bloemfontein 9300; tel. (51) 447-9609; fax (51) 447-6273; f. 1877; Institute for Herpetology, Ornithology, Mammalogy, Arachnology, Palaeontology, Archaeology, Local History, Anthropology, Entomology and Ethnology, Botany, Rock Art; the unique Florisbad human fossil skull housed here; library of 8,000 vols, 2,600 serial titles; Dir Dr C. J. ENGELBRECHT; publs *Navorsinge van die Nasionale Museum / Researches of the National Museum, CULNA.*

Cape Town

Michaelis Collection: The Old Town House, Greenmarket Square, Cape Town; tel. (21) 246367; fax (21) 461-9592; f. 1916; Dutch and Flemish paintings, drawings and prints of the 16th–19th centuries; library of 1,000 vols; Dir Dr HANS FRANSEN.

Museum of Coast and Anti-Aircraft Artillery: Fort Wynyard, POB 14068, Green Point 8051; tel. (21) 419-1765; f. 1987; coast and anti-aircraft guns and relics displayed in a restored coast artillery battery.

South African Cultural History Museum: POB 645, Cape Town 8000; tel. (21) 461-8280; fax (21) 461-9592; e-mail sachm@iafrica.com; f. 1966; decorative arts, archaeology, local history, restored houses illustrating life in the 18th and 19th centuries; library of 12,000 vols; Dir Dr ARON MAZEL; publs *Annals* (annually), *Newsletter* (quarterly).

Attached maritime museum:

South African Maritime Museum: Dock Road, Table Bay Harbour; tel. (21) 419-2505; fax (21) 419-7332; e-mail museum@maritimemuseum.ac.za; contains information about the fishing industry, shipwrecks, shipping lines, raw materials, ship modelling, Table Bay Harbour, Union-Castle Company, a shipwright workshop, trade, and future development plans; includes two floating exhibitions: SAS *Somerset,* boom defence vessel built in 1942.

South African Museum: POB 61, Cape Town 8000; tel. (21) 243330; fax (21) 246716; e-mail mcluver@samuseum.ac.za; f. 1825; archaeology, anthropology, zoology, palaeontology, marine biology, entomology; library of *c.* 12,000 vols and *c.* 4,000 periodical titles; Dir Prof. M. A. CLUVER; publs *Annals* (irregular), *Brochures*.

South African National Gallery: Government Ave, Gardens/POB 2420, Cape Town 8000; tel. (21) 45-1628; fax (21) 461-0045; e-mail sang@gem.co.za; f. 1871; 19th- and 20th-century South African art; African art with special emphasis on southern African beadwork and sculpture; 16th–19th-century British and European art including Sir Abe Bailey collection of British sporting art; 20th-century British, European and American art; Annexe Gallery: exhibitions with an educational emphasis; newspaper cutting collection of South African art; library of 9,000 vols; Dir M. MARTIN.

Administers:

Natale Labia Museum: 192 Main Rd, Muizenberg, Cape Town 7951; tel. (21) 788-4107; f. 1988; built 1929 as residence of first Italian Minister Plenipotentiary in SA, Prince Natale Labia; elaborate Italianate furnishings with 18th- and 19th-century British and European art; special exhibitions and cultural activities.

William Fehr Collection: The Castle, POB 1, Cape Town 8000; tel. (21) 45-4725; fax (21) 462-3750; f. 1965; antique Cape furniture, silver, copper, glass, and Africana oils; at Rust en Vreugd, Buitenkant St, tel. 453628: collection of Africana water colours and prints; Dir P. M. GROBELAAR.

Durban

Durban Museums: City Hall, POB 4085, Durban 4000; tel. (31) 3006911; fax 3006302; f. 1887; South African fauna, flora, ethnography, archaeology, paintings, graphic art, porcelain, sculptures, local history; Dir Museums J. J. OBERHOLZER; publs *Novitates*.

Local History Museum: Old Court House Museum, Aliwal St, Durban; tel. (31) 300-6313; f. 1966; local and KwaZulu Natal historical collections, restored Natal colonial public building; Dir R. H. OMAR (acting).

Selected attached museums:

Kwa Muhle Museum: 130–132 Ordnance Rd, Durban; tel. (31) 3006313; f. 1994; 20th-century urban life with emphasis on the 'Durban System' of administering the African population 1908–1986; Dir R. H. OMAR (acting).

Port Natal Maritime Museum: C/o Old Court House Museum, Aliwal Street, Durban; tel. (31) 3061092; f. 1988; Natal and Durban maritime history, two tugs and a minesweeper; Dir R. H. OMAR (acting).

East London

East London Museum: POB 11021, Southernwood 5213, East London; tel. (431) 430-686; fax (431) 433-127; f. 1921; research departments, reference collections and displays of conchology, ichthyology, ornithology of the Eastern Cape Province, cultural history of the Border region and ethnography of the Southern Nguni peoples; houses type specimen of Coelacanth caught in 1938; educational service; administers Victorian house museum; Chair. Board of Trustees B. W. WATSON; Dir R. M. TIETZ; publs *Cape Provincial Museums Annals* (jointly with 4 other museums), *Annual Report*, *Newsletter* (quarterly).

Franschhoek

Huguenot Memorial Museum: Lambrechts St, POB 37, Franschhoek; tel. (21) 876-2532; fax (21) 876-3649; e-mail hugenoot@museum.co.za; f. 1967; research into Cape Huguenot history, exhibition of over 400 Huguenot pieces and documents; Chair. Prof. P. COERTZEN; Curator J. E. MALHERBE; publ. *Bulletin of the Huguenot Society of South Africa*.

Grahamstown

Albany Museum: Somerset St, Grahamstown 6139; tel. (46) 622-2312; fax (46) 622-2398; e-mail amwh@giraffe.ru.ac.za; f. 1855; archaeology, terrestrial entomology, freshwater ichthyology, freshwater invertebrates, botany, palaeontology, ornithology, history and material cultures of the peoples of the eastern Cape Province; library of 2,000 vols, 1,400 periodicals; Dir W. HOLLEMAN; publs *Annals of the Eastern Cape Provincial Museums* (jointly with 3 other museums, irregular), *Southern African Field Archaeology*† (2 a year).

Johannesburg

Adler Museum of the History of Medicine: University of the Witwatersrand, POB 1038, Johannesburg 2000; SAIMR, Hospital Street, Johannesburg; tel. 489-9482; fax 489-9001; f. 1962; collection of medical, dental and surgical instruments and equipment; reconstructions of early 20th-century pharmacy, doctor's and dentist's surgeries, herbalist shop and traditional medicine display; library of 4,000 vols; Curator A. J. V. Brown; publ. *Adler Museum Bulletin* (3 a year).

Johannesburg Art Gallery: POB 23561, Joubert Park 2044; tel. (11) 725-3130; fax (11) 720-6000; e-mail tmabaso@mj.org.za; f. 1910; indigenous southern African and Western-tradition paintings, sculpture, drawings, prints, textiles, furniture and ceramics; Oriental prints and ceramics; library of 8,700 vols; Dir R. KEENE.

MuseuMAfricA: Old Market Bldg, 121 Bree St, POB 517, Newtown 2113, Johannesburg; tel. (11) 833-5624; fax (11) 833-5636; f. 1935;

life in South Africa since prehistoric times; also Geological Museum, Bensusan Museum of Photography, Museum of South African Rock Art.

Branch museums:

Bernberg Fashion Museum: 1 Duncombe Rd, Forest Town, Johannesburg; f. 1973; tel. (11) 646-0176; costume and accessories since 1750.

George Harrison Park: Main Reef Rd, Johannesburg; tel. (11) 833-5624; f. 1936; Main Reef goldmine workings.

James Hall Museum of Transport: Pioneers' Park, Rosettenville Rd, La Rochelle, Johannesburg; tel. (11) 435-9718; f. 1964; history of land transport in South Africa (excluding public railways).

Kimberley

McGregor Museum: Atlas St, POB 316, Kimberley 8300; tel. 32645; f. 1907; archaeology and rock art, history, geology, zoology and herbarium of N. Cape; ethnological collection housed in Duggan-Cronin Gallery, f. 1938; incorporates Magersfontein Battlefield Museum (f. 1971), Rudd House, Dunluce and Memorial to the Pioneers of Aviation; Dir E. A. VOIGT; publ. *McGregor Miscellany*.

King William's Town

Kaffrarian Museum: Cnr Albert Rd and Alexandra Rd, POB 1434, King William's Town 5600; tel. (433) 24506; fax (433) 21569; e-mail lloyd@huberta.ru.ac.za; f. 1884; studies, collects, houses and exhibits southern Africa mammalogy, Xhosa ethnography, local history and Eastern Cape missionary history; library of 8,200 vols, 150 current periodicals; special collection of 2,300 vols of Africana (Kitton Collection); Dir LLOYD R. WINGATE; publs *Annual Report*, *Newsletter IMVUBU*, *Cape Provincial Museums Annals* (jointly with 4 other museums).

Incorporates:

Missionary Museum: Berkeley St, POB 1434, King William's Town 5600; tel. (433) 24506; f. 1972; missionary history in Eastern Cape.

Pietermaritzburg

Natal Museum: Private Bag 9070, Pietermaritzburg 3200; located at: 237 Loop St, Pietermaritzburg 3201; tel. (331) 451404; fax (331) 450561; e-mail library@nmsa.org.za; f. 1903; extensive natural history exhibits, especially the collections of African mammals, birds, shells and insects; ethnology; KwaZulu-Natal's history; research in Diptera, Myriapoda, Lower Invertebrates (Annelida), Mollusca, herpetology, small mammals, Stone Age and Iron Age KwaZulu-Natal; Zulu anthropology, Natal history; library of 15,000 monographs, 2,300 periodicals, 61,000 pamphlets, 8,000 photographs, 900 maps, special collections; Dir Dr J. LONDT; publs *Annals*, *Natal Museum Journal of Humanities*.

Tatham Art Gallery (Municipal): Commercial Road, opp. City Hall, Pietermaritzburg; tel. (331) 421804; fax (331) 949831; f. 1903; 19th- and 20th-century British and French painting, sculpture and graphics, Southern African painting, sculpture, ceramics, prints and ethnic objets d'art; public reference library of 2,300 vols; Dir BRENDAN BELL.

Port Elizabeth

King George VI Art Gallery: 1 Park Drive, Port Elizabeth; tel. (41) 586-1030; fax (41) 586-3234; f. 1956; municipal art museum; collections of British and South African art, Indian miniatures, international graphics, Southern Nguni art, Chinese textiles; reference library of 2,000 vols; Dir MELANIE HILLEBRAND.

Port Elizabeth Museum (incorporating Snake Park, Oceanarium, Tropical House and Historical Museum): POB 13147, Humewood 6013; tel. (41) 586-1051; fax (41) 586-2175; f. 1856, moved 1959; research on marine archaeology, marine biology, marine mammalogy, herpetology, ornithology and local history; library of 20,000 vols; Museum: whale skeletons, shells and general marine life; fossils, geology, birds and local history; Snake Park: African and worldwide collection of reptiles; Oceanarium; local fish, sharks, sea birds, seals and dolphins; Dir S. VAN ZYL; publs *Cape Provincial Museums Annals* (jointly with 4 other museums), *Annual Reports*, *Otolith* (Port Elizabeth Museum newsletter).

Pretoria

National Cultural History Museum: POB 28088, Sunnyside 0132; tel. (12) 341-1320; fax (12) 341-6146; f. 1892; comprises Pierneef Museum (Vermeulen St), Voortrekker Monument Museum, Paul Kruger Museum (Church St), Willem Prinsloo Agricultural Museum (dist. Pretoria), Pioneer Museum (Silverton), Coert Steynberg Museum (Pretoria North), Sammy Marks Museum (dist. Pretoria), Tswaing Crater Museum (dist. Pretoria) and the Museum of Culture (Visagie St); library of 7,000 vols, 200 periodicals; special collections: Jansen Collection, Hertzog collection; Dir Dr UDO KÜSEL; publ. *Nasko Navorsing* (irregular).

Pretoria Art Museum (Municipal Art Gallery): Arcadia Park, Arcadia, Pretoria 0083; tel. (12) 344-1807; fax (12) 344-1809; e-mail pam@ccp.co.za; f. 1964; South African art, small collection of European graphic art, some 17th-century Dutch art, collection of traditional and contemporary African art; Curator D. OFFRINGA; publ. *Bulletin*.

Transvaal Museum: Paul Kruger St, POB 413, Pretoria 0001; tel. (12) 3227632; fax (12) 322-7939; f. 1893, from 1964 a Natural History museum only; taxonomy, ecology, zoogeography and evolutionary studies with main emphasis on Southern Africa; mammals, birds, herpetology, palaeontology (incl. mammal-like reptiles and early hominids), Coleoptera, Lepidoptera, Orthoptera, lower invertebrates and archaeo-zoology; library of 10,000 vols, 2,000 periodicals and 80,000 reprints; rare book collection; Dir I. L. RAUTENBACH; publs *Transvaal Museum Monographs* (irregular), *Annals of the Transvaal Museum* (irregular), *Transvaal Museum Bulletin* (irregular).

Stellenbosch

Stellenbosch Museum: Private Bag X5048, Stellenbosch; tel. (21) 887-2937; fax (21) 883-2232; f. 1962; comprises 18th-century powder magazine (weaponry, Stellenbosch military history), Village Museum (buildings illustrating life from 1690 to 1890), Toy and Miniature Museums; Dir M. J. LE ROUX; publ. *Stellenbossiana* (quarterly).

Universities

UNIVERSITY OF BOPHUTHATSWANA

Mmabatho Campus:
Private Bag X2046, Mmabatho 8681

Telephone: (140) 892111
Telex: 3072
Fax: (140) 25775

Founded 1979
Autonomous control
Language of instruction: English
Academic year: February to November

Chancellor: Dr T. VAN DER WALT
Vice-Chancellor: Prof. ZAC CHUENYANE (acting)
Deputy Vice-Chancellors:
- Student Affairs: Prof. J. E. SETSHEDI
- Academic Affairs: Prof. M. Z. CHUENYANE
- Administration: (vacant)

Registrar: J. R. BANDA
Librarian: D. BAMPOE

Library of 90,000 vols
Number of teachers: 198
Number of students: 3,846

Publications: *Unibo News* (quarterly), *Dateline* (every 2 weeks), *Inaugural Lecture Series*, *Vice-Chancellor's Report* (annually).

DEANS

Administration and Management: Prof. S. N. TLAKULA
Agriculture: Prof. S. M. FUNNAH
Education: D. RANGAKA
Law: Prof. J. MIHALIK
Health and Social Sciences: P. J. MABETOA

HEADS OF DEPARTMENTS

School of Administration and Management:
- Accounting: Prof. C. R. SNYMAN
- Economics: D. HODGE (acting)
- Industrial Psychology: Prof. N. P. SIBEKO
- Data Processing: Prof. E. J. SIMBO
- Management: Prof. W. P. J. VAN RENSBURG
- Political Studies: E. T. HEDDING
- Public Administration: Prof. S. N. TLAKULA (acting)
- Statistics: D. U. A. GALAGEDERA (acting)
- Internship: C. A. MAYEZA

School of Agriculture:
- Animal Health: Prof. D. E. BEIGHLE
- Animal Production: Dr B. A. KUMAR
- Plant Production: Prof. H. T. OO
- Agricultural Extension and Rural Development: K. YEBOAH-ASUAMAH
- Agricultural Economics: Dr L. H. MALAMBO
- Bio-Mathematics and Statistics: Dr E. R. FALKENHAGEN

School of Education:
- Afrikaans: Prof. T. GOUWS
- English: K. AMUZU (acting)
- Setswana: J. W. P. MASHIKE (acting)
- Teaching and Curriculum: Dr S. A. AWUDETSEY
- Physics: Prof. S. H. TAOLE
- Chemistry: Prof. M. SELVARATNAM
- Biology: Prof. Y. RECHAV
- Mathematics: Prof. T. G. SCHULTZ
- History: Prof. K. BONER
- Geography: Prof. J. W. COWLEY
- Fine Arts: Prof. ESTELLE MARAIS
- Foundations of Education: Prof. M. MAQSUD
- Administration and Planning: E. V. N. MOTSHABI
- Internship: T. L. MAKETE (acting)

School of Health and Social Sciences:
- Communication: K. M. KOTSOKOANE (acting)
- Development Studies: Dr B. C. CHIKULU
- Nursing Science: Prof. M. KAU
- Psychology: Prof. M. C. C. PRETORIUS
- Social Work: Prof. W. W. ANDERSON
- Sociology: Prof. D. B. T. MILAZI

School of Law:
- Jurisprudence: Prof. A. M. DLAMINI
- Customary Law: Prof. D. J. VAN DER POST
- Criminal Law: Prof. J. MIHALIK
- Mercantile Law: Prof. J. BALORO
- Private Law: Prof. L. KAKULA
- Procedural and Clinical Law: C. NDAWENI (acting)
- Public Law: Prof. B. F. NDAKI
- UNIBO Law Clinic: J. STANDER

ATTACHED INSTITUTES

Institute of African Studies: research and development of the African Heritage; Dir Prof. T. SONO.

Institute of Development Research: research on economic and social development of Bophuthatswana; Dir Prof. N. AHMAD.

Institute of Education: educational research, and provides academic control of the courses at the eight colleges of education attached to the university; Dir M. I. MAHAPE.

Centre for Business and Management Development: Prof. A. A. ISMAIL BOOTHA.

International Centre for Medicine and Law: Exec. Chair. D. FRIEDMAN.

UNIVERSITY OF CAPE TOWN

Private Bag, Rondebosch 7700

Telephone: (21) 650-9111
Telex: 522208
Fax: (21) 650-2138

Founded as South African College 1829, established as university 1918

Autonomous, state subsidized
Language of instruction: English
Academic year: March to December (two terms)

Chancellor: (vacant)
Vice-Chancellor: Dr MAMPHELA ALETTA RAMPHELE
Deputy Vice-Chancellors: Prof. WIELAND GEVERS, Prof. JOHN MARTIN, Prof. DANIEL NCAYIYANA, Prof. MARTIN WEST
Registrar: H. T. AMOORE
Librarian: J. RAPP

Library: see Libraries
Number of teachers: 774 full-time, 601 part-time
Number of students: 15,000
Publications: *Contributions from the Bolus Herbarium, Studies in English, Studies in the History of Cape Town, Acta Juridica, Mathematics Colloquium, Jagger Journal, Social Dynamics* (2 a year), *UCT Research Report, Energy Research Unit Research Report, UCT News, Monday Paper, Vice-Chancellor's Report.*

DEANS

Faculty of Humanities: (vacant)
Faculty of Science: (vacant)
Faculty of Engineering and the Built Environment: Prof. C. T. O'CONNOR
Faculty of Law: (vacant)
Faculty of Health Sciences: (vacant)
Faculty of Commerce: Prof. B. S. KANTOR

PROFESSORS

Faculty of Humanities:

ASHLEY, M. J., School of Education
BOADEN, B. G., Construction Economics and Management
BOWEN, P. A. , Construction Economics and Management
BRINK, A., English Language and Literature
BUNTING, I., Philosophy
CHIDESTER, D. S., Religious Studies
COCHRANE, U. R., Religious Studies
COETZEE, J. M., English Language and Literature
COOKE, J., School of Architecture and Planning
CORNILLE, J.-L., French Language and Literature
CUMPSTY, J. S., Religious Studies
DE GRUCHY J., Religious Studies
DEWAR, D., School of Architecture and Planning
DONALD, D. R., School of Education
DRIVER, D. D., English Language and Literature
DUBOW, N. E., Michaelis School of Fine Art
DU PREEZ, P. D., Psychology
DU TOIT, A. B., Political Studies
FOSTER, D. H., Psychology
GILIOMEE, H. B., Political Studies
GITAY, Y., Hebrew and Jewish Studies
GODBY, M. A. P., History of Art
HAYNES, D. J., Drama
HORN, P. R. G., German Language and Literature
LASS, R. G., Linguistics
LOUW, J., Psychology
MAMDANI, M., Centre for African Studies
MAREE, J., Sociology
MEYER, J. H. F., School of Education
MILLAR, C. J., Adult Education and Extra-Mural Studies
MULLER, J. P., School of Education
NASSON, W., History
PRINSLOO, I. C., School of Architecture and Planning
REYNOLDS, P. F., Social Anthropology
SALAZAR, PH.-J., French Language and Literature
SATYO, S. C., African Languages
SCHRIRE, R. A., Political Studies
SEEGERS, A., Political Studies
SHAIN, M., Hebrew and Jewish Studies
SNYMAN, H. J., Afrikaans and Netherlandish Studies
STEVENS, A. J., Construction Economics and Management
SWARTZ, L., Psychology
UNDERWOOD, P. G., School of Librarianship
UYTENBOGAARDT, R. S., School of Architecture and Planning
VILLA-VICENCIO, C., Religious Studies
WELSH, D. J., Political Studies
WEST, M., Social Anthropology
WHITAKER, R. A., Classics
WORDEN, N. A., History
YOUNG, D. N., School of Education

Faculty of Science:

ASCHMAN, D. G., Physics
BECKER, R. I., Mathematics and Applied Mathematics
BEN-AVRAHAM, Z., Geological Sciences
BOND, W., Botany
BRANCH, G. M., Zoology
BRINK, C., Mathematics and Applied Mathematics
BRÜMMER, G. C. L., Mathematics and Applied Mathematics
BRUNDRIT, G. B., Oceanography
BULL, J., Chemistry
BUTTERWORTH, D. S., Mathematics and Applied Mathematics
CLEYMANS, J. W. A., Physics
COWLING, R. M., Botany
DE WIT, M. J., Geological Sciences
DOMINGUEZ, C. A., Physics
DU PLESSIS, M., Zoology
ELLIS, G. F. R., Mathematics and Applied Mathematics
FAIRALL, A. P., Astronomy
FIELD, J. G., Zoology
FUGGLE, R. F., Environmental and Geographical Science
GÄDE, G., Zoology
GURNEY, J. J., Geological Sciences
HALL, M. J., Archaeology
KLUMP, H. H., Biochemistry
KRITZINGER, P. S., Computer Science
LE ROEX, A. P., Geological Sciences
LINDER, P. W., Chemistry
LUTJEHARMS, J. R. E., Oceanography
MACGREGOR, K. J., Computer Science
MINTER, W. E. L., Geological Sciences
MOSS, J. R., Chemistry
NASSIMBENI, L. R., Chemistry
PARKINGTON, J. H., Archaeology
PEREZ, S. M., Physics
RAWLINGS, D. E., Microbiology
REDDY, B. D., Mathematics and Applied Mathematics
SILLEN, A., Archaeology
STEWART, T. J., Statistical Sciences
THOMSON, J. A., Microbiology
TROSKIE, C. G., Statistical Sciences
UNDERHILL, L. G., Statistical Sciences
VAN DER MERWE, N. J., Archaeology
VAUGHAN, C. L., Biomedical Engineering
VIOLLIER, R. D., Physics
VON OPPELL, U., Cardiothoracic Surgery
WARNER, B., Astronomy
WEBB, J. H., Mathematics and Applied Mathematics

Faculty of Engineering and the Built Environment:

ABBOTT, J., Civil Engineering
ALEXANDER, M. G., Civil Engineering
ALLEN, C., Materials Engineering
BALL, A., Materials Engineering
BENNETT, K. F., Mechanical Engineering
BRAAE, M., Electrical Engineering
DE JAGER, G., Electrical Engineering
DOWNING, B. J., Electrical Engineering
DUTKIEWICZ, R. K., Energy Research Institute
EKAMA, G. A., Civil Engineering
HANSFORD, G. S., Chemical Engineering
MARTIN, J. B., Centre for Research in Computational and Applied Mechanics
NURICK, G. N., Mechanical Engineering
O'CONNOR, C. T., Chemical Engineering
REDDY, B. D., Centre for Research in Computational and Applied Mechanics
REINECK, K. M., Electrical Engineering
RÜTHER, H., Geomatics

Faculty of Law:

BENNETT, T. W., Public Law
BLACKMAN, M. S., Commercial Law
BURMAN, S. B., Private Law
CORDER, H. M., Public Law
DAVIS, D. M., Commercial Law
DEVINE, D. J., Public Law
HUTCHISON, D. B., Private Law
JOOSTE, R. D., Commercial Law
LEEMAN, I., Criminal and Procedural Law
MALUWA, T., Public Law
MEYERSON, D., Legal History and Method
MURRAY, C. M., Public Law
SMIT, D. VAN Z., Criminal and Procedural Law
VAN ZYL SMIT, D., Criminal and Procedural Law
VISSER, D. P., Private Law

Faculty of Health Sciences:

BAQWA, D., Primary Health Care
BATEMEN, E. D., Medicine
BEATTY, D. W., Paediatrics and Child Health
BEIGHTON, P., Human Genetics
BELONJE, P. C., Physiology
BENATAR, S. R., Medicine
BENINGFIELD, B., Nuclear Medicine
BENINGFIELD, S., Radiology
BORNMAN, P. C., Surgery
COMMERFORD, P., Medicine
CRUSE, J. P., Anatomical Pathology
DENT, D. M., Surgery
FOLB, P. I., Pharmacology
GEVERS, W., Medical Biochemistry
HARLEY, E. H., Chemical Pathology
IMMELMAN, E. J., Surgery
JACOBS, M. E., Paediatrics and Child Health
JAMES, M. F. M., Anaesthetics
KIRSCH, R. E., Medicine
KNOBEL, G. J., Forensic Medicine
LOUW, J., Medicine
MILLAR, R. P., Chemical Pathology
MOLTENO, C. D., Psychiatry
MURRAY, A. D. N., Ophthalmology
MYERS, J. E., Community Health
NOAKES, T. D., Physiology
NOVITZKY, N., Haematology
OPIE, L. H., Medicine
PARKER, M. I., Medical Biochemistry
PETER, J. C., Neurosurgery
POWER, D. J., Paediatrics and Child Health
RAWDON, B. B., Anatomy and Cell Biology
ROBERTSON, B. A., Psychiatry
RUDE, H., Paediatric Surgery
RYFFEL, B., Immunology
SELLARS, S. L., Otorhinolaryngology
TERBLANCHE, J., Surgery
THOMPSON, R. A. E., Nursing
VAN DER SPUY, Z. M., Obstetrics and Gynaecology
VAN NIEKERK, J. P., Radiology

VAUGHAN, C. L., Biomedical Engineering
VILJOEN, J. F., Anaesthesia
VON OPPELL, U., Cardiothoracic Surgery
WALTERS, J., Orthopaedic Surgery
WERNER, I. D., Radiation Oncology
WILSON, E. L., Clinical Science and Immunology

Faculty of Commerce:

BARR, G. D. I., School of Economics: Statistical Sciences
DORRINGTON, R. E., Management Studies
EVERINGHAM, G. K., Accounting
FAULL, N. H. B., Graduate School of Business
FIRER, C., Management Studies
HORWITZ, F., Graduate School of Business
JOWELL, K., Graduate School of Business
KAHN, S. B., School of Economics
KANTOR, B. S., School of Economics
LICKER, P., Information Systems
MORRIS, J. R. P., Accounting
MORRIS, M., Graduate School of Business
NEL, D., Graduate School of Business
PAGE, M., Graduate School of Business
SIMPSON, J. D., Business Science
SMITH, D. C., Information Systems
STEWART, T. J., Statistical Sciences
STOCKPORT, R., Graduate School of Business
SULCAS, P., Graduate School of Business
SURTEES, P., Accounting
TROSKIE, C. G., Statistical Sciences
ULIANA, E. O., Accounting
UNDERHILL, L. G., Statistical Sciences
VAN WYK, R., Graduate School of Business
WILSON, F. A. H., School of Economics

RESEARCH CENTRES, INSTITUTES, UNITS AND GROUPS

African Gender Institute: Dir Dr A. GOUWE.

Avian Demography Unit: Dir Prof. L. G. UNDERHILL.

Cape Heart Centre: Dir Prof. L. H. OPIE.

Cardiovascular Research Unit: Dir Prof. P. ZILLA.

Catalysis Research Group: Dir Prof. C. T. O'CONNOR.

Centre for Applied Molecular Medicine: Dir Prof. P. ZILLA.

Centre for Conflict Resolution: Dir L. NATHAN.

Centre for Contemporary Islam: Dir Dr E. MOOSA.

Centre for Energy Studies: Chair of the Board Prof. J. B. MARTIN.

Centre for Manufacturing Engineering: Dir Assoc. Prof. J. GRYZAGORIDIS.

Centre for Marine Studies: Dir Prof. A. C. BROWN.

Centre for Research in Engineering Education: Dir J. JAWITZ.

Centre for Rhetoric Studies: Dirs Prof. Y. GITAY, Prof. PH-J. SALAZAR.

CSD/UCT Centre for Socio-legal Research: Dir Prof. S. B. BURMAN.

CSD/UCT Religion and Social Change Research Unit: Dir Prof. J. DE GRUCHY.

CSD/UCT Research Unit for the Archaeology of Cape Town: Dir Prof. M. J. HALL.

CSD/UCT Science and Technology Policy Research Centre: Dir Assoc. Prof. D. KAPLAN.

CSD/UCT Spatial Archaeology Research Unit: Dir Prof. J. PARKINGTON.

Development Policy Research Unit: Dir D. E. LEWIS.

Energy and Development Research Centre: Dir Assoc. Prof. A. A. EBERHARD.

Energy Research Institute: Dir Prof. R. K. DUTKIEWICZ.

Environmental Evaluation Unit: Dir Prof. R. F. FUGGLE.

Equal Opportunities Research Project: Dir F. MOTTENO.

FRD/UCT Archaeometry Research Unit: Dir Assoc. Prof. J. C. SEALY.

FRD/UCT Centre for Research in Computational and Applied Mechanics: Dirs Prof J. B. MARTIN, Prof. B. D. RODDY.

FRD/UCT Coastal Ecology Unit: Dir Prof G. M. BRANCH.

Freshwater Research Unit: Dir Dr J. DAY.

Group for Research Relevant to Agriculture: Convener Prof. J. A. THOMSON.

HSRC/UCT Centre for Gerontology: Dir Dr M. FERREIRA.

Industrial Health Research Group: Dir J. CORNELL.

Institute for Comparative Religion in Southern Africa: Dir Assoc. Prof. D. CHIDESTER.

Institute for Plant Conservation: Dir Prof. R. M. COWLING.

Institute of Child Health: Chair. of Advisory Cttee Prof. D. W. BEATTY.

Institute of Criminology: Dir Prof. D. VAN ZYL SMIT.

Institute of Development and Labour Law: Dir Assoc. Prof. E. KALULA.

Institute of Theoretical Physics and Astrophysics: Dir Prof. C. A. DOMINGUEZ.

Law, Race and Gender Research Unit: Dir Assoc Prof. C. M. MURRAY.

Marine Biology Research Institute: Dir Prof. C. L. GRIFFITHS.

MRC/UCT Bioenergetics of Exercise Research Unit: Dir Prof. T. D. NOAKES.

MRC/UCT Biomembrane Research Unit: Dir Prof. M. C. BERMAN.

MRC/UCT Ischaemic Heart Disease Research Unit: Dir Prof. L. H. OPIE.

MRC/UCT Liver Research Centre: Dirs Prof. J. TERBLANCHE, Prof. R. KIRSCH.

MRC/UCT Research Unit for Medical Genetics: Dir Prof. P. BEIGHTON.

MRC/UCT Research Unit for Molecular Reproductive Endocrinology: Dir Prof. R. P. MILLAR.

Occupational Health Research Unit: Dir Assoc. Prof. J. MYERS.

Percy FitzPatrick Institute of African Ornithology: Dir Prof. M. DU PLESSIS.

Quaternary Research Centre: Dir Dr J. LEE THORPE.

Research Institute on Christianity in South Africa: Dirs Prof. J. W. DE GRUCHY, Prof. C. VILLA-VICENCIO.

South African Bird Ringing Unit: Dir Prof. L. G. UNDERHILL.

Southern Africa Labour and Development Research Unit: Dir Prof. F. A. H. WILSON.

Student Learning Research Group: Dir Prof. J. H. F. MEYER.

Supramolecular Chemistry Unit: Dir Prof. L. R. NASSIMBENI.

UCT Drug Surveillance Research Centre: Dir Dr L. WALTERS.

UCT Leukaemia Centre: Dir Prof. N. NOVITZKY.

UCT/University College, London, Hatter Institute: Dirs Prof. L. H. OPIE, Prof. D. YELLON (London).

Urban Problems Research Unit: Dir V. WATSON.

Women's Health Research Unit: Dirs Dr. D. COOPER, Dr. M. HOFFMAN.

UNIVERSITY OF DURBAN-WESTVILLE

Private Bag X54001, Durban 4000
Telephone: 204-4111
Telex: 6-23338
Fax: 204-4383
E-mail: knaicker@pixie.udw.ac.za

Founded 1961
Language of instruction: English
Autonomous control
Academic year: February to December (four terms)

Chancellor: H. E. MALL
Vice-Chancellor and Principal: Prof. J. B. K. KABURISE (acting)
Vice-Principals: Prof. P. P. NTULI (acting), Prof. D.V. SONI (acting)
Registrar (Administration): M. J. STEWART
Registrar (Academic): Prof. A. BRIMER (acting)

Number of teachers: 450
Number of students: 10,000

Publications: *Con-text* (irregular), *Calendar* (annually).

DEANS

Faculty of Arts: Prof. D. P. MCCRACKEN
Faculty of Commerce and Administration: D. U. C. WINDVOGEL (acting)
Faculty of Dentistry: Dr M. A. SEEDAT (acting)
Faculty of Education: Prof. J. D. JANSEN
Faculty of Engineering: Prof. L. M. MASU
Faculty of Health Sciences: Dr M. A. SEEDAT
Faculty of Law: Prof. L. GERING
Faculty of Science: Prof. R. G. ORI
Faculty of Theology: Prof. H. A. J. KRUGER (acting)

PROFESSORS AND HEADS OF DEPARTMENTS

Faculty of Arts:

COOPOO, Y., Human Movement (acting Head)
ENGEL, A. H., Modern European Languages (acting)
FILATOVA, I. I., History
GOODALL, S., Music
KUMAR, P., Hindu Stories and Indian Philosophy
MATIER, K. O., Classical Languages
MORE, P., Philosophy
NADVI, S. H. H., Arabic, Urdu and Persian
NADVI, S. S., Islamic Studies
NAIDOO, T., Science of Religion
NANACKCHAND, V., Fine Art and History of Art (acting)
OLIVIER, T., English
PAREKH, A. G., Psychology
RAMPHAL, R., Social Work
SCHAUFFER, D. L., Drama
SCHOLTZ, M. G., Afrikaans
SITARAM, R., Indian Languages
STEARS, L.-H. P., Sociology
VAWDA, M., Anthropology
VENKETRATHNAM, S., Political Science
ZUNGU, P. J., Zulu

Faculty of Commerce and Administration:

CONTOGIANNIS, E., Economics
GEACH, W. D., Accountancy
MCCARNEY, L. J., Graduate School of Business
POOVALINGAM, K., Business Economics (acting)
RYAN, K. C., Statistics
THOMSON, E., Industrial Psychology
WALLIS, M. A. H., Public Administration

Faculty of Dentistry:

LAHER, M. H. E. (acting)

Faculty of Education:

JANSEN, J. D., Curriculum Studies
MOODLEY, M., Applied Curriculum Studies
RAMPHAL, A., Psychology of Education

Faculty of Engineering:

BASSA, A. F. C., Chemical Engineering (acting)
MNENEY, S. H., Electrical Engineering
OTIENO, F., Civil Engineering
VADASZ, P., Mechanical Engineering

Faculty of Health Sciences:
- DANGOR, C. M., Pharmacy
- GOUNDEN, P., Physiotherapy
- GOVENDER, C. D., Speech Therapy and Audiology
- HAFFAJEE, M. R., Anatomy
- JOUBERT, R. W. E., Occupational Therapy
- NAIDOO, K., Optometry
- PILLAI, G., Pharmacology

Faculty of Law:
- GERING, L., Mercantile Law
- REDDI, M., Public Law
- ZAAL, F. N., Private Law

Faculty of Science:
- ACHAR, P. N., Microbiology
- ARIATTI, M., Biochemistry
- BABOOLAL, S., Computer Science
- BHARUTH-RAM, K., Physics
- MCCOURT, S., Geology
- NAIDOO, G., Botany
- ORI, R. G., Mathematics and Applied Mathematics
- SANKAR, M., Chemistry
- SOMOVA, L. I., Human Physiology and Physiological Chemistry
- SONI, D. V., Geography
- THANDAR, A. S., Zoology

Faculty of Theology:
- BALIVA, D. M., Church History and Missiology (acting)
- HEUER, N. A. C., Systematic Theology and Ethics, Practical Theology
- MAARTENS, P. J., Biblical Literature

ATTACHED INSTITUTE

Institute for Social and Economic Research: Dir Prof. J. J. MCCARTHY.

UNIVERSITY OF FORT HARE

Private Bag X1314, Alice 5700

Telephone: (404) 22011

Fax: (404) 31643

Founded as 'South African Native College' in 1916 by the United Free Church of Scotland. In 1960 the College was transferred to the Department of Bantu Education to cater specifically for the Xhosa ethnic group; now accepts students from all races; present name 1970.

Language of instruction: English

Academic year: February to December

Chancellor: Dr G. A. MBEKI

Vice-Chancellor and Rector: Prof. M. V. MZAMANE

Vice-Rector: (vacant)

Registrar: G. N. ZIDE

Librarian: M. N. TAU

Library: see Libraries

Number of teachers: 429

Number of students: 5,550

Publications: *Fort Hare Papers, The Fort Harian, Vice-Chancellor's Annual Report, Ardrinews.*

DEANS

Faculty of Law: Prof. P. A. DU PLESSIS
Faculty of Arts: Prof. T. N. MAQASHALALA
Faculty of Science: Prof. J. R. SERETLO
Faculty of Economic Sciences: Prof. T. M. JORDAN
Faculty of Theology: Prof. G. THOM
Faculty of Agriculture: Prof. W. S. W. TROLLOPE
Dean of Research: Prof. J. B. BRAND
Dean of Students: S. MAFANYA

PROFESSORS

Faculty of Agriculture:
- BESTER, B. J., Agricultural Economics
- IGODAN, C. O., Agricultural Extension and Rural Development
- KADZERE, C. T., Livestock and Pasture Science
- MZAMANE, N., Agronomy
- NYAMAPFENE, K., Agronomy
- RAATS, J. G., Livestock and Pasture Science
- TROLLOPE, W. S. W., Livestock and Pasture Science

Faculty of Arts:
- AUCAMP, J. C., History
- BOTHA, C. R., African Languages
- BROUWER, P., Political Science and Public Administration
- DE JAGER, E. J., African Studies
- DE WET, G., Communication
- ELS, J. M., Classical Languages
- ETSIAH, A. K., Political Science and Public Administration
- HALLIER, M. G. T., Fine Arts
- LOSAMBE, L., English
- MAKALLMA, M. W., Sociology
- MAQASHALALA, T. N. V., Social Work
- MKONTO, B. B., African Languages
- PRINS, M. J., Afrikaans and Dutch
- SIMBAYI, L. C., Psychology

Faculty of Economic Sciences:
- JORDAN, T. M., Accountancy
- VAN DAALEN, H. J., Industrial Psychology

Faculty of Education:
- DARGIE, D. J., Music
- DREYER, J. N., Foundations of Education
- FILHA, P. M., Educational Psychology
- JIYA, M. A. Y., Curriculum Studies and Didactics
- LINDEQUE, B. R. G., Curriculum Studies and Didactics

Faculty of Law:
- DU PLESSIS, P. A., Mercantile Law
- LABUSCHAGNE, J., Constitutional and Public International Law
- REMBE, N. S., Oliver Tambo Chair of Human Rights

Faculty of Science:
- BRAND, J. M., Biochemistry and Microbiology
- EVERTSE, L., Nursing Sciences
- FATOKI, O. S., Chemistry
- MAKUNGA, O. H. D., Plant Sciences
- MDEBUKA, A. M., Physics
- MILDENHALL, J., Microbiology
- SADIMENKO, A., Chemistry
- SANYAL, D. K., Chemistry
- SERETIO, J. R., Physics
- VAN DYK, T. J., Mathematics
- VAN HEERDEN, J. W. A., Zoology
- VILJOEN, G. P., Statistics
- WAGENER, P. C., Applied Mathematics

Faculty of Theology:
- ABRAHAMS, S. P., Old Testament and Hebrew
- THOM, G., Historical and Contextual Theology

ATTACHED INSTITUTES

Academic Development Centre: Dr Z. JIYA.

Agricultural and Rural Development Research Institute: (vacant).

Xhosa Dictionary: Prof. B. M. MINI.

Centre for Cultural Studies: Prof. G. T. SIRAYI.

MEDICAL UNIVERSITY OF SOUTHERN AFRICA

PO Medunsa 0204

Telephone: (12) 521-4222

Fax: (12) 521-4343

Founded 1976 predominantly for Black students

Language of instruction: English

Academic year: January to November

Chancellor: Bishop M. S. MOGOBA

Vice-Chancellor and Principal: Prof. E. T. MOKGOKONG

Vice-Principal: Prof. R. A. MOGOTLANE

Vice-Principal, Administration: Prof. T. P. MASHIKLO

Registrar: C. W. BERNDT

Director, Library Services: C. M. VINK

Number of teachers: 455

Number of students: 3,239 undergraduate, 536 postgraduate

Publication: *Research Report.*

DEANS

Faculty of Medicine: Prof. M. D. BOMELA (acting)
Faculty of Dentistry: Prof. J. DE VRIES
Faculty of Veterinary Science: Prof. H. M. TERBLANCHE
Faculty of Basic Sciences: Prof. J. V. GROENEWALD

HEADS OF DEPARTMENTS

Faculty of Medicine:
- Ga-Rankuwa Hospital: Dr R. BROEKMANN
- Anaesthesiology: Prof. M. D. BOMELA
- Anatomical Pathology: Prof. E. J. LANCASTER
- Anatomy: Prof. M. C. BOSMAN
- Cardiology: Dr P. S. MNTLA
- Cardio-Thoracic Surgery: Prof. M. L. MOHLALA
- Chemical Pathology: Prof. H. F. JOUBERT
- Clinical Pharmacology: Prof. W. DU PLOOY
- Clinical Psychology: Prof. E. M. Q. MOKHUANE
- Community Health: Prof. P. W. W. COETZER
- Dermatology: Dr A. H. SHAH
- Diagnostic Radiology: Prof. H. B. BROUDE
- Family Medicine: Prof. G. S. FEHRSEN
- Forensic Pathology: Prof. C. G. H. FOSSEUS
- Gastroenterology: Prof. C. J. VAN DER MERWE
- General Surgery: Prof. C. M. MODIBA
- Haematological Pathology: Prof. D. J. WELGEMOED
- Hand and Microsurgery: Prof. U. MENNEN
- Human Nutrition: Prof. I. I. GLATTHAAR
- Intensive Care: Prof. M. S. MOKGOKONG
- Internal Medicine: Prof. K. P. MOKHOBO
- Medical Physics: Prof. W. J. STRYDOM
- Microbiological Pathology: Prof. C. G. CLAY
- Neurology: Prof. R. F. GLEDHILL
- Neurosurgery: Prof. I. B. COPLEY
- Nuclear Medicine: Prof. W. J. STRYDOM
- Nursing Science: Prof. S. M. MOGOTLANE
- Obstetrics and Gynaecology: Prof. M. MARIVATE
- Occupational Therapy: E. SHIPHAN
- Ophthalmology: Prof. R. C. STEGMANN
- Orthopaedics: Prof. R. GOLELE
- Otorhinolaryngology: Prof. W. F. VORSTER
- Paediatric Surgery: Prof. C. GRANT
- Paediatrics and Child Health: Prof. F. P. DE VILLIERS
- Parasitology: (vacant)
- Pharmacy: Prof. R. S. SUMMERS
- Physiology: Prof. K. A. SMITH
- Physiotherapy: N. P. MBAMBO
- Plastic and Reconstructive Surgery: Prof. J. F. SCHOLTZ
- Psychiatry: Prof. A. E. GANGAT
- Radiography: T. S. M. MOALUSI
- Radiation Oncology: (vacant)
- Urology: Dr A. M. SEGONE
- Virology: Prof. G. LECATSAS

Faculty of Dentistry:
- Medunsa Dental Hospital: Prof. J. DE VRIES
- Community Dentistry: Prof. T. S. GUGUSHE
- Diagnostics and Radiology: Prof. B. BUCH (acting)
- Maxillofacial and Oral Surgery: Prof. F. J. JACOBS
- Operative Dentistry: Dr C. T. BOTHA
- Oral Pathology and Oral Biology: Prof. E. J. RAUBENHEIMER
- Orthodontics: Prof. E. CUMBER
- Periodontology and Oral Medicine: Prof. F. D. VERWAYEN
- Prosthodontics: Prof. B. D. MONTEITH
- Stomatological Studies: Prof. H. V. EXNER

Faculty of Veterinary Sciences:
- Anatomy: Prof. K. K. BOOTH
- Animal Health and Production: Prof. P. A. BOYAZOGLU
- Companion Animal Medicine and Surgery: Prof. P. STADLER
- Herd Health and Reproduction: Prof. K. P. PETTEY
- Infectious Diseases and Public Health: Prof. C. G. STEWART
- Production Animal Medicine: Prof. G. H. RAUTENBACH
- Veterinary Pathology: Dr N. M. DUNCAN
- Veterinary Pharmacology: Prof. C. G. COTTON
- Veterinary Physiology: Prof. S. T. CORNELIUS

Faculty of Basic Sciences:
- Biology: Prof. G. OBERHOLZER
- Chemistry: Prof. J. V. GROENEWALD
- English Language: (vacant)
- Mathematics and Statistics: Prof. H. S. SCHOEMAN
- Physics: D. M. MAFOKWANE
- Psychology: Prof. H. M. VERHAGE

UNIVERSITY OF NATAL

Private Bag X10, Dalbridge, Durban 4014

Telephone: (31) 260-1111
Fax: (31) 260-2214

Founded 1910 as a constituent college of the University of South Africa; independent status 1949

Language of instruction: English
Academic year: February to November

Chancellor: Most Rev. D. E. HURLEY
Vice-Chancellor and University Principal: Prof. BRENDA GOURLEY
Deputy Vice-Chancellor (Academic): Prof. A. C. BAWA
Senior Deputy Vice-Chancellor: Prof. D. A. MAUGHAN-BROWN
Deputy Vice-Chancellor (Students and Transformation): Prof. E. A. NGARA
Deputy Vice-Chancellor (Research and Development): Prof. ELEANOR M. PRESTON-WHYTE
Registrar: Prof. G. J. TROTTER

Number of staff: 2,536
Number of students: 16,357

Publications: *NU Partners* (quarterly), *NU Focus* (quarterly), *NU Info* (monthly), *Current Writing* (annually), *Indicator* (quarterly), *Theoria* (2 a year), *Scholia* (studies in classical antiquity, annually).

RESEARCH INSTITUTES

Natal Institute of Immunology: Pinetown; f. 1968; Dir Dr J. D. CONRADIE.

Oceanographic Research Institute: 2 West St, Durban; f. 1959; Dir Prof. A. J. DE FREITAS.

Research Institute for Diseases in a Tropical Environment (of the South African Medical Research Council): 771 Umbilo Rd, Durban, POB 17120, Congella, 4013; f. 1976; Dir T. F. H. G. JACKSON.

Sugar Milling Research Institute: Francois Rd, Durban; f. 1948; Dir Dr B. S. PURCHASE.

Institute for Commercial Forestry Research: Scottsville, Pietermaritzburg; f. 1946; Dir Prof. P. J. T. ROBERTS.

Plasma Physics Research Institute: University of Natal, Durban; f. 1979; Dir Prof. M. A. HELLBERG.

Institute of Natural Resources: University of Natal, Pietermaritzburg; f. 1980; Dir Prof. C. M. BREEN.

(Note. At the time this chapter went to press, the academic faculties of the University of Natal were about to undergo extensive restructuring.)

Durban Campus

Durban 4014

Telephone: (31) 260-1111
Fax: (31) 260-2214

Librarian: G. H. HAFFEJEE

DEANS

Faculty of Architecture and Allied Disciplines: Prof. M. KHAN
Faculty of Economics and Management: Prof. A. LUMBY
Faculty of Engineering: Prof. L. W. ROBERTS
Faculty of Humanities: Prof. M. J. F. CHAPMAN
Faculty of Law: Prof. A. J. RYCROFT
Faculty of Medicine: Prof. J. R. VAN DELLEN
Faculty of Science: Prof. M. A. HELLBERG
Faculty of of Social Science: Prof. A. SITAS

HEADS OF DEPARTMENT

Faculty of Architecture and Allied Disciplines:
- Architecture: Prof. D. RADFORD
- Property Development and Construction Economics: Prof. R. G. TAYLOR
- Town and Regional Planning: Prof. P. S. ROBINSON

Faculty of Economics and Management:
- Bridging Year Unit: J. HESKETH
- Accounting and Finance: Prof. L. D. MITCHELL
- Business Administration: Prof. D. A. COLDWELL (acting)
- Economics: T. B. JONES (acting)
- Economics Research Unit: Prof. G. G. MAASDORP (Dir)

Faculty of Engineering:
- Bridging Unit: R. F. N. REYNOLDS
- Agricultural Engineering: Prof. P. W. L. LYNE
- Chemical Engineering: Prof. B. K. LOVEDAY
- Civil Engineering: Dr H. D. SCHREINER (acting)
- Electrical Engineering: Prof. R. G. HARLEY
- Electronic Engineering: Prof. A. D. BROADHURST
- Mechanical Engineering: Dr G. D. J. SMITH
- Surveying and Mapping: Prof. H. G. VAN GYSEN

Faculty of Humanities:
- Afrikaans and Dutch: Prof. J. MAARTENS
- Classics: M. ANNE GOSLING
- Economic History: Prof. W. M. FREUND
- English: Prof. MARGARET J. DAYMOND
- European Studies: Prof. B. KYTZLER
- Gender Studies: Dr R. POSEL
- History: Prof. J. J. GUY
- Linguistics: Prof. J. K. CHICK
- Music: J. BRAUNINGER
- Philosophy: Prof. D. HERWITZ
- Politics: Prof. A. McI. JOHNSTON
- Psychology: Dr B. T. GILLMER
- Speech and Drama: Dr M. E. McMURTRY
- Zulu Language and Literature: Prof. N. N. CANONICI
- Language Learning Centre: L. DICKSON
- Tertiary Education: Dr C. MBALI
- School of Education: C. HEMSON (Dir)
  - Education: Prof. C. HARBOR
  - Media Resource Centre: C. CRITICOS
  - Adult and Community Education: Prof. P. S. STANFORD

Faculty of Law:
- Business Law: Prof. ISOBEL E. KONYN
- Institute of Maritime Law: Prof. H. STANILAND (Dir)
- Centre for Socio-Legal Studies: M. A. MOSERY (Dir)
- Private Law: Prof. P. D. GLAVOVIC
- Procedural and Clinical Law: Prof. D. J. McQUOID-MASON
- Public Law: Prof. K. GOVENDER

Faculty of Medicine:
- Anaesthetics: Prof. D. A. ROCKE
- Anatomical Pathology: Prof. R. CHETTY
- Cardiothoracic Surgery: D. F. BLYTH (acting)
- Chemical Pathology: Dr P. J. OJWAMG (acting)
- Community Health: Dr C. C. JINABHAI (acting)
- Experimental and Clinical Pharmacology: Prof. K. D. BHOOLA
- Family Medicine: Dr M. H. CASSIMJEE (acting)
- Forensic Medicine: Prof. A. DADA
- General Surgery: Prof. J. V. ROBBS
- Haematology: Dr D. GAIL KENOYER (acting)
- Human Anatomy: Prof. F. H. GULDNER
- Medicine: Prof. G. M. MODY (acting)
  - Sub-Department of Cardiology: Prof. A. S. MITHA
  - Sub-Department of Dermatology: Dr J. ABOOBAKER
  - Sub-Department of Neurology: Prof. P. L. A. BILL
  - GI Unit: Prof. A. E. SIMJEE
  - Diabetes Unit: Prof. M. A. K. OMAR
  - Nephrology Unit: Dr S. NAICKER
  - Pulmonology Unit: Dr U. G. LALLOO
  - Rheumatology Unit: Prof. G. M. MODY
- Medical Microbiology: Prof. A. W. STURM
- Neurosurgery: Dr K. NAIDOO (acting)
- Obstetrics and Gynaecology: Prof. J. MOODLEY
- Ophthalmology: Prof. A. PETERS
- Otorhinolaryngology: B. SINGH (acting)
- Paediatrics and Child Health: Prof. H. M. COOVADIA
- Paediatric Surgery: Prof. J. P. HADLEY
- Physiology: Prof. M. F. DUTTON
- Plastic and Reconstructive Surgery: Prof. A. MADAREE
- Psychiatry: Dr A. J. LASICH (acting)
  - Sub-Department of Medically Applied Psychology: Prof. L. SCHLEBUSCH
- Radiology: Prof. P. D. CORR
- Radiotherapy and Oncology: Prof. J. P. JORDAAN
- Urology: Z. B. BERECZKY
- Virology: Prof. A. N. SMITH

Faculty of Science:
- Biology: Prof. J. A. COOKE
- Chemistry and Applied Chemistry: Prof. T. M. LETCHER
- Computer Science: Prof. A. G. SARTORI-ANGUS
- Geology and Applied Geology: Prof. F. G. BELL
- Mathematical Statistics: Prof. L. TROSKIE
- Mathematics and Applied Mathematics: Prof. J. H. SWART
- Physics: Prof. J. D. HEY

Faculty of Social Science:
- Centre for Social Development Studies: Prof. M. MORRIS
- Geographical and Environmental Sciences: Prof. ROSEANNE D. DIAB
- Industrial, Organizational and Labour Studies: Dr G. MARÉ
- Nursing: Prof. LEANA R. UYS
- Social Anthropology: Prof. J. KIERNAN
- Social Work: Prof. M. GRAY
- Sociology: Prof. H. CROTHERS

Pietermaritzburg Campus

Private Bag X01, Scottsville 3209

Telephone: (331) 260-5111
Fax: (331) 260-5599

Librarian: C. E. MERRETT

DEANS

Faculty of Agriculture: Prof. F. H. J. RIJKENBERG
Faculty of Commerce: Prof. B. S. STOBIE

Faculty of Law: Prof. J. M. BURCHELL
Faculty of Humanities: Prof. R. NICHOLSON
Faculty of Science: Prof. R. J. HAINES
Faculty of Social Science: Prof. P. STOPFORTH

HEADS OF DEPARTMENT

Faculty of Agriculture:

Agricultural Economics: Prof. W. L. NIEUWOUDT
Agronomy: Prof. M. J. SAVAGE
Animal Science and Poultry Science: Prof. R. M. GOUS
Dietetics and Community Resources: Prof. E. M. MAUNDER
Genetics: Prof. J. W. HASTINGS
Grassland Science: Prof. T. G. O'CONNOR
Horticultural Science: Prof. B. N. WOLSTENHOLME
Microbiology and Plant Pathology: Prof. F. M. WALLIS
School of Rural Community Development: S. LUCKETT (Dir, acting)

Faculty of Commerce:

Accountancy: Prof. L. J. STAINBANK
Business Administration: Prof. T. MCEWAN

Faculty of Law:

School of Law: Prof. J. R. L. MILTON (Dir)

Faculty of Humanities:

Afrikaans and Dutch: Prof. W. F. JONCKHEERE
Applied Language Studies: F. JACKSON
Classics: Prof. Z. M. PACKMAN
Drama Studies: Dr KATHERINE KENDALL
English: Dr A. VAN DER HOVEN
Fine Arts and History of Fine Art: Prof. T. H. KING
French: Prof. S. MENAGER
German: Prof. W. F. JONKHEERE (acting)
Historical Studies: Prof. J. P. C. LEONARD
Philosophy: Dr S. M. BECK (acting)
Religious Studies: P. S. MAXWELL
School of Theology: Prof. J. A. DRAPER
Zulu: M. A. HLENGWA
School of Education: Dr S. KAABWE (Dir)
Education: Prof. K. L. HARLEY
Educational Psychology: Prof. H. ADAMS
Second Language Studies: Prof. R. COMARTY
Curriculum Development Unit: Prof. B. WALLACE-ADAMS
Centre for Adult Education: Prof. J. AITCHISON
Child and Family Centre: Dr R. SCHOEMAN
Midlands Education Development Unit: S. AINSLIE
Open Learning Institute: F. BULMAN

Faculty of Science:

Biochemistry: Prof. C. DENNISON
Botany: Prof. J. VAN STADEN
Chemistry: Prof. J. S. FIELD
Computer Science and Information Systems: Prof. P. R. WARREN
Geography: Prof. R. J. FINCHAM
Geology: (vacant)
Mathematics and Applied Mathematics: Prof. J. MOORI
Physics: Prof. C. GRAHAM
Statistics and Biometry: Prof. G. P. Y. CLARKE
Zoology and Entomology: Prof. G. L. MACLEAN
Science Foundation Programme: Dr D. J. GRAYSON

Faculty of Social Science:

Economics: Prof. M. D. MCGRATH
Information Studies: Prof. A. KANIKI
Political Studies: Prof. R. B. LAWRENCE
Psychology: Prof. L. RICHTER
Sociology: S. I. R. BURTON

UNIVERSITY OF THE NORTH

Private Bag X1106, Sovenga 0727
Telephone: (1521) 68-9111
Telex: 331813
Fax: (1521) 67-0152

Founded 1959 to serve the Tsonga, Sotho, Venda and Tswana peoples
Comprises Main Campus at Turfloop, Qwaqwa Branch at Witzieshoek and Giyani Teaching Centre at Gazankulu (Giyani)
Language of instruction: English
Academic year: February to November

Chancellor: Dr N. R. MANDELA
Vice-Chancellor and Rector: Prof. N. S. NDEBELE
Vice-Rector: M. J. MALATJI
Registrar: (vacant)
Librarian: J. K. TSEBE

Number of teachers: 350
Number of students: 13,110

Publications: *Uninews* (2 a year), *Series A, B and C* (irregular).

DEANS

Faculty of Arts: Prof. S. R. MOTSHOLOGANE
Faculty of Mathematics and Natural Sciences: Prof. S. N. MASHEGO
Faculty of Economics and Administration: Prof. A. J. P. COETZEE
Faculty of Education: Prof M. C. J. MPHAHLELE
Faculty of Theology: Prof. M. C. DIPPENAAR
Faculty of Law: Prof. B. C. MAJOLA
Faculty of Agriculture: Prof. M. S. BURGERS
Faculty of Health Sciences: Prof. P. A. VENTER

HEADS OF DEPARTMENTS

Faculty of Arts:

Afrikaans: Prof. C. J. J. TERBLANCHÉ
Anthropology: Prof. J. S. MALAN
Biblical Studies: Dr M. C. DIPPENAAR
Classical Languages: Prof. F. SAAYMAN
Criminology: Prof. C. J. MOOLMAN
Development Administration: Prof. DE VILLIERS
English: Prof. A. A. ROSCOE
French: R. P. MOLOKO
General Linguistics and General Literary Studies: Dr J. R. LOUW (acting)
Geography: Prof. N. C. TAIT
German: Dr S. R. GOTTWALD (acting)
History: Prof. J. G. PRETORIUS
Library and Information Science: Prof. S. P. MANAKA
Northern Sotho: P. D. SEKHUKHUNE (acting)
Philosophy: Prof. F. J. ENGELBRECHT
Political Science: Prof. A. N. J. HERHOLDT
Psychology: Dr J. A. MEYER (acting)
Semitic Languages: Prof. A. F. CONRADIE
Sesotho: A. M. MOLELEKI (acting)
Setswana: Miss M. C. THUBISI (acting)
Sociology: Prof. S. R. MOTSHOLOGANE
Social Work: Prof. D. W. MALAKA
Venda: Prof. N. A. MILUBI
Xitsonga: Prof. C. P. N. NKONDO

Faculty of Mathematics and Natural Sciences:

Applied Mathematics: Prof. E. D. MALAZA
Biochemistry: Prof. E. M. TYOBEKA
Botany: Prof. D. R. JANSE VAN VUUREN
Chemistry: Prof. C. R. DE WET
Computer Science: Prof. H. J. OOSTHUIZEN
Electron Microscopic Unit: Prof. M. E. LEE (Dir)
Limnological Research Unit: Prof. J. F. PRINSLOO
Mathematical Statistics: Prof. P. C. DU V. OLIVER
Mathematics: Prof. S. P. MASHIKE
Microbiology: Prof. M. M. SIBARA
Physics: Prof. E. O. DE NEIJS
Physiology: Prof. G. L. SMIT
Zoology and Biology: Prof. J. E. SAAYMAN

Faculty of Economics and Administration:

Accounting and Auditing: Prof. N. J. VAN SCHALKWYK
Business Economics: Prof. J. T. VAN NIEKERK
Economics: Prof. W. N. MEYER
Industrial Psychology: Prof. P. E. FRANKS
Public Administration: Prof. V. O. AYENI

Faculty of Education:

Human Movement Science: Prof. L. A. S. DU PLESSIS (acting)
Fundamental Education: Prof. P. M. KGORANE
Language Methodology: Prof. A. L. MAWASHA
Didactics: Dr M. B. MOKGALABONE
History of Education: Prof. S. P. P. MMINELE
Educational Practice: Prof. G. C. PIEK
Psychology of Education: Prof. V. I. CHERIAN
Comparative Education: Prof. S. M. LENYAI

Faculty of Theology:

Church History, Science of Mission and Religion: Prof. G. VAN DER MERWE
Dogmatics and Theological Ethics: Prof. H. VAN DER MERWE
New Testament: Prof. F. S. MALAN
Old Testament: Dr A. AURET
Practical Theology: Prof. A. S. VAN NIEKERK

Faculty of Law:

African Government and Law: Prof. P. H. CLOETE
Criminal Law and Procedure: Prof. J. A. VAN DEN HEEVER
Mercantile Law: Prof. P. F. BREED
Private Law: Prof. P. J. BADENHORST
Public International Law, Constitutional Law and Administrative Law: Prof. B. C. MAJOLA

Faculty of Agriculture:

Agricultural Economics: C. L. MACHETHE (acting)
Animal Production: Prof. P. J. K. MORGAN
Plant Production: Prof. M. S. BURGERS
Soil Sciences: Prof. P. S. FOUCHÉ

Faculty of Health Sciences:

Medical Sciences: Prof. P. A. VENTER
Nursing: Prof. G. T. MNCUBE
Optometry (Academic Section): (vacant)
Optometry (Professional Section): Prof. C. JOUBERT
Pharmaceutical Chemistry: Prof. V. L. M. JALI
Pharmaceutics: Prof. R. H. LOMBARD
Pharmacology: Prof. J. C. LOMBARD

ATTACHED INSTITUTE

Advisory Bureau for Businessmen: Dir M. S. SHOGOLE.

University of the North, Qwaqwa Campus

Private Bag X13, Phuthaditjhaba 9866
Telephone: (58) 713-0211
Fax: (58) 713-0152

Founded 1982

Chancellor: Dr N. R. MANDELA
Vice-Chancellor and Principal: Prof. N. NDEBELE
Vice-Principal: Prof. Dr W. MÖDINGER
Registrars: T. P. MASIHLEHO, A. T. KGABO, N. T. MOSIA
Librarian: C. J. KOK

Library of 30,000 vols
Number of teachers: 85
Number of students: 2,500

DEANS

Faculty of Arts: Prof. L. J. FERREIRA
Faculty of Mathematics and Natural Sciences: Prof. Dr P. C. KEULDER
Faculty of Management Sciences: P. C. MOJET
Faculty of Education: L. E. MOFOKENG
Faculty of Theology: Dr S. P. BOTHA

PROFESSORS

Faculty of Arts:

FERREIRA, L. J., Political Science
JONES, H. J., Afrikaans
MOOLMAN, J. P. F., History

Faculty of Mathematics and Natural Sciences:

DE HAAS, W., Physics
DEN HEYER, J., Zoology
JORDAAN, D. B., Computer Science
KEULDER, P. C., Botany
LUYT, A. S., Chemistry
MOFFETT, R. O., Botany
MTHEMBU, T. Z., Mathematics

Faculty of Management Sciences:

CLOETE, N., Commercial Law
JONKER, L. J. G., Business Economics
VENTER, A. P., Industrial Psychology
WEBSTER, S. A., Accounting

Faculty of Education:

MOLETSANE, R. I. M., Comparative Education

UNIVERSITY OF THE ORANGE FREE STATE

POB 339, Bloemfontein, OFS
Telephone: (51) 401-9111
Fax: (51) 401-2117
Founded 1855 (formerly a Constituent College of the University of South Africa); independent status 1949
Principal languages of instruction: Afrikaans and English
Academic year: February to November
Chancellor: Prof. Dr W. L. MOUTON
Vice-Chancellor and Rector: Prof. S. F. COETZEE
Vice-Rectors: Prof J. G. C. SMALL, B. M. KHOTSENG
Librarian: A. M. DIPPENAAR
Number of teachers: 476
Number of students: 10,459

DEANS

Faculty of Arts: Prof. A. H. SNYMAN
Faculty of Science: Prof. G. N. VAN WYK
Faculty of Social Science: Prof. R. A. VILJOEN
Faculty of Education: Prof. P. F. THERON
Faculty of Law: Prof. D. W. MORKEL
Faculty of Economic and Management Science: Prof. F. C. N. FOUNE
Faculty of Health Sciences: Prof. C. J. C. NEL
Faculty of Agriculture: Prof. P. I. WILKE
Faculty of Theology: Prof. P. C. POTGIETER

PROFESSORS

Faculty of Arts:

BARNARD, S. L., History
CILLIERS, L., Latin
COETZEE, N. A. J., Physical Education
CRONJE, J. V. W., Greek
DE VILLIERS, G. DU T., Geography
LAMPRECHT, G. P., Music
LUBBE, H. J., General Linguistics
MOLEKKI, M. A., African Language
MOLL, J. C., History
MULLER, F. R., English
NEL, C. J., Anthropology
NEL, P. J., Near Eastern Studies
SMIT, J. H., Philosophy
STEYN, J. C., Afrikaans/Dutch
STRAUSS, D. F. M., Philosophy
STRYDOM, L., General Theory of Literature
TEBLANCHE, F. N., Communication Science
ULLYATT, A. G., English
VAN COLLER, H. P., Afrikaans/Dutch
VANDENBERG, D. J., Art History
VAN JAARSVELD, G. J., Afrikaans/Dutch
VENTER, L. S., Afrikaans/Dutch
VON DELFT, K. U. T., German
WESSELS, D. P., Political Science

Faculty of Science:

BASSON, S. S., Chemistry
BERNING, G. L. P., Physics
BOTHA, W. J. H., Urban and Regional Planning
BRANDT, E. V. Chemistry
BRITZ, B. J., Architecture
BRITZ, T. J., Microbiology and Biochemistry
DE WAAL, D. J., Mathematical Statistics and Statistics
DU PLESSIS, J., Physics
DU PREEZ, J. C., Microbiology and Biochemistry
FERREIRA, D., Chemistry
GROBBELAAR, J. U., Botany
GROENEWALD, P. C. N., Mathematical Statistics and Statistics
KOCK, J. L. F., Microbiology and Biochemistry
KOK, O. B., Zoology and Entomology
KOTZE, C. P., Architecture
KUK, D. J., Zoology and Entomology
LAMPRECHT, G. J., Physical Chemistry
MCDONALD, T., Computer Science
MESSERSCHMIDT, H. J., Computer Science
MURRAY, T., Mathematics and Applied Mathematics
NEL, D. G., Statistics
PRIOR, B. A., Microbiology and Biochemistry
ROODT, A., Chemistry
SCOOMBIE, S. W., Applied Mathematics
SCOTT, L., Botany and Genetics
SPIERS, J. J., Botany and Genetics
VAN AS, J. G., Zoology and Entomology
VAN DER MERWE, A. J., Mathematical Statistics and Statistics
VAN WYK, G. N., Physics
VAN ZYL, F. D. W., Town and Regional Planning
VENTER, H. J. T., Botany
VERSTER, J. J. P., Quantity Surveying and Construction Management
VILJOEN, G., Mathematics
VISSER, J. N. J., Geology
WINGFIELD, M. J., Microbiology and Biochemistry

Faculty of Social Science:

BOTHA, Dr D., Social Work
DE KLERK, G. W., Sociology
GROBLER, J. J., Psychology
GROENEWALD, D. C., Sociology
HEYNS, P. M., Psychology
HUYSAMEN, G. K., Psychology
LOUW, D. A., Psychology
MOWAN, G. E., Social Work
PRETOMLIN, C., Sociology
ROSSOUW, P. J., Psychology
VAN RENSBURG, H. C. J., Centre for Health System Research
VILJOEN, M. J., School for Nursing
WEICH, M. J., School for Nursing
WESSELS, S. J., Psychology

Faculty of Education:

BRAYULE, R. R., Historical and Comparative Education
DU FOIT, G. F., Didactics
HENNING, O. A., Philosophy and History of Education
HEYNS, M. G., Historical and Comparative Education
LE ROUR, P. J., Didactics
NIEMAN, G. S., Historical and Comparative Education
PAULSEN, W. J., Psychopedagogics
VAN DER LINDS, H. J., Research Institute for Education Planning

Faculty of Economic and Administrative Science:

BEKKER, J. C. O., Public Administration
BESTER, C. L., Industrial Psychology
CROUS, M. J., Business Management
EKSTEEN, R. B., Transport Economics
LOURENS, J. J., Economics
LUBBE, D. S., Centre for Accounting
STRAUSS, J. M., Centre for Accounting
VAN DER MERWE, W. J. C., Business Management
VAN WYK, H. A., Centre for Accounting
VAN ZYL, H., Money and Banking
VILJOEN, D. A., Development Unit
WESSELS, G. M., Money and Banking

Faculty of Medicine:

ALBERTYN, J., Neurosurgery
BADENHORST, P. N., Haematology
BARRY, R., Unit for Vascular Surgery
BOTHA, J. B. C., Forensic Medicine
BOTHA, P. L., Medical Microbiology
CLAASSEN, A. J., Oto-rhino-laryngology
CRONJE, H. S., Obstetrics and Gynaecology
DE VAAL, J. B., Critical Care
DE VILLIERS, J. F. K., Diagnostic Radiology
DE WET, E. H., Physiology
DIEDERICHS, B. J. S., Anaesthesiology
DU TOIT, R. S., Surgery
GAGIANO, C. A., Psychiatry
GOEDHALS, L., Oncotherapy
HOEK, B. B., Paediatrics and Child Health
HOUGH, J., Cardiosurgery
HUNDT, H. K. L., Pharmacology
KLEYNHANS, P. H. T., Cardiology
KRUGER, A. J., Neurology
KUYL, J. M., Chemical Pathology
LIEBENBURG, S. J., Community Health
LÖTTER, M. G., Biophysics
LOUW, L. DE K., Anatomy and Cell Morphology
MARX, J. D., Cardiology
MEYER, B. H., Hoechst Research Unit
MIDDLECOTE, B. D., Anatomical Pathology
MOLLENTZE, W. F., Internal Medicine
MÜLLER, F. O., Pharmacology
NEL, P. P. C., Anatomy and Cell Morphology
ODENDAAL, C. L., Anaesthesiology
OOSTHUIZEN, J. M. C., Physiology
OTTO, A. C., Nuclear Medicine
PISTORIUS, G. J., Family Practice
PRETORIUS, G. H. J., Haematology
SNOWDOWNE, R. B., Orthopaedics
STULTING, A. A., Ophthalmology
VAN ASWEGEN, A., Biophysics
VENTER, A., Paediatrics and Child Health
VILJOEN, I. M., Urology
VAN RENSBURG, P. H. J. J., Psychiatry
WEICH, D. J. V., Internal Medicine
WESSELS, P. H., Obstetrics and Gynaecology

Faculty of Agriculture:

BENNIE, A. T. P., Soil Science
DE JAGER, J. M., Agricultural Meteorology
DU PREEZ, Soil Science
ERASMUS, G. J., Animal Science
JOOSTE, P. J., Food Science
OOSTHUIZEN, L. K., Agricultural Economics
PRETORIUS, J. C., Agronomy
PRETORIUS, R. A., Plant Pathology
SWART, W. J.
VAN DER MERWE, H. J., Animal Science
VAN DEVENTER, C. S., Plant Breeding
VILJOEN, M. F., Agricultural Economics
VAN WYK, J. B., Animal Science
WALKER, S., Agricultural Meteorology

Faculty of Law:

DU PLESSIS, J. V., Mercantile Law
FICK, G. H., Private Law
HENNING, J. J., Mercantile Law
KELLING, A. S., Mercantile Law
PRETORIUS, J. L., Constitutional Law
VAN SCHALKWYK, J. H., Private Law
VERSCHOOR, T., Criminal Law

Faculty of Theology:

KELLERMAN, J. S., Diaconology
RIEKERT, S. J. P. K., Biblical Studies
STRAUSS, P. J., Ecclesiology
STRAUSS, S. A., Systematic Theology
SNYWAN, S. D., Old Testament
VAN ZYL, H. C., New Testament

ATTACHED INSTITUTES

Institute for Groundwater Studies: Bloemfontein; Dir Prof. F. D. I. HODGSON.

Institute for Contemporary History: Bloemfontein; Dir Prof. J. H. LE ROUX.

Research Institute for Education Planning: Bloemfontein; Dir Prof. H. J. VAN DER LINDE.

UNIVERSITY OF PORT ELIZABETH

POB 1600, Port Elizabeth 6000, Eastern Cape Province

Telephone: (41) 504-2111
Fax: (41) 504-2574
E-mail: postmaster@upe.ac.za

Founded 1964
Languages of instruction: Afrikaans and English
Academic year: February to November (two semesters)

Chancellor: Hon. Mr Justice J. P. G. EKSTEEN
Vice-Chancellor and Principal: Prof. J. M. KIRSTEN
Registrars: J. H. JACOBS (Finance and Works), J. COETZEE (Academic)
Librarian: D. FOKKER

Number of teachers: 224
Number of students: 5,717

Publications: *Calendar, Institute for Planning Research—Research Reports, Obiter, Bureau for Mercantile Law—Research Reports, Bureau for Mercantile Law—Bulletin, Institute for Coastal Research—Research Reports, UPE Publication Series, Industrial Relations Unit—IR Research, Topical Series, Focus.*

DEANS

Faculty of Arts: Prof. P. J. NAUDÉ
Faculty of Science: Prof. C. A. B. BALL
Faculty of Education: Prof. C. A. TAYLOR
Faculty of Economic Sciences: Prof. C. V. R. WAIT
Faculty of Law: Prof. C. VAN LOGGERENBERG
Faculty of Health Sciences: Prof. J. P. P. FULLARD

DIRECTORS

CEDUPE Music Centre: E. ALBERTYN
Institute for Development Planning and Research: Dr D. PRETORIUS
Uranium Chemistry Research Unit: Prof. J. G. H. DU PREEZ
Institute for Science and Mathematics Education: Dr D. J. KRIEL
Institute for Coastal Research: Prof. B. L. ROBERTSON
School for Public Administration and Management: Prof. P. F. A. DE VILLIERS
Centre for Continuing Education: J. A. ERWEE
Bureau for Mercantile Law: Prof. H. J. DELPORT
Computer Centre: C. J. NEL
School of Accounting: Prof. K. S. PRINSLOO
Institute for the Study of Economic Processes: Prof. C. V. R. WAIT
Institute for the Study and Resolution of Conflict: G. J. BRADSHAW
Institute for Statistical Consultation and Methodology: D. J. L. VENTE

HEADS OF DEPARTMENT

Faculty of Arts:

African Languages: Prof. H. M. THIPA
Afrikaans and Dutch: Prof. E. F. KOTZÉ
Anthropology: Prof. P. P. JACOBS
Biblical and Religious Studies: M. J. OOSTHUIZEN
English: Prof. E. T. LICKINDORF
French, German and Classics: Dr H. M. B. THOMAS
Geography: Prof. A. J. CHRISTOPHER
History: Dr T. C. RAUTENBACH
Music: Prof. A. J. J. TROSKIE
Philosophy: Dr C. F. VAN HEERDEN
Political Studies: G. J. BRADSHAW
Public Administration and Management: Prof. P. F. A. DE VILLIERS
Sociology: Prof. R. J. HAINES

Faculty of Science:

Biochemistry and Microbiology: Prof. W. OELOFSEN
Botany: Prof. G. C. BATE
Chemistry: Prof. C. W. MCCLELAND
Computer Science and Information Systems: Prof. G. DE V. DE KOCK
Geology: Prof. R. W. SHONE
Mathematical Statistics: Prof. I. N. LITVINE
Mathematics and Applied Mathematics: Prof. N. J. GROENEWALD
Physics: Prof. J. A. A. ENGELBRECHT
Textile Science: Prof. L. HUNTER
Zoology: Prof. D. BAIRD

Faculty of Education:

Didactics: Prof. C. P. VAN DER WESTHUIZEN
Educational Psychology: Prof. H. J. BADENHORST
Human Movement Science: Prof. F. J. BUYS
Philosophy of Education: Dr S. E. VAN RENSBURG
Teacher Education: Prof. C. P. VAN DER WESTHUIZEN

Faculty of Economic Sciences:

Accounting: Prof. K. S. PRINSLOO
Architectural Subjects: Prof. J. D. THERON
Business Management: Prof. J. K. BOSCH
Construction Management: Prof. B. EKSTEEN
Economics and Economic History: Prof. A. L. MULLER
Industrial and Organizational Psychology: Prof. L. KAMFER
Quantity Surveying Subjects: Prof. G. K. LE ROUX

Faculty of Health Sciences:

Human Movement Science: Prof. F. J. BUYS
Nursing Science: Prof. W. J. KOTZE
Pharmacy: Prof. I. C. WISEMAN
Psychology: Prof. D. M. LUIZ
Social Work: Dr J. L. TSHIWULA

Faculty of Law:

Adjective Law: E. VAN DER BERG
Mercantile Law: Prof. H. J. DELPORT
Private Law: Prof. P. J. BADENHORST
Public Law: Prof. P. H. G. VRANCKEN

POTCHEFSTROOM UNIVERSITY FOR CHRISTIAN HIGHER EDUCATION

Potchefstroom, Transvaal

Telephone: (18) 299-1111
Telex: 346019
Fax: (18) 299-2799

Founded 1869; incorporated in University of South Africa as Constituent College 1921; assumed full university status March 1951
Principal language of instruction: Afrikaans
Academic year: February to November

Chancellor: Dr D. C. CRONJÉ
Vice-Chancellor and Principal: Prof. C. J. REINECKE
Vice-Principals: Prof. A. J. VILJOEN, Prof. P. J. J. PRINSLOO
Chairman of the Council: Dr E. L. GROVÉ
President of Convocation: Prof. P. H. STOKER
Registrars: Prof. C. F. C. VAN DER WALT, Prof. I. J. ROST
Library Director: Prof. C. J. H. LESSING

Library: see Libraries
Number of lecturers: full-time 470, part-time 4, including 109 professors
Number of students: 10,773

Publications: *Koers* (every 2 months), *PU-Kaner, Literator, Orientation, Didaktikom* (all quarterly), *Nuusbrief Rektor* (2 a year), *Fokus, Woord en Daad, Goue Kandelaar, Besembos* (all annually).

DEANS

Faculty of Arts: Prof. J. VAN DER ELST
Faculty of Law: Prof. I. VORSTER
Faculty of Science: Prof. J. C. GEERTSEMA
Faculty of Theology: Prof. A. LE R. DU PLOOY
Faculty of Education: Prof. J. L. VAN DER WALT
Faculty of Economic and Management Sciences: Prof. J. J. D. HAVENGA
Faculty of Engineering: Prof. G. P. GREYVENSTEIN
Faculty of Pharmacy: Prof. H. A. KOELEMAN
Student Dean: Prof. P. J. J. S. POTGIETER
Interfaculty Academic Board: Prof. D. J. MALAN

PROFESSORS

(H = Head of Department)

Faculty of Arts:

CARSTENS, W. A. M., Afrikaans and Dutch (H)
COMBRINK, A. L., English (H)
DE BEER, A. S., Communications (H)
DE VILLIERS, A. B., Geography and Environmental Studies (H)
DU PISANI, J. A., History (H)
DU PLESSIS, H. G. W., ATKV-Skryfskool
GEYER, H. S., Town and Regional Planning (H)
GREEF, M., Nursing Sciences (H)
GROENWALD, H. J., Communications
JOOSTE, S. J., Music (H)
KOTZE, G. J., Social Work (H)
LESSING, C. J. H., Library and Information Science (H)
MEYER C. DU. P., Recreation (H)
MÖLLER, P. H., Sociology
NIEUWOUDT, A., Town and Regional Planning
STRYDOM, G. L., Science of Human Movement (H)
VAN DER WALT, B. J., Philosophy
VAN DER WALT, J. L., English
VAN WYK, W. J., Political Science (H)
VENTER, C. A., Psychology
VENTER, J. J., Philosophy (H)
VILJOEN, H. M., Afrikaans and Dutch
WISSING, M. P., Psychology (H)

Faculty of Law:

COETZEE, T. F., Legal Procedure
DU PLESSIS, W., Legal Pluralism and Roman Law (H)
EISELEN, G. T. S., Private Law
FERREIRA, G. M., Public Law and Philosophy of Law
PIENAAR, G. J., Private Law (H)
ROBINSON, J. A., Private Law
STANDER, A. L., Mercantile Law (H)
VENTER, F., Public Law and Philosophy of Law (H)

Faculty of Science:

BREET, E. L. J., Chemistry
DE JAGER, O. C., Physics
DE JONGH, C. N., Centre for Business Mathematics and Informatics
DU PLESSIS, J. A. K., Chemistry
ERASMUS C. N., Centre for Business Mathematics and Informatics
FOURIE, J. H., Mathematics and Applied Mathematics
GEERTSEMA, J. C., Statistics and Operational Science
GROBLER, J. J., Mathematics and Applied Mathematics
HATTINGH, J. M., Computer Science and Information (H)
JOOSTE, T. DE W., Mathematics and Applied Mathematics
KRUGER, G. H. J., Plant and Soil Science
LOOTS, D. G., Zoology (H)
MALAN, N. T., Physiology (H)
MARTINS, F. J. C., Chemistry
MORAAL, H., Physics (H)
PIETERSE, A. J. H., Plant and Soil Sciences (H)
POTGIETER, M. S., Physics

PRETORIUS, P. J., Biochemistry (H)
RAUBENHEIMER, B. C., Physics
REINECKE, J. P. L., Physics
SMIT, J. J. A., Physics
STEYN, P. S., Chemistry (H)
SWANEPOEL, J. W. H., Statistics and Operational Research
VAN DER WALT, J. J., Physiology
VAN HAMBURG, H., Life Sciences (H)
VAN WYK, D. J., Mathematics and Applied Mathematics (H)
VENTER, C. S., Nutrition and Human Ecology (H)
VENTER, J. H., Statistics and Operational Science (H)
VORSTER, H. H., Nutrition and Human Ecology

Faculty of Theology:
DE BRUYN, P. J., Dogmatics and Ecclesiology
DE KLERK, B. J., Old and New Testament
DENKEMA, F., Diaconology and Missiology
DU PLOOY, A. LE R., Dogmatics and Ecclesiology (H)
JANSE VAN RENSBURG, J. J., Old and New Testaments
JORDAAN, G. J. C., Old and New Testaments
VAN ROOY, H. F., Old and New Testaments (H)
VENTER, C. J. H., Pastoral Subjects and Missiology (H)
VORSTER, J. M., Dogmatics and Ecclesiology

Faculty of Education:
MENTZ, P. J., School for Non-Formal Education (H)
MONTEITH, J. L. DE K., School for Non-Formal Education (H)
STEYN, H. J., School for Graduate Education (H)
VAN DER WESTHUIZEN, P. C., Graduate School for Education
VREKEN, N. J., School for Teacher Training

Faculty of Economic Sciences:
BARNARD, A. L., School for Research Development and Management
COETSEE, L. D., Business Administration
COETZEE, W. N., Business Administration (H)
DE KLERK, G. J., School for Business Management (H)
ELOFF, T., School for Accounting Science (H)
GERICKE, J. S., School for Accounting Science
KOTZE, J. G., Business Administration
KROON, J., School for Business Management
NAUDÉ, W. A., School for Business Management
RADEMEYER, A., Accounting and Auditing
SCHUTTE, P. C., Business Administration
STYGER, P., School for Economics, Money and Banking
VAN HEERDEN, J. H. P., Economics (H)

Faculty of Engineering:
EVERSON, R. C., School for Chemical and Mineral Engineering (H)
GREYVENSTEIN, G. P., Mechanical and Material Engineering
HOFFMAN, A. J., Electrical and Electronic Engineering (H)
ROUSEAU, P. G., Mechanical and Material Engineering (H)

Faculty of Pharmacy:
KOELEMAN, H. A., Pharmaceutics
LOTTER, A. P., Pharmaceutics
OLIVER, D. W., Pharmacology (H)
THOMAS, A. J., Professional Services
VAN DER WATT, J. G., Pharmaceutics (H)
VAN WYK, C. J., Pharmaceutics
VENTER, D. P., Pharmacology (H)

Interfaculty Academic Board (Vaal Triangle Campus):
DE KLERK, P., History
DE WET, A. G., Statistics and Operational Research
LAURIE, D. P., Mathematics
PRETORIUS, J. B., Business Economics
THERON, A. M. C., Education

NON-PROFESSORIAL HEADS OF DEPARTMENTS

Faculty of Arts:
African Languages: G. J. G. VERMEULEN
History: J. A. DU PISANI
Tourism and Free Time Studies: M. SAAYMAN

Faculty of Economic Sciences:
Business Sociology: J. H. VAN DEN BERG

Faculty of Science:
Biochemistry: P. J. PRETORIUS
Nutrition and Family Ecology: C. S. VENTER

Faculty of Pharmacy:
Pharmacy Practice: J. J. GERBER

Interfaculty Academic Board:
Biblical Studies and Philosophy: T. C. RABALI
Psychology: D. J. MALAN
Sociology: C. W. BESTER
Languages: W. H. WILLIES
Computer Science: L. M. VENTER
Business Sociology: C. DE W. VAN WYK
Economics: G. VAN DER WESTHUIZEN
Accounting and Auditing: P. LUCOUW

ATTACHED INSTITUTES

Student Bureau: Prof. P. J. J. S. POTGIETER.

Centre for Faith and Scholarship: Dir Prof. P. G. W. DU PLESSIS.

Bureau for Academic Support Services: Dir Prof. S. J. P. DU PLESSIS.

Institute for Reformatory Studies: Dir Prof. B. J. VAN DER WALT.

ATKV – Skryfskool: Dir Prof. H. G. W. DU PLESSIS.

Institute of Ecological Research: Dir Prof. J. BOOYSEN.

Institute for Biokinetics: Dir Prof. G. L. STRYDOM.

Institute of Industrial Pharmacy: Dir Prof. T. G. DEKKER.

Institute of Psychological and Educational Services and Research: Dir Prof. W. F. DU PLESSIS.

Small Business Advisory Bureau: Dir Prof. P. L. MOOLMAN.

Postgraduate School for Executive Management: Dir Prof. W. N. COETZEE.

Institute for Communication Research: Dir Prof. A. S. DE BEER.

Centre for Regional Development: Exec. Dir Prof. G. J. DU TOIT.

Unit for Development Planning: Dir Prof. A. NIEUWOUDT.

Unit for Strategic Planning: Dir Prof. C. H. BOSHOFF.

Unit for Environmental Management: Dir J. G. NEL.

Institute for Sport Science and Development: Dir Prof. D. D. J. MALAN.

Research Unit for Phonetics and Phonology: Dir Prof. D. P. WISSING.

Space Research Unit: Dir Prof. B. C. RAUBENHEIMER.

Institute for Tourism and Free Time Studies: Dir Dr M. SAAYMAN.

INSTITUTIONS IN CO-OPERATION WITH THE UNIVERSITY

Theological School of the Reformed Church in South Africa: Potchefstroom; Rector Prof. A. LE R. DE PLOOY.

Potchefstroom College of Education: Rector Prof. R. P. VAN ROOYEN.

UNIVERSITY OF PRETORIA

Pretoria 0002
Telephone: (12) 420-4111
Telex: 3-22 723
Fax: (12) 362-5168

Founded as Transvaal University College 1908; granted Charter as University of Pretoria 1930
Private control
Languages of instruction: Afrikaans and English
Academic year: February to December (two semesters)

Chancellor: Dr G. L. STALS
Vice-Chancellor and Principal: Prof. JOHAN VAN ZYL
Vice-Principals: Prof. S. MARX, Prof. T. ERASMUS, Prof. C. R. DE BEER
Executive Director: Prof. J. D. SINCLAIR
Head of Facilities Planning and Business Administration: L. N. BOSHOFF
Head, Academic Administration and Registrar: Dr D. D. MARAIS (acting)
Head, Financial Administration and Director: T. G. KRUGER
Head, Personnel Affairs and Director: Prof. W. VAN DER M. HERHOLDT
Head, Research Administration and Director: Dr Z. M. OFIR
Head, Institutional Research and Planning and Director: Prof. P. J. VERMEULEN
Director of Academic Information Service: Prof. E. D. GERRYTS

Library: see Libraries
Number of teachers: 1,460
Number of students: 26,684

Publications: *Jaarverslag, Tukkie-Werf* (quarterly), *Perdeby* (weekly students' newspaper), *Publikasies van die Universiteit van Pretoria—Nuwe reeks* (Publications of the University of Pretoria—New Series) (I) Research (annually), *Ad-Destinatum: Gedenkboek van die Universiteit van Pretoria, Opvoedkundige Studies* (Educational Studies, 3–4 issues annually), *Openbare Fakulteitslesings* (irregular), *Huldigingsbundels* (irregular).

DEANS

Faculty of Arts: Prof. W. C. VAN WYK
Faculty of Science: Prof. N. SAUER
Faculty of Biological and Agricultural Sciences: Prof. R. M. CREWE
Faculty of Law: Prof. D. G. KLEYN
Faculty of Theology—Dutch Reformed Church of Africa: Prof. C. J. WETHMAR
Faculty of Theology—Dutch Reformed Church: Prof. W. S. PRINSLOO
Faculty of Economic and Management Sciences: Prof. C. THORNHILL
Faculty of Veterinary Science: Prof. R. I. COUBROUGH
Faculty of Education: Prof. M. J. BONDESIO
Faculty of Medicine: Prof. D. J. DU PLESSIS
Faculty of Dentistry: Prof. J. A. LIGTHELM
Faculty of Engineering: Prof. J. A. G. MALHERBE
Student Services: Prof. P. B. VAN DER WATT

PROFESSORS

Faculty of Arts:
ALANT, E., Communication Pathology
ANTONITES, A., Philosophy
BARKHUIZEN, J. H., Ancient Languages
BERGH, J. S., History and Cultural History
BEYERS, D., Psychology
BOON, J. A., Telematic Education
BOTHA, P. J., Ancient Languages
BOTHMA, T. J. D., Information Science
CARSTENS, A., Afrikaans
DE LA REY, R. P., Psychology
DU PLESSIS, A., Political Science
DU PREEZ, M. S. E., Social Work
DU TOIT, A. P., Philosophy
FINN, S. M., English

GRAY, R. A., English
GROENEWALD, P. S., African Languages
HARTMAN, J. B., Anthropology and Archaeology
HOUGH, M., Political Science
HUGO, S. R., Communication Pathology
JANSE VAN RENSBURG, M. C., Afrikaans
LOUW, B., Communication Pathology
MANS, M. J., Latin
MULLER, M. E., Political Science
NOLTE, K. E., Afrikaans
OHLHOFF, C. H. F., Afrikaans
OOSTHUIZEN, J. S., Sociology
PEETERS, L. F. H. M. C., Modern European Languages
POTGIETER, J. H., Ancient Languages
PRETORIUS, F., History and Cultural History
PRETORIUS, R., Criminology
PRINSLOO, D. J., African Languages
ROODT, P. H., Afrikaans
ROOS, N. O., Visual Arts and History of Art
SCHOEMAN, J. B., Psychology
STANDER, H. F., Ancient Languages
STANFORD, H. J., Music
TEMMINGH, H., Music
THERON, A., Criminology
TITLESTAD, P. J. H., English
VAN NIEKERK,C., Music
VAN VUUREN, R. J., Psychology
VAN WYK, G. J., Human Movement Science
WEBB, V. N., Afrikaans
WILKES, A., African Languages

Faculty of Science:

ALBERTS, H. W., Physics
AURET, F. D., Physics
BADENHORST, M. S., Town and Regional Planning
BISHOP, J. M., Computer Science
BOSHOFF, E., Home Economics
BOTHA, P., Home Economics
BOTHA, P. C., Quantity Surveying and Construction Management
BOTHA, W. J., Geology
BRINK, D., Physics
CLOETE, C. E., Quantity Surveying and Construction Management
COETZEE, J., Science
DE WAAL, S. A., Geology
ENGELBRECHT, J. C., Mathematics and Applied Mathematics
ERIKSSON, P. G., Geology
FÖRTSCH, E. B., Geology
FOUCHÉ, W. L., Mathematics and Applied Mathematics
GAIGHER, H. L., Physics
GRÄBE, P. J., Mathematics and Applied Mathematics
HATTINGH, P. S., Geography
HAUPTFLEISCH, A. C., Quantity Surveying and Construction Management
HOLM, D., Architecture
HUGO, M. L., Geography
KLOPPER, C. H., Quantity Surveying and Construction Management
KOURIE, D. G., Computer Science
LE ROUX, S. W., Architecture and Landscape Architecture
LOTZ, S., Chemistry
MALHERBE, J. B., Physics
MILLER, H. G., Physics
MODRO, T. A., Chemistry
PENNING, F. D., Mathematics and Applied Mathematics
PRETORIUS, L. M., Mathematics and Applied Mathematics
RADEMEYER, C., Chemistry
ROHWER, E. R., Chemistry
ROOS, J. D., Computer Science
ROSINGER, E. E., Mathematics and Applied Mathematics
SCHOEMAN, M. J., Mathematics and Applied Mathematics
SIGLÉ, H. M., Quantity Surveying and Construction Management
SNYMAN, C. P., Geology
SWART, J., Mathematics and Applied Mathematics
VAN NIEKERK, F. D., Mathematics and Applied Mathematics
VAN ROOYEN, P. H., Chemistry
VAN SCHALWYK, A., Geology
VAN STADEN, J. F., Chemistry
VLEGGAAR, R., Chemistry
WESSELS, P. L., Chemistry

Faculty of Biological and Agricultural Sciences:

BARNARD, R. O., Plant Production and Soil Technology
BOTHMA, J. DU P., Animal and Wildlife Sciences
BREDENKAMP, G. J., Botany
CASEY, N. H., Animal and Wildlife Sciences
CHOWN, S. L., Zoology and Entomology
CLOETE, T. E., Microbiology and Plant Pathology
DUVEL, G. H., Agricultural Economics, Extension and Rural Development
EICKER, A., Botany
HAMMES, P. S., Plant Production and Soil Technology
HASSAN, R. M., Agricultural Economics, Extension and Rural Development
HASSAN, R. M., Internal Medicine
HUISMANS, H., Genetics
JANSEN VAN RYSSEN, J. B., Animal and Wildlife Sciences
KIRSTEN, J. F., Agricultural Economics, Extension and Rural Development
LAKER, M. C., Plant Production and Soil Technology
LOUW, A. I., Biochemistry
NEITZ, A. W. H., Biochemistry
NEL, L. H., Microbiology and Plant Pathology
REINHARDT, C. F., Plant Production
RETHMAN, N. F. G., Plant Production and Soil Technology
ROBINSON, T. J., Zoology and Entomology
ROUX, C. Z., Genetics
SCHOLTZ, C. H., Zoology and Entomology
SKINNER, J. D., Mammal Research Institute
SMITH, G. A., Animal and Wildlife Sciences
TAYLOR, J. R. N., Food Science
VAN AARDE, R. J., Zoology
VAN DE VENTER, H. A., Botany
VAN JAARSVELD, A. S., Zoology and Entomology
VAN ROOYEN, C. J., Agricultural Economics, Extension and Rural Development
VAN ROOYEN, N., Botany
VAN WYK, A. E., Botany
VERSCHOOR, J. A., Biochemistry
VISSER, L., Biochemistry
WEHNER, F. C., Microbiology and Plant Pathology
WINGFIELD, B. D., Genetics
WINGFIELD, M. J., Biological and Agricultural Sciences (General)

Faculty of Law:

DAVEL, C. J., Private Law
DELPORT, P. A., Mercantile and Labour Law
GROVÉ, N. J., Private Law
HEYNS, C. H., Legal History, Comparative Law and Philosophy of Law
HORN, J. G. G., Procedure and Evidence
KLOPPER, H. B., Mercantile and Labour Law
KOTZE, D. J. L., Procedure and Evidence
LABUSCHAGNE, J. M. T., Indigenous Law
LOTZ, D. J., Mercantile and Labour Law
NAGEL, C. J., Mercantile and Labour Law
SCHOEMAN, M. C., Private Law
SCOTT, T. J., Private Law
THOMAS, P. J., Legal History, Comparative Law and Philosophy of Law
VAN DER MERWE, F. E., Procedure and Evidence
VAN DER WESTHUIZEN, J. V., Legal History, Comparative Law and Philosophy of Law
VAN ECK, B. P. S., Mercantile and Labour Law
VAN JAARSVELD, S. R., Mercantile and Labour Law
VAN OOSTEN, F. F. W., Criminal Law
VAN SCHALKWYK, L. N., Private Law
VILJOEN, H. P., Public Law
VISSER, P. J., Private Law
VORSTER, M. P., Public Law

Faculty of Theology (Dutch Reformed Church of Africa):

BEUKES, M. J. DU. P., Continuing Theological Equipment
BOTHA, S. J., History of Christianity
BREYTENBACH, A. P. B., Old Testament
DREYER, T. F. J., Practical Theology
KOEKEMOER, J. H., Dogmatics and Christian Ethics
PELSER, G. M. M., New Testament
STEENKAMP, L. J. S., Continuing Theological Equipment
VAN AARDE, A. G., New Testament
VAN DER MERWE, P. J., Philosophy of Religion and Missions
VENTER, P. M., Old Testament

Faculty of Theology (Dutch Reformed Church):

BEZUIDENHOUT, L. S., Biblical Studies
DE VILLIERS, D. E., Dogmatics and Christian Ethics
HOFMEYR, J. W., Church History and Church Policy
JOUBERT, S. J., Biblical Studies
KRITZINGER, J. J., Philosophy of Religion and Missions
LE ROUX, J. H., Old Testament
MEIRING, P. G. J., Philosophy of Religion and Missions
MULLER, J. C., Practical Theology
VAN DER WATT, J. G., New Testament
VOS, C. J. A., Practical Theology
WETHMAR, C. J., Dogmatics and Christian Ethics

Faculty of Economic and Management Sciences:

ALBERTS, N. F., Graduate School of Management
BASSON, J. S., Human Resources Management
BOSHOFF, A. B., Graduate School of Management
BRAND, H. E., Human Resources Management
BRÜMMER, L. M., Graduate School of Management
BRYNARD, P. A., School for Public Management and Administration
CROWTHER, N. A. S., Statistics
DE JAGER, H., School of Accountancy
DE LA REY, J. H., Graduate School of Management
DE VILLIERS, C., Informatics
DE VILLIERS, J. A., Business Management
DE WET, J. M., Graduate School of Management
DE WIT, P. W. C., Business Management
DEKKER, G. M., Accountancy
DU PLOOY, N. F., Informatics
GLOECK, J. D., School of Accountancy
GOUWS, D. G., Accountancy
GROENEVELD, H. T., Statistics
HARMSE, C., Economics
HEATH, E. T., Hotel and Tourism Management
KOEN, M., Accountancy
KOORNHOFF, C., Accountancy
LAMBRECHTS, H. A., Graduate School of Management
MAASDORP, E. F. DE V., Business Management
MARX, A. E., Business Management
MARX, G. L., Insurance and Actuarial Science
MENGISTU, B., School for Public Management and Administration
NEL, P. S., Graduate School of Management

OOST, E. J., Business Management
SCHOEMAN, N. J., Economics
SCHREUDER, A. N., Marketing and Communications Management
SMIT, C. F., Statistics
STEYN, F. G., Economics
TRUU, M. L., Economics
VAN HEERDEN, J. H., Economics
VERMEULEN, L. P., Human Resources Management
VIL-NKOMO, S., School for Public Management and Administration
VIVIER, F. L., Statistics
VORSTER, Q., Accountancy

Faculty of Veterinary Science:

BERRY, W. L., Medicine
BERTSCHINGER, H. J., Theriogenology
BEZUIDENHOUT, A. J., Anatomy
COETZER, J. A. W., Veterinary Tropical Diseases
GOTTSCHALK, R. D., Surgery
GUTHRIE, A. J., Equine Research Centre
KIRBERGER, R. M., Surgery
KRECEK, R. C., Veterinary Tropical Diseases
KRIEK, N. P. J., Pathology
LE ROUX, C. D., Poultry Health
LOURENS, D. C., Animal and Community Health
MELTZER, D. G. A., Veterinary Tropical Diseases
ODENDAAL, J. S. J., Veterinary Ethology
PENZHORN, B. L., Veterinary Tropical Diseases
REYERS, F., Medicine
SWAN, G. E., Pharmacology and Toxicology
VAN DEN BERG, J. S., Medicine
VAN DEN BERG, S. S., Surgery
VAN DER WALT, J. G., Veterinary Physiology
VEARY, C. M., Animal and Community Health
VOLKMANN, D. H., Theriogenology

Faculty of Education:

BECKMANN, J. L., Education Management
BERKHOUT, S. J., Education Management
BOUWER, A. C., Orthopedagogics
CALITZ, L. P., Education Management
FERREIRA, G. V., Orthopedagogics
FRASER, W. J., Didactics
JACOBS, L. J., School Guidance
LE ROUX, J., Psycho- and Sociopedagogics
MALAN, S. P. T., Didactics
MAREE, J. G., School Guidance
PRETORIUS, J. W. M., Psycho- and Sociopedagogics
VAN ROOYEN, L., Psycho- and Sociopedagogics

Faculty of Medicine:

ANDERSON, R., Immunology
BARTEL, P. R., Neurology
BECKER, J. H. R., Surgery
BODEMER, W., Psychiatry
CHRISTIANSON, A. L., Human Genetics
DREYER, L., Anatomic Pathology
DU PLESSIS, D. J., Cardiothoracic Surgery
FALKSON, C. I., Medical Oncology
FOURIE, P. J. H. L., Anaesthesiology
GRABOW, W. O. K., Medical Virology
HAY, I. T., Paediatrics
HUGO, J. M., Anaesthesiology
HURTER, P., Chemical Pathology
IJSSELMUIDEN, C. B., Community Health
IONESCU, G. O., Surgery
JACYK, W. K., Internal Medicine
LINDEQUE, B. G., Obstetrics and Gynaecology
MAFOJANE, N. A., Neurology
MARITZ, N. G. J., Orthopaedics
MEDLEN, C. E., Immunology
MEYER, H. P., Family Medicine
MEIRING, J. H., Anatomy
MOKOENA, T. R., Surgery
MULDER, A. A. H., Otorhinolaryngology
MYBURGH, D. P., Cardiology
NEL, J. S., Radiation Oncology
PATTINSON, R. C., Obstetrics and Gynaecology
PRINSLOO, S. F., Radiology
REIF, S., Urology
ROSSOUW, D. S., Internal Medicine
ROUX, P., Ophthalmology
SAAYMAN, G., Forensic Medicine
SLEEP, D. J., Urology
SNYMAN, J. R., Pharmacology
SOMMERS, DE K., Pharmacology
SWART, J. G., Otorhinolaryngology
UBBINK, J. B., Chemical Pathology
VAN DEN BOGAERDE, J. B., Physiology
VAN DER MEYDEN, C. H., Neurology
VAN GELDER, A. L., Internal Medicine
VAN NIEKERK, J. G. P., Nursing
VAN PAPENDORP, D. H., Physiology
VERMAAK, W. J. H., Chemical Pathology
WITTENBERG, D. F., Paediatrics

Faculty of Dentistry:

BECKER, L. H., Restorative Dentistry
BUCH, B., Diagnostics and Rontgenology
BÜTOW, K. W., Maxillo-facial and Oral Surgery
COETZEE, W. J. C., Stomatological Research
DE WET, F. A., Restorative Dentistry
KEMP, P. L., Prosthetics and Dental Mechanics
PETIT, J., Periodontics and Oral Medicine
VAN HEERDEN, W. F. P., Oral Pathology and Oral Biology

Faculty of Engineering:

BAKER, D. C., Electrical and Electronic Engineering
BOTHA, E. C., Electrical and Electronic Engineering
BURDZIK, W. M. G., Civil Engineering
CILLIERS, P. J., Electrical and Electronic Engineering
CLAASSEN, S. J., Industrial and Systems Engineering
CRAIG, I. K., Electrical and Electronic Engineering
DE KLERK, A. M., Engineering and Technology Management
DE VAAL, P. L., Chemical Engineering
DEKKER, N. W., Civil Engineering
DEL MISTRO, R. F., Civil Engineering
DU PLESSIS, H. L. M., Agricultural and Food Engineering
DU PREEZ, R. J., Mechanical and Aeronautical Engineering
FOCKE, W. W., Chemical Engineering
FOURIE, E., Mechanical and Aeronautical Engineering
FOURIE, G. A., Mining Engineering
GELDENHUIS, J. M. A., Materials Science and Metallurgical Engineering
GRIMSEHL, U. H. J., Chemical Engineering
HANCKE, G. P., Electrical and Electronic Engineering
HEYNS, P. S., Mechanical and Aeronautical Engineering
JANSE VAN RENSBURG, B. W., Civil Engineering
JOUBERT, J., Electrical and Electronic Engineering
KRUGER, P. S., Industrial and Systems Engineering
LEUSCHNER, F. W., Electrical and Electronic Engineering
LINDE, L. P., Electrical and Electronic Engineering
MAREE, L., Civil Engineering
MARSHALL, V., Civil Engineering
MATHEWS, E. H., Mechanical and Aeronautical Engineering
ODENDAAL, J. W., Electrical and Electronic Engineering
PIENAAR, G., Material Science and Metallurgical Engineering
PISTORIUS, P. C., Materials Science and Metallurgical Engineering
PRETORIUS, W. A., Chemical Engineering
ROHDE, A. W., Civil Engineering
SANDENBERGH, R. F., Material Science and Metallurgical Engineering
SEEVINCK, E., Electrical and Electronic Engineering
SNYMAN, J. A., Mechanical and Aeronautical Engineering
STEYN, H. DE V., Engineering and Technology Management
STEYN, J. L., Mechanical and Aeronautical Engineering
VAN HEERDEN, J., Civil Engineering
VAN NIEKERK, J. L., Mechanical and Aeronautical Engineering
VAN SCHALKWYK, J. J. D., Electrical and Electronic Engineering
VAN VUUREN, S. J., Civil Engineering
VISSER, A. T., Civil Engineering
VISSER, J. A., Mechanical and Aeronautical Engineering
VISSER, J. K., Engineering and Technology Management
YAVIN, Y., Electrical and Electronic Engineering

ATTACHED RESEARCH INSTITUTES

Forestry and Agricultural Biotechnology Institute: Dir Prof. M. J. WINGFIELD.

Institute of Applied Materials: (vacant).

Centre for Augmentative and Alternative Communication: Dir Prof. E. ALANT.

Centre for Community Education: Dir Prof. J. LE ROUX.

Centre for Eco-tourism: Dir Prof. P. S. HATTINGH.

Centre for Economic and Social Reconstruction: Dir Prof. C. J. VAN ROOYEN.

Centre for Environmental Biology and Biological Control: Dir Prof. M. J. KOTZÉ.

Centre for Equine Research: Dir Prof. A. J. GUTHRIE.

Research Centre for Hetero-atom Chemistry: Dir Prof. T. A. MODRO.

Centre for Human Rights: Dir Prof. J. V. VAN DER WESTHUIZEN.

Centre for Information Development: Dir Prof. T. J. D. BOTHMA.

Mammal Research Institute: Dir Prof. J. D. SKINNER.

Carl and Emily Fuchs Institute for Microelectronics: Dir Prof. M. DU PLESSIS.

Institute for Strategic Studies: Dir Prof. M. HOUGH.

Hans Snyckers Institute (for community directed health research): Dirs Prof. A. L. CHRISTIANSON, Dr P. J. KLOPPERS.

Centre for Stomatological Research: Head Prof. W. J. C. COETZEE.

Institute for Missiological Research: Dir Prof. J. J. KRITZINGER.

Institute for Sports Research: Dir Prof. P. E. KRUGER.

South African Institute for Agricultural Extension: Dir Prof. G. H. DÜVEL.

Glaxo Institute for Clinical Pharmacology: Dir Prof. DE K. SOMMERS.

Atomic Energy Institute for Life Sciences: Dir Prof. I. C. DORMEHL.

Centre for Wildlife Research: Dir Prof. J. DU P. BOTHMA.

Institute for Technological Innovation: Dir Prof. C. W. I. PISTORIUS.

Centre for Continuing Theological Education: Dirs Prof. W. VOSLOO, Prof. M. J. DU P. BEUKES.

RESEARCH BUREAUX

Bureau for Economic Policy and Analysis: Dir (vacant).

Bureau for Financial Analysis: Dir Prof. L. M. BRUMMER.

Bureau for Statistical and Survey Methodology: Dir D. HERBST.

RESEARCH UNITS AND INSTITUTES OF THE MRC

(See under South African Medical Research Council.)

RAND AFRIKAANS UNIVERSITY

POB 524, Auckland Park, Johannesburg 2006

Telephone: (11) 489-2911

Fax: (11) 489-2191

Founded in 1966; the first students were enrolled in 1968

State control

Language of instruction: Afrikaans and English

Academic year: January to November

Chancellor: Dr G. VAN N. VILJOEN

Vice-Chancellor and Rector: Prof. J. C. VAN DER WALT

Vice-Rector: Prof. T. R. BOTHA

Academic Registrar: Prof. P. M. S. VON STADEN

Chief Librarian: J. SANDER

Library of 412,000 vols

Number of teachers: 340

Number of students: 21,181

DEANS

Faculty of Arts: Prof. J. A. NAUDE

Faculty of Economic and Management Science: Prof. I. v. W. RAUBENHEIMER

Faculty of Education and Nursing: Prof. J. C. LAMPRECHT

Faculty of Law: Prof. D. VAN DER MERWE

Faculty of Natural Science: Prof. G. H. DE SWARDT

Faculty of Engineering: Prof. P. VAN DER MERWE

Students: Prof. F. J. DE JAGER

PROFESSORS

ALBERTS, H. L., Physics
ASHWAL, L. D., Geology
BACKER, W., Human Resource Management
BARRIE, G. N., Law
BARTON, J. M., Geology
BESTER, M., Library and Information Science
BEUKES, N. J., Geology
BISSCHOFF, T. C., Education
BOESSENKOOL, A. L., Business Economics
BATES, A. C., Nursing
BOTHA, W. J., Afrikaans
BROERE, I., Mathematics
BUYS, A., Mathematics
CÄSE, M. J., Electrical and Electronic Engineering
COETSEE, D., Accounting
COETZEE, J. H., Biblical Studies
COETZEE, P. P., Chemistry and Biochemistry
CONRADIE, W. M., Business Management
DE BRUYN, H. E. C., Business Management
DE VILLIERS, D. S., Law
DU PLESSIS, J. J., Law
DU RAND, J. A., Biblical Studies
DU TOIT, A., Accountancy
DUBERY, I. A., Chemistry and Biochemistry
EHLERS, E. M., Computer Science
ELOFF, J. H. P., Computer Science
FERREIRA, H. C., Electrical and Electronic Engineering
FERREIRA, J. A., Electrical and Electronic Engineering
FERREIRA, J. T., Optometry
GELDENHUYS, D. J., Political Science
GOUWS, J. S., Sport and Movement Studies
GREYLING, L., Economics
HAARHOFF, J., Civil Engineering
HARRIS, W. F., Optometry
HENDERSON, W. J., Greek and Latin Studies
HENDRICKX, B., Greek and Latin Studies
HEYNS, J. VAN DER S., Economics
HOLZAPFEL, C. W., Chemistry and Biochemistry
JANSE VAN RENSBURG, P. A., Geography and Environmental Studies
JANSE VAN VUREN, J. H., Zoology
JOOSTE, C. J., Business Management
KATZ, Z., Mechanical and Manufacturing Engineering
KNOBLOCH, H. J., German
KOEKEMOER, C. L., Business Management
KOK, J. C., Education
KRIEK, J. H., Accountancy
KRUGER, G. J., Chemistry and Biochemistry
KRUGER, S., Business Management
LACQUET, B. N., Electrical and Electronic Engineering
LEMMER, H. H., Statistics
LESSING, B. C., Human Resource Management
LESSING, N., Business Management
LOMBARD, F., Statistics
LOTTER, H. P. P., Philosophy
MALAN, F. R., Law
MALHERBE, E. F. J., Law
MARITZ, C. J., Development Studies
MARX, B., Accountancy
MEYER, J. P., Mechanical and Manufacturing Engineering
MULLER, M. E., Nursing
MYBURGH, C. P. H., Education
NEL, Z. J., Psychology
NOLTE, A. G. W., Nursing
OLIVIER, M. P., Law
OTTO, J. M., Law
PAUW, D. A., Greek and Latin Studies
POGGENPOEL, M., Nursing
POSTHUMUS, L. C., African Languages
PRETORIUS, L., Mechanical and Manufacturing Engineering
PRETORIUS, W., Transport Economics
RAUBENHEIMER, H.G., Chemistry and Biochemistry
RAUTENBACH, I. M., Law
REINECKE, M. F. B., Law
ROSSOUW, G. J., Philosophy
RYAN, R. P., English
SCHOEMAN, W. J., Psychology
SLABBERT, J. A., Human Resource Management
SMITH, D. P. J., Education
SMITH, T. H. C., Computer Science
SNYMAN, J. J., Philosophy
SONNEKUS, J. C., Law
STEEB, W.-H., Applied Mathematics
STRAUSS, J., Curriculum Studies
STRYDOM, P. D. F., Economics
SWANEPOEL, J. H., Zoology
SWANEPOEL, R., Physics
SWART, P. L., Electrical and Electronic Engineering
TRÜMPELMANN, M. H., Curriculum Studies
UYS, H. H. M., Nursing
UYS, J. M., Sociology
VAN ASWEGEN, H. J., History
VAN BRAKEL, P. A., Information Studies
VAN DEN BERG, G. J., Civil and Urban Engineering
VAN REENEN, D. D., Geology
VAN WARMELO, K. T., Botany
VAN WYK, B. E., Botany
VAN WYK, J. D., Electrical and Electronic Engineering
VAN ZYL, M. A., Social Science
VENTER, A. J., Political Studies
VILLET, C. M., Applied Mathematics
VISSER, J. D., Human Resource Management
VON SOLMS, S. H., Computer Science
VORSTER, D. D., Accountancy
WHITEHEAD, C. S., Botany
WOLFF, E., Psychology

ATTACHED INSTITUTES

Institute for Child and Adult Guidance: Dir Dr H. G. PRETORIUS.

Institute for Energy Studies: Chair. Prof. D. J. KOTZÉ.

Institute for European Studies: Dir Prof. G. C. OLIVIER.

RHODES UNIVERSITY

POB 94, Grahamstown

Telephone: (46) 603-8113

Fax: (46) 622-5049

Telegraphic Address: Rhodescol

Founded 1904

Private control

Language of instruction: English

Academic year: February to November (four terms)

Chancellor: (vacant)

Chairman of the Council: Hon. Mr Justice R. J. W. JONES

Principal and Vice-Chancellor: D. R. WOODS

Vice-Principal and Pro-Vice-Chancellor: M. A. H. SMOUT

Registrar: S. FOURIE

Librarian: F. UBOGU

Library: see Libraries

Number of teachers: 336, including 60 professors

Number of students: 5,142

Publications: *Annual Report, Rhodes Review* (2 a year), *Old Rhodian Newsletter* (2 a year).

DEANS

Faculty of Humanities: I. A. MACDONALD
Faculty of Science: H. R. HEPBURN
Faculty of Education: P. R. IRWIN
Faculty of Commerce: P. VAN DER WATT
Faculty of Law: J. R. MIDGLEY
Faculty of Pharmacy: B. J. WILSON

PROFESSORS

ANTROBUS, G. G., Economics
BAART, E. E., Physics
BARKHUIZEN, G. P., Linguistics and English Language
BERGER, G. J. E. G., Journalism and Media Studies
BERNARD, R. T. F., Zoology
BOSCH, A. B., Afrikaans and Dutch
BOTHA, C. E. J., Botany
BROWN, M. E., Physical Chemistry
CHARTERIS, J., Human Movement Studies
CLAYTON, P. G., Computer Science
COETZEE, J. K., Sociology and Industrial Sociology
DE KLERK, V. A., Linguistics and English Language
DE VILLIERS, P. G. R., New Testament Studies
DE WET, C. J., Anthropology
DUNCAN, J. R., Biochemistry
EDWARDS, D. J. A., Psychology
EDWARDS, F., Contemporary Spirituality
FEIN, P. L.-M., French
GAIN, D. B., Classics
GAYBBA, B. P., Systematic Theology
GILBERT, A. J., Psychology
GORDON, G. E., Drama
GOUWS, J. S., English
HAYWARD, M., Fine Art
HECHT, T., Ichthyology and Fisheries Science
HEPBURN, H. R., Entomology
IRWIN, P. R., Education
IVANOV, A. V., Statistics
JACOB, R. E., Geology
KANFER, I., Pharmaceutics
KAYE, P. T., Organic Chemistry
KIRBY, R., Microbiology
KOTZÉ, W. J., Pure and Applied Mathematics
LEWIS, C. A., Geography
LUCIA, C. E., Music and Musicology
MACDONALD, I.A., Philosophy
MCQUAID, C. D., Zoology
MARSH, J. S., Geology
MAYLAM, P. R., History
MIDGLEY, J. R., Law
MOORE, J. M., Exploration Geology
MQEKE, R. B., Law
MTUZE, P. T., African Languages
NEL, H., Economics
POTGIETER, B., Pharmacology
SCHWIKKARD, P. J., Law

SEWRY, D. A., Information Systems
SOUTHALL, R. J., Political Studies
STACK, E. M., Accounting
STAUDE, G. E., Management
STONES, C. R., Psychology
TERRY, P. D., Computer Science
VAN DER WATT, P., Statistics
VAN WYK SMITH, English
WELZ, D. W., German
WENTWORTH, E. P., Computer Science
WHISSON, M. G., Anthropology

ATTACHED INSTITUTES

Institute for the Study of English in Africa (ISEA): f. 1964; Dir Prof. L. S. WRIGHT.

Institute of Social and Economic Research (ISER): f. 1954; Dir Prof. V. MØLLER.

Rhodes Institute for Water Research: f. 1967; Dir Dr J. H. O'KEEFE.

J. L. B Smith Institute of Ichthyology: f. 1968; Dir Dr P. H. SKELTON.

LIRI Technologies: f. 1941; Dir D. J. SWEETNAM.

National English Literary Museum: f. 1981; Dir M. M. HACKSLEY.

UNIVERSITY OF SOUTH AFRICA

Pretoria 0003
Telephone: 429-3111
Fax: 429-3221

Founded 1873, Royal Charter 1877

Since 1946 the University has been a correspondence and examining institution, accepting only external students; multiracial

Languages of instruction: Afrikaans and English

Academic year: February to November

Chancellor: Dr C. F. GARBERS

Vice-Chancellor and Principal: Prof. M. WIECHERS

Chairperson of the Council: Dr T. B. ROOD

Vice-Principals: Prof. J. A. DÖCKEL (Research), Prof. S. S. MAIMELA (Tuition), Prof. A. P. MELCK (Finance)

Registrars:
- Professional Services: Prof. K. E. MAUER (acting)
- Academic: M. H. STOCKHOFF
- Development: Prof. F. A. MARITZ

Librarian: Prof. J. WILLEMSE

Number of teachers and researchers: 1,392
Number of students: 124,212

Publications: *Unisa Bulletin, Unisa News, Unisa Alumnus, Africanus, Ars Nova, Codicillus, Communicatio, De Arte, Educare, Kleio, Mousaion, Musicus, Politeia, Religion and Theology, Scrutiny*[2], *Unisa Psychologia.*

DEANS

Faculty of Arts: Prof. W. F. MEYER
Faculty of Economic and Management Sciences: Prof. P. A. NEL
Faculty of Education: Prof. L. R. MCFARLANE
Faculty of Law: Prof. J. NEETHLING
Faculty of Science: Prof. G. MCGILLIVRAY
Faculty of Theology and Religious Studies: Prof. J. A. WOLFAARDT

PROFESSORS (with name of department)

ABRIE, A., Accounting
ACKERMANN, P. L. S., Graduate School of Business Leadership
ADLEM, W. L. J., Public Administration
BADENHORST, J. A., Business Management
BEATY, D. T., Graduate School of Business Leadership
BECKER, H. M. R., Applied Accountancy
BEGEMANN, E., Business Management
BEKKER, P. M., Criminal and Procedural Law
BESTER, G., Educational Studies
BEYERS, E., Psychology
BISHOP, N. T., Mathematics, Applied Mathematics and Astronomy
BODENSTEIN, H. C. A., Philosophy of Education
BOOT, G., Accounting
BOOYENS, S. W., Advanced Nursing Sciences
BOOYSE, J. J., Further Teacher Training
BOOYSEN, H., Constitutional and International Law
BORNMAN, C. H., Computer Science
BOTHA, J. E., New Testament
BOTHA, N. J., Constitutional and International Law
BOTHA, P. J. J., New Testament
BRINK, H. I. L., Advanced Nursing Sciences
BRITS, J. P., History
BRYNARD, D. J., Public Administration
BURNS, Y. M., Constitutional and International Law
CALITZ, E., Economics
CANT, M. C., Business Management
CARPENTER, G., Constitutional and International Law
CHURCH, J., Jurisprudence
CILLIERS, C. H., Criminology
CILLIERS, F. VAN N., Industrial Psychology
COETZER, I. A., Educational Studies
CONRADIE, H., Criminology
CRONJE, D. S. P., Private Law
CRONJE, G. DE J., Business Management
CRONJE, P. M., Accounting
CROUS, S. F. M., Educational Studies
DE BEER, C. S., Information Science
DE BEER, F. C., Anthropology and Archaeology
DE BEER, F. C., Development Administration
DE JONGH, M., Anthropology and Archaeology
DRECKMEYER, M., Secondary School Teacher Education
DREYER, J. M., Advanced Nursing Sciences
DU PISANIE, J. A., Economics
DU PLESSIS, I. J., New Testament
DU PLESSIS, P. J., Graduate School of Business Leadership
DU TOIT, C. W., Research Institute for Theology and Religion
DU TOIT, G. S., Business Management
ENGELBRECHT, J., New Testament
ERASMUS, B. J., Business Management
FARIS, J. A., Criminal and Procedural Law
FAURE, A. M., Political Sciences
FINLAYSON, R., African Languages
FLOWERS, J., Industrial Psychology
FOURIE, D. P., Psychology
FOURIE, L. J., Economics
FOURIE, P. J., Communication
FRANZSEN, R. C. D., Mercantile Law
FRASER, W. J., Further Teacher Training
GELDENHUYS, D. G., Musicology
GHYOOT, V. G., Business Management
GRÄBE, R. C., Theory of Literature
GROBBELAAR, A. F., Accounting
GROBBELAAR, J. I., Sociology
GROBLER, G. M. M., African Languages
GROBLER, P. A., Business Management
GRUNDLINGH, A. M., History
HAVENGA, M. K., Mercantile Law
HAVENGA, P. H., Mercantile Law
HAWTHORNE, L., Private Law
HEIDEMA, J., Mathematics, Applied Mathematics and Astronomy
HENDRIKSE, A. P., Linguistics
HIGGS, P., Educational Studies
HOFMEYR, K. B., Graduate School of Business Leadership
HOUGH, J., Business Management
HUBBARD, E. H., Linguistics
HUGO, P. J., Political Sciences
HUGO, W. M. J., Graduate School of Business Leadership
HULLEY, L. D., Systematic Theology and Theological Ethics
JACOBS, L. J., Educational Studies
JANSE VAN RENSBURG, J. B., Applied Accountancy
JORDAAN, R. A., Legal Aid Clinic
JORDAAN, W. J., Psychology
JOUBERT, J. J., Criminal and Procedural Law
JULYAN, F. W., Accounting
KATKOVNIK, V., Statistics
KLERCK, W. G., Graduate School of Business Leadership
KOURIE, C. E. T., New Testament
KRIEK, D. J., Political Sciences
KRITZINGER, J. N. J., Missiology
KRUGER, E. G., Secondary School Teacher Education
KRUGER, J. A., Information Science
KRÜGER, J. S., Religious Studies
LABUSCHAGNE, W. A., Computer Science and Information Systems
LANDMAN, A. A., Mercantile Law
LEMMER, E. M., Further Teacher Training
LESSING, A. C., Educational Studies
LIEBENBERG, E. C., Geography
LIGTHELM, A. A., Bureau for Market Research
LOADER, J. A., Old Testament
LOMBARD, D. B., Classics
LOMBARD, H. A., New Testament
LÖTTER, S., Criminal and Procedural Law
LOUWRENS, L. J., African Languages
LÜBBE, J. C., Semitics
LUCAS, G. H. A., Business Management
MADER, G. J., Classics
MARAIS, A. DE K., Business Management
MARÉ, M. C., Criminal and Procedural Law
MAREE, M. C., Romance Languages
MARKHAM, R., Statistics
MARTINS, J. A., Bureau for Market Research
MARX, J., Business Management
MAUER, K. F., Industrial Psychology
MCKAY, V. I., Institute for Adult Basic Education and Training
MCLEARY, F., Graduate School of Business Leadership
MISCH, M. K. E., German
MOHR, P. J., Economics
MSIMANG, C. T., African Languages
MURPHY, J. J., Graduate School of Business Leadership
MYNHARDT, C. M., Mathematics, Applied Mathematics and Astronomy
NAUDE, C. M. B., Criminology
NELL, V., Psychology
NESER, J. J., Criminology
NTULI, D. B., African Languages
OBERHOLZER, M. O., Educational Studies
OLIVIER, A., Primary School Teacher Education
ORR, M. A., English
PALMER, P. N., Business Management
PAUL, S. O., Chemistry
PAUW, J. C., Public Administration
PELSER, G. P. J., Graduate School of Business Leadership
PIETERSE, H. J. C., Practical Theology
PLUG, C., Psychology
POTGIETER, C., Further Teacher Training
POTGIETER, J. M., Private Law
POTGIETER, T. J. E., Graduate School of Business Leadership
POULOS, G., African Languages
PRETORIUS, E. A. C., New Testament
PRETORIUS, J. C., Sociology
PRETORIUS, J. T., Mercantile Law
PRETORIUS, L., Sociology
PRETORIUS, M. C. C., Industrial Psychology
PRINSLOO, E. D., Philosophy
RABINOWITZ, I. A., English
RADEMEYER, G., Psychology
RALL, P. J., Graduate School of Business Leadership
REID, D. J., Musicology
REYNHARDT, E. C., Physics
ROELOFSE, J. J., Communication
ROOS, H. M., Afrikaans
RUTHERFORD, B. R., Mercantile Law
RYAN, P. D., English
SAAYMAN, W. A., Missiology
SADLER, E., Applied Accountancy
SAENGER, E., Accounting
SCHEFFLER, E. H., Old Testament
SCOTT, S. J., Private Law
SERUDU, S. M., African Languages

SHAHIA, M., Transport Economics and Logistics
SMIT, B. F., Criminology
SMIT, P. J., Business Management
SMITH, J. DU P., Economics
SMITH, K. W., History
SMUTS, C. A., Transport Economics and Logistics
SNYDERS, F. J. A., Psychology
SNYMAN, C. R., Criminal and Procedural Law
SNYMAN, J. W., African Languages
SOFIANOS, S. A., Physics
SÖHNGE, W. F., Educational Studies
STEENEKAMP, T. J., Economics
STEFFENS, F. E., Statistics
STEYN, B. L., Accounting
STOOP, B. C., Jurisprudence
STRIKE, W. N., Romance Languages
STRYDOM, J. W., Business Management
STUART, J. F., Secondary School Teacher Education
SUMMERS, G. J., Chemistry
SWANEPOEL, C. F., African Languages
SWANEPOEL, C. H., Institute for Educational Research
SWANEPOEL, F. A., C. B. Powell Bible Centre
SWANEPOEL, H. J., Development Administration
SWANEPOEL, P. H., Afrikaans
SWANEVELDER, J. J., Accounting
SWART, G. J., Mercantile Law
SWEMMER, P. N., Auditing
TERBLANCHE, S. S., Criminal and Procedural Law
THOMASHAUSEN, A. E. A. M., Institute for Foreign and Comparative Law
TORR, C. S. W., Economics
TROSKIE, R., Advanced Nursing Sciences
VAN ASWEGEN, A., Private Law
VAN BILJON, R. C. W., Social Work
VAN BLERK, A. E., Jurisprudence
VAN DELFT, W. F., Social Work
VAN DEN BERG, P. H., Graduate School of Business Leadership
VAN DER MERWE, C. A., Quantitative Management
VAN DER MERWE, D. P., Criminal and Procedural Law
VAN DER WALT, A. J., Private Law
VAN DYK, P. J., Old Testament
VAN DYK, P. S., Business Management
VAN NIEKERK, E., Systematic Theology, Theological Ethics
VAN NIEKERK, J. P., Mercantile Law
VAN NIEKERK, S. L. H., Secondary School Teacher Education
VAN ROOY, M. P., Educational Studies
VAN ROOYEN, J. H., Criminal and Procedural Law
VAN WYK, A. M. A., Private Law
VAN WYK, C., Educational Studies
VAN WYK, C. W., Jurisprudence
VAN WYK, D. H., Constitutional and International Law
VAN ZYL, A. E., Educational Studies
VAN ZYL, L. J., Jurisprudence
VERWOERD, W. S., Physics
VILJOEN, H. G., Psychology
VISSER, C. J., Mercantile Law
VISSER, P. S., Educational Studies
VORSTER, H. J. S., Auditing
VORSTER, J. N., New Testament
VORSTER, L. P., Indigenous Law
VORSTER, S. J. R., Mathematics, Applied Mathematics and Astronomy
WEINBERG, A. M., English
WESSELS, W. J., Old Testament
WHELPTON, F. P. VAN R., Indigenous Law
WIECHERS, E., Educational Studies
WIECHERS, N. J., Private Law
WILLIAMS, G., Applied Accountancy
WOLFAARDT, J. B., Industrial Psychology
WOLVAARDT, J. S., Quantitative Management

ATTACHED INSTITUTES

Centre for Applied Statistics: Dir Prof. F. E. STEFFENS.

Centre for Business Law: Dir Prof. C. J. VISSER.

Centre for Latin American Studies: Head Z. ROELOFSE-CAMPBELL.

Centre for Women's Studies: Dir Prof. J. R. WILKINSON.

C. B. Powell Bible Centre: Dir Prof. F. A. SWANEPOEL.

Institute for Behavioural Sciences: Dir Prof. C. PLUG (acting).

Institute for Continuing Education: Head E. P. NONYONGO.

Institute for Criminology: Dir Prof. J. H. PRINSLOO.

Institute for Educational Research: Dir Prof. C. H. SWANEPOEL.

Institute for Foreign and Comparative Law: Dir Prof. A. E. A. M. THOMASHAUSEN.

Research Institute for Theology and Religion: Prof. C. W. DU TOIT.

UNIVERSITY OF STELLENBOSCH

Private Bag X1, Matieland 7602, Cape Province

Telephone: (21) 808-9111
Telegraphic Address: University
Fax: (21) 808-4499
E-mail: webinfo@maties.sun.ac.za

Incorporated 1918
Language of instruction: Afrikaans
Academic year: February to December (four terms)

Chancellor: Prof. ELIZE BOTHA
Principal and Vice-Chancellor: Prof. A. H. VAN WYK
Vice-Principals: Dr R. STUMPF, Prof. W. T. CLAASSEN
Registrar: Prof. S. KRITZINGER
Director of Library Services: Prof. J. H. VILJOEN

Number of teachers: 741
Number of students: 16,848

Publications: *Annals of the University, Calendar, Matieland, Maatskaplike Werk* (Social Work, quarterly), *Opinion Survey Report* (Bureau of Economic Research, quarterly), *Survey of Contemporary Economic Conditions and Prospects* (annually), *Research Report* (annually), *Report of the Rector,* faculty and student information brochures.

DEANS

Faculty of Arts: Prof. I. J. VAN DER MERWE
Faculty of Science: Prof. F. J. W. HAHNE
Faculty of Medicine: Prof. J. DE V. LOCHNER
Faculty of Education: Prof. T. PARK
Faculty of Agriculture: Prof. M. J. HATTINGH
Faculty of Law: Prof. J. S. A. FOURIE
Faculty of Theology: Prof. H. J. B. COMBRINK
Faculty of Economic and Management Sciences: Prof. J. A. MATTHEE
Faculty of Engineering: Prof. P. W. VAN DER WALT
Faculty of Forestry: Prof. G. VAN WYK
Faculty of Military Science: C. NELSON
Faculty of Dentistry: Prof. W. P. DREYER

PROFESSORS

Faculty of Arts:

BEKKER, S. B., Sociology
BOTHA, R. P., Linguistics
BREYTENBACH, W. J., Political Science
CLAASSEN, G. N., Journalism
CLAASSEN, W. T., Ancient Near Eastern Studies
DEACON, H. J., Archaeology
DU PLESSIS, J. A., African Languages
GROENEWALD, C. J., Sociology
GROVÉ, I. J., Music
HAUPTFLEISCH, T., Drama
HEYNS, M. W., English
KAPP, P. H., History
KERR, G., Fine Arts
KINGHORN, J., Biblical Studies
KOTZE, H. J., Political Science
KRUIJSSE, H. W., Psychology
KUSSLER, H. R., Modern Foreign Languages
MÖLLER, A. T., Psychology
MOUTON, J., Sociology
NEL, P. R., Political Science
PONELIS, F. A., Afrikaans and Dutch
ROUX, J. C., African Languages
SHARP, J. S., Sociology (Anthropology)
SPIES, L., Afrikaans and Dutch
THOM, J. C., Classics
VAN DER MERWE, I. J., Geography
VAN DER WESTHUYSEN, T. W. B., Psychology
VAN NIEKERK, A. A., Philosophy
WELCH, C. T., Town and Regional Planning
ZIETSMAN, H. L., Geography and Environmental Studies

Faculty of Science:

BURGER, B. V., Chemistry
COWLEY, A. A., Physics
CRUYWAGEN, J. J., Chemistry
DE BRUYN, G. F. C., Mathematics
DE VILLIERS, J. M., Mathematics
ENGELBRECHT, W. J., Physical Chemistry
GEYER, H. B., Physics
HAHNE, F. J. W., Physics
HOFMEYR, J. H. S., Biochemistry
KRZESINSKI, A. E., Computer Science
LOOS, M. A., Microbiology
MORGENTHAL, J. C., Human and Animal Physiology
NEL, J. A. J., Zoology
PRETORIUS, I. S., Microbiology
REINECKE, A. J., Zoology
ROZENDAAL, A., Geology
SANDERSON, R. D., Polymer Science
SCHNEIDER, D. F., Chemistry
SMITH, V. R., Botany
VAN DER WALT, A. P. J., Mathematics
VAN WYK, L., Mathematics
VISSER, E. M., Consumer Studies: Food, Clothing, Housing
WALTERS, P. E., Physics

Faculty of Medicine:

BARDIN, P. G., Internal Medicine
COETZEE, A. R., Anaesthesiology
DOUBELL, A. F., Internal Medicine
DU TOIT, D., Anatomy and Histology
EMSLEY, R. A., Psychiatry
GREGOR, R. T., Otorhinolaryngology
HESSELING, P. B., Paediatrics and Child Health
HEYNS, C. F., Urology
HOUGH, F. S., Internal Medicine
JOUBERT, J. J., Medical Microbiology
JOUBERT, J. R., Internal Medicine
KLOPPER, J. F., Nuclear Medicine
KRUGER, T. F., Obstetrics and Gynaecology
LABADARIOS, D., Human Nutrition
LOCHNER, J. DE V., Medical Physiology and Biochemistry
MEYER, D., Ophthalmology
MOORE, S. W., Surgery
ODENDAAL, H. J., Obstetrics and Gynaecology
SCHAETZING, A. E., Obstetrics and Gynaecology
SCHER, A. T., Radiation Oncology
SMIT, B. J., Radiotherapy
TALJAARD, J. J. F., Chemical Pathology
VAN DER MERWE, P.-L., Paediatrics
VAN DER MERWE, W. L., Anaesthesiology
VAN JAARSVELD, P. P., Pharmacology
VAN WYK, J. A. L., Surgery
VLOK, G. J., Orthopaedic Surgery
WEICH, H. F. H., Internal Medicine
WELMANN, E. B., Nursing Science
WRANZ, P. A. B., Anatomical Pathology

ZEEMAN, B. J. VAN R., Plastic and Reconstructive Surgery

Faculty of Education:

CARL, A. E., Didactics
CILLIERS, C. D., Educational Psychology and Specialized Education
ENGELBRECHT, P., Educational Psychology and Specialized Education
KAPP, C. A., Centre for Higher and Adult Education
PARK, T., Didactics
POTGIETER, J. R., Human Movement Studies
PRINSLOO, N. P., Educational Policy Studies
STEYN, J. C., Educational Policy Studies

Faculty of Agriculture:

AGENBAG, G. A., Agronomy and Pastures
BRITZ, T., Food Science
CROUS, P. W., Plant Pathology
GILIOMEE, J. H., Entomology and Nematology
GOUSSARD, P. G., Oenology and Viticulture
HATTINGH, M. J., Plant Pathology
HAYES, J. P., Animal Sciences
HOLZ, G., Plant Pathology
JACOBS, G., Horticultural Science
MARAIS, G. F., Genetics
RABE, E., Horticultural Science
SCHOEMAN, S. J., Animal Sciences
VINK, N., Agricultural Economics

Faculty of Law:

BUTLER, D. W., Mercantile Law
DE VOS, W., Private Law and Roman Law
DE WAAL, M. J., Private Law and Roman Law
DU PLESSIS, L. M., Public Law
ERASMUS, M. G., Public Law
FOURIE, J. S. A., Mercantile Law
HUGO, C. F. , Mercantile Law
LOUBSER, M. M., Private Law and Roman Law
LUBBE, G. F., Private Law and Roman Law
PIENAAR, J. M., Private Law and Roman Law
RABIE, M. A., Public Law
VAN DER MERWE, C. G., Private Law and Roman Law
VAN DER MERWE, S. E., Public Law
VAN WYK, A. H., Mercantile Law

Faculty of Theology:

BOSMAN, H. L., Old and New Testament
COERTZEN, P., Systematic Theology, Church History and Church Polity
COMBRINK, H. J. B., Old and New Testament
DU TOIT, D. A., Systematic Theology, Church History and Church Polity
LOUW, D. J., Practical Theology and Missiology
PAUW, C. M., Practical Theology and Missiology

Faculty of Economic and Management Sciences:

AUGUSTYN, J. C. D., Industrial Psychology
BENDIX, D. W. F., Business Administration
BROWN, W., Accounting
CLAASEN, M. S., Statistics and Actuarial Science
CLOETE, G. S., Public and Developent Management
DE VILLIERS, J. U., Business Management
DU PLESSIS, P. G., Business Management
DU TOIT, M. A., Business Management
GEVERS, W. R., Business Management and Administration
HAMMAN, W. D., Business Management and Administration
HUMAN, L. N., Business Management and Administration
LAMBRECHTS, I. J., Business Management
LEIBOLD, M., Business Management
MATTHEE, J. A., Accounting
MCCARTHY, C. L., Economics
MOSTERT, F. J., Business Management
OLIVIER, P., Accounting
OOSTHUIZEN, H., Business Administration
PIENAAR, W. J., Transport Economics
SCHOEMAN, A., Statistics and Actuarial Science
SCHWELLA, E., Public and Development Management
SMIT, B. W., Economics
SMIT, E. VAN DER M., Business Management and Administration
STEEL, S. J., Statistics and Actuarial Science
TROMP, D., Industrial Psychology
VAN DER BERG, S., Economics
VAN WYK, A. J., Industrial Psychology

Faculty of Engineering:

BASSON, A. H., Mechanical Engineering
BESTER, C. J., Civil Engineering
CLOETE, J. H., Electrical and Electronic Engineering
DAVIDSON, D. B., Electrical and Electronic Engineering
DUNAISKI, P. E., Civil Engineering
DU PLESSIS, J. J., Electrical and Electronic Engineering
DU PLESSIS, J. P., Applied Mathematics
DU PREEZ, N. D., Industrial Engineering
ENSLIN, J. H. R., Electrical and Electronic Engineering
GÖRGENS, A. H. M., Civil Engineering
KRÖGER, D. G., Mechanical Engineering
LORENZEN, L., Chemical Engineering
MILNE, G. W., Electrical and Electronic Engineering
PEROLD, W. J., Electrical and Electronic Engineering
READER, H. C., Electrical and Electronic Engineering
RETIEF, J. V., Civil Engineering
ROOSEBOOM, A., Civil Engineering
SCHOONWINKEL, A., Electrical and Electronic Engineering
VAN DE VEN, M. F. C., Civil Engineering
VAN DER MERWE, F. S., Electrical and Electronic Engineering
VAN DER WALT, P. W., Electrical and Electronic Engineering
VAN RYNEVELD, W. P., Industrial Engineering
VON BACKSTRÖM, T. W., Mechanical Engineering

Faculty of Forestry:

BREDENKAMP, B. V., Forestry Science
VAN WYK, G., Forestry Science
VERMAAS, H. F., Wood Science

Faculty of Dentistry:

DREYER, W. P., Oral Medicine and Periodontics
GROTEPASS, F. W., Maxillo-facial and Oral Surgery
HARRIS, A. M. P., Orthodontics
LOUW, N. P., Restorative Dentistry
NORTJÉ, C. J., Maxillofacial Radiology
PETERS, R., Restorative Dentistry
PHILLIPS, V. M., Oral Pathology
VAN RENSBURG, B. G. J., Oral Biology

Faculty of Military Science:

NELSON, C., Political Science (Military Context)

ATTACHED RESEARCH INSTITUTES

Institute for Futures Research: Dir Prof A. ROUX.

Institute for Mathematics and Science Teaching: Dir Dr J. H. SMIT.

Institute for Polymer Science: Dir Prof. R. D. SANDERSON.

Institute for Applied Computer Science: Dir Prof. A. E. KRZESINSKI.

Institute for Industrial Engineering: Dir Prof. N. D. DU PREEZ.

Institute for Wine Biotechnology: Dir Prof. I. S. PRETORIUS.

Institute for Sport and Movement Studies: Dir Dr J. H. MALAN.

Institute for Structural Engineering: Dir Prof. J. V. RETIEF.

Institute for Oral and Dental Research: Dir Prof. P. VAN DER BIJL.

Institute for Theoretical Physics: Dir Prof. H. B. GEYER.

Institute for Thermodynamics and Mechanics: Dir Prof. D. G. KRÖGER.

Institute for Transport Technology: Dir Prof. F. HUGO.

Centre for Applied Ethics: Head Prof. A. A. VAN NIEKERK.

Centre for Bible Translation in Africa: Head Dr C. H. J. VAN DER MERWE.

Centre for Children's Literature and Media: Prof. A. E. CARL.

Centre for Contextual Hermeneutics: Head Prof. J. KINGHORN.

Centre for Cost Effective Medicine: Head Prof. J. R. JOUBERT.

Centre for Disabled Care and Rehabilitation: Head J. A. HENDRY.

Centre for Educational Development: Head A. H. MEYER.

Centre for Electrical and Electronic Engineering: Head Prof. F. S. VAN DER MERWE.

Centre for Entrepreneurship: Head Dr J. VENTER.

Centre for Geographical Analysis: Head Dr J. H. VAN DER MERWE.

Centre for Higher and Adult Education: Head Prof. C. A. KAPP.

Centre for Interdisciplinary Studies: Head Prof. J. MOUTON.

Centre for International and Comparative Politics: Head Prof. H. J. KOTZÉ.

Centre for International Business: Head Prof. M. LEIBOLD.

Centre for Leadership Studies (Southern Africa): Head Prof. H. H. SPANGENBERG.

Centre for Military Studies: Head Col L. DU PLESSIS.

Centre for Molecular and Cellular Biology: Head Prof. P. D. VAN HELDEN.

Centre for Theatre and Performance Studies: Head Prof. T. HAUPTFLEISCH.

Advanced Manufacturing Unit: Head C. J. FOURIE.

Cranio-Facial Unit at Tygerberg Hospital: Head Dr C. S. F. SMIT.

Drug Research Unit; Head Prof. J. R. JOUBERT.

Educational Psychology Unit: Head Dr P. J. NORMAND.

Experimental Phonology Unit: Head Prof. J. C. ROUX.

Mathematics Education Unit: Head Prof. P. G. HUMAN.

Perinatal Mortality Research Unit: Head Prof. H. J. ODENDAAL.

UNIVERSITY OF TRANSKEI

Private Bag X1, Unitra
Telephone: 3022111
Fax: (471) 26820

Founded 1976 as branch of Fort Hare University, independent 1977
State control through University Council
Language of instruction: English

Chancellor: T. MBEKI
Vice-Chancellor: Prof. A. T. MOLEAH
Deputy Vice-Chancellor: Prof. J. M. NORUWANA
Registrar: Prof. R. B. MQEKE
Chief Librarian: (vacant)

Number of teachers: 502
Number of students: 6,700

DEANS

Faculty of Arts: Prof. D. N. JAFTA
Faculty of Natural Sciences: Prof. G. L. BOOTH
Faculty of Economic Sciences: Prof. M. MAHABIR
Faculty of Law: Prof. D. S. KOYANA
Faculty of Education: Prof. T. S. MWAMWENDA
Faculty of Medicine and Health Sciences: Prof. E. L. MAZWAI

PROFESSORS

Faculty of Arts:

BROWN, M. J., Social Work
CREHAN, A. S., English
DOWLING, K., Philosophy
JAFTA, D. N., African Languages (Sesotho and Xhosa)
LAWUYI, O. B., Anthropology
MIJERE, N., Sociology
MJOLI, Q. T., Psychology
PHILLIPS-HOWARD, K. D., Geography
THIPA, H. M., African Languages (Sesotho and Xhosa)

Faculty of Natural Sciences:

BOOTH, G. L., Mathematics
DEMANET, C. M., Physics
DYE, A. H., Zoology
JACOBS, T. V., Botany
KULESZA, W., Computer Science
MDODA, G. N., Applied Mathematics

Faculty of Economic Sciences:

WILLIAMS, G., Accountancy

Faculty of Education:

GLENCROSS, M. J., Mathematics and Sciences Education
LWANGA-LUKWAGO, J., Social Studies Education
MWAMWENDA, T. S., Educational Foundations
NGUBENTOMBI, S. V. S., Educational Foundations
PIENAAR, P. T., Language Studies Education

Faculty of Law:

DLOVA, V., Mercantile Law
KOYANA, D. S., Criminal and Adjective Law

Faculty of Medicine and Health Sciences:

GUMBI, R. V., Nursing Science
IPUTO, J. E., Physiology
MEISSNER, O., Pharmacology
MFENYANA, K., Family and Community Medicine
NGANWA-BAGUMAH, A. B., Anatomy
STEPHEN, A., Pathology

VISTA UNIVERSITY

Central Campus, Private Bag X634, Pretoria 0001
Telephone: (12) 322-8967
Fax: (12) 320-0528
Founded 1982
Campuses in Bloemfontein, Mamelodi, Port Elizabeth, Sebokeng, Soweto, Daveyton, Welkom, Pretoria (Distance Education Campus)
Chancellor: (vacant)
Vice-Chancellor: Prof. HUGH P. AFRICA
Deputy Vice-Chancellors: Prof. TSEHLOANE KETO, Prof. KINGSTON NYAMAPFENE
Registrar: K. O. RUSSELL
Librarian: A. LESSING (acting)
Library of 150,000 vols
Number of teachers: 456
Number of students: 32,108

DEANS

Faculty of Arts: Prof. S. R. CHAPHOLE
Faculty of Economic and Management Sciences: Prof. M. LEVIN
Faculty of Education: Prof. P. D. G. STEYN
Faculty of Law: Prof. G. GERTSCH
Faculty of Science: Prof. H. J. DU T. VAN DER LINDE

HEADS OF DEPARTMENTS

Accountancy: Prof. R. P. VOGES
Afrikaans: Prof. G. A. JOOSTE
Business Management: Prof. J. J. A. STEENEKAMP
Chemistry: Prof. H. J. DU T. VAN DER LINDE
Commercial Law: Prof. J. BALORO
Computer Science and Information Systems: S. HAUPT (acting)
Economics: Prof. M. LEVIN
Education: Prof. P. D. G. STEYN
English: Prof. T. B. MHAMBI
Geographical Sciences: Prof. J. H. REYNHARDT
History: Prof. J. S. MOHLAMME
Mathematics: Prof. E. W. STRAEULI
Nguni Languages: B. P. MNGADI (acting)
Physics: Prof. D. RAUBENHEIMER
Postgraduate Education: Prof. P. J. H. SMAL
Private Law: Prof. B. P. WANDA
Procedural Law: K. D. MULLER (acting)
Professional Education J. R. DEBEILA
Psychology: Prof. C. N. HOELSON
Public Administration: Prof. C. A. J. FREYSEN
Public Law: Prof. N. J. C. VAN DEN BERGH
School Subject Education: Prof. C. R. DAVEY
Sociology: Prof. L. S. A. TOGNI
Sotho Languages: N. J. MANYAKA (acting)
Statistics: Prof. J. I. DE WET

ATTACHED UNITS

Centre for Cognitive Development: Dir Prof. G. N. NAUDÉ.
Employment Research Unit: Head Prof. M. LEVIN.

UNIVERSITY OF THE WESTERN CAPE

Private Bag X17, Bellville 7535
Telephone: (21) 959-2911
Telex: 526661
Fax: (21) 959-3627
E-mail: jsmith@uwc.ac.za
Founded 1960
State subsidized, but functions under its own charter
Languages of instruction: Afrikaans and English
Academic year: February to December
Chancellor: Archbishop DESMOND TUTU
Vice-Chancellor and Rector: Prof. C. A. ABRAHAMS
Registrar: Dr J. F. SMITH
Vice-Rectors: Prof. A. REDLINGHUIS, Prof. I. VAN DE RHEEDE, Prof. C. T. JOHNSON (acting)
Librarian: P. E. SEPTEMBER (acting)
Library of 254,000 vols, 2,600 journals, 173,000 microfiche items
Number of teachers: 434
Number of students: 11,211
Publications: *Rector's Annual Report*, *UWC Perspective*, *On Campus*, *Donor Report*.

DEANS

Faculty of Arts: Prof. A. TEMU
Faculty of Natural Sciences: Prof. L. SLAMMERT (acting)
Faculty of Dentistry: Prof. M. H. MOOLA (acting)
Faculty of Education: Prof. H. D. HERMAN
Faculty of Economic and Management Sciences: Prof. A. KRITZINGER
Faculty of Law: Prof. D. DU TOIT
Faculty of Religion and Theology: Prof. W. T. W. CLOETE
Faculty of Community and Health Sciences: Prof T. B. PRETORIUS

DEPARTMENTAL CHAIRPERSONS

Faculty of Arts:

Afrikaans and Dutch: Prof. W. VAN ZYL
Anthropology and Sociology: Dr A. J. HUMPHREYS
Arabic: Drs M. H.HARON
English: Prof. A. PARR
French: Dr J. ALANT
Geography and Environmental Studies: Prof. D. W. MYBURGH
German: A. FLEGG
History: Dr G. MINKLEY
Latin: Dr B. VAN ZYL SMIT
Linguistics: Prof. D H. GOUGH
Library and Information Sciences: Prof. B. NZOTTA
Music: A. PETERSEN (acting)
Philosophy: J. P. ABRAHAMS
Xhosa: A. STUURMAN

Faculty of Community and Health Sciences:

Human Ecology and Dietetics: J. J. CORNELISSEN
Human Movement Studies: A. TRAVILL
Nursing: G. PRINCE
Occupational Therapy: J. DE JONGH
Physiotherapy: Prof. S. L. AMOSUN
Psychology: Prof. L. C. SIMBAYI
Public Health Programme: Prof. D. SANDERS
Social Work: Dr F. G. KOTZE

Faculty of Dentistry:

Anatomical Pathology and Oral Pathology: Prof. J. J. HILLE
Anatomy: Prof. C. J. LEONARD
Community Dentistry: Dr N. MYBURGH
Community Oral Health: C. CAMARA
Conservative Dentistry: Prof. Y. I. OSMAN
Maxillofacial and Oral Surgery: Prof. G. KARRIEM
Medical Microbiology: Prof. A. HALLETT
Oral Medicine and Periodontics: Prof. T. M. ARENDORF
Orthodontics: Dr E. T. L. THEUNISSEN
Prosthetic Dentistry: Dr V. WILSON
Radiology and Diagnostics: Prof. M. E. PARKER

Faculty of Economic and Management Sciences:

Accounting: Prof. D. S. ALBERTYN
Economics: I. ADAMS
Industrial Psychology: Prof. F. ABRAHAMS
Information Systems: K. MATTISON
Management: C. MAY
Political Studies: S. MASEKO
Public Administration: Dr C. J. MPHAISHA

Faculty of Education:

Comparative Education: Dr D. M. SAYED
Didactics: Prof. C. JULIE
Educational Psychology: J. L. ENGELBRECHT
Philosophy of Education: Prof. W. MORROW
School of Science and Mathematics: Prof. M. OGUNNIYI

Faculty of Law:

Comparative Law and International Law: Prof. P. C. SMIT
Mercantile Law: Adv. G. F. KOTZE
Private Law: Prof. L.F. VAN HUYSSTEEN
Public Law and Adjective Law: Prof. L. FERNANDEZ

Faculty of Natural Sciences:

Biochemistry: P. MCLAREN
Botany: Dr L. RAITT
Chemistry: Dr D. L. KEY
Computer Science: Prof. S. W. POSTMA
Earth Sciences: Dr V. TAYLOR
Mathematics: Prof. G. GROENEWALD
Microbiology and Plant Pathology: Dr S. DAVISON
Pharmaceutical Chemistry: Prof. P. F. K. EAGLES
Pharmaceutics: Prof. I. RUSSELL
Pharmacology: Dr. G. AMABEOKU
Pharmacy Practice: Prof. N. C. BUTLER
Physics: Prof. R. LINDSAY
Physiology: Prof. G. MARITZ
Statistics: Dr D. O. CHALTON
Zoology: Dr M. HOFMEYER

Faculty of Religion and Theology:
- Biblical Studies and Biblical Language: Dr J. Daniels
- Christian Studies: Dr A. Phillips
- Christianity and Society: Dr. A. Phillips (acting)
- Religious Studies: J. K. Cornelissen

ATTACHED RESEARCH INSTITUTES

Centre for Southern African Studies: Dir Prof. P. Vale.

Institute for Child and Family Development: Dir Prof. F. C. T. Sonn (acting).

Institute for Historical Research: Dir Prof. H. C. Bredekamp.

Institute for Social Development: Dir Prof. P. J. le Roux.

South African Development Education and Policy Research Unit: Dir V. Taylor.

UNIVERSITY OF THE WITWATERSRAND, JOHANNESBURG

Private Bag 3, Wits 2050
Telephone: (11) 716-1111
Telex: 42 7125
Fax: (11) 716-8030

Founded 1922

State subsidized, but functions under its own charter

Language of instruction: English

Academic year: February to November

Chancellor: Hon. Mr Justice R. Goldstone

Vice-Chancellor and Principal: Prof. Colin J. Bundy

Deputy Vice-Chancellors: Prof. A. R. Kemp (Vice-Principal), Prof. A. F. Ogunrinade

Chairman of the Council: Hon. Mr Justice E. Cameron

Registrar: Dr D. K. Swemmer (Academic)

Librarian: H. Edwards

Library: see Libraries

Number of teachers: 980 full-time, 316 part-time

Number of students: 17,587

Publications: *Calendar, Wits Perspectives, The Research Report, Facts on Wits, Urban Forum, Palaeontologia Africana, African Studies, English Studies in Africa* (2 a year), *Perspectives in Education* (quarterly), *Philosophical Papers* (3 a year), *The Industrial Law Journal* (6 a year), etc.

DEANS

Faculty of Architecture: Prof. J. G. Muller
Faculty of Arts: Prof. G. Olivier
Faculty of Management: Prof. K. Yeomans
Faculty of Commerce: Prof. M. B. Dagut
Faculty of Health Sciences: Prof. M. Price
Faculty of Education: Prof. P. Christie
Faculty of Engineering: Prof. J. P. Reynders
Faculty of Law: Prof. C. M. Lewis
Faculty of Science: Prof. J. R. Hoch

PROFESSORS

Faculty of Architecture:
- Bremner, L., Architecture
- Muller, J. G., Town and Regional Planning
- Schloss, R. I., Building and Quantity Surveying

Faculty of Arts and Faculty of Science:
- Adler, J., Mathematics Education Development
- Alexander, J. J., Microbiology
- Anhaeusser, C. R., Geology
- Asher, A., Statistics and Actuarial Science
- Beavon, K. S. O., Geography and Environmental Studies
- Boeyens, J. C. A., Theoretical Chemistry
- Bonner, P. L., History
- Bozzoli, B., Sociology
- Cawthorn, R. G., Geology
- Cheadle, B. D., English
- Cock, J., Sociology
- Comins, J. D., Physics
- Coplan, D. B., Social Anthropology
- Couzens, T. J., Institute for Advanced Social Research
- Coville, N. J., Organo-Metallic Chemistry
- Crump, A., Fine Arts
- Delius, P. S., History
- Dirr, H. W., Biochemistry
- Du Plessis, P., Physics
- Every, A. G., Physics
- Fabian, B. C., Zoology
- Fatti, L. P., Statistics
- Fisher, J., Psychology
- Glasser, L., Physical Chemistry
- Heiss, W. D., Theoretical Physics
- Hoch, M. J. R., Solid State Physics
- Hofmeyr, I., African Literature
- Huffman, T. N., Archaeology
- Hughes, G. I., English
- Hunt, J. H. V., Mathematics
- Kirchner, W. H., Zoology
- Lewis-Williams, J. D., Archaeology
- Lowther, J. E., Physics
- Lodge, T., Political Studies
- Lubinsky, D. S., Mathematics
- Maake, N. P., African Languages
- Mason, D. P., Applied Mathematics
- Marques, H., Chemistry
- McCarthy, T. S., Geology
- McKendrick, B. W., Social Work
- McLachlan, D. S., Electronic Properties of Solids
- Michael, J. P., Organic Chemistry
- Murray, B. K., Edwardian British History
- Nethersole, R., Comparative Literature
- Olivier, G., Afrikaans and Dutch
- Owen-Smith, N., Zoology
- Pendlebury, M., Philosophy
- Penn, C., Speech Pathology and Audiology
- Pienaar, R. N., Botany
- Prodinger, H., Mathematics
- Robb, L. J., Geology
- Rodrigues, J. A. P., Physics
- Rogers, B. G., French
- Rogers, K. H., Botany
- Rogerson, C. M., Geography
- Rubidge, B. S., Palaeontology
- Rutherford, M., Director, College of Science
- Stadler, A. W., Political Studies
- Straker, G., Applied Psychology
- Stremlau, J. J., International Relations
- Traill, A., Linguistic Phonetics
- Tyson, P. D., Climatology
- Van Onselen, C., Advanced Social Research
- Van Wyk, C., Music
- Viljoen, M. J., Mining Geology
- Webster, E. C., Sociology
- Wright, C., Geophysics
- Wright, C. J., Computational and Applied Mathematics

Faculty of Management:
- Abratt, R., Business Administration
- Ahwireng-Obeng, F., Business Administration
- Douwes-Dekker, L., Industrial Relations
- Duffy, N. M., Management Information Systems
- Klein, S., International Business

Faculty of Commerce:
- Burgess, S., Business Economics
- Dagut, M., Economics
- De Koker, A. P., Accounting
- Reekie, W. D., Business Economics
- Simkins, C., Economics
- Vivian, R., Insurance and Risk Management

Faculty of Education:
- Christie, P.
- Enslin, P. A.
- Russell, D. D.
- Skuy, M. S.

Faculty of Engineering:
- Blight, G. E., Civil Engineering
- Bryson, A. W., Chemical Engineering
- Eric, R. H., Metallurgy and Materials Engineering
- Glasser, D., Chemical Engineering
- Hanrahan, H. E., Electrical Engineering
- Hildebrandt, D., Process and Materials Engineering
- Iwankiewicz, R. M., Applied Mathematics
- Landy, C. F., Electrical Engineering
- MacLeod, I. M., Control Engineering
- McCutcheon, R. T., Project and Construction Management
- Onsongo, W. M., Undergraduate Engineering Education
- Ozbay, M. U., Mining Engineering
- Phillips, H. R., Mining Engineering
- Reynders, J. P., Electrical Engineering
- Sheer, T. J., Mechanical Engineering
- Skews, B. W., Mechanical Engineering
- Stephenson, D., Hydraulic Engineering

Faculty of Law:
- Cheadle, M. H.
- Cockrell, A. H. P.
- Itzikowitz, A.
- Larkin, M. P.
- Lewis, C. H.
- Paizes, A. P.
- Skeen, A. St A.

Faculty of Health Sciences:
- Allwood, C., Psychiatry
- Altini, M., Oral Pathology
- Bezwoda, W. R., Medicine
- Carmichael, T., Ophthalmology
- Carr, L., Prosthetic Dentistry
- Cleaton-Jones, P. E., Experimental Odontology
- Cooper, K., Antomical Pathology
- Cooper, P. A., Paediatrics
- Crewe-Brown, H., Medical Microbiology
- Cronje, S. L., Cardiothoracic Surgery
- Davies, M. R. Q., Paediatric Surgery
- Erken, E. H. W., Orthopaedic Surgery
- Esser, J. D., Nuclear Medicine
- Evans, W. G., Orthodontics
- Exner, H. V., Conservative Dentistry
- Farrell, V. J. R., Neurological Surgery
- Feldman, C., Medicine
- Fritz, V. U., Neurology
- Gear, J. S., Community Health
- George, J. A., Orthopaedic Surgery
- Gray, I. P., Chemical Pathology
- Havlik, I., Pharmacology
- Hofmeyr, G. J., Obstetrics and Gynaecology
- Huddle, K., Medicine
- Joffe, B. I., Medicine
- Kalk, W. J., Clinical Endocrinology
- Kew, M. C., Medicine
- Klugman, K. P., Clinical Microbiology
- Koornhof, H. J., Medical Microbiology
- Kramer, B., Anatomical Sciences
- Laburn, H. P., Physiology
- Lemmer, J., Oral Medicine and Periodontology
- Levin, S. E., Paediatrics
- Lownie, J. F., Maxillo-Facial and Oral Surgery
- McIntosh, W., ENT Surgery
- MacPhail, A. P., Medicine
- Maina, J. N., Anatomical Sciences
- Makgoba, M. W., Human Genetics
- Manga, P., Cardiology
- Mendelow, B. V., Haematology
- Meyers, A. M., Nephrology
- Milne, F. J., Medicine
- Mitchell, D., Physiology
- Mitchell, G., Physiology
- Moodley, I., Pharmacy
- Morrell, D. F., Anaesthesia
- Pantanowitz, D., Surgery
- Paterson, A. C., Anatomical Pathology
- Pettifor, J. M., Paediatrics
- Pick, W., Community Health
- Preston, C. B., Orthodontics
- Rudolph, M. J., Community Medicine
- Saadia, R., Surgery
- Schoub, B. D., Virology

SEGAL, I., Gastro-enterology
SHIPTON, E. A., Anaesthesia
SMEGO, R. A., Infectious Diseases
SONNENDECKER, E. W. W., Obstetrics and Gynaecology
SPARKS, B. L. W., Family Health
VAN GELDEREN, C. J., Obstetrics and Gynaecology
VILJOEN, D., Human Genetics
WADEE, A. A., Immunology

ATTACHED RESEARCH INSTITUTES

Bernard Price Institute of Geophysical Research: f. 1936; Dir Prof. C. WRIGHT.

Bernard Price Institute for Palaeontological Research: f. 1949; Dir Dr B. RUBIDGE.

Bone Research Laboratory: Dir Prof. U. RIPAMONTI.

Centre for Applicable Analysis and Theory: Dir Prof. D. S. LUBINSKY.

Centre for Applied Chemistry and Chemical Technology: Dir Prof. N. COVILLE.

Centre for Applied Legal Studies: Dir Prof. D. UNTERHALTER.

Centre for Continuing Education: Dir Prof. D. D. RUSSELL.

Centre for Differential Equations, Continuing Mechanics and Applications: Dir Dr F. MAHOMED.

Centre for Health Policy: Dir Dr H. SCHNEIDER.

Centre for Molecular Design: Dir Prof. J. BOEYENS.

Centre for Materials Research: Dir Prof. H. ERIC.

Centre for Non-Linear Studies: Dir Prof. W. D. HEISS.

Dental Research Institute: Dir Prof. P. CLEATON-JONES.

Ernest Oppenheimer Institute of Portuguese Studies: Dir (vacant).

Institute for Advanced Social Research: f. 1972; Dir Prof. C. VAN ONSELEN.

Research Centre for Labour Creation in Construction: Dir Prof. R. MCCUTCHEON.

San Heritage Research Centre: Dir Prof. J. LEWIS-WILLIAMS.

Schonland Research Centre for Nuclear Sciences: Dir Prof. V. HNIDZO.

UNIVERSITY OF ZULULAND

Private Bag X1001, KwaDlangezwa, KwaZulu, Natal 3886
Telephone: KwaDlangezwa (351) 93911
Telex: 631311
Fax: (351) 93735

Founded 1960. There is an extra-mural division at Umlazi (Durban)
State control
Language of instruction: English
Academic year: February to December

Chancellor: Hon. Mntwana M. G. BUTHELEZI
Rector: Prof. C. R. M. DLAMINI
Vice-Rectors: Prof. H.J. DREYER (Umlazi), Prof. A. J. THEMBELA (Academic Affairs and Research), J. J. POTGIETER (Financial Planning and Administration)
Librarian: Dr P. MINNAAR

Number of teachers: 293
Number of students: 7,978

Publications: *Paidonomia*, *Journal of Psychology*, *Unizul*.

DEANS

Faculty of Arts: Prof. L. M. MAGI
Faculty of Commerce and Administration: Prof. S. J. ZONDI
Faculty of Education: Prof. P. C. LUTHULI
Faculty of Law: Prof. A. E. B. DHLODHLO
Faculty of Science: Prof. D. N. BOSHOFF
Faculty of Theology: Prof. M. C. KITSHOFF

PROFESSORS

Faculty of Arts:
BURGER, W. D., Afrikaans
CUBBIN, A. E., History
DALRYMPLE, L. I., Drama
DE CLERCQ, J. L. W., Anthropology
DE VILLIERS, J., History
EDWARDS, S. D., Psychology
HLONGWANE, J. B., African Languages
HOOPER, M. J., English
HUTCHINGS, G. J. M., English
KLOPPER, R. M., Afrikaans
MAGI, L. M., Geography
MAKHANYA, E. M., Geography
MAPHALALA, S. J., History
MASHABA, T. G., Nursing Science
MEIHUIZEN, N. C. T., English
NZIMANDE, P. N., Nursing Science
PAKATI, E. R. V., Social Work
POTGIETER, P. J., Criminal Justice
VAN WYK, G. J. C., Philosophy
VERMEULEN, W. H., Library and Information Science
VILAKAZI, H. W., Sociology

Faculty of Commerce and Administration:
DU TOIT, M. K., Industrial Psychology
GORDHAN, Y. N., Accountancy and Auditing
KATONA, E., Economics
NDLOVU, A. M., Public Administration
VILJOEN, H. J., Accountancy and Auditing
ZONDI, S. J., Business Economics

Faculty of Education:
COETSEE, M. F., Human Movement Science
GABELA, R. V., Educational Planning and Administration
JACOBS, M., Didactics
MAGI, N. V., History of Education and Comparative Education
SIBAYA, P. T., Educational Psychology
URBANI, G., Educational Psychology

Faculty of Law:
DHLODHLO, A. E. B., Criminal and Procedural Law
ERASMUS, M. G., Zulu and Roman Law
VOLPE, P. L., Private Law

Faculty of Science:
BERMANSEDER, N., Engineering
BEESHAM, A., Applied Mathematics
BOSHOFF, D. N., Botany
CYRUS, D. P., Zoology
DAVIDSON, A. T., Physics
DUBE, T. A., Statistics
JEKOT, T., Mathematics
KELBE, B. E. M.-L., Hydrology
LUBOUT, P. C., Agriculture
SPOELSTRA, B., Physics
TERBLANCHE, S. E., Biochemistry
WEINERT, C. H. S. W., Chemistry
ZULU, M. M., Chemistry

Faculty of Theology:
KITSHOFF, M. C., Systematic Theology and History of Christianity
LOUBSER, J. A., Bibliological Studies
SONG, A., Missiology, Religious Studies and Practical Theology

ATTACHED INSTITUTE

Institute for Educational and Human Development: Dir S. W. D. DUBE.

Colleges

CAPE TECHNIKON

Tennant St, POB 652, Cape Town 8000
Telephone: (21) 460-3911
Telex: 52-1666
Fax: (21) 461-7564

Founded 1923, present name 1979

Languages of instruction: English and Afrikaans

Rector: Dr M. M. BALINTULO
Vice-Rectors: Prof. N. J. KOK, Dr M. A. TSHABALALA
Registrar: J. VAN ZYL
Director: Library Services: J. A. COETZEE

Library of 53,000 books, 1,596 periodicals
Number of lecturers: 351 full-time, 54 part-time
Number of students: 7,777 full-time, 2,314 part-time

Publication: *Rector's Report* (annually).

Faculties of human sciences, commercial sciences, engineering and natural sciences.

TECHNIKON FREE STATE

Private Bag X20539, Bloemfontein 9300
Telephone: (51) 507-3911
Fax: (51) 507-3199

Founded 1981

Rector: Prof. A. S. KOORTS
Senior Vice-Rector (Academic): Prof. C. A. J. VAN RENSBURG
Vice-Rectors: Prof. L. G. HECHTER (Planning and Development), Prof. J. M. B. HADEBE (Administration), J. J. HAMMAN (Finance)
Registrar: J. J. HAMMAN
Librarian: B. J. ERASMUS

Library of 45,000 vols
Number of teachers: 158 full-time, 331 part-time
Number of students: 7,500

DEANS

Faculty of Applied Sciences: Prof. B. J. FREY
Faculty of Management: Prof. P. G. LE ROUX
Faculty of Engineering: G. D. JORDAAN (acting)
Faculty of Human Sciences: Dr S. M. THULARE

TECHNIKON MANGOSUTHU

POB 12363, Jacobs 4026; Mangosuthu Highway, Umlazi, Durban
Telephone: (31) 907-7111
Fax: (31) 907-2892
E-mail: miken@julian.mantech.co.za

Founded 1978

Principal and Vice-Chancellor: Prof. A. M. NDLOVU
Vice-Principal (Administration): A. B. MAHOMED
Vice-Principal (Academic): Prof. E. C. ZINGU
Vice-Principal (Student Affairs): Prof. L. B. G. NDABANDABA

Library of 39,000 vols
Number of teachers: 154
Number of students: 5,197

DEANS

Faculty of Engineering: B. K. STEWART
Faculty of Human Sciences: Y. M. MBELE
Faculty of Natural Sciences: Dr L. E. OBERHOLSTER

TECHNIKON M.L. SULTAN

41/43 Centenary Rd, POB 1334, Durban 4000
Telephone: (31) 308-5111
Fax: (31) 308-5194

Founded 1946

Principal and Vice-Chancellor: Prof. B. C. GOBA
Deputy Vice-Chancellor (Academic): Prof. A. PADAYACHEE
Deputy Vice-Chancellor (Administration): A. CHEDDIE
Deputy Vice-Chancellor (Resources, Planning and Communications): U. S. PURMASIR
Assistant Vice-Chancellor (Student Services): Dr M. MANDEW

Assistant Vice-Chancellor (Campus Affairs): Dr P. Ndlovu

Library of 40,000 vols
Number of students: 7,500

Publications: *Technikon Calendar* (annually), *Annual Report*.

Tertiary level courses in applied sciences, art and design, building, civil, electrical, mechanical engineering, health sciences, hotel and catering administration, management administration, computer science, secretarial studies, communication and languages, technical teacher training.

TECHNIKON NATAL

POB 953, Durban 4000

Telephone: (31) 204-2111
Fax: (31) 223405
E-mail: postmaster@umfolozi.ntech.ac.za

Founded 1907, present name 1979

Chairman of Council: Rt Rev. R. Phillips
Principal and Vice-Chancellor: Prof. B. A. Khoapa
Vice-Principal (Academic): Dr A. L. Du Preez
Vice-Principal (Administrative): Dr R. Thabede
Vice-Principal (Student Affairs and Development): Adv. R. Jacobus
Vice-Principal (Pietermaritzburg): Prof. S. Zondi
Chief Librarian: N. Muller (acting)

Library of 81,000 vols, 1,001 periodical titles
Number of lecturers: 350 full-time
Number of students: 11,500

Publication: *New Perspectives* (annually).

Faculties of applied science, arts, commerce, design, engineering, health services.

TECHNIKON NORTHERN TRANSVAAL

Private Bag X07, Pretoria-North 0116

Telephone: (1214) 912225
Fax: (1214) 912227
E-mail: wilrey@tnt.ac.za

Founded 1979

Rector: Prof. G. S. K. Lenyai
Vice-Rectors: Dr W. F. Reyneke (Academic), M. A. Mashigo (Finance and Administration), Dr M. E. Collen (Student Services and Development)
Librarian: Ms M. A. Botha

Library of 40,000 vols
Number of teachers: 265
Number of students: 9,200

DEANS

Faculty of Engineering: M. T. Pudikabekwa
Faculty of Health and Food Technology: A. J. Aucamp
Faculty of Arts: L. Mosia
Faculty of Education: Dr L. R. van Staden
Faculty of Commerce: E. Ledwaba (acting)
Faculty of Economics and Management Sciences: A. L. van Staden

PENINSULA TECHNIKON

POB 1906, Bellville 7535, Cape Province

Telephone: (21) 959-6911
Telex: 9515617

Founded 1967

President: Brian Figaji
Vice-Rector (Academic): Dr Johan Tromp
Vice-Rector (Student Affairs): Vuyisa Tanga
Vice-Rector (Administration): Mauritz Slabbert

Library of 88,000 vols
Number of teachers: 221
Number of students: 8,855

Courses in electrical, mechanical and civil engineering, building and architecture, applied sciences, health sciences, business studies, dental technology, and education.

PORT ELIZABETH TECHNIKON

Private Bag X6011, Port Elizabeth 6000

Telephone: (41) 504-3911
Fax: (41) 533644

Founded 1881, present name 1979

Rector: Prof. H. C. Snyman
Vice-Rectors: Prof. I. N. Moutlana, Prof. B. K. Wells
Registrar: M. H. Grimbeek
Chief Director (Finance): S. G. Majiedt
Dean of Students: Dr J. H. Pretorius
Director of Library Services: M. Eales

Library of 42,000 vols
Number of lecturers: 320
Number of students: 10,291

Publications: *Rector's Annual Report, Impetus* (2 a year).

DEANS

Art and Design: Prof. N. Allen
Management: Dr N. J. Dorfling
Commerce and Government Studies: Dr H. Wissink
Communication Studies: Adv. N. G. Wood
Applied Science: D. W. Sharwood
Electrical Engineering: M. W. J. Wilson
Mechanical Engineering: Prof. H. L. T. Jeffery
Civil Engineering: J. J. van Wyk
Computer Studies: Dr E. F. Du Preez
Forestry: J. C. Scriba
Education: Dr J. H. Botha

TECHNIKON PRETORIA

Private Bag X 680, Pretoria 0001

Telephone: (12) 318-5911
Telegraphic Address: Techpret
Fax: (12) 318-5114

Founded 1906, present name 1979

Rector: Prof. D. J. J. van Rensburg
Vice-Rectors: (vacant)
Library Director: M. Swanepoel

Library of 70,000 vols
Number of lecturers: 626 full-time, 152 part-time
Number of students: 16,493

Publications: *Peritus* (4 a year), *School for Chemical Science Newsletter* (quarterly), *Student*.

DEANS

Economic Sciences: M. J. van der Merwe
Engineering: K. Vorster
Human Sciences: E. Dinkelman
Natural Sciences: Prof. R. Uys
Environmental Sciences: Prof. Botha

TECHNIKON SA

Private Bag X6, Florida 1710

Telephone: (11) 471-2000
Fax: (11) 471-2134

Founded 1980

Vice-Chancellor and Principal: Prof. A. J. H. Buitendacht
Vice-Principals: Prof. N. Morgan (Academic), Dr D. Moore (Academic), Prof. T. Links (Registrar)
Library Director: Dr J. C. Henning

Library of 150,000 vols
Number of teachers: 1,022
Number of students: 79,516

VAAL TRIANGLE TECHNIKON

Private Bag X021, Vanderbijlpark, 1900 Gauteng

Telephone: (16) 950-9262
Fax: (16) 950-9787
E-mail: marijke@vtt_nt.tritek.ac.za

Founded 1966, present name 1979

Rector: Prof. A. T. Mokadi
Vice-Rectors: P. A. Swanepoel (Academic), Dr R. Nayagar (Marketing and Development), Prof. I. N. Steyn (Administration)
Librarian: (vacant)

Library of 42,000 vols, 500 periodicals
Number of teachers: 299 full-time, 190 part-time
Number of students: 12,434

Faculties of Applied and Computer Sciences, Management Sciences, Engineering and Humanities.

Publication: *Tempo* (communication journal of the Technikon, 2 a year).

TECHNIKON WITWATERSRAND

POB 17011, Doornfontein 2028

Telephone: (11) 406-2911
Fax: 402-0475

Founded 1925, present name 1979

Chairman: Dr Roy Marcus
Vice-Chancellor and Principal: C. Swanepoel
Deputy Vice-Chancellor and Principal: H. van Ede
Registrars: D. Strauss, F. van den Berg
Library Director: J. van der Klashorst

Library of 35,000 vols
Number of teachers: 344 full-time, 483 part-time
Number of students: 9,498 full-time, 1,824 part-time

Publication: *Technibrief* (quarterly).

DEANS

Art and Design: P. J. Coetzee
Business Management: F. W. Schleicher
Engineering: W. F. Haupt
Health and Biotechnology: A. Hugo
Mining and Metallurgy: Dr R. V. R. Handfield-Jones

SPAIN

Learned Societies

GENERAL

Casa de Velázquez: Ciudad Universitaria, 28040 Madrid; tel. 91-455-15-80; fax 91-544-68-70; f. 1928; French school for research into all aspects of Iberia; grants senior fellowships to French artists or scholars to work in Spain; 34 mems; library of 90,000 vols, 800 current periodicals; Dir JEAN CANAVAGGIO; publ. *Mélanges*.

Dirección General de Relaciones Culturales y Científicas (Cultural and Scientific Relations Department): Ministerio de Asuntos Exteriores, Calle José Abascal 41, 28003 Madrid; tel. 91-441-16-00; fax 91-441-44-17; f. 1926; promotes Spanish culture and science in foreign countries; international cultural and scientific agreements, exchange of professors and lecturers, scholarships, etc.; Dir-Gen. SANTIAGO CABANAS.

Institut d'Estudis Catalans (Institute of Catalan Studies): Carrer del Carme 47, 08001 Barcelona; tel. 93-270-16-20; fax 93-270-11-80; f. 1907; incorporates sections History and Archaeology, Science and Technology, Philology, Philosophy and Social Sciences, and Biological Sciences; 122 ordinary mems, 41 corresp. mems; Pres. MANUEL CASTELLET I SOLANAS; Sec.-Gen. CARLES MIRALLES; publs *Anuari*, *Memòria*, *Arxius de les Seccions de Ciències*, *Estudis Romànics*, *Treballs de la Secció de Filosofia i Ciències Socials*, *Treballs de la Societat Catalana de Biologia*, *Corpus Vasorum Antiquorum*, *Corpus Vitrearum Medii Aevi*, *Cartografia de Briòfits*, *Biblioteca Filològica*, *Arxiu de Textos Catalans Antics*, *Lambard*, *Quaderns Agraris*, *Butlletí de la Institució Catalana d'Història Natural*, *Anuari de la Societat Catalana d'Economia*, *Treballs de Física*, *Treballs de la Societat Catalana de Geografia*, *Llengua i Literatura*, *Còrsia*, *Miscel·lània Litúrgica Catalana*, *Acta Numismàtica*, *Butlletí de les Societats Catalanes de Física, Química, Matemàtiques i Tecnologia*, *Butlletí i Revista de la Societat Catalana de Matemàtiques*.

Instituto de Cooperación con el Mundo Arabe, Mediterráneo y Países en Desarrollo (Institute for Co-operation with the Arab World, the Mediterranean and Developing Countries): Avda Reyes Católicos 4, 28040 Madrid; tel. 91-583-85-65; fax 91-583-82-19; technical assistance, economic co-operation, cultural activities, research grants, scholarships; library of 65,000 vols, 800 periodicals; Dir SENÉN FLORENSA PALAU; publs *Arabismo* (quarterly), *Awraq* (annually).

Instituto de Cooperación Iberoamericana (Institute for Ibero-American Co-operation): Avda de los Reyes Católicos 4, Ciudad Universitaria, 28040 Madrid; tel. 91-583-81-00; fax 91-583-83-10; f. 1946; promotes cultural understanding between Spain and America by organizing conferences, congresses, cultural exhibitions and university exchanges, scholarships for students; finances programmes of cultural, scientific, economic and technical co-operation; information department; Centre for Advanced Hispanic Studies; organizes programmes to diffuse the Spanish language and culture in the USA; radio, cinema and theatre unit; large library open to students; Spanish Library: see Libraries; Pres. FERNANDO VILLALONGA; Dir-Gen. JESÚS MANUEL GRACIA ALDAZ; Sec.-Gen. LUIS ESPINOSA; publs include *Cuadernos Hispanoamericanos* (monthly), *Pensamiento Iberoamericano* (2 a year).

Instituto de España (Institute of Spain): San Bernardo 49, 28015 Madrid; tel. 91-522-48-85; fax 91-521-06-54; f. 1938; the Institute's constituent academies form a 'Senado de la Cultura Española'; Pres. MARGARITA SALAS FALGUERAS; Sec.-Gen. PEDRO GARCÍA BARRENO; publ. *Anuario*.

Constituent academies:

Real Academia Española (Royal Spanish Academy): Calle de Felipe IV 4, 28014 Madrid; tel. 91-420-14-78; f. 1713; 46 mems, 41 Spanish corresp. mems; 4 Spanish-American corresp. mems; 52 foreign mems; Dir FERNANDO LÁZARO CARRETER; Sec. VÍCTOR GARCÍA DE LA CONCHA.

Real Academia de la Historia (Royal Academy of History): León 21, 28014 Madrid; tel. 91-429-06-11; fax 91-369-46-36; f. 1738; 36 mems; library of 350,000 vols, 180,000 MSS; Dir ANTONIO RUMEU DE ARMAS; Sec. ELOY BENITO RUANO; publs *Memorias*, *Memorial Histórico*, *Boletín*.

Real Academia de Bellas Artes de San Fernando (San Fernando Royal Academy of Fine Arts): Alcalá 13, 28014 Madrid; tel. 91-532-15-46; fax 91-523-15-99; f. 1752; 54 mems; library of 40,000 vols; attached museum: see Museums and Art Galleries; Dir RAMÓN GONZÁLEZ DE AMEZÚA; Gen. Sec. ANTONIO IGLESIAS ALVAREZ; publ. *Boletín* (2 a year).

Real Academia de Ciencias Exactas, Físicas y Naturales (Royal Academy of Exact, Physical and Natural Sciences): Valverde 22 y 24, 28004 Madrid; tel. 91-521-25-29; fax 91-532-57-16; f. 1847; sections of Exact Sciences (Pres. GREGORIO MILLÁN BARBANY, Sec. FRANCISCO JAVIER GIRÓN), Physical Sciences (Pres. LUIS GUTIÉRREZ JODRA, Sec. MIGUEL A. ALARIO FRANCO), Natural Sciences (Pres. MANUEL R. LLAMAS MADURGA, Sec. P. GARCÍA BARRENO); 42 mems, 60 Spanish corresp. mems, 80 foreign corresp. mems; Pres. ANGEL MARTÍN MUNICIO; Sec.-Gen. JOSÉ J. ETAYO MIQUEO; publs *Memoria*, *Revista*, *Anuario*.

Real Academia de Ciencias Morales y Políticas (Royal Academy of Moral and Political Sciences): Casa de los Lujanes, Plaza de la Villa 2, 28005 Madrid; tel. 91-548-13-30; fax 91-548-19-75; e-mail secre@racmyp.es; f. 1857; 40 mems, 14 Spanish corresp. mems, 35 foreign corresp. mems; library of 95,000 vols, 340 periodicals; Pres. ENRIQUE FUENTES QUINTANA; Sec. SALUSTIANO DEL CAMPO URBANO; publs *Anales* (1 a year), *Papeles y Memorias* (4 a year).

Real Academia Nacional de Medicina (Royal National Academy of Medicine): Arrieta 12, 28013 Madrid; tel. 91-547-03-18; fax 91-547-03-20; f. 1732; 50 mems, 90 Spanish corresp. mems, 57 foreign corresp. mems; Pres. HIPÓLITO DURÁN SACRISTÁN; Sec. (vacant); publ. *Anales*.

Real Academia de Jurisprudencia y Legislación (Royal Academy of Jurisprudence and Law): Marqués de Cubas 13, 28014 Madrid; tel. 91-522-20-69; fax 91-523-40-21; f. 1730; 40 mems; library of 35,000 vols; Pres. JUAN BERCHMANS VALLET DE GOYTISOLO; Sec. JOSÉ MA. CASTÁN VÁZQUEZ; publ. *Anales*.

Real Academia de Farmacia (Royal Academy of Pharmacy): Farmacia 11, 28004 Madrid; tel. 91-531-03-07; f. 1589; 42 mems; library of 17,600 vols; Dir RAFAEL CADÓRNIGA CARRO; Permanent Sec. ANTONIO PORTOLÉS ALONSO; publ. *Anales* (quarterly).

Instituto de Estudios Norteamericanos (Institute of North American Studies): Vía Augusta 123, 08006 Barcelona; tel. 93-209-27-11; fax 93-202-06-90; f. 1952; cultural exchange programmes, lectures, discussions, musical events, theatre, cinema, art exhibitions, seminars, etc.; courses in English and in American Studies; runs an academic counselling service and is the official centre for examinations for students entering US universities; *c.* 400 mems; 18,000 students; library of *c.* 10,000 vols; Pres. ALFREDO SNEYERS; Exec. Dir MARCIA A. GRANT.

Instituto Egípcio de Estudios Islámicos (Egyptian Institute of Islamic Studies): Francisco de Asís Mendez Casariego 1, 28002 Madrid; tel. 91-563-94-68; fax 91-563-86-40; e-mail iegipcio@mundivia.es; f. 1950; 6 mems; library of 23,000 vols, 300 periodicals; Dir SOLIMAN EL-ATTAR; publ. *Revista* (2 a year).

Real Academia de Bellas Artes y Ciencias Históricas de Toledo (Toledo Royal Academy of Fine Arts and Historical Sciences): Calle Esteban Illán 9, Toledo; tel. 925-21-43-22; f. 1916; 25 mems; library of 4,000 vols; Dir Dr FÉLIX DEL VALLE Y DIAZ; Sec. LUIS ALBA GONZÁLEZ; Librarian MARIO ARELLANO GARCÍA; publ. *Toletum*.

Real Academia de Ciencias y Artes de Barcelona (Barcelona Royal Academy of Science and Arts): Rambla de los Estudios 115, 08002 Barcelona; tel. 93-317-05-36; fax 93-301-16-56; f. 1764; 900 mems; attached observatory: see Research Institutes; library of 100,000 vols; Pres. Dr RAMÓN PARÉS FARRÁS; Vice-Pres. Dr MANUEL BALLESTER BOIX; Sec. Dr MANUEL PUIGCERVER ZANÓN; Librarian Dr J. CASTELLS GUARDIOLA; publs *Nómina*, *Memorias*.

Real Academia de Córdoba de Ciencias, Bellas Letras y Nobles Artes (Royal Academy of Science, Literature and Fine Arts): Ambrosio de Morales 9, 14003 Córdoba; f. 1810; 35 mems, 35 corresp. mems; Dir Dr MANUEL PELÁEZ DEL ROSAL; Sec. JOAQUIN CRIADO COSTA; publs *Boletín* (2 a year), *Anuario* (1 a year), monographs, scientific, historical and literary works.

Real Academia de Doctores: Calle de San Bernardo 49, 28015 Madrid; tel. 91-531-95-22; fax 91-531-95-22; f. 1920; sections of Philosophy and Literature, of Sciences, of Law, of Medicine, of Pharmacy, of Politics, Economics and Commerce, of Engineering, of Architecture, of Theology, of Veterinary Science; 8 hon. mems, 104 mems, 114 national corresp., 86 foreign corresp. mems; Pres. Prof. GUSTAVO VILLAPALOS SALAS; First Vice-Pres. Dr JOSÉ MARÍA BARAJAS GARCÍA ANSORENA; Second Vice-Pres. ANTONIO LÓPEZ GOMEZ; Sec.-Gen. Dr GUILLERMO SUÁREZ FERNÁNDEZ.

Real Academia Gallega (Royal Galician Academy): Tabernas 11, 15001 La Coruña; tel. 981-20-73-08; fax 981-20-73-08; f. 1905; 25 mems; library of 42,000 vols, including valuable collection of books on Galicia; Pres. FRANCISCO FERNANDEZ DEL RIEGO; Sec. CONSTANTINO GARCÍA; Librarian ANTONIO GIL MERINO; publs *Caderna da Lingua*, *Diccionario da Lingua Galega*, etc.

Real Academia Hispano-Americana (Royal Spanish-American Academy): Calle Almirante Vierna 14, Apdo 16, 11009 Cádiz; f. 1910; 29 mems; Dir ANTONIO OROZCO ACUAVIVA; Sec.-Gen. JUAN I. VARELA GILABERT; publ. *Anuario*.

AGRICULTURE, FISHERIES AND VETERINARY SCIENCE

Institut Agrícola Català de Sant Isidre (Catalan Agricultural Institute): Plaça Sant Josep Oriol 4, 08002 Barcelona; tel. 93-301-17-40; fax 93-317-30-05; f. 1851; 2,000 mems; library of 16,000 vols, 200 periodicals; Pres. BALDIRI ROS; Sec.-Gen. FERRAN DE MULLER; publs *La Drecera* (monthly), *Calendari del Pagés* (annually).

Real Academia de Ciencias Veterinarias de España (Royal Academy of Veterinary Sciences of Spain): C/o Prof. Dr Mariano Illera Martín, Departamento de Fisiología, Facultad de Veterinaria, Ciudad Universitaria, 28040 Madrid; tel. 91-394-38-67; fax 91-394-38-64; f. 1975; 113 mems; Pres. Prof. Dr MARIANO ILLERA MARTÍN; Sec. Dr JAIME GARCÍA HERNÁNDEZ; publ. *Anales* (1 a year).

Sociedad Veterinaria de Zootecnia de España (Spanish Veterinary Society of Zootechnics): Isabel la Católica 12, Madrid; tel. 91-247-18-38; fax 91-541-69-02; f. 1945; zootechnical science, animal husbandry, ethology, animal behaviour, animal genetics, economics, animal production; 250 ordinary mems, 3,500 corresp. mems; library of 5,000 vols; Pres. Prof. Dr C. L. DE CUENCA; Technical Sec.-Dir. Prof. Dr J. M. CID DIAZ (acting); publ. *Zootechnia* (quarterly).

ARCHITECTURE AND TOWN PLANNING

Col·legi d'Arquitectes de Catalunya (Association of Catalan Architects): Plaça Nova 5, 08002 Barcelona; tel. 93-301-50-00; fax 93-412-39-64; f. 1931; 5,174 mems; library of 80,392 vols; Sec. PERE SERRA AMENGUAL; publs *Quaderns d'Arquitectura i Urbanisma*, *Informació i debat*.

Subdirección General de Arquitectura: Dirección General de la Vivienda, la Arquitectura y el Urbanismo, Ministerio de Fomento, Paseo de la Castellana 67, 28071 Madrid; tel. 91-597-83-87; fax 91-597-85-10; e-mail jserra@mfom.es; f. 1940; development of technical regulations and recommendations concerning building technology and quality control; test laboratory; technical assistance to the Construction Board of the National Standards Organization; 120 mems; Sub-Dir-Gen. GERARDO MINGO; publs *Normas Tecnológicas de la Edificación*, *Normas Básicas de la Edificación*.

BIBLIOGRAPHY, LIBRARY SCIENCE AND MUSEOLOGY

Asociación Amics dels Museus de Catalunya (Friends of the Catalan Museums Association): Palau de la Virreina, La Rambla 99, Barcelona; tel. 93-301-43-79; fax 93-318-94-21; f. 1933; 800 mems, 6 hon., 81 associates, 52 others; Pres. JOSEP MA GARRUT; Vice-Pres. LOLA MITJANS; Sec.-Gen. FAUSTO SERRA; publs *Historiales*, monographs.

Asociación Español de Archiveros, Bibliotecarios, Museólogos y Documentalistas: Calle Recoletos 5-3°-izqda, 28001 Madrid; tel. 91-575-17-27; fax 91-575-17-27; f. 1949; 1,616 mems; groups all specialists working in the country's archive services, libraries, museums and documentation services; has regional branches in Galicia, Aragón, Castilla-La Mancha and Murcia; Pres. JULIA M. RODRÍGUEZ BARRERO; Sec. CARMEN CAYETANO MARTIN; publs *Boletín*, many irregular works.

ECONOMICS, LAW AND POLITICS

Centro de Estudios Constitucionales (Centre for Constitutional Studies): Plaza de la Marina Española 9, 28071 Madrid; tel. 91-541-50-00; fax 91-247-85-49; f. 1977, having merged with Instituto de Estudios Políticos; organizes courses, lectures and seminars on political, constitutional and administrative questions; library of 80,000 vols; Dir CARMEN IGLESIAS CANO; Man. DANIEL VILLAGRA BLANCO; publs *Revista de Estudios Políticos* (4 a year), *Revista Española de Derecho Constitucional* (3 a year), *Revista de Administración Pública* (3 a year), *Revista de Derecho Comunitario Europeo* (2 a year), *Revista de Derecho Privado y Constitución* (1 a year).

Colegio de Abogados de Barcelona (Barcelona Bar Association): Calle Mallorca 283, 08037 Barcelona; tel. 93-487-28-14; fax 93-487-15-89; f. 1832; 14,000 mems; library: see Libraries and Archives; Dean EUGENI GAY MONTALVO; Sec. XAVIER PUIGDOLLERS NOBLOM; publ. *Revista Jurídica de Catalunya*.

Col·legi de Notaris (College of Notaries): Carrer Notariat 4, 08001 Barcelona; tel. 93-317-48-00; 346 mems; Dean R. FOLLÍA CAMPS.

Instituto Nacional de Administración Pública (National Institute of Public Administration): Atocha 106, 28012 Madrid; tel. 91-349-32-41; fax 91-349-32-87; e-mail biblioteca@inap.map.es; f. 1940; library of 140,000 vols, 2,300 periodicals; Pres. ENRIQUE ALVAREZ CONDE; publs *Gestión y Análysis de Políticas Públicas* (4 a year), *Cuadernos de Derecho Publico* (4 a year), *Revista Iberoamericana de Administración Pública* (2 a year).

Instituto Nacional de Estadística (National Statistical Office): Paseo de la Castellana 183, 28046 Madrid; tel. 91-279-93-00; f. 1945; library of 150,000 vols; Dir JOSÉ QUEVEDO; publs *Anuario Estadístico de España*, *Censos de la Población y de la Vivienda*, *Boletín Mensual de Estadística*, *Censo Agrario*, *Estadística Industrial*, *Indicadores de coyuntura*, *Revista 'Estadística Española'*, etc.

Real Sociedad Económica de Amigos del País de Tenerife (Royal Economic Society of Friends of Tenerife): La Laguna de Tenerife, Calle San Agustín 23, Tenerife, Canary Is; f. 1777; 490 mems; sections: *Intereses Morales, Intereses Materiales, Intereses Culturales, Intereses Económicos, Prensa y Propaganda*; library of 11,000 vols; museum; Dir Marqués de Villanueva del Prado D. MANUEL DE QUINTANA; publs works relating to the Canary Islands.

EDUCATION

Asociación Iberoamericana de Educación Superior a Distancia (Ibero-American Association for Open University Education): UNED, Bravo Murillo 38, 28015 Madrid; tel. 91-398-65-46; fax 91-398-80-86; e-mail relint@bm.uned.es; f. 1981; 53 member universities; Pres. Dr JENARO COSTAS; Dir/Sec. Dr CARLOS RODRIGO ILLERA.

Conferencia de Rectores de las Universidades Españolas (CRUE): UNED – Edificio Interfacultativo, Ciudad Universitaria s/n, 28040 Madrid; tel. 91-398-76-25; fax 91-398-79-06; e-mail sgcrue@cu.uned.es; f. 1978; fosters links between the universities, studies and analyses university problems, acts as link between the University Council and the state universities; 37 mems; library of 497 vols; Pres. Prof. CARLES SOLÀ I FERRANDO; Sec. FELIX GARCÍA LAUSÍN.

Consejo de Universidades: Ciudad Universitaria s/n, 28040 Madrid; tel. 91-449-74-37; f. 1983; consists of the rectors of the 31 public univs and 21 others; Pres. The Min. of Education and Science; Sec.-Gen. FRANCISCO MICHAVILA.

Consejo General de Colegios Oficiales de Doctores y Licenciados en Filosofía y Letras y en Ciencias (National Council of Official Colleges of Doctors and Licentiates in Philosophy, Letters and Science): Bolsa 11, 2°, 28012 Madrid; tel. 91-522-45-97; f. 1944; 55,800 mems; Pres. Dr JOSÉ LUÍS NEGRO FERNÁNDEZ; Sec.-Gen. Dr ROBERTO SALMERÓN SANZ; publs information bulletins of the colleges in Barcelona, Bilbao, Madrid, Seville and Valladolid.

Fundación Juan March: Castelló 77, 28006 Madrid; tel. 91-435-42-40; fax 91-576-34-20; f. 1955; awards scholarships and research grants to Spanish professors and scholars in molecular biology and other fields; organizes cultural, artistic and musical activities; library dealing with 20th-century Spanish theatre and contemporary Spanish music; Pres. JUAN MARCH DELGADO; Gen. Dir JOSÉ LUIS YUSTE GRIJALBA; publs *Boletín Informativo* (monthly), *Anales* (annual report), *Saber Leer* (book review, monthly).

FINE AND PERFORMING ARTS

Asociación Española de Pintores y Escultores (Association of Spanish Artists and Sculptors): Infantas 30, 28004 Madrid; tel. 91-522-49-61; fax 91-522-55-08; e-mail genea@lander.es; f. 1910; Pres. JESÚS CÁMARA; Sec. MARCIA OLIVER; publs *Gaceta de las Bellas Artes*, *Catálogo Salón de Otoño*.

Ateneo Científico, Literario y Artístico (Scientific, Literary and Artistic Athenaeum): Calle Cifuentes 25, Mahón, Minorca, Balearic Is; f. 1905; library of 15,000 vols; 630 mems; Pres. FRANCESC TUTZÓ BENNASAR; Sec. MIGUEL ANGEL LIMÓN PONS; publ. *Revista de Menorca* (quarterly).

Ateneo Científico, Literario y Artístico (Scientific, Literary and Artistic Athenaeum): Calle del Prado 21, 28014 Madrid; tel. 91-429-62-51; f. 1820; 6,500 mems; library of 800,000 vols; Pres. JOSÉ PRAT GARCÍA; Gen. Sec. DAVID M. RIVAS INFANTE.

Ateneu Barcelonès (Barcelona Athenaeum): Carrer Canuda 6, 08002 Barcelona; tel. 93-317-49-04; fax 93-317-15-25; f. 1860; library: see Libraries; 3,100 mems; governed by a Directorate; Pres. HERIBERT BARRERA I COSTA; Sec.-Gen. ISIDOR CONSUL I. GIRIBET.

Comité Nacional Español del Consejo Internacional de la Musica (National Cttee of the International Music Council): Martín de los Héroes 56, 28001 Madrid; Sec.-Gen. ANTONIO IGLESIAS.

Departamento de Historia del Arte 'Diego Velázquez': Centro de Estudios Históricos, Duque de Medinaceli 6, 3°, 28014 Madrid; tel. 91-429-06-26; fax 91-369-09-40; f. 1939; attached to the Consejo Superior de Investigaciones Científicas (CSIC); history of Spanish art, hispanoamerican art and history of European art in Spain; 9 mems; library of *c.* 50,000 vols, 500 periodicals, 200,000 photographs; Head Dr WIFREDO RINCÓN GARCÍA; publ. *Archivo Español de Arte* (quarterly).

Institut Amatller d'Art Hispànic (Institute of Hispanic Art): Passeig de Gràcia 41, 08007 Barcelona; tel. 93-216-01-75; fax 93-487-58-27; f. 1942; library of 22,000 vols; collection of 300,000 photographs; Dir SANTIAGO ALCOLEA-BLANCH.

Institut del Teatre (Theatrical Institute): Carrer Sant Pere més baix 7, 08003 Barcelona;

tel. 93-268-2078; fax 93-268-1070; e-mail i .teatre@diba.es; f. 1913; drama and dance school; documentation and research information centre; library of 150,000 vols; Dir PAU MONTERDE.

Real Academia de Bellas Artes de la Purísima Concepción (Royal Academy of Fine Arts): Calle del Rastro, Casa de Cervantes, 47001 Valladolid; tel. 983-30-88-10; fax 983-39-07-03; f. 1746; 30 mems; Pres. JAVIER LÓPEZ DE URIBE Y LAYA; Sec. JESUS URREA FERNANDEZ.

Real Academia de Bellas Artes de San Telmo (Royal Academy of Fine Arts): Málaga; f. 1849; 28 mems; Pres. JOSÉ LUIS ESTRADA SEGALERVA; Secs BALTASAR PEÑA HINOJOSA, LUIS BONO HERNÁNDEZ DE SANTAOLALLA.

Real Academia de Bellas Artes de Santa Isabel de Hungría (Royal Fine Arts Academy): Abades 14, 41004 Seville; f. 1660; research, courses and exhibitions; 36 mems; library of 3,800 vols; Pres. ANTONIO DE LA BANDA Y VARGAS; Sec.-Gen. RAMÓN CORZO SÁNCHEZ; Librarian IGNACIO OTERO NIETO; publs *Boletín de Bellas Artes* (annually), *Temas de Estética y Arte* (annually).

Real Academia de Nobles y Bellas Artes de San Luis (Royal Academy of Fine Arts): Plaza de Los Sitios 6, Zaragoza; f. 1792; library of 5,517 vols; composed of 28 Academicians, 84 Spanish and 28 foreign corresponding members and variable number of delegates; comprises 5 sections (architecture, sculpture, painting, music, literature) and 3 permanent committees; Pres. ANGEL CANELLAS LÓPEZ; Sec.-Gen. JORGE ALBAREDA AGÜERAS; Librarian FRANCISCO OLIVÁN BAILE; publs *Boletín* (irregularly), catalogues, works.

Real Sociedad Fotográfica Española (Royal Spanish Photographic Society): Calle del Príncipe 16, 28012 Madrid; tel. 91-522-43-00; f. 1899; 1,320 mems; library of 3,780 vols; Pres. MARÍA TERESA GUTIERREZ BARRANCO; Sec.-Gen. ANDRÉS MASCARAQUE SANZ; publ. *Boletín* (monthly).

Reial Acadèmia Catalana de Belles Arts de Sant Jordi (Royal Catalan Academy of Fine Arts): Casa Llotja, Passeig d'Isabel II 1 (2°), 08003 Barcelona; tel. 93-319-24-32; fax 93-319-02-16; f. 1849; library of 8,000 vols; Pres. JOAN BASSEGODA NONELL; Sec.-Gen. LEOPOLDO GIL NEBOT; Librarian EDUARD RIPOLL PERELLO; publs historical, literary and artistic works.

Sociedad de Ciencias, Letras y Artes 'El Museo Canario' (Scientific, Literary and Art Society): Dr Chil 25, 35001 Las Palmas, Canary Is; f. 1879; incorporated in the Consejo Superior de Investigaciones Científicas (*q.v.*); museum: see Museums; laboratories; important library (60,000 vols), archives and periodicals relating to the history and primitive peoples of the Canary Islands; Pres. LOTHAR SIEMENS HERNANDEZ; publ. *El Museo Canario* (annually).

HISTORY, GEOGRAPHY AND ARCHAEOLOGY

Arxiu Històric de la Ciutat de Barcelona: Casa de l'Ardiaca, Carrer Santa Llúcia 1, 08002 Barcelona; tel. 93-318-11-95; fax 93-317-83-27; f. 1917; archives of municipal records and local press; library: see Libraries; the Archives undertake historical research on Barcelona, organize courses, lectures, exhibitions; Dir MANUEL ROVIRA SOLÀ.

Deutsches Archaeologisches Institut (German Archaeological Institute): Serrano 159, 28002 Madrid; tel. 91-561-09-04; fax 91-564-00-54; f. 1943; library of 50,000 vols; archive of photographs; Dir Prof. Dr TILO ULBERT; publs *Madrider Mitteilungen* (annually), *Madrider Forschungen*, *Madrider Beiträge*, *Hispania Antiqua*, *Studien über frühe Tierknochenfunde von der Iberischen Halbinsel*.

Instituto Arqueológico del Ayuntamiento de Madrid (Archaeological Institute of the City of Madrid): Enrique D'Almonte 1, 28028 Madrid; tel. 91-409-61-65; fax 91-409-62-09; f. 1953; conducts research into the archaeology of Madrid and environs; library of 8,500 vols; laboratory and museum; Dir ENRIQUE DE CARRERA HONTANA; publ. *Estudios de Prehistoria y Arqueología Madrileñas* (annually).

Instituto de Historia y Cultura Naval (Institute of Naval History and Culture): Calle Juan de Mena 1, 28071 Madrid; tel. 91-379-50-50; f. 1942; associated with the Consejo Superior de Investigaciones Científicas; for library see entry under Museo Naval; Dir Contralmirante JOSÉ IGNACIO GONZÁLEZ-ALLER HIERRO.

Instituto Geográfico Nacional (National Geographical Institute): Calle del General Ibáñez de Ibero 3, 28003 Madrid; tel. 91-597-94-10; fax 91-579-97-53; f. 1870; 1,200 mems; library of 28,000 vols; geodesy and geophysics, cartography, map printing, seismology, geophysics, astronomy, runs the National Observatory (see under Research Institutes); Dir-Gen. JOSÉ ANTONIO CANAS TORRES; publs *Boletín Astronómico*, *Anuario del Observatorio Astronómico*, *Anuario de Geomagnetismo*, *Boletines Sísmicos*, *Boletín Informativo del IGN*.

Real Sociedad Geográfica (Royal Geographic Society): Calle Pinar 25, 28006 Madrid; tel. 91-561-78-25; fax 91-562-55-67; f. 1876; geography and earth sciences; 433 mems; library of 10,375 vols and 12,525 booklets; Pres. Dr RODOLFO NUÑEZ DE LAS CUEVAS; Perm. Sec. Dr JOAQUÍN BOSQUE MAUREL; publs *Boletin* (annually), *Hoja Informativa* (monthly).

Reial Societat Arqueologica Tarraconense (Archaeological Society): Calle Mayor 35, Apdo 573, Tarragona; tel. 977-23-37-89; fax 977-23-93-07; f. 1844; Iberian, Roman and early Christian archaeology; ancient, medieval, modern and contemporary history of Tarragona; 601 mems; library of 18,000 vols; Pres. RAFAEL GABRIEL COSTA; Sec. MANEL GÜELL JUNKERT; publs *Butlleti Arqueologic* (quarterly), *Citerior*.

Servicio de Investigación Prehistórica de la Excelentísima Diputación Provincial (Prehistoric Research Society of the Province of Valencia): Calle de la Corona 36, 46003 Valencia; tel. 96-388-35-87; f. 1927; palaeolithic, neolithic, Bronze and Iron Ages, Iberian and colonial exhibits, prehistoric Americana; 30 mems; library: specialized 40,000 vols; Dir BEGOÑA CARRASCOSA MOLINER; publs *Serie de Trabajos Varios*, *Archivo de Prehistoria Levantina*.

Societat Arqueològica Lul-liana (Archaeological Society): Monti-Sion 9, 07001 Palma de Mallorca, Balearic Is; tel. 971-21-39-12; f. 1880; 600 mems; library of 20,000 vols; museum; Pres. MARIA BARCELÓ CRESPÍ; Sec. GABRIEL ENSENYAT PUJOL; publ. *Boletín* (annually).

LANGUAGE AND LITERATURE

Asociación de Escritores y Artistas Españoles (Writers' and Artists' Association): Calle de Leganitos 10, 28013 Madrid; tel. 91-559-90-67; fax 91-559-90-67; f. 1872; 1,014 mems; library of 3,000 vols; Pres. JOSÉ GERARDO MANRIQUE DE LARA; Dir and Gen. Sec. JOSÉ LÓPEZ MARTÍNEZ.

Euskaltzaindia/Real Academia de la Lengua Vasca (Academy of the Basque Language): Plaza Barria, 15, 48005 Bilbao; tel. 94-415-81-55; fax 94-415-81-44; delegations in: Hernani 15, 20004 Donostia/San Sebastián 4; Conde Oliveto 2, 31002 Iruñea/Pamplona; San Antonio 41, 01005 Vitoria/Gasteiz; f. 1919; research into and conservation of the Basque language; 24 mems and an indeterminate number of honorary and corresponding mems; library of 70,000 vols specializing in philology and linguistics, principally of the Basque language; Pres. JEAN HARITSCHELHAR; Vice-Pres. ENDRIKE KNÖRR; Sec. PATXI GOENAGA; Vice-Sec. JOSÉ LUIS LIZUNDIA; Treas. JOSÉ ANTONIO ARANA MARTIJA; Librarian JOSÉ ANTONIO ARANA MARTIJA; publs *Euskera* (2 a year), *Iker*, *Jagon*, *Euskararen Lekukoak*, *Onomasticon Vasconiae*, *Hiztegiak eta Izendegiak / Diccionarios y Nomenclator* (occasionally), *Soziolinguistika Saila / Estudios de Sociolingüística* (occasionally), *Gramatika eta Metodoak / Gramáticas y Métodos* (occasionally).

Instituto Aula de 'Mediterráneo': Universidad de Valencia; f. 1942; 545 mems; Dir Dr F. SÁNCHEZ-CASTAÑER; publs *Mediterráneo*, *Unión de Literatura* (quarterly).

Real Academia Sevillana de Buenas Letras (Seville Royal Academy of Belles Lettres): Abades 14, 41004 Seville; tel. 95-422-52-00; f. 1751; 30 mems, 5 honorary, 100 corresponding; library of 10,000 vols; Dir EDUARDO YBARRA HIDALGO; Sec. Dr ROGELIO REYES CANÓ; Librarian ALFREDO JIMÉNEZ NÚÑEZ; publ. *Boletín* (annually); monographs.

Reial Acadèmia de Bones Lletres (Royal Academy of Belles Lettres): Bisbe Caçador 3, 08002 Barcelona; tel. 93-310-23-49; fax 93-310-23-49; f. 1700; 36 mems; Pres. EDUARD RIPOLL; Sec. FREDERIC UDINA; Librarian FRANCISCO MARSÁ; publs *Boletín*, *Memorias*, etc.

Seminario de Filología Vasca 'Julio de Urquijo' ('Julio de Urquijo' Seminary of Basque Philology): Palacio de la Diputación Foral de Guipúzcoa, San Sebastián; f. 1953 to encourage the use and scientific study of the Basque language; attached to the University of País Vasco, Vitoria; Dir IBON SARASOLA; publ. *Anuario*.

Sociedad General de Autores y Editores (General Society of Authors and Publishers): Fernando VI 4, Apdo 484, 28004 Madrid; f. 1932; library of 22,000 vols, relating to the theatre, music (scores) and cinema only; Dir.-Gen. ENRIQUE LORAS GARCÍA; Sec.-Gen. CARLOS FERNÁNDEZ-LERGA GARRALDA; publ. *Boletín* (quarterly).

MEDICINE

Academia de Ciencias Médicas de Bilbao (Academy of Medicine): Lersundi 9-1°, Apdo 5073, 48080 Bilbao; tel. 94-423-37-68; f. 1895; 1,300 mems; library of 9,070 vols; Pres. Dr CIRIACO AGUIRRE ERRASTI; Sec.-Gen. Dr Fco JAVIER GARRÓS GARAY; publ. *Gaceta Médica de Bilbao* (quarterly).

Acadèmia de Ciències Mèdiques de Catalunya i de Balears (Catalonian Academy of Medicine): Paseo de la Bonanova 47, 08017 Barcelona; f. 1898; 14,000 mems; Pres. JOAQUIM RAMIS CORIS; Sec. JOSEP REIG VILALLONGA; publs *Annals de Medicina*, *Monografies Mèdiques*.

Academia Española de Dermatología y Sifilografía (Spanish Academy of Dermatology and Syphilography): Sandoval 7, Madrid; f. 1909; 435 mems, 51 hon., 3 corresp.; library of 900 vols; Hon. Pres Prof. JOSÉ GÓMEZ ORBANEJA, Prof. JOSÉ GAY PRIETO; Pres D. JOSÉ CABRE PIERA; Vice-Pres Dr FÉLIX CONTRERAS DUEÑAS, JOSÉ MASCARO BALLESTER; Sec.-Gen. RAMÓN MORÁN LÓPEZ; Librarian Dr JUAN JOSÉ APELLANIZ FERNÁNDEZ; brs in Catalonia, Valencia, Biscay-Navarre-Aragon, Eastern Andalusia, Western Andalusia and Canary Islands; publ. *Actas Dermosifiliográficas*.

Academia Médico-Quirúrgica Española (Spanish Academy of Medicine and Surgery): Villanueva 11, 28001 Madrid; f. 1891; 492 mems; Pres. Prof. EDUARDO ARIAS VALLEJO; Sec. Dr JULIO MÚÑIZ GONZÁLEZ; publ. *Anales*.

Consejo General de Colegios Oficiales de Farmacéuticos (General Council of Official Colleges of Pharmacists): Villanueva 11-4°, 28001 Madrid; f. 1942; 13,500 mems; Pres. ERNESTO MARCO CAÑIZARES; publ. *Boletín de Información*.

Organización Médica Colegial – Consejo General de Colegios Médicos de España (General Council of Medical Colleges): Villanueva 11, Madrid; f. 1930; 21 mems; Pres. JOSÉ FORNES RUIZ; publs *Boletín Formativo e Informativo* (monthly), *Medicina de España*.

Real Academia de Medicina y Cirugía de Palma de Mallorca (Royal Academy of Medicine and Surgery): Morey 20, Palma de Mallorca; 19 mems; Pres. JOSÉ SAMPOL VIDAL; Sec. SANTIAGO FORTEZA FORTEZA.

Sociedad de Pediatría de Madrid y Castilla La Mancha (Paediatrics Society of Madrid and Castilla La Mancha): Villanueva 11, 28001 Madrid; f. 1913; 750 mems; Pres. M. MORO SERRANO; Sec.-Gen. L. M. ANTON RODRÍGALVAREZ.

Sociedad Española de Patología Digestiva y de la Nutrición (Society of Digestive and Nutritional Diseases): Almagro 38, Madrid; f. 1933; 800 mems; Pres. Dr HELIODORO G. MOGENA; publ. *Revista Española de las Enfermedades del Aparato Digestivo y de la Nutrición*.

Sociedad Española de Radiología Médica (Society of Medical Radiology): Goya 38, 3° piso, 28001 Madrid; f. 1946; 3,250 mems, 200 founder mems; Pres. Dr JOAQUÍN FERNÁNDEZ CRUZ; publ. *Radiología* (every 2 months).

NATURAL SCIENCES

General

Academia de Ciencias Exactas, Físicas, Químicas y Naturales (Academy of Exact, Physical, Chemical and Natural Sciences): Facultad de Ciencias, Ciudad Universitaria, Zaragoza; f. 1916; comprises sections on Exact Sciences, Physics and Chemistry, and Natural Sciences; Pres. HORACIO MARCO MOLL; Sec. MARIANO GASCA; Librarian HORACIO MARCO MOLL; mems 40; corresponding 7; publ. *Revista* (quarterly).

Sociedad de Ciencias 'Aranzadi' Zientzi Elkartea: Museo de San Telmo, Plaza de I. Zuloaga, 20003 San Sebastián; tel. 943-42-29-45; fax 943-42-13-16; f. 1947; to encourage interest in the various branches of natural science, prehistory and ethnology; 1,944 mems; Pres. JESÚS ALTUNA; Sec. FRANCISCO ETXEBERRIA; publs *Munibe Antropologia – Arkeologia*, *Munibe Ciencias Naturales – Natur Zientziak*, *Anuario de Eusko Folklore* (annually), *Aranzadiana* (all annually).

Biological Sciences

Asociación Española de Entomología (Spanish Entomological Association): Facultad de Ciencias Biológicas, Universidad de Valencia, 46100 Burjasot (Valencia); f. 1977; Pres. Dr EDUARDO GALANTE PATIÑO; Sec. Dr RICARDO JIMÉNEZ PEYDRÓ; publ. *Boletín*.

Institut Botànic de Barcelona (Botanical Institute): Parc de Montjuïc, Avinguda dels Muntanyans, 08038 Barcelona; tel. 93-325-80-50; fax 93-426-93-21; e-mail jarbot@ija.csic.es; f. 1917; herbarium of 650,000 specimens; research in systematics, ecology and citology of western Mediterranean vascular plants; library of 20,000 vols and natural history museum; Dir J. M. MONTSERRAT; publs *Collectanea Botanica*, *Treballs*, *Index Seminum*, etc.

Real Sociedad Española de Historia Natural (Royal Spanish Natural History Society): Facultades de Biología y Geología, Ciudad Universitaria, 28040 Madrid; tel. 91-394-50-00; fax 91-394-50-00; e-mail rsehno@eucmax.sim.ucm.es; f. 1871; biological and geological sciences; 800 mems; library of *c.* 10,000 vols, 760 current periodicals; Pres. and Sec. elected every 2 years; publs *Boletín: Sección Biológica*, *Sección Geológica* (both quarterly), *Actas* (annually).

Sociedad Española de Etología (Spanish Ethological Society): Museu de Zoologia, Apdo 593, Parc Ciutadella, 08080 Barcelona; tel. 93-319-69-12; fax 93-310-49-99; e-mail jcsenar@intercom.es; f. 1984; Pres. L. ARIAS DE REYNA; Sec. J. C. SENAR; publs *Etología*, *Etologuía*.

Mathematical Sciences

Real Sociedad Matemática Española (Royal Spanish Mathematical Society): Departamento de Matematicas, Universidad de Murcia, 30100 Murcia; tel. 968-36-41-71; e-mail salsegom@fru.um.es; f. 1911; 800 mems; Pres. ANTONIO M. NAVEIRA; Sec. SALVADOR S. GOMIS; publ. *Gaceta*.

Physical Sciences

Asociación Nacional de Químicos de España (National Association of Chemists): Lagasca 83, 1°, 28006 Madrid; f. 1945; 9,000 mems; a member of the international Federation of Mediterranean Associations and of European Federation of Chemical Engineering; Pres. JOSÉ LUIS NEGRO LÓPEZ; Sec. JOAQUÍN COPADO LÓPEZ; publ. *Química e Industria* (monthly); technical and professional works.

Instituto Nacional de Meteorología (National Meteorological Institute): Ciudad Universitaria, Apdo 285, Madrid; f. 1887; library of 19,500 vols, 2,000 reports; 511 mems, 4,500 correspondents; Dir-Gen. EDUARDO COCA VITA; 4,500 stations; publs *Boletín diario*, *Boletín mensual climatológico*, *Resúmenes anuales*, *Calendario Meteorológico*.

Real Sociedad Española de Física (Royal Spanish Society of Physics): Facultad de Física y Química, Ciudad Universitaria, 28040 Madrid; tel. 91-394-43-59; fax 91-543-38-79; f. 1903; 800 mems; Pres. GERARDO DELGADO BARRIO; Sec.-Gen. JOSÉ M. LOS ARCOS; publs *Anales de Física* (quarterly), *Revista Española de Física* (quarterly).

Real Sociedad Española de Química (Royal Spanish Society of Chemistry): Facultad de Ciencias Químicas, Ciudad Universitaria, 28040 Madrid; tel. 91-394-43-61; fax 91-543-38-79; f. 1903; 2,900 mems; Pres. J. ANTONIO RODRÍGUEZ RENUNCIO; Sec.-Gen. ANTONIO BALLESTER PÉREZ; publ. *Anales de Química* (monthly).

Sociedad Astronómica de España y América (Astronomical Society of Spain and America): Avda Diagonal 377, 08008 Barcelona; f. 1911; 250 mems; library of 2,800 vols; lectures, courses, etc.; Acting Pres. Dr JOSEPH M. CODINA-VIDAL; Sec. ANTONIO PALUZIER-BORRELL; publs *Urania* (quarterly), *Suplemento de Urania* (twice monthly).

Sociedad Geológica de España (Geological Society of Spain): Fundación Gómez Pardo, Alenza 1, 28003 Madrid; tel. 91-441-71-38; f. 1985; 980 mems; Pres. Dr JORGE CIVIS LLOVERA; Sec. Dr JOSÉ MANUEL GONZÁLEZ-CASADO; publs *Geogaceta* (2 a year), *Revista* (2 a year).

RELIGION, SOCIOLOGY AND ANTHROPOLOGY

Federación Española de Religiosos de Enseñanza (FERE) (Spanish Federation of Religious Centres in Education): Hacienda de Pavones 5 (1°), 28030 Madrid; tel. 91-328-80-00; fax 91-328-80-01; e-mail fere@planalfa.es; f. 1957; groups all the centres of elementary, secondary and higher education of the Catholic Church; there are 2,847 centres; library specializing in psychology and pedagogy containing 6,200 vols, 156 specialized periodicals; Pres. ISIDRO GONZÁLEZ MODROÑO; Sec. ANGEL ASTORGANO RUIZ; publs *Educadores* (Teachers' Review, quarterly), *Revista FERE* (monthly).

Institución 'Fernando el Católico' de la Excma Diputación de Zaragoza: Palacio Provincial, Plaza de España 2, 50071 Zaragoza; tel. 976-288878; fax 976-288869; e-mail ifc@mail.sendanet.es; f. 1943; part of CSIC; Sections: Philology, Literature, Art, Archaeology and Numismatics, Folklore, History, Medicine, Geography, Economic and Social Studies, International Studies, Architecture, Culture, Religion, Agricultural Studies, Regional Aragonese Law, Ecology and Environmental Studies, Music for Young People, Ancient Music, Heraldry; Council of 12 representing the University and Municipality; library of 78,000 vols; Pres. JOSÉ IGNACIO SENAO; Dir Prof. GUILLERMO FATÁS; Sec. JOSÉ BARRANCO; publs *Archivo de Filología Aragonesa*, *Cesaraugusta*, *Seminario de Arte Aragonés*, *Cuadernos de Historia 'Jerónimo Zurita'*, *Cuadernos de Aragón*, *Nassarre* (musicology review), *Emblemata*, *Revista de Derecho Civil Aragonés*.

Real Instituto de Estudios Asturianos (Institute of Asturian Studies): Plaza Porlier 9, Oviedo; tel. 98-521-17-60; f. 1946; 50 mems; library of 20,000 vols; Dir FRANCISCO TUERO BERTRAND; publs *Boletín de Humanidades*, *Boletín de Ciencias*.

Real Sociedad Bascongada de los Amigos del País (Royal Society of Friends of the Basque Country): Donostia 20003, San Sebastián, Apartado 3263; tel. 943-42-44-78; f. 1764, the first of such societies in Spain; 24 mems; organized Museo de San Telmo and Museo Naval, also Conservatorio Municipal de Música; f. Editorial Guipuzcoana de Ediciones y Publicaciones, Books in Basque and Biblioteca Vascongada de los Amigos del País, collaborated in archaeological exploration of the prehistoric cave dwellings of the district; is the Guipuzcoan Office of the Consejo Superior de Investigaciones Científicas, Madrid (see below); Dir IGNACIO M. BARRIOLA IRIGOYEN; publs *Boletín* (quarterly), *Egan* (literary supplement), *Munibe* (natural sciences supplement), *Boletín de la Cofradía Vasca de Gastronomía*, *Boletín de Estudios Históricos sobre San Sebastián* (annually), *Anuario de Eusko-Folklore Aranzadiana Orria*.

TECHNOLOGY

Col-legi Oficial d'Enginyers Industrials de Catalunya: Via Laietana 39, 08003 Barcelona; tel. 93-319-23-00; fax 93-310-06-81; f. 1950; 7,200 mems; is an association of engineer-graduates of the Schools of Industrial Engineers of Spain; library of 20,000 vols; Dean ANGEL LLOBET I DIEZ; Sec. JOSEP M. ROVIRA I RAGUÉ.

Instituto de la Ingeniería de España (Spanish Institute of Engineering): General Arrando 38, 28010 Madrid; f. 1905; 20,000 mems; comprises 9 associations of higher engineers and the *Aula de Ingeniería* (training centre), offering courses, seminars, etc. for postgraduate students; Gen. Sec. JAIME TORNOS.

Sociedad Española de Cerámica y Vidrio (Spanish Ceramic and Glass Society): Carretera de Valencia, Km 24,300, Arganda del Rey, Madrid; tel. 91-871-18-00; fax 91-870-05-50; e-mail secv@icv.csic.es; f. 1960; promotes technical progress in ceramic and glass work and disseminates information about manufacture and developments within the field; 730 mems; library of 500 vols; Gen. Sec. EMILIO CRIADO; publ. *Boletin* (every 2 months).

Research Institutes

GENERAL

Consejo Superior de Investigaciones Científicas (CSIC) (Council for Scientific Research): Serrano 117, 28006 Madrid; tel. 91-261-98-00; fax 91-411-30-77; f. 1940; the CSIC is the largest multidisciplinary research body in Spain, to serve culture and technological development. It is a creative instrument and forum for Spanish science; the Council has 100 research centres distributed throughout almost the entire country, institutes directly governed by CSIC, those operated jointly by CSIC and universities, and others in association with regional government or other institutions; 7,500 employees, 2,000 scientists, 1,500 trainees, 3,300 researchers and technicians, 700 administrative staff; maintains office for transfer of technology in co-operation with Spanish supervisory agencies for technological development; Library and two centres for documentation and information comprising 100,000 vols, journals published by the institutes, scientific and cultural dissemination, scientific publishing house, technical facilities and installations; Pres. CÉSAR NOMBELA CANO; Vice-Pres. (Scientific and Technological Research) EMILIO LORA-TAMAYO D'OCON; Vice-Pres. (Administration and Institutional Relations) MIGUEL GARCÍA GUERRERO; Dir JUAN ANTONIO RICHART CHACÓN.

Attached research institutes in the field of Humanities and Social Sciences:

Centro de Estudios: Históricos: C/ Duque de Medinaceli 6, 28014 Madrid; tel. 91-429-06-26; fax 91-369-09-40; Dir MARIA PILAR LÓPEZ GARCÍA.

Centro de Información y Documentación Científica: C/ Joaquín Costa 22, 28002 Madrid; tel. 91-563-54-82; fax 91-564-2644; Dir ROSA VIESCA ESPINOSA DE LOS MONTEROS.

Escuela Española de Historia y Arqueología: Via di Torre Argentina 18, 00186 Rome, Italy; tel. Italy 06-68309043; fax Italy 06-68309047; Dir JESÚS JAVIER ARCE MARTÍNEZ.

Escuela de Estudios Árabes: Cta Cuesta del Chapiz 22, 18010, Granada; tel. 958-22-22-90; fax 958-22-47-54; Dir LUIS MOLINA MARTÍNEZ.

Escuela de Estudios Hispano Americanos: C/ Alfonso XII 16, 41002 Seville; tel. 95-422-28-43; fax 95-422-43-31; Dir CONSUELO VALERA BUENO.

Institución Milá y Fontanals: C/ Egipciaques 15, 08001 Barcelona; tel. 93-442-34-89; fax 93-443-0071; Dir JAUME JOSA LLORCA.

Instituto de Análisis Económico: Universidad Autónoma, 08193 Bellaterra (Barcelona); tel. 93-580-66-12; fax 93-580-14-52; Dir FRANCISCO JAVIER VIVES TORRENTS.

Instituto de Economía y Geografía: C/ Pinar 25, 28006 Madrid; tel. 91-411-10-98; fax 91-562-55-67; Dir MARIA ASUNCIÓN MARTÍN LOU.

Instituto de Estudios Gallegos 'Padre Sarmiento': Rúa do Franco 2, 15702 Santiago de Compostela (La Coruña); tel. 981-58-20-49; fax 981-58-20-49; Dir EDUARDO PARDO DE GUEVARA Y VALDÉS.

Instituto de Estudios Sociales Avanzados en Madrid: C/ Alfonso XII 18–5 Planta, 28014 Madrid; tel. 91-521-90-28; fax 91-521-81-03; Dir LUDOLFO PARAMIO RODRIGO.

Instituto de Estudios Sociales Avanzados en Andalucia: Avda Menéndez Pidal s/n, 14004 Córdoba; tel. 957-21-81-39; fax 957-21-81-40; Dir MANUEL PÉREZ YRUELA.

Instituto de Estudios Sociales Avanzados de Cataluña: C/ Egipciaques 15, 08001 Barcelona; tel. 93-442-35-56; fax 93-443-17-99; Dir MANUEL MANDIANES CASTRO.

Instituto de Estudios Documentales e Históricos sobre la Ciencia: CSIC Universidad de Valencia, C/ Vicente Blasco Ibáñez 17, 46010 Valencia; tel. 96-386-41-64; fax 96-361-39-75; Dir RAFAEL PERIS BONET.

Instituto de Filología: C/ Duque de Medinaceli 6, 28014 Madrid; tel. 91-429-06-26; fax 91-369-09-40; Dir MARIA TERESA ORTEGA MONASTERIO.

Instituto de Filosofía: C/ Pinar 25, 28006 Madrid; tel. 91-411-70-05; fax 91-564-52-52; Dir MANUEL REYES MATE RUPÉREZ.

Centro Marcelino Menendez y Pelayo: Duque de Medinaceli 6, 28014 Madrid; tel. 91-429-06-26; fax 91-369-09-40; Dir MARIA PILAR LOPEZ GARCIA.

Attached research institutes in the field of Biology and Biomedicine:

Instituto de Biología Molecular: Ftad de Ciencias, 28049 Cantoblanco (Madrid); tel. 91-397-50-70; fax 91-397-47-99; Dir JUAN MODOLELL MAINOU.

Centro de Investigaciones Biológicas: C/ Velázquez 144, 28006 Madrid; tel. 91-561-18-00; fax 91-562-75-18; Dir GUILLERMO GIMÉNEZ GALLEGO.

Centro de Investigación y Desarrollo: C/ Jordi Girona Salgado 18–26, 08034 Barcelona; tel. 93-400-61-00; fax 93-204-59-04; Dir PERE PUIGDOMÉNECH ROSELL.

Centro Nacional de Biotecnología: UAM, Campus del Cantoblanco, 28049 Cantoblanco (Madrid); tel. 91-585-45-00; fax 91-585-45-06; Dir MARIANO ESTEBAN RODRÍGUEZ.

Instituto de Biología Molecular y Celular de Plantas 'Eduardo Primo Yúfera': CSIC-Universidad Politécnica, Camino de Vera s/n, 46022 Valencia; tel. 96-387-78-51; fax 96-377-78-59; Dir VICENTE CONEJERO TOMÁS.

Instituto de Bioquímica: CSIC-Universidad Complutense, Facultad de Farmacia, Ciudad Universitaria, 28040 Madrid; tel. 91-394-17-82; fax 91-394-17-82; Dir EVANGELINA PALACIOS ALAIZ.

Instituto de Bioquímica Vegetal y Fotosíntesis: CSIC-Universidad de Sevilla, Americo Vespucio s/n, Isla de la Cartuja, 41092 Seville; tel. 95-448-95-06; fax 95-446-00-65; Dir MIGUEL GARCIA GUERRERO.

Instituto de Farmacología y Toxicología: CSIC-Universidad Complutense, Faculted de Medicina, Ciudad Universitaria, 28040 Madrid; tel. 91-394-14-69; fax 91-394-14-70; Dir JUAN TAMARGO MENÉNDEZ.

Instituto de Investigaciones Biomédicas: C/ Arturo Duperier 4, 28029 Madrid; tel. 91-585-46-00; fax 91-585-45-87; Dir ANA ARANDA IRIARTE.

Instituto de Microbiología Bioquímica: CSIC-Universidad de Salamanca, Edif. Departmental, Avda Campo Charro s/n, 37007 Salamanca; tel. 923-29-44-62; fax 923-22-48-76; Dir MARIA DEL PILAR PEREZ GONZALEZ.

Instituto de Parasitología y Biomedicina 'Lopez Neyra': C/ Ventanilla 11, 18001 Granada; tel. 958-20-38-02; fax 958-20-33-23; Dir ANTONIO GONZÁLEZ AGUILAR.

Instituto Neurobiologica Ramon y Cajal: Doctor Arce 37, 28002 Madrid; tel. 91-585-47-50; fax 91-585-47-54; Dir RICARDO MARTINEZ MURILLO.

Instituto de Investigaciones Biomedicas de Barcelona: Jorge Girona Salgado 18–26, 08034 Barcelona; tel. 93-400-61-00; fax 93-204-59-04; Dir EMILIO GELPI MONTEYS.

Centro Biologica Molecular Severo Ochoa: CSIC-Universidad Autonoma de Madrid, Facultad de Ciencias, Cantoblanco U. Auton., 28049 Madrid; tel. 91-397-50-70; fax 91-397-47-99; Dir MIGUEL ANGEL DE PEDRO MONTALBAN.

Instituto Biomedicina de Valencia: Botanico Cavanilles 26-2 Planta, 46010 Valencia; tel. 96-362-27-57; fax 96-360-02-87; Dir VICENTE RUBIO ZAMORA.

Centro de Investigaciones Científicas Isla de la Cartuja: CSIC-Universidad de Sevilla, Americo Vespucio s/n, Isla de la Cartuja, 41092 Seville; tel. 95-448-95-01; fax 95-446-01-65; Dir ERNESTO CARMONA GUZMÁN.

Attached research institutes in the field of Natural Resources:

Centro de Estudios Avanzados de Blanes: Cam. de Santa Bárbara s/n, 17300 Blanes (Gerona); tel. 972-33-61-01; fax 972-33-78-06; Dir MARIA JESÚS URIZ LESPE.

Estacion Biológica de Doñana: Avda Ma. Luisa s/n, Pabellón Peru, 41013 Seville; tel. 95-423-23-40; fax 95-462-11-25; Dir MIGUEL ANGEL FERRER BAENA.

Estacíon Experimental de Zonas Áridas: C/ General Segura 1, 04001 Almería; tel. 950-27-64-00; fax 950-27-71-00; Dir MARIA DEL MAR CANO PÉREZ.

Instituto de Acuicultura de Torre de la Sal: Planta Pilato de Acuicultura s/n, 12595 C. Torre de la Sal (Castellón); tel. 964-31-95-00; fax 964-31-95-09; Dir FRANCISCO AMAT DOMÉNECH.

Instituto Andaluz de Ciencias de la Tierra: CSIC-Universidad de Granada, Facultad de Ciencias, Avda Fuentenueva s/n, 18002 Granada; tel. 958-24-31-58; fax 958-24-33-84; Dir CARLOS SANZ DE GALDEANO EQUIZA.

Instituto de Astronomía y Geodesia: CSIC-Universidad Complutense, Facultad de Ciencias Matemáticas, 28040 Madrid; tel. 91-394-45-85; fax 91-394-46-07; Dir RICARDO VIEIRA DÍAZ.

Instituto Botánico Municipal: CSIC-Ayuntah de Barcelona, Avda Muntanyans s/n, Parque de Monjuic, 08038 Barcelona; tel. 93-325-80-50; fax 93-426-92-31; Dir JOSE M. MONSERRAT.

Instituto de Ciencias del Mar: Po. Joan de Borbó s/n, 08039 Barcelona; tel. 93-221-64-50; fax 93-221-73-40; Dir ROSA FLOS BASSOLS.

Instituto de Ciencias de la Tierra 'Jaime Almera': C/ Lluis Solé Sabarís s/n, Apdo 30102, 08028 Barcelona; tel. 93-330-27-16; fax 93-411-00-12; Dir ÁNGEL LÓPEZ SOLER.

Centro de Investigaciones sobre Desertificación: Apdo Oficial, 46470 Alba (Valencia); tel. 96-126-01-26; fax 96-127-09-67; Dir JOSÉ L. RUBIO DELGADO.

Instituto de Ciencias Marinas de Andalucía: Poligono Río San Pedro s/n, 11510 Puerto Real (Cádiz); tel. 956-83-26-12; fax 956-83-47-01; Dir LUIS MARIA LUBIÁN CHAICHIO.

Instituto de Geología Económica: CSIC-Universidad Complutense, Facultad de Geólogicas, Ciudad Universitaria, 28040

Madrid; tel. 91-394-48-13; fax 91-394-48-08; Dir ALFONSO SOPEÑA ORTEGA.

Instituto de Investigaciones Marinas: C/ Eduardo Cabello, 36208 Vigo (Pontevedra); tel. 986-23-19-30; fax 986-29-27-62; Dir RICARDO ISAAC PÉREZ MARTIN.

Instituto Mediterraneo de Estudios Avanzados: CSIC-Universidad de las Islas Baleares, Facultad de Ciencias, Carr. de Valldemossa, km. 7,500, 07071 Palma de Mallorca; tel. 971-17-30-00 ext. 3381; fax 971-17-32-48; Dir ENRIQUE TORTOSA MARTORELL.

Instituto Pirenaico de Ecología: Avda Montañana 177, Apdo 202, 50080 Zaragoza; tel. 976-57-58-83; fax 976-57-58-84; Dir JUAN PABLO MARTÍNEZ RICA.

Museo Nacional de Ciencias Naturales: C/ José Gutiérrez Abascal 2, 28006 Madrid; tel. 91-561-86-00; fax 91-564-50-78; Dir ROBERTO FERNANDEZ DE CALEYA ALVAREZ.

Real Jardín Botanico: Pl. de Murillo 2, 28014 Madrid; tel. 91-420-30-17; fax 91-420-01-57; Dir MARIA TERESA TELLERÍA JORGE.

Centro de Ciencias Medioambientales: Serrano 115 bis, 28006 Madrid; tel. 91-562-50-20; fax 91-564-08-00; Dir MARIA DEL ROSARIO FELIPE ANTON.

Instituto de Recurcos Naturales y Agrobiologicos de Salamanca: Apdo 257, Cordel de Merinas 40–52, 37071 Salamanca; tel. 923-21-96-06; fax 923-21-96-09; Dir CLAUDINO RODRIGUEZ BARRUECO.

Instituto de Recurcos Naturales y Agrobiologicos de Sevilla: Apdo 1052, Estafeta-Puerto, 41080 Seville; tel. 954-62-47-11; fax 954-62-40-02; Dir DIEGO DE LA ROSA ACOSTA.

Centro de Edafologia y Biologia Aplicada del Segura: Avda de la Fama 1, Apdo 195, 30080 Murcia; tel. 968-21-76-42; fax 968-26-66-13; Dir ANTONIO CERDA CERDA.

Instituto Agroquimica y Tecnologia Alimentos: Apdo de Correos 73, 46100 Burjassot (Valencia); tel. 96-390-00-22; fax 96-363-63-01; Dir JOSÉ LUIS NAVARRO FABRA.

Instituto de Productos Naturales y Agrobiología: Astrofisico Francisco Sanchez 3, 38205 La Laguna (Tenerife); tel. 922-25-21-44; fax 922-26-01-35; Dir COSME GARCIA FRANCISCO.

Attached research institutes in the field of Agricultural Sciences:

Estación Experimental de Aula Dei: Avda Montañana 177, Apdo 202, 50080 Zaragoza; tel. 976-57-65-11; fax 976-57-56-20; Dir JAVIER ABADÍA BAYONA.

Estación Experimental del Zaidín: C/ Profesor Albareda 1, 18008 Granada; tel. 958-12-10-11; fax 958-12-96-00; Dir JOSÉ MIGUEL BAREA NAVARRO.

Estación Experimental 'La Mayora': Algarrobo-Costa, 29750 Málaga; tel. 952-55-26-56; fax 952-55-26-77; Dir MARIA LUISA GÓMEZ-GUILLAMÓN ARRABAL.

Instituto de Agricultura Sostenible: Alameda del Obispo s/n, Apdo 4084, 14080 Córdoba; tel. 957-49-92-00; fax 957-49-92-52; Dir ELIAS FERERES CASTIEL.

Instituto de Investigaciones Agrobiológicas de Galicia: Avda de Vigo s/n, Apdo 122, 15080 Santiago de Compostela (La Coruña); tel. 981-59-09-58; fax 981-59-25-04; Dir MARIA TARSY CARBALLAS FERNÁNDEZ.

Instituto de Recursos Naturales y Agrobiología: C/ Cordel de Merinas 40–52, Apdo 257, 37071 Salamanca; tel. 923-21-96-06; fax 923-21-96-09; Dir CLAUDINO RODRÍGUEZ BARRUECO.

Instituto de Recursos Naturales y Agrobiología: Apdo 1052, Estafeta-Puerto, 41080 Seville; tel. 95-462-47-11; fax 95-462-40-02; Dir DIEGO DE LA ROSA ACOSTA.

Misión Biológica de Galicia: Apdo 28, 36080 Pontevedra; tel. 986-85-48-00; fax 986-84-13-62; Dir AMANDO ORDÁS PERÉZ.

Estacion Agricola Experimental de León: Finca Marzanas, Apdo 788, 24080 León; tel. 987-31-70-64; fax 987-31-71-61; Dir ANGEL RUIZ MANTECON.

Attached research institutes in the field of the Science and Technology of Physics:

Instituto de Microelectronica: Universidad Autónoma, 08193 Cerdanyola del Valles (Barcelona); tel. 93-580-26-25; fax 93-580-14-96; Dir FRANCISCO SERRA MESTRES.

Instituto de Acústica: C/ Serrano 144, 28006 Madrid; tel. 91-561-88-06; fax 91-411-76-51; Dir JUAN ANTONIO GALLEGO JUÁREZ.

Instituto de Astrofísica de Andalucía: Camino Bajo de Huetor 24, Apdo 3004, 18008 Granada; tel. 958-12-13-11; fax 958-81-45-30; Dir RAFAEL RODRIGO MONTERO.

Instituto de Automática Industrial: Km. 22.800, Ctra Madrid-Valencia, 28500 Arganda del Rey (Madrid); tel. 91-871-19-00; fax 91-871-50-70; Dir JOSÉ ANTONIO CORDERO MARTIN.

Instituto de Estructura de la Materia: C/ Serrano 113 bis, 28006 Madrid; tel. 91-561-94-00; fax 91-564-24-31; Dir FRANCISCO JOSÉ BALTÁ CALLEJA.

Instituto de Física Corpuscular: SCIC-Universidad de Valencia, Avda Doctor Moliner 50, 46100 Burjassot (Valencia); tel. 96-386-45-00; fax 96-386-45-83; Dir JORGE VELASCO GONZÁLEZ.

Instituto de Física de Cantabria: CSIC-Universidad de Cantabria, Facultad de Ciencias, 39005 Santander; tel. 942-20-14-59; fax 942-20-14-59; Dir XAVIER BARCONS JÁUREGUI.

Instituto de Robotica e Informatica Industrial: Gran Capitan 2–4, Edificio Nexus, 08034 Barcelona; tel. 93-401-57-51; fax 93-401-57-50; Dir RAFAEL MARIA HUBER GARRIDO.

Observatorio Fisica Cosmica del Ebro: 43520 Roquetas (Tarragona); tel. 977-50-05-11; fax 977-50-46-60; Dir LUIS FELIPE ALBERCA SILVA.

Instituto de Investigación de Inteligencia Artificial: Universidad Autónoma, 08193 Bellaterra (Barcelona); tel. 93-580-95-70; fax 93-580-96-61; Dir FRANCISCO ESTEVA MASSAGUER.

Instituto de Matemáticas y Física Fundamental: C/ Serrano 113–123, 28006 Madrid; tel. 91-561-68-00; fax 91-585-48-94; Dir ALFREDO TIEMBLO RAMOS.

Instituto de Microelectrónica de Madrid: C/ Isaac Newton 8, Tres Cantos, 28760 Madrid; tel. 91-806-07-00; fax 91-806-07-01; Dir FERNANDO BRIONES FERNÁNDEZ-POLA.

Instituto de Óptica 'Daza de Valdes': Serrano 121, 28006 Madrid; tel. 91-561-68-00; fax 91-564-55-57; Dir CARMEN NIEVES AFONSO RODRÍGUEZ.

Centro Física 'Miguel A. Catalan': Serrano 121, 28006 Madrid; tel. 91-561-68-00; fax 91-564-55-57; Dir FRANCISCO JOSE BALTA CALLEJA.

Centro de Tecnologias Físicas 'L. Torres Quevedo': Serrano 114, 28006 Madrid; tel. 91-561-88-06; fax 91-411-76-51; Dir JUAN ANTONIO GALLEGO JUAREZ.

Instituto de Microelectronica de Sevilla: Avda Reina Mercedes s/n, Edificio Cica, 41012 Seville; tel. 95-423-99-23; fax 95-423-99-40; Dir JOSE LUIS HUERTAS DIAZ.

Attached research institutes in the field of Materials Science and Technology:

Centro Nacional de Investigaciones Metalúrgicas: Avda Gregorio del Amo 8, 28040 Madrid; tel. 91-553-89-00; fax 91-534-74-25; Dir ANTONIO FORMOSO PREGO.

Instituto de Cerámica y Vidrio: Km. 24, Ctra Madrid-Valencia 3, 28500 Arganda del Rey (Madrid); tel. 91-871-18-00; fax 91-870-05-50; Dir ÁNGEL CABALLERO CUESTA.

Instituto de Ciencia de Materiales de Aragón: CSIC-Universidad de Zaragoza, Pl. de S. Francisco s/n, Facultad de Ciencias, 50009 Zaragoza; tel. 976-55-25-28; fax 976-76-12-29; Dir DOMINGO GONZÁLEZ ALVAREZ.

Instituto de Ciencia de Materiales de Barcelona: Campus Universidad Autónoma, 08193 Cerdanyola del Valles (Barcelona); tel. 93-580-18-53; fax 93-580-57-29; Dir CARLOS MIRAVITLLES TORRAS.

Instituto de Ciencia de Materiales de Madrid: Cantoblanco, 28049 Madrid; tel. 91-334-90-00; fax 91-372-06-23; Dir FEDERICO JESUS SORIA GALLEGO.

Instituto de Ciencia de Materiales de Sevilla: CSIC-Universidad de Sevilla, Americo Vespucio s/n, Isla de la Cartuja, 41092 Seville; tel. 95-448-95-27; fax 95-446-06-65; Dir JOSÉ LUIS PÉREZ RODRÍGUEZ.

Instituto de Ciencia y Tecnología de Polímeros: C/ Juan de la Cierva 3, 28006 Madrid; tel. 91-562-29-00; fax 91-564-48-53; Dir MARIA DEL CARMEN MIJANOS UGARTE.

Instituto de Ciencias de la Construccíon 'Eduardo Torroja': C/ Serrano Galvache s/n, Apdo 19002, 28080 Madrid; tel. 91-302-04-40; fax 91-302-07-00; Dir MARIA DEL CARMEN ANDRADE PERDRIX.

Centro de Investigaciones Cientificos de Isla de la Cartuja: Americo Vespucio s/n, Isla de la Cartuja, 41092 Seville; tel. 95-448-95-01; fax 95-446-01-65; Dir ERNESTO CARMONA GUZMÁN.

Attached research institutes in the field of Foodstuff Science and Technology:

Instituto de Agroquímica y Tecnología de Alimentos: Apdo de Correos 73, 46100 Burjassot (Valencia); tel. 96-390-00-22; fax 96-363-63-01; Dir JOSÉ LUIS NAVARRO FABRA.

Instituto de Fermentaciones Industriales: C/ Juan de la Cierva 3, 28006 Madrid; tel. 91-562-29-00; fax 91-564-48-53; Dir MARIA DEL CARMEN POLO SÁNCHEZ.

Instituto del Frío: C/ Ramiro de Maeztu s/n, C. Universitaria, 28040 Madrid; tel. 91-549-23-00; fax 91-549-36-27; Dir JESÚS ESPINOSA MULAS.

Instituto de la Grasa: Avda Padre García Tejero 4, 41012 Seville; tel. 95-461-15-50; fax 95-461-67-90; Dir JOSÉ MANUEL OLÍAS JIMÉNEZ.

Instituto de Nutrición y Bromatología: CSIC-Universidad Complutense, Facultad de Farmacia, Cdad Universitaria, 28040 Madrid; tel. 91-549-00-38; fax 91-394-17-32; Dir JOSÉ LUIS REY DE VIÑAS (acting).

Instituto de Productos Lácteos de Asturias: Ctra de Infiesto s/n, Apdo 85, 33300 Villaviciosa (Oviedo); tel. 98-589-21-31; fax 98-589-22-33; Dir JUAN CARLOS BADA GANCEDO.

Attached research institutes in the field of Chemical Science and Technology:

Centro de Investigación y Desarrollo: C/ Jordi Girona Salgado 18–26, 08034 Barcelona; tel. 93-400-61-00; fax 93-204-59-04; Dir PERE PUIGDOMÉNECH ROSELL.

Instituto de Carboquímica: C/ Poeta Luciano Gracia 5, 50015 Zaragoza; tel. 976-

73-39-77; fax 976-73-33-18; Dir JOSÉ MANUEL ANDRÉS GIMENO.

Instituto de Catálisis y Petrolequímica: Universidad Autónoma, Camino Valdelatas s/n, 28049 Cantoblanco (Madrid); tel. 91-585-48-00; fax 91-585-47-60; Dir JAVIER SORIA RUIZ.

Instituto Nacional del Carbón: C/ La Corredoria s/n, Apdo 73, 33080 Oviedo; tel. 98-528-08-00; fax 98-529-76-62; Dir JESÚS A. PAJARES SOMOANO.

Instituto de Productos Naturales y Agrobiología: Avda Astrofísico Francisco Sánchez 3, 38205 La Laguna; tel. 922-25-21-44; fax 922-26-01-35; Dir COSME GARCIA FRANCISCO.

Instituto de Química Física Rocasolano: C/ Serrano 119, 28006 Madrid; tel. 91-561-94-00; fax 91-564-24-31; Dir JOSÉ ANTONIO GARCÍA DOMÍNGUEZ.

Instituto de Química Médica: C/ Juan de la Cierva 3, 28006 Madrid; tel. 91-562-29-00; fax 91-564-48-53; Dir MARIA TERESA GARCÍA LÓPEZ.

Instituto de Química Orgánica General: C/ Juan de la Cierva 3, 28006 Madrid; tel. 91-562-29-00; fax 91-564-48-53; Dir SERAFÍN VALVERDE LÓPEZ.

Instituto de Tecnología Química: CSIC-Universidad Politécnic, Avda de los Naranjos s/n, 46022 Valencia; tel. 96-387-78-00; fax 96-387-78-09; Dir AVELINO CORMA CANÓS.

Laboratorio de Investigación en Tecnologías de la Combustión: ETSI Industries, C/ Maria de Luna 3, 50015 Zaragoza; tel. 976-73-83-60; fax 976-76-18-82; Dir CÉSAR DOPAZO GARCÍA.

Instituto de Investigaciones Biomedicas de Barcelona: Jorge Girona Salgado 18–26, 08034 Barcelona; tel. 93-400-61-00; fax 93-204-59-04; Dir EMILIO GELPI MONTEYS.

Instituto de Ciencia de Materiales de Aragón: Facultad de Fisicas, Pl. San Francisco s/n, 50009 Zaragoza; tel. 976-55-25-28; fax 976-76-12-29; Dir DOMINGO GONZALEZ ALVAREZ.

Instituto de Investigaciones Químicas: Americo Vespucio s/n, Isla de la Cartuaja, 41092 Seville; tel. 95-448-95-53; fax 95-446-05-65; Dir ERNESTO CARMONA GUZMÁN.

Fundació Catalana per a la Recerca (Catalan Foundation for Research): Pg Lluís Companys 23, 08010 Barcelona; tel. 93-315-23-23; fax 93-268-01-01; f. 1986; promotes scientific and technological research; Pres. XAVIER TRIAS I VIDAL DE LLOBATERA; Dir JOSEP A. PLANA I CASTELLVI; publs *Tecno 2000* (6 a year), newsletter (quarterly).

Instituto de Relaciones Europeo-Latinoamericanas (IRELA) (Institute for European-Latin American Relations): Apdo 2600, 28002 Madrid; tel. 91-561-72-00; fax 91-562-64-99; f. 1984; organization of conferences, etc., for European and Latin American officials, diplomats, journalists, politicians, businessmen, trade-unionists and academics on different aspects of European-Latin American relations; collection and systematization of information on relations between the two regions; advisory activities for regional instns in Europe and Latin America; promotion, coordination and pursuit of specific research on relations between the two regions; Dir WOLF GRABENDORFF.

AGRICULTURE, FISHERIES AND VETERINARY SCIENCE

Departamento de Protección Vegetal (Plant Protection Department): CIT-INIA, Carretera de la Coruña Km 7.5, Apdo 8.111, 28040 Madrid; tel. 91-2-07-00-40; f. 1888; molecular biology and virology, entomology and plant pathology, weed science; attached to the Instituto Nacional de Investigaciones Agrarias; 60 staff; Head Dr JOSÉ M. GARCÍA-BAUDIN; publ. *Investigación Agraria: Producción y Protección Vegetales* (3 a year).

Instituto Nacional de Investigación y Tecnología Agraria y Alimentaria (INIA) (National Institute for Food and Agricultural Research and Technology): Ministerio de Agricultura, José Abascal 56, 28003 Madrid; tel. 91-347-39-00; fax 91-442-35-87; f. 1971; library of 40,000 vols; Pres. JESÚS MIRANDA DE LARRA Y DE ONIS; publs *Investigación Agraria, Comunicaciones*.

ECONOMICS, LAW AND POLITICS

Centro de Investigaciones Sociológicas: Montalbán 8, 28014 Madrid; tel. 91-580-76-00; f. 1973; attached to govt Min. of the Presidency; promotes research in social sciences, arranges courses and seminars, collaborates with similar national and int. orgs, and creates data bases for relevant material; library of 15,000 vols; Dir Dra PILAR DEL CASTILLO; publ. *Revista Española de Investigaciones Sociológicas*.

Instituto de Estudios Fiscales (Institute of Fiscal Studies): Avda de Caredenal Herrera Oria 378, 28035 Madrid; tel. 91-339-88-00; fax 91-339-89-64; f. 1969; public finance; library of 77,000 vols; Dir JUAN ANTONIO GARDE ROCA; Sec.-Gen. JOSÉ IGNACIO CORCES PANDO; publs *Hacienda Pública Española* (quarterly), *Crónica Tributaria* (quarterly), *Presupuesto y Gasto Público* (3 a year), *Revista Española de Economía* (2 a year).

Instituto Universitario Ortega y Gasset: Calle Fortuny 53, 28010 Madrid; tel. 91-310-44-12; fax 91-308-40-07; f. 1986; affiliated with Univ. Complutense; offers postgraduate courses, doctoral programmes in contemporary Latin America, European studies, linguistics, international relations, and public administration, research and training in social studies and the promotion of scholarship on Ortega y Gasset (Spanish philosopher and essayist) as well as contemporary studies; library of 45,000 vols incl. personal library of Ortega y Gasset; archive material concerning Ortega y Gasset; Academic Dir EMILIO LAMO DE ESPINOSA; Sec. CARLOS MALAMUD; publ. *Revista de Occidente* (monthly).

EDUCATION

Centro de Investigación y Documentación Educativa (CIDE): Ciudad Universitaria s/n, 28040 Madrid; tel. 91-549-77-00; fax 91-543-73-90; f. 1983; conducts and co-ordinates educational research; manages the library, archive and documentation centre of the Min. of Education and Science; library of 85,000 vols; Dir (vacant).

FINE AND PERFORMING ARTS

Instituto del Patrimonio Histórico (Institute of National Heritage): Calle del Greco 4, 28040 Madrid; tel. 91-549-56-33; f. 1985; part of Min. of Education and Culture; library of 30,000 vols; Gen. Asst Dir ISABEL CABRERA-KÁBANA.

HISTORY, GEOGRAPHY AND ARCHAEOLOGY

Instituto Germano-Español de Investigación de la Sociedad Görres (German-Spanish Research Institute for History): Calle San Buenaventura 9, 28005 Madrid; tel. 91-366-85-08; fax 91-366-85-09; f. 1926; studies on German-Spanish cultural relations in the 17th, 18th and 19th centuries; library of *c.* 20,000 vols; Dirs Prof. QUINTÍN ALDEA, Prof. HANS JURETSCHKE; publ. *Berichte der diplomatischen Vertreter des Wiener Hofes aus Spanien in der Regierungszeit Karls III und Karls IV*.

MEDICINE

Instituto Cajal (Santiago Ramón y Cajal Institute of Neurobiological Research): Dr Arce 37, 28002 Madrid; tel. 91-585-47-50; fax 91-585-47-54; f. 1906; 30 mems; library of 35,000 vols; Dir ALBERTO FERRÚS; Sec. M. CARMEN GARCÍA; part of CSIC.

Instituto Español de Hematología y Hemoterapía (Institute of Haematology and Haemotherapy): Gral. Oraá 15, Madrid; f. 1940; Dir Dr CARLOS ELÓSEGUI; publ. *Anales*.

Instituto Nacional de Medicina y Seguridad del Trabajo (National Institute of Medicine and Safety): Pabellón 8, Facultad de Medicina, Ciudad Universitaria, 28003 Madrid; Dir Prof. D. MANUEL DOMINGUEZ CARMONA.

Instituto Nacional de Reeducación de Inválidos (National Institute for Retraining Physically Handicapped): Arnedo s/n, Madrid; tel. 91-462-84-44; f. 1922; Dir Dr ANSELMO ALVAREZ CUÉ; publs booklets, films.

NATURAL SCIENCES

General

Instituto Español de Oceanografía (Spanish Institute of Oceanography): Avda del Brasil 31, 28020 Madrid; tel. 91-597-44-43; fax 91-597-47-70; e-mail paloma.barrios@md.ieo.es; f. 1919; comprises Physics, Chemistry, Pollution, Geology, Fishery Biology and Marine Biology sections in Madrid, coastal laboratories at Santander, La Coruña, Vigo, Málaga, San Pedro del Pinatar, Santa Cruz de Tenerife, and Palma de Mallorca; library of 13,000 vols; research vessels 'Cornide de Saavedra' (1,100 tons), 'Jafuda Cresques' (35 tons), 'Argos' (50 tons), 'Naucrates' (100 tons); 121 mems; Dir ALVARO FERNÁNDEZ; publ. *Boletín* (every 2 years).

Physical Sciences

Centro Meteorológico Territorial de Baleares (Meteorological Station): Muelle de Poniente-Porto Pi, Apdo Oficial, 07015 Palma de Mallorca, Balearic Is; tel. 971-40-35-11; fax 971-40-46-26; f. 1934; library of 600 vols; Dir AGUSTÍN JANSA CLAR; publs *Boletín Mensual Climatológico* (monthly), *Boletín PEMMOC* (2 a year).

Instituto de Astrofísica de Canarias (IAC) (Canaries Institute of Astrophysics): Calle Vía Láctea s/n, 38200 La Laguna, Tenerife, Canary Islands; tel. 922-60-52-00; fax 922-60-52-10; e-mail postmaster@ll.iac.es; f. 1982; includes two international observatories on Tenerife and La Palma; library of 10,000 vols; Dir Prof. FRANCISCO SÁNCHEZ; publs newsletter *IAC Noticias*, *Annual Reports*.

Attached observatories:

Observatorio del Teide: Calle Vía Láctea s/n, Tenerife, Canary Islands; tel. 922-32-91-00; fax 922-32-91-17; e-mail teide@ot.iac.es; European Northern Observatory.

Observatorio del Roque de los Muchachos: Apdo 303, Santa Cruz de La Palma, Canary Is; tel. 922-40-55-00; fax 922-40-55-01; e-mail adminorm@orm.iac.es; f. 1985; European Northern Observatory.

Instituto de Astronomía y Geodesía (Institute of Astronomy and Geodesy): Facultad de Matemáticas, Ciudad Universitaria, 28040 Madrid; tel. 91-394-45-86; fax 91-394-46-07; f. 1984; attached to CSIC (See above); library of 2,000 vols, 500 periodicals; Dir Dr R. VIEIRA.

Instituto Nacional de Geofísica (National Institute of Geophysics): Serrano 123, Madrid; f. 1941; 17 mems; Dir LUIS LOZANO CALVO; Sec.

MANUEL RODRÍGUEZ RON; publ. *Revista de Geofísica* (quarterly).

Observatorio Astronómico Meteorológico y Sísmico Fabra: Tibidabo, Barcelona; tel. 93-417-57-36; f. 1905; attached to Real Academia de Ciencias y Artes de Barcelona; Dir Dr JOSÉ MARÍA CODINA.

Observatorio Astronómico Nacional (National Astronomical Observatory): Calle de Alfonso XII 3, 28014 Madrid; f. 1790; attached to the Instituto Geográfico Nacional; library of *c.* 10,000 vols; Dir JOSÉ F. LAHULLA; publs *Anuario*, *Boletín Astronómico*.

Observatorio del Ebro (Ebro Observatory): 43520 Roquetes, Tarragona; tel. 977-50-05-11; fax 977-50-46-60; e-mail ebre.lfalberca@readysoft.es; f. 1904; library of 16,000 vols, rare works dating from 1499; Dir Rev. L. F. ALBERCA; Vice-Dir Rev. E. SANCLEMENT; publs *Boletín* (in five series: (*a*) Heliophysics; (*b*) Meteorology; (*c*) Seismology; (*d*) Terrestrial Magnetism, Atmospheric Electricity; (*e*) Ionosphere), also *Memorias*, *Miscelanea*, etc.

Observatorio Universitario de Cartuja (Observatory of Cartuja): Apdo Universidad, Granada; f. 1902; 9 mems; library of 6,000 vols; Dir J. BIEL; publ. *Publicaciones* (geophysics).

Real Instituto y Observatorio de la Armada (Royal Naval Institute and Observatory): San Fernando, Cádiz; tel. 956-59-93-65; fax 956-59-93-66; f. 1753; positional astronomy, ephemerides, time, geophysics and satellite geodesy; library of 45,000 vols, 1,800 maps and plans; Dir RAFAEL BOLOIX; collaborates with the British and the American Nautical Almanac Offices, Centre National d'Etudes Spatiales, Le Bureau des Longitudes and Das Astronomische Rechen Institut; publs *Almanaque Náutico* (annually), *Efemérides Astronómicas* (annually), *Anales*, *Observaciones Meteorológicas, Magnéticas y Sísmicas*, *Boletín*, *Rotación de la Tierra*, *Fenómenos Astronómicos*, *Boletín de Ocultaciones de Estrellas por la Luna*.

PHILOSOPHY AND PSYCHOLOGY

Instituto de Filosofía: Pinar 25, 28006 Madrid; tel. 91-411-70-05; fax 91-564-52-52; e-mail flvpp01@fresno.csic.es; f. 1985; part of CSIC (*q.v.*); development of research in philosophy in collaboration with the Spanish universities; main fields of activity: logic and philosophy of science, political philosophy, ethics, philosophy of religion, history of philosophy; library of 53,000 vols; Dir MANUEL REYES MATE; publ. *Isegoria* (2 a year).

TECHNOLOGY

Centro de Investigaciones Energéticas, Medioambientales y Tecnológicas: Ciudad Universitaria, Avda Complutense 22, 28040 Madrid; tel. 91-346-60-00; fax 91-346-60-05; f. 1951; controls and directs research and study of nuclear and new and renewable energies, environmental policy and several advanced technologies; library of 30,500 vols, 300,000 reports, 750,000 microcards, 2,000 periodicals; Pres. ALBERTO LAFUENTE FELEZ; Vice-Pres. and Dir-Gen. JOSÉ ANGEL AZUARA SOLÍS; publs reports, books.

Instituto Tecnológico Geominero de España (Geological and Mining Institute): Ministry of the Environment, Ríos Rosas 23, 28003 Madrid; tel. 91-349-57-00; fax 91-442-62-16; f. 1849; library of 42,500 vols; documentation centre of 20,000 items in microfilm; sections: geology, geophysics, mineral resources, subterranean hydrology, laboratories, museum; Dir EMILIO CUSTODIO GIMENA; Sec. FELIPE GARCÍA ORTIZ; publs *Boletín Geológico y Minero* (every 2 months), *Revista Española de Micropaleontología* (3 a year), geological, metallogenic and hydrogeological maps.

Libraries and Archives

Barcelona

Archivo Capitular de la Santa Iglesia Catedral de Barcelona: Catedral de Barcelona, Plaza de la Seu s/n, 08002 Barcelona; tel. 93-310-06-69; f. 9th century; documents from 9th- to 20th-centuries; treatises on Holy Scripture, ecclesiastical history and law; religious and economic history; 250 MSS, *c.* 200 incunabula and various printed books from the original Biblioteca Capitular; 41,000 parchment documents, 20,000 vols; Archives Prefect JOSEP M. MARTÍ BONET; Archivist JOSEP BAUCELLS.

Archivo de la Corona de Aragón (Royal Archives of Aragon): Almogávares 77, 08018 Barcelona; tel. 93-485-42-85; f. 9th century; library: auxiliary 15,000 vols; Dir RAFAEL CONDE; publs publication on unedited MSS, *Colección de Documentos Inéditos del Archivo de la Corona de Aragón*, Guides, Catalogues, Indexes.

Archivo Diocesano (Diocesan Archives): Calle Obispo 5, 08002 Barcelona; tel. 93-318-30-31; f. 11th century; registers (1,200) from 1302; Diocesan Archivist Dr JOSÉ MA MARTI BONET; publ. *El Archivo Diocesano d' Barcelona*.

Biblioteca Balmes (Balmes Library): Durán y Bas 9–11, 08002 Barcelona; f. 1923; specializes in church studies; library of 40,000 vols, 345 periodicals; Dir RAMÓN CORTS BLAY.

Biblioteca 'Bergnes de las Casas': Gran Via de les Corts Catalanes 657 bis, Barcelona; f. 1917; 37,000 vols on bibliography, copyrights, history and technology of books, printing and allied trades, etc.

Biblioteca de Catalunya: Carrer de l'Hospital 56, 08001 Barcelona; tel. 93-270-23-00; fax 93-270-23-04; e-mail infbibl@bnc.es; f. 1914; library of 1,102,000 vols, 33,000 periodicals, MSS, prints, drawings, printed music, maps, and sound and video recordings; Dir MANUEL JORBA.

Biblioteca de l'Arxiu Històric de la Ciutat de Barcelona: Casa de l'Ardiaca, Carrer Santa Llúcia 1, 08002 Barcelona; tel. 93-318-11-95; fax 93-317-83-27; f. 1921; library of 140,000 vols, divided into several sections; general works, books published in Barcelona from the 15th century; the Massana Library, containing works on iconography and the history of costume; other libraries donated by private donors, e.g. Eduardo Toda (British and general books); Dir MANUEL ROVIRA SOLÀ.

Biblioteca de l'Associació d'Enginyers Industrials de Catalunya (Library of the Association of Industrial Engineers of Catalonia): Via Laietana 39, 08003 Barcelona; tel. 93-319-23-00; fax 93-310-06-81; f. 1863; library of 20,000 vols; Librarian (vacant); publ. *Fulls Informatius* (monthly).

Biblioteca de la Cámara Oficial de Comercio, Industria y Navegación de Barcelona (Library of Chamber of Commerce, Industry and Navigation): Avda Diagonal 454, 08006 Barcelona; tel. 93-415-16-00; fax 93-416-09-84; library of 108,824 vols; Sec.-Gen. LUIS SOLÁ VILARDELL (acting); Librarian NURIA SAGALÁ; publs *Boletín de la Cámara* (monthly), *Noticiario de Comercio Exterior*, *Boletín Estadístico Coyuntural*.

Biblioteca de la Delegación Territorial de Barcelona, Organización Nacional de Ciegos (Braille Library): Calabria 66–76, 08015 Barcelona; tel. 93-325-92-00; f. 1939; library of 3,000 vols; loan service; publs 25 monthly magazines.

Biblioteca de la Universitat de Barcelona: Baldiri Reixac 2, 08028 Barcelona; tel. 93-403-57-15; fax 93-440-23-80; e-mail sbib@or.ub.es; f. 1835; general library and 7 special sections; library of 1,100,000 vols, of which 5,000 are 16th-century, 914 incunabula, 2,039 MSS; Dir DOLORS LAMARCA MORELL; publs *Inventario General de Manuscritos*, *Inventario de Incunables*, *Catàleg Collectiu de la Biblioteca de la Universitat de Barcelona* (CD-ROM), *Catàleg Automatitzat de Publicacions en Sèrie* (CD-ROM).

Biblioteca del Centre Excursionista de Catalunya (Library of the Mountaineering Centre): Paradís 10, 08002 Barcelona; tel. 93-315-23-11; fax 93-315-14-08; e-mail cec.centre@mx3.redestb.es; f. 1876; 7,000 mems; library of 28,000 vols, 6,000 maps; Dir FRANCESC OLIVÉ; publs *Muntanya* (every 2 months), *Espeleòleg* (irregular).

Biblioteca del Colegio de Abogados de Barcelona (Barcelona College of Lawyers' Library): Mallorca 283, 08037 Barcelona; tel. 93-487-28-14; fax 93-487-11-28; f. 1832; 150,000 items; Dean JAUME ALONSO-CUEVILLAS SAYROL; publ. *Revista Jurídica de Catalunya*.

Biblioteca del Col-legi de Farmacèutics de la Provincia de Barcelona (Library of Barcelona Province College of Pharmaceutists): Pau Claris 94, 08010 Barcelona; tel. 93-318-04-70; fax 93-01-97-30; f. 1926, reorg. 1985; library of 17,359 vols; Dir RAMON MAGRINYÀ; publs *Circular Farmacèutica*, *Butlletí Informatiu*.

Biblioteca del Col-legi de Notaris i Arxiu Històric de Protocols de Barcelona (Library of College of Notaries): Notariat 4, Barcelona; tel. 93-317-48-00; f. 1862; specializes in law and the medieval history of Catalonia; library of 25,000 vols, 50,000 protocols from 13th century; Archivist LAUREÀ PAGAROLAS SABATÉ; Librarian MONTSERRAT GÓMEZ; publs *Estudios Històrics i Documents dels Arxius de Protocols*, *La Notaría*.

Biblioteca del Fomento del Trabajo Nacional (Library of Dept of Trade Development): Vía Layetana 32, 08003 Barcelona; tel. 93-484-12-00; fax 93-484-12-30; f. 1889; library of 78,500 vols; Librarian NURIA SARDÁ; publ. *Horizonte Empresarial* (monthly).

Bilbao

Biblioteca de la Universidad de Deusto: Avda de las Universidades 24, 48007 Bilbao; tel. 94-413-90-32; fax 94-445-23-58; e-mail ntaranco@biblio.deusto.es; f. 1886; library of 650,000 vols; Dir NIEVES TARANCO; publs *Catálogo de Publicaciones Periódicas*, *Catálogo de Obras Impresas en los Siglos XVI-XVIII*, *Boletín Bibliográfico. Centro de Documentación Europea*, *Boletín Bibliográfico*, *Estudios Cooperativos*.

El Escorial

Real Biblioteca del Monasterio de San Lorenzo de El Escorial (Royal Library of the Monastery of San Lorenzo de El Escorial): 28200 San Lorenzo de El Escorial, Madrid; tel. 91-890-38-89; fax 91-890-54-21; f. 1575; library of 75,000 vols, 650 incunabula; MSS: 2,000 Arabic, 2,090 Latin and vernacular, 72 Hebrew, 580 Greek; many rare and unique editions, including complete copy of the *Biblia Poliglota Complutensis* and of the *Biblia Poliglota* of Antwerp on parchment, and the *Epítome de Anatomía*, by Vesalius, also on parchment; 10,000 engravings and prints; Dir P. JOSÉ LUIS DEL VALLE MERINO.

Granada

Archivo de la Real Chancillería de Granada (Archives of the Royal Chancery of Granada): Plaza del Padre Suárez 1, 18009 Granada; tel. 958-222338; fax 958-222338; f. 1494; 8,810 linear metres of conventional archive material, incl. lawsuits settled by the *Tribunal de la Real Chancillería* from 1490 to 1834; also holds documents issued by the *Audiencia Territorial de Granada* from 1834 to 1970; Dir DAVID TORRES IBÁÑEZ.

Jerez de la Frontera

Biblioteca, Archivo y Colección Arqueológica Municipal (Town Library, Archive and Archaeological Museum): Plaza General Primo de Rivera 7 y 8, Jerez; tel. 956-32-33-00; f. 1873 (library), 1933 (museum); library of 75,000 vols; incunabula, important collections from 17th and 18th centuries, local collections on horses, bullfighting, flamenco; Dir RAMON CLAVIJO PROVENCIO; Librarians CARLA PUERTO CASTRILLON, AMPARO GOMEZ MARTIN; town archive: tel. (56) 32-35-05; documents dating back to the reconquest of Jerez by Alfonso El Sabio, documents on the discovery of America; Dir CRISTOBAL ORELLANA.

Biblioteca de la Facultad de Derecho, Universidad de Cádiz: Avda León de Carranza s/n, Jerez de la Frontera; f. 1979; library of 12,000 vols; Dir (vacant).

La Coruña

Archivo del Reino de Galicia/Arquivo do Reino de Galicia (Archive of the Kingdom of Galicia): Jardín de San Carlos s/n, 15001 La Coruña; tel. 981-20-92-51; fax 981-20-92-51; f. 1775; comprise a total of 82,000 bundles of documents dating back to 867, the most important being 16th- to 20th-century concerning disputes and lawsuits of the 'Real Audiencia de Galicia' and the 'Audiencia Territorial' relative to the clergy, the nobility, villages and private persons; 18th- and 19th-century documents of 'Real Intendencia', concerning government and administration of Galicia; documents 1808-1814 of the 'Junta Superior de Armamento y Defensa' relative to the Peninsular War; 19th- and 20th-century documents of Provincial Administration of La Coruña, concerning the govt, police, education, economy, tourism, finance, health; 12th- to 20-century records of families, labour unions and churches; collection of parchment 876-1652; 2,500 maps, plans and drawings covering years 1583–1985; 24,000 photographs and postcards, 11,000 microforms; library of 17,000 vols, 1,700 reviews and 920 pamphlets closely related to the archives and of special interest for research; Dir GABRIEL QUIROGA BARRO.

Lérida (Lleida)

Arxiu Històric de Lleida: Plaça de Sant Antoni Ma. Claret 5, Casa de Cultura, 25002 Lleida; tel. 973-27-08-67; fax 973-27-31-60; f. 1952; library of 3,000 vols; Dir PILAR FACI LACASTA.

Madrid

Archivo General de la Administración Civil del Estado: Paseo de Aguadores 2, 28804 Alcalá de Henares, Madrid; tel. 91-889-29-50; f. 1969; preserves and makes available for information or scientific research documents on public administration which are no longer of current administrative relevance; library of 2,733 vols; Dir MARÍA LUISA CONDE VILLAVERDE.

Archivo Histórico Nacional (National Historical Archives): Calle Serrano 115, 28006 Madrid; f. 1866; library: private, 21,338 vols; Dir MA CARMEN GUZMÁN PLA; publs catalogues, indexes, historical documents.

Biblioteca Central de Marina (Central Naval Library): Cuartel General de la Armada, Montalbán 2, Madrid 28014; f. 1856; library of 65,540 vols; Librarian MERCEDES DORDA SAINZ.

Biblioteca Central del Ministerio de Hacienda (Central Library of the Ministry of Finance): Calle de Alcalá 11, 28014 Madrid; f. 1852; library of 40,000 vols on economics, finance and Government legislation; Librarian ESPERANZA SALÁN PANIAGUA.

Biblioteca Central Militar (Army Library): Calle Mártires de Alcalá 9, 28071 Madrid; tel. 91-247-03-00; fax 91-559-43-71; f. 1932; library of 250,000 vols on military history; rare books, engravings, photographs, maps and plans; Dir Col. ANTONIO MANZANEDO CERECEDA; publ. *Revista de Historia Militar*.

Biblioteca de la Escuela Técnica Superior de Ingenieros de Caminos, Canales y Puertos (Library of Higher School for Road, Canal and Port Engineers): Ciudad Universitaria, 28040 Madrid; tel. 91-336-67-39; f. 1802; library of 73,000 vols; Dir VICENTE SÁNCHEZ GALVEZ.

Biblioteca de la Escuela Técnica Superior de Ingenieros Industriales (Library of the Higher School for Industrial Engineers): José Gutiérrez Abascal 2, 28006 Madrid; tel. 91-336-30-75; f. 1905; library of 25,000 vols; Librarian MARÍA DOLORES CAMPAÑA.

Biblioteca de la Secretaría de Estado de Cultura (Library of the Office of the Secretary of State for Culture): Plaza del Rey 1, 28004 Madrid; tel. 91-701-70-00 ext. 32500; fax 91-522-93-77; f. 1984; cultural policy, cultural institutions, fine arts, librarianship; library of 22,000 vols, 500 periodicals; Dir PILAR BLANCO MUÑOZ.

Biblioteca de la Universidad Complutense de Madrid (Complutense University of Madrid Library): Antiguo Pabellón de Gobierno, C/ Isaac Peral s/n, 28040 Madrid; tel. 91-394-69-39; fax 91-394-69-26; e-mail buc@buc.ucm.es; f. 1341; second in importance in Spain; one of the most complete in Spain; library of 2,097,000 vols, 175,000 ancient books, 49,000 special materials, 38,000 periodicals; Head MARTA TORRES SANTO DOMINGO.

Biblioteca del Ministerio de Asuntos Exteriores (Library of the Ministry of Foreign Affairs): Plaza de la Provincia 1, 28012 Madrid; tel. 91-366-48-00; fax 91-366-39-53; f. 1900; library of 43,256 vols; works on history, geography, literature, international law, political and civil law; Dir MARIA JOSE ALBO ALVAREZ.

Biblioteca del Ministerio de Educación y Cultura (Library of the Ministry of Education and Culture): San Agustín 5, 28014 Madrid; tel. 91-369-30-26; fax 91-429-94-38; e-mail ernesto.calbetr@educ.mec.es; f. 1912; library of 80,000 vols, 1,800 periodicals, 20,000 microforms; Man. ERNESTO CALBET ROSELLÓ; publs *Boletín de Adquisiciones* (monthly), *Boletín de Sumarios* (monthly), *Catálogo de Publicaciones Periódicas* (irregular).

Biblioteca Hispánica (de la Agencia Española de Cooperación Internacional): Avda de los Reyes Católicos 4, Ciudad Universitaria, 28040 Madrid; tel. 91-583-85-24; fax 91-583-85-25; f. 1946; library of *c.* 520,000 vols and 10,200 periodicals; special collection: Latin American incunabula; Dra CARMEN DIEZ HOYO; publ. *Boletín de Últimas Adquisiciones*.

Biblioteca Nacional (National Library): Paseo de Recoletos 20, 28071 Madrid; tel. 91-580-78-00; fax 91-577-56-34; f. 1712 as Royal Library; library of 4,000,000 vols, 25,000 vols of MSS, 3,000 incunabula, 238,000 rare books, 2,036,000 pamphlets and sheets, 80,000 periodicals, 1,637,000 prints and photographs, 20,000 drawings, 771,000 posters, 462,000 postcards, 114,000 maps, 199,000 music scores, 281,000 sound recordings, 21,000 video recordings, microforms, multimedia, computer files, CD-ROM; deposit library; ISSN national centre; Dir LUIS ALBERTO DE CUENCA.

Centro de Información y Documentación Científica (CINDOC): Joaquín Costa 22, 28002 Madrid; tel. 91-563-54-82; fax 91-564 2644; f. 1953; information section of CSIC (*q.v.*); 7,827 periodical titles, 16,000 books, 75 special collections; Dir ROSA DE LA VIESCA; Sec. M. VILLARREAL; publs *Revista Española de Ciencia y Tecnologia* (quarterly), *Boletín de Traducciones CINDOC*.

Hemeroteca Municipal de Madrid (Periodicals Library of the Corporation of Madrid): Calle Conde Duque 9–11, 28015 Madrid; tel. 91-588-57-71; f. 1918; over 20,000 titles; the library maintains a microfilm service; Dir CARLOS DORADO FERNÁNDEZ.

Real Biblioteca (Royal Library): Palacio Real, Calle Bailén s/n, 28071 Madrid; tel. 91-454-87-33; fax 91-541-21-72; e-mail realbiblioteca@lander.es; f. 1760; 250,000 printed vols; fine collections of MSS, incunabula, music, rare editions dating from the 16th century, engravings and drawings; collection of bookbindings; research library; Dir MARÍA LUISA LÓPEZ-VIDRIERO; publ. *Avisos: Noticias de la Real Biblioteca*.

Subdirección General de los Archivos Estatales (State Archives Section): Plaza del Rey 1, 28071 Madrid; tel. 91-521-56-26; fax 91-521-05-08; f. 1979; Dir ELISA CAROLINA DE SANTOS CANALEJO; publ. *Boletín de Información del Centro de Información Documental de Archivos*.

Subdirección General de Publicaciones del Ministerio de Trabajo y Asuntos Sociales (Publications Section of the Ministry of Labour and Social Affairs): Calle Agustín de Bethencourt 11, 28003 Madrid; tel. 91-554-34-00; fax 91-533-06-91; library of 80,000 vols excluding pamphlets and newspapers; publ. *Revista del Ministerio de Trabajo y Asuntos Sociales* (monthly).

Palma de Mallorca

Archivo del Reino de Mallorca (Historical Archives of Mallorca): Calle Ramón Llull 3, 07001 Palma de Mallorca; tel. 971-72-59-99; fax 971-71-87-81; f. 1851; 13th- to 20th-century public and private archives; library of 11,584 vols, 193 periodicals; Dir RICARD URGELL HERNÁNDEZ.

Peralada

Biblioteca del Palacio de Peralada (Palace of Peralada Library): 17491 Peralada; tel. 972-53-81-25; fax 972-53-80-87; f. 1882 by the Count of Peralada; library contains 80,000 vols, 200 incunabula, 20,000 pamphlets and parchments on history; Librarian INÉS PADROSA; Archivist JOSEP CLAVAGUERA.

Sabadell

Arxiu Històric de Sabadell (Historical Archives): Indústria 32, 08202 Sabadell; tel. 93-726-87-77; fax 93-727-57-03; f. 14th century; documents date from 1111; MS of *Arxius Privats* (Private Records) from 1247, *Fons eclesiàstics* (ecclesiastical archives) from 1334, *Corts Senyorials* (Court of Justice) from 1347, *Escrivania* (Notarial Archives) from 1400, *Actes* (Proceedings of Local Council meetings) from 1449, *Hemeroteca oficial* from 1570, *Fons d'empresa* (Records of 30 Companies) from 19th century; collection of local journals and reviews dating from 1855; library of 9,000 vols, 26,000 photographs and 625 audiovisual records; Dir JOAN COMASÒLIVAS I FONT; publ. *Arraona*.

Santander

Biblioteca de Menéndez Pelayo (Menéndez Pelayo Library): Rubio 6, 39007 Santander; tel. 942-23-45-34; e-mail xjagenjo@sarenet.es; the private library of this writer, 45,000 vols, not to be increased in number, left by him to the town; opened to the public 1915; inaugurated 1923 by Alfonso XIII; Dir XAVIER AGENJO BULLÓN; publ. *Boletín* (annually).

Seville

Archivo de la Casa Ducal de Medinaceli (Medinaceli Archives): Plaza de Pilatos 1, Seville; archives of 9th to 20th centuries; 8,000 files; Archivist ANTONIO SÁNCHEZ GONZÁLEZ; publ. *Histórica*.

Archivo General de Indias (Archives of the Indies): Avda de la Constitución s/n, 41004 Seville; tel. 95-450-05-32; fax 95-421-94-85; f. 1785; documents relating to Spanish colonial administration in America and the Philippines; library of 25,000 vols, 43,000 files; Dir MAGDALENA CANELLAS ANOZ; publs include *Catálogos de Pasajeros a Indias, Catálogos de Mapas y Planos, CD-ROM Tesoros del Archivo General de Indias*.

Biblioteca Capitular y Colombina: Institución Colombina, C/ Alemanes s/n, 41004 Seville; tel. 95-456-27-21; fax 95-421-18-76; f. 13th century; library of 60,500 vols; includes the 3,500-vol. library of Hernando Colón, son of the explorer, Cristóbal; Man. Dir NURIA CASQUETE DE PRADO.

Simancas

Archivo General de Simancas (Simancas General Archives): Simancas; f. 1540; 68,242 filed documents and 4,979 vols of documents; library of 20,000 vols on history; Dir JOSÉ LUIS RODRIGUEZ DE DIEGO.

Toledo

Archivo y Biblioteca Capitulares (Archives and Library of the Cathedral Chapter): Catedral de Toledo; tel. 925-21-24-23; fax 925-21-24-23; the *Archivo Capitular* contains 11,000 documents (mostly medieval) dating from 1086; the library (f. 1383) contains 2,521 MSS, 1,200 printed books; Dirs Dr RAMÓN GONZÁLVEZ RUIZ, Dr ANGEL FERNÁNDEZ COLLADO.

Valencia

Archivo del Reino de Valencia: Alameda 22, 46010 Valencia; tel. 96-360-31-23; fax 96-360-35-67; f. 1419; 71,561 MSS books (13th to 20th centuries), 49,650 files of MSS, 61,483 charters, deeds, etc, from the 13th century onwards; Dir CARLOS LÓPEZ RODRÍGUEZ.

Zaragoza

Biblioteca Moncayo: Mayor 62, Jarque, Zaragoza; f. 1972; library of 15,000 vols by Aragonese authors or on the subject of Aragon; Dir LUIS MARQUINA MARÍN.

Museums and Art Galleries

Barcelona

Museo de Geología (Museo Martorell): Parc de la Ciutadella, s/n, 08003 Barcelona; tel. 93-319-68-95; fax 93-319-93-12; e-mail mgeolbcn@lix.intercom.es; f. 1882; geological library; Dir Dra ALICIA MASRIERA; publ. *Treballs del Museu de Geologia de Barcelona*.

Museo de la Música: Avda Diagonal 373, 08008 Barcelona; tel. 93-416-11-57; fax 93-217-11-06; f. 1946; valuable collections of antique instruments; phonographs and gramophones, historical early recordings; archives of Albéniz, Granados and other Catalan composers; Dir ROMÀ ESCALAS.

Museo Etnológico: Avda Sta Madrona s/n, Parc de Montjuïc, 08038 Barcelona; tel. 93-424-64-02; fax 93-423-73-64; e-mail metno@intercom.es; f. 1948; African, Asiatic, American, Oceanic ethnography and American archaeology; library of 25,000 vols; Dir CARMEN FAURIA ROMA.

Museo Geologico del Seminario de Barcelona (Geological Museum of Barcelona Seminary): Diputación 231, 08007 Barcelona; tel. 93-454-16-00; f. 1874; palaeontology of invertebrates; library of 15,000 vols; collection of 74,000 fossils; Dir Dr S. CALZADA; publ. *Batalleria* (annually).

Museu d'Arqueologia de Catalunya (Archaeological Museum of Catalonia): Passeig de Santa Madrona 39–41, Parc de Montjuïc, 08038 Barcelona; tel. 93-423-21-49; fax 93-425-42-44; e-mail difusio@barcelona.mac.es; f. 1935; collections of pre-historic, Greek, Phoenician, Visigothic and Roman art; library of 40,000 vols; Dir FRANCESC TARRATS-BOU; publs *Empúries* (annually), monographs.

Museu d'Història de la Ciutat: Plaça del Rei s/n, 08002 Barcelona; tel. 93-315-11-11; fax 93-315-09-57; e-mail mhistbcm@lix.intercom.es; f. 1943; 15th-century mansion containing Roman remains *in situ* (1st- to 5th-century Roman wall), 11th- to 15th-century Royal Palace; documentation centre, information service; Dir ANTONÍ NÍCOLAU MARTÍ.

Museu de Zoologia: Parc de la Ciutadella, Apdo 593, 08003 Barcelona; tel. 93-319-69-12; fax 93-310-49-99; e-mail mzoolbcn@intercom.es; f. 1882; permanent exhibitions on systematics and zoological diversity; research on biospeleology and ethology; library of 8,000 vols, 1,200 periodicals, 500 old books; Dir ANNA OMEDES; publs *Treballs, Miscel·lània Zoològica* (2 a year).

Museu Marítim de Barcelona (Barcelona Maritime Museum): Av. Drassanes s/n, 08001 Barcelona; tel. 93-301-18-71; fax 93-318-78-76; e-mail cdb-mmb@taz.feelingst.es; f. 1941; library of 15,000 vols; photographic, cartographic and documental archives, restoration workshop; Dir ELVIRA MATA ENRICH; publ. *Drassana* (2 a year).

Museu Nacional d'Art de Catalunya (National Art Museum): Palau Nacional, Parc de Montjuïc, 08038 Barcelona; tel. 93-423-71-99; fax 93-325-57-73; f. 1934; incl., on various sites, Museum of Art of Catalonia (romanesque to baroque Catalan art, Dir EDUARD CARBONELL I ESTELLER), Museum of Modern Art (19th- and 20th-century art, Dir CRISTINA MENDOZA), Numismatic Division (Dir MARTA CAMPO), Drawings and Engravings Division (Dir CECILIA VIDAL); library of 130,000 vols; Dir ROSA REIXATS.

Museu Picasso: Montcada 15–19, 08003 Barcelona; tel. 93-319-63-10; fax 93-315-01-02; e-mail mpicasso@intercom.es; f. 1963; paintings, pottery, drawings and engravings by Pablo Picasso, 1881–1973, including the series 'Las Meninas' and the artist's donation, in 1970, of 940 works of art; library of 5,000 vols; Dir M. TERESA OCAÑA.

Bilbao

Guggenheim Bilbao Museoa: Abandoibarra 2, 48001 Bilbao; tel. 94-435-90-08; fax 94-435-90-10; f. 1997; 20th-century American and European art; Dir-Gen. JUAN IGNACIO VIDARTE.

Museo de Bellas Artes de Bilbao: Plaza del Museo 2, 48011 Bilbao; tel. 94-439-60-60; fax 94-439-61-45; f. 1913; 1,923 exhibits of paintings, sculpture, furniture, famous works by El Greco, Goya, Velázquez, Jordaens, Teniers, Ribera, Gauguin and many others including an important new collection of early Spanish paintings and a new building containing contemporary art; cinema, bookshop and library; Dir MIGUEL ZUGAZA.

Burgos

Museo de Burgos: Casa Miranda – Casa Angulo, Calle Calera 25, 09002 Burgos; tel. 947-26-58-75; fax 947-27-67-92; f. 1871; Casa Miranda: archaeological collections (from Palaeolithic to Visigothic); Casa Angulo: fine arts collections (from Mozarabic to contemporary painting), enamels, ivories, tomb of Juan de Padilla, Tablas Flamencas (Ecce Homo) and 15th- to 20th-century painting, sculpture, altarpieces; library of 2,000 vols, specializing in archaeology and art; Dir Dr J. C. ELORZA Y GUINEA; publ. *Anales*.

Cartagena

Museo Arqueológico Municipal: Calle Ramón y Cajal 45, 30204 Cartagena; tel. 968-12-88-81; fax 968-12-88-82; f. 1943; important collections of Roman remains found in the area, including mining, submarine, industrial arts exhibits; model sites; Dir Dr MIGUEL MARTÍNEZ ANDREU; publs *Guía, Boletines*.

Chipiona

Museo Misional de Nuestra Señora de Regla: Colegio de Misioneros Franciscanos, Chipiona; f. 1939; about 600 exhibits of early Roman Christian relics, ancient Egyptian and other North African objects, antique coins, etc.; Dir R. P. Rector del Colegio.

Córdoba

Museo Arqueológico Provincial de Córdoba: Palacio de Jerónimo Páez, 14003 Córdoba; tel. 957-47-40-11; f. 1867; 30,200 exhibits; archaeological, prehistoric and local finds, Roman and medieval collections; library of 10,977 vols; Dir FRANCISCO GODOY DELGADO; publ. *Corduba Archaeologica* (annually).

Figueres

Teatre-Museu Dalí: Plaça Gala – Salvador Dalí 5, 17600 Figueres; tel. 972-51-18-00; fax 972-50-16-66; f. 1974; Dir ANTONÍ PITXOT SOLER.

Granada

Museo de Bellas Artes: Palacio de Carlos V, 18009 Granada; tel. 958-22-48-43; f. 1958 (present site); paintings and sculpture by local artists from 16th century to mid-20th century; library of 4,000 vols; Dir ANTONIO GARCÍA BASCÓN; publ. *Guide*.

Ibiza

Museo Arqueológico de Ibiza y Formentera: Plaza de la Catedral 3, 07800 Ibiza; tel. 971-30-12-31; fax 971-30-32-63; f. 1907; prehistoric, Roman, Carthaginian and medieval exhibits; museum has other sections in other buildings; Dir JORGE H. FERNÁNDEZ GÓMEZ; publ. *Trabajos* (2 a year).

Attached museum:

Museo y Necrópolis del Puig des Molins: Via Romana 31, Ibiza; tel. 971-30-17-71; fax 971-30-32-63; f. 1966; Carthaginian and Roman remains from the national monument of Puig des Molins; excavations in Ibiza and Formentera; library of 14,000 vols; Dir JORGE H. FERNÁNDEZ GÓMEZ; publ. *Trabajos del Museo Arqueológico de Ibiza y Formentera*.

La Escala

Museu d'Arqueologia de Cataluyna – Empúries: Ap. Correos 21, 17130 L'Escala; tel. 972-77-02-08; fax 972-77-42-60; f. 1908; collection of excavations of the Greco-Roman city; library of 3,000 vols; Dir XAVIER AQUILUÉ.

Las Palmas

Museo Canario: Dr Chil 25, Las Palmas; tel. 928-31-56-00; fax 928-31-49-98; f. 1879; local archaeology and anthropology, ethnography and natural sciences; library of 60,000 vols; Pres. LOTHAR SIEMENS HERNÁNDEZ; publ. *El Museo Canario* (annually).

Lérida (Lleida)

Gabinet Numismàtic: Institut d'Estudis Ilerdencs, Plaça de la Catedral s/n, 25002 Lérida; e-mail iei@fpiei.es; Roman, Iberian, Ibero-Roman, Medieval and Modern exhibits; local collections.

Restes Monumentals-Museo de la Paeria: Plaça Paeria 1; Lérida; tel. 973-70-02-23; fax 973-23-89-53; f. 1963; historical documents and objects belonging to the municipality; archaeological finds of Lérida.

Museo Diocesano: Jaime Conquistador 67, Lérida; tel. 973-26-86-28; fax 973-27-29-72; f.1893; medieval sculptures; also sub-section at Rambla de Aragón containing religious paintings, metal work and vestments; Dir JESÚS TARRAGONA MURAY; publ. *Catàlog del Museu*.

Museu d'Art Modern 'Jaume Morera': Edificio Roser, Calle Caballeros 15, Lérida; f. 1917; museum of modern paintings mainly by Catalan artists, including works by Morera, C. Haes and others; Dir JESÚS NAVARRO GUITART.

Sala d'Arqueologia de la Fundació Pública: Institut d'Estudis Ilerdencs, Plaça Catedral s/n, 25002 Lérida; tel. 973-27-15-00; fax 973-27-45-38; f. 1954; archaeology (Bronze Age, Iberian, Roman, Visigoth); Dir JOSEP BORRELL I FIGUERA.

Madrid

Instituto de Valencia de Don Juan (Don Juan Institute of Valencia): Fortuny 43, 28010 Madrid; tel. 91-308-18-48; f. 1916; historical archives; library of 10,024 historical and art vols; illuminated MS *Les Statuts de la Toison d'Or* with miniatures; museum of ancient Spanish industrial arts; Pres. CARLOS MARTÍNEZ DE IRUJO; Dir BALBINA MARTÍNEZ CAVIRO.

Museo Arqueológico Nacional (National Archaeological Museum): Serrano 13, 28001 Madrid; tel. 91-577-79-12; fax 91-431-68-40; f. 1867; library of 54,000 vols, 1,493 periodicals; medieval MSS include Huesca Bible of 12th century, *Beato de Liébana, Comentarios al Apocalipsis* (12th–13th-century), *Martirologio y Regla de S. Benito* (13th-century), *Cantorales* (15th-century), 16th-century miniatures; collections relating to Egyptian, Cypriot, Greek and Etruscan Antiquities and to national prehistory, Iron Age, Iberian and Hispano-Roman Art; from medieval and modern times: ivory carvings, Spanish pottery, Islamic pottery, brocades, tapestries, porcelain, furniture, textiles and a numismatic collection; Dir MARTÍN ALMAGRO GORBEA; publ. *Boletín*.

Museo Cerralbo: Ventura Rodríguez 17, 28008 Madrid; tel. 91-547-36-46; fax 91-559-11-71; f. 1924; the seventeenth Marquis of Cerralbo left his house to the nation as a museum, together with his collection of paintings, drawings, engravings, porcelain, arms, carpets, coins, furniture; includes paintings by El Greco, Ribera, Titian, Van Dyck, Tintoretto; library of 12,000 vols; Dir PILAR DE NAVASCUÉS BENLLOCH.

Museo de la Farmacia Hispana: Facultad de Farmacia, Universidad Complutense, Ciudad Universitaria, 28040 Madrid; tel. 91-394-17-97; fax 91-394-17-97; f. 1951; library of *c*. 10,000 vols; Dir FRANCISCO JAVIER PUERTO SARMIENTO.

Museo de la Real Academia de Bellas Artes de San Fernando: Alcalá 13, 28014 Madrid; tel. 91-522-14-91; fax 91-523-15-99; f. 1744; 16th- to 20th-century Spanish paintings (incl. works by Goya, Zurbarán, Murillo, Ribera and Pereda), 16th- to 18th-century European paintings, 17th- to 20th-century Spanish sculpture; Dir ANTONIO BONET CORREA; publ. *Academia* (2 a year).

Museo del Ejército (Army Museum): Méndez Núñez 1, 28071 Madrid; tel. 91-522-06-28; fax 91-531-46-24; f. 1803; some 30,000 exhibits; collections of arms, war trophies, flags and tin soldiers; department at Toledo; library of 8,500 vols; Dir Gen. JUAN MA. DE PEÑARANDA Y ALGAR; publ. *Guía del Museo*.

Museo del Ferrocarril (Railway Museum): Paseo de las Delicias 61, 28045 Madrid; fax 91-506-80-24; f. 1984; steam, diesel and electric trains, models, exhibitions; photographic archive; Dir RAFAEL RUIZ SANCHIDRIAN.

Museo Lázaro Galdiano: Calle Serrano 122, 28006 Madrid; tel. 91-561-60-84; fax 91-561-77-93; e-mail goya@flg.es; f. 1951; 10,000 items: Italian, Spanish and Flemish Renaissance paintings; Primitives; Golden Age, 18th- and 19th-century Spanish paintings; 17th-century Dutch paintings; English 18th-century collection; Golden Age MSS and incunabula; collections of ivory, enamels, watches, jewellery, furniture, weapons and armour, oriental and Spanish tapestries and cloth; Dir ARACELI PEREDA ALONSO; publ. *'Goya' Revista de Arte* (every 2 months).

Museo Municipal de Madrid (Madrid Museum): Calle Fuencarral 78, 28004 Madrid; tel. 91-588-86-72; fax 91-588-86-79; f. 1929; history of Madrid, from its origin to the 20th century; prehistoric finds, portraits, paintings, designs, engravings, sculptures, plans, silversmiths' work, coins, ceramics, porcelain, paintings by Berruguete, Maella, Luca Giordano, Bayeu, Castillo, Goya and other contemporary artists, 1830 Madrid scale model, Ramón de Mesonero Romanos and Ramón Gómez de la Serna studies; Dir CARMEN PRIEGO FERNÁNDEZ DEL CAMPO.

Museo Nacional Centro de Arte Reina Sofía: Calle Santa Isabel 52, 28012 Madrid; tel. 91-467-50-62; fax 91-467-31-63; f. 1986 in a refurbished 18th-century building; contemporary art; Dir JOSÉ GUIRAO CABRERA.

Museo Nacional de Antropología (National Anthropological Museum): Alfonso XII 68, 28014 Madrid; tel. 91-539-59-95; fax 91-467-70-98; f. 1993 through the fusion of Museo Nacional de Etnología and Museo Nacional del Pueblo Español; 30,000 exhibits and about 1,500 skulls; famous collections from Europe, the former Spanish Guinea, the Philippines, South America, Micronesia, Melanesia, the Sahara, Morocco, Asia and West and Central Africa; Inuit and Mesoamerican exhibits; library of 14,000 vols and anthropological periodicals; Dir PILAR ROMERO DE TEJADA; publ. *Catalogues*.

Museo Nacional de Artes Decorativas: Calle Montalbán 12, 28014 Madrid; tel. 91-532-64-99; fax 91-523-20-86; f. 1912; contains collections of interior decorative arts, especially Spanish of 15th to 19th centuries, including carpets, furniture, leatherwork, jewellery, tapestries, ceramics, glass, porcelain, textiles, etc.; library of 12,000 vols; Dir Dr ALBERTO BARTOLOMÉ ARRAIZA.

Museo Nacional de Ciencia y Tecnología (National Museum of Science and Technology): Paseo de las Delicias 61, 28045 Madrid; tel. 91-530-31-21; fax 91-467-51-19; e-mail mhct@mnct.dit.upm.es; f. 1980; library of 7,000 vols; Dir Dra JOSEFA JIMÉNEZ ALBARRÁN (acting).

Museo Nacional de Ciencias Naturales (Natural Science Museum): José Gutiérrez Abascal 2, 28006 Madrid; fax 91-564-50-78; f. 1771 as Gabinete de Historia Natural by Carlos III; attached to CSIC; valuable natural history and scientific collections, mainly from Iberia, Central and South America, Philippines and North Africa; library of 62,300 vols, incl. over 2,000 volumes dating from the 15th-18th centuries and 1 incunabulum; 1,835 periodicals, dating from 1790; Dir ROBERTO FERNÁNDEZ DE CALEYA; publs *Graellsia, Estudios Geológicos*.

Museo Nacional de Reproducciones Artísticas (Reproductions of Works of Art): Ciudad Universitaria, Madrid; tel. 91-549-66-18; f. 1878; library of 8,250 vols; 3,240 reproductions of Oriental, Greek, Roman and Hispano-Roman statuary, medieval and Renaissance art, classical and medieval sculpture and decorative arts; Dir MA JOSÉ ALMAGRO GORBEA.

Museo Nacional del Prado (National Museum of Paintings and Sculpture): Paseo del Prado s/n, 28014 Madrid; tel. 91-330-28-00; fax 91-330-28-56; f. 1819; paintings by Botticelli, Rembrandt, Velázquez, El Greco, Goya, Murillo, Raphael, Bosch, Van der Weyden, Zurbarán, Van Dyck, Tiepolo, Ribalta, Rubens, Titian, Veronese, Tintoretto, Moro, Juanes, Meléndez, Poussin, Ribera, etc.; Classical and Renaissance sculpture; jewels and medals; Dir FERNANDO CHECA CREMADES; publs Catalogues.

Museo Naval (Naval Museum): Paseo del Prado 5, 28014 Madrid; tel. 91-379-52-99; fax 91-379-50-56; f. 1843; library of 18,000 vols; engravings of sea battles, portraits, nautical instruments and armaments; 2,500 vols of MSS; some 6,000 original maps, charts, prints and drawings of many countries dating from 1600; files containing over 17,800 photographs; Dir JOSÉ IGNACÍO GONZÁLEZ-ALLER HIERRO; publ. *Revista de Historia Naval* (quarterly).

Museo Romántico (Museum of the Romantic Period): San Mateo 13, 28004 Madrid; tel. 91-448-10-45; fax 91-594-28-93; f. 1924; paintings, furniture, books and decorations of the Spanish romantic period; Dir MA. BEGOÑA TORRES GONZÁLEZ.

Museo Sorolla (Sorolla Museum): General Martínez Campos 37, 28010 Madrid; tel. 91-310-15-84; fax 91-308-59-25; f. 1931; permanent exhibition of some 350 of the artist's works, including drawings, water-colours, portraits, and his own art collections; library of 4,000 vols; Dir FLORENCIO DE SANTA-ANA Y ALVAREZ OSSORIO.

Museo Thyssen-Bornemisza: Paseo del Prado 8, 28014 Madrid; tel. 91-420-39-44; fax 91-420-27-80; e-mail museo.thyssen-bornemisza@offcampus.es; f. 1992; 13th- to 20th-century paintings and sculpture; Dir CARLOS FERNÁNDEZ DE HENESTROSA.

Patrimonio Nacional: Calle de Bailén s/n, 28071 Madrid; f. 1940 to administer former Crown property; it is responsible for all the museums situated in royal palaces and properties and is governed by an Administrative Council; Dir JOAQUÍN DEL POZO LÓPEZ; publs Guides to all the Museums, *Reales Sitios* (quarterly).

Controls the following:

Palacio Real de Madrid: Calle Bailen s/n, 28071 Madri; tel. 91-542-00-59; special rooms devoted to 16th- to 18th-century tapestries, clocks, paintings and porcelain from the royal palaces and pharmacy; there is also an armoury; library: see Libraries; the archives date from the 12th century.

Palacio Real de Aranjuez: 28300 Aranjuez; tel. 91-891-13-44; former royal palace rich in 18th-century art.

Museo-Monasterio de San Lorenzo de El Escorial: 28200 San Lorenzo de El Escorial; tel. 91-890-59-03; built by Juan de

Herrera; contains many famous works by international artists of the 16th century and 18th century from royal residences.

Museo-Monasterio de las Huelgas: Calle Compás de Adentro s/n, 09001 Burgos; tel. 947-20-16-30; founded by Alfonso VIII in the 9th century.

Museo-Monasterio de Santa Clara: 47100 Tordesillas (Valladolid); tel. 983-77-00-71; 14th century.

Museo-Monasterio de la Encarnación: Plaza de la Encarnación 1, 28013 Madrid; tel. 91-542-00-59; monastic life in the 16th and 17th centuries.

Museo-Monasterio de las Descalzas Reales: Plaza de las Descalzas s/n, 28013 Madrid; tel. 91-542-00-59; showing monastic life in the 16th and 17th centuries; 'European Museum of the Year' 1987.

Palacio Real de El Pardo: Paseo de El Pardo s/n, 24048 El Pardo (Madrid); tel. 91-376-11-36; built for Carlos V in 1547; furniture, porcelain, tapestries, etc.

Palacio de La Granja: Plaza de España 17, 40100 La Granja de San Ildefonso (Segovia); tel. 921-47-00-19; gardens and fountains in imitation of Versailles, tapestry museum.

Palacio de Riofrío: 40420 Riofrío (Segovia); tel. 921-48-01-42; hunting palace built in 1752.

Palacio de la Almudaina: Calle Palau Reial s/n, 07001 Palma de Mallorca, Balearic Is; tel. 971-72-71-45; Arab-gothic palace.

Valle de Los Caídos: Valle de Cuelgamuros, 28209 Madrid; tel. 91-890-55-44; monument to the fallen, begun in 1940 and finished in 1958.

Planetario de Madrid: Parque Tierno Galván, 28045 Madrid; tel. 91-467-34-61; fax 91-468-11-54; e-mail buzon@planetmad.es; f. 1986; exhibition and projection room seating 250 people; Dir ASUNCIÓN SÁNCHEZ JUSTEL; publs brochures.

Real Jardín Botánico (Royal Botanical Garden): Plaza de Murillo 2, 28014 Madrid; tel. 91-420-30-17; fax 91-420-01-57; part of CSIC (*q.v.*); f. 1755; botanical research; herbarium with 1,000,000 specimens; library of 18,000 vols, 2,000 periodicals, 22,000 reprints, 3,200 microfiches, MSS, 13,000 botanical drawings, 6,900 slides; Dir Dra M. T. TELLERÍA; Sec. J. GIL; publs *Anales* (annually), *Ruizia* (irregular).

Mérida

Museo Nacional de Arte Romano: José Ramón Mélida s/n, 06800 Mérida; tel. 924-31-19-12; fax 924-30-20-06; e-mail mnar@mnar.es; f. 1838; Roman archaeology; library of 10,000 specialized vols, periodicals; Dir Dr JOSÉ M. ALVAREZ MARTÍNEZ; publs *Monografías Emeritenses*, *Anas*, *Cuadernos Emeritenses*.

Palma de Mallorca

Museo de Mallorca: Calle Portella 5, 07001 Palma; tel. 971-71-75-40; fax 971-71-04-83; f. 1961; history, ethnology, fine arts; Dir GUILLERMO ROSSELLÓ BORDOY.

Pontevedra

Museo de Pontevedra: Calle Pasantería 10, Apdo 104, 36080 Pontevedra; tel. 986-851455; fax 986-840693; f. 1927, opened 1929; library of 100,000 vols on literature, art and archaeology of Galicia; pottery and ancient industrial and naval history of Galicia; prehistoric jewellery and jet ornaments; Spanish 15th–20th-century paintings; Dir Dr JOSÉ CARLOS VALLE PEREZ; publ. *El Museo de Pontevedra* (annually).

Sabadell

Museu d'Art de Sabadell: Carrer Dr Puig 16, 08202 Sabadell; tel. 93-725-77-47; f. 1978; painting, ceramics, photography; Dir JOSEP SERRANO; Curator ENGRÀCIA TORRELLA; publ. *Arraona*.

Museu d'Història de Sabadell: Carrer Sant Antoni 13, 08201 Sabadell; tel. 93-727-85-55; f. 1931; prehistoric archaeological, numismatic collections, native handicrafts; Iberico-Roman section, and sections on textiles and mineralogy; Dir (vacant); publ. *Arraona* (2 a year).

Sabiñánigo

Museo de Dibujo 'Castillo de Larrés': Apdo 25, 22600 Sabiñánigo, Huesca; tel. 974-48-29-81; f. 1986 by 'Amigos de Serrablo', a cultural asscn specializing entirely in contemporary Spanish and Spanish-American design; Pres. JULIO GAVÍN MOYA.

San Roque

Museo Histórico de San Roque: Ayuntamiento, San Roque, Prov. Cádiz; f. 1956; documents of Gibraltar and museum of Carteyan excavations; Dir RAFAEL CALDELA LÓPEZ; Chief of Archaeological Section FRANCISCO PRESCEDO.

San Sebastián

Museo Municipal de San Telmo: Plaza Ignacio Zuloaga 1, 20003 Donostia-San Sebastián; tel. 943-42-49-70; fax 943-43-06-93; housed in an ancient Convent dating from the reign of Charles V; inaug. 1932 by Alfonso XIII; prehistoric, archaeological, anthropological; paintings by Vicente López, El Greco, José María Sert, etc.; Museo Vasco, Ethnographical Section, shows the rural life of the Basques; weapons, history of San Sebastián; Dir RAFAEL ZULAIKA; governed by a Junta de Patronato.

Museo Naval y Aquarium (Naval Museum and Aquarium): Sociedad de Oceanografía de Guipúzcoa, Paseo del Muelle 34, 20003 Donostia–San Sebastián; tel. 943-44-00-99; fax 943-43-00-92; e-mail aquarium@paisvasco.com; f. 1908; history of seafaring from the 13th century, models of historical ships, portraits of navigators, local fishing tackle, and aquarium; oceanographic museum and marine laboratory.

Santander

Museo de Prehistoria y Arqueología (Prehistoric and Archaeological Museum): Casimiro Saine 4, 39003 Santander; tel. 942-20-71-08; fax 942-20-71-06; f. 1941; palaeolithic to Middle Ages in Cantabria; library of 60,000 vols.

Santiago de Compostela

Museo das Peregrinacions (Pilgrimage Museum): San Miguel 4, 'Casa Gotica', Santiago de Compostela; tel. 981-58-15-58; fax 981-58-19-55; f. 1951, inaugurated 1966; relics and items related to St James and the Pilgrimages; medieval art and history of the 'Camino de Santiago'; library of 4,000 vols; Dir BIEITO PÉREZ OUTERIÑO; Curator MA. ISABEL PESQUERA VAQUERO.

Seville

Museo Arqueológico Provincial: Plaza de América (Parque de María Luisa), Seville; tel. 95-423-24-01; f. 1880; *c.* 10,000 exhibits; Roman statues, mosaics; incorporates the municipal collections; treasures of Tarshish; Dir FERNANDO FERNÁNDEZ GÓMEZ; publs *Catálogo del Museo Arqueológico de Sevilla*, and various monographs.

Museo de Bellas Artes de Sevilla: Plaza del Museo 9, 41001 Seville; tel. 95-422-18-29; fax 95-422-43-24; e-mail mbase@zoom.es; f. 1841; fine arts; library of 9,000 vols, 90 periodicals; Dir ENRIQUE PAREJA LOPEZ.

Sitges

Museu Cau Ferrat: Calle Fonollar s/n, Sitges; tel. 93-894-03-64; fax 93-894-85-29; f. 1933; house and studio of the painter and writer Santiago Rusiñol; contains drawings and paintings by Rusiñol and his friends and contemporaries; (Casas, Picasso, Utrillo, etc.); also woodcarving, sculpture, ancient painting (El Greco), ceramics (14th to 20th centuries), furniture, ironwork (13th to 19th centuries), glass (16th to 19th centuries); Dir MARIA-NADAL SAU I GIRALT.

Soria

Museo Numantino: Paseo del Espolón 8, Soria; tel. 975-22-13-97; fax 975-22-98-72; f. 1916; prehistoric, ethnological, Roman and medieval archaeological collections, comprising 180,000 objects; library of 10,000 vols; Dir JOSÉ LUIS ARGENTE OLIVER; Curator MARÍA ANGELES ARLEGUI SÁNCHEZ.

Tarragona

Museu i Necròpolis Paleocristians: Avda de Ramon y Cajal 80, 43005 Tarragona; tel. 977-21-11-75; fax 977-24-53-93; e-mail mnat@mnat.es; f. 1930; objects discovered during excavation of the Roman-Christian necropolis; Dir J. M. CARRETÉ NADAL.

Museu Nacional Arqueològic de Tarragona (Archaeological Museum): Plaça del Rei 5, 43003 Tarragona; tel. 977-23-62-06; fax 977-24-53-93; f. 1834; archaeological, historical, local Roman exhibits; library of 12,000 vols; Dir FRANCESC TARRATS I BOU; publ. *Forum*.

Toledo

Casa y Museo del Greco: Fundaciones Vega Inclán (El Greco's House): Calle Samuel Leví, Toledo; tel. 925-22-40-46; f. 1911; the artist's house, furniture of the period, and a collection of the artist's paintings and those of his followers; Dir MA ELENA GÓMEZ-MORENO; Curator CONSOLACIÓN PASTOR.

Museo de Santa Cruz: Calle Cervantes 3, 45001 Toledo; tel. 925-22-14-02; fax 925-22-58-62; f. 1958; archaeology, fine arts, industrial and decorative arts; library of 12,000 vols; Dir RAFAEL GARCÍA SERRANO; publs *Memoria del Museo de Santa Cruz* (irregular), catalogues.

Affiliated museums:

Museo de los Concilios y de la Cultura Visigoda: Calle San Román s/n, Toledo; tel. 925-22-78-72; f. 1969; Visigothic art and archaeology.

Museo Taller del Moro: Calle Taller del Moro 4, Toledo; tel. 925-22-71-15; f. 1961; Mudejar art and archaeology.

Museo de Arte Contemporáneo (Museum of Contemporary Art): Calle de las Bulas, Toledo; tel. 925-22-78-71; f. 1973.

Museo Casa de Dulcinea en El Toboso: Toledo; tel. 925-19-72-88; f. 1967; ethnography of La Mancha area and period reconstruction in the 17th-century Casa Solariega.

Museo de Cerámica 'Ruíz de Luna': Calle San Agustín, Talavera de la Reina; tel. 925-80-01-49; f. 1963; local ceramics.

Sinagoga del Tránsito: Calle Samuel Leví, s/n, 45002 Toledo; tel. 925-22-36-65; fax 925-21-58-31; e-mail museo.sefardi@tld.servicom.es; Jewish synagogue built in the 14th century by Samuel Ha-Levi, treasurer to King Don Pedro I, 'The Cruel'; given to the Military Order of Calatrava in 1494 by Ferdinand and Isabella; in 18th century became church of Sta María del Tránsito; national monument; created Sephardic Museum 1964; archaeology, life and costumes of Sephardic Jews; library of 9,000 vols on Judaism, Hebraism and Sephardism; Dir ANA MARÍA LÓPEZ ALVAREZ.

Valencia

Museo de Bellas Artes (Museum of Fine Arts): Calle de San Pío V 9, 46010 Valencia; tel. 96-360-57-93; fax 96-369-71-25; housed in an old palace; f. 1839; more than 3,000 paintings, also sculpture, archaeology, drawing and print sections; library of 12,000 vols on art; Dir FERNANDO BENITO.

Museo Nacional de Cerámica 'González Martí': Poeta Querol 2, 46002 Valencia; tel. 96-351-63-92; fax 96-351-35-12; e-mail jaime_coll@bbs.idg.es; f. 1947; a national museum of ceramics and minor arts, set in the Palace of the Marquis of Dos Aguas; library of 20,000 vols; Dir Dr JAIME COLL CONESA.

Valladolid

Casa de Cervantes (Cervantes' House): Calle del Rastro, 47001 Valladolid; tel. 983-30-88-10; fax 983-39-07-03; furniture and possessions of the writer; Dirs NICOMEDES SANZ Y RUIZ DE LA PEÑA, AMPARO MAGDALENO DE LA CRUZ.

Museo de Valladolid: Palacio de Fabio Nelli, Plaza de Fabio Nelli s/n, Valladolid; tel. 983-35-13-89; fax 983-35-04-22; f. 1879; archaeology and fine art, articles from palaeolithic times to the 18th century; specialized library with restricted access; Dir ELOISA WATTENBERG GARCIA.

Museo Nacional de Escultura: Cadenas de San Gregorio 1, 47011 Valladolid; tel. 983-25-03-75; f. 1933; housed in the old Colegio de San Gregorio, dating from end of 15th century; works by Alonso Berruguete, Juan de Juni, Gregorio Fernández, and others; library of 7,277 vols; Dir LUIS LUNA MORENO; publs *Catálogos*.

Vic

Museu Arqueològic-Artístic Episcopal de Vic (Archaeological and Artistic Episcopal Museum): Pl. Bisbe Oliba 3, Vic, Barcelona; tel. 93-886-22-14; fax 93-889-48-07; f. 1891; medieval arts, provincial Romanesque, Gothic precious metalwork, textiles, embroideries, liturgical vestments, forged iron, etc.; Curator M. S. GROS.

Zamora

Museo de Zamora: Palacio del Cordón, Plaza de Sta Lucía 2, 49002 Zamora; tel. 980-51-61-50; fax 980-53-50-64; f. 1877 and inaugurated 1911 as Museo Provincial de Bellas Artes; housed in 16th-century palace; collections: palaeontology, prehistory and archaeology, fine arts, ethnography; library of 5,000 vols; Dir ROSARIO GARCÍA ROZAS.

Zaragoza

Museo de Zaragoza: Plaza de los Sitios 6, Zaragoza; (Ethnology and Ceramics sections: Parque Primo de Ribera); tel. 976-22-21-81; fax 976-22-23-78; f. 1908; archaeological; prehistory, Roman, Arab, Gothic, Moorish, Romanesque and Renaissance exhibits; primitive arts and crafts, paintings from 14th to 19th centuries, contemporary Aragonese artists; library of 21,000 vols; Dir Dr MIGUEL BELTRÁN LLORIS; Curators MARÍA LUISA CANCELA RAMÍREZ DE ARELLANO, JUAN PAZ PERALTA; publ. *Boletín*.

Museo Pablo Gargallo: Plaza de San Felipe 3, 50003 Zaragoza; tel. 976-39-20-58; fax 976-39-20-76; f. 1982; important collection of sculpture, designs and cartoons by Gargallo; research on his life and works, and modern art in general; documentation centre of 15,000 vols on Gargallo and sculpture in general; Dir MARÍA CRISTINA GIL IMAZ.

Universities

UNIVERSIDAD NACIONAL DE EDUCACIÓN A DISTANCIA (Open University)

Ciudad Universitaria s/n, 28040 Madrid
Telephone: 91-398-60-16
Fax: 91-398-60-37

Founded 1972
State control
Language of instruction: Spanish
Academic year: October to July

Rector: JENARO COSTAS RODRÍGUEZ
Vice-Rectors: MA DOLORES DÍAZ-AMBRONA BARDAJI (Continuing Education), ROGELIO MEDINA RUBIO (Academic Affairs), LUIS TEJERO ESCRIBANO (Associated Centres), ANGEL MUÑOZ MERCHANTE (Economic Affairs), ENRIQUE CANTERA MONTENEGRO (Co-ordination), ALFONSO CONTRERAS LÓPEZ (Students), MARIANO RODRÍGUEZ-AVIAL LLARDENT (Research), EDUARDO RAMOS MÉNDEZ (Methodology, Media and Technology)
Chief of Administration: SANTIAGO JIMÉNEZ BARRULL
Librarian: ISABEL BELMONTE MARTÍNEZ

Number of teachers: 879
Number of students: 109,653 (in faculties), 33,671 (Foundation and Courses)

DEANS

Faculty of Law: GASPAR ESCALONA MARTÍNEZ
Faculty of Psychology: ARACELI MACIÁ ANTÓN
Faculty of Philosophy: ELOY RADA GARCÍA
Faculty of Educational Studies: RAMÓN PÉREZ JUSTE
Faculty of Economics and Business Studies: EDUARDO PÉREZ GORÓSTEGUI
Faculty of Philology: JOSÉ ROMERA CASTILLO
Faculty of Geography and History: JESÚS VIÑUALES GONZÁLEZ
Faculty of Politics and Sociology: SANTOS JULIÁ DÍAZ
Faculty of Sciences: JOSÉ L. FERNÁNDEZ MARRÓN
Technical School of Computer Science: VICTORIANO LÓPEZ RODRÍGUEZ
School of Industrial Engineering: MIGUEL ANGEL SEBASTIÁN PÉREZ
Institute of Educational Sciences: EUSTAQUIO MARTÍN RODRÍGUEZ
Foundation Course: ROSA MARTÍNEZ SEGARRA

The University has 60 associated centres in Spain, and 11 abroad in Brussels, Geneva, Paris, London, Bonn, Caracas, Rosario, Mexico, Sao Paulo and Equatorial Guinea (2).

UNIVERSIDAD DE ALCALÁ

Plaza de San Diego s/n, 28801 Alcalá de Henares (Madrid)
Telephone: 91-885-40-00
Fax: 91-885-40-95

Founded 1977
State control
Language of instruction: Spanish
Academic year: September to June

Rector: Dr MANUEL GALA MUÑOZ
Vice-Rectors: Dr ELADIO MONTOYA MELGAR (Academic Staff), Dr JOSÉ A. GONZALO ANGULO (Economic Affairs), Dr LUIS BELTRÁN (International Relations), Dr JULIO ALVAREZ-BUÍLLA (Scientific and Technological Developments), Dr JUAN CARLOS PRIETO VILLAPÚN (Research), Dra PILAR LÓPEZ LUNA (Student Affairs), Dr CARLOS ALVAR (Extramural Studies), Dr JOSÉ BLÁZQUEZ (Curricula and Centres), Dr MANUEL MAZO (Infrastructure), Dr FRANCISCO BOSCH (Guadalajara Campus)
Secretary-General: Dr JOSÉ ENRIQUE BUSTOS
Administrative Director: OLGA RIUS
Librarian: MA. DEL CARMEN FERNÁNDEZ GALIANO

Number of teachers: 1,314
Number of students: 18,664

Publications: *Paraninfo, Encuentro, Estudios de Historia Económica y Social de América, Henares, Teatro, Polis, Reale, Reden, Las Comarcas Agrarias de España, Signo, Barataria, Idagación, Quodlibet, Cairón*.

DEANS

Faculty of Philosophy and Letters: Dra MARÍA DOLORES CABAÑAS
Faculty of Sciences: Dr FERNANDO JORDÁN DE URRIES
Faculty of Pharmacy: Dr VICENTE VILAS
Faculty of Law: Dr LUIS GARCÍA-SAN MIGUEL
Faculty of Economics and Business Administration: Dr JESÚS PENA TRAPERO
Faculty of Medicine: Dr ANTONIO LÓPEZ
Faculty of the Environment: Dr ANTONIO SASTRE
Faculty of Library Science: Dra PURIFICACIÓN MOSCOSO

DIRECTORS

Polytechnic School: JOSÉ ANTONIO PÁMIES
School of Nursing: Dra MARTA DURÁN ESCRIBANO
School of Business (Guadalajara): Dra ESPERANZA VITÓN
Teacher Training School (Alcalá): Dr ANGEL MARÍA ALCALÁ DEL OLMO
School of Architecture: RICARDO ALEN
School of Tourism: Dr ANTONIO MORA

HEADS OF DEPARTMENTS

Animal Biology: Dr JOSÉ MANUEL VIÉITEZ MARTÍN
Cell Biology and Genetics: Dr NICOLÁS JOUVE DE LA BARREDA
Vegetal Biology: Dr MANUEL PEINADO LORCA
Biochemistry and Molecular Biology: Dra MARÍA NATIVIDAD RECIO
Business Studies: Dr VICENTE GONZÁLEZ CATALÁ
Health and Medico-Social Sciences: Dr ANTONIO PIGA RIVERO
Morphology and Surgery: Dr LUIS GÓMEZ PELLICO
Law and Penal Law: AGUSTÍN MOTILLA
Mathematics: Dr JOAN LLOVET
Private Law: Dr JOSÉ MARÍA SOLAS RAFECAS
Public Law: Dr JUAN JOSÉ GONZÁLEZ ENCINAR
Applied Economics: Dr TOMÁS MANCHA
Education: Dr ALBERTO DEL AMO DELGADO
Medical Specializations: Dr JOSÉ LUIS BARDASANO RUBIO
Pharmacy and Pharmaceutical Technology: Dr EUGENIO SELLÉS FLORES
Philology: Dr ANTONIO ALVAR EZQUERRA
Physics: Dr JUAN SEQUEIROS UGARTE
Physiology and Pharmacology: Dr EDUARDO CUENCA FERNÁNDEZ
Criminal Law and Law Principles: Dr AGUSTÍN MOTILLA DE LA CALLE
Principles of Economics and Economic History: Dr JUAN MURO
Geography: Dr JOSÉ SANCHO COMINS
Geology: Dr IRENE BUSTAMANTE GUTIERREZ
History I and Philosophy: Dr LUIS GARCÍA MORENO
History II: Dr MANUEL LUCENA SALMORAL
Computer Science: Dr LUIS LÓPEZ CORRAL
Medicine: Dr MELCHOR ALVAREZ DE MON
Microbiology and Parasitology: Dra FILOMENA RODRÍGUEZ CAABEIRO
Physical Chemistry: Dra MARÍA MELIA RODRIGO LÓPEZ
Inorganic Chemistry: Dr TOMÁS CUENCA AGREDA
Organic Chemistry: Dr LUIS FUENTES GARRIDO

Computer Engineering: Dr DANIEL MEZIAT LUNA
Electronic Engineering: Dr JESÚS UREÑA UREÑA
Communications Engineering: Dr ROBERTO JIMÉNEZ
Modern Philology: Dr FERNANDO GALVÁN
Analytical Chemistry and Chemical Engineering: Dr ELOY GARCÍA CALVO
Nutrition and Bromatology: Dra AMELIA HERNÁNDEZ GARCÍA
Nursing Studies: Dra MARTA DURÁN ESCRIBANO
Statistics, Economic Structure and International Economic Organization: Dr ANTONIO TORRERO

ATTACHED INSTITUTES

Teacher-Training School: Dir Dr LUIS REBOLLO FERREIRO.

Centre of European Studies: Dir Dr CARLOS MOLINA DEL POZO.

Centre of American (USA) Studies: Dir Dr JOSÉ MORILLA CRITZ.

Institute of Business Organization and Management (IDOE): Dir Dr SANTIAGO GARCÍA ECHEVARRÍA.

Institute of Education: Dir Dra ISABEL BRINCONES.

Foreign Languages Centre: Dir Dr FRANCISCO MORENO.

Bioelectromagnetism Institute 'Alonso de Santa Cruz': Dir Dr JOSÉ LUIS BARDASANO.

Law School: Dir Dr DIEGO MANUEL LUZÓN.

Spanish Institute of Architecture: Dir JOAQUÍN IBÁÑEZ.

Institute of Sephardic and Andalusian Studies: Dir Dr JAIME CONTRERAS.

Centre for Initiatives in Co-operation for Development: Dir MANUEL GUEDAN.

Antonio Machado Euro-American Institute of Culture, Science and Communication: Dir MANUEL NUÑEZ ENCABO.

UNIVERSIDAD ALFONSO X EL SABIO

Avda Universidad 1, Edif. 2A, 28691 Villanueva de la Canada, Madrid

Telephone: 91-810-92-00

Founded 1993

DEANS

Faculty of Health Sciences: (vacant)
Faculty of Social Studies: ANDRÉS TAGLIAVIA LÓPEZ
Faculty of Applied Languages: ÍÑIGO SÁNCHEZ PAÑOS
Polytechnic School: ANDRÉS ARÉVALO MARTÍNEZ (Dir)

UNIVERSIDAD DE ALICANTE

San Vicente del Raspeig, 03690 Alicante
Telephone: 96-590-34-00
Fax: 96-590-36-72

Founded 1979
State control
Languages of instruction: Spanish, Valenciano
Academic year: October to September

Rector: ANDRÉS PEDREÑO MUÑOZ
Vice-Rector for Academic Affairs: SALVADOR ORDÓÑEZ DELGADO
Vice-Rector for Research: JUAN RUIZ MANERO
Vice-Rector for Alumni: MARIO PARDO CASADO
Vice-Rector for University Extension and Cultural Activities: ANTONIO RAMOS HIDALGO
Vice-Rector for Development and Economic Affairs: CARLOS BARCIELA LÓPEZ
Vice-Rector for Advanced Technology Development: MANUEL MARCO SUCH
Vice-Rector for Institutional and International Relations: ANA LAGUNA PÉREZ
Vice-Rector for Courses and Academic Innovation: ARMANDO ALBEROLA ROMÁ
Secretary-General: GUILLERMO BERNABEU PASTOR
Librarian: JOSÉ MATEO MARTÍNEZ

Number of teachers: 1,200
Number of students: 30,000

Publications: *Anales* (all faculties)

DEANS

Faculty of Philosophy and Letters: FRANCISCO AURA JORRO
Faculty of Sciences: FRANCISCO IGNACIO LLORCA ALCARAZ
Faculty of Law: MANUEL SANTANA MOLINA
Faculty of Economics and Business Administration: ANTONIO ESCUDERO GUTIÉRREZ

DIRECTORS

University School of Business Studies: LEONARDO YÁÑEZ MUÑOZ
University School of Professional Studies: JESÚS RAFAEL DE VERA FERRÉ
University School of Labour Relations: MARÍA DEL CARMEN VIQUEIRA PÉREZ
University School of Social Work: MARÍA TERESA MIRA-PERCEVAL PASTOR
University School of Optics: BEGOÑA DOMENECH AMIGOT
University School of Nursing: MARÍA LORETO MACIÁ SOLER
Alicante Polytechnic: FERNANDO VARELA BOTELLA

ATTACHED INSTITUTES

School of Criminology: Dir BERNARDO DEL ROSAL BLASCO.

Research Institute of Geography: Dir ANTONIO GIL OLCINA.

Research Institute of Water and Environmental Sciences: Dir RAMÓN MARTÍN MATEO.

Joint University Institute of Valencian Language Studies: Dir RAFAEL ALEMANY FERRER.

Joint University Institute of International Economics: Dir GLORIA PARDO ALES.

UNIVERSIDAD DE ALMERÍA

Ctra del Sacramento s/n, 04120 Almería
Telephone: 950-21-50-80
State control

UNIVERSIDAD INTERNACIONAL DE ANDALUCÍA

Avda de las Palmeras s/n, 41092 Seville

UNIVERSIDAD ANTONIO DE NEBRIJA

Campus de la Berzosa, Iioya de Manzanares, 28240 Madrid

Telephone: 91-859-37-53

Private control

Director of Academic Affairs: LUIS DÍAZ MARCOS
Chief of External Relations and Publications: JAVIER ESPINIELLA TENDERO
Director of Administration: JESÚS ROBLEDO MONASTERIO

Number of students: 2,356

Departments of Applied Languages, Economics and Business Administration, Law and European Studies, Communication Sciences and Computer Engineering; Institute of Modern Languages; Centre for Hispanic Studies

UNIVERSITAT DE BARCELONA

Gran Via de les Corts Catalanes 585, 08007 Barcelona

Telephone: 93-318-42-66
Fax: 93-302-59-47

Founded 1450
State control
Languages of instruction: Catalan, Castilian
Academic year: October to September

Rector: ANTONI CAPARRÓS I BENEDICTO
Vice-Rectors: MIQUEL MARTÍNEZ MARTÍN (Teaching and Student Affairs), MARIUS RUBIRALTA ALCAÑIZ (Research), ENRIC CANELA CAMPOS (Economics and Organization), JOAN M. MALAPEIRA GAS (Faculty and Academic Affairs), JOSEP M. PONS RÀFOLS (Institutional Relations and Linguistic Policy), JUAN TUGORES QUCS (External Co-operation), MERCEDES MARÍN RAMOS (University Community)
General Secretary: ANNA ROIGÉ BOTÉ
Library Director: DOLORS LAMARCA MARGALEF

Number of teachers: 4,092
Number of students: 72,480

DEANS

Faculty of Philosophy: AGUSTIN GONZÁLEZ GALLEGO
Faculty of Geography and History: PEDRO CLAVERO PARICIO
Faculty of Philology: ESTHER ARTIGAS ÁLVAREZ
Faculty of Fine Arts: PEDRO FALCÓ GOLONDRINA
Faculty of Law: MARIA TERESA DE GISPERT PASTOR
Faculty of Economics and Business Administration: MANUEL ARTÍS ORTUÑO
Faculty of Biology: MIQUEL SALICRÚ PAGÉS
Faculty of Chemistry: FIDEL CUNILL GARCÍA
Faculty of Physics: ROLF TARRACH SIEGEL
Faculty of Mathematics: JOAN ELIAS GARCÍA
Faculty of Geology: JORDI SERRA RAVENTÓS
Faculty of Medicine: JOSEP A. BOMBI LATORRE
Faculty of Pharmacy: JOSEP BOATELLA RIERA
Faculty of Dentistry: RAMON BARTRON BACH (acting)
Faculty of Psychology: CARME GIMENEZ SEGURA
Faculty of Educational Sciences: CARME PANCHÓN IGLESIAS

CHAIRMEN

Division of Human and Social Sciences: JESÚS CONTRERAS HERNANDEZ
Division of Legal, Economic and Social Studies: RICARD PANERO GUTIÉRREZ
Division of Experimental Sciences and Mathematics: CLAUDI MANS TEIXIDÓ
Division of Health Sciences: GLÒRIA BORDONS DE PORRATA-DORIA
Division of Educational Sciences: VICENÇ BENEDITO ANTOLI

DIRECTORS OF UNIVERSITY CENTRES

Centre of Business Administration: ALFREDO ROCAFORT NICOLAU
Centre of Nursing: CARMEN CAJA LÓPEZ
Centre of Education: IGNASI PUIGDELLIVOL AGUADÉ

DIRECTORS OF ATTACHED CENTRES

University School 'Abat Oliba' (Barcelona): FRANCISCO TARRAGÓ
Centre of Nursing 'Nuestra Señora del Mar' (Barcelona): NATIVITAT ESTEVE RIOS
Centre of Nursing 'Sant Joan de Deu' (Barcelona): ROSA MATA ROCH
Centre of Nursing 'Santa Madrona' (Barcelona): MONSERRAT TEIXIDOR FREIXA
University School of Business Administration 'Osona' (Vic): JOAN CARLES SUARI ANIORTE
Faculty of Translation and Interpreting of Osona (Vic): MARTHA TENNENT HAMILTON

Centre of Education 'Jaume Balmes' (Vic): ANTONI TORT BARDOLET
Centre of Social Work: MARTA LLOBET
School of Social Work (Barcelona): JOSEP RIBAS SEIX
University School of Library Science and Documentation: CONCEPCIÓ MIRALPEIX BALLÚS
Catalan National Institute for Physical Education: AUGUSTÍ BOIXEDA DE MIQUEL
University College of Higher Education in Hotel Management (Sitges): AMÈLIA DÍAZ ÁLVAREZ
Centre of Higher Education in Nutrition and Dietetics: PILAR CERVERA RAL
Catalan College of Higher Education in Cinema and Audiovisual Techniques: LLUÍS TORT RAVENTÓS
Faculty of Legal and Economic Sciences of Osona: JOSEP BURGAVA

ATTACHED INSTITUTES

Institute of Educational Sciences (ICE): Dir JESÚS GARANTO ALÓS.

UNIVERSITAT AUTÒNOMA DE BARCELONA

Campus Universitari, 08193 Bellaterra (Barcelona)
Telephone: 93-581-11-00
Fax: 93-581-20-00
Founded 1968
Regional government control
Languages of instruction: Spanish, Catalan
Academic year: September to June

Rector: Dr CARLES SOLÀ I FERRANDO
Vice-Rectors: Dr JULIÀ CUFÍ I SOBREGRAU (Academic), JORDI BERRIO I SERRANO (Studies), Dr ANTONI TULLA I PUJOL (Economics and Administration), Dra M. TERESA ESPINAL I FARRÉ (Research), Dra MONTSERRAT PONSÀ I FONTANALS (Research), Dr TOMÁS IBÁÑEZ GRACIA (Teaching Staff), Dr LOUIS LEMKOW ZETTERLING (International Relations), Dra NÚRIA PUJOL I MOIX (Hospitals), Dra MERCÈ IZQUIERDO I AYMERICH (Students and Cultural Promotion)
Registrar: Dr SALVADOR ALEGRET I SANROMA
Administrative Officer: JOAN TURRÓ VICENS
Librarian: JUAN GÓMEZ ESCOFET

Number of teachers: 2,643
Number of students: 36,856

Publications: *Memòria de la Recerca*, *Anàlisi: Quaderns de Comunicació i Cultura*, *Anuari d'Anglès*, *Cuadernos de Psicología*, *Cuadernos de Traducción e Interpretación*, *Documents d'Anàlisi Geogràfica*, *Educar*, *Enrahonar: Quaderns de Filosofia*, *Estudios de la Antigüedad*, *Faventia*, *Medievalia*, *Orsis: Organismes i Sistemes*, *Papers: Revista de Sociologia*, *Quaderns de Treball*, *Recerca Musicològica*, *Quaderns de Música Històrica Catalana*.

DEANS

Faculty of Letters: Dr JOSEP M. BRUCART MARRACO
Faculty of Medicine: Dr MIQUEL VILARDELL TARRÉS
Faculty of Educational Sciences: Dr PERE DARDER VIDAL
Faculty of Economics: Dr LLUÍS BARBÉ DURAN
Faculty of Science: Dr ANTONI OLIVA CUYAS
Faculty of Law: Dr MANUEL JESÚS CACHÓN CADENAS
Faculty of Communication Science: Dr EMILI PRADO PICÓ
Faculty of Political Sciences and Sociology: Dra JUDITH ASTELARRA BONOMÍ
Faculty of Veterinary Medicine: Dr LLUIS M. FERRER CAUBET
Faculty of Psychology: Dra M. ASSUMPCIÓ MARTÍ CARBONELL
Faculty of Translation and Interpretation: Dr SEAN V. GOLDEN

HEADS OF DEPARTMENTS

Anglo-Germanic Philology: J. OLTRA PONS
Animal and Plant Biology and Ecology: A. MALGOSA MORERA
Antiquity and Middle Ages Sciences: P. L. CANO ALONSO
Applied Economics: J. OLIVER ALONSO
Applied Education: A. FERRÁNDEZ ARENAZ
Art: B. BASSEGODA HUGAS
Audiovisual Communication and Publicity: J. L. TERRÓN BLANCO
Biochemistry and Molecular Biology: X. PARÉS CASASAMPERA
Business Economics: E. GENESCÀ GARRIGOSA
Catalan Philology: J. A. ARGENTÉ GIRALT
Cell Biology and Physiology: J. BALASCH MARTÍN
Chemical Engineering: JOSEP LÓPEZ SANTIN
Chemistry: J. MARQUET CORTÉS
Computing: I. SERRA PUJOL
Economics and Economic History: J. MASSÓ CARRERAS
Educational Psychology: S. ESTAÚN FERRER
Electronic Engineering: J. SUÑÉ TARRUELLA
French and Romance Philology: J. MURILLO PUYAL
Genetics and Microbiology: R. MARCOS DAUDER
Geography: M. D. GARCÍA RAMÓN
Geology: M. LL. ARBOLEYA CIMADEVILLA
Journalism and Communication Science: J. LL. GÓMEZ MOMPART
Mathematics: E. NART VIÑALS
Medicine: J. GUARDIA MASSÓ
Modern and Contemporary History: J. L. MARTÍN RAMOS
Morphological Sciences: A. MORAGAS REDECILLA
Paediatrics, Obstetrics and Gynaecology, and Preventive Medicine: J. VAQUÉ RAFART
Pathology and Animal Production: M. T. PARAMIO NIETO
Pharmacology and Therapeutics: X. CARNÉ CLADELLAS
Philosophy: J. ROVIRA SALLÈS
Physics: F. LÓPEZ AGUILAR
Political Science and Public Law: J. M. MOLINS LÓPEZ-RODO
Private Law: M. C. GETE-ALONSO CALERA
Psychiatry, Toxicology and Health Legislation: A. TOBEÑA PALLARÈS
Psychobiology and Methodology of Health Sciences: M. D. RIBA LLORET
Psychology of Health and Social Psychology: L. EZPELETA ASCASO
Public Law and Historical-Juridical Sciences: S. SOLÉ COT
Social Anthropology and Prehistory: A. GONZÀLEZ ECHEVARRIA
Sociology: M. J. IZQUIERDO BENITO
Spanish Philology: M. L. HERNANZ CARBÓ
Surgery: P. QUESADA MARÍN
Systematic and Social Education: J. M. ASENSIO AGUILERA
Teaching of Language, Literature and Social Sciences: A. NOGUEROL RODRIGO
Teaching of Mathematics and Experimental Sciences: J. DEULOFEU PIQUET
Teaching of Musical, Plastic and Corporal Expression: A. FORRELLAD BRACONS
Translation and Interpretation: M. L. PRESAS CORBELLA

DIRECTORS

School of Business Administration of Sabadell: SANTIAGO GUERRERO BONED
School of Data Processing of Sabadell: JAVIER SERRANO GARCÍA

ATTACHED INSTITUTES

'Vincent Villar i Palasí' Fundamental Biology Institute: Dir Prof. XAVIER AVILÈS PUIGVERT.

Institute of Education: Dir Prof. PILAR BENEJAM ARQUIMBALL.

'Josep Ricard i Mates' Musicological Research and Documentation Institute: Dir Prof. FRANCESC BONASTRE BERTRAN.

Medieval Studies Institute: Dir Prof. JOSÉ ENRIQUE RUIZ DOMÈNEC.

Barraquer Institute: Dir Dr JOAQUIM BARRAQUER.

Social and Political Sciences Institute: Dir Prof. ISIDRE MOLAS BATLLORI.

Dexeus Institute: Dir Dr CARLES FONTCUBERTA.

European Studies Institute: Dir Prof. JORDI BACARIA COLOM.

High-Energy Physics Institute: Dir Prof. ENRIQUE FERNÁNDEZ SÁNCHEZ.

Municipal Medical Research Institute: Dir Dr JORDI CAMÍ MORELL.

Inter-University Institute of Ancient Middle Eastern Studies: Co-ordinator Prof. JORDI CORS MEYA.

Ecological Research and Forestry Centre: Dir Prof. JAUME TERRADAS SERRA.

UNIVERSIDAD DE BURGOS

Burgos

UNIVERSIDAD DE CÁDIZ

C/ Ancha 16, 11001 Cádiz
Telephone: 956-22-26-04
Fax: 956-22-54-01
Founded 1979

Rector: Prof. Dr GUILLERMO MARTÍNEZ MASSANET
Vice-Rectors: Prof. Dr MANUEL GALÁN VALLEJO (Academic Affairs), Prof. Dr ISIDRO GONZÁLEZ COLLADO (Research), Profa Dra PALOMA BRAZA LLORET (Student Affairs), Prof. Dr ENRIQUE RAMOS JURADO (University Extension)
Registrar: Prof. Dr RAFAEL PADILLA GONZÁLEZ
Administration Officer: JOSÉ RAMÓN REPETO GUTIÉRREZ

Number of teachers: 1,600
Number of students: 21,300

DEANS

Faculty of Medicine: Prof. Dr MANUEL ROSETY PLAZA
Faculty of Law: Prof. Dr JOSÉ IGNACIO MORILLO VELARDE
Faculty of Philosophy and Letters: Prof. Dr JUAN LÓPEZ ALVAREZ
Faculty of Sciences: Prof. Dr DOMINGO CANTERO MORENO
Faculty of Marine Sciences: Prof. Dr JAVIER SALVA GARCÍA
Faculty of Economics and Business: Prof. Dr RAMÓN VALLE CABRERA
Faculty of Nautical Sciences: Prof. Dr JUAN LANDETA BILBAO
Faculty of Education: Prof. JOSÉ MARÍA JURADO MAGDALENO

UNIVERSIDAD DE CANTABRIA

Avda de los Castros s/n, 39005 Santander
Telephone: 942-20-10-01
Fax: 942-20-10-70
Founded 1972 as Universidad de Santander
State control
Language of instruction: Spanish
Academic year: October to June

Rector: JAIME VINUESA TEJEDOR

Vice-Rectors: ALFONSO MOURE ROMANILLO (Institutional Relations and Extracurricular Activities), JUAN JOSÉ JORDÁ CATALÁ (Research), JOSÉ MANUEL BAYOD BAYOD (Student and Academic Affairs), JOSÉ IGNACIO FORTEA PÉREZ (International Relations), FEDERICO GUTIÉRREZ-SOLANA SALCEDO (Academic Staff)
Registrar: LUIS GASPAR VEGA ARGÜELLES
Librarian: LUIS J. MARTÍNEZ RODRÍGUEZ

Number of teachers: 965
Number of students: 15,000

DEANS

Faculty of Sciences: MANUEL ARRATE PEÑA
Faculty of Medicine: JUAN ANTONIO GARCÍA-PORRERO PÉREZ
Faculty of Humanities: JUAN E. GELABERT GONZÁLEZ
Faculty of Law: LUIS MARTÍN REBOLLO
Faculty of Economics and Business Studies: CONCEPCIÓN LÓPEZ FERNÁNDEZ

DIRECTORS

School of Civil Engineering: FERNANDO CAÑIZAL BERINI
School of Industrial Engineering and Telecommunications: FERNANDO VIADERO RUEDA
School of Nautical Studies: EMILIO EGUÍA LÓPEZ
School of Teacher Training: DEMETRIO CASCÓN MARTÍNEZ
School of Mining Engineering: EDUARDO PARDO DE SANTAYANA DE LA HIDALGA
School of Nursing: CELIA NESPRAL GAZTELUMENDI
School of Labour Relations: JESÚS RAFAEL MERCADER

HEADS OF DEPARTMENTS

Business Administration: MYRIAN GARCÍA OLALLA
Science and Technique of Navigation and Ship Construction: MARCELINO SOBRON IRURETAGOYENA
Anatomy and Cell Biology: JUAN MARIO HURLE GONZÁLEZ
Molecular Biology: FERNANDO DE LA CRUZ CALAHORRA
Materials Science, Geoscience and Engineering: JOSÉ MARÍA VARONA RUIZ
History: RAMÓN TEJA CASUSO
Water and Environmental Sciences: JOAQUÍN DÍEZ-CASCÓN SAGRADO
Medical and Surgical Sciences: JOSÉ MANUEL REVUELTA SOBA
Public Law: CONCEPCIÓN ESCOBAR HERNÁNDEZ
Private Law: LUIS ROJO AJURIA
Design and Construction of Buildings: JULIAN DÍAZ DEL VALLE
Project and Process Transportation and Technology: FRANCISCO BALLESTER MUÑOZ
Economics: RAFAEL DOMÍNGUEZ MARTÍN
Education: LAURENTINO SALVADOR BLANCO
Electronics and Computers: JOSÉ MA. DRAKE MOYANO
Philology: FÁTIMA CARRERA DE LA RED
Applied Physics: JAIME AMORÒS ARNAU
Modern Physics: RAFAEL BLANCO ALCAÑIZ
Physiology and Pharmacology: JESÚS FLÓREZ BELEDO
Geography and Regional and Town Planning: ANGELA DE MEER LECHA-MARZO
Modern and Contemporary History: GERMÁN RUEDA HERNANZ
Electrical and Energy Engineering: JOSÉ ANTONIO GURRUTXAGA RUIZ
Applied Mathematics and Computer Science: EDUARDO MORA MONTE
Mathematics, Statistics and Computer Science: JOSÉ ANTONIO CORDÓN MUÑOZ
Medicine and Psychiatry: JESÙS GONZÀLEZ MACÍAS
Chemistry: INMACULADA ORTIZ URIBE
Geographical Engineering and Technical Drawing: JESÚS OTI VELASCO
Nursing: MA. DEL PILAR SANTOS ABAUNZA
Electronic Technology in Systems Engineering and Automation: SALVADOR BRACHO DEL PINO
Communications Engineering: JOSE LUIS GARCÍA GARCÍA

ATTACHED INSTITUTES

Institute of Education: Dir (vacant).

Cantabria Physics Institute: Dir X. BARCOUS JAUREGUI.

UNIVERSIDAD CARLOS III DE MADRID

Calle Madrid 126, Getafe 28903, Madrid
Telephone: 91-624-95-00
Fax: 91-624-97-57

Founded 1989
State control
Language of instruction: Spanish
Academic year: September to June

Rector: GREGORIO PECES-BARBA MARTÍNEZ
Registrar: RAFAEL ZORRILLA TORRAS
Librarian: MARGARITA TALADRIZ MÁS

Number of teachers: 607
Number of students: 9,250

Publications: *Derechos y Libertades* (every 6 months), *Boletín III*.

DEANS

Faculty of Social and Juridical Sciences: RAFAEL ILLESCAS ORTIZ
Higher Polytechnical School: JAVIER SANZ FEITO

HEADS OF DEPARTMENTS

Private and Commercial Law: FERNANDO PANTALEÓN PRIETO
Economics: CARLOS HERVÉS BELOSO
Statistics and Economics: ANTONI ESPASA TERRADES
Library and Information Science: JOSÉ ANTONIO MOREIRO GONZÁLEZ
Public Law and Philosophy of Law: JUAN JOSÉ ZORNOZA PÉREZ
Humanities, Political Science and Sociology: EDUARDO LÓPEZ-ARANGUREN QUIÑONES
Company Finance: CARLOS MALLO RODRÍGUEZ
Engineering: CARLOS NAVARRO UGENA
Computing: ARTURO RIBAGORDA GARNACHO
Mathematics: FRANCISCO MARCELLÁN ESPAÑOL
Physics: ROBERTO GONZÁLEZ AMADO

ATTACHED INSTITUTES

Instituto Universitario de Derechos Humanos 'Bartolomé de las Casas': Dir RAFAEL DE ASIS ROIG.

Instituto de Humanidades y Comunicación 'Miguel de Unamuno': Dir JORGE URRUTIA GÓMEZ.

Instituto 'Pascual Madoz' del Territorio, Urbanismo y Medio Ambiente: Dir LUCIANO PAREJO ALFONSO.

Instituto de Derecho y Económica: Dir SANTOS PASTOR PRIETO.

Instituto 'Flores de Lemus' de Estudios Avanzados en Economía: Dir JUAN URRUTIA ELEJALDE.

Instituto 'Francisco de Vitoria' de Estudios Internacionales y Comunitarios: Dir FERNANDO MARIÑO.

UNIVERSIDAD DE CASTILLA–LA MANCHA

Casa-Palacio Medrano, C/ Paloma 9, 13071 Ciudad Real
Telephone: 926-295300
Fax: 926-223894

Founded 1982
State control
Language of instruction: Spanish
Academic year: October to June

Rector: LUIS ARROYO ZAPATERO
Vice-Rectors: ERNESTO MARTÍNEZ ATAZ (Academic), MIGUEL ANGEL COLLADO YURITA (Curriculum), ISIDRO SÁNCHEZ SÁNCHEZ (Centres and Substructures), MIGUEL OLMEDA FERNÁNDEZ (Research), JOAQUIN SAUL GARCÍA MARCHANTE (University Extension), ANTONIO DE LUCAS MARTÍNEZ (Student Affairs), ANGEL CARRASCO PERERA (Institutional Relations), FEDERICO ANDRES RODRÍGUEZ MORATA (Campus of Albacete), ANTONIO OTERO MONTERO (Campus of Ciudad Real)
Registrar: EDUARDO ESPIN TEMPLADO
Chief Administrative Officer: IGNACIO GAVIRA TOMÁS
Librarian: FRANCISCO ALÍA MIRANDA

Number of teachers: 1,170
Number of students: 28,500

Publications: *Multi-campus*, *Universidad*, *Info-Campus*.

DEANS

Faculty of Fine Arts: JOSÉ ANTONIO SÁNCHEZ MARTÍNEZ
Faculty of Letters: MARÍA RUBIO MARTÍN
Faculty of Chemistry: JUAN JOSÉ BERZAS NEVADO
Faculty of Law: NICOLÁS GARCÍA RIVAS
Faculty of Economics and Management Science: OSCAR DE JUAN ASENJO
Faculty of Juridical and Social Sciences: JAVIER CASARES RIPOLL

DIRECTORS

University School of Education, Albacete: PEDRO LOSA SERRANO
University School of Education, Ciudad Real: EMILIO NIETO LÓPEZ
University School of Education, Cuenca: MARTÍN MUELAS HERRÁIZ
University School of Teaching, Toledo: RAIMUNDO DRUDIS BALDRICH
University Polytechnic School, Albacete: FRANCISCO JOSÉ QUILES FLOR
University Polytechnic School, Almadén: LUIS MANSILLA PLAZA
University School of Agricultural Engineering: MARÍA LUISA SORIANO MARTÍN
University School of Nursing, Albacete: ELÍAS ROVIRA GIL
University School of Nursing, Ciudad Real: CARMEN PRADO LAGUNA
University School of Nursing, Cuenca: DOLORES SERRANO PARRA
University School of Nursing and Physiotherapy: MARI PAZ MOMPART GARCÍA
Centre for Business Law Studies: MIGUEL ANGEL COLLADO YURITA
University School of Social Work, Cuenca: FERNANDO CASAS MÍNGUEZ
University School of Information Technology: FRANCISCO RUIZ GONZÁLEZ
University College: SILVIA VALMAÑA OCHAITA
University School of Industrial Engineering: JOSÉ ANTONIO SAMPER LÓPEZ
University College, Toledo (Letters Section): LUIS LORENTE TOLEDO
University College, Toledo (Chemistry Section): JUAN FUERTES GONZÁLEZ
University School of Labour Relations, Albacete: JOAQUÍN APARICIO TOVAR
University School of Labour Relations, Ciudad Real: JULIO SUELA SARRO
University School of Labour Relations, Cuenca: ENRIQUE GASCO GARCÍA
Technical High School of Agricultural Engineering: FRANCISCO MONTERO RIQUELME
Higher Centre for Humanities, Toledo: LOURDES CAMPOS ROMERO

Faculty of Chemistry, Toledo: JUAN FUERTES GONZÁLEZ
Centre for University Studies of Talavera: VIRGILIA ANTÓN ANTÓN

DIRECTORS OF DEPARTMENTS

Agroforestry Science and Technology: LAUREANO GALLEGO MARTÍNEZ
Analytical Chemistry and Food Technology: MARÍA DOLORES CABEZUDO IBÁÑEZ
Applied Mechanics and Project Engineering: CARLOS DE LA CRUZ GÓMEZ
Applied Physics: JOSÉ M. RIVEIRO CORONA
Art: ANA NAVARRETE TUDELA
Chemical Engineering: PABLO CAÑIZARES CAÑIZARES
Economics and Management: JOSÉ VICTOR GUARNIZO GARCÍA
Education: TERESA MARÍN ECED
Electrical and Electronics Engineering: BALDOMERO GONZÁLEZ SÁNCHEZ
Geography and Territory: MIGUEL PANADERO MOYA
Geological and Mining Engineering: JOSÉ MARÍA IRAIZOZ FERNÁNDEZ
Hispanic and Classical Philology: FELIPE PEDRAZA JIMÉNEZ
History: JERÓNIMO LÓPEZ-SALAZAR PÉREZ
History of Art: ALICIA DIEZ DE BALDEÓN GARCÍA
Information Science: FERNANDO CUARTERO GÓMEZ
Juridical Science: ANTONIO BAYLOS GRAU
Mathematics: PABLO PEDREGAL TERCERO
Modern Philology: JUAN BRAVO CASTILLO
Nursing: VICTORIA UNGRÍA CAÑETE
Organic and Inorganic Chemistry and Biochemistry: ENRIQUE DÍEZ BARRA
Philosophy: ATILANO BASALO DOMÍNGUEZ
Physical Chemistry: ANTONIO MUCIENTES BALADO
Psychology: JUAN MONTAÑÉS RODRÍGUEZ
Teaching of Movement, Music and the Plastic Arts: ONOFRE RICARDO CONTRERAS JORDAN
Vegetable Production and Agricultural Engineering: JOSÉ MARÍA TARJUELO MARTIN-BENITO

UNIVERSITAT OBERTA DE CATALUNYA

Avda Tibidabo 39–43, 08035 Barcelona
Telephone: 93-253-23-00
Fax: 93-471-64-95
Founded 1995
Rector: GABRIEL FERRATÉ
Vice-Rectors: FRANCESC PEDRÓ (Academic Affairs), JOSEP COLL
Secretary-General: XAVIER ARAGAY
Librarian: ADORACIÓ PEREZ
Library of 17,900 vols
Number of teachers: 50
Number of students: 4,000

DEANS

Industrial Sciences: JORDI VILASECA
Humanities: ISIDOR MARÍ
Law: JOAQUIM BISBAL
Information Science: CRISTINA NOGUÉS
Educational Psychology: CARLOS FRADE

UNIVERSIDAD PONTIFICIA 'COMILLAS'

Calle Alberto Aguilera 23, 28015 Madrid
Telephone: 91-542-28-00
Fax: 91-559-65-69
E-mail: webmaster@cal.upco.es
Founded by Pope Leo XIII, classes commencing at Comillas, Santander, in 1890. The right to confer degrees was granted in 1904. Moved to Madrid in 1960
Private control (Society of Jesus)
Language of instruction: Spanish
Academic year: October to June
Grand Chancellor: R. P. PETER-HANS KOLVENBACH
Rector: Dr MANUEL GALLEGO DÍAZ
Vice-Rectors: Dr JOSÉ JOAQUÍN ALEMANY BRIZ (Academic Affairs and Academic Staff), Dr LUIS GARCÍA PASCUAL (Research and Postgraduate Studies), Dr ANGEL SARABIA VIEJO (International and Institutional Relations), JOSÉ LÓPEZ FRANCO (University Extension and Development)
Secretary-General: Dr JAVIER BERRIATÚA SAN SEBASTIÁN
Librarian: JUAN BAUTISTA VALERO AGUNDEZ
Number of teachers: 1,161
Number of students: 16,820
Library of 550,000 vols
Publications: *Miscelánea Comillas* (2 a year), *Estudios eclesiásticos*, *Pensamiento* (quarterly), *ICADE* (3 a year).

DEANS

Faculty of Theology: Dr JOSÉ RAMÓN BUSTO SAIZ
Faculty of Canon Law: Dr LUIS VELA SÁNCHEZ
Faculty of Philosophy and Letters: Dr AUGUSTO HORTAL ALONSO
Faculty of Law: Dr JOAQUÍN ALMOGUERA CARRERES
Faculty of Economics: Dra MARGARITA PRAT RODRIGO
Higher Technical School of Engineering: Dr LUIS PAGOLA Y DE LAS HERAS
University School of Social Work: PEDRO CABRERA CABRERA (Dir)
University School of Nursing: CALIXTO PLUMED MORENO (Dir)

Institutes of business administration and management, matrimonial law, spiritual theology, modern languages, and postgraduate training and continuing education.

ATTACHED INSTITUTES

Instituto Superior de Ciencias Morales: Calle Félix Boix 13, 28036 Madrid.

Estudio Teológico Agustiniano: Paseo de Filipinos 7, 47007 Valladolid.

Estudio Teológico del Seminario Mayor de Ciudad Real: Seminario Mayor, 13002 Ciudad Real.

Estudio Teológico Claretiano de Colmenar Viejo (Madrid): Padres Claretianos, 28770 Colmenar Viejo (Madrid).

Centro Teológico de Las Palmas de Gran Canaria: Seminario Mayor, 35001 Las Palmas de Gran Canaria.

Centro Teológico Monseñor Romero: Apdo Postal (01) 168, El Salvador (Central America).

Estudio Teológico del Seminario Mayor de Logroño: Seminario Mayor, Apdo de Correos 150, 26080 Logroño.

Estudio Teológico del Seminario Mayor de Córdoba: Amador de los Ríos 1, 14004 Córdoba.

Estudio Teológico del Seminario Mayor 'Tagaste': Padres Agustinos, Santa Emilia 10, 28409 Los Negrales (Madrid).

Instituto Fe y Secularidad: Diego de León 33, 28006 Madrid.

Instituto Internacional de Teología a Distancia: José Ortega y Gasset 62, 1°, 28006 Madrid.

There are other Theological and Philosophical Faculties in Spain conferring degrees, which are partly associated with the Pontifical Universities, as follows:

Institut de Teologia Fonamental

Sant Cugat del Vallés, Barcelona
Telephone: 93-590-80-88
Founded 1864
Jesuit College forming part of the Faculty of Theology of Barcelona, and is open to non-Jesuit students
Chancellor: Dr RICARD MA. CARLES, Cardinal Archbishop of Barcelona
General Moderator: R. P. JESÚS RENAU
Director: R. P. ORIOL TUÑÍ
Registrar: P. JOSEP MA. ROCAFIGUERA
Librarian: P. ANTONI BORRÁS
Number of teachers: 19
Number of students: 200
Publications: *Pensamiento*, *Estudios Eclesiásticos*, *Manresa*, *Selecciones de Teología*, *Actualidad Bibliográfica*, *Cuadernos de Teología Fundamental*.

PROFESSORS

ALEGRE, X., New Testament Scripture
BADIA, A., Fundamental Theology
BENTUÉ, A., Fundamental Theology
BOADA, J., Fundamental Theology
BORRAS, A., Ecclesiastical History
COLL, J. MA., Fundamental Theology
CORBI, M., History of Religions
DOU, A., History of Science
ESCUDÉ, J., Fundamental Moral Theology
FONDEVILA, J. MA., Systematic Theology
GARCÍA DONCEL, M., Philosophy of Sciences
GONZÁLEZ FAUS, J. I., Systematic Thelogy
MANRESA, F., Fundamental Theology
RAMBLA, J. MA., Spiritual Theology
SALVAT, I., Fundamental Social Morality
TUÑÍ, O., New Testament Scripture
VALL, H., Ecumenical Theology
VIVES, J., Systematic Theology
YOLDI, J. A., Ecclesiastical History

ATTACHED DEPARTMENT

Departamento de Papirología: Dir P. JOSÉ O'CALLAGHAN.

Facultad de Teología

Apdo 2002, 18080 Granada
Telephone: 958-16-02-92
Fax: 958-16-25-59
Founded 1939
Grand Chancellor: R. P. PETER-HANS KOLVENBACH
Vice-Grand Chancellor: R. P. GUILLERMO RODRÍGUEZ-IZQUIERDO
Rector: R. P. ANTONIO M. NAVAS GUTIÉRREZ
Vice-Rector: EDUARDO LÓPEZ AZPITARTE
Secretary: JOSÉ M. CALVO ENRIQUE DÍAZ
Board of Administration: ESTANISLAO OLIVARES D'ANGELO
Librarian: GABRIEL VERD
Library of 350,000 vols
Number of teachers: 36
Number of students: 747
Publications: *Archivo Teológico Granadino* (*Anuario de Teología Postridentina*) (quarterly), *Biblioteca Teológica Grana dina* (collection of textbooks and theses), *Centro de Cultura Religiosa Superior* and *Lecturas de Teología* (textbooks), *Proyección*; in collaboration with other Spanish Jesuit reviews: *Estudios Eclesiásticos, Manresa, Razón y Fe.*

PROFESSORS

BERDUGO VILLENA, T., Latin
BORREGO PIMENTEL, E., Philosophy

CALDERÓN MARTÍNEZ, S., Pastoral Theology
CALVO VARGAS, N., Pastoral Theology
CAMACHO LARAÑA, I., Moral Theology
CARNERERO PEÑALVER, J., Canon Law
CASTÓN BOYER, P., Sociology
CONTRERAS MOLINA, F., Scripture
DOMÍNGUEZ MORANO, C., Psychology
DOMÍNGUEZ PÉREZ, H., Ecumenicism
GARCÍA GÓMEZ, M., Moral Theology
GARCÍA HIRSCHFELD, C., Pastoral Theology
GONZÁLEZ DORADO, A., Dogmatic and Pastoral Theology
GRANADO BELLIDO, C., Patrology and Dogmatic Theology
HERNÁNDEZ MARTÍNEZ, J., Dogmatic Theology
JIMÉNEZ ORTIZ, A., Fundamental Theology
LEÓN, T., Theology
LÓPEZ AZPITARTE, E., Moral Theology
LÓPEZ CUADRADO, E., Philosophy
LÓPEZ CUERVO, T., Greek
MARTÍNEZ MEDINA, J., Ecclesiastical Art
NAVAS GUTIÉRREZ, A., Ecclesiastical History
OLIVARES, E., Canon Law
PEINADO MUÑOZ, M., Scripture
PÉREZ NIETO, J., Philosophy
POZO, C., Dogmatic Theology
RODRÍGUEZ CARMONA, A., Scripture
RODRÍGUEZ IZQUIERDO, J. M., Liturgy
RUIZ PÉREZ, F., Dogmatic Theology
SÁNCHEZ NOGALES, J. M., Liturgy
SANTOS CAMPAÑA, F., Pastoral Theology
SEQUEIROS SANROMÁN, L., Philosophy
SICRE DÍAZ, J. L., Scripture
SOTOMAYOR MURO, M., Ecclesiastical History, Christian Archaeology
VÍLCHEZ LÍNDEZ, J., Dogmatic Theology, Scripture

ATTACHED INSTITUTES

Instituto Superior de Ciencias Religiosas 'Tomás Sánchez': Apdo 2002, 18080 Granada; Rector ANTONIO M. NAVAS GUTIÉRREZ.

Instituto Superior de Ciencias Religiosas 'San Pablo': Santa María 20, 29015 Málaga; Rector GABRIEL LEAL.

Centro Diocesano de Teología de Málaga: Calle Toquero 20, 29013 Málaga; Rector ALFONSO FERNÁNDEZ CASAMAYOR PALACIO.

Centro de Estudios Teológicos: Paseo de María Cristina, 41004 Seville; Rector ANTONIO MARÍA CALERO.

Centro de Estudios Teológicos: Juan Montilla 1, 23002 Jaén; Rector MANUEL RUIZ CARRERO.

UNIVERSIDAD DE CÓRDOBA

Alfonso XIII, 13, 14071 Córdoba
Telephone: 957-21-80-00
Fax: 957-21-80-30

Founded 1972
State control
Language of instruction: Spanish
Academic year: October to June

Rector: EUGENIO DOMINGUEZ VILCHES
Vice-Rectors: MARÍA LUISA CALERO VAQUERA (Academic Staff), ANDRÉS GARCÍA ROMÁN (Academic Co-ordination and Study Plans), JOSÉ ROLDÁN CAÑAS (Management and Resources), FRANCISCO GRACIA NAVARRO (Scientific Research and New Technology), JOSÉ MANUEL ROLDÁN NOGUERAS (Students), MARGARITA CLEMENTE MUÑOZ (Co-ordination of Institutional and International Relations)
Registrar: MANUEL TORRALBO RODRÍGUEZ
Librarian: MARÍA DEL CARMEN LIÑÁN

Number of teachers: 1,066
Number of students: 21,000

DEANS

Faculty of Veterinary Science: Prof. Dr ALFONSO BLANCO RODRIGUEZ
Faculty of Medicine: (vacant)
Faculty of Science: Prof. Dr ANTONIO MARTÍN MARTÍN
Faculty of Philosophy and Letters: Prof. Dr JOSÉ C. MARTÍN DE LA CRUZ
Faculty of Law: Prof. Dr MANUEL TORRES AGUILAR
Faculty of Education: VICENTA PÉREZ FERRANDO

DIRECTORS

Higher Technical School for Agricultural Engineers: JESÚS LÓPEZ GIMÉNEZ
University School of Technical Mining Engineering: CARLOS LAO MORENO
University School of Nursing: PILAR MARTÍNEZ NAVÍA OSORIO
University School of Labour Relations: (vacant)
Polytechnic University School: ANTONIO JOSÉ CUBERO ATIENZA
Centre for Innovation and Personal Studies: EDUARDO RAMOS REAL

HEADS OF DEPARTMENTS

Agricultural and Forestry Science and Resources: LUIS LÓPEZ BELLIDO
Agro-chemistry and Edaphology: ANGEL TRINIDAD MATEOS
Agronomy: JOSÉ ROLDÁN CAÑAS
Anatomy and Pathological Anatomy: EDUARDO AGÜERA CARMONA
Animal Biology: FRANCISCO CASTEJÓN MONTISANO
Animal Health: ANTONIO GARRIDO CONTRERAS
Animal Production: JOSÉ J. RODRÍGUEZ ALCAIDE
Applied Mathematics and Didactics: J. CARLOS DÍAZ ALCAIDE
Applied Physics and Radiology: VICENTE COLOMAR VIADEL
Art and Archaeology: ALBERTO VILLAR MOVELLÁN
Bromatology and Nutrition: FRANCISCO LEÓN CRESPO
Cellular Biology: JOSÉ ANTONIO GONZÁLEZ REYES
Chemical Analysis: MANUEL SILVA RODRÍGUEZ
Chemical and Inorganic Engineering: JULIAN MORALES PALOMINO
Clinical Veterinary Pathology: RAFAEL MAYER VALOR
Didactics: MERCEDES MANZANARES GAVILÁN
Education: ANTONIO ONTORIA PEÑA
French and English Philology: M. ANGEL GARCÍA
Genetics: JOSÉ I. CUBERO SALMERÓN
Graphic Engineering: MANUEL SÁNCHEZ DE LA ORDEN
Historical-Juridical and Social Economic Disciplines: JOSÉ MARÍA CASADO RIAGÓN
Human, Experimental and Territorial Sciences: BARTOLOMÉ VALLE BUENESTADO
International Public Law, Philosophy of Law, Criminal Law: JUAN JOSÉ GONZÁLEZ RUS
Mechanics: JOSÉ MIGUEL MARTÍNEZ JIMENEZ
Medical and Surgical Specializations: PEDRO CARPINTERO BENITEZ
Medicine: RAFAEL FERNÁNDEZ-CREHUET
Microbiology: JOSÉ JUAN AGUILAR GAVILÁN
Mining: RAFAEL HERNANDO LUNA
Modern and Contemporary History and American History: JOSÉ MANUEL DE BERNARDO ARES
Organic Chemistry: JOSÉ MARÍA MARINAS RUBIO
Philology and Teaching of Spanish: RAMÓN MORILLO-VELARDE PÉREZ
Philosophy, Social Anthropology and Sociology: JOSÉ LUIS CANTÓN ALONSO
Physical Chemistry and Applied Thermodynamics: JUAN JOSÉ RUÍZ SÁNCHEZ
Plant Biology and Ecology: JUAN FERNÁNDEZ HALGER
Public and Private Juridic Institutions: JOSÉ MANUEL GONZÁLEZ PORRAS
Rural Engineering: JOSÉ LUIS AYUSO MUÑOZ
Science of Antiquity and Middle Ages: EMILIO CABRERA MUÑOZ
Administration, Finance, Markets and Ventures: MANUEL REBOLLO PUIG
Biochemistry, Molecular and Physiological Biology: JUAN LOPEZ BAREA
Morphological Science: RICARDO VAAMONDE LEMOS
Agrarian Economy, Sociology and Policy: JUAN ANTONIO CAÑAS MADUEÑO
Nursing: FRANCISCA SERRANO PRIETO
Pharmacology and Toxicology: FELIX INFANTE MIRANDA
Electrotechnics and Electronics: ADOLFO PLAZA ALONO
Physiology and Immunology: ENRIQUE AGUILAR BENÍTEZ DE LUGO
Corporal and Artistic Education: FRANCISCA GALLARDO OTERO

ATTACHED INSTITUTES

Faculty of Economic and Management Science (Management Section): Escritor Castilla Aguayo 4, 14012 Córdoba; tel. 957-29-61-33; fax 957-20-36-11; Dir AUGUSTO GÓMEZ CABRERA.

University Teacher Training School 'Sagrado Corazón': Amador de los Ríos s/n, 14012 Córdoba; tel. 957-47-47-50; Dir JUAN BAUTISTA APARICIO MACARRO.

University School of Business Studies: Escritor Castilla Aguayo 4, 14012 Córdoba; tel. 957-29-61-33; Dir AUGUSTO GÓMEZ CABRERA.

University College 'Lucio Anneo Seneca': Avd. Menéndez Pidal s/n, 14004 Córdoba; tel. 957-21-83-92; Dir MARIANO HERRERA GARCÍA.

University College 'Ntra Sra de la Asunción': Avd. Menéndez Pidal s/n, 14004 Córdoba; tel. 957-21-81-48; Dir JOSÉ MANUEL MUÑOZ MUÑOZ.

University College 'Poveda': Vandalino, 4, 14012 Córdoba; tel. 957-27-57-12; Dir FRANCISCA FERIA.

UNIVERSIDADE DA CORUÑA

A Maestranza s/n, 15001 A Coruña
Telephone: 981-16-70-00
Fax: 981-16-70-14

Founded 1989
Languages of instruction: Spanish, Galician

Rector: JOSÉ LUIS MEILÁN GIL
Vice-Rectors: JORGE TEIJEIRO VIDAL (Institutional Relations and Postgraduate Studies), DOLORES ESTHER FERNÁNDEZ FERNÁNDEZ (Research), JUAN J. FERNÁNDEZ CAINZOS (Economic Affairs), MANUEL CASTELEIRO MALDONADO (Academic Affairs), ROSA MA. FERNÁNDEZ ESTELLER (Planning), MANUEL GONZÁLEZ SARCEDA (Students), MANUEL RECUERO ASTRAY (Campus at Ferrol)
Secretary-General: JOSÉ EDUARDO LÓPEZ PEREIRA

Number of teachers: 967
Number of students: 23,426

DEANS

Faculty of Law: ALEJANDRINO FERNÁNDEZ BARREIRO
Faculty of Sciences: JOSÉ LUIS ARMESTO BARBEITO
Faculty of Computing: JOSÉ LUIS FREIRE NISTAL
Faculty of Business and Economics: ANTONIO ERIAS REY
Faculty of Philology: XOSÉ MA. DOBARRO PAZ
Faculty of Humanities: JOSÉ A. FERNÁNDEZ DE ROTA MONTER
Faculty of Science Education: ALFONSO BARCA LOZANO
Faculty of Sociology: BENJAMÍN GONZÁLEZ RODRÍGUEZ

DIRECTORS

Higher Technical School of Architecture: JOSÉ JUAN GONZALEZ-CEBRIAN TELLO
University Medical School: MANUEL ROMERO MARTÍN
Higher School of the Civil Marine: JUAN TRIGO DEL RÍO
University School of Technical Architecture: JOSÉ LUIS RODILLA LÓPEZ
University School of Business Studies: AURELIA BLANCO GONZÁLEZ
University Polytechnical School: JESUS VICTORIA MEIZOSO
University School of Physiotherapy: RAMON FERNANDEZ CERVANTES
Higher Technical School of Roads, Canals and Ports: FERMIN NAVARRINA MARTÍNEZ
Higher Polytechnical School: ENRIQUE CASANOVA

UNIVERSIDAD DE DEUSTO

Avda de las Universidades 24, 48007 Bilbao, Apdo 1, 48080 Bilbao
Telephone: 94-413-90-00
Fax: 94-413-91-10
Founded 1886
Private control, directed by the Jesuits
Languages of instruction: Spanish, Basque
Academic year: October to June
Chancellor: R.P. PETER-HANS KOLVENBACH
Vice-Chancellor: R.P. IGNACIO ECHARTE
Rector: R.P. JOSÉ MARÍA ABREGO DE LACY
Vice-Rectors: R. P. DIONISIO ARANZADI (San Sebastián Campus), ANTONIO YABAR (Academic Studies), R. P. JOSÉ MARÍA ETXEBERRIA (International Relations and Basque Language), JUAN FRANCISCO SANTACOLOMA (Research), LUIS MIGUEL VILLAR (Alumni)
Registrar: R.P. JOSÉ ANTONIO ALDECOA
Librarian: NIEVES TARANCO
Library: see Libraries
Number of teachers: 655
Number of students: 18,338
Publications: *Estudios de Deusto* (2 a year), *Boletín de Estudios Económicos* (3 a year), *Letras de Deusto* (4 a year), *Cuadernos Europeos de Deusto* (2 a year), *Revista de Derecho y Genoma Humano* (2 a year), *Revista Noticias UD Berriak* (4 a year).

DEANS

Faculty of Law: JAVIER CAÑO MORENO
Faculty of Philosophy and Letters: ROBERTO PÉREZ
Faculty of Philosophy and Letters (San Sebastián): ELENA BARRENA OSORO
Faculty of Theology: RAFAEL AGUIRRE
Faculty of Political Sciences and Sociology: FRANCISCO GARMENDIA
Faculty of Philosophy and Education: MARIA LUISA AMIGO
Faculty of Economics and Business Studies: SUSANA RODRÍGUEZ
Faculty of Economics and Business Studies (in San Sebastián): FRANCISCO JOSÉ OLARTE
Faculty of Computer Science: JUAN LUIS GUTIERREZ

DIRECTORS

Institute of Educational Sciences (ICE): AURELIO VILLA
Institute of Modern Languages: WINFRIED ARNOLD
School of Legal Practice: PABLO SESMA
School of Tourism and Secretarial Studies: R.P. JESÚS TERÁN
Institute of Basque Studies: ROSA MIREN PAGOLA
School of Theology: JOSÉ MANUEL ELORRIAGA
International Institute of Business Management: Hermanos Aguirre 2, Apdo 153, 48007 Bilbao; ANTONIO FREIJE
Institute of European Studies: f. 1979; BEATRIZ PÉREZ DE LAS HERAS
Institute of Co-operative Studies: R.P. DIONISIO ARANZADI
Institute of Drug Addiction: LUIS PANTOJA
Institute of Leisure Studies: MANUEL CUENCA
Institute of Fiscal Studies: JUAN IGNACIO APOITA
Institute 'Ignacio de Loyola': R. P. JUAN PLAZAOLA
Pedro Arrope Institute of Human Rights: JAIME ORNÁ
School of Social Work: MARIA LUISA SETIEN
School of Tourism (in San Sebastián): JOSE MARIA PEREZ DE ARENAZA
School of Theology (in San Sebastián): R. P. ALFREDO TAMAYO

UNIVERSIDAD EUROPEA DE MADRID (CEES)

C/ Tajo s/n, Urbanización el Bosque, 28670 Villaviciosa de Odon, Madrid
Telephone: 91-616-71-42
Rector: JUAN SALCEDO MARTÍ
Vice-Rector for Alumni: FRANCISCO JOSÉ VALDERRAMA CANALES
Vice-Rector for Research: GASPAR GARROTE BERNAL
Vice-Rector for Academic Affairs: FERNANDO IBÁÑEZ LÓPEZ-POZAS
Secretary-General: LUIS CRUZ MIRAVET

DEANS AND DIRECTORS

Faculty of Philology: ANTONIO ARGÜESO GONZALEZ
Faculty of Information Sciences: MATILDE EIROA SAN FRANCISCO
Faculty of Sciences: EMILIA GÓMEZ PARDO
Faculty of Law and Administration: FERNANDO IBÁÑEZ LÓPEZ-POZAS
Faculty of Physical Education and Sport: JUAN MAYORGA GARCÍ
Faculty of Economic Sciences and Business Studies: FERNANDO MÉNDEZ IBISATE
Faculty of Health Sciences: JOSÉ ROMERO VIVAS
Faculty of Humanities: (vacant)
Faculty of Psychology: (vacant)
Higher School of Architecture: ANGEL LUIS FERNÁNDEZ MUÑOZ
Higher School of Industrial Engineering: RAFAEL GARCÍA DE LA SEN
Higher School of Computer Science: MANUEL ORTEGA ORTIZ DE APODACA
Higher School of Telecommunications: LUIS VALOR SAN ROMÁN

UNIVERSIDAD DE EXTREMADURA

Avda de Elvas s/n, 06071 Badajoz; and Plaza de los Caldereros 1, 10071 Cáceres
Telephone: 924-28-93-00 (Badajoz); 927-21-20-00 (Cáceres)
Fax: 924-27-29-83 (Badajoz); 927-21-12-68 (Cáceres)
Founded 1973
State control
Language of instruction: Spanish
Academic year: October to June
Rector: CÉSAR CHAPARRO GÓMEZ
Vice-Rectors: JOSÉ MORALES BRUQUE (Academic Affairs), MIGUEL RODRÍGUEZ CANCHO (Extension), CARLOS GUTIÉRREZ MERINO (Research), VICENTE RAMOS ESTRADA (Economic Affairs and Infrastructure), RICARDO HERNÁNDEZ MOGOLLÓN (University and Institutional Co-ordination), FLORENTINO DE LOPE REBOLLO (Teaching Staff and Departments), PATRICIO GONZÁLEZ VALVERDE (Student Affairs and Teaching)
Secretary-General: JOSÉ LUIS BERNAL SALGADO
Number of teachers: 1,057
Number of students: 19,179
Publication: *Boletín*.

DEANS

Faculty of Science (Badajoz): ARSENIO MUÑOZ DE LA PEÑA CASTRILLO
Faculty of Medicine (Badajoz): JOAQUÍN INGELMO FERNÁNDEZ
Faculty of Philosophy and Letters (Cáceres): JOSÉ LUIS SÁNCHEZ ABAL
Faculty of Economics and Business (Badajoz): ANTONIO FERNÁNDEZ FERNÁNDEZ
Faculty of Veterinary Science (Cáceres): MIGUEL ANGEL VIVES VALLÉS
Faculty of Library Science (Badajoz): CARLOS CASTRO CASTRO
Faculty of Sports Science (Cáceres): FERNANDO DEL VILLAR ALVAREZ
Faculty of Education (Badajoz): MA. ROSA LUENGO GONZÁLEZ
Faculty of Law (Cáceres): CASTOR DÍAZ BARRADO

DIRECTORS

School of Agricultural Engineering (Badajoz): JOSÉ MIGUEL COLETO MARTÍNEZ
University School of Industrial Engineering (Badajoz): FRANCISCO QUINTANA GRAGERA
University School of Technology (Cáceres): JOSÉ LUIS CANAL MACÍAS
University School of Teacher Training (Cáceres): JOSÉ MA. CORRALES VÁZQUEZ
University School of Business Studies (Cáceres): JOSÉ ANTONIO PÉREZ RUBIO
University School of Nursing (Cáceres): MA. JOSÉ MORLANS LORIENTE

UNIVERSITAT DE GIRONA

Pl. Sant Domènec 3, 17071 Gerona
Telephone: 972-41-80-28
Fax: 972-41-80-31
Founded 1992
State control
Rector: JOSEP M. NADAL
Vice-Rectors: SEGI BONET (Finance and General Administration, and Secretary-General), MARIA GISPERT (Research, External Co-operation and International Relations), ANNA M. GELI (Academic Affairs), MIQUEL DURAN (Staff Affairs and Information Systems), PILAR MONREAL (Teaching and Students), MIQUEL MARTIN (Campus and Library)
Librarian: ANTONIA BOIX
Library: 132,000 books, 3,500 periodicals
Number of teachers: 735
Number of students: 10,500

DEANS

Faculty of Sciences: DAVID BRUSI
Faculty of Education: JOAQUIM PELACH
Faculty of Arts: JOAN NOGUÉ
Economics and Business Studies: JAUME PORTELLA
Legal Studies: EDUARD ROJO
Higher Polytechnic School: LLUÍS ALBÓ (Dir)
School of Nursing: CARME ARPÍ (Dir)

UNIVERSIDAD DE GRANADA

Hospital Real, Calle Cuesta del Hospicio s/n, 18071 Granada
Telephone: 958-243063
Fax: 958-243066
Founded 1526, established 1536, charter granted 1531
State control
Language of instruction: Spanish
Academic year: October to May
Rector: Prof. LORENZO MORILLAS CUEVA

Vice-Rectors: FLORENTINO GARCÍA SANTOS, PILAR ARANDA RAMÍREZ, JOSÉ LUIS GONZÁLEZ MONTES, JUAN CAMPOS FERNÁNDEZ, FRANCISCO GONZÁLEZ LODEIRO, BLAS GIL EXTREMERA, MANUEL SÁENZ LORITE
Registrar: JOAQUÍN MOLERO MESA
Librarian: CRISTÓBAL PASADAS UREÑA

Library of 686,000 vols, 35 incunabula; faculty libraries: 408,000 vols
Number of teachers: 2,590
Number of students: 58,960

DEANS

Faculty of Science: JOSÉ LUIS ROSUA CAMPOS
Faculty of Pharmacy: MARÍA JOSÉ FAUS DADER
Faculty of Philosophy and Letters: CANDIDA MARTÍNEZ LÓPEZ
Faculty of Medicine: ANTONIO CAMPOS MUÑOZ
Faculty of Law: J. MIGUEL ZUGALDIA ESPINAR
Faculty of Fine Arts: DOMINGO SÁNCHEZ MESA
Faculty of Dentistry: JUAN CARLOS LLODRA CALVO
Faculty of Political Sciences and Sociology: JULIO IGLESIAS DE USELL Y ORDIS
Faculty of Economic and Business Science: JUAN DE DIOS JIMENES AGUILERA
Faculty of Education: VÍCTOR LÓPEZ PALOMO
Faculty of Psychology: FRANCISCO MARTOS PERALES
Faculty of Physical Sciences and Sports: ANTONIO OÑA SICILIA
Faculty of Translation and Interpretation: JOSÉ LUIS VÁZQUEZ MARRUECOS
High School of Social Work: MANUEL MARTÍN JORGE
Higher Technical School of Engineers of Ports and Waterways: JOSÉ ANTONIO GARCÍA SUÁREZ
High School of Health Sciences: JESÚS FLORIDO NAVIO
High School of Quantity Surveying: JOSÉ JIMÉNEZ BENAVIDES
Higher Technical School of Architecture: FRANCISCO JAVIER GALLEGO ROCA
Higher Technical School of Computer Engineering: RAFAEL MOLINA SORIANO
High School of Library Science and Documentation: FÉLIX MOTA ANEGÓN
High School of Social Relations: FRANCISCO ABAD MONTES

AFFILIATED SCHOOLS AND INSTITUTIONS

Instituto Federico Oloriz, Sección de Anatomía (Anatomy Section of the Federico Oloriz Institute): Dir Dr GUIRAO PÉREZ.

Instituto del Agua (Water Institute): Dir JOSÉ JAVIER CRUZ SANJULIÁN.

Instituto de Biotecnología (Biotechnology Institute): Dir Dr OSUNA CARRILLO DE ALBORNOZ.

Instituto Andaluz de Ciencias de la Tierra (Andalusian Institute of Earth Sciences): Dir MARÍA DEL CARMEN COMAS MINONDO.

Instituto Andaluz de Geofísica y Prevención de Desastres Sísmicos (Andalusian Institute of Geophysics and Prevention of Seismic Disasters): Dir Dr GERARDO ALGUACIL DE LA BLANCA.

Instituto de Desarrollo Regional (Regional Development Institute): Dir Dr FRANCISCO RODRÍGUEZ MARTÍNEZ.

Instituto de Física Teórica y Computacional (Institute of Theoretical and Computational Physics): Dir Dr JESÚS SÁNCHEZ-DEHESA MORENO CID.

UNIVERSIDAD DE HUELVA

Plaza de la Merced 11, 21071 Huelva
Telephone: 959-28-42-37
Fax: 959-28-43-05

Founded 1993
State control

Rector: Prof. Dr ANTONIO RAMÍREZ DE VERGER JAÉN
Vice-Rectors: JUAN MANUEL CAMPOS CARRASCO (Research and Third Year), JOSÉ LÓPEZ MEDINA (Students and Teaching Standards), JESÚS ESTEPA GIMÉNEZ (Academic Affairs), JOSÉ LUIS GUZMÁN GUERRERO (Planning and Infrastructure), ROQUE JIMÉNEZ PÉREZ (University Extension), JUAN CARLOS FERRÉ OLIVÉ (Teaching Staff)
Secretary-General: EDUARDO GAMERO CASADO
Librarian: JOSÉ CARLOS MORILLO MORENO

Number of teachers: 643
Number of students: 13,600

DEANS

Faculty of Experimental Sciences: EMILIO PASCUAL MARTÍNEZ
Faculty of Business Studies: JUAN JOSÉ GARCÍA DEL HOYO
Faculty of Law: RAMÓN LÓPEZ ROSA
Faculty of Humanities: LUIS GÓMEZ CANSECO
Faculty of Education: ANA SÁNCHEZ VILLALVA
Higher Polytechnic School: FULGENCIO PRAT HURTADO (Dir)
University School of Social Work: OCTAVIO VÁZQUEZ AGUADO (Dir)
University School of Nursing: ISABEL MARISCAL CRESPO (Dir)
University School of Labour Relations: AGUSTÍN GALÁN GARCÍA (Dir)

ASOCIACIÓN UNIVERSITARIA IBEROAMERICANA DE POSTGRADO

C/ Consuelo 32, Torre del Clavero, 37001 Salamanca
Telephone: 923-21-00-39
Fax: 923-21-49-49

Director-General: VICTOR CRUZ CARDONA
Deputy Director-General: ANGEL ESPINA BARRIO

Publications: *Catálogo General AUIP*, *Boletín Informativo AUIP*, *Estudios Monográficos sobre Educación Superior*.

One hundred universities offer 1,500 postgraduate courses under the aegis of the AUIP.

UNIVERSIDAD DE JAÉN

Paraje Las Lagunillas s/n, 23071 Jaén
Telephone: 953-21-21-21
Fax: 953-21-22-39

Founded 1993
State control

President of the Management Commission: LUIS PARRAS GUIJOSA
Vice-Rectors: JOSÉ FERNÁNDEZ GARCÍA (Students and Recreation), PEDRO ANTONIO GALERA ANDREU (University Extension), ANGEL CONTRERAS DE LA FUENTE (Infrastructure and Planning), ADOLFO SÁNCHEZ RODRIGO (Research), RAFAEL PEREA CARPIO (Academic Affairs)
Secretary-General: JOSÉ GONZÁLEZ GARCÍA
Library Director: MARÍA DOLORES SÁNCHEZ COBOS

Library of 115,000 vols
Number of teachers: 673
Number of students: 15,523

DEANS

Faculty of Science: ANTONIO HAYAS BARRÚ
Faculty of Social Sciences and Law: AGUSTIN MUÑOZ VÁZQUEZ
Faculty of Humanities and Education: ANA RAQUEL ORTEGA MARTÍNEZ
Higher Polytechnic School: FRANCISCO BAENA VILLODRES (Dir)
University School of Nursing: ANTONIO FRÍAS OSUNA (Dir)
University Polytechnic School: PATRICIO LUPIAÑEZ CRUZ (Dir)
University School of Social Work in Linares: PATRICIO LUPIAÑEZ CRUZ (Dir)

UNIVERSIDAD JAUME I DE CASTELLÓN

Campus de Penyeta Roja, 12071 Castellón
Telephone: 964-34-58-32

State control

Rector: FERNANDO ROMERO SUBIRÓN

Library facilities with 153,000 vols
Number of teachers: 979
Number of students: 10,322

UNIVERSIDAD DE LA LAGUNA

Molinas de Agua s/n, 38207 La Laguna, Tenerife, Canary Islands
Telephone: 922-60-30-00
Fax: 922-25-96-28
E-mail: ccti@ull.es

Founded 1792
State control
Language of instruction: Spanish
Academic year: October to June

Rector: MATÍAS LÓPEZ RODRÍGUEZ
Vice-Rectors: LUIS RODRÍGUEZ DOMÍNGUEZ (Research and Postgraduates), MIGUEL A. ESTESO DÍAZ, EDUARDO CAMACHO CABRERA (Programming and Co-ordination), PABLO RÓDENAS UTRAY (Students), JORGE RODRÍGUEZ GUERRA (Teachers), RAFAEL FERNÁNDEZ HERNÁNDEZ (General Affairs)
Registrar: PEDRO YANES YANES
Librarian: JAVIER GONZÁLEZ ANTÓN

Number of teachers: 1,963
Number of students: 25,620

Publications: *Revista de Historia Canaria*, *Anales de la Facultad de Derecho*, *Revista Tabona*, *Revista Canaria de Estudios Ingleses*, *Revista Fortunatae*, *Revista de Filología*, *Revista Alisios*, *Cuadernos de Cemyr*.

DEANS

Faculty of Fine Arts: MIGUEL JUAN AROCHA ISIDRA
Faculty of Biology: ANGEL GUTIÉRREZ NAVARRO
Faculty of Economics and Business Administration: VÍCTOR J. CANO FERNÁNDEZ
Faculty of Journalism: ADRIÁN ALEMÁN DE ARMAS
Faculty of Law: CARMEN SEVILLA GONZÁLEZ
Faculty of Pharmacy: MARÍA LUZ PÉREZ PONT
Faculty of Philology: FRANCISCA DEL MAR PLAZA PICÓN
Faculty of Philosophy: AMPARO GÓMEZ RODRÍGUEZ
Faculty of Physics: JUSTO PÉREZ CRUZ
Faculty of Geography and History: FRANCISCO QUIRANTES GONZÁLEZ
Faculty of Mathematics: PABLO GONZÁLEZ VERA
Faculty of Medicine: CLAUDIO A. OTÓN SÁNCHEZ
Faculty of Psychology: JUAN IGNACIO CAPAFONS BONET
Faculty of Chemistry: FRANCISCO GARCÍA MONTELONGO
Centre of Computer Science: LORENZO MORENO RÚIZ (Dir)
Centre of Nautical and Marine Studies: JOSÉ A. BASTIDE TIRADO (Dir)
Centre of Agrarian Sciences: WOLFREDO WILDPRET DE LA TORRE (Dir)
Centre of Education: JAVIER MARRERO ACOSTA (Dir)

ATTACHED INSTITUTES

Andrés Bello Institute of Linguistics: Dir RAMÓN TRUJILLO CARREÑO.

University Institute of Bio-Organics: Dir VÍCTOR SOTERO MARTÍN GARCÍA.

Institute of Political and Social Sciences: Dir (vacant).

Astrophysics Institute of the Canary Islands: Dir FRANCISCO SÁNCHEZ MARTÍNEZ.

University Business Institute: Dir JUAN RAMÓN OREJA RODRÍGUEZ.

UNIVERSIDAD DE LA RIOJA

C/ Avenida de La Paz 93, 26004 Logroño

Telephone: 941-29-91-18
Fax: 941-29-91-20

State control

Rector: URBANO ESPINOSA RUIZ
Vice-Rectors: ROSARIO GARCÍA GÓMEZ (Academic and Staff Affairs), JOSÉ MARTÍN Y PÉREZ DE NANCLARES (Research), PEDRO ARAÚZ GÓMEZ-CADIÑANOS (Students and University Extension), ANGELA ATIENZA LÓPEZ (Resources for Teaching and Research), FÉLIX SANZ ADÁN (Infrastructure)
Chief Administrative Officer: FERRAN MATEO RUEDA
Secretary-General: LEONOR GONZÁLEZ MENORCA
Librarian: MARTA MAGRIÑÁ CONTRERAS

Library of 103,000 vols
Number of teachers: 335
Number of students: 7,300

DIRECTORS

Centre for Humanities, Law and Social Sciences: MA. JESÚS DE TORRE RESA
Teaching Centre for Science and Technology: MANUEL CELSO JUÁREZ CASTELLÓ

UNIVERSIDAD DE LAS PALMAS DE GRAN CANARIA

Calle Alfonso XIII 2, 35003 Las Palmas de Gran Canaria, Canary Islands

Telephone: 928-45-10-00
Fax: 928-45-10-22

Founded 1980
State control
Language of instruction: Spanish
Academic year: October to September

Rector: FRANCISCO RUBIO ROYO
Vice-Rectors: PABLO SAAVEDRA GALLO (Academic), MANUEL LOBO CABRERA (Research), MIGUEL SÚAREZ DE TANGIL NAVARRO (Finance), SANTIAGO CANDELA SOLA (Students)
Secretary-General: GONZALO PÉREZ MELIÁN
Librarian: ELENA SUÁREZ MANRIQUE DE LARA

Number of teachers: 1,200
Number of students: 19,000

UNIVERSITY CENTRES

Higher Technical School of Industrial Engineering: University Campus of Tafira Baja, 35017 Las Palmas de G.C.; tel. 928-45-19-00; Dir MANUEL RODRÍGUEZ DE RIVERA.

Higher Technical School of Architecture: University Campus of Tafira Baja, 35017 Las Palmas de G.C.; tel. 928-45-13-00; Dir JUAN CARLOS RODRÍGUEZ ACOSTA.

Faculty of Oceanic Science: University Campus of Tafira Baja, 35017 Las Palmas de G.C.; tel. 928-45-13-00; Dean JOSE JUAN SANTANA RODRIGUEZ.

Faculty of Physical Activity Science and Sports: University Campus of Tafira Baja, 35017 Las Palmas de G.C.; tel. 928-45-88-68; Dir JUAN M. GARCÍA MANSO.

Faculty of Computer Science: University Campus of Tafira Baja, 35017 Las Palmas de G.C.; tel. 928-45-87-00; Dir ROBERTO MORENO DÍAZ.

Faculty of Economic and Business Studies: University Campus of Tafira Baja, 35017 Las Palmas de G.C.; tel. 928-45-18-00; Dean ANTONIO MARRERO HERNÁNDEZ.

Faculty of Veterinary Science: Calle Francisco Inglott Artiles 12, 35080 Las Palmas de G.C.; tel. 928-45-11-00; Dean ANTONIO FERNÁNDEZ RODRÍGUEZ.

Higher Technical School of Telecommunications Engineering: University Campus of Tafira Baja, 35017 Las Palmas de G.C.; tel. 928-45-13-00; Dir ANTONIO NUÑEZ ORDÓÑEZ.

Faculty of Law: Avda Marítima del Sur s/n, 35080 Las Palmas de G.C.; tel. 928-45-12-00; Dean MANUEL PEREZ RODRIGUEZ.

Faculty of Philology: Plaza de la Constitución s/n, 35003 Las Palmas de G.C.; tel. 928-45-17-00; Dean YOLANDA ARENCIBIA SANTANA.

Higher Studies in Health Sciences (Medicine, Nursing and Physiotherapy): Avda Marítima del Sur s/n, 35080 Las Palmas de G.C.; tel. 928-45-14-00; Dean PEDRO BETANCOR LEÓN.

Faculty of Geography and History: Plaza de la Constitución s/n, 35003 Las Palmas de G.C.; tel. 928-45-17-00; Dean JOSÉ MIGUEL PÉREZ.

Faculty of Translation and Interpretation: Plaza de la Constitución s/n, 35003 Las Palmas de G.C.; tel. 928-45-17-00; Dean ISABEL PASCUA FEBLES.

UNIVERSITY SCHOOLS

University School of Computer Science: University Campus of Tafira Baja, 35017 Las Palmas de G.C.; tel. 928-45-87-00; Dir LUIS MAZORRA MANRIQUE DE LARA.

University College of Technical Engineering in Telecommunications: University Campus of Tafira Baja, 35017 Las Palmas de G.C.; tel. 928-45-13-00; Dir EDUARDO ROVARIS ROMEROS.

University Polytechnic School: University Campus of Tafira Baja, 35017 Las Palmas de G.C.; tel. 928-45-19-00; Dir JOSÉ MARIA DE LA PORTILLA FERNANDEZ.

University School of Business Studies: University Campus of Tafira Baja, 35017 Las Palmas de G.C.; tel. 928-45-18-00; Dir RAFAEL ESPARZA MACHÍN.

University Teacher Training School: Sta Juana de Arco, 1, 35004 Las Palmas de G.C.; tel. 928-24-69-57; Dir DOLORES CABRERA SUÁREZ.

University School of Labour Relations: Avda Marítima del Sur s/n, 35080 Las Palmas de G.C.; tel. 928-45-12-00; Dir RODOLFO ESPINO ROMERO.

HEADS OF DEPARTMENTS

Biology: ANGEL LUQUE ESCALONA
Architecture and Construction: JOSÉ M. PÉREZ LUZARDO
Electronics and Telecommunications: MANUEL CUBERO ENRICI
Physics: (vacant)
Modern Philology: GISELA WIRNITZER
Morphology: JOSÉ REGIDOR GARCÍA
Economics and Business Management: JUAN MANUEL GARCÍA FALCÓN
Mechanical Engineering: ROQUE CALERO PÉREZ
Applied Mathematics: RAFAEL ALEJANDRO MONTENEGRO ARMAS
Applied Economics: LOURDES TRUJILLO CASTELLANO
Psychology and Sociology: GONZALO MARRERO RODRÍGUEZ
Cartography and Engineering Graphics: ILDEFONSO JIMÉNEZ MESA
Civil Engineering: MIGUEL GALANTE GUILLE
Historical Science: ERNESTO MARTÍN RODRÍGUEZ
Art, City and Territory: EDUARDO CÁCERES MORALES
Computer Science and Systems: (vacant)
Finance and Accountancy: JUAN GARCÍA BOZA
Clinical Science: ZOILO GONZÁLEZ LAMA
Cellular and Molecular Endocrinology: LUISA FERNANDA FANJUL RODRÍGUEZ
Juridical Science: (vacant)
Chemistry: JESÚS PÉREZ PEÑA
Physical Education: RAFAEL REYES ROMERO
Education: SANTIAGO ARENCIBIA
Spanish, Classical and Arabic Philology: JOSÉ ANTONIO SAMPER PADILLA
Process Engineering: SEBASTIÁN OVIDIO PÉREZ BÁEZ
Electrical Engineering: JOSÉ MIGUEL MONZÓN VERONA
Architectural Planning and Graphics: LUIS DOMÍNGUEZ REYES
Special Education: EMIDGIA REPETTO JIMÉNEZ
Animal Pathology, Animal Production, Food Science and Technology: FERNANDO REAL VARCÁRCEL
Nursing: BENEDICTA OJEDA PÉREZ

UNIVERSIDAD DE LEÓN

Campus Universitario Vegazana, 24071 León

Telephone: 987-29-10-00
Fax: 987-29-16-14

Founded 1979
State control
Language of instruction: Spanish
Academic year: October to September

Rector: Prof. Dr JULIO-CÉSAR SANTOYO MEDIAVILLA
Vice-Rectors: JOSÉ VAQUERA ORTE (Academic), ASUNCIÓN ORDEN RECIO (Research), JESÚS SUÁREZ MOYA (Finance), JESÚS CALABOZO MORÁN (University Extension and International Relations), RAMÓN MORALA RODRÍGUEZ (Students)
Administrative Officer: JOSÉ LUIS CARRETERO
Librarian: SANTIAGO ASENJO RODRÍGUEZ

Number of teachers: 624
Number of students: 16,281

Publications: *Anales de la Facultad de Veterinaria*, *Estudios Humanísticos—Filología*, *Estudios Humanísticos—Geografía, Historia y Arte*, *Contextos*, *Livius*, *Polígonos*.

DEANS

Faculty of Veterinary Medicine: ELÍAS RODRÍGUEZ FERRI
Faculty of Biology: HUMILDAD RODRÍGUEZ OTERO
Faculty of Law: FRANCISCO SOSA WAGNER
Faculty of Philosophy and Letters: GUSTAVO PUENTE FELIZ
Faculty of Economics: JOSÉ LUIS FANJUL SUÁREZ
School of Professional Training: JUSTO FERNÁNDEZ OBLANCA
School of Mining: BERNARDO LLAMAS GARCÍA
School of Agricultural Engineering: RAFAEL DE COS JÄRLHING
School of Industrial Engineering: DAVID MARCOS MARTÍNEZ
School of Social Labour Studies: GERMÁN BARREIRO GONZÁLEZ
Institute for Physical Education: GONZALO CUADRADO SÁENZ
University Nursing School: DAVID ORDÓÑEZ ESCUDERO
University School of Social Work: JOAQUÍN MARBÁN ROMÁN

UNIVERSITAT DE LLEIDA

Plaça de Víctor Siurana 1, 25003 Lleida

Telephone: 973-70-20-00
Fax: 973-70-20-62

Founded 1991
State control

Rector: Dr JAUME PORTA CASANELLAS
Vice-Rectors: Dra M. PAU CORNADO TEIXIDO (Vice-Rector attached to the Rector), Dr JOSEP M. VILLAR MIR (Academic Affairs and Innovation in Teaching), Dr JAUME SANUY BURGUÉS (Teaching Personnel), Dra MONTSERRAT PARRA ALBÀ (Cultural Activities and University Promotion), ASSUMPTA ESTRADA ROCA (University Extension), Dr JOAN XAVIER COMELLA CARNICÉ (Research), Dr JOSEP M. TAMARIT SUMALLA (Secretary-General), XAVIER RUESTES SISCART (Director)
Library Director: DOLORES MANCIÑEIRAS VAZ-ROMERO

Library of 138,000 vols
Number of teachers: 597
Number of students: 11,377

DEANS

Faculty of Arts: Dra ÀNGELS SANTA BAÑERES
Faculty of Medicine: Dr JOAN VIÑAS SALAS
Faculty of Law and Economics: Dra TERESA ARECES PIÑOL
Faculty of Education: Dr FIDEL MOLINA LUGUE
University School of Nursing: CARME TORRES PENELLA
University Polytechnic School: JOSEP M. MIRET BIOSCA
Higher Technical School of Agricultural Engineering: Dr IGNACIO ROMAGOSA CLARIANA

UNIVERSIDAD COMPLUTENSE DE MADRID

Ciudad Universitaria, 28040 Madrid
Telephone: 91-549-02-56
Fax: 91-394-34-37

Founded 1508

Rector: Prof. GUSTAVO VILLAPALOS SALAS
Administrator-General: JESÚS CALVO SORIA
Secretary-General: GUILLERMO CALLEJA PARDO
Librarian: Dra CECILIA FERNÁNDEZ FERNÁNDEZ

Library: second in importance in Madrid; 1,500,000 vols, 40,000 periodicals
Number of teachers: 5,312
Number of students: 124,150

Publications: *Memoria de la UCM*, *Gaceta Complutense*, various faculty publications.

DEANS

Faculty of Philosophy: MANUEL MACEIRAS FAFIÁN
Faculty of Education: ANASTASIO MARTÍNEZ NAVARRO
Faculty of Philology: JESÚS SANCHEZ LOBATO
Faculty of Geography and History: FRANCISCO JOSÉ PORTELA SANDOVAL
Faculty of Chemistry: MIGUEL ANGEL ALARIO Y FRANCO
Faculty of Physics: FRANCISCO SÁNCHEZ QUESADA
Faculty of Mathematics: JUAN FERRERA CUESTA
Faculty of Biology: RAFAEL HERNÁNDEZ TRISTÁN
Faculty of Geology: MERCEDES DOVAL MONTOYA
Faculty of Law: JOSÉ ITURMENDI MORALES
Faculty of Medicine: VICENTE MOYA PUEYO
Faculty of Pharmacy: BENITO DEL CASTILLO GARCÍA
Faculty of Veterinary Science: GUILLERMO SUÁREZ FERNÁNDEZ
Faculty of Political Science and Sociology: ALFONSO DE ESTEBAN ALONSO
Faculty of Economics and Management: CARLOS BERZOSA ALONSO-MARTÍNEZ
Faculty of Information Science: ALFONSO FERNANDEZ DEL MORAL
Faculty of Psychology: JOSÉ MA ARREDONDO RODRÍGUEZ
Faculty of Fine Arts: ROSA GARCERÁN PIQUERAS
Faculty of Odontology: CARLO FERNÁNDEZ FRIAS

DIRECTORS OF UNIVERSITY SCHOOLS

Librarianship and Documentation: JOSÉ LÓPEZ YEPES
Ma Díaz Jiménez: ANTONIO MORENO GONZÁLEZ
Management Studies: SERAFÍN PIÑEIRO FERNÁNDEZ
Nursing, Physiotherapy and Paedology: JUAN VICENTE BENEIT MONTESINOS
Optics: GLORIA RICO ARNAIZ DE LAS REVILLAS
Pablo Montesino: ADOLFO F. J. CERMEÑO APARICIO
Social Work: JOSÉ AURELIO PALAFOX BOGDANOVITCH
Statistics: BENJAMÍN HERNÁNDEZ BLÁZQUEZ

UNIVERSIDAD AUTÓNOMA DE MADRID

Carretera de Colmenar Km. 15,000, Canto Blanco, 28049 Madrid
Telephone: 91-397-50-00
Fax: 91-397-41-23

Founded 1968
State control
Language of instruction: Spanish
Academic year: October to June

Rector: RAÚL VILLAR LÁZARO
Vice-Rectors: ALFONSO RUIZ MIGUEL (Research), NICOLÁS ORTEGA CANTERO (Cultural Affairs), MARTA BIZCARRONDO ALBEA (Academic Affairs), ENRIQUE PEÑARANDA RAMOS (Teaching Staff), MERCEDES SALAICES SÁNCHEZ (Student Affairs), CARLOS SIEIRO DE NIESO (Infrastructure for Research), MA. OLIVA MÁRQUEZ SÁNCHEZ (International and Institutional Relations), JOSÉ MIGUEL RODRÍGUEZ ANTON (Community Services)
Secretary-General: GREGORIO TUDELA CAMBRONERO
Chief Administrative Officer: LUCIANO GALAN CASADO
Librarian: (vacant)

Library of 411,000 vols
Number of teachers: 2,000
Number of students: 37,000

Publications: *Revista Edad de Oro*, *Revista Narria*, *Memoria Anual*, *Revista Cuardenos de Prehistoria y Arqueología*, *Revista Manuscrit CAO*.

DEANS

Faculty of Medicine: JOSÉ VILLAMOR LEÓN
Faculty of Economics and Business Studies: FRANCISCO PRIETO PÉREZ
Faculty of Philosophy and Letters: ISIDRO BANGO TORVISO
Faculty of Science: SANTIAGO CARRILLO MENÉNDEZ
Faculty of Law: MANUEL ARAGÓN REYES
Faculty of Psychology: AMALIO BLANCO ABARCA

DIRECTORS

University School of Teacher Training 'Santa Maria': ALBERTO BARCIA DOMÍNGUEZ
University School of Teacher Training 'Virgen de la Fuencisla': SANTIAGO HIDALGO ALONSO
University School of Nursing 'Puerto de Hierro': PILAR ARROYO GORDO
University School of Nursing 'La Paz': CATALINA GARCÍA MARTÍN-CARO
University School of Nursing 'Fundación Jiménez Díaz': MARIANO JIMÉNEZ CASADO
Institute of Educational Sciences: FERNANDO ARROYO LLERA
School of Physiotherapy: 'ONCE': HORACIO OLIVA ALDÁMIZ
School of Nursing 'Cruz Roja': CARMEN BARAGAÑO MORALES
School of Nursing 'Communidad de Madrid': MARÍA VICTORIA ANTÓN NARDIZ

UNIVERSIDAD DE MÁLAGA

El Ejido s/n, 29071 Málaga
Telephone: 95-213-10-00
Fax: 95-226-38-58

Founded 1972
State control
Language of instruction: Spanish
Academic year: October to July

Rector: Prof. JOSÉ M. MARTÍN DELGADO
Vice-Rectors: JOSÉ MARÍA SOUVIRÓN MORENILLA (Academic Affairs), JUAN JOSÉ RODRÍGUEZ JIMÉNEZ (Research), CARLOS CAMACHO PEÑALOSA (Programming and Investment)
Administrative Officer: RAFAEL RIVAS SAUCO
Secretary-General: ENRIQUE SALVO TIERRA

Library of 202,367 vols, 4,300 periodicals
Number of teachers: 1,600
Number of students: 33,000

Publications: *Filosofía Malacitana* (1 a year), *Boletín de Arte* (1 a year), *Histología Médica* (2 a year).

DEANS

Economic and Business Sciences: FRANCISCO GONZÁLEZ FAJARDO
Medicine: Prof. PEDRO GONZÁLEZ SANTOS
Science: ENRIQUE CARO GUERRA
Philosophy and Letters: SIRO VILLAS TINOCO
Law: BLANCA SILLERO CROVETTO
Information Science: FRANCISCO TRIGUERO RUIZ

PROFESSORS

Faculty of Economic and Business Studies:
- AGUIRRE SADABA, A., Economics and Business Administration
- GARCÍA LIZANA, A., Applied Economics (Political)
- GONZÁLEZ PAREJA, A., Applied Economics (Mathematics)
- MOCHON MORCILLO, F., Economic Analysis
- OTERO MORENO, J. M., Applied Economics (Statistics and Econometrics)
- PINO ARTACHO, J. DEL, State Law and Sociology
- REQUENA RODRÍGUEZ, J. M., Financial Economics and Accountancy
- SANCHEZ MALDONADO, J., Applied Economics (Structure and Public Finance)

Faculty of Medicine:
- BROTAT ESTER, M., Radiology, Physical and Psychiatric Medicine
- CASTILLA GONZALO, J., Normal and Pathological Morphology
- FERNÁNDEZ-CREHUET NAVAJAS, J., Preventative Medicine and Public Health
- OCAÑA SIERRA, J., Medicine
- SÁNCHEZ DE LA CUESTA Y ALARCÓN, F., Physiology, Pharmacology and Paediatrics
- SÁNCHEZ DEL CURA, G., Surgery, Obstetrics and Gynaecology

Faculty of Philosophy and Letters:
- ALVAR EZQUERRA, M., Spanish and Romance Philology
- CUEVAS GARCÍA, C., Spanish Philology and Theory of Literature
- ESTEVE ZARAZAGA, J. M., Theory and History of Education
- GARCÍA DE LA FUENTE, O., Classical Philology and Arabic and Islamic Studies
- LAVIN CAMACHO, E., English and French Philology
- MARTÍNEZ FREIRE, P., Philosophy
- MORALES FOLGUERAS, J. M., History of Art
- NADAL SANCHEZ, A., Modern History
- OCANA OCANA, M. C., Geography
- PEREZ GOMEZ, A., Didactics

Rodriguez Oliva, P., Prehistory and Science of Antiquity and Middle Ages
Traines Torres, M. V., Psychology

Faculty of Sciences:

Arenas Rosado, J. F., Physical Chemistry
Cabezudo Artero, B., Plant Biology
Cano Pavón, J. M., Analytical Chemistry
Cuenca Mira, J. A., Algebra, Geometry and Topology
Fernández-Figares Perez, J. M., Cellular and Genetic Biology
Fernández Jimenez, C., Applied Physics
García Raso, E., Animal Biology
Jiménez López, A., Inorganic Chemistry, Crystalography and Mineralogy
Rodríguez Jimenez, J. J., Chemical Engineering
Rodríguez Ortiz, C., Applied Mathematics and Statistics
Serrano Lozano, L., Ecology and Geology
Suau Suárez, R., Biochemistry, Molecular Biology and Organic Chemistry

Faculty of Law:

Aurioles Martin, A., Private Law
Carretero Leston, J. L., Public Law
Ortega Carillo de Albórnoz, A., Civil, Ecclesiastical and State Law
Robles Garzon, J. A., Political Science, International Law

University School of Teacher Training:

del Campo y del Campo, M., Didactics of Expression, Music
García España, J., Didactics, Social Science, Experimental Science
Mantecon Ramirez, B., Didactics of Language and Literature

University Polytechnic:

Ollero Baturone, A., Systems Engineering, Information Science, Electronics
Ruiz Munoz, J. M., Electrical Engineering, Electronic Technology
Simon Mata, A., Mechanical Engineering, Engineering Graphics
Troya Linero, J. M., Language and Science of Computing

AFFILIATED INSTITUTES

Institute of Education Sciences: Dir Miguel Angel Santos Guerra.

University Institute of Technological Research and Control: Dir Francisco Serrano Casares.

UNIVERSIDAD MIGUEL HERNÁNDEZ DE ELCHE

Paseo Melchor Botella s/n, 03206 Elche (Alicante)

MONDRAGON UNIBERTSITATEA

Laramendi 4, Apdo 23 (Esuela Politécnica José Ma. Arizmendjarrieta), 20500 Gipúzcoa
Telephone: 943-79-47-00
Fax: 943-79-15-36
Private control
General Director: Ignacio Lacunza
Director of International Relations: Ignacio Irizar
Director of General Studies: Mila Arregui
Academic Registrar: Miren Irune Murguiondo
Librarian: Obdulia Velez

DIRECTORS

Continuous Training: Javier Retegui
Engineering: Javier Mendiluce
Polytechnic Institute: Luis Ma. Iriarte
School of Economic Sciences: (vacant)
School of Humanities: (vacant)

UNIVERSIDAD DE MURCIA

Avda Teniente Flomesta 5, Edificio Convalecencia, 30071 Murcia
Telephone: 968-36-30-00
Fax: 968-36-36-03
Founded 1915
State control
Language of instruction: Spanish
Academic year: October to June
Rector: Prof. Juan Monreal Martínez
Vice-Rectors: José Serrano Marino (Campus and Infrastructure), Ramón Almela Pérez (Students and Social Services), Jośe Nieto Martínez (Development of the Cartagena Campus), Joaquín Ataz López (Planning), Antonio Calvo-Flores Segura (Finance), César Oliva Olivares (University Extension), Pedro Molina Buendía (Research), Concha Martínez Sánchez (Academic Staff), Manuel Esteban Albert (International and Institutional Relations)
Registrar: José Ramón Torres Ruiz
Librarian: María Carmen Aparicio Fernández
Library of 498,000 vols, 9,635 periodicals
Number of teachers: 1,748
Number of students: 36,368
Publications: *Anales* (quarterly), *Monteagudo*, *Gaceta Universitaria* (monthly).

DEANS

Faculty of Letters: José María Pozuelo Yvancos
Faculty of Law: José Antonio Cobacho Gómez
Faculty of Chemistry: Gabriel García Sánchez
Faculty of Mathematics: José Ma. Ruíz Gómez
Faculty of Medicine: Tomás Quesada Pérez
Faculty of Psychology: Concepción López Soler
Faculty of Economics and Business: Domingo García Pérez de Lema
Faculty of Information Science: Fernando Martín Rubio
Faculty of Veterinary Science: Francisco Moreno Medina
Faculty of Philosophy: Patricio Peñalver Gómez
Faculty of Biology: Francisco García Carmona
Faculty of Education: Diego Guzmán Martínez-Valls

DIRECTORS

University School of Business Studies (in Murcia): Francisco Cremades Bañón
University School of Business Studies (in Cartagena): Eugenio B. Gomaríz Mercader
University School of Nursing (in Murcia): Carmen Isabel Gómez García
University School of Nursing (in Cartagena): Juana Hernández Conesa
University School of Librarianship and Documentation: José Antonio Gómez Hernández
University School of Graduate Social Studies (in Murcia): Antonio Vicente Sempere Navarro
University School of Graduate Social Studies (in Cartagena): Ma. Dolores Fontes Bastos
University School of Social Work: Conrado Navalón Vila
University School of Naval Engineering: José A. Martínez García
University School of Mining Engineering: Andrés Perales Agüera
Higher Technical School of Agricultural Engineering: Miguel A. Martínez Cañadas
Higher Technical School of Industrial Engineering: Pascual Martí Montrull

UNIVERSIDAD DE NAVARRA

Ciudad Universitaria, 31080 Pamplona
Telephone: 948-42-56-00
Fax: 948-42-56-19
Founded 1952
Private control
Language of instruction: Spanish
Academic year: October to June
Chancellor: Javier Echevarria
Vice-Chancellor: Tomás Gutiérrez Calzada
President: José Ma. Bastero Eleizalde
Vice-Presidents: Manuel Casado, Pilar Fernández Otero, Luis Herrera
Secretary-General: Guido Stein
Bursar: José Antonio González
Librarian: David Isaacs
Number of teachers: 2,342
Number of students: 17,700
Publications: *Revista de Medicina*, *Ius Canonicum*, *Nuestro Tiempo*, *Scripta Theologica*, *Redacción*, *Anuario Filosófico*, *Anuario de Derecho Internacional*, *Persona y Derecho*, *Revista de Edificación*, *Comunicación y Sociedad*, *RILCE*.

DEANS

School of Law: Rafael Domingo
School of Public Communication: Alfonso Sánchez Tabernero
School of Medicine: Pedro Gil
School of Canon Law: Eduardo Molano
Faculty of Pharmacy: Edurne Cenarruzabeitia
Faculty of Sciences: Pilar Sesma
School of Theology: Pedro Rodríguez
Faculty of Economics and Business Administration: Luis Ravina
Ecclesiastical Faculty of Philosophy: Mariano Artigas
Higher Technical School of Industrial Engineering: Carlos Bastero
School of Architecture: Juan Miguel Otxotorena
Graduate School of Business Administration (in Barcelona): Carlos Cavallé (see also under Colleges)
School of Humanities and Social Science: Angel Luis González

DIRECTORS OF AFFILIATED COLLEGE, SCHOOLS AND INSTITUTES

College of Liberal Arts: Juan Bosco Amores
Institute of Church History: Domingo Ramos
Institute of Modern Languages: James Leahy
Institute of Secretarial and Administrative Studies: Begoña Taus
Institute of Further Education: David Isaacs
Institute of Spanish Language and Culture: Ma. Victoria Romero
School of Nursing: Isabel Saracibar
Institute of Applied Sciences: Isabel García Jalón

PROFESSORS

Faculty of Law:

Aparisi, M. A., Philosophy of Law
Arechederra, L., Civil Law
Barrios, G., Labour Law
Blanco, M., Canon Law
Calvo, A. L., Private International Law
Cordón, F., Procedural Law
de la Iglesia, M. A., Constitutional Law
Diego, D., Juridical Deontology
Dios, M. V., Administrative Law
Domingo, R., Roman Law
Doral, J. A., Commercial Law
Escriva, J., Natural Law
Fornes de la Rosa, J., Canon Law
Fuenmayor, A., Civil Law
García, A., Political Law
García Pérez, R., History of Law
Galán, M., History of Law
Gonzalez, F., Administrative Law
Hernández, A., International Law

HERVADA, J., Natural Law
LEJEUNE, E., Financial and Tax Law
LÓPEZ JURADO, E., Administrative Law
LÓPEZ SÁNCHEZ, M. A., Commercial Law
MARTÍNEZ, J. M., Administrative Law
MATEO, A., Roman Law
MUERZA, J. J., Penal Law
ORS, A. D', Roman Law
PÉREZ MORIONES, A., Commercial Law
RIVAS, P., Philosophy of Law
SALCEDO, J., History of Law
SAN JULIÁN, V., Civil Law
SÁNCHEZ BELLA, I., History of Law
SEMPERE, A., Labour Law
SERNA, P., Philosophy of Law
SIMON, E., Financial and Tax Law
SUAREZ-LLANOS, L., Commercial Law
VALPUESTA, E., Commercial Law
VÁSQUEZ DEL REY, A., Financial and Tax Law
VELARDE, C., Philosophy of Law
WALTER, P. G., International Law
ZAFRA, J., Political Law

Faculty of Arts, Humanities and Social Sciences:

AGUADO, G., Pedogogy
ALONSO DEL REAL, C., Latin
ALVIRA, R., History of Philosophy
ALTAREJOS, F., History of Education
ARELLANO, I., Spanish Literature
ARTIGAS, M., Philosophy of Nature and Sciences
BAÑALES, J., Latin Language
BASTONS, M., History of Philosophy
BEGUIRISTAIN, M. A., Prehistory and Archaeology
BERIAIN, I., Regional Spanish Geography
BLAZQUEZ, A. M., Latin Language
CASADO, M., Spanish Language
CASTIELLA, A., Archaeology
CASTILLO, C., Latin
CRUZ, A., Philosophy and Practice
CRUZ, J., Psychology
DIZ-LOIS, C., Modern and Contemporary History
ECHAIDE, A. M., Spanish Language
ENTREMONT, A. D', Human Geography
FERNÁNDEZ, A. R., Contemporary Spanish Literature
FERNÁNDEZ, J. L., Fundamental Philosophy
FERNÁNDEZ-LADREDA, C., History of Art
FERRER, M., Geography
FLORISTÁN, A., Geography
GARCIA, A., Pedagogical Diagnosis
GARCÍA ARANCÓN, M. R., Medieval History
GARCÍA GAINZA, C., History of Art
GARCÍA LARRAGUETA, S., Palaeography
GARCÍA RUIZ, V., Spanish Literature
GONZÁLEZ, A. L., Ontology and Theodicy
GONZÁLEZ ENCISO, A., History of Economics
GONZÁLEZ OLLE, F., Spanish Language
GONZÁLEZ SIMANCAS, J. L., Theory of Education, Guidance and Counselling in Education
LABRADA, M. A., Practical Philosophy
LIZARRAGA, M. A., General Geography
LONGARES, J., Contemporary History
LLANO, A., Epistemology
MARTÍN DUQUE, A., Medieval History
MARTÍNEZ, R., Greek Language
MARTÍNEZ FERNÁNDEZ, R., Philosophy
MERIDA-NICOLICH, E., General Pedagogy
MOLINOS, M. DE C., Curriculum Theory and Practice
MUGICA, L. F., Sociology
NARBONA, J., Educational Neuropsychology
NAVARRO, A. M., Sociology of Education
OLABARRI, I., Contemporary History
ORTIZ, J. M., Philosophy
POLO, L., History of Philosophical Systems
PURROY, C., History of America
REDONDO, E., History of Education
SANCHO, J., Spanish Geography
SANTOS, M., Ethics and Sociology
SANZ, V., Metaphysics
SARALEGUI, C., History of Spanish Language
SARRAIS, F., General and Educational Psychology
SEGURA, C., History of Philosophy
SOTO, M. J., Metaphysics
SPANG, K., Literary Criticism
TOURON, F. J., Experimental Pedagogy
VÁZQUEZ DE PRADA, M., Modern and Contemporary History
VÁZQUEZ DE PRADA, V., Modern Spanish History
VERGARA, J., History of Education
ZUBIAUR, F. J., History of Art

Faculty of Medicine:

ALBEROLA, I., Internal Medicine
ALEGRÍA, E., Medical Pathology and Clinics
ARROYO, J. L., Anaesthesiology
BARRAQUER, L., Neurology
BERIAIN, J. M., Internal Medicine
BERJÓN, A., Biology
BORRAS, F., Biotechnology
BRUGAROLAS, A., Oncology
CALVO, F., Radiology and Physical Medicine
CAÑADELL, J. M., Orthopaedic Surgery
CARRASCOSA, F., Anaesthesiology
CERVERA, S., Psychiatry
CIVEIRA, M. P., General Pathology
CONCHILLO, F., Digestive System
DÍAZ, E. J., Physics
DÍAZ, R., Microbiology
ERRASTI, P., Medical Pathology
FORRIOL, F., Orthopaedic Surgery
FUENTE, F. DE LA, Obstetrics and Gynaecology
GAMAZO, C., Microbiology
GARCIA-JALON, I., Microbiology
GARCIA-TAPIA, R., Oto-rhino-laryngology
GIL, P., History of Medicine
GIMÉNEZ, J. M., Anatomy
GONZALO, J. M., Anatomy
HERRANZ, G., Pathological Anatomy
HONORATO, J., Pharmacology
INSAUSTI, R., Anatomy
JURADO, M., Gynaecology and Obstetrics
LÓPEZ, G., Obstetrics and Gynaecology
LÓPEZ, M. J., Biochemistry
LÓPEZ, M. N., Biochemistry
LOZANO, R., Surgery
LUCAS, I., Medical Surgery and Pathology
MARTÍN, A., Clinical Surgery and Pathology
MARTÍNEZ CARO, D., Cardiology
MARTÍNEZ LAGE, J. M., Neurology
MATO DE LA PAZ, J. M., Internal Medicine
MIGUEL, C. DE, Biochemistry
MONCADA, E., Endocrinology
MONREAL, I., Biochemistry
MORIYON, I., Microbiology
MUÑOZ, M. A., Digestion
OEHLING, A., Allergology
OLIVARES, C., Dermatology
PANIAGUA, J. A., History of Medicine
PARDO, F. J., Pathological Anatomy
PELLICER, S., Biochemistry
PRIETO, J. M., General Pathology
PURROY, A., Medical Pathology and Clinics
QUINTANILLA, E., Dermatology
QUIROGA, J. A., Medical Pathology
RIO, J. DEL, Pharmacology
ROCHA, E., Medical Pathology and Clinics
SANCHEZ, A., Immunology
SANTIDRIAN, S., Human Physiology
SANTIAGO, E., Biochemistry
SANTOS, A., Orthopaedic Surgery and Traumatology
SERRA, J. M., Surgery
SERRANO, M., Internal Medicine
SESMA, M. P., Biology
SIERRASESUMAGA, L., Paediatrics
TOSAR, A., Human Physiology
ULLÁN, J., Anatomy
VILLARO, C., Biology
VILLAS, C., Orthopaedic Surgery and Traumatology
ZAPATA, R., Medical Physiology and Psychiatry
ZORNOZA, G., Surgical Pathology

Faculty of Pharmacy:

(Some professors also serve in the Faculty of Sciences)

ALDANA, I., General Chemistry
ASTIASARAN, I., Bromatology
BARBER, A., Animal Physiology
BELLO, J., Bromatology, Toxicology and Chemical Analysis
CENARRUZABEITIA, E., Pharmacodynamics
CID, C., Bromatology
FERNÁNDEZ, M., Pharmacognosis
FERNÁNDEZ OTERO, P., Physiology
FONT, M., Organic Chemistry
GARCÍA, P. J., General Chemistry
GIRÁLDEZ, J., Galenic Pharmacy
IGARTUA, P., Galenic Pharmacy
IRACHE, J. M., Galenic Pharmacy
LARRALDE, J., Animal Physiology
LASHERAS, B., Pharmacodynamics
MARTIN, C., Physical Chemistry
MARTÍNEZ, A., Animal Physiology
MONGE, A., Organic Chemistry
PALOP, J. A., General Chemistry
RENEDO, M. J., Galenic Pharmacy
SANCHEZ, M., Physical Chemistry

Faculty of Sciences:

AGUIRREOLEA, J. M., Phytopathology
ARBEA, J. I., Zoology
ARIÑO, A. H., Ecology
CALASANZ, M. J., Bio-Statistics
CHASCO, M. J., Mathematics
EDERRA, A., Botany
ESCALA, M. DEL C., Zoology
GARCIA, C., Physics
GARCÍA, M., Genetics
GULLON, A., Genetics
HERNÁNDEZ, M. A., Zoology
HERRERA, L., Zoology
JORDANA, R., Animal Physiology and Applied Ecology
LOPEZ, J., Biology
LOPEZ, M. L., Botany
MIGUEL, A. M. DE, Botany
MONTUENGA, L., Deontology
MORAZA, M. L., Zoology
MUÑOZ, M., Dietetics
PALACIOS, C., Physics
PEÑA, J. I., Plant Physiology
PEREZ, C., Physics
SAN MARTÍN, C., Organic Chemistry
SÁNCHEZ, J. M., Analytical Chemistry
SÁNCHEZ, M., Vegetal Physiology
SÁNCHEZ-CARPINTERO, I., Geology

Faculty of Public Communication:

DESANTES, J. M., Mass Media Law
FAUS, A., Broadcasting
GARCÍA-NOBLEJAS, J. J., Mass Media Technology
GÓMEZ ANTON, F., Political Institutions
LÓPEZ-ESCOBAR, E., Mass Media Theory
LOZANO BARTOLOZZI, P., International Relations
NAVAS, A., Sociology
NIETO, A., Journalistic Enterprise
REDONDO, G., Contemporary World History
ROMERO, M. V., Spanish Language
SÁNCHEZ, A., Journalism
SÁNCHEZ, F. J., Spanish Language
SANCHEZ-ARANDA, J. J., History of Spanish Journalism
SORÍA, C., Mass Media Law

School of Architecture:

ALONSO DEL VAL, M. A., Projects
ARAUJO, I., Means of Expression
BASSEGODA, J., Landscaping
BAYO, E., Structures
BAZAL, J. J., Projects
CARVAJAL, J., Projects
DIOS, M. J., Installations
FERNÁNDEZ, A., History of Art

FRIAS, M. A., Humanities
GARCIA DURAN, L., Structures
GONZÁLEZ, M., Form Analysis
GUTIÉRREZ, M. A., Construction
HERNÁNDEZ, R., Consturction
LAHUERTA, J., Construction
LORDA, J., History of Art
OCHOTORENA, J. M., Projects
PELLICER, D., Construction
POZO, J. M., Descriptive Geometry

Faculty of Canon Law:

BAÑARES, J. I., Family Law
CALVO, J., Administrative Canon Law
CATTANEO, A., Fundamental Canon Law Theory
DIEGO, C. DE, Codex Texts
FUENTES, J. A., Administrative Canon Law
HERRANZ, J., Special Disciplines
MARZOA, A., Penal Canon Law
MOLANO, E., Constitutional Canon Law
ORLANDIS, J., History of Canon Law
OTADUY, J., General and Personal Law
OTADUY, J., Ecclesiastical Law
RINCÓN, T., Administrative Canon Law
RODRIGUEZ, R., Procedural Canon Law
TEJERO, E., History of Canon Law
VIANA, A., Ecclesiastical Organization
VILADRICH, P. J., Canon Law

Faculty of Theology:

ADEVA, I., Latin Language
ARANDA, A., Dogmatic Theology
ARANDA, G., Sacred Scripture: New Testament
AUSIN, S., Sacred Scripture: Old Testament
BASEVI, C., Fundamental Dogmatic Theology
BASTERO, J. L., Dogmatic Theology
CASCIARO, J. M., New Testament
CHAPA, J., Sacred Scripture (New Testament)
DOMINGO, F. J., Dogmatic Theology
GARCÍA-MORENO, A., Sacred Theology
GOÑI, J., History of the Church: Middle Ages
ILLANES, J. L., Fundamental Dogmatic Theology
IZQUIERDO, C., Fundamental Theology
LIMBURG, K., Sacred Scripture (New Testament)
LOPEZ, P., Sacred Theology
LOPEZ, T., History of Theology: Middle Ages
LORDA, J. L., Dogmatic Theology
MARTÍN, A., Theology
MATEO-SECO, L. F., Dogmatic Theology
MERINO, M., Patristics
MORALES, J., Dogmatic Theology
ODERO, J. M., Fundamental Theology
PAZOS, A., History of the Church
PUJOL, J., Theological Methodology
QUIROS, A., Moral Theology
RAMOS, D., Latin Patristics
RODRÍGUEZ, P., Dogmatic Theology
SANCHO, J., Dogmatic Theology: The Sacraments
SARANYANA, J. I., History of Theology
SARMIENTO, A., Moral Theology
SESE, F. J., Spiritual Theology
TINEO, P., History of the Early Church
VARO, F., Sacred Scripture (New Testament)
VICIANO, A., Patrology
YANGUAS, J. M., Dogmatic Theology

Graduate School of Business Administration:

ABADIA, L., Business Policy
AGELL, P., Managerial Economics
AGUIRRE, J., Finance
ALVAREZ, J. L., Human Behaviour
ALVAREZ DE MON, S., Human Behaviour
ANDREU, R., Managerial Economics
ANZIZU, J. M., Business Policy
ARGANDOÑA, A., Business Policy
ARIÑO, M. A., Decision Analysis
BALLARÍN, E., Control
BLANC, M., Organizational Behaviour
CANALS, J., Social and Economic Analysis
CARRASCO, R., Financial Management
CAVALLE, C., Production Management
CHIESA, C., Marketing
CHINCHILLA, M. N., Human Behaviour
CORTES, L. J., Social and Economic Analysis
DIONIS, L., Production Management
ELORDUY, J. M., Business Policy
FARRAN, J., Marketing
FATIMA, A. DE, Finance
FAUS, J., Managerial Economics
FERNÁNDEZ LÓPEZ, P., Finance
FERRAZ, R., Control
FONT, V., Marketing
GALLO, M. A., Business Policy
GARCIA, C., Business Policy
GINEBRA, J., Marketing
GOMEZ, P. S., Human Behaviour
GÓMEZ-LLERA, G., Environmental Analysis for Management
GRANDES, M. J., Control
GUAL, J., Social and Economic Analysis
GUILLÉN, F. J., Marketing
HUERTA, F., Financial Management
HUETE, L. M., Production Management
JORDAN, P., Financial Management
KASE, K., Marketing
LACUEVA, F., Business Policy
LEGETT, B., Managerial Communications
LÓPEZ, J., Financial Management
LUCAS, J. L., Business Policy
MARTINEZ, E., Finance
MASIFERN, E., Business Policy
MELE, D., Business Ethics
MONS, J., Finance
NEGRE, A., Financial Management
NUENO, J. L., Marketing
NUENO, P., Production Management
O'CALLAGHAN, R., Information Systems
OCARIZ, J., Environmental Analysis for Management
PALACIOS, J. A., Financial Management
PARES, F., Marketing
PEREIRA, F., Control
PÉREZ LÓPEZ, J. A., Organizational Behaviour
PIN, J. R., Human Behaviour
PONS, J. M., Marketing
POU, V., Environmental Analysis for Management
PREGEL, G., Finance
RABADAN, M., Finance
RENART, L. G., Marketing
RIBERA, J., Production Management
RICART, J. E., Managerial Economics
RIVEROLA, J., Managerial Economics
RODRÍGUEZ, J. M., Organizational Behaviour
ROIG, B., Business Policy
ROSANAS, J. M., Control
ROURE, J., Production Management
SABRIA, F., Production
SANTOMA, J., Financial Management
SCHERK, W., Finance
SEGARRA, J. A., Marketing
SUÁREZ, J. L., Financial Management
SUBIRA, A., Managerial Economics
TAPIES, J., Financial Management
TERMES, R., Financial Management
TORIBIO, J. J., Social and Economic Analysis
TORRES, J., Control
TREVILLE, S., Production
VALERO, A., Business Policy
VALOR, J., Managerial Economics
VÁZQUEZ-DODERO, J. C., Control
VELILLA, M., Control
VILLAMARIN, B., Managerial Economics
WEBER, E., Control
ZANTINGA, J., Production

Institute of Further Education:

CASTILLO, G., Learning Process
GONZÁLEZ SIMANCAS, J. L., Counselling
ISAACS, D., Organization

School of Industrial Engineering:

ALONSO, J., Electricity and Magnetism
ARIZTI, F., Fundamental Electronics
ARRICIBITA, F., Chemistry
BASTERO, J. M., Mechanics
FERNÁNDEZ, J., Mechanical Technology
FLAQUER, J., Linear Algebra
FONTAN, L., Fundamentals of Electrotechnics
FUENTES, M., Metallurgy
GARCÍA DE JALON, J., Kinematics
GARCÍA RICO, A., Electrical Machines
GIL, F. J., Metallurgy
GIMÉNEZ, G., Mechanical Technology
GRACIA, F. J., Electronics
GURRUCHAGA, J. M., Technical Drawing
IRIGARAY, J., Heat Transfer
JIMÉNEZ CONDE, M., General Physics
JORDANA, C., Elementary Electrical Techniques
MARTINEZ ESNAOLA, J. M., Mechanics of Continua
MOZOS, L. M., Industrial Architecture and Structural Engineering
PARGADA, M., Advanced Mathematics
SANCHO REBULLIDA, F., Quantum Mechanics
SANTOS, F., Projects
URCOLA, J., Thermodynamics
VERA, E., Steel Structures

Faculty of Economics and Business Administration:

DIAZ, M. J., Introduction to Economics
FERNANDEZ, C., Applied Economics
GALERA, F., Economics
GARCIA, V., Accountancy
GONZALEZ, A., Economic History
IRASTORZA, J., Economics
MARTIN, E., Sociology
MARTINEZ CHACON, E., Political Economy
MARTINEZ-ECHEVARRIA, M. A., Economics and Finance
MORENO, A., Economic History
PONCE, J. M., Mathematics
RAVINA, L., Economics
SANCHEZ, J. M., Economic Theory
SAN MARTIN, M. DEL C., Economics and Statistics
TOLSA, A., Mathematics
TORRES, R., Economic History

ATTACHED INSTITUTES

Instituto de Estudios Superiores de la Empresa (IESE): Avda Pearson 21, 08034 Barcelona; tel. 93-204-40-00; fax 93-280-11-77; *also at:* Camino del Cerro del Aguila 3 (Ctra. de Castilla km 5.180), 28023 Madrid; tel. (91) 357-08-09; fax (91) 357-29-13; f. 1958; business administration; 80 full-time teachers; 1,200 students; library of 32,000 vols, 370 periodicals; Dean Prof. Dr CARLOS CAVALLÉ.

Instituto Martín Azpilicueta: Biblioteca de Humanidades; Dir EDUARDO MOLANO.

Instituto de Empresa y Humanismo: Dir RAFAEL ALVIRA.

Instituto de Derechos Humanos: Dir JAVIER HERVADA.

Centro de Investigaciones Técnicas de Guipúzcoa: Av. de Tolosa, Ibaeta, 20009 San Sebastián; Dir CARLOS BASTERO.

Escuela Profesional de Medicina Interna: Facultad de Medicina; Dir. JESÚS PRIETO.

Clínica Universitaria: Universidad de Navarra; Dir-Gen. AMADOR SOSA.

Centro de Estudios de Ecología Urbana: Dir MANUEL FERRER.

Centro de Documentación Europea: Dir ENRIQUE BANUS.

Escuela de Práctica Jurídica: Dir FAUSTINO CORDON.

Instituto de Ciencias para la Familia: Dir PEDRO J. VILADRICH.

Centro de Investigaciones Biomédicas: Dir JESUS PRIETO.

Centro de Tecnología Informática: Dir IGNACIO COUPEAU.

Centro de Investigacion en Farmacobiología Aplicada: Dir ANTONIO MONGE.

Escuela Profesional de Dermatología Medico-Quirúrgica y Venereología: Dir EMILIO QUINTANILLA.

Escuela Profesional de Bioquímica Clínica: Dir ESTEBAN SANTIAGO.

Escuela Profesional de Psiquiatría: Dir SALVADOR CERVERA.

Escuela Profesional de Aparato Digestivo: Dir FEDERICO CONCHILLO.

Centro de Investigaciones de Historia Moderna y Contemporánea: Dir VALENTIN VAZQUEZ DE PRADA.

UNIVERSIDAD PÚBLICA DE NAVARRA

Campus de Arrosadía, 31006 Pamplona
Telephone: 948-16-90-01
Fax: 948-16-90-04
E-mail: rector@upna.es

Founded 1987; in process of formation
State control ended September 1993
Language of instruction: Spanish
Academic year: October to June

Rector: Dr ANTONIO PEREZ PRADOS
Vice-Rectors: Dr JORGE NIETO VÁZQUEZ (Academic Affairs), Dr ENRIQUE RUBIO TORRANO (Prospective and Institutional Development), Dr PEDRO APARICIO TEJO (Research), Dr HELIODORO ROBLEDA CABEZAS (University Projection), Dr JOSÉ JAVIER CRESPO GANUZA (Students)
Registrar: Dr JESÚS MA. OSÉS GORRAIZ
Librarian: GUILLERMO SÁNCHEZ MARTÍNEZ

Number of teachers: 670
Number of students: 11,000

DEANS

Faculty of Business and Economics: RAFAEL SANTAMARÍA AQUILUÉ
Faculty of Humanities and Social Sciences: JOSÉ MARIA URIBE OYARBIDE

DIRECTORS OF UNIVERSITY SCHOOLS

Industrial Engineering: PEDRO DIEGUEZ ELIZONDO
Agrarian Engineering: ANTONIO LOPEZ GOMEZ
Health Studies: MILAGROS POLLAN RUFO

HEADS OF DEPARTMENTS

Agrarian Production: ANTONIO GERARDO PISABARRO DE LUCAS
Agrarian Projects and Engineering: JOSÉ LUIS TORRES ESCRIBANO
Applied Chemistry: ANA CASP VANACLOCHA
Automation and Computation: MARÍA VICTORIA MOHEDANO SALILLAS
Business Management: JOSÉ MIGUEL MÚGICA GRIJALBA
Economics: MANUEL RAPÚN GÁRATE
Electrical and Electronic Engineering: MANUEL LÓPEZ-AMO SAINZ
Geography and History: JUAN CARRASCO PÉREZ
Health Sciences: IGNACIO ENCÍO MARTÍNEZ
Mathematics and Informatics: LUIS EZQUERRO MARÍN
Mechanical, Energy and Materials Engineering: JOSE GONZALEZ VIAN
Ecology Sciences: CARMEN LAMSFUS ARRIEN
Philology and Language Teaching: PATRICIO HERNÁNDEZ PÉREZ
Physics: AMAYA EZCURRA GUISASOLA
Private Law: JUAN CARLOS SÁENZ GARCÍA DE ALBIZU
Psychology and Pedagogy: BENJAMÍN ZUFIAURRE GOIKOETXEA
Public Law: JOSÉ ANTONIO CORRIENTE CÓRDOBA
Social Work: CONCEPCIÓN CORERA OROZ
Sociology: IGNACIO SÁNCHEZ DE LA YNCERA
Statistics and Operative Research: ELENA ABASCAL FERNÁNDEZ

UNIVERSIDAD DE OVIEDO

Calle San Francisco 3, 33003 Oviedo
Telephone: 985-510-40-58
Fax: 985-522-71-26

Founded 1608
Language of instruction: Spanish
State control
Academic year: October to June

Rector: JULIO RODRÍGUEZ FERNÁNDEZ
Registrar: LUIS MARTÍNEZ ROLDÁN
Administrative Officer: MA. MERCEDES GARCÍA SAN MILLÁN
Librarian: RAMÓN RODRÍGUEZ ALVAREZ

Library of 650,000 vols
Number of teachers: 1,739
Number of students: 41,070

Publications: *Revista de Ciencias*, *Archivos de la Facultad de Medicina*, *Memorias de Historia Antigua*, *Asturiensía Medievalía*, *Revista de Minas*, *Trabajos de Geología*, *Revista de Biología*, *Brevoria Geológica Astúrica*.

DEANS

Faculty of Law: ANDRÉS CORSINO ALVAREZ CORTINA
Faculty of Education: PALOMA SANTIAGO MARTÍNEZ
Faculty of Chemistry: JULIO BUENO DE LAS HERAS
Faculty of Geology: INMACULADA CORRALES ZARAUZA
Faculty of Philology: JOSÉ RAMÓN FERNÁNDEZ GONZÁLEZ
Faculty of Geography and History: JOSÉ ADOLFO RODRÍGUEZ ASENSIO
Faculty of Medicine: ENRIQUE MARTÍNEZ RODRÍGUEZ
Faculty of Economics and Business Studies: ANA ISABEL FERNÁNDEZ ALVAREZ
Faculty of Biology: MIGUEL A. COMENDADOR GARCÍA
Faculty of Science: SANTOS GONZÁLEZ JIMÉNEZ
Faculty of Psychology: SERAFÍN LEMOS GIRALDEZ
Faculty of Philosophy: ALFONSO GARCÍA SUÁREZ

DIRECTORS OF UNIVERSITY SCHOOLS

Business Studies (Oviedo): MANUEL LAFUENTE ROBLEDO
Business Studies (Gijón): LUIS VALDÉS PELÁEZ
Computer Science (Oviedo): JUAN MANUEL CUEVA LOBELLE
Computer Science (Gijón): JOSÉ MANUEL GONZÁLEZ SARIEGO
Nursing and Physiotherapy: CARMEN FERNÁNDEZ IGLESIAS
Industrial Engineering: ALBERTO SÁNCHEZ RIESGO
Mining Engineering and Topography: ANGEL RAMÓN VIDAL VALDES DE MIRANDA
Teacher Training: FRANCISCO DE ASIS MARTIN DEL BUEY
Industrial Relations: JAIME JOAQUÍN ALBERTI NIETO

DIRECTORS OF HIGHER TECHNICAL SCHOOLS

Industrial and Computer Engineering: JAIME VIÑA OLAY
Mining Engineering: EUGENIO SÁEZ GARCÍA
Civil Marine: ANTONIO MONTESERÍN TORRES

DIRECTOR OF POSTGRADUATE SCHOOL

Stomatology: JUAN SEBASTIÁN LOPEZ ARRANZ

HEADS OF DEPARTMENTS

Energy: JORGE XIBERTA BERNAT
Anglo-Germanic and French Philology: JOSÉ LUIS GONZÁLEZ ESCRIBANO
Electrical, Electronic, Computer and Systems Engineering: JOSÉ GÓMEZ CAMPOMANES
History: PEDRO FLORIANO LLORENTE
Art and Musicology: JULIA MARÍA BARROSO VILLAR
Medicine: JOSÉ M. ARRIBAS CASTRILLO
Business Studies and Accounting: JUAN A. TRESPALACIOS GUTIÉRREZ
Mathematics: BENJAMÍN DUGNOL ALVAREZ
Economics: RAFAEL ANES ALVAREZ
Chemical Engineering: JOSÉ COCA PRADOS
Biology of Organisms and Systems: RICARDO SÁNCHEZ TAMÉS
Spanish Philology: JOSÉ LUIS ROCA MARTÍNEZ
Geology: FRANCISCO JAVIER ALVAREZ PULGAR
Morphology and Cellular Biology: ALFONSO LÓPEZ MUÑIZ
Private and Business Law: JOAQUÍN GARCÍA MURCIA
Construction and Production Engineering: ESTEBAN FERNÁNDEZ RICO
Surgery: JUAN SEBASTIÁN LÓPEZ ARRANZ
Materials Science and Metallurgical Engineering: JOSÉ LUIS IBÁÑEZ LOBO
Philosophy: SANTIAGO GONZÁLEZ ESCUDERO
Psychology: JULIO ANTONIO GONZÁLEZ GARCÍA
Mining: JESÚS JOSÉ MARÍA GARCÍA IGLESIAS
Basic Law: JOSÉ MA. GONZÁLEZ DEL VALLE CIENFUEGOS-JOVELLANOS
Public Law: PAZ ANDRÉS SÁENZ DE SANTA MARIA
Classical and Romance Philology: ANA MARÍA CANO GONZÁLEZ
Physical and Analytical Chemistry: PAULINO TUÑON BLANCO
Biochemistry and Molecular Biology: PAZ SUÁREZ RENDUELES
Geography: ALADINO FERNÁNDEZ GARCÍA
Physics: MARCOS TEJEDOR GANCEDO
Education: JOSÉ VICENTE PEÑA CALVO
Organic and Inorganic Chemistry: VICTOR RIERA GONZÁLEZ
Functional Biology: ANGELES MENÉNDEZ PATTERSON

UNIVERSIDAD PABLO DE OLAVIDE

Carretera de Utrera Km 1, 41013 Seville

UNIVERSIDAD DEL PAÍS VASCO/ EUSKAL HERRIKO UNIBERTSITATEA (University of the Basque Country)

Apdo 1397, 48080 Bilbao
Telephone: 94-464-77-00
Fax: 94-464-74-46

Founded 1968, reorganized 1980
Located on three campuses: Bizkaia Campus, Araba Campus, Gipuzkoa Campus
Basque Regional Government control
Languages of instruction: Spanish, Basque
Academic year: October to June

Rector: PELLO SALABURU
Registrar: MARISOL ESTEBAN
Administrative Director: MOISES GURIDI
Librarian: CARMEN GUERRA

Number of teachers: 3,553
Number of students: 62,159

Publications: *Lección Inaugural*, *Memoria Estadística*, *Catálogo de Biblioteca*, *Recursos Científicos y Lineas de Investigación*, *Nomenclator*, *Memoria de Actividades*, *Cursos Monograficos de Doctorado*, *Resúmenes de Tesis Doctorales*, *Acto de Investidura* (all annually).

DEANS AND DIRECTORS

(The letters A, B, G refer to the three campuses)

Faculty of Chemistry (G): UNAI UGALDE
Faculty of Computer Science (G): IGNACIO MORLAN
Faculty of Economics and Business Administration (B): JOSÉ I. MARTÍNEZ CHURIAQUE
Faculty of Fine Arts (B): ANDER GONZÁLEZ
Faculty of Law (G): ROSA MENTXAKA
Faculty of Social Sciences and Media Studies (B): MANUEL MONTERO
Faculty of Psychology (G): AGUSTÍN ETXEBARRIA

Faculty of Medicine and Dentistry (B): FRANCISCO J. GOIRENA
Faculty of Pharmacy (A): JOSE RUIZ DE LARRAMENDI
Faculty of Philology, Geography and History (A): JOAQUÍN GORROCHATEGUI
Faculty of Philosophy and Education (G): LUIS LIZASOAIN
Faculty of Sciences (B): MANUEL J. TELLO
Higher Technical School of Architecture (G): EDUARDO ARTAMENDI
Higher Technical School of Industrial Engineering and Telecommunications (B): JUAN ANDRÉS LEGARRETA
College of Business Administration (B): PEDRO VELARDE
College of Business Administration (G): VICTORIA ELIZAGARATE
College of Mining Engineering (B): JUAN CLEMENTE RUIZ
College of Nursing (B): LUCÍA CAMPOS
Teacher Training College (A): PATXI SALABERRI
Teacher Training College (B): BINGEN GARAIZAR
Teacher Training College (G): INÉS SANZ
College of Studies in Social Aspects of the Labour Market (B): JUAN HERNÁNDEZ
College of Technical Engineering (A): LUIS M. CAMARERO
College of Technical Engineering (B): JOSÉ SAINZ
College of Technical Engineering (G): RICARDO ECHEPARE

ATTACHED INSTITUTES

Basque Institute of Criminology/Euskal Kriminologi Institutoa: Barrio Ibaeta s/n, 20009 San Sebastián; Dir ANTONIO BERISTAIN.

Institute of Applied Industrial Economics: Campus de Leioa, Edif. Biblioteca Central, 48940 Leioa/Vizcaya; Dir JAVIER FERNANDEZ MACHO.

Institute of Epidemiology and Prevention of Cardiovascular Diseases: Hospital Civil de Bilbao, Gurtubay s/n, 48012 Bilbao; Dir MIGUEL M. IRIARTE.

Institute of Education: Edif. Rectorado, 48940 Leioa/Vizcaya; Dir LONTXO OIHARTZABAL.

Institute of Applied Business Economics: Facultad de Ciencias Económicas y Empresariales, Avda del Ejército 87, 48015 Bilbao; Dir EMILIO SOLDEVILLA.

Institute of Research and Development of Processes: Facultad de Ciencias, 48940 Leioa/Vizcaya; Dir MANUEL DE LA SEN.

Institute of Synthesis and Material Studies: Facultad de Ciencias, 48940 Leioa/Vizcaya; Dir MANUEL J. TELLO.

Institute of Financial and Actuarial Studies: Avda Lehendakari Aguirre 83, 48015 Bilbao; Dir AMANCIO BETZUEN.

Medical Institute in Basurto: Facultad de Medicina y Odontología, 48940 Leioa/Vizcaya.

UNIVERSITAT DE LES ILLES BALEARS

Campus Universitari, Cra. de Valldemossa km 7.5, 07071 Palma de Mallorca
Telephone: 971-17-30-00
Fax: 971-17-28-52
Founded 1978
State control
Languages of instruction: Catalan, Spanish, English
Academic year: October to September
Rector: LLORENÇ HUGUET ROTGER
Vice-Rectors: EDUARD CESARI ALIBERCH (Research), SANTIAGO CAVANILLAS MÚGICA (Academic Affairs), JAUME SUREDA NEGRE (Institutional Relations), MERCÈ GAMBÚS (Extra-mural Activities), JOSEP SERVERA BAÑO (Academic Staff), CARLES MANERA ERBINA (Economic and Administrative Planning), JOANA M. PETRUS BEY (Students and Campus), EUGENI GARCÍA (External Co-operation)
Chief Administrative Officer: SEBASTIÀ ALEMANY FONT
Secretary-General: APOLLÒNIA MARTÍNEZ NADAL
Librarian: ANDREU RIBAS MAURA

Number of teachers: 721
Number of students: 16,328

Publications: *Grama i Cal*, *Educació i Cultura*, *Mayurqa*, *Taula*, *Treballs de Geografia*, *Psicología del Deporte*.

DEANS AND DIRECTORS

Faculty of Arts: PERFECTO CUADRADO FERNÁNDEZ
Faculty of Business Studies: EUGENI AGUILÓ PÉREZ
Faculty of Computer Science: RAMON PUIGJANER TREPAT
Faculty of Law: ISABEL TAPIA FERNÁNDEZ
Faculty of Science: PERE M. DEYÀ SERRA
Faculty of Education: ANTONI COLOM CAÑELLAS
College of Business Studies: JOSEP AGUILÓ FUSTER
Polytechnic College: GABRIEL FIOL ROIG
College of Nursing: JORDI PERICÀS BELTRAN
Official School of Tourism: FRANCESC SASTRE ALBERTÍ

HEADS OF DEPARTMENTS

Environmental Biology: ISABEL MORENO CASTILLO
Fundamental Biology and Health Sciences: ANDREU PALOU OLIVER
Education: JORDI VALLESPIR SOLER
Earth Sciences: ANTONIO RODRÍGUEZ PEREA
History and Theory of the Arts: MIQUEL DURÁN PASTOR
Mathematics and Computer Science: LLORENÇ VALVERDE GARCIA
Private Law: JOSÉ Á. TORRES LANA
Public Law: ROSARIO HUESA VINAIXA
Economics and Business Studies: CATALINA JUANEDA SAMPOL
Catalan Philology and General Linguistics: JOAN MIRALLES MONSERRAT
Spanish, Modern and Latin Philology: M. CARME BOSCH JUAN
Philosophy: FRANCESC TORRES MARÍ
Physics: MONSERRAT CASAS AMETLLER
Psychology: JAVIER PÉREZ PAREJA
Chemistry: ANTONI ROIG MUNTANER

ATTACHED INSTITUTES

Research Institute: Edifici Mateu Orfila i Rotger, Cra. Valldemossa km. 7.5, 07071 Palma; Dir ENRIC TORTOSA.

Institute of Education (Support and extracurricular courses): Rafael Rodríguez Méndez 4, 07010 Palma; Dir GABRIEL JANER MANILA.

UNIVERSITAT POMPEU FABRA

Plaça de la Mercè 10–12, 08002 Barcelona
Telephone: 93-542-20-00
Fax: 93-542-20-02
E-mail: webmaster@upf.es
Founded 1990
Regional govt control
Languages of instruction: Catalan, Spanish
Academic year: September to June
Rector: Dr ENRIC ARGULLOL
Vice-Rectors: Dra TERESA CASTIÑEIRA (Academic Affairs and Teaching Staff), Dr ORIOL AMAT (Economic Affairs and Services), Dr JORDI PERICOT (University Community), Dr ALBERT CARRERAS (Teaching, Programming and Evaluation), Dr JAUME GARCÍA VILLAR (Science Policy and PhD Programmes), Dr JAUME TORRAS (attached to the Rector)
Manager: ALFONSO DE ALFONSO
Librarian: MERCÈ CABO

Library of 220,000 vols
Number of teachers: 781
Number of students: 6,560

DEANS

Faculty of Economics and Business: Dr TERESA GARCIA-MILÀ
Faculty of Law: Dr JOAN EGEA
Faculty of Humanities: Dra DOLORS FOLCH
Faculty of Journalism: Dr JOSEP M. CASASÚS
Faculty of Translation and Interpreting: Dr M. PAZ BATTANER
Faculty of Audiovisual Communication: Dr JOSEP GIFREU
Faculty of Political Sciences and Public Administration: Dr JACINT JORDANA
University School of Business Studies: Dr CARLES MURILLO
University School of Labour Relations: Dra JULIA LÓPEZ

ATTACHED INSTITUTES

Institut Universitari d'Història Jaume Vicens i Vives: Dir Dr JOSEP FONTANA.

Institut Universitari de Lingüística Aplicada: Dir Dra TERESA CABRÉ.

Centre d'Economia Internacional: Dir Dr ANDREU MAS COLELL.

Institut Universitari de l'Audiovisual: Dir XAVIER BERENGUER.

Institut d'Estudis Territorials: Dir Dr DANIEL SERRA.

Institut Universitari de Cultura: Dir Dr FRANCISCO FERNÁNDEZ BUEY.

UNIVERSITAT RAMÓN LLULL

Sant Joan de la Salle 8, 08022 Barcelona
Telephone: 93-253-04-50
Fax: 93-418-80-65
E-mail: urlsc@sec.url.es
Founded 1990
Rector: Dr MIQUEL GASSIOT I MATAS
Vice-Rector for Academic Affairs: Dr JOSEP GALLIFFA I ROCA
Vice-Rector for Research and Technology: Dr JOSEP MARTI I ROCA
Director-General: ANDREU MORILLAS

Library of 247,800 vols, 7,407 periodicals
Publications: *La URL Informa*, *Signes*.

DEANS

Sarrià Chemical Institute: Dr LLUÍS COMELLAS I RIERA
Faculty of Economics: Dr JESÚS TRICÀS PRECKLER
Blanquerna Faculty of Psychology and Educational Sciences: Dr JORDI RIERA I ROMANI
Blanquerna Faculty of Communication Sciences: Dr MIQUEL TRESSARRAS I MAJÓ
Blanquerna University School of Nursing and Physiotherapy: MÀRIUS DURAN I HORTOLÀ
Blanquerna Faculty of Political Sciences and Sociology: MARCEL GABARRÓ (Dir)
La Salle University School of Telecommunications Engineering Technology: Dr DANIEL CABEDO I PUY (Dir)
La Salle Higher Technical School of Electronic Engineering and Computing: Dr DANIEL CABEDO I PUY (Dir)
La Salle Higher Technical School of Architecture: ROBERT TERRADAS MUNTAÑOLA (Dir)

Faculty of Philosophy of Catalonia: Dr JOSEP M. COLL I D'ALEMANY
Faculty of Business at the Higher School of Business Administration and Management (ESADE): Dr ROBERT TORNABELL I CARRIÓ
Faculty of Law at the Higher School of Business Administration and Management (ESADE): Dr MIGUEL TRÍAS SAGNIER
Sant Ignasi School of Tourism at the Higher School of Business Administration and Management (ESADE): ENRIC LÓPEZ VIGURIA (Dir)
University School of Social Work (ICESB): CARLES ARMENGOL I SISCARES (Dir)
Pere Tarres University School of Social Education: CARLES ARMENGOL I SISCARES (Dir)
University Observatory Institute: Dr LUIS FELIPE ALBERCA SILVA (Dir)
Higher School of Design (ESDI): ENRIC TARRIDA I CRUZ (Dir)

UNIVERSIDAD REY JUAN CARLOS I

C/ Independencia 12, 28931 Madrid
Telephone: 916-47-61-93

UNIVERSITAT ROVIRA I VIRGILI

Calle de l'Escorxador s/n, 43003 Tarragona
Telephone: 977-55-80-00
Fax: 977-55-80-22
Founded 1991
State control
Rector: JOAN MARTÍ CASTELL
Registrar: MIQUEL CAMINAL BADIA
Secretary-General: ESTANISLAO PASTOR I MALLOL
Librarian: ESPERANZA MANERA I ROCA
Library of 93,700 vols
Number of teachers: 743
Number of students: 10,309

DEANS

Faculty of Arts: Dr JOAN JOSEP PUJADES
Faculty of Chemistry: Dra ROSA CABALLOL
Faculty of Medicine and Health Sciences: Dr LLUÍS MASANA
Faculty of Law: Dr JAUME VERNET
Faculty of Economics and Business Studies: Dr ANTONI TERCEÑO
Faculty of Education and Psychology: Dr ANGEL-PÍO GONZÁLEZ
School of Engineering: J. A. FERRÉ
School of Nursing: CARME VIVES
School of Oenology: Dr ALBERT MAS

HEADS OF DEPARTMENTS

Faculty of Chemistry:

Department of Chemistry: Dr SERGIO CASTILLÓN
Department of Biochemistry and Biotechnology: Dr ALBERT BORDONS

Faculty of Law:

Department of Law: Dr ÀNGEL DE SOLÀ

Faculty of Arts:

Department of Anthropology: Dra DOLORS COMAS D'ARGEMIR
Department of History and Geography: Dr FRANCISCO-JAVIER FACI
Department of Catalan Studies: Dra MARGARIDA ARITZETA
Department of English and Germanic Studies: Dr JORDI LAMARCA
Department of Hispanic Studies: Dra ESTHER FORGAS

School of Engineering:

Department of Chemical Engineering: Dr XAVIER FARRIOL
Department of Electronic Engineering: Dr XAVIER CORREIG BLANCHAR
Department of Electrical and Mechanical Engineering: Dr FRANCESC-XAVIER GRAU
Department of Computer Engineering: Dr EDUARD MONTSENY

School of Nursing:

Department of Nursing: VIRTUDES RODERO

School of Business Administration and Economics:

Department of Business Administration and Economics: Dr AGUSTÍ SEGARRA

Faculty of Education and Psychology:

Department of Education: Dr VINCENÇ FERRERES
Department of Psychology: Dr JOSÉ-EUGENIO GARCÍA-ALBEA

Faculty of Medicine and Health Sciences:

Department of Basic Medicine: Dr JOAN M. LLOBET
Department of Medicine and Surgery: Dr ALBERTO MARTÍNEZ

UNIVERSIDAD PONTIFICIA DE SALAMANCA

Calle Compañía 1, Apdo 541, 37002 Salamanca
Telephone: 923-21-22-60
Fax: 923-26-24-56
Founded 1134 as the Ecclesiastical School of Salamanca Cathedral; named a University by Alfonso IX of León in 1219. The University had ceased to function by the end of the 18th century, but was restored in 1940 by Pope Pius XII
Private control
Language of instruction: Spanish
Academic year: October to June
Grand Chancellor: FERNANDO SEBASTIÁN AGUILAR (Bishop of Pamplona)
Rector: Excmo. Dr JOSÉ MANUEL SÁNCHEZ CARO
Vice-Rectors: Dr ANTONIO GARCÍA MADRID, Dra MA FRANCISCA MARTÍN TABERNERO
Administrative Officer: P. LUIS RODRÍGUEZ MARTÍNEZ
General-Secretary: Dr MARCELIANO ARRANZ RODRIGO
Director of Library: Dr ENRIQUE LLAMAS MARTÍNEZ
Library of 185,000 vols and numerous MSS
Number of teachers: 351
Number of students: 8,500
Publications: *Salmanticensis*, *Helmántica*, *Boletín de Información*, *Cuadernos Salmantinos de Filosofía*, *Diálogo Ecuménico*, *Colectanea de Jurisprudencia Canónica*, etc.

DEANS

Faculty of Theology: Dr ANGEL GALINDO GARCÍA
Faculty of Canon Law: Dr JULIO MANZANARES MARIJUAN
Faculty of Philosophy: Dr DIONISIO CASTILLO CABALLERO
Faculty of Trilingual Biblical Philology: Dr ALFONSO ORTEGA CARMONA
Faculty of Education: Dra MARÍA JESÚS GARCÍA ARROYO
Faculty of Psychology: Dr LUIS JIMÉNEZ DÍAZ
Faculty of Political and Social Sciences: Dr JUAN GONZÁLEZ-ANLEO
Faculty of Information Sciences: Dr GERARDO PASTOR RAMOS
Faculty of Computer Sciences: Dr MANUEL CAPELO MARTÍNEZ

PROFESSORS

Faculty of Theology:

BOROBIO GARCÍA, D., Liturgy and Sacraments
FERNÁNDEZ RAMOS, F., Scripture
FLECHA ANDRÉS, J., Fundamental Moral Theology
GARCÍA LOPEZ, F., Old Testament Exegesis
GONZÁLEZ HERNÁNDEZ, O., Christology
GONZÁLEZ MONTES, A., Fundamental Theology
PIKAZA IBARRONDO, J., Phenomenology of Religion
SANCHEZ CARO, J. M., Introduction to the Scriptures
TELLECHEA IDÍGORAS, J. I., Church History
TREVIJANO ECHEVERRIA, R., Patrology

Faculty of Canon Law:

ACEBAL LUJÁN, J. L., Procedural Law
AZNAR GIL, F., Matrimonial, Hereditary and Penal Law
GARCÍA Y GARCÍA, A., Canon Law
MANZANARES MARIJUÁN, J., Constitutional Law

Faculty of Philosophy:

ARRANZ RODRIGO, M., Natural Philosophy
CASTILLO CABELLERO, D., Theodicy
PINTOR RAMOS, A., History of Modern Philosophy

Faculty of Trilingual Biblical Philology:

ORTEGA CARMONA, A., Greek Language and Literature

Faculty of Education:

CASTRO POSADA, J. A., Child Psychology
FAUBELL ZAPATA, V., History of Education
FERNÁNDEZ PELLITERO, M., Biological Sciences
HOLGADO SÁNCHEZ, A., General Didactics
SANS VILA, J., Theology of Education

Faculty of Psychology:

FERNÁNDEZ VILLAMARZO, P., Psychology
GONZÁLEZ GONZÁLEZ, J. A., Psychophysiology
JIMENEZ DIAZ, L., Clinical Child Psychology
MÁLAGA GUERRERO, J., Psychopathology of Human Communications
MARTÍN TABERNERO, M. F., Statistics Applied to Human Sciences
PASTOR RAMOS, G., Social Psychology
VÁZQUEZ FERNÁNDEZ, A., General Psychology

Faculty of Political and Social Sciences:

ALVAREZ RICO, M.
BUCETA FACORRO, L., Social Psychology
CAPELO MARTÍNEZ, M., Economic Policy
VALVERDE MUCIENTES, C., Theology of Social Reality

AFFILIATED INSTITUTES AND CENTRES

Higher Institute of Pastoral Studies: Paseo Juan XXIII 3, 28003 Madrid; Dir Dr JUAN MARTIN VELASCO.

Institute of Education Science: Dir Dr MANUEL FERNANDEZ PELLITERO.

Institute of European Studies and Human Rights: Dir Dr ALFONSO ORTEGA CARMONA.

Institute of Clinical Child Psychology: Dir Dr LUIS JIMENEZ DIAZ.

Institute of Iberoamerican Thought: Dir Dr FRANCISCO RODRIGUEZ PASCUAL.

E.S.E.F.A.: Dir Dra MARÍA JESÚS GARCÍA ARROYO.

Logopedia: Dir Dr JESUS MALAGA GUERRERO.

Psychology of Language: Dir Dr JESUS MALAGA GUERRERO.

Family Studies: Dir Dr DIONISIO BOROBIO GARCIA.

Spanish Language and Culture: Dir Dra MARÍA MERCEDES SANDE BUSTAMANTE.

Oriental and Ecumenical Studies: Dir Dr ADOLFO GONZALEZ MONTES.

Institute of History of Theology: Dir Dr ANTONIO GARCIA Y GARCIA.

Higher Institute of Philosophy (Valladolid): Dir Dr FERNANDO VELA LÓPEZ.

'Pius X' Institute of Catechetical Studies (Madrid): Dir Dr LLUIS DIUMENGE I. PUJOL.

Theological Institute of the Religious Life: Dir Dr JOSE CRISTO REY GARCÍA PARADES.

'San Damaso' Higher Institute of Theology (Madrid): Dir (vacant).

'Luis Vives' University Teacher Training College: Dir Dr EMILIO GUTIERREZ TORDABLE.

University School of Nursing (Salamanca): Dir Dr JULIAN BENAVENTE HERRERO.

University School of Nursing 1 (Madrid): Dir Dr LORENZO RUBIO MORALES.

University School of Physiotheraphy (Majadahonda): Dir Dr FRANCISCO GALA SANCHEZ.

Theological Institute of Santiago de Compostela: Dir Dr LUIS QUINTEIRO FIUZA.

Theological Institute of Murcia: Dir Dr JOSE LUIS PARADA NAVAS.

Theological Institute of Oviedo: Dir Dr JORGE JUAN FERNÁNDEZ SANGRADOR.

Theological Institute of Leon: Dir Lic. ANTONIO TROBAJO DIAZ.

Theological Institute of Aragon: Dir Dr CARLOS TARTAJ SÁNCHEZ.

Theological Institute of El Escorial: Dir Dr FERMIN FERNANDEZ BIENZOBAS.

Theological Institute of Pamplona: Dir Dr JULIO GORRICHO MORENO.

Theological Institute of Badajoz: Dir Lic. JUAN GARCIA FRANGANILLO.

Theological Institute of San Fulgencio (Murcia): Dir Dr FERNANDO EGEA ALBADALEJO.

University School of Family Science (Valladolid): Dir Dr JESUS MA. GALDEANO ARAMENDIA.

University School of Family Science (Murcia): Dir Dr PEDRO RIQUELME OLIVA.

University School of Family Science (Sevilla): Dir Dr MANUEL DE BURGOS NUÑEZ.

Spanish Biblico-Archaeological Institute: Dir Lic. ANTONIO MARÍN.

UNIVERSIDAD DE SALAMANCA

Patio de Escuelas 1, Apdo 20, 37008 Salamanca

Telephone: 923-29-44-00
Fax: 923-29-45-02

Founded 1218 by Alfonso IX of León and reorganized 1254 by Alfonso X of Castile
State control
Language of instruction: Spanish
Academic year: October to July

Rector: IGNACIO BERDUGO GÓMEZ DE LA TORRE
Vice-Rectors: JOSÉ ANTONIO FERNÁNDEZ DELGADO (Institutional Relations), MIGUEL ANGEL VERDUGO ALONSO (Postgraduate Studies and Degrees Specific to the University), ANTONIO CARRERAS PANCHÓN (Teaching and Teaching Staff), JESÚS HERNÁNDEZ MÉNDEZ (Research), ENRIQUE CABERO MORÁN (Student Assistance), CARMEN POL MÉNDEZ (Finance)
Administrator: ANTONIO ALONSO SÁNCHEZ

Library of *c.* 140,300 vols and MSS; the Faculty libraries have an additional 365,269 vols
Number of teachers: 2,171
Number of students: 32,338

Publications: *Hojas Universitarias*, and various faculty publs.

DEANS

Faculty of Philology: EMILIANO FERNÁNDEZ VALLINA
Faculty of Geography and History: ANGEL RODRÍGUEZ SÁNCHEZ
Faculty of Philosophy: PABLO GARCÍA CASTILLO
Faculty of Psychology: RAMÓN FERNÁNDEZ PULIDO
Faculty of Chemistry: PEDRO RAMOS CASTELLANOS
Faculty of Biology: FRANCISCO AMICH GARCÍA
Faculty of Law: MARÍA JOSÉ HERRERO GARCÍA
Faculty of Medicine: AGUSTÍN BULLÓN SOPELANA
Faculty of Pharmacy: JUAN MANUEL CACHAZA SILVERIO
Faculty of Fine Arts: ELVIRA DÍAZ MORENO
Faculty of Sciences: FRANCISCO NAVARRO VILÁ
Faculty of Economics and Business: JOSÉ MANUEL PRADO LORENZO
Faculty of Social Sciences: PABLO DEL RIO PEREDA
Faculty of Education: JOSÉ MARÍA HERNANDEZ DÍAZ
Faculty of Translation and Documentation: CARLOS GARCÍA DE FIGUEROLA PANIAGUA

DIRECTORS

Teacher Training College at Zamora: LUIS MELERO MARCOS
College of Education at Avila: ISABEL VALDUNQUILLO CARLÓN
School of Nursing: JOSÉ IGNACIO CALVO ARENILLAS
School of Industrial Engineering at Bejar: FÉLIX REDONDO QUINTELA
Polytechnical College of Zamora: MANUEL DOMÍNGUEZ VALVERDE
Institute of Educational Sciences: MIGUEL ANGEL BAÑARES MUÑOZ
School of Agricultural Engineering: FERNANDO SANTOS FRANCÉS
School of Nursing: MARÍA SOLEDAD SÁNCHEZ ÁRNOSE
School of T.E. in Topography at Avila: CELESTINO LERALTA DE MATÍAS

UNIVERSIDAD SAN PABLO-C.E.U.

Issac Peral 58, 28040 Madrid

Telephone: 91-456-63-00
Fax: 91-553-92-65

Founded 1993
Private control

Rector: Prof. Dr JOSÉ T. RAGA
Vice-Rectors: Prof. Dr JOSÉ LUIS PEREZ DE AYALA (Academic Affairs, Staff Affairs and Research), Prof. Dr JUAN IGLESIAS (Students)
Secretary-General: Prof. Dr JUAN VIVANCOS
Librarian: JOSÉ MORILLO-VELARDE

Library of 42,000 vols
Number of teachers: 636
Number of students: 8,100

DEANS

Faculty of Law and Administration: Prof. Dr JOSÉ LUIS PIÑAR
Faculty of Business and Economics: Prof. Dr JOSÉ MA. GARCÍA
Faculty of Humanities: Prof. Dr LUIS ESCOBAR
Faculty of Science and Technology: Prof. Dr EMILIO HERRERA

UNIVERSIDADE DE SANTIAGO DE COMPOSTELA

Praza do Obradoiro s/n, 15705 Santiago de Compostela

Telephone: 981-56-31-00
Fax: 981-58-85-22

Founded 1495
State control
Languages of instruction: Spanish, Galician

Rector: DARÍO VILLANUEVA PRIETO
Vice-Rectors: JOSÉ RAMÓN LEIS FIDALGO, CELSO RODRÍGUEZ FERNÁNDEZ, CASTOR MÉNDEZ PAZ, FERNANDO DOMÍNGUEZ PUENTE, FRANCISCO MASEDA EIMIL, ANTONIO LÓPEZ DÍAZ, MANUEL CASTRO COTÓN, BLANCA-ANA ROIG RECHOU, JOSÉ M. RIVERA OTERO
Secretary-General: GUMERSINDO GUINARTE CABADA
Administrator: ANA FERNÁNDEZ PULPEIRO
Librarian: CONCEPCIÓN VARELA OROL

General Library of 1,500,000 volumes, over 140 incunabula, prayer book of Fernando I of Castile (11th century); other special libraries in the faculties
Number of teachers: 1,536
Number of students: 35,000

Publications: *Trabajos Compostelanos de Biología*, *Memoria*, *Verba*, *Anuario Gallego de Filología*, *Anejos de la revista Verba*, *Cursos y Congresos de la Universidad de Santiago de Compostela*, *Monografías*, *Acta Científica Compostelana*.

DEANS

Faculty of Philosophy and Education: JUAN VÁZQUEZ SÁNCHEZ
Faculty of Law: JAVIER GÁRATE CASTRO
Faculty of Medicine and Dentistry: ANDRÉS BEIRAS IGLESIAS
Faculty of Pharmacy: ISABEL SUÁREZ GIMENO
Faculty of Economic and Business Science: XAVIER ROJO SÁNCHEZ
Faculty of Philology: EMILIO MONTERO CARTELLE
Faculty of Geography and History: JOSÉ CARLOS BERMEJO BARRERA
Faculty of Sciences (in Lugo): EUGENIO RODRÍGUEZ NÚÑEZ
Faculty of Political and Social Sciences: JOSÉ VILAS NOGUEIRA
Faculty of Information Science: MARGARITA LEDO ANDIÓN
Faculty of Psychology: JOSÉ M. SABUCEDO CAMESELLE
Faculty of Humanities: CONCEPCIÓN DEL BURGO LÓPEZ
Faculty of Chemistry: JUAN M. NAVAZA DAFONTE
Faculty of Physics: JOSÉ M. FDEZ. DE LABASTIDA Y DEL OLMO
Faculty of Mathematics: ENRIQUE MACÍAS VIRGÓS
Faculty of Veterinary Science: ENRIQUE ANTONIO GONZÁLEZ GARCÍA
Faculty of Biology: JOSÉ C. OTERO GONZÁLEZ

DIRECTORS

Higher Polytechnic School: EDUARDO ZURITA DE LA VEGA
University School of Nursing: PILAR SÁNCHEZ SEBIO
University School of Business Studies: MA. ROSA VARELA PUGA
University School of Optics: VICENTE MORENO DE LAS CUEVAS

UNIVERSIDAD S.E.K. DE SEGOVIA

C/ Cardenal Zúñiga s/n, 40003 Segovia

Telephone: 921-44-47-16
Fax: 921-44-55-93
E-mail: sek@sek.edu

Founded 1992
Private control

Faculties of Biological Sciences, Cultural Heritage Studies, Information Science and Psychology; Centre of Integrated Architectural Studies.

UNIVERSIDAD DE SEVILLA

Calle de San Fernando 4, Seville
Telephone: 95-455-11-36
Fax: 95-421-28-03

Founded 1502
State control
Language of instruction: Spanish
Academic year: October to July

Rector: MIGUEL FLORENCIO LORA
Vice-Rectors: JOSÉ MARÍA VEGA PIQUERES (Research), JAVIER HERRERA GOVANTES (Teaching Staff), ADOLFO L. GONZÁLEZ (Extension), ANTONIO QUIJADA JIMENO (Infrastructure), IGNACIO UGALDE (Students and Educational Standards), EMILIO DÍEZ DE CASTRO (Quality), JUAN JOSÉ IGLESIAS (Planning Studies)
Administrator: MANUEL MARTÍNEZ GARCÍA
General Secretary: JUAN IGNACIO FERRARO GARCÍA
Librarian: Lcda SONSOLES CELESTINO

Number of teachers: 3,500
Number of students: 75,000

Publication: *Anales de la Universidad Hispalense* (annually).

DEANS AND DIRECTORS

Faculty of Geography and History: Dr GABRIEL CANO GARCÍA
Faculty of Philology: JESÚS DÍAZ
Faculty of Philosophy: Dr JOSÉ LUIS LÓPEZ LÓPEZ
Faculty of Law: Dr MANUEL RAMÓN ALARCÓN
Faculty of Medicine: Dr PEDRO MANUEL BLASCO HUELVA
Faculty of Biology: Dr FRANCISCO GIL MARTÍNEZ
Faculty of Physics: Dr SATURIO RAMOS VICENTE
Faculty of Mathematics: Dra ROSA ECHEVARRÍA LÍBANO
Faculty of Chemistry: Dr MIGUEL TERNERO
Faculty of Pharmacy: Dr ANTONIO VENTOSA UCERO
Faculty of Economics (Business Studies): FRANCISCO JAVIER LANDA BERCEBAL
Faculty of Fine Arts: Dr FRANCISCO CORTÉS SOMÉ
Faculty of Information Science: Dr CARLOS COLÓN PERALES
Faculty of Psychology: Dra MA. DEL CARMEN MORENO RODRÍGUEZ
Faculty of Education: Dr SANTIAGO ROMERO
Faculty of Odontology: Dr PEDRO BULLÓN FERNÁNDEZ
Faculty of Informatics and Statistics: Dr FRANCISCO PÉREZ GARCÍA

DIRECTORS

University School of Architecture: Dr ANTONIO RAMÍREZ DE ARELLANO
University School of Business Studies: JOSÉ MORENO ROJAS
University School of Health Sciences: JESÚS REBOLLO
University School of Social Science Graduates: CARLOS ARENAS POSADAS
University School of Technical Agricultural Engineering: MANUEL BAENA FERNÁNDEZ
University School of Social Sciences (Seville): JOSÉ LUIS MALAGÓN BERNAL
Polytechnic School (Seville): FRANCISCO AYUSO SACRISTÁN
Higher Technical School of Architecture: Dr FÉLIX ESCRIG PALLARES
Higher Technical School of Industrial Engineering: JOSÉ VALE PARAPAR

UNIVERSITAT DE VALÈNCIA

C/ Antiga Senda de Senent 11, Edificio Alameda, 46023 Valencia
Telephone: 96-386-41-00
Fax: 96-386-42-24

Founded 1502
State control

Rector: Prof. PEDRO RUIZ TORRES
Vice-Rectors: JULI PERETÓ MAGRANER (Research), FRANCISCO MONTES SUAY (Academic), FRANCISCO MORALES OLIVAS (Studies), LLUIS GUIA MARIN (Administration), FRANCISCO POMER MURGUI (External Relations), RICARD MARTÍNEZ MARTÍNEZ (Students), ANTONI TORDERA SAEZ (Culture), JAIME SANMARTÍN ARCE (Planning), JOAQUÍN AZAGRA (Economic Infrastructure)
Secretary-General: ROSA MOLINER
Librarian: MARIA CRUZ CABEZA SÁNCHEZ-ALBORNOZ

Library of 227,453 vols and 2,720 MSS; libraries are also attached to each faculty
Number of teachers: 3,010
Number of students: 63,293

Publication: *Memoria Anual*.

DEANS

Faculty of Geography and History: RAFAEL GIL SALINAS
Faculty of Philosophy and Education: LUIS MIGUEL LÁZARO LORENTE
Faculty of Law: CARMELO LOZANO SERRANO
Faculty of Mathematics: ISABEL SEGURA GARCÍA
Faculty of Medicine and Odontology: JOSÉ MANUEL RODRIGO GÓMEZ
Faculty of Economics and Business: VICENTE LLOMBART ROSA
Faculty of Pharmacy: JORGE MÁÑEZ VINUESA
Faculty of Philology: CARMEN MORENILLA TALENS
Faculty of Physics: JOSÉ ANTONIO MARTÍNEZ LOZANO
Faculty of Biology: VICENTE TORDERA DONDERIS
Faculty of Chemistry: VICENTE SANZ PERSIVA
Faculty of Psychology: JOSÉ MARÍA PEIRÓ SILLA

DIRECTORS

Teacher Training College 'Ausias March': MARÍA LUISA CONTRI SEMPERE
School of Business Studies: VICENTE RAMÓN TORCAL TOMÁS
School of Nursing: AMPARO BENAVENT GARCÉS
School of Physiotherapy: CRISTINA ARAMBURU DE VEGA
School of Social Work: MAGDALENA LÓPEZ PRECIOSO
School of Social Graduates: IGNACIO LERMA MONTERO

UNIVERSIDAD DE VALLADOLID

Plaza de Santa Cruz 8, 47002 Valladolid
Telephone: 983-29-14-67
Fax: 983-42-32-34

Founded 13th century

Rector: Dr FRANCISCO JAVIER ALVAREZ GUISASOLA
Vice-Rectors: ANGEL DE LOS RIOS RODINO (Academic), RAFAEL PEDROSA SAEZ (Research), OLGA OGANDO CANABAL (Finance), FRANCISCO JAVIER SÁNCHEZ TABERNERO (Students), JUAN REPRESA DE LA GUERRA (University Extension), MA JOSÉ CRESPO ALLUE (International Relations), MANUEL BETEGÓN BAEZA (University Campus at Palencia), JOSÉ ANTONIO TEJERO HERNÁNDEZ (University Campus at Soria)
Secretary-General: ELIAS GONZÁLEZ-POSADA MARTINEZ

Library of 300,000 vols
Number of students: 47,000

DEANS

Faculty of Law: Dr ALEJANDRO MENÉNDEZ FERNÁNDEZ
Faculty of Science: CARLOS BALBÁS RUESGAS
Faculty of Philosophy and Letters: Dr BASILIO CALDERON CALDERON
Faculty of Medicine: Dr JUAN JOSÉ MATEOS OTERO
Faculty of Economic and Commercial Sciences: Dr JOSÉ MIGUEL RODRIGUEZ FERNANDEZ
School of Industrial Engineering: Dr FRANCISCO TINAUT FLUIXÁ
School of Telecommunications Engineering: MIGUEL LÓPEZ CORONADO

UNIVERSIDAD VIC

C/ Miramarges 4, 08500 Barcelona

UNIVERSIDAD DE VIGO

C/ Oporto 1, 36201 Vigo
Telephone: 986-81-36-36
Fax: 986-81-35-54

Founded 1990
State control

Rector: Prof. Dr JOSÉ ANTONIO RODRÍGUEZ VÁZQUEZ
Vice-Rectors: Prof. Dr JOSÉ BARREIRO SOMOZA (Planning), Prof. Dr JOSÉ POSE BLANCO (Finance), Prof. JOSÉ ANGEL VÁZQUEZ BARQUERO (Students, and Innovation in Teaching), Prof. Dr CARLOS MARTÍNEZ-PEÑALVER FREIRE (University Administration), Prof. Dr EUSEBIO CORBACHO ROSAS (Staff Affairs), Prof. Dr XULIO PARDELLAS DE BLAS (External Relations), Prof. Dr JOSÉ TOJO SUÁREZ (Research)
Secretary-General: Prof. Dr JOSÉ LEGIDO SOTO
Librarian: MA. DEL CARMEN PÉREZ PAIS

Library of 170,000 vols
Number of teachers: 1,200
Number of students: 30,000

DEANS

Vigo Campus:

Faculty of Humanities: Prof. Dr CELSO RODRÍGUEZ FERNÁNDEZ
Faculty of Science: Prof. Dr MANUEL JOAQUÍN REIGOSA ROGER
Higher Technical School of Industrial Engineering: Prof. Dr MANUEL PÉREZ DONSIÓN
Higher Technical School of Telecommunications Engineering: Prof. Dr JOSÉ MANUEL SANTOS SUÁREZ
University Business School: Prof. Dra MA. PILAR LÓPEZ VIDAL
University School of Industrial Technological Engineering: Prof. JOSÉ ANTONIO GÓMEZ BARBEITO

Orense Campus:

Faculty of Humanities: Prof. Dr XOSÉ MANUEL CID FERNÁNDEZ
Faculty of Science: Prof. Dr FRANCISCO TUGORES MARTORELL
Faculty of Law: Prof. Dr LUIS RODRÍGUEZ ENNES
University Business School: Prof. Dr LUIS GARCÍA LLORÉNS
University School of Engineering Management: Prof. ENRIQUE BARREIRO ALONSO

Pontevedra Campus:

Faculty of Fine Arts: Prof. Dr XOSÉ CHAVETE RODRÍGUEZ
Faculty of Social Sciences: Prof. Dr MANUEL FERNÁNDEZ AREAL
University School of Forestry Engineering: Prof. Dr EDUARDO RUBIALES CAMINO
University School of Physiotherapy: Prof. Dr JUAN SUÁREZ QUINTANILLA

UNIVERSIDAD DE ZARAGOZA

C/ Pedro Cerbuna 12, 50009 Zaragoza
Telephone: 976-76-10-00
Fax: 976-76-10-09

Founded in 1583 by the Emperor Carlos V
State control
Language of instruction: Spanish
Academic year: October to June

Rector: JUAN JOSÉ BADIOLA DÍEZ
Vice-Rectors: FELIPE PÉTRIZ CALVO (Staff), MANUEL JOSÉ LÓPEZ PÉREZ (Academic Affairs), JOSÉ VICENTE GARCÍA ESTEVE (Research), TOMÁS ESCUDERO ESCORZA (Reform and Extension of Studies), MANUEL GARCÍA GUATAS (External Relations), JOSE ANTONIO BIESCAS FERRER (Finance), FIDEL CORCUERA MANSO (International Relations), ANO CASTELLÓ PUIG (Huesca Campus), MONTSERRAT MARTÍNEZ GONZÁLEZ (Teruel Campus)
Registrar: ANTONIO MARTÍNEZ BALLARIN
Librarian: REMEDIOS MORALEJO

Library of 562,000 vols
Number of teachers: 2,424
Number of students: 45,197

Publications: *Temas*, *Archivos de la Facultad de Medicina*, *Anales de la Facultad de Veterinaria*, *Guía*, *Boletín Informativo*, *Revista Universidad*, *Resúmenes de Tesis Doctorales*.

DEANS

Faculty of Arts: LUISA MA. FRUTOS MEJÍAS
Faculty of Law: FRANCISCO JAVIER FERRER ORTÍZ
Faculty of Sciences: JOSÉ ANGEL VILLAR RIVACOBA
Faculty of Medicine: DOLORES SERRÁT MORÉ
Faculty of Veterinary Science: TERESA VERDE ARRIBAS
Faculty of Economics and Business Studies: ELOY FERNÁNDEZ CLEMENTE
Faculty of Humanities and Social Sciences: PASCUAL RUBIO TERRADO
Faculty in Huesca: TERESA CARDESA GARCÍA
Higher Polytechnic Centre: JAVIER MARTÍNEZ RODRÍGUEZ (Dir)

DIRECTORS OF UNIVERSITY SCHOOLS

University College at Huesca: (vacant)
School of Business Studies at Huesca: ESPERANZA MINGUILLÓN CONSTANTE
School of Business Studies at Zaragoza: JOAQUÍN VALENZUELA CASTAÑO
School of Health Sciences at Zaragoza: ARACELLI MONZÓN FERNÁNDEZ
School of Nursing at Huesca: MOYANO DÍEZ
School of Nursing at Teruel: CARMEN GÓRRIZ GONZÁLEZ
'San Vicente de Paúl' School of Social Work at Zaragoza: JAVIER MORERA BETÉS
School of Social Graduates at Teruel: MICAELA MUÑOZ CALVO
School of Industrial Engineering at Zaragoza: DOLORES MARISCAL MASOT
Teacher Training College at Huesca: PILAR BOLEA CATALÁN
Teacher Training College at Teruel: JUAN FÉLIX ROYO GRACIA
Teacher Training College at Zaragoza: ROSA DOMÍNGUEZ CABREJAS
Institute of Education: AGUSTÍN UBIETO ARTETA
School of Social Studies at Zaragoza: FLORENCIO GARCÍA MADRIGAL
Polytechnic at Huesca: J. MANUEL MUNIOZ GUREN ETCHEVERRI
Polytechnic at La Almunia de Doña Godina: MARCUS VICENTE LOBERA
Polytechnic at Teruel: CARLOS HERNANZ PÉREZ

PROFESSORS

Faculty of Philosophy and Letters:
- ALVARO ZAMORA, M. I., History of Art
- ANDRES RUPEREZ, T., Prehistory
- BIELZA DE ORY, V., Human Geography
- BORRAS GUALIS, G. M., History of Art
- CABANES PECOURT, M. D., Palaeography
- CALVO PALACIOS, J. L., Human Geography
- CARRERAS ARES, J. J., Modern History
- CORRIENTE CORDOBA, F., Arabic and Islamic Studies
- EGIDO MARTINEZ, A., Spanish Philology
- FATAS CABEZA, G., Ancient History
- FORCADELL ALVAREZ, C., Modern History
- FRAGO GRACIA, J. A., Spanish Philology
- FRUTOS MEJÍAS, L., Geography
- GUILLEN SELFA, L. M., Greek Philology
- HIGUERAS ARNAL, A., Geography
- ISO ECHEGOYEN, J. J., Latin Philology
- LACARRA DUCAY, M. C., History of Art
- LOMBA FUENTES, J., Philosophy
- MAINER BAQUE, J. C., Spanish Philology
- MARCO SIMON, F., Ancient History
- MARTIN BUENO, M., Archaeology
- MARTIN ZORRAQUINO, M. A., Spanish Philology
- OLIVARES RIVERA, C., English Philology
- ONEGA JAEN, S., English Philology
- PEÑA MONNE, J. L., Physical Geography
- ROMERO TOBAR, L., Spanish Philology
- SÁNCHEZ VIDAL, A., History of Art
- SESMA MUÑOZ, J. A., Medieval History
- UTRILLA Y MIRANDA, P., Prehistory

Faculty of Law:
- ARNAL MONREAL, M., Applied Economics
- BERMEJO VERA, J., Administrative Law
- BERNAD ALVAREZ DE EULATE, M., International Civil Law
- BONET NAVARRO, A., Procedural Law
- CAYON GALIARDO, A., Finance and Tax Law
- CEREZO MIR, J., Criminal Law
- CONTRERAS CASADO, M., Constitutional Law
- CRISTOBAL MONTES, A., Civil Law
- DELGADO ECHEVARRIA, J., Civil Law
- EMBID IRUJO, A., Administrative Law
- FERRER ORTIZ, F. J., Ecclesiastical Law
- GIL CREMADES, J. J., Philosophy of Law
- GONZALEZ DE SAN SEGUNDO, M. A., History of Law and Institutions
- GRACIA MARTIN, L., Criminal Law
- HIGUERA GUIMERA, J. F., Criminal Law
- LACASTA ZABALZA, J. I., Philosophy of Law
- LOPEZ RAMON, F., Administrative Law
- LOZANO CORBI, E., Roman Law
- MARTINEZ DE AGUIRRE ALDAZ, C., Civil Law
- MOREU BALLONGA, J. L., Civil Law
- PEREZ ALVAREZ, M. A., Civil Law
- QUINTANA CARLO, I., Mercantile Law
- RAMÍREZ JIMÉNEZ, M., Constitutional Law
- RIVERO LAMAS, J., Labour and Social Security Law
- ZABALO ESCUDERO, M. E., International Private Law

Faculty of Science:
- ALCALA ARANDA, R., Solid State Physics
- ALONSO BUJ, J. L., Theoretical Physics
- ALVAREZ ABENIA, J. M., Optics
- AZNAREZ ALDUAN, J. L., Analytical Chemistry
- BASTERO ELEIZALDE, J., Mathematical Analysis
- BILBAO DUÑABEITIA, R., Chemical Engineering
- BOYA BALET, L. J., Theoretical Physics
- CACHO PALOMAR, J. F., Analytical Chemistry
- CALVO PINILLA, M., Applied Mathematics
- CARIÑENA MARZO, J. F., Theoretical Physics
- CASTILLO SUÁREZ, J. R., Analytical Chemistry
- CRISTÓBAL CRISTÓBAL, J. A., Statistics and Operational Research
- CRUZ FLOR, A., Theoretical Physics
- CUARTERO RUIZ, B., Mathematical Analysis
- DOMÍNGUEZ MURILLO, E., Computer Science and Artificial Intelligence
- FERNANDEZ-PACHECO PEREZ, A., Terrestrial Physics, Astronomy and Astrophysics
- FORNIES GRACÍA, J. O., Inorganic Chemistry
- GARAY DE PABLO, J., Mathematical Analysis
- GASCA GONZALEZ, M., Applied Mathematics
- GÓMEZ-MORENO CALERA, C., Biochemistry and Molecular Biology
- GONZALEZ ALVAREZ, D., Solid State Physics
- GONZALEZ LOPEZ, J. M., Crystallography and Mineralogy
- GRACÍA TORRECILLA, M., Physical Chemistry
- GUTIÉRREZ ELORZA, M., Geodynamics
- LAGUNA CASTRILLO, A., Inorganic Chemistry
- LIÑAN GUIJARRO, E., Palaeontology
- LISBONA CORTES, F., Applied Mathematics
- LOZANO IMIZCOZ, M. T., Geometry and Topology
- MARTÍNEZ GIL, F. J., Geodynamics
- MARTÍNEZ MARTÍNEZ, P.A., Electronics
- MELÉNDEZ ANDREU, E., Organic Chemistry
- MORAL GAMIZ, A. DEL, Solid State Physics
- MORALES VILLASEVIL, A., Atomic, Molecular and Nuclear Physics
- NAVARRO MARTIN, R., Inorganic Chemistry
- NÚÑEZ-LAGOS ROGLA, R., Atomic, Molecular and Nuclear Physics
- ORO GIRAL, L. A., Inorganic Chemistry
- OTAL CINCA, J., Algebra
- OTIN LACARRA, S. F., Physical Chemistry
- QUINTANILLA MONTÓN, M., Optics
- REBOLLEDO SANZ, M. A., Optics
- SAN MIGUEL MARCO, M., Statistics and Operational Research
- SÁNCHEZ CELA, V. E., Petrology and Geochemistry
- SANTAMARIA RAMIRO, J. M., Chemical Engineering
- SAVIRÓN DE CIDÓN, J. M., Fluid Mechanics
- SESMA BIENZOBAS, J., Theoretical Physics
- TORRES IGLESIAS, M., Algebra
- URIETA NAVARRO, J. S., Physical Chemistry
- VAREA AGUDO, V. R., Algebra
- VILLENA MORALES, J., Stratigraphy

Faculty of Medicine:
- ASIRON IRIBARREN, P. J., Physical and Sport Education
- BARTOLOME RODRIGUEZ, M., Pharmacology
- BUENO GÓMEZ, J., Medicine
- BUENO SÁNCHEZ, M., Paediatrics
- CALATAYUD MALDONADO, V., Surgery
- CARAPETO MÁRQUEZ DE PRADO, F. J., Medicine
- CASTELLANO ARROYO, M., Toxicology and Health Legislation
- CIA GOMEZ, P., Medicine
- CONDE GUERRI, B., Morphology
- FABRE GONZÁLEZ, E., Obstetrics and Gynaecology
- FERREIRA MONTERO, I. J., Medicine
- GÓMEZ LÓPEZ, L. I., Preventive Medicine and Public Health
- GOMEZ LUS, R., Microbiology
- GONZÁLEZ GONZÁLEZ, M., Surgery
- GUILLÉN MARTÍNEZ, G., Medicine
- GUTIERREZ MARTIN, M., Medicine
- LOZANO MANTECÓN, R., Surgery
- MARTINEZ DIEZ, M., Surgery
- MARTÍNEZ HERNÁNDEZ, H., Obstetrics and Gynaecology
- ORTEGO FERNANDEZ DE RETANA, F. J., Pathology
- PEREZ CASTEJON, M. C., Morphology
- PÉREZ GONZÁLEZ, J. M., Paediatrics
- RAMÓN Y CAJAL JUNQUERA, S., Pathology
- RUBIO CALVO, E., Preventive Medicine and Public Health
- RUBIO CALVO, M. C., Microbiology
- SARRAT TORREGUITART, R., Morphology
- SERAL IÑIGO, F., Surgery
- SEVA DÍAZ, A., Psychiatry
- VERA GIL, A., Morphology

Faculty of Veterinary Science:
- BADIOLA DIEZ, J. J., Animal Pathology
- BASCUAS ASTA, J. A., Animal Pathology
- BURGOS GONZALEZ, J., Food Technology
- CLIMENT PERIS, S., Comparative Anatomy and Pathology
- DUCHA SARDAÑA, J. J., Animal Pathology
- ESPINOSA VELÁZQUEZ, E., Animal Pathology
- GARCIA MARIN, J. F., Animal Pathology
- GOMEZ PIQUER, J., Animal Pathology
- GUADA VALLEPUGA, J. A., Animal Production

Herrera Marteache, A., Nutrition and Bromatology
Josa Serrano, A., Animal Pathology
López Pérez, M. J., Biochemistry and Molecular Biology
Ocaña García, M., Agrarian Economics, Sociology and Politics
Rodríguez Moure, A. A., Animal Pathology
Sala Trepat, F. J., Food Technology
Sánchez Acedo, C., Animal Pathology
Sierra Alfranca, I., Animal Production

Faculty of Economics and Business Studies:
Aznar Grasa, A., Principles of Economic Analysis
Biescas Ferrer, J. A., Applied Economics
Broto Rubio, J. J., Finance and Accountancy
Condor López, V. E., Finance and Accountancy
Espitia Escuer, M., Business Organization
Fernández Clemente, E., Economic History and Institutions
Gabas Trigo, F., Finance and Accountancy
Lafuente Felez, A. J. M., Marketing
Lainez Gadea, J. A., Finance and Accountancy
Olave Rubio, P., Applied Economics
Oliver Pérez-Santacruz, E., Principles of Economic Analysis
Polo Redondo, J., Marketing
Sanso Frago, M., Principles of Economic Analysis
Serrano Sanz, J. M., Applied Economics

Higher School of Industrial Engineering:
Camarena Badia, V., Applied Mathematics
Cano Fernández, J. L., Design Engineering
Castany Valeri, J., Mechanical Engineering
Correas Dobato, J. M., Applied Mathematics
Doblare Castellano, M., Theory of Structures
Dopazo García, C., Fluid Mechanics
Martinez Rodriguez, F. J.
Masgrau Gómez, E. J., Transmission and Communications Theory
Navarro Artigas, J., Electronic Technology
Navarro Linares, R., Materials Science and Metallurgical Engineering
Pastor Franco, J. C.
Petriz Calvo, F., Applied Mathematics
Roy Yarza, A., Electronics
Silva Suárez, M., Systems Engineering and Automation
Torres Leza, F., Production Engineering
Valero Capilla, A., Heat Engineering
Zubiaurre Maquinay, E., Graphics in Engineering

Polytechnics

UNIVERSITAT POLITÈCNICA DE CATALUNYA

Avda Gregorio Marañón s/n, 08028 Barcelona
Telephone: 993-401-62-00
Fax: 993-401-62-10

Founded 1971
Autonomous control under Ministry of Universities and Research
Languages of instruction: Spanish, Catalan
Academic year: October to June
Rector: Gabriel A. Ferraté i Pascual
Vice-Rectors: José Luis Andrés Yebra, Albert Corominas i Subias, Antoni Giró Roca, Jaume Pagès i Fita, Albert Prat i Bartés, Vera Pawlowsky Glahn, Rafael Serra Florensa
Administrative Director: Francesc Solà i Busquets
Library: each constituent school has a library attached
Number of teachers: 2,040
Number of students: 47,062
Publications: *Guía del estudiante*, *Boletín UPC*.

CONSTITUENT SCHOOLS

Escuela Técnica Superior de Arquitectura: Dir Santiago Roqueta Matias.

Escuela Técnica Superior de Ingenieros Industriales de Barcelona: Dir Ferran Puerta i Sales.

Escuela Técnica Superior de Ingenieros Industriales de Tarrasa: Dir Ramon Capdevila Pagès.

Escuela Técnica Superior de Ingenieros de Telecomunicación: Dir Lluís Jofre i Roca.

Escuela Técnica Superior de Ingenieros de Caminos, Canales y Puertos: Dir Jesús Carrera.

Escuela Universitaria de Ingenieria Técnica Industrial de Tarrasa: Dir Josep Xercavins i Valls.

Escuela Universitaria de Ingenieria Técnica Industrial de Villanueva y Geltrú: Dir Joan Majó i Roca.

Escuela Universitaria Politécnica de Manresa: Dir Pere Rubió i Diaz.

Escuela Universitaria de Optica de Tarrasa: Dir Joan Salvadó i Arqués.

Escuela Técnica Superior de Arquitectura del Vallès: Dir Xavier Monteys i Roig.

Escuela Universitaria Politécnica del Baix Llobregat: Dir Javier Barà Temes.

Escuela Universitaria Politécnica de Barcelona: Dir Francisco Javier Llovera Sáez.

Facultad de Matemáticas y Estadística: Dir Joan Solà-Morales i Rubio.

Facultad de Náutica: Dir Antoni Vila i Mitjà.

Facultad de Informática: Dir Pere Botella i López.

ATTACHED INSTITUTES

Instituto de Ingeniería Cibernética: Diagonal 647, 08028 Barcelona; Dir Rafael Huber Garrido.

Instituto de Investigación Textil y Cooperación Industrial: Colon 1, 08222 Tarrasa; Dir José Valldeperas i Morell.

Instituto de Ciencias de la Educación: Diagonal 647, 08028 Barcelona; Dir José A. Martín Rioja.

Instituto de Tecnología y Modelzación Ambiental: Ctra Nacional 150, Km 14.500 (Mancomunitat Sabadell-Terrassa); Dir José M. Baldasano Recio.

Instituto de Técnicas Energéticas: Diagonal 647, 08028 Barcelona; Dir Xavier Ortega i Aramburu.

UNIVERSIDAD POLITÉCNICA DE MADRID

Avda Ramiro de Maeztu 7, Ciudad Universitaria, 28040 Madrid
Telephone: 91-336-60-00
Fax: 91-336-61-73

Founded 1971
State control
Language of instruction: Spanish
Academic year: October to July
Rector: Dr Saturnino de la Plaza Pérez
Vice-Rectors: Dr Félix Soriano Santandreu (Academic Affairs), Dr José Luis Maté Hernández (Academic Staff), Dr José Ramón Casar Corredera (Research), Dr Manuel Balgañón Moreno (Development and Economic Planning), Dr Adolfo de Francisco García (Doctorate and Postgraduate Studies)
Chief Administrative Officer: Fernando Lanzaco Bonilla
Secretary-General: Dr Miguel Oliver Alemany
There is a library attached to each constituent school of the University
Number of teachers: 3,266
Number of students: 48,383

CONSTITUENT SCHOOLS

Escuela Técnica Superior de Ingenieros Aeronáuticos: Ciudad Universitaria, 28040 Madrid; tel. 91-336-60-00; fax 91-336-63-70; Dir Pascual Tarín Remohí.

Escuela Técnica Superior de Arquitectura: Ciudad Universitaria, 28040 Madrid; tel. 91-336-65-24; fax 91-544-24-81; Dir Ricardo Aroca Hernández-Ros.

Escuela Técnica Superior de Ingenieros Agrónomos: Ciudad Universitaria, 28040 Madrid; tel. 91-336-56-00; fax 91-543-48-79; Dir Dr José Luis Sainz Vélez.

Escuela Técnica Superior de Ingenieros de Caminos, Canales y Puertos: Ciudad Universitaria, 28040 Madrid; tel. 91-336-60-00; fax 91-549-22-89; Dir Edelmiro Rúa Alvarez.

Escuela Técnica Superior de Ingenieros Industriales: Calle José Gutiérrez Abascal 2, 28006 Madrid; tel. 91-336-60-00; fax 91-561-86-18; Dir Dr Javier Uceda Antolín.

Escuela Técnica Superior de Ingenieros de Minas: Ríos Rosas 21, 28003 Madrid; tel. 91-336-60-00; fax 91-336-70-68; Dir Hermenegildo Mansilla Izquierdo.

Escuela Técnica Superior de Ingenieros de Montes: Ciudad Universitaria, 28040 Madrid; tel. 91-336-60-00; fax 91-543-95-57; Dir Antonio Notario Gómez.

Escuela Técnica Superior de Ingenieros Navales: Ciudad Universitaria, 28040 Madrid; tel. 91-336-60-00; fax 91-544-21-49; Dir José Fernando Núñez Basáñez.

Escuela Técnica Superior de Ingenieros de Telecomunicación: Ciudad Universitaria, 28040 Madrid; tel. 91-336-60-00; fax 91-543-96-52; Dir Dr Jesús Sánchez Miñana.

Facultad de Informática: Campus Montegancedo, Boadilla del Monte 28660, Madrid; tel. 91-336-73-99; fax 91-336-74-12; Dean Dr José Luis Morant Ramón.

Escuela Universitaria de Ingeniería Técnica Aeronáutica: Ciudad Universitaria, 28040 Madrid; tel. 91-336-60-00; fax 91-336-75-11; Dir Manuel Alfonso Ortega Pérez.

Escuela Universitaria de Arquitectura Técnica: Ciudad Universitaria, 28040 Madrid; tel. 91-336-60-00; fax 91-336-76-44; Dir Dr José Luís Moreira Sánchez.

Escuela Universitaria de Ingeniería Técnica Agrícola: Ciudad Universitaria, 28040 Madrid; tel. 91-544-58-00; fax 91-549-30-02; Dir Joaquín García de Martitegui.

Escuela Universitaria de Ingeniería Técnica Forestal: Ciudad Universitaria, 28040 Madrid; tel. 91-336-60-00; fax 91-544-60-25; Dir Rafael Llavero Fernández.

Escuela Universitaria de Ingeniería Técnica Industrial: Ronda de Valencia 3, 28012 Madrid; tel. 91-336-60-00; fax 91-530-92-44; Dir Jesús Pérez Sanz.

Escuela Universitaria de Ingeniería Técnica de Obras Publicas: Alfonso XII 3, 28014 Madrid; tel. 91-336-60-00; fax 91-336-79-58; Dir MANUEL VÁZQUEZ FERNÁNDEZ.

Escuela Universitaria de Ingeniería Técnica de Telecomunicación: Complejo Politécnico de Vallecas, 28031 Madrid; tel. 91-336-60-00; fax 91-331-92-29; Dir JUAN BLANCO COTANO.

Escuela Universitaria Topográfica: Complejo Politécnico de Vallecas, 28031 Madrid; tel. 91-336-60-00; fax 91-336-79-32; Dir Dr PEDRO J. CAVERO ABAD.

Escuela Universitaria de Informática: Complejo Politécnico de Vallecas, 28031 Madrid; tel. 91-336-60-00; fax 91-331-17-67; Dir JESÚS SÁNCHEZ LÓPEZ.

ATTACHED RESEARCH INSTITUTES

Instituto de Ciencias de la Educación: ETS de Ing. de Caminos, Canales y Puertos, Ciudad Universitaria, 28040 Madrid; tel. 91-336-60-00; fax 91-336-68-12.

Instituto de Ampliación de Estudios e Investigación Industrial "Jose Antonio Artigas": E.T.S. de Ingenieros Industriales, Calle José Gutiérrez Abascal 2, 28006 Madrid; tel. 91-336-30-70; fax 91-336-30-11.

Instituto de Control Automatico: E.T.S. de Ingenieros Industriales, Calle José Gutiérrez Abascal 2, 28006 Madrid; tel. 91-262-62-00.

Instituto de Fusión Nuclear: E.T.S. de Ingenieros Industriales, Calle José Gutiérrez Abascal 2, 28006 Madrid; tel. 91-336-31-08.

Instituto de Energia Solar: E.T.S. de Ingenieros de Telecomunicación, Ciudad Universitaria, 28040 Madrid; tel. 91-544-10-60; fax 91-544-63-41.

Instituto de Ingeniería Ambiental 'Agustín de Bethencourt': ETS de Ingenieros de Caminos, Canales y Puertos, Cuidad Universitaria, 28040 Madrid; tel. 91-336-67-35.

Instituto 'Juan de Herrera': ETS de Arquitectura, Cuidad Universitaria, 28040 Madrid; tel. 91-244-54-05.

Instituto de Energías Renovables: ETS de Ingenieros Agrónomos, Cuidad Universitaria, 28040 Madrid; tel. 91-244-48-07.

UNIVERSIDAD POLITÉCNICA DE VALENCIA

Camino de Vera s/n, 46022 Valencia
Telephone: 96-387-70-00
Fax: 96-387-70-09
Founded 1968
State control
Language of instruction: Spanish
Academic year: October to June
Rector: JUSTO NIETO NIETO
Vice-Rectors: PEDRO MIGUEL SOSA, JUAN FRANCISCO JULIÁ IGUAL, ELIAS DE LOS REYES DAVÓ, JOSEP TORNERO I MONTSERRAT, ANTONIO HOSPITALER PÉREZ, JUAN MANUEL GISBERT BLANQUER, AMPARO CARBONELL TATAY, FRANCISCO MORANT ANGLADA
Secretary-General: CARLOS GARCÍA GÓMEZ
Librarian: JOSÉ LLORENS SÁNCHEZ
Number of teachers: 1,612
Number of students: 31,035

CONSTITUENT SCHOOLS

Escuela Técnica Superior de Ingenieros Agrónomos: Campus del Camino de Vera, Valencia; Dir BALDOMERO SEGURA GARCÍA DEL RÍO.

Escuela Técnica Superior de Arquitectura: Campus del Camino de Vera, Valencia; Dir ARTURO MARTÍNEZ BOQUERA.

Escuela Técnica Superior de Ingenieros de Caminos, Canales y Puertos: Campus del Camino de Vera, Valencia; Dir JOAQUÍN ANDREU ALVAREZ.

Escuela Técnica Superior de Ingenieros Industriales: Campus del Camino de Vera, Valencia; Dir ELISEO GÓMEZ-SENENT MARTÍNEZ.

Escuela Técnica Superior de Ingenieros de Telecomunicación: Campus del Camino de Vera, Valencia; Dir MIGUEL FERRANDO BATALLER.

Escuela Universitaria de Ingeniería Técnica Agrícola: Avenida Blasco Ibáñez, 21, Valencia; Dir SANTIAGO GUILLEM PICO.

Escuela Universitaria de Ingeniería Técnica Industrial: Campus del Camino de Vera, Valencia; Dir ENRIQUE BALLESTER SARRIÁS.

Escuela Técnica Superior de Ingenieros en Geodesia, Cartografía y Topografía: Campus del Camino de Vera, Valencia; Dir MANUEL CHUECA PAZOS.

Escuela Universitaria de Arquitectura Técnica: Campus del Camino de Vera, Valencia; Dir JOSÉ LUIS MONTALVÁ CONESA.

Facultad de Bellas Artes: Campus del Camino de Vera, Valencia; Dean JOAN LLAVERIA I ARASA.

Escuela Universitaria de Informática: Campus del Camino de Vera, Valencia; Dir PEDRO BLESA PONS.

Escuela Politécnica Superior de Orihuela: Carretera de Beniel Km. 3, Orihuela (Alicante); Dir Prof. PABLO MELGAREJO MORENO.

Facultad de Informática: Campus del Camino de Vera, Valencia; Dean JOSE FRANCISCO DUATO MARIN.

Escuela Universitaria de Gandía: Carretera Nazaret-Oliva s/n, Grao de Gandía; Dir MIGUEL ALAMAR PENADES.

Escuela Politécnica Superior de Alcoy: Passeig del Viaducte 1, Alcoy; Dir FRANCISCO COLOMINA FRANCES.

Colleges

GENERAL

Schiller International University – Spain: for general details, see entry in Germany chapter.

Madrid Campus: Calle de Rodríguez, San Pedro 10, 28015 Madrid; tel. 91-446-23-49; fax 91-593-44-46; Dir L. BURGUNDE.

Universidad Internacional Menéndez Pelayo: Isaac Peral 23, 28040 Madrid; tel. 91-592-06-00; f. 1932; offers summer courses to Spanish and foreign students and grants fellowships for scientific research; library of 15,200 vols; 700 teachers; 15,000 students; there are campuses in Madrid, Santander, Barcelona, Cuenca, Santa Cruz de Tenerife, La Coruña, Seville, Valencia; Rector JOSÉ L. GARCÍA DELGADO; Vice-Rectors JOSÉ A. RODRÍGUEZ, JUAN A. VÁZQUEZ; Secretary-General JUAN CARLOS JIMÉNEZ; Administrator-General JESÚS GÜEMES MUTILBA.

ECONOMICS AND LAW

Institut d'Estudis Europeus: Via Laietana 32, 08003 Barcelona; f. 1951; studies and information in political, economic, cultural, scientific and judicial aspects of modern Europe; participates in conferences on European themes throughout Spain; Pres. JOSEP SANS; Dir ENRIC PICANOL; publs various.

Real Colegio Universitario 'Escorial-María Cristina': San Lorenzo de El Escorial, Madrid; tel. 91-890-45-45; fax 91-890-66-09; f. 1892; private college of the Augustinian Fathers accredited by Universidad Complutense de Madrid; library of 185,000 vols; 60 teachers; 1,200 students; Rector FRANCISCO JAVIER CAMPOS FERNANDEZ DE SEVILLA; Vice-Rector JESÚS MIGUEL BENÍTEZ SÁNCHEZ; Secretary JOSE RODRÍGUEZ DÍEZ; Dean of the Faculty of Law PROMETEO CEREZO DE DIEGO; Dean of the Faculty of Economics AGUSTÍN ALONSO RODRÍGUEZ; Librarian FLORENTINO DÍEZ FERNÁNDEZ; publs *Anuario jurídico y económico escurialense* (annually), *La Ciudad de Dios* (quarterly), *Nueva Etapa* (annually).

MEDICINE

Escuela Andaluza de Salud Publica: Campus Universitario de Cartuja, Apdo 2070, 18080 Granada; tel. 958-16-10-44; fax 958-16-11-42; f. 1985; master's degree and other courses in public health management and services; library of 17,000 books, 842 current periodicals; 45 teachers.

MILITARY SCIENCE

Escuela de Estado Mayor (Army Staff College): Santa Cruz de Marcenado 25, 28071 Madrid; f. 1842; 60; 180; library of 135,202 vols; Dir Brig.-Gen. LUIS RUIZ DE CONEJO SANCHEZ.

TECHNOLOGY

Escuela Técnica Superior de Ingenieros Industriales (School of Industrial Engineering): José Gutiérrez Abascal 2, 28006 Madrid; tel. 91-261-58-91; fax 91-261-86-18; f. 1850; 350; 3,500; library: see Libraries; Dir JOSÉ M. MARTÍNEZ-VAL.

ETEA: Escritor Castilla Aguayo 4, Apdo 439, 14004 Córdoba; tel. 957-22-21-00; fax 957-22-21-01; f. 1963; undergraduate and postgraduate courses in business administration; research institute; extension courses in management; management consultancy services; 150 teachers; library of 50,000 vols; Dir-Gen. Dr MANUEL CABANES FUENTES.

Institut Químic de Sarriá (Sarriá Institute of Chemistry): Calle Via Augusta 390, 08017 Barcelona; tel. 93-203-89-00; fax 93-205-62-66; f. 1916; 95 teachers; 1,223 students; library of 45,000 vols; Dir Dr ENRIC JULIÀ DANÉS; Sec. MARIA LUISA ESPASA SEMPERE; Librarian NÚRIA VALLMITJANA; publs *Afinidad* (every 2 months), *IQS* (annually).

DIRECTORS

Analytical Chemistry: Dr CARME BROSA BALLESTEROS
Organic Chemistry: Dr JOSEP IRURRE PÉREZ
Chemical Engineering: Dr ROSA NOMEN RIBÉ
Economics (Universitat Ramon Llull): Dr JESÚS TRICÀS PRECKLER
Physical Chemistry: Dr SANTIAGO NONELL MARRUGAT
Applied Statistics: Dr XAVIER TOMÀS MORER

Schools of Art, Architecture and Music

Conservatorio Profesional de Música y Escuela de Arte Dramático: Málaga; 450 students; Dir JOSÉ ANDREU NAVARRO.

Conservatorio Superior de Música: Angel de Saavedra 1, 14003 Córdoba; tel. 957-47-66-61; fax 957-48-77-52; f. 1862; 2,300 students; library of 15,000 vols; Dir MA SOLEDAD NIETO GARCÍA; Sub-Dir CASIMIRO TIRADO ROJAS; Sec. JOAQUÍN CASTELLS CANET.

Conservatorio Superior de Música: Calle Jesús del Gran Poder 49, 41002 Seville; tel. 95-438-10-09; fax 95-438-33-57; f. 1935; teaching and training in music; 92 teachers; library of 8,000 vols, 20,000 scores; Dir FERNANDO PÉREZ HERRERA; Vice-Dir FRANCISCO JAVIER LÓPEZ; Sec. BEGOÑA SÁNCHEZ PEÑA; publ. *Diferencias*.

Conservatorio Superior de Música de San Sebastián: Easo 45, 20006 San Sebastián; tel. 943-46-64-88; fax 943-45-18-92; 45 teachers; library of 3,000 books, 2,500 records, 16,500 scores; Dir ROBERTO NUÑO.

Conservatorio Superior de Música y Escuela de Arte Dramático: Paseo del Malecón s/n, 30004 Murcia; tel. 968-29-47-58; f. 1916; 100 teachers; 3,000 students; library of *c*. 5,000 vols; 1,200 audio materials; Dir CELIA GUIRADO CID; publ. *Cadencia* (3 a year).

Conservatorio Superior de Música y de Valencia: Camino de Vera 29, 46022 Valencia; tel. 96-369-67-32; fax 96-393-37-98; e-mail 46013129@centres.cult.gua.es; f. 1879; 40 teachers; 900 students; library of 10,820 vols; Dir JOSÉ VICENTE CERVERA; Sec. GREGORIO JIMÉNEZ; publ. *Memoria* (annually).

Conservatorio Superior Municipal de Música de Barcelona: Calle Bruc 112, 08009 Barcelona; tel. 93-458-43-02; fax 93-459-31-04; f. 1886; 102 teachers; 1,815 students; library of 27,400 vols and scores; 7,250 items of audio material; Dir ESTHER VILAR TORRENS.

Escuela Superior de Bellas Artes de San Carlos (Valencia School of Fine Arts): San Pio 9, 46010 Valencia; f. 1756; library of 5,105 vols; 26 teachers; 300 students; Dir DANIEL DE NUEDA LLISIONA; Sec. AMANDO BLANQUER PONSODA.

Escuela Técnica Superior de Arquitectura de Sevilla (School of Architecture): Avda Reina Mercedes s/n, 41012 Seville; f. 1964; 2,200 students; 153 teachers; library of 17,000 vols; Dir FELIX ESCRIG PALLARES.

Instituto Formación Profesional 'Islas Filipinas': Calle Jesús Maestro, 28003 Madrid; tel. 91-534-37-08; f. 1985; library of 15,000 vols; 109 teachers; 1,900 students; delineation and graphics; Dir FIDEL HIGUERA GORRIDO.

Real Conservatorio Profesional de Música 'Manuel de Falla': Calle Marqués del Real Tesoro 10, 11001 Cádiz; tel. 956-21-13-23; fax 956-22-39-18; 1,000 students.

Real Conservatorio Superior de Música de Madrid (Royal Academy of Music): Calle Doctor Mata 2, 28012 Madrid; tel. 91-539-29-01; fax 91-527-58-22; f. 1830; 700 registered students and 100 free students; 80 teachers; library of 100,000 vols; Dir MIGUEL DEL BARCO; Sec. JOSE MA. MUÑOZ LÓPEZ; publ. *Musica* (annually).

Real Escuela Superior de Arte Dramático y Danza (Royal Higher School of Dramatic Art): Plaza de Isabel II, Madrid; Dir RICARDO DOMÉNECH YVORRA.

SRI LANKA

Learned Societies

GENERAL

Institute of Sinhala Culture: 375 Bauddhaloka Mawatha, Colombo 7; tel. 687979; f. 1954 for the preservation and development of Sinhala culture: art and architecture, drama, dance, music, folklore, arts and crafts, film, research, traditional embroidery, puppetry; presents cultural programmes; holds seminars and workshops; 680 mems; Pres. L. STANLEY JAYEWARDANE; Hon. Sec. Mrs R. G. SENANAYAKE.

National Academy of Sciences of Sri Lanka: 120/10 Wijerama Mawatha, Colombo 7; f. 1976; 104 mems; Pres. Prof. M. U. S. SULTANBAWA; Gen. Sec. Prof. ERIC H. KARUNANAYAKE; Sec. for Foreign Relations Dr U. PETHIYAGODA.

Royal Asiatic Society of Sri Lanka: 1st Floor, Mahaweli Centre and Royal Asiatic Society Bldg, 96 Ananda Coomaraswamy Mawatha, Colombo 7; tel. and fax 699249; f. 1845; institutes and promotes inquiries into the history, religions, languages, literature, arts, sciences and social conditions of the present and former inhabitants of Sri Lanka, and connected cultures; library contains one of the largest collections of books on Sri Lanka, and others on Indian and Eastern culture in general; 500 mems; Pres. Prof. M. B. ARIYAPALA; Hon. Secs. KALASURI WILFRED M. GUNASEKARA, METHSIRI COORAY; publ. *Journal* (annually).

BIBLIOGRAPHY, LIBRARY SCIENCE AND MUSEOLOGY

Sri Lanka Library Association: The Professional Centre, 275/75 Bauddhaloka Mawatha, Colombo 7; tel. 58-91-03; f. 1960; Pres. P. VIDANAPATHIRANA; Gen. Sec. WILFRED RANASINGHE; publs *Sri Lanka Library Review* (annually), *SLLA Newsletter* (quarterly).

ECONOMICS, LAW AND POLITICS

Ceylon Institute of World Affairs: c/o Mervyn de Silva, 82B Ward Place, Colombo 7; f. 1957; Pres. Maj.-Gen. ANTON MUTTUKUMARU.

EDUCATION

National Education Society of Sri Lanka: Faculty of Education, University of Colombo, Colombo 03; 75 mems; publ. *Education.*

FINE AND PERFORMING ARTS

Arts Council of Sri Lanka: 8th Floor, Sethsiripausa, Battaramulla; tel. 872031; f. 1952 to promote art projects in Sri Lanka; the Council carries out projects in all fields of Arts, i.e. painting, drama, music, film, literature, ballet, dancing, folk song, folklore; Pres. R. A. A. RANAWEERA (acting); Sec. H. K. PREMADASA.

Ceylon Society of Arts (Sri Lanka): Art Gallery, Ananda Coomarassamy Mawatha, Colombo 7; tel. 693067; f. 1887; Pres. KALAPATHI-P. SUNIL; Hon. Gen. Sec. M. D. S. GUNATHILAKE.

HISTORY, GEOGRAPHY AND ARCHAEOLOGY

Archaeological Society of Sri Lanka: c/o Dept of Archaeology, Sir Marcus Fernando Mawata, Colombo 7; f. 1966; Pres. Prof. CHANDRA WIKKRAMAGAMAGE; Co-Secs S. LAKDUSINGHE, W. H. WIJAYAPALA.

Ceylon Geographical Society: 61 Abdul Caffoor Mawatha, Colombo 3; f. 1938; 100 mems; Pres. Prof. K. KULARATNAM; Secs Dr K. U. SIRINANDA, Dr W. P. T. SILVA; publ. *The Ceylon Geographer* (annually).

LANGUAGE AND LITERATURE

English Speaking Union of Sri Lanka: 14A, 16k Lane Galle Road, Colombo 3; tel. 575843; f. 1981; library of 3,000 vols; includes an English Language School; Pres. Dr TERENCE AMERASINGHE; publ. *Open Mind* (quarterly).

MEDICINE

Sri Lanka Medical Association: Wijerama House, 6 Wijerama Mawatha, Colombo 7; tel. 693324; fax 698802; f. 1887; 1,000 mems; Pres. Dr S. RAMACHANDRAN; Hon. Sec. Dr DEVAKA FERNANDO; publs *Newsletter* (monthly), *Medical Journal* (4 a year), *Abstracts of Anniversary Academic Sessions* (annually).

NATURAL SCIENCES

General

Sri Lanka Association for the Advancement of Science: 120/10 Wijerama Mawatha, Colombo 7; tel. 691681; f. 1944 to provide for systematic direction of scientific enquiry in the interests of the country, to promote contact among scientific workers, and to disseminate scientific knowledge, etc; holds annual session; seven sections; 2,600 mems; Gen. Pres. Prof. VALENTINE BASNAYAKE; Gen. Secs Dr W. L. SUMATHIPALA, Dr C. P. D. W. MATHEW; publs *Proceedings*, *Vidya Viyapthi.*

PHILOSOPHY AND PSYCHOLOGY

Ceylon Humanist Society: Rutnam Inst. Bldg, University Lane, Jaffna; Pres. J. T. RUTNAM; Sec. O. M. DE ALWIS.

RELIGION, SOCIOLOGY AND ANTHROPOLOGY

Buddhist Academy of Ceylon: 109 Rosmead Place, Colombo.

Maha Bodhi Society of Ceylon: 130 Rev. Hikkaduwe Sri Sumangala Na Himi Mawatha, Colombo 10; tel. and fax 698079; f. 1891 for propagation of Buddhism throughout the world; 1,000 mems; Pres. RAJA WANASUNDERA; Hon. Sec. RANJIT SAMARASINGHE; publ. *Sinhala Bauddhaya* (monthly).

TECHNOLOGY

Institution of Engineers, Sri Lanka: 120/15 Wijerama Mawatha, Colombo 7; tel. 698426; fax 699202; e-mail iesl@slt.lk; f. 1906; 5,000 mems; library of 9,000 vols; Pres. Eng. A. N. P. WICKREMASURIYA; Exec. Sec. Eng. D. D. S. JAYAWARDENA; publs *Engineer* (every 4 months), *Sri Lanka Engineering News* (monthly), *Transactions* (annually).

Research Institutes

AGRICULTURE, FISHERIES AND VETERINARY SCIENCE

Hector Kobbekaduwa Agrarian Research and Training Institute: POB 1522, 114 Wijerama Mawatha, Colombo 7; f. 1972; research into and policy analysis on agrarian structures and the economic, social and institutional aspects of agricultural development; operates training programmes; library: see Libraries; Dir S. G. SAMARASINGHE; publs *Annual Report, Newsletter, Food Commodities Bulletin, Agroclimatic Bulletin, Farmers' Journal* (in Sinhala and Tamil), *Journal of Agrarian Studies* (in English and Sinhala).

Coconut Research Institute: Bandirippuwa Estate, Lunuwila; tel. (31) 55300; fax (31) 77195; f. 1929; quasi-government research institute serving coconut industry of Sri Lanka; library: see Libraries; Chair. Dr U. P. DE S. WAIDYANATHA; Dir Dr M. DE S. LIYANAGE; publs *COCOS, Coconut Bulletin, Annual Report.*

Fisheries Research Station: Negombo.

Horticultural Research and Development Institute: Gannoruwa, Peradeniya; tel. (8) 88011; f. 1965; research on fruit, vegetables, roots and tubers and other horticultural crops, and soya processing; library of 16,500 vols; Dir Dr S. D. B. G. JAYAWARDANE; publ. *Tropical Agriculturist* (annually).

National Aquatic Resources Agency: Crow Island, Colombo 15; Dir-Gen. M. JAYAREKAR.

Rice Research and Development Institute: Batalagoda, Ibbagamuwa; tel. and fax (37) 22681; e-mail dhane@rrdi.ac.lk; f. 1994; Dir Dr M. P. DHANAPALA.

Rubber Research Institute of Sri Lanka: Dartonfield, Agalawatta; tel. (34) 47426; fax (34) 47427; e-mail director@rri.ac.lk; f. 1910; Colombo office and laboratories: Telawala Rd, Ratmalana, Mt Lavinia; research and advisory services on rubber planting and manufacture; comprises five research depts, extension dept and economic research unit, specification unit and estate dept; about 500 staff; Dir Dr L. M. K. TILLEKERATNE; publs *Annual Report, Annual Review*, journals, bulletins and advisory circulars.

Tea Research Institute of Sri Lanka: St Coombs, Talawakelle; tel. (52) 8385; fax (52) 8311; e-mail postmaster@tri.ac.lk; f. 1925; tea processing, agronomic studies, tissue culture and pest control techniques, fertilizer economy, plant biochemical analysis, economic evaluation; 5 brs; library: see Libraries; Dir W. W. MODDER; publs *Tea Bulletin* (2 a year), *Sri Lanka Journal of Tea Science* (2 a year), *Technical Report* (annually).

Veterinary Research Institute: POB 28, Gannoruwa, Peradeniya; tel. (8) 88311; fax (8) 88125; f. 1967; concerned with research and investigations into health and production problems of livestock and poultry, veterinary vaccine production; 45 scientific officers, 48 technicians; Head Dr M. C. L. DE ALWIS.

ECONOMICS, LAW AND POLITICS

Economic Research Unit: Business Intelligence Dept, Bank of Ceylon, Colombo; Business Intelligence Officer S. E. A. JAYAWICKREMA.

Marga Institute: POB 601, 93/10 Dutugemunu St, Kirullapone, Colombo 6; tel. (1) 828544; fax (1) 828597; f. 1972; non-profit multi-disciplinary research org. undertaking critical, non-partisan study of development issues in Sri Lanka and the Asian region; library of 25,000 vols, 37 periodicals; Chair. GODFREY GUNATILLEKE; Exec. Vice-Chair. Dr G. USWATTE ARATCH; publ. *The Marga Quarterly Journal*.

Wiros Lokh Institute: 81-1A Isipatana Mawatha, Colombo 5; tel. and fax (1) 580817; f. 1981; private research and teaching institute; stockmarkets, commercial law, African studies, sports research; library of 12,000 vols; Dir DARIN C. GUNESEKERA.

HISTORY, GEOGRAPHY AND ARCHAEOLOGY

Archaeological Survey Department of Sri Lanka: Sir Marcus Fernando Rd, Colombo 7; tel. (1) 694727; fax (1) 696250; e-mail gamini@sri.lanka.net; f. 1890; library of 10,000 vols; Dir-Gen. S. U. DERANIYAGALA; publs *Administration Report*, *Ancient Ceylon* (annually), *Memoirs.*

MEDICINE

Medical Research Institute: Baseline Rd, Colombo 8; tel. 693532; f. 1900; comprising departments of Bacteriology, Biochemistry, Chemistry of Natural Products, Entomology, Food and Water Bacteriology, Leptospira, Media, Mycology, Clinical Pathology, Parasitology, Nutrition, Pharmacology, Salmonella, Serology, Vaccines, Virology, Animal Centre, School of Medical Laboratory Technology; Dir Dr MAYA ATTAPATTU; Sec. GEMUNU WIJAYAWARDANA.

NATURAL SCIENCES

Biological Sciences

Department of Wild Life Conservation: 18 Gregory's Road, Colombo 7; tel. 698086; fax 698556; f. 1950; library of 1,962 vols; Dir N. W. DISSANAYAKE; publs *Sri Lanka Wild Life, Vana Divi* (annually), *National Parks of Sri Lanka.*

Physical Sciences

Colombo Observatory: Dept of Meteorology, Bauddhaloka Mawatha, Colombo 7; tel. (1) 684746; fax (1) 691443; e-mail meteo@slt.lk; f. 1907; climatological data for Sri Lanka; time service; astronomical service; weather forecasting; agrometeorological service; library of 18,000 vols; Dir Dr A. W. MOHOTTALA; publ. *Report of the Department of Meteorology* (1 a year), *Agrometeorological Bulletin* (4 a year).

TECHNOLOGY

Industrial Technology Institute: 363 Bauddhaloka Mawatha, Colombo 7; tel. 693807; f. 1955; applied technical research institute working in many fields for industry, government agencies and the public; process research, resource studies, waste material utilization, product testing, standards, calibration and repair of instruments, technical consultation; industrial extension; information services centre: see Libraries and Archives; Dir Dr P. M. JAYATISSA; publs *Annual Reports, Bulletins, Seminar Proceedings.*

Geological Survey and Mines Bureau: Senanayake Building, 4 Galle Road, Dehiwala; tel. (1) 725745; fax (1) 735752; e-mail gsmb@slt.lk; f. 1903; systematic geological mapping of the country; identifies and assesses the mineral resources of Sri Lanka; issues licences to regulate exploration, mining, processing, transport, trading in and export of minerals; Chair. D. M. JAYASEKERA; Dir Dr N. P. WIJAYANANDA; publs *Annual Report, Memoirs, Mineral Information Series, Economic Bulletins, Professional Papers.*

Natural Resources, Energy and Science Authority of Sri Lanka: 47/5 Maitland Place, Colombo 7; tel. (1) 696771; fax (1) 691691; e-mail postmast@naresa.ac.lk; f. 1982 (1968 as Nat. Science Council); advises government on measures for promotion and development of national self-reliance in the application of science and technology; management and development of natural resources and energy; initiates and promotes research, liaises with similar overseas bodies and publishes scientific papers and reports; runs the Sri Lanka Scientific and Technical Information Centre (SLSTIC); the 'Man and the Biosphere' Programme for Sri Lanka works under the auspices of the Authority; library of 5,469 vols; documentation and publications unit; acts as National Research Reports Depository on science and technology; Dir-Gen. Prof. P. E. SOYSA; publs *Journal of the National Science Council* (quarterly), *Annual Report*, *Sri Lanka Journal of Social Science* (2 a year), *Vidurava* (quarterly).

Sri Lanka Water Resources Board: 2A Gregory's Ave, Colombo 7; established 1966; advises the Government on all matters concerning the conservation and utilization of water resources; library of 4,620 vols, 60 periodicals; Chair. K. YOGANATHAN.

Libraries and Archives

Agalawatta

Rubber Research Institute of Sri Lanka Library: Dartonfield, Agalawatta; branch library: Telawala Rd, Ratmalana; tel. (34) 47426; fax (34) 47427; e-mail rublib@rri.ac.lk; f. 1953; 8,000 vols, 236 periodical titles; Librarian (vacant); publs *Annual Review, Journal* (2 a year), *Bulletin* (2 a year), *Rubber Puwath* (1 a year).

Colombo

Centre for Development Information: National Planning Dept, Ministry of Policy Planning and Implementation, POB 1547, Galleface Secretariat, Colombo 1; tel. 449378; telex 21409; fax 448063; f. 1979 to co-ordinate and collate socio-economic information; participates in regional information networks, and maintains an int. exchange programme; 15,000 vols, unpublished reports collection; Dir C. I. KARUNANAYAKE; publs *Bibliography of Economic and Social Development in Sri Lanka, Register of Development Research in Sri Lanka, Press Index* (quarterly), *Guide to current periodical literature in economic and social development* (quarterly), *Current Acquisitions* (quarterly).

Industrial Technology Institute Information Services Centre: 363 Bauddhaloka Mawatha, Colombo 7; tel. 698624; f. 1955; 35,000 vols, 300 journals; several thousand reports, reprints, standards; information service to scientists, industrialists and engineers; computer database of books and articles in periodicals; national centre of Asian and Pacific Information Network on Medicinal and Aromatic Plants; Man. Information Services Centre D. S. T. WARNASURIYA; publs *Bibliographical Series*, State of the Art surveys on spices and essential oilbearing plants, *News Digest, Food Digest, CISIR News Bulletin, S & T News, Management Thought.*

Colombo National Museum Library: POB 854, Colombo 7; f. 1877 (incorporating collection of Government Oriental Library, f. 1870); depository for Sri Lanka publications since 1885; 618,221 items (including 141,703 monographs, 4,500 periodical titles, 3,772 palm leaf MSS in Sinhala and Sanskrit, Pali, Burmese and Cambodian); publs *Sri Lanka Periodicals Index, NML Acquisitions Bulletin, Sri Lanka Periodicals Directory, Bibliographical Series.*

Department of National Archives: POB 1414, 7 Reid Ave, Colombo 7; tel. 694523; f. 1902; contains official records of the Dutch Administration from 1640 to 1796, British Administration from 1796 to 1948; official records of Independent Sri Lanka from 1948 onwards; a few codices of Portuguese Administration prior to 1656 and some documents in French, Sinhalese and Tamil; operates a Presidential Archival Depository and a Reference Service; operates Hon. J. R. Jayewardene Research Centre; deals with documents in private possession; is the legal depository for all printed material in the country, effects the registration of printing presses, printed publications, and newspapers; holds copies of books printed after 1885 and newspapers since 1832; Dir Dr K. D. G. WIMALARATNE; publs *Administration Report of The National Archives, Quarterly Statement of Books printed in Sri Lanka* (quarterly), *Catalogue of Newspapers* (annually), *Sri Lanka Archives* (annually).

Hector Kobbekadwa Agrarian Research and Training Institute Library: POB 1522, 114 Wijerama Mawatha, Colombo 7; tel. 696981; f. 1972; 15,000 vols and 70 periodicals; several hundred reports and reprints; special collection on Sri Lanka; part of Nat. Centre for Information on Agrarian Development; Librarian G. H. KARUNARATNE.

Law Library: Hultsdorp, Colombo 12.

National Library of Sri Lanka: 14 Independence Ave, Colombo 7; tel. (1) 698847; fax (1) 685201; e-mail natlib@slt.lk; f. 1990; 250,000 vols (incl. govt publs), 500 periodical titles, 8,003 microfiches, 1,000 maps, microfilms, computer diskettes, CD-ROMs and sound recordings; special collections: Ola Leaf collection, drama MS collection, library and information science collection, Martin Wickramasinghe collection, folk culture, UNESCO; legal deposit library; ISBN, ISMN and ISSN centres; compiles Union Catalogue; Dir M. S. UPALI AMARASIRI; publs *Sri Lanka National Bibliography* (monthly), *Library News* (quarterly), *Sri Lanka Newspaper Index*, Children's bibliography, *Directory of Social Science Libraries, Information Centres and Databases in Sri Lanka, ISBN Publishers Directory, Natnet Lanka Newsletter* (2 a year), *Conference Index, Directory of Government Publicatiions.*

Public Library: 15 Sir Marcus Fernando Mawatha, Colombo 7; tel. 691968; f. 1925; 13 brs; three mobile libraries; 693,000 vols, 2,000 periodical titles; special collections: Sri Lanka, Buddhism, FAO Depository, fine arts, Braille, Theo Auer collection; Chief Librarian M. D. H. JAYAWARDHANA; publ. *Administration Report* (annually).

University of Colombo Library: Colombo 3; tel. and fax (1) 583043; e-mail scj@liby.cmb.ac.lk; f. 1967; 225,000 vols; Librarian Mrs S. C. JAYASURIYA; publs *University of Colombo Review* (annually), *Ceylon Journal of Medical Science* (2 a year), *Colombo Law Review* (annually), *Sri Lanka Journal of International Law* (annually).

Lunuwila

Coconut Research Institute Library: Lunuwila; tel. (1) 253795; fax (31) 57391; e-mail dircn@sri.lanka.net; f. 1929; 9,000 vols; houses the Int. Coconut Information Centre; special collection of world literature on coconut available in hard copies, microfiche, diskettes; Librarian P. A. S. F. PERERA.

Moratuwa

Centre for Industrial Technology Information Services: I.D.B., 615 Galle Rd, Katubedda, Moratuwa; tel. (1) 605372; fax (1) 607002; e-mail citis@sit.lk; f. 1988; acquisition, processing and dissemination of technology information, reference and enquiry services, networking; library of 13,100 vols, 42 current periodicals; Dir NALINI DE SILVA; publs *Current Awareness Bulletin, Current Contents, Karmantha Bulletin* (2 a year), *Industrial Newsletter* (quarterly).

Peradeniya

University of Peradeniya Library: POB 35, Peradeniya; tel. and fax (8) 388678; e-mail sena@lib.pdn.ac.lk; f. 1921; 595,728 vols; collections include deposit materials obtained under printers' and publishers' ordinance from 1955 onwards, reference collection on Sri Lanka, palmleaf manuscripts and rare materials on Sri Lanka; Librarian N. T. S. A. SENADEERA; publs *Ceylon Journal of Science–Biological Sciences, Ceylon Journal of Science – Physical Sciences, Modern Sri Lanka Studies, Sri Lanka Journal of the Humanities* (2 a year).

Talawakele

Tea Research Institute Library: St Coombs, Talawakele; tel. 052-8385; f. 1925; 15,000 vols and 250 periodicals for reference and loan, including a specialist reference section dealing with tea and allied subjects; Librarian WASANTHA ILLANGANTILAKE.

Museums and Art Galleries

Anuradhapura

Anuradhapura Folk Museum: Anuradhapura; f. 1971; regional museum for North Central Province; tel. (2) 52589.

Colombo

Colombo Dutch Period Museum: Pettah, Colombo; f. 1982; period museum depicting life and times during the Dutch rule 1656–1796; tel. 448466.

Colombo National Museum (Cultural): Colombo; f. 1877; national collection of art, antiquities and folk culture.

Mobile Museum: Colombo; natural and cultural heritage of Sri Lanka.

National Museum (Natural History): Colombo; f. 1985; national collection of natural sciences.

Galle

Galle National Museum: Galle; f. 1986; regional museum for Galle District; tel. (9) 32051.

Kandy

Kandy National Museum: Kandy; f. 1942; regional museum for the Central Province; tel. (8) 23867.

Peradeniya

Royal Botanic Gardens: Peradeniya; f. 1821; Supt D. B. SUMITHRAARACHCHI.

Ratnapura

Ratnapura National Museum: Ratnapura; f. 1942; regional museum for the Sabaragamuwa Province; tel. (4) 52451.

Trincomalee

Regional Museum: Trincomalee.

Universities

BUDDHIST AND PALI UNIVERSITY OF SRI LANKA

214 Bauddhaloka Mawatha, Colombo 7
Telephone: 580609
Fax: 580610

Founded 1982
State control
Languages of instruction: Sinhala and English
Academic year: January to December

Chancellor: Most Ven. POTHTHEWELA PANNASARA MAHA NAYAKE THERA
Vice-Chancellor: Ven. A. NANDA
Registrar: S. WIJESEKERA
Librarian: (vacant)

Library of 13,142 vols
Number of teachers: 64
Number of students: 1,639

Publication: *Sri Lanka Journal of Buddhist Studies* (annually).

DIRECTORS

Buddhist Thought: Prof. Y. KARUNADASA
Buddhist Culture: Prof. T. KARIYAWASAM
Buddhist Social Philosophy: Prof. O. ABEYNAYAKE
Buddhism and Comparative Studies: Prof. P. D. PREMASIRI
Buddhist Art and Archaeology: Prof. P. L. PREMATILLAKE
Sinhala Language and Literature: Ven. Dr H. VAJIRANANA THERA
Pali Language and Literature: Prof. N. A. JAYAWICKREMA
Sanskrit Language and Literature: Prof. M. H. F. JAYASURIYA
English Proficiency Programme: Dr D. WALATARA

AFFILIATED COLLEGES

Maligakanda Vidyodaya Institute: Dir Ven. B. SOBHITA THERA.
Peliyagoda Vidyalankara Institute: Dir Ven. W. DHAMMARAKKHITA THERA.
Pinwatta Saddharmakara Institute: Dir Ven. D. NANALOKA THERA.
Balagalla Saraswathie Institute: Dir Ven. Dr YATAGAMA DHAMMAPALA THERA.

UNIVERSITY OF COLOMBO

94 Cumaratunga Munidasa Mawatha, Colombo 3
Telephone: 81835, 84695, 85509
Telex: 22039
Fax: 583810

Founded 1921, present name 1979
State control
Languages of instruction: Sinhala, Tamil, English
Academic year: October to September

Chancellor: Dr P. R. ANTHONIS
Vice-Chancellor: Prof. W. D. LAKSHMAN
Registrar: K. G. JINASENA (acting)
Librarian: Mrs S. C. JAYASURIYA

Number of teachers: 462
Number of students: 6,744

Publications: *The Ceylon Journal of Medical Science* (2 a year), *University of Colombo Review* (annually), *Annual Report, University Calendar.*

DEANS

Faculty of Arts: Dr A. PARAKRAMA
Faculty of Law: Prof. SHARYA DE SOYSA
Faculty of Medicine: Prof. LALITHA MENDIS
Faculty of Science: Prof. KANTHI ABEYNAYAKE
Faculty of Education: Dr W. G. KULARATHE
Faculty of Graduate Studies: Prof. T. HETTIARACHCHY
Faculty of Management and Finance: Dr P. S. M. GUNARATNE

HEADS OF DEPARTMENTS

Faculty of Arts:

Demography: Dr K. A. P. SIDDHISENA
Economics: S. S. VIDANAGAMA
English: Dr F. NELOUFER S. DE MEL
Geography: Prof. YOGAMBIKAI RASANAYAGAM
History and Political Science: M. G. A. COORAY
Sinhala: Prof. R. P. T. JAYAWARDENA
Sociology: Prof. S. T. HETTIGE

Faculty of Management and Finance:

Commerce: J. A. S. C. JAYASINGHE
Management Studies: R. M. R. B. RAJAPAKSE

Faculty of Education:

Educational Psychology: Dr H. P. R. GUNAWARDENA
Humanities Education: D. R. ATUKORALA
Science and Technical Education: M. W. DISSANAYAKE
Social Science Education: J. D. PATHIRANA

Faculty of Law:

Law: NIRMALA PERERA

Faculty of Medicine:

Anatomy: Prof. M. M. R. W. JAYASEKERA
Biochemistry: Prof. E. H. KARUNANAYAKA
Community Medicine: Prof. DULITHA FERNANDO
Forensic Medicine: Prof. P. R. FERNANDO
Clinical Medicine: Prof. M. H. R. SHERIFF
Microbiology: Prof. A. J. PERERA
Obstetrics and Gynaecology: Prof. H. R. SENEVIRATNA
Paediatrics: Prof. S. P. LAMABADUSURIYA
Parasitology: Dr T. DE S. NAOTUNNE
Pathology: Prof. L. R. AMARASEKARA
Pharmacology: Prof. K. WEERASURIYA
Physiology: Prof. K. H. TENNAKOON
Psychological Medicine: Prof. D. S. SAMARASINGHE
Surgery: Prof. A. H. SHERIFFDEEN

Faculty of Science:

Botany: Prof. R. L. C. WIJESUNDERA
Chemistry: Dr S. HEWAGE
Mathematics: Dr S. T. SAMARATUNGA
Physics: Dr T. R. ARIYARATNE
Radio Isotope Centre: Dr R. HEWAMANNA
Statistics and Computer Science: A. KARUNARATNE
Zoology: Prof. W. D. RATNASOORIYA

ATTACHED INSTITUTES

Institute of Indigenous Medicine: Rajagiriya; Dir R. H. M. PIYASENA
Institute of Postgraduate Medicine: Faculty of Medicine, Kynsey Rd, Colombo 8; Dir Dr J. B. PIERIS
Institute of Workers' Education: Reid Ave, Colombo 3; Dir H. M. N. WARAKAULLE
Institute of Computer Technology: Prof. Dir V. K. SAMARANAYAKE

EASTERN UNIVERSITY

Vantharumoolai, Chenkaladi
Telephone: (65) 40490
Fax: (65) 20302

Founded 1981 as Batticaloa University College, present name 1986
State control
Languages of instruction: English and Tamil
Academic year: August to July

Chancellor: (vacant)
Vice-Chancellor: Prof. G. F. RAJENDRAM
Registrar: V. SHANMUGAM (acting)
Senior Assistant Librarian: T. ARULNANDHY

Library of 33,000 vols
Number of teachers: 96
Number of students: 972 (internal), 521 (external)

DEANS

Faculty of Science: Prof. MANO SABARATNAM
Faculty of Agriculture: K. THEDCHANAMOORTHY
Faculty of Arts and Culture: V. GUNARETNAM (acting)
Faculty of Commerce and Management: J. RAGURAGAVAN

HEADS OF DEPARTMENTS

Faculty of Agriculture:
- Agronomy: Dr T. MAHENDRAN
- Agricultural Economics: Dr J. NADARAJAH
- Animal Science: Dr S. RAVEENDRANATH

Faculty of Science:
- Botany: Dr T. JAYASINGAM
- Chemistry: Dr S. KARUNAKARAN (acting)
- Mathematics: Dr R. VIGNESWARAN
- Physics: Dr N. PATHMANATHAN
- Zoology: Dr P. VINOBABA

Faculty of Commerce and Management:
- Management: (vacant)
- Economics: (vacant)

Faculty of Arts and Culture:
- Islamic Studies: (vacant)
- Languages: (vacant)
- Social Sciences: (vacant)

UNIVERSITY OF JAFFNA

Thirunelvely, Jaffna

Telephone: 2248

Founded 1974, present name 1978
State control
Languages of instruction: Tamil and English
Chancellor: Prof. T. NADARAJAH
Vice-Chancellor: Prof. P. BALASUNDARAMPILLAI
Registrar: Dr K. KUNARASA
Librarian: R. PARARAJASINGAM

Library of 100,000 vols
Number of teachers: 310 full-time, 82 part-time
Number of students: 3,245

Publications: *Cintanai* (quarterly), *Sri Lanka Journal of South Asian Studies* (annually), *Vingnanam, Journal of Science* (2 a year).

DEANS

Faculty of Medicine: Dr R. RAJENDRA PRASAD
Faculty of Science: Prof. V. K. GANESALINGAM
Faculty of Arts: Prof. A. SANMUGADAS
Faculty of Agriculture: R. VIJAYARATNAM

HEADS OF DEPARTMENTS

Faculty of Medicine:
- Anatomy: Dr R. RAJENDRA PRASAD
- Biochemistry: Prof. V. ARASARATNAMY
- Community Medicine: Dr N. SIVARAJAH
- Forensic Medicine: Dr C. S. NACHINARKINIAN
- Medicine: Dr J. GANESHAMOORTHY
- Paediatrics: (vacant)
- Pathology: M. JEYANATHAN (acting)
- Physiology: Dr D. GUNARAJASINGAM (acting)
- Psychiatry: Prof. D. J. SOMASUNDARAM
- Siddha Division: M. C. SRIKANTHAN
- Surgery: Dr V. KUNANANDAM
- Obstetrics and Gynaecology: Prof. M. SIVASURIYA

Faculty of Science:
- Botany: N. SELVARATNAM (acting)
- Chemistry: Prof. R. MAGESWARAN
- Computer Unit: Dr S. MAHESAN
- Mathematics and Statistics: P. MAKINAN
- Physics: Prof. R. KUMARAVADIVEL
- Zoology: Dr KRISHNARAJAH (acting)
- Computer Science: Dr S. MAHESAN

Faculty of Arts:
- Commerce: K. THEVARAJAH
- Management Studies: M. NADARAJASUNDARAM
- Economics: V. P. SIVANATHAN
- Education: Prof. V. ARUMUGAM
- Fine Arts: S. KRISHNARAJAH
- Geography: Dr K. KUGABALAN
- Hindu Civilization: Dr P. GOPALAKRISHNA IYER
- History: S. SATHIYASEELAN
- Linguistics and English: Prof. S. SUSEENDARAJAH
- Philosophy: Dr N. GNANAKUMARAN
- Sanskrit: Prof. V. SIVASAMY
- Tamil: Prof. N. SUBRAMANIAM
- Christian and Islamic Civilization: Rev. R. A. J. MATTHIAS
- English Language Teaching Centre: S. VIGNARAJAH
- Dance: Dr S. JEYARASAH
- Music: S. PATHMALINGAM

Faculty of Agriculture:
- Agricultural Chemistry: Dr S. MOHANADAS
- Agricultural Biology: Dr S. MOHANDAS (acting)
- Animal Science: Dr A. NAVARATNARAJAH
- Agronomy: S. RAJADURAI
- Agricultural Engineering: P. ALVAPILLAI (acting)
- Agricultural Economics: S. RAJADURAI (acting)

UNIVERSITY OF KELANIYA

Dalugama, Kelaniya

Telephone: 911391
Fax: 911485

Formerly Vidayalankara Pirivena; University status 1959; reorganized 1972 as a campus of University of Sri Lanka; present name 1978
State control
Languages of instruction: English and Sinhala
Chancellor: Rev. KUSALADHAMMA DHARMAKEERTHI
Vice-Chancellor: Prof. SENAKE BANDARANAYAKE
Deputy Vice-Chancellor: Prof. K. THILAKARATHNE
Registrar: N. B. AMARASINGHE
Librarian: Dr JAYASIRI LANKAGE

Number of teachers: 325
Number of students: 6,392

Publication: *Kalyani* (1 a year), *Journal of the Faculty of Social Science* (1 a year), *Journal of the Faculty of Humanities* (1 a year).

DEANS

Faculty of Science: Prof. M. J. S. WIJAYARATNE
Faculty of Medicine: Prof. H. J. DE SILVA
Faculty of Humanities: Prof. C. PALLIYAGURU
Faculty of Social Science: A. A. D. AMARASEKERA
Faculty of Commerce and Management Studies: A. PATABENDIGE

PROFESSORS

ARIYARATNE, J. K. P., Chemistry
CHANDRASENA, L. G., Biochemistry
DANGALLA, N. K., Geography
DHARMASENA, K., Economics
EDIRISINGHE, D., Philosophy
GUNASEKERA, S. A., Botany
GUNATHILAKE, D. C. R. A., English
ILANGASINGHE, H. B. M., History
KARUNADASA, Y., Pali and Buddhist Studies
KARUNANAYAKE, K., Economics
KARUNATHILAKE, W. S., Linguistics
LIYANAGAMAGA, A., History
SIRISENA, J. L. G. J., Obstetrics and Gynaecology
THILAK KARIYAWASAM, Pali and Buddhist Studies
VIDANAPATHIRENA, S., Microbiology

ATTACHED INSTITUTES

Postgraduate Institute of Pali and Buddhist Studies: Dir Prof. THILAK KARIYAWASAM.

Postgraduate Institute of Archaeology: Dir S. LAKDUSINGHE.

Institute of Aesthetic Studies: Dir Prof. ANANDA ABEYSIRIWARDENA.

Wickramaarachchi Ayurvedic Institute: Dir Prof. A. S. DISSANAYAKE.

UNIVERSITY OF MORATUWA

Katubedda, Moratuwa

Telephone: 645441

Founded 1966 as Ceylon College of Technology; present name 1978
State control
Language of instruction: English
Academic year: October to September
Chancellor: Dr ARTHUR C. CLARKE
Vice-Chancellor: Prof. SAMARAJEEWA KARUNARATNE
Registrar: K. C. F. SILVA
Librarian: S. RUBASINGHAM

Number of teachers: 180
Number of students: 1,860

Publication: *Development Planning Review* (quarterly).

DEANS

Faculty of Engineering: Prof. L. L. RATNAYAKE
Faculty of Architecture: Prof. L. ALWIS

HEADS OF DEPARTMENTS

Faculty of Engineering:
- Chemical Engineering: Prof. H. D. J. SILVA
- Civil Engineering: Prof. N. A. D. R. DE ALWIS
- Computer Science and Engineering: Dr A. S. INDURUWA
- Electrical Engineering: (vacant)
- Electronic and Telecommunications Engineering: Dr G. S. ATUKORALA
- Materials Engineering: M. PERERA
- Mathematics: Dr M. INDRALINGAM
- Mechanical Engineering: S. R. TITTAGALA
- Mining and Mineral Engineering: S. WEERAWARNAKULA
- Textile Technology: Prof. L. D. FERNANDO
- Technical Studies Division: Dr P. PERERA (acting)

Faculty of Architecture:
- Architecture: Prof. L. BALASURIYA
- Building Economics: D. E. R. C. WEDDIKKARA
- Town and Country Planning: Prof. A. L. S. PERERA

OPEN UNIVERSITY OF SRI LANKA

POB 21, Nawala, Nugegoda

Telephone: (85) 3777
Fax: 436858

Founded 1980
State control
Languages of instruction: Sinhala, Tamil, English
Chancellor: Dr GAMINI COREA
Vice-Chancellor: Prof. N. R. ARTHENAYAKE
Registrar: N. W. S. W. S. DE SILVA
Librarian: S. R. KORALE

Number of teachers: 390
Number of students: 16,763

Publications: monthly newsletters, annual reports, *The Open University Review of Engineering Technology.*

DEANS

Faculty of Humanities and Social Sciences: Prof. G. I. C. GUNAWARDENA
Faculty of Natural Sciences: Prof. J. N. O. FERNANDO
Faculty of Engineering Technology: Dr A. G. K. DE S. ABEYSURIYA

HEADS OF ACADEMIC DIVISIONS

Mathematics: Dr A. S. KARUNANANDA
Textile Technology: G. Y. A. R. JAYANANDA
Management Studies: H. R. GAMAGE
Education: W. A. R. WIJERATNE
Legal Studies: C. E. GUNARATNE
Language Studies: Dr R. RAHEEM
Social Studies: Dr G. AMARASENA
Chemistry: Dr G. M. K. B. GUNAHERATH
Physics: Prof. E. M. JAYASINGHE
Botany: Prof. U. COOMARASWAMY
Zoology: Prof. N. B. RATNASIRI (acting)
Civil Engineering: Dr J. LIYANAGAMA
Electrical and Electronics Engineering: D. L. TALDENA
Mathematics and Philosophy of Engineering: Dr A. P. K. DE ZOYSA
Agricultural and Plantation Engineering: K. D. G. KULATUNGA
Mechanical Engineering: P. D. SARATH CHANDRA

DIRECTORS

Regional Educational Services: Dr T. A. G. GUNASEKERA
Educational Technology: Dr B. WEERASINGHE
Operations: N. JAYASINGHE

UNIVERSITY OF PERADENIYA

University Park, Peradeniya

Telephone and fax: (8) 388151
E-mail: vc@vcoffice.pdn.ac.lk

Founded 1942 by the incorporation of the Ceylon Medical College (f. 1870) and the Ceylon University College (f. 1921); reorganized 1972, present name 1978
State control
Languages of instruction: Sinhala, Tamil, English
Academic year: October to September

Chancellor: Prof. R. G. PANABOKKE
Vice-Chancellor: Prof. R. A. L. H. GUNAWARDANA
Registrar: D. M. W. DISSANAYAKE
Librarian: N. T. S. A. SENADEERA

Number of teachers: 730
Number of students: 9,415

Publications: *Sri Lanka Journal of Humanities, Sri Lanka Journal of Biological Science, Modern Sri Lanka Studies, Sri Lanka Journal of Physical Science.*

DEANS

Faculty of Arts: Prof. K. N. O. DHARMADASA
Faculty of Science: Prof. R. P. GUNAWARDANE
Faculty of Medicine: Prof. A. M. A. N. K. SENANAYAKE
Faculty of Dental Sciences: Dr A. W. RANASINGHE
Faculty of Engineering: Prof. R. J. K. S. K. RANATUNGA
Faculty of Agriculture: Prof. K. G. A. GOONASEKARA
Faculty of Veterinary Medicine and Animal Science: Dr S. MAHALINGAM (acting)

PROFESSORS

Faculty of Arts:

AMARASINGHE, Y. R., Political Science
DHARMADASA, K. N. O., Sinhala
GUNARATNE, R. D., Philosophy
GUNAWARDENA, R. A. L. H., History
HANDURAKANDE, M. R. M., Sanskrit
HEWAVITHARANA, B., Economics
KIRIBAMUNE, S., History
MADDUMA BANDARA, C. M., Geography
MEEGASKUMBURA, P. B., Sinhala
PATHMANATHAN, S., History
PEIRIS, G. H., Geography
PREMASIRI, P. D., Pali and Buddhist Studies
RAJAKARUNA, M. A. D. A., Sinhala
SENEVIRATNE, C. A. D. A., Sinhala
SIRIWEERA, W. I., History
THILLAINATHAN, S., Tamil
WICKRAMASINGHE, A., Geography

Faculty of Science:

ADIKARAM, N. K. B., Botany
AMARASINGHE, F. P., Zoology
BANDARA, B. M. R., Chemistry
BRECKENRIDGE, W. R., Zoology
CAREEM, M. A., Physics
DAHANAYAKE, K. G. A., Geology
DE SILVA, K. H. G. M., Zoology
DE SILVA, P. K., Zoology
DISSANAYAKE, C. B., Geology
DISSANAYAKE, M. A. K. L., Physics
GUNATILLAKE, C. V. S., Botany
GUNATILLAKE, I. A. U. N., Botany
GUNAWARDANE, R. P.
ILLEPERUMA, O. A., Chemistry
KULASOORIYA, S. A., Botany
KUMAR, N. S., Chemistry
KUMAR, V., Chemistry
SENEVIRATNE, H. H. G., Mathematics
TENNAKOON, D. T. B., Chemistry

Faculty of Medicine:

ALUVIHARE, A. P. R., Surgery
BABAPULLE, C. J., Forensic Medicine
GUNARATNE, M., Obstetrics and Gynaecology
MENDIS, P. B. S., Medicine
PERERA, P. A. J., Biochemistry
SENANAYAKE, A. M. A. N. K., Medicine
UDUPIHILLE, M., Physiology
WIJESUNDARA, M. K. DE S., Parasitology
WIKRAMANAYAKE, Mrs E. R., Anatomy

Faculty of Dental Sciences:

AMARATUNGE, N. A. DE S., Oral Surgery
EKANAYAKE, A. N. I., Community Dentistry
MENDIS, B. R. R. N., Oral Pathology

Faculty of Engineering:

EKANAYAKE, E. M. N., Electrical and Electronic Engineering
FERNANDO, W. J. N., Chemical Engineering
GUNAWARDENA, J. A., Computer Science
JAYATILEKE, C. L. V., Mechanical Engineering
RANATUNGA, R. J. K. S. K., Production Engineering
RANAWEERA, M. P., Civil Engineering
SAMUEL, T. D. M. A., Engineering Mathematics
SENEVIRATNE, K. G. H. C. N., Civil Engineering

Faculty of Agriculture:

BANDARA, J. M. R. S., Plant Protection
BOGAHAWATTE, C., Agricultural Economics and Extension
GOONASEKERA, K. G. A., Agricultural Engineering
GUNASENA, H. P. M., Crop Science
RAJAGURU, A. S. B., Animal Science
SAMARAJEEWA, U., Food Science and Technology
SANGAKKARA, U. R., Crop Science

Faculty of Veterinary Medicine and Animal Science:

GUNAWARDENA, Mrs V. K., Veterinary Paraclinical Studies
KURUWITA, V. Y., Veterinary Clinical Studies
WETTIMUNY, S. G. DE S., Veterinary Paraclinical Studies

Postgraduate Institute of Agriculture:
GUNASENA, H. P. M. (Dir)

UNIVERSITY OF RUHUNA

Matara
Telephone: (41) 22681

Founded 1978 as Ruhuna University College, present name 1984
State control
Languages of instruction: Sinhala and English
Academic year: October to September.

Chancellor: Ven. Dr PARAWAHERA PANNANANDA NAYAKA THERO
Vice-Chancellor: Prof. SATYAPALA PINNADUWAGE
Registrar: K. A. RATNATILAKA
Librarian: W. R. G. DE SILVA

Library of 54,500 vols
Number of teachers: 192
Number of students: 3,903

DEANS

Faculty of Science: Dr SANATH HETTIARACHCHI
Faculty of Humanities and Social Sciences: S. WAWWAGE
Faculty of Agriculture: Prof. R. SENARATNE
Faculty of Medicine: Prof. SUSIRITH MENDIS

HEADS OF DEPARTMENTS

Faculty of Agriculture:

GUNAWARDENA, W. W. D. A., Animal Science
PATHIRANA, R., Agricultural Biology
SERASINGHE, P. S. J. W., Crop Science
WEERASINGHE, K. D. N., Agricultural Engineering
WIJERATNE, V., Agricultural Chemistry
WIJERATNE, W. M. M. P., Agricultural Economics

Faculty of Humanities and Social Sciences:

ATAPATTU, D., Economics
EKANAYAKE, P. B., Sinhala
JAYASINGHE, A. K. G., Sociology
NANDAWANSHA, Rev. N., Pali and Buddhist Studies
RAZZAQ, M. M. A., Geography
SILVA, M. U. DE, History and Sociology

Faculty of Medicine:

ARIYANANDA, P. L., Medicine
CHANDRASIRI, N., Forensic Medicine
FERNANDO, A. I., Pharmacology
FONCEKA, P. H. G., Forensic Medicine
GUNAWARDENA, I. M. R., Obstetrics and Gynaecology
JAYAWARDENA, M. K. G. R DE S., Psychiatry
KUMARA, M. M. A J., Surgery
PATHIRANA, C., Biochemistry
SILVA, D. G. H. DE, Paediatrics
SILVA, N. DE, Microbiology
WEERASOORIYA, M. V., Parasitology
WEERASOORIYA, T. R., Anatomy

Faculty of Science:

AMARASINGHE, N. J. DE S., Zoology
CUMARANTUNGE, P. R. T., Fisheries Biology
DHARMARATNE, W. G.D., Physics
JAYAWARDENA, S. C., Computer Science
SILVA, M. P. DE, Botany
WIJAYANAYAKE, R. H., Chemistry
WIJAYASIRI, M. P. A., Mathematics

UNIVERSITY OF SRI JAYEWARDENEPURA

Gangodawila, Nugegoda

Telephone: 852695
Fax: 852604

Founded 1959 as Vidyodaya University of Ceylon; reorganized 1972 as campus of University of Sri Lanka; present name and status 1978

Languages of instruction: Sinhala and English

Chancellor: Dr WIMALA DE SILVA
Vice-Chancellor: Prof. P. WILSON
Registrar: M. ABEYWARDENE
Librarian: (vacant)

Number of teachers: 300
Number of students: 5,000

Publications: *Vidyodaya Journal of Social Sciences, Vidyodaya Journal of Sciences.*

DEANS

Faculty of Arts: Prof. T. KARIYAWASAM
Faculty of Applied Sciences: Prof. R. A. DAYANANDA
Faculty of Management Studies and Commerce: Dr H. M. A HERATH
Faculty of Medical Sciences: Prof. M. T. M. JIFFRY
Faculty of Graduate Studies: Prof. M. M. KARUNANAYAKE

PROFESSORS

ABEYSEKARA, A., Chemistry
ARIYARATNE, S., Sinhala
BAMUNUARACHCHI, A., Chemistry
DAYANANDA, R. A., Statistics
FERNANDO, W. S., Chemistry
JANES, E. R., Biochemistry
JAYATISSA, W. A., Social Statistics
JINADASA, J., Zoology
KARIYAWASAM, T., Sinhala
KARUNANAYAKE, M. M., Geography
MARASINGHE, E. W., Sanskrit
NANDADASA, H. G., Botany
RATNAPALA, B. M., Sociology
TANTRIGODA, D. A., Physics
THILEKERATNE, S., Economics
WARNASOORIYA, N. D.., Paediatrics
WIKRAMAGAMAGE, C., Pali
WITHANA, R. J., Pathology

AFFILIATED INSTITUTE

Post-Graduate Institute of Management: Dir Dr G. NANAYAKKARA.

Colleges

Aquinas College of Higher Studies: Colombo 8; tel. 694014; f. 1954; courses for the external examinations of Universities in Sri Lanka and abroad, for the Aquinas Diplomas and Certificates, and for examinations conducted by professional institutions in Sri Lanka and abroad; faculties of arts and science; institute of technology; school of agriculture; school of English; school of computer studies; school of psychology and counselling; 3,500 students; library of 35,000 vols; experimental farm at Ragama; Rector Rev. Fr W. D. G. CHRISPIN LEO; Registrar M. L. FERNANDO; publ. *Aquinas Journal* (annually).

Ceylon College of Physicians: 6 Wijerama Mawatha, Colombo 7; tel 695418; fax 696632; f. 1967; 340 mems; Pres. Dr NANDA AMARASEKERA; Joint Secs Dr SAMAN GUNATILAKE, Dr SHYAM FERNANDO; publ. *Ceylon College of Physicians Journal* (annually).

In-Service Training Institute: Gannoruwa, POB 21, Peradeniya; tel. (8) 88146; f. 1965; agricultural education and training; 22 staff; Dir HENRY GAMAGE.

Institute of Aesthetic Studies: 21 Albert Crescent, Colombo 7; tel. 686071; fax 686071; f. 1974; attached to University of Kelaniya; dancing, music, art and sculpture; 105 teachers; library of 18,000 vols; Dir Prof. ANANDA ABEYSIRIWARDENA.

Jaffna College: Vaddukoddai; f. 1823, renamed 1872; provides primary, secondary, tertiary and technical education; library of 60,000 vols; Principal G. RAJANAYAGAM; publs *Young Idea, Jaffna College Miscellany*, etc.

Attached Institutes:

Christian Institute for the Study of Religion and Society: Dir C. V. SELLIAH.

Institute of Technology: Vaddukoddai; Dir H. R. G. HOOLE (acting).

Institute of Agriculture: Maruthanamadam; Principal T. KUGATHASAN.

Evelyn Rutnam Institute for Inter-Cultural Studies: University Lane, Thirunelvely; Dir Rev. Dr S. JEBANESAN.

School of Agriculture: Kundasale; tel. (8) 25513; f. 1916; library of 5,000 vols; Principal K. L. JAYATISSA; publs *Annual Magazine of the Students Union, Progress Report* (annual).

Sri Lanka Law College: 244 Hulftsdorp St, Colombo 12; tel. (1) 323759; fax (1) 436040; f. 1900; run by Council of Legal Education; prepares students for admission to the Bar, and conducts the examinations; 1,500 students; library of 11,462 vols; Principal Dr H. J. F. SILVA.

Sri Lanka Technical College: Colombo 10; f. 1893; courses in trades and commerce; 4,525 students; Principal B. P. H. S. MENDIS; Registrar H. V. S. BREMADASA; Librarian A. A. WIJERATNE.

SUDAN

Research Institutes

GENERAL

National Centre for Research: POB 2404, Khartoum; tel. 779040; fax 770701; f. 1991; conducts pure and applied scientific research for the realization of Sudan's economic and social development; incorporates research institutes in renewable energy, environment and natural resources, technology, tropical medicine, medicinal and aromatic plants, economic and social studies, remote sensing, biotechnology and biological engineering.

AGRICULTURE, FISHERIES AND VETERINARY SCIENCE

Agricultural Research Corporation: POB 126, Wad Medani; f. 1904; part of Ministry of Agriculture; includes the following sections: Land and Water, Crop Protection, Forestry, Food, Date Palms; 16 research stations; 3 specialized units (Tissue Culture, Gene Bank, Pesticides Laboratory); library: see Libraries; Dir-Gen. OSMAN AHMED ALI AGEEB.

Animal Production Corporation, Research Division: POB 624, Khartoum; Dir of Research Dr MUHAMMAD EL TAHIR ABDEL RAZIG; Senior Veterinary Research Officer Dr AMIN MAHMOUD EISA.

Forestry Research Centre: POB 7089, Khartoum; f. 1962; Dir Prof. HASSAN A. MUSNAD.

ECONOMICS, LAW AND POLITICS

Sudan Academy for Administrative Sciences: POB 2003, Khartoum; f. 1980; provides post-service training for government officials; conducts studies on current administrative problems; Dir-Gen. Dr OSMAN ELZUBERI AHMED; publ. *Journal of Administration and Development*.

MEDICINE

Sudan Medical Research Laboratories: POB 287, Khartoum; f. 1935; Dir MAHMOUD ABDEL RAHMAN ZIADA.

NATURAL SCIENCES

Physical Sciences

Geological Research Authority: POB 410, Khartoum; tel. (11) 777-939; fax (11) 776-681; f. 1905; attached to Min. of Energy and Mining; applied research and surveys; library: see Libraries; Dir Dr OMER MOHAMER KHEIR.

TECHNOLOGY

Industrial Research and Consultancy Centre: POB 268, Khartoum; tel. 613750; telex 26008; f. 1965 by the Government with assistance from the UN Development Programme; performs tests, investigations, analysis, research and surveys; offers advice and consultation services to industry; Dir Dr MOHAMMED EL-AMIN ABDELRAHMAN.

Libraries and Archives

Juba

University of Juba Library: POB 82, Juba; f. 1977; 38,700 vols, 664 periodicals; acts as a depository library for UN, UNESCO, WHO, FAO and World Bank; Librarian OKENY A. ADALA (acting).

Khartoum

Antiquities Service Library: POB 178, Khartoum; f. 1946; 7,200 vols excluding periodicals; Librarian AWATIF AMIN BEDAWI.

Bakht er Ruda Institute of Education Library: Khartoum; central library, postal library for teachers.

Educational Documentation Centre: POB 2490, Khartoum; tel. 71898; f. 1967; 7 mems; library of 20,000 vols; Dir IBRAHIM M. S. SHATIR; publs *Al-Tawitheq El Tarbawi* (Educational Documentation, 2 a year), annual reports and educational researches.

Flinders Petrie Library: Sudan Antiquities Service, POB 178, Khartoum; f. 1946; 6,000 vols.

Geological Research Authority of the Sudan Library: POB 410, Khartoum; tel. 70934; telex 22168; f. 1904; 2,200 vols, 63 periodicals; special collection: geology of the Sudan; Chief Librarian SALAH ABDEL GADIR MOHMED; publs *Annual Report, Bulletin*.

Khartoum Polytechnic Library: POB 407, Khartoum; f. 1950; 9 libraries on 5 sites: audio visual/education; business studies; fine and applied arts; further education; 2 engineering and science libraries; 3 agricultural libraries; 26,000 vols; Chief Librarian Dr ABBAS EL SHAZALI; publ. *Union Catalogue* (Microfiche, updated every 2 months).

National Chemical Laboratories Library: National Chemical Laboratories, Ministry of Health, POB 287, Khartoum; f. 1904; 2,500 vols, 1,600 pamphlets.

National Records Office: POB 1914, Khartoum; f. 1953; 20,000,000 documents covering Sudanese history since 1870; library of 12,820 vols; Sec.-Gen. Dr M. I. ABU SALEEM; publ. *Majallatal Wathaiq* (Archives Magazine).

Sudan Medical Research Laboratories Library: POB 287, Khartoum; f. 1904 (as part of Wellcome Tropical Research Laboratories); 7,000 pamphlets, 6,000 vols.

University of Khartoum Library: POB 321, Khartoum; f. 1945; contains 209,000 vols and receives 4,200 periodicals and journals; includes a special Sudan and African collection; acts as a depository library for UN, FAO, ILO, WHO and UNESCO publications; both are under the general charge of the University Librarian ABDEL RAHMAN EL NASRI.

Omdurman

Omdurman Central Public Library: Omdurman; f. 1951; 17,650 vols.

Wad Medani

Agricultural Research Corporation Library: POB 126, Wad Medani; tel (51) 42226; fax (51) 43213; e-mail arcsudan@sudanet.net; f. 1931; 15,000 books, 20,000 pamphlets, 250 periodicals; Librarian AHLAM ISMAIL MUSA.

Gezira Research Station Library: Wadi Medani; 6,500 vols on agricultural topics.

Museums and Art Galleries

Khartoum

Sudan National Museum: POB 178, Khartoum; f. 1971; Departments of Antiquities, Ethnology and Sudan Modern History; Dir HASSAN HUSSEIN IDRIS; Curator SIDDIG M. GASM AL-SID; publs *Report on the Antiquities Service and Museums, Kush* (annually), occasional papers, museum pamphlets, etc.

Controls the following museums:

Ethnographical Museum: POB 178, Khartoum; tel. 77052; f. 1956; collection and preservation of ethnographical objects; Curator MOHAMMED HAMED.

Khalifa's House: Omdurman.

Merowe Museum: Merowe, Northern Province; antiquities and general.

Sheikan Museum: El Obeid; archaeological and ethnographic museum.

Sultan Ali Dinar Museum: El Fasher.

Sudan Natural History Museum: University of Khartoum, POB 321, Khartoum; tel. 81873; f. 1920; library of 801 vols; Dir Dr DAWI MUSA HAMED.

Universities

AHFAD UNIVERSITY FOR WOMEN

POB 167, Omdurman

Telephone: 53363

Fax: 452076

Founded 1966, university status 1988

Private control

Languages of instruction: English and Arabic

Academic year: July to April

Chancellor: Prof. YOUSIF BADRI

President: Prof. GASIM BADRI

Vice-President (Academic Affairs): Dr AMNA E. BADRI

Vice-President (Admissions and Student Affairs): Dr AWATIF MUSTAFA

Vice-President (Administrative and Financial Affairs): ABDEL GADIR EL-NASRI

Librarian: IMAN MOHAMMED AHMED

Number of teachers: 150 full-time, 50 part-time

Number of students: 4,300

Library of 1,500 vols

Publications: *Ahfad Journal: Women and Change* (2 a year), *El Nisf el Waeed* (mostly in Arabic, 2 a year).

DEANS

School of Family Sciences: Dr SIDDIGA WASHI

School of Psychology and Pre-school Education: Dr AMNA ABDEL GADIR

School of Organizational Management: Dr ASIA MAKAWI

School of Rural Extension, Education and Development: Dr AMNA RAHHAMA

School of Medicine: Dr FAROUK ABDEL AZIZ

UNIVERSITY OF GEZIRA

POB 20, Wad Medani, 2667 Khartoum

Telex: 22115

Founded 1975
Language of instruction: English
Vice-Chancellor: (vacant)
Secretary-General: Dr MAHMOUD ABDALLA IBRAHIM
Librarian: ABUEL GAITH SANHOURI
Number of teachers: 140
Number of students: 1,000

DEANS

Faculty of Agriculture: Dr OSMAN ALI SID AHMED
Faculty of Economics and Rural Development: Dr EL TAHIR MOHAMED NUR
Faculty of Medicine: Prof. SALAH ELDIN TAHA SALIH
Faculty of Science and Technology: Dr ELNUR KAMAL EL DIN ABU SABAH
Faculty of Education: Prof. ABDEL SALAM MAHMOUD ABDALLA
Graduate Studies and Academic Affairs: ISAM ABDEL RAHMAN AHMED
Preparatory College: Prof. FAYSAL AWAD
Students: Dr ABD EL-MUTAAL GIRSHAB

UNIVERSITY OF JUBA

POB 82, Juba
Telephone: 2113
Founded 1975 with financial help from the EEC; first student admission 1977
Language of instruction: English
Academic year: March to December (two semesters)
Chancellor: (vacant)
Vice-Chancellor: Prof. MAHMOUD MUSA MAHMOUD
Secretary-General: Prof. MOSES MACAR KACUOL
Librarian: ALFRED D. LADO (acting)
Number of teachers: 220
Number of students: 1,200
Publications: *Juvarsity* (monthly), *Library News* (monthly).

DEANS

College of Natural Resources and Environmental Studies: Prof. JOSEPH AWAD MORGAN
College of Social and Economic Studies: Dr VENANSIO TOMBE MULUDIANG
College of Education: Dr ABDEL MONIEM MOHAMED OSMAN
College of Adult Education and Training: GEORGE ISMAIL GABRA
College of Medicine: Dr MATHEW ATEM ADUOL
Dean of Students: AJANG BIOR DUOT

PROFESSORS

College of Medicine:
SUBBARAO, V. V., Physiology
College of Natural Resources and Environmental Studies:
ASHRAF, M., Crop Breeding
MORGAN, J. A., Animal Production
TINGWA, P. O., Horticulture

UNIVERSITY OF KHARTOUM

POB 321, Khartoum
Telephone: 75100
Founded 1956; formerly University College of Khartoum
State control
Language of instruction: Arabic
Academic year: July to April
Chancellor: THE PRESIDENT OF THE REPUBLIC
Vice-Chancellor: Prof. YOUSIF FADL HASSAN
Principal: Prof. SHERIF TAHIR (acting)
Personnel Secretary: Ustaz AHMED A. KHEIRAWI
Librarian: Prof. ABDEL RAHMAN EL NASRI HAMZA
Library: see Libraries
Number of teachers: 685
Number of students: 14,000

DEANS

Faculty of Agriculture: Prof. ELIMAM ELKHIDIR
Faculty of Arts: Prof. HASSAN AHMED
Faculty of Education: Prof. A. GAUU H. A. GANI
Faculty of Economic and Social Studies: Prof. A. HASSAN EL JACK
Faculty of Engineering and Architecture: Dr ABUBA K. A. WAHAB
Faculty of Law: Dr ABDALLA IDRIS
Faculty of Medicine: Prof. A. MUSA
Faculty of Pharmacy: Prof. RIFAAT BUTROS
Faculty of Science: Dr A. OBEID
Faculty of Veterinary Science: Prof. SALAH IMBABI
Graduate College: Dr O. ELAGRA
Institute of African and Asian Studies: Dir Dr SEID HUREIS
Institute of Extra Mural Studies: Dir Dr G. GARANBA
Institute of the Environment: Dir Dr M. D. KHALIFA

NILAYN UNIVERSITY

POB 1055, Khartoum
Founded 1955; until 1993, Cairo University, Khartoum Branch
Secretary-General: (vacant)
Number of teachers: 80
Number of students: 30,000
Faculties of arts, commerce, law, science (mathematics)

ATTACHED INSTITUTE

Higher Institute of Statistics: f. 1969; offers two-year postgraduate course; 10 teachers, 150 students.

OMDURMAN AHLIA UNIVERSITY

POB 786, Omdurman
Telephone: 51489
Founded 1986
President: Prof. ABDUL RAHMAN ABU ZEID
Registrar: Dr MOHAMMED EL HASSAN AHMED
Number of teachers: *c.* 40
Number of students: *c.* 750

HEADS OF DEPARTMENTS

Arabic Language: Prof. FATHI AL MASRI
Management: Dr FAROUK KADUDA
English Language: Dr KHALID HASSEIN AL KID
Secretarial Programme: DYA EL DIN HAYDER
Interior Design: AL FATIH SAAD
Environmental Studies: FATH AL ALIM
Computer Studies: LUBNA MOHAMED IBRHIM
Mathematics and Physics: Dr MOHAMED EL HASSAN SINADA
Library Science: Prof. ABDUL RAHMAN EL NASRI

OMDURMAN ISLAMIC UNIVERSITY

POB 382, Omdurman
Telephone: 54220
Founded 1912; university status 1965
State control
Language of instruction: Arabic
Academic year: July to March
Chairman of University Council: SAYED DAFALLA EL HAG YOUSIF
Vice-Chancellor: (vacant)
Secretary-General: Dr AHMED EL TIGANI OMER
Academy Secretary: AHMED HASSAN IBRAHIM
Librarian: (vacant)
Library of 90,000 vols
Number of teachers: 192
Number of students: 2,010
Publications: *Faculty of Arts Magazine, Faculty of Islamic Studies Magazine.*

DEANS

Faculty of Islamic Studies: Dr MUBARAK IDRIS AHMED
Faculty of Social Studies: Dr YOUSIF HAMID EL A'ALIM
Faculty of Arts: Dr EL TAHIR M. ALI
Girls' College: Dr SOAD EL-FATIH EL-BEDAWI
Dean of Students: Dr ABD ELMONIEM ELGOUSI

SUDAN UNIVERSITY OF SCIENCE AND TECHNOLOGY

POB 407, Khartoum
Telephone: (11) 72508
Founded 1950
State control
Academic year: January to October
Vice-Chancellor: Prof. Dr IZZELDIN MOHAMED OSMAN
Principal: ABDULMONIM AHMAD SALIH

DEANS

College of Agriculture: Dr SADDIG HASSAN AL-SADDIG
College of Commerce: ALI ABDALLA ADAM
College of Engineering: Dr ABDULRAHMAN AL-ZUBAIR
College of Sciences: HAGO AHMAD MOHAMED
College of Radiography and Radiotherapy: ALI A. EL-HAG
College of Music and Drama: Dr AHMAD ABU-LAAL
College of Fine and Applied Arts: MOHAMMED ELAMIN ALI
College of Education: ABDULATIF MOHAMED
College of Further Education: (vacant)

Colleges and Institutes

Faculty of Hygiene and Environmental Studies: POB 205, Khartoum; tel. 72690; f. 1933; 26 staff; 4 depts; awards BSc and MSc in Environmental Health; Librarian M. MOHD. SALIH; Dean B. M. EL-HASSAN.

HEADS OF DEPARTMENTS

Epidemiology and Bio-statistics: Dr A. TIGANI
Environmental Health: Dr M. A. H. ALLOBA
Health Education: MAHMOUD A. RAHMAN
Nutrition and Food Hygiene: ALI NASIR
Field Training Unit: AHMED ABDALLA

Khartoum Nursing College: POB 1063, Khartoum; 3-year diploma course; Principal A. M. OSMAN.

Yambio Institute of Agriculture: Sud 82/002, c/o UNDP POB 913, Khartoum; f. 1972; library of 5,000 vols; 15 staff; 130 students; two-year diploma courses; Principal CHRISTOPHER LADO GALE.

SURINAME

Research Institutes

AGRICULTURE, FISHERIES AND VETERINARY SCIENCE

Centre for Agricultural Research in Suriname: POB 1914, Paramaribo; tel. 60244; telex 311; f. 1965; a branch of the University of Suriname; research in tropical agriculture; Dir R. E. SWEEB; publ. *Celos Bulletins*.

Landbouwproefstation (Agricultural Experiment Station): POB 160, Paramaribo; tel. 472442; fax 478986; f. 1903; attached to the Min. of Agriculture, Animal Husbandry and Fisheries; library of 28,502 vols, including bound periodicals and pamphlets; Dir Drs ELVIS GOEDHART (acting); publs *Annual Report, Suriname Agriculture* (2 to 3 a year), Bulletins (irregular).

TECHNOLOGY

Geologisch Mijnbouwkundige Dienst (Geological Mining Service): 2–6 Kleine Waterstraat, Paramaribo; tel. 75941; telex 364; f. 1943; library of 20,000 vols; Dir Dr R. L. VERWEY; publs contributions in *Mededelingen*, geological maps.

Libraries and Archives

Paramaribo

Bibliotheek van het Cultureel Centrum Suriname (Library of the Suriname Cultural Centre): POB 1241, Paramaribo; tel. 472369; fax 473903; f. 1947; library of 500,000 vols; 7 branches, 1 book-mobile; Librarian G. R. KOORNAAR.

Museums and Art Galleries

Paramaribo

Stichting Surinaams Museum: POB 2306, Abraham Crijnssenweg 1, Paramaribo; tel. 425871; fax 425881; f. 1947; library of 10,000 vols; archaeology, art, history, ethnology; Dir Drs J. H. J. VAN PUTTEN; publ. *Mededelingen* (every 6 months).

University

UNIVERSITEIT VAN SURINAME

Universiteitscomplex Leysweg 26, POB 9212, Paramaribo

Telephone: 465558
Fax: 462291

Founded 1968
Language of instruction: Dutch

President: Dr W. R. ROSEVAL
Vice-President: Dr J. SIETARAM
Secretary: Y. BAAL

Number of teachers: 207
Number of students: 2,585

DEANS

Faculty of Social Sciences: Dr J. BREEVELD
Faculty of Medicine: Prof. Dr M. A. VREDE
Faculty of Technology: Ir D. WIP

SWAZILAND

Learned Societies

GENERAL

Royal Swaziland Society of Science and Technology: c/o The University, Private Bag, Kwaluseni; tel. 84011; telex 2087; fax 85276; f. 1977 to promote science and technology and relevant research; organizes meetings, seminars, etc.; 100 mems; Pres. Prof. L. P. MAKHUBU; Sec. R. MARTIN; publ. *Swaziland Journal of Science and Technology* (2 a year).

BIBLIOGRAPHY, LIBRARY SCIENCE AND MUSEOLOGY

Swaziland Library Association: POB 2309, Mbabane; tel. (c/o British Council) 43101; fax 42641; f. 1984; 120 mems; Chair. L. DLAMINI; Sec. P. MUSWAZI; publs *SWALA Journal, SWALA Newsletter.*

FINE AND PERFORMING ARTS

Swaziland Art Society: POB 812, Mbabane; f. 1970; classes, workshops, exhibitions, films, discussions, etc.; 60 mems; Chair. LIZ STIRLING.

Research Institutes

AGRICULTURE, FISHERIES AND VETERINARY SCIENCE

Lowveld Experiment Station: POB 11, Matata; tel. 36311; telex 2259; fax 36450; f. 1964; agricultural research, cotton breeding, cotton entomology; Chief Research Officer P. MKHATSHWA.

Malkerns Research Station: POB 4, Malkerns; f. 1959; general research on crops, vegetables, fruits, pastures and farming systems research; 14 research sections; library of 5,000 vols; Chief Research Officer P. D. MKHATSHWA.

Mpisi Cattle Breeding Experimental Station: Mpisi; to improve indigenous Nguni cattle; to provide multiplication studs of Brahman, Simmentaler and Friesland cattle for beef, milk and cross breeding; Dir R. A. JOHN; Man. I. A. MORLEY HEWITT.

TECHNOLOGY

Geological Survey and Mines Department: POB 9, Mbabane; f. 1944; activities: mapping of the territory (published at a scale of 1:25,000 and 1:50,000), the investigation of mineral occurrences by prospecting, detailed mapping and diamond drilling, mine and quarry inspections, control of explosives and prospecting; 13 mems; small library; Dir A. S. DLAMINI; publs *Annual Reports, Bulletins*.

Libraries and Archives

Mbabane

Swaziland National Archives: POB 946, Mbabane; tel. 61276; fax 61241; f. 1970; government records from 1880s to the present; reference library of *c.* 3,200 vols; collection of historical photographs, newspapers, maps, coins, stamps; Dir N. N. TWALA.

Swaziland National Library Service: POB 1461, Mbabane; tel. 42633; telex 2270; fax 43863; f. 1971; operates a public library service throughout the country with branch libraries at Manzini, Mpaka, Lomahasha, Nhlangano, Siteki, Pigg's Peak, Big Bend, Bhunya, Tshaneni, Mankayana, Lavumisa, Hlatikulu and Mhlume; mobile library visits; libraries at secondary schools; 80,000 vols, 150 periodicals; a national library was est. in 1986 which will eventually function as the focal point in Swaziland's documentation and information system; Dir D. J. KUNENE; publs *Annual Report, Index to Swaziland Collection* (occasional), *Accessions List* (irregular).

Museums and Art Galleries

Lobamba

Swaziland National Museum: POB 100, Lobamba; tel. 61178; f. 1972, under the patronage of the Swaziland National Trust Commission; museum with extra-mural functions, giving information about Swazi culture as well as other Southern African Bantu groups; reference library; Curator ROSEMARY ANDRADE; publs *Annual Report, Museum Occasional Paper.*

University

UNIVERSITY OF SWAZILAND

Private Bag 4, Kwaluseni
Telephone: 84011
Telex: 2087
Fax: 85276

Founded 1964 as part of University of Botswana, Lesotho and Swaziland, present name 1982

Language of instruction: English
Academic year: August to May

Chancellor: HM King MSWATI III
Vice-Chancellor: Prof. L. P. MAKHUBU
Pro Vice-Chancellor: Prof. B. M. DLAMINI
Registrar: Dr C. W. S. SUKATI
Librarian: M. R. MAVUSO

Number of teachers: 250
Number of students: 3,428

Publications: *Swaziland National Bibliography* (irregular), *Serials in Swaziland University Libraries* (irregular), *University Calendar* (annually), *UNISWA Research Journal, University of Swaziland Staff Directory,* Vice-Chancellor's report (annually), *UNISWA Newsletter* (irregular).

DEANS

Faculty of Agriculture: Dr G. N. SHONGWE
Faculty of Commerce: Prof. M. A. KHAN
Faculty of Education: Dr T. D. MKHATSHWA
Faculty of Humanities: Dr H. S. SIMELANE
Faculty of Social Sciences: Prof. J. K. NGWISHA
Faculty of Science: Prof. V. S. B. MTETWA
Faculty of Postgraduate Studies: Prof. E. C. L. KUNENE
Faculty of Heath Sciences: M. MATHUNJWA

There are also an Institute of Distance Education and a Division of Extra Mural Services.

HEADS OF DEPARTMENTS

Faculty of Agriculture:
- Home Economics: Dr T. SIBIYA
- Agricultural Extension and Education: Dr C. B. MNDEBELE
- Agricultural Economics and Management: Dr P. M. DUAMINI
- Animal Production and Health: Dr B. J. DLAMINI
- Crop Production: Prof. O. T. EDJE
- Land Use and Mechanization: Dr A. M. MAMYATSI

Faculty of Commerce:
- Accountancy: C. A. KYARA
- Business Administration: P. N. JOUBERT

Faculty of Education:
- Curriculum and Teaching: Dr S. E. ZWANE
- Educational Foundations and Management: Dr A. M. NXUMALO
- In-Service Education: Dr S. E. MAMYATSI
- Primary Education: Dr N. S. DLAMINI

Faculty of Humanities:
- African Languages and Literature: Prof. W. D. KAMERA
- English Language and Literature: Dr L. OYEGOKE
- History: Dr KANDUZA
- Theology and Religious Studies: Dr H. L. NDLOVU

Faculty of Social Sciences:
- Economics: V. M. SITHOLE
- Law: N. A. HLATSHWAYO
- Political and Administrative Studies: Dr P. Q. MAGAGULA
- Sociology: P. K. KHUMALO
- Statistics and Demography: Dr S. S. DLAMINI

Faculty of Science:
- Biological Sciences: Dr I. S. KUMENE
- Chemistry: Dr J. THWALA
- Computer Studies: G. K. BOATENG
- Mathematics: Dr P. A. PHIRI
- Geography and Environmental Planning: Dr N. O. SIMELANE
- Physics and Electronic Engineering: Dr M. D. DLAMINI

Faculty of Health Science:
- General Nursing: Dr M. A. SUKATI
- Environmental Health Science: S. V. DLAMINI

Colleges

Swaziland College of Technology: POB 69, Mbabane: tel. 42681; fax 44521; f. 1946 as Trade School, present name 1968; awards the following qualifications: mechanical engineering technician certificate, electrical engineering, automotive engineering, diploma in construction studies, hotel and catering certificate, association of accounting technician, secretarial studies certificate, diploma in technical teaching and diploma in commercial teaching; 129 staff; library of 13,000 vols; Prin. L. B. LUKHELE; Registrar M. S. DLODLO.

Swaziland Institute of Management and Public Administration: POB 495, Mbabane; tel. 42981; fax 44689; f. 1965; 12 full-time, 15 part-time teachers; 400 students; Dir M. H. KHOZA.

SWEDEN

Learned Societies

GENERAL

Kungl. Humanistiska Vetenskaps-Samfundet i Uppsala (Royal Society of Humanities at Uppsala): c/o Prof. Bo Utas, Dept of Asian and African Languages, Box 513, 751 20 Uppsala; f. 1889 to promote the study of humanities; 70 Swedish, 40 foreign mems; Pres. Prof. HARRY LENHAMMAR; Sec. Prof. BO UTAS; publs *Skrifter* (Acta), *Årsbok* (Yearbook, available for exchange through the University Library, Uppsala (*q.v.*)).

Kungl. Vetenskaps- och Vitterhets-Samhället i Göteborg (Göteborg Royal Society of Arts and Sciences): c/o Klassiska institutionen, Göteborg University, Box 200, 405 30 Göteborg; f. 1778; 218 Swedish, 36 foreign mems; Sec. Prof. BIRGER KARLSSON; publs *Acta Regiae Societatis Scientiarum et Litterarum Gothoburgensis* (monographs), *Årsbok*.

Kungl. Vetenskapsakademien (Royal Academy of Sciences): Box 50005, 104 05 Stockholm; tel. (8) 673-95-00; fax (8) 15-56-70; e-mail rsas@kva.se; f. 1739; sections of Mathematics (Chair. H. WALLIN), Astronomy and Space Sciences (Chair. B. GUSTAFSSON), Physics (Chair. P. CARLSON), Chemistry (Chair. B. ANDERSSON), Geosciences (Chair. B. BERGLUND), Biosciences (Chair. B. DANEHOLT), Medical Sciences (Chair. A. BJÖRKLUND), Engineering Sciences (Chair. J. CARLSSON), Economics and Social Sciences (Chair. G. LINDENCRONA), Humanistic and Other Sciences and for Distinguished Services to Scientific Research (Chair. B. ARRHENIUS); 340 Swedish mems, 161 foreign mems; attached research institutes: see Research Institutes; library: see Libraries and Archives; Pres. Prof. JAN S. NILSSON; Sec.-Gen. Prof. ERLING NORRBY; publs *Acta Mathematica*, *Acta Zoologica*, *Arkiv för Matematik*, *Physica Scripta*, *Zoologica Scripta*, *Ambio*, *Documenta*.

Kungl. Vetenskaps-Societeten i Uppsala (Royal Society of Sciences of Uppsala): St Larsgatan 1, 753 10 Uppsala; f. 1710, charter 1728; to promote research principally in mathematics, natural sciences, medicine, Swedish antiquities and topography, by (a) publishing works of scholarship, (b) awarding grants, (c) collecting and making available relevant publications, (d) lectures; mems in four sections: physics and mathematics (40 national, 40 foreign), natural history and medicine (50 national, 40 foreign), history and archaeology (20 national, 10 foreign), technology and economics (20 national, 10 foreign); library of 600 periodicals; Pres. Prof. MÅRTEN CARLSSON; Sec. Prof. LARS-OLOF SUNDELÖF; publs *Nova Acta*, *Årsbok*.

Kungl. Vitterhets Historie och Antikvitets Akademien (Royal Academy of Letters, History and Antiquities): Box 5622, 114 86 Stockholm; tel. (8) 440-42-80; fax (8) 440-42-90; f. 1753; humanities, social sciences, religion, law; 126 Swedish mems, 44 foreign mems; library: see Libraries and Archives; Pres. Prof. INGE JONSSON; Sec.-Gen. Dr ULF ERIK HAGBERG; publs *Fornvännen* (journal), *Handlingar* (acta), *Arkiv* (archives).

Svenska Institutet (The Swedish Institute): Box 7434, S-103 91 Stockholm; tel. 789-20-00; telex 10025; fax (8) 20-72-48; f. 1945; object: to increase knowledge about Swedish society and culture abroad, to promote cultural and informational exchange with other countries, and to contribute to increased international co-operation in the fields of education and research; administers scholarships and grants for study or research in Sweden; Pres. LARS ENGQVIST; Dir PER SÖRBOM.

AGRICULTURE, FISHERIES AND VETERINARY SCIENCE

Kungl. Skogs- och Lantbruksakademien (Royal Swedish Academy of Agriculture and Forestry): Drottninggatan 95B, Box 6806, 113 86 Stockholm; tel. (8) 73-60-900; fax (8) 322 130; f. 1811 to apply science to the development and improvement of agriculture and forestry; 15 hon., 180 working mems, 75 foreign mems; library: see Libraries; Pres. INGEMAR ÖHRN; Deputy Perm. Sec. Prof. SVEN-UNO SKARP; publs *Kungl. Skogs och Lantbruksakademiens Tidskrift* (quarterly), *Acta Agriculturae Scandinavica* (quarterly), *Scandinavian Journal of Forest Research* (quarterly).

ARCHITECTURE AND TOWN PLANNING

Svenska Arkitekters Riksförbund (National Assn of Swedish Architects): Norrlandsgatan 18, 111 43 Stockholm; tel. (8) 679-27-60; fax (8) 611-49-30; f. 1936; objects are to promote the standing of architects in Sweden and maintain the people's right to a good environment by promoting good architecture and planning; 4,000 mems; Chair. PIETRO RAFFONE; Sec.-Gen. KATARINA NILSSON; publ. *Arkitekt Tidningen* (monthly).

Sveriges Arkitekt- och Ingenjörsföretags Förening (Swedish Federation of Architects and Consulting Engineers): Norrlandsgatan 11, Box 7394, 103 91 Stockholm; f. 1910; mems: 400 firms; Pres. LARS HANSSON; Man. Dir MÅRTEN LINDSTRÖM.

BIBLIOGRAPHY, LIBRARY SCIENCE AND MUSEOLOGY

Svenska Bibliotekariesamfundet (Swedish Assn of University and Research Librarians): C/o Vitterhetsakademiens bibliotek, Box 5405, 114 84 Stockholm; tel. (8) 783-93-25; fax (8) 663-35-28; f. 1921; Pres. KERSTIN ASSARSSON-RIZZI; Sec. CHRISTINA FRISTRÖM (Lunds universitetsbibliotek); publs *Svenska bibliotekariesamfundets skriftserie*, *Bibliotekariesamfundet meddelar*.

ECONOMICS, LAW AND POLITICS

Centre for the Study of International Relations: Döbelnsgatan 81, Box 19112, S-104 32 Stockholm 19; tel. (8) 612-07-30; telex 12453; fax (8) 612-05-92; f. 1971; studies social sciences, international politics, law and economy; independent of any political party; organizes lectures and conferences, research seminars; library; Chair. HRH Prince SIGVARD BERNADOTTE; Pres. CLÄES PALME; Vice-Pres. and Dir Prof. Dr RICHARD K. T. HSIEH; Secs Prof. Dr JACOB W. F. SUNDBERG, Prof. Dr LARS HJERNER; publs *Review*, CSIR courses and lecture series.

International Law Association, Swedish Branch: POB 1711, 111 87 Stockholm; tel. (8) 613-55-00; fax (8) 613-55-01; f. 1922; Pres. OVE BRING; Hon. Sec. KAJ HOBÉR.

Kungl. Krigsvetenskapsakademien (Royal Swedish Academy of War Sciences): POB 5435, 114 84 Stockholm; e-mail kkrva@ebox.tninet.se; f. 1796 to promote military sciences, including civil defence, economic defence and psychological defence, security and defence policy; 380 mems; Pres. Vice-Adm. PETER NORDBECK; Sec. Major Gen. LARS ANDERSSON; publ. *Handlingar och Tidskrift* (every 2 months).

Nationalekonomiska Föreningen (Swedish Economic Association): C/o Dept of Economics, Stockholm University, 106 91 Stockholm; tel. (8) 16-30-48; fax (8) 16-14-25; f. 1877; study of economics; 1,200 mems; Chair. ULF DAHLSITEN; Sec. MICHAEL LUNDHOLM; publ. *Ekonomisk Debatt* (8 a year).

Utrikespolitiska Institutet (Swedish Institute of International Affairs): Box 1253, S-111 82 Stockholm; tel. (8) 23-40-60; fax (8) 20-10-49; e-mail siia@ui.se; f. 1938; object: to improve public understanding of current international affairs; research dept; library of 40,000 vols, 400 periodicals; Pres. LEIF LEIFLAND; Man. Dir Dr ANDERS MELLBOURN; publs *Världspolitikens dagsfrågor*, *Internationella studier*, *Länder i fickformat*, *Världens Fakta*, *Conference Papers*, *Research Report*, monograph series, etc.

EDUCATION

Högskoleverket (National Agency for Higher Education): Birger Jarlsgatan 43, POB 7851, 103 99 Stockholm; tel. (8) 453-70-00; fax (8) 453-70-50; govt agency in charge of management of the higher education system; Dir-Gen. AGNETA BLADH; Head of Information ÅSA KLEVARD.

Rådet för grundläggande högskoleutbildning (Council for the Renewal of Undergraduate Education): Box 7285, 103 89 Stockholm; tel. (8) 453-71-61; fax (8) 453-71-92; e-mail hgur@hsv.se; dept of National Agency for Higher Education; promotes and supports efforts to develop the quality and pedagogical renewal of undergraduate education and administers funds provided by the Swedish Parliament for experiments in undergraduate education; Chair. Prof. LARS HAIKOLA; Sec. Dr HANS JALLING.

Sveriges universitets- och högskoleförbund (Swedish Association of Universities and University Colleges): Rådmansgaton 72, 113 60 Stockholm; f. 1995; 37 mems; Chair. Prof. GUSTAF LINDENCRONA; Sec.-Gen. LARS EKHOLM.

FINE AND PERFORMING ARTS

Föreningen Svenska Tonsättare (Society of Swedish Composers): POB 27-327, 102 54 Stockholm; tel. (8) 783-88-00; telex 15591; fax (8) 783-95-40; f. 1918; 215 mems; Pres. THOMAS JENNEFELT.

Fylkingen (Society of Contemporary Music and Intermedia Art): Münchenbryggeriet, Söder Mälarstrand 27, 117 25 Stockholm; POB 4269, 102 66 Stockholm; tel. (8) 84-54-43; fax (8) 669-38-68; f. 1933; new music and intermedia art; 188 mems; Chair. KENT TANKRED; Producer MATS LINDSTRÖM.

Kungl. Akademien för de fria Konsterna (Royal Academy of Fine Arts): Fredsgatan 12, Box 16317, 103 26 Stockholm; tel. (8) 23-29-45; fax (8) 790-59-24; f. 1735 to promote the development of painting, sculpture, architecture and allied arts; 99 Swedish mems, 28 foreign mems, 20 hon. mems; library of 40,000 vols; Pres. HENRY MONTGOMERY; Sec. BO GRANDIEN; publ. *Meddelanden*.

Kungl. Musikaliska Akademien (Royal Swedish Academy of Music): Blasieholmstorg 8, 111 48 Stockholm; tel. (8) 407-18-00; fax (8) 611-87-18; e-mail adm@musakad.se; f. 1771 for the promotion and protection of the art and science of music; 170 mems; Pres. DANIEL BÖRTZ; Sec. BENGT HOLMSTRAND; publs *Årsskrift* (year book), *Musica Sveciae* (record anthology), etc.

Musikaliska Konstföreningen (Musical Art Association): Blasieholmstorg 8, S-111 48, Stockholm; f. 1859 for the publication of Swedish music; Chair. I. MILVEDEN; Sec. G. PERCY.

Statens kulturråd (Swedish National Council for Cultural Affairs): Box 7843, 103 98 Stockholm; tel. (8) 679-72-60; fax (8) 611-13-49; f. 1974 as funding, advisory and investigatory body concerning state grants for cultural purposes; covers theatre, dance, music, literature, cultural journals, public libraries, art, museums and exhibitions; Chair. BRITT THEORIN; Dir GÖRAN LANNEGREN; publ. *Kulturrådet*.

Svensk Form (Swedish Society of Crafts and Design): Renstiernas gata 12, 116 28, Stockholm; tel. (8) 644-33-03; fax (8) 644-22-85; f. 1845; 7,000 mems; Chair. RAGNE BOGHOLT; Man.-Dir JOHAN HULDT; publ. *Form* (every 2 months).

Svenska samfundet för musikforskning (Swedish Society for Musicology): Box 7448, 103 91 Stockholm; f. 1919; 325 mems; Pres. GUNNAR TERNHAG; Sec. CATHARINA DYRSSEN; publs *Svensk Tidskrift för Musikforskning* (Swedish Journal of Musicology, annually), *Monumenta Musicae Sveciae*.

Sveriges Allmänna Konstförening (Swedish General Art Asscn): Rödbodtorget 2, POB 16260, 103 24 Stockholm; f. 1832; 13,000 mems; Pres. JAN-ERIK WIKSTRÖM; Dir JAN MANKER; publ. *Sveriges Allmänna Konstförenings årspublikation* (Swedish General Art Association's annual publication).

HISTORY, GEOGRAPHY AND ARCHAEOLOGY

Kartografiska Sällskapet (Swedish Cartographic Society): c/o Statens Lantmäteriverk, 801 82 Gävle; f. 1908; 1,900 mems; Pres. PETER NYHLÉN; Sec. PATRIK OTTOSON; publs *Kartbladet* (quarterly), *Sveriges Kartläggning* (mapping of Sweden, every 10 years).

Svenska Museiföreningen (Swedish Museums Asscn): Box 24051, 104 50 Stockholm; tel. (8) 660-60-34; fax (8) 660-60-34; f. 1906; association of Swedish museums and members of staff; debates, etc., concerning practical development and museum policy issues; 1,150 mems, 200 institutional mems; Pres. MARGITA BJÖRKLUND; Sec.-Gen. GUNILLA SUNDBLAD; publ. *Svenska Museer* (quarterly).

Svenska Sällskapet för Antropologi och Geografi (Swedish Society for Anthropology and Geography): Naturgeografiska Institutionen, Stockholms Universitet, 106 91 Stockholm; f. 1880; aims: to forward the development of anthropology and geography in Sweden, to communicate with foreign societies with the same objectives, and to support investigations into anthropology and geography; 900 mems; library of 10,000 vols; Pres. THOMAS LUNDÉN; Sec. GUNHILD ROSQVIST; publs *Geografiska Annaler* (series A and B), *Ymer*.

LANGUAGE AND LITERATURE

Samfundet de Nio (Nine Swedish Authors' Society): c/o Anders Öhman, Smålandsgatan 20, 111 46 Stockholm; f. 1913; Pres. INGE JONSSON (professor); Sec. ANDERS R. ÖHMAN (lawyer); mems NINA BURTON (novelist), GUNNAR HARDING (poet and essayist), KERSTIN EKMAN (novelist), ULLA ISAKSSON (novelist), AGNETA PLEIJEL (essayist and novelist), JOHAN SVEDJEDAL (professor), NIKLAS RÅDSTRÖM (novelist).

Svenska Akademien (Swedish Academy): Box 2118, 103 13 Stockholm; tel. (8) 10-65-24; fax (8) 24-42-25; e-mail sekretariat@svenskaakademien.se; f. 1786; Swedish language and literature; awards Nobel Prize for Literature; 18 mems; library: see Libraries and Archives; Permanent Sec. Prof. STURE ALLÉN; publs *Svenska Akademiens Handlingar* (annually), *Artes* (jointly with Acads of Fine Arts and Music and with Soc. of Nine, quarterly).

Svenska PEN-klubben (International PEN, Swedish Centre): c/o Wahlström & Widstrand, POB 5587, 114 85 Stockholm; f. 1922; 500 mems; Pres. MONICA NAGLER; Sec. JONAS MODIG.

Sveriges Författarförbund (The Swedish Writers' Union): Box 3157, Drottninggatan 88B, 103 63 Stockholm; tel. (8) 545-132-00; fax (8) 545-132-10; e-mail sff@forfattarfordundet.se; f. 1893 to protect the intellectual and economic interests of writers and translators; 2,300 mems; Pres. META O. HOSSON; Dir JOHN ERIK FORSLUND; publ. *Författaren*.

MEDICINE

Socialstyrelsen (National Board of Health and Welfare): S-106 30 Stockholm; tel. (8) 783-30-00; telex 16773; fax (8) 783-32-52; public health, medical and social services administration; f. 1663; Dir-Gen. CLAES ÖRTENDAHL; publs *Cancer Incidence in Sweden* (Report of the Board's Cancer Registry), *Nytt fran Socialstyrelsen* (bulletins by fax).

Svenska Läkaresällskapet (Swedish Society of Medicine): Box 738, S-101 35 Stockholm; tel. (8) 440-88-60; fax (8) 440-88-99; f. 1807; *c.* 18,000 mems; Pres. Prof. RAGNAR NORRBY; Exec. Dir LARS ÅKE PELLBORN; Sec. CHRISTER EDLING; publ. *Svenska Läkaresällskapets Handlingar Hygiea*.

NATURAL SCIENCES

General

Wenner-Gren Foundation (WGS): Sveavägen 166, S-113 46 Stockholm; f. 1962; residence and meeting place for foreign and visiting scientists; Pres. of the Board Dr JAN WALLANDER; Sec. Prof. TORVARD LAURENT; publ. *The Wenner-Gren Center International Symposium Series*.

Biological Sciences

Kungl. Fysiografiska Sällskapet i Lund (Royal Physiographical Society of Lund): Stortoget 6, 22223 Lund; tel. (46) 13-25-28; telex 33533; fax (46) 13-19-44; f. 1772; science, medicine and technology; 370 mems; 75 foreign correspondents; Pres. Prof. BIRGER BERGK; Sec. Prof. ROLF ELOFSSON; publ. *Årsbok* (2 a year).

Naturskyddsföreningen (Society for Nature Conservation): Box 4625, 116 91 Stockholm; f. 1909; mem of IUCN; 176,000 mems; Sec. Gen. ULRIKA RASMUSON; publs *Sveriges Natur* (every 2 months), a yearbook.

Mathematical Sciences

Lunds Matematiska Sällskap (Lund Mathematical Society): C/o Matematiska Institutionen, Box 118, 221 00 Lund; fax (46) 222-40-10; f. 1923; 150 mems; Pres. Prof. ANDERS MELIN; Sec. and Treas. ADAM JONSSON.

Matematiska Föreningen, Universitetet, Uppsala (Mathematical Society): Department of Mathematics, Uppsala University, POB 480, 75106 Uppsala; tel. (18) 18-32-00; fax (18) 18-32-01; f. 1853; 50 mems; Pres. WARWICK TUCKER; Sec. JERK MATERO.

Statistiska Föreningen (Statistical Society): Statistiska Centralbyrån, POB 24300, 104 51 Stockholm; f. 1901; forms a link between practising statisticians and laymen interested in statistics, and by means of lectures, discussions and reports contributes to the analysis of problems in this field of science; 600 mems; Pres. BJÖRN HÅRSMAN; Sec. EIWOR HÖGLUND DÁVILA.

Svenska Matematikersamfundet (Swedish Mathematical Society): Luleå University of Technology, Dept of Mathematics, 971 87 Luleå; tel. (920) 911-17; fax (920) 910-73; f. 1950; 540 mems; Chair. Prof. LARS-ERIK PERSSON; Sec. YUANJI CHENG; publs *Nordisk Matematisk Tidskrift*, *Mathematica Scandinavia* (with other Scandinavian Mathematical Societies).

Physical Sciences

Geologiska Föreningen (Geological Society of Sweden): C/o SGU, POB 670, 751 28 Uppsala; tel. (18) 17-92-76; fax (18) 51-67-67; e-mail gff@sgu.se; f. 1871; 650 mems; Pres. JAN BERGSTRÖM; Sec. PER SANDGREN; publs *GFF* (in English, 4 a year), *Geologiskt forum* (in Swedish, 4 a year).

Svenska Fysikersamfundet (Swedish Physical Society): Manne Siegbahn Laboratory, Stockholm University, Frescativ 24, 104 05 Stockholm; tel. (8) 16-10-21; fax (8) 15-86-74; e-mail sfs@atom.msi.se; f. 1920; 900 mems; Chair. Dr ANDERS BÁRÁNY; Secs. Dr PETER GLANS, Dr LOTTEN HÄGG; publs *Kosmos* (annually), *Fysikaktuellt* (quarterly).

Svenska Geofysiska Föreningen (Swedish Geophysical Society): ABEM Instrument AB, Box 20086, 161 02 Bromma; tel. (8) 764-60-60; fax (8) 28-11-09; f. 1920; 200 mems; Pres. PETER LUNDBERG; Sec. JOHAN NISSEN; publ. *Tellus*.

RELIGION, SOCIOLOGY AND ANTHROPOLOGY

Kungl. Gustav Adolfs Akademien för svensk folkkultur (Royal Gustavus Adolphus Academy for Swedish Folk Culture): Klostergatan 2, 753 21 Uppsala; tel. (18) 548783; fax (18) 548783; e-mail gustav.adolfs.akademien@mbox200.swipnet.se; f. 1932; 212 mems (including honorary); Pres. Prof. CARL GÖRAN ANDRÆ; Vice-Pres. Prof. NILS-ARVID BRINGÉUS; Sec. Prof. LENNART ELMEVIK; publs *Saga och Sed*, *Arv. Nordic Yearbook of Folklore*, *Ethnologia Scandinavica*, *Namn och Bygd*, *Svenska Landsmärk och Svenskt Folkliv* (annually), *Acta*.

TECHNOLOGY

Kungl. Ingenjörsvetenskapsakademien (Royal Swedish Academy of Engineering Sciences): Box 5073, S-102 42 Stockholm; tel. (8) 791-29-00; fax (8) 611-56-23; e-mail info@iva.se; f. 1919 to promote engineering and economic science; acts as a clearing house for scientific information; establishes contacts with foreign research organizations by means of lectures and conferences, trade research organizations and research agreements with East European countries, China and the Republic of Korea; 720 Swedish mems, 240 foreign or corresponding mems; Dir Prof. KURT ÖSTLUND; publs *Meddelanden*, *Rapporter*, *IVA-Aktuellt*, *IVA Newsletter* (irregular bulletins).

Sveriges Civilingenjörsförbund (CF) (Swedish Association of Graduate Engineers): Malmskillnadsgatan 48, Box 1419, S-111 84 Stockholm; tel. (8) 61-38-000; f. 1861, present name 1981; 74,000 mems; Pres. GERHARD

RAUNIO; Man. Dir JÖRAN TJERNELL; publs *Civilingenjören* (9 a year), *Ny Teknik-Teknisk Tidskrift* (weekly).

Research Institutes

AGRICULTURE, FISHERIES AND VETERINARY SCIENCE

Jordbrukstekniska institutet (Swedish Institute of Agricultural Engineering): POB 7033, S-750 07 Uppsala; tel. (18) 30-33-00; fax (18) 30-09-56; f. 1945; library of 3,000 vols; Dir BJÖRN SUNDELL; publs *Meddelanden* (bulletins on the various investigations, quarterly), *Agricultural Technology* (5 a year), *JTI-Reports* (irregular).

Skogs- och jordbrukets forskningsråd (Swedish Council for Forestry and Agricultural Research): POB 6488, 113 82 Stockholm; address for visitors: Odengatan 61, 11322 Stockholm; tel. (8) 736-09-10; telex 13433; fax (8) 33-29-15; f. 1945 as the Swedish Agricultural Research Council, re-named 1981; to promote scientific research in natural resources, especially agriculture, forestry and fisheries; Pres. HANS EKELUND; Sec.-Gen. Prof. JAN-ERIK HÄLLGREN.

Statens veterinärmedicinska anstalt (National Veterinary Institute): POB 7073, S-750 07 Uppsala; tel. (18) 67-40-00; fax (18) 30-91-62; e-mail lars-erik.edqvist@sva.se; f. 1911; research, diagnostic work, consultative work concerning control and prophylaxis of animal diseases; national veterinary laboratory; organization: central laboratory, epizootiology unit, animal diseases specialists unit, administration; library of 27,000 vols; Dir-Gen. L.-E. EDQVIST; Admin. Dir L. EHRENGREN.

STFI (Swedish Pulp and Paper Research Institute): Box 5604, S-114 86 Stockholm; tel. (8) 67-67-000; telex 10880; fax (8) 411-55-18; f. 1942; library of 25,000 vols, 250 periodicals; Man. Dir OLLE ALSHOLM; publs *Rapporter*, *STFI-KONTAKT* (quarterly).

ARCHITECTURE AND TOWN PLANNING

Nordregio (Nordic Centre for Spatial Development): Box 1658, 111 86 Stockholm; tel. (8) 463-54-00; fax 463-54-01; f. 1997; administered by Nordic Council of Ministers; urban and regional studies, spatial planning, and regional economic development and policy; Chair. of Board ARVID STRAND; Dir HALLGEIR AALBU; publ. *North* (6 a year).

ECONOMICS, LAW AND POLITICS

Ekonomiska Forskningsinstitutet vid Handelshögskolan i Stockholm (The Economic Research Institute at the Stockholm School of Economics): see under Handelshögskolan i Stockholm.

Humanistisk-samhällsvetenskapliga forskningsrådet, HSFR (Swedish Council for Research in the Humanities and Social Sciences): POB 7120, 103 87 Stockholm; tel. (8) 454-43-10; fax (8) 454-43-20; f. 1977; 11 mems; Chair. Prof. OLOF RUIN; Sec.-Gen. Prof. ANDERS JEFFNER; Dir BJÖRN THOMASSON.

IUI (Research Institute of Industrial Economics): POB 5501, 114 85 Stockholm; tel. (8) 783-84-01; fax (8) 661-79-69; e-mail info@iui.se; f. 1939; industrial economics; 20 research fellows; Dir ULF JAKOBSSON; publs books, research reports, working papers.

Latinamerika-institutet i Stockholm (Institute of Latin American Studies, Univ. of Stockholm): S-106 91 Stockholm; tel. (8) 16-28-82; fax (8) 15-65-82; f. 1951, reorganized 1969; library of 40,000 vols; research on economic, social and political development; information, seminars, courses; Dir WEINE KARLSSON; Librarian BRITT JOHANSSON; publ. *Ibero-Americana: Nordic Journal of Latin American Studies*.

Nordiska Afrikainstitutet (Nordic Africa Institute): POB 1703, 751 47 Uppsala; tel. (18) 56-22-00; fax (18) 69-56-29; e-mail nai@nai.uu.se; f. 1962; documentation and research centre for current African affairs, publication work, lectures and seminars; library of 45,000 vols, 1,000 periodicals; Dir LENNART WOHLGEMUTH; Chief Librarian LOUISE FREDÉN; publs *Seminar Proceedings*, *Research Reports*, *News from Nordiska Afrikainstitutet*, *Annual Report*, *Discussion Paper*, *Current African Issues*.

Statistiska Centralbyrån (Statistics Sweden): Karlavägen 100, POB 24300, 104 51 Stockholm; tel. (8) 783-40-00; fax (8) 661-52-61; and at: Klostergatan 23, 701 89 Örebro; tel. (19) 17-60-00; fax (19) 17-70-80; f. 1858; library: see Libraries; Dir.-Gen. JAN CARLING; publs include *Statistical Abstract of Sweden*, *Journal of Official Statistics*, *Monthly Digest of Swedish Statistics*, *Survey of Living Conditions*, *Statistical Reports*.

Swedish Collegium for Advanced Study in the Social Sciences (SCASSS): Götavägen 4, 752 36 Uppsala; tel. (18) 55-70-85; fax (18) 52-11-09; f. 1985; offers 9 fellowships for study at the Collegium each semester; Admin. Dir Prof. BJÖRN WITTROCK.

HISTORY, GEOGRAPHY AND ARCHAEOLOGY

Riksantikvarieämbetets Gotlandsundersökningar (Gotland Research Institute of the Central Office of Antiquities): Strandgatan 10, S-621 02 Visby; f. 1970; archaeology, particularly prehistory and the middle ages; experimental archaeology and technical development; Dir ANDERS BROBERG; publs *Annual Proceedings*, *Research Reports*.

MEDICINE

Livsmedelsverket (National Food Administration): POB 622, 751 26 Uppsala; fax (18) 10-58-48; f. 1972; central administrative agency in Sweden for foodstuffs and handling of foodstuffs in accordance with the Food Act; library of 11,000 vols; Dir-Gen. B. NORBELIE; publs *Vår Föda* (popular scientific), *Livsmedelsverkets författningar* (The National Food Administration's Regulations), *Livstecknet* (Newsletter).

Medicinska forskningsrådet (Medical Research Council): POB 7151, 103 88 Stockholm; f. 1945, reorganized 1977; established under the Ministry of Education and Science to administer funds provided annually by the Swedish Parliament for the promotion of scientific research in medicine; 10 mems; Chair LENI BJÖRKLUND; Sec. Prof. OLLE STENDAHL.

NATURAL SCIENCES

General

Abisko naturvetenskapliga station (Abisko Scientific Research Station): 981 07 Abisko; tel. (980) 400-21; fax (980) 401-71; f. 1913; belongs to The Royal Swedish Academy of Sciences; research mainly on sub-arctic biology and earth sciences; Dir Prof. TERENCE CALLAGHAN.

Kristinebergs Marina Forskningsstation (Kristineberg Marine Research Station): S-450 34 Fiskebäckskil; tel. (523) 185-00; fax (523) 185-02; f. 1877; belongs to the Royal Swedish Academy of Sciences and Göteborg University; marine ecology, taxonomic, morphological and physiological research on marine animals and plants; Dir ANDERS TÖRNKVIST.

Naturvetenskapliga forskningsrådet (Swedish Natural Science Research Council): POB 7142, 103 87 Stockholm; tel. (8) 454-42-00; fax (8) 454-42-50; f. 1977; objects are to promote basic research in natural sciences in Sweden and to encourage and support international co-operation; offers grants to scientists and scientific institutions; 11 mems; Dir ARNE WITTLÖV; Sec.-Gen. Prof. GUNNAR ÖQUIST; publs *Årsbok* (yearbook), *Annual Report*.

Stockholm Environment Institute (International Institute for Environmental Technology and Management): Box 2142, 103 14 Stockholm; tel. (8) 412-14-00; telex 19580; fax (8) 723-03-48; e-mail postmaster@sei.se; f. 1989; partially core-funded by Swedish Government, but independently governed by an international Board; policy-related research on international environmental technology and management issues, including acidic deposition co-ordinated abatement strategies, climatic change assessment, energy futures, economics and environmental value, water and integrated waste-management, urban environment, common property, energy and development, biotechnology, risk assessment, atmospheric environment, cleaner production, sustainable development planning and computer tools for integrated management; centres in Stockholm, Tallinn (Estonia), York (UK) and Boston (USA); Exec. Dir NICHOLAS SONNTAG.

Biological Sciences

Bergianska stiftelsen (Bergius Foundation): Box 50017, 104 05 Stockholm; tel. (8) 15-68-96; telex 17073; fax (8) 61-29-005; f. 1791; belongs to the Royal Swedish Academy of Sciences; botanical and horticultural research; Flora Nordica project; Dir Prof. Bergianus BENGT JONSELL.

Mathematical Sciences

Makarna Mittag-Lefflers Matematiska Stiftelse (Mittag-Leffler Institute): Auravägen 17, S-182 62 Djursholm; tel. (8) 755-18-09; fax (8) 622-05-89; f. 1916; research institute to promote pure mathematics; belongs to the Royal Swedish Academy of Sciences; *c.* 20 mems; library of 60,000 vols; Dir KJELL OVE WIDMAN; publs *Acta Mathematica* (quarterly), *Arkiv för matematik* (2 a year).

Physical Sciences

Forskningsstationen för astrofysik på La Palma (Astrophysical Research Station at La Palma): c/o Stockholms Observatorium, 133 36 Saltsjöbaden; f. 1951, reorganized 1978; belongs to Royal Swedish Academy of Sciences; solar research; Dir Prof. GÖRAN SCHARMER.

Manne Siegbahn Laboratory (MSL): Stockholm University, Frescativägen 24, 104 05 Stockholm; tel. (8) 16-10-00; fax (8) 15-86-74; f. 1937 as Nobel Institute of Physics, present name 1993; research in nuclear, atomic, elementary particle, molecular and surface physics; accelerator-storage ring for highly charged ions; computer, electronics, detector and theory divisions; library of 10,000 vols; Dir Assoc. Prof. K.-G. RENSFELT; publ. *Annual Report*.

Stockholms Observatorium (Stockholm Observatory): S-133 36 Saltsjöbaden; f. 1753; Dir Prof. HANS OLOFSSON.

Sveriges Geologiska Undersökning (Geological Survey of Sweden): POB 670, 751 28 Uppsala; tel. (18) 179000; fax (18) 179210; f. 1858; library of 100,000 vols; Dir OLOF RYDH.

Swedish Institute of Space Physics: POB 812, S-981 28 Kiruna; tel. (980) 790-00; fax (980) 790-50; e-mail irf@irf.se; f. 1957 as an institute of the Swedish Academy of Sciences; government institute since 1973; research in space physics, atmospheric physics and related fields; library of 6,000 vols; Dir Prof. R. LUNDIN; publs *Kiruna Geophysical Data*, *IRF Reports*, reprints.

TECHNOLOGY

Byggforskningsrådet (Swedish Council for Building Research): St Eriksgatan 46, POB 12866, 112 98 Stockholm; tel. (8) 617-73-00; fax (8) 653-74-62; f. 1960; aim is to promote and finance research in building, energy and town planning; 10 board mems; Chair. OLOF HULTHÉN; Dir-Gen. BERTIL PETTERSSON; publs *Byggforskning* (in Swedish), *Swedish Building Research* (in English).

Cement och Betong Institutet (Swedish Cement and Concrete Research Institute): 100 44 Stockholm; tel. (8) 696-11-00; fax (8) 24-31-37; e-mail cbi@cbi.se; f. 1942; conducts research into and acts as a consultancy for engineering materials based on cement and concrete and allied materials; library of 9,000 vols; Dir Dr ÅKE SKARENDAHL; Librarian TUULA OJALA; publs *CBI rapporter/reports*, *CBI informerar*.

Flygtekniska Försöksanstalten (FFA) (Aeronautical Research Institute of Sweden): Box 11021, 161 11 Bromma; tel. (8) 6341000; fax (8) 253481; f. 1940; Dir-Gen. HANS DELLNER.

Institutet för Fiber- och Polymerteknologi (Swedish Institute for Fibre and Polymer Research): POB 104, 431 22 Mölndal; tel. (31) 706-63-00; fax (31) 706-63-63; e-mail roshan .shishoo@irf.se; f. 1943; library of 6,000 vols; Dir ROSHAN L. SHISHOO; publ. *Struktur* (6 a year).

Institutet för Metallforskning (Swedish Institute for Metals Research): Drottning Kristinas väg 48, S-114 28 Stockholm; tel. (8) 440-48-00; fax (8) 440-45-35; f. 1921; areas of research include: application of instrumental methods for chemical analysis; hot working, cold forming and microscopy; the relationship between microstructure and properties; solidification processes and their industrial applications; continuous casting; powder metallurgy; corrosion problems in connection with microstructure with a special interest in stainless steels; library of 2,000 monographs and 120 periodicals; Pres. Prof. RUNE LAGNEBORG; publ. *Annual Report*.

SIK, Institutet för Livsmedel och Bioteknik (Swedish Institute for Food and Biotechnology): Box 5401, 402 29 Göteborg; tel. (31) 335-56-00; fax (31) 83-37-82; f. 1946; research and development, documentation and education on production, preservation, food safety, biotechnology, structure and rheology, packaging, information and marketing; library of 7,000 vols; Dir Prof. KAJ MÅRTENSSON; publs *SIK-Publikation*, *SIK-Rapport*, *SIK-Dokument*, *SIK-Infood* (in English), *SIK Annual Report* (in English).

Statens Geotekniska Institut (Swedish Geotechnical Institute): 581 93 Linköping; tel. (13) 20-18-00; fax (13) 20-19-14; e-mail sgi@ geotek.se; f. 1944; research, information and consulting work in soil mechanics and foundation engineering, environment and energy geotechnology; computerized library retrieval system; Dir-Gen. H. STRÖMBERG; publs *Report*, *Information*, *SGI Varia*.

Statens Provningsanstalt (Swedish National Testing and Research Institute): POB 857, S-501 15 Borås; tel. (33) 16-50-00; telex 36252; fax (33) 13-55-02; f. 1920 (Testing Institute of the Royal Institute of Technology, 1896–1920); object is to carry out, on behalf of government institutions and private firms, impartial expert tests of raw products and manufactured articles, to investigate and report on their mechanical, physical and chemical properties and their commercial utilization, to test precious metals and to inspect weights and measures; *c.* 500 staff; library of *c.* 17,000 vols; Dir-Gen. CLAES BANKVALL; publs *SP Rapport* (technical reports), *Kontrollbestämmelser*.

STU Styrelsen för teknisk utveckling (Swedish National Board for Technical Development): Liljeholmsvägen 32, 117 86 Stockholm; tel. (8) 775-40-00; telex 10840; fax (8) 19-68-26.

Libraries and Archives

Borås

Borås stadsbibliotek (City Library and County Library of Älvsborgs län): Box 856, S-501 15 Borås; tel. (33) 35-70-00; fax (33) 35-76-75; f. 1860; library of 695,000 vols; Chief Librarian TOMMY OLSSON; publ. *P-läningen*.

Eskilstuna

Eskilstuna stads- och länsbibliotek (City Library and County Library of Södermanland): Kriebsensg. 4, 632 20 Eskilstuna; tel. (16) 10-10-00; fax 46-16-132949; f. 1925; library of 550,000 vols; Chief Librarian BIRGITTA WIDHOLM.

Gävle

Gävle stadsbibliotek (Gävle City Library): Box 801, 801 30 Gävle; tel. (26) 17-80-00; fax (26) 68-85-62; f. 1907; library of 700,000 vols; Dir of Dept of Culture INGA LUNDEN.

Gothenburg

Chalmers Tekniska Högskolas Bibliotek (Chalmers University of Technology Library): 412 96 Göteborg; tel. (31) 772-10-00; telex 2369; fax (31) 16-84-94; f. 1829; library of 540,000 vols; Chief Librarian JAN ROHLIN.

Göteborgs stadsbibliotek (City Library and County Library of Göteborgs och Bohus län): Götaplatsen, Box 5404, S-402 29 Göteborg; tel. (31) 61-65-00; fax (31) 61-66-93; f. 1861; library of 700,000 vols; Chief Librarian ANDERS CLASON.

Göteborgs Universitetsbibliotek (Göteborg University Library): Central Library, POB 5096, 402 22 Göteborg; tel. (31) 773-10-00; fax (31) 16-37-97; Bio-Medical Library, Medicinaregatan 4, 413 90 Göteborg; tel. (31) 773-30-00; fax (31) 773-37-46; Botanical Library, Carl Skottsbergs gata 22, S-413 19 Göteborg; Economics Library, Vasagatan 1, 411 80 Göteborg; Undergraduate and Newspaper Library, Vasagatan 2A, 411 80 Göteborg; Education Library, POB 1010, S-431 26 Mölndal; f. 1891; library of 2,800,000 vols; legal deposit library for Swedish publications; special collections include MSS collection, Women's History Collection, Snoilsky Collection (early Swedish literature), Sound and Video Archives; Chief Librarian JON ERIK NORDSTRAND; publs *Acta*, *Acta Universitatis Gothoburgensis* (monographs), *New Literature on Women* (bibliography).

Halmstad

Halmstads stadsbibliotek (City Library and County Library of Hallands län): Fredsgatan 2, 302 46 Halmstad; tel. (35) 13-71-81; fax (35) 13-71-64; f. 1922; library of 209,000 vols; Chief Librarian (vacant).

Jönköping

Jönköpings stadsbibliotek (City Library and County Library of Jönköpings län): Box 1029, 551 11 Jönköping; tel. (36) 10-50-00; f. 1916; library of 600,000 vols; Chief Librarian INGER JEPSSON.

Kalmar

Kalmar stadsbibliotek (City Library of Kalmar län): Box 610, 391 26 Kalmar; tel. (480) 83563; fax (480) 83596; e-mail bo .eklinder@kommun.kalmar.se; f. 1922; library of 407,000 vols; Chief Librarian BO EKLINDER.

Linköping

Linköpings stadsbibliotek (State County Library, Östergötlands län): Box 1984, 581 19 Linköping 3; f. 1926; library of 722,000 vols; Chief Librarian TANJA LEVIN.

Linköpings universitetsbibliotek (Linköping University Library): S-581 83 Linköping; tel. (13) 28-10-00; fax (13) 28-44-24; f. 1969; library of 477,000 vols; Chief Librarian CHRISTER KNUTHAMMAR; publ. *Publikation*.

Luleå

Luleå Kommuns folkbibliotek (City Library and County Library of Norrbottens län): Kyrkogatan 15, POB 50065, 951 05 Luleå; f. 1903; library of 490,500 vols; special collection of Finnish and Nord-kalotten literature; Chief Librarian GUN-BRITT LINDSKOG.

Lund

Landsarkivet i Lund: Box 2016, 220 02 Lund; tel. (46) 19-70-00; fax (46) 19-70-70; e-mail landsarkivet@landsarkivet-lund.ra.se; f. 1903; holds records of government bodies in the south of Sweden (counties of Halland, Skåne, Blekinge); 27,000 shelf metres of records; special collections: estate archives; library: 36,500 shelf metres, mainly genealogical and topographical; Chief Archivist JAN DAHLIN.

Lunds Universitetsbibliotek (Lund University Library): POB 3, S-221 00 Lund; tel. (46) 222-00-00; f. 1671; legal deposit library and national lending library; library of 5,000,000 vols, 129,000 MSS, 120,000 items of microforms; MSS include *Necrologium Lundense*, the oldest Scandinavian MS; special collections: *Bibliotheca Gripenhielmiana* (6,000 vols 16th- and 17th-century prints), Taussig collection of Schubert MSS, Broman collection of Elsevier prints, De La Gardie collection of prints and MSS; Dir Dr GÖRAN GELLERSTAM.

Malmö

Malmö Stadsbibliotek (City Library, County Library of Malmöhus län and Loan Centre for South Sweden): Regementsgatan 3, S-211 42 Malmö; tel. (40) 6608500; fax (40) 6608681; f. 1905; library of 916,000 vols; Chief Librarian GUNILLA KONRADSSON; publ. *Litteratur om Skåne* (Bibliography of Scania 1974–).

Norrköping

Norrköpings stadsbibliotek (Norrköping City Library): 600 02 Norrköping; f. 1913; 8 branch libraries, 3 bookmobiles; library of 463,665 vols; library of 51,500 vols, special collections; Chief Librarian CONNY ENG.

Nyköping

Studsvikbiblioteket Kungl. Tekniska Högskolans Bibliotek (Royal Institute of Technology): S-611 82 Nyköping; tel. (155) 221000; fax (155) 263044; e-mail stubib@lib .kth.se; f. 1947; energy research, technology and safety, environmental research; library of 80,000 vols, 2 million reports (*c.* 1.5 million as microfiche), 500 periodicals; computerized catalogue on reports in 7 Nordic technical libraries, NTIS (USA) co-operating organization for sale in Nordic countries; Chief Librarian Dr LARS EDVARDSSON.

Örebro

Örebro stadsbibliotek (City Library and County Library of Örebro län): Box 310-10, 701

35 Örebro; tel. (19) 211000; fax (19) 216162; f. 1862; library of 780,000 vols; Chief Librarian CHRISTER KLINGBERG; publ. *Samfundet Örebro Stads- och Länsbiblioteks vänner. Meddelande 1929–*.

Östersund

Jämtlands läns bibliotek (City Library of Östersund and County Library of Jämtlands län): Rådhusgatan 25–27, 831 80 Östersund; tel. (63) 14-30-00; fax (63) 10-98-40; f. 1833; library of 550,000 vols; Chief Librarian LENA MOBERG.

Skara

Stifts- och landsbiblioteket i Skara (State County and City Library of Skaraborgs län): Biblioteksgatan 3, S-532 23 Skara; tel. (511) 32-000; f. 1938; library of 400,000 vols, 200 running metres MSS; Chief Librarian ARNE STRÄNG; publ. *Acta*.

Stockholm

Antikvarisk-topografiska arkivet (Antiquarian Topographical Archives): Box 5405, 114 84 Stockholm; tel. (8) 783-90-50; fax (8) 783-90-88; f. 1786 (1666); archives of the Collegium Antiquitatum and the Royal Archives of Antiquities (1666–1786), archives and collections of the Royal Academy of Letters, History and Antiquities (1786–1975) and of the Central Board of Antiquities and National Historical Museums, archives of the office of monuments (1918–67) of the National Board of Public Buildings; library of 1,100 million vols; 300 private archives; 120,000 maps and drawings; 1,100,000 negatives and photographs; open to the public; Head Dr STEFAN ÖSTERGREN.

Handelshögskolans Bibliotek (Library of the Stockholm School of Economics): Box 6501, S-113 83 Stockholm; tel. (8) 736-90-00; fax (8) 31-82-13; e-mail library@hhs.se; f. 1909; library of 210,000 vols, 1,400 periodicals; Librarian EVA THOMSON-ROOS; publ. *SSE Library Report* (irregular).

Karolinska Institutets Bibliotek (Karolinska Institute Library): Box 200, 171 77 Stockholm; tel. (8) 728-80-00; fax (8) 34-87-93; f. 1810; library of 362,500 vols, 258,600 theses, 2,845 current periodicals, 874 MSS on medicine and dentistry; affiliated libraries at NOVUM research centre and University College of Sodertorn; Chief Librarian PER OLSSON; publs *KIB-Rapport* (irregular), *Contributions from the Karolinska Institute Library and Museum Collections* (irregular).

Konstbiblioteket, Statens konstmuseer (Art Library, Swedish National Art Museums): Box 16176, 103 24 Stockholm; premises at: Hovslagargatan 2, Stockholm; tel. (8) 51-95-43-00; fax (8) 51-95-43-52; f. late 19th century; library of 307,000 vols, 247 serials, 2,390,000 cuttings; speciality: exhibition catalogues; Librarian GRETEL EKLÖF (acting).

Kungl. Biblioteket (Royal Library): Box 5039, S-102 41 Stockholm; f. early 17th century; 3,500,000 vols, National Library of Sweden with the most complete collection of Swedish printed books in the world; foreign holdings in humanities; important collections of Old Swedish and Icelandic MSS; special collections include incunabula, elzeviers, maps, portraits, heraldry; responsible for the union catalogue *LIBRIS* and for co-operation among scientific libraries (BIBSAM); Dir Dr TOMAS LIDMAN; publs *Svensk bokförteckning, Svensk Kartförteckning, Svensk periodicaförteckning, Svensk musikförteckning, Suecana extranea* (all parts of the Swedish national bibliography), *CD-Libris, Acta Bibliothecæ regiæ Stockholmiensis, Rapport/Kungl. biblioteket, Rapport/BIBSAM*.

Kungl. Skogs- och Lantbruksakademiens Bibliotek (Library of the Royal Swedish Academy of Agriculture and Forestry): Box 6806, S-113 86 Stockholm; tel. (8) 30-07-08; fax (8) 33-53-77; e-mail kslab@ksla.se; f. 1811; library of 80,000 vols, 400 periodicals; collection of books on rural and agricultural history, horticulture, forestry and related fields; Chief Librarian LARS LJUNGGREN; publ. *Skogs- och Lantbrukshistoriska Meddelanden*.

Kungl. Tekniska Högskolans Bibliotek (Royal Institute of Technology Library): Valhallavägen 81, S-100 44 Stockholm; tel. (46-8) 790-60-00; telex 10389; fax (46-8) 109199; f. 1826; centre for computerized information and documentation services in science and technology; dept of History of Science and Technology; library of 650,000 vols, 3,500 periodicals (incl. br. libraries), 3,000,000 microforms; Chief Librarian GUNNAR LAGER; publs *List Tech* (list of foreign periodicals and serials in Swedish libraries in technological fields), Report series *Stockholm Papers in Library and Information Science, Stockholm Papers in History and Philosophy of Science and Technology*.

Östasiatiska Biblioteket (Far Eastern Library—library of the Museum of Far Eastern Antiquities): Box 16176, 103 24 Stockholm; tel. (8) 51-95-57-78; f. 1986; library of 120,000 vols, 1,150 current periodicals; unique collection of Chinese periodicals, Japanese collection of A.E. Nordenskiöld, collection of Chinese congshu; Dir JAN WIRGIN; Librarians LARS FREDRIKSSON, KERSTIN WALLIN.

Riksarkivet (National Archives): Fyrverkarbacken 13–17, Box 12541, S-102 29 Stockholm; tel. (8) 737-6350; fax (8) 737-6474; e-mail riksarkivet@riksarkivet.ra.se; f. 1618; 130,000 linear metres of archival holdings, 100,000 vols, special collections on archival science and Swedish history; Dir-Gen. Dr ERIK NORBERG; publs *Årsbok för Riksarkivet och landsarkiven, Nordisk Arkivnyt, Skrifter utgivna av Svenska Riksarkivet, Svenskt diplomatarium, Glossarium till medeltidslatinet i Sverige*.

Riksdagsbiblioteket (Parliamentary Library): S-100 12 Stockholm; tel. (8) 786-40-00; fax (8) 786-58-70; f. 1851; serves the Riksdag, the administrative services and research; library of 700,000 vols; chiefly devoted to political science, administration, social science and law; Chief Librarian MARGARETA BRUNDIN; publs *Fakta om folkvalda: Riksdagen 1985–* (biographical handbook, every 4 years), *Statliga publikationer* (government publications, database only).

Stadsarkivet i Stockholm (Stockholm City Archives): Kungsklippan 6, Box 22 063, S-104 22 Stockholm; e-mail stadsarkivet@ssa.stockholm.se; f. 1930; documents from regional authorities and the municipal government of Stockholm; archives on urban history of Stockholm; library of *c.* 120,000 vols; archives: 65,000 shelf-metres; City Archivist (vacant); publs *Stockholms arkivnämnd och stadsarkiv. Årsberättelse* (annually), *Stockholms tänkeböcker från år 1592* (irregular), *Stadsarkivets småtryck* (irregular).

Statens musikbibliotek (Music Library of Sweden): Box 16326, 103 26 Stockholm; tel. (8) 666-45-12; e-mail exp@muslib.se; f. 1771; 45,000 books on music, 400,000 scores of music, 28,000 MSS and about 15,000 letters; the library is especially rich in 18th-century music and is a documentation centre for Swedish music; Chief Librarian ANDERS LÖNN; publ. *Musik i Sverige: dokument och förteckningar* (Music in Sweden: Documents and Catalogues).

Statens Psykologisk-Pedagogiska Bibliotek (National Library for Psychology and Education): Frescati Hagväg 10, POB 500 63, S-104 05 Stockholm; tel. (8) 441-86-00; fax (8) 441-86-11; e-mail sppb@sppb.se; f. 1885; library of 300,000 vols; Chief Librarian EVA TROTZIG.

Statistiska centralbyråns bibliotek (Statistics Sweden, Library): POB 24300, 104 51 Stockholm; tel. (8) 783-50-66; telex 15261; fax (8) 783-40-45; f. 1858; library of 230,000 vols, 3,200 periodicals; Chief Librarian R.-A. NORRMOSSE; publs *Statistics from Individual Countries* (annually), *Statistics from International Organizations and other Issuing Bodies* (annually).

Stockholms stadsbibliotek (City Library of Stockholm): Box 47601, 117 94 Stockholm; tel. (8) 50-83-11-00; fax (8) 50-83-12-10; f. 1927; library of 2,225,000 vols; Chief Librarian JAN BOMAN.

Svenska Akademiens Nobelbibliotek (Nobel Library of the Swedish Academy): Börshuset, Box 2118, 103 13 Stockholm; f. 1901; library of 200,000 vols; Librarian ÅKE ERLANDSSON.

Sveriges Radio Dokumentarkivet (Archives of the Swedish Broadcasting Corporation): 105 10 Stockholm; tel. (8) 784-1447; f. 1925; documents relating to Swedish broadcasting and television.

Stockholms universitetsbibliotek med Kungl. Vetenskapsakademiens Bibliotek (Stockholm University Library with the Library of the Royal Academy of Sciences): S-106 91 Stockholm; tel. (8) 16-20-00; fax (8) 15-28-00; library of 2,500,000 vols; Librarian Dr GUNNAR SAHLIN.

Utrikesdepartementet (Library of the Ministry for Foreign Affairs): POB 16121, S-103 23 Stockholm; works on modern history and politics, law, international law, economy and statistics; not open to the public.

Vitterhetsakademiens Bibliotek (Library of the Royal Academy of Letters, History and Antiquities): POB 5405, Storgatan 41, S-114 84 Stockholm; tel. (8) 783-90-00; fax (8) 663-35-28; e-mail bibl@raa.se; f. 1786; library of 350,000 vols; special collections on archaeology, medieval art and architecture, numismatics, preservation of cultural heritage; open to the public; Chief Librarian KERSTIN ASSARSSON-RIZZI; publ. *Fornvännen*.

Umeå

Umeå stadsbibliotek (City Library and County Library of Västerbottens län): 901 78 Umeå; tel. (90) 16-33-04; fax (90) 16-33-16; f. 1903; library of 870,000 vols; Chief Librarian INGER SIKSTRÖM.

Umeå Universitetsbibliotek (University Library of Umeå): 901 74 Umeå; tel. (90) 786-54-05; fax (90) 786-96-26; e-mail ub@umu.se; f. 1964; library of 1,000,000 vols; Chief Librarian LARS-ÅKE IDAHL.

Uppsala

Sveriges lantbruksuniversitets bibliotek (Library of the Swedish University of Agricultural Sciences): Box 7071, S-750 07 Uppsala; tel. (18) 67-10-00; fax (18) 67-28-53; f. 1977; consists of Ultunabiblioteket (main library, in Uppsala) and 5 branch libraries; 15,500 shelf-metres including those in branch libraries: Alnarp Library, Garpenberg Library, Skara Veterinary Library, Forestry Library (Umeå), Vet. Medical Library at the Nat. Veterinary Inst. (Uppsala); Dir STEN F. VEDI.

Uppsala Stads- och Länsbibliotek (City Library and County Library of Uppsala län): Box 643, 751 27 Uppsala; f. 1906; library of 791,000 vols; Chief Librarian KERSTIN SJÖGREN FLEISCHER.

Uppsala universitetsbibliotek (Uppsala University Library): Box 510, 751 20 Uppsala; tel. (18) 471-39-00; fax (18) 471-39-13; f. 1620; consists of Main Library and 18 branch libraries; library of 5,000,000 vols, 42,000 MSS, including the famous *Codex argenteus*, the 'Silver Bible' of the 6th century, a translation of the Gospels into the Gothic language, Swedish and Icelandic medieval MSS, the Bibliotheca Walleriana (medical books), a collection of old music books and MSS, a collection of old maps, engravings and drawings, including the *Carta Marina* of 1539 by Olaus Magnus (earliest accurate map of Scandinavia); Librarian ULF GÖRANSON; publs include *Acta Universitatis Upsaliensis, Acta Bibliothecae R. Universitatis Upsaliensis, Bibliotheca Ekmaniana, Scripta Minora Bibliothecae R. Universitatis Upsaliensis, Uppsala universitetsbiblioteks utställnings-kataloger* (exhibition catalogues), etc.

Västerås

Västerås stadsbibliotek (City and County Library of Västmanlands län): Box 717, S-721 20 Västerås; tel. (21) 16-46-00; fax (21) 13-25-12; e-mail stadsbibliotek@mail.vasteras.se; f. 1952; library of 670,000 vols; Chief Librarian STAFFAN RUNE.

Växjö

Landsbiblioteket i Växjö (City and County Library, Kronobergs län): Västra Esplanaden 7-p, 351 12 Växjö; f. 1954; library of 460,000 vols; Chief Librarian CHRISTINA WESTERMAN.

Visby

Gotlands länsbibliotek (Gotlands City and County Library): Hästgatan 24, 621 81 Visby; tel. (498) 269-000; f. 1865; library of 502,000 vols; Chief Librarian ANNA SÖDERBERGH.

Museums and Art Galleries

Gothenburg

Göteborgs Museer (Museums of the City of Göteborg): Norra Hamngatan 14, 411 14 Göteborg; tel. (31) 61-10-00; fax (31) 13-60-97; e-mail kulturnemuden@goteborg.se; f. 1861; Chair. of Trustees VIVI-ANNE NILSSON; Man. Dir ANDERS CLASON; publs *Annual Reports*, special series from various museums.

Comprise:

Museum of the City of Göteborg: Norra Hamngatan 12, Göteborg; tel. (31) 61-27-70; fax (31) 774-03-58; archaeology from prehistoric times to the present, industrial heritage; Dir (vacant).

Museum of Ethnography: Åvägen 24, Göteborg; tel. (31) 61-24-30; fax (31) 773-09; Indian artefacts from North and South America, Paracas textiles from Peru; Dir Dr SVEN-ERIK ISACSSON.

Museum of Art: Götaplatsen, Göteborg; tel. (31) 61-29-80; fax (31) 18-41-19; f. 1861; European paintings, sculpture, prints and drawings from 1500, special collections of French art from 1820 onwards and Scandinavian art; art library; Dir BJÖRN FREDLUND.

Museum of Natural History: Slottsskogen, Göteborg; tel. (31) 775-24-10; fax (31) 12-98-07; f. 1833; Dir GÖRAN ANDERSSON.

Röhss Museum of Arts and Crafts: Vasagatan 37–39, Göteborg; tel. (31) 61-38-50; fax (31) 18-46-92; f. 1916; Dir LESSE BRUNNSTROM.

Maritime Museum and Aquarium: Karl Johansgatan 1–3, Göteborg; tel. (31) 61-29-00; fax (31) 24-61-82; f. 1913; Swedish maritime history; library of 14,000 vols; Dir (vacant); publ. *Unda Maris*.

Karlskrona

Marinmuseum (Naval Museum): Stumholmen, 371 32 Karlskrona; tel. (455) 539-16; fax (455) 539-49; f. 1752; *c.* 40,000 exhibits from 17th to 20th century; library of 22,000 vols, 4,000 maps and drawings, 200,000 negatives and photographs; Dir PER-INGE LINDQVIST; publ. *Aktuellt-Marinmuseum* (yearbook).

Linköping

Flygvapenmuseum (Swedish Air Force Museum): Carl Cederströms Gata, POB 13300, 580 13 Linköping; tel. (13) 28-35-67; fax (13) 29-93-04; f. 1984; library of 10,000 vols; Dir SVEN SCHEIDERBAUER; publs *Meddelanden, Ikaros* (annually).

Lund

Kulturhistoriska Museet (Cultural History Museum): Box 1095, S-221 04 Lund; tel. (46) 35-04-00; fax (46) 35-04-70; f. 1882; ethnography, cultural history, medieval archaeology; open-air museum, town and country houses; applied arts (ceramics, textiles, silver, glass); weapons and uniforms; musical instruments; furniture and fittings; trades; commerce and crafts; fishery; farming; folk art; archaeological finds from medieval Lund; Östarp, old farm with inn, 30 km from Lund; library of 35,000 vols; Dir MARGARETA ALIN; publ. *Kulturen* (yearbook).

Mariefred

Swedish National Portrait Collection: Gripsholm Castle, Mariefred; c/o Magnus Olausson, National Museum, POB 16176, 103 24 Stockholm; tel. (8) 666-42-50; fax (8) 611-37-19); f. *c.* 1550; Curator MAGNUS OLAUSSON.

Stockholm

Armémuseum (Army Museum): Riddargatan 13, POB 14095, 104 41 Stockholm; tel. (8) 788-95-60; fax (8) 662-68-31; f. 1879; library of 60,000 vols; Dir JOHAN ENGSTRÖM; publs *Meddelanden, Skrifter, Småskrifter*; museum closed in 1996 for rebuilding.

Dance Museum: Barnhusgatan 14, 11123 Stockholm; tel. (8) 10-82-43; fax (8) 20-06-02; f. 1932 in Paris as Archives Internationales de la Danse, 1950 in Sweden; unique collection of material from all over the world, notably Ballets Suédois; temporary exhibitions, videotheque, folk dance dept, Rolf de Maré archive; Curator Dr ERIK NÄSLUND.

Folkens Museum Etnografiska (National Museum of Ethnography): POB 27140, Djurgårdsbrunnsvägen 34, 102 52 Stockholm; tel. (8) 666-5000; fax (8) 666-5070; f. 1880; collection of 150,000 artefacts from Africa, America, Asia, Australia and the Pacific; the Museum also houses the Sven Hedin Foundation; Dir PER KÅKS; publs *Ethnos* (2 a year), Monograph Series.

Livrustkammaren, Skoklosters Slott och Hallwylska Museet (Royal Armoury, Skokloster Castle and Hallwyl Museum): Slottsbacken 3, 111 30 Stockholm; Dir BARBRO BURSELL.

Comprise:

Livrustkammaren: Slottsbacken 3, 111 30 Stockholm; tel. (8) 51-95-55-00; fax (8) 51-95-55-11; f. 1628; housed in south-east wing of Royal Palace; historical collections dating from mid-16th century; Swedish royal arms, costumes, jewels, coaches, etc.; library of 40,000 vols; Dir BARBRO BURSELL; Curators NILS DREJHOLT, LENA RANGSTRÖM; publ. *Livrustkammaren*.

Skoklosters Slott: 746 95 Bålsta; baroque castle built 1654 by Count C. G. Wrangel; contains mainly 17th-century furniture, paintings, applied art and armour; library; Dep. Dir KARIN SKEKI; publ. *Skokloster Studies*.

Hallwylska Museet: Hamngatan 4, 111 47 Stockholm; f. *c.* 1900; private residence of Hallwyl family; collection of furniture, paintings, applied art, etc.; Dir EVA HELENA CASSEL-PIHL; publ. *Hallwyliana*.

Musikmuseet: Box 16326, 103 26 Stockholm; tel. (8) 57-95-54-90; fax (8) 663-91-81; e-mail museum@musikmuseet.se; f. 1899; over 6,000 art and folk music instruments; exhibitions, archives and library; Dir KRISTER MALM.

National Maritime Museums (Statens Sjöhistoriska museer): Box 27131, 102 52 Stockholm; tel. (8) 666-49-00; Pres. AGNETA LUNDSTRÖM.

Comprise:

Sjöhistoriska museet (Maritime Museum): Stockholm; tel. (8) 666-49-00; fax (8) 666-49-49; f. 1938; the oldest part of the Royal Naval Section originates from the Royal Chambers in 1752; collections give a view of Swedish naval and merchant history, vessels of the past and of today as well as the history of Swedish shipbuilding; archive of drawings and photographs; library of 60,000 vols; Dir ANDERS BJÖRKLUND; publ. *Sjöhistorisk årsbok*.

Vasamuseet (Vasa Museum): Stockholm; tel. (8) 666-48-00; fax (8) 666-48-88; f. 1961, new museum 1990; the Swedish warship *Vasa*, lost in 1628 and raised in 1961, and associated exhibits; Dir KLAS HELMERSON.

Naturhistoriska Riksmuseet (Swedish Museum of Natural History): Box 50007, S-104 05 Stockholm; tel. (8) 666-40-00; fax (8) 666-40-85; f. 1739; Dir D. EDMAR; The Swedish Omnitheater: Dir S. FORSSELL; Public Department (exhibitions and administration): Head P. LINDAHL; Heads of Departments: Vertebrate, Prof. B. FERNHOLM, Entomology, Senior Curator T. PAPE; Invertebrate, Prof. C. ERSÉUS; Palaeozoology, Prof. J. BERGSTRÖM; Phanerogamic Botany, Prof. B. NORDENSTAM; Cryptogamic Botany, Prof. A. TEHLER; Palaeobotany, Prof. E. M. FRIIS; Mineralogy, Prof. U. HÅLENIUS; Isotope Geology, Prof. S. CLAESSON.

Nordiska Museet: Djurgårdsvägen 6–16, Box 27820, S-115 93 Stockholm; tel. (8) 666-46-00; fax (8) 665-38-53; f. 1873; national museum of cultural history from 16th century to present; ethnological and industrial art collections; *c.* 1,500,000 exhibits; textiles museum in Sandviken; 10m. archive and photographic items; library of 300,000 vols; Dir LARS LÖFGREN; Institute of Folk Life Research Prof. ÅKE DAUN; Chief Librarian BO NILSSON.

Skansen: POB 27807, 115 93 Stockholm; tel. (8) 442-80-00; fax (8) 442-82-80; f. 1891; open-air museum, zoological garden; Dir ANNA-GRETA LEIJON; Keeper of Buildings BO NILSSON; Keeper of Natural History BENGT ROSÉN; publs daily programmes, guides, etc.

Statens försvarshistoriska museer (National Swedish Museums of Military History): Riddargatan 13, POB 14095, 104 41 Stockholm; tel. (8) 788-95-30; fax (8) 662-68-31; administers Armémuseum, Flygvapenmuseum (*qq.v.*), Försvarets Traditions- nämnd (Board of Military Traditions); Dir Col LEIF TÖRNQUIST.

Statens historiska museer (State Historical Museums): Box 5428, 114 84 Stockholm; tel. (8) 51-91-80-00; comprises Museum of National Antiquities, Museum of Mediterranean and Near Eastern Antiquities, and Royal Cabinet of Coins and Medals; Dir.-Gen JANE CEDERQVIST.

Statens konstmuseer (Swedish National Art Museums): Box 16176, 103 24 Stockholm; tel. (8) 51-95-43-00; fax (8) 51-95-44-51; Dir OLLE GRANATH; publ. *Årsbok för Statens konst-*

museer (annual publication of the Swedish National Art Museums).

Comprise:

Nationalmuseum: Södra Blasieholmshamnen, Box 16176, 103 24 Stockholm; tel. (8) 51-95-43-00; fax (8) 51-95-44-50; f. 1792; 12,500 paintings, sculptures and other objects, 500,000 drawings and prints, 30,000 items of applied art; library: see Libraries; also administers collections of several royal castles with 23,000 works of art; Dir OLLE GRANATH; publs *Nationalmuseums skriftserie. N.S.*, *Art Bulletin of Nationalmuseum Stockholm* (annually).

Moderna Museet (Museum of Modern Art): Skeppsholmen, Box 16382, 103 27 Stockholm; tel. (8) 51-95-52-00; fax (8) 51-95-52-10; f. 1958; 4,050 20th-century paintings and sculptures by Swedish and foreign artists; f. 1971; photographs, prints and drawings; Dir DAVID ELLIOTT; publ. *Moderna Museets utställningskatalog* (exhibition catalogues).

Östasiatiska Museet (Museum of Far Eastern Antiquities): Skeppsholmen, Box 16381, 103 27 Stockholm; tel. (8) 51-95-57-50; fax (8) 51-95-57-55; f. 1959; art section containing mostly Chinese paintings, sculptures and ceramics; archaeological section containing Chinese pottery and bronze objects; Japanese, Korean and Indian art; Far Eastern Library; Dir Dr JAN WIRGIN; publs *Bulletin* (annually), *Östasiatiska museet och Föreningen Östasiatiska museets vänner* (every 2 years, with annual reports).

Stockholms Stadsmuseum (City Museum): POB 15025, 104 65 Stockholm; premises at: Ryssgården, Slussen; tel. (8) 70-00-500; f. 1937; permanent exhibitions on the development of the capital from prehistoric times to *c.* 1900; collections include the 'Lohe treasure' and naive 19th-century paintings of Josabeth Sjöberg; *c.* 1,500,000 photographs, 2,000 paintings, 15,000 drawings, sketches and engravings; Dir NANNA HERMANSSON; publs *Stadsvandringar*, *Sankt Eriks årsbok* (year book), *Annual Report*, catalogues.

Affiliated museum:

Stockholms Medeltidsmuseum (Museum of Medieval Stockholm): Strömparterren, Norrbro, S-100 12 Stockholm; f. 1986; archaeological remains of Stockholm, reflecting its foundation and history from *c.* 1250–1550; Dir JONAS FERENIUS; publs catalogues, report series on medieval boats.

Tekniska Museet (National Museum of Science and Technology): Museivägen 7, S-115 27 Stockholm; tel. (8) 663-10-85; telex 10682; fax (8) 660-45-19; f. 1924; history of science and technology; development of Swedish industry and engineering; mining, iron and steel, steam power and machines, cars and aircraft, technology in the home, history of electricity, chemistry, computers, Polhem's collection of engineering models, mechanical workshop and model railway; forest industry, Swedish building technology, Swedish printing over 500 years; Teknorama science centre; archives of drawings and photographs; library of 50,000 vols; Telemuseum: telegraphy, telephony; archives of documents and photographs; library of 50,000 vols; open daily; Dir PETER LARSSON; publ. *Daedalus* (year book).

Uppsala

Upplandsmuseet (Upplands Museum): St Eriksgränd 6, 753 10 Uppsala; tel. (18) 16-91-00; fax (18) 69-25-09; f. 1959; provincial cultural history; Curator STIG RYDH; publ. *Uppland.*

Universities

CHALMERS TEKNISKA HÖGSKOLA (Chalmers University of Technology)

412 96 Gothenburg

Telephone: (31) 772-10-00
Telex: 2369
Fax: (31) 772-38-72

Founded 1829
Private control
Language of instruction: Swedish
Academic year: September to June

President: Prof. A. SJÖBERG
Vice-Presidents: CHR. ULLENIUS (Academic), B. RÖNNÄNG (PhD Programs), B. APPELQVIST (Administration and Resources), F. HJALMERS (Information and External Relations)
Libraries Director: J. ROHLIN

Library: see Libraries
Number of teachers: 480
Number of students (excluding the College of Applied Engineering and Maritime Studies): 4,550 (full-time), 942 PhD students

Publications: *Research Catalogue*, *Annual Report*, *Catalogue of Courses*, *Departmental Reports*.

DEANS

School of Mathematics and Computer Science: P. BRENNER
School of Physics and Engineering Physics: G. NIKLASSON
School of Mechanical and Vehicular Engineering: Prof. G. GERBERT
School of Electrical and Computer Engineering: B. LANNE
School of Civil Engineering: S. BENGTSSON
School of Chemical Engineering: Prof. J.-O. LILJENZIN
School of Architecture: Prof. A. M. WILHELMSEN
School of Technology Management and Economics: Prof. H. BJÖRNSSON
School of Environmental Sciences: E. SELIN

PROFESSORS

School of Mathematics and Computer Science:
ARKERYD, L., Mathematics
DAHLBERG, B., Mathematics
FRIBERG, J., Mathematics
HOLM, S., Biostatistics
HUGHES, J., Computer Science
JAGERS, P., Mathematical Statistics
JOHNSON, C., Applied Mathematics
NORDSTRÖM, B., Computer Science
PERSSON, U., Mathematics
ROOTZÉN, H., Mathematical Statistics
RUHE, A., Numerical Analysis
SJÖGREN, P., Mathematics
THOMÉE, V., Mathematics

School of Physics and Engineering Physics:
ABRAMOWICS, M., Astrophysics
ANDERSSON, S., Physics
BRANDER, O., Mathematical Physics
BRINK, L., Elementary Particle Physics
CLAESON, T., Physics
DUBOIS, J., Physics
ERIKSSON, K.-E., Theoretical Physics
JONSON, B., Physics
JONSON, M., Condensed Matter Physics
KASEMO, B., Chemical Physics
LAGERWALL, T., Experimental Physics
LINDGREN, I., Physics
LODDING, A., Materials Science
LUNDQVIST, B., Mathematical Physics
NILSSON, J., Mathematical Physics
NILSSON, P.-O., Electronic Structure of Condensed Matter
PÁZSIT, I., Reactor Physics
ROSÉN, A., Molecular Physics
THÖLÉN, A., Materials Physics
TORELL, L., Experimental Materials Physics
WALLDÉN, L., Social State Theory
ÖSTLUND, S., Solid State Theory

School of Mechanical and Vehicular Engineering:
BERNTSSON, T., Heat and Power Technology
BOSTRÖM, A., Mechanics
CHOMIAK, J., Thermodynamics and Fluid Dynamics
CRAAFORD, R., Production Engineering
DYNE, G., Marine Hydromechanics
EDBERG, B., Textile Technology
GERBERT, G., Machine Design
HÅLL, U., Turbomachines
KARLSSON, B., Engineering Materials
KLASON, C., Polymer Materials
LARSSON, L., Hydromechanics
LECKNER, B., Energy Conversion
MCHUGH, B., Nuclear Engineering
MÅRTENSSON, N., Factory Automation
MÄGI, M., Vehicle Design
OLEFJORD, I., Engineering Metals
OLSSON, E., Applied Thermodynamics and Fluid Dynamics
RUNESSON, K., Strength of Materials
ULFVARSSON, A., Marine Structural Engineering
WENE, C.-O., Energy Systems Technology
ÅKESSON, B., Strength of Materials

School of Electrical and Computer Engineering:
ASKNE, J., Radio Astronomy
BOOTH, R., Radio Astronomy
DAALDER, J., Electrical Power Systems
EGARDT, B., Control Engineering
ENGSTRÖM, O., Solid State Electronics
HEDELIN, P., Information Theory
HÖGLUND, B., Electron Physics
KILDAL, P.-S., Microwave Antennae
KOLLBERG, E., Microwave Techniques
LARSSON, A., Optoelectronics
LUOMI, J., Electrical Machines
OLSSON, T., Medical Electronics
RÖNNÄNG, B., Radio Electronics
SVENSSON, A., Computer Engineering
SVENSSON, B., Computer Engineering
TAFVELIN, S., Computer Systems
THORBORG, K., Power Electronics
TORIN, J., Computer Engineering
VIBERG, M., Applied Electronics
VLASTOS, A., High Voltage Engineering
WEILAND, J., Plasma Physics
WILHELMSSON, H., Electromagnetic Field Theory

School of Civil Engineering:
ABEL, E., Building Services Engineering
BERGDAHL, L., Hydraulics
CEDERWALL, K., Concrete Structures
EDLUND, B., Steel and Timber Structures
GUSTAFSON, G., Engineering Geology
HAGENTOFT, C.-E., Building Physics
HEDBERG, T., Water Supply and Sewerage Engineering
KIHLMAN, T., Applied Acoustics
LARSSON, S.-Å., Mineralogy and Petrology
LINDBLOM, U., Rock Engineering
MIDDLETON, M., Petrophysics
NILSSON, L.-E., Highway Engineering
NILSSON, L.-O., Building Materials
SAMUELSSON, A., Structural Mechanics
SJÖBERG, A., Hydraulics
SÄLLFORS, G., Geotechnical Engineering
WIBERG, N.-E., Structural Mechanics

School of Chemical Engineering:
ALBERTSSON, J., Inorganic Chemistry
ANDERSSON, B., Chemical Reaction Engineering
CARLSSON, R., Engineering Chemistry
ERICSSON, C., Food Science
HERMANSSON, A.-M., Food Science
HJERTBERG, TH., Polymer Technology
LILJENZIN, J.-O., Nuclear Chemistry
MAURER, F., Polymer Technology

MENON, G., Engineering Chemistry
NILSSON, M., Organic Chemistry
NORDÉN, B., Physical Chemistry
OTTERSTEDT, J.-E., Engineering Chemistry
RASMUSON, A., Chemical Engineering Design
SCHÖÖN, N.-H., Chemical Reaction Engineering
SHISHOO, R., Polymer Engineering
SIMONSSON, R., Forest Products and Chemical Engineering
WESTERMARK, U., Forest Products and Chemical Engineering

School of Architecture:

BJUR, H., Urban Design
BJÖRKMAN, A., Theoretical and Applied Aesthetics
GUNNARSSON, S. O., Urban Transportation Planning
HOLMDAHL, B., Housing Design
LINN, B., Theory and History of Architecture
SACHS, J., Industrial Architecture
WILHELMSEN, A.-M., Building Design and Construction

School of Technology Management and Economics:

BJÖRNSSON, H., Systems Management
GADDE, L.-E., Industrial Marketing
GRANSTRAND, O., Industrial Management and Economics
HAMMARLUND, Y., Building Economics and Construction Management
HULT, J., History of Technology
IGIELSKA, J., Marine Transport Systems
JACOBSSON, S., Technology Policy
KARLSSON, U., Operations Management and Work Organization
LÖVSUND, P., Traffic Safety
ROSENBLAD, E., Consumer Technology
SJÖLANDER, S., Innovative Techniques
SJÖSTEDT, L., Transportation and Logistics
SPERLING, L., User Requirements in Working Life
TINGVALL, C., Epidemiology of Injuries
ÖRTENGREN, R., Injury Prevention

ATTACHED INSTITUTES

Chalmers Science Park: Sven Hultins gata 9, 412 88 Gothenburg; tel. (31) 772-40-00; fax (31) 772-42-40; Man. L. JACOBSON.

Ingenjörs- och sjöbefälsskolan vid Chalmers (College of Applied Engineering and Maritime Studies): 412 96 Gothenburg; tel. (31) 772-10-00; fax (31) 772-57-67; f. 1841 as Nautical College; 1,800 students; Dir E. HULTIN; Man. of Admin. B. CARLSSON.

HEADS OF DEPARTMENTS

ALVELID, B., Mechanical Technology
BERGKVIST, Å., Building Services Technology
JOHANSSON, A., Applied Civil Engineering
LINDHOLM, G., Nautical Technology
MILTHON, E., Applied Electrical Engineering
WADMAN, L., Applied Chemical Engineering

Onsala Space Observatory: 439 00 Onsala; tel. (300) 606-50; fax (300) 626-21; national facility for radio astronomy; Dir Prof. R. S. BOOTH.

GÖTEBORGS UNIVERSITET (Gothenburg University)

POB 100, 405 30 Gothenburg
Telephone: (31) 773-10-00
Fax: (31) 773-10-66

Founded 1891, became state university 1954
Academic year: September to June

Rector: Prof. B. E. SAMUELSSON
Vice-Rectors: Asst Prof. M. FRITZ, Prof. B. SKARIN-FRYKMAN
Head of Administration: B. JÄRBUR
Librarian: J. E. NORDSTRAND
Library: see Libraries
Number of professors: 225
Number of students: 33,000
Publication: *Acta Universitatis Gothoburgensis*.

DEANS

Faculty of Arts: Asst Prof. L. OLAUSSON
Fine and Applied Arts: Prof. B. OLSSON
Faculty of Social Sciences: Prof. L. STRÖMBERG
Faculty of Science: Prof. S. LINDQVIST
Faculty of Medicine: Prof. G. BONDJERS
Faculty of Odontology: Prof. G. DAHLÉN
School of Economics and Commercial Law: Prof. G. BERGENDAHL

PROFESSORS

Faculty of Arts:

AHLSÉN, E., Neurolinguistics
AIJMER, K., English
ALLWOOD, J., General Linguistics
ANDERSSON, L.-G., Modern Swedish
ANDERSSON, S.-G., German
BENSON, K., Spanish
BJÖRK, L., English Literature
COOPER, R., Computational Linguistics
EDSTRÖM, K.-O., Musicology
ELZINGA, A., Theory of Science and Research
FOGELMARK, S., Ancient Greek
GLAESER, B., Human Ecology
GÖRANSSON, A., Women's History
HAGLUND, D., Religious Studies
HANSSON, S., Comparative Literature
HÄGG, R., Classical Archaeology and Ancient History
JANSON, T., African Languages
JOHANNESSON, L., History of Art
JOSEPHSON, F., Sanskrit and Comparative Philology
KRISTIANSEN, K., Archaeology
LASKOWSKI, R., Slavonic Languages
LIEDMAN, S.-E., History of Ideas and Learning
LINDSTRÖM, P., Logic
LINDVALL, L., Romance Languages
LÖNNROTH, L., Comparative Literature
RALPH, B., Northern Languages
RETSÖ, J., Arabic
SKARIN-FRYKMAN, B., Ethnology
TÄNNSJÖ, T., Philosophy
WINBERG, C., History

Fine and Applied Arts:

LINDSTRÖM-CAUDWELL, T., Photography
LÜTZOW-HOLM, O., Composition
OLSSON, B., Music Education (Research)
VERES, F., Drama

Faculty of Social Sciences:

School of Economics and Commercial Law:

ALVSTAM, C.-G., International Economic Geography
BERGENDAHL, G., Managerial Economics
BIGSTEN, A., Economics
CZARNIAWCKA, B., Business Administration
DAHLBOM, B., Informatics
FLOOD, L., Econometrics
FRISÉN, M., Statistics
GUSTAFSSON, K. E., Mass Media Economics
HIBBS, D., Economics
HJALMARSSON, L., Economics
JANSSON, H., International Business
JENSEN, A., Transport Management
LAULAJAINEN, R., Economic Geography
NORDSTRÖM, L., Human Geography
OLSON, O., Accounting and Finance
OLSSON, U., Economic History
POLESIE, T., Accounting and Finance
STERNER, T., Environmental Economics
STJERNBERG, T., Management and Organization
TÖLLBORG, D., Legal Science
WESTERHÄLL, L., Public Law
WIHLBORG, C., Banking and Finance

Division of Social and Behavioural Sciences:

AIJMER, G., Social Anthropology
ARCHER, T., Psychology
ASP, K., Journalism
BJÖRNBERG, U., Sociology
BRORSTRÖM, B., Management Economics
BÄCK, H., Public Administration
BÄCK-WIKLUND, M., Social Work
BÄCKMAN, L., Psychology
FURÅKER, B., Sociology
GÄRLING, T., Psychology
HETTNE, B., Peace Research
HJELMQVIST, E., Behavioural Studies of Disabilities and Handicap
HOLMBERG, S., Political Science
HWANG, P., Psychology
HÖGLUND, L., Library Science
LUNDQVIST, L. J., Political Science
MÅNSSON, S.-A., Social Work
ROMBACH, B., Management Economics
ROTHSTEIN, B., Political Science
STRÖMBERG, L., Political Science
THERBORN, G., Sociology
WEIBULL, L., Mass Communication
ÅRHEM, K., Social Anthropology

Division of Education:

ASKLING, B., Education and Educational Research
EKHOLM, M., Education and Educational Research
EMANUELSSON, I., Special Education and Educational Research
GUSTAFSSON, J.-E., Education and Educational Research
MARTON, F., Education and Educational Research
PRAMLING-SAMUELSSON, I., Education and Educational Science
SÄLJÖ, R., Education and Educational Science

Faculty of Science:

ABRAMOWICZ, M., Astrophysics
AHLBERG, P., Organic Chemistry
ALLENMARK, S., Microbiological Chemistry
ANDERSSON, L., Systematic Botany
ANDERSSON, M., Zooecology
ARKERYD, L., Applied Mathematics
BERGSTRÖM, G., Chemical Ecology
BILLETER, M., Molecular Biophysics
BJURSELL, G., Molecular Biology
CAMPBELL, E., Atomic and Molecular Physics
COQUAND, T., Computer Science
CREMER, D., Theoretical Chemistry
CREMER, E., Theoretical Chemistry, Reaction Dynamics and Reaction Mechanisms
ELWING, H., Surface Biophysics
ERIKSSON, K. E., Theoretical Physics
HOLM, S., Biostatistics
JAGNER, D., Analytical Chemistry
LARSON, S. A., Geology
LEVAN, G., Genetics
LINDQVIST, O., Inorganic Chemistry
LINDQVIST, S., Physical Geography
LUNDQVIST, B., Mathematical Physics
MALMGREN, B., Marine Geology
NILSSON, L.-E., Highway Engineering
NILSSON, S., Zoophysiology
NORDHOLM, S., Physical Chemistry
ROSEN, A., Molecular Physics
ROSENBERG, R., Marine Ecology
RYDSTRÖM, J., Biochemistry
SELIN LINDGREN, E., Environmental Physics
SELLDÉN, G., Tree Physiology, Influence of Air Pollution
SJÖGREN, P., Mathematics
STIGEBRANDT, A., Oceanography
SUNDQVIST, CH., Plant Physiology
TURNER, D. R., Marine Chemistry
VAN VEEN, T., Zoomorphology
WALIN, G., Oceanography
WALLENTINUS, I., Marine Botany
WEIMARCK, G., Systematic Botany and Plant Geography
WILLANDER, M., Experimental Physics

Faculty of Medicine:
AHLMAN, H., Endocrine Surgery
ALBERTSSON-WIKLAND, K., Paediatric Growth Research
ALBREKTSSON, T., Handicap Research
ALLEBECK, P., Social and Preventive Medicine
ALPSTEN, M., Medical Radiophysics
ANDERSSON, H., Clinical Nutrition
AURELL, M., Medicine, especially Nephrology
AXELSSON, R., Psychiatry
BENGTSSON, C., General Medicine
BERTHOLD, C.-H., Anatomy
BETSHOLTZ, CH., Medical Biochemistry
BONDJERS, G., Cardiological Research
DAHLGREN, C., Medical Microbiology
DAHLSTRÖM, A., Histology
EDEBO, L., Clinical Bacteriology
EDÉN, S., Physiology, especially Endocrinology
EKHOLM, S., Neuroradiology
EKMAN, R., Neurochemistry
EKSTRÖM, J., Pharmacology
ENGEL, J., Pharmacology
ERICSON, L., Anatomy
ERIKSSON, B. O., Paediatric Cardiology
FREDHOLM, P., Neurochemistry
FUNA, K., Cell Biology
GILLBERG, CH, Child and Youth Psychiatry and Handicap Research
GUSTAFSSON, B., Neurophysiology
HAGBERG, M., Occupational Medicine
HALJAMÄE, H., Anaesthesiology
HAMBERGER, A., Histology
HAMBERGER, L., Obstetrics and Gynaecology
HANSON, L.-Å., Clinical Immunology
HANSSON, T., Occupational Orthopaedics
HEDNER, T., Clinical Pharmacology
HERBERTS, P., Orthopaedic Prosthetics
HJALMARSON, Å., Cardiology
HOLMGREN, J., Medical Microbiology
HOLMSTRÖM, H., Plastic Surgery
ISAKSSON, O., Endocrinology
IWARSON, S., Infectious Diseases
JANSON, P.-O., Obstetrics and Gynaecology
KARLSSON, K.-A., Medical Biochemistry
KINDBLOM, L.-G., Pathology
KJELLMER, I., Paediatrics
LINDSTEDT, G., Clinical Chemistry
LUNDBERG, CH., Oto-rhino-laryngology
LUNDGREN, O., Physiology
LUNDHOLM, K., Surgery
MÖLLER, C., Oto-rhino-laryngology
NORRBY, K., Pathology
NORRSELL, U., Psychobiology
OLOFSSON, S.-O., Medical Biochemistry
PASCHER, I., Molecular Membrane Research
PETTERSSON, S., Urological Surgery
RISBERG, B., Surgery
RYDEVIK, B.
RYLANDER, R., Hygiene
RYMO, L., Clinical Chemistry
RÖNNBÄCK, L., Neurology
SAMUELSSON, B., Transfusion Medicine
SANDBLOM, J., Medical Physics
SJÖBERG, B., Medical Biochemistry
SJÖSTRAND, J., Ophthalmology
SJÖSTRÖM, L., Clinical Research
SKOOGH, B.-E., Pneumology
SMITH, U., Medicine
STEEN, B., Geriatric and Long-term Care Medicine
STENMAN, G., Pathology
STRANDVIK, B., Paediatrics
STRANNEGÅRD, Ö., Clinical Virology
SVENNERHOLM, A.-M., Infectious Diseases and Immunology
SWANBECK, G., Dermatology and Venereal Diseases
TARKOWSKI, A., Rheumatology
THOMSEN, P., Medical Biomaterials Research
TYLÉN, U., X-Ray Diagnostics
VALLBO, Å., Physiology
WALLGREN, A., Radio Therapeutics
WALLIN, A., Geriatric Neuropsychiatry
WALLIN, G., Clinical Neurophysiology
WIKLUND, O., Medicine
WILHELMSEN, L., Cardiovascular Epidemiology
ÅGREN, H., Psychiatry

Faculty of Odontology:
BERGENHOLTZ, G., Endodontics
BIRKHED, D., Cardiology
DAHLÉN, G., Oral Microbiology
FRIEDE, H., Orthodontics
GRÖNDAHL, H.-G., Oral Diagnostic Radiology
HEYDEN, G., Oral Pathology
KAHNBERG, K.-E., Dental Surgery
KARLSSON, S., Prosthetic Dentistry
LINDE, A., Oral Biochemistry
LINDHE, J., Periodontology

KARLSTADS UNIVERSITET
(Karlstad University)

651 88 Karlstad
Telephone: (54) 83 80-00
Fax: (54) 83-84-60
E-mail: information@hks.se

Founded 1967 as Universitetsfilialen, present name 1977
State control
Academic year: August to June

Rector: CHRISTINA ULLENIUS
Vice-Rector: BENGTOVE GUSTAVSSON
Head of Administration: ALF SUNDIN
Chief Librarian: EVA KLING

Library of 150,000 vols
Number of teachers: 500
Number of students: 9,000

Publications: *Anslaget* (monthly), *Utbilder* (6 a year).

DEANS

Educational Sciences: MATS EKHOLM
Social Sciences and Humanities: MATS DAHLKVIST
Natural Sciences and Engineering: KJELL MAGNUSSON

HEADS OF DEPARTMENTS

BLOMQUIST, L., Department of Social Sciences
ERIKSSON, J.-O., Department of Culture and Communication
ERIKSSON, M., Department of Educational Sciences
FORSHULT, S., Department of Chemistry
HÅKANGÅRD, S., Department of Information Technology
KLOCKARE, R., Department of Environmental Sciences
LANDSTRÖM, B., Department of Engineering Sciences, Physics and Mathematics
ROLANDSSON, M., Department of Health and Caring Sciences
RUNDH, B., Department of Business and Economics

ATTACHED INSTITUTES

Service Research Centre: 651 88 Karlstad; Dir BO EDVARDSSON.

Centre for Gender Studies: Dir LENA MELESJÖ-WINDAHL.

KUNGLIGA TEKNISKA HÖGSKOLAN
(Royal Institute of Technology)

S-100 44 Stockholm
Telephone: (8) 790-60-00
Fax: (8) 790-65-00

Founded 1827
State control
Academic year: September to June

President: Prof. A. FLODSTRÖM
Vice-President: Prof. I. GRENTHE
Chief Administrative Officer: A. LUNDGREN
Chief Librarian: G. LAGER

Library: see Libraries
Number of teachers: 1,900, including 167 professors
Number of students: 10,500

Publications: *Catalogue*, *Study Handbook* (annually).

DEANS

Faculty: Prof. F. INGMAN
School of Engineering Physics: Prof. H. ALFREDSSON
School of Mechanical and Materials Engineering: Prof. B. LINDSTRÖM
School of Electrical Engineering and Information Technology: Prof. J.-O. EKLUNDH
School of Architecture, Surveying and Civil Engineering: Prof. K. ÖDEÉN
School of Chemistry and Chemical Engineering: Prof. I. NERETNIEKS

PROFESSORS

School of Architecture, Surveying and Civil Engineering:
ANDERSSON, R., Real Estate Economics
ATKIN, B., Construction Management
BÅNG, K.-L., Transport and Traffic Planning
BJÖRK, B.-C., Construction Management
CEDERWALL, K., Hydraulic Engineering
CVETKOVIC, V., Water Resources Engineering
ERIKSSON, A., Structural Mechanics and Engineering
HENRIKSSON, J., Architecture
HOLMGREN, J., Concrete Structures
HÖGLUND, T., Steel Structures
ISACSSON, U., Highway Engineering
JACKS, G., Land and Water Resources
JOHANNESSON, G. A., Building Technology
KNUTSSON, G., Land and Water Resources
KRUPINSKA, J., Architecture
LILJEFORS, A., Architecture
LJUNG, B., Business Administration
LUNDEQUIST, J., Design Methodology
MALMSTRÖM, T.-G., Building Services Engineering
MATTSSON, H., Real Estate Planning
MÅRTELIUS, J., History of Architecture
NORLÉN, U., Building Analysis and Housing Quality
QUIEL, F., Environmental and Natural Resources Information Systems
SAMUELSSON, S., Building Engineering
SANDBERG, M., Indoor Environment and Ventilation
SJÖBERG, L. E., Geodesy
SJÖSTRÖM, C., Materials Technology
SNICKARS, F., Regional Planning
STEPHANSSON, O., Engineering Geology
STILLE, H., Rock Mechanics
SUNDQUIST, H., Structural Design and Bridges
TORLEGÅRD, K., Photogrammetry
WARTIANEN, K., Town Planning and Urban Design
VICTORIN, A., Law of Real Estate Buildings Valuation
ÖDEÉN, K., Buildings Materials

School of Electrical Engineering and Information Technology:
ANDERSSON, G., Electric Power Systems
ARNBORG, S., Computing Science
BUBENKO, J., Information Processing, esp. Automatic Data Processing
CARLSON, R., Speech Technique
CEGRELL, T., Industrial Control Systems
CHRISTENSEN, H., Computer Science
DRAKE, J. R., Fusion Plasma Physics
EINARSSON, G., Telecommunication Theory
EKLUNDH, J.-O., Computer Vision
EKSTRÖM, Å., High-power Electronics
ENGQUIST, B., Numerical Analysis

ERIKSSON, R., Electrical Plant Engineering
GRANSTRÖM, B., Speech Technique
HELLSTEN, T., Fusion Plasma Physics
KARLSSON, G., Teletraffic Systems
KLEIJN, B., Speech Technology
LANDGREN, G., Semiconductor Materials
LEIJON, A., Hearing Technique
MAGUIRE, G., Computer Systems
MARKLUND, G., Plasma Physics
OLSSON, H., Radio Electronics
OTTERSTEN, B., Signal Processing
PARROW, J., Distribution Systems
PEHRSON, B., Telecommunication
PETERSSON, S., Solid State Electronics
SADARANGANI, C., Electrical Machines and Drives
SEVERINSON-EKLUNDH, K., Interaction and Presentation
STEMME, G., Electrical Measurement
STRÖM, S., Electromagnetic Theory
SUNDBERG, J., Music Acoustics
TENHUNEN, H., Electronics
THYLEN, L., Photonics and Microwave
TORVEN, S., Plasma Physics
TYUGU, E., Teleinformatics
WAHLBERG, B., Automatic Control
ZANDER, J., Radio Communication

School of Chemistry and Chemical Engineering:

ALBERTSSON, A.-C., Polymer Technology
ENFORS, S.-O., Biotechnology
ERIKSEN, T., Nuclear Chemistry
ERIKSSON, J. C., Physical Chemistry
GELLERSTEDT, G., Wood Chemistry
GRENTHE, I., Inorganic Chemistry
HULT, A., Surface Treatment Technology
HULT, K.-A., Biochemistry
HÄRD, T., Structural Biochemistry
INGMAN, F., Analytical Chemistry
JANSSON, J.-F., Polymeric Materials
JÄRÅS, S., Chemical Technology
MOBERG, C., Organic Chemistry
MÅNSSON, J.-A. E., Polymer Technology
NERETNIEKS, I., Chemical Engineering
NORIN, T., Organic Chemistry
NORMAN, B., Paper Technology
SETTERWALL, F., Transport Phenomena
SJÖBERG, K., Chemical Technology
STILBS, P., Physical Chemistry
SVEDBERG, G., Energy Technology for the Chemical Process Industry
TEDER, A., Pulp Technology
TEERI, T., Biochemistry
UHLEN, M., Biochemistry and Microbiology
ÅKERMARK, B., Organic Chemistry

School of Mechanical and Materials Engineering:

ANDERSSON, S., Machine Elements
ARNSTRÖM, A., Assembly Systems
BLOMSTRAND, J., Nuclear Reactor Engineering
BÄCKLUND, J., Lightweight Structures
CARLSSON, J., Solid Mechanics
ELIASSON, G., Industrial Competence Education
ENLUND, N., Graphic Art Technology
FORSLIN, J., Industrial Management
FRANSSON, T., Heat and Power Technology
FREDRIKSSON, H., Metal Casting
GRANRYD, E., Applied Thermodynamics and Refrigeration Engineering
GUDMUNDSON, P., Materials Mechanics
GUSTAFSSON, C., Industrial Economics and Management
HANNERZ, N. E., Welding Technology
HUML, P., Metal Forming
JÖNSSON, P., Process Metallurgy
LEYGRAF, C., Corrosion Science
LINDSTRÖM, B., Production Engineering
MATTSSON, L., Industrial Metrology
MUHAMMED, M., Inorganic Materials Chemistry
NILSSON, A., Technical Acoustics
NILSSON, F., Solid Mechanics
NISSER, M., History of Science and Technology
NORELL-BERGENDAHL, M., Integrated Product Development
OLSSON, K.-A., Aeronautics
OLSSON, K.-A., Lightweight Structures
PERSSON, J.-G., Machine Design
PETERSON, F., Heating and Ventilation Technology
PETTERSSON, K., Metallography
RINGERTZ, U., Aeronautics
RIZZI, A., Aeronautical Engineering
ROWCLIFFE, D., Ceramic Technology
RUTGERSSON, O., Vehicle Engineering
SANDSTRÖM, R., Applied Materials Technology
SEETHARAMAN, S., Theoretical Metallurgy
SEHGAL, B. R., Nuclear Power Safety
SOHLENIUS, G., Manufacturing Systems
STORÅKERS, B., Solid Mechanics
STÅHLBERG, U., Metal Forming
WENNERSTRÖM, E., Vehicle Engineering
WIKANDER, J., Mechatronics
WIKLUND, M., Carpentry
ÅGREN, J., Metallography
ÅNGSTRÖM, H.-E., Internal Combustion Engineering

School of Engineering Physics:

ALFREDSSON, H., Fluid Physics
BARK, F., Hydromechanics
BENEDICKS, M., Mathematics
BIEDERMANN, K., Optics
BJÖRNER, A., Mathematics
BLOMBERG, C.-O., Theoretical Physics
CARLSON, P., Particle Physics
DAHLBORG, U., Applied Neutron Physics
ELIASSON, H., Mathematics
ERMAN, P., Physics
FLODSTRÖM, A., Materials Physics
FRIBERG, A., Optics
GRIMVALL, G., Theoretical Physics
GRISHIN, A., Materials Physics
HAVILAND, D., Physics of Nanostructures
HERTZ, H., Materials Physics
HOLST, L., Mathematical Statistics
HÅSTAD, J., Theoretical Computer Science
JOHANSSON, A., Mechanics
JOHNSON, A., School of Engineering Physics
KARLSSON, U. H., Material Physics
LAKSOV, D., Applied Mathematics
LESSER, M., Mechanics
LINDQUIST, A., Optimization Theory and Systems Theory
MICKELSSON, J., Mathematical Physics
RAO, V., Condensed-matter Physics
ROSENGREN, A., Condensed Matter Theory
SJÖLIN, P., Mathematical Analysis
STENHOLM, S., Laser Physics and Quantum Optics
STRÖMBERG, J.-O., Computational Harmonics Analysis

LINKÖPINGS UNIVERSITET
(Linköping University)

581 83 Linköping
Telephone: (13) 28-10-00
Fax: (13) 14-94-03

Founded 1970

Rector: Prof. A. FLODSTRÖM

Library: see Libraries

Number of teachers: 1,000, including 115 professors

Number of students: 11,000

DEANS

Faculty of Technology: Prof. M. MILLNERT
Faculty of Medicine: Prof. R. ANDERSSON
Faculty of Arts and Sciences: Prof. B. SANDIN

PROFESSORS

Faculty of Technology:

AHRENBERG, L., Computational Linguistics
ARONSSON, G., Applied Mathematics
ASK, P., Biomedical Engineering
BERGGREN, K.-F., Theoretical Physics
BERGMAN, B., Quality Technology
BJÖRCK, Å., Numerical Analysis
BRANDES, O., Industrial Marketing
BREGE, S., Industrial Marketing
DANIELSSON, P.-E., Computer Engineering
ELDÉN, L., Numerical Analysis
ERICSON, T., Data Transmission
ERICSSON, T., Engineering Materials
ERLANDER, S., Optimization
FRITZSON, P., Computer Science
GLAD, T., Automatic Control
GRANLUND, G., Computer Vision
GRUBBSTRÖM, R. W., Production Economics
HANSSON, G., Experimental Semiconductor Physics
HEDBERG, L. I., Applied Mathematics
HELANDER, M., Industrial Ergonomics
HÄGGLUND, S., Computer Science
INGEMARSSON, I., Information Theory
JANZÉN, E., Semiconductor Physics
KARLSSON, B., Energy Systems
KLARBRING, A., Optimization Models in Structural Mechanics
LAUBER, A., Measurement Technology
LINDBERG, P.-O., Optimization
LJUNG, L., Automatic Control
LOYD, D., Applied Thermodynamics and Fluid Mechanics
LUND, A., Chemical Physics
LUNDSTRÖM, I., Applied Physics
MALUSZYNSKI, J., Programming Theory
MAZ'YA, V., Applied Mathematics
MONEMAR, B., Condensed Matter Physics
NIELSEN, L., Vehicle Systems
NILSSON, G., Biomedical Instrumentation
NILSSON, L., Solid Mechanics
NOVAK, A., Production Engineering
OLSSON, K. O., Machine Design
PALMBERG, J.-O., Fluid Power Technology
PENG, Z., Computer Systems
PETERSSON, L.-G., Chemical Surface Physics
RAPP, B., Economic Information Systems
RISCH, T., Engineering Database Systems
SALANECK, W., Surface Physics and Chemistry
SANDEWALL, E., Computer Science
SANDKULL, B., Industrial Organization
SUNDGREN, J.-E., Experimental Thin Film Physics
SVENSSON, C., Electronic Devices
WANDEL, S., Transportation Systems
WIGERTZ, O., Medical Informatics
WOHLIN, C., Software Engineering
ÅGREN, H., Computational Physics
ÖBERG, Å., Biomedical Engineering

Faculty of Medicine:

ALM-CARLSSON, G., Radiology
ANDERSSON, R., Pharmacology
AXELSSON, O., Occupational Medicine
BJÖRKSTÉN, B., Paediatrics
BRUNK, U., Pathology
FORSUM, U., Clinical Microbiology
GERDLE, B., Rehabilitation Medicine
GILLQUIST, J., Sports Medicine
GRANERUS, A.-K., Long-Term Treatment
HAMMARSTRÖM, S., Cell Biology
HILDEBRAND, C., Cell Biology
KARLBERG, B., Medicine
KJESSLER, B., Obstetrics and Gynaecology
LARSSON, S.-E., Orthopaedic Surgery
LENNQUIST, S., Disaster Medicine and Traumatology
LINDSTRÖM, S., Cell Biology
LISANDER, B., Anaesthesiology
LUDVIGSSON, J., Paediatrics
LUNDBLAD, A., Clinical Chemistry
LUNDQUIST, P.-G., Oto-Rhino-Laryngology
MAGNUSSON, K.-E., Medical Microbiology
MÅRDH, S., Cell Biology
NILSSON, S. E., Ophthalmology
NORDENSKJÖLD, B., Oncology
OLIN, C., Cardiothoracic Surgery
OLSSON, A. G., Medicine

OLSSON, J.-E., Neurology
RAMMER, L., Forensic Science and Medicine
STENDAHL, O., Medical Microbiology
STENMAN, G., Medical Genetics
SVANVIK, J., Surgery
TAGESSON, C., Experimental Medicine
THEODORSSON, E., Neurochemistry
TISELIUS, H.-G., Urology
TRELL, E., Family Medicine
VAHLQVIST, A., Dermatology and Venereology
WASTESON, Å., Cell Biology
WESTERMARK, P., Pathology
WIGERTZ, O., Medical Engineering (Medical Information Processing)
WRANNE, B., Clinical Physiology
WÅLINDER, J., Psychiatry
ÖBERG, Å., Medical Engineering (Instrumentation)
ÖSTRUP, L., Plastic Surgery

Faculty of Arts and Sciences:
ALLARD, B., Water and Environmental Studies
ARONSSON OTTOSSON, K., Child Studies
ASKLING, B., Education
BECKMAN, S., Technology and Social Change
BERNER, B., Technology and Social Change
BORGQUIST, L., Health and Society
CARSTENSEN, J., Health and Society
DAHLGREN, L.-O., Education
EDQUIST, C., Technology and Social Change
ERIKSSON, B. E., Health and Society
GRANINGER, G., Technology and Social Change
HELLGREN, B., Management
HJORT AF ORNÄS, A., Water and Environmental Studies
INGELSTAM, L., Technology and Social Change
JANSSON, J., Transport Economics
LINDKVIST, L., Management
LINELL, P., Communication Studies
LOHM, U., Water and Environmental Studies
LUNDQVIST, J., Water and Environmental Studies
NILSSON, G. B., Technology and Social Change
NORDENFELT, L., Health and Society
QVARSELL, R., Health and Society
RAHM, L., Water and Environmental Studies
RÖNNBERG, J., Psychology
SANDELL, R., Clinical Psychology
SANDIN, B., Child Studies
SUNDIN, E., Technology and Social Change
SUNDIN, J., Health and Society
SVENSSON, B., Water and Environmental Studies
WAERN, Y., Communication Studies

LULEÅ TEKNISKA UNIVERSITET
(Luleå University of Technology)

971 87 Luleå
Telephone: (920) 910 00
Telex: 80447
Fax: (920) 913-99

Founded 1971
State control
Language of instruction: Swedish
President: INGEGERD PALMÉR
Vice-President: (vacant)
Chief Administrative Officer: STAFFAN SARBÄCK
University Librarian: TERJE HÖISETH
Number of teachers: 592
Number of students: 8,300
Publications: *Research Reports, Technical Reports.*

DEANS

Faculty of Technology: ERIK HÖGLUND
Faculty of Humanities and Natural Sciences: GUNNAR PERSSON

PROFESSORS

Faculty of Technology:

Department of Civil and Mining Engineering:
AXELSSON, K., Soil Mechanics and Foundation Engineering
BORGBRANT, J., Construction Management
ELFGREN, L., Structural Engineering
JOHANSSON, B., Steel Structures
KLISINSKI, M., Structural Mechanics
LINDQVIST, P.-A., Geological Engineering
STILLBORG, B., Rock Mechanics

Department of Materials and Manufacturing Engineering:
BERGLUND, L., Polymer Engineering
KINNANDER, A., Manufacturing Engineering
MAGNUSSON, C., Materials Processing
WARREN, R., Engineering Materials

Department of Computer Science and Electrical Engineering:
BÖRJESSON, P.-O., Signal Processing
CARLSSON, S., Computer Science
DELSING, J., Industrial Electronics
JENNINGS, G., Computer Engineering
MEDVEDE, A., Automatic Control
PINK, S., Network Architecture
SCHEFSTRÖM, D., Software Engineering
WERNERSSON, Å., Robotics and Automation

Department of Mechanical Engineering:
FREDRIKSSON, S., Physics
GUSTAVSSON, H., Fluid Mechanics
HÖGLUND, E., Machine Elements
KARLSSON, L., Computer Aided Design
KJELLSTRÖM, B., Energy Engineering
MOLIN, N. E., Experimental Mechanics
STÅHLE, P., Solid Mechanics

Department of Chemical and Metallurgical Engineering:
BJÖRKMAN, B., Process Metallurgy
FORSSBERG, E., Mineral Processing
FORSLING, W., Inorganic Chemistry
STERTE, J., Chemical Technology

Department of Human Work Sciences:
JOHANSSON, J., Industrial Work Environment, Product Design
OLSSON, K., Technical Psychology
SHAHNAVAZ, H., Industrial Ergonomics
SUNDBÄCK, U., Environmental Technology
TELLENBACH, S., Social Psychology of Working Life
TROJER, L., Gender and Technology

Department of Business Administration and Social Sciences:
HENSWOLD, E., Industrial Logistics
HÖRTE, S.-Å., Industrial Organization
KLEFSJÖ, B., Quality Technology and Statistics
ORCI, I., Computer and Systems Sciences

Department of Environmental Planning and Design:
CORDI, I., Traffic Engineering
ELMING, S.-Å., Applied Geophysics
HANAEUS, J., Sanitary Engineering
LÖFGREN, O., Ecology and Environmental Protection
ÖHLANDER, B., Applied Geology
ÖSTMAN, A., Geographical Information Technology
TIBERG, N., Waste Management and Recycling
SELLGREN, A., Water Resources Engineering

Department of Wood Technology:
GRÖNLUND, A., Wood Technology

Department of Mathematics:
PERSSON, L.-E., Applied Mathematics

School of Education:
LINDELL, N. E., Pedagogics

Faculty of Humanities and Natural Sciences:

Department of Business Administration and Social Sciences:
BENGTSSON, B., Jurisprudence
DE RAADT, D., Informatics and Systems Sciences
HACKNER, E., Management Control
LUNDGREN, N.-G., Political Science
RADETZKI, M., Economics
SALEHI-SANGARI, E., Industrial Marketing

Department of Communication and Languages:
PERSSON, G., English
BONNER, M., German

School of Music:
BRÄNDSTRÖM, J., Education and Teaching Methods in Music
ERICSSON, H.-O., Organ
SANDSTRÖM, J., Composition
WESTBERG, E., Choir Singing and Choir Conducting

Centre for Research in Teaching and Learning:
JOHANSSON, H., Education

LUNDS UNIVERSITET

POB 117, S-221 00 Lund
Telephone: (46) 222-00-00
Telex: 33533
Fax: (46) 222-47-20

Founded 1666
Languages of instruction: Swedish, English
State control
Academic year: September to June (two semesters)

Rector: Prof. B. FLODGREN
Vice-Rector: Prof. A. ARDEBERG
Head of Administration: PETER HONETH

Library: see Libraries
Number of teachers: 2,000, including 400 professors
Number of students: 38,000
Publication: *LUM* (14 a year).

DEANS

Faculty of Theology: Prof. G. BEXELL
Faculty of Law: Prof. P. WESTBERG
Faculty of Medicine: Prof. P. BELFRAGE
Faculty of Humanities: Prof. H. ANDERSSON
Faculty of Political and Social Sciences: Prof. L.-G. STENELO
Faculty of Science: Prof. A. ARDEBERG
Faculty of Odontology: Prof. P.-O. GLANTZ
Faculty of Technology: T. JOHANNESSON

PROFESSORS

Faculty of Theology:
BERGLING, K., Psychology of Religion
BEXELL, G., Ethics
GUSTAFSSON, G., Sociology of Religion
HJÄRPE, J., Islamic Studies
JEANROND, W., Systematic Theology
LANDE, A., Missiology with Ecumenical Theology
OLSSON, B., New Testament Exegesis
OLSSON, T., History and Phenomenology of Religions
METTINGER, T., Old Testament Exegesis
SELANDER, S.-Å., Practical Theology
TRAUTNER-KROMANN, H., Jewish Studies

Faculty of Law:
BERGHOLTZ, G., Legal Procedure
BERGSTRÖM, S., Tax Law
BOGDAN, M., Comparative and Private International Law
CHRISTENSEN, A., Private Law
FAHLBECK, R., Labour Law
MELANDER, G., Public International Law
MODÉER, K. Å., Legal History
NUMHAUSER-HENNING, A., Private Law
PECZENIK, A., Jurisprudence
TRÄSKMAN, P. O., Criminal Law

VOGEL, H.-H., Public Law
WESTBERG, P., Legal Procedure

Faculty of Medicine:

ALLING, CH., Medical Neurochemistry
ALM, P., Pathology
ANDERSSON, K.-E., Clinical Pharmacology
ANDERSSON, T., Experimental Pathology
ANDREO, P., Radiotherapy
BERGGREN, P.-O., Cell Physiology
BELFRAGE, P., Medical Biochemistry
BERGLUND, G., Internal Medicine
BERGLUND, M., Clinical Alcohol Research
BJURSTEN, L.-M., Bio-implant Research
BJÖRK, L., Medical Biochemistry
BJÖRKLUND, A., Histology
BÄCK, O., Dermatology
CEDERBLAD, M., Child and Adolescent Psychology
DAHLBÄCK, B., Coagulation Research
DEHLIN, O., Geriatric Medicine
EKHBERG, O., Diagnostic Radiology
EHINGER, B., Ophthalmology
FORSBERG, H., Paediatrics
FORSBERG, J.-G., Anatomy
FORSGREN, A., Clinical Bacteriology
FRANSSON, L.-Å., Cell Biology
FRANZEN, L., Pathology
FÄSSLER, R., Experimental Pathology
GROOP, L., Endocrinology
GRUBB, A., Clinical Biochemistry
GUSTAFSON, L., Geriatric Psychiatry
HAMSTEN, A., Clinical Cardiovascular Research
HEIJL, A., Ophthalmology
HEINEGÅRD, D., Medical Biochemistry
HELLSTRAND, P., Muscle Research
HERMERÉN, G., Medical Ethics
HOLMBERG, L., Paediatrics
HOLMER, N.-G., Biomedical Engineering
HOLTÅS, S., Neuroradiology
HOVELIUS, B., General Practice
HÅKANSSON, R., Experimental Endocrinology
IHSE, I., Surgery
ISACSSON, S.-O., Social Medicine
JANZON, L., Epidemiology
JEPPSSON, B., Surgery
JOHANSSON, B., Neurology
JOHNELL, O., Orthopaedic Surgery
JONSON, B., Clinical Physiology
KARLSSON, S., Gene Therapy in Molecular Medicine
KILLANDER, D., Oncology
LEANDERSON, T., Immunology
LEIRISALO-REPO, M., Rheumatology
LEVANDER, S., Psychiatry
LIDGREN, L., Orthopaedics
LINDGREN, B., Health Economics
LINDVALL, O., Restorative Neurology
LUNDBERG, D., Anaesthesiology
LUNDBORG, G., Hand Surgery
LUNDQUIST, I., Pharmacology
LÖFDAHL, C.-G., Lung Disease
LÖWENHIELM, P., Forensic Medicine
MCNEIL, T., Medical Behavioural Research
MALM, L., Otorhinolaryngology
MARSAL, K., Obstetrics and Gynaecology
MATTIASSON, A., Urology
MATTSSON, S., Medical Radiation Physics
MITELMAN, F., Clinical Genetics
NILSSON, B., Orthopaedic Surgery
NILSSON, J., Experimental Cardiovascular Research
NORRBY, R., Infectious Diseases
OHLSSON, K., Surgical Pathophysiology
OLSSON, B., Cardiology
OLSSON, I., Haematology
OWMAN, CH., Histology
PERSSON, B., Medical Radiation Physics
PESONEN, E., Child Cardiology
PETTERSSON, H., Diagnostic Radiology
PRELLNER, K., Otorhinolaryngology
PÅHLMAN, S., Molecular Medicine
RAHM, H. J., Caring Sciences
RENCK, H., Anaesthesiology
RIPPE, B., Nephrology
RISBERG, J., Neuropsychology
RORSMAN, P., Membrane Physiology
ROSÉN, I., Clinical Neurophysiology
RÅSTAM, L., Applied Public Health
SALFORD, L., Neurosurgery
SJÖBERG, N.-O., Obstetrics and Gynaecology
SJÖGREN, H. A., Tumour Immunology
SKERFVING, S., Occupational Medicine
STEEN, S., Thoracic Surgery
STENFLO, J., Clinical Chemistry
SVANBORG, C., Clinical Immunology
THORNGREN, K.-G., Orthopaedics
WADSTRÖM, T., Bacteriology
WIELOCH, T., Neurobiology
WOLLMER, P., Clinical Physiology
ÖHMAN, R. L., Psychiatry

Faculty of Humanities:

ANDERSSON, G., Musicology
ANDERSSON, H., Medieval Archaeology
ANKARLOO, B., History
BERGH, B., Latin
BLOMQVIST, J., Greek Language and Literature
BROBERG, G., History of Ideas and Sciences
BRUCE, G., Phonetics
FRYKMAN, J., European Ethnology
GÄRDENFORS, P., Cognitive Science
HAETTNER-AURELIUS, E., Literature
HANSSON, B., Theoretical Philosophy
HOLMBERG, B., Semitic Languages
HORNBORG, A., Human Ecology
LARSSON, L., Archaeology
LÖFGREN, O., European Ethnology
NILSSON, S. Å., Art History
PLATZACK, C., Scandinavian Languages
RABINOWICZ, W., Practical Philosophy
RAGVALD, L., Chinese
RIDDERSTAD, P. S., Book and Library History
ROSENGREN, I., German
RYDÉN, P., Literature
RYSTEDT, E., Classical Archaeology and Ancient History
SALOMON, K., International History
SCHLYTER, S., Romance Languages
SJÖLIN, J.-G., History of Contemporary Art
STEENSLAND, L., Slavic Languages
TELEMAN, U., Swedish
THORMÄHLEN, M., English Literature
VIBERG, Å., General Linguistics
WARREN, B., English
WIRMARK, M., Drama, Theatre and Film
ÖSTERBERG, E., History

Faculty of Political and Social Sciences:

ALLWOOD, C.-M., Psychology
ALVESSON, M., Business Administration
ARWIDI, O., Business Administration
ASPLUND, J., Sociology of Culture
BERG, S., Statistics
BORGLIN, A., Public Sector Economics
BRANTE, T., Sociology
CLARK, E., Social Geography
DAHLGREN, P., Sociology of Communication
EDGERTON, D., Econometrics
EHN, P., Information and Computer Sciences
ELIASSON, R.-M., Social Work
FLODGREN, B., Business Law
FRIEDMAN, J., Social Anthropology
GANDEMO, B., Business Administration
GUNNARSSON, CHR., Economic History
HANSSON, G., International Economics
HETZLER, A., Social Policy
HYDÉN, H., Sociology of Law
JACOBSSON, B., Business Administration
JOHANNISSON, B., Business Administration
JOHANSSON, C. R., Industrial and Organizational Psychology
JÖNSSON, CHR., Political Science
LANKE, J., Statistics, especially Biostatistics
LÖFGREN, H., Education
LUNDQUIST, L., Political Science, especially Public Administration
MALM, A., Business Administration
NILSSON, A., Clinical Psychology
OHLSSON, R., Modern Economic and Social History
OXELHEIM, L., International Business
PERSSON, I., Economics, especially Women's Studies
RYDÉN, O., Personality Psychology
SCHÖN, L., Economic History
SELLERBERG, A.-M., Sociology
STENELO, L.-G., Political Science
STÅHL, I., Economics
SÖDERSTEN, B., International Economics
SÖDERSTRÖM, L., Economics, especially Social Policy
STANKIEWICZ, R., Science and Technology Policy
SUNESSON, S., Social Work
SVENSSON, L., Pedagogy
SVENSSON, L.-G., Economics
SVINGBY, G., Education
TÖRNQVIST, G., Economic Geography

Faculty of Science:

ALERSTAM, T., Animal Ecology
ALLEN, J. F., Plant Cell Biology
ANDERSEN, T., Astronomy
ANDERSSON, B., Theoretical Physics
ARDEBERG, A., Astronomy
ARNASON, U., Evolutionary Genetics
ASMUSSEN, S., Mathematical Statistics
BENGTSSON, B. O., Genetics
BENGTSSON, S.-A., Systematic Zoology
BERGLUND, B., Quaternary Geology
BJÖRN, L. O., Plant Physiology
CHAO, K., Theoretical Physics
DRAVINS, D., Astronomy
EDSTRÖM, A., Zoophysiology
ELDING, L. I., Inorganic Chemistry
ERIKSSON, M., Physics
FAGERSTRÖM, T., Theoretical Ecology
FAHLANDER, C., Physics
FREJD, T., Organic Chemistry
GORTON, L., Analytical Chemistry
GRANELI, W., Limnology
GUSTAFSON, G., Theoretical Physics
HEDENMALM, H., Mathematics
HOLMBERG, B., Inorganic Chemistry
JAKOBSSON, B., Physics
JARLSKOG, G., Physics
JERGIL, B., Biochemistry
JOHANSSON, S., Atomic Spectroscopy
KANJE, M., Zoophysiology
LARSSON, C., Plant Biochemistry
LARSSON, K., Historical Geology and Palaeontology
LILJAS, A., Molecular Biophysics
LINDAU, I., Synchrotron Light Research
LINDMAN, B., Physical Chemistry
LINGAS, A., Computer Sciences
MARTINSON, I., Atomic Physics
MATTSSON, S., Radiation Physics
MEURMAN, A., Mathematics
NIHLGÅRD, B., Plant Ecology
NILSSON, D. E., Zoology
NILSSON, N., Mathematics
OTTERLUND, I., Physics
PEETRE, J., Mathematics
PERSSON, B., Radiation Physics
PETTERSON, G., Biochemistry
PRENTICE, H., Systematic Botany
PRENTICE, I. C., Plant Ecology
ROOS, B., Theoretical Chemistry
RUTBERG, L., Microbiology
STRAND, S.-E., Radiation Physics
STYRING, S., Biochemistry
SUNDSTRÖM, V., Chemical Dynamics
SVENSSON, B. E. Y., Theoretical Physics
SÖDERGREN, A., Chemical Ecology and Ecotoxicology
SÖDERLIND, G., Numerical Mathematics
SÖDERSTRÖM, B., Microbial Ecology
TJERNELD, F., Biochemistry
TYLER, G., Plant Ecology
WENNERSTRÖM, H., Physical Chemistry

Faculty of Odontology:

ATTSTRÖM, R., Periodontics
BRATTHALL, D., Cariology

DERAND, T., Dental Technology
EDWARDSSON, S., Oral Microbiology
GLANTZ, P.-O., Prosthetics
KUROL, J., Orthodontics
LARSSON, Å., Oral Pathology
MATSSON, L., Pedodontics
NILNER, S. K., Clinical Dental Material Research
ROHLIN, M., Oral Radiology and Diagnostics
ROSENQUIST, J., Oral and Maxillofacial Surgery
SÖDERFELDT, B., Dental Public Health

Faculty of Technology:

AHLIN, J., Theoretical and Applied Aesthetics
AKSELSSON, R., Working Environment
ALAKÜLA, M., Electrical Engineering
ALDÉN, M., Combustion Diagnostics with Lasers
ASP, N.-G., Applied Nutrition
AXSÄTER, S., Production Management
BENGTSSON, L., Water Resources Engineering
BERGENSTÅHL, B., Food Technology
BJELM, L., Geo-Resource Technology
BOLMSJÖ, G., Robot Technology
BORREBAECK, C., Immunotechnology
BOVIN, J.-O., High-Resolution Electron Microscopy and the Structure of Solids
DALGAS, V., Town Planning
DEJMEK, P., Food Engineering
ELIASSON, A.-C., Cereal Technology
ELMROTH, A., Building Physics
FAGERLUND, G., Building Materials
FREDLUND, B., Construction Science
FUCHS, L., Applied Fluid Mechanics
HAHN-HÄGERDAL, B., Applied Microbiology
HAMMAMOTO-KURODA, I., Mathematical Physics
HOLMBERG, B., Public Transport
HYDÉN, C., Traffic Planning
JACOBSON, B., Machine Design
JARLSKOG, C., Theoretical Particle Physics
JENSEN, L. H., Installations for Heating
JOHANNESSON, R., Information Theory
JOHANNESSON, T., Materials Engineering
JOHANSSON, T.-B., Environmental and Energy Systems Studies
JÖNSON, G., Packaging Logistics
KARLSSON, H., Chemical Engineering Catalysis
KRISTENSSON, G., Electromagnetic Theory
KÖRNER, U., Communication Systems
L'HUILLIER, A., Atomic Physics
LA COUR JANSEN, J., Water and Waste Water Engineering
LIDGREN, K., Environmental Economics
LINDBLAD, S., Engineering Acoustics
LINDGREN, G., Mathematical Statistics
LINDSTRÖM, K., Electrical Measurements
LUNDHOLM, G., Combustion Engines
MAGNUSSON, G., Organic Chemistry
MAGNUSSON, S.-E., Fire Safety Engineering and Building Science
MALMQVIST, K., Nuclear Physics
MATTIASSON, B., Biotechnology
MELIN, A., Mathematics
OLSSON, G., Industrial Automation
OMLING, P., Solid State Physics
PERSSON, W., Atomic Physics
PETERSON, H., Structural Mechanics
PHILIPSON, L., Computer Systems
REUTERSWÄRD, L., Architecture and Development Studies
SAABYE-OTTOSEN, N., Solid Mechanics
SALOMONSSON, G., Signal Processing
SAMUELSSON, L., Solid State Physics
SHERWIN, D. J., Terotechnology
SIEGRIST, T., Solid State Chemistry
SMEETS, B., Computer Engineering
STÅHL, J.-E., Production and Materials Engineering
SUNDÉN, B., Heat Transfer
SVANBERG, S., Atomic Physics
SVERDRUP, H., Environmental Science in connection with Chemical Engineering
SÖDERBERG, J., Construction Management
THAM, K., Architecture
THELANDERSSON, S., Structural Engineering
THÖRNQVIST, L., Energy Economics Planning
TORISSON, T., Power Plant Engineering
WAHLUND, K.-G., Technical Analytical Chemistry
WERNE, F., Building Functions
WIBERG, K., Architecture
WIMMERSTEDT, R., Chemical Engineering
WITTENMARK, B., Automatic Control
WOHLIN, C., Software Systems Engineering
YUAN, J., Circuit Design
ZACCHI, G., Chemical Engineering
ZIGANGIROW, K., Telecommunications Theory
ÅSTRÖM, K. J., Automatic Control

Malmö Academy of Music:

FOLKESTAD, G., Music Education
GEFORS, H., Composition
HARDENBERGER, H., Trumpet
HELLSTEN, H., Organ
LINDROOS, P., Singing
PÅLSSON, H., Piano
SÖLLSCHER, G., Guitar

Malmö Art Academy:

LEIDERSTAM, M., Fine Arts
NILSSON, L., Fine Arts

HÖGSKOLAN I ÖREBRO
(University of Örebro)

701 82 Örebro
Telephone: (19) 30-30-00

Founded 1967
State control
Academic year: September to June

Vice-Chancellor: INGEMAR LIND
Deputy Vice-Chancellor: LENNART HEDBERG
Registrar: EVA FURUHOLM
Information Officer: KAY ISACSON
Librarian: ELISABET ANDERSSON

Library of 150,000 vols
Number of teachers: 600
Number of students: 8,000

DEANS

Caring Sciences: BRITT-MARIE TERNESTEDT
Domestic Science: BIRGITTA ULMANDER
Economics, Statistics and Computer Science: OLLE HÄGGBOM
Humanities: INGRID ÅBERG
Social Sciences: BERNT JOHANSSON
Sports and Physical Training: KJELL SUNESSON
Teacher-Training: KJELL SUNESSON
Technology: LENNART PHILIPSON
Training of Music Teachers: ANITA NILSSON

STOCKHOLMS UNIVERSITET

106 91 Stockholm

Telephone: (8) 16-20-00
Fax: (8) 15-95-22

Founded 1877, became State University 1960
State control
Language of instruction: Swedish
Academic year: August to June

President: Prof. G. LINDENCRONA
Vice-President: Prof. G. ENGWALL
Head of Administration: L. LINDFORS

Library: see Libraries
Number of teachers: (full-time): 1,150, including 200 professors
Number of students: 32,000

Publications: *Katalog*, *Acta Universitatis Stockholmiensis*.

DEANS

Faculty of Humanities: Prof. E. WANDE
Faculty of Law: Prof. P. SEIPEL
Faculty of Social Sciences: Prof. E. WADENSJÖ
Faculty of Natural Sciences: Prof. L. WASTENSON

PROFESSORS

Faculty of Humanities:

History-Philosophy Section:

ALGULIN, I., Literature
BERGLIE, A., Religion
BERGQVIST, B., Ancient Culture and Civilization
BERGSTRÖM, L., Practical Philosophy
BOËTHIUS, U., Literary History, especially Children's Literature
CULLHED, A., Literary History
DAHLBÄCK, G., History of the Middle Ages
DAUN, Å., Ethnology
HALL, T., Scandinavian and Comparative Art History
HVITFELT, H., Journalism
HYENSTRAND, Å., Archaeology
HÄGG, I., Archaeology, with Laboratory Analysis
JARRICK, A., History
JONSSON, K., Numismatics
KÖLL, A. M., Baltic Studies
LINDBERG, B., History of Ideas
LINDROTH, J., History of Athletics
NILSSON, L., History of Municipality
NOWAK, K., Media and Communication
OLSSON, J., Film Studies
PRAWITZ, D., Theoretical Philosophy
ROSSHOLM LAGERLÖF, M., Art History and Theory
SAUTER, W., Theatre Studies
SJØVOLD, T., Historical Osteology
ÅMARK, K., History

Language Section:

ALBERG JENSEN, P., Slavic Languages, especially Russian Language and Literature
BERGMAN, B., Sign Language
BRODDA, B., Computational Linguistics
DAHL, Ö., General Linguistics
EKSELL, K., Arabic Language, especially Modern Arabic
ENGWALL, G., Romance Languages, French
FANT, L., Romance Languages, especially Ibero-Romance Languages
FAWKNER, H., English, especially English Literature
GUNNARSON, B.-L., Swedish Language
HELLBERG, S., Scandinavian Languages
HYLTENSTAM, K., Bilingualism
KANGERE, B., Baltic Languages
LINDBERG-WADA, G., Japanology, especially modern Japanese
LINDBLOM, B., Physiology and Perception of Speech
LJUNG, M., English Language
LODÉN, T., Language and Culture of China
MÜSSENER, H., German, especially German Literature
NILSSON, B., Slavic Languages
NYSTEDT, J., Italian
OETKE, C., Language and Culture of India
ROSÉN, S., Language and Culture of Korea
WANDE, E., Finnish Language
ÖBERG, J., Latin

Faculty of Law:

BERNITZ, U., European Law
BJARUP, J., Jurisprudence
BOHLIN, A., Public Law
BRING, O., International Law
DUFWA, B., Insurance Law
EKLUND, R., Private Law, Labour Law
HANSSON, I., International Economics
HEUMAN, L., Procedure
KLEINEMAN, J., Civil Law
KÄLLSTRÖM, K., Private Law
LEIJONHUFVUD, M., Penal Law
LEVIN, M., Private Law
LINDENCRONA, G., Financial Law
MELZ, P., Financial Law
PETERSON, C., Legal History

PEHRSON, L., Economics and Economic Law
SANDGREN, C., Civil Law
SEIPEL, P., Law and Informatics
VICTORIN, A., Private Law
VOGEL, H.-H., Public Law
WENNBERG, S., Penal Law

Faculty of Social Sciences:

AHRNE, G., Sociology
BERGLUND, B., Perception and Psychophysics
BERGMAN, L., Behavioural Sciences
BERGMARK, A., Social Work
BJÖRKLUND, A., Economics, especially Evaluating Labour Market Research
BOHM, P., Economics
BUBENKO, J., Information Processing
CALMFORS, L., International Economics
DAHL, G., Social Anthropology, Development Research
DAHLERUP, O., Political Science
EDWARDS, M., Political Science
ERIKSON, R., Sociology
FLAM, H., International Economics
FORSBERG, G., Human Geography
FRANK, O., Statistics
FÄGERLIND, I., International and Comparative Education
GOLDMANN, K., Political Science
GUILLET DE MONTHOUX, P., Business Administration
GUMMESSON, E., Business Administration
HANNERZ, U., Social Anthropology
HART, T., Pacific Asia Studies
HEDBERG, B., Business Administration
HEDSTRÖM, P., Sociology, Population Processes
HESSLE, S., Social Work
HOEM, J., Demography
HORN AF RANTZIEN, H., International Economics
JOHANSSON, G., Working Life Psychology
JONSSON, E., Business Administration, Administrative Economics
KORPI, W., Social Politics
KÜHLHORN, E., Sociological Alcoholic Research
LENNTORP, B., Human and Economic Geography
LUNDBERG, B., Information Administration
LUNDBERG, U., Human Biological Psychology
MONTGOMERY, H., Cognitive Psychology
NILSSON, L.-G., Psychology
NORSTRÖM, T., Sociology, Social Politics
NYSTEDT, L., Psychology, Social Perception
OVARSELL, B., Education
PALME, J., Computer and Systems Sciences
PERSSON, M., International Economics
PERSSON, T., International Economics
PREMFORS, R., Political Science
SAHLIN-ANDERSON, K., Public Organization
SARNECKI, J., Criminology
SIVEN, C.-H., Economics, especially Economic Politics
SKÖLDBERG, K., Business Administration
SPORRONG, U., Geography, especially Human Geography
SVEDBERG, P., Development Economics
SVENSON, O., Nuclear Power Safety (Psychology)
SVENSSON, L., International Economics
SWEDBERG, R., Economic Sociology
SÖDERBERG, J., Economic History
TARSCHYS, D., Political Science, especially Planning and Administration
THAM, H., Criminology
THORBURN, D., Statistics
THORSLUND, M., Social Work
TÅHLIN, M., Sociology
WADENSJÖ, E., Employment Policy
WESTIN, C., Immigration Research
WIJKANDER, H., International Economics
WIKANDER, U., Economic History
VÅGERÖ, D., Medical Sociology
WITTROCK, B., Political Science
ÖST, L.-G., Clinical Psychology

Faculty of Natural Sciences:

Mathematics-Physics Section:

BARGHOLTZ, C., Nuclear Physics
BJÖRK, J.-E., Mathematics
BOHM, C., Technology of Physical Systems
EKEDAHL, T., Mathematics
FRANSSON, C., Astrophysics
HANSSON, H., Theoretical Physics
HANSSON, H.-C., Air Pollution
HOLMGREN, S.-O., High-Energy Physics
KÄLLEN, E., Dynamic Meteorology
LARSSON, M., Experimental Molecular Physics
MARTIN-LÖF, A., Actuarial Mathematics and Mathematical Statistics
OLOFSSON, H., Astronomy
PALMGREN, J., Biostatistics
PASSARE, M., Mathematics
RODHE, H., Chemical Meteorology
ROOS, J. E., Mathematics
SCHUCH, R., Atomic Physics
SIEGBAHN, P., Theoretical Physics
SUNDQVIST, H., Meteorology
SVENSSON, R., Astrophysics with Cosmology

Chemistry Section:

ANDERSSON, B., Biochemistry
BARTFAI, T., Neurochemistry
BERGMAN, Å., Environmental Chemistry
BRZEZINSKI, P., Biochemistry, esp. Molecular Energy Research
BÄCKVALL, J.-E., Organic Chemistry
DEPIERRE, J., Biochemistry, especially Enzymological Toxicology
HULTH, P.-O., Experimental Physics
JANSSON, B., Chemical Environmental Analysis
JOSEFSSON, B., Analytical Chemistry
KOWALEWSKI, J., Physical Chemistry
LEVITT, M., Chemical Spectroscopy
LIDIN, S., Inorganic Chemistry
NELSON, D., Biochemistry
NORDLUND, P., Structural Biochemistry
NORRESTAM, R., Structural Chemistry
NYGREN, M., Material Chemistry, Electroceramics
ODHAM, G., Analytical Environmental Chemistry
VON HEIJNE, G., Theoretical Chemistry

Biology Section:

BERGMAN, B., Physiological Botany
BORG, H., Aquatic Environmental Chemistry
BROMAN, D., Aquatic Ecotoxicology
CANNON, B., Animal Physiology
ELMGREN, R., Marine Ecology
ERIKSSON, O., Plant Ecology
FOLKE, C., Management of Natural Resources
GRÄSLUND, A., Biophysics
HAGGÅRD, E., Genetics
ISAKSSON, L., Microbiology
KAUTSKY, N., Marine Ecotoxicology
LINDBERG, U., Zoological Cell Biology
MÖLLER, G., Immunology
NÄSSEL, D., Functional Zoomorphology
RADESÄTER, T., Ethology
RANNUG, U., Toxicological Genetics
SJÖBERG, B.-M., Molecular Biology
WALLES, B., Morphological Botany
WIESLANDER, L., Molecular Genome Research
WIKLUND, C., Ecological Zoology
WULFF, F., Marine Systems Ecology

Earth Sciences Section:

BACKMAN, J., General and Historical Geology
HALLBERG, R., Microbial Chemistry
IHSE, M., Ecological Geography
INGRI, J., Geochemistry and Petrology
KARLÉN, W., Physical Geography
RINGBERG, B., Quaternary Geology
ROSSWALL, T., Water and Environmental Studies
WASTENSON, L., Remote Sensing

AFFILIATED INSTITUTES

Bergianska trädgården (Bergius Garden): Dir Prof. BENGT JONSELL.

Centrum för naturresurs- och miljöforskning (Centre for Natural Resources and Environmental Research): Prof. ANNMARI JANSSON.

Latinamerika-institutet (Institute of Latin American Studies): Dir WEINE KARLSSON; see under Research Institutes.

Manne Siegbahn-laboratoriet: Dir K.-G. RENSFELT.

Tolk- och översättarinstitutet (Institution for Interpretation and Translation Studies): Dir GUNNAR LEMHAGEN.

SVERIGES LANTBRUKSUNIVERSITET (Swedish University of Agricultural Sciences)

750 07 Uppsala
Telephone: (18) 67-10-00
Fax: (18) 67-20-00
E-mail: registrator@stu.se

Founded 1977 by amalgamation of the former *Lantbrukshögskolan, Skogshögskolan,* and *Veterinärhögskolan*

Rector: Prof. T. ROSSWALL
Vice-Rector: J. CARLSTEN
Head of Administration: (vacant)
Director of Library: JAN HAGERLID
Library: see Libraries
Number of teachers: 500
Number of students: 3,300

Publications: *Studia Forestalia Suecica, Collected Papers, Catalogue, List of Publications, Students' Handbook.*

DEANS

Faculty of Agriculture, Landscape Planning and Horticulture: Prof. B. NILSSON
Faculty of Forestry: Prof. K. ROSÉN
Faculty of Veterinary Medicine: G. DALIN

PROFESSORS

(Some professors serve in more than one faculty)

Faculty of Agriculture, Landscape Planning and Horticulture:

ANDERSSON, A., Soil Science
ANDERSSON, I., Plant Biochemistry
ANDRÉN, O., Soil Biology and Agriculture
BANDOLIN, G., Aesthetics in Landscape Architecture
BENGTSSON, B., International Crop Production Science
BENGTSSON, J., Environmental Science and Conservation
BJÖRCK, L., Dairy Products Science
BOLIN, O., Economics of Agriculture, International Trade
BOTHMER, R. VON, Genetics and Breeding of Cultivated Plants
BUCHT, E., Landscape Planning
BYLUND, A.-C., Meat Science
CARLSSON, M., Business Administration
DANELL, B., Animal Breeding
DANELL, Ö., Reindeer Husbandry
EBBERSTEN, S., Organic Farming/Ecological Farming
EKLUND, H., Structural Molecular Biology
ERIKSSON, B., Nematology
ERIKSSON, L.-O., Aquaculture
FLORGÅRD, C., Landscape Architecture
GERHARDSON, B., Plant Pathology
GIBBON, D., Small-Scale Farming
GLIMELIUS, K., Genetics and Plant Breeding
GUSTAFSON, A., Water Quality Management
GUSTAFSSON, M., Plant Disease Resistance

GUSTAFSSON, P., Landscape Architecture
GUSTAVSSON, R., Planting Design and Management
HAVNEVIK, K., Rural Development
HENEEN, W., Genetics and Breeding of Cultivated Plants
HUSS-DANELL, K., Crop Science
ISAKSSON, N.-I., Agricultural Economics
JANSSON, P.-E., Agricultural Hydrotechnics
JARVIS, N., Biogeophysics
JENSÉN, P., Horticultural Science
JIGGINS, J., Human Ecology
JILAR, T., Horticultural Building and Climate Technology
JOHANSON, K. J., Radioecology
JÄGERSTAD, M., Food Chemistry
KENNE, L., Organic Chemistry
LARSEN, R., Greenhouse Production, Horticultural Crops
LILJEDAHL, L.-E., Animal Breeding
LINDBERG, J.-E., Animal Nutrition and Management
LINDBERG, M., Ecological Microbiology
LÖFQVIST, J., Insect Pheromone Systems
MAGNHAGEN, C., Aquaculture
MERKER, A., Plant Breeding
MYRDAL, J., History of Agriculture
MÖLLER, N., Agricultural Engineering
NILSSON, B., Agricultural Engineering
NILSSON, C., Building Science
NILSSON, I., Soil Chemistry and Pedology
NILSSON, J., Co-operation
NILSSON, T., Postharvest Physiology and Handling of Horticultural Produce
NITSCH, U., Agricultural Communication
NYBOM, H., Horticultural Genetics and Plant Breeding
NYBRANT, T., Agricultural Control Engineering
NYSTRÖM, H., Agricultural Marketing
OLOFSSON, C., Entrepreneurial Studies
OLSSON, K., Animal Physiology
PERSSON, I., Inorganic and Physical Chemistry
PERSSON, J., Plant Nutrition
PETTERSSON, J., Applied Entomology
PETTERSSON, S., Plant Physiology
RONNE, H., Molecular Genetics
SEEGER, P., Statistics
SIMÁN, G., Plant Nutrition
SKAGE, O., Comprehensive Landscape Planning
SORTE, G., Landscape Architecture
SÄLLVIK, K., Agricultural Building Functions Analysis
TILLBERG, E., Plant Physiology
UVNÄS-MOBERG, K., Animal Physiology
VALKONEN, J., Virology comprising Plant Viruses
WAGNER, G., Microbiology
WELANDER, M., Horticultural Science
WIKTORSSON, H., Animal Nutrition and Management
ÅMAN, P., Plant Products
ÖHLMER, B., Agricultural Business Administration

Faculty of Forestry:

AHLÉN, I., Forest Vertebrate Ecology
ANDERSSON, F., Terrestrial Ecology
ANDERSSON, S. B., Operational Efficiency
ARNOLD, S. VON, Forest Cell Biology
AXELSSON, S.-Å., Operational Efficiency
BISHOP, K., Environmental Assessment
BORGEFORS, G., Remote Sensing and Image Analysis
BÄCKSTRÖM, P. O., Forestry
CHRISTERSSON, L., Fast-growing Tree Species
CLARHOLM, M., Soil Ecology
DANELL, K., Wildlife Ecology
ELFVING, B., Forest Yield Research
ELOWSON, T., Wood Technology
ERIKSSON, G., Forest Genetics
ERIKSSON, L. O., Forestry Planning
FINLAY, R., Forest Microbiology
GEMMEL, P., Forestry
HANSSON, L., Population Ecology
HAGNER, M., Forest Regeneration
HENNINGSSON, B., Wood Preservation and Protection of Timber
HULTÉN, H., Forest Regeneration
HÄLLGREN, J.-E., Forest Plant Physiology
HÖGBERG, P., Soil Science
JEGLUM, J., Forest Peatland Science
KARDELL, L., Environmental Forestry
KRISTRÖM, B., Natural Resources Economics
LARSSON, S., Forest Entomology
LINDER, S., Forest Ecology
LINDGREN, D., Forest Genetics
LÅNGSTROM, B., Forest Protection from Insects
LÖNNER, G., Marketing of Sawn Timber
LÖNNSTEDT, L., Business Economics
NILSSON, P.-O., Energy System in Forestry
NILSSON, S., Planning
NILSSON, T., Ultrastructure and Disintegration of Wood
NYLINDER, M., Wood Measurement and Cross-Cutting
ODÉN, P. C., Forestry Seed Research
OLSSON, H., Remote Sensing applied to Forestry
OLSSON, M., Forest Soil Chemistry
PERSSON, A., Provenance Research
PERSSON, T., Biology of Forest Soils
RANNEBY, B., Forest Survey
ROSEN, K., Forest Soils
SALLNÄS, O., Forestry Technology
SANDBERG, G., Morphogenesis of Trees
STENLID, J., Pathology of Forest Trees
STÅHL, G., Forest Survey
WIBE, S., Forest Economics
WÄSTERLUND, I., Forestry Technology
ZACKRISSON, O., Forest Vegetation Ecology
ÅGREN, G., Systems Ecology

Faculty of Veterinary Medicine:

ALGERS, B., Animal Hygiene
ALM, G., Immunology
ANDERSSON, L., Genetics
APPELGREN, L.-E., Pharmacology
BJÖRK, I., Medical and Physiological Chemistry
DANIELSSON-THAM, M.-L., Food Hygiene
DREVEMO, S., Anatomy and Histology
EINARSSON, S., Obstetrics and Gynaecology
ENGSTRÖM, W., Pathology
ERIKSSON, S., Medical and Physiological Chemistry
GUSTAVSSON, I., Genetics
HAKKARAINEN, J., Nutritional Pathology
JENSEN, P., Ethology
JONES, B., Clinical Chemistry
JÖNSSON, L., Pathology
KINDAHL, H., Obstetrics and Gynaecology
LORD, P., Clinical Radiology
LUTHMAN, J., Medicine for Ruminants
MOREIN, B., Virology
NARFSTRÖM, K., Surgery and Ophthalmology
NILSSON, G., Physiology
OSKARSSON, A., Food Hygiene
PLÖEN, L., Anatomy and Histology
RODRÍGUEZ-MARTÍNEZ, H., Reproduction Biotechnology
SVENSSON, S., Bacteriology
TJÄLVE, H., Toxicology
UGGLA, A., Parasitology

UMEÅ UNIVERSITET

901 87 Umeå
Telephone: (90) 786-50-00
Telex: 54005
Fax: (90) 786-54-88

Founded 1965
State control

Rector: Prof. S. FRANKE
Vice-Rector: Prof. J.-O. KELLERTH
Director: MATS OLA OTTOSSON
Library: see Libraries
Number of teachers: 2,000, including 168 professors
Number of students: 23,700

DEANS

Faculty of Humanities: Prof. ANDERS PETTERSON
Faculty of Social Sciences: Prof. RUNE ÅBERG
Faculty of Medicine: Prof. THOMAS OLIVECRONA
Faculty of Odontology: Prof. ANNA-KARIN HOLM
Faculty of Mathematics and Natural Sciences: Prof. ULF EDLUND

PROFESSORS

Faculty of Humanities:

AMBJÖRNSSON, R., History of Science and Ideas
BANNERT, R., Phonetics
BROADBENT, N., Archaeology
DANELL, K. J., French Language
EDLUND, L.-E., Scandinavian Languages
EDMAN, M., Philosophy and Science of Humanities
EHN, B., Ethnology
EJERHED, E., General Linguistics
FINDAHL, O., Mass Communication
GROUNDSTROEM, A., Finnish Language
JOHANSSON, E., History of Popular Education
KIHLGREN, S., Graphics
KORHONEN, O., Lapp Language
KRÜGER, A., Free Art in Nordic Contemporary Art
LARSSON, K., Swedish Language
PALMGREN, B., Design
PERSSON, G., English Language
PETTERSSON, A., Comparative Literature
SPOLANDER, R., History of Art
SPÅNBERG, S.-J., English Literature
STEDJE, A., German Language
SUNDIN, B., History of Science and Ideas
SÖRLIN, S., Environmental History
TEDEBRAND, L.-G., Historical Demography
ÅKERMAN, S., History

Faculty of Social Sciences:

ANELL, B., Business Administration and Economics
ARMELIUS, B.-Å., Clinical Psychology
BOJE, T., Sociology
BRÄNNÄS, K., Econometrics
FRANKE, S., Pedagogics
GIDLUND, J.-E., Regional Politics and Administration
GUSTAFSSON, G., Political Science
HAMILTON, D., Pedagogics
HOFSTEN, C. VON, Psychology
HOLM, E., Social and Economic Geography
IVANOV, K., Administrative Data Processing
JOHANSSON, M., Pedagogics (Sports)
KALLÓS, D., Pedagogics
KHAKEE, A., Urban Planning
KRANTZ, O., Economic History
LUNDIN, R., Business Administration and Economics
LÖFGREN, K.-G., Economics
MARKLUND, S., Sociology (Welfare and Social Policy)
MÄNTYLÄ, T., Psychology (Cognitive Science)
NYGREN, L., Social Work
NYQUIST, H., Statistics
PUU, T., Regional Economics
SANDGREN, C., Law
SHARMA, D., Marketing and International Business
TEDEBRAND, L. G., Demography
WEDMAN, I., Pedagogics (Measurement)
WIBERG, U., Economic Geography
ÅBERG, R., Sociology

Faculty of Medicine:

ADOLFSSON, R., Psychiatry
ALSTERMARK, B., Physiology

ASPLUND, K., Medicine
BERGH, A., Pathology
BIBERG, B., Anaesthesiology
BJERMER, L., Pulmonary Medicine
BOQUIST, L., Pathology
BROSTRÖM, L.-A., Orthopaedics
BUCHT, G., Geriatrics
BYGREN, L. O., Preventive and Social Medicine
BÄCKSTRÖM, T., Obstetrics and Gynaecology
DAHLQUIST, G., Paediatrics
DAHLQVIST, R., Clinical Pharmacology
DAMBER, J.-E., Urology
DENEKAMP, J., Radiobiology
EGELRUD, T., Dermatology and Venereology
ERIKSSON, A., Forensic Medicine
FORSGREN, L., Neurology
FOWLER, C., Pharmacology
GROTH, S., Clinical Physiology
GRUNDSTRÖM, T., Tumour Biology
HAFSTRÖM, L., Surgery
HAMMARSTRÖM, S., Immunology
HELLSTRÖM, S., Oto-rhino-laryngology
HENRIKSSON, R., Experimental Oncology
HERNELL, O., Paediatrics
HIETALA, S. O., X-ray and Diagnostics
HOLM, S., Clinical Bacteriology
HOLMGREN, G., Clinical Genetics
HOVELIUS, B., Family Medicine
JACOBSSON, L., Psychiatry
JOHANSSON, R., Physiology
JÄRVHOLM, B., Occupational Medicine
KELLERTH, J.-O., Anatomy
LIBELIUS, R., Clinical Neurophysiology
LITTBRAND, B., Oncology
LORENTZON, R., Sports Medicine
LUNDGREN, E., Applied Cell Biology
MARKLUND, S., Clinical Chemistry
MILLÁN, J. L., Medical Genetics
NORBERG, A., Advanced Nursing
NORDBERG, G., Environmental Medicine
NY, T., Medical and Physiological Chemistry
OLIVECRONA, G., Medical Chemistry
OLIVECRONA, T., Medical and Physiological Chemistry
ROOS, G., Pathology
SANDSTRÖM, T., Pulmonary Medicine
SEHLIN, J., Histology
SELSTAM, G., Physiology
STENDAHL, U., Gynaecological Oncology
STIGBRAND, T., Immunochemistry
SUNDKVIST, K. G., Clinical Immunology
SVENSSON, H., Medical Radiation Physics
THELANDER, L., Medical and Physiological Chemistry
THORNELL, L.-E., Anatomy
TÄLJEDAL, I.-B., Histology
TÄRNVIK, A., Infectious Diseases
UHLIN, B. E., Microbiology
WACHTMEISTER, L., Ophthalmology
WADELL, G., Virology
WAHLSTRÖM, G., Pharmacology
WALDENSTRÖM, A., Cardiology
WALL, S., Epidemiology and Public Health
WIJMENGA, S., Medical Biophysics

Faculty of Odontology:
CARLSSON, J., Oral Microbiology
ERIKSSON, P.-O., Clinical Oral Physiology
HOLM, A.-K., Pedodontics
ISBERG, A., Oral Diagnostic Radiology
LERNER, U., Oral Cell Biology
OLSSON, K. Å., Physiology
PERSSON, M., Orthodontics
STRÖMBERG, N., Cardiology
SUNDQVIST, G., Endodontics

Faculty of Mathematics and Natural Sciences:
BELYAER, Y., Mathematical Statistics
BJÖRK, G., Microbiology
BONSDORFF, R., Marine Biology
CEDERGREN, A., Analytical Chemistry
CEGRELL, U., Mathematics
EDLUND, T., Molecular Genetics
EDLUND, U., Organic Chemistry
EKLUND, P., Computer Science
ERICSSON, L., Plant Ecology
GUSTAFSSON, P., Plant Molecular Biology
HEBY, O., Cellular and Developmental Biology
HÄGGKVIST, R., Discrete Mathematics
JANSSON, M., Physical Geography
KIHLBERG, J., Organic Chemistry
KÅGSTRÖM, B., Numerical Analysis and Parallel Computing
LINDBLOM, G., Physical Chemistry
LINDSKOG, S., Biochemistry
LISZKA, L., Space Physics
LUNDIN, R., Space Physics
MINNHAGEN, P., Theoretical Physics
OPGENOORTH, H., Space Physics
OTTO, CH., Animal Ecology
PERSSON, L., Aquatic Ecology
RAPPE, C., Environmental Chemistry
RENBERG, I., Ecological and Environmental Impact Assessment
ROSÉN, E., High-Temperature Inorganic Chemistry
RÖNNMARK, K., Theoretical Space Physics
SAURA, A., Genetics
SHINGLER, V., Microbiology
SJÖBERG, S., Inorganic Chemistry
STENFLO, L., Plasma Physics
WALLIN, H., Mathematics
WEDIN, P.-Å., Numerical Analysis
WOLD, S., Chemometrics
WOLF-WATZ, H., Molecular Biology
ÖQUIST, G., Plant Physiology

UPPSALA UNIVERSITET

POB 256, 751 05 Uppsala
Telephone: (18) 471-00-00
Fax: (18) 471-20-00

Founded 1477
Academic year: September to June

Rector: Prof. B. U. R. SUNDQVIST
Vice-Rector: Prof. L. MARCUSSON
Head of Administration: J. ANDERSSON
Chief Librarian: U. GÖRANSSON

Library: see Libraries
Number of teachers: 1,800, including 290 professors
Number of students: 28,000 (incl. 3,000 postgraduates)

Publications: *Universen* (10 a year), *Uppsala Accelerator News*, *Uppsala Newsletter in History of Science*, *Multiethnica*, *Acta Universitatis Upsaliensis*.

DEANS

Faculty of Theology: Prof. C. R. BRÅKENNIELM
Faculty of Law: Prof. T. HÅSTAD
Faculty of Medicine: Prof. B. WESTERMARK
Faculty of Arts:
Historical-Philosophical Division: Prof. R. TORSTENDAHL
Linguistic Division: Prof. L. ELMEVIK
Faculty of Social Science: Prof. L. LEWIN
Faculty of Science: Prof. J.-O. CARLSSON
Faculty of Pharmacy: Prof. L. PAALZOW
Division for Education and Teaching Professions: TOR HUDNER (Rector)

PROFESSORS

Faculty of Theology:
BRODD, S.-E., Studies of Churches and Religious Denominations
BRÅKENHIELM, C. R., Studies in Faiths and Ideologies
FRANZÉN, R., Church History
GRENHOLM, C.-H., Ethics
HERRMANN, E., Philosophy of Religions
HULTGÅRD, A., History of Religions
JEFFNER, A., Studies in Faiths and Ideologies
NORIN, S., Old Testament Exegesis
PETTERSSON, T., Sociology of Religion
SCHALK, P., History of Religion
SYREENI, K., New Testament Exegesis
WIKSTRÖM, O., Psychology of Religion

Faculty of Law:
BRING, O., Public International Law
FRÄNDBERG, Å., Jurisprudence
HÅSTAD, T., Private Law
JAREBORG, N. B., Penal Law
LEHRBERG, B., Private Law
LINDBLOM, P. H., Judicial Procedure
LINDELL, B., Judicial Procedure
MARCUSSON, L., Administrative Law
MATTSSON, N., Taxation
NYGREN, R., History of Law
SALDEEN, Å., Private Law
STRÖMHOLM, S., Private Law, International Private Law
STERZEL, F., Constitutional Law
THORELL, P., Business Law
WESTERLUND, S., Environmental Law

Faculty of Medicine:
AKUSJÄRVI, G., Microbiology
ALDSHOGIUS, H., Medical Structural Biology
ALM, A., Ophthalmology
ANDERSSON, A., Diabetes Research
ANDERSSON, J., Immunology
ANNIKO, M., Otorhinolaryngology
AQUILONIUS, S.-M., Neurology
BERGQVIST, D., Vascular Surgery
BLOMBERG, J., Clinical Virology
BOMAN, G., Pulmonary Medicine
CARLSSON, J., Biomedical Radiation Science
CLAESSON-WELSH, L., Medical Biochemistry
DANIELSSON, B., Nephrology
EBENDAL, T., Developmental Biology
EDLING, C., Occupational Medicine
FLEMSTRÖM, G., Physiology
FRIMAN, G., Infectious Diseases
FUGL-MEYER, A., Rehabilitation Medicine
GEBRE-MEDHIN, M., International Child Health
GERDIN, B., Intensive and Burn Care
GRIMELIUS, L., Pathology
GYLFE, E., Secretion Research
GYLLENSTEN, U., Medical Molecular Genetics
HAGLUND, U., Surgery
HAKELIUS, L., Plastic Surgery
HÄLLGREN, R., Rheumatology
HAMBRAEUS, L., Nutrition
HAU, J., Comparative Medicine
HEDENSTIERNA, G., Clinical Physiology
HELDIN, C.-H., Molecular Cell Biology
HEMMINGSSON, A., X-Ray Diagnosis
HENZE, A., Thoracic Surgery
KARLSSON, A., Experimental Endocrinology
KNORRING, A.-L. VON, Child Psychiatry
KNORRING, L. VON, Psychiatry
LANDEGREN, U., Molecular Medicine
LARHAMMAR, D., Molecular Cell Biology
LINDAHL, U., Medical Chemistry
LINDBLOM, B., Obstetrics and Gynaecology
LINDGREN, P. G., X-ray Diagnosis
LINDHOLM, D., Neurobiology
LINDMARH, G., International Mother and Child Health
LITHELL, H., Geriatrics
LJUNGHALL, S., Medicine
MAGNUSSON, G., Virology
MELLSTEDT, H., Experimental Oncology
MÅRDH, P.-A., Clinical Bacteriology
NILSSON, K., Cell Pathology
NILSSON, O., Orthopaedics
NORLÉN, B. J., Urology
OLSSON, Y., Neuropathology
ORELAND, L., Pharmacology
PERSSON, E., Physiology
PERSSON, L., Neurosurgery
PETTERSSON, U. G., Medical Genetics
RAININKO, R., Neuroradiology
RANE, A., Clinical Pharmacology
RASK, L., Medical Biochemistry
ROOMANS, G., Medical Ultrastructure
ROSENQVIST, U., Nursing and Health Care
RUBIN, K., Connective Tissue Biochemistry
SALDEEN, T., Forensic Medicine
SEDIN, G., Perinatal Medicine
SJÖDÉN, P.-O., Clinical Physiology

STÅLBERG, E., Clinical Neurophysiology
SVÄRDSUDD, K., Human Anatomy
TOREBJÖRK, E., Pain Research
TURESSON, J., Oncology
TUVEMO, T., Paediatrics
TÖTTERMAN, T., Clinical Immunology
ULMSTEN, U., Obstetrics and Gynaecology
VAHLQUIST, A., Dermatology and Venereology
VENGE, P., Clinical Chemistry
WALLENTIN, L., Cardiology
WESTERMARK, B., Tumor Biology
WIDE, L., Endocrinologic Biochemistry
WIESEL, F.-A., Psychiatry
WIKLUND, L., Anaesthesiology
ÅKERMAN, K., Cell Physiology
ÅKERSTRÖM, G., Endocrinological Surgery
ÖBERG, K., Oncologic Endocrinology

Faculty of Pharmacy:
ALDERBORN, G., Pharmaceutical Technology
ARTURSSON, P., Biopharmaceutical Dosage Form Design
BOHLIN, L., Pharmacognosy
DENCKER, L., Toxicology
HALLBERG, A., Medicinal Chemistry
LANG, M., Biochemistry with Drug Metabolism
NYBERG, F., Biological Research on Drug Dependence
NYSTRÖM, CHR., Pharmaceutics
PAALZOW, L., Biopharmaceutics
OLIW, E., Biochemical Pharmacology
SKÖLD, O., Pharmaceutical Microbiology
SUNDELÖF, L.-O., Physical Pharmaceutical Pharmacy
WESTERLUND, D., Analytical Pharmaceutical Pharmacy
WIKBERG, J., Pharmacology

Faculty of Arts:
I. Historical-Philosophical Division:
ALANEN, L., History of Philosophy
DANIELSSON, S., Practical Philosophy
FRÄNGSMYR, T., History of Science
GRÄSLUND, B., Archaeology
GUSTAVSSON, A., Ethnology and Folklore
HELLSTRÖM, P., Ancient Culture and Society
JACOBSON WIDDING, H. A., Cultural Anthropology
JANSSON, T., History
JOHANNESSON, K., Rhetoric
JOHANNISSON, K., History of Science and Ideas
KJELLBERG, E., Musicology
LANDGREN, B., Literature
LINDEGREN, J., History
OHLANDER, A.-S., History
PETTERSSON, T., Literature
SEGERBERG, K., Theoretical Philosophy
SINCLAIR, P., African Archaeology
SKALIN, L.-Å., Literature
SVEDJEDAL, J., Literature
TORSTENDAHL, R., History
ÅMAN, A., Art

II. Linguistic Division:
ALVARES CORREA FRYCHSTEDT, M., English Literature
EKLUND, S., Latin
ELMEVIK, L., Scandinavian Languages
GREN-EKLUND, G., Indology
GUSTAVSSON, S. R., Slavic Languages
JONASSON, K., French Language
KINDSTRAND, J. F., Greek Language and Literature
KROHN, D., German
KRONHOLM, T., Semitic Languages
KYTÖ, M., English Language
LARSSON, L.-G., Finno-Ugrian Languages
LUNDÉN, R., American Literature
NORDBERG, B., Sociolinguistics
ROSENQUIST, J. O., Byzantine Studies
STRANDBERG, L. S., Scandinavian Onomastics
SWAHN, S., French Literature
SÅGVALL-HEIN, A., Computational Linguistics
THELANDER, M., Swedish Language
UTAS, B., Iranian Studies
ÖHMAN, S. E. G., Phonetics

Faculty of Social Sciences:
AGELL, J., Economics
BERG, G., Education
BERGLUND, S., Political Science
BERGSTRÖM, R., Econometrics
BLOMQUIST, S., Local Public Economics
BURNS, T. R., Sociology
CHRISTOFFERSSON, A., Statistics
CLARKE, E., Urban Geography
EDIN, P.-A., Labour Market Relations
EKEHAMMAR, B., Psychology
ENGLUND, P., Economics
ENGLUND, T., Education
ENGWALL, L., Business Administration
FOGELKLOU, A., East European Studies
FREDRIKSON, M., Clinical Psychology
GERNER, K., East European Studies
GOTTFRIES, N., Economics
HADENIUS, A., Political Science
HANSSON, Å., Computing Science
HEDLUND, S., East European Studies
HOLMLUND, B., Economics
HOPPE, G., Economic Geography
HULTKRANTZ, L., Economics
HÅKANSSON, H., Business Administration
ISACSON, M., Economic History
JOHANSON, J., International Business Administration
JÖRESKOG, K. G., Statistics
KEMENY, J., Urban Sociology
KLEVMARKEN, N. A., Econometrics
LARSSON, M., Economic History
LEWIN, L., Political Science
LINDBLAD, S., Education
LUNDGREN, E., Women's Studies
MAGNUSSON, L., Economic History
MELIN, L., Clinical Psychology
PETERSSOHN, E., Business Administration
RIIS, U., Education
STATTIN, H., Psychology
SWENSSON, B., Statistics
SÖDER, M., Disability Studies
SÖDERSTEN, J., Economics
TORNSTAM, L., Social Gerontology
VEDUNG, E., Housing Policy
WALLENSTEEN, P., Peace and Conflict Research
WIGREN, R., Economics
ÅBERG, L., Traffic Psychology
ÖBERG, S., Social and Economic Geography

Faculty of Science and Technology:
AHLÉN, A., Signal Processing
ALMGREN, M., Physical Chemistry
ANNERSTEN, H. S., Mineral Chemistry and Petrology
BENGTSSON, E., Computerized Image Analysis
BERG, S., Electronics
BERGSON, G., Organic Chemistry
BERGSTRÖM, Y., Materials Science
BJÖRKLUND, M., Animal Ecology
BOSTROM, R., Geocosmic Physics
BRANDT, I., Ecotoxicology
BREMER, K., Systematic Botany
CALDWELL DAHLGREN, K., Surface Biotechnology
CARLSSON, J.-O., Inorganic Chemistry
CHATTOPADHYAYA, J., Bio-organic Chemistry
EHELÖF, T., Experimental Elementary Particle Physics
EHRENBERG, M., Molecular Biology with Kinetics
EKBLOM, P., Zoophysiology
EKMAN, J., Population Biology
ELLEGREN, H., Evolutionary Biology
ENGSTRÖM, P., Physiological Botany
GEE, D., Orogenic Dynamics
GELIUS, U., Physics
GOSCINSKI, O., Quantum Chemistry
GRANQVIST, C. G., Solid State Physics
GUSTAFSSON, B., Numerical Analysis
GUSTAFSSON, B., Theoretical Astrophysics
GUSTAFSSON, G., Geocosmic Physics
GUT, A., Mathematical Statistics
HAJDU, J., Biochemistry
HALLDIN, S., Hydrology
HEJHAL, D., Mathematics
HOGMARK, S., Materials Science
HÅKANSSON, L., Sedimentology
HÖISTAD, B., Nuclear Physics
JANSON, S., Mathematics
JOHANSSON, B., Condensed Matter Theory
JONES, A., Structural Molecular Biology
JONSSON, B., Computer Systems
JUHL-JÖRICKE, B., Mathematics
KISELMAN, C. O., Mathematics
KOLSTRUP, E., Physical Geography
KULLANDER, S., High Energy Physics
KURLAND, C. G., Molecular Biology
LUNDBERG, B., Solid Mechanics
LUNELL, S., Applied Quantum Chemistry
LÅNGSTROM, B., Organic Chemistry
LÖFBERG, J., Morphology, Zoology
LÖTSTEDT, P., Numerical Analysis
MANNERVIK, B., Biochemistry
MARKIDES, K. E., Analytical Chemistry
MÅRTENSSON, N., Physics of Metals and Metal Surfaces
NIEMI, A., Theoretical Physics
NORDGREN, J., Soft X-ray Physics
NORDSTRÖM, K., Microbiology
OHLSSON, R., Developmental Zoology
OJA, T., Astronomy
OLSSON, E., Experimental Physics
PAMILO, P., Conservation Biology
PEDERSEN, L. B., Solid Earth Physics
PEEL, J. S., Historical Geology and Palaeontology
PISKOUNOV, N., Astronomy
RONQUIST, F., Systematic Zoology
SAXENA, S., Theoretical Geochemistry
SCHWEITZ, J.-Å., Materials Science
SCUKA, V., Electricity
SKÖLD, K., Neutron Scattering Physics
STRÖMQUIST, L., Applied Environmental Impact Analysis
SUNDQVIST, B., Ion Physics
SÖDERHÄLL, K., Physiological Mycology
SÖDERSTRÖM, T., Automatic Control
TALBOT, C. J., Geodynamics and Tectonics
TAPIA-OLIVARES, O., Physical Chemistry
THOMAS, J., Solid State Electro-chemistry
TÄRNLUND, S. A., Computer Science
VIRO, O., Mathematics
ÅGREN, J., Ecological Botany

ATTACHED INSTITUTE

Ludwig Institute for Cancer Research: Uppsala Biomedical Centre BMC, POB 595, 751 23 Uppsala; br. of International Ludwig Institute; Dir Prof. C.-H. HELDIN.

HÖGSKOLAN I VÄXJÖ (Växjö University)

351 95 Växjö
Telephone: (470) 685-00
Fax: (470) 832-17

Founded 1967 as a branch of Lund University; independent status 1977
State control
Languages of instruction: Swedish, English
Academic year: September to June

Rector: Prof. BENGT ABRAHAMSSON
Registrar: BO PAULSSON
Chief Librarian: MARGARETHA JOSEFSSON

Library of 140,000 vols
Number of teachers: 285
Number of students: 7,500

Publications: *Acta Wexionensia* series including: *Växjö Social Studies*, *Växjo Migration Studies*, *Economy and Labour Market*, *Behavioural Science*, *Language and Literature*, *Economics and Politics*.

HEADS OF SCHOOL

Social Sciences: BETTY ROHDIN
Mathematics, Statistics and Computer Science: GÖSTA SUNDBERG
Education: PER GERREVALL
Humanities: ROLF JOHANSSON
Engineering and Natural Sciences: ALF THOMASSON
School of Management and Economics: LARS-OLOF RASK

PROFESSORS

ABRAHAMSSON, B., Sociology
ANDERSEN, J. A., Business Administration
ANDERSSON, G., Business Administration
ANDERSSON, L., Economics
ANGELFORS, C., French
ANGELÖW, B., Sociology
ARONSSON, P., History
BERGFELDT, L., Political Science
BERGSTRÖM, M., Law
BOOK, T., Geography
BREDENLÖW, T., Business Administration
BRUZELIUS, N., Business Administration
BULLE, A., French
BÅNG, B., Civil Engineering
CEDERLING, U., Computer Science
DELANDER, L., Economics
EKBERG, J., Economics
EKLUND, L., Biology
ERIKSSON, B., Sociology
FRISK, H., Mathematics
FRITZELL, C., Education
FÜLE, E., Statistics
GERREVALL, P., Education
GLARNER, J., English
GUSTAFSSON, B.-Å., Business Administration
HEDENBORG, M., Computer Science
HELLSTRÖM, L., Mathematics
HULT, MAGNUS, Business Administration
HULT, MARGARETA, Business Administration
HULTBOM, C., Business Administration
HYTTER, A., Business Administration
HÖJELID, S., Political Science
JAGER, B., German
JENSE, G., Sociology
JESKE, H., German
JOHANNESSON, C., Political Science
JOHANNISSON, B., Business Administration
JOHANSSON, A., Physics
JOHANSSON, L., Physics
JOHANSSON, R., History
JOHNSSON, L.-G., Business Administration
JOHNSSON, P., Psychology
KARLSSON, G., Statistics
KARLSSON, S.
LARSSON, L.-O., History
LARSSON RINGQVIST, E., French
LENELLS, M., Computer Science
LILJA, C., Biology
LINDQVIST, L.-G., Business Administration
LINDVÅG, A., Literature
LIUKKONEN, P., Business Administration
LUNDBERG, B., Education
LUNDBERG, B., Information Systems
LUNDBERG, E., Communication
MARSHALL, J., English
MARTEN, T., German
MATSSON, M., Biology, Chemistry
MATSSON, S.-A., Logistics
NETTERVIK, I., Literature
NIKLASSON, H., Economics
NILSSON, Å., Chemistry
NILSSON, B., Mathematical Physics
OZOLINS, A., Psychology
PALM, O., Education
PÁSTHY, K., English
PETERSSON, O., Computer Science
RASK, L.-O., Business Administration
RING, H., Administration
RINGBLOM, A., Literature
ROMARE, B., Technology
SAMUELSSON, J., History
SHERWIN, D., Terotechnology
SIMON, K., Law
SJÖGERÅS, I., Business Administration
SJÖGREN, C., Physics
SJÖLAND, S., Chemistry
STENBORG, E., Literature
SUNDBERG, G., Computer Science
SVENSSON, O., Electronic Engineering
SÖDERSTRÖM, U., Mathematics
TENGSTRAND, A., Mathematics
THOMASSON, A., Electronic Engineering
TOLLBOM, Ö.
TOLLIN, K., Business Administration
TRONDMAN, M., Sociology
WIESELGREN, A.-M., Scandinavian Languages
WINDAHL, S., Communication
ZANDERIN, L., Sociology

ATTACHED INSTITUTES

Centre for Labour Market Research: 351 95 Växjö; tel. (470) 685-00; Dir LENNART DELANDER.

Centre for Small Business Development: 351 95 Växjö; tel. (470) 685-00; Dir STIG MALM.

Transportation Centre: 351 95 Växjö; tel. (470) 685-00; Dir JONAS MÅNSSON.

Communication Centre: 351 95 Växjö; tel. (470) 685-00; Dir BETTY ROHDIN.

Computer Science Unit: 351 95 Växjö; tel. (470) 685-00; Dir MATHIAS HEDENBORG.

Centre for the Humanities: 351 95 Växjö; tel. (470) 685-00; Dir ROLF JOHANSSON.

Other Institutes of University Standing

GENERAL

Högskolan i Borås: 501 90 Borås; tel. (33) 16-40-00; fax (33) 16-40-03; f. 1977; library of 125,000 vols; 115 teachers; 4,500 students; Rector ANDERS FRANSSON; Vice-Rector PETER APELL; Librarian EVA LILJA.

DEANS

Swedish School of Library and Information Science: ROMULO ENMARK
Department of Computer Science and Business Administration: ARNE SÖDERBOM
Department of Textiles and Clothing: CARL-GUSTAF ELIASSON
Department of Education: ROLF APPELQUIST
School of Engineering: BENGT ANDERSSON

Högskolan Halmstad: Box 823, S-30118 Halmstad; tel. (35) 16-71-00; fax (35) 14-85-33; f. 1983; 291 teachers; 4,500 students; library of 25,000 vols; Rector SVEN-OVE JOHANSSON; Administrative Officer JAN ARVIDSSON; Librarian GÖRAN ERICSSON.

HEADS OF DEPARTMENTS

Technology and Science: MAGNUS LARSSON
Business Administration: MAJ-BRITT BÄCK
Social and Behavioural Sciences: OLE OLSSON
Humanities: URSULA WALLIN
Health Sciences: ULRIKE KYLBERG

Högskolan i Jönköping: POB 1026, 551 11 Jönköping; tel. (36) 15-77-00; fax (36) 15-08-12; f. 1977; library of 100,000 vols; 180 teachers; 6,000 students; Pres. CLAS WAHLBIN; Librarian INGER MELIN.

DEANS

Jönköping International Business School: LEIF LINDMARK
Jönköping School of Education and Communication: LARS-ERIK OLSSON
Jönköping School of Engineering: ROY HOLMBERG

Högskolan i Kalmar (University of Kalmar): Box 905, 391 29 Kalmar; tel. (480) 44-60-00; fax (480) 44-60-32; f. 1977, fmrly teacher training college (f. 1876); library of 65,000 vols; 165 teachers; 4,200 students; Vice-Chancellor ÖRN TAUBE; Administrative Officer BENGT SEDVALL; Librarian BERTIL JANSSON.

HEADS OF DEPARTMENTS

Nautical Sciences: ROLF ZEBERG
Technology Sciences: ULF VEENHUIZEN
Teacher Training: INGBERT KARLSSON
Arts: LARS OREDSSON
Natural Sciences: HÅKAN HALLMER
Economics and Social Sciences: NILS NILSSON
Communication and Media Studies: MAUD SKOOG-BRANDIN
In-service Training of Journalists: ANNELIE EWERS

Högskolan i Skövde: Box 408, 541 28 Skövde; tel. (500) 46-46-00; fax (500) 41-63-25; f. 1983; business administration, economics, engineering science, biosciences, computer science, languages, art, social science; library of 70,000 vols; 160 teachers; 3,000 students; Rector LARS-ERIK JOHANSSON; Librarian LENA OLSSON.

Mitthögskolan (Mid Sweden University): 851 70 Sundsvall; tel. (60) 14-86-00; fax (60) 14-87-00; e-mail info@mh.se; main sites in Härnösand, Sundsvall and Östersund; f. 1993; courses and research in humanities, social sciences, science and engineering, teacher training, and nursing and social care; library of 100,000 vols; 480 teachers; 11,000 students; Rector Dr KARI MARKLUND.

Attached Institutes:

SISY, Centre for Applied Science and Technology: Dir LENNART HJUL.

KVC, Communication Centre for the Promotion of Higher Education and Research: Chair K. G. SVENSSON (acting).

Zenit Foundation (centre for development and education in fields of information technology, electrical engineering and educational assignments in developing countries): Dir JOHNNY HEDBERG.

ART

Högskolan för Design och Konsthantverk (School of Design and Crafts): Kristinelundsgatan 6–8, S-41137 Göteborg; tel. (31) 773-48-72; f. 1848; affiliated to Göteborg University; product design, arts, crafts, industrial, interior and graphic design; library of 20,000 vols; Dean OVE THORSÉN.

Konstfack (University College of Arts, Crafts and Design): POB 24115, Valhallavägen 191, 104 51 Stockholm; tel. (8) 450-41-00; fax (8) 450-41-90; e-mail jbp@konstfach.se; f. 1844; graphic design and illustration, industrial design, interior architecture, furniture design, textile design, ceramics and glass, metalwork design, fine art, art education; library of 110,000 vols; 135 teachers; 550 students; Rector JOHAN BENGT-PÅHLSSON.

Konsthögskolan Valand: Box 9004, S-400 70 Göteborg; f. 1865; affiliated to Göteborg University; 9 teachers; 60 students; Dir SVEN-ROBERT LUNDQUIST.

Kungl. Konsthögskolan (Royal University College of Fine Arts): Flaggmansv. 1, Box 16 315, 103 26 Stockholm; tel. (8) 614-40-00; f. 1735; 215 students; Principal OLLE KÅKS; Admin. Man. EVA BORGSTRÖM; Librarian A. EKSTRÖM; publs *Konsthögskolans Broschyr*, *Konsthögskolan Elevkatalog*.

PROFESSORS

BEDOIRE, F., History of Swedish Architecture, Comparative Architectural History
BOOK, M., Painting
EDHOLM, A., Painting
LISINSKY, J., Restoration
WOLGERS, D., Sculpture

ECONOMICS AND ADMINISTRATION

Handelshögskolan i Stockholm (Stockholm School of Economics): Box 6501, 113 83 Stockholm; tel. (8) 736-90-00; fax (8) 31-81-86; e-mail info@hhs.se; f. 1909; private; library: see libraries; number of teachers and researchers: 200, including 36 professors; 1,700; Pres. Prof. CLAES-ROBERT JULANDER; Dir of Admin. HÅKAN HEDERSTIERNA; Librarian E. THOMSON-ROOS.

PROFESSORS

BERGMAN, L., Economics, especially Environmental and Energy Areas
BERGSTRÖM, C., Finance (Commercial Law)
BJÖRK, T., Finance (Mathematical Finance)
BLOMSTRÖM, M., International Business, Economics
BRUNSSON, N., Business Administration, Public Administration
ELIAESON, P.-J.
ENGLUND, P., Banking and Insurance
HORN, H., International Economics
JENNERGREN, P., Business Administration
JOHANSSON, P.-O., Economics, Health Economics
JONUNG, L., Economics and Economic Policy
JULANDER, C.-R., Business Administration, Retailing and Consumer Behaviour
JÖNSSON, B., Health Economics
KARLSSON, C., Industrial Production
KARNELL, G., Law, Intellectual Property Law
LINDGREN, H., Economic History (Banking and Finance History)
LJUNGQVIST, L., Economics
LUNDAHL, M., Development Economics
LUNDEBERG, M., Information Management
MATTSSON, L.-G., International Marketing
MÄLER, K.-G., Economics, Environmental Economics
NEREP, E., Law, Swedish and International Commercial Law
NÄSLUND, B., Business Administration, Finance
SAMUELSON, L. A., Business Administration
SJÖBERG, L., Psychology, Risk Research
SJÖSTRAND, S.-E., Business Administration, Management and Labour-Related Issues
SKOGSVIK, K., Business Administration, Finance
STYMNE, B., Business Administration, Organization Theory
STÅHL, I., Business Administration, Computer Based Applications of Economic Theory
TERÄSVIRTA, T., Economic Statistics
WEIBULL, J. W., Economics
WESTLUND, A., Economic Statistics
WIMAN, B., International Tax Law
ÖSTMAN, L., Business Administration, Accountancy and Finance

Affiliated Institutes:

Ekonomiska Forskningsinstitutet vid Handelshögskolan i Stockholm (Economic Research Institute at the Stockholm School of Economics): Sveavägen 65, Stockholm; f. 1929; scientific research in management science and economics; 300 research fellows; Dir Assoc. Prof. BO SELLSTEDT; publs *EFI News*, reports, working papers.

Japan Institutet (European Institute of Japanese Studies): POB 6501, 113 83 Stockholm; f. 1992; research and educational programmes concerning Japanese and East-Asian economies and business in relation to Europe; 10 research fellows; Dir Prof. MAGNUS BLOMSTRÖM.

Institutet för Internationellt Företagande (Institute of International Business): Box 6501, 113 83 Stockholm; f. 1975; centre for research and education in international business, particularly the strategy and management of multinational corporations; 20 research fellows; Dir. Ö. SÖLVELL.

Östekonomiska Institutet (Stockholm Institute of East European Economies): Box 6501, 113 83 Stockholm; f. 1989; research into the economic development of Eastern Europe; 10 research fellows; Dir Assoc. Prof. ERIC BERLÖF; publs newsletters, reports.

MEDICINE

Karolinska Institutet: 171 77 Stockholm; tel. (8) 728-64-00; fax (8) 31-11-01; f. 1810; library: see libraries; 400; 2,600; Rector HANS WIGZELL; Head of Administration RUNE FRANSSON; Librarian TEODORA OKOR-BLOM; publs *Computerized Publication Register* (information on all publs issued by the Institute), *Curriculum*, *Students' Handbook*.

DEANS

Faculty of Medicine: Prof. ERLING NORRBY
Faculty of Odontology: Prof. THOMAS MODÉER

PROFESSORS

Faculty of Medicine:

AHLBOM, N. A., Epidemiology
AHLBORG, U. G., General Toxicology
AKUSJÄRVI, K. G. O., Microbial Genetics
ALLANDER, E., Social Medicine
ALVESTRAND, A., Renal Medicine
ANGELIN, B., Metabolism
APERIA, A. CH., Paediatrics
ASPELIN, P., Diagnostic Radiology
BERGLUND, B., Environmental Psychology
BERGMAN, H. O. M., Psychology of Alcoholism
BIBERFELD, G., Clinical Immunology
BJÖRKHEM, J. I., Biochemical Research on Atherosclerosis
BRITTON, S. F. F., Infectious Diseases
BYGDEMAN, M. A., Obstetrics and Gynaecology
CAMNER, P. J. H., Pulmonary Medicine
CARLSÖÖ, B., Otorhinolaryngology
COLLINS, P., Tumour Pathology
DALLNER, G., Pathology
DANEHOLT, P. B. E., Molecular Genetics
DE FAIRE, U., Tumour Pathology
EDSTRÖM, L., Neurology
EFENDIĆ, S., Clinical Diabetes Research
EINARSSON, K., Gastroenterology
EKBLOM, B. T., Exercise Physiology
EKHOLM, J. T., Physical Medicine and Rehabilitation
EKMAN, P., Urology
ELMQVIST, H., Medical Technology
ENEROTH, H. E. P., Hormone Research
ERICSON, K. L., Neuroradiology
ERICSSON, H., Clinical Bacteriology
ERIKSSON, H. A., Reproductive Endocrinology
ERIKSSON, L. A., Neurophysics
FLOCK, K. Å. I., Physiology
FREDHOLM, B., Pharmacology
FUXE, K. G., Histology
GAHRTON, C. A. G., Medicine
GAROFF, P. H., Molecular Biology
GOLDIE, I. R. V. G. F., Orthopaedic Surgery
GRANT, N. G., Anatomy
GRILLNER, S. E., Exercise Physiology
GROTH, C.-G., Transplantation Surgery
GUSTAFSSON, J.-Å., Medical Nutrition
HAGENFELDT, L., Clinical Chemistry
HAKULINEN, T., Epidemiology and Biostatistics
HAMBERGER, K. B., Surgery
HANSSON, G., Experimental Cardiovascular Research
HEDQVIST, P. O., Physiology
HEMMINKI, K. J., Epidemiology
HENRIKSSON, J., Physiology
HOLMGREN, K. A., Medical Protein Chemistry and Enzymology
HÄLLSTRÖM, T., Psychiatry
HÖGLUND, G., Neuromedicine
HÖKFELT, T. G. M., Histology with Cell Biology
JANSSON, B. I., Psychiatry
JANSSON, P. E., Bioanalysis, Analytical Biochemistry
JOHANSSON, S. G. O., Clinical Immunology
JÖRNVALL, H. E., Medical and Physiological Chemistry
KAIJSER, L., Clinical Physiology
KIESSLING, R., Oncology
KLARESKOG, L., Rheumatology
KNUTSSON, E., Clinical Neurophysiology
KOLMODIN-HEDMAN, B., Occupational Medicine
KRISTENSSON, S. K., Pathology (Neuropathology)
KRONVALL, H. C. G., Clinical Bacteriology
KÄRRE, K., Molecular Immunology
LADENSTEIN, R., Structural Biochemistry
LAGERCRANTZ, H., Paediatrics, Neonatology
LAGERLÖF, B. A. M., Pathology
LAMBERT, B. B., Genetic Toxicology
LARSSON, A., Paediatrics
LARSSON, J., Anaesthesiology, Radiology, Orthopaedics
LENNERSTRAND, Å. G., Ophthalmology
LENNERSTRAND, G., Ophthalmology
LERNMARK, Å., Experimental Endocrinology
LIDBERG, L. G., Social and Forensic Psychiatry
LIDÉN, S. S., Dermatology and Venereology
LINDAHL, S. G. E., Anaesthesiology
LINDBERG, A. E. A., Clinical Bacteriology
LINDGREN, J. U., Orthopaedic Surgery
LINDSTEN, J. E., Medical Genetics
LINDVALL, S. T. I., General Hygiene
LINK, H. G., Neurology
LINNARSSON, D., Baromedicine
LJUNGQVIST, A. G., Pathology
LUNDBERG, J., Neurotransmission Research
LUNELL, N.-O., Obstetrics and Gynaecology
MIDTVEDT, T., Medical Microbial Ecology
MOLDÉUS, P. W., Biochemical Toxicology
MÖLLBY, N. R., Bacteriology
MÖLLER, E. B., Transplantation Immunology
NORD, C.-E., Oral Microbiology
NORDBERG, A., Medical Tobacco Research
NORDENSKJÖLD, M., Clinical Genetics
NORMARK, S., Medical Microbiology
NORRBY, E. C. J., Virus Research
OLSON, O. L., Neurobiology
OLSSON, P. I., Experimental Surgery
ORLOVSKI, G., Physiology
ORRENIUS, S. G., Toxicology
OTTING, G., Molecular Biophysics
PERSHAGEN, B. G., Environmental Epidemiology
PHILIPSON, B. T., Ophthalmology
PISCATOR, E. M., Hygiene
RAJS, J., Forensic Medicine
RIGLER, R. H. A., Medical Physics
RINGBORG, U., Oncology
RINGDEN, O., Transplantation Immunology
RINGERTZ, H. G., Diagnostic Radiology
RINGERTZ, N. R., Medical Cell Genetics
RITZÉN, E. M., Paediatric Endocrinology
ROLAND, P. E., Positron Emission Tomography
ROSENHALL, U., Clinical Audiology
RYDBERG, U. S., Clinical Alcohol and Drug Addiction Research
RYDELIUS, P.-A., Child and Adolescent Psychiatry
RYDÉN, L. E., Cardiology
RÄDEGRAN, K., Thoracic Surgery
RÖSNER, S., Health Behaviour Research
SALTIN, B., Physiology
SAMUELSSON, B. I., Medical and Physiological Chemistry
SCHNEIDER, G., Molecular Structural Biology
SEDVALL, C. G., Psychiatry
SEIGER, Å. B., Geriatric Medicine
SJÖQVIST, F. G. F., Clinical Pharmacology
STONE-ELANDER, S., Medical Radiochemistry
SVANSTRÖM, L. O. E., Social Medicine
SVENDGAARD, N.-A., Neurosurgery

SVENSSON, H. T., Pharmacology
TENGROTH, B. M., Ophthalmology
TERENIUS, L., Experimental Alcohol and Drug Addiction Research
THOMASSON, B. H., Paediatric Surgery
THORÉN, P., Physiology
TOFTGÅRD, R., Environmental Toxicology
TRYGGVASON, K., Medical Chemistry
UNGERSTEDT, C. U., Neuropsychopharmacology
VAHLNE, A., Clinical Virology
VAHTER, M. E., Metal Toxicology
VENNSTRÖM, B. R., Molecular Biology
VON SCHOULTZ, B., Obstetrics and Gynaecology
WAHLGREN, M., Parasitology
WAHREN, B., Clinical Virology
WETTERBERG, C. L. E., Psychiatry
WIGZELL, H. L. R., Immunology
WIMAN, B., Clinical Coagulation Research
WINBLAD, B. G., Geriatric Medicine
WRETLIND, B., Clinical Bacteriology
ZETTERBERG, A. H. D., Pathology, Tumour Cytology
ÅBERG, H. E., Family Medicine
ÅSBERG, M., Psychiatry
ÖBRINK, B. J., Medical Cell Biology
ÖHMAN, A., Psychology

Faculty of Odontology:
ANGMAR-MÅNSSON, B., Cariology
EDWALL, L. G. A., Endodontics
FREDHOLM, B. I. B., Pharmacology
HAMMARSTRÖM, L. E., Oral Pathology
HEIMDAHL, A., Oral Surgery
HOLM-PEDERSEN, P., Geriatric Odontology
HUGGARE, J., Orthodontics
KLINGE, B., Paradontology
KOPP, S. F. O., Clinical Oral Physiology
MODÉER, TH., Pedodontics
NORD, C.-E. H., Oral Microbiology
WELAUDER, O., Oral Diagnostic Radiology

MUSIC AND DRAMA

Dramatiska Institutet: Filmhuset, Borgvägen 5, Box 27090, 102 51 Stockholm; tel. (8) 665-13-00; fax (8) 662-14-84; e-mail kansli@draminst.se; f. 1970; instruction in production techniques for theatre, radio, television and film; Pres. KJELL GREDE.

Konstnärliga högskolorna i Malmö (Malmö Academies of Performing Arts): Ystadvägen 25, Box 8203, 200 41 Malmö; tel. (40) 32-54-50; fax (40) 22-54-80; f. 1907; comprises Malmö Academy of Music, Malmö Theatre Academy, Malmö Academy of Art; 230 teachers; 650 students; Dean HÅKAN LUNDSTRÖM.

Kungl. Musikhögskolan (Royal University College of Music): Valhallavägen 103-109, Box 27711, 115 31 Stockholm; tel. (8) 16-18-00; fax (8) 664-14-24; f. 1771; 200 teachers; 650 students; Principal Prof. G. MALMGREN.

Musikhögskolan i Göteborg: POB 5439, 402 29 Göteborg; tel. (31) 773-4001; fax (31) 773-4030; f. 1971; music education, performing, teaching musicology; 175 teachers; 650 students; Pres. (vacant); Dean HENRIK TOBIN; Librarian PIA SHEKHTER.

Teater- och operahögskolan: POB 5439, 402 29, Göteborg; f. 1964; 50 students; affiliated to Göteborg University; Head HARALD EK; Admin. MARGARETA HANNING.

PHYSICAL EDUCATION

Idrottshögskolan (Stockholm University College of Physical Education and Sports): POB 5626, 114 86 Stockholm; f. 1813; library of 40,000 vols; 40 teachers; 500 students; Rector Prof. INGEMAR WEDMAN.

SWITZERLAND

Learned Societies

GENERAL

Institut National Genevois: Promenade du Pin 1, 1204 Geneva; f. 1853; 750 mems; Pres. Francis Strub; Sec.-Gen. Monique Tanner; consists of Moral and Political Sciences Section (Pres. Uli Windisch), Industry and Agriculture Section (Pres. Pierre Kunz), Fine Arts Section (Pres. Giorgio Quadranti); publs *Mémoires*, *Bulletin*.

Schweizerische Akademie der Geistes- und Sozialwissenschaften/Académie Suisse des Sciences Humaines et Sociales (Swiss Academy of Humanities and Social Sciences): Postfach 8160, Hirschengraben 11, 3001 Bern; tel. (31) 311-33-76; fax (31) 311-91-64; f. 1946; 49 mem. socs; Pres. Prof. Dr R. Ris; Sec.-Gen. Prof. Dr Beat Sitter-Liver; publs *Bulletin der SAGW*, *SAGW-Kolloquien*.

Schweizerische Akademie der Naturwissenschaften/Académie suisse des sciences naturelles (Swiss Academy of Sciences): Bärenplatz 2, 3011 Bern; tel. (31) 312-33-75; fax (31) 312-32-91; e-mail sanw@sanw.unibe.ch; f. 1815; promotion of research, international relations; library: see Stadtbibliothek, Bern; mems: 65 scientific societies, 30 commissions, 41 national cttees; Pres. Prof. Dr B. Hauck; Sec.-Gen. A. C. Clottu Vogel; publs *Jahrbuch*, *Denkschriften*, *Bulletin*.

Schweizerische Akademie der Technischen Wissenschaften/Académie Suisse des Sciences Techniques (Swiss Academy of Engineering Sciences): Selnaustr. 16, Postfach, 8039 Zürich; tel. (1) 283-1616; fax (1) 283-1620; f. 1981; 146 individual mems, 58 constituent societies with 67,000 mems; co-operation with similar societies and acts in advisory capacity to the government; Chair. Prof. Dr J.-C. Badoux; Vice-Chair. Prof. Dr H. Leuenberger.

Schweizerischer Nationalfonds zur Förderung der Wissenschaftlichen Forschung/Fonds national suisse de la recherche scientifique (Swiss National Science Foundation): Wildhainweg 20, 3001 Bern; tel. (31) 308-22-22; fax (31) 301-30-09; f. 1952 for the promotion of basic non-commercial scientific research at Swiss universities and other scientific institutions in all branches of science; responsible for National Research Programmes and 3 out of the 6 federal government Swiss Priority Programmes; has a Council of Foundation, on which the Government, the universities and other cultural institutions are represented, and a National Research Council, consisting of scientists; awards grants to promising young researchers; Pres. Council of Foundation Prof. Ralf Hütter; Pres. National Research Council Prof. Heidi Diggelmann; Sec.-Gen. Dr H. P. Hertig; publs *Annual Report*, *Horizonte*.

Schweizerischer Wissenschaftsrat/Conseil Suisse de la Science: Inselgasse 1, 3003 Bern; tel. (31) 322-96-66; fax (31) 322-80-70; e-mail edo.poglia@swr.admin.ch; f. 1965 to co-ordinate and examine national policy on science and research and aid its implementation; 19 mems; Pres. Prof. Verena Meyer; Gen. Sec. Dr Edo Poglia.

AGRICULTURE, FISHERIES AND VETERINARY SCIENCE

Association des Groupements et Organisations Romands de l'Agriculture—AGORA: Ave des Jordils 3, CP, CH-1000 Lausanne 6; tel. (21) 617-74-77; fax (21) 617-76-18; f. 1881; 28,000 mems; library of 200 vols; Dir Christophe Darbellay; publs *Revue suisse de viticulture, d'arboriculture et d'horticulture* (every 2 months), *Revue suisse d'agriculture* (every 2 months).

Gesellschaft Schweizerischer Tierärzte/Société des Vétérinaires Suisses: POB 6324, 3001 Bern; tel. (31) 307-35-35; fax (31) 307-35-39; f. 1813; 2,200 mems; Pres. Dr A. Meisser; Sec.-Gen. B. Josi; publ. *Schweizer Archiv für Tierheilkunde* (monthly).

ARCHITECTURE AND TOWN PLANNING

Bund Schweizer Architekten (BSA)/Fédération des Architectes Suisses (FAS): Pfluggässlein 3, 4001 Basle; tel. (61) 262-10-10; 630 mems; Pres. Dr Frank Krayenbühl; publ. *Werk, Bauen und Wohnen*.

Schweizer Heimatschutz (Swiss National Trust): Merkurstr. 45, Postfach, 8032 Zürich; tel. (1) 252-26-60; fax (1) 252-28-70; e-mail info@heimatschutz.ch; f. 1905; 20,000 mems; Pres. Councillor Caspar Hürlimann; Sec.-Gen. Hans Gattiker; publ. *Heimatschutz* (French and German, quarterly).

Société Suisse des Ingénieurs et des Architectes: Selnaustr. 16, 8039 Zürich; tel. (1) 283-15-15; fax (1) 201-63-35; f. 1837; 12,000 mems; Pres. K. Aellen; Gen. Sec. E. Mosimann; publs *Schweizer Ingenieur und Architekt* (Schweizerische Bauzeitung), *Ingénieurs et architectes suisses* (Bulletin technique de la Suisse romande), *Rivista tecnica della Svizzera italiana*.

BIBLIOGRAPHY, LIBRARY SCIENCE AND MUSEOLOGY

Schweizer Diplombibliothekare, -innen (SDB)/Bibliothécaires diplômé(e)s suisses (BDS) (Association of Swiss Diplomaed Librarians): Postfach 638, 4003 Basel; e-mail sdb-bds@yahoo.com; f. 1988; promotes the professional interests of qualified librarians; publ. *SDB / BDS News*.

Schweizerische Bibliophilen Gesellschaft/Société Suisse des Bibliophiles: Voltastr. 43, 8044 Zürich; f. 1921; 600 mems; Pres. Dr Conrad Ulrich; publs *Stultifera Navis 44–57*, *Librarium 58* (3 a year).

Schweizerische Gesellschaft für die Rechte der Urheber musikalischer Werke (SUISA) (Swiss Society for Rights of Authors of Musical Works): Bellariastr. 82, 8038 Zürich; tel. (1) 485-66-66; fax (1) 482-43-33; f. 1942; 14,000 mems; Pres. Hans Ulrich Lehmann; Gen. Dir Patrick Liechti.

Schweizerische Vereinigung für Dokumentation/Association Suisse de Documentation: Schmidgasse 4, 6301 Zug; tel. (41) 726-45-05; f. 1939; collaboration and representation of Swiss documentation in national and international spheres; consultation on documental problems; training of documentalists; 600 mems (individual and collective); Pres. St. Holländer; Sec. H. Schwenk; publ. *ARBIDO* (11 a year).

Verband der Bibliotheken und der Bibliothekare/innen der Schweiz (BBS)/Association des bibliothèques et bibliothécaires Suisses (Swiss Association of Libraries and Librarians): Effingerstr. 35, 3008 Bern; tel. (31) 382-42-40; f. 1894; 1,850 mems; Pres. Marie-Claude Troehler; Sec. Alain Huber; publ. *ARBIDO* (monthly).

Verband der Museen der Schweiz/Association des Musées Suisses: Baselstr. 7, 4500 Solothurn; tel. (32) 623-67-10; fax (32) 623-85-83; f. 1966; asscn of Swiss museums, zoological and botanical gardens to represent their interests; forms a link between Swiss museums and ICOM (*q.v.*); organizes annual conference and work sessions on museology, conservation, restoration and other related topics; 520 mems; Pres. Dr Joseph Brülisauer; Sec. Verena v. Sury Zumsteg; publ. *Bulletin* (2 a year).

Verein Schweizerischer Archivarinnen und Archivare/Association des archivistes suisses (Association of Swiss Archivists): Archives cantonales vaudoises, rue de la Mouline 32, 1022 Chavannes-près-Renens; tel. (21) 316-37-11; fax (31) 317-37-55; f. 1922; lectures, discussions, etc., concerning archive work; 360 mems; Pres. Gilbert Coutaz; publ. *ARBIDO* (11 a year).

ECONOMICS, LAW AND POLITICS

Bundesamt für Statistik/Office Fédéral de la Statistique (Federal Statistical Office): Espace de l'Europe 10, 2010 Neuchâtel; tel. (32) 713-60-11; fax (32) 713-60-12; e-mail info@bfs.admin.ch; f. 1860; for production and publication of statistics; Dir Dr Carlo Malaguerra; publs *Statistical Yearbook*, other statistical and economics publications.

Gottlieb Duttweiler Institute for Trends and Futures: Langhaldenstr. 21, 8803 Rüschlikon/Zürich; tel. (1) 724-61-11; fax (1) 724-62-62; f. 1963; monitoring of societal change; symposia; management development; Pres. Jules Kyburz; Dir Dr Christian Lutz; publs *gdi-impuls*, occasional publications.

Schweizerische Gesellschaft für Aussenpolitik/Association Suisse de Politique Etrangère: Stapferhaus, Bleicherain 7, 5600 Lenzburg; tel. (62) 891-14-69; fax (62) 891-80-25; f. 1968; 800 mems; Pres. Thomas Wagner; Sec. Gabriela Winkler.

Schweizerische Gesellschaft für Statistik und Volkswirtschaft/Société suisse de Statistique et d'Economie politique: Espace de l'Europe 10, 2010 Neuchâtel; tel. (32) 713-60-53; f. 1864; aims to encourage research, familiarise practicians in the field with recent developments, develop personal contacts, encourage students of economics; 1,290 mems; library: Schweiz. Wirtschaftsarchiv (*q.v.*); Pres. E. Baltensperger; Sec. Gabriel Gamez; publ. *Zeitschrift für Volkswirtschaft und Statistik / Revue suisse d'économie politique et de statistique* (quarterly).

Schweizerische Vereinigung für Internationales Recht/Société Suisse de Droit International: Postfach 690, 8027 Zürich; f. 1914; 990 mems; Pres. Prof. Dr W. Kälin; Sec. Dr Stefan Breitenstein; publs *Schweizerische Zeitschrift für internationales und europäisches Recht*, *Swiss Studies in International Law*.

Schweizerischer Anwaltsverband/ Fédération Suisse des Avocats/ Federazione Svizzera degli Avvocati (Swiss Bar Association): Bollwerk 21, 3011 Bern; tel. (31) 312-25-05; fax (31) 312-31-03; f. 1898; 5,500 mems; Pres. Dr KASPAR SCHILLER; Gen. Sec. F. MEYER; publ. *Bulletin* (every 2 months).

Schweizerischer Notarenverband/ Fédération Suisse des Notaires/ Federazione Svizzera dei Notai: Gerechtigkeitsgasse 50/52, 3000 Bern 8; tel. (31) 310-58-40; fax (31) 310-58-50; f. 1920; 1,500 mems; Pres. Me BERNHARD BURKARD; Sec. Me ANDREAS B. NOTTER.

Zentrale für Wirtschaftsdokumentation (Economic Documentation Centre): Plattenstr. 14, 8032 Zürich; tel. (1) 257-39-11; fax (1) 262-02-76; f. 1910; attached to the University of Zurich; large world-wide collection of annual reports of the main companies; press cuttings, periodicals, OECD collection, daily newspapers, magazines and statistical material available.

EDUCATION

EDK/IDES (Information, Documentation, Education in Switzerland): Zähringerstr. 25, 3001 Berne; tel. (31) 309-51-00; fax (31) 309-51-10; e-mail ides@edk.unibe.ch; f. 1962 (with partial integration of CESDOC 1994); to inform Swiss and foreign services on questions concerning teaching and education in Switzerland; library of 8,000 vols, 400 periodicals, 6,000 documents; Dir ANNEMARIE STREIT.

Institut de Recherche et de Documentation Pédagogique: Faubourg de l'Hôpital 43–45, CP 54, 2007 Neuchâtel 7; tel. (32) 889-69-70; fax (32) 889-69-71; f. 1969; research in French-speaking Switzerland, into educational methods, organization and administration; creation and analysis of teaching aids; documentation; 22 mems; library of 10,000 vols; Pres. (vacant); Dir J. WEISS; publs *Coordination*, *Liste des acquisitions*, reports, textbooks.

Schweizerische Hochschulkonferenz/ Conférence Universitaire Suisse: Sennweg 2, 3012 Bern; tel. (31) 306-60-60; fax (31) 302-17-92; e-mail shk@shk.unibe.ch; f. 1969; co-ordination of Swiss universities and institutes of higher education; 18 mems; representing cantons, universities, National Union of Students, etc.; Pres. AUGUSTIN MACHERET; Sec.-Gen. N. ISCHI; publs *Rapport annuel*, *Info CUS* (6 a year).

Schweizerische Hochschulrektorenkonferenz/Conférence des recteurs des universités suisses: Sennweg 2, 3012 Bern; tel. (31) 306-60-34; fax (31) 302-68-11; f. 1904; a consultative body which meets periodically to examine questions of common interest to universities; 12 mems; Pres. Prof. GEORGES FISCHER; Sec.-Gen. Dr RUDOLF NAEGELI.

Schweizerische Zentralstelle für Hochschulwesen/Office Central Universitaire Suisse (Central Office of the Swiss Universities): Sennweg 2, 3012 Bern; tel. (31) 306-60-45; fax (31) 302-68-11; f. 1920; information service on Swiss and foreign universities; administration of bilateral govt scholarships for Swiss students; Swiss ERASMUS bureau; nat. information service in matters of academic equivalence; secretariat of the Conference of Swiss University Rectors; Dir Dr RUDOLF NAEGELI.

Vereinigung Schweizerischer Hochschuldozenten/Association suisse des professeurs d'université: Hohstalenweg 30, 3047 Bremgarten; tel. (31) 302-03-95; fax (31) 302-03-95; 1,480 mems; Pres. Prof. Dr KLAUS WEGENAST; Sec. (vacant); publ. *Bulletin VSH* (4 a year).

FINE AND PERFORMING ARTS

Fondation Hindemith: c/o Me M. Décombaz, 45 rue du Simplon, 1800 Vevey; f. 1968 to promote and cultivate music, in particular contemporary music; to maintain the musical and literary heritage of Paul Hindemith; to encourage research in the field of music and diffusion of research results; chamber music master classes, Blonay; archives in Hindemith Institute, Eschersheimer Landstrasse 29–39, 60322 Frankfurt/M., Germany; Pres. Dr ANDRES BRINER (Zürich); Vice-Pres. Prof. Dr A. ECKHARDT (Bonn); publs *Hindemith General Original Edition*, *Les Annales Hindemith*.

Gesellschaft für Schweizerische Kunstgeschichte: Pavillonweg 2, 3001 Bern; tel. (31) 301-42-81; fax (31) 301-69-91; f. 1880; 9,500 mems; Dir STEFAN BIFFIGER; publs *Die Kunstdenkmäler der Schweiz*, *Inventar der neueren Schweizer Architektur 1850–1920*, *Schweiz. Kunstführer* (20 a year), *Kunst Architektur in der Schweiz* (quarterly), *Beiträge zur Kunstgeschichte der Schweiz*, *Kunstführer durch die Schweiz*.

Gesellschaft Schweizerischer Maler, Bildhauer und Architekten/Société des Peintres, Sculpteurs et Architectes Suisses: Im Laubegg II, 8045 Zürich; tel. (1) 462-10-30; fax (1) 462-16-10; f. 1865; 2,000 active mems; Pres. BERNARD TAGWERKEN; Dir ROBERTA WEISS-MARIANI; publs *Schweizer Kunst*, *Art Suisse*, *Arte Svizzera*.

Kunstverein St Gallen: Museumstr. 32, CH-9000 St Gallen; tel. (71) 245-33-55; f. 1827; 2,750 mems; Pres. Dr H. P. MÜLLER; Man. CH. KALTHOFF.

Pro Helvetia (Arts Council of Switzerland): Hirschengraben 22, CH-8024 Zürich; tel. (1) 267-71-71; telex 817599; fax (1) 267-71-06; f. 1939; public foundation under the supervision of the Swiss Federal Council to maintain and promote Switzerland's spiritual and cultural heritage and to foster cultural relations with foreign countries. In addition to sending printed material for foreign enquirers, it organizes exhibitions, concerts, lectures and theatrical performances abroad; the Swiss Federal Council appoints the President and the 34 mems of the board of the Foundation; Pres. ROSEMARIE SIMMEN; Dir URS FRAUCHIGER.

Schweizer Blasmusikverband/ Association suisse des musiques: Geschäftsstelle, Postfach, 5001 Aarau; tel. (62) 822-81-11; fax (62) 822-81-10; e-mail gsemv@bluewin.ch; f. 1862; mems: 88,000 musicians in 2,136 local bands, which play concert and marching music; Pres. JOSEF ZINNER; publ. *Blasmusik-Zeitung / Revue des musiques suisses* (fortnightly).

Schweizer Musikrat/Conseil Suisse de la Musique: Haus der Musik, Gönhardweg 32, 5000 Aarau; tel. (62) 822-94-23; fax (62) 822-47-67; e-mail musikrat@aaravonline.ch; f. 1964; mem. of the CIM (UNESCO); membership of various musical organizations; Pres. Prof. JAKOB STÄMPFLI; Exec. Officer URSULA BALLY-FAHR; publ. *Guide for Musical Studies in Switzerland*.

Schweizerische Musikforschende Gesellschaft: Petersgraben 27, 4051 Basel; tel. (61) 257-28-00; e-mail williman@ubaclu.unibas.ch; f. 1916; 700 mems; Pres. Dr JOSEPH WILLIMANN; Sec. Dr DOROTHEA BAUMANN; publs *Schweiz Musikdenkmäler*, *Publikationen der SMG Serie II*, *Jahrbuch* (annually).

Schweizerischer Kunstverein/Société Suisse des Beaux-Arts/Società Svizzera di Belle Arti: Zeughausstrasse 55, 8026 Zürich; tel. (1) 241-63-01; fax (1) 241-63-73; f. 1806; acts as the umbrella organization for 36 member sections; aims to promote and protect the interests of artists and art lovers on a federal level; Pres. REINER PEIKERT (acting); publ. *Das Kunst-Bulletin* (monthly).

Schweizerischer Tonkünstlerverein/ Association Suisse des Musiciens: Ave du Grammont 11 bis, 1000 Lausanne 13; tel. (21) 614-32-90; fax (21) 614-32-99; e-mail asm-stv@span.ch; f. 1900; 820 mems; Pres. ROMAN BROTBECK; Sec. JACQUES LASSERRE; publs *Dissonanz / Dissonance* (4 a year), *Tendances et Réalisations*.

Schweizerischer Werkbund (SWB): Limmatstr. 118, 8031 Zürich; tel. (1) 272-71-76; fax (1) 272-75-06; f. 1913; 1,000 mems; Pres. ELLEN MEYRAT-SCHLEE; publs *SWB-Dokumente*, *SWB-Information* (quarterly).

Schweizerisches Institut für Kunstwissenschaft/Institut Suisse pour l'Etude de l'Art: Zollikerstr. 32, 8032 Zürich; tel. (1) 388-51-51; fax (1) 381-52-50; f. 1951; registration of Swiss works of art—studies in art and technology; 1,500 mems; library of 92,000 books, 78,000 reproductions; Pres. Dr JOHANNES FULDA; Dir Dr HANS-JORG HEUSSER; publs *Jahresbericht*, catalogues of Swiss artists and collections, Technological Reports, etc.

SGD Swiss Graphic Designers: Limmatstr. 63, 8005 Zürich; tel. (1) 272-45-55; fax (1) 272-52-82; f. 1972; 600 mems; Pres. ERIKA REMUND; publ. *SGD Information* (quarterly).

Société Suisse de Pédagogie Musicale: Birchwilerstr. 6, 8303 Bassersdorf; tel. (1) 836-45-35; fax (1) 836-45-73; f. 1893; 5,000 mems; Pres. ROLAND VUATAZ; Sec. ELISABETH EICHERT; publ. *Agenda du musicien*.

HISTORY, GEOGRAPHY AND ARCHAEOLOGY

Allgemeine Geschichtforschende Gesellschaft der Schweiz/Société Générale Suisse d'Histoire: Unitobler 3000, Bern 9; tel. (31) 631-80-93; fax (31) 631-44-10; f. 1841; 1,400 mems; Pres. Prof. Dr Y. COLLART; publs *Schweizerische Zeitschrift für Geschichte*, *Bulletin AGGS*, *Quellen zur Schweizergeschichte*.

Antiquarische Gesellschaft in Zürich: Staatsarchiv, Postfach, 8057 Zürich; tel. (1) 635-69-11; fax (1) 635-69-05; f. 1832; concerned with history of Zürich and Swiss history in general; 500 mems; Pres. Dr JÜRG E. SCHNEIDER; publ. *Mitteilungen der Antiquarischen Gesellschaft in Zürich* (1 a year).

Geographisch-Ethnographische Gesellschaft Zürich: Geographisches Institut, Universität Zürich-Irchel, Winterthurerstr. 190, 8057 Zürich; tel. (1) 257-51-51; e-mail kbrass@geo.unizh.ch; f. 1889; 560 mems; Pres. Prof. Dr K. BRASSEL; Sec. Dr C. DEFILA; publs *Mitteilungen 1899–1945*, *Geographica Helvetica*.

Geographisch-Ethnologische Gesellschaft Basel: Klingelbergstr. 16, 4056 Basel; tel. 267-36-60; fax 267-36-51; f. 1923; 510 mems; Pres. Dr DIETER OPFERKUCH; Sec. JEAN-MARC BOLL; publs *Regio Basiliensis* (3 a year), *Basler Beiträge zur Geographie*, *Basler Beiträge zur Ethnologie*, *Basler Beiträge zur Physiogeographie* (irregular).

Geographische Gesellschaft Bern: Hallerstr. 12, 3012 Bern; tel. (31) 631-88-69; fax (31) 631-85-44; e-mail wiesmann@giub.unibe.ch; f. 1873; 650 mems; Pres. Dr U. WIESMANN; Sec. M. BALZLI; publ. *Berner Geographische Mitteilungen* (1 a year).

Historisch-Antiquarischer Verein: 9410 Heiden; tel. 891-19-56; f. 1874; concerned with the maintenance and preservation of fabrics, furniture, armour, coins, etc., of historical interest; Pres. RUDOLF ROHNER.

Historische und Antiquarische Gesellschaft zu Basel: Universitätsbibliothek, Schönbeinstr. 18/20, CH-4056 Basel; tel. (61) 267-31-11; fax (61) 267-31-03; f. 1836; 750

mems; library of 30,000 vols; Pres. Dr FRITZ NAGEL; publ. *Basler Zeitschrift für Geschichte und Altertumskunde*.

Historischer Verein des Kantons Bern: C/o Burgerbibliothek, Münstergasse 63, CH-3000 Bern 7; tel. (31) 311-18-03; f. 1847; Pres. Dr J. SEGESSER; publs *Archiv des Historischen Vereins*, *Berner Zeitschrift für Geschichte und Heimatkunde*.

Schweizerische Gesellschaft für Kartographie: C/o Wäger & Partner, Juchstr. 27, 8500 Frauenfeld; tel. (52) 722-27-90; fax (52) 722-27-90; f. 1969; educational publications and courses; 250 mems; Pres. Prof. E. SPIESS.

Schweizerische Gesellschaft für Ur- und Frühgeschichte (SGUF)/Société Suisse de Préhistoire et d'Archéologie (SSPA): Petersgraben 9-11, CH-4001 Basel; tel. (61) 261-30-78; fax (61) 261-30-78; f. 1907; 2,600 mems; Sec. Dr URS NIFFELER; publs *Archäologie der Schweiz / Archéologie Suisse* (quarterly), *Jahrbuch / annuaire* (annually).

Schweizerische Numismatische Gesellschaft/Société suisse de numismatique: C/o J.-P. Righetti, 24 rue de Romont, 1700 Fribourg; tel. (26) 321-41-61; fax (26) 322-83-01; f. 1926; 650 mems; Pres. SILVIA HURTER; publs *Schweizer Münzblätter / Gazette numismatique suisse*, *Schweizerische Numismatische Rundschau*, *Revue suisse de numismatique*, *Schweizer Münzkatalog*.

Schweizerische Vereinigung für Altertumswissenschaft / Association suisse pour l'Étude de l'Antiquité: Séminaire des sciences de l'Antiquité classique, Espace L. Agassiz, 2000 Neuchâtel; tel. (38) 20-83-38; f. 1943; 150 mems; Pres. Prof. DENIS KNOEPFLER.

Società Storica Locarnese: C/o Archivio Comunale, Pza de' Capitani, 6600 Locarno; f. 1955; collection and conservation of documents relating to the history of the Locarno area, organizes exhibitions and lectures; 150 mems; Pres. Dr UGO ROMERIO.

Société d'Egyptologie, Genève: Case postale 26, 1218 Grand-Saconnex; e-mail seg-jlc@swissonline.ch; f. 1978; 450 mems; library of 2,000 vols; Pres. PHILIPPE GERMOND; Sec. SANDRA POGGIA; publs *Bulletin de la Société d'Egyptologie, Genève (BSEG)* (annually), *Cahiers de la Société d'Egyptologie, Genève (CSEG)* (irregular).

Société d'Histoire de la Suisse Romande: Bibliothèque Cantonale et Universitaire, Dorigny, 1015 Lausanne; f. 1837; 530 mems; library: see Bibliothèque Cantonale et Universitaire de Lausanne.

Société d'Histoire et d'Archéologie: c/o Bibliothèque publique et universitaire, Les Bastions, 1211 Geneva 4; f. 1838; 550 mems; 1,000 MSS (library of 10,000 vols, C/o Archives de la Ville de Genève, Palais Eynard, 4 rue de la Croix-Rouge, 1211 Geneva 3); Pres. MICHEL GRANDJEAN; Sec. FABIA CHRISTEN KOCH; publs *Bulletin* (annually), *Mémoires et Documents*, *Bibliographie genevoise* (annually).

Société de Géographie de Genève: rue de l'Athénée 2, 1205 Geneva; f. 1858; 250 mems; Pres. PHILIPPE DUBOIS; publ. *Le Globe* (1 a year).

Société vaudoise d'histoire et d'archéologie: 32 rue de la Mouline, 1022 Chavannes-près-Renens; tel. (21) 316-37-11; f. 1902; 900 mems; publ. *Revue historique vaudoise* (annually).

Verband der Schweize Geographen/ Association Suisse de Géographie (Association of Swiss Geographers): Geographisches Institut der Universität Basel, Spalenring 145, 4055 Basel; tel. (61) 272-64-80; fax (61) 272-69-23; f. 1990; co-ordinates six regional and five thematic socs, and nine university institutes; no individual mems; Central Cttee acts as nat. cttee of IGU; Pres. Dr DANIEL SCHAUB; Sec. HELLA MARTI; publ. *GeoAgenda (Mitteilungsblatt der ASG)* (every 2 months).

Vereinigung der Freunde antiker Kunst/ Association des amis de l'art antique (Association of Friends of Classical Art): c/o Archäologisches Seminar der Universität, Schönbeinstr. 20, 4056 Basel; f. 1956; 1,050 mems; Pres. Dr JEAN-ROBERT GISLER; publs *Antike Kunst* (2 a year), *Supplements* (irregular).

LANGUAGE AND LITERATURE

Collegium Romanicum: C/o G. Colón, Universität Basel, Stapfelberg 7, 4051 Basel; tel. (61) 261-61-92; f. 1947; study of Romance languages and literature; 200 mems; Pres. G. COLÓN; Sec. T. BRANDENBERGER; publs *Vox Romanica* (annually), *Romanica Helvetica*, *Versants* (2 a year).

Deutschschweizerisches PEN-Zentrum: POB 403, 3000 Bern 14; tel. (31) 372-40-85; fax (31) 372-30-32; f. 1932, present name 1979; 200 mems; Pres. BEAT BRECHBÜHL; Sec. B. TRABER; publ. *Annals*.

Gesellschaft für deutsche Sprache und Literatur in Zürich: Deutsches Seminar der Universität Zürich, Schönberggasse 9, 8001 Zürich; tel. (1) 634-25-71; e-mail uguenthe@ds.unizh.ch; f. 1894; 210 mems; Pres. Dr ULLA KLEINBERGER GÜNTHER.

Institut et Musée Voltaire: 25 rue des Délices, 1203 Geneva; tel. (22) 344-71-33; f. 1952; library of 25,000 vols and MSS; Curator CHARLES WIRZ.

PEN Club de Suisse Romande: c/o Mme Mantilleri, 217 route de Vovray, 74160 Collonges s/s Salève, France; tel. (France) 50-43-69-35; f. 1949; defends freedom of expression and promotes international cultural exchanges; 70 mems; Pres. JEAN-PIERRE MOULIN; Sec.-Gen. BRIGITTE MANTILLERI; publ. *Newsletter*.

Schweizerische Schillerstiftung/ Fondation Schiller Suisse: Sollrütistr. 18, 3098 Schliern; f. 1905; grants prizes to Swiss authors; 300 mems; Pres. Dr PETER UHLMANN; Vice-Pres. MANUELA CAMPONOVO; publ. *Jahresbericht*.

Schweizerische Sprachwissenschaftliche Gesellschaft/Société suisse de linguistique/Società svizzera di linguistica: Institut de linguistique et des sciences du langage, BFSH 2, 1015 Lausanne; f. 1947; 207 mems; Pres. Prof. Dr ANNE-CLAUDE BERTHOUD; Sec. Dr PASCAL SINGY; publs *Cahiers Ferdinand de Saussure* (annually), *Bulletin CILA* (2 a year).

Schweizerischer Schriftstellerinnen- und Schriftsteller-Verband (Swiss Society of Writers): Kirchgasse 25, 8001 Zürich; tel. (1) 261-30-20; fax (1) 261-31-53; f. 1912; 670 mems; Pres. EDITH GLOOR; Sec. LOU PFLÜGER.

Società Retorumantscha: Ringstr. 34, 7000 Chur; tel. (81) 284-66-42; f. 1885; conservation and research into the Romansch language; *c.* 1,000 mems; library of 18,000 vols; Pres. Dr JACHEN CURDIN ARQUINT; publs *Annalas* (one part a year), *Dicziunari Rumantsch Grischun* (3 parts a year).

MEDICINE

Académie Suisse des Sciences Médicales/ Schweizerische Akademie der Medizinischen Wissenschaften (Swiss Academy of Medicine): Petersplatz 13, 4051 Basel; tel. (61) 261-49-77; f. 1943; 56 mems; Pres. Prof. E. R. WEIBEL; Sec.-Gen. Dr MARGRIT LEUTHOLD; publ. *Bulletin*.

Schweizerische Gesellschaft für Balneologie und Bioklimatologie/Société Suisse de Médecine Thermale et Climatique: c/o Dr R. Eberhard, Heilbadzentrum, 7500 St Moritz; tel. (81) 833-71-71; f. 1902; aims to develop thermal and climate medicine, physical and dietary therapy, and to improve scientific, professional and social links with the medical profession; 126 mems; library of 3,000 vols; Pres. Dr O. KNÜSEL; Sec. Dr R. EBERHARD; publ. Congress report.

Schweizerische Gesellschaft für Chirurgie/Société Suisse de Chirurgie: Service de chirurgie, CHUV, 1011 Lausanne; f. 1913; 1,106 mems; Pres. Prof. Dr T. RÜEDI; Sec. (vacant); publ. *Swiss Surgery*.

Schweizerische Gesellschaft für Geschichte der Medizin und der Naturwissenschaften/Société Suisse d'Histoire de la Médecine et des Sciences Naturelles: Rämistr. 71, 8006 Zürich; f. 1921; 350 mems; Sec. Prof. Dr CH. MÖRGELI; publs *Gesnerus* (quarterly), *Supplements to Gesnerus* (individual monographs).

Schweizerische Gesellschaft für Innere Medizin/Société Suisse de Médecine Interne: C/o Dr V. Briner, Med. Klinik, Kantonsspital, 6004 Luzern; f. 1932; 2,100 mems; Pres. Prof. F. FOLLATH; publs reports of meetings, etc.

Schweizerische Gesellschaft für Neurologie: c/o Prof. P. A. Despland, CHUV Neurologie, 11 rue du Bugnon, 1011 Lausanne; f. 1908; 368 mems; Pres. Prof. K. HESS; Sec. Dr H. STÖCKLI; publ. *Schweizer Archiv für Neurologie und Psychiatrie*.

Schweizerische Gesellschaft für Orthopädie/Société Suisse d'Orthopédie: Rabbentalstr. 83, Postfach, 3000 Bern 25; tel. (31) 332-96-10; fax (31) 332-98-79; e-mail bbscongress@swissonline.ch; f. 1942; professional organization for orthopaedic surgeons which promotes specialization in orthopaedics and safeguards professional interests; 526 mems; Pres. Dr L. DUBS; Sec. Dr B. SIMMEN; publs *Bulletin d'information* (3 a year), report of annual congress.

Schweizerischer Apotheker-Verein/ Société Suisse de Pharmacie: Stationsstr. 12, 3097 Bern-Liebefeld; tel. (31) 978-58-58; fax (31) 978-58-59; f. 1843; 5,200 mems; publs *Schweizer Apothekerzeitung*, *Pharmaceutica Acta Helvetiae* (quarterly), *Index Nominum*.

NATURAL SCIENCES

General

International Academy of the Environment (Académie Internationale de l'Environnement): 4 chemin des Conches, 1231 Conches, Geneva; tel. (22) 702-18-00; fax (22) 702-18-99; f. 1991; independent organization supported by the Swiss government and the Canton of Geneva; aims to provide decision-makers from public and private sectors, NGOs and academia with high-level training and negotiation opportunities based on research; main research programmes cover climate change and international fresh waters; library of 1,000 vols, 100 periodicals; Dir Dr FRANCISCO SZEKELY.

Naturforschende Gesellschaft in Basel: Universitätsbibliothek, CH-4056 Basel; f. 1817; 600 mems; library of 74,000 vols; Pres. Dr L. LANDMANN; Sec. Dr H. MEINDL; publ. *Verhandlungen* (annually).

Naturforschende Gesellschaft in Bern: Stadt- und Universitätsbibliothek, Münstergasse 61, CH-3000 Bern 7; tel. (31) 320-32-31; fax (31) 320-32-99; f. 1786; 478 mems; Pres. R. WEINGART; Sec. K. GROSSENBACHER; publ. *Mitteilungen*.

Naturwissenschaftliche Gesellschaft Winterthur (NGW): Stadtbibliothek Winterthur, Museumstr. 52, 8401 Winterthur; f. 1884; lectures, field trips, publications; 340 mems; Pres. Dr K. F. KAISER; Sec. Dr W. CAPREZ; publ. *Mitteilungen* (every 3 years).

Schweizerische Energie-Stiftung/Fondation Suisse pour l'Energie: Sihlquai 67, 8005 Zürich; tel. (1) 271-54-64; f. 1976; aims to promote an energy policy suitable for human beings and the environment; and the control of energy consumption; promotes alternative sources of energy and the practice of conservation; Pres. ROSMARIE BÄR; Man. A. BRAUNWALDER; publs *Energie Umwelt*, *SES-Reports* (irregular).

Schweizerische Stiftung für Alpine Forschungen (Swiss Foundation for Alpine Research): Binzstr. 23, 8045 Zürich; tel. (1) 461-01-47; fax (1) 287-13-68; f. 1939; 11 mems; Pres. Dr JÜRG MARMET; Sec. Dr F. H. SCHWARZENBACH.

Società ticinese di scienze naturali: c/o Museo cantonale di Storia naturale, viale Cattaneo 4, CH-6900 Lugano; tel. (91) 911-53-80; f. 1903; promotion of scientific research; 300 mems; Pres. Dr C. VALSANGIACOMO; publs *Bollettino* (2 a year), *Memorie*.

Société de Physique et d'Histoire Naturelle de Genève: POB 6434, 1211 Geneva 6; tel. (22) 418-63-00; fax (22) 418-63-01; e-mail jean.wuest@mhn.ville-ge.ch; f. 1790; natural and exact sciences; 237 mems; Pres. PAUL TISSOT; Sec. JEAN WÜEST; publ. *Archives des sciences* (3 a year).

Société Vaudoise des Sciences Naturelles: Palais de Rumine, 1005 Lausanne; tel. (21) 312-43-34; fax (21) 312-43-34; f. 1815; 600 mems; 1,000 periodicals in the library reading-room: see also Bibliothèque Cantonale et Universitaire de Lausanne; Sec. Mme MUNDLER; publs *Bulletin* (2 a year), *Mémoires* (irregular).

Biological Sciences

Bernische Botanische Gesellschaft: Altenbergrain 21, 3013 Bern; tel. (31) 631-49-11; fax (31) 332-20-59; f. 1918; 380 mems; Pres. Dr D. M. MOSER; Sec. RITA GERBER; publ. *Sitzungsberichte* (annually).

Schweizerische Botanische Gesellschaft: C/o Institut de Botanique Systématique et de Géobotanique, Université, 1015 Lausanne; f. 1890; 700 mems; publ. *Botanica Helvetica*.

Schweizerische Entomologische Gesellschaft: C/o CSCF, Terreaux 14, 2000 Neuchâtel; tel. (32) 725-72-57; f. 1858; 325 mems; library of 18,000 vols; Pres. Dr H. BUHOLZER; Sec. G. CARRON; publs *Mitteilungen*, *Fauna Helvetica*; Library and Exchange Agency: Library of the Swiss Federal Institute of Technology, Leonhardstr. 33, 8092 Zürich.

Mathematical Sciences

Schweizerische Mathematische Gesellschaft/Société Mathématique Suisse: Section de Mathématiques, Université de Genève, CP 240, 1211 Geneva 24; f. 1910; 480 mems; Pres. Prof. GERHARD WANNER; Sec. Prof. ROLF JELTSCH; publs *Commentarii Mathematici Helvetici* (quarterly), *Elemente der Mathematik* (quarterly).

Physical Sciences

Neue Schweizerische Chemische Gesellschaft/Nouvelle Société Suisse de Chimie: C/o Novartis, K-25.1.45, 4002, Basel; tel. (61) 696-66-26; fax (61) 696-69-85; f. 1997; 2,200 mems; Pres. Dr H. L. SENTI; Dir Dr R. DARMS; publs *Chimia*, *Helvetica Chimica Acta*.

Physikalische Gesellschaft Zürich: Schönberggasse 9, 8001 Zürich; tel. (1) 257-29-03; fax (1) 261-63-23; f. 1887; 640 mems; Pres. Prof. Dr N. STRAUMANN; Sec. Dr H. KELLER.

Schweizerische Astronomische Gesellschaft/Société Astronomique de Suisse: Gristenbühl 13, 9315 Neukirch; tel. (71) 477-17-43; f. 1938; 3,700 mems; Pres. DIETER SPÄNI; Sec. SUE KERNEN; publ. *Orion* (every 2 months).

Schweizerische Geologische Gesellschaft/Société Géologique Suisse: c/o Dr M. Sartori, Dept de géologie, Université de Genève, 13 rue des Maraîchers, 1211 Geneva 4; tel. (22) 702-66-11; fax (22) 320-57-32; f. 1882; 1,034 mems; promotes geology from a general view-point; regular annual meetings; Pres. Prof. M. BURKHARD; Sec. Dr M. SARTORI; publ. *Eclogae geologicae Helvetiae* (3 a year).

Schweizerische Meteorologische Anstalt: Krähbühlstr. 58, CH-8044 Zürich; tel. (1) 256-91-11; fax (1) 256-92-78; f. 1880; 200 mems; meteorological services; library of 35,000 vols; Dir TH. GUTERMANN.

Schweizerische Paläontologische Gesellschaft/Société Paléontologique Suisse: Muséum d'histoire naturelle, Dr Danielle Decrouez, Route de Malagnou, Case postale 6434, 1211 Geneva 6; f. 1921; 260 mems; Sec. and Treas. Dr D. DECROUEZ; publ. *Bericht*.

Schweizerische Physikalische Gesellschaft/Société Suisse de Physique: Institut für Physik, Klingelbergstr. 82, 4056 Basel; tel. (61) 267-37-13; fax (61) 267-37-16; f. 1908; 1,400 mems; Pres. Prof. PETER OELHAFEN; publ. *Helvetica Physica Acta*.

PHILOSOPHY AND PSYCHOLOGY

Schweizerische Gesellschaft für Psychologie/Société Suisse de Psychologie: c/o Psychologisches Institut der Universität Zürich, Schmelzbergstr. 40, 8044 Zurich; tel. (1) 257-31-04; fax (1) 252-46-45; f. 1943; 430 mems; Pres. Dr R. VOLKART; publ. *Swiss Journal of Psychology*.

Schweizerische Philosophische Gesellschaft/Société suisse de philosophie: 4 rue des Parcs, 2000 Neuchâtel; f. 1940; 800 mems; Pres. Prof. Dr D. SCHULTHESS; Sec. Prof. Dr E. G. KOHLER; publs *Studia philosophica* (annually), *Supplementa* (irregular).

Schweizerische Stiftung für Angewandte Psychologie/Fondation Suisse pour la psychologie appliquée: C/o Dr M. Notter, Schweizerischer Bankgesellschaft, Bahnhofstr. 45, 8021 Zürich; f. 1927; 150 mems; Pres. Dr H. SCHMID; Sec. Dr M. NOTTER.

Schweizerischer Berufsverband für Angewandte Psychologie/Association professionnelle suisse de psychologie appliquée: Winkelweg 3, 8127 Forch; tel. (1) 980-36-20; f. 1952; 420 mems; Pres. URS RÜEGSEGGER; Sec. MAJA HEFTI.

RELIGION, SOCIOLOGY AND ANTHROPOLOGY

Schweizerische Afrika-Gesellschaft/Société Suisse d'Etudes Africaines: POB 8212, 3001 Berne; f. 1974; co-ordinates multi-disciplinary research on Africa; 200 mems; Pres. Dr BEAT SOTTAS; Vice-Pres. Dr NICOLE STAEUBLE-TERCIER; publs *Newsletter* (quarterly), *Swiss Bibliography of Africa* (annually).

Schweizerische Gesellschaft für Soziologie/Société Suisse de Sociologie: Rämistr. 69, 8001 Zürich; f. 1955; 600 mems; Pres. C. HONEGGER; Sec. PETER RUSTERHOLZ; publs *Bulletin* (quarterly), *Schweizerische Zeitschrift für Soziologie / Revue suisse de sociologie / Swiss Journal of Sociology* (3 a year).

Schweizerische Gesellschaft für Volkskunde/Société suisse des traditions populaires: Spalenvorstadt 2, 4051 Basel; tel. (61) 261-99-00; f. 1896; 1,500 mems; Pres. Prof. Dr T. BÜHLER; Sec. Dr R. ANZENBERGER; publs *Schweizerisches Archiv für Volkskunde* (2 a year), *Schweizer Volkskunde / Folklore suisse / Folklore svizzero* (4 a year).

Schweizerische Theologische Gesellschaft/Société suisse de Théologie: Postfach 8204, 3001 Bern; f. 1965; 250 mems; Pres. Prof. Dr M. ROSE; Sec. (vacant).

Schweizerische Trachtenvereinigung/Fédération Nationale des Costumes Suisses: Mühlegasse 13, 3400 Burgdorf, Postfach; tel. (34) 22-22-39; f. 1926; folk dance records and descriptions; 28,000 mems; Pres. HANSRUEDI SPICHIGER; publ. *Tracht und Brauch / Costumes et Coutumes* (quarterly).

Verband Jüdischer Lehrer und Kantoren der Schweiz (Society of Jewish teachers and cantors in Switzerland): Brandschenkesteig 12, 8002 Zürich; f. 1926; 62 mems; Pres. ERICH HAUSMANN; Sec. MICHEL BOLLAG; publ. *Bulletin*.

TECHNOLOGY

Schweizerische Gesellschaft für Automatik/Association Suisse pour l'Automatique (Swiss Federation of Automatic Control): C/o Hörrmann Secretarial Services, Zürcherstr. 15, 5400 Baden; tel. (56) 222-36-66; fax (56) 222-36-62; e-mail sga@aut.ee.ethz.ch; f. 1956; promotes and develops knowledge of techniques of measurement, control and calculation, and their application in the field of automation; 200 individual mems, 20 corporate mems; Pres. Prof. Dr A. H. GLATTFELDER; Sec. J. HOERRMANN-CLARKE; publ. *SGA-ASSPA-Bulletin* (quarterly).

Schweizerische Gesellschaft für Mikrotechnik/Association Suisse de Microtechnique: c/o FRSM, Rue Jaquet-Droz 1, CP 20, 2007, Neuchâtel; tel. (32) 720-09-00; fax (32) 720-09-90; f. 1962; 95 mems; Pres. P. STAUBER; Sec. M. GRÜNIG; publ. *Bulletin* (annually).

Schweizerischer Technischer Verband (Association of Engineers and Architects): Weinbergstr. 41, STV-Haus, 8023 Zürich; tel. (1) 268-37-11; e-mail info@swissengineering.ch; f. 1905; 18,000 mems; Pres. G. WOLF; Sec.-Gen. STEPHAN SCHWITTER; publs *Schweizerische Technische Zeitschrift*, *Revue Technique Suisse*.

Schweizerischer Verband der Ingenieur-Agronomen und der Lebensmittel-Ingenieure/Association suisse des ingénieurs agronomes et des ingénieurs en technologie alimentaire: Länggasse 79, 3052 Zollikofen, Bern; tel. (31) 911-06-68; fax (31) 911-49-25; e-mail svial@pop.agri.ch; f. 1901; 2,370 mems; Pres. D. KOHL; Sec. O. MEYER; publ. *Bulletin* (quarterly).

Verband Schweizer Abwasser- und Gewässerschutzfachleute (Swiss Water Pollution Control Association): Strassburgstr. 10, Postfach 2443, 8026 Zürich; tel. (1) 241-25-85; fax (1) 241-61-29; f. 1944; 1,420 mems; 2,500 reps; Pres. F. CONRADIN.

Verband Schweizerischer Vermessungsfachleute (Association of Swiss Surveyors): C/o Marja Kaempfer, Weissensteinstr. 15, 3400 Burgdorf; tel. (34) 422-98-04; fax (34) 422-98-04; f. 1929; 1,500 mems; Pres. ERICH BRUNNER; Sec. MARJA KAEMPFER; publ. *Vermessung-Mensuration* (12 a year).

Research Institutes

AGRICULTURE, FISHERIES AND VETERINARY SCIENCE

Office fédéral de l'agriculture: Ministry of Public Economy, Mattenhofstr. 5, 3003 Bern; tel. (31) 322-25-11; the centre for federal agricultural research; Dir Dr HANS BURGER; Head of Agricultural Research Prof. Dr JACQUES MOREL.

Federal agricultural research stations:

Station Fédérale de Recherches en Ecologie et Agriculture: 8046 Zürich-Reckenholz; Dir Dr A. BRÖNNIMANN.

Station Fédérale de Recherches Agronomiques de Changins: Château de Changins, 1260 Nyon; Dir Dr ALEXANDRE VEZ.

Station Fédérale de Recherches Laitières: 3097 Liebefeld-Bern; Dir Dr CHRISTIAN STEFFEN.

Station Fédérale de Recherches en Arboriculture, Viticulture et Horticulture de Wädenswil: 8820 Wädenswil; Dir Dr WALTER MÜLLER.

Station Fédérale de Recherches sur la Production animale: 1725 Posieux; Dir DANIELLE GAGNAUX.

Station Fédérale de Recherches d'Economie d'entreprise et de génie rural de Tänikon: 8356 Tänikon b. Aadorf; Dir Prof. Dr WALTER MEIER.

ECONOMICS, LAW AND POLITICS

Institut suisse de droit comparé/Schweizerisches Institut für Rechtsvergleichung/Istituto svizzero di diritto comparato (Swiss Institute of Comparative Law): CH-1015 Lausanne-Dorigny; tel. (21) 692-49-11; fax (21) 692-49-49; e-mail secretariat@isdc-dfjp.unil.ch; f. 1978; provides the Federal Government with the documents and studies necessary for legislation and for the conclusion of international conventions; participates in international efforts towards approximation and unification of law; gives information and consultations to courts, administrations, attorneys and interested persons; conducts its own scientific research, promotes and co-ordinates studies in Swiss universities and furnishes to researchers in Switzerland an appropriate centre for study; library: see Libraries; Dir Prof. P. WIDMER.

Institut Suisse de Recherche sur les Pays de l'Est (Swiss Eastern Institute): Jubiläumsstr. 41, CH-3000 Bern 6; tel. (31) 43-12-12; fax (31) 43-38-91; f. 1959; study and information on the development of Communist countries; library: see Libraries; Dir Dr GEORG J. DOBROVOLNY; Admin. Dir SIMON MAURER; publs *Zeit-bild* (fortnightly), *Le Périscope* (monthly), *Swiss Press Review* (fortnightly), *Schwejzarskij Vestnik* (monthly, in Russian), *SOI-Bilanz* (monthly).

Schweizerisches Institut für Auslandforschung (Swiss Institute of International Studies): Seilergraben 49, 8001 Zürich; tel. (1) 632-63-62; fax (1) 632-19-47; Dir Prof. Dr DIETER RULOFF; publ. *Sozialwissenschaftliche Studien* (annually).

MEDICINE

Institut für Geschichte und Ethik der Medizin: Schönbeinstr. 18/20, 4056 Basel; tel. (61) 267-30-67; fax (61) 267-31-90; f. 1964; library of 10,000 vols; Dir Prof. U. TROEHLER.

Institut für Immunologie: Grenzacherstr. 487, CH-4005 Basel; f. 1970; 55 mems; library of 3,000 monographs and 140 journals; Dir Prof. F. MELCHERS; publ. *Annual Report*.

Institut suisse de recherche expérimentale sur le cancer/Schweizerisches Institut für Experimentelle Krebsforschung (Swiss Institute for Experimental Cancer Research): Ch. des Boveresses 155, 1066 Epalinges s. Lausanne; tel. (21) 692-58-58; fax (21) 652-69-33; f. 1964; 180 mems; library of 5,400 vols, 200 periodicals; Pres. G. MULLER; Dir Dr M. AGUET; Admin. Dir E. CURRAT.

Schweizerisches Tropeninstitut (STI)/Institut Tropical Suisse: 4002 Basel; tel. (61) 284-81-11; telex 96-25-08; fax (61) 271-86-54; f. 1943; library of 4,000 vols; Dir Prof. Dr MARCEL TANNER.

NATURAL SCIENCES

General

Bundesamt für Bildung und Wissenschaft/Office fédéral de l'éducation et de la science (Federal Office for Education and Science): Hallwylstr. 4, 3003 Bern; tel. (31) 322-96-91; fax (31) 322-78-54; e-mail martin.fischer@bbw.admin.ch; f. 1969; prepares policy decisions for education and science and executes scientific policy; co-ordinates activities of Federal bodies concerned with research and education; supports universities and other institutes of higher education and contributes to grants; is responsible for encouragement and general co-ordination of research and higher education; with other Departments deals with international scientific affairs; Dir GERHARD M. SCHUWEY.

Jungfraujoch and Gornergrat Scientific Stations: Secretariat, Sidlerstr. 5, 3012 Bern; tel. (31) 631-40-52; fax (31) 631-44-05; f. 1930; high-altitude research in astronomy, astrophysics, environmental sciences, atmospheric physics, atmospheric chemistry, glaciology, meteorology, physics and biology; international foundation run by scientific organizations of Austria, Belgium, Germany, Great Britain, Italy, Switzerland; Pres. Prof. H. DEBRUNNER; publ. *Review on Activity*.

Stiftung für Humanwissenschaftliche Grundlagenforschung/Fondation pour la Recherche de Base dans les Sciences de l'Homme: Postfach 112, 8030 Zürich; tel. (1) 383-09-22; f. 1970; basic research in human sciences; Pres. Prof. JULES ANGST; Dir Dr WALTER BODMER.

Biological Sciences

Botanische Institute und Botanischer Garten/Instituts et Jardin Botaniques de l'Université: Altenbergrain 21, 3013 Bern; tel. (31) 631-49-11; fax (31) 322-20-59; f. 1862.

Incorporates:

Botanischer Garten: Altenbergrain 21, 3013 Bern; Dir Dr K. AMMANN.

Geobotanisches Institut: Altenbergrain 21, 3013 Bern; Dirs Dr B. AMMANN, Prof. Dr D. M. NEWBERY.

Pflanzenphysiologisches Institut: Altenbergrain 21, 3013 Bern; Dir Prof. Dr CH. BRUNOLD.

Conservatoire et Jardin botaniques de la Ville de Genève: CP 60, 1292 Chambésy; tel. (22) 418-51-00; fax (22) 418-51-01; e-mail jeanmonod@cjb.unige.ch; f. 1817; systematic botany, taxonomy, floristics, ecology, phytogeography; 95 mems, including 15 scientific mems; library of 200,000 vols, 3,500 periodicals; Dir Prof. RODOLPHE SPICHIGER; publs *Candollea*, *Boissiera*, *Index Seminum*, *Série documentaire*, *Série éducative*, etc.

Physical Sciences

Eidgenössisches Institut für Schnee- und Lawinenforschung (Federal Institute for Snow and Avalanche Research): Flüelastrasse 11, 7260 Davos Dorf; tel. (81) 417-01-11; fax (81) 417-01-10; f. 1936; physics and mechanics of snow and snow pack, avalanche formation and mechanics, protective structure, snow and avalanche interaction with forests, and an avalanche warning service; 45 mems; library of 15,000 titles; Dir Dr WALTER AMMANN; publs *Winterbericht* (annually), *Mitteilungen*, *Sonderdrucke*.

Institut für Astronomie: ETH-Zentrum, 8092 Zürich; tel. (1) 632-3813; fax (1) 632-1205; f. 1864; 30 mems; astrophysics, particularly solar physics; Dir Prof. Dr J. O. STENFLO.

Observatoire: 51 Ch. des Maillettes, 1290 Sauverny/ Ge; tel. (22) 755-26-11; telex 419209; fax (22) 755-39-83; f. 1772; astrophysics, galactic structure, photometry, space research; 90 staff; library of 6,000 vols, 500 periodicals; Dr Prof. ANDRÉ MAEDER.

Observatoire Cantonal: 2000 Neuchâtel; tel. (32) 889-68-70; fax (32) 889-62-81; e-mail secretariat.on@on.unine.ch; f. 1858; library of 1,000 vols; research in atomic frequency standards, space clocks and lidar geophysics; dissemination of official time in Switzerland; Dir G. BUSCH; publ. annual report.

Schweizerische Gesellschaft für Astrophysik und Astronomie/Société Suisse d'Astrophysique et d'Astronomie: Astronomisches Institut der Universität Basel, Venusstr. 7, 4102 Binningen; tel. (61) 205-54-54; fax (61) 205-54-55; f. 1968; research in astrophysics; 165 mems; Pres. Prof. ROLAND BUSER; Sec. Dr J.-C. MERMILLIOD.

Specola Solare Ticinese: 6605 Locarno-Monti; tel. (91) 756-23-76; f. 1957; solar observation; library of 400 vols; Dir S. CORTESI.

Libraries and Archives

Aarau

Aargauische Kantonsbibliothek: Aargauerplatz, 5001 Aarau; tel. (62) 835-23-60; fax (62) 835-23-60; e-mail kantonsbibliothek@ag.ch; f. 1803; library of 600,000 vols, 2,000 periodicals; 850 incunabula, 1,500 MSS; special collections: Zurlaubiana (history of Switzerland), literature of and on Karl Barth; Dir Dr JOSEF GEORG BREGENZER.

Staatsarchiv des Kantons Aargau: Obere Vorstadt 6, 5001 Aarau; tel. (62) 835-12-90; fax (62) 835-23-69; f. 1803; State Archivist Dr ROMAN W. BRÜSCHWEILER.

Basel

Allgemeine Bibliotheken der Gesellschaft für das Gute und Gemeinnützige: Rümelinsplatz 6, 4001 Basel; tel. (61) 264-11-11; fax (61) 264-11-90; e-mail abg@ubaclu.unibas.ch; f. 1807; central library, 8 br. libraries; library of 290,000 vols; Dir KURT WALDNER; publ. *Jahresbericht*.

Archiv für Schweizerische Kunstgeschichte: Münzgasse 16, 4051 Basel; tel. (61) 267-29-43; library of 6,000 vols; Dir NIKLAUS MEIER.

Bibliothek des Museums der Kulturen Basel: Augustinergasse 2, 4001 Basel; tel. (61) 266-56-30; library of 70,000 vols on ethnography of the world; Librarians ELISABETH IDRIS-HÖHENER, EILEEN SCHLOTE.

Öffentliche Bibliothek der Universität Basel (Public University Library): Schönbeinstr. 20, 4056 Basel; tel. (61) 267-31-30; fax (61) 267-31-03; f. 1460; library of 3,000,000 vols; scientific works, special collections of MSS, incunabula, maps, portraits; Chief Librarian H. HUG; publs *Bericht über die Verwaltung der Öffentlichen Bibliothek der Universität Basel* (1 a year), *Jahresverzeichnis der Schweizerischen Hochschulschriften*, *Die mittelalterlichen Handschriften der Universitätsbibliothek Basel*, *Die Matrikel der Universität Basel*, *Die Amerbachkorrespondenz*.

Schweizerisches Wirtschaftsarchiv/Archives Economiques Suisses: Petersgraben 51, Postfach 4003 Basel; tel. (61) 267-32-19; fax (61) 267-32-08; e-mail gisler@ubaclu.unibas.ch; f. 1910; library of over 650,000 vols, including business reports, periodicals, statistical publications, reports on social institutions and international conferences, professional societies and law and economics; 2,000,000 newspaper cuttings; the library is open to the public; Dir JOHANNA GISLER.

Staatsarchiv Basel-Stadt: Martinsgasse 2, 4001 Basel; tel. (61) 267-86-01; fax (61) 267-65-71; e-mail stabs@afibs.ch; Dir Dr J. ZWICKER;

publs *Jahresberichte*, *Quellen und Forschungen zur Basler Geschichte*.

Bern

Bibliothek des Konservatoriums für Musik und Theater: Kramgasse 36, 3011 Bern; f. 1917; library of 50,000 vols; Pres. ANNAMARIE ZINSLI.

Bibliothèque Nationale Suisse/Schweizerische Landesbibliothek: Hallwylstr. 15, 3003 Bern; tel. (31) 322-89-11; fax (31) 322-84-63; e-mail iz-helvetica@slb.admin.ch; f. 1895; contains all publications issued in Switzerland and foreign publications if by Swiss authors or if concerning Switzerland; library of 2,890,000 vols, 11,000 current periodicals and newspapers, 298,000 engravings and photos, 75,000 maps, 50,000 posters; Swiss union catalogue, Information Center Helvetica, Swiss Literary Archives, Swiss ISSN Center; Dir Dr J.-F. JAUSLIN; publs *Le Livre suisse*, *Répertoire des périodiques suisses*, *Répertoire des périodiques étrangers dans les bibliothèques suisses*, *Bibliographia scientiae naturalis Helvetica*, *Bibliographie der Schweizergeschichte*, *Bibliographie der deutschsprachigen Schweizerliteratur*, *Bibliographie annuelle des Lettres romandes*.

Burgerbibliothek Bern/Bibliothèque de la Bourgeoisie de Berne: Münstergasse 63, 3000 Bern 7; tel. (31) 311-18-03; fax (31) 320-33-70; f. 1951; 1,200 metres of historical MSS, of which 50 metres medieval MSS; Curators H. WÄBER, M. GERMANN, M. BÄBLER.

Centre de documentation de politique de la science/Dokumentationsstelle für Wissenschaftspolitik (Documentation Centre for Political Science): Inselgasse 1, 3003 Bern; tel. (31) 322-96-55; telex 912981; fax (31) 322-80-70; f. 1972; library of 10,000 vols, 200 periodicals; Head EDITH IMHOF; publ. *Internationale wissenschaftspolitische Presseschau*.

Eidgenössische Parlaments- und Zentralbibliothek (Central Library of Parliament and Federal Administration): Bundeshaus West, 3003 Bern; tel. (31) 322-37-89; fax (31) 322-78-07; e-mail info-epzb@bk.admin.ch; f. 1848; library of 110,000 vols; open to the public for reference only; Dir CHARLES R. PFERSICH.

Gewerbebibliothek: Zeughausgasse 2, 3011 Bern; tel. (31) 311-31-61; f. 1869; trade, applied art; library of 13,000 vols; Dir MAX WERREN.

Schweizerisches Bundesarchiv: Archivstr. 24, 3003 Bern; tel. (31) 322-89-89; fax (31) 322-78-23; f. 1798; Dir Prof. CHRISTOPH GRAF.

Staatsarchiv des Kantons Bern: Falkenplatz 4, 3012 Bern; tel. (31) 633-51-01; fax (31) 633-51-02; contains the archives of the Canton of Bern; Archivist Dr KARL F. WÄLCHLI; publ. *Das Staatsarchiv des Kantons Bern*.

Stadt- und Universitätsbibliothek: Münstergasse 61, 3000, Bern 7; tel. (31) 320-32-11; fax (31) 320-32-99; f. 1528; library of 1,800,000 vols; Chief Librarian Prof. Dr ROBERT BARTH.

Chur

Staatsarchiv des Kantons Graubünden: Karlihofplatz, 7001 Chur; tel. (81) 257-28-03; f. 1803; Archivist Dr S. MARGADANT.

Cologny

Bibliotheca Bodmeriana (Fondation Martin Bodmer): 19–21 route du Guignard, 1223 Cologny; tel. (22) 707-44-33; fax (22) 707-44-30; f. 1972; library of 160,000 vols; special collections of papyrus, MSS, autographs, incunabula, drawings; Dir Dr M. BIRCHER; publs series *Papyri*, *Catalogues*, *Texts*.

Fribourg

Bibliothèque Cantonale et Universitaire/Kantons- und Universitätsbibliothek: rue Joseph-Piller 2, 1701 Fribourg; tel. (26) 305-13-13; fax (26) 305-13-77; e-mail bcu@etatfr.ch; f. 1848; library of 1,800,000 vols; Dir M. NICOULIN.

Geneva

Archives d'Etat: 1 rue de l'Hôtel de Ville, 1211 Geneva 3; tel. (22) 319-33-95; fax (22) 319-33-65; material on history of Geneva; Archivist Miss C. SANTSCHI.

Bibliothèque d'Art et d'Archéologie (annexe of Musées d'Art et d'Histoire): 5 Promenade du Pin, 1204 Geneva; tel. (22) 418-27-00; fax (22) 418-27-01; e-mail info.baa@ville-ge.ch; library of 198,000 vols, 150,000 slides, 5,000 periodicals, 114,000 exhibition and auction catalogues; Head Librarian VERONIQUE ESTÈBE.

Bibliothèque des Nations Unies/United Nations Library: Palais des Nations, 1211 Geneva 10; tel. (22) 917-41-81; telex 412962; fax (22) 917-00-28; f. 1919; library of 1,100,000 vols, 4 million documents and publications of the United Nations and its specialist agencies, 500,000 government documents, 9,000 periodicals; archives of the Société des Nations; Chief Librarian PIERRE PELOU; publs *Monthly Bibliography, Pt. I—Books, Official Publications, Serials, Pt. II—Selected Articles, Weekly Bibliography, Library News / Nouvelles de la Bibliothèque*.

Bibliothèque Publique et Universitaire de Genève: Promenade des Bastions, 1211 Geneva 4; tel. (22) 418-28-00; fax (22) 418-28-01; e-mail info.bpu@ville-ge.ch; f. 1562; library of 1,800,000 vols and pamphlets, 70,000 posters, 23,000 maps, 45,000 engravings, 400 painted portraits, 15,000 MSS; Dir A. JACQUESSON.

Bibliothèques Municipales: 10 rue de la Tour-de-Boël, 1204 Geneva; tel. (22) 418-32-50; fax (22) 418-32-51; f. 1931; adult libraries (7 brs) 400,000 vols, children's libraries (7 brs) 175,000 vols, 5 bookmobiles 60,000 vols, 2 sound-recording libraries 80,000 records; Dir ISABELLE RUEPP.

International Labour Office Library: 1211 Geneva 22; tel. (22) 799-86-75; telex 415647; fax (22) 799-65-16; f. 1919; library of 1,000,000 vols and pamphlets, 5,500 current periodicals (including annuals and official gazettes); open to the public on special request; computerized data base (LABORDOC), containing 210,000 abstracts, available for on-line searching world-wide through the facilities of ESA-IRS and Questel-ORBIT and on CD-ROM; Dir E. FRIERSON; publs *International Labour Documentation* (10 a year), *ILO Thesaurus: labour, employment and training terminology*.

Grand Saint-Bernard

Bibliothèque de l'Hospice du Grand Saint-Bernard: CH-1931 Bourg-Saint-Pierre, Canton de Valais (library of Austin Canons monastery, f. 1050); tel. (26) 4-92-36; works on botany and numismatics, ancient MSS and maps; library of over 30,000 vols and many thousands of brochures.

Lausanne

Bibliothèque Cantonale et Universitaire de Lausanne: Palais de Rumine, 1005 Lausanne; tel. (21) 316-78-80; fax (21) 316-78-70; (Dorigny br.: 1015 Lausanne; tel. (21) 692-11-11; fax (21) 692-48-45); f. 1537; legal deposit library of Vaud Canton; regional documentation; 1,400,000 vols, 150 incunabula; 8,500 CD and 2,500 LP records; the library is open to the public; Dir HUBERT VILLARD; publs *Catalogues des fonds de manuscrits*, *Catalogues des manuscrits musicaux*, *Rapport annuel*.

Bibliothèque centrale de l'École Polytechnique Fédérale de Lausanne: 1015 Lausanne; tel. (21) 693-21-59; fax (21) 693-51-00; e-mail bibliotheque.centrale@epfl.ch; f. 1945; science and technology; library of 300,000 vols, 700 current periodicals; open to the public; Dir JOSETTE NOENINGER.

Bibliothèque de l'Institut Suisse de Droit Comparé/Bibliothek des Schweizerischen Instituts für Rechtsvergleichung: 1015 Lausanne-Dorigny; tel. (21) 692-49-11; fax (21) 692-49-49; e-mail christiane.serkis@isdc-dfjp.unil.ch; f. 1982; collects legal material from all countries in all fields of law, incl. international law; European documentation centre; library of 180,000 vols; Librarians CHRISTIANE SERKIS BISCHOF, JARMILA LOOKS (acting).

Bibliothèque et Centre de Documentation de la Faculté de Médecine: Centre Hospitalier Universitaire Vaudois, 1011 Lausanne; tel. (21) 314-50-82; fax (21) 314-50-70; e-mail bdfm@chuv.hospvd.ch; f. 1968; library of 60,000 vols, 1,300 periodicals; microcomputer facilities, videodiscs, audiovisual library; Librarian ISABELLE DE KAENEL.

Bibliothèque Municipale de la Ville de Lausanne: 11 place Chauderon, 1003 Lausanne; tel. (21) 315-69-11; fax (21) 315-60-07; e-mail bml@lausanne.ch; f. 1934; library of 350,000 vols; Dir PIERRE-YVES LADOR.

Lucerne

Staatsarchiv des Kantons Luzern: Schützenstr. 9, 6000 Luzern 7; tel. (41) 228-53-65; fax (41) 228-66-33; f. 1803; local history; library of 20,000 vols; Archivist Dr A. GÖSSI; publs *Jahresbericht des Staatsarchivs Luzern*, *Luzerner Historische Veröffentlichungen* (irregular).

Zentralbibliothek Luzern: Sempacherstr. 10, CH-6002 Lucerne; tel. (41) 228-53-12; fax (41) 210-82-55; e-mail zbluzern@zbluzern.ch; f. 1951; library of 675,000 vols, 2,650 MSS, 130,000 engravings, photos and maps; collection of Swiss publs prior to 1848; Dir Dr U. NIEDERER.

Lugano

Biblioteca Cantonale: Lugano, Ticino: Viale C. Cattaneo 6, 6900 Lugano; tel. (91) 911-53-50; fax (91) 911-53-59; f. 1852; library of 270,000 vols; only public library of Italian culture in Switzerland; incorporates *Libreria Patria*, special collection of 'Ticinensia', 40,000 vols, also Archivio Prezzolini and collections on contemporary culture; Dir Dott. G. CURONICI.

Neuchâtel

Archives de l'Etat: Le Château, CH-2001 Neuchâtel; tel. (32) 889-60-40; fax (32) 889-60-88; f. 1898; maintains a historical library and an administrative library; Archivist MAURICE DE TRIBOLET.

Bibliothèque des Pasteurs: Fbg de l'Hôpital 41, 2000 Neuchâtel; tel. (32) 725-46-66; f. 1538; theological; library of 70,000 vols, 20,000 pamphlets; Librarian RENÉ PÉTER-CONTESSE.

Bibliothèque Publique et Universitaire: 3 place Numa-Droz, Neuchâtel; tel. (32) 717-73-00; fax (32) 717-73-09; f. 1788; library of 450,000 vols, including vols of periodicals, an Encyclopaedia Library, Swiss theses, many reviews received mostly by exchange; MSS of J.-J. Rousseau (works and correspondence) and Mme de Charrière; archives of Société typographique de Neuchâtel; Dir M. SCHLUP; publs *Bibliothèques et musées*, *Musée neuchâtelois*, and bulletins of chronometry, geography, and natural sciences.

St Gallen

Kantonsbibliothek Vadiana: Notkerstr. 22, CH-9000 St Gallen; tel. (71) 244-78-17; fax (71) 245-93-51; f. 1551; library of 645,000 vols; the library is open to the public; Dir Dr ALOIS STADLER.

Stifts-Bibliothek St Gallen: Klosterhof 6D, 9004 St Gallen; tel. (71) 227-34-16; fax (71) 227-34-18; library of former Benedictine Abbey of St Gall; f. *c.* AD 719; important collection of manuscripts and incunabula, some dating from Irish period; library of 150,000 vols; Dir Prof. Dr PETER OCHSENBEIN.

Solothurn

Schweizerische Volksbibliothek/ Bibliothèque pour tous: Rosenweg 2, 4500 Solothurn; tel. (32) 623-32-31; fax (32) 623-33-80; f. 1920; library of *c.* 300,000 vols, 3 brs; Dir Dr P. WILLE.

Zentralbibliothek: Bielstr. 39, 4502 Solothurn; tel. (32) 624-11-41; fax (32) 624-11-45; f. 1930; library of 800,000 vols, 1,200 incunabula, 13,200 MSS, 7,000 illustrations and graphics, 18,000 music scores, 42,000 records and cassettes, 550 current periodicals and series; Dir Prof. Dr R. M. KULLY; publs *Jahresbericht*, *Veröffentlichungen*.

Winterthur

Stadtbibliothek: Museumstr. 52, 8401 Winterthur; tel. (52) 267-51-45; fax (52) 267-51-40; f. 1660; 730,000 items; special collections of local history, numismatics, music, African languages and literature; open to the public; Dir Dr ROLF WEISS; publ. *Neujahrsblatt* (annually).

Zürich

ETH-Bibliothek (Library of the Swiss Federal Institute of Technology): Rämistr. 101, CH-8092 Zürich; tel. (1) 632-25-49; fax (1) 632-13-57; f. 1855; library of 5,200,000 vols and documents (7,000 current periodicals, 22,000 current serials, 2 m. reports, 250,000 maps, 200,000 documents on history of science); university library specializing in science and technology; affiliated libraries: Geological Inst. Library, Architecture and Civil Engineering Library; Dir Dr W. NEUBAUER; publ. *Theses*.

Schweizerisches Sozialarchiv/Archives sociales suisses: Stadelhoferstr. 12, 8001 Zürich; tel. (1) 251-76-44; fax (1) 251-76-08; f. 1906; Swiss centre of social documentation; library of 100,000 vols and over 300,000 brochures, pamphlets, etc.; 1,300 current newspapers and reviews in the lecture hall; newspaper cuttings; the library is open to the public; Librarian Dr A. ULRICH.

Staatsarchiv des Kantons Zürich: Winterthurerstr. 170, Postfach, 8057 Zürich; tel. (1) 635-69-11; fax (1) 635-69-05; f. 1837; contains the archives of the canton of Zürich since 853 and a specialized library (local publications and collections of statutes; library of 30,000 vols and numerous pamphlets); Dir Dr O. SIGG.

Zentralbibliothek Zürich: Zähringerplatz 6, 8025 Zürich; tel. (1) 268-31-00; fax (1) 268-32-90; f. 1914; city, cantonal and university library, incorporating also the libraries of Naturforschende Gesellschaft in Zürich, Antiquarische Gesellschaft in Zürich, Geographisch-Ethnographische Gesellschaft Zürich, Schweizerischer Alpenclub, Allgemeine Musikgesellschaft Zürich, Bibliotheca Fennica, etc.; 3,000,000 vols, 28,000 MSS and autographs, 1,600 incunabula, 188,000 maps, and special collections of graphic arts (190,000 items), 32,000 records and cassettes, genealogy, heraldry; 12,400 current periodicals and series, 190 newspapers; service for photostats, xerocopies, microfilms; Dir Dr HERMANN KÖSTLER.

Museums and Art Galleries

Aarau

Aargauer Kunsthaus: Aargauer-Platz, 5001 Aarau; tel. (62) 835-23-30; fax (62) 835-23-27; f. 1860; Swiss painting and sculpture from 1750 to the present day; considerable collection of paintings by Caspar Wolf (1735–1783), the first painter of the Alps, and by the landscape painter, Adolf Staebli, and by Auberjonois, Brühlmann, Amiet, G. Giacometti, Hodler, Meyer-Amden, Louis Soutter, Vallotton; Dir BEAT WISMER.

Avenches

Musée Romain Avenches: 1580 Avenches; f. 1824; excavations of Aventicum; library of 15,000 vols; Pres. Prof. P. DUCREY; Dir Dr A. HOCHULI-GYSEL; publs *Bulletin de l'Association Pro Aventico* (annually), *Aventicum* (quarterly).

Basel

Antikenmuseum Basel und Sammlung Ludwig: St Albangraben 5, 4010 Basel; tel. 271-22-02; fax 272-18-61; f. 1961; collections of Greek art (2500–100 BC), Italian art (1000 BC–AD 300) and Etruscan art; Dir Prof. Dr P. BLOME.

Historisches Museum Basel: Verwaltung, Steinenberg 4, 4051 Basel; tel. (61) 271-05-05; fax (61) 271-05-42; f. 1856; 4 brs containing collection of objects from prehistoric times to 20th century, civic culture of Basel in 18th and 19th centuries and collection of old musical instruments, coaches and sleighs; Dir Dr BURKARD VON RODA; publ. *Jahresberichte*.

Museum der Kulturen Basel: Augustinergasse 2, Postfach, 4001 Basel; tel. (61) 266-55-00; fax (61) 266-56-05; f. 1893; ethnographical collections from all parts of the world, especially from Oceania, Indonesia, South America and Europe; textiles; library of 66,000 vols; Dir Dr C. B. WILPERT; publs *Annual Report*, *Basler Beiträge zur Ethnologie*, guides.

Oeffentliche Kunstsammlung Basel Kunstmuseum: St Albangraben 16, 4010 Basel; tel. (61) 271-08-28; fax (61) 271-08-45; f. 1662; pictures from 15th century to present day, notably by Witz, Holbein and contemporary painters; collection includes Grünewald, Rembrandt, 16th- and 17th-century Dutch painting, Cézanne, Gauguin and Van Gogh; large collection of cubist art; sculptures by Rodin and 20th-century artists; American art since 1945; Dept of prints and drawings with old Upper Rhine, German and Swiss masters; library of 100,000 vols; Dir Dr KATHARINA SCHMIDT; Curators Dr DIETER KOEPPLIN, Dr CHRISTIAN MÜLLER, Dr BERND W. LINDEMANN; Librarian NIKOLAUS MEIER.

Has attached:

Museum für Gegenwartskunst: St Alban-Rheinweg 60, CH-4010 Basel; tel. (61) 272-81-83; fax (61) 271-08-45; modern art from 1960 to the present; Head Dr THEODORA VISCHER.

Bern

Bernisches Historisches Museum: Helvetiaplatz 5, 3000 Bern 6; tel. (31) 350-77-11; fax (31) 350-77-99; f. 1881; pre- and early history, history, applied arts, 15th-century tapestries, coin collections, ethnology, folklore.

Kunstmuseum: Hodlerstr. 8–12, 3000 Bern 7; tel. (31) 311-0944; fax (31) 311-7263; f. 1879; Italian paintings from 14th to 16th centuries, works by Swiss masters from 15th to 19th centuries and modern works by Hodler and other Swiss, French and German masters; Paul Klee foundation; Hermann and Margrit Rupf foundation, including paintings by Picasso, Braque, Léger, Gris and Kandinsky; Adolf Wölfli Foundation; paintings, reliefs, water-colours, gouache paintings and illustrations by Sophie Taeuber-Arp; the graphic art collection contains over 38,000 drawings and engravings; library of *c.* 25,000 vols; Dir TONI STOOSS; publs *Berner Kunstmitteilungen* (5 a year), catalogues.

Naturhistorisches Museum: Bernastr. 15, 3005 Bern; tel. (31) 350-71-11; fax (31) 350-74-99; f. 1832; collection includes 220 dioramas of Swiss mammals and birds, big game (especially African), Swiss fish, amphibians and reptiles, minerals of the Swiss Alps, Alpine fossils, insects, vertebrates; Dir Prof. Dr M. GÜNTERT; publ. *Jahrbuch* (every 3 years).

Biel

Museum Schwab: Seevorstadt 50, 2502 Biel; tel. (32) 322-76-03; fax (32) 323-37-68; e-mail muschwab@bielsta.ch; f. 1872; contains prehistoric exhibits, especially of the lake-dwelling culture, the New Stone Age, the Bronze Age, and the second Iron Age; also a collection of the Roman period (Petinesca); Dir (vacant).

Chur

Bündner Kunstmuseum: Postfach 107, 7002 Chur; tel. (81) 257-28-68; f. 1900; contains works by Swiss artists, principally Segantini, Hodler, Alberto, Augusto and Giovanni Giacometti, E. L. Kirchner and Angelica Kauffmann; exhibitions of national and international art; Dir Dr BEAT STUTZER.

Fribourg

Musée d'art et d'histoire: 12 rue de Morat, 1700 Fribourg; tel. (26) 305-51-40; fax (26) 305-51-41; f. 1823; housed in Hotel Ratzé (16th century); collections of prehistoric, Roman and medieval exhibits; important collections of Swiss sculpture and painting from 11th to 20th centuries; works from the Marcello Foundation; monumental pieces by Jean Tinguely; Curator YVONNE LEHNHERR; publs *Annual Report*, exhibition catalogues.

Geneva

Collections Baur: 8 rue Munier Romilly, Geneva; tel. (22) 346-17-29; fax (22) 789-18-45; f. 1944, opened to public 1964; ceramics and works of art from China and Japan; library of 3,700 vols; Pres. OLIVIER REVERDIN; Curator FRANK DUNAND; publ. *Bulletin des Collections Baur* (2 a year).

Musée d'Art et d'Histoire: 2 rue Charles Galland, CP 3432, 1211 Geneva 3; tel. (22) 418-26-00; fax (22) 418-26-01; e-mail cathy.savioz@mah.ville-ge.ch; f. 1910; contains local prehistory section; Mediterranean, Egyptian, Near Eastern, Byzantine and Coptic archaeology; Italian, Dutch, Flemish, German, French, English and Swiss (especially Genevese) paintings, 20th-century paintings, European sculpture, applied art and numismatic collection; library of 95,000 vols; Dir C. MENZ; publs *Genava* (annually), *Journal des Musées d'Art et d'Histoire* (quarterly).

Attached museums:

Musée Ariana: 10 ave de la Paix, 1202 Geneva; tel. (22) 418-54-50; fax (22) 418-54-51; f. 1884; European and Eastern ceramics and glass; Curator ROLAND BLAETTLER.

Musée d'Histoire des Sciences: 128 rue de Lausanne, CH-1202 Geneva; tel. (22) 731-69-85; fax (22) 741-13-08; scientific instruments; f. 1964; library of 10,000 vols; Curator MARGARIDA ARCHINARD.

Musée de l'Horlogerie: 15 route de Malagnou, 1208 Geneva; tel. (22) 418-64-70; fax (22) 418-64-71; f. 1972; European clock and watchmaking; enamels, jewellery and miniatures, 1600–1900; Curator FABIENNE STURM.

Musée Rath: Place Neuve, 1204 Geneva; tel. (22) 418-33-40; fax (22) 418-33-41; f. 1828; temporary exhibitions.

Cabinet des estampes: 5 promenade du Pin, 1204 Geneva; tel. (22) 418-27-70; fax (22) 418-27-71; f. 1952; ancient and modern prints and twentieth-century books; Curator RAINER M. MASON.

Maison Tavel: 6 rue du Puits Saint-Pierre, 1204 Geneva; tel. (22) 310-29-00; f. 1985; history of the city; Curator LIVIO FORNARA.

Musée d'Ethnographie de la Ville de Genève: 65–67 blvd Carl Vogt, 1205 Geneva; tel. (22) 418-45-50; fax (22) 418-45-51; f. 1901; collections of ethnographic artifacts from the five continents; collection of musical instruments and of popular pottery; library of 20,000 vols; also houses the Société Suisse des Américanistes and the Archives internationales de musique populaire; Dir Dr LOUIS NECKER; Curators Dr JERÔME DUCOR (Asia), Dr CLAUDE SAVARY (Africa), DANIEL SCHOEPF (Americas), Dr BERNARD CRETTAZ (Europe), RENÉ FUERST (Oceania), LAURENT AUBERT (Ethnomusic); publs *Bulletin du Centre Genevois d'Anthropologie* (annually), *Totem* (3 a year), *Bulletin de la Société suisse des Américanistes* (annually).

Muséum d'Histoire Naturelle: Route de Malagnou, 1211 Geneva 6; tel. (22) 418-63-00; fax (22) 418-63-01; e-mail volker.mahnert@mhn.ville-ge.ch; f. 1820; 120 mems; departments of mammalogy and ornithology, herpetology and ichthyology, invertebrates, arthropods and insects, entomology, archaeozoology, geology and palaeontology, mineralogy; library of 125,000 vols; Dir Prof. Dr V. MAHNERT; Admin. C. WYLER; Librarian A.-M. DEUSS; publs *Catalogue des Invertébrés de la Suisse*, *Catalogue Illustré de la collection Lamarck* (fossils), *Revue suisse de Zoologie* (quarterly), *Revue de Paléobiologie* (2 a year), *Le Rhinolophe* (annually).

Glarus

Kunsthaus Glarus: Im Volksgarten, 8750 Glarus; tel. (55) 640-25-35; fax (55) 640-25-19; e-mail office@kunsthausglarus.ch; f. 1870; 19th- and 20th-century Swiss art, Swiss and foreign contemporary art; Curator BEATRIX RUF.

La Chaux-de-Fonds

Musée des Beaux-Arts: 33 rue des Musées, 2300 La Chaux-de-Fonds; tel. (32) 913-04-44; fax (32) 913-61-93; f. 1864; comprises paintings and sculpture by Swiss artists, particularly of the Neuchâtel district, and modern European painting and sculpture; Dir EDMOND CHARRIÈRE; publs Catalogues.

Musée International d'Horlogerie: 29 rue des Musées, CP 952, 2301 La Chaux-de-Fonds; tel. (32) 967-68-61; fax (32) 967-68-89; f. 1902; artistic and technical collections of watches, clocks, instruments and objects connected with the measurement of time; time research department; a modern carillon; specialist library of 3,000 vols; Curator CATHERINE CARDINAL.

Lausanne

Musée cantonal des Beaux-Arts: Palais de Rumine, Pl. Riponne 6, 1014 Lausanne; tel. (21) 316-34-45; fax (21) 316-34-46; f. 1841 by the painter Marc-Louis Arlaud; collection of 18th- to 20th-century works mainly by Swiss artists; international exhibitions of classical, modern and contemporary art; Dir Dr J. ZUTTER.

Musée historique de Lausanne: Ancien Evêché, 4 place de la Cathédrale, 1005 Lausanne; tel. (21) 331-03-53; fax (21) 312-42-68; f. 1918; historical collection; library; Curator OLIVIER PAVILLON; publ. *Mémoire vive*.

Musée Olympique: Quai d'Ouchy 1, Case postale, 1001 Lausanne; tel. (21) 621-65-11; fax (21) 621-65-12; f. 1993; Olympic sports and culture; library of 17,000 vols, 200 periodicals; 450 metres of archives; 12,000 hours of audiovisual material, 270,000 photographs; Dir FRANÇOISE ZWEIFEL.

Ligornetto

Museo Vela: 6853 Ligornetto; tel. (91) 647-32-68; fax (91) 647-32-41; f. 1897 by the Vela family; the works of Vincenzo, Lorenzo and Spartaco Vela comprise the basis of the collection, which also includes paintings from Lombard schools (17th to 19th centuries), sketches, drawings and photographs; Curator Dr GIANNA A. MINA; (The museum is closed until 2000.).

Locarno

Museo Civico e Archeologico, Dicastero Musei e Cultura: Via B. Rusca 5, 6600 Locarno; tel. (91) 756-31-80; fax (91) 756-31-70; f. 1970; 14th-century fortress housing an archaeological collection and historical museum; Dir Prof. RICCARDO CARAZZETTI.

Pinacoteca Casa Rusca: Dicastero Musei e Cultura, Via B. Rusca 5, 6600 Locarno; tel. (91) 756-31-85; fax (91) 751-98-71; f. 1987; restored 17th-century building housing the municipal art gallery; includes Jean Arp collection, and works by Calder, Hans Richter, Van Doesburg, etc.; Dir Prof. PIERRE CASÈ.

Lucerne

Historisches Museum: Altes Zeughaus, Pfistergasse 24, POB 7437, 6000 Lucerne 7; tel. (41) 228-54-24; fax (41) 228-54-18; e-mail jbruelisauer@hmluzern.ch; f. 1878; Curator Dr JOSEF BRÜLISAUER; publs *Jahrbuch der Historischen Gesellschaft Luzern*, *Jahresbericht des Historischen Museums*, exhibitions and collections catalogues.

Kunstmuseum: Unter der Egg 10, 6004 Lucerne; tel. (41) 410-90-40; fax (41) 410-90-92; e-mail kunstmuseum@centalnet.ch; f. 1819; Swiss art from ancient times to 20th century, European expressionism, with special international collection of contemporary works; exhibitions of modern art; Dir ULRICH LOOCK; owing to building work, the permanent collection will not be on display until late 1999.

Richard Wagner-Museum: Richard Wagner-Weg 27, 6005 Lucerne-Tribschen; tel. (41) 360-23-70; f. 1933; home of Richard Wagner from 1866 to 1872; contains original scores of *Siegfried-Idyll, Schusterlied (Meistersinger)*, etchings, paintings, busts and the Erard grand piano which accompanied Wagner throughout Europe; also collection of old musical instruments; Dir Dr UELI HABEGGER.

Verkehrshaus der Schweiz (Swiss Transport Museum): Lidostr. 5, 6006 Lucerne; tel. (41) 370-44-44; fax (41) 370-61-68; f. 1942; transport by land, water and air, communication and tourism; transportation archives; IMAX Theatre; Planetarium Longines; Dir FREDY REY.

Lugano

Museo Civico di Belle Arti: Villa Ciani, 6900 Lugano; f. 1903 by Antonio Caccia; works by artists of the Ticino from 17th to 20th centuries, and by French and Italian artists.

Neuchâtel

Musée d'Art et d'Histoire: Esplanade Léopold Robert 1, 2000 Neuchâtel; tel. (32) 717-79-20; fax (32) 717-79-29; f. 1885; pictures, drawings, prints and sculptures by local and other Swiss artists; French 18th- and 19th-century works (Courbet, Corot, and others); French Impressionists; furniture, coins and medals; an exceptional collection of 18th-century automata by Jaquet-Droz; Dir CAROLINE JUNIER-CLERC.

Musée d'Ethnographie: 4 rue Saint-Nicolas, 2000 Neuchâtel; tel. (32) 718-19-60; fax (32) 718-19-69; e-mail men.secr@men.unine.ch; f. 1795; North Africa, Sahara, Angola, Bhutan; non-European musical instruments; library of *c.* 5,000 vols, 175 periodicals; *c.* 100 records of non-European music; Curator JACQUES HAINARD.

Musée d'Histoire Naturelle: Terreaux 14, Neuchâtel; tel. (32) 717-79-60; fax (32) 717-79-69; f. 1835; Curator CHRISTOPHE DUFOUR; publs *Ville de Neuchâtel, Bibliothèques et Musées* (annually).

Olten

Kunstmuseum: Kirchgasse 8, 4600 Olten; tel. (62) 32-86-76; f. 1845; drawings and paintings by Martin Disteli; paintings, drawings and sculptures by Swiss artists; library of 500 vols; Curator PETER KILLER.

St Gallen

Historisches Museum: Museumstr. 50, 9000 St Gallen; tel. (71) 244-78-32; f. 1877; collection of arms, banners, porcelain, painted glass, ancient chambers, ancient stoves; Curator Dr LOUIS SPECKER.

Kunstmuseum: Museumstr. 32, 9000 St Gallen; tel. (71) 245-22-44; fax (71) 245-97-51; f. 1877; works by 19th- and 20th-century masters, incl. Segantini, post-war sculpture; Dir ROLAND WÄSPE.

Museum Kirchhoferhaus: Museumstr. 27, St Gallen; tel. (71) 244-75-21; prehistoric and historic exhibits; 17th- to 19th-century paintings by Graff, Diogg, Stäbli, Hodler, Corot, Renoir and others; peasant art of eastern Switzerland; furniture, silverware.

Naturmuseum St Gallen: Museumstr. 32, CH-9000 St Gallen; tel. (71) 245-22-44; fax (71) 245-97-51; f. 1846; library of 2,000 vols; Curator Dr T. BÜRGIN; publs *Museumsbriefe*, *Jahresberichte*.

Sammlung für Völkerkunde: Museumstr. 50, 9000 St Gallen; tel. (71) 244-88-02; fax (71) 244-73-81; collection of ethnological objects from Africa, America, Asia and Oceania; Curator ROLAND STEFFAN.

Textilmuseum mit Textilbibliothek: Vadianstr. 2, 9000 St Gallen; tel. (71) 222-17-44; f. 1886; lace, embroideries, woven and printed fabrics; Coptic fabrics; period and modern textiles; library of 20,000 vols; special collection of 2m. textile samples; Curators Dr A. WANNER-JEANRICHARD, M. GÄCHTER-WEBER; Head Librarian MONICA STRÄSSLE.

Schaffhausen

Museum zu Allerheiligen: 8200 Schaffhausen; tel. (52) 633-07-77; fax (52) 633-07-88; f. 1938; prehistory, history, natural history and art of the City and Canton of Schaffhausen and district; Dir Dr GÉRARD SEITERLE.

Solothurn

Kunstmuseum Solothurn: Werkhofstr. 30, 4500 Solothurn; tel. (32) 622-23-07; fax (32) 622-50-01; f. 1902; small old master collection including works by Hans Holbein the younger; small international colln, incl. works by Van Gogh, Klimt, Matisse, Picasso and Braque; Swiss art collection from 1850 to 1990, incl. works by Hodler; paintings, drawings, watercolours; primitive art section; Curator Dr CHRISTOPH VÖGELE.

Vevey

Jenisch Museum: 2 ave de la Gare, 1800 Vevey; tel. (21) 921-29-50; comprises Fine Arts

Museum (19th- and 20th-century Swiss and foreign artists; Oskar Kokoschka Foundation) and Cantonal Museum of Prints (16th- to 20th-century prints).

Winterthur

Kunstmuseum: Museumstr. 52, POB 378, 8402 Winterthur; tel. (52) 267-51-62; fax (52) 267-53-17; f. 1864; painting and sculpture from late 19th century to present day, including Monet, Degas, Picasso, Gris, Léger, Klee, Schlemmer, Magritte, Arp, Kandinsky, Bonnard, Maillol, Van Gogh, Rodin, M. Rosso, Lehmbruck, Brancusi, Morandi, Giacometti, de Staël, Guston, Bishop, Marden, D. Rabinowitch, Richter, Merz, etc.; drawings and prints; administered by Kunstverein Winterthur; 2,000 mems; Pres. ALFRED R. SULZER; Dir Dr DIETER SCHWARZ; Sec. C. JAEGGLI; publs *Jahresbericht des Kunstvereins Winterthur*, collection and exhibition catalogues.

Museum Oskar Reinhart am Stadtgarten: Stadthausstr. 6, 8400 Winterthur; tel. (52) 267-51-72; fax (52) 267-62-28; f. 1951; public art gallery; Pres. MARTIN HAAS; Curator PETER WEGMANN.

Zürich

Botanischer Garten und Museum der Universität Zürich: Zollikerstr. 107, 8008 Zürich; tel. (1) 634-84-11; fax (1) 634-84-03; f. 1836; world-wide herbarium, especially of African and New Caledonian Flora; library of *c.* 100,000 vols; Dirs Prof. Dr C. D. K. COOK, Prof. Dr P. K. ENDRESS.

Graphische Sammlung der Eidgenössischen Technischen Hochschule: Rämistr. 101, 8092 Zürich; tel. (1) 632-40-46; f. 1867; 150,000 examples of the graphic art of all periods and schools, with special reference to the development of graphic art in Switzerland; Curator PAUL TANNER; publs catalogues covering the work of individual artists and the exhibitions.

Kunsthaus Zürich: Heimplatz 1, 8024 Zürich; tel. (1) 251-67-65; fax (1) 251-24-64; e-mail info@kunsthaus.ch; f. 1787; chiefly 19th- and 20th-century paintings and sculptures by Swiss and foreign artists; small selection of old masters; extensive collection covering all branches of graphic art from 16th century onwards; library of 209,000 vols; Dir Dr FELIX BAUMANN.

Museum für Gestaltung Zürich, Kunstgewerbemuseum (Museum of Design Zürich): Ausstellungsstr. 60, Postfach, 8031 Zürich; tel. (1) 446-22-11; fax (1) 446-22-33; f. 1875; design collection, graphic art collection, poster collection; public library of 90,000 vols; Dir MARTIN HELLER.

Affiliated museum:

Museum Bellerive: Höschgasse 3, 8008 Zürich; tel. (1) 383-43-76; fax (1) 383-44-68; f. 1968; collection of applied and fine arts in glass, ceramics, textiles, marionettes, musical instruments, etc.; Dir MARTIN HELLER.

Museum Rietberg: Gablerstr. 15, 8002 Zürich; tel. (1) 202-45-28; fax (1) 202-52-01; e-mail museum@rietb.stzh.ch; f. 1952; works of art from Asia, Africa, Oceania and the Americas; E. von der Heydt collection and others.

Paläontologisches Institut und Museum der Universität: Karl Schmid-Str. 4, 8006 Zürich; tel. (1) 634-23-39; fax (1) 634-49-23; f. 1956; Triassic reptiles and fishes, Triassic and Jurassic invertebrates, Tertiary mammals; library of 5,500 vols, 30,000 publs; Dir Prof. Dr H. RIEBER.

Schweizerisches Landesmuseum/Musée National Suisse: Museumstr. 2, 8023 Zürich; tel. (1) 218-65-11; fax (1) 211-29-49; f. 1898; history and development of culture in Switzerland from prehistoric times to the 20th century; library of 90,000 vols, 2,000 periodicals; Dir Dr ANDRES FURGER; publs *Zeitschrift fur Schweizerische Archäologie und Kunstgeschichte* (quarterly), *Jahresbericht* (annually), *Kulturagenda* (monthly).

Zoologisches Museum der Universität: Karl Schmid-Strasse 4, 8006 Zürich; tel. (1) 634-38-38; fax (1) 634-38-39; f. 1837; research in systematics, taxonomy, and population biology; exhibitions of birds, molluscs and mammals of the world and Swiss fauna; public slide shows and films; library of 7,000 vols; Dir Prof. V. ZISWILER; publs *Jahresbericht*, *List of publications* (*c.* 2 a year).

Universities

UNIVERSITÄT BASEL

Petersplatz 1, 4003 Basel
Telephone: (61) 267-30-11
Fax: (61) 267-30-35
Founded 1460
Language of instruction: German
Academic year: October to March, April to July
Rector: Prof. Dr sc. nat. H.-J. GÜNTHERODT
Pro-Rector: Prof. iur. L. WILDHABER
Administrative Director: Dr M. STAUFFACHER
Registrar: H. JOSS
Librarian: Dr F. GRÖBLI

Number of teachers: 786
Number of students: 7,439

DEANS

Faculty of Theology: Prof. Dr theol. E. STEGEMANN
Faculty of Jurisprudence: Prof. Dr iur. E. A. KRAMER
Faculty of Medicine: Prof. Dr med. CH. MORONI
Faculty of Philosophy and History: Prof. Dr phil. G. LÜDI
Faculty of Science: Prof. Dr phil. H. LEUENBERGER

PROFESSORS

Faculty of Theology:

BRÄNDLE, R., New Testament, History of the Early Church
FISCHER, J., Systematic Theology
GÄBLER, U., Ecclesiastical and Dogmatic History
JENNI, E., Old Testament
OTT, H., Systematic Theology
SEYBOLD, K., Old Testament
STEGEMANN, E., New Testament

Faculty of Law:

HASENBÖHLER, F., Civil Law
KRAMER, E. A., Civil Law
PIETH, M., Penal Law
RHINOW, R. A., Public Law
RICHLI, P., Public Law
SCHNYDER, A. K., Civil Law
SCHWENZER, I., Civil Law
SIMONIUS, P., Civil Law
WILDHABER, L., Public Law

Faculty of Medicine:

ACKERMANN-LIEBRIEL, U., Social and Prophylactic Medicine
BATTEGAY, R., Psychiatry
BÜHLER, F. R., Pathophysiology
BÜRGIN, D., Child and Adolescent Psychiatry
FLAMMER, J., Ophthalmology
GRABER, G., Dentistry
GRÄDEL, E., Heart and Thorax Surgery
GRATZL, O., Neurosurgery
GYR, N., Internal Medicine
HARDER, F., Surgery
HERZOG, B., Paediatric Surgery
HÖSLI, L., Physiology
LAMBRECHT, J. TH., Dentistry
LUDWIG, H., Gynaecology and Obstetrics
MEYER, U. A., Pharmacology
MIHATSCH, M. J., General and Special Pathology
MORONI, CHR., Medical Microbiology
MORSCHER, E., Orthopaedics
NICHOLLS, J. G., Pharmacology
PÖLDINGER, W., Psychiatry
PROBST, R., Otorhinolaryngology
RATEITSCHAK, K. H., Dentistry
RUFLI, T., Dermatology and Venereal Diseases
RUTISHAUSER, G., Urology
SASSE, D., Anatomy
SCHAAD, U. B., Paediatrics
SCHEIDEGGER, D. H., Anaesthetics
SCHIFFERLI, J., Internal Medicine
STÄHELIN, H. B., Geriatrics
STAUFFACHER, W., Internal Medicine
STECK, A., Neurology
STEINBRICH, W., Medical Radiology
WALTER, P., Biochemistry
WIESLANDER, L., Dentistry

Faculty of Philosophy and History:

ALLERTON, D. J., English Philology
ANGEHRN, E., Philosophy
ARLT, W., Musicology
BERGER, L. R., Early History
BERNHOLZ, P., Political Economics
BLUM, C., Romance Philology
BOEHM, G., History of Art
BORNER, S., Political Economics
BRENK, B., History of Art
COLÓN, G., Iberoromance Philology
ELMER, W., English Philology
ENGLER, B., English Philology
FREY, R. L., Political Economics
GRAF, F., Latin Philology
GUGGISBERG, H. R., Swiss and Modern History
GUSKI, A., Slavonic Philology
HELLWIG, M. F., Political Economics
HOBI, V., Psychology
HORNUNG, E., Egyptology
ISERNHAGEN, H., English Philology
KOPP, R., Romance Philology
LATACZ, J., Greek Philology
LÖFFLER, H., German Philology
LÜDI, G., Romance Philology
LURATI, O., Romance Philology
MOOSER, J., History of the 20th century
MÜLLER, W. R., Business Administration
MÜLLER, A. VON, Medieval History
OPITZ-BELAKHAL, C., History of the 17th and 18th centuries
OTTMANN, H., Philosophy
PESTALOZZI, K., German Philology
PIEPER, A., Philosophy
POLASEK, W., Statistics and Econometrics
SCHIERENBECK, H., Business Administration
SCHNELL, R., German Philology
SCHOELER, G., Islamic Studies
SCHUSTER, M., Ethnology
STEINER, G., Psychology
STERN, M., German Philology
STUCKY, R., Classical Archaeology
TERZIOLI, M. A., Romance Philology
TRAPPE, P., Sociology
UNGERN-STERNBERG, J. VON, Ancient History

Faculty of Science:

A'CAMPO, N., Mathematics
ALDER, K., Theoretical Physics
ARBER, W., Molecular Microbiology
BACKENSTOSS, G., Physics of Nuclear Structures
BALLI, H., Chemistry of Dyes
BICKLE, T. A., Microbiology
BOLLER, TH., Botany
BURGER, M. M., Biochemistry
CONSTABLE, E. C., Inorganic Chemistry
ENGEL, J., Biophysical Chemistry
FRANKLIN, R. M., Virology

FREY, M., Mineralogy and Petrography
GALLUSSER, W. A., Human Geography
GEHRING, W. J., Physiology of Development and Genetics
GERSON, F., Physical Chemistry
GIESE, B., Organic Chemistry
GÜNTHERODT, H.-J., Experimental Physics
IM HOF, H.-CHR., Mathematics
JANSONIUS, J. N., Structure determination of Biopolymers
KELLER, W., Cell Biology
KIRSCHNER, K., Biophysical Chemistry
KOTSCHICK, D., Mathematics
KRAFT, H., Mathematics
KÖRNER, CHR., Botany
LESER, H., Physical Geography
LETENSORER, J.-M., Early History
LEUENBERGER, H., Pharmaceutical Technology
LINDE, H. H. A., Pharmaceutical Chemistry
MAIER, J. P., Physical Chemistry
MASSER, D., Mathematics
PFALTZ, A., Organic Chemistry
PHILIPPSEN, P., Applied Microbiology
RIEZMANN, H., Biochemistry
ROWELL, C. H. F., Zoology
SCHATZ, G., Biochemistry
SCHMID, S. M., Geology and Palaeontology
SCHWARZ, G., Biophysical Chemistry
SEELIG, J., Structure Biology
SICK, I., Experimental Physics
STEARNS, S. C., Zoology
TAMM, CH., Organic Chemistry
TAMMANN, G. A., Astronomy
THIELEMANN, F. K., Theoretical Physics
THOMAS, H., Theoretical Physics
WIEMKEN, A. M., Botany

UNIVERSITÄT BERN

Hochschulstr. 4, 3012 Bern
Telephone: (31) 631-81-11
Fax: (31) 631-39-39

Founded 1834 (incorporating the Theological School, founded 1528)
State control
Language of instruction: German
Academic year: September to August

Rector: Prof. CHRISTOPH SCHÄUBLIN
Vice-Rectors: Prof. U. WÜRGLER, Prof. ALFRED GEERING
Administrator: ELIAS KÖCHLI
Academic Director: Prof. Dr PETER MÜRNER
Chief Librarian: Prof. Dr ROBERT BARTH

Number of teachers: 1,200, including 500 professors
Number of students: 10,000

DEANS

Faculty of Evangelical Theology: Prof. Dr W. LIENEMANN
Faculty of Old Catholic Theology: Prof. Dr H. ALDENHOVEN
Faculty of Jurisprudence and Economics: Prof. Dr G. WALTER
Faculty of Medicine: Prof. Dr R. SCHOPFER
Faculty of Veterinary Science: Prof. Dr A. FRIESS
Faculty of Philosophy and History: Prof. Dr R. SCHWINGES
Faculty of Pure Science: Prof. Dr H. BUNKE

UNIVERSITÉ DE FRIBOURG

1700 Fribourg
Telephone: (26) 300-71-11
Fax: (26) 300-97-00
E-mail: rectorat@unifr.ch

Founded 1889
Languages of instruction: French, German
State control

Rector: Prof. P.-H. STEINAUER
Vice-Rectors: Prof. L. G. WALSH, Prof. J. KOHLAS, Prof. P. RAMIREZ, Prof. L. SCHLAPBACH
Librarian: M. NICOULIN

Library of over 1,800,000 vols
Number of teachers: 732
Number of students: 8,757

DEANS

Faculty of Theology: Prof. A. HOLDEREGGER
Faculty of Law: Prof. H. W. STOFFEL
Faculty of Economics and Social Sciences: Prof. R. WOLFF
Faculty of Letters: H. A. MARTINI
Faculty of Sciences: Prof. H. B. HIRSBRUNNER

PROFESSORS

Faculty of Theology:

AIMONE, P.-V., Ecclesiastical Law
BEDOUELLE, G.-T., Ecclesiastical History
BERTHOUZOZ, R., Moral Theology
BRANTSCHEN, J. B., Dogmatic Theology
BRUGUÈS, J. L., Moral Theology
BUJO, B., Moral Theology
DELGADO, M., Ecclesiastical Theology
EMERY, G., Dogmatic Theology
HALLENSLEBEN, B., Dogmatic Theology
HOLDEREGGER, A., Moral Theology
IMBACH, R., Philosophy
KARRER, L., Pastoral Theology
KEEL, O., Old Testament
KLÖCKENER, M., Liturgy
KUECHLER, M., New Testament Exegesis
NAYAK, A., Missiology and Science of Religions
O'MEARA, D., Philosophy
SCHENKER, A., Old Testament Exegesis
SELVATICO, P. P., Systematic Theology
VENETZ, H.-J., New Testament
VERGAUWEN, G., Fundamental Theology
VIVIANO, B. T., New Testament
WALSH, L., Dogmatic Theology
WERMELINGER, O., Patristics

Faculty of Law:

BORGHI, M., Public Law
EPINEY, A., Constitutional Law, International Public Law, European Law
FLEINER, T., General and Swiss Public Law
GAUCH, P., Private Law
HAENNI, P., Constitutional and Administrative Law
HURTADO POZO, J., Criminal Law
LE ROY, Y., History of Law, Canon Law
MICHEL, N., International Public Law, European Law
MURER, E., Labour and Social Insurance Law
NIGGLI, M., Criminal Law
PAHUD DE MORTANGES, R., History of Law
QUELOZ, N., Criminal Law
RIKLIN, F., Criminal Law
RUMO, A., Private Law
SCHMID, J., Private Law
STEINAUER, P.-H., Private Law
STOFFEL, W., International Private Law, Trade Law
TERCIER, P., Private Law
VOLKEN, P., Private International Law, Trade Law, Bankruptcy Law
WERRO, F., Private Law
ZUFFEREY, J. B., Administrative Law

Faculty of Economics and Social Sciences:

ASCHINGER, G., Economic Theory
BLUEMLE, E. B., Marketing
BORTIS, H., History of Economic Theory
BOSSHART, L., Journalism
BRACHINGER, H.-W., Statistics
DAFFLON, B., Public Finance
DEISS, J., Economic Theory
DEMBINSKI, P., International Management
DESCHAMPS, P., Econometrics
FRIBOULET, J.-J., Economic History
GAUDARD, G., International Commerce, Regional Economics
GROEFLIN, H., Information Systems
GRUENIG, R., Management
KIRSCH, G., Public Finance
KOHLAS, J., Operations Research
KLEINEWEFFERS, H., Political Economy
LUCCHINI, R., Sociology
PASQUIER-DORTHE, J., Advertising Techniques
PASQUIER-ROCHA, J., Operations Research
PURTSCHERT, R., Management for Non-Profit Organizations
SCHMITT, B., Economic Theory
VANETTI, M., Marketing
VILLET, M., Economic Theory
WIDMER, J., Journalism
WIDMER, M., Computer Integrated Manufacturing
WOLFF, R., Economic Theory

Faculty of Letters:

ALTERMATT, U., General and Swiss Contemporary History
BÉGUELIN, M., French Linguistics
BERRENDONNER, A., French Linguistics
BILLERBECK, M., Classical Philology
BLESS, G., Therapeutic Pedagogy
COMBE, D., French Literature
DAPHINOFF, D., English Literature
DARMS, G., Rhaeto-Romance Language and Culture
FAUDEMAY, A., French Literature
FIEGUTH, R., Slavonic Studies
FRICKE, H., Modern German Literature
FRIEDLI, R., Science of Religions
FUMAGALLI, E., Italian Literature
GIORDANO, C., Ethnology
GIRAUD, Y., French Literature
GODENZI, A., Social Work
GOHARD, F., Practical French
GURTNER, J. L., General Pedagogy
HAAS, W., German Philology
HAEBERLIN, U., Therapeutic Pedagogy
HUBER, O., General Psychology
KNÜSEL, R., Social Work
KÜNG, G., Philosophy
KURMANN, P., History of Art
LADNER, P., Science of History
LAMBERT, J.-L., Therapeutic Pedagogy
LUTZ, E. C., German Philology
MARSCH, E., German Literature
MARTINI, A., Italian Literature
MENICHETTI, A., Romanistic Philology
MORTIMER, A., English Literature
OSER, F., General Pedagogy
PERREZ, M., Clinical Psychology
PIÉRART, M., Ancient History
PYTHON, F., General and Swiss Contemporary History
RAMIREZ-MOLAS, P., Iberian Literature
REHDER, R., English and American Literature
REICHERTS, M., Clinical Psychology
REINHARDT, V., Early Modern History of Europe and Switzerland
RETSCHITZKI, J., General Psychology
SCHAMP, J., Classical Philology
SCHMIDT, H.-J., Medieval History of Europe and Switzerland
SCHNEIDER, G., Practical German
SCHNEIDER, H.-D., Experimental Psychology
SOULET, M.-H., Social Work
SPIESER, J.-M., Early Christian Archaeology
STOICHITA, V., History of Art
SWIDERSKI, E., Philosophy of Culture in Eastern and Central Europe
TAGLIAVINI, L., History of Music
TURCHETTI, M., Early Modern History of Europe and Switzerland
VERNAY, P., Romanistic Philology
WOLF, J.-U., Ethical and Political Philosophy
WÜRFFEL, S. B., German Literature

Faculty of Sciences:

AEBY, P., Experimental Physics
ALLAN, M., Physical Chemistry
ANTILLE, A., Mathematics

BAERISWYL, D., Theoretical Physics
BAGNOUD, X., Theoretical Physics
BALLY, TH., Physical Chemistry
BELSER, P., Inorganic Chemistry
BENISTON, M., Geography
BERGER, J.-P., Geology
BERRUT, J.-P., Mathematics
CARON, C., Geology
CELIO, M., Histology
CONZELMANN, A., Biochemistry
DAUL, CL., Inorganic Chemistry
DOUSSE, J. CL., Experimental Physics
DREYER, J.-L., Biochemistry
DURAND, J., Biochemistry
EMMENEGGER, F. P., Inorganic Chemistry
GABRIEL, J.-P., Mathematics
GOSSAUER, A., Organic Chemistry
GROBETY, B., Mineralogy and Petrography
HASELBACH, E., Physical Chemistry
HIRSBRUNNER, B., Computer Science
HOLMANN, H., Mathematics
HUG, W., Physical Chemistry
INGOLD, R., Computer Science
JENNY, T., Organic Chemistry
JÖRG, A., Biochemistry
KAUP, B., Mathematics
KERN, J., Experimental Physics
KLEISLI, H., Mathematics
KRETZ, R., Anatomy
LAMPEL, G., Zoology
LEIMGRUBER, W., Geography
MAGGETTI, M., Mineralogy and Petrography
MAUCH, F., Botany
METRAUX, J.-P., Botany
MEYER, D., Zoology
MONBARON, M., Geography
MONTANI, J.-P., Physiology
MÜLLER, F., Zoology
MÜLLER-SCHÄRER, H., Botany
RAGER, G., Anatomy
RENAUD, P., Organic Chemistry
ROUILLER, E., Physiology
RÜEGG, D., Physiology
RUH, E., Mathematics
RUMMLER, H.-K., Mathematics
RUSCONI, A., Biochemistry
SCHALLER, L., Experimental Physics
SCHLAPBACH, L., Experimental Physics
SCHLÄPFER, C.-W., Inorganic Chemistry
SCHNEUWLY, H., Experimental Physics
SCHULTZ, W., Physiology
SPRUMONT, P., Anatomy
STOCKER, R., Zoology
STOLIC, E., Anatomy
STRASSER, A., Geology
STREBEL, R., Mathematics
TOBLER, H., Zoology
ZELEWSKY, A. VON, Inorganic Chemistry
ZHANG, Y.-C., Theoretical Physics

ASSOCIATED INSTITUTES

Biblical Institute: Curator C. UEHLINGER.

Institute of Pastoral Theology: Dir L. KARRER.

Institute of Moral Theology: Dir J. L. BRUGUÈS.

Institute for Missions and the Study of Religions: Dir A. NAYAK (acting).

Institute for Ecumenical Studies: Dir G. VERGAUWEN.

Institute of Ecclesiastical Law: Dir R. PAHUD DE MORTANGES.

Institute of Federalism: Dir T. FLEINER.

Institute for European Law: Dir A. EPINEY.

Institute for Swiss and International Construction Law: Dir J. B. ZUFFEREY.

Institute of Informatics: Dir J. PASQUIER.

Institute for Journalism and Social Communications: Dirs L. BOSSHART, J. WIDMER.

Institute for Management of Non-Profit Organizations: Dir E.-B. BLÜMLE.

Institute of Therapeutic Pedagogy: Dirs U. HAEBERLIN, Y.-L. LAMBERT.

Institute for Practical French: Dir F. GOHARD.

Institute for Practical German: Dir G. SCHNEIDER.

Institute of Medieval Studies: Dir R. IMBACH.

Institute of Physical Education and Sport: Dir F. SOTTAS.

Institute of Mathematics: Dir H. HOLMANN.

Institute of Experimental Physics: Dir L. SCHALLER.

Institute of Theoretical Physics: Dir D. BAERISWYL.

Institute of Inorganic Chemistry: Dir A. VON ZELEWSKY.

Institute of Organic Chemistry: Dir A. GOSSAUER.

Institute of Physical Chemistry: Dir E. HASELBACH.

Institute of Mineralogy and Petrography: Dir M. MAGGETTI.

Institute of Geography: Dir M. BENISTON.

Institute of Geology: Dir C. CARON.

Institute of Botany: Dir J.-P. MÉTRAUX.

Institute of Zoology: Dir H. TOBLER.

Institute of Physiology: Dir J. P. MONTANI.

Institute of Anatomy: Dir G. RAGER.

Institute of Histology: Dir M. CELIO.

Institute of Biochemistry: Dir A. CONZELMANN.

Institute of Practical English: Dir (vacant).

Interdisciplinary Institute of Ethics and Human Rights: Dir M. BORGHI.

Interdisciplinary Institute of Research in the Field of the Family: Dir M. PERREZ.

Interdisciplinary Institute of Eastern and Central Europe: Dir EDWARD SWIDERSKI.

UNIVERSITÉ DE GENÈVE

24 rue Général-Dufour, 1211 Geneva 4
Telephone: (22) 705-71-11
Fax: (22) 320-29-27

Founded 1559
Language of instruction: French
Rector: Prof. BERNARD FULPIUS
Administrative Director: L. PALLY
Secretary-General: A. VIFIAN
Library: see Libraries
Number of teachers: 2,900
Number of students: 12,191

Publications: *Guides*, *Catalogue de la recherche*, *Dies Academicus*, *Statistiques*, *Rapport de gestion*.

DEANS

Faculty of Science: Prof. J. WEBER
Faculty of Medicine: Prof. P. SUTER
Faculty of Letters: Prof. C. MÉLA
Faculty of Economics and Social Science: Prof. B. BURGENMEIR
Faculty of Law: L. DALLÈVES
Faculty of Protestant Theology: Prof. O. FATIO
Faculty of Psychology and Educational Sciences: Prof. J.-P. BRONCKART
Institute of Architecture: (vacant)
School of Translation and Interpretation: A. RIBAS-PUJOL

PROFESSORS

Faculty of Science:

ALEXAKIS, A, Organic Chemistry
AMREIN, W., Theoretical Physics
BALLIVET, M., Biochemistry
BENY, J.-L., Animal Biology
BERTRAND, J., Mineralogy
BILL, H., Physical Chemistry
BLECHA, A., Astronomy
BORDIER, C., Biochemistry
BOURQUIN, M., Nuclear Physics
BROUGHTON, W., Botany
BUETTIKER, M., Theoretical Physics
BUFFLE, J., Mineral Chemistry
BURGER, U., Organic Chemistry
BURI, P., Galenic Pharmacy
BURKI, G., Astronomy
CAR, R., Solid State Physics
CHAIX, L., Anthropology
CHAROLLAIS, J.-J., Geology
CLARK, A., Nuclear Physics
COURVOISIER, TH., Astronomy
DAVAUD, E.-J., Geology
DE LA HARPE, P., Mathematics
DELALOYE, M., Mineralogy
DESCOUTS, P., Theoretical Physics
DOELKER, E., Pharmacy
DOMINIK, J., History and Philosophy of Science
DUBOULE, D., Biology
DUNGAN, M., Mineralogy
DURRER, R., Theoretical Physics
ECKMANN, J. P., Theoretical Physics
EDELSTEIN, S., Biochemistry
EXTERMANN, P., Nuclear Physics
FISCHER, Ø., Physics
FLÜKIGER, R.-L., Solid State Physics
FONTBOTE, L., Mineralogy
GALLAY, A., Anthropology
GASPAR, T., Botany
GEOFFROY, M., Physical Chemistry
GIOVANNINI, B., Solid State Physics
GISIN, N., Theoretical Physics
GORIN, G. E., Geology
GREPPIN, H., Botany
GRUENBERG, J., Biochemistry
GUENIN, M., Theoretical Physics
GULAGAR, F., Physical Chemistry
GURNY, R., Pharmacy
GUY, R., Pharmacy
HAIRER, E., Mathematics
HARMS, J., Electronic Computing
HAUSER, A., Physical Chemistry
HAUSMANN, J.-C., Mathematics
HOCHSTRASSER, D., Pharmacy
HUGUENIN, D., Astronomy
KIENZLE, M. N., Solid State Physics
KRAEMER, BILBE, A., Biology
KREIS, T., Biology
KUNDIG, E. P., Organic Chemistry
LACHAVANNE, J.-B., Anthropology
LÄMMLI, U., Biochemistry, Biology
LANGANEY, A., Anthropology
LE LUC, C., Nuclear Physics
LEVRAT, B., Electronic Computing
MAEDER, A., Astronomy
MAHNERT, V., Animal Biology
MARTINET, L., Astronomy
MAYOR, M., Astronomy
MULLER, P., Organic Chemistry
NEESER, J. R., Pharmacy
NIGG, E., Molecular Biology
PEDUZZI, R., Botany
PELLEGRINI, CH., Electronic Computing
PICARD, D., Biology
PIRON, C., Theoretical Physics
PIRROTTA, V., Biology
PONT, J.-C., History and Philosophy of Science
POPA, S. T., Mathematics
PUN, T., Electronic Computing
ROCHAIX, J.-D., Biology
RONGA, F., Mathematics
SCHIBLER, U., Molecular Biology
SHORE, D., Molecular Biology
SIERRO, J., Physics of Condensed Matter
SPICHIGER, R.-E., Botany
SPIERER, P., Animal Biology
STEINIG, J., Mathematics
STRASSER, R., Botany
STREIT, F., Mathematics
THOMAS, R. L., Environmental Sciences
TISSOT, P., Mineral Chemistry
TRISCONE, J.-M., Solid State Physics
TRONCHET, J., Pharmaceutical Chemistry

VEUTHEY, J.-L., Pharmaceutical Chemistry
WAGNER, E. A., Botany
WAGNER, J.-J., Mineralogy
WANNER, G., Mathematics
WEBER, C., Mathematics
WEBER, J., Chemical Physics
WERNLI, R., Micropalaeontology
WILDI, W., Geology
WILLIAMS, A. F., Applied Mineral Chemistry
YVON, K., Structural Crystallography
ZANINETTI, L., Zoology and Palaeontology

Faculty of Medicine:

ANDREOLI, A., Psychiatry
ANTONORAKIS, S., Genetics and Microbiology
ASSAL, J.-P., Medicine
AUBERT, M., Paediatrics
BADER, C., Oto-neuro-ophthalmology
BAEHNI, P., Dentistry
BAERTSCHI, A. J., Physiology
BALANT, L., Psychiatry
BELSER, U., Dentistry
BENAGIANO, G., Gynaecology and Obstetrics
BERNER, M., Paediatrics and Obstetrics
BERTRAND, D., Physiology
BONJOUR, J.-PH., Physiopathology
BORISCH, B., Pathology
BOUNAMEAUX, H., Medicine
BRESLOW, N., Social Medicine
BUDTZ-JORGENSEN, E., Dentistry
BURGER, A, Medicine
CAMPANA, A., Gynaecology and Obstetrics
CAPPONI, A., Endocrinology
CARPENTIER, J.-L., Morphology
CHAPUIS, B., Medicine
CHEVROLET, J.-C., Medicine
CLARKSON, S. G., Genetics, Microbiology
CLERGUE, F., Cardiology
CRAMER, B., Psychiatry
DAYER, J.-M., Medicine
DAYER, P., Pharmacology
DE SOUSA, R., Physiology
DE TORRENTE, A., Medicine
DE TRIBOLET, N., Oto-neuro-ophthalmology
DELAFONTAINE, P., Cardiology
DREIFUSS, J. J., Physiology
DUNANT, Y., Pharmacology
FAIDUTTI, B., Cardiology
FANTINI, B., Medicine
FAVRE, H., Medicine
FERRERO, F., Pharmacology
FRIEDLI, B., Paediatrics
FRYC, O., Legal Medicine
GABBIANI, G., Pathology
GAJISIN, S., Morphology
GARCIA, J., Radiology
GEORGOPOULOS, C. P., Medical Biology
GIACOBINO, J.-P., Medical Biology
GUIMON, J., Psychiatry
HADENGUE, A., Medicine
HALBAN, PH., Medicine
HARDING, T., Legal Medicine
HIRSCHEL, B., Medicine
HOCHSTRASSER, D., Medical Biochemistry
HUMBERT, J. R., Paediatrics
IMHOF, B., Pathology
IZUI, S., Pathology
JATON, J. C., Medical Biochemistry
JEQUIER, S., Paediatrics
JUNOD, A., Pneumology
KATO, A. C., Oto-neuro-ophthalmology
KOLAKOFSKY, D., Microbiology
KRAUER, F., Gynaecology and Obstetrics
KRAUSE, K. H., Medicine
KREJCI, I., Dentistry
KURTZ, J., Radiology
LADAME, F., Psychiatry
LAMBERT, P. H., Medicine
LANDIS, R., Medicine
LANDIS, T., Oto-neuro-ophthalmology
LE COULTRE, C., Surgery
LEHMANN, W., Oto-neuro-ophthalmology
LERCH, R., Medicine
LESKI, M., Medicine
LEUENBERGER, P., Oto-neuro-ophthalmology
LEW, D. P., Microbiology
MANZANO, J., Psychiatry
MARTI, M.-C., Cardiology
MAURON, A., Clinical Ethics
MEDA, P., Morphology
MEYER, J. M., Dentistry
MICHEL, J.-P., Geriatrics
MONTANDON, D., Surgery
MONTANDON, P., Otorhinolaryngology
MONTESANO, R., Morphology
MOREL, D., Cardiology
MOREL, PH., Surgery
MOULIN, A.-M., History of Medicine
MUHLETHALER, M., Neurophysiology
MÜLLER, D., Pharmacology
OFFORD, R., Medical Biochemistry
ORCI, L., Morphology
PANIZZON, R., Oto-neuro-ophthalmology
PASINI, W., Psychiatry, Sexology
PECHERE, J. C., Microbiology
PERRELET, A., Morphology
PERRIN, L., Medicine
PHILIPPE, J., Medicine
PIFFARETTI, N., Genetics, Microbiology
RAPIN, CH. H., Medicine
RATIB, O., Radiology
REGAMEY, C., Medicine
RIGHETTI, A., Cardiology
ROCHAT, T., Medicine
ROUGEMONT, A., Social Medicine
RUEFENACHT, A., Radiology
RYLANDER, R. C., Social Medicine
SAFRAN, A.-B., Oto-neuro-ophthalmology
SAMSON, J., Dentistry
SAPPINO, P., Oncology
SARTORIUS, N., Psychiatry
SAURAT, J.-H., Dermatology
SCHLEGEL, W., Medicine
SCHNIDER, A., Oto-neuro-ophthalmology
SCHORDERET, M., Pharmacology
SEYDOUX, J., Physiology
SLOSMAN, D., Radiology
STALDER, J., Medicine
SUTER, P., Surgery
SUTER, S., Paediatrics
TERRIER, F., Radiology
TRONO, D., Genetics and Microbiology
TSACOPOULOS, M., Ophthalmology
TSCHANTZ, P., Surgery
VASSALLI, J.-D., Morphology
VILLEMURE, J.-G., Oto-neuro-opthalmology
VISCHER, T., Physical Medicine
VU, NU. V., Medicine
WALDVOGEL, F., Microbiology
WOLLHEIM, C., Medicine
ZUBLER, R., Medicine

Faculty of Letters:

AMACKER, R., Latin Literature
BARDAZZI, G., Romance Literature
BARNES, J., Philosophy
BILLETER, J.-F., Chinese Language and Civilization
BLAIR, J., American Literature
BOESCHENSTEIN, R., German Literature
BONNET, C. A., Archaeology
BORGEAUD, P., History of Ancient Religions
BURCKHARDT, A., Modern History
CAVIGNEAUX, A., Oriental Languages
CERQUIGLINI-TOULET, J., Medieval French
CHRISTE, Y., Archaeology
DARBELLAY, E., Musicology
DE LIBERA, A., Philosophy
DE MONTICELLI, R., Philosophy
DESCOEUDRES, J.-P., Archaeology
EIGELDINGER, J. J., Musicology
FAVEZ, J.-C., Contemporary History
FLEURY, A., General History
GENEQUAND, C., Muslim and Arab Civilization
GIOVANNINI, A., History of Antiquity
GODZICH, W., English
GORNI, G., Medieval Italian
GROSRICHARD, A., French Literature
HAEGEMAN DE PAUW, L., English Literature
HURST, A., Classical Greek
IÑIGO-MADRIGAL, L., Spanish Language and Literature
JEANNERET, M., History of French Literature
JENNY, L., French Literature
KOLDE, G., German Linguistics and Stylistics
LOMBARDO, P., French Literature
MANZOTTI, E., Italian Linguistics
MÉLA, CH., Medieval Romance Languages and Literature
MOESCHLER, J., General Linguistics
MULLIGAN, K., Philosophy
MYSYROWICZ, L., Contemporary History
NINOMIYA, M., Japanese
NIVAT, G., Russian Literature and Civilization
PASCHOUD, F., Latin Literature
PAUNIER, D., Ancient History
PERUGI, M., Medieval Latin Language and Literature
PONT, J.-C., History of Sciences
POT, O., French Literature
RAYBAUD, A., French Literature
RIZZI, L., Linguistics
ROULET, E., French Linguistics
SCHRADER, H. J., German Literature and Civilization
TILLETTE, J.-Y., Medieval Latin Language and Literature
VAISSE, P., History of Modern Art
VALLOGGIA, M., Egyptology
WALTER, F., General History
WASWO, R., Modern English Literature
WHERLI, E., French Linguistics and Computer Science
WIRTH, J., History of Art and Architecture in the Middle Ages
ZALIZNIAK, A., Russian Linguistics

Faculty of Economics and Social Science:

ALLAN, P., Political Science
ANTILLE-GAILLARD, G., Economics and Social Science
AYBERK, U., Economics and Social Science
BAILLY, A., Geography
BALASKO, Y., Statistics
BALESTRA, P., Econometry
BALLMER-CAO, T.-H., Political Science
BENDER, A., Industrial Organization
BERGADAA DELMAS, M., Marketing
BIRNBAUM, P., Political Science
BURGENMEIER, B., Political Economy
CARDIA, C., Economics and Social Science
CARLEVARO, F., Econometry
CURZON-PRICE, V., Economics
DE BLASIS, J. P., Industrial Organization
DE LA GRANDVILLE, O., Political Economy
DE LAUBIER, P., Sociology
DE MELO, J., Political Economy
DENIS, J. E., Industrial Organization
DUMONT, P.-A., Industrial Organization
FLUECKIGER, Y., Political Economy
FONTELA, E., Econometry
FRICKER, Y., Econometry
GILLI, M., Electronic Computing
GILLIAND, P., Political Science
GUGGENHEIM, D., Contracts
HAGMANN, H.-M., Econometry
HAURIE, A., Computer Science applied to Management
HEAD, A.-L., Economic History
HORBER, E., Sociology
HUSSY, C., Geography
JARILLO, J.-C., Economic Strategy
KELLERHALS, J., Sociology
KOHLI, U., Political Economy
KRIESI, H., Political Science
KRISHNAKUMAR, J., Econometrics
LALIVE D'EPINAY, C., Sociology
LANE, J. E., Political Science
LEFOLL, J., Industrial Organization
LEONARD, M., Computer Science applied to Business
LOUBERGÉ, H., Political Economy

MAGNENAT-THALMANN, N., Industrial Organization
MORARD, B., Accountancy
OSSIPOW, W., Political Science
PERRENOUD, A., Economic History
PROBST, G., Industrial Organization
RAFFESTIN, C., Geography
RAFFOURNIER, B., Accountancy
RECORDON, P. A., Contracts
RITSCHARD, G., Econometrics
RONCHETTI, E., Industrial Organization
ROYER, D., Statistics
SCHNEIDER, S. C., Industrial Organization
SCHWAB, K., Marketing
STEINER, J., Political Science
SWOBODA, A., Political Economy
TSICHRITZIS, D., Computer Science applied to Business
URIO, P., Political Science
VERNEX, J. C., Geography
VIAL, J.-PH., Industrial Organization
WALTON, P., Industrial Organization
WEBER, L., Political Economy
WINDISCH, U., Sociology
ZIEGLER, J., Sociology

Faculty of Law:

AUBERT, G., Administrative Law
AUER, A., Constitutional Law
BELLANGER, F., Fiscal Law
BOISSON DE CHAZOURNES, L., Public International Law
BOUET, C., Fiscal Law
BUCHER, A., Civil Law
CASSANI, U., Penal Law
CONDORELLI, L., Public International Law
DALLÈVES, L., Swiss Commercial Law
DUFOUR, A., History of Institutions and Law
FOEX, B., Civil Laws
GREBER, P. Y., Administrative Law
HOTTELIER, M., Constitutional Law
KAUFMANN-KOHLER, G., Private International Law
KNAPP, B., Administrative Law
MALINVERNI, G., Constitutional Law, Introduction to the Science of Law
MANAÏ-WEHRLI, D., Civil Law
MORAND, C.-A., Constitutional Law
OBERSON, X. B., Fiscal Law
PERRET, F., Patents, Swiss Civil Law
PERRIN, J.-F., Introduction to the Science of Law, Sociology of Law
PETER, H., Commercial Law
PETERSMANN, E. U., Public International Law
PETITPIERRE, G., Contracts
PETITPIERRE-SAUVAIN, A., Commercial Law
RENS, I., History of Political Doctrines
ROBERT, C. N., Penal Law, Criminology
ROTH, R., Penal Law
STAUDER, B., German Commercial Law
STETTLER, M., Civil Law
TANQUEREL, T., Constitutional Law
THÉVENOZ, L., Civil Law
WILL, M., German Civil Law

Faculty of Protestant Theology:

DE PURY, A., Old Testament Exegesis
DERMANGE, F., Ethics
FATIO, O., History
KNAUF, E. A., Old Testament
MOTTU, H., Practical Theology
NORELLI, E., New Testament Exegesis
RORDORF, B., Systematic Theology
VON GEMUENDEN, P., New Testament Exegesis

Faculty of Psychology and Educational Sciences:

Section of Psychology:

ASSAL, G., Clinical Neuropsychology
BOVET, P., Psychology
BULLINGER, A., Experimental Psychology
DE LANNOY, J., Introduction to Psychology, Experimental Psychology
DE RIBAUPIERRE, A., Psychology
DOISE, W., Social Psychology
ETIENNE-KFOURI, A., Ethology
FLUCKIGER, M., Experimental Psychology
FRAUENFELDER, U. H., Psychology
GILLIÈRON-PALÉOLOGUE, C., Psychology
HAUERT, C. A., Psychology of Development
MENDELSOHN, P., Electronic Computing for Human Sciences
MONTANGERO, J., Psychology
MOUNOUD, P., Psychology of Personality Development
MUGNY, G., Psychology
MUNARI, A., Educational Psychology in the School
SCHERER, K., Social Psychology
STERN, D., Psychopathology
VIVIANI, P., Psychology
VONÈCHE, J., Child and Adolescent Psychology

Section of Educational Sciences:

ALLAL, L., Pedagogical Evaluation
BAYER, E., Research Techniques in Education
BRONCKART, J.-P., Introduction to Language Theories
BRUN, J., Mathematics Education
BUCHEL, F., Pedagogy
CIFALI, M., Psycho-pedagogy
DASEN, P., Introduction to Educational Sciences
DOMINICÉ, P., Adult Education
GIORDAN, A., Psycho-pedagogy in Sciences
MONTANDON, C., School, Family, Society
PERREGUEAUX, C., Cultural and Linguistic Diversity at School
PERRENOUD, P., General Pedagogy
RIEBEN, L., Education and Development of Children
SCHNEUWLY, B., Introduction to Language Theories
SCHUBAUER, M.-L., Social Psychology

Institute of Architecture:

CÈTRE, J.-P., Materials and Structures
DAGHINI, G., Theory and Problems of Land
DESCOMBES, G., Projects
MARIANI, R., Urban History
REICHLIN, B., Theory of Architecture
SCHEIWILLER, A., Architectural Design, and Arts and Crafts
SIMONNET, C., Culture and History of Architecture and Arts and Crafts
WEBER, W., Architecture

School of Translation and Interpretation:

ABDEL HADI, M., Arabic
ARMSTRONG, S., Use of Computers
BOCQUET, C.-Y., French
DANIEL, M., Translation with Computer Assistance
DE BESSE, B., Terminology
GEMAR, J.-C., French
ILG, G., Interpretation
MARCHESINI, G., Italian
MOSER-MERCER, B., German
RIBAS-PUJOL, A., Spanish

Centres of inter-faculty studies:

AYBERK, U., European Studies
BACKUS, I., Theology
BRAILLARD, PH., European Studies
CURZON-PRICE, V., European Studies
GIARINI, V., European Studies
PITASSI, M.C., Theology
RESZLER, A., European Studies
RICQ, C., European Studies

ATTACHED SCHOOLS

School of French Language and Culture: Dirs J. JESPERSEN, F. PRICAM.

School of Physical Education and Sport: Dir P. HOLENSTEIN.

OTHER ASSOCIATED INSTITUTES

Institut Universitaire de Hautes Etudes Internationales (Graduate Institute of International Studies): 132 rue de Lausanne, 1211 Geneva 21; f. 1927; a research and teaching institution studying international questions from the juridical, political and economic viewpoints; Dir F. HEISBOURG.

Institut Universitaire d'Etudes du Développement (Graduate Institute of Development Studies): 24 rue Rothschild, 1202 Geneva; f. 1960; African history, Middle Eastern and Latin American studies, international relations, Switzerland–Third World economic relations; Dir J.-L. MAURER.

Institut Oecuménique de Bossey (Graduate Institute of Ecumenical Studies): Château de Bossey, 1298 Céligny; Dir H. HADSELL.

UNIVERSITÉ DE LAUSANNE

Bâtiment du Rectorat et de l'Administration Centrale, 1015 Lausanne
Telephone: (21) 692-11-11
Telex: 25110
Fax: (21) 692-20-15
Founded 1537
Language of instruction: French
Academic year: October to July

Rector: Prof. E. JUNOD
Vice-Rectors: P. BRIDEL, O. BURLET, J. DIEZI
Administrative Director: JEAN-PAUL DÉPRAZ
Librarian: H. VILLARD

Library: see Libraries
Number of teachers: 770
Number of students: 9,000

Publications: *L'Enseignement*, *La Recherche*, *Uniscope*, *Allez Savoir!*, also essays and documents on the history of the University.

DEANS

Faculty of Theology: Prof. P. GISEL
Faculty of Law: Prof. D. PIOTET
Institute of Forensic Science: Prof. P. MARGOT
Faculty of Letters: Prof. R. JOLIVET
School of Modern French: (vacant)
Faculty of Social and Political Science: Prof. M. KILANI
Business School: Prof. O. BLANC
Faculty of Science: Prof. F. GRIZE
Faculty of Medicine: Prof. B. ROSSIER

PROFESSORS

Faculty of Theology:

BASSET, L., Practical Theology
BLASER, K., Modern Theology and Ecclesiasticism
BURGER, M., Science of Religions
CAMPICHE, R., Sociology of Religion
DE SAUSSURE, T., Psychology of Religion
GISEL, P., Dogmatics and Fundamental Theology
JUNOD, E., Ecclesiastical and Dogmatic History
KAESTLI, J.-D., Intertestamentary and Apocryphal Literature
MARGUERAT, D., New Testament
MÜLLER, D., Fundamental Ethics
REYMOND, B., Practical Theology
RÖMER, T., Old Testament

Faculty of Law:

BIEBER, R., European Law
BRIDEL, P., Political Economics
CHERPILLOD, I., Intellectual Property
COQUOZ, R., Forensic Biology
DESSEMONTET, F., Commercial Law
DUTOIT, B., International Law, Comparative Civil Law
FLAUSS, J.-F., Constitutional Law
GIOVANOLI, M., Swiss Economic Law, Banking Law
GRISEL, E., Constitutional Law
GUISAN, F., Private Insurance Law
HALDY, J., Constitutional Law
KILLIAS, M., Criminology, Penal Law
KRAFFT, M., Foreign Trade Law
KUHN, A., Criminology
MARGOT, P., Criminal Investigation

MARTIN, J.-C., Fire Investigation
MERCIER, P., European Law
MOOR, P., Administrative Law
MOREILLON, L., Penal Procedural Law
MULLER, G., Commercial Law
OYON, D., Accounting
PETER, H., Roman Law
PIOTET, D., Civil Law
POUDRET, J.-F., History of Law, Civil Procedural Law
RAPP, J.-M., Commercial Law
RIVIER, J. M., Tax Law
SANDOZ, S., Civil Law
SORTAIS, J.-P., French Civil and Commercial Law
STURM, F., German Law
TAPPY, D., History of Law

Faculty of Letters:

ADAM, J.-M., French Linguistics
ALBERA, F., History of Cinema
BÉRARD, C., Classical Archaeology
BERTHOUD, A.-C., Applied Linguistics
BOREL, M.-J., General Contemporary Epistemology and Logic
BRIDEL, L., Geography
BRONKHORST, J., Sanskrit, Indian Studies
CALAME, C., Greek Language and Literature
CASSINA, G., History of Art
CÉLIS, R., Philosophy
DUBOIS, A., Modern History
DUCREY, P., Ancient History
EBERENZ, R., Spanish Linguistics and Philology
FORSYTH, N., English Literature
FREI-STOLBA, R., Latin Epigraphy
HALTER, P., American Literature
HART-NIBBRIG, C., German Language and Literature
HELLER, L., Modern Russian Linguistics, Philology and Literature
HICKS, E., Medieval French
JAKUBEC, D., Swiss French Literature
JEQUIER, F., Modern History
JOLIVET, R., Theoretical and Applied Linguistics
JOST, H.-U., Swiss Modern History
JUNOD, P., History of Art
KAEMPFER, J., French Literature
KELLER, E., Speech Synthesis
KIRBY, I., English Medieval Language and Literature
LARA POZUELO, A., Spanish Language and Literature
LENSCHEN, W., German Medieval Language and Literature, German Philology
MAHMOUDIAN, M., Linguistics
MARCHAND, J.-J., Italian Language and Literature
MARTHALER, M., Physical and Geological Geography
MUDRY, P., Latin Language and Literature
MÜHLETHALER, J.-C., Medieval French
NESCHKE HENTSCHKE, A., Philosophy
PAPINI, G., Italian Philology
PARAVICINI, A., Medieval History
PAUNIER, D., Roman Provincial Archaeology
RACINE, J.-B., Geography
REICHLER, C., French Language and Literature
ROMANO G. DI STURMECK, S., History of Art
ROTEN, M., Climatology
SANDOZ, C, Historical Linguistics and Comparative Grammar
SCHERRER-SCHAUB, C., Tibetan and Buddhist Studies
SCHÜSSLER, I., Contemporary and Modern Philosophy
SCHWARZ, A., German Linguistics
SERIOT, P., Russian Linguistics and Philology
STÄUBLE, A., Italian Language and Literature
THÉVOZ, M., History of Art
TILLEMANS, T., Oriental Languages and Civilizations
TRUDGILL, P., English Language and Linguistics
UTZ, P., German Language and Literature
WINISTÖRFER, J., Physical Geography
WYSS, A., Modern French Language and Literature
ZUFFEREY, F., Medieval French

Faculty of Social and Political Science:

BATOU, J., European Political and Social History
BEAUD, P., Sociology
BERTHOUD, G., Cultural and Social Anthropology
BRAUN, D., Political Science
BRIDEL, L., Geography
BUSINO, G., Sociology
CORAJOUD, G, Social Policies
DAUWALDER, J.-P., Applied Pedagogics
DE SENARCLENS, P, International Relations
DESCHAMPS, J.-C., Psychosociology
DROZ, R., Psychology, Experimental Pedagogics
DURUZ, N., Introduction to Psychopathology
ETEMAD, B., Extra-European History
FONTANA, B., History of Political Theory
GAILLARD, F., Psychosociology, Applied Psychology
GROSSEN, M., Clinical Psychosociology
HOFMANN, E., History of Political Theory
KELLER, J.-P., Sociology
KILANI, M., Cultural and Social Anthropology
LEVY, R., Sociology
MASNATA, F., Political Science
MERRIEN, F., Sociology
MESSANT LAURENT, F., Sociology
PAPADOPOULOS, I., Public Policies
PETITAT, A., Pedagogics
SCHENK, F., Psychophysiology
VOELIN, C., Child and General Psychology
VOLKEN, H., Mathematics

Business School:

APOTHÉLOZ, B., Accounting
BACCHETTA, P., Macroeconomy and International Economy
BERGMANN, A., Organization of Behaviour
BLANC, O., Statistics, National Accounting, Demography
BONZON, P., Computer Science
CATRY, B., Finance Management, Planning
CESTRE, G., Marketing
CHAUDET, F., Trade Law
COSSIN, D., Finance
DANTHINE, J.-P., Monetary Theory and Policy, Macroeconomy, Quantitative Methods
DELAY, P., Personnel Management and Organization
DUBEY, A., Actuarial Mathematics
DUFRESNE, F., Economic and Actuarial Mathematics
GARELLI, S., Management
GERBER, H.-U., Economic and Actuarial Mathematics
GHERNAOUTI HÉLIE, S., Computer Science
GIBSON, R., Finance
GUALTIEROTTI, A., Statistical Inference into Decision Making
HENRY, C., Political Economy
HOLLY, A., Econometry
KELLER, P., Tourism
LAMBELET, J.-C., National Economy, Macroeconomy, Economic Analysis
LARA, B., Quantitative Methods Applied to Decision Making
LÉONARD, F., Sales Management, Marketing
MAEDER, P., Actuarial Mathematics
MATHE, H., Production Management
MATTEI, A., Microeconomy and Statistics
MIKDASHI, Z., Banking Systems, Energy Policies
MUNARI, S., System Management
MUSTAKI, G., Introduction to Law
NEUENSCHWANDER, D., Actuarial Mathematics
NEVEN, D., European Studies
OYON, D., Accounting
PIGNEUR, Y., Computer Management
PROBST, A.-R., Computer Science
RACINE, J.-B., Geographical Structures
RUEDIN, R., Commercial Law
SCHÄRLIG, A., Statistics Applied to Management and Decision Making
SCHERLY, F., Tourism
SCHMUTZ, R., Actuarial Mathematics
SCHWARTZ, J.-J., Political Economy, Public Finance
STEINMANN, T., Fiscal Systems
STETTLER, A., Analytical Accounting
TUCHSCHMID, N., Finance
VON THADDEN, L., Macroeconomics
VON UNGERN-STERNBERG, T., Analysis of Industrial Structures, Macroeconomy
WENTLAND FORTE, M., Knowledge Management

Faculty of Science:

ARLETTAZ, D., Algebraic Topology
BAUER, W., Food Products
BAUMGARTNER, P.-O., Sedimentology
BAY, A., Physics of Particles
BODENHAUSEN, G., Organic Chemistry
BOÉCHAT, J., Linear Algebra
BÜNZLI, J.-C., Mineral and Analytical Chemistry
BURLET, O., Differential Geometry
CHAPELLIER, D., Geophysics
CHAPUIS, G., Crystallography
CHERGUI, M., Physics of Condensed Matter
CHERIX, D., Entomology
CLÉMENÇON, H., Systematic Botany
COLLET, G., Plant Physiopathology
DAUL, C., Theoretical Inorganic Chemistry
DERIGHETTI, A., General Topology
DESVERGNE, B., Animal Biology and Genetics
DIETLER, G., Physics
DUBOCHET, J., Ultrastructural Analysis
FARMER, E., Plant Biology
FLORIANI, C., Mineral and Analytical Chemistry
GALLAND, N., Botany
GRIZE, F., Computer Science
GUEX, J., Palaeontology
GUILLEMIN, M., Industrial Hygiene
HAINARD, P., Geobotany
HAUCK, B., Astronomy, Astrophysics
HAUSSER, J., Animal Ecology and Zoology
HERNANDEZ, J., Mineralogy and Petrography
HIRT, B., Biochemistry
HOFER, R.-M., Plant Biology and Physiology
HOSTETTMANN, K., Pharmacognosis and Phytochemistry
HUNZIKER, J. C., Mineralogy
JORIS, H., Mathematics and Advanced Geometry
KELLER, L., Ecology
KESSELRING, U., Pharmaceutical Analysis
LOEFFEL, J.-J., Theoretical Physics
LOUDE, J.-F., Nuclear Electronics
MAIGNAN, M., Geostatistics
MARAZZI, A., Statistics for Biologists
MARILLIER, F., Geophysics
MASSON, H., Tectonics and Sedimentology
MAUMARY, S., Topology
MERBACH, A., Mineral and Analytical Chemistry
MERMOD, N., Molecular Genetics
MUTTER, M., Organic Chemistry
OJANGUREN, M., Algebra
OLIVIER, R., Geophysics
PERRIN, N., Ecology
PFEIFER, H.-R., Thermodynamics
ROSSELET, P., Physics
ROTHEN, F., Solid State Physics
ROULET, R., Mineral and Analytical Chemistry
RÜEGG, U., Pharmacology

SALOMON, J. L., Code of Ethics, Pharmaceutical Organization
SCHLOSSER, M., Organic Chemistry
SCHNEIDER, W.-D., Solid State Physics
SCHWARZENBACH, D., Crystallography
STAMPFLI, G., Geology
STECK, A., Mineralogy and Petrography
TESTA, B., Chemical Therapy
VOGEL, P., Organic Chemistry
VOGEL, P., Zoology and Animal Ecology
WAHLI, W., Animal Biology
WIDMER, F., Plant Biology
WITTEK, R., Applied Zoology
ZRYD, J.-P., Plant Biology

Faculty of Medicine:

ACHA-ORBEA, H., Biochemistry
AEBISCHER, P., Surgical Research
AGUET, M., Molecular Oncology
ALBANESE, A., Neurology
ANDEREGG, A., Ultrasonography
ANSERMET, F., Child Psychiatry
ASSAL, G., Neuropsychology
BACHMANN, C., Clinical Chemistry
BARRAS, V., History of Medicine
BAUMANN, P., Psychopharmacology
BILLE, J., Microbiology
BIOLLAZ, J., Clinical Pharmacology
BISCHOF-DELALOYE, A., Nuclear Medicine
BLUM, A.-L., Gastroenterology
BOGOUSLAVSKY, J., Neurology
BOILLAT, M.-A., Occupational Medicine
BORGEAT, F., Psychiatry
BOSMAN, F. T., Pathology
BRON, C., Biochemistry
BRUNNER, H.-R., Hypertension
BURCKHARDT, P., Internal Medicine
BURNIER, M., General Medicine
CALAME, A., Paediatrics
CATSICAS, S., Cellular Biology, Morphology
CEROTTINI, J.-C., Immunology
COTECCHIA, S., Pharmacology
DARIOLI, R., Insurance Medicine
DE CROUSAZ, G., Neurology
DE GRANDI, P., Gynaecology and Obstetrics
DE RIBAUPIERRE, F., Physiology
DE TRIBOLET, N., Neurosurgery
DEONNA, T., Child Neurology
DESPLAND, P.-A., Neurological Electrophysiology
DIEZI, J., Toxicology
DIGGELMANN, H., Microbiology, Virology
EGLOFF, D. V., Plastic and Reconstructive Surgery
FANKHAUSER, H., Neurosurgery
FANTINI, B., History of Medicine
FASEL, N., Biochemistry
FRANCIOLI, P., Epidemiology of Infectious Diseases
FREI, P.-C., Immunoallergy
GAILLARD, R., Endocrinology
GEERING, K., Pharmacology, Toxicology
GENTON, C.-Y., Pathology
GERSTER, J.-C., Rheumatology
GILLET, M., Surgery
GILLIÉRON, E., Psychiatry
GIVEL, J.-C., Surgical Proctology
GLAUSER, M.P., Internal Medicine
GONVERS, J.-J., Gastroenterology
GONVERS, M., Ophthalmology
GOY, J.-J., Cardiology
GUEX, P., Psychological and Social Medicine
GUIGNARD, J.-P., Child Nephrology
HAAS, D., Microbiology
HALFON, O., Child Psychiatry
HESSLER, C., Radiology
HIRT, B., Oncology
HOHLFELD, P., Obstetrics
HONEGGER, P., Physiology
HORISBERGER, J.-D., Pharmacology
HORNUNG, J.-P., Anatomy
INNOCENTI, G., Anatomy
JANZER, R.-C., Neuropathology
JEQUIER, E., Physiology
KAPPENBERGER, L., Cardiology
KARAMATA, D., Microbiology
KRAEHENBUHL, J.-P., Biochemistry
KROMPECHER, T., Forensic Medicine
KRSTIC, R., Histology and Embryology
KUCERA, P., Physiology
LAURINI, R. N., Child Pathology
LEISINGER, H. J., Urology
LEJEUNE, F., Oncology
LEUENBERGER, P., Pneumology
LEVI, F.-G., Non-Infectious Epidemiology
LEYVRAZ, J.-F., Orthopaedics
LOUIS, J., Immunology
MACH, J.-P., Biochemistry
MAGISTRETTI, P., Physiology
MANGIN, P., Forensic Medicine
MARAZZI, A., Medical Statistics
MATTHIEU, J.-M., Paediatrics
MAUËL, J., Biochemistry
MICHAUD, P.-A., Adolescent Health
MIRIMANOFF, R.-O., Radiotherapy
MOESSINGER, P., Neonatology
MONNIER, P., Otorhinolaryngology
NICOD, P., Internal Medicine
PACCAUD, F. M., Preventive Medicine
PANIZZON, R., Dermatology
PANTALEO, G., AIDS Immunopathology
PÉCOUD, A., General Medicine
PESCIA, G., Medical Genetics
PIOT, P., AIDS Epidemiology
RAVUSSIN, P., Anaesthesiology
REIZ, S., Anaesthesiology
RIVA, C. E., Ophthalmology
ROSSIER, B., Pharmacology
RÜEDI, B., Endocrinology
SAURAT, J. H., Dermatology, Venereology
SAVOLAINEN, H., Labour Medicine
SCHAPIRA, M., Haematology
SCHENK, F., Physiology
SCHNYDER, P.-A., Radiology
SCHORDERET, D., Genetics
SO, A., Rheumatology
STAMENKOVIC, I., Experimental Pathology
THEINTZ, G. E., Child Diabetology
THORENS, B., Pharmacology, Toxicology
TSCHOPP, J., Biochemistry
VALLEY, J.-F., Radioprotection
VILLEMERE, J. G., Neurosurgery
VON SEGESSER, L.-K., Cardiovascular Surgery
WAEBER, B., Hypertension
WAUTERS, J.-P., Nephrology
WELKER, E., Cellular Biology, Morphology
WERTHEIMER, P., Psychogeriatrics
ZOGRAFOS, L., Ophthalmology

UNIVERSITÉ DE NEUCHÂTEL

Ave du 1er Mars 26, 2000 Neuchâtel
Telephone: (32) 718-10-00
Fax: (32) 718-10-01

Founded 1909
Language of instruction: French

Rector: Prof. F. PERSOZ
Vice-Rectors: Prof. D. HAAG, Prof. D. MIÉVILLE
Secretary-General: P. BARRAUD
Librarian: A. JEANNERET

Number of teachers: 360
Number of students: 3,427

Publications: *Recueils, Annales, Informations, Domaines et sujets de recherches.*

DEANS

Faculty of Letters: Prof. A. NAEF
Faculty of Science: Prof. F. STÖKLI
Faculty of Jurisprudence and Economics: Prof. F. HAINARD
Faculty of Theology: Prof. P. L. DUBIED

PROFESSORS

Faculty of Letters:

ANDRÉS-SUÁREZ, I., Spanish Language and Literature
BANDELIER, A., Modern French
BÉGUELIN, M.-J., French Linguistics
BORIE, J., French Literature
BRUNKO-MEAUTIS, A., Modern French
CAPPELLO, G., Italian Language and Literature
CHIFFELLE, F., Geography
ECKARD, G., Medieval French Language and Literature
EGLOFF, M., Archaeology
EIGELDINGER, F., Modern French
GENDRE, A., French Literature
GHASARIAN, C., French Literature
GLAUSER, R., General Philosophy
GRAHAM, K., English Language and Literature
GRIENER, P., History of Art
GROSJEAN, F., Linguistics
HENRY, P., Swiss History
JAQUIER KAEMPFER, C., French Literature
KNÖPFLER, D., Archaeology and Ancient History
KRISTOL, A. M., Gallo-Roman Dialectology
LOSONCZY, A.-M., Ethnology
MARC, P., Pedagogy
MARGUERAT, P., Modern History
MAURICE, A., Journalism
MIEVILLE, D., Logic, History and Philosophy of Science
NAEF, A., German Language
PERRET-CLERMONT, A.-N., Psychology
PY, B., Linguistics
RUBATTEL, CH., General Linguistics
SCHEURER, R., Medieval History
SCHULTHESS, D., Philosophy
SÖRING, J., German Literature
TERRIER, PH., French Language and Literature

Faculty of Science:

ARAGNO, H., Bacteriology
BAER, Y., Physics
BECK, H., Theoretical Physics
BERNAUER, K., Inorganic and Analytical Chemistry
BESSON, O., Mathematics
BETSCHART, B., Animal Biology
BURKHARD, M., Structural Geology
DAENDLIKER, R., Optics
DERENDINGER, J.-P., Theoretical Physics
DE ROOIJ, N., Microelectronics
DESCHENAUX, R., Organic Chemistry
DIEHL, P.-A., Zoology
ERARD, P.-J., Computer Science
FAIST, J., Physics
FÖLLMI, K., Geology
GOBAT, J.-M., Botany
JEANNET, E., Physics
KÜPFER, PH., Systematic Botany
MARTINOIA, A., Vegetal Physiology
MARTINOLI, P., Physics
MERMOD, C., Zoology
MUELLER, J.-P., Computer Science
NAEGELI, H. H., Computer Science
NEIER, R., Organic Chemistry
NEUHAUS, J.-M., Biochemistry
PELLANDINI, F., Electronics
PERSOZ, F., Petrography
REMANE, J., Palaeontology
ROBERT, A., Mathematics
ROWELL-RAHIER, M., Ecology
SHAH, A., Electronics
SIEGENTHALER, P.-A., Vegetal Physiology
SIGRIST, F., Mathematics
STOECKLI, F., Physical Chemistry
SUSS-FINK, G., Chemistry
SUTER, U., Mathematics
TABACCHI, R., Organic Chemistry
VALETTE, A., Mathematics
VUILLEUMIER, J. L., Physics
ZWAHLEN, F., Hydrogeology

Faculty of Jurisprudence and Economics:

AUBERT, J.-F., Constitutional Law
BÉGUIN, F., Financial Strategy
BIRCHER, B., Management
BOLLE, P.-H., Penal and Elementary Law
CANNATA, C.-A., History of Law
DODGE, Y., Statistical Science
DUBOIS, M., Finance

GERN, J.-P., History of Economics
GUILLOD, O., Private Law, Civil Law
HAAG, D., Financial Economics
HAINARD, F., Sociology
JEANRENAUD, C., Public Economics
KNOEPFLER, F., International Private Law
KOSTECKI, M., Marketing
MAILLAT, D., Political Economics
MAVROIDIS, P., International Public Law
PROBST, T., Law for Economists
PUTT, G., Economic Theory
ROUSSON, M., Psychology
RUEDIN, R., Commercial Law
SAVOY, J., Informatics in Economics
SCHUPBACH, H., Civil Law
WEIBEL, E., Political Science
WESSNER, P., Obligatory Law
ZARIN-NEJADAN, M., Political Economics
ZEN-RUFFINEN, P., Law

Faculty of Theology:
BUEHLER, P., Systematic Theology
DETTWILER, A., Theology
DUBIED, P.-L., Practical Theology
HAMMANN, G., Modern Church History
ROSE, M., Old Testament
SIEGERT, V., Medieval Church History

ASSOCIATE INSTITUTE

Seminar of Modern French for Foreigners: 10 professors; 150 students; Dir PH. TERRIER.

UNIVERSITÄT ST GALLEN – HOCHSCHULE FÜR WIRTSCHAFTS-, RECHTS- UND SOZIALWISSENSCHAFTEN
(University of St Gallen – Graduate School of Business Administration, Economics, Law and Social Sciences)

Dufourstr. 50, 9000 St Gallen
Telephone: (71) 2242111
Fax: (71) 2242816
E-mail: unihsg@unisg.ch
Founded 1898
State control
Language of instruction: German
Academic year: April to March
Rector: Prof. Dr G. FISCHER
Vice-Rectors: Prof. Dr A. KEEL, Prof. Dr P. GOMEZ
Administrative Director: Dr H.-R. TROXLER
Librarian: Dr X. BAUMGARTNER
Number of teachers: 180
Number of students: 4,000

Publications: *Vorlesungsverzeichnis* (2 a year), *Studienpläne*, *Prüfungsvorschriften*, *Studentenführer*, *Geschäftsbericht* (1 a year), *HSG-Information* (quarterly), *alma* (quarterly), *Broschüre öffentliche Vorlesungen* (2 a year), *Bibliotheksführer*, *Aulavorträge*.

DEANS

Faculty of Business Administration: Prof. Dr C. BELZ
Faculty of Economics: Prof. Dr H. HAUSER
Faculty of Law: Prof. Dr R. WALDBURGER
Faculty of Cultural Sciences: Prof. Dr J. SILES

PROFESSORS

ANDEREGG, J., German Language and Literature
BACK, A., Information Processing
BAUDENBACHER, C., Private, Commercial and Economic Law
BAUMER, J.-M., Development Policy
BEHR, G., Business Administration
BELZ, C., Marketing
BERNET, B., Business Administration, Banking
BIEGER, T., Business Administration, Tourism
BOURQUI, C., Business Administration
BOUTELLIER, P., Technology
BURMEISTER, K. H., History of Law
CHONG, L., Business Administration
DACHLER, P., Psychology
DOPFER, K., Foreign Trade and Development Theory
DRUEY, J. N., Civil and Commercial Law
DUBS, R., Business Pedagogy
DYLLICK, T., Business Administration
EHRENZELLER, B., Public Law
FICKERT, R., Business Administration
FISCHER, G., Economics
FRAUENDORFER, K., Operations Research
GÄRTNER, M., Economics
GEISER, T., Civil and Commercial Law
GOMEZ, P., Business Administration
GROSS, P., Sociology
GRÜNBICHLER, A., Finance
HALLER, M., Insurance and Business Administration, Risk Management
HAUSER, H., Foreign Trade Theory and Policy
HILB, M., Business Administration
INGOLD, F. P., Russian Language and Literature
JAEGER, F., Economic Policy
KAUFMANN, V., French Language and Literature
KEEL, A., Statistics
KIRCHGÄSSNER, G., Economics
KLEY, R., Political Science
KOLLER, A., Civil and Commercial Law
LECHNER, M., Empirical Economic Research and Econometrics
LEUENBERGER, T., Modern History
MANELLA, J., Economics
MARTINONI, R., Italian Language and Literature
MASTRONARDI, P., Public Law
MEIER, A., Economics
MEIER-SCHATZ, C., Civil and Commercial Law
METZGER, CH., Business Administration
MOHR, E., Economics
MÜLLER, H., Mathematics
MÜLLER-STEWENS, G., Business Administration
NOBEL, P., Private, Commercial and Economic Law
OESTERLE, H., Information Processing
PLEITNER, H. J., Business Administration
REETZ, N., Economics
RIKLIN, A., Political Science
ROBERTO, V., Private, Commercial and Economic Law
ROBINSON, A. D., English Language and Literature
RUIGROK, W., International Management
RUUD, F., Accounting
SCHEDLER, K., Public Management
SCHMID, B., Information Processing
SCHMID, H., Economics
SCHUH, G., Technology
SCHWANDER, I., Civil Law
SCHWEIZER, R., Public Law
SILES, J. R., Spanish Language and Literature
SPREMANN, K., Business Administration
STÄHLY, P., Operations Research
STIER, W., Empirical Social Research and Applied Statistics
TOMCZAK, T., Business Administration
TRECHSEL, ST., Criminal Law and Criminal Case Law
ULRICH, P., Economic Ethics
VALLENDER, C., Public Law and Law of Taxation
VON KROGH, F., Business Administration
WALDBURGER, R., Taxation Law
WINTER, R., Information Processing
WUNDERER, R., Business Administration
ZIMMERMANN, H., Financial Market Analysis

ATTACHED INSTITUTES

Institute for Accounting and Control.
Institute for Agricultural Economics and Agricultural Law.
Institute for Business Ethics.
Institute for Economy and the Environment.
Institute for Empirical Economic Research.
Institute for Information Management.
Institute for Leadership and Human Resources Management.
Institute for Operations Research.
Institute for Public Services and Tourism.
Institute for Technology Management.
Institute for the Teaching of Economics.
Institute of Economics.
Institute of European, Economic and Comparative Law.
Institute of Insurance Economics (with European Centre for Insurance Education and Training).
Institute of Management.
Institute of Political Science.
Institute of Public Finance and Fiscal Law.
Media and Communications Management Institute.
Research Institute for Economic Geography and Regional Planning.
Research Institute for International Management.
Research Institute for Labour Economics and Labour Law.
Research Institute for Legal Sciences.
Research Institute for Marketing and Distribution.
Sociology Seminar.
Swiss Institute for Research in International Economics, Regional Science and Structural Problems.
Swiss Research Institute of Small Business and Entrepreneurship.
Swiss Institute of Banking and Finance.
Swiss Institute of Courses in Public Administration.

UNIVERSITÀ DELLA SVIZZERA ITALIANA

Corso Elvezia 36, 6900 Lugano
Telephone: (91) 923-81-62
Fax: (91) 923-81-63
E-mail: admin@unisi.ch
Founded 1995
State control
Language of instruction: Italian
Academic year: October to June
President: Prof. MARCO BAGGIOLINI
Secretary-General: Dr MAURO DELL'AMBROGIO
Head Librarians: Dr GIUSEPPE ORIGGI (Lugano), SERGIO STEFFEN (Mendrisio)
Library of 70,000 vols
Number of students: 900

DEANS

Faculty of Economics: Prof. PIETRO BALESTRA
Faculty of Communication Sciences: Prof. EDDO RIGOTTI
Faculty of Architecture: Prof. AURELIO GALFETTI

UNIVERSITÄT ZÜRICH

Rämistr. 71, 8006 Zürich
Telephone: (1) 634-11-11
Fax: (1) 634-23-04
Founded 1833
State control
Language of instruction: German
Academic year: October to July (two semesters)
Rector: Prof. H. H. SCHMID

Vice-Rectors: Prof. U. FRIES, Prof. C. C. KUENZLE, Prof. C. MEYER
Director of Administration: P. BLESS
Secretary: Dr K. REIMANN
Librarian: Dr H. KÖSTLER

Library of 2,700,000 vols
Number of teachers: 2,059
Number of students: 19,900

Publications: *Unizürich* (journal (6 a year) and magazine (quarterly)).

DEANS

Faculty of Theology: Prof. T. KRÜGER
Faculty of Law: Prof. D. THÜRER
Faculty of Economics: Prof. P. STUCKI
Faculty of Medicine: Prof. A. BORBÉLY
Faculty of Veterinary Medicine: Prof. M. WANNER
Faculty of Philosophy: Prof. J. WÜEST
Faculty of Science: Prof. V. ZISWILER

PROFESSORS

Faculty of Theology:

BÜHLER, P., Systematic Theology
CAMPI, E., Church History
DALFERTH, I. U., Systematic Theology
FISCHER, J., Theological Ethics
KRÜGER, T., Old Testament
RUH, H., Systematic Theology and Social Ethics
SCHINDLER, A., History of Church and Dogma
SCHMID, H. H., Old Testament and History of Religions
STECK, O. H., Old Testament
STOLZ, F., History and Science of Religions
STUBBE, E., Practical Theology and Psychology of Religion
WEDER, H., New Testament
ZUMSTEIN, J., New Testament

Faculty of Law:

DONATSCH, A., Criminal Law
FÖGEN, M. T., Roman Law and Comparative Law
FORSTMOSER, P., Trade Law
HALLER, W., State and Administrative Law
HONSELL, H., Swiss and European Civil Law, Roman Law
HUGUENIN, C., Private Economic Law and European Law
JAAG, T., State and Administrative Law
KÖLZ, A., Administrative Law
MEIER, I., Civil Case Law, Bankruptcy Law
MÜLLER, G., State and Administrative Law
OTT, W., Philosophical and Swiss Civil Law
PORTMANN, W., Private and Industrial Law
RAUSCH, H., Environmental and Administrative Law
REHBERG, J., Criminal Law
REHBINDER, M., Labour Law, Sociology of Law, Press Law
REICH, M., Tax, Fiscal and Administrative Law
REY, H., Swiss Civil Law
RIEMER, H. M., Swiss Civil Law
SCHMID, N., Criminal Law, Law Instruction
SCHOTT, C. D., History of Swiss and German Law
SENN, M., Philosophical Law
SIEHR, K., Civil Law, International Private Law and Comparative Law
SPÜHLER, K., Civil Law
THÜRER, D., Law of Nations, State and Administrative Law
VON DER CRONE, H. C., Private and Business Law
WEBER, R., European Law
WEBER-DÜRLER, B., State and Administrative Law
WEIMAR, P., Roman and Civil Law
ZÄCH, R., Private Economic Law and European Law
ZOBL, D., Civil Law, Banking and Securities Law

Faculty of Economics:

BAUKNECHT, K., Informatics
BOHLEY, P., Statistics and Finance
DE BONDT, W. F. M., Monetary Economics
DITTRICH, K. R., Computer Science
FEHR, E., Economics
FREY, B. S., Theory and Practice of Social Economics
GARBERS, H., Econometry and Mathematical Statistics
GEIGER, H., Banking and Finance
GLINZ, M., Informatics
HÄSSIG, K., Operations Research
HELBLING, C., Accountancy and Financial Control
HIRSZOWICZ, CH., Banking and Finance
HOTZ-HART, B., Economics
KALL, P., Operations Research and Mathematical Methods of Economics
KLATTE, D., Mathematics for Economists
MEYER, C., Accountancy and Financial Control
OSTERLOH, M., Business Administration
PFAFF, D., Accountancy and Financial Control
PFEIFER, R., Computer Science
RICHTER, L. H., Computer Science
RÜHLI, E., Business Administration
SCHAUER, H., Computer Science
SCHNEIDER, H., Theoretical and Practical Social Economics
STAFFELBACH, B., Business Administration
STUCKI, P., Computer Science
VOLKART, R., Banking and Finance
WEHRLI, H. P., Business Administration
ZWEIFEL, P., Political Economy
ZWEIMÜLLER, J., Macroeconomics

Faculty of Medicine:

AGUZZI, A., Neuropathology
BÄR, W., Forensic Medicine
BAUER, CHR., Physiology
BERGER, E. G., Physiology
BINSWANGER, U., Internal Medicine, Nephrology
BOLTSHAUSER, E., Paediatrics
BORBÉLY, A. A., Pharmacology
BÖSIGER, P., Biomedical Technology
BOSSHARD, H. R., Biochemistry
BOUTELLIER, U., Sports and Human Physiology
BUCHER, H. U., Neonatology
BUDDEBERG, C., Social Psychology
BURG, G., Dermatology and Venereology
CHRISTEN, PH., Biochemistry
DIETZ, V., Paraplegology
DOUGLAS, R. J. D., Theoretical Neuro-informatics
FEHR, J., Haematology
FISCH, U., Oto-Rhino-Laryngology
FISCHER, J. A., Calcium Metabolism and Assimilation in Orthopaedics
FOLLATH, F., Internal Medicine
FONTANA, A., Clinical Immunology
FRIED, M., Gastroenterology
GÄHWILER, B., Neurology and Anatomy
GASSER, T., Biostatistics
GAY, S., Experimental Rheumatology
GERBER, C., Orthopaedics
GLANZMANN, C., Radio-oncolgy
GLOOR, B. R. P., Ophthalmology
GRAEVENITZ, A. VON, Medical Microbiology
GROB, P. J., Immunology
GROSCURTH, P., Anatomy
GRÜSSNER, R., Abdominal Surgery
GRÜTTER, M. G., Biochemistry, Macromolecular Crystallography
GUTTE, B., Biochemistry
GUTZWILLER, F., Social and Preventive Medicine
HALLER, U., Obstetrics and Gynaecology
HAURI, D., Urology
HEITZ, P. U., Pathological Anatomy
HELL, D., Clinical Psychiatry
HENGARTNER, H., Experimental Pathology
HERZKA, H. S., Psychopathology of Infants and Children
HESS, K., Neurology
HUBBELL, J. A., Biomedical Engineering and Medical Informatics
HUCH, A., Gynaecology
HUCH, R., Perinatal Physiology
JENNI, R., Cardiology
JIRICNY, J., Molecular Radiology
KAISSLING, B., Anatomy
KAYSER, F. H., Medical Microbiology
KELLER, P. J., Gynaecology, especially Patho-Physiology of Reproduction
KLEIHUES, P., Neuropathology
KOLLER, E. A., Physiology
KOPPENSTEINER, R., Angiology
LICHTENSTEIGER, W., Neuro-Pharmacology
LIPP, H. P., Anatomy
LÜSCHER, T. F., Cardiology
LÜTOLF, U. M., Radiotherapy
MARINCEK, B., Diagnostic Radiology
MARTIN, K. A. C., Systems Neurophysiology
MEIER-ABT, P., Clinical Pharmacology and Toxicology
MESSMER, E., Ophthalmology
MEYER, V. E., Restorative Surgery
MICHEL, B., Rheumatology
MODESTIN, J., Clinical Psychiatry
MOELLING, K., Virology
MÖHLER, H., Pharmacology
MÜNTENER, M., Anatomy
MURER, H., Physiology
NIEMEYER, G., Ophthalmology and Neurophysiology
PASCH, TH., Anaesthesia
PLÜCKTHUN, A., Biochemistry
REINECKE, M., Anatomy
REMÉ, CH., Ophthalmology
RÖSSLER, W., Clinical Psychiatry
ROTH, J., Cell Molecular Pathology
RUSSI, E., Internal Medicine
RÜTTIMANN, B., History of Medicine
SALLER, R., Naturopathy
SAUTER, CH., Clinical Oncology
SCHAFFNER, A., Molecular Biology
SCHARFETTER, CH., Clinical Psychiatry, Psychopathology
SCHINZEL, A., Medical Genetics
SCHMID, E., Anaesthesia
SCHULTHESS, G. K. VON, Nuclear Medicine
SCHWAB, M. E., Neurology and Anatomy
SEGER, R., Children's Medicine, Immunology and Haematology
SENNHAUSER, F. H., Paediatrics
SONDEREGGER, P., Biochemistry
SPINAS, G. A., Endocrinology, Diabetology and Pathophysiology
STAUFFER, U. G., Children's Surgery
STEFFEN, R., Travel Medicine
STEINHAUSEN, H.-C., Child and Youth Psychiatry
TRENTZ, O., Accident Surgery
TURINA, M., Cardiac Surgery
VALAVANIS, A., Neuroradiology
VETTER, W., Internal Medicine
VONDERSCHMITT, D. J., Clinical Chemistry
WIESER, H.-G., Neurology, Special Epileptology
WILLI, J., Psychiatry and Medical Psychology
WOGGON, B., Pharmacotherapy
WÜTHRICH, B., Dermatology and Venereology
YONEKAWA, Y., Neurology, Surgery
ZAPF, J., Experimental Medicine and Biology
ZINKERNAGEL, R. M., Experimental Pathology

Centre for Dentistry, Oral and Maxillary Medicine:

GUGGENHEIM, B., Oral Microbiology and General Immunology
IMFELD, T., Preventive Dentistry, Periodontology, Cardiology

LUTZ, F., Cariology, Periodontology, Preventive Dentistry
PALLA, S., Dental Prosthesis
SAILER, H., Cranio-maxillofacial Surgery
SCHÄRER, P., Crowns and Bridges
STÖCKLI, P. W., Maxillary Surgery and Children's Dentistry

Faculty of Veterinary Medicine:

ACKERMANN, M., Virology
ALTHAUS, F., Pharmacology and Toxicology
AUER, J. A., Veterinary Surgery
BRAUN, U., Internal Medicine of Ruminants
EHRENSPERGER, F., Immunopathology
FELLENBERG, R.-L. VON, Physiology
FREWEIN, J., Anatomy
HÜBSCHER, U., Biochemistry
ISENBÜGEL, E., Veterinary Medicine
KELLER, H., Swine Diseases
KÖHLER, P., Biochemical and Molecular Parasitology
KUENZLE, C. C., Veterinary Biochemistry
LUTZ, H., Internal Medicine
MONTAVON, P. M., Surgery of Small Domestic Animals
POSPISCHIL, A., Pathology
REUSCH, C., Internal Medicine (Small Animals)
RÜSCH, P., Obstetrics, Veterinary Medicine
SCHARRER, E., Physiology
SPIESS, B., Veterinary Ophthalmology
STRANZINGER, G. F., Breeding Biology
THOMANN, P. E., Laboratory Animal Science
UNTERMANN, F., Veterinary Food Hygiene
WANNER, M., Animal Nutrition
WITTENBRINK, M. M., Veterinary Bacteriology

Faculty of Philosophy (Humanities):

BAECHTOLD, A., Special Pedagogics
BITTERLI, U., Modern History and European Human History
BÖHLER, M., Modern German Literature
BONFADELLI, H., Journalism
BOOTHE, B., Clinical Psychology
BORNSCHIER, V., Economic Sociology
BOSSONG, G., Roman Philology
BRINCKMANN, CH., Cinematography
BRINKER, H., History of East Asian Art
BRONFEN, E., English and American Literature
BUCHMANN, M., Sociology
BURGER, H., German Philology
CLAUSSEN, P. C., Art History of the Middle Ages
DESCOEDRES, G., History of Medieval Art
DOELKER, C., Media Pedagogics
DUNKEL, G. E., Comparative Indo-German Linguistics
EBERT, K. H., General German Philology
FATKE, R., Pedagogics, Special Social Pedagogics
FEND, H., Pedagogic Psychology
FISCH, J., General Modern History
FISCHER, A., English Philology
FRANCILLON, R., History of French Literature from the Renaissance to the Present
FRIES, U., English Philology
FRITZSCHE, B., Swiss History since 19th Century
FRÖHLICHER, P., History of French Literature
FUHRER, T., Classical Philology
GASSMANN, R. H., Sinology
GESER, H., Sociology
GILOMEN, H. J., General Economic and Social History, Swiss History
GLASER, E., German Philology
GLAUSER, J., Nordic Philology
GOEHRKE, C., East European History
GÜNTERT, G., Romance Literature
GÜNTHER, H., History of Modern Art
GUTSCHER, H., Social Psychology
GYR, U., Folklore
HAAS, A., German Literature until 1700
HELBLING, J., Ethnology
HERZOG, U., German Literature to 1700
HESS, M., Computer Linguistics
HIRSIG, R., Psychological Methods
HOFFMANN-NOWOTNY, H.-J., Sociology
HOLZHEY, H., History of Philosophy
HORNUNG, R., Social Psychology
HUGHES, P., English and American Literature
ISLER, H. P., Archaeology
JARREN, O., Publistic Science
JUNG, M. R., History of French and Provençal Literature
KAISER, R., History of the Middle Ages
KELLER, H., General Didactics of Intermediate School Teaching
KELLER, L., History of French Literature
KLOPFENSTEIN, E., Japanese Studies
KLÖTI, U., Political Science, Domestic Policy
KOHLER, G., Philosophy, Political Philosophy
LA FAUCI, N., Romance Philology, Linguistics of Italian
LEIST, A., Ethics
LICHTENHAHN, E., Musicology
LIENHARD, M., Spanish
LOPORCARO, M., Romance Philology, History of Italian
LÜTOLF, M., Musicology
MAREK, CH., Ancient History
MARX, W., General Psychology
MATT, P. VON, German Literature since 1700
MICHEL, P., Ancient German Literature
MOOS, C., General and Swiss Modern History
MOOS, S. VON, Modern and Contemporary Art
MÜLLER, H.-P., Ethnology
NÄF, B., Ancient History
NAUMANN, H.-P., Nordic Philology
OPPITZ, M., Ethnology
PETERS, J.-U., Slavic Philology
PICONE, M., Italian Literature
PRIMAS, Mrs M., Primeval History
REDDICK, A., English Literature
REUSSER, K., Pedagogics
RIEDWEG, C., Classical Philology, Graecistics
ROSSI, L., Romance Literature
RULOFF, D., Political Science
SABLONIER, R., Medieval History
SCHALLBERGER, U., Applied Psychology and Personality Research
SCHELLING, W. A., Psychology
SCHLEY, W., Special Pedagogics
SCHMUGGE, L., Medieval History
SCHREINER, P., Indology
SCHULTHESS, P., Philosophical Theory
SITTA, H., German Language
STADLER, U., German Literature
STOLL, F., Practical Industrial and Professional Psychology
STOTZ, P., Middle Latin Philology
STRAUCH, I., Clinical Psychology
TANNER, J., General and Swiss Modern History
TAROT, R., History of German Literature
TOTTIE, G., English Language
WEIGEL, S., German Literature
WEISS, D., Slavonic Languages
WILKENING, F., General Psychology
WÜEST, J.-TH., Gallo-Romanic Philology
ZELGER, F., Fine Arts

Faculty of Science:

AMANN, H., Mathematics, especially for Natural Scientists
AMSLER, C., Experimental Physics
BACHOFEN, R., General Botany
BARBOUR, A. D., Biomathematics
BASLER, K., Zoology, Molecular Development Genetics
BERKE, H. G. H., Inorganic Chemistry
BERNOULLI, D., Geology
BILLETER, M. A., Molecular Biology
BOLTHAUSEN, E., Mathematics, especially Applied Mathematics
BRASSEL, K., Geography
BRINKMANN, D., Experimental Physics
BRODMANN, M., Mathematics
BURG, J.-P., Geology
CHIPOT, M. M., Mathematics
COOK, C. D. K., Systematic Botany
ELSASSER, H., Geography
ENDRESS, P. K., Systematic Botany
ENGFER, R., Experimental Physics
FISCHER, H., Physical Chemistry
GÜNTER, J. R., Inorganic Chemistry
HAEBERLI, W., Geography
HAEFNER, H., Geography
HAFEN, E., Zoology
HANSEN, H.-J., Organic Chemistry
HEIMGARTNER, H., Organic Chemistry
HEINRICH, CH. A., Crystallography and Petrography
HESSE, M., Organic Chemistry
HUBER, J. R., Physical Chemistry
ITTEN, K. I., Geography
JARCHOW, H., Mathematics
JÜTTNER, F., Limnology
KAPPELER, T., Mathematics
KELLER, B., Plant Molecular Biology
KELLER, H., Physics of Condensed Matter
KÖNIG, B., Zoology, Behavioural Biology
KUBLI, E., Zoology
KÜNDIG, W., Experimental Physics
MARTIN, R. D., Anthropology
MÜLLER-BÖKER, U., Anthropogeography
NAGASAWA, M., Theory of Probability
NOLL, M., Molecular Biology
NÖTHIGER, R., Genetics
OKONEK, CH., Mathematics
OSTERWALDER, J., Experimental Physics
RASCHE, G., Theoretical Physics
REYER, H.-V., Zoology
RIEBER, H., Palaeontology
ROBINSON, J.-A., Organic Chemistry
SCHAFFNER, W., Molecular Biology
SCHARF, G., Theoretical Physics
SCHMID, B., Environmental Science
SCHROEDER, V., Mathematics
STENFLO, J. O., Astronomy
STEURER, W., Crystallography
STORRER, H. H., Mathematics
STRAUMANN, N., Theoretical Physics
THIEL, W., Organic Chemistry
THIERSTEIN, H. R., Micro-Palaeontology
THOMPSON, A. B., Petrology
TROMMSDORFF, V., Petrography
TRUÖL, P., Experimental Physics
WAGNIÈRE, G., Physical Chemistry
WARD, P., Zoology, Ecology
WEHNER, R., Zoological Physiology
WEISSMANN, CH., Molecular Biology
WYLER, D., Theoretical Physics
ZISWILER, V., Zoology

AFFILIATED INSTITUTES

Center for International Studies Zürich: Seilergraben 49, 8001 Zürich; Dirs Prof. D. RULOFF (Universität Zürich), Prof. M. GABRIEL (Eidgenössische Technische Hochschule Zürich), Prof. K. SPILLMAN (Eidgenössische Technische Hochschule Zürich).

Institut für Suchtforschung: Konradstr. 32, 8005 Zürich; drug dependence research; Dir Prof. A. UCHTENHAGEN.

Technical Universities

ÉCOLE POLYTECHNIQUE FÉDÉRALE DE LAUSANNE

Ecublens, 1015 Lausanne
Telephone: (21) 693-11-11
Telex: 454478
Fax: (21) 693-43-80

Founded 1853; present status 1969
Language of instruction: French
State Federal Control
Academic year: October to July

President: Prof. JEAN-CLAUDE BADOUX
Vice-President: Prof. D. DE WERRA
Administrative Director: P. IMMER
Planning and Research Director: J.-J. PALTENGHI
Academic Affairs Director: M. JACCARD
Library Director: J. NOENINGER

Library: see Libraries
Number of teachers: 200
Number of students: 4,700
Publications: *General Prospectus*, *Annual Report*, *Scientific Report*.

HEADS OF DEPARTMENTS

Department of Civil Engineering: Prof. M. HIRT
Department of Rural Engineering: Prof. J.-C. VEDI
Department of Mechanical Engineering: Prof. A. MONKEWITZ
Department of Microengineering: Prof. R. SALATHE
Department of Electrical Engineering: Prof. J.-J. SIMOND
Department of Physics: Prof. A. BALDERESCHI
Department of Chemistry and Chemical Engineering: Prof. T. RIZZO
Department of Mathematics: Prof. P. BUSER
Department of Materials Science and Engineering: Prof. N. SETTER
Department of Architecture: Prof. C. MOREL
Department of Computer Science: Prof. B. FALTINGS

PROFESSORS

Department of Civil Engineering:
BADOUX, M., Institute of Reinforced and Prestressed Concrete
BOVY, P., Institute of Transportation and Planning
BRUEHWILER, E., Maintenance, Construction and Safety of Structures
DESCOEUDRES, F., Road Mechanics
DUMONT, A.-G., Institute of Soils, Rocks and Foundations
FAVRE, R., Institute of Structural Engineering
FREY, FR., Laboratory of Structural and Continuum Mechanics
GRAF, W.-H., Hydraulic Research
HIRT, M., Institute of Steel Structures
JACQUOT, P., Stress Analysis and Measurement
LAFITTE, R., Institute of Hydraulics and Energy
MARCHAND, J.-D., Economics of Infrastructure
NATTERER, J., Timber Construction
PARRIAUX, A., Geology
PERRET, F.-L., Construction Management
PFLUG, L., Optical Stress Analysis Laboratory
RIVIER, R., Institute of Transportation and Planning
SANDOZ, J.-L., Timber Construction
SARLOS, G., Institute of Hydraulics and Energy
SCHLEISS, A., Institute of Hydraulics and Energy
SMITH, I., Institute of Reinforced and Prestressed Concrete
VULLIET, L., Soil Mechanics

Department of Rural Engineering:
GOLAY, F., Institute of Geodesy and Surveying
KÖLBL, O., Institute of Geodesy and Surveying
MERMINOD, B., Institute of Geodesy and Surveying
MERMOUD, A., Institute of Development of Earth and Water
MUSY, A., Institute of Agricultural Engineering
PÉRINGER, P., Institute of Environmental Engineering
SCHLAEPFER, R., Soils and Water
TARRADELLAS, J., Institute of Environmental Engineering
VAN DEN BERGH, H., Institute of Environmental Engineering
VÉDY, J.-C., Institute of Agricultural Engineering

Department of Mechanical Engineering:
AVELLAN, F., Institute of Hydraulic Machinery and Fluid Mechanics
BÖLCS, A., Institute of Thermal Engineering
BONVIN, D., Institute of Automatic Control
BOTSIS, J., Applied Mechanics
CURNIER, A., Laboratory of Applied Mechanics
DEVILLE, M., Institute of Hydraulic Machinery and Fluid Mechanics
FAVRAT, D., Laboratory of Industrial Energy Systems
GIANOLA, J.-C., Laboratory of Industrial Energy Systems
GIOVANOLA, J., Laboratory of Mechanical Systems Design
GLARDON, R., Applied Mechanics and Institute of Machine Design
LONGCHAMP, R., Institute of Automatics
MONKEWITZ, P., Institute of Hydraulic Machinery and Fluid Mechanics
PAHUD, P., Design and Production of Mechanical Systems
THOME, J., Laboratory of Applied Thermodynamics
XIROUCHAKIS, P., Applied Mechanics and Institute of Machine Design
ZYSSET, P., Laboratory of Applied Mechanics

Department of Microengineering:
BLEULER, H., Institute of Microtechnology
CLAVEL, R., Institute of Microtechnology
DÄNDLIKER, R., Microtechnology Laboratory
JACOT-DESCOMBES, J., Institute of Microtechnology
MARQUIS WEIBLE, F., Applied Optics
NICOLLIER, C., Institute of Microtechnology
PELLANDINI, E., Microtechnology Laboratory
PFLUGER, P., Institute of Microtechnology
POPOVIC, R., Institute of Microtechnology
RENAUD, P., Institute of Microtechnology
ROOIJ, N. DE, Microtechnology Laboratory
SALATHÉ, R., Applied Optics
SHAH, A., Microtechnology Laboratory
SIEGWART, R., Institute of Microtechnology

Department of Electrical Engineering:
COULON, F. DE, Signal Processing Laboratory
DECLERCQ, M., Electronics Laboratory
FAZAN, P., Electronics Laboratory
FONTOLLIET, P.-G., Telecommunications Laboratory
GARDIOL, F., Electromagnetism and Microwaves Laboratory
GERMOND, A., Electrical Installations Laboratory
HASLER, M., Circuits and Systems Theory
HUBAUX, J.-P., Telecommunications Laboratory
IANOZ, M., Electrical Energy Networks
JUFER, M., Electromechanics Laboratory
KUNT, M., Signal Processing Laboratory
MLYNEK, D., Electronics Laboratory
MOSIG, J., Electromagnetism and Acoustics
ROBERT, PH., Metrology Laboratory
ROSSI, M., Electromagnetism and Microwaves Laboratory
RUFER, A.-C., Electronics Laboratory
SIMOND, J.-J., Electromechanics and Electrical Machines Laboratory
SKRIVERVIK, A., Electromagnetism and Acoustics
VETTERLI, M., Signal Processing Laboratory
VITTOZ, E., Electronics Laboratory
WAVRE, N., Electromechanics and Electrical Machines Laboratory

Department of Physics:
ANSERMET, J.-P., Experimental Physics Institute
BALDERESCHI, A., Applied Physics Institute
BARÈS, P.-A., Theoretical Physics
BENOIT, W., Nuclear Engineering Institute
BRÜESCH, P., General Physics of Solids
BUTTET, J., Experimental Physics Institute
CHÂTELAIN, A., Experimental Physics Institute
CHAWLA, R., Nuclear Engineering Institute
DEVEAUD-PLEDRAN, B., Micro- and Opto-electronics Institute
FIVAZ, R., Dir, Applied Physics Institute
GRUBER, C., Theoretical Physics Institute
ILEGEMS, M., Dir, Micro- and Opto-electronics Institute
KAPON, E., Micro- and Opto-electronics Institute
KERN, K., Experimental Physics Institute
KUNZ, H., Theoretical Physics Institute
LÉVY, F., Applied Physics Institute
MARGARITONDO, G., Applied Physics Institute
MARTIN, J.-L., Dir, Nuclear Engineering Institute
MARTIN, PH., Theoretical Physics Institute
MEISTER, J.-J., Applied Physics Institute
MONOT, R., Experimental Physics Institute
QUATTROPANI, A., Theoretical Physics Institute
REINHART, F. K., Micro- and Opto-electronics Institute
STERGIOPOULOS, N., Medical Engineering
ZUPPIROLI, L., Nuclear Engineering Institute

Department of Chemistry and Chemical Engineering:
COMINELLIS, CH., General Laboratory of Chemical Reactions
FREITAG, R., Laboratory of Cellular Biotechnology
FRIEDLI, C., Institute of Physical Chemistry
GIRAULT, H., Institute of Physical Chemistry
GRAETZEL, M., Institute of Physical Chemistry
HUNKELER, D., Laboratory of Polymer Chemistry
RENKEN, A., Institute of Chemical Engineering III
RIZZO, T., Institute of Physical Chemistry
STOCKAR, U., VON, Institute of Chemical Engineering II
STOESSEL, F., Safety of Chemical Processes
VOGEL, H., Laboratory of Polymer Chemistry
WURM, F., Institute of Chemical Engineering

Department of Mathematics:
ANDRÉ, M., Algebra and Topology
BEN AROUS, G., Probability Theory
BUSER, P., Geometry
CHATTERJI, S., Probability Theory
DACAROGNA, B., Analysis
DALANG, R., Probability Theory
DAVISON, A.
DESCLOUX, J., Numerical Analysis and Simulation
FROIDEVAUX, H., Numerical Analysis and Simulation
HERTZ, A., Operational Research
LIEBLING, T., Operational Research
MADDOCKS, J., Analysis
MORGENTHALER, S., Statistics
NÜESCH, P., Probability and Statistics
PFISTER, CH.-E., Mathematical Methodology
RAPPAZ, J., Numerical Analysis and Simulation
STUART, C., Numerical Analysis and Simulation
TROYANOV, M., Geometry
WERRA, D. DE, Operational Research
WOHLHAUSER, A., Geometry

ZWAHLEN, B., Numerical Analysis and Simulation

Department of Computer Science:

BOURLARD, H., Artificial Intelligence Laboratory
CORAY, G., Dir, Theoretical Computer Science Laboratory
COULON, F. DE, Dir, Computer-Aided-Learning Laboratory
FALTINGS, B., Dir, Artificial Intelligence Laboratory
GERSTNER, W., Mini- and Micro-Computer Laboratory
HERSCH, R.-D., Dir, Peripheral Systems Laboratory
LE BOUDEC, J.-Y., Dir, Communication Network Laboratory
MANGE, D., Dir, Logic Systems Laboratory
NICOUD, J.-D., Dir, Mini- and Micro-Computer Laboratory
PETITPIERRE, C., Dir, Data Communication Laboratory
SANCHEZ, E., Logic Systems Laboratory
SCHIPER, A., Dir, Operating Systems Laboratory
SPACCAPIETRA, S., Dir, Databases Laboratory
STROHMEIER, A., Dir, Software Engineering Laboratory
THALMANN, D., Dir, Computer Graphics Laboratory
THIRAN, P., Institute of Data Communication
WEGMANN, A., Industrial Computer Engineering Laboratory
ZAHND, J., Dir, Logic Systems Laboratory

Department of Materials Science and Engineering:

AEBISCHER, P., Welding Metallurgy Laboratory
HILBORN, J. G., Polymer Laboratory
HOFMANN, H., Powder Technology Laboratory
HUET, CH., Building Materials Laboratory
KURZ, W., Physical Metallurgy Laboratory
LANDOLT, D., Chemical Metallurgy
MANSON, J. A., Technology of Composites and Polymers
MATHIEU, H. J., Chemical Metallurgy Laboratory
MORTENSEN, A., Mechanical Metallurgy Laboratory
RAPPAZ, M., Physical Metallurgy Laboratory
SETTER, N., Ceramics Laboratory

Department of Architecture:

ABOU-JAOUDÉ, G., Computer-Aided Design
BASSAND, M., Sociology
BERGER, P., Architecture
BEVILACQUA, M., Architecture
BOTTA, M., Architecture
CANTAFORA, A., Architecture
CHUARD, P., Building Techniques
FAIST, A., Solar Energy Research Building
GUBLER, J., History of Architecture
LAMUNIÈRE, I., History and Theory of Architecture
LUCAN, J., Architectural Theory
MANGEAT, V., Architecture
MARCHAND, B., History and Theory of Architecture
MEISS, P. VON, Architectural Experimentation Laboratory
MESTELAN, P., Architecture
MOREL, C., Building Techniques
ORTELLI, L., Architectural Theory
RUHLEY, P. A., Regional Planning
SCARTEZZINI, J.-L., Solar Energy Research Building
STEINMANN, M., Architecture
THALMANN, P., Economics

Communications Systems Section:

HUBAUX, J.-P.
KUNT, M.
LE BOUDEC, J.-Y.
NUSSBAUMER, H.
PETITPIERRE, C.
VETTERLI, M.

INTERDISCIPLINARY UNITS

Centre for Electron Microscopy: Dir Prof. P. BUFFAT.

Plasma Physics Research Centre: Dir Prof. MINH QUANG TRAN (from April 1999).

Pedagogy and Didactics: Dir Prof. M. GOLDSCHMID.

Special Mathematics: Dir ISABELLE DUSTIN.

Interdisciplinary Group for Analytical Chemistry: Head R. HOURIET.

Community Studies for Urban and Rural Planning: Gen. Sec. M. REY.

Western Swiss Research Institute for Computational Physics of Condensed Matter: Dir Prof. R. CAR.

International Institute of Management (IML): Dir Prof. J.-L. PERRET.

Centre for Technology and Management: Co-ordinator Prof. J.-L. PERRET.

EIDGENÖSSISCHE TECHNISCHE HOCHSCHULE ZÜRICH
(Swiss Federal Institute of Technology)

Rämistr. 101, ETH-Zentrum, 8092 Zürich
Telephone: (1) 632-11-11
Telex: 817-379
Fax: (1) 632-35-25

Founded 1855
Language of instruction: German (some basic lectures are given in French)
Federal State control
Academic year: October to July (two semesters)

President: Prof. OLAF KÜBLER
Rector: Prof. KONRAD OSTERWALDER
Vice-President for Research: Prof. ALBERT WALDVOGEL
Vice-President for Planning and Logistics: Prof. GERHARD SCHMITT
Secretary-General: Dr PETER KOTTUSCH

Library: see Libraries
Number of teachers: 347
Number of students: 12,096

Publications: *Semesterprogramm* (2 a year), *ETH Bulletin* (quarterly), *Annual Report, Research Report*, etc.

HEADS OF DIVISIONS (TEACHING)

Architecture: Prof. V. MAGNAGO LAMPUGNANI
Civil Engineering: Prof. H. R. SCHALCHER
Mechanical Engineering: Prof. P. R. VON ROHR
Electrical Engineering: Prof. A. KÜNDIG
Computer Science: Prof. W. GANDER
Materials Science: Prof. P. SMITH
Industrial Production Engineering: Prof. U. MEYER
Chemistry: Prof. R. PRINS
Pharmacy: Prof. H. WUNDERLI-ALLENSBACH
Forestry: Prof. L. J. KUCERA
Agriculture: Prof. M. TEUBER
Rural Engineering and Surveying: Prof. G. KAHLE
Mathematics and Physics: Prof. C. BLATTER
Environmental Natural Sciences: Prof. H. FLÜHLER
Biology: Prof. N. AMRHEIN
Earth Sciences: Prof. W. LOWRIE
Military Science: Prof. J. M. GABRIEL
Training of Physical Education and Sports Teachers: Dr K. MURER
Liberal Studies: Dr R. KAPPEL

HEADS OF DEPARTMENT (RESEARCH)

Agriculture and Food Science: Prof. W. LANGHAUS
Architecture: Prof. V. MAGNAGO LAMPUGNANI
Civil and Environmental Engineering: Prof. M. FONTANA
Biology: Prof. K. WÜTHRICH
Chemistry: Prof. R. PRINS
Electrical Engineering: Prof. P. NIEDERER
Mechanical and Process Engineering: Prof. G. YADIGAROGLU
Earth Sciences: Prof. W. LOWRIE
Geodetic Sciences: Prof. H. INGENSAND
Human Sciences: Prof. L. DÄLLANBACH
Computer Science: Prof. W. GANDER
Management and Production: Prof. H. KRUEGER
Mathematics: Prof. G. MISLIN
Pharmacy: Prof. H. WUNDERLI-ALLENSBACH
Physics: Prof. J. FRÖHLICH
Law and Economy: Prof. R. SCHUBERT
Environmental Sciences: Prof. H. FLÜHLER
Forest and Wood Sciences: Prof. L. J. KUCERA
Materials: Prof. P. SMITH

PROFESSORS

Architecture:

ANGELIL, M., Architectural Design
CAMPI, M., Architectural Design
DANIELS, K., HVAC Engineering
DEPLAZES, A., Architecture and Construction
ENGELI, M., Architecture and CAAD
FLÜCKIGER, H., Spatial Development
FORSTER, K. W., History of Architecture and Art
JENNY, P., Basic Design
KELLER, B., Building Physics
KIENAST, D., Landscape Architecture
KÖHLER, History and Theory of Architecture
KOLLHOFF, H., Architectural Design
KRAMEL, H. E., Architectural Design
KUENZLE, O., Building Management
MAGNAGO, V., History of Architecture and Art
MEYER, A., Architectural Design
MEYER, P., Building Management (Structural Design and Building Implementation)
MÖRSCH, G., Preservation of Monuments and Sites; Art History
OECHSLIN, W., History of Architecture and Art
OSWALD, F., Architectural Design
RUCHAT-RONCATI, F., Architectural Design
RÜEGG, A., Architectural Design
SCHETT, W., Architectural Design
SCHMID, W. A., Regional Planning and Methodology
SCHMITT, G., Computer-aided Architectural Design
TROPEANO, R., Architectural Design

Civil and Environmental Engineering:

AMANN, P., Soil Engineering and Soil Mechanics
ANDERHEGGEN, E., Applied Computer Science
BACCINI, P., Material Flux and Waste Management
BACHMANN, H., Concrete Constructions
BÖHNI, H., Materials Science
BRÄNDLI, H., Traffic Engineering
BURLANDO, P., Hydrology and Water Resource Management
DIETRICH, K., Traffic Engineering
FLURY, U., Rural Engineering Management
FONTANA, M., Structural Engineering
FRITSCH, M., Rural Engineering
GIRMSCHEID, G., Construction Management and Process Technology
GUJER, W., Sanitary Engineering
HERMANNS STENGELE, R., Geotechnics
KINZELBACH, W., Hydromechanics
KOVARI, K., Tunnelling
MARTI, P., Structural Engineering
MINOR, H.-E., Hydraulic Structures
SCHALCHER, H.-R., Planning and Construction Management

SCHMID, W. A., Rural Engineering and Planning
SCHNEIDER, J., Statics and Concrete Constructions
SPRINGMAN, S., Geotechnical Engineering
VIRTANEN, S., Metallic High-Performance Materials
VOGEL, TH., Structural Engineering
WITTMANN, F., Materials Science

Mechanical and Process Engineering:

BRAUCHLI, H., Theoretical Mechanics
BUSER, R., Theoretical Mechanics
DUAL, J., Theoretical Mechanics
EBERLE, M., Internal Combustion Engines
ERMANNI, P., Design and Construction
GEERING, H. P., Control Systems
GUZZELLA, L., Internal Combustion Engines
GYARMATHY, G., Turbomachinery
KLEISER, L., Fluid Dynamics
KOUMOUTSAKOS, P., Fluid Dynamics
KRÖGER, W., Safety Engineering
MAZZOTTI, M., Process Engineering
MEIER, M., Mechanical Design
MEYER-PIENING, H.-R., Lightweight Structures and Cableway Technology
POUBLIKAKOS, D., Thermodynamics
PRASINIS, S. E., Process Engineering
RÖSGEN, T., Fluid Dynamics
RUDOLF VON ROHR, PH., Process Engineering
SAYIR, M., Mechanics
SCHWEITZER, G., Robotics
SEILER, A., Operations Research
STEINER, M., Control Systems
STEMMER, A., Nanotechnology
WIDMER, F., Process Engineering
WINTERMANTEL, E., Biocompatible Materials Science and Engineering
YADIGAROGLU, G., Nuclear Engineering

Computer Science:

ALONSO, G., Computer Systems
GANDER, W., Scientific Computing
GONNET, G., Scientific Computing
GROSS, M., Scientific Computing
GROSS, T., Computer Systems
GUTKNECHT, J., Computer Systems
MAURER, U., Theoretical Computer Science
NIEVERGELT, J., Theoretical Computer Science
NORRIE, M., Computer Science
RICHTER-GEBERT, J., Theoretical Computer Systems
SCHÄUBLE, P., Information Systems
SCHEK, H.-J., Information Systems
STRICKER, T., Computer Systems
WELZL, E., Computer Science
WIDMAYER, P., Theoretical Computer Science
WIRTH, N., Computer Systems
ZEHNDER, C. A., Information Systems

Electrical Engineering:

ALLGÖWER, F., Non-linear Systems
BACHER, R., Electric Power Transmission and High Voltage Technology
BÄCHTOLD, W., Electromagnetic Fields and Microwaves
EGGIMANN, F., Signal and Information Processing
FICHTNER, W., Integrated Systems
FRÖHLICH, K., Electric Power Transmission and High Voltage Technology
GLAVITSCH, H., Electric Power Transmission and High Voltage Technology
GUNZINGER, A., Electronics
GUT, J., Military Security Technology
HUANG, Q., Integrated Systems
HUBBELL, J. A., Biomedical Engineering and Medical Informatics
HUGEL, J., Electrical Engineering Design
JAECKEL, H., Electronics
KÜNDIG, A., Computer Engineering and Communications Networks
KUSTER, N., Electromagnetic Fields and Microwaves
LEUTHOLD, P., Communication Technology
MORARI, M., Automatic Control
MOSCHYTZ, G., Signal and Information Processing
NIEDERER, P., Biomedical Engineering and Medical Informatics
PLATTNER, B., Computer Engineering and Communications Networks
SCHAUFELBERGER, W., Automatic Control
STEMMLER, H., Power Electronics and Electrometrology
THIELE, L., Computer Engineering
TROESTER, G., Electronics
VAHLDIECK, R., Field Theory

Materials:

GAUCKLER, L. J., Inorganic Non-metallic Materials
HUBBELL, J. A., Biomedical Engineering
ÖTTINGER, H. C., Theoretical Polymer Physics
SMITH, P., Polymer Technology
SPEIDEL, M., Metals and Metallurgy
SPENCER, N. D., Surface Technology
STÜSSI, E., Biomechanics
SUTER, U. W., Macromolecular Chemistry
VIRTANEN, S., Metallic High-performance Materials
WINTERMANTEL, E., Biocompatible Materials

Management and Production:

ABELL, D. F., Leadership and Technology Programme
ENGELI, M., Machine Tools and Manufacturing
FRAUENFELDER, P., Industrial Engineering and Management
GROTE, G., Work Psychology
HUBER, F., Industrial Engineering and Management
KELLER, T., Hygiene and Applied Physiology
KRUEGER, H., Hygiene and Applied Physiology
MEYER, U., Textile Machinery and Textile Industries
REHSTEINER, F., Machine Tools and Manufacturing
REISSNER, J., Forming Technology
SCHÖNSLEBEN, P., Industrial Engineering and Management
TSCHIRKY, H., Industrial Engineering and Management
WEHNER, T., Work and Organizational Psychology
ZÜST, R., Industrial Engineering and Management

Chemistry:

BAIKER, A., Chemical Engineering and Catalysis
BAUDER, A., Physical Chemistry
CHEN, P., Physical-organic Chemistry
DIEDERICH, F. N., Organic Chemistry
GRÜTZMACHER, H., Inorganic Chemistry
HARTLAND, S., Chemical Engineering
HILVERT, D., Organic Chemistry
HUNGERBÜHLER, K., Safety and Environmental Protection
KUPPENOL, W. H., Inorganic Chemistry
LUISI, P. L., Macromolecular Chemistry
MEIER, B., Physical Chemistry
MERKT, F., Physical Chemistry
MORBIDELLI, M., Chemical Reaction Engineering
NESPER, R., Inorganic Chemistry
QUACK, M., Physical Chemistry
RÖTHLISBERGER, U., Computer-aided Inorganic Chemistry
SCHWEIGER, A., Physical Chemistry
SEEBACH, D., Organic Chemistry
TOGNI, A., Inorganic Chemistry
VAN GUNSTEREN, W. F., Computer-aided Chemistry
VASELLA, A., Organic Chemistry
WILD, U., Physical Chemistry
WOKAUN, A., Chemistry
ZENOBI, R., Analytical Chemistry

Pharmacy:

BECK-SICKINGER, A., Pharmaceutical Biochemistry
FOLKERS, G., Medicinal Chemistry
MERKLE, H. P., Pharmaceutics
MÖHLER, H., Pharmacology
MÜNTENER, M., Anatomy
SCHUBIGER, P. A., Radiopharmacy
STICHER, O., Pharmacognosy and Phytochemistry
WUNDERLI-ALLENSPACH, H., Biopharmacy

Forest and Wood Sciences:

BACHMANN, P., Forest Inventory and Planning
EWALD, K., Nature and Landscape Conservation
GEHRI, E., Wood Technology
HEINIMANN, H. R., Forestry Engineering
HOLDENRIEDER, O., Forest Pathology and Dendrology
KISSLING-NÄF, I., Forest Resource Economics
KUCERA, L., Wood Science
SCHMITHÜSEN, F., Forestry Policy and Forestry Economics
SCHÜTZ, J.-P., Silviculture

Agriculture and Food Science:

AMADÒ, R., Food Chemistry
AMRHEIN, N., Biochemistry and Plant Physiology
APEL, K., Plant Science
DORN, S., Applied Entomology
ESCHER, F., Food Technology
FROSSARD, E., Plant Nutrition
HURRELL, R. F., Human Nutrition
KREUZER, M., Animal Nutrition
KÜNZI, N., Animal Breeding
LANGHANS, W., Physiology and Animal Husbandry
LEHMANN, B., Farm and Agrobusiness Management
NÖSBERGER, J., Fodder Production and Crop Physiology
POTRYKUS, I., Plant Science
PUHAN, Z., Dairy Science
RIEDER, P., Agricultural Market and Policy
STAMP, P., Agronomy and Plant Breeding
STRANZINGER, G., Breeding Biology
TEUBER, M., Food Microbiology
WENK, C., Biology of Nutrition
WINDHAB, E., Food Engineering

Geodetic Sciences:

CAROSIO, A., Geodesy
GRÜN, A., Photogrammetry
HURNI, L., Cartography
INGENSAND, H., Geodesy
KAHLE, H.-G., Geodesy

Mathematics:

BLATTER, CH., Mathematics
BÜHLMANN, H., Mathematics
BURGER, M., Mathematics
DELBAEN, F., Financial Mathematics
EMBRECHTS, P., Mathematics
FELDER, G., Mathematics
GROTE, M. J., Mathematics
HAMPEL, F., Statistics
IMAMOGLU, O., Mathematics
JELTSCH, R., Mathematics
KIRCHGRABER, U., Mathematics
KNÖRRER, H., Mathematics
KNUS, M., Mathematics
KÜNSCH, H., Mathematics
LANG, U., Mathematics
LÜTHI, H.-J.
MARTI, J., Mathematics
MISLIN, G., Mathematics
OSTERWALDER, K., Mathematics
SALMHOFER, M., Mathematics
SCHWAB, C., Applied Mathematics
STAMMBACH, U., Mathematics
STRUWE, M., Mathematics
SZNITMAN, A.-S., Mathematics
TRUBOWITZ, E., Mathematics

WÜSTHOLZ, G., Mathematics
ZEHNDER, E., Mathematics

Biology:
AEBI, M., Microbiology
AMRHEIN, N., Plant Biochemistry
APEL, K., Plant Genetics
BAILEY, J. E., Biotechnology
BOUTELLIER, U., Exercise Physiology
CARAFOLI, E., Biochemistry
DIMROTH, P., Microbiology
EPPENBERGER, H. M., Cell Biology
FELDON, J., Behavioural Biology
GLOCKSHUBER, R., Molecular Biology and Biophysics
HELENIUS, A., Biochemistry
HENGARTNER, H., Experimental Immunology
HENNECKE, H., Microbiology
LEISINGER, TH., Microbiology
MARTIN, K. A. C., Systematic Neurophysiology
NERI, D., Molecular Biology and Biophysics
POTRYKUS, I., Development Biology of Plants
RICHMOND, T. J., Molecular Biology and Biophysics
SCHWAB, M. E., Neuroscience
SUTER, U., Cell Biology
WINTERHALTER, K. H., Biochemistry
WITHOLT, B., Biotechnology
WÜRGLER, F., Toxicology
WÜTHRICH, K., Molecular Biology and Biophysics

Environmental Sciences:
DAVIES, H. C., Atmospheric Physics, Dynamic Meteorology
EDWARDS, P., Plant Ecology
FLÜHLER, H., Soil Physics
IMBODEN, D., Environmental Physics
KAISER, F. G., Human–Environmental Relations
KOLLER, TH., Cell Biology
MIEG, H., Human–Environmental Relations
OHMURA, A., Climatology
ROY, B. A., Plant Biodiversity
SCHÄR, C., Climate Dynamics
SCHMID-HEMPEL, P., Experimental Ecology
SCHOLZ, R. W., Environmental Sciences
SCHULIN, R., Soil Protection
SCHWARZENBACH, R., Organic Environmental Chemistry
STEINER, D., Human Ecology, Cultural Evolution
STICHER, H., Soil Chemistry
WALDVOGEL, A., Atmospheric Physics
WARD, J. V., Aquatic Ecology
WEHRLI, B., Aquatic Chemistry
ZEHNDER, A. J. B, Environmental Biotechnology
ZEYER, J., Soil Biology

Earth Sciences:
BERNOULLI, D., Geology
BURG, J. P., Structural Geology
GIARDINI, D., Seismology and Geodynamics
GREEN, A., Applied and Environmental Geophysics
HALLIDAY, A., Isotope and Trace Element Geochemistry
HEINRICH, CH. A., Mineral Resources and Processes of the Earth's Interior
KUNZ, M., Crystallography
LÖW, S., Engineering Geology
LOWRIE, W., Geophysics
MCKENZIE, J., Earth System Sciences
SEWARD, T., Geochemistry
STEURER, W., Crystallography
THIERSTEIN, H. R., Micropalaeontology
THOMPSON, A. B., Petrology
TROMMSDORFF, V., Petrography

Human Sciences:
BERGIER, J.-F., General History
BESOMI, O., Italian Language and Literature
BUCHMANN, M., Sociology
DÄLLENBACH, L., French Language and Literature
DELHEES, K., Psychology
EISNER, M., Sociology
ELKANA, Y., Philosophy and Social Studies
FREY, K., Education
GUGERLI, D., History of Technology
HOLENSTEIN, E., Philosophy
KAPPEL, R., Problems for Developing Studies
MUSCHG, A., German Literature
NOWOTNY, H., Philosophy and Social Studies
RIS, R., German Language and Literature
SUTER, C., Sociology
TOBLER, H. W., General History
VICKERS, B., English Language and Literature

Physics:
BALTES, H., Quantum Electronics
BLATTER, G., Theoretical Physics
EICHLER, R., Experimental Particle Physics
ENSSLIN, K., Solid State Physics
FRÖHLICH, J., Theoretical and Mathematical Physics
GRAF, G. M., Theoretical Physics
GÜNTER, P., Quantum Electronics
HEPP, K., Theoretical Physics
HOFER, H., Experimental Particle Physics
HUNZIKER, W., Theroretical Physics
KELLER, U., Quantum Electronics
KOSTORZ, G., Applied Physics
LANG, J., Experimental Particle Physics
MELCHIOR, H., Quantum Electronics
OTT, H. R., Solid State Physics
PAUSS, F., Experimental Particle Physics
PESCIA, D., Solid State Physics
RICE, T. M., Theoretical Physics
RUBBIA, A., Experimental Particle Physics
SCHMID, CH., Theoretical Physics
SIEGMANN, H.-CH., Solid State Physics
STENFLO, J. O., Astrophysics
WACHTER, P., Solid State Physics

Law and Economics:
BERNOUER, T., International Relations
GABRIEL, J. M., International Relations
HERTIG, G., Jurisprudence
NEF, U., Law
RUCH, A., Law
SCHIPS, B., Economics
SCHUBERT, R., Economics
SPILLMANN, K., Security Studies and Conflict Research

INSTITUTES AFFILIATED TO BOTH TECHNICAL UNIVERSITIES

Eidgenössische Materialprüfungs- und Forschungsanstalt (EMPA) (Federal Laboratories for Materials Testing and Research): Überlandstr. 129, 8600 Dübendorf; tel. (1) 823-55-11; fax (1) 821-62-44; Dir Prof. Dr F. EGGIMANN.

Eidgenössische Forschungsanstalt für Wald, Schnee und Landschaft (WSL) (Federal Research Institute for Forest, Snow and Landscape): 8903 Birmensdorf; tel. (1) 739-21-11; fax (1) 739-22-15; Dir Prof. R. SCHLÄPFER.

Eidgenössische Anstalt für Wasserversorgung, Abwasserreinigung und Gewässerschutz (EAWAG) (Federal Institute for Water Resources and Water Pollution Control): Überlandstr. 133, 8600 Dübendorf; tel. (1) 823-55-11; fax (1) 823-50-28; Dir Prof. Dr A. ZEHNDER.

Paul Scherrer Institut (PSI): Würenlingen und Villigen; tel. (56) 310-21-11; fax (56) 310-21-99; Dir Prof. Dr M. EBERLE.

Colleges

Staatsunabhängige Theologische Hochschule Basel (Independent Theological Seminary Basel): Mühlestiegrain 50, 4125 Riehen BS; tel. (61) 641-11-88; fax (61) 641-37-98; f. 1970; masters and doctoral degree programmes in theology; Rector Prof. Dr S. KÜLLING; publ. *Fundamentum*.

C. G. Jung Institute Zürich: Hornweg 28, 8700 Küsnacht; tel. (1) 910-53-23; fax (1) 910-54-51; f. 1948; private teaching and research institute for analytical psychology as conceived by C. G. Jung; clinical and professional training programme leading to a Diploma; courses and seminars in German and English for qualified auditors; special training in child-psychotherapy (for German-speaking students); counselling centre; international picture archive and library; 100 teachers; 380 students; Pres. Dr B. SPILLMANN; Dir of Studies IRENE LÜSCHER.

Franklin College, Switzerland: Via Ponte Tresa 29, 6924 Sorengo (Lugano); tel. (91) 993-01-01; fax (91) 994-41-17; f. 1969; mem. of Asscn of American International Colleges and Universities; Associate in Arts and BA degree courses; accred. by Middle States Asscn; library of 26,000 vols; 28 teachers; 225 students; Pres. ERIK O. NIELSEN; Dean of Academic Affairs TIMOTHY J. KEATING.

Institut de Hautes Etudes en Administration Publique: Rte de la Maladière 21, 1022 Chavannes/Lausanne; tel. (21) 691-06-56; fax (21) 691-08-88; f. 1981; autonomous institution affiliated with Univ. of Lausanne and Federal Polytechnic; postgraduate courses; library of 9,000 vols and 100 periodicals; Pres. ARTHUR DUNKEL; Dir PETER KNOEPFEL; publs *Bulletin* (quarterly), *Cahiers*.

International Institute for Management Development (IMD): 23 chemin de Bellerive, POB 915, 1001 Lausanne; tel. (21) 618-01-11; fax (21) 618-07-07; f. 1989 in a merger between IMEDE in Lausanne and IMI in Geneva; one-year post-experience MBA course; 10-week course for middle managers, and various short-term general management courses; research activities in international management issues; 42 full-time faculty mems; Pres. Prof. PETER LORANGE.

Schiller International University – Switzerland: for general details, see entry in Germany chapter.

American College of Switzerland Campus: 1854 Leysin VD-WL; tel. (25) 342223; telex 453227; fax (25) 341346; f. 1963; degree courses in liberal arts and business administration; French and English Language Institute for EFL/ESL students (programme certificate); library of 48,000 vols; Pres. WALTER LEIBRECHT.

Engelberg Campus: Dorfstrasse 40, 6390 Engelberg; tel. (41) 637-43-43; telex 866461; fax (41) 637-22-55; Dir MAXIMILLIAN FRIEDLI.

Schools of Art and Music

ART

Ecoles d'art de Genève:

Ecole supérieure d'art visuel: 9 blvd Helvétique, 1205 Geneva; tel. (22) 311-05-10; fax (22) 310-13-63; f. 1748; painting, drawing, sculpture, etching, mixed media, audio-visual depts; 320 students; library of 6,000 vols; Dir BERNARD ZUMTHOR.

Ecole des arts décoratifs–Ecole supérieure d'arts appliqués: Rue Jacques-Necker 2, 1201 Geneva; tel. (22) 732-04-39; fax (22) 731-87-34; f. 1876; jewellery, ceramics, stylism, interior architecture, dressmaking, graphic art, art expression; *c.* 400 students; Dir ROGER FALLET.

Ecole Cantonale d'Art de Lausanne: 4 ave de l'Elysée, 1006 Lausanne; tel. (21) 617-75-23; fax (21) 616-39-91; e-mail manuela.marti@ecal

.vd.ch; f. 1821; departments of fine arts, audio-visual studies, graphic design, multimedia and industrial design; 60 teachers; 200 students; Dir P. KELLER.

MUSIC

Conservatoire de Musique: 8 route Louis Braille, 1700 Fribourg; tel. (26) 466-22-22; fax (26) 466-65-17; e-mail sennm@etatfr.ch; f. 1904; music, singing, dance, theatre; Dir M. SENN.

Conservatoire de Musique de Lausanne: 2 rue de la Grotte, 1003 Lausanne; tel. (21) 321-35-35; f. 1861 under the auspices of the State and of the City of Lausanne; 1,400 students; Dir OLIVIER CUENDET.

Conservatoire de Musique: Place Neuve, 1204 Geneva; tel. (22) 311-76-33; fax (22) 312-18-10; f. 1835; all branches of music, dramatic art and classical ballet; organizes a yearly International Competition for musical performers which attracts young virtuosi of all countries; library of 80,000 music scores and 10,000 vols; 100 teachers; 500 full-time students; Dir PHILIPPE DINKEL; Librarian XAVIER BOUVIER; publ. *Bulletin* (monthly).

Conservatoire de Musique de Neuchâtel: Clos-Brochet 30–32, 2007 Neuchâtel; tel. (32) 25-20-53; fax (32) 25-70-24; f. 1918; Dir FRANÇOIS-XAVIER DELACOSTE; publ. *Duetto* (10 a year).

Konservatorium für Musik und Theater in Bern: Kramgasse 36, 3011 Bern; tel. (31) 311-62-21; fax (31) 312-20-53; f. 1858; 170 teachers; library of 50,000 vols; Pres. E. ZÖLCH; Dir Prof. J. STÄMPFLI.

Konservatorium und Musikhochschule Zürich: Florhofgasse 6, 8001 Zürich; tel. (1) 268-30-40; fax (1) 251-89-54; f. 1876; controlled by the public authorities; professional school, providing comprehensive musical courses for teachers, performers, composers, leading to State diplomas; department for children and amateurs; 240 teachers; 500 students; 2,000 amateurs; library of *c.* 15,000 vols; Dir DANIEL FUETER; publ. *Der Bindebogen* (quarterly).

Musik-Akademie der Stadt Basel: Postfach, Leonhardsstr. 6, 4003 Basel; tel. (61) 264-57-57; fax (61) 264-57-13; e-mail musakabas@ubaclu.unibas.ch; f. 1867; comprises 3 institutes: music school providing non-professional musical education, conservatory providing professional musical education, Schola Cantorum Basiliensis providing specialized education in early music; library of 250,000 vols; 430 staff; 9,000 students; Dir HANS LINNARTZ.

Musikschule und Konservatorium (Musikhochschule) Winterthur: Tössertobelstr. 1, 8400 Winterthur; tel. (52) 213-36-23; fax (52) 213-36-33; f. 1873; 170 teachers; 250 students (Konservatorium), 1,700 students (Musikschule); Dir FRITZ NÄF.

SYRIA

Learned Societies

GENERAL

Arabic Language Academy of Damascus: POB 327, Damascus; fax 3733363; f. 1919; Arabic Islamic legacy and linguistic studies and terminology; 20 mems; Pres. Dr SHAKER FAHAM; Sec.-Gen. Dr A. WASSEK CHAHID; publ. *Majallat Majmaa al-Lughah al-Arabiyyah bi-Dimashq* (review, quarterly).

Research Institutes

GENERAL

Institut Français d'Etudes Arabes: BP 344, Damascus; tel. (11) 3330214; fax (11) 3327887; f. 1922; study of the classical Arab world; library of 70,000 vols, 1,000 periodicals; Dir DOMINIQUE MALLET; Scientific Secs NADINE MÉOUCHY, SARAB ATTASSI; Librarian MICHEL NIÉTO; publ. *Bulletin d'Etudes Orientales*.

AGRICULTURE, FISHERIES AND VETERINARY SCIENCE

Arab Center for the Study of Arid Zones and Dry Lands (ACSAD): POB 2440, Damascus; tel. 5323087; fax 5323063; e-mail ruacsad@rusys.eg.net; f. 1971 by the Arab League; studies problems of management conservation and development of agricultural resources, including water, soil, plant and animal resources; emphasis on resources survey and assessment, causes of degradation and desertification, processes of conservation and development, economic evaluation and social implications, proper management through appropriate technologies, technical training, processing and dissemination of pertinent scientific and technical knowledge and information; mems: 16 Arab countries; 300 staff; library of 1,500 vols, 152 periodicals, 65,000 references; Dir-Gen. Dr HASSAN SEOUD; publs *Agriculture and Water in Arid Regions of the Arab World* (2 a year), *The Camel Newsletter* (2 a year), annual reports of divisions, technical reports, scientific papers.

EDUCATION

Arab Centre for Arabization, Translation, Authorship and Publication: Al-Afif St, 2 Senbul Jadet, POB 3752, Damascus; tel. 3334876; fax 3330998; f. 1990; attached to ALECSO; translates and prints recent educational, medical and scientific titles in Arabic; organizes seminars and workshops; library of 3,500 items; Dir Prof. Dr GADEER IBRAHEEM ZAYZAFOON; publ. *Arabization* (2 a year).

Libraries and Archives

Aleppo

Al Maktabah Al Wataniah: Bab El-Faradj, Aleppo; f. 1924; Librarian YOUNIS ROSHDI.

Damascus

Al Zahiriah (Public Library): Bab el Barid, Damascus; f. 1919; main subjects are miscellaneous sciences, literature and language, history, biography, religion; 100,000 vols, 50,000 periodicals; special collection: rare pre-1900 Arabic books; Librarian SAMA EL MAHASSINI; publ. brochure of new additions (quarterly).

Assad National Library: Malki St, POB 3639, Damascus; tel. 338255; telex 419143; f. 1984, in process of formation; national deposit library; publishes National Bibliography, trains librarians; 280 staff; 147,124 vols, 19,000 Arabic MSS; Gen. Dir GHASSAN LAHHAM; publs *National Bibliography* (annually), *Analytical Index of Syrian Periodicals*, *Index of Syrian University Theses*.

University of Damascus Library: Damascus; f. 1919; 150,000 vols; 2,700 scientific, literary and specialized journals and magazines; Librarian Dr NIZAR OYOUN EL-SOUD; publs *Conférences Générales* (annually), *Statistic Collection* (annually).

Homs

Dar al-Kutub al-Wataniah (Public Library): Homs.

Latakia

Public Library of Latakia: Latakia; f. 1944; 12,000 vols; Dir MOHAMAD ALI NTAYFI.

Museums and Art Galleries

Aleppo

Aleppo National Museum: Aleppo; tel. 212400; f. 1931; archaeology and modern art; library of 4,000 vols; Head Curator Dr SHAWQI SHAATH.

Busra

Busra Museum: Busra; traditional arts and crafts; Dir of Archaeological Research Dr SULEIMAN MOGHDAD.

Damascus

Adnan Malki Museum: Damascus.

Agricultural Museum: Damascus.

Military Museum: Damascus.

Museum of Arabic Epigraphy: Damascus; f. 1974; Dir FAYEZ HOMSI.

National Museum: Syrian University St, Damascus 4; tel. 2214854; telex 412491; fax 2247983; f. 1919; Sections: Prehistory; Ancient Oriental; Greek, Roman and Byzantine; Arab and Islamic; Modern Art; of special interest is the reconstruction of the Palmyrene Hypogeum of Yarhai (2nd century A.D.), of the Dura Synagogue (3rd century A.D.), of the Umayyad Qasr El-Hair El-Gharbi (8th century A.D.) and of the Damascus Hall (18th century A.D.); houses the Directorate-General of Antiquities and Museums, established by decree in 1947 to conserve Syrian antiquities and to supervise the archaeological museums and the excavations; Dir-Gen. of Antiquities and Museums Prof. Dr SULTAN MUHESEN; publ. *Les Annales Archéologiques Arabes Syriennes*.

Popular Traditions Museum Qasrelazem: Bzourieh St, Damascus; tel. 226160; f. 1954; traditions and crafts; library of 3,000 vols; Curator HASSAN KAMAL.

Deir ez-Zor

Deir ez-Zor Museum: Deir ez-Zor; f. 1974; archaeology; library of 1,000 vols; Dir ASSAD MAHMOUD; publ. *Les Annales Archéologiques de Syrie*.

Hama

Hama Museum: Hama; f. 1956; history and folklore.

Homs

Homs Museum: Homs dar Al-Thakafa; f. 1974; archaeology, folk and modern art; Curator MAJED EL-MOUSSLI.

Palmyra

Palmyra National Museum: Palmyra; f. 1961; archaeological finds from pre-history to 16th century; attached is the museum of Syrian desert folklore, traditional handcraft industry and agriculture; Dir KHALED AL-AS'AD.

Sweida

Sweida Museum: Sweida.

Tartos

Tartos Museum: Tartos; Islamic history.

Universities

AL-BAATH UNIVERSITY

POB 77, Homs

Telephone: 431440
Telex: 441133
Fax: 426716

Founded 1979
State control
Language of instruction: Arabic
Academic year begins September

President: Dr ABDUL MAJID SHEIKH HUSSEIN
Vice-President: Dr MOHAMMED EL-ISA
Administrative Officer: KASSEM HAMMOUD
Librarian: LINA MAASRANI

Library of 63,000 vols
Number of teachers: 505
Number of students: 16,274

DEANS

Faculty of Chemical and Petroleum Engineering: Dr MAHER SAADEH
Faculty of Veterinary Science (in Hama): Dr TAMER HADDAD
Faculty of Sciences: Dr YASSIN KHALLOUF
Faculty of Literature: Dr SARMI MANSOUR
Faculty of Civil Engineering and Architecture: Dr TAMER AL-HAJI (Civil Engineering), Dr HOUSAM BARAKAT (Architecture)
Faculty of Dentistry: MOUHAMED SABEH ARAB
Faculty of Agriculture: Dr ABDULA AL-ISA
Faculty of Medicine: Dr ABDUL KARIM AYYUP
Faculty of Mechanical and Electrical Engineering: Dr NADEEM SLAIMAN
Intermediate Institute of Engineering: Dr WALID IBRAHIM
Intermediate Institute of Industry: Dr HASSAN FARAH
Intermediate Institute of Veterinary Medicine: Dr IBRAHIM HAJO

UNIVERSITY OF ALEPPO

Aleppo

Telephone: (21) 236130
Telex: 331018
Fax: (21) 229184

Founded 1960
State control
Languages of instruction: Arabic, French and English
Academic year: September to June

Rector: Dr MOHAMMAD ALI HOURIEH
Vice-Rectors: Dr TAJEDDIN DIA (Academic Affairs), Dr MAHMOUD KARROUM (Administrative and Student Affairs)
Chief Administrator and Secretary: MOHAMMAD WATTAR
Registrar: MAHMUD ELWANI
Librarian: MUSTAFA JASSOUMEH

Number of teachers: 3,377
Number of students: 53,465

Publications: *Journal for the History of Arabic Science, Newsletter of the Institute for the History of Arabic Science, Research Journal of Aleppo University (comprises the following series: Arts and Humanities; Medical Sciences; Agricultural Sciences; Basic Sciences; Engineering Sciences; Adiyat Halab).*

DEANS

Faculty of Civil Engineering: Dr SAMEH JAZMATI
Faculty of Electrical and Electronic Engineering: Dr MISHEL HALLAK
Faculty of Mechanical Engineering: Dr SALMAN SAGHBINI
Faculty of Architectural Engineering: Dr ABDUL GHANI AL-SHEHABI
Faculty of Agriculture: Dr JEMMA IBRAHIM
Second Faculty of Agriculture: Dr MUHIEDDEEN QARAWANI
Faculty of Arts and Humanities: Dr MOUSTAFA JATAL
Faculty of Medicine: Dr MOUNZER BARAKAT
Faculty of Sciences: Dr NASSUH ALAYA
Faculty of Economics: Dr AHMAD ASHKAR
Faculty of Dentistry: Dr MOHAMMAD IKBAL MUSHREF
Faculty of Law: Dr KHALED AL-HAMOUD
Faculty of Pharmacy: Dr SAMEER SA'AD

HEADS OF DEPARTMENTS

Faculty of Civil Engineering:

Principal Sciences: Dr N. NABGHALI
Engineering Management and Construction: Dr M. HINDIEH
Geotechnical Engineering: Dr MARWAN HAMZEH
Communications and Transport: M. SATEH AL-HUSARI
Hydraulic Engineering: M. NIZAR KAZAN
Topographical Engineering: MICHAEL ASWAD
Environmental Engineering: Dr AMJAD MURAD AGHA
Structural Engineering: Dr A. KATKHUDA

Faculty of Mechanical Engineering:

Agricultural Machines: I. DAMERJI
Applied Mechanics: Dr G. SALLUM
Mechanical Power: Dr YASER HAYANI
Principal Sciences: A. NADIM AKKAD
Production Engineering: Dr H. ABU SALEH

Faculty of Architectural Engineering:

Architectural Design: Dr GEORGE TUMA
Environment and Planning: Dr FATINA KURDI
Construction and Implementation: A. AL-DAKAR
History and Theories of Architecture: Dr JAMAL MUSELMANI

Faculty of Electrical and Electronic Engineering:

Electrical Power Systems: M. SHAABAN
Principal Sciences: Dr DALAR BAYA'A
Communication Engineering: W. HABBAL
Information Engineering: Dr FADI FOWZ
Machinery and Electrical Conducting: ABDUL KARIM MANOUK
Mechanical Control and Electronics: Dr M. SAID AKIL
Electronic Engineering: M. G. TURMANINI

Faculty of Agriculture:

Field Products: A. HAITHAM MUSHANTAT
Plant Protection: Dr A. AMER Hadj KASEM
Animal Production: F. AL-YASIN
Rural Engineering: S. BARBARA
Nutritional Sciences: Dr A. ZIAD KEYALI
Soils: Dr ZUHAIR ABBASI
Economic and Agricultural Instruction: M. SAID FUTAYEH
Forestry: M. NABEEL SHALABI
Basic Sciences: Dr WALID ASWAD
Horticulture: Dr H. AL-WARA'

Second Faculty of Agriculture:

Animal Production: Dr ALI AL-ALI
Economy and Agricultural Instruction: Dr FAROUK BAKDASH
Field Products: Dr AHMED EL-FARHAN
Nutritional Science: Dr ABOUD EL-SALEH
Pasture and Field Products: Dr ZIAD AL-HOUSSEIN
Plant Protection: Dr ISAM AL-MUGHIR
Rural Engineering: Dr ZIB IBRAHIM
Soil and Soil Reclamation: Dr A. AL-IBRAHIM
Forestry and Ecology: Dr A. AL-JUM'A AL-DAKHIL

Faculty of Medicine:

Dermatology: Dr H. BALABAN
Paediatrics: A. MATTAR
General Surgery: A. DAWLI
Gynaecology and Obstetrics: B. NASIF
Cerebral Diseases: S. AL-SAYED
Internal Medicine: R. ASFARI
Biochemistry: A. KARAZEH
Anaesthesiology and Resuscitation: M. TAHA AL-JASER
Anatomy: Dr A. ZAIDEH
Pathology: Dr B. BAZERBASHI

Faculty of Sciences:

Physics: RIAD AL-RASHIH
Chemistry: S. AL-KADRI
Plant Physiology: Dr A. KASHLAN
Mathematics: Dr M. KHER AHMAD
Geology: A. FUAD IBRAHIM BASHA
Animal Physiology: M. ADEL HAKIM

Faculty of Economics:

Business Administration: Dr M. KHARSHUM
Economics and Planning: Dr J. BASH AGHA
Statistics: Dr A. RAFIK KASEM
Accounting: Dr M. DABBAGHIYEH

Faculty of Arts and Humanities:

Arabic Literature: Dr S. KAZZARA
English Literature: Dr A. Y. KOTOB
French Literature: Dr N. ISMAEL
Education and Psychology: Dr H. ABU HAMMUD

ATTACHED INSTITUTES

Agricultural Research Centre: Meselmieh, Aleppo.

Institute for the History of Arabic Science: Dir Dr KHALED MAGOUT.

Intermediate Institute for Agriculture: Dir Dr MUSTAFA AL-JADDER.

Intermediate Institute for Commerce: Dir Dr A. RAHMAN AL-OBEID.

Intermediate Institute for Engineering: Dir Dr N. SHEHADEH.

Intermediate Institute for Mechanical and Electrical Engineering: Dir Dr A. NAHHAS.

Intermediate Institute for Medicine: Dir Dr Y. KHANJI.

Intermediate Institute for Dentistry: Dir Dr ADEL AJAM.

Intermediate Institute for Secretariat: Dir Dr H. IBRAHIM.

School of Nursing: Dir Dr B. NASSIF.

UNIVERSITY OF DAMASCUS

Damascus
Telephone: 215100
Telex: 411971

Founded 1903
State control
Language of instruction: Arabic
Academic year: September to June

President: Prof. Dr ABDUL GHANI MAA BARED
Vice-Presidents: Dr MWAFFAQ SAYYED HASSAN (Academic), Dr FEISAL DAYYOUB (Administrative)
Secretary General: FAYEZ TUBAJI
Registrar: AHMAD AL-SHAM'A
Librarian: Dr THABET JARI

Number of teachers: 2,609
Number of students: 81,175

Publications: *Aljami'a Journal, Historical Studies Journal, Statistical Collections, Damascus University Bulletin.*

DEANS

Faculty of Agriculture: Prof. MAHMOUD YASSEEN
Faculty of Architecture: Prof. M. TALAL UQEILI
Faculty of Dentistry: Prof. Dr M. ADNAN MASSASATI
Faculty of Civil Engineering: Prof. MAHMOUD WARDEH
Faculty of Economics: Prof. SAFI FALLOUH
Faculty of Education: Prof. MAHMOUD AL-SAYYED
Faculty of Fine Arts: Prof. KHALED ALMAZ
Faculty of Islamic Studies: Prof. M. FAROUQ AL-AKKAM
Faculty of Law: Prof. M. AZIZ SHOKRI
Faculty of Letters: Prof. HAMED KHALIL
Faculty of Mechanical and Electrical Engineering: Dr N. MOKHEIBER
Faculty of Medicine: Prof. Dr M. ADNAN SOUMAN
Faculty of Pharmacy: Prof. M. NABIL SHARIF
Faculty of Science: Prof. GHADIR ZAYZAFOON

ATTACHED INSTITUTES

Intermediate Institute of Agriculture: Dir Dr AKRAM KHOURI.

Intermediate Institute of Commerce: Dir Dr M. JAMIL OMAR.

Intermediate Institute of Dentistry: Dir Dr FOU'AD MALQO.

Intermediate Institute of Engineering: Dir Dr FAROUQ AL-'ADILI.

Intermediate Institute of Industry: Dir Dr ALI ISSA (acting).

Medical Intermediate Institute: Dir Dr M. SA'D EDDEEN ZEITOUN.

Secretarial Intermediate Institute: Dir Dr TAREQ AL-KHAYYER.

Nursing School: Dir Dr HEYYAM AL RAYYES.

Institute of Computers: Dir Dr NIZAR AL-HELOU.

TISHREEN UNIVERSITY (University of October)

Lattakia

Telephone: 36311

Founded 1971 as University of Latakia
Language of instruction: Arabic
Academic year: September to June

President: Prof. Dr Eng. KHALED HALLAJE
Vice-President for Academic Affairs: Dr HASSAN ISMAIL
Vice-President for Students and Administrative Affairs: Dr SOULEIMAN AL-KHODER

Secretary: Miss NAJAT OSMAN
Librarian: ADIB KHOURY

Number of teachers: 214
Number of students: 18,130

DEANS

Faculty of Science: Dr MOUHAMMAD AL-HOSHI
Faculty of Agriculture: Dr AHMAD JALLOUL
Faculty of Arts: Dr NAJIB GHAZAWI
Faculty of Civil Engineering: Dr GEORGE DAGHER
Faculty of Medicine: Dr ZOOHER HALLAJE
Faculty of Electrical and Mechanical Engineering: Dr ABEDALLA SAID
Faculty of Dentistry: Dr HASSAN NASER ED-DINE
Faculty of Architecture: Dr NUHAD ABDALLA
Faculty of Economics: Dr IBRAHIM AL-ALI

Colleges

Aleppo Institute of Music: Aleppo; f. 1955; departments of Eastern and Western music.

Higher Institute of Applied Sciences and Technology: POB 31983, Barzeh, Damascus; tel. (11) 5124639; fax (11) 2237710; awards BSc, MSc, PhD; depts of Informatics, Systems Engineering, Mathematics, Physics, Electronics, Management; Dir Prof. Dr DUREID AZZOUZ.

Institute of Electrical Engineering and Electronics: Damascus; f. 1974 with aid from Germany.

Institute of Technical Training: Damascus; f. 1978 with aid from Germany; 2-year courses.

TAJIKISTAN

Learned Societies

GENERAL

Tajik Academy of Sciences: 734025 Dushanbe, Pr. Rudaki 33; tel. (3772) 22-50-83; fax (3772) 23-49-17; f. 1951; depts of Physical-Mathematical, Chemical and Technical Sciences (Chair. D. N. PACHADZANOV, Scientific Sec. K. H. AKHMEDOV), Earth Sciences (Chair. M. R. DZHALILOV, Scientific Sec. R. I. KOSTOVA), Biological and Medical Sciences (Chair. K. K. MANSUROV, Scientific Sec. A. G. KOLTUNOVA), Social Sciences (Chair. T. N. NAZAROV, Scientific Sec. T. A. BAIMATOVA); 26 mems, 43 corresp. mems; attached research institutes: see Research Institutes; library: see Libraries and Archives; Pres. S. K. NEGMATULLAEV; Chief Academic Sec. G. H. SALIBAEV; publs *Doklady* (Reports), *Problemy gastroenterologii, Izvestiya* (bulletins: Physical-Engineering and Geological Sciences, Biological Sciences, History and Philology, Philosophy, Economics and Law).

Research Institutes

GENERAL

Khudzhand Scientific Centre: Khudzhand; tel. 5-12-78; attached to Tajik Acad. of Sciences; Chair. M. R. DZHALILOV; Scientific Sec. M. SUBKHONOV.

Pamir Research Station: 736000 Khorog, Gorno-Badakhshan Autonomous Region; attached to Tajik Acad. of Sciences; Chair. U. KH. KHOLDOROV.

ARCHITECTURE AND TOWN PLANNING

Institute of Seismic Resistant Construction and Seismology: 734029 Dushanbe, Ul. Aini 121; tel. 25-06-69; attached to Tajik Acad. of Sciences; Dir S. K. NEGMATULLAEV.

BIBLIOGRAPHY, LIBRARY SCIENCE AND MUSEOLOGY

Institute of Manuscripts: 734025 Dushanbe, Kirov 35; tel. 27-34-04; attached to Tajik Acad. of Sciences; Dir D. NAZRIEV.

ECONOMICS, LAW AND POLITICS

Institute of Philosophy and Law: 734025 Dushanbe, Pr. Rudaki 33; tel. 22-67-21; attached to Tajik Acad. of Sciences; Dir M. DINORSHOEV.

Institute of World Economics and International Relations: 734000 Dushanbe, Ul. Aini 44; tel. 23-27-32; attached to Tajik Acad. of Sciences; Dir R. K. RAKHIMOV.

HISTORY, GEOGRAPHY AND ARCHAEOLOGY

Donish Institute of History, Archaeology and Ethnography: 734025 Dushanbe, Pr. Rudaki 33; tel. 22-37-42; attached to Tajik Acad. of Sciences; Dir R. M. MASOV.

LANGUAGE AND LITERATURE

Rudaki Institute of Language and Literature: 734025 Dushanbe, Pr. Rudaki 21; tel. 22-37-73; attached to Tajik Acad. of Sciences; Dir A. M. MANIYAZOV.

MEDICINE

Institute of Gastroenterology: 734002 Dushanbe, Parvin 12; tel. (3772) 24-81-47; fax (3772) 23-49-17; e-mail mansurov@academy.td.silk.org; f.1959; attached to Tajik Acad. of Sciences; library of 5,000 vols; Dir H. H. MANSUROV; publ. *Problems of Gastroenterology* (4 a year).

NATURAL SCIENCES

Biological Sciences

Institute of Botany: 734017 Dushanbe, Ul. Karamova 27; tel. 24-43-57; attached to Tajik Acad. of Sciences; Dir U. I. ISMOILOV.

Institute of Plant Physiology and Biophysics: 734063 Dushanbe, Ul. Aini 299/2; tel. (3772) 23-36-09; fax (3772) 24-45-05; e-mail akotibbm@academy.td.silk.org; f. 1964; attached to Tajik Acad. of Sciences; Dir Prof. KHURSHED KARIMOV.

Pavlovskii, E.N., Institute of Zoology and Parasitology: 734025 Dushanbe, Post Office 70; tel. 27-66-41; attached to Tajik Acad. of Sciences; Dir A. K. GAFUROV.

Mathematical Sciences

Institute of Mathematics and Computer Centre: 734063 Dushanbe, Akademgorodok; tel. 25-16-00; attached to Tajik Acad. of Sciences; Dir Z. D. USMANOV.

Physical Sciences

Institute of Astrophysics: 734670 Dushanbe, Ul. Sviridenko 22; tel. 22-59-73; attached to Tajik Acad. of Sciences; Dir P. B. BABADZHANOV.

Institute of Geology: 734063 Dushanbe, Akademgorodok; tel. 25-30-59; attached to Tajik Acad. of Sciences; Dir M. R. DZHALILOV.

Nikitin, V. I., Institute of Chemistry: 734063 Dushanbe, Akademgorodok; tel. 25-10-87; attached to Tajik Acad. of Sciences; Dir U. M. MIRSAIDOV.

RELIGION, SOCIOLOGY AND ANTHROPOLOGY

Institute of Humanities: Khorog, Lenin 33; tel. 43-28; attached to Tajik Acad. of Sciences; Dir H. DODKHUDOEV.

TECHNOLOGY

Umarov, S.U., Physical-Engineering Institute: 734063 Dushanbe, Akademgorodok; tel. 25-11-65; attached to Tajik Acad. of Sciences; Dir R. M. MARUPOV.

Libraries and Archives

Dushanbe

Central Scientific Library of the Tajik Academy of Sciences: 734025 Dushanbe, Pr. Rudaki 33; tel. (3772) 22-42-24; f. 1933; 1,500,000 vols; Dir Dr A. A. ASLITDINOVA.

Firdousi State Public Library of Tajikistan: 734025 Dushanbe, Pr. Rudaki 36; tel. 27-47-26; 2,995,000 vols; Dir S. MUKHIDDINOV.

Republican Scientific and Technical Library of Tajikistan: 734042 Dushanbe, Ul. Aini 14A; tel. (3772) 27-58-77; fax (3772) 21-71-54; f. 1965; 13,000,000 vols (incl. 11,000,000 patents); Dir K. I. ISMAILOV.

Tajik State University Library: 734016 Dushanbe, Pr. Rudaki 17; tel. 23-39-81; f. 1948; 1,039,000 vols; Dir RUSTAM YARBABAEV; publ. *Vestnik* (annually).

Museums and Art Galleries

Dushanbe

Tajik Historical State Museum: 734012 Dushanbe, Ul. Aini 31; tel. 23-15-44; history, culture, art; library of 14,000 vols; Dir M. MAKHMUDOV.

University

TAJIK STATE UNIVERSITY

734025 Dushanbe, Pr. Rudaki 17

Telephone: 22-77-11

Founded 1948

Languages of instruction: Tajik and Russian

Academic year: September to July

Rector: Prof. F. T. TAKHIROV

Vice-Rectors: A. A. AMINJANOV (Scientific), Prof. KH. M. SAFAROV (Educational), N. N. JUMAEV (International Relations and Courses)

Librarian: R. I. YARBABAEV

Number of teachers: 864

Number of students: 6,196 (full-time), 1,467 (evening) 3,811 (extra-mural)

DEANS

Faculty of Mechanics and Mathematics: Dr H. M. MALIKOV
Faculty of Physics: Prof. F. H. KHAKIMOV
Faculty of Chemistry: Dr Z. N. YUSUPOV
Faculty of Geology: Prof. A. R. FAIZIEV
Faculty of Biology: Prof. B. G. GAFUROV
Faculty of History: Dr N. M. MIRZOEV
Faculty of Tajik Philology: Dr H. SH. SHARIPOV
Faculty of Oriental Languages: S. SH. SHUKROEVA
Faculty of Russian Language and Literature: Dr V.S. USHAKOVSKY
Faculty of Law: M. A. MAKHMUDOV
Faculty of Commerce and Management: Prof. G. B. BOBOSADIKOVA
Faculty of Finance and Credit: Prof. B. I. ISOMATOV
Chair of English Language: Dr A. KH. MAMADNAZAROV
Faculty of Accounting: D. U. UROKOV

Other Higher Educational Institutes

Tajik Abu-Ali Ibn-Cina (Avicenna) State Medical Institute: 734003 Dushanbe, Pr. Rudaki 139; tel. 24-12-53; f. 1939; library of 128,000 vols; Rector Prog. Acad. K. T. TADZHIEV.

Tajik Agricultural University: 734017 Dushanbe, Pr. Rudaki 146; tel. 24-72-07; f. 1931; depts: agrochemistry and soil science, agronomy, fruit and vegetable growing, plant protection, veterinary, animal husbandry, mechanization, electrification and automation, irrigation and land reclamation, economics and management, accounting, extramural and qualification improvement faculties; 482 teachers; 6,960 students; library of 400,000 vols; Rector Acad. Prof. Yu. S. Nasyrov.

Tajik Technical University: 734042 Dushanbe, Pr. Acad. Rajabovs 10; tel. 21-35-11; fax 21-71-35; e-mail chief@tecuni2.td.silk.glas.org; f. 1956; faculties: Power Engineering, Mechanical Technology, Chemical Technology and Metallurgy, Transport and Road Engineering, Construction and Architecture, Engineering Business and Management; 8,000 students; Rector Prof. Khisrav R. Sadykov.

Tajik State Institute of Fine Arts: 734032 Dushanbe, Ul. Borbada 73A; tel. 31-18-21; piano, orchestral instruments, folk instruments, singing, choral conducting, musicology, dancing, theatre and cinema acting.

TANZANIA

Learned Societies

GENERAL

Tanzania Society: Box 511, Dar es Salaam; f. 1936; a non-profit society catering for the geographical, ethnological, historical, and general scientific interests of Tanzania; *c.* 1,200 mems; publ. *Tanzania Notes and Records* (annually).

AGRICULTURE, FISHERIES AND VETERINARY SCIENCE

Tanzania Veterinary Association: POB 3174, Morogoro; tel. (56) 4979; telex 53308; fax (56) 3177; f. 1968; 350 mems; Chair. Prof. U. M. MINGA; Sec. Dr A. PEREKA; publs *Tanzania Veterinary Journal, Annual Proceedings of the Tanzania Veterinary Association Scientific Conferences*.

BIBLIOGRAPHY, LIBRARY SCIENCE AND MUSEOLOGY

Tanzania Library Association: POB 2645, Dar es Salaam; f. 1965 as a branch of the East African Library Association, reorganized 1972 as an independent body; 200 mems; Chair. T. E. MLAKI; Sec. Miss M. NGAIZA; publs *Someni* (2 a year), *Matukio* (Newsletter, irregular).

HISTORY, GEOGRAPHY AND ARCHAEOLOGY

Historical Association of Tanzania: POB 35050, Dar es Salaam; f. 1966; 2,000 mems; Chair. Prof. I. N. KIMAMBO; Sec. M. L. SAGO; publ. *Tanzania Zamani*, seasonal pamphlets.

Research Institutes

GENERAL

Tanzania Commission for Science and Technology: POB 4302, Dar es Salaam; tel. 75311; f. 1968; advises the government on science and technology policy and on all matters pertaining to the development of science and technology and their application to socio-economic development in the country; executive functions: co-ordinates all research in the country, promotes documentation and dissemination of information on science and technology and scientific research, collaborates with other research organizations; 60 mems; library of 8,000 vols; Chair. Hon. BEN W. MKAPA; Dir.-Gen. Dr Y. M. KOHI: publ. *Tanzania Science and Technology Newsletter* (quarterly).

AGRICULTURE, FISHERIES AND VETERINARY SCIENCE

Agricultural Research Institute (Mlingano): Ministry of Agriculture, Livestock Development and Co-operatives, Private Bag, Ngomeni, Tanga; telex 45030; fax (53) 46168; f. 1934; research on cultivation of sisal and other crops, soils, resourcing of efficient farming methods, horticulture; germplasm collection of tropical and subtropical fruits, spices and essential oils; Dir Dr K. L. HAULE.

Forest Division Headquarters: POB 426, Dar es Salaam; forest surveying, mapping, industrial development, economics, management and education; library of 2,500 vols; Dir E. M. MNZAVA.

Livestock Production Research Institute: POB 202, Mpwapwa, Dodoma; tel. 21; fax (61) 24526; f. 1905; research in dairy science, breeding and nutrition of livestock, pasture agronomy and multidisciplinary research; library of 4,000 vols, 40 periodicals; Dir Dr J. K. K. MSECHU; publs *Progressive Stockman* (quarterly), *Annual Research Report*.

Tanzania Forestry Research Institute: Silviculture Research Centre, POB 95, Lushoto; f. 1951; library of 3,000 vols; Officer-in-Charge T. H. MSANGI; publs *Technical Notes, Tanzania Silviculture Research Notes* (4 a year), *TAFORI Newsletter*.

Tropical Pesticides Research Institute: POB 3024, Arusha; tel. (57) 8813; telex 42002; fax (57) 8217; f. 1962; research into all aspects of pesticide application and behaviour; library of 5,000 vols; Dir Dr F. W. MOSHA; publ. *Annual Report*.

HISTORY, GEOGRAPHY AND ARCHAEOLOGY

Ministry of Energy and Minerals: POB 903, Dodoma; tel. (61) 24945; fax (61) 24943; e-mail mrd@twiga.com; f. 1925; regional mapping, mineral exploration and assessment; supporting laboratory facilities; library of 4,000 books, 2,100 bound vols; reprints and maps; publs *Bulletins, Memoirs, Annual Reports, Records of the Geological Survey of Tanzania, Reprints,* geological maps.

LANGUAGE AND LITERATURE

Eastern African Centre for Research on Oral Traditions and African National Languages (EACROTANAL): POB 600, Zanzibar; tel. 30786; f. 1979 as a regional and intergovernmental organization to encourage research and develop means of collection, analysis, conservation and diffusion of oral traditions and promotion of national languages; provides short-term training courses on these subjects; library of 3,000 vols (incl. 148 old Arabic MSS from Zanzibar); one of 3 African regional centres, set up by Burundi, Comoros, Ethiopia, Madagascar, Mauritius, Mozambique, Somalia, Sudan, Tanzania; Exec. Dir HENRI RAHAINGOSON; publs *EACROTANAL Information, Studies and Documents*, collection series, annotated bibliography of the Arabic MSS.

Institute of Kiswahili Research: POB 35110, Dar es Salaam; tel. 410757; telex 410327; f. 1970; initiates and conducts fundamental research in all aspects of Kiswahili language; co-operates with local public authorities and int. organizations; promotes the standardization of orthography and the development of language generally; preparing new standard dictionary, technical dictionaries, grammars, monographs on oral literature; research library of 3,000 vols; Dir Prof. S. A. K. MLACHA; publs *Kiswahili, Mulika* (annually), Supplements.

MEDICINE

National Institute for Medical Research, Amani Centre: POB 4, Amani, Tanga; f. 1949 (fmrly East African Institute of Malaria and Vector-borne diseases); investigation into human vector-borne diseases, especially malaria, bancroftian filariasis, and onchocerciasis; Dir Dr S. G. M. IRARE; publs *Annual reports, research papers*.

National Institute for Medical Research, Mwanza Centre: POB 1462, Mwanza; tel. 50189; f. 1949; investigations into various tropical diseases with emphasis on bilharziasis, and other soil-transmitted helminths, bacterial diseases, sanitation and water, diarrhoeal diseases, sexually transmitted diseases, HIV/AIDS; library of 2,300 vols; Dir Dr R. M. GABONE; publs *Annual Report, Proceedings of the Annual NIMR Joint Scientific Conference, NIMR Bulletin*.

Libraries and Archives

Dar es Salaam

National Archives: India/Chusi St, POB 2006, Dar es Salaam; f. 1963; German and British Colonial archives, post-independence archives; Chief Archivist JOSEPH KARUGILA; publs *Annual Report, Guide to Archives*.

Tanzania Information Services Library: POB 9142, Dar es Salaam; e-mail maelezo@raha.com; reference books on Tanzania, journalism, photography, social sciences, geography and history; newspapers and periodicals.

Tanzania Library Services Board: Bibi Titi Mohamed Rd, POB 9283, Dar es Salaam; tel. 150048; 16 brs; Dir-Gen. ELIEZER A. MWINYIMVUA.

University of Dar es Salaam Library: POB 35092, Dar es Salaam; tel. and fax (51) 410241; e-mail libdirec@udsm.ac.tz; f. 1961; legal deposit library; 600,000 vols; special collections: East Africana Collection, UN Collection, Law Collection; 8,000 periodicals; Dir Prof. J. NAWE.

Mwanza

Ladha Maghji Indian Public Library: POB 70, Mwanza; tel. 500482; f. 1935; 6,000 vols; runs English, French and oriental languages classes; Librarian RAMAN DESAI.

Zanzibar

Agricultural Department Library: POB 159, Zanzibar; agriculture in general; 1,100 vols, 50 periodicals.

Museum Library: POB 116, Zanzibar; free public lending service; 3,000 vols and 41 periodicals.

Zanzibar National Archives: POB 116, Zanzibar; tel. 30342; f. 1956; history and administration; 3,500 vols; Archivist HAMAD OMAR.

Museums and Art Galleries

Dar es Salaam

National Museums of Tanzania: POB 511, Dar es Salaam; f. 1937 as King George V Memorial Museum, name changed 1963; ethnography, palaeoanthropology, history and marine biology; houses the *Zinjanthropus* skull and other material from Olduvai Gorge and other Palaeolithic sites; also houses reference library; Dir M. L. MBAGO; publs *Annual Report*, occasional papers.

Branch museums:

Arusha Declaration Museum: POB 7423, Arusha; political photographs and MSS.

Arusha Natural History Museum: POB 2160, Arusha.

Village Museum: POB 511, Dar es Salaam; traditional house styles and crafts.

Zanzibar

Zanzibar Government Museum: POB 116, Zanzibar; local collection, items relating to exploration in East Africa; library; Archivist and Curator SAIS HILAL EL-BAULY.

Universities

OPEN UNIVERSITY OF TANZANIA

POB 9123, Dar es Salaam

Telephone: (51) 668445
Fax: (51) 668759

Founded 1992
State control
Languages of Instruction: English, Kiswahili
Academic year: January to December

Chancellor: Dr JOHN SAMWEL MALECELA
Vice-Chancellor: Prof. G. R. V. MMARI
Deputy Vice-Chancellor: Prof. ABDU M. KHAMISI
Registrar: Dr EGINO M. CHALE
Librarian: A. S. SAMZUGI

Library of 5,000 vols
Number of teachers: 33 full-time, 80 part-time
Number of students: 3,811

Publication: *HURIA Journal*.

DEANS

Faculty of Arts and Social Sciences: S. S. KAPALATU
Faculty of Education: SYDNEY MKUCHU (acting)
Faculty of Science, Technology and Environmental Studies: Dr J. R. MHOMA
Faculty of Law: Dr M. C. MUKOYOGO

SOKOINE UNIVERSITY OF AGRICULTURE

POB 3000, Chuo Kikuu, Morogoro

Telephone: (56) 3511
Telex: 55308
Fax: (56) 4088
E-mail: sua@hnettan.gn.apc.org;

Founded 1984, previously a faculty of University of Dar es Salaam
State control
Language of instruction: English
Academic year: September to June

Chancellor: AL NOOR KASSUM
Vice-Chancellor: Prof. A. B. LWOGA
Deputy Vice-Chancellor: Prof. P. M. MSOLLA
Registrar: S. P. MKOBA
Librarian: A. M. CHAILLA

Library of 100,000 vols, 150 current periodicals
Number of teachers: 218
Number of students: 1,253

Publications: *Annual Record of Research*, *Annual Report*, Prospectus, *SUA Convocation Newsletter* (1 a year), *Library Accessions Bulletin* (monthly), etc.

DEANS

Faculty of Agriculture: Dr N. HATIBU
Faculty of Forestry: Prof. R. C. ISHENGOMA
Faculty of Veterinary Medicine: Prof. R. D. MOSHA

HEADS OF DEPARTMENT

Faculty of Agriculture:

Agricultural Education and Extension: Dr D. F. RUTATORA
Agricultural Engineering and Land Planning: Dr N. I. KIHUPI
Animal Science and Production: Prof. N. A. URIO
Crop Science and Production: Dr S. O. W. REUBEN
Food Science and Technology: Dr A. B. GIDAMIS
Agricultural Economics and Agribusiness: Prof. M. E. MLAMBITI
Soil Science: Dr J. P. MREMA

Faculty of Forestry:

Forest Biology: Dr S. M. S. MALIONDO
Forest Engineering: Assoc. Prof. R. E. L. OLE-MEILUDIE
Forest Economics: Dr G. MONELA
Forest Mensuration and Management Planning: Assoc. Prof. R. E. MALIMBWI
Wood Utilization: Dr F. K. S. HAMZA

Faculty of Veterinary Medicine:

Veterinary Anatomy: Dr R. J. ASSEY
Veterinary Medicine and Public Health: Assoc. Prof. D. M. KAMBARAGE
Veterinary Microbiology and Parasitology: Prof. A. A. KASSUKU
Veterinary Pathology: Assoc. Prof. J. A. MATOVELO
Veterinary Physiology, Biochemistry, Pharmacology and Toxicology: Dr A. E. PEREKA
Veterinary Surgery, Obstetrics and Reproduction: Prof. M. N. MGASSA

ATTACHED INSTITUTES

Institute of Continuing Education: Dir Dr R. M. WAMBURA.
Development Studies Institute: Dir Dr B. J. KASIMILA.
Research and Postgraduate Studies: Prof. L. D. B. KINABO.

UNIVERSITY OF DAR ES SALAAM

POB 35091, Dar es Salaam

Telephone: 410500
Telex: 41561
Fax: 43078

Founded 1961
University status 1970; Unesco-aided
Language of instruction: English
Academic year: October to June (four terms)

Chancellor: Ambassador P. BOMANI
Vice-Chancellor: Prof. M. L. LUHANGA
Chief Academic Officer: Prof. P. O. MLAMA
Chief Administrative Officer: Prof. D. J. MKUDE

Library: see Libraries
Number of teachers: 902
Number of students: 3,901

Publications: *Calendar, Prospectus, Research Bulletin, Annual Report.*

DEANS

Faculty of Law: Assoc. Dr S. E. A. MVUNGI
Faculty of Arts and Social Sciences: Prof. R. S. MUKANDALA
Faculty of Science: Prof. M. H. H. NKUNYA
Faculty of Medicine: Prof. F. S. MHALU
Faculty of Engineering: Prof. J. R. MASUHA
Faculty of Commerce and Management: Prof. L. H. K. RUTASHOBYA

PROFESSORS

BAREGU, M., Political Science and Public Administration
BESHA, R. M., Kiswahili
HOWELL, K. M., Zoology
ISHUMI, A. G., Education
KAMUZORA, C. L., Statistics
KAUZENI, A. S., Institute of Resource Assessment
KAYUMBO, H. Y., Zoology and Marine Biology
KHAMISI, A. M., Institute of Kiswahili Research
KIMAMBO, I. N., History
KLAASEN, G., Mathematics
KWEKA, A., Development Studies
LIHAMBA, A., Fine and Performing Arts
MAHALU, C. R., International Law
MASCARENHAS, O. C., Library Studies
MASENGE, R. W. P., Mathematics
MASUHA, J. R., Mechanical Engineering
MBILINYI, Mrs M. J., Institute of Development Studies
MBUNDA, F. L., Curriculum and Teaching
MGOMBELO, H. R., Electrical Engineering
MHALU, F. S., Microbiology and Immunology
MLAMA, P. O., Fine and Performing Arts
MLAWA, H., Development Studies
MOSHA, H. J., Educational Administration
MSAMBICHAKA, L. A., Economic Research Bureau
MSHANA, J. S., Mechanical Engineering
MSHIGENI, K. E., Botany
MSHIMBA, A. S. A., Mathematics
MULOKOZI, A. M., Chemistry
MUSHI, S. S., Political Science and Public Administration
MWANDOSYA, M. J., Electrical Engineering
NJAU, E. C., Physics
NKONOKI, S. R., Institute of Development Studies
OMARI, C. K., Sociology
OMARI, I. M., Educational Research and Evaluation
OTHMAN, H., Institute of Development Studies
RWEZAURA, B. A., Constitutional and Administrative Law
SANGAWE, J. L. F., Ophthalmology
SEMESI, A. K., Botany
SHIJA, J. K., Surgery
SHIVJI, I. G., Legal Theory
SOKOL, W., Chemical and Process Engineering
STALLMAN, R. K., Physical Education, Sport and Culture

ATTACHED INSTITUTES

Institute of Development Studies: POB 35169, Dar es Salaam; Dir Prof. I. F. SHAO.

Institute of Kiswahili Research: see Research Institutes.

Institute of Marine Sciences: POB 668, Zanzibar; f. 1950 as East African Marine Fisheries Research Organization; postgraduate studies and research; Dir Dr J. FRANCIS.

Institute of Resource Assessment: POB 35097, Dar es Salaam; Dir Dr E. K. SHISHIRA.

Institute of Production Innovation: POB 35075, Dar es Salaam; Dir Dr O. KAUNDE.

Colleges

College of African Wildlife Management, Mweka: POB 3031, Moshi; tel. Kibosho 18; f. 1963; library of 10,000 vols; 14 teachers, 140 students; Principal Dr D. N. MANYANZA; publ. *Newsletter*.

College of Business Education: POB 1968, Dar es Salaam; tel. 31056; f. 1965; 55 teachers; 1,300 students; two- and three-year diploma courses in business administration and metrology; Principal G. A. M. CHALE.

Co-operative College: POB 474, Sokoine Rd, Moshi; tel. 54401; fax 50806; e-mail iswcl@form.net.com; f. 1963; 70 teachers; 600 students; library of 29,000 vols; special collection: Women's Documentation Centre on co-operatives and development; Principal S. A. CHAMBO; publ. *Tushirikiane Journal* (quarterly).

Dar es Salaam Technical College: Private Bag 2958, Dar es Salaam; tel. 23406; f. 1957;

civil, mechanical, electrical, electronics and telecommunications engineering courses; 110 staff; 865 full-time students; library of 17,000 vols; Principal S. H. MSOMA.

Eastern and Southern African Management Institute: POB 3030, Arusha; tel. 8383; telex 42076; fax 8285; e-mail esamihq@yako.habar.co.tz; f. 1974, reconstituted 1980; field offices in Kenya, Malawi, Mozambique, Namibia, Swaziland, Tanzania, Uganda, Zambia, Zimbabwe; conducts management development programmes; library of 12,000 vols, 15,000 pamphlets; 30 consultants and advisers; Dir-Gen. Dr BONARD MWAPE; publs *African Management Development Forum* (every 6 months), *ESAMI Newsletter* (quarterly).

Institute of Development Management (IDM): POB 1, Mzumbe, Morogoro; tel. (56) 4380; fax (56) 4011; f. 1972; 110 teachers; 1,000 students; library of 30,000 vols; Principal Dr MOSES M. D. WARIOBA.

Institute of Finance Management: Shaaban Robert St, POB 3918, Dar es Salaam; tel. (51) 112931; telex 41969; fax (51) 112935; e-mail ifm@costech.gn.apc.org; f. 1972; financial management, accountancy, banking, insurance, taxation, social security administration, computing and information technology; 60 teachers; 1,400 students; library of 30,000 vols; Principal H. S. MADOFFE; publs *African Journal of Finance and Management*, *IFM Newsletter*.

Kivukoni Academy of Social Sciences: POB 9193, Dar es Salaam; tel. 820019; f. 1961; depts of economic studies, political studies, and social studies; library of 27,000 vols; 30 teachers; 250 students; Principal Dr JOHN M. J. MAGOTTI; publs *Mbioni* (in English, monthly), *Ujamaa* (in Swahili, monthly), *Kivuko* (in Swahili, annually).

Korogwe Teachers' College: POB 533, Korogwe, Tanga Region; f. 1863; 1,200 students; Prin. S. K. MGOMA.

National Social Welfare Training Institute: POB 3375, Dar es Salaam; tel. 74443; f. 1974; 20 teachers; 180 students; library of 7,172 vols; Principal T. F. NGALULA: publ. *Jamii Journal*.

University College of Lands and Architectural Studies: POB 35176, Dar es Salaam; tel. 71264; fax 75444; e-mail ihsbr@ud.co.tz; f. 1996; architecture, building economics, land management and valuation, land surveying, environmental engineering, urban and rural planning; Institute of Housing Studies and Building Research (applied research and documentation services in housing, building and planning); 100 teachers; 365 students; library of 15,000 vols; special collections of UN publications, theses and masterplans; Principal Prof. A. M. NIKUNDIWE; publ. *Journal of Building and Land Development* (2 a year).

Usambara Trade School: Lushoto; f. 1961; 70 students.

THAILAND

Learned Societies

GENERAL

Office of the National Culture Commission: Ratchadapisek Rd, Huay Khwang, Bangkok 10320; tel. 2470013; fax 248-5841; f. 1979; advises the Ministerial Council on cultural policy, and promotes co-ordination and co-operation in cultural activities (e.g. ASEAN projects, UNESCO programmes, intra-regional music workshop, cultural exchanges, varied research); 335 staff; library of 27,627 vols; Sec.-Gen. ARTORN CHANDAVIMOL; publ. *Thai Cultural Newsletter* (monthly).

Royal Institute: The Royal Grand Palace Grounds, Thanon, Na Phra Lan Rd, Bangkok 10200; tel. 2214822; fax 2249910; e-mail royal_institute@mozart.inet.co.th; f. 1933 for the investigation and encouragement of all branches of knowledge, the exchange of knowledge and for advice to the Government; 151 mems; library of 25,000 vols; Pres. Prof. Dr PRAYOON KANCHANADUL; Sec.-Gen. CHAMNONG TONGPRASERT.

Siam Society: 131 Soi Asoke, Sukhumvit 21, Bangkok 10110; tel. (2) 6616470; fax 2583491; f. 1904; under royal patronage; *c.* 1,500 mems; for the investigation and encouragement of art, science and literature of Thailand and neighbouring countries; Pres. BANGKOK CHOWKWANYUN; Hon. Sec. VIRGINIA M. DI CROCCO; library of 27,000 vols; publs *Journal, Natural History Bulletin* (2 a year).

BIBLIOGRAPHY, LIBRARY SCIENCE AND MUSEOLOGY

Thai Library Association: 273 Vibhavadee Rangsit Rd, Phyathai, Bangkok 10400; tel. 271-2084; f. 1954; 1,524 mems; Pres. M. CHAVALIT; Sec. K. SUCKCHAROEN; publs *TLA Bulletin, The World of Books.*

EDUCATION

Rectors' Conference of Thailand: Planning Division, Ministry of University Affairs, Si-Ayuthya Rd, Bangkok 10400; f. 1971; to exchange ideas and discuss problems of common concern to universities; 14 mems; Chair. Prof. Dr NATTH BHAMARAPRAVATI; Sec. Asst Prof. Dr UTHAI BOONPRASERT.

UNESCO Principal Regional Office for Asia and the Pacific: 920 Sukhumvit Rd, POB 967, Prakanong PO, Bangkok 10110; tel. (2) 391-0879; telex 20591; fax (2) 391-0866; f. 1961; permanent secretariat to Conferences of Ministers of Education and Those Responsible for Economic Planning in Asia and the Pacific and the Advisory Cttee on Regional Co-operation in Education in Asia and the Pacific; supports and plans programmes for the development of education, promotion of social and human sciences, preservation of cultural heritage; cultural studies and policies; regional projects carried out through Asia and Pacific Programme of Educational Innovation for Development (APEID); works towards universal primary education, eradication of illiteracy and continuing education through Asia-Pacific Programme of Education for All (APPEAL); supports higher education, educational planning and management and educational facilities services through a network of centres, institutions and national development groups; clearing house service collects information on education and other areas within UNESCO's fields of competence in Asia and the Pacific and makes them available to member states, governments, institutions in the Asia-Pacific region covering libraries, researchers and educational workers; General Information Programme Unit (PGI) provides services on the use of information and promotes int. co-operation in information exchange; Dir V. ORDONEZ; publs *Bulletin* (annually), *Education in Asia and the Pacific, Education in Asia and the Pacific, ACEID Newsletter, Population Education Newsletter, International Law* (Asia-Pacific Newsletter).

MEDICINE

Medical Association of Thailand: 3 Silom St, Bangkok; f. 1921; 3,057 mems; Pres. Prof. Dr SONGKRANT NIYOMSEN; Hon. Sec. Prof. Dr SANONG UNAKOL; publ. *Journal.*

NATURAL SCIENCES

General

Science Society of Thailand: Faculty of Science, Chulalongkorn University, Phya Thai Rd, Bangkok 10330; tel. and fax (2) 2527987; telex 20217; f. 1948; aims to promote education and research in all branches of natural science; 2,500 mems; Pres. Prof. Dr MONTRI CHULAVATNATOL; Sec.-Gen. Dr PIAMSOOK PONGSAWASDI; publs *Journal* (quarterly in English), *Science* (fortnightly).

Research Institutes

AGRICULTURE, FISHERIES AND VETERINARY SCIENCE

Fishery Technological Development Division: Dept of Fisheries, Ministry of Agriculture and Co-operatives, Charoen Krung Rd, Yannawa, Bangkok 10120; tel. (2) 2111261; f. 1954; fish handling, processing and utilization; analytical and sanitary certificate for export; Dir UDOM SUNDRARAVIPAT.

Forest Products Research and Development Division: Royal Forest Dept, Ministry of Agriculture and Co-operatives, 61 Paholyothin Rd, Jatujak, Bangkok 10900; f. 1935; wood and non-wood products research and utilization; library of 20,000 vols; Dir of Division WANIDA SUBANSENEE.

Rubber Research Centre: Hat Yai, Songkhla, Dept of Agriculture, Ministry of Agriculture, Bangkok.

NATURAL SCIENCES

Biological Sciences

Marine Biology Centre: Marine Fisheries Division, 89/1 Sapanpla, Yanawa, Bangkok 12; f. 1968; research and training of marine biologists; Dir DEB MENASWETA.

RELIGION, SOCIOLOGY AND ANTHROPOLOGY

Buddhist Research Centre: Wat Benchamabopitr, Bangkok; f. 1961; sponsored by Department of Religious Affairs, Ministry of Education; publ. *Pali-Thai-English Dictionary,* vol. 1.

TECHNOLOGY

Department of Energy Affairs: Kasatsuk Bridge, Rama I Rd, Bangkok 10330; tel. 2260021; telex 20524; fax 2261416; f. 1953; conducts research and inspection, surveys and gathers data on energy resources; lays down safety regulations, sets up standards for the sale of energy, promotes the use of energy to improve the economy; library of 10,000 vols; Dir Gen. Dr PRATHES SUTABUTR; publs *Thailand Energy Situation, Oil Thailand, Electric Power in Thailand* (annually).

Department of Mineral Resources: Ministry of Industry, Rama VI Rd, Bangkok 10400; geological mapping, mineral prospecting, mining, mineral dressing and metallurgical research; Dir-Gen. Dr PRABHAS CHAKKAPHAK.

Department of Science Service: Rama VI Rd, Bangkok 10400; tel. 2461387-95; f. 1891; testing, calibration and analysis services; research in food technology, industrial fermentation, pulp and paper raw materials, chemical engineering processes, air and water pollution control; research in ceramics; scientific and technological information service; library: see Libraries; Dir-Gen. CHODCHOI EIUMPONG; publs *Annual Report, Journal* (3 a year).

Office of Atomic Energy for Peace: Vibhavadi Rangsit, Chatuchuk, Bangkok 10900; tel. 579-5230; fax 561-3013; f. 1961; 401 staff; library of 11,000 vols, 265 periodicals; Sec.-Gen. KRIENGSAK BHADRAKOM; publs *OAEP Newsletter* (quarterly), technical reports.

Thailand Institute of Scientific and Technological Research: 196 Phahonyothin Rd, Chatuchak, Bangkok 10900; tel. (2) 579-1121; telex 21392; fax 561-4771; f. 1963; principal govt research agency; research depts: Pharmaceuticals and Natural Products, Food Industry, Chemical Industry, Biotechnology, Building Technology, Electronics Industry, Engineering Industry, Metals and Materials Technology, Agricultural Technology, Energy Technology, Environmental and Resources Management, Ecological Research, Thai Packaging Centre, Special Programme Centre; 748 staff; Governor CHALERMCHAI HONARK.

Libraries and Archives

Bangkok

Asian Institute of Technology, Center for Library and Information Resources (CLAIR): POB 4, Klong Luang, Pathumthani 12120; tel. (2) 5160110-29; telex 84276; fax (2) 5245870; e-mail ref@ait.ac.th; f. 1959; provides services and training in library and information services; 200,000 vols, 1,200 periodicals; four specialized information centres in: geotechnical engineering, ferrocement, renewable energy resources and environmental systems; Dir Dr FRANCIS J. DEVADASON (acting); publs *Geotechnical Engineering Bulletin* (quarterly), *AGE Current Awareness Service* (4 a year), *RERIC News* (quarterly), *RERIC International Energy Journal* (2 a year), *ENFO* (newsletter, quarterly), *Environmental Systems Reviews* (2 a year), *Journal of Ferrocement* (quarterly).

Chulalongkorn University, Centers of Academic Resources: Phya Thai Rd,

Bangkok 10330; tel. 218-2905; fax 215-3617; f. 1910; six centres: Central Library (711,000 vols), Thailand Information Center (60,000 vols), Audio-Visual Center (50,000 vols), International Information Center (12,300 vols), the Chula-Internet Service Center and the Art Center; Dir Dr KAMALES SANTIVEJKUL.

Kasetsart University, Main Library: Bangkok 10903; fax 5611369; f. 1943; 313,000 vols, 4,700 periodicals, 55,000 theses, 93,000 sheets of microfiche, 5,700 titles of audiovisual materials; Dir Mrs PIBOONSIN WATANAPONGSE; publs *Buffalo Bulletin* (quarterly), *Thai Agricultural Bibliography* (annually).

Library of the Scientific and Technological Information Division, Department of Science Service: Ministry of Science, Technology and Environment, Rama VI St, Bangkok 10400; f. 1918; 450,000 vols; special library and technical information services including patents, standards and trade literature; Dir MAYUREE PONGPUDPUNTH.

National Archives of Thailand: Fine Arts Department, Samsen Rd, Bangkok 10300; tel. 2811599; f. 1952; historical and research resources services for official agencies, scholars and the public; four major classes of documentary material: textual (313,000 dossiers of public and personal records), 408,000 photos, 4,000 videos, 1,700 tapes, 51,000 posters, 5,600 microfilm reels, cartographic (24,000 maps and 1,753 aerial photographs), govt publs (3,660 titles), 1,026,000 film negatives and slides, 54,000 films and newsreels; Dir SAGARINDRA VISESHABANDHU.

National Library: Samsen Rd, Bangkok 10300; tel. 2815212; fax 2810263; e-mail suwaksir@emiscmoc.go.th; f. 1905; 2,028,000 vols, 125,000 MSS, 2,100 periodicals, 69,000 audiovisual items; national research and deposit library; controls International Standard Serial Number (ISSN–Thailand), ISSN Regional Centre for Southeast Asia (ISSN-SEA); Dir KONGKAEW VEERAPRAJAK (acting); publs *National Bibliography, ISSN-SEA Bulletin*.

Neilson Hays Library: 195 Suriwongse Rd, Bangkok; f. 1869; Librarian Mom Rajwongse NAPACHARI THONGTHAM.

Siriraj Medical Library, Mahidol University: Siriraj Hospital, Bangkok 10700; tel. 411-3112; fax 412-8418; f. 1897; 159,600 vols, 3,918 periodicals; Librarian K. CHOLLAMPE; publs *Siriraj Hospital Gazette, Journal of the Medical Association of Thailand, Newsletter* (monthly).

Srinakharinwirot University Library: Sukhumvit 23, Bangkok 10110; telex 72270; f. 1954; 196,011 vols (emphasis on education), 1,157 periodicals; audio-visual centre; Head Librarian NONGNUAL PONGPAIBOOL; brs in Bangkhen, Bang Saen, Patoom Wan, Pitsanuloke, Songkla; publs *New Books of the Month—A Bibliography*.

Thai National Documentation Centre: 196 Phahonyothin Rd, Chatuchak, Bangkok 10900; tel. 579-112130; telex 21392; fax 579-8594; f. 1961; documentation services to science and technology; monographs in English 28,275 vols, monographs in Thai 9,866 vols, periodicals (369 in English, 152 in Thai); Dir Mrs. NONGPHANGA CHITRAKORN.

Thammasat University Libraries: 2 Prachand Rd, Bangkok 10200; tel. (2) 6235176; fax (2) 6235173; f. 1934; 684,000 vols (social sciences and humanities, medical science, science and technology); 3,476 periodicals; 11 br. libraries; Librarian NUALCHAWEE SUTHAMWONG; publ. *Dom That* (2 a year).

United Nations Economic and Social Commission for Asia and the Pacific Library: United Nations Bldg, Rajdamnern Ave, Bangkok 10200; tel. (2) 288-1360; fax (2) 288-1000; e-mail library-escap@un.org; economic and social development; 150,000 vols; Librarian JA-KYUNG YOO; publs *Asian Bibliography* (2 a year), *ESCAP Documents and Publications* (1 a year), *Register of Serials* (irregular).

Museums and Art Galleries

Bangkok

National Museum: Na Phra That Rd, Bangkok 10200; tel. 2241396; f. 1926; prehistoric artefacts, bronze and stone sculptures, costumes, textiles, ancient weapons, coins, wood-carvings, ceramics, royal regalia, theatrical masks and dresses, marionettes, shadow-play figures, funeral chariots, illustrated books, musical instruments; Dir Mrs CHIRA CHONGKOL; publs *Guide to the National Museum, Official Guide to Ayutthaya and Bang Pa-in, Guide to Old Sukhothai, Thai Cultural Series,* etc.

Universities and Technical Institutes

ASIAN INSTITUTE OF TECHNOLOGY

POB 2754, Bangkok 10501

Telephone: 5160114
Telex: 84276
Fax: 5162126

Founded 1959
Independent graduate school, open to graduates from all Asian countries; 3-term (1 year) course leading to Diploma; 5-term (20 months) course leading to a Master's degree; further 3 years leading to Doctoral degree
Language of instruction: English
Academic year: three annual admissions (January, May, September)

President: Prof. ALASTAIR M. NORTH
Vice-President for Academic Affairs: Prof. RICARDO P. PAMA
Vice-President for Development: Prof. PISIDHI KARASUDHI
Academic Secretary and Dean of Student Affairs: Dr ROGER HAWKEY

Library: see Libraries
Number of teachers: 157
Number of students: 1,000
Publications: *Annual Report on Research and Activities, AIT Annual Report, AIT Review* (3 a year).

DEANS

School of Advanced Technologies: Prof. M. T. TABUCANON
School of Civil Engineering: Prof. PRINYA NUTALAYA
School of Environment, Resources and Development: Prof. KARL E. WEBER
School of Management: Prof. JYOTI GUPTA

DIRECTORS

Continuing Education Center: Dr N. C. AUSTRIACO
Centre for Language and Educational Technology: Dr MICHAEL CONNELLY (Chair.)
Centre for Library and Information Resources: Prof. ROBERT D. STUEART
Regional Computer Center: Dr CHAROON CHIRAPAISARNKUL
Asian Disaster Preparedness Center: JOHN BARRETT

ASSUMPTION UNIVERSITY

Huamark, Bangkok 10240

Telephone: (2) 300-4553
Fax: (2) 300-4563

Founded 1969; became university in 1990; formerly Assumption Business Administration College
Private control
Language of Instruction: English
Academic year: June to March

President: Rev. Dr PRATHIP M. KOMOLMAS
Vice-President for Academic Affairs: Rev. Dr BANCHA SAENGHIRAN
Vice-President for Student Affairs: Rev. Dr VISITH SRIVICHAIRATANA
Vice-President for Financial Affairs: Rev. ANUPATT P. YUTTACHAI
Vice-President for Planning and Development: Prof. Dr SRISAKDI CHARMONMAN
Vice-President for Research: Asst Prof. Dr JIRAWAT WONGSWADIWAT
Vice-President for Administrative Affairs: Dr CHEVALIT MEENNUCH
Registrar: KAMOL KIDSAWAD
Director of Central Library: SUPRATA SINCHAISUK

Library of 92,000 vols
Number of teachers: 889
Number of students: 16,158
Publications: *ABAC Journal, ABAC Newsletter, ABAC Today, IJCEM, Journal of Philosophy, Culture and Religion, Journal of Risk Management and Insurance, AU Journal of Technology, AU Tech Note, ABAC Periodical.*

DEANS

Graduate School of Computer Information Systems: Air Marshall Dr CHULIT MEESAJJEE
Graduate School of Computer Information Systems (PhD Programme): Asst Prof. Dr VICHIT AVATCHANAKORN
Graduate School of Computer and Engineering Management: Asst Prof. Dr BOONMARK SIRINAOVAKUL (Senior Dean), Dr CHAMNONG JUNGTHIRAPANICH
Graduate School of Computer and Engineering Management (PhD Programme): Asst Prof. Dr PRAPON PHASUKYUD
Graduate School of Counselling Psychology: Dr DOLORES DE LEON
Graduate School of Philosophy and Religious Studies: Prof. KIRTA BUNCHUA
School of Management: Dr VINDHAI COCRACUL
Faculty of Risk Management and Industrial Services: Prof. CHUKIAT PRAMOOLPOL
Faculty of Arts: Dr EDWARD P. VARGO
School of Nursing Science: SIRIANAN CHUTHATAMEE
School of Science and Technology: Asst Prof. Dr PRATIT SANTIPRABHOB
School of Engineering: Dr SUDHIPORN PATUMTAEWAPIBAL
School of Law: Assoc. Prof. Dr VIRA LOCHAYA
School of Biotechnology: Dr CHURDCHAI CHEOWTIRAKUL
School of Architecture: PISIT VIRIYAVADHANA
School of Humanities: Dr SOMPIT PORSUTYARUK

ATTACHED RESEARCH INSTITUTES

Insurance Research Centre: Dir SUNDARARAJAN PARTHASARATHY.

ABAC-KSC Internet Poll Research Centre: Dir NOPPADON KANNIKA.

Virtual Reality Research Centre: Dir KITTI PHOTHIKITTI.

Centre for Research in Social Science: Dir PREECHA BOONRORD.

CHIANG MAI UNIVERSITY

239 Huay Kaew Rd, Muang District, Chiang Mai 50200

Telephone: (53) 943661

Fax: (53) 217143

Founded 1964
State control
Languages of instruction: Thai and English
Academic year: June to May

President: Prof CHOTI THEETRANONT
Vice-Presidents: Dr NIPON TUWANON (Administrative Affairs), Assoc. Prof. Dr WICHIT SRISUPHAN (Academic), Asst Prof. SAMPAN SRISUWAN (Planning and Development Affairs), Assoc. Prof. Dr LUECHAI CHULASAI (Foreign Relations), Assoc. Prof. Dr NORKUN SITTHIPHONG (Research and Property), Asst Prof. Dr CHAWALIT PUTHAWONGS (Student Affairs), THERDSAK KOSAIYAKANONT (Welfare)
Registrar: Assoc. Prof. PRATEEP CHANKONG
Librarian: Asst Prof. PRASIT MALUMPONG

Number of teachers: 1,926
Number of students: 20,635

Publications: *Chiang Mai Medical Bulletin* (4 a year), *Journal of the Asian Studies Center, Journal of Social Sciences, Women's Studies News* (2 a year), *Journal of Economics, Journal of Agriculture, Journal of the Science Faculty, Engineering Journal.*

DEANS

Faculty of Humanities: Dr WATTANA SUKSAMAI
Faculty of Social Sciences: Asst Prof. Dr PONG-IN RAKARIYATHAM
Faculty of Science: Prof. Dr KITTICHAI WATLANANIKORN
Faculty of Associated Medical Sciences: Assoc. Prof. DECHA ROMCAI
Faculty of Agriculture: Assoc. Prof. Dr PONGSAK ANGKASITH
Faculty of Education: Assoc. Prof. Dr SIRMSREE CHAISORN
Faculty of Engineering: Assoc. Prof. Dr AKACHAI SANG-IN
Faculty of Nursing: Asst Prof. WILAWAN SENARATANA
Faculty of Dentistry: Assoc. Prof. VIRUSH PATANAPORN
Faculty of Medicine: Prof. KUMPOL KLUNKLIN
Faculty of Fine Arts: Assoc. Prof. PONGDEJ CHAIYAKUT
Graduate School: Prof. Dr TAVISAKDI RAMINGWONG
Faculty of Pharmacy: Assoc. Prof. JARATBHAN SANGUANSERMSRI
Faculty of Agro-Industry: Assoc. Prof. Dr NAIYATAT POOSARAN
Faculty of Economics: Dr SANGKOM SUWANNARAT
Faculty of Business Administration: Asst Prof. PONGSA VIBOONSANTI
Faculty of Veterinary Medicine: Assoc. Prof. Dr TED TESAPRATEEP

ATTACHED RESEARCH INSTITUTES

Social Research Institute: Dir Prof. Dr SIDDHI BUTR-INDR.
Research Institute for Health Sciences: Dir Assst Prof. VINAI SURIYANONT.
Institute for Science and Technology Research and Development: Dir Dr ANUSORN INTARANGSI.

CHULALONGKORN UNIVERSITY

Phyathai Rd, Bangkok 10330
Telephone: (662) 215-0871
Telex: 20217
Fax: (662) 215-4804

Founded 1917
State control
Language of instruction: Thai
Academic year: June to March

Chancellor: Prof. Dr BOONROD BINSON
President: Prof. CHARAS SUWANWELA
Vice-President for Administrative Affairs: Assoc. Prof. RABIN RATTANAPHANI
Vice-President for Academic Affairs: Assoc. Prof. Dr PRANEE KULLAVANIJAYA
Vice-President for Research Affairs: Assoc. Prof. Dr AMARA PONGSAPICH
Vice-President for Planning and Development: Assoc. Prof. SUCHATA JINACHITRA
Vice-President for Property Management: Assoc. Prof. PRIDA TASANAPRADIT
Vice-President for Student Affairs: Asst Prof. SOMKIAT RUJIRAWAT
Vice-President for International Affairs: Assoc. Prof. Dr SUPACHAI YAVAPRABHAS
Vice-President for Intellectual Property: Assoc. Prof. Dr SALAG DHABANANDANA
Vice-President for Cultural Affairs: Assoc. Prof. Dr SURAPONE VIRUNRAK
Registrar: Assoc Prof. PRADISTHA INTARAKOSIT
Library: see Libraries
Number of teachers: 2,427
Number of students: 13,858 undergraduate, 5,135 postgraduate

Publications: *University Newsletter* (quarterly), *'Pra Keaw' Students' Handbook* (annually), *Data on Freshmen Entering Chulalongkorn University, Annual Report, Research Journal* (annually), *Fact Book* (annually), *Chula Samphan* (every 2 weeks).

DEANS

Faculty of Arts: Assoc. Prof. Dr PRAPIN MANOMAIVIBOOL
Faculty of Science: Prof. CHAIYUDH KHANTAPRAB
Faculty of Architecture: Assoc. Prof. TORPONG YOMNAK
Faculty of Commerce and Accountancy: Assoc. Prof. Dr SUCHADA KIRANANDANA
Faculty of Political Science: Prof. Dr SUCHIT BUNBONGKARN
Faculty of Economics: Prof. Dr THIENCHAI KIRANANDANA
Faculty of Education: Assoc. Prof. Dr PAITOON SINLARAT
Faculty of Engineering: Assoc. Prof. Dr NARONG YOOTHANOM
Faculty of Fine and Applied Arts: CHUNNONG SANGVICHIEN
Faculty of Medicine: Prof. SUPAWAT CHUTIVONGSE
Faculty of Nursing: Assoc. Prof. Dr PRANOM OTHAGANONT
Faculty of Veterinary Science: Assoc. Prof. SONGKRAM LUANGTONGKUM
Faculty of Dentistry: Assoc. Prof. Dr JEERASAK NOPAKUN
Faculty of Communication Arts: Assoc. Prof. Dr DARUNEE HIRUNRAK
Faculty of Law: Assoc. Prof. Dr SURAKIART SATHIRATHAI
Faculty of Pharmaceutical Science: Assoc. Prof. Dr SUNIPHOND PAMMANGURA
Faculty of Allied Health Sciences: Asst Prof. Dr BYAPON NA NAGARA

HEADS OF DEPARTMENTS

Faculty of Arts:

English: CHARURAT TANTRAPORN
Thai: Assoc. Prof. Dr NAVAVAN BANDHUMEDHA
Eastern Languages: Asst Prof. Dr KANLAYANEE SITASUWAN
Western Languages: Asst. Prof. PANITI HOONSWAENG
Philosophy: Assoc. Prof. Dr MARK TANTHAI
Geography: Assoc. Prof. NAROTE PALAKAWONGSA NA AYUDHYA
History: Prof. Dr PIYANART BUNNAG
Linguistics: Assoc. Prof. Dr THERAPHAN LUANGTHONGKUM
Dramatic Arts: NALINEE SITASUWAN
Library Science: Assoc. Prof. Dr PRAPAVADEE SUEBSONTHI

Faculty of Science:

Chemistry: Assoc. Prof. Dr SIRI VAROTHAI
Chemical Technology: Assoc. Prof. KUNCHANA BUNYAKIAT
Physics: Asst Prof. SOMPHONG CHATRAPHORN
Biology: Assoc. Prof. Dr VITHAYA YODYINGYUAD
Geology: Assoc. Prof. SOMPOP VEDCHAKANCHANA
General Science: SA-ARD VIROCHRUT
Mathematics: Asst Prof. LA-OR CHONVIRIYA
Marine Science: Assoc. Prof. MANUWADEE HUNGSPREUGS
Biochemistry: Asst Prof. TIPAPORN LIMPASENI
Microbiology: Assoc. Prof. PRAKITSIN SIHANONTH
Material Science: Asst Prof. WERASAK UDOMKICHDECHA
Food Technology: Assoc. Prof. Dr CHAIYUTE THUNPITHAYAKUL
Photographic Science and Printing Technology: Assoc. Prof. PONTAWEE PUNGRASSAMEE
Botany: Assoc. Prof. Dr PREEDA BOON-LONG

Faculty of Architecture:

Architecture: Assoc. Prof. VIRA BURANAKARN
Industrial Design: Asst Prof. Dr AURAPIN PANTONG
Urban and Regional Planning: Asst Prof. Dr NIPAN VICHIENNOI
Landscape Architecture: Asst Prof. NILUBOL KLONGVESSA
Interior Architecture: Asst Prof. SURACHAI CHOLPRASERD
Housing Development: Assoc. Prof. MANOP BONGSADADT

Faculty of Commerce and Accountancy:

Accountancy: ORAPIN CHARTABSORN
Commerce: Dr ACHARA CHANDRACHAI
Statistics: Assoc. Prof. PAKAVADI SIRIRANGSI
Banking and Finance: Asst Prof. VIRACH APHIMETEETAMRONG
Marketing: Assoc. Prof. SURAPAT VACHARAPRATIP

Faculty of Political Science:

Government: Assoc. Prof. Dr PRAYAD HONGTONGKUM
International Relations: Asst Prof. Dr CHAIWAT KHAMCHOO
Sociology and Anthropology: Assoc. Prof. SUPATRA SOOPHARB
Public Administration: Asst Prof. Dr THOSAPORN SIRISUMPHAND

Faculty of Education:

Psychology: Assoc. Prof. Dr SOMPOCH IAMSUPASIT
Educational Administration: Asst Prof. Dr WEERAWAT UTAIRAT
Elementary Education: Assoc. Prof. Dr DUANGDUEN ANNUAM
Physical Education: Asst Prof. Dr LAWAN SUKKRI
Secondary Education: Asst Prof. Dr THERACHAI PURANAJOTI
Educational Research: Assoc. Prof. Dr VANNA PURANAJOTI
Art Education: Asst Prof. SANYA WONG-ARAM
Foundations of Education: Assoc. Prof. Dr RERNGRATCHANEE NIMNUAL
Audio-Visual Education: Asst Prof. SUGREE RODPOTHONG
Higher Education: Asst Prof. Dr THIDARAT BOONNUJ

Faculty of Engineering:

Civil Engineering: Prof. VATTANA THAMMONGKOL
Electrical Engineering: Prof. Dr SOMSAK PANYAKEOW
Mechanical Engineering: Assoc. Prof. Dr WITHAYA YONGCHAREON
Industrial Engineering: Prof. Dr SIRICHAN THONGPRASERT
Mining Engineering and Mining Geology: Assoc. Prof. SARITHDEJ PATHANASETHPONG
Metallurgical Engineering: Asst Prof. Dr CHATCHAI SOMSIRI

Chemical Engineering: Dr PIYASAN PRASERTHDAM
Survey Engineering: SANYA SOWAPARB
Computer Engineering: Assoc. Prof. DUAN SINTUPUNPRATUM
Nuclear Technology: Asst Prof. NARES CHANKOW
Environmental Engineering: Assoc. Prof. SUREE KHAODHIAN

Faculty of Fine and Applied Arts:
Visual Arts: Asst Prof. PRAMUAN BURUSPHAT
Creative Arts: SUCHINTANA SANGAUNMU
Music: CHUMNONG SANICHIEN (acting)
Dance: PUSADEE LIMSAKUL

Faculty of Medicine:
Anatomy: Asst Prof. ORASRI ROMYANAN
Physiology: BUNGORN CHOMDEJ
Biochemistry: Dr JERAPAN KRUNGKAI
Pharmacology: Assoc. Prof. SOPIT THAMAREE
Pathology: Assoc. Prof. CHOOSAK VIRATCHAI
Laboratory Medicine: Assoc. Prof. PAILIN UJJIN
Microbiology: Assoc. Prof. SOMJAI REINPRAYOON
Parasitology: Assoc. Prof. MEDHI KULKUMTHORN
Forensic Medicine: Assoc. Prof. VIRATT PANICHABHONGSE
Medicine: Prof. CHAIVEJ NUCHPRAYOON
Preventative and Social Medicine: Asst Prof. MUNEE SRESHTHABUTRA
Psychiatry: Prof. SUWATANA ARIBARG
Surgery: Assoc. Prof. YOD SUKOTHAMAN
Orthopaedic Surgery: Assoc. Prof. CHAITHAVAT NGARMUKOS
Anaesthesiology: Assoc. Prof. POGCHIT PRAMUAN
Obstetrics and Gynaecology: Prof. PRAMUAN VIRUTAMASEN
Radiology: Prof. NITAYA SUWANWELA
Paediatrics: Prof. VIROJNA SUEBLINVONG
Ophthalmology: Prof. PRACHAK PRACHAKVEJ
Otolaryngology: Prof. AMNUAY CUTCHAVAREE

Faculty of Veterinary Science:
Veterinary Anatomy: Assoc. Prof. PAYATTRA TANTILIPIKARA
Veterinary Pathology: Assoc. Prof. MANOP MUANGYAI
Veterinary Physiology: Prof. Dr NARONGSAK CHAIYABUTR
Veterinary Pharmacology: Assoc. Prof. Dr WARA PANICHKRIANGKRAI
Veterinary Surgery: Asst Prof. Dr PHAIWIPA KAMOLRAT
Veterinary Medicine: Asst Prof. Dr JIROJ SASIPREEYAJAN
Animal Husbandry: Assoc. Prof. SUCHIN JALAYANAGUPTA
Veterinary Obstetrics, Gynaecology and Reproduction: Assoc. Prof. PRACHIN VIRAKUL

Faculty of Dentistry:
Anatomy: Assoc. Prof. DOLLY METHATHRATHIP
Physiology: Asst Prof. Dr CHOOKIAT SUCANTHAPREE
Biochemistry: Asst Prof. LAMOONYONG POVATONG
Microbiology: Asst Prof. RATANA SERINIRACH
Oral Pathology: VICHADE LEELAPRUTE
Pharmacology: WATANA KONTHIKAMEE
Operative Dentistry: Asst Prof. SAICHI MATHURASAI
Prosthodontics: Asst Prof. SUPABOON BURNAVEJA
Orthodontics: Asst Prof. KANOK SORATHESN
Oral Surgery: Assoc. Prof. SITHICHAI TUDSRI
Radiology: PAIRAT DHIRAVARANGKURA
Paediatric Dentistry: Asst Prof. DHANIS HEMINDRA
Oral Medicine: Asst Prof. VILAIWAN ANEKSUK
Community Dentistry: Assoc. Prof. SOMPOL LEKFUANGFU
Periodontology: Assoc. Prof. NOPHADOL SUPPIPAT
Occlusion: Asst Prof. SUKNIPA VICHAICHALERMVONG

Faculty of Communication Arts:
Public Relations: Assoc. Prof. Dr THANAVADEE BOONLUE
Mass Communications: Assoc. Prof. Dr NUNTHAWAN SUCHATO
Motion Picture and Still Photography: Asst Prof. Dr YUTHAWAT PATHARAPANUPATH
Speech Communication and Performing Arts: Dr SAKDA PANNENGPETCH

Faculty of Law:
Civil and Commercial Law: Assoc. Prof. PHIJAISAKDI HORAYANGKURA
Procedural and Court Law: Assoc. Prof. PAITOON KONGSOMBOON
International Law: Prof. VITIT MUNTARBHORN
Administrative Law: Assoc. Prof. Dr BORWORNSAK UWANNO
Criminal Law and Criminology: Assoc. Prof. VIRAPHONG BOONYOBHAS

Faculty of Pharmaceutical Science:
Pharmacy: Assoc. Prof. PRAPAPUCK SILAPACHOTE
Pharmaceutical Chemistry: Assoc. Prof. SUTTATIP CHANTARASKUL
Pharmacognosy: Assoc. Prof. CHAIYO CHAICHANTIPYUTH
Pharmaceutical Botany: Assoc. Prof. RAPEEPOL BAVOVADA
Pharmacology: Assoc. Prof. Dr PORNPEN PREMYOTHIN
Food Chemistry: SUTHEE SUNTHORNTHUM
Physiology: Asst Prof. SUMLEE JAIDEE
Biochemistry: Assoc. Prof. SUNATA PONGSAMART
Microbiology: Assoc. Prof. Dr VIMOLMAS LIPIPUN
Manufacturing Pharmacy: Asst Prof. Dr POJ KULVANICH

Faculty of Allied Health Sciences:
Clinical Microscopy: Assoc. Prof. Dr PORNTHEP TIENSIWAKUL
Clinical Chemistry: Assoc. Prof. Dr RACHANA SANTIYANONT
Transfusion Medicine: Asst Prof. Dr WINAI DAHLAN

DIRECTORS

Institute of Social Research: Prof. Dr KRAIYUDHT DHIRATAYAKINAN
Institute of Health Research: Assoc. Prof. VICHAI POSHYACHINDA
Institute of Environmental Research: Assoc. Prof. Dr SUTHIRAK SUJARITTANONTA
Institute of Population Studies: Assoc. Prof. Dr KUO WONGBOONSIN
Language Institute: Assoc. Prof. CHANIGA SILPA-ANAN
Computer Service Center: Assoc. Prof. KRAIVIJIT TANTIMEDH
Academic Resource Centre: Assoc. Prof. Dr PRACHAK POOMVISES
Scientific and Technological Research Equipment Centre: Asst Prof. CHYAGRIT SIRIUPATHAM
Energy Research and Training Center: Assoc. Prof. Dr KULTHORN SILAPABANLENG
Institute of Asian Studies: Assoc. Prof. Dr WITHAYA SITHAYA SUCHARITHANARUGSE
Institute of Biotechnology and Genetic Engineering: Assoc. Prof. Dr NALINE NILUBOL
Sasin Graduate Institute of Business Administration: Prof. TOEMSAKDI KRISHNAMRA
Merchant Marine Institute: Assoc. Prof. Dr ITTIPHOL PAN-NGUM
Institute of Middle East and Muslim World Studies: Asst Prof. Dr ARONG SUTHASASNA
Public Enterprise Institute: Asst Prof. Dr PIPAT THAIAREE
Institute of Security and International Studies: Assoc. Prof. SUKHUMBHAND PARIBATRA
American Studies Program: PRANEE TIPPAYARATANA
Institute of Thai Studies: Assoc. Prof. Dr PRAKONG NIMMANHAEMINDA
General Education Project: Assoc. Prof. Dr PIRAWAN BHANTHUMNAVIN
Metallurgy and Materials Science Research Institute: Asst Prof. Dr LEK UTTAMASIL
Chula Unisearch: Assoc. Prof. Dr PRASIT PRAPINMONGKOLKARN
Cultural Center of Chulalongkorn University: CHUMNONG SANGVICHIEN
Toban-N.E. Thai Project: Assoc. Prof. Dr PRAPANT SVETANANT
Petroleum and Petrochemical College: Assoc. Prof. Dr KAMCHAD MONGKOLKUL

DHURAKIJPUNDIT UNIVERSITY

110/1-4 Prachacheun Rd, Donmuang, Bangkok 10210
Telephone: 9547300
Fax: 5899605

Founded 1968
Private Control
Language of instruction: Thai
Academic year: June to October, November to February

President: Prof. PAITOON PONGSABUTRA
Registrar: THANU UTHAIPUN
Librarian: Assoc. Prof. Dr NAVANIT INTRAMA

Library of 116,442 vols
Number of teachers: 1,500
Number of students: 19,000

Publication: *Sudhiparidhasna* (University journal).

DEANS

Graduate School: Dr PHIRAPHAN PHAUSUK
Faculty of Business Administration: Asst Prof. THANIDA CHITNOMRATH
Faculty of Accounting: Asst Prof. WANVIPA TAPWONG
Faculty of Economics: Dr PIMOL CHITMAN
Faculty of Law: Asst Prof. NUCHTIP P. BANCHONGSILPA
Faculty of Humanities: Asst Prof. Dr VINIT PHINIT-AKSON
Faculty of Communication Arts: Assoc. Prof. Dr SOMKUAN KAVIYA
Faculty of Engineering: Dr ARCHAMPHON KHAMBANONDA

KASETSART UNIVERSITY

Chatuchak, Bangkok 10900
Telephone: (2) 942-8171
Fax: (2) 942-8170

Founded 1943
State control
Languages of instruction: Thai and English
Academic year: June to March (two semesters)

President: Prof. Dr THIRA SUTABUTRA
Vice-Presidents: Assoc. Prof. VIROCH IMPITHUKSA (Planning and Development), Prof. SOMPIAN KASEMSAP (Academic Affairs), Prof. Dr CHAREINSAK ROJANARIDPICHED (Administration and Student Development), Dr JEERASAK PONGPISANUPICHT (Property Management), Assoc. Prof. Dr VICHAI KORPRADITSKUL (Kamphaengsaen Campus), Assoc. Prof. Dr THANONG PUKRUSHPAN (Bangkhen Campus), Prof. Dr TORKUL KANCHANALAI (Development), Assoc. Prof. VINICH VEERAYANGKUR (Personnel Development), Assoc. Prof. RUNGCHAROEN KANCHANOMAI (Finance), Assoc. Prof. Dr SUPOT FAUNGFUPONG (Research and Academic Services), Assoc. Prof. Dr SUREE BHUMIBHAMON (International Affairs), Assoc. Prof. KHUNGYING SUCHADA SRIPEN (Special Affairs)
Registrar: BAWPIT CHARUBHUN
Librarian: PIBOONSIN WATANAPONGSE

Library: see Libraries
Number of teachers: 1,800

Number of students: 20,064 undergraduates, 5,551 graduates

Publications: *Kasetsart Journal* (annually), and many faculty and institute publs.

DEANS

Faculty of Agriculture: SUPAMARD PANICHSAKPATANA
Faculty of Agro-Industry: PREEYA VIBULSRESTH
Faculty of Fisheries: YONT MUSIG
Faculty of Forestry: UTIS KUTINTARA
Faculty of Science: VINIJ JIAMSAKUL
Faculty of Humanities: KAMALA NAKASIRI
Faculty of Engineering: VUDTECHAI KAPILAKANCHANA
Faculty of Business Administration: PREYANUCH APIBUNYOPAS
Faculty of Social Sciences: SOMKIAT WANTHANA
Faculty of Veterinary Medicine: THAVEEWAT TASSANAWAT
Faculty of Education: SUPITR SAMAHITO
Faculty of Economics: RUANGDEJ SRIVARDHANA
Faculty of Liberal Arts and Science: SANGSURI SINTHUVANIK
Graduate School: THAMMASAK SOMMARTYA

DIRECTORS

Regional Community Forestry Training Center: SOMSAK SUKWONG
National Agricultural Extension and Training Center: CHUKIAT RUKSORN
National Corn and Sorghum Research Center: YUPAPAN CHUTATHONG
National Agricultural Machinery Center: MONGKOL KWANGWAROPAS
National Biological Control Research Center: BANPOT NAPOMPETCH
Inseechandrasatitya Institute for Crop Research and Development: PORN RUNGCHANG
Industrial Entomology Research and Development Center: NIT KIRITIBUTR
Dairy Research and Development Center: BOONLUA RENGSIRIKUL
Sugar and Sugarcane Research and Development Center: KOSOL CHARERNSOM
Tropical Vegetable Research Center: SUTEVEE SUKPRAKARN
Suwanvajokkasikit Animal Research and Development Institute: CHANVIT VAJRABUKKA
Central Laboratory and Greenhouse Complex: TEERANUD ROMPHOPHAK
Central Scientific Equipment Laboratory: VICHIEN YONGMANITCHAI
Research and Development Center for Agriculture under Adverse Conditions: PIYA DUANGPATRA

PROFESSORS

AKSORNKOAE, S., Silviculture
ATTANANDANA, T., Soil Science
CHANDRAPATYA, A., Entomology
CHIENGKUL, P., History
CHUNKAO, K., Conservation
DUANGPATRA, P., Soil Science
KANCHANALAI, T., Civil Engineering
KANCHANOMAI, P., History
KAPILAKANCHANA, N., History
KASEMSAP, S., Horticulture
KETSA, S., Horticulture
KIATGRAJAI, P., Forest Products
KIRDPITUGSA, C., Water Resources
LAMSEEJAN, S., Applied Radiation and Isotopes
LAUSUNTHORN, N., Literature
LIMPOKA, M., Veterinary Pharmacology
LOTONG, N., Microbiology
PRUGSASRI, P., Animal Science
ROJANARIDPICHED, C., Agronomy
SAHUNALU, P., Silviculture
SOMMARTYA, T., Plant Pathology
SONGPRASERT, P., History
SRINIVES, P., Agronomy
SUBHADRABANDHU, S., Horticulture
SUKUMOLANANDANA, C., Horticulture
SURATANAKAVIKUL, P., History
SUTABUTRA, T., Plant Pathology
SUWANARIT, A., Soil Science
SUWANKETNIKORN, R., Agronomy
TARNCHALANUKIT, W., Aquaculture
TONGPAN, S., Agricultural Economics
VAJRABUKKA, C., Animal Science
WANLEELAG, N., Entomology
YINJAJAVAL, S., Soil Science

KHON KAEN UNIVERSITY

123 Friendship Highway, Amphoe Muang, Khon Kaen 40002

Telephone: (43) 242331
Telex: 55303
Fax: (43) 241216

Founded 1964
State control
Language of instruction: Thai
Academic year: June to March (two semesters)

Chairman of University Council: Police Gen. PAO SALASIN
President: Assoc. Prof. Dr PRINYA CHINDAPRASIRT
Vice-President for Academic Affairs: Assoc. Prof. Dr SUCHITRA LUANGAMORNLERT
Vice-President for Administrative Affairs: Asst Prof. Dr SUCHART AREEMIT
Vice-President for Student Affairs: Asst Prof. Dr AMNOUY KAMTUO
Vice-President for Planning and Development: Assoc. Prof. RANGSAN NIAMSANIT
Vice-President for Welfare Affairs: Assoc. Prof. Dr TANOO PHOLAWADANA
Vice-President for Research Affairs: Assoc. Prof. Dr WINIT CHINSUWAN
Vice-President for Personnel Affairs: Assoc. Prof. ARNONE YAMTREE
Vice-President for International Relations and Information: Assoc. Prof. Dr SUMON SAKOLCHAI

Library of 339,614 vols
Number of teachers: 1,718
Number of students: 12,300

Publications: *Architecture Journal* (quarterly), *Bulletin of Medical Technology and Physical Therapy* (quarterly), *Khon Kaen Agriculture Journal* (6 a year), *Srinagarind Hospital Medical Journal* (quarterly), *Humanities and Social Sciences Journal, Khon Kaen University Daily News, Khon Kaen University Newsletter* (fortnightly), *Kaen Kaset* (quarterly), *Science Journal* (quarterly), *Khon Kaen University Engineering Quarterly, Journal of Nursing* (quarterly), *Khon Kaen University Health Sciences Center Newsletter* (weekly), *Khon Kaen University Health Sciences Center Bulletin* (6 a year), *Academic Services Newsletter* (monthly).

DEANS

Faculty of Agriculture: Assoc. Prof. Dr ARAN PATHANOTHAI
Faculty of Education: Assoc. Prof. RAJIT TREEPUTTARAT
Faculty of Engineering: Assoc. Prof. DAMRONG HORMDEE
Faculty of Fine and Applied Arts: Assoc. Prof. SUWIT SATHITWITHAYANAN
Faculty of Medicine: Assoc. Prof. Dr SOMPORN PHOTHINAM
Faculty of Nursing: Asst Prof. KULAYA PATTANASRI
Faculty of Science: Asst Prof. WANCHAI SOOMLEG
Faculty of Humanities and Social Sciences: Assoc. Prof. Dr YUPIN TECHAMANEE
Faculty of Associated Medical Sciences: Asst Prof. JIRAPORN SITTITHAWORN
Faculty of Public Health: Assoc. Prof. AROON JIRAWATKUL
Faculty of Dentistry: Asst Prof. Dr NITIPAVEE SRISUK
Faculty of Pharmaceutical Sciences: Asst Prof. Dr WONGWIWAT TASSANEEYAKUL
Faculty of Technology: Asst Prof. Dr KASEM NANTACHAI
Faculty of Architecture: Assoc. Prof. WEERAWAN SATISARA
Faculty of Veterinary Medicine: Assoc. Prof. PICHET LUENGTHONGCOME
Faculty of Management Sciences: Assoc. Prof. PORNSIRI THIVAVARNVONGS
Graduate School: Assoc. Prof. Dr WINIT CHINSUWAN (acting)

KING MONGKUT'S INSTITUTE OF TECHNOLOGY LADKRABANG

Chalongkrung Rd, Ladkrabang District, Bangkok 10520

Telephone: (2) 3269157
Telex: 84967
Fax: (2) 3267333

Founded 1960
State control

President: Prof. PAIRASH THAJCHAYAPONG
Vice-Presidents: TEERAMON WAIROCHANAKICH (Planning and Development), SUWAN KUSAMRAN (Administration), SUPACHAI RATANOPAS (International Affairs), WILAIWAN WONYODPUN (Finance and Property), WANLOP SURAKAMPOLTHON (Academic and Research Affairs), KRIENGSAK SUWANPOSRI (Student Affairs)
Administrative Officer: RUAMPORN INTARAPRASONG
Director of Central Library: UAIN PIN-NGERN

Library of 47,144 vols
Number of teachers: 571
Number of students: 8,663

DEANS AND HEADS OF DEPARTMENTS

Faculty of Engineering: PRAKIT TANGTISANON
- Telecommunications Engineering: KOBCHAI DEJHAN
- Electrical Engineering: MONTHON LEERAJINDAKRAIRERK
- Industrial Technology: UTHAI SRITHEERAVIROJANA
- Electronics: PRAPAKORN SUWANNA
- Mechanical Engineering: MING LOKITSANGTONG
- Computer Engineering: PRATHEEP BUNYATNOPARAT
- Control Engineering: SUTHIAN KIATSUNTHON
- Industrial Instrumentation: VIRIYA KONGRATANA
- Civil Engineering: AMNOUY PANITKULPONG
- Agricultural Engineering: SONGVOOT SANGCHAN

Faculty of Architecture: WICHIAN SUWANARAT
- Architecture: SOMCHAI SRISOMPONG
- Interior Architecture: SIRICHAI THANATIT
- Industrial Design: SURAPOL PLEEKRAM
- Communication Arts and Design: CHIRAPHONG BHUMICHITR
- Fine Arts: KIATTISAK CHANONNART
- Urban and Regional Planning: SOPARK PASUKNIRANT

Faculty of Industrial Education: PREEYAPORN WONGANUTROHD
- Industrial Education: OWAT POOLSIRI
- Languages and Social Sciences: AMNART TUNGJAROENCHAI
- Architectural Education: PICHAI SODBHIBAN
- Engineering Education: THEERAPHON THEPHASADIN NA AYUTHYA
- Agricultural Education: SOMJITTA KLUMGLIN

Faculty of Science: THEERAWAT MONGKOLAUSSAWARATNA
- Chemistry: PACHERNCHAI CHAIYASITH
- Mathematics and Computer Science: PAKKINEE CHITSAKUL
- Applied Physics: PREECHA TEANSOMPRASONG
- Applied Statistics: VEERASAK SURAPAT
- Applied Biology: OUNREAN SIRIVANITCHAGUL

Faculty of Agricultural Technology: AROM SRIPIJIT
Plant Production Technology: PANYA PHOTHITIRAT
Animal Production Technology: SRISAKUL VORACHANTRA
Agri-Business and Administration: NITTAYA SITHICHOKE
Agro-Industry: WARAWUT KRUSONG
Agricultural Technique: SANONG NILPETCH
Pest Management Technology: SUMRERNG KUMTHONG
Soil Science: SUMITRA POOVARODOM
Graduate School: MANAS SANGWORASIL
Computer Research and Service Centre: Dir CHOM KIMPAN
Faculty of Information Technology: Dir SURASIT VANNAKRAIROJN (acting)
Chumphorn Study and Research Center: Dir WITHYA BUAJARERN (acting)
International Education Center: Dir SUPACHAI RATANOPAS (acting)

KING MONGKUT'S INSTITUTE OF TECHNOLOGY NORTH BANGKOK

1518 Pibulsongkram Rd, Bangsue, Bangkok 10800
Telephone: (2) 913-2500
Fax: (2) 587-4350
Founded 1959
State control
Languages of instruction: Thai and English
Academic year: begins in June
President: Assoc. Prof. BANLENG SORNIL
Vice-President (Administration): Asst Prof. AMNUAY SANGSAWANG
Vice-President (Academic Affairs): Assoc. Prof. NARONG VARONGKRIENGKRAI
Vice-President (Planning and Development): Prof. Dr TERAVUTI BOONYASOPON
Vice-President (Student Affairs): Dr TIRACHOON MUANGNAPOH
Vice-President (Finance and Properties): Asst Prof. Dr PRANOM UTAKRIT
Vice-President (Special Affairs): CHATREE RATANAWONG
Registrar: SANGOB KONGKA
Director of Central Library: Assoc. Prof. TANAKORN KIETBANLUE
Number of teachers: 547
Number of students: 12,370
Publications: *Annual Report, Journal of King Mongkut's Institute of Technology North Bangkok, Educational Statistical Report, Report on the Status of Graduate Job Placement, New Enrolments, International News* (all annually).

DEANS

Faculty of Engineering: Asst Prof. Dr BUNDIT FUNGTAMMASAN
Faculty of Technical Education: SAMER ROENGANAN
Faculty of Applied Science: Asst Prof. Dr UTOMPORN PHALAVONK
Faculty of Technology and Industrial Management: WORAWIT CHATURAPANICH
Graduate College: Asst Prof. Dr SOMCHAI CHATRATANA

HEADS OF DEPARTMENT

Faculty of Engineering:
Chemical and Process Engineering: SANGNUAN SRIRATHCHATCHAWARN
Mechanical Engineering: Dr SUWAT KUNTANAPREEDA
Electrical Engineering: ITTHITHEP AMATYAKUL
Production Engineering: Asst Prof. SOMNUK WATANASRIYAKUL
Industrial Engineering: SOMKIAT JONGPRASITHPORN
Civil Engineering: VISIT PRATOOMSUWAN
Material Handling Technology: CHAIPORN VONGPISAL
Production Technology: THAWEEP NGAMSOM
Industrial Electrical Technology: Asst Prof. TEERASILAPA DUMAWIPATA

Faculty of Technical Education:
Computer Education: Assoc. Prof. Dr MONCHAI TIENTONG
Teacher Training in Mechanical Engineering: SUTTIPHAN KHUNIN
Teacher Training in Electrical Engineering: PRAMUAL KONGSAKORN
Teacher Training in Civil Engineering: NOPPADOL SRISUPARP
Technological Education: Asst Prof. PALLOP PIRIYASURAWONG
Language and Social Science: Assoc. Prof. ROSSUKON SRIVARAKAN
Technical Education Management: Dr SUPORN PANRAT-ISRA

Faculty of Applied Science:
Mathematics: Asst Prof. SUPORN RATANAPUN
Applied Statistics: WICHAI SURACHERDKIATI
Computer and Information Science: SOMCHAI PRAKANCHAROEN
Industrial Chemistry: RANUT SIRICHOTI
Agro-Industrial Technology: Asst Prof. GANNIKAR DISYAWONGS
Industrial Physics and Medical Instrumentation: Asst Prof. THONGCHAI SIRIPRAYOOK

Faculty of Technology and Industrial Management:
Industrial Management: TIKAMPORN THAWEEDECH
Information Technology: ANIRACH MINGKHWAN
Construction Technology: TOOL SRIMANTA

College of Industrial Technology:
Mechanical Technology: Asst Prof. CHALIE TRAGANGOON
Electrical Technology: ANAN WETWATANA
Civil Construction and Woodworking: Asst Prof. SOMNOEK WISSUTTIPAT
Social and Applied Science: Asst Prof. SIVILAI THANOMSUAY

ATTACHED INSTITUTES

College of Industrial Technology: Dir Asst Prof. CHAMNONG PHUMKAN.
Institute for Technical Education Development: Dir Asst Prof. BHAISAL HOONKEO.
Institute of Technological Development for Industry: Dir PONGTORN MANUPIPATPONGSE.
Institute of Computer and Information Technology: Dir NARONG WESNARAT.
Thai-French Innovation Centre: Dir PANARIT SETAKUL.

MAEJO UNIVERSITY

Sansai, Chiang Mai 50290
Telephone: (53) 878-038
Fax: (53) 498-861
Founded 1934, present name *c.* 1992 (fmrly Maejo Institute of Agricultural Technology)
State control
Language of instruction: Thai
Academic year: June to October, November to March
President: Prof. Dr KAMPHOL ADULAVIDHAYA
Vice-Presidents: SARAN PERMPOOL (Administration and Property), Asst Prof. Dr PISOT NUMSUP (Academic Affairs), Assoc. Prof. KITTIPONG VUTTIJUMNONK (Planning), Assoc. Prof. NIPON JAYAMANGKALA (International and Special Affairs), NARONGRIT PUSADEE (Student Affairs)
Registrar: KRISSADA BHACKDEE
Librarian: Dr BOONRAWD SUPA-UDOMLERK
Library of 72,300 vols, 42,700 periodicals
Number of teachers: 267
Number of students: 5,903
Publications: *Maejo Journal* (every 2 months, in Thai), *Journal of Agricultural Research and Extension* (every 2 months, in Thai with English summaries).

DEANS

Faculty of Agricultural Business: Assoc. Prof. Dr THEP PHONGPARNICH
Faculty of Agricultural Production: Asst Prof. Dr CHAMNIAN YOSRAJ
Faculty of Science: PRASAN WONGMANEERUNG
Faculty of Engineering and Agro-Industry: Assoc. Prof. KITTIPONG VUTIJUMNONK

HEADS OF DEPARTMENTS

Faculty of Agricultural Production:
Horticulture: Dr SAEKSAN USSAHATANANONT
Ornamentals: RAEWADEE WUTTIJUMNONK
Pomology: SUMET KETVARAPORN
Vegetable Technology: DAMKERNG PONGPAL
Agronomy: Dr ANAN PINTARAK
Plant Protection: Asst Prof. Dr DUMRE ROONGSOOK
Landscape and Environmental Conservation: SIRICHAI HONGVITYAKORN
Animal Technology: Dr VINAI YOTHINSIRIKUL
Farm Machinery: RATCHATA CHEUVIROJ
Soils and Fertilizers: Asst Prof. Dr PITOON KITTICHAICHANANONT
Fisheries Technology: Asst Prof. KRIANGSAK MENG-UMPUN

Faculty of Agricultural Business:
Agricultural Economics and Co-operatives: Asst Prof. CHOOSAK JANTANOPSIRI
Business Administration and Agricultural Marketing: WALAPA LIMSAKUI
General Education: ADISORN KHUNTAROSE
Agricultural Extension: Assoc. Prof. Dr WITTAYA DAMRONGKIATTISAK

Faculty of Science:
Biology: TUREAN THACHAROEN
Chemistry: SIRIRAT PAISANSUTHICOL
Computer Science: Assoc. Prof. CHARAS KAYAI
Mathematics and Statistics: YAOWALUCK KONGTHAM
Physics: WITTAYA WARASAWAS

Faculty of Engineering and Agro-Industry:
Food Technology: Asst Prof. UMAPORN SIRIPIN
Post-harvest Technology: SUJITRA RATANAMANO
Agriculture and Food Engineering: Asst Prof. TIENCHAI SANDUSADEE

MAHIDOL UNIVERSITY

198/2 Somdejpra Pinklao Rd, Bangyikhan, Bangplad, Bangkok 10700
Telephone: (2) 433-0140
Telex: 84770
Fax: (2) 433-7083
President: Prof. ATHASIT VEJJAJIVA
Vice-Presidents: Prof. CHANIKA TUCHINDA, Prof. PRASERT SOBHON (Academic Affairs), Asst Prof. MANAS WATANASAK (Student Affairs), Assoc. Prof. ORAPHAN MATANGKASOMBUT (International Relations), Assoc. Prof. BOONRAT AURSUDKIJ (Finance), Prof. SOMPOL PONGTHAI (Policy and Planning), Assoc. Prof. WIJITR FUNGLADDAR (Administration), Prof. SURAPOL ISSARAGRISIL (Research)
Number of teachers: 2,464
Number of students: 13,893
Publications: *MU Annual Information Booklets, MU Annual Research Abstracts, Spectrum* (newsletter).

DEANS

Faculty of Medicine, Siriraj Hospital: Prof. ARUN PAUSAWASDI
Faculty of Dentistry: Asst Prof. SOMSAK CHUCKPAIWONG
Faculty of Pharmacy: Assoc. Prof. CHANTRA CHAIPANICH

Faculty of Public Health: Assoc. Prof. PORNPAN PUNUARATABUNDHU
Faculty of Medical Technology: Assoc. Prof. VIRAPONG PRACHAYASITTIKUL
Faculty of Medicine, Ramathibodi Hospital: Prof. BOONCHOB PONGPANICH
Faculty of Tropical Medicine: Prof. SORNCHAI LOAREESUWAN
Faculty of Social Sciences and Humanities: Assoc. Prof. SUBARN PANVISAVAS
Faculty of Environmental and Resource Studies: Assoc. Prof. RUANGJARAT HUTACHAROEN
Faculty of Nursing: Assoc. Prof. TASSANA BOONTHONG
Faculty of Graduate Studies: Assoc. Prof. ADULYA VIRIYAVEJAKUL
Faculty of Engineering: PIROJANA SUVANSUTHI
Faculty of Science: Prof. PORNCHAI MATANGKASOMBUT

DIRECTORS

Institute for Population and Social Research: Assoc. Prof. BENCHA YODDUMMNERN-ATTIG
Institute of Nutrition: Prof. Dr KRAISID TONTISIRIN
Institute of Language and Culture for Rural Development: Prof. Dr KUNYING SURIYA RATANAKUL
Institute of Science and Technology for Development: Prof. SAKOL PANYIM
ASEAN Institute for Health Development: Asst Prof. SOM-ARCH WONGKHOMTHONG
College of Sports Science and Technology: Assoc. Prof. VICHAI VANADURONGWAN
College of Music: Assoc. Prof. SUGREE CHAROENSOOK
Mahidol University International College: Prof. CHARIYA BROCKELMAN
College of Management: Asst Prof. OHM HUWANUNTA
Rachasuda College: Assoc. Prof. POONPIT AMATYAKUL

NATIONAL INSTITUTE OF DEVELOPMENT ADMINISTRATION

118 Sereethai Rd, Klong Chan, Bangkapi, Bangkok 10240

Telephone: 377-7400
Fax: 375-8798

Founded 1966
State control
Languages of instruction: Thai and English
Academic year: June to May (3 semesters)

President: Assoc. Prof. Dr ANUMONGKOL SIRIVEDHIN
Vice-President for Academic Affairs: Asst Prof. Dr WUTTITHEP INDHAPANYA
Vice-President for Administration: Assoc. Prof. Dr SUCHITRA PUNYARATABANDHU
Vice-President for Planning: Assoc. Prof. NAREEWAN CHINTAKANOND
Library Director: SUTANNEE KEESIRI

Library of 202,300 vols
Number of teachers: 173
Number of students: 10,474

Publications: *Thai Journal of Development Administration* (quarterly), *Index to Thai Periodical Literature* (annually), *Index to Siamrath Weekly Review and Matichon Weekend* (annually), *NIDA Bulletin* (6 a year), *NIDA Annual Report*.

DEANS

School of Public Administration: Assoc. Prof. Dr VINIT SONGPRATOOM
School of Business Administration: Assoc. Prof. Dr CHIRADET OUSAWAT
School of Development Economics: Asst Prof. Dr WISARN PUPPHAVESA
School of Applied Statistics: Assoc. Prof. Dr SOOMBOONWAN SATYARAKWIT
School of Social Development: Assoc. Prof. Dr SAGOL JARIYAVIDYANONT

DIRECTORS

Training Center: Asst Prof. PHIN PANKHAO
Research Center: Assoc. Prof. Dr KANIKAR SOOKASAME
Language Center: SAVALEE NITITHAM
Library and Information Center: SUTANNEE KEESIRI
Information Systems Education Center: Asst Prof. CHAMIPORN KUNAKEMAKORN
Graduate Programme in Human Resource Development: Assoc. Prof. Dr CHARTCHAI NA CHIANGMAI
Graduate Development Center: Assoc. Prof. Dr CHARTCHAI NA CHIANGMAI

PROFESSORS

School of Public Administration:

Political Science: Prof. Dr PHAIBUL CHANGRIEN
Public Administration: Prof. Dr ARUN RACTHAM
Public Administration: Prof. Dr VORADEJ CHANDARASORN
City and Regional Planning: Prof. Dr GRIT PERMTANJIT
Human Behaviour in Urban Development: Prof. Dr BOONTON DOCKTHAISONG

School of Business Administration:

Organization Behaviour: Prof. Dr VUDHICHAI CHAMNONG

School of Applied Statistics:

Statistics: Prof. Dr PRACHOOM SUWATTEE

School of Social Development:

Social Psychology: Prof. Dr DUANGDUEN BHANTHUMNAVIN

Training Center:

Demography: Prof. Dr SUCHART PRASITHRATHSINT

PAYAP UNIVERSITY

Amphur Muang, Chiang Mai 50000
Telephone: (53) 304-805
Fax: (53) 241-983
E-mail: intexch@payap.ac.th

Founded 1974
Private control
Language of instruction: Thai
Academic year: June to March

President: Dr BOONTHONG POOCHAROEN
Vice-Presidents: NIPA TOTSPARIN (Academic Affairs), Dr BOONRATANA BOAYEN (Religious Affairs), CHOOWIT WOOTIKARN (Student Affairs), BOONSAK CHONGWATTANA (Administration)
Librarian: SUNTREE RATAYA-ANANT

Library of 125,100 vols
Number of teachers: 359
Number of students: 9,276

DEANS

Faculty of Accountancy and Finance: MANIT PABUT
Faculty of Business Administration: YUVALUCK CHIVAKIDAKARN
Faculty of Humanities: VIRA SAKDIVIRAVONGSA
Faculty of Science: DUANGDUEN POOCHAROEN
Faculty of Social Science: Dr NARONG PRACHADEJSUWAT
McCormick Faculty of Nursing: RUJIRA INDRATULA
Graduate School: Dr RANTANAPORN SETHAKUL
McGilvary Faculty of Theology: Rev. WILLIAM J. YODER
Faculty of Law: KASAMA DECHRUXSA

ATTACHED INSTITUTES

Christian Communications Institute: Dir Dr BOONRATANA BOAYEN.
Research and Development Institute: Dir Dr SINTH SARABOL.

PRINCE OF SONGKLA UNIVERSITY

71/1 Moo. 5 Thanon Karnjanavanich Tambon Kor-Hong, POB Hat-Yai, Hat-Yai District, Songkla 90110

Telephone: (74) 211030 (Hat-Yai Campus)
Fax: (74) 212828

Founded 1967
State control
Languages of instruction: Thai, English
Academic year: June to March (two semesters)

President: Assoc. Prof. Dr SUNTHORN SOTTHIBANDHU
Vice-President for Planning and Development: Assoc. Prof. UDOM CHOMCHAN
Vice-President, Hat-Yai Campus: Asst Prof. Dr METHI SUNBHANICH
Vice-President for Academic Affairs (Hat-Yai Campus): Dr PAIRAT SA-NGUANSAI
Vice-President for Research and International Relations: Assoc. Prof. Dr PRASERT CHITAPONG
Vice-President, Pattani Campus: Asst Prof. PRAPAN WISETRATTAKAM
Vice-President for Academic Affairs (Pattani Campus): Asst Prof. Dr SUWIMON KIEWKAEW
Vice-President for Special Affairs (Pattani Campus): PANN YAUNLAIE
Vice-President for Development Affairs (Pattani Campus): PRAMOTE KRAMUT
Vice-President for Development: Asst Prof. Dr SUJITRA JARAJIT
Assistant Presidents (Hat-Yai Campus): Asst Prof. Dr SUJITRA JORAJIT (Academic Affairs), PARIPON PATTANASATTAYAVONG (Physical Facilities), Asst Prof. SUPOTE KOVITAVA (Student Activities), JEDSADA MOKHAGUL (Student Development), WINIT JUNGCHAROENTHAM (System Development)
Assistant Presidents (Pattani Campus): SOMKIAT SUKNUNPONG (Administration), Asst Prof. WERA MANUSAVANICH (Student Affairs), Asst Prof. SUTHEP SANTIVARANON (Academic Affairs), PHAYAM PHETKLA (International Relations)

Number of teachers: 1,428
Number of students: 13,048

Publications: *PSU Newsletter, PSU Arts and Culture.*

DEANS AND HEADS OF DEPARTMENTS

Hat-Yai Campus

Faculty of Engineering: PICHIT RERNGSANGVATANA
Chemical Engineering: Asst Prof. CHAKRIT THONGURAI
Civil Engineering: Asst Prof. Dr VACHARA THAONGCHAROEN
Electrical Engineering: Dr PRAKARN KURAHONGSA
Industrial Engineering: SANE THANTHADALUGSANA
Mechanical Engineering: PAIROJ KIRIRAT
Mining and Metallurgical Engineering: Asst Prof. Dr DANUPON TANNAYOPAS
Computer Engineering: WEERAPANT MUSIGASARN

Faculty of Science: Prof. PUANGPEN SIRIRUGSA
Anatomy: ARAYA ADUNTRAKOOL
Mathematics: Asst Prof. BUNCHERD PUDTIKTI
Chemistry: Assoc. Prof. CHANITA PONGLIMANONT
Microbiology: VIVID SOMSARN
Biology: Assoc. Prof. JUTAMARD PHOLPUNTIN
Biochemistry: Assoc. Prof. PRAPAPORN UTARAPHUN
Physics: Dr WORAVUT LOHAVIJARN
Foreign Languages: ADISA SAETEAU
Pharmacology: PERARATCH THAINA
Physiology: Assoc. Prof. PRADUP PRASARTKAEW
General Science: Asst Prof. MANIDA PETCHARAT

Faculty of Medicine: Assoc. Prof. PUNTIPYA SANGUANCHUA
- Internal Medicine: Asst Prof. UTHAI KHOW-EAN
- Pathology: Asst Prof. SINEENART KALANUWAKUL
- Ophthalmology: Asst Prof. SUCHITRA KANOKKANTAPONG
- Otolaryngology: Asst Prof. SUMATE PERAVUT
- Paediatrics: Asst Prof. NARUMON PATARAKITVANICH
- Orthopaedic Surgery and Physical Therapy: Assoc. Prof. NIRAN KIATSIRIROJE
- Radiology: SOMCHAI WATTANAARPORNCHAI
- Obstetrics and Gynaecology: Asst Prof. VERAPOL CHANDEYING
- Anaesthesiology: Asst Prof. LUKSAMEE CHARNVATE
- Psychiatry: CHARNVIT NGENSRITRAKUL
- Surgery: Dr PRASERT VASINANUKORN
- Community Medicine: Asst. Prof. Dr THAWAN BENJAWONG
- Biomedical Sciences: SUVINA RATANACHAIYAVONG

Faculty of Management Science: Asst Prof. Dr SOMPORN FUANGCHAN
- Business Administration: Asst Prof. PRALOM CHAIRATANAPONG
- Public Administration: Asst Prof. TEERACHAI POOPAIBOOL
- Educational Foundation: SUNUNTRA CHUSCHART

Faculty of Natural Resources: Assoc. Prof. Dr SOMKIAT SAITANOO
- Plant Science: Asst Prof. Dr PRAVIT SOPANODON
- Animal Science: Asst Prof. PEERASAK SUTTIYOTIN
- Agricultural Development: Assoc. Prof. KRIANGSAK PATTAMARAKHA
- Aquatic Science: Dr KIDCHAKAN SUPAMATTAYA
- Earth Science: NIPA PANAPITUKKUL
- Pest Management Unit: Asst Prof. Dr SURAKRAI PERMKAM
- Agricultural Economics and Agricultural Projects: Asst Prof. SOMBOON CHARERNJIRATRAGUL

Faculty of Pharmaceutical Science: Asst Prof. Dr PITI TRISDIKOON
- Pharmaceutical Technology: Asst Prof. ARUNSRI SUNTHORNPIT
- Pharmaceutical Chemistry: Dr VIMON TANTISHAIYAKUL
- Pharmacognosy and Pharmaceutical Botany: Asst Prof. ARUNPORN ITHARAT
- Pharmacy Administration: AUTTAPORN SORNLERTLAMVANICH
- Clinical Pharmacy: Asst Prof. WANTANA LIANGMONGKOL

Faculty of Nursing: Asst. Prof. Dr SUNUTTRA TABOONPONG
- Paediatric Nursing: Dr LADDA PRATEEPCHAIKOOL
- Psychiatric Nursing: TIPPA CHETCHAOVALIT
- Administration in Nursing Education and Nursing Service: SAWITEE LYMCHAIARUNNRUNG
- Fundamental Nursing: SIRIRATANA KOSALWATANA
- Surgical Nursing: PINTIPAYA NARKDUM
- Public Health Nursing: Asst Prof. SUPANEE ONCHUNCHIT
- Obstetrical-Gynaecological Nursing and Midwifery: WATTANA SRIPOTEJANARD
- Medical Nursing: JARUWAN MANASURAKAM

Faculty of Dentistry: KRASSANAI WONGRANGSIMAKUL
- Oral Biology and Occlusion: Asst Prof. SITTICHAI KUNTHONGKAWE
- Prosthetic Dentistry: Asst. Prof. POTJANARAT BENJAKUL
- Preventive Dentistry: SUPANEE SUNTHORNLOHANAKUL
- Conservative Dentistry: PRATINYA RATANACHONT
- Surgery: Asst Prof. PRISANA PRIPATNANONT
- Stomatology: Asst Prof. RAWE TEANPAISAN

Faculty of Environmental Management Establishment Project: Asst. Prof. Dr CHADCHAI RATANACHAI

Faculty of Agro-Industry: Assoc. Prof. PAIBOON THAMMARATWASIK
- Food Technology: Dr SUANYA CHANTHACHUM
- Industrial Biotechnology: Assoc. Prof. Dr POONSUK PRASERTSUB
- Material Product Technology: Dr CHAIRAT SIRIPATANA
- Agro-industrial Technology: Assoc. Prof. PAIBOON THAMMARATWASIK (acting)
- Graduate School: Asst Prof. Dr KHARN CHANPROMMA

Pattani Campus

Faculty of Education: Asst Prof. Dr WIRAT THUMMARPORN
- Education: WITHADA SINPRAJUKPOL
- Educational Administration: SOMKIAT PUANGROD
- Educational Evaluation and Research: THAWEE THONGKUM
- Educational Technology: Asst Prof. PORNTHEP MUANGMAN
- Psychology and Guidance: PRASERT CHUSING
- Physical Education: CHARUS CHOOMUANG
- Demonstration School: Asst Prof. NONGNAT SATHAWARODOM (Dir)

Faculty of Humanities and Social Sciences: Asst Prof. PRAPAN WISETRATAKAM
- Eastern Languages: WORAWIT BARU
- Western Languages: CHAILERT KITPRASERT
- Thai Language: Assoc. Prof. WANNAO YUDEN
- Social Sciences: Asst Prof. NIPA CHAISAVATE
- Library Science: Assoc. Prof. Dr DHIDA BODHIBUKKANA
- Philosophy and Religion: Asst Prof. Dr PAITOON PATYAIYING
- History and Art: SOMBOON THANASOOK
- Geography: Asst Prof. PERM NILRAT

Faculty of Science and Technology: Asst Prof. PREECHA PONGBHAI
- Science: NOPPORN REINTHONG
- Home Economics: SUEBSAK GLINSORN
- Technology and Industry: SOMSAK LAOCHAREONSUK
- Rubber Technology and Polymer Science: ADISAI RUNGVICHANIWAT
- Mathematics and Computer Science: KANDA YANSAN

College of Islamic Studies: Dr ISMA-AE ALEE (Dir)
- Islamic Studies: ROHEEM NIYOMDECHA

Phuket Community College: Asst Prof. PUVADON BUTTRAT (Dir)

Faculty Establishment Project of Hotel and Tourism Management: Assoc. Prof. MANAT CHAISAWAT (Dir)

Surat Thani Community College: SORAT MAGBOON (Dir, acting)

Trang Province Educational Extension Project: Assoc. Prof. SOMKAEW RUNGIERDKRIENGKRAI (Dir)

RAMKHAMHAENG UNIVERSITY

Ramkhamhaeng Rd, Huamark, Bangkok 10241
Telephone: (2) 3180867
Telex: 72515
Fax: (2) 3180917
E-mail: admin@ram1.ru.ac.th

Founded 1971
State control
Language of instruction: Thai
Academic year: June to March (two semesters)

Rector: Prof. RANGSAN SAENGSOOK
Vice-Rector for Financial Affairs: Assoc. Prof. SOMCHINTANA SIVALI
Vice-Rector for General Affairs: Assoc. Prof. ARUNTAVADEE PHATNIBUL
Vice-Rector for Welfare: Assoc. Prof. NOPPAKUN KUNACHEEWA
Vice-Rector for Policy and Planning: Assoc. Prof. SUVAT SRIVITHAYARAKS
Vice-Rector for Business Affairs: Assoc. Prof. THEERA SINGHAPANDA
Vice-Rector for Academic Affairs and Research: Prof. Dr CHUTA THIANTHAI
Vice-Rector for International Affairs: Assoc. Prof. Dr KHOSIT INTAWONGSE
Vice-Rector for Administration: Assoc. Prof. SITTIPAN BUDDHAHUN
Vice-Rector for Student Affairs: Assoc. Prof. Dr PIT SOMPONG
Vice-Rector for Campus Affairs: Assoc. Prof. MATAYA INGKANART
Vice-Rector for Regional Centres Affairs: Assoc. Prof. VISIT TAWESETH
Vice-Rector for Arts and Cultural Affairs: Assoc. Prof. WIWATCHAI KULLAMARD
Director of Admissions and Records Office: SOMCHAI NOICHUM
Director of the Central Library Office: REANOO KANCHANABHOKIN

Number of teachers: 805
Number of students: 337,471

Publication: *Ramkhamhaeng University Newsletter* (weekly).

DEANS

Faculty of Business Administration: Assoc. Prof. VACHARAKORN SHEVASOPHIT
Faculty of Economics: Assoc. Prof. VANCHAI RIMVITAGAYORN
Faculty of Education: Assoc. Prof. PIMPUN TEPSUMETHANON
Faculty of Humanities: Assoc. Prof. NONTANA PUAKPONG
Faculty of Law: Assoc. Prof. JARAL LENGVITTAYA
Faculty of Political Science: Assoc. Prof. Dr NIYOM RATHAMARIT
Faculty of Science: Assoc. Prof. Dr PIBOON PURIVETH

HEADS OF DEPARTMENTS

Business Administration:
- General Management: Assoc. Prof. Dr NAPAPORN KANNAPHA
- Money and Banking: Assoc. Prof. ARUNEE NARINTRAKU NA AYUTHAYA
- Marketing: Assoc. Prof. BANYAT JUNNAPHAN
- Accounting: Assoc. Prof. SUKKAJIT NANAKORN
- Advertising and Public Relations: KANNOPAN IAM-OPAS
- Service Industries: SUVANNEE DEJVORACHAI

Economics:
- Economic Theory: Assoc. Prof. SOMRUX RAKSASUB
- Industrial Economics: MALEEWAN PONGAWASDI
- Monetary Economics: Assoc. Prof. SUPARIRK SRINATE
- Development Economics: Assoc. Prof. Dr BENJAPORN THONGKASEMVATHANA
- Economic History: Assoc. Prof. Dr YADA PRAPAPUN
- Quantitative Economics: Asst Prof. PAPAI TRAKARNVACHIRAHUT
- Agricultural Economics: Assoc. Prof. CHALEO CHATKEAO
- Human Resource Economics: Assoc. Prof. Dr NANTHAWAN ANTARASENA
- Public Finance: BOONTHAM RACHARAK
- International Economics: VASANT PHUVAPATTARAPORN

Education:
- Physical Education: Asst Prof. SUMETH KAEWPRAG
- Curriculum and Instruction: Assoc. Prof. RAVIWAN SRIKRAMKRAN
- Educational Foundation: Assoc. Prof. WINITA SUTTISOMBOON

Evaluation and Research: Assoc. Prof. Dr Boonmee Punthai
Psychology: Asst Prof. Lt Teerachai Hongyantarachai
Educational Technology: Tuangsang Nanakorn
Geography: Asst. Prof. Paitoon Piyapakorn
Home Economics: Assoc. Prof. Anukool Polsiri
Educational Administration and Higher Education: Assoc. Prof. Wattana Kurusawat
Continuing Education: Dr Sumana Charanasomboon

Humanities:
English and Linguistics: Assoc. Prof. Emorn Dispanya
Thai and Oriental Languages: Assoc. Prof. Saowaluk Anantasan
History: Assoc. Prof. Athaya Kamolkanchana
Library Science: Asst Prof. Yupa Saimala
Western Languages: Asst Prof. Dr Orapin Kampanthong
Philosophy: Assoc. Prof. Nongyao Channarong
Sociology and Anthropology: Asst Prof. Dr Chongcit Soponkanaporn
Mass Communication: Assoc. Prof. Arunee-prabhahomsettee

Law:
Public Law: Assoc. Prof. Dr Sirivat Supornpaibul
Civil Law: Surasak Iamboonyarit
Commercial Law: Assoc. Prof. Dr Kalaya Tansiri
General Law: Assoc. Prof. Chatuphorn Vongthongson
International Law: Assoc. Prof. Dr Mallika Pinijchan
Procedural Law: Assoc. Prof. Nakorn Setpuriwat
Legal Practice: Assoc. Prof. Nimit Chinkrua
Development Law: Assoc. Prof. Padungsak Noranitipadungkarn

Political Science:
Government: Assoc. Prof. Dr Usa Baiyoke
International Relations: Assoc. Prof. Karunlak Bhaholyotin
Public Administration: Assoc. Prof. Piyanush Ngernklay

Science:
Mathematics: Assoc. Prof. Dr Patchara Chaisuriya
Statistics: Assoc. Prof. Puntipa Sundarajun
Chemistry: Asst Prof. Preecha Paholdeph
Physics: Asst Prof. Dr Nipon Thangprasert
Biology: Ampawan Balankura
Computer Science: Assoc. Prof. Rapeepun Piriyakul
Materials Technology: Pakamas Sadindhammasak
Food Technology: Parichart Boonpikum

SIAM UNIVERSITY

235 Petchkasem Rd, Phasi-Charoen, Bangkok 10160
Telephone: (2) 457-0068
Fax: (2) 457-3982

Founded 1973
Private control

President: Dr Pornchai Mongkhonvanit
Vice-Presidents: Assoc. Prof. Dr Twee Hormchong (Academic Affairs), Prof. Dr Smith Kampempool (Research), Buncha Pornprapa (Student Affairs), Dr Prasert Luangaram (Planning and Development), Dr Subordas Warmsingh (Assistant for International Affairs)
Registrar: Suradej Prugsamatz
Librarian: Kannika Sirikhet

Library of 108,900 vols
Number of teachers: 588
Number of students: 17,897

Publications: *Siam University Review* (every 2 months), *Siam Business Review* (every 4 months), *Siam University Law School Journal* (annually)

DEANS
Faculty of Engineering: Prof. Dr Smith Kampermpool
Faculty of Law: Prof. Boonpraw Sangtien
Faculty of Liberal Arts: Prof. Dr Niphone Kanthasevi (acting)
Faculty of Communication Arts: Prof. Pratan Rangsimaporn
Faculty of Science: Assoc. Prof. Dr Twee Hormchong
Faculty of Nursing Science: Assoc. Prof. Panan Boon-Laung
Faculty of Graduate Studies: Assoc. Prof. Dr Sompong Janposri
School of Business Administration: Prof. Priya Vonkorporn

SILPAKORN UNIVERSITY

22 Boromrachachonnani Rd, Taling-Chan, Bangkok 10170
Telephone: (2) 880-7374
Fax: (2) 880-7372

Founded 1943
State control
Language of instruction: Thai
Academic year: June to March (2 semesters)

President: Assoc. Prof. Dr Trungjai Buranasomphob
Vice-Presidents:
Administrative Affairs: Asst Prof. Dr Nikom Tangkapipop
Academic Affairs: Prof. Dr Theera Nuhpiam
Planning and Development: Assoc. Prof. Sindhchai Kceokitichai
Special Affairs: Asst Prof. Pongsak Arayangkoon
International Affairs: Asst Prof. Dr Sompid Kattiyapikul
Student Affairs: Assoc. Prof. Kanit Kheovichai
Art and Culture: Panya Vijinthanasarn
Registrar: Pranee Toadithap
Librarian: Chirayoo Darsri

Number of teachers: 698
Number of students: 6,024

Publications: *Annual Report, Veridian* (newsletter).

Thapra Palace Campus: 31 Na-Pra Lan Rd, Bangkok 10200; tel. (2) 623-6115; fax (2) 225-7258

Vice-President: Asst Prof. Somchai Ekpanyakul

DEANS AND HEADS OF DEPARTMENTS
Faculty of Painting, Sculpture and Graphic Arts: Nonthivath Chandhanaphalin
Painting: Roong Trirapichit
Sculpture: Vichai Sithiratn
Graphic Arts: Yanawit Kunchaethong
Thai Arts: Thongchai Srisukprasert
Art Theory: Manop Isaradej
Faculty of Architecture: Chaicharn Thavaravet
Architecture: Suriya Rantanaputh
Related Arts and Architecture: Sathit Choosang
Architectural Technology: Charunpat Puvanant
Urban Design and Planning: Amara Juangbhanich
Faculty of Archaeology: Pibul Supakitvilekagarn
Archaeology: Pacharee Sarikabutara
Art History: Chittima Amornpichetkul
Anthropology: Maneewan Pewnim
Oriental Languages: Chirapat Prabandvidya
Western Languages: Poonsuk Temiyanon
Faculty of Decorative Arts: Teera Palprame
Interior Design: Niranr Krairiksh
Visual Communication Design: Nopadon Yudhamontri
Product Design: Pradit Kanchana-Akradej
Applied Art Studies: Pairoj Jumani
Ceramics: Supphaka Palprame

Sanamchand Palace Campus: Rajmankhanakana Rd, Muang District, Nakhon Pathom 73000; tel. (34) 253840; fax (34) 255099

Vice-President: Asst Prof. Dr Narong Chimpalee
Librarian: Kanchana Sukonthamanee

DEANS AND HEADS OF DEPARTMENTS
Faculty of Arts: Maneepin Phromsuthirak
Thai: Kanyarat Vechasat
English: Lakana Glinkong
French: Yaowadee Patanothai
German: Wanpen Banchongtad
History: Manas Kiattitharai
Geography: Worapot Chobthum
Philosophy: Tirasak Opasbutr
Social Science: Suwida Thammaneewong
Library Science: Rabiab Supawiree
Musical Art: Chollada Thongtawee
Faculty of Education: Likhit Karnchanaporn
Educational Administration: Pragob Kunarak
Foundations of Education: Manee Sriwiboon
Psychology and Guidance: Somsap Sookanan
Educational Technology: Thapanee Thammetar
Non-formal Education: Chidchong Nantananate
Curriculum and Instruction: Prasert Mongkol
Faculty of Science: Jarungsang Laksanaboonsong
Mathematics: Suda Tragantalengsak
Biology: Vilaiporn Boonyakitjinda
Chemistry: Puangnoi Aksorntong
Physics: Sa-guansiri Roongkeadsakoon
Environmental Science: Guntharee Sripongpan
Faculty of Pharmacy: Wanchai Sutananta
Biopharmaceutical: Rochaporn Wacharotayankun
Community Pharmacy: Rapeepun Chalongsuk
Pharmaceutical Chemistry: Lawan Sripong
Pharmaceutical Technology: Praneet Opanasopit
Pharmacognosy: Chavalit Sittisombut
Pharmacology and Toxicology: Pajaree Chotnopparatpat
Pharmaceutics: Intira Kanchanaphibool
Faculty of Industrial Technology: Amnard Sittattrakul
Materials Technology: Chanpen Anuratananon
Food Technology: Suchet Samuhasaneetoo
Biotechnology: Pittaya Liewsaree

SRINAKHARINWIROT UNIVERSITY

Sukhumvit Rd Soi 23, Bangkok 10110
Telephone: (2) 258-0310
Fax: (2) 258-4006

Founded 1954, University status 1974
State control
Language of instruction: Thai
Academic year: June to October, November to February, March to May

President: Prof. Dr Pote Sapianchai
Vice-Presidents: Assoc. Prof. Dr Boon-earn Milindasuda (Administration), Assoc. Prof. Dr Sumonta Promboom (Academic), Assoc. Prof. Dr Prapart Brudhiprabha (Research and International Relations), Asst Prof. Chalat Chongsubphant (Planning and Development), Dr Somsuke Terapijitra (Student Affairs), Dr Sakchai Tabsuwan (Special

Affairs), Asst Prof. Dr Piroj Intarasirisawat (Southern Campus), Assoc. Prof. Dr Phaisal Wangpanich (Ongkharak Campus)
Registrar: Urai Sanghkanand
Librarian: Assoc. Prof. Chaleo Pansida

Library: see Libraries
Number of teachers: 1,173
Number of students: 8,682 full-time, 4,282 evening

Publications: *Newsletters* (monthly), *Thesis Abstracts Series* (annually), faculty and campus periodicals, etc.

DEANS

Graduate School: Prof. Dr Siriyupa Poonsuwan
Faculty of Education: Assoc. Prof. Dr Sakchai Nirunthawee
Faculty of Social Sciences: Asst Prof. Dr Tumrong Udompaijitkul
Faculty of Sciences: Assoc. Prof. Dr Suthep Thongyoo
Faculty of Physical Education: Assoc. Prof. Dr Sujin Preechamart
Faculty of Humanities: Vinai Bhurahongse
Faculty of Pharmaceutical Science: Asst Prof. Dr Chavee Tongroach
Faculty of Medicine: Dr Thamoon Vaniyapong
Faculty of Engineering: Assoc. Prof. Dr Phaisal Wangpanich (acting)
Faculty of Dentistry: Assoc. Prof. Dr Yuttana Panya-Ngarm
Faculty of Fine Arts: Assoc. Prof. Dr Wiroon Tangcharoen

DIRECTORS

Behavioural Science Research Institute: Asst Prof. Dr Pachongchit Intasuwan
Institute of Asia Pacific Studies: Assoc. Prof. Piboon Duangchan
Institute of Eco-Tourism: Assoc. Prof. Dr Payom Dhamabuta
Institute of Southern Thai Studies: Asst Prof. Plubplung Kongchana

SUKHOTHAI THAMMATHIRAT OPEN UNIVERSITY

Bangpood, Pakkred, Nonthaburi 11120

Telephone: (2) 503-2121
Telex: 72353
Fax: (2) 503-3607

Founded 1978
State control
Language of instruction: Thai
Academic year: July to April (2 semesters), Summer Session May to July

President: Prof. Dr Iam Chaya-Ngam
Vice-President for Academic Affairs: Assoc. Prof. Dr Jumpol Nimpanich
Vice-President for Development: Prof. Dr Nipone Sookpreedee
Vice-President for Planning: Assoc. Prof. Dr Chow Rojanasang
Vice-President for Administration: Assoc. Prof. Natee Khlibtong
Vice-President for Operations: Assoc. Prof. Chutima Sacchanand
Vice-President for Special Affairs: Assoc. Prof. Dr Makha Khittasangka
Vice-President for Services: Assoc. Prof. Dr Tasanee Limsuwan
Registrar: Asst Prof. Somsak Meesap-Lak

Library of 608,100 vols, 1,078 periodicals
Number of teachers: 378
Number of students: 222,995

DEANS

School of Liberal Arts: Assoc. Prof. Dr Paitoon Mikusol
School of Educational Studies: Assoc. Prof. Dr Somprasong Wittayagiat
School of Management Science: Assoc. Prof. Suna Sithilertprasit
School of Law: Thienchai Na Nakorn
School of Economics: Dr Somchin Suntavaruk
School of Health Science: Asst Prof. Dr Adisak Sattam
School of Home Economics: Assoc. Prof. Dr Makha Kittasangka
School of Political Science: Assoc. Prof. Rosarin Siriyaphan
School of Agricultural Extension and Co-operatives: Assoc. Prof. Dr Pornchulee Nilvises
School of Communication Arts: Assoc. Prof. Sumon Yuesin
School of Science and Technology (pending official approval): Assoc. Prof. Dr Jumpol Nimpanich (acting)

THAMMASAT UNIVERSITY

2 Prachan Rd, Bangkok 10200
Telephone: 221-6111
Telex: 72432
Fax: 224-8099

Founded 1934
State control
Languages of instruction: Thai and English
Academic year: June to February (two semesters), Summer Session March to May

Rector: Assoc. Prof. Noranit Setabutr
Vice-Rector for General Administration: Dr Udom Rathamarit
Vice-Rector for Academic Affairs: Assoc. Prof. Dr Anek Laothamatas
Vice-Rector for Planning and Development: Assoc. Prof. Gasinee Witoonchart
Vice-Rector for Student Affairs: Assoc. Prof. Dr Kundhol Srisermbhok
Vice-Rector for Personnel Administration: Assoc. Prof. Dr Chintana Damronglerd
Vice-Rector for International Affairs: Dr Kajit Jittasevi
Vice-Rector for Finance and Property Management: Asst Prof. Jaruporn Viyanant
Vice-Rector for Administration at Rangsit Center: Assoc. Prof. Dr Twekiat Menakanist
Vice-Rector for Academic Affairs at Rangsit Centre: Asst Prof. Dr Boonhong Chongkid
Registration Office Director: Asst Prof. Sakon Varanyuwatana
Librarian: Nualchwee Suthamwong

Library: see Libraries
Number of teachers: 955
Number of students: 19,983

Publications: *Journal of Political Science, Thammasat University Journal, Thammasat Law Journal, Journal of Business Administration, Faculty Bulletin, Social Work Journal*, etc.

DEANS

Faculty of Law: Asst Prof. Sutee Supanit
Faculty of Commerce: Assoc. Dr Thanet Norabhoompipat
Faculty of Economics: Assoc. Prof. Dr Sirilaksana Khoman
Faculty of Political Science: Assoc. Prof. Dr Corrine Phuangkasem
Faculty of Social Administration: Dr Decha Sungkawan
Faculty of Liberal Arts: Asst Prof. Dr Sirinee Chenvidyakam
Faculty of Journalism and Mass Communication: Assoc. Prof. Piyagul Lawansiri
Faculty of Sociology and Anthropology: Pornchai Trakulwaranont
Faculty of Science and Technology: Assoc. Prof. Venus Peachavanich
Faculty of Engineering: Julsiri Jaroenpuntaruk
Faculty of Medicine: Prof. Suchati Indraprasit
Faculty of Dentistry: Assoc. Prof. Dr Prathip Phantumvanit
Faculty of Nursing: Asst Prof. Dr Siriporn Khamplikit
Faculty of Allied Health Science: Prof. Dr Vithoon Viyanant
Graduate School: Assoc. Prof. Manoon Pahirah
Sirindhon International Institute of Technology: Prof. Dr Sawasd Tantaratana

ATTACHED INSTITUTES

Language Institute: Dir Asst Prof. Dr Pratin Pimsarn
Thai Khadi Research Institute: Dir Assoc. Prof. Sumitr Pitiphat
Human Resources Institute: Dir Assoc. Prof. Dr Chulacheeb Chinwanno
Institute of East Asian Studies: Dir Assoc. Prof. Dr Medhi Krongkeaw
Information Processing Institute for Education and Development: Dir M. R. Pongsvas Svativat
Centre for Continuing Education and Social Service: Dir Assoc. Prof. Somchai Srisutthiyakorn
College of Innovative Education: Dir Assoc. Prof. Dr Naris Chaiyasoot

Colleges and Institutes

AGRICULTURE

Ayuthaya Agricultural College: Ayuthaya.

Bang Phra Agricultural College: Bang Phra, Cholburi; f. 1957; teacher training; 8,000 vols; Dir Dr Suraphol Sanguansri.

Surin Agricultural College: Surin.

TECHNOLOGY

Mahanakorn University of Technology: 51 Chuem Sampan Rd, Krathumrai, Nong Chok, Bangkok 10530; tel. 988-3655; fax 988-3687; f. 1990; private institution; masters degrees in engineering and business administration, bachelor degrees in science, engineering and veterinary medicine; Pres. Assoc. Prof. Dr Sitthichai Pookaiyaudom: publ. *Engineering Transactions* (3 a year).

Rajamangala Institute of Technology, Bangkok Technical Campus: 2 Nang Linchee Rd, Bangkok 10120; tel. 2863991; f. 1952; degree courses, 2- to 5-year certificate and diploma courses; 431 teachers; 6,111 students; library of 61,048 vols; Dir Skul Vejakorn; publs *Bulletin, Annual Report*.

DEANS

Faculty of Agriculture: T. Sarasophorn
Faculty of Engineering Technology: S. Povatong
Faculty of Business Administration: P. Chottikhun
Faculty of Home Economics: A. Chareonchai
Faculty of Fine Arts: B. Plawongse
Faculty of Music and Drama: P. Lapkesorn
Faculty of Liberal Arts: S. Pichyapaiboon
Faculty of Education: M. Kittipong

Rajamangala Institute of Technology, Khon Kaen Campus: 150 Srichan Rd, Khon Kaen; tel. (43) 236-451; f. 1963 (fmrly Thai-German Technical Institute); specializes in industrial technology; 3-year vocational certificate course, 2-year higher vocational diploma, 2-year BS; library of 11,186 vols (mainly industrial education); Dir Subhan Tuengsook.

Northern Technical Institute: Huay Kaew Rd, Chiangmai; f. 1957; library of 50,777 vols; 2–3-year diploma courses; Dir C. Suwathee.

Southern Technical Institute: Songkla.

TOGO

Learned Societies

BIBLIOGRAPHY, LIBRARY SCIENCE AND MUSEOLOGY

Association togolaise pour le développement de la documentation, des bibliothèques, archives et musées: s/c Bibliothèque de l'Université de Bénin, BP 1515, Lomé; f. 1959; promotes research in the field of documentation and library science; participates in the education of adults and young people; holds conferences, etc.; 60 mems; Pres. KOFFI ATTIGNON; Sec.-Gen. EKOUE AMAH.

Research Institutes

GENERAL

Institut Français de Recherche Scientifique pour le Développement en Coopération (ORSTOM): BP 375, Lomé; tel. 21-23-44; fax 21-03-43; f. 1949; agronomy, geology, pedology, geography, sociology, hydrology, geophysics, library; Dir J. L. LIERDEMAN. (See main entry under France.)

AGRICULTURE, FISHERIES AND VETERINARY SCIENCE

Institut de Recherches Agronomiques Tropicales et des Cultures Vivrières (IRAT): BP 1163, Lomé; tel. 21-21-48; Dir M. SARAGONI. (See main entry under France.)

Institut de Recherches du Café, du Cacao et Autres Plantes Stimulantes (IRCC): BP 90, Kpalimé; tel. 41-00-34; fax 410060; f. 1967; research to improve quality and production of coffee, cocoa and other stimulants; experimental unit at Tové; Dir K. EDEM DJIEKPOR.

Institut Togolais de Recherche Agronomique: BP 01, Kolokopé Anié; f. 1948; Dir M. LAODJASSONDO; publ. *Rapports annuels Coton et Fibres Tropicales*. (See main entry under France.)

NATURAL SCIENCES

General

Institut National de la Recherche Scientifique: BP 2240, Lomé; tel. 21-01-39; f. 1965; initiation of national scientific research; rural development research; 12 permanent staff; library of 5,000 vols; publ. *Etudes Togolaises* (2 a year).

TECHNOLOGY

Service des Mines du Togo: c/o Ministère des Mines, Ave de la Marina, Lomé; Dir-Gen. ANKOUM P. AREGBA.

Libraries and Archives

Lomé

Archives Nationales du Togo: POB 1002, Lomé; tel. 21-04-10; f. 1976; administered by the Nat. Ministry for Education and Scientific Research; library of 2,500 vols, specializing in colonial history, tropical agronomy, stock breeding, health; Curator SENGHOR MOUSSA.

Bibliothèque du Ministère de l'Intérieur: Rue Albert Sarraut, Lomé; Librarian KWAOVI GABRIEL JOHNSON.

Bibliothèque Nationale: BP 1002, Lomé; German and French archives; 13,600 vols, 650 periodicals; Dir ZAKARI MAMAH.

Museums and Art Galleries

Lomé

Direction du Musée National, des Sites et Monuments: BP 12156, Lomé; tel. 21-68-07; fax 21-43-80; f. 1974; Curator of the National Museum NAYONDJOUA DJANGUENANE.

University

UNIVERSITÉ DU BÉNIN

BP 1515, Lomé

Telephone: 21-30-27
Telex: 5258
Fax: 21-85-95

Founded 1965 as a College; university status 1970; includes all the institutions of higher education in the country
State control
Language of instruction: French
Academic year: October to June (three terms)
Rector: Prof. K. SEDDOH
Vice-Rector: Prof. O. TIDJANI
Secretary-General: A. TABO
Librarian: E.E. AMAH
Library of 70,000 vols
Number of teachers: 650
Number of students: 11,000

Publications: *Livret de l'Etudiant, Annales (Lettres, Sciences, Médecine, Droit-Economie), Actes des Journées Scientifiques, Annuaire*.

DEANS AND DIRECTORS

Faculty of Medicine: Prof. K. KESSIE
Faculty of Letters and Humanities: Prof. L. PH. BOLOUVI
Faculty of Sciences: Prof. M. GBEASSOR
Faculty of Law: Prof. M. FOLI
Faculty of Economics and Business Management: K. AYASSOU
National Higher School of Engineering: E. K.-S. BEDJA
Higher School of Agriculture: K. AGBEKO
University Technical Institute of Food and Biological Sciences: K. DOGBA
Medical Training School: Prof. K. TATAGAN-AGBI
National Institute of Education: A. KOMLAN
University Technical Institute of Management: N. BIGOU-LARE
Higher Secretarial School: N. A. SEDDOH

Colleges

Centre de Formation Professionnelle Agricole de Tove: BP 401, Kpalimé; f. 1901; 21 teachers, 230 students; library of 3,500 vols; Dir S. N. KANKARTI; Sec.-Gen. I. KUEVI.

Ecole Africaine des Métiers d'Architecture et d'Urbanisme: BP 2067, Lomé; tel. 21-62-53; telex 5322; fax 22-06-52; f. 1975; specialist courses in architecture and town planning; in-service courses for trained architects; library of 1,957 vols; 23 staff; 102 students; Dir AHMED ASKIA SIDI.

Ecole Nationale d'Administration: Ave de la Libération, Lomé; f. 1958; provides training for Togolese civil servants; *c.* 50 students; library of over 1,000 vols; Dir FOUSSÉNI MAMA; Sec.-Gen. NICOLAS ADJETEY.

Technical College: Sokodé; apprentice training.

TONGA

Learned Societies

BIBLIOGRAPHY, LIBRARY SCIENCE AND MUSEOLOGY

Tonga Library Association: c/o USP Tonga Centre, POB 278, Nuku'alofa; tel. 29-055; fax 29-249; e-mail judy@tonga.usp.ac.fj; f. 1981; training courses and library-related activities for children; 40 mems; Pres. JUDY MATILEI; Sec. LOMALANI KAVAPALU.

Libraries and Archives

Nuku'alofa

Ministry of Education Library: POB 123, Nuku'alofa; tel. 21-588; f. 1976; provides supplementary reading and text books for students and public library service; 12,432 vols; special collection: Pacific (1,515 vols); Librarian Miss TUILOKAMANA TUITA.

University of the South Pacific, Tonga Centre Library: POB 278, Nuku'alofa; tel. 29-240; fax 29-249; e-mail judy@tonga.usp.ac.fj; 10,000 vols; Librarian JUDITH MATILEI.

Museums and Art Galleries

Nuku'alofa

Tupou College Museum: POB 25, Nuku'alofa; tel. 32-240; f. 1866; museum within Tupou College; artifacts from Tonga's history; Principal Rev. SIOSAIA PELE.

Colleges

Atenisi Institute: POB 220, Nuku'alofa; private control; language, literature, mathematics, philosophy, sociology; Founder/Dir Prof. FUTA HELU.

Hango Agricultural College: Ohonua, Eua; tel. 50044; fax (676) 50128; f. 1968; part of Free Wesleyan Church Education System; 1-year diploma course in para-veterinary studies, 1-year diploma course in horticulture/cropping, 2-year certificate course; 7 teachers; 55 students; library of 1,200 vols.

Tonga Maritime Polytechnical Institute: POB 485, Nuku'alofa; tel. 22-667; fax 24-334; f. 1985; maritime and technical divisions; library of 300 vols; 20 teachers, 160 students; Principal MELINO KUPU.

University of the South Pacific, Tonga Centre: POB 278, Nuku'alofa; tel. 29-240; fax 29-249; e-mail salote@tonga.usp.ac.fj; library: see Libraries and Archives; Dir SALOTE FUKOFUKA.

Includes:

Tonga Centre: extension centre with responsibilities for distance education, adult non-formal education; interests in village and community development and appropriate technology; Dir SALOTE FUKOFUKA.

TRINIDAD AND TOBAGO

Learned Societies

AGRICULTURE, FISHERIES AND VETERINARY SCIENCE

Agricultural Society of Trinidad and Tobago: POB 256, 112 St Vincent St, Port-of-Spain; f. 1894; 528 mems; Pres. AINSLEY NICHOLS; Sec. J. S. HANNIBAL; publ. *Journal* (1 a year).

Sugar Manufacture Association of Trinidad and Tobago: 80 Abercromby St, POB 230, Port-of-Spain; tel. 62–36106; f. 1967; to promote information of interest to the sugar industry; 272 mems; Pres. T. N. SKINNER; Sec. M. Y. KHAN; publ. *Proceedings*.

Tobago District Agricultural Society: Main St, Scarborough; Pres. Capt. R. H. HARROWER; Sec. Miss S. A. DAVIES.

ARCHITECTURE AND TOWN PLANNING

Trinidad and Tobago Institute of Architects: POB 585, Port-of-Spain; tel. 625-5982; fax 624-5217; f. 1954; present name 1982; 65 mems (incl. overseas); Pres. GEOFFREY MACLEAN; Hon. Sec. LINDA LOIUSON; publ. *Journal* (annually).

BIBLIOGRAPHY, LIBRARY SCIENCE AND MUSEOLOGY

Library Association of Trinidad and Tobago: POB 1275, Port-of-Spain; e-mail latt@ttemail.com; f. 1960; Pres. ESAHACK MOHAMMED; Sec. SHAMIN RENWICK; publ. *Bulletin*.

ECONOMICS, LAW AND POLITICS

Law Association of Trinidad and Tobago: 62 Sackville St, Port-of-Spain; f. 1986; Pres. FRANK SOLOMON; Sec. STEPHANIE DALY; publ. *The Lawyer* (every 6 months).

EDUCATION

Congress of Adult Education of Trinidad and Tobago: c/o School of Continuing Studies Unit, University of the West Indies, St Augustine; tel. 663-1364, ext. 2516; f. 1980; Hon. Pres. H.E. NOOR HASSANALI; Chair. CAROL KELLER; Sec.-Treas. ALTHEA CLIFFORD; publs reports of seminars, workshops.

FINE AND PERFORMING ARTS

Trinidad Music Association: Bishop Anstey High School, Abercromby St, Port-of-Spain; f. 1941; 102 mems; Pres. Mrs ROBERT JOHNSTONE; Hon. Sec. Mrs VELMA JARDINE.

HISTORY, GEOGRAPHY AND ARCHAEOLOGY

Historical Society of Trinidad and Tobago: c/o POB 780, Port-of-Spain; f. 1932; 45 mems; Pres. MAX B. IFILL; Hon. Sec. and Treas. KENT VILLAFANA.

MEDICINE

Pharmaceutical Society of Trinidad and Tobago: c/o Ministry of Health, Welfare and Status of Women, 35–37 Sackville St, Port-of-Spain; f. 1899; 300 mems; Pres. (vacant); Hon. Sec. W. E. WILLIAMS.

Libraries and Archives

Port-of-Spain

Central Library of Trinidad and Tobago: POB 547, corner Duke and Pembroke Sts, Port-of-Spain; tel. 624-3120; fax 625-5369; e-mail nalis@trinidad.net; f. 1941; a division of the Office of the Prime Minister; 442,000 vols; public library; Heritage Library held jointly with Trinidad Public Library; 13 brs; Dir PAMELLA BENSON; publ. *Trinidad and Tobago National Bibliography.*

National Archives: The Government Archivist, POB 763, 105 St Vincent St, Port-of-Spain; tel. 625-2689; f. 1960; government and private archives; microfilm copies of Trinidad and Tobago records in other countries; Dir EDWINA PETERS; publ. *Select Documents*.

Trinidad Public Library: corner Duke and Pembroke Sts, Port-of-Spain; tel. 624-3409; fax 624-1130; f. 1851; 70,000 vols; Heritage Library held jointly with Central Library of Trinidad and Tobago; 2 brs; Librarian LYNETTE COMISSIONG.

St Augustine

University of the West Indies, Main Library: St Augustine; tel. 662-2002 ext. 2132; fax 662-9238; e-mail mainlib@library.uwi.tt; f. 1926; 324,000 vols, 16,000 serials, 769,000 unbound serial parts, 27,000 audiovisual items, 3,000 MSS, 318 archives, 33,000 microtexts, 27,000 other non-book items; West Indiana, Oral and Pictorial Records Collections; Campus Librarian Dr MARGARET ROUSE-JONES; publs *CARINDEX: Science and Technology* (2 a year), *CARINDEX: Social Sciences and Humanities* (2 a year), *OPReP Newsletter*. (See also under Jamaica.)

San Fernando

San Fernando Carnegie Free Library: Harris Promenade, San Fernando; tel. 652-2921; fax 653-9645; f. 1919; lending and reference service for children and adults; 36,109 vols; special collection: West Indies, Carnival; Librarian REYNOLD BASSANT.

Museums and Art Galleries

Port-of-Spain

National Museum and Art Gallery: 117 Frederick St, Port-of-Spain; tel. 623-5941; fax 623-7116; f. 1898 as Royal Victoria Inst., present status 1962; art, archaeology, history, Carnival, petroleum technology; Curator VEL A. LEWIS; publs occasional papers on Folk Arts, History, etc.

University

UNIVERSITY OF THE WEST INDIES, ST AUGUSTINE CAMPUS

St Augustine, Trinidad

Telephone: 663-1334

Fax: 662-2002

Founded 1948 by the Governments of the Caribbean Commonwealth Territories with the co-operation of the British Government. The University serves Jamaica, Trinidad and Tobago, Barbados and the Commonwealth Territories in the Caribbean

Autonomous control

Language of instruction: English

Academic year: September to June

Chancellor: Sir SHRIDATH RAMPHAL

Vice-Chancellor: Sir ALISTER MCINTYRE

Pro-Vice-Chancellor and Principal at St Augustine: Prof. C. BOURNE

Deputy Principal: Prof. B. MOOTOO

Registrar of St Augustine: Z. ALI

Librarian at St Augustine: Dr MARGARET ROUSE-JONES

Number of teachers: 413

Number of students: 6,007

Publications: *Caribbean Dialogue* (policy bulletin of Caribbean affairs), *Journal of Tropical Agriculture, St Augustine News,* departmental reports.

DEANS

Faculty of Agriculture and Natural Sciences: Dr C. R. MCDAVID

Faculty of Humanities and Education: V. SINGH

Faculty of Engineering: Prof. G. S. KOCHHAR

Faculty of Medical Sciences: Prof. G. N. MELVILLE

Faculty of Social Sciences: Dr P. WATSON

PROFESSORS

BACON, P., Zoology
BOURNE, C., Economics
BRERETON, B., History
BUTLER, D., Cocoa Research
CARRINGTON, L. D., School of Continuing Studies
DEOSARAN, R., Behavioural Sciences
DUNCAN, J., Plant Sciences
DUROJAIYE, M. D. A., Teacher Education
EZEOKOLI, D., Veterinary Surgery
FARRELL, E. J., Mathematics
FEYTMANS, E., Biochemistry (Pre-Clinical Sciences)
GEORGIEV, G., Community Health
HAYNES, S., Dentistry
KAMINJOLO, J. S., Veterinary Microbiology
KING, ST. C., Electronics and Instrumentation
KOCHHAR, G. S., Mechanical Engineering
MCGAW, D. R., Chemical Engineering
MELVILLE, G. N., Physiology
MOOTOO, B., Chemistry
NARAYAN, C. V., Mechanical Engineering
NJOKU, C. O., Veterinary Anatomical Pathology
POSTHOFF, C., Computer Science
RAMCHAND, K., English
RAE, A., Human Anatomy (Pre-Clinical Sciences)
ROHLEHR, D. G., West Indian Literature
ROOPNARINESINGH, S., Obstetrics and Gynaecology
RYAN, S., Social and Economic Research
SAUNDERS, R. M., Physics
SUITE, W., Civil Engineering
TELANG, B. V., Pharmacology
THOMSON, E. R., Oral and Maxillofacial Surgery
WILSON, L. A., Crop Science

ATTACHED INSTITUTES

Caribbean Agricultural Research and Development Institute: St Augustine; Exec. Dir HAYDEN BLADES. (Field units in Barbados and Jamaica.)

Institute of Business: St Augustine; tel. 624-4356; fax 624-8753; Dir B. TEWARIE.

Institute of International Relations: St Augustine; tel. 66-22002, ext. 2011; f. 1966; diplomatic training, postgraduate teaching and research in int. relations; Dir CARL PARRIS.

Institute of Social and Economic Research: St Augustine; Assoc. Dir S. RYAN.

TUNISIA

Learned Societies

GENERAL

Comité Culturel National: 105 ave de la Liberté, Tunis; central body co-ordinating national and international cultural activities, sponsored by the Ministry of Culture and by foreign embassies; Regional and Local Cultural Committees throughout the country; Pres. MOHAMED TALBI; Sec.-Gen. AMARA SKHIRI.

BIBLIOGRAPHY, LIBRARY SCIENCE AND MUSEOLOGY

Association Tunisienne des Bibliothécaires, Documentalistes et Archivistes: BP 380, 1015 Tunis; f. 1965; information sciences; 150 mems; Pres. KSIBI AHMED; publ. *Newsletter* (in Arabic, quarterly).

Comité National des Musées: Musée National du Bardo, Tunis; f. 1961; Pres. HABIB BEN YOUNES; publ. *Les musées de Tunisie.*

EDUCATION

Arab League Educational, Cultural and Scientific Organization (ALECSO)/ Organisation de la Ligue Arabe pour l'Education, la Culture et la Science: BP 1120, Ave Mohamed V, Tunis; tel. 784-466; telex 18825; f. 1970 for the development of education, culture and sciences in Arab countries; mems: 21 Arab countries; library of 5,000 vols; Dir Gen. MOHAMED EL-MILI BRAHIMI; publs *Arab Journal of Culture, Arab Journal of Science, Arab Journal of Language Studies, Arab Journal of Education, Arab Journal of Information, Arab Magazine of Information Science, Statistical Yearbook of Education in Arab Countries, Analytical Studies on Education, Culture, Science and Literacy.*

FINE AND PERFORMING ARTS

Union Nationale des Arts Plastiques: Musée du Belvédère, Tunis.

LANGUAGE AND LITERATURE

Institut des Belles Lettres Arabes: 12 rue Jamâa el Haoua, 1008 Tunis Bab Menara; tel. (1) 560-133; fax (1) 572-683; f. 1930; cultural centre; library of Tunisian studies (31,000 vols); Dir A. FERRE; publs *IBLA* (2 a year), various studies on Tunisian, Arab and Islamic studies.

Union des Ecrivains Tunisiens: 20 ave de Paris, 1000 Tunis; f. 1970; 200 mems; Pres. MOHAMED LAROUSSI MÉTOUI; Sec. Gen. SOUF ABIOL; publ. *El Masson.*

Research Institutes

GENERAL

Centre d'Etudes Maghrebines à Tunis: Impasse Menabrea, 19 bis rue d'Angleterre, BP 404, 1049 Tunis-Hached; tel. (1) 326-219; fax (1) 328-378; e-mail cemat@planet.tn; f. 1985; operated by American Institute for Maghrib Studies, Univ. of Wisconsin, Milwaukee; sponsors research by American scholars in all disciplines; gives research grants; facilitates liaison with North African scholars; holds annual research conference and frequent lectures; research library of 1,600 vols, 800 dissertations; Dir JEANNE JEFFERS MRAD; publs *Newsletter*, conference proceedings, occasional papers.

Institut Français de Recherche Scientifique pour le Développement en Coopération Mission ORSTOM: 5 impasse Chahrazed, BP 434, 1004 Tunis El Menzah; tel. 750-009; fax 750-254; f. 1958; pedology, hydrology, microbiology, medical entomology, agricultural economics, archaeology, desertification, remote detection; library; Dir J. CLAUDE. (See main entry under France.)

Institut National de Recherche Scientifique et Technique (INRST): BP 95, Hammam-Lif 2050; premises at: Route Touristique, Borj-Cedria, Soliman; tel. 430-215; telex 15453; fax 430-934; f. 1969; applied physics, biology, chemistry, biotechnology, earth sciences, development of the use of domestic and industrial waste; library of 1,500 vols, 100 in special collections; Dir MOHAMED ENNABLI; Sec.-Gen. MESSAOUD CHAHTOUR.

AGRICULTURE, FISHERIES AND VETERINARY SCIENCE

Centre de Recherche du Génie Rural: BP 10, Ariana 2080; tel. (1) 718-055; f. 1959; agronomy, irrigation, etc.; Dir MOHAMED NEJIB REJEB; publ. *Cahier du CRGR.*

Institut de la Recherche Vétérinaire de Tunisie: Rue Djebel Lakhdhar La Rabta, 1006 Tunis; tel. (1) 562-602; fax (1) 569-692; f. 1897; veterinary research; library of 3,000 vols; Dir Dr MALEK ZRELLI.

Institut National de la Recherche Agronomique de Tunisie: Rue Hédi Karray 2080, Ariana; tel. 230-024; f. 1914 as the Service Botanique et Agronomique de Tunisie; improvement of vegetable and livestock production through the use of appropriate agroecological and socioeconomic methods; library of 7,300 vols, 1,500 periodicals; Dir Dr M. S. MEKNI; publs *Annales*, and miscellaneous reprints: *Documents techniques.*

Institut National de Recherches Forestières de Tunisie: BP 2-2080, Ariana; f. 1967 under present title; research in all aspects of forestry; 130 staff, of whom 13 are research workers; Documentation Centre comprises 2,981 vols and 3,144 documents; Dir M. DAHMAN; publs *Bulletin d'Information* (2 or 3 a year), *Annales, Notes de Recherches.*

Institut National des Sciences et Technologies de la Mer: 28 rue 2 Mars 1934, 2025 Salammbô; tel. (1) 73-05-48; fax (1) 73-26-22; f. 1924; fisheries research, aquaculture, fishing technology, marine environment; library of 35,000 vols; marine museum; Dir-Gen. Prof. AMOR EL-ABED; publs *Notes* (3 a year), *Bulletin* (annually).

BIBLIOGRAPHY, LIBRARY SCIENCE AND MUSEOLOGY

Institut National du Patrimoine: 4 place du Château, 1008 Tunis; tel. 261-622; f. 1957; library of 25,000 vols; archaeology, museography, ethnography, research, protection and evaluation of the national heritage; Dir ABDELAZIZ DAOULATLI; publ. *Africa.*

EDUCATION

Institut National des Sciences de l'Education: 17 rue d'Irak, 1002 Tunis-Belvédère; tel. 287-722; fax 795-423; f. 1969; conducts research, undertakes assessment of curricula, books, students and teaching techniques, develops the use of audiovisual aids in education, organizes seminars and conferences; library of 30,000 vols; Dir NEJIB AYED; publs *Revue Tunisienne des Sciences de l'Education, Cahiers de l'INSE, Bulletin pédagogique.*

MEDICINE

Institut Pasteur: BP 74, 13 place Pasteur, 1002 Tunis Belvédère; tel. (1) 789-608; telex 14391; fax (1) 791-833; f. 1893; research in health sciences; library of 4,500 vols, 200 periodicals; Dir Prof. K. DELLAGI; publ. *Archives* (quarterly).

TECHNOLOGY

Centre National de l'Informatique: 17 rue Belhassen Ben Chaâbane, El-Omrane, 1005 Tunis; tel. 783-055; fax 781-862; e-mail mongi .miled@e-mail.ari.tn; f. 1976; assistance, training, development of computer applications and software, management of processing centres; library of 4,000 vols; Dir MONGI MILED.

Office National des Mines: BP 215, 1080 Tunis Cedex; premises at: 24 rue 8601, La Charguia, Tunis; tel. (1) 788-842; fax (1) 794-016; f. 1962; geological research and mapmaking; bibliographic database on geology of Tunisia; library of 10,000 vols, 450 periodicals; Pres. and Dir-Gen. ABDERRAHMAN TOUHAMI; publs *Annales des Mines et de la Géologie, Notes du service géologique.*

Libraries and Archives

Tunis

Archives Nationales: Le Premier Ministère, La Casbah, 1020 Tunis; tel. 560556; fax 569-175; f.1874; MSS in Arabic, Turkish, French, Italian and English; library of 5,000 vols; Dir MONCEF FAKHFAKH; publ. *Inventaires des documents d'archives conservés.*

Bibliothèque Nationale: BP 42, 20 Souk-el-Attarine, Tunis; tel. 245–338; fax 342-700; f. 1885; 1,500,000 vols in 12 languages; 15,000 periodicals; 40,000 Arabic and Oriental MSS; depository of books published in Tunisia; documentation and information dept; Curator DJOMA'A CHIKHA; publs *Bibliographie Nationale* (annually), *Catalogue général des manuscrits* (annually).

Bibliothèques Publiques: Head Office: 39 rue Asdrubal, Lafayette, 1002 Tunis; tel. 782-552; fax 797-752; f. 1965; 2,746,678 vols in 293 public libraries throughout the country, notably at Tunis, Béjà, Bizerte, Gabès, Gafsa, Jendouba, Kairouan, Kasserine, El Kef, Medenine, Monastir, Nabeul, Sfax, Sousse, Siliana, Mahdia, Ariana, Ben Arous, Zagnouan, Sidi Bouzid, Tozeur, Kébili and Tetaouine; 233 children's libraries, 266 local and community libraries and 27 mobile libraries; Dir ALI FETTAHI; publs *Statistics of public libraries, Répertoire, Bulletin* (annually).

Centre de Documentation Nationale: 4 rue Ibn Nadim, 1002 Tunis-Belvédère; tel. (1) 894-266; fax (1) 792-241; f. 1966; library of 8,000 monographs, 2,400 periodicals, 10,000 press articles, 50,000 photographs; Dir-Gen. MOHAMED MAHFOUDH.

Museums and Art Galleries

Carthage

Musée National de Carthage: BP 3, 2016 Carthage; tel. 730-036; fax 730-099; f. 1964; archaeology; library of 5,000 vols (special collection: antiquity); Dir ABDELMAJID ENNABLI.

El Jem

Musée Archéologique d'El Jem: El Jem.

Kairouan

Musée d'Art Islamique: Kairouan.

Makthar

Musée Archéologique de Makthar: Makthar; Punic and Roman.

Monastir

Musée d'Art Islamique du Ribat: Monastir.

Sbeïtla

Musée de Sbeïtla: Sbeïtla; Roman antiquities.

Sfax

Musée Archéologique de Sfax: Sfax.

Sousse

Musée Archéologique de Sousse (Kasbah): Sousse.

Tunis

Maison des Arts: Parc du Belvédère, 1002 Tunis; tel. 283-749; fax 795-860; f. 1992; art exhibition, musical and cultural activities; library of 6,000 vols; Dir ALI LOUATI.

Musée National du Bardo: 2000 Le Bardo, Tunis; tel. 513-650; fax 514-050; f. 1888; contains prehistoric collections, relics of Punic, Greek and Roman art, and ancient and modern Islamic arts, largest collection in the world of Roman mosaics; library of 4,700 vols; Dir HABIB BEN YOUNES; publs *Les Nécropoles Puniques de Tunisie*, and occasional publications.

Universities

UNIVERSITÉ DES LETTRES, DES ARTS ET DES SCIENCES HUMAINES (TUNIS I)

29 rue Asdrubal, 1002 Tunis

Telephone: 788-068
Fax: 786-776

Founded 1988 from existing faculties

President: ABDERRAOUF MAHBOULI
Secretary-General: LAMJED MESSOUSSI

Number of teachers: 1,025
Number of students: 25,782

Publications: *Les Annales de l'Université* (in Arabic), *Les Cahiers de Tunisie* (multilingual), *La Revue des Langues* (multilingual), *La Revue Tunisienne des Sciences de la Communication.*

DEANS AND DIRECTORS

Faculty of Letters: HEDI TRABELSI
Faculty of Human and Social Sciences: HASSEN ANNABI
Institute of Journalism and Information Sciences: MUSTAPHA HASSEN
Bourguiba Institute of Modern Languages: AYATOLLAH LABADI
Higher Documentation Institute: HENDA HAJAMI BEN GHZALA
Higher Institute of Education and Training: MALIKA AYADI
Higher Institute of the History of the National Movement: NOURDDINE DOGUI
Higher Institute of Drama: MOHAMED MESSAOUD DRISS
Higher Institute of Music: MUSTAPHA ALOULOU
Higher Institute of Childhood Research: TAHAR ABID
Higher Institute for Youth and Cultural Activity: TAOUFIK HAWAT
National Institute of Heritage: BOUBAKER BEN FREDJ
Higher Normal School of Tunis: SAMIR MARZOUKI
Tunis National School of Architecture and Town Planning: MOULDI CHAABANI
Tunis Higher Institute of Fine Arts: AÏCHA FILALI

UNIVERSITÉ DES SCIENCES, DES TECHNIQUES ET DE MÉDECINE DE TUNIS (TUNIS II)

Campus Universitaire, Manar II, 2092 Tunis
Telephone: 873-366
Fax: 872-055

Founded 1988 from existing faculties

President: Prof. RAFÂA BEN ACHOUR
Secretary-General: ISMAIL KHELIL

Number of teachers: 2,733
Number of students: 23,488

DEANS AND DIRECTORS

Faculty of Mathematics, Physics and Natural Sciences: HABIB ZANGER
Faculty of Sciences at Bizerte: HECHMI SAID
Faculty of Medicine: CHELBI BELKAHIA
Sidi Thabet National School of Veterinary Medicine: ATEF MALEK
Higher School of Health Sciences and Technology: HABIB JAAFOURA
National School of Engineering: KHELIFA MAALEL
National School of Computer Science: FAROUK KAMMOUN
Nabeul Preparatory Institute of Engineering: MONCEF HADDED
Higher School of Posts and Telecommunications: NACEUR AMMAR
National Institute of Agronomy: MONCEF EL-HARRABI
Kef Higher School of Agriculture: BOUZID NASRAOUI
Mograne Higher School of Agriculture: TIJANI MAHOUACHI
Medjez el Bab Higher School of Rural Engineering: ABDERRAZEK SUISSI
Mateur Higher School of Agriculture: HEDI ABDOULI
Tabarka Forestry School: HAMDA SAOUDI
Higher School of Food Technology: ABDELKADER CHERIF
Preparatory Institute of Scientific Studies and Technology: FAOUZIA CHARFI
Institute for the Advancement of Disabled People: RAOUF BEN AMMAR
Higher Institute for Sport and Physical Education: ABDELAZIZ SFAR
Kef Institute for Sport and Physical Education: YOUSSEF FEKIH
El Khawarizmi Computer Centre: KAMEL BERHOUMA
Higher School of Science and Technology: SLAHEDDINE EL-GHRISSI
National Institute of Applied Sciences and Technology: MOHAMED AMARA
Polytechnic Institute: TAIEB HADHRI
Tunis Preparatory School of Engineering: EZZEDDINE TRIKI
Mateur Preparatory School of Engineering: MOHAMED BEJAOUI
National Research Institute of Rural Engineering for Water and Forests: NEJI RAJEB
Veterinary Research Institute: MALEK ZRELLI
National Agricultural Research Institute: SALAH MEKNI

UNIVERSITÉ DE DROIT, D'ÉCONOMIE ET DE GESTION (TUNIS III)

29 rue Asdrubal, BP 106, 1002 Tunis

Founded 1988 from existing faculties

President: AFIF HENDAOUI

DIRECTORS

Institute of Higher Commercial Studies (Carthage): RIDHA FERCHIOU
Higher Institute of Business Management (Le Bardo): ABDESSATAR GRISSA

UNIVERSITÉ DE SFAX

Route de l'Aéroport, Sfax

Telephone: 40200
Fax: 40913

Founded 1986 from existing faculties
State Control
Languages of instruction: Arabic, French

President: MOHAMED HEDI KTARI
Secretary-General: MOHSEN BEN MANSOUR

Number of teachers: 556
Number of students: 8,895

DEANS

Faculty of Medicine: Prof. HABIB MOKHTAR JEDDI
Faculty of Economics and Administration: Prof. SALMA ZOUARI-BOUATTOUR
Faculty of Arts and Humanities: Prof. FATHI TRIKI
Faculty of Law: Prof. NEJI BACCOUCHE
Faculty of Science: Prof. SALEM MANSOUR

CONSTITUENT INSTITUTES

National School of Engineering: route Soukra, Sfax 3038; Dir Prof. YOUSSEF MLIK.

National School of Engineering: route de Medenine, Gabes 6029; Dir Prof. MOHIEDDINE ALOUI.

Higher Institute of Technology: route de Medenine, Gabes 6011; Dir Dr SLAH ROUMDHANE.

Higher Institute of Industry and Mining Technology: Cité des Jeunes, 2119 Gafsa; Dir Dr SAIED LAATAR.

RESEARCH CENTRE

Biotechnology Centre: route Soukra, 3038 Sfax; Dir Prof. RADHOUANE ELLOUZ.

UNIVERSITÉ ZITOUNA

Abou-Zakaria El Hafsi, Montfleury, Tunis

Founded 1988 from existing faculties

President: TOUHAMI NEGRA

Faculties of theology and religious studies.

Other Institutions of Higher Education

Centre Culturel International d'Hammamet: Ave des Nations Unies, 8050, Hammamet; tel. 280-410; fax 280-722; f. 1962; theatrical techniques, history and sociology of the theatre and video; Dir TAOUFIK BESBÈS.

Conservatoire National de Musique, de Danse et d'Arts Populaires: 20 ave de Paris, Tunis.

Ecole Nationale d'Administration: 24 ave du Docteur Calmette, Mutuelleville, Tunis;

tel. 288-300; f. 1964; library of 53,000 vols; 1,050 students; Dir MAHER KAMOUN; publ. *Revue Tunisienne d'Administration Publique* (3 a year).

Ecole Nationale de la Statistique: BP 65, Tunis; f. 1969; 1- and 2-year diploma courses.

Institut d'Economie Quantitative: 27 rue de Liban, 1002 Tunis; tel. 283-633; fax 787-034; f. 1964; methodological research in planning and documentation in social and economic fields; library of 7,500 vols, 300 periodicals; Dir Gen. GHORBEL HÉDI.

Institut National du Travail et des Etudes Sociales: Z. I. Charguia II, BP 692, 1080 Tunis Cedex; tel. 706-207; fax 703-464; 34 full-time teachers, 76 part-time teachers; library of 5,000 vols; Dir Prof. MUSTAPHA NASRAOUI; publ. *Travail et Développement*.

TURKEY

Learned Societies

AGRICULTURE, FISHERIES AND VETERINARY SCIENCE

Türk Veteriner Hekimleri Derneği (Turkish Veterinary Medicine Association): Saglik Sok. 21–3, Yenisehir, Ankara; f. 1930.

BIBLIOGRAPHY, LIBRARY SCIENCE AND MUSEOLOGY

Türk Kütüphaneciler Derneği (Turkish Librarians' Association): Elgün Sok. 8/8, 06440 Yenişehir, Ankara; tel. (312) 230-13-25; fax (312) 232-04-53; f. 1949; *c.* 1,500 mems; Pres. A. BERBEROGLU; Sec.-Gen. A. KAYGUSUZ; publ. *Türk Kütüphaneciliği*.

ECONOMICS, LAW AND POLITICS

Türk Hukuk Kurumu (Turkish Law Association): 2 Cad. 55/6 Bahçelievler, Ankara; f. 1934; publs *La Turquie* (Vie Juridique des Peuples, Paris), *Türk Hukuk Lûgati* (Turkish Law Dictionary).

EDUCATION

Türk Üniversite Rektörleri Komitesi (Cttee of Turkish University Rectors): Yükseköğretim Kurulu, Bilkent, Ankara; tel. (312) 266-47-25; telex 42839; fax (312) 266-51-53; f. 1967; rectors of all Turkish universities, with five former rectors; advises the Higher Education Ccl and the Interuniversity Board on university affairs, promotes co-operation between universities; Pres. Prof. Dr KEMAL GÜRÜZ; Sec. Prof. Dr UĞUR BÜGET.

HISTORY, GEOGRAPHY AND ARCHAEOLOGY

Türk Tarih Kurumu (Turkish Historical Society): Kızılay Sok. 1, 06100 Sıhhiye, Ankara; tel. 3102368; fax 3101698; e-mail yusuf@ttk.gov; f. 1931; 40 mems; library of 212,000 vols; Pres. Prof. Dr YUSUF HALAÇOĞLU; publs *Belleten* (3 a year), *Belgeler* (annually).

LANGUAGE AND LITERATURE

PEN Yazarlar Derneği (Turkish PEN Centre): General Yazgan, Sok 10/10, 80050 Tünel, Istanbul; tel. and fax (212) 292-00-26; f. 1989; 200 mems; Pres. ALPAY KABACALI; Sec.-Gen. SUAT KARANTAY; publ. *Turkish PEN Reader* (every 6 months, in English).

Türk Dil Kurumu (Turkish Language Institute): Kavaklıdere, 06680 Ankara; tel. (312) 428-61-00; fax (312) 428-52-88; e-mail tdili @tdk.gov.tr; f. 1932; 40 mems; library of 35,000 vols; Pres. Prof. Dr AHMET B. ERCİLASUN; Sec.-Gen. HALİL SELÇUK; publ. *Türk Dili Araştırmaları Yıllığı* (Yearbook of Turkic Studies), *Tercüme Yıllığı* (Yearbook of Translation).

MEDICINE

Türk Cerrahi Cemiyeti (Turkish Surgical Society): Valikonagi Cad. 10, Harbiye, Istanbul; f. 1931.

Türk Mikrobiyoloji Cemiyeti (Turkish Microbiological Society): PK 57, Beyazit, Istanbul; fax (216) 349-55-94; f. 1931; Pres. Prof. Dr OZDEM ANĞ; Sec. Gen. Assoc. Prof. Dr CANDAN BOZOK JOHANSSON; publs *Türk Mikrobiyoloji Cemiyeti Dergisi* (Journal, quarterly), *Infeksiyon Dergisi* (quarterly).

Türk Nöropsikiyatri Derneği (Turkish Neuropsychiatric Society): İ.Ü. Istanbul Tıp Fakültesi Psikiyatri Kliniği, 34390 Topkapı/ Istanbul; f. 1914; 1,200 mems; meetings to discuss aspects of psychiatry and neurology; Pres. Prof. ÖZCAN KÖKNEL; Sec.-Gen. Dr RAŞIT TÜKEL; publ. *Nöropsikiyatri Arşivi* (Archives of Neuropsychiatry) (quarterly).

Türk Ortopedi ve Travmatoloji Derneği (Turkish Association of Orthopaedics and Traumatology): Istanbul Tıp Fakültesi Ortopedi, Kliniği Topkapı, 34390 Istanbul; tel. (212) 524-10-53; fax (212) 635-28-35; f. 1939; 867 mems; library of 3,700 vols; Pres. Prof. Dr FAHRİ SEYHAN; Sec.-Gen. Dr I. R. TÖZÜN; publ. *Acta Orthopaedica et Traumatologica Turcica* (5 a year).

Türk Oto-Rino-Larengoloji Cemiyeti (Turkish Oto-Rhino-Laryngological Society): c/o Cerrahpaşa Tip Fakültesi Kulak, Burun, Boğaz Anabilim Dali Cerrahpaşa, Istanbul; tel. 5861575; f. 1930; 1,500 mems; Pres. Prof. Dr ORHAN SUNAR; Gen. Sec. Prof. Dr NURETTIN SÖZEN; publ. *Turkish Archives of Otolaryngology* (quarterly).

Türk Tıb Cemiyeti (Turkish Medical Society): Valikonagi Cad. 10, Harbiye, Istanbul; f. 1856; 312 mems; Pres. Dr KAZIM İSMAİL GÜRKAN; Sec. Dr ASİL MUKBİL ATAKAM; publs *Türk Tıp Cemiyeti Mecmuası, Anadolu Klinigi* (Turkish Medical Journal).

Türk Tibbi Elektro Radyografi Cemiyeti (Turkish Electro-Radiographical Society): Valikonagi Cad. 10, Harbiye, Istanbul; f. 1924.

Türk Tıp Tarihi Kurumu (Turkish Medical History Society): Tıp Tarihi Enstitüsü, Istanbul University, Istanbul; f. 1938; 48 mems; library of 70,000 vols; Dirs Prof. BEDI N. ŞEHSUVAROĞLU, Prof. FERIDUN FRIK.

Türk Tüberküloz Cemiyet (Turkish Tuberculosis Society): Selime Hatun, Sağlik Sok., Taksim, Istanbul; f. 1937.

Türk Uroloji Derneği (Turkish Urological Society): c/o Dr Cafer Yildiran, Tâlimhane Lâmartin Cad. 46/4, Eren ap. Taksim, Istanbul; f. 1933; 180 mems; Pres. Dr SEDAT TELLALOGLU; Vice Pres. Dr CAFER YILDIRAN; publs *Türk Uroloji Dergisi* (Turkish Journal of Urology, quarterly).

NATURAL SCIENCES

Mathematical Sciences

Türk Matematik Derneği (Turkish Society of Mathematics): i.ü. Fen Fakültesi Matematik Bölümü, 34459 Vezneciler, Istanbul; f. 1948; development of mathematics among young people; 420 mems; Pres. Prof. TOSUN TERZIOĞLU.

Physical Sciences

Türkiye Kimya Derneği (Chemical Society of Turkey): Harbiye, Halaskârgazi Cad. 53, Uzay Apt D.8, PK 829, Istanbul; tel. 1407331; f. 1919; 1,500 mems; Pres. Prof. Dr ALI RIZA BERKEM; Sec. Chem. Eng. ERDEM TARGUL; publ. *Kimya ve Sanayi* (Chemistry and Industry).

PHILOSOPHY AND PSYCHOLOGY

Türkiye Felsefe Kurumu (Philosophical Society of Turkey): f. 1974 to promote philosophy and philosophical education in Turkey, to encourage philosophical thinking in public life, and to secure international co-operation through seminars, symposia, courses etc.; 123 individual mems; Pres. IOANNA KUÇURADI; Sec.-Gen. ISMAIL DEMIRDÖVEN, P.K. 176, Yenişehir, 06442 Ankara; tel. 2351219; fax 4410297; publ. *Bülteni* (3 a year).

Yeni Felsefe Cemiyeti (New Philosophical Society): Işık Lisesi, Nişantaşı, Istanbul; f. 1943.

TECHNOLOGY

TMMOB Jeoloji Mühendisleri Odası (Chamber of Geological Engineers of Turkey): PK 464-Yenişehir, 06444 Ankara; tel. (312) 434-36-01; fax (312) 434-23-88; e-mail tmmobj-o@servis2.net.tr; f. 1974; 6,600 mems; library of 14,000 vols; Pres. AYHAN KÖSEBALABAN; Sec.-Gen. MUTLU GÜRLER; publs *Geological Bulletin of Turkey* (2 a year), *Abstracts of the Geological Congress of Turkey* (annually), *Journal of Geological Engineering* (2 a year), *Bulletin News* (4 a year), *Abstracts of Geological Research in Turkey* (annually), *Energy Bulletin of Turkey* (2 a year).

Research Institutes

GENERAL

Milletlerarasi Şark Tetkikleri Cemiyeti (International Society for Oriental Research): Türkiyat Enstitüsü, Bayezit, Istanbul; f. 1947; Pres. Prof. FUAD KÖPRÜLÜ.

Research Centre for Islamic History, Art and Culture (IRCICA): POB 24, 80692 Beşiktaş, İstanbul; tel. (212) 259-17-42; telex 26484; fax (212) 258-43-65; f. 1979; a subsidiary of the Organisation of the Islamic Conference; research and publication, organization of conferences, symposia and exhibitions; library of 50,000 vols, 62,000 photographs; Dir-Gen. Prof. Dr EKMELEDDİN İHSANOĞLU; publ. *IRCICA Newsletter* (3 a year).

Türk Kültürünü Araştırma Enstitüsü (Turkish Cultural Research Institute): 17° Sok. 38, Bahçelievler, Ankara; tel. (312) 213-31-00; fax (312) 213-41-35; f. 1961; scholarly research into all aspects of Turkish culture; Dir Dr ŞÜKRÜ ELÇİN; publs *Türk Kültürü* (monthly), *Cultura Turcica* (annually), *Türk Kültürü Araştırmaları* (annually).

Türkiye Bilimsel ve Teknik Araştırma Kurumu (Scientific and Technical Research Council of Turkey): Atatürk Bulvarı 221, 06100 Kavaklıdere, Ankara; tel. (312) 468-53-00; telex 43186; fax (312) 427-74-89; f. 1963; library of 19,000 vols, 426 periodicals; government body which carries out, sponsors, promotes and co-ordinates research activities in pure and applied sciences; Pres. Prof. Dr TOSUN TERZIOĞLU; Sec.-Gen. SALIH ZEKI TOKDEMIR: publs *Bilim ve Teknik* (Science and Technology, monthly), (Turkish Journals of Agriculture and Forestry, Medical Sciences, Physics, Chemistry, Engineering and Environmental Sciences, Mathematics, Biology, Botany, Zoology, Veterinary and Animal Sciences, Earth Sciences, Electrical Engineering and Computer Sciences), *Tübitak Bulteni* (Tübitak Bulletin, 6 a year), *Tokten* (bulletin, 3 a year), *Eureka* (bulletin, 3 a year), *Informatics Bulletin* (6 a year).

Attached institutes:

Ankara Electronics Research and Development Institute: İnönü Bulv., Middle East Technical University Campus, 06531 Ankara; tel. (312) 210-1310; fax (312) 210-1315; Dir Prof. Dr AYHAN TÜRELI.

Defence Research and Development Institute: PK 16 Mamak, 06261 Ankara; tel. (312) 399-0338; fax (312) 212-3749; Dir Prof. Dr ERES SÖYLEMEZ.

Marmara Research Centre: PK 21, Gebze, Kocaeli; tel. (262) 641-2300; fax (262) 641-7250; Dir ÖMER KAYMAKÇALAN.

AGRICULTURE, FISHERIES AND VETERINARY SCIENCE

Çay Başkanliği Enstitüsü (Tea Research Institute): Zihniderin Cad., PK 23, 53100 Rize; tel. 30284; telex 83306; fax 30239; f. 1958; tea cultivation; library of 1,500 vols; Pres. HAYRİ PİRİMOĞLU; publ. *Annual Report*.

Kavak ve Hızlı Gelişen Tür Orman Ağaçları Araştırma Müdürlüğü (Poplar and Fast Growing Forest Trees Research Institute): PK 93, 41001 Izmit; tel. (262) 335-08-70; fax (262) 335-08-85; f. 1962; attached to the Ministry of Forests; development of forest nursery and reafforestation techniques, introduction of new forest tree species, increase of wood production, research in poplar cultivation and management techniques; library of 3,700 vols; Dir ALİ SENCER BİRLER; publs *Annual Bulletin, Magazine, Technical Bulletin*.

Tarım ve Köyişleri Bakanliğı, Zirai Mücadele Araştırma Enstitüsü (Ministry of Agricultural and Rural Affairs, Plant Protection Research Institute): Bağdat Cad. 250, PK 49, Yenimahalle, Ankara; tel. (312) 344-74-30; fax (312) 315-15-31; f. 1934; depts dealing with research into combating plant diseases, pests and weeds; engaged in phytopathology, entomology, insect taxonomy and toxicology, nematology; analyses pesticides and crop pesticide residues; library of 5,000 vols; Dir Dr ZİYA ŞİMŞEK; publ. *Bitki Koruma Bülteni* (Plant Protection Bulletin, English, French or German summary, irregularly).

HISTORY, GEOGRAPHY AND ARCHAEOLOGY

British Institute of Archaeology at Ankara: Tahran Cad. 24, Kavaklıdere, 06700 Ankara; tel. 426-5487; fax 428-0159; f. 1947 with the object of furthering archaeological research by British and Commonwealth students or scholars in Turkey; London Office: c/o Gina Coulthard, British Institute of Archaeology at Ankara, Senate House, Malet St, London WC1E 7HU, England; library of *c*. 20,000 vols; Pres. Prof. O. R. GURNEY; Dir Dr ROGER MATTHEWS; publs *Anatolian Studies* (annually), *Occasional Publications, Monograph Series*.

Deutsches Archäologisches Institut: Gümüşsuyu/Ayazpaşa Camii Sk. 48, 80090 Istanbul; tel. 2440714; fax 2523491; f. 1929; research into archaeology and cultural history in Turkey from prehistory to the Ottoman period; library of 60,000 vols; Dir Prof. Dr HARALD HAUPTMANN; publs *Istanbuler Mitteilungen des DAI* (annually), *Istanbuler Forschungen, Istanbuler Beihefte*.

Hollanda Tarih ve Arkeoloji Enstitüsü (Netherlands Historical and Archaeological Institute): Istiklâl Cad. 393, Beyoğlu, Istanbul; tel. (212) 293-92-83; fax (212) 251-38-46; f. 1958; library of 12,500 vols; Dir H. E. LAGRO; Sec. Y. ERDEMLİ; publ. *Anatolica*.

Institut Français d'Etudes Anatoliennes d'Istanbul: PK 54, Palais de France, 80072 Beyoğlu-Istanbul; tel. (212) 244-17-17; fax (212) 252-80-91; f. 1930; Anatolian studies from prehistory to contemporary period; library of 18,000 vols; 11 mems; Dir STÉPHANE YERASIMOS; publs *Travaux et Recherches en Turquie, Varia Turcica, Varia Anatolica, Anatolia antiqua* (annually), *Anatolia moderna* (annually).

MEDICINE

Çocuk Sağlığı Enstitüsü (Institute of Child Health): Hacettepe University Children's Hospital, 06100 Ankara; tel. (312) 324-42-91; fax (312) 324-32-84; f. 1958; library incorporated in Medical Faculty Library; Dir Dr A. MURAT TUNCER; publs *Turkish Journal of Paediatrics* (quarterly), *Çocuk Sağlığı ve Hastalıkları Dergisi* (abstracts in English, quarterly).

NATURAL SCIENCES

General

İstanbul Üniversitesi Deniz Bilimleri ve İşletmeciliği Enstitüsü (University of Istanbul, Institute of Marine Sciences and Management): Müsküle Sok. Vefa 1, 34470 Istanbul; tel. (212) 528-25-39; fax (212) 526-84-33; f. 1993; 14 mems; library of 11,243 vols; Dir Prof. Dr ERTUĞRUL DOĞAN; publ. *Turkish Journal of Marine Science* (3 a year).

Türk Bilim Tarihi Kurumu (Turkish Society for History of Science): POB 234, 80692 Beşiktaş, Istanbul; tel. (212) 260-07-17; fax (212) 258-43-65; e-mail ircica@superonline.com; f. 1989; research and publication on history of science with emphasis on Ottoman history of science, organization of symposia; Pres. Prof. Dr EKMELEDDİN İHSANOĞLU; publ. *Newsletter* (2 a year).

Physical Sciences

Maden Tetkik ve Arama Genel Müdürlüğü (MTA) (General Directorate of Mineral Research and Exploration): İsmet İnönü Bulvarı, Ankara; f. 1935; conducts the Geological Survey of Turkey and evaluates mineral resources; library: see Libraries; Dir-Gen. CENGİZ ATAK; publs *Bulletin* (2 a year, in English), monographs, annual reports and maps.

RELIGION, SOCIOLOGY AND ANTHROPOLOGY

İslâm Araştırmaları Merkezi (Centre for Islamic Studies): Bağlarbaşı, Gümüşyolu Caddesi 38, 81200 Üsküdar, İstanbul; tel. (216) 474-08-50; f. 1988; library of 100,000 vols, 1,700 periodicals; Chair. Doç. Dr AZMİ ÖZCAN; Sec.-Gen. SÜLEYMAN N. AKÇEŞME; publ. *Turkish Journal of Islamic Studies*.

TECHNOLOGY

Ankara Nükleer Araştırma ve Eğitim Merkezi (Ankara Nuclear Research and Training Centre): 06105 Saray, Ankara; tel. (312) 815-43-00; fax (312) 815-43-07; f. 1967; attached to the Turkish Atomic Energy Authority; applied research in radiation chemistry and physics, electronics, nuclear agriculture, materials sciences and plasma physics; library of periodicals and technical reports; Dir O. GÜVEN; publ. *Turkish Journal of Nuclear Sciences* (2 a year).

Araştirma Dairesi Başkanliği (Dept of Research and Materials, General Directorate of Turkish Highways): Yücetepe, Ankara; tel. 188016; f. 1948; road materials testing, pavement design, soil and rock mechanics and geotechnical investigations; 60 staff; library of 2,467 vols; Dir TANKUT BALKIR; publ. *Research Bulletin*.

Deprem Araştırma Dairesi (Earthquake Research Dept): Yüksel Cad. 7/B, Yenişehir, Ankara; f. 1969; 78 staff; attached to the Ministry of Public Works and Resettlement; establishment, operation and maintenance of nationwide strong ground motion recorder network; earthquake prediction; preparation of codes and regulations for earthquake resistant design and construction; research on earthquake hazard minimization; education and information of the public; Pres. OKTAY ERGÜNAY; publ. *Bulletin* (quarterly).

Devlet Su İşleri Teknik Araştırma ve Kalite Kontrol Dairesi, DSİ (State Hydraulic Works, Technical Research and Quality Control Department): 06100 Ankara; f. 1958; research and laboratory work on hydraulic engineering, soil mechanics, construction materials and concrete, chemistry, isotopes for hydrology; *in situ* research on water works; library; Dir Assoc. Prof. ERGÜN DEMİRÖZ; publ. *DSI Teknik Bülteni* (original papers, some in foreign languages).

Marmara Scientific and Industrial Research Centre: POB 21, Gebze-Kocaeli; f. 1972; research on basic and applied sciences, and industrial research; library of 90,000 vols, 746 periodicals; Dir Prof. ÖMER KAYMAKÇALAN; publs research reports.

Libraries and Archives

Afyon

Gedik Ahmed Paşa Library: Afyon; f. 1785; 30,000 vols.

Akseki

Yegen Mehmet Paşa Library: Akseki; f. 1926; 6,000 vols.

Ankara

Ankara University Library: Ankara; the main library has 50,000 vols; there are also separate faculty, institute and higher school libraries, with a total of over 750,000 vols; Librarian Dr H. SEKINE KARAKAŞ.

Grand National Assembly Library and Documentation Centre: T.B.M.M. Kütüphane ve Dokümantasyon Merkezi, Ankara; tel. (312) 420-68-35; fax (312) 420-75-48; e-mail library@tbmm.gov.tr; f. 1920; 255,000 vols in social sciences including 138,000 in Turkish, 68,000 in European languages, 1,000 in Arabic and Persian, 500 MSS, 50,000 vols of periodicals; Dir ALI RIZA CİHAN; publ. *Bilgi* (quarterly).

Library of National Defence: Ankara; f. 1877; 8,678 vols in Turkish, 5,820 vols in other languages; State-governed.

Library of the Mineral Research and Exploration General Directorate: İsmet İnönü Bulvarı, Ankara; f. 1935; 180,000 vols in various languages; Librarian ÜMİT ERKMEN; publs *Bulletin*, monographs, annual reports and maps (in Turkish and English).

Middle East Technical University Library: İsmet İnönü Bulvarı, 06531 Ankara; tel. (312) 210-27-80; fax (312) 210-11-19; e-mail lib-hot-line@metu.edu.tr; f. 1956; maintains custody of the university's recording, microfilm and projection equipment; 284,000 vols; 1,818 current periodicals received mainly in English; Dir Prof. Dr BÜLENT KARASÖZEN.

Milli Kütüphane (National Library): Bahçelievler, Ankara; tel. (312) 2223812; fax (312) 2230451; f. 1946; 936,847 vols, 243,170 vols of periodicals, 11,417 MSS, 94,325 microfiches, 79,453 non-book items; Pres. TUNCEL ACAR; publs *Türkiye Bibliyografyası* (Turkish National Bibliography, monthly), *Türkiye Makaleler Bibliyografyası* (Bibliography of articles in Turkish periodicals, monthly).

Public Library: Ankara; f. 1922; 21,000 vols in Turkish, 10,200 vols in European languages, over 1,200 MSS in Arabic and Persian.

Antalya

Tekelioğlu Library: Antalya; f. 1924; 5,000 vols, nearly 2,000 MSS in Persian, Arabic and Turkish.

Balıkeşir

Il Halk Kütüphanesi (Provincial Public Library): Balıkeşir; f. 1901; 1,286 MSS in Turkish, Arabic and Persian, 49,000 vols in Turkish, Arabic and English, 766 in other languages, 5,088 periodicals; Dir A. Ercan Tığ.

Bor

Halil Nuri Bey Library: Bor; f. 1932; 12,000 vols, nearly 500 MSS in Persian, Arabic and Turkish.

Darende

Mehmet Paşa Library: Darende; f. 1776; 4,000 vols, 800 MSS.

Edirne

Selimiye Library: Edirne; f. 1575; 36,113 vols (including 3,172 MSS and 3,894 vols in Arabic); Librarian Mrs Ozlem Ağirgan.

Isparta

Halil Hamit Paşa Library: Isparta; f. 1783; 20,200 vols, over 850 MSS; Dir Mahmut Kayici.

Istanbul

Atatürk Kitaplığı (Ataturk Library): Mete Caddesi 45, Taksim, Istanbul; tel. (212) 249-56-83; fax (212) 251-79-72; f. 1929; public library; 184,000 vols.

Beyazit Devlet Kütüphanesi (Beyazit State Library): İmaret Sok. 18, Beyazit, Istanbul; tel. 522-24-88; fax 526-11-33; f. 1882; legal deposit library; 500,000 vols in various languages, 11,120 MSS, 32,992 photographs, 21,616 periodicals; Dir Yusuf Tavaci.

Boğaziçi University Library: Bebek, 80815, İstanbul; f. 1863; 235,000 vols in English and other languages, including a special collection of over 27,000 vols on the Near East; Librarian Ender Altuğ.

Ecumenical Patriarchate Library: Istanbul; foundation dates from beginning of Patriarchate, reorganization 1890; 25,000 vols in main library, and 1,500 MSS; 45,000 vols in branch library at Orthodox Seminary of Heybeliada; Dir Rev. Panağhiotis Theodoridis, under the jurisdiction of the Holy Synod.

Hüsrev Paşa Library: Eyüp, Istanbul; f. 1839; public library; 13,468 vols, over 300 MSS, 562 periodicals; Dir Şükrü Yaman.

Institute of Turkology Library: Istanbul University, Beyazıt, Istanbul; f. 1924; over 50,000 vols relating to Turkish language, literature, history and culture.

İstanbul Teknik Üniversitesi Kütüphanesi (Istanbul Technical University Libraries): Ayazağa, Maslak 80626, Istanbul; tel. (212) 276-35-96; fax (212) 276-17-34; f. 1795; five separate libraries on different campuses of the university; 372,000 vols; Dir of Libraries Nurten Atalik.

Istanbul University Library and Documentation Centre: University PTT 34452, Beyazit, Istanbul; tel. (212) 514-03-80; fax (212) 511-12-19; e-mail alpay-ed@mam.net.tr; f. 1925; comprises the central university library and 15 faculty libraries; 400,000 vols, 18,606 MSS, 18,000 periodicals (3,000 current), 30,000 theses; Dir Prof. Dr Meral Alpay.

Köprülü Library: Istanbul; f. 1677; 3,000 vols, 2,755 MSS, of which 193 are from early Ottoman presses, and 42 handwritten works over 1,000 years old.

Millet Kütüphanesi (Public Library): Fatih, Istanbul; f. 1916; 33,980 vols, 8,844 MSS.

Nuruosmaniye Library: Istanbul; f. 1755; 6,000 vols, 5,000 MSS.

Süleymaniye Library: Istanbul; f. 1557; 113,068 vols and 66,117 MSS in Turkish, Uyghur, Arabic and Persian; 109 different collections including those from Ayasofya and Fatih; MS restoration service; brs at Atif Efendi, Hacı Selim Ağa, Köprülü, Nuru-Osmaniye, Ragıppaşa; Dir Muammer Ülker.

Women's Library and Information Center Foundation: Fener Mahallesi, Fener Vapur İskelesi Karşısı, Fener Haliç, 34220 Istanbul; tel. (212) 534-95-50; fax (212) 523-74-08; 6,500 vols.

Izmir

National Library of İzmir: Milli Kütüphane Cad. 39, Konak-İzmir; f. 1912; 295,000 vols in Turkish, 39,100 vols in European languages, 19,000 vols in Oriental scripts, 4,000 MSS; 4,700 periodicals; dir by the National Library of İzmir Foundation; Dir Ali Riza Atay.

Konya

Public Library: Konya; f. 1947; 20,000 vols, over 6,000 MSS.

Nevşehir

Damat Ibrahim Paşa Library: Nevşehir; f. 1727; 5,500 vols, 600 MSS.

Museums and Art Galleries

Adana

Adana Bölge Müzesi (Adana Regional Museum): Adana; f. 1926; depts of archaeology and ethnography; conference hall, laboratories, library and administrative sections; over 107,000 items from the Neolithic to Roman and Byzantine periods; unique statue of a god made from natural crystal dating from Hittite Empire.

Amasya

Amasya Müzesi: Amasya; f. 1926, moved 1961 to the Gök Medrese Mosque; archaeological finds from the early Bronze Age to Ottoman period; includes mummies dating from the Imperial period.

Ankara

Anadolu Medeniyetleri Müzesi (Museum of Anatolian Civilizations): Samanpazarı, Ankara; tel. 3243160; fax 3112839; f. 1921; exhibits cover the palaeolithic, Neolithic, Chalcolithic, Early Bronze Age, Hittite, Phrygian, Urartian and Classical periods; Hittite reliefs from Alaca, Carchemish, Sakcagözü and Aslantepe and Ankara regions; collections represent excavations at Karain, Çatalhöyük, Hacılar, Can Hasan, Alacahöyük, Ahlatlıbel, Karaz, Alişar, Karaoğlan, Karayavşan, Oymaağaç, Merzifon, Beycesultan, Kültepe, Acemhöyük, İnandık, Boğazköy, Eskiyapar, Patnos, Adilcevaz, Uşak-İkiztepe, Pazarlı, Gordion, Altıntepe, with special sections for cuneiform tablets and coins; library of 6,567 vols; Dir İlhan Temizsoy, publs *The Anatolian Civilizations Museum Periodical, Museum Annual, Museum Lectures* (annually), *Museum News* (2 a year), *Museum Conference Annual.*

Anıtkabir Müzesi (Ataturk's Mausoleum and Museum): Ankara; tel. (312) 231-18-61; fax (312) 231-53-80; f. 1953; Ataturk's official and civil possessions: documents, medals, plaques, albums, etc.; library of 6,543 vols.

Ethnographical Museum: Ankara; tel. 311-30-07; f. 1930; specimens of Turkish and Islamic art, archives and Islamic numismatics; library of 6,245 vols; Dir Mrs Sema Koç.

Kurtuluş Savaşl ve Cumhuriyet Müzeleri (Museums of the Turkish Independence War and Turkish Republic): Cumhuriyet Bulvari No. 14–22, Ulus, Ankara; f. 1961; located in former Grand National Assembly buildings; library of 60,000 vols and 20,000 documents; Dir Mustafa Süel.

Turkish Natural History Museum: Ankara; f. 1968 by the Institute of Mineral Research.

Antakya

Hatay Museum: Gündüz Cad. 1, Antakya, Hatay; tel. (326) 214-61-67; f. 1934; collection of mosaics from Roman Antioch, also finds from Al-Mina, Atchana, Çatal Hüyük, Judeidah and Tainat excavations; Dir Mehmet Erdem.

Antalya

Antalya Müzesi (Antalya Museum): Konyaaltı Caddesi, Antalya; tel. (242) 241-45-28; fax (242) 241-53-86; f. 1922; prehistory, archaeology, numismatics, ethnography, children's section; library of 7,500 vols; Dir Kayhan Dörtlük.

Aydın

Aydın Müzesi: Aydın; f. 1959; archaeology, ethnography, historical coins.

Bergama

Pergamon Museum: Bergama; houses the historical relics discovered as the result of excavations conducted at Pergamon; Dir Osman Bayatli.

Bodrum

Bodrum Sualtı Arkeoloji Müzesi (Bodrum Museum of Underwater Archaeology): Bodrum; f. 1964 in the castle of Bodrum built in 15th century by the Knights of St John from Rhodes; finds from land and underwater.

Bursa

Bursa Arkeoloji Müzesi: Kültürpark, Bursa; tel. 234-49-18; f. 1902; archaeological finds from Bursa, Balıkesir and Bilecik; prehistoric, Roman and Byzantine finds, stone, ceramic, glass and metal objects, coins; library of 3,824 vols; Chief Officer Salih Kütük.

Bursa Türk ve Islâm Eserleri Müzesi (Bursa Turkish and Islamic Art Museum): Yeşil, Bursa; tel. 277679; f. 1975 in the Yeşil Medrese which was built by the Ottoman Emperor Çelebi Mehmet; items from 12th century to late Ottoman period; illuminated MSS, samples of calligraphy, woodwork, metalwork, embroidery, costumes, ceramics; open-air museum of gravestones.

Çanakkale

Truva Müzesi (Troy Museum): Çanakkale; at the entrance to the ruins of Troy in Çanakkale is a small museum exhibiting pottery, figurines, statues, glass objects.

Eskişehir

Eskişehir Arkeoloji Müzesi: Akarbaşı, Eskişehir; tel. (222) 230-13-71; fax (222) 230-17-49; f. 1935; plant and animal fossils; prehistory (ceramics, idols, stone and bone objects); the walls are decorated with the late Roman mosaics found in excavations at Doryleum.

Istanbul

Âsiyan Museum: Aşiyan Yokuşu, 80810 Bebek, Istanbul; tel. (212) 263-69-86; home of Turkish poet and artist T. Fikret.

Askeri Müze ve Kültür Sitesi Komutanlığı (Military Museum and Cultural Centre): Harbiye, Istanbul; tel. (212) 233-71-15; fax (212) 296-86-18; f. 1846; military uniforms, weapons and trophies from the earliest times; library of 12,000 vols; Dir Col Erdal Güleç.

Ayasofya (Saint Sophia) Museum: Sultan Ahmet, Istanbul; tel. 522-09-89; telex 4; f. 1934; the Museum is housed in the Byzantine Basilica; built by Justinian and dedicated in AD 537, it was a church until 1453, after which it became a mosque; in 1935 it was made a state museum; contains Byzantine and Turkish antiquities; Dir CANSEL URAL; publ. *The Annual of St Sophia*.

İstanbul Arkeoloji Müzeleri (Archaeological Museums of Istanbul): Gülhane, 34400 Istanbul; tel. (212) 5207740; fax (212) 5274300; f. 1891; includes Archaeological, Turkish Tiles and Ancient Orient museums, with Sumerian, Akkadian, Hittite, Assyrian, Egyptian, Urartu, Phrygian, Greek, Roman and Byzantine works of art; over 1 million exhibits; library of 80,000 vols; Dir Dr ALPAY PASİNLI.

İstanbul Deniz Müzesi (Istanbul Naval Museum): Beşiktaş-Istanbul; tel. (212) 261-00-40; fax (212) 260-60-38; f. 1897; cannons, important collection of historical caiques, models, torpedoes and mines, Turkish standards, medals, costumes, paintings; library of 20,000 vols, 22,436 archives files (Ottoman Empire period); Dir Comdr A. MUHLIS ERGİN.

İstanbul Resim ve Heykel Müzesi (Museum of Painting and Sculpture): Beşiktaş, Istanbul; tel. (212) 2614298; telex 24723; fax (212) 2440398; f. 1937; 19th- and 20th-century Turkish paintings and sculptures; international art exhbns; Dir Prof. KEMAL İSKENDER.

Tanzimat Müzesi (Museum of the 1839 Turkish Revolution): Gülhane Parkı, 34400 Sirkeci, Istanbul; tel. (212) 512-63-84.

Topkapı Palace Museum: Istanbul; palace built by Muhammad II; collections of Turkish armour, cloth, embroidery, glass and porcelain, copper- and silver-ware, treasure, paintings, miniatures, illuminated manuscripts, royal coaches, collections of Sèvres and Bohemian crystal and porcelain, clocks, important collection of Chinese and Japanese porcelain amassed by the Sultans, collection of manuscripts, Ottoman tent; library of 18,000 MSS and 200,000 archive documents; Audience Hall, Council Hall of Viziers, Baghdad and Revan Köşks, Harem; Dir FİLİZ ÇAĞMAN.

Türk ve Islam Eserleri Müzesi (Museum of Turkish and Islamic Art): İbrahim Paşa Sarayı, Sultanahmet, Istanbul; tel. 528-5158; f. 1914; exhibitions, research and educational dept; fine collection of Turkish and Islamic rugs, illuminated MSS, sculpture in stone and stucco, woodcarvings, metalwork and ceramics, traditional crafts and ethnographical material, all gathered from Turkish mosques and tombs; 37 scientific staff; library of 4,142 MSS and 3,279 vols; Dir NAZAN TAPAN ÖLCER.

Izmir

İzmir Arkeoloji Müzesi: Kültür Park, Izmir; f. 1927; works from the Archaic, Classical and Hellenistic periods of the Ionian civilization.

Konya

Konya Museums: Konya Valiliği, İl Kültür Müdürlüğü, Müze Müdürlüğü; 1. Mevlâna: founded in Mevlâna Turbe—Seljuk, Ottoman and Turkish collections, clothing, carpets, and Turkish collections, clothing, carpet, coins, library; 2. Classical Museum: founded in new classical museum–collections of Neolithic, early Bronze Age, Hittite, Phrygian, Greek, Roman and Byzantine monuments; 3. Turkish Ceramics Museum: founded in Karatay Medresseh–contains ceramics of the 13th–18th century; 4. Seljuk Museum: founded in İnce Minare–contains stone and wooden works of the Seljuk period; 5. Sirçali Medresseh–Sarcophagus and inscription, collections of Seljuk and Ottoman period; 6. Atatürk Museum–collection of documents and objects connected with Atatürk, also Konya clothing and other ethnographic exhibits; Dir of Museums Dr ERDOĞAN EROL.

Polatlı

Gordion Museum: Polatlı, Ankara; f. 1965; built near the Great Tumulus believed to be that of the Phrygian king Midas; archaeological items found during excavations at Gordion (now Yassıhöyük).

Selçuk

Efes Müzesi Müdürlügü (Ephesus Museum): Selçuk-Izmir; tel. 54511010; f. 1929; of art (mostly statues and reliefs) excavated from Ephesus; library of 2,100 vols; Dir SELAHATTIN ERDEMGIL; publ. *Efes Müzesi Yilligı* (annually).

Selimiye

Side Müzesi: Manavgat-Antalya, Side (Selimiye); f. 1962; museum is located in a Late Roman bath; statues and busts of Roman gods, goddesses and emperors; library of 985 vols; Dir ORHAN ATVUR.

Van

Van Müzesi: Van; f. 1947; archaeological finds from the Urartu Civilization.

Universities

AKDENİZ ÜNİVERSİTESİ

Dumlupınar Bulvarı Kampus, 07003 Antalya

Telephone: 227-52-66
Fax: 227-55-40

Founded 1982; previously affiliated to Ankara University
State control
Language of instruction: Turkish
Academic year: October to June

Rector: Prof. Dr TUNCER KARPUZOĞLU
Vice-Rectors: Prof. Dr OKTAY YEĞEN, Prof. BEKIR ÖZER, Prof. Dr METİN SEVÜK
Chief Administrative Officer: H. C. OĞUZ
Librarian: L. TEKİN

Number of teachers: 809
Number of students: 7,558

Publications: *Journal of the Faculty of Medicine* (quarterly), *University Bulletin, Journal of the Faculty of Agriculture.*

DEANS

Faculty of Medicine: Prof. Dr İFFET BIRCAN
Faculty of Agriculture: Prof. Dr TEVFİK AKSOY
Faculty of Arts and Sciences: Prof. Dr EFRAİM AVŞAR
Faculty of Social and Administrative Sciences: (vacant)
Faculty of Law: Prof. Dr A. NECİP ORTAN

HEADS OF DEPARTMENT (PROFESSORS)

Faculty of Medicine:
- Basic Medical Sciences: Prof. Dr T. ASLAN AKSU
- Internal Medicine: Prof. Dr YILMAZ BAYKAL
- Surgery: Prof. Dr MELİHA ERMAN

Faculty of Agriculture:
- Horticulture: Prof. Dr MUSTAFA PEKMEZCİ
- Plant Protection: Prof. Dr İRFAN TUNÇ
- Food Science and Technology: Prof. Dr HASAN YAYGIN
- Agricultural Mechanization: Prof. Dr AZİZ ÖZMERZİ
- Irrigation and Agricultural Structures: Prof. Dr FERIDUN HAKGÖREN
- Agronomy: Dr M. İLHAN ÇAĞIRGAN
- Soil Sciences: Assoc. Prof. Dr TURGUT KÖSEOĞLU
- Animal Sciences: Prof. Dr SALİM MUTAF
- Animal Husbandry and Fodder: Prof. Dr NİHAT ÖZEN

Faculty of Arts and Sciences:
- Mathematics: Prof. Dr NURI ÜNAL
- Biology: Prof. Dr MUSTAFA GÖKÇEOĞLU
- Chemistry: Prof. Dr EROL AYRANCI
- Physics: Prof. Dr ZEKİ ARSLAN
- History: Prof. Dr M. FUAT BOZKURT
- Archaeology and History of Art: Prof. Dr FAHRİ IŞIK

ATTACHED INSTITUTES AND CENTRES

Computer Sciences Research and Development Centre: Dumlupınar Bulvarı Kampus, 07003 Antalya; Dir Assoc. Prof. OSMAN SAKA.

Environmental Problems Research and Development Centre: Dumlupınar Bulvarı Kampus, 07003 Antalya; Dir Assoc. Prof. Dr BÜLENT TOPKAYA.

Health Sciences Research and Development Centre: Morfoloji Binası, 07003 Antalya; Dir Prof. Dr GÜLSEN ÖNER.

Institute of Science and Technology: Dumlupınar Bulvarı Kampus, 07003 Antalya; Dir Assoc. Prof. Dr TEVFİK BARDAKÇI.

Institute of Social Sciences: Topçular, PK 750, 07200 Antalya; Dir Dr METIN GÜRKANLAR.

Likya Civilization Research and Development Centre: Topçular, 07200 Antalya; Dir Assoc. Prof. Dr HAVVA YILMAZ.

Principles of Ataturk Research and Development Centre: Topcular, 07200 Antalya; Dir Prof. Dr M. FUAT BOZKURT.

Transplantation-Education Research Centre: Dumlupınar Bulvarı Kampus, 07003 Antalya; Dir Prof. Dr TUNCER KARPUZOĞLU.

University Research and Development Hospital: Dumlupınar Bulvari Kampus, 07003 Antalya; Dir Assoc. Prof. Dr KEMAL EMEK.

ANADOLU ÜNİVERSİTESİ
(University of Anatolia)

Yunus Emre Kampüsü, 26470 Eskişehir

Telephone: (222) 3350580
Fax: (222) 3353616

Founded 1958
State control
Languages of instruction: Turkish, English
Academic year: October to June

Rector: Prof. Dr AKAR ÖCAL
Vice-Rectors: Prof. Dr SEMİH BÜKER, Prof. Dr ŞAN ÖZ-ALP, Prof. Dr ENGİN ATAÇ, Prof. Dr FEVZİ SÜRMELİ, Prof. Dr ERCAN GÜVEN.
Registrar/Secretary General: ALİ RIZA ÖNDER
Librarian: ADNAN YILMAZ

Number of teachers: 1,112
Number of students: 446,800 (including open-education students)

Publications: various faculty journals.

DEANS

Faculty of Economics and Administrative Sciences: Prof. Dr SABRİ BEKTÖRE
Faculty of Sciences: Prof. Dr MUHSİN ZOR
Faculty of Education: Prof. Dr AHMET KONROT
Faculty of Engineering and Architecture: Prof. Dr ATİLA BARKANA
Faculty of Open Education: Prof. Dr HİKMET SEÇİM
Faculty of Pharmacy: Prof. Dr HÜSNÜ CAN BAŞER
Faculty of Communication Sciences: Prof. Dr DURSUN GÖKDAĞ
Faculty of Fine Arts: Prof. Dr M. TURGAY EREM
Faculty of Letters: Prof. Dr İHSAN GÜNEŞ
Faculty of Economics: Prof. Dr NÜVİT GEREK
Faculty of Business Administration: Prof. Dr ÖZCAN UÇKAN
Faculty of Law: Prof. Dr ERHAN TÜRKER

HEADS OF DEPARTMENTS

Faculty of Economics and Administrative Sciences:

Labour Economics and Industrial Relations: Prof. Dr ERCAN GÜVEN
Business Administration: Prof. Dr BİROL TENEKECİOĞLU
Economics: Prof. Dr ERGÜL HAN
Public Finance: Prof. Dr AYKUT HEREKMAN

Faculty of Sciences:

Mathematics: Prof. Dr ŞAHİN KOÇAK
Physics: Prof. Dr KUDRET ÖZDAŞ
Chemistry: Prof. Dr LALE ZOR
Biology: Prof. Dr MERİH KIVANÇ
Statistics: Prof. Dr ERSOY CANKÜYER

Faculty of Education:

French Language Teaching: Prof. Dr GÜLNİHAL GÜLMEZ
English Language Teaching: Prof. Dr ZÜLAL BALPINAR
German Language Teaching: Assoc. Prof. Dr MUSTAFA GAKIR
Educational Sciences: Assoc. Prof. Dr BEKİR ÖZER
Teacher Training in Arts and Crafts: Prof. OYA KINIKLI
Science Teacher Training: Assoc. Prof. Dr AYNUR ÖZDAŞ
Special Education: Prof. Dr SÜLEYMAN ERİPEK

Faculty of Engineering and Architecture:

Ceramics Engineering: Prof. Dr ERSAN PÜTÜN
Environmental Engineering: Prof. Dr SERAP KARA
Industrial Engineering: Prof. Dr MUSA ŞENEL
Architecture: Asst Prof. Dr TÜRKAN GÖKSAL
Computer Engineering: Prof. Dr ALİ GUNEŞ

Faculty of Open Education:

Economics and Administration: Prof. Dr SEMİH BÜKER
Distance Education: Prof. Dr YILMAZ BÜYÜKERŞEN
Continuing Education: Prof. Dr ŞAN ÖZ-ALP
Health Care: Prof. Dr HİKMET SECİM

Faculty of Pharmacy:

Basic Pharmaceutical Sciences: Prof. Dr MUZAFFER TUNÇEL
Pharmaceutical Technology: Prof. Dr ERDEN GÜLER
Professional Pharmaceutical Sciences: Prof. Dr YUSUF ÖZTÜRK

Faculty of Communication Sciences:

Cinema and Television: Prof. YALÇIN DEMİR
Communication Arts: Assoc. Prof. HALUK GÜRGEN
Educational Communication and Planning: Prof. Dr MURAT BARKAN
Printing and Publishing: Prof. Dr UĞUR DEMİRAY

Faculty of Fine Arts:

Graphics: Prof. MEHMET T. EREM
Ceramics: Prof. ZEHRA ÇOBANLI
Interior Design: Asst Prof. GÜRSOY BACAKSIZ
Animation: Assoc. Prof. HİKMET SOFUOĞLU
Sculpture: Assoc. Prof. AYTAÇ KATI
Painting: Prof. ABDULLAH DEMİR

Faculty of Letters:

History: Assoc. Prof. Dr CAHİT BİLİM
Classical Archaeology and Art History: Assoc. Prof. Dr EBRU PARMAN
Sociology: Asst Prof. Dr NADİR SÜGUR

Faculty of Economics:

Labour Economics and Industrial Relations: (vacant)
Economics: Prof. Dr ÖNDER ÖZKAZANÇ
Public Administration: Assoc. Prof. Dr RAMAZAN GEYLAN
Public Finance: Assoc. Prof. Dr NEZİH VARCAN

Faculty of Business Administration:

Accounting and Finance: Prof. Dr DAVUT AYDIN
Marketing: Prof. Dr YAVUZ ODABAŞI
Management and Organization: (vacant)

Faculty of Law:

Public Law: Prof. Dr ÖZCAN UÇKAN
Special Law: Prof. Dr AKAR ÖCAL
Public Finance and Economics: Asst Prof. Dr RANA EŞKİNAT

ATTACHED SCHOOLS

School of Drama and Music: Dir Prof. Dr BAHADIR GÜLMEZ.

College for the Handicapped: Dir Assoc. Prof. Dr ÜMRAN TÜFEKÇİOĞLU.

School of Tourism and Hotel Management: Dir Prof. Dr İLHAN ÜNLÜ.

School of Physical Education and Sports: Dir Prof. Dr FETHİ HEPER.

School of Civil Aviation: Dir Asst Prof. Dr MUSTAFA ÖÇ.

School of Industrial Arts: Assoc. Prof. Dr YAŞAR HOŞCAN.

ATTACHED RESEARCH CENTRES

Research Centre for Folklore: Dir Asst Prof. Dr HASAN ISLATİNCE.

Research Centre for the Education of Hearing Impaired Children: Dir Assoc. Prof. Dr ÜMRAN TÜFEKÇİOĞLU.

Research Centre for Computer Studies: Dir Prof. Dr ÖNDER ÖZKAZANÇ.

Research Centre for Continuous Education: Dir Prof. Dr İLHAN ÜNLÜ.

Research Centre for Environmental Studies: Dir Prof. Dr SERAP KARA.

Research Centre for Archaeology and Art History: Dir Assoc. Prof. Dr EBRU PARMAN.

Research Centre for the European Community: Dir Prof. Dr AKAR ÖCAL.

Research Centre for Culture and the Environment: Dir Prof. Dr İNAL C. AŞKUN.

Research Centre for Foreign Languages: Dir Prof. Dr ZÜLAL BALPINAR.

Research Centre for Medicinal and Aromatic Plants and Drugs: Dir Prof. Dr HÜSNÜ C. BAŞER.

Centre for Health and Social Services: Dir Dr HAMDİ SARIKARDEŞOĞLU.

Research Centre for Televised Distance Learning: Dir Assoc. Prof. Dr SİNAN BOZOK.

Atatürk Research Centre for Music: Dir Asst Prof. Dr ALİ CEMALCILAR.

Research Centre for Modern Turkish History: Dir Prof. Dr ERCAN GÜVEN.

Research Centre for Economics and Social Studies: Dir Prof. Dr DAVUT AYDIN.

Research Centre for Civil Aviation: Dir Asst Prof. Dr MUSTAFA OÇ.

GRADUATE SCHOOLS

Graduate School of Social Sciences: Dir Prof. Dr ENVER ÖZKALP.

Graduate School of Science: Dir Prof. Dr ERSAN PÜTÜN.

Graduate School of Health Sciences: Dir Prof. Dr MUZAFFER TUNÇEL.

Institute of Educational Sciences: Dir Assoc. Prof. Dr AYHAN HAKAN.

Institute of Communication Sciences: Dir Prof. Dr YILMAZ BÜYÜKERŞEN.

Handicapped Research Institute: Dir Assoc. Prof. Dr GÖNÜL İFTAR.

Institute of Fine Arts: (vacant).

Institute of Satellite and Space Sciences: Dir Assoc. Prof. Dr CAN AYDAY.

Institute of Transport Economics: Dir Prof. Dr MEHMET ŞAHİN.

ANKARA ÜNİVERSİTESİ

06100 Tandoğan, Ankara

Telephone: (312) 223-43-61
Telex: 44066
Fax: (312) 223-60-70

Founded 1946
State control
Language of instruction: Turkish
Academic year: October to June

Rector: Prof. Dr GÜNAL AKBAY
Vice-Rectors: Prof. Dr EMİN TEKELİ, Prof. Dr ALİ ERKAN EKE, Prof. Dr CEMAL TALUĞ
General Secretary: Prof. Dr YAVUZ OKAN
Registrar: Mrs DILEK KAYRAN
Librarian: Y. KAYA SARICIOĞLU

Number of teachers: 3,393
Number of students: 42,438

Publications: *Ankara Üniversitesi Yıllığı* (Annals of the University), and faculty and research institute publications.

DEANS

Faculty of Agriculture: Prof. Dr YETKİN GÜNGÖR
Faculty of Communication: Prof. Dr EROL MUTLU
Faculty of Dentistry: Prof. Dr AHMET DURU PAMİR
Faculty of Divinity: Prof. Dr SAİT YAZICIOĞLU
Faculty of Education: Prof. Dr BELKA ÖZDOĞAN
Faculty of Education Health Sciences: Prof. Dr SEZAİ YAMAN
Faculty of Law: Prof Dr RAMAZAN ARSLAN
Faculty of Letters: Prof. Dr MELEK DELİLBAŞI
Faculty of Medicine: Prof. Dr NUSRET ARAS
Faculty of Pharmacy: Prof. Dr SEÇKİN ÖZDEN
Faculty of Political Science: Prof. Dr CELAL GÖLE
Faculty of Science: Prof. Dr CEMAL AYDIN
Faculty of Veterinary Medicine: Prof. Dr ERGÜN ÖZALP

HEADS OF DEPARTMENTS

Faculty of Agriculture:

Horticulture: Prof. Dr HASAN ÇELİK
Plant Protection: Prof. Dr GÜRSEL ERDİLLER
Farm Structures and Irrigation: Prof. Dr CENGİZ OKMAN
Landscape Architecture: Prof. Dr HAYRAN ÇELEM
Fisheries: Prof Dr DOĞAN ATAY
Agricultural Economics: Prof. Dr MEHMET BÜLBÜL
Agricultural Machinery: Prof. Dr BAHA GALİP TUNALIGİL
Food Engineering: Prof. Dr M. EKİN ŞAHİN
Dairy Technology: Prof. Dr EMEL SEZGİN
Agronomy: Prof. Dr CELAL ER
Soil Science: Prof. Dr NURİ MUNSUZ
Animal Science: Prof. MURAT ZİNCİRLİOĞLU

Faculty of Communication:

Radio, Television and Cinema: Prof. Dr NİLGÜN ABİSEL
Journalism: Prof. Dr TÜRKER ALKAN
Public Relations: Prof. Dr METİN KAZANCI

Faculty of Dentistry:

Basic Dental Sciences: Prof. Dr AYKUT MISIRLIOĞLU
Clinical Dentistry: Prof. Dr AHMET DURU PAMİR

Faculty of Divinity:

Basic Islamic Sciences: Prof. Dr HÜSEYİN ATAY
Philosophy and the Science of Religion: Prof. Dr HAYRANİ ALTINTAŞ
Islamic History and Arts: Prof. Dr SABRİ HİZMETLİ

Faculty of Education:

Curriculum Development and Teaching: SABRİ BÜYÜKDÜVENCİ
Psychological Services in Education: Prof. Dr UĞUR ÖNER
Educational Administration and Planning: Prof. Dr MAHMUT ADEM
Adult Education: Assoc. Prof. Dr SERAP AYHAN
Special Education: Prof. Dr LATİFE BIYIKLI

Faculty of Law:

Public Law: Prof. Dr ADNAN GÜRİZ
Public Finance and Economics: Prof. Dr GÜRGEN ÇELEBİCAN
Private Law: Prof. Dr TURGUT KALPSÜZ

Faculty of Letters:

Linguistics: Prof. Dr ÖZER ERGENÇ
Archaeology and History of Art: Prof. Dr KUTLU EMRE
Western Languages and Cultures: Prof. Dr ÜNAL AYTÜR
Eastern Languages and Cultures: Prof. Dr İNCI KOÇAK
Geography: Prof. Dr ERDOĞAN AKKAN
Physical Anthropology and Palaeoanthropology: Prof. Dr ERKSİN GÜLEÇ
Social Anthropology and Ethnology: Prof. Dr ZAFER İLBARS
History: Prof. Dr YÜCEL ÖZKAYA
Philosophy: Prof. Dr ESİN KAHYA
Sociology: Prof. Dr AYKUT KASAPOĞLU
Library Sciences: Prof. Dr MUSTAFA AKBULUT
Drama: Prof. Dr NURHAN KARADAĞ
Turkish Language and Literature: Prof. Dr İSMAİL ÜNVER

Faculty of Medicine:

Basic Medicine: Prof. Dr CANAN AKBAY
Internal Medicine: Prof. Dr İSFENDİYAR CANDAN
Surgery: Prof. Dr ERTEKİN ARASIL

Faculty of Pharmacy:

Basic Pharmaceutical Sciences: Prof. Dr SERPİL NEBİOĞLU
Professional Pharmaceutical Sciences: Prof. Dr MEKİN TANKER
Pharmaceutical Technology: Prof. Dr KANDEMİR CANEFE

Faculty of Political Science:

Management: Prof. Dr YÜKSEL KOÇ YALKIN
Business Administration: Prof. Dr YÜKSEL KOÇYALKIN
Public Finance: Prof. Dr ÜREN ARSAN
Labour Economics and Industrial Relations: Prof. Dr ALPASLAN IŞIKLI
International Relations: Prof. Dr FÜSUN ARSAVA
Public Administration: Prof. Dr SİNA AKŞİN

Faculty of Science:

Astronomy and Space Sciences: Prof. Dr CEMAL AYDIN
Chemical Engineering: Prof. Dr ARAL OLCAY
Mathematics: Prof. Dr HİLMİ HACISALİHOĞLU
Statics: Prof. Dr ÖMER L. GEBİZLİOĞLU
Geophysical Engineering: Prof. Dr TURAN KAYIRAN
Biology: Prof. Dr GÖNÜL ALGAN
Physics: Prof. Dr ARSIN ARDINURAZ
Engineering Physics: Prof. Dr ZEKERİYA AYDIN
Geological Engineering: Prof. Dr BAKİ VAROL
Chemistry: Prof. Dr ATİLLA ÖKTEMER
Electronic Engineering: Prof. Dr ÖNDER TÜZÜNALP

Faculty of Veterinary Medicine:

Basic Sciences of Veterinary Medicine: Prof. Dr ATİLLA TANYOLAÇ
Diseases and Clinical Sciences: Prof. Dr ERDOĞAN SAMSAR
Animal Husbandry and Animal Nutrition: Prof. Dr AHMET ERGİN

DIRECTORS OF APPLIED RESEARCH CENTRES

Atatürk's Principles: Prof. Dr ÜNSAL YAVUZ.
Biotechnology: Prof. Dr TUNCER ÖZDAMAR.
Cardiology: Prof. Dr DERVİŞ ORAL.
Education-Rehabilitation: Prof. Dr EFSER KERİMOĞLU.
Environmental Problems: Prof. Dr RUŞEN KELEŞ.
European Communities: Prof. Dr NECDET SERİN.
Foreign Language Teaching: Prof. Dr ERSİN ONULDURAN.
Gastroenterology: Prof. Dr ÖZDEN UZUNALİMOĞLU.
Oncology: Prof. Dr FİKRİ İÇLİ.
Ottoman History: Prof. Dr YAVUZ ERCAN.
Psychiatric Crisis: Prof. Dr IŞIL SAYIL.
Journalism and Communication: Prof. Dr EROL MUTLU.
Turkish Geography: Doç. Dr ALİ FUAT DOĞRU.
Turkish Language Teaching Centre: Dr MEHMET HENGİRMEN.

ATTACHED INSTITUTES

Graduate Institute of Science: Dir Prof. Dr AZİZ EKŞİ.
Graduate Institute of Medical Sciences: Dir Prof. Dr MEKİN TANKER.
Graduate Institute of Social Sciences: Dir Prof. Dr CAN HAMAMCI.
Graduate Institute of Medical Jurisprudence: Dir Prof. Dr BAHATTİN KORUCU.
Graduate Institute of the History of the Turkish Revolution: Dir Prof. Dr HASAN KÖNİ.
Graduate Institute of Hepatology: Dir Prof. Dr ÖZDEN UZUNALİMOĞLU.

ATTACHED SCHOOLS AND COLLEGES

School of Home Economics (Faculty of Agriculture): Dir Prof. Dr SENİHA HASİPEK.
School of Justice (Faculty of Law): Dir Doç. Dr ERDAL ONAR.
School of Başkent: Dir Prof. Dr ORHAN BİNGÖL.
School of Çankırı: Dir Prof. Dr SABAHATTİN BALCI.
School of Dörtyol Health Services: Dir Prof. Dr CİHAT ÜNLÜ.
School of Dikimevi Health Services: Dir Prof. Dr İLKSEN TURHANOĞLU.
School of Kalecik: Dir Prof. Dr ERDOĞAN ERDOĞAN.
School of Kastamonu: Dir Prof. Dr BAHRİ GÖKÇEBAY.
School of Cebeci Health Services: Dir Doç. Dr MEHMET KIYAN.
School of Beypazarı: Dir Prof. Dr İLHAN KARAÇAL.

ATATÜRK ÜNİVERSİTESİ

Erzurum

Telephone: (442) 218-41-20
Fax: (442) 218-71-40

Founded 1957
State control
Language of instruction: Turkish
Academic year: October to June

Rector: Prof. Dr EROL ORAL
Vice-Rectors: Prof. Dr YILMAZ OZBEK, Prof. Dr HAMZA AKTAN
Chief Administrative Officer: YAŞAR GÖK
Librarian: ADNAN ÇINARLIOĞLU

Library of 296,141 vols
Number of teachers and assistants: 1,629
Number of students: 24,000

Publications: *Ziraat Fakültesi Dergisi, Tıp Fakültesi Dergisi, Edebiyat Fakültesi Dergisi, İktisadi ve İdari Bilimler Fakültesi Dergisi, İlahiyat Dergisi, Enstitü Dergisi.*

DEANS

Faculty of Agriculture: Prof. Dr AYHAN AKSOY
Faculty of Medicine: Prof. Dr DURKAYA ÖREN
Faculty of Arts and Sciences: Prof. Dr ENVER KONUKÇU
Faculty of Economics and Administrative Sciences: Prof. Dr CEVAT GERNİ
Faculty of Education: Prof. Dr MANSUR HARMANDAR
Faculty of Engineering: Prof. Dr SABRİ ÇOLAK
Faculty of Dentistry: Prof. Dr MUZAFFER GÜLYURT
Faculty of Theology: Prof. Dr NACİ S. OKÇU
Faculty of Fine Arts: Prof. Dr SEVİM SAĞSÖZ
Faculty of Education (Erzincan): Prof. Dr MUHARREM GÜLERYÜZ
Faculty of Education (Ağrı): Prof. Dr YAŞAR SÜTBEYAZ
Faculty of Law School (Erzincan): Prof. Dr RECAİ ÇINAR

HEADS OF DEPARTMENTS

Faculty of Agriculture:

Horticulture: Prof. Dr M. GÜLERYÜZ
Entomology: Prof. Dr H. ÖZBEK
Engineering: Prof. Dr A. ÖZDENGİZ
Agricultural Economics: Prof. Dr C. KARAGÖLGE
Food Science and Technology: Prof. Dr S. SERT
Field Crops: Prof. Dr SEVIM SAĞSÖZ
Soil Science: Prof. Dr G. ŞİMŞEK
Animal Feeding and Husbandry: Prof. Dr H. EMSEN
Agricultural Mechanization: Prof. Dr N. TURGUT
Aquaculture: Prof. Dr S. ARAS
Landscape Architecture: Prof. Dr I. KIRZIOĞLU

Faculty of Arts and Sciences:

Mathematics: Prof. Dr A. DÖNMEZ
Biology: Prof. Dr M. OZKAN
Physics: Prof. Dr Y. K. YOĞURTÇU
Chemistry: Prof. Dr M. BALCI
History: Prof. Dr E. KONUKÇU
German Language and Literature: Assoc. Prof. Dr Y. ÖZBEK
French Language and Literature: Assoc. Prof. Dr S. AKTEN
English Language and Literature: Prof. Dr Y. AKSOY
Geography: Assoc. Prof. Dr K. ARINÇ
Archaeology and Fine Arts: Prof. Dr H. GÜNDOĞDU
Oriental Languages and Literature: Prof. Dr A. SAVRAN
Philosophy: Prof. Dr A. BİNGÖL
Turkish Language and Literature: Prof. Dr E. GEMALMAZ
Sociology: Assoc. Prof. Dr E. KEMERLİOĞLU
Theatre: Assoc. Prof. S. GÜLLÜLÜ

Faculty of Dentistry

Clinical Sciences: Prof. Dr M. GÜLERYÜZ

Faculty of Economics and Administrative Sciences:

Business Management: Prof. Dr M. TÜRKO
Economics: Prof. Dr C. GERNİ

Faculty of Education:

Physical Sciences: Assoc. Prof. Dr B. DÜZGÜN
Biology: Prof. Dr N. AYYILDIZ
Chemistry: Assoc. Prof. Dr A. GÜRSES
Mathematics: Prof. Dr R. OCAK
German Language: Assoc. Prof. Dr M. YAMAN
French Language: Assoc. Prof. Dr M. BAŞTÜRK
English Language: Assoc. Prof. Dr B. DÜZGÜN
Geography: Prof. Dr H. DOĞANAY
History: Assoc. Prof. Dr M. DEMİREL
Turkish Language and Literature: Prof. Dr Ş. AKTAŞ
Educational Sciences: Prof. Dr N. ÖREN
Drawing: Assoc. Prof. Dr N. KÜLEKÇİ
Philosophy: Assoc. Prof. Dr A. O. GÜNDOĞDU

Physical Training: Assoc. Prof. Dr A. KIRKKILIÇ
Music: Prof. Dr M. AŞKIN

Faculty of Theology:
- Basic Islamic Sciences: Prof. Dr L. CEBECİ
- Philosophy and Theology: Assoc. Prof. Dr A. V. İMAMOĞLU
- Islamic History and Arts: Prof. Dr A. ÇUBUKÇU

Faculty of Medicine:
- Basic Medicine: Prof. Dr M. BABACAN
- General Surgery: Prof. Dr S. ŞİRİN
- Internal Medicine: Prof. Dr S. KOT

Faculty of Engineering:
- Machinery: Assoc. Prof. Dr Ö. ÇOMAKLI
- Civil Engineering: Prof. Dr N. YARDIMCI
- Chemistry: Assoc. Prof. Dr M. KOCAKERİM
- Environmental Engineering: Prof. Dr N. TOPÇU

Faculty of Law:
- Economy: Assoc. Prof. Dr N. KARAKADILAR
- Law: Assoc. Prof. C. HACIOĞLU

Faculty of Fine Arts:
- Design and Architecture: Prof. Dr S. SAĞSÖZ
- Fine Arts: Prof. Dr S. SAĞSÖZ
- Environmental Design: Prof. Dr S. SAĞSÖZ
- Landscape Architecture and Urban Design: Assoc. Prof. Dr M. KAVUKÇU

ATTACHED INSTITUTES

Medical Sciences: Dir Prof. Dr E. BAKAN
Sciences: Dir Prof. Dr Y. K. YOGURTCU
Social Sciences: Dir Prof. Dr B. SEYITOĞLU
History of the Turkish Republic: Dir Prof. Dr E. KONUKÇU
Research on Turkology: Dir Prof. Dr E. GEMALMAZ
Fine Arts: Prof. Dr H. GÜNDOĞDU

BİLKENT ÜNİVERSİTESİ

06533 Bilkent, Ankara
Telephone: (312) 266-41-25
Fax: (312) 266-41-27

Founded 1984
Private control (educational foundations)
Language of instruction: English
Academic year: September to June

President, Board of Trustees: Prof. İHSAN DOĞRAMACI
Rector: Prof. ALİ DOĞRAMACI
Vice-Rectors: Prof. ABDULLAH ATALAR, Prof. EROL ARKUN, Prof. ÜMİT BERKMAN, Dr PHYLLIS L. ERDOĞAN
General Secretary: Prof. ÜMİT BERKMAN
Librarian: Dr PHYLLIS L. ERDOĞAN

Number of teachers: 900
Number of students: 10,000

DEANS

Faculty of Art, Design and Architecture: Prof. BÜLENT ÖZGÜÇ
Faculty of Business Administration: Assoc. Prof. KÜRŞAT AYDOĞAN
Faculty of Economic, Administrative and Social Sciences: Prof. METIN HEPER
Faculty of Engineering: Prof. MEHMET BARAY
Faculty of Humanities and Letters: Prof. BÜLENT BOZKURT
Faculty of Music and Performing Arts: Prof. ERSİN ONAY
Faculty of Science: Prof. HASAN ERTEN
School of Applied Foreign Languages: Prof. TANJU İNAL
School of English Language: JOHN O'DWYER
Vocational School of Tourism and Hotel Services: KAMER RODOPLU
School of Tourism and Hotel Management: KAMER RODOPLU
Vocational School of Computer Programming and Office Management: KAMER RODOPLU

HEADS OF DEPARTMENTS

Faculty of Art, Design and Architecture:
- Fine Arts: Prof. BÜLENT ÖZGÜÇ
- Graphic Design: Prof. BÜLENT ÖZGÜÇ
- Interior Architecture and Environmental Design: Asst Prof. HALİME DEMİRKAN
- Landscape Architecture and Urban Design: Asst Prof. ZUHAL ULUSOY

Faculty of Business Administration:
- Management: Assoc. Prof. KÜRŞAT AYDOĞAN

Faculty of Economic, Administrative and Social Sciences:
- Economics: Assoc. Prof. ERINÇ YELDAN
- International Relations: Prof. ALİ KARAOSMANOĞLU
- Political Science and Public Administration: Prof. METİN HEPER
- History: Dr AKŞİN SOMEL

Faculty of Engineering:
- Computer Engineering and Information Science: Prof. MEHMET BARAY
- Electrical and Electronics Engineering: Prof. BÜLENT ÖZGÜLER
- Industrial Engineering: Assoc. Prof. OSMAN OĞUZ

Faculty of Humanities and Letters:
- American Culture and Literature: Asst Prof. İREM BALKIR
- English Language and Literature: Prof. BÜLENT BOZKURT
- Archaeology and History of Art: Assoc. Prof. İLKNUR ÖZGEN

Faculty of Music and Performing Arts:
- Music: Prof. ERSİN ONAY
- Performing Arts: Prof. CÜNEYT GÖKÇER

Faculty of Science:
- Chemistry: Prof. ŞEFİK SÜZER
- Mathematics: Prof. MEFHARET KOCATEPE
- Physics: Prof. ATİLLA AYDINLI
- Molecular Biology and Genetics: Prof. MEHMET ÖZTÜRK

ATTACHED INSTITUTES

Economics and Social Sciences: Dir Prof. ALİ KARAOSMANOĞLU.
Engineering and Science: Dir Prof. Dr MEHMET BARAY.
Graduate School of Business Administration: Dir Prof. SÜBİDEY TOGAN.
Fine Arts: Dir Prof. BÜLENT ÖZGÜÇ.
Music and Performing Arts: Dir Prof. ERSİN ONAY.
World Systems, Economies and Strategic Research: Dir (vacant).
Centre for Studies in Society and Politics: Dir Prof. ERGUN ÖZBUDUN.
Bilkent Centre for Advanced Studies: Dir Prof. SALİM GIRACI.

BOĞAZİÇİ ÜNİVERSİTESİ
(University of the Bosphorus)

80815 Bebek, İstanbul
Telephone: (212) 263-15-00
Fax: (212) 265-63-57

Founded 1863; formerly Robert College
State control
Language of instruction: English
Academic year: September to July

Rector: Prof. Dr ÜSTÜN ERGÜDER
Vice-Rectors: Prof. Dr YILMAZ ESMER, Prof. Dr ÖKTEM VARDAR
Secretary-General: GÜLÇİN ATARER
Registrar: Doç. Dr ZEYNEP ATAY
Librarian: Doç. Dr TAHA PARLA

Number of teachers: 899
Number of students: 9,162

Publications: *Boğaziçi University Journal* (annually), *Biomedical Engineering Bulletin* (annually), *Education Bulletin, Economics and Administration Studies, Engineering Bulletin, Science and Engineering Bulletin, MİMESİS Theatre Research Journal, Folklora Doğru.*

DEANS

Faculty of Engineering: Prof. Dr SABİH TANSAL
Faculty of Arts and Sciences: Prof. Dr AYŞE SOYSAL
Faculty of Economics and Administrative Sciences: Prof. Dr GÜVEN ALPAY
Faculty of Education: Prof. Dr CEM ALPTEKİN

HEADS OF DEPARTMENTS

Faculty of Engineering:
- ALTAY, G., Civil Engineering
- ISTEFANOPULOS, Y., Electrical Engineering
- KURU, S., Computer Engineering
- ÖNSAN, Z. İ., Chemical Engineering
- OR, İ., Industrial Engineering
- TEZEL, A., Mechanical Engineering

Faculty of Arts and Sciences:
- BAŞAK, O., Western Languages and Literature
- BİRTEK, F., Sociology
- ESENBEL, S., History
- İNEL, Y., Chemistry
- IRZIK, G., Philosophy
- IŞIK, N., Mathematics
- KOÇ, A., Psychology
- KUT, G., Turkish Language and Literature
- OĞUZ, Ö., Physics
- TOLUN, A., Molecular Biology and Genetics

Faculty of Economics and Administrative Sciences:
- ARAT, Y., Political Science
- BODUR, M., Management
- ÖZMUCUR, S., Economics

Faculty of Education:
- AKYEL, A., English Teaching
- ERKTİN, E., Science Teaching
- GÜLERCE, A., Educational Science

ATTACHED INSTITUTES

Biomedical Engineering: Dir Prof. Dr YORGO ISTEFANOPULOS.
Earthquake Research: Dir Prof. Dr A. METE IŞIKARA.
Environmental Sciences: Dir Prof. Dr EROL GÜLER.
Sciences: Dir Prof. Dr AKIN TEZEL.
Social Sciences: Dir Prof. Dr CEVZA SEVGEN.
History of the Turkish Republic: Dir Prof. Dr ZAFER TOPRAK.

ATTACHED SCHOOLS AND COLLEGES

School of Foreign Languages: Dir Prof. Dr ERSİN KALAYCIOĞLU.
School of Vocational Education: Dir AYFER HORTAÇSU.
School of Applied Disciplines: Dir SEMA TAPAN.

ÇUKUROVA ÜNİVERSİTESİ

Balcalı Kampüsü, 01330 Adana
Telephone: (322) 3386084
Telex: 62934
Fax: (322) 3386945

Founded 1973
State control
Language of instruction: Turkish
Academic year: September to July

Rector: Prof. Dr CAN ÖZSAHİNOĞLU
Vice-Rectors: Prof. Dr İBRAHİM GENÇ, Prof. Dr ÜNAL ZORLUDEMİR, Prof. Dr YUSUF ÜNLÜ
Secretary-General: MUSTAFA BERBEROĞLU
Librarian: TURHAN YILMAZ

Number of teachers: 1,540
Number of students: 19,000

Publications: *University Bulletin* (2 a year), faculty journals (all 3 a year).

DEANS

Faculty of Agriculture: Prof. Dr AYTEKİN BERKMAN
Faculty of Medicine: Prof. Dr IŞIK OLCAY
Faculty of Arts and Sciences: Prof. Dr MELİH BORAL
Faculty of Engineering and Architecture: Prof. Dr HAMIT SERBEST
Faculty of Education Sciences: Prof. Dr ADİL TÜRKOĞLU
Faculty of Fisheries: Prof. Dr ERCAN SARUHAN
Faculty of Dentistry: Prof. Dr İLTER UZEL
Faculty of Theology: Prof. Dr KERIM YAVUZ
Faculty of Economics and Administrative Sciences: Prof. Dr MUSTAFA MAZLUM

HEADS OF DEPARTMENTS

Faculty of Agriculture:

ABAK, K., Horticultural Science
BAŞÇETİNÇELİK, A., Agricultural Mechanization
ÇEVİK, B., Farm Structures and Irrigation
FENERCİOĞLU, H., Food Science and Technology
GENÇ, İ., Field Crops
ÖZBEK, H., Soil Science
ÖZKÜTÜK, K., Animal Science
UYGUN, N., Plant Protection
UZUN, G., Landscape Architecture
YURDAKUL, O., Agricultural Economics

Faculty of Medicine:

ACARTÜRK, S., Plastic Surgery
AKGALI, C., Oto-Laryngology
AKAN, E., Microbiology
AKBABA, M., Public Health
AKKIZ, H., Gastroenterology
ARIDOĞAN, N., Obstetrics and Gynaecology
BAYSAL, F., Pharmacology
BAYTOK, G., Orthopaedics-Traumatology
BİRAND, A., Cardiology
BOZDEMİR, N., Family Practice
DERE, F., Anatomy
DOĞAN, A., Physiology
ERKOÇAK, E. U., General Surgery
ERSOZ, T. R., Ophthalmology
IŞIK, G., Anaesthesiology
KARADAYI, A., Neurosurgery
KASAP, H., Medical Biology
KOCABAŞ A., Thoracic Surgery
KOÇAK, R., Haematology
KÜMİ, M., Paediatric Haematology
LEVENT, B. A., Psychiatry
MEMİŞOĞLU, H., Dermatology
OĞUZ, M., Radiology
SAĞLIKER, Y., Nephrology
SARICA, Y., Neurology
TUNCER, I., Forensic Medicine and Pathology
TÜRKYILMAZ, R., Urology
YÜREĞİR, G., Biochemistry
ZORLUDEMİR, Ü., Paediatric Surgery

Faculty of Arts and Sciences:

AKDENİZ, F., Mathematics
ÇOLAK, Ö., Biology
ERBATUR, G., Chemistry
KIYMAÇ, K., Physics
MENGİ, M., Turkish Language and Literature

Faculty of Engineering and Architecture:

ANIL, M., Mining Engineering
EROL, R., Industrial Engineering
ERTEN, E., Architecture
ERTUNÇ, A., Geological Engineering
GÜRÇINAR, Y., Interior Design
KIRKGÖZ, S., Civil Engineering
KOÇ, E., Textile Engineering
SERBEST, H., Electrical and Electronic Engineering
YILMAZ, T., Mechanical Engineering
YÜCEER, A., Environmental Engineering

Faculty of Economics and Administrative Sciences:

CANBAŞ, S., Management
ÇABUK, A., Econometrics
ÖZSOYLU, A. F., Finance
TEKEOĞLU, M., Economics

Faculty of Education:

BALCI, T., Teaching of German Language
EKMEKÇİ, Ö., Teaching of English Language
ERALDEMİR, B., Arts and Crafts
GÖMİEKSİZ, M., Primary School Teaching
İNANÇ, B., Educational Sciences
KAYRA, E., Teaching of French Language
ÖNGEL, Ü., Philosophy

ATTACHED INSTITUTES

Institute of Social Sciences: Dir Prof. Dr N. ERK.

Institute of Health: Dir Prof. Dr G. YÜREĞİR.

Institute of Science: Dir Prof. Dr U. DİNÇ.

CUMHURİYET ÜNİVERSİTESİ
(Republic University)

58140 Campus-Sivas

Telephone: (346) 226-15-27
Fax: (346) 226-15-13

Founded 1974, reorganized 1982
State control
Language of instruction: Turkish
Academic year: October to June

Rector: Prof. Dr FERİT KOÇOĞLU
Vice-Rectors: Prof. Dr ERDOĞAN GÜRSOY, Prof. Dr ALİ ÖZTÜRK, Prof. Dr MEHMET AKÇAY
Secretary-General: Dr EROL ŞANLI
International Relations: Dr SEDAT TÖREL
Librarian: FİLİZ DENER

Number of teachers: 983
Number of students: 10,855

Publications: faculty bulletins.

DEANS

Faculty of Arts and Sciences: Prof. Dr FARUK KOCACIK
Faculty of Engineering: Prof. Dr MEHMET CAMBAZOĞLU
Faculty of Medicine: Prof. Dr YENER GÜLTEKİN
Faculty of Economic and Administrative Sciences: Prof. Dr İBRAHIM YILDIRIM
Faculty of Theological Studies: Prof. Dr ALİ YILMAZ
Faculty of Education: Prof. Dr VAHAP SAĞ
Faculty of Dentistry: Prof. Dr DERVİŞ YILMAZ

DIRECTORS OF INSTITUTES

Medical Sciences: Prof. Dr AHMET ÇOLAK
Social Sciences: Prof. Dr ALİ ERKUL
Basic Sciences: Prof. Dr NECATİ ÇELİK

ATTACHED RESEARCH CENTRES

Atatürk's Principles Research Centre: Dir Prof. Dr MEHMET AKÇAY.
Environmental Problems Research Centre: Dir Asst Prof. Dr ORHAN CERİT.

DİCLE ÜNİVERSİTESİ
(Tigris University)

21280 Diyarbakır

Telephone: 2488202
Fax: 2488216

Founded 1966 as branch of Ankara University, independent 1973
State control
Academic year: October to June

Rector: Prof. Dr MEHMET ÖZAYDIN
Vice-Rectors: Prof. Dr OMER METE, Prof. Dr MASUM ŞIMŞEK
General Secretary: MEHMET TEKDÖŞ
Librarian: SEVGI EKMEKÇİLER

Number of teachers: 1,007
Number of students: 10,370

Publications: *University Annual*, *Medical Faculty Journal*.

DEANS

Faculty of Medicine: Assoc. Prof. Dr RECEP IŞIK
Faculty of Arts and Sciences: Prof. Dr BAHATTİN GÜNİGÜNİ
Faculty of Dentistry: Prof. Dr FATMA ATAKUL
Faculty of Education: Prof. Dr RECEP ZİYADANOĞULLARI
Faculty of Law: Assoc. Prof. Dr AYDIN TÜRKBAL
Faculty of Architecture and Engineering: Assoc. Prof. ZÜLKÜF GÜNELİ
Faculty of Agriculture: Prof. Dr D. ALİ ATALAY
Faculty of Theology: Prof. Dr ABDÜLBAKI TURAN
Faculty of Veterinary Medicine: Prof. Dr ÖMER METE
Faculty of Education (Siirt): Prof. Dr HÜSEYİN MISIRDALI

PROFESSORS

Faculty of Medicine:

ARIKAN, E., Microbiology
AYDINOL, B., Biochemistry
BAHÇECİ, M., Internal Diseases
BAYHAN, N., Anaesthesiology
BUDAK, T., Medical Biology
CANORUÇ, F., Internal Diseases
ÇELİK, S., Biophysics
DEĞERTEKİN, H., Internal Diseases
DERİCİ, M., Dermatology
ERDOĞAN, F., Physical Rehabilitation
GÜL, T., Gynaecology and Obstetrics
GÜRGEN, F., Psychiatry
IŞIKOĞLU, B., Internal Diseases
İLÇİN, E., Public Health
KELLE, A., Medical Biology
METE, Ö., Microbiology
MÜFTÜOĞLU, E., Internal Diseases
NERGİS, Y., Histology
ÖZAYDIN, M., Pathology
ÖZGEN, G., Cardiovascular and Thoracic Surgery
TAŞ, M. A., Public Health
TOPCU, I., Otorhinolaryngology
TOPRAK, N., Internal Diseases
YILMAZ, N., Gynaecology and Obstetrics

Faculty of Arts and Sciences:

BAŞARAN, D., Botany
BİLGİN, F. H., Zoology
GÜLSÜN, Z., Atomic and Molecular Physics
GÜMGÜM, B., Inorganic Chemistry
GÜNİGÜNİ, B., Inorganic Chemistry
TEZ, Z., Physical Chemistry
YILMAZ, A., General Physics

Faculty of Education:

ASLAN, E., Turkish Language and Literature
SÖNMEZ, A., Physics

ATTACHED INSTITUTES

Institute of Medical Sciences: Dir Prof. Dr ALİ KELLE.

Institute of Social Sciences: Dir Prof. Dr ABDÜLBAKİ TURAN.

Institute of Sciences: Dir Prof. Dr DAVUT BAŞARAN.

College of Health: Dir ZEKİ YILDIRIM.

DOKUZ EYLÜL ÜNİVERSİTESİ
(Ninth September University)

Cumhuriyet Bul. 144, 35210 Alsancak, İzmir

Telephone: (232) 421-55-90
Fax: (232) 422-09-78
E-mail: webadmin@deu.edu.tr

Founded 1982 from existing faculties and schools
State control
Academic year: October to June

President: Prof. Dr FETHİ İDİMAN
Vice-Presidents: Prof. Dr NUSRET SEFA KURALAY, Prof. Dr KEMAL AÇIKGÖZ
Secretary-General: İSMAİL HAKKI KARATAŞ
Librarian: HALE BALTEPE

Library of 203,000 vols

Number of teachers: 2,207
Number of students: 32,592

DEANS

Faculty of Arts and Sciences: Prof. Dr GÜZİN GÖKMEN
Faculty of Education: Prof. Dr HÜSEYİN ALKAN
Faculty of Medicine: Prof. Dr EMİN ALICI
Faculty of Law: Prof. Dr ZAFER GÖREN
Faculty of Economics and Administrative Sciences: Prof. Dr ALP TİMUR
Faculty of Theology: Prof. Dr MEHMET AYDIN
Faculty of Engineering: Prof. Dr HALİL KÖSE
Faculty of Fine Arts: Prof. Dr FARUK KALKAN
Faculty of Architecture: Prof. Dr MEHMET TÜREYEN
Faculty of Business Administration: Prof. Dr CEYHAN ALDEMİR

DIRECTORS

Vocational School of Juridical Practice: Prof. Dr BAHRİ ÖZTÜRK
School of Maritime Business and Management: Asst Prof. Dr GÜLDEM CERİT
Vocational School of Religion: Prof. Dr CEMAL SOFUOĞLU
İzmir Vocational School: Prof. Dr MACİT TOKSOY
Torbalı Vocational School: Prof. Dr FARUK ÇALAPKULU
Vocational School of Health Services: Prof. Dr NEDİM GAKIR
Conservatory: Prof. MÜFİT BAYRAŞA
School of Nursing: Prof. Dr GÜLSEREN KOCAMAN
School of Physical Therapy and Rehabilitation: Prof. Dr CANDAN TÜREYEN
Graduate School of Health Sciences: Prof. Dr SEVİN ERGİN
Graduate School of Social Sciences: Prof. Dr ALİ NAZIM SÖZER
Graduate School of Science and Engineering: Prof. Dr CAHİT HELVACI
Graduate School of Atatürk Principles and Turkish Revolution: Prof. Dr ERGÜN AYBARS
Graduate School of Marine Sciences and Technology: Prof. Dr ORHAN USLU
Institute of Oncology: Prof. Dr CAVİT GEHRELİ
Institute of Education: Prof. Dr HÜSAMETTİN AKÇAY

HEADS OF DEPARTMENTS

Faculty of Medicine:

- Basic Medicine: Prof. Dr İ. NURAN YUHIĞ
- Internal Medicine: Prof. Dr SEMA ÖNCEL
- Surgical Medicine: Prof. Dr EMEL SAĞIROĞLU

Faculty of Education:

- Foreign Languages: Prof. Dr GÜLDEN ERTUĞRUL
- Educational Sciences: Prof. Dr İHSAN TURGUT
- Science: Prof. Dr TEOMAN KESERCİOĞLU
- Social Sciences: Prof. Dr İBRAHİM ATALAY
- Painting and Crafts: Prof. İBRAHİM BOZKUŞ
- Turkish Language and Literature: Assoc. Prof. Dr KEMAL YÜCE
- Music: Prof. TAHSİN KILIÇ

Faculty of Law:

- Public Law: Prof. Dr DURMUŞ TEZCAN
- Finance and Economics: Prof. Dr POLAT SOYER
- Private Law: Prof. Dr AYDIN ZEVKLİLER

Faculty of Economics and Administrative Sciences:

- Business Administration: Prof. Dr MUAMMER DOĞAN
- Economics: Prof. Dr TEVFİK PEKİN
- Public Finance: Prof. Dr AYTAÇ EKER
- Econometrics: Assoc. Prof. Dr MUSTAFA GÜNEŞ
- Public Administration: Prof. Dr ALPAY ATAOL
- Labour Economics and Industrial Relations: Prof. Dr FEVZİ DEMİR
- Business Administration (English): Prof. Dr CEYHAN ALDEMİR

Faculty of Business:

- Business Administration: Prof. Dr CENGİZ PINAR
- Economics: Prof. Dr MEHMET A. CİVELEK
- International Relations: Prof. Dr METE OKTAV
- Tourism Administration: Prof. Dr SAİME ORAL

Faculty of Theology:

- Basic Islamic Sciences: Prof. Dr KADİR ŞENER
- Philosophy and Religion: Prof. Dr RAHMİ AYAL
- History of Islam and Islamic Arts: Prof. Dr HAKKI ÖNKAL

Faculty of Engineering:

- Electronics and Electrical Engineering: Prof. Dr KEMAL ÖZMEHMET
- Civil Engineering: Prof. Dr ERTUĞRUL BENZEDEN
- Mechanical Engineering: Prof. Dr TÜLAY HARZADIN
- Industrial Engineering: Prof. Dr DEMİR ASLAN
- Environmental Engineering: Prof. Dr FÜSUN ŞENGÜL
- Mining Engineering: Prof. Dr ÜNER İPEKOĞLU
- Geological Engineering: Prof. Dr ÖZKAN PIŞKIN
- Geophysical Engineering: Prof. Dr GÜNGÖR TAKTAK

Faculty of Architecture:

- Architecture: Prof. Dr ÇETİN TÜRKÇÜ
- Urban and Regional Planning: Prof. Dr ÇINAR ATOY

Faculty of Fine Arts:

- Drama and Theatre Arts: Prof. Dr ÖZDEMİR NUTKU
- Cinema and Television: Prof. Dr OĞUZ ADANIR
- Photography: Assoc. Prof. Dr SİMBER ATAY
- Painting: Assoc. Prof. ADEM GENÇ
- Sculpture: Assoc. Prof. CENGİZ ÇEKİL
- Ceramics and Glass: Assoc. Prof. Dr SEVİM CİZEL
- Turkish Traditional Handicrafts: Assoc. Prof. Dr İSMAİL ÖZTÜRK
- Musicology: Prof. Dr TURGUT ALDEMİR

Faculty of Arts and Sciences:

- American Studies: Prof. Dr AZİZE ÖZGÜVEN
- Statistics: Prof. Dr MEHMET ŞAHİNOĞLU
- Mathematics: Prof. Dr GÜZİN GÖKMEN

EGE ÜNİVERSİTESİ
(Aegean University)

Bornova, İzmir
Telephone: (232) 180110
Telex: 953610
Fax: (232) 182867

Founded 1955
State control
Languages of instruction: Turkish and, in some departments, English
Academic year: October to June

Rector: Prof. Dr SERMET AKGÜN
Vice-Rectors: Prof. Dr REFET SAYGILI, Prof. Dr ERDAL SAYGIN, Prof. Dr ASLI ÖZER
General Secretary: ABDÜRRAHİM İNCEKARA
Librarian: NURCAN ESLİK BAYKAL

Number of teachers and assistants: 992
Number of students: 20,988

Publications: *Tıp Fakültesi Mecmuası, Ziraat Fakültesi Dergisi, Fen Dergisi, Aegean Medical Journal,* and faculty publications.

DEANS

Faculty of Medicine: Prof Dr TURAN ÖRNEK
Faculty of Dentistry: Prof. Dr BERRAN ÖZTÜRK
Faculty of Pharmacy: Prof. Dr AYSEN KARAN
Faculty of Agriculture: Prof. Dr İBRAHİM KARACA
Faculty of Science: Prof. Dr İSMET ERTAŞ
Faculty of Engineering: Prof. Dr TEMEL ÇAKALOZ
Faculty of Literature: Prof. Dr GÖNÜL ÖNEY

DIRECTORS

Press and Publications School: Prof. Dr ÖZCAN ÖZAL
Water Products School: Prof. Dr ATİLLA ALPBAZ
School of Nursing: Prof. Dr İNCİ EREFE
Institute for Solar Energy: Prof. Dr MEHMET AYDIN
Institute for Science: Prof. Dr FERİDUN TOPALOĞLU
Institute for Medical Sciences: Prof. Dr NECMETTİN ZEYBEK
Institute for Nuclear Sciences: Prof. Dr SELMAN KINACI
Professional School: Prof. Dr MEHMET DOKUZOĞUZ
Conservatory of Turkish Music: Prof. Dr REFET SAYGILI

RESEARCH CENTRES

Data Processing Research and Application Centre: Dir Prof. Dr OĞUZ MANAS.

Organ Transplantation and Research Centre: Prof. Dr ÖZDEMİR YARARBAŞ.

Audiovisual Research and Application Centre (Medical Faculty): Dir Prof. Dr İSMET KÖKTÜRK.

Centre of Textile and Apparel Manufacturing Research Application: Prof. Dr IŞIK TARAKÇIOĞLU.

ERCİYES ÜNİVERSİTESİ

PK 275, Kayseri
Telephone: (352) 4374922
Fax: (352) 4374931

Founded 1978
State control
Language of instruction: Turkish
Academic year: November to June

Rector: Prof. Dr MEHMET ŞAHİN
Vice-Rectors: Prof. Dr RECEP KILIK, Prof. Dr OSMAN UNUTULMAZ
Registrar: Dr İLHAMİ VURAL
Librarian: BECAHAT ELKOVAN

Number of teachers: 1,094
Number of students: 17,807

Publications: *Medical School Journal, Business Administration and Management Journal,* journals of the Theology Faculty.

DEANS

Faculty of Medicine: Prof. Dr ZEKİ YILMAZ
Faculty of Business Administration and Management: Prof. Dr CEMAL ÖZGÜVEN
Faculty of Engineering: Prof. Dr İBRAHİM UZMAY
Faculty of Theology: Prof. Dr ALİ TOKSARI
Faculty of Arts and Science: Prof. Dr MEHMET GÜNDÜZ
Faculty of Fine Arts: Prof. Dr ZAFER BAYBURTLUOĞLU
Faculty of Architecture: Prof. Dr HÜSEYİN YURTSEVER
Faculty of Engineering and Architecture (Yozgat): Prof. Dr RECEP KILIK
Faculty of Veterinary Science: Prof. Dr NEJAT AYDIN
Faculty of Business Administration (Yozgat): Prof. Dr MÜMİN ERTÜRK
Faculty of Arts and Science (Yozgat): Prof. Dr YUNUS AKÇAMUR
Faculty of Business Administration and Management (Nevşehir): Prof. Dr RIFAT YILDIZ

PROFESSORS

Faculty of Medicine:

AKTAŞ, E.
ARITAŞ, Y.
ARMAN, F.
AŞÇIOĞLU, Ö.
AYDOĞAN, S.

AYKUT, M.
BAKTIR, A.
BALKANLI, S.
BAYKAL, M. E.
CANER, Y.
CEMİLOĞLU, R.
CEYHAN, O.
ÇETİN, N.
ÇETİN, S.
DEMİR, R.
DEMIRTAŞ, H.
DOĞANAY, M.
DÜŞÜNSEL, R.
ERSOY, A. Ö.
FAZLI, Ş. A.
GÜLEÇ, M.
GÜLMEZ, İ.
GÜNAY, O.
GÜNEY, E.
KARACAGİL, M.
KARAKAŞ, E. S.
KELEŞTİMUR, F.
KURTOĞLU, S.
KÜÇÜKAYDIN, M.
MİRZA, E.
MİRZA, M.
OĞUZ, A.
ÖKTEN, T.
ÖZBAL, Y.
ÖZDEMİR, M. A.
ÖZESMİ, Ç.
ÖZESMİ, M.
ÖZTÜRK, M. A.
ÖZTÜRK, M. K.
ÖZTÜRK, Y.
ÖZÜGÜL, Y.
PATIROĞLU, T.
PATIROĞLU, T. E.
SAĞLAM, A.
SOFUOĞLU, S.
SOYUER, A.
SÖZÜER, E. M.
ŞAHİN, İ.
TATLIŞEN, A.
TEKALAN, Ş. A.
TEKOL, Y.
ÜNVER, U.,
ÜSTDAL, K. M.
ÜSTÜNBAŞ, H. B.
YEŞİLKAYA, Y.
YILMAZ, Z.
YÜCESOY, M.

Faculty of Business Administration and Management:

AKDOĞAN, M. Ş.
ANDAÇ, F.
ATALAY, M.
BİLGİNOĞLU, M. A.
ÇINAR, M.
ÇİVELEK, M.
DURA, C.
ERTÜRK, M.
ÖZGÜVEN, C.
SAATÇİ, M.
SÖNMEZ, İ. H.
ŞAHİN, M.
ÜNUTULMAZ, O.
YILDIZ, R.

Faculty of Engineering:

ATLI, V.
HAKTANIR, T.
KARAMIŞ, M. B.
KILIK, R.
SÖNMEZ, A. İ.
UZMAY, İ.

Faculty of Theology:

AKSU, Z.
APAYDIN, H. Y.
ATİK, M. K.
BAĞÇECİ, M.
COŞKUN, A.
DEMİRCİ, A.
DUMAN, M. Z.
GÜNAY, Ü.
GÜNGÖR, H.
KIRCA, C.
KUZGUN, Ş.
POLAT, S.
ŞAHİN, H.
TOKSARI, A.
TUNÇ, C.
UĞUR, A.
ÜNAL, H.

Faculty of Arts and Science:

AKÇAMUR, Y.
AKTAN, A.
BAYBURTLUOĞLU, Z.
BOR, H.
ÇOBAN, A.
ELÇİ, L.
GÜLENSOY, T.
GÜNDÜZ, M.
KARTAL, Ş.
KESKİN, M.
KESKİN, M.
KÖK, T. R.
OKUYUCU, C.
ÖNEM, A.
ÖZTÜRK, E.
ÜLGEN, A.
YILGOR, İ.
YUVALI, A.

Faculty of Fine Arts:

BAYBURTLUOĞLU, Z.

Faculty of Veterinary Science:

AYDIN, N.

Faculty of Architecture:

YURTSEVER, H.

Yozgat Faculty of Arts and Science:

AKÇAMUR, Y.

Yozgat Faculty of Business Administration and Management:

ERTÜRK, M.

Yozgat Faculty of Engineering and Architecture:

KILIK, R.

Nevşehir Faculty of Business Administration and Management:

YILDIZ, R.

ATTACHED INSTITUTES

Institute of Health: Dir Prof. Dr SAMİ AYDOĞAN.
Institute of Science: Dir Prof. Dr LATİF ELÇİ.
Gevher Nesibe Institute of Medicine History: Dir (vacant).
Institute of Social Science: Dir Prof. Dr CİHAT TUNÇ.
Halil Bayraktar Health Services Vocational School: Dir Prof. Dr YUSUF ÖZTÜRK.
Foreign Languages Institute: Chair. HALİL YÜCEL.

FIRAT ÜNİVERSİTESİ
(Euphrates University)

23119 Elaziğ
Telephone: 17930
Telex: 64538
Fax: 22717

Founded 1975
Language of instruction: Turkish

Rector: Prof. Dr M. ARİF ÇAĞLAR
General Secretary: HÜSEYİN AŞAN
Librarian: HALE BALTEPE

Number of teachers: 531
Number of students: 6,302

DEANS

Faculty of Arts and Sciences: Prof. Dr ŞENER BALTEPE
Faculty of Engineering: Prof. Dr MUTLU BAŞAKMAN
Faculty of Medicine: Prof. Dr OKTAY ÖZKARAKAŞ
Faculty of Technical Education: Prof. Dr ŞEREF KUNÇ
Faculty of Veterinary Medicine: Prof. Dr ŞENDOĞAN GÜLEN

HEADS OF DEPARTMENTS

Faculty of Arts and Sciences:

Biology: Prof. Dr NİYAZI ÖZDEMİR
Chemistry: Prof. Dr ŞEREF KUNÇ
History: Asst Prof. Dr ABDÜLKADIR YUVALI
Mathematics: Assoc. Prof. Dr SALİH ÖZÇELIK
Physics: Assoc. Prof. Dr MEHMET AYDOĞDU
Sociology: Assoc. Prof. Dr ZEKİ ERDOĞMUŞ
Turkish Language and Literature: Asst Prof. Dr A. BERAT ALPTEKIN

Faculty of Engineering:

Chemical Engineering: Asst Prof. Dr. EMIN ONAT
Civil Engineering: Prof. Dr MUTLU BAŞAKMAN
Electrical and Electronic Engineering: Asst Prof. Dr MUSTAFA POYRAZ
Environmental Engineering: Prof. Dr SUCAATTIN KIRIMHAN
Geological Engineering: Prof. Dr YUSUF TATAR
Mechanical Engineering: Assoc. Prof. Dr KAZIM PIHTILI

Faculty of Medicine:

Fundamental Medical Sciences: Prof. Dr HALUK ARVAS
Internal Medicine: Assoc. Prof. Dr NADL ARSLAN
Surgical Medicine: Prof. Dr YAVUZ BURDURLU

Faculty of Technical Education:

Automative Education: Asst Prof. Dr ASAF VAROL
Construction Education: Assoc. Prof. Dr MEHMET KÜLAHÇI
Education: Assoc. Prof. Dr ŞADLYE KÜLAHÇI
Metallurgical Education: Assoc. Prof. Dr MUSTAFA YILDIRIM

Faculty of Veterinary Medicine:

Animal Husbandry: Assoc. Prof. Dr MUSTAFA SARI
Fundamental Veterinary Sciences: Assoc. Prof. Dr ALI OTLU
Internal Diseases and Surgical Sciences: Prof. Dr SİTKİ GÜLER

ATTACHED INSTITUTES (GRADUATE SCHOOLS)

Health Sciences: Dir Prof. Dr ŞENDOĞAN GÜLEN.
Natural and Applied Sciences: Dir Assoc. Prof. Dr TÜRKER AŞAN.
Social Sciences: Dir Assoc. Prof. Dr ZEKL ERDOĞMUŞ.

ATTACHED SCHOOLS AND COLLEGES

School of Aquaculture: Dir Prof. Dr TEKIN MENGI.
College of Vocational Education (Bingöl): Dir CELAL ÖZTÜRK.
College of Vocational Education (Elazığ): Dir Prof. Dr ŞEREF KUNÇ.
College of Vocational Education (Muş): Dir Prof. Dr SÜCAATTIN KIRIMHAN.
College of Vocational Education (Tunceli): Dir ŞINASI ELÇI.

ATTACHED DEPARTMENTS

Fine Arts: Dir HIMMET GÜMRAH.
History of Turkish Revolution: Dir ERDAL AÇIKSES.
Foreign Languages: Dir BEKIR ÜSTÜNDAĞ.
Physical Education and Sports: Dir BEYTULLAH SÖNMEZ.
Turkish: Dir Ismail GÖRKEM.

GAZİ ÜNİVERSİTESİ

Teknikokullar, Ankara
Telephone: 2126840
Fax: 2213202

Founded 1982
State control
Language of instruction: Turkish

Academic year: October to June
Rector: Prof. Dr ENVER HASANOĞLU
Vice-Rectors: Prof. Dr EMİN TÜRKÖZ, Prof. Dr MUSTAFA KURU, Prof. Dr TUNCEL ÖZDEN
Chief Administrative Officer: Assoc. Prof. EYÜP BEDİR
Librarian: PINAR ERZURUMLUOĞLU

Number of teachers: 2,364
Number of students: 44,226 undergraduates, 4,611 postgraduates

Publication: *Gazi Üniversitesi Bülteni* (6 a year).

DEANS

Faculty of Architecture and Engineering: Prof. Dr ESEN ONAT
Faculty of Arts and Sciences: Prof. Dr MUSTAFA İSEN
Faculty of Dentistry: Prof. Dr İ. LEVENT TANER
Faculty of Economic and Administrative Sciences: Prof. Dr NEJAT TENKER
Gazi Faculty of Education: Prof. Dr MUSTAFA TAN
Faculty of Medicine: Prof. Dr M. ALİ GÜRER
Faculty of Pharmacy: Prof. Dr FETHİ ŞAHİN
Faculty of Technical Education: Prof. Dr YALÇIN ÖRS
Faculty of Vocational Education: Prof. Dr REFET YİNANÇ
Faculty of Commerce and Tourism: Prof. Dr RAUF ARIKAN
Faculty of Vocational Extension Education: Prof. Dr H. ÖRCÜN BARIŞTA
Faculty of Industrial Arts Education: Prof. Dr NALAN AKDOĞAN
Faculty of Law: Prof. Dr ZEHRA ODYAKMAZ
Faculty of Communication: Prof. Dr ERTAN OKTAY
Çorum Faculty of Theology: Prof. Dr HÜSEYİN ALGÜL
Kırşehir Faculty of Education: Prof. Dr SELAHATTİN SALMAN
Kastamonu Faculty of Education: Prof. Dr REFİK TURAN
Kastamonu Faculty of Forestry: Prof. Dr HASAN VURDU
Çorum Faculty of Economics and Administrative Sciences: Prof. Dr BURHAN AYKAÇ

GRADUATE SCHOOLS

Graduate School of Accident Research and Prevention: Teknikokullar, Ankara; Dir Prof. Dr M. ALİ BUMİN.

Graduate School of Health Sciences: Teknikokullar, Ankara; Dir OKTAY ÜNER.

Graduate School of Natural Sciences: Maltepe, Ankara; Dir Prof. Dr SÜLEYMAN PAMPAL.

Graduate School of Social Sciences: Kavaklıdere, Ankara; Dir Prof. Dr KAZIM YAŞAR KOPRAMAN.

Graduate School of Educational Sciences: Teknikokullar, Ankara; Dir Prof. Dr HÜSEYİN SOYLU.

GAZIANTEP ÜNİVERSİTESİ

POB 300, 27310 Gaziantep
Telephone: 180189
Telex: 69146
Fax: 181749

Rector: Prof. Dr UGUR BÜGET

HACETTEPE ÜNİVERSİTESİ

Hacettepe, 06100 Ankara
Telephone: (312) 310-3545
Telex: 4418
Fax: (312) 310-5552

Founded 1206 in Kayseri; chartered 1967
State control
Languages of instruction: Turkish and English
Academic year: September to August
Rector: Prof. Dr SÜLEYMAN SAĞLAM
Vice-Rectors: Prof. Dr MUSTAFA İLHAN, Prof. Dr OKTAY BEŞKARDEŞ, Prof. Dr NİHAT BOZCUK
Secretary-General: Prof. Dr SADIK KIRBAŞ
Registrar: MÜCELLA MERDOL
Director of Libraries: Dr HANSIN TUNÇKANAT

Beytepe campus library of 150,000 vols, central library of 125,000 vols
Number of teachers: 2,844
Number of students: 29,223

Publications: *Hacettepe Tıp / Cerrahi Bülteni* (quarterly), and several faculty bulletins.

DEANS

Hacettepe Campus:
Faculty of Medicine: Prof. Dr A. YAVUZ RENDA
Faculty of Dentistry: Prof. Dr FERDA TAŞAR
Faculty of Pharmacy: Prof. Dr MURAT ŞUMNU

Beytepe Campus:
Faculty of Economics and Adminstrative Sciences: Prof. Dr DOĞAN TUNCER
Faculty of Engineering: Prof. Dr K. ERÇIN KASAPOĞLU
Faculty of Education: Prof. Dr İLHAMI KIZIROĞLU
Faculty of Fine Arts: Prof. ZAFER GENÇAYDIN
Faculty of Letters: Prof. Dr ÖZKAN İZGI
Faculty of Science: Prof. Dr AYŞE BOŞGELMEZ

DIRECTORS

School of Foreign Languages: Prof. Dr DENIZ BOZER
School of Health Administration: Prof. Dr TEVFIK DINÇER
School of Health Technology: Prof. Dr PERIHAN ASLAN
School of Home Economics: Prof. Dr MEZIYET ARI
School of Nursing: Prof. Dr NEBAHAT KUM
School of Physical Therapy and Rehabilitation: Prof. Dr HÜLYA ARIKAN
School of Social Work: Prof. Dr SEMA KUT
Ankara State Conservatoire: Prof. EROL GÖMÜRGEN
Vocational School of Woodwork Technology: Prof. Dr N. KUTER ATAÇ
Vocational School (Ankara): Prof. Dr ABIDIN AYPAR
Vocational School of Sports Sciences and Technology: Dr CANER AÇIKADA
Vocational School of Health Services: Prof. Dr EROL BELGIN

PROFESSORS

Faculty of Medicine:
ADALAR, N., Internal Medicine
ADALIOĞLU, G., Paediatrics
AKAN, H. T., Dermatology
AKIN, A., Community Health
AKŞİT, D., Anatomy
AKYOL, F. H., Oncology
ALAÇAM, R., Microbiology
ALPARSLAN, M., Orthopaedics
ALPAY, M., Obstetrics and Gynaecology
ALTAY, Ç., Paediatrics
ANDAÇ, O., Physiology
ANLAR, B. F., Paediatrics
ARAN, Ö., Surgery
ARIOĞLU, S., Internal Medicine
AŞAN, E., Morphology
ATAHAN, İ. L., Oncology
ATAKAN, Z. N., Dermatology
AYAS, K., Ear, Nose and Throat Surgery
AYHAN, A., Pathology
AYHAN, A., Obstetrics and Gynaecology
AYPAR, Ü., Anaesthesiology
AYSUN, S., Neurophysiology
AYTAR, Ş., Medical Biology
BAKKALOĞLU, A., Paediatrics
BAKKALOĞLU, A. M., Urology
BALCI, S., Paediatrics
BALKANCI, F., Radiology
BALTALI, A. E., Internal Medicine
BALTALI, E., Oncology
BARIŞ, İ., Internal Medicine
BAŞGÖZE, O., Physical Therapy and Rehabilitation
BATMAN, F., Internal Medicine
BAYRAKTAR, Y., Internal Medicine
BEKDİK, F. C., Nuclear Medicine
BEKSAÇ, S., Obstetrics and Gynaecology
BELGİN, E., Ear, Nose and Throat Surgery
BENLİ, K., Neurosurgery
BERKEL, A. İ., Paediatrics
BERTAN, M., Community Medicine
BERTAN, V., Neurosurgery
BEŞBAŞ, N., Paediatrics
BESİM, A., Radiology
BİLGİÇ, A., Paediatrics
BİLGİÇ, S., Ophthalmology
BİLİR, N., Community Health
BÖKE, E., Cardiovascular and Thoracic Surgery
BOZKURT, A., Pharmacology
BÜYÜKPAMUKÇU, M., Oncology
BÜYÜKPAMUKÇU, N., Paediatric Surgery
ÇAĞLAR, M., Paediatrics
ÇAĞLAR, S., Internal Medicine
ÇAKAR, A. N., Morphology
ÇAKMAK, F., Urology
ÇALGÜNERİ, M., Internal Medicine
ÇEYHAN, M., Paediatrics
ÇİLİV, G., Biochemistry
ÇOSKUN, T., Paediatrics
CUMHUR, M., Morphology
DALKARA, N. E. T., Institute of Neurological Sciences
DEMİRCİN, M., Cardiovascular and Thoracic Surgery
DİNÇER, F., Physical Therapy and Rehabilitation
DORAL, M. N., Orthopaedics
DUMAN, O., Physiology
DURUKAN, T., Obstetrics and Gynaecology
DÜNDAR, S., Internal Medicine
ERBENGİ, A., Neurosurgery
ERCAN, B. M., Nuclear Medicine
ERDEM, G., Paediatrics
ERDEM, K., Anaesthesiology and Reanimation
EREN, N., Community Health
ERGEN, A., Urology
ERKAN, İ., Urology
ERK, Y., Plastic Surgery
ERSOY, F. N., Paediatrics
ERSOY, Ü., Cardiovascular and Thoracic Surgery
FIRAT, D., Internal Medicine
GEDİK, O., Internal Medicine
GÖÇMEN, A., Paediatrics
GÖĞÜŞ, A., Psychiatry
GÖĞÜŞ, S., Child Health and Paediatrics
GÖĞÜŞ, T., Orthopaedics
GÖKLER, B., Psychiatry
GÖKÖZ, A., Pathology
GÖKŞİN, E., Obstetrics and Gynaecology
GÜLEÇ, C., Institute of Neurological Sciences
GÜNALP, A., Microbiology
GÜNDOĞAN, N., Physiology
GÜNGEN, Y. Y., Pathology
GÜRÇAY, O., Neurosurgery
GÜRGAN, T., Obstetrics and Gynaecology
GÜRGERY, A., Paediatrics
GÜRSEL, B., Ear, Nose and Throat Surgery
GÜRSEL, G., Internal Medicine
GÜRSU-HAZARLI, K. G., Plastic Surgery
HASÇELİK, H. Z., Physical Therapy and Rehabilitation
HERSEK, E., Surgery
HIÇSÖNMEZ, A., Paediatric Surgery
HIÇSÖNMEZ, G., Paediatrics
HOŞAL, N., Ear, Nose and Throat Surgery
İLHAN, M., Pharmacology
İLGİ, N. S., Morphology
İRKEÇ, M., Ophthalmology
KALE, G., Paediatrics
KANRA, G., Paediatrics
KANSU, E., Oncology

KANSU, T., Institute of Neurological Sciences
KARAMEHMETOĞLU, M., Anaesthesiology
KART, A., Medical Biology
KAYA, S., Ear, Nose and Throat Surgery
KAYAALP, O., Pharmacology
KAYHAN, B., Internal Medicine
KEÇİK, A., Plastic Surgery
KENDİ, S., Urology
KES, S., Internal Medicine
KILINÇ, K., Biochemistry
KINIK, E., Child Health and Paediatrics
KOÇAK, N., Child Health and Paediatrics
KOŞAL, A. C., Urology
KÖLEMEN, F., Dermatology
KÜÇÜKALİ, T., Pathology
KUTLUK, M. T., Paediatrics
MEMİKOĞLU, S., Orthopaedics
MOCAN, G., Pathology
MUŞDAL, Y., Orthopaedics and Traumatology
NAZLI, N., Internal Medicine, Cardiology
ONUR, E. R., Pharmacology
ORAM, A., Internal Medicine, Cardiology
ORAN, M. B., Radiology
ORAN, O., Child Health and Paediatrics
ORHON, A., Psychiatry
OTO, M. A., Internal Medicine
ÖNER, Z. N., Surgery
ÖRS, U., Histology and Embryology
ÖZALP, I., Child Health and Paediatrics
ÖZCAN, E. O., Neurosurgery
ÖZDEMİR, N., Orthopaedics and Traumatology
ÖZDİRİM, E., Paediatrics
ÖZEN, H. A., Urology
ÖZENÇ, A. M., Surgery
ÖZER, E. S., Paediatrics
ÖZER, N., Biochemistry
ÖZERKAN, K., Haematology
ÖZGEN, T., Institute of Neurological Sciences
ÖZGÜÇ, M., Medical Biology
ÖZGÜNEŞ, N., Biochemistry
ÖZKAN, S., Ear, Nose and Throat Surgery
ÖZKUTLU, H., Internal Medicine
ÖZKUTLU, S., Paediatrics
ÖZMEN, F., Internal Medicine
ÖZMEN, S., Child Health and Paediatrics
ÖZTEK, A. Z., Community Medicine
ÖZTÜRK, N., Biophysics
ÖZYAZICI, A., Morphology
PAŞAOĞLU, İ., Cardiovascular and Thoracic Surgery
PEKCAN, H., Community Health
REMZİ, D., Urology
RENDA, N., Biochemistry
RENDA, Y., Paediatrics
RIDVANAĞAOĞLU, A. Y., Physiology
RUAÇAN, S., Oncology
SAATÇİ, Ü., Paediatrics
SAĞLAM, S., Neurosurgery
SANAÇ, A. Ş., Ophthalmology
SANAÇ, Y., Surgery
SANAL, S. Ö., Paediatrics
SANCAK, B., Anatomy
SARAÇLAR, M., Paediatrics
SARAÇLAR, Y., Paediatrics
SARIBAŞ, O., Neurosurgery
SARIKAYALAR, F., Paediatrics
SAVAŞIR, I., Psychiatry
SAVAŞIR, Y., Psychiatry
SAYEK, İ., Surgery
SEÇMEER, G., Paediatrics
SELEKLER, K., Neurology
SÖZEN, T., Internal Medicine
SÖZER, A. B., Ear, Nose and Throat Surgery
SÜMBÜLOĞLU, K., Medical Biology
SURAT, A., Orthopaedics
ŞAHİN, A. A., Internal Medicine
ŞEFTALİOĞLU, A., Histology
TANER, D., Anatomy
TANYEL, F. C., Paediatric Surgery
TASAR, C., Oncology
TEKİNALP, G., Paediatrics
TEKUZMAN, G., Oncology
TELATAR, E. F., Internal Medicine
TEZCAN, F., Biochemistry
TEZCAN, S., Community Medicine
TINAZTEPE, K., Paediatrics
TOKGÖZOĞLU, N., Orthopaedics
TUNCER, A., Paediatrics
TUNCER, A. M., Paediatrics
TUNCER, M., Pharmacology
TURAN, E., Ear, Nose and Throat Surgery
TURGAN, Ç., Internal Medicine
TUNÇBİLEK, E., Paediatrics
UNGAN, P., Biophysics
USMAN, A., Internal Medicine
USTAÇELEBİ, S., Microbiology
USTAY, K., Obstetrics and Gynaecology
UZUNALİMOĞLU, B., Pathology
ÜNAL, S., Internal Medicine
ÜNSAL, M., Radiology
YALAZ, K., Paediatrics
YASAVUL, Ü., Internal Medicine
YAZICIOĞLU, B., Community Medicine
YETKİN, S., Paediatrics
YOLAÇ, S. P., Psychiatry
YORDAM, N., Paediatrics
YÖRÜKAN, S., Physiology
YURDAKÖK, M., Paediatrics
YURDAKUL, Y., Cardiovascular and Thoracic Surgery
YÜCE, K., Obstetrics and Gynaecology

Faculty of Dentistry:

AKSOY, A. Ü., Orthodontics
ALPARSLAN, M. G., Oral Dental Therapeutics
ARAS, K., Dental Surgery
ASLAN, Y., Prosthesis
BATIRBAYGİL, Ş. Y., Pedodontics
BERKER, A. E., Periodontics
BİLGE, A., Prosthesis
ÇAĞLAYAN, F., Periodontics
ÇAĞLAYAN, G., Periodontics
ÇELENLİGİL, H., Periodontics
ÇİĞER, S., Orthodontics
DAYANGAÇ, B., Oral and Dental Therapeutics
DURMAZ, V., Oral and Dental Therapeutics
ENACAR, A., Orthodontics
ERATALAY, Y. K., Periodontics
ETİKAN, I., Endodontics
GÖKALP, S., Oral and Dental Therapeutics
GÜRGAN, S., Oral and Dental Therapeutics
HERSEK, N. E., Prosthesis
KANSU, H., Oral and Dental Therapeutics
KARABIYIKOĞLU, T., Oral and Dental Therapeutics
KÖPRÜLÜ, H., Oral and Dental Therapeutics
KÖSEOĞLU, O. T., Dental Surgery
KURAL, O., Prosthesis
KURANER, T., Oral and Dental Therapeutics
ÖKTEMER, M., Prosthesis
ÖNEN, A., Oral and Dental Therapeutics
ÖZÇELİK, B., Oral and Dental Therapeutics
SÖYLEV, İ., Oral and Dental Therapeutics
ŞAHİN, E., Prosthesis
ŞENGÜN, F. D., Periodontics
TAŞAR, F., Dental Surgery
TUNCER, M., Periodontics
TURGUT, E., Oral and Dental Therapeutics
URAN, N., Dental Surgery
USMEN, E., Pedodontics
YENİĞÜL, M., Prosthesis
YUKAY, F. E., Orthodontics

Faculty of Engineering:

ACAR, J., Food
ALPER, E., Chemistry
APAYDIN, F., Physics
ARIKAN, A., Hydrogeology
ATEŞ, S. I., Chemistry
BALCIOĞLU, N., Chemistry
BATMAN, B., Geology
BAYHAN, H., Geology
BAYRAKTAR, İ., Mining Engineering
BEŞKARDEŞ, O., Chemistry
BİRGÜL, Ö., Nuclear Physics
CANKURTARAN, M., Physics
ÇAĞLAR, A., Chemistry
ÇELEBİ, S. S., Chemistry
ÇELİK, H., Physics
ÇELİK, E. T., Physics
DEMİREL, H., Mining Engineering
EFGÜER, E., Chemistry
ERGİN, G., Food
ERGİN, M., Chemistry
ERKAN, Y., Geology
FIRAT, T., Physics
GEÇİM, S., Electrical Engineering
GENÇ, O., Chemistry
GİRGİN, İ, Mining Engineering
GÜNAY, G., Hydrogeology
GÜNDOĞDU, M. N., Earth Sciences
GÜNDÜC, Y., Electrical Engineering
GÜRBÜZ, H., Geology
GÜVEN, O., Chemistry
GÜVENÇ, T., General Geology
İMAMOĞLU, Y., Chemistry
İNAN, İ. D., Physics
IŞIN, A., Physics
KADİROĞLU, K. E., Nuclear Physics
KARAKAŞ, M. Ü., Computer Science Engineering
KASAPOĞLU, K. E., Geology
KENDİ, E., General Physics
KIŞ, M., Physics, Chemistry
KORKMAZ, M., Physics
KULAKSIZ, S., Mining
KUTSAL, T., Chemistry
OKAY, G., Chemistry
ÖKTÜ, Ö., General Physics
ÖNDER, M., Physics
ORAL, B., Physics
ÖZBEY, T., Physics
ÖZDURAL, A. R., Chemistry
ÖZKOL, S., Mining Engineering
ÖZTEKİN, E., Physics
PIŞKİN, E., Chemistry
SAATÇI, A., Computer Science Engineering
SALANCI, B., Earth Sciences
SALDAMLI, İ., Food
SANALAN, Y., Physics
ŞAFAK, M., Electrical Engineering
ŞIMŞEK, S., Hydrogeology
TABAK, F., Physics
TÖRECİ, E., Computer Science Engineering
URAZ, A., Electrical Engineering
ÜLKÜ, D., Physics
YARIMAĞAN, Ü., Computer Science Engineering
YAZGAN, E., Electrical Engineering
YILDIRIM, S., Chemistry
YILDIZ, A., Chemistry
YÜRÜM, Y., Chemistry

Faculty of Pharmacy:

BİLGİN, A., Pharmaceutical Chemistry
ÇALIŞ, İ., Pharmacognosy
ÇAPAN, Y., Pharmaceutical Technology
DALKARA, S., Pharmaceutical Chemistry
DEMİRDAMAR, S. R., Pharmacy
DİNÇ, A., Pharmacy
DURU, S., Pharmaceutical Toxicology
ERDOĞAN, H., Pharmaceutical Chemistry
ERTAN, M., Pharmaceutical Chemistry
HINCAL, A., Galenic Pharmacy
HINCAL, F., Pharmaceutical Toxicology
KAŞ, S., Pharmaceutical Technology
OSKAY, E., Pharmacy
ÖNER, A. F., Pharmaceutical Chemistry
ÖNER, L., Pharmaceutical Chemistry
ÖZER, A. Y., Pharmaceutical Chemistry
ÖZER, İ., Biochemistry
ÖZGÜNES, H., Pharmaceutical Toxicology
SAKAR, M. K., Pharmaceutical Chemistry
SUNGUR, R., Physics
ŞAFAK, C., Pharmaceutical Toxicology
ŞAHİN, G., Pharmaceutical toxicology
ŞUMLU, M., Pharmaceutical Technology
TAMER, A., Analytical Chemistry
TEMİZER, A., Analytical Chemistry
ÜSTEL, İ., Pharmacy

Faculty of Economics and Administrative Sciences:

AKALIN, G., Public Finance
AKINCI, E., Economics
AKTAN, O. H., Economics
ARSAN, Y., Public Finance
ATAÇ, N. K., Economics
AYHAN, D. Y., Economics

Bağış, A. İ., Economics
Can, H., Economics
Çarıkcı, E., Accounting and Finance
Çingi, S., Economics
Çubukcu, N. T., Economics
Dener, H. I., Economics
Erdost, C., Economics
Ergün, İ., Economics
Gökçe, B., Sociology
Hacıhasanoğlu, B., Economics
İpçi, M. Ö., Accounting and Finance
Kahraman, N., Tourism Management
Kayım, H., Economics
Kırbaş, S., Accounting and Finance
Lalik, Ö., Accounting and Finance
Morgil, O., Economics
Oygur, H. L., Economics
Özer, İ., Sociology
Şahinöz, A., Economics
Şişik, Ü., Economics
Tanyeri, İ, Economics
Tekelioğlu, Y., Accounting and Finance
Timur, H., Economics
Tokgöz, E., Economics
Tuncer, D., Economics
Türkel, S., Economics
Türkkan, E., Economics

Faculty of Letters:

Akkoyunlu, Z., Folklore Studies
Aksoy, E., Western Language and Literature
Arıcı, H., Psychology
Aydın, O., Experimental Psychology
Babür, S., Philosophy
Batum, O., English Studies
Baydur, K. G., Librarianship
Bayraktar, R., Psychology
Bear, A. C., English Studies
Canlı, G., Western Languages and Literature
Çakın, İ., Librarianship
Dikeçliğil, F. B., Sociometry
Durukan, A. A., History of Art
Ercilasun, B., Literature
Erkenal, A., History of Art
Günay, U., Turkish
İçli, T., Sociology
İnal, T., French Studies
İzgi, Ö., General Turkish History
Karakaş, S., Experimental Psychology
Karamağaralı, B., History of Art
Kocaman, A., Linguistics
Kongar, E. R., Sociology
König, G., Linguistics
Kucuradi, I., Philosophy
Ocak, A. Y., History
Ocak, F. T., History
Ötüken, S. Y., Archaeology
Özbek, M., Social Anthropology
Özer, S., American Culture and Literature
Özgen, E., Archaeology
Özger, N., German Studies
Özönder, M. C., Sociology
Özünlü, Ü., Linguistics
Renda, G., History of Art
Sağlamtunç, Z. T., Librarianship
Sümer, N., Philosophy
Topçu, S., Psychology
Tuncer, N., Librarianship
Uçele, G., American Culture and Literature
Yediyıldız, B., History
Yenişehirlioğlu, F., History of Art
Yıldırım, D., Literature
Yıldız, S., German Studies
Yörükoğlu, A., Sociology

Faculty of Fine Arts:

Aydınöz, A. A., Art
Bilgin, H., Graphic Art
Büyükişleyen, Z., Fine Arts
Çolakoğlu, H., Ceramic Art
Gencaydın, Z., Fine Arts
Günay, V., Fine Arts
Pekmezci, H., Fine Arts
Savaş, R., Sculpture

Faculty of Science:

Aksöz, E., Molecular Biology
Aksöz, N., General Biology
Altıntaş, O., Mathematics
Boşgelmez, A., Zoology
Bozcuk, A. N., Biology
Bozcuk, S., Biology
Çağatay, N., Zoology
Cansunar, E., General Biology
Çırakoğlu, Ç., Molecular Biology
Çingi, H., Statistics
Demirsoy, A., Zoology
Erdemir, C., Statistics
Erik, S., Botany
Erk, A. F., Hydrobiology
Esensoy, Ö., Statistics
Günay, S., Statistics
Harmancı, A., Mathematics
İnal, C., Statistics
Karaçay, T., Topology
Kazancı, N., Hydrobiology
Kolankaya, N., General Biology
Muluk, F. Z., Statistics
Oral, G., Statistics
Öğüş, A., Molecular Biology
Özden, H., Experimental Mathematics
Şişli, N., Zoology
Tatlıdil, H., Statistics
Terzioğlu, S., Botany
Tümer, M. A., General Biology
Yıldırımlı, Ş., Botany

Faculty of Education:

Acar, N., Counselling and Guidance
Açıkalın, A., Education
Akhun, İ., Educational Measurement and Evaluation
Baykul, Y., Educational Measurement and Evaluation
Bozer, A., English
Bülbül, E. S., Education
Çoker, D., Mathematics
Demirel, Ö., Education
Demirezen, M., Language Studies
Eratalay, N., French
Eren, A., Physics
Ersever, O. G., Counselling and Guidance
Ertem, C., Language and Literature
Kıran, A., Language Studies
Kıran, Z., French
Kiziroğlu, İ, Biology
Morgil, I., Analytical Chemistry
Önalp, B., Biology
Özgüven, E., Counselling and Guidance
Salihoğlu, H., Language Studies
Soran, H., Biology
Sönmez, V., Education
Sunel, A., Language and Literature
Tosun, C., English
Umunc, H., English

Zonguldak Engineering Faculty:

Atalay, T., Mining Engineering
Dağlı, F., Mechanical Engineering
Dılmaç, M., Mechanical Engineering
Kişioğlu, E. İ, Mining Engineering
Pelin, S., Mining Engineering
Yiğit, E., Mining Engineering

ATTACHED INSTITUTES

Institute of Ataturk Principles and History of the Turkish Revolution: Dir Prof. Dr Bahaeddin Yediyıldız.

Institute of Child Health: Dir Prof. Dr Murat Tuncer.

Institute of Health Sciences: Dir Prof. Dr Atilla Hincal.

Institute of Neurological Sciences and Psychology: Dir Prof. Dr Özdemir Gürçay.

Institute of Nuclear Sciences: Dir Prof. Dr Özgen Birgül.

Institute of Oncology: Dir Prof. Dr Dinçer Fırat.

Institute of Population Studies: Dir Prof. Dr Sunday Üner.

Institute of Science: Dir Prof. Dr Gültekin Günay.

Institute of Social Sciences: Dir Assoc. Prof. Dr Hüsnü Arıcı.

Institute of Public Health: Dir Prof. Dr Münevver Bertan.

Institute of Turkish Research: Dir Prof. Dr A. Yaşar Ocak.

Institute of Fine Arts: Prof. Dr Ayhan Azzem Aydınöz.

İNÖNÜ ÜNİVERSİTESİ

Malatya
Telephone: (422) 341-00-10
Telex: 66140
Fax: (422) 341-00-34

Founded 1975
State control
Language of instruction: Turkish (but English in Faculty of Medicine)
Academic year: October to July

Rector: Prof. Dr Mehmet Yücesoy
Vice-Rectors: Prof. Dr Eyyüp Aktepe, Prof. Dr Aslan Aksoy, Prof. Dr Osman Kazancı
Secretary-General: Asst Prof. Dr Emir Erden
Librarian: Abuzer Bulut
Number of teachers: 552
Number of students: 8,913

DEANS

Faculty of Science and Literature: Prof. Dr Bekir Çetinkaya
Faculty of Economics and Administrative Sciences: Prof. Dr Eyyüp Aktepe
Faculty of Education: Prof. Dr Hikmet Y. Celkan
Faculty of Medicine: Prof. Dr Mustafa Paç
Faculty of Engineering: Prof. Dr Muhammet Köksal

HEADS OF DEPARTMENTS

Faculty of Science and Literature:

Biology: Prof. Dr Eşref Yüksel
Chemistry: Prof. Dr Engin Çetinkaya
Mathematics: Prof. Dr Sadık Keleş
Physics: Prof. Dr Hikmet Uslu
Sociology: Prof. Dr Fügen Berkay

Faculty of Economics and Administrative Sciences:

Business Studies: Prof. Dr Şener Dilek
Economics: Prof. Dr A. Naim Akman
Public Administration: Assoc. Prof. Dr Ali Öztekin
Econometrics: Asst Prof. Dr Yavuz Cömert

Faculty of Education:

Education in Social Sciences: Assoc. Prof. Dr Salim Cöhçe
Educational Sciences: Prof. Dr Mustafa Aydın
Turkish Language and Literature: Asst Prof. Dr Zeki Kaymaz
Science: Prof. Dr Aslan Aksoy
Drawing: Prof. Dr Hikmet Y. Celkan
Music: Asst Prof. Dr Cemal Yurga
Physical Training: Asst Prof. Dr Faruk Yamaner

DIRECTORS

Institute of Science: Prof. Dr Eşref Yüksel
Institute of Social Sciences: Prof. Dr A. Naim Akman
Institute of Health Sciences: Prof. Dr Ahmet Acet

İSTANBUL ÜNİVERSİTESİ

Beyazıt, Istanbul
Telephone: (212) 5280701
Telex: 22062
Fax: (212) 5205473

Founded 1453, reorganized 1933 and 1946

State control
Languages of instruction: Turkish, English
Academic year: November to February, March to July

Rector: Prof. Dr KEMAL ALEMDAROĞLU
Vice-Rectors: Prof. Dr ÖZDEM ANĞ, Prof. Dr NUR SERTER
Administrative Officer: NURETTİN ERDEM

Number of teachers and assistants: 4,364
Number of students: 73,061

DEANS

Faculty of Letters: Prof. Dr SÜHA GÖNEY
Faculty of Science: Prof. Dr DİNÇER GÜLEN
Faculty of Law: Prof. Dr AYSEL ÇELİKEL
Faculty of Economics: Prof. Dr MÜNİR KUTLUATA
Faculty of Forestry: Prof. Dr MELİH BOYDAK
Faculty of Medicine: Prof. Dr ÖZDEM ANĞ
Faculty of Pharmacy: Prof. Dr HAKAN BERKKAN
Faculty of Dentistry: Prof. Dr ALTAN ÖZERKAN
Faculty of Medicine at Cerrahpaşa: Prof. Dr AHMET N. ÖZBAL
Faculty of Political Science: Prof. Dr ALİ ÜLKÜ AZRAK
Faculty of Management: Prof. Dr HAYRİ ÜLGEN
Faculty of Veterinary Science: Prof. Dr AHMET ALTINEL
Faculty of Engineering: Prof. Dr REŞAT APAK
Faculty of Communication: Prof. Dr NÜKHET GÜZ
Faculty of Fisheries: Prof. Dr MUSTAFA KARABATAK
Faculty of Theology: Prof Dr YAŞAR NURİ ÖZTÜRK

ATTACHED INSTITUTES:

Institute of Cardiology: Dir Prof. Dr MUZAFFER ÖZTÜRK.

Institute of Social Sciences: Dir Prof. Dr ALİ ÜLKÜ AZRAK.

Institute of Natural Sciences: Dir Prof. Dr MEHMET ALİ GÜRKAYNAK.

Institute of Health Sciences: Dir Prof. Dr PERİHAN BASLO.

Institute of Child Health: Dir Prof. Dr GÜNAY SANER.

Institute of Forensic Medicine: Dir Prof. Dr SEVİL ATASOY.

Institute of Oncology: Dir Prof. Dr ERKAN TOPUZ.

Institute of Marine Sciences and Geography: Dir Prof. Dr ERTUĞRUL DOĞAN.

Institute of Atatürk's Principles and Reforms: Dir Prof. Dr EROL CİHAN.

Institute of Turcology: Dir Prof. Dr OSMAN FİKRİ SERTKAYA.

Institute of Application and Research in Experimental Medicine: Dir Prof. Dr ÖZDEM ANĞ.

Institute of Neurological Sciences: Dir Prof. Dr CENGİZ KUNDAY.

Institute of Thoracic Diseases and Tuberculosis: Dir Prof. Dr MÜZEYYEN ERK.

Institute of Accounting: Dir Prof. Dr ERSİN GÜREDİN.

Institute of Management: Dir Prof. Dr HAYRİ ÜLGEN.

İSTANBUL TEKNİK ÜNİVERSİTESİ

Ayazağa, Istanbul 80626
Telephone: (212) 285-30-00
Telex: 28186
Fax: (212) 285-29-10
Founded 1773
State control
Languages of instruction: Turkish and English
Academic year: October to July (2 semesters)

Rector: REŞAT BAYKAL
Vice-Rectors: FERİDUN DİKEÇ, EMİN KARAHAN, GÜLSÜN SAĞLAMER
Secretary-General: NEVZAT ÖZKÖK
Registrar: MEHMET TÜRKSEZER
Librarian: NURTEN ATALIK

Library: see Libraries
Number of teachers: 1,866
Number of students: 20,999

Publications: *Bulletin* (quarterly), *Dergisi* (quarterly), *Haberleri* (quarterly), *Catalog* (biennially).

DEANS

Faculty of Civil Engineering: NADİR YAYLA
Faculty of Architecture: UĞUR ERKMAN
Faculty of Mechanical Engineering: NİLÜFER EĞRİCAN
Faculty of Electrical and Electronics Engineering: AHMET DERVİŞOĞLU
Faculty of Mining Engineering: ŞİNASİ ESKİKAYA
Faculty of Chemical-Metallurgical Engineering: ALİ FUAT ÇAKIR
Faculty of Naval Architecture and Ocean Engineering: ALİ İHSAN ALDOĞAN
Faculty of Sciences and Letters: SEZAİ SARAÇ
Faculty of Management: ATAÇ SOYSAL
Faculty of Aeronautics and Astronautics: OĞUZ BORAT
Faculty of Maritime Studies: OSMAN KAMİL SAĞ

HEADS OF DEPARTMENTS

Faculty of Civil Engineering:
- Civil Engineering: VURAL CİNEMRE
- Geodesy and Photogrammetry: ORHAN ALTAN
- Environmental Engineering: DERİN ORHON

Faculty of Architecture:
- Architecture: MİNE İNCEOĞLU
- Urban and Regional Planning: CENGİZ GİRİTLİOĞLU
- Industrial Design: NİGAN BEYAZIT

Faculty of Mechanical Engineering:
- Mechanical Engineering: KAAN EDİS
- Textile Engineering: BAYRAM YÜKSEL

Faculty of Electrical and Electronics Engineering:
- Electronics and Communications Engineering: ERGÜL AKÇAKAYA
- Electrical Engineering: R. NEJAT TUNÇAY
- Control and Computer Engineering: EMRE HARMANCI

Faculty of Mining Engineering:
- Mining Engineering: SENAİ SALTOĞLU
- Geological Engineering: ATASEVER GEDİKOĞLU
- Geophysical Engineering: MUZAFFER SANVER
- Petroleum Engineering: ARGUN GÜRKAN

Faculty of Chemical-Metallurgical Engineering:
- Chemical Engineering: AYŞE AKSOY
- Metallurgical Engineering: H. ERMAN TULGAR
- Food Engineering: F. ARTEMİS KARAALİ

Faculty of Naval Architecture and Ocean Engineering:
- Naval Construction: ALİM YILDIZ
- Ocean Engineering: MACİT SÜKAN

Faculty of Sciences and Letters:
- Mathematics: ABDULKADİR ÖZDEĞER
- Physics: YILDIRIM ÖNER
- Chemistry: AHMET AKAR
- Engineering Sciences: ERDOĞAN ŞUHUBİ

Faculty of Management:
- Industrial Engineering: HALUK ERKUT
- Management: ÖNER EYRENCİ

Faculty of Aeronautics and Astronautics:
- Aeronautics: M. FEVZI ÜNAL
- Meteorological Engineering: ZEKAİ ŞEN
- Space Science and Technology: UMUR DAYBELGE

Faculty of Maritime Studies:
- Marine Engines: AHMET BAYÜLKEN
- Deck Engineering: SÜREYYA ÖNEY

ATTACHED CONSERVATORY AND DEPARTMENTS

State Conservatory of Turkish Music: Dir FİKRET DEĞERLİ.

Department of Languages and the History of the Turkish Revolution: Dir SELİME SEZGİN.

Department of Fine Arts: Dir SEMRA AYDINLI.

Department of Physical Education: Dir YALÇIN AKÖZ.

ATTACHED GRADUATE INSTITUTES

Institute of Science and Technology: Dir HAKKI İSMAİL ERDOĞAN.

Institute of Nuclear Energy: Dir A. HASBİ YAVUZ.

Institute of Social Sciences: Dir ALTAN ÖKE.

ATTACHED RESEARCH CENTRES

Construction and Earthquake Research Centre: Dir REMZİ ÜLKER.

Earth Sciences and Resources Research Centre: Dir AYTİN GÖKTEKİN.

Electronics and Control Systems Research Centre: Dir OSMAN PALAMUTÇUOĞULLARI.

Energy Sciences and Production Technology Research Centre: Dir METE ŞEN.

Environmental and Urban Planning Research Centre: Dir AYTEN ÇETİNER.

Machinery Manufacturing and Production Research Centre: Dir MEHMET ÇAPA.

Material Sciences and Production Technology Research Centre: Dir ERMAN TULGAR.

Transport Research Centre: Dir NADİR YAYLA.

Water and Marine Sciences Research Centre: Dir MEHMETÇİK BAYAZIT.

Computer Centre: A. EMRE HARMANCI.

Visual Education Centre: MELİH PAZARCI.

Bio-Engineering Centre: ERTUĞRUL YAZGAN.

Aerospace and Space Technologies Research Centre: BİNGÜL YAZGAN.

KARADENİZ TEKNİK ÜNİVERSİTESİ (Karadeniz Technical University)

61080 Trabzon
Telephone: (462) 325-32-23
Fax: (462) 325-31-85
E-mail: head@jbsd.ktu.edu.tr
Founded 1955
State control
Language of instruction: Turkish
Academic year: October to July

Rector: Prof. Dr TÜRKAY TÜDES
Vice-Rectors: Prof. Dr ZAFER ERTÜRK, Prof. Dr HASAN BASRİ ŞENTÜRK, Prof. Dr ERSAN BOCUTOĞLU
General Secretary: Assoc. Prof. Dr TAHSİN YOMRALIOĞLU
Librarian: İ. HİLMİ ŞEŞEN

Library of 82,000 vols
Number of teachers: 1,398
Number of students: 24,759

Publications: *Karadeniz Teknik Üniversitesi Haber Bülteni* (Newsletter, weekly), faculty bulletins (monthly).

DEANS

Faculty of Forestry: Prof. Dr ZİYA GERÇEK
Rize Faculty of Theology: Prof. Dr KEMAL SANDIKÇI
Rize Faculty of Water Resource Sciences: Prof. Dr OSMAN BEYAZOĞLU
Gümüşhane Faculty of Engineering: Prof. Dr AHMET DURMUŞ

Ordu Faculty of Agriculture: Prof. Dr Y. N. İSMAİLÇELEBİOĞLU
Ünye Faculty of Economics and Administrative Sciences: Prof. Dr FETHİ BAYRAKLI
Sürmene Faculty of Marine Sciences: Prof. Dr M. SALİH ÇELİKKALE
Faculty of Arts and Sciences: Prof. Dr YAŞAR GÖK
Fatih Faculty of Education: Prof. Dr MUSTAFA ÖZDEMİR
Faculty of Medicine: Prof. Dr CELAL BAKİ
Faculty of Engineering and Architecture: Prof. Dr RAGIP ERDÖL
Faculty of Economics and Administrative Sciences: Prof. Dr HASAN ÖZYURT
Giresun Faculty of Education: Prof. Dr SALİM KOCA
Rize Faculty of Arts and Sciences: Prof. Dr NAZMİ TURAN OKUMUŞOĞLU
Rize (Çayeli) Faculty of Education: Prof. Dr ADULLAH DEMİRTAŞ
Giresun Faculty of Arts and Sciences: (vacant)

PROFESSORS

Faculty of Forestry:

ANŞİN, R., Forestry Engineering
GERÇEK, Z., Forestry Botany
KALAY, H. Z., Forestry Engineering
KAPUCU, F., Forestry Engineering
KÖSE, S., Forestry Engineering
MEREV, N., Forestry Botany
ÖZBİLEN, A., Landscape Design
TÜRÜDÜ, Ö. A., Forestry Engineering
YAHYAOĞLU, Z., Forestry Engineering

Rize Faculty of Theology:

SANDIKCI, S. K., Islamic Education

Gümüşhane Faculty of Engineering:

DURMUS, A., Civil Engineering
SEYMEN, İ., Geology

Ordu Faculty of Agriculture:

İSMAİLÇELEBİOĞLU, Y. N., Agriculture

Sürmene Faculty of Marine Sciences:

ÇELİKKALE, M. S., Fisheries Technology Engineering
DÜZGÜNEŞ, E., Fisheries Technology Engineering
KARAÇAM, H., Fisheries Technology Engineering

Faculty of Arts and Sciences:

ALTUNBAŞ, M., Physics
BAYSAL, A., Biology
BEYAZOĞLU, O., Biology
BÜLBÜL, A., Mathematics
EROĞLU, M. S., Mathematics
GÜRSOY, O., Geometry
GÖK, Y., Inorganic Chemistry
İKİZLER, A. A., Organic Chemistry
KADIOĞLU, A., Biology
KOPYA, A. İ., Physics
ÖZDEMİR, M., Chemistry
ŞENTÜRK, H., Analytical Chemistry
TUNÇER, S., Biology
YAPAR, Z., Geometry

Fatih Faculty of Education:

BAYDAR, S., Biology
ÇAPA, M., History
DEMİRBAŞ, A., Chemistry
GÖKÇAKAN, A. Z., Education
ÖZÇELİK, İ., Social Sciences

Faculty of Medicine:

ALHAN, E., Medical Surgery
ALPAY, K., Dermatology
ARVAS, A. H., Basic Medicine
BAKİ, A., Paediatrics
BAKİ, C., Orthopaedics
BAYRAM, A., Internal Medicine
BEKAROĞLU, M., Psychiatry
BOZKAYA, H., Gynaecology
ÇALIK, A., Medical Surgery
ÇETİNKAYA, K., Medical Surgery
DEĞER, O., Biochemistry
ERCİYES, H. N., Anaesthesiology
GEDİK, Y., Paediatrics
GÖR, A., Urology
GÜLER, M., Physical Rehabilitation
GÜMELE, H. R., Diagnostic Radiology
KAPICIOĞLU, S., Internal Medicine
KARAGÜZEL, A., Medical Biology
KEHA, E. E., Biochemistry
MOCAN, H., Paediatrics
MOCAN, M. Z., Internal Medicine
MUHTAR, H., Medical Surgery
ÖNCÜ, M., Internal Medicine
ÖNDER, E., Biochemistry
ÖNDER, C., Orthopaedics
ÖZEN, İ., Anaesthesiology
ÖZGÜR, G. K., Urology
ÖZMENOĞLU, M., Neurology
ÖZORAN, Y., Pathology
PİŞKİN, B., Medical Surgery
SOLAK, Z. M., Anaesthesiology
TELATAR, M., Internal Medicine
ULUUTKU, N., Psychiatry
YILDIZ, K., Pathology

Faculty of Engineering and Architecture:

AKPINAR, A. S., Electrical and Electronic Engineering
ARSLAN, F., Mechanical Engineering
ASLANER, M., Geology
AYDEMİR, S., Architecture
AYDEMİR, Ş., Architecture
AYHAN, T., Mechanical Engineering
BEKTAŞ, O., Geology
BERKÜN, M., Civil Engineering
BIYIKLIOĞLU, A., Construction
ÇAKIROĞLU, A. O., Mechanical Engineering
DİLEK, R., Geology
DUMANOĞLU, A. A., Civil Engineering
DURGUN, O., Energy
DURMUŞ, A., Civil Engineering
ERDÖL, R., Civil Engineering
ERTÜRK, D. Z., Architecture
ERTÜRK, S., Architecture
GEDİK, İ. Geology
GENÇ, S., Geology
GÜR, Ş., Architecture
GÜRLEYİK, M. Y., Mechanical Engineering
GÜRÜNLÜ, C., Electronics and Electrical Engineering
KALENDER, A., Hydraulics
KANDİL, M., Architecture
KARADENİZ, S., Mechanical Engineering
ÖNSOY, H., Civil Engineering
ÖZDENİZ, M. B., Civil Engineering
ÖZTÜRK, E., Geodesy and Photogrammetry
ÖZTÜRK, K., Architecture
SAVAŞKAN, T., Mechanical Engineering
TANYOLU, E., Geology
TARHAN, F., Geology
TÜDEŞ, T., Geodesy and Photogrammetry
UZUNER, B. A., Civil Engineering
ÜLKÜ, Z. A., Mechanical Engineering
YAVUZ, T., Mechanical Engineering

Faculty of Economics and Administrative Sciences:

ALPUGAN, O., Management
BOCUTOĞLU, E., Economics
ÇIKRIKÇI, M., Finance
KESİM, A., Economics
ÖZYURT, H., Economics
TANDOĞAN, A., Economics
TÜREDİ, H., Finance
YAZICI, K., Management

GRADUATE SCHOOLS

Graduate School of Social Sciences: Prof. Dr ALÂETTİN TANDOĞAN
Graduate School of Natural and Applied Sciences: Prof. Dr ASIM KADIOĞLU
Graduate School of Health Sciences: Assoc. Prof. Dr MURAT ERTÜRK

KOÇ UNIVERSITY

Çayir Cad. Istinye, 80860 Istanbul
Telephone: (212) 229-30-06
Fax: (212) 229-36-02

Founded 1993
Private control
Language of instruction: English
Academic year: October to June

President: Prof. Dr SEHA M. TİNİÇ
Provost: Prof. Dr ATTİLA AŞKAR
Vice-President for Administration: Prof. Dr AYŞEGÜL SOMERSAN
Registrar: ŞERMİN EROL
Librarian: JANE ANN LINDLEY

Library of 82,000 vols
Number of teachers: 126
Number of Students: 1,054

DEANS

College of Arts and Sciences: Prof. Dr ÇIĞDEM KAĞITÇIBAŞI
College of Administrative Sciences and Economics: Prof. Dr SEHA M. TİNİÇ (acting)
Graduate School of Business: Prof. ŞAYESTE DAŞER

MARMARA ÜNİVERSİTESİ

Sultanahmet, 34413 Istanbul
Telephone: (212) 518-16-00
Fax: (212) 518-16-15

Founded 1883, reorganized 1982
State control
Languages of instruction: Turkish, English, French and German
Academic year: September to July

Rector: Prof. Dr ÖMER FARUK BATIREL
Vice-Rector: Prof. Dr AHMET HAYRİ PURMUŞ
General Secretary: Dr ALTAN KİTAPÇI
Librarian: SEVINC KAZAZ

Number of teachers: 2,443
Number of students: 37,243
Publications: various faculty journals.

DEANS

Faculty of Science and Letters: Prof. Dr MUSTAFA ÇETİN VARLIK
Faculty of Law: Prof. Dr BULENT TAHIROĞLU
Atatürk Faculty of Education: Prof. Dr HİKMET SAVCI
Faculty of Technical Education: Prof. Dr İHSAN GÖK
Faculty of Economics and Business Administration: Prof. Dr AHMET HAYRİ DURMUŞ
Faculty of Dentistry: Prof. Dr NESRİN EMEKLİ
Faculty of Pharmacology: Prof. Dr MERAL KEYER UYSAL
Faculty of Theology: Prof. Dr MUSTAFA FAYDA
Faculty of Fine Arts: Prof. Dr HUSAMETTİN KOCAN
Faculty of Medicine: Prof. Dr NURDAN TÖZÜN
Faculty of Communication: Prof. Dr ATEŞ VURAN
Faculty of Engineering: Prof. Dr NÜKET YETİŞ

ATTACHED INSTITUTES

Institute of Social Sciences: Dir Prof. Dr ORHAN SEZGİN.

Institute of Sciences: Dir Prof. Dr AHMET ALP SAYAR.

Institute of Health Sciences: Dir Prof. Dr SEVİM ROLLAS.

Institute of Neurology: Dir Prof. Dr NECMETTİN PAMİR.

Institute of Gastroenterology: Dir Prof. Dr NURDAN TÖZÜN.

Institute of Turkic Studies: Dir Prof. Dr NADİR DEVLET.

Institute of European Community Studies: Dir Prof. Dr ASLAN GÜNDÜZ.

Institute of Banking and Insurance: Dir Prof. Dr ILHAN ULUDAĞ.

Institute of Middle Eastern and Islamic Country Studies: Dir Prof Dr. AHMET TABAKOĞLU.

Institute of Fine Arts: Dir Prof. Dr ŞERMİN ALYANAK.

Institute of Educational Studies: Dir Prof. Dr AYLA OKTAY.

MİMAR SİNAN ÜNİVERSİTESİ

Fındıklı, 80040 Istanbul

Telephone: (212) 145-00-00
Telex: 24723

Founded 1883, university status 1982
State control
Language of instruction: Turkish

Rector: Prof. GÜNDÜZ GÖKÇE
Chief Administrative Officer: ERDAL KÜPELİ
Librarian: ASİYE ALAGÖZOĞLU

Library of 51,200 vols
Number of teachers: 420
Number of students: 3,509

DEANS

Faculty of Architecture: Prof. ÖNDER KÜÇÜKERMAN
Faculty of Fine Arts: Prof. SADI DİREN
Faculty of Sciences and Literature: Prof. Dr GÜLÇİN ÇANDARLIOĞLU

HEADS OF DEPARTMENTS

Faculty of Architecture:

Architecture: Prof. ESAD ŞUHER
Industrial Design: Prof. Ö. KÜÇÜKERMAN
Urban and Regional Planning: Prof. M. ÇUBUK

Faculty of Fine Arts:

Applied Arts: Prof. B. SALDIRAY
Painting: Prof. S. DİREN
Sculpture: Prof. TAMER BAŞOĞLU
Stage and Visual Arts: Prof. S. ÖZİŞ
Traditional Turkish Arts: Prof. İLHAMI TURAN

Faculty of Sciences and Literature:

Archaeology and History of Art: Prof. Dr NERMIN SİNEMOĞLU
Mathematics: Doc. Dr BELGIN MAZLUMOĞLU
Statistics: Prof. Dr K. YOĞURTÇUGIL
Turkish Language and Literature: Prof. Dr ZEYNEP KERMAN
Sociology: Prof. Dr N. TURHAN

ATTACHED INSTITUTES

State Museum of Painting and Sculpture: Istanbul; Dir Prof. B. MUTLU.

State School of Music: Istanbul; Dir ERCIVAN SAYDAM.

ONDOKUZ MAYIS ÜNİVERSİTESİ (Nineteenth of May University)

Üniversite Kampusu, Kurupelit, Samsun 55139

Telephone: (362) 457-60-00
Fax: (362) 457-60-91

Founded 1975
State control
Language of instruction: Turkish
Academic year: October to June

Rector: Prof. Dr OSMAN ÇAKIR
Vice-Rectors: Prof. Dr NURİ KURUOĞLU, Prof. Dr ALİ GÜLÜMSER, Prof. Dr KAYHAN ÖZKAN
Registrar: NAZIM ALKAN
Librarian: ÖMER BOZKURT

Number of teachers: 1,158
Number of students: 24,365

Publications: various faculty bulletins, *News from Ondokuz Mayıs University.*

DEANS

Faculty of Medicine: Prof. Dr CEMİL RAKUNT
Faculty of Arts and Sciences: Prof. Dr HABİP ÖZKAPLAN
Faculty of Agriculture: Prof. Dr ERDOĞAN SELÇUK
Faculty of Education (Samsun): Prof. Dr DURSUN ALİ AKBULUT
Faculty of Education (Amasya): Prof. Dr ALİ ENGİN
Faculty of Water Products (Sinop): Prof. Dr ŞEVKET BÜYÜKHATİPOĞLU
Faculty of Engineering: Prof. Dr M. ORHAN BÜYÜKGÜNGÖR
Faculty of Theology: Prof. Dr HÜSEYİN PEKER
Faculty of Dentistry: Prof. Dr PERUZE ÇELENK

PROFESSORS AND HEADS OF DEPARTMENTS

(H=Head of Dept)

Faculty of Medicine:

ALVUR, M., Biochemistry (H)
BAĞCI, H., Medical Biology (H)
BAŞOĞLU, A., Thoracic Surgery (H)
BAYSAL, M. K., Paediatrics
BİLGİÇ, S., Anatomy (H)
CENGİZ, K., Internal Medicine (H)
ÇELİK, C., Biochemistry
ÇELİK, F., Neurosurgery (H)
ÇELİK, S., Pharmacology (H)
ÇİFTÇİ, N., Morphology (H)
DURUPINAR, B., Microbiology (H)
ERKAN, M. L., Thoracic Diseases (H)
ERZURUMLU, K., General Surgery
GÜLMAN, B., Orthopaedics and Traumatology (H)
GÜRSES, N., Paediatric Surgery (H)
KANDEMİR, B., Pathology (H)
KARAGÖZ, F., Pathology
KESİM, M., General Surgery
KESİM, Y., Pharmacology
KÖKÇÜ, A., Obstetrics and Gynaecology (H)
KOYUNCU, M., Oto-rhino-laryngology
KÜÇÜKÖDÜK, Ş., Paediatrics (H)
MARANGOZ, C., Physiology (H)
ONAR, M. K., Neurosurgery
ÖGE, F., Ophthalmology (H)
ÖGE, İ., Ophthalmology
ÖKTEN, G., Medical Biology
ÖZKAN, A., Psychiatry (H)
ÖZKAN, K., General Surgery (H)
ÖZREN, N., General Surgery
PEKŞEN, Y., Public Health (H)
RAKUNT, C., Neurosurgery
SAĞKAN, O., Cardiology (H)
ŞAHİNOĞLU, H., Anaesthesiology
ŞESEN, T., Oto-rhino-laryngology (H)
TANYERİ, F., Internal Diseases
TANYERİ, Y., Oto-rhino-laryngology
TUNALI, G., Neurology (H)
TURANLI, A. Y., Dermatology (H)
TÜR, A., Anaesthesiology (H)
ULUSOY, N., General Surgery
UYSAL, O. A., Plastic and Reconstructive Surgery (H)
ÜNAL, R., Oto-rhino-laryngology
ÜSTÜN, F. E., Anaesthesiology
YILDIZ, S., Urology (H)
YILMAZ, A. F., Urology
YÜCEL, İ, Internal Diseases

Faculty of Arts and Sciences:

BÜYÜKGÜNGÖR, O., Solid State Physics
ÇAKIR, O., Physical Chemistry
DALCI, M., Biology
DİNÇER, M., Solid State Physics
ERDÖNMEZ, A., Solid State Physics
GÖNÜLOL, A., Botany
GÜLEL, A., Biology
GÜMRÜKÇÜOĞLU, İ. E., Organic Chemistry
GÜMÜŞ, H., General Physics (H)
GÜRKANLI, A. T., Mathematics
KARACAN, T., Turkish Language and Literature
KARTAL, V., Zoology
KILINÇ, M., Biology (H)
KÖKSAL, F., Atomic and Molecular Physics
KURUOĞLU, N., Mathematics (H)
OKUMUŞOĞLU, N. T., Physics
ONAR, N. A., Analytical Chemistry
ÖLMEZ, H., Chemistry (H)
ÖZKAPLAN, H., Solid State Physics
POLAT, N., Biology
SHAHBAZOV, A., Mathematics
TARAKÇI, C., Turkish Language and Literature

Faculty of Agriculture:

APAN, M., Agricultural Engineering (H)
BAYRAKLI, F., Soil Science
ECEVİT, O., Entomology (H)
GÜLÜMSER, A., Field Crops
KORKMAZ, A., Soil Science (H)
KÖYCÜ, C., Field Crops (H)
ODABAŞ, F., Horticulture (H)
PINAR, Y., Agricultural Machines (H)
SELÇUK, E., Animal Sciences (H)

Faculty of Education:

AKBULUT, D. A., Primary Teaching
DİNDAR, B., Education and Educational Programmes (H)
ENGİN, A., Biology (H)
ERSANLI, K., Education
NİŞANCI, A., Geography (H)

Faculty of Theology:

CİHAN, S., Basic Islamic Sciences
DAĞ, M., The Words of the Scriptures
KOÇAK, M., Basic Islamic Sciences
PEKER, H., Psychology of Religion
SARIKÇIOĞLU, E., Philosophy and Religion (H)
TERZİ, M. Z., Islamic History and Arts (H)
TURAN, A., Basic Islamic Sciences (H)
YAZICI, İ., Koranic Interpretation

Faculty of Water Products (Sinop):

BİRCAN, R., Breeding
BÜYÜKHATİOĞLU, Ş., Technology of Processing, Biology of Drinking Water (H)
ERDEM, M., Breeding (H)
ERKOYUNCU, İ., Technology of Fishing (H)
KALMA, M., Breeding

Faculty of Engineering:

BÜYÜKGÜNGÖR, H., Environmental Technology (H)
EFENDİYEV, Ç. A., Telecommunications
ERGUN, O. N., Environmental Sciences
KASUMOV, A. A., Building
ÖNBİLGİN, G., Electrical Machines (H)

Faculty of Dentistry:

ÇELENK, P., Clinical Sciences (H)

DIRECTORS

Graduate School of Social Sciences: Assoc. Prof. Dr MUSTAFA ÖZBALCI
Graduate School of Sciences: Prof. Dr FERHAT ODABAŞ
Graduate School of Health Sciences: Prof. Dr SAİT BİLGİÇ

ORTA DOĞU TEKNİK ÜNİVERSİTESİ (Middle East Technical University)

Ismet İönü Bulvarı, Ankara 06531

Telephone: 210-20-00
Fax: 210-11-05
E-mail: sevuk@rorqual.cc.metu.edu.tr

Founded 1956
State control
Language of instruction: English
Academic year: October to June (two semesters)

President: Prof. Dr SUHA SEVÜK
General Secretary: Prof. Dr MEHMET ÇALIŞKAN
Registrar: NESRİN ÜNSAL (acting)
Librarian: BÜLENT KARASÔZEN (acting)

Library: see Libraries
Number of teachers and assistants: 1,744
Number of students: 19,020 (Ankara and İçel campuses)

Publications: *METU Studies in Development* (quarterly), *METU Journal of Faculty of Architecture* (2 a year), *METU Journal of Human Sciences* (2 a year).

DEANS

Faculty of Economic and Administrative Sciences: Prof. Dr A. ACAR
Faculty of Architecture: Prof. Dr N. TEYMUR
Faculty of Education: Prof. Dr D. ALPSAN
Faculty of Engineering: Prof. Dr Y. UÇTUĞ
Faculty of Arts and Sciences: Prof. Dr M. TOMAK

DIRECTORS

Graduate School of Natural and Applied Sciences: Prof. Dr T. ÖZTÜRK
Graduate School of Social Sciences: Prof. Dr B. AKŞIT
Graduate School of Marine Sciences: Prof. Dr ÜMİT ÜNLÜATA
School of Foreign Languages: B. BARUTLU
Informatics Institute: Prof. Dr N. YALABIK
Food Engineering and Biotechnology Institute: Prof. Dr H. HAMAMCI

PROFESSORS

Faculty of Economic and Administrative Sciences:

ACAR, A., Management
ACAR, F., Political Sciences and Public Administration
AKDER, H., Economics
AKSOY, Ş., Political Sciences and Public Administration
ATEŞ, H., Management
AYATA, A., Political Sciences and Public Administration
CELASUN, M., Economics
ERALP, A., International Relations
ERLAT, H., Economics
EROL, C., Management
GITMEZ, A. S., Management
GÖKTAN, E., Management
GÖRÜN, F., Economics
GÜRKAYNAK, M. R., Public Administration
İNAN, H., Economics
KASNAKOĞLU, H., Economics
KASNAKOĞLU, Z., Economics
KAYA, R., Political Sciences and Public Administration
KEPENEK, Y., Economics
KEYDER, N., Economics
OLGUN, H., Economics
ŞENSES, F., Economics
SOYSAL, M., Management
TANSEL, A., Economics
TİLEYLİOĞLU, A., Management
TUNCOKU, A. M., International Relations
TÜREL, O., Economics
YAZICI, A., Management

Faculty of Architecture:

AKTÜRE, S., City and Regional Planning
ASLANOĞLU, İ. N., Architecture
BADEMLİ, R., City and Regional Planning
BAKIRER, Ö., Industrial Design
ERAYDIN, A., City and Regional Planning
ERDER, C., Architecture
ERSOY, M., City and Regional Planning
ERZEN, A. J., Architecture
EVYAPAN, G., Architecture
GEDİK, A., City and Regional Planning
İMAMAĞLU, V., Architecture
KORTAN, E., Architecture
PAMİR, H., Architecture
SALTIK, E., Architecture
ŞENYAPILI, T., City and Regional Planning
TANKUT, G., City and Regional Planning
TARAKLI, D., City and Regional Planning
TEKELİ, İ, City and Regional Planning
TEYMUR, N., Architecture
TÜREL, A., City and Regional Planning
YAVUZ, A., Architecture
YAVUZ, Y., Architecture

Faculty of Education:

AKKÖK, F., Educational Sciences
AKSU, M., Educational Science
ALPSAN, D., Science Education
AŞKAR, P., Science Education
AYDIN, A., Educational Sciences
BERBEROĞLU, G., Educational Sciences
BEZEL, N., Foreign Language Education
ENGİNARLAR, H., Foreign Language Education
ERSOY, Y., Science Education
ERTEPINAR, H., Science Education
GÜÇLÜOL, K., Educational Science
GÜNÇER, B., Educational Science
İÇÖZ, N., Foreign Language Education
KARABAŞ, S., Foreign Language Education
KAŞ, A. D., Foreign Language Education
KOÇ, S., Foreign Language Education
KONIG, W., Foreign Language Education
KOYUNCU, İ., Educational Science
ÖZKAN, I., Science Education
PAYKOÇ, F. A., Educational Science

Faculty of Arts and Sciences:

ALAADDİNOĞLU, N. G., Biological Sciences
AKBULUT, U., Chemistry
AKGÜN, S., History
AKOVALI, G., Chemistry
AKSİT, B., Sociology
AKYILDIZ, E., Mathematics
ALPAR, A., Physics
ALPAY, Ş., Mathematics
ALYÜRÜK, K., Chemistry
ARAS, L., Chemistry
ARAS, N. K., Chemistry
ARINÇ, E., Biological Sciences
ATAMAN, Y. O., Chemistry
AYATA, S., Sociology
AYDIN, R., Physics
AYHAN, Ö., Statistics
AYTUNA, A., Mathematics
BAYIN, S., Physics
BAYRAMLI, E., Chemistry
BİLHAN, M., Mathematics
BİLİKMEN, S. K., Physics
ÇELEBİ, O., Mathematics
ÇEYLAN, Y., Philosophy
DEMİR, A. S., Chemistry
DEMOKAN, O., Physics
DERELİ, T., Physics
DOĞAN, M., Biology
DURGUT, M., Physics
ECEVİT, A., Physics
EKER, D., Psychology
ELLİALTIOĞLU, Ş., Physics
ERGÜDEN, A., Philosophy
ERKİP, A. K., Mathematics
ERKOÇ, Ş., Physics
ERTÜRK, Y., Sociology
GÖKMEN, A., Chemistry
GÖKMEN, İ., Chemistry
GÖKTÜRK, E. H., Chemistry
GÜLER, Y., Physics
GÜLOĞLU, İ. Ş., Mathematics
GÜNDÜZ, U., Biological Sciences
HACALOĞLU, İ., Chemistry
HACALOĞLU, İ., Chemistry
HASIRCI, N., Chemistry
HASIRCI, V. N., Biological Sciences
HORTAÇSU, N., Psychology
İMAMOĞLU, O., Psychology
İNAM, A., Philosophy
IŞCAN, M., Biology
IŞÇİ, H., Chemistry
KARANCI, N., Psychology
KARASÖZEN, B., Mathematics
KATIRCIOĞLU, B., Physics
KAYA, A., Mathematics
KAYA, Z., Biology
KENCE, A., Biological Sciences
KILDIR, M., Chemistry
KIRBIYIK, H., Physics
KISAKÜREK, D., Chemistry
KIZILOĞLU, N., Physics
KIZILOĞLU, Ü, Physics
KIZILYALLI, M., Chemistry
KOCABAŞOĞLU, U., History
KOCABIYIK, S., Biology
KOÇ, C., Mathematics
KURAT, Y. T., History
KÜÇÜKYAVUZ, S., Chemistry
KÜÇÜKYAVUZ, Z., Chemistry
MUTLU, K., Sociology
NALBANTOĞLU, Ü., Sociology
NURLU, Z., Mathematics
ÖNAL, A., Chemistry
ÖNDER, T., Mathematics
ÖNSİPER, H., Mathematics
ÖZDEMİR, S., Physics
ÖZER, A., Physics
ÖZKAN, H., Physics
ÖZKAR, S., Chemistry
ÖZSAN, E., Physics
PAK, N. K., Physics
PAMUK, Ö., Chemistry
PEYNİRCİOĞLU, N. B., Chemistry
SAYRAÇ, T., Chemistry
SEVER, R., Physics
SEVERCAN, F., Biology
ŞAHIN, N., Psychology
TALASLI, U., Psychology
TANYELİ, C., Chemistry
TARHAN, O., Chemistry
TAŞELİ, H., Mathematics
TATLI, A., Physics
TEZER, C., Mathematics
TEZER, M., Mathematics
TİNCER, T., Chemistry
TOGAN, İ, Biology
TOGAN, İ, History
TOLUN, P., Physics
TOMAK, M., Physics
TOPUZOĞLU, A., Mathematics
TUNÇEL, S., Chemistry
TUNCER, Y., Statistics
TÜRKER, L., Chemistry
ULA, A. T., Statistics
USANMAZ, A., Chemistry
YALÇIN, C., Physics
YILDIRIM, F., Statistics
YÜCEL, M., Biology

Faculty of Engineering:

AKGÖZ, Y. C., Engineering Sciences
AKKAŞ, N., Engineering Sciences
AKKÖK, M., Mechanical Engineering
AKMAN, K. I., Computer Engineering
AKSEL, H., Mechanical Engineering
AKYILMAZ, Ö., Civil Engineering
ALEMDAROĞLU, N., Aeronautical Engineering
ALTINBİLEK, D. H., Civil Engineering
ALTINER, D., Geological Engineering
ANKARA, A., Metallurgical Engineering
ANLAĞAN, Ö., Mechanical Engineering
ARIKAN, M. S., Mechanical Engineering
ARINÇ, F., Mechanical Engineering
ASKAR, M., Electrical Engineering
ATALA, H., Metallurgical Engineering
ATALAY, Ü. M., Mining Engineering
ATIMTAY, A., Environmental Engineering
ATIMTAY, E., Civil Engineering
AYDIN, Y., Engineering Science
BAÇ, N., Chemical Engineering
BALKAŞ, B. T., Environmental Engineering
BAYKA, A. D., Mechanical Engineering
BİLGEN, S., Electrical and Electronic Engineering
BİLİR, Ö. G., Mechanical Engineering
BİRAND, A. A., Civil Engineering
BİRAND, T., Electrical Engineering
BİRLİK, G., Engineering Sciences
BOR, Ş., Metallurgical Engineering
BOZOĞLU, F. T., Food Engineering
BÖLÜKBAŞI, N., Mining Engineering
CANATAN, F., Electrical Engineering
ÇALIŞKAN, M., Mechanical Engineering
ÇİLİNGİR, C., Industrial Engineering
ÇIRAY, C., Aeronautical Engineering
ÇITIPITIOĞLU, E., Civil Engineering
ÇULFAZ, A., Chemical Engineering
DEMİRBAŞ, K., Electrical and Electronic Engineering
DEMİREKLER, M., Electrical Engineering
DOĞAÇ (FER), A., Computer Engineering
DOĞAN, T., Engineering Sciences
DOĞU, T., Chemical Engineering
DORUK, M., Metallurgical Engineering

DOYURAN, V., Geological Engineering
ERALP, O. C., Mechanical Engineering
ERBATUR, F., Civil Engineering
ERDEN, A., Mechanical Engineering
ERDOĞAN, T., Civil Engineering
ERGİN, A., Civil Engineering
ERGÜL, R., Electrical Engineering
ERGUN, U., Civil Engineering
ERKİP, N., Industrial Engineering
ERLER, A., Geological Engineering
ERMIŞ, M., Electrical and Electronic Engineering
EROĞLU, I., Chemical Engineering
EROL, O. A., Civil Engineering
ERSAK, A., Electrical and Electronic Engineering
ERSOY, U., Civil Engineering
ERTAN, B., Electrical Engineering
ERTAŞ, A., Electrical Engineering
ERTEPINAR, A., Civil Engineering
ESİN, A., Food Engineering
ESİN, A., Mechanical Engineering
ESKİCİOĞLU, H., Mechanical Engineering
GEÇİT, M. R., Engineering Sciences
GENÇ, F. P., Computer Engineering
GER, M., Engineering Sciences
GEVECİ, A., Metallurgical Engineering
GÖĞÜŞ, A. Y., Aeronautical Engineering
GÖĞÜŞ, M., Civil Engineering
GÖKÇAY, C. F., Environmental Engineering
GÖNCÖĞLU, M. C., Mining Engineering
GÜLKAN, P., Civil Engineering
GÜNALP, N., Electrical and Electronic Engineering
GÜNDÜZ, G., Chemical Engineering
GÜRAN, H., Electrical Engineering
GÜRKAN, T., Chemical Engineering
GÜRÜZ, G., Chemical Engineering
GÜVEN, Ç., Industrial Engineering
GÜVEN, N., Electrical and Electronic Engineering
GÜYAGÜLER, T., Mining Engineering
HALICI, U., Electrical Engineering
HAMAMCI, H., Food Engineering
HIÇYILMAZ, C., Mining Engineering
HIZAL, A., Electrical Engineering
HIZAL, M., Electrical Engineering
HOŞTEN, Ç., Mining Engineering
İDER, K., Mechanical Engineering
İDER, Y. Z., Electrical Engineering
İLERİ, A., Mechanical Engineering
İNAL, A., Civil Engineering
İNAN, K., Electrical Engineering
KAFTANOĞLU, B., Mechanical Engineering
KARAHANOĞLU, N., Geological Engineering
KARAKAYA, I., Metallurgical Engineering
KARPUZ, C., Mining Engineering
KEYDER, E., Civil Engineering
KILIÇ, E. S., Mechanical Engineering
KINCAL, N. S., Chemical Engineering
KIRCA, Ö., Industrial Engineering
KISAKÜREK, B., Chemical Engineering
KİPER, A., Computer Engineering
KOCAOGLAN, E., Electrical Engineering
KOÇYİĞİT, A., Geological Engineering
KÖKSALAN, M., Industrial Engineering
MEHMETOĞLU, T., Petroleum Engineering
MENGİ, Y., Engineering Science
MİRATA, T., Civil Engineering
NAKİPOĞLU, M., Geological Engineering
NORMAN, T., Geological Engineering
OĞURTANI, T., Metallurgical Engineering
OKANDAN, E., Petroleum Engineering
ORAL, S., Mechanical Engineering
OSKAY, R., Mechanical Engineering
ÖNAL, I., Chemical Engineering
ÖNDER, H., Civil Engineering
ÖZAY, N., Electrical and Electronic Engineering
ÖZBAYOĞLU, G., Mining Engineering
ÖZBELGE, Ö., Chemical Engineering
ÖZBELGE, T., Chemical Engineering
ÖZENBAŞ, M., Metallurgical Engineering
ÖZGEN, C., Chemical Engineering
ÖZGENOĞLU, A., Mining Engineering
ÖZGÖREN, K., Mechanical Engineering
ÖZGÜVEN, N., Mechanical Engineering
ÖZHAN, E., Civil Engineering
ÖZKAN, Y., Civil Engineering
ÖZTÜRK, T., Metallurgical Engineering
PAŞAMEHMETOĞLU, G., Mining Engineering
PAYKOÇ, E., Mechanical Engineering
PLATİN, B. E., Mechanical Engineering
RUMELİ, A., Electrical Engineering
SAATÇİOĞLU, Ö., Industrial Engineering
SELÇUK, E., Metallurgical Engineering
SELÇUK, N., Chemical Engineering
ŞENDİL, U., Civil Engineering
SEVAİOĞLU, O., Electrical and Electronic Engineering
SEVERCAN, M., Electrical Engineering
SEVİNÇ, N., Metallurgical Engineering
SEVÜK, A. S., Civil Engineering
SÖYLEMEZ, E., Mechanical Engineering
SOYLU, R., Mechanical Engineering
SOYUKPAK, S., Environmental Engineering
SUCUOĞLU, H., Civil Engineering
SÜRÜCÜ, G., Environmental Engineering
ŞORMAN, A. Ü., Civil Engineering
TANIK, Y., Electrical Engineering
TANKUT, A. T., Civil Engineering
TEKİN, E., Metallurgical Engineering
TEKKAYA, E., Mechanical Engineering
TİMUÇİN, M., Metallurgical Engineering
TOKDEMİR, T. Engineering Sciences
TOKER, C., Electrical Engineering
TOPKAYA, Y., Metallurgical Engineering
TOSUN, H., Electrical and Electronic Engineering
TULUNAY, E. S., Electrical Engineering
TULUNAY, Y., Aeronautical Engineering
TUNCEL, G., Environmental Engineering
TÜMER, T. S., Mechanical Engineering
TÜRELİ, A., Electrical Engineering
ULUATAM, S., Civil Engineering
ULUĞ, E. S., Environmental Engineering
UNAN, C., Geological Engineering
UNGAN, S., Food Engineering
UTKU, M., Civil Engineering
ÜÇER, A. Ş., Mechanical Engineering
ÜÇTUĞ, Y., Electrical and Electronic Engineering
ÜNLÜSOY, Y. S., Mechanical Engineering
ÜNVER, Z., Electrical Engineering
VURAL, F. Y., Computer Engineering
WASTİ, Y., Civil Engineering
YAHŞİ, O. S., Mechanical Engineering
YALABIK, N., Computer Engineering
YAZICIGİL, H., Geological Engineering
YEĞİNOBALI, A., Civil Engineering
YEŞİN, O., Mechanical Engineering
YEŞİN, T., Mechanical Engineering
YILDIRIM, N., Electrical Engineering
YILDIRIM, R. O., Mechanical Engineering
YILDIZ, F., Food Engineering
YILMAZ, Ç, Civil Engineering
YILMAZ, L., Chemical Engineering
YILMAZER, Ü., Chemical Engineering
YÜCE, R., Civil Engineering
YÜCEL, B., Mechanical Engineering
YÜCEMEN, M. S., Civil Engineering
YÜCEOĞLU, U., Aeronautical Engineering
YÜKSEL, Y. Ö., Electrical Engineering
YÜNCÜ, H., Mechancial Engineering
YÜCEL, H., Chemical Engineering
YURTERI, C., Environmental Engineering

Graduate School of Marine Scienes:

BAŞTÜRK, Ö., Marine Sciences
BİNGEL, F., Marine Sciences
MOHAMMED, A., Marine Sciences
OĞUZ, T., Marine Sciences
ÖZSOY, E., Marine Sciences
SALİHOĞLU, İ, Marine Sciences
SAYDAM, C., Marine Sciences
TUGRUL, S., Marine Sciences
ÜNLÜATA, Ü., Marine Sciences
ÜNSAL, M., Marine Sciences
YILMAZ, A., Marine Sciences

ATTACHED RESEARCH CENTRES

Audiovisual Systems Research and Application Centre: Dir Prof. Dr ALIKAŞ.
Centre for the Preservation and Evaluation of Historical Artefacts: Dir Assoc. Prof. Dr NUMAN TUNA.
Centre for Computer-Aided Design, Manufacture and Robotics Research and Application: Dir Prof. Dr METİN AKKÖK.
Centre for Welding and Non-Destructive Testing: Dir Prof. Dr ALPAY ANKARA.
Centre for Continuing Education: Dir Prof. Dr SABRİ KOÇ.
Southeast Anatolia Project Research and Application Centre: Dir Prof. Dr SEMRA SIBER SULUATAM.
Centre for Black Sea and Central Asia: Dir Prof. Dr AYŞE AYATA.

SELÇUK ÜNİVERSİTESİ

Vali İzzetbey Caddesi, 42151 Konya

Telephone: (332) 350-70-05
Fax: (332) 350-96-93

Founded 1975
State control
Language of instruction: Turkish
Academic year: October to May (2 terms)

Rector: Prof. Dr ABDURRAHMAN KUTLU
Vice-Rectors: Prof. Dr MEHMET KARA, Prof. Dr MEHMET NİZAMLIOĞLU, Prof. Dr ERŞAN AYGÜN
Secretary-General: BEHIC COSKUN
Librarian: Dr ALİ ÖZGÖKMEN

Number of teachers: 1,781
Number of students: 42,136 undergraduates, 2,445 postgraduates

Publications: *Journal of Veterinary Science* (every 2 months), *Journal of the Faculty of Medicine* (quarterly).

DEANS

Faculty of Agriculture: Prof. Dr MEHMET KARA
Faculty of Dentistry: Prof. Dr ADNAN ÖZTÜRK
Faculty of Economics and Administrative Sciences (Konya): Prof. Dr ORHAN GÖKÇE
Faculty of Economics and Administrative Sciences (Karaman): Prof. Dr MAHMUT TEKİN
Faculty of Education: Prof. Dr AKİF AKKUŞ
Faculty of Engineering and Architecture: Prof. Dr ALİ SİNAN
Faculty of Law: Prof. Dr OKTAY YAZGAN
Faculty of Medicine: Prof. Dr UĞUR ERONGUN
Faculty of Science and Humanities: Prof. Dr RAMAZAN MİRZAOĞLU
Faculty of Theology: Prof. Dr MEHMET AYDIN
Faculty of Veterinary Sciences: Prof. Dr VEYSİ ASLAN
Faculty of Communication: Doç. Dr NURETTİN GÜZ
Faculty of Vocational Education: Prof. Dr FİLİZ GÜNDÜZ

ATTACHED INSTITUTES

Institute of Health Sciences: Dir Prof. Dr OSMAN ERGANİŞ
Institute of Natural and Applied Sciences: Dir Prof. Dr ALİ SİNAN
Institute of Social Sciences: Dir Prof. Dr HAŞİM KARPUZ
Institute of Turkish Studies: Dir Prof. Dr AHMET SEVGİ

TRAKYA ÜNİVERSİTESİ

22100 Edirne

Telephone: (284) 214-40-04
Fax: (284) 214-42-03

Founded 1982 from existing faculties in Edirne

Rector: Prof. Dr OSMAN İNCİ
Vice-Rectors: Prof. Dr ÖMER YİĞİTBAŞI, Prof. Dr ULKÜ OYMAN

Administrative Director: ALİ SUCU
Librarian: ENDER BİLAR
Number of teachers: 1,104
Number of students: 19,868

DEANS

Faculty of Medicine: Prof. Dr AHMET KARASALİHOĞLU
Faculty of Arts and Sciences: Prof. Dr İSMAİL HAKKI DURU
Faculty of Engineering and Architecture: Prof. Dr CEM ECE
Faculty of Agriculture: Prof. Dr AHMET NEDİM YÜKSEL
Faculty of Education: Prof. Dr MEHMET İŞCAN
Faculty of Administrative Sciences: Prof. Dr SABAHAT AVŞAR
Faculty of Engineering in Çorlu: Prof. Dr H. METE ŞEN

HEADS OF DIVISIONS

Faculty of Medicine:

Basic Medical Sciences: Prof. Dr ÇETİN ALGÜNEŞ
Internal Medicine: Prof. Dr MURAT TUĞRUL
Surgery: Prof. Dr M. AYDIN ALTAN

Faculty of Agriculture:

Agricultural Economics: Prof. Dr İ. HAKKI İNAN
Agricultural Machinery: Prof. Dr POYRAZ ÜLGER
Animal Science: Prof. Dr SABAHATTİN ÖĞÜN
Crop Production: Prof. Dr SEZEN ŞEHİRALİ
Farm Buildings and Irrigation: Prof. Dr A. NEDİM YÜKSEL
Food Engineering: Prof. Dr MEHMET DEMİRCİ
Horticulture: Prof. Dr SALİH ÇELİK
Landscape Architecture: Prof. Dr ASLI BOZKUR
Plant Protection: Asst Prof. Dr AHMET ÇITIR
Soil Science: Prof. Dr CEMİL CANGİR

Faculty of Arts and Sciences:

Biology: Prof. Dr CENGİZ KURTONUR
Physics: Prof. Dr ASKERİ BARAN
Mathematics: Prof. Dr İSMAİL HAKKI DURU
Chemistry: Prof. Dr ÜLKÜ OYMAN
Turkish Language and Literature: Prof. Dr H. KEMAL BAYATLI
History: Prof. Dr İLKER ALP
Archaeology and History of Art: Asst Prof. Dr ÖZKAN ERTUĞRUL

Faculty of Engineering and Architecture:

Mechanical Engineering: Prof. Dr M. CEM ECE
Architecture: Prof. Dr VEYİS ÖZEK
Computer Engineering: Asst Prof. Dr CAVİT TEZCAN

Faculty of Education:

Educational Science: Assoc. Prof. Dr CEVAT CELEP
Primary Education: Prof. Dr SERVET EKMEKÇİ
Foreign Languages: Asst Prof. Dr SEVİNÇ SAKARYA
Fine Arts: Asst Prof. Dr MEHTAP ÜLKÜCÜ

Faculty of Administrative Sciences:

Public Administration: Asst Prof. Dr ÜLKÜ VARLIK
Business Administration: Asst Prof. Dr SEFER GÜMÜŞ
Econometrics: Asst Prof. Dr ADİL OĞUZHAN
International Relations: Asst Prof. Dr SİBEL TURAN
Finance: Prof. Dr SEBAHAT AVŞAR
Economics: Asst Prof. Dr DERMAN KÜÇÜKALTAN
Labour Economics and Industrial Relations: Assoc. Prof. Dr RIZA BÜYÜKUSLU
Computers and Teaching Technology: Prof. Dr MEHMET İŞCAN

Faculty of Engineering in Çorlu:

Electronics and Telecommunications: Asst Prof. Dr RAFET AKDENİZ
Computer Engineering: Assoc. Prof. Dr ABDURRAHMAN GÜNER
Environmental Engineering: Asst Prof. Dr FİSUN UYSAL
Textile Engineering: Asst Prof. Dr NEVİN KAPTANOĞLU
Civil Engineering: Prof. Dr ABDURRAHMAN GÜNER
Mechanical Engineering: Asst Prof. Dr HAVVA AKDENİZ

ATTACHED INSTITUTES

Health Sciences Institute: Dir Prof. Dr İSMET DÖKMECİ.
Sciences Institute: Dir Prof. Dr CENGİZ KURTONUR.
Social Sciences Institute: Dir Prof. Dr CEVAT CELEP.

ULUDAĞ ÜNİVERSİTESİ

Görükle Kampüsü, 16059 Bursa

Telephone: (224) 442-80-01
Fax: (224) 442-80-12
E-mail: ulu.rek@uubim.bim.uludag.edu.tr

Founded 1975
State control
Language of instruction: Turkish
Academic year: October to June

Rector: Prof. Dr AYHAN KIZIL
Vice-Rectors: Prof. Dr ERHAN OĞUL, Prof. Dr ATİLLA ERİŞ, Prof. Dr ALİ YAŞAR SARIBAY
Secretary-General: Prof. Dr A. HAMDİ AYTEKİN
Head of Libraries and Documentation Centre: NEŞE ARAT

Number of professors: 1,470
Number of students: 33,127

Publications: several faculty journals.

DEANS

Faculty of Medicine: Prof. Dr METE CENGİZ
Faculty of Economics and Administrative Sciences: Prof. Dr ÖZER SERPER
Faculty of Engineering and Architecture: Prof. Dr İBRAHİM YÜKSEL
Faculty of Veterinary Medicine: Prof. Dr RECEP TINAR
Faculty of Agriculture: Prof. Dr ABDURRAHİM KORUKÇU
Faculty of Education: Prof. Dr ALİ ÖZÇELEBİ
Faculty of Theology: Prof. Dr İZZET ER
Faculty of Science and Letters: Prof. Dr ULVİYE ÖZER

HEADS OF DEPARTMENT

Faculty of Medicine:

Basic Medical Sciences: Prof. Dr İSMET KAN
Internal Medical Sciences: Prof. Dr MÜNİR KERİM KARAKAYA
Surgical Sciences: Prof. Dr ENDER KORFALI

Faculty of Economics and Administrative Sciences:

Economics: Prof. Dr ZEYNEL DİNLER
Management: Prof. Dr ERHAN KOTAR
Finance: Prof. Dr NİHAT EDİZDOĞAN
Labour Economics and Industrial Relations: Prof. Dr NURHAN AKÇAYLI
International Relations: Prof. Dr MEHMET GENÇ
Public Administration: Prof. Dr ALİ YAŞAR SARIBAY
Econometrics: Prof. Dr MUSTAFA AYTAÇ

Faculty of Engineering and Architecture:

Mechanical Engineering: Prof. Dr RECEP YAMANKARADENİZ
Textile Engineering: Prof. Dr HALİL RIFAT ALPAY
Electronics Engineering: Prof. Dr ALİ OKTAY
Environmental Engineering: Prof. Dr H. SAVAŞ BAŞKAYA
Industrial Engineering: Prof. Dr ERDAL EMEL
Architecture: Assoc. Prof. Dr NESLİHAN DOSTOĞLU
Civil Engineering: Prof. Dr İBRAHIM YÜKSEL

Faculty of Veterinary Medicine:

Basic Sciences of Veterinary Medicine: Prof. Dr AYTEKİN ÖZER
Diseases and Clinics: Prof. Dr OSMAN SACİT GÖRGÜL
Animal Husbandry and Feeding: Prof. Dr HASAN BAŞPINAR

Faculty of Agriculture:

Horticulture: Prof. Dr ATİLLA ERİŞ
Plant Protection: Prof. Dr NECATİ BAYKAL
Agricultural Construction and Irrigation: Prof. Dr İSMET ARICI
Agricultural Economics: Prof. Dr ERKAN REHBER
Agricultural Machines: Prof. Dr KAMİL ALİBAŞ
Field Crops: Prof. Dr NEVZAT YÜRÜR
Food Science and Technology: Prof. Dr İSMET ŞAHİN
Soil Science: Prof. Dr VAHAP KATKAT
Animal Husbandry: Prof. Dr ALİ KARABULUT

Faculty of Education:

Education: Prof. Dr LEYLA KÜÇÜKAHMET
Foreign Language Education: Prof. Dr MUSTAFA DURAK
Fine Arts: Prof. Dr AYTEN SÜRÜR
Physical Training and Sports: Assoc. Prof. Dr FEVZİ TOKER
Primary School Teacher Training: Prof. Dr SUZAN ERBAŞ
Primary School Teaching of Turkish: Assoc. Prof. Dr MUSTAFA CEMİLOĞLU
Computer Teaching Appliances: Assoc. Prof. Dr FİKRET YARCI

Faculty of Theology:

Basic Islamic Sciences: Prof. Dr MEHMET ALİ SÖNMEZ
Philosophy and Science of Religion: Prof. Dr HAYATİ HÖKELEKLİ
Islamic History and Arts: Assoc. Prof. Dr MEFAİL HIZLI
Primary School Religion and Teaching of Ethics: Assoc. Prof. Dr M. EMIN AY

Faculty of Science and Letters:

Mathematics: Prof. Dr MUSTAFA BAYRAKTAR
Physics: Prof. Dr AYTAÇ YALÇINER
Chemistry: Prof. Dr ŞEREF GÜÇER
Biology: Prof. Dr RAHMİ BİLALOĞLU
Turkish Language and Literature: Prof. Dr COŞKUN AK
History: Assoc. Prof. Dr YUSUF OĞUZOĞLU
Philosophy: Assoc. Prof. Dr SEVGİ İYİ
Sociology: Prof. Dr FÜGEN BERKAY
Psychology: Assoc. Prof. Dr YUSUF OĞUZOĞLU
Archaeology and History of Art: Prof. Dr ZEREN TANINDI

YILDIZ TEKNİK ÜNİVERSİTESİ

Yıldız, 80750 Istanbul

Telephone: (212) 259-70-70
Fax: (212) 261-42-84

Founded 1911; reorganized 1982 (fmrly State Academy of Engineering and Architecture)

Rector: Prof. Dr AYHAN ALKIŞ

Deputy Rectors: Prof. Dr Emre Aysu, Prof. Dr Şeniz Kaban, Prof. Dr Ahmet Ulvi Avci
Secretary-General: Prof. Dr Mehmet Sümer
Number of teachers: 835
Number of students: 14,244
Publication: *Periodical* (4 a year).

DEANS

Faculty of Structural Engineering: Prof. Dr İbrahim Ekiz
Faculty of Mechanical Engineering: Prof. Nurullah Gültekin
Faculty of Architecture: Prof. Hakki Önel
Faculty of Science and Literature: Prof. Dr Behiç Çağal
Faculty of Electrical and Electronics Engineering: Prof. Dr Çelik Aktaş
Faculty of Metallurgy and Chemical Engineering: Prof. Dr Ahmet Topuz
Faculty of Economics and Organizational Science: Prof. Dr Murat Demircioğlu

ATTACHED INSTITUTES

Sciences: Dir Prof. Dr Hüseyin Demirel.
Social Sciences: Dir Prof. Dr Naci Kepkep.

ATTACHED COLLEGES

School of Vocational Sciences: Dir Prof. Mehmet Bayhan.

YÜZÜNCÜ YİL ÜNİVERSİTESİ
(Centennial University)

Van
Telephone: 12305
Founded 1982
State control
Language of instruction: Turkish
Academic year: October to July

Rector: Prof. Dr Nihat Bayşu
Vice-Rectors: Prof. Dr Cemalettin Köküüslu, Prof. Dr Ataman Güre
Secretary-General: M. Salih Mercan
Librarian: Dursun Öztürk
Number of teachers: 204
Number of students: 2,338

DEANS

Faculty of Arts and Sciences: Prof. Dr Nurhan Akyüz
Faculty of Veterinary Science: Prof. Dr Hayati Çamaş
Faculty of Agriculture: Prof. Dr Ahmet Güncan

PROFESSORS

Akyürek, A., Agronomy and Genetics
Andiç, C., Forage Crops
Günel, E., Plant Production and Breeding
Karacal, İ., Soil Science
Şen, S. M., Horticulture
Vanli, Y., Animal Breeding and Genetics

ATTACHED INSTITUTES

Social Sciences
Sciences

ATTACHED COLLEGES

College of Education
College of Vocational Education: Hakkari
College of Vocational Education: Tatvan

TURKMENISTAN

Learned Societies

GENERAL

Turkmen Academy of Sciences 744000 Ashkhabad, Ul, Gogolya 15; 17 mem, 38 corresp. mems; attached research institutes: see Research Institutes; library: see Libraries and Archives; Pres. A. G. BABAEV; Chief Learned Sec. V. N. NIKOLAEV; publs *Izvestiya* (bulletins, series: technical sciences, biological sciences, humanities), *Problemy osvoyeniya pustyn* (Problems of Desert Development).

Research Institutes

GENERAL

Desert Institute: 744000 Ashkhabad, Neutral Turkmenistan St 15; tel. 39-54-27; fax 35-37-16; e-mail babaev@desert.ashgabad.su; f. 1962; attached to Min. of National Resources; Dir A. G. BABAEV; publ. *Problems of Desert Development* (6 a year).

AGRICULTURE, FISHERIES AND VETERINARY SCIENCE

Research Institute of Agricultural Economics: Ashkhabad.

Research Institute of Hydrotechnology and Land Reclamation: Ashkhabad.

ECONOMICS, LAW AND POLITICS

Institute of Economics: 744032 Ashkhabad, Bikrova sad keshi 28; tel. 24-02-52; attached to Turkmen Acad. of Sciences; Dir G. M. MURADOV.

Institute of Philosophy and Law: 744000 Ashkhabad, Ul. Gogolya 15; tel. 25-41-69; attached to Turkmen Acad. of Sciences; Dir O. MUSAEV.

HISTORY, GEOGRAPHY AND ARCHAEOLOGY

Batyrov, S., Institute of History: 744000 Ashkhabad, Ul. Gogolya 15; tel. 25-31-38; attached to Turkmen Acad. of Sciences; Dir N. V. ATAMAMEDOV.

Southern Turkmen Multidisciplinary Archaeological Expedition: Ashkhabad, Ul. Gogolya 15; tel. 25-15-25; attached to Turkmen Acad. of Sciences; Man. K. KURBANSAKHATOV.

LANGUAGE AND LITERATURE

Bailyev Institute of Linguistics: 744000 Ashkhabad, Ul. Gogolya 15; tel. 25-27-73; attached to Turkmen Acad. of Sciences; Dir M. SOEGOV.

Makhtumkuli Institute of Literature: 744000 Ashkhabad, Ul. Gogolya 15; tel. 25-35-09; attached to Turkmen Acad. of Sciences; Dir A. ORAZOV.

MEDICINE

Institute of Oncology: 744012 Ashkhabad, Pervomaiskaya ul. 53; tel. 24-66-45.

Turkmen Eye Diseases Research Institute: Ashkhabad, Soyuznaya ul. 32/2.

Turkmen Research Institute of Preventive and Clinical Medicine: 744006 Ashkhabad, Gorogly St 31; tel. 29-01-88; fax 24-11-93; f. 1989; Dir Dr NINA KERIMI.

NATURAL SCIENCES

Biological Sciences

Institute of Botany: 744000 Ashkhabad, Makhtumkuli 79; tel. 25-37-58; attached to Turkmen Acad. of Sciences; Dir K. M. MURADOV.

Institute of Physiology: 744011 Ashkhabad, Ul. Ostrovskogo 30; tel. 24-74-18; f. 1959; attached to Turkmen Acad. of Sciences; Dir K. AMANNEPESOV.

Institute of Zoology: 744000 Ashkhabad, Ul. Engelsa 6; tel. 25-37-91; attached to Turkmen Acad. of Sciences; Dir T. TOGKAEV.

Physical Sciences

Institute of Chemistry: 744012 Ashkhabad, Ul. Sovetskikh Pogranichnikov 92; tel. 24-05-08; attached to Turkmen Acad. of Sciences; Dir A. KHODZHAMAMEDOV.

Institute of Geology: 744000 Ashkhabad, Ul. Gogolya 15; tel. 29-14-85; attached to Turkmen Acad. of Sciences; Dir O. A. ODEKOV.

Institute of Seismology: 744000 Ashkhabad, Komsomolskaya ul. 20; tel. and fax 39-06-13; e-mail ashirov@icca.cat.glasnet.ru; f. 1959; attached to Turkmen Acad. of Sciences; Dir Prof. TACHMET A. ASHIROV.

TECHNOLOGY

Institute of Mathematics and Mechanics: 744000 Ashkhabad, Ul. Gogolya 15; tel. 29-87-13; attached to Turkmen Acad. of Sciences; Dir M. B. ORAZOV.

Physical Engineering Institute: 744000 Ashkhabad, Ul. Gogolya 15; tel. 25-42-85; attached to Turkmen Acad. of Sciences; Dir A. BERKELIEV.

Libraries and Archives

Ashkhabad

Central Scientific Library of the Turkmen Academy of Sciences: 744007 Ashkhabad, Bitarap Turkmenistan St 15A; tel. 35-65-71; f. 1941; 2,130,000 vols; Dir A. B. YAZBERDIEV.

National Library of Turkmenistan: 744000 Ashkhabad, Pl. Karla Marxa; tel. 25-32-54; f. 1895; 5,500,000 vols; Dir S. A. KURBANOV.

Republican Scientific and Technical Library of Turkmenistan: Ashkhabad, Pr. Svobody 106; 900,000 vols; Dir Z. I. CHEREPANOVA.

Turkmen A. M. Gorkii State University Library: 744014 Ashkhabad, Pr. Lenina 31; tel. 5-39-22; about 542,000 vols; Dir. A. T. VOROBEVA.

Museums and Art Galleries

Ashkhabad

Central Botanical Garden: 744012 Ashkhabad, Ul. Timiryazeva 17; tel. 24-18-57; attached to Turkmen Acad. of Sciences; Dir D. KURBANOV.

National Museum of History and Ethnography of Turkmenistan: 744000 Ashkhabad, Ul. Shevchenko 1; tel. 25-51-38; f. 1899; library of 3,000 vols; Dir A. ATAKARIYEV.

Turkmen State Museum of Fine Art: 744000 Ashkhabad, Ul. Pushkina 9; tel. 25-63-71; f. 1938; art of the former USSR and Western Europe, Turkmenian carpets; library of 6,000 vols; Dir N. SHABUNTS.

University

TURKMEN A. M. GORKII STATE UNIVERSITY

744014 Ashkhabad, Pr. Lenina 31

Telephone: 5-11-59

Founded 1950

Rector: Prof. S. N. MURADOV

Pro-Rectors: G. M. MYALIK-KULIEV, A. A. KURBANOV, T. R. REDZHEPOV

Number of students: 11,000

Faculties of Russian philology, Turkmen philology, foreign languages, history, law physics, mathematics, biology, geography.

Other Higher Educational Institutes

Ashkhabad Institute of National Economy: 744000 Ashkhabad, Ul. Khudaiberdyeva 46; tel. 46-98-06; faculties: economic planning, trade economics, accounting.

Turkmen Agricultural Institute: 744000 Ashkhabad, Pervomaiskaya ul. 62; tel. 4-25-22; depts: agrochemistry, fruit and vegetable growing, viticulture, veterinary, animal husbandry, mechanization, accounting; library of 136,000 vols; Rector A. K. RUSTAMOV.

Turkmen Polytechnic Institute: 744025 Ashkhabad, 8-i Mikroraion, Ul. Kotovskogo 1; tel. 9-37-10; faculties: construction, oil, chemical technology, energy, economics and sanitation technology.

Turkmen State Medical Institute: 744000 Ashkhabad, GSP-19, Ul. Shaumyana 58; tel. 25-40-96; f. 1932; library of 191,000 vols; Rector D. N. NEPESOV.

Turkmen State Pedagogical Institute of Fine Arts: 744007 Ashkhabad, Pr. V. I. Lenina 3; tel. 5-36-66, 5-41-35; piano, orchestral instruments, folk instruments, singing, choral conducting, composition, musicology.

UGANDA

Learned Societies

GENERAL

Uganda Society: POB 4980, Kampala; f. 1933; premises in the Uganda Museum, Kira Rd, Kampala; membership open to persons of all races and institutions, to promote interest in literary, historic, scientific and general cultural matters, discovering and recording facts about the country, arranging lectures and establishing contacts; library of 1,600 vols and periodicals; publ. *The Uganda Journal.*

BIBLIOGRAPHY, LIBRARY SCIENCE AND MUSEOLOGY

Uganda Library Association: POB 5894, Kampala; f. 1972; 140 mems; Chair. P. BIRUNGI; Sec. L. M. SSENGERO; publ. *Ugandan Libraries*.

EDUCATION

Association for Teacher Education in Africa: c/o Assoc. Prof. J. C. B. Bigala, Makerere University, POB 7062, Kampala; f. 1970; to develop and co-ordinate syllabi and materials to be used in teacher education insts; 50 mem. insts in anglophone Africa; Pres. Prof. M. MOHAPELOA; Sec. Assoc. Prof. J. C. B. BIGALA; publs *Journal of West African Education, Education in Eastern Africa*.

Inter-University Council for East Africa: POB 7110, Kampala; tel. (41) 256251; telex 61572; fax (41) 342007; f. 1980 as a corporate body to succeed the Inter-University Cttee for East Africa; aims to facilitate contact and co-operation between the universities of Kenya, Tanzania and Uganda, and to provide a forum for discussion on academic matters, and to maintain comparable academic standards; also provides secretariat for the Asscn of Eastern and Southern African Universities (see under International); Exec. Sec. E. K. KIGOZI; publs *Report* (annually), *Newsletter*.

MEDICINE

Uganda Medical Association: POB 2243, Kampala; tel. (41) 236539; fax (41) 532591; f. 1961; 850 mems; library of 500 vols; Pres. Dr FRANK MWESIGYE; Sec. Dr FRANCIS O. ORIOKOT; publ. *Uganda Medical Journal*.

Research Institutes

AGRICULTURE, FISHERIES AND VETERINARY SCIENCE

Animal Health Research Centre: POB 24, Entebbe; f. 1926; research and field work in animal diseases, husbandry and nutrition; herbarium; library of 13,950 vols; Dir Veterinary Research Services Prof. O. BWANGAMOI; Librarian H. R. KIBOOLE; publs *Research Index* (irregular), *Research Bulletin* (irregular), *Annual Report*.

Cotton Research Station (Namulonge): (Cotton Research Corporation): POB 7084, Kampala; pure and applied aspects of cotton culture and technology; library of 4,000 vols.

Kawanda Agricultural Research Institute: POB 7065, Kampala; tel. 567649; fax (42) 21070; f. 1937; research on bananas and coffee, horticulture, post-harvest soil and soil fertility management, integrated pest management, biometrics, plant breeding, plant pathology; library of 2,600 vols; plant herbarium; insect museum; Dir of Research Dr ISRAEL KIBIRIGE-SEBUNYA.

Nakawa Forestry Research Centre: POB 1752, Kampala; tel. 56261; f. 1952; logging, milling and building research; preservation and seasoning tests; small specialized library.

Namulonge Agricultural and Animal Production Research Institute: POB 7084, Kampala; tel. (41) 342554; e-mail naari@naro.bushnet.net; f. 1950; library of 1,700 vols, 155 periodicals.

ECONOMICS, LAW AND POLITICS

Centre for Basic Research: POB 9863, Kampala; premises at 15 Baskerville Ave, Kololo; tel. (041) 342987; fax (041) 235413; f. 1988; non-governmental organization active in social research; library of 2,500 vols; Exec. Dir Dr JOHN JEAN BARYA.

Makerere Institute of Social Research: POB 16022, Kampala; tel. 554582; fax 532821; f. 1948; conducts independent research into social, political and economic problems of East Africa; 6 Research Fellows, University staff in Departments of Economics, Political Science, Rural Economy and Extension, Environmental Studies, Women's Studies, Sociology, Social Work and Social Administration; library of 10,000 vols. 300 current periodicals and extensive pamphlets, etc.; Dir APOLO NSIBAMBI; Research Sec. PATRICK MULINDWA; publs *East African Studies* (irregularly), *East Africa Linguistic Studies* (occasional), working papers, USSC Conference papers (annually), *Policy Abstracts and Research Newsletter, Mawazo Journal* (2 a year), library catalogues.

MEDICINE

Child Malnutrition Unit: Medical Research Council, Mulago Hospital, POB 7051, Kampala; Dir Dr R. G. WHITEHEAD. (See also under Medical Research Council, UK.)

NATURAL SCIENCES

Physical Sciences

Geological Survey and Mines Department: POB 9, Entebbe; f. 1919; library of 22,900 vols; Commissioner C. E. TAMALE-SSALI.

Government Chemist Department: POB 2174, Kampala; forensic chemical examination, bacteriological examination of foods and water, chemical analysis of water, food and drugs, pollution control, identification and assay of drugs, general chemical analysis of soils and ores, isolation and identification of active principles of medicinal plants.

Libraries and Archives

Kampala

Cabinet Office Library: POB 7168, Kampala; tel. 254881; fax 235459; f. 1920; for government officials and for research workers; 10,000 vols; Librarian HERBERT R. KIBOOLE; publ. *Catalogue*.

Forest Department Library: POB 7124, Kampala; tel. 259626; telex 61196; fax 254423; f. 1904; specialized library (open to students by special arrangement with the Commissioner for Forestry): literature on forestry and related sciences; 20,000 vols; Librarian W. M. BWIRUKA; publs *Forest Department Annual Report, The Woodsman Newsletter*.

Makerere University, Albert Cook Library: Makerere Medical School, POB 7072, Kampala; tel. (41) 534149; fax (41) 530024; f. 1946; 55,000 vols, 210 periodicals, covering all medical subjects, especially East African and tropical medicine; special collections: Albert Cook, Mengo Notes, WHO publications; Librarian EUNICE N. N. SENDIKADIWA (acting); publs *Uganda Medical Bibliography* (3 a year), *Library Bulletin and Accessions List* (irregular), *Annual Report, Uganda Health Information Digest* (4 a year).

Makerere University Library Service: POB 16002, Kampala; f. 1940; comprises Main Library functioning as National Reference Library, with five sub-libraries for the faculties of medicine (functioning as National Library of Medicine), technology, education, social science research and farm management; main library of over 400,000 vols, over 240,000 periodicals, special collections of East Africa, Uganda legal deposit, and private archives; Librarian J. MUGASHA; publs incl. *East African Studies, Mawazo, Makerere Law Journal, Makerere Political Review*, etc.

Public Libraries Board: Buganda Rd, POB 4262, Kampala; tel. (41) 233633; fax (41) 348625; e-mail library@imul.com; f. 1964 to establish, equip, manage and maintain libraries in Uganda; 20 branch libraries, book box and postal services are administered; library of 157,000 vols, 200 serial titles; Dir P. BIRUNGI; publs *Annual Report, Quarterly Newsletter*.

Museums and Art Galleries

Entebbe

Entebbe Botanic Gardens: POB 40, Entebbe; f. 1898; conservation and development of native and exotic plants, collection and planting of local medicinal plants; Curator JOHN MULUMBA-WASSWA; publ. *Index Seminum* (annually).

Game and Fisheries Museum, Aquarium and Library: POB 4, Entebbe; collections of heads of game animals, reptiles, fish and butterflies, hunting and fishing implements and weapons; library of 1,100 vols; Commissioner for Wildlife MOSES OKUA; Commissioner for Fisheries CHRISTOPHER DHATEMWA.

Geological Survey Museum and Library: POB 9, Entebbe; about 37,500 specimens of rocks and minerals; library of over 9,850 vols and 3,850 periodicals.

Wildlife Education Centre: POB 369, Entebbe; tel. (42) 20520; fax (42) 20073; e-mail uweczoo@imul.com; zoological colln of mammals, birds and reptiles; Dir WILHELM MOELLER.

Kampala

Uganda Museum: 5–7 Kira Rd, POB 365, Kampala; f. 1908; natural history, geology, ethnology, archaeology, palaeontology; science and industry pavilion; special collection of African musical instruments; centre for archaeological research in Uganda; library of 4,000 vols; Curator Dr E. KAMUHANGIRE; publs occasional papers, *Annual Report*.

Universities

MAKERERE UNIVERSITY

POB 7062, Kampala

Telephone: 542803

Telex: 61351

Founded as technical school 1922, became University College 1949, attained University status 1970

Language of instruction: English

Academic year: October to June (three terms)

Chancellor: H. E. The President of Uganda

Vice-Chancellor: Prof. J. P. SEBUWUFU

Deputy Vice-Chancellor: Prof. J. EPELO-OPIO

Secretary: A. K. M. TIBARIMBASA

Academic Registrar: MUKWANASON A. HYUHA

Librarian: J. MUGASHA

Number of teachers: 650

Number of students: 15,500

Publication: *Mawazo*.

DEANS

Faculty of Arts: Dr O. NDOLERIIRE
Faculty of Social Sciences: Dr JOY KWESIGA
Faculty of Agriculture and Forestry: Assoc. Prof. E. SABRITI
Faculty of Science: Prof. L. S. LUBOOBI
Faculty of Medicine: Assoc. Prof. N. SEWANKEMBO
Faculty of Law: Assoc. Prof. J. OLOKA-ONYANGO
Faculty of Veterinary Medicine: Assoc. Prof. E. KATUNGA-RWAKISHAYA
Faculty of Technology: Dr J. HIGENYI
Faculty of Commerce: WASWA-BALUNYWA
School of Education: Assoc. Prof. J. C. SSEKAMWA

PROFESSORS

Faculty of Agriculture and Forestry:

KITUNGULU-ZAKE, Y. J., Soil Science
OSIRU, D. O., Crop Science
RUBAIHAYO, P. R.
RUYOOKA, D., Forestry

Faculty of Arts:

BYARUHANGA-AKIIKI, A. B. T., Religious Studies and Philosophy
DALFOVO, A. T., Philosophy
MUKAMA, R.
TIBENDERANA, P. K., History

Faculty of Law:

BAKIBINGA, D. J., Commercial Law
KAKOOZA, J. M. N., Law and Jurisprudence

Faculty of Medicine:

ANOKBONGGO, W. W., Pharmacology and Therapeutics
BULWA, F. M., Obstetrics and Gynaecology
MMIRO, F. A., Obstetrics and Gynaecology
MUGERWA, J. W., Pathology
OTIM, M. A., Medicine
OWOR, R., Pathology

Faculty of Science:

ILUKOR, J. O., Physics
KAHWA, Y., Physics
LUBOOBI, L. S., Mathematics
MUGAMBE, P. E., Physics
MUGAMBI, P. E., Mathematics
POMEROY, D. E., Zoology
SEKAALO, H.
TALIGOOLA, H. K., Botany
TUKAHIRWA, E., Environmental Science

Faculty of Social Sciences:

AKIIKI-MUJAJU, A. B., Political Science
GINGYERA-PINYCWA, A. C. G., Political Science
MWAKA, V. M.

School of Education:

OCITTI, J., Geography
ODAET, C. F., Educational Foundations and Management
OPOLOT, J. A., Psychology

Institute of Statistics and Applied Economics:

NTOZI, S. P. N.
TULYA-MUHIKA

HEADS OF DEPARTMENT

Faculty of Agriculture and Forestry:

Agricultural Engineering: J. S. KIBALAMA
Agricultural Extension: Dr W. DENTON (acting)
Animal Science: Prof. F. B. BAREEBA
Food Science and Technology: C. MAGALA-NYAGO (acting)
Crop Science: Prof. D. O. OSIRU
Forestry: Dr J. R. S. KABOGGOZA
Soil Science: Dr J. R. F. ANIKU
Agricultural Economics: T. HYUHA (acting)

Faculty of Arts:

Geography: Dr H. SSENGENDO (acting)
History: Prof. TIBENDERANA
Music, Dance and Drama: D. I. KISENSE (acting)
Literature: A. KIYIMBA
Languages: Dr M. J. K. MURANGA
Philosophy: Rev. Prof. A. T. DALFOVO
Religious Studies: Rev. Canon KATAHWEIRE

Faculty of Commerce:

Accounting, Banking and Finance: J. KAKURU
Marketing and Management: Mr SEJAKA

Faculty of Law:

Commercial Law: JOHN KIGULA
Law and Jurisprudence: F. W. JJUUKO
Public and Comparative Law: Dr J. J. BARYA

Faculty of Medicine:

Anaesthesia: Dr W. H. BUKWIRWA (acting)
Anatomy: Dr NZARUBARA
Biochemistry: J. P. KABAYO
Medical Microbiology: (vacant)
Medicine: Dr R. D. MUGERWA
Obstetrics and Gynaecology: Prof. F. A. MPIRO
Ophthalmology: Dr A. MEDI KIWUMA
Orthopaedics: (vacant)
Paediatrics: Dr J. S. MUKASA
Pathology: Prof. J. BYARVGABA
Pharmacology and Therapeutics: Prof. W. W. ANOKBONGGO
Physiology: J. N. NAKIBONEKA
Institute of Public Health: Dr F. WABWIRE MANGENI
Psychiatry: Dr E. B. L. OVUGA
Surgery: S. KIJJAMBO
Oto-rhino-laryngology (E.N.T.): Dr TUMWEHEIRE
Radiology: M. G. KAWOOYA
Dentistry: Dr S. ECEC
Pharmacy: Dr R. ODOI-ADOME (acting)

Faculty of Science:

Biochemistry: J. P. KABAYO
Botany: H. BURUGA
Chemistry: Dr B. T. KIREMIRE
Geology: A. MUWANGA
Physics: E. M. TWESIGOMWE
Mathematics: Dr P. MANGHENI
Zoology: Dr P. KASOMA

Faculty of Social Sciences:

Economics: Dr J. ODUMBA-SENTAMU
Political Science: Prof. AKIIKI-MUJAJU
Social Work and Social Administration: Dr PENINA DUFITE (acting)
Sociology: E. K. KIRUMIRA
Women's Studies: GRACE BANTEBYA (acting)

Faculty of Technology:

Civil Engineering: Dr B. M. KIGGUNDU
Architecture: Dr B. NAWANGWE
Surveying: N. A. BATUNGI
Mechanical Engineering: J. B. TURYAGYENDA
Electrical Engineering: L. KALUUBA

Faculty of Veterinary Medicine:

Veterinary Anatomy: Dr R. T. MUWAZI (acting)
Veterinary Medicine: Asst Prof. E. KATUNGUKA
Veterinary Parasitology and Microbiology: Dr R. AKIIKI
Veterinary Pathology: Dr OJOK-LONZY
Veterinary Physiological Sciences: (vacant)
Veterinary Public Health and Preventive Medicine: Dr OPUDA-ASIBO
Veterinary Surgery and Reproduction: Dr K. KOMA

School of Education:

Curriculum, Teaching and Media: P. MUGOMA (acting)
Educational Foundations and Management: J. M. NSEREKO
Educational Psychology: VICKY OWENS
Language Education: M. BUKENYA
Science and Technical Education: P. OLANGO
Social Science and Arts Education: Mr MAZINGA-KALYEMKOLO

ATTACHED INSTITUTES AND SCHOOLS

Centre for Continuing Education: Kampala; f. 1953; reorganized into three divisions: Adult Education and Communication Studies, Community Education and Extra-Mural Studies, Distance Education; one-year post-secondary school courses; shorter courses are also arranged both at the Centre and up-country; Dir Mr NUWA SENTONGO.

East African School of Librarianship: Kampala; f. 1963 to train librarians for all parts of East Africa; 3-year course leads to degree in Library and Information Science; Dir S. A. H. ABIDI.

Institute of Environment and Natural Resources: Dir P. KASOMA (acting).

Institute of Statistics and Applied Economics: Kampala; a joint enterprise of the Government of Uganda and the United Nations Development Programme; depts of Planning and Applied Statistics, Population Studies, and Statistical Methods; 3-year degree courses; Dir G. W. KIBIRIGE.

Makerere Institute of Social Research: see under Research Institutes.

School of Fine Art: Head P. K. KWESIGA.

School of Postgraduate Studies: Head Prof. J. MUGERWA.

MBARARA UNIVERSITY OF SCIENCE AND TECHNOLOGY

POB 1410, Mbarara

Telephone: (485) 21623

Fax: (485) 20782

E-mail: must@uga.healthnet.org

Founded 1989

Language of instruction: English

Academic year: October to August

Chancellor: President of Uganda

Vice-Chancellor: Prof. F. I. B. KAYANJA

Registrar: S. B. BAZIRAKE

Librarian: L. KAMIHANDA

Library of 11,900 vols

Number of teachers: 60

Number of students: 404

DEANS

Faculty of Medicine: Prof. E. MUTAKOOHA
Faculty of Science Education: Prof. J. BARANGA

PROFESSORS

BEGUMYA, Y. R., Physiology
DOBREVA, V., Paediatrics and Child Health
EL BAZ, E., Surgery
HERPAY, G., Obstetrics and Gynaecology
KAYANJA, F. I. B., Histology
PADILLA, E., Pathology
PEPPER, L., Medicine
SING Y-DING, Community Health

ATTACHED INSTITUTE

Institute of Tropical Forest Conservation: POB 7487, Kampala; fax 245597; Dr R. MALENKY.

UGANDA MARTYRS UNIVERSITY

POB 5498, Kampala
Telephone: (481) 21894
Fax: (481) 21898
E-mail: vmu@imul.com

Founded 1993
Private Control
Academic year: October to June

Chancellor: Rt Rev. Bishop PAUL KALANDA
Vice-Chancellor: Prof. MICHEL LEJEUNE
Deputy Vice-Chancellor: Dr PETER KAUYAUDAGO
Assistant Librarian: AARON LUSWEJJE

Library of 20,000 vols
Number of teachers: 25
Number of students: 240

DEANS

Faculty of Business Administration and Management: Dr ESTHER M-HAPLETT
Institute of Ethics and Development Studies: Dr DEIRDRE CARABINE
Extra-Mural Department: Dr CECILIA NGANDA

ATTACHED RESEARCH INSTITUTE

African Research and Documentation Centre: all aspects of African cultures; Dir Dr PETER KANYANDAGO.

College

Uganda Polytechnic Kyambogo: POB 7181, Kampala; tel. 285211; fax 222643; f. 1954; formerly Uganda Technical College; 118 teachers; 1,000 students; technical education offered at High and Ordinary diploma level; Principal Dr B. MPANDEY (acting); Registrar S. MULINDWA; Chief Librarian R. E. NGANWA.

UKRAINE

Learned Societies

GENERAL

National Academy of Sciences of Ukraine: 252601 Kiev, Volodymirska 54; tel. (44) 224-51-67; fax (44) 224-32-43; f. 1918; depts of Mathematics (Academician-Sec. I. V. SKRYPNIK), Informatics (Academician-Sec. I. V. SERGIENKO), Mechanics (Academician-Sec. V. V. PYLYPENKO), Physics and Astronomy (Academician-Sec. M. S. BRODYN), Earth Sciences (Academician-Sec. V. I. STAROSTENKO), Physical and Technical Problems of Materials Science (Academician-Sec. I. K. POKHODNYA), Physical and Technical Problems of Power Engineering (Academician-Sec. A. K. SHIDLOVSKY), Chemistry (V. D. POKHODENKO), Molecular Biology, Biochemistry and Experimental and Clinical Physiology (Academician-Sec. G. KH. MATSUKA), General Biology (Academician-Sec. YU. YU. GLEBA), Economics (Academician-Sec. I. I. LUKINOV), History, Philosophy and Law (Academician-Sec. YA. D. ISAYEVYCH), Literature, Language and Art Studies (Academician-Sec. I. M. DZUBA; 195 mems, 285 corresp. mems, 95 foreign mems; attached research institutes: see Research Institutes; libraries; see Libraries and Archives; Pres. B. E. PATON; Chief Scientific Sec. A. P. SHPAK; publs in Ukrainian and Russian: *Dopovidi NAN Ukrainy* (Reports of National Academy of Sciences of Ukraine), *Ekonomika Ukrainy* (Economy of Ukraine), *Filosofska i Sotsiologichna Dumka* (Philosophy and Sociological Thought); *Arkheologiya* (Archaeology), *Bibliotechnyi Visnyk* (Library Journal), *Movoznavstvo* (Linguistics), *Narodna Tvorchist ta Etnografiya* (Folk Art and Ethnography), *Ukrainskii Botanichnyi Zhurnal* (Ukrainian Botanical Journal), *Avtomaticheskaya Svarka* (Automatic Welding), *Biopolimery i Kletka* (Biopolymers and the Cell), *Eksperimentalnaya Onkologiya* (Experimental Oncology), *Electronnoe Modelirovanie* (Electronic Modelling), *Fizika Nizkikh Temperatur* (Low-Temperature Physics), *Fizyko-khimichna Mekhanika Materialiv* (Physical and Chemical Mechanics of Materials), *Fiziologicheskii Zhurnal* (Physiological Journal), *Fiziologiya i Biokhimiya Kulturnykh Rastenii* (Physiology and Biochemistry of Cultivated Plants), *Geofizicheskyi Zhurnal* (Geophysical Journal), *Geologicheskyi Zhurnal* (Geological Journal), *Gidrobiologicheskyi Zhurnal* (Hydrobiological Journal), *Khimiya i Tekhnologiya Vody* (Water Chemistry and Engineering), *Kibernetika i Sistemnyi Analiz* (Cybernetics and Systems Analysis), *Metallofizika i Noveishie Tekhnologii* (Metal Physics and Advanced Technology), *Mikrobiologicheskyi Zhurnal* (Microbiological Journal), *Mineralogichesky Zhurnal* (Mineralogical Journal), *Morskoy Gidrofizicheskyi Zhurnal* (Marine Hydrophysical Journal), *Prikladnaya Mekhanika* (Applied Mechanics), *Problemy Prochnosti* (Problems of Strength), *Problemy Spetsyalnoi Elektrometallurgii* (Problems of Special Electrometallurgy), *Promyshlennaya Teplotekhnika* (Industrial Thermal Engineering), *Sverkhtverdye Materialy* (Superhard Materials), *Tekhnicheskaya Diagnostika i Nerazrushayushchii Kontrol* (Technical Diagnostics and Non-destructive Testing), *Tekhnicheskaya Elektrodinamika* (Technical Elektrodynamics), *Teoreticheskaya i Eksperimentalnaya Khimiya* (Theoretical and Experimental Chemistry), *Tsitologiya i Genetika* (Cytology and Genetics), *Ukrainskii Biokhimicheskii Zhurnal* (Ukrainian Biochemical Journal), *Ukrainskii Fizychnyi Zhurnal* (Ukrainian Physics Journal), *Ukrainskii Khimichnyi Zhurnal* (Ukrainian Chemical Journal), *Ukrainskii Matematychnyi Zhurnal* (Ukrainian Mathematical Journal), *Upravlyayuschie Sistemy i Mashiny* (Control Systems and Computers), *Vestnik Zoologii* (Zoological Journal), *Algologiya* (Algology), *Ekotekhnologiya i Resursosberezhenie* (Ecotechnologies and Resource Saving), *Fizika i Tekhnika Vysokikh Davleniy* (High Pressure Physics and Engineering), *Fiziologichnyi Zhurnal* (Physiological Journal), *Funktsinalnye Materialy* (Functional Materials), *Geologiya i Geokhimiya Goriuchykh Kopalyn* (Geology and Geochemistry of Mineral Fuels), *Kinematika i Fizika Nebesnykh Tel* (Kinematics and Physics of Heavenly Bodies), *Kosmichna Nauka i Tekhnologiya* (Space Science and Engineering), *Matematicheskaya Fizika, Analiz, Geometriya* (Mathematical Physics, Analysis, Geometry), *Nauka i Naukovedenie* (Science and Science History), *Neirofiziologiya* (Neurophysiology), *Problemy Energosberezheniya* (Problems of Energy Saving), *Problemy Kriobiologii* (Problems of Cryobiology), *Problemy Upravleniya i Informatiki* (Problems of Control and Informatics), *Protsessy Litiya* (Casting Processes), *Radiofizika i Astronomiya* (Radiophysics and Astronomy), *Skhidnyi Svit* (Eastern World), *Termoelektrichestvo* (Thermoelectricity), *Ukrainskii Geograficnyi Zhurnal* (Ukrainian Geographical Journal); in Ukrainian: *Kyivska Starovyna* (Kiev Antiquities), *Slovo i Chas* (Word and Time), *Ukrainskii Istorychnyi Zhurnal* (Ukrainian Historical Journal), *Pravo Ukrainy* (Ukrainian Law), *Regionalna Ekonomika* (Regional Economics), *Visnyk NAN Ukrainy* (Journal of the National Academy of Sciences of Ukraine); in Russian: *Poroshkovaya Metallurgiya* (Powder Metallurgy).

AGRICULTURE, FISHERIES AND VETERINARY SCIENCE

Ukrainian Academy of Agricultural Sciences: 252010 Kiev, Vul. Suvorova 9; tel. 290-10-85; attached research institutes: see Research Institutes.

EDUCATION

Academy of Pedagogical Sciences of Ukraine: 252601 Kiev, Tryokhsvyatytelska vul. 8; tel. (44) 226-31-80; fax (44) 228-38-34; f. 1992; 38 mems, 63 corresp. mems; Pres. Prof. MYKOLA D. YARMACHENKO; publs *Pedahohichna Hazeta* (Pedagogical Newspaper, 12 a year), *Pedahohika i Psykholohiya* (Pedagogy and Psychology, 4 a year), *Pochatkova Shkola* (Primary School, 12 a year), *Mystetstvo i Osvita* (Arts and Education, 4 a year).

MEDICINE

Academy of Medical Sciences of Ukraine: 254050 Kiev, Vul. Gertsena 12; tel. (44) 213-34-11; fax (44) 219-39-81; f. 1993; 31 mems, 44 corresp. mems, 5 foreign mems; attached research institutes: see Research Institutes; Pres. Prof. ALEKSANDR F. VOZIANOV; Chief Scientific Sec. Prof. VOLODIMYR A. MIHNOV; publ. *Journal* (4 a year).

Gerontology and Geriatrics Society: 252655 Kiev 114, Vyshgorodska vul. 67; tel. 430-40-68; fax 432-99-56; f. 1963; 200 mems; library of 75,000 vols; Chair. V. V. BEZRUKOV; Chief Learned Sec. A. A. BELY; publ. *Problems of Ageing and Longevity* (quarterly).

NATURAL SCIENCES

General

Scientific and Technical Societies—National Headquarters: 252053 Kiev, Vul. Artema 21; tel. 212-42-34.

Research Institutes

AGRICULTURE, FISHERIES AND VETERINARY SCIENCE

Central Research, Design and Technological Institute of the Mechanization and Electrification of Livestock Production: 330017 Zaporozhe, Ostrov Khortitsa; tel. 2-73-44; attached to Ukrainian Acad. of Agricultural Sciences; Dir Y. F. NOVIKOV.

Dairy and Meat Technology Institute: 252660 Kiev, M. Raskovoi 4A; tel. (44) 517-17-37; fax (44) 517-02-28; f. 1959; attached to Ukrainian Acad. of Agricultural Sciences; library of 27,000 vols; Dir G. A. ERESKO; publ. *Meat and Milk* (6 a year).

Institute for Fisheries: 252164 Kiev, Obukhivska 135; tel. (44) 452-50-86; fax (44) 452-66-85; e-mail ifr@mail.kar.net; attached to Ukrainian Acad. of Agricultural Sciences; library of 50,000 vols; Dir Dr MYKOLA GRYNZHEVSKY; publ. *Rybne Gospodarstvo* (1 a year).

Institute of Agricultural Engineering and Electrification: 255133 Kievska oblast, Vasilkovsky raion, pos. Glevakha; tel. (4498) 3-52-00; fax (44298) 3-56-79; Dir I. P. MASLO.

Institute of Crop Growing: 320027 Dnepropetrovsk, Vul. Dzerzhinskogo 14; tel. and fax (562) 45-02-36; f. 1930; attached to Ukrainian Acad. of Agricultural Sciences; maize, winter wheat, other cereals and leguminous plants; library of 110,000 vols; Dir Dr EUGENY LEBED; publ. *Bulletin* (2 a year).

Mironovka Institute of Wheat: 256816 Kievska oblast, P/o Mironovka; tel. (4474) 7-41-35; fax (4474) 7-41-60; f. 1911; attached to Ukrainian Acad. of Agricultural Sciences; library of 51,000 vols; Dir L. A. ZHIVOTKOV; publ. *Annual Collected Papers*.

National Research Institute of the Sugar Industry: 252601 Kiev, Vul. Engelsa 20; tel. 225-05-08; telex 132163; Dir P. V. POLTORAK.

National Research Institute of Viticulture and its Products: 334200 Krymska republika, Yalta, Vul. Kirova 31; tel. 32-55-91; telex 187148; Dir S. YU. DZHANEEV.

Plant Breeding and Genetics Institute: 270036 Odessa, Ovidiopolska dor. 3; tel. (482) 656187; fax (482) 657084; e-mail vsokolov@paco.net; attached to Ukrainian Acad. of Agricultural Sciences; Dir V. M. SOKOLOV; publs *Collected Scientific Papers* (2 a year), *Scientific and Technical Bulletin* (3 or 4 a year).

Poltava Research Institute of Pig Breeding: 314006 Poltava, Shvedska Mogila; tel. 2-88-98; f. 1930; library of 54,000 vols; Dir

Prof. VALENTIN P. RYBALKO; publ. *Pig Breeding* (annually).

Prokopovych, P. I., Beekeeping Institute: 252022 Kiev, Zabolotnogo 19; tel. and fax (44) 266-67-98; f. 1989; attached to Ukrainian Acad. of Agricultural Sciences; library of 4,000 vols; Dir L. I. BODNARCHUK; publs *Beekeeping* (1 a year), *Ukrainian Beekeeper, Apiary* (monthly).

Research and Design Institute for Land Use: 252151 Kiev, Narodnogo Opolcheniya 3; tel. 277-73-44; fax 277-73-33; e-mail kyiv@zempro.relc.com; f. 1961; attached to Ukrainian Acad. of Agricultural Sciences; Dir (vacant).

Research, Design and Technological Institute of Hop Growing: 267007 Zhitomir, Vul. Lenina 291; tel. 6-62-31; Dir A. A. GODOVANY.

Research Institute of Agricultural Radiology: 252205 Kiev, Selo Chabani, Mashinobudivnikiv 7; tel. 266-45-02; fax 266-71-75; attached to Ukrainian Acad. of Agricultural Sciences; Dir (vacant).

Research Institute of Agriculture: 252205 Kievska oblast, Kievo-Svyatoshinsky raion, P/o Chabani; tel. 266-23-27; fax 266-20-25; attached to Ukrainian Acad. of Agricultural Sciences; Dir (vacant).

Research Institute of Plant Protection: 252022 Kiev, Vasilkivska 33; tel. 263-11-24; attached to Ukrainian Acad. of Agricultural Sciences; Dir M. P. LESOVOI.

Research Institute of the Economics and Organization of Agriculture: 252067 Kiev, Vul. Geroev Oborony; tel. 261-48-21; attached to Ukrainian Acad. of Agricultural Sciences; Dir (vacant).

Sugar Beet Institute: Kiev 110, Klinichna vul. 25; tel. (44) 277-50-00; fax (44) 277-53-66; f. 1922; attached to Ukrainian Acad. of Agricultural Sciences; library of 28,000 vols, 30,000 periodicals; Dir M. V. ROIK; publ. *Tsukrovi buryaky* (Sugar Beet, 6 a year).

Ukrainian Research Institute of Water Management and Ecological Problems: 252010 Kiev, Inzhenerny per. 4B; tel. and fax 290-03-02; e-mail undiwep@ukrwecol.kiev.ua; f. 1974; library of 10,000 vols; Dir Prof. A. V. YATSYK.

Ukrainian Scientific Research Institute of Ecological Problems: 310166 Kharkov, Vul. Bakulina 6; tel. (572) 14-20-66; fax (572) 45-50-47; e-mail mnts@uscpw.kharkov.ua; Dir Prof. Dr ANATOLY V. GRITSENKO.

Veterinary Research Institute: 252020 Kiev, Vul. Donetska 30; tel. 272-35-63; attached to Ukrainian Acad. of Agricultural Sciences; Dir (vacant).

Zakarpatsky Institute of Agroindustrial Production: 295520 Zakarpatska oblast, Beregovo raion, Selo V. Bakhta; tel. 2-38-47; f. 1989; library of 40,000 vols; Dir V. V. SHEPA; publ. *Problems of Agroindustrial Production* (every 2 years).

ARCHITECTURE AND TOWN PLANNING

Construction Research Institute: 252180 Kiev, Krasnozvezdny pr. 51; tel. 276-52-75; telex 131380; Dir V. I. SNISARENKO.

Donetsk Research and Design Institute of Industrial Construction: 340004 Donetsk, Krasnoarmeiska vul. 19; tel. 93-18-15; telex 115142; Dir A. P. SERDYUK.

Research and Development Institute for Municipal Facilities and Services: 252035 Kiev, Vul. Uritskogo 35; tel. (44) 276-31-89; fax (44) 276-81-21; f. 1963; library of 75,000 vols; Dir GENNADY P. SHCHERBINA.

Research Institute of Automated Systems of Planning and Management in Construction: 252180 Kiev, Vul. Krivonosa 2A; tel. 276-23-53; telex 131420; Dir E. P. DUBROVA.

Research Institute of Building Construction: 252680 Kiev, Vul. Klimenko 5/2; tel. (44) 276-23-65; fax (44) 276-62-69; f. 1956; library of 30,000 vols, 72,000 patents; Dir P. I. KRIVOSHEYEV; publ. *Building Construction* (annually).

Ukrainian Zonal Scientific and Research Design Institute of Civil Engineering: 252133 Kiev, Bul. L. Ukrainka 26; tel. (44) 296-36-72; fax (44) 295-74-81; f. 1963; library of 125,000 vols; Dir VLADIMIR B. SHEVELEV.

ECONOMICS, LAW AND POLITICS

Council for the Study of the Productive Forces of the Ukraine: 252011 Kiev, Bul. T. Shevchenko 60; attached to Nat. Acad. of Sciences of Ukraine; Dir A. N. ALYMOV.

Economics Research Institute: 252601 Kiev, Bul. Druzhby 28; tel. 296-96-33.

Institute of Economics: 252011 Kiev, Vul. Panasa Mirnogo 26; tel. 290-84-44; fax 290-86-63; attached to Nat. Acad. of Sciences of Ukraine; Dir I. I. LUKINOV.

Institute of Industrial Economics: 340048 Donetsk, Universitetska vul. 77; tel. 55-85-42; attached to Nat. Acad. of Sciences of Ukraine; Dir N. G. CHUMACHENKO.

Institute of State and Law: 252601 Kiev, Vul. Geroev Revolyutsii 4; tel. 228-51-55; attached to Nat. Acad. of Sciences of Ukraine; Dir YU. S. SHEMSHUCHENKO.

Institute of the Social and Economic Problems of Foreign Countries: 252030 Kiev, Vul. Leontovicha 5; tel. 225-51-27; fax 225-22-31; attached to Nat. Acad. of Sciences of Ukraine; Dir A. N. SHLEPAKOV.

EDUCATION

Institute of Pedagogics: 252151 Kiev, Povitroflotsky pr. 53; tel. (44) 226-31-80; fax (44) 228-38-34; f. 1926; attached to Acad. of Pedagogical Sciences of Ukraine; library of 500,000 vols; Dir Prof. VASYL M. MADZIHON.

HISTORY, GEOGRAPHY AND ARCHAEOLOGY

Institute of Archaeology: 252014 Kiev, Vydubetska vul. 40; tel. 295-35-81; fax 295-43-17; attached to Nat. Acad. of Sciences of Ukraine; Dir P. P. TOLOCHKO.

Institute of Ukrainian Studies: 290026 Lviv, Kozelnytska vul. 4; tel. (322) 42-70-22; fax (322) 42-74-42; e-mail svitlo@litech.lviv.ua; f. 1951; attached to Nat. Acad. of Sciences of Ukraine; archaeology, history, philology; library of 10,000 vols; Dir IA. D. ISAIEVYCH; publs *Ukraina: kulturna, spadshchyna, natsionalna svidomist, derzhavnist* (1 a year), *Shashkevychiana* (1 a year), *Ukrainian Studies Abstracts* (1 a year).

Ukrainian Institute of History: 252001 Kiev, Vul. Grushevskogo 4; tel. and fax (44) 229-63-62; attached to Nat. Acad. of Sciences of Ukraine; Dir V. A. SMOLY.

LANGUAGE AND LITERATURE

Potebnya, A. A., Institute of Linguistics: 252601 Kiev, Vul. Kirova 4; tel. 229-02-92; attached to Nat. Acad. of Sciences of Ukraine; Dir V. M. RUSANOVSKII.

Shevchenko, T. G., Institute of Literature: 252601 Kiev, Vul. Kirova 4; tel. 229-10-84; fax 228-52-81; attached to Nat. Acad. of Sciences of Ukraine; Dir I. A. DZEVERIN.

MEDICINE

Donetsk Institute of Industrial Physiology: Donetsk, 2-a linia 50.

Donetsk Scientific Research Institute of Traumatology and Orthopaedics: Donetsk, Vul. Artema 106.

Filatov Institute for Eye Diseases and Tissue Therapy: 270061 Odessa, Vul. Frantsi 49–51; tel. (482) 22-20-35; fax (482) 68-48-51; f. 1936; library of 81,000 vols; Dir Prof. IVAN M. LOGAI; publ. *Ophthalmological Journal* (8 a year).

Institute of Clinical and Experimental Surgery: 252180 Kiev, Vul. Geroev Sevastopolya 30; tel. 488-13-74; fax 488-19-09; f. 1972; abdominal and vascular surgery; library of 25,000 vols; Dir VALERY SAYENKO; publ. *Clinical Surgery* (monthly).

Institute of Clinical Radiology: 252075 Kiev, Pushcha-Voditsa, Vul. Gamarnikova 42; attached to Ukrainian Acad. of Medical Sciences; Dir V. G. BEBESHKO.

Institute of Epidemiology and the Prevention of Radiation Injury: 252075 Kiev, Pushcha-Voditsa, Vul. Gamarnikova 42; attached to Ukrainian Acad. of Medical Sciences; Dir V. A. BUZUNOV.

Institute of Experimental Radiology: 252050 Kiev, Vul. Melnikova 53; attached to Ukrainian Acad. of Medical Sciences; Dir M. I. RUDNEV.

Institute of Gerontology: 252655 Kiev, Vishgorodska vul. 67; tel. 430-40-68; attached to Ukrainian Acad. of Medical Sciences; Dir V. V. BEZRUKOV.

Institute of Medical Radiology: 310024 Kharkov, Pushkinska 82; tel. (572) 43-15-42; fax (572) 43-11-25; f. 1920; library of 70,000 vols; Dir Prof. NIKOLAI I. PILIPENKO; publ. *Ukrainian Journal of Radiology* (quarterly).

Institute of Microbiology and Immunology: 310057 Kharkov, Pushkinska 14; tel. (572) 12-73-47; fax (572) 22-52-33; f. 1887; library of 54,000 vols; Dir Prof. YU. L. VOLYANSKY; publ. *Proceedings* (annually).

Institute of Occupational Health: 252033 Kiev, Vul. Saksaganskogo 75; tel. 220-80-30; fax 220-66-77; f. 1928; library of 42,000 vols; Dir Prof. Y. I. KUNDIEV; publ. *Gigiyena Truda* (annually).

Institute of the Problems of Cryobiology and Cryomedicine: 310015 Kharkov, Pereyaslovska vul. 23; tel. 72-41-43; fax 72-00-84; e-mail cryo@online.kharkov.ua; f. 1972; attached to Nat. Acad. of Sciences of Ukraine; library of 53,000 items; Dir V. I. GRISHCHENKO; publ. *Problems of Cryobiology* (in Russian and English, 4 a year).

Institute of Urology and Nephrology: 252053 Kiev, Yu. Kotsyubinskoi 9A; tel. 216-67-31; fax 244-68-62; f. 1965; attached to Ukrainian Acad. of Medical Sciences; library of 45,690 vols; Dir A. F. VOZIANOV.

Kavetsky, R. E., Institute of Experimental Pathology, Oncology and Radiobiology: 252022 Kiev, Vasilkovska vul. 45; tel. 266-75-98; fax 267-16-56; e-mail iepor@onconet.kiev.ua; f. 1960; attached to Nat. Acad. of Sciences of Ukraine; library of 20,000 vols, 238 periodicals; Dir Prof. V. F. CHEKHUN; publ. *Experimental Oncology* (4 a year).

Kharkiv M. I. Sitenko Research Institute of Orthopaedics and Traumatology: Kharkiv 24, Pushkinska vul. 80; tel. (57) 43-02-86; fax (57) 43-11-05; e-mail hniiot@kharkov.com; f. 1907; library of 40,500 vols; Dir Prof. M. A. KORZH; publ. *Orthopaedics, Traumatology and Prosthetics* (quarterly).

Kharkiv Psycho-Neurological Research Institute: Kharkiv; Dir O. R. STEPANENKO.

Kharkiv Research Institute of Endocrinology and Hormone Chemistry: 310002 Kharkiv, Vul. Artema 10; tel. and fax 47-51-21; f. 1919; library of 44,800 vols; Dir V. V. NATAROV.

Kharkiv Research Institute of General and Emergency Surgery: Kharkiv, Chernyshevska vul. 7/9.

Kharkiv Research Institute of Industrial Hygiene and Occupational Diseases: Kharkiv 22, Vul. Trinklera 6; f. 1923; library of 36,547 vols; publ. *Bulletin* (every 2 years).

Kharkiv Tuberculosis Research Institute: Kharkiv, Chernyshevska vul. 83.

Kiev Haematology and Blood Transfusion Research Institute: 252060 Kiev, Vul. M. Berlinskogo 12; tel. 440-27-44.

Kiev N. D. Strazhesko Research Institute of Cardiology: 252151 Kiev, Vul. Narodnogo Opolchenia 5; tel. 277-66-22; telex 131498; fax 228-72-72; f. 1936; 650 mems; library of 65,000 vols; Dir Prof. V. A. BOBROV.

Kiev Research Institute of Oncology: Kiev, Vul. Lomonosova 33/43; tel. 266-75-67; f. 1920; library of 27,000 vols; Dir V. L. GANUL.

Kiev Research Institute of Otolaryngology: 252057 Kiev, Zoologichna 3; tel. 213-22-02; fax 213-73-68; f. 1960; library of 33,000 vols; publ. *Journal of Ear, Nose and Throat Diseases* (6 a year).

L. V. Gromashevsky Institute of Epidemiology and Infectious Diseases: 252601 Kiev, Vul. S. Razina 4; tel. 277-37-11; Dir A. F. FROLOV.

Lviv Institute of Haematology and Blood Transfusion: 290044 Lviv, Vul. Pushkina 45, tel. 35-22-76; telex 234141; f. 1945; library of 12,000 vols, 21,000 periodicals; Dir Prof. B. KACHOROVSKY.

Lviv Scientific Research Institute of Hereditary Pathology: 290000 Lviv, Vul. Lysenko 31A; tel. (322) 76-54-99; fax (322) 75-38-44; f. 1940; library of 28,000 vols; Dir O. Z. HNATEIKO; publ. *Medychna Genetyka* (every 2 years, in Ukrainian with Russian and English abstracts).

Lviv State Tuberculosis Research Institute: Lviv, Vul. Engelsa 22.

Medved, L.I., Institute of Ecohygiene and Toxicology: 252022 Kiev, Vul. Heroiv Oborony 6; tel. and fax (44) 261-74-66; e-mail postmaster@him.kiev.ua; f. 1964; library of 34,000 vols; publs *Ukrainian Journal of Health Protection* (4 a year), *Ukrainian Medical and Ecological Journal* (4 a year).

National Research Centre of Radiation Medicine: 254050 Kiev, Vul. Melnikova 53; tel. (44) 213-06-37; fax (44) 213-72-02; e-mail sam@rcrm.freenet.viaduk.net; f. 1986; attached to Ukrainian Acad. of Medical Sciences; library of 30,000 vols; Dir Prof. A. E. ROMANENKO.

Odessa Glavche Research Institute of Dermatology and Venereal Diseases: Odessa, Krasna slobodka, Poleva vul. 3.

Odessa Research Institute of Virology and Epidemiology: 270031 Odessa, Yubileina vul. 6; tel. and fax (482) 33-03-38; f. 1886; library of 20,000 vols; Dir G. S. SKRIPCHENKO.

Odessa Tuberculosis Research Institute: Odessa, Vul. Belinskogo 11.

Research Institute of Cardiovascular Surgery: 252110 Kiev, Uzviz Protasiv Yar 11; tel. 277-43-22.

Research Institute of Neurology and Psychiatry: 252034 Kiev, Lisenka 1; tel. 229-36-30; fax 229-36-30.

Research Institute of Paediatrics, Obstetrics and Gynaecology: 252052 Kiev, Manuilska vul. 8; tel. 213-80-67.

Research Institute of Pharmacology and Toxicology: 252057 Kiev, E. Pote 14; tel. (44) 446-42-56; fax (44) 446-41-08; f. 1934; library of 80,000 vols; Dirs A. V. STEFANOV, V. S. DANILENKO.

Research Institute of Psychology: 252037 Kiev, Pankivska 2; tel. 224-90-68.

Romodanov, A., Institute of Neurosurgery: 254050 Kiev, Vul. Manuilskogo 32; tel. and fax (44) 213-95-73; f. 1950; library of 70,000 vols; Dir Prof. Y. ZOZULIA.

Sechenov, I. M., Crimean Scientific Research Institute of Physical Methods of Treatment and Medical Climatology: 334203 Yalta, Polikurovska vul. 25; tel. 32-75-91; f. 1914; non-medical treatment and prophylaxis of lung diseases and diseases of the cardiovascular and nervous systems; Dir Prof. S. S. SOLDATCHENKO.

State Scientific Centre of Drugs: Kharkov 310085, Astronomicheska vul. 33; tel. 44-10-33; fax 44-11-18; f. 1920; production and development of finished drugs and technologies for preparation of phytochemicals; library of 28,000 vols; Dir Prof. V. P. GEORGIEVSKY; publ. *Pharmacom* (in Russian and Ukrainian, monthly).

Tuberculosis and Pulmonology Research Institute: 252000 Kiev, GSP-650, Uzviz Protasiv Yar 7; tel. (44) 277-04-02; fax (44) 277-21-18; e-mail admin@pulmo.freenet.kiev.ua; f. 1922; Dir YURI I. FESCHENKO; publ. *Ukrainian Journal of Pulmonology* (4 a year).

Ukrainian Institute of Mother and Child Care: Kiev, Vozdukhoflotske shosse 24.

Ukrainian Institute of Public Health: 252054 Kiev, Vul. O. Gonchara 65; tel. (44) 216-81-51; fax (44) 216-71-00; e-mail uiph@health.freenet.vladuk.net; f. 1997; attached to Min. of Health; Dir Prof. V. M. PONOMARENKO.

Ukrainian Research Institute of Dermatology and Venereology: 310057 Kharkov, Chernyshevska vul. 7/9; tel. (572) 43-17-83; fax (572) 47-65-82; f. 1924; library of 40,000 vols; Dir Prof. IVAN I. MAVROV.

Ukrainian Research Institute of Endocrinology and Metabolism: 254114 Kiev, Vyshgorodska vul. 69; tel. (44) 430-36-94; fax (44) 430-37-18; f. 1965; library of 18,510 vols, 38,900 periodicals; Dir Prof. NIKOLAI D. TRONKO; publ. *Endokrinologia* (annually).

Ukrainian Research Institute of Traumatology and Orthopaedics: 252054 Kiev, Vul. Vorovskogo 27; tel. 216-42-49; fax 216-44-62; f. 1919; library of 57,000 vols; Dir G. V. GAIKO; publ. *Ortopediya, travmatologiya i protezirovanie* (annually).

Ukrainian Scientific Centre of Hygiene: 253660 Kiev 94, Vul. Popudrenko 50; tel. (44) 559-73-73; fax (44) 559-90-90; f. 1931; incl. Institute of General and Communal Hygiene, Institute of Nutrition Hygiene, Institute of Medical Genetics; library of 102,213 vols; Dir Dr A. M. SERDIUK.

NATURAL SCIENCES

Biological Sciences

Bogomolets, A. A., Institute of Physiology: 252601 Kiev, Vul. Bogomoltsa 4; tel. 293-20-13; fax 293-64-58; attached to Nat. Acad. of Sciences of Ukraine; Dir P. G. KOSTYUK.

Institute of Cellular Biology and Genetic Engineering: 252143 Kiev, Vul. Zabolotnogo 148; tel. 266-96-14; attached to Nat. Acad. of Sciences of Ukraine; Dir YU. YU. GLEBA.

Institute of Hydrobiology: 252216 Kiev, Pr. Geroev Stalingrada 12; tel. 419-39-81; attached to Nat. Acad. of Sciences of Ukraine; Dir V. D. ROMANENKO.

Institute of Molecular Biology and Genetics: 252143 Kiev, Vul. Zabolotnogo 150; tel. (44) 266-11-69; fax (44) 266-07-59; e-mail matsuka@imbig.kiev.ua; f. 1973; attached to Nat. Acad. of Sciences of Ukraine; library of 85,000 vols; Dir G. KH. MATSUKA; publ. *Biopolymers and Cells* (6 a year).

Institute of Plant Physiology and Genetics: 252627 Kiev, Vasilkovska vul. 31/17; tel. 263-51-60; attached to Nat. Acad. of Sciences of Ukraine; Dir V. V. MORGUN.

Institute of Sorption and Problems of Endoecology: 252164 Kiev, Pr. Generala Naumova 13; tel. (44) 452-93-36; fax (44) 293-06-39; f. 1991; attached to Nat. Acad. of Sciences of Ukraine; Dir V. V. STRELKO.

Kholodny, M. G., Institute of Botany: 252601 Kiev, Tereshchenkivska vul. 2; tel. (44) 224-40-41; fax 224-10-64; e-mail inst%botan.kiev.ua@relay.ua.net; f. 1937; attached to Nat. Acad. of Sciences of Ukraine; library of 106,000 vols; Dir K. M. SYTNIK.

Kovalevsky, A. O., Institute of Biology of Southern Seas: 335000 Sevastopol, Pr. Nakhimova 2; tel. 52-41-10; telex 187124; attached to Nat. Acad. of Sciences of Ukraine; Dir S. M. KONOVALOV.

Palladin, O. V., Institute of Biochemistry: 252650 Kiev, Vul. Leontovicha 9; tel. 224-59-74; fax 224-50-36; attached to Nat. Acad. of Sciences of Ukraine; Dir S. V. KOMISSARENKO.

Shmalgauzen, I. I., Institute of Zoology: 252030 Kiev, Vul. Lenina 15; tel. 225-10-70; attached to Nat. Acad. of Sciences of Ukraine; Dir I. A. AKIMOV.

Zabolotny Institute of Microbiology and Virology: 252143 Kiev, Vul. Akademika Zabolotnogo 154; tel. (44) 266-11-79; fax (44) 266-23-79; e-mail smirnov@imv.kiev.ua; f. 1928; attached to Nat. Acad. of Sciences of Ukraine; library of 128,000 vols; Dir V. V. SMIRNOV; publ. *Mikrobiologichny Zhurnal* (6 a year).

Mathematical Sciences

Institute of Mathematics: 252601 Kiev, Vul. Repina 3; tel. 224-53-16; attached to Nat. Acad. of Sciences of Ukraine; Dir A. M. SAMOILENKO.

Physical Sciences

Bogatsky, A. V., Physico-Chemical Institute: 270080 Odessa, Lustdorfskaya doroga 86; tel. 66-51-55; e-mail physchem@paco.odessa.ua; attached to Nat. Acad. of Sciences of Ukraine; Dir S. A. ANDRONATI.

Bogolyubov Institute of Theoretical Physics: 252143 Kiev, Metrologichna vul. 14B; tel. 266-53-62; fax 266-59-98; e-mail itp@gluk.apc.org; f. 1966; attached to Nat. Acad. of Sciences of Ukraine; Dir A. G. SITENKO; publ. *Ukrainian Journal of Physics* (monthly).

Coal Research Institute: Donetsk.

Dumansky, V. A., Institute of Colloid Chemistry and Water Chemistry: 252680 Kiev 142, Vernadsky pr. 42; tel. (44) 444-01-96; fax (44) 452-02-76; e-mail honch@iccwc.kiev.ua; f. 1968; attached to Nat. Acad. of Sciences of Ukraine; Dir V. V. GONCHARUK; publ. *Khimiya i Tekhnologiya Vody* (Water Chemistry and Technology, 6 a year).

Gas Institute: 252113 Kiev, Degtiarivksa vul. 39; tel. (44) 446-44-71; fax (44) 446-88-30; f. 1949; attached to Nat. Acad. of Sciences of Ukraine; library of 110,000 vols; Dir Prof. I. N. KARP; publ. *Eco-Technologies and Resource Saving*† (6 a year).

International Physics Centre: 252143 Kiev, Metrologicheska vul. 14B; e-mail icp@gluk.apc.org; attached to Nat. Acad. of Sciences of Ukraine; Dir A. G. SITENKO.

Institute of Bio-organic Chemistry and Petrochemistry: 253660 Kiev, Vul. Murmanska; tel. (44) 558-53-88; fax (44) 543-51-52; f. 1987; attached to Nat. Acad. of Sciences of Ukraine; Dir Prof. V. P. KUKHAR.

Institute of General and Inorganic Chemistry: 252680 Kiev, Pr. Akademika Palladina 32/34; tel. 444-34-61; telex 131750; fax 444-30-70; attached to Nat. Acad. of Sciences of Ukraine; Dir S. V. VOLKOV.

Institute of Geochemistry, Mineralogy and Ore Formation: 252680 Kiev 142, Pr. Akademika Palladina 34; tel. (44) 444-15-70; fax (44) 444-12-70; f. 1969; attached to Nat. Acad. of Sciences of Ukraine; library of 30,000 vols, 35 periodicals; Dir N. P. SHCHERBAK; publ. *Mineralogichesky Zhurnal* (6 a year).

Institute of Geology: 252650 Kiev, Vul. Chkalova 55B; tel. 216-94-46; telex 131444; attached to Nat. Acad. of Sciences of Ukraine; Dir E. F. SHNYUKOV.

Institute of Geology and Geochemistry of Mineral Fuels: 290047 Lviv, Nauchna vul. 3A; tel. 63-15-03; attached to Nat. Acad. of Sciences of Ukraine; Dir V. E. ZABIGAILO.

Institute of Geophysics: 252680 Kiev, Pr. Akademika Palladina 32; tel. (44) 444-01-12; fax (44) 450-25-20; attached to Nat. Acad. of Sciences of Ukraine; Dir V. I. STAROSTENKO.

Institute of Nuclear Research: 252028 Kiev, Pr. Nauki 47; tel. 265-23-49; fax 265-44-63; attached to Nat. Acad. of Sciences of Ukraine; Dir V. I. SUGAKOV.

Institute of Organic Chemistry: 252094 Kiev, Murmanska vul. 5; tel. 552-71-50; telex 132687; fax 552-83-08; Dir V. V. MALOVIK.

Institute of Physics: 252650 Kiev, Pr. Nauki 46; tel. 265-12-20; attached to Nat. Acad. of Sciences of Ukraine; Dir M. S. BRODIN.

Institute of Physics of Metals: 252680 Kiev, Pr. Vernadskogo 36; tel. 444-10-05; fax 444-34-20; attached to Nat. Acad. of Sciences of Ukraine; Dir V. G. BARYAKHTAR.

Institute of Semiconductor Physics: 252650 Kiev, Pr. Nauki 45; tel. 265-40-20; fax 265-83-42; attached to Nat. Acad. of Sciences of Ukraine; Dir O. V. SNITKO.

Institute of Single Crystals: 310141 Kharkov, Pr. Lenina 60; tel. and fax 232-02-73; attached to Nat. Acad. of Sciences of Ukraine; Dir V. P. SEMINOZHENKO.

Institute of Surface Chemistry: 252022 Kiev, Pr. Nauki 31; tel. (44) 265-41-60; fax (44) 264-04-46; e-mail Ogenko%silar.kiev.ua@relay.ua.net; f. 1986; attached to Nat. Acad. of Sciences of Ukraine; library of 20,000 vols; Dir Prof. V. M. OGENKO; publ. *Chemistry, Physics and Surface Technology*.

Institute of the Chemistry of Higher Molecular Compounds: 252660 Kiev, Darnitsa, Kharkovske shosse 48; tel. 559-13-94; telex 132223; fax 552-40-64; attached to Nat. Acad. of Sciences of Ukraine; Dir E. V. LEBEDEV.

Institute of the Ionosphere: 310002 Kharkov, Chervonopraporna vul. 16; tel. (572) 47-55-83; fax (572) 45-11-23; e-mail iion@kpi.kharkov.ua; f. 1991; attached to Nat. Acad. of Sciences of Ukraine; Dir Prof. VITALY TARAN.

Litvinenko, L. M., Institute of Physical-Organic Chemistry and Coal Chemistry: 340114 Donetsk, Vul. R. Lyuksemburga 70; tel. and fax (622) 55-85-24; e-mail postmast@infou.donesk.ua; f. 1975; attached to Nat. Acad. of Sciences of Ukraine; library of 34,000 vols, 44 periodicals; Dir ANATOLY F. POPOV.

Main Astronomical Observatory: 252127 Kiev, Goloseevo; tel. 266-31-30; attached to Nat. Acad. of Sciences of Ukraine; Dir YA. S. YATSKIV.

Marine Hydrophysical Institute: 335005 Sevastopol, Vul. Lenina 28; tel. (69) 52-04-52; attached to Nat. Acad. of Sciences of Ukraine; Dir VALERY N. EREMEEV.

Pisarzhevsky, L. V., Institute of Physical Chemistry: 252039 Kiev, Pr. Nauki 31; tel. (44) 265-11-90; fax (44) 265-62-16; e-mail ipcukr@sovamsu.sovusa.com; f. 1927; attached to Nat. Acad. of Sciences of Ukraine; Dir Prof. V. D. POKHODENKO; publ. *Theoretical and Experimental Chemistry* (6 a year).

Poltava Gravimetric Observatory: 314029 Poltava, Vul. Myasoedova 27/29; tel. 7-20-39; fax 7-49-03; e-mail geo@geo.kot.poltava.ua; f. 1926; attached to Nat. Acad. of Sciences of Ukraine; library of 25,000 vols; Dir V. G. BULATSEN.

Radio-Astronomy Institute: 310002 Kharkov, Krasnoznamenna vul. 4; tel. 245-10-09; fax 232-23-70; attached to Nat. Acad. of Sciences of Ukraine; Dir L. N. LITVINENKO.

Research and Design Institute of Basic Chemistry: 310002 Kharkov, Mironositska vul. 25; tel. (572) 43-07-23; fax (572) 43-60-60; f. 1923; library of 185,000 vols; Dir V. I. MOLCHANOV.

Ukrainian Natural Gas Research Institute: 310125 Kharkov, Krasnoshkilna nab. 20; tel. (572) 21-29-14; fax (572) 21-53-28; f. 1959; library of 65,000 vols; Dir ILYA M. FYK.

Ukrainian State Geological Research Institute: 290601 Lviv, Pl. Mitskevicha 8; tel. (322) 72-20-90; fax (322) 72-56-14; Dir MYROSLAV M. IVANYUTA.

PHILOSOPHY AND PSYCHOLOGY

Institute of Philosophy: 252001 Kiev, Vul. Trekhsviatytelska 4; tel. 228-06-05; attached to Nat. Acad. of Sciences of Ukraine; Dir V. I. SHINKARUK.

RELIGION, SOCIOLOGY AND ANTHROPOLOGY

Institute of Sociology: 252053 Kiev, Observatorna 11/1; tel. 212-11-35; attached to Nat. Acad. of Sciences of Ukraine; Dir (vacant).

Rylsky, M. F., Institute of Art, Folklore and Ethnography: 252601 Kiev, Vul. Kirova 4; tel. 228-34-54; attached to Nat. Acad. of Sciences of Ukraine; Dir A. G. KOSTYUK.

TECHNOLOGY

Donetsk Physical-Engineering Institute: 340114 Donetsk, Vul. R. Lyuksemburga 72; tel. (622) 55-14-33; fax (622) 55-01-27; e-mail var@hpress.dipt.donetsk.ua; f. 1965; attached to Nat. Acad. of Sciences of Ukraine; solid-state physics; library of 10,000 vols; Dir V. N. VARYUKHIN.

East Ukraine Institute of Engineering Technical Research: 310731 Kharkov, Pr. Lenina 38; tel. 32-23-74; Dir V. G. TABOTA.

Electrical Engineering Research Institute: 310816 Kharkov, Moskovsky pr. 199; tel. (572) 26-00-71; fax (572) 26-01-74; Dir M. A. DOLGIN.

Frantsevich Institute of Problems of Materials Science: 252142 Kiev, Vul. Krzhizhanovskogo 3; tel. 444-01-02; telex 131257; fax 444-20-78; attached to Nat. Acad. of Sciences of Ukraine; Dir V. I. TREFILOV.

Glushkov, V. M., Institute of Cybernetics: 252207 Kiev, Pr. Glushkova 20; tel. 266-60-08; telex 131272; fax 226-64-07; attached to Nat. Acad. of Sciences of Ukraine; Dir V. S. MIKHALEVICH.

Institute of Applied Mathematics and Mechanics: 340114 Donetsk, Vul. R. Lyuksemburga 74; tel. (622) 55-23-94; fax (622) 55-22-65; f. 1965; attached to Nat. Acad. of Sciences of Ukraine; Dir I. V. SKRYPNIK; publs *Mekhanica Tverdogo Tela, Nelineinye Granichnye Zadachi, Teoriya Sluchainykh Protsessov, Teoriya i Modelirovanie Upravliauschikh System*.

Institute of Applied Problems of Mechanics and Mathematics: 290047 Lviv, Nauchna vul. 3B; tel. 35-25-97; attached to Nat. Acad. of Sciences of Ukraine; Dir YA. S. PIDSTRYGACH.

Institute of Automation: 252655 Kiev 107, Hagirna 22; tel. 213-01-61; telex 131401; Dir N. A. RYUMSHIN.

Institute of Electrical Dynamics: 252057 Kiev, Pr. Pobedy 56; tel. and fax 446-01-51; telex 132310; attached to Nat. Acad. of Sciences of Ukraine; Dir. A. K. SHIDLOVSKII.

Institute of Energy Saving Problems: 252070 Kiev, Pokrovska vul. 11; tel. 417-01-42; telex 131392; fax 417-07-37; attached to Nat. Acad. of Sciences of Ukraine; Dir V. E. TONKAL.

Institute of Engineering Mechanics: 320005 Dnepropetrovsk, Vul. Leshko-Popelya 9; tel. 45-12-38; attached to Nat. Acad. of Sciences of Ukraine; Dir V. V. PILIPENKO.

Institute of Engineering Thermal Physics: 252057 Kiev, Vul. Zhelyabova 2A; tel. 446-62-82; telex 131283; fax 446-60-91; attached to Nat. Acad. of Sciences of Ukraine; Dir A. A. DOLINSKII.

Institute of Geotechnical Mechanics: 320095 Dnepropetrovsk, Simferopolska vul. 2A; tel. 46-01-51; fax 46-24-26; e-mail nanu@igtm.dp.ua; f. 1962; attached to Nat. Acad. of Sciences of Ukraine; library of 109,000 vols; Dir A. F. BULAT.

Institute of Hydromechanics: 252057 Kiev, Vul. Zhelyabova 8/4; tel. 446-43-13; fax 446-42-29; attached to Nat. Acad. of Sciences of Ukraine; Dir V. T. GRINCHENKO.

Institute of Mining and the Chemical Industry: 290026 Lviv, Striiska vul. 98; tel. (322) 97-13-77; fax (322) 34-40-61; Chair. I. I. ZOZULIA.

Institute of Modelling Problems in Energetics: 252680 Kiev, Vul. Generala Naumova 15; tel. 444-10-63; fax 444-05-86; attached to Nat. Acad. of Sciences of Ukraine; Dir V. F. EVDOKIMOV.

Institute of Problems of Engineering: 310046 Kharkov, Vul. Pozharskogo 2/10; tel. 94-55-14; telex 125579; attached to Nat. Acad. of Sciences of Ukraine; Dir V. N. PODGORNYI.

Institute of Pulse Research and Engineering: 327018 Nikolaev, Oktyabrsky pr. 43A; tel. (512) 22-41-13; fax (512) 22-61-40; e-mail ipre@iipt.aip.mk.ua; f. 1962; attached to Nat. Acad. of Sciences of Ukraine; library of 131,000 vols; Dir A. I. VOVCHENKO; publ. *Theory, Experiment, Practice of Electrical Discharge Technologies* (in Russian, 1 a year).

Institute of Radiophysics and Electronics: 310085 Kharkov, Vul. Akademika Proskury 12; tel. (572) 44-11-29; fax (572) 44-11-05; e-mail ire@ire.kharkov.ua; f. 1955; attached to Nat. Acad. of Sciences of Ukraine; Dir VLADIMIR M. YAKOVENKO.

Institute of Registration of Information: 252113 Kiev, Vul. Shpaka 2; tel. 446-33-18; fax 446-14-91; f. 1987; attached to Nat. Acad. of Sciences of Ukraine; telecommunications; Dir V. V. PETROV.

Institute of Strength Problems: 252014 Kiev, Timiryazevska vul. 2; tel. 295-16-87; fax 296-16-84; attached to Nat. Acad. of Sciences of Ukraine; Dir V. T. TROSHCHENKO.

Institute of Supraresistant Materials: 252153 Kiev, Avtozavodska vul. 2; tel. 435-13-21; telex 131372; fax 435-32-91; attached to Nat. Acad. of Sciences of Ukraine; Dir N. V. NOVIKOV.

Iron and Steel Institute: 320050 Dnepropetrovsk, Pl. Akademika Starodubova 1; tel.

(562) 76-53-15; telex 143513; fax (562) 76-59-24; attached to Nat. Acad. of Sciences of Ukraine; Dir VITALY L. PILUSHENKO.

National Research and Design Institute of Recycled Non-ferrous Metals: 340103 Donetsk, Pr. Lagutenko 14; tel. 92-54-43; Dir V. A. ZOLOTUKHIN.

National Research and Design Institute of the Technology of Electrical Engineering: 310831 Kharkov, GSP, Vul. Ak. Pavlova 82; tel. 26-49-51; Dir V. F. SAMARCHANTS.

National Research, Design and Technological Institute of Low Voltage Equipment: 310037 Kharkov, Moskovsky pr. 138A; tel. 92-31-00; Dir YU. S. BRUS.

National Research Institute of Reagents and Chemically Pure Materials for Electronic Technology: 340087 Donetsk, Vul. Bakinskikh Komissarov 17A; tel. 53-36-57.

National Research Institute of Refractory Metals and Hard Alloys: 317000 Kirovogradska oblast, Svetlovodsk, Observatorna vul. 12; tel. 2-85-80.

National Research Institute of Safety in the Chemical Industry: Luganska oblast, Severodonetsk.

NIIconditioner JSC: 310818 Kharkov, Moskovsky pr. 257; tel. (572) 92-00-01; fax (572) 92-33-15; f. 1967; air-conditioning systems; Dir V. B. GORELIK; publ. *Air-Conditioning Equipment* (annually).

Oil Research and Design Institute: 252054 Kiev, Kudryavsky spusk 7; tel. (44) 417-12-93; fax (44) 212-53-93; e-mail root@ukrngi.freenet.kiev.ua; f. 1966; library of 30,000 vols, 40 periodicals; Pres. V. K. MELNICHUK.

Ore-mining Research Institute: 324086 Krivoi Rog, Pr. Gagarina 57; tel. 71-72-52; telex 143474; fax 74-28-48; f. 1933; library of 100,000 vols; Dir B. I. RIMARTSCHUK; publs *Collected Scientific Works*, *The Mining Industry of Ferrous Metal Ores* (annually).

Paton, E. O., Institute of Electrical Welding: 252650 Kiev, Vul. Bozhenko 11; tel. 227-31-83; telex 131139; attached to Nat. Acad. of Sciences of Ukraine; Dir B. E. PATON.

Physical-Engineering Institute: 310108 Kharkov, Akademicheska vul. 1; tel. 235-19-93; telex 115175; fax 235-17-38; attached to Nat. Acad. of Sciences of Ukraine; Dir V. F. ZELENSKII.

Physical-Mechanical Institute: 290601 Lviv, Nauchna vul. 5; tel. 63-70-49; attached to Nat. Acad. of Sciences of Ukraine; Dir V. V. PANASYUK.

Physico-Technological Institute of Metals and Alloys: 252680 Kiev, Pr. Vernadskogo 34/1; tel. 444-35-15; fax 444-12-10; e-mail metal@ptima.kiev.ua; f. 1958; attached to Nat. Acad. of Sciences of Ukraine; library of 200,000 vols; Dir Prof. V. L. NAYDEK; publs *Protsessy Litiya* (Casting Processes, in Russian, 4 a year), *Metal and Casting of Ukraine* (in Russian, monthly), *Metal Science and Treatment of Metals* (in Ukrainian, 4 a year).

Radioengineering Research Institute: 290060 Lviv, Nauchna vul. 7; tel. 64-59-44; telex 234213; Dir R.-A. B. OBUKHANICH.

Research and Design Institute for the Enrichment and Agglomeration of Ferrous Metal Ores: 324039 Krivoi Rog, Televizionna vul. 3; tel. (564) 71-61-36; fax (564) 71-48-42; f. 1956; library of 65,000 vols; Dir N. K. VOROBEV; publs *Mining Journal, Mineral Processing Journal.*

Research and Design Institute of Chemical Engineering: 310126 Kharkov, Vul. Marshala Koneva 21; tel. 22-84-75; Dir O. T. STOROZHENKO.

Research and Design Institute of Electronics and Computer Technology: 290005 Lviv, Vul. Knjaza Romana 5; tel. (322) 74-21-79; fax (322) 72-88-47; f. 1945; Dir VICTOR F. TKACHENKO.

Research and Design Institute of the Metallurgical Industry: 310059 Kharkov, Pr. Lenina 9; tel. 40-90-25; telex 131487; Dir E. V. DYACHENKO.

Research and Development Institute of the Impuls Joint Stock Co.: 349940 Luganska oblast, Severodonetsk, Pl. Pobedy 2; tel. (6452) 2-77-15; fax (6452) 4-13-23; f. 1954; development and manufacture of computers for industrial automation; library of 120,000 books and periodicals; Dir GRIGORY Y. PIVOVAROV.

Research and Development Institute of the Merchant Marine: 270026 Odessa, Lanzheronovska vul. 15; tel. (482) 25-20-35; fax (482) 25-04-57; f. 1947; Dir Dr SERGEY NUNUPAROV.

Research, Design and Technological Institute of Robot Engineering: 252150 Kiev, Predslavinska vul. 28; tel. 268-71-88; telex 132559; Dir M. G. PRIMACHENKO.

Research, Experimental and Design Institute of Electrical Consumer Appliances: Kiev, Vul. Parkhomenko 36.

Research Institute for the Automation of Management and Production: 310034 Kharkov, Vul. Sverdlova 188A; tel. 72-01-32; Dir V. A. PILIPENKO.

Research Institute of Large-Size Tyres: 320600 Dnepropetrovsk, Vul. Krotova 16; tel. 96-05-05; telex 127497; fax 96-70-44; Dir E. S. SKORNYAKOV.

Research Institute of Machine Tools and Tooling: 270001 Odessa, Vul. R. Lyuksemburga 30, tel. 22-61-09; Dir N. I. RESHETNEV.

Research Institute of Metals: 310002 Kharkov, Vul. Darvina 20; tel. 40-31-39; telex 125071; fax 47-20-61; f. 1928; library of 130,000 vols; Dir D. K. NESTEROV; publs *Theory and Technology of Shaped Rolled Steel and Formed Section Production, Rail Production* (both annually).

Research Institute of Non-ferrous Metallurgy: 340017 Donetsk, Bul. Shevchenko 26; tel. 95-34-07; telex 232398; Dir L. A. NEZDOIMINOGA.

Research Institute of Special Steels, Alloys and Ferroalloys: 330600 Zaporozhe, Patrioticheska vul. 74A; tel. 39-48-52; telex 127348; Dir G. I. KAPLANOV.

Research Institute of Television Equipment: 290601 Lviv, Vul. Storozhenko 12; tel. 33-61-46; telex 234125; fax 22-02-20; Dir E. G. BELOUSOVA.

Research Institute of the Sewn Goods Industry: 252022 Kiev, Vul. P. Lyubchenko 15; tel. (44) 268-55-41; fax (44) 269-71-72; f. 1961; library of 27,500 vols; Dir V. P. KRYSKO.

Research Institute of Transformer Manufacture: Zaporozhe, Dnepropetrovske shosse 11; tel. 7-21-63; Dir I. D. VOEVODIN.

Scientific and Research Institute of Fluid Power Drives and Automation: 310145 Kharkov, Vul. Shatilova dacha 4; tel. and fax (572) 14-20-23; f. 1951; library of 30,000 vols; Dir A. YA. OKSENENKO.

Southern Cement Research and Design Institute: 310022 Kharkov, Pr. Pravdy 10; tel. 47-80-18; telex 273134; Dir Z. I. GORLOVSKY.

Southern Gas Research and Design Institute: 340121 Donetsk, Vul. Artema 169G; tel. (622) 55-10-68; fax (622) 58-20-67; f. 1933; library of 38,000 vols; Chair. V. D. BATOZSKY.

State Research and Design Institute of Chemical Engineering: 349940 Lugansk oblast, Severodonetsk, Vul. Dzerzhinskogo 1; tel. (6452) 2-33-88; fax (6452) 2-50-42; f. 1950; library of 97,000 vols; Gen. Dir P. P. BORISOV; publ. collected research papers (monthly).

State Research and Development Institute of Consumer Radio and Electronic Equipment: 290060 Lviv, Vul. Naukova 7A; tel. (322) 64-74-55; telex 234120; fax (322) 63-70-58; f. 1987; library of 22,000 vols; Dir V. I. SHULIPA.

State Research Institute for the Agrobiochemical, Chemical and Pharmaceutical Industries: 253090 Kiev, Prazhska vul. 5; tel. 552-51-23; fax 559-23-45; Dir M. K. MESHKOV.

State Scientific Research Institute of Sanitary Engineering and the Equipment of Buildings and Constructions: 252110 Kiev, Vul. Mekhanizatorov 9; tel. 276-83-34; fax 276-81-14; f. 1957; library of 19,000 vols; Dir A. S. MAKAROV.

State Titanium Research and Design Institute: 330600 Zaporozhe, GSP 314, Pr. Lenina 180; tel. (612) 33-23-23; telex 127462; fax (612) 33-42-17; f. 1956; titanium, magnesium and other non-ferrous metals; Dir A. N. PETRUNKO.

State Tube Research Institute: 320600 Dnepropetrovsk, Vul. Pisarzhevskogo 1A; tel. and fax (562) 46-11-92; f. 1937; library of 84,000 vols; Dir V. V. SERGEEV.

'Storm' Research Institute: 270876 Odessa, Vul. Tereshkovoi 27; tel. 66-81-80; Dir I. D. KONOPLEV.

Thermal Power Research Institute: 338046 Donetsk oblast, Gorlovka, Pl. Lenina 3; tel. (6242) 4-42-29; fax (6242) 4-44-88; f. 1972; Dir ALEKSANDR N. GRECHANY.

Timoshenko, S. P., Institute of Mechanics: 252057 Kiev, Vul. Nesterova 3; tel. 446-93-51; fax 446-03-19; e-mail ang@imech .freenet.kiev.ua; attached to Nat. Acad. of Sciences of Ukraine; Dir A. N. GUZ.

Ukrainian Pulp and Paper Research Institute: 252133 Kiev, Vul. Kutuzova 18/7; tel. (44) 295-21-66; fax (44) 295-82-46; f. 1931; library of 21,200 vols; Dir N. T. LOZOVIK.

Ukrainian Research Institute for Alcohol and the Biotechnology of Foodstuffs: 252190 Kiev, Prov. Babushkina 3; tel. (44) 442-02-32; telex 331192; fax (44) 449-03-11; f. 1945; library of 44,000 vols; Dir VICTOR YANCHEVSKY.

Ukrainian Research Institute of Artificial Fibres: 253094 Kiev, Krasnotkatska vul. 61; tel. 559-07-77; telex 131505; fax 559-17-72; Dir A. I. NIKISHENKO.

Ukrainian Scientific Research Institute of Power Electronics 'Preobrazovatel': 330600 Zaporozhe, GSP-187, Kremlevska vul. 63A; tel. 52-55-09; fax 52-60-09; f. 1969; Dir Prof. P. D. ANDRIENKO.

Ukrainian State Research and Design Institute of Rock Geology, Geomechanics and Mine Surveying: 340121 Donetsk, Vul. Chelyuskintsev 291; tel. (622) 55-54-49; telex 115226; fax (622) 55-78-86; f. 1932; Dir Prof. N. YA. AZAROV.

Verkin, B., Institute of Low-Temperature Physics and Engineering: 310164 Kharkov, Pr. Lenina 47; tel. (572) 32-12-23; fax (572) 32-23-70; e-mail ilt@ilt.kharkov.ua; attached to Nat. Acad. of Sciences of Ukraine; Dir Prof. V. V. EREMENKO; publs *Low-Temperature Physics* (monthly), *Mathematical Physics, Analysis, Geometry* (4 a year).

Vniichimprojekt Institute: 253002 Kiev, Vul. M. Raskovoi 11; tel. (44) 517-05-81; fax (44) 517-15-18; f. 1970; develops synthetic detergents, personal care products, packaging materials; library of 48,200 vols; Pres. VALERY N. KRIVOSHEI; publs *Khimichna Promyslovist Ukrainy* (6 a year), *Upakovka* (4 a year).

Libraries and Archives

Chernivtsi

Chernivtsi State University Scientific Library: Chernivtsi, Vul. Lesi Ukrainki 23; tel. 2-93-91; 1,722,000 vols; Dir A. Y. VOLOSHCHUK.

Dnepropetrovsk

Dnepropetrovsk State University Library: Dnepropetrovsk, Vul. Libknekhta 3A; tel. 44-17-07; 1,200,000 vols; Dir L. S. KUBISHKINA.

Donetsk

Donetsk State University Library: 340055 Donetsk, Universitetska vul. 24; tel. 3-30-28; 782,000 vols; Dir A. N. KHARCHENKO.

Kharkiv

Kharkiv State University Central Scientific Library: 310077 Kharkiv, Pl. Svobody 4; tel. (57) 245-74-20; e-mail cnb@library.univer.kharkov.ua; 3,400,000 vols; Dir E. V. BALLA.

Kiev

Main Archival Administration of Ukraine: 252601 Kiev 110, Solomyanska vul. 24; tel. 277-27-77; fax 277-36-55.

Supervises:

Central State Archives of the Highest Governmental Bodies of Ukraine: 252601 Kiev 110, Solomyanska vul. 24; tel. 277-36-66.

Central State Historical Archives of Ukraine: 252601 Kiev 110, Solomyanska vul. 24; tel. 277-30-02.

Central State Historical Archives of Ukraine: 290008 Lviv 8, Pl. Sobornosti 3A; tel. 72-35-08.

Central State Archives of Public Organizations of Ukraine: 252011 Kiev 11, Vul. Kutuzova 8; tel. 295-73-22; former Party archive.

Central State Archives of Audiovisual Documents of Ukraine: 252601 Kiev 110, Solomyanska vul. 24; tel. 277-37-77.

Central State Archives of Scientific-Technical Documentation of Ukraine: 310003 Kharkiv 3, Universitetska vul. 4; tel. 22-75-66.

Central State Archives of Literature and Art of Ukraine: 252601 Kiev 25, Volodymirska 22A; tel. 228-22-81.

National Agricultural Library of the Ukrainian Academy of Agricultural Sciences: 252127 Kiev, Ul. Geroev Oborony 10; tel. (44) 266-05-09; fax (44) 290-42-55; e-mail dir@ucsal.nauu.kiev.ua; f. 1921; 973,000 vols; Dir MICHAEL SLOBODIANIK; publs *Novi Silskogospodarski Knyhy* (4 a year), *Genetyka i Selektsia Silskogospodarskykh Kultur* (2 a year).

National Medical Library: 252017 Kiev, Vul. L. Tolstogo 7; tel. 224-51-97.

National Parliamentary Library of Ukraine: 252001 Kiev, Vul. M. Grushevskogo 1; tel. 228-85-12; fax 228-42-16; e-mail npbu@alpha.rada.kiev.ua; f. 1866; 4,000,000 vols; Dir A. P. KORNIENKO; publ. *Kalendar znamennikh i pamyatnikh dat* (quarterly).

Scientific and Technical Library of the Ukraine: 252171 Kiev, Vul. Gorkogo 180; tel. 269-42-04; f. 1935; 4,000,000 books, 15,500,000 periodicals and patents; Dir G. M. TISHCHENKO.

State History Library: 252601 Kiev 15 MSP, Vul. Yanvarskogo Vasstaniya 21, Kor. 24; tel. 290-46-17.

Taras Shevchenko University of Kiev Library: 252601 Kiev, Vladimirska vul. 58; tel. 266-54-77; 2,708,000 vols; Dir V. G. CHUBUK.

Ukrainian Institute of Scientific-Technical and Economic Information: 252171 Kiev, Vul. Gorkogo 180; tel. (44) 268-25-79; fax (44) 268-25-41; Dir N. N. ERMOSHENKO.

Vernadsky Central Scientific Library of the National Academy of Sciences of Ukraine: 252650 Kiev 34, Pr. 40-richya Zhovtnya 3; tel. 265-81-04; fax 264-33-98; f. 1919; 12,500,000 vols; Dir M. I. SENCHENKO.

Lviv

Lviv Ivan Franko State University Library: 290602 Lviv, Vul. Dragomanova 5; tel. 3-04-94; 2,500,000 vols; Dir V. K. POTAICHUK.

Lviv V. Stefanyk Scientific Library of the National Academy of Sciences of Ukraine: 290601 Lviv, Vul. Stefanyka 2; tel. (322) 72-57-20; fax (322) 76-51-58; e-mail library@lsl.lviv.ua; f. 1940; 6,000,000 vols; Dir L. I. KRUSHELNYTSKA.

Odessa

Odessa I. I. Mechnikov State University Library: 270100 Odessa, Vul. Sovetskoi Armii 24; tel. 26-04-01; 3,510,000 vols; Dir S. M. STARITSKAYA.

Simferopol

Simferopol State University Library: Simferopol 36, Yaltinska vul. 4; 776,000 vols; Librarian V. I. DRYAGINA.

Uzhgorod

Uzhgorod State University Library: Uzhgorod, Kremlevska vul. 9; tel. 41-01; 1,160,000 vols; Dir YU. V. SABADOSH.

Museums and Art Galleries

Alupka

Alupka State Palace and Park Preserve: Alupka, Dvortsove shosse 10; tel. (654) 72-29-51; f. 1921; Russian noble culture and way of life in 19th century; library of 10,000 vols; spec. colln of 17th-century maps of Europe and America; Dir K. K. KASPEROVICH.

Alushta

Alushta S. M. Sergeev-Tsensky Literary Museum: Alushta, Vul. Sergeeva-Tsenskogo 15; house where the author lived; Dir T. A. FEFYUZA.

Bakhchisarai

Bakhchisarai Historical and Cultural State Preserve: Krymska republika, Bakhchisarai; tel. and fax 4-28-81; f. 1917; works of art, architectural monuments, cave towns; library of 12,000 vols; Dir YE. V. PETROV.

Chernigiv

Chernigiv M. M. Kotsyubinsky Literary Museum: 250000 Chernigiv, Vul. Kotsyubinskogo 3; tel. (4622) 4-04-59; f. 1934; life and work of Kotsyubinsky; library of 11,000 books; Dir YULY KOTSYUBINSKY; publ. *Collections* (every 5 years).

Chernivtsi

Chernivtsi Yu. A. Fedkovich Memorial Museum: Chernivtsi, Vul. Pushkina 17; tel. 2-56-78; f. 1945; life and work of the writer A. Fedkovich; Dir D. FYLYPCHUK.

Dneprodzerzhinsk

Dneprodzerzhinsk Museum of Town History: 322600 Dneprodzerzhinsk; tel. 3-02-24; f. 1931; library of 10,000 vols; Dir NINA TSIGANOK.

Dnepropetrovsk

Dnepropetrovsk Historical Museum: Dnepropetrovsk, Vul. K. Marksa 16.

Dnepropetrovsk State Art Museum: Dnepropetrovsk, Vul. Shevchenko 21.

Donetsk

Botanical Gardens: 340059 Donetsk, Pr. Ilicha 110; tel. (622) 94-12-80; fax (622) 94-61-57; e-mail sad@botgar.donetsk.ua; attached to Nat. Acad. of Sciences of Ukraine; Dir A. Z. GLUCHOV.

Donetsk Museum of Art: Donetsk, Vul. Artema 84.

Kamyanets-Podilsk

Kamyanets-Podilsk State Historical Museum-Preserve: Khmelnitska oblast, Kamyanets-Podilsk, Vul. K. Marksa 20; Dir K. G. MIKOLAIOVICH.

Kerch

Kerch State Archaeological Museum: 334501 Krymska republika, Kerch, Sverdlova 7; tel. 2-04-75; f. 1826; library of 20,000 vols; Dir P. I. IVANENKO; publ. *Arkheologiya i istoriya Bospora* (irregular).

Kharkiv

Kharkiv State Art Museum: Kharkiv, Sovnarkomovska vul. 11; tel. and fax (57) 43-35-85; f. 1934; Ukrainian, Russian and Western European artists; library of 18,000 vols; Dir V. V. MYZGINA.

Kharkiv State Historical Museum: Kharkiv, Universitetska vul. 10; Dir N. A. VOEVODIN.

Khomutovo

Ukrainian State Steppe Reservation: Donetsk oblast, Novoazov Raion, Khomutovo; attached to Nat. Acad. of Sciences of Ukraine; Dir A. P. GENOV.

Kiev

Central Botanical Garden: 252014 Kiev, Timiryazevska vul. 1; tel. (44) 295-41-05; fax (44) 295-26-49; e-mail gaponenko@botanical-garden.kiev.ua; f. 1935; attached to Nat. Acad. of Sciences of Ukraine; library of 46,000 vols; Dir Prof. Dr T. M. CHEREVCHENKO.

Kiev Lesya Ukrainka State Literary Museum: 252032 Kiev, Vul. Saksaganskogo 97; tel. 220-57-52; f. 1962; life and work of the Ukrainian poets and artists of the 19th and early 20th centuries; library of 5,000 vols; Dir IRINA L. VEREMEYEVA.

Kiev Museum of Russian Art: 252004 Kiev, Tereshchenkovska vul. 9; tel. (44) 224-62-18; fax (44) 224-61-07; f. 1922; library of 17,000 vols; Dir T. N. SOLDATOVA.

Kiev Museum of Ukrainian Art: 252004 Kiev, Vul. Kirova 6; painting and wood-carving since the Middle Ages; Dir V. F. YATSENKO.

Kiev Shevchenko, T. G., State Museum: Kiev, Bul. Shevchenko 12; life and work of the poet T. G. Shevchenko; Dir E. P. DOROSHENKO.

Kiev State Historical Museum: Kiev, Vladimirska 2; tel. 228-65-45; Dir I. E. DUDNIK.

Kiev-Pechersky National Museum: Kiev, Vul. Yanvarskogo Vosstaniya 21; tel. 290-66-46; fax 290-46-48; ancient monastery, icons.

St Sophia of Kiev National Architectural Conservation Area: 252034 Kiev, Volodymyrska vul. 24; tel. 228-67-06; fax 229-77-28; e-mail info@sophia.kiev.ua; f. 1934; comprises 11th-century St Sofia cathedral (with early frescoes and mosaics) and other, 18th-century bldgs; attached museums incl. St Cyril Church Museum, St Andrew Church Museum, Golden Gates Museum (11th-century town gatehouse) and, in the Crimea, 6th- to 15th-century Sudak fortress; Curator VALENTYNA N. ACHKASOVA.

Museum of Western and Oriental Art: Kiev, Tereshchenkivska vul. 15–17; tel. (44) 225-02-25; Dir V. I. VINOGRADOVA.

Ukrainian Museum of Folk and Decorative Art: Kiev, Vul. Yanvarskogo Vosstaniya 21; f. 1954; library of 3,180 vols; Dir V. G. NAGAI; publ. *Folk Creative Work and Ethnography*.

Ukrainian State Museum of Theatrical, Musical and Cinematographic Art: Kiev 15, Sichnevoho Povstanya 21/24; tel. and fax (44) 290-51-31; library of 29,000 vols; Dir L. N. MATAT.

Kolomya

Kolomya State Museum of Folk Art: Ivano-Frankivska oblast, Kolomya, Teatralna vul. 25; tel. 2-39-12; f. 1926; library of 6,000 vols; Dir Y. TKACHUK; publ. *People's House* (6 a year).

Lviv

Lviv Historical Museum: Lviv, Pl. Rynka 4/6; tel. 74-33-04; f. 1893; Dir BOGDAN N. CHAIKOWSKII.

Lviv National Museum: 290005 Lviv, Vul. Dragomanova 42; tel. 72-57-45; Dir VASYL OTKOVYCH.

Lviv State Picture Gallery: Lviv, Vul. Stefanika 3; tel. 72-39-48; f. 1907; West European and Ukrainian contemporary art; library of 29,390 vols; Dir BORIS VOZNITSKY.

State Museum of Ethnography and Arts and Crafts: Lviv, Pr. Lenina 15; f. 1873; attached to Nat. Acad. of Sciences of Ukraine.

State Museum of Natural History: 290008 Lviv, Teatralna vul. 18; tel. (322) 72-89-17; fax (322) 74-23-07; f. 1868; library of 62,000 vols; Dir Dr YU. CHERNOBAI; publ. *Scientific Notes*.

Odessa

Odessa Archaeological Museum: Odessa, Vul. Lastochkina 4; tel. 22-01-71; f. 1825; history of the Northern Black Sea Coast area; library of 26,000 vols; Dir V. P. VANCHUGOV.

Odessa Fine Arts Museum: Odessa, Sofievska vul. 5A; tel. (482) 23-82-72; fax (482) 23-83-93; f. 1899; Ukrainian and Russian art from 15th century to the present; library of 15,000 vols; Dir NATALYA S. POLISHCHUK.

Odessa Museum of Western and Eastern Art: 270026 Odessa, Pushkinsha vul. 9; tel. (482) 22-48-15; fax (482) 24-67-47; f. 1920; library of 14,000 vols; Dir VICTOR S. NIKIFOROV.

Poltava

Poltava Art Museum: 314020 Poltava, Spaska 11; tel. 7-27-11; f. 1919; library of 4,000 vols; Curator KIM SKALATSKY.

Poltava State Museum: Poltava, Pl. Lenina 2; life and work of the writers P. Mirnyi, J. Kotlyarevsky, V. G. Korolenko, N. V. Gogol; library of 80,000 vols; Dir Y. P. BELOUS.

Sevastopol

Khersones Museum of History and Archaeology: Sevastopol 45; f. *c.* 1860; incl. material from the ancient Greek colony of Khersones; library of 20,000 vols; Dir L. V. MARCHENKO.

Shevchenkovo

Shevchenko, T. G., State Memorial Museum: Cherkasska oblast, Zvenigorodsky raion, Shevchenkovo; f. 1939; life and work of T. G. Shevchenko; library of 3,000 vols; Dir T. V. GULAK.

Sumy

Sumy State Art Museum: Sumy, Vul. Lenina 67; Dir M. M. KOMAROV.

Yalta

State Nikitsky Botanical Gardens: Krymska republika, 334267 Yalta, Nikita; tel. (654) 33-55-30; fax (654) 33-53-86; e-mail flora@gnbs.crimea.ua; f. 1812; attached to Ukrainian Acad. of Agricultural Sciences; library of 214,000 vols; Dir Dr A. I. LISHCHUK; publs *Bulletin* (3 a year), *Collected Scientific Works* (3 a year).

Universities

CHERNIVTSI STATE UNIVERSITY

274012 Chernivtsi, Ul. Kotsyubinskogo 2
Telephone: (3722) 2-62-35
Fax (3722) 5-38-36

Founded 1875
State control
Language of instruction: Ukrainian
Academic year: September to June

President: S. S. KOSTYSHYN
Academic Vice-President: V. I. VASHCHENKO
Vice-President (Research): M. V. TKACH
Librarian: A. Y. VOLOSHCHUK

Library: see Libraries
Number of teachers: 675
Number of students: 5,850 full-time, 4,290 part-time

Publications: *Scientific University Annual, Universitetsky Visnyk* (monthly), *Pytannia Literaturoznavstva, Bukovynsky Zhurnal* (monthly).

DEANS

Faculty of Physics: M. D. RARANSKY
Faculty of Engineering and Technology: G. K. KUREK
Faculty of Mathematics: V. V. KREKHIVSKY
Faculty of Chemistry: O. E. PANCHUK
Faculty of Biology: V. I. STEFANYK
Faculty of Geography: V. O. DZHAMAN
Faculty of History: Y. I. MAKAR
Faculty of Slavic Philology: B. I. BUNCHUK
Faculty of Foreign Languages: V. I. KUSHNERYK
Faculty of Education: I. S. RUSNAK
Faculty of Economics: Y. K. ZAITSEV
Faculty of Law: P. S. PATSURKIVSKY
Faculty of Philosophy and Theology: M. M. SYDORENKO

HEADS OF DEPARTMENT

Agrochemistry: I. I. NAZARENKO
Algebra and Geometry: R. F. DOMBROVSKY
Analytical and Organic Chemistry: Y. S. MAZURKEVYCH
Ancient and Medieval History: V. O. BALUKH
Applied Mathematics and Mechanics: Y. Y. BIHUN
Biochemistry: S. S. KOSTYSHYN
Botany and Plant Physiology: B. K. TERMENA
Calculus: P. P. NASTASIEV
Computer Science: Z. M. MYKHAILETSKY
Constitutional Law: M. K. YAKYMCHUK
Correlation Optics: O. V. ANGELSKY
Differential Equations: M. I. MATIYCHUK
Economic Geography: V. P. RUDENKO
Economics and Accounting: V. P. DUDKO
Education: D. I. PENISHKEVYCH
English: V. V. MYKHAILENKO
Finance: V. G. OKHRIMOVSKY
French: M. M. POPOVYCH
General Physics: R. D. VENGRENOVYCH
German and General Linguistics: V. V. LEVYTSKY
Mathematical Modelling: S. D. IVASYSHEN
Microelectronics: I. M. RARENKO
Modern History: Y. I. MAKAR
Modern Ukrainian Language: N. V. GUIVANYUK
Music: A. I. KUSHNIRENKO
Non-organic Chemistry: O. E. PANCHUK
Optics and Spectroscopy: B. M. NITSOVYCH
Optoelectronics: L. A. KOSIACHENKO
Philosophy: B. V. POCHYNOK
Physical Chemistry: V. V. NECHYPORUK
Physical Education: M. T. GONZHA
Physical Electronics: M. P. HAVALESHKO
Physical Geography and Natural Resources: M. I. KYRYLYUK
Radio-engineering: L. F. POLITANSKY
Romanian and Latin Philology: G. K. BOSTAN
Russian: O. S. BILA
Solid State Physics: M. D. RARANSKY
Spectroscopy: B. M. NITSOVYCH
Thermoelectrics and Physical Metrology: L. I. ANATYCHUK
Theoretical Physics: M. V. TKACH
Theory and History of State and Law: V. P. MARCHUK
Theory and History of World Literature: A. R. VOLKOV
Ukrainian Geography and Cartography: Y. I. ZHUPANSKY
Ukrainian History: V. M. BOTUSHANSKY
Ukrainian Language, History and Culture: N. D. BABYCH
Ukrainian Literature: M. I. YURIYCHUK
Zoology and Physiology: I. M. PAVLIUK

DNEPROPETROVSK STATE UNIVERSITY

320625 Dnepropetrovsk, Nauchnyi 13
Telephone: (562) 46-00-95
Telex: 143452
Fax: (562) 46-55-23

Founded 1918
Languages of instruction: Ukrainian, Russian
Academic year: September to July

President: V. F. PRISNYAKOV
Vice-President (Research): V. V. SKALOZUB
Vice-Presidents (Academic): N. V. POLYAKOV, V. G. MUSYAKA
Librarian: L. S. KUBISHKINA

Library: see Libraries
Number of teachers: 1,100
Number of students: 11,168

DEANS

Faculty of Mechanics and Mathematics: N. V. POLIAKOV
Faculty of Physics: R. S. TUTIK
Faculty of Radio Physics: V. M. DOLGOV
Faculty of Philology: I. I. MENSHIKOV
Faculty of History: A. G. BOLEBRUCH
Faculty of Applied Economics: A. F. SANIN
Faculty of Biology and Medicine: A. N. VINICHENKO
Faculty of Chemistry: V. F. VARGALYUK
Faculty of Applied Mathematics: I. I. MISCHISCHIN
Faculty of Geology and Geography: G. V. PASECHNY
Faculty of Ukrainian Philology and Art History: I. S. POPOVA
Faculty of Education and Psychology: I. V. RASPOPOV
Faculty of Finance and Credit: S. A. SMIRNOV
Faculty of Law and Sociology: P. I. GNATENKO
Institute of Physics and Technology: E. A. DZUR

ATTACHED RESEARCH INSTITUTES

Scientific and Research Institute of Biology: Dir A. N. VINNICHENKO
Scientific and Research Institute of Geology: Dir V. M. IVANOV
Scientific and Research Institute of Engineering: Dir I. N. STATSENKO

DONETSK STATE UNIVERSITY

340055 Donetsk, Ul. Universitetskaya 24

Telephone: 93-30-28
Telex: 115102

Founded 1965
Languages of instruction: Ukrainian and Russian
Academic year: September to July

Rector: V. P. Shevchenko
Vice-Rector: N. P. Ivanitsin
Librarian: A. N. Kharchenko

Library: see Libraries
Number of teachers: 900
Number of students: *c.* 12,000

Publication: *Universitetskie Visti* (in Ukrainian, weekly).

DEANS

Faculty of Biology: G. P. Lipnitskaya
Faculty of Chemistry: A. N. Nikolaevsky
Faculty of Economics: G. A. Chernichenko
Faculty of Finance: P. V. Egorov
Faculty of Foreign Languages: B. D. Kaliushchenko
Faculty of History: V. F. Burnosov
Faculty of Law: V. D. Volkov
Faculty of Mathematics: P. M. Velichko
Faculty of Physics: A. B. Stupin
Faculty of Russian and Ukrainian Philology: E. S. Otin
Preparatory Faculty: A. I. Bilobrova

KHARKIV STATE UNIVERSITY

310077 Kharkiv, Pl. Svobody 4

Telephone: 43-61-96
Fax: 43-33-93

Founded 1805
Academic year: September to June
Languages of instruction: Russian, Ukrainian

Rector: V. A. Svich
Pro-Rectors: O. F. Tyrnov, I. I. Zalyubovskii, V. K. Mikheev, N. I. Dudka.
Librarian: E. V. Balla

Number of teachers: 2,000
Number of students: 12,000

Publications: *Vestnik Kharkovskogo Universiteta* (16 issues a year), *Collected Articles* (mathematics, physics, chemistry, 2–3 issues a year).

DEANS

Faculty of Biology: Asst Prof. V. I. Gluschenko
Faculty of Chemistry: Prof. V. D. Orlov
Faculty of Geology and Geography: Asst Prof. K. A. Nemets
Faculty of Economics: Asst Prof. V. V. Alexandrov
Faculty of Foreign Languages: Asst Prof. V. G. Pasynok
Faculty of Basic Medicine: Prof. N. I. Yabluchansky
Faculty of History: Asst Prof. Yu. V. Buinov
Faculty of Mathematics and Applied Mathematics: Asst Prof. V. V. Zolotarev
Faculty of Philology: Asst Prof. Yu. N. Bezkhutry
Faculty of Physics: Prof. V. P. Lebedev
Faculty of Physics and Technology: Prof. N. A. Azarenkov
Faculty of Radiophysics: Asst Prof. M. P. Perepechai
Faculty of Sociology: Asst Prof. V. N. Nikolaevsky
Preparatory Faculty for Foreign Students: Asst Prof. V. A. Shalaev

ATTACHED INSTITUTES

Institute of Biology: Dir Prof. V. V. Lemeshko
Institute of Chemistry: Dir Prof. V. I. Larin

UNIVERSITY OF KIEV-MOHYLA ACADEMY

254070 Kiev, Vul. Skovorodi 2

Telephone: (44) 416-45-16
Fax: (44) 416-45-16
E-mail: rec@ukma.kiev.ua

Founded 1632, closed 1817, re-established 1992
State control
Languages of instruction: Ukrainian and English
Academic year: September to June

President: Viacheslav Briukhovetsky
Rector: Serhiy Ivanyuk
Registrar: Vira Doroschenko
Librarian: Tetiana Yaroshenko

Library of 200,000 vols
Number of teachers: 300
Number of students: 1,500

DEANS

Faculty of Humanities and Social Sciences: Dr Valentin Gusev
Faculty of Natural Sciences: Dr Alla Bezusko
Faculty of Law: Dr Volodymyr Sushchenko
School of Social Work: Prof. Volodymyr Poltavets
Department of Computer Engineering: Dr Mykola Glybovets
Department of Social Sciences and Technology: Prof. Volodymyr Poltavets
Department of Economics: Prof. Oleksandr Yastremsky

LVIV STATE IVAN FRANKO UNIVERSITY

290602 Lviv, Universitetskaya vul. 1

Telephone: (322) 74-12-62
Fax: (322) 72-28-01

Founded 1661
Language of instruction: Ukrainian
Academic year: September to June

Rector: Prof. I. Vakarchuk
Pro-Rectors: V. Vysochansky, M. Pavlun, V. Kyrylych
Librarian: M. Bozhko

Library: see Libraries
Number of teachers: 1,042
Number of students: 16,000

Publications: *Visnyk* (Journal, 12 series), *Inozemna Filologiya* (Foreign Philology), *Ukrainske Literaturoznavstvo* (Ukrainian Literature Studies), *Teoretychna Elektrotekhnika* (Theoretical Electrical Engineering), *Mineralogichniy Zbirnyk* (Proceedings on Mineralogy), *Paleontologichniy Zbirnyk* (Proceedings on Palaeontology), *Matematychni Studii* (Mathematical Studies).

Faculties of history, philology, philosophy, journalism, foreign languages (English, German, French, Spanish, Latin, Greek), international relations, law, economics, physics, mechanico-mathematics, applied mathematics and programming, chemistry, biology, geology, geography

ODESSA I. I. MECHNIKOV STATE UNIVERSITY

270026 Odessa, Dvoryanska vul. 2

Telephone: (482) 23-52-54
Fax: (482) 23-35-15
E-mail: oguint@paco.net

Founded 1865
State control
Languages of instruction: Ukrainian, Russian
Academic year: September to July

Rector: Prof. V. A. Smyntyna
First Pro-Rector: Prof. N. P. Kovalenko (Academic)
Pro-Rectors: Prof. E. L. Streltsov (Academic and Methodological Work), Prof. V. A. Ivanitsa (Scientific Research), Assoc. Prof. S. S. Fedorko (International Relations and External Economic Affairs, acting), V. A. Foros (Building and Maintenance)
Librarian: S. M. Staritskaya

Library: see Libraries
Number of teachers: 1,803
Number of students: 11,078

Publications: *Fisika aerodispersnikh sistem* (annually), *Fotoelektronika* (annually), *Studies in Literature* (annually), *Odessa State University Herald* (4 a year).

DEANS

Faculty of Biology: Prof. V. D. Taranenko
Faculty of Chemistry: Assoc. Prof. V. I. Nikitin
Faculty of Geology and Geography: Assoc. Prof. Y. M. Bilanchin
Faculty of History: Prof. V. N. Stanko
Faculty of Romance and Germanic Philology: Assoc. Prof. L. N. Golubenko
Faculty of Physics: Prof. G. G. Chemeresyuk
Faculty of Philology: Prof. N. M. Shlyakhovaya
Faculty of Business and Management: Assoc. Prof. V. T. Mak
Faculty of Economics and Law: Prof. A. S. Vasiliev
Institute of Mathematics, Economics and Mechanics: Assoc. Prof. V. E. Kruglov
Institute of Social Studies: Assoc. Prof. I. N. Koval

ATTACHED INSTITUTES

Astronomical Observatory: Dir Prof. V. G. Karetnikov.

V. I. Lipsky Botanical Garden: Dir A. S. Bonetsky.

Institute for the Protection of Nature and Man from Physical and Chemical Hazards: Scientific Advisor Prof. A. A. Ennan.

Institute of Physics: Dir Prof. V. M. Belous.

Centre for International Educational and Cultural Programmes: Dir Assoc. Prof. S. S. Fedorko.

SIMFEROPOL STATE UNIVERSITY

333036 Simferopol, Yaltinskaya ul. 4

Telephone: (652) 23-22-80
Fax: (652) 23-23-10

Founded 1918
State control
Language of instruction: Russian
Academic year: September to July

Rector: Vyacheslav G. Sidyakin
Vice-Rectors: Viktor F. Sharapa, Nikolay A. Groshenko, Yuri M. Ilyin
Registrar: Vladimir N. Oparin
Librarian: Viktoria I. Dryagina

Number of teachers: 600
Number of students: 6,600

Publications: *Ecological Study of the Mountainous Crimea* (annually), *Ecosystems of the Mountainous Crimea in Studies of Nature Protection* (annually), *Ecological Aspects of Nature Protection in the Crimea* (annually), *Dynamic Systems* (annually).

DEANS

Faculty of Mathematics: Vladimir F. Ignatenko
Faculty of Physics: Tamara A. Korostelina
Faculty of Natural Sciences: Vassily Ya. Chirva
Faculty of Geography: Ivan G. Gubanov
Faculty of History: Leonid A. Pashkovsky
Faculty of Philology: Yevgeny S. Regushevsky
Faculty of Romance-Germanic Languages: Alexander D. Petrenko
Faculty of Physical Training: Nikolai V. Korolyov
Faculty of Preparatory Training: Valentin N. Kasatkin

PROFESSORS

AKULOV, M. R., Politics
APATOVA, N. V., Information Systems in Economics
APOSTOLOV, L. G., Ecology and Rational use of Nature
ARIFOV, L. YA., Theoretical Physics
BEREZOVSKAYA, D. A., History of World Culture
BERZHANSKY, V. N., Experimental Physics
BOKOV, V. A., Geography
BUROV, G. M., Ancient and Middle Ages History
CHEKHOV, V. N., Theoretical and Applied Mechanics
CHIRVA, V. YA., Organic and Analytical Chemistry
DEMENTIEV, N. E., History of Ukraine and USSR
DONSKOI, V. I., Informatics
DUBLYANSKY, V. N., General Land Science
EMIROVA, A. M., Russian Language
FEDORENKO, A. M., Physical Chemistry
FILIMONOV, S. B., History of Ukraine
GARCHEV, P. I., History of Ukraine and USSR
IGNATENKO, V. F., Geometry and Topology
KALIN, V. K., General Psychology, History of Psychology
KASCHENKO, S. G., History of Ukraine and USSR
KAZARIN, V. P., Russian and General Literature
KHLYSTOV, A. S., General Physics
KIRICHEK, P. M., Literature
KOLESOV, M. S., History of Philosophy
KOPACHEVSKY, N. D., Mathematical Analysis
KORENYUK, I. I., Human and Animal Physiology
KOZLOV, A. S., Russian and General Literature
KUDRYASHOV, A. P., Political Economy
KUZHEL, A. V., Theory of Functions and Functional Analysis
LEIKIN, M. G., Gymnastics
LYSENKO, N. I., General Land Science
MANANKOV, M. K., Physiology of Plants
MARTYNYUK, YU. N., Philosophy
MELNIKOV, G. I., Scientific Socialism
MESCHERYAKOV, V. P., Russian and General Literature
MISHNEV, V. G., Botany
MITZAY, YU. N., Theoretical Physics
NIKOLKO, V. N., Philosophy
NOVIKOVA, M. A., Russian and General Literature
OLIFEROV, A. N., Oceanology
OREKHOVA, L. A., Russian Literature
PERSIDSKY, S. K., Differential and Integral Equations
PODSOLONKO, V. A., Economics
PONOMARENKO, V. I., Experimental Physics
REGUSHEVSKY, E. S., Languages of the Nations of the Former USSR
SELEZNEV, V. N., Solid State Physics
SHEVLYAKOV, YU. M., Applied Mathematics
SIDYAKIN, V. G., Human and Animal Physiology
SKRYABIN, A. S., Zoology
STADNIK, I. P., Theoretical Physics
STASHKOV, A. M., Animal and Biophysics
TEMURYANTZ, N. A., Human and Animal Physiology
TEREZ, E. K., Astronomy and Teaching Methods of Physics
TOLKACHEVA, N. V., Biochemistry
URSU, D. P., Modern and Contemporary History
VOLYAR, A. V., Physics
YEFIMENKO, A. M., Theoretical Foundations of Physical Culture
YURAKHNO, M. V., Zoology

TARAS SHEVCHENKO UNIVERSITY OF KIEV

252601 Kiev, Volodymyrska vul. 64

Telephone: (44) 225-20-82
Fax: (44) 224-61-66

Founded 1834

Rector: Prof. VICTOR VASSYLYOVYCH SKOPENKO
Pro-Rector (Research): Prof. VOLODYMYR ARSENOVYCH MAKARA
First Vice-Rector: Prof. OLEG VASSYLYOVYCH TRETYAK
Vice-Rector: Prof. LEONID VASSYLYOVYCH GUBERSKIY

Library: see Libraries
Number of teachers: 1,850
Number of students: 18,000

Publications: *Vestnik Kievskogo Universiteta*, etc.

DEANS

Faculty of Biology: Prof. N. YE. KUCHERENKO
Faculty of Chemistry: Prof. V. V. SUKHAN
Faculty of Cybernetics: Prof. O. K. ZAKUSILO
Faculty of Economics: Prof. D. M. CHERVANYOV
Faculty of Foreign Philology: Prof. O. I. CHEREDNYCHENKO
Faculty of Geography: Prof. M. M. PADUN
Faculty of Geology: Prof. V. S. SHABATIN
Faculty of History: Prof. A. G. SLYUDARENKO
Faculty of Law: Prof. V. G. GONCHARENKO
Faculty of Mechanics and Mathematics: Prof. M. O. PERESTYUK
Faculty of Philology: Prof. N. K. NAYENKO
Faculty of Philosophy: Prof. A. YE. KONVERSKIY
Faculty of Physics: Prof. L. A. BULAVIN
Faculty of Radiophysics: Prof. G. A. MELKOV
Faculty of Sociology and Psychology: Prof. V. I. VOLOVYCH

ATTACHED INSTITUTES

Institute of International Relations: Dir Prof. L. V. GUBERSKIY.

Institute of Journalism: Dir Prof. A. Z. MOSKALENKO.

Institute of Ukrainian Studies: Dir Prof. P. P. KONONENKO.

UZHGOROD STATE UNIVERSITY

294000 Uzhgorod, Vul. Pidhirna 46
Telephone: (3122) 3-33-41
Fax: (3122) 3-61-36

Founded 1945
State control
Language of instruction: Ukrainian
Academic year: September to July

Rector: Prof. V. Y. SLIVKA
Vice-Rectors: Prof. YU. V. VOROSHILOV, Prof. YU. M. VYSOCHANSKY, Asst Prof. V. I. OPIYARY
Registrar: R. V. ROMANYUK
Librarian: O. I. POCHEKUTOVA

Number of teachers: 600
Number of students: 8,000

Publications: *Bulletin* (series: Biology, Medicine, Romance and Germanic Philology, Philology, Mathematics, Physics, Chemistry, 1 each a year).

DEANS

Faculty of History: Asst Prof. I. O. MANDRYK
Faculty of Philology: Asst Prof. V. V. BARCHAN
Faculty of Law: Prof. V. I. YAREMA
Faculty of Romance and Germanic Philology: Asst Prof. S. S. BOBYNETS
Faculty of Economics: Prof. V. P. MIKLOVDA
Faculty of Mathematics: Prof. V. V. MARINETS
Faculty of Physics: Prof. L. L. SHIMON
Faculty of Medicine: Asst Prof. V. M. BORA
Faculty of Biology: Asst Prof. V. I. NIKOLAYCHUK
Faculty of Chemistry: Asst Prof. V. G. LENDEL
Faculty of Engineering: Asst Prof. YU. YU. RUBISH

ATTACHED INSTITUTES

Institute for Solid State Physics and Chemistry: Dir Prof. YU. M. VYSOCHANSKI.

Institute of Herbal Medicine: Dir Prof. O. M. HANICH.

Carpathian Institute: Dir Asst Prof. M. P. MAKARA.

Hungarian Philology Centre: Dir Prof. P. M. LIZANETS.

ZAPOROZHE STATE UNIVERSITY

330600 Zaporozhe, Ul. Zhukovskogo 66

Telephone: (612) 64-45-46
Telex: 127447
Fax: (612) 62-71-61

Founded 1985
State control
Languages of instruction: Russian and Ukrainian
Academic year: September to July

Rector: Prof. V. A. TOLOK
Pro-Rectors: A. N. GORBAN, V. Z. GRISHCHAK, T. A. PAKHOMOVA, O. L. SKIDIN, G. P. BREKHARYA, I. G. YAKUSHEV
Registrar: YA. F. PIKHULYA
Librarian: V. A. GERASIMOVA

Number of teachers: 500
Number of students: 7,412

Publication: *Zaporizkiy universytet* (weekly).

DEANS

Faculty of Physics and Mathematics: Prof. N. G. TAMUROV
Faculty of Physics: Doc. A. YE. OSIPOV
Faculty of Foreign Languages: Doc. YE. M. RUZHIN
Faculty of Philology: Prof. V. A. CHABANENKO
Faculty of Biology: Prof. L. I. OMELYANCHIK
Faculty of Physical Training: Doc. S. S. VOLKOVA
Faculty of History: Prof. F. G. TURCHENKO
Faculty of Law: Dr V. V. VASILCHENKO
Faculty of Economics: Dr I. I. KOLOBERDYANKO
Faculty of Social Pedagogics: Dr L. I. MISCHIK
Faculty of Foreign Economic Activity: Doc. I. G. SHAVKUN
Faculty of Undergraduate Education: Prof. S. N. BESHENKOV

PROFESSORS

BESHENKOV, S. N., Mathematics
BESSONOVA, V. P., Biology
CHABANENKO, V. A., General Linguistics
CHERNYSH, A. M., Politics
FALKEVICH, E. S., Semiconductors
FROLOV, A. K., Physiology of Man
GORBAN, A. N., Physics of Semiconductors
GRISHCHAK, V. Z., Mathematics
IVANENKO, B. K., Russian Language
KARAGODIN, A. I., History of the Russian Empire before 1917
KOLESNIK, N. V., Biology
KUDLAI, T. P., Law
LYAKH, S. R., History of Ukraine
MOROZOV, L. V., Economics
OMELYANCHIK, L. I., Pharmacology
PAKHOMOVA, T. A., Philology
PEREPELITSA, V. A., Mathematical Methods in Economics
PRIKHODKO, N. I., Teaching
PRIVARNIKOV, A. K., Algebra and Geometry
PSARYOV, V. I., Physics of Solid Matter
ROITMAN, A. B., Mathematics
ROZENBAUM, YE. M., French Language
SERGEEV, L. N., Philosophy
TAMUROV, N. G., Mathematics
TERNOVOI, YU. F., Physics
TOLOK, V. A., Applied Mathematics
TURCHENKO, F. G., History of Soviet Society
VOLKOVA, S. S., Physical Training
VOLOVIK, V. I., Philosophy
YESHENKO, V. A., Human Anatomy

ATTACHED INSTITUTE

Azov Regional Institute of Management and Administration: Rector Dr M. B. KOTLIAREVSKI.

Polytechnics

Donetsk Technical University: 340000 Donetsk, Ul. Artema 58; tel. (622) 92-20-04; telex 115183; fax (622) 92-12-78; f. 1921; faculties: mechanical, geology, mining, mining engineering, metallurgy, electrical engineering, chemical technology, automated management systems, computer technology, engineering economics, automobile transport, roads; brs in Gorlovka and Krasnoarmeisk; 17,000 students; library of 1,500,000 vols; Rector A. A. MINAEV; publ. *Development of Mining Minerals*.

Kharkiv V. I. Lenin Polytechnic Institute: 310002 Kharkiv, Ul. Frunze 21; tel. 247-80-68; f. 1885; faculties: mechanics and metallurgy, engineering, technical physics, power machine building, electrical engineering, automation and instrument building, power engineering, technology of inorganic substances, technology of organic substances, technology of organic chemicals, chemical engineering, transport engineering, engineering physics; teachers' training department; brs in Sumy and Kremenchug; Rector YU. T. KOSTENKO.

Kherson State Technical University: 325008 Kherson, Bereslavskoe shosse 24; tel. (552) 55-40-11; fax (552) 51-84-43; e-mail adm@kherson.niiit.kiev.ua; f. 1957; faculties: engineering and automation, mechanics, mechanical technology of fibrous materials, technology, economics; library of 400,000 vols; Rector YURI N. BARDACHEV; publ. *Proceedings* (2 a year).

Kiev Polytechnic Institute: 252056 Kiev, Pr. Peremokhy 37; tel. (44) 274-69-13; telex 131434; fax (44) 274-09-54; f. 1898; faculties: mechanical engineering, precision instruments, chemical machine-building, welding, radio engineering, electronics, informatics and computer engineering, chemical engineering, electrical power engineering and automatics, heat power engineering, mining engineering, physical engineering, publishing and printing, applied mathematics, physics and technology, linguistics, law, physics and mathematics, sociology, management and marketing, air and spacecraft systems, physical training and sport; 27,729 students; library of 3,000,000 vols; Rector M. Z. ZGUROVSKY; publs *Vesti* (2 a year), *Kyivsky Politekhnik* (newspaper, weekly).

Lviv Polytechnic Institute: 290646 Lviv, Ul. St Bandery 12; tel. 72-47-33; telex 234139; f. 1844; faculties: geodesy, mechanical technology, mechanics and machine building, energy, electrical engineering, radio engineering, automation, electrical physics, engineering economics, chemical technology, technology of organic materials, civil and industrial construction, architecture, heat engineering, general engineering, computer engineering and information technology; 2,000 teachers; 17,000 students; library of 3,000,000 vols; Rector Prof. Dr YURY RUDAVSKY; publ. *Journal* (15 series annually).

Odessa Polytechnic Institute: 270044 Odessa, Pr. Shevchenko 1; tel. 22-34-74; f. 1918; faculties: mechanical technology, thermal power, nuclear power, radio engineering, automation and electrification of industry, robot systems, automation and computer technology, engineering economics, chemical technology; Rector V. P. MALAKHOV.

Vinnitsa State Technical University: 286021 Vinnitsa, Khmelnitske shosse 95; tel. (0432) 32-57-18; telex 119384; fax (0432) 46-57-72; f. 1960; faculties: power engineering, civil engineering, automation and computer control systems, computer engineering and software, radio engineering and microelectronics, radio instrumentation design, machine-building technology, transport and tribotechnology, fundamental and economics training; 600 teachers; 7,000 students; library of 722,000 vols; Rector B. I. MOKIN; publs *University News* (monthly), *Proceedings* (quarterly).

Other Higher Educational Institutes

ENGINEERING AND INDUSTRY

Dneprodzerzhinsk M. I. Arsenichev Industrial Institute: 322618 Dneprodzerzhinsk, Dneprostroevskaya ul. 2; tel. 3-21-23; faculties: technology, metallurgy, mechanics; Rector V. I. LOGINOV.

Dnepropetrovsk Metallurgical Institute: 320635 Dnepropetrovsk, Pr. Gagarina 4; tel. (562) 45-31-56; telex 143412; fax (562) 47-44-61; f. 1899; faculties: metallurgy, technological engineering, electrometallurgy, thermophysics, engineering economics, power and mechanical engineering; 600 teachers; 7,000 students; library of 520,000 vols; Rector YU. N. TARAN-ZHOVNIR.

Dnepropetrovsk Mining Institute: 320600 Dnepropetrovsk, Pr. K. Marksa 19; tel. 45-43-44; faculties: mining, prospecting, engineering, electrical engineering, construction of mines; library of 495,000 vols; Rector A. A. RENGEVICH.

Dnepropetrovsk State Technical University of Railway Transport: 320700 Dnepropetrovsk, Ul. Akademika Lazaryana 2; tel. (562) 76-59-47; fax (562) 47-18-66; f. 1930; faculties: mechanical engineering, electrification of railways, railway construction and track maintenance, technical cybernetics, economics and transport management, traffic management, industrial and civil engineering, bridges and transport tunnels; 4,200 students; library of 800,000 vols; Rector V. A. KABLUKOV.

Donbass Mining and Metallurgical Institute: 349104 Alchevsk, Pr. Lenina 16; tel. 2-31-23; fax 2-68-87; e-mail rector@dgmi.lugansk.ua; f. 1957; depts: mining, electrical and mechanical mining engineering, metallurgy and machine-building, automation of production processes, construction; library of 695,000 vols; Rector Prof. V. N. DOROFEEV; publ. *Impulse* (weekly).

Donbass State Engineering Academy: 343913 Kramatorsk, Ul. Shkadinova 72; tel. (626) 41-67-94; fax (626) 41-63-15; e-mail postmaster@dgma.edu.donetsk.ua; faculties: engineering and economics, machine-building, automation, automation of metal-shaping processes, economics and humanities.

East Ukrainian State University: 348034 Lugansk, Kvartal Molodezhnyi 20A; tel. (642) 46-12-30; fax (642) 46-13-64; e-mail root@vugu.lumsi.lugansk.ua; f. 1921; fields covered: engineering, economics, law, archives, ecology, informatics, robotics, journalism, transport, international economics, finance and credit, management of production, physics, machine building, applied mathematics, foundry, welding, materials-handling equipment, automobiles, hydraulics, hydrodrives, internal combustion engines, electric machines, electronics, automation of production systems; library of 700,000 vols; Rector A. L. GOLUBENKO; publ. *Bulletin* (6 a year).

Ivano-Frankivsk State Technical University of Oil and Gas: 284018 Ivano-Frankivsk, Karpatskaya ul. 15; tel. (3422) 4-22-64; fax (3422) 4-21-39; f. 1967; faculties: geological prospecting, gas and oil industry, gas and oil pipelines, automation and electrification, mechanical, economics and management, mechanics and technology, engineering ecology; 413 teachers; 4,453 students; library of 668,000 vols; Rector Y. I. KRYZHANIVSKY; publ. *Collected Works 'Prospecting and Exploitation of Oil and Gas Deposits'* (annually).

Kharkiv Civil Engineering Institute: 310002 Kharkiv, Sumskaya ul. 40; tel. 47-72-79; fax 43-20-17; faculties: construction, sanitary engineering, architecture, machinery and manufacturing, library of 218,000 vols; Rector N. S. BOLOTSKIH.

Kharkiv N. Y. Zhukovsky Aviation Institute: 310070 Kharkiv, Ul. Chkalova 17; tel. 44-98-56; telex 440153; fax 44-11-31; f. 1930; faculties: aircraft building, aircraft engines, aircraft vehicles, control systems, radio engineering, management; library of 990,000 vols; Rector Prof. N. T. BEREZYUK.

Kharkiv State Academy of Railway Transport: 310050 Kharkiv, Pl. Feierbakha 7; tel. 21-20-67; f. 1930; faculties: traffic management, mechanics, automation, telemechanics and communication, construction, economics; library of 700,000 vols; brs in Donetsk, Kiev; Rector YU. V. SOBOLOEV.

Kharkiv State Municipal Academy: 310002 Kharkiv, Ul. Revolyutsii 12; tel. (572) 43-21-62; telex 311038; fax (572) 47-65-00; f. 1930; faculties: management, of public services and municipal finances, electric and underground transport, urban electric power supply and lighting, urban planning and development, engineering ecology; library of 890,000 vols; Rector Prof. L. N. SHUTENKO.

Kharkiv State Road Construction University: 310078 Kharkiv, Ul. Petrovskogo 25; tel. (572) 43-30-65; fax (572) 43-30-62; e-mail admin@khadi.kharkov.ua; f. 1930; depts: road building, motor vehicles, mechanics, business and management; college of motor vehicle construction; library of 450,000 vols; 450 teachers; 5,500 students; Rector ANATOLY N. TURENKO.

Kharkiv State Technical University of Radioelectronics: 310726 Kharkiv, Pr. V. I. Lenina 14; tel. 43-30-53; telex 3113009; fax 40-91-33; f. 1933 (as Kharkov M. K. Yangel Institute of Radioelectronics, present name 1993); depts: computing, electronics, control systems, design of radio and computer equipment, radio engineering; 600 teachers; 6,000 students; library of 900,000 vols; Rector Prof. V. V. SVIRIDOV.

Kiev International University of Civil Aviation: POB at 252601 Kiev; premises at: 252058 Kiev, Kosmonavta Komarova 1; tel. (44) 483-31-41; telex 131362; fax (44) 488-30-27; f. 1933 (as Kiev Institute of Civil Aviation Engineers, renamed 1994); faculties: preparatory, mechanics, avionics, aircraft equipment, airports, automation and computer technology, engineering economics and management, aviation ground machinery; 7,000 students; library of 2m. vols; Rector P. V. NAZARENKO.

Kiev State Technical University of Construction and Architecture: 252180 Kiev 37, Vozdukhoflotskii pr. 31; tel. (44) 276-53-30; fax (44) 276-92-82; f. 1930; faculties: architecture, construction, constructional technology, urban construction, sanitary engineering, construction industry automation; 684 teachers; 6,400 students; library of 1,096,000 vols; Rector A. M. TUGAY.

Kirovograd Higher Flying School of Civil Aviation: 316005 Kirovograd oblastnoi, Ul. Dobrovolskogo 1; tel. 2-38-64; faculties: flying, air navigation, air traffic control.

Krivoi Rog Ore Mining Institute: 324027 Krivoi Rog, Ul. XXII Partsezda 11; tel. (564) 23-22-30; telex 143433; fax (564) 74-84-12; f. 1922; faculties: geology and dressing, mine surveying and geodesy, underground mining, open-cast mining, electrical engineering, engineering, construction; geological museum; 4,500 students; library of 1.2m. vols; Rector V. F. BIZOV; publ. *Collection of Works* (2 a year).

Makeevka Civil Engineering Institute: 339023 Makeevka, pos. Dzerzhinskogo; tel. 90-29-38; faculties: metal structures, industrial and civil construction, technology, sanitary engineering.

Mariupol Metallurgical Institute: 341000 Mariupol, Republic Lane 7; tel. 34-30-97; telex 115243; f. 1929; faculties: metallurgy, technology, welding, industrial energy, mechanical engineering; library of 580,000 vols; 444 teachers; 5,600 students; Rector I. V. ZHEZHELENKO.

Odessa Hydrometeorological Institute: 270016 Odessa, Lvovskaya ul. 15; tel. (482) 63-62-09; fax (482) 63-63-08; f. 1932; faculties: ecology, hydrology, meteorology, agrometeorology, military hydrometeorology, oceanology; 200 teachers; 2,000 students; library of 250,000 vols; Rector S. STEPANENKO; publs *Meteorology, Climatology, Hydrology* (annual collection of papers).

Odessa Marine Academy: 270029 Odessa, Ul. Didrikhsona 8; tel. 23-40-88; fax 33-49-31; f. 1944; faculties: navigation, ship engineering, electrical engineering, automation; 3,000 mems; library of 450,000 vols; Rector Prof. V. M. ZALETOV; publ. *Transactions of Navigation and Marine Engineering* (annually).

Odessa State Academy of Civil Engineering and Architecture: 270029 Odessa, Ul. Didrikhsona 4; tel. 23-33-42; fax 32-32-29; f. 1930; faculties: architecture, industrial and civil construction, technical engineering, construction engineering, power engineering, sanitary engineering; library of 600,000 vols; Rector Prof. L. V. MAZURENKO.

Odessa State Academy of Food Technologies: 270039 Odessa, Ul. Kanatnaya 112; tel. (482) 25-32-84; fax (482) 25-32-84; f. 1902; faculties: mechanics, mechanical technology and automation, grain technology, canning and bottling technology, meat and dairy products technology, nutrition, bread, confectionery, pasta products, ecology, fish processing, engineering economics; 450 teachers; 6,500 students; library of 600,000 vols; Rector Prof. N. D. ZACHAROV; publ. *Scientific Works* (every 6 months).

Odessa State Academy of Refrigeration: 270026 Odessa, Ul. Dvoryanska 1/3; tel. (482) 23-22-20; fax (482) 23-89-31; e-mail admin@osar.odessa.ua; f. 1930; faculties: refrigeration engineering, automation and robot engineering, systems of automatized projection, environment protection and rational use of natural resources, heat technology, thermophysics, mechanical engineering, cryogenic engineering; 288 teachers; 3,500 students; library of 487,173 vols; Rector I. G. CHUMAK; publ. *Refrigeration Engineering and Technology* (every 6 months).

Poltava State Technical University: 314601 Poltava, Pervomaiskii pr. 24; tel. 2-28-50; f. 1930; faculties: industrial and civil construction, architecture, economics, electromechanics, sanitary engineering; 387 teachers; 3,020 students; library of 400,000 vols; Rector A. G. ONISHCHENKO.

Pridneprovsk State Academy of Civil Engineering and Architecture: 320600 Dnepropetrovsk, Ul. Chernyshevskogo 24A; tel. (562) 45-23-72; fax (562) 47-07-88; f. 1930; faculties: industrial and residential construction, building technology, economics, mechanics, architecture, building structures; 589 teachers; 5,500 students; library of 600,000 vols; Rector Prof. V. I. BOLSHAKOV.

Sevastopol State Technical University: 335053 Sevastopol, Streletsky Bay, Studgorodok; tel. (690) 24-35-90; fax (690) 24-45-30; f. 1963; machine-building, automation, computers, shipbuilding, radio-engineering; 550 teachers; 7,000 students; library of 1,200,000 vols, special collections on machine-building and environmental monitoring; Rector M. Z. LAVRINENKO.

State Academy of Food Technology and Management: 310051 Kharkov, Klochkivska ul. 333; tel. (572) 36-89-79; fax (572) 37-85-35; e-mail hdatoh@kharkov.com; f. 1967; faculties: food technology, food science and food trade, economics, accountancy and audit, industrial management, services management, food industry machines and equipment; 308 teachers; 4,000 students; library of 360,000 vols; Rector A. I. CHEREVKO; publ. *Zbirnyk naukovykh prats* (annually).

Technological University of Podolye: 280016 Khmelnitsky, Institutskaya 11; tel. (322) 2-20-05; telex 291220; fax (322) 2-32-65; f. 1967; faculties: mechanics, engineering economics, technology, radio electronics, business and law, humanities and education; 450 teachers; 8,500 students; library of 700,000 vols; Rector Prof. R. SILIN.

Ukrainian Engineering Pedagogics Academy: 310003 Kharkov, Universitetskaya Ul. 16; tel. (572) 12-78-62; fax (572) 22-72-36; e-mail docents@uenpa.kharkov.ua; f. 1958; faculties: power engineering, mechanical and technological, electrical and mechanical, machine-building, chemical and technological, chemical and mechanical, mining engineering; 350 teachers; 8,000 students; library of 1,000,000 vols; Rector S. F. ARTYUKH.

Ukrainian Institute of Printing: 290020 Lviv, Ul. Podgolosko 19; tel. (322) 59-94-01; faculties: mechanics, technology, economics, book illustration, editorial; library of 384,000 vols; Rector Dr STEPAN HUNKO; publ. *Journal of Printing and Publishing*.

Ukrainian State Academy of Light Industry: 252601 Kiev, Ul. Nemirovicha-Danchenko 2; tel. (44) 290-05-12; fax (44) 290-10-02; f. 1930; depts: light industry technology, chemical technology, engineering and economics, technological equipment and control systems; 504 teachers; 6,294 students; library of 1,015,300 vols; Rector DMITRIY B. GOLOVKO.

Ukrainian State Maritime Technical University: 327025 Nikolaev, Pr. Geroev Stalingrada 9; tel. (512) 35-91-48; fax (512) 39-73-26; f. 1920; faculties: shipbuilding, mechanical engineering, electrical engineering, economics; library of 750,000 vols; Rector Prof. GEORGI F. ROMANOVSKY; publ. *Report* (monthly).

Ukrainian State Telecommunications Academy: 270021 Odessa, Kyznechna vul. 1; tel. (482) 23-22-44; fax (482) 26-19-63; f. 1930; faculties: radio broadcasting and television, automatic electrical communication, information technology, multi-channel electrical communication, posts, management and economics; library of 919,000 vols; br. in Kiev; Rector I. P. PANFILOV.

Ukrainian State University of Chemical Technology: 320005 Dnepropetrovsk 5, Ul. Gagarina 8; tel. 47-46-70; fax 47-33-16; f. 1930; faculties: inorganic chemistry technology, organic chemistry technology, silicate technology, technology of high molecular compounds, engineering; 470 teachers; 5,300 students; library of 753,000 vols; br. in Rubezhnoe.

Ukrainian State University of Food Technology: 252033 Kiev, Volodimyrska vul. 68; tel. and fax (44) 220-95-55; f. 1930; faculties: sugar technology, baking/brewing technology, meat, fat and dairy industry technology, engineering economics, power, food industry machinery and equipment; 8,281 students; 506 teachers; library of 977,000 vols; Rector Prof. I. S. GULYI; publs *Scientific Works* (every 6 months), *Food Industry* (annually), *The Problems of Friction and Wearing* (2 a year).

Ukrainian State University of Forestry and Wood Technology: 290057 Lviv, Ul. Pushkina 103; tel. 35-24-11; f. 1945; faculties: economic engineering, mechanics, woodworking technology, forestry; 300 teachers; 3,500 students; library of 300,000 vols; Rector YU. YU. TUNYTSIA; publ. *Ukrainski lis* (Ukrainian Forest).

Ukrainian Transport University: 252601 Kiev, Ul. Suvorova 1; tel. and fax 290-82-03; f. 1944; faculties: road building, transport management, mechanical; 400 teachers; 5,500 students; library of 440,000 vols; Rector V. YE. KANARCHUK.

Zaporozhe State Engineering Academy: 330600 Zaporozhe, Pr. Lenina 226; tel. (612) 22-64-34; fax (612) 22-31-83; f. 1959; faculties: thermal power engineering, metallurgy, environmental protection, industrial and civil engineering, electronics, management and economics; 350 teachers; 4,500 students; library of 473,000 vols; Rector Dr M. P. REVUN; publs collections of scientific papers (annually).

Zaporozhe State Technical University: 330600 Zaporozhe, Ul. Zhukovskogo 64; tel. (612) 64-25-06; fax (612) 64-21-41; e-mail rector@zstu.zaporizhzhe.ua; 1900; faculties: machine construction, automobile and mechanical engineering, radio engineering, physical engineering, electrical engineering, economics and management; 600 teachers; 6,000 students; library of 1,000,000 vols; Rector Prof. S. B. BELIKOV.

MEDICINE

Chernivtsi Medical Institute: 274000 Chernivtsi, Teatralnaya pl. 2; tel. 2-70-09; library of 174,000 vols.

Crimean Medical Institute: 333670 Simferopol, Bul. Lenina 5/7; tel. 27-44-62; f. 1931; medical training of general practitioners, paediatricians and dentists; library of 550,000 vols; Rector Prof. I. V. BOGADELNIKOV; publ. *Proceedings of the Crimea Medical Institute* (annually).

Dnepropetrovsk State Medical Academy: 320044 Dnepropetrovsk, Vul. Dzerzhinskoho 9; tel. (562) 45-22-68; fax (562) 46-41-91; e-mail root@dma.dnepropetrovsk.ua; f. 1916; library of 650,000 vols; Rector Dr GEORGY V. DZYAK.

Donetsk Medical Institute: 340098 Donetsk, Pr. Ilicha 16; tel. 95-55-41; library of 381,000 vols.

Ivano-Frankovsk Medical Institute: 284000 Ivano-Frankovsk, Galitskaya ul. 2; tel. 2-33-25; library of 109,000 vols.

Kharkiv State Medical University: 310022 Kharkiv, Pr. Lenina 4; tel. 43-07-26; fax 43-06-81; e-mail gnd@khmu.kharkov.ua; f. 1805; 590 teachers; 4,600 students; library of 830,800 vols; Rector Prof. ANATOLY YA. TSYGANENKO; publ. *Medicine Today and Tomorrow* (1 a year).

Kiev Medical Institute: 252004 Kiev, Bul. Shevchenko 13; tel. and fax 224-40-62; library of 400,000 vols.

Lugansk State Medical University: 348045 Lugansk, Vul. 50-let Oborony Luganska; tel. (642) 54-84-03; fax (642) 53-20-36; f. 1956; faculties: medicine, pharmacy, stomatology; library of 420,000 vols; Rector Prof. V. G. KOVESHNIKOV.

Lviv Medical Institute: 290010 Lviv, Pekarskaya ul. 69; tel. 79-64-19; library of 240,000 vols.

Odessa N. I. Pirogov Medical Institute: 270100 Odessa, Per Nariman Narimanova 2; tel. 23-35-67; library of 433,000 vols.

Poltava Medical Stomatological Institute: 314024 Poltava, Ul. Shevchenko 23; tel. 2-88-25; Rector N. S. Skripnikov.

Ternopil Medical Institute: 282000 Ternopil, pl. Svobody 6; tel. 5-15-72.

Ukrainian Academy of Pharmacy: 310002 Kharkov, Pushkinskaya ul. 53; tel. and fax (572) 47-01-64; e-mail root@ukrfa.kharkov.ua; f. 1921; faculties: pharmacy, industrial pharmacy, economics; 350 teachers; 3,000 students; library of 300,000 vols; Rector V. P. Chernykh; publ. *Visnik Farmatsii* (Pharmacy Bulletin, 4 a year), *Klinichna Farmatsiya* (Clinical Pharmacy, 4 a year), *Liki i Zdorovya* (Drugs and Health, 2 a month).

Vinnitsa Medical Institute: 286018 Vinnitsa, Ul. Pirogova 54; tel. 2-06-85; library of 187,000 vols.

Zaporozhe Medical Institute: 330074 Zaporozhe, Ul. Mayakovskogo 26; tel. 33-01-49; f. 1965; Rector I. I. Tokarenko.

AGRICULTURE

Belotserkovsky Agricultural Institute: 256400 Kievskaya obl., Belaya Tserkov, Pl. Svobody 8/1; tel. 5-12-88; f. 1920; faculties: agronomy, veterinary science, animal husbandry; Rector Prof. N. S. Palamar; publ. *Nauchnye Zapiski* (Scientific Notes).

Crimean M. I. Kalinin Agricultural Institute: 330030 Simferopol, Vuzgorodok; tel. 26-31-45; depts: agronomy, fruit and vegetable growing, viticulture, economics, book-keeping; library of 304,450 vols; Rector A. M. Lukyanchenko.

Dnepropetrovsk State Agrarian University: 320027 Dnepropetrovsk, Vul. Voroshilova 25; tel. (562) 44-81-32; fax (562) 45-53-57; f. 1922; faculties: agronomy, agricultural mechanization, economics, veterinary medicine, machinery reclamation; library of 317,000 vols; Rector Prof. N. T. Masyuk; publs *Transactions* (2 a year), *Bulletin* (2 a year).

Kamyanets-Podilsk Institute of Agriculture: 281900 Khmelnytska region, Kamyanets-Podilsk, Ul. Shevchenko 13; tel. 2-52-18; fax 3-92-20; f. 1920; depts: agronomy, animal husbandry, veterinary medicine, economics, mechanization of agriculture; library of 600,000 vols; Rector M. I. Samokish.

Kharkiv Animal Husbandry and Veterinary Institute: 312050 Kharkiv oblast, Dergachevskii raion, P/O Malaya Danilovka; tel. 32-00-03; library of 320,000 vols.

Kharkiv Institute of Agricultural Mechanization and Electrification: 310078 Kharkiv, Ul. Artema 44; tel. 22-37-86; f. 1929; library of 150,000 vols; Rector M. K. Evseev.

Kharkiv State Agricultural University: 312131 Kharkiv, P/O 'Kommunist-1'; tel. 93-71-46; fax 93-60-67; f. 1816; depts: agronomy, plant protection, agrochemistry and soil science, land organization, plant genetics and plant breeding, economics and management, accounting; 378 teachers; 5,182 students; library of 602,000 vols; Rector Prof. N. I. Laktionov; publs *Scientific Reports on Crop Production, Agrochemistry and Soil Science, Land Organization, Plant Protection, Economics and Management, Plant Genetics and Plant Breeding.*

Kherson A. D. Tsuryupa Agricultural Institute: 325006 Kherson, Ul. Rozy Lyuksemburg 23; tel. 2-64-71; f. 1874; faculties of agronomy, animal husbandry, economics and agrobusiness jurisdiction, agricultural construction and hydromelioration; library of 300,000 vols; Rector V. A. Ushkarenko.

Kirovograd Institute of Agricultural Engineering: 316050 Kirovograd, Pr. Pravdy 70A; tel. 55-92-43; f. 1967; faculties: automatics and energetics, economics, engineering and maintenance, fundamental training, mechanical engineering; 308 teachers; 4,680 students; library of 420,000 vols; Rector V. A. Kondratets.

Lugansk Agricultural Institute: 348008 Lugansk 8; tel. 95-20-40; depts: agronomy, mechanization, economics, accounting.

Lviv Academy of Veterinary Medicine: 290010 Lviv, vul. Pekarska 50; tel. 75-67-84; fax 75-67-85; f. 1881; faculties: veterinary medicine, zoo-engineering, sanitary and technological; 250 teachers; 3,400 students; library of 333,000 vols; Rector Prof. Dr R. J. Kravtsiv.

Lviv State Agricultural University: 292040 Lviv oblast, Zhovkva raion, Misto Dublyany; tel. 79-33-45; f. 1856; depts: agronomy, mechanization, organization of land exploitation, farm building, architecture, economics and management, accounting; 390 teachers; 5,000 students; library of 521,000 vols; Rector V. V. Snitynsky; publ. *Transactions*.

Melitopol Institute of Agricultural Mechanization: 332319 Zaporozhe oblast, Melitopol, Pr. B. Khmelnitskogo 18; tel. 2-21-32; telex 337807; f. 1932; 315 teachers; 4,045 students; library of 330,000 vols; Rector N. L. Krizhachkovskii; publs collections of scientific articles (quarterly).

Odessa Agricultural Institute: 270039 Odessa, Ul. Sverdlova 99; tel. (482) 22-37-23; fax (482) 24-01-84; f. 1918; depts: agronomy, fruit and vegetable growing, viticulture, animal husbandry, veterinary medicine, land management, mechanization, economics and management, accounting; 1,000 teachers; 5,200 students; library of 280,000 vols; br. in Nikolaev; Rector Yu. S. Tsukanov.

Poltava State Agricultural Institute: 314003 Poltava, Vul. Skovorody 1/3; tel. (5322) 2-26-10; (5322) fax 2-29-57; f. 1920; depts: agronomy, veterinary science, agro-management, accounting and auditing, mechanization; library of 315,000 vols; Rector V. N. Pisarenko; publ. *Poltava Agrarian News* (4 a year).

Ukrainian Agricultural Academy: 252041 Kiev, Ul. Geroev oborony 15; tel. 263-51-75; depts: agrochemistry and soil science, agronomy, plant protection, mechanization, electrification, economics and management, forestry, animal husbandry, veterinary, accounting; library of 486,000 vols; br. in Vinnitsa; Rector V. V. Yurchishin.

Ukrainian State Academy of Water Management: 266000 Rivne, vul. Soborna 11; tel. 22-10-86; fax 22-21-97; f. 1922; land improvement, water supply and drainage, land reclamation and hydraulic engineering, environmental engineering, industrial and civil engineering, building materials production, land management, town planning and development, hoisting, building, road-making machinery and equipment, automobiles and automobile facilities, mining, automated control of technological processes and production, accounting and audit, production management, business economics, administrative management, topical problems of the water economy, education technology, power-saving materials; 600 teachers; 8,500 students; library of 600,000 vols; Rector Prof. Stepan T. Vozniuk; publ. *Proceedings* (in Ukrainian, 1 a year).

Uman A. M. Gorkii Agricultural Institute: 258900 Cherkasskaya oblast, Uman, P/O 'Sofievka'; tel. 5-33-65; f. 1844; depts: agronomy, fruit and vegetable growing, economics and management of agricultural production, 184 teachers; 1,800 students; library of 200,000 vols; Rector A. Zdorovtsov.

State Academy of Agriculture and Ecology: 262001 Zhitomir, Stary bul. 7; tel. (412) 37-49-31; fax (412) 22-14-02; f. 1922; depts: agricultural ecology, economics and agribusiness, animal husbandry, agricultural engineering, veterinary medicine; 276 teachers; 2,859 students; library of 370,000 vols; Rector V. P. Slavov.

ECONOMICS

Donetsk Institute of Trade: 340050 Donetsk, Ul. Shchorsa 31; tel. 93-18-14; f. 1920; library of 600,000 vols; Rector V. M. Filippov.

Institute of National Economy: 252057 Kiev, Pr. Pobedy 54/1; tel. (44) 446-50-55; fax (44) 226-25-73; f. 1912; depts: economics and management, marketing, engineering economics, finance, agricultural management, accounting and audit, international relations; br. in Krivoi Rog; 600 teachers; 11,000 students; library of 800,000 vols; Rector Anatoly Pavlenko.

Kharkiv State University of Economics: 310001 Kharkiv, Pr. Lenina 9A; tel. (572) 30-23-04; f. 1930; faculties: economics, finance, management, marketing, information systems, accounting and auditing, international economic relations, human resources; 331 teachers; 7,800 students; library of 700,000 vols; Rector N. A. Seroshtan.

Kiev State University of Trade and Economics: 253156 GSP Kiev 156, Ul. Kioto 19; tel. (44) 513-33-48; fax (44) 544-39-74; e-mail mazaraki@kdteu.niiit.kiev.ua; f. 1966; faculties: economics, management and law, science of commodities, accounting and finance, public catering, hospitality service and tourism, banking, postgraduate, preparatory; 593 teachers; library of 434,000 vols; Rector Anatoly Mazaraki; publ. *Bulletin* (monthly).

Lviv Commercial Academy: 290008 Lviv, vul. Tuhan-Baranovskogo 10; tel. 75-65-50; f. 1899; faculties: economics, management, international economic relations, law, commodity science and commerce; 300 teachers; 5,740 students; library of 600,000 vols; Rector Ya. A. Goncharuk.

Odessa State Economic University: 270100 Odessa, Preobrazhenska vul. 8; tel. 23-61-58; fax 23-44-24; f. 1921; faculties: economics and management of production, international economics, credit and economics, financial economics, economics and accounting, commercial economics; 420 teachers; 7,255 students; library of 359,000 vols; Rector V. P. Borodaty.

Poltava Consumers' Co-operative Institute: 314601 Poltava, Ul. Kovalya 3; tel. (5322) 2-09-29; fax (5322) 7-45-42; e-mail root@pki.septor.net.ua; f. 1974; depts: international economics, accounting and auditing, business economics, business management, international management, finance, commodity research and commerce, commodity research and customs, quality control, fruit and vegetables processing and canning technology, meat preservation and processing and canning technology, catering technology; 255 teachers; 3,651 students; library of 356,000 vols; Rector Acad. Viktor A. Dorokhin.

Ternopil Academy of National Economy: 282000 Ternopil, Lvivska 11; tel. and fax (3522) 3-11-02; telex 234146; f. 1971; faculties: international business and management, accountancy and audit, finance, banking, economy and management, agricultural business; 400 teachers; 8,000 students; library of 300,000 vols; Rector Prof. O. Ustenko.

ARTS

Kharkiv Institute of Industrial and Applied Arts: 310002 Kharkiv, Ul. Krasnoznamennaya 8; tel. 43-10-56; f. 1927 and renamed 1963; faculties: industrial design, interior design; library of 88,000 vols; Rector V. I. TORKATYUK.

Kiev State Institute of Fine Arts: 252053 Kiev, Ul. Smirnova-Lastochkina 20; tel. (44) 212-15-40; telex 13156; fax (44) 212-19-46; f. 1917; faculties: sculpture, painting, theatrical decorative art, graphic art, architecture, restoration, art history, arts management; 130 teachers; 800 students; library of 130,000 vols; Rector Prof. ANDREI V. CHEBYKIN.

Lviv State Institute of Applied and Decorative Art: 290011 Lviv, Vul. Kubiyovycha 38; tel. 76-14-77; f. 1946; faculties: decorative and applied art, interior design, monumental and easel painting, sculpture, textile fashion, glass, ceramics, interior decoration, furniture, wood and metal carving, artistic skin products, history and theory of art; 140 teachers; 640 students; library of 90,000 vols; Rector E. P. MYSKO.

LANGUAGES

Gorlovka State Pedagogical Institute of Foreign Languages: 338001 Donetsk oblast, Gorlovka, Ul. Rudakova 25; tel. 4-65-01; f. 1956; library of 213,000 vols; Rector Prof. I. A. KLITSAKOV.

Kiev State Linguistic University: 252650 Kiev, Chervonoarmeiskaya vul. 73; tel. (44) 227-33-72; fax (44) 227-67-88; e-mail lit@kslu.cfrriar.kiev.ua; f. 1948; depts of English, German, French, Spanish, Ukrainian, Russian, translation and interpretation, divisions of Chinese, Japanese, Turkish, Arabic, Korean, Persian, Italian; 500 teachers; library of 650,000 vols; Rector Dr. G. I. ARTEMCHUK; publs *Methods in Foreign Language Teaching*, *Philology of Foreign Languages* (both in Ukrainian and other languages, 4 a year).

LAW

Kharkiv Law Institute: 310024 Kharkiv, Pushkinskaya ul. 77; tel. 47-36-49; library of 256,000 vols.

LIBRARIANSHIP

Kharkiv State Academy of Culture: 310003 Kharkiv, Bursatskii Uzviz 4; tel. and fax (572) 12-81-05; e-mail sheiko@ic.ac.kharkov.ua; f. 1929; departments: library and information science, folk art, cultural studies; 200 teachers; library of 400,000 vols; Rector Prof. VASYL M. SHEIKO; publs *Kultura Ukrainy*, *Bibliotekoznavstvo, dokumentoznavstvo, informatyka*.

Kiev State Institute of Culture: 252195 Kiev, Ul. Shchorsa 36; tel. 269-98-44; fax 212-10-48; departments: library science, folk culture.

Rovno State Institute of Culture: 260000 Rovno, Moskovskaya ul. 12; tel. 2-41-20; librarianship, educational and cultural work.

MUSIC AND THEATRE

Donetsk Musical-Pedagogical Institute: 340086 Donetsk, Ul. Artema 44; tel. 93-81-22; departments: piano, orchestral instruments, folk instruments, choral conducting, singing, composition, musicology.

Kharkiv State Institute of Arts: 310003 Kharkiv, Pl. Sovetskoi Ukrainy 11/13; tel. 22-56-28; piano, orchestral instruments, singing, choral conducting, composition, musicology, acting (puppets), directing (puppets), theatre studies; library of 100,000 vols.

Kiev I. K. Karpenko-Kary State Institute of Theatrical Art: 252034 Kiev, Yaroslavov Val 40; tel. 212-02-00; f. 1918; drama, cinema and television, stage management, choreography, sound direction, film and television direction, scriptwriting; library of 72,000 vols; Rector ROSTISLAV PYLYPCHUK.

Mykola Lysenko Higher State Institute of Music: 290005 Lviv, vul. Nyzhankivsky 5; tel. (322) 74-31-06; fax (322) 72-36-13; f. 1903; faculties: piano, orchestral instruments, folk instruments, operatic and symphonic conducting, choral conducting, musicology, composition, singing; 175 teachers; 550 students; library of 196,000 vols; Rector MARIA KRUSHELNYTSKA.

Odessa State Conservatoire: 270000 Odessa, Ul. Ostrovidova 63; tel. 23-69-68; f. 1913; piano, orchestral and folk instruments, singing, choral conducting, composition, musicology; 140 teachers; 680 students; library of 100,000 vols; Rector V. P. POVZUN.

Ukrainian National Tchaikovsky Academy of Music: 252001 Kiev, Gorodetska vul. 1–3/11; tel. (44) 229-07-92; fax (44) 229-35-30; f. 1913; faculties: piano, orchestral instruments, folk instruments, singing, choral conducting, opera and symphony orchestra conducting, composition, theory and history of music, music production, music education; 304 teachers; 1,156 students; library of 355,000 vols; Rector OLEG TIMOSHENKO; publ. *Ukrainian Musicology* (1 a year).

UNITED ARAB EMIRATES

Research Institutes

GENERAL

Centre for Documentation and Research: Old Palace, POB 2380, Abu Dhabi; f. 1968; attached to the Ministry of Foreign Affairs; collects manuscripts, documents, books, maps and articles relevant to the Arabian Gulf and the Arabian peninsula, and carries out research on subjects related to this area; library of 10,000 vols in many languages; Dir Dr MOHAMMAD MORSI ABDULLAH; publ. *Arabian Gulf Research Review* (quarterly).

AGRICULTURE, FISHERIES AND VETERINARY SCIENCE

Agricultural Research Centre: POB 176, Ras Al Khaimah; tel. 41428; telex 99240; f. 1975 as a UNDP-FAO assisted project, present name 1984; run by Ministry of Agriculture and Fisheries; conducts research into irrigation, plant protection, vegetable varieties, vegetables under plastic houses, soil fertility; *c.* 48 staff; library of 500 vols; Research Dir MOHAMMED HASSAN AL SHAMSI.

Libraries and Archives

Abu Dhabi

National Archives: POB 2380, Abu Dhabi; tel. 447797; fax 445639; f. 1985; attached to the Cultural Foundation, an independent government body; cares for current and historical public records; Dir Dr ABDULLAH ABU EZZAH.

National Library: POB 2380, Abu Dhabi; tel. 215300; telex 22414; fax 217472; f. 1981; 900,000 vols, 1,500 periodical titles, 8,000 audiovisual items; UN Deposit Centre; Dir JUMAA ALQUBAISI; publs *Risalaat Al-Maktbah* (newsletter), *National Bibliography* (in Arabic and English), *Union Catalogue of Periodicals in the UAE* (in Arabic and English).

Dubai

Dubai Municipality Public Libraries: POB 67, Dubai; tel. (4) 262788; fax (4) 266226; f. 1963; 140,000 vols, 537 periodicals; special collection of Arab Islamic art books; Head MOHAMMAD JASSIM AL-ORAIDI.

Museums and Art Galleries

Al Ain

Al-Ain Museum: POB 15715, Al Ain; tel. (3) 641595; fax (3) 658311; f. 1971; archaeology and ethnography; library of 150 vols; archaeological sites at Al-Ain and Umm Al Nar island; Dir SAIF BIN ALI AL-DARMAKI WALID YASIN.

University

UNITED ARAB EMIRATES UNIVERSITY

POB 15551, Al Ain

Founded 1976

State control

Languages of instruction: Arabic and English

Academic year: two semesters

Chancellor: H. H. Sheikh NAHYAN BIN MUBARAK AL-NAHYAN

Vice-Chancellor: Dr YEHIA A. EL-EZABI

Secretary-General: SHABEEB M. AL-MARZOOQI

Librarian: SALEH HUSSEIN HUDEIR

Library of 300,000 vols

Number of teachers: 842

Number of students: 9,394

DEANS

Faculty of Arts: Dr FUAD SHAABAN

Faculty of Sciences: Dr SALAH EL-NAHAWY

Faculty of Economics and Administrative Sciences: Dr AHMED A. ABDEL-HALIM

Faculty of Sharia and Law: Dr MUSTAPHA EL-GAMMAL

Faculty of Education: Dr SAYED KHEIRALLA

Faculty of Engineering: Dr IHAB KAMEL

Faculty of Agricultural Sciences: Dr NUHAD DAGHIR

Faculty of Medicine and Health Sciences: Dr IAIN MCA. LEDINGHAM

RESEARCH CENTRE

Desert and Marine Environment Research Centre.

Colleges

Ajman University College of Science and Technology: POB 346, Ajman; tel. 455299; telex 69619; fax 446355; f. 1988; Chair. Founding Cttee HE Dr SAEED ABDULLAH SALMAN; Vice-Chair. Exec. Cttee Dr AHMED NASIR AL-NUAIMI.

Etisalat College of Engineering: POB 980, Sharjah; tel. (6) 355355; fax (6) 378987; f. 1989; awards B.Eng. degree in Communications; 23 teachers; 130 students; library of 7,000 vols; College Man. SALIM MOHAMMAD AL-OWAIS.

Higher Colleges of Technology: POB 25026, Abu Dhabi; tel. (2) 341-153; fax (2) 328-074; f. 1988; library of 120,000 vols; 900 teachers, 7,000 students; Chancellor H. E. Sheikh NAHAYAN MABARAK AL-NAHAYAN; Vice-Chancellor JOHN WATSON; Librarian FREIDE WIEBE.

DIRECTORS

Abu Dhabi Men's College: JEFF GUNNINGHAM.

Abu Dhabi Women's College: Dr GRADDON R. ROWLANDS.

Al Ain Men's College: NANCY LYNCH.

Al Ain Women's College: DAVID GROSS.

Dubai Men's College: NORMAN J. GRAY.

Dubai Women's College: Dr HOWARD E. REED.

Ras Al Khaimah Men's College: EDWARD MCLEAN.

Ras Al Khaimah Women's College: EDWARD MCLEAN.

Sharjah Men's College: Dr FARID OHAN.

Sharjah Women's College: Dr FARID OHAN.

UNITED KINGDOM

Learned Societies

GENERAL

British Academy: 10 Carlton House Terrace, London, SW1Y 5AH; f. 1901; sections of Classical Antiquity, of African and Oriental Studies, Theology and Religious Studies, of Linguistics and Philology, of Early Modern Languages and Literature, of Modern Languages, Literature and Other Media, of Archaeology, of Medieval Studies, of Early Modern History to 1800, of Modern History from 1800, of History of Art and Music, of Philosophy, of Law, of Economics and Economic History, of Social Anthropology and Human Geography, of Sociology, Psychology, Demography and Social Statistics, of Political Studies; 650 mems; Pres. Sir TONY WRIGLEY; Sec. P. W. H. BROWN; Foreign Sec. Prof. B. E. SUPPLE; publs *Proceedings*, *Annual Report*, *Schweich Lectures on Biblical Archaeology*.

British Council: 10 Spring Gardens, London, SW1A 2BN; tel. (171) 930-8466; fax (171) 839-6347; f. 1934; principal purposes of the British Council are the promotion of a wider knowledge of Britain and the English language abroad and the development of closer cultural relations with other countries; operates in 109 countries; maintains English Teaching Centres in 53 countries, and 209 overseas libraries and information centres; Central Bureau facilitates academic exchange and interchange; British Council arranges for the invigilation overseas of British examinations and, in collaboration with the University of Cambridge Local Examinations Syndicate, offers service to test English-language proficiency of foreign students seeking admission to British instns; gives scholarships and other awards to overseas scholars and research workers to enable them to pursue their studies in Britain, and is responsible for administering in Britain a number of Fellowships schemes on behalf of other bodies including the UN and the Foreign and Commonwealth Office; promotes liaison between scientists in Britain and abroad and provides information on British science, medicine and technology; promotes British writers, actors and other artists abroad; organizes overseas exhibitions of British books and periodicals; Chair. HELENA KENNEDY; Dir-Gen. Dr DAVID DREWRY; publs *British Medical Bulletin*, *Media in Education and Development*, *Writers and their Work*, *English Language Teaching Journal*, *Language Teaching*, *Video English*, *Working Holidays*, *A Year Between*, *Home from Home*, *Volunteer Work*, *Teach Abroad*, *Workplace*.

Commonwealth Institute: Kensington High St, London, W8 6NQ; tel. (171) 603-4535; fax (171) 602-7374; e-mail info@commonwealth.org.uk; aims to promote and to celebrate the Commonwealth; specialist Commonwealth Resource Centre and literature library; Dir-Gen. DAVID FRENCH.

English-Speaking Union (of the Commonwealth): Dartmouth House, 37 Charles St, Berkeley Square, London, W1X 8AB; tel. (171) 493-3328; fax (171) 495-6108; e-mail esu@esu.org; f. 1918; international voluntary organization which through its educational programme is devoted to the promotion of understanding and friendship; 35,000 mems worldwide; library of 13,000 vols; Pres. HRH The Prince PHILIP, Duke of EDINBURGH; Chair. Baroness BRIGSTOCKE; Dir-Gen. VALERIE MITCHELL; publs *Page Memorial Library Accessions List* (quarterly), *Concord* (2 a year), *Newsletter* (monthly).

Royal Society: 6 Carlton House Terrace, London, SW1Y 5AG; tel. (171) 839-5561; fax (171) 930-2170; f. 1660; science, technology and engineering; 1,150 fellows, 108 foreign mems; library: see Libraries and Archives; Pres. Sir AARON KLUG; Biological Sec. Prof. P. J. LACHMANN; Physical Sec. Prof. J. S. ROWLINSON; Foreign Sec. Prof. BRIAN HEAP; Exec. Sec. S. J. COX; publs *Philosophical Transactions*, *Proceedings*, *Annual Report*, *Bulletin*.

Royal Society for the encouragement of Arts, Manufactures and Commerce (RSA): 8 John Adam St, London, WC2N 6EZ; tel. (171) 930-5115; f. 1754 for the promotion of arts, manufactures and commerce; 21,000 Fellows; library of 8,000 vols, 11,000 MSS; Pres. HRH Prince PHILIP Duke of EDINBURGH; Chair. DICK ONIANS; Dir PENNY EGAN; publ. *Journal* (monthly).

Royal Society of Edinburgh: 22 & 24 George St, Edinburgh, EH2 2PQ; tel. (131) 240-5000; fax (131) 240-5024; e-mail rse@rse.org.uk; f. 1783; arts and sciences; 1,200 fellows, 70 hon. fellows; Pres. Prof. MALCOLM JEEVES; Gen. Sec. Prof. P. N. WILSON; Exec. Sec. Dr WILLIAM DUNCAN; publs *Proceedings*, *Transactions*, *RSE News*.

Saltire Society: 9 Fountain Close, 22 High St, Edinburgh, EH1 1TF; branches throughout Scotland; f. 1936 to conserve and foster the Scottish way of life through education, literature, arts and crafts, and architecture; 1,640 mems; Pres. PAUL SCOTT; Administrator KATHLEEN MUNRO.

AGRICULTURE, FISHERIES AND VETERINARY SCIENCE

Agricultural Economics Society: Dept of Agricultural and Food Economics, The Queen's University of Belfast, Newforge Lane, Belfast, BT9 5PX; tel. (1232) 255204; fax (1232) 255327; e-mail john.davis@qub.ac.uk; f. 1926 to promote the study and teaching of all disciplines relevant to agricultural economics as they apply to the agricultural, food and related industries; approx. 700 mems; Hon. Sec. Dr J. DAVIS; publ. *Journal of Agricultural Economics* (3 a year).

British Agricultural History Society: Dept of Economic and Social History, University of Exeter, Amory Building, Rennes Drive, Exeter, EX4 4RJ; f. 1952; 800 mems; Pres. Prof. E. J. T. COLLINS; publ. *Agricultural History Review* (2 a year).

British Society of Animal Science: POB 3, Penicuik, Midlothian EH26 0RZ; tel. (131) 445-4508; fax (131) 535-3120; e-mail bsas@ed.sac.ac.uk; f. 1944; 1,300 mems; United Kingdom member organization of the European Association for Animal Production; Pres. Prof. C. T. WHITTEMORE; Sec. M. A. STEELE; publ. *Animal Science* (every 2 months).

British Society of Soil Science: c/o Dr J. H. Gauld, Macaulay Land Use Research Institute, Craigiebuckler, Aberdeen, AB15 8QH; tel. (1224) 318611; fax (1224) 208065; e-mail j.gauld@mluri.sari.ac.uk; f. 1947 to advance the study of the soil itself and its management in agriculture, forestry, environmental matters and other fields; 950 mems; Pres. Prof. K. SMITH; publs *European Journal of Soil Science*, *Soil Use and Management* (quarterly).

British Veterinary Association: 7 Mansfield Street, London, W1M 0AT; tel. (171) 636-6541; f. 1881 to advance the veterinary art by means of publications and conferences, and to forward and protect the interests of mems of the veterinary profession; 9,000 mems; Pres. KEITH BAKER; Chief Exec. J. H. BAIRD; publs *The Veterinary Record* (weekly), *In Practice* (10 a year).

Institute of Chartered Foresters: 7A St Colme St, Edinburgh EH3 6AA; tel. (131) 225-2705; fax (131) 220-6128; f. 1925, Royal Charter 1982; to maintain and improve the standards of practice and understanding of forestry, and to be the representative body of the forestry profession; 1,440 mems; Pres. G. M. MCROBBIE; Exec. Dir M. W. DICK; publ. *Forestry*.

Institution of Agricultural Engineers: West End Rd, Silsoe, Bedford, MK45 4DU; tel. (1525) 861096; fax (1525) 861660; f. 1938; professional body aiming to advance all those branches of engineering relevant to agriculture, horticulture, forestry and related industries; 2,000 mems; Sec. JOHN NEVILLE; publ. *Landwards* (quarterly).

Royal Agricultural Society of England: National Agricultural Centre, Stoneleigh, Warwicks, CV8 2LZ; tel. (1203) 696969; fax (1203) 696900; f. 1838 (Royal Charter 1840); 14,000 mems; established National Agricultural Centre at Stoneleigh in 1963 to promote advancements in British Agriculture and disseminate information; organizes the Royal Show; arranges regular courses, conferences etc.; agricultural history library; Chief Exec. CHARLES RUNGE; publ. *RASE Journal*.

Royal College of Veterinary Surgeons: Belgravia House, 62 – 64 Horseferry Rd, London, SW1P 2AF; tel. (171) 222-2001; fax (171) 222-2004; f. 1844; the governing body of the veterinary profession in the United Kingdom, which maintains the Statutory Registers and the discipline of the profession and has supervisory functions in relation to veterinary education in the universities; possesses the foremost veterinary library in the UK, open to veterinary surgeons and *bona fide* scientific workers; Pres. Dr L. A. BROWN; Registrar J. C. HERN.

Royal Forestry Society of England, Wales and Northern Ireland: 102 High Street, Tring, Herts HP23 4AF; tel. (1442) 822028; fax (1442) 890395; e-mail rfshq@rfs.org.uk; f. 1882 as the English Arboricultural Society to advance the knowledge and practice of forestry and arboriculture, and to disseminate knowledge of the sciences on which they are based; 4,500 mems; library of 1,500 vols; Pres. J. B. HOWELL; Dir Dr J. E. JACKSON; publ. *Quarterly Journal of Forestry*.

Royal Highland and Agricultural Society of Scotland: Ingliston, Edinburgh EH28 8NF; tel. (131) 335-6200; fax (131) 333-5236; f. 1784, inc. by Royal Charter 1787, for the promotion of agriculture and related industries and education; 14,000 mems; library of 6,000 vols; Chief Exec. H. DAVIES; Sec. J. R. GOOD; publs *Review of the Royal Highland and Agricultural Society of Scotland*, *Royal Highland Spring News*.

Royal Horticultural Society: Exhibition Halls, Library and Offices, 80 Vincent Square, London, SW1P 2PE; tel. (171) 834-4333; Gardens and School, Wisley, Woking, Surrey; Gardens at Rosemoor, Great Torrington, Devon, and Hyde Hall, Chelmsford, Essex; f. 1804; 230,000 mems; library of 50,000 vols (Lindley Library); Pres. Sir SIMON HORNBY; Dir-Gen. GORDON RAE; Sec. D. P. HEARN; publs *The Garden* (monthly), *The New Plantsman*, *Proceedings*, *Wisley Handbooks*, etc.

Royal Scottish Forestry Society: The Stables, Dalkeith Country Park, Dalkeith, Midlothian, EH22 2NA; tel. (131) 660-9480; fax (131) 660-9490; f. 1854; 1,400 mems; Pres. ALAN BLOOMFIELD; Dir M. OSBORNE; publ. *Scottish Forestry* (quarterly).

Royal Welsh Agricultural Society: Llanelwedd, Builth-Wells, Powys LD2 3SY; tel. (1982) 553683; fax (1982) 553563; f. 1904; 12,000 mems; organizes Royal Welsh Show and Royal Welsh Agricultural Winter Fair; Chief Exec. D. WALTERS; publs annual journal, schedules, etc.

Society of Dairy Technology: 72 Ermine St, Huntingdon, Cambs., PE18 6EZ; tel. (1480) 450741; fax (1480) 431800; f. 1943 for the advancement of dairy technology and for the encouragement of technical education and scientific enquiry in the dairy industry; 1,000 mems; Pres. R. MCC. HAMILTON; Sec. ROS GALE; publ. *Journal* (quarterly).

ARCHITECTURE AND TOWN PLANNING

Architects and Surveyors Institute: St Mary House, 15 St Mary St, Chippenham, Wilts, SN15 3WD; tel. (1249) 444505; fax (1249) 443602; f. 1989 by amalgamation of the Faculty of Architects and Surveyors with the Construction Surveyors Institute; aims to promote and extend the practice, knowledge and study of disciplines related to architecture and surveying; maintains standards of technical education; acts as a professional examining body; 6,000 mems; Chief Exec. IAN NORRIS; publ. *ASI Journal* (6 a year).

Architectural Association (Inc.): 34 – 36 Bedford Square, London, WC1B 3ES; tel. (171) 887-4000; fax (171) 414-0782; f. 1847; 3,000 mems; library of 23,000 vols, 49,000 classified periodical articles, 120,000 slides; school of architecture offers facilities for architectural studies; Pres. Sir MICHAEL HOPKINS; Sec. EDOUARD LE MAISTRE; publs *AA Files* (3 a year), Exhibition Catalogues, Weekly Events List, etc.

Association of Building Engineers: Jubilee House, Billing Brook Rd, Weston Favell, Northampton NN3 8NW; tel. (1604) 404121; fax (1604) 784220; f. 1925; examining and qualifying professional body for those specializing in the technology of building; 4,800 mems; Pres. D. PHYTHIAN; Hon. Sec. W. A. BLACK; publ. *Building Engineer* (monthly).

Civic Trust, The: 17 Carlton House Terrace, London, SW1Y 5AW; tel. (171) 930-0914; fax (171) 321-0180; f. 1957 to improve and regenerate the environment where people live and work; registered charity; supports over 1,000 local amenity societies; Dir MICHAEL GWILLIAM; publ. *Civic Focus* (quarterly).

Council for the Care of Churches: Fielden House, Little College St, London, SW1P 3SH; tel. (171) 222-3793; fax (171) 222-3794; f. 1921 to maintain the highest standards in the preservation, restoration and alteration of Anglican churches and their contents by making available sound artistic and technical advice; library of 12,000 vols; Chair. Bishop of Hulme; Sec. THOMAS COCKE; publs *Churchscape* (annually), series on various aspects of caring for churches and their furnishings.

Council for the Protection of Rural England: Warwick House, 25 Buckingham Palace Rd, London, SW1W 0PP; tel. (171) 976-6433; fax (171) 976-6373; e-mail cpre@gn.apc.org; f. 1926; nat. charity which helps people to protect and enhance their local countryside; 45,000 mems; Pres. PRUNELLA SCALES; Dir KATE PARMINTER; publs *CPRE Voice* (3 a year), *Annual Report*, leaflets, reports.

Landscape Institute, The: 6/8 Barnard Mews, London, SW11 IQU; tel. (171) 738-9166; f. 1929; objects: advancement of the art of landscape architecture, theory and practice of landscape design, promotion of research and education therein, maintenance of a high standard of professional qualification, promotion of the highest standard of professional service; the Institute is the chartered institute in the UK for landscape architects, incorporating designers, scientists and managers; 4,100 mems; reference library; Dir-Gen. STUART ROYSTON; publ. *Landscape Design* (10 a year).

London Society: 4th floor, Senate House, Malet St, London, WC1E 7HU; tel. (171) 580-5537; f. 1912 to stimulate a wider concern for the beauty of the capital city, the preservation of its charms and the careful consideration of its development; collection of books and manuscripts including journals since 1912, now housed at London University Library; 520 mems; Pres. HRH the Duke of GLOUCESTER; Chair. Exec. Cttee G. A. WELLS; Hon. Sec. B. R. JONES; publ. *Journal* (2 a year).

National Housing and Town Planning Council: 14 – 18 Old St, London, EC1V 9AB; tel. (171) 251-2363; fax (171) 608-2830; f. 1900 as the National Housing Reform Council to secure the abolition of unhealthy and socially undesirable houses; name changed 1907; a campaigning organization with mems in both public and private sectors, seeking to promote the best standards of housing and planning; and to disseminate information on housing conditions and standards of planning; Dir KELVIN MACDONALD; publ. *Housing and Planning Review* (every 2 months).

National Trust for Places of Historic Interest or Natural Beauty: 36 Queen Anne's Gate, London, SW1H 9AS; tel. (171) 222-9251; fax (171) 222-5097; f. 1895 for the purpose of promoting the permanent preservation of, and public access to, land of natural beauty and buildings of historic interest; 2,300,000 mems; Chair. CHARLES NUNNELEY; Dir-Gen. MARTIN DRURY; publs include, *Members' and Visitors' Handbook*, *Annual Report*, *Newsletter*.

National Trust for Scotland: 5 Charlotte Square, Edinburgh, EH2 4DU; tel. (131) 226-5922; fax (131) 243-9501; f. 1931; promotes the preservation of places of historical or architectural interest or natural beauty in Scotland; 230,000 mems.

Open Spaces Society: 25A Bell St, Henley-on-Thames, RG9 2BA; tel. (1491) 573535; f. 1865; 2,500 mems; Chair. RODNEY LEGG; Sec. KATE ASHBROOK; publ. *Open Space* (3 a year).

Oxford Preservation Trust: 10 Turn Again Lane, St Ebbes, Oxford, OX1 1QL; tel. (1865) 242918; fax (1865) 251022; f. 1927 to combine together Oxford City and University, to work for the beauty of Oxford and its surroundings; it is particularly concerned with planning problems which will affect future development; *c.* 1,000 mems; Chair. Sir DAVID YARDLEY; Sec. MOYRA HAYNES; publ. *Annual Report*.

Royal Incorporation of Architects in Scotland: 15 Rutland Square, Edinburgh, EH1 2BE; tel. (131) 229-7545; fax (131) 228-2188; f. 1916 as a professional organization; 3,300 mems; library of 3,000 vols; Pres. GEORGE WREN; Sec. SEBASTIAN TOMBS; publs *Prospect* (quarterly), *Practice Information* (quarterly), *Newsletter* (10 a year).

Royal Institute of British Architects: 66 Portland Place, London, W1N 4AD; tel. (171) 580-5533; fax (171) 255-1541; e-mail admin@inst.riba.org; f. 1834; 28,000 corporate mems; library: see Libraries; Pres. DAVID ROCK; Dir-Gen. Dr ALEXANDER REID; publs *Journal* (monthly), *RIBA Directory of Members*, *Directory of Practices*, *RIBA International Directory of Practices* (all annually).

Royal Institution of Chartered Surveyors, The: 12 Great George St, Parliament Square, London, SW1P 3AD; tel. (171) 222-7000; fax (171) 222-9430; f. 1868 as the Institution of Surveyors, received Royal Charter 1881; proclaimed as a Royal Institution 1946; unified with the Chartered Land Agents' Society and the Chartered Auctioneers' & Estate Agents' Inst. 1970, with Inst. of Quantity Surveyors 1983; 92,000 mems; library of 35,000 vols; Pres. RICHARD LAY; Chief Exec. JOHN ARMSTRONG; publs *Chartered Surveyor Monthly*, *Library Information Service Weekly Briefing*, *Abstracts and Reviews* (all monthly).

Royal Town Planning Institute: 26 Portland Place, London, W1N 4BE; tel. (171) 636-9107; fax (171) 323-1582; e-mail online@rtpi.org.uk; f. 1914 to further the science and art of town planning for the benefit of the public; 17,000 mems; library of 10,000 vols; Pres. TREVOR ROBERTS; Sec.-Gen. ROBERT UPTON; publs *The Planner* (quarterly), *Planning Week*, *Planning* (weekly).

Society for the Protection of Ancient Buildings: 37 Spital Square, London, E1 6DY; tel. (171) 377-1644; fax (171) 247-5296; f. 1877 by William Morris to prevent the destruction of old buildings and to advise on their conservative repair through courses, campaigns, etc.; *c.* 6,000 mems; Pres. The Duke of GRAFTON; Sec. PHILIP VENNING; publs *Annual Report*, *Newsletter* (quarterly), technical pamphlets.

Town and Country Planning Association: 17 Carlton House Terrace, London, SW1Y 5AS; tel. (171) 930-8903; fax (171) 930-3280; e-mail tcpa@tcpa.org.uk; f. 1899 to campaign for garden cities; now concerns itself with all aspects of planning and the environment; campaigns for improvement to the environment by effective planning, community participation and sustainable development; holds conferences and study tours; 1,300 mems; Chair. Prof. PETER HALL; Dir GRAEME BELL; publ. *Town and Country Planning* (monthly).

Victorian Society, The: 1 Priory Gardens, Bedford Park, London W4 1TT; tel. (181) 994-1019; fax (181) 995-4895; f. 1958; aims to preserve the best of Victorian and Edwardian architecture, and to study the art and history of the period; makes suggestions to the Dept of the Environment for buildings to be added to the statutory list; comments on the applications for listed building consent to demolish or alter buildings of the period; represented at public inquiries on preservation of buildings; 3,500 mems; Chair. Dr CHRIS BROOKS; Dir Dr WILLIAM FILMER-SANKEY; publs *Annual Journal*, *Campaigne Reports*.

BIBLIOGRAPHY, LIBRARY SCIENCE AND MUSEOLOGY

Arlis UK and Ireland/Art Libraries Society of United Kingdom and Ireland: 18 College Rd, Bromsgrove, Worcs, B60 2NE; tel. (1527) 579298; fax (1527) 579298; e-mail sfrench@arlis.demon.co.uk; f. 1969; aims to promote art librarianship particularly by acting as a forum for the interchange of information and materials; 325 mems, 345 overseas mems; Chair. DEBORAH SHORLEY; Admin. SONIA FRENCH; publs *Art Libraries Journal* (quarterly), *News-sheet* (every 2 months), *Directory* (annually).

Aslib: Asscn for Information Management, 20 – 24 Old St, London EC1V 9AP; tel. (171) 253-4488; fax (171) 430-0514; f. 1924; an association of industrial and commercial firms, government departments, research associations and institutions, universities and learned societies in the UK and 80 other countries; provides an enquiry service covering areas such as on-line information retrieval methods, library automation and modern library/information resources management; short courses on all aspects of information work; organizes national and international conferences and meetings; membership of 2,100 organizations; library: see Special Libraries; Chief Exec. R.N. BOWES; publs *The Journal of Documentation* (quarterly), *Aslib Proceedings* (monthly), *Managing Information* (monthly), *Aslib Book Guide* (monthly), *Program* (quarterly), *Forthcoming International Scientific and Technical Conferences* (quarterly), *Records Management Journal* (quarterly), *Current Awareness Abstracts* (monthly), *Online & CD Notes* (monthly), *International Journal of Electronic Library Research* (4 a year), handbooks, reports, directories, bibliographies.

Association of Independent Libraries: C/o The Leeds Library, 18 Commercial St, Leeds, LS1 6AL; tel. (113) 245-3071; f. 1989; 21 mems; Pres. Prof. PETER ISAAC; publs *Newsletter* (annually), *Directory*.

Bibliographical Society: C/o Wellcome Institute, 183 Euston Road, London, NW1 2BE; f. 1892; 1,100 mems; Pres. M. FOOT; Hon. Sec. D. PEARSON; publs *The Library* (quarterly), various books on bibliographical subjects.

Book Trust: Book House, 45 East Hill, London, SW18 2QZ; tel. (181) 516-2977; an independent educational charity; f. 1925 as The National Book Council to extend the use and enjoyment of books, which is still its aim; provides book lists and a book information service; administers 9 literary prizes; over 1,000 mems; houses Young Book Trust, including a reference library containing all children's books published over the past 2 years; Pres. DORIS LESSING; Chief Exec. BRIAN PERMAN.

Cambridge Bibliographical Society: University Library, Cambridge, CB3 9DR; tel. (1223) 333000; telex 81395; fax (1223) 333160; e-mail cbs@ula.cam.ac.uk; f. 1949; historical bibliography and history of the book trade; 500 mems; Hon. Treas. N. THWAITE; publs *Transactions* (annually), *Monographs* (irregular).

Edinburgh Bibliographical Society: C/o Rare Books Division, National Library of Scotland, George IV Bridge, Edinburgh, EH1 1EW; tel. (131) 226-4531; fax (131) 220-6662; e-mail r.ovenden@nls.uk; f. 1890 (the oldest bibliographical society in Great Britain) for discussion and elucidation of questions connected with books, printed or manuscript, especially Scottish, the promotion and encouragement of bibliographical studies, and the printing of bibliographical works; *c.* 210 mems; Hon. Sec. R. OVENDEN; publ. *Transactions* (every 2 years).

Friends of the National Libraries: C/o The British Library, Great Russell St, London, WC1B 3DG; tel. (171) 412-7559; f. 1931 to promote the acquisition of printed books and MSS of historical, literary or archaeological significance for libraries and record offices; 900 mems; Chair. Lord EGREMONT; Hon. Sec. MICHAEL BORRIE; publ. *Annual Report*.

Library Association: 7 Ridgmount St, London, WC1E 7AE; tel. (171) 636-7543; fax (171) 436-7218; e-mail info@la-hq.org.uk; f. 1877; advice and publs on librarianship and information management in all sectors; 26,000 mems; Chief Exec. ROSS SHIMMON; publs include *Library Association Record, Year Book*.

Museum Training Institute: Glyde House, Glydegate, Bradford, BD5 0UP; tel. (1274) 391056; fax (1274) 394890; f. 1989 to promote training and develop competence-based standards and vocational qualifications; Dir CHRIS NEWBERY; publ. *News* (every 2 months).

Museums & Galleries Commission: 16 Queen Anne's Gate, London, SW1H 9AA; tel. (171) 233-4200; fax (171) 233-3686; f. 1931; advises the Govt on museum affairs; executive functions: allocates grants to Area Museum Ccls, co-ordinates funding and monitoring of Museum Documentation Asscn, administers grant scheme for non-national museums; administers arrangements for govt indemnities, and acceptance of works of art in lieu of inheritance tax; has responsibility for the two purchase funds for local museums which are managed on its behalf by the V & A and Science Museums; maintains register of conservators; 15 mems; Chair. JAMES JOLL; Dir TIMOTHY MASON; publs *Annual Report*, various reports, newsletters and reviews.

Museums Association: 42 Clerkenwell Close, London, EC1R 0PA; tel. (171) 608-2933; fax (171) 250-1929; e-mail info@museumsassociation.org; f. 1889 to promote and improve museums and galleries and the training of museum staff; 5,028 mems; Pres. BARBARA WORONCOW; Dir MARK TAYLOR; publs *Museums Journal* (monthly), *Museums Yearbook* (annually), *Museums Practice* (3 a year).

Scottish Library Association: 1 John St, Hamilton, ML3 7EU; tel. (1698) 458888; fax (1698) 458899; f. 1908; affiliated to the Library Asscn; 2,200 mems; Pres. IAN McGOWAN; Dir ROBERT CRAIG; publs *Annual Conference Proceedings*, *Scottish Libraries* (every 2 months), *Library and Information Resources in Scotland*, etc.

Standing Conference of National and University Libraries (SCONUL): 102 Euston St, London, NW1 2HA; tel. (171) 387-0317; f. 1950 to promote the work of the national and university libraries of the UK and Ireland; mems: 120 institutions; Chair. G. FORD; Sec. A. J. C. BAINTON.

Welsh Library Association: Executive Officer, D. I. L. S., University College of Wales, Llanbadarn Fawr, Aberystwyth, Dyfed, SY23 3AS; tel. (1970) 622174; fax (1970) 622190; e-mail ggc995@aber.ac.uk; f. 1933; a branch of the Library Association; a professional body of librarians in Wales concerned with all aspects of librarianship and related matters; 980 mems; Chair. ANDREW GREEN; publs *News / Newyddion* (monthly), *Y Ddolen* (quarterly).

ECONOMICS, LAW AND POLITICS

Association of Chartered Certified Accountants, The: 29 Lincoln's Inn Fields, London, WC2A 3EE; tel. (171) 242-6855; fax (171) 831-8054; f. 1904; inc. by Royal Charter; 55,000 mems; Pres. D. N. LEONARD; Chief Exec. A. L. ROSE; publs *Certified Accountant* (monthly), *List of Members*, *Students' Newsletter* (monthly), *Accountants' Guide*.

British Academy of Forensic Sciences: Anaesthetics Unit, The Royal London Hospital, Whitechapel, London, E1 1BB; tel. (171) 377-9201; f. 1959 to advance forensic science in all its aspects to the benefit of justice and the law; annual meetings; over 500 mems; Sec.-Gen. Dr PATRICIA J. FLYNN; publ. *Medicine, Science and the Law* (quarterly).

British Institute of International and Comparative Law: Charles Clore House, 17 Russell Square, London, WC1B 5DR; tel. (171) 636-5802; fax (171) 323-2016; e-mail biicl@dial.pipex.com; f. 1958 by the amalgamation of the Grotius Society and the Society of Comparative Legislation and International Law; organizes the Commonwealth Legal Advisory Service and research in comparative law, international law, and law of the European Communities; holds conferences, meetings and lectures in international and comparative law; Chair. Lord GOFF; Dir J. P. GARDNER; publs *International and Comparative Law Quarterly*, *Bulletin of Legal Developments* (fortnightly), and other occasional publications on international and comparative law.

Chartered Institute of Bankers: Emmanuel House, 4–9 Burgate Lane, Canterbury, Kent, CT1 2XJ; tel. (1227) 762600; fax (1227) 763788; f. 1879; provides the educational foundation and qualifications for a career in banking, building societies or other financial services; publishes textbooks for the financial sector; 67,000 mems; library of 30,000 vols; Pres. J. M. BLACKBURN; Chief Exec. GAVIN SHREEVE; publs *CIB News* (monthly), *Chartered Banker* (monthly).

Chartered Institute of Bankers in Scotland: Drumsheugh House, 38B Drumsheugh Gardens, Edinburgh, EH3 7SW; tel. (131) 473-7777; fax (131) 473-7788; f. 1875 to improve the qualifications of those engaged in banking, and to raise their status and influence; 13,000 mems; Chief Exec. Dr C. W. MUNN; publ. *The Scottish Banker* (quarterly).

Chartered Institute of Management Accountants: 63 Portland Place, London, W1N 4AB; tel. (171) 637-2311; fax (171) 631-5309; e-mail pr@cima.org.uk; f. 1919, Royal Charter granted 1975; professional management accountants' body for the UK; membership is gained through examination and practical experience; 47,000 mems; Sec. J. S. CHESTER; publ. *Management Accounting*.

Chartered Institute of Public Finance and Accountancy: 3 Robert St, London, WC2N 6BH; tel. (171) 543-5600; fax (171) 543-5700; f. 1885; professional accountancy body for public services; provides education and training in accountancy and financial management, and sets and monitors professional standards; 12,000 mems; 3,000 students; library of 3,500 vols and 100 journals and collection of CIPFA's own publs; Dir D. H. ADAMS; publs *Public Finance* (weekly), *Public Money and Management* (quarterly).

Chartered Insurance Institute: The Hall, 20 Aldermanbury, London, EC2V 7HY; tel. (181) 989-8464; fax (171) 726-0131; inc. by Royal Charter 1912 with the object of providing and maintaining a central organization for the promotion of professionalism and progress among insurance and financial services employees; primarily an educational and examining body; 70,000 mems; library of 15,000 vols; Dir-Gen. D. E. BLAND; Librarian R. L. CUNNEW; publ. *Journal* (every 2 months).

David Davies Memorial Institute of International Studies: 2 Chadwick St, Westminster, London, SW1P 2EP; tel. (171) 222-4063; fax (171) 233-2863; e-mail munwin@ddmi.org.uk; f. 1951 to commemorate and continue the work of Lord Davies (1880 – 1944), on the means of establishing a viable world order; aims: to advance and promote the development of international relations in the political, economic, legal, social, educational, ecological and other fields, and to carry out and instigate research; works through *ad hoc* groups, seminars, conferences, bringing together experts in the relevant fields and publishing its findings; 1,000 mems; Pres. The Rt Hon. Lord HEALEY OF RIDDLESDEN; Dir and Editor MARY UNWIN; publ. *International Relations* (3 a year).

Economics and Business Education Association: 1A Keymer Rd, Hassocks, W. Sussex, BN6 8AD; tel. (1273) 846033; fax (1273)

844646; f. 1948 to promote and extend the study of economics, business studies and related subjects in schools and colleges, to act as a representative body for economics and business studies teachers in educational matters and to promote knowledge of and interest in economics and related subjects among the general public; 2,800 mems; Pres. IAN BYATT; Chair. JENNY WALES; publ. *Teaching Business and Economics* (3 a year).

Electoral Reform Society of Great Britain and Ireland Ltd: 6 Chancel St, Blackfriars, London, SE1 0UU; tel. (171) 928-1622; fax (171) 401-7789; f. 1884 to secure an effective vote for every parliamentary and local government elector by the adoption of the single transferable vote form of proportional representation for all elections of representative bodies, and similarly for elections in all voluntary organizations; 2,000 mems; comprehensive reference library and archive; Electoral Reform (Ballot Services) Ltd (tel. (181) 365-8909, fax (181) 365-8587) provides advice and electoral administration service for UK organizations; Electoral Reform (International Services) (tel. (171) 620-3794, fax (171) 928-4366) provides advice for overseas organizations; Pres. (vacant); Chair. Rev. DAVID MASON; Chief Exec. E. M. SYDDIQUE; publs *ERS News* (quarterly), *Representation* (quarterly).

European Movement, The (British Council): Dean Bradley House, 52 Horseferry Rd, London, SW1P 2AF; tel. (171) 233-1422; fax (171) 799-2817; f. 1948 to help individuals, especially students and pupils, industrial and commercial companies, banks, trade unions, political parties, professional organizations to keep abreast of developments in the field of European integration; Dir STEPHEN WOODARD; publ. *Britain in Europe* (quarterly).

Fabian Society: 11 Dartmouth St, London, SW1H 9BN; tel. (171) 222-8877; fax (171) 976-7153; e-mail fabian-society@geo2.poptel.org.uk; f. 1884; public policy think-tank and socialist society; 5,400 mems; Gen. Sec. MICHAEL JACOBS; publs *Fabian Review* (4 a year), *Fabian Pamphlets* (16 a year).

Faculty of Actuaries: MacLaurin House, 18 Dublin St, Edinburgh, EH1 3PP; tel. (131) 240-1300; fax (131) 240-1313; e-mail faculty@actuaries.org.uk; f. 1856; 946 Fellows; 576 students; library of 9,000 vols; Sec. W. W. MAIR; publ. *British Actuarial Journal*.

Faculty of Advocates: Advocates Library, Parliament House, Edinburgh, EH1 1RF; tel. (131) 226-5071; fax (131) 225-3642; f. *c.* 1532; the sole professional body for Advocates (Barristers) in Scotland; it maintains professional standards, examines Intrants and represents its members; 605 mems; copyright library in respect of Legal works of *c.* 100,000 Law books associated with National Library of Scotland (*q.v.*); Dean Hon. NIGEL EMSLIE; Clerk IAIN G. ARMSTRONG; Keeper of the Library ANGUS STEWART.

Federal Trust for Education and Research: Dean Bradley House, 52 Horseferry Road, London, SW1P 2AF; tel. (171) 799-2818; fax (171) 799-2820; e-mail andrewduff@fedtrust.co.uk; f. 1945 to promote and carry out research and education into federal solutions to national, European and global problems, in particular the European Union; Dir ANDREW DUFF; Chair. JOHN PINDER.

General Council of the Bar: 3 Bedford Row, London, WC1R 4DB; tel. (171) 242-0082; fax (171) 831-9217; f. 1894, present constitution 1987; governing body for the barristers' profession in England and Wales; Chief Exec. NIALL MORISON; publs *Counsel* (quarterly), *Code of Conduct*.

Hansard Society for Parliamentary Government: St Philip's Bldg, Sheffield St, London, WC2A 2EX; tel. (171) 955-7478; fax (171) 955-7492; f. 1944; promotes political education, political research and the informed discussion of all aspects of modern parliamentary government; 400 mems; Chair. Dr DAVID BUTLER; Dir SHELAGH DIPLOCK; publ. *Parliamentary Affairs* (quarterly).

Institute for Fiscal Studies: 7 Ridgmount St, London, WC1E 7AE; tel. (171) 291-4800; fax (171) 323-4780; e-mail mailbox@ifs.org.uk; f. 1969 to improve the quality of public discussion and policy making in the fiscal system; organizes conferences, lectures, seminars, undertakes original research, publishes reports; *c.* 750 individual mems, 250 corporate and institutional mems; Dir ANDREW DILNOT; Research Dir RICHARD BLUNDELL; publ. *Fiscal Studies* (quarterly).

Institute of Actuaries: Staple Inn Hall, High Holborn, London, WC1V 7QJ; tel. (171) 632-2100; fax (171) 632-2111; Education Service and Library: Napier House, 4 Worcester St, Oxford, OX1 2AW; tel. (1865) 268200; fax (1865) 268211; e-mail institute@actuaries.org.uk; f. 1848, Royal Charter 1884, for the elevation of the attainments and status of all who are engaged in actuarial pursuits, etc.; 9,000 mems; library of 15,000 vols (Oxford), collection of rare books (London); Pres. P. N. THORNTON; Hon. Secs M. R. KIPLING, N. B. MASTERS; Sec.-Gen. G. B. L. CAMPBELL; publ. *British Actuarial Journal* (with Faculty of Actuaries, 5 a year).

Institute of Chartered Accountants in England and Wales: Chartered Accountants' Hall, Moorgate Place, London, EC2P 2BJ; tel. (171) 920-8100; fax (171) 920-0547; f. 1880 by Royal Charter; 112,000 mems; library of 40,000 vols; special collection of early European books on bookkeeping; Pres. C. SWINSON; Sec. J. COLLIER; publs *Accountancy* (monthly), *Accountants Digests* (irregular), *Accounting and Business Research* (quarterly), *List of Members* (annually), *Auditing Standards and Guidelines* (annually), *Accounting Standards* (annually), *Tax Digests* (irregular), *Update* (monthly).

Institute of Chartered Accountants of Scotland: 27 Queen St, Edinburgh, EH2 1LA; tel. (131) 225-5673; fax (131) 225-3813; f. 1854 to deal with professional matters concerning its members; 14,000 mems; libraries with 18,000 books; Pres. A. S. HUNTER; Chief Exec. and Sec. P. W. JOHNSTON; publs *Annual Report*, *Official Directory of Members* (annually), *CA Magazine* (monthly), various occasional publications.

Institute of Chartered Secretaries and Administrators: 16 Park Crescent, London, W1N 4AH; tel. (171) 580-4741; fax (171) 323-1132; f. 1891 as a professional organization for secretaries of incorporated bodies; over 44,000 mems; Librarian/Information Officer M. P. NOLAN; publs *Company Secretarial Practice*, *Chartered Secretary* (monthly).

Institute of Economic Affairs: 2 Lord North St, Westminster, London, SW1P 3LB; tel. (171) 799-3745; fax (171) 799-2137; f. 1955; to improve understanding of economics and its application to business and public policy; Gen. Dir JOHN BLUNDELL; publs *Hobart Papers*, *Research Monographs*, *IEA Readings*, *Occasional Papers*, *Current Controversies*, *Choice in Welfare*, *Economic Affairs*, *Journal* (quarterly), *IEA Studies in Education*, *IEA Studies on the Environment*.

Law Society: 113 Chancery Lane, London, WC2A 1PL; tel. (171) 242-1222; telex 261203; fax (171) 831-0344; f. 1825; governing body of solicitors in England and Wales; 62,439 mems; library: see Libraries; Sec.-Gen. JANE BETTS; publ. *Gazette* (weekly).

Political Studies Association of the United Kingdom: C/o Victoria Leach, Dept of Politics, University of Nottingham, Nottingham, NG7 2RD; tel. (115) 951-4797; fax (115) 951-4797; e-mail psa@nottingham.ac.uk; f. 1950 to promote the development of political studies; 1,000 mems; Chair. Prof. IAN FORBES; Hon. Sec. Dr MOYA LLOYD; publs *Political Studies* (5 a year), *Politics* (3 a year), *British Journal of Politics and International Relations* (4 a year), *PSA Directory* (annually), *PSA Media Register* (annually), *Newsletter* (quarterly).

Royal Economic Society: Dept of Economics, London Business School, Sussex Place, Regents Park, London, NW1 4SA; tel. (171) 262-5050; fax (171) 724-1598; e-mail eburke@lbs.ac.uk; f. 1890; 3,500 mems; Pres. Prof. P. DASGUPTA; Sec.-Gen. Prof. R. PORTES; publ. *Economic Journal* (quarterly).

Royal Faculty of Procurators in Glasgow, The: 12 Nelson Mandela Place, Glasgow, G2 1BT; inc. long prior to 1668, and by Royal Charter 1796; a legal society; 500 mems; library of over 20,000 vols; Dean CAMPBELL WHITE; Clerk, Treasurer and Fiscal A. J. CAMPBELL; Librarian E. M. PEIRCE.

Royal Institute of International Affairs: Chatham House, 10 St. James's Square, London, SW1Y 4LE; tel. (171) 957-5700; fax (171) 957-5710; f. 1920 to facilitate the scientific study of international questions; mems, all categories, approx. 3,500; research programme: studies of broad economic, political and security trends in international relations and research into Middle East, Asia-Pacific, Europe, Russia and CIS regions and into energy and the environment; library: see Libraries and Archives; Pres Lord CARRINGTON, Lord CALLAGHAN, Lord JENKINS OF HILLHEAD; Dir Sir TIMOTHY GARDEN; Dir of Studies GEORGE JOFFÉ; publs *International Affairs* (quarterly), *The World Today* (monthly).

Royal Statistical Society: 12 Errol St, London, EC1Y 8LX; tel. (171) 638-8998; fax (171) 256-7598; f. 1834; 6,000 mems; Pres. Prof. A. F. M. SMITH; Hon. Secs G. M. CLARKE, P. V. ALLIN, T. SWEETING; publs *Journal* (Series A *Statistics in Society*, Series B *Methodology*, Series C *Applied Statistics*, Series D *The Statistician*, 3 or 4 parts annually).

Selden Society: c/o Faculty of Laws, Queen Mary and Westfield College, Mile End Rd, London, E1 4NS; tel. (171) 975-5136; fax (181) 981-8733; e-mail selden-society@qmw.ac.uk; f. 1887; 1,700 mems; Pres. Rt Hon. Lord MUSTILL; Hon. Treas. CHRISTOPHER WRIGHT; Literary Dir Prof. J. H. BAKER; Sec. VICTOR TUNKEL; publs over 130 vols on sources and other aspects of English legal history.

Stair Society: Saltire Court, 20 Castle Terrace, Edinburgh, EH1 2ET; tel. (131) 228-9900; fax (131) 228-1222; f. 1934 to encourage the study and advance the knowledge of the history of Scots Law; 535 mems; Pres. Lord HOPE; Chair. of Council Sheriff PETER G. B. MCNEILL; Sec. LORNA M. SMITH.

EDUCATION

Advisory Centre for Education (ACE) Ltd: 1B Aberdeen Studio, 22 – 24 Highbury Grove, London, N5 2DQ; tel. (171) 354-8321; fax (171) 354-9069; e-mail ace-ed@easynet.co.uk; f. 1960; aims to provide information on education for parents and others, to encourage close home-school relationships, and to arouse discussion on education issues; publs *ACE Bulletin* (every 2 months), *Stop Press* (monthly).

British Educational Communications and Technology Agency: Milburn Hill Rd, Science Park, Coventry, CV4 7JJ; tel. (1203)

416994; fax (1203) 411418; e-mail becta@becta.org.uk; f. 1998; aims to ensure that technology supports the Government's objectives to raise standards, in particular to provide the professional expertise needed to support the development of the National Grid for Learning.

British Educational Management and Administration Society: 12 Coleraine Rd, Blackheath, London, SE3 7PQ; tel. (171) 403-1990; fax (171) 378-1590; f. 1971; to advance the practice of and research into educational administration; to maintain close contact with national and international organizations and to encourage the foundation of local groups; *c.* 1,400 mems; Hon. Pres. (vacant); Chair. L. E. WATSON; Hon. Sec. L. C. MARTIN; publs *Educational Management and Administration*, *Management in Education* (both quarterly).

City & Guilds: 1 Giltspur St, London, EC1A 9DD; tel. (171) 294-2468; fax (171) 294-2400; f. 1878; awards vocational qualifications in 500 subjects, at all levels from basic skills to professional; 3.8 million entries a year; Dir-Gen. Dr NICHOLAS CAREY; publs *Broadsheet* (3 a year), *Report and Accounts* (annually).

College of Teachers: Theydon Bois, Epping, Essex CM16 7DN; tel. (1992) 81-2727; fax (1992) 81-4690; e-mail collegeofteachers@mailbox.ulcr.ac.uk; f. 1846, incorporated by Royal Charter 1849; offers membership to educationists, awards qualifications by examination to experienced teachers of Associate, Licentiate (equivalent to university first degree), Diploma in the Advanced Study of Education, and Fellow; Pres. Prof. JOHN D. TURNER; publ. *Education Today* (quarterly).

Committee of Vice-Chancellors and Principals of the Universities of the United Kingdom: Woburn House, 20 Tavistock Square, London, WC1H 9HQ; tel. (171) 419-4111; fax (171) 388-8649; e-mail info@cvcp.ac.uk; aims to promote, encourage and develop UK universities, and to promote understanding of the role, achievements and objectives of universities; mems: exec. heads of all UK univs; Chair. Prof. MARTIN HARRIS; Chief Exec. D. WARWICK.

Council for Education in World Citizenship: 15 St Swithin's Lane, London, EC4N 8AL; tel. (171) 929-5090; fax (171) 929-5091; e-mail cewc@campus.bt.com; f. 1939; an independent, non-political organization to assist schools and colleges in the teaching of international affairs and promote a more global perspective in curricula; 1,000 mem. schools; library of resources and reference material; Dir PATRICIA ROGERS; publs *Broadsheet*, *Broadsheet Digest*, *Activities Sheet*, *Newsletter* (all 5 a year).

Educational Institute of Scotland, The: 46 Moray Place, Edinburgh, EH3 6BH; tel. (131) 225-6244; f. 1847; to promote sound learning and advance the interests of teachers in Scotland; 50,800 mems; Pres. MOIRA MCCROSSAN; Gen. Sec. RONALD A. SMITH; publ. *Scottish Educational Journal* (*c.* 8 per session).

Higher Education Funding Council for England: Northavon House, Coldharbour Lane, Bristol, BS16 1QD; tel. (117) 931-7317; fax (117) 931-7203; e-mail hefce@hefce.ac.uk; f. 1992; responsible under the Further and Higher Education Act 1992 for the distribution of funds made available by the Secretary of State for Education and Employment for the provision of education and the undertaking of research by institutions of higher education in England; Chair. Sir MICHAEL CHECKLAND; Chief Exec. BRIAN FENDER.

National Conference of University Professors: c/o Prof. W. J. Cram, Biological and Nutritional Sciences, University of Newcastle upon Tyne, NE1 7RU; tel. (191) 222-7886; fax (191) 222-6720; f. 1989 to support university professors in carrying out their special responsibilities for the maintenance of academic standards, to provide a forum for discussion and a corporate voice on matters of concern to the nation's university system, to improve public perceptions about the work of universities, and to act as a means of collecting and disseminating information relevant to universities; mems: 640 univ. profs; Pres. Prof. J. E. WALSH; Sec. Prof. W. J. CRAM.

National Institute of Adult Continuing Education (England and Wales): 21 De Montfort St, Leicester; tel. (116) 204-4200; fax (116) 285-4514; e-mail niace@niace.org.uk; f. 1921 by incorporation of the British Institute of Adult Education and the National Foundation for Adult Education to promote understanding and co-operation between bodies and individuals engaged in adult education, to encourage research and training and serve as a centre of information; conferences and meetings; library; develops co-operative relations with foreign and international organizations; both corporate and individual membership; Dir ALAN TUCKETT; publs *Adults Learning* (monthly), *Year Book of Adult Continuing Education*, *Time to Learn*, *Studies in the Education of Adults* (2 a year), research studies.

National Society for Education in Art and Design: The Gatehouse, Corsham Court, Corsham, Wilts., SN13 0BZ; tel. (1249) 714825; fax (1249) 716138; f. 1888; the recognized professional body and trade union for principals, lecturers and teachers employed in colleges and schools of art and all specialist teachers of art, craft and design; Gen. Sec. JOHN STEERS; publ. *Journal of Art and Design Education* (3 a year).

Open and Distance Learning Quality Council Ltd: 25 Marylebone Rd, London, NW1 5JS; tel. (171) 935-5391; fax (171) 935-2540; e-mail odlqc@dial.pipex.com; f. 1968; only organization in the UK officially recognized as responsible for the award of Accreditation to Colleges offering open and distance learning; recognized as a Registered Charity; 43 colleges accredited; Chair. JOHN AINSWORTH; Sec. DAVID MORLEY.

Standing Conference of Arts and Social Sciences: c/o Dr S. Delamont, University of Wales, SOCAS, 50 Park Place, Cardiff, CF1 3AT; tel. (1222) 874803; fax (1222) 874436; f. 1984 to interpret, explain and safeguard the role of university teaching and research in the Arts and Social Sciences; organizes conferences; Convenor Prof. J. BIRKETT.

UK Council for Graduate Education: C/o CEDAR, University of Warwick, Coventry, CV4 7AL; tel. (1203) 524847; fax (1203) 524472; f. 1994; promotes a distinct identity for graduate education and research in higher education; 127 institutional mems; Chair Prof. ROBERT BURGESS; Hon. Gen. Sec. Dr JOHN HOGAN.

University Association for Contemporary European Studies: King's College London, Strand, London, WC2R 2LS; tel. (171) 240-0206; fax (171) 836-2350; f. 1968; to bring together academics from different disciplines (law, politics, economics, languages, etc.) with a common interest in European studies and specifically in European integration; circulates information to mems about developments in European studies; holds conferences and seminars; provides documentation on European Studies; 600 individual, 110 corporate mems; Chair. Prof. G. GEORGE; Sec. J. GOWER; publs *Register of Current Research in European Integration*, *Register of Courses in European Studies in British Universities & Colleges* (every 2 years).

Workers' Educational Association: Temple House, 17 Victoria Park Sq., London, E2 9PB; tel. (181) 983-1515; fax (181) 983-4840; e-mail info@wea.org.uk; f. 1903 to stimulate public interest in education and to provide opportunities for adults to pursue liberal studies and to encourage them to render effective service to the community; co-operates with universities and other voluntary asscns through its districts and brs for the provision of classes; these classes, although provided independently, are grant-aided by the Further Education Funding Council in England, the Scottish Office Education Dept, local education authorities and other funding bodies; 100,000 students; Gen. Sec. R. LOCHRIE.

FINE AND PERFORMING ARTS

Arts Council of England: 14 Great Peter St, London, SW1P 3NQ; tel. (171) 333-0100; f. 1940 as the Council for the Encouragement of Music and the Arts (CEMA), in 1945 became the Arts Council of Great Britain, present name 1994; develops and improves the knowledge, understanding and practice of the arts, to increase the accessibility of the arts to the public throughout England, and advises and co-operates with govt depts, local authorities and other bodies concerned with these objects; 10 mems; Chair. GERRY ROBINSON; Chief Exec. PETER HEWITT; publs *Annual Report*, *Development Funds*.

Arts Council of Wales: 9 Museum Place, Cardiff, CF1 3NX; tel. (1222) 376500; fax (1222) 221447; funded by the Welsh Office; Chair. Sir RICHARD LLOYD JONES; Chief Exec. JOANNA WESTON.

British Federation of Festivals: Festivals House, 198 Park Lane, Macclesfield, Cheshire, SK11 6UD; tel. (1625) 428297; fax (1625) 503229; e-mail festivals@compuserve.com; inc. 1921; headquarters of the Amateur Festival Movement; Patron HM The QUEEN; Gen. Sec. E. WHITEHEAD; publ. *Year Book*.

British Film Institute: 21 Stephen St, London, W1P 1PL; tel. (171) 255-1444; telex 27624; fax (171) 436-7950; f. 1933; nat. agency with responsibility for encouraging the arts of film and television and conserving them in the nat. interest; among its divisions are the National Film and Television Archive (*q.v.*), the National Cinema Centre, the Museum of the Moving Image, Information and Education, BFI Films, a Research Division, and BFI Production; 29,000 mems; in receipt of annual government grant; Dir W. STEVENSON; publs *Sight and Sound* (monthly, illustrated), *BFI Film and Television Handbook* (annually).

British Institute of Professional Photography: Fox Talbot House, Amwell End, Ware, Herts, SG12 9HN; tel. (1920) 464011; f. 1901; professional qualifying body; awards the designatory letters FBIPP, ABIPP and LBIPP; represents professional photographers and photographic technicians; to improve the quality of photography; to establish recognized examinations and standards of conduct; to safeguard the interests of the public and the profession; 4,000 mems; publs *The Photographer* (monthly), *The Directory of Professional Photography* (annually).

British Society of Painters in Oil, Pastels and Acrylic: c/o Leslie Simpson, 2 The Brambles, Ilkley, West Yorks, LS29 9DH; tel. (1943) 609075; f. 1986; 12 fellows, 50 mems; holds two exhibitions annually; awards prizes; Dir LESLIE SIMPSON.

British Watercolour Society: c/o Leslie Simpson, 2 The Brambles, Ilkley, West Yorks, LS29 9DH; tel. (1943) 609075; f. 1911; holds two exhibitions annually; awards prizes; Pres. KENNETH ELMSLEY; Dir LESLIE SIMPSON.

Composers' Guild of Great Britain: The Penthouse, 4 Brook St, London, W1Y 1AA; tel. (171) 629-0886; fax (171) 629-0993; f. 1944 to further the artistic and professional interests of its members, and to nurture the art of composition; 500 mems; Pres. Sir PETER MAXWELL DAVIES; Vice-Pres Sir MALCOLM ARNOLD, RICHARD ARNELL, THEA MUSGRAVE, JOHN TAVENER; publs *Composer News* (3 a year), *First Performances* (annually).

Contemporary Art Society: 17 Bloomsbury Square, London, WC1A 2LP; tel. (171) 831-7311; fax (171) 831-7345; f. 1910 to promote the development of contemporary art and to acquire works by living artists for loan or gift to public galleries; 1,500 mems; Chair. OLIVER PRENN; Exec. Dir GILL HEDLEY.

English Folk Dance and Song Society, The: Cecil Sharp House, 2 Regent's Park Rd, London, NW1 7AY; tel. (171) 485-2206; fax (171) 284-0534; f. 1932 (Folk Song Society 1898, English Folk Dance Society 1911); to collect, study and preserve English folk dances and songs and other folk music, and to encourage their performance; 5,000 mems; library: see Vaughan Williams Memorial Library; Chief Exec. MARTIN FROST; publs *Folk Music Journal* (annually), *English Dance and Song* (quarterly), *Folk Directory* (annually).

Federation of British Artists: 17 Carlton House Terrace, London, SW1Y 5BD; tel. (171) 930-6844; fax (171) 839-7830; The Federation administers The Mall Galleries, The Mall, London SW1 and holds annual exhibitions, open to all artists, for mem. socs.

Member societies include:

Hesketh Hubbard Art Society: London; f. 1930 by the Royal Soc. of British Artists; annual open exhibition; Pres. SIMON WHITTLE.

New English Art Club: London; f. 1886; exhibition held in November, open to all artists; 51 mems, 4 hon. mems; Hon. Sec. WILLIAM BOWYER; publ. *Catalogue of Annual Exhibition*.

Pastel Society: London; 60 mems; annual open exhibition; Pres. TOM COATES.

Royal Institute of Oil Painters: London; f. 1882; annual exhibition (Dec.); Pres. RICHARD MANWARING BAINES.

Royal Institute of Painters in Water Colours: London; f. 1831; annual exhibition (March) open to all artists; 61 mems, including 2 hon. retd mems; also 1 hon. sculptor mem.; Pres. RONALD MADDOX; publ. *Catalogue of Exhibition*.

Royal Society of British Artists: London; annual open exhibition (September); 97 mems, 16 assoc. mems, 6 hon. mems; Pres. ROMEO DI GIROLAMO.

Royal Society of Marine Artists: London; annual open exhibition (November); 49 mems; Pres. MARK MYERS.

Royal Society of Portrait Painters: London; f. 1891; 41 mems; mems limited to 50; annual exhibition; Pres. DAPHNE TODD; publ. *Catalogue of Annual Exhibition*.

Society of Wildlife Artists: London; f. 1963; annual open exhibition (July–August); 66 mems; Pres. BRUCE PEARSON.

Guild of Church Musicians: c/o John Ewington, 'Hillbrow', Godstone Rd, Blechingley, Surrey; tel. (1883) 741854; fax (1883) 741854; f. 1888; runs courses and seminars, conducts examinations for the Archbishops' Certificate in Church Music; Pres. Dr MARY ARCHER; Warden Very Rev. Dr RICHARD FENWICK; Gen. Sec. JOHN EWINGTON; publs *Year Book* (January), *Laudate* (2 or 3 a year).

Incorporated Association of Organists: C/o Richard Popple, 11 Stonehill Drive, Bromyard, Herefordshire, HR7 4XB; tel. (1885) 483155; fax (1885) 488609; f. 1913 as the National Union of Organists' Associations and inc. 1929; 93 associations, with 6,500 mems throughout the Commonwealth; aims to improve and advance the knowledge of organ music and teaching methods by organising an Annual Organ Week, residential and day courses, master-classes, recitals and lectures; administers a Benevolent Fund for organists; Pres. MARGARET PHILLIPS; Hon. Sec. RICHARD POPPLE; publ. *The Organists' Review* (quarterly).

Incorporated Society of Musicians: c/o Neil Hoyle, 10 Stratford Place, London, W1N 9AE; tel. (171) 629-4413; fax (171) 408-1538; e-mail membership@ism.org; f. 1882; professional association for all musicians (performers, teachers and composers); 5,000 mems; Pres. JOHN HOSIER; Chief Exec. NEIL HOYLE; publs *Yearbook and Register of Members*, *Register of Specialist Teachers* (annually), *Music Journal* (monthly), etc.

Institute of Contemporary Arts: Nash House, The Mall, London, SW1Y 5AH; tel. (171) 930-0493; fax (171) 873-0051; f. 1947; contemporary cultural centre; organizes exhibitions, lecture series, films, performances and musical events, etc.; *c*. 6,000 mems; Dir PHILIP DODD; publs *Monthly Bulletin of Events*, *ICA Documents*.

Oriental Ceramic Society: 30B Torrington Square, London, WC1E 7JL; f. 1921 to increase knowledge and appreciation of Eastern Ceramics and other arts; Pres. Dr OLIVER IMPEY; Sec. JEAN MARTIN.

Plainsong and Mediaeval Music Society: c/o Dr S. Farmer, Magdalene College, Cambridge, CB3 OAG; f. 1888 for the promotion of the study and appreciation of plainsong and medieval music, especially by publication and performance; *c*. 320 mems; Pres. Prof. Revd Sir HENRY CHADWICK; Chair. Dr C. PAGE; Sec. Dr S. FARMER; publ. *Plainsong & Medieval Music* (every 6 months).

Royal Academy of Arts in London: Burlington House, Piccadilly, London, W1V 0DS; tel. (171) 439-7438; fax (171) 434-0837; f. 1768; fine arts; 18 senior academicians, 78 academicians; runs an art school; Pres. Sir PHILIP DOWSON; Sec. DAVID GORDON; Keeper LEONARD MCCOMB; publs *RA Magazine* (quarterly), *RA Illustrated* (summer exhibition souvenir, annually).

Royal Cambrian Academy of Art: Crown Lane, Conwy, LL32 8BH; tel. (1492) 593413; fax (1492) 593413; f. 1882 for the promotion of the arts of painting, engraving, sculpture, and other forms of art in Wales; 100 mems; Pres. KYFFIN WILLIAMS; Hon. Sec. ANN LEWIS; Curator VICKY MACDONALD.

Royal Fine Art Commission: 7 St James's Square, London, SW1Y 4JU; tel. (171) 839-6537; fax (171) 839-8475; appointed by Royal Warrant, 1924; independent body which advises central government, local government and others on all matters affecting the visual environment; concerned mainly with architectural design, but also advises on the design of bridges, roads, major landscaping proposals and art in public places; principal aim: to improve the quality of new architecture and design in England and Wales; Chair. The Rt Hon. The Lord ST JOHN OF FAWSLEY; Sec. FRANCIS GOLDING; publ. *Annual Report*.

Royal Fine Art Commission for Scotland: Bakehouse Close, 146 Canongate, Edinburgh, EH8 8DD; tel. (131) 556-6699; fax (131) 556-6633; e-mail rfacscot@gtnet.gov.uk; f. 1927; advises Government Depts and local planning authorities on all questions affecting public amenity, especially the development of the built environment; holds annual exhibitions of its work during the Edinburgh International Festival; Sec. CHARLES PROSSER.

Royal Musical Association, The: c/o Jonathan King, 77 Kings Rd, Surbiton, KT6 5JE; f. 1874, inc. 1904, for the investigation and discussion of subjects connected with the art and science of music; 900 mems; Pres. JULIAN RUSHTON; Sec. JONATHAN KING; publs *Journal* (2 a year), *Research Chronicle* (annually).

Royal Photographic Society of Great Britain: The Octagon, Milsom St, Bath, BA1 1DN; tel. (1225) 462841; fax (1225) 448688; e-mail rps@rps.org; f. 1853 for the advancement of the science and art of photography; 10,500 mems; library of 20,000 vols and periodicals; permanent collection of 100,000 photographs and 8,000 items of photographic equipment; Pres. JOHN BIRKETT; Sec. BARRY LANE; publs *The Photographic Journal* (monthly), *The Imaging Science Journal*, *Imaging Abstracts* (every 2 months).

Royal Scottish Academy: The Mound, Edinburgh, EH2 2EL; tel. (131) 225-6671; fax (131) 225-2349; f. 1826; painting, sculpture, architecture, printmaking; 9 senior academicians, 36 academicians, 3 senior associates, 43 associates; Pres. W. J. L. BAILLIE; Sec. IAN MCKENZIE SMITH; publ. *Annual Report*.

Royal Society of British Sculptors: 108 Old Brompton Rd, London, SW7 3RA; tel. (171) 373-8615; fax (171) 370-3721; f. 1904 for the promotion and advancement of the art of sculpture; Pres. JOHN MILLS; Administrator DONNA LOVEDAY; publ. *Sculpture97*.

Royal Watercolour Society: Bankside Gallery, 48 Hopton St, Blackfriars, London, SE1 9JH; tel. (171) 928-7521; fax (171) 928-2820; f. 1804; exhibitions confined to the work of its members are held twice yearly; annual open exhibition (summer); 76 mems; 13 assocs; small archive and diploma collection; Pres. JOHN DOYLE; Sec. JUDY DIXEY; publ. *Bankside Bulletin* (quarterly).

Royal West of England Academy: Queen's Rd, Clifton, Bristol, BS8 1PX; tel. (117) 9735129; fax (117) 9237874; f. 1844 to encourage, advance and promote the appreciation of the fine arts by exhibitions and occasional lectures and meetings; 160 Academicians; small library, mainly exhibition catalogues; Pres. and Chair. of Council PETER THURSBY; Academy Sec. RACHEL FEAR; publs catalogues of exhibitions.

Scottish Arts Council: 12 Manor Place, Edinburgh, EH3 7DD; tel. (131) 226-6051; fax (131) 225-9833; funded by the Scottish Office; Chair. MAGNUS LINKLATER; Dir SEONA REID.

Society for the Promotion of New Music: Francis House, Francis St, London, SW1P 1DE; tel. (171) 828-9696; fax (171) 931-9928; e-mail spnm@spnm.org.uk; f. 1943; 1,300 mems; concert and workshop performances of new music selected from scores submitted by composers resident in Great Britain, and British composers living abroad; Pres. Sir PETER MAXWELL DAVIES; Vice-Pres RICHARD RODNEY BENNETT, Sir HARRISON BIRTWISTLE, Sir WILLIAM GLOCK, Prof. ALEXANDER GOEHR, JANE MANNING, MICHAEL RUBINSTEIN; Exec. Dir GILL GRAHAM; publ. *New Notes* (monthly).

Society for Theatre Research, The: c/o Theatre Museum, 1E Tavistock St, London, WC2E 7PA; f. 1948; acts as a clearing house for information concerning the history and technique of the British theatre and encourages research in these subjects; holds monthly lectures in the winter season; distributes up to £4,000 in research grants annually; 800 individual and corporate mems; Pres. Prof. GLYNNE WICKHAM; publs *Theatre Notebook* (3 a year), and an annual publication.

Society of Architectural Illustrators: POB 22, Stroud, Glos., GL5 3DH; tel. (1453) 882563; f. 1975; has established a professional body and a recognized qualification for mems of the design professions who specialize in architectural illustration; confers SAI (Member), FSAI (Fellow), Hon.FSAI (Hon. Fellow); 359 mems;

Pres. PHILIP CROWE; Admin. ERIC MONK; publs *Newsletter*, *Yearbook*, journals, etc.

Society of Miniaturists: c/o Leslie Simpson, 2 The Brambles, Ilkley, West Yorks, LS29 9DH; tel. (1943) 609075; f. 1895; holds two exhibitions annually; awards prizes.

Society of Scribes and Illuminators: C/o 6 Queen Square, London, WC1N 3AR; e-mail scribe@calligraphy.org; f. 1921; aims to re-establish and perpetuate the tradition of craftsmanship, calligraphy and fine lettering; meetings and exhibitions; 65 fellows, 1,000 lay mems; reference library; publs *Journal* (3 a year), *The Scribe* (2 a year).

HISTORY, GEOGRAPHY AND ARCHAEOLOGY

Ancient Monuments Society: St Ann's Vestry Hall, 2 Church Entry, London, EC4V 5HB; tel. (171) 236-3934; f. 1924 for the study and conservation of ancient monuments, historic buildings and fine old craftsmanship; 2,000 mems; Pres. Dame JENNIFER JENKINS; Chair. Prof. R. W. BRUNSKILL; Sec. M. J. SAUNDERS; publs *Transactions* (annually, in conjunction with the Friends of Friendless Churches), and three newsletters.

Baptist Historical Society, The: Baptist House, POB 44, 129 Broadway, Didcot, OX11 8RT; e-mail slcopson@dial.pipex.com; f. 1908 to promote the study of and record the history of the Baptists; assists researchers, and gives advice to Churches on care and preservation of records; library administered jointly with Angus Library, Regent's Park College, Oxford; 602 mems; Pres. Rev. Dr W. M. S. WEST; Sec. Rev. S. L. COPSON; publ. *The Baptist Quarterly*.

British Archaeological Association: c/o Dr W. Filmer-Sankey, Victorian Society, 1 Priory Gardens, Bedford Park, London, W4 1TT; Hon. Sec. Dr W. FILMER-SANKEY; f. 1843; 700 mems; Pres. L. KEEN; publs *Journal* (annually), *Conference Transactions* (annually).

British Cartographic Society: C/o Royal Geographic Society, 1 Kensington Gore, London, SW7 2AR; tel. (1703) 781519; fax (1703) 781519; e-mail admin@cartography.org.uk; f. 1963; 940 mems; Pres. Dr A. F. TATHAM; Hon. Sec. KEN ATHERTON; publs *The Cartographic Journal* (2 a year), *Newsletter* (quarterly).

British Numismatic Society: c/o Dr J. D. Bateson, Hunterian Museum, Glasgow University, Glasgow, G12 8QQ; tel. (141) 330-4221; f. 1903; 535 mems; Pres. G. P. DYER; Sec. Dr J. D. BATESON; publ. *British Numismatic Journal* (annually).

British Records Association: C/o London Metropolitan Archives, 40 Northampton Rd, London, EC1R 0HB; tel. (171) 833-0428; fax (171) 833-0416; f. 1932 for the preservation and use of records (archives), and for the co-ordination of the work of institutions and individuals interested in the subject; 1,000 mems; conferences; Pres. Rt Hon. Sir THOMAS BINGHAM; Hon. Sec. ELIZABETH HUGHES; publs *Archives* (2 a year), *Archives and the User* (occasional).

Cambrian Archaeological Association: c/o Peter Llewellyn, Coch Willan, Tal-y-Bont, Bangor, Gwynedd, LL57 3AZ; f. 1846; 832 mems; Pres. Prof. GLYN L. JONES; Gen. Sec. PETER LLEWELLYN; publ. *Archaeologia Cambrensis*.

Canterbury and York Society: c/o Prof. C. Harper-Bill, 15 Cusack Close, Twickenham, TW1 4TB; tel. (181) 892-0500; f. 1904; 289 mems; Pres. The ARCHBISHOPS OF CANTERBURY and YORK; Treas. Prof. C. HARPER-BILL; Gen. Editor Prof. R. L. STOREY; publ. *Medieval Bishops' Registers*.

Catholic Record Society: c/o 114 Mount St, London, W1Y 6AH; f. 1904; publishes documentary material on Catholic history in England and Wales since the reformation; international membership; Sec. Dr L. GOOCH; publs *Journal*, *Recusant History* (2 a year).

Council for British Archaeology: Bowes Morrell House, 111 Walmgate, York, YO1 9WA; tel. (1904) 671417; fax (1904) 671384; e-mail archaeology@compuserve.com; f. 1944; works to promote the study and safeguarding of Britain's historic environment, to provide a forum for archaeological opinion, and to improve public knowledge of Britain's past; 485 institutional mems, 4,300 individual mems; Pres. P. DIXON; Dir R. K. MORRIS; publs *British and Irish Archaeological Bibliography* (2 a year), *British Archaeological Yearbook* (annually), *British Archaeology* (10 a year), *Research Reports*, *Practical Handbooks* (occasional), etc.

Council of British Geography: c/o Royal Geographical Society, 1 Kensington Gore, London SW7 2AR; tel. (171) 591-3000; f. 1988 to provide a formal organization linking all British geographical societies for the advancement of British geography; co-ordinates policies of mem. societies, and takes initiatives in educational, academic, research or policy matters; Chair. Prof. R. J. BENNETT; Hon. Sec. N. M. SIMMONDS.

Dugdale Society for the Publication of Warwickshire Records: The Shakespeare Centre, Stratford-upon-Avon, Warwickshire, CV37 6QW; f. 1920; 330 mems; Pres. Sir WILLIAM STRATFORD DUGDALE, Bt; Chair. Dr LEVI FOX.

Ecclesiastical History Society: c/o M. J. Kennedy, Dept of Medieval History, University of Glasgow, G12 8QQ; tel. (141) 339-8855; fax (141) 330-5056; f. 1961; aims to further the study of ecclesiastical history and to maintain relations between British ecclesiastical historians and scholars abroad; over 900 mems; Pres. Rev. Prof. COLIN MORRIS; Sec. M. J. KENNEDY; publs *Studies in Church History* (annually), *Subsidia*.

Economic History Society: Department of Economics and Social History, University of Glasgow, 4 University Gardens, Glasgow, G12 8QQ; tel. (141) 330-4662; fax (141) 330-4889; e-mail ehsoc@arts.gla.ac.uk; f. 1927; 1,700 mems; Pres. Prof. P. K. O'BRIEN; Hon. Sec. Prof. R. H. TRAINOR; publs *The Economic History Review* (quarterly), *ReFRESH: Recent Findings of Research in Economic and Social History* (every 6 months), *Newsletter of the Economic History Society* (quarterly).

Egypt Exploration Society: 3 Doughty Mews, London, WC1N 2PG; tel. (171) 242-1880; fax (171) 404-6118; e-mail eeslondon@compuserve.com.uk; f. 1882; excavation in Egypt and publication of work; 3,000 mems; library: see Libraries; Sec. PATRICIA SPENCER; publs *Excavation Memoirs*, *Archaeological Survey*, *Graeco-Roman Memoirs*, *Texts from Excavations*, *The Journal of Egyptian Archaeology*, *Occasional Publications*, *Egyptian Archaeology* (etc.).

English Place-Name Society: School of English Studies, University of Nottingham, Nottingham, NG7 2RD; f. 1923 for the publication of a yearly volume on the place-names of a county, or part of a county; 650 mems; Hon. Dir VICTOR WATTS; publ. *Journal* (annually).

Friends Historical Society: c/o Friends House, Euston Rd, London, NW1 2BJ; f. 1903; 400 mems; Clerk of Exec. HOWARD F. GREGG; publ. *Journal* (annually).

Geographical Association, The: 160 Solly St, Sheffield, S1 4BF; tel. (114) 2960088; fax (114) 2967176; f. 1893 to further the interests of teachers of geography and the study and teaching of geography generally; 11,400 mems; Pres. R. C. CARTER; Joint Hon. Secs C. HARRIS, K. FLINDER, J. KRAUSE; publs *Geography* (quarterly), *Teaching Geography* (quarterly), *Primary Geographer* (quarterly).

Hakluyt Society: c/o Map Library, British Library, 96 Euston Road, London, NW1 2BD; tel. (1986) 788359; fax (1986) 788181; e-mail haksoc@paston.co.uk; f. 1846; 2,300 mems; Pres. SARAH TYACKE; Hon. Sec. ANTHONY PAYNE; publs early voyages and travel and other geographical records.

Harleian Society: c/o College of Arms, Queen Victoria St, London, EC4V 4BT; tel. (171) 236-7728; f. 1869, inc. 1902, for the transcribing, printing and publishing of the Heraldic Visitations of Counties, Parish Registers or any MSS relating to genealogy, family history and heraldry; *c.* 300 subscribers; Chair. J. P. BROOKE-LITTLE; Hon. Sec. and Treas. T. H. S. DUKE, Chester Herald of Arms.

Heraldry Society: POB 32, Maidenhead, Berks., SL6 3FD; tel. (118) 932-0210; f. 1947 to further the study of heraldry, armory, chivalry, genealogy and kindred subjects; 1,000 mems; Patron The Duke of NORFOLK; publs *The Coat of Arms* (quarterly), *The Heraldry Gazette* (quarterly).

Historical Association: 59A Kennington Park Rd, London, SE11 4JH; tel. (171) 735-3901; fax (171) 582-4989; f. 1906; aims to advance the study and teaching of history at all levels, to increase public interest in all aspects of the subject and to develop it as an essential element in the education of all; 72 branches in the UK and overseas; 8,500 mems; history textbook collection; CEO Mrs M. STILES; publs *History* (3 a year), *Teaching History* (quarterly), *The Historian* (quarterly), *Primary History* (3 a year), *Annual Bulletin of Historical Literature*, *Helps for Students of History* (series), *Appreciations in History* (series), *Teaching of History* (series), *Historical Association Studies* (series), *New Appreciations in History* (series).

Honourable Society of Cymmrodorion: 30 Eastcastle St, London, W1N 7PD; f. 1751; Royal Charter 1951; 1,000 mems; Patron HM THE QUEEN; Pres. Prof. EMRYS JONES; Hon. Sec. JOHN SAMUEL; publs *Transactions*, *The Dictionary of Welsh Biography*.

Huguenot Society of Great Britain and Ireland: The Huguenot Library, University College, Gower St, London, WC1E 6BT; tel. (171) 380-7094; f. 1885; 7 Hon. Fellows, 1,350 Ordinary Fellows, 8 Junior Fellows, 126 subscribing libraries, 17 societies in correspondence; Pres. Lady MONSON; Hon. Sec. Mrs MARY BAYLISS; publs *Proceedings* (annually), *Quarto Series*, *New Series* (occasional).

Institute of Heraldic and Genealogical Studies: Northgate, Canterbury, Kent; tel. (1227) 768664; fax (1227) 765617; e-mail ihgs@dial.pipex.com; f. 1961 for education and research in family history, degree and correspondence courses, training and professional qualification; research services; genetical research group assisting medical teams; library of 35,000 vols, 20,000 case studies; special collections; Pres. Major-Gen. The Viscount MONCKTON OF BRENCHLEY; Principal C. R. HUMPHERY-SMITH; Reg. JEREMY PALMER; publs *Family History*, *Atlas and Index of Parishes*, *Syllabus of Study*, *Teacher's Aids*.

Jewish Historical Society of England: 33 Seymour Place, London, W1H 5AP (Office); tel. (171) 723-5852; fax (171) 723-5852; e-mail jhse@dircon.co.uk; Jewish Studies Library, University College, London; f. 1893; 900 mems; Pres. Dr GERRY BLACK; Hon. Sec. C. M. DRUKKER; publs *Transactions*, etc.

London and Middlesex Archaeological Society: c/o Museum of London, London Wall, London, EC2Y 5HN; tel. (171) 600-3699; f. 1855; promotes and publishes archaeological and historical research and conservation in London area; 556 mems; Pres. MARK HASSEL; Hon. Sec. KAREN FIELDER; publs *Transactions* (annually), *Special Papers* (occasional).

London Record Society: c/o Institute of Historical Research, Senate House, Malet Street, London, WC1E 7HU; e-mail creaton@sas.ac.uk; f. 1964 to publish the original sources for the history of London and generally to stimulate public interest in archives relating to London; *c.* 380 mems; Hon. Sec. HEATHER CREATON; publ. *Annual Series*.

London Topographical Society: 36 Old Deer Park Gardens, Richmond, Surrey, TW9 2TL; tel. (181) 940-5419; f. 1880; 900 mems; Patron HRH The Duke of EDINBURGH; Hon. Sec. PATRICK FRAZER; publs *Newsletter* (2 a year), *London Topographical Record* (every 5 years), and maps, views and books, annually.

Manchester Geographical Society: Friends' Meeting House, 6 Mount St, Manchester, M2 5NS; tel. (161) 834-2965; f. 1884 to promote the study of all branches of geographical science; 120 mems; library of 6,500 vols (now on permanent loan to the University of Manchester); Hon. Sec. Dr B. P. HINDLE; publ. *The North West Geographer* (2 a year).

Maritime Trust: 2 Greenwich Church St, London SE10 9BG; tel. (181) 858-2698; an independent trust; f. 1969 to restore, preserve and display historic British ships; maintains *Cutty Sark* (at Greenwich); 550 mems (Friends); Pres. HRH The Duke of EDINBURGH; Chair. Adm. of the Fleet Sir JULIAN OSWALD; publ. *Newsletter* (2 a year).

Monumental Brass Society: c/o H. M. Stuchfield, Lowe Hill House, Stratford St Mary, Suffolk, CO7 6JX; f. 1887 to promote the study of and interest in, better preservation of monumental brasses, and to compile and publish a full and accurate list of all extant and lost brasses, English and foreign; Hon. Sec. H. M. STUCHFIELD; publs *Transactions* (annually), *Portfolio* (occasional), *Bulletin* (3 a year).

Palestine Exploration Fund: 2 Hinde Mews, Marylebone Lane, London, W1M 5RR; tel. (171) 935-5379; f. 1865; 900 subscribers; to obtain and disseminate non-political information about ancient and modern Syria (Syria, Lebanon, Jordan, Israel); library of 5,000 vols; Pres. The Archbishop of CANTERBURY; Hon. Sec. Y. HODSON; publ. *Palestine Exploration Quarterly* (2 a year).

Prehistoric Society: c/o Institute of Archaeology, University College London, 31-34 Gordon Square, London WC1H 0PY; f. 1908; furthers prehistoric archaeology; 2,000 mems; Pres. Prof. P. MELLARS; Hon. Sec. Dr R. H. BEWLEY; publs *Proceedings* (annually), *Past* (3 a year).

Regional Studies Association: Wharfdale Projects, 15 Micawber St, London N1 7TB; tel. (171) 490-1128; fax (171) 253-0095; f. 1965; an interdisciplinary group exclusively concerned with regional issues; provides a forum for the exchange of ideas and information on regional problems, publishes the results of regional research, and stimulates studies and research in regional planning and related fields; holds meetings, conferences and seminars; organizes study groups; 14 branches; 600 individual, 200 corporate mems, including government depts, ministries, local authorities, educational institutions, etc; Chair. GORDON DABINETT; Dir SALLY HARDY; Hon. Sec. ANNE GREEN; publs *Regional Studies* (9 a year), *Newsletter* (every 2 months).

Royal Archaeological Institute: c/o Society of Antiquaries, Burlington House, Piccadilly, London, W1V 0HS; f. 1843; Pres. Prof. A. P. QUINEY; Hon. Sec. J. G. COAD; publ. *Archaeological Journal*.

Royal Commission on Historical Manuscripts: Quality House, Quality Court, Chancery Lane, London, WC2A 1HP; tel. (171) 242-1198; fax (171) 831-3550; e-mail nra@hmc.gov.uk; f. 1869, reconstituted 1959; locates, reports on, and publishes guides to papers of value for the study of British history outside of public records; advises researchers, owners and custodians of archives, government and public agencies, grant-awarding bodies and other professional and archival organizations concerning the care and use of historical records; maintains the central *National Register of Archives*, containing 41,000 indexed unpublished lists of manuscripts; Sec. C. J. KITCHING.

Royal Geographical Society (with the Institute of British Geographers): 1 Kensington Gore, London, SW7 2AR; tel. (171) 591-3000; fax (171) 591-3001; e-mail info@rgs.org; f. 1830; furtherance of geographical research, teaching and expeditions; Expedition Advisory Centre for scientific expeditions overseas; 11,000 mems; major collection of 800,000 individual maps and charts, 4,500 atlases, 130,000 books and 100,000 pictures and photographs dating back to the mid-19th century; Pres. Earl SELBORNE; Dir and Sec. Dr RITA GARDNER; publs *Geographical Journal* (3 a year), *Geographical Magazine* (monthly), *Transactions* (quarterly), *Area* (quarterly).

Royal Historical Society: University College London, Gower St, London, WC1E 6BT; tel. (171) 387-7532; fax (171) 387-7532; f. 1868; library of 3,000 vols; Pres. Prof. P. J. MARSHALL; Exec. Sec. Mrs J. MCCARTHY; publ. *Transactions*.

Royal Numismatic Society: c/o Dept of Coins and Medals, British Museum, London, WC1B 3DG; f. 1836; 1,000 mems; Pres. D. M. METCALF; Secs V. H. HEWITT, B. J. COOK; publs *Numismatic Chronicle* (annually), *Monographs*.

Royal Philatelic Society, London: 41 Devonshire Place, London, W1N 1PE; f. 1869; 1,600 mems; Pres. J. M. MOUBRAY; Sec. Prof. B. S. JAY; publ. *The London Philatelist* (10 a year).

Royal Scottish Geographical Society: Graham Hills Bldg, 40 George St, Glasgow, G1 1QE; tel. (141) 552-3330; fax (141) 552-3331; f. 1884 to further the science of geography in all its branches; symposia, illustrated talks and schools conferences; provides support to scientific expeditions; library of 20,000 vols, 30,000 maps, 200 current periodicals, special collection of early maps of Scotland; 2,200 mems; Pres. Viscount YOUNGER OF LECKIE; Dir DAVID M. MUNRO; publs *The Scottish Geographical Magazine* (4 a year), *Geogscot* (newsletter, 3 a year).

Scottish History Society: Dept of Scottish History, University of Aberdeen, Aberdeen, AB9 1FX; f. 1886 for the printing of unpublished documents illustrating the history of Scotland; 800 mems; Pres. Dr G. G. SIMPSON; Hon. Sec. Dr S. I. BOARDMAN.

Society for Army Historical Research: c/o National Army Museum, Royal Hospital Rd, London, SW3 4HT; f. 1921; 1,000 mems; Pres. Field Marshal Sir JOHN CHAPPLE; Hon. Sec. G. J. EVELYN; publ. *Journal* (quarterly).

Society for Medieval Archaeology: C/o 'Devonia', Forton Heath, Shrewsbury, SY4 1EY; tel. (1743) 850736; f. 1957 for the study of archaeology of the post-Roman period; 1,500 mems; Pres. Prof. M. BIDDLE; Sec. Dr P. STAMPER; publs *Medieval Archaeology* (annually), *Monograph Series* (occasional).

Society for Nautical Research: c/o National Maritime Museum, Greenwich, London, SE10 9NF; tel. (171) 218-5449; f. 1910; *c.* 2,000 mems; Pres. Admiral of the Fleet Lord LEWIN; Chair. Rear-Adm. R. HILL; Sec. W. J. R. GARDNER; publs *The Mariners' Mirror* (quarterly), *Newsletter* (quarterly).

Society for Post-Medieval Archaeology Ltd: c/o Dr David Gaimster, British Museum, Great Russell St, London, WC1B 3DG; tel. (171) 323-8734; fax (171) 323-8496; f. 1967; 820 mems; Pres. D. BARKER; Sec. Dr DAVID GAIMSTER; publs *Post-Medieval Archaeology* (annually), *Newsletter and Conferences* (2 a year).

Society for Renaissance Studies, The: c/o Emma Rose Flett, 3 Penpoll Rd, London, E8 1EX; tel. (181) 986-1168; f. 1967 to further the aims of scholarship in the Renaissance field, including literature, philosophy, art and history; 550 mems; Chair. Prof. GORDON CAMPBELL; Sec. EMMA ROSE FLETT; publs *Renaissance Studies* (quarterly), *Bulletin* (2 a year).

Society of Antiquaries of London: Burlington House, Piccadilly, London, W1V 0HS; tel. (171) 734-0193; fax (171) 287-6967; e-mail soc.antiq.lond@dial.pipex.com; f. 1707; 2,100 Fellows; library: see Libraries; Pres. S. S. JERVIS; Sec. JEAN COOK; publs *Archaeologia*, *The Antiquaries Journal*, *Research Reports*, *Occasional Papers*.

Society of Antiquaries of Scotland: National Museums of Scotland, York Buildings, Queen St, Edinburgh, EH2 1JD; tel. (131) 225-7534 ext. 327; f. 1780; study of Scottish antiquities and history, particularly by archaeological research; grants and awards available for research; reference library open to the public; 3,000 mems; Pres. G. S. MAXWELL; Dir F. M. ASHMORE; publs *Proceedings* (annually), *Monographs* (irregular).

Society of Archivists: 40 Northampton Rd, London, EC1R 0HB; tel. (171) 278-8630; fax (171) 278-2107; e-mail societyofarchivists@archives.org.uk; f. 1947; 1,500 mems; Pres. A. J. E. ARROWSMITH; Exec. Sec. PATRICK S. CLEARY; publs *Journal* (2 a year), *Newsletter* (monthly).

Society of Genealogists: 14 Charterhouse Bldgs, Goswell Rd, London, EC1M 7BA; tel. (171) 251-8799; fax (171) 250-1800; e-mail info@sog.org.uk; f. 1911; 14,000 mems; library of 100,000 vols; Pres. HRH Prince MICHAEL OF KENT; Dir ROBERT I. N. GORDON; publs *Genealogists' Magazine* (quarterly), *Computers in Genealogy* (quarterly).

United Reformed Church History Society: Westminster College, Madingley Rd, Cambridge, CB3 0AA; f. 1972 to incorporate the Congregational Historical Society (f. 1899) and the Presbyterian Historical Society of England (f. 1913); 600 mems; library of 7,000 vols; Hon. Sec. Rev. ELIZABETH J. BROWN; publ. *Journal* (2 a year).

Wesley Historical Society: c/o Dr E. D. Graham, 34 Spiceland Rd, Birmingham, B31 1NJ; tel. (121) 475-4914; f. 1893 to promote the study of the history and literature of all branches of Methodism; 820 mems; library (Bretherton collection); Pres. Rev. Dr JOHN A. NEWTON; Gen. Sec. Dr E. D. GRAHAM; publ. *Proceedings* (3 a year).

Wiltshire Record Society: c/o County Record Office, County Hall, Trowbridge, Wilts, BA14 8JG; f. 1938; to publish the documentary sources for the history of Wiltshire and the means of reference thereto; 310 mems; Pres. C. ELRINGTON; Hon. Sec. J. N. D'ARCY; Hon. Editor Dr J. CHANDLER.

LANGUAGE AND LITERATURE

Academi Gymreig/Welsh Academy: 3rd Floor, Mount Stuart House, Mount Stuart Square, Cardiff, CF1 6DQ; tel. (1222) 492025; e-mail dafr@celtic.co.uk; f. 1959; Welsh-language section (promotes literature in the Welsh language; 100 mems; Pres. J. E. C. WILLIAMS; Chair. NESTA WYN JONES; Dir

DAFYDD ROGERS; publs *Taliesin*, *Cyfres Cyfieithiadau'r Academi*); English-language section (promotes Anglo-Welsh literature; 200 mems; Pres. DANNIE ABSE; Chair. SALLY ROBERTS JONES; Dir KEVIN THOMAS).

Association for Language Learning: 150 Railway Terrace, Rugby, CV21 3HN; tel. (1788) 546443; fax (1788) 544149; e-mail langlearn@aol.com.uk; f. 1990; offers help, in-service training and support to language teachers; promotes the learning and use of foreign languages; Dir BRIGITTE BOYCE; publs *Language Learning Journal*, *Rusistika*, *Tuttitalia*, *Vida Hispánica*, *Deutsch: Lehren und Lernen*, *Francophonie* (all 2 a year), *Language World* (quarterly).

Association of British Science Writers: c/o British Asscn for the Advancement of Science, 23 Savile Row, London W1X 2NB; tel. (171) 439-1205; fax (171) 973-3051; f. 1947 for the promotion of science writing; 500 mems; Chair. RICHARD STEVENSON; Administrator BARBARA DRILLSMA; publ. *Newsletter* (monthly).

British Association for Applied Linguistics: Frankfurt Lodge, Clevedon Hall, Victoria Rd, Clevedon, Avon, BS21 7SJ; tel. (1275) 876519; f. 1968 to promote the study of language in use, to foster interdisciplinary collaboration and to provide a common forum for those engaged in the theoretical study of language and those interested in its practical use; *c.* 500 mems; Chair. ROSAMOND MITCHELL; Sec. ULRIKE MEINHOF; publs *Newsletter*, *Applied Linguistics* (3 a year, in asscn with American Asscn for Applied Linguistics), *British Studies in Applied Linguistics* (Edited Proceedings of Annual Meetings).

British Association of Academic Phoneticians: Phonetics Laboratory, Dept of English Language, The University, Glasgow G12 8QQ; tel. (141) 330-4596; fax (141) 330-3531; e-mail m.macmahon@englang.arts.gla.ac.uk; f. 1984, fmrly Colloquium of British Academic Phoneticians; 75 mems; Sec. and Archivist Prof. M. K. C. MACMAHON.

Brontë Society: The Brontë Parsonage Museum, Haworth, Keighley, West Yorks, BD22 8DR; tel. (1535) 642323; fax (1535) 647131; f. 1893, inc. 1902, to collect and act as guardian of Brontë letters, MSS, and personal belongings which are housed in the Brontë Parsonage Museum, former home of the Brontës and now in the care of the Society; 3,000 mems; Pres. Lord MORRIS OF CASTLEMORRIS; Chair. Prof. ROBERT BARNARD; publs *Brontë Society Transactions* (2 a year), *Brontë Society Gazette* (2 a year).

Charles Lamb Society, The: 1A Royston Rd, Richmond, Surrey, TW10 6LT; f. 1935; to promote the study of the lives and works of Charles Lamb and his circle and to form a collection of Eliana; library housed in the Guildhall Library, City of London; Pres. Prof. JOHN BEER; Hon. Sec. Mrs M. R. HUXSTEP; publ. *The Charles Lamb Bulletin* (quarterly).

Classical Association: c/o Dr Malcolm Schofield, St John's College, Cambridge, CB2 1TP; f. 1903; 4,000 mems; Pres. Prof. OLIVER TAPLIN; Joint Secs Dr MALCOLM SCHOFIELD, BARBARA FINNEY; publs *Classical Review*, *Classical Quarterly*, *Greece and Rome* (2 a year), *CA News* (2 a year), *Proceedings* (annually).

Dickens Fellowship: Dickens House, 48 Doughty St, London, WC1N 2LF; tel. (171) 405-2127; fax (171) 831-5175; f. 1902 to knit together in a common bond of friendship lovers of Charles Dickens, and to assist in the preservation and purchase of buildings and objects associated with Dickens or mentioned in his works; approx. 7,000 mems; Pres. GABRIEL WOOLF; Hon. Gen. Sec. EDWARD G. PRESTON; publs *The Dickensian* (3 a year), *Mr Dick's Kite* (3 a year).

Early English Text Society: Christ Church, Oxford; f. 1864; 1,260 mems; Hon. Dir Prof. JOHN BURROW; Exec. Sec. R. F. S. HAMER; texts published annually.

English Association: University of Leicester, University Rd, Leicester, LE1 7RH; tel. (116) 252-3982; fax (116) 252-2301; f. 1906 to promote the knowledge and appreciation of the English language and of English literature, through conferences, lectures and publications; 1,500 mems; Pres. ROGER KNIGHT; Chair. MARTIN BLOCKSIDGE; Chief Exec. HELEN LUCAS; publs *English* (3 a year), *Essays and Studies*, *The Year's Work in English Studies*, *The Use of English* (3 a year), *English 4–11* (3 a year), *English Association Newsletter* (3 a year), *The Year's Work in Critical and Cultural Theory*.

English Centre of International PEN: 7 Dilke St, London, SW3 4JE; tel. (171) 352-6303; fax (171) 351-0220; f. 1921; 990 mems; Pres. RACHEL BILLINGTON; Gen. Sec. GILLIAN VINCENT.

English Speaking Board (International) Ltd: 26A Princes St, Southport, Merseyside, PR8 1EQ; tel. (1704) 501730; f. 1953; brings together people from educational, professional and industrial spheres who are concerned with oral education as a means of communication; individual and corporate mems in 34 countries; arranges lectures, courses, etc; examinations in spoken English at all levels of education from primary to higher education students, certificates and diplomas awarded to teachers, professional speakers; Pres. CHRISTABEL BURNISTON; Chair. RICHARD ELLIS; publ. *Spoken English* (every 6 months).

Francis Bacon Society Inc., The: C/o T. D. Bokenham, 56 Westbury Rd, New Malden, Surrey, KT3 5AX; f. 1886; registered charity; for the study of the works and life of Francis Bacon and evidence in respect of the authorship of the plays attributed to Shakespeare; library; Pres. Sir GEORGE TREVELYAN; Chair T. D. BOKENHAM; publ. *Baconiana*.

Institute of Linguists: Saxon House, 48 Southwark Street, London, SE1 1UN; tel. (171) 940-3100; fax (171) 940-3101; e-mail info@iol.org.uk; f. 1910; professional body for practising linguists; conducts examinations in languages; over 6,500 mems; library of *c.* 6,000 vols; Pres. Prof. J. DREW; Chair. Dr J. M. MITCHELL; Dir H. PAVLOVICH; publ. *The Linguist* (every 2 months).

Institute of Translation and Interpreting: 377 City Rd, London, EC1V 1NA; tel. (171) 713-7600; fax (171) 713-7650; e-mail iti@compuserve.com; f. 1986; 2,500 mems; Office Man. JANE HIBBERT; publ. *ITI Bulletin* (every 2 months).

Kipling Society: Tree Cottage, 2 Brownleaf Rd, Brighton, Sussex, BN2 6LB; tel. (1273) 303179; f. 1927 to honour and extend the influence of Rudyard Kipling; 800 mems; Pres. Dr MICHAEL BROCK; Hon. Sec. J. W. MICHAEL SMITH; publ. *The Kipling Journal* (quarterly).

Linguistics Association of Great Britain: c/o Dr D. Adger, Language and Linguistic Science, University of York, YO1 5DD; f. 1959 to promote the study of linguistics and provide a forum for discussion and facilities for co-operation in furtherance of this interest in linguistics; annual spring and autumn meetings; 611 mems; Pres. Prof. R. HUDSON; Hon. Sec. Dr D. ADGER; publ. *Journal of Linguistics* (2 a year).

Malone Society: c/o Anne Ashby, Arts and Reference Division, Oxford University Press, Walton St, Oxford, OX2 6DP; tel. (1865) 558229; e-mail j.creaser@holl.u-net.com; f. 1906 for the study, editing and publishing of early English drama; 680 mems; Chair. Prof. RICHARD PROUDFOOT; Exec. Sec. Prof. JOHN CREASER.

Philological Society: School of Oriental and African Studies, University of London, London, WC1H 0XG; fax (171) 691-3424; f. 1842, inc. 1879, to investigate and promote the study and knowledge of the structure, affinities, and history of languages; over 500 mems; Pres. Prof. R. POSNER; Secs Prof. NICHOLAS SIMS-WILLIAMS, Prof. K. BROWN; publ. *Transactions* (2 a year).

Poetry Society: 22 Betterton St, London, WC2H 9BU; tel. (171) 240-4810; fax (171) 240-4818; f. 1909 to promote the study and appreciation of poetry; poetry reading, educational activities; 3,000 mems; Dir CHRIS MEADE; publs *Poetry Review*, *Poetry News* (quarterly).

Royal Society of Literature of the United Kingdom: 1 Hyde Park Gardens, London, W2 2LT; tel. (171) 723-5104; fax (171) 402-0199; f. 1823; lectures and literary discussions; 850 fellows and mems; Pres. Lord JENKINS; Sec. M. FERGUSSON.

Society for the Promotion of Hellenic Studies: Senate House, Malet St, London, WC1E 7HU; tel. (171) 862-8730; fax (171) 862-8731; e-mail hellenic@sas.ac.uk; f. 1879; 3,000 mems; library: see Libraries; Pres. Prof. P. E. EASTERLING; Hon. Sec. Prof. B. A. SPARKES; publs *Journal of Hellenic Studies*, with supplement *Archaeological Reports*.

Society for the Promotion of Roman Studies: Senate House, Malet St, London, WC1E 7HU; tel. (171) 862-8727; fax (171) 862-8728; e-mail romansoc@sas.ac.uk; f. 1910; 4,000 mems; library: see Libraries; Pres. Rev. Prof. J. S. RICHARDSON; publs *Journal of Roman Studies* (annually), *Britannia* (annually).

Society for the Study of Medieval Languages and Literature: c/o Dr Carolyne Larrington, 32 Great Clarendon St, Oxford, OX2 6AT; fax (1865) 438394; e-mail carolyne@patrol.i-way.co.uk; f. 1932; Pres. Prof. NICHOLAS MANN; Sec. Dr CAROLYNE LARRINGTON; publs *Medium Ævum* (2 a year), monographs (occasional).

Society of Authors: 84 Drayton Gardens, London, SW10 9SB; tel. (171) 373-6642; fax (171) 373-5768; e-mail authorsoc@writers.org.uk; f. 1884 to promote and protect the rights of authors in all the media; 6,000 mems; Gen. Sec. MARK LE FANU; publ. *The Author* (quarterly).

Wells, H. G., Society: c/o J. R. Hammond, 49 Beckingthorpe Drive, Bottesford, Notts, NG13 0DN; f. 1960 to promote an active interest in and an appreciation of the life, work and thought of H. G. Wells; library of 300 vols (H. G. Wells Collection, Library, Polytechnic of North London); Sec. J. R. HAMMOND; publs *Newsletter*, *Wellsian*.

MEDICINE

Anatomical Society of Great Britain and Ireland: c/o Prof. G. M. Morriss-Kay, Dept of Human Anatomy and Genetics, South Parks Road, Oxford, OX1 3QX; tel. (1865) 272165; e-mail morrissk@ermine.ox.ac.uk; f. 1887; 700 mems; Pres. Prof. J. A. FIRTH; Hon. Sec. Prof. G. M. MORRISS-KAY; publ. *Journal of Anatomy* (8 a year).

Apothecaries of London, Worshipful Society of: Apothecaries' Hall, Black Friars Lane, London, EC4V 6EJ; f. 1617 by King James I; grants a registrable medical qualification (LMSSA Lond.), also the post-graduate diplomas in Medical Jurisprudence (DMJ), in Genito-Urinary Medicine (Dip. GUM), in Sports Medicine (DSMSA), in History of Medicine (DHMSA), Philosophy of Medicine (DPMSA), Musculo Skeletal Medicine (DMSM), Medical Care of Catastrophes

(DMCC), Regulatory Toxicology (Dip. Reg. Tox.), Clinical Pharmacology (DCPSA), Mastership in Medical Jurisprudence (MMJ); 1,600 mems; Master I. T. FIELD; Clerk Lt-Col R. J. STRINGER; Registrar A. M. WALLINGTON-SMITH.

Association for the Study of Medical Education: 4th Floor, Hobart House, 80/82 Hanover St, Edinburgh, EH2 1EL; tel. (131) 225-9111; fax (131) 225-9444; e-mail info@asme.org.uk; f. 1957 to exchange information and promote research into medical education; over 800 mems; Pres. Prof. DAVID SHAW; Chair Prof. JOHN BIGGS; Gen. Sec. Dr GRAHAM BUCKLEY; publs *Medical Education* (every 2 months), *Medical Education Booklets*, *Annual Report*.

Association of Anaesthetists of Great Britain and Ireland: 9 Bedford Square, London, WC1B 3RA; tel. (171) 631-1650; fax (171) 631-4352; e-mail aagbi@compuserve.com; f. 1932 to promote the development and study of anaesthetics and their administration and to maintain the high standard of this branch of medicine; 6,300 mems; Pres. Dr W. L. M. BAIRD; Hon. Sec. Dr D. J. WILKINSON; publ. *Anaesthesia*.

Association of British Neurologists: 9 Fitzroy Square, London, W1P 5AH; f. 1933; 860 mems; Pres. Dr R. B. GODWIN-AUSTEN; Hon. Sec. Dr P. R. D. HUMPHREY.

Association of Surgeons of Great Britain and Ireland: at The Royal College of Surgeons, 35/43 Lincoln's Inn Fields, London, WC2A 3PN; tel. (171) 973-0300; f. 1920 for the advancement of the science and art of surgery; Pres. R. C. N. WILLIAMSON; Hon. Sec. R. H. S. LANE.

British Dental Association: 63/64 Wimpole St, London, W1M 8AL; tel. (171) 935-0875; fax (171) 487-5232; f. 1880 as a professional asscn; 16,000 mems; library of 10,000 vols; Chief Exec. J. M. G. HUNT; Librarian R. FARBEY; publ. *British Dental Journal* (fortnightly).

British Diabetic Association: 10 Queen Anne St, London, W1M 0BD; tel. (171) 323-1531; fax (171) 637-3644; f. 1934 to help all people with diabetes and those interested in diabetes, to promote greater public understanding of the condition and to support diabetic research; 160,000 mems; Chair. of Exec. Council Prof. HARRY KEEN; Dir-Gen. MICHAEL COOPER; publs *Balance Magazine* (every 2 months), *Diabetes Update* (2 a year), *Diabetic Medicine* (10 a year), *Balance for Beginners* (updated annually).

British Dietetic Association: 7th Floor, Elizabeth House, 22 Suffolk St, Queensway, Birmingham, B1 1LS; tel. (121) 643-5483; fax (121) 633-4399; e-mail bda@dial.pipex.com; f. 1936; 4,000 mems; Chair. A. M. DOBSON; Sec. J. C. J. GRIGG; publ. *Journal of Human Nutrition and Dietetics* (every 2 months).

British Geriatrics Society: c/o Dr D. Lubel, 1 St Andrew's Place, Regent's Park, London NW1 4LB; tel. (171) 935-4004; fax (171) 224-0454; e-mail info@bgs.org.uk; f. 1947 to improve standards of medical care for elderly patients and to encourage research in the problems of old age; 2,000 mems; Pres. Dr B. O. WILLIAMS; Hon. Sec. Dr D. LUBEL; publ. *Age and Ageing*.

British Institute of Radiology: 36 Portland Place, London, W1N 4AT; tel. (171) 580-4085; fax (171) 255-3209; e-mail admin@bir.org.uk; f. 1897; a centre for consultation on the medical, physical and biological applications of radiology; current and historic radiological library; 2,000 mems; Pres. Prof. M. A. SMITH; Chief Exec. MARY-ANNE PIGGOTT; publ. *The British Journal of Radiology*.

British Institute of Surgical Technologists: Room 888, School of Dentistry, St Chad's, Queensway, Birmingham, B4 6NN; tel. (121) 237-2914; f. 1935; 350 mems; Chair. L. B. WARD; Sec. G. D. THOMAS; publ. *Journal* (annually).

British Medical Association: Tavistock Square, London, WC1H 9JP; tel. (171) 387-4499; fax (171) 383-6400; f. 1832; 116,888 mems; library: see Libraries; Pres. Lord KILPATRICK OF KINCRAIG; Sec. Dr MAC ARMSTRONG; publs *British Medical Journal* (weekly), *BMA News Review* (General Practitioners' edition 20 a year, hospital doctors' edition monthly), and numerous journals on specialized medical subjects.

British Nutrition Foundation: High Holborn House, 52 – 54 High Holborn, London WC1V 6RQ; tel. (171) 404-6504; fax (171) 404-6747; f. 1967; Hon. Pres. Sir DOUGLAS BLACK; Dir-Gen. Prof. R. S. PICKARD; Sec. N. S. PORTER; publ. *Bulletin* (3 a year).

British Orthodontic Society: c/o David Barnett, BOS Office, Eastman Dental Hospital, Grays Inn Rd, London, WC1X 8LD; tel. (171) 837-2193; fax (171) 837-2193; f. 1994; Chair. DAVID LAWTON; Sec. DAVID BARNETT; publ. *British Journal of Orthodontics* (quarterly).

British Orthopaedic Association: c/o The Royal College of Surgeons, 35-43 Lincoln's Inn Fields, London, WC2A 3PN; tel. (171) 405-6507; fax (171) 831-2676; f. 1918; the advancement of the science and art of orthopaedic surgery; 3,034 mems; Pres. D. J. DANDY; Hon. Sec. D. H. A. JONES; publ. *Journal of Bone and Joint Surgery*.

British Pharmacological Society: 16 Angel Gate, City Road, London, EC1V 2PT; tel. (171) 417-0113; fax (171) 417-0114; e-mail sjs@bphs.org.uk; f. 1931; 2,500 mems; Gen. Sec. Dr T. P. BLACKBURN; publs *British Journal of Pharmacology* (2 a month), *British Journal of Clinical Pharmacology* (monthly).

British Psycho-Analytical Society: 63 New Cavendish St, London, W1M 7RD; tel. (171) 580-4952; f. 1913 for the advancement of psychoanalysis as a science; 400 mems; library of 50,000 vols; Pres. I. BRENMAN PICK; Hon. Sec. S. WEINTROBE; publ. *The International Journal of Psycho-Analysis* (every 2 months).

British Society for Research on Ageing: c/o Dr I. Davies, University of Manchester School of Biological Sciences, 1.124 Stopford Bldg, Oxford Rd, Manchester, M13 9PT; tel. (161) 275-5252; e-mail ioan.davies@man.ac.uk; f. 1945 to encourage gerontological research in Great Britain by acting as a forum for the report and discussion of new advances in ageing research; open to all who are actively engaged in experimental gerontology; Chair. Prof. T. KIRKWOOD; Sec. Dr I. DAVIES; publ. *Lifespan* (2 a year).

British Society for Rheumatology: 41 Eagle St, London, WC1R 4AR; tel. (171) 242-3313; fax (171) 242-3277; f. 1984 to promote the development of rheumatology and scientific knowledge of musculo-skeletal diseases; 1,400 mems; Pres. Prof. R. D. STURROCK; Exec. Sec. C. F. BAILLIE; publ. *British Journal of Rheumatology*.

British Society of Gastroenterology: 3 St Andrews Place, Regent's Park, London NW1 4LB; tel. (171) 387-3534; fax (171) 487-3734; 2,400 mems; Pres. Prof. M. J. S. LANGMAN; Sec. Dr T. DANESHMOND.

Cancer Research Campaign: 10 Cambridge Terrace, London, NW1 4JL; tel. (171) 224-1333; f. 1923 as British Empire Cancer Campaign for Research with the object of attacking and defeating the disease of cancer in all its forms by research into its causes, distribution, symptoms, pathology and cure; Pres. HRH The Duke of GLOUCESTER; Dir-Gen. Prof. J. G. MCVIE; publs *British Journal of Cancer* (monthly), *Annual Report*, *CRC News* (quarterly).

Central Council of Physical Recreation: Francis House, Francis St, London, SW1P 1DE; tel. (171) 828-3163; fax (171) 630-8820; f. 1935 to formulate and promote measures to improve and develop sport and physical recreation; Pres. HRH The Prince PHILIP, Duke of EDINBURGH; Chair. of Exec. Cttee DAVID OXLEY; Gen. Sec. MALCOLM DENTON.

Chartered Society of Physiotherapy: 14 Bedford Row, London, WC1R 4ED; tel. (171) 306-6666; fax (171) 306-6611; f. 1894, inc. by Royal Charter 1920; 34,000 mems; Chief Exec. PHIL GREY; publs *Physiotherapy* (monthly), *Frontline* (2 a month).

College of Optometrists: 42 Craven St, London, WC2N 5NG; tel. (171) 839-6000; fax (171) 839-6800; e-mail optometry@coptom.demon.co.uk; f. 1980 (by The British Optical Association, The Scottish Association of Opticians and The Worshipful Company of Spectacle Makers) for the improvement and conservation of human vision; the advancement for the public benefit of the study of and research into optometry and related subjects and the publication of the results thereof; the promotion and improvement for the public benefit of the science and practice of optometry; the maintenance for the public benefit of the highest possible standards of professional competence and conduct; 10,560 mems; library of 10,000 vols; museum; Pres. G. J. MORGAN; Sec. PETER D. LEIGH; publ. *Ophthalmic and Physiological Optics* (6 a year).

Harveian Society of London: 11 Chandos St, London, W1M 0EB; tel. (171) 580-1043; f. 1831 to promote the advance of medical science; 448 mems; Pres. Dr STEPHEN LOCK; Hon. Sec. ROBIN PRICE; Exec. Sec. M. C. GRIFFITHS.

Hunterian Society: c/o Michael Laurence, Brampton House, 60 Grove End Rd, London, NW8 9NH; f. 1819; 450 mems; Hon. Sec. MICHAEL LAURENCE; publ. *Transactions* (annually).

Institute of Biomedical Science: 12 Coldbath Square, London, EC1R 5HL; tel. (171) 636-8192; fax (171) 436-4946; e-mail 101771.3572@compuserve.com; inc. 1942 to promote and develop biomedical science and its practitioners, and establish and maintain professional standards; 14,000 mems; Chief Exec. ALAN R. POTTER; publs *British Journal of Biomedical Science* (quarterly), *Biomedical Scientist* (monthly).

Medical Society for the Study of Venereal Diseases: C/o Sarah Carney, 1 Wimpole St, London, W1M 8AE; tel. (171) 290-2968; fax (171) 290-2989; f. 1922 to study sexually transmitted and allied diseases, incl. AIDS; 600 mems; Pres. Prof. MICHAEL ADLER; Hon. Sec. Dr ANGELA ROBINSON; publ. *Sexually Transmitted Infections* (6 a year).

Medical Society of London: Lettsom Ho., 11 Chandos St, London, W1M 0EB; tel. (171) 580-1043; f. 1773; 558 mems; library of 4,500 vols; Pres. ELLIOT PHILIPP; Hon. Secs Dr P. MITCHELL-HEGGS, Dr MARTIN SEIFERT.

MIND: Granta House, 15–19 Broadway, London, E15 4BQ; tel. (181) 519-2122; fax (181) 522-1725; f. 1946; charity which works for a better life for people in mental distress, campaigns for rights to better services; 1,600 mems, 223 local asscns, 7 regional offices; Chair. DAVID PERYER; Chief Exec. JUDI CLEMENTS; publs *OPENMind* (6 a year), books and leaflets.

Nutrition Society: 10 Cambridge Court, 210 Shepherds Bush Rd, London, W6 7NJ; tel. (171) 602-0228; fax (171) 602-1756; f. 1941 to advance the scientific study of nutrition and its application to the maintenance of human and animal health; over 1,350 mems; Pres. Prof. M. J. GIBNEY; publs *Proceedings*, *British Journal of Nutrition*, *Nutrition Research Reviews*.

Pathological Society of Great Britain and Ireland: 2 Carlton House Tce, London SW1Y 5AF; tel. (171) 976-1260; fax (171) 976-1267; f. 1906; 1,600 mems; Chair. Prof. F. WALKER; Meetings Secs Prof. M. WELLS, Dr C. G. GEMMELL; publs *Journal of Pathology*, *Journal of Medical Microbiology*, *Reviews in Medical Microbiology*.

Royal Association for Disability and Rehabilitation: 12 City Forum, 250 City Rd, London, EC1V 8AF; tel. (171) 250-3222; fax (171) 250-0212; f. 1977; covers the whole field of disability; a co-ordinating organization concerned with the needs and rights of disabled people; Chair. TREVAN HINGSTON; Dir BERT MASSIE.

Royal College of Anaesthetists: 48/49 Russell Square, London WC1B 4JY; tel. (171) 813-1900; fax (171) 813-1875; f. 1948 to advance the science and art of anaesthesia; it is an academic, educational and examining body; Pres. Prof. LEO STRUNIN; publ. *Newsletter* (6 a year).

Royal College of General Practitioners: 14 Princes Gate, London, SW7 1PU; tel. (171) 581-3232; fax (171) 225-3047; f. 1952 to ensure the highest possible standards in general medical practice; 18,500 mems; Chair. Dr JOHN TOBY; Hon. Sec. Dr BILL REITH; publs *British Journal of General Practice*, *Connection* (monthly).

Royal College of Nursing of the United Kingdom: 20 Cavendish Square, London, W1M 0AB; tel. (171) 409-3333; fax (171) 355-1379; f. 1916; library of 60,000 vols; Gen. Sec. CHRISTINE HANCOCK; publ. *Nursing Standard* (weekly).

Royal College of Obstetricians and Gynaecologists: 27 Sussex Place, Regent's Park, London, NW1 4RG; tel. (171) 772-6200; fax (171) 723-0575; f. 1929; 4,400 Fellows, 4,300 mems; library of 11,000 vols; Pres. Dr Sir NARENDRA PATEL; College Administrator P. A. BARNETT; publs *British Journal of Obstetrics and Gynaecology* (monthly), *The Diplomate* (quarterly).

Royal College of Ophthalmologists: 17 Cornwall Terrace, London, NW1 4QW; tel. (171) 935-0702; fax (171) 935-9838; f. 1988 for the cultivation and promotion of ophthalmology; *c.* 2,800 mems; Pres. Dr JEFFREY JAY; Hon. Sec. MICHELLE BEACONSFIELD; publ. *Eye* (6 parts per year).

Royal College of Paediatrics and Child Health: 5 St Andrews Place, Regent's Park, London, NW1 4LB; tel. (171) 486-6151; fax (171) 486-6009; f. 1928 to advance for the benefit of the public, education in paediatrics and to relieve sickness by promoting the improvement of paediatric practice; 4,107 mems; Pres. Prof. DAVID BAUM; Hon. Sec. Dr K. L. DODD; publ. *Archives of Disease in Childhood* (monthly, with British Medical Association).

Royal College of Pathologists: 2 Carlton House Terrace, London, SW1Y 5AF; tel. (171) 930-5863; fax (171) 321-0523; f. 1962; 7,500 Fellows and Mems; library (special collection) of 2,100 vols; Pres. Prof. R. N. M. MACSWEEN; Sec. K. LOCKYER.

Royal College of Physicians: 11 St Andrew's Place, London, NW1 4LE; tel. (171) 935-1174; fax (171) 487-5218; f. 1518; membership consists of Fellows, Members and Licentiates; library: see Libraries; Pres. Prof. K. G. M. M. ALBERTI; Registrar Prof. DAVID R. LONDON; Sec. A. P. MASTERTON-SMITH; publs *Journal* (quarterly), *College Reports*, etc.

Royal College of Physicians and Surgeons of Glasgow: 232 – 242 St Vincent St, Glasgow, G2 5RJ; tel. (141) 221-6072; fax (141) 221-1804; f. 1599; a medical licensing corporation; 6,500 Mems and Fellows, incl. Fellows in Dental Surgery; library of 150,000 vols; Pres. Prof. NORMAN MACKAY; Hon. Sec. Dr S. D. SLATER.

Royal College of Physicians of Edinburgh: 9 Queen St, Edinburgh EH2 1JQ; tel. (131) 225-7324; fax (131) 220-3939; e-mail h.robinson@rcpe.ac.uk; f. 1681; library: see Libraries; Pres. Prof. J. C. PETRIE; Sec. Dr JEREMY ST JOHN THOMAS.

Royal College of Psychiatrists: 17 Belgrave Square, London, SW1X 8PG; tel. (171) 235-2351; fax (171) 245-1231; e-mail rcpsych@rcpsych.ac.uk; f. 1971 by Charter, previously Royal Medico-Psychological Association; 8,000 Fellows and mems; Pres. Dr R. E. KENDELL; Registrar Dr M. SHOOTER; Sec. Mrs V. CAMERON; publ. *British Journal of Psychiatry*.

Royal College of Radiologists: 38 Portland Place, London, W1N 4JQ; tel. (171) 636-4432; fax (171) 323-3100; f. 1939 as the Faculty of Radiologists; practice of radiology; 4,800 mems; Pres. Dr M. J. BRINDLE; Registrar Dr I. W. MCCALL; publs *Clinical Radiology* (monthly), *Clinical Oncology* (every 2 months).

Royal College of Surgeons of Edinburgh: Nicolson St, Edinburgh, EH8 9DW; tel. (131) 527-1600; fax (131) 557-6406; f. 1505; postgraduate education and assessment in surgery; 12,000 Fellows; Pres. Prof. A. G. D. MARAN; Exec. Sec. A. S. CAMPBELL; publ. *Journal* (every 2 months).

Royal College of Surgeons of England: 35-43 Lincoln's Inn Fields, London, WC2A 3PN; tel. (171) 405-3474; fax (171) 831-9438; f. 1800; 12,900 Fellows; Pres. BARRY JACKSON; Sec. CRAIG DUNCAN; publs *Annals* (every 2 months), *Annual Report*.

Royal Institute of Public Health and Hygiene and Society of Public Health: 28 Portland Place, London, W1N 4DE; tel. (171) 580-2731; fax (171) 580-6157; 3,000 mems; Sec. Group Capt. R. A. SMITH; publs *Health and Hygiene* (quarterly), *Public Health* (6 a year).

Royal Medical Society: Students' Centre, Bristo Square, Edinburgh, EH8 9AL; f. 1737; 2,000 mems; library of 2,000 vols; Pres. ANDREW SUTHERLAND; Sec. EMMA-JANE DAWSON.

Royal Pharmaceutical Society of Great Britain: 1 Lambeth High St, London, SE1 7JN; tel. (171) 735-9141; e-mail info.rpsgb@dial.pipex.com; f. 1841; 1,284 fellows, 40,676 mems; library of *c.* 66,000 vols, pamphlets and MSS, *c.* 500 journals; Pres. A. M. LEWIS; Sec. and Registrar J. FERGUSON; publs *The Pharmaceutical Journal* (weekly), *Journal of Pharmacy and Pharmacology* (monthly), *Annual Register of Pharmaceutical Chemists*, *Pharmaceutical Codex*, *Medicines and Ethics*, *Martindale: The Extra Pharmacopoeia*, *Pharmaceutical Sciences* (monthly), *The International Journal of Pharmacy Practice* (quarterly), *The Hospital Pharmacist* (6 a year), *British National Formulary* (published jointly with the British Medical Association), etc.

Royal Society of Health: RSH House, 38A St George's Drive, London, SW1V 4BH; tel. (171) 630-0121; fax (171) 976-6847; e-mail rsh@cygnet.co.uk; f. 1876 for the protection and preservation of health and the advancement of health-related sciences; 10,000 mems; an examining body; holds conferences, lectures, etc; Patron HM THE QUEEN; Chief Exec. (vacant); publ. *Journal* (every 2 months).

Royal Society of Medicine: 1 Wimpole St, London, W1M 8AE; tel. (171) 290-2900; f. 1805; first Royal Charter 1834, supplemental Charter 1907; world-wide membership, over 17,000; library: see Libraries; 40 Sections cover whole field of medicine and surgery; major publishers of own material, journals for other organizations and proceedings of sponsored meetings; Pres. Sir CHRISTOPHER PAINE; Exec. Dir (vacant); publs *Annual Report*, *Journal* (monthly), *Tropical Doctor* (quarterly), *International Journal of STD and AIDS* (every 2 months), *International Congress and Symposium Series*, occasional papers.

Royal Society of Tropical Medicine and Hygiene: Manson House, 26 Portland Place, London, W1N 4EY; tel. (171) 580-2127; fax (171) 436-1389; e-mail mail@rstmh.org; f. 1907 for the stimulation of inquiry and research into causes, treatment, and prevention of human and animal diseases in warm climates; 3,000 mems; Pres. Prof. D. A. WARRELL; Hon. Secs Dr D. C. BARKER, Dr S. B. SQUIRE; publs *Transactions* (every 2 months), *Year Book* (every 2 years), *Bulletin of Tropical Medicine and International Health* (3 a year).

St John's Hospital Dermatological Society: St John's Institute of Dermatology, St Thomas' Hospital, London SE1; meeting at St John's Hospital for Diseases of the Skin; f. 1911 to promote the knowledge and study of dermatology by presentation and discussion of rare and interesting cases; 250 Fellows; Pres. Dr CHARLES DARLEY; Hon. Sec. Dr NEIL WALKER; publ. *Clinical and Experimental Dermatology* (every 2 months).

Society for Endocrinology: 17/18 North Court, The Courtyard, Woodlands, Bradley Stoke, Bristol, BS32 4NQ; tel. (1454) 619036; fax (1454) 616071; e-mail info@endocrinology.org; f. 1946 to promote the advancement of public education in endocrinology; 1,700 mems, incl. 13 hon. mems; Chair. S. G. HILLIER; publs *Journal of Endocrinology* (monthly), *Journal of Molecular Endocrinology* (every 2 months), *The Endocrinologist*, *Endocrine-Related Cancer* (quarterly).

Society of British Neurological Surgeons: C/o University Dept of Neurosurgery, Institute of Neurology, National Hospital for Neurology and Neurosurgery, Queen Square, London, WC1N 3BG; tel. (171) 837-3611 ext. 3153; fax (171) 278-7894; f. 1926; 384 mems; Pres. J. BARTLETT; Hon. Sec. D. G. T. THOMAS; publs *Proceedings* (in *British Journal of Neurosurgery*), *Safe Neurosurgery*.

Society of Occupational Medicine: 6 St. Andrew's Place, London, NW1 4LB; tel. (171) 486-2641; fax (171) 486-0028; f. 1935; concerned with the protection of the health of people at work and the prevention of occupational diseases and injuries; stimulates research and education in occupational medicine; 2,000 mems; Pres. Dr D. O. TODD; Hon. Sec. Dr P. J. J. RYAN; publ. *Occupational Medicine* (8 a year).

Stroke Association: Stroke House, Whitecross St, London, EC1Y 8JJ; tel. (171) 566-0300; f. 1899, fmrly The Chest, Heart and Stroke Association; aims to provide practical support to people who have had strokes and to their families, through community services and welfare grants, and to prevent strokes through education; Chair. of Council Lord SKELMERSDALE; Sec. I. W. PRATT.

Tavistock Institute of Medical Psychology: 12 Keswick Close, Camberley, Surrey, GU15 1RN; tel. (1276) 675266; fax (1276) 675266; f. 1929; promotes the study and practice of psychotherapy and sponsors research and preventive measures in the field of mental health; assists those training in psychotherapy at the Tavistock Clinic; administers the Tavistock Marital Studies Institute which offers a professional service to those experiencing difficulty in marriage, trains practitioners in the helping services, conducts relevant research, publishes its own series of papers; also administers Career and Educational Consultation which offers a vocational and educational counselling service for individuals and their families; provides training in the application of a psychodynamic approach to work and educational settings; Sec. G. C. HUME.

NATURAL SCIENCES

General

Association for Science Education: College Lane, Hatfield, Herts., AL10 9AA; tel. (1707) 283000; fax (1707) 266532; e-mail ase@asehq.telme.com; organizes meetings and workshops locally and nationally; aims to improve science teaching and to provide a medium of expression for science teachers; 23,000 mems; Chief Exec. Dr D. S. MOORE; publs *School Science Review* (quarterly), *Education in Science* (5 a year), *Primary Science Review* (5 a year), *ASE Primary Science* (3 a year), *Post-Sixteen Science Forum* (3 a year).

British Association for the Advancement of Science: 23 Savile Row, London, W1X 2NB; tel. (171) 973-3500; fax (171) 973-3051; e-mail baadmin@britassoc.org.uk; f. 1831; national institution offering membership to all; aims to promote and enhance public understanding and awareness of science and technology and their impact on society; 2,000 mems; Pres. Sir RICHARD SYKES; Chair. Sir WALTER BODMER; Chief Exec. Dr PETER BRIGGS; publs *Science and Public Affairs* (quarterly), *SCAN* (Science Awareness Newsletter, monthly).

British Society for the History of Science: 31 High St, Stanford in the Vale, Faringdon, Oxon, SN7 8LH; tel. (1367) 718963; fax (1367) 718963; e-mail bshs@hidex.demon.co.uk; f. 1947; *c.* 850 mems; Pres. Prof. J. H. BROOKE; publs *British Journal for the History of Science* (quarterly), *Monographs in the History of Science*, *Lists of Theses in History of Science in British Universities* (annually), *Newsletter* (3 a year), *Guide to History of Science Courses in Britain* (annually).

Cambridge Philosophical Society: Bene't St, Cambridge CB2 3PY; tel. 334743; f. 1819 to promote scientific enquiry and to facilitate the communication of facts connected with the advancement of science; 1,900 mems; library of 96,000 vols, mainly periodicals, covering most branches of science, but especially mathematics, physics and general biology; Exec. Sec. Miss J. M. WINTON THOMAS; publs *Mathematical Proceedings* (every 2 months), *Biological Reviews* (quarterly).

Council for Environmental Education: University of Reading, London Rd, Reading, RG1 5AQ; tel. (118) 975-6061; fax (118) 975-6264; e-mail info@cee.i-way.co.uk; f. 1968 to increase the effectiveness of the environmental education movement by developing and influencing policy and supporting and encouraging good practice; reference library and resource centre; Dir LIBBY GRUNDY; publs *Newsheet* (10 a year), *Earthlines* (4 a year), *Update* (quarterly).

Environment Council: 212 High Holborn, London, WC1V 7VW; tel. (171) 836-2626; fax (171) 242-1180; e-mail environment.council@ukonline.co.uk; f. 1969, fmrly Ccl for Environmental Conservation; protects and enhances Britain's environment by promoting awareness, dialogue, understanding and effective action; Chief Exec. STEVE ROBINSON; publ. *Habitat* (10 a year).

Field Studies Council: Preston Montford, Montford Bridge, Shrewsbury, SY4 1HW; tel. (1743) 850674; f. 1943 to provide facilities for every aspect of field work and to set up for this purpose field study centres in localities selected for the richness and variety of their ecological features and their geological, geographical, archaeological and artistic interest; operates 12 field centres; 4,000 mems; Pres. Prof. I. D. MERCER; Chair. Prof. T. P. BURT; Dir A. D. THOMAS; publs *Programmes of Courses*, *Annual Report*, *Field Studies* (annually).

Institute of Information Scientists: 44 Museum St, London, WC1A 1LY; tel. (171) 831-8003; fax (171) 430-1270; f. 1958; professional body for information scientists; aims to promote and maintain high standards in information work and to establish qualifications for those engaged in the profession; organizes annual conference, meetings and courses; 2,750 mems; Pres. MICHAEL F. LYNCH; Dir ELSPETH B. HYAMS; publs *Journal of Information Science* (1 vol of 6 issues a year), *Journal of Document and Text Management* (annually), *Inform* (10 a year).

Institution of Environmental Sciences: 14 Princes Gate, Hyde Park, London, SW7 1PU; tel. (1778) 394846; fax (1778) 394846; f. 1971 for consultation in matters of an environmental nature; aims to promote interdisciplinary studies of the environment, to diffuse information relating to environmental sciences at national and international levels, and to bring together into a corporate professional body all persons throughout the world possessing responsibilities for environmental affairs; 820 individual, 7 collective mems; Chair. J. BAINES; publ. *The Environmental Scientist*.

London Natural History Society: c/o P. C. Holland, Flat 9, Pinewood Ct, London, SW4 8LB; f. 1858 for the study of natural history, archaeology and kindred subjects, especially within a radius of 20 miles from St Paul's Cathedral; library of 3,000 vols; 1,250 mems; Mem. Sec. P. C. HOLLAND; publs *The London Naturalist*, *London Bird Report* (both annually).

Royal Institution of Great Britain: 21 Albemarle St, London, W1X 4BS; tel. (171) 409-2992; fax (171) 629-3569; promotes science to the public through lectures and discussions; 2,300 mems and subscribers; Davy Faraday Research Laboratory conducts research in solid-state chemistry; library: see Libraries and Archives; museum: see Museums and Art Galleries; Pres. HRH The Duke of KENT; Sec. Prof. R. J. H. CLARK; Dir Prof. SUSAN GREENFIELD; publs *Proceedings*, *Record* (annually).

Scottish Field Studies Association: Kindrogan Field Centre, Enochdhu, Blairgowrie, Perthshire, PH10 7PG; tel. (1250) 881286; fax (1250) 881433; f. 1945; provides residential courses at the Association's Kindrogan Field Centre in Perthshire; 400 mems; Chair. Dr ALAN PIKE; publ. *Newsletter*.

United Kingdom Science Park Association: Aston Science Park, Love Lane, Aston Triangle, Birmingham, B7 4BJ; tel. (121) 359-0981; fax (121) 333-5852; f. 1984 to act as a forum for those concerned with the planning and management of science parks, and to promote awareness of science parks and provide information on their objectives and achievements; linked with Int. Asscn of Science Parks; mems: 45 science parks; Chair. Dr G. HUNTER; Sec. W. HERRIOT; publs *Directory*, *The Development and Operation of Science Parks*.

Wildlife Trusts: The Green, Witham Park, Waterside South, Lincoln, LN5 7JR; tel. (1522) 544400; fax (1522) 511616; f. 1912 as Royal Society for Nature Conservation; inc. by Royal Charter 1916 and 1976, to promote the conservation of nature for study and research and to educate the public in the understanding and appreciation of nature, the awareness of its value and the need for its conservation; acts as the national office for the 46 Wildlife Trusts, Urban Wildlife Groups and Wildlife Watch (junior branch); Pres. Prof. DAVID BELLAMY; publs annual report, *Natural World* (3 a year).

Biological Sciences

Association of Applied Biologists: c/o M. May, IACR Broom's Barn, Higham, Bury St. Edmunds, Suffolk, IP28 6NP; f. 1904 to promote the study and advancement of all branches of biology, with special reference to their applied aspects; 1,000 mems; Pres. Dr C. DUFFAS; Hon. Sec. M. MAY; publ. *Annals of Applied Biology* (every 2 months).

Biochemical Society, The: 59 Portland Place, London, W1N 3AJ; tel. (171) 580-5530; fax (171) 637-7626; e-mail genadmin@biochemsoc.org.uk; f. 1911 for the advancement of the science of biochemistry; 9,000 mems; Chair. Prof. R. B. FREEDMAN; Exec. Sec. G. D. JONES; publs *The Biochemical Journal* (fortnightly), *Biochemical Society Transactions* (quarterly), *Clinical Science* (in conjunction with Medical Research Society, monthly), *Essays in Biochemistry* (annually), *Symposia* (annually), *The Biochemist* (every 2 months), *Biotechnology and Applied Biochemistry* (monthly).

Botanical Society of Scotland: C/o Royal Botanic Garden, Edinburgh, EH3 5LR; tel. (131) 552-7171; f. 1836, fmrly Botanical Society of Edinburgh; incorporates the Cryptogamic Soc. of Scotland; 400 Mems and Fellows; Pres. Prof. E. G. CUTTER; Hon. Gen. Sec. R. GALT; publs *Botanical Journal of Scotland* (every 6 months), *Newsletter* (every 6 months).

Botanical Society of the British Isles: c/o Dept. of Botany, Natural History Museum, London, SW7 5BD; f. 1836 for study of British native flowering plants and ferns; exhibitions, conferences, field meetings; 2,800 mems; Hon. Gen. Sec. R. GWYNN ELLIS; publs *Watsonia* (2 a year), *BSBI Abstracts* (annually), *BSBI News* (3 a year).

British Biophysical Society: C/o Dr W. A. Thomas, 28 Milton Ave, Eaton Ford, St Neots, Cambs., PE19 3LE; f. 1960; 800 mems; Sec. Dr W. A. THOMAS.

British Ecological Society: 26 Blades Court, Deodar Rd, Putney, London, SW15 2NU; tel. (181) 871-9797; fax (181) 871-9779; e-mail general@ecology.demon.co.uk; f. 1913; 5,000 mems; Exec. Sec. Dr HAZEL J. NORMAN; publs *Symposium* (annually), *Journal of Ecology*, *Journal of Animal Ecology*, *Journal of Applied Ecology* (6 a year), *Functional Ecology* (6 a year).

British Lichen Society: c/o Dr O. W. Purvis, Dept of Botany, Natural History Museum, Cromwell Rd, London SW7 5BD; tel. (171) 938-8852; telex 929437; fax (171) 938-9260; f. 1958; 520 mems; library of 500 vols, 5,000 reprints; Sec. Dr O. W. PURVIS; publs *The Lichenologist* (6 a year), *Bulletin* (2 a year).

British Mycological Society: c/o Dr S. T. Moss, School of Biological Sciences, University of Portsmouth, King Henry I St, Portsmouth, Hants, PO1 2DY; tel. (1705) 842024; fax (1705) 525902; e-mail steve.moss@port.ac.uk; f. 1896; 1,206 mems and 644 assocs; Sec. Dr S. T. MOSS; publs *Mycological Research* (monthly), *Mycologist* (quarterly).

British Ornithologists' Union: c/o The Natural History Museum, Akeman St, Tring, Herts, HP23 6AP; tel. (1442) 890080; f. 1858 for the advancement of the science of ornithology; 1,800 ordinary mems, plus hon. mems and corresp. mems; Pres. Dr J. P. CROXALL; Sec. N. BUCKNELL; publ. *Ibis* (quarterly).

British Society for Plant Pathology: c/o Plant Breeding International Cambridge, Maris Lane, Trumpington, Cambridge, CB2 2LQ; tel. (1223) 849368; fax (1223) 844425; e-mail graham.j.jellis@unilever.com; f. 1981; 700 mems; Pres. Prof. D. S. INGRAM; Sec. Prof. G. J. JELLIS; publs *Plant Pathology* (6 a year), *BSPP Newsletter* (2 a year).

British Trust for Ornithology: The Nunnery, Thetford, Norfolk, IP24 2PU; tel. (1842) 750050; fax (1842) 750030; e-mail bto.staff@bto.org; f. 1933; promotes and encourages the wider understanding, appreciation and conservation of birds through scientific studies using the combined skills and enthusiasm of its members, other bird watchers and staff; projects include National Bird Ringing Scheme, Nest Records Scheme, Common Birds Census, Wetland Bird Survey, Breeding Bird Survey, Garden Bird Watch; offers advisory services to ecologists, land use planners, conservationists, developers; 10,000 mems; library; Pres. Sir FRED HOLIDAY; Dir Dr J. J. D. GREENWOOD; publs *BTO News* (every 2 months), *Bird Study* (3 a year), *Ringing and Migration* (2 a year), *Bird Table* (4 a year).

Fauna and Flora International: Great Eastern House, Tenison Rd, Cambridge, CB1 2DT; tel. (1223) 571000; fax (1223) 461481; e-mail info@fauna-flora.org; f. 1903; world's oldest international wildlife conservation society working to save endangered species from extinction; especially concerned with the prevention of illegal trade; publishes information and news about wildlife conservation throughout the world; *c.* 5,000 mems; Chair. of Council LINDSAY BURY; publ. *Oryx* (quarterly).

Freshwater Biological Association: The Ferry House, Ambleside, Cumbria, LA22 0LP; tel. (15394) 42468; fax (15394) 46914; e-mail csr@wpo.nerc.ac.uk; f. 1929 to promote the investigation of the biology of the animals and plants found in fresh (including brackish) water, and to establish and maintain a laboratory or laboratories equipped with boats and other necessary apparatus for the investigation of freshwater life; 1,500 mems; library: 150,000 books and reprints and 10,000 vols. of scientific periodicals; River Laboratory of East Stoke, Wareham, Dorset; Pres. and Chair. of Council Prof. Sir F. G. T. HOLLIDAY; Sec. and Dir Prof. C. S. REYNOLDS (acting); publs *Freshwater Forum* (includes *Annual Report*), *Scientific Publications*, *Membership Newsletter*.

Genetical Society: c/o Dr J. F. Burke, School of Biological Sciences, University of Sussex, Brighton, BN1 9QG; tel. (1273) 678308; fax (1273) 678535; f. 1919; all aspects of genetics, both pure and applied; 1,600 mems; Pres. Prof. M. ASHBURNER; Sec. Dr J. F. BURKE; publs *Heredity* (monthly), *Genes and Development* (fortnightly).

Institute of Biology: 20 – 22 Queensberry Place, London, SW7 2DZ; tel. (171) 581-8333; fax (171) 823-9409; f. 1950 to advance the science and practice of biology; 18 regional brs; 75 affiliated socs; 16,000 mems; Pres. Dr J. R. NORRIS; Chief Exec. Prof. A. D. B. MALCOLM; publs *Biologist*, *Journal of Biological Education*, *New Studies in Biology*, handbooks, registers, occasional publs.

Linnean Society of London: Burlington House, Piccadilly, London, W1V 0LQ; tel. (171) 434-4479; fax (171) 287-9364; f. 1788; 1,942 Fellows, 50 Foreign Members and 20 Hon. Fellows, 18 Associates (under the age of 30) and 4 Student Associates (under the age of 25); library: see Libraries; Pres. Prof. Sir GHILLEAN PRANCE; Secs Dr C. J. HUMPHRIES (Botany), Dr V. R. SOUTHGATE (Zoology), Dr D. F. CUTLER (Editorial); publs *Botanical, Zoological and Biological Journals of the Linnean Society*, *Synopses of the British Fauna*, *Symposium* (volumes); possesses the unique collection of Linnaeus's plants and animals.

Malacological Society of London: c/o Dr G. B. J. Dussart, Canterbury Christ Church College, North Holmes Rd, Canterbury, Kent, CT1 1QU; f. 1893 to promote all aspects of the study of Mollusca; 300 mems; Radley Library deposited at University College London; Pres. Dr D. REID; Sec. Dr G. B. J. DUSSART; publ. *Journal of Molluscan Studies* (4 parts a year).

Marine Biological Association of the United Kingdom: The Laboratory, Citadel Hill, Plymouth, Devon, PL1 2PB; tel. (1752) 633331; fax (1752) 669762; e-mail sec@mba.ac.uk; f. 1884 to promote scientific research into all aspects of life in the sea and to make public the results; the Assn receives grants from universities, research charities and other public bodies and an annual grant-in-aid from the Natural Environment Research Council; 1,539 mems; library: National Marine Biological Library of 60,000 vols; Pres. Sir CRISPIN TICKELL; Sec. and Dir Dr M. WHITFIELD; publ. *Journal* (quarterly).

Physiological Society: Administration & Publications Office, POB 506, Oxford, OX1 3XE (regd. office); tel. (1865) 798498; fax (1865) 798092; f. 1876 to promote the advancement of physiology and facilitate communication between physiologists at home and abroad; 1,795 mems; Sec. Dr C. A. R. BOYD; publs *The Journal of Physiology* (monthly), *Experimental Physiology* (every 2 months), *The Physiological Society Magazine* (quarterly).

Ray Society: c/o Natural History Museum, Cromwell Rd, London, SW7 5BD; f. 1844 to publish works primarily concerned with the natural history of the British Isles and north-west Europe; 370 mems; Pres. D. MACFARLANE; Hon. Sec. Dr N. J. EVANS.

Royal Entomological Society of London: 41 Queens Gate, London, SW7 5HR; tel. (171) 584-8361; fax (171) 581-8505; e-mail reg@royensoc.demon.co.uk; f. 1833; 2,025 Fellows; library of 29,000 vols and 70,000 separates; Pres. Prof. W. M. BLANEY; Registrar G. G. BENTLEY; publs *Ecological Entomology*, *Physiological Entomology*, *Systematic Entomology*, *Medical and Veterinary Entomology*, *Insect Molecular Biology*, *Antenna* (quarterly bulletin), *Handbooks for the Identification of British Insects* (irregular), *Symposium Volumes* (every 2 years).

Royal Society for the Protection of Birds: The Lodge, Sandy, Bedfordshire, SG19 2DL; tel. (1767) 680551; telex 82469; fax (1767) 692365; f. 1889 (inc. 1904) to protect wild birds and the environment; 925,000 mems; library of 9,000 vols; Chair. JOHN LAWTON; Chief Exec. BARBARA YOUNG; publs *Birds* (every 3 months), *Bird Life* (every 2 months), *Annual Report*, and occasional titles.

Royal Zoological Society of Scotland: Scottish National Zoological Park, Edinburgh, EH12 6TS; tel. (131) 334 9171; fax (131) 316-4050; f. 1909, inc. by Royal Charter 1913, to promote, through the presentation of the society's living collections, the conservation of animal species and wild places by captive breeding, environmental education and scientific research; 13,000 mems; Pres. JOHN GRANT OF ROTHIEMURCHUS; Dir Dr DAVID WALSH; publs *Annual Report*, *Illustrated Park Guides*, *Arkfile* (quarterly).

Scottish Association for Marine Science: POB 3, Oban, Argyll, PA34 4AD; tel. (1631) 562244; fax (1631) 565518; f. 1897 for research and education in marine science; 446 mems; Dir Dr GRAHAM SHIMMIELD; publs *Annual Report*, *Newsletter*.

Selborne Society: c/o R. J. Hall, 89 Daryngton Drive, Greenford, Middx, UB6 8BH; f. 1885 to perpetuate the memory of Gilbert White of Selborne and to promote the study of natural history, especially amongst schoolchildren; 900 mems; Hon. Sec. R. J. HALL; publ. *Newsletter* (3 a year).

Society for General Microbiology: Marlborough House, Basingstoke Road, Spencers Wood, Reading RG7 1AE; tel. (118) 988-1800; fax (118) 988-5656; e-mail admin@socgenmicrobiol.org.uk; f. 1945 to promote the advancement of microbiology, providing a common meeting ground for those working in specialized fields including medical, veterinary, agricultural and economic microbiology; 5,300 mems; Pres. Prof. H. DALTON; Exec. Sec. Dr R. S. S. FRASER; publs *Microbiology* (monthly), *Journal of General Virology* (monthly), *Society for General Microbiology Quarterly* (quarterly), *International Journal of Systematic Bacteriology* (quarterly).

Systematics Association: C/o Dr Z. Lawrence, CABI Bioscience UK Centre (Egham), Bakeham Lane, Egham, Surrey, TW20 9TY; tel. (1784) 470111; fax (1784) 470909; e-mail z.lawrence@cabi.org; f. 1937 to study systematics in relation to biology and evolution; 500 mems; Pres. Dr P. FOREY; Secs Dr Z. LAWRENCE, Dr D. M. WILLIAMS (Botany), D. L. J. QUICKE (Zoology); publ. *Newsletter* (3 a year).

Zoological Society of London: Regent's Park, London, NW1 4RY; tel. (171) 722-3333; fax (171) 586-5743; f. 1826; 20,000 mems; library of *c.* 180,000 vols, 1,300 periodicals; Pres. Sir MARTIN HOLDGATE; Sec. Prof. R. MCNEILL ALEXANDER; publs *Animal Conservation* (quarterly), *Journal of Zoology* (3 vols, annually), *Zoological Record* (annually), *International Zoo Yearbook* (annually), *Nomenclator Zoologicus* (9 vols), *Symposia* (irregular).

Mathematical Sciences

British Society for the History of Mathematics: c/o Dr Eleanor Robson, 30A Marsh Lane, Oxford, OX3 0NG; tel. (1865) 278236; e-mail eleanor.robson@wolfson.ox.ac.uk; f. 1971; provides a forum for all interested in the history and development of mathematics and related disciplines; organizes conferences, workshops, visits; 450 mems; Hon. Sec. Dr ELEANOR ROBSON.

Institute of Mathematics and its Applications: Catherine Richards House, 16 Nelson St, Southend-on-Sea, Essex, SS1 1EF; tel. (1702) 354020; fax (1702) 354111; e-mail post@ima.org.uk; f. 1964 to extend and diffuse knowledge of mathematics and of the applications of mathematics in science, engineering, economics, etc; to promote education in mathematics; 6,000 mems; Pres. Prof. H. J. BEKER; publs *IMA Journal of Applied Mathematics* (every 2 months), *IMA Journal of Numerical Analysis* (quarterly), *IMA Journal of Mathematics Applied in Medicine and Biology* (quarterly), *IMA Journal of Mathematical Control and Information* (quarterly), *IMA Journal of Mathematics Applied in Business and Industry* (quarterly), *Mathematics Today: Bulletin of the IMA* (every 2 months), *Teaching Mathematics and its Applications* (quarterly).

London Mathematical Society: 57–58 Russell Square, London, WC1B 4HP; tel. (171) 323-3686; fax (171) 323-3655; e-mail lms@lms.ac.uk; f. 1865 for the promotion and extension of mathematical knowledge; 2,300 mems; Pres. Prof. J. M. BALL; Hon. Secs Prof. J. S. PYM, Dr D. J. H. GARLING; publs *Journal*, *Proceedings*, *Bulletin*, *Nonlinearity* (every 2 months).

Physical Sciences

Association of Public Analysts: Burlington House, Piccadilly, London W1V 0BN; f. 1953 for the furtherance of analytical chemistry in relation to the composition of foodstuffs, fertilizers, animal feeding stuffs, other areas of consumer protection; water, air and land pollution and other environmental matters; 100 mems; Pres. E. B. REYNOLDS; Hon. Sec. P. LENARTOWICZ; publ. *Journal* (quarterly).

British Astronomical Association: Burlington House, Piccadilly, London, W1V 9AG;

tel. (171) 734-4145; f. 1890; amateur astronomers asscn; 3,250 mems; publ. *Journal* and *Handbook*.

British Cryogenics Council, The: c/o Institution of Mechanical Engineers, 1 Birdcage Walk, London, SW1 7BU; tel. (115) 931-2896; fax (115) 931-2896; f. 1967 to foster and stimulate the development and application of cryogenics in Britain by means of contacts, education and research; 10 mem. instns; Chair. N. P. HEGARTY; Hon. Sec. J. S. HARRIS; publ. *British Cryogenics Council Newsletter* (quarterly).

British Horological Institute: Upton Hall, Upton, Newark, Notts. NG23 5TE; tel. (1636) 813795; fax (1636) 812258; f. 1858 to promote the cultivation of the science of horology; library; *c*. 3,400 mems; Pres. THE MASTER OF THE WORSHIPFUL COMPANY OF CLOCKMAKERS; Sec. H. BARTLETT; publ. *The Horological Journal* (monthly).

British Interplanetary Society: 27/29 South Lambeth Rd, London, SW8 1SZ; tel. (171) 735-3160; fax (171) 820-1504; e-mail bis .bis@virgin.net; f. 1933 to promote the science, engineering and technology of astronautics, to support and engage in research studies and to disseminate the results thereof; inc. 1945; mem. International Astronautical Federation; 1,800 Fellows, 1,500 Mems; Pres. C. M. HEMPSELL; Exec. Sec. S. A. JONES; publs *Spaceflight* (monthly), *Journal* (monthly).

British Nuclear Energy Society: 1-7 Great George St, London, SW1P 3AA; tel. (171) 665-2241; fax (171) 799-1325; e-mail tillbrook_a@ ice.org.uk; f. 1962 in succession to British Nuclear Energy Conference to provide a forum for discussion, and directed to the broader aspects of nuclear energy, covering engineering and scientific disciplines; 12 constituent institutions; 1,200 mems; Sec. ANDREW TILLBROOK; publs *Nuclear Energy* (every 2 months), *Conference Proceedings*.

Challenger Society for Marine Science: C/o Southampton Oceanography Centre, Empress Dock, Southampton, SO14 3ZH; tel. (1703) 596097; fax (1703) 596149; e-mail jxj@ soc.soton.ac.uk; f. 1903 for the promotion of the study of oceanography; 500 mems; Pres. Prof. M. WHITFIELD; Hon. Sec. Dr C. ROBINSON; publs *Ocean Challenge* (3 a year), occasional papers.

Geological Society: Burlington House, Piccadilly, London, W1V 0JU; tel. (171) 434-9944; fax (171) 439-8975; f. 1807 to investigate the mineral structure of the Earth; 8,600 mems; library: see Libraries; Pres. Dr L. R. M. COCKS; Exec. Sec. E. NICKLESS; publs *Journal*, *Quarterly Journal of Engineering Geology*, *Petroleum Geoscience*, *Geoscientist*, *Special Reports*, *Special Publications*, *Memoirs*, *Annual Report*, miscellaneous papers.

Geologists' Association: Burlington House, Piccadilly, London, W1V 9AG; tel. (171) 434-9298; fax (171) 287-0280; f. 1858 to foster the progress and diffusion of the science of geology and to encourage research and the development of new methods; *c*. 2,500 mems; Pres. Dr BOB SYMES; Exec. Sec. SARAH STAFFORD; publs *Proceedings* (quarterly), *Circular* (every 8 weeks).

Institute of Physics: 76 Portland Place, London, W1N 4AA; tel. (171) 470-4800; fax (171) 470-4848; f. 1918, amalgamated with the Physical Society 1960; Chartered 1970; professional body for physicists in the UK and Ireland; 22,000 mems; Pres. Sir G. ROBERTS; Hon. Sec. Prof. ERIC JAKEMAN; Chief Exec. Dr ALUN JONES; publs *Journal of Physics Series A to G*, etc.

Mineralogical Society of Great Britain and Ireland: 41 Queen's Gate, London, SW7 5HR; tel. (171) 584-7516; fax (171) 823-8021; f. 1876; *c*. 1,000 mems; Pres. Prof. A. H. RANKIN; Gen. Sec. Dr B. A. CRESSEY; publs *Mineralogical Magazine*, *Mineralogical Abstracts*, *Clay Minerals*, *Mineral Deposits of Europe* and monographs.

Palaeontographical Society: Dept of Palaeontology, Natural History Museum, Cromwell Rd, London, SW7 5BD; tel. (171) 938-8902; e-mail p.ensom@nhm.ac.uk; f. 1847 for the illustration and description of British fossils; Pres. Prof. C. R. C. PAUL; Sec. P. C. ENSOM; publs *Annual Volume*, monographs.

Quekett Microscopical Club: c/o Natural History Museum, Cromwell Rd, London, SW7 5BD; f. 1865 to encourage the study of every branch of microscopical science; 600 mems; library of *c*. 1,000 vols; publ. *Quekett Journal of Microscopy* (2 a year).

Royal Astronomical Society: Burlington House, Piccadilly, London, W1V 0NL; tel. (171) 734-4582; fax (171) 494-0166; f. 1820; granted Royal Charter in 1831; *c*. 2,800 mems; library: see Libraries; Pres. Prof. M. S. LONGAIR; Secs Prof. A. M. CRUISE, Dr M. J. PENSTON, Dr K. A. WHALER; publs *Monthly Notices* (monthly), *Geophysical Journal International* (monthly), *Quarterly Journal* (quarterly).

Royal Meteorological Society: 104 Oxford Rd, Reading, Berks, RG1 7LS; tel. (1734) 568500; fax (1734) 568571; f. 1850; 3,000 mems; library of 1,200 archival books; Pres. Prof. J. E. HARRIES; Sec Dr D. J. GRIGGS; publs *Quarterly Journal*, *International Journal of Climatology* (monthly), *Weather* (monthly), *Meteorological Applications* (quarterly).

Royal Microscopical Society: 37/38 St Clements, Oxford, OX4 1AJ; tel. (1865) 248768; fax (1865) 791237; e-mail info@rms .org.uk; f. 1839 for the promotion of Microscopical Science and its applications; granted Royal Charter in 1866; 1,900 mems; Pres. Prof. G. W. LORIMER; Administrator P. B. HIRST; publs *Journal of Microscopy* (monthly), *Proceedings* (quarterly).

Royal Society of Chemistry: Thomas Graham House, Science Park, Milton Rd, Cambridge, CB4 4WF; tel. (1223) 420066; fax (1223) 423623; f. 1980 from unification of the Chemical Society and the Royal Institute of Chemistry (f. 1841 and 1877 respectively); 45,000 mems (Fellows and Members (designated Chartered Chemists), Licentiates, Graduate Members and Assoc. mems, incl. 3,755 students); library: see Libraries; Pres. EDWARD ABEL; Sec.-Gen. Dr T. D. INCH; publs *Chemistry in Britain* (monthly), *Journal of the Chemical Society* (including *Dalton, Faraday and Perkin Transactions and Chemical Communications*), *Journal of Materials Chemistry*, *Education in Chemistry*, translation of *Russian Chemical Reviews*, series of *Specialist Periodical Reports*, *The Analyst*, *Analytical Abstracts*, *Chemical Business Newsbase*, *Chemical Engineering and Biotechnology Abstracts*, *Laboratory Hazards Bulletin*, *Mass Spectrometry Bulletin*, *Natural Product Updates*, *Journal of Chemical Research*, *Faraday Discussions*, *Mendeleev Communications*, *Chemical Society Reviews*, *Journal of Analytical Atomic Spectroscopy*, *Contemporary Organic Synthesis*.

SCI (Society of Chemical Industry): 14/15 Belgrave Square, London, SW1X 8PS; tel. (171) 235-3681; fax (171) 823-1698; e-mail secretariat@chemind.demon.co.uk; f. 1881; Royal Charter 1907; 6,000 mems; Pres. KEN MINTON; Gen. Sec. RICHARD DENYER; publs *Chemistry and Industry* (2 a month), *Journal of Chemical Technology and Biotechnology* (monthly), *Journal of the Science of Food and Agriculture* (monthly), *Pesticide Science* (monthly), *Polymer International* (monthly), *SCI Bulletin* (monthly).

Yorkshire Geological Society: C/o W. J. VARKER, Dept of Earth Sciences, The University, Leeds, LS2 9JT; f. 1837; 1,200 mems; library of 5,000 vols; Pres. G. HOLLIDAY; Gen. Sec. W. J. VARKER; publ. *Proceedings* (2 a year).

PHILOSOPHY AND PSYCHOLOGY

Aristotelian Society: c/o A. C. Grayling, Dept of Philosophy, Birkbeck College, Malet St, London, WC1E 7HX; tel. (171) 255-1724; f. 1870 for the systematic study of philosophy, its historic development and its methods and problems; 1,140 mems and 741 subscribing libraries; Hon. Sec. A. C. GRAYLING; publs *Proceedings* (annually, and as a journal 3 a year), *Supplementary Volume* (annually), *Monographs* (occasional).

British Psychological Society: St Andrews House, 48 Princess Rd East, Leicester, LE1 7DR; tel. (116) 254-9568; fax (116) 247-0787; e-mail mail@bps.org.uk; f. 1901; 30,000 mems; Pres. Dr INGRID LUNT; Hon. Gen. Sec. Prof. TONY GALE; publs *The Psychologist*, *British Journal of Medical Psychology*, *British Journal of Educational Psychology*, *British Journal of Mathematical & Statistical Psychology*, *British Journal of Social Psychology*, *British Journal of Clinical Psychology*, *Journal of Occupational & Organisational Psychology*, *British Journal of Developmental Psychology*, *British Journal of Psychology*, *Selection & Development Review*, *Legal and Criminological Psychology*, *British Journal of Health Psychology*.

British Society of Aesthetics: Lancaster University, Lancaster, LA1 4YG; tel. (1524) 592495; fax (1524) 592503; f. 1960 to promote study, research and discussion in aesthetics and the growth of artistic taste among the public, and to facilitate communications between scholars at an international and European level; Pres. RICHARD WOLLHEIM; Sec. EMILY BRADY; publs *Newsletter* (every 6 months), *British Journal of Aesthetics* (quarterly).

Experimental Psychology Society: Dept of Psychology, University of Glasgow, 56 Hillhead St, Glasgow, G12 8QB; f. 1946; to further scientific enquiry within the field of psychology; 480 mems; Pres. Prof. J. MORTON; Hon. Sec. Prof. A. MICHAEL BURTON; publs *Quarterly Journal of Experimental Psychology*, Sections A and B.

Leeds Philosophical and Literary Society Ltd: City Museum, Leeds, LS1 3AA; tel. (113) 245-2894; f. 1820 for the advancement of knowledge in all its branches, excepting religion, politics and ethics; 140 mems; Sec. J. LYDON; publs *Proceedings*, etc.

Manchester Literary and Philosophical Society: Churchgate House, 56 Oxford St, Manchester, M60 7HJ; tel. (161) 228-3638; fax (161) 228-3571; f. 1781 for the advancement of literature and science; 500 mems; library of 4,000 vols; Pres. D. E. WILSON; Hon. Sec. Dr R. E. CATLOW; publ. *Manchester Memoirs* (annually).

Mind Association: C/o All Souls College, University of Oxford, Oxford, OX1 4AL; f. 1900 to publish the journal *Mind* (f. 1876; quarterly), and help organize annual conferences jointly with the Aristotelian Society (*q.v.*); Hon. Sec. J. BUTTERFIELD.

Philosophical Society of England, The: King George VI Bldg, University of Newcastle upon Tyne, Newcastle upon Tyne, NE1 7RU; tel. (191) 222-6796; fax (191) 222-7090; f. 1913 to spread a knowledge of philosophy among the general public; Sec. MICHAEL BAVIDGE; publ. *The Philosopher* (2 a year).

Royal Institute of Philosophy: 14 Gordon Square, London, WC1H 0AG; tel. (171) 387-130; f. 1925; *c*. 850 mems; Pres. Lord QUINTON;

Chair. Prof. Sir S. R. SUTHERLAND; Dir Prof. A. O'HEAR; Sec. INGRID PURKISS; publs *Philosophy* (quarterly), collection of lectures given in preceding session (annually), *Conference Proceedings* (annually).

Royal Philosophical Society of Glasgow: C/o Dept of Philosophy, West Quadrangle, University of Glasgow, Glasgow, G12 8QQ; tel. (141) 334-4144; fax (141) 330-4112; e-mail rphil@arts.gla.ac.uk; f. 1802; principal activity: lectures; 200 mems; Pres. GEORGE GORMAN; Sec. E. J. BOROWSKI.

Society for Psychical Research: 49 Marloes Rd, London, W8 6LA; tel. (171) 937-8984; f. 1882 for the purpose of making an organized and systematic attempt to investigate certain paranormal phenomena which are *prima facie* inexplicable on any generally recognized hypothesis; 1,180 mems; Pres. Prof. D. J. WEST; publs *Proceedings* (irregular), *Journal* (quarterly), *Newsletter* (quarterly).

Victoria Institute, The, or Philosophical Society of Great Britain: 41 Marne Ave, Welling, Kent, DA16 2EY; tel. (181) 303-0465; f. 1865; Pres. Dr DAVID J. E. INGRAM; publs *Faith and Thought Bulletin*, and jointly with Christians in Science, *Science and Christian Belief*.

William Morris Society: Kelmscott House, 26 Upper Mall, London, W6 9TA; tel. (181) 741-3735; f. 1955; to stimulate wider appreciation and deepen understanding of the life, work and influence of William Morris and his friends; 1,800 mems; library of 2,000 vols; Hon. Sec. PETER FAULKNER; publs *Journal* (2 a year), *Newsletter* (quarterly), occasional monographs.

RELIGION, SOCIOLOGY AND ANTHROPOLOGY

African Studies Association of the United Kingdom: c/o SOAS, Thornhaugh St, London, WC1H 0XG; f. 1963 to advance academic studies relating to Africa by providing facilities for the interchange of information and ideas; holds inter-disciplinary conferences, symposia; 600 mems; Hon. Pres. Prof. J. D. Y. PEEL; Hon. Sec. Dr NICI NELSON.

Arab Research Centre: 76 – 78 Notting Hill Gate, London, W11 3HS; tel. (171) 221-2425; fax (171) 221-5899; f. 1979 to promote study of problems and issues in the Arab world; commissions academic papers and holds international symposia; 50 mems; library of *c.* 2,500 vols; Chair. ABDEL MAJID FARID; Man. A. ARNALL; publ. *The Arab Researcher*.

British Association for the Study of Religions: c/o Dr Kim Knott, Dept of Theology and Religious Studies, University of Leeds, Leeds, LS2 9JT; f. 1954; affiliated to IAHR; 200 mems; organizes an annual conference; Pres. Dr KIM KNOTT; Sec. PEGGY MORGAN, Westminster College, Oxford, OX2 9AT; publ. *Bulletin* (3 a year).

British Society for Middle Eastern Studies: Centre for Middle Eastern and Islamic Studies, University of Durham, South End House, South Rd, Durham, DH1 3TG; tel. (191) 374-7989; fax (191) 374-2830; e-mail a.l.haysey@durham.ac.uk; f. 1973; to promote the study of the Middle Eastern region from the end of classical antiquity and the rise of Islam, encouraging discussion and debate and fostering co-operation among teachers, researchers and students of the Middle East, both within the UK and internationally; co-operation with similar societies is being consolidated and expanded; 700 mems; Pres. Sir ROGER TOMKYS; Sec. Dr C. HILLENBRAND; publs *British Journal of Middle Eastern Studies* (2 a year), *Newsletter* (3 a year).

British Sociological Association, The: Unit 3G, Mountjoy Research Centre, Stockton Rd, Durham, DH1 3UR; tel. (191) 383-0839; fax (191) 383-0782; e-mail britsoc@dial.pipex.com; f. 1951 to promote interest in sociology, to advance its study and application in Britain, and to encourage contacts between workers in all relevant fields of enquiry; Pres. Prof. DAVID MORGAN; Hon. Gen. Sec. Prof. PAMELA ABBOTT; publs *Sociology*, *Work Employment and Society* (quarterly), *Network* (3 a year).

Ecclesiological Society: C/o 'Underedge', Back Lane, Hathersage, via Sheffield, S32 1AR; f. 1839 as The Cambridge Camden Society; object: to study the arts, architecture and liturgy of the Christian Church; programme of lectures, tours, conferences, etc.; 900 mems; collections of books, pamphlets and photographs; Pres. D. R. BUTTRESS, Surveyor of Westminster Abbey; Chair. PAUL VELLUET; Hon. Sec. Prof. K. H. MURTA; publs papers (up to 3 a year), journal (3 a year).

Folklore Society: c/o University College, Gower St, London, WC1E 6BT; f. 1878; about 1,000 mems and subscribers; library of 11,000 vols; Pres. Dr JULIETTE WOOD; Hon. Sec. Dr JACQUELINE SIMPSON; publ. *Folklore* (annually).

Galton Institute: 19 Northfields Prospect, Northfields, London, SW18 1PE; tel. (181) 874-7257; f. 1907 to promote the study of eugenics, genetics, population problems; approx. 400 mems; Pres. ROBERT PEEL; Gen. Sec. B. NIXON; publs *Symposium Proceedings* (annually) and occasional papers.

Henry Bradshaw Society: School of Music, University of East Anglia, Norwich, NR4 7TJ; tel. (1603) 592454; telex 975197; fax (1603) 250454; f. 1890; publishes facsimiles and editions of rare texts relating to the liturgy of the Christian church; 190 institutional mems, 110 individual mems; Chair. H. E. J. COWDREY; Sec. D. F. L. CHADD.

Institute of Community Studies: 18 Victoria Park Square, London, E2 9PF; tel. (181) 980-6263; f. 1954; social research on poverty, deprivation and comparative social policy; housing, urban planning and community; education; Dir M. YOUNG.

Institute of Race Relations: 2 – 6 Leeke St, King's Cross Rd, London, WC1X 9HS; tel. (171) 837-0041; fax (171) 278-0623; f. 1958 to promote scientific study and publication on race and racism, and to make information and proposals available on race relations; library of 20,000 books and pamphlets, 900 journals, extensive press cuttings; Dir A. SIVANANDAN; publ. *Race and Class* (quarterly).

Maghreb Studies Association: c/o The Maghreb Bookshop, 45 Burton St, London, WC1H 9AL; tel. (171) 388-1840; f. 1981 to promote the study of and interest in the Maghreb (North Africa) through lectures, conferences, occasional publs and co-operation with the current periodical, *The Maghreb Review*; Chair. Prof. HÉDI BOURAOUI; Exec. Sec. M. BEN-MADANI.

Modern Churchpeople's Union: c/o Rev. Nicholas Henderson, MCU Office, 25 Birch Grove, London, W3 9SP; tel. (181) 932-4379; fax (181) 993-5812; e-mail modchurchunion@btinternet.com; f. 1898 for the advancement of liberal religious thought; fmrly Modern Churchmen's Union; 1,600 mems; Pres. Rt Revd JOHN SAXBEE; Chair. Rev. RICHARD TRUSS; Gen. Sec. Rev. NICHOLAS HENDERSON; publ. *Modern Believing* (quarterly).

National Institute for Social Work: 5 Tavistock Place, London, WC1H 9SN; tel. (171) 387-9681; fax (171) 387-7968; e-mail info@nsw.org.uk; f. 1961 to advance study, research and development in social work and social care; library of 20,000 vols; Pres. Sir WILLIAM UTTING; Chair. DENISE PLATT; Dir DAPHNE STATHAM.

National Society (Church of England) for Promoting Religious Education: Church House, Great Smith St, Westminster, SW1P 3NZ; tel. (171) 222-1672; fax (171) 233-2592; e-mail info@natsoc.org.uk; f. 1811; promotes religious education in accordance with the principles of the Church of England; Chair. The Bishop of Ripon; Gen. Sec. Rev. Canon JOHN HALL; publ. *Together with Children* (9 a year).

Royal African Society: SOAS, Thornhaugh St, Russell Square, London, WC1H 0XG; tel. (171) 323-6253; fax (171) 436-3844; f. 1901; *c.* 800 mems; Pres. Sir MICHAEL CAINE; Sec. LINDSAY ALLAN; publs *Journal* (quarterly), *African Affairs*.

Royal Anthropological Institute of Great Britain and Ireland: 50 Fitzroy St, London W1P 5HS; tel. (171) 387-0455; fax (171) 383-4235; e-mail rai@cix.compulink.co.uk; f. 1843; 2,400 mems; library with borrowing rights to 110,000 vols; film-hire library and video sales; photographic archive; conferences and film festivals; manages various trust and scholarship funds; awards medals and prizes; raises funds for research; Pres. Dr JOHN DAVIS; Dir JONATHAN BENTHALL; Hon. Sec. Dr MICHAEL O'HANLON; publs *The Journal of the Royal Anthropological Institute* (incorporating *Man*, quarterly), *Anthropology Today* (every 2 months), occasional papers, Teachers' Resource Guide, etc.

Royal Asiatic Society of Great Britain and Ireland: 60 Queen's Gardens, London, W2 3AF; tel. (171) 724-4742; f. 1823 for the study of the history, religions, institutions, customs, languages, literature and art of Asia; *c.* 800 mems; *c.* 600 subscribing libraries; branches in various Asian cities; library: see Libraries; Sec. T. N. GUINA; publ. *Journal*, and monographs on Oriental subjects.

Royal Commonwealth Society: 18 Northumberland Ave, London, WC2N 5BJ; tel. (171) 930-6733; fax (171) 930-9705; e-mail rcslondon@compuserve.com; f. 1868.

Royal Society for Asian Affairs: 2 Belgrave Square, London, SW1X 8PJ; tel. (171) 235-5122; fax (171) 259-6771; e-mail info@rsaa.org.uk; f. 1901; 1,100 mems with knowledge of, and interest in, Central Asia, Middle and Far East; library of about 7,000 vols; Pres. Lord DENMAN; Chair. Sir DONALD HAWLEY; Sec. D. J. EASTON; publ. *Journal* (3 a year).

Society for South Asian Studies: c/o Dept of Oriental Antiquities, British Museum, London, WC1B 3DG; f. 1972; research in cultural history and archaeology of South Asia; 250 mems; Chair. Dr D. W. MACDOWALL; Sec. Dr M. WILLIS; publ. *South Asian Studies* (annually).

Swedenborg Society: 20–21 Bloomsbury Way, London, WC1A 2TH; tel. (171) 405-7986; e-mail swed.soc@netmatters.co.uk; f. 1810 for the translation and publication of the writings of Emanuel Swedenborg, Swedish scientist, philosopher and theologian; approx. 1,000 mems; Pres. NANCY DAWSON; Sec. MADELINE G. WATERS.

TECHNOLOGY

British Computer Society, The: 1 Sanford St, Swindon, Wilts., SN1 1HJ; tel. (1793) 417417; fax (1793) 480270; f. 1957; a Chartered Engineering Instn, promoting knowledge of the development of information systems, engineering of information technology and business and scientific applications; professional qualifications from 1968; 34,000 mems; joint library with Instn of Electrical Engineers (*q.v.*); Chief Exec. JUDITH M. SCOTT; Registrar ANDREW LEWIS; publs *The Computer Journal* (10 a year), *The Computer Bulletin* (6 a year), *Software Engineering Journal* (6 a year, in conjunction with IEE).

British Masonry Society: C/o British Ceramic Research Ltd, Queens Road, Penkhull, Stoke on Trent, ST4 7LQ; tel. (1782) 845431; f. 1986; 400 mems; Pres. Dr H. W. H. WEST; publ. *Masonry International* (3 a year).

British Society of Rheology: c/o Dr G. J. Brownsey, Institute of Food Research, Norwich Research Park, Colney, Norfolk, NR4 7UA; tel. (1603) 255201; fax (1603) 507723; f. 1940; 600 mems; Pres. Prof. P. TOWNSEND; Sec. Dr G. J. BROWNSEY; library held at Univ. of Wales, Aberystwyth; publs *Rheology Abstracts*, *Bulletin* (quarterly).

BSI (British Standards Institution): 389 Chiswick High Rd, London, W4 4AL; tel. (181) 996-9000; fax (181) 996-7400; formed 1901 as Engineering Standards Committee; inc. 1918 as British Engineering Standards Asscn, f. under Royal Charter in 1929 and Supplemental Charter in 1931 when scope was extended and present name adopted; organization for the preparation and promulgation of all national standards for industry, science and technology and for the presentation of the UK viewpoint on such standards internationally; over 26,000 subscribing mems; over 500,000 British and foreign standards and regulations; Man. Dir KEITH TOZZI; Sec. S. K. WILLIAMS; publs *BSI Catalogue* (annually), *Business Standards*, *Standards Update* (monthly), *Annual Report*, *British Standards*.

Chartered Institute of Building, The: Englemere, Kings Ride, Ascot, Berks, SL5 7TB; tel. (1344) 630700; fax (1344) 630777; e-mail irc@ciob.org.uk; f. 1834, inc. by Royal Charter 1980; professional institution for those who are (a) practising building production and engaged in the construction, alteration, maintenance and repair of buildings, (b) teaching building technology and management in educational establishments, (c) engaged in building research, and (d) undergoing training for a career in building production; 33,000 mems; Pres. JOE DWYER; Chief Exec. KEITH BANBURY; publs *Chartered Builder* (monthly), *Construction Computing* (quarterly), *Construction Manager* (10 a year), *Campus Construction*, technical information and occasional papers, monographs, etc.

Chartered Institute of Patent Agents: Staple Inn Bldgs, High Holborn, London, WC1V 7PZ; tel. (171) 405-9450; fax (171) 430-0471; f. 1882, chartered 1891; professional and examining body; 2,500 mems; Sec. MICHAEL C. RALPH; publs *CIPA* (monthly), *Register of Patent Agents* (annually).

Chartered Institute of Transport: 80 Portland Place, London, W1N 4DP; tel. (171) 467-9400; fax (171) 467-9440; e-mail gen@citrans.org.uk; f. 1919, inc. by Royal Charter 1926 to promote, encourage, and co-ordinate the study and advancement of the science and art of transport in all its branches, and to provide a source of authoritative views on transport; distance-learning tuition provided for professional transport qualifications and MSc degree; *c.* 20,000 mems; brs in Argentina, Australia, Bangladesh, Canada, Cyprus, Ghana, Greece, Hong Kong, India, Ireland, Kenya, Malawi, Malaysia, Malta, Mauritius, New Zealand, Nigeria, Pakistan, Singapore, South Africa, Spain, Sri Lanka, Thailand, Uganda, West Indies, Zambia and Zimbabwe; 53,000 items; Pres. Tan Sri Dato ABDUL AZIZ BIN ABDUL RAHMAN; Dir-Gen. GRAHAM GREAVES; publs *Global Transport* (quarterly), *Proceedings* (quarterly), *Pegasus* (newsletter, monthly).

Chartered Institution of Building Services Engineers: 222 Balham High Rd, London, SW12 9BS; tel. (181) 675-5211; fax (181) 675-5449; e-mail info@cibse.org; promotes the science and practice of such engineering services as are associated with the built environment and industrial processes and the advancement of education and research in building services engineering; 15,000 mems; Chief Exec. and Sec. RICHARD JOHN; publs *Building Services* (monthly), *Lighting Research and Technology* (quarterly), *Building Services Engineering Research and Technology* (quarterly), technical guides and codes (irregular).

Chartered Institution of Water and Environmental Management: 15 John St, London WC1N 2EB; tel. (171) 831-3110; fax (171) 405-4967; e-mail admin@ciwem.org.uk; f. 1895; to advance the science and practice of water and environmental management for the public benefit and to promote education, training, study and research in those areas; 12,000 mems; Pres. PETER MATTHEWS; Exec. Dir NICK REEVES; publs *Journal* (6 a year), *Water and Environment Manager Magazine* (6 a year).

Chartered Society of Designers: 32/38 Saffron Hill, London, EC1N 8FH; tel. (171) 831-9777; fax (171) 831-6277; e-mail csd@csd.org.uk; f. 1930, incorporated by Royal Charter 1976; professional body for designers practising in product design, fashion and textiles design, interiors and graphics, design management, education and professional development; 7,000 mems; Pres. ADRIANNE LEMAN; publ. *Chartered Designers' Newsletter* (6 a year).

Confederation of British Industry: Centre Point, 103 New Oxford St, London, WC1A 1DU; tel. (171) 379-7400; telex 21332; fax (171) 240-1578; *Education Panel and Training Panel:* to keep under review policies in the whole field of education and training as they affect industry and commerce and to take any necessary action; Pres. Sir BRYAN NICHOLSON; Dir-Gen. HOWARD DAVIES; publs *CBI Distributive Trades Survey* (monthly), *Employment Affairs Report* (every 2 months), *Economic Situation Report* (monthly), *Industrial Trends Survey* (quarterly/monthly).

Crafts Council: 44A Pentonville Rd, London, N1 9BY; tel. (171) 278-7700; fax (171) 837-6891; e-mail reference@craftscouncil.org.uk; f. 1971 as the Crafts Advisory Committee, present name 1979; directly funded by the Dept of Culture, Media and Sport; national org. for contemporary crafts in Great Britain, offering exhibition and education programmes; maintains an Index of Selected Makers, electronic picture library, a National Register of Makers, Reference Library, Loan Collection, Reference Desk; offers maintenance and/or equipment grants; 15 mems; library of 3,000 vols, 142 periodicals; Chair. Sir NICHOLAS GOODISON; Dir TONY FORD; publ. *Crafts* (every 2 months).

Design Council: 34 Bow St, London, WC2E 1DL; tel. (171) 420-5200; fax (171) 420-5300; f. 1944 to inspire, in the world context, the best use of design by the UK to improve prosperity and well-being; Chair. of Council JOHN SORRELL; Chief Exec. ANDREW SUMMERS; publ. *Design* (quarterly).

Engineering Council, The: 10 Maltravers St, London, WC2R 3ER; tel. (171) 240-7891; fax (171) 240-7517; f. 1981 by Royal Charter; to advance the education and training of engineers and technologists, and to promote the science and practice of engineering for the public benefit; three objectives to increase public awareness of the role of engineering in society, and to demonstrate the beneficial impact of good engineering on everyday life; to improve the supply of qualified engineers and technologists; to set up and maintain relevant professional, educational and training standards; Senate Chair ALAN RUDGE; Dir-Gen. MALCOLM SHIRLEY; publs *Annual Report and Accounts*, brochures.

Ergonomics Society: Devonshire House, Devonshire Sq., Loughborough, Leics., LE11 3DW; tel. (1509) 234904; fax (1509) 234904; e-mail ergsoc@ergonomics.org.uk; f. 1949 to promote learning and advance education concerning the relation between man and his environment, and particularly the application of anatomical, physiological and psychological knowledge to the problems arising therefrom; 1,196 mems; Pres. D. A. STUBBS; Hon. Gen. Sec. J. G. SCRIVEN; publs *Ergonomics*, *Applied Ergonomics*, *Work and Stress*, *Behaviour and Information Technology*.

Faculty of Royal Designers for Industry: RSA, 8 John Adam St, London, WC2N 6EZ; tel. (171) 930-5115; fax (171) 839-5805; e-mail general@rsa.demon.co.uk; f. 1936 to further the development of design and in particular its application to industrial purposes; number of holders of RDI limited to 100 (85 at present plus 39 Hon.); Pres. DICK ONIANS; Master MARSHALL MEEK; Sec. HELEN AUTY (acting).

Gemmological Association and Gem Testing Laboratory of Great Britain: 27 Greville St, London, EC1N 8SU; tel. (171) 404-3334; fax (171) 404-8843; e-mail gagtl@btinternet.com; f. 1931 for promotion of the study of gemmology and the scientific and industrial study of all materials and articles used or dealt in by persons interested in the science of gems; 4,000 mems; publs *Journal of Gemmology* (quarterly), *Gem and Jewellery News* (quarterly).

Institute of Corrosion: 4 Leck House, Lake St, Leighton Buzzard, Beds, LU7 8TQ; tel. (1525) 851771; fax (1525) 376690; e-mail admin@icorr.demon.co.uk; f. 1975; 1,600 mems; Pres. BILL COX; Hon. Sec. EDDIE FIELD; publ. *Corrosion Management* (6 a year).

Institute of Energy: 18 Devonshire St, London, W1N 2AU; tel. (171) 580-7124; fax (171) 580-4420; f. 1927, Royal Charter 1946, to promote the advancement of energy technology; nominated body of The Engineering Council; 5,000 mems; Sec. J. LEACH; publs *Journal* (quarterly), *Energy World* (monthly), *Energy World Yearbook* (annually), conference proceedings, etc.

Institute of Food Science and Technology: 5 Cambridge Court, 210 Shepherd's Bush Rd, London, W6 7NJ; tel. (171) 603-6316; fax (171) 602-9936; f. 1964 to promote the knowledge, development and application of science and technology of food, and the provision of a professional body for food scientists and technologists; 3,500 mems; Pres. D. HICKS; Hon. Sec. V. D. ARTHEY; Chief Exec. H. G. WILD; publs *International Journal of Food Science and Technology* (every 2 months), *Food Science and Technology Today* (quarterly).

Institute of Management: 2 Savoy Court, Strand, London, WC2R 0EZ; tel. (171) 497-0580; fax (171) 497-0463; e-mail savoy@inst-mgt.org.uk; and Management House, Cottingham Rd, Corby, Northants., NN17 1TT; tel. (1536) 204222; fax (1536) 201651; e-mail member@inst-mgt.org.uk; f. 1947 as British Inst. of Management, name changed 1992; promotes the development, recognition and exercise of professional management; mems: 600 companies, 84,000 individuals; library of 80,000 items, 200 periodicals; Dir-Gen. MARY M. CHAPMAN; Sec. CHRISTINE HAYHURST; publs *Professional Manager* (6 a year), *Management Today* (monthly), surveys, reports, occasional papers, etc.

Institute of Management Services: 1 Cecil Court, London Rd, Enfield, Middx, EN2 6DD; tel. (181) 363-7452; fax (181) 367-8149; f. 1941; professional and examining body; 6,000 mems; library of 2,000 vols and 20 journals; Pres.

Lord CHILVER; Dir Gen. PAUL SYMES; publ. *Management Services* (monthly).

Institute of Marine Engineers: 76 Mark Lane, London, EC3R 7JN; tel. (171) 481-8493; fax (171) 488-1854; e-mail mem@imare.org.uk; f. 1889 to promote the scientific development of maritime engineering in all its branches; 17,000 mems; library and Marine Information Centre; Sec. J. E. SLOGGETT; publs *Marine Engineers' Review* (monthly), *Journal of Offshore Technology* (4 a year).

Institute of Materials: 1 Carlton House Terrace, London, SW1Y 5DB; tel. (171) 839-4071; fax (171) 839-2078; inc. 1993 by merger of Inst. of Ceramics, Inst. of Materials (fmrly Metals) and Plastics and Rubber Inst.; acts as professional qualifying body for materials engineers and scientists and is actively concerned with the development and study of all aspects of the science, technology and use of engineering materials; 18,000 mems; library: see Libraries; Pres. Sir ROBIN NICHOLSON; Sec. Dr B. A. RICKINSON; publs *Materials World* (monthly), *Surface Engineering* (quarterly), *Materials Science and Technology* (monthly), *International Materials Reviews* (every 2 months), *Ironmaking and Steelmaking* (every 2 months), *British Corrosion Journal* (quarterly), *Powder Metallurgy* (quarterly), *Plastics, Rubber and Composites Processing and Applications* (10 a year), *Interdisciplinary Science Reviews* (quarterly).

Institute of Measurement and Control: 87 Gower St, London, WC1E 6AA; tel. (171) 387-4949; fax (171) 388-8431; e-mail instmc-sec@mailbox.ulcc.ac.uk; f. 1944 as Society of Instrument Technology; inc. by Royal Charter 1975; to promote the advancement of the science and practice of measurement and control and its application; to co-ordinate and disseminate information and to conduct examinations; 5,500 mems; Pres. C. R. HOWARD; Sec. M. J. YATES; publs *Measurement and Control* including *Inst MC Interface* (monthly), *Transactions* (5 a year), *Instrument Engineer's Yearbook*.

Institute of Petroleum: 61 New Cavendish St, London, W1M 8AR; tel. (171) 467-7100; fax (171) 255-1472; e-mail lp@petroleum.co.uk; f. 1913 to promote, encourage, and co-ordinate the study of petroleum and its allied products, and to accumulate and disseminate information and knowledge relating thereto; 8,350 individual and 350 corporate mems; library of 15,000 books and 200 journals; Pres. C. M. MOORHOUSE; Dir-Gen. I. WARD; publs *Petroleum Review* (monthly), *IP Standards for Petroleum and its Products* (annually), *Safety Codes*, etc.

Institute of Physics and Engineering in Medicine: 4 Campleshon Rd, York, YO2 1PE; tel. (1904) 610821; fax (1904) 612279; e-mail office@ipem.org.uk; objective is to promote, for the public benefit, the advancement of physics and engineering applied to medicine and biology and to advance public education in the field; 2,300 mems; Pres. Prof. PETER SHARP; Gen. Sec. ROBERT NEILSON; publs *Medical Engineering and Physics* (every 2 months), *Physiological Measurement* (quarterly), *Physics in Medicine and Biology* (monthly).

Institute of Quarrying: 7 Regent St, Nottingham, NG1 5BS; tel. (115) 941-1315; f. 1917; professional body to provide a professional qualification, to improve science and practice of quarrying and to provide a forum for technical discussion; over 5,000 home and overseas mems; Exec. Dir J. BERRIDGE; Sec. M. J. ARTHUR; publ. *Quarry Management* (monthly).

Institute of Refrigeration: Kelvin House, 76 Mill Lane, Carshalton, Surrey, SM5 2JR; tel. (181) 647-7033; fax (181) 773-0165; f. 1899 (as the Cold Storage and Ice Association) for the general advancement of refrigeration in all its applications; *c.* 2,600 mems; Pres. R. HEAP; Sec. M. J. HORLICK; publ. *Proceedings*.

Institute of Science Technology: Mansell House, 22 Bore St, Lichfield, Staffs, WS13 6LP; tel. (1543) 251346; fax (1543) 415804; f. 1954 from the Science Technologists' Asscn (f. 1948); professional and qualifying body for laboratory technicians; 2,000 mems; Pres. Lord PERRY OF WALTON; Chair. R. C. DOW; Hon Sec. D. C. J. SAYERS; publs *Annual Science Review*, *Science Technology* (quarterly).

Institute of Scientific and Technical Communicators: Blackhorse Road, Letchworth, Herts, SG6 1YY; e-mail istc@istc.org.uk; f. 1972; aims to establish and maintain professional codes of practice for people engaged in all branches of scientific and technical communication; 1,500 mems; Pres. GERRY GENTLE; Sec. PETER LIGHTFOOT.

Institution of Chemical Engineers, The: 165 – 189 Railway Terrace, Rugby, CV21 3HQ; tel. (1788) 578214; fax (1788) 560833; e-mail tjevans@icheme.org.uk; f. 1922, inc. by Royal Charter to promote the science and practice of chemical engineering, to improve the standards and methods of education therein, and to act as a qualifying body for chemical engineers, etc.; 23,000 mems; library of 6,000 vols; Pres. GORDON CAMPBELL; Chief Exec. and Sec. Dr T. J. EVANS; publs *Chemical Engineering Research and Design* (every 2 months), *Process Safety and Environmental Protection*, *Food and Bioproducts Processing* (quarterly), *The Chemical Engineer* (every 2 weeks).

Institution of Civil Engineers: 1 Great George St, Westminster, London, SW1P 3AA; tel. (171) 222-7722; fax (171) 222-7500; e-mail library@ice.org.uk; f. 1818; inc. by Royal Charter in 1828 for the general advancement of mechanical science and more particularly for promoting the acquisition of that species of knowledge which constitutes the profession of a Civil Engineer, being the art of directing the great sources of power in Nature for the use and convenience of man; two principal roles: i) that of being the qualifying body for all three levels of registration, Chartered Engineers, Incorporated Engineers and Engineering Technicians, ii) that of a learned Society; as a qualifying body the Institution is concerned with academic and professional achievements and with continuing education, and as a Learned Society it is concerned with the acquisition and dissemination of knowledge; 80,000 corporate and non-corporate mems; library of 95,000 vols; Pres. ROGER SAINSBURY; Dir-Gen. and Sec. S. R. DOBSON; publs *Proceedings* (in 6 parts: *Civil Engineering, Geotechnical Engineering, Structures & Building, Municipal Engineer, Transport, Water, Maritime & Energy*), (quarterly), *Geotechnique* (quarterly), *Nuclear Energy*, *Advances in Cement Research*, *Magazine of Concrete Research*, *Ground Improvement*.

Institution of Electrical Engineers: Savoy Place, London, WC2R 0BL; tel. (171) 240-1871; telex 261176; fax (171) 240-7735; e-mail postmaster@iee.org.uk; f. in 1871 and inc. by Royal Charter in 1921; inc. the Instn of Radio and Electronic Engineers 1988, and Instn of Manufacturing Engineers 1991; to promote the advancement of electrical, manufacturing and information engineering, and to facilitate the exchange of information and ideas on those subjects; 138,000 mems; library: see Libraries; Pres. D. G. JEFFERIES; Sec. Dr J. C. WILLIAMS; publs *IEE Proceedings* (every 2 months), *Electronics Letters* (fortnightly), *Electronics & Communication Engineering Journal*, *Software Engineering Journal*, *Computer-Aided Engineering Journal*, *Power Engineering Journal*, *Engineering Management Journal*, *Manufacturing Engineer*, *Engineering Science and Education Journal* (all every 2 months), etc.

Institution of Electronics: Devonia House, 659 Oldham Rd, Rochdale, Lancs, OL16 4PE; f. 1930, inc. 1935, for the furtherance of the science of electronics and other scientific subjects; over 2,500 mems; Gen. Sec. W. BIRTWISTLE; publ. *Proceedings* (quarterly).

Institution of Engineering Designers: Courtleigh, Westbury Leigh, Westbury, Wilts, BA13 3TA; tel. (1373) 822801; fax (1373) 858085; f. 1945 to advance education in engineering, particularly in engineering and product design and to constitute a body of members qualified to a recognized high standard; a nominated body of the Engineering Council; 5,300 mems; Sec. M. J. OSBORNE; publ. *Engineering Designer* (every 2 months).

Institution of Engineers and Shipbuilders in Scotland: 1 Atlantic Quay, Broomielaw, Glasgow, G2 8JE; tel. (141) 248-3721; f. 1857 to facilitate the exchange of information and ideas amongst its mems, and to promote the advancement of the science and practice of engineering and shipbuilding; 800 mems; Pres. I. C. BROADLEY; Exec. Sec. E. W. BELL; publs *Transactions* (annually), *Year Book and List of Members* (every 2 years).

Institution of Fire Engineers: 148 New Walk, Leicester, LE1 7QB; tel. (116) 255-3654; fax (116) 247-1231; f. 1918, inc. 1924, to promote, encourage, and improve the science of fire engineering and technology; 11,000 home and overseas mems; Pres. P. YOUNG; Sec. D. W. EVANS; publ. *The Fire Engineer's Journal*.

Institution of Gas Engineers: 21 Portland Place, London, W1N 3AF; tel. (171) 636-6603; fax (171) 636-6602; f. 1863; Royal Charter 1929, to promote by research, discussion, education or otherwise as may seem to the Institution desirable each and all of the sciences of which knowledge may from time to time be required for the better production, distribution or utilization of gas and of the by-products of its production; 6,000 mems; library of over 10,000 vols; Sec. SANDRA RAINE; publ. *Gas Engineering and Management* (monthly).

Institution of Highways and Transportation: 6 Endsleigh St, London, WC1H 0DZ; tel. (171) 387-2525; fax (171) 387-2808; f. 1930 to promote the furtherance, consideration and discussion of all questions affecting the profession of Highway and Transportation Planning and Engineering; 10,500 mems; Pres. W. J. MCCOUBREY; Sec. Dr M. R. CRAGG; publ. *Monthly Journal*.

Institution of Incorporated Engineers in Electronic, Electrical and Mechanical Engineering (IIE): Savoy Hill House, Savoy Hill, London, WC2R 0BS; tel. (171) 836-3357; fax (171) 497-9006; e-mail iie@dial.pipex.com; Sec. and Chief Exec. PETER F. WASON.

Institution of Lighting Engineers: Lennox House, 9 Lawford Rd, Rugby, Warwicks., CV21 2DZ; tel. (1788) 576492; fax (1788) 540145; f. 1924, inc. 1928, to promote, encourage, and improve the science and art of efficient lighting, and to facilitate the exchange of information and ideas on this subject; 1,900 mems; Pres. C. LANE; Chief Exec. RICHARD FROST; publ. *Lighting Journal* (6 a year).

Institution of Mechanical Engineers: 1 Birdcage Walk, London, SW1H 9JJ; tel. (171) 222-7899; fax (171) 222-4557; f. 1847, inc. by Royal Charter 1930; education, training and professional development of engineers; acts as an int. centre for technology transfer in mechanical engineering; 78,000 mems; library of 155,000 vols; Pres. PAM LIVERSIDGE; Dir-Gen. and Sec. Dr R. A. PIKE; publs *Automotive Engineer* (10 a year), *Journal of Strain Anal-*

ysis, *Professional Engineering* (22 a year), *Environmental Engineering* (quarterly), *Institution of Diesel and Gas Turbine Engineers* (6 a year).

Institution of Mining and Metallurgy (incorporating the Institution of Mining Engineers): Danum House, South Parade, Doncaster, DN1 2DY; tel. (1302) 320486; fax (1302) 340554; f. 1892 for the advancement of the science and practice of economic and engineering geology, mining and associated technologies, mineral and petroleum engineering and extraction metallurgy; to facilitate the acquisition and preservation of knowledge pertaining to the associated professions; to establish, uphold and advance the industry standards of education, training and competence; organizes meetings and conferences worldwide; administers scholarships and fellowships; library of 50,000 vols, and offers information services; mems in *c.* 100 countries; Pres. Prof. P. A. DOWD; Sec. G. J. M. WOODROW; publs *Transactions of the Institution of Mining and Metallurgy* (9 a year), *International Mining and Minerals*, *IMM Abstracts* (4 a year).

Institution of Nuclear Engineers: Allan House, 1 Penerley Rd, London, SE6 2LQ; tel. (181) 698-1500; fax (181) 695-6409; f. 1959; 1,700 mems; Pres. M. C. ROBBINS; Sec. W. J. HURST; publ. *The Nuclear Engineer* (every 2 months).

Institution of Plant Engineers: 77 Great Peter St, London SWIP 2EZ; tel. (171) 233-2855; fax (171) 233-2604; f. 1946: professional body; 6,000 mems; Pres. K. SANDERSON; Sec. P. F. TYE; publ. *The Plant Engineer* (every 2 months).

Institution of Structural Engineers: 11 Upper Belgrave St, London, SW1X 8BH; tel. (171) 235-4535; fax (171) 235-4294; e-mail istructe.lon@mail.bogo.co.uk; f. 1908, inc. by Royal Charter 1934, to promote the general advancement of the science and art of structural engineering; library of 15,000 vols; 23,000 mems; Pres. Prof. L. A. CLARK; Sec. Dr J. W. DOUGILL; publs *The Structural Engineer* (2 a month), *Sessional Yearbook and Directory of Members* (annually), *Directory of Firms* (annually).

National Society for Clean Air and Environmental Protection: 136 North St, Brighton, East Sussex, BN1 1RG; tel. (1273) 326313; fax (1273) 735082; e-mail info@usca .org.uk; f. 1899 as Coal Smoke Abatement Society and amalgamated with the Smoke Abatement League of Great Britain in 1929; air pollution and noise control, environmental protection; 1,500 mems, incl. learned societies, local authorities, industrial concerns, etc.; library of 1,000 vols, educational material; Pres. Sir CRISPIN TICKELL; Sec.-Gen. RICHARD MILLS; publs *Clean Air* (2 a year), *NSCA Environmental Protection Yearbook*, *Proceedings of Annual Conferences and Workshops*, *NSCA Pollution Handbook*, *NSCA Pollution Glossary*, reports.

Newcomen Society for the Study of the History of Engineering and Technology: Science Museum, South Kensington, London, SW7 2DD; tel. (171) 589-1793; fax (171) 589-1793; e-mail thomas@newcomen.demon.co .uk; f. 1920 to encourage and foster study of the history of engineering and technology in all parts of the world; 1,100 mems; Exec. Sec. COLIN ARMSTRONG; publs *Transactions* (2 a year), *Bulletin* (3 a year).

Oil and Colour Chemists' Association: Priory House, 967 Harrow Rd, Wembley, Middx, HA0 2SF; tel. (181) 908-1086; fax (181) 908-1219; f. 1918 to promote by discussion and scientific investigation the technology of the paint, oil, printing ink, and allied industries; 2,400 mems; Pres. S. LAWRENCE; Gen. Sec. C. PACEY-DAY; publs *Journal* (monthly), *Introduction to Paint Technology*, *Paint Technology Manual 'Works Practice'*, *Monographs*, *UV Polymerization 1 + 2*.

Photogrammetric Society, The: Dept of Geomatic Engineering, University College London, Gower St, London, WC1E 6BT; tel. (171) 504-2741; f. 1952; theory, techniques, instrumentation, applications in surveying, engineering, etc; 650 mems; library of 2,000 vols; Pres. R. P. KIRBY; Hon. Sec. S. ROBSON; publ. *The Photogrammetric Record* (2 a year).

Radio Society of Great Britain: Lambda House, Cranborne Rd, Potters Bar, EN6 3JE; tel. (1707) 659015; fax (1707) 45105; e-mail sales@rsgb.org.uk; f. 1913 to promote interest in the science of radio-communication by amateurs, and to safeguard the interests of those of its members who operate or aspire to operate amateur transmitting stations; 30,000 mems; Gen. Man. PETER A. KIRBY; publs *Radio Communication* (monthly), *Radio Today* (monthly).

Royal Academy of Engineering: 29 Great Peter St, London, SW1P 3LW; tel. (171) 222-2688; fax (171) 233-0054; f. 1976; conducts engineering and educational studies, sponsors links between industry and higher education, co-sponsors with industry academic posts at higher education instns; 1,096 fellows, 71 foreign mems, 18 hon. fellows; Pres. Sir DAVID DAVIES; Exec. Sec. J. R. APPLETON; publs *Annual Report*, *Newsletter* (quarterly).

Royal Aeronautical Society: 4 Hamilton Place, London, W1V 0BQ; tel. (171) 499-3515; fax (171) 499-6230; f. 1866; 17,500 mems; library of 115,000 vols; Pres. Capt. W. D. LOWE (1998/99), L. A. EDWARDS (1999/2000); Dir K. MANS; publs *Aeronautical Journal* (10 a year), *Aerospace International* (monthly).

Royal Institution of Naval Architects, The: 10 Upper Belgrave St, London, SW1X 8BQ; tel. (171) 235-4622; fax (171) 245-6959; f. 1860, to advance maritime engineering; 5,200 mems; Pres. Dr T. JOHN PARKER; Chief Exec. TREVOR BLAKELEY; publs *Transactions* (annually), *The Naval Architect*, *Ship and Boat International* (10 a year), *Ship Repair and Conversion Technology* (quarterly), *Significant Ships* (1 a year), occasional publications and symposium proceedings.

Royal Television Society: Holborn Hall, 100 Gray's Inn Rd, London, WC1X 8AL; tel. (171) 430-1000; fax (171) 430-0924; e-mail royaltvsociety@btinternet.com; f. 1927 for the furtherance of the arts and sciences of television; over 3,000 mems; Chair. TONY HALL; Exec. Dir MICHAEL BUNCE; publ. *Television* (8 a year).

Scottish Design Ltd: Stock Exchange House, 7 Nelson Mandela Place, Glasgow, G2 7JN; tel. (141) 221-6121; fax (141) 221-8799; inc. 1994 to promote best practice in design within Scottish industry; Chief Exec. ANDY TRAVERS.

Society for Underwater Technology: 76 Mark Lane, London, EC3R 7JN; tel. (171) 481-0750; fax (171) 481-4001; f. 1966; to promote the further understanding of the underwater environment, and to advance the development of the techniques and tools needed to explore, study and exploit the oceans; provides sponsorship for undergraduate and 1-year postgraduate students studying in an appropriate subject area; 1,000 individual and 90 corporate mems; Exec. Sec. I. N. L. GALLETT; publs *Underwater Technology* (quarterly), *SUT News* (8 a year).

Society of Consulting Marine Engineers and Ship Surveyors: The Italian Building, Little London, 41 Dockhead, London, SE1 2BS; tel. (171) 237-3034; fax (171) 237-3888; f. 1920 to provide a central organization for consulting marine engineers, naval architects and ship surveyors, and generally to elevate the status and procure the advancement of the interests of the profession; Pres. EUAN D. DAVIDSON; Sec. P. R. HICKS.

Society of Designer Craftsmen: 24 Rivington St, London, EC2A 3DU; tel. (171) 739-3663; fax (171) 739-3663; e-mail richard@ society.designcraft.org.uk; f. 1888; 750 mems; Pres. Prof. CHRISTOPHER FRAYLING; Chair. JOHN WEISS; Hon. Sec. RICHARD O'DONOGHUE; publ. *The Designer Craftsman* (annually).

Society of Dyers and Colourists: Perkin House, POB 244, 82 Grattan Rd, Bradford, W. Yorks, BD1 2JB; tel. (1274) 725138; fax (1274) 392888; f. 1884 to promote the advancement of the science and technology of colour and coloration; examining and awarding body for chartered qualifications; colour museum; 2,500 mems and 800 subscribers; Pres. V. BELL; Chief Exec. and Gen. Sec. K. MCGHEE; publs *Journal* (10 a year), *Review of Progress in Coloration and Related Topics* (annually), *Colour Index*, *Additions and Amendments* (quarterly), various textbooks.

Society of Engineers Inc.: Guinea Wiggs, Nayland, Colchester, Essex, CO6 4NF; tel. (1206) 263332; fax (1206) 262624; f. 1854; library of 2,000 vols; Pres. J. H. WILKINSON; Sec. L. C. A. WRIGHT; publ. *Engineering World* (quarterly).

Society of Glass Technology: 'Thornton', 20 Hallam Gate Rd, Sheffield, S10 5BT; tel. (114) 266-3168; fax (114) 266-5252; f. 1916 to promote the association of persons interested in glass technology; approx. 1,100 mems; library of 9,000 vols; Hon. Sec. W. SIMPSON; publs *Glass Technology*, *Physics and Chemistry of Glasses* (every 2 months).

South Wales Institute of Engineers: Empire House, Mount Stuart Square, Cardiff, CF1 6DN; tel. (1222) 481726; fax (1222) 451953; e-mail swie@celtic.co.uk; f. 1857 for the encouragement and advancement of engineering science and practice; 272 mems; Pres. G. T. POWELL; Hon. Sec. R. E. LINDSAY; publ. *Proceedings* (every 2 years).

Steel Construction Institute, The: Silwood Park, Ascot, Berks, SL5 7QN; tel. (1344) 23345; fax (1344) 22944; f. 1986; to develop and promote the proper and effective use of steel as a construction material; 800 mems; library of 11,000 vols; Dir Dr G. W. OWENS; publ. *New Steel Construction* (every 2 months).

Textile Institute, The: see under International.

TWI: Abington Hall, Cambridge, CB1 6AL; tel. (1223) 891162; fax (1223) 892588; e-mail twi@twi.co.uk; f. 1968 to undertake general and contract research, to advance welding technology in all aspects, to provide consultancy and laboratory services, to provide education and training and to improve the professional status and qualification of members; 2,500 research mems, 5,000 professional mems; library of 10,000 vols in library; specialized information services; Chief Exec. A. B. M. BRAITHWAITE; publs *Connect* (6 a year), *The Welding Institute News Video* (2 a year).

Research Institutes

AGRICULTURE, FISHERIES AND VETERINARY SCIENCE

Animal Health Trust: Lanwades Park, Kentford, Newmarket, Suffolk, CB8 7UU; tel. (1638) 751000; fax (1638) 750410; f. 1942; aims to advance veterinary knowledge for the welfare of horses, dogs and cats; Pres. HRH THE PRINCESS ROYAL; Chair. Lord FAIRHAVEN; Dir Dr ANDREW HIGGINS.

Biotechnology and Biological Sciences Research Council (BBSRC) (fmrly Agricultural and Food Research Council): Polaris House, North Star Ave, Swindon, Wilts, SN2 1UH; tel. (1793) 413200; fax (1793) 413201; f. 1994; responsible to the Office of Science and Technology; supports fundamental and strategic multidisciplinary research, with emphasis on the biological sciences, biotechnology and engineering, in its institutes and universities; Chair. Dr PETER DOYLE; Chief Exec. Prof. R. BAKER; publs *Handbook*, *Annual Report*, *Corporate Plan*.

Institutes and units:

Babraham Institute: Babraham Hall, Babraham, Cambridge, CB2 4AT; tel. (1223) 832312; fax (1223) 836122; f. 1948; research to advance understanding of function in animal cells and systems, with emphasis on cell signalling, recognition mechanisms and mammalism development; Dir Dr R. G. DYER; publ. *Annual Review*.

Institute for Animal Health: Compton, Nr Newbury, Berks., RG20 7NN; tel. (1635) 578411; fax (1635) 577237; undertakes basic, strategic and applied research required for the understanding of the aetiology, pathogenesis, epidemiology and diagnosis of diseases of farm animals, including those exotic diseases that could spread to the UK, the study of newly recognized diseases and the influence of disease control measures on food safety and quality; Dir of Research Dr C. J. BOSTOCK.

Sites:

Institute for Animal Health—Compton Laboratory: Compton, Nr Newbury, Berks., RG20 7NN; tel. (1635) 578411; fax (1635) 577237.

Institute for Animal Health—Pirbright Laboratory: Ash Rd, Pirbright, Woking, Surrey, GU24 0NF; tel. (1483) 232441; fax (1483) 232448; Head Dr A. I. DONALDSON.

Institute for Animal Health—Neuropathogenesis Unit: Ogston Bldg, West Mains Rd, Edinburgh, EH9 3JF; tel. (131) 667-5204; fax (131) 668-3872; Head Dr C. J. BOSTOCK.

Institute of Arable Crops Research (IACR): Rothamsted, Harpenden, Herts., AL5 2JQ; tel. (1582) 763133; fax (1582) 760981; basic, strategic and applied research on soils and crop plants; Dir Prof. B. MIFLIN.

Sites:

IACR—Rothamsted: Harpenden, Herts, AL5 2JQ; tel. (1582) 763133; fax (1582) 760981; Head Prof. B. J. MIFLIN.

IACR—Long Ashton Research Station: Univ. of Bristol, Long Ashton, Bristol, BS18 9AF; tel. (1275) 392181; fax (1275) 394007; Head Prof. P. R. SHEWRY.

IACR—Broom's Barn: Higham, Bury St Edmunds, Suffolk, IP28 6NP; tel. (1284) 810363; fax (1284) 811191; Head Dr J. PIDGEON.

Institute of Food Research: Earley Gate, Whiteknights Rd, Reading, RG6 6BZ; tel. (118) 935-7055; fax (118) 926-7903; investigates the relationship between diet and health and seeks to improve the safety, quality and nutritional value of foods for consumers; contributes to the improvement of dietary guidelines and advice and generates and evaluates new options for safe and efficient food manufacture; Dir Prof. H. J. H. MACFIE (acting).

Sites:

Institute of Food Research—Norwich Laboratory: Norwich Research Park, Colney Lane, Norwich, NR4 7UA; tel. (1603) 255000; fax (1603) 507723; Head Prof. P. S. BELTON.

Institute of Food Research—Reading Laboratory: Earley Gate, Whiteknights Rd, Reading, RG6 6BZ; tel. (118) 935-7000; fax (118) 926-7917; Head Prof. H. J. H. MACFIE.

Institute of Grassland and Environmental Research: Plas Gogerddan, Aberystwyth, SY23 3EB; tel. (1970) 828255; fax (1970) 828357; basic and strategic research into grassland and environmental research related to non-arable agriculture; seeks to increase understanding of genetic and competitive processes in pastures and natural plant populations in response to grazing and climatic variables, to elucidate processes controlling intake, growth, body composition and lactation in ruminants, to investigate consequences of climatic and management changes on grassland agriculture and the opportunities for alternative animals and crops, and to study the fluxes of nutrients and utilization efficiencies of inputs with reference to losses and environmental pollution; Research Dir Prof. C. J. POLLOCK.

Sites:

Institute of Grassland and Environmental Research—Aberystwyth Research Centre: Plas Gogerddan, Aberystwyth, Dyfed, SY23 3EB; tel. (1970) 828255; fax (1970) 828357; Dir (vacant).

Institute of Grassland and Environmental Research—North Wyke Research Station: Okehampton, Devon, EX20 2SR; tel. (1837) 82558; fax (1837) 82139; Head of Site Prof. R. J. WILKINS.

Institute of Grassland and Environmental Research—Bronydd Mawr Research Centre: Trecastle, Brecon, Powys, LD3 8RD; tel. (1874) 636480; fax (1874) 636542; Officer in charge J. M. M. MUNRO.

John Innes Centre: Colney Lane, Norwich, NR4 7UH; tel. (1603) 452571; fax (1603) 456844; aims to assist the agricultural and biotechnological industries by carrying out fundamental research on plants and bacteria; to understand and describe the basis of the control of plant and bacterial form, behaviour and metabolism so that genetically modified plants and bacteria may be improved or changed to offer new industrial potentialities; Dir Prof. R. B. FLAVELL.

Roslin Institute (Edinburgh): Roslin, Midlothian, EH25 9PS; tel. (131) 527-4200; basic and strategic research on farm animals; Dir Prof. G. BULFIELD.

Silsoe Research Institute: Wrest Park, Silsoe, Bedford, MK45 4HS; tel. (1525) 860000; fax (1525) 860156; research in engineering and physical sciences for the agricultural, food and biology-based production and processing industries; Dir Prof. B. J. LEGG.

Central Science Laboratory: Sand Hutton, N. Yorks., YO41 1LZ; tel. (1904) 462000; fax (1904) 462111; e-mail science@csl.gov.uk; an exec. agency of the Min. of Agriculture, Fisheries and Food; research and advice in the fields of crop pests and diseases, pesticide safety and the effects of agriculture on the environment, and food safety; research laboratories at Sand Hutton and Norwich; Chief Exec. Prof. P. I. STANLEY.

Centre for the Environment, Fisheries and Aquaculture Science (CEFAS): Pakefield Rd, Lowestoft NR33 0HT; tel. (1502) 562244; fax (1502) 513865; e-mail library@cefas.co.uk; an exec. agency of the Min. of Agriculture, Fisheries and Food; provides contract research, consultancy and training services in environmental impact assessment, environmental research and monitoring, aquaculture health and hygiene, and fisheries science and management; extensive research library; brs at Conwy, Weymouth and Burnham-on-Crouch; Dir Dr P. W. GREIG-SMITH.

Forest Research: Alice Holt Lodge, Wrecclesham, Farnham, Surrey, GU10 4LH; tel. (1420) 22255; fax (1420) 23653; f. 1919 to advance forest technology; library of 20,000 vols; comprises two research stations with biological sections for silviculture and seeds, tree improvement, woodland ecology, entomology, pathology, environmental research, development of forest machinery and working methods, woodland surveys, and service sections for statistics and computing, mensuration, photography, library, research information and technical support; publ. *Report on Forest Research* (annually).

Research stations:

Forest Research Station: Alice Holt Lodge, Wrecclesham, Farnham, Surrey, GU10 4LH; tel. (1420) 22255; fax (1420) 23653; e-mail j.parker@forestry.gov.uk; Chief Research Officer P. H. FREER-SMITH.

Northern Research Station: Roslin, Midlothian, Scotland, EH25 9SY; tel. (131) 445-2176; fax (131) 445-5124; Chief Exec. J. DEWAR.

National Institute of Agricultural Botany: Huntingdon Rd, Cambridge, CB3 0LE; tel. (1223) 276381; fax (1223) 277602; f. 1919 to promote the improvement of existing varieties of seeds, plants and crops in the United Kingdom; includes the Official Seed Testing Station for England and Wales, and other depts which are particularly concerned with crop variety testing and description, seed certification and seed production techniques; library of 10,000 vols; Dir J. MACLEOD; publs *Annual Report*, *Plant Varieties and Seeds*, booklets and leaflets.

Oxford Forestry Institute: University of Oxford, Dept of Plant Sciences, South Parks Rd, Oxford OX1 3RB; tel. (1865) 275000; fax (1865) 275074; f. 1924 (as Imperial, later Commonwealth Forestry Inst.), for research and higher studies in forestry; library of 200,000 vols, in conjunction with CAB International; Dir Prof. J. BURLEY.

Scottish Agricultural Science Agency: Scottish Office Agriculture, Environment and Fisheries Department, East Craigs, 82 Craigs Rd, Edinburgh, EH12 8NJ; tel. (131) 244-8890; fax (131) 244-8940; scientific executive work, associated research and consultation on: seed testing, testing of candidate cultivars of crop plants for National Listing and Plant Breeders' Rights, certification of seed and planting stock, production of disease-tested clonal stocks of potatoes, statutory aspects of pest and disease control, pesticide usage assessment, pesticide residues, ecology of mammals and birds of actual or potential pest status; Dir Dr R. K. M. HAY.

Scottish Office Agriculture, Environment and Fisheries Department: Pentland House, 47 Robb's Loan, Edinburgh, EH14 1TW; tel. (131) 556-8400; e-mail ceu@isd01.scotoff.gov.uk.

Research institutes:

Hannah Research Institute: Ayr, KA6 5HL, Scotland; tel. (1292) 674000; fax (1292) 674003; f. 1928; research to improve the efficiency of milk production and increase the scope for the use of milk and its components in food products; Dir Prof. M. PEAKER.

Macaulay Land Use Research Institute: Craigiebuckler, Aberdeen AB15 8QH;

tel. (1224) 311556; f. 1987; research in marginal land use and resource management; Dir Prof. T. J. MAXWELL.

Moredun Research Institute: Pentlands Science Park, Bush Loan, Penicuik, Midlothian, EH26 0PZ; tel. (131) 445-5111; fax (131) 445-6235; f. 1920; research on livestock diseases that undermine biological efficiency, impair welfare or threaten public health; Dir Prof. Q. MCKELLAR.

Rowett Research Institute: Greenbank Rd, Bucksburn, Aberdeen, AB21 9SB; tel. (1224) 715349; research on nutritional aspects of animals and man with particular emphasis on the biochemical and physiological aspects of nutrition and their interaction with reproduction relevant to agriculture, food and health; Dir Prof. W. P. T. JAMES.

Scottish Crop Research Institute: Invergowrie, Dundee, DD2 5DA; tel. (1382) 562731; fax (1382) 562426; f. 1981; Dir Prof. J. R. HILLMAN; publs *Annual Report*, *Bulletin* (irregular).

Veterinary Laboratories Agency: Woodham Lane, Addlestone, Surrey, KT15 3NB; tel. (1932) 341111; fax (1932) 347046; an exec. agency of the Min. of Agriculture, Fisheries and Food; f. 1917; Dir T. W. A. LITTLE.

Woburn Experimental Station (Lawes Agricultural Trust): Husborne Crawley, Bedford; f. 1876 for the investigation of manurial and other problems of British crops; run as outstation of Rothamsted Experimental Station; Dir L. FOWDEN; publ. *Annual Report*.

ARCHITECTURE AND TOWN PLANNING

Prince of Wales's Institute of Architecture: 14 – 15 Gloucester Gate, Regent's Park, London, NW1 4HG; tel. (171) 916-7380; fax (171) 916-7381; f. 1992; research into all areas of architecture, building, methods of construction and the crafts; public lectures, seminars and exhibitions; educational courses; library of 5,000 vols.

ECONOMICS, LAW AND POLITICS

Economic Research Council: 239 Shaftesbury Ave, London, WC2H 8PJ; tel. (171) 439-0271; f. 1943 as a non-profit-making research and educational organization in the field of economics and monetary practice; Pres. Lord EZRA; Chair. DAMON DE LASZLO; Hon. Secs J. BOURLET, Prof. P. DAVISON; publ. *Britain and Overseas* (quarterly).

Henley Centre for Forecasting: 9 Bridewell Place, London, EC4V 6AY; tel. (171) 353-9961; fax (171) 353-2899; f. 1974 to promote and develop business and environmental forecasting; aims to make its research available to a wide audience in business, education and government; forecasts based on specific sets of assumptions about changes in political, social and environmental factors; holds seminars and training programmes; Chief Exec. R. J. TYRRELL; publs *UK Economic Forecasts* (monthly), *Global Economic Forecasts* (quarterly), *The Directors' Report* (monthly), *Frontiers* (annually), *Leisure Futures* (quarterly), *Planning Consumer Markets* (quarterly), *Planning for Social Change* (annually), and other titles.

International Institute for Strategic Studies, The: 23 Tavistock St, London, WC2E 7NQ; tel. (171) 379-7676; fax (171) 836-3108; e-mail iiss@iiss.org.uk; f. 1958; aims to promote discussion and research on the problems of international security arising from all causes; international membership, Council, and staff; 1,800 mems, 220 corporate mems, 500 assoc. mems, 120 student mems; Chair. of the Council Prof. ROBERT O'NEILL; Dir Dr JOHN CHIPMAN; publs *Strategic Comments* (monthly), *Survival* (quarterly), *The Military Balance*, *Strategic Survey* (annually), *Adelphi Papers* (8 a year).

National Institute of Economic and Social Research: 2 Dean Trench St, Smith Square, London, SW1P 3HE; tel. (171) 222-7665; fax (171) 654-1900; e-mail jkirkland@niesr.ac.uk; f. 1938; library of 10,000 vols, 300 periodicals; Pres. Sir BRIAN CORBY; Dir M. WEALE; publs *National Institute Economic Review* (quarterly), *Annual Report*.

Overseas Development Institute: Portland House, Stag Place, London, SW1E 5DP; tel. (171) 393-1600; fax (171) 393-1699; e-mail odi@odi.org.uk; f. 1960 to act as a research and information centre on overseas development issues; library of 20,000 vols; Chair. Earl CAIRNS; Dir SIMON MAXWELL; publs *Development Policy Review* (quarterly), *Disasters: The Journal of Disaster Studies and Management* (quarterly), research work in the form of books, pamphlets, working and briefing papers.

Research Institute for the Study of Conflict and Terrorism: POB 1179, Leamington Spa, CV32 6ZY; tel. (1926) 833307; fax (1926) 833307; e-mail risct_potts@compuserve.com; f. 1970 for the advancement of research into the causes and manifestations of insurgency, subversion and political violence; Chair. DUNCAN SLATER; Dir Prof. WILLIAM GUTTERIDGE; publs *Conflict Studies*, special reports.

EDUCATION

Institute for Cultural Research: POB 13, Tunbridge Wells, Kent; f. 1966; to promote and conduct research and advance public education in man's heritage of knowledge; Chair. of Council DAVID WADE; Hon. Sec. HENRI BORTOFT; publs intercultural monographs.

National Foundation for Educational Research in England and Wales: The Mere, Upton Park, Slough, Berks., SL1 2DQ; tel. (1753) 574123; fax (1753) 691632; f. 1946; to study problems arising within the national educational system, to disseminate information on its findings and to collaborate on a national and international basis with other educational and research bodies; Pres. Sir JAMES HAMILTON; Chair. N. HARRISON; Dir Dr SEAMUS HEGARTY; publs *Educational Research* (3 a year), *Educational Research News*, *Research Reports* (various), etc.

Society for Research into Higher Education Ltd: 3 Devonshire St, London, W1N 2BA; tel. (171) 637-2766; fax (171) 637-2781; e-mail srhe@mailbox.ulcc.ac.uk; f. 1964 to collect and disseminate information about research into and development in higher education and to encourage research into higher education; 622 individual mems, 237 corporate mems; Chair. Prof. DIANA GREEN; Dir HEATHER EGGINS; publs *Abstracts* (3 a year), *Studies in Higher Education* (3 a year), *Higher Education Quarterly*, *News* (quarterly), monographs, occasional publications, pamphlets.

HISTORY, GEOGRAPHY AND ARCHAEOLOGY

German Historical Institute: 17 Bloomsbury Square, London, WC1A 2LP; tel. (171) 404-5486; fax (171) 404-5573; e-mail ghil@ghil.prestel.co.uk; f. 1976; research in modern and comparative British history; study of international, especially Anglo-German relations; seven research fellows; library: reference, 50,000 vols, 227 periodicals; Dir Prof. Dr PETER WENDE.

Institute of Contemporary British History: Senate House (Room 357), Malet St, London, WC1E 7HU; tel. (171) 436-2478; fax (171) 436-2480; f. 1986; ind. instn; Exec. Dir Dr PETER CATTERALL; publs *Contemporary Record* (3 a year), *Modern History Review* (4 a year).

Leo Baeck Institute: 4 Devonshire St, London, W1N 2BH; f. 1955; an international research institute for the history of German-speaking Jewry; Dir Dr Dr h.c. ARNOLD PAUCKER; publs *Year Book*, symposium volumes, monographs, etc.

Scott Polar Research Institute: Lensfield Rd, Cambridge, CB2 1ER; tel. (1223) 336540; fax (1223) 336549; f. 1920; research and information centre on the Polar regions (glaciology, geophysics, oceanography, remote sensing, history, anthropology, socio-economics); archives; exhibits; library of 50,000 vols, 1,000 periodicals; Dir Dr J. HEAP; publs *Polar Record*, *Polar and Glaciological Abstracts*, *Iceberg Research*.

LANGUAGE AND LITERATURE

Centre for Information on Language Teaching and Research (CILT): 20 Bedfordbury, London, WC2N 4LB; tel. (171) 379-5101; fax (171) 379-5082; e-mail library@cilt.org.uk; f. 1966; independent charitable educational foundation, supported by govt grants; national centre for information on learning and teaching languages; has an enquiry service, specialized library and audio-visual collection, conference programme; Dir Dr E. KING; publs reports, papers, guides, etc.

Modern Humanities Research Association: c/o Prof. D. A. Wells, Birkbeck College, Malet St, London, WC1E 7HX; f. at Cambridge in 1918 with the object of encouraging advanced studies in modern and medieval languages and literatures; approx. 700 mems; Hon. Sec. Prof. D. A. WELLS; publs *Modern Language Review* (quarterly), *Annual Bibliography of English Language and Literature*, *Yearbook of English Studies*, *The Year's Work in Modern Language Studies*, *The Slavonic and East European Review* (quarterly), *Portuguese Studies*, *Publications Series*, *MHRA Texts and Dissertations*, *Annual Bulletin*, *MHRA Style Book*.

MEDICINE

Arthritis Research Campaign: POB 177, Chesterfield, Derbyshire, S41 7TQ; tel. (1246) 558033; fax (1246) 558007; e-mail info@arc.org.uk; f. 1936 to organize research into the causes and means of treatment of rheumatism, arthritis, and allied diseases; to encourage teaching, and to enhance the service to the patient; Chief Exec. F. LOGAN; publ. *Arthritis Today* (3 a year).

Beatson Institute for Cancer Research: Garscube Estate, Switchback Rd, Bearsden, Glasgow, G61 1BD, Scotland; tel. (141) 942-9361; fax (141) 942-6521; f. 1910, renamed 1967, and in 1989 inc. as the major component of the Cancer Research Campaign Beatson Laboratories (with Glasgow Univ. Depts of Medical and Radiation Oncology); research in molecular and cell biology of cancer and related diseases; library of 1,000 textbooks, 83 journals; Dir Prof. J. A. WYKE; publ. *Scientific Report* (annually).

Burden Neurological Institute: Stoke Lane, Stapleton, Bristol, BS16 1QT; tel. (117) 956-7444; f. 1939 to conduct research in neurology, neurophysiology, neuropsychology and psychiatry; library of 4,000 vols; Dir Dr S. R. BUTLER; Sec. R. C. NORTH.

Central Public Health Laboratory: 61 Colindale Ave, London, NW9 5HT; tel. (181) 200-4400; telex 8953942; fax (181) 200-7874; f. 1946; central laboratory of the Public Health Laboratory Service, 61 Colindale Ave, London, NW9 5DF, providing a microbiological reference service (incl. specialist tests) for the control of the spread of infectious diseases; library of 35,000 vols; Dir Prof. PETER BORRIELLO; publs *PHLS Library Bulletin* (weekly), *PHLS HIV Bulletin*, *PHLS Food and Environment Bulletin* (monthly), *PHLS Microbiology Digest* (quarterly).

Centre for Applied Microbiology and Research: Porton Down, Salisbury, Wilts, SP4 0JG; tel. (1980) 612100; fax (1980) 611096; f. 1979; Special Health Authority administered by the Microbiological Research Authority; WHO Reference Laboratory for pathogenic viruses; undertakes research and development in health care and environmental fields; also production and consultancy contracts in all its principal activities, and maintains strong links with government, academia and industry, in the UK and overseas; AIDS research; biotechnology; pharmaceutical manufacturing; role of microorganisms in chronic diseases; vaccine research and development (and production at clinical trial level); molecular genetics of bacteria and yeast; microbiological safety; European Collection of Cell Cultures; protein isolation and characterization; manufactures a number of biologically derived drug compounds from both wild-type and recombinant microorganisms; has specialist facilities for work with pathogenic microorganisms and their products; library of 5,000 vols, 200 periodicals; Dir Dr R. H. GILMOUR.

Imperial Cancer Research Fund: POB 123, Lincoln's Inn Fields, London, WC2A 3PX; tel. (171) 242-0200; fax (171) 269-3101; f. 1902; library of 4,000 vols, 300 periodicals; Chair. Prof. R. D. COHEN; Dir-Gen. Dr PAUL NURSE; publs *Annual Report*, *Scientific Report* (annually), *Cancer Surveys* (quarterly).

Institute of Ageing and Health (West Midlands): c/o Moseley Hall Hospital, Alcester Rd, Moseley, Birmingham, BI3 8JL; f. 1971; the first institute of its kind in the UK; to promote and advance science and medicine relating to the development of gerontology and of medicine in old age; 200 mems; small specialist library; Dir Dr P. P. MAYER.

Institute of Cancer Research: see under University of London.

Lister Institute of Preventive Medicine, The: The White House, 70 High Rd, Bushey Heath, Herts., WD2 3JG; tel. (181) 421-8808; fax (181) 421-8818; e-mail secretary@lister-institute.org.uk; inc. 1891 to support research into biomedicine; Chair. Dr ANNE MCLAREN; Sec. F. K. COWEY.

Liverpool School of Tropical Medicine: Pembroke Place, Liverpool, L3 5QA; tel. (151) 708-9393; fax (151) 708-8733; e-mail robbinsv@liverpool.ac.uk; f. 1898 and received its Charter of Incorporation 1905; affiliated to the University of Liverpool; its objects are to train medical and paramedical personnel in all aspects of individual or community medicine in the tropics, to conduct original research into tropical diseases and their control, and to organize and conduct clinical and prophylactic measures against tropical diseases; also undertakes research and technical assistance work in other health sector areas; library of 50,000 vols and periodicals, incl. Ronald Ross collection; Dir Prof. D. H. MOLYNEUX; publs *Annals of Tropical Medicine and Parasitology*, *Annals of Tropical Paediatrics*.

Mathilda and Terence Kennedy Institute of Rheumatology: 1 Aspenlea Rd, London, W6 8LH; tel. (181) 383-4444; fax (181) 383-4499; f. 1966; conducts research into the causes and cure of the rheumatic diseases; Dir Prof. R. N. MAINI; Gen. Sec. C. R. L. BODEN.

Medical Research Council (MRC): 20 Park Crescent, London, W1N 4AL; tel. (171) 636-5422; telex 24897; fax (171) 436-6179; inc. 1920; its principal objectives are to promote the balanced development of medical and related biological research and to advance knowledge that will lead to improved health care; it employs its own research staff in 40 establishments; also provides grants to enable individual scientists to undertake research programmes and projects, thus complementing the research resources of the universities and hospitals; research training is supported by means of fellowships and studentships; Chair. Sir ANTHONY CLEAVER; Chief Exec. Prof. GEORGE K. RADDA; publs *Annual Report*, *Scientific Strategy*, *MRC News*.

Attached research establishments:

National Institute for Medical Research: The Ridgeway, Mill Hill, London, NW7 1AA; Dir Sir JOHN SKEHEL.

MRC Laboratory of Molecular Biology: Hills Rd, Cambridge, CB2 2QH; Dir Dr R. HENDERSON.

MRC Clinical Sciences Centre: Royal Postgraduate Medical School, Hammersmith Hospital, Du Cane Rd, London, W12 0NN; Dir Prof. C. HIGGINS.

MRC Anatomical Neuropharmacology Unit: Mansfield Rd, Oxford, OX1 3TH; Dir Prof. P. SOMOGYI.

MRC Biochemical and Clinical Magnetic Resonance Unit: Magnetic Resonance Spectroscopy, John Radcliffe Hospital, Headington, Oxford, OX1 9DU; Dir Dr P. STYLES (acting).

MRC Biostatistics Unit: Institute of Public Health, University Forvie Site, Robinson Way, Cambridge, CB2 2SR; Hon. Dir Prof. N. E. DAY.

MRC Brain Metabolism Unit: University Dept of Pharmacology, University of Edinburgh, 1 George Square, Edinburgh, EH8 9JZ; Dir Prof. G. FINK.

MRC Cancer Trials Office: 5 Shaftesbury Rd, Cambridge, CB2 2BW.

MRC Cell Mutation Unit: University of Sussex, Falmer, Brighton, Sussex, BN1 9RR; Dir Prof. B. A. BRIDGES.

MRC Cellular Immunology Unit: Sir William Dunn School of Pathology, University of Oxford, OX1 3RE; Dir Dr D. W. MASON (acting).

MRC Centre, Cambridge: Hills Rd, Cambridge, CB2 2QH; Head Dr M. B. DAVIES.

MRC Centre, Oxford: Manor House, John Radcliffe Hospital, Headington, Oxford, OX3 9DU; Head Dr D. MCLAREN.

MRC Centre for Brain Repair: E. D. Adrian Building, University Forvie Site, Robinson Way, Cambridge, CB2 2PY; Chair. Prof. D. A. S. COMPSTON.

MRC Centre for Mechanisms of Human Toxicity: Hodgkin Building, University of Leicester, POB 138, Lancaster Rd, Leicester, LE1 9HN; Dir Prof. G. C. K. ROBERTS.

MRC Centre for Molecular Sciences: New Chemistry Laboratory, South Parks Rd, Oxford, OX1 3QT; Dir Prof. J. E. BALDWIN.

MRC Centre for Protein Engineering: Hills Rd, Cambridge, CB2 2QH; Dir Prof. A. FERSHT.

MRC Child Psychiatry Unit: Institute of Psychiatry, De Crespigny Park, Denmark Hill, London, SE5 8AF; Hon. Dir Prof. Sir MICHAEL RUTTER.

MRC Cognition and Brain Sciences Unit: 15 Chaucer Rd, Cambridge, CB2 2EF; Dir Prof. W. MARSLEN-WILSON.

MRC Cyclotron Unit: Royal Postgraduate Medical School, Hammersmith Hospital, Du Cane Rd, London, W12 0NN; Dir Prof. C. HIGGINS.

Dunn Nutrition Unit: Downhams Lane, Milton Rd, Cambridge, CB4 1XJ; Dir Dr J. WALKER.

MRC Environmental Epidemiology Unit: Southampton General Hospital, Southampton, SO16 6YD; Dir Prof. D. J. P. BARKER.

MRC Epidemiology and Medical Care Unit: Wolfson Institute of Preventive Medicine, St Bartholomew's and the Royal London Hospital School of Medicine and Dentistry, Charterhouse Square, London, EC1M 6BQ; Dir Prof. T. W. MEADE.

MRC Health Services Research Collaboration: University of Bristol, Canynge Hall, Whiteladies Road, Bristol, BS8 2PR; Dir Prof. P. DIEPPE.

MRC Human Biochemical Genetics Unit: The Galton Laboratory, University College London, Wolfson House, 4 Stephenson Way, London, NW1 2HE; Dir Prof. D. A. HOPKINSON.

MRC Human Genetics Unit: Western General Hospital, Crewe Rd, Edinburgh, EH4 2XU; Dir Prof. N. D. HASTIE.

UK Human Genome Mapping Project Resource Centre: Hinxton Hall, Cambridge, CB10 1SB; Dir Dr D. CAMPBELL.

MRC Human Movement and Balance Unit: Institute of Neurology, The National Hospital for Neurology and Neurosurgery, Queen Square, London, WC1N 3BG; Hon. Dir Prof. C. D. MARSDEN.

MRC Immunochemistry Unit: University Dept of Biochemistry, South Parks Rd, Oxford, OX1 3QU; Dir Prof. K. B. M. REID.

MRC Institute for Environment and Health: University of Leicester, POB 138, Lancaster Rd, Leicester, LE1 7DD; Dir (vacant).

MRC Institute of Hearing Research: University of Nottingham, Nottingham, NG7 2RD; Dir Prof. M. P. HAGGARD.

MRC Institute of Molecular Medicine: John Radcliffe Hospital, Headington, Oxford, OX3 9DU; Hon. Dir Prof. Sir DAVID WEATHERALL.

MRC Interdisciplinary Research Centre for Cognitive Neuroscience: University Laboratory of Physiology, Parks Rd, Oxford, OX1 3PT; Dir Prof. C. BLAKEMORE.

MRC Interdisciplinary Research Centre in Cell Biology: MRC Laboratory for Molecular Cell Biology, University College London, Gower St, London, WC1E 6BT; Dir Prof. C. R. HOPKINS.

MRC Laboratories, The Gambia: POB 273, Banjul, The Gambia, W. Africa; Dir Prof. K. P. W. J. MCADAM.

MRC Laboratories, Jamaica: University of the West Indies, Mona, Kingston 7, Jamaica, West Indies; Dir Prof. G. R. SERJEANT.

MRC Harwell (Mammalian Genetics Unit): Chilton, Didcot, Oxon., OX11 0RD; Dir Prof. S. BROWN.

MRC Medical Sociology Unit: 6 Lilybank Gardens, Glasgow, G12 8QQ; Dir Prof. SALLY MACINTYRE.

MRC Molecular Haematology Unit: Institute of Molecular Medicine, John Radcliffe Hospital, Headington, Oxford, OX3 9DU; Hon. Dir Prof. Sir DAVID WEATHERALL.

MRC Harwell (Mouse Genome Centre): Chilton, Didcot, Oxon., OX11 0RD; Dir Prof. S. BROWN.

MRC Muscle and Cell Motility Unit: Division of Biophysics, King's College London, 26 – 29 Drury Lane, London, WC2B 5RL; Hon. Dir Prof. R. M. SIMMONS.

MRC Neurochemical Pathology Unit: Newcastle General Hospital, Westgate Rd, Newcastle upon Tyne, NE4 6BE; Dir Prof. J. A. EDWARDSON.

MRC/BBSRC Neuropathogenesis Unit: Ogston Bldg, University of Edinburgh, West Mains Rd, Edinburgh, EH9 3JF; Dir Dr C. BOSTOCK.

MRC Protein Phosphorylation Unit: Dept of Biochemistry, Medical Sciences Institute, University of Dundee, Dundee, DD1 4HN; Hon. Dir Prof. P. COHEN.

MRC Harwell (Radiation and Genome Stability Unit): Chilton, Didcot, Oxon., OX11 0RD; Dir Prof. D. GOODHEAD.

MRC Reproductive Biology Unit: Centre for Reproductive Biology, 37 Chalmers St, Edinburgh, EH3 9EW; Dir Prof. A. S. MCNEILLY.

MRC Social, Genetic and Developmental Psychiatry Research Centre: Institute of Psychiatry, De Crespigny Park, Denmark Hill, London, SE5 8AF; Dir Prof. Sir MICHAEL RUTTER.

MRC Toxicology Unit: Hodgkin Bldg, University of Leicester, POB 138, Lancaster Rd, Leicester, LE1 9HN; Dir (vacant).

MRC Virology Unit: Institute of Virology, Church St, Glasgow, G11 5JR; Dir Prof. D. J. MCGEOCH.

National Asthma Campaign: Providence House, Providence Place, London, N1 0NT; tel. (171) 226-2260; fax (171) 704-0740; funds research into asthma, hay fever and related allergy and provides advice and information; 40,000 mems; Chair. Sir PETER EMERY; Chief Exec. ANNE BRADLEY; publ. *Asthma News* (quarterly).

Paterson Institute for Cancer Research: Christie Hospital (NHS) Trust, Manchester, M20 9BX; tel. (161) 446-3000; fax (161) 446-3109; f. 1932; conducts basic and clinical cancer research; Dir Prof. D. G. HARNDEN.

Strangeways Research Laboratory: Wort's Causeway, Cambridge, CB1 4RN; tel. (1223) 243231; fax (1223) 411609; f. 1912; research into cell biology, developmental biology, cancer, rheumatoid arthritis; Dirs Prof. N. DAY, Prof. B. PONDER.

NATURAL SCIENCES

General

Engineering and Physical Sciences Research Council: Polaris House, North Star Ave, Swindon, SN2 1ET; tel. (1793) 444000; telex 449466; fax (1793) 444010; f. 1994; supports basic, strategic and applied research in the natural sciences and engineering, and provides trained manpower; Chair. Dr ALAN RUDGE; Chief Exec. Prof. RICHARD BROOK.

Natural Environment Research Council (NERC): Polaris House, North Star Ave, Swindon, SN2 1EU; tel. (1793) 411500; fax (1793) 411501; established by Royal Charter 1965 to support research, monitoring and postgraduate training in: terrestrial, marine and freshwater biology; earth, atmospheric, hydrological, oceanographic and polar sciences; Earth observation; Chair. JAMES SMITH; Chief Exec. Prof. JOHN KREBS.

The component institutes of the Council are:

British Antarctic Survey: High Cross, Madingley Rd, Cambridge, CB3 0ET; tel. (1223) 221400; fax (1223) 362616; Dir Prof. C. RAPLEY.

British Geological Survey: Kingsley Dunham Centre, Nicker Hill, Keyworth, Nottingham, NG12 5GG; tel. (115) 936-3100; fax (115) 936-3200; Dir Dr D. FALVEY.

Centre for Coastal and Marine Sciences: Prospect Place, Plymouth, PL1 3DH; Dir Prof. J. MCGLADE; (based at Plymouth), comprises three laboratories.

Constituent laboratories:

Proudman Oceanographic Laboratory: Bidston Observatory, Birkenhead, Merseyside, L43 7RA; tel. (151) 653-8633; fax (151) 653-6269; Dir Prof. J. HUTHNANCE (acting).

Dunstaffnage Marine Laboratory: POB 3 Oban, Argyll, PA34 4AD; tel. (1631) 562244; fax (1631) 565518; Dir Dr G. B. SHIMMIELD.

Plymouth Marine Laboratory: Prospect Place, Plymouth, PL1 3DH; tel. (1752) 633100; fax (1752) 633101; Dir Prof. R. F. MANTOURA.

Centre for Ecology and Hydrology: Maclean Bldg, Crowmarsh Gifford, Wallingford, Oxon., OX10 8BB; Dir Prof. BRIAN WILKINSON; comprises four institutes.

Constituent institutes:

Institute of Hydrology: Maclean Bldg, Crowmarsh Gifford, Wallingford, Oxon., OX10 8BB; tel. (1491) 838800; fax (1491) 629424; Dir Prof. JIM WALLACE.

Institute of Freshwater Ecology: The Ferry House, Far Sawry, Ambleside, Cumbria, LA22 0LP; tel. (15394) 42468; Dir Prof. ALAN PICKERING.

Institute of Terrestrial Ecology: Monks Wood, Abbots Ripton, Huntingdon, Cambs PE17 2LS; tel. (1487) 773381; fax (1487) 773467; Dir Prof. T. M. ROBERTS.

Institute of Virology and Environmental Microbiology: Mansfield Rd, Oxford, OX1 3SR; tel. (1865) 512361; fax (1865) 59962; Dir Prof. P. NUTTALL.

Southampton Oceanography Centre: University of Southampton, Empress Dock, Southampton, SO14 3ZH; tel. (1703) 596666; fax (1703) 592865; Dir Prof. JOHN SHEPHERD.

Centre for Population Biology: Imperial College, Silwood Park, Ascot, SL5 7PY; tel. (1344) 294354; fax (1344) 873173; Dir Prof. J. H. LAWTON.

Environmental Systems Science Centre: Dept of Geography, University of Reading, Whitenights, POB 227, Reading, RG6 2AB; tel. (1734) 318741; fax (1734) 755865; Head Prof. R. J. GURNEY.

Centre for Global Atmospheric Modelling: Dept of Meteorology, University of Reading, POB 243, Earley Gate, Reading, RG6 6BB; tel. (118) 931-8315; fax (118) 935-2604; Dir Prof. A. O'NEILL.

Atmospheric Chemistry Modelling Support Unit: Dept of Chemistry, University of Cambridge, Lensfield Rd, Cambridge, CB2 1EP; tel. (1223) 336473; fax (1223) 336473; Dir Dr J. A. PYLE.

Sea Mammal Research Unit: Gatty Marine Laboratory, Univ. of St Andrews, St Andrews, Fife, KY16 8LB; tel. (1334) 463472; fax (1334) 463443; Dir Prof. P. HAMMOND.

Biological Sciences

Bristol University Botanic Garden: Bracken Hill, North Rd, Leigh Woods, Bristol, BS8 3PF; tel. (117) 973-3682; fax (117) 973-3682; f. 1882 to advance public education in and promote research into botany and its related subjects; Supt NICHOLAS WRAY; publs *Annual Report*, *Guide*, *Annual Seed List*.

Cambridge University Botanic Garden: Cory Lodge, Bateman St, Cambridge, CB2 1JF; tel. (1223) 336265; fax (1223) 336278; f. 1762 (1846 on present site); teaching and research in botany and horticulture; library of 7,700 vols (incl. early vols of *Gardeners Chronicle* annotated by Charles Darwin); Dir Prof. J. S. PARKER; publ. *Seed List* (annually).

Chelsea Physic Garden: 66 Royal Hospital Rd, London SW3 4HS; tel. (171) 352-5646; fax (171) 376-3910; f. 1673; botanic garden and centre for research and education on plants, conservation of rare plants, and a public amenity; library: (restricted access) *c.* 300 vols, incl. Society of Apothecaries Dale bequest; Curator S. A. MINTER; publ. *Index Seminum* (annually).

Institute of Zoology: Zoological Society of London, Regent's Park, London, NW1 4RY; tel. (171) 722-3333; fax (171) 586-2870; f. 1977; studies aimed at the scientific advancement of conservation, breeding and management of animals in the wild and in captivity; research groups in reproductive biology (gamete biology, endocrinology, physiological ecology), genetics (population genetics, molecular genetics), veterinary science (incl. wildlife disease and comparative medicine), ecology (behavioural ecology and population dynamics); incorporates Nuffield Laboratories of Comparative Medicine and Wellcome Laboratories of Comparative Physiology; library and publs: see Zoological Society of London; Dir L. M. GOSLING.

National Institute for Biological Standards and Control: Blanche Lane, South Mimms, Potters Bar, Herts, EN6 3QG; tel. (1707) 654753; fax (1707) 646730; e-mail enquiries@nibsc.ac.uk; f. 1976; the National Biological Standards Board is responsible for control and standardization of biological substances used in human medicine, and its functions are executed through the Institute; biological substances include all vaccines such as poliomyelitis, measles, rubella and whooping cough, also blood products, certain hormones and a number of antibiotics; research and development work is an important part of the Institute's activities; designated a WHO Int. Laboratory for Biological Standards; library of 4,000 vols, 200 periodicals; Dir Dr G. C. SCHILD; publs *Annual Report*, *Biological Reference Materials*.

Oxford University Botanic Garden: Rose Lane, Oxford, OX1 4AX; tel. (1865) 276920; f. 1621 for teaching purposes; 12 staff; library of *c.* 1,000 vols on horticulture; Supt T. WALKER; publ. *Guide*.

Royal Botanic Garden: Edinburgh, EH3 5LR; tel. (131) 552-7171; fax (131) 248-2901; f. 1670; int. centre for the study of plant biodiversity and conservation; courses leading to HND in horticulture with plantsmanship; MSC course in plant taxonomy; Inverleith House Gallery with art exhibitions inspired by nature; specialist gardens—Younger Botanic Garden, near Dunoon, Argyll; Logan Botanic Garden, Stranraer, Wigtownshire; Dawyck Botanic Garden, Stobo, Peebles; Herbarium of *c.* 2,000,000 specimens; library: see Special Libraries; Regius Keeper Prof. DAVID INGRAM; publ. *Edinburgh Journal of Botany*.

Royal Botanic Gardens, Kew: Richmond, Surrey, TW9 3AB; tel. (181) 940-1171; telex 296694; fax (181) 332-5197; e-mail information@rbgkew.org.uk; f. 1759, became a public institution in 1841; taxonomic botany, horticulture, conservation, economic aspects, biochemistry, genetics, propagation and seed storage; library: see Libraries; Dir Prof. Sir G. T. PRANCE; publs *Kew Index* (annually), *Kew Record of Taxonomic Literature* (quarterly), *Kew Bulletin*, *Kew Magazine*, floras, generic monographs.

University Marine Biological Station: Millport, Isle of Cumbrae, Scotland; tel. (1475) 530581; fax (1475) 530601; e-mail j

.davenport@udcf.gla.ac.uk; f. 1884; reorganized 1970 as University Station for provision of teaching and research facilities, for supply of marine specimens, to UK universities, etc.; library of 2,600 vols; Dir Prof. J. DAVENPORT; Sec. DAVID MURDEN; publs *Annual Report*, occasional publs.

Wildfowl & Wetlands Trust: Slimbridge, Glos. GL2 7BT; tel. (1453) 890333; fax (1453) 890827; e-mail research@wwt.org.uk; f. 1946; 75,000 mems; concerned with all aspects of biology/ecology of wetlands and wildfowl, particularly those related to conservation, research, education and recreation; the world's largest comparative collection of living wildfowl is maintained at Slimbridge; other centres open to the public all year round at Arundel, Sussex; Castle Espie, Co. Down; Martin Mere, Lancs.; Washington, Tyne and Wear; Welney, Norfolk; Llanelli, Dyfed; Caerlaverock, Dumfriesshire; education staff and facilities at all centres; research library at Slimbridge; Man. Dir TONY RICHARDSON; publs *Wildfowl* (annually), *Wildfowl and Wetlands* (quarterly).

Mathematical Sciences

National Computing Centre Ltd., The: Oxford Rd, Manchester, M1 7ED; tel. (161) 228-6333; fax (161) 242-2400; f. 1966; a membership organization run on a commercial basis; acts as a focus for its mems and represents their views at nat. and int. level; provides consultancy and training services, software packages and products to promote open systems; co-operates with other bodies to foster standards and best practices in Information Technology; Chair. J. M. OCKENDEN; Man. Dir CHRISTOPHER PEARSE; publ. *NCC Interface* (monthly).

Physical Sciences

Cambridge University Institute of Astronomy: The Observatories, Madingley Rd, Cambridge, CB3 0HA; tel. (1223) 337548; fax (1223) 337523; incorporating former Observatory f. 1824; Solar Physics Observatory f. 1913; Institute of Theoretical Astronomy f. 1967; library of 17,500 vols; work on observational and theoretical astrophysics; Dir Prof. R. S. ELLIS.

Central Laboratory of the Research Councils: Chilton, Didcot, Oxon., OX11 0QX; tel. (1235) 821900; fax (1235) 445808; provides advanced and large-scale laboratory facilities, and expertise, to support univ. and industrial research; Chair. of governing ccl Dr BERT WESTWOOD; publs *Annual Report*, *Newsletter* (3 a year).

Laboratories:

Daresbury Laboratory: Keckwick Lane, Daresbury, Warrington, Cheshire, WA4 4AD; tel. (1925) 603000; fax (1925) 603100; f. 1958; operates synchrotron X-ray source; provides advanced surface science and other materials facilities, and computational support in a broad range of disciplines; Chief Exec. Dr BERT WESTWOOD.

Rutherford Appleton Laboratory: Chilton, Didcot, Oxon., OX11 0QX; tel. (1235) 821900; fax (1235) 445808; f. 1957; operates pulsed source of neutrons and muons (ISIS), high-power lasers, microelectronic design and microengineering facilities, and space engineering and data centres; provides supercomputing, detector technology and particle physics support; Chief Exec. Dr BERT WESTWOOD.

Fulmer Materials Technology: Wantage Business Park, Wantage, Oxon, OX12 9BJ; tel. (1235) 772992; fax (1235) 771144; owned by BNF Metals Technology Centre; carries out contract research, principally in the fields of metallurgy, composites, ceramics, chemistry, physics, engineering, industrial computer applications and transducer design and instrumentation, for Government and industrial sponsors, both British and Overseas; 135 staff; library of 10,000 vols; Chief Exec. Dr W. H. BOWYER; publ. *FRI Newsletter* (quarterly).

Meteorological Office: London Rd, Bracknell, Berks, RG12 2SZ; tel. (1344) 420242; telex 849801; fax (1344) 854942; f. 1854; the Exec. Agency that provides a national meteorological service and is responsible for implementing the objectives of the World Meteorological Organisation (*q.v.*); provides comprehensive forecasting and consultative services; involved with major research into all aspects of meteorology, climatology and atmospheric science, partly in co-operation with universities and other national and international agencies; work on the physics and dynamics of the atmosphere ranges in scale from global numerical analyses and forecasts to the microphysics of clouds; library: see Libraries; Chief Exec. P. D. EWINS; publs *Annual Report*, *Scientific and Technical Review*, *Marine Observer* (quarterly), *Outlook*.

Mullard Radio Astronomy Observatory: Astrophysics Group, Cavendish Laboratory, Madingley Rd, Cambridge, CB3 0HE; tel. (1223) 337295; fax (1223) 354599; f. 1945; Dir Prof. R. E. HILLS; publ. numerous scientific papers.

Nuffield Radio Astronomy Laboratories —Jodrell Bank (University of Manchester): Macclesfield, Cheshire; tel. (1477) 571321; fax (1477) 571618; the station uses seven large steerable radio telescopes, including the Lovell (fmrly Mark 1A) 250-ft diameter radio telescope; these can be connected into MERLIN array which now extends to Cambridge (baseline: 230 km) to study radio objects in any part of the sky; research on galactic and extragalactic astrophysical continuum and spectral line radio emissions and cosmic micro-wave background; observations of radio emission from quasars, pulsars and stars; multi-telescope interferometry and very long base-line interferometry; tracking of lunar and planetary space probes; Dir Prof. A. G. LYNE (acting).

Particle Physics and Astronomy Research Council (PPARC): Polaris House, North Star Ave, Swindon, SN2 1SZ; tel. (1793) 442000; fax (1793) 442002; Chief Exec. Prof. IAN HALLIDAY.

The Council is responsible for:

Astronomy Technology Centre: Blackford Hill, Edinburgh, EH9 3HJ; f. 1818; manages the 3.8-metre infra-red telescope and the James Clerk Maxwell millimetre wave telescope in Hawaii; responsible for the optical telescope at La Palma Observatory; houses the Dept of Astronomy of Edinburgh Univ.; has a Starlink data processing centre and a Super-COSMOS high-speed plate scanning machine; Head STUART PITT.

United Kingdom Atomic Energy Authority: Harwell, Didcot, Oxon., OX11 0RA; tel. (1235) 436900; telex 83135; fax (1235) 436899; f. 1954; has responsibility for the safe management and decommissioning of the nuclear reactors and other research and development facilities used to develop the UK's nuclear power programme, together with the safe disposal of the radioactive waste; implements the UK's contribution to the European fusion programme; sites at Dounreay (Caithness), Windscale (Cumbria), Risley (Cheshire), Culham (Oxfordshire), Harwell (Oxfordshire), Winfrith (Dorset); Chair. Sir KENNETH EATON; Chief Exec. Dr JOHN MCKEOWN.

University of London Observatory: 553 Watford Way, Mill Hill Park, London, NW7 2QS; tel. (181) 959-0421; fax (181) 906-4161; e-mail vmp@star.ucl.ac.uk; f. 1929; part of Dept of Physics and Astronomy, University College, London; teaching and research in astronomy; 15 mems; specialized astronomical library; Dir Dr M. DWORETSKY; publ. *Communications* (occasionally).

PHILOSOPHY AND PSYCHOLOGY

Institute of Psychophysical Research: 118 Banbury Rd, Oxford, OX2 6JU; tel. (1865) 558787; fax (1865) 558064; f. 1961; carries out academic research in the fields of philosophy, psychology and theoretical physics, and their inter-relationships; Dir C. E. GREEN; publ. *Proceedings* (irregular).

RELIGION, SOCIOLOGY AND ANTHROPOLOGY

Centre for Orcadian Studies: 8 Broad St, Kirkwall, Orkney, KW15 1NX; tel. (1856) 875747; fax (1856) 876284; f. 1994; aims to promote the study of all aspects of Orkney, including post-Ice-Age development, Pictish and Norse culture, traditional cosmology; Dir HOWARD FIRTH.

Economic and Social Research Council: Polaris House, North Star Ave, Swindon, SN2 1UJ; tel. (1793) 413000; fax (1793) 413001; f. 1965; ind. org. funded mainly by Govt; research and training agency; aims to provide research on issues of importance to business, public sector and govt; Chair. Dr BRUCE SMITH; Chief Exec. Prof. RON AMANN; publs *Social Sciences* (quarterly), *Annual Report*.

Institute for the Study and Treatment of Delinquency: King's College London, Strand, London, WC2R 2LS; tel. (171) 873-2822; fax (171) 873-2823; e-mail istd.enq@kcl.ac.uk; f. 1931; is an independent objective forum for all criminal justice professionals and those with a lay interest in crime; arranges conferences, courses and visits; Pres. The Baroness HILTON OF EGGARDON; Chair. of Council Sir HENRY BROOKE; Dir JULIA BRAGGINS; publs *British Journal of Criminology* (quarterly), *Annual Report*, *Criminal Justice Matters* (quarterly).

Muslim Institute for Research and Planning, The: 109 Fulham Palace Rd, London, W6 8JA; tel. (181) 563-1995; fax (181) 563-1993; f. 1972; research in early history of Islam, Islamic economics, philosophy of science, international relations, global Islamic movement; teaching (short courses) in political thought, philosophy of science, Arabic language, journalism; 18 staff; library of 600 vols; Dir Dr M. G. U. SIDDIQUI; publs *Issues in the Islamic Movement* (annually), *Crescent International* (2 a month).

Tavistock Institute: 30 Tabernacle St, London, EC2A 4DD; tel. (171) 417-0407; fax (171) 417-0566; incorporated 1947; study of human relations in conditions of well-being, conflict or breakdown in the family, the work group, the community and the larger organization; disciplines range from social science to organizational development; Sec. JOHN MARGARSON; publs *Human Relations* (monthly), *Evaluation*.

TECHNOLOGY

BHR Group Ltd: Cranfield, Beds., MK43 0AJ; tel. (1234) 750422; fax (1234) 750074; f. 1947; provides research, development and consultancy on all aspects of fluid engineering and process technology, for a wide range of industries; specializes in abrasive water-jet cutting, fluid power, filtration, hydraulics, mixing, separation, pumping, process intensification, multiphase flow, pipe networks, sealing and containment, slurry transport; knowledge-based software systems; field studies; conferences and specialist training courses; technical information services; Chief Exec. I. COOPER.

British Ceramic Research Ltd: Queens Rd, Penkhull, Stoke-on-Trent, Staffs., ST4 7LQ; tel. (1782) 764444; fax (1782) 412331; e-mail info@ceram.co.uk; f. 1948; research into properties of raw materials and products of the pottery, refractories and clay building materials industries; manufacturing processes; materials engineering and processing; design and performance of machinery and kilns; performance and high-temperature physics and chemistry of refractories; production and properties of advanced industrial ceramics; strength of brick masonry; improved methods of chemical and physical testing; library of 13,000 vols and 60,000 pamphlets; Chair. J. K. SYKES; Chief Exec. Dr N. E. SANDERSON; publ. *World Ceramics Abstracts* (monthly).

British Maritime Technology Ltd: Orlando House, 1 Waldegrave Rd, Teddington, TW11 8LZ; tel. (181) 943-5544; fax (181) 943-5347; f. 1985; provides industry with high level research and technical assistance; solutions to the problems of designers and operators of structures and vehicles on land, coast and sea; 22 subsidiary and assoc. operating companies; Chair. DAVID GOODRICH; publ. *Focus*.

British Technology Group plc: 101 Newington Causeway, London, SE1 6BU; tel. (171) 403-6666; telex 894397; fax (171) 403-7586; f. 1981 from merger of Nat. Research Development Corpn and Nat. Enterprise Board; identifies commercially viable technologies from universities and companies worldwide, protects the technologies through patenting, and negotiates licences with industrial partners for commercialization; Chair. JACK LEONARD.

British Textile Technology Group (BTTG): Wira House, West Park Ring Rd, Leeds, LS16 6QL; tel. (113) 259-1999; fax (113) 278-0306; e-mail info@bttg.co.uk; f. 1918; engaged in research, development, testing and evaluation for textile and related industries; undertakes product development and testing, international consulting work, etc; Man. Dir A. J. KING.

Building Research Establishment Ltd: Bucknalls Lane, Garston, Watford, Herts., WD2 7JR; tel. (1923) 664000; fax (1923) 664010; e-mail enquiries@bre.co.uk; f. 1921; research and consultancy covering building, construction and the prevention and control of fire; library of 20,000 books and 250,000 pamphlets, and a database on construction; Man. Dir Dr M. J. WYATT; publ. *BRE News of Construction Research* (4 a year).

CBD Porton Down: Porton Down, Salisbury, Wilts., SP4 0JQ; tel. (1980) 613000; f. 1916; defence-related chemical and biological research; Dir-Gen. Dr D. A. ANDERSON.

Centre for Marine and Petroleum Technology: Offshore Technology Park, Exploration Drive, Aberdeen, AB23 8GX; tel. (870) 608-3400; fax (870) 608-3480; non-profit organization; broker of technology, co-ordinating research and innovation in the oil and gas industry; CEO ROGER LANE-NOTT.

Construction Industry Research and Information Association (CIRIA): 6 Storey's Gate, London, SW1P 3AU; tel. (171) 222-8891; fax (171) 222-1708; e-mail enquiries@ciria.org.uk; research and information on building and civil engineering; Dir-Gen. Dr P. L. BRANSBY; publs *Annual Report*, *CIRIA News Letter* (quarterly), books, reports, technical notes.

Defence Evaluation and Research Agency—Farnborough: DERA Farnborough, Hants, GU14 0LX; tel. (1252) 392000; fax (1252) 394777; f. 1995; Chief Exec. JOHN CHISHOLM; publ. *Annual Report*.

Defence Evaluation and Research Agency—Malvern: St Andrews Rd, Malvern, Worcs, WR14 3PS; tel. (1684) 894000; fax (1684) 894540; Dirs Dr N. APSLEY (Electronics), A. MIDDLETON (Command Information Systems).

Defence Research Agency—Winfrith: A22 Winfrith Technology Centre, Dorchester, Dorset, DT2 8XJ; tel. (1305) 212448; fax (1305) 212444; 80,000 reports.

Laboratory of the Government Chemist: Queens Rd, Teddington, Middx, TW11 0LY; tel. (181) 943-7000; fax (181) 943-2767; f. 1842; provision of analytical services to the public and private sectors; research in analytical chemistry; library of *c.* 8,000 vols, 500 periodicals; Government Chemist Dr R. D. WORSWICK; publs occasional reports.

National Physical Laboratory: Teddington, Middx, TW11 0LW; tel. (181) 977-3222; fax (181) 943-6458; f. 1900; national standards laboratory; establishes measurement standards, and undertakes research into improved techniques, engineering materials and information technology; Dir Dr JOHN RAE; publs various.

National Remote Sensing Centre Ltd: Delta House, Southwood Crescent, Farnborough, Hants., GU14 0NL; tel. (1252) 362000; fax (1252) 375016; f. 1989 to commercialize the National Remote Sensing Centre and Earth Observation Centre; supplier of products and services based on information extracted from data acquired by Earth observation satellites and aerial photography; consultancy services; Marketing Dir TRISTRAM CARY.

Natural Resources Institute: University of Greenwich, Central Ave, Chatham Maritime, Kent, ME4 4TB; tel. (1634) 880088; fax (1634) 880066; e-mail reception@nri.org; f. 1987; became an institute of the Univ. of Greenwich 1996; supplier of research, consultancy and training services in the environment and natural resources sector to support development assistance programmes, sustainable management of natural resources, environmental sciences, cost-effective and environmentally safe pest management, development and transfer of technologies to improve food security, social, economic and institutional analysis to enhance the impact of development projects and policies; training (some courses accredited for postgraduate qualifications); library of 300,000 vols and information service; Dir Prof. JOHN PERFECT; publ. *NRI Bulletin*.

NEL: East Kilbride, Glasgow, G75 0QU; tel. (13552) 20222; fax (13552) 72999; e-mail info@ncl.uk; f. 1947; applied engineering research, development; calibration, consultancy and prototype manufacture for private and public sectors; Gen. Man. Dr F. KINGHORN; publs *Conference Proceedings*, technical papers, reports.

Pera International: Melton Mowbray, Leics., LE13 0PB; tel. (1664) 501501; fax (1664) 501264; f. 1946; a multi-disciplinary technology centre specializing in all aspects of manufacture, incl. materials, quality training, methods, computer applications, human resources and manufacturing integration.

Scottish Universities Research and Reactor Centre: East Kilbride, Glasgow, G75 0QF; tel. (1355) 223332; fax (1355) 229898; e-mail Director@surrc.gla.ac.uk; f. 1963; provides research and teaching facilities in radioactive and stable isotopes in the environment, ultratrace analysis, radiation mapping, nuclear waste disposal, thermoluminescence dating and dosimetry, food irradiation, reactor physics, radiochemistry, nuclear physics, radiation chemistry, nuclear medicine, radiation protection, environmental studies, geochronology, isotope geology, stable isotope geochemistry and carbon dating; Dir Prof. R. D. SCOTT.

Smith Institute: POB 183, Guildford, Surrey, GU2 5GG; tel. (1483) 579108; fax (1483) 568710; e-mail office@smithinst.ac.uk; f. 1993; non-profit organization; mathematics depts of univs of Cambridge and Oxford; joint industry/academic institute for research in industrial mathematics and system engineering; Dir Dr LINCOLN WALLEN.

Transport Research Laboratory: Crowthorne, Berks, RG45 6AU; tel. (1344) 773131; fax (1344) 770356; e-mail info@lib.trl.co.uk; establ. 1933, fmrly Transport and Road Research Laboratory; independent research-and-development and consultancy organization specializing in road materials and construction, structures, road safety and traffic, vehicle safety, environment; library of 200,000 books and pamphlets, 400 current journals, and int. roads and transport database; Chief Exec. G. CLARKE; publ. *Current Topics in Transport*.

Tun Abdul Razak Research Centre: Brickendonbury, Hertford, SG13 8NL; tel. (1992) 584966; fax (1992) 554837; f. 1938; research and development on natural rubber; 3,000 books and 200 periodicals, information retrieval system containing 100,000 items; Dir of Research Dr C. S. L. BAKER; publs *Annual Report*, *Rubber Developments*.

WRc PLC: Henley Rd, Medmenham, Marlow, Bucks., SL7 2HD; tel. (1491) 571531; fax (1491) 579094; independent research and development and consultancy organization specializing in water and environmental management; two main technology centres in Medmenham and Swindon; liaison offices in Stirling and Hong Kong; subsidiary cos in Rome, Italy and Philadelphia, USA; national research centre for the UK water industry; libraries at each lab; Man. Dir J. MOSS.

Libraries and Archives

Aberdeen

Aberdeen City Council Arts and Recreation Department Library and Information Services: Central Library, Rosemount Viaduct, Aberdeen, AB25 1GW; tel. (1224) 652500; fax (1224) 641985; f. 1884; adult lending, reference, local studies, business and technical, children's, cassettes, compact discs, videos, arts equipment lending service, online information retrieval; 17 brs; housebound service; library of 495,495 vols; CD-ROMs; special collections: Scottish genealogy, local photographs, North Sea oil, British patent abstracts, 10,000 standard specifications; Principal Officer, Library and Information Services NEIL M. BRUCE.

Robert Gordon University Library: Garthdee Road, Aberdeen, AB10 7QE; tel. (1224) 263450; fax (1224) 262889; library of 181,000 vols; Chief Librarian DIANE DEVINE (acting).

University of Aberdeen Library: Queen Mother Library, Meston Walk, Aberdeen, AB24 3UE; tel. (1224) 272579; telex 73458; fax (1224) 487048; f. 1495; library of 1,200,000 vols; McBean Jacobite Collection, O'Dell railway collection, Biesenthal Hebrew collection, Taylor psalmody collection, G. W. Wilson photographic collection, Gregory, Melvin and other special collections; Librarian R. V. PRINGLE.

Aberystwyth

Ceredigion County Library: Public Library, Corporation St, Aberystwyth, SY23 2BU; tel. (1970) 617464; fax (1970) 625059; library of 168,000 vols; 6 brs; County Librarian WILLIAM H. HOWELLS.

National Library of Wales: Aberystwyth, Dyfed, SY23 3BU; tel. (1970) 632800; fax (1970) 615709; f. 1907; one of the six copyright libraries of the British Isles; 5,000,000 printed books, 30,000 MSS, over 3,500,000 deeds and documents and 200,000 maps, prints and drawings, including the finest existing Welsh collection; diaries and correspondence of David Lloyd George; Librarian ANDREW M. W. GREEN; publ. *The National Library of Wales Journal* (2 a year).

University of Wales, Aberystwyth, Hugh Owen Library: Penglais, Aberystwyth, Dyfed, SY23 3DZ; tel. (1970) 622391; fax (1970) 622404; f. 1872; library of 740,000 vols, 4,568 periodicals; Thomas Parry Library incl. Welsh Institute of Rural Studies Library; special collections include: Celtic Collection (13,000 vols); Gregynog Press books and 20th-century private press books; George Powell Collection (19th-century English and French literature, fine art and music); James Camden Hotten Collection; Rudler Collection of geological pamphlets; Duff Collection of pamphlets (Classics); League of Nations and UN Documents; microforms such as Early American Imprints 1639 – 1800; David De Lloyd Papers (Welsh folksongs); Lily Newton Papers (water pollution); Thomas Webster letters (19th-century geologist); British Soc. of Rheology Library; Horton Collection (early children's books), Appleton Collection (Victorian colour printing and binding); Dir of Information Services Dr M. HOPKINS.

Aldershot

Prince Consort's Library: Knollys Rd, Aldershot, Hants., GU11 1PS; tel. (1252) 349381; f. 1860; library facilities with 25,000 vols on military studies, and Army historical library of 35,000 vols.

Ashton under Lyne

Tameside Metropolitan Borough Council Leisure Services Department: Council Offices, Wellington Rd, Ashton under Lyne, OL6 6DL; tel. (161) 342-8355; fax (161) 342-3744; f. 1974; library of 504,226 vols; special collections: local studies and archives, sound recordings, video cassettes, computer software; Asst Dir (Libraries and Heritage) B. DELVE.

Aylesbury

Buckinghamshire County Library: County Offices, Walton St, Aylesbury, Bucks., HP20 1UU; tel. (1296) 383206; fax (1296) 382259; f. 1918; library of 1,272,094 vols; 35 brs; Asst Dir of Education (Life-Long Learning) J. WHITTER.

Bangor

National Educational Video Library: Arts and Crafts Building, University of Wales (Bangor), Hen Goleg Site, Siliwen Rd, Bangor, Gwynedd, LL57 2DY; tel. (1248) 353053; fax (1248) 370144; f. 1949; educational and training videos; Library Man. JOHN LOVELL.

University of Wales, Bangor, Information Services: Bangor, LL57 2DG; tel. (1248) 382961; fax (1248) 382979; f. 1884; library of 500,000 vols; Bangor Cathedral Library; local Estate archives; Dir P. R. BRADY; publ. *Annual Report.*

Barry

Vale of Glamorgan Council Education and Libraries Department: Civic Offices, Holton Road, Barry, CF63 4RU; tel. (1446) 709104; fax (1446) 701820; 10 brs; Vale Librarian SIAN E. JONES.

Bath

University of Bath Library: Claverton Down, Bath, BA2 7AY; tel. (1225) 826826; fax (1225) 826229; library of 400,000 vols; contains Sir Isaac Pitman's Library; University Librarian H. D. NICHOLSON.

Bedford

Bedfordshire Libraries: County Hall, Bedford MK42 9AP; tel. (1234) 363222; fax (1234) 228993; f. 1925; 20 brs; 4 mobile libraries; special services for hospitals, housebound readers, prisons, local government, schools and young people; special collections: Mott-Harrison collection of Bunyan life and works, Fowler collection of historical source material (Bedford Central Library); aeronautics, agriculture, slides, audio-visual including videos, records, cassettes, compact discs and computer software; library of 950,000 vols; Head of Libraries and Communications B. S. GEORGE.

Birmingham

Aston University Library and Information Services: Aston Triangle, Birmingham, B4 7ET; tel. (121) 359-3611; fax (121) 359-7358; e-mail library@aston.ac.uk; f. 1895; library of 253,000 vols, 1,608 periodicals; Dir Dr N. R. SMITH; publs *Current Contents Bulletins* (fortnightly), *Special Subject Guides*, *Library Fact Sheets*.

Birmingham Library Services: Central Library, Chamberlain Sq., Birmingham, B3 3HQ; tel. (121) 235-4511; fax (121) 233-4458; f. 1861; 45 community libraries; Reference Library f. 1866; Departments: Archives (incl. Diocesan Record Office and Boulton & Watt collection); Arts, Business Information, Language and Literature (including John Ash Oberammergau Passion Play Collection, King's Norton Parish Library, Sheldon Rector's Library, Parker Collection of early children's books and games, Samuel Johnson, Milton, Cervantes, Baskerville and War Poetry Collections, Early Printed Books, Fine Bindings and Private Press Books, and Shakespeare Library (f. 1864, 45,000 vols in 90 languages)), Local Studies and History (including Priestley Collection, Sir Benjamin Stone Collection of photographs, Marston Rudland Collection of Engraved Portraits, Francis Frith Negative Archive, Bedford Photographic Collection, and Warwickshire Photographic Survey), Music Library, Science and Technology (including Patents), Social Sciences (incl. railways colln and United Nations depository); library of 1,162,000 vols including 134 incunabula; Dir VIVIEN GRIFFITHS.

Orchard Learning Resources Centre: Hamilton Drive, Weoley Park Rd, Selly Oak, Birmingham, B29 6QW; tel. (121) 415-2255; fax (121) 415-2273; e-mail olrc@westhill.ac.uk; f. 1921; anthropology and world area studies, communications, development aid, Islamics, Judaism, social studies, world religions, missions, education; library of 160,000 vols, 3,000 Arabic and Syriac MSS; Greek papyri; spec. collns incl. Harold W. Turner Colln on New Religious Movements; Dir GORDON HARRIS.

University of Birmingham Library: Edgbaston, Birmingham, B15 2TT; tel. (121) 414-5816; fax (121) 471-4691; f. 1880 (as Mason Science College Library); library of 2,100,000 vols, 7,500 current periodicals, 3,000,000 MSS; special collections include: archives of Joseph, Austen and Neville Chamberlain, Anthony Eden, W. H. Dawson, Francis Brett Young, Harriet Martineau, Bishop E. W. Barnes, Sir Oliver Lodge, Church Missionary Society Archives (pre-1950); St Mary's, Warwick and Bengeworth parish libraries, Wigan Library from Bewdley, Worcs, Baskerville collection; Birmingham and Midland Institute pamphlet collection; Librarian Dr C. FIELD; publs *Annual Report*, *Research Libraries Bulletin*.

Blackburn

Blackburn with Darwen Borough Libraries: Central Library, Town Hall St, Blackburn, BB2 1AG; tel. (1254) 661221; Head of Cultural Services N. MONKS.

Blackpool

Blackpool Borough Libraries: Central Library, Queen St, Blackpool, FY1 1PX; tel. (1253) 478111; fax (1253) 478071; Head of Cultural Services P. HANSELL.

Bournemouth

Bournemouth Libraries: Leisure and Tourism Directorate, Town Hall, Bourne Ave, Bournemouth, BH2 6DY; tel. (1202) 454614; fax (1202) 454620; Head of Libraries SHELAGH LEVETT.

Bracknell

Bracknell Forest Borough Libraries: Bracknell Library, Town Square, Bracknell, RG12 1BH; tel. (1344) 423149; fax (1344) 411392; 7 brs; Head of Libraries, Arts and Information RUTH BURGESS.

National Meteorological Library and Archive: London Rd, Bracknell, Berks., RG12 2SZ; tel. (1344) 854841; fax (1344) 854840; e-mail metlib@meto.gov.uk; f. 1870; library of 250,000 vols, 53,000 pamphlets and 32,000 pictures; the national library for meteorology, climatology; and includes comprehensive records of data published by British and foreign institutions; early weather diaries; official weather records and charts; ships' weather log books; open to the public; Librarian ALAN HEASMAN; publ. *Monthly Accessions List*.

Bradford

Bradford Libraries: Prince's Way, Bradford, BD1 1NN; tel. (1274) 753600; fax (1274) 395108; library of 1,000,000 vols; 32 libraries and 3 mobile libraries, provide general collections; Central Library specializes in: local history, business information, Asian languages, and audio and video services; Head of Service PAUL LAWSON.

University of Bradford Library: Bradford, Yorks., BD7 1DP; tel. (1274) 233400; fax (1274) 233398; f. 1966; library of 520,000 vols; J. B. Priestley Library; Librarian M. B. STEVENSON; publs *Annual Report*, occasional bibliographies and guides.

Bredbury

National Library for the Blind: Cromwell Rd, Bredbury, Stockport, SK6 2SG; tel. (161) 494-0217; fax (161) 406-6728; f. 1882; library contains 400,000 vols, including music, in Braille and Moon types; Austin collection of large-type books; Chief Exec. MARGARET BENNETT; publs *Hands On* (3 a year), *NLB Bulletin* (4 a year).

Bridgend

Bridgend County Borough Library and Information Service: Coed Parc, Park St, Bridgend, Mid Glam., CF31 4BA; tel. (1656) 767451; fax (1656) 645719; 13 brs; County Borough Librarian JOHN WOODS.

Bridgwater

Somerset County Library: Mount St, Bridgwater, Somerset, TA6 3ES; tel. (1278) 451201; fax (1278) 452787; e-mail lbhq.gen@somerset.gov.uk; f. 1919; library of 1,135,429 vols and sound recordings; 34 brs, 8 mobile libraries; County Librarian R. N. FROUD.

Brighton

Brighton and Hove Libraries: C/o Brighton Central Library, Church St, Brighton, BN1 1UE; tel. (1273) 290800; Chief Librarian SARAH PLAYFORTH.

University of Sussex Library: Falmer, Brighton, BN1 9QL; tel. (1273) 606755; fax (1273) 678441; f. 1961; library of 750,000 vols; Librarian ADRIAN PEASGOOD.

Bristol

Bristol City Council Leisure Services Department: Central Library, College Green, Bristol, BS1 5TL; tel. (117) 927-6121; telex 44200; fax (117) 922-6775; 26 brs, 2 mobile libraries (including 2 for schools); reference library; business, fine art, music; library of 876,332 vols; Dir S. WRAY.

University of Bristol Library: Tyndall Ave, Bristol, BS8 1TJ; tel. (117) 928-9000; fax (117) 925-5334; f. 1909; library of 1,500,000 vols and pamphlets; special collections include the English novel to 1850, the Sir Allen Lane Penguin collection, business histories, early geology, medicine, mathematics, chemistry and physics, Pinney Papers (17th – 19th centuries), Brunel workbooks and papers, British philosophers, landscape gardening, courtesy books, General Election addresses (part of the National Liberal Club Library), Wiglesworth Ornithological Library, EDC, Addington Symonds Papers, Papers of the Somerset Miners' Association; Librarian M. G. FORD.

Brynmawr

Blaenau Gwent Libraries: Central Depot, Barleyfields Industrial Estate, Brynmawr, NP3 4YF; tel. (1495) 355311; fax (1495) 355468; e-mail bglibs@dial.pipex.com; library of 94,000 vols; 7 brs, 2 mobile libraries; County Borough Librarian MARY JONES.

Caernarfon

Gwynedd Library and Information Service: Dept of Education and Culture, Gwynedd County Council, Shirehall St, Caernarfon, LL55 1SH; tel. (1286) 679465; fax (1286) 671137; library of 530,000 vols; 22 brs; Dir DAFYDD WHITTALL.

Cambridge

British and Foreign Bible Society's Library: c/o Cambridge University Library, West Rd, Cambridge, CB3 9DR; tel. (1223) 333000, ext. 33075; fax (1223) 333160; f. 1804; largest collection of printed Bibles (over 35,000 vols of Scripture in more than 2,500 languages); Librarian ALAN F. JESSON; publs *Word in Action* (3 a year), *library guide, sectional catalogues*.

Cambridgeshire Education, Libraries and Heritage: Castle Court, Shire Hall, Cambridge, CB3 0AP; tel. (1223) 717067; fax (1223) 717079; e-mail community.services@libraries.camcnty.gov.uk; f. 1974; library of 1,155,000 vols; 40 brs, 7 mobile libraries; Head of Libraries and Information MIKE HOSKING.

Needham Research Institute: East Asian History of Science Library, 8 Sylvester Rd, Cambridge, CB3 9AF; tel. (1223) 311545; telex 81240; fax (1223) 362703; f. 1976 from collections originally assembled since 1942 by Dr Joseph Needham and Dr Lu Gwei-Djen, from sources in China and the West, primarily intended for the researches on which is based the series 'Science and Civilisation in China' (c. 30 volumes planned, of which 16 already published); governed by the East Asian History of Science Trust (f. 1968), an educational charity; a unique collection specialized in works in the history of science, technology and medicine in East Asia and consisting of books, periodicals, off-prints, MSS in Asian and European languages, also archival and iconographic material (notes, photographs, maps, microfilms, etc.); open to research scholars by appointment; Librarian JOHN P. C. MOFFETT.

Tyndale Library: 36 Selwyn Gardens, Cambridge, CB3 9BA; tel. (1223) 566601; fax (1223) 566608; e-mail librarian@tyndale.cam.ac.uk; f. 1944; a residential centre for biblical research; intended for postgraduate study in biblically-related fields, with a view to promoting evangelical scholarship; library of *c.* 35,000 vols; Librarian D. INSTONE BREWER; publ. *Tyndale Bulletin* (2 a year).

University of Cambridge Library: West Rd, Cambridge, CB3 9DR; tel. (1223) 333000; fax (1223) 333160; a Copyright library; 6,050,000 printed books, numerous special collections, 142,000 MSS, large collections of papers and correspondence, 1,076,000 maps, 1,196,000 microforms; the collections have been accumulating since the beginning of the 15th century; incl. Royal Commonwealth Society Colln (250,000 vols and pamphlets relating to the countries of the Commonwealth); Librarian P. K. FOX.

College libraries:

Christ's College Library: Cambridge, CB2 3BU; tel. (1223) 334950; fax (1223) 334973; f. 1448, refounded 1505; library of 100,000 vols, incunabula, periodicals; special collections: works of John Milton, including items published before 1700, Charles Lesingham Smith collection of early mathematical and scientific books, William Robertson Smith Oriental Library, Sir Stephen Gaselee collection of Coptic studies, A. H. Wratislaw collection of Slavonic language and literature, W. H. D. Rouse collection of Indian studies and 16th-century English books; Librarian Dr V. COX.

Churchill College Library: Cambridge, CB3 0DS; tel. (1223) 336138; fax (1223) 336160; f. 1960; library of 45,000 vols; special collections, extensive political, military and scientific archives mainly of the late 19th and 20th centuries; Librarian Miss M. KENDALL; Keeper of Archives Dr PIERS BRENDON.

Clare College Library: Cambridge, CB3 9AJ; tel. (1223) 333202; f. 1326; comprises Fellows' Library (8,000 vols) and Forbes Mellon Library (28,000 vols); special collections: Cecil Sharp MSS; Forbes Librarian and Fellows' Librarian Dr R. S. SCHOFIELD.

Corpus Christi College Library: Trumpington St, Cambridge, CB2 1RH; tel. (1223) 338025; fax (1223) 338041; e-mail parker.library@corpus.cam.ac.uk; f. 14th century; library of 30,000 vols (8,000 in Parker Library, 22,000 in Butler Library); special collections: Parker bequest of MSS and early printed books, Lewis collection of coins, gems and other antiquities, Stokes collection on Jewish history; Librarian Dr F. W. RATCLIFFE.

Downing College: The Maitland Robinson Library: Cambridge, CB2 1DQ; tel. (1223) 334829; f. 1800; library of 40,000 vols; special collections of Bowtell MSS relating to the city and university of Cambridge; library of 500 vols of naval history and navigation and large collection of law, Civil War and Interregnum newspapers; Librarian Dr J. H. SCOTT.

Emmanuel College Library: Cambridge, CB2 3AP; tel. (1223) 334233; f. 1584; 400 MSS from 12th century to the present; library of 72,000 vols with large number of pre-18th century works; Librarian P. J. SPREADBURY.

Fitzwilliam College Library: Cambridge, CB3 0DG; tel. (1223) 332042; library of 35,000 vols; Librarian M. A. MACLEOD.

Girton College Library: Cambridge, CB3 0JG; tel. (1223) 338970; f. 1869; library of 76,000 vols, 120 periodicals; special collections: Newall collection of Scandinavian material, Frere collection of Hebrew MSS, Crews collection of Judeo-Spanish material, Somerville collection of mathematics, Bibas collection of 18th-century French works, Blackburn collection of women's rights materials; College Archive covers history of higher education for women; Librarian FRANCES GANDY.

Gonville and Caius College Library: Cambridge, CB2 1TA; tel. (1223) 332419; fax (1223) 332430; f. 1348; library of 60,000 vols, 1,000 MSS related to medieval law and science; Librarian J. H. PRYNNE.

Jesus College Old Library: Cambridge, CB5 8BL; tel. (1223) 339414; fax (1223) 324910; f. 1500; library of *c.* 8,600 vols, 39 incunabula, 80 medieval MSS from north-country monasteries, 17 Oriental MSS; special collections: Civil War tracts, military science, library of T. R. Malthus, large theological collection; Keeper of the Old Library P. R. GLAZEBROOK.

King's College Library: Cambridge, CB2 1ST; tel. (1223) 331232; f. 1441; library of 125,000 vols; special collections: MSS of Sir Isaac Newton (available on microfilm in the University Library), 20th-century MSS, notably major collections of Rupert Brooke, E. M. Forster, T. S. Eliot, J. M. Keynes, Joan Robinson; includes the Rowe Music Library; f. 1928; library of 25,000 vols; Librarian P. M. JONES.

Magdalene College Old Library: Cambridge, CB3 0AG; tel. (1223) 332100; MSS of works by Thomas Hardy, Rudyard Kipling, T. S. Eliot, I. A. Richards and 38 MSS, including a 13th-century Apocalypse; incunabula, foreign-printed books of 16th, 17th and 18th centuries, early theological works; Diaries of A. C. Benson and W. R. Inge; library of 17,000 vols; Keeper Dr R. LUCKETT.

Newnham College Library: Cambridge, CB3 9DF; tel. (1223) 335740; f. 1897; 8 medieval MSS, incunabula, early editions of poets, dramatists and chroniclers of 16th and 17th centuries; Librarian D. HODDER.

Pembroke College Library: Cambridge, CB2 1RF; tel. (1223) 338121; fax (1223) 338163; f. 1347; library of 45,000 vols, 317 medieval MSS; special collections: papers of Gray, C. Smart, William Mason, R. Storrs; Librarian T. R. S. ALLAN.

Pepys Library (Magdalene College): Cambridge, CB3 0AG; tel. (1223) 332115; fax (1223) 332187; f. 1724 in its present location; library of 3,000 vols in original bookcases; Pepys's own collection (MSS, books, music, maps, prints and drawings), not added to since 1703; Pepys's own catalogue; special collections: Pepys MSS (including Diary), medieval MSS, naval and historical MSS (mostly English, 16th- and 17th-century), collection of calligraphy, prints of London and Westminster, incunabula, broadside ballads, plays, etc.; Librarian Dr R. LUCKETT.

Peterhouse (Perne) Library: Cambridge, CB2 1RD; tel. (1223) 338200; fax (1223) 337578; f. 1594; 280 medieval MSS, 16th- and 17th-century musical MSS (on permanent deposit in University Library); library of 4,000 vols, 70 incunabula; special collections: first editions of classics in science, 16th-century theological books; Librarian Dr R. W. LOVATT.

Queens' College Old Library: Cambridge, CB3 9ET; tel. (1223) 335549; fax (1223) 335522; f. 1448; 22 medieval MSS, 31 incunabula,; library of over 28,000 vols; catalogue by Thomas Hartwell Horne (1827); Milner collection of works on history of Reformation and 18th-century science and mathematics; Thomas Smith collection of Renaissance humanist writings; Keeper of the Old Library C. J. POUNTAIN.

St Catharine's College Library: Cambridge, CB2 1RL; tel. (1223) 338343; fax (1223) 338340; e-mail cth1@ula.cam.ac.uk; f. 18th century; library of 42,000 vols in undergraduate library; MSS, 30 incunabula; library of 25,000 vols in special collections: 17th-century political and religious tracts, 184 vols of 18th-century medical works (Addenbrooke collection), medieval Romance literature, Spanish books and MSS of 16th and 17th centuries; Librarian J. R. SHAKESHAFT.

St John's College Library: Cambridge, CB2 1TP; tel. (1223) 338662; fax (1223) 337035; f. 1511; MSS; special collections: 15th-century books, Matthew Prior bequest, Sir Soulden Lawrence law collection, Thomas Baker's collection of printed books and MSS, Samuel Butler collection, Smith collection of Rabelais literature, Wordsworthiana, papers of Sir Cecil Beaton, mathematical works of historical interest from libraries of Adams, Todhunter and Pendlebury, Udny Yule collection of Thomas à Kempis editions, Hugh Gatty collection, Sparrow bequest of Samuel Parr books; Librarian AMANDA SAVILLE.

Selwyn College Library: Grange Rd, Cambridge, CB3 9DQ; tel. (1223) 335880; f. 1930; library of 40,000 vols, MSS, incunabula; special collections: diaries and papers of George Augustus Selwyn (1809 – 78) Primate of New Zealand and later Bishop of Lichfield, large collection of theological works including 19th-century sermons, 19th-century missionary collection with particular emphasis on Melanesia and New Zealand, and 3,000 19th-century English ecclesiastical pamphlets; Librarian Dr J. D. RAY.

Sidney Sussex College Library: Cambridge, CB2 3HU; tel. (1223) 338852; fax (1223) 338884; e-mail hel20@cam.ac.uk; f. 16th century; library of 35,000 vols, 70 periodicals; Muniment Room: 7,300 vols, 106 MSS, incunabula; special collections: 18th and 19th century mathematical books; Taylor Mathematical Library (separately administered); Librarian HEATHER E. LANE.

Trinity College Library: Cambridge, CB2 1TQ; tel. (1223) 338488; fax (1223) 338532; e-mail trin-lib@lists.cam.ac.uk; f. 1546; library of 300,000 vols; spec. collns incl. medieval western and oriental MSS; literary MSS of Milton, Tennyson, Housman, etc., Capell collection of Shakespeareana; Rothschild library of 18th-century English literature; Isaac Newton's library; papers of 19th- and 20th-century economists, philosophers, politicians; Librarian D. MCKITTERICK.

Trinity Hall Library: Cambridge, CB2 1TJ; tel. (1223) 332546; f. 1350; library of 15,000 vols, 31 MSS; special collections: early canon law, Larman Bequest of books and MSS relating to Reformation and Tudor periods, particularly heraldry, ecclesiastical history and theology; Librarian Dr P. HUTCHINSON.

Special libraries:

Balfour and Newton Library: Department of Zoology, Downing St, Cambridge, CB2 3EJ; tel. (1223) 336648; fax (1223) 336676; Balfour Library f. 1883, Newton Library f. 1907; library of 19,000 vols, 18,000 periodicals, over 110,000 reprints; Librarian C. D. OSBOURN.

Marshall Library of Economics: Sidgwick Ave, Cambridge, CB3 9DB; tel. (1223) 335217; f. 1925; library of 97,000 vols; Librarian ROWLAND THOMAS.

Squire Law Library: 10 West Rd, Cambridge, CB3 9DZ; tel. (1223) 330077; fax (1223) 330048; f. 1904; library of 130,000 vols; special collections: Roman law, legal history, comparative law, conflict of laws, international law, environmental law, intellectual property, political biographies; research library; Librarian D. F. WILLS.

Canterbury

Canterbury Cathedral Archives and Library: Canterbury, Kent, CT1 2EH; tel. (1227) 463510 (Archives), (1227) 458950 (Library); fax (1227) 762897; e-mail (Library) catlib@ ukc.ac.uk; f. probably *c.* 597; in continuous existence since 11th century; *c.* 50,000 printed books, administrative MSS of the Dean and Chapter, Canterbury Diocesan Archives, Canterbury City archives; East Kent parish records; early printed books: bibles, prayer books, natural science, travel, theology, history, 17th- and 19th-century pamphlets, slavery material; Canon-Librarian Rev. Canon R. SYMON; Archivist Dr M. STANSFIELD; Librarian Mrs S. HINGLEY.

University of Kent, The Templeman Library: Canterbury, CT2 7NU; tel. (1227) 764000; telex 965449; fax (1227) 823984; library of 700,000 vols; special collections include Pettingell, Melville and Reading-Rayne (MSS and printed plays, mainly 19th century), Maddison collection (history of science), Cartoon Centre (original political cartoons), C. P. Davies Wind and Watermill collection, the papers of Lord Weatherill; Librarian M. M. COUTTS.

Cardiff

Cardiff County Libraries: Central Library, St David's Link, Frederick St, Cardiff, CF1 4DT; tel. (1222) 382116; fax (1222) 238642; library of 750,000 vols; 19 br libraries, 2 mobile libraries; County Librarian PAUL SAWYER.

Central library:

Cardiff Central Library and County Library Headquarters: f. 1862; main library includes lending and reference books; music and sound recordings library; children's library; local studies library includes maps, prints and MSS, large collection of Welsh history; facilities for disabled.

National Museums and Galleries of Wales Library: Cathays Park, Cardiff, CF1 3NP; tel. (1222) 573202; f. 1907; books and periodicals relevant to the Museum collections; library of 168,000 vols; special collections: Tomlin (conchology), Willoughby Gardner (early natural history), Vaynor (James) Collection (early works on astronomy); also houses libraries of Cardiff Naturalists' Society and Cambrian Archaeological Association; Librarian J. R. KENYON.

University of Wales College of Cardiff Library: POB 430, Cardiff, CF1 3XT; tel. (1222) 874795; telex 498635; fax (1222) 371921; f. 1883; library of 750,000 vols; Salisbury Library (Welsh and Celtic Studies), EEC Documentation Centre, Brett collection of Tennysoniana, Ifor Powell collection of pamphlets on 20th-century affairs, Mazzini collection, Architecture library and technical reference bureau, Law library, Morse, Ayleward, Mackworth, Population Studies, Victorian Children's Literature, Company Information; Librarian J. K. ROBERTS.

University of Wales College of Medicine Library: Heath Park, Cardiff, CF4 4XN; tel. (1222) 742875; fax (1222) 743651; f. 1931; library of 150,000 vols, including Dental Hospital and Nursing and Allied Health libraries plus Historical Collection; Dir of Information Services J. M. LANCASTER.

Carlisle

Cumbria County Library: County Heritage Services, Arroyo Block, The Castle, Carlisle, CA3 8UR; tel. (1228) 607300; fax (1228) 607299; e-mail herithq@dial.pipex.com.

Carmarthen

Carmarthenshire County Library: Public Library, St Peter's St, Carmarthen, SA31 1LN; tel. (1267) 224830; fax (1267) 221839; library of 762,000 vols; 34 brs, 5 mobile libraries; special collections: coal mine plans, Theodore Nichol Collection, the library of the Carmarthenshire Antiquarian Society; Cultural Services Man. DAVID F. GRIFFITHS.

Chelmsford

Anglia Polytechnic University Library: Rivermead Campus, Bishop Hall Lane, Chelmsford, CM1 1SQ; tel. (1245) 493131; fax (1245) 490835; library of 250,000 vols; Librarian NICOLA KERSHAW.

Essex County Libraries Department: County Library Headquarters, Goldlay Gardens, Chelmsford, Essex, CM2 0EW; tel. (1245) 284981; fax (1245) 492780; e-mail essexlib@essexcc.gov.uk; library of 3,037,000 vols, 487,000 audiovisual items; Head of Libraries, Information, Heritage and Cultural Services GRACE KEMPSTER.

Chester

Cheshire Libraries: Goldsmith House, Hamilton Place, Chester, CH1 1SE; tel. (1244) 606034; fax (1244) 602805; f. 1922; library of 1,500,000 vols; 34 full-time, 17 part-time, 5 dual use brs, 6 mobile libraries and 3 research libraries; HQ special collections; Education Library Service; County Libraries Officer I. DUNN.

Chichester

West Sussex County Council Library Service: Tower St, Chichester, West Sussex, PO19 1QJ; tel. (1243) 756700; fax (1243) 756714; e-mail countylibraries@westsussex.gov.uk; f. 1925; library of 1,254,000 vols; 35 full-time, 4 mobile libraries; County Librarian R. A. KIRK.

Colchester

University of Essex, The Albert Sloman Library: Wivenhoe Park, Colchester, CO4 3SQ; tel. (1206) 873333; fax (1206) 872289; f. 1964; library of 600,000 vols, 135,000 microforms, 3,000 current periodicals; special collections: Latin America, fmr Soviet Union, Social Democratic Party (SDP) archives, Tawney Society archives, Nat. Viewers' and Listeners' Asscn archives, Boundary Commission for England archives (1992–93 public enquiries), papers and publications of the Committee on Standards in Public Life (Nolan Committee), Sigmund Freud and related collections (papers and publications); Librarian R. BUTLER.

Conwy

Conwy County Borough Council Library, Information and Archive Service: Bodlandeb, Conwy, LL32 8DU; tel. (1492) 576140; fax (1492) 592061; e-mail conlibhq@netcomuk.co.uk; f. 1996; library of 200,000 vols; 13 libraries, mobile library service for housebound; special collections: local history, Welsh language and literature; County Librarian and Archivist RONA ALDRICH.

Coventry

Coventry City Libraries: Central Library, Smithford Way, Coventry, CV1 1FY; tel. (1203) 832314; fax (1203) 832440; e-mail covinfo@discover.co.uk; library of 480,000 vols; special collections on the motor industry, cycle industry, local history, George Eliot, trade unions and industrial relations; Head of Cultural Services RICHARD MUNRO.

University of Warwick Library: Gibbet Hill Rd, Coventry, CV4 7AL; tel. (1203) 523523; fax (1203) 524211; f. 1963; library of 900,000 vols; special collections: British and foreign statistical serials (trade, finance, production), current and retrospective, Economics Working Papers, pre-1948 collections of Howard League for Penal Reform, Modern Records Centre (labour history, employers' records, industrial relations), Modern German Literature; Librarian Dr J. A. HENSHALL.

Cwmbran

Monmouthshire Libraries and Information Service: County Hall, Cwmbran, NP44 2XH; tel. (1633) 644550; fax (1633) 644545; e-mail mlis@dial.pipex.com; 6 brs; Head of Libraries and Culture KEVIN SMITH.

Darlington

Darlington Libraries: 11 Houndgate, Darlington, DL1 5RF; Head of Leisure, Libraries and Community Safety N. MALTBY.

Derby

Derby City Libraries: Celtic House, Heritage Gate, Friary St, Derby, DE1 1QX; tel. (1332) 716607; fax (1332) 715549; City Librarian RAY RIPPINGALE.

Dorchester

Dorset County Library: Colliton Park, Dorchester, Dorset, DT1 1XJ; tel. (1305) 251000; fax (1305) 224344; f. 1920, reorganized 1997; 720,000 items; 34 brs; 6 mobile libraries; special collections: Dorset Collection, Thomas Hardy Collection, Powys Collection; Head of Libraries and Arts Service I. J. LEWIS; publs *Subject Index*, *Hardy Catalogue*, *Lawrence Catalogue*.

Dundee

Dundee City Council Central Library: The Wellgate, Dundee, DD1 1DB; tel. (1382) 434318; fax (1382) 434036; e-mail library@dundeecity.gov.uk; f. 1869; 13 brs, mobile library; special collections: local history and genealogy, commerce, music, Wighton Collection of National Music (620 vols), British Standards, Audio Library, video library; Chief Neighbourhood Resource Officer FRASER PATRICK.

University of Dundee Library: Dundee, DD1 4HN; tel. (1382) 344087; fax (1382) 229190; f. 1881; library of 500,000 vols; Librarian J. M. BAGNALL.

Durham

Durham Arts, Libraries and Museums Department: PO Box, County Hall, Durham, DH1 5TY; tel. (191) 383-3595; fax (191) 384-1336; e-mail alm@durham.gov.uk; f. 1923; library of 876,000 vols; 38 full-time brs, 2 trailers, 4 mobile and 3 travelling libraries, 1 bookbus for the elderly; Dir PATRICK CONWAY.

University of Durham Library: Main University Library, Stockton Rd, Durham, DH1 3LY; tel. (191) 374-3018; fax (191) 374-7481; f. 1833; 1m. printed items on four sites, incl. European Documentation Centre, Middle East Documentation Unit; dept of Archives and Special Collections houses extensive special collections of early printed books, MSS, maps, prints, photographs; printed book special collections include those formed by Bishop Cosin, M. J. Routh, Bishop Maltby, Dr Winterbottom, and the Sharp Library from Bamburgh Castle; 200 incunabula, 2,200 STC, 10,000 Wing; collections of MSS and archives include medieval MSS, modern literary MSS (C. C. Abbott, Basil Bunting, William Plomer Collections), Earl Grey Papers, Malcolm MacDonald Papers, Durham Cathedral Archives, Durham diocesan and probate records, Howard of Naworth Papers and other collections of local family and estate records, Sudan Archive; Librarian Dr J. T. D. HALL; publ. *Durham University Library Publications* (occasional).

Edinburgh

Edinburgh City Libraries: Central Library, George IV Bridge, Edinburgh, EH1 1EG; tel. (131) 225-5584; fax (131) 225-8783; f. 1890; 1,376,494 items; 24 brs, 5 mobile libraries; Central Reference (incl. business information, British Standards, online information service; 304,374 items); special collections: Edinburgh Room (contains information on life in Edinburgh and on Scott, Stevenson, Ballantyne; press cuttings; 94,395 items), Scottish (especially genealogy; 92,815 items), Music (includes indexes to songs and instrumental music; 70,000 items), Fine Art (includes costume; large collection of prints; 81,413 items); Audio library: 78,000 items; City Librarian Mrs M. SHARP.

Edinburgh University Library: George Square, Edinburgh, EH8 9LJ; tel. (131) 650-3384; telex 727442; fax (131) 667-9780; e-mail library@ed.ac.uk; f. 1580; 2,700,000 printed items, MSS, maps, microforms, theses and audiovisual packages, 10,000 current periodicals; Drummond (of Hawthornden) Collection; Laing Charters and MSS; Halliwell-Phillipps Collection; MSS on Scottish history and the Scottish literary renaissance; Arthur Koestler MSS and part library; Corson Sir Walter Scott Collection; New Zealand Studies Collection; MSS and printed books on early 20th-century English literature; Scottish Enlightenment; history of science and medicine; African, East Asian, Islamic and Middle Eastern studies; includes the Erskine Medical Library, Law and Europa Library, New College Library (Divinity), Reid Music Library, Science Libraries and Royal (Dick) School of Veterinary Studies Libraries; Librarian IAN R. M. MOWAT; publs *Annual report*, *Union list of current serials in Edinburgh libraries* (on fiche).

Heriot-Watt University, Cameron Smail Library: Riccarton, Edinburgh, EH14 4AS; tel. (131) 451-3570; fax (131) 451-3164; f. 1821; library of 145,000 vols, 1,500 periodicals; Librarian M. L. BREAKS.

National Archives of Scotland: HM General Register House, Edinburgh, EH1 3YY; tel. (131) 535-1314; national archives of Scotland; local and church records and records of Scottish government and law from 12th to 20th centuries; contains also many groups of deposited private and business muniments; Keeper of the Records of Scotland PATRICK M. CADELL.

National Library of Scotland: George IV Bridge, Edinburgh, EH1 1EW; tel. (131) 226-4531; fax (131) 622-4803; e-mail enquiries@nls.uk; f. 1680s as the Advocates' Library; library contains 6,000,000 vols and pamphlets and a large collection of MSS; under Copyright legislation may claim any book, etc., published in the United Kingdom and Ireland; Library's Lending Services (33 Salisbury Pl., Edinburgh, EH9 1SL) maintain a stock (120,000 vols) of scarce books to supplement the reserves of Scottish public libraries, act as the headquarters for Scottish inter-library co-operation, and house Scottish Union Catalogue; Chair. of the Trustees The Rt Hon. The Earl of CRAWFORD AND BALCARRES; Librarian I. D. MCGOWAN; Sec. of the Library M. C. GRAHAM; Keeper of MSS, Maps and Music I. C. CUNNINGHAM; Keeper of Printed Books A. MATHESON.

Incorporates:

National Library of Scotland Map Library: 33 Salisbury Pl., Edinburgh, EH9 1SL; f. 1958; modern topographic and thematic map coverage of most parts of the world; particular interest in early/modern maps with Scottish association.

Scottish Science Library: 33 Salisbury Pl., Edinburgh, EH9 1SL; f. 1989.

Royal Botanic Garden Library: Edinburgh, EH3 5LR; tel. (131) 522-7171; f. 1670; incorporates the botanical libraries of the Plinian (1841), Wernerian (1858) and Botanical (1872) societies of Edinburgh, Dr John Hope (1899), Cleghorn Memorial Library (1941) and Mr Robert Scarlett (1975); compiles indexes to Monographs, Floras, Gardens, botanists, botanical expeditions, etc.; library of 100,000 vols, including pre-Linnean literature on botany, horticulture, agriculture and medicine; 80,000 pamphlets and separates; 3,500 (1,800 current) periodicals; extensive collection of botanical drawings and prints, photographs, cuttings, etc., correspondence, diaries, maps, plans, MSS, etc., relating to the early Regius Keepers and Curators and botanists and horticulturists in Britain and abroad; Librarian C. D. WILL; publs *Edinburgh Journal of Botany* (3 a year), *British Fungus Flora* (irregular), *RBG Edinburgh Departmental Publication Series*, *Periodicals Holding List* (irregular), *Catalogue of Plants*, various guides.

Royal College of Physicians of Edinburgh Library: 9 Queen St, Edinburgh, EH2 1JQ; tel. (131) 225-7324; fax (131) 220-3939; e-mail library@rcpe.ac.uk; f. 1681; library of 50,000 vols; open to all *bona fide* enquirers; particularly rich in the early sources of medical knowledge; colln of periodicals; library of 1,000 vols of MSS; Librarian I. A. MILNE.

Royal College of Surgeons of Edinburgh Library: Nicolson St, Edinburgh, EH8 9DW; tel. (131) 527-1630; fax (131) 557-6406; e-mail library@rcsed.ac.uk; library of 35,000 vols, 170 periodicals; current texts and CD-ROM; historical collection; College Archive; mainly a private library for Fellows; Hon. Librarian A. A. GUNN.

Signet Library: Parliament Square, Edinburgh, EH1 1RF; tel. (131) 225-4923; fax (131) 220-4016; f. date of foundation 1722, but there were Writers to Her Majesty's Signet as early as 1460; library of 75,000 vols; the Library of the Society of Writers to Her Majesty's Signet is devoted chiefly to Scots law and Scottish history and genealogy; Librarian AUDREY R. WALKER.

Eton

Eton College Library: Eton College, Windsor, Berks SL4 6DB; tel. (1753) 671221; f. 1440; 85,000 items, incl. 200 medieval MSS, 200 incunabula; important collections of editions of classical writers and related material (XVIth – XVIIIth centuries), early science, Elizabethan, Jacobean and Restoration drama, large collection of Civil War and early XVIIIth-century English pamphlets, XVIth-century Italian books; bindings, English and Continental, XIIth – XXth centuries; Topham collection of drawings and engravings after the antique (*c.* 2,500 items); Etoniana collection (*c.* 5,000 printed books, drawings, prints, scrapbooks, MSS); School Books collection; Parikian collection of Armenian printed books 1500 – 1900; 19th- and 20th-century English literature, incl. Elizabeth Barrett Browning, Anne Thackeray Ritchie, Thomas Hardy, Edward Gordon Craig, Moelwyn Merchant collections; mezzotint collection (1,000 items); for archives see Foster, J. and J. Sheppard, *British Archives*, Macmillan 1982, no. 693 (Eton College Records); Librarian M. C. MEREDITH; Archivist Mrs P. C. HATFIELD.

Exeter

Devon Library Services: Barley House, Isleworth Rd, Exeter, EX4 1RQ; tel. (1392) 384300; fax (1392) 384316; f. 1974; library of 1,500,000 vols; 57 brs, 11 mobile libraries; Head of Library and Information Services L. OSBORNE.

Exeter Cathedral Library: Diocesan House, Palace Gate, Exeter, EX1 1HX; tel. (1392) 272894; fax (1392) 263871; e-mail p.w.thomas@exeter.ac.uk; f. 11th century when Bishop Leofric gave 66 MS volumes to the Cathedral Church; library of 25,000 vols including *Exeter Book of Old English Poetry* and *Exon Domesday*; special collections: Cathedral MSS and archives, early printed books in medicine and science, Cook Collection (16th- to 19th-century, early linguistics), printed tracts (mainly Civil War period), Harington Collection (16th- to 19th-century, theology, ecclesiastical history, history); Librarian A. T. PATERSON; Asst Librarian in charge P. W. THOMAS.

University of Exeter Library: Stocker Rd, Exeter, EX4 4PT; tel. (1392) 263869; f. 1937; library of 950,000 vols; administers Exeter Cathedral Library (*q.v.*), and Library of Devon and Exeter Institution (36,000 vols); Librarian A. T. PATERSON.

Falkirk

Falkirk Council Library Services: Public and Schools Library Service, Victoria Bldgs, Queen St, Falkirk, FK2 7AF; tel. (1324) 506800; fax (1324) 506801; library of 365,319 vols, 28,123 audio and 4,260 video items; local history collection; Libraries Man. SUE ALLISON; publ. *Current Awareness Bulletin* (weekly).

Glasgow

Glasgow Caledonian University Library: City Campus, Cowcaddens Road, Glasgow, G4 0BA; tel. (141) 331-3000; library of 220,000 vols; Librarian Prof. J. HAYTHORNTHWAITE.

Glasgow City Libraries and Archives: Glasgow, G3 7DN; tel. (141) 287-2999; fax (141) 287-2815; 32 district libraries; library of 2,145,000 vols; special collections of foreign literature and local history; Dir (vacant).

Attached library:

Mitchell Library: North St, Glasgow, G3 7DN; f. 1874; library of 1,235,000 vols; special collections: on Glasgow (20,000 vols), music (43,000 vols), Robert Burns (5,000 vols), Scottish poetry (12,000 vols) and Patent Depositary Library; business users' service; receives a copy of every publication issued by HMSO, and is also a Depository Library for the unrestricted publications of the United Nations, Unesco and FAO; Librarian F. MACPHERSON.

Royal College of Physicians and Surgeons of Glasgow Library: 234 St Vincent St, Glasgow, G2 5RJ; tel. (141) 221-6072; fax (141) 221-1804; f. 1599; library of 150,000 vols; Librarian JAMES BEATON; publ. *Scottish Medical Journal*.

University of Glasgow Library: Hillhead St, Glasgow, G12 8QE; tel. (141) 330-6704; fax (141) 330-4952; e-mail library@lib.gla.ac.uk; f. 15th century; library of 1,600,000 vols; incorporates Trinity College Glasgow Library (Church of Scotland); Hunterian Books and MSS, Euing Collections of the Bible and music, Farmer Music Collection, Laver, MacColl and Wright Papers on fine art, Hamilton Collection of philosophy, Ferguson Collection of the history of chemistry, Stirling Maxwell Collection of Emblem books, J. M. Whistler archive, David Murray regional history collection, Scottish Theatre Archive, Edwin Morgan Papers, Trotsky Collection; Librarian H. J. HEANEY.

University of Strathclyde Library: 101 St James' Rd, Glasgow, G4 0NS; tel. (141) 552-3701; fax (141) 552-3304; f. 1796; library of 880,000 vols, 5,300 periodicals; special collections include Anderson collection (founder's library), Young collection (alchemy and early chemistry), Laing collection (18th- and 19th-century mathematics), Robertson collection (Scottish history and topography); Librarian DEREK LAW; publ. *Annual Report*.

Gloucester

Gloucestershire County Library, Arts and Museums Service: Shire Hall, Quayside House, Gloucester, GL1 2HY; tel. (1452) 425020; fax (1452) 425042; e-mail clams@glosc.gov.uk; spec. collns incl. Gloucestershire Colln, Hartland Herbals colln; County Library, Arts and Museums Officer LINDA HOPKINS.

Grays

Thurrock Libraries: Grays Central Library, Orsett Rd, Grays, RM17 5DX; tel. (1375) 383611; fax (1375) 370806; 8 brs, 1 mobile library; Head of Libraries ALEC KENNEDY.

Guildford

University of Surrey Library: Guildford, Surrey, GU2 5XH; tel. (1483) 300800; telex 859331; fax (1483) 259500; f. 1894; library of 400,000 vols, 3,800 current periodicals; Librarian T. J. A. CRAWSHAW.

Hatfield

Hertfordshire Libraries, Arts and Information: Library HQ, New Barnfield, Travellers Lane, Hatfield, Herts., AL10 8XG; tel. (1707) 281581; fax (1707) 281589; f. 1925; library of 1,932,393 vols, other media 270,631 items; 53 brs, 13 mobile libraries, 6 hospital libraries, one prison library; special collections: drama, music, local history; Head of Service SUE REEDER.

Haverfordwest

Pembrokeshire County Library: Dew St, Haverfordwest, Pembs., SA61 1SU; tel. (1437) 762070; fax (1437) 769218; 9 brs; Cultural Services Officer MARY JOHN.

Hawarden

St Deiniol's Residential Library: Hawarden, Deeside, Flintshire, CH5 3DF; tel. (1244) 532350; fax (1244) 520643; f. 1896 by W. E. Gladstone; library of 200,000 vols, 50,000 pamphlets, and MSS material; theology, philosophy, history (esp. 19th century), classics, English and European literature; accommodation for 47 residents; Warden Rev. PETER B. FRANCIS.

Hereford

Herefordshire Council Libraries: Shire Hall, Hereford; tel. (1432) 359830; 11 brs; Policy and Communications Man. ALAN BLUNDELL; Library Services Man. JENNY WILLIAMS.

Huddersfield

Kirklees Cultural Services: Headquarters, Red Doles Lane, Huddersfield, West Yorks., HD2 1YF; tel. (1484) 226300; fax (1484) 446842; f. 1974; library of 1,250,000 vols; Head of Cultural Services JONATHAN DRAKE.

University of Huddersfield Library: Queensgate, Huddersfield, HD1 3DH; tel. (1484) 472040; fax (1484) 517987; library of 450,000 vols; Dir of Library Services PHIL SYKES.

Ipswich

Suffolk County Council—Libraries and Heritage: St Andrew House, County Hall, Ipswich, IP4 1LJ; tel. (1473) 583000; fax (1473) 584549; e-mail amanda.arrowsmith@libher.suffolkcc.gov.uk; f. 1974 by amalgamation of former Suffolk library authorities; County Dir of Libraries and Heritage A. J. E. ARROWSMITH.

Keele

University of Keele Library: Keele, Staffs., ST5 5BG; tel. (1782) 584159; fax (1782) 711553; f. 1949; library of 460,000 vols; Librarian and Dir of Information Services A. J. FOSTER.

Keyworth

British Geological Survey Library: British Geological Survey, Keyworth, Nottingham, NG12 5GG; tel. (115) 936-3205; telex 378173; fax (115) 936-3200; f. 1837; incorporating the libraries of the Geological Survey and Museum and Overseas Geological Surveys; library of 500,000 vols, over 3,000 current periodicals, over 200,000 maps, 20,000 archives, national collections of 75,000 photographs illustrating British scenery and geology; regional office library at Edinburgh; Chief Librarian and Archivist G. MCKENNA.

Kingston upon Hull

Hull City Council Libraries: Central Library, Albion St, Hull, HU1 3TF; tel. (1482) 210000; fax (1482) 883024; Head of Libraries BRIAN CHAPMAN.

University of Hull, Academic Services Library: Cottingham Rd, Hull, North Humberside, HU6 7RX; tel. (1482) 465436; fax (1482) 466205; e-mail library@hull.ac.uk; f. 1929; library of 850,000 vols; special collections: South East Asia, India, British Labour history; Dir of Academic Services and Librarian R. G. HESELTINE.

Kirkcaldy

Fife Council Libraries, Central Area: East Fergus Place, Kirkcaldy, Fife, KY1 1XT; tel. (1592) 412930; fax (1592) 412941; library of 400,000 vols; Librarian DOROTHY MILLER.

Lampeter

University of Wales, Lampeter Library: Lampeter, Ceredigion, SA48 7ED; tel. (1570) 422351; telex 48475; fax (1570) 423875; library of 200,000 vols, including Tract collection of 11,000 items; Librarian M. PERRETT (acting); publ. *Trivium*.

Lancaster

University of Lancaster Library: Bailrigg, Lancaster, LA1 4YH; tel. (1524) 592515; fax (1524) 63806; f. 1963; library of 936,000 vols, pamphlets and other items, 3,000 current serials; special collections: business history, Quaker, Redlich (music), Socialist, European Documentation Centre; Librarian JACQUELINE WHITESIDE; publ. *Report of the Librarian*.

Leeds

Leeds City Libraries: Central Library, Municipal Bldgs, Calverley St, Leeds, LS1 3AB; tel. (113) 2478274; fax (113) 2478268; 2 million vols; 57 brs, 8 mobile libraries; numerous special collections including early botanical books, fine arts, Jewish and Hebrew books, military history, music books, scores and audio, patents, HMSO publications, business information, family and local history, maps and photographic prints, Braille and large print transcription service; Chief Librarian CATHERINE BLANSHARD.

Leeds University Library: Leeds, LS2 9JT; tel. (113) 233-6388; fax (113) 233-5561; f. 1874; library of 2,500,000 vols, pamphlets and microforms including the Brotherton Collection which contains over 50,000 vols and pamphlets and a large number of MSS, deeds and letters; includes fmr Ripon Cathedral Library containing early MSS, Service Books, Books of Hours, 13th – 20th-century MSS, important

15th – 18th-century printed books, etc; Liddle Collection of First World War archive materials; Librarian LYNNE J. BRINDLEY; publs *Al-Masaq, Journal of Educational Administration and History, Leeds Studies in English, Leeds Texts and Monographs, Northern History, Proceedings of the Leeds Philosophical and Literary Society: literary and historical section, Proceedings of the Leeds Philosophical and Literary Society: scientific section, Proceedings of the Yorkshire Geological Society, Publications of the Thoresby Society, University of Leeds Review*.

Leicester

De Montfort University Library: Kimberlin Library, The Gateway, Leicester, LE1 9BH; tel. (116) 255-1551; fax (116) 255-0307; Head of Library Services KATHRYN ARNOLD.

Leicester City Libraries: New Walk Centre, Welford Place, Leicester, LE1 6ZG; tel. (116) 252-7348; fax (116) 255-9257; e-mail clarmooz@leicester.gov.uk; Head of Library and Information Services MICHAEL CLARKE.

Leicestershire Libraries and Information Service: County Hall, Glenfield, Leicester, LE3 8SS; tel. (116) 265-7372; fax (116) 265-7370; e-mail poldroyd@leics.gov.uk; f. 1974; library of 912,000 vols; sound recordings, video recordings, talking books; 53 libraries, 8 mobile libraries; Chief Librarian PETER OLDROYD; publs local studies, reports, booklists.

University of Leicester Library: POB 248, University Rd, Leicester, LE1 9QD; tel. (116) 252-2042; fax (116) 252-2066; e-mail libdesk@le.ac.uk; f. 1921; 1,000,000 items; special collections of local history of England and Wales, Transport History, papers of Joe Orton; Librarian Dr T. HOBBS.

Lewes

East Sussex Libraries, Information and Arts: Southdown House, 44 St Anne's Crescent, Lewes, East Sussex, BN7 1SQ; tel. (1273) 481870; fax (1273) 481716; library of 1,409,700 vols; 30 full-time and part-time brs; Head of Libraries, Information and Arts DINA THORPE.

Lichfield

Dean Savage Reference Library: 19B The Close, Lichfield, Staffs., WS13 7LD; tel. (1543) 306240; f. 1924; library of 6,000 vols, mostly theology and ecclesiastical history; for use, apply to above address.

Lincoln

Lincolnshire County Council Education and Cultural Services Directorate—Libraries: County Offices, Newland, Lincoln, LN1 1YL; tel. (1522) 553207; fax (1522) 552820; f. 1974 from 7 former Lincolnshire library authorities; library of 1,765,835 vols; 50 brs, 11 mobile libraries, 2 trailer libraries; special collections: Music, Drama, Lincolnshire material, Alfred Lord Tennyson; Library Services Man. LORRAINE M. JUBB.

Liverpool

Liverpool Libraries and Information Services: Central Library, William Brown St, Liverpool, L3 8EW; tel. (151) 225-5429; fax (151) 207-1342; f. 1852; library of 1,500,000 vols, pamphlets, MSS etc; reference services (includes Hornby Library: rare books, fine bindings, MSS, prints etc. and patents library), services to business, record office, family history service; EU depository library; Head of service PAUL CATCHESIDE.

University of Liverpool Library: POB 123, Liverpool, L69 3DA; tel. (151) 794-2674; fax (151) 794-2681; e-mail library@liverpool.ac.uk; f. 1881; library of over 1,400,000 vols, 4,900 current periodicals; special collections include 254 incunabula, the T. G. Rylands collection (early cartography, Lancashire and Cheshire history), the William Blake collection, the Scott Macfie collection (gypsy studies), the William Noble collection (Kelmscott and other private presses), the Knowsley collection (17th – 19th-century English pamphlets), the Peers collection (Spanish Civil War), and the Fraser collection (*c.* 900 books and pamphlets on tobacco; also much material on positivism and secularism) Robert Graves Collection, Merseyside poets; modern MS holdings include the Rathbone, Blanco White, Brunner and Glasier papers, Science Fiction Foundation Collection, Olaf Stapledon collection; the Education Library contains an important collection of children's books; Librarian F. M. THOMSON; publs *Guide to Special Collections, Annual Report*.

Llandrindod Wells

Powys County Library: Cefnllys Rd, Llandrindod Wells, Powys, LD1 5LD; tel. (1597) 826860; f. 1974; library of 521,000 vols; 19 brs; special local history collection; County Librarian Miss T. L. ADAMS.

Llangefni

Isle of Anglesey County Library: Llangefni Library, Lon-y-Felin, Llangefni, Anglesey, LL77 7RT; tel. (1248) 752093; fax (1248) 750365; Asst Dir, Libraries, Information and Archives JOHN REES THOMAS.

London

Aslib – The Association for Information Management Information Service: Staple Hall, Stone House Court, London, EC3A 7PB; tel. (171) 903-0000; fax (171) 903-0011; e-mail aslib@aslib.co.uk; library of *c.* 16,000 vols on information management, incl. documentation, information science, special libraries and related subjects, 370 current periodicals of the world and about 25,000 references to articles, reports, etc., on library and information science; publs *Aslib Guide to Copyright* (3 a year), *Aslib Book Guide* (monthly), *Aslib Proceedings* (10 a year), *Current Awareness Abstracts* (10 a year), *Forthcoming International Scientific and Technical Conferences* (4 a year), *Journal of Documentation* (5 a year), *Managing Information* (10 a year), *Online and CD Notes* (10 a year), *Program: Electronic Library and Information Systems* (4 a year), *Records Management Journal* (3 a year).

Barking and Dagenham Public Libraries: Central Library, Barking, Essex, IG11 7NB; tel. (181) 517-8666; fax (181) 594-1156; f. 1888; library of 432,000 vols; Librarian ALAN J. HILL.

Barnet Libraries, Arts and Museums: Educational Services, Friern Barnet Lane, London, N11 3DL; tel. (181) 359-3164; fax (181) 359-3171; f. 1965; library of 1,134,000 vols; special collection of Sociology; Head of Libraries and Arts P. J. USHER.

Bexley Public Libraries: Hall Place, Bourne Road, Bexley, Kent, DA5 1PQ; tel. (1322) 523509; fax (1322) 522921; library of 607,000 vols; 13 brs; 2 mobile libraries, ref. library; Local History library; Librarian R. ALSTON.

Bray Libraries (SPCK): Holy Trinity Church, Marylebone Rd, London, NW1 4DU; tel. (171) 387-5282; fax (171) 387-3411; e-mail spckww@spck.org.uk; f. 1730 by Dr Thomas Bray (1658 – 1730) to assist the establishment of small libraries within parochial, deanery or diocesan groups in UK and overseas.

Brent Library Service: Chesterfield House, 9 Park Lane, Wembley, Middx, HA9 7RW; tel. (181) 937-3144; fax (181) 937-3023; f. 1965; library of 580,000 vols; 12 brs, mobile library, housebound service, Grange Museum of Local History; Head of Library Service KAREN TYERMAN.

British Architectural Library: RIBA, 66 Portland Place, London, W1N 4AD; tel. (891) 234400; fax (171) 631-1802; f. 1834; library of 135,000 vols, 700 current serials, 1,400 dead runs, 400,000 photographic images, 175,000 negatives, 700 metres of MSS, and an important collection of 450,000 drawings (housed at 21 Portman Square, W1H 9HF), is one of the most complete architectural libraries; Dir RUTH H. KAMEN; publs *Architectural Periodicals Index and Books catalogued by the British Architectural Library* (quarterly), *RIBA List of Recommended Books* (annually), *APId: Architectural Publications Index* (on disc, quarterly).

British Geological Survey London Information Office: Natural History Museum (Earth Galleries), Exhibition Rd, London, SW7 2DE; tel. (171) 589-4090; fax (171) 584-8270; f. 1986; information and advisory service; public reference collection of British Geological Survey publs including geological maps, memoirs, reports, technical reports and photographs illustrating the geology of the British Isles; online access to British Geological Survey databases; sales point (BGS publs); some overseas maps and textbooks; Mineral Exploration and Investment Grants Act reports; Officer in Charge SYLVIA J. BRACKELL; publs *Guide to London Office*, catalogues.

British Library: 96 Euston Rd, London, NW1 2DB; tel. (171) 412-7000; f. 1973; legal deposit library; among the Library's divisions and services are Reader Services and Collection Development (15 million vols; incorporates Newspaper Library and National Sound Archive), Science Reference and Information Service (science, technology, business, commerce; colln of books, journals, business reports and patents), Special Collections (separate colls: Western manuscripts, oriental collection, India Office collection, maps, music, philately), Bibliographic Services and Document Supply (Boston Spa, Wetherby, West Yorks., LS23 7BQ; maintains British National Bibliography and other products); Chair. Dr JOHN ASHWORTH; Chief Exec. B. LANG; Deputy Chief Exec. D. RUSSON; Dir-Gen. D. BRADBURY; publs *British Library Journal* (2 a year), *British Library News* (monthly).

British Library of Political and Economic Science: London School of Economics, 10 Portugal St, London, WC2A 2HD; tel. (171) 955-7219; fax (171) 955-7454; f. 1896; 4 million bibliographic items covering economics, political science, law (especially international), sociology, history, geography, etc., legislative and administrative reports, important deposits of official documents, and special collections, including MSS; Librarian and Dir of Information Services JEAN SYKES; publ. *The International Bibliography of the Social Sciences* (annually, also on-line).

British Medical Association Library: Tavistock Square, London, WC1H 9JP; tel. (171) 383-6625; fax (171) 388-2544; e-mail bma-library@bma.org.uk; f. 1887; library of 50,000 vols, 3,000 periodicals, 3,500 films and videos; Librarian TONY MCSEÁN; publ. *BMA Library Bulletin* (irregular).

Bromley Public Libraries: Central Library, High St, Bromley, BR1 1EX; tel. (181) 460-9955; fax (181) 313-9975; f. 1894; library of 763,375 vols; 63,004 audiovisual items; special collections: Crystal Palace, Walter de la Mare, H. G. Wells; Librarian BARRY WALKINSHAW.

Camden Leisure Community Services (Libraries, Arts and Tourism): The Crowndale Centre, 218 – 220 Eversholt St, London, NW1 1BD; tel. (171) 911-1557; fax (171) 911-1587; library of 759,537 vols; Chief Officer FRANCES MORGAN.

Canning House Library: The Hispanic and Luso-Brazilian Council, Canning House, 2 Belgrave Square, London, SW1X 8PJ; tel. (171) 235-2303; fax (171) 235-3587; f. 1943;

library of 55,000 vols on Latin America, Caribbean, Spain and Portugal; Librarian C. SUÁREZ; publs *British Bulletin of Publications on Latin America, the Caribbean, Portugal and Spain* (2 a year).

City of Westminster Libraries and Archives: Dept of Education and Leisure, Westminster City Hall, Victoria St, London, SW1E 6QP; tel. (171) 641-2496; 11 community libraries; health information service at Marylebone Library; total stock of books and other materials 1,245,000; Asst Dir, Leisure and Libraries DAVID RUSE.

Constituent libraries include:

Westminster Reference Library: 35 St Martin's St, WC2H 7HP; tel. (171) 641-4636; library of 563,000 vols covering the humanities, pure sciences, business and technology; British and foreign directories; over 1,000 current periodicals; access to CD-ROM online databases; Art and Design Library; 21,000 maps.

Westminster Music Library: 160 Buckingham Palace Rd, SW1W 9UD; tel. (171) 641-5180; 71,000 items on music (not recordings).

Archives and Local History Centre: 10 St Ann's St, London, SW1P 2XR; tel. (171) 641-4292; 200,000 archive items.

College of Arms: Queen Victoria St, London, EC4V 4BT; tel. (171) 248-2762; fax (171) 248-6448; library of *c.* 30,000 vols; genealogical and heraldic collections; Archivist R. C. YORKE.

Congregational Library: 15 Gordon Square, London, WC1H 0AG; f. 1831; library of *c.* 40,000 vols, mainly relating to Church history, the history and activities of the Nonconformists, theology, religious liberty and hymnology; administered by Dr Williams's Library (see below).

Croydon Public Libraries: Katharine St, Croydon, CR9 1ET; tel. (181) 760-5400; fax (181) 253-1004; f. 1888; library of 695,017 vols; 23,592 audio items; Libraries Officer C. BATT.

Department for Education and Employment, Information and Library Network: Sanctuary Bldgs, Great Smith St, London, SW1; f. 1896; library of 210,000 vols; Librarian PATRICK RYAN; publ. *Education Publications* (monthly).

Department of the Environment, Transport and the Regions Library and Information Services: Ashdown House, 123 Victoria Street, London, SW1E 6DE; tel. (171) 890-3333; fax (171) 890-6098; provides information to the staff of the Department on environmental protection, roads, planning, local transport, countryside, railways, aviation, shipping, and local and regional government.

Department of Trade and Industry, Information and Library Services: 1 Victoria St, London, SW1H 0ET; tel. (171) 215-5006; telex 8813148; fax (171) 215-5665; Head of Information Management Services M. A. BRIDGE; Head of Information and Library Services A. RAISIN; publ. *Publications* (annual list of non-HMSO Departmental documents).

Constituent libraries:

Information Centre Victoria Street: 1 Victoria St, London, SW1H 0ET; tel. (171) 215-5006; telex 8813148; fax (171) 215-5665; f. 1950; current material in the social sciences and archival collection of Board of Trade and Ministry of Technology publs; material on energy resources, technology, use and efficiency and archival collection of publs of the Department of Energy and its predecessors; Man. A. COTTERILL.

Information Centre Buckingham Palace Road: Fifth Floor, 151 Buckingham Palace Rd, London, SW1W 9SS; tel. (171) 215-1930; telex 8813148; fax (171) 215-1932; industrial policy, industrial development, the manufacturing industries, science and technology policy, information technology and telecommunications; the emphasis is on material published commercially in the last 10 years; Man. G. J. TATE.

Export Market Information Centre: Kingsgate House, 66 – 74 Victoria St, London, SW1E 6SW; tel. (171) 215-5444; fax (171) 215-4231; e-mail emic@xpd3.dti.gov.uk; f. 1962; compilations of overseas statistics of trade, production, price, employment, population and other economic topics; foreign trade and telephone directories; overseas market surveys; development plans and overseas mail order catalogues; Multicultural Aid project documentation; Man. A. STRACHAN.

British National Space Centre Information Unit: 151 Buckingham Palace Rd, London, SW1W 9SS; tel. (171) 215-0901; fax (171) 215-0936; European Space Agency documentation; information on space projects, programmes and companies and on satellites and remote sensing; open to public by appointment only; Librarian KERRY SEELHOFF.

Monopolies and Mergers Commission Library: New Court, 48 Carey St, London, WC2A 2JT; tel. (171) 324-1467; fax (171) 324-1400; f. 1970; material on monopoly, competition and anti-trust; industrial economics; Librarian Miss L. FISHER.

Office of Fair Trading Library: Room 501, Field House, Breams Bldgs, London, EC4A 1PR; tel. (171) 269-8938; fax (171) 269 8940; f. 1973; material on consumer affairs; competition; consumer credit; monopolies; mergers and restrictive practices; Librarian M. DITRI.

Office of Gas Supply Library: Stockley House, 130 Wilton Rd, London, SW1V 1LQ; tel. (171) 932-1604; fax (171) 630-8164; f. 1986; Librarian B. M. SCOTT.

Office of Telecommunications Library: 50 Ludgate Hill, London, EC4M 7JJ; tel. (171) 634-8700; fax (171) 634-8946; f. 1984; material on all aspects of telecommunications; Library Man. (vacant).

Radiocommunications Agency Information and Library Service: New King's Beam House, 22 Upper Ground, London, SE1 9SA; tel. (171) 211-0502; fax (171) 211-0507; f. 1986; material on all aspects of radio communications; Librarian Ms J. FRASER.

Departments of Health and Social Security Library: Skipton House, Elephant and Castle, London, SE1 6LW; tel. (171) 972-6541; fax (171) 972-5976; f. 1834; library of over 200,000 vols and pamphlets and 2,000 current periodicals on public health, health services, medicine, hospitals, social security and social welfare; produces DHSS-Data: online database; Chief Librarian IAN SNOWLEY; publs *Health Service Abstracts, Social Security Library Bulletin, Social Service Abstracts* (all monthly).

Dr Williams's Library: 14 Gordon Square, London, WC1H 0AG; tel. (171) 387-3727; fax (171) 388-1142; e-mail 101340.2541@compuserve.com; f. opened 1729; library of *c.* 150,000 vols; a lending and reference library of theological, philosophical and historical works; Dir DAVID L. WYKES; publs *Catalogue of Accessions, Bulletin of Accessions* (annually), *Lectures of Friends of Dr Williams's Library* (annually), occasional papers.

Ealing Library and Information Service: Perceval House, 14/16 Uxbridge Rd, London, W5 2HL; tel. (181) 579-2424; f. 1965; library of 650,000 vols; Borough Librarian ANDREW SCOTT.

Enfield Libraries: Central Library, Cecil Rd, Enfield, Middx, EN2 6TW; tel. (181) 366-2244; fax (181) 379-8401; e-mail webmaster@efirstop.demon.co.uk; f. 1965; library of 649,677 vols; 14 brs, 3 reference libraries, mobile library, 2 welfare delivery vans; special collections: linguistics, local history; Head of Library Services CLAIRE LEWIS.

Foreign and Commonwealth Office Library: King Charles St, London, SW1A 2AH; tel. (171) 270-3925; the library serving the Dept for International Development is situated in Abercrombie House, Eaglesham Rd, East Kilbride, Glasgow, G75 8EA; tel. (1355) 843599; the library specializes in publications on international relations and diplomacy and the history, economy, politics and law of foreign countries; includes books on early travel, diplomatic memoirs, treaty collections and material on all aspects of overseas development and technical assistance; written and telephone enquiries only; Librarian JOY HERRING.

Friends' Library: Friends House, Euston Rd, London, NW1 2BJ; tel. (171) 663-1135; fax (171) 663-1001; e-mail library@quaker.org.uk; f. 1673; the official library of the Society of Friends (Quakers) in Great Britain and the repository of its central archives; library of *c.* 14,000 vols, 20,000 pamphlets, and 4,000 vols of MSS, as well as prints and photographs; Librarian MALCOLM J. THOMAS.

Geological Society Library: Burlington House, Piccadilly, London, W1V 0JU; tel. (171) 734-5673; fax (171) 439-3470; e-mail library@geolsoc.org.uk; f. 1807; library of *c.* 300,000 vols, 35,000 maps; lending restricted to the UK only via British Library Document Supply Centre; reference access by appointment; Librarian Miss S. MEREDITH.

Gray's Inn Library: South Square, Gray's Inn, London, WC1R 5EU; f. *c.* 1522; library of 40,000 vols; Legal Reference Library, for members of Gray's Inn, others admitted on application; special collections: 12th – 14th century MSS, Baconiana; Librarian Mrs T. L. THOM.

Greenwich Public Libraries: Greenwich Library, Woolwich Rd, London, SE10 0RL; tel. (181) 858-6656; f. 1905; library of 750,833 vols, 85,213 sound recordings; Borough Librarian (vacant).

Guildhall Library (Corporation of London): Aldermanbury, London, EC2P 2EJ; tel. (171) 332-1868; telex 887955; fax (171) 600-3384; f. *c.*1425; contains 194,000 printed books, etc., more than 95,000 series of MSS, 30,000 prints and 30,000 maps; public reference library, particularly rich in books on all aspects of London history; the MSS collection consists mainly of City parochial records, records of the City Livery Companies, London diocesan records, and records of major London commercial institutions; Guildhall Librarian and Dir of Libraries and Art Galleries MELVYN P. K. BARNES.

Branch library:

City Business Library (Corporation of London): 1 Brewers' Hall Gardens, London, EC2V 5BX; tel. (171) 638-8215; telex 887955; contains British and foreign directories, newspapers, trade papers, statistics and is strong in most aspects of commerce and management; Business Librarian G. P. HUMPHREYS.

Guy's, King's College and St Thomas's Hospitals' School of Medicine and Dentistry, Libraries: Lambeth Palace Rd, London, SE1 7EH; Dir FELICITY GRAINGER.

Constituent libraries:

Guy's Campus Library: St Thomas's St, London, SE1 9RT; Wills Library (Medical); tel. (171) 955-4234; fax (171) 357-0458; f. 1903; F. S. Warner Library (Dental); tel.

(171) 955-4238; f. 1975; library of 30,000 vols.

St Thomas's Campus Library: Lambeth Palace Rd, London, SE1 7EH; STC Library; tel. (171) 928-9292, ext. 2367; fax (171) 401-3932; Inst. of Dermatology Library: tel. (171) 928-9292, ext. 1313; library of 17,000 vols.

Hackney Library Services: Edith Cavell Bldg, Enfield Rd, London, N1 5AZ; tel. (171) 214-8400; f. 1965; library of *c.* 900,000 vols; 14 brs, ref. library; special collections: mechanic trades, woodwork and furniture, local history, John Dawson Collection; Exec. Librarian BETHAN WILLIAMS.

Hammersmith and Fulham Public Libraries: Central Library, Shepherds Bush Rd, London, W6 7AT; tel. (181) 576-5055; fax (181) 576-5022; f. 1888; library of 550,000 vols, 48,000 audio items; special collections: law, politics, Christianity, HMSO publs since 1970, videos; Librarian NIGEL E. BOUTTELL.

Haringey Libraries: Central Library, High Rd, Wood Green, London, N22 6XD; tel. (181) 888-1292; Head of Libraries JEAN EARLEY.

Harrow Public Library Service: PO Box 4, Civic Centre, Station Rd, Harrow, HA1 2UU; tel. (181) 424-1055; fax (181) 424-1971; f. 1965; library of 433,000 vols; 10,000 audio recordings; 15,000 records, cassettes and compact discs; 10 brs; special collections: architecture and building; Librarian R. J. R. MILLS.

Havering Public Libraries: Central Library, St Edward's Way, Romford, Essex, RM1 3AR; tel. (1708) 772389; library of *c.* 500,000 vols; 9 brs, Arts Centre; Chief Librarian G. H. SADDINGTON.

Hillingdon Borough Libraries: High St, Uxbridge, Middx, UB8 1HD; tel. (1895) 250600; fax (1895) 239794; f. 1965; library of 706,000 vols; Chief Officer TRISHA GRIMSHAW.

Home Office Information and Library Services: 50 Queen Anne's Gate, London, SW1H 9AT; tel. (171) 273-3398; telex 24986; fax (171) 273-3957; library of 42,000 vols, 100,000 microforms, 3,400 periodicals; social sciences, especially official publications, criminal law and justice, criminology, police, emergency planning services, immigration, nationality, probation and community relations; available to researchers for reference by appointment; Librarian P. GRIFFITHS; publ. *Home Office List of Publications* (annually).

Hounslow Library Services: Community Initiatives Partnership, The Civic Centre, Lampton Rd, Hounslow, Middx, TW3 4DN; tel. (181) 862-5797; f. 1965; Librarian G. C. ALLEN.

House of Commons Library: London, SW1A 0AA; tel. (171) 219-4272; f. 1818; contains over 150,000 volumes, plus Parliamentary Papers; the reference library files contain more than 1,500 periodicals and newspapers; the research division issues internal reference sheets and background papers on subjects of current interest to Members; library private to MPs; the Public Information Office handles enquiries on Parliament from the general public; Librarian JENNIFER TANFIELD; publs *Weekly Information Bulletin*, *Sessional Digest*, *Factsheets*.

House of Lords Library: London, SW1A 0PW; tel. (171) 219-5242; fax (171) 219-6396; f. 1826; library of *c.* 120,000 vols, legal and Parliamentary, history, general literature and reference; Librarian DAVID L. JONES.

Imperial College of Science, Technology and Medicine Libraries: South Kensington, London, SW7 2AZ; tel. (171) 594-8820; fax (171) 584-3763; e-mail library@ic.ac.uk; Central Library (Lyon Playfair Library),; f. 1962, shares some collections with Science Museum Library, includes Haldane Collection of non-scientific literature; 13 departmental libraries, 4 School of Medicine libraries; library of 750,000 vols; Dir of Library and Audiovisual Services MAGDA CZIGANY.

Imperial College School of Medicine at St Mary's Library: Norfolk Place, Paddington, London, W2 1PG; tel. (171) 594-3692; f. 1854; library of 31,000 vols; Librarian N. D. PALMER.

Inner Temple Library: Temple, London, EC4Y 7DA; tel. (171) 797-8217; e-mail enquiries@innertemplelibrary.org.uk; f. *c.* 1500; library of 100,000 vols; mostly legal and historical; contains, in addition to UK law and legal history, an extensive collection of law relating to the Commonwealth. Collection of 10,000 MSS, including Petyt MSS, available to the public (on special application) for historical research; Librarian MARGARET CLAY.

Institute of Advanced Legal Studies Library: 17 Russell Square, London, WC1B 5DR; tel. (171) 637-1731; fax (171) 436-8824; e-mail ials.lib@sas.ac.uk; f. 1947; library of 230,000 vols, 2,800 current serials; comprehensive collection of legal literature (except for Oriental laws and literature of East European law in East European languages), with special emphasis on English law, the legal systems of the Commonwealth, United States law, Western European law, Latin American law, international law; special collection: Foreign and Commonwealth Office Commonwealth Law Library; Librarian JULES WINTERTON.

Institute of Contemporary History—Wiener Library: 4 Devonshire St, London, W1N 2BH; tel. (171) 636-7247; fax (171) 436-6428; e-mail lib@wl.u-net.com; f. in Amsterdam in 1933 by Dr Alfred Wiener, moved to London 1939; library of about 50,000 vols, 2,500 periodicals, 2,000 microfilms, magazines, press archives, photos and other documents on Nazism, Fascism, anti-Semitism, racialism, refugee and minority problems. Jewish history and contemporary European, Jewish and Middle Eastern history; Dir Prof. DAVID CESARANI; Librarian MARGOT TRASK; publs *The Wiener Library Catalogue Series*, *Journal of Contemporary History*.

Institute of Historical Research Library: University of London, Senate House, London, WC1E 7HU; tel. (171) 636-0272; e-mail ihrlib@sas.ac.uk; f. 1921; library of 157,000 vols; Librarian ROBERT LYONS.

Institute of Materials Library: 1 Carlton House Terrace, London, SW1Y 5DB; tel. (171) 451-7360; fax (171) 451-7349; e-mail hilda_kaune@materials.org.uk; f. 1869; library of 5,000 vols, 50 current periodicals; Information Officer HILDA KAUNE.

Institution of Electrical Engineers' Library: Savoy Place, London, WC2R 0BL; tel. (171) 344-5461; fax (171) 497-3557; e-mail libdesk@iee.org.uk; f. 1871; the main collection contains over 70,000 books, 200,000 bound volumes of periodicals, 20,000 reports, pamphlets, etc.; 1,100 periodicals are received; special collections of historical electrical works; Sir Francis Ronalds Collection (6,000 vols and pamphlets), Silvanus P. Thompson Library (4,500 vols and 8,000 pamphlets), Faraday MSS, and library, notebooks and MSS of Oliver Heaviside; holds Library of British Computer Society (5,000 vols and 100 periodicals); produces INSPEC database and provides specialised information services; Librarian JOHN W. COUPLAND; publs numerous journals, books and abstracting services on physics, electronics, electrical engineering, computing and manufacturing engineering control.

Islington Libraries: Central Library, 2 Fieldway Crescent, London, N5 1PF; tel. (171) 619-6900; fax (171) 619-6939; f. 1905; library of 544,357 vols; Borough Librarian E. ROBERTS.

Kensington and Chelsea Libraries and Arts Service: Central Library, Phillimore Walk, London, W8 7RX; tel. (171) 937-2542; fax (171) 361-2976; f. 1888; library of 620,000 vols; the system includes the Chelsea Library, Chelsea Old Town Hall, Kings Rd, London, SW3 5EZ; 4 brs, mobile library, art gallery at Leighton House, 12 Holland Park Rd, London, W14 8LZ; Linley Sambourne House, 18 Stafford Tce, London W8 7BH; special collections: genealogy and heraldry, biography, languages, folklore, costume and local history; Dir of Libraries and Arts C. J. KOSTER.

King's College London Library: Strand, London, WC2R 2LS; tel. (171) 873-2139; fax (171) 872-0207; f. 1829; library of 1,200,000 vols; Dir of Library Services A. E. BELL.

Kingston-upon-Thames Public Libraries: Fairfield Rd, Kingston-upon-Thames, Surrey, KT1 2PS; tel. (181) 547-6413; fax (181) 547-6426; f. 1882; library of 230,000 vols; Head of Cultural Services SCOTT HERBERTSON.

Lambeth Directorate of Environmental Services, Libraries: 5th Floor, Courtenay House, 9–15 New Park Road, London, SW2 4DU; tel. (171) 926-7124; fax (171) 926-0161; f. 1888; library of over 600,000 vols; Library Services Man. (vacant).

Lambeth Palace Library: Lambeth, London, SE1 7JU; tel. (171) 928-6222; fax (171) 928-7932; f. 1610; wide-ranging collections, especially for church history; 200,000 printed items and 4,000 vols of MSS dating from 9th to 20th centuries; Sion College Library MSS and early printed books; also large archival collections; Librarian and Archivist Dr R. J. PALMER.

Law Society Library: 113 Chancery Lane, London, WC2A 1PL; tel. (171) 320-5946; fax (171) 831-1687; e-mail lib-enq@lawsociety.org.uk; f. 1828; library of 45,000 vols, primarily English legal material; Librarian LYNN QUINEY.

Lewisham Library Service: Education and Community Services, C/o 3rd Floor, Laurence House, Catford, London SE6 4RU; tel. (181) 695-6000 ext. 8024; fax (181) 690-4392; f. 1890; library of 700,000 vols; 12 brs, Central Reference Library, Local Studies Centre, Open Learning Centre; Head of Libraries JULIA NEWTON (acting); publs *Looking Back at Lewisham*, local history publs.

Library Association Library: see British Library.

Library of Anti-Slavery International: The Stableyard, Broomgrove Rd, London, SW9 9TL; tel. (171) 924-9555; fax (171) 738-4110; e-mail antislavery@gn.apc.org; historical literature of anti-slavery movement and human rights issues; 3,000 books, and journals, pamphlets, reports; Librarian CAROLINE MOORHEAD.

Library of the Theosophical Society in England: 50 Gloucester Place, London, W1H 4EA; tel. (171) 935-9261; f. 1875; library of 12,500 vols; publ. *Insight*.

Lincoln's Inn Library: Holborn, London, WC2A 3TN; tel. (171) 242-4371; fax (171) 404-1864; in existence 1475; library of 130,000 vols and 2,000 vols of MSS, including the Hale Collection; the oldest law library in London; Librarian G. F. HOLBORN.

Linnean Society Library: Burlington House, Piccadilly, London, W1V 0LQ; tel. (171) 434-4479; fax (171) 287-9364; f. 1788; library of 90,000 vols on natural history, including Linnaeus's own library and a collection of MSS, engravings and portraits; Librarian GINA DOUGLAS; publs *Biological Journal* (monthly), *Botanical Journal* (8 a year), *Zoological Journal* (monthly), *The Linnean Newsletter and Proceedings* (3 a year), *Annual Report*,

Synopses of the British Fauna, *Symposium* volumes.

London Library: 14 St James's Square, London, SW1Y 4LG; tel. (171) 930-7705; fax (171) 766-4766; e-mail membership@londonlibrary.co.uk; f. 1841; library of *c*. 1,000,000 vols mainly in the humanities and social sciences; open to subscribing members; an educational charity; Librarian A. S. BELL.

London Oratory Library: Brompton Rd, South Kensington, London, SW7; f. 1854; library contains 40,000 vols and 3,000 pamphlets on Theology and Church History; separate library (4,000 vols) of David Lewis, Tractarian convert.

London School of Hygiene and Tropical Medicine Library: Keppel St, Gower St, London, WC1E 7HT; tel. (171) 927-2283; telex 8953474; fax (171) 927-2273; e-mail library@lshtm.ac.uk; f. 1924; library of *c*. 72,000 vols, 800 current periodicals; tropical and preventive medicine in all aspects, many series of medical reports; Librarian R. B. FURNER; publs *Dictionary Catalogue*, *Ross Archives Catalogue*.

Marx Memorial Library: Marx House, 37A Clerkenwell Green, London, EC1R 0DU; tel. (171) 253-1485; f. 1933; library of over 100,000 vols; pamphlets, files of Labour, Socialist and Communist periodicals; special collections: Peace Movement, Spanish Civil War, USA, and the Hunger Marches; James Klugmann collection of Chartist and early British working-class history; research, reading and lending; lectures and discussion conferences; Librarian T. NEWLAND; publ. *Bulletin*.

Merton Libraries and Heritage Service: Merton Civic Centre, London Rd, Morden, Surrey, SM4 5DX; tel. (181) 545-3771; fax (181) 545-4037; f. 1887; library of 500,000 vols; special collections: William Morris, Nelson; Head of Libraries and Heritage Services JOHN PATEMAN.

Middle Temple Library (The Hon. Society of the): Middle Temple Lane, London, EC4Y 9BT; tel. (171) 427-4830; fax (171) 427-4831; f. 1641; library: contains *c*. 125,000 vols of works on British, Commonwealth, American, Public International and European Communities law; special collections: 80 incunabula, miscellaneous tracts, mainly 17th-century, 83 vols from John Donne's library; Librarian and Keeper of the Records Mrs J. EDGELL.

Ministry of Defence Whitehall Library: 3-5 Great Scotland Yard, London SW1A 2HW; tel. (171) 218-4445; fax (171) 218-5413; library: main library contains 750,000 vols; covers defence policy, defence forces, military, naval and aviation history and technology, politics, economics, biography, science and technology, management and computer science; 1,100 periodical titles; Chief Librarian R. H. SEARLE; publ. *MoD Library Bulletin*.

National Art Library: Victoria and Albert Museum, Cromwell Rd, London, SW7 2RL; tel. (171) 938-8315; fax (171) 938-8461; e-mail enquiry@nal.vam.ac.uk; f. 1837; a reference library for the int. documentation of art and design; *c*. 1 million vols on art and allied subjects; special collections: Dyce (1869) and Forster (1876) literary libraries, Clements Collection of armorial book-bindings, Piot Collection of festival literature, and many others; administers Archive of Art and Design (23 Blythe Rd, Olympia, London; tel. (171) 603-1514; fax (171) 602-6907; collection of principally 20th-century archives of designers, design associations and companies involved in the design process); Keeper and Chief Librarian JAN VAN DER WATEREN.

National Film and Television Archive: 21 Stephen St, London, W1P 1PL; tel. (171) 255-1444; telex 27624; fax (171) 580-7503; f. 1935 as a division of the British Film Institute; 350,000 film and TV titles; preserves for posterity, and makes available for study, cinematograph films and TV programmes, stills, posters and set designs of artistic and historical value; includes J. Paul Getty Jr Conservation Centre (in Berkhamsted); Curator ANNE FLEMING.

Natural History Museum Library and Archives: Cromwell Rd, London, SW7 5BD; tel. (171) 938-9191; fax (171) 938-9290; e-mail library@nhm.ac.uk; f. 1881; library of 1,000,000 vols covering botany, entomology, museum techniques, palaeontology, mineralogy, parasitology, physical anthropology; special collections: Carl Linnaeus, Sir Joseph Banks; 1,800 MS colln, 100,000 original works of art; Head, Dept of Library and Information Services Dr R. LESTER; publs *Bulletin* (4 series: *Botany, Entomology, Geology, Zoology*), scientific books, leaflets, special publs.

Newham Public Libraries: East Ham Library, High St South, London, E6 4EL; tel. (181) 472-1430; f. 1965; library of 500,530 vols, 57,243 reference stock, 14,031 audio items; Chief Librarian (vacant).

Partnership House Mission Studies Library: 157 Waterloo Rd, London, SE1 8XA; tel. (171) 928-8681; fax (171) 928-3627; e-mail c.rowe@mailbox.ulcc.ac.uk; f. 1988 from post-1945 collections of fmr Church Missionary Society and United Society for the Propagation of the Gospel libraries; houses the CMS Max Warren collection; library of 25,000 vols on missiology, growth of the Church worldwide and its social concerns, comparative religion, ecumenical movement; Librarian COLIN E. ROWE.

Public Record Office: Ruskin Ave, Kew, Richmond, Surrey, TW9 4DU; tel. (181) 876-3444; fax (181) 878-8905; f. 1838; National Repository for records of central government of the United Kingdom and the Law Courts of England and Wales; over 50 million documents on 92 miles of shelving; incorporates commercial Image Library; Keeper of Public Records S. TYACKE.

Queen Mary and Westfield College Library: Mile End Rd, London, E1 4NS; tel. (171) 775-3300; fax (181) 981-0028; f. 1887; library of 600,000 vols on the arts, sciences, engineering, medicine, social studies and law; European Documentation Centre; Librarian B. MURPHY.

Medical libraries:

St Bartholomew's and the Royal London School of Medicine and Dentistry Libraries: Turner St, London, E1 2AD; tel. (171) 295-7110; fax (171) 295-7113.

Redbridge Public Libraries: Central Library, Clements Rd, Ilford, Essex, IG1 1EA; tel. (181) 478-7145; fax (181) 553-3299; e-mail martin.timms@redbridge.gov.uk; library: adult and reference 470,000 vols, children's 126,000 vols, recorded sound 40,517 items; 8 brs, 3 mobile libraries; special collection: social problems and services; Chief Librarian M. TIMMS; publ. *Introduction to Service* (irregularly).

Richmond upon Thames Public Libraries: Central Lending Library, Little Green, Richmond, Surrey TW9 1QL; tel. (181) 940-0981; fax (181) 940-7516; Central Reference Library: Old Town Hall, Whittaker Ave, Richmond, Surrey, TW9 1TP; tel. (181) 940-5529; fax (181) 940-6899; f. 1880; library of 371,780 vols; includes Richmond Local Studies Collection and Twickenham Local Studies Collection; Head of Libraries and Resources JOHN WRIGHT.

Royal Academy of Arts Library: Burlington House, London, W1V 0DS; tel. (171) 300-5737; telex 21812; fax (171) 300-5765; e-mail 106003.1303@compuserve.com; f. 1768; library of 35,000 vols on the fine arts and standard reference books; also original drawings, MSS and engravings; Librarian NICHOLAS SAVAGE.

Royal Academy of Music Library: Marylebone Rd, London, NW1 5HT; tel. (171) 873-7323; fax (171) 873-7322; e-mail library@ram.ac.uk; f. 1822; library of 150,000 vols, 5,500 sets of orchestral parts, sound recordings; special collections include MSS and early editions, Sir Henry Wood Library, Angelina Goetz Library, David Munrow Library, Sullivan Archive, Robert Spencer Collection; Librarian KATHRYN ADAMSON (acting).

Royal Asiatic Society Library: 60 Queen's Gardens, London, W2 3AF; tel. (171) 724-4741; f. 1823; library of *c*. 100,000 vols dealing with Asia, and 2,000 Oriental MSS; Librarian M. J. POLLOCK; publs *Journal of the Royal Asiatic Society* (3 a year), monographs.

Royal Astronomical Society Library: Burlington House, Piccadilly, London, W1V 0NL; tel. (171) 734-4582; fax (171) 494-0166; e-mail info@ras.org.uk; f. 1820; library of 31,000 vols, plus archives, dealing with astronomy, history of astronomy and geophysics; Librarian P. D. HINGLEY.

Royal Botanic Gardens, Kew, Library and Archives: Kew, Richmond, Surrey, TW9 3AE; tel. (181) 332-5414; telex 296694; fax (181) 332-5278; f. 1852; library of over 120,000 vols, 4,000 periodicals, 140,000 pamphlets, 175,000 plant illustrations; approved place of deposit for own records; botany (especially taxonomic, floristic and economic aspects), horticulture, conservation, also biochemistry, anatomy, genetics, molecular systematics, propagation and seed storage; registered files and 250,000 letters and MSS; Head of Library and Archives S. M. D. FITZGERALD.

Royal College of Art Library: Kensington Gore, London, SW7 2EU; tel. (171) 590-4444; fax (171) 590-4500; f. 1953; library of 70,000 vols on the visual arts, history and philosophy of design, history and criticism of the arts; Colour Reference Library: a comprehensive collection of books and articles on all aspects of colour; Head of Information Services and Librarian ANNE GEORGE.

Royal College of Music Library: Prince Consort Rd, South Kensington, London, SW7 2BS; tel. (171) 589-3643; fax (171) 589-7740; e-mail pthompson@rcm.ac.uk; f. 1883; library of *c*. 200,000 vols, incl. MSS and early printed music; admission for reference only; Chief Librarian PAMELA THOMPSON.

Royal College of Physicians' Library and Archives: 11 St Andrew's Place, Regent's Park, London, NW1 4LE; tel. (171) 935-1174; fax (171) 487-5218; e-mail info@rcplondon.ac.uk; f. 1518; library of 60,000 vols (mostly related to history of medicine, but some on current medical issues), 100 incunabula, 200 linear metres of MSS, 30,000 portrait photographs and other pictorial items; Historical Resources Man. GEOFFREY DAVENPORT; publs *Munk's Roll* (Lives of Fellows of the College, 9 volumes 1878 – 1994), *Evan Bedford Library of Cardiology: catalogue*, exhibition catalogues, etc.

Royal College of Surgeons of England Library: 35-43 Lincoln's Inn Fields, London, WC2A 3PN; tel. (171) 973-2137; fax (171) 405-4438; e-mail library@rcseng.ac.uk; f. 1800; medical and surgical books and 400 current periodicals; 150,000 volumes; Librarian I. F. LYLE; publs *English Books before 1701* (1963), *Annals*.

Royal College of Veterinary Surgeons' Wellcome Library: Belgravia House, 62 – 64 Horseferry Rd, London, SW1P 2AF; tel. (171) 222-2021; fax (171) 222-2004; e-mail library@

rcvs.org.uk; f. 1842; open to all qualified veterinary surgeons; library of 30,000 vols; Librarian TOM ROPER.

Royal Geographical Society (with the Institute of British Geographers) Library: Kensington Gore, London, SW7 2AR; tel. (171) 591-3000; fax (171) 591-3001; e-mail info@rgs.org; f. 1830; library of 150,000 vols on geography, 800 periodicals; Map Room: 800,000 maps and charts, 3,000 atlases, large selection of gazetteers and expedition reports; Librarian R. M. ROWE; Map Curator F. HERBERT.

Royal Institute of International Affairs Library: 10 St James's Square, London, SW1Y 4LE; tel. (171) 957-5723; fax (171) 957-5710; e-mail libenquire@riia.org; f. 1920; library of 130,000 vols, 450 current periodicals and newspapers; over 5 million classified cuttings from the international press from 1924 to 1939 (on microfilm) and 1972 to July 1997: (further 5 million cuttings for 1940 – 71 at British Library Newspaper Library); Librarian SUSAN J. BOYDE.

Royal Institution of Great Britain Library: 21 Albemarle St, London, W1X 4BS; tel. (171) 409-2992; fax (171) 629-3569; e-mail ril@ri.ac.uk; f. 1799; library of 50,000 vols on all branches of science; 150 periodicals currently received; special collections: solid state chemistry, catalysis, scientific biography, social relations of science, popular science, history of science, early scientific books and journals especially of 18th and 19th centuries; archives and MSS of many scientists who have worked at the Institution, including Davy, Faraday, Tyndall, Dewar and the Braggs; Head of Collections Dr FRANK JAMES.

Royal National Institute for Deaf People (RNID) Library: 330 – 332 Gray's Inn Rd, London, WC1X 8EE; tel. (171) 915-1553; f. 1911; 16,000 books and 200 current journals on all aspects of deafness and other communication disorders; Librarian MARY PLACKETT.

Royal Society Library: 6 Carlton House Terrace, London, SW1Y 5AG; tel. (171) 451-2606; fax (171) 930-2170; e-mail library@royalsoc.ac.uk; f. 1660; history of science and scientists, science policy, science education, public understanding of science; library of *c.* 150,000 vols.

Royal Society of Chemistry Library and Information Centre: Burlington House, Piccadilly, London, W1V 0BN; tel. (171) 437-8656; fax (171) 287-9798; f. 1841; library of 70,000 vols; Librarian P. O'N. HOEY.

Royal Society of Medicine Library: 1 Wimpole St, London, W1M 8AE; tel. (171) 290-2940; fax (171) 290-2939; f. 1805; library of *c.* 500,000 vols, *c.* 2,000 current periodicals; lending restricted to members; back-up library to British Library; worldwide mail order photocopy service; Dir of Information Services DAVID STEWART.

Royal United Services Institute for Defence Studies Library: Whitehall, London, SW1A 2ET; tel. (171) 930-5854; fax (171) 321-0943; e-mail defence@rusids.demon.co.uk; f. 1831; library of 20,000 vols, 200 periodicals on British defence and related subjects, international affairs; Dir Rear Adm. RICHARD COBBOLD.

St Bride Printing Library: Bride Lane, Fleet St, London, EC4Y 8EE; tel. (171) 353-4660; fax (171) 583-7073; f. 1895; printing, papermaking, bookbinding, illustration, graphic design; 40,000 books and pamphlets, 2,000 periodicals; early technical literature, drawings, MSS, prospectuses, patents, materials for printing and type founding; Librarian JAMES MOSLEY.

St Paul's Cathedral Library: London, EC4M 8AE; tel. (171) 246-8345; fax (171) 248-3104; f. 1707; containing old works on theology and Greek and Latin classics, also some interesting MSS; library of 13,500 vols and 11,500 pamphlets; Librarian J. WISDOM.

School of Oriental and African Studies Library: University of London, Thornhaugh St, Russell Square, London, WC1H 0XG; tel. (171) 323-6109; fax (171) 636-2834; f. 1916; library of 859,000 vols and pamphlets, 4,500 periodicals, 2,700 MSS and archive collections dealing with Asian and African languages, literature, philosophy, religions, history, law, cultural anthropology, art and archaeology, social sciences; back-up library to the British Library for loans; Librarian MARY AUCKLAND.

School of Slavonic and East European Studies Library: University of London, Senate House, London, WC1E 7HU; tel. (171) 637-4934; fax (171) 436-8916; e-mail ssees-library@ssees.ac.uk; f. 1915; library of 330,000 vols on the history, language, literature, politics, economics and contemporary life of Russia, Finland, and the countries of eastern and south-eastern Europe; Librarian J. E. O. SCREEN.

Science Museum Library: Imperial College Rd, South Kensington, London, SW7 5NH; tel. (171) 938-8234; fax (171) 938-9714; e-mail smlinfo@nmsi.ac.uk; f. 1883; a national library of pure and applied science specializing in the history and public understanding of science and technology; shares collections and services with the Central Library of Imperial College of Science, Technology and Medicine; library of 600,000 vols including 21,000 periodicals, of which some 2,500 titles are current; archival collections; Comben collection of early veterinary books; photocopying, photographic and information services; Head of Library P. DINGLEY.

Sir John Soane's House and Museum Library: 13 Lincoln's Inn Fields, London, WC2A 3BP; tel. (171) 405-2107; fax (171) 831-3957; f. 1837; library: contains Sir John Soane's collection of some 8,000 vols on art, antiquities, architecture, classical and general literature, architectural drawings, personal and business archive; Archivist SUSAN PALMER.

Societies for the Promotion of Hellenic and Roman Studies Joint Library: Senate House, Malet St, London, WC1E 7HU; tel. (171) 862-8709; fax (171) 862-8735; e-mail ch.annis@sas.ac.uk; f. 1879; since 1953 run in association with London University's Institute of Classical Studies Library; 82,000 books and 17,000 periodicals, vols on classical archaeology, art, history, religion, philosophy, language and literature; 530 current periodicals; classified collection of 6,500 coloured slides; Librarian C. H. ANNIS.

Society of Antiquaries Library: Burlington House, Piccadilly, London, W1V 0HS; tel. (171) 734-0193; fax (171) 287-6967; e-mail soc.antiq.lond@dial.pipex.com; f. 1707; contains more than 130,000 books and 650 current periodicals on British and foreign archaeology and history, heraldry, genealogy, etc.; MSS, prints, drawings, early printed books, brass rubbings, seal casts; Librarian E. B. NURSE; publs *Antiquaries Journal* (annually), *Archaeologia*, research reports (occasionally).

Southwark Libraries: Headquarters, 15 Spa Rd, London, SE16 3QW; tel. (171) 525-1993; fax (171) 525-1505; library of 600,000 vols; special collection: computer science; 50,000 tapes, CDs, videos; 13 brs; Art Gallery; 2 museums; Arts, Libraries and Museums Man. ADRIAN OLSEN.

Supreme Court Library: Royal Courts of Justice, Strand, London, WC2A 2LL; tel. (171) 936-6587; fax (171) 936-6661; f. 1970; library of 300,000 vols; special collections: Court of Appeal (Civil Division) Transcripts 1950 – ; Immigration Appeal Tribunal Determinations 1970 – ; old editions of legal textbooks (in Supreme Court Library (Bar), f. 1883); Librarian Mrs S. PHILLIPS.

Surrey County Libraries and Leisure Service: Weston House, 7 Penrhyn Rd, Kingston upon Thames, KT1 2DN; tel. (181) 541-9911; fax (181) 541-9871; library of 1,913,000 vols, 78,400 audiovisual items; Dir J. A. SAUNDERS.

Sutton Leisure Services: Central Library, St Nicholas Way, Sutton, Surrey, SM1 1EA; tel. (181) 770-4700; fax (181) 770-4777; f. 1936; 9 libraries; library of 537,472 vols; 46,577 audio items, 11,037 visual items; special collection: genealogy and heraldry; Head of Libraries and Heritage T. J. KNIGHT.

Thames Valley University Learning Resource Centres: University Centre for Complementary Learning, St Mary's Rd, London, W5 5RF; tel. (181) 231-2246; fax (181) 231-2631; f. 1992; library of 160,000 vols; Learning Resources Man. P. R. MOUNTJOY.

Tower Hamlets Public Libraries: C/o Head of Libraries, Bancroft Library, Bancroft Rd, London, E1 4DQ; tel. (181) 980-4366; f. 1965; library of 627,564 vols; special collections: General, American, French, German, Portuguese literature and texts; Local History library; collection of books in Urdu, Bengali, Punjabi, Hindi, Gujerati, Chinese and Vietnamese; gramophone records and tape cassettes; video cassettes, compact discs; Head of Libraries ANNE CUNNINGHAM.

Treasury and Cabinet Office Library: Parliament St, London, SW1P 3AG; tel. (171) 270-5290; fax (171) 270-5681; library of 120,000 vols; 1,500 periodicals; covers economics, finance and public administration; Librarian JEAN CLAYTON.

United Nations Information Centre Library: 21st Floor, Millbank Tower 21/24 Millbank, London, SW1P 4QH; tel. (171) 630-1981; fax (171) 976-6478; e-mail info@uniclondon.org; f. 1946; maintains collection of official United Nations documents and publications, and selected specialized agency publications; Librarian ALEXANDRA MCLEOD.

University College London Library: Gower St, London, WC1E 6BT; tel. (171) 380-7700; fax (171) 380-7373; e-mail library@ucl.ac.uk; f. 1828; *c.* 1.25 million books and periodicals, and includes several important collections of research interest, e.g. manuscripts of Jeremy Bentham, papers of Sir Edwin Chadwick, C. H. Barlow Dante collection augmented by libraries of Sir John Rotton and Mr H. St John Brooks, J. T. Graves mathematical library, Whitley Stokes Celtic library, C. K. Ogden library including correspondence of Lord Brougham, and scripts and letters of George Orwell; houses Mocatta library of Anglo-Judaica, and libraries of British Society of Franciscan Studies, Folklore Society, Geologist's Association, Hertfordshire Natural History Society, Huguenot Society, London Mathematical Society, Malacological Society, Philological Society, Royal Historical Society, Royal Statistical Society, Viking Society for Northern Research; Dir of Library Sevices PAUL AYRIS.

Includes the following institute libraries:

Institute of Archaeology Library: 31-34 Gordon Square, London, WC1H 0PY; tel. (171) 380-7485.

Institute of Child Health Library: 30 Guildford St, London, WC1N 1EH; tel. (171) 242-4789.

Institute of Laryngology and Otology Library: Royal National Throat, Nose & Ear Hospital, Gray's Inn Rd, London, WC1X 8EE; tel. (171) 837-8855.

Institute of Neurology: The National Hospital, Queen Square, London, WC1N 3BG; tel. (171) 829-8709.

Institute of Ophthalmology Library: Bath St, London, EC1V 9EL; tel. (171) 608-6814.

Institute of Orthopaedics Library: Royal National Orthopaedic Hospital, Brockley Hill, Stanmore, HA7 4LP; tel. (181) 954-2300.

University of Greenwich Library: Woolwich Campus, Beresford St, Woolwich, London, SE18 6BU; tel. (181) 331-8192; fax (181) 331-9084; Librarian DENIS HEATHCOTE.

University of London Library: Senate House, Malet St, London, WC1E 7HU; tel. (171) 862-8500; fax (171) 862-8400; e-mail ull@ull.ac.uk; f. 1838; library of 2,000,000 vols, principally in the arts, humanities and social sciences, for reference and loan, including special collections, e.g., Goldsmiths' Library of Economic Literature, Harry Price Collection, Sterling Library, Durning-Lawrence Library, Eliot-Phelips Collection, Bromhead Library, Carlton Shorthand Collection, Porteus Library, Malcolm Morley Theatre Collection and the Libraries of the Canadian and Australian High Commissions; Librarian EMMA ROBINSON.

Upper Norwood Joint Library: Westow Hill, London, SE19 1TJ; tel. (181) 670-2551; fax (181) 670-5468; f. 1900; library of 90,000 vols; collections on the Crystal Palace and its historical background, the Gerald Massey collection; Librarian CHRISTOPHER DOBB.

Vaughan Williams Memorial Library: Cecil Sharp House, 2 Regents Park Rd, London, NW1 7AY; tel. (171) 284-0523; fax (171) 284-0523; f. 1930; maintained by the English Folk Dance and Song Society (*q.v.*); England's main source of information on traditional song, dance, customs and folk culture; contains books and pamphlets, periodicals, MS collections, photographs and slides, films and videos, records and tapes, wax cylinders, phonographic recordings, microfilms, press cuttings, broadsides; open to the public for reference; Librarian MALCOLM TAYLOR.

Victoria and Albert Museum, Library of the: see National Art Library.

Waltham Forest Public Libraries: Central Library, High St, Walthamstow, London, E17 7JN; tel. (181) 520-3031; fax (181) 509-9539; f. 1893; library of 448,427 vols; special collections: Cookery, Domestic Economy, Fiction Authors U, V; Librarian COLIN RICHARDSON.

Wandsworth Public Libraries: Town Hall, Wandsworth High St, London, SW18 2PU; tel. (181) 871-6364; fax (181) 871-7630; f. 1883; library of 929,113 vols; 12 brs; 2 reference libraries, 2 music libraries, local history library, mobile services; special collections: architecture, town planning, European history, geography and travel, occult sciences, local history, early children's books, G. A. Henty; Librarian D. F. PARKER.

Warburg Institute Library: Woburn Square, London, WC1H 0AB; tel. (171) 580-9663; fax (171) 436-2852; f. 1922; library of 300,000 vols, 1,260 current serials; cultural and intellectual history of Europe from Classical Antiquity to modern times, including history of art, literature, science, religion, humanism; houses libraries of the Royal and British Numismatic Societies; Librarian Dr W. F. RYAN.

Wellcome Institute for the History of Medicine Library: 183 Euston Rd, London, NW1 2BE; tel. (171) 611-8582; fax (171) 611-8369; f. *c.* 1890, opened to public 1949; over 600 incunabula; 600,000 books; broadsides; 50,000 pamphlets, 2,700 periodical titles; 7,000 Western MSS; 11,000 Oriental MSS in 43 languages; 100,000 autograph letters; 100,000 prints, drawings, photographs, paintings; medical imprints of the colonial Americas 1557 – 1833; 450 collections of medical archives; Librarian DAVID R. S. PEARSON; publs *Medical History* (quarterly), *Current Work in the History of Medicine* (bibliographical quarterly).

Westminster Abbey Library and Muniment Room: London, SW1P 3PA; tel. (171) 222-5152 ext. 228; fax (171) 222-6391; f. 1623 – 25; library of *c.* 14,000 vols, mainly 16th- to 18th-century, predominantly theological but with general literature and music; Abbey Records and other documents, of 11th to 20th centuries; Librarian Dr T. TROWLES; Keeper of Muniments Dr R. MORTIMER.

Zoological Society Library: Regent's Park, London, NW1 4RY; tel. (171) 449-6293; fax (171) 586-5743; f. 1826; library: contains about 180,000 vols, 1,300 current periodicals connected with zoology and animal conservation; photograph library; Librarian A. SYLPH.

Loughborough

Loughborough University: Pilkington Library: Loughborough, Leics, LE11 3TU; tel. (1509) 222360; fax (1509) 223993; f. 1911; library of 550,000 vols, 4,000 periodicals; includes the University Archives; University Librarian M. D. MORLEY.

Luton

Luton Libraries, Information and Communications Service: Luton Central Library, St George's Square, Luton, LU1 2NG; tel. (1582) 547440; fax (1582) 547461; e-mail evansr@luton.gov.uk; Libraries, Information and Communications Man. JEAN GEORGE.

Maidenhead

Royal Borough of Windsor and Maidenhead Libraries: Maidenhead Library, St Ives Rd, Maidenhead, SL6 1QU; tel. (1628) 625657; fax (1628) 770054; Head of Library Services MARK TAYLOR.

Maidstone

Kent Arts and Libraries Department: Springfield, Maidstone, Kent, ME14 2LH; tel. (1622) 696511; fax (1622) 690897; f. 1921; library of 3,300,000 vols; Dir of Arts and Libraries YINNON EZRA.

Manchester

Chetham's Library: Long Millgate, Manchester, M3 1SB; tel. (161) 834-7961; fax (161) 839-5797; f. 1653 as a free public reference library; library of *c.* 100,000 vols including many 17th and 18th century works; local history records; Librarian Dr M. R. POWELL.

John Rylands University Library of Manchester: University of Manchester, Oxford Rd, Manchester, M13 9PP; tel. (161) 275-3738; fax (161) 273-7488; f. 1972 by merger of John Rylands Library (f. 1900) with Manchester University Library (f. 1851); 3,500,000 printed books, over 1,000,000 MS or archival items, 800,000 titles on microform, 6,800 serials currently received; numerous special collections, several of international renown such as Althorp Library of 2nd Earl Spencer and manuscript portion of Bibliotheca Lindesiana, containing, *inter alia*, 220,000 books printed before 1801, amongst them *c.* 4,500 incunabula and 1,500 Aldines; Librarian C. J. HUNT; publs include *Bulletin* (3 a year), *John Rylands Research Institute Prospectus*.

Manchester Libraries and Theatres: Central Library, St Peter's Square, Manchester, M2 5PD; tel. (161) 234-1900; fax (161) 234-1963; f. 1852; library of 2,430,000 vols, 141,000 audio-visual items; includes social sciences, commercial, arts, music, Chinese, languages and literature, technical, local studies, European information and general libraries, and a unit for the visually impaired; two library theatres with resident company; 23 brs, offering Afro-Caribbean, Asian, Vietnamese and community resource services, with 3 mobile libraries and a housebound readers' service; libraries in old people's homes, hospitals and prisons; special collections incl. the Newman Flowers, Henry Watson, and Gaskell; Dir D. OWEN.

Manchester Metropolitan University Library: All Saints Library, All Saints Bldg, Manchester Metropolitan University, Manchester, M15 6BH; tel. (161) 247-6104; fax (161) 247-6349; library of 1,000,000 vols; Librarian Prof. COLIN HARRIS.

Matlock

Derbyshire County Council Libraries and Heritage: County Hall, Matlock, Derbyshire, DE4 3AG; tel. (1629) 580000; fax (1629) 585363; f. 1923; library of 1,100,000 vols; 46 brs; Dir of Libraries and Heritage MARTIN MOLLOY.

Merthyr Tydfil

Merthyr Tydfil County Borough Library: Central Library, High St, Merthyr Tydfil, CF47 8AF; tel. (1685) 723057; fax (1685) 370690; library of 175,000 vols; 4 brs; Libraries and Arts Officer GERAINT H. JAMES.

Middlesbrough

Middlesbrough Borough Libraries: Central Library, Victoria Square, Middlesbrough, TS1 2AY; tel. (1642) 263358; fax (1642) 230690; library of 500,000 vols; central library, 11 brs; Head of Libraries and Information Services NEIL BENNETT.

University of Teesside Library: Library and Information Services, Borough Road, Middlesbrough, TS1 3BA; tel. (1642) 342103; fax (1642) 342190; library of 290,000 vols; Dir IAN C. BUTCHART.

Milton Keynes

Milton Keynes Council Library Service: Milton Keynes Central Library, 555 Silbury Blvd, Central Milton Keynes, MK9 3HL; tel. (1908) 835010; fax (1908) 835028; Chief Librarian WILLIAM PEARSON.

Open University Library: Walton Hall, Milton Keynes, MK7 6AA; tel. (1908) 653138; fax (1908) 653571; f. 1969; library of 161,000 vols; Dir of Library Services NICKY WHITSED.

Mold

Denbighshire County Council, Library and Information Service: County Hall, Mold, CH7 6GR; tel. (1824) 706773; fax (1824) 706775; library of 349,665 vols; 9 libraries, 2 mobile libraries, 1 library for the housebound; special collections: Welsh music, local history; Chief Officer W. GWYN WILLIAMS.

Flintshire Library and Information Service: County Hall, Mold, CH7 6NW; tel. (1352) 704400; fax (1352) 753662; e-mail flintslib@dial.pipex.com; 20 libraries, 2 mobile libraries, 1 library for the housebound; special collections: Arthurian literature, local studies; Wales Euro Information Centre; Head of Libraries and Archives LAWRENCE RAWSTHORNE.

Morpeth

Northumberland County Library: The Willows, Morpeth, Northumberland, NE61 1TA; tel. (1670) 511156; fax (1670) 518012; f. 1924; library of 635,000 vols; 35 brs, 5 mobile libraries; special collections: local history, vocal scores, cinema, drama, poetry, technical and commercial; Divisional Dir (Libraries, Arts and Heritage) D. E. BONSER.

Newbury

West Berkshire Libraries: Sundial House, Cheap St, Newbury, Berks, RG14 5BT; tel. (1635) 519830; Library and Information Man. KEN RICHARDSON.

Newcastle upon Tyne

Newcastle Libraries and Information Service: Princess Square off New Bridge St, NE99 1DX; tel. (191) 2610691; fax (191) 261-1435; f. 1880; library of 764,900 vols, 45,009 audiovisual items, 299,000 other items; Thomas Bewick Collection (wood engravings), Thomlinson Library (theological), local collections, music, business and science collections; Asst Dir (Education and Libraries) D. R. GUNN.

University of Newcastle upon Tyne, The Robinson Library: Newcastle upon Tyne, NE2 4HQ; tel. (191) 2226000; f. 1871 as Library of Durham College of Physical Science; library of 1,000,000 vols; special collections include: Pybus (medical history), Robert White, Gertrude Bell, Runciman Papers, Trevelyan Papers, Catherine Cookson, Library of Japanese Science and Technology, Wallis; Librarian Dr T. W. GRAHAM; Library publications issued occasionally.

Newport (Isle of Wight)

Isle of Wight Council Library Services: Guildhall, High St, Newport, Isle of Wight, PO30 1TY; tel. (1983) 823822; fax (1983) 823841; 11 brs; Head of Libraries and Information Services TIM BLACKMORE.

Newport (South Wales)

Newport Libraries: Central Library, John Frost Square, Newport, NP9 1PA; tel. (1633) 265539; fax (1633) 222615; e-mail centrallibrary@newport.gov.uk; 11 brs; Borough Librarian HELEN OSBORN.

Northallerton

North Yorkshire County Library: County Library Headquarters, Grammar School Lane, Northallerton, North Yorks., DL6 1DF; tel. (1609) 776271; fax (1609) 780793; library of 1,059,000 vols; 45 brs; Head of Libraries and Arts R. DE GRAFF; publs occasional.

Northampton

Northamptonshire Libraries and Information Service: POB 259, 27 Guildhall Rd, Northampton, NN1 1BA; tel. (1604) 20262; fax (1604) 26789; f. 1927; library of 1,512,196 vols; 107,960 sound recordings and videotapes; 36 brs, 8 mobile libraries; County Librarian VERNA TAYLOR; publs *LOG* (weekly list of local government articles), *What the Papers Say* (daily).

Norwich

Norfolk Library and Information Service: County Hall, Norwich, NR1 2DH; tel. (1603) 222049; fax (1603) 222422; f. 1925, reorganised 1974; library of 1,307,000 vols; 4 core libraries; 44 brs; 3 shop libraries; 13 mobile libraries; Dir of Arts and Libraries H. HAMMOND.

Norwich Cathedral Dean and Chapter Library: Norwich, Norfolk; tel. (1603) 760285; fax (1603) 766032; a medieval monastic (Benedictine) foundation; library of over 8,000 vols, some incunabula and MSS; houses 450 vols of the Swaffham Parochial Church Library; Librarian Cathedral Office, The Close, Norwich, NR1 4EH.

University of East Anglia Library: Norwich, NR4 7TJ; tel. (1603) 592425; fax (1603) 259490; f. 1962; library of 725,000 vols; Dir of Library and Learning Resources JEAN STEWART.

Nottingham

Nottinghamshire County Library: Central Library, Angel Row, Nottingham, NG1 6HP; tel. (115) 9412121; fax (115) 950-4207; f. 1868; library of 480,000 vols, 33,000 sound recordings; special collections include local history, D. H. Lawrence, Byron and Robin Hood; Asst Dir of Leisure Services (Libraries) DAVID LATHROPE.

University of Nottingham Library: University Park, Nottingham, NG7 2RD; tel. (115) 951-4555; fax (115) 951-4558; f. (University College) 1881; *c.* 1 million vols and pamphlets; 4,600 current periodicals; MSS and archives (Portland, Newcastle, Middleton, Manvers, etc.) 3,000,000 items; special collections include D. H. Lawrence, early children's books, French Revolution, meteorology, ornithology; includes Hallward Library (arts, social sciences and education), George Green Library of Science and Engineering, Law Library, James Cameron Gifford Library of Agricultural and Food Sciences (Sutton Bonington) and Greenfield Medical Library; Dir R. E. OLDROYD.

Oakham

Rutland County Libraries: Oakham Library, Catmose St, Oakham, LE15 6HW; tel. (1572) 722918; fax (1572) 757138; Head of Libraries and Museums ROY KNIGHT.

Oxford

Bodleian Library: Oxford, OX1 3BG; tel. (1865) 277000; telex 83656; fax (1865) 277182; the library of Oxford University; f. 1602; contains 6.1 million printed vols, 154,000 MSS; includes the Old Library, the Radcliffe Camera, New Library and seven dependent libraries: the Radcliffe Science Library, the Bodleian Law Library, the Indian Institute Library, Rhodes House Library (for the history of the Commonwealth and of the United States), the Bodleian Japanese Library, the Philosophy Library and the Oriental Institute Library; a Copyright library, entitled to a free copy of every book published in the UK; Librarian R. P. CARR; publ. *The Bodleian Library Record* (every 6 months).

College libraries of the University of Oxford:

Balliol College Library: Oxford, OX1 3BJ; tel. (1865) 277709; f. 1263; library of 100,000 vols; Librarian Dr P. A. BULLOCH.

Brasenose College Library: Oxford, OX1 4AJ; tel. (1865) 277827; library of 60,000 vols; Librarian J. W. DAVIES.

Christchurch Library: Oxford, OX1 1DP; tel. (1865) 276169; e-mail library@christ-church.ox.ac.uk; library of 130,000 vols; Librarian R. F. S. HAMER.

Codrington Library (All Souls College): Oxford, OX1 4AL; tel. (1865) 279318; fax (1865) 279299; e-mail codrington.library@all-souls.ox.ac.uk; f. 1710; library of 110,000 vols; special collections: medieval and modern history, military history, strategic studies and law; Librarian Prof. I. MACLEAN.

Corpus Christi College Library: Oxford, OX1 4JF; tel. (1865) 276744; f. 1517; library of 80,000 vols, MSS; special collections: incunabula, early English printed books, 17th- and 18th-century Italian books, English, French and German books on 19th-century philosophy; Fellow Librarian J. HOWARD-JOHNSTONE; Librarian-in-Charge S. NEWTON.

Exeter College Library: Oxford, OX1 3DP; tel. (1865) 279600; Librarian Dr J. R. MADDICOTT.

Green College Library: Oxford, OX2 6HG; tel. (1865) 274770; fax (1865) 274796; e-mail gill.edwards@green.ox.ac.uk; f. 1979; library of 7,000 vols; Medicine and Social Science Librarian GILL EDWARDS.

Hertford College Library: Oxford, OX1 3BW; tel. (1865) 279409; library of 43,000 vols; 17th-century collection from Magdalen Hall (forerunner of Hertford College); Fellow Librarian Dr S. R. WEST; Librarian S. M. GRIFFIN.

Jesus College Library: Oxford, OX1 3DW; tel. (1865) 279704; Fellows' Library, f. 1571; 12,000 early printed books, 150 MSS; special collections: library of Lord Herbert of Cherbury, material relating to T. E. Lawrence (of Arabia); Meyricke Library, f. 1865; undergraduate library; library of 42,000 vols, incl. periodicals; Celtic collection; Fellow Librarian Dr T. HORDER; College Librarian Miss S. A. COBBOLD; Archivist Dr B. ALLEN.

Keble College Library: Oxford, OX1 3PG; tel. (1865) 272797; f. 1876; library of *c.* 40,000 vols in working library; special collections: medieval MSS, incunabula and early printed books, Brooke collection, Millard collection, Hatchett-Jackson collection, Port-Royal, John Keble's own library, part of Henry Liddon's library, 19th-century archive material; Librarian M. M. SZURKO.

Lincoln College Library: Oxford, OX1 3DR; tel. (1865) 279831; e-mail library@lincoln.ox.ac.uk; f. 1427; library of 30,000 vols; Librarian Mrs F. M. PIDDOCK.

Magdalen College Library: Oxford, OX1 4AU; tel. (1865) 276045; f. 1458; library of 100,000 vols; special collections: 16th- to 18th-century books, late medieval English history; Fellow Librarian C. Y. FERDINAND.

Merton College Library: Oxford, OX1 4JD; tel. (1865) 276380; fax (1865) 276361; e-mail library@merton.oxford.ac.uk; f. 1264; library of 70,000 vols; Librarian Dr A. S. BENDALL.

New College Library: Holywell St, Oxford, OX1 3BN; tel. (1865) 279580; fax (1865) 279590; f. 1379; library of 90,000 vols; special collections: medieval MSS (deposited in Bodleian Library), incunabula, early archives, modern papers of Milner Collection (deposited in Bodleian Library); Librarian S. CROMEY.

Nuffield College Library: Oxford, OX1 1NF; tel. (1865) 278550; f. 1937; library of 70,000 vols; special collections: social sciences, modern political MSS; Librarian J. LEGG.

Oriel College Library: Oxford, OX1 4EW; tel. (1865) 276558; f. 1326; library of 100,000 vols; special collection of personages who attended Oriel College; Fellow Librarian A. M. VOLFING.

Pembroke College (McGowin) Library: Oxford, OX1 1DW; tel. (1865) 276409; fax (1865) 276418; f. 1624; library of 40,000 vols; Chandler collection of Aristotelia; Fellow Librarian Prof. M. GODDEN.

Queen's College Library: Oxford, OX1 4AW; tel. (1865) 279130; fax (1865) 790819; e-mail queenlib@ermine.ox.ac.uk; library of 140,000 vols; Librarian J. B. BENGTSON.

St Edmund Hall Library: Queen's Lane, Oxford, OX1 4AR; tel. (1865) 279062; f. 17th century; library of 54,000 vols; special collections: Emden (naval and American history), Aularian (Hall members' publications), John Oldham, Thomas Hearne; Librarian DEBORAH EATON.

St John's College Library: Oxford, OX1 3JP; tel. (1865) 277300; library of 75,000 vols; Librarian Dr P. HACKER.

Trinity College Library: Oxford, OX1 3BH; tel. (1865) 279863; Librarian J. MARTIN.

University College Library: Oxford, OX1 4BH; tel. (1865) 276621; fax (1865) 276987;

f. 1249; library of 40,000 vols; special collections, including the Attlee Papers, are deposited in the Bodleian Library (see above); Librarian C. M. RITCHIE.

Wadham College Library: Oxford, OX1 3PN; tel. (1865) 277900; f. 1613; library of 55,000 vols; special collections: 16th-century theology, 17th-century science; Persian history and literature; Fellow Librarian Dr R. H. ROBBINS.

Worcester College Library: Oxford, OX1 2HB; tel. (1865) 278354; fax (1865) 278387; f. 1714; library of 75,000 vols; special collections: Clarke Papers (Civil War and Commonwealth documents), architectural books and drawings (Inigo Jones, Hawksmoor), English poetry and drama from 1550 – 1750, Pottinger collection of 19th century pamphlets; Librarian JOANNA PARKER.

Special libraries:

Ashmolean Library: Beaumont St, Oxford, OX1 2PH; tel. (1865) 278088; f. 1969, but fmrly dept of Ashmolean Museum, f. 1683; library of 180,000 vols; archaeology, ancient history and ancient Near Eastern studies, and Byzantine studies, numismatics, classical languages and literature, Western art and architecture. Special collections include Grenfell and Hunt Papyrological Library, Griffith Egyptological Library, Haverfield and Richmond Archives and original documentation of principal archaeological expeditions and explorations and classification of artefacts; Librarian B. MCGREGOR.

Taylor Institution Library: St Giles, Oxford, OX1 3NA; tel. (1865) 278158; e-mail enquiries@taylib.ox.ac.uk; f. 1849; library of 500,000 vols; Continental European languages and literature, medieval and modern, including general and historical background material and in particular older and modern editions of French, German, Italian, Spanish and Portuguese literature; Russian and other Slavonic languages and literatures; literature of modern Latin American, Celtic studies, modern Greek; philology and general linguistics; Yiddish; special collections: Voltaire and the French Enlightenment, Anglo-German literary relations, B. Constant, G. B. Guarini, East German literature; Librarian E. A. CHAPMAN.

Indian Institute Library: Broad St, Oxford, OX1 3BG; tel. (1865) 277081; fax (1865) 277182; e-mail indian.institute@bodley.ox.ac.uk; f. 1883; dept of the Bodleian Library; classical and modern South Asian studies; library of 100,000 vols, including government reports and periodicals; Librarian Dr G. A. EVISON; see also Bodleian Library.

Oxfordshire County Libraries: Holton, Oxford, OX33 1QQ; tel. (1865) 810200; fax (1865) 810207; library of 1,036,000 vols; 10,000 maps, 3,070 prints, 4,750 slides, 69,640 photographs of local history; 13,000 scores, 38,200 sound recordings and 9,500 videos; 17 full-time and 26 part-time libraries; 8 mobile libraries; 248 school libraries; County Librarian TOM FORREST.

Paisley

Renfrewshire Libraries: Marchfield Ave, Paisley, Renfrewshire, PA3 2RJ; tel. (141) 887-2468; fax (141) 848-0583; library of 418,000 vols; 20 brs; Dir of Leisure Services HOWARD HANN.

University of Paisley Library: High St, Paisley, PA1 2BE; tel. (141) 848-3758; fax (141) 887-0812; e-mail library@paisley.ac.uk; library of 200,000 vols; Chief Librarian STUART JAMES.

Peterborough

Peterborough Cathedral Library: Peterborough; tel. (1733) 562125; f. *c.* 1670 by Dean Duport; library of 8,000 vols, some important medieval MSS and many early printed books; books printed before 1800 are now deposited in the Cambridge University Library, save those of local concern; Librarian Canon J. HIGHAM.

Peterborough City Libraries: Peterborough Central Library, Broadway, Peterborough, PE1 1RX; tel. (1733) 348343; 8 brs, 2 mobile libraries; Library Man. RICHARD HEMMINGS.

Plymouth

City of Plymouth Libraries and Information Services: Central Library, Drake Circus, Plymouth, Devon, PL4 8AL; tel. (1752) 305921; fax (1752) 305929; 20 brs, 1 mobile library; City Librarian ALASDAIR MACNAUGHTAN.

Pontypool

Torfaen Libraries: Torfaen County Borough Council, Civic Centre, Pontypool, NP4 6YB; tel. (1495) 762200; library of 116,000 vols; 4 brs; Principal Librarian SUE JOHNSON.

Poole

Borough of Poole Libraries: Poole Central Library, Dolphin Centre, Poole, Dorset, BH15 1QE; tel. (1202) 673910; fax (1202) 670253; Head of Cultural Services OLIVER GREEN.

Port Talbot

Neath, Port Talbot County Borough Library: Reginald St, Velindre, Port Talbot, SA13 1YY; tel. (1639) 899829; fax (1639) 899152; library of 391,000 vols; 19 brs; County Librarian and Head of Information Services J. L. ELLIS.

Porth

Rhondda Cynon Taff County Borough Library Services: Educational Resources Centre, Grawen St, Porth, CF39 0BU; tel. (1443) 687666; fax (1443) 680286; library of 550,000 vols; 30 brs; County Borough Librarian JULIE JONES.

Portsmouth

Portsmouth City Libraries: Central Library, Guildhall Square, Portsmouth, PO1 2DX; tel. (1705) 819311; fax (1705) 839855; City Librarian JOHN THORN.

University of Portsmouth Library: Frewen Library, University of Portsmouth, Cambridge Road, Portsmouth, PO1 2ST; tel. (1705) 843222; fax (1705) 843233; library of 500,000 vols; Librarian IAN BONAR (acting).

Preston

Lancashire County Library: 143 Corporation St, Preston, PR1 2UQ; tel. (1772) 254868; fax (1772) 264880; f. 1924; library of 3,018,000 vols; 84 brs, 12 mobile libraries, 2 trailer libraries; Library Man. DAVID G. LIGHTFOOT.

Reading

Reading Borough Libraries: Central Library, Abbey Square, Reading, RG1 3BQ; tel. (118) 901-5955; fax (118) 901-5954; e-mail reading.ref@dial.pipex.com; f. 1883; library of 250,000 vols; 7 brs, 2 mobile libraries; Business Library, Local Studies Library, Music and Drama Library; Head of Libraries SARA LETT.

University of Reading Library: POB 223, Whiteknights, Reading, RG6 6AE; tel. (118) 931-8770; fax (118) 931-6636; f. 1892; library of 950,000 vols, 4,500 current periodicals; special collections include Overstone Library, Stenton Library on English history, Cole Library on early zoology, Finzi collections of music and English poetry, Turner collection of French Revolution pamphlets, Stendhal collection, agricultural history, children's books, archives of British publishers; Librarian S. M. CORRALL.

Rochester

Medway Towns Council Directorate of Leisure, Arts and Libraries: Annex A, Civic Centre, Strood, Rochester, Kent, ME2 4AU; tel. (1634) 727777; 16 brs, 1 mobile library; Asst Dir for Arts, Libraries and Heritage JANICE MASKORT.

Runcorn

Halton Borough Libraries: Halton Lea Library, Shopping City, Runcorn, WA7 2PF; tel. (1928) 715351; fax (1928) 790221; 4 brs; Head of Libraries PAULA RILEY-COOPER.

St Andrews

University of St Andrews Library: North St, St Andrews, Fife KY16 9TR; tel. (1334) 462280; fax (1334) 462282; e-mail library@st-and.ac.uk; f. 1412; library of 780,000 vols, MSS, maps and numerous special collections, including Donaldson (Classics and Education), J. D. Forbes (Science), and Von Hügel (Theology and Philosophy); Librarian N. F. DUMBLETON.

Salford

HM Customs and Excise Library: Ralli Quays, 3 Stanley St, Salford, M60 9LA; tel. (161) 827-0444; fax (161) 827-0491; f. 1991; also at New King's Beam House, 22 Upper Ground, London, SE1 9PJ; tel. (171) 865-5668; fax (171) 865-5670; f. 1671; library of *c.* 35,000 vols; Chief Librarian TONY ALBROW.

University of Salford Library: Clifford Whitworth Building, Salford, M5 4WT; tel. (161) 295-5846; fax (161) 745-5888; f. 1957; library of 500,000 vols, 2,200 periodicals; Dir of Academic Information Services Prof. M. J. CLARK.

Salisbury

Salisbury Cathedral Library: The Cathedral, Salisbury, Wilts.; f. 11th century; contains printed books and medieval MSS; open only to *bona fide* research students by appointment; an exhibition of books and documents including an original Magna Carta is on show in the Chapter House from March to December; Librarian SUZANNE EWARD.

Sheffield

Sheffield Hallam University Learning Centre: Adsetts Centre, City Campus, Sheffield, S1 1WB; tel. (114) 225-2109; fax (114) 225-3859; e-mail learning.centre@shu.ac.uk; library of 498,000 vols, 2,600 journal titles; Dir GRAHAM BULPITT.

Sheffield Libraries and Information Services: Central Library, Surrey St, Sheffield, S1 1XZ; tel. (114) 273-4711; fax (114) 273-5009; f. 1856; library of 1,333,000 vols (excluding MSS); 26 br. libraries, 5 mobile libraries and 1 travelling library; Central Library (incl. private press books, books printed in England 1765 – 79); Business and Technology Standards, Local Studies, Circulation Services (incl. Whitworth Collection of organ books, Sports Library and Information Service), Sheffield Archives (incl. Strafford papers, Edmund Burke papers, Edward Carpenter papers, Fairbank map collection); Head of Service DAVE SPENCER.

University of Sheffield Library: Western Bank, Sheffield, S. Yorks, S10 2TN; tel. (114) 222-7200; fax (114) 273-9826; library of over 1,000,000 vols; special collections include Sir Charles Firth's collection of 17th-century tracts and 19th-century broadside ballads; the Samuel Hartlib Papers; the papers of Sir Hans Krebs, FRS and Nobel Laureate; National

Fairground Archive; Sir Thomas Beecham Music Library; Librarian M. S.-M. HANNON.

Shrewsbury

Shropshire County Library Service: Column House, 7 London Rd, Shrewsbury, Shropshire, SY2 6NW; tel. (1743) 255000; fax (1743) 255050; f. 1925; library of 820,000 vols, audio-visual collections; 33 brs, 8 mobile and 1 trailer library; County Librarian TIM WILLIAMS.

Slough

Slough Borough Council Libraries and Information Service: Slough Library, High St, Slough, SL1 1EA; tel. (1753) 535166; 3 brs, 1 mobile library; Head of Libraries and Information YVONNE COPE.

Southampton

Southampton City Libraries: Central Library, Civic Centre, Southampton, SO14 7LW; tel. (1703) 832459; fax (1703) 336305; City Librarian H. A. RICHARDS.

University of Southampton Library: Southampton, SO17 1BJ; tel. (1703) 592180; fax (1703) 593007; main and branch libraries; library of 950,000 vols, 6,500 current periodicals, Wessex Medical Library, Ford Collection of Parliamentary Papers (1801 to date), Wellington Papers, Broadlands Archives (Palmerston, Shaftesbury, Mountbatten), Cope collection of Hampshire material, Perkins Agricultural Library, Parkes Library (relationship between Jewish and non-Jewish worlds), archive collections relating to Anglo-Jewry, Hampshire Field Club Library; Librarian B. NAYLOR.

Southend on Sea

Southend on Sea Borough Council Education and Libraries Department: Box 6, The Civic Centre, Victoria Ave, Southend on Sea, Essex, SS2 6DU; tel. (1702) 215921; 7 brs; Dir of Education and Libraries STEPHEN HAY.

Stafford

Staffordshire Library and Information Services: Friars Terrace, Stafford, ST17 4AY; tel. (1785) 278334; fax (1785) 278309; f. 1916; library of 1,650,000 vols; 19,800 cassettes, 63,200 compact discs, 12,000 videos; 43 static libraries; 12 mobile libraries; schools service provides books, project collections, cassettes, videos, and 2 mobile libraries; Young People's Service; Community Care Service; Information Service; County Librarian RAY HYDE.

Stirling

Stirling Library Services: Borrowmeadow Rd, Stirling, FK7 7TN; tel. (1786) 432383; library of 380,000 vols; Head of Service A. GILLIES.

University of Stirling Library: Stirling, FK9 4LA; tel. (1786) 467227; fax (1786) 466866; f. 1966; library of 450,000 vols, 2,500 periodicals; collection of works of Sir Walter Scott and contemporaries, John Grierson archive, Howietoun Fish Farm archive, labour history collection; facilities for on-line information retrieval; electronic access to databases, CD-ROMs, bulletin boards, catalogues of other libraries; Dir of Information Services and Univ. Librarian (vacant).

Stoke on Trent

Staffordshire University Library: POB 664, College Rd, Stoke on Trent, ST4 2XS; tel. (1782) 294443; fax (1782) 744035; library of 300,000 vols; Librarian KEVIN ELLARD.

Stoke on Trent City Council Libraries, Information and Archives: Civic Offices, POB 816, Glebe Street, Stoke on Trent, ST4 1HF; tel. (1782) 236923; fax (1782) 232544; e-mail margaret.green@stoke01.stoke-cc.gov.uk; library of 460,000 vols; Solon ceramics colln; Asst Dir (Libraries, Information and Archives) MARGARET GREEN.

Stratford upon Avon

Shakespeare Centre Library: Henley St, Stratford upon Avon, Warwicks., CV37 6QW; tel. (1789) 201813; fax (1789) 296083; e-mail library@shakespeare.org.uk; f. 1964; library of *c*. 50,000 vols, comprising the collections of the Shakespeare Birthplace Trust and the Royal Shakespeare Theatre Library; Dir ROGER PRINGLE.

Swansea

City and County of Swansea Library and Information Service: Library HQ, 12 Orchard St, Swansea, SA1 5AZ; tel. (1792) 516720; fax (1792) 516737; library of 986,546 vols; special collections: Dylan Thomas, Deffett Francis, Welsh and Local History; County Librarian MICHAEL ALLEN.

University of Wales, Swansea Library: Singleton Park, Swansea, SA2 8PP; tel. (1792) 295697; fax (1792) 295851; f. 1920; library of 700,000 vols and pamphlets; Librarian A. M. W. GREEN.

Swindon

Swindon Borough Council Libraries: Swindon Central Library, Regent Circus, Swindon, SN1 1QG; tel. (1793) 463231; fax (1793) 541319; Principal Librarian DAVID ALLEN.

Telford

Telford and Wrekin Libraries: Telford Town Centre Library, St Quentin Gate, Telford, TF3 4JG; tel. (1952) 292151; fax (1952) 292078; 9 brs, 1 mobile library; Libraries and Heritage Services Man. PAT DAVIS.

Torquay

Torbay Library Services: Torquay Central Library, Lymington Rd, Torquay, TQ1 3DT; tel. (1803) 208300; 3 brs, 1 mobile library; Head of Library Services P. J. BOTTRILL.

Trowbridge

Wiltshire Libraries and Heritage: Bythesea Rd, Trowbridge, Wilts, BA14 8BS; tel. (1225) 713700; fax (1225) 713993; f. 1919; library of 869,000 vols, cassettes, compact discs, videos, etc.; 31 brs, 4 mobile libraries; special collections: Wiltshire, agriculture, cricket, life of Christ, anthropology and sociology of the family; public and private archives for Wiltshire and the Diocese of Salisbury; Head of Service PAULINE DYER; publ. *Annual Report*.

Truro

Cornwall Library Service: County Hall, Truro, Cornwall, TR1 3AY; tel. (1872) 322184; fax (1872) 323836; f. 1925; library of 835,000 vols; 29 brs, 9 mobile libraries; Information Sevices Dir M. BARTZ.

Warrington

Warrington Borough Libraries: Warrington Library, Museum St, Warrington, WA1 1JB; tel. (1925) 442889; 13 brs, 1 mobile library; Head of Libraries JANET HILL.

Warwick

Warwickshire Department of Libraries and Heritage: Barrack St, Warwick, CV34 4TH; tel. (1926) 412166; fax (1926) 412471; e-mail warcolib@dial.pipex.com; f. 1920; library of 1,105,000 vols; 34 brs; 5 mobile libraries; one community service vehicle; County Records Office; special collections: Warwick, George Elliot; Libraries and Heritage ; Dir MICHAEL HENRY.

West Bretton

National Arts Education Archive, Lawrence Batley Centre for: University College, Bretton Hall, West Bretton, Wakefield, West Yorks., WF4 4LG; tel. (1924) 830261; fax (1924) 832077; f. 1985; to establish an illustrated 'trace' of work in art and design education 1880 to date, to make this available to scholars and the general public, and to promote academic research and more informed teaching through its use; includes many thousands of original papers, letters and examples of children's work, also slides, films, videos, tapes and books; Dir Prof. R. GEORGE.

Winchester

Hampshire County Library: 81 North Walls, Winchester, Hampshire, SO23 8BY; tel. (1962) 846057; fax (1962) 856615; f. 1974; library of 2,840,000 vols; 54 brs; 18 mobile libraries; County Librarian P. H. TURNER.

Worcester

Worcestershire County Libraries: Cultural Services, Corporate Services Directorate, County Hall, Spetchley Rd, Worcester, WR5 2NP; tel. (1905) 766233; 22 brs; Library Services Man. CATHY EVANS.

Wrexham

Wrexham County Borough Council, Library and Information Service: Education and Leisure Services Directorate, Roxburgh House, Hill St, Wrexham, LL11 1SN; tel. (1978) 297430; fax (1978) 297422; library of 214,746 vols; 12 libraries, 2 mobile libraries, 1 library for the housebound; special collections: open learning, Japanese life and culture; business information centre; Chief Officer ALAN WATKIN.

York

City of York Libraries: York Library, Museum St, York, YO1 2DS; tel. (1904) 655631; fax (1904) 611025; Principal Librarian ALISON HENESEY.

University of York Library: Heslington, York, YO10 5DD; tel. (1904) 433865; fax (1904) 433866; e-mail aemh1@york.ac.uk; f. 1963; library of 720,000 vols; Librarian A. ELIZABETH M. HEAPS.

York Minster Library: Dean's Park, York, YO1 7JQ; tel. (1904) 625308; fax (1904) 611119; f. 7th/8th century; library of 120,000 vols, 80 incunabula, 80 medieval MSS; 200 music MSS; special collections include Civil War Tracts and Yorkshire local history (120,000 vols); Librarian Canon J. TOY.

Ystrad Mynach

Caerphilly Libraries: District Education Office, Caerphilly Rd, Ystrad Mynach, Hengoed, CF81 7EP; tel. (01443) 816016; fax (01443) 816998; 20 brs; Principal Officer Libraries MARY PALMER.

Museums and Art Galleries

Aberdeen

Aberdeen Art Gallery and Museums: Arts and Recreation Division, Schoolhill, Aberdeen, AB10 1FQ; tel. (1224) 646333; fax 632133.

Selected museums and galleries:

Aberdeen Art Gallery: Schoolhill, Aberdeen, AB10 1FQ; tel. (1224) 646333; f. 1884; fine and decorative arts; major collections of 18th- to 20th-century British art.

Aberdeen Maritime Museum: Shiprow, Aberdeen, AB11 5BY; tel. (1224) 337700; f. 1984; displays covering all aspects of Aberdeen and the North East of Scotland's maritime heritage.

Tolbooth Museum: Castle St, Aberdeen; tel. (1224) 621167; f. 1995; civic history.

Alloway

Burns Cottage and Museum: Alloway, Ayrshire; tel. (1292) 443700; birthplace of the poet Robert Burns; MSS and correspondence; Curator JOHN MANSON.

Anstruther

Scottish Fisheries Museum, The: St Ayles, Harbourhead, Anstruther, Fife; tel. (1333) 310628; f. 1969; visual historical record of every aspect of the Scottish Fishing Industry and modern methods and trends; reference ; library of 1,000 vols; Man. J. K. LINDSAY; publ. *Newsletter* (annually).

Bangor

Bangor Museum and Art Gallery: Ffordd Gwynedd, Bangor, Gwynedd; tel. (1248) 353368; f. 1884; artefacts relating to North Wales; archaeology, furniture, crafts, costumes, prints and maps; art gallery; Curator PAT BENNEYWORTH.

Barnard Castle

Bowes Museum, The: Barnard Castle, Co. Durham, DL12 8NP; tel. (1833) 690606; fax (1833) 637163; collections formed 1840 – 75 by John and Josephine Bowes mainly of all forms of Continental Fine and Decorative Arts; f. at Barnard Castle 1869, since when there have been additions of British Decorative Arts, including series of English rooms from 16th to 19th centuries, music, costumes, local history and archaeology galleries; administered by Durham County Council; Curator Mrs E. CONRAN.

Bath

American Museum in Britain: Claverton Manor, nr Bath, BA2 7BD; tel. (1225) 460503; fax (1225) 480726; f. 1959, opened 1961; first American museum in Europe; aims at illustrating the development of American decorative arts from 17th to 19th centuries; library; Dir WILLIAM MCNAUGHT.

Holburne Museum and Crafts Study Centre: Great Pulteney St, Bath, Avon BA2 4DB; tel. (1225) 466669; fax (1225) 333121; f. 1893; Crafts Study Centre ; f. 1977; paintings, miniatures, silver, ceramics, glass, furniture, and work by 20th-century artist craftsmen in an 18th-century building; Dir BARLEY ROSCOE.

Beamish

Beamish, The North of England Open Air Museum: Beamish, Co. Durham, DH9 0RG; tel. (1207) 231811; fax (1207) 290933; f. 1970 to study, collect, preserve and exhibit buildings, machinery, objects and information illustrating the development of industry and way of life in the North of England; the museum covers over 200 acres and includes a colliery village, railway station, a working farm and The Town of around 1913; Pockerley Manor and Horse yard illustrate yeoman farming lifestyle in early 19th century; library of 10,000 vols; photographic archive containing 250,000 photos; Dir PETER LEWIS; publ. guide book.

Birmingham

Birmingham Museums and Art Gallery: Chamberlain Sq., Birmingham, B3 3DH; tel. (121) 235-2834; f. 1867; Departments of Fine and Applied Art (foreign schools from Renaissance, English from 17th century, early English watercolours and Pre-Raphaelite paintings and drawings, sculpture, silver, metalwork, costume, glass, stained glass, ceramics and textile collections); Archaeology, Ethnography and Local History (collections from Ancient Egypt, Ur, Nineveh, Jericho, Nimrud, Vinca, Jerusalem, Petra and Vounos (Cyprus) in the Old World, Mexico and Peru in the New, Prehistoric, Roman and British Medieval antiquities); Pacific ethnography collection; British coin collection; Natural History; comprehensive collections of minerals, gemstones and molluscs, British birds, lepidoptera and coleoptera; Midlands flora; br. museums incl. Aston Hall, Blakesley Hall, Weoley Castle, Sarehole Mill, Soho House, Jewellery Quarter Discovery Centre; Asst Dir (Museums and Arts) GRAHAM ALLEN.

Bishop's Stortford

Rhodes Memorial Museum and Commonwealth Centre: South Rd, Bishop's Stortford, Herts., CM23 3JG; tel. (1279) 651746; f. 1938; Cecil Rhodes' birthplace preserved, with 15 rooms of exhibits relating to his life and times; Curator DAVID PARRY.

Blackburn

Blackburn Museum and Art Gallery: Museum St, Blackburn, Lancs, BB1 7AJ; tel. (1254) 667130; fax (1254) 695370; f. 1862; local history, Indian and Pakistani textiles and jewellery, military history, icons, coins, books, MSS, fine and decorative arts.

Bradford

National Museum of Photography, Film and Television: Pictureville, Bradford, West Yorks., BD1 1NQ; tel. (1274) 727488; fax (1274) 723155; f. 1983 as a joint venture between the Science Museum and the City of Bradford; explores the art and science of photography, film and television; through working models, equipment, dramatic reconstructions and the pictures themselves, visitors can explore from the first cameras and photographs to the latest satellite television images; permanent exhibitions on television, photojournalism, camera obscura; portrait studios, electronic imaging, moving pictures and lenses, 'History of Cinema' presentations; Kodak museum, 'The Story of Popular Photography'; Daily Herald archive; transmitting television studio doubling as walk-through display; Education Unit arranges workshops, lectures, etc.; resident theatre company; the Museum houses IMAX projection system, with cinema screen; also incorporates Pictureville Cinema, screening world cinema old and new, and Cinerama Theatre; Head AMANDA NEVILL.

Brighton

Booth Museum of Natural History: 194 Dyke Road, Brighton, BN1 5AA; tel. (1273) 292777; fax (1273) 292778; displays of British birds in recreated natural settings, and galleries of World butterflies, geology and vertebrate evolution; reference collections of eggs, insects, minerals, palaeontology, osteology, skins and herbaria.

Brighton Museum and Art Gallery: Church St, Brighton, Sussex, BN1 1UE; tel. (1273) 290900; fax (1273) 292841; collection of 15th- to 20th-century paintings, drawings and prints; English pottery and porcelain, including the Willett Collection; decorative art and furniture of Art Nouveau and Art Deco periods; fashion gallery; ethnography and archaeology; local history.

Royal Pavilion: Brighton, BN1 1EE; tel. (1273) 290900; fax (1273) 292871; Regency seaside palace of King George IV.

Bristol

Bristol City Museums and Art Gallery: Queen's Rd, Bristol, BS8 1RL; tel. (117) 922-3571; fax (117) 922-2047; also Red Lodge, Park Row (16th century), Georgian House, Blaise Castle House Museum, Bristol Industrial Museum (Princes Wharf); Kingsweston Roman Villa and Sea Mills Roman Site, Fairbairn Steam Crane (City Docks); Dir of Leisure Services STEPHEN WRAY; publs guides, catalogues, *Events* (quarterly), etc.

Burnley

Towneley Hall Art Gallery and Museums: Towneley Hall, Burnley, Lancs; tel. (1282) 424213; fax (1282) 436138; e-mail nathist@gn.apc.org; f. 1902; 17th- to 20th-century oils; early English watercolours; collections of period furniture, ivories, 18th-century glassware and oriental ceramics; archaeological specimens and militaria; Hall built from *c.* 1350; attached Museum of Local Crafts and Industries and Natural History Centre; Curator J. SUSAN BOURNE.

Cambridge

Fitzwilliam Museum: Trumpington St, Cambridge, CB2 1RB; tel. (1223) 332900; fax (1223) 332923; f. 1816; art collections of the University; paintings, drawings, prints, sculpture; coins and medals; ceramics, glass, textiles, arms and armour, and other applied arts; Greek, Roman, Cypriot, western Asiatic and Egyptian antiquities; library of 250,000 vols and medieval, literary and music MSS, autograph letters; early printed books, printed music, books on history of art; Dir DUNCAN ROBINSON; publ. *Annual Report*.

University Museum of Archaeology and Anthropology: Downing St, Cambridge, CB2 3DZ; tel. (1223) 333516; f. 1883; anthropology and prehistoric archaeology of all parts of the world; also local archaeology of all periods; Dir and Curator D. W. PHILLIPSON.

University Museum of Zoology: Downing St, Cambridge CB2 3EJ; tel. (1223) 336650; fax (1223) 336676; f. 1815; zoological collection for teaching and research purposes; Dir M. AKAM.

Cardiff

National Museums and Galleries of Wales: Cathays Park, Cardiff, CF1 3NP; tel. (1222) 397951; fax (1222) 373219; e-mail post@nmgw.ac.uk; f. 1907; a museum of the natural sciences, archaeology, ethnography, industry and art with special reference to Wales; Pres. MATTHEW PRICHARD; Dir COLIN FORD; publ. *Amgueddfa Yearbook*.

Associated museums:

Museum of Welsh Life: St Fagans, Cardiff.

Cardiff Docks Gallery: Cardiff Bay.

Turner House: Penarth; art gallery.

Roman Legionary Museum: Caerleon.

Museum of the Welsh Woollen Industry: Drefach Felindre, Dyfed.

Welsh Slate Museum: Llanberis, Gwynedd.

Segontium Roman Fort Museum: Caernarfon, Gwyned.

Carmarthen

Carmarthenshire County Museum: Abergwili, Carmarthen, SA31 2JG; tel. (1267) 231691; fax (1267) 223830; local authority museum; archaeology, ceramics, art, costume, folk life, geology, social history; County Museums Officer C. J. DELANEY.

Chawton

Jane Austen's House: Chawton, Alton, Hampshire; tel. (1420) 83262; f. 1949; portraits, documents, furniture and objects relating to Jane Austen and her family; Dir T. F. CARPENTER; Curator JEAN K. BOWDEN.

Cirencester

Corinium Museum: Park St, Cirencester, Glos; tel. (1285) 655611; fax (1285) 643286;

important collection of Roman material; mosaic pavements, sculpture, military and civil tombstones, household domestic utensils, personal ornaments, and Samian and coarse pottery, all giving ample evidence of the importance and wealth of Corinium, which was the second largest town in Roman Britain; regional museum for the Cotswolds; br. museums incl. Cirencester Lock-Up and Cotswold Countryside Collection; Museums Service Man. Dr JOHN PADDOCK.

Colchester

Colchester Museums: Museum Resource Centre, 14 Ryegate Rd, Colchester, Essex, CO1 1YG; tel. (1206) 282931; fax (1206) 282925; f. 1860 from the collections of Essex Archaeological Society; local human and natural history; the large collections in the Norman Castle are from Colchester and Essex, and the Roman section is particularly extensive; three branch museums (covering Natural History, Decorative Arts, Colchester Clocks); Head of Museums PETER BERRIDGE.

Devizes

Devizes Museum (Wiltshire Archaeological and Natural History Society): The Museum, 41 Long St, Devizes, Wilts, SN10 1NS; tel. (1380) 727369; fax (1380) 722150; f. 1853; Neolithic, Bronze Age, Iron Age, Roman, Saxon and Natural History collections; local history gallery; library of over 8,000 vols; picture gallery; Curator P. H. ROBINSON; publ. *Wiltshire Archaeological and Natural History Magazine* (annually).

Doncaster

Doncaster Museum and Art Gallery: Chequer Rd, Doncaster, Yorks, DN1 2AE; tel. (1302) 734293; fax (1302) 735409; f. 1909; regional natural history, geology, archaeology and local history collections; permanent art collection, paintings, ceramics and glass; Regimental collection of the King's Own Yorkshire Light Infantry; frequent temporary exhibitions; Curator G. PREECE; publs *Museum and Art Gallery Publications* (8vo and 4to series, irregular), *Catalogues*.

Dorchester

Dorset County Museum and Dorset Natural History and Archaeological Society: Dorchester; tel. (1305) 262735; f. Museum 1846, Society f. 1875, merged in 1928; natural history, palaeontology, archaeology, fine arts, geology, literature (incl. Thomas Hardy), and the local history of Dorset; lectures, conferences and seminars are held in the Museum in winter and spring; Pres. ALAN SWINDELL; publ. *The Proceedings of the Dorset Natural History and Archaeological Society* (annually).

Dumfries

Dumfries Museums: The Observatory, Dumfries, DG2 7SW; tel. 253374; fax 265081; e-mail postmaster@dumfriesmuseum.demon.co.uk; building erected as a windmill *c.* 1790; f. 1835 as an observatory; exhibits Roman relics, Stone and Bronze Age artefacts, natural and local history from Dumfries and Galloway; incorporates Dumfries Museum, Thornhill Museum, Langholm Museum and Myrseth Museum collections; MSS concerning Carlyle and Barrie; camera obscura; period rooms at Old Bridge House (1660) nearby; Robert Burns Centre in Dumfries Town Mill (1781): exhibitions on Burns and his life in South West Scotland; Burns House: period house occupied by Burns 1793–6, and where he died; Sanquhar Museum in Adam-designed Town House (1735) covers local history and geology; Museums Man. D. LOCKWOOD.

Dundee

Dundee Art Galleries and Museums: McManus Galleries, Albert Square, Dundee, DD1 1DA; tel. (1382) 432020; f. 1873; Victorian Scottish paintings, contemporary art and photography, decorative arts; local history displays from time of earliest settlers to modern era; costume gallery; br. museums incl. Barrack Street Museum (natural history, local geology), Broughty Castle Museum (history of Broughty Ferry, Dundee's whaling industry, natural history of the seashore), Mills Observatory; Dir A. B. RITCHIE; publs works on archaeology, history, natural history, etc.

Durham

University of Durham, Oriental Museum: Elvet Hill Rd, Durham, DH1 3TH; tel. (191) 374-7911; fax (191) 374-7911; e-mail oriental.museum@durham.ac.uk; f. 1960; Duke of Northumberland's collection of Egyptian antiquities; MacDonald collection of Chinese ceramics; Charles Hardinge collection of Chinese jades; Henry de Laszlo collection of Chinese art and other examples of oriental art and archaeology covering Ancient Egypt and the Near East, the Indian sub-continent, Japan and S. E. Asia; Curator L. M. BREWSTER.

Edinburgh

Edinburgh City Museums and Art Galleries: City Art Centre, 2 Market St, Edinburgh, EH1 1DE; tel. (131) 529-3993; fax (131) 529-3977; comprise Huntly House, 142 Canongate (local history), People's Story, Canongate Tolbooth (life and work of Edinburgh's people), Museum of Childhood, 42 High St, Writers' Museum, Lawnmarket (collection of Scott, Burns and Stevenson), City Art Centre (museum headquarters), Market St (temporary exhibitions and 19th- and 20th-century artists), Lauriston Castle, Cramond Rd South (furniture collection), Queensferry Museum, South Queensferry (local history); Newhaven (local history); Head of Heritage and Arts HERBERT COUTTS.

National Galleries of Scotland: The Mound, Edinburgh, EH2 2EL; tel. (131) 624-6200; e-mail pressinfo@natgalscot.ac.uk; Dir TIMOTHY CLIFFORD; publs *Bulletin* (describing new acquisitions and exhibitions of the 3 National Galleries, every 2 months), *Triennial Report*.

Constituent galleries:

National Gallery of Scotland: The Mound, Edinburgh, EH2 2EL; tel. (131) 624-6200; fax (131) 220-0917; f. 1859; European and Scottish paintings etc. up to 1900; Dir as above; Keeper MICHAEL CLARKE.

Scottish National Portrait Gallery: Queen St, Edinburgh, EH2 1JD; tel. (131) 624-6200; fax (131) 558-3691; f. 1882; portraits of Scottish historical interest; an extensive reference section of engravings and photographs of portraits; the national photography collection; Dir as above; Keeper JAMES HOLLOWAY.

Scottish National Gallery of Modern Art: Belford Rd, Edinburgh, EH4 3DR; tel. (131) 624-6200; fax (131) 343-2802; f. 1960; paintings, drawings, prints and sculptures, Scottish and Continental, 20th-century; Dir as above; Keeper RICHARD CALVOCORESSI.

Dean Gallery: Belford Rd, Edinburgh, EH4; tel. (131) 624-6200; due to open in spring 1999; Paolozzi gift of sculpture and graphic art, works from the Penrose colln; library and archive.

National Museums of Scotland: Royal Museum, Chambers St, Edinburgh, EH1 1JF; tel. (131) 247-4260; fax (131) 247-4308; e-mail mj@nms.ac.uk; f. 1985; Dir M. E. P. JONES.

Comprise:

Royal Museum of Scotland: Chambers St, Edinburgh, EH1 1JF; f. 1854; collections covering decorative arts, archaeology, ethnography, natural history, geology, science and technology.

Scottish United Services Museum: Edinburgh Castle; collections covering the armed forces in Scotland.

Scottish Agricultural Museum: Ingliston, Edinburgh; displays on life and work in rural Scotland.

Museum of Flight: East Fortune Airfield, North Berwick; collection of aircraft, rockets and aeroengines displayed in the hangars of a former RAF wartime station.

Shambellie House Museum of Costume: New Abbey, Dumfries; mid 19th-century house; changing exhibitions of costume.

Glasgow

Glasgow Museums: The Art Gallery and Museum, Kelvingrove, Glasgow, G3 8AG; tel. (141) 287-2000; fax (141) 287-2690; art collection f. 1854, now extensive, with pictures representative of Italian, Dutch, Flemish and French Schools, including Rembrandt, Rubens, Giorgione and a particularly strong group of French Impressionists; collection of British, especially Scottish, art; British domestic, Colonial and Scandinavian silver and Scottish communion plate; sculpture, ceramics, glass, furniture and costume; good collections of European arms and armour; archaeological and ethnographic collections; the Natural History department contains a wide range of botanical, zoological and geological collections and displays; library of 50,000 vols, and periodicals; Dir JULIAN SPALDING; publ. *Preview Magazine* (quarterly).

Branch museums:

Burrell Collection: Pollok Country Park, 4060 Pollokshaws Rd, Glasgow G43 1AT; tel. (141) 649-7151; fax (141) 636-0086; antiquities from Iraq, Egypt, Greece and Italy; Oriental art, including Chinese ceramics, bronzes and jades, Japanese prints, Near Eastern carpets, rugs, ceramics and metal work; European decorative arts of 14th – 18th centuries including tapestries, stained glass, sculpture, furniture, glass, silver and ceramics; fine art, especially French 19th-century works by Degas, Boudin, Monet and Daumier.

McLellan Galleries: 270 Sauchiehall St, Glasgow; tel. (141) 331-1854; fax (141) 332-9957; temporary exhibition gallery.

Museum of Transport: Kelvin Hall, 1 Bunhouse Rd, Glasgow, G3 8DP; tel. (141) 287-2000; f. 1988; history of transport; displays include Glasgow trams and buses, Scottish-built cars, commercial vehicles, cycles and motor cycles, railway locomotives, horse-drawn vehicles, ship models and reproduction of typical Glasgow street of 1938.

People's Palace Museum: Glasgow Green, Glasgow; tel. (141) 554-0223; fax (141) 550-0892; local and social history collection f. 1898; history of Glasgow, and important collections of Glasgow paintings, stained glass, labour, trade union, church and women's history.

Pollok House: Pollok Country Park, 4060 Pollokshaws Rd, Glasgow; tel. (141) 632-0274; 18th-century Palladian house with Edwardian additions, furnished *c.* 1750 – 1820 and with Stirling Maxwell collection of Spanish and European paintings.

Provand's Lordship: 3 Castle St, Glasgow; tel. (141) 552-8819; built 1471, the oldest house in Glasgow, with period room displays.

St Mungo Museum of Religious Life and Art: 2 Castle St, Glasgow, G4 0RH; tel. (141) 553-2557; f. 1993; art objects associated with religious faiths; displays on religion in art, world faiths, religion in Scottish history.

Gallery of Modern Art: Queen St, Glasgow; tel. (141) 221-9600; f. 1996; Scottish and foreign art (incl. the 'Glasgow Boys').

Hunterian Museum: University of Glasgow Main Bldg, Glasgow, G12 8QQ; tel. (141) 330-4221; fax (141) 330-3617; f. 1807; geological, prehistoric, Roman, ethnographical and coin collections; art collection in Hunterian Art Gallery; zoological, anatomical and pathological collections in university depts of Zoology, Anatomy and Pathology; books and MSS in university library; Dir MALCOLM D. MCLEOD.

Attached gallery:

Hunterian Art Gallery: University of Glasgow, 82 Hillhead St, Glasgow, G12 8QQ; tel. (141) 330-5431; fax (141) 330-3618; collections of C. R. Mackintosh and J. M. Whistler; works by Chardin, Stubbs and Reynolds; Scottish painting from the 18th century to the present; Old Master and modern prints; Dir MALCOLM D. MCLEOD.

Gloucester

City Museum and Art Gallery: Brunswick Rd, Gloucester, GL1 1HP; tel. (1452) 524131; f. 1859; natural history, archaeology (before AD 1500), fine and applied art; temporary art exhibitions.

Gloucester Folk Museum: 99 – 103 Westgate St, Gloucester, GL1 2PG; tel. (1452) 526467; history of the city from AD 1500; bygone crafts and industries of Gloucestershire.

Grasmere

Dove Cottage and the Wordsworth Museum, The Wordsworth Trust (Centre for British Romanticism): Dove Cottage, Grasmere, Ambleside, Cumbria, LA22 9SH; tel. (15394) 35547; fax (15394) 35748; f. 1890; former home of William and Dorothy Wordsworth and, later, of Thomas de Quincey; contains original furniture and personal effects, and a museum containing MSS, books, paintings, objects relating to the poet, and to Grasmere life of the period; major research library for the Romantic period; Dir Dr R. S. WOOF; publ. *Friends of the Wordsworth Trust—Newsletter* (4 a year).

Grays

Thurrock Museum: Orsett Rd, Grays, Essex, RM17 5DX; tel. (1375) 382555; fax (1375) 392666; f. 1956; archaeology and history of Thurrock with accent on the growth of technology in a Thamesside landscape; ; Deputy Curator T. CARNEY.

Haverfordwest

Pembrokeshire County Museum Service: Cultural Services Dept, Scolton Manor Museum, Spittal, Haverfordwest, Pembs., SA62 5QL; tel. (1437) 731328; fax (1437) 731743; County Museums Officer MARK THOMAS.

Incorporates:

Scolton Manor Museum: Spittal, Haverfordwest; tel. (1437) 731328; f. 1972; regional history of Pembrokeshire; includes period rooms in early Victorian mansion, World War II exhibition, railway exhibits, geology, river fishing.

Penrhos Cottage: Llanycefn, Clunderwen; f. 1971; traditional thatched Welsh cottage with original furniture.

High Wycombe

Disraeli Museum: Hughenden Manor, High Wycombe, Bucks, HP14 4LA; tel. (1494) 532580; contains Disraeli's books, furniture, paintings and personal effects; property of the National Trust (*q.v*).

Huddersfield

Tolson Memorial Museum: Ravensknowle Park, Wakefield Rd, Huddersfield, HD5 8DJ, West Yorks; tel. (1484) 223830; fax (1484) 223843; opened 1922; illustrates natural and human history of the district; prehistory, folklife, development of woollen industry, collection of vehicles.

Ironbridge

Ironbridge Gorge Museums: Ironbridge, Telford, Shropshire, TF8 7AW; tel. (1952) 433522; fax (1952) 432204; f. 1968; explain and interpret the industrial and social history of the East Shropshire Coalfield, regarded as the 'Birthplace of the Industrial Revolution'; 6-mile site on the River Severn comprising: Coalbrookdale Museum of Iron and Darby Furnace, Ironbridge with the Museum of the River/Visitor Centre, the world's first Iron Bridge (built 1779), Blists Hill Victorian Town, Coalport China Museum, Jackfield Tile Museum, Ironbridge Institute at Coalbrookdale, Rosehill and Dale House (restored home of the Darby family), Tar Tunnel (200-year-old source of natural bitumen); designated a World Heritage Site by UNESCO; library of 50,000 vols; Chief Exec. GLEN R. LAWES.

Kendal

Abbot Hall Art Gallery and Museum of Lakeland Life and Industry: Kendal, Cumbria, LA9 5AL; tel. (1539) 722464; f. 1962 (gallery), 1971 (museum); gallery provides changing exhibitions of local and international interest; houses permanent collections of 18th-century furniture, paintings and *objets d'art*, modern paintings, sculpture and drawings; museum features the working and social life of the area; Arthur Ransome Room; John Cunliffe Room; talks and tours provided; Dir EDWARD KING.

Attached museum:

Kendal Museum of Natural History and Archaeology: Kendal, Cumbria; tel. (1539) 721374; f. 1796 (redesigned 1986); Westmorland Gallery of local history and archaeology, World Wildlife gallery, Natural History gallery of geology, flora and fauna of the district; owned by South Lakeland District Council and managed by Abbot Hall; Dir EDWARD KING.

Kirkcaldy

Kirkcaldy Museum and Art Gallery: War Memorial Gardens, Kirkcaldy, Fife, KY1 1YG; tel. (1592) 412860; fax (1592) 412870; f. 1925; local history, archaeology, earth and natural sciences, industrial history, decorative arts, costume, ceramics; 19th- and 20th-century Scottish paintings; Curator D. M. MECHAN.

Leeds

Leeds Museums and Galleries: The Town Hall, The Headrow, Leeds, LS1 3AD; tel. (113) 247-7241; fax (113) 247-7747; f. 1820; Dir Dr E. SILBER; publ. *Museums and Galleries Review* (1 a year).

Selected museums and galleries:

City Museum: The Headrow, Leeds, LS1 3AA; tel. (113) 247-8275; fax (113) 234-2300; natural history, archaeology, ethnology; Curator ADRIAN NORRIS.

Abbey House Museum: Kirkstall Rd, Leeds, LS5 3EH; tel. (113) 275-5821; fax (113) 274-9439; gatehouse of Kirkstall Abbey, street scenes, toys and games, costume; Curator SAMANTHA FLAVIN; closed for restoration until 2000.

Armley Mills Industrial Museum: Canal Rd, Armley, Leeds, LS12 2QF; tel. (113) 263-7861; fax (113) 263-7861; textiles, printing, cinematography, manager's and mill-workers' houses; Curator DARU ROOKE.

Temple Newsam House: Temple Newsam Rd, off Selby Rd, Leeds, LS15 0AE; tel. (113) 264-7321; fax (113) 260-2285; opened to the public 1923; Tudor-Stuart house, birthplace of Lord Darnley; contains extensive collections of old master and Ingram family paintings and the decorative arts; Curators ANTHONY WELLS-COLE, JAMES LOMAX.

Leeds City Art Gallery: Municipal Bldgs, Leeds, LS1 3AA; tel. (113) 247-8248; fax (113) 244-9689; f. 1888; 19th-century English and European paintings; early English watercolours, including Kitson and Lupton collections; modern paintings and sculpture; Print Room and Art Library; Henry Moore Centre for the Study of Sculpture; Curator CORINNE MILLER.

Lotherton Hall: Aberford, Leeds, LS25 3EB; tel. (113) 281-3259; fax (113) 281-2100; opened to the public 1969; 19th- and 20th-century country house; Gascoigne Collection of 17th – 19th-century furniture, silver, ceramics, costume and paintings; modern crafts; oriental gallery; Curator ADAM WHITE.

Leicester

Leicestershire Museums, Arts and Records Service: County Hall, Glenfield, Leicester, LE3 8TB; tel. (116) 265-6781; fax (116) 265-6788; f. 1849; sections of archaeology, natural sciences, dress and textiles, working life, Leicestershire history, education, Leicestershire Record Office Repository for official and private archives, Leicestershire Environmental Resources Centre, Sherrier Resources Centre – Lutterworth, Melton Museum, The Manor House – Donington Le Heath, Harborough Museum, Snibston Discovery Park, Century Theatre; Head H. E. BROUGHTON.

Lincoln

Lincolnshire Heritage Services: Education and Cultural Services, County Offices, Newland, Lincoln, LN1 1YQ; tel. (1522) 552806; Heritage Services Man. JOANNA MILFORD.

Selected museums and galleries:

City and County Museum: Friary Lane, Lincoln; tel. (1522) 530401; Curator and Man. T. PAGE.

Museum of Lincolnshire Life: Burton Rd, Lincoln; tel. (1522) 528448; f. 1969; displays illustrating the social, agricultural and industrial history of Lincolnshire over the last three centuries; Curator and Man. P. R. COUSINS.

Usher Gallery: Lindum Rd, Lincoln; tel. (1522) 527980; f. 1927; exhibits the Usher collection of watches, miniatures, porcelain, *objets d'art*, etc.; special collection of works by Peter De Wint and a general collection of paintings, sculpture and decorative art objects; extensive collection of coins and tokens from Lincolnshire; Curator and Man. R. H. WOOD.

Gainsborough Old Hall: Parnell St, Gainsborough; tel. (1427) 612669; f. 1974; 15th-century manor house with great hall, medieval kitchen, etc.; Curator and Man. HEATHER CUMMINS.

Grantham Museum: St Peter's Hill, Grantham; tel. (1476) 568783; local prehistoric, Roman and Saxon archaeology, Grantham local history, trades and industries, and a collection devoted to Isaac Newton and Margaret Thatcher; Curator and Man. KATIE PAGE (acting).

Skegness Church Farm Museum: Church Rd South, Skegness, Lincs; tel. (1754) 766658; f. 1976; a complex of 18th- and 19th-century farmhouse and agricultural buildings with displays of agricultural equipment typical of the area; farmhouse furnished to period *c.* 1900; Curator and Man. P. R. COUSINS.

Stamford Museum: Broad St, Stamford; tel. (1780) 766317; local archaeology and history; exhibits include Daniel Lambert's clothing; Curator and Man. KATIE PAGE (acting).

Liverpool

Lady Lever Art Gallery: Port Sunlight Village, Bebington, Wirral; tel. (151) 478-4136; fax (151) 478-4140; outstanding collection of English 18th-century paintings and furniture, Chinese porcelain, Wedgwood pottery and Victorian paintings.

Liverpool Museum: William Brown St, Liverpool, L3 8EN; tel. (151) 478-4399; fax (151) 478-4390; f. 1851, rebuilt 1964-69; special collections include the Mayer-Fejérvàry Gothic ivories, the Bryan Fausset group of Anglo-Saxon antiquities, the Lord Derby and Tristram ornithological collections; Vivarium, Aquarium, Historic Transport, Archaeology, Ethnology, Time and Space Gallery, Planetarium, National History Centre.

Merseyside Maritime Museum: Albert Dock, Liverpool, L3 4AA; tel. (151) 478-4499; fax (151) 478-4590; set in Liverpool's docklands; displays about the region's maritime past; incorporates H.M. Customs & Excise National Museum and the Museum of Liverpool Life, Pier Head.

Sudley House: Mossley Hill Rd, Liverpool; tel. (151) 724-3245; former home of 19th-century shipowner; 18th- and 19th-century art including works by Gainsborough, Landseer and the Pre-Raphaelites.

Walker Art Gallery: William Brown St, Liverpool, L3 8EL; tel. (151) 478-4199; fax (151) 478-4190; collections of European art from 1300, sculpture gallery.

London

Bank of England Museum: Threadneedle St, London, EC2R 8AH; tel. (171) 601-5545; fax (171) 601-5808; f. 1988; to illustrate the history of the Bank and to explain its work today; Curator JOHN KEYWORTH.

British Museum: Great Russell St, London, WC1B 3DG; tel. (171) 636-1555; fax (171) 323-8480; f. 1753 in pursuance of the will of Sir Hans Sloane, and with the addition of the Cottonian and Harleian Libraries; opened 1759; present buildings begun 1823, completed 1852; collections and exhibitions of prehistoric, Egyptian, Assyrian, medieval, oriental and other archaeological collns, ethnography, prints, drawings, ceramics, coins, medals and banknotes; many catalogues and reproductions are published; Chair. of Board of Trustees G. C. GREENE; Dir Dr ROBERT G. W. ANDERSON; Sec. C. N. PARKER; Keepers of Departments: Prints and Drawings A. V. GRIFFITHS; Egyptian Antiquities W. V. DAVIES; Western Asiatic Antiquities Dr J. E. CURTIS; Greek and Roman Antiquities Dr D. J. R. WILLIAMS; Medieval and Later Antiquities J. CHERRY; Japanese Antiquities V. T. HARRIS; Oriental Antiquities J. R. KNOX; Ethnography Dr J. B. MACK; Prehistoric and Romano-British Antiquities Dr T. W. POTTER; Coins and Medals Dr A. M. BURNETT; Scientific Research Dr S. BOWMAN; Conservation Dr W. A. ODDY.

Carlyle's House: 24 Cheyne Row, Chelsea, London, SW3 5HL; tel. (171) 352-7087; built 1708; occupied by the Carlyles 1834 – 81; National Trust property; contains books, paintings, furniture, and personal relics.

Courtauld Gallery: Courtauld Institute of Art, Somerset House, Strand, London, WC2R ORN; tel. (171) 873-2526; f. 1958; collection of Impressionist and Post-Impressionist paintings; masterpieces by Botticelli, Tiepolo, Rubens, Goya, Manet, Van Gogh and Renoir; Dir JOHN MURDOCH.

Cuming Museum (Borough of Southwark): 157 Walworth Rd, London, SE17 1RS; tel. (171) 701-1342; fax (171) 703-7415; f. 1902; worldwide collections of the Cuming family joined with the local history of Southwark, from Roman times to the present; Man. SOPHIE PERKINS.

Design Museum: Butler's Wharf, 28 Shad Thames, London, SE1 2YD; tel. (171) 403-6933; fax (171) 378-6540; f. 1981, opened 1989; independent museum set up by the Conran Foundation, to promote awareness of the importance of design in education, industry, commerce and culture; collection of mass-produced design; Dir PAUL THOMPSON.

Dulwich Picture Gallery: College Rd, London, SE21 7AD; tel. (181) 693-5254; built 1814 by Sir John Soane to house collection of Old Masters including Rembrandt, Rubens, Cuyp, Van Dyck, Teniers, Poussin, Claude, Watteau, Raphael, Tiepolo, Gainsborough, Murillo, etc.; Dir DESMOND SHAWE-TAYLOR.

Geffrye Museum: Kingsland Rd, London, E2 8EA; tel. (171) 739-9893; f. 1914; English furniture and domestic objects arranged in a series of period rooms from 1600 to the present day; herb garden; reference library of books and periodicals on the arts and social history, temporary exhibitions, family workshops and regular teaching sessions for schools.

Hampton Court Palace: East Molesey, Surrey, KT8 9AU; tel. (181) 781-9500; fax (181) 781-9509; contains a collection of paintings and tapestries, including Andrea Mantegna's nine great tempera paintings of 'The Triumphs of Julius Caesar'; Palace Dir ROBIN EVANS; Superintendent of the Royal Collection J. COWELL.

Horniman Museum and Gardens: London Rd, Forest Hill, London, SE23 3PQ; tel. (181) 699-1872; f. 1901; ethnographical collection from all parts of the world (including tools, musical instruments, the arts, magic and religion), and exhibits related to the natural history of animals; education centre; Aquarium; library of 35,000 vols, mainly on anthropology, prehistory, art, ethnomusicology and natural history; free lectures and concerts on subjects connected with the exhibits are given in autumn and winter; Dir MICHAEL HOULIHAN.

Imperial War Museum: Lambeth Rd, London, SE1 6HZ; tel. (171) 416-5000; fax (171) 416-5374; a national museum and picture gallery; f. in 1917, illustrating and recording many aspects of the various operations in which the Armed Forces of the British Commonwealth have been engaged since 1914; contains many exhibits, 15,000 works of art, 5,000,000 photographs, archive on British and foreign documents, more than 125 million feet of film and a growing collection of sound records; library of 100,000 vols, 25,000 pamphlets, 15,000 sets of periodicals, 15,000 maps and drawings; Vice-Pres. and Chair. of the Board of Trustees Prof. ROBERT O'NEILL; Dir ROBERT CRAWFORD; publ. *Imperial War Museum Review* (annually).

Branches:

Duxford Airfield: Duxford, Cambridge, CB2 4QR; tel. (1223) 835000; fmr Battle of Britain airfield housing historic collection of aircraft, military vehicles, tanks and artillery; Dir E. O. INMAN.

HMS Belfast: Morgans Lane, Tooley St, London, SE1 2JH; tel. (171) 407-6434; Second World War cruiser moored in the Pool of London; Dir E. J. WENZEL.

Cabinet War Rooms: Clive Steps, King Charles St, London SW1A 2AQ; tel. (171) 930-6961; Churchill's underground headquarters; Curator P. REED.

Iveagh Bequest: Kenwood, Hampstead Lane, London, NW3 7JR; tel. (181) 348-1286; left to the nation by Edward Cecil Guinness, first Earl of Iveagh, in 1927; includes paintings of British, Dutch, Flemish and French Schools, housed in an 18th-century mansion designed by Robert Adam containing a fine library; exhibitions on aspects of 18th-century art; Admin. Trustee English Heritage (HBMC); Dir of E.H. London Region PHILIP DAVIES; publs catalogues.

Livesey Museum (Borough of Southwark): 682 Old Kent Rd, London, SE15 1JF; tel. (171) 639-5604; fax (171) 277-5384; f. 1974; variety of changing interactive exhibitions for children; Keeper N. BOYD.

London Transport Museum: Covent Garden, London, WC2E 7BB; tel. (171) 379-6344; fax (171) 836-4118; f. 1978, opened on present site 1980; governing body: London Regional Transport; exhibition relating to the establishment and development of public passenger transport in London; small library (*c.* 5,000 vols); film and photo library; historic poster archive; Dir SAM MULLINS; publ. *Annual Report*.

Museum of London: London Wall, London, EC2Y 5HN; tel. (171) 600-3699; fax (171) 600-1058; formed from amalgamation of London Museum and Guildhall Museum; social history of London from prehistory to 20th century; exhibits include the Lord Mayor's coach, 18th-century prison cell, Victorian shop fronts; Chair. of Board of Govs PETER REVELL-SMITH; Dir Dr SIMON THURLEY.

National Army Museum: Royal Hospital Rd, Chelsea, London, SW3 4HT; tel. (171) 730-0717; fax (171) 823-6573; e-mail nam@enterprise.net; f. 1960; displays depicting the history of the British Army since 1485, the Indian Army until Independence in 1947, and colonial land forces; reference collections of 43,000 books, 30,000 pamphlets, 1,000 ft of archives, 40,000 prints and drawings, 1,000,000 photographs; uniforms including decorations and badges; weapons; painting, silver, china, models; personal relics; Dir IAN ROBERTSON; publ. *Army Museum*.

National Gallery: Trafalgar Square, London, WC2N 5DN; tel. (171) 747-2885; fax (171) 930-4764; f. 1824; contains examples of all the principal schools of European painting from 1260 to 1900; a selection of British painters from Hogarth to Turner; guided tours and public lectures; various educational events; Chair. PHILIP HUGHES; Dir NEIL MACGREGOR; Keeper Dr NICHOLAS PENNY; Senior Curator DAVID JAFFÉ; Scientific Adviser Dr ASHOK ROY; Chief Restorer MARTIN WYLD.

National Maritime Museum: Romney Rd, Greenwich, London, SE10 9NF; tel. (181) 858-4422; fax (181) 312-6632; established 1934, opened 1937; illustrates British maritime history; the collection includes portraits and sea pieces, models, instruments, maps and charts, weapons, medals, a library of books and MSS; photo library of 140,000 historic photographs; Maritime Information Centre for researchers; Nelson Gallery; 20th-century Gallery; Queen's

House: 17th-century royal apartments of Queen Henrietta Maria; Dutch paintings; also the Old Royal Observatory, where the displays illustrate themes concerned with astronomy, time and navigation, the meridian line, and a planetarium; Dir RICHARD ORMOND.

National Portrait Gallery: St Martin's Place, London, WC2H 0HE; tel. (171) 306-0055; f. 1856; collection contains over 10,000 portraits of eminent British men and women of the last 500 years; activities include lectures, exhibitions; Dir Dr CHARLES SAUMAREZ SMITH; Chair. of Trustees HENRY KESWICK; publ. *Annual Report*.

National Postal Museum: King Edward Bldg, King Edward St., London, EC1A 1LP; fax (171) 600-3021; f. 1966, reopened in new premises 1969; collection of stamps, essays, drawings and official documents dating back to Rowland Hill's proposals for Uniform Penny Postage in 1837 – 39; also the Post Office collection of stamps of the world and of British 20th-century stamps, and the philatelic archives (1855 – 1965) of Thomas De La Rue and Co., security printers, on microfilm; post-boxes and other postal exhibits; Man. (vacant); the Museum was expected to close to the public in 1999 and to re-open on new premises in 2001.

Natural History Museum, The: Cromwell Rd, South Kensington, London, SW7 5BD; tel. (171) 938-9123; originates from the Natural History Departments of the British Museum, and a branch comprising the Zoological Museum at Tring, Herts; separate institution 1963; incorporates the Geological Museum; Chair. of the Board of Trustees Prof. Sir ROBERT MAY; Dir Dr N. CHALMERS; Science Dir Prof. P. HENDERSON; Keeper of Zoology Dr C. R. CURDS; Keeper of Entomology Dr R. LANE; Keeper of Palaeontology Dr L. R. M. COCKS; Keeper of Mineralogy Dr A. FLEET; Keeper of Botany Prof. S. BLACKMORE; Head of Dept of Exhibitions and Education Dr G. CLARKE; Head of Dept of Administrative Services C. J. E. LEGG; library: see Special Libraries.

Polish Institute and Sikorski Museum: 20 Princes Gate, London, SW7 1PT; tel. (171) 589-9249; f. 1945; archives, museum, research centre and publishing house; includes the Sikorski Collection (personal belongings, memorabilia, wartime diary, etc.), militaria (over 10,000 items), maps, paintings and engravings, also sculptures, porcelain, miniatures, coins and medals.

Royal Air Force Museum: Grahame Park Way, London, NW9 5LL; tel. (181) 205-2266; fax (181) 200-1751; f. 1963, opened 1972; grant-aided through the Ministry of Defence; exhibits almost 70 full-size British and foreign aircraft from 1909 to the present day, together with supporting material recording the history of the Royal Air Force and the development of aviation generally; activities cover many aspects of aviation, including military, civil, artistic, scientific, industrial and political; library of 100,000 vols, and archives and photographic collection; Dir Dr MICHAEL FOPP.

Royal Armouries: HM Tower of London, London, EC3N 4AB; tel. (171) 481-6358; fax (171) 481-2922; and Royal Armouries Museum, Armouries Drive, Leeds, W. Yorks., LS10 1LT; tel. (113) 220-1999; fax (113) 220-1995; the nat. museum of arms and armour and museum of the Tower of London, originating from the working arsenal at the Tower and the collection of royal armours begun by Henry VIII; first open to the public *c.* 1660; the national and royal collections cover the development of arms and armour from *c.* 1000 to the present day; Tower-based reference library of 25,000 MSS and vols, photographic collection of 120,000 prints and transparencies. The Royal Armouries artillery collection is housed at Fort Nelson, Down End Road, Portsdown Hill, Fareham, PO17 6AN; tel. (1329) 233734; fax (1329) 822092; Master of the Armouries GUY WILSON.

Royal College of Music Museum of Instruments: Prince Consort Rd, South Kensington, London, SW7; tel. (171) 591-4346; fax (171) 589-7740; e-mail museum@rcm.ac.uk; f. 1883; includes Donaldson, Tagore, Hipkins, Ridley and Hartley collections; Curator Mrs ELIZABETH WELLS.

Royal College of Surgeons of England Museums: 35 – 43 Lincoln's Inn Fields, London, WC2A 3PN; tel. (171) 405-3474, ext. 3011; formed upon the Hunterian Collection purchased by Parliament in 1799; opened in 1813; Keeper of the College Collections STELLA MASON; Senior Curator (vacant); Qvist Curator of the Hunterian Museum ELIZABETH ALLEN; Head of Conservation Unit MARTYN COOKE.

Royal Institution of Great Britain Faraday Museum: 21 Albemarle St, London, W1X 4BS; tel. (171) 409-2992; fax (171) 629-3569; Michael Faraday's Magnetic Laboratory, where many of his most important discoveries were made, was restored in 1972 to the form it was known to have in 1845; the adjacent museum has a unique collection of original apparatus, diaries, notebooks and personal effects; it was anticipated that the museum might be closed to the public for refurbishment for a part of 1999.

Science Museum: South Kensington, London, SW7 2DD; tel. (171) 938-8000; fax (171) 938-8118; f. 1857; the National Museum of Science & Industry; Dir Sir NEIL COSSONS; Science Library: see Libraries (London).

Sir John Soane's House and Museum: 13 Lincoln's Inn Fields, London, WC2; tel. (171) 430-0175; fax (171) 831-3957; built in 1812 by Sir John Soane, Architect of Bank of England; est. by Act of Parliament 1833, for the promotion of the study of architecture and allied arts; collection includes paintings by Hogarth, the Egyptian Sarcophagus of Seti I, Italian bronzes, paintings, antique sculpture, 18th-century English sculpture, models, 30,000 architectural drawings; Curator MARGARET RICHARDSON; library: see Special Libraries.

South London Gallery (Borough of Southwark): 65 Peckham Rd, London, SE5 8UH; tel. (171) 703-6120; f. 1891; frequent exhibitions of innovative contemporary art; supplementary events and workshops; Dir DAVID THORP.

Tate Gallery: Millbank, London, SW1P 4RG; tel. (171) 887-8000; fax (171) 887-8007; f. 1897 by Sir Henry Tate; comprises the national collections of British art and 20th-century painting and sculpture; the Historic British collection consists of works from the 16th century to about 1900, incl. works by Hogarth, Blake, Constable and the Pre-Raphaelites, with the Turner Collection housed in the Clore Gallery; the Modern Collection incorporates the most extensive survey of British art of its period in any public collection, incl. selected examples of very recent art; the development of art abroad is traced from Impressionism onwards; Dir NICHOLAS SEROTA.

Incorporates:

Barbara Hepworth Museum: St Ives, Cornwall; tel. (1736) 796226; opened 1976, became part of Tate Gallery 1981; studio and garden of the sculptor.

Tate Gallery Liverpool: Liverpool; tel. (151) 709-3223; opened 1988; displays of 20th-century painting and sculpture from the Tate Gallery collection, also temporary exhibitions and events.

Tate Gallery St Ives: St Ives; tel. (1736) 796226; opened 1993; displays of painting and sculpture (*c.* 1925 – 75) by artists associated with St Ives from the Tate Gallery collection, supplemented by loans, including ceramics.

Victoria and Albert Museum – The National Museum of Art and Design: S. Kensington, London, SW7 2RL; tel. (171) 938-8500; fax (171) 938-8379; f. 1852; a museum of Fine and Applied Arts of all countries, periods and styles; Dir Dr ALAN BORG; Curators Dr O. WATSON (Ceramics and Glass), R. KERR (Far Eastern), C. WILK (Furniture and Woodwork), Dr D. A. SWALLOW (Indian and South-East Asian), P. GLANVILLE (Metalwork), S. B. LAMBERT (Prints, Drawings and Paintings), Dr P. WILLIAMSON (Sculpture), V. MENDES (Textiles and Dress); publ. *Report of the Board of Trustees* (every 3 years); library: see National Art Library.

Branch museums:

Apsley House (Wellington Museum): Hyde Park Corner, 149 Piccadilly, London, W1V 9FA; tel. (171) 499-5676; fax (171) 493-6576; London home of the first Duke of Wellington (1769–1852); built by Robert Adam and enlarged by Benjamin Dean Wyatt; opened to the public 1952; contains fine paintings, sculpture, silver, porcelain, orders and decorations, and personal relics of the first Duke; Head ALICIA ROBINSON.

Bethnal Green Museum of Childhood: Cambridge Heath Rd, London, E2 9PA; tel. (181) 980-2415; fax (181) 983-5225; f. 1872; toys, dolls' houses, model theatres, optical toys, games, puppets, children's costumes, nursery furniture, children's books; Head Dr SUE LAURENCE (acting).

Theatre Museum – National Museum for the Performing Arts: Russell St, London, WC2E 7PA; tel. (171) 836-7891; fax (171) 836-5148; f. 1974, opened to the public 1987; nat. colln of archive and documentary materials relating to all branches of the live performing arts; library of 100,000 vols (incorporating British Theatre Association colln and library of the Society for Theatre Research); spec. archive collns incl. D'Oyly Carte Company, English Stage Company, Diaghilev's Ballets Russes and Edward Gordon Craig; spec. photographic archives incl. Houston Rogers, Gordon Anthony and Anthony Crickmay; Head MARGARET BENTON.

Wallace Collection: Hertford House, Manchester Square, London, W1M 6BN; tel. (171) 935-0687; fax (171) 224-2155; f. 1900; outstanding collections of pictures, miniatures, sculpture, French furniture, clocks, ceramics, Sèvres porcelain, bronzes, arms and armour and *objets d'art*, bequeathed to the nation in 1897 by Lady Wallace; Dir ROSALIND SAVILL.

Whitechapel Art Gallery: Whitechapel High St, London, E1 7QX; tel. (171) 377-5015; fax (171) 377-1685; f. 1901; temporary exhibitions, principally of modern or contemporary art; no permanent collection; charitable trust supported by the Arts Council, local authorities, charitable bodies and the business community; Chair. of Trustees STEPHEN KEYNES; Dir CATHERINE LAMPERT.

Manchester

Manchester City Art Galleries: corner of Mosley St and Princess St, Manchester, M2 3JL; tel. (161) 236-5244; f. 1823; British paintings, drawings, sculpture, old masters and decorative arts; other galleries: Gallery of Costume, Platt Hall (clothes since the 17th century), Wythenshawe Hall and Heaton Hall; Dir RICHARD GRAY; closed until 2001.

Manchester Museum: The University, Manchester, M13 9PL; tel. (161) 275-2634; f. 1821; archaeology, Egyptology, ethnology, geology, botany, zoology, entomology, archery, numismatics; education and exhibition services; Dir TRISTRAM BESTERMAN.

Museum of Science and Industry in Manchester: Liverpool Rd, Manchester, M3 4FP; tel. (161) 832-2244; fax (161) 833-2184; f. 1983; housed in the world's oldest passenger railway station; displays of computers, microscopes; large display of stationary steam engines running on live steam; gas engines, early motor cars, steam and diesel locomotives; National Electricity Gallery; Air and Space Gallery; exhibitions: Underground Manchester, The Making of Manchester; Xperiment! (inter-active science centre); 'Out of this World' Space Gallery; National Gas Gallery; 'Fibres, Fabrics and Fashion' Gallery; Dir Dr J. PATRICK GREENE.

Newcastle upon Tyne

Museum of Antiquities of the University and the Society of Antiquaries of Newcastle upon Tyne: Department of Archaeology, The University, Newcastle upon Tyne, NE1 7RU; tel. (191) 222-7849; fax (191) 222-8561; f. 1813; prehistoric, Roman and medieval collections, scale models of Hadrian's Wall, reproductions of Roman arms and armour, and reconstruction of a Temple of Mithras; departmental library of 18,000 items relating to Hadrian's Wall, British, Continental and Mediterranean archaeology; Museums Officer L. ALLASON-JONES.

Tyne and Wear Museums: Newcastle Discovery Museum, Blandford Square, Newcastle upon Tyne, NE1 4JA; tel. (191) 232-6789; fax (191) 230-2614; Dir DAVID FLEMING.

Selected museums and galleries:

Laing Art Gallery: Higham Place, Newcastle upon Tyne, NE1 8AG; f. 1904; British oil paintings and watercolours from 1700 (incl. works by Reynolds, Gainsborough, Turner, Landseer, Burne-Jones, Holman Hunt, Spencer, etc.) and a special display of works by John Martin; British and Newcastle silver, ceramics and glass (incl. display of enamelled glass by William Beilby); British textiles; temporary exhibitions (Egyptian, Greek and Roman antiquities, Oriental collection).

Newcastle Discovery: Blandford Square, Newcastle upon Tyne; f. 1981; eight galleries with displays of fashion, military history, social history and maritime history, and regular temporary exhibitions; Inter-Active Science Centre; Great City! and People's Galleries, and ship 'Turbina'.

Sunderland Museum and Art Gallery: Borough Rd, Sunderland; local history; English pottery, silver, paintings and glass; natural history.

Shipley Art Gallery: Prince Consort Rd, Gateshead; contemporary craft; also British paintings and old masters.

South Shields Museum and Art Gallery: Ocean Rd, South Shields; local history.

Hancock Museum: Barras Bridge, Newcastle upon Tyne, NE2 4PT; tel. (191) 2227418; f. 1829; general zoology, ornithology, geology, botany and ethnology; also temporary exhibitions; headquarters and property of the Natural History Society of Northumbria; Curator A. COLES.

Newport (Gwent)

Borough of Newport Museum and Art Gallery: John Frost Square, Newport, Gwent, NP9 1PA; tel. (1633) 840064; f. 1888; special collections of Roman material from Caerleon and Caerwent; oils, early English watercolours and prints; teapot displays; natural and local history collections; Museum Officer R. TRETT.

Norwich

Norfolk Museums Service: Norwich, Norfolk, NR1 3JU; tel. (1603) 493624; Dir (vacant).

Selected museums:

Castle Museum: Norwich; Norman Keep; fine art, ceramics, social history, natural history, archaeology.

Royal Norfolk Regimental Museum: Norwich; social history of the county regiment from 1685.

Bridewell Museum: Norwich; local industries and crafts in medieval house.

Maritime Museum for East Anglia: Great Yarmouth; various aspects of East Anglian maritime history.

Tolhouse Museum: Great Yarmouth; history of Great Yarmouth and brass-rubbing centre.

Elizabethan House Museum: Great Yarmouth; domestic life, toys, porcelain, glassware.

Lynn Museum: King's Lynn; social history, natural history, archaeology and geology of West Norfolk.

Town House: King's Lynn; history of King's Lynn.

Ancient House Museum: White Hart St, Thetford; 15th-century timber-framed building; Breckland life, natural history, brass rubbing centre.

Norfolk Rural Life Museum and Union Farm: Gressenhall; farm tools and implements, engines; workshop reconstruction; working farm.

Cromer Museum: Cromer; local history, archaeology, geology, natural history.

Sainsbury Centre for Visual Arts: University of East Anglia, Norwich, Norfolk, NR4 7TJ; tel. (1603) 592467; fax (1603) 259401; f. 1978; modern European art and art of other cultures and periods; library of 13,000 vols (mainly non-Western art and anthropology); Dir of Galleries N. JOHNSON; Librarian P. HEWITT.

Nottingham

Castle Museum: Nottingham, NG1 6EL; tel. (115) 915-3700; fax (115) 915-3653; f. 1878; archaeology and ethnography, fine and applied arts, military and social history; temporary exhibitions and educational activities; Dir MICHAEL WILLIAMS.

Nottingham Natural History Museum: Wollaton Hall, Nottingham; f. 1867; collections of botanical, zoological, and geological material; extensive British and foreign herbaria, Crowfoot collection of exotic butterflies, Pearson collection of European butterflies, Fowler collection of British Coleoptera, Hollier collection of Wenlock Limestone fossils, Carrington series of Mountain Limestone fossils; library of 3,500 vols; Nottinghamshire environmental database; controlled by Nottingham City Council; Senior Keeper G. WALLEY.

Oxford

Ashmolean Museum, University of Oxford: Beaumont St, Oxford; tel. (1865) 278000; fax (1865) 278018; f. 1683; contains the art and archaeological collections of the University of Oxford; British, European, Mediterranean, Egyptian and Near Eastern archaeology; Italian, Dutch, Flemish, French and English oil paintings; Old Master and modern drawings, water-colours and prints; miniatures; European ceramics; sculpture and bronzes; English silver; objects of applied art; Hope collection of engraved portraits; coins and medals of all countries and periods; Chinese and Japanese porcelain, paintings and lacquer; Chinese bronzes, Tibetan art; Indian sculpture and painting; Islamic pottery and metalwork; Dir Dr CHRISOPHER BROWN; publs *Annual Report*, *The Ashmolean* (2 a year).

Museum of Modern Art Oxford: 30 Pembroke St, Oxford, OX1 1BP; tel. (1865) 722733; fax (1865) 722573; f. 1965; major exhibitions of 20th-century painting, sculpture, design, photography, architecture, film and video; lectures, seminars, films, workshops; Dir KERRY BROUGHER.

Pitt Rivers Museum, University of Oxford: South Parks Rd, Oxford, OX1 3PP; tel. (1865) 270927; f. 1884; part of the School of Anthropology and Museum Ethnography of the University; teaching and research on the ethnology, prehistory and cultures of the whole world from man's emergence; library of 30,000 vols, 250 periodicals, photographic and documentary archives; Dir Dr MICHAEL O'HANLON; publs occasional papers, monographs (irregular).

Plymouth

Plymouth City Museum and Art Gallery: Drake Circus, Plymouth, Devon PL4 8AJ; tel. (1752) 264878; f. 1897 to illustrate the arts and sciences of the West Country; comprises the Cottonian Collection of early printed and illuminated books, Old Master engravings and drawings, and portraits by Sir Joshua Reynolds; general collections of Fine Art (16th – 20th-century) and of Decorative Arts including Plymouth silver and William Cookworthy's Plymouth and Bristol porcelain; natural history, archaeology and local history; the Museum provides displays and interpretation in Buckland Abbey, owned and administered by the National Trust, originally a medieval monastery and subsequently Sir Francis Drake's home, the Merchant's House (f. 1977), 33 St Andrew's St (16 – 17th-century); Curator NICOLA MOYLE.

Portsmouth

Portsmouth City Museum and Records Office: Museum Rd, Portsmouth, Hants, PO1 2LJ; tel. (1705) 827261; fax (1705) 875276; f. 1972; local history, art; City Museums and Records Officer SARAH QUAIL.

Branch museums:

Charles Dickens Birthplace: 393 Old Commercial Rd, Portsmouth, Hants, PO1 4QL; f. 1903; built *c.* 1800; decorated and furnished in style of the period.

D-Day Museum and Overlord Embroidery: Clarence Esplanade, Southsea, Hants; f. 1984; houses the Overlord Embroidery; displays of original archive material, vehicles, uniforms and artefacts.

Natural History Museum: Eastern Parade, Southsea, Portsmouth, Hants, PO4 9RF; f. 1930; wildlife dioramas and geology of the Portsmouth area; freshwater aquarium and European butterflies flying free.

Southsea Castle: Clarence Esplanade, Southsea, Hants, PO5 3PA; f. 1967; built 1544 by Henry VIII; exhibition on the military history of Portsmouth and life in the castle.

Preston

Harris Museum and Art Gallery: Market Square, Preston, Lancs, PR1 2PP; tel. (1772) 258248; fax (1772) 886764; e-mail pbch@harris.demon.co.uk; f. 1882; specialist collections in the fields of fine art, decorative art, archaeology, local history; temporary exhibitions of contemporary art and local history; workshops, children's activities; watercolour and costume galleries; Dir ALEXANDRA WALKER.

Reading

Museum of Reading: Blagrave St, Reading, Berks, RG1 1QH; tel. (118) 939-9800; f. 1883 to collect, preserve and exhibit objects of art, archaeology and science, especially of the district; special collections: Silchester collection of Romano-British remains; Blake's Lock Branch Museum treats Reading's industry, commerce and waterways; Dir K. HULL.

Rural History Centre/Museum of English Rural Life: University of Reading, Whiteknights, POB 229, Reading, Berks., RG6 6AG; f. 1951; national collection of objects, photographs and records of English rural and agricultural history; special collection of archives and publications of agricultural engineering firms and national agricultural institutions; bibliographical index of classified references to the printed literature of British agricultural history; *c.* 1 million photographic prints and negatives; library of 70,000 vols incl. large sections on agricultural sciences and technology and pre-1950 agricultural development overseas; Dir Prof. E. J. T. COLLINS.

St Helens

Pilkington Glass Museum: Prescot Rd, St Helens, Merseyside, WA10 3TT; tel. (1744) 692499; fax (1744) 692727; f. 1964; illustrates the evolution of glassmaking techniques, and how the product has been used since Phoenician times; private museum, forming an integral part of the head office complex of Pilkington PLC; f. 1826 (as St Helens Crown Glass Co); library: reference 1,500 vols; Curator I. M. BURGOYNE.

St Peter Port (Guernsey)

Guernsey Museum and Art Gallery: Candie Gardens, St Peter Port, Guernsey; tel. (1481) 726518; fax (1481) 715177; f. 1978 (as Lukis Museum 1909); tells story of the island and its people; includes art gallery displaying pictures of Guernsey and by Guernsey painters, and audio visual theatre; offers education service; maritime and military brs at Fort Grey and Castle Cornet; Dir PETER SARL; publs museum guides, *Guernsey Museum Monographs*.

Salisbury

Salisbury and South Wiltshire Museum: The King's House, 65 The Close, Salisbury, Wilts; tel. (1722) 332151; fax (1722) 325611; f. 1860; archaeology, local history, ceramics, costume, Pitt Rivers collection; Dir P. R. SAUNDERS; publ. *Annual Report*.

Selborne

Gilbert White's House and Garden and the Oates Museum: The Wakes, High St, Selborne, Alton, Hants; tel. (1420) 511275; f. 1954; private collections funded by the Oates Memorial Trust; furnished period rooms, original MS of Natural History of Selborne, plants of 18th century grown in the garden; exploration in Africa by Frank Oates and in Antarctica by Capt. Lawrence Oates; Oates Memorial Library.

Sheffield

Kelham Island Museum: Alma St, Sheffield, S3 8RY; tel. (114) 272-2106; f. 1982; shows past 300 years of Sheffield's industries (12,000 hp steam engine, Bessemer converter, cutlery workshops, etc.); Exec. Dir JOHN HAMSHERE.

Sheffield City Museum and Mappin Art Gallery: Weston Park, Sheffield, Yorks, S10 2TP; tel. (114) 276-8588; fax (114) 275-0957; e-mail sheffmu@mag.demon.co.uk; f. 1875; collections of Sheffield cutlery, Old Sheffield Plate, British and European cutlery, coins and medals, ceramics, local archaeology, natural sciences, local geology, etc.; Victorian paintings; Senior Principal Keeper JANET BARNES.

Singleton

Weald and Downland Open Air Museum: Singleton, Chichester, W. Sussex, PO18 0EU; tel. (1243) 811348; fax (1243) 811475; e-mail wealddown@mistral.co.uk; f. 1967 to save interesting examples of vernacular architecture from South East England which have been threatened with demolition; so far more than 35 buildings ranging from medieval times to 19th century have been re-erected on the site; research library and educational material available; Dir C. ZEUNER; Research Dir R. HARRIS; publ. Guide Books.

Southampton

Southampton City Art Gallery: Civic Centre, Southampton, Hants., SO14 7LP; tel. (1703) 632601; f. 1916 by a bequest fund for purchase and display of works of art; opened 1939; collections include Old Masters, French 19th- and 20th-century School, British painting from the 18th century to present day, with emphasis on the Camden Town School; large collection of British contemporary painting and sculpture; library of 1,500 vols; activities include a temporary exhibition programme, Education Service and community outreach programme, Artshop; City Arts Man. STEPHEN SNODDY.

Southport

Atkinson Art Gallery: Lord St, Southport, Merseyside; tel. (1704) 533133, ext. 2110; f. 1878 for the exhibition of the town's permanent collection; 18th-, 19th- and 20th-century British oils and watercolours, contemporary sculpture, paintings and prints; Keeper of Art Galleries and Museums ANTHONY K. WRAY.

Stoke on Trent

Chatterley Whitfield Mining Museum: Tunstall, Stoke on Trent, North Staffs, ST6 8UN; tel. (1782) 813337; f. 1979 at a former colliery; aims to demonstrate the realities of mining development; recreation of surface and underground conditions; reference library; mining artefacts, photographs, films, documents, maps and plans, and oral history recordings; Dir JAMES HUTCHINSON; publs *Schools Roadshow Pack, Primary Teachers' Pack, Chatterley Whitfield News*.

Potteries Museum and Art Gallery: Hanley, Stoke on Trent, Staffs, ST1 3DE; tel. (1782) 232323; fax (1782) 232500; Staffordshire pottery and porcelain, art, natural history, archaeology, local history; also administers Ford Green Hall, Smallthorne, a timber-framed building of *c.* 1624; and Etruria Industrial Museum: the last steam-powered potter's mill in Britain; Gladstone Working Pottery Museum; Asst Dir (Cultural Services) I. LAWLEY; publs *Journal of Ceramic History, Staffordshire Archaeological Studies*.

Wakefield

Wakefield Museums, Galleries and Castles: Wakefield Art Gallery, Wentworth Terrace, Wakefield, W. Yorks; tel. (1924) 305796; fax (1924) 305770; museums and sites incl. Wakefield Art Gallery, Wakefield Museum, Pontefract Museum, Castleford Museum Room, Pontefract Castle, Sandal Castle; Museums and Galleries Officer GORDON WATSON.

Widnes

Catalyst—The Museum of the Chemical Industry: Gossage Bldg, Mersey Rd, Widnes, Cheshire, WA8 0DF; tel. (151) 420-1121; fax (151) 495-2030; f. 1987; to inform the public about the role of the chemical industry in society past and present, including its relationship to the environment; reference library on history of the chemical industry; archive of historical photographs; collection of relevant artefacts; Dir Dr G. RINTOUL.

Wolverhampton

Wolverhampton Art Gallery and Museum: Lichfield St, Wolverhampton, W. Midlands, WV1 1DU; tel. (1902) 552055; fax (1902) 552053; f. 1884; collections of 18th-, 19th- and 20th-century fine art, oriental art and weapons, geology, local history; Branch museums: Bantock House (English enamels, porcelain, japanned ware); Bilston Art Gallery and Museum (English enamels and local history exhibits); Arts and Museums Officer NICHOLAS DODD; Bantock House and Bilston Art Gallery and Museum were expected to be closed until Spring 1999.

York

Jorvik Viking Centre: Coppergate, York, YO1 1NT; tel. (1904) 643211; fax (1904) 627097; e-mail jorvik@jvcyork.demon.co.uk; f. 1984; exhibits excavated by York Archaeological Trust; full-scale reconstruction of the excavated street, vendors, craftsmen, a Viking home, etc.; *c.* 500 excavated items are displayed in the Skipper Gallery.

National Railway Museum: Leeman Road, York, YO2 4XJ; tel. (1904) 621261; fax (1904) 611112; f. 1975; part of the Science Museum (*q.v.*); houses a large part of the National Railway Collection reflecting over 150 years of British railway heritage; full-size rolling stock of diesel, electric and steam locomotives, carriages and wagons, models, signalling equipment, railway relics, posters, prints, films, technical drawings, photographs and paintings; library of 15,000 vols; Head ANDREW SCOTT.

York Castle Museum: York; tel. (1904) 653611; fax (1904) 671078; f. 1938; England's first major folk museum; Kirk collection illustrates English life in the 17th – 20th centuries, including reconstructed shops and streets; also costumes, arms and armour, craft workshops; nearby is the 'York Story' at the Heritage Centre, Castlegate, depicting the social and architectural history of the City of York; Dir (vacant).

York City Art Gallery: Exhibition Square, York, YO1 2EW; tel. (1904) 551861; fax (1904) 551866; f. 1879; permanent collection consists of paintings of the Italian, Dutch, Flemish, German, French, Spanish and British Schools and includes the Lycett Green Collection (presented through the NACF 1955); there is a collection of works by William Etty, and other York artists; a collection of modern stoneware pottery and an extensive collection of prints and drawings, largely devoted to the topography of York; temporary art exhibitions throughout the year; library of 7,000 vols; Curator RICHARD GREEN.

Yorkshire Museum: Museum Gardens, York, YO1 2DR; tel. (1904) 629745; fax (1904) 651221; e-mail yorkshire.museum@york.gov.uk; f. 1822; important and extensive collections of archaeology (Roman, Anglo-Saxon and Viking life), natural history, geology, numismatics and ceramics; Curator PAUL HOWARD.

Universities

UNIVERSITY OF ABERDEEN

Aberdeen, AB24 3FX

Telephone: (1224) 272000

Telex: 73458

Fax: (1224) 276054

Founded 1495

Chancellor: Lord WILSON OF TILLYORN

Vice-Chancellor and Principal: Prof. C. DUNCAN RICE
Senior Vice-Principal: Prof. I. R. MACDONALD
Vice-Principals: Prof. A. R. FORRESTER, Prof. G. R. D. CATTO
Secretary: S. CANNON
Director of Information Systems and Services: G. H. S. PRYOR
Library: see Libraries
Number of teachers: 842
Number of students: 11,292
Publications: *Aberdeen University Calendar*, *Aberdeen University Review*, *Staff Lists*, *Undergraduate Prospectus*, *Postgraduate Prospectus*.

VICE-PRINCIPALS AND DEANS

Faculty of Arts and Divinity: Dr G. ROBERTS
Faculty of Social Sciences and Law: Prof. P. J. SLOANE
Faculty of Science and Engineering: Prof. D. F. HOULIHAN
Faculty of Medicine and Medical Sciences: Prof. S. D. LOGAN

PROFESSORS

Faculty of Arts and Divinity:
BRIDGES, R. C., History and Economic History
BRITTON, C. M., French
CAMERON, J. R., Philosophy
DUKES, P., History and Economic History
FERGUSSON, D. A. S., Divinity with Religious Studies
GRAHAM, L. G., Moral Philosophy
HARRIS, D., Spanish
HEWITT, D. S., English
IRWIN, D. G., History of Art
JOHNSTONE, W., Divinity with Religious Studies
MACDONALD, I. R., Spanish
MACINESS, A. I., History and Economic History
MARSHALL, I. H., Divinity with Religious Studies
MATTHEWS, E. H., Philosophy
MEEK, D. M., Celtic
PAYNE, P. L., History and Economic History
PORTER, J. W., English (Elphinstone Institute)
ROUSSEAU, G. S., English
SAUNDERS, A. M., French
STEPHENS, Rev. W. P., Divinity with Religious Studies
THOMANECK, J., German
THROWER, J. A., Divinity with Religious Studies

Faculty of Social Sciences and Law:
ADAMS, C. D., Land Economy
ARTER, D., Politics and International Relations
BEAUMONT, P. R., Law (European and Private International Law)
BRUCE, S., Sociology
BRYDEN, J., Geography (Arkleton Centre)
BUCKLAND, R., Accountancy
CAREY-MILLER, D. L., Law (Jurisprudence)
CHAPMAN, K., Geography
CLAPPERTON, C., Geography
CLARK, B., Geography
CUSINE, D. J., Law (Conveyancing and Professional Practice of Law)
DUFF, P. R., Law
ELLIOTT, R., Economics
EVANS-JONES, R., Law (Jurisprudence)
FORTE, A. D. M., Law (Commercial Law)
FRASER, P., Accountancy
GANE, G. H. W., Law (Scots Law)
HEALD, D., Accountancy
HENDRY, L. B., Education
HOESLI, M., Accountancy
JORDAN, A. G., Politics and International Relations
KEMP, A. G., Economics
LEE, C. H., Economics
LYALL, F., Law (Public Law)
MACGREGOR, B., Land Economy
MATHER, A., Geography
ROBERTS, C., Accountancy
ROWAN-ROBINSON, R. J., Land Economy
SALMON, T., Politics and International Relations
SHEEHAN, M. J., Politics and International Relations
SHUCKSMITH, D. M., Land Economy
SLOANE, P. J., Economics
URWIN, D., Politics and International Relations

Faculty of Science and Engineering:
ALEXANDER, I., Plant and Soil Science
ARCHBOLD, R. J., Mathematical Sciences
BAKER, M. J., Engineering
BOYLE, P. R., Zoology
CAMERON, G. G., Chemistry
CHANDLER, H. M., Engineering
CRESSER, M. S., Plant and Soil Science
DELLA SALA, S. F., Psychology
DEREGOWSKI, J. B., Psychology
DUFFY, J. A., Chemistry
FLIN, R., Psychology
FORRESTER, A. R., Chemistry
GLASSER, F. P., Chemistry
GORMAN, D. G., Engineering
GRAY, P. M. D., Computing Science
HALL, G. S., Mathematical Sciences
HOULIHAN, D. F. J., Zoology
HUBBUCK, J. R., Mathematical Sciences
HURST, A., Geology and Petroleum Geology
INGRAM, M. D., Chemistry
JOLLIFFE, I., Mathematical Sciences
KILLHAM, K. S., Plant and Soil Science
LOGIE, R. H., Psychology
LOMAX, M. A., Agriculture
MILLER, H. G., Forestry
MORDUE, W., Zoology
NAYLOR, R. E. L., Agriculture
PENMAN, J., Engineering
PLAYER, M. A., Engineering
RACEY, P. A., Zoology
RODGER, A. A., Engineering
SALZEN, E. A., Psychology
SLEEMAN, D. H., Computing Science
SPRACKLEN, C. T., Engineering
THOMSON, K. J., Agriculture
VAS, P., Engineering
WEST, A. R., Chemistry
WILLETTS, B. B., Engineering
WILLIAMS, B. P. J., Geology and Petroleum Geology

Faculty of Medicine and Medical Sciences:
ALEXANDER, D. A., Mental Health
ASHFORD, M. L. J., Biomedical Sciences
BOOTH, I. R., Microbiology
CASSIDY, J., Medicine and Therapeutics (Oncology)
CATTO, G. R. D., Medicine and Therapeutics
DOCHERTY, K., Molecular and Cell Biology (Biochemistry)
DONALDSON, C. R., Public Health
EREMIN, O., Surgery
FORRESTER, J. V., Ophthalmology
FOTHERGILL, J. E., Molecular and Cell Biology (Biochemistry)
GILBERT, F. J., Radiology
GOLDEN, M. H. N., Medicine and Therapeutics
GOODAY, G. W., Molecular and Cell Biology
GOW, N. A. R., Molecular and Cell Biology
GREAVES, M., Medicine and Therapeutics (Haematology)
HAITES, N. E., Medicine and Therapeutics, and Molecular and Cell Biology
HAMILTON, W. A., Medical Microbiology
HANNAFORD, P., Primary Care
HARRIS, W. J., Molecular and Cell Biology (Genetics)
HAWKSWORTH, G. M., Biomedical Sciences, and Medicine and Therapeutics
HELMS, P. J. B., Child Health
HUKINS, D. W. L., Biomedical Physics and Bioengineering
HUTCHISON, J. D., Surgery (Orthopaedics)
JEFFERY, J., Molecular and Cell Biology
KIDD, C., Biomedical Sciences (Physiology)
LITTLE, J., Medicine and Therapeutics (Epidemiology)
LOGAN, S. D., Biomedical Sciences (Neuroscience)
MAUGHAN, R. J., Environmental and Occupational Medicine
MILTON, A. S., Biomedical Sciences (Pharmacology)
NORMAN, J. N., General Practice and Primary Care
OGSTON, D., Medicine and Therapeutics
PENNINGTON, T. H., Medical Microbiology
PETRIE, J. C., Medicine and Therapeutics
PORTER, R. W., Surgery
PROSSER, J. I., Molecular and Cell Biology
RALSTON, S. H., Medicine and Therapeutics
REES, A. J., Medicine and Therapeutics
RITCHIE, L. D., General Practice and Primary Care
RUSSELL, E. M., Public Health
SEATON, A., Environmental and Occupational Medicine
SEYMOUR, D. G., Medicine and Therapeutics, and General Practice and Primary Care
SHARP, P. F., Biomedical Physics and Bioengineering
SHAW, D. J., Molecular and Cell Biology
TEMPLETON, A. A., Obstetrics and Gynaecology
WALKER, F., Pathology
WEBSTER, N. R., Medicine and Therapeutics (Anaesthesia and Intensive Care)
WEIR, J., Radiology
WHALLEY, L. J., Mental Health
WISCHIK, C. M., Mental Health
WOOD, R. A., Medicine and Therapeutics

DIRECTORS

Centre for Defence Studies: D. E. GREENWOOD
Centre for Soviet and East European Studies: Prof. P. DUKES
Centre for the Study of Religions: J. A. THROWER
Language Laboratory: G. R. TRENGOVE
Thomas Reid Institute for Research in the Humanities: G. S. ROUSSEAU

ASSOCIATED INSTITUTES

Macaulay Land Use Research Institute: see under Research Institutes.

Marine Laboratory of the Department of Agriculture and Fisheries for Scotland: Dir Prof. A. D. HAWKINS.

Rowett Research Institute: see under Research Institutes.

Institute of Terrestrial Ecology (NERC): see under Natural Environment Research Council.

UNIVERSITY OF ABERTAY DUNDEE

Bell St, Dundee, DD1 1HG
Telephone: (1382) 308000
Fax: (1382) 308877

Founded 1888 as Dundee Technical Institute, present name and status 1994
Academic year: October to June

Chancellor: Rt Hon. Earl of AIRLIE
Vice-Chancellor and Principal: Prof. B. KING
Vice-Principal: Prof. J. MCGOLDRICK
Assistant Principal (External Relations): G. A. WRIGHT
Assistant Principal (Finance and Administration): D. J. HOGARTH
Chief Librarian: I. G. LLOYD

Library of 100,000 items
Number of teachers: 230 full-time, 150 part-time

Number of students: 3,800 full-time, 750 part-time

HEADS OF SCHOOL

School of Accountancy and Law: R. JELLY
School of Construction and Environment: Dr J. MUNDAY
School of Engineering: Prof. P. MARTIN
School of Computing: Dr I. MARSHALL
School of Management: Dr W. S. HOWE
School of Molecular and Life Sciences: Prof. D. A. ROSS
School of Social and Health Sciences: Prof. M. SWANSTON

ATTACHED RESEARCH INSTITUTES

Waste Water Technology Centre: Co-ordinator Prof. R. M. ASHLEY.

Scottish Institute for Wood Technology: Senior Research Dir Dr J. W. PALFREYMAN.

Sino-Scottish Institute: Dir Dr YIFA CAI.

Tayside Economic Research Centre: Dr M. HEAFEY.

ATTACHED SCHOOL

Dundee Business School: Dudhope Castle, Dundee, DD3 6HF; Dir G. MARTIN.

ANGLIA POLYTECHNIC UNIVERSITY

Chelmsford Campus: Rivermead Campus, Bishop Hall Lane, Chelmsford, CM1 1SQ
Cambridge Campus: East Rd, Cambridge, CB1 1PT
Danbury Campus: Danbury Park, Chelmsford, CM3 4AT

Telephone: (1245) 493131 (Chelmsford); (1223) 63271 (Cambridge); (1245) 222141 (Danbury)
Fax: (1245) 490835

University status 1992
Academic year: September to July

Chancellor: Lord PRIOR
Vice-Chancellor: MICHAEL MALONE-LEE
Deputy Vice-Chancellor: Prof. ANTHONY POWELL
Librarian: NICOLA KERSHAW

Number of teachers: 709
Number of students: 14,000

DEANS

Applied Sciences: Prof. MICHAEL DAVIES
Arts and Letters: Prof. IAN GORDON
Business: Prof. HUGH JENKINS
Design and Communication Systems: RICHARD WOOLLEY
Education: Prof. BRIAN UNDERWOOD
Languages and Social Science: ERICA MORGAN
Law: Prof. JOHN WHITE
Health-Care Practice: DAWN HILLIER
Community Health and Social Studies: LESLEY DOBREE

ASTON UNIVERSITY

Aston Triangle, Birmingham, B4 7ET
Telephone: (121) 359-3611
Fax: (121) 333-6350
E-mail: support@aston.ac.uk

Founded as Birmingham Municipal Technical School 1895, Central Technical College 1927, College of Advanced Technology 1956, University Charter 1966
Academic year: October to June

Chancellor: Sir ADRIAN CADBURY
Pro-Chancellor: Sir MICHAEL BETT
Vice-Chancellor: Prof. M. T. WRIGHT
Senior Pro-Vice-Chancellor: Prof. B. J. TIGHE
Pro-Vice-Chancellors: Prof. N. B. R. REEVES, Dr F. HEWITT
University Secretary and Registrar: R. D. A. PACKHAM
Director of Library and Information Services: Dr N. R. SMITH

Library: see Libraries and Archives
Number of teachers: 343
Number of students: 5,222 full-time, 923 part-time

Publications: *Undergraduate Studies, Postgraduate Studies, Calendar, Guide for Overseas Students, Annual Report and Accounts, Regulations.*

DEANS

Faculty of Engineering and Applied Science: Dr J. D. MILLER
Faculty of Management, Languages and European Studies: Prof. E. W. DAVIS
Faculty of Life and Health Sciences: Prof. W. J. IRWIN

PROFESSORS

AGER, D. E., Languages and European Studies
BENNETT, D., Aston Business School
BENNION, I., Electronic Engineering and Computer Science
BILLINGTON, D., Pharmaceutical Sciences
BOOTH, R. T., Civil and Mechanical Engineering
BRIDGWATER, T., Chemical Engineering and Applied Chemistry
CARDWELL, M. J., Electronic Engineering and Computer Science
CHILTON, P. A., Languages and European Studies
DAVIS, E. W., Aston Business School
DORAN, N. J., Electronic Engineering and Computer Science
FOSTER, D. H., Vision Sciences
GÖRNER, R., Languages and European Studies
GREENLEY, G. E., Aston Business School
HARDING, G. F. A., Psychology and Human Biology
HAYNS, M. R., Civil and Mechanical Engineering
HOMER, J., Chemical Engineering and Applied Chemistry
HOOLEY, G. J., Aston Business School
IRWIN, W. J., Pharmaceutical Sciences
KETTLE, R., Civil and Mechanical Engineering
KNOWLES, F. E., Languages and European Studies
LATHAM, R. V., Computer Science and Applied Mathematics
LEWIS, C. D., Aston Business School
LOVERIDGE, R. J., Aston Business School
LOWE, D., Electronic Engineering and Computer Science
MCWHINNIE, W. R., Chemical Engineering and Applied Chemistry
MARTIN, I., Pharmaceutical Sciences
NORRIS, T., Civil and Mechanical Engineering
PAGE, C. L., Civil and Mechanical Engineering
PARKER, D., Aston Business School
REEVES, N. B. R., Languages and European Studies
SAUNDERS, J., Aston Business School
SLATER, N. K. H., Chemical Engineering and Applied Chemistry
TIGHE, B. J., Chemical Engineering and Applied Chemistry
TISDALE, M. J., Pharmaceutical Sciences
WRIGHT, M. T., Civil and Mechanical Engineering

AFFILIATED INSTITUTE

Aston Science Park (Birmingham Technology Ltd): Chief Exec. D. W. HARRIS.

UNIVERSITY OF BATH

Claverton Down, Bath, BA2 7AY
Telephone: (1225) 826826
Telex: 449097
Fax: (1225) 62508 (Group 3)

Founded 1856, designated College of Advanced Technology 1960, independent institution with direct-grant status 1962, University Charter 1966

Chancellor: Lord CHRISTOPHER TUGENDHAT
Vice-Chancellor: Prof. V. D. VANDELINDE
Secretary and Registrar: J. A. BURSEY
Librarian: H. NICHOLSON

Library: see Libraries
Number of teachers: 400
Number of students: 7,835

DEANS

Faculty of Humanities and Social Sciences: Prof. I. M. JAMIESON
Faculty of Engineering and Design: Prof. C. R. BURROWS
Faculty of Management: Prof. B. T. BAYLISS
Faculty of Science: Prof. D. J. G. DAVIES

DIRECTORS

Centre for Continuing Education: T. D. BILHAM
Bath Institute of Medical Engineering: Prof. S. C. LILLICRAP
Computing Services: J. HARLOW

PROFESSORS

ALMOND, D. P., Materials Science
BARNES, M. R., Civil Engineering
BAYLISS, B. T., Management
BIRD, D. M., Physics
BOARD, R. G., Biological Sciences
BRAMLEY, A. N., Mechanical Engineering
BUDD, C. J., Applied Mathematics
BULL, A., Modern Languages
BULLETT, D. W., Physics
BURROWS, C. R., Systems Engineering
CALDERHEAD, J., Education
CAMPBELL, M. M., Chemistry
CARLEN, P. C., Social Sciences
COLLARD, D., Economics
CRITTENDEN, B. D., Chemical Engineering
CRONIN, N. J., Physics
DANSON, M. J., Biochemistry
DAVENPORT, J. H., Information Technology
DAVIES, D. J. G., Pharmacy
EASTHAM, J. F., Power Engineering
EDGE, K. A., Mechanical Engineering
FINEMAN, S., Management
FITCH, J. P., Software Engineering
FORD, I. D., Management
FRAENKEL, L. E., Mathematical Sciences
FRANKS, N. R., Biology
FREWER, R. J. B., Architecture
GOUGH, I. R., Social Sciences
GRAVES, A. P., Management
GREEN, M., Inorganic Chemistry
HAMMOND, G. P., Environmental Engineering
HARRIS, B., Materials Science
HEADY, C. J., Applied Economics
HENSHAW, G. G., Plant Biology
HOLMAN, G. D., Biochemistry
HORROCKS, M., Surgical Science
HOWELL, J. A., Biochemical Engineering
HOWORTH, J. M., Modern Languages
HUNT, G. W., Mechanical Engineering
HURST, L. D., Biology
JAMIESON, I. M., Education
JENNISON, C., Statistics
JOHNS, A. T., Electrical Engineering
KLEIN, R. E., Social Policy and Administration
KOLACZKOWSKI, S. T., Chemical Engineering
LAMMING, R. C., Purchasing and Supply Management
LAUDER, H., Education
LILLICRAP, S. C., Medical Engineering
LUNT, G. G., Biochemistry
MADDISON, P. J., Pharmacy
MANN, S., Chemistry
MARKANDYA, A., Economics and International Development
MARSH, R. J., Modern Languages
MARSHALL, J., Management
MCENANEY, B., Materials Science

MEDLAND, A. J., Design Engineering
MILLAR, J., Social Policy
MILNER, P. C., Public Health
MONRO, D. M., Electronics
OWEN, J. M., Mechanical Engineering
PETER, L. M., Physical Chemistry
PICKERING, J., Business Strategy
POTTER, B. V. L., Pharmacy
PURCELL, J., Management
REDFERN, P., Pharmacy
REES, A. R., Biochemistry
REES, J. E., Pharmaceutics
REYNOLDS, S. E., Biology
RODGER, D., Electronic and Electrical Engineering
ROGERS, C., Probability
ROOM, G. J., Social Sciences
RUSSELL, P. ST. J., Physics
RYAN, E. P., Mathematical Sciences
SAINSBURY, M., Chemistry
SAUNDERS, G. A., Physics
SHALEV, D., Architecture
SLACK, J. M. W., Cell and Molecular Biology
SPENCE, A., Numerical Analysis
STANIFORTH, J. N., Pharmacy
STEVENS, R., Materials Science
TARGETT, D., Management
TAVERNOR, R. W., Architecture
THOMPSON, J. J., Education
TOLAND, J. F., Mathematics
TOMKINS, C. R., Business Finance
TYRELL, R. M., Pharmacy and Pharmacology
WALLACE, I., German
WARHURST, A., Management
WESTWICK, J., Pharmacy
WHITE, I. H., Physics
WILKINSON, B., Management
WILLIAMS, D., Mathematical Sciences
WILLIAMS, I., Chemistry
WILLIAMS, J. M. J., Chemistry
WILLIS, P. J., Mathematical Sciences

UNIVERSITY OF BIRMINGHAM

Edgbaston, Birmingham, B15 2TT
Telephone: (121) 414-3344
Telex: 333762
Fax: (121) 414-3971

Founded 1900
Academic year: September to June

Chancellor: Sir ALEX JARRATT
Vice-Chancellor and Principal: Prof. MAXWELL IRVINE
Vice-Principal: Prof. D. R. WESTBURY
Pro-Vice-Chancellors: Prof. M. S. SNAITH, Prof. F. M. YOUNG, Prof. M. G. CLARKE
Registrar and Secretary: D. J. ALLEN
Librarian: Dr C. D. FIELD

Library: see Libraries
Number of teachers: 1,241
Number of students: full-time 17,993

Publications: *Annual Report* (annually), *Annual Accounts* (annually), *Court Reporter* (annually), *Postgraduate Prospectus* (annually), *Undergraduate Prospectus* (annually), *The Birmingham Magazine* (annually), *Bulletin* (fortnightly, in termtime), *Medlines* (2 a year).

DEANS

Arts and Social Sciences: Prof. C. P. RICKWOOD
Engineering: Prof. J. F. KNOTT
Medicine, Dentistry and Health Sciences: Prof. W. F. DOE
Science: Prof. J. R. BLAKE

PROFESSORS

Arts:
BANFIELD, S. D., Music
BARKER, A., Classics
BIRKETT, J., French Studies
BREUILLY, J. J., Modern History
BRIGGS, A. D. P., Russian Language and Literature
BROOKS, N. P., Medieval History
BRYER, A. A. M., Byzantine Studies
BUTLER, M. G., Modern German Literature
CAESAR, M. P., Italian Studies
COSTA, C. D. N., Classics
COULTHARD, R. M., English Language and Linguistics
CROSSLEY, E. C. D., 19th-Century French Studies
DADSON, T. J., Hispanic Studies
DAVIES, L. A., English
DENT, N. J. H., Philosophy
DYER, C. C., Medieval Social History
EDGAR, D., Playwriting Studies
ELLIS, S., English Literature
FAULKES, A. R., Old Icelandic
GARSIDE, W. R., Economic and Social History
GOLDSTEIN, E. D., International History
HALDON, J. F., Byzantine History
HOLLAND, P., Shakespeare Studies
HUGHES, A., African Politics
HUNTER, J. R., Ancient History and Archaeology
JONES, P. M., French History
KAPLAN, J., Drama and Theatre Arts
LIMBREY, S., Environmental Archaeology
MCCULLOCH, G. W., Philosophy
MCLEOD, D. H., Church History
RANDALL, A. J., English Social History
SIMMONS, R. C., American History
SINCLAIR, J. M., Modern English Language
SMALL, I. C., English Literature
SPEIRS, R. C., German
STOREY, M. G., English Literature
TIMMS, C. R., Music
THORNTON, R. K. R., English Studies
TOOLAN, M., Applied English Linguistics
TURNER, D. A., Theology
TZIOVAS, D. P., Modern Greek Studies
USTORF, W., Mission
VERDI, R., Fine Art
WHENHAM, J., Music History
WICKHAM, C. J., Early Medieval History
WOOD, D. M., French Literature
VAN DER WILL, W., Modern German Studies
YOUNG, F. M., Theology

Commerce and Social Science:
BACKHOUSE, R. E., History and Philosophy of Economics
BATLEY, R. A., Development Administration
BURTON, J., Business Administration
CLARK, P. A., Commerce
CLARKE, M. G., Local Government Management
COOPER, J. M., Russian Economic Studies
COX, A. W., Strategic Procurement Management
CROFT, S. J., International Relations
DAVEY, K. J., Development Administration
DAVIS, A., Social Work
DEAKIN, N. D., Social Policy and Administration
DOLING, J. F., Housing Studies
FENDER, J., Macroeconomics
FRY, M. J., International Finance
HAM, C. J., Health Policy and Management
HANSON, P., Soviet Economics
JENNINGS, J., Political Theory
JONES, R. H., Public Sector Accounting
KELSEY, D., Economic Theory
LARRAIN, J., Social Theory
MARSH, D., Political Science and International Studies
MULLINEUX, A. W., Money and Banking
MURIE, A., Urban and Regional Studies
PATERSON, W. E., Institute for German Studies
RAFTERY, J. P., Health Economics
RAINE, J., Management in Criminal Justice
REDMOND, J., European Studies
RICHARDS, S., Public Management
RICKWOOD, C. P., Management Accounting
SAMUELS, J. M., Business Finance
SEN, S., Development Economics
SIEBERT, W. S., Labour Economics
SINCLAIR, P. J. N., Economics
SPENCER, K. M., Local Policy
SPURGEON, P. C., Health Services Management
SUGDEN, R., Industrial Economics
THEOBALD, M. F., Accounting
WILKES, F. M., Business Investment and Management

Education and Continuing Studies:
BURTON, L. M., Education
DANIELS, H. R. J., Special Education and Educational Psychology
DAVIES, M. L., International Education
HULL, J. M., Religious Education
MARTIN, G. R., Avian Sensory Science
RANSON, P. R. S., Education
RIBBINS, P. M., Education Management
THOMAS, H. R., Economics of Education
TOBIN, M. J., Special Education
WADE, C. B., English in Education

Engineering:
ABELL, S., Functional Materials
BAKER, C., Environmental Fluid Mechanics
BALL, A. A., Engineering Design
BELL, T., Metallurgy
BIDDLESTONE, A. J., Chemical Engineering
BOWEN, P., Mechanical Metallurgy
CAMPBELL, J., Casting Technology
CLARK, L. A., Structural Engineering
COATES, R. F. W., Environmental Electronics
DAWE, D. J., Structural Mechanics
DEAN, T. A., Manufacturing Engineering
EVANS, P. D., Electrical Engineering
FRYER, P. J., Chemical Engineering
HALEY, K. B., Operational Research
HALL, P. S., Communications Engineering
HARRIS, I. R., Materials Science
JONES, I. P., Physical Metallurgy
KING, T. G., Mechanical Engineering
KNIGHT, D., Water Engineering
KNOTT, J. F., Metallurgy and Materials
LORETTO, M. H., Materials Science and Technology
LYDDIATT, A., Process Biotechnology
MACKAY, G. M., Transport Safety
MADELIN, K. B., Civil Engineering
MARQUIS, P. M., Biomaterials
NEAL-STURGESS, C. E., Automotive Engineering
NIENOW, A. W., Biochemical Engineering
NORTON, J. P., Control Engineering
OATES, G., Principles of Industrial Design
PERRY, J. G., Civil Engineering
ROGERS, C., Geotechnical Engineering
RUSHTON, K. R., Civil Engineering
SEVILLE, J. P. K., Chemical Engineering
SNAITH, M. S., Highway Engineering
THOMAS, C. R., Biochemical Engineering
WALTON, D., Mechanical Engineering
WARNER, N. A., Minerals Engineering

Law:
ARNULL, A. M., European Law
BALDWIN, J., Judicial Administration
ELLIS, E. D., Public Law
FELDMAN, D. J., Jurisprudence
HARVEY, B. W., Property Law
MILLER, C. J., English Law
SCOTT, I. R., Law
WOODMAN, G., Comparative Law

Medicine, Dentistry and Health Sciences:
ADAMS, D. H., Hepatology
ANDERSON, R. J., Dental Public Health
BACON, P. A., Rheumatology
BARNETT, A. H., Diabetic Medicine
BEEVERS, D. G., Medicine
BOOTH, I. W., Paediatric Gastroenterology and Nutrition
BOWERY, N. G., Pharmacology
BROCKINGTON, I. F., Psychiatry
CHENG, K. K., Public Health and Epidemiology
CLIFFORD, C. M., Nursing

COOTE, J. H., Physiology
CORBETT, J. A., Developmental Psychiatry
CRADDOCK, N., Molecular Psychiatry
CRUIKSHANK, G. S., Neurosurgery
DAVENPORT, J. C., Primary Dental Care
FRAME, J. W., Oral Surgery
FRANKLYN, J. A., Medicine
GALLIMORE, P. H., Cancer Studies
GEDDES, A. D., Infection
GORDON, J., Cellular Immunology
GRAY, R., Medical Statistics
HARRINGTON, J. M., Occupational Health
HOBBS, F. D. R., General Practice
HUTTON, P., Anaesthetics and Intensive Care
JEFFERIS, R., Molecular Immunology
JEFFERYS, J. G. R., Neuroscience
JENKINSON, E. J., Experimental Immunology
JOHNS, E., Renal Science
JONES, E. L., Pathology
KEIGHLEY, M. R. B., Surgery
KENDALL, M., Classical Pharmacology
KERR, D. J., Clinical Oncology
LAIRD, W. R. E., Prosthetic Dentistry
LANGMAN, M. J. S., Medicine
LITTLER, W. A., Cardiovascular Medicine
LUESLEY, D. M., Gynaecological Oncology
MACLENNAN, I. C. M., Immunology
MAHER, E., Medical Genetics
MARQUIS, P. M., Biomaterials
MARSHALL, J. M., Cardiovascular Science
MORTON, D. B., Biomedical Science and Biomedical Ethics
MOSS, P. A. H., Haematology
MURRAY, P. I., Ophthalmology
NEWTON, J. R., Obstetrics and Gynaecology
OWEN, J. J. T., Anatomy
RICKINSON, A. B., Cancer Studies
SASHIDHARAN, S., Community Psychiatry
SAVAGE, C., Nephrology
SHEPPARD, M. C., Medicine
SINCLAIR, A. J., Geriatric Medicine
SMITH, A., Oral Biology
STEVENS, A., Public Health
STEWART, P. M., Medicine
TAYLOR, A. M. R., Cancer Genetics
TEMPLE, J. G., Surgery
TRAUB, R., Mathematical Neuroscience
TURNER, B. M., Experimental Genetics
WAKELAM, M. J. O., Molecular Pharmacology
WESTBURY, D. R., Physiology
WHITTLE, M. J., Fetal Medicine
WILLIAMS, A. C., Clinical Neurology
YOUNG, L. S., Cancer Biology

Science:

BALE, J. S., Environmental Biology
BARNDEN, J., Computer Science
BEYNON, T. D., Applied Physics
BLAKE, J. R., Applied Mathematics
BOCCA, J. B., Computer Science
BOONS, G. J., Bio-Organic Chemistry
BOOTH, D. A., Psychology
BROWN, K., Forensic and Family Psychology
BROWN, N. L., Molecular Genetics and Microbiology
BUSBY, S. J. W., Biochemistry
BUTLER, P. J., Comparative Physiology
CALLOW, J. A., Botany
CARROLL, D., Applied Psychology
CHIPMAN, K., Cell Toxicology
COCHRANE, R., Psychology
COLE, J. A., Microbial Physiology
COLEMAN, R., Medical Biochemistry
CRITCHLEY, F., Statistics
CRUISE, A. M., Astrophysics and Space Research
CUNINGHAME-GREEN, R. A., Industrial Mathematics
CURTIS, R., Combination Algebra
DANIELS, P. W., Geography
DOWELL, J. D., Elementary Particle Physics
EDWARDS, P. P., Inorganic Chemistry
FORGAN, E. M., Condensed Matter Physics
GARVEY, J., Particle Physics
GEORGESON, M. A., Psychology
GOUGH, C. E., Condensed Matter Physics
GREAVES, C., Solid State Chemistry
GUNN, J. M. F., Theoretical Physics
GURNELL, A. M., Physical Geography
HALLAM, A., Geology
HARRIS, K. D. M., Structural Chemistry
HARRISON, R. M., Environmental Health
HAWKES, D. D., Geological Sciences
HEATH, J. K., Biochemistry
HUMPHREYS, G. W., Cognitive Psychology
HUTTON, D. W., Earth Sciences
ISAAK, G. R., Physics
JACKSON, J. B., Bioenergetics
JARRATT, P., Computer Science
JONES, D. A., Sport and Exercise Sciences
JUNG, A., Computer Science
KEARSEY, M., Biometrical Genetics
KING, A. C., Applied Mathematics
KINSON, J. B., High Energy Physics
KNOWLES, P. J., Theoretical Chemistry
LAWRANCE, A. J., Statistics
LERNER, I., Theoretical Physcis
LLOYD, J. W., Hydrogeology
MACKAY, R., Hydrogeology
MICHELL, R. H., Biochemistry
NELSON, J. M., Nuclear Physics
ORFORD, J. F., Clinical and Community Psychology
PALMER, R. E., Experimental Physics
PETTS, G., Physical Geography
RIDDOCH, J., Cognitive Neuropsychology
ROBINSON, E. J., Developmental Psychology
SIMNETT, G. M., High-Energy Astrophysics
SLOMAN, A., Artificial Intelligence and Cognitive Science
SMITH, I. W. M., Chemistry
TAYLOR, E. W., Animal Physiology
THOMAS, C. M., Molecular Genetics
THOMAS, G. V., Psychology
TRAYER, I. P., Biochemistry
WALKER, R. T., Bio-organic Chemistry
WESTBROOK, G. K., Geophysics
WHITEHAND, J. W. R., Urban Geography
WILSON, J. S., Pure Mathematics
WING, A. M., Human Movement

DIRECTORS

Assessment Research Unit: R. J. RIDING
Automotive Engineering Centre: Prof. J. N. RANDLE
Barber Institute of Fine Arts: Prof. R. VERDI
Biochemical Engineering Research: Prof. C. R. THOMAS
Centre for Byzantine, Ottoman and Modern Greek Studies: Prof. J. F. HALDON
Centre for Educational Management and Policy Studies: P. R. S. RANSON
Centre for English Language Studies: C. J. KENNEDY
Centre for Religious Education Development and Research: M. H. GRIMMITT, J. H. HULL
Centre for Russian and East European Studies: Prof. J. M. COOPER
Centre for Strategic Procurement Management: Prof. A. W. COX
Centre for Urban and Regional Studies: Prof. A. MURIE
Centre of West African Studies: Prof. A. HUGHES
Dental School: Prof. R. J. ANDERSON
English for International Students Unit: M. J. HEWINGS
Field Archaeology Unit: S. BUTEUX, I. M. FERRIS, P. J. LEACH
Graduate Centre for Business Administration: J. R. SLATER
Health Services Management Centre: Prof. C. J. HAM
Information Services: C. D. FIELD
Institute for Advanced Research in the Humanities: Prof. J. T. BOULTON
Institute for German Studies: Prof. W. E. PATERSON
Institute of Child Health: Prof. I. W. BOOTH
Institute of European Law: Dr J. L. LONBAY
Institute of Judicial Administration: Dr J. BALDWIN
Institute of Surgery, Anaesthesia and Intensive Care: Prof. P. HUTTON
Shakespeare Institute: Prof. P. D. HOLLAND
Infection Research Division: D. CATTY
International Development: D. M. E. CURTIS
International Unit: M. L. DAVIES
IRC in Materials for High Performance Applications: Prof. M. H. LORETTO
Japan Centre: C. J. WATSON
Language Technology Research and Development Unit: Prof. R. M. COULTHARD
Modern Languages Unit: J. M. KLAPPER
Research Centre for the Education of the Visually Handicapped: Prof. M. J. TOBIN
Research Centre for Industrial Strategy: Dr C. P. OUGHTON

ATTACHED INSTITUTE

Institute of Research and Development: University of Birmingham Research Park, Vincent Drive, Edgbaston, Birmingham, B15 2SQ; tel. (121) 471-4977; opened 1986; aims to provide support and accommodation for commercial projects and companies arising from research in the University, or closely associated with University research; to assist in the transfer of technology from the University to commerce and industry; Chief Exec. Dr D. J. BURR.

BOURNEMOUTH UNIVERSITY

Fern Barrow, Poole, Dorset, BH12 5BB
Telephone: (1202) 524111
Fax: (1202) 595287
E-mail: marketing@bournemouth.ac.uk

Founded 1976 as Dorset Institute of Higher Education; became Bournemouth Polytechnic 1990; present name and status 1992

Academic year: September to July

Chancellor: Baroness COX
Vice-Chancellor: Prof. GILLIAN SLATER
Registrar: NOEL RICHARDSON
Librarian: DAVID BALL

Library of 150,000 vols
Number of teachers: 391
Number of students: 9,000 full-time, postgraduate and sandwich, 2,500 part-time

UNIVERSITY OF BRADFORD

Bradford, West Yorkshire, BD7 1DP
Telephone: (1274) 232323
Telex: 896827
Fax: (1274) 305340

Founded 1957 as Bradford Institute of Technology; University Charter 1966

Academic year: September to June (two semesters)

Chancellor: Baroness LOCKWOOD OF DEWSBURY
Vice-Chancellor and Principal: COLIN BELL
Deputy Vice-Chancellor: B. COSTALL
Pro-Vice-Chancellors: J. N. GREEN, C. MELLORS
Registrar and Secretary: N. J. ANDREW
Librarian: M. B. STEVENSON

Library: see Libraries
Number of teachers: 434
Number of students: 10,002

Publications: *University Undergraduate Prospectus, University Postgraduate Prospectus, Course and Research Booklets, Vice-Chancellor's Annual Report, Calendar, News and Views* (monthly in term-time).

DEANS

Engineering: J. G. GARDINER
Natural and Applied Sciences: G. ALDERSON
Social Sciences: A. WATON

PROFESSORS

(H = Head of Department)

ALDERSON, G., Medical Microbiology
BAKER, T. G., Biomedical Sciences (H)
BARRY, B. W., Pharmaceutical Technology
BENKREIRA, H., Coating and Polymer Processing
BIBBY, M. C., Cancer Biology
BUTLER, R. J., Organizational Analysis
CAVAZZA, M. O. C., Digital Media
CHRYSTYN, H., Pharmacy Practice
COATES, P. D., Polymer Engineering
COSTALL, B., Neuropharmacology
DANDO, M., International Security
DAY, A. J., Quality Engineering
DOUBLE, J. A., Experimental Cancer Chemotherapy
DYSON, K. H. F., European Studies
EARNSHAW, R. A., Electronic Imaging (H)
EDWARDS, H. G. M., Molecular Spectroscopy
FEATHERSTONE, K., European Politics
FELL, A. F., Pharmaceutical Chemistry
GALLAGHER, T. G. P., Ethnic Conflict and Peace
GARDINER, J. G., Electronic Engineering (H)
GARDNER, M. L. G., Physiological Biochemistry
GRAVES-MORRIS, P. R., Numerical Analysis
GREEN, J. N., Romance Linguistics
HIDEN, J. W., Modern European History
HUSBAND, C. H., Social Analysis
JAMES, A. L., Applied Social Studies
JOBBER, D., Marketing
KEYZER, D. M., Nursing
KOUVATSOS, D. D., Computer Systems Modelling
LLOYD, D. W., Industrial Technology (H)
LUCAS, J., Health Studies (H)
MCCOLM, I. J., Ceramic Materials (H)
MEINHOF, U. H., Cultural Studies
MELLORS, C., Political Science
MIRZA, H. R., International Business
MUHLEMANN, A. P., Operations Management
NAYLOR, R. J, Pharmacology (H)
O'HEAR, A., Philosophy
PIKE, R. H., Finance and Accounting
POLLARD, A. M., Archaeological Sciences (H)
ROGERS, P. F., Peace Studies (H)
SCHALLREUTER, K. U., Clinical and Experimental Dermatology
SEAWARD, M. R. D., Environmental Biology
SPARKES, J. R., Business Economics
STYLIOS, G., Industrial Systems Engineering
TAYLOR, W. A., Business Information Systems
THEW, M. T., Fluid Technology
TORSUN, I. S., Information Technology (H)
WALLS, J. R., Chemical Engineering
WEISS, J., Development Economics
WHALLEY, R., Mechanical Engineering (H)
WILLIAMS, A., Contemporary German Studies
WILSON, N., Credit Management
WINN, B., Optometry (H)
WOOD, J. M., Medical Biochemistry
WOODCOCK, L. V., Chemical Engineering Science
WRONSKI, A., Materials Science
YORK, P., Physical Pharmaceutics
ZAIRI, M., Best Practice Management

NON-PROFESSORIAL HEADS OF DEPARTMENT

Applied Social Studies: E. MOXON
Chemical Engineering: P. J. BAILES
Civil and Environmental Engineering: S. W. GARITY
Development and Project Planning Centre: J. W. CUSWORTH
Environmental Science: M. J. FRENCH
European Studies: R. ESPINOLA
Interdisciplinary Human Studies: D. R. FELLOWS
Modern Languages: J. RUSSELL
Social and Economic Studies: G. M. LITTLEJOHN

ATTACHED INSTITUTE

Development and Project Planning Centre: University of Bradford, Bradford, BD7 1DP, West Yorks.; f. 1969; 26 teachers; post-experience courses, in UK and overseas, for project planning and management and aspects of development policy and related issues, including management, decentralization, resource management, privatization; 12-month taught Master's courses in National Development and Project Planning, Macroeconomic Policy and Planning for Developing Countries, International Development Studies, Agricultural Development and Rural Finance, Project Planning and Management; Master's degrees and Doctorates by Research; Head J. W. CUSWORTH.

UNIVERSITY OF BRIGHTON

Lewes Rd, Brighton, BN2 4AT
Telephone: (1273) 600900
Fax: (1273) 642607
Founded 1970 as Brighton Polytechnic, present name and status 1992
Academic year: September to June
Director: Prof. D. WATSON
Deputy Director: D. E. HOUSE
Assistant Director (Academic): Dr S. LAING
Academic Registrar: P. J. REYNOLDS
Head of Learning Resources: C. MOON
Library of 550,000 vols
Number of teachers: 600 (full-time)
Number of students: 9,500 (full-time)

DEANS

Faculty of Arts and Architecture: Prof. B. BROWN
Faculty of Business: Prof. J. BAREHAM
Faculty of Education and Sport: PAUL GRIFFITHS
Faculty of Health: Prof. M. WHITING
Faculty of Information Technology: Prof. G. BULL
Faculty of Science and Engineering: Prof. F. MAILLARDET

HEADS OF SCHOOL

Faculty of Arts and Architecture:
School of Architecture and Design: (vacant)
School of Arts and Communication: BILL BEECH
School of Historical and Critical Studies: (vacant)

Faculty of Business:
Brighton Business School: Prof. AIDAN BERRY
School of Service Sector Management: Dr PAUL FROST
Centre for Research in Innovation Management: Prof. JOHN BESSANT

Faculty of Education and Sport:
School of Education: MAGGIE CARROLL
School of Languages: Prof. BRIAN HILL
Chelsea School: PAUL MCNAUGHT-DAVIS

Faculty of Health:
Institute of Nursing and Midwifery: SUE BERNHAUSER
School of Healthcare Professions: Dr LINDA LANG
School of Applied Social Science: (vacant)

Faculty of Information Technology:
School of Computing and Mathematical Sciences: Prof. DAN SIMPSON
School of Information Management: Dr PETER ENSER
Information Technology Research Institute: Prof. DONIA SCOTT

Faculty of Science and Engineering:
School of Engineering: Prof. ALAN JOHNS
School of the Environment: Prof. PETER GARDINER
School of Pharmacy and Biomolecular Sciences: Prof. STEPHEN DENYER

UNIVERSITY OF BRISTOL

Bristol BS8 1TH
Telephone: (117) 928-9000
Fax: (117) 925-1424
Founded 1909, previously established as University College, Bristol, 1876
Visitor: H.M. THE QUEEN
Chancellor: Sir JEREMY MORSE
Pro-Chancellors: Sir ROBERT WALL, T. P. DURIE, STELLA CLARKE
Vice-Chancellor: Sir JOHN KINGMAN
Deputy Vice-Chancellor: Prof. B. T. PICKERING
Pro-Vice-Chancellors: Prof. D. V. EVANS, Prof. T. M. PARTINGTON
Registrar: J. H. M. PARRY
Librarian: M. G. FORD
Library: see Libraries
Number of teachers: 1,058 including 208 professors
Number of students: (full-time and part-time): 12,577
Publications: *Calendar*, Prospectuses.

DEANS

Faculty of Arts: M. J. H. LIVERSIDGE
Faculty of Science: Prof. J. E. BERINGER
Faculty of Medicine: Prof. J. J. HOLBROOK
Faculty of Engineering: Prof. D. I. BLOCKLEY
Faculty of Law: Prof. R. J. BAILEY-HARRIS
Faculty of Social Sciences: Prof. R. HODDER-WILLIAMS

PROFESSORS

(some professors serve in more than one faculty)

Faculty of Arts:
ALFORD, B. W. E., Economic and Social History
ASTON, M. A., Landscape Archaeology
BRYCE, J. H., Italian
BUXTON, R. G. A., Greek Language and Literature
CLAY, C. G. A., Economic History
CORNWELL, N. J., Russian and Comparative Literature
COSTELOE, M. P., Hispanic and Latin American Studies
DOYLE, W., History
FORBES, J. E., French Language and Literature
FOWLER, R. J., Greek
FREEMAN, M. J., French Language and Literature
GRAHAM, K., Philosophy
HARRISON, R. J., European Prehistory
HUTTON, R. E., History
KING, U. M., Theology and Religious Studies
LOWE, R., Contemporary History
MCVAY, G., Russian Literature
MARTINDALE, C. A., Latin
MORTON, A., Philosophy
OFFORD, D. C., Russian Intellectual History
SAMSON, T. J., Music
SKRINE, P. N., German
WARREN, P. M., Ancient History and Classical Archaeology
WEBB, E. T., English
WHITE, M. E., Theatre
WILLIAMS, P. M., Indo-Tibetan Studies

Faculty of Science:
ALDER, R. W., Organic Chemistry
ALLEN, G. C., Materials Science
ALLEN, M. P., Theoretical Physics
ANDERSON, M. G., Geography
ASHFOLD, M. N. R., Chemistry
ATKINS, E. D. T., Physics
BALINT-KURTI, G. G., Theoretical Chemistry
BENTON, M. J., Vertebrate Palaeontology
BERINGER, J. E., Molecular Genetics
BERRY, Sir MICHAEL, Physics
BIRKINSHAW, M., Cosmology and Astrophysics
BRIGGS, D. E. G., Palaeontology

CLOKE, P. J., Geography
CONNELLY, N. G., Inorganic Chemistry
CONWAY, M. A., Psychology
COSGROVE, T., Physical Chemistry
CUTHILL, I. C., Behavioural Ecology
DENTON, R. M., Biochemistry
DOWDESWELL, J. A., Physical Geography
DRAZIN, P. G., Mathematics
EVANS, D. V., Applied Mathematics
EVANS, R., Physics
FOSTER, B., Physics
GALLAGHER, T. C., Organic Chemistry
GATHERCOLE, S. E., Psychology
GREEN, P. J., Statistics
GYORFFY, B. L., Physics
HALESTRAP, A. P., Biochemistry
HALFORD, S. E., Biochemistry
HALL, L., Biochemistry
HANCOCK, P. L., Neotectonics
HARRIS, S., Environmental Sciences
HENSHAW, D. L., Physics
HOLBROOK, J. J., Biochemistry
HOUSTON, A. I., Theoretical Biology
KEATING, J. P., Mathematics
KNOX, S. A. R., Inorganic Chemistry
LONGLEY, P. A., Geography
McCLEVERTY, J. A., Inorganic Chemistry
McNAMARA, J. M., Mathematics and Biology
MILLER, P. J., Zoology
ORPEN, A. G., Structural Chemistry
PARKES, R. J., Geomicrobiology
PEREGRINE, D. H., Applied Mathematics
RAYNER, J. M. V., Zoology
ROBERTS, A. M., Zoology
SCHOFIELD, A. H., Pure Mathematics
SHEWRY, P. R., Agricultural Sciences
SILVERMAN, B., Statistics
SIMPSON, T. J., Organic Chemistry
SMART, P. L., Geography
SMITH, A. P., Psychology
SPARKS, R. S. J., Geology
SPRINGFORD, M., Physics
STEEDS, J. W., Physics
STOBART, A. K., Plant Biochemistry
TANNER, M. J. A., Biochemistry
TINSLEY, R. C., Zoology
VAN DEN BERG, M., Pure Mathematics
VINCENT, B., Physical Chemistry
WALSBY, A. E., Botany
WOOD, B. J., Earth Sciences
WOODS, A. W., Applied Mathematics
WRAITH, D. C., Pathological Sciences

Faculty of Medicine:

ADDY, M., Periodontology
ALDERSON, D., Gastrointestinal Surgery
ANGELINI, G., Cardiothoracic Surgery
ARMSTRONG, D. M., Physiology
BAUM, J. D., Child Health
BERRY, P. J., Paediatric Pathology
BRADLEY, B. A., Transplantation Sciences
BROWN, M. W., Anatomy and Cognitive Neuroscience
CAMPBELL, A. V., Ethics in Medicine
COLLINGRIDGE, G., Neuroscience in Anatomy
COWPE, J. G., Oral Surgery
DAVEY SMITH, G., Clinical Epidemiology
DIEPPE, P. A., Health Services Research
DUFFUS, W. P. H., Veterinary Medicine
EASTY, D. L., Ophthalmology
ELSON, C. J., Immunology
FARNDON, J. R., Surgery
FRANKEL, S. J., Epidemiology and Public Health Medicine
GALE, E. A. M., Diabetic Medicine
GOLDING, M. J., Paediatric and Perinatal Epidemiology
HANKS, G. W. C., Palliative Medicine
HARRISON, A., Dental Care of the Elderly
HARRISON, G. L., Mental Health
HEADLEY, P. M., Physiology
HENDERSON, G., Pharmacology
HIRST, T. R., Microbiology
HOLLY, J. M. P., Clinical Sciences
HOWS, J. M., Clinical Haematology
HULL, M. R. G., Reproductive Medicine and Surgery
JENKINSON, H. F., Oral Microbiology
JOHNSON, K. A., Companion Animal Studies
LEARMONTH, I. D., Orthopaedic Surgery
LIGHTMAN, S. L., Medicine
MATHIESON, P. W., Renal Medicine
MATTHEWS, B., Physiology
MOTT, M. G., Paediatric Oncology
MURPHY, D., Experimental Medicine
NEWBY, A. C., Vascular Cell Biology
NUTT, D. J., Psychopharmacology
PARASKEVA, C., Experimental Oncology
PRIME, S. S., Experimental Pathology
PRYS-ROBERTS, C., Anaesthesia
REES, M. R., Clinical Radiology
ROBERTS, P. J., Neurochemical Pharmacology
SHARP, D. J., Primary Health Care
SOOTHILL, P. W., Maternal and Foetal Medicine
STEPHENS, C. D., Child Dental Health
STIRRAT, G. M., Obstetrics and Gynaecology
STOKES, C. R., Mucosal Immunology
THRIFT, N. J., Geography
WATERMAN-PEARSON, A. E., Veterinary Anaesthesia
WEBSTER, A. J. F., Animal Husbandry
WEST, R. J., Postgraduate Medical Education
WHITELAW, A. G. L., Neonatal Medicine
WILCOCK, G., Care of the Elderly

Faculty of Engineering:

ADAMS, R. D., Applied Mechanics
BALDWIN, J. F., Artificial Intelligence
BLOCKLEY, D. I., Civil Engineering
BOWES, S., Electrical and Electronic Engineering
BULL, D. R., Digital Systems Processing
CLUCKIE, I. D., Worldwide Water Management
DAGLESS, E. L., Microelectronics
FIDDES, S. P., Aerodynamics
HOGAN, S. J., Mathematics
LOWSON, M. V., Aerospace Engineering
LLOYD, J. W., Computer Science
McGEEHAN, J. P., Communications Engineering
MAY, M. D., Computer Science
MUIR WOOD, D., Civil Engineering
QUARINI, G. L., Process Engineering
SMITH, D. J., Mechanical Engineering
STOTEN, D. P., Dynamics and Control
THOMAS, B. T., Computer Science
WHITE, I. H., Optical Communication Systems
WISNOM, M. R., Aerospace Structures

Faculty of Law:

ANNAND, R. E., Law
BAILEY-HARRIS, R. J., Law
CLARKE, D. N., Law
DAVIS, G. C., Socio-Legal Studies
FUREY, N. E., Finance Law
HILL, J. D., Law
MORGAN, R. E., Criminal Justice
PARKINSON, J. E., Law
PARTINGTON, T. M., Law
SANDERS, A. H. L., Criminal Law and Criminology
STANTON, K. M., Law

Faculty of Social Sciences:

ASHTON, D. J., Accountancy and Finance
ATTFIELD, C. L. F., Econometrics
BODDY, M. J., Urban and Regional Studies
BREWER, A. A., Economics
BROADFOOT, P. M., Education
BULLOCK, R., Child Welfare Research
BURGESS, S. M., Economics
CARVER, T. F., Political Theory
CHESHER, A. D., Econometrics
DOYAL, L., Health and Social Care
FORREST, R. S., Urban Studies
FURLONG, V. J., Education
GROUT, P. A., Economics
HODDER-WILLIAMS, R., Politics
JEWITT, I. D., Economics
JOHNSON, M. L., Health and Social Policy
JOHNSTON, R. J., Geography
LAND, C. M. H., Family Policy and Child Welfare
LITTLE, R., International Politics
MACDONALD, G. M., Social Work and Applied Social Studies
McLENNAN, G., Sociology
MODOOD, T., Sociology, Politics and Public Policy
NICHOLS, W. A. T., Sociology
POLLARD, A. J., Education
PRIDHAM, G. F. M., European Politics
PROPPER, C., Economics of Public Policy
QUINTON, D. L., Psychosocial Development
REES, T. L., Labour Market Studies
SMITH, A. P., Psychology
SMITH, R. J., Economics
SUTHERLAND, R. J., Education

Continuing Education:

THOMAS, E. J., Continuing Education

ASSOCIATED INSTITUTIONS

Long Ashton Research Station: see under Research Institutes.

Baptist College: The Promenade, Clifton, Bristol, BS8 3NF; f. 1679; Principal Rev. Dr B. HAYMES.

Wesley College: Henbury Hill, Bristol, BS10 7QD; f. 1842; Methodist; Principal Dr N. G. RICHARDSON.

Trinity College: Stoke Hill, Bristol, BS9 1JP; f. 1971; Anglican; Principal Rev. Canon D. K. GILLETT.

Cheltenham and Gloucester College of Higher Education: Cheltenham, Glos.; Principal JANET TROTTER.

BRUNEL UNIVERSITY

Uxbridge, Middlesex, UB8 3PH
Telephone: (1895) 274000
Fax: (1895) 232806

Founded 1957 as Brunel College of Technology; College of Advanced Technology 1962; University Charter 1966; incorporated West London Institute into the University in 1995

Academic year: September to June

Chancellor: Lord WAKEHAM
Pro-Chancellor: P. E. TRIER
Vice-Chancellor and Principal: Prof. M. J. H. STERLING
Vice-Principal: Prof. M. CAVE
Pro-Vice-Chancellors: Prof. E. H. BILLETT, Prof. M. SARHADI
Secretary General and Registrar: (vacant)
Librarian: B. A. THOMPSON

Number of teachers: 639
Number of students: 13,070

Publications: *Undergraduate Prospectus*, *Postgraduate Prospectus*, *Vice-Chancellor's Report*, *Graduates Newsletter* (all annually), *Brunel and Business* (2 a year).

DEANS

Arts: Prof. D. WOOTTON
Professional Education: Prof. L. THOMAS
Science: Prof. R. F. NEWBOLD
Technology: Prof. N. LADOMMATAS
Social Sciences: Prof. A. WOOD

PROFESSORS

ANTONIOU, A., Economics and Finance
ARRAND, J. E., Biology and Biochemistry
BALACHANDRAN, W., Manufacturing
BILLETT, E. H., Design
BRICKWOOD, A., Design
BURNETT, J., Government
BUXTON, M., Economics and Finance
CAVE, M., Economics and Finance

CHOO, A., Law
CLARK, C., Manufacturing and Engineering Systems
DONALDSON, J. D., Centre for Environmental Research
ESAT, I. I., Mechanical Engineering
FOLKES, M. J., Materials Engineering
HENSHALL, J. L., Mechanical Engineering
HINDI, K., Manufacturing and Engineering Systems
HODKINSON, S., Education
IRVING, M. R., Electrical Engineering
IRWIN, G. A., Sociology
ISHERWOOD, P. W., Design
JONES, B. E., Manufacturing and Engineering Systems
KING, M., Law
KOGAN, M., Government
KUPER, A. J., Human Sciences
LADOMMATOS, N., Mechanical Engineering
LEA, R. M., Electrical Engineering and Electronics
LOVELAND, I., Law
LYNCH, M., Human Sciences
MARSLAND, D., Health Studies
MIDDLEDITCH, A. E., Manufacturing and Engineering Systems
MITRA, G., Mathematics and Statistics
MORRIS, G., Law
MUSGRAVE, G., Electrical Engineering and Electronics
NEWBOLD, R., Biology and Biochemistry
O'KEEFE, R. M., Information Systems and Computing
PAUL, R., Information Systems and Computing
POLLITT, C., Government
RADFORD, P., Sports Sciences
RALPH, B., Materials Technology
REYNOLDS, A. J., Mechanical Engineering
RICHARDSON, J. T. E., Human Sciences
SARHADI, M., Manufacturing and Engineering Systems
SERMON, P. A., Chemistry
SHARP, N. C. C., Sport Sciences
SIMS, D., Management Studies
SONG, Y. H., Electrical Engineering
SOUZA, L. H. DE, Health Studies
STOLARSKI, T. A., Mechanical Engineering
STONHAM, T. J., Electrical Engineering
SUMPTER, J. P., Biology and Biochemistry
TERRY, P. C., Sports Sciences
THOMAS, L., Education
TOMLINSON, J., Government
TWIZELL, E. H., Mathematics and Statistics
WHITEMAN, J. R., Mathematics and Statistics
WOODROFFE, G. F., Law
WOODS, A., Management Studies
WOOLGAR, S., Human Sciences
WRIGHT, M. J., Human Sciences
WROBEL, L. C., Mechanical Engineering
YELLOLY, M. A., Social Work
YETTRAM, A. L., Mechanical Engineering

ATTACHED INSTITUTES

Brunel Able Child Education Centre: Dir Dr V. KOSHY.

Centre for Evaluation of Public Policy and Practice: Dirs Prof. M. KOGAN, Prof. C. POLLITT.

Centre for Manufacturing Metrology: Dir Prof. B. JONES.

Centre for Research into Innovation, Culture and Technology: Dir Prof. S. WOOLGAR.

Centre for the Study of Health, Sickness and Disablement: Dir I. ROBINSON.

Wolfson Centre for Materials Processing: Dir Prof. M. BEVIS.

Institute for Bioengineering: Dir Prof. I. SUTHERLAND.

Institute of Computational Mathematics: Dir Prof. J. R. WHITEMAN.

Centre for Applied Simulation Modelling: Dir Prof. R. PAUL.

Centre for Youth Work Studies: Dir Dr M. L. DAY.

Centre for Consumer and Commercial Law Research: Dir Prof. G. WOODROFFE.

Centre for Criminal Justice Research: Dirs Prof. E. STANKO, Dr C. CORBETT.

Centre for the Study of Law, the Child and the Family: Dirs Dr C. PIPER, M. KING.

Design for Life Centre: Dir C. CHAPMAN.

Design Research Centre: Dir T. INNS.

Health Economics Research Group: Dir Prof. M. J. BUXTON.

Lifelong Learning Centre: Head Prof. A. JONES.

Brunel Institute for Power Systems: Dir Prof. M. R. IRVING.

Industrial Regulation, Innovation and Standards Research Centre: Dir Prof. M. CAVE.

Centre for Organisational and Professional Ethics: Dir K. DICKINSON.

Water Operational Research Centre: Dir Dr R. POWELL.

Electronic Systems Research Centre: Dir Prof. W. BALACHANDRAN.

Centre for Information Systems: Dir Prof. R. PAUL.

Centre for Information Environments: Dir Dr D. ROSENBERG.

Centre for Neural and Evolutionary Systems: Dir Dr D. DRACOPOULOUS.

Economics Education Research Centre: Dir Prof. S. HODKINSON.

Centre for Neural Computing Applications: Dir T. HARRIS.

Centre for Research in Rehabilitation: Dir L. DE SOUZA.

Neotectonics Research Centre: Dir C. FIRTH.

UNIVERSITY OF BUCKINGHAM

Buckingham, MK18 1EG
Telephone: (1280) 814080
Fax: (1280) 822245
E-mail: admissions@buck.ac.uk
Founded 1973 (first student intake 1976); Royal Charter 1983
Private control
Academic year: January to December (4 10-week terms)
Chancellor: Sir MARTIN JACOMB
Chairman of Council: ROBERT TOMKINSON
Vice-Chancellor: Prof. ROBERT TAYLOR
Pro-Vice-Chancellor: Prof. ROBERT PEARCE
Secretary and Registrar: STEPHEN COOKSEY
Librarian: JOAN HOLAH
Number of teachers: 65 full-time, 25 part-time
Number of students: 798
Publication: *Prospectus* (annually).

DEANS OF ACADEMIC DEPARTMENTS

Accounting, Business, and Economics: Prof. M. J. RICKETTS
Humanities: Dr J. C. CLARKE
Law: ALISTAIR ALCOCK
Sciences: Dr FRANCES ROBINSON

PROFESSORS

ADAMS, C. J., Computer Science
BARRY, N. P., Politics
CAWTHORNE, M. A., Metabolic Research
DANIEL, R. C., Business Studies
MILLMAN, A., International Business and Marketing
PEARCE, R., Law of Equity and Property
PENDRILL, D., Accounting and Financial Management
RICKETTS, M. J., Economic Organization
ROSE, F. D., Commercial and Common Law
SHAW, G. K., Economics
STACEY, R., Management Accounting
WATSON, P. L., Accounting and Financial Management

NON-PROFESSORIAL HEADS OF DEPARTMENTS

Economics: M. J. MCCROSTIE
English Literature and Modern History: Dr J. C. CLARKE

UNIVERSITY OF CAMBRIDGE

Cambridge CB2 1TN
Telephone: (1223) 337733 (Central Switchboard); (1223) 332200 (Central Administration)
Founded in the 13th Century
Chancellor: HRH The Prince PHILIP, Duke of EDINBURGH
Vice-Chancellor: Prof. Sir ALEC BROERS
Pro Vice-Chancellor: Prof. R. M. NEEDHAM
High Steward: The Rt Rev. Lord RUNCIE
Registrar: Dr T. J. MEAD
Treasurer: J. M. WOMACK
Secretary-General of the Faculties: D. A. LIVESEY
Librarian: P. K. FOX
Fitzwilliam Museum: see Museums
Number of teachers: 1,500
Number of students: 14,500
Publications: *Admissions Prospectus*, *Graduate Studies Prospectus* (annually), *Statutes and Ordinances of the University*, *Cambridge University Reporter* (weekly during full-term and occasionally at other times), *Guide to Courses* (annually), *List of Members*, Supplements to the *Historical Register*.

PROFESSORS

Faculty of Archaeology and Anthropology:
HODDER, I. R., Archaeology (Darwin College)
JONES, M. K., Archaeological Science (Peterhouse)
MACFARLANE, A. D. J., Anthropological Science (King's College)
MELLARS, P. A., Prehistory and Human Evolution (Corpus Christi College)
RENFREW, Lord, Archaeology (Jesus College)
STRATHERN, A. M., Social Anthropology (Girton College)

Faculty of Architecture and History of Art:
CAROLIN, P. B., Architecture (Corpus Christi College)
ECHENIQUE, M., Land Use and Transport Studies (Churchill College)
SAINT, A. J., Architecture

Faculty of Biology:
AKAM, M. E., Zoology
ASHBURNER, M., Genetics (Churchill College)
BATESON, P. P. G. B., Ethology (King's College)
BLUNDELL, TOM, Biochemistry
BURROWS, M., Zoology (Jesus College)
CLUTTON BROCK, T. A., Zoology (King's College)
CRAWFORD, A. C., Neurophysiology (Trinity College)
CUTHBERT, A. W., Pharmacology (Jesus College)
DAVIES, N. B., Behavioural Ecology (Pembroke College)
EVANS, M. J., Mammalian Genetics (Christ's College)
EVERITT, B. J., Behavioural Neuroscience (Downing College)
FERGUSON-SMITH, M. A., Pathology (Peterhouse)

GRAY, J. C., Plant Molecular Biology (Robinson College)
GURDON, Sir J., Cell Biology (Magdalene College)
HARRIS, B. A., Anatomy
IRVINE, R. F., Molecular Pharmacology (Corpus Christi College)
JACKSON, S. P., Wellcome/CRC
JOHNSON, M. H., Anatomy (Christ's College)
LAMB, T. D., Physiology (Darwin College)
LASKEY, R. A., Wellcome/CRC (Darwin College)
MACKINTOSH, N. J., Experimental Psychology (King's College)
MACROBBIE, Miss E. A. C., Plant Biophysics (Girton College)
METCALFE, J. C., Mammalian Cell Biochemistry (Darwin College)
MINSON, A. C., Virology (Wolfson College)
MOORE, B. C. J., Experimental Psychology (Wolfson College)
PARKER, J. S., Biochemistry (St. Catharine's College)
PERHAM, R. N., Structural Biochemistry (St John's College)
ROBBINS, T. W., Experimental Psychology (Downing College)
SALMOND, G. P. C., Biochemistry
SHACKLETON, N. J., Earth Sciences
SURANI, M. A. H., Wellcome/CRC (Queens' College)
THOMAS, J. O., Macromolecular Biochemistry (New Hall)
THOMAS, R. C., Physiology (Downing College)
TROWSDALE, J., Pathology

Faculty of Classics:

DIGGLE, J., Greek and Latin (Queens' College)
EASTERLING, P. E., Greek—Regius (Newnham College)
HOPKINS, M. K., Ancient History (King's College)
HORROCKS, G. C., Comparative Physiology (St John's College)
KILLEN, J. T., Mycenaean Greek (Jesus College)
LLOYD, Sir GEOFFREY, Ancient Philosophy and Science (Darwin College)
REEVE, M. D., Latin (Pembroke College)
SEDLEY, D. N., Ancient Philosophy (Christ's College)
SNODGRASS, A. M., Classical Archaeology (Clare College)
STRIKER, G., Ancient Philosophy (Trinity College)

Faculty of Clinical Medicine:

ALLAIN, J. P., Transfusion Medicine
BARTON, A., Genetics (Trinity College)
BLACKWELL, J. M., Molecular Parasitology (Newnham College)
BOBROW, M., Medical Genetics
BRADLEY, J. A., Surgery
BROWN, M. J., Clinical Pharmacology (Gonville and Caius College)
CALNE, Sir ROY, Surgery (Trinity Hall)
CARRELL, R. W., Haematology (Trinity College)
COMPSTON, D. A. S., Neurology (Jesus College)
COX, T. M., Medicine (Sidney Sussex College)
DAY, N. E., Community Medicine (Churchill College)
DIXON, A. D., Radiology (Peterhouse)
FEARON, D. T., Medicine
GARETH JONES, J., Anaesthesia
GASTON, J. S. H., Rheumatology
GOODYER, I. M., Child and Adolescent Psychiatry (Wolfson College)
HALES, C. N., Clinical Biochemistry (Downing College)
HALL, L. D., Medicinal Chemistry (Emmanuel College)
HIMSWORTH, R. L., Institute of Public Health (Girton College)
HUGHES, I. A., Paediatrics (Clare Hall)
JONES, J. G., Anaesthesia
KHAW, K.-T., Clinical Gerontology (Gonville and Caius College)
KINMONTH, A.-L., General Practice (New Hall)
O'RAHILLY, S., Metabolic Medicine
PAYKEL, E. S., Psychiatry (Gonville and Caius College)
PETERS, Sir KEITH, Physic—Regius (Christ's College)
PICKARD, J. D., Neurosurgery (St. Catharine's College)
PONDER, B. A. J., Pathology (Jesus College)
SIDDLE, K., Clinical Biochemistry (Churchill College)
SISSONS, J. G. P., Haematology (Darwin College)
SMITH, S. K., Obstetrics and Gynaecology (Fitzwilliam College)
WEISSBERG, Cardiovascular Medicine (Wolfson College)

Faculty of Clinical Veterinary Medicine:

ALLEN, W. R., Equine Reproduction (Robinson College)
BROOM, D. M., Animal Welfare (St. Catharine's College)
JEFFCOTT, L. B., Veterinary Clinical Studies
LACHMANN, P. J., Immunology (Christ's College)
MCCONNELL, I., Veterinary Science (Clare Hall)
MASKELL, D. J., Farm Animal Health, Food Science and Food Safety (Gonville and Caius College)

Faculty of Divinity:

FORD, D. F., Divinity—Regius (St John's College)
HOOKER, M. D., Divinity (Robinson College)
LASH, N. L. A., Divinity—Norris-Hulse (Clare Hall)

Faculty of Earth Sciences and Geography:

BENNETT, R. J., Geography (St. Catharine's College)
CLIFF, A. D., Theoretical Geography (Christ's College)
CONWAY MORRIS, S., Evolutionary Palaeobiology (St John's College)
MCCAVE, I. N., Geology (St John's College)
MCKENZIE, D. P., Earth Sciences (King's College)
RICHARDS, K. S., Geography (Emmanuel College)
SALJE, E. K. H., Mineralogy and Petrology (Darwin College)
SHACKLETON, N. J., Quaternary Palaeoclimatology (Clare Hall)
WHITE, R. S., Geophysics (St Edmund's College)

Faculty of Economics and Politics:

BROWN, W. A., Industrial Relations (Wolfson College)
BUITER, W. H., International Macroeconomics (Emmanuel College)
DASGUPTA, P., Economics (St John's College)
HARRIS, C. J., Economics (King's College)
HARVEY, A. C., Econometrics (Corpus Christi College)
MIRRLEES, Sir JAMES, Political Economy (Trinity College)
NEWBERY, D. M. G., Applied Economics (Churchill College)
PESARAN, M. H., Economics (Trinity College)
ROWTHORN, R. E., Economics (King's College)
SINGH, A., Economics (Queens' College)
WHITTINGTON, G., Financial Accounting (Fitzwilliam College)

Faculty of Education:

HARGREAVES, D. H., Education (Wolfson College)
MCINTYRE, D. I., Education

Faculty of Engineering:

CALLADINE, C. R., Structural Mechanics (Peterhouse)
CARROLL, J. E., Engineering (Queens' College)
CUMPSTY, N. A., Aerothermal Technology (Peterhouse)
DAWES, W. N., Aeronautical Engineering (Churchill College)
DENTON, J. D., Turbomachinery, Aerodynamics (Trinity Hall)
DOWLING, A. P., Mechanical Engineering (Sidney Sussex College)
FFOWCS WILLIAMS, J. E., Engineering (Emmanuel College)
FLECK, N. A., Mechanics of Materials (Pembroke College)
GLOVER, K., Engineering (Sidney Sussex College)
GREGORY, M. J., Manufacturing Engineering (Churchill College)
MILNE, W. I., Electrical Engineering (Churchill College)
NEWLAND, D. E., Engineering (Selwyn College)
SCHOFIELD, A. N., Engineering (Churchill College)
YOUNG, S. J., Information Engineering (Emmanuel College)

Faculty of English:

BEER, G. P. K., English (Clare Hall)
BROWN, G., English as an International Language (Clare College)
DONALDSON, C. I. E., Classics (King's College)
DUMVILLE, D. N., Anglo-Saxon, Norse, Celtic (Girton College)
ERSKINE-HILL, H. H., Literary History (Pembroke College)
LAPIDGE, M., Anglo-Saxon (Clare College)
MANN, J. L., Medieval and Renaissance English (Girton College)
TANNER, P. A., English and American Literature (King's College)

Faculty of History:

ANDREW, C. M., Modern and Contemporary History (Corpus Christi College)
BADGER, A. J., American History (Sidney Sussex College)
BAYLY, C. A., South Asian Studies Centre (St. Catharine's College)
BLANNING, T. C. W., Modern European History (Sidney Sussex College)
BURKE, U. P., Cultural History (Emmanuel College)
CLARKE, P. F., Modern British History (St John's College)
DAUNTON, M. J., Economic and Social History
DOBSON, R. B., Medieval History (Christ's College)
GARNSEY, P. D. A., History of Classical Antiquity (Jesus College)
HATCHER, M. J., Economic and Social History (Corpus Christi College)
HOPKINS, A. G., Commonwealth History (Pembroke College)
ILIFFE, J., African History (St John's College)
MCKITTERICK, R. D., Early Medieval European History (Newnham College)
RILEY-SMITH, J. S. C., Ecclesiastical History (Queens' College)
SKINNER, Q. R. D., Modern History—Regius (Christ's College)
STEDMAN JONES, G., Political Economy (King's College)

Faculty of Law:

BAKER, J. H., English Legal History (St. Catharine's College)
BEATSON, J., English Law – Rouse Ball (St John's College)
BOTTOMS, A. E., Criminology (Fitzwilliam College)
CHEFFINS, B. R., Corporate Law (Trinity Hall)
CORNISH, W. R., International Property Law (Magdalene College)
CRAWFORD, J. R., International Law (Jesus College)
DASHWOOD, A. A., European Law (Sidney Sussex College)
FARRINGTON, D. P., Psychological Criminology (Darwin College)
GRAY, K. J., Law (Trinity College)
HEPPLE, B. A., Law (Clare College)
JOHNSTON, D. E. L., Civil Law – Regius (Christ's College)
JONES, G. H., Laws of England (Trinity College)
SEALY, L. S., Corporate Law (Gonville and Caius College)
SMITH, A. T. H., Criminal and Public Laws (Gonville and Caius College)
SPENCER, J. R., Law (Selwyn College)
TILEY, J., Law of Taxation (Queens' College)
WILLIAMS, Sir DAVID, Law (Emmanuel College)

Faculty of Mathematics:

BAKER, A., Pure Mathematics (Trinity College)
COATES, J. H., Pure Mathematics (Emmanuel College)
CRIGHTON, D. G., Applied Mathematics (St John's College)
GIBBONS, G. W., Theoretical Physics (Clare College)
GODDARD, P., Theoretical Physics (St John's College)
GREEN, M. B., Theoretical Physics (Clare Hall)
GRIMMETT, G. R., Mathematical Statistics (Peterhouse)
HAWKING, S. W., Mathematics (Gonville and Caius College)
HITCHIN, N. J., Mathematics (Gonville and Caius College)
HUPPERT, H. E., Theoretical Geophysics (King's College)
KELLY, F. R., Mathematics of Systems (Christ's College)
LANDSHOFF, F. V., Mathematical Physics (Christ's College)
LICKORISH, W. B. R., Geometric Topology (Pembroke College)
MCINTYRE, M. E., Atmospheric Dynamics (St John's College)
MACKAY, R. S., Nonlinear Dynamics (Trinity College)
MOFFATT, H. K., Mathematical Physics (Trinity College)
PEDLEY, T. J., Fluid Mechanics (Gonville and Caius College)
POWELL, M. J. D., Applied Numerical Analysis (Pembroke College)
SEGAL, G. B., Astronomy and Geometry (St John's College)
SMITH, R. L., Statistical Science
TUROK, N., Mathematical Physics
WEBER, R. R., Mathematics for Operational Research (Queens' College)
WEISS, N. O., Mathematical Astrophysics (Clare College)
WHITESIDE, D. T., History of Mathematics and Exact Sciences (Churchill College)
WILLIS, J. R., Theoretical Solid Mechanics (Fitzwilliam College)

Faculty of Modern and Medieval Languages:

BAYLEY, P. J., French (Gonville and Caius College)
BOYDE, P., Italian (St John's College)
CROSS, A. G., Slavonic Studies (Fitzwilliam College)
DRONKE, E. P. M., Medieval Latin Literature (Clare Hall)
MATTHEWS, P. H., Linguistics (St John's College)
NISBET, H. B., Modern Languages (Sidney Sussex College)
PAULIN, R. C., German (Trinity College)
PRENDERGAST, C. A. J., Modern French Literature (King's College)
SMITH, P. J., Spanish (Trinity Hall)

Faculty of Music:

GOEHR, A., Music (Trinity Hall)

Faculty of Oriental Studies:

BOWRING, R. J., Modern Japanese Studies (Downing College)
GORDON, R. P., Hebrew—Regius (St. Catharine's College)
KHALIDI, T., Arabic (King's College)
MCMULLEN, D. L., Chinese (St John's College)
POSTGATE, J. N., Assyriology (Trinity College)

Faculty of Philosophy:

MELLOR, D. H., Philosophy (Darwin College)
SMILEY, T. J., Philosophy (Clare College)

Faculty of Physics and Chemistry:

AHMED, H., Microelectronics (Corpus Christi College)
BALDWIN, J. E., Radio Astronomy (Queens' College)
BROWN, L. M., Physics (Robinson College)
ELLIS, R. S., Astronomy and Experimental Philosophy (Magdalene College)
FERSHT, A. R., Organic Chemistry (Gonville and Caius College)
FIELD, J. E., Applied Physics (Magdalene College)
FRAY, D. J., Materials Chemistry (Fitzwilliam College)
FREEMAN, R., Magnetic Resonance (Jesus College)
FRIEND, R. H., Physics (St John's College)
GOUGH, D. O., Theoretical Astrophysics (Churchill College)
HANDY, N. C., Quantum Chemistry (St. Catharine's College)
HANSEN, J.-P., Chemistry (Corpus Christi College)
HILLS, R. E., Radio Astronomy (St Edmund's College)
HOWIE, A., Physics (Churchill College)
HUMPHREYS, C. J., Materials Science (Selwyn College)
JOHNSON, B. F. G., Chemistry (Fitzwilliam College)
JOSEPHSON, B. D., Physics (Trinity College)
KING, D. A., Physical Chemistry (Downing College)
KIRBY, A. J., Bio-organic Chemistry (Gonville and Caius College)
LEY, S. V., Organic Chemistry (Trinity College)
LIANG, W. Y., Superconductivity (Gonville and Caius College)
LITTLEWOOD, P. B., Physics (Trinity College)
LONGAIR, M. S., Natural Philosophy (Clare Hall)
LONZARICH, G. G., Condensed-Matter Physics (Trinity College)
LYNDEN-BELL, D., Astrophysics (Clare College)
PEPPER, M., Physics (Trinity College)
SANDERS, J. K., Inorganic Chemistry (Selwyn College)
WILLIAMS, D. H., Biological Chemistry (Churchill College)
WINDLE, A. H., Materials Science (Trinity College)

Faculty of Social and Political Sciences:

DUNN, J. M., Political Theory (King's College)
RICHARDS, M. P. M., Family Research (Trinity College)

Department of Chemical Engineering:

BRIDGWATER, J., Chemical Engineering (St. Catharine's College)

Computer Laboratory:

GORDON, M. J. C., Computer Assisted Reasoning (King's College)
MILNER, A. J. R. G., Computer Science (King's College)
NEEDHAM, R. M., Computer Systems (Wolfson College)

Department of History and Philosophy of Science:

JARDINE, N., History and Philosophy of the Sciences (Darwin College)
LIPTON, P., History and Philosophy of Science (King's College)

Department of Land Economy:

GRANT, M. J., Land Economy (Clare College)

Judge Institute of Management Studies:

CHILD, J., Management Studies (St John's College)
DAWSON, J. N., Management Studies
DEMPSTER, M. A. H., Management Studies
NOLAN, P. H., Chinese Management (Jesus College)

WOMEN'S COLLEGES

Lucy Cavendish College: Lady Margaret Rd, Cambridge, CB3 0BU; tel. (1223) 332190; f. 1964 (Approved Foundation 1965); Pres. Lady PERRY.

New Hall: Cambridge, CB3 0DF; tel. (1223) 362100; f. 1954; Pres. A. LONSDALE.

Newnham College: Cambridge, CB3 9DF; tel. (1223) 335700; f. 1871; Principal O. S. O'NEILL.

MIXED COLLEGES

Christ's College: Cambridge, CB2 3BU; tel. (1223) 334900; f. 1505 for men; women admitted 1978; Master Dr A. J. MUNRO.

Churchill College: Cambridge, CB3 0DS; tel. (1223) 336000; f. 1960 for men; women admitted 1972; Master Sir JOHN BOYD.

Clare College: Cambridge, CB2 1TL; tel. (1223) 333200; f. 1326 for men; women admitted 1972; Master Dr B. A. HEPPLE.

Corpus Christi College: Cambridge, CB2 1RH; tel. (1223) 338000; f. 1352 for men; women admitted 1983; Master Prof. Sir TONY WRIGLEY.

Downing College: Cambridge, CB2 1DQ; tel. (1223) 334800; f. 1800 for men; women admitted 1978; Master Prof. D. A. KING.

Emmanuel College: Cambridge, CB2 3AP; tel. (1223) 334200; f. 1584 for men; women admitted 1978; Master Prof. J. E. FFOWCS WILLIAMS.

Fitzwilliam College: Cambridge, CB3 0DG; tel. (1223) 332000; f. 1966 for men; women admitted 1978; Master Prof. A. W. CUTHBERT.

Girton College: Cambridge, CB3 0JG; tel. (1223) 338999; f. 1869 for women; men admitted 1977; Mistress Prof. MARILYN STRATHERN.

Gonville and Caius College: Cambridge, CB2 1TA; tel. (1223) 332400; f. 1348 for men; women admitted 1978; Master N. MCKENDRICK.

Homerton College: Cambridge, CB2 2PH; tel. (1223) 507111; f. 1824 as a Training College (Approved Society 1977); men re-admitted 1978; Principal Dr K. B. PRETTY.

Hughes Hall: Cambridge, CB1 2EW; tel. (1223) 334898; f. 1885 as the Cambridge Training College for Women (Approved Foundation 1968); Pres. Prof. PETER RICHARDS.

Jesus College: Cambridge, CB5 8BL; tel. (1223) 339339; f. 1496 for men; women admitted 1978; Master Prof. D. G. CRIGHTON.

King's College: Cambridge, CB2 1ST; tel. (1223) 331100; f. 1441 for men; women admitted 1972; Provost Dr J. D. BARBER.

Magdalene College: Cambridge, CB3 0AG; tel. (1223) 332100; f. 1542 for men; women admitted 1987; Master Prof. Sir JOHN GURDON.

Pembroke College: Cambridge, CB2 1RF; tel. (1223) 338100; f. 1347 for men; women admitted 1983; Master Sir ROGER TOMKYS.

Peterhouse: Cambridge, CB2 1RD; tel. (1223) 338200; f. 1284 for men; women admitted 1984; Master Sir JOHN MEURIG THOMAS.

Queens' College: Cambridge, CB3 9ET; tel. (1223) 335511; f. 1448 for men; women admitted 1979; Pres. Lord EATWELL.

Robinson College: Cambridge, CB3 9AN; tel. (1223) 339100; f. 1977; Warden Prof. Lord LEWIS.

St Catharine's College: Cambridge, CB2 1RL; tel. (1223) 338300; f. 1473 for men; women admitted 1978; Master Prof. Sir TERENCE ENGLISH.

St Edmund's College: Cambridge, CB3 0BN; tel. (1223) 336250; f. 1896 for men; (Approved Foundation 1975); women admitted 1978; Master Dr B. HEAP.

St John's College: Cambridge, CB2 1TP; tel. (1223) 338600; f. 1511 for men; women admitted 1981; Master Prof. P. GODDARD.

Selwyn College: Cambridge, CB3 9DQ; tel. (1223) 335846; f. 1882 for men; women admitted 1976; Master Sir DAVID HARRISON.

Sidney Sussex College: Cambridge, CB2 3HU; tel. (1223) 338800; f. 1596 for men; women admitted 1976; Master Prof. G. HORN.

Trinity College: Cambridge, CB2 1TQ; tel. (1223) 338400; f. 1546 for men; women admitted 1977; Master Dr A. K. SEN.

Trinity Hall: Cambridge, CB2 1TJ; tel. (1223) 332500; f. 1350 for men; women admitted 1977; Master Sir JOHN LYONS.

MIXED COLLEGES FOR GRADUATE STUDENTS

Clare Hall: Cambridge, CB3 9AL; tel. (1223) 332360; f. 1966 (Approved Foundation); Pres. Prof. G. P. K. BEER.

Darwin College: Cambridge, CB3 9EU; tel. (1223) 335660; f. 1964; Master Prof. Sir GEOFFREY LLOYD.

Wolfson College: Cambridge, CB3 9BB; tel. (1223) 335900; f. 1965; Pres. Dr G. JOHNSON.

ATTACHED INSTITUTES

Committee for Aerial Photography: Cambridge; Curator D. R. WILSON (Wolfson College).

Centre of African Studies: Cambridge; Dir Dr A. QUAYSON (acting) (Girton College).

McDonald Institute for Archaeological Research: Cambridge; Dir Lord RENFREW (Jesus College).

Wellcome Trust and Cancer Research Campaign, Institute of Biotechnology: Cambridge; Dir C. R. LOWE (Trinity College).

Brain Repair: MRC Cambridge Centre; Chair. D. A. S. COMPSTON (Jesus College).

Business Research Centre, ESRC: Dir A. HUGHES (Sidney Sussex College).

Institute of Cancer and Developmental Biology: Cambridge; Chair. Sir JOHN GURDON (Magdalene College).

Research Centre for English and Applied Linguistics: Cambridge; Dir G. BROWN (Clare College).

Wolfson Industrial Liaison Office: Dir R. C. JENNINGS.

Research Centre for International Law: Cambridge; Dir E. LAUTERPACHT.

Centre of International Studies: Cambridge; Dir Dr P. A. TOWLE.

Language Centre: Cambridge; Dir E. M. ESCH.

Centre of Latin American Studies: Cambridge; Dir A. D. LEHMANN (St Edmund's College).

Isaac Newton Mathematical Sciences Institute: Cambridge; Dir H. K. MOFFATT (Trinity College).

Centre for Medical Genetics: Cambridge; Dir M. A. FERGUSON-SMITH (Peterhouse).

Centre of Middle Eastern Studies: Cambridge; Dir T. KHALIDI (King's College).

Institute of Public Health: Cambridge; Dir Dr J. POWLES (acting) (Churchill College).

Advanced Religious and Theological Studies Centre: Dir D. M. THOMPSON (Fitzwilliam College).

Centre of South Asian Studies: Cambridge; Dir G. JOHNSON (Wolfson College).

Superconductivity Research Centre: Cambridge; Dir W. Y. LIANG (Gonville and Caius College).

UNIVERSITY OF CENTRAL ENGLAND IN BIRMINGHAM

Perry Barr, Birmingham, B42 2SU

Telephone: (121) 331-5000

Founded 1971 as City of Birmingham Polytechnic, later became Birmingham Polytechnic, present name and status 1992

Chancellor: SYBIL SPENCE
Vice-Chancellor: Dr P. C. KNIGHT
Pro Vice-Chancellors: Prof. D. TIDMARSH, Prof. P. WALKLING
Secretary and Registrar: M. PENLINGTON
Library of 900,000 vols
Number of teachers: 700
Number of students: 10,750 full-time, 9,900 part-time

DEANS

Institute of Art and Design: Prof. M. DURMAN
Faculty of the Built Environment: Prof. J. LOW
Faculty of Computing and Information Studies: Prof. J. ELKIN
Faculty of Education: Prof. S. BUCHANAN
Faculty of Engineering and Computer Technology: Prof. G. ROGERS
Faculty of Health and Community Care: Prof. J. HITCHEN
Faculty of Law and Social Services: Prof. JOHN ROUSE
UCE Business School: Prof. U. PARDESI
Birmingham Conservatoire: Prof. G. CAIRD (Principal)

HEADS OF DEPARTMENTS AND SCHOOLS

Accountancy: Prof. G. WHITE
Architecture: P. MADDEN
Art: Prof. A. A. HUGHES
Birmingham Conservatoire Junior School Administrator: H. SLADE-LIPKIN
Building Surveying: R. GRIMSHAW
Business: J. JOHNSON
Clinical Nursing: Prof. L. WILLIAM
Community Care Nursing: Prof. E. PAJAK
Computing: R. RILEY
Creative Studies: Prof. A. DOWNES
Economics: D. RAMSAY
Electronic and Software Engineering: M. WILKES
Engineering Systems and Information Technology: Prof. P. HALLAM
English: Prof. H. JACKSON
Environmental Studies and Humanities (Teacher Training): A. CHOLMONDELEY
Fashion and Textiles: Prof. R. POTTER
Finance: D. WINSTONE
Foundation and Community Studies (Art and Design): Prof. T. JONES
Health and Policy Studies: M. FILBY
Housing: V. COATHAM
Information Studies: G. MATTHEWS
International Development: Prof. A. T. WHITEHOUSE
Jewellery: Prof. N. CHERRY
Keyboard Studies: Prof. M. WILSON
Landscape: Prof. D. CASSIDY
Language (Teacher Training): C. HILL
Law: M. TIGHE
Management: Prof. L. MEACHAM
Marketing and Languages: Prof. P. CLARKE
Mathematics, Science and Technology (Teacher Training): C. BENSON
Mechanical and Manufacturing Engineering: R. MCCAFFERTY
Media and Communication: R. PILLING
Music Studies in Art (Teacher Training): H. COLL
Nursing Studies: C. MALLABER
Orchestral Studies: Prof. J. ROSS
Planning: Prof. D. CHAPMAN
Podiatry: R. ASHFORD
Property and Construction: J. BADMAN
Quantity Surveying: J. BADMAN
Radiography: R. KLEM
Social Work: M. DOEL
Sociology: R. VANNELLI
Speech Therapy: J. NETTLETON
Three-Dimensional Design: Prof. R. W. POTTER
Visual Communication: Prof. D. KNIGHT
Vocal Operatic Study: Prof. K. DARLINGTON
Women's Health Studies: S. HUNT

UNIVERSITY OF CENTRAL LANCASHIRE

Preston, PR1 2HE

Telephone: (1772) 201201
Telex: 677409
Fax: (1772) 892911

Founded 1956 as Harris College, 1973 as Preston Polytechnic, 1984 as Lancashire Polytechnic; present name and status 1992
Academic year: September to July

Chancellor: Sir FRANCIS KENNEDY
Vice-Chancellor: Dr MALCOLM MCVICAR
Deputy Vice-Chancellor: ALAN ROFF
Librarian: (vacant)

Number of teachers: 601 full-time, 63 part-time

Number of students: 11,379 full-time, 8,314 part-time

Publications: *Prospectus of Full-time Courses, Prospectus of Part-time Courses, Prospectus of Post Graduate Courses, Annual Report.*

DEANS

Lancashire Business School: ALAN FRANCE
Faculty of Cultural, Legal and Social Studies: ANGELA MURPHY
Faculty of Design and Technology: Prof. NORMAN BURROW
Faculty of Health: EILEEN MARTIN
Faculty of Science: Prof. PETER YOUNG

HEADS OF DEPARTMENTS

Lancashire Business School:
- Accounting and Financial Services: Prof. HENRY LUNT
- International Business: PHIL BAUGH
- Business Information Management: Prof. PHIL HEWITT
- Hospitality and Tourism: DIANE DAVIS
- Management Development: Prof. GRAHAM KELLY
- Organization Studies: MARTIN GIBSON
- Journalism: PETER COLE

Faculty of Cultural, Legal and Social Studies:
Education Studies: KEN PHILLIPS
Languages: PAUL GENTLE
Legal Studies: Prof. RICHARD TAYLOR
Historical and Critical Studies: JOE POPE
Social Studies: JOY FOSTER
Cultural Studies: Dr DANIEL LAMONT
European Studies and Politics: Prof. STANLEY HENIG

Faculty of Design and Technology:
Art and Fashion : GLENDA BRINDLE
Visual Communication and Three Dimensional Design: PAUL COYLE
Electrical and Electronic Engineering: TREVOR TERELL
Engineering and Product Design: ROB PAINE
The Built Environment: Prof. JOHN ROBERTS
Computing: NIMAL JAYARATNA

Faculty of Health:
Health Studies: MAUREEN ROBINSON
Midwifery Studies: LASZLO HALLDORA
Nursing Practice Development: SUE ANTROBUS
Nursing Studies: DOROTH JONES
Social Work: LAURA MIDDLETON

Faculty of Science:
Applied Biology: PETER GACESCA
Chemistry: Dr JOHN HOLDER
Mathematics and Statistics: Prof. MIKE GRANNELL
Physics and Astronomy: Prof. MIKE HOLMES
Centre for Environmental Management: NIGEL SIMONS
Psychology: PAUL POLLARD
Centre for Toxicology: Prof. IAN SHAW

CITY UNIVERSITY

Northampton Square, London, EC1V 0HB
Telephone: (171) 477-8000
Fax: (171) 477-8560

Founded 1894 as Northampton Institute, Northampton College of Advanced Technology 1957, University Charter 1966

Academic year: September to July

Chancellor: The Lord Mayor of London
Vice-Chancellor and Principal: Prof. D. W. RHIND
Pro-Vice Chancellors: F. J. CHARLWOOD, C. R. HAINES, M. DOCKRAY, C. TH. GRAMMENOS
Academic Registrar: Dr A. H. SEVILLE
Librarian: J. A. MCGUIRK

Library of 338,000 vols
Number of teachers: 460
Number of students: 8,053

Publications: *Undergraduate Prospectus*, *Postgraduate Prospectus*, *Annual Report*.

DEANS AND HEADS OF DEPARTMENTS

Schools:

School of Mathematics, Actuarial Science and Statistics: Prof. S. HABERMAN
Actuarial Science and Statistics: Dr L. C. WOLSTENHOLME
Mathematics: Prof. J. MATHON
Business Systems Applications: Prof. O. J. HANSON

School of Engineering: Prof. L. R. WOOTTON
Civil Engineering: Dr L. F. BOSWELL
Electrical, Electronic and Information Engineering: Prof. K. T. V. GRATTAN
Mechanical Engineering and Aeronautics: Prof. A. R. D. THORLEY

School of Informatics: Prof. P. E. OSMON
Computing: (vacant)
Information Science: Dr D. NICHOLS
Human Computer Interface Design: Prof. A. G. SUTCLIFFE
Centre for Software Reliability: Prof. B. LITTLEWOOD

Business School: Prof. L. HANNAH
Accounting and Finance: Prof. M. LEVIS
Banking and Finance: Prof. C. GEMMIL (acting)
Human Resource Management and Organizational Behaviour: Prof. C. HENDRY
Management Systems and Information: Prof. C. W. HOLTHAM
Investment and Risk Management: Dr E. DINENIS
Marketing: Prof. F. A. JOHNE
Property Valuation and Management: W. H. RODNEY
Shipping, Trade and Finance: Prof. C. TH. GRAMMENOS
Strategy and International Business: Prof. C. CHOI

School of Social and Human Sciences: Dr S. H. MILLER
Clinical Communication Studies: Prof. S. BYNG
Economics: Prof. D. GLYCOPANTIS
Health Management: V. ILES
Psychology: Prof. J. HAMPTON
Rehabilitation Resources Centre: M. FLOYD
Sociology: Dr H. TUMBER

St Bartholomew School of Nursing and Midwifery: S. STUDDY
Adult Nursing: Dr C. COX
Applied Behavioural and Biological Science: D. YARWOOD
Children's Nursing: M. LANE
Community and Primary Health Care Nursing: V. MAYOR
Educational Development and Academic Standards: D. HOLROYD
Mental Health and Learning Difficulties Nursing: S. SOURIAL
Midwifery: D. OPOKU

Departments:
Optometry and Visual Science: M. FAHLE
Law: Prof. C. L. RYAN
Journalism: R. ALLEN
Arts Policy and Management: Dr E. MOODY
Music: Prof. D. SMALLEY
Continuing Education: A. J. LEWIS
Radiography: R. W. HICKS

Institute:
Institute of Health Sciences and Centre for Measurement and Information in Medicine: Prof. E. R. CARSON

PROFESSORS

ATKINSON, J. H., Soil Mechanics
BADEN-FULLER, C., Business Strategy
BARBUR, J. L., Optics and Visual Science
BARRETT, M. V., Sociology
BATCHELOR, R., Banking and Finance
BOR, R., Psychology
BOSWELL, L. F., Civil Engineering
BOWERS, L., Psychiatric Nursing
BOYLAN, P. J., Arts Policy and Management
BUCKLEY, R. J., Ocular Medicine
BURN, E. H., Law
BYNG, S., Communication Disability
CAPIE, F. H., Economic History
CARSON, E. R., Systems Science
CHAPLIN, J. R., Hydraulics
CHOI, C., Internal Business Policy
CHRYSTAL, K. A., Monetary Economics
COHEN, B., Computing
COLLINS, M. A., Marketing Research
CONNELL, T. J., Languages for the Professions
COOPER, M. A. R., Engineering Surveying
COYLE, A., Sociology
CUBBIN, J., Economics
DANIELS, P. G., Applied Mathematics
DICKINSON, G. M., International Insurance
DOCKRAY, M. S., Law
DONE, G. T. S., Aeronautics
FAHLE, M., Optometry
FENTON, N. E., Computing Science
FINKELSTEIN, L., Measurement and Instrumentation
FITZGERALD, L., Health Services Research
GARDINER, J. M., Psychology
GEMMILL, G. T., Finance
GLYCOPANTIS, D., Economics
GOLOMBOK, J. M., Psychology
GRAMMENOS, C. TH., Shipping, Trade and Finance
GRATTAN, K. T. V., Measurement and Instrumentation
HABERMAN, S., Actuarial Science
HAMPTON, J., Psychology
HANNAH, L., Business
HANSON, O. J., Business Computing
HEFFERNAN, S. A., Banking and Finance
HENDRY, C., Organizational Behaviour
HILLS, J., Sociology
HINES, M., Psychology
HOLTHAM, C. W., Information Management
JOHNE, F. A., Marketing
KARCANIAS, N., Control Theory and Design
LEVIS, M., Finance
LITTLEWOOD, B., Software Engineering
MCGUIRE, A. J., Economics
MARTIN, P. P., Mathematical Physics
MATHON, J., Mathematical Physics
MINTZ, B., Engineering Materials
NEWBY, J., Statistical Science
OSMON, P. E., Computer Systems
PALMER, A. W., Electrical Engineering
PEAKE, D. J., Aero and Fluid Dynamics
PEPPER, G., Financial Markets
PRICE, S., Economics
PURDUE, H. M., Law
ROBERTS, P. D., Control Engineering
RYAN, C. L., Law
SALMON, M., Financial Markets
SAMUEL, R., Music
SELIM, G., Internal Auditing
SMALLEY, D., Music
SMITH, I. K., Applied Thermodynamics
STEPHENSON, H., Journalism
STOSIC, N., Positive Displacement Compressor Technology
SUDARSANUM, P. S., Finance and Accounting
SUTCLIFFE, A. G., Systems Engineering
TAFFLER, R. J., Accounting and Finance
TAYLOR, R. N., Geotechnical Engineering
THORLEY, A. R. D., Fluid Engineering
TUNSTALL, C. J., Sociology
VENMORE-ROWLAND, P., Property Valuation and Finance
VIRDI, K. S., Structural Engineering
WILLIAMS, A. P. O., Organizational and Occupational Psychology
WOLL, B., Sign Language and Deaf Studies
WOOD, G., Economics
WOODWARD, E. G., Optometry and Visual Science
WOOTTON, L. R., Engineering

COVENTRY UNIVERSITY

Priory St, Coventry, CV1 5FB
Telephone: (1203) 631313
Fax: (1203) 838793

Founded 1970 as Lanchester Polytechnic, later became Coventry Polytechnic; present name and status 1992

Vice-Chancellor: Dr M. GOLDSTEIN
Pro-Vice-Chancellors: Prof. N. W. BELLAMY, Prof. R. J. PRYCE, Prof. D. G. THOMAS
Academic Registrar: J. GLEDHILL
Librarian: P. NOON

Library of 200,000 vols
Number of teachers: 600
Number of students: 16,000

HEADS OF SCHOOL

Art and Design: Prof. M. TOVEY
The Built Environment: Prof. C. J. PRATT
Business: Dr D. MORRIS
Engineering: Prof. E. H. SMITH
Health and Social Sciences: Dr D. PENNINGTON

International Studies and Law: Dr P. D. HARTLEY
Mathematical and Information Sciences: Prof. D. J. G. JAMES
Natural and Environmental Sciences: P. V. O'CONNOR

CRANFIELD UNIVERSITY

Cranfield campus: Cranfield, Beds., MK43 0AL
Silsoe campus: Silsoe, Bedford, MK45 4DT
Shrivenham campus: RMCS Shrivenham, Swindon, Wilts., SN6 8LA

Telephone: (1234) 754025 (Cranfield); (1525) 860428 (Silsoe); (1793) 782551 (Shrivenham)

Fax: (1234) 750972 (Cranfield); (1525) 861527 (Silsoe); (1793) 783878 (Shrivenham)

Founded 1946 as College of Aeronautics; became Cranfield Institute of Technology 1969; incorporated National College of Agricultural Engineering (Silsoe) 1975; took responsibility for academic work at Royal Military College of Science, Shrivenham, 1984; present name 1993

Chancellor: Lord VINCENT OF COLESHILL
Vice-Chancellor: Prof. F. R. HARTLEY
Secretary: (vacant)

Library of 100,000 vols, 200,000 reports

Number of students: 2,700 degree-course (mostly postgraduate), 10,000 short-course

Schools: at Cranfield, Aeronautics, Industrial and Manufacturing Science, Bioscience and Technology, Mechanical Engineering, Management; at Silsoe, Agriculture, Food and Environment; at Shrivenham, Defence Technology.

PROFESSORS

ALLEN, P. M., Evolutionary Complex Systems
ALLERTON, D. J., Avionics
ASHWELL, G. J.
BAILEY, A., Applied Chemistry
BILLINGHAM, J., Marine Technology
BOWMAN, C. C., Business Strategy
BREWSTER, C. J., European Human Resource Management
BROWN, A., Power Plants and Propulsion
BUCKLEY, A. A., International Financial Management
BUCKNALL, C. B., Polymer Science
CARR, M. K. V., Agricultural Water Management
CHRISTOPHER, M. G., Marketing and Logistics
CORBETT, J., Precision Engineering
CORDEY-HAYES, M., Technology Policy
CROWLEY, A. B., Ballistics
DAVIES, I. R., Development and Disaster Management
DEASLEY, P. J., Mechatronics
EDWARDS, C., Management Information Systems
ELDER, R. L., Compressor Technology
FIELDING, J. P., Aircraft Design
FLETCHER, R. S., Thermal Power
FRIEND, C. M., Materials and Medical Sciences
GODWIN, R. J., Agricultural Machinery Technology
GREENHALGH, D. A., Non-Intrusive Measurement of Combustion and Flow
HANCOCK, P., Engineering Metallurgy
HATCH, M. J., Organization Theory
HETHERINGTON, J. G., Engineering Design
HILL, P. C. J., Information Systems Engineering
HOLMES, E. R., Military and Security Studies
HUFF, A., Strategic Management
HUTCHINSON, P., Statistical Fluid Mechanics
IRVING, P. E., Helicopter Damage Tolerance
JAMES, J. R., Electromagnetic Systems Engineering
JOHNSON, G. N., Strategic Management
KAKABADSE, A., Management Development
KAY, J. M., Manufacturing Systems Engineering
KNOX, S., Brand Marketing
MCDONALD, M. H. B., Marketing Strategy
MAYS, G. C., Civil Engineering
MORGAN, R. P. C., Soil Erosion Control
MORRIS, A. J., Computational Structural Analysis
MORRIS, E. R., Food Structure and Processing
MOSS, J. B., Thermofluids and Combustion
MOULDING, M. R., Software Engineering
MUIR, H. C., Aerospace Psychology
MURRAY, L. G., Director of Cranfield School of Management
MYDDELTON, D. R., Finance and Accounting
NELLIS, J. G., International Management Economics
NEW, C. C., Manufacturing Strategy
NICHOLLS, J. R., Coatings Technology
ORMONDROYD, R. F., Communications and Wireless Network
PAYNE, A. F. T., Services and Relationship Marketing
POLL, D. I. A., Aerospace Engineering
RADLEY, R. W., Agricultural Production Technology
ROGERSON, J. H., Quality Systems
SACKETT, P. J., Integrated Systems
SAMMES, A. J., Computer Science
SANDERSON, M. L., Fluid Instrumentation
SHARP, R. S., Automotive Product Engineering
SINGH, R., Gas Turbine Engineering
SPOOR, G., Applied Soil Physics
SPRAGUE, L.
STEPHENSON, D. J., Materials Processing
STEPHENSON, T., Water Sciences
SWEENEY, M. T., Operations Management
TAYLOR, J. C., Land Resources Monitoring
TAYLOR, T., Head of Defence Analysis and Security Management
TURNER, A. P. F., Biosensor Technology
TYSON, S. J. J., Human Resource Management
WARD, J. M., Strategic Information Systems
WARNER, P. J., Industrial Molecular Biology
WHATMORE, R. W., Engineering Nanotechnology
WHITE, B. A., Control and Guidance

DE MONTFORT UNIVERSITY

The Gateway, Leicester, LE1 9BH
Telephone: (116) 255-1551
Fax: (116) 255-0307

Founded 1969 as City of Leicester Polytechnic, later became Leicester Polytechnic; present name and status 1992

Chancellor: Sir CLIVE WHITMORE
Chief Executive and Vice-Chancellor: Prof. K. BARKER
Executive Pro-Vice-Chancellors: Prof. B. SWANICK (Academic Affairs), Prof. M. BROWN (Resources), Prof. D. CHIDDICK (Development)
Academic Registrar: E. CRITCHLOW
Chief Librarian: R. J. ADAMS

Number of teachers: 1,500
Number of students: 21,500 full-time, 6,000 part-time

DEANS OF FACULTY

Faculty of Applied Sciences: Prof. R. G. LINFORD
Faculty of Business and Law: Prof. J. COYNE
Faculty of Computing and Engineering: Prof. P. LUKER
Faculty of Art and Design: (vacant)
Faculty of Humanities: Prof. J. SIMONS
Faculty of Health and Community Studies: Prof. M. SAKS

UNIVERSITY OF DERBY

Kedleston Rd, Derby, DE22 1GB
Telephone: (1332) 622222
Fax: (1332) 294861

Founded 1851 with college status, later Derbyshire College of Higher Education; present name and status 1993

Academic year: September to June

Chancellor: Sir CHRISTOPHER BALL
Vice-Chancellor: Prof. ROGER WATERHOUSE
Deputy Vice-Chancellor: MICHAEL HALL
Pro Vice-Chancellors: ROBERT FAITHORN, MICHAEL TAYLOR, FREDA TALLANTYRE
Pro Vice-Chancellor and Registrar: JENNIFER FRY
Librarian: GORDON BREWER

Library of 275,000 vols
Number of teachers: 450
Number of students: 9,193 full-time, 3,580 part-time

Publications: *Sphere* (monthly), *Annual Review*.

DEANS

Derbyshire Business School: TONY FITZSIMONS
School of Art and Design: DAVID MANLEY
School of Health and Community Studies: DAWN FORMAN
School of Education and Social Science: MIKE WISER
School of Mathematics and Computing: Dr DAVID KNIBB
School of Engineering: Prof. RAY BAINES
School of Environmental and Applied Sciences: Dr JOHN THOMAS (acting)
School of European and International Studies: SUE WALL

UNIVERSITY OF DUNDEE

Dundee, DD1 4HN
Telephone: (1382) 344000
Fax: (1382) 201604

Founded 1881 as University College, Dundee, Royal Charter 1967

Academic year: October to June

Chancellor: Sir JAMES BLACK
Rector: TONY SLATTERY
Principal and Vice-Chancellor: Dr I. J. GRAHAM-BRYCE
Vice-Principal: Prof. D. B. SWINFEN
Secretary: R. SEATON
Librarian: J. M. BAGNALL

Library: see Libraries
Number of teachers: 616 full-time, including 124 professors
Number of students: 8,412 full-time

Publications: *University Calendar*, *Prospectus*, *Graduate Prospectus*, *Diary*, *Contact*.

DEANS

Faculty of Medicine and Dentistry: Prof. D. A. LEVISON
Faculty of Science and Engineering: Prof. D. H. BOXER
Faculty of Law and Accountancy: R. A. LYON
Faculty of Arts and Social Sciences: Prof. H. R. JONES
Faculty of Duncan of Jordanstone College: W. W. BARR

PROFESSORS

Faculty of Medicine and Dentistry:

BAIN, D. J. G., General Practice
BELCH, J. J. F., Vascular Medicine
BURCHELL, B., Medical Biochemistry
CHISHOLM, D. M., Dental Surgery
CUSCHIERI, Sir ALFRED, Surgery
FLOREY, C. DU V., Epidemiology and Public Health
FORBES, C. D., Medicine
GLEN, S., Nursing and Midwifery
GRIEVE, A. R., Conservative Dentistry
HALL, P. A., Cellular Pathology
HARDEN, R. M., Medical Education
HAYES, J. D., Molecular Carcinogenesis
HOWIE, P. W., Obstetrics and Gynaecology

KERR, M. A., Infection and Immunity
LAMBERT, J. J., Neuropharmacology
LEDINGHAM, I. M., Clinical Skills
LEVISON, D. A., Pathology
MCDEVITT, D. G., Clinical Pharmacology
MCGHEE, C. N. J., Ophthalmology
MCMURDO, M. E. T., Ageing and Health
MATTHEWS, K., Psychiatry
MUNRO, A. J., Radiation Oncology
NICHOLLS, D. G., Neurochemistry
OLVER, R. E., Child Health
PIPPARD, M. J., Haematology
PITTS, N. B., Dental Health
POUNDER, D. J., Forensic Medicine
RANKIN, E. M., Cancer Medicine
REID, I. C., Psychiatry
ROWLEY, D. I., Orthopaedic and Trauma Surgery
SCHOR, S. L., Oral Cell Biology
STEELE, R. J., Surgical Oncology
STEVENSON, I. H., Pharmacology
STIRRUPS, D. R., Orthodontics
STRUTHERS, A. D., Clinical Pharmacology
SULLIVAN, F. M., General Practice and Primary Care
TUNSTALL PEDOE, H. D., Cardiovascular Epidemiology
WILDSMITH, J. A. W., Anaesthesia
WOLF, C. R., Molecular Pharmacology
YEMM, R., Dental Prosthetics

Faculty of Science and Engineering:
BOXER, D. H., Microbial Biochemistry
BRIMACOMBE, J. S., Chemistry
CAIRNS, J. A., Microelectronics and Materials Science
CODD, G. A., Microbiology
COHEN, Sir PETER, Enzymology
CRACKNELL, A. P., Physics
DAVIES, M. C. R., Civil Engineering
DAVIES, P. A., Fluid Dynamics
DHIR, R. K., Concrete Technology
DOWNES, C. P., Biochemistry
FAIRLAMB, A. H., Biochemistry
FERGUSON, M. A J., Molecular Parasitology
FITZGERALD, A. G., Analytical Electron Microscopy
FLETCHER, R., Mathematics
GADD, G. M., Microbiology
GLOVER, D. M., Molecular Genetics
GOODMAN, T. N. T., Applied Analysis
HARDIE, D. G., Cellular Signalling
HERBERT, R. A., Microbial Ecology
HEWIT, J. R., Mechanical and Manufacturing Engineering
HORNER, R. M. W., Engineering Management
HUNTER, G., Chemistry
JONES, H. G., Plant Ecology
LAMOND, A. I., Biochemistry
LANE, D. P., Molecular Oncology
LANE, E. B., Anatomy and Cell Biology
LILLEY, D. M. J., Molecular Biology
MAKIN, B., Electrical Engineering
NEWELL, A. F., Electronics and Microcomputer Systems
PROUD, C. G., Biochemical Physiology
RAVEN, J. A., Biology
RENNIE, M. J., Physiology
ROCHESTER, C. H., Chemistry
STURROCK, R. R., Anatomy
TICKLE, C. A., Developmental Biology
VARDY, A. E., Civil Engineering
WATSON, G. A., Numerical Analysis
WATTS, C., Immunobiology
WILLIAMS, J. A., Developmental Biology

Faculty of Law and Accountancy:
BISSETT-JOHNSON, A., Private Law
CAMERON, P. D., International Energy Law and Policy
GRAY, R. H., Accountancy and Information Systems
GRINYER, J. R., Accountancy and Business Finance
INNES, J., Accountancy
MCBRYDE, W. W., Scots Law
PAGE, A. C., Public Law
PALMER, K. F., Energy Finance
POWER, D. M., Business Finance
REID, C. T., Environmental Law
STEVENS, P., Petroleum Law and Economics
WALDE, T. W., International Economic, Energy and Natural Resources Law
WARD, I., Law

Faculty of Arts and Social Sciences:
BALDWIN, N., Child Care and Protection
BLACK, A. J., History of Political Thought
CHATTERJI, M., Applied Economics
FINDLAY, A. M., Geography
HARTLEY, J. D., Educational Theory and Policy
HOGG, J., Profound Disabilities
JONES, H. R., Population Geography
KEMAL, S., Philosophy
KENNEDY, R. A., Psychology
MACDONALD, M., History of Scottish Art
MACHIN, G. I. T., British History
MOLANA, H. H., Economics
NEWTON, K. M., Literary Theory
SEYMOUR, P. H. K., Cognitive Psychology
SIANN, G., Gender Relations
SMITH, S. W., English
SWINFEN, D. B., Commonwealth History
WADE, N. J., Visual Psychology
WARD, G. C., English
WERRITTY, A., Physical Geography
WHATLEY, C. A., Scottish History
WILLIAMS, B. P., Social Work

Faculty of Duncan of Jordanstone College:
ANDERSON, A. S., Food Choice
FOLLET, G. L. P., Design
HOWARD, I. A., Fine Art
LLOYD, M. G., Planning Research
MCKEAN, C. A., Scottish Architectural History
MACLEAN, W., Fine Art
PARTRIDGE, S., Media Art
ROBERTS, P. W., European Strategic Planning
ROBB, A., Fine Art
STARSZAKOWNA, N., Design

UNIVERSITY OF DURHAM

Old Shire Hall, Durham, DH1 3HP
Telephone: (191) 374-2000
Fax: (191) 374-7250

Founded 1832

Academic year: October to June (three terms)

Chancellor: Sir PETER USTINOV
Vice-Chancellor: Sir KENNETH CALMAN
Pro-Vice-Chancellors: Prof. M. C. PRESTWICH, B. S. GOWER, Prof. J. H. ANSTEE
Registrar and Secretary: J. C. F. HAYWARD

Library: see Libraries
Number of teachers: 503
Number of students: 8,392 full-time, 2,204 part-time

DEANS

Arts: Prof. P. D. MANNING
Science: Prof. A. UNSWORTH
Social Sciences: Prof. J. A. PALMER

PROFESSORS

Faculty of Arts:
BAGULEY, D., French
BARNES, G. L., Japanese
BRITNELL, R., History
BROWN, D. W., Divinity
COOPER, D. E., Philosophy
DUNN, J. D. G., Divinity
EMONDS, J. E., English Language
GOOD, C. H., German
GREER, D. C., Music
KNIGHT, D. M., History and Philosophy of Science
LOADES, A. L., Divinity
LOWE, E. J., Philosophy
MANNING, P. D., Music
MOLES, J. L., Classics
MOSS, J. A., French
O'NEILL, M. S. C., English Studies
PROVINE, R. C., Music
RHODES, P. J., Ancient History
ROWE, C. J., Greek
SANDERS, A. L., English Studies
SELBY, P. S. M., Theology
WATSON, J. R., English
WAUGH, P., English
WOODMAN, A. J., Latin

Faculty of Social Sciences:
AMIN, A., Geography
ANDERSON, E. W., Middle Eastern and Islamic Studies
ARMSTRONG, J. D., Politics
BILSBOROUGH, A., Anthropology
BLAKE, G. H., Geography
BRITNELL, R. H., History
BOYNE, R. D., Sociology and Social Policy
BURT, T. P., Geography
BYRAM, M. S., Education
CARPENTER, J. S. W., Applied Social Studies
CARRITHERS, M. B., Anthropology
CHANEY, D. C., Sociology and Social Policy
COCKERILL, T. A. J., Business Management and Economics
DARNELL, A. C., Economics
FITZ-GIBBON, C. T., Education
FRAME, R. F., History
FULLER, S. W., Sociology and Social Policy
GALLOWAY, D. M., Education
GIBB, A. A., Small Business Studies
GOTT, R., Education
GRAY, A. G., Public Sector Management
GREAVES, R.-M., Law
HALL, R., Operations and Procurement Strategy
HARDING, A. F., Archaeology
HASELGROVE, C. C., Archaeology
HUDSON, R., Geography
JOHNSON, P. S., Economics
LAYTON, R. H., Anthropology
MICHIE, R. C., History
MILLETT, M. J., Archaeology
NIBLOCK, T. C., Middle Eastern and Islamic Studies
O'BRIEN, D. P., Economics
PRESTWICH, M. C., History
ROLLASON, D. W., History
SHENNAN, I., Geography
SILLITOE, P., Anthropology
SIMMONS, I. G., Geography
SMITH, D., Management
TEFF, H., Law
TODD, M., Archaeology
WARBRICK, C., Law
WILLIAMSON, B., Continuing Education
WILSON, R. J. A., Economics

Faculty of Science:
ABRAM, R. A., Physics
ANGELIDES, K. J., Animal Cell Biology
ANSTEE, J. H., Biological Sciences
APPLETON, E., Manufacturing Systems Engineering
BADYAL, J. P., Chemistry
BENNETT, K. H., Computer Science
BETTESS, P., Engineering
BLOOR, D., Applied Physics
BOWLER, K., Animal Physiology
BRYCE, M. R., Chemistry
CHAMBERS, R. D., Chemistry
COOPER, S. J., Psychology
CORRIGAN, F. E., Mathematics
DAVIES, R. L., Astronomy
EVANS, P. R., Zoology
FAIRLEY, D. B., Mathematical Sciences
FEAST, W. J., Chemistry
FINDLAY, J., Psychology
FLOWER, D. R., Physics
FRENK, C. S., Astronomy
GARIGLIANO, R., Computer Science
GOLDSTEIN, M., Statistics
HARRIS, R. K., Chemistry

HOWARD, J. A. K., Chemistry
HUNTLEY, B., Biological Sciences
HUTSON, J. M., Chemistry
LINDSEY, K., Plant Molecular Biology
LITTLE, H. J., Psychopharmacology
MARDER, T., Inorganic Chemistry
MARS, P., Electronics
MARTIN, A. D., Theoretical Physics
PARKER, D., Chemistry
PENNINGTON, M. R., Mathematical Sciences and Physics
PETTY, M. C., Engineering
PURVIS, A., Engineering
RAN, Z., Pure Mathematics
RICHARDS, R. W., Chemistry
SCHOLL, A. J., Pure Mathematics
SEARLE, R. C., Geophysics
SLABAS, A. R., Plant Sciences
SPOONER, E., Engineering
STIRLING, W. J., Mathematical Sciences and Physics
TANNER, B. K., Physics
THOMPSON, R. N., Geology
TUCKER, M. E., Geological Sciences
TURVER, K. E., Physics
UNSWORTH, A., Engineering
WADE, K., Chemistry
WARD, R. S., Mathematics
WILLIAMS, D. L. H., Chemistry
ZAKRZEWSKI, W. J., Mathematics

COLLEGES

University College: Durham; f. 1832; Master Dr E. C. SALTHOUSE.

Hatfield College: Durham; f. 1846; Master Prof. T. P. BURT.

Grey College: Durham; f. 1959; Master V. E. WATTS.

Van Mildert College: Durham; f. 1963; Principal Dr JUDITH TURNER.

Collingwood College: Durham; f. 1972; Principal Prof. G. H. BLAKE.

College of St Hild and St Bede: Durham; f. 1975; Principal Prof. D. J. DAVIES.

St Chad's College: Durham; f. 1904; Principal Rev. Dr J. P. M. CASSIDY.

St John's College with Cranmer Hall: Durham; f. 1909; Principal D. V. DAY.

Ushaw College: Durham; f. 1808; President Rev. J. O'KEEFE.

St Cuthbert's Society: Durham; f. 1888; known as non-Collegiate until 1947; Principal S. G. C. STOKER.

St Mary's College: Durham; f. 1899; Principal Miss JOAN M. KENWORTHY.

St Aidan's College: Durham; f. 1895; known as St Aidan's Society until 1961; Principal Dr A. YARWOOD (acting).

Trevelyan College: Durham; f. 1965; Principal Prof. M. TODD.

Graduate Society, The: Durham; f. 1965; Principal Dr M. RICHARDSON.

University College Stockton: f. 1992, to award joint qualifications of Universities of Durham and Teesside; now constituent college of University of Durham; students entering from October 1996 have studied for qualifications of University of Durham; Principal J. C. F. HAYWARD.

AFFILIATED COLLEGE

Codrington College: Barbados, West Indies; theological college; Principal Canon N. F. TITUS.

UNIVERSITY OF EAST ANGLIA

Norwich, Norfolk NR4 7TJ
Telephone: (1603) 456161
Telex: 97154
Fax: (1603) 458553
Founded 1964

Chancellor: Prof. Sir GEOFFREY ALLEN
Vice-Chancellor: V. WATTS
Pro-Vice-Chancellors: Prof. F. W. O. WOODHAMS, Prof. C. DAVIS, Prof. D. BRIDGES
Registrar and Secretary: M. G. E. PAULSON-ELLIS
Librarian: Dr D. M. BAKER

Number of teachers: 491
Number of students: 9,725 (incl. 2,200 graduate students)

Publications: *The University of East Anglia Prospectus, Postgraduate Prospectus, Calendar, Vice-Chancellor's Annual Report, Overseas Students' Guide, Ziggurat* (2 a year), individual school prospectuses.

DEANS

School of World Arts Studies and Museology: Dr R. COCKE
School of Biological Sciences: Dr A. DAWSON
School of Chemical Sciences: Prof. D. L. ANDREWS
School of Developmental Studies: Dr R. O. JENKINS
School of Economic and Social Studies: Dr A. KEMP-WELCH
School of Education and Professional Development: R. ASPLAND
School of English and American Studies: Prof. R. SALES
School of Environmental Sciences: Prof. F. VINE
School of Social Work: Prof. M. DAVIES
School of Health: Prof. S. PEARCE
School of History: Prof. R. A. CHURCH
School of Information Systems: Dr J. R. W. GLAUERT
School of Law: Prof. J. G. MILLER
School of Management: Prof. K. P. FLETCHER
School of Mathematics: Dr A. R. CAMINA
School of Modern Languages and European Studies: M. G. CARR

PROFESSORS

School of World Art Studies and Music:
ASTON, P. G., Music
HODGES, R. A.
JORDANOVA, L.
ONIANS, J. B., Visual Arts

School of Biological Sciences:
EDWARDS, D. R.
FLAVELL, G., Biology
GREENWOOD, C., Biology
HEWITT, G. M., Biology
HOPWOOD, Sir DAVID, Genetics
JOHNSTON, A. W. B., Biology
MURPHY, G., Biology
SUTHERLAND, W. J., Biology
WATKINSON, A. R., Biology

School of Chemical Sciences:
COLEMAN, P. G., Experimental Physics
COOK, M. J., Chemistry
DAVIES, J. J., Experimental Physics
McKILLOP, A., Chemistry
MOORE, G. R., Chemistry
ROBINSON, B. H., Chemistry
THOMSON, A. J., Chemistry

School of Developmental Studies:
BARNETT, A. A., Development Studies
BLAIKIE, P. M., Development Studies
ELLIS, F. T., Development Studies
LIVINGSTONE, I., Development Studies
SEDDON, J. D., Development Studies
STOCKING, M. A., Development Studies

School of Economic and Social Studies:
DAVIES, S. W., Economics
GOODWIN, B., Politics
LAWSON, S., Politics
LYONS, B. R., Economics
PARIKH, A., Economics
SUGDEN, R., Economics

School of Education and Professional Development:
BRIDGES, D.
ELLIOTT, J.
GOODSON, I. F.
SCHOSTAK, J. F.
THORNE, B. J.

School of English and American Studies:
BIGSBY, C. W. E., American Studies
FAIRCLOUGH, A., American History
LAWTON, D. A., English Literature
MOTION, A., Creative Writing
SAGE, L., English Literature
SALES, R., English Literature
THOMPSON, R., American History
TODD, J., English Literature

School of Environmental Sciences:
BRIMBLECOMBE, P., Environmental Sciences
DAVIES, T. D., Environmental Sciences
LISS, P. S., Environmental Sciences
O'RIORDAN, T., Environmental Sciences
PENKETT, S. A., Enviromental Sciences
TURNER, R. K., Environmental Studies
VINE, F. J., Environmental Sciences
WATKINSON, A. R., Ecology
WATSON, A. J., Environmental Sciences
WIGLEY, T. M. L., Environmental Sciences

School of Social Work:
DAVIES, M. B., Social Work
HOWE, D. K., Social Work
THOBURN, J., Social Work

School of Health:
PEARCE, S., Health Psychology

School of History:
ACTON, E. D. J., Modern European History
DAVIS, J. C.
JOHN, M. F., European History
SEARLE, G. R., English History

School of Information Systems:
ARNOLD, D. B., Computing Science
FORREST, A. R., Computing Science
RAYWARD-SMITH, V. J., Computing Science
SLEEP, M. R., Computing Science
WOODHAMS, F. W. D.

School of Law:
MILLER, J. G.
PRIME, T.
SMITH, I. T.
THOMAS, D. R.

School of Management:
FLETCHER, K. P.
JONES, C. S., Accountancy

School of Mathematics:
JOHNSON, J. A., Mathematics
MORLAND, L. W., Mathematics
RILEY, N., Applied Mathematics
ZALESSKII, A., Pure Mathematics

School of Modern Languages and European Studies:
FLETCHER, J. W. J., European Literature
PIPE-FOWLER, R. G., Linguistics
ROBINSON, M. G., Scandinavian Studies
SCOTT, C., European Literature (French)
SEBALD, W. G., European Literature (German)

ASSOCIATED RESEARCH INSTITUTES

British Sugar Technical Centre: Norwich Research Park, Colney, Norwich, NR4 7UB; tel. (1603) 250000.

Fisheries Laboratory (Ministry of Agriculture, Fisheries and Food): see under Research Institutes.

Institute of Food Research Norwich Laboratory: Norwich Research Park, Colney, Norwich NR4 7UA; tel. (1603) 255000.

John Innes Centre: see under Research Institutes.

Ministry of Agriculture, Fisheries and Food, Food Science Laboratory: See under Research Institutes.

Norfolk and Norwich Institute for Medical Education: Norfolk and Norwich Hospital, Norwich, NR1 3SR; tel. (1603) 628377.

Sainsbury Laboratory: Norwich Research Park, Colney, Norwich, NR4 7UH; tel. (1603) 452571.

CSL Food Science Laboratory: Norwich Research Park, Colney, Norwich, NR4 7UA; tel. (1603) 259350.

UNIVERSITY OF EAST LONDON

Romford Rd, Stratford, London, E15 4LZ

Telephone: (181) 590-7722
Fax: (181) 590-7799

Founded 1970 as North East London Polytechnic, later became Polytechnic of East London; present name and status 1992

Organized in three campuses: Stratford Campus, Romford Rd, Stratford, London, E15 4LZ (management and science); Barking Campus, Longbridge Rd, Dagenham, Essex, RM8 2AS (arts and social sciences, business, engineering); Docklands Campus, Royal Albert Way, London, E16 (opening in 1999)

Chancellor: BRIAN RIX
Vice-Chancellor: Prof. F. W. GOULD
Registrar: A. INGLE
Librarian: J. DOUST

Library of 248,000 vols and 1,400 current periodicals
Number of teachers: 390 full-time, 27 part-time
Number of students: 9,150 full-time, 2,850 part-time

DEANS

Faculty of Design, Engineering and the Built Environment: Dr C. ELLIS
East London Business School: P. KNOWLES
Faculty of Science and Health: Prof. SHAWN DOONAN
Faculty of Social Sciences: Prof. M. RUSTIN

HEADS OF DEPARTMENTS

Faculty of Design, Engineering and the Built Environment:
- Architecture: Prof. PETER SALTER
- Art and Design: G. ELINOR
- Civil Engineering: S. K. AL NAIB
- School of Electrical and Manufacturing Engineering: R. PERRYMAN
- School of Surveying: Dr ALLAN BRIMICOMBE

East London Business School:
- Postgraduate Programmes: T. HONOUR
- Post-Experience Programmes: T. HONOUR
- Undergraduate Programmes: G. CURTIS
- Corporate Programmes: D. NEEDLE

Faculty of Science and Health:
- Environmental and Mathematical Sciences: Prof. K. SNOW
- Health Sciences: S. BEESTON
- Life Sciences: D. HUMBER
- Psychology: Dr D. ROSE

Faculty of Social Sciences:
- Economics: F. SKUSE
- Cultural Studies: A. O'SHEA
- Education Studies: J. GRAHAM
- Human Relations: Prof. BARRY RICHARDS
- School of Law: C. SUMNER
- Sociology: Dr BARBARA HARRISON
- Social Politics, Language and Linguistics: D. ROBBINS

UNIVERSITY OF EDINBURGH

Old College, South Bridge, Edinburgh, EH8 9YL

Telephone: (131) 650-1000
Telex: 727442
Fax: (131) 650-2147

Founded 1583
Private control
Academic year: October to September

Chancellor: HRH The Prince PHILIP, Duke of EDINBURGH
Vice-Chancellor and Principal: Prof. Sir STEWART SUTHERLAND
Rector: J. COLQUHOUN
Secretary: Dr M. J. B. LOWE
Librarian: I. R. MOWAT

Library: see Libraries
Number of teachers: 2,589 including 272 professors
Number of students: 17,845 including 1,921 part-time
Publication: *The University of Edinburgh Calendar*.

DEANS AND PROVOSTS

Provost of Arts, Divinity and Music and Dean of Arts: Dr F. D. DOW
Dean of Divinity: Rev. Prof. D. B. FORRESTER
Dean of Music: Prof. D. R. B. KIMBELL
Provost of Law and Social Sciences and Dean of Social Sciences: Prof. A. P. COHEN
Dean of Law: Prof. J. A. USHER
Provost of Medicine and Veterinary Medicine and Dean of Medicine: Prof. C. C. BIRD
Dean of Veterinary Medicine: Prof. H. R. P. MILLER
Provost and Dean of Science and Engineering: Prof. G. S. BOULTON

PROFESSORS

Faculty of Divinity:
- AULD, A. G., Hebrew Bible
- BROWN, S. J., Ecclesiastical History
- FORRESTER, D. B., Christian Ethics and Practical Theology
- HURTADO, D. A., New Testament Language, Literature and Theology
- KEE, A. A., Religious Studies
- KERR, D. A., Christianity in the Non-Western World
- MACKEY, J. P., Systematic Theology
- SUTHERLAND, S. R., Philosophy of Religion
- WHALING, F., Study of Religion

Faculty of Law:
- BANKOWSKI, Z., Legal Theory
- BLACK, R., Scots Law
- BOYLE, A. E., Public International Law
- GARLAND, D. W., Penology
- GILMORE, W. C., International Criminal Law
- GRETTON, G. L., Law
- MCCALL SMITH, R. A. A., Medical Law
- MACCORMICK, D. N., Public Law
- MACQUEEN, H. L., Private Law
- MUNRO, C. R., Constitutional Law
- MURRAY, J., Company Law
- REID, K. G. C., Property Law
- SMITH, D. J., Criminology
- USHER, J. A., European Institutions

Faculty of Medicine:
- AMYES, S. J. B., Microbial Chemotherapy
- ANSELL, J. D., Experimental Haematology
- BAIRD, D. T., Reproductive Endocrinology
- BEST, J. J. K., Medical Radiology
- BIRD, C. C., Pathology
- BONTHRON, D. T., Medical Genetics
- BROCK, D. J. H., Human Genetics
- BUSUTTIL, A., Forensic Medicine
- BUTLER, P. C., Diabetic Medicine
- CALDER, A. A., Obstetrics and Gynaecology
- CARTER, Sir D. C., Surgery
- CRAWFORD, D. H., Bacteriology
- DONALDSON, I. M. L., Neurophysiology
- DOUGLAS, N. J., Respiratory and Sleep Medicine
- EBMEIER, K. P., Psychiatry
- FERGUSON, A., Gastroenterology
- FOWKES, F. G. R., Epidemiology
- FOX, K. A. A., Cardiology
- GARDEN, O. J., Hepatobiliary Surgery
- GILLESPIE, W. J., Orthopaedic Surgery
- GOVAN, J. R. W., Microbial Pathogenecity
- HASLETT, C., Respiratory Medicine
- HAYES, P. C., Hepatology
- HILLIER, S. G., Reproductive Endocrinology
- HOOPER, M. L., Molecular Pathology
- HOWIE, J. G. R., General Practice
- HUNTER, J. A. A., Dermatology
- JAMES, K., Immunology
- JOHNSTONE, E. C., Psychiatry
- KAUFMAN, M. H., Anatomy
- KELLY, J. S., Pharmacology
- LAMB, J. R., Respiratory Science
- LENG, G., Experimental Physiology
- MCARDLE, C. S., Surgery
- MCDICKEN, W. N., Medical Physics and Medical Engineering
- MCINTOSH, N., Child Life and Health
- MACNEE, W., Respiratory and Environmental Medicine
- MARAN, A. G. D., Otolaryngology
- MASON, J. I., Clinical Biochemistry
- MILLER, W. R., Experimental Oncology
- MORRIS, R. G. M., Neuroscience
- MUIR, A. L., Postgraduate Medical Education
- MURRAY, G. D., Medical Statistics
- NUKI, G., Rheumatology
- PHILLIPS, J. H., Biology Teaching
- POWER, M. J., Clinical Psychology
- PRICE, A., Radiation Oncology
- RUCKLEY, C. V., Vascular Surgery
- SAVILL, J. S., Medicine
- SECKL, J. R., Molecular Medicine
- SMYTH, J. F., Medical Oncology
- SPENCE, A. A., Anaesthetics
- SUTCLIFFE, P., Preventive Dentistry
- TURNER, A. N., Nephrology
- WALKINSHAW, M. D., Structural Biochemistry
- WARLOW, C. P., Medical Neurology
- WATSON, W. E., Physiology
- WEBB, D. J., Clinical Pharmacology
- WHITTLE, I. R., Surgical Neurology
- WILL, R. G., Clinical Neurology
- WYLLIE, A. D. H., Experimental Pathology
- YOUNG, A., Geriatric Medicine

Faculty of Arts:
- ANDERSON, J. M., English Language
- ANDERSON, R. D., Modern History
- ANGOLD, M. J., Byzantine History
- BARKER, A. W., Austrian Studies
- BROCKINGTON, J. L., Sanskrit
- CAMPBELL, I., Scottish and Victorian Literature
- DICKINSON, H. T., History
- ERMARTH, E., English Literature
- GIEGERICH, H. J., English Linguistics
- GILLIES, W., Celtic
- GOODMAN, A. E., Medieval and Renaissance History
- HILLENBRAND, R., Islamic Art
- HURFORD, J. R., General Linguistics
- JACK, R. D. S., Scottish and Medieval Literature
- JEFFREYS-JONES, R., American History
- JONES, C., English Language
- JONES, P. H., Philosophy
- JOSEPH, J. E., Applied Linguistics
- LADD, D. R., Linguistics
- LARKIN, M. J. M., History
- LAVER, J. D. M. H., Phonetics
- LYNCH, M., Scottish History
- MCDOUGALL, B. S., Chinese
- MACMILLAN, J. D., History of Scottish Art
- MILLER, J. E., Linguistics and Spoken Language
- RENWICK, J. P., French

RICHARDSON, J. S., Classics
SCHEUNEMANN, D., German
SULEIMAN, M. Y. I. H., Arabic and Islamic Studies
THOMSON, R., Fine Art
USHER, J., Italian
WILLIAMSON, E. H., Hispanic Studies
WILLIAMSON, T., Logic and Metaphysics

Faculty of Science and Engineering:
ABRAMSKY, S., Theoretical Computer Science
AMBLER, R. P., Protein Chemistry
BARRY, A., Environmental Engineering
BIRD, A. P., Genetics
BISHOP, C. M., Computer Science
BISHOP, J. O., Molecular Cell Biology
BOULTON, G. S., Geology
BOWNES, M., Developmental Biology
BRAND, P. W. J. L., Astrophysics
BUNDY, A. R., Automated Reasoning
BURSTALL, R. M., Computer Science
CARBERY, A., Mathematics
CATES, M., Natural Philosophy
CHAPMAN, S. K., Biological Inorganic Chemistry
DAVIE, A. M., Mathematical Analysis
DENYER, P. B., Integrated Electronics
DONACHIE, W. D., Bacterial Genetics
DONOVAN, R. J., Chemistry
DRYSDALE, D. D., Fire Safety Engineering
FINNEGAN, D. J., Molecular Genetics
FLITSCH, S. L., Protein Chemistry
FORDE, M. C., Civil Engineering Construction
FOURMAN, M. P., Computer Systems – Software
FRY, S. C., Plant Biochemistry
GILLESPIE, T. A., Mathematical Analysis
GRACE, J., Environmental Biology
GRAHAM, C. M., Experimental Geochemistry
GRANT, P. M., Electronic Signal Processing
GREATED, C. A., Fluid Dynamics
HANLEY, N., Agricultural Resource Management
HARLEY, S. L., Lower Crustal Processes
HARTE, B., Metaphorism
HARWOOD, R. S., Atmospheric Physics
HEGGIE, D. C., Mathematical Astronomy
HILL, W. G., Animal Genetics
IBBETT, R. N., Computer Science
JACK, M. A., Electronic Systems
JARVIS, P. G., Forestry and Natural Resources
JORDAN, J. R., Electronic Instrumentation
KENWAY, R. D., Mathematical Physics
KILBEY, B. J., Molecular Parasitology
LAWRENCE, A., Astronomy
LEONARD, T., Statistics
MCCOMB, W. D., Statistical Physics
MCGEOUGH, J. A., Engineering
MACINTYRE, A. J., Mathematical Logic
MAIZELS, R. M., Zoology
MANNING, A. W. G., Natural History
MELTON, D. W., Somatic Cell Genetics
METCALFE, I. S., Chemical Engineering
MOORE, J. D., Artificial Intelligence
MURRAY, A. F., Neural Electronics
MURRAY, Sir K., Molecular Biology
MURRAY, N. E., Molecular Genetics
NELMES, R. J., Physical Crystallography
PARKER, D. F., Applied Mathematics
PARSONS, I., Mineralogy
PAWLEY, G. S., Computational Physics
PEACH, K., Particle Physics Experiment
PEACOCK, J. A., Cosmology
PLOTKIN, G. D., Computation Theory
PONTON, J. W., Chemical and Process Systems Engineering
PUSEY, P. N., Physics
RAMAGE, R., Organic Chemistry
RANICKI, A. A., Algebraic Surgery
RANKIN, D. W. H., Structural Chemistry
REES, E. G., Mathematics
ROBERTSON, A. H. F., Geology
ROTTER, J. M., Civil Engineering
SADLER, P. J., Chemistry
SALTER, S. H., Engineering Design
SANNELLA, D. T., Computer Science
SAUNDERS, D. S., Insect Physiology
SEATON, N. A., Interfacial Engineering
SHOTTER, A. C., Experimental Physics
SINCLAIR, A. M., Operator Algebras and Mathematical Analysis
STENNING, K., Human Communications
STIRLING, C., Computation Theory
SUTHERLAND, I. W., Microbial Physiology
TASKER, P. A., Industrial Chemistry
TATE, A., Knowledge Based Systems
THOMPSON, R., Environmental Geophysics
TREWAVAS, A. J., Plant Biochemistry
TURNER, N., Biological Chemistry
UNDERHILL, J. R., Seismic and Sequence Stratigraphy
UPTON, B. G. J., Petrology
WALTON, A. J., Microelectronic Manufacturing
WEBBER, B., Artificial Intelligence
WHALER, K. A., Geophysics
WHITTEMORE, C. T., Agriculture and Rural Economy
WHITTINGTON, H. W., Electrical Power Engineering
ZIOLKOWSKI, A. M., Petroleum Geoscience

Faculty of Music:
KIMBELL, D. R. B., Music
OSBORNE, N., Music

Faculty of Social Sciences:
ADLER, M. E., Socio-Legal Studies
ANDERSON, M., Economic History
BECHHOFER, F., Social Research
BLANCHARD, I. S. W., Medieval Economic History
BLOOR, D., Sociology of Science
BROWN, A., Politics
COHEN, A. P., Social Anthropology
COKE, S., International Business
COYNE, A. R., Architectural Computing
DAWSON, J. A., Marketing
DEARY, I. J., Differential Psychology
DRAPER, P., Finance and Investment
ENTWISTLE, N. J., Education
FLECK, J., Organization of Industry and Commerce
FRANSMAN, M., Economics
FURLEY, P. A., Tropical Biogeography
GRIEVE, R., Psychology
HARDING, D. W., Archaeology
HATHERLY, D. J., Accounting
HENLEY, J. S., International Management
JEFFERY, P. M., Sociology
JEFFERY, R., Sociology of South Asia
JONATHAN, R. M., Educational Theory and Policy
KEAT, R. N., Political Theory
KING, K. J., International and Comparative Education
KOOP, G., Political Economy
LAPSLEY, I. MCL., Accountancy and Finance
LEE, D. N., Perception, Action and Development (Psychology)
MCCRONE, D., Sociology
MACKENZIE, D. A., Sociology
MAIN, B. G. M., Economics
MARTIN, G., Canadian Studies
MELIA, K. M., Nursing Studies
MITCHELL, F., Management Accounting
MORRIS, R. J., Economic and Social History
MORRIS, R. L., Parapsychology
ORR, J. M., Sociology
PELTENBURG, E. J., Archaeology
RAFFE, D. J., Sociology of Education
RALSTON, I., Prehistoric European Archaeology
SINFIELD, R. A., Social Policy
SMITH, S. J., Geography
STEEL, M., Economics
SUGDEN, D. E., Geography
SUMMERFIELD, M. A., Geography
THOMAS, L. C., Management Science
THOMPSON, P. I., Management
THOMSON, G. O. B., Educational Psychology
TIERNEY, A. J., Nursing Research
WALKER, S. P., Accounting History
WATERHOUSE, L. A. M., Social Work
WHYTE, I. B., Architectural History
WITHERS, C. W. J., Geography

Faculty of Veterinary Medicine:
BROPHY, P. J., Veterinary Anatomy and Cell Biology
BROWN, A. G., Veterinary Physiology
BUNNETT, N., Veterinary Physiology
DUGGAN, A. W., Veterinary Pharmacology
HALLIWELL, R. E. W., Veterinary Clinical Studies
HOPKINS, J., Veterinary Immunology
MARTIN, R. J., Veterinary Pharmacology
MAYHEW, I. G., Veterinary Clinical Science
MILLER, H. R. P., Veterinary Clinical Studies
NASH, A. A., Veterinary Pathology
TAYLOR, D. W., Tropical Animal Health
WOOLHOUSE, M. E. J., Veterinary Public Health and Quantitive Epidemiology

Non-Faculty based:
SCHULLER, T. E., Continuing Education

CONSTITUENT COLLEGE

New College: The Mound, Edinburgh, EH1 2LX; f. 1846; Principal RUTH PAGE.

ATTACHED INSTITUTES

Artificial Intelligence Applications Institute: 80 South Bridge, Edinburgh EH1 1HN; Man. Dir Prof. J. HOWE.

Institute for Advanced Studies in the Humanities: Hope Park Square, Edinburgh, EH8 9NW; Dir Prof. P. H. JONES.

Institute for Applied Language Studies: 21 Hill Place, Edinburgh EH8 9BP; Dir E. H. GLENDINNING.

Scottish Agricultural College Edinburgh: see under Colleges.

UNIVERSITY OF ESSEX

Wivenhoe Park, Colchester, CO4 3SQ
Telephone: (1206) 873333
Fax: (1206) 873598

Founded 1961

Chancellor: Lord NOLAN
Pro-Chancellor and Chairman of Council: Rt Rev. JOHN WAINE
Vice-Chancellor: Prof. I. M. CREWE
Pro-Vice-Chancellor (Research): Prof. D. J. SANDERS
Pro-Vice-Chancellor (Resources): Prof. R. E. MASSARA
Pro-Vice-Chancellor (Academic): Prof. G. J. CROSSICK
Registrar and Secretary: A. F. WOODBURN
Librarian: R. BUTLER

Library: see Libraries
Number of teachers: 365
Number of students: 5,710

Publications: *Calendar* (annually), *Undergraduate Prospectus* (annually), *Annual Review* (annually), *Postgraduate Prospectus* (annually), *Course Catalogue* (every 2 years).

DEANS

School of Humanities and Comparative Studies: Prof. A. RADFORD
School of Law: Prof. G. MCCORMACK
School of Science and Engineering: Prof. T. R. G. GRAY
School of Social Sciences: Prof. J. RICHMOND
Graduate School: Prof. M. J. SHERER

PROFESSORS

ADAMS, M. J., Physics
ADES, J. D., Art History and Theory
ANDERMAN, S. D., Law

ARNOLD, A. J., Accounting, Finance and Management
ATKINSON, R. M., Language and Linguistics
BABIKER, M. E. H., Physics
BAKER, N. R., Biological Sciences
BARKER, F. A., Literature
BENTON, E., Sociology
BERTHOUD, R., Institute for Social and Economic Research
BHASKAR, V., Economics
BOOTH, A. L., Institute for Social and Economic Research
BOYLE, C. K., Law
BUDGE, I., Government
BURDETT, K., Economics
BUSFIELD, N. J., Sociology
CHAMBERS, M. J., Economics
CHIA, R. C. H., Accounting, Finance and Management
CLAHSEN, H., Language and Linguistics
COLES, M. G., Economics
COXON, A. P. M., Sociology
CRAIB, I. E., Sociology
CROSSICK, G. J., History
DEWS, P. K., Philosophy
DINE, J. M., Law
DORAN, J. E., Computer Science
DOWDEN, J. M., Mathematics
DOWNTON, A. C., Electronic Systems Engineering
ERMISCH, J. F., Institute for Social and Economic Research
FLETCHER, A., History
FOWERAKER, J. W., Government
GERSHUNY, J. I., Institute for Social and Economic Research
GHANBARI, M., Electronic Systems Engineering
GILBERT, G. S., Law
GLUCKSMANN, M. A., Sociology
GOBERT, J. J., Law
GRAY, R. J., Literature
HAMNETT, B. R., History
HAMPSON, F. J., Law
HANLEY, J. R., Psychology
HATTON, T. J., Economics
HAWKSFORD, M. J., Electronic Systems Engineering
HOLT, A. R., Mathematics
HULME, P. D., Literature
JENKINS, S. P., Institute for Social and Economic Research
KEEN, M. J., Economics
KING, A., Government
KIRCHNER, E. J., Government
LAHIRI, S., Economics
LAUGHLIN, R. C., Accounting, Finance and Management
LEADER, S. L., Law
LIEVESLEY, D. A., Data Archive
LIND, L. F., Electronic Systems Engineering
LONG, S. P., Biological and Chemical Sciences
MCCORMACK, G., Law
MCKAY, D. H., Government
MARSDEN, D., Sociology
MASSARA, R. E. Electronic Systems Engineering
MAZUMDAR, R., Mathematics
MEDDIS, R., Psychology
MORRIS, L. D., Sociology
MUTHOO, A., Economics
NEARY, I. J., Government
NEDWELL, D. B., Biological Sciences
NEWTON, K., Government
OLIVER, J., Computer Science
O'MAHONY, M. J., Electronic Systems Engineering
PARKER, T. J., Physics
PATRICK, P., Language and Linguistics
PEARSON, D. E., Electronic Systems Engineering
PLUMMER, K. J., Sociology
PUTTFARKEN, T., Art History and Theory
RADFORD, A., Language and Linguistics
RICHARDSON, J. J., Government
RICHMOND, J., Economics
ROCA, I. M., Language and Linguistics
RODLEY, N. S., Law
ROSE, D. I., Institute for Social and Economic Research
SANDERS, D. J., Government
SCOTT, J. P., Sociology
SEAL, W. B., Accounting, Finance and Management
SHERER, M. J., Accounting, Finance and Management
SIKKA, P. N., Accounting and Financial Management
SMITH, S. A., History
SORELL, T. E., Philosophy
SOUTH, N., Sociology
SUNKIN, M. S., Law
TATHAM, M. A. A., Language and Linguistics
TEMPLE, C. M., Psychology
THORNALLEY, P. J., Biological Sciences
TURNER, R., Computer Science
VERGO, P. J., Art History and Theory
WEALE, A. P., Government
WILKINS, A. J., Psychology
WILSON, M. T., Biological and Chemical Sciences
WOODWISS, A. B., Sociology

ATTACHED INSTITUTES

Data Archive: computerized social science data archive; Dir Prof. D. A. LIEVESLEY.

Institute for Social and Economic Research: annual panel survey of 5,000 British households, examines income distribution etc., labour market behaviour, household formation and dissolution; Dir Prof. J. I. GERSHUNY.

UNIVERSITY OF EXETER

Exeter, EX4 4QJ
Telephone: (1392) 263263
Telex: 42894
Fax: (1392) 263108

University College

Founded 1922, University 1955

Chancellor: Lord ALEXANDER OF WEEDON
Vice-Chancellor: Sir GEOFFREY HOLLAND
Deputy Vice-Chancellors: Prof. K. ATKINSON, Dr P. A. COLLIER, Prof. S. NEVILLE BENNETT
Registrar and Secretary: I. H. C. POWELL
Librarian: ALASDAIR PATERSON

Library: see Libraries

Number of teachers: 665 full-time, 166 part-time

Number of students: 8,514 full-time, 1,888 part-time

Publications: *Annual Report*, *Calendar*, prospectuses, *Extra* (4 a year).

DEANS

Faculty of Undergraduate Studies: Dr AJIT NARAYANAN
Faculty of Postgraduate Studies: Prof. MARK OVERTON
Faculty of Academic Partnerships: Dr WILLIAM J. FORSYTHE

PROFESSORS

School of Biological Sciences:
ANDERSON, J. M., Ecology
BRYANT, J. A., Biological Sciences
HUGHES, S. G., Biological Sciences
KENNEDY, C. R., Parasitology
MACNAIR, M. R., Evolutionary Genetics

School of Business and Economics:
BULKLEY, I. G., Business and Economics
COOKE, T. E., Accounting
DE MEZA, D. E., Business and Economics
ELLIOTT, R. H., Marketing
GREGORY, A., Business and Economics
HODGKINSON, G. P., Organizational Behaviour and Strategic Management
MARIOTTI, M., Economics
MYLES, G. D., Business and Economics
PHILLIPS, G. D. A., Econometrics
TIPPETT, M., Accounting
WREN-LEWIS, S., Business

Camborne School of Mines:
ATKINSON, K., Mining Geology
SCOTT, P. W., Industrial Geology
STEAD, D., Geomechanics
WILLIAMS, R. A., Minerals Engineering

School of Chemistry:
BRUCE, D. W., Inorganic Chemistry
FOWLER, P. W., Theoretical Chemistry
LEGON, A. C., Physical Chemistry
MOODY, C. J., Organic Chemistry

School of Classics and Theology:
BRAUND, D. C., Mediterranean and Black Sea History
CATCHPOLE, D. R., Theology
GILL, C. J., Ancient Thought
GORRINGE, T., Theology
SEAFORD, R. A. S., Greek Literature
WISEMAN, T. P., Classics and Ancient History

Department of Continuing Education:
FIELDHOUSE, R. T., Adult Education

School of Drama and Music:
SANDON, N. J., Music
THOMSON, P. W., Drama

School of Education:
BENNETT, S. N., Education
BURDEN, R. A., Applied Educational Psychology
BURGHES, D. N., Education
COPLEY, T. D., Religious Education
DAVIS, N. E., Educational Telematics
DESFORGES, C. W., Education
ERNEST, P., Philosophy of Mathematics Education
HUGHES, M., Education
PREECE, P. F. W., Education
WRAGG, E. C., Education

School of Engineering and Computer Science:
DAVIES, T. W., Thermofluids Engineering
EVANS, K. E., Materials Engineering
HARVEY, W. J., Civil Engineering
OWENS, D. H., Systems and Control Engineering
PARTRIDGE, D., Computer Science
WOOLLONS, D. J., Engineering Science
WRAGG, A. A., Electrochemical Engineering

School of English:
GAGNIER, R., English Literature
HENRY, A. K., English Medieval Culture
PURKISS, D., English
SWANTON, M. J., English Medieval Studies
TAYLOR, H. R., English

School of Geography and Archaeology:
COLES, B. J., Prehistoric Archaeology
COLES, J. M., Archaeology
KAIN, R. J. P., Geography
WALLING, D. E., Geography
WEBB, B. W., Physical Geography
WILLIAMS, A. M., Human Geography and European Studies

School of Historical, Political and Sociological Studies:
BARNES, S. B., Sociology
BLACK, J. M., History
BURT, R., Mining History
DOERN, G. B., Public Policy
HAMPSHER-MONK, I. W., Political Theory
NOAKES, J. D., History
ORME, N. I., History
OVERTON, M., History
RUSH, M. D., Politics
SNOWDEN, R., Family Studies
SZAJKOWSKI, B., Pan-European Politics
WILKS, S. R. M., Politics
WITKIN, R. W., Sociology

School of Law:

BETTEN, L., European Law
BRIDGE, J. W., Public Law
TETTENBORN, A. M., Law

Centre for Legal Practice:

SHRUBSALL, V. J.

School of Mathematical Sciences:

JONES, C. A., Applied Mathematics
KRZANOWSKI, W. J., Statistics
SOWARD, A. M., Applied Mathematics
VAMOS, P., Pure Mathematics
ZHANG, K., Fluid Dynamics

School of Modern Languages:

CAMERON, K. C., French and Renaissance Studies
COOK, M. C., French 18th-Century Studies
DIFFLEY, P. B., Italian
HAYWARD, S., French
LONGHURST, C. A., Spanish
SHARPE, L., German
YATES, W. E., German

School of Physics:

INKSON, J. C., Theoretical Physics
SAMBLES, J. R., Experimental Physics
WYATT, A. F. G., Physics

School of Postgraduate Medicine and Health Sciences:

ARMSTRONG, N., Health and Exercise Science
ERNST, E., Complementary Medicine
PEREIRA GRAY, D. J., General Practice
SHELDON, B., Evidence-based Social Services
SPARKES, A. C., Social Theory
TOOKE, J. E., Vascular Medicine

School of Psychology:

EISER, J. R., Psychology
HOWE, M. J. A., Psychology
LEA, S. E. G., Psychology
WEBLEY, P., Economic Psychology

ATTACHED INSTITUTES

Centre for Arab Gulf Studies: Exeter; f. 1979; Dir Dr K. MAHDI.

Institute of Population Studies: Hoopern House, 101 Pennsylvania Rd, Exeter, EX4 6DT; f. 1978; Dir (vacant).

Institute of Cornish Studies: Truro; f. 1970; Dir Dr P. J. PAYTON.

Centre for Energy and the Environment: Exeter; f. 1975; Dir Prof. A. F. G. WYATT.

Centre for Complementary Health Studies: Exeter; f. 1987; Dir S. Y. MILLS.

Earth Resources Centre: Exeter; f. 1989; Dir Dr P. GRAINGER.

Centre for European Studies: Exeter; f. 1979; Dir Prof. B. SZAJKOWSKI.

Centre for Management of Industrial Reliability, Cost and Effectiveness: Exeter; f. 1988; Dir Dr J. KNEZEVIC.

Dictionary Research Centre: f. 1984; Dir Dr R. R. K. HARTMANN.

Centre for European Legal Studies: Dir Prof. L. BETTEN.

English Language Centre: f. 1991; Dir J. NUTTALL.

Foreign Language Centre: Dir D. LEWIS (acting).

Centre for Legal Practice: f. 1992; Dir Prof. V. J. SHRUBSALL.

Centre for Mediterranean Studies: Dir Dr J. M. WILKINS.

Centre for Children's Health and Exercise Research: f. 1987; Dir Prof. N. ARMSTRONG.

Centre for Continuing Education Research: f. 1993; Dir Prof. R. FIELDHOUSE.

Centre for Educational Development and Cooperation: f. 1985; Dir Dr J. M. BLOOMER.

Centre for South West Historical Studies: f. 1985; Dir Prof. R. BURT.

Centre for Systems and Control Engineering: f. 1991; Dir Prof. D. H. OWENS.

Centre for Research on Teaching and Learning: f. 1987; Dir Prof. N. BENNETT.

Centre for Women's Studies: f. 1993; Dir Dr G. E. HANSCOMBE.

Centre for Innovation in Mathematics Teaching: Dir Prof. D. N. BURGHES.

Centre for Maritime Historical Studies: Dir Dr M. DUFFY.

Bill Douglas Centre for the History of Cinema and Popular Culture: f. 1996; Dir Dr D. PETRIE.

Centre for Leadership Studies: f. 1997; Dir A. HOOPER.

Centre for Medical History and Related Social Studies: f. 1997; Dir J. MELLING.

Centre for Wetland Research: f. 1997; Dir Prof. B. COLES.

Centre of Telematics for Education: f. 1997; Dir Prof. N. DAVIS.

Centre for Evidence-Based Social Services: f. 1997; Dir Prof. B. SHELDON.

UNIVERSITY OF GLAMORGAN

Pontypridd, Mid Glamorgan, CF37 1DL

Telephone: (1443) 480480
Fax: (1443) 480558

Founded 1913 as South Wales and Monmouth School of Mines; in 1956 became Glamorgan College of Technology; became Glamorgan Polytechnic in 1970, later Polytechnic of Wales; present name and status 1992

Chancellor: Lord MERLYN-REES
Vice-Chancellor: Prof. A. WEBB
Deputy Vice-Chancellor (Academic): Prof. L. HOBSON
Deputy Vice-Chancellor (Resources): J. PORTER
Academic Registrar: J. O'SHEA
Librarian: J. ATKINSON
Library of 245,000 vols, 1,745 current periodicals
Number of teachers: 560
Number of students: 10,931 full-time, 6,217 part-time
Includes degree, HND and B/TEC courses, sandwich course

HEADS OF DEPARTMENTS

Built Environment: Prof. R. NEALE
Applied Sciences: Prof. J. R. DIXON
Computer Studies: P. J. HODSON
Electronics and Information Technology: Prof. P. WITTING
Accounting and Mathematics: Prof. A. RYLEY
Design and Advanced Technology: Prof. J. WARD
Business School: Prof. M. CONNOLLY
School of Humanities and Social Science: Dr F. MANNSAKER
Law: M. GRIFFITHS
Nursing and Midwifery: Prof. D. MEAD

UNIVERSITY OF GLASGOW

Glasgow, G12 8QQ

Telephone: (141) 339-8855

Founded 1451, reconstituted 1577

Academic year: October to June

Chancellor: Sir WILLIAM KERR FRASER
Vice-Chancellor and Principal: Prof. Sir GRAEME DAVIES
Vice-Principals: Prof. J. D. BONE, Prof. R. H. TRAINOR, Prof. A. C. ALLISON, Prof. D. R. GREEN, Prof. P. H. HOLMES, Dr R. V. EMANUEL
Rector: R. WILSON
Secretary: D. MACKIE
Librarian: (vacant)
Library: see Libraries
Number of teachers: 1,606 (plus 1,141 honorary clinical staff)
Number of students: 17,175

Publications: *University of Glasgow Calendar*, *Undergraduate Prospectus*, *Undergraduate Catalogue of Courses*, *Postgraduate Catalogue*, *Annual Report of the University Court*, *Newsletter* (monthly during term), *Avenue* (2 a year).

DEANS

Faculty of Arts: Prof. M. G. WARD
Faculty of Science: Prof. G. WEBB
Faculty of Medicine: Prof. B. WHITING
Faculty of Law and Financial Studies: Prof. J. M. THOMSON
Faculty of Divinity: Prof. D. JASPER
Faculty of Engineering: Prof. D. J. MURRAY-SMITH
Faculty of Veterinary Medicine: Prof. N. G. WRIGHT
Faculty of Social Sciences: Prof. A. SLAVEN

PROFESSORS (CHAIRHOLDERS)

Faculties of Arts:

BATES, D. R., Medieval History
BONE, J. D., English Literature
BROADIE, A., Logic and Rhetoric
CAIE, G. D., English Language
CAUGHIE, J. M., Film and Television Studies
COHN, S. K., Medieval History
COWAN, E. J., Scottish History
DOWNIE, R. S., Philosophy
GARVIE, A. F., Greek
GIFFORD, T. D., Scottish Literature
GREEN, R. P. H., Humanity
HAIR, G. B., Music
HALE, R. L. V., Metaphysical Philosophy
KAY, C. J., English Language
KENNEDY, A. J., French Language and Literature
MACCALLUM, C. H. A., Architecture
MCDONALD, J. B. I., Drama
MACDOWELL, D. M., Greek
MACKENZIE, A. L., Spanish
MCLEOD, M. D., African Studies
MACMAHON, M. K. C., Phonetics
MILLER, W. L., Politics
MORRIS, C. D., Archaeology
MOSS, M. S., Archives
O'DOCHARTAIGH, C. N. O., Celtic
PEACOCK, N. A., French Language and Literature
PRICKETT, S., English Literature
SLOWEY, M., Adult and Continuing Education
SMITH, A G. R., Early Modern History
STALLEY, R. F., Ancient Philosophy
STEPHENSON, R. H., German Language and Literature
STRACHAN, H. F. A., Modern History
TAIT, A. A. H., History of Art
THOMSON, J. A. F., Medieval History
WALTERS, D. G., Hispanic Studies
WARD, M. G., German Language and Literature
WILKINSON, J. E., Education

Faculty of Science:

ADAMS, R. L. P., Nucleic Acid Biochemistry
ALLEN, J. M., Molecular Medicine
ALLISON, A. C., Computing Science
ATKINSON, M. P., Computing Science
BARRON, L. D., Physical Chemistry
BARRY, J. D., Molecular Parasitology
BISHOP, P. M., Geography
BLUCK, B. J., Sedimentation and Tectonics
BOWMAN, A. W., Statistics

Briggs, J. A., Geography
Brown, J. C., Astronomy
Brown, K. A., Mathematics
Browning, G. K., Publishing
Campbell, A. M., Biochemical Immunology
Chapman, J. N., Physics
Clements, J. B., Virology
Cogdell, R. J., Botany
Coggins, J. R., Molecular Enzymology
Connolly, J. D., Organic Chemistry
Coombs, G. H., Biochemical Parasitology.
Cooper, A., Biophysical Chemistry
Craven, A., Physics
Crompton, D. W. T., Zoology
Curtis, A. S. G., Cell Biology
Davies, R. W., Biotechnology
Dickson, J. H., Archaeobotany and Plant Systematics
Doyle, C. J., Agricultural Economics
Fallick, A. E., Isotope Geosciences
Fearn, D. R., Applied Mathematics
Ferrier, R. P., Natural Philosophy
Fewson, C. A., Microbial Biochemistry
Ford, I., Statistics
Freer, J. H., Bacterial Toxicology
Furness, R., Seabird and Fishing Interactions
Gilmore, C., Crystallography
Gould, G. W., Membrane Biology
Hough, J., Physics
Houslay, M. D., Biochemistry
Huntingford, F. A., Functional Ecology
Isaacs, N. W., Protein Crystallography
Johnson, K. J., Genetics
Johnson, C. W., Computing Science
Kennedy, M. W., Infection Biology
Kocienski, P. J., Chemistry
Kusel, J. R., Cellular Biochemistry
La Thangue, N. B., Biochemistry
Leake, R. E., Endocrine Oncology
Lindsay, J. G., Medical Biochemistry
McGrath, J. C., Physiology
Martin, W., Cardiovascular Pharmacology
Maudlin, I., Molecular Entomology
Melham, T., Computing Science
Milligan, G., Molecular Pharmacology
Mitchell, T. J., Microbiology
Monaghan, P., Animal Ecology
Morris, A. S., Geography
Nimmo, H. G., Plant Biochemistry
Odoni, R. W. K., Mathematics
Ogden, R. W., Mathematics
Owens, R. O., Physics
Paddison, R., Geography
Peaker, M., Dairy Science
Peyton-Jones, S. L., Computing Science
Phillips, R. S., Parasitology
Philo, C., Geography
Pride, S. J., Mathematics
Robins, D. J., Bio-organic Chemistry
Rosenberg, J. R., Neurophysiology
Russell, M. J., Applied Geology
Saxon, D. H., Physics
Scott, R. D., Nuclear Science
Smith, H., Forensic Medicine
Smith, K. M., Physics
Smith, P. F., Mathematics
Smythe, D. K., Geophysics
Spurway, N. C., Exercise Physiology
Stewart-Tull, D. E. S., Microbial Immunology
Stone, T. W., Pharmacology
Straughan, B., Mathematics
Thomas, P. C., Agriculture
Thompson, I. B., Geography
Titterington, D. M., Statistics
van Rijsbergen, C. J., Computing Science
Watt, D. A., Computing Science
Webb, G., Catalytic Science
Webb, J. R. L., Mathematics
Whitehead, R. R., Theoretical Physics
Wilkins, M. B., Botany
Winfield, J. M., Inorganic Chemistry

Faculty of Medicine:

Barrett, A., Radiation Oncology
Behan, P. O., Neurology
Bond, Sir M. R., Psychological Medicine
Browning, G. G., Otorhinolaryngology
Burke, F. J. T., Dental Primary Care
Cameron, I. T., Obstetrics and Gynaecology
Cobbe, S. M., Medical Cardiology
Connell, J. M. C., Endocrinology
Connor, J. M., Medical Genetics
Cooke, T. G., Surgery
Dominiczak, A. F., Cardiovascular Medicine
Elliott, A. T., Clinical Physics
Fitch, W., Anaesthesia
Franklin, I. M., Transfusion Medicine
George, W. D., Surgery
Graham, D. I., Neuropathology
Greer, I. A., Obstetrics and Gynaecology
Hamblen, D. L., Orthopaedics
Hillan, E. M., Midwifery
Hillis, W. S., Cardiovascular and Exercise Medicine
Kaye, S. B., Medical Oncology
Kennedy, P. G. E., Neurology
Kenny, G. N. C., Anaesthesia
Kerr, W. J. S., Orthodontics
Kinane, D. F., Periodontology and Oral Immunology
Kirkness, C. M., Ophthalmology
Lean, M. E. J., Human Nutrition
Liew, F. Y., Immunology
Lowe, G. D. O., Vascular Medicine
McColl, K. E. L., Gastroenterology
McCulloch, J., Neuroscience
MacDonald, D. G., Oral Pathology
McEwen, J., Public Health
MacFarlane, P. W., Electrocardiology
MacFarlane, T. W., Oral Microbiology
McGowan, D. A., Oral Surgery
MacKay, N., Postgraduate Medical Education
MacKie, R. M., Dermatology
McKillop, J. H., Medicine
MacSween, R. N. M., Pathology
Millar, K., Behavioural Science
Murray, T. S., General Practice
O'Dwyer, P. J., Gastrointestinal Surgery
Payne, A. P., Anatomy
Percy-Robb, I. W., Pathological Biochemistry
Reid, J. L., Medicine and Therapeutics
Saunders, W. P., Endodontology
Shepherd, J., Pathological Biochemistry
Smith, L. N., Nursing Studies
Stephen, K. W., Dental Public Health
Stott, D. J., Geriatric Medicine
Sturrock, R. D., Rheumatology
Teasdale, G. M., Neurosurgery
Vanezis, P., Forensic Medicine and Science
Watt, G. C. M., General Practice
Weaver, L. T., Child Health
Welsh, J., Palliative Medicine
Wheatley, D., Cardiac Surgery
Whiting, B., Clinical Pharmacology
Wray, D., Oral Medicine
Young, D. G., Surgical Paediatrics

Faculty of Veterinary Medicine:

Bennett, D., Small Animal Clinical Studies
Boyd, J. S., Veterinary Clinical Anatomy
Duncan, J. L., Clinical Veterinary Parasitology
Griffiths, I., Comparative Neurology
Holmes, P. H., Veterinary Physiology
Jarrett, J. O., Comparative Virology
Love, S., Equine Clinical Studies
Murray, M., Veterinary Medicine
Nash, A. S., Small Animal Medicine
Neil, J. C., Virology and Molecular Oncology
Nolan, A., Veterinary Pharmacology
O'Shaughnessy, P. J., Reproductive Biology
Onions, D. E., Veterinary Pathology
Parkins, J. J., Animal Health
Pirie, H. M., Systemic Veterinary Pathology
Reid, J., Veterinary Anaesthesia
Reid, S. W. J., Veterinary Informatics and Epidemiology
Solomon, S. E., Poultry Science
Tait, A. A., Veterinary Parasitology
Wright, N. G., Veterinary Anatomy

Faculty of Law and Financial Studies:

Burrows, N., European Law
Crerar, L. D., Banking Law
Davidson, F. P., Law
Emmanuel, C. R., Accountancy
Garrod, N., Accountancy
Gordon, W. M., Jurisprudence
Grant, J. P., Public International Law
Holland, J. B., Accountancy
McLean, S. A. M., Law and Ethics in Medicine
Orucu, A. E., Comparative Law
Prosser, J. A. W., Law
Rees, W. P., Accountancy
Rennie, R., Conveyancing
Thomson, J. M., Law

Faculty of Divinity:

Carroll, R. P., Hebrew Bible and Semitic Studies
Jasper, D., Literature and Theology
Newlands, G. M., Divinity
Riches, J. K., Divinity and Biblical Criticism

Faculty of Engineering:

Arnold, J. M., Applied Electromagnetics
Barker, J. R., Electronics
Barlow, A. J., Electronics
Barltrop, N. D. P., Naval Architecture and Ocean Engineering
Beaumont, S. P., Nanoelectronics
Bicanic, N. J. D., Civil Engineering
Cartmell, M. P., Mechanical Engineering
Cooper, J. M., Bioelectronics and Bioengineering
Cowling, M. J., Marine Technology
De La Rue, R. M., Optoelectronics
Ervine, D. A., Water Engineering
Galbraith, R. A. M., Aerospace Systems
Gawthrop, P. J., Mechanical Engineering
Green, D. R., Structural Engineering
Hancock, J. W., Mechanical Engineering
Hunt, K. J., Mechanical Engineering
Laybourn, P. J. R., Electronic Engineering
Marsh, J. H., Optoelectronic Systems
Miller, T. J. E., Electrical Engineering
Murray-Smith, D. J., Engineering Systems and Control
O'Reilly, J., Control Engineering
Richards, B. E., Aeronautics and Fluid Mechanics
Scott, B. F., Mechanical Engineering
Sewell, J. I., Electronic Systems
Wheeler, S. J., Civil Engineering
Wilkinson, C. D. W., Electrical Engineering

Faculty of Social Sciences:

Anderson, A. H., Psychology
Asquith, S., Centre for the Child and Society
Beaumont, P. B., Employee Relations
Berry, C. J., Political Theory
Burton, A. M., Psychology
Crowther, M. A., Social History
Eldridge, J. E. T., Sociology
Espie, C. A., Clinical Psychology
Flynn, P., Latin American Studies
Frisby, D. P., Sociology
Garrod, S. C., Cognitive Psychology
Goodlad, R., Housing and Urban Studies
Hill, M., Social Work
Hunter, Sir Laurie, Applied Economics
Jones, B. T., Psychology
Kellas, J. G., Politics
Kemp, P. A., Housing and Urban Studies
Lever, W. F., Urban Studies
Lowenhardt, J. H. L., Russian and East European Studies
Macbeth, D. K., Supply Chain Management
Maclennan, D., Urban Economics and Finance
McGregor, A. M., Housing and Urban Studies
McKeganey, N., Drug Misuse Research
Martin, R., Organizational Behaviour
Miles, R. F., Sociology

MILLER, W. L., Politics
MOUTINHO, L. A. M., Marketing
MUSCATELLI, V. A., Economics
PARR, J. B., Regional and Urban Economics
PETCH, A. J., Community Care Studies
RIDDELL, S. I., Social Policy
SANFORD, A. J., Psychology
SLAVEN, A., Business History
TAYLOR, R. C., Social Policy and Social Work
TRAINOR, R. H., Social History
TUROK, I. N., Urban Economic Development
WHITE, S. L., Government
WOOTON, I., Economics

ASSOCIATED COLLEGES

Glasgow School of Art: see under Colleges.

St Andrew's College.

Scottish Agricultural College, Auchincruive: see under Colleges.

ATTACHED INSTITUTIONS

Scottish Universities Research and Reactor Centre: see under Research Institutes.

Medical Research Council Virology Unit: see under MRC.

Medical Research Council Medical Sociology Unit: see under MRC.

Particle Physics and Astronomy Research Council Particle Physics Unit (Physics and Astronomy).

Beatson Institute for Cancer Research: see under Research Institutes.

Public Health Research Unit: 1 Lilybank Gardens, Glasgow, G12 8RZ.

Wellcome History of Medicine Unit: 5 University Gardens, Glasgow, G12.

Wellcome Surgical Institute: Garscube Estate, Bearsden Rd, Bearsden, Glasgow, G61.

Institute of Russian and East European Studies: 28/29 Bute Gardens, Glasgow, G12; f. 1963; research, teaching and editorial activities on Russia and Eastern Europe in all fields of social sciences; library of 16,000 vols and pamphlets; Dir J. H. L. LOWENHARDT; publ. *Soviet Studies* (quarterly).

GLASGOW CALEDONIAN UNIVERSITY

Cowcaddens Rd, Glasgow, G4 0BA
Telephone: (141) 331-3000
Fax: (141) 331-3005
E-mail: rhu@gcal.ac.uk

Founded 1971 as Glasgow Polytechnic; merged with The Queen's College; present name and status 1993
State control
Academic year: September to June

Chancellor: Lord NICKSON
Principal: Dr I. JOHNSTON
Vice-Principals: Prof. P. W. BUSH, Prof. J. C. PHILLIPS
Senior Assistant Principal: P. B. FINCH
Head of Academic Administration: E. B. FERGUSON
Librarian: Prof. J. HAYTHORNTHWAITE

Number of teachers: 560
Number of students: 10,562 full-time, 2,881 part-time

Publications: *Prospectus of Full-time Undergraduate Programmes*, *Prospectus of Part-time Programmes*, *Prospectus of Postgraduate Programmes*, *Research Report* (annually), *Annual Report*.

DEANS

Faculty of Business: Prof. J. TAYLOR
Faculty of Health: Prof. G. DICKSON
Faculty of Science and Technology: Prof. C. CHISHOLM

HEADS OF DEPARTMENTS

Faculty of Business:
Business Administration: (vacant)
Consumer Studies: G. CAMPBELL
Economics: Prof. A. C. DOW
Entrepreneurial Studies: Prof. R. Y. WEAVER
Finance and Accounting: Prof. A. D. GODFREY
Hospitality, Tourism and Leisure Management: J. FLANNERY
Language and Media: Prof. W. T. SCOTT
Law and Public Administration: J. CHARLTON
Management: J. MCKAY
Risk and Financial Services: (vacant)

Faculty of Health:
Biological Sciences: Prof. J. T. KNOWLER
Nursing and Community Health: Prof. B. PARFITT
Physiotherapy, Podiatry and Radiography: Prof. S. MYLES
Psychology: Prof. D. PARKER
Social Sciences: Prof. D. WALSH
Vision Sciences: Prof. A. TOMLINSON

Faculty of Science and Technology:
Building and Surveying: Prof. C. HARDCASTLE
Computer Studies: E. GRAY
Energy and Environmental Technology: Dr E. TAYLOR
Engineering: Prof. D. KIRKWOOD
Mathematics: Prof. R. BRADLEY
Physical Sciences: Prof. J. R. PUGH

UNIVERSITY OF GREENWICH

Bexley Rd, Eltham, London, SE9 2HB
Telephone: (181) 331-8000
Fax: (181) 331-8145

Founded 1890, later became Thames Polytechnic; present name and status 1992

Chancellor: Baroness YOUNG OF FARNWORTH
Vice-Chancellor: Dr DAVID FUSSEY
Deputy Vice-Chancellor (Strategy): J. D. A. MCWILLIAM
Pro-Vice-Chancellor: Prof. J. HUMPHREYS
Academic Registrar: C. H. ROSE
Librarian: D. A. HEATHCOTE

Library of 500,000 vols
Number of teachers: 560
Number of students: 17,000

Publication: *Computational Fluid Dynamics News*.

DEANS

Avery Hill Faculty: Dr ROBERT ALLEN
Dartway Faculty: Prof. DAVID WILLS
Designate Greenwich Faculty: Dr ROGER FINNEY
Woolwich Faculty: PAUL STIGANT

HEADS OF SCHOOLS

Avery Hill Faculty:
Education: (vacant)
Health: Prof. L. MEERABEAU
Humanities: (vacant)
Law: Prof. DAVID CHAMBERS
PCET: Prof. IAIN MCNAY
Social Sciences: Prof. MIKE KELLY

Dartway Faculty:
Architecture and Landscape: CORINNE DELARGE
Earth and Environmental Sciences: Dr ALISTAIR BAXTER
Engineering: Prof. ALAN REED
Land and Construction Management: LEWIS ANDERSON

Woolwich Faculty:
Business School: SUE MILLAR
Chemical and Life Sciences: Prof. EDWIN METCALFE
Computing and Mathematical Sciences: Prof. MARTIN EVERETT

ATTACHED INSTITUTE

Greenwhich Maritime Institute: Dir SARAH PALMER.

HERIOT-WATT UNIVERSITY

Edinburgh, EH14 4AS
Telephone: (131) 449-5111
Fax: (131) 449-5153

Founded 1821 as Edinburgh School of Arts, Heriot-Watt College 1885, University Charter 1966

Chancellor: The Rt Hon. The Lord MACKAY OF CLASHFERN
Principal and Vice-Chancellor: Prof. JOHN S. ARCHER
Vice-Principal: Prof. C. N. BROWN
Secretary: P. L. WILSON
Librarian: M. L. BREAKS

Number of teachers: 750
Number of students: 9,500

Publications: *Guide for Applicants*, *Guide to Postgraduate Study and Research*, *Annual Report*.

DEANS

Faculty of Science: Prof. J. C. EILBECK
Faculty of Engineering: Prof. D. G. OWEN
Faculty of Economic and Social Studies: Prof. I. MASON
Faculty of Environmental Studies: W. E. ANDERSON
Faculty of Art and Design: M. DOCHERTY

PROFESSORS/HEADS OF DEPARTMENTS

Faculty of Art and Design:
FRANKS, A. M., Design and Crafts
SCOTT, G. W., Sculpture

Faculty of Economic and Social Studies:
CRAIG, V., Business School
HARE, P. G., Economics
HART, S., Business Organization
HIRST, I. R. C., Finance
KEENAN, A., Business Organization
LANG, M., Languages
LOTHIAN, N., Accounting
MAIR, D., Economics
MASON, I., Interpreting and Translating
SCHAFFER, M., Economics
STANFORTH, A. W., Languages
WEETMAN, P., Accounting

Faculty of Engineering:
CLARKE, R. J., Electronic Engineering
CRAIK, R. J. M., Acoustics
GRANT, I., Offshore Engineering
HELSZAJN, J., Microwave Engineering
JOWITT, P. W., Civil Engineering Systems
KILGOUR, A. C., Computing
LEITCH, R. R., Computing and Electrical Engineering
MAY, I., Civil Engineering
MAYES, T., Computer-based Learning
MURRAY, J. L., Computer-aided Engineering
OWEN, D. G., Offshore Engineering
PEDEN, J. M., Petroleum Engineering
RUSSELL, G. T., Electrical and Electronic Engineering
SANGSTER, A. J., Electrical and Electronic Engineering
SIMMONS, J. E. L., Mechanical Engineering
SMART, B. D. G., Petroleum Engineering
SORBIE, K. S., Petroleum Engineering
STEWART, G., Petroleum Engineering
SWAFFIELD, J. A., Building Services Engineering
TODD, A. C., Petroleum Engineering
TOPPING, B. H. V., Structural Engineering
WALDIE, B., Chemical Engineering
WILLIAMS, B. W., Electrical Engineering
WILLIAMS, M. H., Computing

WOLFRAM, J., Offshore Research and Development
YANG, S. J., Electrical and Electronic Engineering

Faculty of Environmental Studies:
BRAMLEY, G. R., Planning and Housing
DENTON, T., Architecture
MURIE, A. S., Planning and Housing

Faculty of Science:
AUSTIN, B., Biological Sciences
BAILEY, P., Organic Chemistry
BALL, J. M., Applied Analysis
BEEVERS, C. E., Mathematics
BROWN, K. J., Mathematics
CARR, J., Mathematics
CAVENETT, B. C., Optoelectronic Materials
COWIE, J. M. G., Chemistry of Materials
EILBECK, J. C., Applied Numerical Analysis
HALL, D. R., Optoelectronics
HARRISON, R. G., Physics
HOWIE, J., Mathematics
JONES, J. D. C., Physics
MCCUTCHEON, J. J., Actuarial Studies
MOLLISON, D., Applied Probability
PALMER, G. H. O., Brewing
PECKHAM, G. E., Physics
PENROSE, O., Mathematics
PFAB, J., Chemistry
PIDGEON, C. R., Semiconductor Physics
SMITH, S. D., Physics
VAN DEN BERG, M., Mathematics
WALKER, A. C., Modern Optics
WATERS, H. R., Actuarial Mathematics and Statistics
WHERRETT, B. S., Theoretical Physics

Institute of Education:
CAMERON-JONES, M., Teacher Education
MUNN, P., Curriculum Research
PATERSON, L. J., Educational Policy Studies

NON-PROFESSORIAL HEADS OF DEPARTMENTS

Faculty of Art and Design:
Design and Crafts: D. C. J. BROWN
Drawing and Painting: K. MAIN
Humanities: C. J. BAILEY

Faculty of Economic and Social Studies:
Business Organisation: W. N. SHAW

Faculty of Engineering:
Building Engineering and Surveying: P. G. CHEESMAN

Faculty of Environmental Studies:
Architecture: A. NAPPER
Landscape Architecture: C. J. WARD THOMPSON
Planning and Housing: C. B. HAGUE

Institute of Education:
Community Education: L. TETT
International Education: J. W. MORRISON
Physical Education: D. M. BAYMAN
Social Work: I. MALLINSON

ATTACHED INSTITUTES

Esmée Fairbairn Research Centre, The: Heriot-Watt University, Riccarton, Edinburgh, EH14 4AS; Dir Prof. K. G. LUMSDEN.

Heriot-Watt Business School: Heriot-Watt University, Riccarton, Edinburgh, EH14 4AS; Dir Prof. I.R.C. HIRST.

Institute for Computer-Based Learning: Heriot-Watt University, Riccarton, Edinburgh, EH14 4AS; Dir (vacant).

Institute of Offshore Engineering: Heriot-Watt University, Research Park, Riccarton, Edinburgh, EH14 4AS; Dir Prof. A. R. HALLIWELL.

Institute of Technology Management: Heriot-Watt University, Riccarton, Edinburgh, EH14 4AS; Dir Prof. J. L. MURRAY.

International Centre for Brewing and Distilling: Heriot-Watt University, Riccarton, Edinburgh, EH14 4AS; Dir G. G. STEWART.

International Centre for Island Technology: Old Academy Building, Back Road, Stromness, Orkney, KW16 2AW; Dir J. C. SIDE.

IOE Group: Heriot-Watt University, Riccarton, Edinburgh, EH14 4AS; Dir Prof. C. S. JOHNSTON.

Orkney Water Test Centre: Flotta, Orkney; Dir T. J. G. HARTMANN.

Scottish Centre for Education Overseas: Heriot-Watt University, Institute of Education, Moray House College, Holyrood Rd, Edinburgh, EH8 8AQ; Dir J. W. MORRISON.

Scottish Centre for Physical Education, Movement and Leisure Studies: Heriot-Watt University, Institute of Education, Moray House College, Cramond Rd North, Edinburgh, EH4 6JD; Dir D. M. BAYMAN.

ASSOCIATED INSTITUTION

Edinburgh College of Art: see under Colleges.

UNIVERSITY OF HERTFORDSHIRE

College Lane, Hatfield, Herts AL10 9AB
Telephone: (1707) 284000
Telex: 262413
Fax: (1707) 284870

Founded 1952 as Hatfield College of Technology, became Hatfield Polytechnic in 1969; present name and status 1992

Campuses also at Hertford, Watford and St Albans

Chancellor: Lord MACLAURIN OF KNEBWORTH
Vice-Chancellor: Prof. N. K. BUXTON
Pro-Vice-Chancellors: R. J. T. WILSON, Prof. H. R. HANAHOE, Prof. P. D. LINES
Secretary and Registrar: P. G. JEFFREYS
Librarian: D. MARTIN

Library of 350,000 vols
Number of teachers: 699
Number of students: 17,000

DEANS

Faculty of Art and Design: C. MCINTYRE
Business School (Hertford Campus): Prof. B. FLETCHER
Faculty of Interdisciplinary Studies: A. C. WEIR
Faculty of Engineering and Information Sciences: (vacant)
Faculty of Health and Human Sciences: P. R. TURNER
Faculty of Humanities and Education (Watford Campus): Prof. G. HOLDERNESS
Faculty of Law (St Albans Campus): Prof. D. TRIBE
Faculty of Natural Sciences: (vacant)

UNIVERSITY OF HUDDERSFIELD

Queensgate, Huddersfield, W. Yorkshire, HD1 3DH
Telephone: (1484) 422288
Telex: 518299
Fax: (1484) 516151

Founded 1841, formerly Huddersfield College of Technology, became Polytechnic of Huddersfield in 1970; present name and status 1992

Chancellor: Sir ERNEST HALL
Vice-Chancellor and Principal: Prof. J. TARRANT
Pro Vice-Chancellors: Prof. F. ARTHUR, Dr D. A. KIRBY
Registrar and Secretary: M. H. ANDREW

Library of 380,000 vols
Number of teachers: 450
Number of students: 8,100 full-time, 6,200 part-time

DEANS OF SCHOOLS

Business: D. SMITH
Music and Humanities: Prof. B. J. EVANS
Education: Prof. B. SOMEKH
Engineering: Prof. K. STOUT
Computing and Mathematics: Prof. B. S. LEE
Human and Health Sciences: Prof. S. FROST
Applied Sciences: Prof. M. I. PAGE
Design Technology: G. CALDERBANK

UNIVERSITY OF HULL

Cottingham Road, Hull, HU6 7RX
Telephone: (1482) 346311
Telex: 592592
Fax: (1482) 465936

Founded 1927 as University College of Hull, University Charter 1954

Academic year: September to June

Chancellor: The Rt Hon. Lord ARMSTRONG
Vice-Chancellor: Prof. D. N. DILKS
Pro-Vice-Chancellors: P. E. KOPP, Prof. R. WALKER, Prof. V. T. KING, Prof. H. A. LLOYD
Registrar and Secretary: D. J. LOCK
Academic Registrar: (vacant)
Librarian and Academic Services Director: R. G. HESELTINE

Library: see Libraries
Number of teachers: 466 full-time, 64 part-time
Number of students: 8,100 full-time, 5,375 part-time

Publications: *Calendar*, *Annual Report*, *Prospectuses*, *Departmental Pamphlets*.

DEANS

Faculty of Arts: Dr ALAN BEST
Faculty of Engineering and Mathematics: Prof. CHRIS D. COLLINSON
Faculty of Health: Prof. TONY HORSMAN
Faculty of Science and the Environment: Prof. DAVID BARTRAM
Faculty of Social Sciences: Prof. FERDINAND VON PRONDZYNSKI

PROFESSORS

ALASZEWSKI, A. M., Health Studies
ALMOND, B. M., Philosophy
ARMSTRONG, W., Biological Sciences
ASHWORTH, J., American Studies
AVEYARD, R., Chemistry
BEARDSELL, P. R., Hispanic Studies
BIRKINSHAW, P. J., Law
BOTTOMLEY, A. K., Comparative and Applied Social Sciences
BRISTON, R. J., Accounting, Business and Finance
BROOKES, G. R., Computer Science
BRYAR, R. M., Nursing
CAMPION, P. D., Medicine
CARVALHO, G., Biological Sciences
CHAMBERS, A., Accounting, Business and Finance
CHESTERS, G., French
COLLINSON, C. D., Applied Mathematics
CUMMINGS, A., Engineering Design and Manufacture
CUTLAND, N. J., Pure Mathematics
DYER, P. E., Physics
ELTIS, D., Economic Studies
FLETCHER, P. D., Chemistry
FLINT, V. I. J., History
FLOOD, R. L., Management
FREESTONE, D. A., Law
FROSTICK, L. E., Geography and Earth Resources
GIBBS, D. C., Geography and Earth Resources
GOODBY, J. W., Chemistry
GRABBE, L. L., Theology
GRAHAM, C., Law
GRAY, C., Politics and Asian Studies
HAGSTON, W. E., Physics
HARDISTY, J. H., Geography and Earth Resources

HARRIS, R. J., Politics and Asian Studies
HOCKEY, G. R., Psychology
HOPPEN, T., History
HORSMAN, A., Medicine
HUTSON, L. M., English
KILLICK, S. R., Medicine
KING, V. T., Politics and Asian Studies
LAMARQUE, P. V., Philosophy
LEIGHTON, A., English
LIND, M. J., Medicine
LLOYD, H. A., History
MCCLELLAND, V. A., Educational Studies
MCCOLLUM, P. T., Medicine
MCCOUBRAY, H., Law
MCNAMARA, D. R., Educational Studies
MATTHEWS, A., Engineering Design and Manufacture
MAUNDERS, K. T., Accounting, Business and Finance
MONSON, J. R. T., Medicine
MORICE, A. H., Medicine
MORTIMER, A., Medicine
NEWBOULD, B. R., Music
NORTON, Lord P., Politics and Asian Studies
OKELY, J. M., Comparative and Applied Social Sciences
O'SULLIVAN, P., Politics and Asian Studies
PAGE, E. C., Politics and Asian Studies
PAREKH, B. K., Politics and Asian Studies
PATTON, R. J., Electronic Engineering
PEARSON, D. B., Applied Mathematics
PHILLIPS, R., Computer Science
PURDIE, D. W., Medicine
RICHARDSON, P. D., Economic Studies
RIGBY, B., French
SCHLUDERMANN, B., Dutch Studies
SINN, E., Chemistry
SMITH, P. M., French
STAFFORD, N., Medicine
SWIFT, K. G., Engineering Design and Manufacture
THOMPSON, A. D., Italian
THRELFALL, D. R., Biological Sciences
TOWNSHEND, A., Chemistry
TOYNE, K., Chemistry
TURNBULL, L. W., Medicine
TURNER, M. E., Economic Studies
VON PRONDZYNSKI, F., Law
WALKER, R. W., Chemistry
WALLMAN, S., Sociology
WALTON, J. M., Drama
WELLS, P. B., Chemistry
WESTWOOD, R., Chemistry
WHITEHEAD, D. G., Electronic Engineering
WILKINSON, S. G., Chemistry
WILLIAMS, D. A., French
WOODWARD, D. M., Economic Studies

ATTACHED INSTITUTES AND CENTRES

Language Institute: Dir Dr G. E. AUBBUSCHER.

Institute of Estuarine and Coastal Studies: Dir Dr M. ELLIOTT.

Centre for Magnetic Resonance Investigations: Dir Prof. L. W. TURNBULL.

Institute for Chemistry in Industry: Dir Prof. R. WESTWOOD.

University of Hull International Fisheries Institute (HIFI): Dir K. CREAN.

Institute of European Public Law: Dir M. J. FEINTUCK.

Interdisciplinary Research Institute on City and Regional Studies: Dir Prof. D. GIBBS.

Research Institute for Environmental Science and Management: Dir Prof. L. FROSTICK.

Family Assessment and Support Unit: Dir J. PARKER.

Institute for Health Studies: Dir Prof. A. ALASZEWSKI.

Centre for Metabolic Bone Disease: Dir Prof. D. PURDIE.

Institute of Rehabilitation: Dir Dr J. K. MOFFETT (acting).

Centre for Lifelong Learning: Head D. VULLIAMY (acting).

Centre for Professional Development and Training in Education: Head Prof. G. CHESTERS.

Graduate Research Institute: Dir Dr A. W. BOWER.

Computers in Teaching Initiative Centre for Modern Languages: Dir Prof. G. CHESTERS.

KEELE UNIVERSITY

Keele, Staffordshire, ST5 5BG
Telephone: (1782) 621111
Telex: 36113
Fax: (1782) 613847

Founded as University College of North Staffordshire 1949, University of Keele 1962
Academic year: September to June

Chancellor: Sir CLAUS MOSER
Vice-Chancellor: Prof. JANET FINCH
University Secretary and Registrar: SIMON MORRIS
Library: see Libraries
Number of teachers: 418
Number of students: 4,000 undergraduates, 1,400 postgraduates

Publication: *University Calendar*.

DEANS

Faculty of Humanities: Prof. IAN BELL
Faculty of Social Sciences: Prof. ALEX DANCHEV
Faculty of Natural Sciences: Prof. CHRISTOPHER ARME
Faculty of Health: (vacant)

PROFESSORS

ADAMS, D. K., American Studies
AINSWORTH, W. A., Communication and Neuroscience
ANDREW, J., Russian
ARME, C., Biological Sciences
BELL, I. F. A., American Studies
BLADEN-HOVELL, R. C., Economics
BONWICK, C. C., American Studies
BUDGEN, D., Computer Science
BURCHILL, F., Human Resource Management and Industrial Relations
BURLEY, S. D., Earth Sciences
CANOVAN, M. E., Politics
CHALLIS, R. E., Electronic Engineering
CLAYTON, R. N., Medicine
COCKS, R. C. J., Law
COOPER, D., Law
COOPER, R., Social Theory
CORNES, R. C., Economics
COX, J. L., Psychiatry
CROFT, P., Epidemiology
CROME, P., Geriatric Medicine
CULLEN, C., Psychology
DANCHEV, A., International Relations
DEEN, S. M., Computer Science
DEVEREUX, M. P., Economics
DOBSON, A. N. H., Politics
DUGDALE, A. M., Law
DYSON, R., Health Planning and Management
ELDER, J. B., Medicine
EVANS, A., Physics
EVANS, E. F., Communication and Neuroscience
FAIRCHILD, I. J., Earth Sciences
FRASCINA, F. A., Visual Arts
FULLER, W., Physics
GAFFNEY, J., French
GALLOIS, A., Philosophy
GILLAN, M. J., Physics
GLEESON, D., Education
GODDEN, R. L., American Studies
HACKNEY, C., Auditory Neuroscience
HARRISON, M., Politics
HARTLEY, J., Psychology
HARTLEY, R., Economics
HASSARD, J. S., Management
HERMAN, D. K., Law
HEYWOOD, B. R., Inorganic Chemistry
HOLMES, D., Modern Languages
HOWELL, J. A. S., Organometallic Chemistry
HUGHES, A. L., Early Modern History
JAMES, A. M., International Relations
JEFFERSON, T., Criminology
JONES, P., Mathematics
KEMPA, R. F., Education
KENDALL, K., Materials Science
KOLINSKY, E. W., German
LAINÉ, D. C., Physics
LARRISSY, E. T., English
LAW, J., Sociology and Social Anthropology
LEE, K., Health Planning and Management
LINKLATER, A., International Relations
MCCALL, I., Medicine
MCEWAN, J. A., Law
MCGUINNESS, B. W., Primary Health Care
MACKENZIE, G., Medical Statistics
MCNAUGHTON, D. A., Philosophy
MADEN, M., Education
MORGAN, N. G., Biology
MYERS, K., Professional Development in Education
NICHOLLS, D. R., Music
O'BRIEN, P. M. S., Medicine
OZGA, J., Education
PATON, C. R., Health Policy
PHILLIPSON, C. R., Applied Social Studies
POLUKHINA, V., Russian Studies
PROOPS, J. L. R., Environmental Social Sciences
RAMSDEN, C. A., Chemistry
REDCLIFT, M. R., Environmental Social Sciences
ROGERS, G. A. J., History of Philosophy
SCRIVENS, E. E. J., Health Policy
SEIFERT, R. V., Industrial Relations
SIM, J. W., Physiotherapy Studies
SLOBODA, J. A., Psychology
SMITH, P., Mathematics
SOUTHALL, D. P., Paediatrics
SPARKS, J. R., Criminology
STRANGE, R., Medicine
TEMPLETON, J. J., Orthopaedic Surgery
THORNBERRY, P., International Relations
TOWNSHEND, C. J. N., History
TRUSCOTT, T. G., Chemistry
VINCENT, D. M., History
WALKER, I., Economics
WALLER, D. M., Politics
WALLER, M., European Studies
WARD, R. D., Biological Sciences
WHITE, E. G., Nursing
WILKS, G., Mathematics
WILLIAMS, G. D., Earth Sciences
WILLIAMS, G. T., Biochemistry
WILLMOTT, A. J., Mathematics
WORBOYS, M. F., Computer Science
WORRALL, T. S., Economics
YOUNG, R. P., Geology

UNIVERSITY OF KENT AT CANTERBURY

The Registry, Canterbury, Kent, CT2 7NZ
Telephone: (1227) 764000
Fax: (1227) 452196

Founded 1965
State control
Academic year: October to June

Chancellor: Sir CRISPIN TICKELL
Vice-Chancellor: Prof. ROBIN SIBSON
Deputy Vice-Chancellor: Prof. ROBERT FREEDMAN
Secretary and Registrar: NICK MCHARD
Librarian: MARGARET COUTTS

Number of teachers: 850
Number of students: 9,904

Publications: *Undergraduate Prospectus*, *Postgraduate Prospectus*, *Annual Report*.

DEANS

Faculty of Humanities: (vacant)
Faculty of Social Sciences: Prof. CHRISTOPHER HALE
Faculty of Science, Technology and Medical Studies: URSULA FULLER

PROFESSORS

Faculty of Humanities:

ANDERSON, G., Classics
ANDREWS, M. Y., Victorian and Visual Studies
ARMSTRONG, W. A., Economic and Social History
BANN, S., Modern Cultural Studies
BAUGH, C., Drama
BIRMINGHAM, D., Modern History
BOLT, C. A., American History
CARDINAL, R. T., Literary and Visual Studies
CHRISTIE, I., Film Studies
CUNNINGHAM, H. S. C., Social History
DOCHERTY, T., English
DURRANI, O., German
ELLIS, D., English
FLOWER, J., French
GILL, R., Theology
INNES, C. L., Post Colonial Literatures
IRWIN, M., English Literature
JAMES, L., Victorian and Modern Literature
NORMAN, R. J., Moral Philosophy
RADFORD, C. J., Philosophy
WELCH, D. A., Modern European History

Faculty of Science, Technology and Medical Studies:

BEEZER, T., Applied Chemistry
BROWN, H., Electronic Publishing
BROWN, P. J., Computer Science
BROWN, P. J., Medical Statistics
BULL, A. T., Microbial Technology
BURNS, R. G., Environmental Microbiology
CHADWICK, A. V., Physical Chemistry
CLARKSON, P., Mathematics
COMMON, A. K., Applied Mathematics
CONNOR, J. A., Inorganic Chemistry
COOK, C. C. H., Psychiatry of Alcohol Misuse
DAVIDSON, S., Applied Chemistry
DAVIES, P. A., Optical Communications
DORE, J., Condensed-Matter Physics
FAIRHURST, M. C., Computer Vision
FLEISCHMAN, P., Mathematics
FREEDMAN, R. B., Biochemistry
HALE, A., General Adult Psychiatry
JACKSON, D. A., Applied Optics
JOHNSON, L., Information Management
LANGLEY, R. J., Antenna Systems
LININGTON, P. F., Computer Communication
LITTLE, L. T., Millimetre Wave Astronomy
MCDONNELL, J. A. M., Space Physics
MORGAN, B. J. T., Applied Statistics
NEWPORT, R., Materials Physics
PARKER, E. A., Radio Communications
PREECE, D., Statistics
SLATER, J. B., Computing
SOBHY, M. I., Electronic Engineering
STRANGE, J. H., Experimental Physics
TONG, H., Statistics
TUITE, M., Molecular Biology
WELCH, P. H., Parallel Computing

Faculty of Social Sciences:

ABRAMS, W. D. J., Social Psychology
ARMSTRONG, W. A., Economic and Social History
BROWN, R. J., Social Psychology
BUTLER, J., Health Services Studies
CALNAN, M., Sociology of Health Studies
CARRUTH, A., Economics
CHENG, R., Operational Research
CHURCH, C., European Studies
ELLEN, R. F., Anthropology and Human Ecology
EVANS, M. S., Women's Studies
FROST, M., International Relations
GEORGE, V., Social Administration and Social Work
GREEN, F., Economics
GROOM, A. J. R., Government
HALE, C., Criminology
HANN, C. M., Social Anthropology
HARROP, S., Wildlife Management Law
HOWARTH, W., Environmental Law
HUGHES, J. J., Industrial Relations
LEADER-WILLIAMS, N., Biodiversity Management
MCLELLAN, D. T., Political Theory
MANSELL, J., Applied Psychology of Learning Disability
PAHL, J., Social Policy
PICKVANCE, C. G., Urban Studies
RAY, L., Sociology
RUBIN, G., Law
RUCHT, D., Sociology
RUTHERFORD, B. A., Accounting
RUTTER, D., Health Psychology
SAKWA, R., Russian and European Politics
SAMUEL, G., Law
SAYERS, J., Psychoanalytic Psychology
SCASE, R., Sociology and Organizational Behaviour
SEYMOUR-URE, C. K., Government
SHARP, J. A., Management
STEPHENSON, G. M., Social Psychology
SWINGLAND, I., Conservation Biology
TAYLOR-GOOBY, P., Social Policy
THIRLWALL, A. P., Applied Economics
VICKERMAN, R. W., Regional and Transport Economics

ATTACHED INSTITUTES

Kent Institute of Medicine and Health Sciences: Dean Dr M. RAKE.

Personal Social Services Research Unit: Dir Prof. B. DAVIES.

Centre for American Studies: Dir Dr D. TURLEY.

Centre for Applied Ethic: Dir Prof. R. GILL.

Centre for Colonial and Postcolonial Research: Dir R. EDMOND.

Centre for History and Cultural Studies of Science: Dir Dr CROSBIE SMITH.

Centre for Medieval and Tudor Studies: Dir Dr P. BROWN.

Centre for Modern Cultural Studies: Dir Prof. S. BANN.

Centre for the Study of Propaganda: Dir Prof. D. WELCH.

Centre for Materials Research: Dir Dr R. JONES.

Unit for Space Sciences and Astrophysics: Dir Prof. T. MCDONNELL.

Centre for European, Regional and Transport Economics: Dir Prof. R. VICKERMAN.

Kent Energy Economics Research Group: Dir Dr J. PIERSON.

Centre for Criminal Justice Studies: Dr S. UGLOW.

Centre for Research in Health Behaviour: Dir Prof. D. RUTTER.

Centre for the Study of Group Processes: Dir Prof. D. ABRAMS.

European Institute of Social Services: Dir B. MUNDAY.

Urban and Regional Studies Unit: Dir C. PICKVANCE.

Centre for Social Anthropology and Computing: Dir Dr M. FISCHER.

Centre for the Study of Social and Political Movements: Dir C. ROOTES.

Centre for Women's Studies: Dir Prof. M. EVANS.

Centre for Geography: Dir Dr J. WHYMAN.

Centre for Economic History: Dir Prof. W. A. ARMSTRONG.

Institute for Social Research: Dir D. MORGAN.

London Centre for International Relations: Dir Dr H. A. SMITH.

Tizard Centre: Dir Prof. J. MANSELL.

Centre for Health Service Studies: Dir Prof. M. CALNAN.

Centre for the Study of Psychotherapy: Dir Dr A. CARTWRIGHT.

KINGSTON UNIVERSITY

River House, 53 – 57 High St, Kingston upon Thames, Surrey, KT1 1LQ
Telephone: (181) 547-2000
Fax: (181) 547-7178

Founded 1970 as Kingston Polytechnic, present name and status 1992
Academic year: October to July

Chancellor: Sir FRANK LAMPL
Vice-Chancellor: Prof. PETER SCOTT
Deputy Vice-Chancellor: Prof. CAROLINE GIPPS
University Secretary: RAFICQ ABDULLA
Librarian: NIK POLLARD

Library of 400,000 vols
Number of teachers: 603
Number of students: 13,299

DEANS

Faculty of Business: Prof. DAVID MILES
Faculty of Design: KEITH GRANT
Faculty of Human Sciences: Dr GAIL CUNNINGHAM
Faculty of Science: Prof. REG DAVIS
Faculty of Technology: Prof. JOHN ROBERTS
Faculty of Healthcare Sciences: Prof. MIKE PITTILO

HEADS OF SCHOOL/DEPARTMENT

Accounting and Finance: ROBIN JARVIS
Applied Chemistry: Prof. CLIFF WELLS
Applied Physics: Prof. DAVID BRIERS
Architecture: Prof. PETER JACOB
Business Strategy and Operations: PHIL SAMOUEL
Civil Engineering: Prof. MIKE O'REILLY
Computer Science and Electronic Systems: GRAHAM WILKINSON
Economics: VINCENT DALY
Education: Prof. MIKE GIBSON
Fashion: Prof. IAN GRIFFITHS
Fine Art: Prof. BRUCE RUSSELL
Foundation Studies: PAUL STAFFORD
Geography: Prof. GUY ROBINSON
Geological Sciences: Prof. ANDY RANKIN
Graphic Design: PENNY HUDD
History of Art: FRAN LLOYD
Humanities: JOHN IBBETT
Human Resource Management: Prof. CHRISTINE EDWARDS
Information Systems Design: BRIAN SAXBY
Kingston University Enterprises Ltd: Dr CHET DYMEK
Languages: TERESA LAWLOR
Law: Prof. HUGH BRAYNE
Life Sciences: Dr RALPH MANLY
Marketing: ANNIK HOGG
Mathematics: PATRICK MCCABE
Mechanical, Aeronautical and Production Engineering: Prof. ANDREW SELF
Music: Prof. EDWARD HO
Operations Management and Quantitive Methods: Prof. RICHARD ENNALS
Postgraduate and In-Service Teacher Training: PETER STAMMERS
Social Science: Prof. JOE BAILEY
Social Work: PAUL DONNELLY
Surveying: SARAH SAYCE
Three-Dimensional Design: NIGEL ORDISH

UNIVERSITY OF LANCASTER

Lancaster, LA1 4YW
Telephone: (1524) 65201
Fax: (1524) 843087

Founded 1964

Chancellor: HRH Princess ALEXANDRA, The Hon. Lady OGILVY
Pro-Chancellor: J. B. HERON
Vice-Chancellor: Prof. W. RITCHIE
Deputy Vice-Chancellor: (vacant)
Pro-Vice-Chancellors: Prof. N. ABERCROMBIE, Prof. R. B. DAVIES, A. WHITAKER
Secretary: S. A. C. LAMLEY
Librarian: J. M. WHITESIDE

Library: see Libraries
Number of teachers: 900
Number of students: (full-time) 7,630 undergraduates, 2,703 postgraduates

Publications: *Undergraduate Prospectus*, *Graduate Studies Prospectus*, *Annual Report*, *Calendar* (all annually).

The university has five faculty boards

PROFESSORS

ABERCROMBIE, N., Sociology
ALDERSON, J. C., Linguistics and English Language Education
AYRES, P. G., Biological Sciences
BALASUBRAMANYAM, V. N., Economics
BELLANY, I., Politics
BLACKLER, F. H. M., Behaviour in Organizations
BLAIR, G. S., Distributed Systems
BLINKHORN, R. M., History
BRADSHAW, A., Mechanical Engineering
BRAY, R. W., Music
BREMNER, J. G., Developmental Psychology
BROOKES, J. H., History of Science
BURGOYNE, J. G., Management Learning
CARLING, P. A., Physical Geography
CARTER, R. G., Electronic Engineering
CHAPMAN, G. P., Geography
CHECKLAND, P. B., Systems and Information Management
CLAPHAM, C. S., Politics and International Relations
DAVIES, R. B., Social Statistics
DAVIES, W. J., Environmental Physiology
DAVISON, W., Environmental Chemistry
DEEM, R., Educational Research
DENVER, D. T., Politics
DIGGLE, P. J., Mathematics and Statistics
DILLON, G. M., Politics
EASTERBY-SMITH, M. P. V., Management Learning
EASTON, G., Marketing
EBDON, J. R., Polymer Chemistry
EVANS, E. J., Social History
FAIRCLOUGH, N. L., Linguistics
FILDES, R. A., Management Science
GATRELL, A. C., Health
GOODYEAR, P. M., Educational Research
GRAHAM, H., Social Policy
GUÉNAULT, A. M., Physics
HANLEY, K. A., English Literature
HEELAS, P. L. F., Religion and Modernity
HETHERINGTON, A. M., Plant Cell Physiology
HEWITT, C. N., Atmospheric Chemistry
HITCH, G. J., Psychology
HONARY, B., Engineering
HOPKINS, J. B., Psychology
HUGHES, J. A., Sociological Analysis
HUTCHISON, D., Computing
JESSOP, R. D., Sociology
JONES, K., Environmental Chemistry and Ecotoxicology
KATAMBA, F. X., Linguistics
KEEFE, T., Modern Languages
KING, P., Politics and International Relations
KINGSMAN, B. G., Management Science
KIRBY, M. W., Economic History
LAMBERT, C. J., Theoretical Condensed Matter Physics
LEA, P. J., Biological Sciences
LEECH, G. N., Linguistics
MCCLINTOCK, P. V. E., Physics
MACDONALD, R., Environmental Science
MACKENZIE, J. M., Imperial History
MCKINLAY, Politics and International Relations
MCMILLAN, T. J., Cancer Biology
MANSFIELD, T. A., Biological Sciences
MERCER, A., Operational Research and Operations Management
MORRIS, P. E., Psychology
NIEDUSZYNSKI, I. A., Biological Science
OTLEY, D. T., Accounting and Finance
PEASNELL, K. V., Accounting and Finance
PENN, R. D., Economic Sociology and Statistics
PERCY, K. A., Adult Continuing Education
PICCIOTTO, S., Law
PICKETT, G. R., Physics
PIDD, M., Management Science
POOLEY, C. G., Geography
POPE, P. F., Accounting and Finance
POWER, S. C., Mathematics
REED, M. I., Organizational Theory
RICHARDS, J. M., History
ROBERTS, R., Religious Studies
RODDEN, T., Interactive Systems
RODWELL, J. S., Plant Ecology
ROWE, P., Law
SAPSFORD, D. R., Economics
SAYER, R. A., Sociology
SHAPIRO, D. Z., Sociology
SHEPHERD, W. D., Computing
SHEVTSOVA, M., Theatre Studies
SHORT, M.H., Linguistics
SIEWIERSKA, A. M., Linguistics
SLOAN, T., Nuclear Physics
SOMMERVILLE, I. F., Computing
SOOTHILL, K., Social Research
SOUTAR, I., Chemistry
STAPLETON, R. C., Accounting and Finance
STEWART, M. A., History of Philosophy
SUGARMAN, D., Law
SUMMERFIELD, A. P., Women's History
TAWN, J. A., Statistics
TAYLOR, J., Economics
TAYLOR, S. J., Finance
THORPE, D. H., Applied Social Science
TUCKER, R. W., Theoretical Physics
TWYCROSS, M. A., English Medieval Studies
URRY, J. R., Sociology
WATSON, S. R., Management
WELLBURN, A. R., Biochemistry
WHEELER, M. D., English
WHITELEY, N. S., Visual Arts
WHITTAKER, J. B., Biological Sciences
WHITTON, D. W., French Theatre
WHYTE, I. D., Historical Geography
WILSON, L., Environmental Science
WILSON, R. F., Renaissance Studies
WYNNE, B. E., Science Studies
YOUNG, P. C., Environmental Science

UNIVERSITY OF LEEDS

Leeds, LS2 9JT
Telephone: (113) 243-1751
Telex: 556473
Fax: (113) 233-6017

Founded 1874 as Yorkshire College of Science, University Charter 1904

Chancellor: HRH The Duchess of KENT
Pro-Chancellor: Col A. C. ROBERTS
Vice-Chancellor: Prof. ALAN WILSON
Registrar and Secretary: Dr D. S. ROBINSON
Librarian: L. BRINDLEY

Library: see Libraries
Number of teachers: 1,113 full-time, 128 part-time
Number of students: 17,811 undergraduates, 5,193 postgraduates

Publications: *University Calendar*, *Undergraduate Prospectus*, *Postgraduate Prospectus*, *University of Leeds Review*, *Annual Report*.

DEANS

Faculty of Arts: Dr G. R. RASTALL (Teaching and Learning), Prof. J. J. MACKLIN (Research)
Faculty of Business, Law, Education and Social Sciences: Prof. R. K. S. TAYLOR (Teaching and Learning), Prof. A. D. PEARMAN (Research)
Faculty of Biological Sciences: Dr E. J. WOOD (Teaching and Learning), Prof. P. J. F. HENDERSON (Research)
Faculty of Earth and Environment: Dr S. M. MACGILL (Teaching and Learning), Prof. A. C. MCDONALD (Research)
Faculty of Mathematics and Physical Sciences: Dr C. J. HATTON (Teaching and Learning), Prof. J. E. DYSON (Research)
Faculty of Engineering: Prof. M. J. HOWES (Teaching and Learning), Prof. J. FISHER (Research)
Faculty of Medicine, Dentistry, Psychology and Health: Prof. R. H. S. MINDHAM (Teaching and Learning), Prof. M. A. SMITH (Research)

PROFESSORS AND HEADS OF DEPARTMENTS

(H = Non-professorial Head of Department)

Faculty of Arts:

ANDREWS, R. A., Italian
ATACK, M. K., French
BARBER, G. D., Music (H)
BARNARD, J., English Literature
BENTON, G., Chinese Studies
BRIDGE, F. R., Diplomatic History
CAIRNS, D. L., Classics (H)
CAIRNS, F., Latin Language and Literature
CANTOR, G. N., History of Science
CHEW, S., Commonwealth and Post Colonial Literature
CHILDS, J. C. R., Military History
COLLINS, D. N., Russian and Slavonic Studies (H)
DAVIN, D., East Asian Studies (H)
DONALD, S. G., German (H)
ELLIOTT, J. K., New Testament Textual Criticism
FOX, A. T. C., Linguistics and Phonetics (H)
GOOCH, J., International History
GIDLEY, C. M., American Literature
HAMMOND, P., 17th-century English Literature
HAY, K. G., Fine Art
HILL, J. M., Old and Middle English Language and Medieval English Literature
HOLMAN, M. J. DE K., Russian and Slavonic Studies (H)
HUNTER, L. C., History of Rhetoric
KILLICK, R., French Language and Romance Philology
KNOTT, K., Theology and Religious Studies (H)
LARRISSY, E., English Literature
LINDLEY, D., Renaissance Literature (H)
MACKLIN, J. J., Spanish and Portuguese
MORISON, J. D., History (H)
NETTON, I. R., Arabic Studies
PALLISER, D. M., Medieval History
POIDEVIN, R. LE, Philosophy (H)
POLLOCK, G. F. S., Social and Critical Histories of Art
RICHARDSON, B. F., Italian
RIFKIN, A., Fine Art
ROBERTS, P., Drama and Theatre Studies
RUSHTON, J. G., Music
SIEGFRIED, S. L., Art History
SIMONS, P. M., Philosophy
SPIERS, E. M., Strategic Studies
WALES, K., Modern English Language
WOOD, I. N., Early Medieval History

Faculty of Business, Law, Education and Social Sciences:

ANNING, A. J. E., Early Childhood Education
BATES, I., Education and Work
BAYLIES, C., Development Studies (H)

BEETHAM, D., Politics
BELL, D. S., French Government and Politics
BELL, J. S., Public and Comparative Law
BUCKLEY, P. J., International Business
BUSH, R. C., Politics (H)
CERNY, P. G., International Political Economy
CHARTRES, J. A., Business and Economic Studies
CLIFFE, L. R., Development Studies
COLLINS, M., Financial History
DEACON, A. J., Social Policy
DYER, H. C., International Studies (H)
EDWARDS, A., Primary Education
FRY, G. K., British Government and Administration
GLAISTER, K. W., International Strategic Management
HARDING, L. M., Social Policy and Sociology (H)
HAYES, J., Management Studies
JENKINS, E. W., Science Education Policy
KEASEY, K., Financial Services
LODGE, J., European Studies
LYNCH, J. E., Marketing and Strategic Management
MCGEE, A., Business Law
MCMULLEN, J., Labour Law
MACKIE, P. J., Transport Studies (joint post)
MICHELL, P. C. N., Marketing and Media
MOIZER, P., Accounting
NASH, C. A., Transport Economics (joint post)
NOLAN, P. J., Industrial Relations
OGDEN, S. G., Accounting and Organizational Analysis
PEARMAN, A. D., Management Decision Analysis
SAWYER, M. C., Economics
SELF, J. A., Knowledge-based Systems
SHARP, P. R., Education (H)
SHAW, J., European Law
SHORROCKS-TAYLOR, D., Assessment and Evaluation in Education
SMART, C. C., Sociology
SUGDEN, D. A., Special Needs in Education
TAYLOR, P. M., International Communications
TAYLOR, R. K. S., Continuing Education
TOLLIDAY, S. W., Economic History
WALBY, S., Sociology
WALKER, C. P., Criminal Justice
WHEELER, S., Law, Business and Society
WILLIAMS, F., Social Policy
WILSON, N., Credit Management
WOOLMER, K. J., Business School (H)
ZUKAS, M., Continuing Education (H)

Faculty of Biological Sciences:

ALEXANDER, R. MCN., Zoology
ATKINSON, H. J., Nematology
BALDWIN, S. A., Biochemistry
BAUMBERG, S., Bacterial Genetics
BOYETT, M. R., Physiology
BROWN, S B., Biochemistry
CHOPRA, I., Microbiology
COVE, D. J., Genetics
EVANS, E. G. V., Medical Mycology
FINDLAY, J. B. C., Biochemistry
FORBES, J. M., Agricultural Sciences
HAWKEY, P. M., Medical Microbiology
HENDERSON, P. J. F., Biochemistry
HOLDEN, A. V., Physiology
HOLLAND, K. T., Microbiology
HOLLINGDALE, M. R., Parasitology
KNOWLES, P. F., Biophysical Chemistry
MEYER, P., Plant Genetics
ORCHARD, C. H., Physiology
PHILLIPS, S. E. V., Biophysics
RAYFIELD, K. M., Physiology (H)
ROWLANDS, D. J., Molecular Virology
SHORROCKS, B., Population Biology
SOAMES, R. W., Human Biology (H)
STOCKLEY, P. G., Biological Chemistry
TRINICK, J. A., Animal Cell Biology
TURNER, A. J., Biochemistry
TURNER, J. R. G., Evolutionary Genetics
WOOD, E. J., Biochemistry
WRAY, D. A., Pharmacology

Faculty of Earth and Environment:

BAKER, P. E., Earth Sciences
BONSALL, P. W., Transport Planning (joint post)
CANN, J. R., Earth Sciences
CLARKE, G. P., Geography (H)
CLARKE, M. C., Geographic Modelling
FAIRHEAD, J. D., Applied Geophysics
GUBBINS, D., Geophysics
KAY, D., Environmental Science
KIRKBY, M. J., Physical Geography
KNIPE, R. J., Structural Geology
LEEDER, M. R., Sedimentology
LEIGH, C. M., Virtual Working Environments
MCDONALD, A. T., Environmental Management
MACKIE, P. J., Transport Studies (joint post)
MAY, A. D., Transport Engineering (joint post)
MOBBS, S. D., Atmospheric Dynamics
NASH, C. A., Transport Economics (joint post)
OPENSHAW, S., Human Geography
RAISWELL, R. W., Sedimentary Geochemistry
REES, P. H., Population Geography
WILSON, A. G., Urban and Regional Geography
WILSON, B. M., Igneous Petrology
YARDLEY, B. W. D., Metamorphic Geochemistry

Faculty of Mathematics and Physical Sciences:

BARTLE, K. D., Chemistry
BATCHELDER, D. N., Physics
BEDDARD, G., Chemical Physics
BLOOR, M. I. G., Applied Mathematics
BOCHMANN, M., Inorganic and Structural Chemistry
BODEN, N., Chemistry
BRINDLEY, J., Applied Mathematics
CLIFFORD, A. A., Chemical Technology
COOPER, S. B., Pure Mathematics
DALES, H. G., Pure Mathematics
DAVIES, G. R., Polymer Science
DICKINSON, E., Food Colloids
DYSON, J. E., Astronomy
FALLE, S. A. E. G., Astrophysical Fluid Dynamics
FORDY, A. P., Nonlinear Mathematics
GREIG, D., Physics
GRIFFITHS, J. F., Combustion Chemistry
GRIGG, R. E., Organic Chemistry
GUTHRIE, J. T., Polymer and Surface Coatings, Science and Technology
HILLAS, A. M., Physics
HOWSON, M. A., Condensed Matter Physics
HUGHES, D. W., Applied Mathematics
INGHAM, D. B., Applied Mathematics
JOHNSON, A. F., Polymer Science and Technology
JOHNSON, A. P., Computational Chemistry
KENT, J. T., Statistics
LANCE, E. C., Pure Mathematics
LEWIS, D. M., Colour Chemistry and Dyeing
MCCONNELL, J. C., Pure Mathematics
MCLEISH, T. C. B., Polymer Physics
MARDIA, K. V., Applied Statistics
MERKIN, J. H., Applied Mathematics
MORGAN, G. J., Theoretical Physics
PILLING, M. J., Physical Chemistry
ROBINSON, D. S., Food Science
ROBSON, J. C., Pure Mathematics
SAVAGE, M. D., Thin Liquid Films and Coatings
SCOTT, S. K., Mathematical Chemistry
SHAW, B. L., Chemistry
SLEEMAN, B. D., Applied Mathematics
WAINER, S. S., Pure Mathematics
WARD, I. M., Physics
WATSON, A. A., Physics
WEDZICHA, B. L., Food Science
WOOD, J. C., Pure Mathematics

Faculty of Engineering:

AMOOIE-FOUMEY, E., Process Modelling
ANDREWS, G. E., Combustion Engineering
BARTON, S. K., Integral Information Systems
BEEBY, A., Structural Design
BIRTWISTLE, G. M., Formal Methods
BONSALL, P. W., Transport Planning (joint post)
CABRERA, J. G., Civil Engineering Materials
CHILDS, T. H. C., Manufacturing Engineering
COCHRANE, R. C., Metallurgy
COHN, A. G., Automated Reasoning
CROLLA, D. A., Automotive Engineering
DALY, P., Electronic and Electrical Engineering
DARNELL, M., Electronic Engineering
DEW, P. M., Computer Science
DOWD, P. A., Mining Engineering
DYER, M. E., Theoretical Computer Science
EDMONDS, D. V., Metallurgy
FISHER, J., Mechanical Engineering
GASKELL, P. H., Fluid Mechanics
HOGG, D. C., Artificial Intelligence
HOWES, M. J., Electronic Engineering
HOYLE, B. S., Vision and Image Systems
HUGHES, A., Electronic and Electrical Engineering
JOHNSON, D. J., Fibre Science
KING, T., Textile Mechatronics
LAWRENCE, C. A., Textile Engineering
MCGREAVY, C., Chemical Engineering
MALE, S. P., Building Engineering and Construction Management
MARA, D., Civil Engineering
MAY, A. D., Transport Engineering (joint post)
DE PENNINGTON, A., Computer-Aided Engineering
POLLARD, R. D., High-Frequency Measurements
RAND, B., Ceramics
RHODES, J. D., Electronic and Electrical Engineering
RILEY, F. L., Ceramic Processing
SHEPPARD, C. G. W., Applied Thermodynamics and Combustion Science
SMITH, N. J., Construction Project Management
SNOWDEN, C. M., Microwave Engineering
STEER, M. B., Microwave/Millimetre Engineering
STENTIFORD, E. I., Public Health Engineering
TAYLOR, C. M., Tribology
WILLIAMS, A., Fuel and Combustion Science
WREN, A., Scheduling and Constraint Management

Faculty of Medicine, Dentistry, Psychology and Health:

ALIMO-METCALFE, B. M., Leadership Studies
BALL, S. G., Cardiology
BASKER, R. M., Dental Prosthetics
BIRD, H. A., Pharmacological Rheumatology
BLUNDELL, J. E., Psychobiology
BOYLSTON, A. W., Pathology
CARTWRIGHT, R. A., Cancer Epidemiology
CHAMBERLAIN, M. A., Rheumatological Rehabilitation
CHAPMAN, A. J., Psychology
COOK, P. A., Child Dental Health (H)
CORRIGAN, A. M., Dental Surgery (H)
COTTRELL, D. J., Child and Adolescent Psychiatry
CUCKLE, H. S., Reproductive Epidemiology
CURZON, M. E. J., Children's and Preventative Dentistry
DAVIES, J. A., Clinical Education
DICKSON, R. A., Orthopaedic Surgery
DIXON, M. F., Gastrointestinal Pathology
DRIFE, J. O., Obstetrics and Gynaecology
ELLIS, F. R., Anaesthesia

EMERY, P., Rheumatology
FORMAN, D., Cancer Epidemiology
GOSDEN, R., Reproductive Biology
GRANT, P. J., Molecular Vascular Medicine
GUILLOU, P. J., Surgery
HAINSWORTH, R., Applied Physiology
HAWARD, R., Cancer Studies
HOWDLE, P. D., Clinical Education
HUME, W. J., Oral Pathology
HUNTER, D. J., Health Policy and Management
JONES, J. C. G., Restorative Dentistry (H)
KNOWLES, M., Experimental Cancer Research
LEVENE, M. I., Paediatrics and Child Health
MCMAHON, M. J., Surgery
MARKHAM, A. F., Medical Research Trust
MARSH, P. D., Oral Microbiology
MINDHAM, R. H. S., Psychiatry
MORLEY, S. J., Clinical Psychology
PRENTICE, C. R. M., Medicine
QUIRKE, P., Pathology
RENFREW, M., Midwifery Studies
ROBINSON, C., Oral Biology
RODGERS, R. J., Behavioural Pharmacology
ROWLANDS, D. J., Molecular Virology
SELBY, P. J., Cancer Medicine
SHAPIRO, D. A., Clinical Psychology
SIMS, A. C. P., Psychiatry
SMITH, M. A., Medical Physics
WALKER, J. J., Obstetrics and Gynaecology
WILD, C., Molecular Epidemiology
WILLIAMS, D. R. R., Epidemiology and Public Health
WILLIAMS, S. A., Oral Health Services Research
WISTOW, G., Health and Social Care

COLLEGES OF THE UNIVERSITY

Bretton Hall: West Bretton, Wakefield, WF4 4LG; tel. (1924) 830261; 2,203 students; Principal Prof. G. H. BELL.

College of Ripon and York St John: Lord Mayor's Walk, York, YO31 7EX; tel. (1904) 656771; f. 1841; 4,094 students; Principal Prof. R. BUTLIN.

Trinity and All Saints College: Brownberrie Lane, Horsforth, Leeds, LS18 5HD; tel. (113) 283-7100; 2,140 students; Principal Dr M. J. COUGHLAN.

LEEDS METROPOLITAN UNIVERSITY

Calverley St, Leeds, LS1 3HE
Telephone: (113) 283-2600
Founded 1970 as Leeds Polytechnic; present name and status 1992
Vice-Chancellor: Prof. L. WAGNER
Deputy Vice-Chancellors: Dr D. G. HITCHINS, F. GRIFFITHS
Head of Learning Support Services: JOHN HEAP
Library of 366,000 vols, 3,000 periodicals
Number of teachers: 1,091
Number of students: 10,985 full-time and sandwich, 11,421 part-time

DEANS

Faculty of Business: D. M. GREEN
Faculty of Cultural and Education Studies: A. OSBORNE
Faculty of Health and the Environment: Prof. J. BALE
Faculty of Information and Engineering Systems: Prof. G. E. TAYLOR

UNIVERSITY OF LEICESTER

University Road, Leicester, LE1 7RH
Telephone: (116) 252-2522
Telex: 34 11 98
Fax: (116) 252-2200
University College founded 1918, Charter 1950, University Charter 1957
Chancellor: Sir MICHAEL ATIYAH
Vice-Chancellor: Dr K. J. R. EDWARDS
Registrar: K. J. JULIAN
Librarian: T. D. HOBBS
Library: see Libraries
Number of teachers: 540
Number of students: (full-time): 8,657
Publications: *Calendar*, *Prospectus* (annually), *Annual Report*.

DEANS

Faculty of Arts: Prof. S. M. PEARCE
Faculty of Science: Prof. J. H. HOLLOWAY
Faculty of the Social Sciences: Prof. D. J. PYLE
Faculty of Law: J. C. WOODLIFFE
Faculty of Medicine and Biological Sciences: Prof. F. HARRIS
Faculty of Education and Continuing Studies: Prof. K. R. FOGELMAN

PROFESSORS

Faculty of Arts:
BARKER, G. W., Archaeology
BONNEY, R. J., Modern History
CAMPBELL, G. R., Renaissance Literature
CULL, N. J., American Studies
HOUSLEY, N. J., History
LITTLEJOHNS, R., Modern Languages
MATTINGLY, D. J., Roman Archaeology
MYERS, W. F. T., English Literature
NEWEY, V., English
PEARCE, S. M., Museum Studies
SHATTOCK, E. J., Victorian Literature
STANNARD, M. J., Modern English Literature
WALKER, G. M., Early Modern Literature and Culture
YARRINGTON, A., Art History

Faculty of Education and Continuing Studies:
BUSH, A. W., Educational Management
FOGELMAN, K. R., Education
GALTON, M. J., Education

Faculty of Science:
ALDRIDGE, R. J., Palaeontology
BEEBY, J. L., Theoretical Physics
BLANDAMER, M. J., Physical Chemistry
COCKS, A. C. F., Mechanical Engineering
COWLEY, S. W. H., Solar-Planetary Physics
CULLIS, P. M., Organic Chemistry
DAVIS, E. A., Experimental Physics
DISSADO, L. A., Engineering
FISHER, P. F., Geographical Information
GOSTELOW, J. P., Engineering
HILLMAN, A. R., Physical Chemistry
HOLLOWAY, J. H., Inorganic Chemistry
HUDSON, J. D., Geology
JONES, N. B., Engineering
KING, A. R., Astrophysics
LEWIS, G. T., Human Geography
LIDDINGTON, R. C., Macromolecular Crystallography
LIGHT, W. A., Mathematics
LLEWELLYN-JONES, D. T., Earth Observation Science
MILLINGTON, A. C., Physical Geography
NORRIS, C., Surface Physics
PARRISH, R. R., Isotope Geology
PARSONS, A. J., Physical Geography
PONTER, A. R. S., Engineering
POSTLETHWAITE, I., Engineering
POUNDS, K. A., Space Physics
ROBINSON, G. R., Mathematics
ROBINSON, T. R., Space Plasma Physics
SAUNDERS, A. D., Geochemistry
STEWART, A., Computer Science
TARNEY, J., Geology
THOMAS, R. M., Mathematics and Computer Science
WARD, M. J., X-Ray Astronomy
WELLS, A. A., Space Technology
WINDLEY, B. F., Geology

Faculty of the Social Sciences:
ALDGATE, P. J., Social Work
ASHTON, D. N., Sociology
BENYON, J. T., Political Studies
BERRIDGE, G. R., International Politics
CHAREMZA, W., Economics
CLARK, P. A., Economic and Social History
COTTRELL, P. L., Economic and Social History
CROMPTON, R., Sociology
FEARON, P. S., Modern Economic and Social History
FRASER, C. D., Economics
JACKSON, P. M., Economics; Public Sector Economics
LAYDER, D. R., Social Theory
LEE, K. C., Economics
MONAR, J., Politics
PHIZACKLEA, A. M., Sociology
PUDNEY, S. E., Economics
PYLE, D. J., Applied Economics
SCARBROUGH, H., Organizational Analysis
SREBERNY, A., Mass Communications
THOMPSON, R. S., Economics
WESTWOOD, S., Sociology
YOUNG, J. W., Politics

Faculty of Law:
CLARKSON, C. M. V., Law
NEAL, A. C., Law
SHAW, M. N., International Law
THOMPSON, M. P., Law
WHITE, R. C. A., Law

Faculty of Medicine and Biological Sciences:
ANDREW, P. W., Microbial Pathogenesis
BARNETT, D. B., Clinical Pharmacology
BELL, P. R. F., Surgery
BLAKELEY, A. G. H., Applied Physiology
BRAMMAR, W. J., Biochemistry
CAMP, R. D. R., Dermatology
CASTLEDEN, C. M., Medicine for the Elderly
CHERRYMAN, G. R., Radiology
CLARKE, M., Epidemiology
COLLEY, A. M., Psychology
CRITCHLEY, D. R., Biochemistry
CUNDLIFFE, E., Biochemistry
DAVIES, G. M., Psychology
DE BONO, D., Cardiology
DOVER, G., Genetics
EVANS, D. H., Medical Physics
FIELD, D. J., Neonatal Medicine
FRASER, R. C., General Practice
GRANT, W. D., Environmental Microbiology
HALLIGAN, A. W. F., Foetal-Maternal Medicine
HARRIS, F., Paediatrics
HOLLIN, C. R., Criminological Psychology
JEFFREYS, Sir ALEC, Genetics
JONES, D. R., Medical Statistics
JOSEPH, M. H., Behavioural Neuroscience
KYRIACOU, C. P., Behavioural Genetics
LAUDER, I., Pathology
LINDESAY, J. E. B., Psychiatry for the Elderly
LONDON, N. J. M., Surgery
LUNEC, J., Chemical Pathology
MAXWELL, A., Biochemistry
MILLER, E., Clinical Psychology
MYINT, S. H., Clinical Microbiology
NAHORSKI, S. R., Pharmacology and Therapeutics
NICHOLSON, M. L., Transplant Surgery
PARKER, G., Community Care
PETERSEN, S. A., Medical Education
PLAYFORD, R. J., Gastroenterology
POTTER, J. F., Medicine for the Elderly
REVELEY, M. A., Psychiatry
ROBERTS, G. C. K., Biochemistry
ROWBOTHAM, D. J., Anaesthesia and Pain Management
SAMANI, N. J., Cardiovascular Medicine
SILVERMAN, M., Child Health
SMITH, G., Anaesthesia
SMITH, H., Botany
SMITH, R. H., Environmental Biology
STACE, C. A., Plant Taxonomy
STANDEN, N. B., Physiology
STANFIELD, P. R., Physiology
STEWARD, W. P., Oncology
SWALES, J. D., Medicine

TAYLOR, D. J., Obstetrics and Gynaecology
THURSTON, H., Medicine
TREMBATH, R. C. P., Medical Genetics
WHALEY, K., Immunology
WHITELAM, G. C., Plant Molecular Physics
WILLIAMS, B., Medicine
WILLIAMS, P. H., Microbiology
WOODS, K. L., Therapeutics

ATTACHED INSTITUTES

Centre for Mass Communication Research: Dir Prof. A. SREBERNY-MOHAMMADI.

Centre for the Study of Public Order: Dir Prof. J. T. BENYON.

Public Sector Economics Research Centre: Dir Prof. P. M. JACKSON.

Centre for Labour Market Studies: Dir Prof. D. ASHTON.

Management Centre: Dir Prof. P. M. JACKSON.

International Centre for Management, Law and Industrial Relations: Dir Prof. A. C. NEAL.

Centre for Mechanisms of Human Toxicity: Dir Prof. G. C. K. ROBERTS.

UNIVERSITY OF LINCOLNSHIRE AND HUMBERSIDE

Humberside University Campus, Kingston upon Hull: Cottingham Road, Hull, HU6 7RT
Lincoln University Campus: Brayford Pool, Lincoln, LN6 7TS
Telephone: (1482) 440550 (Hull); (1522) 882000 (Lincoln)
Fax: (1482) 463310 (Hull); (1522) 882088 (Lincoln)

Founded 1861 as School of Art and Design; became Humberside College of Higher Education 1978, Humberside Polytechnic 1990, University of Humberside 1992; present name 1996

Vice-Chancellor: Prof. R. P. KING
Senior Deputy Vice-Chancellor (Provost, Lincoln Campus): J. HOLT
Deputy Vice-Chancellor (Provost, Hull Campus): Prof. K. BARDON
Pro-Vice-Chancellors: Dr J. WHITTINGHAM, D. CROTHALL
Director of Learning Support: Dr MIKE FOSTER

Libraries with a total of 224,000 vols
Number of teachers: 377 (both campuses)
Number of students: 11,724 (both campuses)

DEANS

Arts and Technology: Prof. PETER ARNOLD
Business and Management: Prof. MICHAEL JACKSON
Social and Life Sciences: JOHN LOCKWOOD

ATTACHED RESEARCH INSTITUTES

International Educational Leadership and Management Centre: Dir Prof. B. DAVIES.

Food Research Centre: Dir Dr P. QUANTICK.

Policy Research Centre: Dir Prof. GARY CRAIG.

Centre for Health and Medical Psychology: Head Dr JON SLACK.

Centre for Management Systems: Head EDGAR NEVILL.

Economic Development Partnership and Innovation Centre: Dir GARY COOK.

UNIVERSITY OF LIVERPOOL

Liverpool, L69 3BX
Telephone: (151) 794-2000
Fax: (151) 708-6502

Founded 1881 as University College, Royal Charter 1903

Chancellor: Rt Hon. Lord OWEN
Pro-Chancellor: A. M. MOULD
Vice-Chancellor: Prof. P. N. LOVE
Pro-Vice-Chancellors: Prof. P. J. GOODHEW, Prof. J. N. TARN, Prof. D. F. WILLIAMS
Registrar: M. D. CARR
Librarian: F. M. THOMSON

Library: see Libraries
Number of teachers: 993 including 197 professors
Number of students: 13,579

Publications: *Town Planning Review* (quarterly), *Bulletin of Hispanic Studies* (quarterly), *Third World Planning Review* (quarterly), *Calendar* (annually), *Recorder* (annually).

DEANS

Faculty of Arts: Prof. K. D. EVEREST
Faculty of Science: Prof. A. L. HARRIS
Faculty of Medicine: Prof. P. M. JOHNSON
Faculty of Law: Prof. B. J. DOYLE
Faculty of Engineering: Prof. D. J. BACON
Faculty of Veterinary Science: Prof. C. J. GASKELL
Faculty of Social and Environmental Studies: Prof. P. W. J. BATEY
College Studies: Dr J. C. CHUBB
Dental Studies: Prof. J. SCOTT
School of Tropical Medicine: Prof. D. H. MOLYNEUX (Dir)

PROFESSORS

Faculty of Arts:
AINSWORTH, P. F., French
BATE, A. J., English Literature
BELCHEM, J. C., History
BURGESS, G. S., French
CLARK, S. R. L., Philosophy
DAVIES, J. K., Ancient History and Classical Archaeology
ELLIOTT, M., Irish Studies
EVEREST, K. D., Modern English
FISHER, J. R., Latin-American History
HIGGINS, J., Latin American Literature
HOEY, M. P., English Language
LEE, W. R., Economic and Social History
MILLARD, A. R., Hebrew and Ancient Semitic Languages
MILLS, A. D., English Language and Literature
ORLEDGE, R. F. N., Music
SAUL, N. D. B., German
SEVERIN, D. S., Spanish
SHAW, J., Archaeology, Classics and Oriental Studies
SLATER, E. A., Archaeology
TALBOT, M. O., Music
UNWIN, T. A., French
WRIGHT, R. H. P., Hispanic Studies

Faculty of Science:
ABRAHAM, R. J., Chemistry
APPLEBY, P. G., Mathematical Sciences
BEGON, M. E., Biological Sciences
BETHELL, D., Physical Organic Chemistry
BHANSALI, R. J., Mathematical Sciences
BOOTH, P. S. L., Experimental Physics
BRUCE, J. W., Pure Mathematics
CANTER, D. V., Psychology
CHESTER, R., Oceanography
COSSINS, A. R., Biological Sciences
CRAMPTON, J. M., Molecular Biology
DAINTON, J. B., Physics
DEROUANE, E. G., Chemistry, Innovative Catalysis
DUNBAR, R. I. M., Psychology
DUNCAN, C. J., Zoology
ELLIOTT, T. J., Geology
FLINT, S. S., Earth Sciences
GABATHULER, E., Experimental Physics
GIBBONS, A. M., Computer Science
HARRIS, A. L., Earth Sciences
HEATON, B. T., Inorganic Chemistry
HOLLOWAY, S., Chemical Physics
JOHNSON, M. S., Biological Sciences
JONES, D. R. T., Mathematical Sciences
KUSZNIR, N. J., Geophysics
MADEN, B. E. H., Biochemistry
MARRS, R. H., Applied Plant Biology
MICHAEL, C., Theoretical Physics
MOSS, B., Botany
NORTON, T. A., Marine Biology
PARKER, G. A., Zoology
PAUL, C. R. C., Earth Sciences
REES, H. H., Biological Sciences
RITCHIE, D. A., Genetics
ROBERTS, S. M., Organic Chemistry
RUDLAND, P. S., Biochemistry
RYTTER, W., Computer Science
SAUNDERS, J. R., Genetics and Microbiology
SCHIFFRIN, D. J., Physical Chemistry
SHAVE, M. J. R., Computer Science
SHAW, J., Earth Sciences
STIRLING, W. G., Experimental Physics
STRIKE, P., Biological Sciences
TOMSETT, A. B., Biological Sciences
TWIN, P. J., Experimental Physics
WALL, C. T. C., Pure Mathematics
WEIGHTMAN, P., Physics

Faculty of Medicine:
ASHFORD, R. W., Parasite and Vector Biology
BACK, D. J., Pharmacology and Therapeutics
BENTALL, R. P., Clinical Psychology
BIANCO, A. E., Parasitology
BLACKBURN, R., Clinical and Forensic Psychological Studies
BLIGH, J. G., Primary Care Education
BRECKENRIDGE, A. M., Clinical Pharmacology
BRODIE, D. A., Movement Science and Physical Education
BURGOYNE, R. D., Physiology
CALVERLEY, P. M. A., Rehabilitation Medicine
CARTY, H. M. L., Paediatric Radiology
CAWLEY, J. C., Haematology
CHADWICK, D. W., Neurology
CRAMPTON, J. M., Molecular Biology
COBBOLD, P. H., Human Anatomy and Cell Biology
COOKE, R. W. I., Paediatric Medicine
DOCKRAY, G. J., Physiology
DOWRICK, C. F., Primary Care
FOSTER, C. S., Pathology
FROSTICK, S. P., Orthopaedics
GOSDEN, C. M., Medical Genetics
GOWERS, S. G., Adolescent Psychiatry
GRIERSON, I., Experimental Ophthalmology
HART, C. A., Medical Microbiology
HART, G., Medicine
HILL, J., Child and Development Psychiatry
HOMMEL, M., Tropical Medicine
IRELAND, R. S., Primary Dental Care
JACKSON, M. J., Cellular Pathophysiology
JOHNSON, P. M., Immunology
JONES, A. S., Oto-rhino-laryngology
JONES, R. S., Anaesthesia
KROEGER, A., International Community Health
LEINSTER, S. J., Surgery
LENNON, M. A., Periodontology and Preventative Dentistry
LLOYD, D. A., Paediatric Surgery
LYE, M. D. W., Geriatric Medicine
MOLYNEUX, D. H., Tropical Health Sciences
MOLYNEUX, M. E., Tropical Medicine
NEILSON, J. P., Obstetrics and Gynaecology
NEOPTOLEMOS, J. P., Surgery
PARK, B. K., Pharmacology and Therapeutics
PETERSEN, O. H., Physiology
RHODES, J. M., Medicine
SALMON, P., Clinical Psychology
SCHULZ, T. F., Urinary Medicine
SCOTT, J., Oral Diseases
SHENKIN, A., Clinical Chemistry
SLOANE, J. P., Pathology

THEAKSTON, R. D. G., Tropical Medicine
TOWNSON, H., Medical Entomology
WALLEY, T. J., Clinical Pharmacology
WARENIUS, H. M., Research Oncology
WATSON, A. J. M., Medicine
WATTS, A., Restorative Dentistry
WEINDLING, A. M., Child Health
WHITEHOUSE, G. H., Diagnostic Radiology
WILKINSON, D. G., Liaison Psychiatry
WILLIAMS, D. F., Clinical Engineering
WILLIAMS, G., Medicine
WILSON, K. C. M., Psychiatry of Old Age
WRAY, S. C., Physiology

Faculty of Law:
ARORA, A., Law
DOYLE, B. J., Law
JONES, M. A., Law
LYON, C. M., Common Law
MCGOLDRICK, D., Law
MACLEOD, J. K., Law
NEUWAHL, N. A. E. M., European Law

Faculty of Engineering:
BACON, D. J., Materials Science and Engineering
BUNGEY, J. H., Civil Engineering
BURROWS, R., Environmental Hydraulics
ECCLESTON, W., Electronic Engineering
ESCUDIER, M. P., Mechanical Engineering
FANG, M. J. C., Applied Electromagnetism
GOODHEW, P. J., Materials Engineering
HON, K. K. B., Manufacturing Systems
JONES, G. R., Electrical Engineering and Electronics
JONES, N., Mechanical Engineering
LUCAS, J., Electrical Engineering and Electronics
MOTTERSHEAD, J. E., Applied Mechanics
O'CONNOR, B. A., Maritime Civil Engineering
OWEN, I., Mechanical Engineering
POND, R. C., Materials Science and Engineering
TEMPLEMAN, A. B., Civil Engineering
WU, Q. H., Electrical Engineering

Faculty of Veterinary Science:
DOBSON, H., Veterinary Reproduction
EDWARDS, G. B., Equine Studies
EISNER, D. A., Veterinary Biology
GASKELL, C. J., Small Animal Studies
GASKELL, R. M., Veterinary Pathology
HURST, J. L., Animal Science
JONES, R. S., Veterinary Anaesthesia
KELLY, D. F., Veterinary Pathology
MORGAN, K. L., Epidemiology
TREES, A. J., Veterinary Parasitology

Faculty of Social and Environmental Studies:
BATEY, P. W. J., Town and Regional Planning
CORNER, J., Politics and Communication Studies
DAVIES, M. R., Public Administration and Management
DEARING, J. A., Geography
DRUMMOND, H., Decision Sciences
DUNSTER, D., Architecture
GIBBS, B. M., Acoustics
GOULD, W. T. S., Geography
HILLIER, B, Economic Science
JONES, C., Social Policy and Social Work
KAVANAGH, D. A., Politics and Communication Studies
LLOYD, P. E., Urban Geography
MCCABE, B., Economics
MADDEN, M., Planning and Regional Science
MOORE, R. S., Sociology
MORRIS, R. C., Accounting
MUNSLOW, B., Politics and Communication Studies
OLDHAM, D. J., Building Engineering
PADGETT, S. A., Politics
PEPPER, S. M., Architecture and Building Engineering
POLLACK, B., Latin-American and Spanish Politics
ROBERTS, K., Sociology
RUSSELL, T., Centre for Research into Primary Science and Technology
SHARPE, K. A., Education
SMITH, D. W., Economic Geography
SMITHERS, A. G., Education
TARN, J. N., Architecture
THISTLEWOOD, D. J., Architecture and Building Engineering
WOODS, R. I., Geography

AFFILIATED INSTITUTION

Liverpool School of Tropical Medicine: see Research Institutes.

LIVERPOOL JOHN MOORES UNIVERSITY

Roscoe Court, 4 Rodney St, Liverpool L1 2TZ
Telephone: (151) 231-5090
Fax: (151) 231-3194

Founded 1970 as Liverpool Polytechnic, present name and status 1992

Chancellor: Sir JOHN MOORES
Vice-Chancellor: Prof. PETER TOYNE
Provost: Prof. JENNIFER LATTO
Registrar and Secretary: ALISON WILD
Number of teachers: 2,800
Number of students: 20,000

DIRECTORS OF ACADEMIC DIVISIONS AND SCHOOLS

Division of Arts and Professional Studies:
Built Environment: Prof. PETER MORGAN
Liverpool Art School: CECILIA CREIGHTON
Law and Applied Social Studies: Prof. ROGER EVANS
Liverpool Business School: Prof. FRANK SANDERSON
Media, Critical and Creative Studies: Prof. ROGER WEBSTER
Modern Languages: Dr LINDA ARCHIBALD

Division of Education, Health and Social Science:
Education and Community Studies: Prof. LESLIE BELL
Health Care: Prof. JANE JACKS
Human Sciences: Prof. PAM JAMES
Social Science: Prof. DAVID MCEVOY

Division of Engineering and Science:
Biological and Earth Sciences: Prof. PETER WHEELER
Biomolecular Sciences: Prof. HILARY EVANS
Computing and Mathematical Sciences: Dr DAVID CLEGG
Engineering: DAVE BURTON
Pharmacy and Chemistry: Prof. MIKE RUBINSTEIN

UNIVERSITY OF LONDON

Senate House, London, WC1E 7HU
Telephone: (171) 636 8000
Fax: (171) 636-5841

Founded 1836 as an examining body; became also a teaching body in 1898

Chancellor: HRH The PRINCESS ROYAL
Vice-Chancellor: Prof. GRAHAM ZELLICK
Deputy Vice-Chancellor: Prof. A. LUCAS
Chairman of Convocation: D. D. A. LESLIE
Academic Registrar: G. F. ROBERTS

Library: see Libraries
Number of teachers: 7,381
Number of internal students: 95,754
Number of external students: 22,135

COLLEGES OF THE UNIVERSITY

Birkbeck College

Malet St, London, WC1E 7HX
Telephone: (171) 631-6000

Founded 1823; Charter of Incorporation 1926
State control
Academic year: September to July

Master: Prof. TIM O'SHEA
Vice-Master: Prof. JULIA GOODFELLOW
Dean of College: Prof. PAUL BARNES
Dean of the Faculty of Continuing Education: Prof. TIM SCHULLER
Secretary: CHRISTINE MABEY
Registrar: B. A. HARWOOD
Librarian: PHILIPPA DOLPHIN

Number of teachers: 1,060 (incl. 800 part-time)
Number of students: 5,762

Publications: *Undergraduate Prospectus*, *Postgraduate Prospectus*, *Annual Report*, *Calendar*.

PROFESSORS

ARMSTRONG, I., English
BARNES, P., Applied Crystallography
BEGG, D., Economics
BINGHAM, N. H., Statistics
CONNOR, S., Modern Literature and Theory
DOUZINAS, C., Law
DUPRÉ, J. A., Philosophy
FIGES, O., History
FLINT, C. D., Chemistry
GOLDSWORTHY, G. J., Biology
GOODFELLOW, J. M., Biomolecular Sciences
GOODRICH, P., Law
GUEST, D., Occupational Psychology
HILEY, B., Physics
HIRST, P., Social Theory
HORNSBY, J., Philosophy
HUNTER, M., History
JOHNSON, M. H., Psychology
LABANYI, J., Modern Spanish Literature and Cultural Studies
LEADER, E., Physics
LOIZOU, G., Mathematics of Computation
MCAUSLAN, J. P., Law
MICHIE, J., Business Studies
PERRAUDIN, W., Financial Economics
PRICE, G. D., Mineral Physics
SCHULLER, T., Continuing Education
SELINKER, L., Applied Linguistics
SHEPHERD, J., Geography
SHORT, I., French
SLATER, M., Victorian Literature
SMITH, R., Applied Economics
SNOWER, D. J., Economics
SPENCER, P., Financial Economics
THORNTON, J. M., Biomolecular Structure
UNWIN, D. J., Geography
VAUGHAN, W. H. T., History of Art
WALKER, R. M., Spanish
WELLS, D. A., German
WHITE, R. E., Geology

Goldsmiths College

New Cross, London SE14 6NW
Telephone: (171) 919-7171
Fax: (171) 919-7113

Founded 1891

Undergraduate and postgraduate internal degrees; professional and postgraduate diploma and certificate courses in visual and performing arts, design, social and mathematical sciences, humanities, languages, media and communication studies, cultural studies, educational studies, art and group psychotherapy, and professional and community education

Warden: Prof. BEN PIMLOTT
Pro-Warden (Academic): Prof. ALAN DOWNIE
Pro-Warden (Research): Prof. CHRIS JENKS
Pro-Warden (Students): Dr BOB AYLETT
Secretary: SHANE GUY
Director of Information Services and Librarian: RON HORRILL

Library of 230,000 vols
Number of teachers: 310
Number of students: 4,669 full-time, 1,716 part-time

Publications: *Undergraduate Prospectus, Postgraduate Prospectus, PGCE Prospectus, Part-time Courses Programme, Study in London.*

PROFESSORS

ALEXANDER, S., History and Cultural Studies
ANDERSON, N., European Languages
BALDICK, C., English
CHU, C.-H., Mathematics and Computer Science
CRAIG-MARTIN, M., Visual Arts
CURRAN, J. P. P., Media and Communications
DAVIDOFF, J., Psychology
DE VILLE, N., Visual Arts
DOWNIE, A., English
DRYDEN, W., Psychology
FLETCHER, C., Psychology
GABER, I., Media and Communications
GILROY, P., Sociology
GOTTLIEB, V., Drama
HALPIN, D., Educational Sudies
HEIDENSOHN, F. M., Social Policy and Politics
JACKSON, B., Mathematics and Computer Science
JENKS, C., Sociology
KILLINGRAY, D., History and Cultural Studies
KIMBELL, R. A., Design Studies, Technology Education Unit
LAWSON, C., Music
MAHARAJ, S., History and Cultural Studies
MCROBBIE, A., Media and Communications
MORRIS, B., Anthropology
NEWBURN, T., Social Policy and Politics
PEARSON, G., Professional and Community Education
ROGOFF, I., History and Cultural Studies
ROSE, N., Sociology
SEIDLER, V., Sociology
SILVERMAN, D., Sociology
SMITH, P. K., Psychology
STEPHENS, N. M., Mathematics and Computer Science
TOMLINSON, S., Educational Studies
VALENTINE, T., Psychology
WOOLLEY, M., Design Studies

Heythrop College

Kensington Square, London, W8 5HQ
Telephone: (171) 795-6600
Fax: (171) 795-4200

Courses lead to the BD, Dip Th, MTh, PhD in the Faculty of Theology, BA in Philosophy and Theology, BA in Biblical Studies, BA in Theological Studies, BA in Theology and Society, BA in Theology for Ministry, BA in Philosophy, MA in Christian Spirituality, MA in Pastoral Liturgy, MA in Pastoral Studies, MA in Philosophy, MA in Philosophy and Religion, PhD in the Faculty of Arts

The college does not receive an HEFCE grant

Principal: Rev. BRENDAN CALLAGHAN
Secretary: ROSALIE BOLLAND
Academic Registrar: ANNABEL CLARKSON

Library of 250,000 vols
Number of teachers: 30
Number of students: 350

Imperial College of Science, Technology and Medicine

South Kensington, London, SW7 2AZ
Telephone: (171) 589-5111
Fax: (171) 584-7596
E-mail: webmaster@ic.ac.uk

Formed 1907 by federation of Royal College of Science, Royal School of Mines, and City and Guilds College, (1988) St Mary's Hospital Medical School, (1995) National Heart and Lung Institute and (1997) Charing Cross and Westminster Medical School and Royal Postgraduate Medical School

Rector: Prof. Sir RONALD OXBURGH
Deputy Rector: Prof. W. A. WAKEHAM
College Secretary: K. A. MITCHESON

Number of teachers: 1,192
Number of students: 8,824 full-time, 894 part-time

DEANS

Royal College of Science: Prof. D. M. P. MINGOS
Royal School of Mines: Prof. R. D. RAWLINGS
City and Guilds College: Prof. B. BRISCOE
School of Medicine: Prof. C. R. W. EDWARDS (Principal)

PROFESSORS

Science and Technology:

ALEKSANDER, I., Electrical Engineering
ARCOUMANIS, C., Internal Combustion Engines
ATKINSON, A., Materials Chemistry
ATKINSON, C., Applied Mathematics
BALOGH, A., Space Physics
BARBER, J., Biochemistry
BARRETT, A. G. M., Organic Chemistry
BEARMAN, P. W., Experimental Aerodynamics
BEDDINGTON, J. R., Applied Population Biology
BELL, A. R., Physics
BELL, J. N. B., Environmental Pollution
BESANT, C. B., Computer-Aided Manufacture
BIRLEY, S., Management
BRADFORD, H. F., Neurochemistry
BRISCOE, B. J., Interface Engineering
BUCHANAN, D. L., Mining Geology
BUCK, K. W., Plant and Fungal Virology
BURLAND, J. B., Soil Mechanics
CAPLIN, A. D., Physics
CASH, J. R., Numerical Analysis
CAWLEY, P., Mechanical Engineering
CHANDLER, R. J., Geotechnical Engineering
CHRISTOFIDES, N., Operational Research
CLARK, K. L., Computational Logic
CONNERADE, J. P., Atomic and Molecular Physics
CONSTANTINIDES, A. G., Signal Processing
CRAWLEY, M. J., Plant Ecology
CRISFIELD, M. A., Computational Mechanics
CRONAN, D. S., Marine Geochemistry
CUTHBERTSON, K., Finance
DAINTY, J. C., Applied Optics
DARLINGTON, J., Programming Methodology
DAVIES, G. A. O., Aeronautical Structures
DELL, A., Carbohydrate Biochemistry
DJAMGOZ, M., Neurobiology
DOLLY, J. O., Molecular Neurobiology
DORNAN, P. J., Experimental Particle Physics
DOUGAN, G., Physiological Biochemistry
DURANT, J. R., Public Understanding of Science
EDALAT, A., Computer Science and Mathematics
EDWARDS, D. M., Mathematical Physics
ELGIN, J. N., Applied Mathematics
ELNASHI, A. S., Earthquake Engineering
ENGLAND, G. L., Mechanics and Structures
EVANS, A. W., Transport Safety
EVANS, J., Tropical Forestry
EWINS, D. J., Vibration Engineering
FENNER, R. T., Engineering Computation
FLOWER, H. M., Materials Science
FOKAS, A. S., Applied Mathematics
FRANKS, N. P., Biophysics
GIBBON, J. D., Applied Mathematics
GIBSON, V. C., Polymer Synthesis
GODDARD, A. J. H., Environmental Safety with special reference to Nuclear Power
GODFRAY, H. C. J., Evolutionary Biology
GOODGAME, D. M., Chemistry
GOODLAD, J. S. R., Sociology and Higher Education
GOSMAN, A. D., Computational Fluid Dynamics
GRAHAM, J. M. R., Unsteady Aerodynamics
GRAHAM, N. J. D., Environmental Engineering
GRIFFITH, W. P., Inorganic Chemistry
GRINGARTON, A., Petroleum Engineering
HAINES, M. G., Physics
HALL, P., Applied Mathematics
HALL, S., Economics
HANKIN, C., Computing Science
HARRIES, J. E., Earth Observation
HARRISON, P. G., Computing Science
HARVEY, J. K., Gas Dynamics
HASSELL, M. P., Insect Ecology
HENCH, L. L., Ceramic Materials
HEWITT, G. F., Chemical Engineering
HIGGINS, J. S., Polymer Science
HILLIER, R., Compressible Flow
HOBBS, R. E., Structural Engineering
HOLMES, P., Hydraulics
HYNDS, R. J., Computing Management
ISHAM, C. J., Theoretical Physics
JAMES, G. D., Pure Mathematics
JOHNSON, H. D., Petroleum Geology
JONES, A. R., Combustion Engineering
JONES, W. P., Combustion Engineering
JOYCE, B. A., Semiconductor Materials
KANDIYOTI, R., Chemical Engineering
KARAKITSOS, E., Economics
KELSALL, G. H., Electrochemical Engineering
KERSHENBAUM, L. S., Chemical Engineering
KILNER, J., Materials Science
KINLOCH, A. J., Adhesion
KITNEY, R. I., Biomedical Systems Engineering
KNIGHT, P. L., Quantum Optics
KOWALSKI, R. A., Computational Logic
KRAMER, J., Distributed Computing
LAWTON, J. H., Community Ecology
LEPPINGTON, F. G., Applied Mathematics
LESTER, J. N., Water Technology
LIEBECK, M. N., Pure Mathematics
LIMEBEER, D. J. N., Control Engineering
LOCKWOOD, F. C., Combustion
LUCKHAM, P. F., Particle Technology
LYONS, T. J., Mathematics
MACCHIETO, S., Process Systems Engineering
MACKINNON, A., Physics
MCLEAN, M., Materials
MACRORY, R. B., Environmental Law
MAIBAUM, T. S. E., Foundations of Software Engineering
MAMDANI, E. H., Telecommunications Strategy and Services
MANTLE, P. G., Microbial Biochemistry
MANZ, A., Analytical Chemistry
MATTHEWS, G. A., Pest Management
MILES, D., Finance
MINGOS, D. M. P., Inorganic Chemistry
MONHEMIUS, A. J., Environmental Engineering
MORGAN, B. L., Physics
MORRIS, H. R., Biological Chemistry
NEW, G. H. C., Non-Linear Optics
NEWMAN, R. C., Semiconductor Materials
NORBURN, D., Management
O'BRIEN, P., Inorganic Chemistry
OXBURGH, E. R., Mineralogy and Petrology
PALMER, J. M., Plant Biochemistry
PANTELIDES, C. C., Chemical Engineering
PARRY, G., Electro-Optic Engineering
PAVLOVIC, M., Structural Engineering and Mechanics
PENDRY, J. B., Theoretical Solid-State Physics
PERKINS, J. D., Chemical Engineering
PHILLIPS, D., Physical Chemistry
POTTS, D. M., Analytical Soil Mechanics
QUENBY, J. J., Physics
RAWLINGS, R. D., Materials Science
RICHARDS, B., Computing Science
RICHARDSON, S. M., Chemical Engineering
RIDLEY, T. M., Transport Engineering
ROWAN-ROBINSON, G. M., Astrophysics

RUSTEM, B., Computational Methods in Operations
SCHROTER, R. C., Biological Mechanics
SELLEY, R. C., Applied Sedimentology
SHAW, C. T., Mining
SINDEN, R. E., Parasite Cell Biology
SLOMAN, M. S., Distributed Systems Management
SMITH, A. F. M., Statistics
SMITH, R., Physics
SOUTHWOOD, D. J., Physics
SPENCE, R., Information Engineering
SPIKES, H., Lubrication
SQUIRE, J. M., Structural Biophysics
STEELE, K., Physics
STRADLING, R. A., Physics
SYMS, R. R., Microsystems Technology
THORNTON, I., Environmental Geochemistry
TOUMAZOU, C., Analogue Circuit Design
TURNER, L. F., Digital Communications
VANDERMERWE, S., International Marketing and Design
VAN HEEL, M., Structural Biology
VINTER, R. B., Control Theory
VIRDEE, T. S., Physics
VVEDENSKY, D., Theoretical Solid-State Physics
WAKEHAM, W. A., Chemical Physics
WALDEN, A. T., Statistics
WEBSTER, G. A., Engineering Materials
WHEATER, H. S., Hydrology
WHITELAW, J. H., Convective Heat Transfer
WILLI, O., Physics
WILLIAMS, D. J., Structural Chemistry
WILLIAMS, J. G., Mechanical Engineering
WISE, C. M., Civil Engineering
WOODS, J. D., Oceanography
WORTHINGTON, M. H., Geophysics
ZEGARLINSKI, B., Pure Mathematics

School of Medicine:

ADAMS, L., Respiratory Physiology
ALLISON, D. J., Diagnostic Radiology
ANDERSON, R. H., Cardiac Morphology
ARCHARD, L. C., Molecular Pathology
ARST, H. N., Microbial Genetics
BANGHAM, C., Immunology
BARNES, P. J., Thoracic Medicine
BENNETT, P. R., Obstetrics and Gynaecology
BLOOM, S., Metabolic Medicine
BOOBIS, A. R., Biochemical Pharmacology
BOSANQUET, N. F. G., Health Policy
BROOKS, D. J., Neurology
BUCKINGHAM, J. C., Pharmacology
BULPITT, C. J., Geriatric Medicine
CALAM, J., Gastroenterology
CALDWELL, J., Biochemical Toxicology
CHUNG, K. F., Respiratory Medicine
CLARK, T. J. H., Pulmonary Medicine
COATS, A. J. S., Clinical Cardiology
COHEN, J., Infectious Diseases
COLE, P. J., Respiratory Medicine
COLEMAN, D. V., Cell Pathology
COLLINGE, J., Molecular Neurogenetics
CORRIN, B., Histopathology
COSGROVE, D. O., Clinical Ultrasound
COUTELLE, C.
DAVIES, D. S., Biochemical Pharmacology
DAWSON, P., Diagnostic Radiology
DE BELLEROCHE, J. S., Neurochemistry
EDWARDS, A. D., Neonatology
EDWARDS, C. R. W., Medicine
ELDER, M. G., Obstetrics and Gynaecology
ELLAWAY, P. H., Physiology
ELLIOTT, P., Epidemiology and Public Health Medicine
EVANS, D. J., Histopathology
EVANS, T., Intensive Care Medicine
FARRELL, P. J., Tumour Virology
FELDMANN, M., Cellular Immunology
FIELDER, A., Ophthalmology
FIRTH, J. A., Anatomy
FISK, N. M., Obstetrics and Gynaecology
FRANKS, S., Reproductive Endocrinology
GAREY, L. J., Anatomy
GARRALDA, M. E., Child and Adolescent Psychiatry
GEDDES, D., Respiratory Medicine
GILLON, E. Z. R., Medical Ethics
GOLDMAN, J. M., Leukaemia Biology and Therapeutics
GORDON, M. Y., Experimental Haematology
GOTCH, F., Immunology
GREENHALGH, R. M., Surgery
GRUZELIER, J. G., Psychology
HALL, R. J., Clinical Cardiology
HARVEY, D. R., Paediatrics and Neonatal Medicine
HASKARD, D. O., Cardiovascular Medicine
HENRY, J. A., Accident and Emergency Medicine
HODGSON, H. J., Medicine
HODSON, M. E., Respiratory Medicine
HOLDEN, D. W., Molecular Microbiology
HUGHES, S. P. F., Orthopaedic Surgery
JARMAN, B., Primary Health Care
JOHNSTON, D. G., Clinical Endocrinology
JONES, R. M., Anaesthetics
KAY, A. B., Clinical Immunology
KESSLING, A., Community Genetics
KRAUSZ, T., Surgical Pathology
KROLL, J. S., Paediatrics and Molecular Infectious Diseases
LAB, M. J., Physiology
LANE, D. A., Molecular Haematology
LANT, A. F., Clinical Pharmacology and Therapeutics
LECHLER, R. I., Immunology
LEVIN, M., Paediatrics
MACDERMOT, J., Clinical Pharmacology
MARSTON, S. B., Cardiovascular Biochemistry
MASON, R. M., Biochemistry
MATHIAS, C. J., Neurovascular Medicine
MICHEL, C. C., Physiology
MONJARDINO, J. P., Molecular Hepatology
NICHOLSON, J. K., Biological Chemistry
OPENSHAW, P. J. M., Experimental Medicine
PASVOL, G., Infection and Tropical Medicine
PEPYS, M. B., Immunological Medicine
PETERS, A. M., Diagnostic Radiology
POLAK, J. M., Histochemistry
POOLE-WILSON, P., Cardiology
POWELL, J. T., Vascular Biology
PUSEY, C. D., Renal Medicine
REDINGTON, A. N., Congenital Heart Disease
REED, M. J., Steroid Biochemistry
REGAN, L., Obstetrics and Gynaecology
REISER, M., Immunology
RITTER, M. A., Immunology
ROBOTHAM, J. L., Anaesthesia
ROYSTON, J. P., Medical Statistics
SAKLATVALA, J., Experimental Pathology
SEED, W. A., Medicine
SEVER, P. S., Clinical Pharmacology and Therapeutics
SEVERS, N. J., Cell Biology
SHAW, R. J., Thoracic Medicine
SHERIDAN, D. J., Clinical Cardiology
SIKORA, K., Clinical Oncology
STAMP, G. W. M., Histopathology
STEER, P. J., Obstetrics and Gynaecology
STIMSON, G. V., Sociology of Health Behaviour
SUGDEN, P. H., Cellular Biochemistry
SUMMERFIELD, J. A., Experimental Medicine
TAYLOR, K. M., Cardiac Surgery
THOMAS, H. C., Medicine
THOMPSON, S. G., Medical Statistics and Epidemiology
TYRER, P. J., Community Psychiatry
UNDERWOOD, S. R., Cardiac Imaging
WALPORT, M. J., Medicine
WASTELL, C., Surgery
WEBER, J. N., Genito-Urinary Medicine and Communicable Diseases
WHITEHOUSE, J. M. A., Medical Oncology
WICKRAMASINGHE, S. N., Haematology
WIGGLESWORTH, J. S., Perinatal Pathology
WILLIAMS, A. J., Membrane Biophysics
WILLIAMS, T. J., Applied Pharmacology
WILLIAMSON, R. C., Surgery
WINSTON, L. R. M. L., Fertility Studies
WOOD, D. A., Clinical Epidemiology
WRIGHT, N. A., Histopathology
YACOUB, M. M., Cardiothoracic Surgery
YOUNG, D. B., Medical Microbiology

Institute of Education

20 Bedford Way, London, WC1H 0AL
Telephone: (171) 580-1122
Fax: (171) 612-6097
E-mail: overseas.liaison@ioe.ac.uk

Founded as London Day Training College in 1902, transferred to control of University of London in 1932, became a School of the University in 1987

Advanced studies and research in education and related areas; higher degrees; Associateship; advanced diploma courses and short courses for teachers and others working in the education service; postgraduate teacher training

Director: Prof. PETER MORTIMORE
Secretary: D. J. WARREN
Academic Registrar: Dr L. G. LOUGHRAN
Librarian: A. PETERS

Number of teachers: 180
Number of students: 4,400 (1,600 full-time, 2,850 part-time)

Library of *c*. 320,000 vols, 2,160 periodicals

Publications: *London Educational Studies* (monographs), *Bedford Way Papers* (occasional papers), *Inaugural and Special Lectures*, *London File*, and supplements (occasional).

PROFESSORS

AGGLETON, P., Education
ALDRICH, R., Education
BARNETT, R., Higher Education
BRANNEN, J., Sociology of the Family
GIPPS, C. V., Education
GOLDSTEIN, H., Statistical Methods
HOYLES, C. M., Mathematics Education
KRESS, G., Education with special reference to the teaching of English
LAWTON, D., Education
LITTLE, A., Education with special reference to Developing Countries
MORTIMORE, P. J., Education
MOSS, P., Early Childhood Provision
NORWICH, B., Educational Psychology with reference to Children with Special Needs
NOSS, R., Mathematics Education
NUNES, T. N., Education
OAKLEY, A. R., Sociology and Social Policy
SWANWICK, K., Music Education
WHITE, J. P., Philosophy of Education
WHITTY, G. J., Sociology of Education
WIDDOWSON, H. G., Education
WILLIAMS, G. L., Educational Administration
WOLF, A., Education
YOUNG, M., Education

ATTACHED INSTITUTE

Thomas Coram Research Unit: 27/28 Woburn Sq., London WC1; f. 1974 with support from the Dept of Health and Social Security, Thomas Coram Fndn, and other bodies; now a Dept of Health Designated Research Centre; research in health, education and development of children; Dir Prof. PETER AGGLETON.

King's College London

Strand, London WC2R 2LS
Guy's campus: London Bridge, London, SE1 9RT
St Thomas' campus: Lambeth Palace Rd, London, SE1 7EH
King's Denmark Hill campus: Bessemer Rd, London, SE5 9PJ

Telephone: (171) 836-5454 (Strand), (171) 955-5000 (Guy's), (171) 928-9292 (St Thomas'), (171) 737-4000 (King's Denmark Hill)

Founded 1829; merged with Queen Elizabeth College and Chelsea College 1985, and with United Medical and Dental Schools of Guy's and St Thomas' Hospitals 1998

Principal: Prof. A. LUCAS
Vice-Principals: Prof. Sir CYRIL CHANTLER, Prof. B. W. IFE, W. C. SLADE
Secretary and Registrar: H. T. MUSSELWHITE
Academic Registrar: B. E. SALTER
Library: see Libraries
Number of teachers: 1,535
Number of students: (incl. School of Medicine and Dentistry): 16,515

HEADS OF SCHOOLS

School of Education: Dr DYLAN WILLIAMS
School of Humanities: Prof. LINDA A. NEWSON
School of Law: Prof. C. G. J. MORSE
Guy's, King's and St Thomas' School of Medicine: Prof. ADRIAN L. W. F. EDDLESTON
Guy's, King's and St Thomas' School of Dentistry: Prof. FRANK P. ASHLEY
Guy's, King's and St Thomas' School of Biomedical Sciences: Prof. SIMON L. HOWELL
School of Health and Life Sciences: Prof. ROBERT C. HIDER
School of Physical Sciences and Engineering: Prof. COLIN BUSHNELL
Institute of Psychiatry: Prof. STUART CHECKLEY

PROFESSORS

School of Education:

BALL, S. J.
BROWN, M. L.
DRIVER, R. H.
JOHNSON, O. C.
STREET, B. U.

School of Humanities:

ADLER, J. D., German
BANNER, M. C., Theology and Religious Studies
BEATON, R. M., Modern Greek
BIRTWISTLE, H., Music
BOND, B. J., War Studies
BUSH, C., American Literature
BUTT, J. W., Spanish and Spanish-American Studies
CHABAL, P. E., Portuguese and Brazilian Studies
CLARKE, M., Centre for Defence Studies
CLARKE, P. B., Theology and Religious Studies
DANAEKER, C., War Studies
DEATHRIDGE, J. W., Music
DREYFUS, L., Music
FREEDMAN, L. D., War Studies
GANZ, D., English and Classics
GILLIES, D. A., Philosophy
GRIFFITHS, R. M., French
GUNTON, C. E., Theology and Religious Studies
HAMNETT, C., Geography
HEATH, M. J., French
HELM, P., Theology and Religious Studies
HERRIN, J. E., Byzantine Studies
HOOK, D., Spanish and Spanish-American Studies
IFE, B. W., Spanish and Spanish-American Studies
KARSH, E., War Studies
KNIBB, M. A., Theology and Religious Studies
MACEDO, Portuguese and Brazilian Studies
MAYER, R. G. M., Classics
NELSON, J. L., History
NEWSON, L. A., Geography
ORMOND, L., English
OVERY, R. J., History
PAPINEAU, D. C., Philosophy
PORTER, A. N., History
PROUDFOOT, G. R., English
ROBERTS, J. A., English
ROSEVEARE, H. G., History
ROWE, W. W., Spanish and Spanish-American Studies
RUSSELL, C. S. R., History
SAINSBURY, R. M., Philosophy
SAVILE, A. B., Philosophy
SCHIESARO, A., Classics
SILK, M. S., Classics
SORABJI, R. R. K., Philosophy
STANTON, G. N., Theology and Religious Studies
STOKES, J., English
THORNES, J. B., Geography
WAYWELL, G. B., Classics
WHITE, J. J., German

School of Law:

BLACKBURN, R., Constitutional Law
EWING, K. D.
GEARTY, C. A.
GRUBB, A.
GUEST, A. G.
HAYTON, D. J.
KENNEDY, I. M.
LOMNICKA, E. Z.
MARTIN, J. E.
MATTHEWS, P.
MORSE, C. G. J.
MULLERSON, R.
PHILLIPS, J. C.
WHISH, R.

Guy's, King's and St Thomas' School of Medicine:

ADAM, A., Interventional Radiology
ADAMS, A. P., Anaesthetics
AMIEL, S., Medicine
BANATVALA, J. E., Clinical Virology
BENJAMIN, I., Surgery
BINNIE, C., Clinical Neurosciences
BLACK, Sir JAMES, Analytical Pharmacology
BRAUDE, P. R., Obstetrics and Gynaecology
BURNAND, K. G., Vascular Surgery
BURNEY, P. G. J., Public Health Medicine
CARDOZO, L., Obstetrics and Gynaecology
CHANTLER, C., Paediatric Nephrology
COLLINS, W. P., Obstetrics and Gynaecology
CRAIG, T. K., Community Psychiatry
DAVID, A., Psychological Medicine
DAVIS, H. M., Child Health Psychology
DOHERTY, P., Cell Biology
DOWLING, R. H., Gastroenterology
EADY, R. A., Experimental Dermatopathology
EDDLESTON, A. L. W. F., Liver Studies
EYKYN, S. J., Clinical Microbiology
FABRE, J., Clinical Sciences
FARZANEH, F., Molecular Medicine
FENTIMAN, I. S., Surgical Oncology
FOGELMAN, I., Nuclear Medicine
FORSLING, M. L., Neuroendocrinology
FRENCH, G. L., Medical Microbiology
GARETY, P. A., Clinical Psychology
GIANNELLI, F. B., Molecular Genetics
GLEESON, M. J., Otolaryngology
GREAVES, M. W., Dermatology
GREENOUGH, A., Child Health
HART, I. R., Cancer Research
HAWKES, D. J., Computing Imaging
HAY, R. J., Cutaneous Medicine
HAYCOCK, G. B., Paediatrics
HAYDAY, A. C., Immunobiology
HEATLEY, F. W., Orthopaedic Surgery
HENDRY, B., Medicine
HIGGINSON, I., Palliative Care and Policy
HIGGS, R., General Practice
HOWARD, E., Surgery
HUGHES, R. A. C., Neurology
JACKSON, S., Health Care of the Elderly
JONES, R. H., General Practice
KALRA, L., Stroke Medicine
KEMENY, D. M., Immunology
KERWIN, R., Psychological Medicine
KOPELMAN, M. D., Neuropsychiatry
LEE, T. H., Allergy and Respiratory Medicine
LEHNER, T., Basic and Applied Immunology
LEIGH, N., Neurology
LUCAS, S. B., Clinical Histopathology
McCOLL, I., Surgery
MACDONALD, A. J. D., Old-Age Psychiatry
MCGREGOR, A., Medicine
MAISEY, M. N., Radiological Sciences
MALLET, A. I., Analytical Chemistry
MARTEAU, T. M., Health Psychology
MELDRUM, B., Neurology
MIELI-VERGANI, G., Child Health
MILNER, A. D., Neonatology
MOXHAM, J., Respiratory Medicine
MUFTI, G., Haematological Medicine
MUNDY, A. R., Urology
MURRAY, R., Psychological Medicine
NICOLAIDES, K., Obstetrics and Gynaecology
PAGE, C., Respiratory Medicine
PANAYI, G. S., Rheumatology
PEARSON, T. C., Haematology
PETERS, T. J., Clinical Biochemistry
POLKEY, C., Clinical Neurosciences
POSTON, L., Foetal Health
PRICE, J., Child Health
RAMIREZ, A. J., Liaison Psychiatry
RICHARDS, M. A., Palliative Medicine
ROBERTS, V. C., Medical Engineering and Physics
ROBINSON, R. O., Paediatric Neurology
ROSS, E., Community Paediatrics
RUBENS, R. D., Clinical Oncology
SACKS, S. H., Nephrology
SAVIDGE, G. F., Coagulation Medicine
SCOTT, D. L., Rheumatology
SHEPHERD, G. W., Mental Health Rehabilitation
SIMONOFF, E. A., Child and Adolescent Psychiatry
SOLOMON, E., Human Genetics
SONKSEN, P. H., Endocrinology
SWAMINATHAN, R., Clinical Biochemistry
SWIFT, C., Health Care of the Elderly
TYNAN, M. J., Paediatric Cardiology
VIBERTI, G., Diabetes and Metabolic Medicine
WATSON, J. P., Psychiatry
WEINMAN, J. A., Psychology Applied to Medicine
WESSELEY, S., Psychological Medicine
WILLIAMS, D. G., Medicine

Guy's, King's and St Thomas' School of Dentistry:

ASHLEY, F. P., Periodontology and Preventive Dentistry
BEIGHTON, D., Dental Science
CHALLACOMBE, S. J., Oral Medicine
GELBIER, S., Dental Public Health
GIBBONS, D. E., Oral Health Services Research
JOHNSON, N., Dental Sciences
KIDD, E. A., Cariology
LANGDON, J., Oral and Maxillofacial Surgery
LINDEN, R., Craniofacial Biology
McGURK, M., Oral and Maxillofacial Surgery
MEIKLE, M. C., Orthodontics
PALMER, R. M., Implant Dentistry and Periodontology
PITT-FORD, T. R., Endodontology
SHARPE, P. T., Craniofacial Biology
SMITH, B. G. N., Conservative Dental Surgery
WADE, W. G., Oral Microbiology
WATSON, R., Prosthetic Dentistry

Guy's, King's and St Thomas' School of Biomedical Sciences:

BERRY, M., Anatomy
BUCKLAND-WRIGHT, J. C., Radiological Anatomy
CAMMACK, R., Biochemistry
CICLITIRA, P. J., Gastroenterology
DIPLOCK, A. T., Biochemistry
FILE, S. E., Psychopharmacology

FRASER, L. R., Anatomy
GOULD, H. G., Biophysics
HALLIWELL, B., Biochemistry
HEARSE, D. J., Cardiovascular Biochemistry
HOLDER, N. H., Anatomy
HOWELL, S. L., Physiology
JENNER, P. G., Pharmacology
LITTLETON, J. M., Pharmacology
LUMSDEN, A. G. S., Developmental Neurobiology
MCMAHON, S. B., Physiology
MCNAUGHTON, P. A., Physiology
MARSHALL, J., Ophthalmology
NAFTALIN, R. J., Physiology
NEAL, M. J., Pharmacology
PAGE, C. P., Pharmacology
PEARSON, J. D., Physiology
PRICE, R. G., Biochemistry
QUINN, P. J., Biochemistry
RICE-EVANS, C., Biochemistry
RITTER, J. M., Clinical Pharmacology
SIMMONS, R., Biophysics
STANDRING, S. M., Applied Neurobiology
WEBSTER, K., Anatomy

School of Health and Life Sciences:

GEISSLER, C. A., Nutrition
HIDER, R. C., Pharmacy
MACLEOD CLARK, J. L., Nightingale Institute
MARRIOTT, C., Pharmacy
NEWHAM, D. J., Physiotherapy
POOLE, R. K., Microbiology
REDFERN, S. J., Nursing Studies
ROSS MURPHY, S. B., Life Sciences
SANDERS, T. A., Nutrition
STAINES, N. A., Immunology
TINKER, A. M., Gerontology
WHILE, A. E., Nursing Studies
WILSON-BARNETT, J., Nursing Studies

School of Physical Sciences and Engineering:

AGHVAMI, A. H., Electrical Engineering
BURGE, R. E., Physics
BUSHNELL, C. J., Mathematics
CLARKSON, T. G., Electrical Engineering
COLEMAN, D., Computer Science
DAVIES, A. C., Electrical Engineering
DAVIES, E. B., Mathematics
DAVIES, G., Physics
GAUNT, D. S., Physics
HALL, T. J., Electrical Engineering
HIBBERT, F., Chemistry
HOWE, P. S., Mathematics
HUGHES, M. N., Chemistry
LIGHTOWLERS, E. C., Physics
MACDONALD, J. S., Management Studies
ROBB, M. A., Chemistry
ROGERS, A. J., Electrical Engineering
SANDLER, M. B., Electrical Engineering
SAUNDERS, P. T., Mathematics
STREATER, R. F., Mathematics
SWANSON, J. G., Electrical Engineering
TAYLOR, J. G., Mathematics
TURNER, C. W., Electrical Engineering
UFF, J., Engineering Law
ULLMANN, J. R., Computer Science
WEST, P. C., Mathematics

London Business School

Sussex Place, Regent's Park, London NW1 4SA
Telephone: (171) 262-5050
Fax: (171) 724-7875

Founded 1965

Principal and Dean: Prof. JOHN QUELCH

Number of teachers: 100
Number of students (postgraduate): 1,000

PROFESSORS

BARWISE, P., Management and Marketing
BRENNAN, M. J., Finance
BUNN, D. W., Decision Science
CABRAL, L., Economics
COOPER, I. A., Finance
CURRIE, D. A., Economics
DIMSON, E., Finance
DOW, J., Finance
EARL, M. J., Information Management
ESTRIN, S., Economics
FRANKS, J. R., Finance
GEROSKI, P. A., Economics
GHOSHAL, S., Strategic Leadership
GOFFEE, R. E., Organizational Behaviour
HILL, T., Operations Management
MARKIDES, C., Strategic and International Management
MARSH, P. R., Finance
NICHOLSON, A., Operations Management
NICHOLSON, N., Organizational Behaviour
PORTES, R., Economics
ROBERTSON, T. S., Marketing
SCHAEFER, S. M., Finance
SERVAES, H., Finance
SIMMONDS, K., Marketing and International Business
STOPFORD, J. M., International Business
VOSS, C., Total Quality Management
WILLMAN, P. W., Organizational Behaviour, Industrial Relations

London School of Economics and Political Science

Houghton St, London WC2A 2AE
Telephone: (171) 405-7686
Telex: 24655
Fax: (171) 242-0392

Founded 1895

Director: Prof. ANTHONY GIDDENS
Secretary: Dr CHRISTINE CHALLIS

Library: see Libraries

Number of teachers: 677
Number of research staff: 141
Number of students: 6,549

Publications: *Economica* (quarterly journal of economics, economic history, and statistics), *The British Journal of Sociology* (quarterly), *British Journal of Industrial Relations* (quarterly), *Journal of Transport Economics and Policy* (3 a year), *Millennium: Journal of International Studies* (3 a year), *The International Bibliography of the Social Sciences* (1 a year), *Government and Opposition* (quarterly), *Journal of Public Economics* (monthly), *Population Studies* (3 a year), *Russian Economic Trends* (quarterly).

PROFESSORS

ABELL, P., Institute of Management/CEP/Sociology
ALPERN, S., Mathematics
ANGELL, I. O., Information Systems
ATKINSON, A. C., Statistics
BALDWIN, R., Law
BARKER, E. V., Sociology
BARRY, B. M., Government
BARTHOLEMEW, D., Statistics
BEAN, C. R., Economics/CEP
BESLEY, T. J., Economics
BHATTACHARYA, S., Accounting and Finance
BIGGS, N. L., Mathematics
BLOCH, M. E. F., Anthropology
BROMWICH, M., Accounting and Finance
CARTWRIGHT, N., Philosophy, Logic and Scientific Method
CHARVET, J., Government
CHESHIRE, P. C., Geography
CHINKIN, C., Law
COHEN, S., Sociology
COLEMAN, J., Government
COLLEY, L., European Institute
COLLINS, H., Law
COWELL, F. A., Economics
CRAFTS, N. F. R., Economic History/CEP
DAVIES, B. P., Personal Social Services Research Unit
DAVIES, P., Law
DE MEZA, D., Management
DESAI, LORD, Economics
DOWNES, D. M., Social Policy and Administration
DUNLEAVY, P., Government
DYSON, T., Population Studies, Social Policy and Administration
FARR, R. M., Social Psychology
FREEMAN, R. B., CEP
FULLER, C. J., Anthropology
GILLINGHAM, J. B., International History
GLENNERSTER, H., Social Policy and Administration/STICERD
GOODHART, C., Economics
GRAY, J., European Institute
GREENWOOD, C. J., Law
HALLIDAY, F., International Relations
HARDMAN MOORE, J., Economics/Financial Markets
HARLOW, C. R., Law
HARPER, D., Institute of Management
HARTLEY, T. C., Law
HILL, C., International Relations
HILL, S. R., Sociology/Institute of Management
HILLS, J., CASE
HOBCRAFT, J., Population Studies
HOOD, C. C., Government
HOWSON, C., Philosophy
HUMPHREY, P. C., Social Psychology
JACKMAN, R., Economics
JONES, D. K. C., Geography
JONES, G. W., Government
KNAPP, M. R. J., Personal Social Services Research Unit
KNOX, M., International History
LACEY, N., Law
LAYARD, P. R. G., Economics/CEP
LE GRAND, J., Social Policy and Administration
LEIFER, M., International Relations
LIEVEN, D. C. B., Government
LOIZOS, P., Anthropology
MACVE, R. H., Accounting and Finance
MANNING, A., Economics
MAYALL, J. B. L., International Relations
MAYNARD, A., LSE Health
METCALF, D., Industrial Relations/CEP
MILLER, P. B., Accounting and Finance
MOORE, H., Anthropology
MOUZELIS, N. P., Sociology
MURPHY, M., Social Policy and Administration
NICKELL, S., Economics/CEP
O'LEARY, B., Government
PARRY, J. P., Anthropology
PIACHAUD, D. F. J., Social Policy and Administration
PISSARIDES, C. A., Economics/CEP
POWER, M. K., Accounting and Finance
PRESTON, P., International History
PUTTNAM, Lord, Media and Communications
QUAH, D., Economics/CEP
REES, J. A., Geography
REINER, R., Law
ROBERTS, K. W. S., Economics
ROBERTS, S. A., Law
ROBINSON, P. M., Economics
ROCK, P. E., Sociology
RODRIGUEZ-SALGADO, M., International History
ROSENHEAD, J. V., Operational Research
RUBEN, D.-H., Philosophy, Logic and Scientific Method
SAITH, A., Development Studies Institute
SILVERSTONE, R., Media and Communications
SMITH, A. D. S., European Institute
SUTTON, J., Economics
TAYLOR, P., International Relations
TEUBNER, G., Law
TSOUKALIS, L., European Institute
VENABLES, A. J., Economics/CEP
WEBB, D. C., Accounting and Finance/Financial Markets
WORRALL, J., Philosophy, Logic and Scientific Method

ATTACHED INSTITUTES

Asia Research Centre: f. 1995; conducts social science research on Asia; Dir Dr A. HUSSAIN.

Business History Unit: f. 1978 jointly with Imperial College of Science and Technology to promote research into business history, including technological aspects; Dir Dr T. GOURVISH.

Centre for Discrete and Applicable Mathematics: f. 1995 to promote mathematical research within LSE and in collaboration with other European sites; Dir Prof. N. BIGGS.

Centre for Economic Performance: f. 1990 to conduct interdisciplinary research on economic performance, focussing particularly on the performance of firms; Dir Prof. P. R. G. LAYARD.

Centre for Educational Research: f. 1990 to carry out research into current educational topics including choice of schools, schools' admissions, the National Curriculum, the funding of education, and European and international issues; Dir Dr A. WEST.

Centre for International Studies: f. 1967 to promote research in all aspects of international studies; Chair. of Steering Committee Prof. J. MAYALL.

Centre for Philosophy of Natural and Social Science: f. 1990 to promote the study of philosophical and methodological issues; Dir Prof. NANCY CARTWRIGHT.

Centre for Research into Economics and Finance in Southern Africa: f. 1989; undertakes research into the management of international finance, foreign-exchange policy and domestic financial policy in South Africa, and macroeconomic and financial issues in the southern African region; Dir Dr J. LEAPE.

Centre for Research on the USA: f. 1993; social science analysis of contemporary USA and its relations with the rest of the world, with emphasis on US-Europe relations; Dir (vacant).

Centre for the Study of Global Governance: f. 1992 to investigate the origin and nature of urgent problems amenable to a multinational co-operative solution and to promote debate and propose solutions; Dir Prof. Lord DESAI.

Centre for Voluntary Organisation: f. 1987 to conduct research on problems and issues in the management of voluntary agencies and non-governmental organizations; Dir Dr M. HARRIS.

City Policy, Architecture and Engineering Programme: f. 1996; undertakes design-based teaching and research on the social, technical and economic aspects of cities and urban systems; Dir R. BURDETT.

Computer Security Research Centre: f. 1991 to study computer security issues from organizational, management, social and technical perspectives; Dir Dr J. BACKHOUSE.

Development Studies Institute: f. 1990; a multi-disciplinary centre for teaching economic research and development studies, covering problems from around the globe, of the third world and Eastern Europe; Head Prof. A. SAITH.

European Institute: f. 1991 to co-ordinate and develop research and research training on European issues; Dir Dr H. MACHIN.

Financial Markets Group: f. 1987 to undertake first rate basic research into the nature and operation of financial markets; Dir Prof. D. WEBB.

Greater London Group: f. 1958 to undertake research and publication on the government and economy of Greater London and the South-East Region; consists of academic teachers of the School with a small professional research staff; Chair. Prof. G. W. JONES.

Interdisciplinary Institute of Management: f. 1990; concerned with promoting interdisciplinary research into management; research is closely linked with the Centre for Economic Performance; Dir Prof. PETER ABELL.

Joint Centre for Survey Methods: established at LSE in 1989 jointly with external research bodies, to research methodological aspects of social surveys; LSE co-ordinator C. O'MUIRCHEARTAIGH.

LSE Gender Institute: f. 1993; a multi-disciplinary centre established to address the major intellectual challenges posed by contemporary changes in gender relations; Dir Prof. H. L. MOORE.

LSE Health: f. 1994; undertakes research, consultancy and training in international comparative health policy; co-ordinates the European Health Policy Research Network; Dir Dr E. MOSSIALOS.

LSE Housing: f. 1989; a centre for research, development and consultancy work in the areas of housing policy and management; residents' consultation and involvement, tenant involvement, inner-city problems, difficult estates; European housing issues; Co-ordinator Dr ANNE POWER.

Mannheim Centre for Criminology and Criminal Justice: f. 1990 to co-ordinate research in the field of criminology and criminal justice; Dir Prof. R. REINER.

Methodology Institute: f. 1991 to co-ordinate methodologic activities in teaching and research; Dir Dr G. GASKELL.

Personal Social Services Research Unit: f. 1974 at the University of Kent, transferred to LSE 1996; to conduct research in efficiency and equity in social and long-term care; Dir Prof. M. KNAPP.

Population Investigation Committee: f. 1936 to promote and undertake research into population questions and to promote the study of demography in both its quantitative and qualitative aspects; Chair. Prof. J. HOBCRAFT.

Suntory and Toyota International Centres for Economics and Related Disciplines: f. 1978 to promote research into applied economics and related fields; incl. Centre for the Analysis of Social Exclusion; Chair. Prof. H. GLENNERSTER.

London School of Hygiene & Tropical Medicine

Keppel St, London, WC1E 7HT

Telephone: (171) 636-8636

Telex: 8953474

Fax: (171) 436-5389

Founded 1924, opened 1929

Dean: Prof. H. C. SPENCER

Secretary and Registrar: WENDY SURRIDGE

Library: see Libraries

Number of teaching and research staff: 325

Number of students: 627

Publications: *Annual Report*, *Research Report*, *Prospectus*, *Health Policy and Planning*, *Journal of Tropical Medicine and Hygiene*.

PROFESSORS

BERRIDGE, V., History
BLACK, N. A., Health Services Research
BRADLEY, D. J., Tropical Hygiene
BRYCESON, A. D. M., Tropical Medicine
CLELAND, J., Medical Demography
COLEMAN, M. P., Epidemiology and Vital Statistics
DRASAR, B. S., Bacteriology
FINE, P. E. M., Communicable Disease Epidemiology
GREENWOOD, B. M., Communicable Diseases
HAYES, R. J., Epidemiology
KENDALL, C., Medical Anthropology and International Health
KIRKWOOD, B. R., Epidemiology and International Health
MABEY, D., Communicable Diseases
MCADAM, K. P. W., Clinical Tropical Medicine
MCKEE, C. M., European Public Health
MCMICHAEL, A. J., Epidemiology
MCPHERSON, K., Public Health
MILES, M. A., Medical Protozoology
MILLS, A. J., Health Economics and Policy
NORMAND, C. E. M., Health Policy
POCOCK, S. J., Medical Statistics
SHETTY, P. S., Human Nutrition
SMITH, P. G., Tropical Epidemiology
SPENCER, H. C., Public Health and Tropical Medicine
STEWARD, M. W., Immunology
SWERDLOW, A. J., Epidemiology
TARGETT, G. A. T., Immunology of Protozoal Diseases
TAYLOR, M. G., Medical Helminthology

ATTACHED INSTITUTE

Ross Institute of Tropical Hygiene: Dir Prof. D. J. BRADLEY.

Queen Mary and Westfield College

Mile End Road, London, E1 4NS

Telephone: (171) 975-5555

Fax: (171) 975-5500

Established 1989 after merger of Queen Mary College (f. 1887) and Westfield College (f. 1882)

Principal: Prof. ADRIAN SMITH

Warden, St Bartholomew's and the Royal London School of Medicine and Dentistry: Prof. ALEXANDER MCNEISH

Library: see Libraries

Number of teachers: 960

Number of students: 8,029

Publications: *Prospectuses*, *Bulletin*.

DEANS

Faculty of Arts: Dr R. J. KUHN
Faculty of Natural Sciences: Dr P. HEATHCOTE
Faculty of Engineering: Dr R. J. CROOKES
Faculty of Law: Prof. G. M. RICHARDSON
Faculty of Social Sciences: Prof. P. E. OGDEN
Faculty of Informatics and Mathematical Sciences: Prof. M. A. H. MACCULLUM
School of Medicine and Dentistry: Prof. DAVID WILLIAMS (Deputy Warden)

PROFESSORS

Faculty of Arts:

CHESHIRE, J. L., Linguistics
DEYERMOND, A. D., Spanish
DUNKERLEY, J. C., Political Studies
EVANS, P. W., Hispanic Studies
HAMILTON, P. W. A., English
HENNESSY, P. J., Contemporary History
HOBSON JEANNERET, M. E., French Language and Literature
IGNATIEFF, M., English and Drama
JARDINE, L. A., English and Drama
KAY, S., Medieval Studies
MILLER, J. L., History
MORIARTY, M. M., French Literature and Thought
OLSCHNER, L. M., German
PARSONS, D. W., Public Policy
PENNY, R. J., Romance Philology
RAMSDEN, J. A., Modern History
RANAWAKE, S. A., German
RAYFIELD, D., Russian
ROSE, J., English
SASSOON, D., History
TERRY, A. H., Catalan
VAREY, J. E., Hispanic Studies and Italian
WHITFORD, M. L., Modern French Thought
WILLIAM, J., History
WOODWARD, S., History
YOUNG, K., Political Studies

Faculty of Engineering:

ANDREWS, E. H., Materials
BENTLEY, G., Materials
BERRY, C., Materials
BONFIELD, W., Materials
CLARRICOATS, P. J. B., Electrical and Electronic Engineering
COLLINS, W. J. M., Engineering Design
CUTHBERT, L. G., Electronic Engineering
DAVIES, C. K. L., Materials
GASTER, M., Experimental Aerodynamics
GIBSON, R. E., Research Engineering
HENCH, L. L., Materials
JONES, J. G., Aerospace
KIRK, G. E., Engineering Design
LAUGHTON, M. A., Electrical and Electronic Engineering
LAWN, C. J., Thermo-Fluids Engineering
LOXHAM, M., Civil Engineering
OLVER, A. D., Electrical and Electronic Engineering
REVELL, P. A., Materials
ROSE, J. W., Mechanical Engineering
STARK, J. P. W., Aeronautical Engineering
WHITE, C. G., Engineering Design
WHITE, J. K., Civil Engineering

Faculty of Informatics and Mathematical Sciences:

ARROWSMITH, D. K., Mathematics
BAILEY, R. A., Statistics
BORNAT, R., Computer Programming
CAMERON, P. J., Mathematics
CARR, B. J., Mathematics and Astronomy
DONKIN, S., Pure Mathematics
GLENDINNING, P. A., Applied Mathematics
GOLDSHEID, I., Probability Theory
HODGES, W. A., Mathematics
JOHNSON, P., Human Computer Interaction
LEEDHAM-GREEN, C. R., Pure Mathematics
LIDDELL, H. M., Parallel Computing Applications
MACCALLUM, M. A. H., Applied Mathematics
MURRAY, C. D., Mathematics and Astronomy
PAKER, Y., Parallel Computing
PAPALOIZOU, J. C. B., Mathematics and Astronomy
ROBINSON, E., Computer Science
ROXBURGH, I. W., Mathematics and Astronomy
SCHWARTZ, S. J., Space Plasma Physics
WEHRFRITZ, B. A. F., Pure Mathematics
WILLIAMS, I. P., Mathematics and Astronomy

Faculty of Law:

ADAMS, J. E., Law
BLAKENEY, M., Intellectual Property Law
COTTERRELL, R. B. M., Legal Theory
FITZPATRICK, P., Law
FLETCHER, I. F., Commercial Law
LAHORE, J. C., Intellectual Property Law
MCCONVILLE, S. D. M., Criminal Justice
MUCHLINSKI, P. T., Drapers' Law
NORTON, J. J., Banking Law
O'DONOVAN, K., Law
RICHARDSON, G. M., Public Law
VAN BUEREN, G., International Human Rights Law
YELLAND, J. L., Law

Faculty of Natural Sciences:

ADE, P. A. R., Experimental Astrophysics
AYLETT, B. J., Chemistry
BONNETT, R., Research Chemistry
BRADLEY, D. C., Chemistry
BUGG, D. V., Nuclear Physics
CARTER, A. A., Particle Physics
CHARAP, J. M., Theoretical Physics
CLEGG, P. E., Astrophysics
CLYMO, R. S., Ecology
DUCKETT, J. G., Botany
DUNSTAN, D. J., Experimental Physics
EDGINGTON, J. A., Physics
HILDREW, A. G., Ecology
HULL, C. M., Theoretical Physics
LICHTENSTEIN, C. P., Molecular Biology
PRITCHARD, J., Chemistry
PYE, J. D., Biological Sciences
QUIRKE, N., Physical Chemistry
RANDALL, E. W., Research Chemistry
THOMPSON, G., Physics
THORPE, A., Biology
UTLEY, J. H. P., Organic Chemistry
VLCEK, A., Inorganic Chemistry
WHITE, G. J., Physics and Astronomy
WILSON, E. G., Physics

Faculty of Social Sciences:

ATKINSON, B. W., Geography
BAILLIE, R. T., Economics
LEE, R., Geography
OGDEN, P. E., Geography
SMITH, D. M., Geography
SPENCE, N. A., Human Geography

School of Medicine and Dentistry:

ANSEAU, M. R., Institute of Dentistry
ARMSTRONG, P., Haematology, Oncology and Imaging
ARMSTRONG-JAMES, M. A., Biomedical Sciences
ASHBY, D., Wolfson Institute of Preventive Medicine
BENJAMIN, N., Pharmacology
BERRY, C. L., Molecular Pathology, Infection and Immunity
BESSER, G. M., Metabolism
BRADLEY, P. F., Institute of Dentistry
BRITTON, K. E., Haematology, Oncology and Imaging
BROCKLEHURST, K., Biomedical Sciences
BURRIN, J., Metabolism
CARTER, Y. H., Community Sciences
CHARD, T., Haematology, Oncology and Imaging
CLARK, A. J. L., Metabolism
COHEN, R. D., Metabolism
COID, J. W., Community Sciences
COSTELOE, K., Metabolism
DAVIES, R. J., Molecular Pathology, Infection and Immunity
DAYAN, A. D., Wolfson Institute of Preventive Medicine
DOYAL, L., Metabolism
ELLIOTT, J. C., Institute of Dentistry
FARTHING, M. J., Metabolism
FELDMAN, R. A., Surgery, Clinical Neuroscience and Intensive Care
FLOWER, R. J., Pharmacology
GALTON, D., Metabolism
GOODE, A. W., Surgery, Clinical Neuroscience and Intensive Care
GOWLAND, G., Pharmacology
GROSSMAN, A., Metabolism
GRUDZINSKAS, J. G., Community Sciences
HARDIE, J. M., Institute of Dentistry
HAJ, M., Metabolism
HEATH, M., Institute of Dentistry
HILLIER, S. M., Community Sciences
HITMAN, G. A., Metabolism
ILES, R. A., Metabolism
JEFFRIES, R. A., Molecular Pathology, Infection and Immunity
KOPELMAN, P. G., Metabolism
LEIGH, I. M., Haematology, Oncology and Imaging
LESLIE, R. D. G., Metabolism
LILLEYMAN, J. S., Metabolism
LISTER, T. A., Haematology, Oncology and Imaging
LOWE, D. G., Molecular Pathology, Infection and Immunity
LUMLEY, J. S., Surgery, Clinical Neurosurgery and Intensive Care
MACDONALD, T. T., Metabolism
MARTIN, J. E., Molecular Pathology, Infection and Immunity
MILLER, N. E., Metabolism
NEWLAND, A. C., Haematology, Oncology and Imaging
OLIVER, R. T. D., Haematology, Oncology and Imaging
OXFORD, J., Molecular Pathology, Infection and Immunity
PAINE, A. J., Wolfson Institute of Preventive Medicine
PERRETT, D., Metabolism
PHILLIPS, I. R., Biomedical Sciences
PINCHING, A. J., Molecular Pathology, Infection and Immunity
PRICE, C. P., Metabolism
PRIEBE, S., Community Sciences
PRIESTLEY, J. V., Biomedical Sciences
REES, L. H., Metabolism
REZNEK, R., Haematology, Oncology and Imaging
SANDERSON, I. R., Metabolism
SAVAGE, M., Metabolism
STRUNIN, L., Surgery, Clinical Neuroscience and Intensive Care
SUGDEN, M. C., Biomedical Sciences
SWASH, M., Surgery, Clinical Neuroscience and Intensive Care
TABAQCHALI, S., Molecular Pathology, Infection and Immunity
TOMLINSON, D. R., Biomedical Sciences
TROTT, K. R., Haematology, Oncology and Imaging
VINSON, G. P., Biomedical Sciences
WALD, N. J., Wolfson Institute of Preventive Medicine
WHITTLE, B. J., Pharmacology
WILLIAMS, D. M., Institute of Dentistry
WILLIAMS, N. S., Surgery, Clinical Neuroscience and Intensive Care
WILLOUGHBY, D. A., Pharmacology
WINGATE, D. L., Metabolism

ATTACHED CENTRES

Centre for Commercial Law Studies: f. 1980; serves as focus for advanced teaching and research in commercial and business law; specializations: General Commercial and Comparative Law, Intellectual Property Law, Banking and Finance Law, Taxation Law, Information Technology Law, Insolvency Law, School of International Arbitration and European Law.

Environmental Science Unit: an interdisciplinary unit that co-ordinates and administers Environmental Science teaching (BSc) within the College; the programme comprises courses by Unit academic staff and courses from Biology, Geography, Physics and Chemistry depts; the Unit is also a centre for environmental research in the College.

Interdisciplinary Research Centre in Biomedical Materials: f. 1991; funded by EPSRC as the national centre; innovation of analogue biomaterials for tissue and joint replacement; second generation implants and prostheses for medical and dental applications; offers PhD, MD and MS degrees.

Centre for Medieval and Renaissance Studies: interdisciplinary modular taught courses in Medieval and Renaissance Studies, leading to MA.

Centre for Modern European Studies: administers MA in European Languages, Literatures and Thought and holds regular colloquia and research seminars; also encourages original development in language and literature.

Astronomy Unit: a national centre in receipt of five rolling block grants from the PPARC providing funds for theoretical astronomy, visitors for observational astronomy and space experiments. Research into most areas of astronomy. The UK Cluster Science Centre is located in the Unit.

Health and Health Care Research Centre: f. 1985; links researchers in several disciplines working on health service research, including assessment of local need for health care, health and service utilization of particular population groups, and health policy evaluation procedures.

Public Policy Research Unit: f. 1988 as a vehicle for research grants and contracts and policy discussion within the Dept of Political Studies; oversees the MSc degree in Policy Studies.

Centre for the Study of Migration: f. 1994, as a focal point for those engaged in the study of migration locally, nationally and internationally.

Royal Holloway, University of London

Egham, Surrey, TW20 0EX
Telephone: (1784) 434455
Fax: (1784) 437520
E-mail: liaison-office@rhbnc.ac.uk

Founded 1985 by merger of Bedford College (f. 1849) and Royal Holloway College (f. 1886)

Principal: Prof. N. GOWAR
Academic Registrar: A. PRICE
Librarian: SARAH E. GERRARD

Library of over 497,000 vols
Number of teachers: 339
Number of students: 5,361

Publications: *Prospectus, Annual Report, Academic and Research Record.*

DEANS

Faculties of Arts and Music: Prof. C. CAREY
Faculty of Science: Prof. J. LOWE

PROFESSORS

Faculty of Arts and Music:
ARMOUR, P. J., Italian
BRADBY, D. H., Drama and Theatre Studies
BRATTON, J. S., Theatre and Cultural History
BRAUND, S., Latin
BROADBENT, P. J., Management
BROWN, A. M., Italian Renaissance History
BURY, M., Sociology
CAREY, C., Classics
CARTER, T., Music
CAVE, R. A., Drama and Theatre Studies
CLAEYS, G. R., History of Political Thought
CORFIELD, P. J., History
CREASER, J. W., English Literature
CROOK, J. M., History of Victorian Art and Architecture
DODSWORTH, J. M., English Literature
DREWRY, G., Public Administration
EDWARDS, J. R., Social Policy
FRANK, J. L., Economics
GOULD, W. L., English Literature
HARVEY, C. E., Business History and Management
HASLAM, C. J., Accounting and Business Strategy
JONES, W. J., German
LETHBRIDGE, R. D., French Language and Literature
PILBEAM, P., Modern European History
ROBINSON, F. C. R., History of Southeast Asia
RYAN, K. J., English Language and Literature
SAUL, N. E., Medieval History
SHERINGHAM, M. H., French
SMITH, C. D., Organization Studies
STOCKWELL, A. J., Imperial and Commonwealth History
TOSI, A., Italian Studies
TUNSTILL, Applied Social Studies
TURNER, J. A., Modern History and Politics

Faculty of Science:
BERGER, M., Psychology
BLUNDELL, D. J., Environmental Geology
BOLWELL, G. P., Plant Biochemistry
BOSENCE, D. W. J., Carbonate Sedimentology
BOWYER, J. R., Plant Biochemistry
BRADLEY, C., Health Psychology
BRAMLEY, P. M., Biochemistry
BREWIN, C. R., Psychology
CATCHPOLE, C. K., Animal Behaviour
COOKE, M., Analytical Chemistry
COSGROVE, D., Geography
DAVIES, E. R., Machine Vision
DICKSON, J. G., Molecular Cell Biology
DODGE, J. D., Botany
ESSAM, J. W., Mathematics
EYSENCK, M. W., Psychology
FUNNELL, E., Neuropsychology
GAMMERMAN, A., Computer Science
GREEN, M. G., Particle Physics
HALL, R., Geology
LEA, M. J., Physics
LEWIS, J. W., Zoology
LOWE, J. J., Geography
MALTBY, E., Environmental Geography
MATHER, J. D., Geology
MCCLAY, K. R., Structural Geology
MENZIES, M. A., Geochemistry
MITCHELL, C. J., Computer Science
NISBET, E. G., Geology
PETRASHOV, V. T., Nanotechnology
PIPER, F. C., Mathematics
POTTER, R. B., Geography
RICE-EVANS, P., Experimental Physics
ROSE, J., Geography
SAUNDERS, J., Low Temperature Physics
SCOTT, A. C., Applied Palaeobotany
SHAWE-TAYLOR, J., Computer Science
SMITH, A. T., Psychology
STRONG, J. A., Experimental Physics
THORNDYKE, M. C., Comparative Endocrinology
WALKER, M., Mathematics
WILD, P. R., Mathematics

Royal Veterinary College

Royal College St, London, NW1 0TU
Telephone: (171) 468-5000
Fax: (171) 388-2342

Founded 1791

Principal: Prof. L. E. LANYON
Secretary and Registrar: A. N. SMITH
Academic Registrar: P. PROBYN

Number of teachers: 70
Number of students: 526

PROFESSORS

BAYLISS, M. T., Connective Tissue Biochemistry
BEDFORD, P. G. C., Canine Medicine and Surgery
BROWNLIE, J., Veterinary Pathology
CHANTLER, P. D., Veterinary Molecular and Cellular Biology
EDINGTON, N., Veterinary Virology
GOODSHIP, A. E., Orthopaedic Sciences
HOWARD, C. R., Veterinary Microbiology and Parasitology
JACOBS, D. E., Veterinary Parasitology
LEES, P., Veterinary Pharmacology
LLOYD, D. H., Veterinary Dermatology
MAY, S. A., Equine Medicine and Surgery
NOAKES, D. E., Veterinary Obstetrics and Diseases of Reproduction
SCARAMUZZI, R. J., Veterinary Physiology
STICKLAND, N. C., Veterinary Anatomy
WATHES, D. C., Veterinary Reproduction
WATSON, P. F., Reproductive Cryobiology

St George's Hospital Medical School

Cranmer Terrace, London, SW17 0RE
Telephone: (181) 725-5000
Fax: (181) 725-3426

Founded 1751

Principal: Prof. R. D. H. BOYD
Secretary: Prof. F. C. HAY
Academic Secretary: G. JONES

Library of 150,000 vols
Number of teachers: 520
Number of students: 1,805

Publications: *School Prospectus, Report.*

PROFESSORS

ANDERSON, H. R., Epidemiology and Public Health
AUSTEN, B. M., Protein Science
BELL, B. A., Neurosurgery
BLAND, J. M., Medical Statistics
BOLTON, T. B., Pharmacology
BURNS, T. P., Community Psychiatry
CAMM, A. J., Clinical Cardiology
CAMPBELL, S., Obstetrics and Gynaecology
CARTER, N. D., Developmental Biochemistry
CHALMERS, R. A., Paediatric Metabolism
CHAMBERS, T. J., Tissue Pathology
CLEMENS, M. J., Biochemistry
COATES, A. R. M., Medical Microbiology
DALGLEISH, A. G., Oncology
DAVIES, M. J., Cardiovascular Pathology
DILLY, P. N., Structural Biology
DORMANDY, J. A., Vascular Sciences
FISHER, L. M., Biochemistry
GHODSE, A. H., Psychiatry of Addictive Behaviour
GORDON-SMITH, E. C., Haematology
GRIFFIN, G. E., Infectious Diseases and Medicine
GRIFFITHS, J. R., Medical Biochemistry
HALL, G. M., Anaesthesia
HAY, F. C., Immunology
HERMON-TAYLOR, J., Surgery
HILL, P. D., Child Mental Health
HILTON, S. R., General Practice and Primary Care
HOLLINS, S. C., Psychiatry of Learning Disability
HOWLIN, P. A., Clinical Psychology
JOHNSTONE, A. P., Molecular Immunology
JONES, P. W., Medicine
LACEY, J. H., Psychiatry
LARGE, W. A., Pharmacology
LEVICK, J. R., Physiology
LITTLEJOHNS, P., Public Health
MACGREGOR, G. A., Cardiovascular Medicine
MCKENNA, W. J., Cardiac Medicine
MALIK, M., Cardiology
MILLARD, P. H., Geriatric Medicine
NORTHFIELD, T. C., Gastroenterology
OLIVEIRA, D. B. G., Renal Medicine
RICHES, P. G., Immunopathology
SEYMOUR, C. A., Clinical Biochemistry and Metabolism
SPRY, C. J. F., Cardiovascular Immunology
STANTON, S. L. R., Pelvic Surgery and Urogynaecology
STEPTOE, A. P. A., Psychology
STOCK, M. J., Physiology
STRACHAN, D. P., Public Health
TREASURE, T., Cardiothoracic Surgery
WALTERS, D. V., Child Health
WEST, R. J., Psychology
WHIPP, B. J., Physiology
WILSON, A. G., Diagnostic Radiology
WILSON, C. A. J., Reproductive Physiology

School of Oriental and African Studies

Thornhaugh St, Russell Sq., London, WC1H 0XG
Telephone: (171) 637-2388
Fax: (171) 436-3844

Founded 1916

Director: Sir TIM LANKESTER
Secretary: F. L. DABELL
Registrar: T. HARVEY

Library: see Libraries
Number of teachers: 220
Number of students: 3,220

Publications: *The Bulletin, The China Quarterly, Journal of African Law, Prospectus, Calendar, Annual Report.*

PROFESSORS

ABDEL-HALEEM, M. A. S., Islamic Studies
ABU-DEEB, K. M., Arabic
ALLAN, J. A., Geography (Middle East and North Africa)
ARNOLD, D., History of South Asia
BAKER, H. D. R., Chinese
BARRETT, T. H., East Asian History
BERNSTEIN, H., Development Studies (Africa)
BOOTH, A. E., Economics (South East Asia)
BRAGINSKY, V. I., South East Asian Languages and Literatures
BRENNER, L., Religions in Africa
BROWN, I., History
BYRES, T., Political Economy (South Asia)
CROLL, E., Chinese Anthropology
CRUISE O'BRIEN, D. B., Politics of Africa
DEUCHLER, M., Korean Studies
DICKS, A. R., Chinese Law
FARDON, R., African Anthropology
FINE, B., Economics (Africa)
GERSTLE, C. A., Japanese Studies
HAFEZ, S., Modern Arabic
HARDING, A., Law
HARRIS, L., Economics (Africa)
HAWKINS, J. D., Ancient Anatolian Languages
HAYWARD, R. J., Ethiopian Linguistic Studies
HEWITT, B. G., Caucasian Languages
HOWE, C. B., Economics (Asia)
KAYE, J. D., General Linguistics
KEMPSON, R. M., General Linguistics
LAPPIN, S., Linguistics
MARKS, S., History (Southern Africa)
PEEL, J. D. Y., Anthropology and Sociology (Africa)
PIATIGORSKY, A., Study of Religions
RATHBONE, R. J. A. R., Modern African History
ROBB, P. G., History of India
ROGERS, J. M., Islamic Art and Archaeology
SENDER, J., Economics (Africa)
SHACKLE, C., Modern Languages of South Asia
SIMS-WILLIAMS, N., Iranian and Central Asian Studies
SMITH, R. B., International History of Asia
STOTT, P., Biogeography (South East Asia)
TAPPER, R., Anthropology and Sociology
WEEKS, J., Development Economics (Africa and Latin America)
WHITFIELD, R., Chinese and East Asian Art
WRIGHT, J., South Asia
WRIGHT, O., Musicology of the Middle East

School of Pharmacy

29-39 Brunswick Square, London, WC1N 1AX
Telephone: (171) 753-5800
E-mail: registry@ulsop.ac.uk

Founded 1842

Dean: Prof. A. T. FLORENCE
Clerk to the Council and Secretary: B. D. ROBERTS

Number of teachers: 38
Number of students: 800

PROFESSORS

BARBER, N. D., Pharmacy Practice
BUCKTON, G., Pharmaceutics
DUNCAN, R., Polymer Therapeutics
GIBBONS, W. A., Pharmaceutical and Biological Chemistry
GREGORIADIS, G., Drug Delivery
MOFFAT, A. C., Pharmaceutical Analysis
NEWTON, J. M., Pharmaceutics
SIMMONDS, M. A., Pharmacology
SMART, T. G., Pharmacology
STARR, M. S., Neuropharmacology
STEPHENSON, F. A., Pharmaceutical and Biological Chemistry

University College London

Gower St, London, WC1E 6BT
Telephone: (171) 387-7050
Fax: (171) 387-8057

Founded 1826; merged with Royal Free Hospital School of Medicine 1998

Provost: Sir DEREK ROBERTS (until April 1999), Prof. CHRIS LLEWELLYN SMITH (from April 1999)
Vice-Provosts: M. J. GALLYER (Finance, Personnel and Estates), Prof. J. J. JOWELL (Head of Graduate School), Prof. J. R. PATTISON (Dean of Medical School), D. V. BOWLES, Prof. F. W. BULLOCK, Prof. J. E. MIDWINTER
Registrar: M. H. BUTCHER
Library: see Libraries
Number of teachers: 1,437
Number of students: 13,487

Publications: *Undergraduate Prospectus, Graduate School Prospectus, UCL Universe, The World of UCL.*

DEANS

Faculty of Arts: Prof. M. J. WORTON
Faculty of Social and Historical Sciences: Prof. H. D. CLOUT
Faculty of Mathematical and Physical Sciences: Prof. A. R. LORD
Faculty of Laws: Prof. D. OLIVER
Faculty of Engineering: Prof. R. COLLINS
Faculty of Clinical Sciences: Prof. Sir JOHN PATTISON
Faculty of Life Sciences: Prof. A. R. LIEBERMAN
Faculty of Environmental Studies: Prof. P. E. O'SULLIVAN
Royal Free and University College Medical School: A. J. ZUCKERMAN

PROFESSORS

ADAMS, J. G. U., Geography
ADINOLFI, M., Biology
ADLER, M. W., Sexually Transmitted Diseases
AGHION, P., Economics
AICARDI, J., Child Health
AIELLO, L. C., Anthropology
AIKEN, J., Fine Art
ALI, Y. S., Orthopaedics
ALLSOP, R. E., Transport Studies
ANDERSON, D., Economics
ANDERSON, J. M., Mathematics
ANDREWS, D. J., Mechanical Engineering
ANDREWS, J., Architecture
AQUILECCHIA, G., Italian
ASHMORE, J. F., Physiology
ASHTON, R. D., English
ATKINSON, J., Psychology
ATTANASIO, O. P., Economics
ATTWELL, D. I., Physiology
AUDLEY, R. J., Psychology
AYNSLEY-GREEN, A., Child Health
BALL, K. M., Mathematics
BANISTER, D. J., Architecture
BANKS, B. E. C., Physiology
BANNER, F. T., Geological Sciences
BARENDT, E. M., Law
BARKER, J. A., Geological Sciences
BARLOW, M. J., Physics and Astronomy
BARNARD, E., Molecular Neurobiology
BARNES, M. P., Scandinavian Studies
BARRATT, T. M., Child Health
BATTARBEE, R. W., Geography
BATTY, J. M., Advanced Spatial Analysis
BATTY, M., Geography
BAUM, M., Surgery
BEACH, D., Child Health
BEBBINGTON, P. E., Psychiatry and Behavioural Sciences
BEDI, R., Eastman Dental Institute
BEGENT, R. H. J., Oncology
BELLAIRS, R., Anatomy and Developmental Biology
BENTLEY, G. R., Orthopaedic Surgery
BERGER, M. A., Mathematics
BERRY, R. J., Biology
BETTERIDGE, D. J., Medicine
BEVERLEY, P. C. L., Tumour Immunology
BHATTACHARYA, S. S., Ophthalmology
BINDMAN, D., History of Art
BIRD, A. C., Ophthalmology
BIRKS, H. J. B., Geography
BLACK, C., Rheumatology
BOLSOVER, N. R., Physiology
BOSTOCK, H., Neurology
BOULDS, P. B., Surgery
BOWMAKER, J., Visual Research
BOWN, S. G., Laser Medicine and Surgery
BOYD, I. W., Electronic Materials
BOYDE, A., Mineralised Tissue Biology
BRABEN, D. W., Geological Sciences
BRADDICK, O. J., Psychology
BRAY, W. M., Latin American Archaeology
BRISLEY, S., Fine Art
BROOK, C. D. G., Paediatric Endocrinology
BROOME, D. R., Mechanical Engineering
BROSTOFF, J., Immunology
BROWN, D. A., Pharmacology
BROWN, E. H., Geography
BROWN, S. N., Mathematics
BRUCKDORFER, R., Biochemistry and Molecular Biology
BUDD, M. J., Philosophy
BUNKER, J. P., Epidemiology and Public Health Medicine
BURGESS, A. R., Chemical and Biochemical Engineering
BURK, K. M., Modern and Contemporary History
BURNHAM, P. C., Anthropology
BURNSTOCK, G., Anatomy
BUTLER, W. E., Comparative Law
BUTTERWORTH, B. L., Cognitive Neuropsychology
BUXTON, B. F., Information Processing
CADMAN, D., Public Policy
CALLARD, R., Child Health
CALLOMON, J. H., Chemistry
CAMPBELL, J. A., Computer Science
CAMPBELL, P. N., Biochemistry
CAMPBELL, R., Human Communication Science
CHAIN, B. M., Immunology
CHARLES, I. G., Cruciform Project
CLARK, J. B., Neurology
CLARK, R. J. H., Chemistry
CLARY, D., Chemistry
CLOUT, H. D., Geography
COCKCROFT, S., Cell Physiology
COHEN, B., Fine Art
COHN, P. M., Mathematics
COLE, R. S., Electrical Engineering
COLLINS, M. K. L., Immunology
COLLINS, P. M., Chemistry
COLLINS, R., Mechanical Engineering
COLQUHOUN, D., Pharmacology
CONTRERAS, M., Transfusion Medicine
COOK, P. F. C., Architecture
COOKE, B. A., Endocrine Biochemistry
COPP, A., Child Health
CORNISH, A. R. H., Chemical Engineering
CRAWFORD, M. H., Ancient History
CROLL, J. G. A., Civil and Environmental Engineering
CROSS, P. A., Geomatic Engineering
CROWCROFT, J. A., Networked Systems
CULHANE, J. L., Space and Climate Physics
CULL-CANDY, S. G., Pharmacology
CULLEN, A. L., Electronic and Electrical Engineering
CURZON, G., Neurology
CUZNER, M. L., Neurology
DALE, P. F., Geomatic Engineering
DANPURE, C. J., Biology
DAVIDSON, B. R., Surgery
DAVIES, A. G., Chemistry
DAVIES, J. B., Electrical Engineering
DAVIES, W. E., History
DAVIS, D. H., Physics
D'AVRAY, D. L., History
DAWID, A. P., Statistics
DEAN, M. C., Anatomy and Developmental Biology
DEEMING, A. J., Chemistry
DELHANTY, J. D. A., Biology
DELPY, D. T., Medical Photonics

DENNIS, I. H., English Law
DENZA, E., Law
DI BISCEGLIE, M., Electronic and Electrical Engineering
DICKENSON, A. H., Neuropharmacology
DOLAN, R., Neuropsychiatry
DOLPHIN, A., Pharmacology
DONOVAN, D. T., Geological Sciences
DOVER, W. D., Mechanical Engineering
DOWD, P. M., Medicine
DOWMAN, I. J., Photogrammetry and Remote Sensing
DREWRY, G., Law
DU BOULAY, E. P. G. H., Neurology
DUFF, M. J. B., Applied Physics
DUNNILL, P., Biochemical Engineering
DUSHEIKO, G. M., Medicine
EDWARDS, J. C., Medicine
EDWARDS, Y. H., Biology
EKINS, R. P., Molecular Endocrinology
ELL, P. J., Nuclear Medicine
ELLISON, M., Architecture
ELTON, L., Higher Education
EVANS, A. W., Transport Safety
EVANS, M. C. W., Plant Chemistry
FABRE, J., Child Health
FALLOWFIELD, L., Oncology
FAREWELL, V. T., Medical Statistics
FERGUSSON-PELL, M., Neuromuscular Restoration and Rehabilitation
FINE, L. G., Medicine
FINKELSTEIN, A. C. W., Computer Science
FINNEY, J. L., Physics
FITZGERALD, M., Developmental Neurobiology
FLINT, C. D., Chemistry
FONAGY, P., Psychoanalysis
FOOTE, P. G., Scandinavian Studies
FOREMAN, J. C., Immunopharmacology
FOURCIN, A. J., Phonetics
FRACKOWIAK, R. S. J., Neurology
FREEMAN, M. D. A., English Law
FRENCH, D. W., History
FRITH, C. D., Neurology
FRITH, C. D., Psychology
FRITH, U., Cognitive Development
FRY, C. H., Cellular Physiology
FULBROOK, M. J. A., German History
FULLER, J. H., Public Health
FURNHAM, A. F., Psychology
GABELLA, G., Histology and Cytology
GADIAN, D., Neurology
GADIAN, D., Child Health
GALIS, A., Electronic and Electrical Engineering
GALLIVAN, S., Statistical Science
GANELLIN, C. R., Medicinal Chemistry
GARCIA, A. M., Hispanic Studies
GARDINER, R. M., Paediatrics
GARRATT, P. J., Chemistry
GARTHWAITE, J., Experimental Neuroscience
GELLER, M. J., Semitic Languages
GENN, H. G., Socio-Legal Studies
GIBILARO, L. G., Chemical and Biochemical Engineering
GILBERT, A. G., Geography
GLICKSTEIN, M., Neuroscience
GOLDSPINK, G., Anatomy and Developmental Biology
GOMPERTS, B. D., Physiology
GOODWIN, P. B., Transport Studies
GOSWAMI, U., Child Health
GRAHAM-CAMPBELL, J. A., Medieval Archaeology
GRASS, A. J., Fluid Mechanics
GREEN, R., Anatomy and Developmental Biology
GREGORY, J., Water Chemistry
GRIEVE, D., Human Performance
GRIFFITHS, H. D., Electronics
GRIFFITHS, P. D., Virology
GROSSMAN, S., Mathematics
GUEST, J. E., Planetary Science
GUILLEBAUD, J., Family Planning and Reproductive Health
GURLING, H. M., Psychiatry
HAINES, A. P., Primary Health Care

HALE, K. J., Chemistry
HALL, A., Molecular Biology
HALL, P. G., Planning
HAMBLETON, K. G., Defence Engineering
HAMILTON-MILLER, J. W. T., Medical Microbiology
HANNOOSH, M., French
HANSON, M., Fetal and Neonatal Physiology
HARRIS, D. R., Archaeology
HARRIS, M., Dentistry
HARRIS, N., Development Planning
HARRIS, R., Geography
HARRISON, M. J. G., Clinical Neurology
HARTLEY, J. A., Oncology
HASSAN, F. A., Archaeology
HATCH, D., Child Health
HATTORI, T., Computer Science
HAWLEY, C., Architectural Studies
HAWORTH, S. G., Child Health
HENDERSON, B., Dentistry
HENDERSON, P., Geological Sciences
HEPHER, D., Fine Art
HERMANS, T. J., Dutch and Comparative Literature
HILLIER, W. R. G., Architectural and Urban Morphology
HOARE, M., Biochemical Engineering
HOBSLEY, M., Surgery
HOBSON, R. P., Developmental Psychopathology
HOCKING, L. M., Mathematics
HOLDER, N. H. K., Anatomy and Developmental Biology
HOMEWOOD, K. M., Anthropology
HONDERICH, E. D. R., Philosophy of Mind and Logic
HOPKINS, C. R., Molecular Cell Biology
HOPKINSON, D., Biochemical Genetics
HORTON, M. A., Bone Biology and Mineral Metabolism
HORWICH, P., Philosophy
HOWARTH, I. D., Astronomy
HOWARTH, R. J., Geological Sciences
HOWELL, P., Experimental Psychology
HUDSON, R. A., Linguistics
HUMPHRIES, S. E., Cardiovascular Genetics
HUNT, D. M., Ophthalmology
HYAMS, J. S., Cell Biology
INGRAM, D., Health Informatics
ISAACSON, P. G., Morbid Anatomy
ISENBERG, D. A., Rheumatology
ISHAM, V. S., Probability and Statistics
ISRAEL, J. I., Dutch History and Institutions
IVES, K. J., Civil and Environmental Engineering
JACOBS, H. S., Reproductive Endocrinology
JANKO, R. C. M., Greek
JANOSSY, G., Clinical Immunology
JAYNE, J. E., Mathematics
JEHIEL, P., Economics
JENKINSON, D. H., Pharmacology
JESSEN, K. R., Developmental Neurobiology
JOHNSON, E. R., Mathematics
JOHNSON, G. J., Preventive Ophthalmology
JOHNSTONE, A. D., Space Science
JONES, A. G., Chemical Engineering
JONES, J. S., Genetics
JONES, S. J., Anatomy
JONES, T. W., Physics
JOWELL, J. L., Public Law
JUDAH, J. D., Physiology
KAPFERER, B., Anthropology
KARLIN, D. R., English
KARTUN-BLUM, R., Hebrew and Jewish Studies
KATONA, C. L. E., Psychiatry of the Elderly
KATZ, Sir BERNARD, Physiology
KATZ, D. R., Immunology
KEMP, D. T., Auditory Biophysics
KENNEDY, I. M., Public Policy
KETTERER, B., Oncology
KING, M., Psychiatry
KIRSTEIN, P. T., Computer Systems
KLIER, J. D., Hebrew and Jewish Studies
KORAH, V., Law
KUHRT, A. T. L., History

KULKA, R., Biochemistry and Molecular Biology
LAKE, B., Child Health
LANDON, D. N., Neurology
LARMAN, D. G., Mathematics
LAST, D. M., Anthropology
LATCHMAN, D. S., Molecular Pathology
LAURENT, G. J., Pulmonary Biochemistry
LAVERS, A. C. M., French Language and Literature
LEE, C., Haemophilia
LEMON, R. N., Neurology
LEONARD, J., Child Health
LEPSCHY, A. L. M., Italian
LEVINSKY, R. J., Child Health
LIEBERMAN, A. R., Anatomy
LIGHTMAN, S., Ophthalmology
LILLY, M. D., Biochemical Engineering
LIM, L., Neurology
LINCH, D. C., Clinical Haematology
LINDON, J. C., Chemistry
LINDON, J. M. A., Italian
LITTLEWOOD, R., Anthropological Psychiatry
LONG, J. B., Cognitive Ergonomics
LORD, A. R., Micropalaeontology
LOWENTHAL, D., Geography
LUCAS, A., Child Health
LUND, J., Visual Research
LUND, R., Ophthalmology
LUND, V. J., Rhinology
LUTHERT, P. J., Ophthalmology
LUXON, L. M., Audiological Medicine
LYDYARD, P. M., Immunology
MACHIN, S. J., Haematology
MACKETT, R. L., Transport Studies
MACKINTOSH, I., Technical Innovation
MACLEAN, A. B., Obstetrics and Gynaecology
MADRIGAL, A., Haematology
MAEHLER, H. G. T., Papyrology
MALCOLM, S., Child Health
MALONE-LEE, J. G., Geriatric Medicine
MANDLER, G., Psychology
MANNERS, G., Geography
MARMOT, M. G., Epidemiology and Public Health
MARSDEN, C. D., Neurology
MARTIN, B. R. C., Physics
MARTIN, J. F., Cruciform Project
MASON, K. O., Astronomy
MASON, M. Y., English
MATHEWS, T. P., French
MCAUSLAN, J. P. W. B., Urban Management
MCCARTHY, M., Epidemiology and Public Health
MCDONALD, W. I., Neurology
MCGREGOR, S., Child Health
MCGROUTHER, D. A., Plastic and Reconstructive Surgery
MCGUIRE, W. J., Geological Sciences
MCILWAINE, I. C., Library, Archive and Information Studies
MCINTYRE, N., Medicine
MCKENDRICK, E. G., English Law
MCLEAN, A. E. M., Toxicology
MCLEAN, P., Fine Art
MCMANUS, I. C., Psychology
MCMULLEN, P., Mathematics
MEAD, W. R., Geography
MENDELSOHN, M. H., International Law
MEREDITH, P. G., Rock Physics
MERRIMAN, N. J., Archaeology
MICHAEL, D. H., Mathematics
MICHAELS, L., Histopathology
MIDWINTER, J. E., Electrical Engineering
MILLER, A. I., History and Philosophy of Science
MILLER, D. H., Neurology
MILLER, D. J., Physics
MILLER, K. F. C., English
MIRSKY, R., Neurobiology
MJOS, O. D., Cardiology
MODELL, C. B., Community Genetics
MODELL, M., Primary Health Care
MONCADA, S., Experimental Biology and Therapeutics
MONK, M., Child Health

MORGAN, M. J., Visual Psychophysics
MORTON, J., Cognitive Development
MOSS, J., Medical Physics and Bioengineering
MOTHERWELL, W. B., Chemistry
MULLER, J.-P. A. L., Image Understanding and Remote Sensing
MULLIN, J. W., Chemical and Biochemical Engineering
MUNDY, A. R., Urology
MUNTON, R. J. C., Geography
MURRELL, S. A. F., Geological Sciences
NAHAPIET, H., Architecture
NEILD, G. H., Nephrology
NEVILLE, B., Child Health
NEWMAN, H. N., Dentistry
NEWMAN, S. P., Health Psychology
NICHOLSON, J. K., Chemistry
NORTH, J. A., History
NUTT, B. B., Facility and Environment Management
O'DALY, G. J. P., Latin
O'KEEFE, J., Cognitive Neuroscience
O'KEEFFE, D., European Law
O'NEILL, M. E., Mathematics
O'REILLY, J. J., Telecommunications
O'RIORDAN, J. L. H., Metabolic Medicine
O'SULLIVAN, P. E., Environmental Engineering and Design
ODA, H., Japanese Law
OKA, T., Economics
OLIVER, A. D. H., Constitutional Law
ORDIDGE, R. J., Medical Physics
PALMER, N. E., Commercial Law
PARNAVELAS, J. G., Neuroanatomy
PARRY, M. L., Geography
PARTRIDGE, L., Biometry
PATEL, M. H., Mechanical Engineering
PATTISON, Sir JOHN, Medical Microbiology
PEARCE, D. W., Economics
PEARCE, F. L., Biological Chemistry
PEARL, L. H., Biochemistry and Molecular Biology
PEARSON, G. J., Dentistry
PECKHAM, C., Child Health
PECKHAM, Sir MICHAEL J., Public Policy
PEMBREY, M., Child Health
PHILLIPS, A., Epidemiology and Biostatistics
PITT, C. W., Electrical Engineering
PLATT, J. P., Geology
PLOTKIN, H. C., Psychology
PORAKISHVILI, N., Immunology
PORTER, S. R., Dentistry
POULTER, L. W., Clinical Immunology
POUNDER, R. E., Medicine
POVEY, M. S., Human Somatic Cell Genetics
POWELL, K., Virology and Cell Biology
POWER, E. A., Mathematics
POWIS, S., Nephrology
PREECE, M., Child Health
PREISS, D., Pure Mathematics
PRENTICE, H. G., Haematological Oncology
PRICE, G. D., Mineral Physics
PRICHARD, B. N. C., Clinical Pharmacology
QUINN, N. P., Neurology
QUIRK, Lord RANDOLPH., English
RADEMACHER, T. W., Molecular Medicine
RAFF, M. C., Molecular Cell Biology
RANG, H. P., Pharmacology
RAWSON, P. F., Geology
REVELL, P. A., Histopathology
REYNOLDS, E. O. R., Neonatal Paediatrics
RICH, P. R., Biology
RICHARDSON, W. D., Molecular Cell Biology
RICHMOND, Sir MARK H., Public Policy
RIDD, J. H., Chemistry
RIDEOUT, R. W., Labour Law
RILEY, P. A., Cell Pathology
RISDON, R. A., Child Health
ROBERTS, G. J., Dentistry
RODECK, C. H., Obstetrics and Gynaecology
ROITT, I. M., Immunology
RON, A., Physics and Astronomy
RON, M. A., Neurology
ROOK, G. A. W., Medical Microbiology
ROSEN, F. R., History of Political Thought
ROSEN, S., Speech and Hearing Sciences
ROSNER, R. A., Education and Information Support
ROSSER, R., Psychiatry
ROTHENBERG, B., Archaeology
ROWBURY, R. J., Microbiology
ROWLANDS, M. J. J., Anthropology
RUGG, M., Neurology
SAGGERSON, E. D., Biochemistry
SALT, J., Geography
SALVERDA, R., Dutch Language and Literature
SAMET, P. A., Computer Science
SANDLER, J., Psychology
SAYERS, J. E., Archive Studies
SCAMBLER, P., Child Health
SCARAVILLI, F., Neurology
SCHAPIRA, A. H. V., Neurology
SCULLY, C., Dentistry
SEATON, M. J., Astronomy
SEEDS, A. J., Opto-Electronics
SEGAL, A. W., Medicine
SENN, S. J., Pharmaceutical and Health Statistics
SHALLICE, T., Psychology
SHARPE, A., Mechanical Engineering
SHARPLES, R. W., Classics
SHEIHAM, A., Dental Public Health
SHENNAN, S. J., Theoretical Archaeology
SHEPHARD, E. A., Biochemistry and Molecular Biology
SHORVON, S. D., Neurology
SILLITO, A. M., Visual Science
SINGER, A., Gynaecological Research
SLATER, M., Computer Science
SMITH, C. A. B., Biology
SMITH, F. T., Applied Mathematics
SMITH, N. V., Linguistics
SMITH, S. R., Economics
SOUHAMI, R. L., Clinical Oncology
SOUTHGATE, L. J., Primary Care and Education
SPEIGHT, P. M., Dentistry
SPITZ, L., Child Health
SPYER, K. M., Physiology
STANFORD, J., Bacteriology
STEIN, A., Child and Family Mental Health
STEPHENS, J. A., Physiology
STONEHAM, A. M., Physics
STROBEL, S., Child Health
SUTHERLAND, J. A., Modern English Literature
SWALES, M. W., German
SWALLOW, D. M., Biology
SWANN, P. F., Biochemistry and Molecular Biology
SWANSON, T. M., Economics
TAIT, W. J., Egyptology
TALLANDINI-SHALLICE, M., Psychology
TAYLOR, B., Community Child Health
TAYLOR, I., Surgery
TEDDER, R. S., Medical Virology
TENNYSON, J., Physics
THOMAS, D. G. T., Neurology
THOMPSON, E. J., Neurology
THOMPSON, J. M. T., Nonlinear Dynamics
THORNTON, J. M., Biomolecular Structure
THOROGOOD, P., Child Health
TICKLE, C. A., Developmental Biology
TILLEY, C. Y., Anthropology
TODD, C. J., Network Science
TODD-POKROPEK, A. E., Medical Physics
TOMKINS, A., Child Health
TRELEAVEN, P. C., Computer Science
TRIMBLE, M. R., Neurology
TROTTER, W. D., English Language and Literature
TRUTER, M. R., Chemistry
TURNER, M., Child Health
TURNER, M. K., Biochemical Engineering
TURNER, R., Anthropology
TWINING, W. L., Jurisprudence
UCKO, P. J., Comparative Archaeology
UNWIN, R., Urology and Nephrology
VALLANCE, P., Clinical Pharmacology and Therapeutics
VERGANI, D., Hepatology
VITA-FINZI, C., Neotectonics
VRBOVA, G., Anatomy and Developmental Biology
WADSWORTH, M. E. J., Health and Development
WAKELY, P. I., Urban Development
WALKER, P. S., Biomedical Engineering
WALKER-SMITH, J., Paediatric Gastroenterology
WALLACE, P., Primary Health Care
WALLMAN, S. S., Anthropology
WARD, K. E., Electronic and Electrical Engineering
WARDLE, J., Epidemiology and Public Health
WARNER, A. E., Developmental Biology
WARREN, A., Geography
WATERFIELD, M. D., Biochemistry
WELLER, I. V. D., Genito-Urinary Medicine
WELLS, J. C., Phonetics
WHARTON, B. A., Child Health
WHELAN, H., History
WHITE, R. E., Geology
WILBUR, S. R., Distributed Systems
WILKES, J. J., Greek and Roman Archaeology
WILKIE, D., Biology
WILKIN, C., Physics
WILLIAMS, D. A., Astronomy
WILLIAMS, D. E., Chemistry
WILLIAMS, J. G., Molecular Cell Biology
WILLIAMS, R. S., Hepatology
WILLIS, A. J., Astronomy
WILSON, D. S. M., Linguistics
WILSON, M., Dentistry
WILSON, M. G. F., Electrical Engineering
WINCHESTER, B., Child Health
WINDER, A. F., Chemical Pathology
WINGHAM, D. J., Space and Climate Physics
WINSLET, M. C., Surgery
WINTER, R., Child Health
WOLEDGE, R. C., Experimental Physiology
WOLPERT, L., Biology as applied to Medicine
WOO, P., Paediatric Rheumatology
WOO, PATRICIA, Molecular Pathology
WOOD, P. A., Geography
WOOLF, N., Histopathology
WORTON, M. J., French
WOUDHUYSEN, H. R., English
WRIGHT, A., Otorhinolaryngology
WRONG, O. M., Medicine
WYATT, J. S., Paediatrics
YAARI, M. E., Economics
YATES, J. G., Chemical Engineering
YELLON, D. M., Cellular Cardiology
YUDKIN, J. S., Medicine
ZEITLIN, H. M., Child Adolescent and Family Psychiatry
ZEKI, S. L. S., Anatomy and Developmental Biology
ZUCKERMAN, A. J., Medical Microbiology

INSTITUTES OF THE COLLEGE

Centre for Allergy Research and Environmental Health: Dir Prof. JONATHAN BROSTOFF.

Institute of Child Health: 30 Guilford St, London, WC1N 1EH; tel. (171) 242-9789; is the Medical School of the Hospitals for Sick Children, Great Ormond Street, and the Queen Elizabeth Hospital for Children, Hackney Road; Dean Prof. R. J. LEVINSKY; Sec. I. R. MIDDLETON.

Institute of Neurology: The National Hospital, Queen Square, London, WC1N 3BG; tel. (171) 837-3611; library of 16,000 vols; Dean Prof. D. N. LANDON; Sec. R. P. WALKER; publ. *Annual Report*.

Institute of Ophthalmology: Bath Street, London, EC1V 9EL; tel. (171) 608-6800; (associated with Moorfields Eye Hospital); f. 1947; postgraduate teaching and research in eye disease and prevention of blindness; library of 13,000 vols; Dir of Research and Teaching Prof. A. M. SILLITO; Sec. CHRISTINE GRIFFITHS; publ. *Annual Report*.

ASSOCIATED INSTITUTE

Eastman Dental Institute: Eastman Dental Hospital, Gray's Inn Rd, London, WC1X 8LD;

tel. (171) 915-1000; fax (171) 915-1012; Dean Prof. C. B. A. SCULLY; Sec. R. N. TAYLOR.

Wye College

Wye, Ashford, Kent, TN25 5AH
Telephone: (1233) 812401
Fax: (1233) 813320
E-mail: registry@wyeac.uk

Founded 1447, a School of the Univ. of London since 1900

Undergraduate, postgraduate, distance learning and continuing professional development, in business management and marketing, biological sciences, the environment, rural development, and horticulture and agriculture

Principal: Prof. J. H. D. PRESCOTT
Director: T. M. QUIRKE
Academic Registrar: N. EVANS
Librarian: E. MARY LUCAS

Library of 35,000 vols
Number of teachers: 70
Number of students: 800

Publications: *Undergraduate Prospectus*, *Postgraduate Prospectus*, *Departmental and External Programme Guides*, *Principal's Annual Report*, *Wye World*, *Research Interests*, *Research Co-operation*.

PROFESSORS

BAKER, D. A., Agricultural Botany
BLATT, M., Plant Physiology and Biophysics
BUCKWELL, A. E., Agricultural Economics
GILLER, K., Soil Microbiology
GREEN, B. H., Countryside Management
HUGHES, D. R., Agribusiness Management and Marketing
LEAVER, J. D., Agriculture
MANSFIELD, J. W., Plant Pathology
PRESCOTT, J. H. D., Animal Production
RUSSELL, N. J., Food Microbiology
SWINBURNE, T. R., Horticultural Development
WEBSTER, J. P. G., Agricultural Business Management

ATTACHED INSTITUTES

Centre for European Agricultural Studies Ltd.
Biological Crop Protection Ltd.
Natural Resources Institute.
Horticulture Research International–Hop Research Unit.

UNIVERSITY INSTITUTES

British Institute in Paris

11 rue de Constantine, 75340 Paris Cedex 07
Premises at: University of London, Senate House, London, WC1E 7HU
Telephone: (1) 44-11-73-73 (Paris); (171) 862-8656 (London)
Fax: (1) 45-50-31-55
E-mail: campos@ext.jussieu.fr

Founded in 1894 as 'Guilde Franco-Anglaise', attached to University of Paris 1927, now an inst. of advanced study of University of London

Director: Prof. C. L. CAMPOS
Head of French Department: Dr E. WILLIAMSON
Head of English Department: Dr S. FOSTER-COHEN
Administrative Officer: S. STONE
London Secretary: CHRISTINE BUCHANAN

Centre for Defence Studies

King's College London, Strand, London, WC2R 2LS
Telephone: (171) 873-2338
Fax: (171) 873-2748

Founded 1990

Provides a focus for academic research in the fields of defence and security studies

Executive Director: M. CLARKE

PROFESSORS

CLARKE, M., Defence Studies
FREEDMAN, L., War Studies

Courtauld Institute of Art

Somerset House, Strand, London, WC2R ORN
Telephone: (171) 873-2777
Fax: (171) 873-2657

Founded 1932

Undergraduate and postgraduate courses in the history of Western art; diploma courses in conservation of paintings, textiles and wall paintings, and the history of art; MA degree course in History of Art

Director: Prof. E. C. FERNIE
Secretary and Registrar: J. A. HEARNSHAW
Academic Registrar: Dr R. J. WALKER
Librarian: Dr S. PRICE

Number of teachers: 27
Number of students: 322 full-time, 78 part-time

Publication: *Journal of the Warburg and Courtauld Institutes* (annually).

PROFESSORS

CORMACK, R., History of Art
FERNIE, E. C., History of Art
GREEN, C., History of Art
HOUSE, J., History of Art

School of Slavonic and East European Studies

University of London, London, WC1E 7HU
Telephone: (171) 636-8000

Founded 1915

Director: Prof. M. A. BRANCH
Clerk to the Council: M. WIDDOWSON
Academic Registrar: CAROL PEARCE

Number of teachers: 60
Number of students: 460 full-time, 40 part-time

Publication: *The Slavonic and East European Review* (quarterly).

University Marine Biological Station Millport

Millport, Isle of Cumbrae, Scotland, KA28 0EG
Telephone: (1475) 530581
Fax: (1475) 530601
E-mail: j.davenport@udcf.gla.ac.uk

Founded 1970 in assen with Univ. of Glasgow for teaching and research in marine biology

Director: Prof. J. DAVENPORT

PROFESSORS

DAVENPORT, J., Marine Biology
MOORE, P. G., Marine Biology

CONSTITUENT INSTITUTES OF THE SCHOOL OF ADVANCED STUDY

Dean of the School of Advanced Study: Prof. T. C. DAINTITH

Institute of Advanced Legal Studies

Charles Clore House, 17 Russell Sq., London, WC1B 5DR
Telephone: (171) 637-1731
Fax: (171) 580-9613

Founded 1947

Provides a centre for postgraduate legal studies, professional legal education and legal research

Director: Prof. B. A. K. RIDER
Administrative Secretary: D. E. PHILLIPS
Library: see Libraries

Publications: *IALS Bulletin* (3 a year), *IALS Working Papers*, *Annual Report*.

PROFESSORS

DAINTITH, T. C., EU Law, Public Law, Energy and Natural Resources Law
RIDER, B. A. K., Company Law, Commercial Criminal Law
SHERR, A. S., Legal Education, the Legal Profession

Institute of Classical Studies

Senate House, London, WC1E 7HU
Telephone: (171) 636-8000
Fax: (171) 636-5841

Founded 1953

Director: Prof. R. R. K. SORABJI
Secretary: MARGARET PACKER

Library of basic research books complemented by the library of the Hellenic and Roman Societies (joint library of 90,000 volumes); research courses and seminars held for postgraduate students

Publications: *Bulletin* (annually), *Bulletin Supplements*.

Institute of Commonwealth Studies

28 Russell Sq., London, WC1B 5DS
Telephone: (171) 262-8844
Fax: (171) 262-8820

Founded 1949; for postgraduate research in social sciences and recent history relating to the Commonwealth

Director: Prof. P. CAPLAN
Administrative Secretary: Mrs R. M. KOCHANOWSKA
Librarian: D. S. BLAKE

Library of 17,000 vols

ATTACHED INSTITUTE

Sir Robert Menzies Centre for Australian Studies: Head Prof. C. R. BRIDGE.

Institute of Germanic Studies

29 Russell Sq., London, WC1B 5DP
Telephone: (171) 580-2711
Fax: (171) 436-3497
E-mail: igs@sas.ac.uk

Founded 1950 for advanced study and research

Director: (vacant)
Deputy Director: Prof. J. L. FLOOD
Secretary: KARIN HELLMER
Librarian: W. ABBEY

Number of members: 1,303
Library of 87,000 vols

Publications: *Annual Report*, *Research in Germanic Studies at British Universities* (annually), *Publications* (monograph series), *Bithell Series of Dissertations*, *Bithell Memorial Lectures*.

Institute of Historical Research

Senate House, London, WC1E 7HU
Telephone: (171) 862-8740
Fax: (171) 862-8811
E-mail: ihr@sas.ac.uk

Founded 1921 as the University's centre for postgraduate study in history, it is also a national and int. meeting place for scholars of history and related disciplines

Director: Prof. DAVID CANNADINE
Secretary: Dr STEVEN R. B. SMITH

Library: see Libraries

Publications: *Annual Report*, *Historical Research Bulletin*, *Historical Research for Higher Degrees in the United Kingdom*, etc.

Institute of Latin American Studies

31 Tavistock Sq., London, WC1H 9HA

Telephone: (171) 387-5671
Fax: (171) 388-5024

Founded 1965 to promote Latin American studies at graduate level and to provide for discussion and collaboration between members of the University and other interested persons

Director: Prof. J. DUNKELLEY
Secretary: A. BELL
Librarian: A. BIGGINS

Publications: *Latin American Monographs*, *Research Papers*, *Information on Latin American and Caribbean Studies in the UK*.

PROFESSORS

BULMER-THOMAS, V., Economics
DUNKERLEY, J., Politics

Institute of Romance Studies

Senate House, Malet St, London WC1E 7HU

Telephone: (171) 636-8000, ext. 3054
Fax: (171) 436-4533

Founded 1989 to encourage scholarship and research in the field of Romance languages and literature, and for interdisciplinary discussion in the humanities

Director: Prof. J. LABANYI
Administrative Secretary: A. C. BUCKLE

Institute of United States Studies

Room 305, Senate House, Malet St, London, WC1E 7HU

Telephone: (171) 862-8693
Fax: (171) 862-8696
E-mail: iuss@sas.ac.uk

Founded 1965 to promote and co-ordinate graduate work in American studies in the University and to assist liaison between teachers of American studies in other universities

Director: Prof. GARY L. MCDOWELL

Warburg Institute

Woburn Sq., London, WC1H 0AB

Telephone: (171) 580-9663
Fax: (171) 436-2852
E-mail: warburg@sas.ac.uk

Founded 1921 for the study of cultural and intellectual history and the history of the classical tradition

Director: Prof. C. N. J. MANN
Secretary and Registrar: ANITA C. POLLARD
Librarian: W. F. RYAN

Number of teachers: 4
Number of students: 30

Library: see Libraries

Publications: *Studies* (monographs), *Journal of the Warburg and Courtauld Institutes*, *Corpus Platonicum Medii Aevi*, *Mediaeval and Renaissance Studies*, *Warburg Institute Surveys and Texts*, *Warburg Institute Colloquia*.

PROFESSORS

MANN, C. N. J., History of the Classical Tradition

ASSOCIATE INSTITUTIONS

The following institutions have recognized teachers of the University of London on their staffs and offer courses leading to degrees of the University.

Institute of Cancer Research: 17A Onslow Gardens, London, SW7 3AL; tel. (171) 352-8133; library of 25,000 vols; Chief Exec. Prof. P. B. GARLAND; Sec. J. M. KIPLING.

Jews' College: Schaller House, Albert Rd, Hendon, London, NW4 2SJ; tel. (181) 203-6427; Hebrew and Jewish studies; Dir Prof. D. H. RUBEN.

Royal Academy of Music: see under Colleges.

Royal College of Music: see under Colleges.

Trinity College of Music: see under Colleges.

LONDON GUILDHALL UNIVERSITY

31 Jewry St, London EC3N 2EY

Telephone: (171) 320-1000
Fax: (171) 320-3424

Founded 1970; university status 1992
Academic year: September to July

Provost: Prof. RODERICK FLOUD
Deputy Provost: MAX WEAVER
Academic Registrar: JILL GRINSTEAD
Director of Finance: NICHOLAS MAUDE
Head of Academic Services: MAUREEN CASTENS

Number of teachers: 345 full-time, 400 part-time

Number of students: 15,000 (incl. part-time)

Publications: *Undergraduate Prospectus* (annually), *Postgraduate Prospectus* (annually).

HEADS OF DEPARTMENTS

Accounting and Financial Services: F. SMITH
Art, Design, Silversmithing, Jewellery and Communications: M. A. HUNT
Business Studies: B. GREENHILL
Civil Aviation Studies: D. BARBOUR
Computing and Information Systems: J. T. NAYLOR
Economics: Prof. G. HADJIMATHEOU
Furniture and Interiors, and Musical Instrument Technology: P. COYLE
Language Services Centre: D. FALVEY
Language Studies: C. OSTMANN
Law: F. WEBB
Management and Professional Development: S. PROUDFOOT
Politics and Modern History: Dr I. W. MORGAN
Psychology: Prof. S. MILLAR
Sociology and Applied Social Studies: Prof. J. GABRIEL

LOUGHBOROUGH UNIVERSITY

Loughborough, Leics., LE11 3TU

Telephone: (1509) 263171
Fax: (1509) 223901

Formerly Loughborough College of Advanced Technology; University Charter 1966

Academic year: September to June

Chancellor: Sir DENIS ROOKE
Senior Pro-Chancellor: S. C. MILLER
Pro-Chancellor: J. K. GREEN
Vice-Chancellor: Prof. DAVID WALLACE
Senior Pro-Vice-Chancellor: Prof. R. MCCAFFER
Pro-Vice-Chancellors: Prof. J. P. FEATHER, Prof. C. WILLIAMS, Prof. H. THOMASON
Registrar: D. E. FLETCHER
Librarian: MARY MORLEY

Library of 600,000 vols
Number of teachers: 552
Number of students: 10,506

Publications: *Calendar*, *Undergraduate Prospectus*, *Postgraduate Prospectus*, *Annual Report*.

DEANS

Faculty of Engineering: Prof. N. A. HALLIWELL
Faculty of Science: Prof. J. V. DAWKINS
Faculty of Social Sciences and Humanities: Prof. I. C. MORISON

PROFESSORS

ALEXANDROV, A. S., Theoretical Physics
ALLEN, D., Management Studies (Industrial Professor)
ALTY, J. L., Computer Science
ASHFORD, N. J., Transport Planning
BABITSKY, V. I., Dynamics
BEAN, P. T., Criminology
BELL, R., Manufacturing Technology
BILLIG, M. G., Social Sciences
BROOKS, B. W., Chemical Engineering
BRYMAN, A E., Social Research
BUFFHAM, B. A., Chemical Engineering
BURNS, N. D., Manufacturing Systems
CALLOW, G., Aeronautical and Automotive Engineering and Transport Studies
CAMERON, H., Human Biology
CARPENTER, K. J., Chemical Engineering
CASE, K., Computer Aided Engineering
COX, S. J., Health and Safety Management
DAMODARAN, L., Participative Design and Change Management
DAWKINS, J. V., Polymer Chemistry
DIAMANTOPOULOS, A., Marketing and Business Research
EASON, K. D., Cognitive Ergonomics
EDMONDS, E. A., Computer Studies
EMMONY, D. C., Applied Optics
EVANS, J., Physical Education
EVANS, M., Information Studies
FAULKNER, R. G., Physical Metallurgy
FEATHER, J. P., Library and Information Studies
FINLAY, P. N., Strategic Information Systems
GABE, D., Materials Engineering
GALER-FLYTE, M. D., Vehicle Safety
GHARAVI, M., Communications Engineering
GOLDING, P., Sociology
GOODALL, R. M., Control Systems Engineering
GREEN, C. J., Banking and Finance
GRIFFITHS, J. B., Applied Mathematics
HALLIWELL, N. A., Optical Engineering
HANBY, V. I., Building Services Engineering
HANTRAIS, L., Modern Languages
HARGREAVES, A. G., French and Francophone Studies
HILL, M. R., Russian and East European Industrial Studies
HORNE, J. A., Psychophysiology
HOURSTON, D. J., Polymer Technology
HOWSON, R. P., Applied Physics
JONES, S. R., Electronic Systems Design
KALAWSKY, R. S., Human Computer Integration
KEARNEY, M. J., Electronic Device Engineering
KING, M., Management Sciences
LAWRENCE, P. A., International Management
LISTER, M. R. A., Social Policy
LLEWELLYN, D. T., Money and Banking
LUCAS, G. G., Automotive Engineering
MCCAFFER, R., Construction Management
MCGUIRK, J. J., Aerodynamics
MARPLES, B.A., Organic and Medicinal Chemistry
MEADOWS, A. J., Library and Information Studies
MILLER, J. N., Analytical Chemistry
MILLS, T. C., Economics
MORISON, I. C., Banking and Finance
PAGE, P., Organic Chemistry
PARKIN, R. M., Mechatronics
PARSONS, K. C., Environmental Ergonomics
PETERSSON, B. A. T., Structural Dynamics
PORTER, J. M., Design Ergonomics
POTTER, J. A., Discourse Analysis
PRESLEY, J. R., Economics

PRESTON, M. E., Engineering Design
RAOOF, M., Structural Engineering
REID, I., Physical Geography
REID, I., Education
ROBERTS, P. H., Design and Technology
SAUNDERS, J. A., Marketing
SCHRODER, H., Computing
SHAW, M., English
SLATER, D., Human Geography
SMITH, I. R., Electrical Power Engineering
SMITH, M., European Politics
SMITH, R., Mathematical Engineering
SMITH, R. M., Analytical Chemistry
SMITH, R. W., Applied Mathematics
STREAT, M., Chemical Engineering
TAYLOR, P. J., Geography
THOMASON, H., Physical Education and Recreation Science
THOMASON, H., External Relations
THORPE, A., Construction Information Technology
VESELOV, A. P., Mathematics
WAKEMAN, R. J., Chemical Engineering
WALKER, R. L., Social Policy Research
WALLACE, D. J.
WESTON, R. H., Flexible Automation
WEYMAN-JONES, T. G., Industrial Economics
WHEATLEY, A. D., Water Technology
WICKENS, A. H., Mechanical Engineering
WILKINSON, F., Physical Chemistry
WILLIAMS, C., Sports Science
WILLIAMS, D. J., Manufacturing Processes
WILSON, R. M. S., Business Administration and Financial Management
WOODWARD, B., Underwater Acoustics
WOOLLINS, J. D., Inorganic Chemistry
ZIEBECK, K. R. A., Physics

ATTACHED INSTITUTES

Institute of Polymer Technology and Materials Engineering: Dir Dr M. GILBERT.

Centre for Hazard and Risk Management: Dir Prof. S. J. COX.

Institute for Consumer Ergonomics: Dir M. E. PAGE.

Library and Information Statistics Unit: Dir D. SPILLER.

HUSAT (Human Sciences and Advanced Technology) Research Institute: Dir Prof. L. DAMODARAN.

Centre for Research in Social Policy: Dir Prof. R. L. WALKER.

Banking Centre: Dir J. B. HOWCROFT.

Computer-Human Interaction Research Centre: Dirs Prof. E. A. EDMONDS, Prof. J. L. ALTY.

Institute of Surface Science and Technology: Head Dr D. E. SYKES.

Parallel Algorithm Research Centre (PARC): Dir Prof. H. SCHRÖDER.

Midlands Centre for Criminology and Criminal Justice: Dir Prof. P. T. BEAN.

Communications Research Centre: Dirs Prof. M. BILLIG, Prof. P. GOLDING.

European Construction Institute: Chair. C. J. MARCHANT.

Institute of Development Engineering: Dir D. W. J. MILES.

Centre for Renewable Energy Systems Technology: Dir D. G. INFIELD.

UNIVERSITY OF LUTON

Park Square, Luton, Bedfordshire, LU1 3JU
Telephone: (1582) 734111
Fax: (1582) 418677
E-mail: elizabeth.slater@luton.ac.uk

Founded 1993; fmrly Luton College of Higher Education

Vice-Chancellor: Dr DAI JOHN
Pro-Vice-Chancellors: Prof. PAUL BIRCH, Prof. KATE ROBINSON
Registrar: RON DRIVER
Librarian: TIM STONE

Library of 200,000 vols
Number of teachers: 1,000
Number of students: 14,000

DEANS

Faculty of Health Care and Social Studies: Prof. KATE ROBINSON
Luton Business School: Dr STEPHEN PETTITT
Faculty of Science, Technology and Design: STEPHEN MORTIMER
Faculty of Humanities: TIM BOATSWAIN

UNIVERSITY OF MANCHESTER

Oxford Rd, Manchester, M13 9PL
Telephone: (161) 275-2000

Founded 1851 as Owens College, University Charter 1903

Academic year: September to June (2 semesters)

Chancellor: Prof. The Lord FLOWERS
Vice-Chancellor: Prof. M. B. HARRIS
Pro-Vice-Chancellors: Prof. HOWARD BARRINGER, Prof. KATHERINE PERERA, Prof. P. J. GUMMETT, Prof. N. H. F. WILSON
Registrar and Secretary: E. NEWCOMB
Academic Registrar: A. MCMENAMY
Librarian: C. J. HUNT

Library: see John Rylands University Library of Manchester

Number of teachers: 1,307 full-time
Number of students: 19,508 full-time

Publications: *Calendar*, *Undergraduate Prospectus*, *Postgraduate Courses*.

DEANS

Faculty of Arts: Prof. J. D. ELLSWORTH
Faculty of Business Administration: Prof. B. HARVEY
Faculty of Economic and Social Studies: Prof. M. J. MORAN
Faculty of Education: Prof. T. CHRISTIE
Faculty of Law: Prof. M. LOUGHLIN
Faculty of Medicine, Dentistry and Nursing: Prof. R. GREEN
Faculty of Science and Engineering: Prof. P. R. MEUDELL
Dental School: Prof. W. C. SHAW
School of Biological Sciences: Prof. A. P. J. TRINCI

PROFESSORS

(H = Head of Department)
(Some staff serve in more than one faculty)

Faculty of Arts:

ALEXANDER, P. S., Post-Biblical Jewish Literature
BAIN, D. M., Greek
BERGIN, J. A., History
BRADFORD, M. G., Geography
BROOKE, G. J., Biblical Studies
CASKEN, J., Music
CAUSEY, A. G., Art History
CORNELL, T. J., Ancient History
CROWLEY, A. E., Modern English Literature
CRUTTENDEN, A., Phonetics
DAVIES, C., Spanish
DENISON, D. M. B., English Linguistics
DICKEN, P., Geography (H)
DURRELL, M., German (H)
ELSWORTH, J. D., Russian Studies (H)
FALLOWS, D. N., Music
GATRELL, P. W., Economic History
HAMMOND, G., English Literature (H)
HANDLEY, J. F., Land and Restoration Management
HEALEY, J. F., Semitic Studies
HEBBERT, M. J., Town Planning
HOGG, R. M., English Language and Medieval English Literature
JACKSON, B. S., Modern Jewish Studies
JONES, G. D. B., Archaeology (H)
JOYCE, P., History
LAWRANCE, J. N. H., Spanish Studies (H)
LINDOP, G. C. G., Romantic and Early Victorian Studies
LING, R. J., Classical Art and Archaeology
O'GORMAN, F., History
PAILIN, D. A., Philosophy of Religion
PECK, J. A., Geography
PERERA, K. M., Educational Linguistics
PHILLIPS, J. H., French
POINTON, M. R., History of Art
PULLAN, B. S., Modern History
RICHARDS, K. R., Drama
ROBSON, B. T., Geography
SCRAGG, D. G., Anglo-Saxon Studies
STONEHOUSE, R. J., Architecture
SYMES, M. S., Urban Renewal
VINCENT, N. B., Comparative Philology
WETHERILL, P. M., French
WOOD, C. M., Planning and Landscape

Faculty of Business Administration:

ARNOLD, J. A., Accounting and Financial Management (H)
BARRAR, P. R. N., Operations Management
DAVIES, G., Retailing
EASINGWOOD, C. J., Marketing
HARVEY, B., Corporate Responsibility
HENDERSON, J. W., Economic Sociology
OAKEY, R. P., Business Development
PAXSON, D. A., Finance
PEARSON, A. W., Research and Development Management
RICKARDS, T., Creativity and Organizational Change
STARK, A. W., Accounting
SWANN, G. M. P., Economics
WHITLEY, R. D., Organizational Sociology
WOOD, D., Business Economics

Faculty of Economic and Social Studies:

ARTIS, M. J., Economics
BEYNON, H., Sociology
BLACKBURN, K., Macroeconomics
BULMER, S. J., Government
COATES, D., Government
COLMAN, D. R., Agricultural Economics (H)
DALE, A., Quantitive Social Research
DOBASH, R. E., Social Work
DOBASH, R. P., Criminology Studies
ELSON, D., Development Studies
EZZAMEL, M., Accounting and Finance
GEORGHIOU, L., Science and Technology Management
GERAS, N. M., Government
GLEDHILL, J., Social Anthropology
GUMMETT, P. J., Government and Technology Policy
HALFPENNY, P. J., Sociology (H)
HOPPER, T. M., Management Accounting
INGOLD, T., Social Anthropology (H)
KARN, V. A., Housing Studies
MADDEN, P. J., Mathematical Economics
METCALFE, J. S., Economics
MILLWARD, R., Economic History
MORAN, M. J., Government
MORGAN, D. H. J., Sociology
NIXSON, F. I., Development Economics
ORME, C. D., Econometrics
OSBORN, D. R., Econometrics
PARKER, H., Social Work
PARRY, G. B., Government
ROSE, M. E., Modern Social History
SAVAGE, M., Sociology
SCAPENS, R. W., Accounting
SHANIN, T., Sociology
SHARROCK, W. W., Sociology
STANLEY, L., Sociology and Women's Studies
STEINER, H. I., Political Philosophy
STRONG, N. C., Accounting and Finance
SWANN, G. M. P., Economics and Management of Innovation
TURLEY, W. S., Accounting
WALKER, M., Finance and Accounting
WERBNER, R. P., African Anthropology

WILLIAMS, K. H., Accounting and Political Economy
WRIGHT, M. W., Government

Faculty of Education:
AINSCOW, M., Special Needs and Educational Psychology
BAMFORD, J. M., Audiology and Education of the Deaf
BOREHAM, N. C., Educational Assessment and Evaluation
CHRISTIE, T., Education
CONTI-RAMSDEN, G. M., Child Language and Learning
HARRIS, J., Clinical Bioethics
NEWTON, V. E., Audiological Medicine
REID, D. J., Education
VERMA, G. K., Education

Faculty of Law:
BERCUSSON, B., Law
BRAZIER, M. R., Law
BRAZIER, R. J., Law
DUXBURY, N. T., Law
LOUGHLIN, M., Law
MILMAN, D., Corporate and Commercial Law (H)
OGUS, A. I., Law
WASIK, M., Law

Faculty of Medicine, Dentistry and Nursing:
ADAMS, J. E., Diagnostic Radiology (H)
APPLEBY, L., Psychiatry
BIRCH, J. M., Cancer Research Campaign, Paediatric and Familial Cancer Research Group
BLINKHORN, A. S., Oral Health
BOULTON, A. J. M., Medicine
BROOKER, C. G. D., Nursing
BURNIE, J. P., Medical Microbiology (H)
BURNS, A. S., Psychiatry of Old Age
BUTTERWORTH, C. A., Community Nursing
CASE, R. M., Physiology
CHALLIS, D., Psychiatric Social Work and Community Care
CHERRY, N. M., Epidemiology and Occupational Health (H)
CREED, F. H., Community Psychiatry (H)
CROSSMAN, A. R., Anatomy
DAVID, T. J., Child Health and Paediatrics (H)
DAVIS, J. R. E., Medicine
DEAKIN, J. F. W., Psychiatry
DIXON, M. J., Dental Genetics
DOUGLAS, K. T., Medicinal Chemistry
DUNN, G., Biomedical Statistics
DURRINGTON, P. N., Medicine
EDEN, O. B., Paediatric Oncology
EMERSON, E., Clinical Psychology in Intellectual Disability
FERGUSON, M. W. J., Basic Dental Sciences
FREEMONT, A. J., Tissue Pathology
GALASKO, C. S. B., Orthopaedic Surgery (H)
GALLAGHER, S. T., Oncology
GARROD, D. R., Developmental Biology
GRANT, M. E., Medical Biochemistry
GREEN, R., Physiology
GRENCIS, R. K., Immunology
GRIFFITHS, C. E. M., Dermatology
HARRINGTON, R. C., Child and Adolescent Psychiatry
HAWKINS, R. E., Medical Oncology
HEAGERTY, A., Medicine (H)
HICKMAN, J., Molecular Pharmacology
HORAN, M. A., Geriatric Medicine (South) (H)
HOWELL, A., Medical Oncology
HUTCHINSON, I. V., Immunology
HUXLEY, P. J., Psychiatric Social Work
IRVING, M. H., Surgery
JACKSON, A., Neuroradiology
KERFOOT, M. J., Psychiatric Social Work
KIERNAN, C. C., Behavioural Studies in Mental Handicap
KIRKWOOD, T. B. L., Biological Gerontology
KITCHENER, H. C., Gynaecological Oncology (H)
LEWIS, S. W., Adult Psychiatry
LOWENSTEIN, P. R., Molecular Medicine and Gene Therapy
LUKER, K. A., Nursing
MALLICK, N. P., Renal Medicine
MCALLISTER, I., Medicine
MCCLURE, J., Pathology
MCCOLLUM, C. N., Surgery (H)
MCCORD, J. F., Restorative Care of the Elderly
MCLEOD, D., Ophthalmology (H)
MAWER, E. B., Bone and Mineral Metabolism
O'BRIEN, K. D., Orthodontics
OLDHAM, J. A., Nursing
OLLIER, W. E. R., Immunogenetics
POLLARD, B. J., Anaesthesia
READ, A. P., Human Genetics
RECTOR, A. L., Medical Informatics
ROLAND, M. O., General Practice
SCARFFE, J. H., Oncology
SHAW, W. C., Orthodontics and Dentofacial Development
SIBBALD, B. S., Health Services Research
SIBLEY, C. P., Child Health and Physiology
SILMAN, A. J., Rheumatic Diseases Epidemiology
SLOAN, P., Experimental Oral Pathology
STANLEY, J. K., Hand Surgery
STRATFORD, I. J., Pharmacology
TALLIS, R. C., Geriatric Medicine (Salford) (H)
TARRIER, N., Clinical Psychology
TAYLOR, C. J., Medical Biophysics (H)
THATCHER, N., Oncology
THOMPSON, D. G., Gastroenterology
THORNHILL, M. H., Medicine in Dentistry (H)
TOMLINSON, S., Medicine
VADGAMA, P., Clinical Biochemistry (H)
WATERS, K. R., Nursing
WHITEHOUSE, C. R., Teaching Medicine in the Community
WILKIN, D., Health Services Research (H)
WILSON, N. H. F., Restorative Dentistry
WOODMAN, C. B. J., Cancer Epidemiology and Public Health
YATES, D. W., Accident and Emergency Surgery

Faculty of Science and Engineering:
ACZEL, P. H. G., Mathematical Logic and Computer Science
AUCKLAND, D. W., Electrical Engineering
BAKER, C., Mathematics (H)
BALMENT, R. J., Zoology
BARRINGER, H., Computer Science
BEATTIE, G. W., Psychology
BRAY, A. J., Theoretical Physics
BREE, D. S., Artificial Intelligence
CLARKE, D. J., Drug Delivery
CONNOR, J. N. L., Theoretical Chemistry
CURTIS, C. D., Geochemistry
DAVIES, J. M., Structural Engineering
DONEY, R. A., Probability Theory
EMES, M. J., Botany
FRENCH, S., Manchester School of Informatics
FURBER, S. B., Computer Engineering
GARNER, C. D., Inorganic Chemistry (H)
GREGORY, R. D., Mathematics
GULL, K., Molecular Biology
GURD, J. R., Computer Science
HARDINGHAM, T. E., Biochemistry
HELLIWELL, J. R., Structural Chemistry
HIGHAM, N. J., Applied Mathematics
HILLIER, I. H., Chemistry
HODGE, P., Polymer Chemistry
HOOK, J. R., Low Temperature Physics
HUMPHRIES, M. J., Biochemistry
JACKSON, J. D., Nuclear/Mechanical Engineering
KAHN, H. J., Computer Science
KING, T. A., Applied Physics
LEUNG, A. Y. T., Engineering
LORIMER, G. W., Physical Metallurgy and Materials Science
LOUDON, A. S. I., Animal Biology
LYNE, A. G., Radio Astronomy
MARSHALL, R., Experimental Particle Physics
MCDONOUGH, W. R., Information Systems
MEABURN, J., Astronomy
MEUDELL, P. R., Neuropsychology (H)
MIDDLETON, B. K., Electrical Engineering
MILES, I., Science and Technology Policy
MOORE, M. A., Theoretical Physics
MORRIS, G. A., Physical Chemistry
MULLIN, T., Condensed Matter Physics
NOYCE, P., Pharmacy (H)
OWEN, F., Neuroscience
PARIS, J. B., Mathematics
PICKSTONE, J. V., History of Science, Technology and Medicine (H)
PLYMEN, R. J., Pure Mathematics
POLLICOTT, M., Pure Mathematics
PREMET, A., Algebra
PRICE, C., Polymer Chemistry (H)
RAY, J. N., Pure Mathematics
READ, F. H., Physics
REASON, J. T., Psychology
ROBERTS, I. S., Microbiology
ROTHWELL, N. J., Physiology
ROWLAND, M., Pharmacy
RUBAN, A. I., Fluid Dynamics
RUTTER, E. H., Structural Geology (H)
SALE, F. R., Chemical Metallurgy and Materials Science
SANDOZ, D. J., Industrial Control Engineering
SMITH, I. M., Geotechnical Engineering (H)
STANSBY, P. K., Engineering Hydrodynamics
THOMAS, E. J., Organic Chemistry
THORNTON, G., Surface Science
TRINCI, A. P. J., Cryptogamic Botany (H)
TURNER, G., Isotope Geochemistry
VAUGHAN, D. J., Mineralogy
WARBOYS, B. C., Software Engineering (H)
WATSON, I., Computer Science
WEARDEN, J. H., Psychology
WESTON, A. H., Pharmacology
WOOD, N. J., Aerospace Engineering
WRIGHT, J. R., Mechanical Engineering
XYDEAS, C., Electrical Engineering

Departments not assigned to Faculties:
HULME, D., Development Studies
KIRKPATRICK, C., Development Economics
RABBITT, P. M., Cognitive Psychology and Gerontology

ATTACHED SCHOOL

Manchester Business School: Booth St West, Manchester, M15 6PB; tel. (161) 275-6333; includes the Faculty of Business Administration in the University, but is governed by its own Council, which includes business representatives; postgraduate and post-experience courses and research projects; University courses for DipBA, MBA, MBM, also research facilities for MBSc and PhD; Dir JOHN ARNOLD.

MANCHESTER METROPOLITAN UNIVERSITY

All Saints, Manchester, M15 6BH
Telephone: (161) 247-2000
Fax: (161) 236-6390
Founded 1970 as Manchester Polytechnic; present name and status 1992
Academic year: September to July
Chancellor: The Duke of WESTMINSTER
Pro-Chancellor: TOM BOOTH
Vice-Chancellor: ALEXANDRA V. BURSLEM
Academic Director and Pro-Vice-Chancellor: Prof. B. S. PLUMB
Academic Registrar: J. D. M. KARCZEWSKI-SLOWIKOWSKI
Librarian: Prof. C. HARRIS
Number of teachers: 1,249

Number of students: 17,850 full-time, 2,925 sandwich, 10,493 part-time

PRO-VICE-CHANCELLORS AND DEANS OF FACULTY

Art and Design: Prof. R. WILSON
Community Studies, Law and Education: Prof. K. L. OGLESBY
Crewe and Alsager Faculty: Dr G. WILSON
Hollings Faculty: Prof. R. MURRAY
Humanities and Social Science: Prof. S. KIRBY
Management and Business: Prof. A. R. LOCK
Science and Engineering: Prof. P. GACESA

HEADS OF DEPARTMENTS

Faculty of Art and Design:
Architecture, Landscape and Three Dimensional Design: M. STARLING
Communication Media: A. WOOD
Fine Arts: Prof. J. HYATT
History of Art and Design: Prof. L. A. HUNT
Textiles/Fashion: M. WAYMAN

Faculty of Community Studies, Law and Education:
Applied Community Studies: Dr J. DONE (acting)
Arts and Humanities Education: I. S. KANE
Health Care Studies: Dr D. SKIDMORE
Law: Prof. P. E. LEIGHTON
Psychology and Speech Pathology: Dr C. KAGAN (acting)
Sciences Education: A. J. GOODWIN

Crewe and Alsager Faculty:
Arts, Design and Performance: Prof. L. LANDY
Business and Management Studies: Dr R. L. RITCHIE
Education: Prof. D. WOODROW
Humanities and Applied Social Studies: Prof. G. M. HEATHCOTE
Exercise and Sports Science: Prof. L. BURWITZ
Environmental and Leisure Studies: Dr I. W. EASTWOOD
Modular Studies: Dr J. S. PIPER

Hollings Faculty:
Clothing Design and Technology: C. FAIRHURST (acting)
Food and Consumer Technology: Prof. R. C. MOODY
Hotel, Catering and Tourism Management: Prof. K. JOHNSON

Faculty of Humanities and Social Science:
Economics: Dr J. VINT
English: Prof. J. BEER
History and Economic History: Dr D. NICHOLLS
Sociology: B. LEACH
Languages: P. G. MOREY
Information and Communications: R. J. HARTLEY
Politics and Philosophy: Prof. J. M. BELL

Faculty of Management and Business:
Accounting and Finance: J. M. BROADBENT
Business Information Technology: D. DUNN
Business Studies: Prof. N. M. HEALEY
Management: S. SHAW (acting)
Retailing and Marketing: R. SCHMIDT (acting)

Faculty of Science and Engineering:
Biological Sciences: Prof. T. LOOKER
Chemistry and Materials: Prof. J. B. LEACH
Computing and Mathematics: S. OAKEY
Electrical and Electronic Engineering: Prof. J. M. SENIOR
Environmental and Geographical Studies: Prof. S. A. DALTON
Mathematics and Physics: T. J. RANDALL
Mechanical Engineering, Design and Manufacture: Prof. J. MATHER
Combined Honours and Foundation Studies: E. G. HUBERT

MIDDLESEX UNIVERSITY

White Hart Lane, London, N17 8HR
Telephone: (181) 362-5000
Fax: (181) 362-6878
E-mail: admissions@mdx.ac.uk

Designated 1973 as Middlesex Polytechnic, present name and status 1992; comprises the former Enfield and Hendon Colleges of Technology, Hornsey College of Art, New College of Speech and Drama, Trent Park College of Education, the College of All Saints, London College of Dance and North London College of Health Studies

Academic year: September to July

Chancellor: Baroness PLATT OF WRITTLE
Vice-Chancellor: Prof. MICHAEL DRISCOLL
Deputy Vice-Chancellor: Prof. KEN GOULDING
Assistant Vice-Chancellor and Director of Finance: ANNIE HORNE
Assistant Vice-Chancellor and Director of Corporate Services: TERRY BUTLAND
Pro-Vice-Chancellors: Prof. DENNIS HARDY (Students), Prof. EDMUND PENNING-ROWSELL (Research), Prof. GEOFFREY ALDERMAN (Quality and Standards)
Academic Registrar: G. W. JONES
Head of Information and Learning Resource Service: WILLIAM MARSTERSON

Library of 450,000 vols
Number of teachers: 653 (f.t.e.)
Number of students: 18,019 (full-time and sandwich courses), 3,541 (part-time)

DEANS

School of Art, Design and Performing Arts: Prof. MARTIN PITTS
Middlesex University Business School: Prof. DAVID KIRBY
School of Computing Science: Prof. NORMAN REVELL
School of Engineering Systems: Dr TONY WHITE
School of Health, Biological and Environmental Sciences: Prof. RON HAMILTON
School of Humanities and Cultural Studies: Prof. GABRIELLE PARKER
School of Lifelong Learning and Education: Prof. RICHARD TUFFNELL
School of Social Science: DENNIS PARKER

NAPIER UNIVERSITY

Craiglockhart: 219 Colinton Rd, Edinburgh, EH14 1DJ
Merchiston: 10 Colinton Rd, Edinburgh, EH10 5DT
Sighthill: Sighthill Court, Edinburgh, EH11 4BN
Craighouse: Craighouse Rd, Edinburgh, EH10 3LG
Canaan Lane: 74 Canaan Lane, Edinburgh, EH10 4TB
Telephone: (131) 455-4330

Founded 1964 as Napier College of Science and Technology, later became Napier Polytechnic, present name and status 1992

Academic year: September to July

Chancellor: Lord YOUNGER OF PRESTWICK
Principal: Prof. JOHN MAVOR
Deputy Principal: Prof. MICHAEL THORNE
Secretary and Academic Registrar: I. MILLER
Librarian: Prof. A. R. MCELROY

Number of teachers: 576 f.t.e.
Number of students: 11,000

DEANS

Faculty of Arts and Social Sciences: C. BRYCE (acting)
Faculty of Engineering and Computing: Prof. A. SIBBALD
Faculty of Science: Prof. C. F. A. BRYCE
Napier Business School: J. WORDEN
Faculty of Health Studies: J. ROSS

HEADS OF DEPARTMENTS

Faculty of Applied Arts:
Design: Dr M. TURNER
Music: P. SAWYER
Photography, Film and Television: Prof. D. BELL
Print Media, Publishing and Communication: Prof. A. MCCLEERY
Economics: J. TROY
Law: Prof. R. WALLACE
Social Sciences: Dr N. BONNEY

Faculty of Engineering:
Building and Surveying: Prof. R. MCKENZIE
Civil and Transportation Engineering: Prof. M. MAHER
Electrical, Electronic and Computer Engineering: Prof. D. LIDGATE
Mechanical, Manufacturing and Software Engineering: Prof. J. KUBIE
Computer Studies: Prof. L. BEDDIE

Faculty of Science:
Applied Chemical and Physical Sciences: Dr M. BARROW
Biological Sciences: Dr C. HOUGHTON
Mathematics: Dr J. T. WISE

Napier Business School:
Accounting and Finance: D. YOUNG
Operations and General Management: L. TULLY
Human Resource Management: M. WALLACE
Information Management: S. RAEBURN
Marketing: J. ENSOR
Corporate Strategy: P. BRYANS
Hospitality and Tourism Management: M. ALLARDYCE
Languages: T. WIGHT

Faculty of Health Studies:
Foundation Studies: J. JONES
Adult Physical Health: I. MACINTOSH
Maternal and Child Health, Mental Health and Handicap: A. GIBBS
Advanced Nursing and Midwifery Studies: S. BRIEDITIS

UNIVERSITY OF NEWCASTLE UPON TYNE

Newcastle upon Tyne, NE1 7RU
Telephone: (191) 222-6000

Founded 1851, incorporated as separate University in 1963

Chancellor: (vacant)
Vice-Chancellor: J. R. G. WRIGHT
Pro-Vice-Chancellors: Prof. L. A. HAMNETT, Prof. A. R. ARCHIBALD, Prof. J. B. GODDARD
Registrar: D. E. T. NICHOLSON
Librarian: T. W. GRAHAM

Number of teachers: 1,968
Number of students: 16,107

Publications: *Calendar*, *Undergraduate Prospectus*, *Postgraduate Prospectus*, *Annual Report*.

DEANS

Faculty of Medicine: Prof. P. H. BAYLIS (Medicine), Prof. J. J. MURRAY (Dentistry)
Faculty of Arts: E. G. N. CROSS
Faculty of Science: B. P. STRAUGHAN
Faculty of Engineering: Prof. P. J. HILLS
Faculty of Law, Environment and Social Sciences: Prof. J. B. GODDARD
Faculty of Agriculture and Biological Sciences: Prof. C. RITSON
Faculty of Education: M. J. ATKINS

PROFESSORS

Faculty of Arts:
BAILEY, G. N., Archaeology
BATCHELOR, J. B., English Literature
BURTON-ROBERTS, N. C., English Language and Linguistics

CAMERON, E. K., Early Modern History
DERRY, J. W., Modern British History
LAZENBY, J. F., Ancient History
MIDDLETON, R., Music
MILNER, J., History of Art
MOORE, R. I., Medieval History
NEWMAN, J. A., American and Post-Colonial Literature
PERRIAM, C. G., Hispanic Studies
PORTER, B. J., Modern History
POWELL, J. G. F., Latin
POWRIE, P. P., French Cultural Studies
PUGH, M. D., Modern British History
READER, K. A., French Studies
RIORDAN, C. B., German
SALMON, P. J. K., International History
SAUNDERS, T. J., Greek
VAN DER EIJK, P. J., Greek
WRIGHT, T. R., English Literature

Faculty of Law, Environment and Social Sciences:

ALDER, J. E., Law
ALLEN, M. J., Law
ANDERSON, J., International Development
APPLEYARD, A. R., Accounting and Finance
CAMPBELL, D., International Politics
CHAMPION, A. G., Population Geography
CHELL, E., Management Studies
COOMBES, M. G., Geographic Information
DOLTON, P. J., Economics
DRIFTE, R., Japanese Studies
FOTHERINGHAM, A. S., Quantitative Geography
GILLESPIE, A. E., Communications Geography
GODDARD, J. B., Regional Development Studies
GRAY, T. S., Political Thought
HEALEY, P., Town and Country Planning
JONES, P. N., Political Philosophy
JONES-LEE, M. W., Economics
LOOMES, G. C., Economics
MARSHALL, J. N., Economic Geography
NEWSON, M. D., Physical Geography
RHODES, R. A. W., Politics
RICHARDS, I. J., Architecture
ROBINS, K., Cultural Geography
SEIDMANN, D. J., Economic Theory
STEVENSON, A. C., Environmental Geography
TREMAYNE, A. R., Economics
WALKER, J. A., Family Policy
WILLIS, K. G., Economics of the Environment
WILTSHIRE, T. J., Architectural Science

Faculty of Medicine:

ALBERTI, K. G. M. M., Medicine
ALLEN, A., Physiological Biochemistry
ARCHIBALD, A. R., Microbiological Chemistry
ARGENT, B. E., Cell Physiology
BARER, D. H., Stroke Medicine
BARKER, P. J., Psychiatric Nursing Practice
BARNES, M. P., Neurological Rehabilitation
BARTLETT, K., Paediatric Biochemistry
BASSENDINE, M. F., Hepatology
BAYLIS, P. H., Experimental Medicine
BHOPAL, R. S., Epidemiology and Public Health
BLAIN, P. G., Environmental Medicine
BODDY, K., Medical Physics
BOND, J., Health Services Research
BOND, S., Nursing Research
BURN, J., Clinical Genetics
BURT, A. D., Hepatopathology
CALVERT, A. H., Medical Oncology
CAMPBELL, F. C., Gastroenterological Surgery
CAMPBELL, R. W. F., Cardiology
CAWSTON, T. E., Medicine
CONNOLLY, B. A., Biochemistry
CRAFT, A. W., Paediatric Oncology
DAVISON, J. M., Obstetric Medicine
DIFFEY, B. L., Photobiology
DONALDSON, L. J., Applied Epidemiology
DUNLOP, W., Obstetrics and Gynaecology
ECCLES, M. P., Clinical Effectiveness
EDWARDSON, J. A., Neuroendocrinology
EMMERSON, P. T., Molecular Biology
EYRE, J. A., Paediatric Neuroscience
FERRIER, I. N., Psychiatry
GIBSON, G. J., Respiratory Medicine
GREGG, P. J., Orthopaedic Surgery
GRUBIN, D., Forensic Psychiatry
HARRIS, J. B., Experimental Neurology
HAWKINS, A. R., Molecular Genetics
HILL, P. M., Postgraduate Medical Education
HIRST, B. H., Cellular Physiology
HOME, P. D., Diabetes Medicine
HORMAECHE, C. E., Microbiology
HUGHES, M. A., Plant Molecular Genetics
JAMES, O. F. W., Geriatric Medicine
JARVIS, S. N., Community Child Health
JORDAN, R. K., Medical Education
KEHOE, M. A., Microbiology
KENDALL-TAYLOR, P. A., Endocrinology
KENNY, R. A., Geriatric Medicine
LE COUTEUR, A. S., Child and Adolescent Psychiatry
LEAPER, D. J., Surgery
MCAVOY, B. R., Primary Health Care
MCCABE, J. F., Dental Materials Science
MCKEITH, I. G., Old Age Psychiatry
MALCOLM, A. J., Clinical Pathology
MENDELOW, D., Neurosurgery
MILLER, J. S. G., Anatomy
MURRAY, A., Cardiovascular Physics
MURRAY, J. J., Child Dental Health
NEAL, D. E., Surgery
NEWELL, D. R., Cancer Therapeutics
OSWALD, N. T. A., Primary Health Care
PEARSON, A. D. J., Paediatric Oncology
PERRY, E. K., Neurochemical Pathology
PROCTOR, S. J., Haematological Oncology
RAWLINS, M. D., Clinical Pharmacology
REES, J. L., Dermatology
ROBINSON, N. J., Molecular Genetics
ROBSON, S. C., Fetal Medicine
RUGG-GUNN, A. J., Preventive Dentistry
RUSSELL, R. B. B., Oral Biology
SCOTT, J. L., Community Psychiatry
SELF, C. H., Clinical Biochemistry
SEYMOUR, R. A., Restorative Dentistry
SHAW, P. J., Neurological Medicine
SIMMONS, N. L., Epithelial Physiology
SNASHALL, P. D., Medicine
SOAMES, J. V., Oral Pathology
STRACHAN, T., Human Molecular Genetics
TAYLOR, R., Medicine and Metabolism
THOMSON, P. J., Oral and Maxillofacial Surgery
TURNBULL, D. H., Neurology
VAN ZWANENBERG, T. D., Postgraduate General Practice
WALLS, A. W. G., Restorative Dentistry
WESTLEY, B. R., Molecular Pathology
WHITAKER, M. J., Physiological Sciences
WILKINSON, R., Renal Medicine
WILSON, J. A., Otolaryngology and Head and Neck Surgery
YEAMAN, S. J., Molecular Enzymology
YOUNG, M. P., Psychology

Faculty of Science:

AITKIN, M., Statistics
ANDERSON, T., Computing Science
BARENGI, C. F., Fluid Dynamics
BLEWITT, G., Space Geodesy
BRANDENBURG, A., Applied Mathematics
CLEGG, W., Structural Crystallography
CROWE, A., Physics
DICKINSON, A. S., Theoretical Atomic Physics
DOBSON, J. E., Information Management
DYE, R. H., Pure Mathematics
GLAZEBROOK, K. D., Applied Probability
GOLDING, B. T., Organic Chemistry
HAMNETT, A., Physical Chemistry
HORROCKS, G., Pure Mathematics
JACKSON, R. F., Synthetic Organic Chemistry
JAROS, M., Theoretical Physics
JOHNSON, B. E., Pure Mathematics
LARTER, S. R., Geology
LEE, P. A., Computing Science
MCFARLANE, W., Magnetic Resonance
MATTHEWS, J. N. S., Medical Statistics
MINNIKIN, D. E., Microbial Chemistry
MITRANI, I., Computing Science
RANDELL, B., Computing Science
SHRIVASTAVA, S. K., Computing Science
SNOWDON, K. J., Physics
SYKES, A. G., Inorganic Chemistry
THOMAS, K. M., Carbon Science
WHITFIELD, H., Computing and Data Processing
YOUNG, N. J., Pure Mathematics

Faculty of Engineering:

ACARNLEY, P. P., Electric Drives
AKAY, G., Chemical Engineering
ANDERSON, G. K., Environmental Engineering
BELL, M. G. H., Transport Operations
BRAIDEN, P. M., Manufacturing Engineering
BURDESS, J. S., Engineering Dynamics
CLARKE, B. G., Geotechnical Engineering
DONNELLY, T., Integrated Pollution Control
FAWCETT, J. N., Machine Dynamics
GIBSON, A. G., Composite Materials Engineering
HEARN, G. E., Hydrodynamics
HILLS, P. J., Transport Engineering
HINTON, O. R., Signal Processing
INCECIK, A., Offshore Engineering
JACK, A. G., Electrical Engineering
JAMIESON, D. G., River Basin Management
JOHNSON, G. R., Rehabilitation Engineering
JONES, C. J. F. P., Geotechnical Engineering
KNAPTON, J., Structural Engineering
MECROW, B. C., Electrical Power
MONTAGUE, G. A., Bioprocess Control
MORRIS, A. J., Process Control
O'CONNELL, P. E., Water Resources Engineering
O'NEILL, A. G., Microelectronics
PAGE, T. F., Engineering Materials
PESCOD, M. B., Environmental Control Engineering
PETRIE, C. J. S., Non-Newtonian Fluid Mechanics
RAMSHAW, C., Responsive Processing
RITCHEY, I., Engineering Design
SCOTT, K., Electrochemical Engineering
SEN, P., Marine Design and Construction
SERGEEV, Y. A., Engineering Mathematics
TAYLOR, P. M., Mechanical Engineering
THOMPSON, D. P., Engineering Ceramics
WHITE, J. R., Polymer Science and Engineering

Faculty of Agriculture and Biological Sciences:

BURBRIDGE, P. R., Marine Sciences and Coastal Management
CAIN, R. B., Environmental Microbiology
CRAM, W. J., Plant Biology
DAVISON, A. W., Environmental Biology
GILBERT, H. J., Agricultural Biochemistry and Nutrition
GOODFELLOW, M., Microbial Systematics
GRIFFITHS, H., Plant Ecophysiology
HARVEY, D. R., Agricultural Economics
LOWE, P. D., Rural Economy
MATHERS, J. C., Human Nutrition
O'DONNELL, A. G., Soil Microbiology and Molecular Ecology
OWENS, N. J. P., Marine Sciences
PETHICK, J., Coastal Sciences
RITSON, C., Agricultural Marketing
SYERS, J. K., Soil Science

Faculty of Education:

COFFIELD, F. J., Education
DODD, B. J., Speech and Language Pathology
DYSON, D. A., Special Needs Education
HOWARD, D., Speech
MILROY, A. L., Sociolinguistics

Reynolds, D., Education
Tooley, J. N., Policy Studies in Education

UNIVERSITY OF NORTH LONDON

166 – 220 Holloway Rd, London, N7 8DB
Telephone: (171) 607-2789
Fax: (171) 753-3271

Founded 1896 as Northern Polytechnic Institution; became Polytechnic of North London 1971; present name and status 1992

Schools at: Holloway Rd, London, N7; Highbury Grove, London, N5

Vice-Chancellor: B. Roper
Academic Director: George Holmes
University Secretary: J. McParland
Academic Registrar: M. Storey
Head of Library Services: R. Williams

Library of over 300,000 vols
Number of teachers: 422
Number of students: 9,770 full-time, 5,033 part-time

DEANS

Business School: J. Fawcett
Faculty of Environmental and Social Studies: J. Somerville
Faculty of Humanities and Teacher Education: G. Condry
Faculty of Science, Computing and Engineering: L. I. B. Haines

HEADS OF SCHOOL

Accounting and Information Systems: F. Blewett
Architecture and Interior Design: H. Mallinson
Biological and Applied Sciences: A. Sharma
Business Strategy: R. Morgan
Communications Technology and Mathematical Sciences: (vacant)
Community Health, Psychology and Social Work: S. Pike
Education: I. Menter
European and Language Studies: J. Kidman
Health and Sports Science: B. Bointon
Historical, Philosophical and Contemporary Studies: P. Holmes
Informatics and Multimedia Technology: (vacant)
Law, Governance and Information Management: L. Sheinman
Leisure, Tourism and Hospitality Management: A. Curson
Life Sciences: B. Bointon
Literary and Media Studies: L. Fitzsimmons
Management: M. Bickerton
Polymer Technology: M. O'Brien
Social Sciences: D. Phillips

UNIVERSITY OF NORTHUMBRIA AT NEWCASTLE

Ellison Building, Ellison Place, Newcastle upon Tyne, NE1 8ST
Telephone: (191) 232-6002
Fax: (191) 227-4017

Founded 1969 as Newcastle upon Tyne Polytechnic, present name and status 1992
Language of instruction: English
Academic year: September to July

Chancellor: The Lord Glenamara of Glenridding
Vice-Chancellor and Chief Executive: Prof. Gilbert Smith
Pro-Vice-Chancellor (Resources): Gordon C. Campbell
Pro-Vice-Chancellor (Academic): Prof. Tony Dickson
Head of Carlisle Campus: Prof. R. Smith
Academic Registrar: Cheryl Penna
Director of Information Services: Ian R. Winkworth

Library of 500,000 vols
Number of teachers: 750 (f.t.e.)
Number of students: 13,000 full-time and sandwich, 10,000 part-time

DEANS

Faculty of Arts and Design: Prof. K. McConkey
Newcastle Business School: Prof. D. Weir
Faculty of Social Sciences: Prof. M. Shaw
Faculty of Engineering, Science and Technology: Prof. J. Wilson
Faculty of Health, Social Work and Education: Prof. R. Stephens

HEADS OF DEPARTMENTS AND SCHOOLS

Faculty of Arts and Design:
- Design: Prof. J. More
- Historical and Critical Studies: Prof. C. Bailey
- Information and Library Management: Prof. J. M. Day
- Modern Languages: Prof. D. W. Head
- Visual and Performing Arts: Prof. G. Roper

Faculty of Social Sciences:
- Behavioural and Environmental Sciences: Prof. R. J. Buswell
- Law: Prof. P. H. Kenny
- Social, Political and Economic Sciences: Prof. P. Garrahan

Faculty of Engineering, Science and Technology:
- Built Environment: Prof. A. J. Newall
- Chemical and Life Sciences: Prof. D. Gardiner
- Computing: Prof. R. S. Burgess
- School of Engineering: Prof. R. A. Cryan
- Mathematics and Statistics: Prof. M. J. Giles

Faculty of Health, Social Work and Education:
- Education: Prof. H. Bines
- Health Sciences: Prof. D. W. Watson
- Social Work and Social Policy: Prof. R. Firth

UNIVERSITY OF NOTTINGHAM

University Park, Nottingham, NG7 2RD
Telephone: (115) 951-5151
Telex: 37346
Fax: (115) 951-3666

Founded as University College 1881, University Charter 1948

Chancellor: Sir Ron Dearing
Pro-Chancellors: Prof. S. H. Bailey, Prof. B. R. Clayton, Prof. D. Greenaway, Prof. G. Pattenden
Vice-Chancellor: Sir Colin Campbell
Registrar: K. H. Jones
Librarian: R. E. Oldroyd

Library: see Libraries
Number of teachers: 1,000
Number of students: 16,200

Publications: *Calendar*, *Prospectuses*, *Gazette*, *Annual Report*, *Newsletter*.

DEANS

Arts: Prof. N. Hewitt
Education: Prof. D. W. R. Hopkins
Engineering: Prof. J. V. Wood
Law and Social Sciences: Prof. C. R. Thorne
Medicine and Health Sciences: Prof. P. C. Rubin
Science: Prof. C. A. Bates
Graduate School: Prof. C. E. D. Chilvers

PROFESSORS

Aitkenhead, A. R., Anaesthesia
Armour, E. A., Applied Mathematics
Arulkumaran, S., Obstetrics and Gynaecology
Ashkenazi, V., Engineering Surveying
Azzopardi, B. J., Chemical Engineering
Bailey, S. H., Public Law
Baker, P. N., Obstetrics and Gynaecology
Ball, F. G., Applied Probability
Barnard, C. J., Animal Behaviour
Barnett, V., Mathematics
Bates, C. A., Theoretical Physics
Bath, P. M., Stroke Medicine
Batstone, G. F., Postgraduate Medical Education
Beckett, J. V., English Regional History
Belavkin, V., Applied Mathematics
Benford, S. D., Collaborative Computing
Bennett, T., Physiology
Benson, T. M., Opto-Electronics
Berry, R. H., Accounting and Finance
Birch, D. J., Criminal Justice and Evidence
Birchall, J. P., Otorhinolaryngology
Blamey, R. W., Surgical Science
Bleaney, M. F., Economics
Blumhardt, L. D., Clinical Neurology
Boa, E. J., German
Bossert, W., Economic Theory
Bowley, R. M., Physics
Bradshaw, C. M., Neuropsychology
Brailsford, D. F., Computer Science
Bridge, M. G., Commercial Law
Brincat, M. P., Reproductive Medicine
Britton, J. R., Respiratory Medicine
Brook, J. D., Genetics
Broughton-Pipkin, F., Perinatal Physiology
Brown, S. F., Civil Engineering
Burgess, D. A., Pure Mathematics
Buttery, P. J., Applied Biochemistry
Bycroft, B. W., Pharmaceutical Chemistry
Cardwell, R. A., Modern Spanish Literature
Carmichael, J., Clinical Oncology
Carter, R. A., Modern English Language
Challis, L. J., Low Temperature Physics
Chesters, M. A., Physical Chemistry
Chilvers, C. E. D., Epidemiology
Chiplin, B., Industrial Economics
Choonara, I. A., Child Health
Christopoulos, C., Electrical Engineering
Clayton, B. R., Mechanical Engineering
Cox, T. R., Organizational Psychology
Davies, M. C., Biomedical Surface Chemistry
Davis, S. S., Pharmacy
Day, C. W., Education
Denby, B., Minerals Computing
Derrington, A. M., Psychology
Dingwall, R. W. J., Social Studies
Dodson, A. H., Geodesy
Doherty, M., Rheumatology
Donnelly, R., Vascular Medicine
Drinkwater, J. F., Roman Imperial History
Dua, H. S., Ophthalmology
Dunham, R. K., Rock Mechanics
Eaves, L., Physics
Elliman, D. G., Applied Computing
Emmerson, A. M., Microbiology
Ennew, C. T., Marketing
Evetts, J. A., Sociology
Falvey, R., Economics
Fawcett, A. P., Architecture
Fawcett, T. J., Law
Fenn, P. T., Insurance Studies
Fesenko, I. B., Mathematics
Finch, R. G., Infectious Diseases
Flint, A. P. F., Animal Physiology
Forbes, I., Politics
Ford, P. H., Information Technology and Computing Practice
Foxon, C. T., Physics
Gardiner, S. M., Cardiovascular Physiology
Geary, R. J., Modern History
Gemmell, N., Development Economics
Gillies, P. A., Public Health
Gindy, M. N. Z., Advanced Manufacturing Technology
Glass, R. E., Biochemistry
Gravells, N. P., English Law
Greenwood, D., Antimicrobial Sciences
Greenaway, D., Economics
Gregory, C. D., Cell Death and Survival
Grierson, D., Plant Physiology
Hampton, J. R., Cardiology
Hardcastle, J. D., Surgery
Harding, S. E., Physical Biochemistry

HARRIS, D. J., Public International Law
HARRIS, S. J., Metallurgy
HARRISON, C., Literary Studies in Education
HAWKEY, C. J., Gastroenterology
HEPTINSTALL, S. M., Haemostasis and Thrombosis
HEWITT, N., French
HEYWOOD, P., Politics
HILL, S. J., Molecular Pharmacology
HOPKINS, D. W. R., Education
HOPKINSON, B. R., Vascular Surgery
HYDE, T. H., Mechanical Engineering
JAKEMAN, E., Applied Statistical Optics
JAMES, D. K., Foeto-Maternal Medicine
JAMES, V. C., Nursing
JOHNSON, I. R., Obstetrics and Gynaecology
JONES, M. C. E., Medieval French History
JONES, P. B., Psychiatry and Community Mental Health
JORDAN, T. R., Psychology
KALSHEKER, N., Chemical Pathology and Human Metabolism
KING, J. R., Theoretical Mechanics
KING, R. H., American Intellectual History
KIRK, R., Philosophy
KNIGHT, D. M., French
KNIGHTS, D., Management of Financial Services
LAYBOURN-PARRY, J. E. M., Environmental Biology
LEWIS, J. E., Social Policy/Sociology
LLOYD, R. G., Genetics
LOGAN, R. F., Clinical Epidemiology
LOWE, J. S., Neuropathology
MCCARTHY, M. J., Applied Linguistics
MACDONALD, I. A., Metabolic Physiology
MCGUIRK, B. J., Romance Literatures and Literary Theory
MADELEY, R. J., Public Health Medicine
MAIN, P. C., Physics
MANNING, N. P., Sociology
MARLOW, N., Neonatal Medicine
MARSDEN, C. A., Neuropharmacology
MATHER, P. M., Geographical Information Systems
MAYER, R. J., Molecular Cell Biology
MAYHEW, T. M., Human Morphology
MELLER, H. E., Urban History
MIDDLETON, V., Mechanical Engineering
MILLINGTON, M. I., Hispanic Studies
MILNER, C. R., International Economics
MITCHELL, J. R., Food Rheology
MOREHEN, J. M., Music
MORGAN, W. J., Continuing Education
MORRIS, P. G., Physics
MORSE, G. K., Company Law
MURPHY, R. J. L., Education
MURRAY-RUST, P., Virtual Molecular Science
NETHERCOT, D. A., Civil Engineering
NEWBOLD, P., Econometrics
O'BRIEN, C., Production Engineering
O'HAGAN, A., Statistics
PACKER, K. J., Chemistry
PARKER, S., Adult Education
PARKIN, D. T., Avian Genetics
PATTENDEN, G., Organic Chemistry
PEARCE, J. B., Child and Adolescent Psychiatry
PEBERDY, J. F., Life Science
PHILLIPS, D. R., Human Geography
PIERSON, C., Politics
POLIAKOFF, M., Chemistry
POLNAY, L., Community Paediatrics
PRINGLE, M. A. L., General Practice
PRITCHARD, D. I., Immunoparasitology
RAEBURN, J., Clinical Genetics
RAYNER, A. J., Agricultural Economics
RIFFAT, S. B., Architectural Technology and Energy
RILEY, D. S., Theoretical Mechanics
ROBERTSON, J. F., Surgery
ROWLANDS, B. J., Gastroenterological Surgery
RUBIN, P. C., Therapeutics
RUDD, C. D., Mechanical Engineering
RUSSELL, N. H., Haematology
RUTTER, N., Paediatric Medicine
SARRE, P. J., Chemistry
SAVILL, J. S., Renal and Inflammatory Diseases
SCHOFIELD, R. V., Art History
SCHRODER, M., Inorganic Chemistry
SCOTT, R. K., Agriculture
SEWELL, H., Immunology
SHADBOLT, N. R., Intelligent Systems
SHARP, P. M., Genetics
SHAW, P., Biochemistry
SHAYLER, P. J., Mechanical Engineering
SHEARD, F. W., Physics
SIMPKINS, N. S., Chemistry
SOMEKH, M. G., Electrical Engineering
SOMMERSTEIN, A. H., Classics
STARKEY, K. P., Strategic Management
STEPHENSON, T. J., Child Health
STEVENS, M. F. G., Experimental Cancer Chemotherapy
STEWART, G. S. A. B., Applied Molecular Biology
STILL, J. M., French
SZABADI, E., Psychiatry
TALLACK, D. G., American Studies
TATTERSFIELD, A. E., Respiratory Medicine
TAYLOR, A. J., Flavour Technology
TENDLER, S. J., Biophysical Chemistry
THISELTON, A. C., Christian Theology
THORNE, C. R., Physical Geography
TUCK, B., Physical Electronics
TURVILLE-PETRE, T. F. S., English
UNDERWOOD, G., Cognitive Psychology
USHERWOOD, P. N. R., Life Science
WAITES, W. M., Food Microbiology
WAKELIN, D., Life Science
WALLACE, W. A., Orthopaedic and Accident Surgery
WARD, C. D., Rehabilitation Medicine
WEBB, R., Animal Production
WIEDEMANN, T. E. J., Classics
WHYNES, D. K., Health Economics
WILCOX, R. G., Cardiovascular Medicine
WILLIAMS, B. T., Public Health Medicine
WILLIAMS, H. C., Dermato-Epidemiology
WILLIAMS, P., Molecular Microbiology
WILSON, J. R., Occupational Ergonomics
WILSON, R. J. A., Archaeology
WOOD, D. J., Psychology
WOOD, J. V., Materials Engineering and Materials Design
WOODS, R. A., German
WORTHEN, J., D.H. Lawrence Studies
WRIGHT, D. M., Financial Studies
WRIGLEY, C. J., History

NOTTINGHAM TRENT UNIVERSITY

Burton St, Nottingham, NG1 4BU
Telephone: (115) 941-8418
Telex: 377534
Fax: (115) 948-6503
E-mail: marketing@ntu.ac.uk

Founded 1970; university status 1992
Academic year: September to July

Vice-Chancellor: Prof. R. COWELL
Deputy Vice-Chancellor: Prof. K. C. SHORT
Pro-Vice-Chancellors: Prof. J. D. STANCER, Prof. G. H. THOMPSON
Registrar: D. W. SAMSON
Librarian: E. LINES

Library of 400,000 vols, 2,500 periodicals
Number of teachers: 753 full-time, 91 part-time
Number of students: 23,410

DEANS

Faculty of Art and Design: Prof. E. NEWTON
Nottingham Business School: Prof. M. REYNOLDS
Faculty of Education: Prof. N. HASTINGS
Faculty of Engineering and Computing: Prof. R. WHITROW
Faculty of Construction and the Environment: Prof. R. HAWKINS
Faculty of Economics and Social Sciences: Prof. D. R. WEBB
Faculty of Humanities: Prof. S. CHAN
Nottingham Law School: Prof. A. T. P. JONES
Faculty of Science and Mathematics: Prof. T. PALMER

HEADS OF DEPARTMENTS

Academic Legal Studies: Prof. M. J. GUNN
Accounting: Dr A. T. A. LOVELL
Building and Environmental Health: Prof. T. J. LANE
Civil and Structural Engineering: Dr R. K. HAWKINS
Computing: Prof. R. J. WHITROW
Design: Prof. G. KENNEDY
Economics and Politics: P. D. PERITON
Electrical and Electronic Engineering: Prof. C. B. THOMAS
English and Media Studies: Prof. S. J. HARRIS
Fashion and Textiles: Prof. E. W. NEWTON
Finance and Business Information Systems: Prof. M. REYNOLDS
Health and Human Services: Dr P. E. HIGHAM
Human Resource Management: Prof. J. W. LEOPOLD
International Studies: Prof. S. CHAN
Life Sciences: Prof. T. PALMER
Mathematics, Statistics and Operational Research: Prof. A. BENDELL
Mechanical and Manufacturing Engineering: Prof. J. B. HULL
Modern Languages: Prof. M. HOWARTH
Primary Education: Prof. N. HASTINGS
Professional Legal Studies: Prof. P. F. KUNZLIK
Secondary and Tertiary Education: Prof. S. LAW
Strategic Management and Marketing: Prof. P. FRANKLIN
Surveying: Prof. P. GALLIMORE
Visual and Performing Arts: Prof. S. E. LEWIS

OPEN UNIVERSITY

Walton Hall, Milton Keynes, MK7 6AA, Buckinghamshire
Telephone: (1908) 274066
Telex: 825061
Fax: (1908) 653744

Founded 1969
Academic year: February to October (for undergraduate studies); teaching takes place over nine months, with examinations in October

Distance learning courses supported by personal tuition and, where appropriate, fully integrated with broadcasts on BBC television and radio, audio and video cassette material, computing, and residential summer schools. Students are over the age of 18, resident in the UK, the European Union, or certain other countries where the Open University has agreed to register students, mainly in full-time employment and studying in their spare time. Courses can be taken as single entities or accumulated towards a BA or BSc degree. Short courses in professional and vocational areas are also available, leading to advanced and professional diplomas and certificates. There is also a higher degrees programme for the BPhil, MPhil and PhD by research, and 11 taught masters degrees (incl. MBA). Apart from the headquarters, there are 13 regions administering 290 study centres throughout the UK and in parts of Europe

Chancellor: Rt Hon. BETTY BOOTHROYD
Pro-Chancellor: Sir BRYAN NICHOLSON
Vice-Chancellor: Sir JOHN DANIEL
Pro-Vice-Chancellors: R. LEWIS (Student, Tutorial and Regional Services), Dr A. FLOYD (Curriculum Development), G. PETERS (Strategy and Planning), Prof. D. LAURILLARD (Technology Development)
Secretary: D. J. CLINCH
Director of Library Services: N. J. WHITSED

Number of teachers: 700 full-time, 7,600 part-time
Number of students and clients: 195 full-time, 210,000 part-time
Publications: *Studying with the Open University, Courses, Diplomas and BA/BSc Degrees, Research Degree Prospectus, Taught Master's Degree Prospectuses, Open Business School Brochure, PGCE Brochure.*

DEANS

Faculty of Arts: T. J. BENTON
Faculty of Mathematics: Prof. D. BRANNAN
Faculty of Science: Dr A. BASSINDALE
Faculty of Social Sciences: Dr P. SARRE
Faculty of Technology: Dr M. MEADE
School of Education: Dr R. T. D. GLAISTER
School of Health and Social Welfare: Dr L. JONES
School of Management: D. ASCH

DIRECTORS OF UNITS

Institute of Educational Technology: M. THORPE
Student Services: Prof. D. SEWART
Centre for Modern Languages: A. STEVENS

REGIONAL DIRECTORS

London Region: J. FAGE
South Region: S. WATTS
South East Region: G. W. RUMBLE
South West Region: J. EMMS
West Midlands Region: Dr G. F. HANCOCK
East Midlands Region: G. LAMMIE
East Anglia Region: A. R. MILLS
Yorkshire Region: Dr P. H. K. SMITH
North West Region: H. HORNER
North Region: J. SHIPLEY
Wales: Dr J. MCGRATH
Scotland: P. G. SYME
Ireland: Dr R. HAMILTON

PROFESSORS

ATTENBOROUGH, K., Acoustics
BASSINDALE, A., Organometallic Chemistry
BELL-BURNELL, S. J., Physics
BENTON, T. J., History of Arts
BERRY, F., Inorganic Chemistry
BLOWERS, A. T., Social Sciences
BRADLEY, K., International Management
BRANNAN, D. A., Mathematics
BROWN, H., Social Care
BROWN, J., Educational Guidance
BROWN, S. C., Philosophy
BURROWS, D. J., Music
CHAPMAN, P. F., Energy Systems
CHERNATONY, L. DE, Brand Marketing
COHEN, G. M., Psychology
CRAMPIN, M., Mathematics
CROSS, N. G., Design (Technology)
DAVIES, C., Health Care
EISENSTADT, M., Artificial Intelligence
EMSLEY, C., History
FINNEGAN, R. H., Comparative Social Institutions
GLATTER, R., Educational Policy and Management
GRANT, J., Education in Medicine
GREENE, J. M., Psychology
HALL, P. A. V., Computer Science
HALL, S. M., Sociology
HALLIDAY, T. R., Biology
HAMMERSLEY, M., Educational and Social Research
HAND, D. J., Statistics
HARRISON, C. T., History of the Theory of Art
HAWKESWORTH, C. J., Geochemistry
HAWKRIDGE, D. G., Applied Educational Sciences
HELD, D. A. J., Politics and Sociology
HENDERSON, E. S., Educational Technology
HOUSDEN, R. J., Computer Science
INCE, D. C., Computer Science
ISON, R. L., Systems
JONES, R. C. F., Organic Chemistry
KAYE, G. R., Information Management
LAURILLARD, D., Educational Technology
LAWLESS, C. J., Educational Technology
LEWIS, V., Human Development and Learning
MACKINTOSH, M., Economics
MARWICK, A. J. B., History
MASON, J. H., Mathematics Education
MASSEY, D. B., Geography
MONK, J., Electronics
MOON, R. E., Teaching Studies
PARKINSON, A. G., Engineering Mechanics
PILLINGER, C. T., Planetary Sciences
PLUMRIDGE, W. J., Materials
PORTEOUS, A., Environment Engineering
PRESCOTT, W., Educational Development
ROSE, S. P. R., Biology
ROWNTREE, D. G. F., Educational Development
RUTTERFORD, J., Financial Management
RZEVSKI, G., Engineering Design
SEWART, D., Distance Education
SOLOMON, A. I., Mathematical Physics
SPICER, R. A., Earth Sciences
STANNARD, F. R., Physics
STEADMAN, J. P., Architectural and Urban Morphology (Technology)
STOREY, J., Human Resource Management
THOMSON, A. W. J., Management
THOMPSON, K., Sociology
VINCENT, A. T., Educational Technology
WILSON, R. C. L., Earth Sciences
WOODS, P. E., Education

UNIVERSITY OF OXFORD

University Offices, Wellington Square, Oxford, OX1 2JD
Telephone: (1865) 270000
Fax: (1865) 270708

Originated 12th century
Academic year: October to June

Chancellor: The Rt Hon Lord JENKINS
High Steward: Rt Hon. Lord GOFF
Vice-Chancellor: Dr COLIN R. LUCAS
Registrar: D. R. HOLMES
Secretary of the Chest: J. R. CLEMENTS
Secretary of Faculties: A. P. WEALE
Deputy Registrar (Administration): P. W. JONES

Library: see Bodleian Library
Ashmolean Museum: see Museums
Number of teachers: 1,500
Number of students: 15,600

Publications: *Oxford University Gazette* (weekly during term-time), *Undergraduate Prospectus* (annually), *Graduate Studies Prospectus* (annually), *Statutes, Decrees and Regulations, Examination Decrees, University Calendar* (annually).

PROFESSORS

Faculty of Anthropology and Geography:
BRIDEN, J. C., Environmental Studies (Linacre College)
CLARK, G. L., Geography (St Peter's College)
CUNLIFFE, B. W., European Archaeology (Keble College)
GOUDIE, A. S., Geography (Hertford College)
PARKIN, D. J., Social Anthropology (All Souls College)
PEACH, G. C. K., Social Geography (St Catherine's College)
WARD, R. H., Biological Anthropology (Linacre College)

Committee for Archaeology:
TITE, M. S., Archaeological Science (Linacre College)

Faculty of Biological Sciences:
ANDERSON, R. M., Zoology (Merton College)
BURLEY, J., Forestry (Green College)
CAMPBELL, I. D., Structural Biology (St John's College)
DAVIES, K. E., Anatomy (Hertford College)
DICKINSON, H. G., Botany (Magdalen College)
DWEK, R. A., Glycobiology (Exeter College)
GARDNER, R. L., Zoology (Royal Society's Henry Dale Research) (Christ Church)
GRAHAM, C. F., Animal Development (St Catherine's College)
HAMILTON, W. D., Zoology (Royal Society Research) (New College)
HARVEY, P., Zoology (Jesus College)
JOHNSON, L. N., Molecular Biophysics (Corpus Christi College)
KREBS, J. R., Zoology (Royal Society Research) (Pembroke College)
LEAVER, C . J., Plant Sciences (St John's College)
MAY, Sir ROBERT, Zoology (Royal Society Research) (Merton College)
PERRINS, C. M., Ornithology (Wolfson College)
RADDA, G. K., Molecular Cardiology (Merton College)
REID, K. B. M., Immunochemistry (Green College)
SHERRATT, D. J., Microbiology (Linacre College)
SOUTHERN, E. M., Biochemistry (Trinity College)
SOUTHWOOD, Sir RICHARD, Zoology (Merton College)
STUART, D. I., MRC Structural Biology (Hertford College)

Faculty of Clinical Medicine:
BARLOW, D. H., Obstetrics and Gynaecology (Oriel College)
BELL, J. I., Clinical Medicine (Magdalen College)
BRON, A. J., Ophthalmology (Linacre College)
FOËX, P., Anaesthetics (Pembroke College)
GOODWIN, G. M., Psychiatry (Merton College)
GRAHAME-SMITH, D. G., Clinical Pharmacology (Corpus Christi College)
GRIMLEY EVANS, Sir JOHN, Clinical Geratology (Green College)
HARRIS, A. L., Clinical Oncology (St Hugh's College)
HIGGINS, C. F., Clinical Biochemistry (Hertford College)
KENWRIGHT, J., Orthopaedic Surgery (Worcester College)
MCGEE, J. O'D., Morbid Anatomy (Linacre College)
MCMICHAEL, A. J., MRC Immunology (Trinity College)
MORRIS, Sir PETER, Surgery (Balliol College)
MOXON, E. R., Paediatrics (Jesus College)
NEWSOM-DAVIS, J., Clinical Neurology (St Edmund Hall)
PETO, R., Medical Statistics and Epidemiology (Green College)
REDMAN, C. W. G., Obstetric Medicine (Lady Margaret Hall)
TOWNSEND, A. R. M., Molecular Immunology (Linacre College)
VESSEY, M. P., Public Health (St Cross College)
WARRELL, D. A., Tropical Medicine and Infectious Diseases (St Cross College)
WATKINS, H. C., Cardiovascular Medicine (Exeter College)
WEATHERALL, Sir DAVID, Medicine—Regius (Christ Church)

Continuing Education:
DAWKINS, C. R., Public Understanding of Science (New College)

Educational Studies:
PRING, R. A., Educational Studies (Green College)

Faculty of English Language and Literature:
AITCHISON, J. M., Language and Communication (Worcester College)
BUSH, R. L., American Literature (St John's College)

CAREY, J., English Literature (Merton College)
EAGLETON, T. F., English Literature (St Catherine's College)
FENTON, J., Poetry (Magdalen College)
GODDEN, M. R., Anglo-Saxon (Pembroke College)
HUDSON, A. M., Medieval English (Lady Margaret Hall)
JONES, E. L., English Literature (New College)
LEE, H., English Literature (New College)
LONSDALE, R. H., English Literature (Balliol College)
NUTTALL, A. D., English Literature (New College)
ROMAINE, S., English Language (Merton College)
STALLWORTHY, J. H., English Literature (Wolfson College)
STROHM, P., English Language and Literature (St Anne's College)

Inter-faculty Committee for Japanese Studies:
STOCKWIN, J. A. A., Modern Japanese Studies (St Antony's College)

Faculty of Law:
ASHWORTH, A. J., English Law (All Souls College)
BIRKS, P. B. H., Civil Law - Regius (All Souls College)
BROWNLIE, I., Public International Law (All Souls College)
CRAIG, P. P., English Law (St John's College)
DWORKIN, R. M., Jurisprudence (University College)
FINNIS, J. M., Law and Legal Philosophy (University College)
GALLIGAN, D. J., Socio-Legal Studies (Wolfson College)
MARKESINIS, B. S., European Law (Lady Margaret Hall)
PRENTICE, D. D., Corporate Law (Pembroke College)
RAZ, J., Philosophy of Law (Balliol College)
REYNOLDS, F. M. B., Law (Worcester College)
RUDDEN, B. A., Comparative Law (Brasenose College)
TAPPER, C. F. M., Law (Magdalen College)
VAVER, D., Intellectual Property and Information Technology Law (St Peter's College)
WEATHERILL, S. R., European Community Law (Somerville College)

Faculty of Literae Humaniores:
DAVIES, A. E., Comparative Philology (Somerville College)
FREDE, M., History of Philosophy (Keble College)
GRIFFIN, J., Classical Literature (Balliol College)
GRIFFIN, J. P., Moral Philosophy (Corpus Christi College)
MILLAR, F. G. B., Ancient History (Brasenose College)
PARKER, R. C. T., Ancient History (New College)
PARSONS, P. J., Greek—Regius (Christ Church)
PEACOCKE, C. A. B., Metaphysical Philosophy (Magdalen College)
SMITH, R. R. R., Classical Archaeology and Art (Lincoln College)
STEINBY, E. M., Archaeology of the Roman Empire (All Souls College)
WIGGINS, D. R .P., Logic (New College)
WINTERBOTTOM, M., Latin Language and Literature (Corpus Christi College)

Committee for the School of Management Studies:
HOPWOOD, A. G., Operations Management (Christ Church)
KAY, J. A., Management Studies (St Edmund Hall)
MAYER, C. P., Management Studies (Wadham College)
SAKO, M., Management Studies (Templeton College)

Faculty of Mathematical Sciences:
BALL, J. M., Natural Philosophy (The Queen's College)
BIRCH, B. J., Arithmetic (Brasenose College)
BRENT, R. P., Computing Science (St Hugh's College)
DONALDSON, S. K., Mathematics (St Anne's College)
DONNELLY, P. J., Statistical Science (St Anne's College)
GRANT, I. P., Mathematical Physics (Pembroke College)
HITCHIN, N. J., Geometry (New College)
HOARE, C. A. R., Computation (Wolfson College)
PENROSE, Sir ROGER, Mathematics (Wadham College)
QUILLEN, D. G., Pure Mathematics (Magdalen College)
RIPLEY, B. D., Applied Statistics (St Peter's College)
TREFETHEN, L. N., Numerical Analysis (Balliol College)
WELSH, J. A. D., Mathematics (Merton College)

Faculty of Medieval and Modern European Languages and Literatures other than English:
BOWIE, M. M., French Literature (All Souls College)
CAVE, T. C., French Literature (St John's College)
CHARLES-EDWARDS, T. M. O., Celtic (Corpus Christi College)
EARLE, T. F., Portuguese Studies (St Peter's College)
HIGGINBOTHAM, J. T., General Linguistics (Somerville College)
JEFFERYS, E. M., Byzantine and Modern Greek Language and Literature (Exeter College)
MAIDEN, M. D., Romance Languages (Trinity College)
MICHAEL, I. D. L., Spanish Studies (Exeter College)
PALMER, N. F., German Medieval and Linguistic Studies (St Edmund Hall)
REED, T. J., German Language and Literature (The Queen's College)
SMITH, G. S., Russian (New College)
VIALA, A., French Studies (Wadham College)
WOODHOUSE, J. R., Italian Studies (Magdalen College)

Faculty of Modern History:
BROWN, J. M., History of the British Commonwealth (Balliol College)
BURROW, J. W., European Thought (Balliol College)
DAVIES, R. R., Medieval History (All Souls College)
EVANS, R. J. W., Modern History (Regius) (Oriel College)
FEINSTEIN, C. H., Economic History (All Souls College)
FOSTER, R. F., Irish History (Hertford College)
FOX, R., History of Science (Linacre College)
HARRIS, J. F., Modern History (St Catherine's College)
HOWE, D. W., American History (St Catherine's College)
KEMP, M. J., History of Art (Trinity College)
KNIGHT, A. S., History of Latin America (St Antony's College)
LANGFORD, P., Modern History (Lincoln College)
LEWIS, J. E., History of Medicine (All Souls College)
MATTHEW, H. C. G., Modern History (St Hugh's College)
MAYR-HARTING, H. M. R. E., Ecclesiastical History (Regius) (Christ Church)
O'NEILL, R. J., History of War (All Souls College)

Committee for Modern Middle Eastern Studies:
HOLES, C. D., Contemporary Arab World (Magdalen College)

Faculty of Music:
STROHM, R., Music (Wadham College)

Faculty of Oriental Studies:
BAINES, J. R., Egyptology (The Queen's College)
DUDBRIDGE, G., Chinese (University College)
GOMBRICH, R. F., Sanskrit (Balliol College)
SANDERSON, A. G. J. S., Eastern Religions and Ethics (All Souls College)
SHEIKHOLESLAMI, A. R., Persian Studies (Wadham College)
THOMSON, R. W., Armenian Studies (Pembroke College)
VAN GELDER, G., Arabic (St John's College)
WILLIAMSON, H. G. M., Hebrew (Regius) (Christ Church)

Faculty of Physical Sciences:
BALDWIN, Sir JACK, Organic Chemistry (Magdalen College)
BRADY, J. M., Information Engineering (Keble College)
BROOK, R. J., Materials Science (St Cross College)
CANTOR, B., Materials (St Catherine's College)
CASHMORE, R. J., Experimental Physics (Balliol College)
CHILD, M. S., Theoretical Chemistry (University College)
CLARKE, D. W., Control Engineering (New College)
COOPER, S., Experimental Physics (St Catherine's College)
COWLEY, R. A., Experimental Philosophy (Wadham College)
DEWEY, J. F., Geology (University College)
DOBSON, C. M., Chemistry (Lady Margaret Hall)
EATOCK-TAYLOR, W. R., Mechanical Engineering (St Hugh's College)
GREEN, M. L. H., Inorganic Chemistry (St Catherine's College)
HILL, H. A. O., Bioinorganic Chemistry (The Queen's College)
HOULSBY, G. T., Engineering Science (Brasenose College)
JONES, T. V., Turbomachinery (St Catherine's College)
LLEWELLYN SMITH, C. H., Theoretical Physics (St John's College)
LOWE, G., Biological Chemistry (Lincoln College)
O'NIONS, R. K., Physics and Chemistry of Minerals (St Hugh's College)
PETTIFOR, D. G., Metallurgy (St Edmund Hall)
RAYNES, E. P., Optoelectronic Engineering (St Cross College)
ROSS, G. G., Theoretical Physics (Wadham College)
SANDARS, P. G. H., Experimental Physics (Christ Church)
SHERRINGTON, D., Theoretical Physics (New College)
SIMONS, J. P., Chemistry (Exeter College)
TARASSENKO, L., Electrical and Electronic Engineering (St John's College)
TAYLOR, F. W., Atmospheric Physics (Jesus College)
TITCHMARSH, J., Microanalytical Techniques for Structural Integrity Problems (St Anne's College)
WATTS, A. B., Marine Geology and Geophysics (Wolfson College)
WEBB, C. E., Laser Physics (Jesus College)

WOODHOUSE, J., Geophysics (Worcester College)

Faculty of Physiological Sciences:

BLAKEMORE, C. B., Physiology (Magdalen College)
BROWNLEE, G. G., Chemical Pathology (Lincoln College)
GORDON, S., Cellular Pathology (Exeter College)
NOBLE, D., Cardiovascular Physiology (Balliol College)
SMITH, A. D., Pharmacology (Lady Margaret Hall)
WALDMANN, H., Pathology (Lincoln College)

Faculty of Psychological Studies:

BRYANT, P. E., Psychology (Wolfson College)
COWEY, A., Physiological Psychology (Lincoln College)
IVERSON, S. D., Psychology (Magdalen College)

Committee for Queen Elizabeth House:

PETERS, G. H., Agricultural Economics (Wolfson College)
STEWART, F. J., Development Economics (Somerville College)

Committee for the Ruskin School of Drawing and Fine Art:

FARTHING, S. F. G., Ruskin Master (St Edmund Hall)

Faculty of Social Studies:

BEINHART, W., Race Relations (St Antony's College)
BLISS, C. J., International Economics (Nuffield College)
BROWN, A. H., Politics (St Antony's College)
COHEN, G. A., Social and Political Theory (All Souls College)
COLLIER, P., Economics (St Antony's College)
HAYWARD, J. E. S., European Studies (St Antony's College)
HENDRY, D. F., Economics (Nuffield College)
HESSE, J. J., European Institutions and Politics (Nuffield College)
KLEMPERER, P. D., Economics (Nuffield College)
MACFARLANE, S. N., International Relations (St Anne's College)
NICKELL, S. J., Economics (Nuffield College)
RINGEN, S., Sociology and Social Policy (Green College)
ROBERTS, E. A., International Relations (Balliol College)
SHAFER, B. E., American Government (Nuffield College)
STEPAN, A. C., Government (All Souls College)
VICKERS, J. S., Political Economy (All Souls College)

Faculty of Theology:

BARTON, Rev. J., Interpretation of Holy Scripture (Oriel College)
MAYR-HARTING, H. M. R. E., Ecclesiastical History (Christ Church)
O'DONOVAN, Rev. O. M. T., Moral and Pastoral Theology (Christ Church)
ROWLAND, C. C., Exegesis of Holy Scripture (The Queen's College)
SWINBURNE, R. G., Philosophy of the Christian Religion (Oriel College)
WARD, Rev. J. S. K., Divinity—Regius (Christ Church)
WEBSTER, J. B., Divinity (Christ Church)
WILLIAMSON, H. G. M., Hebrew – Regius (Christ Church)

DIRECTORS AND HEADS OF UNIVERSITY INSTITUTIONS AND DEPARTMENTS

Nuffield Department of Anaesthetics:
Head P. FOEX (Pembroke College)

Department of Applied Social Studies and Social Research:
Dir T. SMITH (St Hilda's College)

Institute of Archaeology:
Dir E. M. STIENBY (All Souls College)

Research Laboratory for Archaeology and the History of Art:
Dir M. S. TITE (Linacre College)

University Archives:
Keeper D. G. VAISEY (Exeter College)

Ashmolean Museum:
Dir C. P. H. B. BROWN (Worcester College)

Department of Biochemistry:
Head P. C. NEWELL (St Peter's College)

Institute of Biological Anthropology:
Head R. H. WARD (Linacre College)

Bodleian Library:
Dir of University Library Services and Bodley's Library R. P. CARR (Balliol College)

Botanic Garden:
Keeper H. G. DICKINSON (Magdalen College)

Brazilian Studies Centre:
Dir L. BETHELL (St Anthony's College)

Department of Cardiovascular Medicine:
Head H. C. WATKINS (Exeter College)

Cellular Science:
Head K. C. GATTER (St John's College)

Chemical Crystallography Laboratory:
Head C. K. PROUT (Oriel College)

Department of Chemistry:
Chair W. G. RICHARDS (Brasenose College)

Institute of Chinese Studies:
Dir G. DUXBRIDGE (University College)

Nuffield Department of Clinical Biochemistry:
Head C. F. HIGGINS (Hertford College)

Nuffield Department of Clinical Medicine:
Head J. I. BELL (Magdalen College)

Department of Clinical Neurology:
Head J. NEWSOM-DAVIS (St Edmund Hall)

Department of Clinical Pharmacology:
Head D. G. GRAHAM-SMITH (Corpus Christi College)

Computing Laboratory:
Dir C. A. R. HOARE (Wolfson College)

Department for Continuing Education:
Dir G. P. THOMAS (Kellogg College)

Centre for Criminological Research and Probation Studies Unit:
Head R. G. HOOD (All Souls College)

Dyson Perrins Laboratory:
Head Sir JACK BALDWIN (St Catherine's College)

Department of Earth Sciences:
Head R. K. O'NIONS (St Hugh's College)

Institute of Economics and Statistics:
Dir S. J. NICKELL (Nuffield College)

Department of Educational Studies:
Dir R. A. PRING (Green College)

Department of Engineering Science:
Head D. W. CLARKE (New College)

Environmental Change Unit:
IBM Dir J. C. BRIDEN (Linacre College)

Centre for the Advanced Study of European and Comparative Law:
Dir B. S. MARKESINIS (Lady Margaret Hall)

Centre for European Politics, Economics and Society:
Dir J. E. S. HAYWARD (St Antony's College)

Institute for European Studies:
Dir J. E. S. HAYWARD (St Antony's College)

Genetics Unit:
Head K. E. DAVIES (Keble College)

School of Geography:
Head G. L. CLARK (St Peter's College)

Glycobiology Unit:
Head R. A. DWEK (Exeter College)

Department of the History of Art:
Head M. J. KEMP (Trinity College)

Wellcome Unit for the History of Medicine:
Dir J. E. LEWIS (All Souls College)

Museum of the History of Science:
Keeper J. A. BENNETT (Linacre College)

Department of Human Anatomy:
Head K. E. DAVIES (Keble College)

Inorganic Chemistry Laboratory:
Head M. L. H. GREEN (St Catherine's College)

Nissan Institute of Japanese Studies:
Dir J. A. A. STOCKWIN (St Anne's College)

Language Centre:
Dir R. N. VANDERPLANK

Latin America Centre:
Dir A. E. ANGELL (St Antony's College)

Centre for Linguistics and Philology:
Curator J. T. HIGGINBOTHAM (Somerville College)

Department of Materials:
Head B. CANTOR (St Catherine's College)

Mathematical Institute:
Chair. J. A. D. WELSH (Merton College)

Department of Medical Illustration:
Dir P. L. C. DOVE

Department of Medical Oncology:
Head A. L. HARRIS (St Hugh's College)

Molecular Physics Laboratory:
Head L. N. JOHNSON (Corpus Christi College)

Molecular Medicine:
Dir Sir DAVID WEATHERALL (Christ Church)

Interdisciplinary Research Centre for Molecular Science:
Dir J. E. BALDWIN (Magdalen College)

Microbiology Unit:
Head D. J. SHERRATT (Linacre College)

MRC Biochemical and Clinical Magnetic Resonance Unit:
Head P. STYLES (Merton College)

MRC Immunochemistry Unit:
Head K. B. M. REID (Green College)

University Museum of Natural History:
Dir K. S. THOMSON (Kellogg College)

Nuffield Department of Obstetrics and Gynaecology:
Head D. H. BARLOW (Oriel College)

Nuffield Laboratory of Ophthalmology:
Head A. J. BRON (Linacre College)

Oriental Institute:
Chair. of Curators J. A. J. RABY (St Hugh's College)

Nuffield Department of Orthopaedic Surgery:
Head J. KENWRIGHT (Worcester College)

Department of Paediatrics:
Head E. R. MOXON (Jesus College)

Sir William Dunn School of Pathology:
Head H. WALDMANN (Lincoln College)

Nuffield Department of Pathology and Bacteriology:
Head J. O'D. MCGEE (Linacre College)

Department of Pharmacology:
Head A. D. SMITH (Lady Margaret Hall)

Philosophy Centre:
Curator H. R. BROWN (Wolfson College)
Physical and Theoretical Chemistry Laboratory:
Head J. P. SIMONS (Exeter College)
Department of Physics:
Chair. R. J. CASHMORE (Balliol College)
Department of Physiology:
Head J. C. ELLORY (Corpus Christi College)
Pitt Rivers Museum:
Dir M. O'HANLON (Linacre College)
Department of Plant Sciences:
Head C. J. LEAVER (St John's College)
Department of Psychiatry:
Head G. M. GOODWIN (Merton College)
Department of Experimental Psychology:
Head S. D. IVERSEN (Magdalen College)
Department of Radiology:
Head B. J. SHEPSTONE (Wolfson College)
Ruskin School of Drawing and Fine Art:
Master S. G. FARTHING (St Edmund Hall)
Said Business School:
Peter Moores Dir J. A. KAY (St Edmund Hall)
Institute of Social and Cultural Anthropology:
Head D. J. PARKIN (All Souls College)
Social Studies Faculty Centre:
Chair. M. D. DEAS (St Antony's College)
Centre for Socio-Legal Studies:
Dir D. J. GALLIGAN (Wolfson College)
Department of Statistics:
Head P. J. DONNELLY (St Anne's College)
Nuffield Department of Surgery:
Head Sir PETER MORRIS (Balliol College)
Transport Studies Unit:
Dir J. M. PRESTON (St Anne's College)
Department of Zoology:
Head R. ANDERSON

COLLEGES

All Souls College: Oxford, OX1 4AL; tel. (1865) 279379; f. 1438; for Fellows only; Warden Prof. JOHN DAVIES.

Balliol College: Oxford, OX1 3BJ; tel. (1865) 277777; f. 1263; Master ANDREW GRAHAM (acting).

Brasenose College: Oxford, OX1 4AJ; tel. (1865) 277830; f. 1509; Principal The Rt. Hon. Lord WINDLESHAM.

Christ Church: Oxford, OX1 1DP; tel. (1865) 276150; f. 1546; Dean The Very Rev. J. H. DRURY.

Corpus Christi College: Oxford, OX1 4JF; tel. (1865) 276700; f. 1517; Pres. Sir KEITH THOMAS.

Exeter College: Oxford, OX1 3DP; tel. (1865) 279600; f. 1314; Rector Dr MARILYN BUTLER.

Green College: Oxford, OX2 6HG; tel. (1865) 274770; f. 1979, for graduates; Warden Sir JOHN HANSON.

Harris Manchester College: Oxford, OX1 3TD; tel. (1865) 271006; f. 1786; Principal The Rev. Dr R. WALLER.

Hertford College: Oxford, OX1 3BW; tel. (1865) 279400; f. 1874; Principal Sir WALTER BODMER.

Jesus College: Oxford, OX1 3DW; tel. (1865) 279700; f. 1571; Principal Dr Sir PETER NORTH.

Keble College: Oxford, OX1 3PG; tel. (1865) 272727; f. 1870; Warden Prof. AVERIL CAMERON.

Kellogg College: Oxford, OX1 2JA; tel. (1865) 270383; f. 1990; Pres. Dr G. P. THOMAS.

Lady Margaret Hall: Oxford, OX2 6QA; tel. (1865) 274300; f. 1878; Principal Sir BRIAN FALL.

Linacre College: Oxford, OX1 1SY; tel. (1865) 271650; f. 1962, as Linacre House, for graduates; Principal Dr PAUL SLACK.

Lincoln College: Oxford, OX1 3DR; tel. (1865) 279800; f. 1427; Rector Dr E. K. ANDERSON.

Magdalen College: Oxford, OX1 4AU; tel. (1865) 276000; f. 1458; Pres. A. D. SMITH.

Mansfield College: Oxford, OX1 3TF; tel. (1865) 270999; f. 1885; Principal Prof. D. I. MARQUAND.

Merton College: Oxford, OX1 4JD; tel. (1865) 276310; f. 1264; Warden Dr JESSICA RAWSON.

New College: Oxford, OX1 3BN; tel. (1865) 279555; f. 1379; Warden Dr A. J. RYAN.

Nuffield College: Oxford, OX1 1NF; tel. (1865) 278500; f. 1937, for graduates; Warden Prof. ANTHONY ATKINSON.

Oriel College: Oxford, OX1 4EW; tel. (1865) 276555; f. 1326; Provost Dr E. W. NICHOLSON.

Pembroke College: Oxford, OX1 1DW; tel. (1865) 276444; f. 1624; Master Dr R. STEVENS.

Queen's College, The: Oxford, OX1 4AW; tel. (1865) 279120; f. 1340; Provost Dr G. MARSHALL.

St Anne's College: Oxford, OX2 6HS; tel. (1865) 274800; f. 1893 (as Society of Oxford Home Students); Principal Mrs R. DEECH.

St Antony's College: Oxford, OX2 6JF; tel. (1865) 284700; f. 1950, for graduates; Warden Sir MARRACK GOULDING.

St Catherine's College: Oxford, OX1 3UJ; tel. (1865) 271700; f. 1868, reconstituted as a full College 1962; Master Lord PLANT OF HIGHFIELD.

St Cross College: Oxford, OX1 3LZ; tel. (1865) 278490; f. 1965, for graduates; Master Dr R. C. REPP.

St Edmund Hall: Oxford, OX1 4AR; tel. (1865) 279000; f. *c.* 1278; Principal J. P. D. DUNBABIN (acting).

St Hilda's College: Oxford, OX4 1DY; tel. (1865) 276884; f. 1893; Principal E. M. LLEWELLYN-SMITH.

St Hugh's College: Oxford, OX2 6LE; tel. (1865) 274900; f. 1886; Principal D. WOOD.

St John's College: Oxford, OX1 3JP; tel. (1865) 277300; f. 1555; Pres. Dr W. HAYES.

St Peter's College: Oxford, OX1 2DL; tel. (1865) 278900; f. 1929 as St Peter's Hall; Master Dr J. P. BARRON.

Somerville College: Oxford, OX2 6HD; tel. (1865) 270600; f. 1879; Principal Dame FIONA CALDICOTT.

Templeton College: Oxford, OX1 5NY; tel. (1865) 422500; fax (1865) 425501; f. 1995; Pres. Sir DAVID ROWLAND.

Trinity College: Oxford, OX1 3BH; tel. (1865) 279900; f. 1554; Pres. Hon. MICHAEL J. BELOFF.

University College: Oxford, OX1 4BH; tel. (1865) 276602; f. 1249; Master Sir ROBIN BUTLER.

Wadham College: Oxford, OX1 3PN; tel. (1865) 277900; f. 1612; Warden J. S. FLEMMING.

Wolfson College: Oxford, OX2 6UD; tel. (1865) 274100; f. 1965, for graduates; Pres. Sir DAVID SMITH.

Worcester College: Oxford, OX1 2HB; tel. 1(1865) 278300; f. 1714; Provost R. G. SMETHURST.

PERMANENT PRIVATE HALLS

Blackfriars: Oxford, OX1 3LY; tel. (1865) 278400; f. 1921; Regent Very Rev. Dr P. PARVIS.

Campion Hall: Oxford, OX1 1QS; tel. (1865) 286100; f. 1896; Master Rev. G. J. HUGHES.

Greyfriars: Oxford, OX4 1SB; tel. (1865) 243694; f. 1910; Warden The Rev. Dr M. SHEEHAN.

Regent's Park College: Oxford, OX1 2LB; tel. (1865) 288120; f. 1810; Principal Rev. P. S. FIDDES.

St Benet's Hall: Oxford, OX1 3LN; tel. (1865) 515006; f. 1897; Master Rev. H. WANSBROUGH.

Wycliffe Hall: Oxford, OX2 6PW; tel. (1865) 274200; Principal Rev. A. E. MCGRATH.

ASSOCIATED INSTITUTIONS

Maison Française d'Oxford: Norham Road, Oxford, OX2 6SE; f. 1946; Dir JEAN-CLAUDE VATIN.

NERC Institute of Virology and Environmental Microbiology: see under Research Institutes.

Oxford Institute for Energy Studies: 57 Woodstock Road, Oxford, OX2 6FA; f. 1982; Dir R. E. MABRO.

Oxford Centre for Hebrew and Jewish Studies: Yarnton Manor, Yarnton, Oxford, OX5 1PY; Pres. B. WASSERSTEIN.

Oxford Centre for Islamic Studies: George St, Oxford, OX1 2AR; f. 1985; Dir Dr FARHAN AHMAD NIZAMI.

Institute of Legal Practice: joint venture of Oxford and Oxford Brookes univs; Dir NICK JOHNSON.

Oxford International Centre for Palliative Care: Churchill Hospital, Oxford OX3 7LJ.

OXFORD BROOKES UNIVERSITY

Gipsy Lane, Headington, Oxford, OX3 0BP
Telephone: (1865) 741111
Founded 1865 as Oxford School of Art; became Oxford Polytechnic 1970; university status 1992
State control
Academic year: September to July
Chancellor: H. KENNEDY
Vice-Chancellor: G. UPTON
Deputy Vice-Chancellors: J. R. BRADSHAW, Prof. P. FIDLER, B. SUMMERS
Academic Secretary: E. WINDERS
Librarian: H. WORKMAN
Library of 314,000 vols
Number of teachers: 700
Number of students: 8,772 full-time and sandwich, 4,934 part-time

HEADS OF DEPARTMENTS

Architecture: C. CROSS
Biological and Molecular Sciences: Prof. D. BEADLE
Business: Prof. M. BENWELL
Computing and Mathematical Sciences: J. L. NEALON
Education: S. CATLING
Engineering: D. MORREY
Health Care: LINDA CHALLIS
Hotel and Restaurant Management: C. ROBERTSON
Humanities: J. PERKINS
Languages: S. HAND
Modular Course: D. SCURRY
Planning: Prof. J. GLASSON
Social Sciences: Prof. SUSAN MCRAE
Art, Publishing and Music: P. RICHARDSON

UNIVERSITY OF PAISLEY

High St, Paisley, Renfrewshire, PA1 2BE
Telephone: (141) 848-3000
Fax: (141) 887-0812

Founded 1897 as Paisley College of Technology, present name and status 1992
Academic year: October to June

Chancellor: Sir ROBERT EASTON
Principal and Vice-Chancellor: Prof. RICHARD W. SHAW
Vice-Principal: Prof. SEAMUS MCDAID
Assistant Principals: Prof. JOHN A. LITTLE, Prof. CAROLINE MACDONALD
Secretary: JAMES M. FRASER
Registrar: DAVID RIGG
Librarian: STUART JAMES

Number of teachers: 455 full-time
Number of students: 6,378 full-time, 2,523 part-time

Publications: *University Prospectus*, *Annual Report*, *Postgraduate Prospectus*.

DEANS

Faculty of Education: P. LOWRIE
Faculty of Engineering: Prof. J. A. LITTLE (acting)
Faculty of Science and Technology: Prof. R. O. MCLEAN
Faculty of Business: Prof. J. J. STRUTHERS
Faculty of Health and Social Sciences: Dr T. P. CLARKE

HEADS OF DEPARTMENTS

Accounting, Economics and Languages: A. I. M. FLEMING
Applied Social Studies: Prof. J. O. FOSTER
Biological Sciences: Prof. R. O. MCLEAN
Chemistry and Chemical Engineering: Prof. A. C. ROACH
Civil, Structural and Environmental Engineering: Prof. P. SMITH
Computing and Information Systems: Prof. M. K. CROWE
Curricular Studies: J. ROBERTSON
Electronic Engineering and Physics: Prof. R. CHAPMAN
Land Economics: Prof. W. D. FRASER
Management and Marketing: Prof. R. VON ZUGBACH
Mathematics and Statistics: Prof. R. R. BURNSIDE
Mechanical and Manufacturing Engineering and the Quality Centre: G. MUIR (acting)
Professional Studies: D. L. GULLAND

ATTACHED INSTITUTES

Centre for Alcohol and Drug Studies: Dir K. BARRIE.

Technology and Business Centre: Manager B. G. CROSS.

Materials and Components Developing and Testing Association: Dir M. ARTHUR.

Network and Information Management Services: Dir A. SHAW.

Land Value Information Unit: Dir D. MARTIN.

Centre for Environmental and Waste Management: Chief Exec. Prof. R. WILLEY.

Centre for Gerontology and Health Studies: Dir Prof. M. GILHOOLY.

Centre for Particle Characterization and Analysis: Man. Dr A. HURSTHOUSE.

Electromagnetic Compatability Centre: Dir F. GALBRAITH.

Enterprise Research Centre: Dir Prof. D. DEAKINS.

Microelectronics in Business Unit: Man. Dr A. WATT.

Environmental Technologies: Dir Prof. P. TUCKER.

UNIVERSITY OF PLYMOUTH

Drake Circus, Plymouth, PL4 8AA
Telephone: (1752) 600600
Fax: (1752) 232293

Founded 1970 as Plymouth Polytechnic; name changed to Polytechnic South West in 1989; present name and status 1992

Vice-Chancellor: Prof. R. J. BULL
Deputy Vice-Chancellor (Academic): Prof. L. EBDON
Deputy Vice-Chancellor (Resources): Prof. N. REID
Secretary and Academic Registrar: J. HOPKINSON
Library and Media Services: J. PRIESTLEY

Number of staff: 2,200
Number of students: 16,000 full-time and sandwich, 8,000 part-time

Publications: *Annual Review*, *Research Report*, prospectuses.

DEANS

Agriculture, Food and Land Use: C. BROOM
Plymouth Business School: Prof. P. JONES
Arts and Education: Prof. M. NEWBY
Science: Dr P. O'NEILL
Human Sciences: Prof. M. BEVERIDGE
Technology: Prof. R. COPE
Postgraduate Medical School: Prof. K. ROGERS

HEADS OF DEPARTMENTS

Agriculture, Food and Land Use:
- Agriculture and Food Studies: Prof. R. BLACKSHAW
- Land Use and Rural Management: M. F. WARREN

Arts and Education:
- Arts and Design: D. BUSS
- Education: G. PAYNE
- Graduate Studies in Arts and Education: Dr G. TAYLOR
- Humanities and Cultural Interpretation: Dr R. GEE

Human Sciences:
- Institute of Health Studies: Prof. M. WATKINS
- Politics: ADRIAN LEE
- Psychology: Dr IAN DENNIS
- Social Work and Social Policy: ANN JEFFRIES
- Sociology: Dr JOAN CHANDLER

Science:
- Biological Sciences: Dr C. B. MUNN
- Environmental Sciences: Dr S. HILL
- Geographical Sciences: Prof. M. BLACKSELL
- Geological Sciences: Dr J. GRIFFITHS
- Institute of Marine Studies: Dr J. CHUDLEY

Technology:
- Architecture: Prof. M. WIGGINTON
- Civil and Structural Engineering: Prof. G. BULLOCK
- Computing: Prof. P. PEARCE
- Electronic, Communication and Electrical Engineering: Prof. E. IFEACHOR
- Mathematics and Statistics: Prof. P. DYKE
- Manufacturing, Materials and Mechanical Engineering: D. SHORT

UNIVERSITY OF PORTSMOUTH

University House, Winston Churchill Ave, Portsmouth, PO1 2UP
Telephone: (1705) 876543
Fax: (1705) 843319

Founded 1869 as Portsmouth School of Science and Art, became Portsmouth Polytechnic in 1969; present name and status 1992

Chancellor: Lord PALUMBO
Vice-Chancellor: Prof. J. CRAVEN
Pro-Vice-Chancellors: C. T. MONK, Dr M. MCVICAR, Dr M. BATEMAN
Academic Registrar: A. REES
Librarian: I. BONAR

Library of 600,000 vols
Number of teachers: 862
Number of students: 11,863 full-time and sandwich, 3,241 part-time

DEANS

Portsmouth Business School: M. DUNN
Faculty of Technology: Dr D. ARRELL
Faculty of the Environment: L. SHURMER-SMITH
Faculty of Humanities and Social Sciences: M. MITCHELL
Faculty of Science: Prof. D. ROGERS

HEADS OF DEPARTMENTS

Business School:
- Business and Management: G. OLIVER
- Accounting and Management Science: A. RIDLEY
- Economics: Prof. L. HUNT
- Management Development: L. BALTHAZOR

Faculty of Technology:
- Electrical and Electronic Engineering: Prof. M. D. CRIPPS
- Mechanical and Manufacturing Engineering: Dr M. BEDFORD
- Information Systems: Dr S. HAND
- Computer Science and Mathematics: Prof. D. MATRAVERS

Faculty of the Environment:
- Architecture: WENDY POTTS
- Art, Design and Media: M. DENNIS
- Civil Engineering: Prof. B. LEE
- Geography: Prof. K. JONES
- Land and Construction Management: R. BELCHER

Faculty of Humanities and Social Sciences:
- Education and English: Dr R. BIRCH
- Health Studies: NEIL LINDFIELD
- Languages and Area Studies: I. KEMBLE
- Social and Historical Studies: F. CARR

Faculty of Science:
- Biological Sciences: Dr R. GREENWOOD
- Geology: Prof. M. E. JONES
- Pharmacy, Biomedical and Physical Sciences: Dr J. SMART
- Psychology: Dr J. MACDONALD
- Radiography: DEREK ADRIAN-HARRIS
- Sport and Exercise Science: G. REID

UNIVERSITY OF READING

Reading, Berkshire, RG6 6AH
Telephone: (118) 987-5123
Telex: 847813
Fax: (118) 931-4404

University Extension College established 1892; University Charter granted 1926

Chancellor: The Rt Hon. Lord CARRINGTON
Vice-Chancellor: Prof. R. WILLIAMS
Deputy Vice-Chancellor: Prof. R. MEAD
Pro-Vice-Chancellors: Prof. M. G. FULFORD, Prof. P. J. GREGORY
Registrar: D. C. R. FRAMPTON
Librarian: SHEILA CORRALL

Library: see Libraries
Number of teachers: 814, including 157 professors
Number of students: 12,320

Publication: *Annual Report*.

DEANS

Faculty of Letters and Social Sciences: Prof. T. A. DOWNES
Faculty of Science: Prof. K. D. BAKER
Faculty of Agriculture and Food: Prof. R. SUMMERFIELD
Faculty of Urban and Regional Studies: Prof. B. GOODALL

Faculty of Education and Community Studies: Prof. MAUREEN POPE

PROFESSORS

(Some professors serve in more than one faculty)

Faculty of Letters and Social Sciences:

ADAMS, J. N., Classics
ALLUM, P. A., Italian Politics
BARAŃSKI, Z., Italian Studies
BARBER, M. C., History
BERRY, D., Psychology
BIDDISS, M. D., History
BLUTH, C., European and International Studies
BRADLEY, R. J., Archaeology
BUCKLEY, R. A., Law
BUCKLEY, S., Fine Art
BULLEN, J. B., English
CANTWELL, J. A., International Economics
CASSON, M. C., Economics
COOPER, P. J., Psychology
COTTINGHAM, J. G., Philosophy
DAVIES, J. C. H., Sociology
DOWNES, T. A., Law
DUNSBY, J. M., Music
EMDEN, W. G. VAN, French
EVANS, A. W., Environmental Economics
FLETCHER, P., Language Pathology
FUDGE, E. C., Linguistic Science
FULFORD, M. G., Archaeology
GARDNER, J. F., Ancient History
GARMAN, M. A. G., Linguistic Science
GREGORY, R. G., Politics
GURR, A. J., English
JACKSON, P., Law
JAMES, E. F., History
JONES, G. G., Business History
JONES, R., International Relations
KEMP, B. R., Medieval History
KNOWLSON, J. R., French
LEPSCHY, G. C., Italian
MCKENNA, F. P., Psychology
MOSLEY, P., Economics
MURRAY, L., Psychology
NOBES, C. W., Accounting
NOBLE, P., Medieval and Quebec Literature
PARRINDER, J. P., English
PATTERSON, K. D., Econometrics
PEMBERTON, J., Economics
PHILIPPAKI WARBURTON, I., Linguistic Science
PILLING, J., English
POTTS, A., History of Art
REDFERN, W. D., French
ROACH, P. J., Phonetics
SALVESEN, C. G., English
SANDFORD, J. E., German
SCOTT-QUINN, B., Investment Banking
SEGAL, N., French Studies
SMITH, P. T., Psychology
TWYMAN, M. L., Typography and Graphic Communication
UNGER, G., Typography
UTTON, M. A., Economics
WADDINGTON, P. A. J., Sociology
WARBURTON, D. M., Psychology
WARBURTON, I. P., Linguistic Science
WILKINS, D. A., Linguistic Science
WOODWARD, P. R., Politics

Faculty of Science:

ALLEN, J. R. L., Geology
ALLOWAY, B., Soil Science
ALMOND, J. W., Microbiology
ATKINS, A. G., Mechanical Engineering
BAINES, M. J., Applied Mathematics
BAKER, K. D., Computer Science
BALDING, D., Applied Statistics
BASSETT, D. C., Physics
BOWKER, M., Physical Chemistry
BROWNING, K. A., Meteorology
BURCH, R., Catalytic Chemistry
CARDIN, D. J., Inorganic Chemistry
CHAPLIN, C. R., Engineering
CODLING, K., Atomic and Molecular Physics
COLEMAN, M. L., Sedimentology
COOPER, P. J., Psychology
CRABBE, M. J. C., Protein Biochemistry
CUNNINGHAM, F. J., Reproductive Physiology
CURNOW, R. N., Applied Statistics
DICK, M. W., Botany
DILS, R. R., Biochemistry and Physiology
GILBERT, A., Photochemistry
GREGORY, P. J., Soil Science
HERRINGTON, T., Colloid Science
HILTON, A. J. W., Pure Mathematics
HOLLAND, P. W., Zoology
HOSKINS, B. J., Meteorology
JERONIMIDIS, G., Composite Materials Engineering
LETTINGTON, A. H., Physics
LOWRY, P. J., Biochemistry and Physiology
MCCANN, C., Geophysics
MANN, J., Organic Chemistry
MEAD, R., Applied Statistics
MEGSON, G. M., Computer Science
MITCHELL, G. R., Polymer Physics
NASH-WILLIAMS, C. ST J. A., Pure Mathematics
NEEDHAM, D. J., Applied Mathematics
NICHOLS, N. K., Applied Mathematics
O'NEILL, A., Meteorology
PARKER, J. S., Botany
PYE, K., Environmental Sedimentology
RICE, D. A., Inorganic Chemistry
ROBSON, R. L., Microbiology
SELLWOOD, B. W., Applied Sedimentology
SEWELL, M. J., Applied Mathematics
SIBLY, R. M., Behavioural Ecology
SIMKISS, K., Zoology
SINHA, P. K., Electronic Engineering
THORPE, A. J., Meteorology
WALKER, C. H., Biochemical Toxicology
WALSH, R., Chemistry
WARWICK, K., Cybernetics
WHITEHEAD, J. R., Applied Statistics
WORSLEY, P., Quarternary Sedimentology
WRIGHT, A., Amorphous Solid State Physics
WRIGHT, J. D. M., Pure Mathematics

Faculty of Agriculture and Food:

BEEVER, D. E., Animal Production
BIRCH, G. G., Food Chemistry
CALIGARI, P. D. S., Agricultural Botany
CAMPBELL-PLATT, G., Food Technology
ELLIS, R. H., Crop Physiology
EMDEN, H. F. VAN, Applied Entomology
HADLEY, P., Horticultural Crop Physiology
JOHN, P., Plant Science
KEATINGE, J. D. H., Agricultural and Rural Systems
LEDWARD, D. A., Food Science
MARSH, J. S., Agricultural Economics and Management
PYLE, D. L., Biotechnology
SCHOFIELD, J. D., Food Biochemistry
SUMMERFIELD, R. J., Crop Physiology
SWINBANK, A., Agricultural Economics
TRAILL, B., Food Management and Marketing
UPTON, M., Agricultural Economics
WILLIAMS, C. M., Nutrition

Faculty of Urban and Regional Studies:

BAUM, A. E., Land Management
BENNETT, J., Quantity Surveying
BON, R., Construction Management and Economics
BREHENY, M. J., Applied Geography
CROOME, D. J., Construction Engineering
CROSBY, F. N., Land Management
DAVIES, H. W. E., Planning
FISHER, G. N., Construction Project Management
FLANAGAN, R., Construction Management
GOODALL, B., Geography
GORDON, I. R., Geography
GURNEY, R., Geography
LANSLEY, P., Construction Management
WARD, C. W. R., Property Investment and Finance
WHITEHEAD, P. G., Geography

Faculty of Education and Community Studies:

ADELMAN, C. L., Education Studies and Management
CROLL, P., Education
EDWARDS, V., Education
GARFORTH, C. J., Extension Systems
GELLERT, C. E., Arts and Humanities in Education
GILBERT, J. K., Science and Technology Education
KEMP, A. E., Arts and Humanities in Education
POPE, M. L., Community Studies and Education
ROLLS, M. J., Rural Extension
STRAUGHAN, R. R., Education
WATSON, J. K. P., Education Studies and Management

CONSTITUENT INSTITUTION

Institute of Food Research, Reading Laboratory: see under Research Institutes.

AFFILIATED INSTITUTION

College of Estate Management: see under Colleges.

ROBERT GORDON UNIVERSITY

Schoolhill, Aberdeen, AB10 1FR
Telephone: (1224) 262000
Fax: (1224) 263000

Founded 1903, present name and status 1992

Chancellor: Sir ROBERT REID
Principal and Vice-Chancellor: Prof. WILLIAM STEVELY
Vice-Principal: (vacant)
Secretary: DAVID C. CALDWELL
Academic Registrar: HILARY DOUGLAS
Chief Librarian: DIANE DEVINE (acting)

Library of 202,109 vols, 2,170 periodicals
Number of teachers: 476 (f.t.e.)
Number of students: 7,079 full-time, 2,276 part-time

Publication: *Prospectus – Annual Report.*

DEANS

Faculty of Science and Technology: Prof. FRANCIS G. MCINTOSH
Faculty of Health and Food: Prof. JOHN HARPER
Faculty of Design: Prof. ERIC SPILLER
Faculty of Management: P. WILLIAM MCINTOSH

HEADS OF SCHOOLS

Faculty of Science and Technology:

Applied Science: Prof. ROBERT BRADLEY
Computer and Mathematical Sciences: ERNEST FORREST (acting)
Electronic and Electrical Engineering: Prof. NORMAN D. DEANS
Mechanical and Offshore Engineering: Prof. IAN BRYDEN

Faculty of Health and Food:

Applied Social Studies: Prof. JOYCE LISHMAN
Food and Consumer Studies: Dr VERONICA HOUSTON
Health Sciences: Dr VALERIE A. MAEHLE
Associate Faculty of Nursing, Midwifery and Community Studies: THOMAS MOORE
Pharmacy: Prof. C. MACKIE

Faculty of Design:

Architecture: Prof. ROBIN G. M. WEBSTER
Art: BARBARA MILLIGAN
Surveying: ROBERT W. POLLOCK

Faculty of Management:

Business School: HECTOR DOUGLAS (acting)

Information and Media: IAN M. JOHNSON
Public Administration and Law: Prof. ROGER P. LEVY

UNIVERSITY OF ST ANDREWS

St Andrews, Fife, KY16 9AJ
Telephone: (1334) 476161
Founded 1411
Chancellor: Sir KENNETH J. DOVER
Principal and Vice-Chancellor: Prof. STRUTHER ARNOTT
Master: Prof. C. A. VINCENT
Secretary: D. J. CORNER
Proctor: Prof. J. J. SANDERSON
Provost: (vacant)
Controller and Factor: A. M. MENZIES
Library: see Libraries
Number of teachers: 350
Number of students: 5,000

DEANS

Faculty of Arts: A. J. KETTLE
Faculty of Science: Prof. P. J. B. SLATER
Faculty of Divinity: Prof. P. F. ESLER

PROFESSORS

Faculty of Arts:

ALEXANDER, M. J., English Literature
BARTLETT, R. J., Medieval History
BEATH, A. J., Economics
BENTLEY, M. J., Modern History
BROWN, K. M., Scottish History
CORCORAN, C. D., English
CRAWFORD, R., English
DENNIS, N., Spanish
DUNN, D. E., English
FITZROY, F. R., Economics
FURNESS, R. S., German Language and Literature
GIFFORD, P., French
GIVEN-WILSON, C. J., Medieval History
GRATWICK, A., Classical Philology
GUY, J. A., Modern History
HALDANE, J. J., Moral Philosophy
HALLIWELL, F. S., Greek
HARDMAN MOORE, J. H., Economics
HARRIES, J. D., Ancient History
HINE, H. M., Humanity
HINNEBUSCH, R., Arabic Studies
HOUSTON, R. A., Modern History
HUMFREY, P., Art History
JENSEN-BUTLER, C. N., Economics
KENNEDY, H. N., Medieval History
LENMAN, B. P., Modern History
LODDER, C. A., Art History
LODGE, R. A., French
MCKIERNAN, P., Management
MCKINLAY, A., Management
MALEK, M., Management
OVERING, J. A., Social Anthropology
PATERSON, A. K. G., Spanish
PETTEGREE, A. D. M., Modern History
PLOBERGER, W., Economics
PRESS, J. I., Russian
REID, G. C., Economics
ROE, N. H., English
SCOTT, M., French
SELLERS, S. C., English
SKORUPSKI, J., Moral Philosophy
SMITH, G., Art History
SMITH, P. G., Management
WALKER, D. M., Art History
WALKER, W. M., International Relations
WILKINSON, P., International Relations
WOOLF, G. D., Greek, Latin and Ancient History
WRIGHT, C. J. G., Logic and Metaphysics

Faculty of Science:

ATKINSON, M. J., Mathematics and Computer Science
BALLANTYNE, C. K., Geography
BLYTH, T. S., Pure Mathematics
BROOME, J. R., Moral Philosophy
BRUCE, P. G., Chemistry
BUCKLAND, S. T., Mathematics and Computational Science
BYRNE, R. W., Psychology
CAIRNS, R. A., Applied Mathematics
COLE-HAMILTON, D. J., Chemistry
CORNWELL, J. F., Theoretical Physics
CRAIK, A. D. D., Mathematics
CRAWFORD, R. M. M., Plant Ecology
CYWINSKI, R., Physics and Astronomy
DAVIES, A. M., Medical Science
DUNN, M. H., Photonics
FALCONER, K. J., Mathematics and Computational Science
FEDAK, M. A., Environmental and Evolutionary Biology
GANI, D., Organic Chemistry
HARWOOD, J., Environmental and Evolutionary Biology
HAY, R. T., Biochemistry
HAY, R. W., Chemistry
HOMANS, S. W., Biomedical Sciences
HORNE, K. D., Physics and Astronomy
JOHNSTON, D., Psychology
JOHNSTON, I. A., Comparative Physiology
JOHNSTON, M., Psychology
MACCALLUM, J. R., Chemistry
MCMANUS, J., Geology
MAGURRAN, A. E., Environmental and Evolutionary Biology
MARTIN, U. H. M., Mathematics and Computer Science
MILLER, A., Physics
MILNER, A. D., Neuropsychology
MORRISON, R., Software Engineering
PERRETT, D. I., Psychology
PRIEST, E. R., Theoretical Solar Physics
RAPPORT, N. J., Social Anthropology
RICHARDSON, N. V., Chemistry
RIEDI, P. C., Chemistry
ROBERTS, B., Mathematics
ROBERTSON, E. F., Mathematics
SANDERSON, J. J., Theoretical Plasma Physics
SIBBETT, W., Natural Philosophy
SLATER, P. J. B., Natural History
STEEL, C. M., Medical Science
TOOLEY, M. J., Geography
TUCKER, J. B., Cell Biology
WALTON, J. C., Chemistry
WHITEN, D. A., Psychology

Faculty of Divinity:

PIPER, R. A.
SEITZ, C. R.

UNIVERSITY OF SALFORD

Salford, M5 4WT
Telephone: (161) 295-5000
Fax: (161) 295-5999
Founded 1896 as the Royal Technical Institute, later Royal College of Advanced Technology, University Charter granted 1967
Academic year: October to July
Chancellor: Sir WALTER BODMER
Pro-Chancellor: R. M. C. SHIELDS
Vice-Chancellor: Prof. M. HARLOE
Deputy Vice-Chancellor: (vacant)
Pro-Vice-Chancellors: Prof. P. BRANDON, Dr C. EMMOTT, Prof. D. J. SANGER, Prof. P. WHEELER, Prof. M. GOLDSMITH
Registrar: Dr M. D. WINTON
Director Academic Information Services and Librarian: Prof. M. J. CLARK
Number of teachers: 835
Number of students: 12,539 (full-time), 4,356 (part-time)
Publications: *Undergraduate Prospectus*, *Postgraduate Prospectus*, *Part-time Prospectus*, *Calendar*, *Vice-Chancellor's Report* (annually).

DEANS

Art and Design Technology: A. GUNNER
Business Management and Consumer Studies: N. HALL
Engineering: Dr B. PARDOE
The Environment: C. G. MARCH
Health Care and Social Work Studies: Prof. P. BOWKER
Media, Music and Performance: Dr K. WILSON
Science: Dr J. T. RICHARDS
Social Sciences, Languages and Humanities: C. HARRISON

PROFESSORS

ALEXANDER, M. S., Politics and Contemporary History
ALSHAWI, M., Surveying
ARMOUR, D. G., Physics
ARNELL, R. D., Aeronautical, Mechanical and Manufacturing Engineering
BARIC, L. F., Information Technology Institute
BARRETT, P. S., Surveying
BETTS, M. P., Surveying
BOARDMAN, A. D., Physics
BOOTH, J. G., Physics
BOWKER, P., Rehabilitation
BRANDON, P. S., Surveying
BROWN, G. R., Surveying
BRYANT, C. G. A., Sociology
BULL, M. J., Politics and Contemporary History
CARTER, G., Physics
CHRISTER, A. H., Computer and Mathematics Science
COLLIER, C. G., Civil and Environmental Engineering
COLLIGON, J. S., Electronic and Electrical Engineering
COLQUHOUN, H. M., Chemistry and Applied Chemistry
CRAIG, P. S., Biological Sciences
CROSSLEY, T. R., Aeronautical, Mechanical and Manufacturing Engineering
DAVIES-COOPER, R., Art and Design Technology
DONNELLY, S. E., Physics
EASSON, A. W., English
EDGELL, S. R., Sociology
EDWARDS, J., Rehabilitation
GARSIDE, P. L., European Studies Research Institute
GEE, K. P., Business Studies
GERBER, R., Physics
GLEAVE, M. B., Geography
GOLDSMITH, M. J. F., Politics and Contemporary History
GRAY, J. O., Electronic and Electrical Engineering
GRUNDY, P. J., Physics
HARRIS, G. T., Modern Languages
HICKEY, L. D., Modern Languages
HUGHES, R., Chemistry and Applied Chemistry
KEIGER, J. F. V., Modern Languages
LARMOUTH, J., Information Technology Institute
LAWSON, R., Biological Sciences
LINGE, N., Electronic and Electrical Engineering
LIVESEY, J. L., Aeronautical, Mechanical and Manufacturing Engineering
LORD, P., Acoustics and Audio Engineering
MASON, R. S., Business Studies
MELBOURNE, C., Civil and Environmental Engineering
MORGAN, C. G., Biological Sciences
NAGY, F. L. N., Information Technology
NEAL, F., European Studies
PEMBLE, M. E., Chemistry and Applied Chemistry
POPAY, J., Public Health Research and Resource Centre
POWELL, J. A., Information Technology
PROCTER, G., Chemistry and Applied Chemistry
ROSS, D. K., Physics
SAMPSON, A. A., Economics

SANGER, D. J., Aeronautical, Mechanical and Manufacturing Engineering
STOREY, D. M., Biological Sciences
TAYLOR, I. R., Sociology
THOMAS, N. L., Modern Languages
TOPHAM, N., Economics
TOWELL, R. J., Modern Languages
VILLIERS, T. A., Biological Sciences
WALKDEN, F., Computer and Mathematics Science
WEBSTER, P. J., Civil and Environmental Engineering
WHEELER, P. D., Acoustics and Audio Engineering
WHITEHEAD, C., Physics
WOOD, J. R. G., Information and Educational and Materials Development, Computer and Mathematical Sciences
WOOD-HARPER, A. T., Computer and Mathematics Science
WYN JONES, E., Chemistry and Applied Chemistry

CONSTITUENT COLLEGE

Research and Graduate College: Head Prof. P. S. BRANDON

Graduate School: Dir Prof. J. A. POWELL
European Studies Research Institute: Dir Prof. G. T. HARRIS
Science Research Institute: Dir Prof. D. K. ROSS
Institute for Social Research: Prof. C. G. A. BRYANT
Telford Research Institute: Dir Prof. C. G. COLLIER (acting)
TIME (Technology, Information, Management, Economics) Research Institute: Dir Prof. P. BARRETT
Health Research Institute: Dir Prof. J. POPAY

UNIVERSITY OF SHEFFIELD

Sheffield, S10 2TN
Telephone: (114) 222-2000
Fax: (114) 273-9826

Founded 1897 as University College, Royal Charter 1905

Chancellor: (vacant)
Pro-Chancellors: R. A. DOUGLAS, P. W. LEE
Vice-Chancellor: Prof. Sir GARETH ROBERTS
Pro-Vice-Chancellors: Prof. A. M. GAMBLE, Prof. I. T. M. GOW, Prof. P. WALDRON, Prof. D. H. LEWIS
Registrar and Secretary: Dr J. S. PADLEY
Librarian: M. S.-M. HANNON

Library: see Libraries
Number of full-time teaching staff: 1,048
Number of students: 16,683 full-time, 3,872 part-time

Publications: *Calendar*, *Annual Report*, *Undergraduate Prospectus*, *Graduate Prospectus*.

DEANS

Faculty of Arts: Prof. W. J. LEATHERBARROW
Faculty of Pure Science: Prof. F. H. COMBLEY
Faculty of Medicine: Prof. H. F. WOODS
Faculty of Law: P. JONES
Faculty of Engineering: Prof. C. M. SELLARS
Faculty of Social Sciences: P. K. ELSE
Faculty of Architectural Studies: Prof. P. R. TREGENZA
Faculty of Educational Studies: Dr P. W. WRIGHT

PROFESSORS

(Some staff serve in more than one faculty)

Faculty of Arts:

BELL, D. A., Philosophy
BLAKE, N. F., English Language
BRANIGAN, K., Archaeology and Prehistory
BURNLEY, J. D., English Language and Linguistics
CARRUTHERS, P. M., Philosophy
CARWARDINE, R. J., History
CLARKE, E. F., Music
CLINES, D. J. A., Biblical Studies
COLLIS, J. R., Archaeology and Prehistory
DAVIES, P. R., Biblical Studies
DENNELL, R. W., Archaeology and Prehistory
DUFFY, J. H., French
EDWARDS, K. J., Palaeoecology
EXUM, J. C., Biblical Studies
GREENGRASS, M., History
HAFFENDEN, J., English Literature
HATTAWAY, M., English Literature
HILL, P. H. A. W., Music
HOLMES, C., History
HOOKWAY, C. J., Philosophy
KERSHAW, I., Modern History
KING, E. J., History
LEATHERBARROW, W. J., Russian and Slavonic Studies
LUSCOMBE, D. E., Medieval History
MCGOWAN, N. M., Germanic Studies
ROBERTS, P. E., English Literature
ROUND, N. G., Hispanic Studies
RUSSELL, R., Russian and Slavonic Studies
SHEPHERD, D. G., Russian and Slavonic Studies
SHUTTLEWORTH, S. A., English Literature
WALKER, D. H., French
WIDDOWSON, J. D. A., English Cultural Tradition and Language
WILLIAMS, D., French
YATES, A., Catalan

Faculty of Pure Science:

ANDERSON, C. W., Mathematics and Statistics
ANDREWS, P. W., Biomedical Science
ANGEL, A., Physiology
ARMSTRONG, H. W., Geography
BAILEY, E., Molecular Biology and Biotechnology
BAILEY, G. J., Mathematics and Statistics
BIGGINS, J. D., Probability and Statistics
BIRKHEAD, T. R., Animal and Plant Sciences
BLACKBURN, G. M., Chemistry
BRADLEY, D. D. C., Physics
BURTON, D. R., Molecular Biology and Biotechnology
CALLAGHAN, T. V., Animal and Plant Sciences
CALOW, P., Zoology
CANNINGS, C., Probability and Statistics
CHAPMAN, N., Earth Sciences
CHATWIN, P. C., Applied and Computational Mathematics
COMBLEY, F. H., Physics
CONNOLLY, K. J., Psychology
COOK, R. J., Pure Mathematics
DUNSMORE, I. R., Probability and Statistics
FENTON, D. E., Chemistry
FERGUSON, R. I., Physical Geography
FRISBY, J. P., Psychology
GEHRING, G. A., Solid State Physics
GREENLEES, J. P. C., Probability and Statistics
GRIME, J. P., Animal and Plant Sciences
GUEST, J. R., Microbiology
HAINING, R. P., Human Geography
HENDERSON, I. W., Zoology
HOLCOMBE, W. M. L., Computer Science
HORTON, P., Molecular Biology and Biotechnology
HUNTER, C. N., Molecular Biology and Biotechnology
HUTSON, V. C. L., Applied and Computational Mathematics
INGHAM, P. W., Biomedical Science
JACKSON, P. A., Human Geography
LEDWITH, A., Chemistry
LEE, J. A., Animal and Plant Sciences
LEEGOOD, R. C., Animal and Plant Sciences
LEWIS, D. H., Botany
LOYNES, R. M., Probability and Statistics
MCLEOD, C. W. M., Earth Sciences
MAITLIS, P. M., Inorganic Chemistry
MANN, B. E., Chemistry
MAYHEW, J. E. W., Psychology
MOFFETT, R. J., Applied and Computational Mathematics
MOORE, H. D. M., Molecular Biology and Biotechnology
NICOLSON, R. I., Psychology
OUTHWAITE, C. W., Mathematics and Statistics
OWENS, B., Earth Sciences
PEARSON, R. C. A., Neuroscience
POOLE, R. K., Molecular Biology and Biotechnology
PYM, J. S., Pure Mathematics
QUEGAN, S., Applied and Computational Mathematics
READ, D. J., Animal and Plant Sciences
REYNOLDS, G. P., Biomedical Science
RICE, D. W., Molecular Biology and Biotechnology
RYAN, A. J., Chemistry
SHARKEY, N. E., Computer Science
SHARP, R. Y., Pure Mathematics
SIEGAL, M., Psychology
SKOLNICK, M. S., Experimental Condensed Matter
SMYTHE, C., Computer Science
SOZOU, C., Applied and Computational Mathematics
SPEARS, D. A., Geology
STIRLING, C. J. M., Organic Chemistry
THOMAS, D. S. G., Geography
TURNER, G., Genetics
WALL, T. D., Psychology
WARR, P. B., Psychology
WHITE, P. E., Geography
WILKS, Y., Computer Science
WOODWARD, F. I., Plant Ecology
ZINOBER, A. S. I., Probability and Statistics

Faculty of Medicine:

AHMEDZAI, S., Palliative Medicine
AKEHURST, R. L., Health Economics
BROOK, A. H., Child Dental Health
BROOK, I. M., Oral and Maxillofacial Surgery
BROWN, B. H., Medical Physics and Clinical Engineering
BROWN, B. L., Human Metabolism and Clinical Biochemistry
CAMPBELL, M. J., Medical Statistics
CLARK, D., Surgery
COOKE, I. D., Obstetrics and Gynaecology
CORDESS, C., Forensic Pathology
CROSSMAN, D. C., Cardiology
CUMBERLAND, D. C., Interventional Cardiology
DOWER, S. K., Medical Physics and Clinical Engineering
DUCKWORTH, T., Orthopaedic Surgery
DUFF, G. W., Molecular Medicine
EASTELL, R., Human Metabolism and Clinical Biochemistry
EDWARDS, B., Health Care Development
EL-NAHAS, A. M., Nephrology
ENDERBY, P. M., Health Care for the Elderly
GRANT, G. W. B., Cognitive Disability
GREEN, M. A., Forensic Pathology
GRIFFITHS, P. D., Diagnostic Radiology
HALE, A. S., Psychiatry
HALL, D. M. B., Community Paediatrics
HANCOCK, B. W., Clinical Oncology
HIGENBOTTAM, T. W., Medical Physics and Clinical Engineering
HUTCHINSON, A., Public Health Medicine
JENNINGS, R., Medical Microbiology
JOHNSON, A. G., Surgery
JONES, D., Gerontological and Continuing Care Nursing
KANIS, J. A., Human Metabolism and Clinical Biochemistry
KIRKHAM, M. J., Midwifery
LOCKE, J. L., Human Communication Sciences
MAYES, A. R., Cognitive Neuroscience

MOORE, H. D. M., Obstetrics and Gynaecology
NICHOLL, J. P., Medical Care Research Centre
NOLAN, M. R., Gerontological and Continuing Care Nursing
PEAKE, I. R., Molecular Medicine
PHILP, I., Health Care for Elderly People
POTTER, C. W., Virology
RAMSAY, L. E., Medicine and Pharmacology
READ, N. W., Gastro-intestinal Physiology and Nutrition
REILLY, C. S., Surgery
RENNIE, I. G., Ophthalmology and Orthoptics
ROBINSON, P. P., Oral and Maxillo-facial Surgery
ROTHWELL, P. S., Dental Services
RUSSELL, R. G. G., Human Metabolism and Clinical Biochemistry
SALEH, M., Surgical Sciences
SHARP, F., Obstetrics and Gynaecology
SMALLWOOD, R. H., Medical Physics and Clinical Engineering
SMITH, C. J., Oral Pathology
UNDERWOOD, J. C. E., Pathology
TANNER, M. S., Paediatrics
TANTAM, D. J. H., Psychotherapy
TAYLOR, C. J., Paediatric Gastroenterology
TUCKER, G. T., Clinical Pharmacology and Therapeutics
VAN NOORT, R., Restorative Dentistry
WALSH, T. F., Restorative Dentistry
WARD, J. D., Medicine
WARNES, A. M., Social Gerontology
WEETMAN, A. P., Medicine
WELLS, M., Gynaecological Pathology
WELSH, C. L., Regional Postgraduate Dean
WHYTE, M. K. B., Medical Physics and Clinical Engineering
WOOD, R. F. M., Surgery
WOODS, H. F., Pharmacology and Therapeutics
YOUNG, R. M., Psychotherapeutic Studies

Faculty of Law:

ADAMS, J. N., Intellectual Property
BATTERSBY, G., Property, Equity, Conveyancing
BEYLEVELD, D., Law
BIRDS, J. R., Commercial Law, Company Law
BROWNSWORD, R., Law, Jurisprudence, Legal Theory, Contract
DITTON, J., Criminology
HARDEN, I., Law
HAYES, P. M., Law
LEWIS, N., Constitutional Law, Sociology of Law
MCCLEAN, J. D., Conflict of Laws, Air Law
MERRILLS, J. E. G., International Law
SHAPLAND, J. M., Criminal Justice
WILES, P. N. P., Criminology

Faculty of Engineering:

ALLEN, R. W. K., Chemical and Process Engineering
ANDERSON, W. F., Civil and Structural Engineering
BANKS, S. P., Automatic Control and Systems Engineering
BEYNON, J. H., Mechanical and Process Engineering
BILLINGS, S. A., Control Engineering
BROWN, M. W., Mechanical Engineering
CULLIS, A. G., Electronic and Electrical Engineering
DAVIES, H. A., Materials
FLEMING, P. J., Automatic Control and Systems Engineering
FREESTON, I. L., Electronic and Electrical Engineering
HOWE, D., Electrical Engineering
IVEY, P. A., Electronic and Electrical Engineering
JAMES, P. F., Materials
JONES, F. R., Materials
JONES, H., Materials
LINKENS, D. A., Automatic Control and Systems Engineering
MILLER, K. J., Mechanical Engineering
PATTERSON, E. A., Mechanical Engineering
RIDGWAY, K., Mechanical Engineering
SAUL, A. J., Civil and Structural Engineering
SELLARS, C. M., Iron and Steel Technology
SHARP, J. H., Materials
SMITH, R. A., Mechanical and Process Engineering
SWITHENBANK, J., Chemical Engineering and Fuel Technology
TOMLINSON, G. R., Engineering Dynamics
WALDRON, P., Civil and Structural Engineering
WHITEHOUSE, C. R., Electronic and Electrical Engineering

Faculty of Social Sciences:

ARMSTRONG, P. J., Accounting
BOOTH, T. A., Social Policy
CHAPPEL, D., Mathematical Economics
CLEGG, C. W., Organizational Behaviour
CURRIE, W. L., Management
DOWD, K., Economics
GAMBLE, A. M., Politics
GEORGE, S. A., Politics
GOW, I. T. M., East Asian Studies
GUNTER, B., Journalism
HOLDAWAY, S. D., Sociology
HOOK, G. D., Japanese Studies
HUMPHREY, C. G., Accounting
JENKINS, R., Sociology
MACDONALD, S., Management
MEIDAN, A., Marketing
NORMAN, J. M., Management Studies
OWEN, D. L., Accounting
PAYNE, A. J., Politics
SEYD, P., Politics
TAYLOR, P. D., Leisure Management
TRELFORD, D. G., Journalism
TYLECOTE, A. B., Strategic Management
UNDERDOWN, B., Accounting
WALKER, A. C., Social Policy
WEST, M. A., Organizational Psychology
WHITELEY, P. F., Politics
WILKINSON, R. K., Economics
WILLETT, P., Information Studies
WILSON, T. D., Information Studies

Faculty of Architectural Studies:

BLUNDELL JONES, P. M., Architecture
CROOK, A. D. H., Town and Regional Planning
LAWSON, B. R., Architecture
PLANK, R. J., Architecture
SWANWICK, C. A., Landscape
TREGENZA, P. R., Architecture

Faculty of Educational Studies:

BARTON, L. F., Education
CAMERON, R. A. D., Continuing Education
CARR, W., Education
CHIVERS, G. E., Continuing Education
HEY, D. G., Continuing Education
INGLIS, F., Education
MAC AN GHAILL, M., Education
MCCULLOCH, G. J., Education
QUICKE, J. C., Education

SHEFFIELD HALLAM UNIVERSITY

Howard St, Sheffield S1 1WB
Telephone: (114) 225-5555
Telex: 54680
Fax: (114) 225-3398

Founded 1969 as Sheffield Polytechnic, later Sheffield City Polytechnic; present name and status 1992
Academic year: September to June

Vice-Chancellor: Prof. DIANA GREEN
Assistant Principals: Dr J. M. HOBBS, Prof. DIANNE WILLCOCK
Director of Finance: R. LANE
Director of Human Resources: M. ORTON
University Secretary: S. NEOCOSMOS
Academic Registrar: J. TORY

Library of 500,000 vols
Number of teachers: 816
Number of students: 15,992 full-time and sandwich, 6,591 part-time

DIRECTORS OF SCHOOLS

Business and Management: GRAHAM WORSDALE

Computing and Management Sciences: Rev. Prof. I. DRAFFAN

(Divisions of Applied Statistics; Computing Mathematics; Information Systems, Networks and Technologies; Software Engineering; Management Sciences.)

Construction: Prof. D. BALMFORTH

(Divisions of Architectural Technology; Building Surveying; Environmental Management; Quantity Surveying; Civil Engineering; Construction Management.)

Cultural Studies: Prof. ELAINE THOMAS

(Divisions of Art and Design; Film and Media, History of Art and Design; English, Historical and Communication Studies.)

Education: Prof. D. BENTLEY

Engineering: D. EATON

(Divisions of Manufacturing, Material and Management Engineering; Design Analysis and Environmental Engineering; Engineering Systems; Electronic and Information Technology.)

Financial Studies and Law: K. HARRISON

(Divisions of Accountancy; Law; Banking and Finance.)

Health and Community Studies: MARTIN KING

(Divisions of Applied Social Studies; Nursing and Social Work; Professions allied to Medicine.)

Leisure and Food Management: V. E. RICK

(Divisions of Tourism; Hospitality; Recreation, Sports and Arts; Countryside and Environment; Food Industries Management and Consumer Studies.)

Science and Mathematics: Prof. JOHN PARKINSON

(Divisions of Applied Physics; Biomedical Sciences; Chemistry; Centre for Science Education.)

Sheffield Business School: GLYN OWEN (acting)

Urban and Regional Studies: Prof. TED KITCHEN (acting)

(Divisions of Housing; Surveying; Planning and Urban Policy.)

SOUTH BANK UNIVERSITY

103 Borough Rd, London, SE1 0AA
Telephone: (171) 928-8989
Fax: (171) 815-8155

Founded 1970 as South Bank Polytechnic; present name and status 1992
State control
Academic year: September to July

Chancellor: C. MCLAREN
Vice-Chancellor: Prof. G. BERNBAUM
Deputy Vice-Chancellors: Prof. T. WATKINS (Academic), R. PHILLIPS (Resources)
Registrar: R. PHILLIPS
Librarian: J. AKEROYD

Library of 280,000 vols

Number of teachers: 652
Number of students: 20,281
Publication: *Prospectuses* (annually).

DEANS

Faculty of the Built Environment: Prof. L. WOOD
Business School: Prof. N. ROWE
Faculty of Engineering and Science: Prof. C. CLARE
Faculty of Health and Social Sciences: Prof. L. GOLDSTONE

HEADS OF SCHOOL/AREA

Faculty of the Built Environment:
Construction: Prof. R. HOWES
Urban Design and Policy: Prof. B. REDDING
Faculty of Engineering and Science:
Computing, Information Systems and Mathematics: Prof. A. HASHIM
Electrical, Electronic and Information Engineering: Prof. B. BRIDGE
Engineering Systems and Design: Prof. R. MATTHEWS
Applied Science: T. G. EVANS
Faculty of Health and Social Sciences:
Health and Social Care: Prof. W. COUCHMAN
Education, Politics and Social Sciences: Prof. J. WEEKES
Redwood College: Prof. K. AGBOLEGBE
Business School:
Undergraduate Office: N. RICHARDS
Postgraduate Office: D. GREEN

UNIVERSITY OF SOUTHAMPTON

Highfield, Southampton, SO17 1BJ
Telephone: (1703) 595000
Fax: (1703) 593939

Founded 1952; opened as the Hartley Institution 1862; incorporated as the Hartley University College 1902

Chancellor: LORD SELBORNE
Vice-Chancellor: Prof. HOWARD NEWBY
Deputy Vice-Chancellors: Prof. R. A. FARRAR, Prof. A. M. ULPH, Dr P. C. LANCHESTER
Secretary and Registrar: J. F. D. LAUWERYS
Academic Registrar: R. KNIGHT
Librarian: B. NAYLOR

Library: see Libraries
Number of full-time teaching staff: 959 including 160 professors
Number of students: 13,480 full-time, 4,190 part-time
Publications: *Calendar*, *Undergraduate Prospectus*, *Postgraduate Prospectus and Study Booklets* (by subject), *Departmental Reports and Research Reports*, *Annual Report*.

DEANS

Faculty of Arts: Prof. N. COOK
Faculty of Science: Prof. J. EVANS
Faculty of Engineering and Applied Science: Prof. C. G. RICE
Faculty of Social Sciences: Prof. I. DIAMOND
Faculty of Educational Studies: Prof. C. J. BRUMFIT
Faculty of Law: Prof. N. WIKELEY
Faculty of Medicine: Prof. E. J. THOMAS
Faculty of Mathematical Studies: Prof. R. C. KING

PROFESSORS

Faculty of Arts:
BANCE, A. F., German
CESARANI, D., History
CHAMPION, T. C., Archaeology
COOK, N. J., Music
COOK, P., Film and Media Studies
CROUAN, K. M., Winchester School of Art
ETTINGHAUSEN, H. M., Spanish and Latin-American Studies
EVERIST, M. E., Music
GAMBLE, C. S., Archaeology
GIBBONS, J., Winchester School of Art
KAPLAN, C., English
KEAY, S. J., Archaeology
KELLY, M. H., French
LIVINGSTONE, R. S., German
MCLUSKIE, K. E., English
PALMER, A., Philosophy
PEACOCK, D. P. S., Archaeology
PILGRIM, P. J., Winchester School of Art
PLATT, C. P. S., History
REUTER, T. A., History
RULE, J. G., History
SHARPE, K. M., History
TAYLOR, B., Winchester School of Art

Faculty of Science:
BARNES, K. J., Physics and Astronomy
BARTLETT, P. N., Chemistry
BRADLEY, M., Chemistry
BROWN, T., Chemistry
CARRINGTON, A., Chemistry
CLARK, M. J., Geography
COLES, H. J., Physics and Astronomy
COLLINS, M. B., Oceanography
CURRAN, P. J., Geography
DEAN, A. J., Physics and Astronomy
DYKE, J. M., Chemistry
EMSLEY, J. W., Chemistry
EVANS, J., Chemistry
FOODY, G., Geography
HAMILTON, N., Geology
HANNA, D. C., Physics and Astronomy
HAYDEN, B. E., Chemistry
HENDRA, P. J., Chemistry
HOLLIGAN, P. M., Oceanography
JENKINS, W., Chemical Oceanography
LUCKHURST, G. R., Chemistry
MASON, C., Geography
MELLOR, J., Chemistry
MURRAY, J. W., Geology
NESBITT, R. W., Geology
PLETCHER, D., Chemistry
RAINFORD, B. D., Physics and Astronomy
ROSS, D. A., Physics and Astronomy
SACHRAJDA, C. T. C., Physics and Astronomy
SANDERSON, D. J., Geology
SHEPHERD, J. G., Southampton Oceanography Centre
THORPE, S. A., Oceanography
TICKELL, A., Geography
TYLER, P. A., Oceanography
WAGSTAFF, J. M., Geography
WELLER, M. T., Chemistry
WRIGLEY, N., Geography

Faculty of Engineering and Applied Science:
ASHBURN, P., Electronics and Computer Science
BAILEY, A. G., Electrical Engineering
BARRON, D. W., Electronics and Computer Science
BRIGNELL, J. E., Electronics and Computer Science
DAVIES, A. E., Electrical Engineering
ELLIOTT, S. J., Institute of Sound and Vibration Research
FAHY, F. J., Institute of Sound and Vibration Research
FARRAR, R. A., Mechanical Engineering
GREGSON, P. J., Engineering Materials
GRIFFIN, M. J., Institute of Sound and Vibration Research
HALL, W., Electronics and Computer Science
HAMMOND, J. K., Institute of Sound and Vibration Research
HARRIS, C. J., Electronics and Computer Science
HENDERSON, P., Electronics and Computer Science
HEY, A. J. G., Electronics and Computer Science
HOLMES, R., Mechanical Engineering
HUGHES, J. F., Electrical Engineering
KEANE, A. J., Mechanical Engineering
KEMHADJIAN, H. A., Electronics and Computer Science
LANGLEY, R. S., Aeronautics and Astronautics
LUTMAN, M. E., Institute of Sound and Vibration Research
MCDONALD, M., Civil and Environmental Engineering
MCLEAN, D., Aeronautics and Astronautics
MORFEY, C. L., Institute of Sound and Vibration Research
NELSON, P. A., Institute of Sound and Vibration Research
PAYNE, D. N., Opto-electronics Research Centre
PETYT, M., Institute of Sound and Vibration Research
POWRIE, W., Civil and Environmental Engineering
PRICE, W. G., Ship Science
RICE, C. G., Institute of Sound and Vibration Research
RUTT, H. N., Electronics and Computer Science
STEELE, R., Electronics and Computer Science
SYKULSKI, J. K., Electrical Engineering
TANTON, T. W., Civil and Environmental Engineering
TURNER, J. D., Mechanical Engineering
WHITE, R. G., Aeronautics and Astronautics
WILLOUGHBY, A. F. W., Engineering Materials

Faculty of Social Sciences:
ARMSTRONG, M., Economics
AVISON, D. E., Management
BAGLEY, C., Social Work Studies
BROWN, C. J., Politics
CALVERT, P. A. R., Politics
CHAMBERS, R., Social Statistics
CHAPMAN, C. B., Management
CLARK, J. W., Sociology and Social Policy
COLEMAN, P. G., Social Work Studies
COLLINS, H. M., Sociology and Social Policy
DALE, R. S., Management
DIAMOND, I. D., Social Statistics
DOMINELLI, L. R., Social Work Studies
DRIFFILL, E. J., Economics
HAMLIN, A., Economics
HARNAD, S. R., Psychology
HILL, D. M., Politics
HILLIER, G. H., Economics
HOLT, D., Social Statistics
LIGHT, P., Psychology
LOVENDUSKI, J., Politics
MALCOMSON, J. M., Economics
MCCORMICK, B., Economics
MCKENZIE, G. W., Management
MIZON, G. E., Economics
NAPIER, C. J., Management
PRITCHARD, C., Social Work Studies
REMINGTON, R. E., Psychology
ROBINSON, R. F., Institute for Health Policy Studies
SIMPSON, J., Politics
SKINNER, C. J., Social Statistics
SOLOMOS, J. N., Sociology and Social Policy
SONUGA-BURKE, E., Psychology
STEVENSON, J. E., Psychology
SUTCLIFFE, C. M. S., Management
THOMAS, C. A., Politics
THOMAS, S. H., Management
ULPH, A. M., Economics
UNGERSON, C. E., Sociology and Social Policy
WALLER, G. C., Psychology

Faculty of Educational Studies:
BENTON, M., Education
BRUMFIT, C. J., Education
DAVIS, G. L., Education
SIMONS, H., Education

Faculty of Law:
GASKELL, N. J., Law
GRIME, R. P., Law
LUSTGARTEN, L., Law

RUTHERFORD, A. F., Law
TRIDIMAS, T., European Community Law
WIKELEY, N. J., Law

Faculty of Medicine:

(Some professors also serve in the Faculty of Science)

AKHTAR, M., Biochemistry
ANTHONY, C., Biochemistry
ARTHUR, M. J. P., Medicine
BARKER, D. J. P., Clinical Epidemiology
BRIGGS, R. S. J., Geriatric Medicine
CHURCH, M. K., Experimental Immunopharmacology
COGGAN, D., Environmental Epidemiology
COLEMAN, P. G., Social Gerontology
ELKINGTON, A. R., Ophthalmology
FRIEDMAN, P., Dermatology
GABBAY, J., Public Health Medicine
GEORGE, C. F., Clinical Pharmacology
GLASPER, E. A., Nursing Studies
GRIMBLE, R. F., Nutrition
HALL, J. L., Biology
HAMBLIN, T. J., Immunohaematology
HAWKINS, S. J., Biology
HOLGATE, S. T., Immunopharmacology
JACKSON, A. A., Human Nutrition
JOHNSON, P., Medical Oncology
JORDAN, P. M., Biochemistry
KENDRICK, T., Primary Medical Care
KINMONTH, A.-L., Primary Medical Care
LEE, A. G., Biochemistry
LEE, H. A., Renal Medicine
LUTMAN, M., Audiology
MACLEAN, N., Biology
MCLELLAN, D. L., Rehabilitation
MANT, D., Primary Care Epidemiology
NORMAN, J., Anaesthetics
PRIMROSE, J. N., Surgery
RENWICK, A., Clinical Pharmacology
SCHUMACHER, U. H., Human Morphology
SEDGWICK, E. M., Neurophysiology
SHEARER, J. R., Orthopaedic Surgery
SHELLEY, T., Medical Physics
SHOOLINGIN-JORDAN, P. M., Biochemistry
SLEIGH, M. A., Biology
STEVENSON, F., Medicine
STEVENSON, G. T., Immunochemistry
THOMAS, E. J., Obstetrics and Gynaecology
THOMPSON, C., Psychiatry
THOMPSON, R. J., Clinical Biochemistry
WALKER, R. J., Physiology and Pharmacology
WARD, M. E., Medical Microbiology
WARNER, J. O., Child Health
WATT, P. J., Microbiology
WELLER, R. O., Neuropathology
WHEAL, H. V., Physiology and Pharmacology
WHITEHOUSE, J. M. A., Medical Oncology
WRIGHT, D. H., Pathology

Faculty of Mathematical Studies:

CLARKE, C. J. S., Mathematics
DUNWOODY, M. J., Mathematics
KING, R. C., Mathematics
ROBERTSON, S. A., Mathematics
SLUCKIN, T. J., Mathematics
SMITH, T. M. F., Mathematics
SNAITH, V., Mathematics
WESTCOTT, B. S., Mathematics
WHEELER, A. A., Mathematics
WILLIAMS, H. P., Mathematics

STAFFORDSHIRE UNIVERSITY

College Rd, Stoke on Trent, ST4 2DE
Telephone: (1782) 294000
Fax: (1782) 292796
E-mail: a.m.edge@staffs.ac.uk

Founded 1970 as North Staffordshire Polytechnic, became Staffordshire Polytechnic 1988; present name and status 1992

Chancellor: Rt Hon. Lord ASHLEY OF STOKE
Vice-Chancellor: Prof. C. E. KING
Executive Academic Director: SUSAN O'BRIEN
University Secretary: K. B. G. SPROSTON
Academic Registrar: F. FRANCIS
Librarian: K. ELLARD

Library of 300,000 vols, 2,000 periodicals
Number of teachers: 589
Number of students: 11,705 full-time and sandwich, 3,993 part-time

Publications: *Prospectuses*, *Research Report*, *Annual Review* (all annually), *University News* (2 a month), *Horizon* (former students; 3 a year).

DEANS

School of Humanities and Social Sciences: Prof. D. LONGHURST
Business School: C. J. BROWNLESS
School of Computing: Prof. R. W. NEWTON
School of Art and Design: D. WEIGHTMAN
School of Engineering and Advanced Technology: Prof. T. RUXTON
Law School: Prof. R. W. PAINTER
School of Sciences: Prof. P. ROWBOTHAM
School of Health: N. MCKELLAR
Graduate School: Prof. D. W. JARY

UNIVERSITY OF STIRLING

Stirling, FK9 4LA
Telephone: (1786) 473171
Fax: (1786) 463000

Founded 1967

Academic year: September to May (two semesters)

Chancellor: Dame DIANA RIGG
Principal and Vice-Chancellor: Prof. A. MILLER
Deputy Principals: Prof. M. P. JACKSON, Prof. S. A. BROWN, Prof. V. BRUCE
Secretary: K. CLARKE
Deputy Secretary and Clerk to the Court: Dr D. J. FARRINGTON
Director of Information Services and University Librarian: Dr PETER KEMP

Library: see Libraries
Number of teachers: 380
Number of students: 7,000

Publications: *Annual Prospectuses*, *Annual Report*, *Calendar*.

DEANS

Faculty of Arts: S. MARSHALL
Faculty of Human Sciences: Prof. R. J. WATT
Faculty of Management: Prof. L. SPARKS
Faculty of Natural Sciences: Dr L. ROSS

PROFESSORS AND HEADS OF DEPARTMENT

(H=Head of Department)

School of Arts:

CORMACK, M. J., Film and Media (H)
CRUMP, J., Japanese Studies
DRAKAKIS, J., English Studies
DUFF, R. A., Philosophy
INGLE, S. J., Political Studies
KEEBLE, N. H., English Studies (H)
LAW, R. C., History
LOW, D. A., English Studies
MARSHALL, S. E., Philosophy (H)
MURDOCH, B. O., German
PEDEN, G. C., History (H)
PERTAUB, W., Spanish (acting H)
REYNOLDS, S., French (H)
SMITH, G. F., English Studies
TRAVIS, C., Philosophy
WATSON, R., English Studies
WHITELAM, K., Religious Studies (H)

School of Human Sciences:

BROWN, S. A., Education
BRUCE, V., Psychology
HALLETT, C., Applied Social Science (H)
JARVIE, G., Sports Studies
JOHNSTONE, R. M., Education (H)
MARKOVA, I., Psychology (H)
MARSHALL, M. T., Dementia Services Development Centre (H)
NIVEN, C., Nursing and Midwifery (H)
NIXON, J., Education
PHILLIPS, W., Psychology
ROWLINGS, C., Applied Social Science
SCOTT, S., Applied Social Science
TIMMS, D. W. G., Applied Social Science
TURNER, C., Applied Social Science
WATT, R. J., Psychology (H)

School of Management:

BEATTIE, V., Accountancy and Finance
BELL, D. N. F., Economics
DEARLE, A., Computing Science
GREENMAN, J. V., Computing and Mathematics
HART, R. A., Economics
HUGHES, M. D., Business Studies (H)
JACKSON, M. P., Human Resources Management
LIMMACK, R. J., Accountancy and Finance
MCINNES, W. M., Accountancy (H)
SAREN, M., Marketing
SPARKS, L., Marketing
STOPFORTH, D., Revenue Law
TURNER, K. J., Computing Science
WESTHEAD, P., Entrepreneurship

School of Natural Sciences:

BROMAGE, N., Aquaculture
BRYANT, D. M., Biological and Molecular Sciences
DAVIDSON, D. A., Environmental Science (H)
PRICE, N. C., Biological Science
REID, J., Biological Science
RICHARDS, R. H., Aquaculture (H)
SARGENT, J. R., Biological Science
SMITH, K., Environmental Science
TEALE, A., Aquatic Molecular Genetics
THOMAS, M. F., Environmental Science

NON-PROFESSORIAL HEADS OF DEPARTMENT

School of Arts:

KIDD, W., French
KILBORN, R. W., Film and Media Studies
THOMPSON, B., German (H)

School of Management:

RATTRAY, C., Computing Science and Mathematics

School of Natural Sciences:

MCLUSKY, D. S., Biological and Molecular Sciences

NON-SCHOOL PROFESSOR

LOCKERBIE, S. I. J., Educational Policy and Development

ATTACHED INSTITUTES

Centre for Publishing Studies: Dir Dr I. D. MCGOWAN.

Centre for English Language Teaching: Dir Prof. S. I. LOCKERBIE.

Centre of Commonwealth Studies: Dir Dr A. M. SMITH.

Centre for Scottish Literature and Culture: Dir (vacant).

Centre for Physical Education and Sports Development: Dir A. NICHOLS.

Dementia Services Development Centre: Dir Prof. M. T. MARSHALL.

Institute of Aquaculture: Dir Prof. R. J. RICHARDS.

Institute of Retail Studies: Dir Prof. J. FERNIE.

Research Institute for Film and Media Studies: Dir Prof. P. SCHLESINGER.

Scottish Centre for Information on Language Teaching and Research: Dir Prof. R. M. JOHNSTONE.

Centre for Cognitive and Computational Neuroscience: Dir Dr W. A. PHILLIPS.

Drugs Training Unit: P. R. YATES.

UNIVERSITY OF STRATHCLYDE

16 Richmond St, Glasgow, G1 1XQ
Telephone: (141) 552-4400
Telex: 77472
Fax: (141) 552-0775

Founded 1796 under the title of Anderson's Institution; affiliated to the University of Glasgow between 1913 and 1964; University Charter 1964; merged with Jordanhill College of Education 1993

Academic year: September to June

Chancellor: The Rt Hon. Lord HOPE
Principal and Vice-Chancellor: Prof. Sir JOHN ARBUTHNOTT
Vice-Principal: Prof. JOHN SPENCE
Secretary: P. W. A. WEST
Librarian: D. LAW

Number of teachers: 942 (full-time)
Number of students: 12,600 (full-time)

Publications: *Annual Report*, *University Calendar*, *Undergraduate Prospectus*, *Postgraduate Prospectus*, *Continuing Education Programme.*

DEANS

Faculty of Science: Dr J. STUART BRAMLEY
Faculty of Engineering: Prof. ALAN HENDRY
Faculty of Arts and Social Sciences: Prof. ARTHUR MIDWINTER
Faculty of Education: Prof. DOUGLAS WEIR
Strathclyde Business School: Prof. DOUGLAS C. PITT

PROFESSORS

ALEXANDER, A., Management in Local Government
ALEXANDER, J., Immunology
ASHCROFT, B. K., Economics
BACHTLER, J., European Policy
BAKER, M. J., Marketing
BAKER, T. N., Metallurgy
BANKS, W. M., Advanced Materials
BARBENEL, J. C., Bioengineering
BARNETT, S., Quantum Optics
BAUM, T. G., Hospitality Management
BIRCH, D. J. S., Photophysics
BLACKIE, J. W. G., Scots Law
BOYLE, J. T., Mechanics of Materials
BRYCE, T. G. K, Education
BUCHANAN, J. T., Computer Science
CADDY, B., Forensic Science
CAMERON, D., English
CARRIE, A. S., Advanced Manufacturing Technology
CHAKRABARTI, M., Social Work
CHALMERS, I. D., Electrical and Mechanical Engineering
CLARK, N., Environmental Studies
CLARKE, J. A., Energy Systems
CLUNIES-ROSS, A. I., Economics
CORCORAN, M., Architecture
COURTNEY, J. M., Bioengineering
CROSS, R. B., Economics
CULSHAW, B., Optoelectronics
DAVIES, J. B., Psychology
DEVINE, T. M., Scottish History
DIANI, M., Sociology
DONALDSON, G. B., Applied Physics
DUNLOP, J., Communications Engineering
DURRANI, T., Signal Processing
DUXBURY, G., Chemical Physics
EDEN, C., Management Science
FARISH, O., Power Engineering
FERGUSON, A. I., Photonics
FERGUSON, J., Fibre and Textile Research
FIRTH, W. J., Experimental Physics
FLEMING, G., Civil Engineering
FOOT, H. C., Psychology
FRASER, S. M., Energy Systems
FRASER, W. H., History
FRITH, S. W., English Studies
GENNARD, J., Human Resource Management
GETTINBY, G. C., Statistics
GORDON, G., Academic Practice
GRAHAM, N. B., Research in Chemistry
GRANT, C. D., Chemical Engineering
GRAY, T. G. F., Fracture Mechanics
GREENSTED, C. S., Business Administration
GRIMBLE, M. J., Industrial Systems
GURNEY, A., Pharmacology
GURNEY, W. S. C., Mathematical Ecology
HALLETT, A. H., Macroeconomics
HALLING, P. J., Biocatalyst Science
HARPER, J. R., Law
HARVEY, A. L., Pharmacology
HASTINGS, G., Marketing
HAYTON, K., Planning
HAYWARD, G., Signal Processing
HENDRY, A., Metallurgy and Engineering Materials
HITCHMAN, M. L., Chemistry
HOGWOOD, B. W., Politics
HOOD, N., Business Policy
HOWE, C., Psychology
HUDSON, S., Pharmaceutical Care
HUGHES, J., Prosthetics and Orthotics
HUGHES-HALLETT, A., Macroeconomics
HUNTER, I., Molecular Microbiology
HUXHAM, C., Management Science
JACKSON, M., Environmental Health
JENKINS, C. L., International Tourism
JUDGE, D., Politics
JUSTER, N., Design and Manufacture
KARTVEDT, P., Architecture
KAY, N. M., Business Economics
KUO, C., Shipbuilding and Naval Architecture
LANGFORD, D. A., Construction
LESLIE, F. M., Mathematics
LITTLEJOHN, D., Analytical Chemistry
LLOYD, I. J., Law
LO, K. L., Power Engineering
LOVE, J., Economics
MACBEATH, J. E. C., Quality on Education
MCCALL, J., Education
MACDONALD, J., Power Engineering
MACDONALD, R., International Finance
MACFARLANE, C. J., Subsea Engineering
MCGETTRICK, A. D., Computer Science
MCGOWN, A., Civil Engineering
MCGREGOR, D. R., Computer Science
MCKEE, S., Mathematics
MACLEOD, I. A., Structural Engineering
MCMILLAN, J. F., European History
MCNICOLL, I. H., Applied Economics
MACROSSON, W. D. K., Management of Technology
MAHER, G., Private Law
MANGAN, J. A., Cultural Studies in Education
MAVER, T. W., Computer-Aided Design
MIDGLEY, J. M., Pharmacy
MIDWINTER, A., Politics
MILLAN, C. G., French Studies
MILLER, K., Employment Law
MULVEY, R. E., Inorganic Chemistry
MURPHY, J., Preparative Chemistry
NIMMO, M., Exercise Physiology
NORRIE, K., Law
PACIONE, M., Geography
PARRATT, J. R., Cardiovascular Pharmacology
PATERSON, A. A., Law
PAUL, J. P., Bioengineering
PETHRICK, R. A., Physical Chemistry
PHELPS, A., Plasma Physics
PITT, D. C., Organisational Analysis
PITTOCK, M., English Literature
RAMSAY, H., Human Resource Managment
REED, P. A., Architecture
REID, S., Veterinary Informatics
RENSHAW, E., Statistics and Modelling Science
RHODES, J., Mechanics of Materials
ROBSON, P., Law
RODGERS, E. J., Spanish Studies
ROSE, R., Politics of Public Policy
SHAW, S. A., Marketing
SHERRINGTON, D. C., Polymer Chemistry
SHERWOOD, J. N., Physical Chemistry
SINCLAIR, J. H., Conveyancing Practice
SLOAN, D. MCP., Numerical Analysis
SMITH, D. G., Communications Engineering
SMITH, J. E., Applied Microbiology
SMITH, J. R., Power Engineering
SMITH, W. E., Inorganic Chemistry
SNAPE, C., Clinical Technology
SPENCE, J., Mechanics of Materials
STEPHEN, F. H., Economics
STIMSON, W. H., Immunology
STOKER, G., Politics
SUCKLING, C. J., Chemistry
SUMMERS, H. P., Theoretical Atomic Physics
SUPPLE, J., French
THOMAS, M. J., Marketing
TOMLINSON, B. R., Economic History
TOOTH, A. S., Pressure Vessel Technology
TOTH, A. G., European Law
TOWERS, B., Industrial Relations
VAN DER HEIJDEN, C. A. J. M., Business Administration
WAIGH, R. D., Pharmacy
WALKER, F. A., Architecture
WATERMAN, P. G., Pharmaceutical Chemistry
WATSON, J., Biochemistry
WEIR, A. D., Education
WILKIE, W. R., Administration
WILLIAMS, H., Management Science
WILSON, C. G., Pharmacy
WOOD, R. C., Hospitality Management
WRIGHT, G., Business Administration
WRIGHT, H. D., Structural Engineering
YADAV, P. K., Accounting and Finance
YOUNG, S., Marketing
YUILL, D., European Policies
ZIETLIN, I. J., Pharmacology

UNIVERSITY INSTITUTES

John Logie Baird Centre for Research in Television and Film: Livingstone Tower, 26 Richmond St, Glasgow G1 1XH; Dir Prof. S. W. FRITH.

Centre for Electrical Power Engineering: Royal College Bldg, 204 George St, Glasgow, G1 1XW; Dir Prof. O. FARISH.

Centre for Professional Legal Studies: Stenhouse Bldg, 173 Cathedral St, Glasgow, G4 0RQ; Dir Prof. R. HARPER.

Centre for Scottish Cultural Studies: Level 6, Livingstone Tower, 26 Richmond St, Glasgow, G1 1XA; Dir Dr K. G. SIMPSON.

Centre for Social Marketing: Stenhouse Bldg, 173 Cathedral St, Glasgow, G4 0RQ; Dir Dr G. HASTINGS.

Centre for the Study of Public Policy: McCance Bldg, 16 Richmond St, Glasgow, G1 1XQ; Dir Prof. R. ROSE.

David Livingstone Institute of Overseas Development Studies: McCance Bldg, 16 Richmond St, Glasgow, G1 1XQ; Dir Prof. J. PICKETT.

European Policies Research Centre: EAC Bldg, 141 St James' Rd, Glasgow, G4 0LT; Dirs Prof. D. M. YUILL, Prof. K. J. ALLEN.

Fraser of Allander Institute for Research on the Scottish Economy (Dept of Economics): Curran Bldg, 131 St James' Rd, Glasgow, G4 0LS; Dir B. K. ASHCROFT.

Graduate School of Environmental Studies: Level 7, Graham Hills Bldg, 50 Richmond St, Glasgow, G1; Dir Ms J. FORBES.

Industrial Control Centre: Marland House, 40 George St, Glasgow, G1 1BA; Dir Prof. M. GRIMBLE.

Institute of Photonics Wolfson Centre: Chief Exec. Dr KAREN NESS.

National Centre for Training and Education in Prosthetics and Orthotics: Curran Bldg, 131 St James' Rd, Glasgow G4 0LS; Dir Prof. J. HUGHES.

Scottish Local Authorities Management Centre: Curran Bldg, 131 St James's Rd, Glasgow, G4 0LS; Dir Prof. A. ALEXANDER.

Scottish Transputer Centre & DTI Centre for Parallel Signal Processing: Royal College Bldg, 204 George St, Glasgow, G1 1XW; Dir Prof. T. DURRANI.

Senior Studies Institute: McCance Bldg, 16 Richmond St, Glasgow, G1 1XQ; Dir L. A. HART.

Smart Structures Research Institute: Royal College Bldg, 204 George St, Glasgow, G1 1XW; Dir P. GARDINER.

Strathclyde Fermentation Centre: Royal College Bldg, Glasgow, G1 1XW; Dir Prof. B. KRISTIANSEN.

Strathclyde Formulation Research Unit: Royal College Bldg, 204 George St, Glasgow, G1 1XW; Dir Dr A. J. BAILLIE.

Strathclyde Institute for Drug Research: Royal College Bldg, 204 George St, Glasgow G1 1XW; Dir Prof. A. L. HARVEY.

UNIVERSITY OF SUNDERLAND

Langham Tower, Ryhope Rd, Sunderland, SR2 7EE

Telephone: (191) 515-2000
Fax: (191) 5152960

Founded 1969 as Sunderland Polytechnic; present name and status 1992
Language of instruction: English
Academic year: September to June

Chancellor: Lord PUTTNAM OF QUEENSGATE
Vice-Chancellor and Chief Executive: Prof. JEFF BROWN (acting)
Pro-Vice-Chancellor: IAN BURNS
Secretary and Clerk to the Board: J. D. PACEY
Director of Information Services: Prof. ANDREW MACDONALD

Library of 280,000 vols
Number of teachers: 494
Number of students: 11,151 full-time and sandwich, 3,753 part-time

DIRECTORS

School of Arts, Design and Communications: Prof. F. SWANN
Sunderland Business School: Prof. G. HENDERSON
School of Computing and Information Systems: R. BELL
School of Education: Dr G. SHIELDS
School of Engineering and Advanced Technology: Dr M. NEWTON (acting), Dr D. TAYLOR (acting)
School of the Environment: Prof. R. HARRISON (acting)
School of Health Sciences: Dr J. M. SNEDDON
School of Social and International Studies: Prof. A. C. HEPBURN (acting), Dr C. STUBBS (acting)
Centre for Independent and Combined Programmes: M. RAMSHAW

PROFESSORS

ARTHUR, W. W., Population Biology
COLBY, J., Biotechnology
CONSTABLE, H., Education
COX, C. S., Control Engineering
CRAGGS, S. R., Music Bibliography
HEPBURN, A., Modern Irish History
FLETCHER, E. J., Applied Computing
HARRISON, R., Renewable Energy
METH-COHN, O., Organic Chemistry
MOSCARDINI, A. O., Mathematical Modelling
OVER, D. E., Philosophical Logic
ROWELL, F. J., Analytical Chemistry
RYAN, H. M., Electrical and Electronic Engineering
SIM, S., English Studies
SMITH, P., Computing

UNIVERSITY OF SURREY

Guildford, Surrey, GU2 5XH
Telephone: (1483) 300800
Telex: 859331
Fax: (1483) 300803

Founded as Battersea Polytechnic Institute 1891; designated a College of Advanced Technology 1956; University Charter 1966
Academic year: September to May

Chancellor: HRH The Duke of KENT
Vice-Chancellor: Prof. PATRICK J. DOWLING
Pro-Vice-Chancellors: Prof. PETER H. W. BUTTERWORTH (senior), Prof. GLYNIS M. BREAKWELL (Research and Enterprise), Prof. G. NIGEL GILBERT (Staff Development), Prof. JOHN E. HARDING (Teaching and Learning)
University Secretary and Registrar: H. W. B. DAVIES
Librarian and Dean of Information Services: T. J. A. CRAWSHAW

Number of teachers: 458 full-time, 71 part-time
Number of students: 8,472

Publications: *Prospectus*, *Prospectus of Research and Postgraduate Studies*, *Report of the Vice-Chancellor* (annually), *Surrey Matters*.

HEADS OF SCHOOL

School of Biological Sciences: Prof. JIM LYNCH
School of Electronic Engineering, Information Technology and Mathematics: Prof. MICHAEL KELLY
School Engineering in the Environment: Prof. HANS MÜLLER-STEINHAGEN
School of Mechanical and Materials Engineering: Prof. MIKE GORINGE
School of Physical Sciences: Prof. WILLIAM GELLETLY
School of Human Sciences: Prof. GLYNIS BREAKWELL
School of Language and International Studies: Prof. PETER LUTZIER
School of Management Studies for the Service Sector: Prof. MICHAEL KIPPS
School of Performing Arts: Prof. JANET LANSDALE
School of Educational Studies: Prof. LENI OGLESBY
European Institute of Health and Medical Sciences: Prof. JIM BRIDGES
Surrey European Management School: Prof. PAUL GAMBLE

PROFESSORS

School of Biological Sciences:

ARENDT, J., Endocrinology
BRIDGES, J. W., Toxicology
BUSHELL, M. E., Microbial Physiology
BUTTERWORTH, P. H. W., Molecular Biology
DALE, J. W., Molecular Microbiology
FERNS, G. A. A., Metabolic and Molecular Medicine
GIBSON, G. G., Molecular Toxicology
GOLDFARB, P., Molecular Biology
HINDMARCH, I., Human Psychopharmacology
KING, L. J., Biochemistry
KITCHEN, I., Neuropharmacology
LYNCH, J. M., Biotechnology
MILLWARD, D. J., Nutrition
SPIER, R. E., Science and Engineering Ethics
WALKER, R., Food Science

School of Electronic Engineering, Information Technology and Mathematics:

CROWDER, M. J., Statistics
EVANS, B. G., Information Systems Engineering
KELLY, M. J.
KITTLER, J. V., Machine Intelligence
KONDOZ, A. M.
PETROV, M., Engineering
SCHUMAN, S. A., Computing Science
SEALY, B. J., Solid State Devices and Ion Beam Technology
SHAIL, R., Mathematics
STEPHENS, K. G.
SWEETING, M. N., Satellite Engineering
SWEETING, T. J., Statistics
UNDERHILL, M. J.
WEISS, B. L., Microelectronics

School of Engineering in the Environment:

CLAYTON, C. R. I., Geotechnical Engineering
CLIFT, R., Environmental Technology
GHADIRI, M., Particle Technology
HANNANT, D. J., Construction Materials
HARDING, J. E., Structural Engineering
HOLLAWAY, L. C., Composite Structures
HUXLEY, M.
LLOYD, B.
MÜLLER-STEINHAGEN, H. M., Chemical and Process Engineering
NOOSHIN, H., Space Structures
SIMONS, N. E., Civil Engineering
SMITH, J. M., Process Engineering
TOY, N., Fluid Mechanics
TÜZÜN, U., Process Engineering

School of Mechanical and Materials Engineering:

CASTLE, J. E., Materials Science
CASTRO, I. P., Fluid Dynamics
GORINGE, M. J., Materials
PARKER, G. A., Mechanical Engineering
POLLARD, D. J.
ROBINS, A. G., Environmental Fluid Mechanics
SMITH, P. A., Composite Materials
TSAKIROPOULOS, P., Metallurgy
VOKE, P., Computational Fluid Dynamics

School of Physical Sciences:

ADAMS, A. R.
BALARAJAN, R., Epidemiology
CROCKER, A. G.
GELLETLY, W.
JOHNSON, R. C.
JONES, J. R., Radiochemistry
O'REILLY, E. P., Physics
SAMMES, P. G.
SERMON, P. A.
SLADE, R. T. C.
WALKER, P.
WEBB, G. A.

School of Human Sciences:

ARBER, S. L., Sociology
BARRETT, M. D., Psychology
BIRD, G. R.
BREAKWELL, G. M., Psychology
BULMER, M. I. A., Sociology
DAVIES, I. R. L.
FIELDING, N. G., Sociology
GILBERT, G. N., Sociology
GROEGER, J. A., Cognitive Psychology
HAMPSON, S. E., Psychology and Health
HORNSBY-SMITH, M. P., Sociology
LEVINE, P.
MCMILLAN, T. M., Clinical Psychology
MORAY, N. P., Applied Cognitive Psychology
REISMAN, D. A., Economics
ROBINSON, C.
TARLING, R., Sociology

School of Language and International Studies:

ANDERMAN, G. M.
CORBETT, G. G., Linguistics and Russian Language
FULCHER, N. G.
JUDGE, A., French
LUTZEIER, P. R., German
RIORDAN, J. W., Russian Studies
SANDERS, C., French
THACKER, M. J.

School of Management Studies for the Service Sector:

AIREY, D. W., Tourism Management
ARCHER, G. S. H., Financial Management
BUTLER, R. W., Tourism
KIPPS, M.

PARLETT, G. R.
RILEY, M. R.
WITT, S.

School of Performing Arts:
FORBES, S., Music
LANSDALE, J. H.
MESSENGER, T., Music

School of Educational Studies:
EVANS, K. M., Post-Compulsory Education
JARVIS, P., Continuing Education
MIDDLEHURST, R. M.
OGLESBY, K. L., Education

European Institute of Health and Medical Sciences:
BRIDGES, J. W., Toxicology and Environmental Health
BUCKLE, P.
CLARKE, M., Nursing Studies
CROW, R. A., Nursing Sciences
HAWKINS, L.
MARKS, V.
STUBBS, D. A., Ergonomics

Surrey European Management School:
GAMBLE, P. R., European Management Studies
STONE, M.

ATTACHED INSTITUTES

Centre for Communication Systems Research: Dir Prof. B. G. EVANS.

Centre for Environmental Strategy: Dir Prof. R. CLIFT.

Centre for Postgraduate Studies: Dir Prof. P. JARVIS.

Centre for Satellite Engineering Research: Dir Prof. M. N. SWEETING.

Centre for the Advancement of Clinical Practice: Dir Prof. R. A. CROW.

Centre for Translation Studies: Dir Prof. G. M. ANDERMAN.

Centre for Vision, Speech and Signal Processing: Dir Prof. J. V. KITTLER.

English Language Institute: Dir Prof. N. G. FULCHER.

Environmental Flow Research Centre: Dir Prof. I. P. CASTRO.

European Institute of Health and Medical Sciences: Dir Prof. J. W. BRIDGES.

European Language Teaching Centre: Dir Prof. M. J. THACKER.

Institute of Health and Medical Sciences: Dir Prof. J. W. BRIDGES.

National Institute of Epidemiology: Dir Prof. R. BALARAJAN.

Surrey Centre for Ion Beam Applications: Dir Prof. B. J. SEALY.

Surrey European Management School: Dir Prof. P. R. GAMBLE.

Surrey Satellite Technology Ltd: CEO Prof. M. N. SWEETING.

UNIVERSITY OF SUSSEX

Falmer, Brighton, Sussex, BN1 9RH
Telephone: (1273) 606755
Fax: (1273) 678335

Founded 1961
Academic year: October to June

Chancellor: Lord ATTENBOROUGH OF RICHMOND UPON THAMES
Vice-Chancellor: Prof. M. A. M. SMITH (acting)
Pro-Vice-Chancellor (Science): Prof. B. ROBERTS
Pro-Vice-Chancellors: Dr C. BROOKS, Prof. A. J. MCCAFFERY
Registrar: B. GOOCH
Librarian: A. N. PEASGOOD
Library: see Libraries
Number of teachers: 522
Number of students: 9,085

Publications: *Undergraduate Prospectus*, *Postgraduate Prospectus*, *Study Abroad Prospectus*, *Annual Report*, etc.

DEANS

School of African and Asian Studies: Dr D. ROBINSON
School of Biological Sciences: Prof. T. MOORE
School of Cognitive Sciences: Prof. R. COATES
School of Cultural and Community Studies: Dr B. SHORT
School of Engineering and Applied Sciences: Prof. E. POWNER
School of English and American Studies: Dr A. CROZIER
School of European Studies: Prof. R. KING
School of Mathematical Sciences: Prof. C. GOLDIE
School of Chemistry, Physics and Environmental Science: Prof. J. N. MURKELL
School of Social Science: Dr J. N. DEARLOVE

PROFESSORS

ATHERTON, D. P., Electrical Engineering
BARROW, J. D., Astronomy
BARTON, G., Physics
BATHER, J. A., Mathematics and Statistics
BENJAMIN, P. R., Animal Physiology
BENNINGTON, G., French
BLISS, J., Education
BODEN, M. A., Philosophy and Social Psychology; Computer Science and Artificial Intelligence
BRIDGES, B. A., Prof. Fellow, Dir MRC Cell Mutation Unit
BURTON, R. D. E., French
BUTTERWORTH, G., Psychology
BUXTON, H., Computer Science
CAWSON, A., Politics
CLARKE, T., Physical Electronics
CHATWIN, C., Manufacturing Systems
CHERRY, D., Art History
CLOKE, G., Chemistry
CLUNAS, C., Art History
COATES, R. A., Linguistics
DARWIN, C. J., Experimental Psychology
DAVEY, G., Psychology
DOMBEY, N. D., Theoretical Physics
DU BOULAY, J. B. H., Artificial Intelligence
DUNFORD, M. F., Economic Geography
EDMUNDS, D. E., Mathematics
ELLIOTT, C. M., Mathematics
ELLIOTT, J. P., Theoretical Physics
ERAUT, M. R., Education
FENDER, S. A., American Literature
FIELDING, A., Geography
FLOWERS, T. J., Plant Physiology
GAZDAR, G. J. M., Linguistics; Computer Science and Artificial Intelligence
GOLDIE, C., Statistics
GRILLO, R. D., Social Anthropology
GRIMSDALE, R. L., Electronics
HARRISON, B. J., Philosophy
HARWIN, J., Social Welfare Studies
HENNESSY, M., Computer Science
HINDS, E. A., Experimental Physics
HOWKINS, A., History
JAYAWANT, B. V., Electrical and Systems Engineering
JENKINS, A. D., Polymer Science
JOSIPOVICI, G. D., English
KAHN, J., Social Anthropology
KEDWARD, H. R., History
KING, R., Geography
KROTO, Sir H. W., Molecular Sciences
LAMONT, W. M., History and Education
LAND, M. F., Neurobiology
LAPPERT, M. F., Chemistry
LEWIN, K., Education
LIPTON, M., Development Economics
LISTER, P., Electronic Engineering
MCCAFFERY, A. J., Molecular Sciences
MCCAPRA, F., Chemistry
MANSELL, R., Technology Policy
MIDDLEMAS, R. K., History
MILNER-GULLAND, R., Russian Studies
MOORE, A., Biochemistry
MURRELL, J. N., Chemistry
NICHOLLS, P., American Studies
NICHOLSON, M., International Relations
NIXON, J. F., Chemistry
O'SHEA, M., Neuroscience
OSMOND-SMITH, D., Music
OUTHWAITE, W., Sociology
PARKIN, A., Experimental Psychology
PARSONS, P., Organic Chemistry
PAVITT, K. L. R., Science and Technology Policy Studies
PENDLEBURY, M., Physics
POWNER, E. T., Electrical, Electronic and Control Engineering
PLATT, J. A., Sociology
RAYAK, H., Law
RENDELL, H., Geography
ROBERTS, J. B., Mechanical Engineering
RÖHL, J. C. G., History
ROPER, T., Biological Sciences
RUSSELL, I. J., Neurobiology
RYAN, C., Italian
SAUNDERS, P. R., Sociology
SINFIELD, A. J., English
SMITH, M. A. M., Economics
SMITH, P., Social Psychology
STACE, A., Chemistry
STEPHENS, D., Psychology
SUMNER, M. T., Economics
TEMKIN, J., Law
THANE, C., History
TIMMS, E. F., German
TOWNSEND, P. D., Experimental Physics
TRASK, L., Linguistics
TURNER, A. B., Mechanical Engineering
VAN GELDEREN, M., Intellectual History
VANCE, N., English
VASSILIER, D., Mathematics
WAGSTAFF, A., Economics
WALLACE, H., Contemporary European Studies
WALLIS, M., Biochemistry
WATTS, C. T., English
WAY, P., American Studies
WILKINSON, R. H., American History
WINCH, D. N., Economics
WINTERS, A., Economics
WORDEN, B., History
YOUNG, D. W., Chemistry

ATTACHED INSTITUTES

Science Policy Research Unit: Dir Prof. B. MARTIN.

Medical Research Council Cell Mutation Unit: see under Research Institutes.

Institute of Development Studies: University of Sussex, Falmer, Brighton, Sussex, BN1 9RE; tel. (1273) 606261; telex 877997; f. 1966; national centre concerned with Third World development and the relationships between rich and poor countries; offers teaching and supervision for university graduate degrees; library of 200,000 vols; an official depository for United Nations publications; Dir KEITH BEZANSON; publ. *IDS Bulletin* (quarterly).

Institute of Employment Studies: University of Sussex, Falmer, Brighton, Sussex, BN1 9RH; Dir R. PEARSON.

Trafford Centre for Medical Research: University of Sussex, Falmer, Brighton, Sussex, BN1 9RH; Dir Prof. R. VINCENT.

UNIVERSITY OF TEESSIDE

Middlesbrough, TS1 3BA
Telephone: (1642) 218121
Fax: (1642) 342067

Founded 1929 as Constantine College of Technology, became Teesside Polytechnic 1970, present name and status 1992

Vice-Chancellor: Prof. DEREK FRASER

Pro-Vice-Chancellors: G. CRISPIN, H. PICKERING

University Secretary: J. M. McCLINTOCK

Academic Registrar: JENETH SLATER

Director, Library and Information Services: I. C. BUTCHART

Library of 330,000 vols

Number of teachers: 494

Number of students: 13,483

DIRECTORS OF SCHOOLS

Business and Management: Dr N. HODGE

Computing and Mathematics: Dr D. MEEHAN

Health: Dr M. HOLMES

Law, Arts and Humanities: Prof. S. BASKERVILLE

Science and Technology: Prof. J. BAINBRIDGE

Social Sciences: Prof. P. ABBOTT

THAMES VALLEY UNIVERSITY

St Mary's Road, Ealing, London, W5 5RF

Telephone: (181) 579-5000

Wellington St, Slough, Berks, SL1 1YG

Telephone: (1753) 534585

Founded as Ealing College of Higher Education, Thames Valley College of Higher Education, Queen Charlotte's College of Health Care Studies and the London College of Music; merged to become Polytechnic of West London in 1991; present name and status 1992

Campuses in Ealing and Slough

Vice-Chancellor: Dr MIKE FITZGERALD

Head of Registry Services: PAUL HEAD

Library of 232,000 vols, 2,274 periodicals

Number of teachers: 560

Number of students: 11,500 full-time and sandwich, 13,800 part-time, 2,100 distance learning

COLLEGE DIRECTORS

Further Education: SUE THURSTON

Undergraduate: ANDY ROSS

Postgraduate: GRAHAM HANKINSON

DEANS OF SCHOOL

School of Business, Management and Accountancy: NICK PRATT

School of English Language Teaching: HELEN THOMAS

School of European, International and Social Studies: PETER McCAFFREY

School of Hospitality Studies: PAUL HAMBLETON

School of Law: TONY FOWLES, GEORGE WEBSTER

London College of Music and Media: RUSSELL PEARSON

Wolfson School of Health Sciences: LOIS CROOKE

Centre for Information Management: ANN IRVING (Dir)

UMIST

POB 88, Manchester, M60 1QD

Telephone: (161) 236-3311

Fax: (161) 228-7040

Founded 1824 as Manchester Mechanics' Institute; became Faculty of Technology in the University of Manchester in 1905, and later University of Manchester Institute of Science and Technology; became independent of the University of Manchester, with university status, in 1994

Academic year: September to June

Chancellor: Prof. Sir ROLAND SMITH

Principal and Vice-Chancellor: Prof. R. BOUCHER

Pro-Vice Chancellors: Prof. I. ROBERTSON, Prof. J. GARSIDE, Prof. C. COOPER, Prof. R. PROCTOR

Secretary and Registrar: P. STEPHENSON

Librarian: M. DAY

Library of 132,000 vols, 1,100 periodicals

Number of teachers: 475

Number of students: 5,835

PROFESSORS

ALDER, J. F., Instrumentation and Analytical Science
AL-HASSANI, S. T. S., Mechanical Engineering
ALLEN, R. N., Electrical Engineering and Electronics
ALLINSON, N. M., Electronic Systems Engineering
BELL, D. J., Applied Mathematics
BEYNON, R. J., Biochemistry
BIRRELL, G. S., Property Development, Finance and Management
BISHOP, R. F., Theoretical Physics
BOSWORTH, D. L., Economics
BROOMHEAD, D. S., Applied Mathematics
BRUCE, M. A., Textile Management
BRYANT, R. M., Pure Mathematics
BURDEKIN, F. M., Civil and Structural Engineering
BUSH, S. F., Polymer Engineering
CHALMERS, B. J., Electrical Engineering
CHARMAN, W. N., Visual Optics
CHOULARTON, T. W., Cloud and Aerosol Physics
CLARKE, J. H. R., Computational Chemistry
COOMBS, R. W., Technology Management
COOPER, C. L., Organizational Psychology
CRONLY-DILLON, J. R., Ophthalmic Optics
DALE, B. G., Quality Management
DAVEY, R. J., Molecular Engineering
DAVIES, G. A., Chemical Engineering
DAVIS, L. E., Electronic Engineering
DEWHURST, R. J., Instrumentation
DODSON, C. T. J., Paper Science
DOLD, J. W., Applied Mathematics
EFRON, N., Optometry and Vision Science
GARSIDE, J., Chemical Engineering
GASKELL, S. J., Mass Spectrometry
GOODMAN, J. F. B., Industrial Relations
GOTT, G. F., Electrical Engineering
GRIFFITHS, R. F., Environmental Technology Centre
HAMILTON, B., Solid State Physics
HAYHURST, D. R., Design Manufacture and Materials
HEGGS, P. J., Chemical Engineering
HICKS, P. J., Electrical Engineering
HOFF, W. D., Building Engineering
HOSKIN, K. W., Accounting and Finance
HUGILL, J., Plasma Physics
HUMPHREYS, F. J., Materials Science
JONAS, P., Atmospheric Physic
KNIGHTS, D., Organizational Analysis
KOCHHAR, A. K., Manufacturing Systems Engineering
KULIKOWSKI, J. J., Optometry and Vision Sciences
LAUNDER, B. E., Mechanical Engineering
LAYZELL, P., Software Management
LESCHZINER, M. A., Computational Fluid Dynamics
LETHERMAN, K. M., Building Engineering
LITTLER, D. A., Marketing
LOUCOPOULOS, P., Computation
McAULIFFE, C. A., Inorganic Chemistry
McCANN, H., Process Tomography
McCARTHY, J. E. G., Molecular Life Sciences
McGOLDRICK, P. J., Retailing
MANN, R., Chemical Reaction Engineering
MARCHINGTON, M., Human Resource Management
MAVITUNA, F., Chemical Engineering
MILLAR, T. J., Astrophysics
MOLENKAMP, F., Civil and Structural Engineering
MORRIS, P., Project Management
MUNN, R. W., Chemical Physics
MUNRO, I. H., Synchrotron Radiation
MUNRO, N., Applied Control Engineering
NEWMAN, R. C., Corrosion and Protection
OLIVER, S. G., Biotechnology
PAYNE, P. A., Instrumentation
PEAKER, A. R., Electrical Engineering and Electronics
PHILLIPS, D. A. S., Textile Chemistry
PHIPPS, M. E., Civil and Structural Engineering
PORAT, I., Clothing Engineering
PROCTER, R. P. M., Science and Technology
RAMSAY, A., Language Engineering
REID, S. R., Mechanical Engineering
RICHARDS, B., Computation
ROBERTSON, I. T., Management
RUBERY, J., Comparative Employment Systems
SINGER, K. E., Solid State Electronics
SINGH, M. G., Information Engineering
SINNOTT, M. L., Paper Science
SMITH, R., Process Integration
SNOOK, R. D., Analytical Science
STEPTO, R. F., Polymer Science
STOODLEY, R. J., Organic Chemistry
STOTT, F. H., Corrosion Science and Engineering
SUBBA RAO, T., Mathematics
TAYLOR, M. J., Pure Mathematics
THOMPSON, G. E., Corrosion and Protection
THOMPSON, P. A., Civil Engineering
TSUJJI, J. I., Computational Linguistics
TURNBULL, P., Marketing
VICKERMAN, J. C., Surface Chemistry
WAUGH, K. C., Physical Chemistry
WEBB, C., Grain-Processing Engineering
WELLSTEAD, P. E., Electrical Engineering and Electronics
WHETTON, A. D., Cell Biology
WILLMOTT, H, C., Organizational Analysis
WINTERBONE, D. E., Mechanical Engineering
WISEMAN, N., Paper Science
YOUNG, R. J., Polymer Science and Technology

ATTACHED SCHOOL

Manchester-Sheffield-UMIST School of Probability and Statistics: c/o Dept of Mathematics, UMIST, POB 88, Sackville St, Manchester, M60 1QD; Dir Prof. M. B. PRIESTLEY.

UNIVERSITY OF WALES

University Registry, King Edward VII Ave, Cathays Park, Cardiff, CF1 3NS

Telephone: (1222) 382656

Fax: (1222) 396040

Founded 1893

Chancellor: HRH The Prince CHARLES, Prince of WALES

Pro-Chancellor: Lord WILLIAMS OF MOSTYN

Senior Vice-Chancellor: Prof. KEITH G. ROBBINS

Secretary-General: J. D. PRITCHARD

Library: see Libraries

The University of Wales Press publishes learned works and periodicals in Welsh and English.

CONSTITUENT COLLEGES

University of Wales, Aberystwyth

Old College, King St, Aberystwyth, Ceredigion, SY23 2AX

Telephone: (1970) 623111

Telex: 35181

Fax: (1970) 611446

Founded 1872

Language of instruction: English, with some courses in Welsh
Academic year: October to December; January to March; April to June
President: Lord ELYSTAN MORGAN
Vice-Presidents: Prof. Emer. R. GERAINT GRUFFYDD, HUW WYNNE-GRIFFITH
Vice-Chancellor: Prof. D. LLWYD MORGAN
Pro-Vice Chancellors: Prof. N. LLOYD, Prof. B. HAMMOND
Registrar: D. GRUFFYDD JONES
Library: see Libraries
Number of teachers: 319
Number of students: 7,333
Publications: *University of Wales Calendar*, *Prospectus*, *Postgraduate Prospectus*, *Abernews*.

DEANS

Faculty of Arts: Prof. DAVID TROTTER
Faculty of Science: Prof. NEIL JONES
Faculty of Economic and Social Studies: JOHN WILLIAMS

PROFESSORS

AITCHISON, J., Geography
BARRETT, J., Biological Sciences
BATTEN, D. J., Earth Studies
BAYLIS, J., International Politics
BEECHEY, R. B., Biological Sciences
BOOTH, K., International Politics
CABLE, J. R., Managerial Economics
CLARK, I., International Politics
COX, M., International Politics
DAUGHERTY, R. A., Education
DAVIES, A. R., Mathematics
DODGSHON, R. A., Geography
DRAPER, J., Biological Sciences
EDWARDS, G., Spanish
FOLEY, M., International Politics
GARNETT, J. C., International Politics
GILBERTSON, D. D., Earth Studies
GOODWIN, M. A., Earth Sciences
GREAVES, G. N., Physics
GWILLIAM, D. R., Accounting
HAINES, M., Agricultural Marketing
HALL, M. A., Botany
HAMMOND, B. S., English
HARDING, C., Law
HARESIGN, W., Agriculture
HARVARD, R. G., European Languages
HARVEY, J., Art
HENLEY, A., Economics
HINCHLIFFE, J. R., Zoology
JONES, A., History and Welsh History
JONES, G. L., European Languages
JONES, R. N., Agricultural Botany
KELL, D. B., Microbiology
KELLY, S. L., Biological Sciences
KIDNER, R. A. W., Law
KERSLEY, L., Physics
LEE, M. H., Computer Science
LLOYD, N. G., Mathematics
MIDMORE, P. R., Rural Studies
MOORE-COLYER, M., Rural Studies
MORRIS, A. O., Pure Mathematics
MORRIS, J. G., Microbiology
PYKETT, L., English
ROBERTS, D. H. R., Information and Library Services
RODGERS, C., Law
ROGERS, L. J., Biochemistry
ROWLANDS, J., Welsh Language
RUBENSTEIN, W. D., History and Welsh History
SIMS-WILLIAMS, P., Welsh Language
SMITH, S. M., International Politics
TEDD, M. D., Computer Science
TROTTER, D., European Languages
WALTERS, K., Applied Mathematics
WARREN, L., Law
WATHERN, P., Biological Sciences
WHATELY, R. C., Geology
WILLIAMS, G. A., Welsh Language and Literature
WILLIAMS, H. L., International Politics
WILLIAMS, I., Theatre, Film and Television Studies
WILLIAMS, P. J. S., Physics
WINTLE, A. G., Geography and Earth Sciences
YOUNG, M., Biological Sciences

HEADS OF DEPARTMENTS

BOTT, M. F., Computer Science
EVANS-WORTHING, L., Physical Education

University of Wales, Bangor

Bangor, Gwynedd, LL57 2DG
Telephone: (1248) 351151
Fax: (1248) 370451
Founded 1884
Academic year: September to June
Chancellor: HRH THE PRINCE OF WALES
President: Rt Hon. Lord CLEDWYN OF PENRHOS
Vice-Chancellor: Prof. ROY EVANS
Pro-Vice-Chancellors: Prof. A. E. UNDERHILL, Dr H. G. FF. ROBERTS, Prof. R. M. JONES, Prof. J. M. G. WILLIAMS
Secretary and Registrar: G. R. THOMAS
Library: see Libraries
Number of teaching staff: 459 including 54 professors
Number of students: 7,200
Publications: *Annual Report*, *Prospectus*, *Postgraduate Prospectus*, *Research Report*.

DEANS

Faculty of Arts and Social Sciences: Dr D. D. MORGAN
Faculty of Science and Engineering: Dr R. WHITBREAD
Faculty of Health Studies: P. J. PYE
Faculty of Education: Dr J. P. M. JONES

PROFESSORS

Faculty of Arts and Social Sciences:

BARSLEY, R. D., English and Linguistics
BUSHELL, A., Modern Languages
BUSST, A. J. L., Modern Languages
CORNS, T. N., English and Linguistics
COX, W. M., Psychology
DAVIS, H., Sociology and Social Policy
ELLIS, N. C., Psychology
FIELD, P. J. C., English and Linguistics
GARDENER, E. P. M., Accounting, Banking and Economics
HARDY, J. P. L., Sport, Health and Physical Education Sciences
JONES, G. LLOYD, Theology and Religious Studies
JONES, R. M., History and Welsh History
JONES, W. G., Modern Languages
KING, R. D., Sociology and Social Policy
LOWE, C. F., Psychology
MACE, F. C., Psychology
MCLEAY, S. J., Accounting, Banking and Economics
MOLYNEUX, P., Accounting, Banking and Economics
PASCAL, R.-J., Music
TANNER, D. M., History and Welsh History
THOMAS, G., Welsh
THOMAS, J. A., English and Linguistics
TIPPER, S. P., Psychology
TREBLE, J. G., Accounting, Banking and Economics
VIHMAN, M. M., Psychology
WENGER, C., Sociology and Social Policy
WILLIAMS, J. M. G., Psychology
WOODS, R. T., Psychology

Faculty of Science and Engineering:

BAIRD, M. S., Chemistry
BROWN, R., Mathematics
CHANTRELL, R. W., Electronic Engineering and Computer Systems
DANDO, P. R., Ocean Sciences
EDWARDS-JONES, G., Agricultural and Forest Sciences
ELLIOTT, A. J., Ocean Sciences
FARRAR, J. F., Biological Sciences
GODBOLD, D. L., Agricultural and Forest Sciences
HUGHES, R. N., Biological Sciences
LAST, J. D., Electronic Engineering and Computer Systems
O'GRADY, K. D., Electronic Engineering and Computer Systems
PAYNE, J. W., Biological Sciences
PETHIG, R., Electronic Engineering and Computer Systems
PORTER, T., Mathematics
PRICE, C., Agricultural and Forest Sciences
SEED, R., Ocean Sciences
SHORE, K. A., Electronic Engineering and Computer Systems
SIMPSON, J. H., Ocean Sciences
TAYLOR, D. M., Electronic Engineering and Computer Systems
THORPE, R. S., Biological Sciences
TOMOS, A. D., Biological Sciences
TYRRELL, A. M., Electronic Engineering and Computer Systems
UNDERHILL, A. E., Chemistry
WILLIAMS, P. A., Biological Sciences
WILLIAMS, P. J. LE B., Ocean Sciences

Faculty of Education:

BAKER, C. R., Education

ATTACHED INSTITUTES

Biocomposites Centre: f. 1991; Dir Dr A. J. BOLTON.

Centre for Applicable Mathematics: f. 1988; Dir Dr G. W. ROBERTS.

Centre for Arid Zone Studies: f. 1984; Dir W. I. ROBINSON.

Centre for Comparative Criminology and Criminal Justice: f. 1992; Dir Prof. R. D. KING.

Centre for Social Policy Research and Development: f. 1986; Dir Prof. C. WENGER.

Institute of Economic Research: Bangor; f. 1969; research in regional economics, economics of developing countries, tourism and economics of ports, policy-making and planning; data analysis; Dir Prof. R. R. MACKAY.

Institute of European Finance: Bangor; f. 1973; Prof. E. P. M. GARDENER.

Industrial Development Bangor (UCNW) Ltd: f. 1968; an engineering company owned by the College which carries out design, development and manufacture of a range of electrical and electronic equipment; Man. Dir E. D. JONES.

Institute for Medical and Social Care Research: f. 1998; Dir Prof. J. M. G. WILLIAMS.

Institute of Molecular and Biomolecular Electronics: f. 1983; Dir Prof. R. PETHIG.

Menai Technology Enterprise Centre (MENTEC): f. 1986; Dir D. V. JONES.

Research Centre Wales: f. 1985; Dir Prof. C. R. BAKER.

Unit for Coastal and Estuarine Studies: f. 1977; Prof. A. J. ELLIOTT.

Welsh National Centre for Religious Education: f. 1980; Dir RH. THOMAS.

University of Wales, Cardiff

POB 68, Cardiff, CF1 3XA
Telephone: (1222) 874000
Telex: 498635
Fax: (1222) 371921
Founded 1988 by merger of University College, Cardiff and University of Wales Institute of Science and Technology (f. 1883)
President: Rt. Hon. NEIL KINNOCK
Vice-Presidents: Sir RICHARD LLOYD-JONES, W. H. JOHN, Sir DONALD WALTERS, K. S. HOPKINS, V. KANE
Vice-Chancellor: Prof. E. BRIAN SMITH

Pro-Vice-Chancellors: Prof. A. CRYER, Prof. H. D. ELLIS, Prof. J. KING, Prof. R. MANSFIELD, Prof. J. PERCIVAL
Library: see Libraries
Number of teaching staff: 1,000
Number of students: 15,000
Publications: *Undergraduate Prospectus*, *Postgraduate Prospectus* (annually), *Annual Report*.

DEANS

Faculty of Health and Life Sciences: Prof. B. J. MOXHAM
Faculty of Physical Sciences: Dr M. J. E. HEWLINS
Faculty of Engineering and Environmental Design: Dr E. S. HAMDI
Faculty of Business Studies and Law: Prof. R. MANSFIELD
Faculty of Humanities and Social Studies: Prof. D. J. SKILTON

HEADS OF DEPARTMENTS/SCHOOLS

Faculty of Health and Life Sciences:
- School of Biosciences: (vacant)
- Welsh School of Pharmacy: Prof. D. K. LUSCOMBE
- Department of Optometry and Vision Sciences: Dr C. WIGHAM
- School of Psychology: Prof. H. D. ELLIS

Faculty of Physical Sciences:
- Department of Chemistry: Prof. G. J. HUTCHINGS
- Department of Physics and Astronomy: Prof. P. BLOOD
- Department of Earth Sciences: Prof. D. T. RICKARD
- School of Mathematics: Prof. J. D. GRIFFITHS
- Department of Computer Science: Dr N. J. FIDDIAN

Faculty of Engineering and Environmental Design:
- Cardiff School of Engineering: Prof. D. V. MORGAN
- Department of City and Regional Planning: Prof. J. D. ALDEN
- Department of Maritime Studies and International Transport: Prof. J. KING
- Welsh School of Architecture: C. PARRY

Faculty of Business Studies and Law:
- Cardiff Business School: Prof. R. MANSFIELD
- Cardiff Law School: Prof. R. G. LEE

Faculty of Humanities and Social Studies:
- School of English, Communication and Philosophy: Prof. D. J. SKILTON
- School of European Studies: Prof. D. L. HANLEY
- School of History and Archaeology: Prof. J. OSMOND
- School of Journalism, Media and Cultural Studies: Prof. J. HARTLEY
- Department of Welsh: Prof. S. M. DAVIES
- Department of Religious and Theological Studies: Rev. P. H. BALLARD
- Department of Music: Prof. A. THOMAS
- School of Social and Administrative Studies: Dr S. DELAMONT
- School of Education: Prof. R. BOLAM
- Department for Continuing Education and Professional Development: (vacant)

OTHER PROFESSORS

Welsh School of Architecture:
DAVIES, C.
HAWKES, D. U.
JONES, P. J.
SILVERMAN, H. R.

Cardiff Business School:
ANTHONY, D. W.
BLYTON, P. R.
CLARKE, R.
COPELAND, L.
DAVIDSON, J. E. H.
EDWARDS, J. R.
FOSH, P.
FOXALL, G. R.
GROVES, R. E. V.
HEERY, E. J.
HINES, P. A.
JONES, D. T.
JONES, M. J.
KATSIKEAS, C. S.
MAKEPEACE, G. H.
MATTHEWS, K. G. P.
MINFORD, A. P. L.
PEEL, D. A.
PENDLEBURY, M. W.
PIERCY, N. F.
PITT, L. F.
POOLE, M. J. F.
RHYS, D. G.
SILVER, M. S.
TURNBULL, P. J.
WHIPP, R. T. H.

Department of Chemistry:
EDWARDS, P. G.
GILLARD, R. D.
HELLER, H. G.
HURSTHOUSE, M. B.
KNIGHT, D. W.
ROBERTS, M. W.
WILLIAMS, D. R.

Cardiff Law School:
FELSTINER, W. L. F.
GRUBB, A.
LEWIS, R. K.
LOWE, N. V.
MERKIN, R. M.
MIERS, D. R.
MURCH, M.
NELKEN, D.
SMITH, K. J. M.
THOMAS, P. A.
WELLS, C. K.
WYLIE, J. C. W.

Department of City and Regional Planning:
CLAPHAM, D. F.
COOKE, P. N.
LOVERING, J.
MARSDEN, T. K.
MORGAN, K. J.
PHILLIPS, A.
PUNTER, J. V.
RAKODI, C. I.
WILLIAMS, H. C. W. L.

Department of Computer Science:
BATCHELOR, B. G.
GRAY, W. A.
JONES, A. J.
WALKER, D. W.

School of Education:
DAVIES, W. B.
MELHUISH, E. C.
REES, G. M.
WALLACE, A. M.

School of Engineering:
BARR, B. I. G.
BOLTON, W. R.
FALCONER, R. A.
KARIHALOO, B. L.
MOSES, A. J.
PHAM, D. T.
POOLEY, F. D.
ROWE, D. M.
SYRED, N.
TASKER, P. J.
THOMAS, H. R.
TILLEY, R. J. D.
WATTON, J.
WILLIAMS, F. W.
YONG, R. N.

School of English, Communication and Philosophy:
ATTFIELD, R.
BELSEY, C.
COUPLAND, N. J. R.
ELAM, D. M.
HUNT, P. L.
KELSALL, M. M.
KNIGHT, S. T.
NORRIS, C. C.
THOMAS, D. S.

School of European Studies:
LOUGHLIN, J. P.
PEITSCH, H. E.
VINCENT, A. W.

Department of Earth Sciences:
BOWEN, D. Q.
EDWARDS, D.
O'HARA, M. J.
WRIGHT, V. P.

School of History and Archaeology:
BURLEIGH, M. C. B.
COSS, P. R.
EVANS, J. G.
HUDSON, P.
JONES, J. G.
MANNING, W. H.
PERCIVAL, J.
WHITTLE, A. W. R.

School of Journalism, Media and Cultural Studies:
HARGREAVES, I. R.
TULLOCH, J. C.

Department of Maritime Studies and International Transport:
BARSTON, R. P.
BROWN, E. D.
DAVIES, A. J.
LANE, A. D.
TOWILL, D. R.
WONHAM, J.

School of Mathematics:
EVANS, D. E.
EVANS, W. D.
HARMAN, G.
HOOLEY, C.
HUXLEY, M. N.
WICKRAMASINGHE, N. C.
WIEGOLD, J.
ZHIGLJAVSKY, A. A.

Cardiff School of Biosciences:
ARCHER, C. W.
BODDY, L.
BOWEN, I. D.
CATERSON, B.
CLARIDGE, M. F.
COAKLEY, W. T.
CRUNELLI, V.
ECCLES, R.
HARWOOD, J. L.
HEMINGWAY, J.
JACOB, T. J. C.
JOHN, R.
KAY, J.
LANGLEY, P. A.
LLOYD, D.
MOXHAM, B. J.
RICHARDS, R. J.
ROBERTS, M. H. T.
SLATER, J. H.
WALLIS, D. I.
WIMPENNY, J. W. T.

Department of Music:
STOWELL, R.

Department of Optometry:
HODSON, S. A.
ROVAMO, J. M.

School of Pharmacy:
BROADLEY, K. J.
HADGRAFT, J.

KELLAWAY, I. W.
MCGUIGAN, C.
NICHOLLS, P. J.
RUSSELL, A. D.
SPENCER, P. S. J.
WALKER, R. D.

Department of Physics and Astronomy:
DISNEY, M. J.
EDMUNDS, M. G.
GRISHCHUK, L.
INGLESFIELD, J. E.
SCHUTZ, B. F.

School of Psychology:
AGGLETON, J. P.
FINCHAM, F. D.
HEWSTONE, M. R. C.
JONES, D. M.
OAKSFORD, M. R.
PAYNE, J. M.
PEARCE, J. M.

Department of Religious and Theological Studies:
PALMER, H.

School of Social and Administrative Studies:
ATKINSON, P.
BROWN, P.
BLOOR, M. J.
COLLINS, H. M.
FEVRE, R. W.
LEVI, M.
MAGUIRE, E. M. W.

Department of Welsh:
JONES, G. E.
WILLIAMS, C. H.

University of Wales, Swansea

Singleton Park, Swansea, SA2 8PP
Telephone: (1792) 205678
Founded 1920
Academic year: September to December; January to March; April to June
President: Lord PRYS-DAVIES
Vice-Chancellor: Prof. R. H. WILLIAMS
Pro-Vice-Chancellors: Prof. R. A. GRIFFITHS, Prof. D. T. HERBERT, Prof. R. WILLIAMS, Prof. B. WILSHIRE
Dean of Student Admissions: Prof. R. A. GRIFFITHS
Registrar and Pro-Vice-Chancellor: Prof. P. TOWNSEND
Library: see Libraries
Number of teaching staff: 800
Number of students: 10,400

DEANS

Faculty of Arts and Social Studies: Prof. D. S. EASTWOOD
Faculty of Science: Prof. A. ROWLEY
Faculty of Engineering: Prof. K. MORGAN
Faculty of Educational and Health Studies: Dr S. SANDERS
Faculty of Business, Economics and Law: Dr G. C. JACOBS

PROFESSORS AND HEADS OF DEPARTMENTS

(H = non-professorial head of department)

Faculty of Arts and Social Studies:
BEDANI, G. L. C., Italian
BELL, I., English Language and Literature
BOUCHER, D., Political Theory and Government
BOYCE, D. G., Political Theory and Government
BYRON, R., Social Services and International Development
CARDY, M. J., French
CLARK, D. S., History
CONNON, D., French
EASTWOOD, D. S., History and Philosophy
GAGEN, D. H., Hispanic Studies
GRIFFITHS, R. A., Medieval History
HARDING, G. N., Political Theory and Government
JACKSON, S., Applied Social Studies
JOHNSTON, D. R., Welsh Language and Literature
LLOYD, A. B., Classics and Ancient History
MILTON, J. L., Applied Language Studies (H)
MITCHELL, S., Classics and Ancient History
RAYNOR, P., Social Sciences and International Development
REW, A. W., Development Studies
ROPER, J. R., American Studies (H)
TAYLOR, R., Political Theory and Government
THOMAS, M. W., English Language and Literature
WILLIAMS, R. W., German

Faculty of Education and Health Studies:
CLARK, J., Community Nursing
FRANCIS, D. H., Adult Continuing Education
GREEN, B. F., Nursing, Midwifery and Health Care (H)
LOWE, R. A., Education
MCGANN, O. A., Institute of Health Care Studies (H)
WILLIAMS, A. M., Nursing

Faculty of Science:
BARNSEY, M. J., Physical Geography
BENTON, D., Psychology
BRAIN, P. F., Zoology
BRENTON, A. G., Mass Spectrometry
BROWN, E. G., Biochemistry
DAVIES, A. J., Physics
FOLKARD, S., Psychology
GALLON, J., Biochemistry
GAMES, D. E., Mass Spectrometry
HARRIS, F. M., Mass Spectrometry
HERBERT, D. T., Geography
JONES, W. J., Chemistry
MATTHEWS, J. A., Physical Geography
MILLS, A., Chemistry
MORLEY, J. O., Computational Chemistry
OBORNE, D. J., Psychology
OLIVE, D. I., Mathematics
PARRY, J. M., Genetics
RATCLIFFE, N. A., Zoology
ROWLEY, A. F., Immunology
SKIBINSKI, D. O. F., Biological Sciences
SMITH, K., Chemistry
STREET-PERROTT, F. A., Physical Geography
TELLE, H. H., Physics
TRUMAN, A., Mathematics
TUCKER, J. V., Computer Science
WATERS, R., Genetics
WILLIAMS, J. G., Postgraduate Studies in Medical and Health Care (H)
WILLNER, P. J., Psychology

Faculty of Engineering:
BOARD, K., Electrical Engineering
BOWEN, W. R., Chemical Engineering
EVANS, R. W., Materials Engineering
EVANS, W. J., Materials Engineering
HALSALL, F., Electrical Engineering
HINTON, E., Civil Engineering
LEWIS, R. W., Mechanical Engineering
MARSHALL, J. M., Electronic Materials
MORGAN, K., Civil Engineering
OWEN, D. R. J., Civil Engineering
PANDE, G. N., Civil Engineering
PARKER, J. D., Materials Engineering
PREECE, P. E., Chemical Engineering
WEATHERILL, N. P., Civil Engineering
WILLIAMS, D. J. A., Chemical Engineering
WILSHIRE, B., Materials Engineering

Faculty of Business, Economics and Law:
BENNETT, J. S., Economics
GEORGE, K. D., Economics
HAWKES, A. G., Statistics
KAYE, P., European Law and Legal Process
LEVIN, J., Law
MAINWARING, L., Economics
SIMINTIRAS, A., Business Management

University of Wales College of Medicine

Heath Park, Cardiff, CF4 4XN
Telephone: (1222) 747747
Fax: (1222) 742914
E-mail: turnercb@cardiff.ac.uk
Incorporated as an Independent Constituent Institution of the University of Wales by Royal Charter in 1931, present name 1984
President: Lord ROBERTS OF CONWY
Provost and Vice-Chancellor: Prof. I. R. CAMERON
Vice-Provost and Vice-Chancellor: Prof. N. H. WHITEHOUSE
Registrar: L. F. J. REES
Secretary: C. B. TURNER
Library: see Libraries
Number of teaching staff: 483, including 37 clinical professors
Number of students: 2,691

DEANS

Medicine: Prof. G. M. ROBERTS
Dental School: Prof. N. H. WHITEHOUSE
School of Nursing Studies: Prof. B. D. DAVIS
School of Healthcare Studies: N. PALASTANGA
Postgraduate Studies: Prof. T. N. HAYES

PROFESSORS

Medicine:
BORYSIEWICZ, L. K., Medicine
BURNETT, A. K., Haematology
CAMPBELL, A. K., Medical Biochemistry
COLES, G. A., Medicine
COOPER, D. N., Human Molecular Genetics
DAVIES, D. P., Child Health
DAVIS, B. D., Nursing Studies
DUERDEN, B. I., Medical Microbiology
EDWARDS, R. H. T., Office of Research and Development for Health and Social Care
ELDER, G. H., Medical Biochemistry
EVANS, W. H., Medical Biochemistry
FARMER, A. E., Psychological Medicine
FELCE, D., Mental Handicap Research
FINLAY, I. G., Palliative Care
FRASER, W. I., Mental Handicap
FRENNEAUX, N. P., Cardiology
GRIFFITH, T. M., Medical Imaging
GRIFFITHS, K., Cancer Research (Steroid Biochemistry)
HARDING, K. G., Rehabilitation Medicine
HARMER, M., Anaesthetics and Intensive Care Medicine
HARPER, P. S., Medical Genetics
HAYES, T. M., Medical Education
LAI, F. A., Cell Signalling
LEWIS, G. H., Community and Epidemiological Psychiatry
LEWIS, M. J., Cardiovascular Pharmacology
LYNE, P. A., Nursing Research
MAC CULLOCH, M. J., Forensic Psychiatry
MANSEL, R. E., Surgery
MARKS, R., Dermatology
MASON, M., Clinical Oncology
MORGAN, B. P., Medical Biochemistry
MORTON, R. A., Media Resources
MCGUFFIN, P., Psychological Medicine
OWEN, M. J., Neuropsychiatric Genetics
PALMER, S. R., Centre for Applied Public Health Medicine
PILL, R., General Practice
RHODES, J., Medicine
ROBERTS, G. M., Medical Imaging
ROUTLEDGE, P., Clinical Pharmacology
ROWE, M., Cell Biology
SCANLON, M. F., Endocrinology
SHALE, D. J., Respiratory and Communicable Diseases
SHAW, R. W., Obstetrics and Gynaecology
SIBERT, J. R., Community Child Health
SMITH, P. J., Cancer Biology
STOTT, N. C. H., General Practice
WHEELER, M. H., Surgery
WILES, C. M., Neurology
WILLIAMS, B. D., Rheumatology

WILLIAMS, G. T., Pathology
WILLIAMS, J. D., Nephrology
WOODCOCK, J. P., Bioengineering
WOODHOUSE, K. W., Geriatric Medicine
WYNFORD-THOMAS, D., Pathology

Dentistry:
DUMMER, P. M. H., Adult Dental Health
EMBERY, G., Basic Dental Science
JONES, M. L., Dental Health and Development
RICHMOND, S., Dental Health and Development
SHEPHERD, J. R., Oral Surgery and Pathology
WHITEHOUSE, N. H., Dental Public Health
WILTON, J. M. A., Adult Dental Health

University of Wales, Lampeter

Lampeter, Ceredigion, SA48 7ED
Telephone: (1570) 422351
Fax: (1570) 423423

Founded 1822

College opened St David's Day 1827; first Royal Charter granted 1827, with later Charters 1852, 1865, 1896, 1963 and 1990; affiliated to Oxford Univ. 1880 and Cambridge Univ. 1883; inc. as constituent college of the University of Wales 1971 and as constituent institution 1987

Academic year: October to December; January to March; April to June

Visitor: The Bishop OF ST DAVIDS
Vice-Chancellor: Prof. K. ROBBINS
Pro-Vice-Chancellor: Prof. D. P. DAVIES
Academic Registrar: Dr T. D. RODERICK

Library: see Libraries
Number of teaching staff: 90
Number of students: 1,600

Publications: *Prospectus*, *Annual Report*, *Trivium*.

PROFESSORS

Faculty of Arts:
AUSTIN, D., Archaeology
BADHAM, B., Theology and Religious Studies
BEAUMONT, P., Geography
COHN-SHERBOK, D., Jewish Studies
DAVIES, D. P., Theology and Religious Studies
FRANCIS, L., Theology and Religious Studies
MANNING, J., English
PEACH, T., French
WALKER, M. J. C., Geography
WRIGHT, R., Classics

University of Wales Institute, Cardiff

POB 377, Llandaff Centre, Western Ave, Cardiff, CF5 2SG
Telephone: (1222) 506070
Fax: (1222) 506911
E-mail: uwicinfo@uwic.ac.uk

Principal and Chief Executive: Prof. ANTHONY CHAPMAN

DEANS

Faculty of Community Health Sciences: Prof. TONY HAZELL
Faculty of Business, Leisure and Food: (vacant)
Faculty of Art, Design and Engineering: Prof. ROBERT BROWN
Faculty of Education and Sport: Dr JOHN PUGH

University of Wales College, Newport

Caerleon Campus, POB 179, Newport, NP6 1YG
Telephone: (1633) 430088
Fax: (1633) 432006
E-mail: uic@newport.ac.uk

Principal: Prof. K. J. OVERSHOTT

HEADS OF DEPARTMENTS

Art and Design: ANN CARLISLE
Business and Management: H. WILLIAMS
Education and Training: VIV DAVIES
Engineering: LYN OELMANN
Health and Social Care: AMELIA LYONS
Humanities and Science: Dr IAN FISHER
Media Arts: ANDREW DEWDNEY
Teacher Education: Dr MURIEL ADAMS

UNIVERSITY OF WARWICK

Coventry, CV4 7AL
Telephone: (1203) 523523
Telex: 317472
Fax: (1203) 461606

Charter granted March 1965

Academic year: October to December; January to March; April to June (three terms)

Chancellor: Sir SHRIDATH RAMPHAL
Pro-Chancellor: R. J. WILLIAMS
Vice-Chancellor: Sir BRIAN FOLLETT
Pro-Vice-Chancellors: R. BURGESS, S. BASSNETT, S. PALMER
Registrar: M. L. SHATTOCK
Librarian: J. A. HENSHALL

Number of teachers: 700
Number of students: 15,630 (incl. part-time)

Publications: *Undergraduate Prospectus*, *Graduate School Prospectus*, *Annual Report*, *Calendar*, *Part-time Degrees Prospectus*.

PROFESSORS

Faculty of Arts:
BASSNETT, S. E., Centre for British and Comparative Cultural Studies
BEACHAM, R. C., Theatre Studies
BELL, M., English
BERG, M., History
CAPP, B. S., History
CLARKE, History
DABYDEEN, D., Caribbean Studies
DOLLIMORE, J., English
DYER, R., Film and Television Studies
EDWARDS, M., English
GARDNER, J. R., History of Art
HILL, L. J., French Studies
JONES, C. D. H., History
KING, J., History
LAZARUS, N., English
MALLETT, M. E., History
MULRYNE, J. R., English
OSBORNE, J., German Studies
STEEDMAN, C. K., Social History
THOMAS, D. B., Theatre Studies
THOMPSON, C. W., French Studies
TREGLOWN, J., English
VINCENDEAU, G., Film and Television Studies
WHITBY, L. M., Classics

Faculty of Science:
ANDERSON, D., Engineering
AYRES, J. G., Biological Sciences
BALL, R. C., Physics
BHATTACHARYYA, S. K., Manufacturing Systems
BOWEN, D. K., Engineering
BROWN, D., Psychology
BRYANSTON-CROSS, P. J., Engineering
CARPENTER, P. W., Mechanical Engineering
CARTER, R. W., Mathematics
CHATER, N., Psychology
COPAS, J. B., Statistics
CROUT, D. H. G., Organic Chemistry
CULLYER, W. J., Electronics
DALE, J., Medical Education
DALTON, H., Biological Sciences
DERRICK, P. J., Chemistry
DIMMOCK, N. J., Biological Sciences
DOWSETT, M. G., Physics
DUPREE, R., Physics
ELWORTHY, K. D., Mathematics
EPSTEIN, D. B. A., Mathematics
FLOWER, J., Engineering
FULFORD, K. W. M., Philosophy and Mental Health
GARDNER, J. W., Engineering
GODFREY, K. R., Engineering
HARRISON, P. J., Statistics
HEARN, E. J., Engineering
HILLHOUSE, E. W., Medicine
HUTCHINS, D. A., Engineering
JENNINGS, K. R., Chemistry
JONES, G. V., Psychology
JONES, J. D. S., Mathematics
KEMP, T. J., Chemistry
KENDALL, W. S., Statistics
LEWIS, M. H., Physics
LORD, J. M., Biological Sciences
MCCRAE, M. A., Biological Sciences
MOORE, P., Chemistry
MURRELL, J. C., Biological Sciences
NEWELL, A. C., Mathematics
NUDD, G., Computer Science
PALMER, S. B., Experimental Physics
PARKER, E. H. C., Semiconductor Physics
PARRY, W., Mathematics
PATERSON, M. S., Computer Science
PAUL, D. MCK., Physics
PRITCHARD, T., Mathematics
RAND, D. A., Mathematics
REID, M. A., Mathematics
ROBINSON, C., Biological Sciences
ROWLANDS, G., Physics
SALAMON, D. A., Mathematics
SCHONEICH, C., Chemistry
SERIES, C. M., Mathematics
SMITH, J. Q., Statistics
SPENCER, N. J., Community Child Health
STEWART, I. N., Mathematics
STRIEN, S. VAN, Mathematics
WALTERS, P., Mathematics
WHALL, T. E., Physics
WHITEHOUSE, D. J., Mechanical Engineering
WHITTENBURY, R., Biological Sciences
WOODLAND, H. R., Biological Sciences
WOODRUFF, D. P., Physics
WYNN, H., Statistics

Faculty of Social Studies:
ALEXANDER, R. J., Primary Education
ANWAR, M., Politics and International Studies
ARCHER, M. S., Sociology
BAXI, U., Law
BEALE, H. G., Law
BECKFORD, J. A., Sociology
BENINGTON, J., Business School
BENJAMIN, A., Philosophy
BROADBERRY, S. N., Economics
BULPITT, J. G., Politics
BURGESS, R. G., Sociology
BURRELL, W. G., Organizational Behaviour
CAMPBELL, R. J., Institute of Education
CLARKE, S. R. C., Sociology
COHEN, R., Sociology
COWLING, K. G., Industrial Economics
CRIPPS, M., Economics
DAVIDSON, I., Accounting and Finance
DEVEREUX, M., Economics/Business School
DICKENS, L. J., Business Studies
DOYLE, P., Marketing and Strategic Management
DYSON, R. G., Business School
EDWARDS, P. K., Business School
EGGLESTON, J., Education
ELIAS, D. P. B., Employment Research
FAUNDEZ, J., Law
FIELD, J., Lifelong Learning
GALLIERS, R. D., Business Systems
GRANT, W., Politics and International Studies
GUTKIND, P., Sociology
HARRISON, R. M., Economics

HIGGOTT, R. A., Politics and International Studies
HODGES, S. D., Financial Management
HOULGATE, S., Philosophy
HURLEY, S., Politics and International Studies
HYMAN, R., Business School
IRELAND, N. J., Economics
JACKSON, R. M. D., Institute of Education
JOHNSTON, R., Business School
KELLY, D. O., Institute of Education
LAYTON-HENRY, Z., Politics and International Studies
LEGGE, K., Business School
LINDLEY, R. M., Employment Research
LINDSAY, G. A., Special Education
LOCKWOOD, B., Politics and International Studies
MCCONVILLE, M. J., Law
MCGEE, J., Strategic Marketing
MASSON, J. M., Law
MILLER, M. H., Economics
MULLENDER, A., Social Work
ORMEROD, R. S., Operational Research
OSWALD, A., Economics
PETTIGREW, A. M., Organizational Behaviour
REEVE, A., Politics and International Studies
ROBINSON, K., Institute of Education
SKIDELSKY, R., Political Economy
SLACK, N. D. C., Manufacturing Strategy and Policy
STEELE, A. J., Accounting
STEWART, M. B., Economics
STONEMAN, P. L., Business School
STOREY, D., Business School
STRANGE, S., Politics and International Studies
TALL, D. O., Institute of Education
TERRY, M., Business School
THOMAS, J. P., Economics
TRIGG, R. H., Philosophy
WADDAMS, C. A., Business School
WAGNER, P., Sociology
WALLIS, K. F., Econometrics
WATERSON, M. J., Economics
WENSLEY, J. R. C., Marketing and Strategic Management
WHALLEY, J., Development Economics

ATTACHED RESEARCH CENTRES

Advanced Technology Centre: Dir Prof. S. K. BHATTACHARYYA.

Centre for Advanced Materials Technology: f. 1984; Dir Prof. M. H. LEWIS.

Centre for British and Comparative Cultural Studies: f. 1992; Dir Dr P. KUHIWCZAK.

Centre for Caribbean Studies: f. 1984; Dir Dr G. J. HEUMAN.

Centre for Comparative Labour Studies: f. 1994; Dir Dr P. FAIRBROTHER.

Centre for Corporate Strategy and Change: f. 1985; Dir Prof. J. MCGEE.

Centre for Education and Industry: f. 1986; Dir P. HUDDLESTON (acting).

Centre for Educational Development, Appraisal and Research: f. 1986; Dir Prof. R. G. BURGESS.

Centre for English Language Teacher Education: f. 1983; Dirs T. HENDERSON, J. KHAN.

Centre for Health Service Studies: f. 1994; Dir Dr A. K. SZCZEPURA.

Centre for Management under Regulation: f. 1998; Dir Prof. C. A. WADDAMS.

Centre for Nanotechnology and Microengineering: f. 1992; Dir Dr J. W. GARDNER.

Centre for Nuclear Magnetic Resonance: f. 1985; Dir Prof. R. DUPREE.

Centre for Research in East Roman Studies: f. 1993; Dir Prof. M. WHITBY.

Centre for Research in Elementary and Primary Education: f. 1995; Dir Prof. R. J. ALEXANDER.

Centre for Research in Philosophy and Literature: f. 1985; Dir Prof. A. E. BENJAMIN.

Centre for Small and Medium Sized Enterprises: f. 1985 as the Small Business Centre; Dir Prof. D. J. STOREY.

Centre for Social Theory: f. 1996; Dirs Prof. P. WAGNER, Dr R. FINE.

Centre for the Study of Democratisation: f. 1994; Dir Dr C. I. P. FERDINAND.

Centre for the Study of the Renaissance: f. 1993; Dir Prof. J. R. MULRYNE.

Centre for the Study of Sport in Society: f. 1994; Dir L. ALLISON.

Centre for the Study of Women and Gender: f. 1993; Dir T. A. LOVELL.

Development Technology Unit: f. 1991; Dir Dr T. THOMAS.

ESRC Centre for Research in Ethnic Relations: f. 1985 (fmrly ESRC Research Unit on Ethnic Relations, University of Aston); Dir Dr D. JOLY.

ESRC Industrial Relations Research Unit: f. 1970; Dir Prof. P. K. EDWARDS.

Humanities Research Centre: f. 1985; Dir Dr A. F. JANOWITZ.

Fluid Dynamics Research Centre: f. 1996; Dir Prof. P. W. CARPENTER.

Institute for Employment Research: f. 1981; Dir Prof. R. M. LINDLEY.

International Centre for Education in Development: f. 1990; Dir Dr R. PRESTON.

Institute of Mass Spectrometry: f. 1988; Dir Prof. P. J. DERRICK.

Legal Research Institute: f. 1978; Dir Prof. M. MCCONVILLE.

Local Government Centre: f. 1989; Dir Prof. J. BENINGTON.

ESRC Macroeconomic Modelling Bureau: f. 1983; Prof. K. WALLIS.

Mathematics Education Research Centre: f. 1979; Dir Dr E. M. GRAY.

Mathematics Research Centre: f. 1965; Dir Dr J. D. S. JONES.

Non-Linear Systems Laboratory: f. 1986; Dir Prof. D. A. RAND.

Risk Initiative: f. 1996; Dir Prof. H. P. WYNN.

ESRC Centre for the Study of Globalisation and Regionalisation: f. 1997; Dir Prof. R. HIGGOTT.

UNIVERSITY OF THE WEST OF ENGLAND, BRISTOL

Frenchay Campus, Coldharbour Lane, Bristol, BS16 1QY

Telephone: (117) 965-6261

Founded 1969 as Bristol Polytechnic; present name and status 1992

Vice-Chancellor: ALFRED C. MORRIS
Deputy Vice-Chancellor: P. E. WOOKEY
Assistant Vice-Chancellors: J. M. BONE (Programmes), R. E. CUTHBERT (Planning and Resources)
Registrar (Academic): M. J. CARTER
Librarian: M. HEERY

Library of 500,000 vols
Number of teachers: 914
Number of students: 15,215 full-time and sandwich, 6,017 part-time

DEANS

Faculty of Accounting, Business and Management (Bristol Business School): (vacant)
Faculty of Applied Sciences: Prof. C. HAWKES
Faculty of Art, Media and Design: Prof. P. J. VAN DER LEM
Faculty of the Built Environment: Prof. C. FUDGE
Faculty of Computer Studies and Mathematics: Prof. K. A. JUKES
Faculty of Economics and Social Science: Prof. A. ASSITER
Faculty of Education: Prof. K. ASHCROFT
Faculty of Engineering: Prof. S. E. J. HODDELL
Faculty of Health and Social Care: Prof. S. WEST
Faculty of Humanities: Prof. G. CHANNON
Faculty of Languages and European Studies: Prof. M. SCRIVENS
Faculty of Law: Prof. A. R. BENSTED

UNIVERSITY OF WESTMINSTER

309 Regent St, London, W1R 8AL

Telephone: (171) 911-5000
Fax: (171) 911-5858
E-mail: regent@wmin.ac.uk

Founded 1838 as Polytechnic Institution; became Royal Polytechnic Institution 1839 and Polytechnic of Central London 1970; present name and status 1992

Academic year: September to August

Vice-Chancellor and Rector: Dr GEOFFREY COPLAND

Deputy Rector: Dr MAUD TYLER
Academic Registrar: EVELYNE GREEN
Provosts: Prof. MICHAEL TREVAN (Cavendish Campus), Dr MAUD TYLER (Harrow Campus), Prof. MICHAEL ROMANS (Marylebone Campus), Prof. MARGARET BLUNDEN (Regent Campus)

Library of 388,000 vols
Number of teachers: 584 (full-time)
Number of students: 9,825 full-time, 9,646 part-time

Publications: prospectuses, *Development Review*.

HEADS OF SCHOOL

School of Biosciences: Prof. JENNIFER GEORGE
School of Computer Science (Cavendish Campus): Prof. STEPHEN WINTER
School of Computer Science (Harrow Campus): VASSILIS KONSTANTINON
Harrow Business School: PETER STEIN
School of Communication, Design and Media: BRIAN WINSTON
School of the Built Environment: Prof. ALAN JAGO
Westminster Business School: Prof. LEN SHACKLETON
School of Languages: HILARY FOOTITT
School of Law: ANDY BOON
School of Social and Behavioural Sciences: Prof. KEITH PHILLIPS

ATTACHED INSTITUTES

Diplomatic Academy of London: University of Westminster, 309 Regent St, London, W1R 8AL; postgraduate diploma in Diplomatic Studies, MA, MPhil, PhD; Dir NABIL AYAD.

Policy Studies Institute (PSI): 100 Park Village East, London, NW1 3SR; tel. (171) 468-0468; fax (171) 388-0914; f. 1978; wholly-owned subsidiary company of Univ. of Westminster; studies questions of economic and social policies and the working of political institutions; Jt Pres Sir CHARLES CARTER, Sir RICHARD O'BRIEN; Chair. of Council Sir LEONARD PEACH; Dir Prof. JIM SKEA; publs *PSI Reports*, *Discussion Papers*, *Occasional Papers*, *Policy Studies* (quarterly).

UNIVERSITY OF WOLVERHAMPTON

Molineux St, Wolverhampton, WV1 1SB

Telephone: (1902) 321000
Fax: (1902) 322680

Founded 1969 as Wolverhampton Polytechnic; present name and staus 1992
Constituent Colleges: Wolverhampton College of Arts, Wolverhampton College of Technology, Dudley College of Education, Wolverhampton Teachers' College for Day Students, Wolverhampton Technical Teachers' College and West Midlands College of Higher Education
Vice-Chancellor: Prof. J. S. BROOKS
Pro-Vice-Chancellors: N. V. WYLIE (Academic Planning), Prof. G. F. BENNETT (Marketing and Development)
Registrar: JON BALDWIN
Librarian: MARY HEANEY

Library of 453,000 vols
Number of teachers: 822
Number of students: 13,300 full-time, 11,000 part-time

Publications: *West Midland Studies*, *Journal of Industrial Affairs*.

DEANS OF SCHOOLS

Art and Design: ANDREW BREWERTON
Humanities and Social Sciences: Prof. GEOFFREY HURD
Applied Sciences: Dr EDWARD MORGAN
Computing and Information Technology: ROBERT REEVE
Engineering and the Built Environment: Prof. MUSA MIHSEIN
Health Sciences: Dr JAMES LOGAN
Wolverhampton Business School: Dr BRYONY CONWAY
Languages and European Studies: Prof. STEPHEN HAGEN
Legal Studies: ROBERT CLARK
Education: JEAN MCKAY
Nursing and Midwifery: ISOBEL BARTRAM

UNIVERSITY OF YORK

Heslington, York, YO10 5DD
Telephone: (1904) 430000
Telex: 57933
Fax: (1904) 433433

Founded 1963
Academic year: October to June (three terms)
Chancellor: Dame JANET BAKER
Pro-Chancellors: Sir MICHAEL CARLISLE, K. H. M. DIXON, R. C. WHEWAY
Vice-Chancellor: Prof. R. U. COOKE
Registrar: D. J. FOSTER
Librarian: A. E. M. HEAPS (acting)

Library: see Libraries
Number of teachers: 430
Number of students: 7,800

Publications: *Annual Review*, *Undergraduate Prospectus*, *Graduate Prospectus* (annually).

PROFESSORS

ABADIR, K., Mathematics, Economics
ARTHURS, A. M., Mathematics
ATTRIDGE, D., English
BALDWIN, S. M, Social Policy
BALDWIN, T. R., Philosophy
BARRELL, J. C., English
BERTHOUD, J. A., English
BESSEL, R., History
BLAKE, D. L., Music
BOSSY, J. A., History
BOWLES, D. J., Biology
BRADSHAW, J. R., Social Policy
BROTHWELL, D. G., Archaeology
BURNS, A., Computer Science
CALLINICOS, A., Politics
CARVER, M. O., Archaeology
CLARK, J. H., Chemistry
CROSS, M. C., History
CULYER, A. J., Economics
CURREY, J. D., Biology
DITCH, J. S., Social Policy and Social Work
DIVALL, C., Railway Studies
DIXON, H. D., Economics
DODSON, G. G., Chemistry
DRUMMOND, M. F., Health Economics
ELLIS, A. W., Psychology
EVERARD, J. K. A. E., Electronics
FIDLER, J. K., Electronics
FITTER, A.H., Biology
FLETCHER, R., History
FORD, J. R., Housing Policy
FORREST, A. I., History
FOUNTAIN, J., Mathematics
GARNER, R. C., Biology
GILBERT, B. C., Chemistry
GODBY, R., Physics
GODFREY, C., Health Services, Centre for Health Economics
GODFREY, L. G., Social and Economic Statistics
GRAVELLE, H. S. E., Economics
HALL, G., Psychology
HALL, R. R., Mathematics
HARRISON, M. D., Computer Science
HARTLEY, K., Economics
HESTER, R. E., Chemistry
HEY, J. D., Social and Economic Statistics
HOWARD, D., Electronics
HOWELL, D., Politics
HUBBARD, R., Chemistry
HULME, C., Psychology
HUTTON, J. P., Economics and Econometrics
JACKSON, S. F., Women's Studies
KLEIJNEN, J. E., Centre for Reviews and Dissemination
LAMBERT, P., Economics
LE FANU, N., Music
LEECH, R. M., Biology
LEESE, H. J., Biology
LEWIN, R. J., Health Studies
LINDSAY SMITH, J., Chemistry
LISTER, I., Education
LOCAL, J. K., Linguistics
MCDERMID, J. A., Computer Science
MACPHAIL, E., Psychology
MAITLAND, N. J., Biology
MARKS, R., English, History
MARVIN, A. C., Electronics
MATTHEW, J. A. D., Physics
MAYNARD, A. K., Social Policy
MAYNARD, M. A., Social Policy and Social Work
MAYSTON, D. J., Public Sector Economics
MENDUS, S., Politics
MILLAR, R., Educational Studies
MILNER, A. J., Biology
MINNIS, A. J., Medieval Literature
MOODY, A. D., English
MUGGLETON, S. H., Computer Science
MULKAY, M., Sociology
MULLER-DETHLEFS, C., Chemistry
ORMROD, M., History
PARISH, R., Health Studies
PARRY, G., English
PEARSON, M. A., Health Studies
PEGG, D., Biology
PERRINGS, C., Environment
PERT, G. J., Computational Physics
PERUTZ, R. N., Chemistry
PRUTTON, M., Physics
RAINEY, L. S., English
RIDDY, F J., English
ROBARDS, A. W., Biology
RUSSELL, I. T., Health Sciences
SANDERS, D., Biology
SHARPE, J. A., History
SHEIL-SMALL, T. B., Mathematics
SHELDON, T.
SIMMONS, P. J., Economics
SINCLAIR, I. A. C., Social Work
SKERRY, T. M., Biology
SMITH, D. M., Borthwick Institute
SMITH, P. C., Economics
SNOWLING, M. S., Psychology
STEIN, M., Social Work
SUDBERY, A., Mathematics
SUTCLIFFE, B. T., Chemistry
SUTHERLAND, A. J., Economics
TAYLOR, R. J. K., Chemistry
THOMPSON, D. R., Health Studies
TYRRELL, A. M., Electronics
WADDINGTON, D. J., Chemical Education
WALVIN, J., History
WAND, I. C., Computer Science
WARD, N. A.-M. F., English
WARNER, A. R., Language
WATT, I. S., Health Studies, Economics
WELLINGS, A. J., Computer Science
WICKENS, M. R., Economics
WILLIAMS, A. H., Economics
WILSON, K., Chemistry
WILSON, R. A., Biology
WOOLHOUSE, R., Philosophy
YEARLEY, S., Sociology
YOUNG, A. W., Psychology
YOUNG, J. P. W., Biology

ATTACHED INSTITUTES

(Unless otherwise stated, institutes are based at the University)

Borthwick Institute of Historical Research: St Anthony's Hall, Peaseholme Green, York, YO1 2PW; Dir Prof. D. M. SMITH.

Institute for Research in the Social Sciences: Dir Prof. T. SHELDON.

Centre for Eighteenth Century Studies: King's Manor, York, YO1 2EP; Co-Dirs Prof. J. C. BARRELL, Dr J. RENDALL.

Centre for Medieval Studies: King's Manor, York, YO1 2EP; Dir Prof. W. H. ORMROD.

Centre for Health Economics: Dir Prof. M. DRUMMOND.

Social Policy Research Unit: Dir Prof. S. M. BALDWIN.

Centre for Women's Studies: Dir Prof. S. JACKSON.

York Health Economics Consortium: Dir Dr J. W. POSNETT.

Centre for Defence Economics: Dir Prof. K. HARTLEY.

Centre for Experimental Economics: Dir Prof. J. D. HEY.

Centre for Housing Policy: Dir Prof. J. FORD.

Centre for Cell and Tissue Research: Man. Dr A. J. WILSON.

Microbiology Research Unit: Dir Dr W. B. BETTS.

Stockholm Environment Institute at York: Dr J. KUYLENSTIERNA.

Jack Birch Unit for Environmental Carcinogenesis: Dir Prof. R. C. GARNER.

Cancer Research Unit: Dir Prof. N. J. MAITLAND.

Environmental Archaeology Unit: Dir H. K. KENWARD.

Tropical Marine Research Unit: Dir Dr R. F. G. ORMOND.

Institute of Railway Studies: Dir Prof. C. DIVALL.

NHS Centre for Reviews and Dissemination: Dir Prof. J. E. KLEIJNEN.

Centre for Management: Dir A. B. SANDERS.

York Cancer Research Group P53: Dir Prof. J. MILNER.

York Electronics Centre: Man. P. G. LONG.

Colleges

Due to space limitations, we are restricted to giving a selection of colleges in the UK.

GENERAL

Cheltenham & Gloucester College of Higher Education: POB 220, The Park, Cheltenham, Glos, GL50 2QF; tel. (1242) 532700; fax (1242) 532810; f. 1990 from existing colleges; postgraduate, degree, HND, HNC and professional level qualifications; modular degree courses; full range of part-time modes of study for degrees within the modular scheme; 293 teachers; 5,525 full-time and sandwich, 3,567 part-time students; Dir J. TROTTER; publs *Landscape Issues* (2 a year), *Research Papers* (occasional), *Contexts* (2 a year), *Journal of Learning and Teaching* (2 a year), *Business School Research Journal* (quarterly), *Research Register* (every 2 years).

QUEEN MARGARET COLLEGE

Clerwood Terrace, Edinburgh, EH12 8TS

Telephone: (131) 317-3000

Fax: (131) 317-3256

Founded 1875

A Scottish University-Sector Institution

Principal and Vice-Patron: Dr JOAN STRINGER

Vice-Principals: ROSALYN MARSHALL (Strategic Planning and Development), Dr AUSTIN REID (Academic Development), Dr GEOFF KING (Resource Planning and Development)

Head of Registry: (vacant)

External Relations Director: Dr GORDON DUNCAN

Librarian: PENNY AITKEN

Library of 95,000 vols

Number of teachers: 172

Number of students: 2,500 full-time, 1,000 part-time and short-course students

HEADS OF DEPARTMENTS

Applied Consumer Studies: Prof. D. KIRK (acting)

Podiatry and Radiography: P. SHENTON

Communication and Information Studies: Dr R. G. FIELDING

Dietetics and Nutrition: Prof. A. DE LOOY

Drama: Prof. I. BROWN

English Language Unit: S. BANNERMAN (Dir)

Health and Nursing: LINDA SYDIE

Hospitality and Tourism Management: Prof. D. KIRK

Management and Social Sciences: Dr A. GILLORAN (acting)

Occupational Therapy: Prof. A. STEWART

Physiotherapy: Prof. P. SALTER

Speech and Language Sciences: Prof. W. HARDCASTLE

Ravensbourne College of Design and Communication: Walden Rd, Chislehurst, Kent, BR7 5SN; tel. (181) 289-4900; fax (181) 325-8320; e-mail info@rave.ac.uk; f. 1962; degree courses in graphic design, product design, furniture design, interior design, fashion design, interaction design, professional broadcasting, broadcast engineering and communication and technology; BTEC HNDs in broadcast operations, engineering and production; foundation course in art design and media; MA in Design for Digital Technology; Dir Prof. ROBIN BAKER; Head of Academic Affairs SARAH GERSHON.

Richmond College, The American International University in London: Queens Road, Richmond upon Thames, Surrey, TW10 6JP; tel. (181) 332-9000; fax (181) 332-1596; f. 1972; campuses in Richmond upon Thames and Kensington, and study centres in Italy and Japan; liberal arts college accredited in the UK (by the Open University) and in the USA; licensed to award BA, BS, AA and MBA degrees by the Dept of Public Instruction in Delaware (USA); all degrees designated by Dept for Education (UK); library of 52,000 books; 1,200 students; President WALTER MCCANN.

Schiller International University – UK: for general details, see entry in Germany chapter.

Central London Campus: Royal Waterloo House, 51 – 55 Waterloo Road, London SE1 8TX; tel. (171) 928-8484; fax (171) 620-1226; Dir Dr R. H. TAYLOR.

AGRICULTURE

Harper Adams University College: Newport, Shropshire; tel. (1952) 820280; fax 814783; est. 1901; Undergraduate and postgraduate taught courses and research degrees in agriculture, animal health, agri-business marketing and managment, agricultural engineering, rural enterprise and land management, rural environmental management; also HND, HNC and Foundation courses; 1,600 students; Principal Prof. E. W. JONES.

Myerscough College: Myerscough Hall, Bilsborrow, Preston, PR3 0RY; tel. (1995) 640611; fax (1995) 640842; e-mail mailbox@myerscough.ac.uk; f. 1894; agriculture, horticulture, arboriculture, veterinary nursing, animal welfare, equine science, ecology and conservation, sport and leisure; 65 teachers; 1,250 students; library of 20,000 vols; Principal Prof. J. MOVERLEY.

Royal Agricultural College: Cirencester, Glos. GL7 6JS; tel. (1285) 652531; fax (1285) 650219; e-mail admissions@royagcol.ac.uk; f. 1845; courses at certificate, diploma, degree and postgraduate levels in agriculture, agribusiness, horticulture, land management, equine and related subjects; library of 26,500 vols; 550 full-time students; Principal Prof. J. B. DENT; publ. *Royal Agricultural College Journal* (annually).

Scottish Agricultural College: Auchincruive, Ayr, KA6 5HW; tel. (1292) 525350; fax (1292) 525349; e-mail etsu@sac.ac.uk; centres at Auchincruive (associated with univs of Glasgow and Strathclyde), Aberdeen (associated with Univ. of Aberdeen) and Edinburgh (associated with Univ. of Edinburgh); courses in production industries, horticulture, business and resource managment, science and technology, environment, leisure and tourism; 250 teachers; 1,200 students; Principal Prof. P. C. THOMAS.

Seale-Hayne, Faculty of Agriculture, Food and Land Use: University of Plymouth, Newton Abbot, Devon TQ12 6NQ; tel. (1626) 325606; fax (1626) 325605; f. 1912; 1,000 students; BSc courses in Agriculture, Rural Resource Management, Agriculture with Rural Estate Management, Hospitality Management, Tourism Management, Agriculture and Countryside Management, Rural Estate Management, Food Biology, Agriculture and the Environment, Animal Production, Crop Science, Food and Hospitality Management, Food Production and Quality, Food Quality with Management, Food Quality with Product Development and Nutrition; HND courses in Agriculture, Rural Resource Management; MSc, Postgraduate Diplomas and short courses in Agricultural Business Management and Rural Development; Dean Prof. CLARE BROOM.

University College Writtle: Lordship Rd, Chelmsford, CM1 3RR; tel. (1245) 424200; fax (1245) 420456; e-mail postmaster@writtle.ac.uk; f. 1893; courses at MSc, BSc, BEng, HND, HNC and ND levels in agriculture, horticulture and related subjects; 1,500 full-time students; Principal Prof. M. D. ALDER.

Welsh Institute of Rural Studies: University of Wales, Llanbadarn Fawr, Aberystwyth, Dyfed, SY23 3AL; tel. (1970) 624471; fax (1970) 611264; f. 1971; BSc (Hons) courses in agriculture (business studies, food marketing, economics), countryside management, equine science, rural resource management; HND sandwich courses in agriculture, countryside management, equine studies; PhD and MPhil research degrees; MSc and MBA one-year courses; library of 53,000 vols; 50 lecturers; 742 students; Dir Prof. MICHAEL HAINES.

Wye College: see under University of London.

ART AND DESIGN

The colleges listed below (unless otherwise stated) are those which run courses leading to the Diploma in Art and Design.

Camberwell College of Arts: Peckham Rd, London, SE5 8UF; tel. (171) 514-6300; fax (171) 514-6310; a constituent college of the London Institute; MA in Conservation, Printmaking and Book Arts; Hons degree courses in Ceramics, Conservation, Drawing, History Theory and Interpretation, Graphic Design, Painting, Sculpture and Silversmithing and Metalwork; Foundation Studies in Art and Design, BTEC ND in Design; Head Prof. ROGER BREAKWELL.

Central Saint Martin's College of Art and Design: Southampton Row, London, WC1B 4AP; tel. (171) 514-7000; fax (171) 514-7024; annexes: 27 Long Acre, London WC2E; 107 Charing Cross Rd, London WC2H 0DU; Back Hill, Clerkenwell, London EC1R 5EN; f. 1896; a constituent college of the London Institute; degree courses in Fine Art, Graphic Design, Product Design, Ceramic Design, Textiles, Fashion, Jewellery, Theatre, Art and Design; course in Foundation Studies; MA courses in Fine Art, Fashion, Design Studies, Industrial Design, Scenography; postgraduate diploma/MA in Textiles, Communication Design with study routes in Illustration, Graphic Design and Multimedia; 1,945 (full-time and sandwich course) students; library of 80,000 vols; Head MARGARET BUCK.

Chelsea College of Art and Design: Manresa Rd, London, SW3 6LS; tel. (171) 514-7751; fax (171) 514-7777; f. 1891; a constituent college of the London Institute; degree courses in fine art and design (options in textile, design, design and public art and interior design); Head COLIN CINA.

City and Guilds of London Art School: 124 Kennington Park Rd, London, SE11 4DJ; tel. (171) 735-2306; fax (171) 582-5361; e-mail cgartsc@rmplc.co.uk; f. 1879; 1-year foundation course; 3-year BA (Hons) degrees in Fine Arts, in Painting and Sculpture; 3-year graduate diploma course in Applied Arts: Illustration, Decorative Arts, Architectural Glass; 3-year BA (Hons) degrees in Conservation Studies; 3-year graduate diploma courses in Wood-carving and Gilding, Stone Carving; 60 part-time teachers; Principal MICHAEL KENNY.

Courtauld Institute of Art: see under University of London.

Edinburgh College of Art: Lauriston Place, Edinburgh, EH3 9DF; tel. (131) 221-6000; fax (131) 221-6001; f. 1907; Schools of Architecture, Planning and Housing, and Landscape Architecture; Schools of Drawing and Painting, Design and Applied Arts, Visual Communication and Sculpture; Principal Prof. ALISTAIR ROWAN; Sec. MICHAEL W. WOOD.

Falmouth College of Arts: Woodlane, Falmouth, Cornwall TR11 4RA; tel. (1326) 211077; fax (1326) 211205; f. 1902; BTEC Diploma in Foundation Art and Design; BA (Hons) programmes in Broadcasting Studies, English with Media Studies, Fine Art, Graphic Design, Illustration, Journalism Studies, Photographic Communication, Studio Ceramics, 3D Design, Visual Culture; Postgraduate Diplomas in Broadcast Journalism, Creative Advertising, Professional Writing; PG Dip/MA in History of Modern Art and Design; PG Dip/MA Integrated Masters programme; 80 teachers; library of 25,000 vols, 200 periodicals; Principal Prof. ALAN LIVINGSTON.

Glasgow School of Art: 167 Renfrew St, Glasgow, G3 6RQ; tel. (141) 353-4500; fax

(141) 353-4746; f. 1845; BA, MA and MPhil courses in Architecture, Fine Art and Design; all degree courses validated by University of Glasgow; 1,400 full-time students; library of 50,000 vols, 59,000 slides; Dir Prof. D. CAMERON.

Hamilton Kerr Institute: Whittlesford, Cambridge, CB2 4NE; tel. (1223) 832040; fax (1223) 837595; f. 1976; dept of Fitzwilliam Museum, Univ. of Cambridge; postgraduate course in conservation and restoration of easel paintings; 5 teachers; 4 full-time students; 4 interns; Dir I. McCLURE.

Kent Institute of Art & Design: Oakwood Park, Maidstone, Kent, ME16 8AG; tel. (1622) 757286; fax (1622) 621100; f. 1987 by merger of existing colleges; Dir Prof. VAUGHAN GRYLLS; Chief Admin. Officer RAY MOON.

Constituent colleges:

Kent Institute of Art & Design at Canterbury: New Dover Rd, Canterbury, Kent, CT1 3AN; tel. (1227) 769371; fax (1227) 817500; f. 1882; BA (Hons) in fine art, architecture; BArch (RIBA Part 2); BTEC ND in general art and design; BTEC Foundation Studies; MA in art and architecture, art criticism and theory, painting, sculpture and graphic fine arts, architecture, foundry practice; 27 full-time, 74 part-time teachers; 752 students; library of *c.* 33,000 vols, 70,000 slides; Admin. Man. NICK JONES.

Kent Institute of Art & Design at Maidstone: Oakwood Park, Maidstone, Kent, ME16 8AG; tel. (1622) 757286; fax (1622) 621100; CNAA BA (Hons) course in visual communication, BTEC Foundation Studies, MA in time-based media with electronic imaging, illustration, photography, graphic design, visual theory, BTEC HND in graphic design, foundation course; 20 full-time, 75 part-time teachers; 699 students; Admin. Man. PAT YARNTON.

Kent Institute of Art & Design at Rochester-upon-Medway: Fort Pitt, Rochester, Kent, ME1 1DZ; tel. (1634) 830022; fax (1634) 820300; BTEC, ND and HND design courses, fashion design and technology, precious metalwork, model-making, interior design; BTEC Foundation Studies; BA in Interior Design, Interior Architecture, Ceramics, Modelmaking, Product Design, Fashion Technology, European Fashion, Fashion Design, Editorial and Advertising Photography, Silversmithing, Goldsmithing and Jewellery Design; MA in Interior Architecture, Interior Design, Ceramics, Product Design, Design Model-making, Silversmithing and Goldsmithing, Jewellery Design; 26 full-time, 98 part-time teachers; 820 students; Admin. Man. JULIET THOMAS.

London Institute, The: 65 Davies St, London W1Y 2DA; tel. (171) 514-6000; fax (171) 514-6131; e-mail marcom@linst.ac.uk; f. 1986 as an amalgamation of existing art and design colleges: Camberwell College of Arts, Central Saint Martins College of Art and Design, Chelsea College of Art and Design (see above), London College of Fashion, London College of Printing; Rector Sir WILLIAM STUBBS.

Norwich School of Art and Design: St George St, Norwich, Norfolk, NR3 1BB; tel. (1603) 610561; fax (1603) 615728; e-mail info@nsad.ac.uk; f. 1846; degree courses in Fine Art, Graphic Design, Cultural Studies, Visual Studies, Textiles; BTEC Advanced GNVQ and BTEC Diploma in Foundation Studies in Art and Design; 45 full-time lecturers; Principal Prof. BRUCE BLACK.

Royal Academy Schools: Burlington House, Piccadilly, London, W1V 0DS; f. 1768; Schools of Painting and Sculpture; Keeper LEONARD McCOMB; Sec. LAURA SCOTT.

Royal College of Art: Kensington Gore, London, SW7 2EU; tel. (171) 590-4444; fax (171) 590-4500; f. 1837, awarded Charter 1967 empowering it to grant its own degrees; postgraduate institution receiving direct grant from HEFCE; 770 students; library of 70,000 vols, 200 periodicals; Visitor HRH The Duke of EDINBURGH; Provost Lord SNOWDON; Rector and Vice-Provost Prof. CHRISTOPHER FRAYLING; Registrar ALAN SELBY; publs *Prospectus*, *Court Report*, *Research Papers*.

COURSE DIRECTORS

Animation: JOAN ASHWORTH
Architecture and Interiors: Prof. NIGEL COATES
Ceramics and Glass: MARTIN SMITH
Computer-Related Design: Prof. GILLIAN CRAMPTON SMITH
Conservation: ALAN CUMMINGS
Menswear, Womenswear, Printed Textiles and Constructed Textiles: JAMES PARK
Furniture: Prof. RON ARAD
Graphic Design: Prof. DAN FERN
History of Design: Prof. PENNY SPARKE
Illustration: Prof. DAN FERN
Industrial Design: Prof. RON ARAD
Industrial Design Engineering: Prof. JOHN DRANE
Goldsmithing, Silversmithing, Metalwork and Jewellery: Prof. DAVID WATKINS
Painting: Prof. PAUL HUXLEY
Photography: OLIVIER RICHON
Printmaking: Prof. CHRIS ORR
Sculpture: Prof. GLYNN WILLIAMS
Vehicle Design: Prof. KEN GREENLEY
Visual Arts Administration: TERESA GLEADOWE

Ruskin School of Drawing and Fine Art: 74 High St, Oxford, OX1 4BG; f. 1871; dept of the University of Oxford; 3-year degree course in Fine Art; 60 students; Principal STEPHEN FARTHING.

School of Architecture, Architectural Association: 34–36 Bedford Square, London, WC1B 3ES; tel. (171) 887-4000; fax (171) 414-0782; instituted 1847; 1-year foundation course; 5-year course leading to AA Dipl. and exemption from the RIBA Parts 1 and 2 exam; postgraduate courses and research in Architecture; 450 students; 2,500 mems; library of 29,000 vols; Chair. MOHSEN MOSTAFAVI; publs *AA Files*, *Projects Review*, exhibition catalogues.

Slade School of Fine Art: University College London, Gower St, London, WC1E 6BT; tel. (171) 504-2313; f. 1871; undergraduate degree courses in Fine Art (painting, sculpture or fine art media) with instruction in History of Art and Theoretical Studies; postgraduate courses in Fine Art (painting, sculpture, theatre design, fine art media (including printmaking, electronic media, photography, film and video)); BA Hons degree in Fine Art; MFA in Fine Art; MA in Fine Art; MPhil and PhD in Fine Art; 260 students; Slade Prof. BERNARD COHEN; Admissions Officer CAROLINE NICHOLAS.

Surrey Institute of Art and Design: Falkner Rd, Farnham, Surrey GU9 7DS; tel. (1252) 722441; fax (1252) 733869; honours degree courses in Fine Art, Printed and Woven Textiles, Photography, Film and Video, Animation, Fashion, Fashion Promotion and Illustration, Media Studies, Three-Dimensional Design, Design Management, Graphic Design, Packaging Design, Interior Design, Visual Communication, Journalism; ND in General Art and Design; foundation course; library of 60,000 vols; 3,000 students; Dir N. J. TAYLOR.

Wimbledon School of Art: Merton Hall Rd, Wimbledon, London, SW19 3QA; tel. (181) 408-5000; fax (181) 408-5050; f. 1890; MA in Critical Studies in Visual Art and Theatre, in Site Specific Sculpture, in Theatre Design, Scenography, in Drawing, in Fine Art Practice; MA and Postgraduate Diploma in Printmaking; BA (Hons) in Fine Art, in Theatre; BTEC Foundation Diploma; library of 28,000 vols; 640 students; Principal Prof. R. BUGG.

BUSINESS AND COMMERCE

Aberdeen College: Gallowgate Centre, Gallowgate, Aberdeen, AB25 1BN; tel. (1224) 612000; fax (1224) 612001; f. 1959; courses include English as a foreign language, EX training (electrical work in hazardous environments), interpreter/translator, business studies, journalism, communication, hospitality, social studies, offshore industries, mechanical engineering, electrical and electronic engineering, art and design, systems analysis and design, sports coaching and development, agriculture; 266 full-time teachers; 6,000 full-time, 18,000 part-time students; library of 25,000 vols; Principal RAE ANGUS; Librarian DAVID MORLEY.

Central College of Commerce: 300 Cathedral St, Glasgow, G1 2TA; tel. (141) 552 3941; f. 1962; courses in accounting, computing, office studies, business studies, distribution, marketing, advertising, librarianship, art and design, sports therapy, hairdressing and beauty therapy;; 120 full-time, 50 part-time teachers; 1,980 full-time, 3,750 part-time students; library of 30,000 vols; Principal P. W. DUNCAN.

College of Estate Management: Whiteknights, Reading, Berks, RG6 6AW; tel. (118) 986-1101; fax (118) 975-0188; e-mail cem_info@compuserve.com; f. 1919; undergraduate and professional distance learning courses include the BSc degree in Estate Management of the University of Reading and CEM Diplomas in Surveying and Construction; courses meet fully the academic requirements of the Royal Instn of Chartered Surveyors, the Incorporated Society of Valuers and Auctioneers and the Chartered Inst. of Building; MBA in Construction and Real Estate (University of Reading) and diplomas in Project Management, Facilities Management, Property Investment, Building Conservation and Arbitration; Principal P. E. GOODACRE; Dir of Student Services E. D. MOIR.

Dundee College: Old Glamis Rd, Dundee, DD3 8LE; tel. (1382) 819021; fax (1382) 88117; f. 1956; 300 full-time and 80 part-time teachers; 9,500 students; library of 65,000 vols; professional courses in management and financial accountancy, postgraduate courses in management and personnel management, HND and HNC and NC courses; Principal C. M. BROWN.

European Business School London: Regent's College, Inner Circle, Regent's Park, London, NW1 4NS; tel. (171) 487-7507; fax (171) 487-7425; e-mail ebs@regents.ac.uk; f. 1979 in UK, centres also in Germany, France, Italy, Japan, Russia, Spain and USA; BA (Hons) degree in European Business Administration, and other degrees with business and language mix; summer courses; 750 full-time students in London; library of 25,500 vols; Academic Dir Prof. ERIC DE LA CROIX.

Henley Management College: Greenlands, Henley-on-Thames, Oxfordshire, RG9 3AU; tel. (1491) 571454; fax (1491) 571635; f. 1945 as the Administrative Staff College; residential courses for managers and administrators already holding important positions to prepare them for still greater responsibilities; special courses; research projects; higher degrees and postgraduate courses; 60 teachers; 121 residential course mems; library of 18,000 vols; Principal Prof. RAY WILD; Librarian GAIL THOMAS; publs *Journal of General Management*, Occasional and College Papers.

Regents Business School: Inner Circle, Regent's Park, London, NW1 4NS; tel. (171) 487-7654; fax (171) 487-7425; e-mail rbs@regents.ac.uk; BA (Hons) degrees (validated by Open University Validation Services) awarded in International Business, in International Finance and Accounting, and in International Marketing; also courses leading to Certificate of Higher Education and Diploma of Higher Education; 16 teachers; 100 students; Academic Dir Dr EDWIN KERR.

Roffey Park Management Institute: Forest Rd, Horsham, West Sussex RH12 4TD; tel. (1293) 851644; fax (1293) 851565; e-mail info@roffey-park.co.uk.; f. 1946; issues MBA degree (validated by University of Sussex) and MSc in management development (validated by Univ. of Salford); 70 students on two-year courses and 45 per week on short courses; 17 teachers; Chief Exec. VALERIE HAMMOND.

LAW

College of Law: Braboeuf Manor, St Catherines, Guildford, Surrey, GU3 1HA; tel. (1483) 460200; fax (1483) 460305; postgraduate courses; brs in Guildford, London, Chester and York; Chief Exec. of Board of Management Prof. NIGEL SAVAGE.

MUSIC AND DRAMATIC ART

Bristol Old Vic Theatre School: 1 and 2 Downside Rd, Clifton, Bristol, BS8 2XF; tel. (117) 925-4495; fax (117) 923-9371; e-mail enquiries@oldvic.drama.ac.uk; f. 1946; courses in acting, theatre design, wardrobe, stage management and technical aspects of the theatre; Principal CHRISTOPHER DENYS.

Central School of Speech and Drama: Embassy Theatre, 64 Eton Ave, London, NW3 3HY; tel. (171) 722-8183; fax (171) 722-4132; f. 1906; 90 staff; 750 students; courses in art, design and the performing arts, in education and in therapy; Principal ROBERT S. FOWLER; Registrar NEIL EMMERTON.

Guildhall School of Music and Drama: Barbican, London, EC2Y 8DT; tel. (171) 628-2571; fax (171) 256-9438; f. by the Corporation of London in 1880 and administered by the Music and Drama Cttee; 300 professorial staff; 700 students; Principal IAN HORSBRUGH; Dir of Music DAMIAN CRANMER; Dir of Drama PETER CLOUGH; Dir of Technical Theatre Studies SUE THORNTON; Dir of Administration DAVID IMRIE.

London Academy of Music and Dramatic Art: Tower House, 226 Cromwell Rd, London, SW5 0SR; tel. (171) 373-9883; f. 1861; professional theatrical training, acting and stage management; Principal PETER JAMES.

National Film and Television School: Beaconsfield Studios, Station Rd, Beaconsfield, Bucks HP9 1LG; tel. (1494) 671234; fax (1494) 674042; f. 1970; professional training for film and television production across a wide range of fields for 150 students; professional facilities; small information library; Chair. DAVID ELSTEIN; Dir HENNING CAMRE.

Royal Academy of Dramatic Art (RADA): 18 Chenies St, London, WC1E 7EX; tel. (171) 636-7076; fax (171) 323-3865; f. 1904; courses: Acting (9 terms), Technical Theatre and Stage Management (6 terms), Scene Painting, Scenic Construction, Stage Electrics, Property Making (each 4 terms); library of 17,500 vols; Principal NICHOLAS BARTER.

Royal Academy of Music: Marylebone Road, London, NW1 5HT; tel. (171) 873-7373; fax (171) 873-7374; f. 1822; inc. by Royal Charter 1830; 4-year B Mus. (London) course, 2-year M Mus. (London) course; training also at junior and intermediate levels; Performance Course; professorial staff 155, students 600 full-time study only; Pres. HRH The Duchess of GLOUCESTER; Principal CURTIS PRICE; Academic Registrar PHILIP WHITE; publs *Prospectus* (annually), *RAM Magazine* (2 a year).

Royal College of Music: Prince Consort Rd, South Kensington, London, SW7 2BS; tel. (171) 589-3643; fax (171) 589-7740; f. 1883; 4-year B Mus in performance, 1-year M Mus, 1 – 2 year PGDip, DMus; 200 professorial staff; 500 students; library: see Libraries; Pres. HRH The Prince of WALES; Dir Dr JANET RITTERMAN; Sec. and Registrar KEVIN PORTER.

Royal College of Organists: 7 St Andrew St, Holborn, London, EC4A 3LQ; tel. (171) 936-3606; fax (171) 353-8244; f. 1864, inc. by Royal Charter 1893; Senior Exec. ALAN DEAR.

Royal Military School of Music: Kneller Hall, Twickenham, Middlesex; a military school established 1857 to train non-commissioned officers as bandmasters and young soldiers as musicians; 42 students; 120 pupils; Commandant Col M. J. N. RICHARDS; Principal Dir of Music (Army) Lt-Col. S. A. WATTS.

Royal Northern College of Music: 124 Oxford Rd, Manchester, M13 9RD; tel. (161) 273-6283; fax (161) 273-7611; 590 students; library contains extensive collection of MSS, reference works, gramophone records, tape cassettes, CDs, videos, periodicals, and important archive material including an historical instrument collection; Pres. HRH The Duchess of KENT; Principal Prof. EDWARD GREGSON.

Royal School of Church Music: Cleveland Lodge, Westhumble St, Dorking, Surrey, RH5 6BW; tel. (1306) 877676; fax (1306) 887260; f. 1927, inc. 1930; centre for training church musicians; world-wide membership of affiliated churches; Chair. of Council Sir DAVID HARRISON; Dir Prof. JOHN HARPER; publ. *Church Music Quarterly*.

Royal Scottish Academy of Music and Drama: 100 Renfrew St, Glasgow G2 3DB; tel. (141) 332-4101; fax (141) 332-8901; f. 1847 as The Glasgow Athenaeum, became The Scottish National Academy of Music 1928, The Royal Scottish Academy of Music 1944 and the Royal Scottish Academy of Music and Drama 1968; library of 46,000 music vols, 19,000 books, 10,000 sound recordings, 2,000 choral and orchestral sets; 200 teachers (incl. part-time); 450 students; Principal PHILIP LEDGER.

Trinity College of Music: 11–13 Mandeville Place, London, W1M 6AQ; tel. (171) 935-5773; fax (171) 224-6278; f. 1872; full-time 4-year BMus. (TCM) course; MMus, MA (Music Education), Postgraduate Certificate and Special courses; 490 full-time and 25 part-time students; Patron HRH The DUKE OF KENT; Pres. Lord MENUHIN; Principal GAVIN HENDERSON; publ. *The Trinity Magazine* (3 a year).

Welsh College of Music and Drama: Castle Grounds, Cathays Park, Cardiff, CF1 3ER; tel. (1222) 342854; fax (1222) 237639; full- and part-time courses for performers, and degree and diploma courses validated by the Univ. of Wales; Principal EDMOND FIVET.

SCIENCE AND TECHNOLOGY

Camborne School of Mines: Pool, Redruth, Cornwall, TR15 3SE; tel. (1209) 714866; fax (1209) 716977; e-mail k.atkinson@csm.ex.ac.uk; f. 1859; under Faculty of Engineering at Univ. of Exeter; 30 teachers; 400 students; library of 30,000 vols; Dir Prof. K. ATKINSON; publs *Annual Journal*, annual prospectus.

Glasgow College of Building and Printing: 60 North Hanover St, Glasgow, G1 2BP; tel. (141) 332-9969; fax (141) 332-5170; f. 1972 by amalgamation of Colleges of Building (f. 1927) and Printing (f. 1925); library of 30,000 vols; 142 teachers; 2,100 full-time and 2,800 part-time students; Principal T. B. WILSON; Academic Registrar M. BURGESS.

Wessex Institute of Technology: Ashurst Lodge, Ashurst, Southampton, Hants, SO40 7AA; tel. (1703) 293223; fax (1703) 292853; f. 1986; 17 teachers; 25 students; library of 4,700 vols; Dir Prof. C. A. BREBBIA; Registrar Dr W. BLAIN; Librarian Mrs R. BARRETT.

HEADS OF DEPARTMENTS

Advanced Computing: Dr H. POWER
Damage Tolerance: Dr M. ALIABADI
Computational Mechanics: Dr M. ZERROUKAT

NORTHERN IRELAND

Learned Societies

FINE AND PERFORMING ARTS

Arts Council of Northern Ireland: 185 MacNeice House, 77 Malone Rd, Belfast, BT9 6AQ; tel. (1232) 385200; fax (1232) 661715; f. 1943; the Council is charged with developing the practice and appreciation of the arts throughout Northern Ireland. It subvents the Ulster Orchestra, galleries, Theatre, Ballet and Opera Companies, literary publications and festivals; Chair. DONNELL DEENY; Chief Exec. Dir BRIAN FERRAN; publs *Annual Report*, catalogues.

HISTORY, GEOGRAPHY AND ARCHAEOLOGY

Ulster Archaeological Society: Environment and Heritage Service, 5-33 Hill St, Belfast, BT1 2LA; tel. (1232) 543045; fax (1232) 543111; e-mail hmb.ehs@nics.gov.uk; f. 1852; local archaeology and history; 370 mems; Pres. R. WARNER; Hon. Sec. D. P. HURL; publ. *Ulster Journal of Archaeology* (annually).

Research Institutes

AGRICULTURE, FISHERIES AND VETERINARY SCIENCE

Agricultural Research Institute of Northern Ireland: Hillsborough, Co. Down; Dir Prof. F. J. GORDON; Sec. G. W. C. TROUGHTON.

Veterinary Sciences Division: Stormont, Belfast; tel. (1232) 545690; fax (1232) 525755; e-mail mcnultys@dani.gov.uk; part of Department of Agriculture, and of Faculty of Agriculture and Food Science, Queen's University Belfast; library of 11,000 vols; Dir Prof. M. S. MCNULTY.

ECONOMICS, LAW AND POLITICS

Northern Ireland Economic Research Centre: 46-48 University Rd, Belfast, BT7 1NJ; tel. (1232) 325594; fax (1232) 439435; f. 1985; independent, funded by Queen's University Belfast, NI Govt and private industry; research and detailed studies into all aspects of the Northern Ireland economy and related issues in regional economics with a view to improving Northern Ireland's growth and employment prospects; library with special emphasis on NI economy; Dir Dr G. GUDGIN.

NATURAL SCIENCES

Physical Sciences

Armagh Observatory: College Hill, Armagh BT61 9DG; tel. (1861) 522928; fax (1861) 527174; f. 1790 by Primate Robinson; library of 15,000 vols; Dir Prof. MARK E. BAILEY; Administrator LAWRENCE YOUNG.

Libraries and Archives

Armagh

Armagh Public Library: Abbey St, Armagh, BT61 7DY; tel. (1861) 523142; fax (1861) 524177; e-mail armroblib@aol.com.uk; f. 1771 by Primate Richard Robinson; library includes Ref. Dept with about 30,000 vols; Dean Swanzy's special collection of genealogical works and Army Lists; history, theology, philosophy; largely antiquarian; MSS include copies of Primatial Registers from 1362 (genealogical research not undertaken); Keeper Very Rev. H. CASSIDY.

Southern Education and Library Board, Library Service: Library HQ, 1 Markethill Rd, Armagh, BT60 1NR; tel. (1861) 525353; fax (1861) 526879; f. 1973; 23 brs, 11 mobile libraries; library of 1,450,000 vols; Chief Librarian A. MORROW.

Ballymena

North-Eastern Education and Library Board, Library Service: Demesne Ave, Ballymena, Co. Antrim; tel. (1266) 664100; fax (1266) 632038; f. 1922, reorganized 1973; library of 2,000,000 vols; 37 brs, 13 mobile libraries; Chief Librarian P. VALENTINE; publ. *Public Services Information Bulletin* (monthly).

Ballynahinch

South-Eastern Education and Library Board: Windmill Hill, Ballynahinch, Co. Down, BT24 8DH; tel. (1238) 566400; fax 565072; f. 1973; 26 brs, 5 mobile libraries; library of 554,000 vols, 4,000 maps, 18,000 microforms, 21,000 sound recordings, 3,000 video recordings; Chief Librarian B. PORTER; publs *Public Services Information Bulletin* (monthly), *News from Hansard*, (monthly) in co-operation with other N. Ireland library services.

Belfast

Belfast Public Libraries: Central Library, Royal Ave, Belfast, BT1 1EA; tel. (1232) 243233; fax 332819; f. 1888; 16 branch libraries, 4 part-time centres and 2 mobile libraries; Central Lending Library 57,000 vols; Central Reserve Collection 100,000 vols; Humanities and General Reference Library 120,000 vols; Irish Library 40,000 books, pamphlets and MSS on all aspects of Ireland, Ulster and Belfast; Fine Arts and Literature 74,000 vols; Music Library 12,000 vols, 24,000 scores, 24,000 records/cassettes; Business, Science and Technology Library 68,000 vols; other special collections: Bibliographies, Government and Agency Publications, Patents, Rare Books, microfilms; holdings, reader/printers; Chief Librarian J. N. MONTGOMERY.

Linen Hall Library (Belfast Library and Society for Promoting Knowledge): Donegall Sq. N., Belfast, BT1 5GD; tel. (1232) 321707; fax (1232) 438586; f. 1788; library of *c.* 200,000 vols; 3,500 mems; noted for its Irish collection of *c.* 70,000 vols, including early Ulster printing and major collection of political ephemera relating to troubles from 1968; *c.* 5,000 17th-century pamphlets, 18th- and 19th-century travel, biography; Librarian J. GRAY; publ. *Annual Report*.

Public Record Office of Northern Ireland: 66 Balmoral Ave, Belfast, BT9 6NY; tel. 251318; fax 255999; e-mail proni@nics.gov.uk; f. 1923; an exec. agency within the Dept of the Environment for Northern Ireland; retains official and private records relating mainly to the history of Northern Ireland; Deputy Keeper of the Records Dr A. P. W. MALCOMSON; publ. *Statutory Reports*.

Queen's University Library: Belfast, BT7 1LS; tel. (1232) 245133; fax (1232) 323340; f. 1849; 996,000 books, periodical vols, pamphlets, manuscripts, theses and microforms; special collections: Hibernica Collection (incl. R. M. Henry Collection, O'Rahilly Collection), Antrim Presbytery Library, MacDouall Collection (Philology), Hamilton Harty Music Collection, Thomas Percy Library; Librarian N. J. RUSSELL; publs *Irish Naturalists Journal* (quarterly), *Northern Ireland Legal Quarterly*, *Wiles Lectures* (annually), *Inaugural Lectures*, *Statistical and Social Inquiry Society of Ireland Journal* (annually).

Londonderry

University of Ulster Library: Coleraine, Co. Londonderry, BT52 1SA; tel. (1265) 44141 ext. 4245; telex 747597; fax (1265) 324934; f. 1968; also at Jordanstown, Co. Antrim, BT37 0QB; tel.(1232) 36531 ext. 8993; telex 747493; fax (1232) 366093; f. 1970; library of *c.* 526,000 vols (incl. 210,000 at Coleraine and 220,000 at Jordanstown, with smaller collections at the Art and Design Faculty in Belfast, and Magee College in Londonderry), 5,600 periodicals; European Documentation Centre; special collections: World Wars I and II, Henry Davis Gift of incunabula, American and women's studies, radical newspapers and periodicals on microfilm; Dir of Educational Services Prof. WALLACE EWART (acting).

University of Ulster, Magee College Library: Northland Rd, Londonderry, BT48 7JL; tel. (1504) 375240; fax (1504) 375626; f. 1865; 100,000 books and pamphlets, 550 periodicals; special collections: Irish Collection, 18th Century Collection (5,000 vols, incl. Irish printing); College Librarian PATRICK TESKEY.

Omagh

Western Education and Library Board: 1 Spillars Place, Omagh, Co. Tyrone, BT78 1HL; tel. (1662) 244821; fax (1662) 246716; e-mail librarian@omalib.demon.co.uk; Chief Librarian R. T. A. FARROW.

Museums and Art Galleries

Armagh

Armagh County Museum: The Mall East, Armagh; tel. (1861) 523070; fax (1861) 522631; f. 1935; collection of material illustrative of local history, antiquities and natural history; Curator CATHERINE MCCULLOUGH.

Belfast

Ulster Museum: Botanic Gardens, Belfast, BT9 5AB; tel. (1232) 383000; fax (1232) 383003; national museum administered by Board of Trustees; fine and applied arts, archaeology, ethnography, history, botany, geology, zoology.

Holywood

Ulster Folk and Transport Museum: Cultra, Holywood, Co. Down; tel. (1232) 428428; fax (1232) 428728; a national museum comprising: open-air museum with authentic buildings illustrating Ulster folk life, both rural and urban; a separate transport museum; library of 18,000 vols; Chair. of Board of Trustees M. ELLIOTT; Dir M. HOULIHAN; publs *Ulster Folklife* (annually), *Ulster Folk and Transport Museum Year Book*.

Universities

QUEEN'S UNIVERSITY OF BELFAST

University Rd, Belfast, BT7 1NN
Telephone: (1232) 245133
Telex: 74487
Fax: (1232) 247895

Founded as Queen's College in 1845, original University Charter 1908, present Charter 1982
State control
Language of instruction: English
Academic year: September to September
Chancellor: Sir DAVID ORR
Pro-Chancellors: J. MCGUCKIAN, C. MACMAHON
President and Vice-Chancellor: Prof. G. BAIN
Pro-Vice-Chancellors: Prof. R. G. SHANKS, Prof. L. CLARKSON, Prof. R. J. CORMACK
Librarian: N. J. RUSSELL
Library: see Libraries
Number of teachers: 1,152 full-time
Number of students: 12,656 full-time, 2,787 part-time
Publications: *Calendar*, *Undergraduate Prospectus*, *Postgraduate Prospectus*, *Adult Education Prospectus*, *Student Accommodation Handbook*, *Vice-Chancellor's Report*.

DEANS

Faculty of Arts: Prof. M. R. ANDREW
Faculty of Science: Prof. A. KINGSTON
Faculty of Law: Prof. J. P. JACKSON
Faculty of Medicine: Prof. R. W. STOUT
Faculty of Engineering: Prof. B. W. HOGG
Faculty of Agriculture and Food Science: Prof. A. GILMAR
Faculty of Theology: Prof. A. HIBBERT
Faculty of Education: Prof. J. GARDNER

PROFESSORS

Faculty of Arts:
ANDREW, M. R., English Language and Literature
BALES, R. M., French
BOWLER, P. J., History and Philosophy of Science
BROOME, P., French
CAMPBELL, B. M., Medieval Economic History
CARAHER, B., English
CONNOLLY, S. J., Irish History
CULLEN, B. A., Philosophy
EVANS, J. D. G., Logic and Metaphysics
GORMAN, J. L., Moral Philosophy
GREEN, I., History
HEMPTON, D., Modern History
JOHNSTON, D. W., Hispanic Studies
JUPP, P. J., British History
LONGLEY, E., English
SMACZNY, J. A., Music
TONKIN, J. E., Social Anthropology
WALKER, B. M., Irish Studies
WHITEHEAD, D., Classics
WILLIAMS, F. J., Greek

Faculty of Science:
ARMITAGE, D. H., Pure Mathematics
BAILLIE, M. G. L., Palaeoecology
BATES, B., Physics
BELL, K. L., Theoretical Physics
BOYD, D. R., Organic Chemistry
BROWN, K., Psychology
BURKE, P. G., Mathematical Physics
BURNS, D. T., Analytical Chemistry
CLINT, M., Computer Science
CROTHERS, D. S. F., Theoretical Physics
DAVIES, R. J. H., Biochemistry
DE SILVA, A. P., Chemistry
DUFTON, P. L., Physics
EARNSHAW, J. C., Physics
FERGUSON, A., Biology
FINNIS, M. W., Atomistic Theory of Materials
GEDDES, J., Pure and Applied Physics
GRAHAM, W. G., Physics
HALTON, D. W., Parasitology
HEPPER, P. G., Psychology
HIBBERT, A., Applied Mathematics
KEENAN, F. P., Physics
KINGSTON, A. E., Theoretical Atomic Physics
LATIMER, C. J., Pure and Applied Physics
LEWIS, C. L., Experimental Physics
LIVINGSTONE, D. N., Geography
LYNDEN-BELL, R. M., Condensed Matter Simulation
MCGARVEY, J., Chemistry
MCKERVEY, M. A., Organic Chemistry
MONTGOMERY, W. I., Biology
ORFORD, J. D., Physical Geography
PATTERSON, T. L., Numerical Analysis
PILCHER, J. R., Palaeoecology
RIMA, B., Molecular Biology
ROONEY, J. J., Catalytic Chemistry
SEDDON, K. R., Inorganic Chemistry
SHEEHY, N., Psychology
SIMPSON, D. D. A., Archaeology
SWAIN, S., Quantum Optics
TAYLOR, K., Physics
WALKER, B., Biochemistry
WALMSLEY, D. G., Physics
WHALLEY, W., Physical Geography
WICKSTEAD, A. W., Pure Mathematics
WRIGHT, A. D., Geology

Faculty of Law:
BROGDEN, M. E., Criminology and Criminal Justice
DAWSON, N. M., Law
GREER, D. S., Common Law
HADDEN, T. B., Law
HADFIELD, B. V. A. M. M., Public Law
JACKSON, J. D., Public Law
MORISON, J. W. E., Jurisprudence
SARTOR, G., Jurisprudence

Faculty of Medicine:
ALLEN, I. V., Neuropathology
ARCHER, D. B., Ophthalmology
BENINGTON, I. C., Dental Prosthetics and Materials
BUCHANAN, K. D., Metabolic Medicine
CARR, K. E., Anatomy
EVANS, A. E., Epidemiology and Public Health
FEE, J. P. H., Anaesthetics
GORMAN, S. P., Pharmaceutical Microbiology
HAYES, J. R., Medicine
JOHNSTON, G. D., Therapeutics and Pharmacology
JOHNSTON, P. G., Oncology
KING, D. J., Clinical Psychopharmacology
LAMEY, P.-J., Oral Medicine
LAPPIN, T. R. J., Haematology
LOVE, A. H. G., Medicine
MCCLELLAND, R. J., Mental Health
MCCLURE, B. G., Neonatal Medicine
MCELNAY, J. C., Pharmacy
MCGIMPSEY, J. G., Dental Surgery
MCHALE, N. G., Physiology
MARSH, D. R., Orthopaedic Surgery
MEBAN, C., Anatomy
MIRAKHUR, R. K., Anaesthetics
NEVIN, N. C., Medical Genetics
ORR, J. A., Nursing Studies
PARKS, T. G., Surgical Science
REILLY, P. M., General Practice
RICHARDSON, A., Orthodontics
SHANKS, R. G., Therapeutics and Pharmacology
SHAW, C., Medicine
SIMPSON, D. I. H., Microbiology
STOUT, R. W., Geriatric Medicine
THOMPSON, W., Obstetrics and Gynaecology
TONER, P. G., Pathology
TRIMBLE, E. R., Clinical Biochemistry
WALLACE, W. F. M., Applied Physiology
WOOLFSON, A. D., Pharmacy
WOOTTON, R., Telemedicine and Telecare

Faculty of Economics and Social Sciences:
BARRETT, T. F., Accounting
BEW, P. A. E., Irish Politics
BREEN, R. J., Sociology
BREWER, J. D., Sociology
BROWN, K. D., Economic and Social History
CLARKSON, L. A., Social History
CORMACK, R. J., Sociology
DONNAN, H. S. C., Social Anthropology
ECCLESHALL, R. R., Politics
FORKER, J. J., Accounting and Finance
GEOGHEGAN, V., Political Theory
GUELKE, A. B., Politics
HITCHINS, D. M. W., Applied Economics
IWANIEC, ST., Social Work
MCKILLOP, D. G., Accounting and Finance
MCLAUGHLIN, E., Social Policy
MEEHAN, E. M., Politics
MOORE, M. J., Finance
O'DOWD, L. G., Sociology and Social Policy
PHILIP, G., Information Management
SANGSTER, A., Accounting
SPENCER, J. E., Economics
VELUPILLAI, K., Economics

Faculty of Engineering:
ARMSTRONG, C. G., Mechanical and Manufacturing Engineering
CLELAND, D. J., Civil Engineering
COWAN, C., Telecommunications Systems Engineering
CRAWFORD, R. J., Engineering Materials
CROOKES, D., Computer Engineering
DUNWOODY, J., Theoretical Mechanics
FLECK, R., Mechanical and Manufacturing Engineering
FUSCO, V. F., High Frequency Electronic Engineering
GAMBLE, H. S., Microelectronics Engineering
HENDRY, J., Town and Country Planning
HOGG, B. W., Electrical Engineering
IRWIN, G. W., Control Engineering
LONG, A. E., Civil Engineering
MCCANNY, J. V., Micro-electronics Engineering
MURPHY, W. R., Chemical Engineering
PERROTT, R. H., Software Engineering
RAGHUNATHAN, S. R., Aeronautical Engineering
SMITH, F. J., Computer Science
STEWART, J. A. C., Communications Engineering
STORRAR, A. M., Manufacturing Systems Engineering
WEATHERLEY, L. R., Process Engineering
WHITTAKER, T. J. T., Coastal Engineering
WOOLLEY, T. A., Architecture

Faculty of Agriculture and Food Science:
BLAKEMAN, J. P., Mycology and Plant Pathology
ELWOOD, R. W., Animal Behaviour
GARRETT, M. K., Agricultural and Environmental Science
GILMOUR, A., Food Microbiology
GORDON, F., Crop and Animal Production
HARPER, D. B., Microbial Biochemistry
LEDWARD, D. A., Food and Agricultural Chemistry
MCNULTY, M. S., Veterinary Science
MARKS, R. J., Agricultural Zoology
PEARCE, J., Food Science

Faculty of Education:
FULTON, J. F., Dir of Development
GARDNER, J. R., Education
MCEWEN, A., Education

UNIVERSITY INSTITUTES

Institute of Continuing Education: Dir P. M. PATTEN.

Institute of European Studies: Dir M. L. SMITH.

Institute of Irish Studies: Dir B. M. WALKER.

Institute of Professional Legal Studies: Dir (vacant).

Institute of Computer-Based Learning: Dir F. V. MCBRIDE.

Institute of Criminology and Criminal Justice: Dir M. E. BROGDEN.

Institute of Telemedicine and Telecare: Dir Prof. R. WOOTTON.

RECOGNIZED COLLEGES

Belfast Bible College: Glenburn House, Glenburn Rd South, Dunmorry, BT17 9JP; tel. (1232) 301551; Principal Rev. G. J. CHEESEMAN.

Edgehill Theological College: Lennoxvale, Belfast BT9 5BY; tel. (1232) 665870; Methodist; Principal Rev. W. D. D. COOKE.

Irish Baptist College: 67 Sandown Rd, Belfast BT5 6GU; tel. (1232) 471908; Principal Rev. H. MOORE.

Loughry College of Agriculture and Food Technology: Cookstown, Co. Tyrone BT80 9AA; tel. (16487) 62491; Principal J. G. S. SPEERS.

St Mary's College: 191 Falls Rd, Belfast BT12 6FE; tel. (1232) 327678; Principal Rev. M. O'CALLAGHAN.

Stranmillis College: Stranmillis Rd, Belfast BT9 5DY; tel. (1232) 381271; courses in education; Principal J. R. MCMINN.

Union Theological College: Botanic Ave, Belfast BT7 1JT; tel. (1232) 325374; Presbyterian; Principal Rev. Prof. T. S. REID.

UNIVERSITY OF ULSTER

Cromore Rd, Coleraine, Co. Londonderry BT52 1SA

Telephone: (1265) 44141

Fax: (1265) 324927

Founded 1984 by merger of the New University of Ulster and the Ulster Polytechnic.

State control

Academic year: October to June

Chancellor: Rabbi JULIA NEUBERGER

Vice-Chancellor: Prof. Sir TREVOR SMITH

Pro-Vice-Chancellors: Prof. P. ROEBUCK, Prof. F. C. MONDS, A. TATE

Academic Registrar: Dr K. I. MILLAR

Number of teachers: 850

Number of students: 13,131 full-time, 6,812 part-time

DEANS

Faculty of Business and Management: Prof. R. R. BARNETT

Faculty of Engineering: Prof. B. NORTON

Faculty of Humanities: Prof. T. O'KEEFFE

Faculty of Informatics: Prof. J. G. HUGHES

Faculty of Social and Health Sciences with Education: Prof. J. M. ALLEN

Faculty of Science: Prof. W. E. WATTS

Ulster Business School: Prof. S. PARKINSON

PROFESSORS

(H = Head of School)

Faculty of Business and Management:

BOREHAM, C. A., Sport and Exercise
BOROOAH, V. K., Applied Economics
BROWN, S., Retailing
CAREY, M., Management Science
CARSON, D., Marketing
CLARKE, W. M., Management (H)
COLLINS, C. A., Public Policy
DICKSON, S. B., Law
FITZPATRICK, T., Law
GLASS, J. C., Applied Financial Studies
HARRISON, R., Strategy and Organization
HUTCHINSON, R. W., Business Finance
KINSELLA, R., Banking and Finance
KIRK, R. J., Accounting and Finance
KNOX, C. G., Comparative Public Policy
MCALEER, W. E., Management
MCALISTER, D. A., Public Policy, Economics and Law (H)
MCDOWELL, D. A., Leisure and Tourism (H)
MCNAMEE, P. B., International Business Studies
OSBORNE, R. D., Applied Policy Studies
OSMANI, S. R., Applied Economics
PALMER, A. J., Tourism
SAUNDERS, E. D., Specialist Studies
TEAGUE, P., Industrial Relations
THAIN, C., Comparative Public Policy
WARD, J. D., Commerce and International Business Studies

Faculty of Humanities:

AGNEW, K. M., Design
ALCOCK, A. E., Languages and Literature
ARTHUR, P. J., History, Philosophy and Politics
BAREHAM, T., Languages and Literature
BRADFORD, R. W., Literature History
DUNN, J. A., Conflict Studies
FRASER, T. G., History, Philosophy and Politics (H)
JEFFERY, K. J., Modern History
JONES, G. J., History, Philosophy and Politics
MCBRIDE, R., Modern Languages
MCCARTHY, G. F., Theatre Studies
MCCLELLAND, B, Design and Communication (H)
MCKEAG, D., Product Development
MACLENNAN, A. M., Fine Applied Arts
MACMATHÚNA, S., Irish Studies
MCMINN, J. M., Anglo-Irish Literature
MORGAN, V., History, Philosophy and Politics
PATTERSON, H. H., History, Philosophy and Politics
PEARSON, R., History, Modern European History
SHARP, A. J., History
WELCH, R. A., English
YORK, R. A., Languages and Literature (H)

Faculty of Social and Health Sciences with Education:

BALL, M. J., Phonetics and Linguistics
BAMFORD, D. R., Social Work
BAXTER, G. D., Rehabilitation Sciences
BIRRELL, W. D., Social and Community Sciences (H)
BOORE, J. R. P., Nursing
CAIRNS, S. E., Behavioural and Communication Sciences
CHAMBERS, M. G., Mental Health Nursing
EAKIN, P. A., Health Sciences
EVASON, E. M. T., Social Administration
HARGIE, O. D. W., Behavioural and Communication Sciences
KERNOHAN, W. G., Health Research
LESLIE, J., Psychology
MCCONKEY, R. A., Health Scienes
MCCOY, M. P., Physiotherapy
MCKENNA, H. P., Nursing
MCWILLIAMS, M. M., Women's Studies
MURPHY, P., Social Inclusion
PARIS, C. T., Housing Studies
RAE, G., Psychology
SINES, D. T., Health Sciences (H)
WEINREICH, P., Behavioural and Communication Sciences
WILSON, J., Behavioural and Communication Sciences (H)

Faculty of Engineering:

ADAIR, A. S., Built Environment (H)
ANDERSON, J. MC C., Electrical and Mechanical Engineering (H)
BLACK, N. D., Digital Communication
HEPBURN, C., Polymer Engineering
MCGREAL, W. S., Property Research
MCILHAGGER, R., Engineering Components
MITCHELL, R. H., Electronics
SHIELDS, T. J., Built Environment
SMYTH, A., Transport Studies
WOODSIDE, A. R., Built Environment

Faculty of Informatics:

ANDERSON, T. J., Computing and Mathematics
BELL, D. A., Information and Software Engineering (H)
BUSTARD, D. W., Computing Science
DUNTSCH, I., Computing Science
HOUSTON, S. K., Mathematical Studies
HULL, M. E. C., Computing and Mathematics
MCCLEAN, S. I., Mathematics
MCTEAR, M., Information and Software Engineering
MURTAGH, F., Computing Science

Faculty of Science:

BEST, G. T., Physics
BROWN, N. M. D., Applied Biological and Chemical Sciences
DOWNES, C. S., Cancer Biology
EASTWOOD, D. A., Environmental Studies (H)
FLATT, P. R., Biomedical Sciences
GRAHAM, B. J., Human Geography
HANNIGAN, B. M., Biomedical Sciences (H)
HIRST, D. G., Radiation Science
KNIPE, A. C., Applied Biological and Chemical Sciences
MARCHANT, R., Applied Biological and Chemical Sciences (H)
MCMULLAN, J. T., Environmental Studies
ROWLAND, I. R., Human Nutrition
STRAIN, J. J., Human Nutrition
THURNHAM, D. I., Biomedical Sciences
WILCOCK, D. N., Environmental Studies

Ulster Business School:

CROMIE, S.
FOX, A. F., Financial Management
O'NEILL, K. E., Enterprise and Small Businesses
PARKINSON, S. T.
REED, T. F., Business

Initiative and Conflict Resolution and Ethnicity:

DARBY, J. P., Ethnic Studies
FITZDUFF, M. C., Initiative and Conflict Resolution and Ethnicity

College

BELFAST INSTITUTE OF FURTHER AND HIGHER EDUCATION

Park House, Great Victoria St, Belfast, BT2 7AG

Telephone: (1232) 265000

Fax: (1232) 265451

Founded 1991 from College of Technology (f. 1901), College of Business Studies and Rupert Stanley College

Director: Prof. PATRICK MURPHY

Number of students: 9,800 f.t.e.

Faculties of general and continuing education, business and management, creative and personal services, hospitality, health and social studies, and technology.

BERMUDA

Learned Societies

GENERAL

Bermuda National Trust: POB HM 61, Hamilton HM AX; tel. (441) 236-6483; fax (441) 236-0617; f. 1970; promotes the preservation of lands, buildings and artefacts of natural or historic interest; 4,000 mems; Pres. HUGH A. C. DAVIDSON; Dir AMANDA OUTERBRIDGE.

FINE AND PERFORMING ARTS

Bermuda Society of Arts: West Gallery, City Hall, POB HM 1202, Hamilton HM FX; tel. (441) 292-3824; fax (441) 296-0699; f. 1956; 700 mems; Pres. ELDON TRIMINGHAM III; Curator NANCY ACTON.

HISTORY, GEOGRAPHY AND ARCHAEOLOGY

Bermuda Historical Society: 13 Queen St, Hamilton HM 11; tel. (441) 295-2487; f. 1895; 130 mems; Pres. ANDREW BERMINGHAM.

St George's Historical Society: Cnr Duke of Kent St and Featherbed Alley, POB 279, St George's GE BX; 186 mems; Pres. ANN SPURLING.

MEDICINE

Bermuda Medical Society: C/o POB HM 1023, Hamilton HM DX; f. 1970; 70 mems; Pres. Dr ANDREW J. WEST; Sec. Dr FIONA ROSS.

NATURAL SCIENCES

Biological Sciences

Bermuda Audubon Society: POB 1328, Hamilton HM FX; tel. (441) 297-2623; f. 1960; 300 mems; environmental education and acquisition and maintenance of land for nature reserves; Pres. JEREMY MADEIROS; publ. *Newsletter*.

Physical Sciences

Astronomical Society of Bermuda: POB HM 1046, Hamilton 5; Pres. MORLEY E. B. NASH; Sec. C. MCGONAGLE; publs *Bermuda Sky Watch*, *Cosmos*.

Research Institutes

AGRICULTURE, FISHERIES AND VETERINARY SCIENCE

Bermuda Department of Agriculture and Fisheries: POB HM 834, Hamilton HM CX; tel. (441) 236-4201; fax (441) 236-7582; f. 1898; management and development of agricultural and fishing industries; Dir JOHN A. BARNES; publs *Annual Report*, *Monthly Bulletin*, occasional special reports.

NATURAL SCIENCES

Biological Sciences

Bermuda Biological Station for Research, Inc: Ferry Reach, St George's GE 01; tel. (441) 297-1880; fax (441) 297-8143; f. 1903; research in most aspects of marine sciences and oceanography and environmental sciences; summer courses organized in marine invertebrates, ecology, pollution, etc., and high school and college facilities for instruction in marine sciences; library of 20,000 vols; Pres. CHRISTOPHER DUP. ROOSEVELT; Dir Dr ANTHONY H. KNAP; publs *Contributions*, *Special Publications*, *Currents* (newsletter), *BBSR Annual Report*.

Libraries and Archives

Hamilton

Bermuda Archives: Government Administration Bldg, Hamilton HM 12; f. 1949; repository for official and non-governmental records; Archivist KARLA HAYWARD (acting).

Bermuda National Library: 13 Queen St, Par-la-Ville, Hamilton HM 11; tel. (441) 295-2905; fax (441) 292-8443; f. 1839; national and public library services; library of 149,834 vols; special collection of Bermudiana; Islandwide bookmobile service; Librarian GRACE E. RAWLINS; publ. *Bermuda National Bibliography* (quarterly).

Museums and Art Galleries

Flatts

Bermuda Aquarium, Museum and Zoo: POB FL 145, Flatts, FL BX; tel. (441) 293-2727; fax (441) 293-3176; f. 1928; live zoological collection, local natural history and other exhibits; 8,500 individual mems, 4,500 mems (Bermuda Zoological Soc.); library of 3,000 vols; Prin. Curator RICHARD J. WINCHELL; publ. *Critter Talk* (quarterly).

Mangrove Bay

Bermuda Maritime Museum: POB MA 273, Mangrove Bay, MA 133; tel. (441) 234-1333; fax (441) 234-1735; e-mail marmuse@ibl.bm; f. 1975; area includes fortress of Bermuda Dockyard and exhibits representing Bermuda maritime history; Dir Dr E. C. HARRIS; Curator LYNNE THORNE; publs *Maritimes*, *Bermuda Journal of Archaeology and Maritime History*.

St George's

National Trust Museum: POB HM-61, Hamilton HM AX; located at: King's Square, St George's; tel. (441) 236-6483; fax (441) 236-0617; displays depicting Bermuda's role in the American Civil War; collection of antique furniture; Dir AMANDA OUTERBRIDGE.

President Henry Tucker House: POB HM-61, Hamilton HM AX; located at: Water St, St George's; tel. (441) 236-6483; fax (441) 236-0617; administered by the Bermuda National Trust: 18th-century house with period furniture; Dir AMANDA OUTERBRIDGE.

Smith's Parish

Verdmont Museum: Collector's Hill, Smith's Parish (POB HM-61, Hamilton HM AX); tel. (441) 236-6483; fax (441) 236-0617; administered by Bermuda National Trust; 18th-century house with period furniture; Dir AMANDA OUTERBRIDGE.

Universities and Colleges

Bermuda College: POB PG 297, Paget PG BX; tel. (441) 236-9000; fax (441) 236-8888; f. 1974; 70 teachers; 550 day students; 3,500 evening students; library of 30,000 vols; faculties of arts and science, continuing and applied studies, hotel and business administration; Pres. G. L. COOK.

GIBRALTAR

Learned Societies

NATURAL SCIENCES

Biological Sciences

Gibraltar Ornithological and Natural History Society: Gibraltar Natural History Field Centre, Jews' Gate, Upper Rock Nature Reserve; tel. 72639; fax 74022; e-mail gonhs@gibnet.gi; f. 1978; research, conservation, education; 450 mems; Sec. J. E. CORTES; publs *Alectoris* (1 a year), *Gibraltar Nature News* (2 a year), *Report of the Strait of Gibraltar Bird Observatory* (2 a year).

Libraries and Archives

Gibraltar

Gibraltar Garrison Library: POB 374; tel. A77418; f. 1793; Gibraltar section; library of 1,740 vols; Sec. JON M. SEARLE.

Gibraltar Government Archives: 6 Convent Place; tel. 79461; fax 79461; f. 1969; repository for official Government records; Archivist T. J. FINLAYSON.

John Mackintosh Hall Library: 308 Main St; tel. 78000; fax 40843; e-mail gfjmh@gibnet.gi; f. 1964; library of 33,000 vols; Librarian Dr J. C. FINLAYSON.

Museums and Art Galleries

Gibraltar

Gibraltar Museum: 18 – 20 Bomb House Lane; tel. 74289; fax 79158; e-mail jcfinlay@gibnet.gi; f. 1930; collection of local natural history, archaeology and palaeontology (especially Palaeolithic, Neolithic and Phoenician) and military history; Dir Dr J. C. FINLAYSON.

UNITED STATES OF AMERICA

Learned Societies

GENERAL

American Academy of Arts and Letters: 633 West 155th St, New York, NY 10032-7599; tel. (212) 368-5900; fax (212) 491-4615; f. 1898; 250 mems; Pres. LOUIS AUCHINCLOSS; Exec. Dir VIRGINIA DAJANI; publ. *Proceedings* (annually).

American Academy of Arts and Sciences: Norton's Woods, 136 Irving St, Cambridge, MA 02138; tel. (617) 576-5000; fax (617) 576-5050; e-mail aaas@amacad.org; f. 1780; 3,900 mems; Pres. DANIEL TOSTESON; Sec. DUDLEY HERSCHBACH; Senior Exec. Officer LESLIE C. BERLOWITZ; publs *Daedalus* (quarterly), *Bulletin* (monthly), *Records* (annually).

American Council of Learned Societies: 228 East 45th St, New York, NY 10017; tel. (212) 697-1505; telex 798921; fax (212) 949-8058; f. 1919; 61 societies concerned with the humanities and the humanistic aspects of the social sciences; Pres. Dr JOHN H. D'ARMS; publs *Annual Report*, *Newsletter* (quarterly), *Occasional Papers*.

American Philosophical Society: 104 South Fifth St, Philadelphia, PA 19106-3387; f. 1743 by Benjamin Franklin, the oldest learned society in the United States; mems (590 US citizens and 130 foreign) are elected by the Society on the basis of distinction in any field of learning; there are five classes of membership: mathematical and physical sciences, biological sciences, social sciences, humanities, and the professions, arts and affairs; the Society meets twice a year (April, November) for symposia, lectures and presenting awards; it makes grants for research, operates a distinguished library rich in historical MSS, chiefly relating to the history of science in America (see Special Libraries), and awards prizes including the Magellanic Premium, the oldest American scientific award; publishes several books each year and engages in community service; it owns three buildings: Philosophical Hall (1789, a National Historical Landmark), Library Hall (105 S. Fifth St), and Benjamin Franklin Hall (427 Chestnut St); the first two buildings contain numerous valuable portraits (paintings and statuary) of distinguished former members; Pres. ARLIN M. ADAMS; Exec. Officer ALEXANDER G. BEARN; publs *Transactions*, *Proceedings*, *Memoirs*, *Year Book*.

Asia Foundation: POB 3223, San Francisco, CA 94119 (Main Office); tel. (415) 982-4640; fax (415) 392-8863; telex 278726; offices in Washington, DC, and 13 Asian and Pacific island countries; f. 1954; 3,370 vols on current Asian and world affairs; assists Asian economic and social development through private American support to Asian institutions, organizations and individuals working towards constructive social change, stable political development and equitable economic growth within their societies; provides small grants, primarily in fields of law and public administration, rural and community development, communications and libraries, Asian regional co-operation; Books for Asia Program distributes books and journals to libraries and institutions in Asia; Pres. WILLIAM P. FULLER; Exec. Vice-Pres. BARNETT F. BARON; publ. *Annual Report*.

Connecticut Academy of Arts and Sciences: POB 208211, Yale University, New Haven, CT 06520-8211; tel. (203) 432-3113; f. 1799; 400 mems; library merged with Yale University Library; Pres. JARED COHEN; Sec. DOLORES GALL; publs *Transactions, Memoirs, A Manual of the Writings in Middle English* (all irregular).

English-Speaking Union of the United States: 16 East 69th St, New York, NY 10021; tel. (212) 879-6800; fax (212) 772-2886; f. 1920; to increase communication and understanding among people of all nationalities through the medium of the English language; initiates and implements innovative educational programmes; non profit; 18,000 mems; library of 6,000 vols; 85 brs in USA; Chair. J. SINCLAIR ARMSTRONG; Pres. D. ROBERT THORNBURG; Exec. Dir DAVID OLYPHANT; publ. *E-SU Today*.

Hispanic Society of America: 613 West 155th St, New York, NY 10032; f. 1904; 400 mems; professional research staff; reference library and museum; Dir MITCHELL A. CODDING; numerous publs.

National Academies of Sciences and Engineering, Institute of Medicine and National Research Council: 2101 Constitution Ave, Washington, DC 20418; established by Congressional charter; linked group of instns, co-ordinating their advice to fed. govt.

Individual institutions:

National Academy of Sciences: 2101 Constitution Ave, Washington, DC 20418; f. 1863; sections of Mathematics, of Astronomy, of Physics, of Chemistry, of Geology, of Geophysics, of Biochemistry, of Cellular and Developmental Biology, of Physiology and Pharmacology, of Neurobiology, of Plant Biology, of Genetics, of Population Biology, Evolution and Ecology, of Engineering Sciences, of Applied Mathematical Sciences, of Applied Physical Sciences, of Medical Genetics, Haematology and Oncology, of Medical Physiology and Metabolism, of Microbiology and Immunology, of Anthropology, of Psychology, of Social and Political Sciences, of Economic Sciences, of Animal Sciences and Human Nutrition, of Plant, Soil and Microbial Sciences; 1,800 mems, 300 foreign assocs; Pres. BRUCE M. ALBERTS; Home Sec. PETER RAVEN; Foreign Sec. F. SHERWOOD ROWLAND; Exec. Dir KENNETH R. FULTON; Exec. Officer E. WILLIAM COLGLAZIER; publ. *Proceedings* (fortnightly).

National Academy of Engineering: 2101 Constitution Ave, Washington, DC 20418; f. 1964; 1,622 mems; Pres. WILLIAM A. WULF; Home Sec. SIMON OSTRACH; Foreign Sec. HAROLD FORSEN.

Institute of Medicine: 2101 Constitution Ave, Washington, DC 20418; f. 1970; 1,060 mems; Pres. Dr KENNETH I. SHINE; Exec. Officer Dr KAREN HEIN; publ. *IOM News* (quarterly).

National Research Council: 2101 Constitution Ave, Washington DC 20418; f. 1916; governed by reps of Acads of Sciences and Engineering and of Institute of Medicine; carries out studies by means of appointed cttees of scientists and engineers; comms on Behavioural and Social Sciences and Education (Chair. NEIL J. SMELSER), Engineering and Technical Systems (Chair. W. DALE COMPTON), Geosciences, Environment and Resources (Chair. GEORGE M. HORNBERGER), Life Sciences (Chair. THOMAS D. POLLARD), Physical Sciences, Mathematics and Applications (Co-Chairmen ROBERT J. HERMANN, W. CARL LINEBERGER), Scientific and Engineering Personnel (Chair. M. R. C. GREENWOOD), Science, Mathematics and Engineering Education (Chair. DONALD KENNEDY); boards of Transportation Research (Chair. DAVID N. WORMLEY), Agriculture (Chair. DALE E. BAUMAN); Chair. BRUCE M. ALBERTS.

National Foundation on the Arts and the Humanities: Washington, DC 20506; f. 1965 as an independent agency in the Executive Branch of Government to develop and promote a broadly conceived national policy of support for the humanities and the arts in the United States.

Constituent institutions:

National Endowment for the Arts: Washington, DC 20506; f. 1965 to establish and carry out a programme of grants-in-aid to non-profit groups, individuals of exceptional talent and state art agencies, which will promote progress in the arts; Chair. JANE ALEXANDER.

National Endowment for the Humanities: Washington, DC 20506; f. 1965 to establish and carry out a programme supporting projects of research, education and public activity in the humanities; Chair. SHELDON HACKNEY.

National Council on the Arts: Washington, DC 20506; appointed 1964, advises the Chairman of the National Endowment for the Arts on policies, programmes and procedures and reviews applications for financial assistance; 26 private citizen mems appointed by the President for six-year terms (*c.* one-third of the appointments expire every two years); Chair. of Council is Chair. of the Arts Endowment.

National Council on the Humanities: Washington, DC 20506; f. 1966; advises the Chairman of the National Endowment for the Humanities on policies, programmes and procedures and reviews applications for financial assistance; 26 private citizen mems appointed by the President for six-year terms (approx. one-third of the appointments expire every two years); Chair. of Council is Chair. of the Humanities Endowment.

Federal Council on the Arts and the Humanities: Washington, DC 20506; f. 1965 to co-ordinate the activities of the two Endowments with related federal agencies and to carry out the federal indemnity programme; mems include the Chairmen of the two Endowments; the Secs of the Depts of Education, Interior, Commerce, Transportation, Housing and Urban Development, and Labor; the Commissioners of the Fine Arts Commission, Administration on Aging, and Public Buildings Service; the Administrators of the Veterans Administration and the General Services Administration; the Dirs of the National Science Foundation, United States Information Agency, and Institute of Museum Services; the Librarian of Congress; the Archivist of the United States;

and the Chairman of the National Museum Services Board; mems who do not vote on indemnity include the Dir, National Gallery of Art; Sec. of the Senate; Sec., Smithsonian Institution; Member, House of Representatives.

New York Academy of Sciences: 2 East 63rd St, New York, NY 10021; tel. (212) 838-0230; fax (212) 888-2894; f. 1817; sections of Anthropology, Atmospheric Sciences, Biochemistry, Biological Sciences, Biomedical Sciences, Chemical Sciences, Computer and Information Sciences, Economics, Engineering, Environmental Sciences, Geological Sciences, History and Philosophy of Science, Inorganic Chemistry and Catalytic Science, Linguistics, Mathematics, Microbiology, Neuroscience, Physics and Astronomy, Psychology, Science and Public Policy, Science Education, Women in Science; 40,000 mems; Chair. MARTIN L. LEIBOWITZ; Pres. and CEO RODNEY W. NICHOLS; publs *The Annals, The Sciences, Academy Update*.

North American Spanish Language Academy/Academia Norteamericana de la Lengua Española: GPO Box 349, New York, NY 10116; f. 1973; mem. of Asociación de Academias de la Lengua Española; corresp. of Real Academia, Spain; 36 Academicians; Dir ODÓN BETANZOS-PALACIOS; Sec. GUMERSINDO YÉPEZ; publs *Boletín, Glosas*.

Smithsonian Institution: Washington, DC 20560; tel. (202) 357-2700; f. 1846 for the 'increase and diffusion of knowledge' by bequest of James Smithson; responsible for many national museums and art galleries, and for the Archives of American Art, the National Zoological Park, the Smithsonian Astrophysical Observatory, the Smithsonian Environmental Research Center and the Smithsonian Tropical Research Institute; library: see Libraries and Archives; Chancellor The Chief Justice of the United States; Secretary (Presiding Officer) IRA MICHAEL HEYMAN; Provost J. DENNIS O'CONNOR; Under-Secretary CONSTANCE BERRY NEWMAN; the Board of Regents consists of the Smithsonian Secretary, Under-Secretary and Provost and the President of the United States, Vice-President of the United States, Chief Justice of the United States, Secretary of State, Secretary of the Treasury, Secretary of Defense, Attorney General, Secretary of the Interior, Secretary of Agriculture, Secretary of Commerce, Secretary of Labor, Secretary of Health and Human Services, Secretary of Housing and Urban Development, Secretary of Transportation, Secretary of Energy, Secretary of Education; publs: *Smithsonian Year, Smithsonian Contributions to Astrophysics, Smithsonian Studies in Air and Space, Smithsonian Contributions to Botany, Smithsonian Contributions to the Earth Sciences, Smithsonian Contributions to the Marine Sciences, Smithsonian Contributions to Paleobiology, Smithsonian Contributions to Zoology, Smithsonian Studies in History and Technology,* also exhibit catalogues, pamphlets, books and special publications.

AGRICULTURE, FISHERIES AND VETERINARY SCIENCE

Agricultural History Society: Business Office: Economic Research Service, Room 2103, 1800 M St NW, Washington, DC 20036-5831; tel. (202) 694-5348; f. 1919 to stimulate interest in, promote the study of, and facilitate research and publication on the history of agriculture; incorporated 1924 as a non-profit organization; 1,400 mems; Pres. LORENA S. WALSH; Sec. LOWELL K. DYSON; publ. *Agricultural History* (quarterly).

American Dairy Science Association: 1111 N. Dunlap Ave, Savoy, IL 61874; tel. (217) 356-3182; fax (217) 398-4119; f. 1906; 4,654 mems; Pres. L. MULLER; Exec. Dir M. KELLEY; publ. *Journal of Dairy Science* (monthly).

American Forests: POB 2000, Washington, DC 20013; f. 1875; 35,000 mems; Exec. Vice-Pres. DEBORAH GANGLOFF.

American Society for Horticultural Science: 600 Cameron St, Alexandria, VA 22314-2562; tel. (703) 836-4606; fax (703) 836-2024; f. 1903; 5,000 mems; field of activities: to promote and encourage scientific research and education in all branches of horticulture; Pres. DONALD N. MAYNARD; Exec. Dir CHARLES H. EMELY; publs *Hort Science* (every 2 months), *Journal* (every 2 months), *HortTechnology* (quarterly).

American Society of Agricultural Engineers: 2950 Niles Rd, St Joseph, MI 49085; tel. (616) 429-0300; fax (616) 429-3852; f. 1907; 9,000 mems; Exec. Vice-Pres. MELISSA MOORE; publs *Resource Magazine* (monthly), *Transactions* (every 2 months), *Standards* (annually).

American Society of Agronomy: 677 South Segoe Rd, Madison, WI 53711; tel. (608) 273-8080; fax (608) 273-2021; f. 1907; 12,600 mems; Exec. Vice-Pres. ROBERT F BARNES; publs *Agronomy Journal* (every 2 months), *Journal of Production* (quarterly), *Agronomy Monographs, Agronomy News* (monthly), *Agronomy Abstracts* (annually), *ASA Special Publication Series, Journal of Environmental Quality* (6 a year), *Journal of Natural Resources and Life Sciences Education* (every six months).

American Society of Animal Science: c/o Carl D. Johnson, 1111 N. Dunlap St, Savoy, IL 61874-9604; tel. (217) 356-3182; fax (217) 398-4119; f. 1908; promotes development of sciences beneficial to animal production; 4,500 mems; Pres. ELTON D. ABERLE; Sec. BARBARA GLENN; publ. *Journal of Animal Science* (monthly).

American Veterinary Medical Association: 1931 N. Meacham Rd, Schaumburg, IL 60173-4360; tel. (847) 925-8070; fax (847) 925-1329; f. 1863; 58,000 mems; Exec. Vice-Pres. Dr BRUCE LITTLE; library of 5,000 vols, 400 periodicals; publs *Journal of the AVMA* (fortnightly) and *American Journal of Veterinary Research* (monthly).

Association for International Agricultural and Extension Education: c/o Dept of Agricultural and Extension Education, Room 409, Ag Hall, Michigan State University, East Lansing, MI 48824-1039; f. 1984 to provide a professional association and network of agricultural educators with the aim of improving and strengthening agricultural education programs and institutions, especially in developing countries; c. 200 mems; Chair. Dr ROGER STEELE; Sec. Dr TOM TRAIL; publ. *Newsletter* (quarterly).

Council for Agricultural Science and Technology: 4420 West Lincoln Way, Ames, IA 50014-3447; tel. (515) 292-2125; fax (515) 292-4512; inc. 1972; non-profit consortium of scientific societies, organizations, companies, scientists and citizens interested in public policy and the science of food and agriculture; compiles scientific information for Congress, the public, journalists and educators; 4,000 mems; Pres. Dr DAVID L. LINEBACK; Exec. Vice-Pres. Dr RICHARD E. STUCKEY; publ. *NewsCAST*.

Poultry Science Association Inc.: 1111 N. Dunlap St, Savoy, IL 61874; tel. (217) 356-3182; fax (217) 398-4119; f. 1908; 1,800 mems; Pres. HENRY MARKS; publ. *Poultry Science* (monthly).

Society of American Foresters: 5400 Grosvenor Lane, Bethesda, MD 20814-2198; tel. (301) 897-8720; fax (301) 897-3690; f. 1900; 18,000 mems; Pres. HARRY V. WIANT, Jr; Exec. Vice-Pres. WILLIAM H. BANZHAF; publs *Journal of Forestry* (monthly), *Forest Science* (quarterly), *Southern Journal of Applied Forestry* (quarterly), *Northern Journal of Applied Forestry* (quarterly), *Western Journal of Applied Forestry* (quarterly).

Soil Science Society of America: f. 1936; 6,300 mems; associated with the American Society of Agronomy; Exec. Vice-Pres. ROBERT F BARNES, 677 South Segoe Rd, Madison, WI 53711; tel. (608) 273-8080; fax (608) 273-2021; publs *Soil Science Society of America Journal* (every 2 months), *Journal of Production Agriculture* (quarterly), *Journal of Environmental Quality* (6 a year).

ARCHITECTURE AND TOWN PLANNING

American Institute of Architects: 1735 New York Ave, NW, Washington, DC 20006; tel. (202) 626-7300; fax (202) 626-7426; f. 1857; 62,000 mems; library of 30,400 vols; Exec. Vice-Pres. and CEO Dr MARK W. HURWITZ; publ. *AIArchitect*.

American Planning Association: 122 S. Michigan Ave, Suite 1600, Chicago, IL 60603-6101; tel. (312) 431-9100; fax (312) 431-9985; f. 1909; non-profit research, educational and professional organization for city planners and others involved in land use and community development; 30,000 mems; includes American Institute of Certified Planners; Exec. Dir FRANK S. SO; publs *APA Journal* (quarterly), *Planning* (monthly), *PAS reports and memos, Land Use Law and Zoning Digest* (monthly), *Zoning News* (monthly).

National Trust for Historic Preservation in the United States: 1785 Massachusetts Ave, NW, Washington, DC 20036; tel. (202) 673-4000; fax (202) 673-4038; f. 1949 to encourage preservation of buildings, sites and objects significant in American history and culture; 250,000 mems; library (at Architecture School, Univ. of Maryland, College Park) of 14,000 vols, 400 periodicals; Pres. RICHARD MOE; Chair. ROBERT M. BASS; publs *Historic Preservation* (every 2 months), *Historic Preservation News* (monthly), *Preservation Law Reporter, Historic Preservation Forum*, etc.

Society of Architectural Historians: 1365 N. Astor St, Chicago, IL 60610-2144; tel. (312) 573-1365; fax (312) 573-1141; e-mail info@sah.org; f. 1940; 4,000 mems; Pres. RICHARD LONGSTRETH; Sec. DENNIS MCFADDEN; Exec. Dir PAULINE SALIGA; publs *Journal* (quarterly), *Newsletter* (every 2 months).

BIBLIOGRAPHY, LIBRARY SCIENCE AND MUSEOLOGY

American Association of Law Libraries: 53 West Jackson Blvd, Chicago, IL 60604; tel. (312) 939-4764; f. 1906; 5,000 mems; Pres. FRANK G. HOUDEK; Sec. SUSAN P. SIEBERS; publs *Law Library Journal* (quarterly), *Index to Foreign Legal Periodicals* (quarterly), *Directory of Law Libraries* (annually), *AALL Spectrum* (10 times a year).

American Association of Museums: 1575 I St NW, Suite 400, Washington, DC 20005; tel. (202) 289-1818; fax (202) 289-6578; f. 1906; promotes museums as cultural resources and represents interests of museum profession; 15,000 mems; programmes include Accreditation, Museum Assessment, Technical Information Service, Continuing Education, Government Affairs, international programs and AAM/ICOM; the Association is governed by a board of dirs, who are museum professionals; Pres. and CEO EDWARD ABLE, Jr.; Chair. W. RICHARD WEST; publs *Museum News* (every 2 months), *Aviso* (monthly), *The Official Museum Directory* (annually), *Annual Report*.

American Library Association: 50 East Huron St, Chicago, IL 60611; tel. (312) 944-6780; telex 4909992000; fax (312) 440-9374; f. 1876; 55,000 mems; library of c. 24,000 vols; Exec. Dir WILLIAM R. GORDON; publs *American Libraries* (monthly), *Booklist* (fortnightly), *Choice* (monthly), *Information Technology and Libraries* (quarterly), *College and Research Libraries* (every 2 months), *Library Resources and Technical Services* (quarterly), *School Library Media Quarterly, Journal of Youth Services* (quarterly), *Library Technology Reports* (every 2 months), *RQ* (quarterly), *Newsletter on Intellectual Freedom* (every 2 months), monographs, reference works and over 20 other serial publications.

American Society for Information Science (ASIS): 8720 Georgia Ave, #501 Silver Spring, MD 20910; tel. (301) 495-0900; fax (301) 495-0810; f. 1937; concerned with the development of advanced methodologies and techniques that contribute to the more efficient use of information; acts as a bridge between research and development and the requirements of diverse types of information systems; comprises managers, designers and users of information systems and technology; over 4,700 mems; Pres. DEBORA SHAW; Exec. Dir RICHARD HILL; publs *Journal, Bulletin* (every 2 months), *Annual Review of Information Science and Technology, Annual Proceedings.*

American Theological Library Association: fax (847) 869-8513; f. 1947, inc. 1973; 750 mems; Pres. M. PATRICK GRAHAM; Exec. Dir DENNIS A. NORLIN, ATLA, 820 Church St, Suite 400, Evanston, IL 60201; tel. (847) 869-7788; publs *Proceedings* (annually), *Newsletter* (quarterly), *Religion Index I: Periodical Literature* (2 a year), *Religion Index II: Multi-Author Works* (annually), *Index to Book Reviews in Religion* (quarterly), *Research in Ministry: an Index to Doctor of Ministry Reports, ATLA Religion Database* (CD-ROM, 2 a year), etc.

Art Libraries Society of North America (ARLIS/NA): 4101 Lake Boone Trail, Suite 201, Raleigh, NC 27607-7509; tel. (919) 787-5181; fax (919) 787-4916; f. 1972; sponsors conferences and workshops, distributes publications, grants awards for art book publishing and student essays on visual librarianship; 20 US and Canadian chapters; 1,365 mems worldwide; affiliated with ARLIS (UK), ARLIS (Australia-New Zealand), ARLIS (Norge), ARLIS (Norden), American Library Asscn, Visual Resources Asscn and College Art Asscn; Pres. JACK ROBERTSON; Exec. Dir PENNEY DEPAS; publs *Art Documentation* (2 a year), *ARLIS/NA Update* (6 a year), *Occasional Papers* (irregular), *Topical Papers* (irregular), *Handbook and List of Members* (annually).

Association for Library and Information Science Education: C/o UM School of Information, 550 E. University Ave (Room 304 West Hall), Ann Arbor, MI 48109-1092; tel. (313) 936-9812; fax (313) 764-2475; f. 1915; 83 institutional mems, 650 personal mems; Exec. Dir EMILY LENHART; publs *Journal of Education for Library and Information Science* (quarterly), *Library and Information Science Education Statistical Report* (annually).

Association of Academic Health Sciences Library Directors: c/o Houston Academy of Medicine—Texas Medical Center Library, 1133 M. D. Anderson Blvd, Houston, TX 77030; tel. (713) 790-7060; fax (713) 790-7052; f. 1978; 125 mems; Pres. JUDITH MESSERLE; Sec. SANDRA WILSON; publs *AAHSLD News, Annual Report, Annual Statistics of Medical School Libraries in the United States and Canada, Membership Directory.*

Association of Art Museum Directors: POB 10082, Savannah, GA 31412; f. 1916 to promote the development of a scholarly and creative role for art museums and their directors in the cultural life of the nation; to apply its members' knowledge and experience in the field of art to the promotion of the public good; to encourage communication among art museums and their directors; 150 mems; Pres. RALPH T. COE; Sec. THOMAS N. MAYTHAM.

Association of Research Libraries: 21 Dupont Circle, Suite 800, Washington, DC 20036; tel. (202) 296-2296; f. 1932; 121 institutional members: Exec. Dir DUANE E. WEBSTER; publs *ARL Newsletter, ARL Salary Survey, ARL Statistics, ARL Proceedings.*

Association of Visual Science Librarians: f. 1968 to foster collective and individual acquisition and dissemination of visual science information, to improve services to those seeking such information and to develop libraries' standards; 70 mems of which 15 outside the USA; Chair. JUDITH SCHAEFFER-YOUNG, Wills Eye Hospital, A. Bedell Library, 900 Walnut St, Philadelphia, PA 19107; tel. (215) 928-3287; publs *Vision Union List of Serials, PhD Theses in Physiological Optics, Guidelines and Standards for Visual Science Libraries serving Optometric Institutions.*

Bibliographical Society of America: POB 1537, Lenox Hill Station, New York, NY 10021; tel. and fax (212) 452-2710; f. 1904, inc. 1927; 1,250 mems; Exec. Sec. MICHELLE RANDALL; publ. *Papers* (quarterly).

Bibliographical Society of the University of Virginia: c/o University of Virginia Library, Charlottesville, VA 22903; f. 1947; an international society of bibliographers; 600 mems; Sec.-Treas. PENELOPE WEISS; publ. *Studies in Bibliography* (annually).

California Library Association: 717 K St, Suite 300, Sacramento, CA 95814-3477; tel. (916) 447-8541; f. 1896; 3,000 mems; Exec. Dir MARY SUE FERRELL; Pres. JANET K. MINAMI; publ. *California Libraries* (monthly).

California School Library Association: 1499 Old Bayshore Hwy, Suite 142, Burlingame, CA 94010; Pres. SUSAN MARTIMO CHOI; publ. *CSLA Journal* (2 a year).

Catholic Library Association: f. 1921; 1,000 mems; Exec. Dir. JEAN R. BOSTLEY; 100 North St, Suite 224, Pittsfield, MA 01201-5109; tel. (413) 443-2CLA; fax (413) 442-2CLA; e-mail cla@vgernet.net; publs *Catholic Library World* (quarterly), *Catholic Periodical and Literature Index* (quarterly).

Commission on Preservation and Access: 1400 16th St, NW, Suite 740, Washington, DC 20036-2217; tel. (202) 939-3400; fax (202) 939-3407; f. 1986 to foster, develop and support systematic and purposeful collaboration among libraries, archives and allied organizations in order to insure the preservation of the human record in all formats and to provide enhanced access to scholarly information; Pres. DEANNA MARCUM; publ. *Newsletter* (monthly).

Council on Library Resources: 1400 16th St NW, Suite 510, Washington, DC 20036-2217; tel. (202) 483-7474; fax (202) 483-6410; f. 1956; to develop resources and services of libraries and information services; Pres. W. DAVID PENNIMAN; publs *Annual Report, CLR Reports* (irregular).

Medical Library Association: Six N Michigan Ave, Suite 300, Chicago, IL 60602; tel. (312) 419-9094; fax (312) 419-8950; f. 1898; 5,000 mems; serves society by improving health through the provision of information for the delivery of health care, the education of health professionals, the conduct of research, and the public's understanding of health; 3,600 individual, 1,400 institutional mems; Exec. Dir CARLA J. FUNK; publs *Bulletin* (quarterly), *MLA News* (monthly), *Directory* (annually), etc.

Music Library Association: POB 487, Canton, MA 02021-0487; tel. (617) 828-8450; fax (617) 828-8915; e-mail acadsvc@aol.com; f. 1931; 2,900 mems; Exec. Sec. BONNA BOETTCHER; publs *Notes* (quarterly), *Music Cataloging Bulletin* (monthly), *MLA Newsletter* (quarterly), *Index Series* (irregular), *Brief Rules for the Cataloging of Music, Technical Reports—Information for Music Media Specialists* (irregular).

Society of American Archivists: f. 1936; a professional association for archivists and institutions interested in the preservation and use of archives, manuscripts and current records; 3,800 mems (international); Pres. NICHOLAS BURCKEL; Exec. Dir SUSAN E. FOX, 600 S. Federal, Suite 504, Chicago, IL 60605; tel. (312) 922-0140; fax (312) 347-1452; publs *The American Archivist* (quarterly), *Archival Outlook* (6 a year).

Special Libraries Association: 1700 18th St, NW, Washington, DC 20009; tel. (202) 234-4700; f. 1909; activities: professional development, resume referral service, employment clearing-house and career advisory service (at annual conference only), chapters and division services, book publishing, government relations, public relations; Information Resources Center provides telephone reference service; research; 14,000 mems; specialized library of 3,000 vols; Exec. Dir D. R. BENDER; publs include *Information Outlook* (monthly).

Theatre Library Association: f. 1937; 500 mems; Pres. GERALDINE DUCLOW; Treas. RICHARD M. BUCK, NYPL for the Performing Arts, 111 Amsterdam Ave, New York, NY 10023; tel. (212) 870-1670; publs *Broadside* (quarterly), *Performing Arts Resources* (annually).

ECONOMICS, LAW AND POLITICS

Academy of Political Science: 475 Riverside Drive, Suite 1274, New York, NY 10115-1274; tel. (212) 870-2500; fax (212) 870-2202; f. 1880; 8,000 mems; Pres. and Exec. Dir DEMETRIOS CARALEY; publ. *Political Science Quarterly*.

American Academy of Political and Social Science: 3937 Chestnut St, Philadelphia, PA 19104; f. 1889; 5,000 mems; Pres. (vacant); Business Man. MARY PARKER; publ. *The Annals* (every 2 months).

American Accounting Association: 5717 Bessie Drive, Sarasota, FL 34233-2399; tel. (813) 921-7747; fax (813) 923-4093; f. 1916; professional society for educators, practitioners and students of accounting; 13,000 mems; Pres. KATHERINE SCHIPPER; Exec. Dir PAUL L. GERHARDT; publs *The Accounting Review, Accounting Horizons, Issues in Accounting Education,* monographs, surveys.

American Arbitration Association: 140 West 51st St, New York, NY 10020; tel. (212) 484-4000; telex 12463; fax (212) 765-4874; f. 1926; a public-service, not-for-profit org. offering a broad range of dispute resolution services to business executives, attorneys, individual employees, trade asscns, unions, management, consumers, families, communities and all levels of govt; also conducts seminars, conferences, etc.; 5,400 mems, over 50,000 arbitrators on national panel; library of 16,000 vols, 330 periodical titles; Pres. ROBERT COULSON; publs *Arbitration Journal, Arbitration Times, The Claims Forum, Forum New York, Lawyers' Arbitration Letter* (quarterly), *Summary of Labor Arbitration Awards, Arbitration in the Schools, Labor Arbitration in Government, New York No-Fault Arbitration Reports* (monthly), *Annual Report.*

American Bar Association: 750 North Lake Shore Dr., Chicago, IL 60611; f. 1878; 310,700 mems; library of 50,000 vols; Chief Operating Officer THOMAS H. GONSER; publs *Journal* (monthly), *Reports* (annually), *Bar Leader* (every 2 months).

American Economic Association: 2014 Broadway, Suite 305, Nashville, TN 37203-2418; f. 1885 to encourage economic discussion, research and the issue of publications on economic subjects; 19,000 mems and 6,000 subscribers; Sec. JOHN SIEGFRIED; publs *American Economic Review, Papers and Proceedings, Journal of Economic Literature, Index of Economic Articles, Journal of Economic Perspectives, Job Openings for Economists.*

American Finance Association: c/o Stern School of Business, New York University, 44 W. Fourth St, Suite 9–19°, New York, NY 10012; f. 1940 to make available knowledge on current developments in the field of finance; 4,000 mems; Sec-Treas. Dr MICHAEL KEENAN; publ. *Journal of Finance* (5 a year).

American Judicature Society: 180 N. Michigan Ave, Suite 600, Chicago, IL 60601; tel. (312) 558-6900; f. 1913 to promote the effective administration of justice; 10,000 mems; Exec. Dir SANDRA RATCLIFF DAFFRON; publ. *Judicature* (every two months).

American Law Institute: 4025 Chestnut St, Philadelphia, PA 19104; tel. (215) 243-1600; fax (215) 243-1664; f. 1923; promotes the clarification and simplification of the law; research work; publishes Restatements of the Law, and model and uniform codifications; 3,685 mems; library of 15,000 vols; Pres. CHARLES ALAN WRIGHT; Dir GEOFFREY C. HAZARD, Jr; publ. *Proceedings of ALI Annual Meetings* (annually).

American Law Institute-American Bar Association Committee on Continuing Professional Education: 4025 Chestnut St, Philadelphia, PA 19104; tel. (215) 243-1600; fax (215) 243-1664; f. 1947 to organize, develop and carry out a national programme of continuing education of the bar; library of 15,000 vols; Exec. Dir RICHARD E. CARTER; publs *AILTO Insider* (quarterly), *The Practical Lawyer* (8 a year), *ALI-ABA CLE Review* (monthly), *ALI-ABA Course Materials Journal, ALI-ABA Estate Planning Course Materials Journal, CLE Journal and Register, The Practical Real Estate Lawyer, The Practical Litigator* (all every 2 months), *The Practical Tax Lawyer* (quarterly), *The Audio Litigator* (audiocassettes) (quarterly).

American Peace Society: 1319 Eighteenth St, NW, Washington, DC 20036-1802; f. 1828; Pres. Dr EVRON M. KIRKPATRICK; Sec. L. EUGENE HEDBERG; publ. *World Affairs* (quarterly).

American Political Science Association: 1527 New Hampshire Ave, NW, Washington, DC 20036; tel. (202) 483-2512; fax (202) 483-2657; e-mail apsa@apsanet.org; f. 1903; 14,500 mems; Exec. Dir CATHERINE E. RUDDER; publs *The American Political Science Review* (quarterly), *PS: Political Science and Politics* (quarterly).

American Society for Political and Legal Philosophy: c/o The Sec., Prof. JUDITH WAGNER DECEW, Philosophy Department, Clark University, Worcester, MA 01610; f. 1955; 500 mems; Pres. FRANK MICHELMAN; publ. *NOMOS* (Yearbook).

American Society for Public Administration: 1120 G St NW, Suite 700, Washington, DC 20005; tel. (202) 393-7878; fax (202) 638-4952; f. 1939; 11,000 mems; national and regional conferences, management institutes; chapters in local centres; Exec. Dir MARY HAMILTON; publs *PA Times* (monthly), *Public Administration Review* (every 2 months).

American Society of International Law: 2223 Massachusetts Ave, NW, Washington, DC 20008; f. 1906, inc. 1950; 4,300 mems; library of 22,000 vols; Pres. THOMAS M. FRANCK; Exec. Dir CHARLOTTE KA; publs *International Legal Materials* (every 2 months), *The American Journal of International Law* (quarterly), *Proceedings* (annually), *Newsletter,* books and occasional publications.

American Statistical Association: 1429 Duke St, Alexandria, VA 22314; tel. (703) 684-1221; fax (703) 684-7037; f. 1839; 18,200 mems; Exec. Dir RAY A. WALLER; publs (all journals are quarterly) *Journal of the American Statistical Association, The American Statistician, Technometrics, Amstat News* (11 a year), *Journal of Educational and Behavioral Statistics, Current Index to Statistics, Journal of Business and Economic Statistics, Journal of Computational and Graphical Statistics, Journal of Agricultural, Biological and Environmental Statistics, Chance Magazine* (quarterly), *Stats Magazine for Students* (3 a year).

Association of American Law Schools: 1201 Connecticut Ave NW, Suite 800, Washington, DC 20036; tel. (202) 296-8851; fax (202) 296-8869; f. 1900 for the improvement of the legal profession through legal education; 160 institutional mems; Exec. Dir CARL C. MONK; publs *Proceedings* (annually), *Directory of Law Teachers* (annually), *Journal of Legal Education* (quarterly), *Newsletter* (quarterly), *Placement Bulletin* (irregular).

Atlantic Council of the United States: 910 17th St NW, Suite 1000, Washington, DC 20006; fax (202) 463-7241; e-mail info@acgate.acus.org; f. 1961; national, non-partisan, non-profit public policy centre that addresses the advancement of U.S. global interests within the Atlantic and Pacific communities; the council engages the U.S. executive and legislative branches, the national and international business community, media and academia, and diplomats and other foreign leaders in an integrated programme of policy studies and round-table discussions, briefings, dialogues and conferences, designed to encourage its selected membership and other constituencies to reflect and plan for the future; funded by corporations, foundations, private individuals, and government grants and contracts; Pres. DAVID C. ACHESON; publs *Bulletin, Policy and Occasional Papers.*

Carnegie Endowment for International Peace: 1779 Massachusetts Ave NW, Washington, DC 20036; tel. (202) 862-7900; fax (202) 332-0925; f. 1910; an operating foundation that conducts its own programmes of research, discussion and education in international affairs and American foreign policy; library of *c.* 8,000 vols; has established Center for Russian and Eurasian Programs in Moscow; Pres. JESSICA T. MATHEWS; 27 trustees; publ. *Foreign Policy* (quarterly).

Century Foundation: 41 East 70th St, New York, NY 10021; tel. (212) 535-4441; f. 1919 by the late Edward A. Filene as an endowed foundation for public policy research on major economic, political and social institutions and issues; Chair. of the Board of Trustees THEODORE D. SORENSEN; Vice-Chair. of the Board and Chair. of Exec. Cttee JAMES A. LEACH; Pres. RICHARD C. LEONE; publs *Annual Report.*

Council for European Studies: 807–807A, International Affairs Bldg, Columbia University, New York, NY 10027; tel. (212) 854-4172; fax (212) 854-8808; f. 1970; a consortium of European studies programs at over 80 universities in the USA; affiliated with Columbia Univ.; aims to encourage greater scholarly interest in Europe, to emphasize the commonality of problems that face the nations of Europe and North America; sponsors research, information services, graduate student training; holds conferences, etc.; mems: 850 individuals, 84 universities; Exec. Dir Dr IOANNIS SINANOGLOU; publs *European Studies Newsletter* (every 2 months), *Fellowship Guide to Western Europe,* Guides to libraries and archives of Germany, France and Italy.

Council of State Governments: 2760 Research Park Drive, POB 11910, Lexington, KY 40578; tel. (606) 244-8000; fax (606) 244-8001; f. 1933; offices in Washington, DC, New York, Atlanta, Chicago and San Francisco; a non-partisan organization established by the States for service to the States; Exec. Dir DANIEL M. SPRAGUE; publs *State Government News* (monthly), *Suggested State Legislation* (annually), *State Government Research Checklist* (every 2 months), *CSG State Directories* (annually).

Council on Foreign Relations, Inc.: 58 East 68th St, New York, NY 10021; tel. (212) 734-0400; telex 239852; fax (212) 861-1789; f. 1921; 2,905 mems; Foreign Relations Library of 18,000 vols, 300 periodicals, clippings files; Chair. PETER G. PETERSON; Pres. LESLIE H. GELB; publs *Foreign Affairs* (6 a year), *Critical Issues*, and books on major issues of US foreign policy.

Economic History Association: c/o Dept of Economics, University of Kansas, 226A Summerfield Hall, Lawrence, KS 66045; f. 1940 to encourage and promote teaching, research and publication in all fields of economic history; 1,200 individual mems, 2,210 library mems; Exec. Dir THOMAS WEISS; publ. *Journal of Economic History* (quarterly).

Federal Bar Association: 1815 H St, NW, Suite 408, Washington, DC 20006; tel. (202) 638-0252; fax (202) 775-0295; f. 1920; 15,000 mems; 99 Chapters; over 100 committees in fields of federal law; Exec. Dir MICHAEL E. CAMPIGLIA; publ. *The Federal Lawyer.*

Foreign Policy Association, Inc.: 470 Park Ave South, New York, NY 10016; tel. (212) 481-8100; fax (212) 481-9275; f. 1918; object: to promote citizen education in world affairs, to assist organizations, communities and educational institutions, to develop programmes for citizen understanding and constructive participation in world affairs, and to advance public understanding of foreign policy problems through national programmes and publications of a non-partisan character based upon the principles of freedom, justice and democracy; publs *Headline Series* (quarterly), *Great Decisions* (yearly).

History of Economics Society: c/o Sec.-Treas. Prof. J. PATRICK RAINES, Dept of Economics, University of Richmond, Richmond, VA 23173; f. 1973 to promote interest and inquiry into the history of economics and related parts of intellectual history; 750 mems in the USA and other countries; publ. *Bulletin* (2 a year).

Institute for Mediterranean Affairs: 428 East 83rd St, New York, NY 10028; established under charter of the University of the State of New York to evolve a better understanding of the historical background and contemporary political and socio-economic problems of the nations and regions that border on the Mediterranean Sea; to analyse the various tensions in the Eastern Mediterranean and to investigate the basic problems of the area; special attention is given to the Israeli-Arab conflict; 250 Academic Advisory mems; Pres. Prof. SEYMOUR M. FINGER; Chair. (vacant); Dir SAMUEL A. MERLIN; publ. *The Mediterranean Survey* (bulletin, irregular).

Institute of Management Sciences, The (TIMS): 2 Charles St, Suite 300, Providence, RI 02904; f. 1953; 8,000 mems; Pres. GARY LILIEN; publs *Management Science* (monthly), *Interfaces* (every 2 months), *Mathematics of Operations Research* (quarterly), *Marketing*

Science (quarterly), *Information Systems Research* (quarterly), *Organization Science* (quarterly).

Society of Actuaries: 475 Martingale Rd, Suite 800, Schaumburg, IL 60173; tel. (847) 706-3541; fax (847) 706-3599; f. 1949; educational, research and professional membership society for actuaries in life and health insurance and pension planning; 16,541 mems; library of 3,900 vols; special collections reports and transactions from U.S., Canadian and international actuarial organizations; Dir of Communications LINDA M. DELGADILLO; publs *The North American Actuarial Journal* (4 a year), *The Actuary* (newsletter, monthly), *The Future Actuary* (newsletter, 3 a year).

World Peace Foundation: One Eliot Square, Cambridge, MA 02138-4952; tel. (617) 491-5085; fax (617) 491-8588; f. 1910; an operating foundation which does not give outside grants; policy-oriented studies in world affairs; international organization; Pres. ROBERT I. ROTBERG; sponsors publ. *International Organization* (quarterly).

EDUCATION

Alfred P. Sloan Foundation: 630 Fifth Ave, New York, NY 10111; f. 1934; makes grants for projects in science and technology, standard of living and economic performance, and education and careers in science and technology; Pres. RALPH E. GOMORY; publ. *Report* (annually).

American Association for Higher Education: One Dupont Circle, Suite 360, Washington, DC 20036; tel. (202) 293-6440; fax (202) 293-0073; f. 1969; sponsors projects and programs that will improve the quality of American higher education; 9,000 mems; Pres. MARGARET A. MILLER; publs *Change* (every 2 months), *AAHE Bulletin* (monthly Sept. to June).

American Association of State Colleges and Universities: One Dupont Circle NW, Suite 700, Washington, DC 20036-1192; tel. (202) 293-7070; fax (202) 296-5819; f. 1961 to improve higher education within its member institutions through co-operative planning, through studies and research on common educational problems, and through the development of a more unified programme of action; 375 mems; 30 assoc. mems; Pres. JAMES B. APPLEBERRY; publs *Memo* (monthly), *OFP Reports* (*Office of Federal Programs*).

American Association of University Professors: 1012 14th St, NW, Washington, DC 20005; tel. and fax (202) 737-5900; f. 1915; 44,000 mems; Pres. JAMES E. PERLEY; Gen. Sec. MARY BURGAN; publ. *Academe: Bulletin of the AAUP* (every 2 months).

American Council on Education: One Dupont Circle, Washington, DC 20036; tel. (202) 939-9300; fax (202) 833-4760; f. 1918; 1,800 member institutions and associations; Pres. ROBERT H. ATWELL; publs *Educational Record* (quarterly), *Higher Education and National Affairs* (fortnightly); *ACE/Oryx Series on Higher Education*.

American Vocational Association, Inc.: 1410 King St, Alexandria, VA 22314; tel. (703) 683-3111; fax (703) 683-7424; f. 1925; 40,000 mems; Exec. Dir BRET LOVEJOY; publs *Techniques* (magazine), *Vocational Education Weekly, School To Work Reporter*.

Association of American Colleges and Universities: 1818 R St, NW, Washington, DC 20009; tel. (202) 387-3760; fax (202) 265-9532; f. 1915 to improve undergraduate curriculum through research, projects, publications and meetings; 675 mems; Pres. PAULA P. BROWNLEE; publ. *Liberal Education* (quarterly).

Association of American Universities: One Dupont Circle, NW, Washington, DC 20036; tel. (202) 466-5030; f. 1900; 60 mems; Pres. Dr C. J. PINGS.

Carnegie Corporation of New York: 437 Madison Ave, New York, NY 10022; tel. (212) 371-3200; f. 1911 by Andrew Carnegie for the advancement and diffusion of knowledge and understanding among peoples of the US and, with subsequent amendment of the charter, of some of the current or former British overseas Commonwealth; primary interests: education, international affairs, democracy; 16 trustees; Pres. VARTAN GREGORIAN; Sec. DOROTHY WILLS KNAPP; publs *Annual, Carnegie Quarterly, Carnegie Newsline*.

Council for Basic Education: 1319 F St NW, Suite 900, Washington, DC 20004-1152; tel. (202) 347-4171; fax (202) 347-5047; f. 1956; a private, non-profit organization dedicated to strengthening the teaching and learning of the basic subjects of the liberal arts; 7,500 mems; Pres. CHRISTOPHER CROSS; publs *Basic Education* (monthly), *Perspectives* (quarterly), reports.

Ford Foundation: 320 East 43rd St, New York, NY 10017; f. 1936; a non-profit corporation, dedicated to the advancement of human welfare, principally by granting funds to institutions and organizations for experimental, demonstration and developmental efforts; Chair. of Board HENRY B. SCHACHT; Pres. SUSAN V. BERRESFORD; publs *Annual Report, Ford Foundation Report, Current Interests of the Ford Foundation*.

Foundation Center, The: 79 Fifth Ave, New York City, NY 10003; tel. (212) 620-4230; offices in Washington, San Francisco, Cleveland, Atlanta; f. 1956; makes available information about philanthropic foundations; maintains a full collection of foundation reports; library of 2,500 vols, 3,250 pamphlets and articles, 500 foundation reports, computer files of foundation grants, aperture card system containing foundation IRS returns; Pres. SARA ENGELHARDT; publs *Foundation Grants Index* (quarterly, and annual cumulation), *Foundation Directory* (annually), *Foundation 1000* (annually), *Guide to US Foundations, Their Officers, Trustees and Donors* (annually), *Foundation Grants to Individuals* (every 2 years), *Foundation Fundamentals, Grant Guides in 30 Subjects* (annually).

Institute of International Education: 809 United Nations Plaza, New York, NY 10017; tel. (212) 883-8200; telex 175977; fax (212) 984-5452; f. 1919; private non-profit agency which develops, administers and programs educational and cultural exchange between the USA and more than 150 other countries; conducts special studies and seminars to analyse and evaluate development in the field of educational exchange; six regional offices, overseas offices in Bangkok, Budapest, Jakarta, Hong Kong, Mexico City and Moscow; library of 5,000 vols; information centre; Pres. RICHARD KRASNO; publs *Annual Report, Open Doors, Vacation Study Abroad, Academic Year Abroad* (all annually), *Funding for US Study, Financial Resources for International Study, English Language and Orientation Programs*.

International Montessori Society: 912 Thayer Ave, Silver Spring, MD 20910; tel. (301) 589-1127; f. 1979 to support the effective application of Montessori principles throughout the world; teacher training, consultation, information dissemination, conferences; 300 mems; small library; Exec. Dir LEE HAVIS; publs *Montessori Observer* (quarterly), *Montessori News* (2 a year).

Kellogg, W.K., Foundation: One East Michigan Avenue, Battle Creek, MI 49017-4005; tel. (616) 968-1611; telex 4953028; fax (616) 968-0413; f. 1930; administers funds for non-partisan, non-profit youth, higher education, leadership, health and agricultural activities in the public interest; Pres./Chief Exec. Officer WILLIAM C. RICHARDSON; publ. *Annual Report*.

National Academy of Education: New York University, School of Education, 726 Broadway (5th Floor), New York, NY 10003-9580; tel. (212) 998-9035; fax (212) 995-4435; f. 1965; 138 mems; Pres. ELLEN CONDLIFFE LAGEMANN; Exec Dir BEVERLY O. FONNOR.

National Education Association of the United States: 1201 16th St, NW, Washington, DC 20036; f. 1857; 2,000,000 mems, 100,000 life mems; Exec. Dir DON CAMERON; Dir in each State; publs *Today's Education* (annually), *NEA Today* (9 a year), *NEA Now* (weekly).

National Society for the Study of Education: 5835 Kimbark Ave, Chicago, IL 60637; tel. (773) 702-1582; fax (773) 702-0248; f. 1901; 1,500 mems; Sec. KENNETH J. REHAGE; publ. *Yearbook*.

Philosophy of Education Society: c/o Sec.-Treas. PAUL WAGNER, Jr, Box 269, University of Houston–Clear Lake, 2700 Bay Area Blvd, Houston, TX 77058; f. 1941; 550 mems; exists to promote discussion and analysis of philosophy and education and to improve the teaching and research in philosophy and education; publs *Educational Theory* (quarterly), *Proceedings of the PES* (annually), *Philosophy of Education Newsletter* (every 6 months).

Rockefeller Foundation: 420 Fifth Ave, New York, NY 10018; tel. (212) 869-8500; f. 1913 to promote the well-being of mankind; makes grants in the fields of: agriculture, health, population sciences, the global environment, African initiatives, organized under the Int. Program to Support Science-Based Development; arts and humanities; equal opportunity; school reform; Chair. of Board ALICE STONE ILCHMAN; Pres. GORDON CONWAY. publs *Annual Report, Program Guidelines*.

Woodrow Wilson International Center for Scholars: 1000 Jefferson Drive SW, Washington, DC 20560; tel. (202) 357-2429; telex 264729; fax (202) 357-4439; f. 1968 'to symbolize and strengthen the fruitful relation between the world of learning and the world of public affairs'; residential fellowships offered for projects in the humanities and social sciences for up to 40 scholars, approx. half from the USA, of both academic and non-academic occupations; periods of study of up to one year; library of 22,000 vols, 400 periodicals; Chair. of Board of Trustees JOSEPH H. FLOM; Dir DEAN W. ANDERSON (acting). See also Smithsonian Institution.

FINE AND PERFORMING ARTS

American Council for the Arts: 1 East 53rd St, New York, NY 10022-4201; tel. (212) 223-2787; fax (212) 223-4415; f. 1960 to promote the interests of the arts; 1,500 mems; library of 5,000 items; Pres. and CEO LUIS R. CANCEL; Chair. DONALD R. GREENE; publ. *ACA UpDate* (monthly).

American Federation of Arts: 41 East 65th St, New York, NY 10021; tel. (212) 988-7700; fax (212) 861-2487; f. 1909; non-profit art museum service organization; aims to broaden the knowledge and appreciation of the arts of the past and present; organizes art exhibitions, with accompanying catalogues, which travel throughout the USA and abroad; specialized support services to more than 500 mem. institutions; management training through the Getty Leadership Institute for Museum Management; Pres. JAN MAYER; Chair. ROBERT M. MELTZER; Dir SERENA RATTAZZI; publ. *Memo to Members* (6 a year).

American Musicological Society: 201 South 34th St, Philadelphia, PA 19104-6313; tel. (215) 898-8698; fax (215) 573-3673; e-mail ams@sas.upenn.edu; f. 1934; 3,500 mems; Pres. RUTH SOLIE; Exec. Dir ROBERT JUDD; publs *Journal* (3 a year), *Newsletter* (2 a year), *Directory* (annually).

American Society for Aesthetics: Marquette University, Cudahy Hall (Room 404), POB 1881, Milwaukee, WI 53201-1881; tel. (414) 288-7831; fax (414) 288-7889; f. 1942; aesthetics and the arts; 1,000 mems; Pres. TED COHEN; Sec. CURTIS L. CARTER; publs *Journal of Aesthetics and Art Criticism* (quarterly), *Newsletter*.

American Society for Theatre Research: c/o Dept of Theatre, Brown University, Providence, RI 02912; tel. (401) 521-6293; f. 1956; serves needs of theatre historians and fosters knowledge of the theatre in the USA and overseas; 806 mems; Pres. Prof. MARGARET KNAPP; Sec. Prof. DON WILMETH; publs *ASTR Newsletter*, *Theatre Survey* (2 a year).

American Society of Composers, Authors and Publishers (ASCAP): 1 Lincoln Plaza, New York, NY 10023; tel. (212) 621-6000; telex 710-581-2084; fax (212) 595-3342; f. 1914; issues licences for public performance of members' copyright works; mems: 40,000 songwriters and composers, 20,000 music publishers; a non-profit-making society; Pres. MARILYN BERGMAN; publs *ASCAP in Action*, *ASCAP Biographical Dictionary*.

Archives of American Art: Smithsonian Institution, 8th and G Sts, NW, Washington, DC 20560; tel. (202) 357-2781; fax (202) 786-2608; f. 1954; collection and preservation of documents relating to the history of art in America; interviewing programme; microfilm interlibrary loan scheme; 1,900 mems, 10,000,000 items; regional centres in Boston, Detroit, New York City and Los Angeles; Dir RICHARD J. WATTENMAKER; publ. *Journal* (quarterly).

Association for Communication Administration: 5105 Backlick Rd, F, Annandale, VA 22003; tel. (703) 750-0533; fax (703) 914-9471; f. 1971; 325 mems; Exec. Dir. JAMES L. GAUDINO; publ. *Journal of the Association for Communication Administration (JACA)* (3 a year).

Center for Creative Photography: University of Arizona, Tucson, AZ 85721-0103; tel. (520) 621-7968; fax (520) 621-9444; e-mail oncenter@ccp.arizona.edu; f. 1975; a unique resource for the study and history of photography; extensive collection of prints and other materials related to the life and works of 20th-century photographers; comprises a computer-catalogued archive; houses the lifetime archives of Ansel Adams, Wynn Bullock, Harry Callahan, Dean Brown, Louise Dahl-Wolfe, Andreas Feininger, Sonya Noskowiak, Aaron Siskind, Frederick Sommer, W. Eugene Smith, Edward Weston, etc.; open to the public; library of 11,000 vols, 100 periodicals; Dir TERENCE PITTS; publs *The Archive*, guide series, bibliography series, catalogues.

College Art Association: 275 Seventh Ave, New York, NY 10001; tel. (212) 691-1051; fax (212) 627-2381; f. 1911 to further scholarship and excellence in the teaching and practice of art and art history; 13,000 individual, 2,000 institutional mems; Exec. Dir SUSAN BALL; publs *Art Bulletin* (quarterly), *Art Journal* (quarterly), *CAA News*, monographs.

Graphic Arts Technical Foundation: 4615 Forbes Ave, Pittsburgh, PA 15213-3796; tel. (412) 621-6941; fax (412) 621-3049; f. 1924; 7,000 mems; library of over 6,000 vols and periodicals; non-profit scientific research and technical education organization serving the international graphic communications community; conducts technical workshops, inplant assessments, seminars worldwide on various aspects of graphic communications; Pres. GEORGE H. RYAN; publs *GATFWORLD* (every 2 months), *SecondSight* (technical reports), *Learning Modules*.

National Academy of Design: 1083 Fifth Ave, New York, NY 10128; tel. (212) 369-4880; fax (212) 360-6795; f. 1825; membership composed exclusively of artists; sections: painting, sculpture, water colour, graphic arts, architecture; art museum, art library and art school attached; Pres. WILLIAM KING; Corresp. Sec. MORTON KAISH; Dir EDWARD P. GALLAGHER.

National Sculpture Society: 1177 Avenue of the Americas, New York, NY 10036; tel. (212) 764-5645; fax (212) 764-5651; f. 1893, inc. 1896; to disseminate knowledge of American sculpture through research, exhibitions, educational programmes and prize-giving; 4,500 mems, 320 professional mems; Exec. Dir GWEN PIER; publ. *Sculpture Review* (quarterly).

Society for Ethnomusicology, Inc.: Morrison Hall 005, Indiana University, Bloomington, IN 47405-2501; 2,300 mems; Pres. KAY K. SHELEMAY; Sec. JUDITH GRAY (tel. (812) 855-6672, fax (812) 855-6673); publs *Ethnomusicology*, *Newsletter* (quarterly), special series.

HISTORY, GEOGRAPHY AND ARCHAEOLOGY

American Antiquarian Society: 185 Salisbury St, Worcester, MA 01609; tel. (508) 755-5221; f. 1812; a learned society and research library concerned with American history before 1877; 680,000 vols, 2,000 linear ft MSS collections, 3 million newspaper issues, 200,300 items of graphic art; 656 mems; Pres. ELLEN S. DUNLAP; publs *Proceedings* (2 a year), *Almanac* (society newsletter), *The Book: Newsletter of the Program in the History of the Book in American Culture*, monographs, etc.

American Association for State and Local History: 530 Church St, Suite 600, Nashville, TN 37219; tel. (615) 255-2971; f. 1940; 6,000 mems; successor to Conference of Historical Societies; objects: exchange of information on local and regional history and historical societies, and dissemination in scholarly and popular publications of professional material and interpretative articles; Exec. Dir TERRY L. DAVIS; publs *History News* (quarterly; professional news), *History News Dispatch* (monthly).

American Catholic Historical Association: The Catholic University of America, Washington, DC 20064; tel. and fax (202) 319-5079); e-mail cua-chracha@cua.edu; f. 1919 to promote interest in the history of the Catholic Church broadly considered; research work; 1,105 mems; Sec.-Treas. ROBERT TRISCO; publ. *Catholic Historical Review* (quarterly).

American Historical Association: 400 A St, SE, Washington, DC 20003; tel. (202) 544-2422; fax (202) 544-8307; f. 1884; 16,000 mems; Pres. JOSEPH C. MILLER; Exec. Dir SANDRIA B. FREITAG; publs *American Historical Review* (5 a year), *Perspectives* (9 a year), *Annual Report, Program*, various historical pamphlets.

American Irish Historical Society: 991 Fifth Ave, New York, NY 10028; tel. (212) 288-2263; fax (212) 628-7927; f. 1897; research in the history of the Irish in America; 800 mems; library of 10,000 vols; Dir PAUL RUPPERT; Librarian Fr JOS. O'HARE; publ. *The Recorder* (2 a year).

American Jewish Historical Society: 2 Thornton Rd, Waltham, MA 02154; tel. (617) 891-8110; e-mail ajhs@ajhs.org; f. 1892 to collect and publish material bearing upon the history of Jews in America and to promote the study of American-Jewish history; 3,200 mems; library of 40,000 vols, 30,000,000 MSS, contains many rare and valuable MSS, some of the 16th, 17th and 18th centuries, American-Jewish periodicals of the 18th, 19th and 20th centuries; Pres. JUSTIN L. WYNER; Chair. SHELDON S. COHEN; Exec. Dir MICHAEL J. FELDBERG; publs *American Jewish History*, monographs, *Heritage* (occasional newsletter).

American Numismatic Society: Broadway at 155th St, New York, NY 10032; tel. (212) 234-3130; fax (212) 234-3381; f. 1858; 2,077 mems; collecting encompasses all periods and fields of interest; specialized library of over 100,000 vols; Pres. ARTHUR A. HOUGHTON; Exec. Dir and Sec. LESLIE A. ELAM; Chief Curator WILLIAM E. METCALF; publs *American Journal of Numismatics* (annually), *Numismatic Literature* (2 a year), *Numismatic Notes and Monographs, Numismatic Studies, Sylloge Nummorum Graecorum, The Collection of the American Numismatic Society, Ancient Coins in the North American Collections, Proceedings of the Coinage of the Americas Conference* (all irregular).

American Society for Eighteenth-Century Studies: Wake Forest University, Winston-Salem, NC 27109; tel. (801) 797-4065; f. 1969, inc. 1970; independent society; works through publications and meetings to foster interest and encourage investigation in the achievements of the 18th century in America and Europe; mems: 50 institutions, 1,077 libraries, 2,500 individuals; Exec. Sec. BYRON R. WELLS; publs *Eighteenth-Century Studies* (quarterly), *Studies in Eighteenth-Century Culture* (annually), *ASECS News Circular* (quarterly).

American Society of Church History: POB 8517, Red Bank, NJ 07701; f. 1888, reorganized 1906; 1,500 mems and 1,475 subscribers; Sec. HENRY W. BOWDEN; publ. *Church History* (quarterly).

Archaeological Institute of America: 656 Beacon St, Boston, MA 02215; tel. (617) 353-9361; fax (617) 353-6550; f. 1879; 11,000 mems; Pres. STEPHEN DYSON; Dir MARK J. MEISTER; publs *American Journal of Archaeology* (quarterly), *Archaeology* (illustrated, every 2 months).

Arizona Archaeological and Historical Society: Arizona State Museum, Univ. of Arizona, Tucson, AZ 85721; f. 1916; 1,150 mems; Pres. MARK SLAUGHTER; Vice-Pres. ALAN FERG; publs *Kiva* (quarterly), *Glyphs* (monthly).

Association of American Geographers: 1710 16th St, NW, Washington, DC 20009-3198; tel. (202) 234-1450; fax (202) 234-2744; e-mail gaia@aag.org; f. 1904; 7,300 mems; Exec. Dir RONALD F. ABLER; publs *Annals* (quarterly), *The Professional Geographer* (quarterly), *AAG Newsletter* (monthly).

Brooklyn Historical Society: 128 Pierrepont St, Brooklyn, NY 11201; tel. (718) 624-0890; fax (718) 875-3869; f. 1863; exhibitions, lectures, tours; includes Shellens Gallery of Brooklyn History; research library of 125,000 vols; 1,250 mems; Pres. JESSIE M. KELLY. (Closed for renovation until spring 2000.)

California Historical Society: 678 Mission St, San Francisco, CA 94105; tel. (415) 357-1848; fax (415) 357-1850; f. 1871; non-profit-making institution; 5,700 mems; library of 55,000 vols, rare MSS, pamphlets and maps, 575,000 historic photographs; Exec. Dir MICHAEL MCCONE; Pres. Board of Trustees STEPHEN L. TABER; publs *California History*, *California Chronicle*.

Dallas Historical Society: Hall of State, Fair Park, Dallas, TX 75226; f. 1922; collection of historical materials; the Society has the custody of the Hall of State (see under Museums), which it operates as a museum and archives of Southwestern United States, Texas and Dallas history; 1,500 mems; library of 14,000 vols, 2,000,000 archive items and 15,000 museum artifacts; Dir NANCY NELSON.

Historical Society of Pennsylvania: 1300 Locust St, Philadelphia, PA 19107; tel. (215) 732-6200; fax (215) 732-2680; e-mail hsppr@aol.com; f. 1824; 2,700 mems; library of 500,000 vols and pamphlets, over 15 million MSS; archives; Pres. SUSAN STITT; Chair. HOWARD H. LEWIS; publ. *The Pennsylvania Magazine of History and Biography* (quarterly).

Maryland Historical Society: 201 West Monument St, Baltimore, MD 21201; tel. (410) 685-3750; fax (410) 385-2105; f. 1844; 5,000 mems; museum and library: see under Museums; Pres. STANARD T. KLINEFELTER; Dir DENNIS A. FIORI; publs *Maryland Historical Magazine* (quarterly), *News and Notes, Maryland Magazine of Genealogy* (2 a year).

Massachusetts Historical Society: 1154 Boylston St, Boston, MA 02215; f. 1791; oldest historical society in US; library: see Libraries; Dir WILLIAM M. FOWLER; Librarian PETER DRUMMEY; publs *Proceedings*, etc.

Medieval Academy of America: 1430 Massachusetts Ave, Cambridge, MA 02138; tel. (617) 491-1622; fax (617) 492-3303; inc. 1925 for the promotion of research, publication and instruction in medieval records, literature, languages, art, archaeology, history, philosophy, science, life, and all other aspects of medieval civilization; 4,100 mems; Pres. THEODORE M. ANDERSSON; Exec. Dir LUKE H. WENGER; publ. *Speculum: A Journal of Medieval Studies* (quarterly).

Minnesota Historical Society: 345 Kellogg Blvd W, St Paul, MN 55102-1906; tel. (612) 296-6126; fax (612) 297-3343; f. 1849; history museum; state historic preservation office; state archives; collection of artefacts; archaeology; 8,000 mems; library of over 500,000 vols; newspaper and audio-visual library, 78,000 cu.ft of MSS; 23 historic sites; Pres. KAREN HUMPHREY; Sec. and Dir NINA ARCHABAL; publs *Minnesota History* (quarterly), *Member News* (6 a year).

National Geographic Society: 17th and M Streets, NW, Washington, DC 20036; f. 1888; organized for the increase and diffusion of geographic knowledge; library: see Libraries; Pres. and CEO REG MURPHY; publs *National Geographic* (monthly), *National Geographic World* (monthly), *National Geographic Traveler* (every 2 months).

New York Historical Society: 2 West 77th St, New York, NY 10024-5194; tel. (212) 873-3400; fax (212) 874-8706; f. 1804; 3,300 mems (all grades); museum of 17th–19th-century American art, antiques and history including portraits, landscapes and genre paintings; library of 630,000 vols, 2,000,000 MSS, 35,000 maps and atlases, large collection of pre-1820 newspapers, sheet music, 25,000 broadsides, *c.* 1 million prints and photographs; Dir B. GOTBAUM.

Omohundro Institute of Early American History and Culture: POB 8781, Williamsburg, VA 23187; tel. (757) 221-1110; fax (757) 221-1047; e-mail ieahc1@facstaff.wm.edu; f. 1943; awards post-doctoral fellowships; library of 7,000 vols, 880 periodicals, 2,000 microfilms; Dir RONALD HOFFMAN; publs *William and Mary Quarterly*, monographs, documents and bibliographies on American history to 1815, *Uncommon Sense* (2 a year).

Oregon Historical Society: 1200 SW Park Ave, Portland, OR 97205-2483; tel. (503) 222-1741; fax (503) 221-2035; e-mail orhist@ohs.org; f. 1873; 8,350 mems; 100,000 books, 2,000,000 photographs, 15,000 maps, thousands of pamphlets, serials and newspapers; original MSS; museum artefacts from neolithic period to discovery, settlement of Oregon Country, Pacific Northwest; Dir CHET ORLOFF; publs *Oregon Historical Quarterly*, *Oregon History Magazine*.

Organization of American Historians: 112 North Bryan St, Bloomington, IN 47408; tel. (812) 855-7311; fax (812) 855-0696; f. 1907 to promote historical study in American history; attached to Indiana University; 9,000 indiv. mems, 2,700 institutional mems; Pres. WILLIAM H. CHAFE; Exec. Dir ARNITA A. JONES; publs *Journal of American History*, *Program for Annual Meeting*, *Newsletter*, *Magazine of History*.

Pilgrim Society: 75 Court St, Plymouth, MA 02360; tel. (508) 746-1620; f. 1820; 850 mems; library of 12,000 vols and Rare Manuscript Collections dealing with the Plymouth Colony; the Society maintains Pilgrim Hall Museum, the oldest public museum in North America; collections of Pilgrim decorative arts, furnishings, prehistoric Native American collections; maintains the National Monument to the Forefathers; Dir PEGGY M. BAKER.

Presbyterian Historical Society: 425 Lombard St, Philadelphia, PA 19147; f. 1852; library of 200,000 vols and 15,000 cu. ft MSS; Exec. Dir FREDERICK J. HEUSER, Jr; publ. *American Presbyterians* (quarterly).

Renaissance Society of America: 24 West 12 St, New York, NY 10011; tel. (212) 998-3797; fax (212) 995-4205; f. 1954; 2,400 individual mems, 1,100 library mems; Exec. Dir JOHN MONFASANI; publs *Renaissance Quarterly*, *Renaissance News & Notes*.

Rhode Island Historical Society: 110 Benevolent St, Providence, RI 02906; tel. (401) 331-8575; fax (401) 351-0127; f. 1822; administers: John Brown House, 52 Power St: 18th-century museum house, RI; decorative arts, furniture, paintings, silver and pewter; library, 121 Hope St, 200,000 vols; historical and genealogical; large graphics and MSS collection; Museum of Rhode Island History: Aldrich House, 110 Benevolent St; 2,100 mems; Dir ALBERT T. KLYBERG; publ. *Rhode Island History* (quarterly).

Society of American Historians: Butler Library, Box 2, Columbia University, New York, NY 10027; f. 1939; 350 fellows; Pres. DAVID MCCULLOUGH; Sec. MARK C. CARNES.

State Historical Society of Wisconsin: 816 State St, Madison, WI 53706-1488; tel. (608) 264-6400; fax (608) 264-6404; f. 1846; 7,200 mems; 1,085,000 vols including pamphlets and government documents; 1,888,000 microforms, 39,000 cu. ft MSS, 49,000 cu. ft public records, 25,000 maps and atlases, 1,000,000 pictures and negatives, 14,000 motion picture and TV films from major Hollywood Studios, 2,000,000 motion picture and theatre promotional graphics; Dir GEORGE VOGT; publs *Wisconsin Magazine of History* (quarterly), *Columns, Wisconsin Public Documents* (both every 2 months).

Vermont Historical Society: 109 State St, Pavilion Building, Montpelier, VT 05609-0901; tel. (802) 828-2291; f. 1838; objects: educational work in Vermont and American history; collection of books, documents, and MSS relating to Vermont; publication of historical magazines and books; maintenance of State Museum; 2,500 mems; library of 40,000 vols, early Vermont imprints; Pres. DOROTHY MITCHELL; Dir GAINOR B. DAVIS; publs *Vermont History in Context* (quarterly), *Booklist* (annually).

Western Reserve Historical Society: 10825 East Blvd, Cleveland, OH 44106; tel. (216) 721-5722; fax (216) 721-0645; f. 1867; maintains a historical museum, auto-aviation museum, five historical sites; 6,400 mems; library of 235,000 vols, 25,000 vols of newspapers, 30,500 rolls of microfilm, 1,000,000 prints and photos, 6,000,000 MSS; Pres. PATRICK H. REYMANN; Exec. Dir RICHARD L. EHRLICH; publ. *News* (6 a year).

LANGUAGE AND LITERATURE

American Center of PEN: 568 Broadway, New York, NY 10012; f. 1922 to promote friendship and intellectual co-operation among writers, the exchange of ideas and freedom of expression; conferences, workshops, emergency fund for writers, translation prize; administers Ernest Hemingway Foundation Award for first novels; sponsors 4 prizes for distinguished literary translation and the PEN/Faulkner Award for distinguished American fiction; PEN/Norma Klein Award for children's fiction; PEN/Spielvogel-Diamondstein Award for books of essays; programme for inmate-writers in American prisons; 2,800 mems; library of 1,000 vols; Pres. MICHAEL SCAMMELL; Exec. Sec. KAREN KENNERLY; publs *Grants and Awards Available to American Writers* (every 2 years), *Newsletter* (6 a year), various books and reports.

American Classical League: Miami University, Oxford, OH 45056 tel. (513) 529-7741; fax (513) 529-7742; f. 1918; 3,400 mems; Sec. GERI DUTRA; publ. *The Classical Outlook* (quarterly).

American Comparative Literature Association: Box 870262, University of Alabama, Tuscaloosa, AL 35487-0262; tel. (205) 348-8425; fax (205) 348-2042; e-mail info@acla.org; f. 1960 to further the growth of comparative literature in the USA; 1,000 mems; Pres. SUSAN SULEIMAN; Sec.-Treas. ELAINE MARTIN; publ. *Comparative Literature Journal* (4 a year).

American Dialect Society: c/o Exec. Sec., Dept of English, MacMurray College, Jacksonville, IL 62650; tel. (217) 479-7049; fax (217) 245-0405; f. 1889; 750 mems; study of the English language in North America, together with other languages or dialects of other languages influencing it or being influenced by it; sponsor of *Dictionary of American Regional English*; Pres. WALT WOLFRAM; Exec. Sec. ALLAN METCALF; publs *Newsletter* (3 a year), *American Speech* (quarterly), *PADS* (occasional monographs).

American Philological Association: c/o Department of Classics, Holy Cross College, Worcester, MA 01610-2395; tel. (508) 793-2203; fax (508) 793-3428 f. 1869; study of classical languages, literatures and history; 3,000 mems; Sec. WILLIAM J. ZIOBRO; publs *Transactions* (annually), *Newsletters* (every 2 months), *Philological Monographs, American Classical Studies, Text Series, Classical Resources* (series), special publications.

Linguistic Society of America: 1325 18th St, NW, Suite 211, Washington, DC 20035-6501; tel. (202) 835-1714; fax (202) 835-1717; e-mail isa@isadc.org; f. 1924; annual meetings, linguistic institute; *c.* 7,000 mems; 2,100 libraries, foreign and domestic; Pres. D. TERENCE LANGENDOEN; Sec.-Treas. ELIZABETH C. TRAUGOTT; publs *Language* (quarterly), *LSA Bulletin* (quarterly).

Modern Language Association of America: 10 Astor Place, New York, NY 10003; tel. (212) 475-9500; fax (212) 477-9863; f. 1883; 32,000 mems; Exec. Dir Prof. PHYLLIS FRANKLIN; publs *PMLA* (every 2 months), *MLA International Bibliography of Books and Articles on the Modern Languages and Literatures* (annually), *MLA Directory of Periodicals* (every 2 years).

National Communication Association: 5105 Backlick Rd, Building E, Annandale, VA 22003; tel. (703) 750-0533; fax (703) 914-9471; f. 1914; 7,000 mems; Exec. Dir JAMES L. GAUDINO; publs *Quarterly Journal of Speech*, *Com-*

munication Monographs (quarterly), *Communication Education* (quarterly), *Critical Studies in Mass Communication* (quarterly), *Directory* (annually), *International and Intercultural Communication Annual, Text and Performance Quarterly, Speech Communication Teacher* (quarterly), *Journal of Applied Communication Research* (quarterly).

Poetry Society of America: 15 Gramercy Park, New York, NY 10003; tel. (212) 254-9628; fax (212) 673-2352; e-mail poetrysocy@aol.com; f. 1910; 2,000 mems; service organization for poets and readers of poetry; sponsor readings, lectures, workshops and annual prize giving; library of 8,000 vols of American poetry; Pres. JOHN BARR; Dir ELISE PASCHEN; publ. *Journal* (2 a year).

Society of Biblical Literature: 1201 Clairmont Ave, Suite 300, Decatur, GA 30030-1228; tel. (404) 636-4744; fax (404) 248-0815; f. 1880; study of biblical and related literature, language, history, religions; 7,000 mems; Exec. Dir KENT RICHARDS; publs *Journal of Biblical Literature* (quarterly), *Semeia* (quarterly), *Semeia Studies,* and monographic series.

MEDICINE

Aerospace Medical Association: 320 So. Henry St, Alexandria, VA 22314; tel. (703) 739-2240; fax (703) 739-9692; f. 1929; advancement of aerospace medicine, life sciences, bio-astronautics and environmental medicine; annual awards; 4,000 mems; Exec. Dir Dr RUSSELL B. RAYMAN; publ. *Aviation, Space and Environmental Medicine* (monthly).

American Academy of Allergy, Asthma and Immunology: 611 East Wells St, Milwaukee, WI 53202; f. 1943; 5,200 mems; Pres. Dr STEPHEN I. WASSERMAN; publ. *The Journal of Allergy and Clinical Immunology.*

American Academy of Family Physicians, The: 8880 Ward Parkway, Kansas City, MO 64114; tel. (816) 333-9700; fax (816) 822-0580; f. 1947; promotes and maintains high standards in the general/family practice of medicine; 85,000 mems; Pres. NEIL H. BROOKS; Exec. Vice-Pres. ROBERT GRAHAM; publs *American Family Physician,* (20 a year), *Family Practice Management* (10 a year), *FP Report* (both monthly).

American Academy of Ophthalmology: 655 Beach St, POB 7424, San Francisco, CA 94120; tel. (415) 561-8500; fax (415) 561-8533; f. 1896; 20,777 mems; Exec. Vice-Pres. H. DUNBAR HOSKINS, Jr; publs *Ophthalmology, Argus* (monthly).

American Academy of Otolaryngology–Head and Neck Surgery: 1 Prince St, Alexandria, VA 22314; tel. (703) 836-4444; f. 1896; offers more than 250 continuing medical educational courses at annual meetings, correspondence courses, and Annual Otolaryngology Examination throughout the US and abroad; 8,000 mems; Exec. Vice-Pres. MICHAEL D. MAVES; publs *Otolaryngology-Head and Neck Surgery* (monthly), *The Bulletin* (monthly), *Membership Directory,* monographs, patient education leaflets.

American Academy of Pediatrics: 141 Northwest Point Blvd, Elk Grove Village, IL 60007-1098; e-mail kidsdocs@aap.org; f. 1930; 53,000 mems; Exec. Dir Dr JOE M. SANDERS, Jr; publs *Pediatrics, Pediatrics in Review.*

American Academy of Periodontology: 737 N. Michigan Ave, Chicago, IL 60611; tel. (312) 787-5518; fax (312) 787-3670; f. 1914; 7,200 mems; Pres. S. TIMOTHY ROSE; publ. *Journal of Periodontology* (monthly).

American Association of Anatomists: Department of Anatomy, Tulane Medical Center, 1430 Tulane Ave, New Orleans, LA 70112; f. 1888; 2,753 mems; Pres. Dr CHARLES E. SLONECKER; Sec-Treas. Dr ROBERT D. YATES; publs *Anatomical Record, Developmental Dynamics.*

American Association of Immunologists: 9650 Rockville Pike, Bethesda, MD 20814; tel. (301) 530-7178; fax (301) 571-1816; e-mail infoaai@aai.faseb.org; f. 1913; independent body for the exchange of information and advancement of knowledge in immunology and related fields; 6,000 mems; Pres. Dr JONATHAN SPRENT; Exec. Dir M. MICHELE HOGAN; publ. *Journal of Immunology.*

American Cancer Society Inc.: 19 W. 56th St, New York, NY 10019; f. 1913; voluntary health agency; library of over 16,000 vols (located at 4 West 35th St, New York, NY 10001); Exec. Vice-Pres. G. ROBERT GADBERRY; publs *Cancer* (2 a month), *Ca-A Cancer Journal for Clinicians* (every 2 months), *Cancer News* (2 a year), *Cancer News* (3 a year), *World Smoking & Health* (3 a year).

American College of Obstetricians and Gynecologists: 409 12th St, SW, POB 96920, Washington, DC 20090-6920; tel. (202) 638-5577; f. 1951; 38,000 mems; Exec. Dir Dr RALPH HALE; publ. *Obstetrics and Gynecology* (monthly).

American College of Physicians: Independence Mall West, Sixth St at Race, Philadelphia, PA 19106; f. 1915; 21,467 Fellows, 239 Masters, 39,712 mems, 19,264 Associates; Exec. Vice-Pres. JOHN R. BALL; publ. *Annals of Internal Medicine* (fortnightly).

American College of Surgeons: 55 East Erie St, Chicago, IL 60611; f. 1913; 53,513 Fellows; Dir Dr PAUL A. EBERT; Sec. Dr KATHRYN D. ANDERSON; publs *Journal of the American College of Surgeons* (monthly), *Bulletin* (monthly).

American Dental Association: 211 East Chicago Ave, Chicago, IL 60611; fax (312) 440-2707; f. 1859; 146,000 mems; library of 50,000 vols; Exec. Dir JOHN S. ZAPP; publs *Journal* (monthly), *ADA News* (fortnightly), *Washington News Bulletin* (irregular), *Index to Dental Literature* (quarterly), *American Dental Directory* (annually).

American Dietetic Association, The: 216W Jackson Blvd, Chicago, IL 60606-6995; tel. (312) 899-0040; fax (312) 899-0008; e-mail membrshp@eatright.org; f. 1917 to improve the nutrition of human beings; to advance the science of dietetics; to promote education in these and allied fields; 70,000 mems; library of 1,000 vols; publ. *Journal* (monthly).

American Geriatrics Society, Inc.: 770 Lexington Ave, Suite 300, New York, NY 10021; tel. (212) 308-1414; fax (212) 832-8646; e-mail info.amger@americangeriatrics.org; f. 1942; 6,500 mems; holds Annual Meeting, runs postgraduate courses; Pres. Dr JEFFREY B. HALTER; Exec. Vice-Pres. LINDA HIDDEMEN BARONDESS; publs *Journal of the American Geriatrics Society,* (monthly), *Newsletter* (every 2 months), *Geriatrics Review Syllabus.*

American Gynecological and Obstetrical Society: f. 1993; 200 Fellows, 92 Life Fellows, 43 Hon. Fellows; Sec. Dr PAUL B. UNDERWOOD, University of Virginia. Charlottesville, VA 22908.

American Heart Association: 7272 Greenville Ave, Dallas, TX 75231; tel. (214) 373-6300; fax (214) 706-1341; f. 1924; 3,629,000 mems; dedicated to the reduction of disability and death from cardiovascular diseases and stroke; supports cardiovascular research and brings its benefits to the public through professional education and community service programmes, to co-ordinate efforts of all medical and lay groups in combating cardiovascular diseases, and to inform the public of progress in the cardiovascular field; Exec. Vice-Pres. DUDLEY H. HAFNER; publs *Arteriosclerosis, Thrombosis and Vascular Biology, Circulation, Circulation Research, Currents in Emergency Cardiac Care* (4 a year), *Hypertension, Stroke.*

American Hospital Association: One N. Franklin, Chicago, IL 60606; tel. (312) 422-3000; e-mail webmaster@aha.com; f. 1898 to advance the health of individuals and communities; represents and serves health care provider organizations that are accountable to the community; 35,000 personal mems; 5,300 institutional mems; library of 63,000 vols; Pres. RICHARD J. DAVIDSON; publs *Hospitals and Health Networks* (2 a month), *AHA News* (weekly), *Trustee* (monthly).

American Institute of Nutrition: 9650 Rockville Pike, Bethesda, MD 20814; tel. (301) 530-7050; fax (301) 571-1892; f. 1928 to develop and extend knowledge of nutrition and to facilitate personal contact between investigators in nutrition and related fields of interest; 3,100 mems; Pres. J. DWYER; Sec. R. J. MARTIN; publ. *The Journal of Nutrition* (monthly).

American Institute of the History of Pharmacy: Pharmacy Bldg, 425 North Charter St, Madison, WI 53706; tel. (608) 262-5378; e-mail aihp@macc.wisc.edu; f. 1941; 1,000 mems; conserves the MS and printed records of pharmacy and provides an information and slide-talk service; presents awards, sponsors historical seminars, provides grants-in-aid to scholars, etc.; Dir GREGORY J. HIGBY; publs *Pharmacy in History* (quarterly), newsletters, booklets and pamphlets.

American Laryngological, Rhinological and Otological Society, Inc., The (Triological Society): f. 1895; *c.* 750 mems; Exec. Sec. Dr ROBERT H. MILLER; Exec. Dir DANIEL HENROID Sr, 10 S Broadway, Suite 1401, St Louis, MO 63102; tel. (314) 621-6550; fax (314) 621-6688; publ. *The Laryngoscope.*

American Lung Association: 1740 Broadway, New York, NY 10019-4374; tel. (212) 315-8700; fax (212) 265-5642; f. 1904; 115 affiliated associations throughout the country; Man. Dir JOHN R. GARRISON; the Medical Section of the ALA, the American Thoracic Society, has a membership of over 11,000, including some 2,000 pulmonary physicians in foreign countries; Exec. Dir MARILYN HANSEN; publs *American Journal of Respiratory and Critical Care Medicine, American Journal of Respiratory Cell and Molecular Biology* (monthly).

American Medical Association: 515 North State St, Chicago, IL 60610-4377; tel. (312) 464-5000; f. 1847; 296,000 mems; Exec. Vice-Pres. Dr P. JOHN SEWARD; publs *Jama* (weekly), *American Medical News* (weekly), 11 special journals (monthly), *American Medical Directory* (irregular).

American Medical Technologists: 710 Higgins Rd, Park Ridge, IL 60068; f. 1939; 29,000 mems; Pres. LINDA CROMEANS; publ. *AMT Events–Continuing Education Quarterly.*

American Neurological Association: Administrative Office, 5841 Cedar Lake Rd 108, Minneapolis, MN 55416; tel. (612) 545-6284; f. 1875; 1,000 mems; Pres. Dr JOHN N. WHITAKER; Sec. S. RICHARD BARINGER; publ. *Annals of Neurology.*

American Occupational Therapy Association, Inc.: 4720 Montgomery Lane, Bethesda, MD 20814; f. 1917; 60,000 mems; library of 4,000 items; Pres. KAREN JACOBS; Exec. Dir JEANETTE BAIR; publs *The American Journal of Occupational Therapy* (10 a year), *OT Practice* (monthly), *OT Week,* eleven special interest section newsletters (quarterly).

American Optometric Association, Inc.: 243 N. Lindbergh Blvd, St. Louis, MO 63141; tel. (314) 991-4100; fax (314) 991-4101; f. 1898 to promote the art and science of optometry, to improve vision care and health of the public; 31,000 mems; Exec. Dir Dr MICHAEL D. JONES; Pres. Dr JOHN A. MCCALL Jr; publs *Journal* (quarterly), *News* (fortnightly).

American Pediatric Society: 3400 Research Forest Drive, Suite B7, The Woodlands, TX 77381; tel. (281) 296-0244; fax (281) 296-0255; e-mail info@aps-spr.org; f. 1888; 855 active mems; Sec.-Treas. DAVID GOLDRING.

American Physical Therapy Association: 1111 N. Fairfax St, Alexandria, VA 22314; f. 1921, inc. 1930; to develop and improve physical therapy education, practice and research; 75,000 mems; CEO FRANCIS J. MALLON; publs *Physical Therapy* (journal), *PT – The Magazine of Physical Therapy.*

American Physiological Society: 9650 Rockville Pike, Bethesda, MD 20814-3991; tel. (301) 530-7164; fax (301) 571-8305; e-mail info@aps.faseb.org; f. 1887; 8,700 mems; Exec. Dir MARTIN FRANK; publs *American Journal of Physiology* (consolidated; Cellular Physiology; Endocrinology and Metabolism; Gastrointestinal and Liver Physiology; Heart and Circulatory Physiology; Lung Cellular and Molecular Physiology; Regulatory, Integrative and Comparative Physiology; Renal Physiology; Advances in Physiology Education), *Journal of Applied Physiology, Journal of Neurophysiology, Physiological Reviews, News in Physiological Sciences, The Physiologist, APStracts, Physiological Genomics.*

American Psychiatric Association: 1400 K St, NW, Washington, DC 20005; tel. (202) 682-6000; fax (202) 682-6114;. f. 1844; 40,050 mems; library of 10,000 vols; Med. Dir MELVIN SABSHIN; publs *American Journal of Psychiatry* (monthly), *Psychiatric News* (every 2 weeks), *Psychiatric Services* (monthly).

American Public Health Association: 1015 15th St, NW, Washington, DC 20005; fax (202) 789-5661; f. 1872; interests include environment, personal health services, social factors, manpower and training in public health; 32,000 mems; Exec. Dir Dr FERNANDO M. TREVIÑO; publs *American Journal of Public Health* (monthly), *The Nation's Health* (monthly).

American Rheumatism Association: 1314 Spring St, NW, Atlanta, GA 30309; tel. (404) 872-7100; 4,000 mems; Exec. Sec. LYNN BONFIGLIO.

American Roentgen Ray Society: 1891 Preston White Drive, Reston, VA20191; tel. (703) 648-8992; fax (703) 264-8863; f. 1900; educational and scientific society for radiologists; 12,400 mems; Exec. Dir PAUL R. FULLAGAR; publ. *American Journal of Roentgenology* (monthly).

American Society for Clinical Laboratory Science (formerly ASMT): 7910 Woodmont Ave, Suite 530, Bethesda, MD 20814; tel. (301) 657-2768; fax (301) 657-2909; f. 1933; 20,000 mems; local, state and regional societies; activities include education, education and research funding, professional affairs and membership services; Exec. Dir ELISSA PASSIMENT; publs. *Clinical Laboratory Science* (every 2 months), *ASCLS Today* (monthly).

American Society for Investigative Pathology, Inc.: 9650 Rockville Pike, Bethesda, MD 20814-3993; tel. (301) 530-7130; f. 1976; 2,200 mems; Pres. Dr VINAY KUMAR; Sec.-Treas. Dr LINDA M. MCMANUS; publ. *American Journal of Pathology* (monthly).

American Society for Microbiology: 1325 Massachusetts Ave N.W., Washington, DC 20006; f.1899, under present name 1961; 37,000 mems; Exec. Dir MICHAEL I. GOLDBERG; publs *Journal of Bacteriology, Applied and Environmental Microbiology, Journal of Virology, Infection and Immunity* (monthly), *ASM News, Antimicrobial Agents and Chemotherapy, Journal of Clinical Microbiology, Molecular and Cellular Biology* (monthly), *International Journal of Systematic Bacteriology, Microbiological Reviews* (quarterly), *Abstracts of the Annual Meeting* (annually).

American Society for Pharmacology and Experimental Therapeutics, Inc.: 9650 Rockville Pike, Bethesda, MD 20814-3995; f. 1908; 4,117 mems; Pres. KENNETH E. MOORE; Exec. Officer CHRISTINE K. CARRICO; publs *Journal of Pharmacology and Experimental Therapeutics* (monthly), *Clinical Pharmacology and Therapeutics* (monthly), *Drug Metabolism and Disposition* (monthly), *Molecular Pharmacology* (monthly), *Pharmacological Reviews* (4 a year), *The Pharmacologist* (4 a year).

American Society of Clinical Hypnosis: 2200 East Devon Ave, Suite 291, Des Plaines, IL 60018; tel. (708) 297-3317; fax (708) 297-7309; f. 1957; an independent organization of professional people in medicine, dentistry, and psychology who share scientific and clinical interests in hypnosis; aims to provide educational programmes to further understanding and acceptance of hypnosis as an important tool of ethical clinical medicine and scientific research; 4,200 mems; Pres. Dr RICHARD P. KLUFT; Sec. Dr MOSHE S. TOREM; publ. *The American Journal of Clinical Hypnosis* (quarterly).

American Society of Clinical Pathologists: 2100 West Harrison St, Chicago, IL 60612; tel. (312) 738-1336; fax (312) 738-1619; e-mail info@ascp.org; f. 1922; 77,200 mems; library of 25,500 vols; Pres. Dr JAMES LINDER; Sec. Dr ANNA R. GRAHAM; publs *American Journal of Clinical Pathology, Laboratory Medicine.*

American Society of Tropical Medicine and Hygiene: 60 Revere Drive, Suite 500, Northbrook, IL 60062; tel. (847) 480-9592; fax (847) 480-9282; f. 1951; 3,000 mems; Exec. Dir JOYCE L. PASCHALL; publs *American Journal of Tropical Medicine and Hygiene, Tropical Medicine and Hygiene News.*

American Speech-Language-Hearing Association: 10801 Rockville Pike, Rockville, MD 20852; tel. (301) 897-5700; fax (301) 571-0457; f. 1925; 93,000 mems; Exec. Dir FREDERICK T. SPAHR; publs *Journal of Speech, Language, and Hearing Research* (every 2 months), *Asha* (quarterly), *Language Speech and Hearing Services in Schools* (quarterly), *American Journal of Audiology* (3 a year), *American Journal of Speech-Language Pathology* (quarterly).

American Surgical Association: f. 1880; 1,000 mems; Sec. JOHN L. CAMERON, 13 Elm St, Manchester, MA 01944; tel. (978) 526-8330; fax (978) 526-4018; e-mail asa@prri.com; publs *Transactions* (annually), *Annals of Surgery.*

American Urological Association, Inc.: 1120 North Charles St, Baltimore, MD 21201; tel. (410) 727-1100; fax (410) 223-4370; f. 1902; 11,304 mems; Pres. Dr JACK W. MCANINCH; Sec. Dr WILLIAM R. TURNER, Jr; publs *The Journal of Urology* (monthly), *AUA News* (6 a year).

Armed Forces Institute of Pathology: 6825 16th St, NW, Washington, DC 20306-6000; est. 1862 as Army Medical Museum, present name 1949; it is the central laboratory of pathology for the Department of Defense serving both the military and civilian sectors in education, consultation and research in the medical, dental and veterinary sciences; research on leprosy, malaria, AIDS, sickle cell disease, radiation injury, trauma, drug toxicity and aerospace pathology; organized into: Center for Advanced Pathology, Center for Clinical Laboratory Medicine, Center for Administrative Services, Center for Education, Repository and Research Services, Office of the Armed Forces Medical Examiner, and National Museum of Health and Medicine; Dir Col MICHAEL J. DICKERSON, USAF.

Association of American Medical Colleges: 2450 N St, NW, Washington, DC 20037-1126; tel. (202) 828-0400; fax (202) 828-1125; f. 1876; 126 US and 16 Canadian medical schools, over 400 teaching hospitals and 87 academic and professional societies; Pres. Dr JORDAN J. COHEN; publs *Academic Medicine* (monthly), *AAMC Directory of Medical Education* (annually), *AAMC Curriculum Directory* (annually), *AAMC Reporter* (monthly), *Medical School Admission Requirements* (annually).

Association of American Physicians: f. 1886; 1,200 mems; Sec. D. HATHAWAY, Krannert Institute of Cardiology, Indiana University School of Medicine, 1111 West 10th St, Indianapolis, IN 46202-4800; publ. *Transactions* (annually).

Center for the Study of Aging and Human Development: Duke University, Durham, NC 27710; f. 1955; trains researchers and clinicians with emphasis on post-doctoral training in all aspects of normal aging (gerontology) as well as diseases and disorders of human aging (geriatrics); lectures, seminars and publications; Geriatric Evaluation and Treatment Clinic for direct service and in-service professional training; geriatric training for health professionals; co-sponsors Duke Institute for Learning in Retirement; Dir HARVEY JAY COHEN.

College of Physicians of Philadelphia: 19 South 22nd St, Philadelphia, PA 19103; f. 1788 (College, f. 1787); library of 340,000 vols; 1,860 Fellows; Pres. ALFRED P. FISHMAN; publs *Transactions and Studies, Fugitive Leaves, Consumer Health Resources.*

Commonwealth Fund, The: 1 East 75th St, New York, NY 10021; tel. (212) 535-0400; fax (212) 249-1276; f. 1918; to enhance the common good through its efforts to help Americans live healthy and productive lives and to assist specific groups with serious and neglected problems; current fund initiatives include helping young people realize their potential through mentoring and educational enhancement programmes, improving health care services, promoting healthier life styles and bettering the health care of minorities; awards Harkness Fellowships which enable future leaders of the UK, Australia and New Zealand to study social issues in the USA; Chair. of Board CHARLES SANDERS; Pres. KAREN DAVIS; publ. *Annual Report.*

Gerontological Society of America, The: 1275 K St, NW, Suite 350, Washington, DC 20005-4006; tel. (202) 842-1275; fax (202) 842-1150; e-mail geron@geron.org; f. 1945; multidisciplinary sciences; 6,000 mems; Exec. Dir CAROL A. SCHUTZ; publs *Journals of Gerontology, The Gerontologist.*

Industrial Health Foundation, Inc.: 34 Penn Circle West, Pittsburgh, PA 15206; f. 1935; a non-profit organization for the advancement of healthy working conditions in industry; 120 member companies and associations; library of 2,000 vols; publs *Industrial Hygiene Digest* (monthly), special technical bulletins.

John A. Hartford Foundation, Inc.: 55 East 59th St, New York, NY 10022; tel. (212) 832-7788; fax (212) 593-4913; f. 1929 by John A. Hartford and George L. Hartford; ageing and health programme; Chair. of the Board JAMES D. FARLEY; Exec. Dir CORINNE H. RIEDER; publ. *Annual Report.*

John and Mary R. Markle Foundation: 75 Rockefeller Plaza, New York, NY 10019-6908; tel. (212) 489-6655; fax (212) 765-9690; f.

1927 by an endowment given by John Markle, chartered by the State of New York; seeks to improve mass media and realize the potential of communications technology; Pres. LLOYD N. MORRISETT; Sec. DOLORES E. MILLER; publ. *Annual Report*.

Medical Society of the State of New York: POB 5404, Lake Success, New York, NY 11042; tel. (516) 488-1267; f. 1807; 27,000 mems; library of 45,000 vols; Exec. Vice-Pres. Dr CHARLES N. ASWAD; publs *News of New York* (fortnightly), *Medical Directory of New York State* (every 2 years).

National Association for Biomedical Research: 818 Connecticut Ave, Suite 303, Washington, DC 2006; tel. (202) 857-0540; fax (202) 659-1902; f. 1979; 350 institutional mems; Pres. FRANKIE L. TRULL; Exec. Vice-Pres. BARBARA RICH; publs *NABR Alert, NABR Update* (both fortnightly), *State Laws, NABR Annual Report*.

National Mental Health Association: 1021 Prince St, Alexandria, VA 22314-2971; tel. (703) 684-7722; fax (703) 684-5968; f. 1950; 40 State Divisions, 400 Local Chapters; Chair. of the Board DAN AKENS; Pres./CEO MICHAEL M. FAENZA; publs *FOCUS, Legislative Alert*.

New York Academy of Medicine: 1216 Fifth Ave, New York, NY 10029; tel. (212) 876-8200; fax (212) 876-6620; f. 1847; 2,700 mems; library: see Libraries; Pres. Dr JEREMIAH A. BARONDESS.

Radiological Society of North America, Inc.: 2021 Spring Rd, Suite 600, Oak Brook, IL 60521; tel. (708) 571-2670; f. 1915; continuing medical education in radiology; 30,000 mems; Pres. Dr ERNEST FERRIS; Sec.-Treas. C. DOUGLAS MAYNARD; publs *Radiology* (monthly), *RadioGraphics* (every 2 months).

Society of Medical Jurisprudence: POB 20678, New York, NY 10021-0073; org. and inc. 1883; investigation, study and advancement of the science of medical jurisprudence, and the attainment of a higher standard of medical testimony; members must be physicians, lawyers, chemists, forensic odontologists or health professionals of good standing in their respective professions, or teachers in approved Law or Medical Schools; 250 mems; publ. *Proceedings* (monthly, October-June).

NATURAL SCIENCES

General

Academy of Natural Sciences of Philadelphia, The: 1900 Benjamin Franklin Parkway, Philadelphia, PA 19103-1195; tel. (215) 299-1000; fax (215) 299-1028; f. 1812; natural history museum; research in systematics and evolutionary biology, ecology, limnology and geology, and environmental monitoring; 24m. specimen collections of plants, animals and fossils of world-wide scope; teaching at all levels; 9,000 mems; library: see Libraries and Archives; Pres. PAUL HANLE; publs *Proceedings, Notulae Naturae, Monographs*, special publications.

American Association for the Advancement of Science: 1200 New York Ave, NW, Washington, DC 20005; tel. (202) 326-6400; fax (202) 289-4958; f. 1848; fed. of 285 scientific and engineering socs, with 144,000 mems; Pres. MILDRED DRESSELHAUS; Exec. Officer RICHARD S. NICHOLSON; publs *Science* (weekly), *AAAS Science Books & Films* (9 a year), *Science and Technology in Congress* (monthly).

American Society of Limnology and Oceanography: f. 1936; 3,500 mems; Sec. P. A. PENHALE, Virginia Institute of Marine Science, College of William and Mary, Gloucester Point, VA 23062; tel. (804) 642-7242; publ. *Limnology and Oceanography* (every 2 months).

Buffalo Society of Natural Sciences: 1020 Humboldt Parkway, Buffalo, NY 14211; tel. (716) 896-5200; org. 1861; administers the Buffalo Museum of Science and Tifft Nature Preserve; samples of natural life in US; cultures from other eras to the present; Insect World and Edward G. Gibson Hall of Space, Endangered Species, Dinosaurs and Company; research in anthropology, botany, entomology, geology, mycology, ornithology, palaeontology, vertebrate zoology, with collections in these fields; 11,000 mems; library of 40,000 vols; Pres. MICHAEL J. SMITH; Chair. MARY ANN KRESSE; publs. *Collections* (quarterly), *Scientific Bulletins* (irregular).

California Academy of Sciences: Golden Gate Park, San Francisco, CA 94118; tel. (415) 221-5100; fax (415) 750-7346; f.1853 for the advancement of natural sciences through public education and research, incorporated under the laws of the State of California 1871; 20,000 mems incl. 300 Fellows; maintains a public museum of natural history, the Steinhart Aquarium (Dir ROBERT JENKINS), the Morrison Planetarium (Chair. STEVEN B. CRAIG), a scientific library of 100,000 vols (Librarian THOMAS MORITZ), and research departments with large scientific collections; Departments: Anthropology (Curator NINA JABLONSKI), Aquatic Biology (Curator JOHN E. McCOSKER), Botany (Curator TOM DANIEL), Entomology (Curator CHARLES GRISWOLD), Exhibits (Chair. LINDA KULIK), Herpetology (Curator ROBERT DREWES), Invertebrate Zoology and Geology (Curator GARY WILLIAMS), Ornithology and Mammalogy (Curator LUIS BAPTISTA), Ichthyology (Curator WILLIAM ESCHMEYER); Pres. Dr WILLIAM CLEMENS; Exec. Dir Dr EVELYN E. HANDLER; publs *Proceedings, Newsletter* (monthly), *Pacific Discovery* (quarterly), *Annual Report, Occasional Papers, Memoirs*.

Chicago Academy of Sciences: 2060 North Clark St, Chicago, IL 60614; tel. (312) 549-0606; fax (312) 549-5199; f. 1857; 2,200 mems; exhibits on the natural history of the Chicago region; study collections of many areas in North America; a technical scientific library of 3,000 vols, 2,000 periodicals; Pres. PAUL G. HELTNE; Sec. LEWIS CRAMPTON; Chair DAVID VOSS; publs *Natural History Miscellanea, Bulletin*.

Cranbrook Institute of Science: 1221 N. Woodward Ave, POB 801, Bloomfield Hills, MI 48303-0801; tel. (810) 645-3259; fax (810) 645-3050; f. 1930; a non-profit-making organization with exhibits and educational programmes in astronomy, mineralogy, geology, botany, zoology, ecology, anthropology, mathematics and physics; 4,000 mems; library of 18,000 vols; Dir DANIEL E. APPLEMAN; publs *Bulletins, Newsletter, Annual Reports*, etc.

Franklin Institute: 222 North 20th St, Philadelphia, PA 19103; f. 1824; a non-profit science centre dedicated to public science education and to advancing knowledge in the physical sciences; its committee on Science and the Arts awards several medals, including the Franklin Medal, for contributions to science and technology; also administers the Bower Awards for science and business; the Institute incorporates the Franklin Institute Science Museum (q.v.), the Fels Planetarium (q.v.), The Tuttleman Omniverse Theater and the Musser Choices Forum, and houses the Benjamin Franklin National Memorial; there is an observatory open to the public; Chair. JAMES A. UNRUH; publs *Journal*.

History of Science Society: f. 1924; Exec. Sec. KEITH R. BENSON, University of Washington, POB 351330, Seattle, WA 98195-1330; tel. (206) 543-9366; fax (206) 685-9544; Pres. FREDERICK GREGORY; publs *Isis* (quarterly), *Osiris* (annually), *HSS Newsletter* (quarterly).

Maryland Academy of Sciences: 601 Light St, Baltimore, MD 21230; tel. (410) 685-2370; fax (410) 545-5974; f. 1797, as an educational and scientific institution, and for the diffusion and explanation of scientific information to the public; controls Maryland Science Center; (10,000 mems); Chair. THOMAS S. BOZZUTO; Pres. (vacant); Exec. Dir GREGORY P. ANDORFER; publ. *Maryland Science Center News* (quarterly).

Mellon Institute: see Carnegie-Mellon University under Universities.

National Science Teachers Association: 1840 Wilson Blvd, Arlington, VA 22201-3000; est. 1895, reorganized 1944, to advance science teaching and science education at elementary, secondary and college levels; 53,000 mems; Pres. FRED D. JOHNSON; Exec. Dir GERALD WHEELER; publs *The Science Teacher, Science and Children, Journal of College Science Teaching, Science Scope, Quantum, Dragonfly*.

Ohio Academy of Science: 1500 West Third Ave, Suite 223, Columbus, OH 43212-2817; tel. and fax (614) 488-2228; e-mail oas@iwaynet.net; f. 1891; 2,000 mems; CEO LYNN E. ELFNER; publs *The Ohio Journal of Science, The Ohio Academy of Science News*.

Sigma Xi, the Scientific Research Society: 99 Alexander Drive, POB 13975, Research Triangle Park, NC 27709; tel. (919) 549-4691; fax (919) 549-0090; e-mail memberinfo@sigmaxi.org; f. 1886 for the encouragement of scientific research; over 90,000 mems; Pres. ROBERT A. FROSCH; Exec. Dir PETER D. BLAIR; publ. *American Scientist* (every 2 months).

Southern California Academy of Sciences: c/o Natural History Museum of Los Angeles County, 900 Exposition Blvd, Los Angeles, CA 90007; f. 1891; 400 mems; publs *Bulletin* (3 a year), *Memoirs* (irregularly).

World Future Society: 7910 Woodmont Ave, Suite 450, Bethesda, MD 20814; tel. (301) 656-8274: fax (301) 951-0394; e-mail wfsinfo@wfs.org; f. 1966; private, non-profit organization promoting free discussion and study of alternative futures especially on technological and social themes; 30,000 mems; Pres. EDWARD S. CORNISH; publs *The Futurist* (10 a year), *Futures Research Quarterly, Future Survey* (monthly).

Biological Sciences

American Genetic Association: POB 257, Buckeystown, MD 21717; tel. (301) 695-9292; fax (301) 695-9292; f. 1903; publ. *Journal of Heredity* (every 2 months).

American Institute of Biological Sciences: 730 11th St, NW, Washington, DC 20001-4521; tel. (202) 628-1500; telex 209061; fax (202) 628-1509; f. 1947; mems: 34 professional societies and 6 industrial firms; 6,900 individual mems; Pres. W. HARDY ESHBAUGH; Exec. Dir CLIFFORD J. GABRIEL; publs *BioScience* (monthly), *Forum* (every 2 months), *Membership Directory and Handbook* (every 2 years).

American Malacological Union Inc., The: Dept of Zoology, University of Rhode Island, Kingston, RI 02881; f. 1931; study of phylum Mollusca–systematics, ecology, functional morphology, evolution; medical, neotological and palaeontological aspects; 750 mems; Pres. ROBERT C. BULLOCK; Sec./Treas. RICHARD PETIT; publ. *American Malacological Bulletin* (2 a year), *Newsletter* (3 a year).

American Ornithologists' Union: Division of Birds, MRC-116, National Museum of Natural History, Washington, DC 20560; tel. (202) 357-2051; fax (202) 633-8084; e-mail aou@sivm.si.edu; f. 1883; scientific study of birds; 5,000 mems; Pres. FRANK GILL; Sec. MARY V.

McDonald; publs *The Auk* (quarterly), *Ornithological Monographs* (irregular), *Check-List of North American Birds, Ornithological Newsletter* (every 2 months).

American Phytopathological Society: f. 1908; 5,000 mems; detection and control of plant diseases; plant health management; Pres. Laurence V. Madden; Exec. Vice-Pres. Steven C. Nelson, 3340 Pilot Knob Rd, St Paul, MN 55121; tel. (612) 454-7250; telex 6502439657; fax (612) 454-0766; publs *Phytopathology* (monthly), *Plant Disease* (monthly), *Molecular Plant-Microbe Interactions* (every 2 months), *Phytopathological Classics, Phytopathological Monographs, Plant Disease Compendia Series.*

American Society for Photobiology: Biotech Park, Suite 9, 1021 15th St, Augusta, GA 30901; tel. (706) 722-7511; fax (706) 722-7515; e-mail maps@csranet.com; f. 1972; 1,600 mems; Exec. Sec. Dr Sherwood M. Reichard; publs *Photochemistry and Photobiology* (monthly), *Newsletter* (every 2 months).

American Society of Human Genetics: 9650 Rockville Pike, Bethesda, MD 20814; tel. (301) 571-1825; fax (301) 530-7079; f. 1948; 6,000 mems; Pres. Larry J. Shapiro; Sec. Ann C. M. Smith; Exec. Dir Elaine Strass; publ. *American Journal of Human Genetics* (monthly).

American Society of Ichthyologists and Herpetologists: C/o Dean Hendrickson, University of Texas J. J. Pickle Research Campus, Texas Natural History Collections, Building 176, 10100 Burnet Rd, Austin, TX 78758-4445; tel. (512) 471-0998; fax (512) 471-9775; e-mail asih@mail.utexas.edu; f. 1913; 3,600 mems and subscribers; Sec. Dean A. Hendrickson; publ. *Copeia* (quarterly).

American Society of Mammalogists: f. 1919, inc. 1920; 3,600 mems; object of the Society is the promotion of interest in mammalogy by holding meetings, issuing serial or other publications, and aiding research; five classes of mems, all elective: Annual, Life, Patron, Honorary and Emeritus; the Society is affiliated with the American Institute of Biological Sciences, the American Association for the Advancement of Science and the International Union for the Conservation of Nature; Sec-Treas. Dr H. Duane Smith, Monte L. Bean Life Science Museum, Brigham Young University, Provo, UT 84602; tel. (801) 378-2492; publs *Journal of Mammalogy* (quarterly), *Mammalian Species* (irregular) and occasional monographs.

American Society of Naturalists: f. 1883; 1,835 mems; Pres. Montgomery Slatkin; Sec. Nancy T. Burley, Dept of Ecology and Evolutionary Biology, University of California, Irvine, CA 92717; tel. (714) 856-8130; publ. *The American Naturalist* (monthly).

American Society of Parasitologists: POB 1897, Lawrence, KS 66044; f. 1924; 1,800 mems; publ. *The Journal of Parasitology* (every 2 months).

Biophysical Society: 9650 Rockville Pike, Room L-0512, Bethesda, MD 20814; fax (301) 530-7133; e-mail society@biophysics.faseb.org; f. 1957; 5,200 mems; Pres. Ken Dill; Sec. Sarah Hitchcock-DeGregori; publs *Biophysical Journal*, abstracts of annual meetings.

Botanical Society of America, Inc.: f. 1906; 3,000 mems; Sec. Pamela Soltis, Dept of Botany, Washington State University, Pullman, WA 99164; publs *American Journal of Botany* (monthly), *Plant Science Bulletin* (quarterly), *Guide to Graduate Study in the US and Canada* (irregular), *Directory* (every 2 years).

Ecological Society of America: Massachusetts Ave NW, Suite 420, Washington, DC 20036; tel. (202) 833-8773; fax (202) 833-8775; f. 1915; 7,200 mems; Exec. Dir Dr Brian D. Keller; publs *Bulletin* (quarterly), *Ecology* (8 a year), *Ecological Monographs* (quarterly), *Ecological Applications* (quarterly).

Entomological Society of America: f. 1953 by the union of the American Association of Economic Entomologists (f. 1889) and the former Entomological Society of America (f. 1906); 9,000 mems; Exec. Dir Harry A. Bradley, 9301 Annapolis Rd, Suite 300, Lanham, MD 20706-3115; publs *Newsletter* (monthly), *Annals, Journal of Economic Entomology, Environmental Entomology. Journal of Medical Entomology* (all every 2 months), *American Entomologist* (quarterly), *Arthropod Management Tests* (annually), *Thomas Say Proceedings* (irregular).

Environmental Mutagen Society: 11250 Roger Bacon Drive, Suite 8, Reston, VA 22090-5202; f. 1969; 1,150 mems; promotion of basic and applied studies of mutagenesis; makes an annual award; Admin. Officer Richard A. Guggolz; publ. *Environmental and Molecular Mutagenesis* (8 a year).

Federation of American Societies for Experimental Biology: 9650 Rockville Pike, Bethesda, MD 20814; tel. (301) 530-7000; fax (301) 530-7001; f. 1912; member societies: American Physiological Society, American Society for Biochemistry and Molecular Biology, American Society for Pharmacology and Experimental Therapeutics, American Society for Investigative Pathology, American Society for Nutritional Sciences, American Association of Anatomists, the Protein Society, American Association of Immunologists; American Society for Cell Biology, Biophysical Society, American Society for Bone and Mineral Research, American Society for Clinical Investigation; associate members: Society for Developmental Biology, American Peptide Society, Association of Biomolecular Resource Facilities, Teratology Society, Society for the Study of Reproduction; library of 2,500 vols; Exec. Dir Michael J. Jackson; publ. *The FASEB Journal* (monthly).

Genetics Society of America: 9650 Rockville Pike, Bethesda, MD 20814; tel. (301) 571-1825; fax (301) 530-7079; f. 1932; 4,400 mems; Pres. Dr David Bottstein; Sec. Thomas D. Petes; Exec. Dir Elaine Strass; publ. *Genetics* (monthly).

Mycological Society of America: f. 1931; 1,300 mems; Sec. Dr Maren A. Klich, USDA, ARS, SRRC, 1100 Robert E. Lee Blvd, New Orleans, LA 70124; e-mail mklich@nola.srrc.usda.gov; publs *Mycologia* (every 2 months), *Inoculum* (newsletter, every 2 months), *Mycologia Memoirs* (irregular).

National Audubon Society: 700 Broadway, New York, NY 10003-9562; tel (212) 979-3000; f. 1905; membership: 550,000, 518 local chapters; Pres. John Flicker; publs *Audubon* (every 2 months), *Audubon Field Notes* (quarterly).

National Wildlife Federation: 8925 Leesburg Pike, Vienna, VA 22184; tel. (703) 790-4000; fax (703) 790-4075; f. 1936; 4 million mems; Pres. and CEO Mark Van Putten; publs *National Wildlife Magazine, International Wildlife Magazine, Ranger Rick, Conservation Directory, Your Big Backyard.*

Nature Conservancy, The: 1815 North Lynn St, Arlington, VA 22209; tel. (703) 841-5300; fax (703) 841-1283; f. 1951; international non-profit organization committed to preserving biological diversity by protecting lands and waters; 920,000 mems; Pres. John C. Sawhill; publ. *Nature Conservancy* (every 2 months).

Society for Developmental Biology: 9650 Rockville Pike, Bethesda, MD 20814-3998; tel. (301) 571-0647; fax (301) 571-5074; e-mail sdb@faseb.org. f. 1939; 1,900 mems; publs *Developmental Biology* (fortnightly), *SDB Newsletter* (4 a year).

Society for Economic Botany: Dept of Anthropology, Univ. of Missouri, Columbia, MO 65211; tel. (314) 882-3038; f. 1959; 700 mems; Pres. Dr Douglas Kinghorn; Sec. Dr Deborah Pearsall; publ. *Economic Botany* (quarterly).

Society for Experimental Biology and Medicine: 162 West 56th St, Suite 203, New York, NY 10019; f. 1903; 1,500 mems; 1,300 subscribers; Exec. Dir Felice O'Grady; publ. *Proceedings* (11 a year).

Society of Vertebrate Paleontology: 401 N. Michigan Ave, Chicago, IL 60611-4267; tel. and fax (312) 321-3708; f. 1941; 1,700 mems; Pres. Louis L. Jacobs; Sec. Catherine Badgley; publs *SVP News Bulletin, Journal of Vertebrate Paleontology, Bibliography of Fossil Vertebrates.*

Wildlife Conservation Society: Bronx Zoo/Wildlife Conservation Park, Fordham Rd and Bronx River Parkway, Bronx, NY 10460; tel. (718) 220-5100; f. 1895; 68,000 mems; operates the Bronx Zoo/Wildlife Conservation Park, New York Aquarium for Wildlife Conservation, Central Park Wildlife Center, Queens Wildlife Center, Prospect Park Wildlife Center; library of 6,000 vols; Chair. David Schiff; Pres. and Gen. Dir Dr William Conway; publ. *Wildlife Conservation* (every 2 months).

Wildlife Management Institute: 1101 Fourteenth St, NW, Suite 801, Washington, DC 20005; tel. (202) 371-1808; fax (202) 408-5059; e-mail wmihq@aol.com; inc. 1946; Pres. Rollin D. Sparrowe; Sec. Richard E. McCabe; publs *North American Wildlife and Natural Resources Conference Transactions* (annually), *Outdoor News Bulletin* (monthly).

Wildlife Society, Inc., The: 5410 Grosvenor Lane, Bethesda, MD 20814; tel. (301) 897-9770; fax (301) 530-2471; e-mail tws@wildlife.org; f. 1937 to develop and promote sound stewardship of wildlife resources and of the environments upon which wildlife and humans depend, to undertake an active role in preventing human-induced environmental degradation, to increase awareness and appreciation of wildlife values, and to seek the highest standards in all activities of the wildlife profession; over 9,700 mems; Exec. Dir Harry E. Hodgdon; publs *Journal of Wildlife Management, Wildlife Society Bulletin* (quarterly), *Wildlife Monographs.*

Mathematical Sciences

American Mathematical Society: POB 6248, Providence, RI 02940; tel. (401) 455-4000; fax (401) 331-3842; f. at Columbia Univ. in 1888 as the New York Mathematical Society; inc. 1923 as American Mathematical Society; sponsors meetings, symposia, seminars and institutes, and provides employment services in the mathematical sciences; membership 27,000; Sec. Robert Fossum; Exec. Dir John Ewing; publs *Bulletin, Journal* (quarterly), *Proceedings, Transactions, Mathematical Reviews* (monthly), *Mathematics of Computation* (quarterly), *Abstracts* (every 2 months), *Current Mathematical Publications* (every 3 weeks), Employment Information in the Mathematical Sciences (every 2 months), *Memoirs, Notices* (11 a year), translations of foreign journals.

Dozenal Society of America: Math. Dept, Nassau Community College, Garden City, NY 11530; tel. (516) 669-0273; inc. 1944; 144 mems; library of 120 vols; Chair. Dr Patricia Zirkel; Pres. Prof. Jay Schiffman; publ. *Duodecimal Bulletin* (every 6 months).

Industrial Mathematics Society: POB 159, Roseville, MI 48066; f. 1949 to promote a better understanding of how mathematics may be used in the solution of complex problems in industry and various professions; 100 mems; Pres. LEONARD G. JOHNSON; Sec. LEO S. PARRY; publ. *Industrial Mathematics* (2 a year).

Mathematical Association of America, Inc.: 1529 18th St, NW, Washington, DC 20036; tel. (202) 387-5200; f. 1915; 30,000 mems; Pres. DONALD L. KREIDER; Sec. GERALD L. ALEXANDERSON; Exec. Dir Dr MARCIA P. SWARD; publs *American Mathematical Monthly* (10 a year), *Mathematics Magazine* (5 a year), *College Mathematics Journal* (5 a year), *Focus* (newsletter, 6 a year), *Math Horizons* (quarterly).

Physical Sciences

Acoustical Society of America: 500 Sunnyside Blvd, Woodbury, NY 11797; tel. (516) 576-2360; fax (516) 576-2377; e-mail asa@aip.org; f. 1929; 6,900 mems; Pres. LAWRENCE A. CRUM; Exec. Dir CHARLES E. SCHMID; publ. *Journal* (monthly).

American Association of Petroleum Geologists: Box 979, Tulsa, OK 74101-0979; tel. (918) 584-2555; telex 49-9432; fax (918) 584-0469; f. 1917; world's largest professional geoscience organization; 31,995 mems; Exec. Dir LYLE BAIE; publs *Bulletin*, *AAPG Explorer* (monthly).

American Astronomical Society: Dept of Physics and Astronomy, Louisiana State University, Baton Rouge, LA 70803-4001; tel. (504) 388-1160; fax (504) 334-1098; f. 1899, inc. 1928; 6,570 mems; Sec. Dr ARLO U. LANDOLT; publs *The Astronomical Journal* (monthly), *Bulletin* (quarterly), *The Astrophysical Journal* (3 a month).

American Chemical Society: 1155 16th St, NW, Washington, DC 20036; tel. (202) 872-4600; fax (202) 872-4615; f. 1876; 155,000 mems; Pres. PAUL H. L. WALTER; Exec. Dir Dr JOHN K CRUM; publs include: *Journal of the ACS, CHEMTECH, Chemical and Engineering News, Analytical Chemistry, Chemical Abstracts and its various services, Journal of Physical Chemistry* and others.

American Crystallographic Association: c/o POB 96, Ellicott Station, Buffalo, NY 14205-0096; tel. (716) 856-9600; fax (716) 852-4846; e-mail aca@hwi.buffalo.edu; f. 1949; 2,000 mems; crystallography and the application of diffraction methods to the study of the arrangement of atoms in matter; Pres. PENELOPE CODDING; Sec. VIRGINIA PETT; publs *Newsletter* (quarterly), *Program and Abstracts* (annually), Transactions (annually).

American Geological Institute: 4220 King St, Alexandria, VA 22302-1502; tel. (703) 379-2480; fax (703) 379-7563; e-mail agi@agiweb.org; f. 1948; comprises 32 earth science societies; Exec. Dir MARCUS E. MILLING; publs *Geotimes* (monthly), *Bibliography and Index of Geology* (monthly).

American Geophysical Union: 2000 Florida Ave, NW, Washington, DC 20009; tel. (202) 462-6900; fax (202) 328-0566; f. 1919; publishes journals and books; sponsors scientific meetings; 35,000 mems; sections: Geodesy; Seismology; Atmospheric Sciences; Geomagnetism and Paleomagnetism; Ocean Sciences; Volcanology, Geochemistry and Petrology; Tectonophysics; Planetology; Space Physics and Aeronomy; Hydrology; Pres. JOHN A. KNAUSS; Exec. Dir A. F. SPILHAUS, Jr; publs *Journal of Geophysical Research,* (5 sections, monthly), *Eos* (weekly), *Reviews of Geophysics* (quarterly), *Geophysical Research Letters* (fortnightly), *Water Resources Research* (monthly), *Tectonics* (6 a year), *Global Biogeochemical Cycles* (quarterly), *Paleoceanography* (6 a year), *Radio Science* (6 a year), *Earth in Space* (9 a year), *Geomagnetism and Aeronomy International* (6 a year), *Nonlinear Processes in Geophysics* (4 a year), *Computational Seismology and Geodynamics* (1 a year), *Earth Interactions* (electronic journal).

American Institute of Chemists: 501 Wythe St, Alexandria, VA 22314-1917; tel. (703) 836-2090; fax (703) 836-2091; f. 1923; professional aspects of chemical practice, including national certification programme, involvement in governmental activities, awards, and sponsorship, through the AIC Foundation, of unique programme annually to honour top college chemistry seniors; 6,000 mems; Pres. ROGER R. FESTA; Exec. Dir SHARON DOBSON; publs *The Chemist* (9 a year), *AIC Professional Directory* (annually).

American Institute of Physics: 335 East 45th St, New York, NY 10017; tel. (212) 661-9404; telex 960-960-983; f. 1931; composed of ten mem. societies with total membership of 95,000; 18 affiliated socs, 94 Corporate Assocs, *c.* 550 student chapters; Niels Bohr Library; Exec. Dir KENNETH W. FORD; Sec. RODERICK M. GRANT; 46 publs including *Physics Today*, journals, bulletins, translated Russian and Chinese journals and secondary information services.

American Meteorological Society: f. 1919, inc. 1920; 11,850 mems; Pres. EUGENE M. RASMUSSON; Exec. Dir Dr RICHARD E. HALLGREN, 45 Beacon St, Boston, MA 02108; tel. (617) 227-2425; fax (617) 742-8718; publs *Bulletin of the American Meteorological Society, Meteorological Monographs, Meteorological and Geoastrophysical Abstracts, Journal of Physical Oceanography, Journal of the Atmospheric Sciences, Journal of Climate, Journal of Applied Meteorology, Monthly Weather Review, Journal of Atmospheric and Oceanic Technology, Weather and Forecasting, Historical Monographs.*

American Microscopical Society: Dept of Biology, Washington College, Chestertown, Maryland 21620; tel. (410) 778-2800; f. 1878; 695 mems and 645 subscribers; Treas. D. A. MUNSON; publ. *Invertebrate Biology* (quarterly).

American Nuclear Society: 555 North Kensington Ave, La Grange Park, IL 60526; tel. (708) 352-6611; telex 4972673; e-mail nucleus@ans.org; f. 1954; 18 professional divisions: Fusion Energy, Education and Training, Environmental Sciences, Isotopes and Radiation, Materials Science and Technology, Mathematics and Computation, Nuclear Criticality Safety, Fuel Cycle and Waste Management, Human Factors, Nuclear Reactor Safety, Power, Radiation Protection and Shielding, Reactor Operations, Reactor Physics, Robotics and Remote Systems Technology, Thermal Hydraulics, Biology and Medicine, Decommissioning, Decontamination and Reutilization, Accelerator Applications Technical Group; 52 local sections, 8 overseas local sections (Japan, South Korea, Latin America, Austria, Switzerland, Italy, France, Taiwan); 51 student branches; 13,930 mems; 120 organization mems; Pres. STANLEY HATCHER; Exec. Dir BRIAN HAJEK (acting); publs *Nuclear Science and Engineering, Nuclear News* (9 a year), *ANS News* (every 2 months), *Nuclear Technology* (monthly), *Fusion Technology* (8 a year), *Transactions* (2 a year), *Proceedings of the Remote Systems Technology, Buyers' Guide* (annually), nuclear standards, technical monographs and topical meeting proceedings.

American Pharmaceutical Association: 2215 Constitution Ave, NW, Washington, DC 20037; tel. (202) 628-4410; f. 1852; 50,000 mems; library of 6,000 vols; Exec. Vice-Pres./Chief Exec. Officer Dr JOHN A. GANS; publs *Journal of the American Pharmaceutical Association, Journal of Pharmaceutical Sciences* (monthly), *Pharmacy Today* (monthly).

American Physical Society: One Physics Ellipse, College Park, MD 20740; tel. (301) 209-3629; fax (301) 209-0865; f. 1899; 43,000 mems; Pres. Dr ANDREW SESSLER; Exec. Officer Dr JUDY R. FRANZ; publs *Bulletin, Physical Review, Reviews of Modern Physics, Physical Review Letters.*

American Society for Biochemistry and Molecular Biology: 9650 Rockville Pike, Bethesda, MD 20814; tel. (301) 530-7145; fax (301) 571-1824; e-mail asbmb@asbmb.faseb.org; f. 1906; 9,700 mems; Exec. Officer C. C. HANCOCK; publ. *Journal of Biological Chemistry* (weekly).

Electrochemical Society, Inc.: 10 South Main St, Pennington, NJ 08534; tel. (609) 737-1902; f. 1902; 7,000 mems; conducts two international meetings annually on various topics in electrochemistry, solid-state science and related fields; Exec. Dir R. J. CALVO; publs *Journal* (monthly), *Interface* (quarterly).

Geochemical Society: Dept of Terrestrial Magnetism, Carnegie Inst. of Washington, 5241 Broad Branch Rd, NW, Washington, DC 20015; tel. (202) 686-4370; f. 1955; 1,800 mems; Pres. A. LASAGA; Sec. S. B. SHIREY; publ. *Geochimica et Cosmochimica Acta.*

Geological Society of America, Inc.: POB 9140, 3300 Penrose Place, Boulder, CO 80301; tel. (303) 447-2020; fax (303) 447-1133; f. 1888; total membership 15,500; Exec. Dir DONALD M. DAVIDSON, Jr; publs *Geology* (monthly), *Bulletin* (monthly), *G. S. A. Today* (monthly), *Special Papers, Maps and Charts, Memoirs, Treatise on Invertebrate Paleontology* (irregular), *Abstracts with Programs* (1 a year), *Decade of North American Geology* publs.

Microscopy Society of America: 4 Barlows Landing Rd, Suite 8, Pocasset, MA 02559; tel. (508) 563-1155; fax (508) 563-1211; f. 1942; annual meeting, presenting technical papers and exhibits; aims to increase and diffuse knowledge of microscopy and related instruments and results obtained through their use; 5,000 mems; Sec. BARBARA REINE; publs *Proceedings* (annually), *Journal* (every 2 months).

Mineralogical Society of America: 1015 Eighteenth St NW, Suite 601, Washington, DC 20036-5274; tel. (202) 775-4344; fax (202) 775-0018; e-mail business@minsocam.org; f. 1919; mineralogy, petrology, crystallography, geochemistry; 2,200 mems; publs *The American Mineralogist* (every 2 months), *Reviews in Mineralogy* (1 or 2 a year), and others.

Oak Ridge Associated Universities, Inc.: POB 117, Oak Ridge, TN 37831-0117; tel. (423) 576-3000; fax (423) 576-3643; f. 1946; consortium of 88 universities; manages and operates the Oak Ridge Institute for Science and Education for the US Department of Energy; carries out research and development, training and education, technical assistance and technology transfer activities for DOE and other federal and private organizations; concentrates on four major areas: science/engineering education, training and management systems, medical sciences, and energy/environment systems; manages educational programmes for pre-college and postdoctoral students; develops training processes that encompass the design, delivery and evaluation of training networks; assesses environmental impacts of a variety of energy technologies; develops, analyzes and evaluates policies and regulations affecting energy and environmental issues; manages University Isotope Separator at Oak Ridge (UNISOR) user facility; maintains medical, training and energy/environment libraries; Pres. Dr RONALD D. TOWNSEND; publs *Annual Report, Trader, Medical Research Report* (annually), *REAC/TS Newsletter* (irregular).

Optical Society of America: 2010 Massachusetts Ave, NW, Washington, DC 20036; tel.

(202) 223-8130; fax (202) 223-1096; f. 1916; a national organization devoted to the advancement of optics and the service of all who are interested in any phase of that science; member American Institute of Physics; 10,250 mems; Pres. DUNCAN MOORE; Exec. Dir DAVID HENNAGE; publs *Journal* (2 series): *A (Optics and Image Science), B (Optical Physics), Optics and Photonics News, Optics Letters* (2 a month), *Applied Optics* (3 a month), *Journal of Lightwave Technology, Optics and Spectroscopy, Journal of Optical Technology.*

Palaeontological Society: f. 1908 to publish and disseminate palaeontological research; 1,710 mems, 1,000 institutional subscribers; associated with the Geological Society of America; Sec. DONALD L. WOLBERG, Jurupa Mountains Cultural Center, 7621 Granite Hill Drive, Riverside, CA 92509; tel. (714) 685-5818; publs *Journal of Paleontology* (every 2 months), *The Paleontological Society Memoirs* (irregular), *Paleobiology* (quarterly), *Short Course Notes* (annually), *Newsletter* (2 a year).

Seismological Society of America: 201 El Cerrito Plaza Professional Bldg, El Cerrito, CA 94530; tel. (510) 525-5475; fax (510) 525-7204; e-mail info@seismosoc.org; f. 1906; 1,900 mems; seismology, earthquake engineering, earthquake geology, etc.; Sec. JOE J. LITEHISER, Jr; publs *Bulletin* (every 2 months), *Seismological Research Letters* (every 2 months).

Society for Sedimentary Geology (SEPM): 1731 E. 71st St, Tulsa, OK 74136-5108; tel. (918) 493-3361; fax (918) 493-2093; f. 1926; 5,260 mems; Pres. LEE F. KRYSTINIK; publs *PALAIOS* (every 2 months), *Journal of Sedimentary Research* (every 2 months).

Society of Economic Geologists: 185 Estes St, Lakewood, CO 80226; f. 1920; 1,500 mems; Sec. A. L. BROKAW; publ. *Economic Geology* (8 a year).

PHILOSOPHY AND PSYCHOLOGY

American Philosophical Association: tel. (302) 831-1112; fax (302) 831-8690; e-mail apaonline@udel.edu; f. 1900; 10,000 mems; to promote the exchange of ideas among philosophers, to encourage creative and scholarly activity in philosophy and to facilitate the professional work of teachers of philosophy; Chair. PHILIP L. QUINN; Exec. Dir ERIC HOFFMAN, Univ. of Delaware, Newark, DE 19716; publs *Proceedings and Addresses of APA, Jobs for Philosophers*, newsletters.

American Psychological Association: f. 1892; 155,000 mems; Exec. Vice-Pres. and CEO RAYMOND D. FOWLER, 750 First Street, NE, Washington, DC 20002-4242; tel. (202) 336-5500; library of 2,500 vols; publs *American Psychologist, APA Monitor, Psychological Abstracts* (monthly), and 33 others.

Metaphysical Society of America: c/o Sec.-Treas. BRIAN MARTINE, Dept of Philosophy, University of Alabama in Huntsville, AL 35899; f. 1950 to study metaphysical problems without regard to sectarian divisions; 700 mems; Pres. MARY CLARK.

Philosophy of Science Association: C/o George Gale, Dept of Philosophy, University of Missouri, Kansas City, MO 64110-2499; f. 1934 to further studies and free discussion in the field of philosophy of science; 1,000 mems; Pres. ABNER SHIMONY; publs *Philosophy of Science* (quarterly), *Newsletter* (quarterly), *Proceedings of Biennial Meetings.*

Psychometric Society: C/o Terry Ackerman, University of Illinois, 260 Education Bldg, 1310 S. Sixth St, Champaign, IL 61820; tel. (217) 244-3361; fax (217) 244-7620; e-mail tackerma@uiuc.edu; f. 1935; 750 mems; Sec. TERRY ACKERMAN; publ. *Psychometrika* (quarterly).

RELIGION, SOCIOLOGY AND ANTHROPOLOGY

African Studies Association: Rutgers University, 132 George St, New Brunswick, NJ 08901-1400; tel. (732) 932-8173; fax (732) 932-3394; e-mail callasa@rci.rutgers.edu; f. 1957; encourages research and collects and disseminates information on Africa; 3,400 mems; Pres. Prof. SANDRA GREENE; Exec. Dir CHRISTOPHER KOCH; publs *African Studies Review* (3 a year), *ASA News* (quarterly), *Issue* (2 a year), *History in Africa* (annually).

American Academy of Religion: 825 Houston Mill Rd, Suite 300, Atlanta, GA 30333; f. 1909; society for teachers of and researchers into religion and religious studies; informs members of current developments within the field and of new materials and opportunities for study grants and research funds; 8,000 mems; Pres. JUDITH PLASKOW; Sec. RONALD M. GREEN; Exec. Dir BARBARA DECONCINI; publ. *Journal.*

American Anthropological Association: 4350 N. Fairfax Drive, Suite 640, Arlington, VA 22203-1620; tel. (703) 528-1902; f. 1902; 10,000 mems; Pres. JANE HILL; publs *City and Society* (2 a year), *American Anthropologist, American Ethnologist, Ethos, Cultural Anthropology, Medical Anthropology Quarterly, Anthropology and Education Quarterly* (all quarterly), *Anthropology Newsletter* (9 a year), *Guide to Departments of Anthropology* (annually), *Journal of Linguistic Anthropology* (2 a year), Special Publs series.

American Counseling Association: 5999 Stevenson Ave, Alexandria, VA 22304; tel. (703) 823-9800; f. 1952; counselling, guidance and student personnel services; 57,000 mems; divisions: American College Counseling Asscn, Asscn for Counselor Education and Supervision, National Career Development Asscn, Asscn for Humanistic Education and Development, American School Counselor Asscn, American Rehabilitation Counseling Asscn, Asscn for Assessment in Counseling, National Employment Counseling Asscn, Asscn for Multicultural Counseling and Development, Asscn for Spiritual, Ethical and Religious Values in Counseling, Internat. Asscn of Addictions and Offender Counselors, American Mental Health Counselors Asscn, Asscn for Counselors and Educators in Government, Asscn for Adult Development and Aging, Asscn for Gay, Lesbian and Bisexual Issues in Counseling, Internat. Asscn of Marriage and Family Counselors; Exec. Dir RICHARD YEP (acting); publs 16 periodicals on aspects of counselling, guidance and human development.

American Folklore Society, Inc.: 4350 N. Fairfax Drive, Suite 640, Arlington, VA 22203-1620; tel. (703) 528-1902; f. 1888; 1,536 mems; Sec.-Treas. SHALOM STAUB; publs *Journal of American Folklore* (quarterly), *Newsletter.*

American Oriental Society: Room 110D, Hatcher Graduate Library, University of Michigan, Ann Arbor, MI 48109-1205; e-mail jrodgers@umich.edu; f. 1842; 1,350 mems; library of 22,000 vols; Pres. STANLEY INSLER; Sec.-Treas. J. RODGERS; publs *Journal* (quarterly), *Monograph Series.*

American Society for Ethnohistory: Dept of Anthropology, McGraw Hall, Cornell University, Ithaca, NY 14853; tel. (607) 277-0109; f. 1954; 1,300 mems; scholarly organization devoted to the study of the histories of cultures and societies in all areas of the world; Sec.-Treas. FREDERIC W. GLEACH; publ. *Ethnohistory* (quarterly).

American Sociological Association: 1722 N St, NW, Washington, DC 20036; tel. (202) 833-3410; fax (202) 785-0146; f. 1905; 13,000 mems; Pres. JILL QUADAGNO; Exec. Officer FELICE J. LEVINE; publs *Employment Bulletin* (monthly), *The American Sociological Review* (6 a year), *Sociology of Education* (quarterly), *Journal of Health and Social Behavior* (quarterly), *Social Psychology Quarterly, Contemporary Sociology* (every 2 months), *Teaching Sociology* (quarterly), *Footnotes* (9 a year), *Sociological Theory* (2 a year), *Sociological Methodology* (annually).

Association for Asian Studies, Inc.: 1 Lane Hall, University of Michigan, Ann Arbor, MI 48109; f. 1941; 7,500 mems; Sec.-Treas. JOHN CAMPBELL; publs *Bibliography of Asian Studies* (annually), *Journal of Asian Studies* (quarterly), *Asian Studies Newsletter* (5 a year), *Journal of Asian Business, Doctoral Dissertations on Asia* (annually), *Membership Directory* (annually), to members and libraries only.

Association for the Study of Afro-American Life and History, Inc.: 1407 14th St, NW, Washington, DC 20005; tel. (202) 667-2822; fax (202) 387-9802; f. 1915; 2,200 mems; publs *The Negro History Bulletin* (quarterly), *The Journal of Negro History* (quarterly).

National Institute of Social Sciences: 150 Amsterdam Ave, New York, NY 10023; f. 1899; 850 mems; Pres. J. SINCLAIR ARMSTRONG; Sec. BRUCE E. BALDING.

Pacific Sociological Association: Dept of Sociology, California State University, Sacramento, CA 95819-6005; tel. (916) 278-5254; f. 1930; 900 mems; Sec.-Treas. DEAN S. DORN; publs *Sociological Perspectives* (quarterly), *The Pacific Sociologist.*

Population Association of America, Inc.: 721 Ellsworth Drive, Suite 300, Silver Spring, MD 20910; f. 1931; 3,000 mems; Pres. ANDREW J. CHERLIN; publs *Demography, PAA Affairs, Applied Demography* (4 a year).

Population Council, The: 1 Dag Hammarskjold Plaza, New York, NY 10017; tel. (212) 339-0500; telex 234722; fax (212) 755-6052; f. 1952; international nonprofit nongovernmental organization; analyses population issues and trends; conducts research in the reproductive sciences; develops new contraceptives; works with public and private agencies to improve the quality and outreach of family planning and reproductive health services; helps governments to design and implement effective population policies; disseminates the results of research in the population field; has four regional and 14 country offices overseas; Pres. MARGARET CATLEY-CARLSON; Chair. MCGEORGE BUNDY; Dir Center for Biomedical Research ELOF JOHANSSON; Dir Programs Division GEORGE F. BROWN; Dir Research Division JOHN BONGAARTS; publs *Studies in Family Planning* (every 2 months), *Population and Development Review* (quarterly), *Annual Report*, newsletters.

Religious Research Association: Marist Hall, Room 108, CUA, Washington, DC 20064; tel. (202) 319-5447; f. 1959; aims to increase understanding of the function of religion in persons and society through application of social scientific and other scholarly methods; to promote religious research; to co-operate with other societies and individuals interested in the study of religion; 600 mems; Pres. (vacant); Exec. Sec. W. SWATOS, Jr; publ. *Review of Religious Research* (quarterly).

Russell Sage Foundation: 112 East 64th St, New York, NY 10021; tel. (212) 750-6000; inc. 1907 to promote improvement of social and living conditions in the United States; supports projects on social analysis of poverty, immigration and the social psychology of cultural contact; Chair. PEGGY C. DAVIS; Pres. ERIC WANNER; Sec. MADELINE SPITALERI; publ. *Biennial Report.*

Society for Applied Anthropology: POB 24083, Oklahoma City, OK 73124-0083; tel. (405) 843-5113; fax (405) 843-8553; e-mail sfaa@telepath.com; f. 1941; application of the social and behavioural sciences to contemporary problems; 2,500 mems; Pres. JOHN YOUNG; publs *Human Organization* (quarterly), *Practicing Anthropology* (quarterly), *SfAA Newsletter* (quarterly), Monograph Series.

Society for the Scientific Study of Religion Inc.: 1365 Stone Hall, Sociology Dept, Purdue University, W. Lafayette, IN 47907-1365; tel. (765) 494-6286; f. 1949; dedicated to research and scholarly publs relating to religious phenomena; examining the consequences of religious beliefs on individual and social behaviour, the impact of religious organizations on other institutions, and problems of continuity and change within religious groups; *c.* 1,500 mems; Pres. N. JAY DEMERATH; Exec. Sec. MAIRE CORNWALL; publs *Journal* (quarterly), monograph series, *Newsletter*.

Society for the Study of Evolution: C/o Allen Press, POB 1897, Lawrence, KS 66044; f. 1946 to promote the study of organic evolution and the integration of the various fields of science concerned with evolution; Exec. Vice-Pres. KENT HOLSINGER; publ. *Evolution*.

TECHNOLOGY

American Ceramic Society, Inc.: POB 6136, Westerville, OH 43086-6136; tel. (614) 890-4700; fax (614) 899-6109; f. 1899; 11,614 mems; library of 11,000 vols; Exec. Dir W. PAUL HOLBROOK; runs Ceramic Correspondence Inst.; publs *Ceramic Society Bulletin* (monthly), *Ceramic Abstracts* (5 a year), *Ceramic Engineering and Science Proceedings* (5 a year), *Ceramic Source* (annually), *Journal of the American Ceramic Society* (monthly), *Ceramics Monthly*.

American Consulting Engineers Council: 1015 15th St, NW, Washington, DC 20005; tel. (202) 347-7474; fax (202) 898-0068; f. 1956; 5,000 mems; Exec. Vice-Pres. HOWARD M. MESSNER; publs *Directory, American Consulting Engineer*.

American Institute of Aeronautics and Astronautics: 1801 Alexander Bell Drive, Suite 500, Reston, VA 20191; f. 1930; 35,000 professional, 10,000 student mems; Pres. ROBERT A. FUHRMAN; Exec. Dir CORT DUROCHER; publs *Aerospace America* (includes *AIAA Bulletin*), *Journal of Spacecraft and Rockets, Journal of Aircraft, AIAA Journal, AIAA Student Journal, Journal of Guidance, Control and Dynamics, Journal of Propulsion and Power, Journal of Thermophysics and Heat Transfer, Progress Series* and *Education Series* books.

American Institute of Chemical Engineers: 345 East 47th St, New York, NY 10017; tel. (800) 242-4363; fax (212) 752-3294; f. 1908; 57,000 mems; Pres. THOMAS EDGAR; Exec. Dir GLENN TAYLOR; publs *AIChE Journal* (monthly), *Chemical Engineering Progress* (monthly), *Biotechnology Progress* (every 2 months), *Environmental Progress* (quarterly), *Process Safety Progress* (quarterly), *Chemical Engineering Faculty Directory* (annually), *ChAPTER One* (8 a year).

American Institute of Mining, Metallurgical and Petroleum Engineers, Inc.: 345 East 47th St, New York, NY 10017; f. 1871; Exec. Dir ROBERT H. MARCRUM.

Member societies:

Society for Mining, Metallurgy and Exploration, Inc.: POB 625002, Littleton, CT 80162-5002; publs *Mining Engineering, Transactions*.

Minerals, Metals and Materials Society: 420 Commonwealth Drive, Warrendale, PA 15086; publs *Journal of Metals, Metallurgical Transactions A* (monthly), *B* (quarterly).

Iron and Steel Society: 410 Commonwealth Drive, Warrendale, PA 15086; publ. *Iron and Steel maker*.

Society of Petroleum Engineers: POB 833836, Richardson, TX 75083-3836; publs *Journal of Petroleum Technology, Journal, Transactions, OTC Preprint*.

American Iron and Steel Institute: 1101 17th St, NW, Washington, DC 20036; f. 1908; 50 corporate mems; Pres. ANDREW G. SHARKEY.

American National Standards Institute: 11 West 42nd St, New York, NY 10036; tel. (212) 642-4900; telex 42-42-96; fax (212) 398-0023; f. 1918; co-ordinates the development of voluntary national standards, approves American National Standards, and represents US interests in the ISO and the IEC; mems: 1,500 companies, 275 organizations; Chair. LAWRENCE WILLS; Pres. SERGIO MAZZA; publ. *Reporter* (monthly), *Standards Action* (every 2 weeks).

American Society for Engineering Education: f. 1893; for the improvement of higher and continuing education for engineers and engineering technologists including teaching, counselling, research, ethics, etc.; 10,200 individual mems; 500 institutional mems; Exec. Dir FRANK L. HUBAND, Suite 600, 1818 N St NW, Washington, DC 20036; tel. (202) 331-3500; publs *ASEE Prism, Journal of Engineering Education, Chemical Engineering Education, Civil Engineering Education, Computers in Education Journal, The Engineering Economist, Mechanical Engineering News, Engineering Design Graphics Journal, Directory of Engineering and Engineering Technology, Journal of Engineering Technology*.

American Society for Photogrammetry and Remote Sensing: 5410 Grosvenor Lane, Suite 210, Bethesda, MD 20814-2160; tel. (301) 493-0290; fax (301) 493-0208; f. 1934; aerial photography, photogrammetry, photo-interpretation, remote sensing, geographic information systems (GIS), surveying, mapping, cartography; 7,000 mems; Pres. ROGER E. CRYSTAL; Exec. Dir WILLIAM D. FRENCH; publs *Manuals of Photogrammetry, Non-Topographic Photogrammetry, GIS Compendiums, Photogrammetric Engineering and Remote Sensing* (monthly), technical papers from meetings and symposia.

American Society for Testing and Materials (ASTM): 1916 Race St, Philadelphia, PA 19103; tel. (215) 299-5400; fax (215) 977-9679; inc. 1902; voluntary consensus standards; 35,000 mems; Pres. JAMES A. THOMAS; publs *ASTM Book of Standards* (annually), *Journal of Testing and Evaluation* (every 2 months), *Standardization News* (monthly), *Journal of Forensic Sciences* (quarterly), *Composites Technology Review* (quarterly), *Geotechnical Testing Journal* (quarterly), *Cement, Concrete and Aggregates* (2 a year).

American Society of Civil Engineers: 1801 Alexander Bell Drive, Reston, VA 20191-4400; f. 1852; 105,000 mems; Exec. Dir JAMES E. DAVIS; publs *Journals* (monthly), *Transactions* (annually), *Civil Engineering, ASCE* (monthly), *ASCE News, Publications Information* (every 2 months), books, manuals, standards.

American Society of Heating, Refrigerating and Air-Conditioning Engineers, Inc.: 1791 Tullie Circle NE, Atlanta, GA 30329; tel. (404) 636-8400; fax (404) 321-5478; e-mail ashrae@ashrae.org; f. 1959 by merger of the American Society of Heating and Ventilating Engineers and the American Society of Refrigerating Engineers; *c.* 50,000 mems; Sec. and Exec. Vice-Pres. FRANK M. CODA; publs *ASHRAE Journal* (monthly), *ASHRAE Handbook* (annually), *Standards, Transactions* (2 a year), *Research Bulletins, International Journal of Heating, Ventilating, Air-Conditioning and Refrigerating Research* (4 a year).

American Society of Mechanical Engineers: United Engineering Center, 345 East 47th St, New York, NY 10017; tel. (212) 705-7722; telex 710-581-5267; fax (212) 705-7674; f. 1880; 122,000 mems; Pres. J. A. FALCON, Jr.; Exec. Dir DAVID L. BELDEN; publs *Mechanical Engineering* (monthly), *Applied Mechanics Reviews* (monthly), Transactions (divided into 17 periodicals, each published quarterly): *Journal of Applied Mechanics; Biomechanical Engineering; Dynamic Systems, Measurement and Control; Energy Resources Technology; Engineering for Industry; Engineering for Gas Turbines and Power; Engineering Materials and Technology; Fluids Engineering; Heat Transfer; Mechanisms, Transmissions and Automation in Design; Pressure Vessel Technology; Solar Energy Engineering; Tribology; Vibration and Acoustics; Electronic Packaging; Turbomachinery; Manufacturing Review* (quarterly).

American Society of Naval Engineers, Inc.: 1452 Duke St, Alexandria, VA 22314-3458; tel. (703) 836-6727; fax (703) 836-7491; f. 1888; 6,000 mems; Pres. J. F. YURSO; Exec. Dir Capt. DENNIS KRUSE; publ. *Naval Engineers Journal* (every 2 months).

American Welding Society: 550 NW Le Jeune Rd, Miami, FL 33126; tel. (305) 443-9353; telex 51-9245; fax (305) 443-7559; f. 1919; welding education seminars and conferences, qualification and certification, annual int. exposition; 46,000 mems; Exec. Dir F. G. DELAURIER; publs *Welding Journal* (monthly), *Inspection Trends* (4 a year), *Welding Handbook* (every 3 years), 200 welding standards, references, training guides.

ASM International: 9639 Kinsman Rd, Materials Park, OH 44073-0002; tel. (440) 338-5151; fax (440) 338-4634; e-mail cust-srv@po.asm-intl.org; f. 1913; 43,000 mems; technical society concerned with advanced materials technology; Man. Dir Dr MICHAEL J. DE HAEMER; publs *Advanced Materials and Processes* (monthly, containing *ASM News*), *Metallurgical Transactions A* (monthly), *& B* (6 a year) (with TMS–AIME), *International Materials Reviews* (6 a year, with Institute of Materials), *Journal of Materials Engineering, and Performance* (6 a year), *Alloy Digest* (monthly), *Journal of Phase Equilibria* (6 a year), *Journal of Thermal Spray Technology* (4 a year).

Association of Consulting Chemists and Chemical Engineers, Inc.: 40 West 45th St, New York, NY 10036; tel. (212) 983-3160; fax (212) 983-3161; f. 1928; 160 mems; Exec. Sec. LINDA B. TOWNSEND; publ. *Consulting Services Directory*.

Edison Electric Institute: 701 Pennsylvania Ave, NW, Washington, DC 20004-2696; tel. (202) 508-5000; fax (202) 508-5360; f. 1933; mems US shareholder-owned electric power companies, int. affiliates and associates; Pres. THOMAS R. KUHN.

Illuminating Engineering Society of North America: 120 Wall St, New York, NY 10005; f. 1906; 10,000 mems; Exec. Vice-Pres. W. HANLEY; publs *Lighting Design and Application* (monthly), *Journal* (2 a year), *IES Lighting Handbooks*.

Industrial Designers Society of America, Inc.: 1142 Walker Rd, Great Falls, VA 22066; tel. (703) 759-0100; fax (703) 759-7679; e-mail idsa@erols.com; f. 1965; 2,300 mems; Exec. Dir ROBERT T. SCHWARTZ; publs *Design Perspectives* (newsletter, monthly), *Innovation* (quarterly).

Institute of Electrical and Electronics Engineers, Inc.: 345 East 47th St, New York, NY 10017; tel. (212) 705-7900; telex 236411; fax (212) 752-4929; f. 1884; 320,000 mems; Exec. Dir JOHN H. POWERS; publs *IEEE Spectrum / The Institute, IEEE Potentials* (monthly), *Proceedings* (monthly), *Society and Council Transactions, etc.*

Institute of Food Technologists: 221 North La Salle St, Suite 300, Chicago, IL 60601; tel. (312) 782-8424; fax (312) 782-8348; e-mail info@ift.org; f. 1939; 28,000 mems; Pres. BRUCE STILLINGS; Exec. Dir DANIEL E. WEBER; publs *Food Technology* (monthly), *Journal of Food Science* (every 2 months).

Institute of Industrial Engineers: 25 Technology Park/Atlanta, Norcross, GA 30092; tel. (770) 449-0460; fax (770) 263-8532; f. 1948; 30,000 mems; Dir of Operations DAVID LEVY; publs *IIE Solutions* (monthly), *Industrial Management* (every 2 months), *IIE Transactions* (monthly), *The Engineering Economist* (quarterly).

Instrument Society of America: POB 12277, 67 Alexander Drive, Research Triangle Park, NC 27709; tel. (919) 549-8411; telex 802540; fax (919) 549-8288; f. 1945; 47,000 mems; Exec. Dir G. F. HARVEY, Pres. HUGH N. ROSER; conferences and exhibitions, symposia, special interest divisions, training, certification, consensus standards; publs *InTech* (monthly), *Industrial Computing* (monthly), *Motion Control* (8 a year), *ISA Directory of Instrumentation* (annually).

International Communication Association: formerly National Society for the Study of Communication; f. 1950 to bring together academics and professionals concerned with research and application of human communication; 3,200 mems; Pres. PETER MONGE; Exec. Dir ROBERT L. COX, POB 9589, 8140 Burnet Rd, Austin, TX 78757-7799; tel. (512) 454-8299; fax (512) 454-4221; publs *A Guide to Publishing in Scholarly Communication Journals, Human Communication Research, Communication Theory, Journal of Communication, Membership Directory, Annual Conference Program* (annually), *The ICA NEWSLETTER, The Communication Yearbook.*

National Society of Professional Engineers: 1420 King St, Alexandria, VA 22314; tel. (703) 684-2800; f. 1934; professional aspects of engineering; 69,000 mems; Exec. Dir RUSSELL C. JONES; publ. *Engineering Times* (monthly).

Society for the History of Technology: Dept. of History, Auburn University, Auburn, AL 36849-5207; tel. (334) 844-6645; fax (334) 844-6673; f. 1958; concerned with history of technological devices and processes, relations of technology with science, politics, social change, the arts and humanities, and economics; affiliated to the American Association for the Advancement of Science, the American Council of Learned Societies; 2,600 mems; Pres. Dr ROBERT POST, Sec. Dr LINDY BIGGS; publs *Technology and Culture, SHOT Newsletter* (both quarterly).

Society of Automotive Engineers, Inc.: 400 Commonwealth Drive, Warrendale, PA 15096; tel. (724) 776-4841; fax (724) 772-1851; e-mail magazines@sae.org; f. 1905; 75,000 mems; Exec. Vice-Pres. MAX E. RUMBAUGH, Jr. publs *SAE Transactions, SAE Handbook* (annually), *Automotive Engineering International* (monthly), *Off-Highway Engineering* (6 a year), *Aerospace Engineering* (monthly), *SAE Update* (monthly).

Society of Manufacturing Engineers: POB 930, Dearborn, MI 48121-0930; tel. (313) 271-1500; fax (313) 271-2861; f. 1932 to advance scientific knowledge in the field of manufacturing and to apply its resources to research, writing, publishing and disseminating information; 65,000 mems in 70 countries; library of 7,000 vols; Exec. Dir/Gen. Man. PHILIP TRIMBLE; publs *Manufacturing Engineering* (monthly), *Forming and Fabricating* (monthly), *Molding Systems* (monthly), *Integrated Design and Manufacturing* (monthly), *Journal of Manufacturing Systems, Composites in Manufacturing, Electronics Manufacturing Engineering, Finishing Line, Vision, Robotics Today, Machining Technology* (all quarterly).

Society of Naval Architects and Marine Engineers: 601 Pavonia Ave, Suite 400, Jersey City, NJ 07306; tel. (201) 798-4800; fax (201) 798-4975; f. 1893; 10,000 mems; Exec. Dir FRANCIS M. CAGLIARI; publs *Transactions* (annually), *Journal of Ship Research* (quarterly), *Journal of Ship Production* (quarterly), *Marine Technology* (quarterly).

Society of Rheology: 500 Sunnyside Blvd, Woodbury, NY 11797; f. 1929; Pres. R. G. LARSON; Sec. A. M. KRAYNIK; publs *Rheology Bulletin* (2 a year), *Journal of Rheology* (every 2 months).

Research Institutes

GENERAL

Getty Research Institute for the History of Art and the Humanities: 1200 Getty Center Drive, Suite 1100, Los Angeles, CA 90049-1688; tel. (310) 440-7335; f. 1983; institute for advanced research; library of 487,000 books, 133,000 periodicals, 122,000 auction sales catalogues; 3,100 archives and MSS collns; 1,700,000 study photographs; Dir SALVATORE SETTIS.

National Humanities Center: 7 Alexander Drive, POB 12256, Research Triangle Park, NC 27709; tel. (919) 549-0661; f. 1977; an institute for advanced study created to encourage scholarship in the humanities and to enhance the usefulness and influence of the humanities in the USA; awards Fellowships (30 a year) to pursue advanced post-doctoral research and writing at the Center, organizes seminars, lectures, conferences; library has reference works, bibliographical aids, microfilm catalogue; Chair. JOHN BIRKELUND; Pres/Dir W. ROBERT CONNOR; Sec. JOHN ADAMS; publs annual report, conference proceedings.

RAND: 1700 Main St, Santa Monica, CA 90406-2138; f. 1948; brs in Washington and in Delft (Netherlands); research on matters affecting the public interest; education, civil and criminal justice, health sciences, int. affairs, labour and population, science and technology, national security, information processing systems; non-profit instn receiving funds from federal, state and local government, foundations and the private sector; 550 research professionals; Pres. Dr JAMES A. THOMSON; Chair. G. G. MICHELSON; publs research reports, *Rand Research Review* (3 a year).

AGRICULTURE, FISHERIES AND VETERINARY SCIENCE

Agricultural Research Institute: 236 Massachusetts Ave NE, Suite 401, Washington, DC 20002; tel. (202) 544-5534; fax (202) 544-5749; f. 1951; 100 mems; forum for agricultural research administrators to discuss agricultural research programmes and needs; Exec. Dir RICHARD A. HERRETT; publs *Newsletter* (every 2 months), *Proceedings* (annually).

Forest Products Society: 2801 Marshall Court, Madison, WI 53705; tel. (608) 231-1361; fax (608) 231-2152; f. 1947; Technology transfer concerning all areas of the forest products industry; 3,000 mems from over 50 countries; Exec. Vice-Pres. ARTHUR B. BRAUNER; publ. *Forest Products Journal* (10 a year), *Wood Design Focus* (quarterly).

BIBLIOGRAPHY, LIBRARY SCIENCE AND MUSEOLOGY

Getty Conservation Institute: 1200 Getty Center Drive, Los Angeles, CA 90049-1684; tel. (310) 440-7325; f. 1983; a programme of the J. Paul Getty Trust; works internationally for the preservation of the world's cultural heritage; library of 25,000 vols; Dir Dr MIGUEL ANGEL CORZO; publs *Art and Archaeology Technical Abstracts* (2 a year), *GCI Newsletter* (3 a year), *Research in Conservation* (annually).

Institute for Scientific Information: 3501 Market St, Philadelphia, PA 19104; f. 1960; periodicals library of 8,000 titles; Pres. and CEO MICHAEL TANSEY, publs *Science Citation Index, Social Sciences Citation Index, Arts and Humanities Citation Index, CompuMath Citation Index, Index to Scientific and Technical Proceedings, Index to Scientific Reviews, Index to Social Sciences and Humanities Proceedings, Index Chemicus, Current Chemical Reactions, Index to Scientific Book Contents; Current Contents* in the following editions: *Agriculture, Biology and Environmental Sciences; Social and Behavioural Sciences; Arts and Humanities; Engineering, Technology and Applied Sciences; Life Sciences; Clinical Medicine; Physical, Chemical and Earth Sciences; Biotechnology Citation Index, Neuroscience Citation Index, Mathematical Science Citation Index, Chemistry Citation Index, Materials Science Citation Index, Biochemistry and Biophysics Citation Index*; online databases include: *Scisearch, Social Scisearch, Arts & Humanities Search, Computer & Mathematics Search, Current Contents Search, ISTP Search, ISTP & B Search, Research Alert Direct.* (Products available in print and in electronic form.)

National Federation of Abstracting and Information Services: 1518 Walnut St, Suite 307, Philadelphia, PA 19102; tel. (215) 893-1561; fax (215) 893-1564; e-mail nfais@nfais.org; f. 1958; aims to serve the world's information community through education, research, and publication; *c.* 70 mems; Pres. JAMES E. LOHR; Dir RICHARD T. KASER; publ. *NFAIS Newsletter* (monthly).

ECONOMICS, LAW AND POLITICS

Brookings Institution: 1775 Massachusetts Ave, NW, Washington, DC 20036; tel. (202) 797-6000; fax (202) 797-6004; f. 1916; 61 professional mems; library of 80,000 vols, 700 periodical titles, files of pamphlets and govt documents, selected UN documents; research, education, and publishing in the fields of economics, government, and foreign policy; Pres. MICHAEL H. ARMACOST, Chair. JAMES A. JOHNSON; publs *The Brookings Review* (quarterly), *Brookings Papers on Economic Activity* (3 a year).

Center for the Study of Democratic Institutions: 10951 West Pico Blvd, Suite 300, Los Angeles, CA 90064; tel. (310) 474-0011; fax (310) 474-8061; f. 1959, fmrly Robert Maynard Hutchins Center for the Study of Democratic Institutions; Exec. Dir NATHAN GARDELS; publ. *New Perspectives Quarterly.*

Counterpart Foundation: 910 17th St NW (Suite 328), Washington, DC 20006-2601; tel. (202) 296-9676; fax (202) 296-9679; f. 1965 to assist human development; to protect tropical forests; to provide technical assistance in assessment, planning, implementation and evaluation of projects; library of 300 vols; offices in Washington, DC, New York, California, Hawaii; programs in Fiji, Kiribati, Papua New Guinea, Tonga, Vanuatu, Samoa, Solomon Islands, Russia, Ukraine, Moldova, Belarus, Kazakhstan, Kyrgyzstan, Uzbekistan, Vietnam; Chair./Pres. ELIZABETH B. SILVERSTEIN; Exec. Dir STANLEY W. HOSIE; publ. *Annual Report*.

East-West Center: 1601 East-West Rd, Honolulu, HI 96848; e-mail ewcinfo@ewc.hawaii.edu; f. 1960; a public, nonprofit educational institution with an international board of governors; *c.* 2,000 research fellows, graduate students, and professionals in government, academia and business each year work with the Center's international staff in cooperative study, training, and research; they examine major issues related to international relations, journalism, population, resources, economic development, the environment, culture, and communication in Asia, the Pacific and the United States; Pres. KENJI SUMIDA (acting); publs *Asia-Pacific Report* (annually), *Centerviews* (every 2 months), *Annual Report of President*, various scholarly publs.

International Center for Economic Growth: One Sansome St, Suite 2000, San Francisco, CA 94104; tel. (415) 984-3193; fax (415) 984-3196; e-mail rhodam@iceg.org; f. 1985 to promote economic growth and human development in the developing and post-socialist countries by strengthening the capacity of local research institutes to provide leadership in policy debates; operates in conjunction with a network of 370 mem. institutes worldwide; sponsors conferences and seminars; CEO ROBERT HODAM; publ. *Newsletter*.

International Marketing Institute, The: 314 Hammond St, Suite 52, Chestnut Hill, MA 02167-1206; tel. (617) 552-8690; fax (617) 552-2590; f. 1960; affiliated to Boston College Graduate School of Management; international executive development and management training programmes in management education, with marketing as the primary focus; Exec. Dir JOSEPH B. GANNON.

Marketing Science Institute: 1000 Massachusetts Ave, Cambridge, MA 02138; tel. (617) 491-2060; fax (617) 491-2065; e-mail msi@msi.org; f. 1961; non-profit marketing consortium that stimulates, supports, and reports research in order to advance marketing knowledge and practice; sponsors and publishes academic research on all areas of marketing; 57 mem. companies; Pres. H. PAUL ROOT; Exec. Dir ROHIT DESHPANDÉ.

National Bureau of Economic Research: 1050 Massachusetts Ave, Cambridge, MA 02138; f. 1920; fundamental qualitative analysis of the US economy; 50 Dirs; Pres. MARTIN FELDSTEIN.

Scripps Foundation for Research in Population Problems and Gerontology Center: Miami University, 396 Upham, Oxford, OH 45056; f. 1922; 20 mems; library of 4,000 vols; Dir SUZANNE R. KUNKEL.

EDUCATION

American Educational Research Association: 1230 17th St, NW, Washington, DC 20036-3078; tel. (202) 223-9485; fax (202) 775-1824; f. 1915; 23,000 mems; Exec. Officer WILLIAM J. RUSSELL; publs *American Educational Research Journal, Review of Educational Research, Educational Researcher, Review of Research in Education, Journal of Educational and Behavioral Statistics, Educational Evaluation and Policy Analysis.*

Office of Educational Research and Improvement (OERI): 555 New Jersey Ave NW, Washington, DC 20208; f. 1980 by Congress; part of the US Dept of Education; main government agency supporting educational research; aims to improve the quality of educational practice; consists of five principal components: Fund for the Improvement and Reform of Schools and Teaching, Library Programs, Program for the Improvement of Practice, Office of Research, and National Center for Education Statistics; publs statistical and research reports.

HISTORY, GEOGRAPHY AND ARCHAEOLOGY

Center for Reformation Research: 6477 San Bonita Ave, St Louis, MO 63105; tel. (314) 505-7199; fax (314) 505-7198; e-mail cslcrr@crf.cuis.edu; f. 1957; microfilm library of original MSS and printed materials of the 15th and 16th centuries; reference library; Exec. Dir ROBERT ROSIN; publ. *Newsletter*.

Leo Baeck Institute, Inc.: 129 East 73rd St, New York, NY 10021; tel (212) 744-6400; fax (212) 988-1305; f. 1955; research and publication about the history of German-speaking Jews; library of 60,000 vols, archives, photographs and art collection; 1,100 mems; Pres. Dr ISMAR SCHORSCH; Exec. Dir CAROL KAHN STRAUSS; publs *LBI Yearbook, LBI News, Library and Archives News.*

Mississippi Office of Geology: POB 20307, Jackson, MS 39289; tel. (601) 961-5500; fax (601) 961-5521; f. 1850; research into the geology and mineral resources of the State; library of 60,000 vols; Dir S. CRAGIN KNOX; publs *Mississippi Geology,* bulletins.

Paleontological Research Institution: 1259 Trumansburg Rd, Ithaca, NY 14850; tel. (607) 273-6623; fax (607) 273-6620; f. 1932; 1,000 mems; library of 50,000 vols; collection of 2 m. specimens; Dir Dr WARREN D. ALLMON; publs *Bulletins of American Paleontology* (2 a year), *Palaeontographica Americana* (irregular), *American Paleontologist* (quarterly).

School of American Research: Box 2188, Santa Fé, NM 87504; tel. (505) 954-7200; fax (505) 989-9809; f. 1907; centre for advanced studies in anthropology; grants to five resident scholars annually; two native American fellows annually; advanced seminars in anthropology; anthropological publications; extensive collections in Southwest Indian art; 2,000 mems; library of 6,000 vols; Pres. DOUGLAS W. SCHWARTZ; Chair. DAVID D. CHASE.

MEDICINE

American Association for Cancer Research, Inc.: c/o Exec. Dir Dr MARGARET FOTI, Public Ledger Bldg, Suite 826, 150 South Independence Mall West, Philadelphia, PA 19106-3483; tel. (215) 440-9300; fax (215) 440-9313; e-mail meetings@aacr.org; f. 1907; to facilitate communication and dissemination of knowledge among scientists and others dedicated to cancer research; 14,000 mems; Pres. WEBSTER K. CAVENEE; publs *Cancer Research* (fortnightly), *Cell Growth and Differentiation* (monthly), *Cancer Epidemiology, Biomarkers & Prevention* (monthly), *Clinical Cancer Research* (monthly).

American Federation for Medical Research: 1200 19th St NW, Suite 300, Washington, DC 20036; tel. (202) 429-5161; fax (202) 223-4579; e-mail afmr@dc.sba.com; f. 1940; 5,300 mems; Pres. MONICA FARLEY; Exec. Administrator LINDA S. CHRENO; publ. *Journal of Investigative Medicine* (6 a year).

Association for Research in Nervous and Mental Disease, Inc.: c/o Secretary, Dr JAMES E. GOLDMAN, 630 West 168th St, New York, NY 10032; tel. (212) 740-7608; fax (212) 305-4548; f. 1920; annual meeting for continuing medical education credits on research topics of interest to neurologists and psychiatrists; 850 mems.

Association for Research in Vision and Ophthalmology, Inc.: 9650 Rockville Pike, Bethesda, MD 20814-3998; f. 1928; 10,198 mems; Exec. Vice-Pres. Dr JANET C. BLANKS; publ. *Investigative Ophthalmology and Visual Science*.

California Pacific Medical Center Research Institute: 2340 Clay St (5th Floor), San Francisco, CA 94115; tel. (415) 561-1601; fax (415) 561-1753; f. 1959; non-profit research division of medical centre conducting patient-oriented research in arthritis, AIDS, cancer, including leukemia and monoclonal antibodies, heart disease, immunology and infectious diseases, artificial heart research, organ transplantation and preservation, neurology, maternal foetal medicine, child health and human development; Vice-Pres. for Research DAVID R. FIELDER.

Fox Chase Cancer Center: 7701 Burholme Ave, Philadelphia, PA 19111; tel. (215) 728-6900; fax (215) 728-3655; f. 1926; library of 22,000 vols including 5,000 monographs and 440 scientific journals; Pres. Dr ROBERT C. YOUNG.

Huntington Medical Research Institutes: 734 Fairmount Ave, Pasadena, CA 91105; tel. (818) 397-5436; fax (818) 397-3330; f. 1952; oncology, cell biology, differentiated cell culture, cancer genetics, prostatic cancer, immunotherapy, biomedical magnetic resonance spectroscopy, cardiology, development of neural prosthetic devices; Exec. Dir WILLIAM OPEL; publ. *Newsletter*.

Jackson Laboratory: 600 Main St, Bar Harbor, Maine 04609-1500; f. 1929; research in molecular genetics, cell biology, biochemistry, immunology and physiological genetics; library of 3,000 books, 20,000 bound journals, 370 current journals and 46,000 article reprints; Dir Dr KENNETH PAIGEN; publs *Scientific Report, Training for Research* (annually), *Inside the Jackson Laboratory* (quarterly), *Annual Report*.

Lovelace Institutes: 2425 Ridgecrest Drive, SE, Albuquerque, NM 87108-5127; fax (505) 262-7043; f. 1947 to conduct biomedical research and technology development; 300 mems; library of 13,700 books and 486 journals; CEO Dr DAVID J. OTTENSMEYER; Vice-Pres. for Admin. Dr ROBERT F. BESTGEN; publs *Annual Report, Advances*.

Mayo Foundation: Rochester, MN 55905; tel. (507) 284-2658; f. 1919; clinical medicine, medical research, graduate and undergraduate education; library of 275,000 vols and 3,500 periodicals; Chair. Board of Trustees E. W. SPENCER; Pres. R. R. WALLER; Admin. J. H. HERRELL; publ. *Mayo Clinic Proceedings* (monthly).

Menninger: 5800 SW 6th Ave, Box 829, Topeka, KS 66601-0829; tel. (785) 350-5000; fax (785) 273-8625; e-mail webmaster@menninger.edu; f. 1925 as a non-profit mental health centre for inpatient and outpatient treatment of mental illness through preventive psychiatry, clinical treatment, research and professional education; medical library of 50,000 vols; Pres. Dr EFRAIN BLEIBERG; CEO Dr W. WALTER MENNINGER; publs *Menninger Perspective* (quarterly), *Bulletin of the Menninger Clinic* (quarterly).

National Institutes of Health: US Department of Health and Human Services, Public Health Service, Bethesda, MD 20892; principal agency of DHHS for biomedical research, research training, and biomedical communications; National Library of Medicine: see Libraries and Archives; Dir HAROLD E. VARMUS.

Constituent institutes:

National Institute of Child Health and Human Development: C/o US Department of Health and Human Services, Public Health Service, Bethesda, MD 20892; f. 1963; supports, fosters and co-ordinates research and training in areas of maternal health, child health and human development, focusing on the continuing process of growth and development, biological and behavioural; also supports research in the population sciences, incl. contraceptive development and evaluation, reproductive health, behavioural and demographic research, and medical rehabilitation; Dir DUANE ALEXANDER.

National Institute of Arthritis and Musculoskeletal and Skin Diseases: C/o US Department of Health and Human Services, Public Health Service, Bethesda, MD 20892; f. 1986; basic and clinical research and training on the causes, prevention, diagnosis and treatment of rheumatic diseases such as rheumatoid arthritis, osteoarthritis and lupus; musculoskeletal diseases such as osteoporosis, Paget's disease of bone, and skin diseases such as psoriasis, acne, ichthyosis and blistering disorders; information and education activities; Dir LAWRENCE E. SHULMAN.

National Institute of Diabetes and Digestive and Kidney Diseases: C/o US Department of Health and Human Services, Public Health Service, Bethesda, MD 20892; f. 1950, renamed 1986; conducts and supports research into diabetes, endocrinology, metabolic diseases, digestive diseases, nutrition, kidney and urologic diseases and haematology; information and education activities; Dir PHILLIP GORDEN.

National Heart, Lung and Blood Institute: C/o US Department of Health and Human Services, Public Health Service, Bethesda, MD 20892; f. 1948 as National Heart Institute, redesignated 1969 and 1976; performs and supports research in diseases of the heart, blood vessels, lungs (exclusive of pulmonary malignancies) and blood; Dir CLAUDE J. M. LENFANT.

National Cancer Institute: C/o US Department of Health and Human Services, Public Health Service, Bethesda, MD 20892; f. 1937; supports broad research programmes into the causes, detection and diagnosis, and treatment of cancer; co-operates with State and local health agencies and voluntary bodies; Dir SAMUEL BRODER.

National Institute of Allergy and Infectious Diseases: C/o US Department of Health and Human Services, Public Health Service, Bethesda, MD 20892; f. 1955; conducts and supports research in the fields of AIDS, allergy, immunology, molecular biology, and infectious diseases; aimed at understanding acquired and inherited immune deficiencies, furthering molecular genetic studies and controlling viral, parasitic, fungal and bacterial diseases; Dir ANTHONY S. FAUCI.

National Institute of Dental Research: C/o US Department of Health and Human Services, Public Health Service, Bethesda, MD 20892; f. 1948; conducts and supports research on the diseases and disorders that affect oral and facial tissues across the lifespan; includes research on the relationship between oral and general health, also basic and clinical research on pain; Dir (vacant).

National Institute of Neurological Disorders and Stroke: C/o US Department of Health and Human Services, Public Health Service, Bethesda, MD 20892; f. 1950; conducts, fosters, and co-ordinates research on the causes, prevention, diagnosis and treatment of disorders of the brain and nervous system; Dir (vacant).

National Institute of Nursing Research: C/o US Department of Health and Human Services, Public Health Service, Bethesda, MD 20892; f. 1993; supports and conducts scientific research and research training to strengthen nursing practice and health care for prevention and amelioration of disease and disability.

National Institute on Deafness and Other Communication Disorders: C/o US Department of Health and Human Services, Public Health Service, Bethesda, MD 20892; f. 1988; supports research and training on disorders of hearing and other communication processes including balance, smell, taste, voice, speech and language; Dir JAMES D. SNOW, Jr.

National Institute of General Medical Sciences: C/o US Department of Health and Human Services, Public Health Service, Bethesda, MD 20892; f. 1962; supports a programme of research and training in the basic medical sciences; Dir RUTH L. KIRSCHSTEIN.

National Institute of Environmental Health Sciences: C/o US Department of Health and Human Services, Public Health Service, Bethesda, MD 20892; f. 1969; conducts, fosters and co-ordinates research on the biological effects of chemical, physical, and biological substances present in or introduced into the environment; Dir KENNETH OLDEN.

National Eye Institute: C/o US Department of Health and Human Services, Public Health Service, Bethesda, MD 20892; f. 1968; conducts and supports research and training relating to blinding eye diseases and visual disorders, including research and training in the special health problems and requirements of the blind; conducts and supports investigations into the basic sciences relating to the mechanisms of sight and visual functions; Dir CARL KUPFER.

National Institute on Aging: C/o US Department of Health and Human Services, Public Health Service, Bethesda, MD 20892; f. 1974; conducts and supports biomedical, social and behavioural research and training related to the ageing process and diseases and other special problems and needs of the aged; Dir RICHARD J. HODES.

Naval Aerospace and Operational Medical Institute: Pensacola, FL 32508-1047; f. 1939; training in aviation and aerospace medicine; library of 20,000 vols; Commanding Officer Capt. R. E. HAIN.

Radiation Research Society: 2021 Spring Rd, Suite 600, Oak Brook, IL 60523; tel. (630) 571-2881; fax (630) 571-7837; f. 1952; 1,990 mems; Pres. WILLIAM A. BERNHARD; Exec. Sec. LISE STEY SWANSON; publs *Radiation Research* (monthly), *Newsletter* (quarterly).

Schepens Eye Research Institute: 20 Staniford St, Boston, MA 02114; tel. (617) 912-0100; fax (617) 912-0101; e-mail geninfo@vision.eri.harvard.edu; f. 1950; basic and clinical research on causes, prevention and treatment of eye diseases, development of diagnostic and therapeutic devices, instruments and techniques for ophthalmology, study of the processes of vision; library of 200 vols, 100 journals; Pres. Dr J. WAYNE STREILEIN; publ. *Sundial*.

Sloan-Kettering Institute for Cancer Research: 1275 York Ave, New York, NY 10021; tel (212) 639-5818; f. 1945; research in physical and biological sciences relating to cancer; postdoctoral research training in laboratory investigations with scientific staff; graduate instruction with Cornell University; research unit of Memorial Sloan-Kettering Cancer Center; Graduate School Dir Dr R. A. RIFKIND; publ. *Annual Report*.

Society for Pediatric Research: 3400 Research Forest Drive, Suite B7, The Woodlands, TX 77381; tel. (281) 296-0244; fax (281) 296-0255; e-mail info@aps-spr.org; f. 1929; Pres. DEBBIE ANAGNOSTELIS; Exec. Sec. KATHY CREWS; publs *Pediatric Research Program, Abstracts* (annually).

Southwest Foundation for Biomedical Research: POB 760549, San Antonio, TX 78425-0549; tel. (210) 674-1410; e-mail fledford@icarus.sfbr.org; f. 1941; basic research in biomedical sciences; library of 70,000 vols; Pres. FRANK F. LEDFORD, Jr; Scientific Dir Dr John L. VANDEBERG, publs *Progress in Biomedical Research* (quarterly), *Annual Report*.

Wistar Institute of Anatomy and Biology: 36th and Spruce Sts, Philadelphia, PA 19104; tel. (215) 898-3700; fax (215) 573-2097; f. 1892; cellular and subcellular research in human diseases; library of 5,000 vols; Dir GIOVANNI ROVERA.

Worcester Foundation for Biomedical Research: 222 Maple Ave, Shrewsbury, MA 01545; tel. (508) 842-8921; fax (508) 842-9632; f. 1944; independent biomedical research centre; emphasis on cell biology, molecular biology, neurobiology and developmental-reproductive biology; conducts joint PhD programme with Clark University, Worcester Polytechnic Inst. and the University of Massachusetts Medical School; library of 25,000 vols; special collections: cellular/molecular biology, developmental biology, neurobiology, endocrine/reproductive biology; Pres. and Dir THORU PEDERSON; publs *Research Reporter* (quarterly), *Annual Report, Scientific Report*.

NATURAL SCIENCES

General

Battelle Memorial Institute: 505 King Ave, Columbus, OH 43201-2693; tel. (614) 424-3304; fax (614) 424-5263; e-mail solutions@battelle.org; f. 1929; serves industry and Government in the generation, application and commercialization of technology; supports research and development activities of clients in 30 countries; major areas of activity are health and environment, products and processes, technology management consulting, national security, energy; research operations in the USA and Europe; offices worldwide; library of more than 150,000 vols; Pres. and Chief Exec. Dr DOUGLAS E. OLESEN.

Carnegie Institution of Washington: 1530 P St, NW, Washington, DC 20005; tel. (202) 387-6400; fax (202) 387-8092; f. 1902 'to encourage, in the broadest and most liberal manner, investigation, research, and discovery, and the application of knowledge to the improvement of mankind'; research and education in the biological and physical sciences; 80 faculty mems; Chair. Board of Trustees THOMAS N. URBAN; Pres. MAXINE F. SINGER; publs *Year Book, Academic Catalog*.

Attached departments:

Observatories of the Carnegie Institution: 813 Santa Barbara St, Pasadena, CA 91101; f. 1904 as Mount Wilson Observatory; Dir AUGUSTUS OEMLER.

Geophysical Laboratory: 5251 Broad Branch Rd, NW, Washington, DC 20015; f. 1906; Dir CHARLES T. PREWITT.

Department of Terrestrial Magnetism: 5241 Broad Branch Road, NW, Washington, DC 20015; f. 1904; Dir SEAN C. SOLOMON.

Department of Plant Biology: 290 Panama St, Stanford, CA 94305; f. 1903 as Desert Laboratory; Dir CHRISTOPHER SOMERVILLE.

Department of Embryology: 115 West University Parkway, Baltimore, MD 21210; f. 1914; Dir ALLAN C. SPRADLING.

Center for Short-Lived Phenomena: POB 199, Harvard Square Station, Cambridge, MA 02238; f. 1968; collects information about oil spills worldwide, incl. details of sites, sources, substances, amounts, causes, clean-up action and environmental impact; Dir RICHARD GOLOB; publs *Golob's Oil Pollution Bulletin* (2 a month), *Hazardous Materials Intelligence Report* (weekly).

Midwest Research Institute: 425 Volker Blvd, Kansas City, MO 64110; tel. (816) 753-7600; fax (816) 753-8420; f. 1944; 1,000 mems; specialization in chemistry, biological sciences, toxicology, health sciences, environmental sciences, engineering, energy, economics, management sciences, human services, applied mathematics, safety; Pres. JOHN MCKELVEY; Exec. Vice-Pres. Dr JAMES SPIGARELLI; publ. *Annual Report*.

Southern Research Institute: POB 55305, Birmingham, AL 35255-5305; tel. (205) 581-2000; fax (205) 581-2726; f. 1941; contract scientific research in the areas of pharmaceutical discovery and development, engineering, environmental and energy-related sciences; library of 40,000 vols; Pres. GILBERT E. DWYER; Sec. BOB COSTON; publ. *Annual Report*.

World Resources Institute: 1709 New York Ave, NW, Suite 700, Washington, DC 20006; tel. (202) 638-6300; f. 1982; provides information about global resources and environmental conditions, analysis of emerging issues, and development of creative yet workable policy responses; seeks to deepen public understanding by publishing a variety of reports and papers, undertaking briefings, seminars and conferences, and offering material for use in the press and on the air; Pres. JONATHAN LASH; Sec.-Treas. MARJORIE BEANE.

Biological Sciences

Boyce Thompson Institute for Plant Research, Inc.: Cornell University, Tower Rd, Ithaca, NY 14853; tel. (607) 254-1234; fax (607) 254-1242; f. 1924; non-profit affiliate of Cornell University; research on plants and human health, including molecular biology, biochemistry, plant physiology, plant pathology, entomology, air and water pollution; library of 4,700 vols; Pres. CHARLES J. ARNTZEN; publ. *Annual Reports*.

Cold Spring Harbor Laboratory: POB 100, Cold Spring Harbor, NY 11724; tel. (516) 367-8397; fax (516) 367-8496; f. 1890, chartered under present title 1962; research on cancer biology, molecular neuroscience, structural biology, plant genetics, professional education, DNA literacy; library of 30,000 vols; special collections on history of science and genetics; Pres. Dr J. D. WATSON; Admin. Dir Dr BRUCE W. STILLMAN; publs *Symposia on Quantitative Biology* (annually), *CSH Monographs* (irregular), *Abstracts of Papers, Annual Report, CSH Current Communications in Cell and Molecular Biology, Banbury Reports* (irregular), *Cancer Surveys, Genes and Development* (every 2 months), *Genome Research* (monthly), *Learning and Memory* (every 2 months).

Marine Biological Laboratory: Woods Hole, Cape Cod, MA 02543; inc. 1888; research and teaching instn; offers courses and seminars on ecology, behaviour, developmental biology, microbiology, neurobiology, parasitology, cell and molecular biology and biological techniques; library of over 150,000 vols, 3,000 periodicals; Dir JOHN E. BURRIS; Chair. of Board SHELDON J. SEGAL; publs *Guide to Research and Education, Annual Report, Lab Notes, Biological Bulletin*.

Missouri Botanical Garden: POB 299, St Louis, MO 63166-0299; tel. (314) 577-5100; fax (314) 577-9595; f. 1859; botanical research, exploration, education and display, with emphases on monographic and floristic studies in North America, tropical Latin America and Africa; library of 123,000 vols, special collections: Pre-Linnaean, Linnaean, Rare Books; archives and non-book materials, herbarium collection (4.3 million vascular plants and 300,000 bryophytes); Dir PETER H. RAVEN; publs *Annals* (quarterly), *Herbarium News* (monthly), *Bulletin* (7 a year), *Monographs in Systematic Botany* (irregular), *Novon* (quarterly), *Flora of North America Newsletter* (every 2 months), *Flora of China Newsletter*.

Moss Landing Marine Laboratories: POB 450, Moss Landing, CA 95039; tel. (408) 633-8650; fax (408) 753-2826; f. 1966; research, undergraduate and postgraduate education in the marine sciences; library of 10,000 vols; Dir Dr KENNETH COALE.

Mote Marine Laboratory, Inc.: 1600 Thompson Parkway, Sarasota, FL 34236; tel. (941) 388-4441; fax (941) 388-4312; f. 1955; independent, non-profit marine research organization; research includes environmental assessment, estuarine and coastal ecology, marine chemistry, toxicology, biology and behaviour of fishes, marine mammals, sea turtles and biomedical research; Aquarium and environmental education programs; 4,000 mems; library of 3,000 vols, 21,000 reprints; Chair. ALFRED GOLDSTEIN; Exec. Dir KUMAR MAHADEVAN; publs *Collected Papers* (every 3 years), *Mote News* (quarterly).

New England Aquarium: Central Wharf, Boston, MA 02110; tel. (617) 973-5200; f. 1969; 11,000 mems; public aquarium, research programmes; library of 3,000 vols; Pres. JOHN F. KEANE; Exec. Dir JOHN H. PRESCOTT; publ. *Aqualog* (quarterly).

New York Botanical Garden: Bronx, NY 10458-5126; tel. (718) 817-8721; fax (718) 817-8842; e-mail scipubs@nybg.org; f. 1891; 10,800 mems; 250 acres of gardens, plant collections and wild areas, including a National Landmark conservatory, museum building includes 6 million-specimen herbarium; library of over 1 million items, inc. 196,000 vols; Pres. GREGORY LONG; publs *Economic Botany* (quarterly), *Botanical Review* (quarterly), *North American Flora* (irregular), *Memoirs* (irregular), *Brittonia* (quarterly), *Contributions* (irregular), *Advances in Economic Botany* (irregular), *Flora Neotropica* (irregular), *Intermountain Flora* (irregular).

Salk Institute for Biological Studies: POB 85800, San Diego, CA 92186; tel. (619) 453-4100; telex 910-337-1283; fax (619) 552-8285; f. 1960; 550 mems; advanced biological research in AIDS, cancer, neuroendocrinology, developmental neurobiology, peptide biology, molecular biology, plant biology, prebiotic chemistry, language studies, neuropsychology, immunology, molecular neurobiology and neurophysiology; library of 15,000 vols; Pres. Dr BRIAN E. HENDERSON.

World Life Research Institute: 23000 Grand Terrace Rd, Grand Terrace, CA 92313; tel. (909) 825-4773; fax (909) 783-3477; f. 1959; research into marine biotoxicology, terrestrial phytochemistry, chemoprevention, immunomodulation, Chinese traditional medicine and environmental pollution; Dir BRUCE W. HALSTEAD.

Physical Sciences

Argonne National Laboratory: 9700 South Cass Ave, Argonne, IL 60439; tel. (630) 252-2000; telex 910-258-3285; f. 1946; multipurpose research laboratory with primary focuses on basic research in the physical, life and environmental sciences, and on technology-directed research in fission, fossil and fusion energy as well as conservation and renewable energy; staff of 4,600; library of 65,000 vols and *c.* 1,000,000 technical reports; Laboratory Dir Dr DEAN E. EASTMAN; publs *Frontiers* (annually), *LOGOS* (4 a year).

Arthur J. Dyer Observatory: Vanderbilt University, Nashville, TN 37235; tel. (615) 373-4897; telex 554323; fax (615) 371-3904; e-mail hall@astro.dyer.vanderbilt.edu; f. 1952; specializes in research on local structure of the Milky Way, photo-electric photometry of eclipsing binaries and variable stars, pre-planetary disks around young stars; equipped with combination 60-cm reflecting and Baker-Schmidt telescope, 40-cm computer controlled automatic telescope, 30-cm and 40-cm Cassegrain reflecting telescopes and 15-cm refracting telescope; Observatory Library of 12,000 vols; Dir DOUGLAS S. HALL; publ. *IAPPP Communications* (quarterly).

Association of Universities for Research in Astronomy, Inc. (AURA): 1625 Massachusetts Ave, NW, Suite 550, Washington, DC 20036; f. 1957; operates the Space Telescope Science Institute, Baltimore, MD, and the National Optical Astronomy Observatories, Tucson, AZ, which consist of the Kitt Peak National Observatory, AZ, the National Solar Observatory, AZ and NM; and Cerro Tololo Inter-American Observatory, Chile; manages the International Gemini Project, Tucson, AZ; library of 30,000 vols; Pres. Dr GOETZ K. OERTEL; Vice-Pres. HARRY W. FEINSTEIN.

Byrd Polar Research Center: 1090 Carmack Road, Ohio State University, Columbus, OH 43210; tel. (614) 292-6531; telex 4945696; fax (614) 292-4697; f. 1960; geology, glaciology, atmospheric sciences, pedology, history, palaeontology, geophysics and remote sensing, palaeoclimatology and environmental policy in polar regions; 60 mems; library of 12,000 vols; papers and memorabilia of Richard E. Byrd, Sir Hubert Wilkins and other polar explorers; Dir K. C. JEZEK; publs *Report* (irregular), *Technical Report* (irregular), *Goldthwait Polar Library Accessions List* (irregular).

Fermi National Accelerator Laboratory: POB 500, Batavia, IL 60510-0500; tel. (708) 840-3000; telex 3736609; fax (708) 840-4343; f. 1967; research in high energy physics; run by Universities Research Asscn, Inc for US Dept of Energy; library of 15,000 vols, 250 periodicals; Dir Dr JOHN PEOPLES; publ. *Fermilab Report*.

Goddard Institute for Space Studies: 2880 Broadway, New York, NY 10025; tel. (212) 678-5500; fax (212) 678-5552; f. 1961; global climate, biogeochemical cycles, cloud studies, planetary atmospheres, global habitability; library of 15,000 vols; Dir Dr JAMES HANSEN.

Lamont-Doherty Earth Observatory of Columbia University: POB 1000, Palisades, NY 10964-8000; tel. (914) 359-2900; telex 710-576-2653; e-mail director@ldeo.columbia.edu; f. 1948; research in earth and ocean sciences; library of *c.* 25,000 vols; *c.* 600 staff; Dir PETER EISENBERGER (acting); publs *Newsletter, Year Book, List of Scientific Publications*.

Lick Observatory: Mount Hamilton, CA 95140; attached to the University of California, Santa Cruz Campus; f. 1888; optical astronomy and astrophysics; Dir J. S. MILLER.

Lowell Observatory: Mars Hill Rd, 1400 West, Flagstaff, AZ 86001; tel. (520) 774-3358; fax (520) 774-6296; f. 1894; astronomical research library of 12,000 vols; Dir R. L. MILLIS; publs *Bulletin, The Lowell Observer*.

Lunar and Planetary Institute: 3600 Bay Area Blvd, Houston, TX 77058; tel. (281) 486-2139; f. 1968 to promote and support research in lunar and planetary studies; library of 17,000 vols, 215 periodicals, also photos, maps and CD-ROMs from planetary missions including Ranger, Surveyor, Lunar Orbiter, Apollo, Mariner, Viking, Voyager, Magellan,

Galileo and Clementine; library is a NASA Regional Planetary Image Facility; Dir DAVID C. BLACK; publ. *Lunar and Planetary Information Bulletin* (quarterly).

Maria Mitchell Observatory: The Nantucket Maria Mitchell Asscn, Vestal St, Nantucket, MA 02554; tel. (508) 228-9273; fax (508) 228-1031; e-mail vladimir@mmo.org; f. 1902; astronomical research, research training, public lectures and viewings; library of 4,000 vols; Dir Dr VLADIMIR STRELNITSKI; publ. *Annual Report*.

National Astronomy and Ionosphere Center: Space Sciences Building, Cornell University, Ithaca, NY 14853; tel. (607) 255-3735; fax (607) 255-8803; f. 1971; national research centre funded by the US National Science Foundation and operated by Cornell Univ.; Arecibo Observatory: see chapter Puerto Rico; Dir Prof. PAUL F. GOLDSMITH; Admin. Dir EUGENE F. BARTELL; publs reports of experiments and observations.

National Center for Atmospheric Research (NCAR): POB 3000, Boulder, CO 80307-3000; tel. (303) 497-1000; fax (303) 497-1194; f. 1960; sponsored by National Science Foundation; operated by the University Corpn for Atmospheric Research (UCAR); research in weather prediction, causes of climatic trends, solar processes and influences of the sun on weather and climate, convective storms, and global air quality; library of 100,000 items, 900 journals received regularly; Dir Dr ROBERT J. SERAFIN; publs *UCAR* (quarterly), *Biannual Report*, *Annual Scientific Report*.

National Radio Astronomy Observatory: 520 Edgemont Rd, Charlottesville, VA, and POB 2, Green Bank, WV, and 949 N. Cherry Ave, Tucson, AZ, and POB O, Socorro, NM; f. 1956; a facility of the National Science Foundation, operated by Associated Universities Inc.; research in radio astronomy, radio astronomy electronics, design of radio telescopes; observing radio telescopes include a 27-element array of 82-ft radio telescopes in New Mexico, a 12-m millimetre-wave radio telescope and a 10-element array of 82-ft radio telescopes located in 7 states and the Virgin Islands, dedicated to very long baseline interferometry; library of 27,000 vols; Dir PAUL VANDEN BOUT.

National Solar Observatory—Sacramento Peak: Sunspot, NM 88349; tel. (505) 434-1390; f. 1952; operated by AURA, Inc. (*q.v.*); national centre for solar research; offers telescope use to astronomical community; 50 staff, including 11 astrophysicists; library of 8,000 vols; Dir J. W. LEIBACHER; publs research papers.

Rare-earth Information Center (RIC): Institute for Physical Research and Technology, Iowa State University, Ames, IA 50011-3020; tel. (515) 294-2272; fax (515) 294-3709; e-mail ric@ameslab.gov; f. 1966; emphasis on metallurgy and solid state physics of rare earth metals, alloys and compounds; Dir R. W. MCCALLUM; publs *Rare-earth Information Center News* (quarterly), *RIC Insight* (monthly), occasional bibliographies, compilations, and critical reviews.

Scripps Institution of Oceanography: Mail Code 0233, La Jolla, CA 92093; tel. (619) 534-3624; telex 910-337-1271; fax (619) 534-5306; f. 1903; graduate school and research division of Univ. of California, San Diego; main depts: Geosciences Research, Marine Biology Research, Physical Oceanography, Marine Physical Laboratory, Center for Marine Biotechnology and Biomedicine, Marine Life Research Group, Center for Coastal Studies, Climate Research, Marine Research, Center for Atmospheric Sciences, Scripps Graduate Department; associated Univ. of California institutes: Institute of Geophysics and Planetary Physics, California Space Institute; special facilities include hydraulics laboratory; operates four research vessels and one platform; public aquarium and museum; library of 225,000 vols, 3,800 periodicals; Dir CHARLES F. KENNEL; publs *Bulletin* (irregular), *Contributions* (annually), *Explorations* (quarterly).

Smithsonian Astrophysical Observatory: 60 Garden St, Cambridge, MA 02138; tel. (617) 495-7461; fax (617) 495-7468; f. 1890 as a bureau of the Smithsonian Institution (see under Learned Societies); mem. of the Harvard-Smithsonian Center for Astrophysics; research in radio and geo-astronomy, theoretical astrophysics, planetary science, atomic and molecular physics, high-energy astrophysics, optical and infra-red astronomy, solar and stellar physics; library of 80,000 vols and 40,000 items on microfiche/microfilm; Dir I. I. SHAPIRO.

Sproul Observatory: Swarthmore, PA 19081; tel. (610) 328-8272; f. 1911; attached to Swarthmore College; 61-cm Long Focus Refractor, 61-cm reflector and echelle spectrometer; astrometry and stellar spectroscopy; library of 9,000 vols.

United States Naval Observatory: 3450 Massachusetts Ave, NW, Washington, DC 20392-5420; tel. (202) 762-1437; fax (202) 762-1461; f. 1830; positional astronomy, astrometry, proper motions, stellar parallaxes, photometry, double stars, earth rotation, master clock, precise time measurement, celestial mechanics; library of 75,000 vols; substation at Flagstaff, Ariz.; Superintendent Capt. K. W. FOSTER; Scientific Dir Dr KENNETH JOHNSTON; publs *Astronomical Almanac, Nautical Almanac, Air Almanac, Multi-year Interactive Computer Almanac, Astronomical Phenomena, NavObs Circulars, Astronomical Papers, Time Service Bulletins,* star catalogs.

Warner and Swasey Observatory: Case Western Reserve University, Cleveland, OH 44106; tel. (216) 368-3728; fax (216) 368-5203; f. 1920; astronomical research and education (observational facility of the department of astronomy at Case Western Reserve University); staff: 3 academic, 7–10 others; library of 15,000 vols; Dir R. EARLE LUCK; publs *Publications*, *Reprints*.

Woods Hole Oceanographic Institution: Woods Hole, MA 02543; tel. (508) 457-2000; telex 951679; fax (508) 457-2156; f. 1930; research in physical, chemical and biological oceanography, marine geology and marine geophysics, ocean acoustics, ocean engineering and marine policy; conducts joint PhD programme with Massachusetts Inst. of Technology, postdoctoral fellowship programme and summer student fellowship programme; joint library with Marine Biological Laboratory of 150,000 vols and 5,000 periodical titles; Pres. JAMES M. CLARK; Dir ROBERT B. GAGOSIAN; publs *Abstracts of Papers* (annually), *Oceanus* (quarterly).

Yale Observatory: Yale University, Dept of Astronomy, 260 Whitney Ave, POB 208101, New Haven, CT 06520-8101; publs *Transactions, Bright Star Catalogue* (and supplement), *General Catalogue of Trigonometric Stellar Parallaxes.*

Yerkes Observatory: POB 258, Williams Bay, WI 53191; tel. (414) 245-5555; fax (414) 245-9805; Department of Astronomy and Astrophysics of the Univ. of Chicago; f. 1897; astronomy and astrophysics; library of 25,000 monographs and journals; Dir Dr R. G. KRON.

PHILOSOPHY AND PSYCHOLOGY

American Society for Psychical Research, Inc.: 5 West 73rd St, New York, NY 10023; tel. (212) 799-5050; fax (212) 496-2497; f. 1885; study of paranormal phenomena such as telepathy, clairvoyance, precognition, psychokinesis etc.; 2,000 mems; library of 9,000 vols; Chester Carlson Research Fellow Emeritus Dr KARLIS OSIS; Exec. Dir PATRICE KEANE; publs *Journal*, *Newsletter* (quarterly), *Proceedings* (occasional).

Institute for Philosophical Research: 555 Laurel, Suite 510, San Mateo, CA 94401; f. 1952; for the study of philosophy from ancient Greek times to the present day; library of 10,000 vols; Pres. and Dir MORTIMER J. ADLER; publ. *Concepts in Western Thought*.

RELIGION, SOCIOLOGY AND ANTHROPOLOGY

American Institutes for Research in the Behavioral Sciences: 3333 K St, NW, Washington, DC 20007; tel. (202) 342-5000; fax (202) 342-5033; f. 1946; independent, non-profit organization conducting research, development, analysis and evaluation studies in the behavioural and social sciences for clients in government and the private sector; Pres. and Chief Exec. Officer Dr DAVID A. GOSLIN, publ. *Newsletter* (1 a year).

American Research Center in Egypt: 30 E. 20th St, Suite 401, New York, NY 10003-1310; tel. (212) 529-6661; fax (212) 529-6856; Cairo office: 2 Midan Qasr el-Doubara, Garden City, Cairo; tel. 3548239; f. 1948; independent, non-profit-making; promotes research on Egypt and the Middle East in the fields of archaeology, art, architecture, history, culture, social sciences; library (in Cairo) of 25,000 vols; *c.* 1,200 mems; Pres. Dr CHARLES D. SMITH; Exec.-Dir TERRY WALZ; Cairo Dir MARK M. EASTON; publs *Newsletter* (quarterly), *Journal* (annually).

American Schools of Oriental Research: 656 Beacon St, 5th Floor, Boston, MA 02215-2010; tel. (617) 353-6570; fax (617) 353-6575; e-mail asor@bu.edu; f. 1900; 1,500 mems; support activities of independent archaeological institutions abroad: The Albright Institute of Archaeological Research, Jerusalem, Israel, the American Center of Oriental Research in Amman, Jordan and the Cyprus American Archaeological Research Institute, Nicosia, Cyprus; Pres. JOE SEGER; publs *Near Eastern Archaeology* (quarterly), *Bulletin* (quarterly), *Journal of Cuneiform Studies* (2 a year), *The Annual, ASOR Newsletter* (quarterly).

Center for Advanced Study in the Behavioral Sciences: 75 Alta Rd, Stanford, CA 94305; tel. (650) 321-2052; fax (650) 321-1192; f. 1954; Dir Dr NEIL J. SMELSER; publ. *Annual Report*.

Harry Ransom Humanities Research Center, The University of Texas at Austin: PO Drawer 7219, Austin, TX 78713; tel. (512) 471-8944; fax (512) 471-9646; f. 1957; specializes in 19th- and 20th-century American, British and French literature and art; library of 1m. vols, 30m. MSS, 5,000,000 photographs; Dir THOMAS STALEY; publ. *Library Chronicle*.

Middle American Research Institute: Tulane University, New Orleans, LA 70118; f. 1924; for research, education, and publications related to Mexico and Central America; supports publication, archaeological excavation and research in humanities and social sciences; small museum gallery; anthropological collections; Dir E. WYLLYS ANDREWS V.

Middle East Institute: 1761 N St, NW, Washington, DC 20036; tel. (202) 785-1141; fax (202) 331-8861; f. 1946; a non-profit, non-advocating resource centre; promotes American understanding of the Middle East, North Africa, the Caucasus and Central Asia; coordinates cultural presentations; library of

25,000 vols; 1,300 mems; Pres. ROSCOE S. SUDDARTH; publ. *Middle East Journal* (quarterly).

Social Science Research Council: 810 Seventh Ave, New York, NY 10019; tel. (212) 377-2700; fax (212) 377-2727; f. 1923; to advance research in the social sciences by: appointment of committees of scholars to set priorities and make plans for critical areas of social research; improvement of research training through training institutes and fellowship programmes; support of individual research through postdoctoral grants; sponsorship of research conferences, often interdisciplinary and international; sponsorship of books and other research publications that may result from these activities; Pres. KEN PREWITT; publ. *Items* (quarterly).

Wenner-Gren Foundation for Anthropological Research, Inc.: 220 Fifth Ave, New York, NY 10001-7708; tel. (212) 683-5000; f. 1941 as the Viking Fund; supports research in all branches of anthropology and closely related disciplines concerned with human origins, development and variation; Small Grants Program to aid individual research, including dissertation research; Conference Grants Program; Historical Archives Program; offers Developing Countries Training Fellowships and International Collaborative Research Grants; Pres. Dr SYDEL SILVERMAN.

TECHNOLOGY

Brookhaven National Laboratory: POB 5000, Upton, Long Island, NY 11973-5000; tel. (516) 344-2345; f. 1947; operated by Brookhaven Science Assocs, under contract with the US Dept of Energy; basic and applied research by staff and visiting scientists in the fields of energy, particle accelerators, physics, medicine, biology, chemistry, applied sciences, mathematics, and the environment, including the design, development, acquisition and operation of large-scale facilities too costly or complex for an individual university; training of scientists and engineers; dissemination of scientific and technical knowledge; library of 82,000 vols; staff: 644 research, 621 professional, 759 technicians, 1,129 general; Dir Dr JOHN MARBURGER; publs *Brookhaven Highlights, Brookhaven Bulletin*.

Building Research Board: 2101 Constitution Ave, NW, Washington, DC 20418; tel. (202) 334-3376; f. 1949 as a unit of the Nat. Academy of Sciences—Nat. Research Council; undertakes activities concerned with the development and application of technology to serve society's needs for the built environment: infrastructure, housing, building and related community and environmental design and development; Chair. HAROLD J. PARMELEE; Dir Dr ANDREW C. LEMER.

Combustion Institute: 5001 Baum Blvd, Pittsburgh, PA 15213-1851; tel. (412) 687-1366; fax (412) 687-0340; f. 1954; 3,600 mems; Pres. Prof. ROBERT F. SAWYER; Exec. Sec. SUE S. TERPACK; publs *Combustion and Flame* (monthly), *Proceedings of Symposium (International) on Combustion* (every 2 years).

Herty Foundation: POB 7798, Savannah, GA 31418-7798; tel. (912) 963-2600; fax (912) 963-2614; f. 1938; non-profit contractual research and development of wood, non-wood and synthetic fibres; Dir Dr MICHAEL J. KOCUREK.

Industrial Research Institute, Inc.: 1550 M St NW, Suite 1100, Washington, DC 20005-1712; f. 1938; 280 mem. companies; Exec. Dir CHARLES F. LARSON; publ. *Research-Technology Management* (every 2 months).

Institute of Textile Technology: 2551 Ivy Rd, Charlottesville, VA 22903-4614; tel. (804) 296-5511; fax (804) 977-5400; f. 1944; research, graduate education and information programmes for the textile industry; library of 50,000 vols; Pres. M. T. WAROBLAK; Dean WILLIAM FORNADEL; publ. *Textile Technology Digest* (monthly).

National Aeronautics and Space Administration (NASA): 300 E St SW, Washington, DC 20546.

Main research centres:

Lyndon B. Johnson Space Center: NASA, Houston, TX 77058; f. 1961; the Johnson Space Center is responsible for the design, development and testing of manned spacecraft and associated systems, for the selection and training of astronauts and for the operation of manned space flights; operates White Sands Test Facility at Las Cruces, NM; Johnson Space Center Technical Library of 49,000 vols, 550,000 technical reports, 600 periodicals; Dir AARON COHEN.

Goddard Space Flight Center: NASA, Greenbelt, MD 20771; f. 1959; space research; 3,500 mems; library of 57,000 vols, 35,000 periodicals; Dir Dr JOHN M. KLINEBERG.

Ames Research Center: NASA, Moffet Field, Calif. 94035; Dir Dr DALE L. COMPTON.

John F. Kennedy Space Center: NASA, FL 32899; f. 1962; previously Launch Operations Center; space vehicle launch facility; library of 32,000 vols, 106,000 documents and reports, 589 periodicals; 160,000 specifications and standards; Dir ROBERT CRIPPEN.

Langley Research Center: NASA, Hampton, VA 23665; Dir JOHN HOLLOWAY.

Lewis Research Center: NASA, 21000 Brookpark Road, Cleveland, OH 44135; Dir LAWRENCE J. ROSS.

George C. Marshall Space Flight Center: National Aeronautics and Space Administration, AL 35812; f. 1960; Dir Dr THOMAS J. LEE.

National Institute of Standards and Technology: Gaithersburg, MD 20899-0001; and at Boulder, CO 80303-3328; tel. (301) 975-3057; fax (301) 926-1630; f. 1901; a non-regulatory agency of the Commerce Department's Technology Administration; works with industry to develop and apply technology, measurements and standards; laboratory research focused on infrastructural technologies; Dir Dr ROBERT HEBNER (acting).

National Renewable Energy Laboratory: 1617 Cole Blvd, Golden, CO 80401; tel. (303) 275-4099; fax (303) 275-4091; f. 1977; a national centre for federally-sponsored long-range high-risk renewable energy research and development; library of 105,000 books and reports, 350 journals; Dir RICHARD H. TRULY; publs *In Review, AFDC Update, Biofuels Update, Detox Update*.

Southwest Research Institute: 6220 Culebra Rd, Post Office Drawer 28510, San Antonio, TX 78228-0510; tel. (210) 684-5111; telex 244846; fax (210) 522-3547; f. 1947; independent non-profit organization conducting research and development in the engineering and physical sciences for government, business and industry around the world; library of 50,000 vols; Pres. MARTIN GOLAND; Exec. Vice-Pres. (Operations) RICHARD B. CURTIN; publ. *Technology Today* (3 a year).

SRI International: 333 Ravenswood Ave, Menlo Park, CA 94025; tel. (415) 326-6200; telex 334486; f. 1946 (fmrly Stanford Research Institute); non-profit-making; centres for diversified research for industry and government in pure and applied science and engineering; br in Washington, DC; overseas offices in London, Cambridge, Zurich, Tokyo, Seoul; Pres. WILLIAM P. SOMMERS.

TRI Princeton: POB 625, Princeton, NJ 08542; tel. (609) 924-3150; fax (609) 683-7836; f. 1930; basic research and graduate education in the physical and engineering sciences relating to fibrous materials; 80 corporate mems, 169 individual mems; library of 5,000 vols; Exec. Dir Dr GAIL R. EATON; publ. *Textile Research Journal*.

Libraries and Archives

Alabama

Birmingham Public Library: 2100 Park Place, Birmingham, AL 35203; tel. (205) 226-3743; f. 1909; 1,094,390 vols; special collections: Agee Cartographical Collection (including Joseph H. Woodward Collection), Catherine Collins Collection of the Dance, Scruggs Philately Collection, Tutwiler Collection of Southern History and Literature, government documents, archives, manuscripts, musical recordings, film and video; DIALOG Online Computer Reference Service, Books by Mail Service; 19 brs; Dir (vacant).

University of Alabama Library: Tuscaloosa, AL 35487-0266; f. 1831; regional depository for federal documents; departmental libraries for business, education, engineering, sciences; special collections on Alabama and Southern history and literature; 1,814,178 vols; Librarian CHARLES B. OSBURN.

Alaska

Alaska State Library: POB 110571, Juneau, AK 99811-0571; tel. (907) 465-2910; fax (907) 465-2151; e-mail asl@muskox.alaska.edu; f. 1956; 15,000 vols; Historical Collections of 32,000 vols, 110,000 photographs, and MSS and Alaska newspapers; State Librarian KAREN R. CRANE.

Arizona

Arizona Department of Library, Archives and Public Records: State Capitol, 1700 W. Washington, Phoenix, AZ 85007; f. 1864; law, government, Arizona and Southwest history, genealogy, federal and state documents; library extension, archives, library for the blind and physically handicapped, museums, public records; 1,127,196 vols; Dir GLADYSANN WELLS.

City of Phoenix Public Library: 1221 North Central, Phoenix, AZ 85004; tel. (602) 262-4636; fax (602) 495-5841; f. 1901; 1,754,000 vols, 4,315 periodical titles; also A/V material; Arizona/Southwest materials; Dir TONI GARVEY.

University of Arizona Library: Tucson, AZ 85721; tel. (602) 621-2101; fax (602) 621-4619; f. 1891; 3,549,281 vols; Librarian CARLA J. STOFFLE; publs occasional papers.

California

California State Library: POB 942837, Sacramento, CA 94237-0001; tel. (916) 654-0183; fax (916) 654-0241; f. 1850; 696,000 vols, 3,011,835 government publications; library service to State Government; preservation of California materials; government document depository; law library; books for the blind, and physically handicapped service; administrator of the state and federal aid to public libraries; State Librarian KEVIN STARR; publs *California State Publications* (monthly), *California Library Directory* (annually), *California Library Statistics* (annually).

Hoover Institution on War, Revolution and Peace: Stanford, CA 94305; tel. (650) 723-1754; fax (650) 723-1687; f. 1919; centre of documentation and research on international and domestic political, social and economic change in the 20th century; 1.6 million vols and 4,772 archival units on the causes and consequences of war and revolutionary movements, and on efforts to achieve peace; with emphasis on international rivalries and global co-operation; research programme on political, economic and social problems in the United States; independent, within the framework of Stanford University; Dir Dr JOHN RAISIAN.

Huntington Library, Art Collections and Botanical Gardens: San Marino, CA 91108; tel. (818) 405-2191; fax (818) 405-0225; e-mail webmaster@huntington.org; estab. 1919 by the late Henry E. Huntington as a free research library, art gallery, museum, and botanical garden; library collections include 500,000 rare books, 3,500,000 MSS, a large print collection and a working reference library of 317,184 vols; available to scholars and others engaged in research work, on application to the Registrar; the collections concentrate on British and American history and literature; particular strengths include English medieval and Renaissance, British drama, American colonial, American Civil War, American frontier, 19th- and 20th-century literary MSS, early science; separate reference libraries are located in the Botanical Department and Art Gallery, the latter including 75,000 photographs of paintings and 6,000 British drawings; public programmes, lectures, exhibitions; research programme includes fellowships, grants, and publication of the *Huntington Library Quarterly* and other scholarly works; Pres. ROBERT A. SKOTHEIM; Librarian DAVID S. ZEIDBERG. See also Museums and Art Galleries.

Los Angeles County Law Library: 301 West First St, Los Angeles, CA 90012-3100; tel. (213) 629-3531; fax (213) 613-1329; e-mail lacll@lalaw.lib.ca.us; f. 1891; 782,000 vols; Dir RICHARD T. IAMELE.

Los Angeles Public Library: Mailing Address: 630 West 5th St, Los Angeles, CA 90071; tel. (213) 228-7000; fax (213) 228-7429; e-mail cenadmin@lapl.org; f. 1872; 5,388,480 vols; 67 brs, 5 bookmobiles; Californiana, children's literature, cookery, genealogy, North American Indians, modern languages, orchestral scores, US patents, standards and specifications, English language, theatre, congressional documents and hearings, business and finance, corporate annual reports, videos, talking books, telephone and trade directories; Librarian SUSAN GOLDBERG KENT.

Sacramento Public Library: 828 I St, Sacramento, CA 95814; tel. (916) 264-2700; fax (916) 264-2755; central library, 23 brs, 3 mobile units; 1,468,000 vols; special collections: Sacramento current and historical information, California collection, business collection, printing history, Sacramento area authors, art and music collection; Dir RICHARD M. KILLIAN.

San Diego County Public Law Library: 1105 Front St, San Diego, CA 92101-3999; tel. (619) 531-3900; fax (619) 238-7716; e-mail cdyer@sdcll.org; f. 1891; 319,000 vols; Dir CHARLES DYER.

San Diego Public Library: 820 E St, San Diego, CA 92101; tel. (619) 236-5800; fax (619) 236-5878; f. 1882; 2,335,811 vols; City Librarian WILLIAM W. SANNWALD.

San Francisco Law Library: 401 Van Ness Ave, Rm 400, San Francisco, CA 94102; 246,000 vols, main library; 30,367 vols, branch library; Librarian MARCIA R. BELL.

San Francisco Public Library: Civic Center, San Francisco, CA 94102; tel. (415) 557-4236; fax (415) 557-4239; 2,309,166 vols; City Librarian REGINA MINUDRI.

Stanford University Libraries: Stanford, CA 94305; f. 1885; 6.1 million vols, including the Green Library (2,163,985 vols), Hoover Institution on War, Revolution and Peace (1,507,016 vols), the J. Henry Meyer Memorial Library for undergraduates (152,222 vols) and 45 departmental and school libraries, of which the major ones are: Lane Medical Library (314,956 vols), Robert Crown Law Library (343,260 vols), Cubberley Education Library (144,668 vols), Branner Earth Sciences Library (95,609 vols), J. Hugh Jackson Business Library (397,908 vols), Food Research Institute Library (76,752 vols), Linear Accelerator Center Library (14,354 vols), Falconer Biology Library (92,687 vols), Hopkins Marine Station Library (27,482 vols), Mathematical and Computer Sciences Library (57,179 vols), Swain Chemistry Library (47,806 vols), Art and Architecture (130,661 vols), Music (78,159 vols), Archive of Recorded Sound (4,285), Physics (46,948 vols), Engineering (88,355 vols); special collections: Transportation, Music, British and American Literature, History of Science, Book Arts and History of the Book, Children's Literature, Judaica and Hebraica; Vice-Pres. of Libraries and Information Resources ROBERT L. STREET.

University of Southern California Library: Los Angeles, CA 90089-0182; tel. (213) 740-2543; fax (213) 749-1221; f. 1880; 2,600,000 vols; Dir of Libraries LYNN SIPE (acting).

Colorado

Boulder Laboratories Library: Boulder, CO 80302; f. 1851; 112,000 vols and 212,000 microfiche; Librarian JOHN J. WELSH.

Denver Public Library: 10 W. 14th Ave, Pkwy, Denver, CO 80204-2731; tel. (303) 571-2000; f. 1889; 1,911,000 vols; specializes in Western US history, conservation of natural resources, energy and the environment, genealogy, Napoleon, fine printing, folk music; City Librarian RICK J. ASHTON.

University of Colorado Libraries: Boulder, CO 80309-0184; tel. (303) 492-7511; fax (303) 492-1881; f. 1876; 2,575,290 vols; special collections: mountaineering, photobooks, human rights; Dir JAMES F. WILLIAMS II.

Connecticut

Connecticut State Library: 231 Capitol Ave, Hartford, CT 06106; tel. (203) 566-4971; f. 1850; 879,060 vols, 1,000,000 government documents, 19,000 cu. ft. of MSS and state archives; Connecticut newspapers, genealogy, history, law, legislative reference; State Librarian RICHARD G. AKEROYD, Jr; publ. *Checklist of Publications of Connecticut State Agencies* (monthly).

University of Connecticut Library: Storrs, CT 06269-1005; tel. (203) 486-2219; f. 1881; 2,210,528 vols; Dir PAUL J. KOBULNICKY; publ. *University of Connecticut Bibliography Series* (irregular).

Yale University Library: New Haven, CT 06520; tel. (203) 432-1775; fax (203) 432-7231; e-mail smlref@yale.edu; f. 1701; 10,500,544 vols; each of the 12 Undergraduate Colleges has its own library; Librarian SCOTT BENNETT.

Delaware

Delaware Division of Libraries, Department of State: 43 S DuPont Highway, Dover, DE 19901; tel. (302) 739-4748; f. 1901; special collections: books by mail, US govt documents, talking books; State Librarian TOM SLOAN.

District of Columbia

Department of Commerce Library: 14th and Constitution Ave, NW, Washington, DC 20230; f. 1913; 50,000 vols, 2,000 vols microform; Dir ANTHONY J. STEINHAUSER.

Independent libraries within the Dept of Commerce include:

Bureau of the Census Library: Federal Office Bldg No. 3, Room 2455, Washington, DC 20233; f. 1952; 250,000 vols; Project Man. JEANE BOTHE.

National Oceanic and Atmospheric Administration, Environmental Data and Information Service, Environmental Science Information Center, Library and Information Services Division: 1315 East-West Highway, 2nd Floor, SSMC3, Silver Spring, MD 20910; 1,000,000 vols; 35 libraries and information centres holding spec. collns; Dir CAROL B. WATTS.

Department of Energy Library: 1000 Independence Ave, SW, Washington, DC 20585; tel. (202) 586-6022; f. 1947; 35,000 titles, 1,000,000 technical reports, 1,700 journal subscriptions; collection includes books, journals, reports and government documents relating to all aspects of energy; Librarian DENISE B. DIGGIN; publs *Data Bases Available at the Energy Library* (irregular), *Guide to Services* (irregular), *New at the Energy Library* (monthly).

Department of Justice Library: 950 Pennsylvania Ave NW, Washington, DC 20530-0001; tel. (202) 514-3775; fax (202) 305-1589; f. 1831; 300,000 vols, principally Anglo-American legal and related materials, over 1 m items of microfiche and microfilm; seven br. libraries (total 300,000 vols); specialized areas of American law; Library Director DAPHNE B. SAMPSON.

Department of Labor Library: Room N2445, 200 Constitution Ave, NW, Washington, DC 20210; tel. (202) 219-6992; fax (202) 219-4187; f. 1885; 550,000 vols, 300 current periodical titles; Librarian DOROTHY FISHER WEED.

Department of the Interior Libraries: Washington, DC 20240.

Constituent libraries:

Library of the US Department of the Interior: Room 1151 Interior Building, 18th and C Streets, NW, Washington, DC 20240; f. 1949 by amalgamation of 8 existing Interior Libraries at Washington; 850,000 vols; 15,000 serials and 2,500 periodicals received; subjects include the conservation and development of natural resources; automated information services; interlibrary loans service; copy facilities; open to the public; Dir VICTORIA NOZERO; publs Bibliographies, available from US National Technical Information Service.

Geological Survey Library: National Center, mail stop 950, 12201 Sunrise Valley Drive, Reston, VA 22092; f. 1879; 600,000 vols, 250,000 maps, 250,000 pamphlets; 8,500 serial and periodical titles received; comprehensive working and research library; interlibrary loan service; open to the public; Chief Librarian BARBARA CHAPPELL.

Department of the Navy Library: Bldg 44, Washington Navy Yard, DC 20374; tel. (202) 433-4132; f. 1800; 170,000 vols; Dir JEAN HORT.

Department of the Treasury Library: 1500 Pennsylvania Ave NW, Washington, DC 20220; tel. (202) 622-0990; fax (202) 622-2611; e-mail treasury.libraryref@treas.sprint.com; f. *c.* 1817; 74,000 vols, 495,000 microfiches and 7,800 reels of microfilm; special collections: taxation, public finance, international economic affairs, Treasury history.

District of Columbia Public Library: 901 G St, NW, Washington, DC 20001; tel. (202) 727-1111; f. 1896; Martin Luther King Memorial Library, 27 brs, Library for the Blind and the Physically Handicapped; special collections: Washingtoniana, Washington Star Collection, Black Studies, Musical Scores, etc; 1,507,000 vols; Dir MARY RAPHAEL (acting).

Dumbarton Oaks Research Library and Collection: 1703 32nd St, Washington, DC

20007; tel. (202) 339-6400; donated in 1940 to Harvard University by Mr and Mrs Robert Woods Bliss as a research centre in the Byzantine and Medieval Humanities; research library of 125,000 vols; collections of early Christian and Byzantine art, and of Pre-Columbian art of Mexico, Central and South America; research programmes in Byzantine and Pre-Columbian studies, and studies in landscape architecture; Dir ANGELIKI LAIOU; publs *Dumbarton Oaks Papers* (Byzantine, annually), *Dumbarton Oaks Studies* (Byzantine, irregular), *Studies in Pre-Columbian Art and Archaeology* (irregular), *Conference Proceedings* (Pre-Columbian, irregular), *Colloquium Papers* (Landscape Architecture, irregular).

Folger Shakespeare Library: Washington, DC 20003; tel. (202) 544-4600; dedicated 1932; collns incl.: the world's largest collection of original editions and reprints of Shakespeare; almost 50 per cent of the extant titles of English Renaissance books, 1475–1640; one of the most significant collections in the Western Hemisphere for the study of British civilization between 1500 and 1700; Continental books of 16th and 17th centuries; 199 vols 17th- and 18th-century Strozzi MSS; a Dryden collection; English plays, 1641–1700; approximately 250,000 play bills; some 55,000 MSS of 16th to 20th centuries relating to the life and times of Shakespeare and the history of drama and Shakespearean scholarship; approximately 50,000 literary and theatrical prints and engravings; Fellowships; Folger Institute; public and educational programmes; theatre; lectures; poetry readings; concerts; exhibitions; administered by Trustees of Amherst College; Dir Dr WERNER GUNDERSHEIMER; publs *Shakespeare Quarterly*, *Folger News* (2 a year).

House of Representatives Library: Cannon House Office Bldg B-18, Washington, DC 20515; f. 1792; 250,000 vols, and special bound collections of all House of Representatives publications since *c.* 1800; Librarian E. RAYMOND LEWIS.

Library of Congress: Washington, DC 20540; tel. (202) 707-5000; f. 1800; Library's priority is service to the Congress of the United States, but it now performs, in its role as the national library, services to other libraries, which include (among other things): (i) the development of scientific schemes of classification (Library of Congress and Dewey Decimal), subject headings, and cataloguing embracing the whole field of printed matter, (ii) a centralized acquisition and cataloguing programme in which publications are acquired worldwide and cataloguing data distributed to other libraries, (iii) a 755-vol. *National Union Catalog: Pre-1956 Imprints*, (iv) an inter-library loan system (only within USA); registers creative work for copyright; 29,000,000 books and pamphlets (incl. Orientalia colln, with 139,000 vols in Hebraic, 175,000 vols in other Near Eastern languages and 2,000,000 vols in Chinese, Japanese, Korean and languages of southern Asia, colln of 1,000,000 vols on Hispanic and Portuguese culture, and colln of Russian literature), newspapers and periodicals, 750,000 rare books and incunabula, 45,301,000 MSS relating to American history and civilization, 4,346,000 maps, 10,316,000 microforms, colln of books and recordings for the blind and physically handicapped (copies available through co-operating regional and sub-regional libraries), Folklife colln (incl. 45,000 hours of recordings dating back to 1890, and 625,000 selections of folk song, folk music, folk tales and oral history), Law colln (American and foreign material), Music colln (8,000,000 items), colln of Motion Pictures, Broadcasts and Sound Recordings (incl. film dating back to 1894, 720,000 moving image items, 3,000,000 sound recordings, copyright deposits of recordings since 1972, jazz and popular music on 78 rpm discs, NBC radio colln of 75,000 broadcasts, House of Representatives debates), colln of Prints and Photographs (15,676,000 items, incl. early daguerreotypes); Librarian of Congress JAMES H. BILLINGTON.

Moorland-Spingarn Research Center: Howard University, Washington, DC 20059; tel. (202) 806-7239; f. 1914; one of the world's largest and most comprehensive repositories for collections documenting the history and culture of people of African descent in the Americas, Africa and Europe; 152,000 vols, 500 MSS and archival collections, many thousands of microforms, sheet music, tapes, transcripts, photographs, records and artifacts; Dir Dr THOMAS C. BATTLE.

National Archives and Records Administration: National Archives Bldg, 700 Pennsylvania Ave NW, Washington, DC 20408; tel. (202) 501-5400; National Archives at College Park, 8601 Adelphi Road, College Park, MD 20740-6001; tel. (301) 713-6800; ensures, for citizens and Federal officials, ready access to essential evidence that documents the rights of American citizens, the actions of Federal officials, and the national experience; establishes policies and procedures for managing US Government records and assists Federal agencies in documenting their activities, administering record management programmes, scheduling records, and retiring non-current records; obtains, arranges, describes, preserves, and provides access to the essential documentation of the three branches of Government, manages the Presidential Libraries system, and publishes the laws, regulations, and Presidential and other public documents; assists the Information Security Oversight Office, which manages Federal classification and declassification policies, and the National Historical Publications and Records Commission, which makes grants nationwide to help nonprofit organizations identify, preserve, and provide access to materials that document American history; consists of 33 facilities nationwide, incl. 18 Regional Records Services Facilities and 10 Presidential Libraries; on permanent display in the Exhibition Hall are the Declaration of Independence, the Constitution of the United States, and the Bill of Rights; Archivist of the United States JOHN W. CARLIN; publ. *Prologue: The Journal of the National Archives*.

National Geographic Society Library: 1145 17th St, NW, Washington, DC 20036; tel. (202) 857-7787; telex 892398; fax (202) 429-5731; f. 1920; 50,000 books, 2 million newspaper clippings, 300 periodical titles; reference reading room open to the public for research by appointment; special collections: polar, NGS publs; Dir SUSAN FIFER CANBY.

Patent and Trademark Office Scientific and Technical Information Center: CP3/4 Room 2C01, Washington, DC 20231; f. 1836; 200,000 vols; foreign patent documents from 1617 to present; Program Man. HENRY ROSICKY.

Pentagon Library: Department of the Army, Service Center of the Armed Forces, 6605 Army Pentagon, Washington, DC 20310-6605; tel. (703) 695-5346; fax (703) 693-6543; f. 1944; combines the resources of 28 former War Dept libraries into one central collection in the Pentagon; 100,000 vols, 1,800 periodicals and 1,000,000 documents; special collections on military arts and sciences, unit histories, military law; and Army administrative, training and technical publications.

Ralph J. Bunche Library of the Department of State: 2201 C St, NW, Washington, DC 20520; tel. (202) 647-1062; f. 1789; 650,000 vols; materials relate primarily to the economic, political and social conditions in foreign areas, international relations and diplomatic history; Librarian DAN O. CLEMMER.

Senate Library: Capitol Building, Washington, DC 20510; tel. (202) 224-7106; fax (202) 224-0879; f. 1871; 250,000 vols, including special collection of legislative proceedings and documents from 1774; the work of the Senate Library is essentially that of research and reference for the use of the Senate and its committees; principal services rendered include legislative and general reference, automated information retrieval, Micrographics Center and photoduplication facilities; Librarian ROGER K. HALEY.

Smithsonian Institution Libraries: National Museum of Natural History Building, 10th and Constitution Ave, NW, Washington, DC 20560; tel. (202) 357-2240; fax (202) 786-2866; e-mail libmail@sil.si.edu; 1,120,740 vols in 17 branches, at many bureaux of Smithsonian administration (see under Learned Societies); Dir Dr NANCY E. GWINN; publs *Information* (newsletter, every 6 months), Research Guide Series (occasional).

Veterans Administration, Library Division: 142D, 810 Vermont Ave, NW, Washington, DC 20420; tel. (202) 565-7337; fax (202) 565-4539; planning, policy, development, training, centralized support services for the VA Library Network (VALNET); this comprises 176 library services at 172 VA facilities (combined holdings *c.* 1,398,000 vols, *c.* 145,000 audio visuals, 75,655 journal subscriptions) and network access to bibliographic data bases through 176 VA Online Centers; Chief WENDY CARTER.

Florida

Broward County Division of Libraries: 100 South Andrews Ave, Fort Lauderdale, FL 33301; tel. (305) 357-7464; f. 1974; 919,048 vols; operates 27 libraries; special collections: Black Heritage, Spanish Language, Floridiana; Main Library is a depository for government documents; Dir SAMUEL F. MORRISON.

Florida State University Library: Tallahassee, FL 32306; tel. (904) 644-5211; fax (904) 644-5016; f. 1853; 2,176,000 books and bound serials; Dir C. E. MILLER.

Miami-Dade Public Library System: 101 West Flagler St, Miami, FL 33130; tel. (305) 375-2665; fax (305) 372-6428; f. 1942; 3,554,437 vols; 4 regional libraries; 26 brs; specializes in Florida history, Spanish books, urban affairs, genealogy; Dir MARY R. SOMERVILLE.

University of Florida Libraries: Gainesville, FL 32611; tel. (352) 392-0342; f. 1905; 3,000,000 vols; special collections: children's literature in English before 1900, contemporary American and British poetry, contemporary American creative writing, Floridiana, history of printing and book arts, Judaica, Latin Americana, New England literature before 1900, performing arts, United States Borderlands (Florida); Dir DALE B. CANELAS.

Georgia

Atlanta-Fulton Public Library: 1 Margaret Mitchell Sq., NW, Atlanta, GA 30303; tel. (404) 688-4636; f. 1867; 2,200,000 vols, 70,000 recordings and cassettes; 24 brs; Dir (vacant).

Hawaii

Hawaii State Public Library System: 465 South King St, Room B-1, Honolulu, HI 96813; tel. (808) 586-3704; 3,328,602 vols; State Librarian VIRGINIA LOWELL.

Illinois

American Medical Association. Department of Library Services: 515 North State St, Chicago, IL 60610; tel. (312) 464-4855;

telex 280248; fax (312) 464-5226; f. 1911; 8,000 vols; 1,200 journal titles, CD-ROMs; special collection: history of US medicine; Dir SANDRA R. SCHEFRIS.

Chicago Public Library: 400 S. State St, Chicago, IL 60605-1203; f. 1872; 4,764,000 vols; Dir SAM MORRISON.

Cook County Law Library: 2900 Richard J. Daley Center, Chicago, IL 60602; f. 1966; 234,000 vols; Exec. Librarian BENNIE E. MARTIN; publs *CCLL Newsletter*, *CCLL Selected New Acquisitions*.

Illinois State Historical Library: Old State Capitol, Springfield, IL 62701; tel. (217) 524-6358; f. 1889; 171,000 books and pamphlets, 3,000 maps, 1,000,000 MSS; special collections: Illinois history and biography, Illinois newspapers and Lincolniana, Mormon history; Library Dir KATHRYN M. HARRIS.

Illinois State Library: 300 So. Second, Springfield, IL 62701-1796; tel. (217) 782-2994; f. 1839; 5 million items and documents; State Librarian GEORGE H. RYAN; publ. *Illinois Libraries* (quarterly).

John Crerar Library of the University of Chicago: 5730 South Ellis Ave, Chicago, IL 60637; tel. (773) 702-7715; fax (773) 702-3317; f. 1892, merged with Univ. of Chicago 1984; 1,250,000 vols on the biomedical and physical sciences, including the history of science and medicine; Photocopy services (tel (773) 702-7031); rare books and MSS from the Crerar collections are in the University's Joseph Regenstein Library (see University Libraries section); Asst Dir for Science Libraries KATHLEEN A. ZAR.

Library of International Relations: 565 W Adams, Chicago, IL 60661; tel. (312) 906-5622; fax (312) 906-5685; f. 1932; non-profit institution supported by voluntary contributions; founded to stimulate interest and research in international affairs; specialized library of 175,000 books, serials and periodicals; official depository of the UN and EC; open to the public; Pres. HOKEN SEKI; Dir MICKIE A. VOGES.

Newberry Library: 60 West Walton St, Chicago, IL 60610; f. 1887; independent research institution of over 1,400,000 vols in the humanities, with special collections on the American Indians, the history of printing, music, American and English history and literature, exploration and early cartography, Portugal, the Renaissance in England and Europe, European history from the Renaissance to 1815, the Philippine Islands; Latin American history and literature of the colonial period; maintains research and educational programmes in its Center for the History of Cartography, Center for the History of the American Indian, Center for Renaissance Studies and Family and Community History Center; Pres. and Librarian CHARLES T. CULLEN.

Northwestern University Libraries: Evanston, IL 60208; tel. (847) 491-7658; fax (847) 491-8306; f. 1856; 3,893,000 vols; Northwestern University Library (humanities and social sciences, with special collections on Africa: comprehensive historically on sub-Sahara, francophone, West Africa and South Africa; extensive holdings in Art Nouveau, Dada, Surrealism, Futurism and Expressionism, Samuel Johnson, Siege and Commune of Paris 1870–71, Women's Liberation movement; libraries for music and transportation); branch libraries for science-engineering, geology and mathematics; professional libraries (dentistry, law, medicine) and the Schaffner Library in Chicago; University Librarian DAVID F. BISHOP.

University of Chicago Library: Chicago, IL 60637; tel. (773) 702-8740; f. 1892; over 6,000,000 vols, included in the Regenstein (humanities and social sciences), Crerar (science, medicine, technology), Harper (college), D'Angelo Law, and 4 other departmental libraries; research collections (including special collections), for research in most areas in the humanities, law, business, and the social, biological and physical sciences; Dir MARTIN RUNKLE. (See also John Crerar Library in Special Libraries section.)

University of Illinois (Urbana-Champaign) Library: Urbana, IL 61801; f. 1867; 8,840,000 vols, 7,457,000 manuscripts, maps, microtexts and other items; special collections in classical literature and history, English literature including Milton and Shakespeare, Western U.S. history, Lincolniana, Italian history, music, architecture, science and technology; University Librarian ROBERT WEDGEWORTH.

Indiana

Allen County Public Library: 900 Webster St, POB 2270, Fort Wayne, IN 46801; tel. (219) 424-7241; fax (219) 422-9688; f. 1894; 2,000,000 vols; Fred J. Reynolds Historical Genealogy Collection; 13 brs; Dir JEFFREY R. KRULL.

Indiana State Library: 140 North Senate Ave, Indianapolis, IN 46204-2296; tel. (317) 232-3675; fax (317) 232-3728; f. 1825; to provide library service to state government, advice and counsel to the libraries and librarians of the state, reference service and materials for local school, public, special, and academic libraries; genealogy and special research collections; Indiana history collection; service to the blind and physically handicapped; library for Indiana Academy of Science; 1,703,621 items; Dir C. RAY EWICK; publs *Indiana Libraries* (quarterly), *Focus on Indiana Libraries* (monthly).

Indiana University Libraries: Bloomington, IN 47405; tel. (812) 855-3403; f. 1829; 5,677,326 vols, 3,623,090 microforms, 6,837,243 MSS, 192,250 music scores, 306,599 slides, 575,434 maps and charts, 268,110 audio recordings, 41,233 serials, 103,000 photographs and pictures, 1,012,188 government publications; Dean of Libraries SUZANNE THORIN.

Indianapolis-Marion County Public Library: 40 East St Clair St, POB 211, Indianapolis, IN 46206; tel. (317) 269-1700; fax (317) 269-1768; f. 1873; 1,815,942 vols; 22 brs, 3 bookmobiles; Dir ED SZYNAKA; publ. *Reading in Indianapolis* (monthly).

Purdue University Libraries: West Lafayette, IN 47907; f. 1869; 2,200,000 vols; Dean EMILY R. MOBLEY.

University of Notre Dame Libraries: Notre Dame, IN 46556; tel. (219) 631-5252; f. 1873; 2,500,000 vols; special collections: Ambrosiana, American Catholic Studies, O'Neill Irish Music, Joyce Sports Research, medieval education, Descartes, Jacques Maritain, Dante, orchids, historical botany, Irish Maps and Sea Charts, Irish Rebellion of 1798, Irish postage stamps; Dir JENNIFER A. YOUNGER.

Iowa

Herbert Hoover Presidential Library and Museum: West Branch, IA 52358; tel. (319) 643-5301; fax (319) 643-5825; e-mail library@hoover.nara.gov; f. 1962; official and personal papers of 31st President of USA; also 150 MS collections; 18,000 vols, 8,247,000 MSS, 43,000 photos, 522 hours sound recordings and 156,000 ft of film, 2,770 rolls of microfilm, 11,864 pages of oral history, 5,300 museum objects covering 20th-century history, economics and political science; Dir TIMOTHY WALCH; publ. *Historical Materials in the Herbert Hoover Presidential Library.*

Iowa State University Library: Ames, IA 50011-2140; tel. (515) 294-3642; f. 1870; 2,125,000 vols, 2,888,000 microforms, 22,000 serials, special collections: Archives of American Agriculture, Archives of American Veterinary Medicine, American Archives of the Factual Film, Women in Science and Engineering Archives, University Archives; federal depository; books on agriculture, entomology, botany, ornithology and veterinary medicine; Dean OLIVIA M. A. MADISON.

University of Iowa Libraries: Iowa City, IA 52242; tel. (319) 335-5867; f. 1847; 3,823,000 vols, 11 departmental libraries; special collection: Iowa Women's Archives; University Librarian SHEILA D. CRETH; publs *Libraries News* (2 a year), *Bindings* (newsletter, 2 a year).

Kansas

Dwight D. Eisenhower Library: Abilene, KS 67410; tel. (785) 263-4751; e-mail library@eisenhower.nara.gov; f. 1962; manuscripts, presidential and personal papers related to former President Eisenhower, and manuscripts of important persons in the Eisenhower administration and in the General's military career; 22,000,000 manuscript materials, 31,500 pages oral history transcripts, 24,000 vols, 211,000 still photographs, audio tapes and films; Dir DAN HOLT; publ. *Overview* (quarterly).

Kansas State Historical Society: 6425 SW 6th St, Topeka, KS 66615-1099; tel. (913) 272-8681; fax (913) 272-8682; f. 1875; 300,000 vols; state archives, newspapers and census, archaeology; manuscript, photograph and maps dept, museum, folk arts dept, education dept; 3,000 mems; Exec. Dir Dr RAMON POWERS; publs *Kansas History: A Journal of the Central Plains* (quarterly), *Kansas Heritage* (quarterly).

Kansas State University, Farrell Library: Manhattan, KS 66506; tel. (913) 532-6516; f. 1863; 1,209,000 vols, 31,867 serials, 3,000,000 microforms, 1,840,000 government documents, 100,000 maps, 8,400 scores, 32,000 pieces of audio visual material, 4 brs (Veterinary Medical, Chemistry, Physics, Architecture and Design); special collections in cookbooks, Linnaeana, Robert Graves; Dean of Libraries BRICE G. HOBROCK; publs *Library Bibliography Series* (irregular), *KSU Library Cassette Series on Library Technology* (irregular).

University of Kansas Libraries: Lawrence, KS 66045-2800; tel. (785) 864-3956; fax (785) 864-5311; e-mail watson-ref@ukans.edu; f. 1866; 3,099,000 vols, 318,000 maps, 2,643,000 microforms, 2,710,000 graphics (mostly photographs), 27,000 sound recordings, 678,000 government documents, 15,000 linear ft MSS; includes Watson (central) Library, Anschutz Library, Kenneth Spencer Research Library (Kansas Collection, Special Collections, University Archives), Government Documents and Maps, Engineering, Music, Art and Architecture, East Asian and Regents Center Libraries; Dean of Libraries WILLIAM CROWE; publs *Currents from the University of Kansas Libraries, Books and Libraries at the University of Kansas, University of Kansas Publications, Library Series*.

Kentucky

Kentucky Department for Libraries and Archives: Box 537, 300 Coffee Tree Rd, Frankfort, KY 40602; tel. (502) 564-8300; 116,000 vols; 3,400 films, 5,000 videos; 646 periodicals; 44,000 federal documents; State Librarian JAMES A. NELSON.

Louisville Free Public Library: 301 York St, Louisville, KY 40203-2257; tel. (502) 561-8600; fax (502) 561-8657; f. 1902; 976,500 vols; 36,000 phono-discs, 70,000 programmes on electronic tape, operates two FM radio stations for music and educational programmes; 14 brs, 1 bookmobile; special Kentucky History Collection; houses a 'Louisville Art Gallery'; Talking Book Library for the blind and physically handicapped; Dir CRAIG BUTHOD; publs *Book Paths, Alivebrary.*

University of Kentucky Libraries: Lexington, KY 40506; tel. (606) 257-3801; f. 1909; 2,634,000 vols, 5,539,000 microforms, 181,423 maps, 26,000 current serials, 237,000 maps; 16 branch and collegiate libraries; UN, federal and state depositories; King Library Press; University and audio-visual archives; large collection of Kentuckiana, special collections in 19th-century British literature, French and Spanish drama 1600–1900, modern political manuscript collections, broadside ballads and chapbooks, Cortot collection of music theory, typography, history of books, Appalachian Regional Commission archives; Dir PAUL A. WILLIS.

Louisiana

Louisiana State University Library: Baton Rouge, LA 70803; f. 1860; 2,270,617 vols, 2,200,045 microforms; UN, federal and state depositories; special collections include E. A. McIlhenny Natural History Collection, Louisiana Collection, sugar technology, Southern history, agriculture, plant pathology, petroleum, bibliography collection, aquaculture, incl. crawfish, wetlands research and marine biology; archives on Lower Mississippi Valley; Dean JENNIFER CARGILL; publs *Statistics of Southern College and University Libraries, Library Lectures.*

New Orleans Public Library: 219 Loyola Ave, New Orleans, LA 70140; tel. (504) 596-2550; fax (504) 596-2609; f. 1843; 952,047 vols; 11 brs; special collections: city archives collection, civil and criminal courts collection, carnivals, maps, photographs, rare books, early sheet music, early jazz recordings and manuscripts; Librarian C. DANIEL WILSON, Jr.

Tulane University of Louisiana Libraries: New Orleans, LA 70118; tel. (504) 865-5131; fax (504) 865-6773; f. 1834; 2,200,000 vols (incl. law, medicine and six other collections); special collections on New Orleans, Louisiana and Southern US history; Latin American archaeology, architecture and jazz; Librarian PHILIP E. LEINBACH.

Maryland

Enoch Pratt Free Library: 400 Cathedral St, Baltimore, MD 21201-4484; tel. (410) 396-5430; fax (410) 837-5837; f. 1886; special H. L. Mencken collection and Maryland history collection; 2,290,042 vols, 91,000 maps, 5,000 films, 19,094 video cassettes, 38,450 slides, 486 filmstrips, 34,802 recordings; Dir CARLA HAYDEN; publs *Menckeniana* (quarterly), *Staff Reporter* (monthly), *Pratt Matters* (quarterly).

Johns Hopkins University Libraries: Baltimore, MD 21218; tel. (410) 516-8325; f. 1876; total of 2,961,160 vols; Dir JAMES NEAL.

National Agricultural Library: US Dept of Agriculture, Beltsville, MD 20705; tel. (301) 504-5248; fax (301) 504-5472; f. 1862; 2,100,000 vols; agriculture and the related sciences; special collections: Layne R. Beaty Papers (farm radio & television broadcasting); foreign and domestic nursery seed trade catalogues; flock, herd and stud books; AV collection on food and nutrition; apiculture; Forest Service and USDA Photo Collection on optical laser discs; M. Truman Fossum Collection (floriculture); James M. Gwin Collection (poultry); Charles E. North Collection (milk sanitation); Pomology Collection (original pomological art); Charles Valentine Riley Collection (entomology); plant exploration photo collection; food and nutrition micro-computer software; MAPP collection of family life education materials; computer database (AGRICOLA) of 3 million records for books and journal articles in agriculture; information centres on agricultural trade and marketing, alternative farming systems, animal welfare, aquaculture, biotechnology, food and nutrition, plant genome, rural information, technology transfer, water quality and youth development; Dir PAMELA ANDRE; publs *Agriculture Libraries Information Notes* (monthly), *Quick Bibliography* (irregular).

National Institute of Standards and Technology Research Library: Administration Bldg, Room E01, Route 70 S and Quince Rd, Gaithersburg, MD 20899; f. 1912; 175,000 vols; Librarian PAUL VASSALLO.

National Institutes of Health Library: Bldg 10, Room 1L25, 10 Center Drive, Bethesda, MD 20892-1150; tel. (301) 496-2447; fax (301) 402-0254; f. 1903; serves the specialized research programs of the NIH; 70,000 books, 160,000 periodicals, 26,500 microforms; biology, medicine, health sciences, chemistry, physiology, physics; Chief Librarian SUZANNE GREFSHEIM.

National Library of Medicine: 8600 Rockville Pike, Bethesda, MD 20894; tel. (301) 496-6308; f. 1836; 5,109,000 vols, journals, theses on medicine and health-related sciences; 600,000 vols on the history of medicine, plus 2,200,000 MSS; 59,000 prints and photographs; the library possesses a computerized information retrieval system; Dir DONALD A. B. LINDBERG; publs *Index Medicus, Cumulated Index Medicus.*

University of Maryland at College Park Libraries: College Park, MD 20742; f. 1856; consist of 7 campus libraries: McKeldin Library, Hornbake Library, Art Library, Architecture Library, Engineering and Physical Sciences Library, Music Library, White Memorial (Chemistry) Library, and a number of special collections; 2,288,796 vols; Dir H. JOANNE HARRAR.

Massachusetts

Boston Athenaeum: 10½ Beacon St, Boston, MA 02108-3777; tel. (617) 227-0270; fax (617) 227-5266; f. 1807; independent research library; 750,000 vols; history, biography, English and American literature, fine and decorative arts; special collections include Confederate States imprints, books from libraries of George Washington, Gen. Henry Knox and the Adams Family, the King's Chapel Collection (1698), Gypsy literature, private press publications, 19th-century tracts, early US Government documents, maps, charts and atlases, and the Charles E. Mason print collection; Bartlett Hayes poster collection; 19th-century photographs; conservation dept for restoration of library materials; Dir and Librarian RICHARD WENDORF.

Boston Public Library: Copley Square, Boston, MA 02117-0286; f. 1852; believed to be the oldest free municipal library supported by taxation in any city of the world; 6,007,000 vols; Pres. BERNARD MARGOLIS.

Boston University Libraries: Boston, MA 02215; f. 1839; 1,920,000 vols, 28,000 periodicals; University Librarian JOHN LAUCUS.

Francis A. Countway Library of Medicine: 10 Shattuck St, Boston, MA 02115; tel. (617) 432-2142; fax (617) 432-0693; f. 1965; a combination of the Harvard Medical Library and Boston Medical Library; 610,000 vols, 3,700 serials; Librarian JUDITH MESSERLE.

Harvard University Library: Cambridge, MA 02138; f. 1638; the oldest library in the USA; the total of 13,143,330 vols is divided among some 90 libraries; the central collections are housed in the Widener, Houghton, Pusey, Lamont, Hilles, Cabot Science, Harvard-Yenching, Littauer, Loeb Music, Tozzer, Fine Arts and Geological Sciences Libraries; important collections in nearly every field of learning, and 4,000 vols printed before 1501; Dir SIDNEY VERBA; Harvard College Librarian NANCY CLINE; publ. *Harvard Library Bulletin.*

Massachusetts Historical Society Library: 1154 Boylston St, Boston, MA 02215; tel. (617) 536-1608; fax (617) 859-0074; e-mail library@masshist.org; f. 1791; 250,000 vols; 3500 MSS collections; Librarian PETER DRUMMEY; publs *Proceedings* (1 a year), *Miscellany* (4 a year).

Massachusetts Institute of Technology Libraries: Cambridge, MA 02139; tel. (617) 253-5651; fax (617) 253-8894; f. 1861; 2,300,000 books and pamphlets, 21,000 periodicals; Dir of Libraries ANN J. WOLPERT.

Springfield City Library: 220 State St, Springfield, MA 01103; f. 1857; 696,000 vols; 8 brs; Dir EMILY BADER; publ. *Bulletin.*

State Library of Massachusetts: 341 State House, Boston, MA 02133; tel. (617) 727-2590; fax (617) 727-5819; f. 1826; 822,083 vols; a government and public affairs library serving the information and research needs of the executive and legislative branches of Massachusetts State government; depository for printed documents of the same and for selected federal documents; collections especially strong in public law, public affairs, state and local history; State Librarian GASPER CASO; publ. *Commonwealth of Massachusetts Publications Received by the State Library* (quarterly).

Worcester Public Library: 3 Salem Square, Worcester, MA 01608; tel. (508) 799-1655; fax (508) 799-1713; f. 1859; 586,000 vols; Librarian PENELOPE B. JOHNSON.

Michigan

Detroit Public Library: 5201 Woodward Ave, Detroit, MI 48202; f. 1865; 2,655,156 vols, 163,158 maps, 754,397 microforms, 788,464 pictures, 20,000 videos; special collections on Automotive history, Burton Historical Collection (Michigan, Great Lakes and Old Northwest Territory), Labor History Collection, Azalia Hackley Memorial Collection of Negro Music, Dance and Drama; Dir Mrs JEAN T. CURTIS.

Library of Michigan: 717 W. Allegan, POB 30007, Lansing, MI 48909; tel. (517) 3731300; fax (517) 373-5700; f. 1828; 5.5 million vols; operates a main library, Law Library Division, Service for the Blind and Physically Handicapped; specializes in Michigan history and current information, public policy issues, genealogy; State Librarian GEORGE M. NEEDHAM; publs *Directory of Michigan Libraries, Michigan Library Statistics, Michigan Documents, Library Law Handbook, Access.*

Michigan State University Libraries: East Lansing, MI 48824; f. 1855; 4m. vols and 14 departmental libraries and special collections; Dir CLIFFORD H. HAKA.

University of Michigan Libraries: Ann Arbor, MI 48109-1205; tel. (313) 764-9356; fax (313) 763-5080; 6,700,000 vols, including special collections in ancient papyri, early economics, early military science, Elsevier imprints, English and American drama, Frost and Faulkner collections, fine printing, French historical pamphlets (16th–17th centuries), imaginary voyages, music and musicology (17th–19th centuries); William L. Clements Library of American History;

Michigan Historical Collections; Dean DONALD E. RIGGS.

Wayne State University Libraries: Detroit, MI 48202; tel. (313) 577-4023; fax (313) 577-5525; 2,600,000 vols in 4 library units: general, law, medicine, science; Dean P. SPYERS-DURAN.

Minnesota

James Jerome Hill Reference Library: 80 West 4th St, Saint Paul, MN 55102; tel. (612) 227-9531; fax (612) 222-4139; f. 1916; 140,000 vols; applied business and commerce; business papers of James Jerome Hill and Louis W. Hill, Sr; Exec. Dir (vacant).

Minneapolis Public Library: 300 Nicollet Mall, Minneapolis, MN 55401; tel. (612) 630-6000; fax (612) 630-6210; f. 1885; 3,271,000 vols; 14 brs; special collections include Heffelfinger Aesop's and Others' Fables, 19th-century American studies, Kittleson World War II, Minneapolis history, Mark Twain, Huttner Abolition and Anti-Slavery, Environmental Conservation Library, Foundations, US Patents, Early American Exploration and Travel, North American Indians, Spencer Natural History; Dir MARY LAWSON.

Minnesota Historical Society Library: 345 Kellogg Blvd, Saint Paul, MN 55102-1906; tel. (612) 296-2143; f. 1849; 300,000 vols; North American history particularly relating to Minnesota and the Upper Midwest (especially travel accounts, fur trade, Scandinavian and other immigration, labour, political and church history, railroad records, local history and genealogy); several million pamphlets, documents, newspapers, films, maps, photographs, tapes, artifacts and MSS; Head of Reference DENISE CARLSON.

Office of Library Development and Services, Minnesota Department of Education: 440 Capitol Square, 550 Cedar St, St Paul, MN 55101; tel. (612) 296-2821; fax (612) 296-5718; f. 1899; state library agency for Minnesota; *c.* 10,000 vols, 200 periodicals, films, cassettes; inter-agency resource and information centre with *c.* 4,500 computer search services, periodicals, reports, on education, planning, vocational rehabilitation and related fields; Dir WILLIAM G. ASP; publ. *Minnesota Libraries*.

Saint Paul Public Library: 90 West 4th St, Saint Paul, MN 55102; tel. 292-6311; fax 292-6141; f. 1882; 1,341,254 vols; Dir CAROLE L. WILLIAMS.

University of Minnesota Libraries: 309–19 Ave S, Minneapolis, MN 55455; tel. (612) 624-4520; fax (612) 626-9353; f. 1851; 5,176,536 vols, 36,000 current journals; general and 15 departmental libraries; special collections: law, immigration history, social welfare history, data processing, medicine, children's literature, horticulture, literary MSS; Dir Dr THOMAS SHAUGHNESSY.

Missouri

Harry S. Truman Library: Independence, MO 64050; tel. (816) 833-1400; fax (816) 833-4368; dedicated 1957; manuscripts, printed materials, photographs, sound recordings, oral history interviews and 30,000 museum objects relating to the career and administration of former President Truman; 15,000,000 MSS, 100,000 photographs, 38,102 vols, 93,750 other printed items; administered by the National Archives and Records Administration; Dir LARRY J. HACKMAN.

Kansas City Public Library: 311 East 12th St, Kansas City, MO 64106-2454; f. 1873; 2,007,420 vols; Dir DANIEL J. BRADBURY.

Linda Hall Library: 5109 Cherry St, Kansas City, MO 64110-2498; tel. (816) 363-4600; fax (816) 926-8727; f. 1946; independent, non-profit science and technology library, specializing in periodicals and scientific and technical research materials; open to the public; collections: 1,000,000 vols, 15,000 current periodicals, 42,200 total serial titles, 225,000 monographs, 1,550,000 government documents, incl. 70,000 maps, 150,000 standards and specifications, History of Science Collection (6,000 vols); also holds US Patent Specifications 1946 to date, and patent searching materials; Pres. C. LEE JONES.

Missouri State Library & Wolfner Library for the Blind and Physically Handicapped: 600 W. Main St, Jefferson City, MO 65102; tel. (314) 751-3615; f. 1945; 87,000 vols, 495 periodicals; special collection: Missouri state documents; Wolfner Library holds 242,000 vols and 93 periodicals; State Librarian SARA PARKER; publs *Missouri Library World* (quarterly), *Newsline* (monthly).

St Louis County Library: 1640 S. Lindbergh Blvd, St Louis, MO 63131; f. 1946; 2,028,498 vols; 17 brs and 19 bookmobiles; Dir DONELL J. GAERTNER.

St Louis Public Library: 1301 Olive St, St Louis, MO 63103-2389; tel. (314) 241-2288; fax (314) 241-3840; f. 1865; 4,895,532 vols; 14 brs; Librarian and Exec. Dir GLEN E. HOLT; publ. *Missouri Union List of Serial Publications*.

St Louis University Libraries: 3650 Lindell Blvd, St Louis, MO 63108; tel. (314) 977-3100; fax (314) 977-3108; f. 1818; 1,688,000 vols; Vatican Microfilm Collection; Dir Dr FRANCES BENHAM; publ. *Manuscripta* (3 a year).

University of Missouri Libraries: Columbia, MO 65201; tel. (314) 882-4701; f. 1839; 2,600,000 vols in general and 7 departmental libraries on Columbia Campus; 925,453 vols in general and departmental libraries on Kansas City Campus; 452,000 vols on the Rolla Campus; 590,000 vols in one library on the St Louis Campus; special collections of Western Historical MSS and Missouriana; Dirs of Libraries: MARTHA ALEXANDER, Columbia; TED SHELDON, Kansas City; JANE EISENMAN (acting), Rolla; JOAN RAPP, St Louis.

Nebraska

University of Nebraska Libraries: Lincoln, NE 68588-0410; tel. (402) 472-2526; fax (402) 472-5131; f. 1869; 2,000,000 vols in combined libraries plus UN and federal and map depositories; 20,000 serials; microfacsimile and archive depts; collections supporting 9 colleges, 5 schools and 42 PhD programmes; Dean JOAN R. GIESECKE.

New Hampshire

New Hampshire State Library: 20 Park St, Concord, NH 03301-6314; tel. (603) 271-2144; fax (603) 271-6826; 600,000 vols; special collections: historical children's books, New Hampshire government, town records and history; Librarian KENDALL F. WIGGIN; publ. *Granite State Libraries* (every 2 months).

New Jersey

New Jersey State Library: 185 W State St, CN 520, Trenton, NJ 08625-0520; tel. (609) 292-6200; f. 1796; 503,000 vols, 367,000 US documents, 551,000 microfiche items, 26,000 microfilm items; Dir JOHN H. LIVINGSTONE (acting).

Newark Public Library: POB 630, Newark, NJ 07101; f. 1888; 1,180,492 catalogued vols, 924,814 catalogued non-book items, 1,696,441 uncatalogued items, 411,531 periodicals, 1,015,095 prints, pictures, and art slides; collections: art, music, science, technology, business, depository for U.S. patents, U.S. government documents, New Jersey documents, New Jersey history, fine printing, black studies, Newark Evening News Morgue; Dir ALEX BOYD.

Princeton University Libraries: Princeton, NJ 08544; tel. (609) 258-3180; f. 1746; 5,000,000 vols; special collections include 450 medieval and Renaissance codices, 10,000 Islamic MSS, cuneiform tablets, stone seals and papyri, pre-Columbian indigenous materials, especially Mayan, George Cruikshank and Aubrey Beardsley, American Theatre (incl. papers of Max Gordon and Otto Kahn), archives of American publishers, especially Charles Scribner's Sons, the Morris L. Parrish Collection of Victorian Novelists, early American family papers, especially Edward Livingston and Blair-Lee, 20th-century public policy papers, especially John Foster Dulles, Adlai Stevenson and the American Civil Liberties Union, 'Boom' period Latin American writers (incl. Mario Vargas Llosa); Librarian KARIN A. TRAINER; publ. *Princeton University Library Chronicle*.

Rutgers University Libraries: New Brunswick, NJ 08903; tel. (908) 932-7505; f. 1766; *c.* 3,000,000 vols; 17 additional libraries on Rutgers campuses in New Brunswick, Camden and Newark with specialized collections in medicine, physics, chemistry, mathematics, microbiology, art, alcohol studies, labour/management relations, urban research, law and music; University Librarian FRANK POLACH.

New Mexico

New Mexico State Library: 1209 Camino Carlos Rey, Santa Fe, NM 87505; tel. (505) 476-9700; fax (505) 476-9701; f. 1929; provides state agencies with library resources and services, and serves as a primary reference source for libraries in the state; 800,000 vols; special collections: *Southwest Resources* (books, journals and newspapers on the history of the southwestern area of the US), *New Mexico Documents* (publs of the various depts, agencies, commissions comprising the state govt); State Librarian HAROLD BOGART (acting); publs *Directory of New Mexico Libraries*, *Hitchhiker* (weekly).

New York

American Museum of Natural History Library: Central Park West at 79th St, New York, NY 10024; tel. (212) 769-5400; fax (212) 769-5009; f. 1869; 444,000 vols, 19,000 periodicals, 1,000,000 photographs, 3,000 films, 13,000 rare vols; Dir NINA J. ROOT; publs *Bulletin*, *Novitates*, *Anthropological Papers* (all irregular).

Association of the Bar of the City of New York Library: 42 West 44th St, New York, NY 10036; tel. (212) 382-6666; fax (212) 302-8219; f. 1870; 600,000 vols; law; Dir NATHAN A. ROSEN.

Brooklyn Public Library: Grand Army Plaza, Brooklyn, NY 11238; tel. (212) 780-7700; f. 1896; consolidated with the Brooklyn Library 1902; Brooklyn history; special programs include: A/V dept, Education and Job Information Centers, prison service and literacy program; 5,474,809 items; borough-wide library system of 58 brs, Business Library, Central Library and bookmobile; Dir Exec. Dir MARTÍN GÓMEZ.

Buffalo and Erie County Public Library: Lafayette Square, Buffalo, NY 14203; tel. (716) 858-8900; fax (716) 858-6211; f. 1954 as an amalgamation of three libraries; 5,216,000 vols; Dir DANIEL L. WALTERS.

Columbia University Libraries: 535 West 114th St, New York, NY 10027; tel. (212) 854-2247; fax (212) 222-0331; f. 1754; 6,600,000 vols; 22 departmental and professional school libraries with important collections in architecture, business, humanities, history, law, medicine, engineering, the sciences and social sciences; Vice-Pres. for Information Services/ University Librarian ELAINE SLOAN.

Cornell University Library: Ithaca, NY 14853; tel. (607) 255-4144; fax (607) 255-9091; f. 1865; 5,300,000 vols, 5,500,000 microforms; special collections: French Revolution, East Asia, South and Southeast Asia, Iceland, history of science, Dante, Petrarch, slavery, Wordsworth, witchcraft; Librarian SARAH E. THOMAS.

Franklin D. Roosevelt Library: 511 Albany Post Rd, Hyde Park, New York 12538; tel. (914) 229-8114; dedicated 1941; manuscripts, photographs, printed and museum materials concerning life and times of Franklin and Eleanor Roosevelt, incl. 4,700 lin. ft of his papers, many papers of his contemporaries and associates; 17 million MSS pages, 130,000 photographs, 45,000 books, 78,000 other printed items, 22,000 museum items; administered by the National Archives and Records Administration; Dir VERNE W. NEWTON.

Hispanic Society of America Library: Broadway, between 155th and 156th Streets, New York, NY 10032; tel. (212) 926-2234; f. 1904; over 200,000 manuscripts; 18,000 books printed before 1701, including 300 incunabula; 250,000 later books; art, history and literature of Spain, Portugal and colonial Hispanic America; Curator of Modern Books GERALD J. MACDONALD; Curator of MSS and Rare Books JOHN O'NEILL.

Jewish Theological Seminary of America Library: 3080 Broadway, New York, NY 10027; tel. (212) 678-8075; fax (212) 678-8998; 320,000 vols, 11,000 MSS, *c.* 23,000 leaves of Cairo Genizah, Archives, Louis Ginzberg Microfilm library (foreign collections of Hebrew MSS); incunabula; Bible, Rabbinics, Jewish History, Liturgy, Theology, Early Yiddish, Hebrew Literature, History of Science and Medicine; Haggadahs; Megillot (Esther scrolls); Ketuboth (marriage contracts); Prints and Photographs; Musical Scores; Librarian Dr MAYER E. RABINOWITZ.

Medical Research Library of Brooklyn: 450 Clarkson Ave, Brooklyn, NY 11203; tel. (718) 270-7400; the joint library of the Academy of Medicine of Brooklyn, Inc., f. 1845, and the State University of New York Downstate Medical Center, f. 1860; 238,181 vols; Dir RICHARD E. WINANT.

New York Academy of Medicine Library: 1216 Fifth Ave, New York, NY 10029; tel. (212) 876-8200; fax (212) 423-0275; f. 1847; 696,951 vols, 182,910 catalogued pamphlets, 275,788 catalogued illustrations and portraits, 2,700 serials; special collections: Medical Americana, history of medicine, medical biography, rare medical books and incunabula, food and cookery; Librarian ARTHUR DOWNING; publ. *Bulletin of the New York Academy of Medicine*.

New York Law Institute Library: 120 Broadway, New York, NY 10271; tel. (212) 732-8720; f. 1828; 230,000 vols; 1,450 reels of microfilm; 16,300 microfiches; law library for practising attorneys; Librarian NANCY G. JOSEPH; publ. *New Acquisitions Bulletin*.

New York Public Library: Fifth Ave and 42nd St, New York, NY 10018; f. 1895 by the consolidation of Astor, Tilden and Lenox Libraries; 11,300,000 vols (not including over 26,000,000 manuscripts, maps, microfilms, films, video and audio cassettes, phonorecords, prints and sheet music), over 40,000 periodicals and newspapers; 82 brs with 4,400,000 vols and 5,900,000 non-book items; special collections include Berg collection of English and American literature, Arents collection of books on tobacco and books in parts, and the Spencer collection of illustrated books; Research Libraries: 10 million vols, 8 million manuscripts; Pres. PAUL LECLERC.

New York State Library: Albany, NY 12230; tel. (518) 474-5355; fax (518) 474-5786; American and New York State History, law, medicine, education, technology and genealogy; MSS and special collections; US govt depository; Talking Book and Braille Library; 19 million items; State Librarian JANET WELCH; Dir LIZ LANE; publs *Checklist of Official Publications of the State of New York* (monthly). Reference Services: Principal Librarian LEE STANTON; Collection Management/Network Services: Principal Librarian JOHN VAN DER VEER JUDD; Collection Acquisition and Processing: Principal Librarian MARY REDMOND (acting).

New York University Libraries: New York, NY 10012; tel. (212) 998-2505; fax (212) 995-4070; e-mail libweb@nyu.edu; f. 1835; 4,057,000 vols; special collections: Tamiment Library, Robert F. Wagner Labor Archives, Fales Library; Dean CARLTON C. ROCHELL.

Queens Borough Public Library: 89-11 Merrick Blvd, Jamaica, NY 11432; tel. (718) 990-0700; fax (718) 291-8936; organized 1896, inc. 1907; central reference and research centre with 62 branch libraries and 8m. vols; special collection Long Island history and genealogy; 500,000 pictures; Dir GARY STRONG.

Pierpont Morgan Library: 29 East 36th St, New York, NY 10016; tel. (212) 685-0008; fax (212) 685-4740; f. 1924; public museum and research library; collections formed by Pierpont Morgan, with additions made by his son and subsequent directors; among its treasures are: Medieval and Renaissance MSS from 5th to 16th centuries; a collection of 10,000 drawings by artists of the 15th to the 20th centuries; major collection of Rembrandt prints; major monuments in the history of printing and typography, from Gutenberg and Caxton to modern times; comprehensive group of fine bindings; literary and historical MSS, incl. Dickens, Ruskin, the Brontës, Austen, Thoreau and Steinbeck; large collection of autograph scores, incl. works by Beethoven, Mahler, Mozart and Stravinsky; extensive Gilbert & Sullivan archive; regular public lectures and exhibitions; Dir CHARLES ELIOT PIERCE, Jr.

Rochester Public Library: 115 South Ave, Rochester, NY 14604; tel. (716) 428-7300; f. 1912; 1,344,621 vols; A/V dept; pictures and photographs on 2,000 subjects; local history archive collection of MSS, directories, histories, newspapers, city and county publs; 11 brs, 1 bookmobile; Dir RICHARD PANZ; publs *Rochester History* (quarterly), *Human Services Directory* (annually).

Syracuse University Library: 222 Waverly Ave, Syracuse, NY 13244-2010; tel. (315) 443-2573; fax (315) 443-2060; f. 1870; 2,650,000 vols; special collections: Leopold von Ranke, Kipling, Crane, 20th-century letters and publishing history, cartoon art; Dir DAVID H. STAM; publ. *Associates Courier* (annually).

Union Theological Seminary Library (The Burke Library): 3041 Broadway at 121st St, New York, NY 10027; tel. (212) 280-1505; fax (212) 280-1456; f. 1836; 580,000 vols, 147,000 pieces in microform, 1,800 periodical subscriptions, 1,740 audio tapes, etc.; incorporates Missionary Research Library; Dir MILTON GATCH.

United Nations Library—Dag Hammarskjöld Library: United Nations Plaza, New York, NY 10017; tel. (212) 963-7443; fax (212) 963-2388; f. 1945, dedicated 1961; comprehensive collections of documents on the UN, Specialized Agencies and the League of Nations; collections of books, periodicals and government documents on topics of concern to the UN; activities and history of the UN; international affairs since 1918; official gazettes of all countries and newspapers of most member states in their official languages; 5m. documents, 600,000 vols, 15,000 serials, 80,000 maps; Head Librarian TAHANI SAID EL-ERIAN.

United States Military Academy Library: West Point, NY 10996-1799; tel. (914) 938-2230; f. 1802; 500,000 bound vols; military-historical, academic, government documents, MSS, rare books and special collections; Library Dir KENNETH W. HEDMAN.

University of Rochester Libraries: Rochester, NY 14627; tel. (716) 275-4461; f. 1850; 2,750,000 vols; 11 dept libraries including Sibley Music Library and Edward G. Miner Library (medicine and dentistry); Dean RONALD DAW.

North Carolina

Duke University Library: Durham, NC 27708; tel. (919) 660-5800; fax (919) 660-5923; f. 1838; 4,534,000 vols, 9,500,000 MSS; British history and literature of 17th to 19th centuries; general European history since 1870; French Revolution; Church history of Reformation; advertising history; American and Latin American history; Southern Americana; French, English, Italian and American literature; international law; ten special libraries; Librarian DAVID S. FERRIERO; publ. *Duke University Libraries* (3 a year).

Public Library of Charlotte and Mecklenburg County: 310 N Tryon St, Charlotte, NC 28202; tel. (704) 336-2801; fax (704) 336-2002; f. 1903; 1.3 million vols; collection of local history and genealogy; Dir ROBERT E. CANNON; publs *PLCMC News, Info Source* (both quarterly), *Annual Report*.

University of North Carolina Library: Chapel Hill, NC 27599; tel. (919) 962-1301; fax (919) 962-0484; f. 1795; 4,263,684 vols, 3,897,013 microforms; special collections on North Carolina, Southern Americana, on the history of the book, incunabula, 16th-century books, including a large collection of Estienne imprints, *crónicas* of the discovery and conquest of the New World, also Johnson, Boswell, Dickens, Shaw and selected contemporary authors, Napoleon and the French Revolution, World War I and World War II materials, early Americana, Confederate imprints, Spanish, Catalan and Portuguese drama, John Murray and Smith, Elder & Co imprints, Afro-American materials, Federal and State documents, Latin America, Mazarinades, Music, and Southern historical MSS; 10 departmental libraries in scientific and other fields; Institute of Government Library; separate libraries in Law, Health Sciences, Population, and a Data Library; Librarian JOE A. HEWITT.

Ohio

Akron-Summit County Public Library: 55 South Main St, Akron, OH 44326; tel. (330) 643-9000; f. 1874; 1,118,000 vols; Librarian/ Dir STEVEN HAWK; publs *Annual Report*, *Shelf Life*.

Case Western Reserve University Libraries: Cleveland, OH 44106; tel. (216) 368-3530; f. 1826; 1,871,260 vols, 13,945 current periodicals and 2,141,154 microforms; special collections include Early American Children's Books, German Literature and Philology, History of Medicine, History of Printing, History of Science and Technology, Environmental Sciences, Natural History, Public Housing and Urban Development.

Cleveland Public Library: 325 Superior Ave, Cleveland, OH 44114-1271; f. 1869; 3,471,000 vols; 27 neighbourhood brs; Books-By-Mail service; the John G. White endowed collection of Folklore, Orientalia and Chess; large circulating collection of video cassettes, films and sound recordings; services to hospitals, the homebound, the physically handicapped and the blind; telephone reference service; fee-based research service; Dir MARILYN GELL MASON; publ. *Cleveland News Index* (monthly).

Columbus Metropolitan Library: 96 S. Grant Ave, Columbus, OH 43215; tel. (614) 645-2800; fax (614) 645-2050; 2,434,000 vols; 20 brs; Dir LARRY D. BLACK.

Dayton and Montgomery County Public Library: 215 East Third St, Dayton, OH 45402; tel. (513) 227-9500; f. 1805; 1,509,623 vols, 19 brs; bookmobile service; service to homebound, elderly and blind; circulating collection of 16 mm. films, records and cassettes; Dir JOHN S. WALLACH; publs *Annual Report, Business Industry Technology Service, Spotlight on your Library.*

Ohio State University Libraries: 1858 Neil Ave. Mall, Columbus, OH 43210; tel. (614) 292-6151; f. 1873; Main (Thompson) Library and 26 departmental and affiliated libraries; 4.9 m. vols; 4.0 m. microforms, 33,368 serials; special collections include American fiction, theatre, cartoons and cartooning, medieval Slavic MSS on microfilm; Dir of Libraries WILLIAM J. STUDER.

Public Library of Cincinnati and Hamilton County: 800 Vine St, Library Square, Cincinnati, OH 45202-2071; tel. (513) 369-6900; fax (513) 369-6993; f. 1853; 4,667,000 vols; 134,000 maps; 41 brs; Regional Library for the Blind and Physically Handicapped, Institutions/ Books-by-Mail dept; specializes in local history, genealogy, theology, art, music, theatre, oral history, inland rivers, US patents; Dir ROBERT D. STONESTREET.

State Library of Ohio: 65 South Front St, Columbus, OH; tel. (614) 644-7061; fax (614) 466-3584; f. 1817; 1.4 m. vols; a special library for state government, incl. periodicals, documents, pamphlets, services and microforms; special collection of management, genealogy, local history, education and health; State Librarian MICHAEL S. LUCAS.

Toledo-Lucas County Public Library: 325 Michigan St, Toledo, OH 43624-1614; tel. (419) 259-5200; consolidated 1970; 1,900,000 vols; 19 brs; Dir CLYDE SCOLES.

University of Cincinnati Libraries: Cincinnati, OH 45221-0033; f. 1819; 2,268,000 vols; comprises a general library, medical, law, departmental and branch libraries; includes special collections on classics, modern Greek, medicine, fine arts, 20th-century poetry, 18th-century literature; Dean and University Librarian DAVID F. KOHL.

Oklahoma

University of Oklahoma Library: Norman, OK 73019; tel. (405) 325-2611; f. 1892; 2,500,000 vols; special collections in western history, business and economic history and history of science; Librarian SUL H. LEE.

Oregon

Multnomah County Library: 205 North East Russell St, Portland, OR 97212-3708; tel. (503) 248-5402; fax (503) 248-5441; f. 1864; 1,587,291 vols; 14 branches; Librarian GINNIE COOPER.

Oregon State Library: State Library Building, Salem, OR 97310-0640; tel. (503) 378-4243; f. 1905; 1,762,877 vols; provides service to state agencies and print-disabled persons; develops local library services; special collections: Oregon and Oregon authors; State Librarian JIM SCHEPPKE.

University of Oregon Library: Eugene, OR 97403-1299; tel. (541) 346-3056; fax (541) 346-3485; f. 1876; 2,083,000 vols; 468,000 government documents; 816,000 maps; 1,889,000 microfilm units; 141 computer files; Librarian G. W. SHIPMAN.

Pennsylvania

American Philosophical Society Library: 105 South 5th St, Philadelphia, PA 19106-3386; tel. (215) 440-3400; fax (215) 440-3423; f. 1743; 250,000 vols, 6,300,000 MSS microfilm; special collections on Benjamin Franklin, history of science, genetics, quantum physics, Darwinism, American Indian linguistics, Thomas Paine; Librarian EDWARD C. CARTER II; publs *Annual Report, Library Publications* (irregular), *Mendel Newsletter* (irregular).

Carnegie Library of Pittsburgh: 4400 Forbes Ave, Pittsburgh, PA 15213-4080; tel. (412) 622-3100; fax (412) 622-6278; f. 1895; part of The Carnegie Institute; 3,304,674 vols, 3,306,849 other materials; 18 brs, all with their own collections, and 3 mobile libraries; Dir (vacant).

Ewell Sale Stewart Library of the Academy of Natural Sciences: 1900 Benjamin Franklin Parkway, Philadelphia, PA 19103-1195; tel. (215) 299-1040; fax (215) 299-1144; e-mail library@acnatsci.org; f. 1812; 170,000 vols, 2,000 current periodicals; Library Dir C. DANIAL ELLIOTT.

Free Library of Philadelphia: 1901 Vine St, Philadelphia, PA 19103-1189; tel. (215) 686-5322; 49 brs throughout the city and 3 regional libraries; f. 1891; 7,881,335 vols; special collections include: Fleisher orchestral music; Carson history of the common law; Widener incunabula; Drinker Choral Library; Lewis Illuminated MSS, European and Oriental; History of the Automobile; Elkins Americana, Dickens, Goldsmith, Gimbel Poe; Lewis cuneiform tablets; Rosenbach children's books of the 18th and 19th centuries; children's illustrators, Beatrix Potter, Kate Greenaway, Arthur Rackham; theatre collection; map collection (over 130,000 single sheet maps, also atlases, etc.); Pres. and Dir E. L. SHELKROT.

Pennsylvania State University Libraries: University Park, PA 16802; tel. (814) 865-0401; f. 1859; 3,743,000 vols; 3,300,000 microforms, 352,000 maps, 1,355,000 government documents, 32,000 serials; comprises Central Library, 6 departmental brs, 12 Commonwealth College Libraries, Penn State Erie, The Behrend College, Penn State Great Valley, Penn State Abington, Abington College, Penn State Altoona, Altoona College, Berks-Lehigh Valley College, Capital College, Dickinson School of Law; special collections; American Literature; Australian Art and Literature; Gift Books, Emblem Books; German Literature in translation (Allison-Shelley); Joseph Priestley; Renaissance; Williamscote Library (18th-century English, History, Theology and Classics); Utopian Literature; Labour History; Australiana; Vance Packard; John O'Hara; Conrad Richter, Theodore Roethke, Kenneth Burke, Arnold Bennett, C. R. Carpenter; Nunzio J. Palladino Nuclear Regulatory Commission Papers; University Archives; US Steel Workers of America Archives; United Mineworkers of America; Stapleton Collection of Pennsylvania Imprints; Dean of Libraries NANCY EATON.

State Library of Pennsylvania: POB 1601, Harrisburg, PA 17105; tel. (717) 787-2646; fax (717) 783-2070; f. 1745; 983,000 vols; American history, education, political science, sociology, library science, law, genealogy; Pennsylvania history, newspapers, maps, original Pennsylvania Assembly Collection; State Librarian GARY WOLFE; publ. *Checklist of Official Pennsylvania Publications* (monthly).

University of Pennsylvania Library: Philadelphia, PA 19104; tel. (215) 898-7555; f. 1750; 3,756,762 vols; central library and 12 departmental and affiliated libraries; Archaeology, Leibniz, Descartes, History of Philosophy and Science, Lithuanian History and Literature (especially Saulys Collection), History of Chemistry (Edgar Fahs Smith collection), French Revolution, Judaica, Modern Jewish History, Modern Hebrew Literature, Aristotelianism, Occam, Medieval History, Medieval Church History, Inquisition (Henry C. Lea Library), English and European Bibles, Italian Renaissance Literature (Macauley Collection), Spanish Literature of the Golden Age (Rennert and Crawford Collections), Spanish Linguistics (Gillet Collection), Shakespeareana (Furness Library), Restoration Drama, 18th- and early 19th-century English fiction, Jonathan Swift, Thomas Paine, American drama, fiction, and poetry: Walt Whitman, Washington Irving, Robert Montgomery Bird, Theodore Dreiser, James Farrell; Middle-High German (Bechstein and part of Ehrismann Collection), Old French, Friesian, Indic MSS., South Asia, History of Economics (especially 18th and early 19th centuries), History of Education, Cryptography, Spiritualism, Programmschriften, Elzevir Imprints, Franklin Imprints, early Americana, the American West, Canadiana; Dir PAUL H. MOSHER.

University of Pittsburgh Libraries: Pittsburgh, PA 15260; tel. (412) 648-7710; fax (412) 648-7887; f. 1873; 22 separate libraries on or near Main Campus and 4 regional campus libraries in Bradford, Greensburg, Johnstown and Titusville; 3,700,000 vols, 3,700,000 micro-units; Dir RUSH MILLER.

Rhode Island

Brown University Library: Providence, RI 02912; tel. (401) 863-2167; f. 1767; 2,933,000 vols; Librarian M. E. TAYLOR.

John Carter Brown Library: POB 1894, Providence, RI 02912; tel. (401) 863-2725; e-mail jcbl_information@brown.edu; f. 1904; independent centre for advanced research in the humanities at Brown University; contains primary historical sources pertaining to the colonial period of the Americas *c.* 1492–*c.* 1825; 45,000 rare books and 15,000 reference books; Dir Dr NORMAN FIERING.

Providence Public Library: 225 Washington St, Providence, RI 02903; tel. (401) 455-8000; fax 455-8080; 1 million vols; Dir M. DALE THOMPSON.

Tennessee

Memphis and Shelby County Public Library and Information Center: 1850 Peabody Ave, Memphis, TN 38104; tel. (901) 725-8855; fax (901) 725-8883; f. 1893; 4.5 m. vols; CATV and colour videotaping studio; information and referral service (LINC-Library Information Center); Dir J. A. DRESCHER; publs *Kaleidoscope* (monthly), *Staff Newsline* (monthly).

University of Tennessee, Knoxville Libraries: Knoxville, TN 37996-1000; tel. (423) 974-4171; f. 1794; 1,876,618 vols; special collections: Tennesseana, North American Indians; Dean PAULA T. KAUFMAN.

Vanderbilt University Library: Nashville, TN 37203; tel. (615) 322-7100; estab. 1873; over 1,800,000 vols incl. Central/Science Library, 5 professional school libraries (Divinity, Education, Law, Management and Medical); special collections: music library, Vanderbilt Television News Archive; Dir MALCOLM GETZ.

Texas

Austin Public Library: 800 Guadalupe St, Box 2287, Austin, TX 78768-2287; tel. (512) 499-7300; fax (512) 499-7403; f. 1926; 1,425,930 vols; 20 facilities; system maintains a comprehensive collection of books, magazines, newspapers, recordings, audio cassettes and videocassettes; Austin History Center contains materials on history of Austin and Travis County; Dir BRENDA BRANCH.

Dallas Public Library: 1515 Young St, Dallas, TX 75201-5499; tel. (214) 670-1400; f. 1901; 5,712,337 system holdings, 2,417,994 catalogue items; Dir RAMIRO SALAZAR.

Fort Worth Public Library: 300 Taylor St, Fort Worth, TX 76102; tel. (817) 870-7701; fax (817) 871-7734; f. 1901; 2,066,000 vols; 11 brs; special collections: genealogy, local history, sheet music, postcards, bookplates; US and Texas govt depository; Dir LINDA ALLMAND.

Houston Public Library: 500 McKinney Ave, Houston, TX 77002; tel. (713) 236-1313; fax (713) 247-3531; f. 1901; 4,220,000 vols; 34 brs; special collections: Bibles, Civil War, Salvation Army posters, early Houston photographs, early printing and illuminated MSS, juvenile literature, petroleum, sheet music, Texana, US and Texas depository; specialises in genealogy, art, architecture, business, management; jazz, Afro-American and Hispanic archives; Dir BARBARA A. B. GUBBIN; publ. *Houston Review*.

University of Texas System Libraries: Austin, TX 78712; f. 1883; 6,835,983 vols; also Arlington 893,155 vols; El Paso 746,308 vols; Permian Basin 215,945 vols; San Antonio 367,583 vols; Health Science Center, Houston 54,000 vols; Health Science Center, Dallas 224,732 vols; Health Science Center, San Antonio 173,143 vols; Medical Branch, Galveston 291,326.

Utah

Family History Library of the Church of Jesus Christ of Latter-day Saints: 35 North West Temple St, Salt Lake City, UT 84150; tel. (801) 240-2331; fax (801) 240-5551; f. 1894; 280,000 bound vols, 2,000,000 reels of microfilm; Man. JIMMY B. PARKER.

University of Utah Library: Salt Lake City, UT 84112; tel. (801) 581-6273; f. 1850; 2,000,000 vols, 13,000 serial titles; special collections: archives, Middle East, MSS, rare books, Western Americana, oral history; US State and UN documents depository; Dir R. K. HANSON.

Virginia

Fairfax County Public Library: 12000 Government Center Parkway, Suite 324, Fairfax, VA 22035; tel. (703) 222-3155; f. 1939; 2,093,000 vols; 19 brs; also CD-ROMs, microfilm, audio and video cassettes, periodicals, recorded and talking books, CATV hookup; Dir EDWIN S. CLAY III.

Library of Virginia: 800 East Broad St, Richmond, VA 23219-1905; f. 1823; 700,000 vols, 834 current periodicals; Virginiana, Southern US History, Civil War, genealogy; archive collection of 55,000 cu. ft; Librarian NOLAN T. YELICH; publ. *Virginia Cavalcade* (quarterly).

Mariners' Museum Research Library and Archives, The: 100 Museum Drive, Newport News, VA 23606-3759; tel. (757) 596-2222; fax (757) 591-7310; f. 1930 by Archer M. and Anna H. Huntington; library of materials related to human interaction with the world's waterways; over 75,000 vols, 350,000 photographs, 1,000,000 archival items such as ships' logs, charts, manuscripts, blueprints and memorabilia; special collections: Edwin Levick Collection of photographs of passenger ships, yachts, and America's Cup Races; A. Aubrey Bodine Collection of images of life on the Chesapeake Bay; Chris-Craft Collection documenting the construction of boats by one of America's most important pleasure boat builders; Librarian BENJAMIN H. TRASK; Archivist R. THOMAS CREW, Jr.

Richmond Public Library: 101 East Franklin St, Richmond, VA 23219-2193; f. 1924; 810,066 vols; City Librarian ROBERT RIEFFEL.

University of Virginia Library: Charlottesville, VA 22903-2498; tel. (804) 924-3026; f. 1819; 4,434,000 vols; special collections: American history and literature, including McGregor Library of American History and the Barrett Library of American Literature, Massey-Faulkner collection, Streeter collection on Southeastern Railways, Optics, Evolution, Thomas Jefferson, Scott Sporting Collection, Victorian fiction, Greek and Latin literature, Music, International Law, History of Printing, Gothic novels, Matthew Arnold, Jorge Luis Borges collection, Gordon collection of French books, Tibetan collection, *inter alia*; Librarian KARIN WITTENBORG.

Washington

Seattle Public Library: 1000 4th Ave, Seattle, WA 98104; tel. (206) 386-4100; f. 1891; 1,668,000 vols; special collections: Aeronautics, Pacific Northwest Americana; 23 br. libraries; Librarian DEBORAH JACOBS.

University of Washington Libraries: Box 352900, Seattle, WA 98195-2900; tel. (206) 543-0242; fax (206) 685-8727; f. 1862; 5,471,784 vols; 56,793 current serials, 6,255,761 microforms; includes Law Library (separately administered; Librarian PENNY HAZELTON), Health Sciences Library, Odegaard Undergraduate Library, East Asia Library, Special Collections and Preservation Division and 15 br. libraries; Dir BETTY G. BENGTSON.

Washington State Library: POB, 42460, Olympia, WA 98504-2460; tel. (360) 753-5592; fax (360) 586-7575; f. 1853; 488,916 books and periodicals, 1,545,899 federal and state documents; 483,118 microfiche, 42,734 microfilm, 8,914 films, 8,744 audio and video tapes; special collections: Washington Authors, Pacific Northwest, Washington State Documents, Washington State Newspapers, Transportation, Labor and Industries, Utilities; State Librarian NANCY L. ZUSSY.

West Virginia

West Virginia University Libraries: Morgantown, WV 26506-6069; tel. (304) 293-4040; f. 1867; 1,497,710 vols; special collections: W. Virginia, Appalachian region, coal; 1,900,000 microforms; 4,000,000 archives; Dean RUTH M. JACKSON.

Wisconsin

American Geographical Society Collection of the University of Wisconsin–Milwaukee Library: POB 399, Milwaukee, WI 53201; tel. (414) 229-6282; 210,000 vols, 479,400 maps, 8,800 atlases, 81 globes, 33,676 pamphlets, 207,320 Landsat images, 158,823 photographs and slides, 1,227 CD-ROMs; publs *Current Geographical Publications* (10 a year).

Milwaukee Public Library: 814 West Wisconsin Ave, Milwaukee, WI 53233; tel. (414) 286-3000; fax (414) 286-2794; f. 1878; 2,441,427 vols; special collections include Great Lakes marine collection, cookbooks, H. G. Wells, definitive editions of collected works of British and American authors, Charles King collection, Harry Franck collection, genealogy; depository for US Federal Documents, US Geologic Survey, US Defense Mapping Agency maps and US Patent Office; 12 br. libraries, Wisconsin Regional Library for the Blind and Physically Handicapped headquarters, 1 mobile library, 2 library vans; City Librarian KATHLEEN M. HUSTON.

University of Wisconsin Library: Madison, WI 53706; f. 1848; 5,535,392 vols; special collections on pharmacy, Scandinavian literature, Gaelic literature and history, modern Polish literature, history of science, history of Calvinism, socialist and labour movements; English, American, French, German, Icelandic, Irish, Spanish literature and history, etc.; Dir KENNETH FRAZIER.

Museums and Art Galleries

Alabama

Alabama Museum of Natural History, University of Alabama: Box 870340, Tuscaloosa, AL 35487-0340; Dir Dr IAN W. BROWN.

Alaska

Alaska State Museum: 395 Whittier St, Juneau, AK 99801-1718; tel. (907) 465-2901; fax (907) 465-2796; f. 1900, opened to the public 1920; collection of Alaskan history, art, natural history and ethnographic materials; state-wide assistance to museums in Alaska; Chief Curator BRUCE KATO.

Attached museum:

Sheldon Jackson Museum: 104 College Drive, Sitka, AK 99835-7657; tel. (907) 747-8981; fax (907) 747-3004; f. 1888; collection of Alaska Native artefacts; Chief Curator BRUCE KATO.

Arizona

Arizona State Museum: Univ. of Arizona, Tucson, AZ 85721-0026; tel. (520) 621-6281; fax (520) 621-2976; f. 1893; devoted to the study of south-western archaeology and the living Indians of the region, and engaged in archaeological, enthnohistoric and ethnological research, excavation and field work in Arizona; library of 43,000 vols; *c.* 22,000 specimens of US southwestern and northwest Mexican ethnographic items; *c.* 150,000 specimens of US southwestern archaeological items, notably Hohokam and Mogollon materials; 10,000 cu ft of Archive Research collections; 225,000 photographic items, largely archaeology and ethnology of the US southwest and northwest Mexico; *c.* 3,000 specimens of osteological remains; *c.* 2,000 vertebrate zooarchaeological specimens, largely from the US southwest and Middle America; 5,000 herbarial specimens primarily from Arizona; Dir GEORGE J. GUMERMAN; publs archaeological series.

California

Asian Art Museum of San Francisco, The Avery Brundage Collection: Golden Gate Park, San Francisco, CA 94118-4598; tel. (415) 668-8921; fax (415) 668-8928; f. 1969; museum and centre of research on outstanding collections of Chinese, Japanese, Korean, Indian, Southeast Asian, Himalayan and Islamic art; library of 20,000 vols; Dir Dr EMILY SANO.

California Palace of the Legion of Honor: Lincoln Park, San Francisco, CA 94121; tel. (415) 863-3330; fax (415) 750-7686; f. 1924; museum of fine arts; ancient art; 16th–20th-century European paintings; French original room interiors; French and Flemish tapestries; sculpture by Auguste Rodin; Achenbach Foundation for Graphic Arts has largest collection of prints and drawings in the Western US; Dir HARRY S. PARKER III; publ. *Fine Arts Magazine* (quarterly). (See also M. H. de Young Memorial Museum.)

Fine Arts Museums of San Francisco, M. H. de Young Memorial Museum: Golden Gate Park, San Francisco, CA 94118; tel. (415) 863-3330; f. 1895; large collection of American art with outstanding paintings, sculpture and decorative arts from colonial times to the 20th century; important textile collection; gallery of the Americas; African art; Dir HARRY S. PARKER III; publ. *Fine Arts Magazine* (quarterly). (See also California Palace of the Legion of Honor.)

Getty Center: 1200 Getty Center Drive, Los Angeles, CA 90049-1681; tel. (310) 440-7300; ancient and modern fine and applied art; Dir JOHN WALSH.

Getty, J. Paul, Museum: 17985 Pacific Coast Highway, Malibu, CA 90265-5799; tel. (310) 459-7611; telex 820268; f. 1953; permanent collection of Greek and Roman antiquities, pre-20th-century Western European paintings, drawings, sculpture, illuminated MSS, decorative arts, and 19th-20th-century American and European photographs; housed in a re-creation of a Roman seaside villa, the Villa dei Papiri, which was destroyed by the eruption of Vesuvius in AD 79; Dir JOHN WALSH, Jr; publ. *Publications*.

Griffith Observatory and Planetarium: 2800 East Observatory Rd, Los Angeles, CA 90027; tel. (213) 664-1181; fax (213) 663-4323; opened 1935; three main divisions; the Observatory, with Zeiss twin 12-inch and 9-inch refracting telescopes and three solar telescopes; the Hall of Science, with over 100 exhibits; the Theatre of the Heavens, with its Zeiss planetarium and space travel projectors; Dir Dr E. C. KRUPP; publ. *The Griffith Observer* (illustrated, monthly).

Huntington Library, Art Collections and Botanical Gardens: 1151 Oxford Rd, San Marino, CA 91108; tel. (818) 405-2100; fax (818) 405-0225; e-mail webmaster@huntington.org; f. 1919; 18th-century British and European paintings, 18th-century French sculpture, 18th-century European decorative arts, American painting, furniture and decorative arts from 1730s to 1930s; botanical gardens; library: see Libraries and Archives; Pres. ROBERT A. SKOTHEIM.

Natural History Museum of Los Angeles County: 900 Exposition Blvd, Los Angeles, CA 90007; f. 1910; Western USA and American History, New World ethnology and archaeology, palaeontology, geology, mineralogy, botany, ichthyology, mammalogy, entomology, herpetology, invertebrate zoology, ornithology; 15,000 mems; library of 100,000 vols; Pres. Board of Governors ED N. HARRISON; Chair. Museum Foundation STEPHEN R. ONDERDONK; Dir JAMES L. POWELL; publs *Science Series* (irregular), *Terra* (every 2 months), Contributions in Science (irregular).

San Diego Museum of Art: Balboa Park, POB 2107, San Diego, CA 92112; Renaissance and Baroque paintings of Spanish, Italian, Dutch, Flemish and French schools; major works by Greco, Zurbaran, Goya, Crivelli, Tiepolo, Guardi, Rubens, Rembrandt, Ruysdael, Hals, Matisse, Braque; early and contemporary American artists; Asiatic arts and sculpture, graphics and decorative arts from many countries; art library of several thousand vols; lectures, concerts, and classes are provided; Dir STEVEN BREZZO.

San Diego Society of Natural History Museum: POB 1390, San Diego, CA 92112; founded 1874 to further the knowledge of natural history and the conservation of natural resources; departments of botany, herpetology, birds and mammals, entomology, palaeontology and marine invertebrates; Laurence Klauber Herpetology Collection; library of 90,000 vols, 900 journals and series; archives; Dir Dr MICHAEL W. HAGER; publ. *Proceedings*.

San Francisco Museum of Modern Art: 151 Third St, San Francisco, CA 94103; tel. (415) 357-4000; fax (415) 357-4158; f. 1935 by the San Francisco Art Association; 20th-century contemporary art; permanent collection: American Abstract Expressionism and other major 20th-century schools; also German Expressionism, Fauvism, Latin American art, art of the San Francisco Bay area; important photography dept; dept of architecture and design; dept of media arts; dept of education; library of 80,000 vols, periodicals, exhibition catalogues; Chair. ELAINE MCKEON; Dir DAVID A. ROSS; publs calendar of events (every 2 months), catalogues of special exhibitions.

University of California, Berkeley, Art Museum & Pacific Film Archive: 2626 Bancroft Way, Berkeley, CA 94720-2250; tel. (510) 642-0808; fax (510) 642-4889; f. 1970; 10 exhibition galleries, sculpture garden; permanent collection of Asian and western art; Hans Hofmann collection; film collection and programme; serves the university community with exhibitions, study collections, etc.; organizes and receives travelling exhibitions from major museums; Dir JACQUELYNN BAAS.

Colorado

Denver Art Museum: 13th Ave and Acoma St, Denver, CO 80204; tel. (303) 640-4433; fax (303) 640-5627; f. 1893 as Artists' Club of Denver; art education programmes for children and adults; permanent collections include Architecture, Design and Graphics, Asian, Pre-Columbian and Spanish Colonial, Modern and Contemporary, Native Arts including American Indian artworks; Painting and Sculpture including American and Western; Dir LEWIS I. SHARP; publ. *On and Off the Wall* (newsletter, every 2 months).

Denver Museum of Natural History: 2001 Colorado Blvd, Denver, CO 80205-5798; tel (303) 370-6387; fax (303) 331-6492; f. and incorporated 1900; departments: anthropology/archaeology, archives/photoarchives, earth sciences, zoology, conservation, exhibitions, youth programmes, adult programmes; Gates Planetarium, Hall of Life, IMAX® Theater, auditorium; library of 30,000 vols, 800 periodicals; Chair. PAMELA D. BEARDSLEY, Pres. and CEO RAYLENE DECATUR; Sec. MARIJKE SWIERSTRA; publs *Annual Reports, Museum Quarterly, Museum Monthly* (newsletter).

Connecticut

Peabody Museum of Natural History: 170 Whitney Ave, New Haven, CT 06511; tel. (203) 432-3750; fax (203) 432-9816; affiliated with Yale University; f. by a gift of George Peabody, 1866; extensive collections in the fields of anthropology, meteorites, botany, palaeobotany, invertebrate palaeontology, mineralogy, vertebrate palaeontology, invertebrate zoology and vertebrate zoology, historic scientific instruments, each with its own Curator; also Yale Peabody Museum Field Station; Dir RICHARD L. BURGER; publs *Bulletin, Postilla, Discovery*.

Wadsworth Atheneum: 600 Main St, Hartford, CT 06103; tel. (860) 278-2670; fax (860) 527-0803; f. 1842; the nation's oldest continuously operating art museum; works of art spanning 5,000 years, incl. early American furniture, Hudson River School colln, Renaissance and Baroque paintings, African-American art; changing temporary exhibitions; MATRIX Gallery for Contemporary Art; Auerbach library of 30,000 vols; Dir PETER C. SUTTON; publs *What's On* (every 2 months), annual report, exhibition catalogues.

Delaware

Winterthur Museum and Gardens: Winterthur, DE 19735; tel. (302) 888-4600; fax (302) 888-4880; f. 1951; collection of early American furniture and domestic objects arranged in 175 period room settings from 17th century to 1860; 200 acres of naturalistic garden; library of 500,000 vols, MSS, microfilm, periodicals, photographs; pre- and postdoctoral research fellowship program; Dir DWIGHT P. LANMON; publs. *Winterthur Portfolio* (3 a year), *Winterthur Newsletter* (quarterly).

District of Columbia

Arthur M. Sackler Gallery: Smithsonian Institution, 1050 Independence Ave, SW, Washington, DC 20560; tel. (202) 357-4880; fax (202) 357-4911; part of the Smithsonian Institution (see under Learned Societies); f. 1982, opened 1987; international loan exhibitions and displays of permanent collection; research, public programmes and publications aim to promote artistic and cultural traditions of Asia; initial collection gift of Arthur M. Sackler; library of 50,000 vols; Dir MILO C. BEACH; publ. *Asian Art and Culture*.

Freer Gallery of Art: Jefferson Drive at 12th St, SW, Washington, DC 20560; tel. (202) 357-4880; fax (202) 357-4911; part of the Smithsonian Institution (see under Learned Societies); established 1906, opened 1923; devoted to research and exhibition of the outstanding collections of Chinese, Japanese, Korean, Indian, Near Eastern and late 19th- and early 20th-century American art; growing collection, based on gift of the late Charles L. Freer, of Detroit (1854-1919); works of James McNeill Whistler; library of 50,000 vols; Dir MILO C. BEACH; publs *Annual Report, Occasional Papers, Oriental Studies, Ars Orientalis*, etc.

Hirshhorn Museum and Sculpture Garden: Independence Ave at 7th St, SW, Washington, DC 20560; tel. (202) 357-3091; fax (202) 786-2682; est. 1966, opened 1974; administered by the Smithsonian Institution; contemporary international art; 19th- and 20th-century sculpture; research library of 40,000 vols; Dir JAMES T. DEMETRION.

National Air and Space Museum: 6th and Independence, Washington, DC 20560; tel. (202) 357-2700; administered by the Smithsonian Institution (see under Learned Societies); f. 1946 to record the national development of aeronautics and astronautics; to collect, preserve, and display aeronautical and astronautical equipment of historical interest and significance; and to provide educational material for the historical study of aeronautics and astronautics. The collection contains original full-size aircraft, spacecraft, recovered space exploration vehicles, engines, instruments, flight clothing, accessories of technical, historical, and biographical interest, scale models, and extensive reference data; includes a Center for Earth and Planetary Studies; library of 24,000 vols and journals; photographic collection; Dir DONALD D. ENGEN.

National Gallery of Art: Between 3rd and 7th Sts NW, on Constitution Ave, Washington, DC 20565; tel. (202) 737-4215; fax (202) 789-2681; independent establishment of the United States govt; estab. 1937, West Building opened 1941, East Building 1978; European and American paintings, sculpture and graphic arts from 13th to 20th centuries; library of 161,538 vols, 2,321 periodicals; photographic archives; slide collection; Pres. ROBERT H. SMITH; Dir EARL A. POWELL III; Administrator DARRELL R. WILLSON; publs *Studies in the History of Art, The A. W. Mellon Lectures in the Fine Arts*, catalogues, etc.

National Museum of African Art: 950 Independence Ave, SW, Washington, DC 20560; tel. (202) 357-4600; f. 1964, merged with Smithsonian Institution 1979; 7,000 items from throughout Africa, incl. traditional and contemporary art; research facilities include the library of 20,000 vols and the Eliot Elisofon Photographic Archives (300,000 photographic prints and transparencies, 120,000 ft of motion picture film and videotape; dept of education organizes workshops, lectures, films, etc.; Dir ROSLYN A. WALKER.

National Museum of American Art and its Renwick Gallery: 8th and G Sts, NW, Washington, DC 20560; tel. (202) 357-2247; fax (202) 357-3108; e-mail nmaainfo@nmaa.si.edu; administered by the Smithsonian Institution (see under Learned Societies); f. 1829; 38,000 American paintings, sculptures, photographs, prints and drawings, folk art, and crafts; specialized library of 100,000 vols; collection of 90,000 slides and 200,000 photographs and negatives; computerized Inventory of American Painting and Sculpture; index of pre-1877 art exhibition catalogues; Smithsonian Art Index; Peter A. Juley and Son Collection of photographs documenting art and artists; research and educational programmes; Dir ELIZABETH BROUN; Chief of Research and Scholars Center RACHEL ALLEN; publ. *American Art* (quarterly).

National Museum of American History: 14th St and Constitution Ave, NW, Washington, DC 20560; tel. (202) 357-2700; telex 264-729; fax (202) 357-1853; administered by the Smithsonian Institution (see under Learned Societies); devoted to the collection, care, study and exhibition of objects which reflect the experience of the American people; programme of lectures and concerts; Dir SPENCER R. CREW.

National Museum of Natural History: Washington, DC 20560; tel. (202) 357-2661; telex 264729; fax (202) 357-4779; f. 1846; a branch of the Smithsonian Institution (see Learned Societies); depository of the national collections, containing over 120m. catalogued items; it is especially rich in the natural science and anthropology of the Americas, including zoology, entomology, botany, geology, palaeontology, archaeology, ethnology, and physical anthropology; also houses exhibits relating to the natural sciences and anthropology; research staff of *c.* 135 scientists; Dir ROBERT W. FRI; publs *Smithsonian Contributions* (separate series for Anthropology, Botany, Earth Sciences, Paleobiology, Zoology and Marine Sciences).

National Portrait Gallery: 8th at F St, NW, Washington, DC 20560; tel. (202) 357-2700; fax (202) 786-2565; administered by the Smithsonian Institution (see under Learned Societies); f. 1962; portraits of persons who have made significant contributions to the history, development or culture of the people of the United States; library of 90,000 vols; Dir ALAN FERN; publ. *Calendar of Events* (every 2 months).

Florida

Marineland Foundation Inc. (Marineland of Florida): 9507 Ocean Shore Blvd, Marineland, FL 32086; tel. (904) 460-1275; fax (904) 460-1330; f. 1938; includes two Oceanariums, 11 marine and fresh water exhibits; houses C. V. Whitney Laboratory; ref. library on aquatic sciences (not open to the public); Gen. Man. ROBIN B. FRIDAY Sr.

Georgia

Roosevelt's Little White House: Route 1, Box 10, Warm Springs, GA 31830; tel. (706) 655-5870; f. 1946; remains as it was when the President died here in 1945; exhibits and film of Roosevelt in Georgia; under direction of Georgia Dept of Natural Resources; Superintendent CHARLES G. BARNES.

Hawaii

Bernice P. Bishop Museum: POB 19000A, 1525 Bernice St, Honolulu, HI 96817-0916; tel. (808) 847-3511; fax (808) 841-8968; f. 1889; devoted to the study of natural and cultural history in the Pacific; depts of anthropology (ethnology and archaeology), botany, entomology, zoology (ichthyology, malacology, vertebrate and invertebrate zoology), education; applied research group, Greenwell Ethnobotanical Garden (island of Hawaii); lectures, films, education programs, permanent and temporary exhibits; library of 100,000 vols, 1,000,000 historic photographs; maps and art works; Dir Dr W. DONALD DUCKWORTH; publs *Ka'Elele* (monthly), bulletins, occasional papers, special publications and annual reports.

Museum of the Honolulu Academy of Arts: 900 South Beretania St, Honolulu, HI 96814; tel. (808) 532-8700; fax (808) 532-8787; f. 1927; museum and art school; Western and Asian art collections; educational programmes for adults and young people; theatre with frequent programmes; special exhibitions; 5,000 mems; 30,000 vols; Pres. HENRY B. CLARK, Jr; Dir GEORGE ELLIS; Sec. Mrs L. B. HALL; publ. *Calendar News* (bulletin for members, 6 a year).

Illinois

Adler Planetarium, The: 1300 South Lake Shore Drive, Chicago, IL 60605; tel. (312) 322-0500; fax (312) 322-2257; f. 1930 by Max Adler; the circular planetarium chamber seats 450 persons, with a hemispherical dome 68 feet wide and Zeiss VI projector; the exhibition areas contain a comprehensive collection of astronomical instruments, mostly ranging from the 15th century; exhibits in astronomy and related sciences; uni-directional Universe Theatre; library of about 5,000 vols; lecture hall seating 120 persons; classrooms; photographic laboratories; optical shop; art, wood, and metal shops; solar telescope; several telescopes including a 20-inch diam. Cassegrain reflector equipped with a charge-coupled device (in the Doane Observatory, east of the planetarium). Programme includes two-part sky shows, classes in astronomy, navigation and telescope making; grade school programme; public observation sessions, demonstrations, lectures and films; Pres. Dr PAUL H. KNAPPENBERGER, Jr; publs *Visitor Guide*, *Course Brochures*.

Art Institute of Chicago: Michigan Avenue at Adams St, Chicago, IL 60603; Tel. (312) 443-3600; f. 1879; American painting and sculpture; 13th- to 20th-century European painting, medieval and Renaissance art; prints and drawings; sculpture; Asian arts (of 5,000 years); African and Amerindian art; textiles; decorative arts; photography; architecture; School of Art; Ryerson Library, f. 1901; Burnham Library of Architecture, f. 1912; total of 180,000 vols and 340,000 slides on art and architecture; also Kraft Education Center; Dir JAMES N. WOOD; publs *News and Events* (every 2 months), *Annual Report, Museum Studies* (2 a year), exhibition catalogues. See also under Colleges.

Field Museum: Roosevelt Rd, at Lake Shore Drive, Chicago, IL 60605; tel. (312) 922-9410; fax (312) 427-7269; f. by Marshall Field in 1893; departments: anthropology, botany, geology, zoology (birds, fishes, insects, invertebrates, mammals, reptiles and amphibians); library of 215,000 vols; large collection of books on China, including several thousand in Chinese; Ornithological Section includes many rare and beautifully illustrated vols; Pres. JOHN W. MCCARTER Jr; publs *The Field Museum Bulletin, General Guide, Fieldiana* (technical publications in anthropology, botany, geology, and zoology), exhibition catalogues, various other publs.

Illinois State Museum: Spring and Edwards Sts, Springfield, IL 62706; tel. (217) 782-7386; fax (217) 782-1254; f. 1877; natural history and anthropology (recreations of American Indian villages and natural habitats); 'At Home in the Heartland' exhibition of decorative arts in Illinois from the 1750's to present day; historic and contemporary works by Illinois artists are exhibited in the fine and applied arts galleries, and *A Place for Discovery* is a 'hands on' learning centre; library of over 10,000 vols mainly relative to collections; Dir R. BRUCE MCMILLAN; publs *The Living Museum* (quarterly), *Impressions* (quarterly).

John G. Shedd Aquarium: 1200 South Lake Shore Drive, Chicago, IL 60605; opened 1930; businessman John Graves Shedd, shortly before his death in 1926, presented $3,000,000 to the people of Chicago with which to build an aquarium; exhibits both fresh- and salt-water species; oceanarium re-creates a Pacific Northwest Coast environment and a Falkland Islands habitat; 90,000-gallon Coral Reef exhibit; Dir TED A. BEATTIE; publ. *WaterShedd* (every 2 months).

Lincoln Park Zoological Gardens: 2200 North Cannon Drive, Chicago, IL 60614-3895; tel. (312) 742-2000; fax (312) 742-2137; f. 1868; specimens of mammals, birds, reptiles, and amphibians; farm; specialities: great apes, primates, perching birds, snakes, big cats; special programmes: Farm in the Zoo, Travelling Zoo and Endangered Species educational programmes; scientific studies include nutrition, behaviour, reproductive biology, physiology, South American field work; reference library and archives of 2,000 vols; Dir KEVIN J. BELL; publs *Guide Book* (irregular), *Lincoln Park Zoo Review* (quarterly), *Annual Report, Animal Inventory* (annually).

Museum of Science and Industry: 57th St and Lake Shore Drive, Chicago, IL 60637; tel. (773) 684-1414; fax (773) 684-7141; f. by Julius Rosenwald, chartered 1926, opened 1933; metals, power, physics, chemistry, electronics, transportation, petroleum, food, space engineering, communications and medical sciences; over 2,000 exhibit units include re-creation of a coal mine, German submarine, walk-through model of human heart, Colleen Moore's Fairy Castle, 'Yesterday's Main Street', actual Apollo 8 spacecraft, Henry Crown Space Center, 'Omnimax' theater, and exhibits on space exploration and energy research; Pres. and CEO TED BEATTIE.

Oriental Institute Museum: 1155 East 58th St, Chicago, IL 60637; tel. (773) 702-9521; fax (773) 702-9853; f. 1894; holds 100,000 objects from Egypt, Iran, Iraq, Israel, Jordan, Palestine, Syria and Turkey; library of 60,000 vols; Museum Dir KAREN L. WILSON.

Kansas

Snow Entomological Museum: University of Kansas, Lawrence, KS 66045; tel. (913) 864-3065; fax (913) 864-5321; f. 1870; primarily North American insects, with worldwide representation of bees, aquatic Hemiptera, Mecoptera, Holarctic and Neotropical Staphylinidae and other beetles; Dir J. S. ASHE; publ. *University of Kansas Science Bulletin*.

Spencer Museum of Art, University of Kansas: Lawrence, KS 66045; tel. (785) 864-4710; fax (785) 864-3112; f. 1928; specializes in medieval art, European painting and sculpture, American painting and graphics, photography, Japanese Edo prints and painting and modern Chinese painting; 105,000 vols in Murphy Library of Art History; Dir ANDREA NORRIS; publs *Register* (annually), the Franklin D. Murphy Lectures Series and exhibition catalogues.

Louisiana

New Orleans Museum of Art: 1 Collins Diboll Circle, City Park, New Orleans, LA 70124; tel. (504) 488-2631; fax (504) 484-6662; e-mail webmaster@noma.org; f. 1911; paintings, sculpture, prints, drawings, photographs and decorative arts; special collections include: history of glass; 150-year collection of photographs; Japanese paintings of the Edo Period; Chinese pottery and stone sculpture; 17th- to 20th-century French paintings; Italian and Spanish paintings from Renaissance and Baroque periods; 16th- to 18th century Low Countries paintings; tribal arts of sub-Saharan Africa; 18th- and 19th-century French porcelain; 20th-century American art and pottery; Spanish colonial Latin American paintings and sculpture; English and Continental portrait miniatures; P. C. Fabergé jewelled objects; 18th- to 20th-century American and English silver; arts of pre-Columbian Mexico, and of Central and South America; North American Indian arts; library of 30,000 vols; Dir E. JOHN BULLARD; publs *Arts Quarterly*, occasional papers and catalogues.

Maryland

Baltimore Museum of Art: 10 Art Museum Drive, Baltimore, MD 21218; tel. (410) 396-7100; fax (410) 396-7153; f. 1914; collections include 2nd–6th-century Antioch Mosaics, Epstein and Jacobs collection of Old Masters, 17th–20th-century American paintings, Cone Collection of 19th- and 20th-century French paintings, drawings and sculptures (special collection of Matisse), George A. Lucas Collection of 19th-century French art, May collection of 20th-century European paintings and sculptures, 65,000 prints, drawings and photographs from 15th century to late 20th century, Gallagher Memorial Collection of modern American paintings, Wurtzburger collection of the arts of Africa, the Americas and Oceania; Levi and Wurtzburger sculpture gardens; collections of American and European decorative arts; library of 50,000 vols; Chair. Dr DOREEN BOLGER; Dir (vacant); publ. *BMA Today* (members' calendar, 6 a year).

Maryland Historical Society, Museum and Library of Maryland History: 201 West Monument St, Baltimore, MD 21201; f. 1844; exhibits Francis Scott Key's original MS of The Star-Spangled Banner and the war of 1812; 3,000 paintings and miniatures; 700 pieces of furniture; sculpture, drawings, silver; ceramics; jewellery, textiles; library of over 90,000 vols, etc.; manuscript room includes Calvert Papers, papers of Benjamin Henry Latrobe, over 1,300 letters and documents of the Lords Baltimore and their families, genealogical collection and many hundreds of prints and drawings; maritime collection emphasizing crafts of Chesapeake Bay; Dir DENNIS A. FIORI; publs *News and Notes* (quarterly), *Maryland Historical Magazine* (quarterly).

Walters Art Gallery: 600 North Charles St, Baltimore, MD 21201; tel. (410) 547-9000; fax (410) 783-7969; f. 1931; 22,000 objects; Chinese, Japanese and Indian art, Ancient Egyptian, Greek and Roman art, Byzantine art, Romanesque, early Gothic art, later Gothic art, Renaissance sculpture and decorative arts, manuscript illumination, incunabula, arms and armour, old master paintings, 19th-century paintings, decorative arts; library of 75,000 vols; Dir GARY VIKAN; publs *Journal* (annually), *Annual Report, Bulletin* (10 a year).

Massachusetts

Adams National Historic Site: 135 Adams St, Quincy, MA 02169; tel. (617) 773-1177; donated to the US in December 1946, by the Adams Memorial Society; designated a national historic site under the administration of the National Park Service of the Department of the Interior; built in 1731 by Major Leonard Vassall of Boston; bought by John Adams in 1787. At the end of his term he lived in the house until his death in 1826. The house then passed to his son, John Quincy Adams, in the middle of his term as sixth President. After his death in 1848 the house passed to his son, Charles Francis Adams, Minister to England during the Civil War. The Adams family continued to live there until the death in 1927 of Brooks Adams, the fourth son of Charles Francis Adams. The house, contents, and garden are as the Adams family left them. The separate stone library, standing in the garden, was built in 1870 by Charles Francis Adams. It contains an estimated 14,000 volumes, comprising most of the libraries of John Quincy Adams and Charles Francis Adams and some of the libraries of John Adams, Charles Francis Adams II, Henry Adams and Brooks.

Concord Museum: 200 Lexington Rd, Concord, MA 01742; tel. (978) 369-9763; fax (978) 369-9660; e-mail cm1@concordmuseum.org; f. 1886; history and decorative arts museum with 16 period rooms and galleries, with artifacts from Concord area; museum rooms chronicle life in Concord from Native American habitation to the 20th century; special collections include relics from the battle at North Bridge, the largest collection of Thoreau artifacts from his stay at Walden Pond, and the contents of Emerson's study; programme of lectures, concerts and films; Dir DESIRÉE CALDWELL; publs *Handbook, Exhibition Catalogs, Newsletter* (quarterly).

Harvard University Art Museums: Harvard University, Cambridge, MA 02138; tel. (617) 495-9400; fax (617) 495-9936; f. 1891; incorporate the Fogg Art Museum, Busch-Reisinger Museum, Arthur M. Sackler Museum; fine arts collection covering prehistoric to modern Eastern and Western art; houses Harvard's Dept of the History of Art and Architecture, and serves as a laboratory for training museum professionals, art historians and conservators; houses Harvard's Fine Arts Library of 225,000 vols, 1,500,000 photographs and slides; Dir JAMES CUNO; publs exhibition catalogues.

Museum of Fine Arts, Boston: 465 Huntington Ave, Boston, MA 02115; tel. (617) 267-9300; fax (617) 267-0280; a private instn; f. 1870; departments of Asiatic art with outstanding collection of Chinese and Japanese sculpture, painting, and ceramics, Indian and Islamic art; Egyptian art with important Old Kingdom Collection; Classical art with Greek and Roman sculpture, coins, and seals; American and European decorative arts with American furniture, silver Medieval and Renaissance European sculpture, English and American silver; paintings of Europe and America, stressing French Impressionist, American Colonial and 19th-century works; art of Africa, Oceania and the ancient Americas, including masks, sculpture, ceramics, jades, textiles and gold; large department of Prints and Drawings; department of Textiles with Coptic, 17th–19th century European and American textiles, costumes, and tapestries; Contemporary Art (since 1955); department of education; Art School; library of 200,000 books and catalogues; Dir MALCOLM ROGERS; publ. *MFA Preview* (calendar of events, 6 a year).

Museum of Science: Science Park, Boston, MA 02114; fax (617) 589-0454; f. 1830; exhibits on astronomy, natural history, physical science, technology, medicine, etc.; houses the Charles Hayden Planetarium, the Mugar Omni Theater and the Lyman Library; library of 40,000 vols and journals; Pres. and Dir DAVID W. ELLIS; publ. *Magazine* (2 a year).

Peabody Essex Museum: East India Sq., Salem, MA 01970; tel. (508) 745-9500; f. 1799; maritime art and history, Asian, Oceanic, African and Native American art; American art and architecture; library of 100,000 vols; Dir DAN L. MONROE; publs *American Neptune* (quarterly), *Quarterly Review of Archaeology.*

Peabody Museum of Archaeology and Ethnology: Harvard University, Cambridge, MA 02138; tel. (617) 495-2248; fax (617) 495-7535; f. 1866 by George Peabody. The Museum works in the closest co-operation with the Department of Anthropology of Harvard, and much of the research is jointly determined. Since its founding more than 800 expeditions have been sent to every continent, resulting, with the addition of important gifts and purchases, in the building up of one of the most comprehensive collections of ethnology, archaeology and physical anthropology in the United States. The first scientific studies of Maya archaeology were made under its direction, and its collections from this area, and from Middle America generally, are extremely important. There are also collections of Old World archaeology. In ethnology, the material from the Pacific Islands is important, and the Museum is also rich in material representing the native tribes of Africa, of South America, and of the Plains and North-west Coast Indians of North America, where some of the objects date from the Lewis and Clark expedition of 1806. The archaeology of the south-western United States, including the Pueblo Indian area, is also strongly represented. The Tozzer Library with its 200,000 books and pamphlets, covers the entire field of anthropology. Dir RUBIE WATSON; publs *Papers, Memoirs, Bulletins, Monographs*, American School of Prehistoric Research *Bulletins* and special publications of the Peabody Museum Press.

Smith College Museum of Art: Northampton, MA 01063; tel. (413) 585-2770; fax (413) 585-2782; e-mail artmuseum@ais.smith.edu; f. 1879; collections include examples from most periods and cultures with special emphasis on European and American paintings, sculpture, drawings, prints and photographs of the 17th–20th centuries; Dir SUZANNAH FABING.

Worcester Art Museum: 55 Salisbury St, Worcester, MA 01609; tel. (508) 799-4406; fax (508) 798-5646; f. 1896; illustrates the evolution of art from early Egyptian civilization to modern times; especially notable are ancient Egyptian, Greek, Roman, Asian and medieval sculpture; mosaics from Antioch; a French Romanesque Chapter House; Italian and other European schools of painting of the 13th to 20th centuries; American collections from the 17th century to the present day; pre-Columbian art; Japanese and Western prints; photographs and drawings; library of 40,000 vols; Pres. JOHN M. NELSON; Dir JAMES A. WELU; publ. *Calendar* (3 a year).

Michigan

Detroit Institute of Arts: 5200 Woodward Ave, Detroit, MI 48202; tel. (313) 833-7900; fax (313) 833-2357; f. 1885; comprehensive fine arts collection from prehistoric to contemporary times; collection of American, Dutch, Flemish, French, Italian and German Expressionist painting; Ancient, African, Oceanic and New World Cultures; Asian, Native American, Islamic and twentieth-century art; graphic arts; twentieth-century American and European decorative arts; theatre arts collection; library of 160,000 vols; Dir MAURICE D. PARRISH; publs *Bulletin of the DIA* (2 a year), *DIA Views* (monthly).

Henry Ford Museum and Greenfield Village: 20900 Oakwood Blvd, POB 1970, Dearborn, MI 48121; tel. (313) 271-1620; f. 1929; indoor/outdoor museum of American history covering 260 acres; domestic life, agriculture and industry, leisure and entertainment, transportation and communication; historic structures; archival and library holdings include 37,600 books, 146,000 periodicals, 18,500 trade catalogues, 22,000 linear feet of archival material including records of the Ford Motor Co, 1,000,000 photographic images and 50,000 graphic items; Chair. of Board WILLIAM CLAY FORD, Jr; Pres. STEVEN K. HAMP; publs exhibition catalogues, etc.

Minnesota

Minneapolis Institute of Arts, The: 2400 Third Ave South, Minneapolis, MN 55404; tel. (612) 870-3046; fax (612) 870-3004; f. 1883; library of 20,000 vols; collection of 80,000 objects representing nearly every school and period of art, including European and American paintings, sculpture, decorative arts, period rooms, prints and drawings, photography, Oriental, African, Oceanic, North and South American Arts from 1500 BC to the present; Minnich collection of botanical, zoological and fashion prints, paintings by Poussin, Rembrandt, El Greco, Goya, Manet, Monet, Renoir, Van Gogh, Matisse; Alfred F. Pillsbury collection of ancient Chinese jades and bronzes, etc.; Dir EVAN M. MAURER.

Science Museum of Minnesota: 30 East 10th St, St. Paul, MN 55101; tel. (612) 221-9488; fax (612) 221-4777; f. 1907; research in anthropology, biology, palaeontology, ethnology, zoology, archaeology, geology and geography; collections in the field of biology, anthropology, palaeontology, geology; outdoor research center; a 300-seat omnitheater; nature centre; Pres. Dr JAMES L. PETERSON.

Walker Art Center: Vineland Place, Minneapolis, MN 55403; tel. (612) 375-7577; fax (612) 375-7618; f. 1879; 20th-century paintings, drawings, prints, sculpture, photography; extensive music, dance, film/video, theatre and education programmes; library of 35,000 vols; audio and film/video archive; Dir KATHY HALBREICH; publ. *Monthly Calendar of Events*.

Missouri

Kansas City Museum: 3218 Gladstone Blvd, Kansas City, MO 64123; tel. (816) 483-8300; fax (816) 483-9912; f. 1939; administered by Kansas City Museum Association; Science and technology exhibitions, American Indian artifacts, costume and textile collection, natural history exhibits, planetarium, Challenger Learning Center; archives and reference library; Pres. DAVID A. UCKO.

Nelson-Atkins Museum of Art: 4525 Oak St, Kansas City, MO 64111; tel. (816) 561-4000; fax (816) 561-7154; estab. 1933 under the will of William Rockhill Nelson for the purchase of works of fine arts such as paintings, engravings, sculptures, tapestries and decorative arts; departments: Oriental Art, Prints, Drawing and Photography, 20th-century and Modern Art, American Art, European Art, Decorative Arts, Ancient Art, The Arts of Africa, Oceania and the Americas, Medieval Art, Education, Henry Moore Sculpture Garden and Kansas City Sculpture Park; library of 75,000 vols; Dir MARC F. WILSON; publ. *Calendar of Events*.

St Louis Art Museum, The: Forest Park, St Louis, MO 63110; f. 1907; publicly owned collection of about 30,000 art objects; important collections of American, European and Asian painting, sculpture and decorative arts, pre-Columbian and Oceanic art; library of 35,000 vols; Dir JAMES D. BURKE; publs *Bulletin*, *Annual Report*.

New Hampshire

Currier Gallery of Art: 201 Myrtle Way, Manchester, NH; tel. (603) 669-6144; f. 1929; galleries devoted to oils, water colours, prints, furniture, decorative arts and sculpture; permanent collection contains works by Copley, Degas, G. B. Tiepolo, Stuart, Homer, Raeburn, Monet, Tintoretto, Constable, Corot, Ruisdael, Mabuse, van Cleve, Rouault, Matisse, Perugino, Picasso and contemporary American painters; 17th- to 19th-century American furniture, silver, pewter, textiles; 18th- and 19th-century European and American art glass; frequent loan exhibitions, lectures, concerts, children's programmes; Dir SUSAN STRICKLER; publ. *Calendar*.

New Jersey

Montclair Art Museum: 3 South Mountain Ave, Montclair, NJ 07042; tel. (973) 746-5555; fax (973) 746-9118; e-mail mail@montclair-art.com; opened 1914; mid-18th- to 20th-century American art incl. paintings, sculpture, works on paper, costumes and bookplates; Native American art and artefacts; LeBrun library of 14,000 vols; 20,000 colour slides; Dir ELLEN S. HARRIS; publ. *Members Bulletin* (every 2 months).

New Mexico

Museum of New Mexico: POB 2087, Santa Fé, NM 87504-2087; f. 1909; a state agency, under Board of Regents appointed by Governor, divisions in anthropology, history, fine arts, international folk art, Indian arts and culture, state monuments located in separate buildings; custody of combined libraries approx. 26,000 vols; Dir THOMAS A. LIVESAY; publs *El Palacio* (quarterly), popular and scientific books, monographs, reports.

Wheelwright Museum of the American Indian: 704 Camino Lejo, POB 5153, Santa Fé, NM 87502; tel. (505) 982-4636; fax (505) 989-7386; f. by Mary C. Wheelwright and Hastiin Klah; incorp. 1937; access by appointment; houses collections of artifacts, archives, sound recordings and photographs, documenting native American (especially Navajo) culture, both historic and contemporary; Dir JONATHAN BATKIN.

New York

American Museum of Natural History: Central Park West at 79th St, New York, NY 10024; inc. 1869; departments: anthropology, earth and planetary sciences, entomology, herpetology, ichthyology, invertebrates, mammalogy, mineral sciences, ornithology, vertebrate palaeontology; library: see Libraries; Chair. Board of Trustees ANNE SIDAMON-ERISTOFF; Pres. ELLEN V. FUTTER, Jr.; publs *Natural History, American Museum Novitates, AMNH Bulletin, Curator, Anthropological Papers, Rotunda.*

Has attached:

Hayden Planetarium: 81st St and Central Park West, New York, NY 10024; f. 1935; Zeiss Star Projector and over 250 special effects projectors are used on a 75-foot diameter dome; *c.* 9,000 stars are projected in the Planetarium heavens; new sky-show several times a year; lectures, educational courses; Chair. Dr WILLIAM A. GUTSCH, Jr. (In 1997 the Planetarium was reported to be closed for renovation.)

Brooklyn Botanic Garden: 1000 Washington Ave, Brooklyn, NY 11225; tel. (718) 622-4433; fax (718) 857-2430; e-mail publicaffairsoffice@bbg.org; f. 1910; living colln of 12,000 species and varieties; herbarium with 200,000 specimens; education programs, children's garden, art and horticulture classes, cultural programs, guided tours, plant information service; library of 55,000 vols; Pres. JUDITH D. ZUK; publs *Plants & Gardens News*, *Annual Report.*

Brooklyn Children's Museum: 145 Brooklyn Ave, Brooklyn, NY 11213; tel. (718) 735-4400; fax (718) 604-7442; f. 1899; world's first children's museum; teaching collection of more than 27,000 ethnographic objects and natural science specimens, interactive technological exhibits on science and culture; Children's Resource Library; Portable Collection Loan Program for schools; special cultural performances, participatory activities for general public, school classes, groups, workshops; Exec. Dir BOBYE G. LIST; publ. *Newsletter* (4 a year).

Brooklyn Museum of Art: 200 Eastern Parkway, Brooklyn, NY 11238; tel. (718) 638-5000; fax (718) 638-3731; e-mail bklynmus@echonyc.com; estab. 1890; native American art; Peruvian textiles; pre-Columbian gold; Costa Rican sculpture; collections from Africa, Melanesia and Polynesia; collections from China, Korea, Southeast Asia, Japan, India and Persia; Colonial South American art; American period rooms; sculpture garden; American and European paintings; Prints and Drawings; Ancient art of the Near East, Egypt, Greece and Rome; American and European costumes; American glass, pewter and silver; contemporary paintings and sculpture; art reference library and Egyptological library (170,000 books and periodicals); Dir Dr ARNOLD L. LEHMAN.

Buffalo Fine Arts Academy: 1285 Elmwood Ave, Buffalo, NY 14222; tel. (716) 882-8700; fax (716) 882-1958; f. 1862; incorporates Albright-Knox Art Gallery (dedicated 1905); collection of 19th- and 20th-century paintings, with emphasis on American and European contemporary artists; sculpture 3000 BC to present day; prints and drawings; Dir (Art Gallery) DOUGLAS G. SCHULTZ; Curator CHERYL BRUTVAN; Curator of Education JENNIFER L. BAYLES.

Buffalo Museum of Science: 1020 Humboldt Parkway, Buffalo, NY 14211; building opened 1929; administered by Buffalo Society of Natural Sciences (*q.v.*); Exhibits halls deal with insects, endangered species, dinosaurs and other fossils, birds, wild flowers and fungi, vertebrates, minerals, flora and fauna of the Niagara Frontier, life in ancient Egypt, solar system and space exploration; library of 50,000 vols; solar and lunar observatory; loan collections, lectures, motion pictures, day and evening classes, etc.; Pres. and CEO MICHAEL J. SMITH.

Cooper-Hewitt, National Design Museum, Smithsonian Institution: 2 East 91st St, New York, NY 10128; tel. 860-6868; fax (212) 860-6909; administered by the Smithsonian Institution (see under Learned Societies); formerly Cooper Union Museum; f. 1895; 250,000 items, including collections of original drawings and designs for architecture and the decorative arts; 15th- to 20th-century prints; textiles, lace, woodwork and furniture, ceramics, glass, etc.; drawings and paintings by F. E. Church, W. Homer and other 19th-century American artists; exhibitions change regularly, each one focussing on aspects of contemporary or historical design; library of 50,000 vols, incl. 6,000 rare books; Dir DIANNE H. PILGRIM.

Frick Collection: 1 East 70th St., New York, NY 10021; tel. (212) 288-0700; fax (212) 628-4417; e-mail info@frick.org; opened 1935; important collection of 13th- to 19th-century European paintings; Italian Renaissance bronzes and furniture; Limoges enamels of the Renaissance; French 18th-century sculpture, furniture and porcelains; Oriental porcelains; the works of art, most of them assembled by the late industrialist Henry Clay Frick, are arranged with a freedom and flexibility that retain the atmosphere of his former residence; Dir SAMUEL SACHS II.

Guggenheim, Solomon R., Museum: 1071 Fifth Ave, New York, NY 10128-0173; tel. (212) 423-3500; fax (212) 423-3650; f. 1937; building designed by Frank Lloyd Wright; the permanent collection of *c.* 6,000 works since the

Post-Impressionist era, augmented by the Justin K. Thannhauser Collection of Impressionist and Post-Impressionist masterpieces, includes large collections of Brâncuși sculptures, Kandinsky paintings and graphics, and works by Klee, Braque, Chagall, Delaunay, Dubuffet, Léger, Marc, Mondrian and Picasso, and the Panza Collection of American Minimalist paintings and sculptures and Conceptual pieces; a continuous programme of loan exhibitions is presented, drawn from its own collection and from leading public and private collections throughout the world; research library of *c.* 20,000 vols; Dir THOMAS KRENS; Deputy Dir and Senior Curator DIANE WALDMAN; publs exhibition catalogues.

Has attached:

Guggenheim Museum SoHo: 575 Broadway, New York, NY 10012-4233; tel. (212) 423-3500.

Hispanic Society of America Museum, The: Broadway, between 155th and 156th Streets, New York, NY 10032; f. 1904; free museum concentrated on the culture of the Iberian Peninsula: paintings, prints and drawings (14th to 20th centuries), sculpture (13th to 20th centuries), archaeology, decorative arts (ceramics, textiles, metalwork, furniture); reference library and photograph files; Dir Dr MITCHELL A. CODDING; Curators MARCUS BURK (Paintings and Drawings), PATRICK LENAGHAN (Iconography).

Jewish Museum, The: 1109 Fifth Avenue, New York, NY 10128; tel. (212) 423-3200; fax (212) 423-3232; f. 1904; most comprehensive collection of Judaica in the US; changing contemporary art and other exhibits of Jewish interest; special events, films, lectures, etc.; Dir JOAN ROSENBAUM; publs catalogues of exhibits, etc.

Metropolitan Museum of Art, The: Fifth Ave and 82nd St, New York, NY 10028; tel. (212) 879-5500; f. 1870; curatorial departments: Art of Africa, Oceania and the Americas, American Paintings and Sculpture, American Decorative Arts, Ancient Near Eastern Art, Asian Art, Costume Institute, Drawings and Prints, European Paintings, European Sculpture and Decorative Arts, Greek and Roman Art, Islamic Art, Robert Lehman Collection, Medieval Art, Musical Instruments, Photographs, Twentieth-century Art; the Museum Library contains 240,000 books, 1,400 periodical titles; Photograph and Slide Library; Pres. WILLIAM H. LUERS; Dir PHILIPPE DE MONTEBELLO; publs *The Bulletin, Calendar, Annual Report.*

Museum of Modern Art, The: 11 West 53rd St, New York, NY 10019; tel. (212) 708-9400; fax (212) 708-9889; f. 1929; collection and changing exhibitions, international in scope, of paintings, drawings, prints, sculptures, industrial and graphic design, photographs and architecture dating from 1880s; large collection of American, British, French, German and Russian films, 1,200 of which are available to educational organizations; daily film showings; modern art library of 140,000 vols; organizes exhibitions in all the visual arts for circulation all over the world; Dir GLENN D. LOWRY; publs monographs, catalogues, etc.

Museum of Television and Radio: 25 West 52 St, New York, NY 10019; tel. (212) 621-6600; fax (212) 621-6700; fmrly Museum of Broadcasting; collection and exhibition reflecting more than seventy years of radio and television history; Pres. Dr ROBERT M. BATSCHA.

Museum of the City of New York: Fifth Avenue at 103rd St, New York, NY 10029; tel. (212) 534-1672; f. 1923; history museum; exhibits include The Big Apple, Marine Gallery, New York paintings, dolls' houses, photographs, costumes, photograph archives, decorative arts, prints; Dir ROBERT R. MACDONALD; publs *Report* (annually), *Quarterly.*

National Museum of the American Indian, Smithsonian Institution: Alexander Hamilton US Custom House, One Bowling Green, New York, NY 10004; f. 1916; dedicated to the preservation, study, exhibition and collection of the material culture of the native peoples of the Western Hemisphere; Resource Center of current information on American Indians; library of 40,000 vols, 100,000 photographs and negatives; Dir RICHARD WEST, Jr.

Rochester Museum and Science Center: 657 East Ave at Goodman St, Rochester, NY 14607; f. 1912; natural science, anthropology, history, and technology; library of 25,000 vols; Strasenburgh Planetarium: computerized, Zeiss projector, exhibits, daily astronomy and space-science shows in Star Theater; 800-acre Cumming Nature Center in the nearby Bristol Hills; environmental education facility; Gannett School of Science and Man; Pres. KATE BENNETT.

Whitney Museum of American Art: 945 Madison Ave, New York, NY 10021; tel. (212) 570-3676; fax (212) 570-1807; f. 1930; established for the encouragement and advancement of contemporary American art; special exhibitions include Whitney biennial and historical surveys; highlights from the permanent collection of over 8,500 paintings, sculptures and works on paper; Dir DAVID A. ROSS.

North Carolina

Morehead Planetarium: University of North Carolina at Chapel Hill, Chapel Hill, NC 27599; tel. (919) 549-6863; f. 1947; Carl Zeiss Model VI Planetarium Instrument, Memorial Rotunda, Copernican Orrery, Scientific and Art Exhibitions, etc.; daily public programmes; Dir Dr LEE T. SHAPIRO; publ. *Sundial.*

Ohio

Cincinnati Art Museum: Eden Park, Cincinnati, OH 45202; tel. (513) 721-5204; fax (513) 721-0129; inc. 1881; permanent collections grouped in 88 galleries: Art of the Ancient World, Near Eastern Art, Far Eastern Art, Medieval Art, Arts of Africa and the Americas, Musical Instruments, Continental and English Decorative Arts, American Decorative Arts, European Painting and Sculpture, American Painting and Sculpture, Prints, Drawings and Photographs, Costumes and Textiles; Nabataean antiquities from Khirbet Tannur; large collection of Old Master prints and modern Japanese and East European prints; contemporary art; temporary exhibitions; library of 52,000 vols with 250,000 pamphlets and clippings; Pres. LAWRENCE H. KYTE, Jr; Dir BARBARA GIBBS; publs *Annual Report, CANVAS* (every 2 months).

Cleveland Museum of Art: 11150 East Blvd, Cleveland, OH 44106; tel. (216) 421-7340; telex MUSART; fax (216) 421-0411; e-mail info@cma-oh.org; inc. 1913, opened 1916; collections include paintings, sculpture, prints and drawings, textiles and decorative arts from the ancient world, Asia, Europe, the Americas, Africa and Oceania; library of 215,000 books and periodicals; Pres. MICHAEL J. HORVITZ; Dir Dr ROBERT P. BERGMAN; publs *Cleveland Studies in the History of Art* (annually), *Members' Magazine* (10 a year), *Annual Report.*

Cleveland Museum of Natural History: 1 Wade Oval Drive, University Circle, Cleveland, OH 44106-1767; tel. (216) 231-4600; fax (216) 231-5919; f. 1920; comprises Natural History Museum, Mueller Planetarium and Observatory, Kelley's Island, Mentor Marsh (and Marsh House), Koelliker Fen, Groves Woods, Medina Sanctuary, Cottonwood Hollow, Grand River Terraces, Fern Lake Bog, North Kingsville Sand Barrens, Pymatuning Creek Fen, Cathedral Woods and Chamberlin Woods; collections in all fields with particular emphasis on the northern half of Ohio, including Upper Devonian Fossil Fishes; also vertebrates, insects, shells, minerals, precious and semi-precious stones, and botanical and ethnological materials; dept. of physical anthropology responsible for the discovery and naming of new species of early man, *A. afarensis*; the Museum has sponsored or participated in several expeditions to Africa, islands of the South Atlantic, Antarctica, the Azuero Peninsula of Panama, and various parts of North America; many study collections, including herbarium, the Hamann-Todd Skeletal collection; mounted Jurassic cetiosaurid, Haplocanthosaurus; library of 50,000 vols; Dir Dr J. JAMES E. KING; publs *The Explorer* (quarterly), *Kirtlandia* (scientific papers), *The Cleveland Bird Calendar, Tracks* (every 2 months, members' newsletter).

Health Museum: 8911 Euclid Ave, Cleveland, OH 44106; tel. (216) 231-5010; fax (216) 231-5129; opened 1940; permanent exhibitions and interactive displays to educate the public in decision-making for healthy lifestyle choices; formalized youth education in 13 laboratory classrooms and 'Health on Wheels' travelling programme; adult education programme of seminars, lectures and health promotion activities; permanent installations include: Juno, the Museum's symbol, a transparent woman who talks to visitors about body systems and functions; 'Wonder of New Life' depicted by Dickinson Birth Models; the 'Giant Tooth' complex; and the participatory Family Discovery centre; Pres. Dr BERNADINE HEALY; Dir MICHAEL J. MARKS; publs *Healthwise* (quarterly), *Classes and Services Booklet* (annually).

United States Air Force Museum: Wright-Patterson Air Force Base, OH 45433-7102; tel. (937) 255-3286; f. 1923; displays of historical events, individuals and materials incl. aircraft and missiles; preservation of milestones in aerospace technology; study of aviation and aerospace history; Research Center with 400,000 photographs, and 4,500,000 video tapes, technical orders, books, drawings, logbooks, diaries, periodicals and other documents); Dir Maj.-Gen. CHARLES D. METCALF (retd); publ. *Friends' Journal.*

Pennsylvania

American Swedish Historical Museum: 1900 Pattison Ave, Philadelphia, PA 19145; tel. (215) 389-1776; f. 1926; contributions by Swedes and Swedish-Americans through the past 350 years; 14 galleries dedicated to all major historical and cultural aspects of Swedish accomplishments; exhibition on New Sweden Colony (1638-1655); research library of 11,000 vols, primary source genealogical documents and sources; collection of letters, documents and designs by John Ericsson; Chair. AGNETA BAILEY; Dir BIRGITTA W. DAVIS (acting); publ. *Newsletter.*

Barnes Foundation Collection: Merion, Montgomery County, PA 19066; tel. (610) 667-3067; fax (610) 664-4026; f. 1922 by Dr Albert C. Barnes; offers courses in the philosophy and appreciation of art; collection of 1,000 paintings, including works by El Greco, Titian, Goya, Rubens, Cézanne, Renoir, Modigliani, Soutine, Picasso, Matisse and Van Gogh; also sculpture, antique furniture and wrought iron; Arboretum, with courses in botany and horticulture.

Carnegie Science Center: One Allegheny Ave, Pittsburgh, PA 15212-5850; tel. (412) 237-3400; fax (412) 237-3375; opened 1991; Rangos

Omnimax Theater, with images projected on a wrap-around screen, Henry Buhl Jr Planetarium and Observatory, Second World War diesel-electric submarine USS Requin, and The Works, featuring a working foundry, the Tesla coil and Van de Graaff generator and experiences with robotics, cryogenics and lasers; informal science and computer classes for children and adults, professional development workshops for educators, outreach programmes, high school science apprenticeships and other specialized science programmes; Dir SEDDON BENNINGTON.

Franklin Institute Science Museum: Benjamin Franklin Parkway at 20th St, Philadelphia, PA 19103; tel. (215) 448-1200; fax (215) 448-1235; f. 1824; planetarium, Omnimax Theater, interactive theatre; exhibits and demonstrations in physical sciences and technology; workshops and teacher training; Pres. and CEO DENNIS WINT.

Pennsylvania Academy of the Fine Arts, Museum of American Art: Broad and Cherry Sts, Philadelphia, PA 19102; tel. (215) 972-7600; fax (215) 972-5564; f. 1805; collection of 18th–20th-century American paintings, sculpture, graphics; special exhibitions yearly; important archive; library of 12,000 vols; Dir DANIEL ROSENFELD; publ. *Newsletter*.

Philadelphia Museum of Art: 26th St and the Benjamin Franklin Parkway, Philadelphia, PA 19101-7646; tel. (215) 763-8100; fax (215) 236-4465; incorp. 1876; *c.* 300,000 pieces of art, including paintings, prints, sculpture and silver from medieval to contemporary times representing European, American, and Far Eastern Art; Dir and CEO ANNE D'HARNONCOURT; publs *Bulletin* (quarterly), *Newsletter* (monthly), *Annual Report,* exhibition catalogues.

University of Pennsylvania Museum of Archaeology and Anthropology: University of Pennsylvania, 33rd and Spruce Sts, Philadelphia, PA 19104; tel. (215) 898-4000; fax (215) 898-0657; f. 1887; archaeological collection from Old and New Worlds; ethnology from the New World, Oceania and Africa; Near Eastern tablet collection of 30,000 documents; Museum Applied Science Center for Archaeology (MASCA) carries out research in physical sciences, especially dating techniques, ancient metallurgical processes and ceramic analyses; the museum also acts as a teaching organization and sends research expeditions around the world; library of 82,000 vols; archives with over 300,000 photographic items; Dir JEREMY SABLOFF; publs *Expedition* (3 a year), *MASCA Research Papers* (annually), monographs, books.

Tennessee

American Museum of Science and Energy: 300 South Tulane Ave, Oak Ridge, TN 37830; tel. (615) 576-3200; f. 1949; operated for the US Department of Energy by Enterprise Advisory Services, Inc.; one of the world's largest energy exhibitions, with live demonstrations, computers and films on all energy forms and uses; Dir DAVID SINCERBOX.

Texas

Dallas Museum of Art: 1717 North Harwood, Dallas, TX 75201; tel. (214) 922-1200; fax (214) 954-0174; f. 1903; owned by City of Dallas; arts of Africa, Asia and Pacific; Indonesian textiles; architectural and shrine objects from S. Asia; Egyptian antiquities; post-1945 contemporary art; American art from pre-Columbian period to mid-1900s; 19th-century and early modern European paintings and sculpture; American and European decorative arts, The Wendy and Emery Reves Collection, The Faith and Charles Bybee Collection of American Furniture; prints, drawings, photographs; reference library of 25,000 vols, special collections: ethnography, artists' files; Dir JAY GATES.

Hall of State: 3939 Grand Ave, Dallas, TX 75226; tel. (214) 421-4500; fax (214) 421-7500; f. 1922; museum and archives of Southwestern United States, Texas and Dallas history; operated by Dallas Historical Society (see Learned Societies); library of 14,000 vols, 15,000 museum artifacts and 2,000,000 archival items; Dir NANCY NELSON.

Museum of Fine Arts, The: 1001 Bissonnet St, Houston, TX 77005; tel. (713) 639-7300; telex 775232; fax (713) 639-7399; incorporated in 1900; art of the ancient world; European painting and sculpture; Far Eastern art; art of Africa, Oceania and the Americas; decorative arts; prints and drawings; film and video; 20th-century art; photography; textiles and costume; the Bayou Bend Collection of American decorative arts, the Cullen Sculpture Garden and the Glassell School of Art; reference library of 80,000 vols, 83,000 slides; Dir PETER C. MARZIO; publ. *MFA Today* (6 a year).

San Jacinto Museum of History: San Jacinto Monument, 3800 Park Rd 1836, La Porte, TX 77571; f. 1939; exhibits revisualize the history of Texas region from 1519 to 1900; library of 25,000 vols; MSS and documents from 15th century to the present day; Pres. PAUL G. BELL, Jr; Dir J. C. MARTIN.

Texas Memorial Museum: 2400 Trinity, Campus of the University of Texas, Austin, TX 78705; tel. (512) 471-1604; fax (512) 471-4794; f. 1936; civic and natural history of Texas, the Southwest and Latin America, minerals, fossils, palaeontology, vertebrate and invertebrate zoology, geology, anthropology, archaeology, radiocarbon, materials conservation, and vertebrate palaeontology laboratories; Dir Dr EDWARD THERIOT; publs *Bulletin, Pearce-Sellards Series, Miscellaneous Papers, Museum Notes, Conservation Notes* (all irregular).

Virginia

Colonial Williamsburg Foundation: POB 1776, Williamsburg, VA 23187-1776; tel. (804) 229-1000; fax (804) 220-7398; f. 1926; preservation project and 173-acre outdoor museum with nearly 500 preserved, restored and reconstructed buildings open to public; more than 90 acres of period gardens and greens; collection of 18th-century English and American furniture and domestic objects displayed in 225 period rooms throughout the Historic Area and in the 10 galleries of the DeWitt Wallace Gallery; library of 65,000 books, 50,000 MSS, 50,000 architectural drawings, 630,000 photographs, negatives and slides; demonstration of 17 historic trades; operates Carter's Grove Plantation (incl. 1754 mansion), Abby Aldrich Rockefeller Folk Art Center, and Bassett Hall (original 18th-century house, local residence of John D. Rockefeller, Jr when instrumental in restoring 18th-century capital of Virginia colony); Chair. COLIN CAMPBELL; Pres. ROBERT C. WILBURN; publs *Annual Report, Colonial Williamsburg* (quarterly magazine).

Mariners' Museum, The: 100 Museum Drive, Newport News, VA 23606; tel. (757) 596-2222; fax (757) 591-7310; e-mail info@mariner.org; f. 1930; international maritime collection; library and archives: see Libraries; Pres. and Chief Exec. JOHN B. HIGHTOWER; publs *Pipe* (quarterly), *Journal* (annually).

Virginia Museum of Fine Arts: 2800 Grove, Richmond, VA 23221-2466; tel. (804) 367-0844; fax (804) 367-9393; e-mail webmaster@vmfa.state.va.us; f. 1936; statewide network of local and regional arts organizations and loan programme offering exhibition material to affiliated groups; film programmes; permanent collections include Russian Imperial jewelled objects by Fabergé, ancient Greek, Roman and Byzantine objects and sculptures; Indian, Chinese, Japanese, medieval, renaissance, and baroque paintings and sculptures; Himalayan collection; Art Nouveau and Art Deco collection; European and American decorative arts, prints, sculpture and paintings; contemporary art; library of 74,000 vols; Dir KATHARINE LEE; publ. *Calendar* (every 2 months).

Universities and Colleges

(Arranged alphabetically by State)

Due to space limitations we give a selection only, which is based mainly on the list of accredited institutions as published by the American Council on Education

ALABAMA

ALABAMA AGRICULTURAL AND MECHANICAL UNIVERSITY

POB 1357, Normal, AL 35762

Telephone: (205) 851-5230
Fax: (205) 851-5244

Founded 1875

President: Dr VIRGINIA CAPLES (acting)
Vice-President for Academic Affairs: Dr JAMES H. HICKS (acting)
Vice-President for Research Administration: Dr JEANETTE JONES
Vice-President for Business and Finance: Dr JOHN T. GIBSON
Vice-President for Student Affairs: Dr OSCAR L. MONTGOMERY
Comptroller: ARTHUR HENDERSON
Registrar: Mrs SHIRLEY CLEMONS (acting)

Library of 339,272 vols
Number of teachers: 360
Number of students: 5,000

DEANS

School of Agriculture and Home Economics: Dr JAMES H. SHUFORD
School of Business: Dr STANLEY V. SCOTT
School of Engineering and Technology: Dr ARTHUR J. BOND
University College: Dr EVELYN ELLIS

ALABAMA STATE UNIVERSITY

915 South Jackson St, POB 271, Montgomery, AL 36101-0271

Telephone: (205) 293-4100
Fax: (205) 834-6861

Founded 1867 as college, attained university status 1969

President: WILLIAM H. HARRIS
Vice-President for Academic Affairs: Dr ROOSEVELT STEPTOE
Vice-President for Fiscal Affairs: WILLIE THOMAS (acting)
Director, Communications and Public Affairs: JOHN KNIGHT, Jr
Vice-President for Student Affairs: Dr JACQUELINE WILLIAMS
Vice-President for Administrative Services: Dr LEON FRAZIER
Vice-President for Planning and Advancement: Dr WILLIAM BROCK (acting)

Library of 218,850 vols
Number of students: 5,608

Publications: *Alabama State University Bulletin* (annually), *ASU Today.*

DEANS

College of Education: Dr Daniel Vethen
College of Business Administration: Dr Percy Vaughn
College of Arts and Sciences: Dr William Lawson
University College: Dr Alma Freeman
School of Graduate Studies: Dr Philip Rosen
Division of Aerospace Studies: Lt-Col J. Wilson
School of Music: Dr Horace Lamar.

ATHENS STATE COLLEGE

Athens, AL 35611

Telephone: (205) 233-8100

Founded 1822

President: Dr Jerry F. Bartlett
Director of Admissions: John King
Librarian: Robert Burkhardt

Library of 94,000 vols
Number of teachers: 69
Number of students: 3,200

AUBURN UNIVERSITY

Auburn University, AL 36849

Telephone: (334) 844-4000
Fax: (334) 844-6179

Land grant State University
Founded in 1856 as The East Alabama Male College, became Alabama Agricultural and Mechanical College 1872, Alabama Polytechnic Institute 1899, Auburn University 1960

President: Dr William V. Muse
Vice-Presidents: Dr C. Michael Moriarty (Research), Dr Bettye B. Burkhalter (Student Affairs, acting), Donald L. Large (Business and Finance), Dr David Wilson (University Outreach), Jimmy D. Ferguson (Administrative Services)
Provost: Dr Paul F. Parks
Librarian: Dr Stella Bentley

Library: of 2,465,000 bound vols, 2,248,000 microforms, numerous special collections and government document collections
Number of teachers: 1,145
Number of students: 21,505

Publications: *The Auburn Plainsman, AU Report* (weekly), *Auburn Magazine, AES Highlights* (monthly), *Southern Humanities Review, Public Sector, Circle, The Auburn Pharmacist, The Auburn Veterinarian* (all quarterly), *Glomerata, Engineering Research Activities, Auburn University Research, The Auburn Bulletin, The Auburn Graduate Bulletin, The Tiger Cub* (all annually), *Facts & Figures* (every 2 years).

DEANS

Agriculture: Dr James E. Marion
Architecture: John T. Regan
Liberal Arts: John Heilman, Rebeka Pindzola (Co-Deans)
Business: Dr C. Wayne Alderman
Education: Dr Richard C. Kunkel
Engineering: Dr William F. Walker
Human Sciences: Dr June M. Henton
Nursing: Dr Charlotte Pitts (acting)
Pharmacy: Dr R. Lee Evans
Veterinary Medicine: Dr Timothy R. Boosinger
Graduate School: Dr John F. Pritchett
Science and Mathematics: Dr Stewart W. Schneller
Forestry: Dr Richard W. Brinker

BIRMINGHAM-SOUTHERN COLLEGE

900 Arkadelphia Rd, Birmingham, AL 35254

Telephone: (205) 226-4600
Fax: (205) 226-4627

Southern University founded in Greensboro 1856, Birmingham College opened 1898; consolidated as Birmingham-Southern College 1918

President: Neal R. Berte
Vice-President for Academic Affairs: Dr Irvin Penfield
Vice-President for Student Affairs: Dudley Long
Vice-President of Administration: Ed Lamonte
Vice-President for Business and Finance: Johnny Johnson
Dean of Admission and Financial Aid: Deedee Barnes Bruns
Vice-President for Development and Public Relations: George Jenkins
Librarian: Billy Pennington

Library of 200,000 vols
Number of teachers: 98
Number of students: 1,492

HUNTINGDON COLLEGE

1500 E. Fairview Ave, Montgomery, AL 36106

Telephone: (334) 833-4222
E-mail: info@huntingdon.edn

Founded 1854

President: Dr Wanda D. Bigham
Dean: Dr William F. Pollard
Librarian: Eric A. Kidwell

Library of 101,505 vols
Number of teachers: 68
Number of students: 673

JACKSONVILLE STATE UNIVERSITY

700 Pelham Rd North, Jacksonville, AL 36265-1602

Telephone: (205) 782-5781

Founded 1883

President: Dr Harold J. McGee
Vice-President for Academic and Student Affairs: Dr David Watts
Vice-President for Administrative and Business Affairs: Don Thacker
Vice-President for Institutional Advancement: William A. Meehan (acting)
Librarian: William Hubbard

Library of 583,365 vols
Number of teachers: 290
Number of students: 7,619

LIVINGSTON UNIVERSITY

Livingston, AL 35470

Telephone: (205) 652-9661

Founded 1835

President: Asa N. Green
Registrar: Clarence Egbert

Library of 115,000 vols
Number of teachers: 92
Number of students: 2,100

UNIVERSITY OF MOBILE

POB 13220, Mobile, AL 36663-0220

Telephone: (334) 675-5990
Fax: (334) 675-6293

Founded 1963
Private control

President: Dr Mark Foley
Registrar: Barbara Smith
Librarian: Jeff Calametti

Library of 117,121 vols
Number of teachers: 102
Number of students: 2,117

DEANS

School of Business: Dr Anne Lowery
School of Education: Dr Lynda Walden
College of Arts and Sciences: Dr Larry Allums
School of Nursing: Dr Rosemary Adams
School of Religion: Dr Cecil Taylor
School of Special Programmes: Dr Kaye F. Brown

OAKWOOD COLLEGE

Huntsville, AL 35896

Telephone: (205) 726-7000

Founded 1896

President: Dr Delbert W. Baker
Vice-President for Academic Affairs: Dr Ella S. Simmons
Registrar: Shirley P. Scott
Librarian: Jannith Lewis

Library of 117,000 vols
Number of teachers: 81
Number of students: 1,666

SAMFORD UNIVERSITY

800 Lakeshore Drive, Birmingham, AL 35229

Telephone: (205) 870-2011

Founded 1841

President: Thomas E. Corts
Provost: James S. Netherton
Dean of Academic Services: Paul G. Aucoin
Librarian: M. Jean Thomason

Number of teachers: 238
Number of students: 4,473

Publication: *Bulletin.*

DEANS

Cumberland School of Law: Barry A. Currier
School of Business: Carl J. Bellas
School of Education: Ruth C. Ash
School of Music: S. Milburn Price
College of Arts and Sciences: J. Roderick Davis
School of Pharmacy: Joseph O. Dean, Jr
Ida V. Moffett School of Nursing: Marian K. Baur
Beeson School of Divinity: Timothy F. George

SPRING HILL COLLEGE

Mobile, AL 36608

Telephone: (205) 460-2011

Founded 1830

President: Rev. Gregory F. Lucey
Academic Vice-President: Dr Barbara S. Nolan (acting)
Vice President for Development: C. Ray Lauten (acting)
Vice-President for Finance: Lee H. Covey
Dean of Students: John Balog
Librarian: Dr Alice Harrison Bahr

Library of 118,000 vols
Number of teachers: 80
Number of students: 1,000

TROY STATE UNIVERSITY SYSTEM

Troy, AL 36082

Telephone: (334) 670-3000

Founded 1887

Chancellor: Dr Jack Hawkins, Jr
Vice-Chancellor: Dr Douglas C. Patterson
Provost: Dr Owen C. Elder
President (Montgomery): Dr Glenda Curry
President (Dothan/Fort Rucker): Dr Mike Malone
Vice-Presidents: Clint Carlson, Dr Charlotte Davis, John Schmidt
Registrar: Vickie Miles
Librarian: Dr Henry Stewart

Library of 334,000 vols
Number of teachers: 365
Number of students: 17,627

TUSKEGEE UNIVERSITY

Tuskegee, AL 36088

Telephone: (334) 727-8011

Founded 1881

President: Dr Benjamin F. Payton
Provost: Dr William L. Lester

Vice-President for University Advancement: MICHAEL B. HILL
Dean of Students: PETER J. SPEARS
Business Affairs: BILLY R. OWENS
Registrar: EDRICE LEFTWICH
Librarian: JUANITA ROBERTS (acting)

Library of 250,000 vols, 1,000 periodicals
Number of teachers: 260
Number of students: 3,300

DEANS

College of Agriculture and Environmental and Natural Sciences: Dr WALTER HILL
College of Liberal Arts and Education: Dr MARY ANN JONES
College of Business, Organization and Management: Dr BENJAMIN NEWHOUSE
College of Engineering, Architecture and Physical Science: Dr BEN ONI (acting)
College of Veterinary Medicine, Nursing and Allied Health: Dr ALBERT DADE (acting)

UNIVERSITY OF ALABAMA

Tuscaloosa, AL 35487

Telephone: (205) 348-6010

Founded 1831

President: ANDREW A. SORENSEN
Provost and Vice-President for Academic Affairs: NANCY S. BARRETT
Vice-President for Financial Affairs and Treasurer: ROBERT A. WRIGHT
Vice-President for Student Affairs: (vacant)
Vice-President for Advancement: GARY ROUNDING
Dean of Libraries: CHARLES B. OSBURN

Library: see Libraries
Number of teachers: 1,057
Number of students: 19,046

Publications: *Alabama Business*, *Alabama Law Review*, *Alabama Heritage*, *Alabama Review*, *Alabama Alumni Magazine*, *Law and Psychology Review*, *Alabama Research Magazine*.

DEANS

College of Arts and Sciences: JAMES YARBROUGH
College of Commerce and Business Administration: J. BARRY MASON
College of Communication and Information Sciences: E. CULPEPPER CLARK
College of Community Health Sciences: ROBERT CENTOR (acting)
College of Continuing Studies: JOHN C. SNIDER
College of Education: JOHN P. DOLLY
College of Engineering: RAYMOND W. FLUMERFELT
Graduate School: RONALD ROGERS
College of Human Environmental Sciences: JUDY BONNER
School of Law: KENNETH RANDALL
Capstone College of Nursing: SARA E. BARGER
School of Social Work: LUCINDA LEE ROFF

UNIVERSITY OF ALABAMA AT BIRMINGHAM

U.A.B. Station, Birmingham, AL 35294

Telephone: (205) 934-4011

Founded 1969

President: W. ANN REYNOLDS
Vice-President for University Advancement: FRED BROOKE LEE
Vice-President for Financial Affairs and Administration: RICHARD MARGISON
Vice-President for Student Affairs: VIRGINIA D. GAULD
Vice-President for Planning and Information Management: JOHN M. LYONS
Provost: PETER V. O'NEIL (acting)
Director and CEO, U.A.B. Health System: MICHAEL A. GEHEB

Library of 1.5 million vols
Number of teachers: 1,863 (1,719 full-time)
Number of students: 16,252

Publications: *UAB Magazine* (quarterly), *UAB Reporter* (weekly), catalogues, bulletins.

DEANS

Graduate School: JOAN F. LORDEN
School of Medicine: WILLIAM DEAL
School of Dentistry: MARY LYNNE CAPILOUTO (acting)
School of Optometry: AROL AUGSBURGER
School of Nursing: RACHEL Z. BOOTH
School of Health Related Professions: CHARLES L. JOINER
School of Business: JACK DUNCAN (acting)
School of Education: CLINT E. BRUESS
School of Engineering: STEPHEN SZYGENDA
School of Arts and Humanities: THEODORE M. BENDITT
School of Natural Sciences and Mathematics: MICHAEL J. NEILSON
School of Public Health: ELI I. CAPILOUTO
School of Social and Behavioral Sciences: TENNANT S. MCWILLIAMS

UNIVERSITY OF ALABAMA IN HUNTSVILLE

Huntsville, AL 35899

Telephone: (800) 824-2255
Fax: (256) 890-6538

Founded 1950

President: Dr FRANK A. FRANZ
Provost and Vice-President for Academic Affairs: Dr SAMUEL P. MCMANUS

Number of teachers: 306
Number of students: 6,464

Publications: *Bulletins, Postscripts, Insight, Exponent, UAH Magazine.*

DEANS

College of Liberal Arts: Dr SUE W. KIRKPATRICK
College of Administrative Science: Dr C. DAVID BILLINGS
College of Engineering: Dr RICHARD WYSKIDA
College of Nursing: Dr C. FAYE RAINES
College of Science: Dr RICHARD MCNIDER (acting)
School of Graduate Studies: Dr JAMES JOHANNES

UNIVERSITY OF MONTEVALLO

Montevallo, AL 35115

Telephone: (205) 665-6000

Founded 1896

President: Dr ROBERT M. MCCHESNEY
Academic Vice-President: Dr WAYNE SEELBACH
Vice-President for Student Affairs: (vacant)
Director of Admissions: WILLIAM C. CANNON
Librarian: LEE K. VAN ORSDEL

Library of 239,000 vols, 1,815 magazines, 28 newspapers
Number of teachers: 129
Number of students: 3,125

UNIVERSITY OF NORTH ALABAMA

Florence, AL 35632-0001

Telephone: (205) 765-4100
Fax: (205) 765-4329

Founded 1830 as a private institution; became a state institution 1872

President: ROBERT L. POTTS
Vice-President for Academic Affairs/Provost: Dr JOSEPH C. THOMAS
Dean of Enrollment Management: Dr SUE J. WILSON
Librarian: Dr GARRY WARREN

Library of 250,000 vols
Number of teachers: 200 full-time, 28 part-time
Number of students: 5,600

UNIVERSITY OF SOUTH ALABAMA

307 University Blvd, Mobile, AL 36688-002

Telephone: (334) 460-6101

Founded 1963

President: V. GORDON MOULTON
Senior Vice-President for Academic Affairs: PATSY C. COVEY (interim)
Vice-President for Finance: M. WAYNE DAVIS
Vice-President for Health Affairs: Dr WILLIAM GARDNER (interim)
Vice-President for Student Affairs: Dr DALE ADAMS
Director of Admissions: CATHERINE KING
Registrar: CAROLYN PARHAM
Librarian: (vacant)

Library of 437,451 vols
Number of teachers: 854
Number of students: 12,386

DEANS

College of Education: Dr G. UHLIG
College of Business and Management Studies: Dr CARL C. MOORE
College of Arts and Sciences: Dr LAWRENCE D. ALLEN
College of Medicine: Dr WILLIAM GARDNER (interim)
College of Engineering: Dr DAVID T. HAYHURST
College of Allied Health: Dr P. COVEY
College of Nursing: Dr DEBRA C. DAVIS
School of Computer and Information Sciences: V. GORDON MOULTON
School of Continuing Education and Special Programs: Dr TOM WELLS
Graduate School: Dr JAMES L. WOLFE

ALASKA

ALASKA PACIFIC UNIVERSITY

4101 University Drive, Anchorage, AK 99508

Telephone: (907) 561-1266
Fax: (907) 564-8317

Founded 1957

President: Dr DOUGLAS MCKAY NORTH
Academic Dean: Dr CHARLES FAHL
Dean of Students: LYN DE MARTIN

Library of 330,000 vols
Number of teachers: 80
Number of students: 500

UNIVERSITY OF ALASKA STATEWIDE SYSTEM

John Butrovich Building, 910 Yukon Drive, Fairbanks, AK 99775

Telephone: (907) 474-7311

Founded 1917 as Alaska Agricultural College and School of Mines; university status 1935; consists of 3 multi-campus four-year universities, one community college

President: MARK R. HAMILTON
Vice-President for Finance: JIM LYNCH
Vice-President for University Relations: WENDY REDMAN

Number of teachers: 2,006 (statewide)
Number of students: 31,184 (statewide)

Publications: program catalogues from various units of the university.

UNIVERSITY CAMPUSES

University of Alaska Fairbanks: 3rd floor, Signers' Hall, Fairbanks, AK 99775; tel. (907) 474-7112; Chancellor Dr JOAN WADLOW.

University of Alaska Anchorage: 3211 Providence Drive, Anchorage, AK 99508; tel. (907) 786-4620; Chancellor LEE GORSUCH.

University of Alaska Southeast: 11120 Glacier Highway, Juneau, AK 99801; tel. (907) 465-6472; Chancellor Dr MARSHALL LIND.

ARIZONA

ARIZONA STATE UNIVERSITY

Tempe, AZ 85287

Telephone: (602) 965-9011

Founded 1885

President: Dr LATTIE F. COOR

Provost and Senior Vice-President: Dr MILTON D. GLICK

Vice-President for Student Affairs: Dr CHRISTINE K. WILKINSON

Vice-President for Institutional Advancement: ALLAN H. PRICE

Provost ASU West: Dr ELAINE MAIMON

Provost ASU East: Dr CHARLES BACKUS

Vice-Provost for Administrative Services: MERNOY HARRISON

Vice-Provost for Research: Dr JONATHAN FINK (acting)

Dean, University Libraries: Dr SHERRIE SCHMIDT

Library of 2,500,000 vols

Number of teachers: 1,800 full-time, 800 part-time

Number of students: 43,000

Publications: various.

DEANS

College of Architecture: JOHN MEUNIER

College of Business: Dr LARRY E. PENLEY

College of Education: Dr LEONARD VALVERDE

College of Engineering and Applied Sciences: Dr PETER CROUCH

College of Fine Arts: J. ROBERT WILLS

College of Law: PATRICIA WHITE

College of Liberal Arts: GARY KRAHENBUHL

College of Nursing: Dr BARBARA DURAND

College of Public Programs: ANNE L. SCHNEIDER

School of Social Work: Dr EMILIA MARTINEZ-BRAWLEY

College of Extended Education: Dr BETTE DEGRAW

Graduate College: Dr BIANCA BERNSTEIN

Honors College: Dr TED HUMPHREY

NORTHERN ARIZONA UNIVERSITY

Flagstaff, AZ 86011

Telephone: (602) 523-9011

Founded 1899

President: Dr CLARA M. LOVETT

Provost: Dr CHARLES W. CONNELL

Associate Provost for Student Affairs: Dr SARAH L. BICKEL

Vice-President for Business Affairs: Dr DAVE LORENZ (acting)

Vice-President for Institutional Advancement: Dr TED FORD

Dean of Students: RICK BRANDEL

Director of Libraries: JEAN COLLINS

Library of 1,335,476 vols

Number of teachers: 650

Number of students: 19,618

DEANS

College of Arts and Science: Dr SUZANNE SHIPLEY

College of Business Administration: Dr PATRICIA MEYERS

College of Social and Behavioral Sciences: Dr SUZANNE MAXWELL

College of Engineering and Technology: Dr MASON SOMERVILLE

School of Forestry: Dr DAVID PATTON

College of Health Professions: Dr JIM BLAGG

Center for Excellence in Education: Dr MELVIN HALL

School of Hotel and Restaurant Management: RON EVANS

School of Performing Arts: Dr GARRY OWENS

School of Communication: Dr SHARON PORTER

Museum Faculty of Fine Arts: Dr RANDY ROHTON

UNIVERSITY OF ARIZONA

Tucson, AZ 85721

Telephone: (602) 621-2211

Fax: (602) 621-9118

Founded 1885

Academic year: August to May (two terms)

President: PETER LIKINS

Senior Vice-President for Academic Affairs and Provost: PAUL S. SYPHERD

Vice-President for Business Affairs: JOEL VALDEZ

Vice-President for Research: MICHAEL A. CUSANOVICH

Vice-President for Undergraduate Education: MICHAEL GOTTFREDSON

Vice-President for Campus Life: SANDRA LAWSON TAYLOR

Dean, Arizona International College: PAUL ROSENBLATT

Registrar: GARY WAGNER (acting)

Dean of University Libraries: CARLA STOFFLE

Library: see Libraries

Number of teachers: 1,723

Number of students: 30,810

Publications: *Arizona Quarterly* (Literature), *Arizona Law Review, Arizona and the West* (Quarterly Journal of History), *Hispanic American Historical Review* (quarterly), *Record, Bulletin, Business and Economic Review* (monthly), *Books of the Southwest*, agricultural publications.

DEANS

College of Agriculture: EUGENE SANDER

College of Architecture: RICHARD ERIBES

College of Arts and Sciences:

- Faculty of Fine Arts: MAURICE SEVIGNY
- Faculty of Humanities: CHARLES TATUM
- Faculty of Sciences: GENE LEVY
- Faculty of Social and Behavioural Sciences: HOLLY SMITH

College of Business and Public Administration: MARK ZUPAN

College of Education: JOHN TAYLOR

College of Engineering and Mines: TOM PETERSON (acting)

College of Law: JOEL SELIGMAN

College of Medicine: JAMES DALEN

College of Nursing: SUZANNE VAN ORT

College of Pharmacy: LYLE BOOTMAN

Graduate College: THOMAS HIXON

Students: MELISSA VITO

Extended University: ANITA MCDONALD

PROFESSORS

(H=Head of Department)

College of Agriculture:

ALLEN, R. E., Nutritional Sciences
APOSHIAN, H. V., Molecular and Cellular Biology
AX, R. L., Animal Science (H)
BEATTIE, B. R., Agricultural and Resource Economics
BOHN, H. L., Soil, Water and Environmental Sciences
BOHNERT, H. J., Biochemistry
BOURQUE, D. P., Biochemistry
BOWERS, W. S., Entomology
BYRNE, D. N., Entomology
CALDWELL, R. L., Soil, Water and Environmental Sciences
CHANDLER, V. L., Plant Science
CHAPMAN, R. F., Entomology
COLBY, B. G., Agricultural and Resource Economics
CORTNER, H. J., Renewable Natural Resources
CORY, D. C., Agricultural and Resource Economics (H)
DEBANO, L. F., Renewable Natural Resources
DIECKMANN, C. L., Biochemistry
FEYEREISEN, R., Entomology
FFOLLIOTT, P. F., Watershed Management
FOSTER, K. E., Arid Lands Studies
FOX, R. W., Agricultural and Resource Economics
GALBRAITH, D. W., Plant Science
GAY, L. W., Watershed Management
GERBA, C. P., Soil, Water and Environmental Sciences
GILLIES, R. J., Biochemistry
GOLL, D. E., Nutritional Sciences
GRIMES, W. J., Biochemistry
HAGEDORN, H. H., Entomology
HALLICK, R. B., Biochemistry
HALVORSON, W. L., Renewable Natural Resources
HARTSHORNE, D. J., Nutritional Sciences
HATCH, K. L., Family and Consumer Resources
HAUSSLER, M. R., Biochemistry
HAVENS, W. H., Landscape Architecture
HAWKINS, R. H., Watershed Management
HEYN, M. P., Biochemistry
HOFFMANN, J. J., Arid Lands Studies
HUBER, R. T., Agricultural Education (H)
HUETE, A. R., Soil, Water and Environmental Sciences
INNES, R. D., Agricultural and Resource Economics
JOENS, L. A., Veterinary Science
JORDAN, K. A., Agricultural and Biosystems Engineering
JORGENSEN, R. A., Plant Science
KENNEDY, C. K., Plant Pathology
KIGHT, M. A., Nutritional Sciences
KRAUSMAN, P., Wildlife and Fisheries Science
KUEHL, R. O., Agricultural and Resource Economics
LAFRANCE, J. T., Agricultural and Resource Economics
LAI, K. W., Physics
LARKINS, B. A., Plant Science
LEAVITT, S. W., Dendrochronology
LEONARD, R. T., Plant Science (H)
LIGHTNER, D. V., Veterinary Science
LITTLE, J. W., Molecular and Cellular Biology
MANNAN, R. W., Wildlife and Fisheries Science
MARCHELLO, J. A., Animal Science
MARÉ, C. J., Veterinary Science
MAUGHAN, O. E., Wildlife and Fisheries Science
MCCLURE, M. A., Plant Pathology
MCDANIEL, R. G., Plant Science
MENDELSON, N. H., Molecular and Cellular Biology
MEYER, T. E., Biochemistry
MONKE, E. A., Agricultural and Resource Economics
MORAN, N. A., Ecology and Evolutionary Biology
MOUNT, D. W., Molecular and Cellular Biology
MULDER, J. B., Veterinary Science
NELSON, M. R., Plant Pathology (H)
NEWCOMB, R. T., Agricultural and Resource Economics
OEBKER, N. F., Plant Science
O'LEARY, J. W., Plant Science
PEPPER, I. L., Soil, Water and Environmental Sciences
POST, D. F., Soil, Water and Environmental Sciences
REID, C. P., Renewable Natural Resources
RICE, R. W., Animal Science

RIDLEY, C. A., Family and Consumer Resources
ROHRBAUGH, M. J., Family and Consumer Resources
ROWE, D. C., Family and Consumer Resources
RUPLEY, J. A., Biochemistry
SANDER, E. G., Biochemistry
SELKE, M. R., Animal Science
SHAW, W. W., Wildlife and Fisheries Science
SHIM, S., Family and Consumer Resources
SILVERTOOTH, J. C., Plant Science
SLACK, D. C., Agricultural and Biosystems Engineering (H)
SMITH, N. S., Wildlife and Fisheries Science
SONGER, J. G., Veterinary Science
STAUSS, J. H., Family and Consumer Resources
STERLING, C. R., Veterinary Science (H)
STOCKTON, C. W., Dendrochronology
STRELKOFF, T. S., Agriculture and Biosystems Engineering
SUBRAMANIAN, A. P., Biochemistry
TABASHNIK, B., Entomology (H)
TAYLOR, L. D., Agricultural and Resource Economics
TISCHLER, M. E., Biochemistry
TOLLIN, G., Biochemistry
VANETTEN, H. D., Plant Pathology
VIERLING, E., Biochemistry
WARD, S., Molecular and Cellular Biology (H)
WARRICK, A. W., Soil, Water and Environmental Sciences
WELLS, M. A., Biochemistry
WHITING, F. M., Animal Science
WIERENGA, P. J., Soil, Water and Environmental Sciences
WILSON, P. N., Agricultural and Resource Economics
WOLFE, W. L., Nutritional Sciences (H)
ZWOLINSKI, M. J., Watershed Management

College of Architecture:

ALBANESE, C. A.
CLARK, K. N.
ERIBES, R. A.
HERSHBERGER, R. G.
MATTER, F. S.
MEDLIN, R. L.
NEVINS, R. L.
ROSENBLOOM, S.
STAMM, W. P.

College of Arts and Sciences:

ADAMEC, L. W., Near Eastern Studies
AIKEN, S. H., English
ANDERSON, K. S., History
ANDREWS, G. R., Computer Science
ANGEL, J. R. P., Astronomy
ANNAS, J. E., Philosophy
APOSHIAN, H. V., Molecular and Cellular Biology
ARCHANGELI, D. B., Linguistics
ARIEW, R. A., French and Italian
ARMSTRONG, N. R., Chemistry
ARNETT, W. D., Astronomy
ASIA, D. I., Music
ATKINSON, G. H., Chemistry
AUSTIN, N. J., Classics (H)
BABCOCK, B. A., English
BAKER, V. R., Hydrology and Water Resources
BARFIELD, M., Chemistry
BARNES, C. A., Psychology
BARRETT, B. R., Physics
BARTELS, P. H., Optical Sciences
BARTON, M. D., Geosciences
BASSO, E. B., Anthropology
BATES, R. B., Chemistry
BAYLES, K. A., Speech and Hearing Science
BECHTEL, R. B., Psychology
BECK, J., French and Italian
BERGESEN, A. J., Sociology
BERGSOHN, I. P., Dance
BERNSTEIN, A. E., History
BERNSTEIN, G. L., History
BEVER, T. G., Cognitive Science
BICKEL, W. S., Physics
BIRKY, C. W., Jr, Ecology and Evolutionary Biology
BOELTS, J. G., Art
BONINE, M. E., Near Eastern Studies
BOOTZIN, R. R., Psychology
BOWEN, R., English
BOYNTON, W. V., Lunar and Planetary Laboratory
BRILLHART, J. D., Mathematics
BROWER, D. L., Molecular and Cellular Biology
BROWN, M. F., Chemistry
BROWN, R. H., Planetary Sciences
BURGOON, H. M., Communication
BURGOON, J. K., Communication
BURROWS, A. S., Astronomy
BUTLER, R. F., Geosciences
CALDER, W. A., III, Ecology and Evolutionary Biology
CANFIELD, J. D., English
CHAMBERS, R. H., Physics
CHAN, M. C., East Asian Studies
CHANDOLA, A. C., East Asian Studies
CHASE, C. G., Geosciences
CHISHOLM, D. H., German
CLARKE, J. N., Political Science
CLARKE, J. W., Political Science
CLASSEN, A., German
COHEN, A. S., Geosciences
COMPITELLO, M. A., Spanish and Portuguese (H)
CONEY, P. J., Geosciences
COOK, G. D., Music
CORTNER, R. C., Political Science
COSGROVE, R. A., History
CRANO, W. D., Communication
CROFT, M. F., Art
CULBERT, T. P., Anthropology
CURLEE, R. F., Speech and Hearing Science
CUSHING, J. M., Mathematics
CUTIETTA, R. A., Music
DAHOOD, R., English
DANIEL, T. C., Psychology
DAVIS, G. H., Geosciences
DAVIS, O. K., Geosciences
DAYAN, J., English
DEAN, J. S., Dendrochronology
DECKER, P. A., Music
DEMERS, R. A., Linguistics
DEMING, C. J., Media Arts
DENTON, M. B., Chemistry
DERENIAK, E. L., Optical Sciences
DEVER, W. G., Near Eastern Studies
DICKINSON, R. E., Atmospheric Physics
DIETZ, W. D., Music
DINNERSTEIN, L., History
DIXON, H. W., Theatre Arts
DIXON, W. J., Political Science
DOMINO, G., Psychology
DONAHUE, D. J., Physics
DONOGHUE, M. J., Ecology and Evolutionary Biology
DOOGAN, M. B., Art
DOYLE, M. P., Chemistry
DRAKE, M. J., Lunar and Planetary Laboratory
DRYDEN, E. A., English
EATON, R. M., History
ENEMARK, J. H., Chemistry
ENGLAND, P. S., Sociology
EPSTEIN, W. H., English
ERCOLANI, M. N., Mathematics
ERLINGS, B. R., Music
ERVIN, T. R., Music
EVERS, L. J., English (H)
FALCO, C. M., Physics
FAN, P., Music
FANG, L. Z., Physics
FARIS, W. G., Mathematics
FERNÁNDEZ, C., Sociology
FERNANDEZ, N., Music
FERNANDO, Q., Chemistry
FIELDER, G. E., Russian and Slavic Languages
FINK, U., Lunar and Planetary Laboratory
FLASCHKA, H., Mathematics (H)
FLESSA, K. W., Ecology and Evolutionary Biology (H)
FORSTER, K. I., Psychology
FRANKEN, P. A., Optical Sciences
FREISER, H., Chemistry
FRIEDEN, B. R., Optical Sciences
GAMAL, A. S., Near Eastern Studies
GANGULY, T., Geosciences
GARCIA, J. A., Political Science
GARCIA, J. D., Physics
GARRARD, J., Russian and Slavic Languages
GARRETT, M. F., Psychology
GASKILL, J. D., Optical Sciences
GAY, D. A., Mathematics
GEHRELS, A. M. J. T., Lunar and Planetary Laboratory
GEHRELS, G. E., Geosciences
GEOFFRION, M. M., Art
GIBBS, H. M., Optical Sciences
GIBSON, L. J., Geography
GILABERT, J. J., Spanish and Portuguese
GILLETTE, J. M., Media Arts
GIMELLO, R. M., East Asian Studies
GLASS, R. S., Chemistry
GLATTKE, T. J., Speech and Hearing Science
GOLDMAN, A. I., Philosophy
GONZALEZ, R. D., English
GORNICK, V., English
GREENBERG, J. L., Psychology
GREENBERG, R. J., Planetary Sciences
GREENLEE, W. M., Mathematics
GREER, W. D., Art
GREIVENKAMP, J. E., Jr, Optical Sciences
GROVE, L. C., Mathematics
GUTSCHE, G. J., Russian and Slavic Languages
GUY, D. J., History
GYURKO, L. A., Spanish and Portuguese
HAMMOND, H., Art
HANCOCK, J. L., Dance
HANSON, G. I., Music
HARALOVICH, M. B., Media Arts (H)
HARNISH, R. M., Philosophy
HARRIS, DE V. P., Geosciences
HASKELL, J. R., Music
HAYNES, C. V., Geosciences
HEALEY, R. A., Philosophy
HECHTER, M., Sociology
HERMAN, B. M., Atmospheric Physics
HILL, J. H., Anthropology
HITNER, C. V., Art
HOFFMANN, W. F., Astronomy
HOGLE, J. E., English
HOLLAND, A. L., Speech and Hearing Science
HOLM, T. M., American Indian Studies
HOUSTON, R. W., English
HRUBY, V. J., Chemistry
HSIEH, K. C., Physics
HUBBARD, W. B., Lunar and Planetary Laboratory
HUFFMANN, D. R., Physics
HUNTEN, D. M., Planetary Sciences
HURT, C. D., Library Science
JACKSON, S. A., Communication
JOKIPII, J. R., Planetary Sciences
JONES, D. L., Art
JONES, H. H., Art
JUST, K. W., Physics
KASHY, J. L., Music
KASZNIAK, A., Psychology
KELLER, P. C., Chemistry
KENNEDY, T. G., Mathematics
KENNICUTT, R. C., Astronomy
KIDWELL, M. G., Ecology and Evolutionary Biology
KIEFER, F. P., Jr, English
KILKSON, R., Physics
KING, J. E., Psychology
KINGERY, W. D., Anthropology
KINKADE, R. P., Spanish and Portuguese
KOHLER, S., Physics
KOLODNY, A., English
KOLOSICK, J. T., Music
KOVACH, T. A., German (H)

KRAMER, C., Anthropology
KRIDER, E. P., Atmospheric Sciences
KUKOLICH, S. G., Chemistry
LANG, W. A., II, Theatre Arts
LANGENDOEN, D. T., Linguistics
LARSON, H. P., Lunar and Planetary Laboratory
LEHMAN, P. R., Media Arts
LEHRER, A., Linguistics
LEHRER, K. E., Philosophy
LEI, K. Y., Nutritional Sciences
LEONARD, A., Jr, Classics
LEVERMORE, C. D., Mathematics
LEVY, E. H., Planetary Sciences (H)
LEWIS, J. S., Planetary Sciences
LICHTENBERGER, D. L., Chemistry (H)
LIEBERT, J. W., Astronomy
LOMEN, D. O., Mathematics
LONG, A., Geosciences
LONGACRE, W. A., Anthropology (H)
LOVELOCK, D., Mathematics
LUNDBERG, J. G., Ecology and Evolutionary Biology
LUNINE, J. I., Lunar and Planetary Laboratory
LYTLE, C. M., Political Science
MAHER, M. Z., Theatre Arts
MALONEY, J. C., Philosophy (H)
MANBER, U., Computer Science
MANN, L. D., Planning
MANSURIPUR, M., Optical Sciences
MARATHAY, A. S., Optical Sciences
MARCHALONIS, J. J., Microbiology and Immunology (H)
MARTINEZ, O., History
MARTINSON, S. D., German
MATKIN, N. D., Speech and Hearing Science
MAY, W. L., Mathematics
MAZUMDAR, S., Physics
MCADAM, D. J., Sociology
MCCALLUM, W. G., Mathematics
MCCULLEN, J. D., Physics
MCELROY, J. H., English
MCGREW, B. E., Art
MCINTYRE, L., Jr, Physics
MCKNIGHT, B. E., East Asian Studies (H)
MCLAUGHLIN, C. M., Music
MCNAUGHTON, B. L., Psychology
MCPHERSON, J. M., Sociology
MEDINE, P. E., English
MELIA, F., Physics
MELOSH, H. J., Lunar and Planetary Laboratory
MENDELSON, N. H., Cellular and Developmental Biology
MÉNDEZ, M. M., Spanish and Portuguese
MEYSTRE, P., Optical Sciences
MICHOD, R. E., Ecology and Evolutionary Biology
MILLER, J. R., English
MISHLER, W. T., II, Political Science (H)
MITTAL, Y. D., Mathematics
MOLM, L. D., Sociology
MOLONEY, J. V., Mathematics
MOMADAY, N. S., English
MONSMAN, G. C., English
MORBECK, M. E., Anthropology
MOSHER-KRAUS, E., Music
MOUNT, D. W., Molecular and Cellular Biology
MULLIGAN, G. F., Geography
MURPHY, E. W., Music
MYERS, D. E., Mathematics
MYERS, E. W., Jr, Computer Science
NADEL, L., Psychology (H)
NADER, H., History (H)
NELSON, D. A., Spanish and Portuguese
NEVINS, R. L., Architecture
NICHOLS, R. L., History
NICHTER, M., Anthropology
NUNAMAKER, J. F., Jr, Management Information Systems
OBERMAN, H. A., History
O'BRIEN, D. F., Chemistry
O'BRIEN, J. P., Music
OEHRLE, R. T., Linguistics (H)
OLSEN, J. W., Anthropology
ORLEN, S. L., English
PACHOLCZYK, A. G., Astronomy
PALMER, J. N., Mathematics
PARRISH, J. T., Geosciences
PARRY, E. C., III, Art
PATCHETT, P. J., Geosciences
PATRASCIOIU, A. N., Physics
PEMBERTON, J. E., Chemistry
PENNER, J. D., English
PETERSON, L. L., Computer Science (H)
PEYGHAMBARIAN, N. N., Optical Sciences
PHILIPS, S. U., Anthropology
PLANE, D., Geography and Regional Development
POLK, A. W., Art (H)
POLLOCK, J. L., Philosophy
POMEAU, Y., Mathematics
POVERMAN, C. E., English
POWELL, W. W., Sociology
PROMIS, J. M. O., Spanish and Portuguese
QAFISHEH, H. A., Near Eastern Studies
RAFELSKI, J., Physics
RAGSDALE, L., Political Science
RATHJE, W. L., Anthropology
RAVAL, S. S., English
REEVES, R. W., Geography and Regional Development
REID, J. J., Anthropology
REITER, J. S., Music
RIEKE, G. H., Astronomy
RIEKE, M. J., Astronomy
RIVERO, E. S., Spanish and Portuguese
ROE, C., Music
ROGERS, B. J., Art
ROSENBLATT, P., English
ROSENZWEIG, M. L., Ecology and Evolutionary Biology
RUIZ, J., Geosciences (H)
RUSK, J. G., Political Science
RUTHERFOORD, J. P., Physics
SALES, B. D., Psychology
SALZMAN, W. R., Chemistry
SARGENT, M., III, Optical Sciences
SARID, D., Optical Sciences
SAVILLE-TROIKE, M., English
SCADRON, M. D., Physics
SCHAFFER, W. M., Ecology and Evolutionary Biology
SCHALLER, M., History
SCHIFFER, M. B., Anthropology
SCHLEGEL, A. E., Anthropology
SCHLICHTING, R. D., Computer Science
SCHNEIDAU, H. N., English
SCHOTLAND, R. M., Atmospheric Sciences
SCHULZ, R. A., German
SCHWARTZ, G. E., Psychology
SCHWARZ, J. E., Political Science
SCOTT, A. C., Mathematics
SCRUGGS, C. W., English
SECHREST, L., Psychology
SELLERS, W. D., Atmospheric Sciences
SEVIGNY, M. J., Art
SHACK, R. V., Optical Sciences
SHAKED, M., Mathematics
SHARKEY, J. E., Journalism
SHELTON, R. L., Speech and Hearing Science
SHELTON, R. W., English
SHOEMAKER, R. L., Optical Sciences
SHUPE, M. A., Physics
SKINNER, M. B., Classics
SMILEY, S. M., Theatre Arts
SMITH, C. D., Jr, Near Eastern Studies (H)
SMITH, M. A., Chemistry
SMITH-LOVIN, D. L., Sociology
SNODGRASS, R. T., Computer Science
SNOW, D. A., Sociology (H)
SOBEL, M. E., Sociology
SOLOMON, J., Classics
SOREN, H. D., Classics
STEELE, S. M., Linguistics
STEIN, D. L., Physics
STEVENSON, F. W., Mathematics
STINI, W. A., Anthropology
STOFFLE, C. J., Library Science
STONER, J. O., Jr, Physics
STRITTMATTER, P. A., Astronomy (H)
STROM, R. G., Lunar and Planetary Laboratory
SULLIVAN, M. P., Political Science
SUTHERLAND, R. W., Music
TABOR, M., Applied Mathematics (H)
TAO, J., East Asian Studies
TATUM, C. M., Spanish and Portuguese (H)
THOMPSON, R. I., Astronomy
THOMSON, D. A., Ecology and Evolutionary Biology
TIFFT, W. G., Astronomy
TITLEY, S. R., Geosciences
TOUBASSI, E., Mathematics
TOUSSAINT, W. D., Physics
TROIKE, R. C., English
TUCCI, A. D., Theatre Arts (H)
ULREICH, J. C., Jr, English
UNDERWOOD, J. H., Anthropology
VELEZ, W. Y., Mathematics
VENABLE, D. L., Ecology and Evolutionary Biology
VOLK, T. J., Political Science
VUILLEMIN, J. J., Physics
WALKER, F. A., Chemistry
WALLACE, T. C., Jr, Geosciences
WARD, S., Molecular and Cellular Biology (H)
WEARING, J. P., English
WEAVER, T., Anthropology
WELLS, M. A., Biochemistry
WELSH, W. A., Political Science
WENK, G. L., Psychology
WETZEL, M. C., Psychology
WHITE, R. E., Jr, Astronomy
WHITE, S. E., Astronomy
WHITING, A. S., Political Science
WIGLEY, D. E., Chemistry
WILD, P. T., English
WILLIAMS, E. J., Political Science
WILLIAMS, J. M., Psychology
WILLOUGHBY, S. S., Mathematics
WILSON, J. M., Dance
WIMMER, G., Art
WINFREE, A. T., Ecology and Evolutionary Biology
WING, W. H., Physics
WITTIG, M. M., French and Italian
WOOLF, N. J., Astronomy
WRENN, R. L., Psychology
WYANT, J. C., Optical Sciences
YAMAMURA, H. I., Pharmacology
ZAKHAROV, V. E., Mathematics
ZALEWSKI, E. F., Optical Sciences
ZEGURA, S. L., Anthropology
ZUMBRO, N. L., Music

College of Business and Public Administration:

BEACH, L. R., Management and Policy
BLOCK, M. K., Economics
BRUCKS, M. L., Marketing
CARLETON, W. T., Finance
CONNOLLY, T., Management and Policy
COX, J. C., Economics
DHALIWAL, D. S., Accounting (H)
DROR, M., Management Information Systems
DYL, E. A., Finance (H)
FELIX, W. L., Accounting
FISHBACK, P. V., Economics
GOODMAN, S., Management Information Systems
GOTTFREDSON, M. R., Management and Policy
GUTEK, B. A., Management and Policy (H)
ISAAC, R. M., Economics (H)
KOFF, T. H., Public Administration and Policy
LASALLE, J. F., Management Information Systems
LEVY, S. J., Marketing (H)
MITTAL, Y., Statistics
NUNAMAKER, J. F., Jr, Management Information Systems
OAXACA, R. L., Economics

PINGRY, D. E., Management Information Systems
PROVAN, K. G., Public Administration and Policy
PUTO, C. P., Marketing
RAM, S., Management Information Systems
RAPOPORT, A., Management and Policy
REYNOLDS, S. S., Economics
RIEBER, M., Economics
SHENG, O. R. L., Management Information Systems (H)
SILVERS, A. L., Public Administration and Policy
SMITH, K. R., Economics
SMITH, V. L., Economics
TAYLOR, L. D., Economics
TULLOCK, G., Economics
VOGEL, R. J., Public Administration and Policy
WALKER, M. A., Economics
WALLENDORF, M., Marketing
WALLER, W. S., Accounting
WELLS, D. A., Economics
ZAJAC, E. E., Economics

College of Education:
ALEAMONI, L. M., Special Education and Rehabilitation
AMES, W. S., Teaching and Teacher Education
ANDERS, P. L., Language, Reading and Culture
ANTIA, S. D., Special Education and Rehabilitation
BOS, C. S., Special Education and Rehabilitation
BRAINERD, C. J., Educational Psychology
CARTER, K. J., Teaching and Teacher Education
CHALFANT, J. C., Special Education and Rehabilitation
CLARK, D. C., Educational Administration
DINHAM, S. M., Educational Psychology
DOYLE, W., Teaching and Teacher Education
GOOD, T. L., Educational Psychology
GOODMAN, K. S., Language, Reading and Culture
GOODMAN, Y. M., Language, Reading and Culture
KIRBY, D. R., Teaching and Teacher Education
LESLIE, L., Higher Education
MAKER, C. J., Special Education and Rehabilitation
MISHRA, S. P., Special Education and Rehabilitation
MOLL, L. C., Language, Reading and Culture
MORRIS, R. J., Special Education and Rehabilitation
OBRZUT, J. E., Special Education and Rehabilitation
RHOADES, G. D., Higher Education (H)
RUIZ, R., Language, Reading and Culture
SABERS, D. L., Educational Psychology (H)
SALES, A. P., Special Education and Rehabilitation
SLAUGHTER, S. A., Higher Education
SMITH, K. J., Educational Psychology
TAYLOR, J. L., Teaching and Teacher Education
TURECHEK, A. G., Special Education and Rehabilitation
VALMONT, W. J., Language, Reading and Culture
WOODARD, D. B., Jr, Higher Education

College of Engineering and Mines:
ARNOLD, R. G., Chemical Engineering
ASKIN, R. G., Systems and Industrial Engineering
BAHILL, A. T., Systems and Industrial Engineering
BALES, R. C., Hydrology and Water Resources
BALSA, T. F., Aerospace and Mechanical Engineering
BASSETT, R. L., Hydrology and Water Resources
BREWS, J. R., Electrical and Computing Engineering
BUDHU, M., Civil Engineering
BURAS, N., Hydrology and Water Resources
CALVERT, P. D., Materials Science and Engineering
CELLIER, F. E., Electrical and Computer Engineering
CHAMPAGNE, F. H., Aerospace and Mechanical Engineering
CHEN, C. F., Aerospace and Mechanical Engineering
CONTRACTOR, D., Civil Engineering and Engineering Mechanics
CROW, S. C., Aerospace and Mechanical Engineering
DAVENPORT, W. G., Materials Science and Engineering
DAVIS, D. R., Hydrology and Water Resources
DESAI, C., Civil Engineering (H)
DEYMIER, P. A., Materials Science and Engineering
DIETRICH, D. L., Systems and Industrial Engineering
DUCKSTEIN, L., Systems and Industrial Engineering
EHSANI, M. R., Civil Engineering and Engineering Mechanics
FARMER, I. W., Mining and Geological Engineering
FASEL, H. F., Aerospace and Mechanical Engineering
GALLAGHER, R. H., Aerospace and Mechanical Engineering
GANAPOL, B. D., Hydrology and Water Resources
GERHARD, G. C., Electrical and Computer Engineering
HALDAR, A., Civil Engineering and Engineering Mechanics
HEINRICH, J. C., Aerospace and Mechanical Engineering
HILL, F. J., Electrical and Computer Engineering
HISKEY, J. B., Materials Science and Engineering
HUMPHREY, J., Aerospace and Mechanical Engineering (H)
HUNT, B. R., Electrical and Computer Engineering
INCE, S., Civil Engineering and Engineering Mechanics
JACKSON, K. A., Materials Science and Engineering
KECECIOGLU, D. B., Aerospace and Mechanical Engineering
KINGERY, W. D., Materials Science and Engineering
KOSTUK, R. K., Electrical and Computer Engineering
KUNDU, T., Civil Engineering and Engineering Mechanics
LYNCH, D. C., Materials Science and Engineering
MADDOCK, T., III, Hydrology and Water Resources
MIRCHANDANI, P. B., Systems and Industrial Engineering (H)
MOFFAT, R. J., Aerospace and Mechanical Engineering
MYLREA, K. C., Electrical and Computer Engineering
NEUMAN, S. P., Hydrology and Water Resources
NIKRAVESH, P. E., Aerospace and Mechanical Engineering
OHANLON, J. F., Electrical and Computer Engineering
PALUSINSKI, O. A., Electrical and Computer Engineering
PATTISON, K. M., Aerospace and Mechanical Engineering
PERKINS, H. C., Jr, Aerospace and Mechanical Engineering
PETERS, W. C., Mining and Geological Engineering
PETERSON, T. W., Chemical Engineering (H)
POIRIER, D. R., Materials Science and Engineering
PRINCE, J. L., III, Electrical and Computer Engineering
RAGHAVAN, S., Materials Science and Engineering
RAMBERG, J. S., Systems and Industrial Engineering
RAMOHALLI, K. N. R., Aerospace and Mechanical Engineering
REAGAN, J. A., Electrical and Computer Engineering (H)
ROUNTREE, J. C., Electrical and Computer Engineering
SCHOOLEY, L. C., Electrical and Computer Engineering
SCOTT, L. B., Jr, Aerospace and Mechanical Engineering
SEN, S., Systems and Industrial Engineering
SHADMAN, F., Chemical Engineering
SHUTTLEWORTH, W. J., Hydrology and Water Resources
SIERKA, R. A., Chemical Engineering
SIMON, B. R., Aerospace and Mechanical Engineering
SOROOSHIAN, S., Hydrology and Water Resources
STERNBERG, B. K., Mining and Geological Engineering (H)
SUNDARESHAN, M. K., Electrical and Computer Engineering
SZIDAROVSZKY, F., Systems and Industrial Engineering
SZILAGYI, M. N., Electrical and Computer Engineering
UHLMANN, D. R., Materials Science and Engineering (H)
VALDES, J. B., Civil Engineering and Engineering Mechanics (H)
VINCENT, T. L., Aerospace and Mechanical Engineering
WEINBERG, M. C., Materials Science and Engineering
WENDT, J. O. L., Chemical Engineering
WILLIAMS, J. G., Nuclear and Energy Engineering
WIRSCHING, P. H., Aerospace and Mechanical Engineering
WYGNANSKI, I. J., Aerospace and Mechanical Engineering
YAKOWITZ, S. J., Systems and Industrial Engineering
ZEIGLER, B. P., Electrical and Computer Engineering
ZIOLKOWSKI, R. W., Electrical and Computer Engineering

College of Law:
ANDREWS, A. W.
ATWOOD, B. A.
BOYD, W. E.
CHERRY, R. L.
DOBBS, D. B.
GLENNON, R. J., Jr
HEGLAND, K. F.
HENDERSON, R. C.
KORN, J. B.
KOZOLCHYK, B.
MASSARO, T. M.
MAUET, T. A.
RATNER, J. R.
SCHNEYER, T. J.
SPECE, R. G., Jr
STRONG, J. W.
WEISS, E. J.
WEXLER, D. B.
WILLIAMS, R. A., Jr
WOODS, W. D., Jr

College of Medicine:
ALBERTS, D. S., Internal Medicine
ALEPA, F. P., Paediatrics
ALPERT, J. S., Internal Medicine (H)
ANGEVINE, J. B., Jr, Cell Biology and Anatomy

BARBEE, R., Internal Medicine
BARBER, H. B., Radiology
BARKER, S. J., Anaesthesiology (H)
BARRETT, H. H., Radiology
BARTON, L. L., Paediatrics
BENSON, B., Cell Biology and Anatomy
BERNSTEIN, H., Microbiology and Immunology
BINKIEWICZ, A., Paediatrics
BOWDEN, G. T., Radiation Oncology
BOYER, J. T., Internal Medicine
BRAUN, E. J., Physiology
CALKINS, J. M., Anaesthesiology
CARLSON, R. W., Clinical Medicine
CARMODY, R. F., Radiology
CETAS, T. C., Radiation Oncology
COHEN, M. W., Paediatrics
COPELAND, J. G., Surgery
COULL, B. M., Neurology (H)
CRAIG, A. D., Jr, Cell Biology and Anatomy
CRESS, A. E., Radiation Oncology
DALLAS, W. J., Radiology
DANTZLER, W. H., Physiology (H)
DAVIS, J. R., Pathology
DAVIS, T. P., Pharmacology
DELGADO, P. L., Psychiatry
DENNY, W. F., Internal Medicine
DOBSON, M. V., Ophthalmology
DRESNER, M. L., Surgery
DUNCAN, B. R., Paediatrics
EARNEST, D. L., Internal Medicine
ERICKSON, R. P., Paediatrics
ESCOBAR, P. L., Clinical Medicine
ESKELON, C. D., Surgery
EWY, G. A., Internal Medicine
FEINBERG, W. M., Neurology
FELICETTA, J. V., Clinical Medicine
FISHER, R. S., Neurology
FLINK, I. L., Medicine
FORTUNE, J. B., Surgery
FRIEDMAN, R. L., Microbiology and Immunology
GALGIANI, J. N., Internal Medicine
GANDOLFI, A. J., Anaesthesiology
GAREWAL, H. S., Internal Medicine
GELENBERG, A. J., Psychiatry (H)
GERNER, E. W., Radiation Oncology
GLASSER, L., Pathology
GLICKMAN, S. I., Surgery
GMITRO, A. F., Radiology
GOLDBERG, S. J., Paediatrics
GOLDMAN, S., Internal Medicine
GOODWIN, M. H., Family and Community Medicine
GORE, R. W., Physiology
GRAHAM, A. R., Pathology
GROGAN, T. M., Pathology
GRUENER, R. P., Physiology
HALE, F. A., Family and Community Medicine
HALONEN, M. J., Pharmacology
HAMEROFF, S. R., Anaesthesiology
HANSEN, R. C., Internal Medicine
HARRIS, D. T., Microbiology and Immunology
HATCH, K., Obstetrics and Gynaecology (H)
HEFFNER, J. E., Clinical Medicine
HEINE, M. W., Obstetrics and Gynaecology
HERSH, E. M., Internal Medicine
HODES, B. L., Ophthalmology
HOYER, P. B., Physiology
HUNTER, T. B., Radiology
HUTTER, J. J., Paediatrics
HUXTABLE, R. J., Pharmacology
ISERSON, K. V., Surgery
ITO, J., Microbiology and Immunology
JARRELL, B. E., Surgery (H)
JOHNSON, D. G., Internal Medicine
JOHNSON, M. I., Paediatrics
KALIVAS, J., Clinical Medicine
KAMEL, W. W., Family and Community Medicine
KATZ, M. A., Internal Medicine
KAY, M. M. B., Microbiology and Immunology
KERN, K. B., Internal Medicine
KOLDOVSKY, O., Paediatrics
KRISHNAMURTHY, G., Clinical Radiology
LEIBOWITZ, A. I., Clinical Medicine
LEMEN, R. J., Paediatrics
LESLIE, J. B., Clinical Anaesthesiology
LEVENSON, A. I., Psychiatry
LEVINE, N., Internal Medicine
LEVINE, R. B., Neurobiology
LIGHTNER, E. S., Paediatrics
LOHMAN, T. G., Physiology
MARCHALONIS, J. J., Microbiology and Immunology (H)
MARCUS, F. I., Internal Medicine
MARSHALL, C. L., Family and Community Medicine
MARSHALL, W. N., Jr, Clinical Paediatrics
MCCARTY, R. J., Clinical Medicine
MCCLURE, C. L., Family and Community Medicine
MCCUSKEY, R. S., Cell Biology and Anatomy (H)
MCDONAGH, P. F., Surgery
MEISLIN, H. W., Surgery
MICHAEL, U. F., Internal Medicine
MOHER, L. M., Family and Community Medicine
MORKIN, E., Internal Medicine
NAGLE, R. B., Pathology
NICHOLS, A. W., Family and Community Medicine
NUGENT, C. A., Internal Medicine
OBER, R. R., Ophthalmology
OLESON, J. R., Radiation Oncology (H)
ORTIZ, A., Family and Community Medicine
OTTO, C. W., Anaesthesiology
OVITT, T. W., Radiology (H)
PALMER, J. D., Pharmacology
PATTON, D. D., Radiology
PEIRCE, J. C., Clinical Medicine
PETERSEN, E. A., Internal Medicine
PHIBBS, B. P., Clinical Medicine
PHILIPPS, A. F., Paediatrics
POND, G. D., Radiology
PORRECA, F., Pharmacology
POTTER, R. L., Psychiatry
POWIS, G., Pathology
PUST, R. E., Family and Community Medicine
PUTNAM, C. W., Surgery
QUAN, S. F., Internal Medicine
RACY, J. C., Psychiatry
RAMSAY, E. G., Surgery
REARDON, D. F., Paediatrics
REICHLIN, S., Medicine
REED, K. L., Obstetrics and Gynaecology
RIMSZA, M. E., Paediatrics
RIZKALLAH, T. H., Obstetrics and Gynaecology
ROEHRIG, H., Radiology
ROESKE, W. R., Internal Medicine
RUBENS, A. B., Neurology
RYAN, K. J., Pathology
SAMPLINER, R. E., Internal Medicine
SANDERS, A. B., Surgery
SCHUMACHER, M. J., Paediatrics
SECOMB, T. W., Physiology
SEEGER, J. F., Radiology
SETHI, G. K., Surgery
SHAH, J. H., Internal Medicine
SHAPIRO, W. R., Neurology
SHEHAB, Z. M., Paediatrics
SHIMM, D. S., Radiation Oncology
SIBLEY, W. A., Neurology
SKINNER, P. H., Family and Community Medicine
SMITH, J. W., Internal Medicine
SNYDER, R. W., Ophthalmology (H)
SOBONYA, R. E., Pathology
SONNTAG, V. K. H., Surgery
SPAITE, D. W., Surgery
SPEER, D. P., Surgery
SPETZLER, R. F., Surgery
STANDEN, J. R., Radiology
STERN, L. Z., Internal Medicine
STONE, H. H., Surgery
STRAUSFELD, N. J., Neurobiology
STUART, D. G., Physiology
SURWIT, E., Obstetrics and Gynaecology
SZIVEK, J. A., Surgery
TAETLE, R., Internal Medicine
TOLBERT, L. P., Neurobiology
UNGER, E. C., Radiology
VALENZUELA, T. D., Surgery
VILLAR, H. V., Surgery
WEINSTEIN, R. S., Pathology
WEISS, J. C., Paediatrics
WILLIAMS, S. K., III, Surgery
WITTE, C. L., Surgery
WITTE, M. H., Surgery
WOOLFENDEN, J. M., Radiology
WRIGHT, S. H., Physiology
YOCUM, D. E., Clinical Medicine

College of Nursing:

GLITTENBERG, J. E.
PARSONS, L. C.
PHILLIPS, L. R.
REED, P. G.
VAN ORT, E. S.
VERRAN, J. A.
WOODTLI, M. A.

College of Pharmacy:

BLANCHARD, J., Pharmaceutical Sciences
BOOTMAN, J. L., Pharmacy Administration
CARTER, D. E., Pharmacology and Toxicology
CONSROE, P. F., Pharmacology and Toxicology
DAVIS, T. P., Pharmacology
HALPERT, J. R., Pharmacology and Toxicology
HERMAN, R. M., Pharmacology
LUCAS, R. J., Pharmacology
MARTIN, A. R., Pharmacology and Toxicology
MAYERSOHN, M., Pharmaceutical Sciences
MURPHY, J. E., Pharmacy Practice (H)
REMERS, W. A., Pharmaceutical Sciences
SCHRAM, K. H., Pharmaceutical Sciences
SIPES, G. I., Pharmacology and Toxicology (H)
SLOVITER, R. S., Pharmacology
TIMMERMANN, B., Pharmacology and Toxicology
TONG, T. G., Pharmacy Administration
TRANG, J., Pharmacy Practice
YALKOWSKY, S. H., Pharmaceutical Sciences

General Departments:

ATWATER, A. E., Exercise and Sport Sciences
CREIGHTON, L. J., Military Science
LOHMAN, T. G., Exercise and Sport Sciences
SCIABARRA, J., Naval Science (H)
THOMPSON, T. N., Military Aerospace Studies (H)

Arizona International Campus:

BIXBY, B. R.
CLAUSEN, E. G.
CONTERIS, H. J.
GRIJALVA, M. A.
LOCKHART, M. A.
PAULSON, C. R.

University of Arizona Prevention Center:

CAMPBELL, C. C.
KOSS, M. P.
LEBOWITZ, M. D.
MARSHALL, J. R.
MATTOX, J. H.
WATSON, W. R.

Arizona Research Laboratories:

DOWNING, T. E.
HILDEBRAND, J. G.
LAMB, W. E.
LAW, J. H.
PAYNE, C. M.

ARKANSAS

ARKANSAS STATE UNIVERSITY

State University, AR 72467
Telephone: (870) 972-3030
Founded 1909
President: LESLIE WYATT
Registrar: GERALD JONES

Librarian: Mary Moore
Library of 1,465,484 vols
Number of teachers: 481
Number of students: 9,828

ARKANSAS TECH UNIVERSITY

Russellville, AR 72801
Telephone: (501) 968-0389
Fax: (501) 964-0839
Founded 1909
President: Bob Brown
Registrar: Ronald D. Harrell
Librarian: William A. Parton
Library of 840,000 vols
Number of teachers: 176
Number of students: 4,500

DEANS

School of Business: Tom Tyler
School of Education: Dennis Fleniken
School of Liberal and Fine Arts: Earl Schrock
School of Physical and Life Sciences: Richard Cohoon
School of Systems Science: Jack Hamm

HARDING UNIVERSITY

POB 2256, 900 E Center, Searcy, AR 72149
Telephone: (501) 279-4000
Fax: (501) 279-4865
Founded 1924
President: Dr David B. Burks
Vice-President for Academic Affairs: Neale T. Pryor
Registrar: Ron Finley
Librarian: Miss Suzanne Spurrier
Library of 366,053 vols
Number of teachers: 183
Number of students: 3,566

DEANS:

College of Arts and Sciences: Dean Priest
School of Business: David Tucker
School of Education: Bobby Coker
School of Nursing: Cathleen Schultz
College of Bible and Religion: Carl Mitchell

HENDERSON STATE UNIVERSITY

Arkadelphia, AR 71999-0001
Telephone: (501) 230-5000
Founded 1890 as church-related college; became a state institution in 1929
President: Dr Charles D. Dunn
Vice-President: Dr Robert Houston
Registrar: Tom Gattin
Librarian: Robert Yehl
Library of 250,000 vols
Number of teachers: 175
Number of students: 3,636

HENDRIX COLLEGE

Conway, AR 72032
Telephone: (501) 329-6811
Fax: (501) 450-1200
Founded 1876
President: Dr Ann H. Die
Registrar: J. T. Brown
Librarian: Robert Frizzell
Library of 191,919 vols
Number of teachers: 80
Number of students: 1,030

LYON COLLEGE

POB 2317, Batesville, AR 72503
Telephone: (870) 793-9813
Fax: (870) 698-4622
Founded 1872; name changed from Arkansas College 1994
President: Dr Walter B. Roettger
Provost: Dr J. William Moncrief
Vice-President for Institutional Advancement: John Willey
Dean of Student Services: Dr Bruce Johnston
Director of Admissions: Kristine A. Penix
Library of 140,000 vols
Number of teachers: 45
Number of students: 600

UNIVERSITY OF ARKANSAS

Fayetteville, AR 72701
Telephone: (501) 575-2000
Fax: (501) 575-7515
E-mail: uafadmis@comp.uark.edu
Established 1871. Opened 1872
Chancellor: John A. White
Vice-Chancellor for Academic Affairs: Donald O. Pederson
Vice-Chancellor for Finance and Administration: Dr Farris Womack (acting)
Vice-Chancellor for Student Services: Dr Suzanne Gordon (acting)
Vice-Chancellor for University Advancement: Dr David Gearhart
Director of Libraries: John A. Harrison
Director of Museum: Johnnie Gentry
Library of 1,460,000 vols
Number of teachers: main campus 900
Number of students: main campus 14,322

DEANS

Dale Bumpers College of Agricultural, Food and Life Sciences: Charles J. Scifres
J. W. Fulbright College of Arts and Sciences: Bernard L. Madison
College of Business Administration: Doyle Z. Williams
College of Education and Health Professions: Charles Stegman
College of Engineering: Otto J. Loewer
Graduate School: Collis R. Geren
School of Law: Len Strickman
School of Architecture: Daniel D. Bennett
Division of Continuing Education: Donnie Dutton

UNIVERSITY OF ARKANSAS AT LITTLE ROCK

2801 South University Ave, Little Rock, AR 72204
Telephone: (501) 569-3000
Founded 1927
Chancellor: Dr Charles E. Hathaway
Provost and Vice-Chancellor for Academic Affairs: Dr Joel E. Anderson
Vice-Chancellor for Educational and Student Services: Dr Charles Donaldson
Vice-Chancellor for Finance and Administration: Barbara Richards
Vice-Chancellor for Advancement: Bill Walker
Librarian: Kathy Saunders
Library of 405,422 vols
Number of teachers: 497 full-time, 304 part-time
Number of students: 10,959

UNIVERSITY OF ARKANSAS AT MONTICELLO

Monticello, AR 71655
Telephone: (501) 460-1020
Founded 1909
Chancellor: Dr Fred J. Taylor
Registrar: Janet Danley
Librarian: William F. Droessler
Library of 136,938 vols
Number of teachers: 100
Number of students: 1,900

UNIVERSITY OF ARKANSAS AT PINE BLUFF

Pine Bluff, AR 71601
Telephone: (501) 543-8000
Founded 1873
Liberal arts and land-grant institution
Chancellor: Lawrence A. Davis, Jr
Vice-Chancellor for Academic Affairs: Dr Mary E. Benjamin
Vice-Chancellor for Student Affairs: Dr Bobbie A. Irvins
Vice-Chancellor for Finance: Hugh A. Blaney
Library of 220,000 vols
Number of students: 3,710

UNIVERSITY OF THE OZARKS

Clarksville, AR 72830-2880
Telephone: (501) 979-1000
Fax: (501) 979-1355
Founded 1834
President: Richard Niece
Registrar: Becky Haynes
Librarian: Stuart Stelzer
Library of 61,547 vols
Number of teachers: 49
Number of students: 576

CALIFORNIA

ARMSTRONG UNIVERSITY

2222 Harold Way, Berkeley, CA 94704
Telephone: (510) 848-2500
Fax: (510) 848-9438
Founded 1918
President: Ronald R. Hook
Registrar: Owais Qureshi
Librarian: Sara O'Keefe
Library of 15,000 vols
Number of teachers: 28
Number of students: 200
Graduate and undergraduate courses in accounting, international business, marketing, finance, management and computer management science.

ART CENTER COLLEGE OF DESIGN

1700 Lida St, Pasadena, CA 91103
Telephone: (626) 396-2200
Fax: (626) 405-9104
Founded 1930
President: David R. Brown
Admissions Director: Catherine Baron
Registrar: Jerry Allen
Librarian: Elizabeth Galloway
Number of teachers: 250
Number of students: 1,150

AZUSA PACIFIC UNIVERSITY

901 E Alosta, Azusa, CA 91702
Telephone: (626) 969-3434
Fax: (626) 969-7180
Founded 1899
President: Dr Richard Felix
Provost: Dr Patricia Anderson
Dean of Admissions: Deanna Porterfield
Librarian: Dr Paul Gray
Library of 140,000 vols
Number of teachers: 406
Number of students: 4,547

BETHANY COLLEGE

800 Bethany Drive, Scotts Valley, CA 95066

Telephone: (408) 438-3800
Fax: (408) 438-1621

Founded 1919

President: Dr EVERETT WILSON
Registrar: SCOTT HUTTON
Academic Dean: Dr WILLIAM SNOW
Librarian: ARNOLD MCLELLAN

Library of 57,704 vols
Number of teachers: 45 (including 22 part-time)
Number of students: 595

BIOLA UNIVERSITY

13800 Biola Avenue, La Mirada, CA 90639

Telephone: (562) 903-6000
Fax: (562) 903-4761

Founded 1908

President: Dr CLYDE COOK
Provost: Dr SHERWOOD LINGENFELTER
Director of Enrolment: GREG VAUGHAN

Library of 190,000 vols
Number of teachers: 252
Number of students: 3,447

CONSTITUENT SCHOOLS

School of Arts and Sciences
Rosemead School of Psychology
Talbot School of Theology
School of Intercultural Studies
School of Business
School of Continuing Studies

CALIFORNIA BAPTIST COLLEGE

8432 Magnolia Ave, Riverside, CA 92504

Telephone: (909) 689-5771
Fax: (909) 351-1808

Founded 1950

President: Dr RONALD L. ELLIS
Dean: Dr BONNIE METCALF
Registrar: ERLINDA MARTINEZ

Library of 103,000 vols
Number of full-time teachers: 51
Number of students: 1,687

CALIFORNIA COLLEGE OF ARTS AND CRAFTS

5212 Broadway, Oakland, CA 94618-1487

Telephone: (510) 594-3630
Fax: (510) 594-3797

Founded 1907

President: LORNE M. BUCHMAN
Provost: STEPHEN BEAL
Dean of Humanities and Sciences: MARTIN VAN BUREN
Vice-President (Development): MARGIE SHURGOT
Director of Admissions: SHERI MCKENZIE
Librarian: MARY MANNING

Library of 35,000 vols
Number of teachers: 200
Number of students: 1,175

CALIFORNIA COLLEGE OF PODIATRIC MEDICINE

1210 Scott St, San Francisco, CA 94115

Telephone: (415) 563-3444

Founded 1914

President and Chief Executive Officer: ROBERT D. ROBERTS (acting)
Dean of Academic Affairs: JEFFREY PAGE
Librarian: RONALD SCHULTZ

Library of 4,500 vols, 18,000 bound periodicals
Number of teachers: 45
Number of students: 400

CALIFORNIA INSTITUTE OF INTEGRAL STUDIES

9 Peter Yorke Way, San Francisco, CA 94109

Telephone: (415) 674-5500
Fax: (415) 674-5555

Founded 1968

President: ROBERT MCDERMOTT
Dean of Students: RICHARD BUGGS
Registrar: STEPHANIE SMITH
Librarian: OLIVE JAMES

Library of 50,000 vols
Number of teachers: 70
Number of students: 1,200

MA and PhD in Eastern/Western philosophy and religion, clinical and counselling psychology, East-West psychology, integral health, women's spirituality, social and cultural anthropology, drama therapy, transformative learning, undergraduate completion.

CALIFORNIA INSTITUTE OF TECHNOLOGY

Pasadena, CA 91125
Telephone: (626) 395-6811
Telex: 675425

Founded 1891
Private

President: Dr DAVID BALTIMORE
Vice-President and Provost: STEVEN E. KOONIN
Vice-President for Business and Finance: JOHN R. CURRY
Vice-President for Institute Relations: JERRY NUNNALLY
Vice-President for Student Affairs: CHRISTOPHER E. BRENNEN
Director of Admissions: CHARLENE LIEBAU
Dean of Students: JEAN-PAUL REVEL
Controller: (vacant)
Secretary: M. L. WEBSTER
Registrar: J. GOODSTEIN
Librarian: ANNE MARIE BUCK

Library of 340,000 vols
Number of teachers: 328
Number of students: 1,925

Publications: *Engineering and Science*, *Caltech News*.

CHAIRMEN OF DIVISIONS

Biology: MELVIN I. SIMON
Chemistry and Chemical Engineering: P. B. DERVAN
Engineering and Applied Science: JOHN H. SEINFELD
Geological and Planetary Sciences: EDWARD M. STOLPER
Humanities and Social Sciences: JOHN O. LEDYARD
Physics, Mathematics and Astronomy: THOMAS A. TOMBRELLO

PROFESSORS

ABELSON, J. N., Biology
ABU-MOSTAFA, Y. S., Computer Science
AHRENS, T. J., Seismology
ALBEE, A. L., Geological and Planetary Science
ALLMAN, J. M., Biology
ANDERSEN, R. A., Biology
ANDERSON, D. J., Biology
ANDERSON, D. L., Geophysics
ANSON, F. C., Chemistry
ANTONSSON, E. K., Mechanical Engineering
ARNOLD, F. H., Chemical Engineering
ASCHBACHER, M., Mathematics
ATTARDI, G., Biology
BALDESCHWIELER, J. D., Chemistry
BALTIMORE, D., Biology
BANKS, J. S., Political Science
BARISH, B. C., Physics
BARR, A. H., Computer Science
BARTON, J. K., Chemistry
BEAUCHAMP, J. L., Chemistry
BECK, J. L., Civil Engineering
BELLAN, P. M., Applied Physics
BERCAW, J. E., Chemistry
BLAKE, G. A., Cosmochemistry
BLANDFORD, R. D., Theoretical Astrophysics
BORDER, KIM C., Economics
BOSSAERTS, P. L., Finance
BOWER, J.M., Biology
BRADY, J. F., Chemical Engineering
BRENNEN, C. E., Mechanical Engineering
BRIDGES, W. B., Engineering
BROKAW, C. J., Biology
BRONNER-FRASER, M., Biology
BRUCK, J., Computation and Neural Systems and Electrical Engineering
BRUNO, O. P., Applied Mathematics
BURNETT, D. S., Geochemistry
CAMERER, C. F., Economics
CAMPBELL, J. L., Chemical Biology
CARREIRA, E. M., Chemistry
CASS, G. R., Engineering Science
CHAN, S. I., Chemical Physics
CHANDY, K. M., Computer Science
CLAYTON, R. W., Geophysics
COHEN, D. S., Applied Mathematics
COHEN, J. G., Astronomy
CORNGOLD, N. R., Applied Physics
CROSS, M. C., Theoretical Physics
CULICK, F. E. C., Applied Physics and Jet Propulsion
DAVIDSON, E. H., Cell Biology
DAVIS, L. E., Social Science
DAVIS, M. E., Chemical Engineering
DERVAN, P. B., Chemistry
DIMOTAKIS, P. E., Aeronautics
DJORGOVSKI, S. G., Astronomy
DOUGHERTY, D. A., Chemistry
DOYLE, J. C., Electrical Engineering
DREVER, R. W. P., Physics
DREYER, W. J., Biology
EISENSTEIN, J. P., Physics
EVERHART, T. E., Electrical Engineering
FILIPPONE, B. W., Physics
FLAGAN, R. C., Chemical Engineering
FRANKLIN, J. N., Applied Mathematics
FRASER, S. E., Biology
FRAUTSCHI, S. C., Theoretical Physics
FULTZ, B. T., Materials Science
GABAI, D., Mathematics
GAVALAS, G. R., Chemical Engineering
GHARIB, M., Aeronautics
GODDARD, W. A., III, Chemistry Applied Science
GOLDREICH, P. M., Applied Physics and Planetary Science
GOODMAN, R. M. F., Electrical Engineering
GOODSTEIN, D. L., Physics
GRAY, H. B., Chemistry
GRETHER, D. M., Economics
GRUBBS, R. H., Chemistry
GURNIS, M. C., Geophysics
HALL, J. F., Civil Engineering
HEATON, THOMAS H., Engineering Seismology
HELMBERGER, D. V., Geophysics
HITLIN, D. G., Physics
HOFFMAN, PHILIP T., Humanities and Social Science
HOFFMANN, M. R., Environmental Science
HORNUNG, H. G., Aeronautics
HOU, YIZHAO T., Applied Mathematics
IMPERIALI, B., Chemistry
INGERSOLL, A. P., Planetary Science
IWAN, W. D., Applied Mechanics
JACKSON, M. O., Economics
JENNINGS, P. C., Civil Engineering
JOHNSON, W. L., Materials Science
KAMB, W. B., Geology and Geophysics
KANAMORI, H., Geophysics
KAVANAGH, R. W., Physics
KECHRIS, A. S., Mathematics
KELLER, H. B., Applied Mathematics
KENNEDY, M. B., Biology
KEVLES, D. J., History
KIEWIET, D. R., Political Science
KIMBLE, H. J., Physics
KIRSCHVINK, J. L., Geobiology
KNAUSS, W. G., Aeronautics and Applied Mechanics

KOCH, C., Computation and Neural Systems
KONISHI, M., Behavioural Biology
KOONIN, S. E., Theoretical Physics
KOUSSER, J. M., Humanities and Social Science
KULKARNI, S. R., Astronomy
KUPPERMANN, A., Chemical Physics
LA BELLE, J., English
LANGE, A. E., Physics
LEDYARD, J. O., Economics and Social Science
LEONARD, A., Aeronautics
LESTER, H. A., Biology
LEWIS, N. S., Chemistry
LIBBRECHT, K. G., Physics
LORDEN, G. A., Mathematics
LUXEMBURG, W. A. J., Mathematics
MCELIECE, R. J., Electrical Engineering
MCGILL, T. C., Applied Physics
MCKELVEY, R. D., Political Science
MCKEOWN, R. D., Physics
MCKOY, B. V., Theoretical Chemistry
MAKAROV, N. G., Mathematics
MANDEL, O., English
MARCUS, R. A., Chemistry
MARSDEN, J. E., Control and Dynamic Systems
MARTIN, A. J., Computer Science
MARTIN, C. R., Physics
MEAD, C. A., Computer Science
MEIRON, D. I., Applied Mathematics
MEYEROWITZ, E. M., Biology
MORGAN, J. J., Environmental Engineering Science
MURRAY, B. C., Planetary Science
MYERS, A. G., Chemistry
NEUGEBAUER, G., Physics
NEWMAN, H. B., Physics
ORDESHOOK, P. C., Political Science
ORTIZ, M., Aeronautics and Applied Mechanics
PALFREY, T. R., Economics and Political Science
PARKER, C. S., Chemical Biology
PATTERSON, P. H., Biology
PECK, C. W., Physics
PERONA, P., Electrical Engineering
PHILLIPS, T. G., Physics
PHINNEY, E. S., III, Theoretical Astrophysics
PIGMAN, G. W., Literature
PINE, J., Physics
PLOTT, C. R., Economics and Political Science
POLITZER, H. D., Theoretical Physics
PORTER, FRANK C., Physics
PRESKILL, J. P., Theoretical Physics
PRINCE, T. A., Physics
PSALTIS, D., Electrical Engineering
PULLIN, D. I., Aeronautics
RAICHLEN, F., Civil Engineering and Mechanical Engineering
RAMAKRISHNAN, D., Mathematics
READHEAD, A. C. S., Astronomy
REES, D. C., Chemistry
REVEL, J.-P., Biology
RICHARDS, J. H., Organic Chemistry
ROSAKIS, A. J., Aeronautics
ROSENSTONE, R. A., History
ROSSMAN, G. R., Geology
ROTHENBERG, E., Biology
ROUKES, M. L., Physics
RUTLEDGE, D. B., Electrical Engineering
SAFFMAN, P. G., Applied Mathematics
SALEEBY, J. B., Geological and Planetary Science
SARGENT, A. I., Astronomy
SARGENT, W. L. W., Astronomy
SCHERER, A., Electrical Engineering and Applied Physics
SCHWARZ, J. H., Theoretical Physics
SCOTT, R. F., Civil Engineering
SCOVILLE, N. Z., Astronomy
SCUDDER, T., Anthropology
SEINFELD, J. H., Chemical Engineering
SIEH, K. E., Geology
SIMON, B. M., Mathematics and Theoretical Physics
SIMON, M. I., Biology
SOIFER, B. T., Physics
STEIDEL, C. C., Astronomy
STERNBERG, P. W., Biology
STEVENSON, D. J., Planetary Science
STOLPER, E. M., Geology
STONE, E. C., Physics
STRAUSS, J. H., Biology
STURTEVANT, B., Aeronautics
TAYLOR, H. P., Geology
THORNE, K. S., Theoretical Physics
TIRRELL, D. A., Chemical Engineering
TOMBRELLO, T. A., Physics
VAHALA, K. J., Applied Physics
VAIDYANATHAN, P. P., Electrical Engineering
VARSHAVSKY, A. J., Cell Biology
VOGT, R. E., Physics
WALES, D. B., Mathematics
WASSERBURG, G. J., Geophysics
WERNICKE, B. P., Geology
WIGGINS, S. R., Applied Mechanics
WILSON, R. M., Mathematics
WISE, M. B., Theoretical Physics
WOLD, B. J., Biology
WOLFF, T. H., Mathematics
WOODWARD, J. F., Philosophy
WYLLIE, P. J., Geological and Planetary Science
YARIV, A., Applied Physics
YEI, N.-C., Physics
YUNG, Y. L., Geological and Planetary Science
ZACHARIASEN, F., Theoretical Physics
ZEWALL, A. H., Chemical Physics

ATTACHED INSTITUTE

Jet Propulsion Laboratory: 4800 Oak Grove Drive, Pasadena, Calif. 91109; planetary exploration and related research; Dir Dr EDWARD C. STONE.

CALIFORNIA INSTITUTE OF THE ARTS

24700 McBean Parkway, Valencia, CA 91355

Telephone: (805) 255-1050
Fax: (805) 254-8352

Incorporated 1961

President: Dr STEVEN D. LAVINE
Senior Vice-President (Administration): JOHN FULLER
Vice-President (Planning and Advancement): JEFFREY H. JAMES
Provost: BEVERLY O'NEILL
Dean of Library: FREDERICK GARDNER

Library of 70,000 vols
Number of teachers: 201
Number of students: 1,051

DEANS

Art: TOM LAWSON
Critical Studies: RICHARD HEBDIGE
Dance: CRISTYNE LAWSON
Film and Video: HARTMUT BITOMSKY
Music: DAVID ROSENBOOM
Theatre: SUSAN SOLT

CALIFORNIA LUTHERAN UNIVERSITY

Thousand Oaks, CA 91360

Telephone: (805) 492-2411
Fax: (805) 493-3513

Founded 1959

President: Dr LUTHER S. LUEDTKE
Provost: Dr PAMELA JOLICOEUR
Vice-President for Administration and Finance: DENNIS GILLETTE
Vice-President for Institutional Advancement: GEORGE ENGDAHL
Vice-President for Student Affairs and Dean of Students: WILLIAM ROSSER
Registrar: DAMON BLUE
Librarian: KENNETH PFLUEGER

Library of 110,416
Number of teachers: 96 full-time, 95 part-time
Number of students: 2,586

CALIFORNIA SCHOOL OF PROFESSIONAL PSYCHOLOGY

2749 Hyde St, San Francisco, CA 94109

Telephone: (415) 346-4500
Fax: (415) 931-8322

Founded 1969

Non-profit corporation

President: Dr JUDITH ALBINO
Chancellor, Alameda Campus: Dr KATSUYUKI SAKAMOTO
Chancellor, Fresno Campus: Dr MARY BETH KENKEL
Chancellor, Los Angeles Campus: Dr LISA PORCHÉ-BURKE
Chancellor, San Diego Campus: Dr RAYMOND J. TRYBUS
Number of teachers: 450
Number of students: 2,400

CALIFORNIA STATE UNIVERSITY SYSTEM

401 Golden Shore, Long Beach, CA 90802

Telephone: (562) 985-2500

Co-ordinating headquarters for 23 state universities

Chancellor: CHARLES REED

CALIFORNIA POLYTECHNIC STATE UNIVERSITY

San Luis Obispo, CA 93407

Telephone: (805) 756-1111

Founded 1901

President: WARREN J. BAKER
Provost and Vice-President for Academic Affairs: PAUL ZINGG
Vice-President for Student Affairs: JUAN C. GONZALEZ
Vice-President for University Advancement: WILLIAM G. BOLDT
Dean of Library Services: HIRAM DAVIS
Library of 625,000 vols and 420,000 govt documents
Number of teachers: 1,096
Number of students: 16,735

Publications: *Mustang Daily, Cal Poly Today* (quarterly).

DEANS

College of Agriculture: JOSEPH JEN
College of Architecture and Environmental Design: MARTIN HARMS
College of Business: WILLIAM BOYNTON
College of Liberal Arts: HAROLD HELLENBRAND
College of Engineering and Technology: PETER LEE
College of Science and Mathematics: PHILIP S. BAILEY

CALIFORNIA STATE POLYTECHNIC UNIVERSITY, POMONA

3801 West Temple Ave, Pomona, CA 91768

Telephone: (714) 869-2000

Founded 1938

President: Dr BOB H. SUZUKI
Registrar: ROSE BEARDSLEY KUKLA
Librarian: HAROLD B. SCHLEIFER

Library of 607,241 vols and 2,870 periodicals
Number of teachers: 958
Number of students: 16,605

DEANS

College of Agriculture: WAYNE R. BIDLACK
College of Business: RONALD W. EAVES
College of Engineering: CARL E. RATHMAN (acting)
College of Environmental Design: SPYROS AMOURGIS (acting)
College of Science: SIMON J. BERNAU

College of Letters, Arts and Social Sciences: BARBARA J. WAY
School of Hotel and Restaurant Management: PATRICIA M. HOPKINS (acting)
School of Education and Integrative Studies: SHEILA J. MCCOY (acting)

CALIFORNIA STATE UNIVERSITY, BAKERSFIELD

9001 Stockdale Highway, Bakersfield, CA 93311-1099
Telephone: (805) 664-2011
Fax: (805) 664-3194
Founded 1965
President: Dr TOMAS A. ARCINIEGA
Provost and Vice-President for Academic Affairs: Dr FRED DORER
Vice-President for Business and Administrative Services: MIKE NEAL
Vice-President for Student Affairs: Dr GEORGE B. HIBBARD
Vice-President, Information Resources: WENDELL BARBOUR
Library of 340,000 vols
Number of teachers: 305
Number of students: 5,435
Schools of Arts and Sciences, Education, Business and Public Administration.

CALIFORNIA STATE UNIVERSITY, CHICO

Chico, CA 95929
Telephone: (530) 898-6116
Founded 1887
President: Dr MANUEL A. ESTEBAN
Provost and Vice-President for Academic Affairs: Dr SCOTT G. MCNALL
Vice-Provost for Enrolment Management: ROBERT HANNIGAN
Vice-President for Business and Finance: DENNIS C. GRAHAM
Vice-President for University Advancement and Student Affairs: Dr PAUL MOORE
Library Director: FRED RYAN
Library of 627,466 vols
Number of teachers: 1,077
Number of students: 14,000

DEANS

College of Agriculture: Dr THOMAS E. DICKINSON
College of Engineering, Computer Science and Technology: Dr KENNETH DERUCHER
College of Behavioral and Social Sciences: Dr JAMES JACOB
College of Business: (vacant)
College of Communication and Education: Dr STEPHEN KING
College of Humanities and Fine Arts: Dr DONALD HEINZ
College of Natural Sciences: Dr ROGER LEDERER
Graduate School: Dr ROBERT JACKSON
Information Services: FRED RYAN
Regional and Continuing Education: Dr RALPH MEUTER

CALIFORNIA STATE UNIVERSITY, DOMINGUEZ HILLS

Carson, CA 90747
Telephone: (310) 243-3300
Founded 1960
President: Dr ROBERT C. DETWEILER
Vice-Presidents: SAMUEL BOICE BOWMAN, AMER EL-AHRAF, YORAM NEUMANN
Registrar: HELEN BATCHELOR
Librarian: BETTY BLACKMAN
Library of 427,000 vols
Number of teachers: 331
Number of students: 10,400

DEANS

Arts and Sciences: SELASE WILLIAMS
Health: ALLAN HOFFMAN
Education: JAMES HARRIS (acting)
Management: R. BRYANT MILLS (acting)
Graduate Studies: CECILE LINDSAY

CALIFORNIA STATE UNIVERSITY, FRESNO

5241 N. Maple, Fresno, CA 93740-0048
Telephone: (209) 278-4240
Founded 1911
President: JOHN WELTY
Associate Vice-President of Enrollment Services: JOSEPH MARSHALL
Librarian: MICHAEL GORMAN
Library of 783,695 vols
Number of teachers: 670
Number of students: 17,277

CALIFORNIA STATE UNIVERSITY, FULLERTON

Fullerton, CA 92634
Telephone: (714) 773-2011
Founded 1957
President: Dr MILTON A. GORDON
Registrar: CAROLE JONES
Library Director: RICHARD POLLARD
Library of 600,000 vols
Number of teachers: 700
Number of students: 24,000

CALIFORNIA STATE UNIVERSITY, HAYWARD

Hayward, CA 94542
Telephone: (510) 885-3000
Fax: (510) 885-3808
Founded 1957
President: NORMA S. REES
Director of Admissions and Assistant Vice-President: BETTY HUFF
Librarian: NOREEN ALLDREDGE
Library of 700,000 vols
Number of teachers: 654
Number of students: 12,825

DEANS

School of Arts, Letters and Social Sciences: JAMES FAY
School of Business and Economics: JAY TONTZ
School of Education: ARTHURLENE TOWNER
School of Science: MICHAEL LEUNG

CALIFORNIA STATE UNIVERSITY, LONG BEACH

1250 Bellflower Blvd, Long Beach, CA 90840-0115
Telephone: (213) 985-4111
Founded 1949
President: Dr CURTIS L. MCCRAY
Provost and Senior Vice-President for Academic Affairs: KARL W. E. ANATOL
Vice-President for University Relations and Development: JERRY MANDEL
Vice-President for Student Services: JUNE COOPER
Vice-President for Administration and Finance: WILLIAM H. GRIFFITH
Director of Admissions and Records: JAMES MENZEL
Library Director: JORDAN SCEPANSKI
Library of 1,010,219 vols
Number of teachers: 932 full-time, 853 part-time
Number of students: 32,875

CALIFORNIA STATE UNIVERSITY, LOS ANGELES

5151 State University Drive, Los Angeles, CA 90032
Telephone: (213) 343-3000
Fax: (213) 343-2670
Founded 1947
President: JAMES M. ROSSER
Provost and Vice-President for Academic Affairs: MARGARET HARTMAN
Vice-President for Information Resources Management: DESDEMONA CARDOZA
Vice-President for Institutional Advancement: KYLE BUTTON
Vice-President for Administration and Finance: STEVE GARCIA
Vice-President for Student Affairs: GEORGE TAYLOR
Librarian: DOUGLAS DAVIS
Library of *c.* 1,000,000 vols
Number of teachers: 888
Number of students: 18,000

CALIFORNIA STATE UNIVERSITY, NORTHRIDGE

18111 Nordhoff St, Northridge, CA 91330
Telephone: (818) 677-1200
Founded 1958
President: BLENDA J. WILSON
Director of Admissions and Records: LORRAINE NEWLON
Librarian: SUE CURZON
Library of 900,000 vols, 175,000 maps
Number of teachers: 1,900
Number of students: 30,000

DEANS

College of Arts, Media and Communication: PHIL HANDLER
College of Business Administration and Economics: WILLIAM HOSEK
College of Education: CAROLYN ELLNER
College of Engineering and Computer Science: LAURENCE CARETTO
College of Health and Human Development: ANN STUTTS
College of Humanities: JORGE GARCIA
College of Science and Mathematics: EDWARD CARROLL Jr
College of Social and Behavioural Sciences: WILLIAM FLORES
College of Extended Learning: JOYCE FEUCHT-HAVIAR

CALIFORNIA STATE UNIVERSITY, SACRAMENTO

6000 J St, Sacramento, CA 95819
Telephone: (916) 278-6011
Fax: (916) 278-6664
Founded 1947
President: DONALD R. GERTH
Director of Admissions and Records: LARRY GLASMIRE
Librarian: PATRICIA LARSEN
Library of 1 m. vols
Number of teachers: 800
Number of students: 23,316

DEANS

College of Arts and Sciences: WILLIAM J. SULLIVAN Jr
College of Business Administration: FELICIENNE H. RAMEY
College of Education: DIANE CORDERO DE NORIEGA
College of Engineering and Computer Science: BRAJA M. DAS
College of Health and Human Services: MICHAEL HARTER

College of Natural Sciences and Mathematics: MARION H. O'LEARY
College of Social Sciences and Interdisciplinary Studies: JOSEPH SHELEY

CALIFORNIA STATE UNIVERSITY, SAN BERNARDINO

5500 University Parkway, San Bernardino, CA 92407
Telephone: (909) 880-5000
Fax: (909) 880-5903
Founded 1960
Liberal Arts college with several applied programmes offering a broad range of first degrees, several teaching credentials and master degrees in selected fields
President: ALBERT K. KARNIG
Vice-President for Academic Affairs: LOUIS FERNANDEZ
Vice-President for Student Services: FRANK RINCON
Librarian: JOHNNIE ANN RALPH
Library of 580,000 vols
Number of teachers: 450
Number of students: 12,153

CALIFORNIA STATE UNIVERSITY, STANISLAUS

801 W. Monte Vista Ave, Turlock, CA 95382
Telephone: (209) 667-3201
Fax: (209) 667-3333
Founded 1957
President: Dr MARVALENE HUGHES
Provost and Vice-President for Academic Affairs: Dr RICHARD A. CURRY
Vice-President for Business and Finance: Dr MAYNARD ROBINSON
Vice-President for Student Affairs and Dean of Students: Dr DAVID KEYMER
Executive Director of University Advancement: LORRAINE GONSALVES (acting)
Senior Director, Admissions and Records: EDWARD AUBERT
Dean, Library Services: JOHN K. AMRHEIN
Library of 310,000 vols
Number of teachers: 371
Number of students: 5,900

CHAPMAN UNIVERSITY

333 North Glassell St, Orange, CA 92866
Telephone: (714) 997-6711
Fax: (714) 997-6887
Founded 1861
Private (Disciples of Christ) Liberal Arts
President: Dr JAMES L. DOTI
Vice-President for Academic Affairs: Dr HARRY HAMILTON
Dean of Student Life: JOE KERTES
Dean of Enrollment: SASKIA KNIGHT
Librarian: MARY SELLEN
Library of 155,000 vols
Number of teachers: 116 full-time, 180 part-time
Number of students: 2,930

CLAREMONT GRADUATE UNIVERSITY

150 E. Tenth St, Claremont, CA 91711
Telephone: (909) 621-8028
Fax: (909) 621-8390
Founded 1925
President: STEADMAN UPHAM
Vice-President for Academic Affairs and Dean of Faculty: ANN W. HART
Librarian: BONNIE J. CLEMENS
Library of 2,000,000 vols
Number of teachers: 85 (augmented by 250 faculty members from The Claremont Colleges)
Number of students: 2,035
Post-baccalaureate degrees in 19 disciplines.

CLAREMONT McKENNA COLLEGE

Claremont, CA 91711-6400
Telephone: (909) 621-8000
Founded 1946
Liberal arts college with emphasis on public affairs
President: JACK L. STARK
Number of teachers: 130
Number of students: 953

COLLEGE OF NOTRE DAME

Ralston Ave, Belmont, CA 94002
Telephone: (415) 593-1601
Fax: (415) 637-0493
Founded 1851; chartered 1868
President: Dr MARGARET HUBER
Registrar: CHIP GOLDSTEIN
Director of Admissions: Dr GREG SMITH
Academic Dean: Dr JANIFER STACKHOUSE
Librarian: RICHARD BRADBERRY
Library of 105,910 vols
Number of teachers: 195
Number of students: 1,687

FRESNO PACIFIC UNIVERSITY

1717 South Chestnut Ave, Fresno, CA 93702
Telephone: (209) 453-2000
Fax: (209) 453-2007
Founded 1944
President: Dr ALLEN CARDEN
Academic Vice-President: Dr HOWARD LOEWEN
Registrar: Dr NORMAN REMPEL
Librarian: STEVE BRANDT
Library of 145,000 vols
Number of teachers: 70
Number of students: 1,600

GOLDEN GATE UNIVERSITY

536 Mission St, San Francisco, CA 94105
Telephone: (415) 442-7000
Fax: (415) 543-2779
Founded 1853
President: THOMAS M. STAUFFER
Vice-President, Academic Affairs: PHILIP FRIEDMAN
Vice-President, Operations: SHARON K. MEYER
Vice-President, University Advancement: DONALD MOYER
Vice-President for Enrollment Services: ARCHIE PORTER
Librarian: JOSHUA ADARKWA
Library of 300,000 vols
Number of teachers: 750
Number of students: 7,000

HARVEY MUDD COLLEGE

Kingston Hall, Claremont, CA 91711
Telephone: (909) 621-8120
Fax: (909) 621-8360
Founded 1955
Courses in science and engineering
President: HENRY E. RIGGS
Registrar: B. LUMPKIN
Dean of Faculty: S. WETTACK
Dean of Students: J. NODA
Dean of Admission: P. COLEMAN
Library Director: B. CLEMENS
Library of over 1,000,000 vols (shared with the Claremont Colleges)
Number of teachers: 78
Number of students: 630

HOLY NAMES COLLEGE

3500 Mountain Blvd, Oakland, CA 94619-1699
Telephone: (510) 436-1000
Fax: (510) 436-1199
Founded 1868
Four-year, co-educational liberal arts college
President: Dr NEIL THORBURN (acting)
Dean of Academic Affairs: Dr DAVID FIKE
Dean of Undergraduate Admissions: JOANN BERRIDGE
Dean of Graduate Admissions: JEAN ANN FLAHERTY
Librarian: FRANCES HUI
Library of 111,000 vols
Number of teachers: 121
Number of students: 861

HUMBOLDT STATE UNIVERSITY

Arcata, CA 95521-8299
Telephone: (707) 826-3011
Founded 1913
President: Dr ALISTAIR W. MCCRONE
Director of Admissions and Records: DENNIS GEYER.
Librarian: RENA K. FOWLER
Library of 479,000 vols
Number of teachers: 613
Number of students: 7,684

JOHN F. KENNEDY UNIVERSITY

12 Altarinda Rd, Orinda, CA 94563
Telephone: (510) 254-0200
Fax: (510) 254-6964
Founded 1964
President: CHARLES E. GLASSER
Dean of Students: GWEN SWENSON
Librarian: ANN PATTERSON
Library of 68,300 vols
Number of teachers: 687
Number of students: 1,900

DEANS

Graduate School of Professional Psychology: RONALD LEVINSON
Graduate School for Holistic Studies: DAVID GOLDBERG
School of Management: CRAIG ZACHLOD
Liberal Arts: JEREMIAH HALLISEY
School of Law: MELINDA THOMAS

LA SIERRA UNIVERSITY

4700 Pierce, Riverside, CA 92515
Telephone: (909) 785-2000
Fax: (909) 785-2901
Founded 1922
President: LAWRENCE GERATY
Registrar: FAYE SWAYZE
Librarian: MAYNARD LOWRY
Number of teachers: 112
Number of students: 1,500

DEANS

College of Arts and Sciences: GARY BRADLEY
School of Education: DAVID PENNER
School of Business and Management: HENRY FELDER
School of Religion: JOHN JONES

CHAIRMEN OF DEPARTMENTS

Art: SUSAN PATT
Biology: LAWRENCE MCCLOSKEY
Chemistry: H. RAYMOND SHELDEN
English and Communications: ROBERT DUNN
Health, Physical Education and Recreation: WALTER HAMMERSLOUGH

History and Political Science: RENNIE SCHOEPFLIN
Liberal Studies: JAMES BEACH
Music: JEFFRY KAATZ
Mathematics and Computing: VERNON HOWE
Modern Languages: LOURDES MORALES-GUDMUNSSON
Physics: IVAN ROUSE
Psychology: GLORIA HICINBOTHAM
Sociology and Anthropology: GARLAND DULAN
Honors Program: DONALD THURBER (Co-ordinator)

LOMA LINDA UNIVERSITY

Loma Linda, CA 92350
Telephone: (909) 824-4300
Fax: (909) 824-4577
Founded 1905
President: B. LYN BEHRENS
Vice-Presidents: DAVID MOORHEAD, BRIAN BULL, AGUSTUS CHEATHAM, DONALD G. PURSLEY, IAN M. FRASER
Director, Admissions and Records: JANELLE PYKE
Director of Libraries: DAVID RIOS
Libraries of 300,946 vols and periodicals
Number of teachers: 1,162
Number of students: 3,319
Publications: bulletins, handbooks, *Courier, LLU Today, Scope.*

DEANS

Faculty of Religion: GERALD WINSLOW
School of Public Health: RICHARD HART
School of Medicine: BRIAN BULL
School of Dentistry: CHARLES GOODACRE
Graduate School: W. BARTON RIPPON
School of Nursing: HELEN KING
School of Allied Health Professions: JOYCE HOPP

LOYOLA MARYMOUNT UNIVERSITY

7900 Loyola Blvd, Los Angeles, CA 90045-8300
Telephone: (310) 338-2700
Founded by Jesuit Fathers 1911, present name 1973
President: Rev. THOMAS P. O'MALLEY
Chancellor: Rev. DONALD P. MERRIFIELD
Academic Vice-President: Dr JOSEPH G. JABBRA
Vice-President for Student Affairs: Dr LANE BOVE
Vice-President for Business and Finance: JOHN R. OESTER
Vice-President for Facilities Management: DAVID G. TRUMP
Associate Vice-President for Academic Affairs: Dr JOSEPH MERANTE
Registrar: ROSE ST. ONGE
Director of Admissions: MATTHEW FISSINGER
Director of Campus Ministry: FERNANDO MORENO
Director of Financial Aid: DONNA PALMER
Director of Institutional Research: Dr BRIAN HU
Library of 324,484 vols (main campus), 440,227 vols (Law School)
Number of teachers: 558 (main campus), 123 (Law School)
Number of students: 5,569 (main campus), 1,321 (Law School)

DEANS

Business: Dr JOHN T. WHOLIHAN
Science and Engineering: Dr GERARD S. JAKUBOWSKI
Loyola Law School: GERALD T. MCLAUGHLIN
Liberal Arts: Dr KENYAN CHAN
Communication and Fine Arts: Prof. THOMAS KELLY

MILLS COLLEGE

Oakland, CA 94613
Telephone: (510) 430-2255
Founded as a Seminary 1852, as a College 1885
President: JANET L. HOLMGREN
Dean of the Faculty: MARYANN KINKEAD
Dean of Students: MURIEL WHITCOMB
Director of Graduate Study: DAVID BERNSTEIN
Librarian: RENEE JADUSHLEVER
Library of 194,000 vols
Number of teachers: 94
Number of students: 1,169
Publications: *The Mills Weekly, Mills Now, Mills Quarterly* (alumnae).

MONTEREY INSTITUTE OF INTERNATIONAL STUDIES

425 Van Buren St, Monterey, CA 93940
Telephone: (408) 647-4123
Fax: (408) 647-6405
E-mail: admit@miis.edu
Founded 1955
Independent international graduate school
President: Dr RICHARD M. KRASNO
Provost: Dr STEVEN J. BAKER
Co-ordinator of Student Affairs: CAROL MCHAMER
Library of 70,000 vols
Number of students: 800

DEANS

Graduate School of International Management: Dr WILLIAM PENDERGAST
Graduate School of International Policy Studies: Dr PHILIP MORGAN
Graduate School of Translation and Interpretation: Dr DIANE DE TERRA
Graduate School of Language and Educational Linguistics: Dr RUTH LARIMER

MOUNT ST MARY'S COLLEGE

12001 Chalon Rd, Los Angeles, CA 90049-1599
Telephone: (310) 954-4000
Fax: (310) 954-4379
Founded 1925
President: Sister KAREN M. KENNELLY
Academic Vice-President: Dr JACQUELINE DOUD
Director of Admissions: KATY MURPHY
Library of 140,000 vols
Number of teachers: 185
Number of students: 1,970
Doheny Campus: 10 Chester Place, Los Angeles, Calif. 90007; tel. (213) 477-2500; f. 1962; graduate and evening college programs; Vice-President Sister KATHLEEN KELLY.

NAVAL POSTGRADUATE SCHOOL

Monterey, CA 93943
Telephone: (408) 656-2512
Fax: (408) 656-2337
Founded 1909
Superintendent: Rear Admiral ROBERT C. CHAPLIN
Chief Faculty Administrative Officer: Dr RICHARD S. ELSTER
Librarian: Dr MAXINE RENEKER
Library of 1,063,696 vols (including microform)
Number of teachers: 353
Number of students: 1,237
Publications: *Catalog, Library Periodical Holdings List* (annually).
Courses in engineering (mechanical, electrical, aeronautical, astronautical), science (oceanography, meteorology, physics, computer science), mathematics, policy science (systems management, operations research, national security affairs), operationally oriented programs (undersea warfare, space systems operations, command, control and communications, intelligence, electronic warfare systems).

NORTHROP UNIVERSITY

Los Angeles, CA 90045
Telephone: (213) 337-4413
Telex: 181000
Fax: (213) 645-4120
Founded 1942
President: JOHN R. BELJAN
Vice-President and Provost: BONNIE NEUMANN
Director of Admissions: (vacant)
Librarian: (vacant)
Library of 126,100 bound vols
Number of teachers: 50 full-time, 75 part-time
Number of students: 1,500
Departments of Aeronautical Engineering and Civil Engineering; Arts and Sciences; Business and Management; Computer and Information Sciences; Electrical Engineering, Engineering Technology; Aviation Technician Program.

OCCIDENTAL COLLEGE

Los Angeles, CA 90041
Telephone: (213) 259-2500
Founded 1887
President: JOHN B. SLAUGHTER
Vice-President for Institutional Advancement: TOBY BETHEA
Vice-President for Student Services: HAZEL J. SCOTT
Dean of the Faculty: DAVID L. AXEEN
Registrar: EVELYNE B. GLASER
Dean of Admissions: WILLIAM TINGLEY
Library of 467,000 vols
Number of teachers: 140
Number of students: 1,534

OTIS COLLEGE OF ART AND DESIGN

9045 Lincoln Blvd, Los Angeles, CA 90045
Telephone: (310) 665-6800
Founded 1918
President: NEIL HOFFMAN
Gallery Director: ANN AYRES
Registrar: RIVER MONTIJO
Library of 25,000 vols
Number of teachers: 200
Number of students: 800

PACIFIC OAKS COLLEGE

5 Westmoreland Place, Pasadena, CA 91103
Telephone: (626) 397-1300
Founded 1945
President: KATHERINE GABEL
Registrar: ELENA ROTUNNO
Academic Vice-President: MARK SCHULMAN
Librarian: DOTTY GRANGER
Library of 30,000 vols
Number of teachers: 30
Number of students: 600

PACIFIC UNION COLLEGE

Angwin, CA 94508
Telephone: (707) 965-6311
Founded 1882
President: D. MALCOLM MAXWELL
Dean: CHARLES V. BELL
Registrar: H. SUSI MUNDY
Business Manager: JOHN I. COLLINS
Chief Librarian: ADUGNAW WORKU
Library of 148,000 vols

Number of teachers: 110
Number of students: 1,800

Publications: *College Bulletin, Student Handbook, PUC Viewpoint* (quarterly).

PEPPERDINE UNIVERSITY

24255 Pacific Coast Highway, Malibu, CA 90263

Telephone: (310) 456-4000

Founded 1937 as college, attained university status 1970

President: Dr DAVID DAVENPORT
Chancellor: Dr CHARLES B. RUNNELS
Provost: Dr STEVEN CEMLEY
Librarian: NANCY KITCHEN

Library of 760,429 vols
Number of teachers: 281 full-time, including 145 professors
Number of students: 7,466

Publication: *Pepperdine People* (quarterly).

Comprises: Seaver College of Letters, Arts and Sciences; School of Law; Graduate School of Education and Psychology; School of Business and Management.

PITZER COLLEGE

1050 N. Mills Ave, Claremont, CA 91711-6110

Telephone: (909) 621-8000

Founded 1963

President: Dr MARILYN CHAPIN MASSEY
Vice-President of College Advancement: J. TERRY JONES
Dean of Admission: Dr PAUL B. RANSLOW
Dean of Faculty: Dr RONALD L. COHEN
Dean of Students: JACQUELINE DANSLER PETERSON
Registrar: VICTOR EGITTO
Librarian: Dr BONNIE CLEMENS

Library of 1,090,000 vols
Number of teachers: 65
Number of students: 740

POMONA COLLEGE

Alexander Hall, Claremont, CA 91711

Telephone: (909) 621-8000

Founded 1887

President: PETER W. STANLEY
Vice-President and Dean: LAURA MAYS HOOPES
Vice-President for Development: GARY DICOVITSKY
Vice-President and Treasurer: CARLENE MILLER
Vice-President and Dean of Students: ANN G. QUINLEY
Dean of Admissions: BRUCE POCH
Registrar: MARGARET ADORNO

Library of 1,900,000 vols
Number of teachers: 164
Number of students: 1,379

Publication: *Pomona College Magazine* (quarterly).

ST MARY'S COLLEGE OF CALIFORNIA

Moraga, CA 94575

Telephone: (510) 631-4000

Founded 1863

President: Bro. CRAIG J. FRANZ
Vice-President for Academic Affairs: Dr WILLIAM HYNES
Vice-President for Student Affairs: Bro. JACK CURRAN
Vice-President for College Relations: Bro. JEROME WEST
Vice-President for Administration and CFO: LIONEL CHAN
Vice-President for Advancement: MICHAEL A. FERRIGNO
Vice-President for Enrollment Services: MICHAEL BESEDA
Registrar: (vacant)
Library Director: STEPHANIE R. BANGERT

Library of 188,000 vols, 1,100 current periodicals
Number of teachers: 274
Number of students: 4,204

Schools of liberal arts, science, economics and business administration; graduate programs in theology, education, business, psychology and health, physical education and recreation; intercollegiate nursing course.

SAN DIEGO STATE UNIVERSITY

San Diego, CA 92182

Telephone: (619) 594-5200

Founded 1897

President: STEPHEN L. WEBER
Vice-President, Academic Affairs: NANCY A. MARLIN
Vice-President, Research, and Dean of the Graduate Division: JAMES W. COBBLE
Vice-President, Business Affairs: SALLY F. ROUSH
Vice-President, Student Affairs: DANIEL B. NOWAK
Vice-President, University Advancement: THERESA M. MENDOZA
Chair of Senate: GENE G. LAMKE
Director of Admissions and Records: CAROLYN MARLAND (acting)
Librarian: KAREN KINNEY (acting)

Library of 1,195,027 vols, 614,900 govt documents
Number of teachers: 2,386 full- and part-time
Number of students: 30,137 undergraduate and graduate

Publications: *SDSU Magazine, The Daily Aztec* (student newspaper), *Fiction International, Poetry International, Journal of Borderland Studies.*

DEANS

Business Administration: MICHAEL L. HERGERT
Engineering: PIETER A. FRICK
Arts and Letters: PAUL J. STRAND
Education: ANN I. MOREY
Extended Studies: PAULA KELLY (acting)
Health and Human Services: DOLORES A. WOZNIAK
Professional Studies and Fine Arts: JOYCE M. GATTAS
Sciences: STEPHEN B. W. ROEDER (acting)
Undergraduate Studies: CAROLE A. SCOTT
Imperial Valley Campus: KHOSROW FATEMI

SAN FRANCISCO CONSERVATORY OF MUSIC

1201 Ortega St, San Francisco, CA 94122

Telephone: (415) 564-8086

Founded 1917

President: COLIN MURDOCH
Dean: TIMOTHY BACH
Admissions Officer: Mrs COLLEEN KATZOWITZ

Library of 25,000 vols and 6,500 recordings and tapes
Number of teachers: 80
Number of students: 250

SAN FRANCISCO STATE UNIVERSITY

1600 Holloway Ave, San Francisco, CA 94132

Telephone: (415) 338-1111
Fax: (415) 338-2514

Founded 1899

President: ROBERT A. CORRIGAN
Vice-President for Student Affairs: JESSELYN SAFFOLD
Vice-President, Business and Finance: DON SCOBLE
Vice-President for Academic Affairs: THOMAS LA BELLE
Director of Enrolment Services: THOMAS RUTTER
Librarian: DEBORAH MASTERS

Library of 793,557 vols
Number of teachers: 1,331
Number of students: 27,420

SAN JOSÉ STATE UNIVERSITY

San José, CA 95192

Telephone: (408) 924-1000

Founded 1857

President: ROBERT L. CARET
Director of Admissions: JOHN BRADBURY
Director of Records: MARILYN RADISCH
Library Director: C. JAMES SCHMIDT

Library of 1,000,000 vols
Number of teachers: 1,800
Number of students: 25,000

SANTA CLARA UNIVERSITY

Santa Clara, CA 95053

Telephone: (408) 554-4764
Fax: (408) 554-2700

Founded 1851
Private control

President: PAUL L. LOCATELLI
Provost: STEPHEN A. PRIVETT
Vice-President for Administration and Finance: ROBERT D. WARREN
Vice-President for University Relations: JAMES M. PURCELL
Librarian: ELIZABETH SALZER

Library of 608,000 vols
Law library of 127,000 vols
Number of teachers: 346 full-time, 214 part-time
Number of students: 7,802

Publications: *Santa Clara, Redwood, Santa Clara Review, Santa Clara Today.*

DEANS

College of Arts and Sciences: PETER FACIONE
School of Engineering: TERRY E. SHOUP
School of Law: MACK A. PLAYER
School of Business: BARRY Z. POSNER

SAYBROOK INSTITUTE

Rollo May Center for Humanistic Studies, 450 Pacific Ave, 3rd Floor, San Francisco, CA 94133

Telephone: (415) 441-5034
Fax: (415) 441-7556

Founded 1971

President: BRUCE FRANCIS
Faculty Chair: (vacant)
Director of Admissions: KATHY TRIMBLE

Number of teachers: 39
Number of students: 260

A graduate school of psychology and human science

Publication: *Saybrook Review* (annually).

SCRIPPS COLLEGE

1030 N. Columbia Ave, Claremont, CA 91711

Telephone: (909) 621-8148

Founded 1926

President: NANCY Y. BEKAVAC
Vice-President for Development and College Relations: LINDA DAVIS TAYLOR
Dean of Faculty: RICHARD FADEM
Dean of Students: PATRICIA GOLDSMITH (acting)
Registrar: CAROL ENTLER
Director of Admissions: PATRICIA GOLDSMITH

Librarian: JUDY B. HARVEY-SAHAK

Library: 110,000 vols in Denison Library, Scripps College; 1,905,102 vols in the Honnold Library of The Claremont Colleges

Number of teachers: 92

Number of students: 704

SIMON GREENLEAF SCHOOL OF LAW

3855 E. La Palma Ave, Anaheim, CA 92807

Telephone: (714) 632-3434

Fax: (714) 630-6109

Founded 1980

Chief Executive Officer: SHANNON J. VERLEUR

Dean: WINSTON FROST

Enrollment Services: JOE WYSE

Librarian: MICHAEL BRYANT

Library of 35,000 vols

Number of teachers: 2 full-time, 21 adjunct

Number of students: 136

Graduate and Law school, evening classes only. Courses in law, Christian apologetics and international human rights; MA in faith and culture.

SONOMA STATE UNIVERSITY

Rohnert Park, CA 94928

Telephone: (707) 664-2880

Fax: (707) 664-2505

Founded 1960

President: RUBEN ARMINANA

Provost Vice-President for Academic Affairs: BERNIE GOLDSTEIN (acting)

Associate Vice-President for Enrollment Services: FRANK TANSEY

Librarian: SUSAN HARRIS

Library of 416,000 vols, 93,247 periodicals

Number of teachers: 240 (full-time), 244 (part-time)

Number of students: 6,998

SOUTHERN CALIFORNIA COLLEGE

55 Fair Drive, Costa Mesa, CA 92626

Telephone: (714) 556-3610

Fax: (714) 957-9317

Founded 1920

President: WAYNE E. KRAISS

Academic Dean: MURRAY DEMPSTER

Librarian: MARY WILSON

Library of 115,828 vols

Number of teachers: 44 full-time

Number of students: 1,200

SOUTHERN CALIFORNIA COLLEGE OF OPTOMETRY

2575 Yorba Linda Boulevard, Fullerton, CA 92831-1699

Telephone: (714) 870-7226

Founded 1904

President: LESLEY L. WALLS

Vice-President: ROBERT A. BAIRD

Dean of Academic Affairs: Dr MORRIS S. BERMAN

Dean of Student Affairs: Dr LORRAINE I. VOORHEES

Comptroller: LISA EINCK

Librarian: Mrs PATRICIA CARLSON

Library of 8,808 vols and 6,019 bound vols of journals

Number of teachers: 97

Number of students: 381

Publications: *The Alumniscope* (quarterly), *The Reflex* (annually), *SCCO Admissions Catalog* (every 2 years).

STANFORD UNIVERSITY

Stanford, CA 94305

Telephone: (415) 723-2300

Founded 1885

President: GERHARD CASPER

Provost: CONDOLEEZZA RICE

Academic Secretary: SUSAN SCHOFIELD

Dean of Admissions: JAMES MONTOYA

Dean of Student Affairs: MARC WAIS

Registrar: ROGER PRINTUP

Chief Information Officer: GLEN MUELLER

Library: see Libraries

Number of teachers: 1,455

Number of students: 14,044

Publications: *Stanford Law Review, Stanford Observer* (8 a year), *Alumni Almanac* (quarterly).

DEANS

Graduate School of Business: A. MICHAEL SPENCE

School of Earth Sciences: FRANKLIN ORR

School of Education: RICHARD SHAVELSON

School of Engineering: JOHN HENNESSY

School of Humanities and Sciences: JOHN SHOVEN

School of Law: PAUL BREST

School of Medicine: EUGENE BAUER

DIRECTORS

Hoover Institution: JOHN RAISIAN (see also under Libraries)

Stanford Linear Accelerator Center: BURTON RICHTER

PROFESSORS

ABERNETHY, D., Political Science
ADAMS, J., Mechanical Engineering, Industrial Engineering
ADMATI, A. R., Business
AGRAS, W. S., Psychiatry
ALDERMAN, E., Medicine
ALDRICH, R. W., Molecular and Cell Physiology
ALEXANDER, J. C., Law
AMEMIYA, T., Economics
ANDERSEN, H., Chemistry
ANDERSSON, T. M., German Studies
AOKI, M., Economics
APOSTOLIDES, J. M., French and Italian Drama
ARVIN, A. M., Microbiology and Immunology, Paediatrics
ATKIN, J. M., Education
AZIZ, K., Petroleum Engineering
BABCOCK, B., Law
BADEN, J., Anaesthesia
BAGANOFF, D., Aeronautics and Astronautics
BAKER, B. S., Developmental Biology, Biological Sciences
BAKER, K., History
BALDWIN, R., Biochemistry
BANDURA, A., Psychology
BANKMAN, J., Law
BARKER, L., Political Science
BARNETT, C., Anthropology
BARNETT, D., Materials Science and Mechanical Engineering
BARON, D. P., Political Science, Economics, Business
BARON, J. N., Business
BARTON, J., Law
BASCH, P., Health Research and Policy
BAUER, E. A., Dermatology
BAUGH, J., Linguistics, Education
BAYLOR, D., Neurobiology
BEASLEY, M., Electrical Engineering, Applied Physics
BEAVER, W. H., Business
BEINEN, J. S., History
BENDER, J., English, Comparative Literature
BENDOR, J., Business, Political Science
BENSCH, K. G., Pathology
BERG, P., Biochemistry
BERGER, K., Music
BERMAN, R. A., German Studies, Comparative Literature
BERNHARDT, E., German Studies
BERNHEIM, B. D., Economics
BERNSTEIN, B., History
BERTRAND, M., French and Italian
BIENENSTOCK, A. I., Applied Physics, Materials Science
BLANKENBECLER, R., Stanford Linear Accelerator Center
BLASCHKE, T., Medicine
BLAU, H. M., Molecular Pharmacology
BLOOM, D. M., Electrical Engineering
BLOOM, E., Stanford Linear Accelerator Center
BLUME, K., Medicine
BONINI, C., Business
BOOTHROYD, J. C., Microbiology and Immunology
BOSKIN, M., Economics
BOTSTEIN, D., Genetics
BOWER, G. H., Psychology
BOWMAN, C., Mechanical Engineering
BOXER, S., Chemistry
BOYD, S. P., Electrical Engineering
BOYER, A. L., Radiation Oncology
BRADY, D., Political Science, Business
BRATMAN, M., Philosophy
BRAUMAN, J. J., Chemistry
BRAVMAN, J. C., Materials Science
BREIDENBACH, M., Stanford Linear Accelerator Center
BREITROSE, H. S., Communication
BRESNAHAN, T., Business, Economics
BRESNAN, J., Linguistics
BREST, P. A., Law
BRIDGES, E. M., Education
BRODSKY, S., Stanford Linear Accelerator Center
BROWN, B., Health Research and Policy
BROWN, G. H., Classics, English
BROWN, G. E., Geology, Environmental Sciences
BROWN, J. M., Radiation Oncology
BRUMFIEL, G., Mathematics
BULOW, J. T., Business
BUMP, D. W., Mathematics
BURGELMAN, R. A., Business
BURKE, D. L., Stanford Linear Accelerator Center
BYER, R., Applied Physics
CABRERA, B., Physics
CALFEE, R. C., Education
CAMARILLO, A. M., History
CAMPBELL, A. M., Biological Sciences
CAMPBELL, T. J., Law
CANTWELL, B., Aeronautics, Mechanical Engineering
CAPELLETTI, M., Law
CARLSON, R., Business, Industrial Engineering
CARLSSON, G., Mathematics
CARNOY, M., Education
CARSON, C., History
CARTER, D., Functional Restoration, Mechanical Engineering
CASE, R., Education
CASEY, E. B., English
CASPER, G., Political Science, Law
CASPER, R., Psychiatry
CASTLE, T., English
CAVA, R. J.
CAZELLES, B., French and Italian
CHAFFEE, S., Political Science, Communication
CHAO, A. W., Stanford Linear Accelerator Center
CHERITON, D. R., Computer Science, Electrical Engineering
CHU, S., Physics
CLAERBOUT, J. F., Geophysics
CLARK, E., Linguistics
CLARK, H. H., Psychology
CLAYTON, D. Developmental Biology
COHEN, A., Music
COHEN, E. G., Education, Sociology
COHEN, H. J., Paediatrics
COHEN, P. J., Mathematics
COHEN, R. L., Mathematics

COHEN, S. N., Genetics, Medicine
COHEN, W., Law
COLLIER, G., Anthropology
COLLIER, J. F., Anthropology
COLLMAN, J. P., Chemistry
CONLEY, F., Neurosurgery
COOPER, A., Medicine
CORK, L., Comparative Medicine
CORN, W., Art
COTTLE, R. W., Operations Research
COVER, T. M., Electrical Engineering, Statistics
COX, D. R., Paediatrics, Genetics
COX, D., Electrical Engineering
CRABTREE, G., Developmental Biology, Pathology
CUBAN, L., Education
CUTKOSKY, M. R., Mechanical Engineering
CUTLER, R. W. P., Neurology
DATAR, S. M., Business
DAVID, P. A., Economics
DAVIS, M. M., Microbiology and Immunology
DAVIS, R., Biochemistry, Genetics
DE MICHELI, G., Electrical Engineering, Computer Science
DEBUSK, R. F., Medicine
DEKKER, G. G., English
DEMENT, W. C., Psychiatry
DENNY, M. W., Mechanical Engineering, Biological Sciences
DEVINE, A., Classics
DI PIERO, S., English
DICKSON, L., Law
DICKSON, L. E., Law
DIMOPOULOS, S., Physics
DJERASSI, C., Chemistry
DONALDSON, S., Radiation Oncology
DONIACH, S., Applied Physics, Physics
DONOHO, D., Statistics
DONOHUE, J. J., III, Law
DORFAN, J., Stanford Linear Accelerator Center
DORFMAN, L., Neurology
DORFMAN, R. F., Pathology
DRETSKE, F., Philosophy
DUFFIE, J. D., Business
DUPRE, J. A., Philosophy
DUPUY, J.-P., French and Italian
DURHAM, W., Anthropology
DUTTON, R., Electrical Engineering
DUUS, P., History
EATON, J. K., Mechanical Engineering
EAVES, B. C., Operations Research
ECKERT, P., Linguistics
EFRON, B., Statistics, Health Research and Policy
EGBERT, P., Ophthalmology
EHRLICH, P. R., Biological Sciences
EINAUDI, M., Geological and Environmental Sciences
EISEN, A. M., Religious Studies, Sociology
EISENHARDT, K. M., Industrial Engineering
EISNER, E. W., Education
ELIASHBERG, Mathematics
EMMONS, T., History
ENGLEMAN, E., Pathology, Medicine
ENTHOVEN, A., Health Research and Policy, Business
ENZMANN, D., Radiology
EPEL, D., Biological Sciences
ERNST, W. G., Geology, Environmental Sciences
ETCHEMENDY, J. W., Philosophy
EVANS, J. M., English
FAINSTAT, T., Gynaecology and Obstetrics
FAJARDO, L., Pathology
FALCON, W. P., Food Research Institute, Economics
FALKOW, S., Microbiology and Immunology, Medicine
FARQUHAR, J. W., Health Research and Policy, Medicine
FATHMAN, C., Medicine
FAURE, B. R., Religious Studies
FAYER, M., Chemistry
FEE, W., Surgery
FEFERMAN, S., Mathematics, Philosophy
FEIGENBAUM, E. A., Computer Science
FELDMAN, D., Medicine
FELDMAN, M. W., Biological Sciences
FELSTINER, L. J., English
FEREJOHN, J. A., Business Economics, Political Science
FERNANDEZ, R., Sociology, Business
FERZIGER, J. H., Mechanical Engineering
FETTER, A. L., Physics, Applied Physics
FIELDS, K., English
FLANAGAN, R., Business
FLAVELL, J., Psychology
FLEISHMAN, L., Slavic Languages and Literatures
FLIEGELMAN, J. W., English
FLYNN, M., Computer Science, Electrical Engineering
FOLLESDAL, D., Philosophy
FOSTER, G., Business
FRANCKE, U., Genetics, Paediatrics
FRANK, C., Materials Science, Chemistry, Chemical Engineering
FRANKLIN, M. A., Law
FREDRICKSON, G., History
FREEDMAN, E., History
FREIDIN, G., Slavic Languages and Literature
FREIHA, F., Urology
FRIED, B., Law
FRIEDMAN, J. H., Statistics
FRIEDMAN, L. M., Political Science, Law
FRIES, J. F., Medicine
FULLER, G. G., Chemical Engineering
FURTHMAYR, Pathology
GAGNIER, R., English
GARCIA-MOLINA, H., Computer Science, Electrical Engineering
GAST, A. P., Chemical Engineering, Chemistry
GELPI, A. J., English
GELPI, B. C., English
GIBBONS, J. F., Electrical Engineering
GIBBS, J., Anthropology
GILLESPIE, G., German Studies, Comparative Literature
GILSON, R. J., Law
GLADER, B. E., Paediatrics
GLAZER, G. M., Radiology
GLOVER, G. H., Electrical Engineering, Radiology
GLYNN, P. W., Operations Research
GOFFINET, D., Radiation Oncology
GOLDSTEIN, P. L., Law
GOLUB, G. H., Computer Science
GOODE, R., Surgery
GOODMAN, J. W., Electrical Engineering
GOODWIN, D., Radiology
GORELICK, S. M., Geological and Environmental Sciences, Geophysics
GORIS, M., Radiology
GOULD, W. B., Law
GRAHAM, S. A., Petroleum Engineering, Geological and Environmental Sciences
GRANOVETTER, M., Sociology
GRAY, G., Medicine
GRAY, R., Electrical Engineering
GREELY, H. T., Law
GREEN, P. B., Biology
GREENBERG, H., Medicine, Microbiology and Immunology
GREENBERG, P., Medicine
GREENO, J., Psychology, Education
GREY, T. C., Law
GRUMET, F. C., Pathology
GRUNDFEST, J. A., Law
GUIBAS, L. J., Computer Science
GUILLEMINAULT, C., Psychiatry
GUMBRECHT, French and Italian, Comparative Literature
HABER, S. H., History
HAERTEL, E. H., Education
HAKUTA, K., Education
HALL, R., Economics
HALLEY, J. E., Law
HALLIBURTON, D., English, Comparative Literature
HAMMOND, P., Economics
HANAWALT, P. C., Dermatology, Biological Sciences
HANNAH, D., Art
HANNAN, M., Sociology, Business
HANRAHAN, P. M., Electrical Engineering, Computer Science
HANSON, R., Aeronautics and Astronautics, Mechanical Engineering
HARBAUGH, J. W., Geological and Environmental Sciences, Petroleum Engineering
HARRIS, D. J., Economics
HARRIS, E., Medicine
HARRIS, J. S., Applied Physics, Electrical Engineering
HARRIS, S. E., Electrical Engineering, Applied Physics
HARRISON, J. M., Business
HARRISON, R. P., French and Italian
HARRISON, W. A., Applied Physics
HARVEY, J., Music
HAUSMAN, W., Business, Industrial Engineering
HEATH, S. B., English, Linguistics, Education
HELLER, H. C., Biological Sciences
HELLER, T. C., Law
HENNESSY, J., Computer Science, Electrical Engineering
HENTZ, V. R., Functional Restoration
HERZENBERG, L. A., Genetics
HESSELINK, Applied Physics, Electrical Engineering, Aeronautics
HESTER, R. M., French and Italian
HEWETT, T., Petroleum Engineering
HIMEL, T. M., Stamford Linear Accelerator Center
HINTZ, R., Paediatrics
HLATKY, M. A., Health Research and Policy, Medicine
HODGSON, K., Chemistry
HOFFMAN, A. R., Medicine, Molecular and Cell Biology
HOFFMAN, B. B., Medicine
HOFMANN, W., Neurology
HOGNESS, D. S., Biochemistry, Developmental Biology
HOLLOWAY, C., Business
HOLLOWAY, D., Political Science
HOLMAN, H. R., Medicine
HOMSY, G., Petroleum Engineering, Chemical Engineering
HOPPE, R., Radiation Oncology
HORNE, R. N., Petroleum Engineering
HOROWITZ, L., Psychology
HOWARD, R. A., Business
HOWELL, J. E., Business
HSUEH, A., Gynaecology and Obstetrics
HUESTIS, W., Chemistry
HUGHES, T. J., Civil Engineering, Mechanical Engineering
IGLEHART, D. L., Operations Research
INAN, U. S., Electrical Engineering
INGLE, J., Geological and Environmental Sciences
JACOBS, C. D., Medicine
JAMISON, R. L., Medicine
JARDETZKY, O., Molecular Pharmacology
JAROS, J. A., Stanford Linear Accelerator Center
JEFFREY, R. B., Radiology
JOHNSTONE, I. M., Statistics, Health Research and Policy
JONES, P., Biological Sciences
JOSLING, T. E., Food Research Institute
JOURNEL, A. G., Geological and Environmental Sciences, Petroleum Engineering
JUCKER, J., Industrial Engineering
KAHN, H., History
KAHN, M. S., Art
KAILATH, T., Electrical Engineering
KAISER, A. D., Developmental Biology, Biochemistry
KALLOSH, R., Physics, Mathematics
KAPITULNIK, A., Applied Physics, Physics
KAPP, D. S., Radiation Oncology
KATCHADOURIAN, H. A., Psychiatry
KATZNELSON, Y., Mathematics
KAY, M., Computer Science, Linguistics
KAZOVSKY, L., Electrical Engineering

KELMAN, M. G., Law
KELSEY, J., Health Research and Policy
KEMPSON, R. L., Pathology
KENDIG, J., Anaesthesia
KENNEDY, D. M., History
KENNEDY, DONALD, Education, Biological Sciences
KERCKHOFF, S. P., Mathematics
KINO, G. S., Applied Physics, Electrical Engineering
KIPARSKY, R. P., Linguistics
KIREMIDJIAN, A. S., Civil Engineering
KIRST, M., Education, Business
KITANIDIS, P. K., Civil Engineering
KLEIN, R. G., Anthropology
KNORR, W., Philosophy, Classics
KNUDSEN, E. I., Neurobiology
KOLLMAN, N. S., History
KOPITO, R. R., Molecular and Cell Physiology, Biological Sciences
KORN, D., Pathology
KORNBERG, R. D., Structural Biology
KOSEFF, J. R., Civil Engineering
KOVACH, R. L., Geophysics
KRAEMER, H., Psychiatry
KRASNER, S., Political Science
KRAWINKLER H., Civil Engineering
KRAWITZ, J. Communication
KREHBIEL, K., Business, Political Science
KRENSKY, A. M., Paediatrics
KREPS, D., Economics, Business
KRUEGER, A. O., Economics
KRUGER, C. H., Mechanical Engineering
KRUGMAN, P. R., Economics
KRUMBOLTZ, J. D., Education, Psychology
KURZ, M., Economics
L'HEUREUX, English
LAI, T., Statistics
LAL, R., Business
LAMB, E., Gynaecology and Obstetrics
LAMBERT, R., Business
LAPIDUS, G. W., Political Science
LATCOMBE, J.-C., Computer Science
LAU, L. J., Economics
LAUGHLIN, R., Physics, Applied Physics
LAZEAR, E. P., Business
LEBEN, W., Linguistics
LECKIE, J., Geological and Environmental Sciences, Civil Engineering
LEE, H., Industrial Engineering, Business
LEHMAN, I. R., Biochemistry
LEIFER, L., Mechanical Engineering
LEITH, D. W. G. S., Stanford Linear Accelerator Center
LENOIR, T., History
LEPPER, M., Psychology, Education
LERER, S., English
LEVIN, H. M., Education
LEVITT, M., Cell Biology
LEVITT, R.E., Civil Engineering
LEVY, R., Medicine
LEWIS, J. W., Political Science
LEWIS, S., Art
LINDE, A., Physics
LINDENBERGER, H. S., Comparative Literature, English
LINK, M., Paediatrics
LIOU, J., Geology and Environment Sciences
LITT, I., Paediatrics
LIU, T.-P., Mathematics
LONG, S., Biochemistry, Biological Sciences
LOUGEE, C., History
LOWE, D. R., Geology and Environmental Sciences
LUENBERGER, D. G., Operations Research, Electrical Engineering
LYONS, C. R., English, Drama, Comparative Literature
MACCORMACK, R., Aeronautics and Astronautics
MACURDY, T., Economics
MADIX, R. J., Chemistry, Chemical Engineering
MANCALL, M., History
MANLEY, J. F., Political Science
MANNA, Z., Computer School
MANSOUR, T. E., Molecular Pharmacology
MARKMAN, E., Psychology
MARKUS, H., Psychology
MARMOR, M., Ophthalmology
MARTIN, J., Sociology, Business
MASS, J., History
MATIN, A., Microbiology and Immunology
MAZE, M., Anaesthesia
MAZZE, R. I., Anaesthesia
MCCALL, M., Continuing Studies, Classics
MCCARTHY, J., Electrical Engineering, Computer Science
MCCARTY, P. L., Civil Engineering
MCCLUSKEY, E. J., Electrical Engineering and Computer Science
MCCONNELL, H. M., Chemistry
MCDERMOTT, R., Education
MCDEVITT, H. O., Microbiology and Immunology, Medicine
MCDONALD, J. G., Business
MCDOUGALL, I. R., Radiology, Medicine
MCGUIRE, J., Paediatrics, Dermatology
MCKAY, D., Structural Biology
MCKINNON, R. I., Economics
MCLAUGHLIN, M. W., Education
MCMAHAN, U. J., Neurobiology
MEIER, G. M., Business
MELMON, K., Molecular Pharmacology, Medicine
MENDELSON, H., Business
MENDEZ, M. A., Law
MERIGAN, T., Medicine
MEYER, J. W., Education, Sociology
MIDDLEBROOK, D., English
MILGRAM, R. J., Mathematics
MILGROM, P., Business, Economics
MILLER, D. C., Cardiothoracic Surgery
MILLER, W. F., Computer Science, Business
MINTS, G., Computer Science, Philosophy
MOCARSKI, E. S., Microbiology and Immunology
MOE, T. M., Political Science
MOIN, P., Mechanical Engineering
MONTGOMERY, D. B., Business
MOONEY, H. A., Biological Sciences
MOOS, R. H., Psychiatry
MORAVCSIK, J. M., Philosophy
MORRIS, I., History, Classics
MUDIMBE, V. Y., Classics, Comparative Literature, French and Italian
MYERS, B., Medicine
MYERS, R. M., Genetics
NAIMARK, N., History
NEALE, M. A., Business
NELSON, D. V., Mechanical Engineering
NELSON, W. J., Molecular and Cell Physiology
NEWSOME, W. T., Neurobiology
NIEDERHUBER, J., Surgery, Microbiology and Immunology
NIX, W. D., Materials Science
NODDINGS, N., Education
NOLL, R., Business, Political Science, Economics
NORTHWAY, W. H., Radiology, Paediatrics
NOYES, H. P., Stanford Linear Accelerator Center
NUR, A., Geophysics
NUSSE, R., Developmental Biology
OKIMOTO, D. I., Political Science
OKIN, S., Political Science
OKSENBERG, M. C., Political Science
OLIGER, J., Computer Science
OLKIN, I., Education, Statistics
OLSHEN, R., Electrical Engineering, Statistics, Health Research and Policy
O'REILLY, C. A., Business
O'REILLY, R., Medicine
ORGEL, S., English
ORNSTEIN, D., Mathematics
ORR, F., Chemical Engineering, Petroleum Engineering
ORTOLANO, L., Civil Engineering
OSGOOD, B. G., Mathematics
OSHEROFF, D., Physics, Applied Physics
OYER, P. E., Cardiothoracic Surgery
PACKENHAM, R., Political Science
PADILLA, A., Education
PAPANICOLAOU, G. C., Mathematics
PARHAM, P., Structural Biology, Microbiology and Immunology
PARKER, P., English, Comparative Literature, French and Italian
PARKINSON, B. W., Aeronautics
PATE-CORNELL, E., Industrial Engineering
PATELL, J., Business
PAULSON, B., Civil Engineering
PEARSON, S., Food Research Institute, Economics
PEASE, R., Electrical Engineering
PECK, A., Food Research Institute
PECORA, R., Chemistry
PENCAVEL, J., Economics
PERKASH, I., Urology
PERL, M. L., Stanford Linear Accelerator Center
PERLOFF, M., English, Comparative Literature
PERRY, J., Philosophy
PERRY, W., Engineering, Organizational Research
PESKIN, M., Stanford Linear Accelerator Center
PETERS, P. S., Linguistics
PETROSIAN, V., Physics, Applied Physics
PFEFFER, J., Business
PFEFFERBAUM, A., Psychiatry
PFLEIDERER, P., Business
PHILLIPS, D., Philosophy, Education
PINSKY, P. M., Mechanical Engineering, Electrical Engineering
PLUMMER, J., Electrical Engineering
POLAN, M., Gynaecology and Obstetrics
POLHEMUS, R., English
POLINSKY, A., Law
POLLARD, D. D., Geological and Environmental Sciences, Geophysics
POPP, R., Medicine
PORRAS, J., Business
PORTEUS, E., Business
POWELL, J., Aeronautics, Mechanical Engineering
POWERS, D. A., Biological Sciences
PRATT, M., Spanish and Portuguese, Comparative Literature
PRATT, V. R., Computer Science
PREDMORE, M., Spanish and Portuguese
PRESCOTT, C., Stanford Linear Accelerator Center
PRINCE, D. A., Neurology
PRINZ, F. B., Mechanical Engineering, Materials Science
PROBER, C. G., Microbiology and Immunology, Paediatrics
RABIN, R. L., Law
RABKIN, R., Medicine
RADIN, M., Law
RAFFIN, T. A., Molecular and Cell Physiology, Medicine
RAKOVE, J., History
RAMIREZ, F., Sociology, Education
RANDELL, R., Art
RATNER, M., Mathematics
RAY, M. L., Business
RAY, P. M., Biological Sciences
REBHOLZ, R., English
REEVES, B., Communication
REISS, P. C., Business
REITZ, B., Cardiothoracic Surgery
REMINGTON, J. S., Medicine
REYNOLDS, W. C., Mechanical Engineering, Aeronautics and Astronautics
RHODE, D. L., Law
RICE, C., Political Science
RICHTER, B., Stanford Linear Accelerator Center
RICKFORD, J., Education, Linguistics
RIDGEWAY, C., Sociology
RIGGS, D., English
RISCH, N. J., Genetics
RIVERS, D., Political Science
ROBERTS, D. F., Communication
ROBERTS, D. J., Economics, Business
ROBERTS, P., Civil Engineering

ROBERTS, R. L., History
ROBERTSON, C. R., Chemical Engineering
ROBINSON, O., German Studies
ROBINSON, P., History
ROBINSON, W. S., Medicine
RODRIGUE, A., History
ROHLEN, T. P., Education
ROMER, P.
ROSALDO, R., Anthropology
ROSENBERG, N., Economics
ROSENHAN, D., Law and Psychology
ROSS, J., Chemical Engineering, Chemistry
ROSS, L., Psychology
ROTH, B., Mechanical Engineering
ROTH, R. A., Molecular Pharmacology
ROTH, W., Psychiatry
ROUGHGARDEN, J., Geophysics, Biological Sciences
RUFFINELLI-ALTESOR, J., Spanish and Portuguese
RUGAR, D.
RUMELHART, D. E., Computer Science, Psychology
SAG, I. A., Linguistics
SALDIVAR, R., English, Comparative Literature
SALONER, G., Business
SAMUELSON, K., Communication
SAPOLSKY, R. M., Biological Sciences
SARASWAT, K., Electrical Engineering
SCHATZBERG, Psychiatry
SCHELLER, R. H., Molecular and Cell Physiology, Biological Sciences
SCHIMKE, R. T., Biological Sciences
SCHMITTER, R., Political Science
SCHNAPP, J. T., French and Italian, Comparative Literature
SCHNEIDER, S., Civil Engineering, Biological Sciences
SCHOEN, R., Mathematics
SCHOLES, M. S., Business, Law
SCHOOLNIK, G. K., Microbiology and Immunology, Medicine
SCHRIER, S. L., Medicine
SCHULMAN, H., Neurobiology
SCHUPBACH, Slavic Languages and Literatures
SCHURMAN, D., Functional Restoration
SCHWETTMAN, H. A., Physics
SCOTT, M. P., Developmental Biology, Genetics
SCOTT, W. R., Education, Health Research and Policy, Business, Sociology
SEAVER, P., History
SERRES, M., French and Italian
SHAPIRO, L., Developmental Biology, Genetics
SHARPE, W. F., Business
SHAVELSON, R., Psychology, Education
SHEEHAN, J. J., History
SHOOTER, E. M., Neurobiology
SHORTLIFFE, Medicine, Computer Science
SHORTLIFFE, L., Urology
SHOVEN, J., Humanities and Sciences, Economics
SHULMAN, L., Education
SIBLEY, R. K., Pathology
SIEGMAN, A. E., Applied Physics, Electrical Engineering
SIEGMUND, D. O., Statistics
SIEMANN, R., Stanford Linear Accelerator Center
SILVERBERG, G. D., Neurosurgery
SIMON, L., Mathematics
SIMON, W., Law
SIMONI, R., Biological Sciences
SIMONSON, I., Business
SINCLAIR, R., Materials Science
SINGLETON, K., Business
SLEEP, N., Geophysics
SMITH, M., Education
SMITH, S. J., Molecular and Cell Physiology
SNIDERMAN, P., Political Science
SNIPP, C. M.
SNOW, R. E., Psychology, Education
SOLOMON, E., Chemistry
SOMERO, G., Biological Sciences
SOMERVILLE, C., Biological Sciences
SORRENTINO, G., English
SPENCE, A. M., Business
SPIEGEL, D., Psychiatry
SPRINGER, G., Mechanical Engineering, Civil Engineering, Aeronautics
SPUDICH, J. A., Biochemistry, Developmental Biology
SRINIVASAN, V., Business
STAMEY, T. A., Urology
STANSKI, D. R., Anaesthesia
STANSKY, P. D. L., History
STARRETT, D. A., Economics
STEBBINS, J., Geological and Environmental Sciences
STEELE, C., Psychology
STEELE, C. H., Mechanical Engineering, Aeronautics and Astronautics
STEELE, C. M., Psychology
STEINMAN, L., Neurology, Paediatrics
STEPHENS, S., Classics
STEVENS, D., Medicine
STEVENSON, D., Gynaecology and Obstetrics, Paediatrics
STIGLITZ, J., Economics
STINSON, E., Cardiothoracic Surgery
STOCKDALE, F., Biological Sciences, Medicine
STREET, R. L., Mechanical Engineering, Civil Engineering
STROBER, M., Education
STROBER, S., Medicine
STRYER, L., Neurobiology
STURROCK, P. A., Physics, Applied Physics
SULLIVAN, K., Law
SUNG, R. J., Medicine
SUSSKIND, L., Physics
SUSSMAN, H., Pathology
SUTTON, R. I., Business, Industrial Engineering
SWEENEY, J., Engineering, Economic Systems
SWITZER, P., Statistics, Geological and Environmental Sciences
TALLENT, E., English
TATUM, C. B., Civil Engineering
TAYLOR, C., Psychiatry
TAYLOR, J. B., Economics
TAYLOR, R. E., Physics, Stanford Linear Accelerator Center
THOMAS, E. A. C., Psychology
THOMPSON, B. H., Law
THOMPSON, S., Biological Sciences
THORESEN, C. E., Psychology, Education
TINKLENBERG, J., Psychiatry
TOBAGI, F., Electrical Engineering, Computer Science
TRAUGOTT, E. C., Linguistics, English
TREGGIARI, S., History, Classics
TROST, B., Chemistry
TSIEN, R., Molecular and Cellular Physiology
TUMA, N., Sociology
TUNE, B., Paediatrics
TURNER, P., Art
TVERSKY, A., Psychology
TYACK, D. B., Education, History
TYLER, G., Electrical Engineering
UEDA, M., Comparative Literature, Asian Languages
ULLMAN, J. D., Electrical Engineering, Computer Science
VALDES, G., Education, Spanish and Portuguese
VAN BENTHEM, J. F., Philosophy
VAN HORNE, J. C., Business
VEINOTT, A., Operations Research
VITOUSEK, P., Biological Sciences
WAGONER, R. V., Physics
WALBOT, V., Biological Sciences
WALD, M. S., Sociology, Law
WALKER, A., Applied Physics, Physics
WALKER, D., Education
WANDELL, B. A., Psychology
WANG, J., Comparative Literature, Asian Languages
WANG, T. S.-F., Pathology
WARNKE, R., Pathology
WASOW, T., Linguistics, Philosophy
WATT, W., Biological Sciences
WEBER, C., Drama
WEINGAST, B. R., Political Science, Economics
WEISBERG, R., Law
WEISSMAN, I., Biological Sciences, Developmental Biology, Pathology
WENDER, P., Chemistry
WEXLER, L., Radiology
WHITLOCK, J., Molecular Pharmacology
WHITTEMORE, A., Health Research and Policy
WIDROW, B., Electrical Engineering
WILLIAMS, J. C., Food Research Institute
WILSON, R. B., Economics, Business
WINE, J., Molecular and Cell Physiology, Psychology
WINOGRAD, T., Computer Sciences
WIRTH, J. D., History
WOJCICKI, S. G., Physics
WOLF, A., Anthropology
WOLFSON, M., Economics, Business
WOOLEY, B. A., Electrical Engineering
WRIGHT, G., History, Economics
WRIGHT, P., Business
YAMAMOTO, Y., Electrical Engineering, Applied Physics
YANAGISAKO, S. J., Anthropology
YANOFSKY, C., Biological Sciences
YARBRO-BEJARANO, Y., Spanish and Portuguese
YEARIAN, M. R., Physics
YEARLEY, L., Religious Studies
YESAVAGE, J., Psychiatry
YOTOPOULOS, P. A., Food Research Institute
ZAJONC, R. B., Psychology
ZARE, R. N., Physics, Chemistry
ZARINS, C. K., Surgery
ZIMBARDO, P. G., Psychology
ZIPPERSTEIN, S. J., History
ZOBACK, M., Geophysics

THOMAS AQUINAS COLLEGE

10000 N. Ojai Rd, Santa Paula, CA 93060
Telephone: (805) 525-4417

Founded 1971
Private control

President: THOMAS E. DILLON
Dean: KEVIN D. KOLBECK
Vice-President of Finance and Administration: PETER L. DE LUCA
Vice-President for Development: DANIEL J. GRIMM
Librarian: VILTIS A. JATULIS

Number of students: 216

UNITED STATES INTERNATIONAL UNIVERSITY

10455 Pomerado Rd, San Diego, CA 92131
Telephone: (619) 635-4772
Fax: (619) 635-4739

Founded 1952
Private university

President: Dr GARRY D. HAYS
Vice-Presidents: ALTHIA DEGRAFT-JOHNSON, JOHN SCHAEDLER, JOSEPH MARRON, RICHARD ABBOTT

INTERNATIONAL CAMPUSES

USIU—Mexico (Universidad Internacional de Mexico, A.C.): Alvaro Obregon 110, Colonia Roma, 06700 México, DF, Mexico; Dir SUSANNE WAGNER.

USIU—Africa: POB 14634, Nairobi, Kenya; Dir Dr FREIDA BROWN.

UNIVERSITY OF CALIFORNIA

Office of the President: University Hall, Berkeley, CA 94720

Founded 1868

Campuses at Berkeley, Davis, Irvine, Los Angeles, Riverside, San Diego, San Francisco, Santa Barbara, and Santa Cruz

UNIVERSITY-WIDE OFFICERS

President: RICHARD ATKINSON
Senior Vice-President, Academic Affairs: C. JUDSON KING
Senior Vice-President, Business and Finance: V. WAYNE KENNEDY
Vice-President (Agriculture and Natural Resources): W. R. GOMES
Vice-President (University and External Relations): WILLIAM B. BAKER
Vice-President (Health Affairs): CORNELIUS L. HOPPER

OFFICERS OF THE REGENTS

General Counsel of the Regents: JAMES E. HOLST
Secretary to the Regents: LEIGH TRIVETTE
Treasurer of the Regents: HERBERT M. GORDON

Library: see Libraries
Number of teachers: 8,776
Number of students: 157,331

University of California, Berkeley

Berkeley, CA 94720

Telephone: (510) 642-6000

Established 1868

Chancellor: ROBERT M. BERDAHL
Vice-Chancellor and Provost: CAROL T. CHRIST
Vice-Chancellor for Research: JOSEPH CERNY
University Librarian: PETER LYMAN

Number of teachers: 1,783
Number of students: 31,123

DEANS

Graduate Division: JOSEPH CERNY
College of Environmental Design: HARRISON FRAKER
College of Chemistry: ALEXIS T. BELL
College of Engineering: PAUL GRAY
College of Letters and Science: CAROL T. CHRIST (Provost)
College of Natural Resources: GORDON RAUSSER
Institute of International and Area Studies: RICHARD M. BUXBAUM
School of Business Administration: WILLIAM HASLER
School of Education: EUGENE GARCIA
School of Journalism: ORVILLE SCHELL
School of Law: HERMA HILL KAY
School of Information Management and System: HAL VARIAN
School of Optometry: ANTHONY ADAMS
School of Public Health: PATRICIA BUFFLER
Graduate School of Public Policy: EUGENE SMOLENSKY
School of Social Welfare: JAMES MIDGLEY
University Extension: MARY METZ

CHAIRMEN OF DEPARTMENTS

College of Letters and Science:

Afro-American Studies: PERCY HINTZEN
Anthropology: NANCY SHEPER-HUGHES
Art, History: HARVEY STAHL
Art, Practice: JAMES BRESLIN
Asian-American Studies: MICHAEL OMI
Astronomy: JOHN ARONS
Classics: MARK GRIFFITH (acting)
Comparative Literature: RALPH J. HEXTER
Demography, Graduate Group: EUGENE A. HAMMEL
Economics: ROBERT M. ANDERSON
English: RALPH RADER
Ethnic Studies: ELAINE KIM
French: VINCENT KAUFMAN
Geography: RICHARD WALKER
Geology and Geophysics: WALTER ALVAREZ
German: ROBERT HOLUB
History: REGINALD ZELNIK
Human Biodynamics: GEORGE A. BROOKS (acting)
Integrative Biology: ROY CALDWELL
Italian: STEVEN BOTTERILL
Linguistics: LARRY HYMAN
Mathematics: CALVIN C. MOORE
Molecular and Cell Biology: JOHN GERHART, ALEXANDER GLAZER
Music: OLLY WILSON
Near Eastern Studies: DAVID STRONACH
Philosophy: BRUCE VERMAZEN
Physics: ROGER FALCONE
Political Science: ROBERT M. PRICE
Psychology: SHELDON ZEDECK
Rhetoric: ANTHONY CASCARDI
Scandinavian: JOHN LINDOW
Slavic Languages and Literatures: DAVID FRICK
Sociology: MICHAEL BULRAWOY
South and Southeast Asian Studies: ROBERT GOLDMAN
Spanish and Portuguese: GWEN KIRKPATRICK
Statistics: PETER BICKEL
Women's Studies: CAROL B. STACK

College of Chemistry:

Chemical Engineering: SIMON GOREN

School of Education: EUGENE GARCIA

College of Engineering:

Civil Engineering: DAVID ASHLEY
Electrical Engineering and Computer Sciences: RANDY H. KATZ
Industrial Engineering and Operations Research: CANDACE YANO
Materials Science and Mineral Engineering: THOMAS M. DEVINE
Mechanical Engineering: DAVID BOGY
Naval Architecture and Offshore Engineering: R. W. YEUNG
Nuclear Engineering: WILLIAM KASTENBERG

College of Environmental Design:

Architecture: DONLYN LYNDON
City and Regional Planning: MICHAEL SOUTHWORTH
Landscape Architecture: MICHAEL LAURIE

Graduate School of Journalism: ORVILLE SCHELL

Law School: HERMA HILL KAY

College of Natural Resources:

Agricultural and Resource Economics: DAVID ZILBERMAN
Environment Science, Policy and Management: JOE R. MCBRIDE
Nutritional Sciences: BARRY SHANE
Plant Biology: WILHELM GRUISSEN

School of Public Health: PATRICIA BUFFLER

School of Social Welfare: JAMES MIDGELEY

Graduate School of Public Policy: EUGENE SMOLENSKY

School of Business Administration: WILLIAM HASLER

Ethnic Studies: ELAINE KIM

Asian-American Studies: (vacant)
Chicano Studies: (vacant)
Native American Studies: (vacant)

Optometry: ANTHONY ADAMS

Peace and Conflict Studies: (vacant)

University Extension: MARY METZ

University of California, Davis

1 Shields Ave, Davis, CA 95616

Telephone: (530) 752-1011
Telex: 5310785
Fax: (530) 752-6363

Established 1905
State Control

Chancellor: LARRY N. VANDERHOEF
Provost and Executive Vice-Chancellor: ROBERT D. GREY
Vice-Chancellor (Administration): JANET C. HAMILTON
Vice-Chancellor (University Relations and Development): CELESTE ROSE
Vice-Chancellor (Research): KEVIN SMITH
Vice-Chancellor (Student Affairs): CAROLYN F. WALL
Registrar: JACK R. FARRELL
Librarian: MARILYN SHARROW

Library: see Libraries
Number of teachers: 1,425
Number of students: 23,473

DEANS

College of Agriculture and Environmental Sciences: BARBARA O. SCHNEEMAN
College of Letters and Science:
Division of Humanities, Arts and Cultural Studies: JO-ANN CANNON
Division of Mathematical and Physical Sciences: PETER ROCK
Division of Social Sciences: STEVEN SHEFFRIN
College of Engineering: ALAN LAUB
School of Law: REX PERSCHBACKER
School of Medicine: JOSEPH SILVA
School of Veterinary Medicine: BENNIE OSBORN
Graduate Studies: CRISTINA GONZALES
Graduate School of Management: ROBERT H. SMILEY
Division of Biological Sciences: MARK MCNAMEE

CHAIRPERSONS AND DIRECTORS OF FACULTY

College of Agricultural and Environmental Science:

Agricultural Economics: Chair. RICHARD SEXTON
Agronomy and Range Science: Chair. JAMES HILL
Animal Science: Chair. EDWARD PRICE
Biological and Agricultural Engineering: Chair. DAVID HILLS
Entomology: Chair. MICHAEL PARRELLA
Environmental Design – Landscape Architecture: DEAN MACCONNELL
Environmental Design – Design: JO-ANN STABB
Environmental Horticulture: Chair. DAVID BURGER
Environmental Science and Policy: ALAN HASTINGS (Chair.)
Environmental Toxicology: Chair. FUMIO MATSUMURA
Food Science and Technology: Chair. CHARLES SHOEMAKER
Human and Community Development: Chair. LAWRENCE V. HARPER
Land, Water and Air Resources: Chair. DENNIS ROLSTON
Nematology: Chair. HOWARD FERRIS (acting)
Nutrition: Chair. CARL W. KEEN
Plant Pathology: Chair. JAMES MACDONALD
Pomology: Chair. THEODORE DEJONG
Textiles and Clothing: Chair. MARGARET H. RUCKER
Vegetable Crops: Chair. KENT BRADFORD
Viticulture and Enology: Chair. JAMES WOLPERT
Wildlife, Fish and Conservation Biology: Chair. DEBORAH ELLIOTT-FISK

Division of Biological Sciences:

Evolution and Ecology: THOMAS W. SCHOENER
Microbiology: STEPHEN C. KOWALCZYKOWSKI
Molecular and Cellular Biology: CARL W. SCHMID
Neurobiology, Physiology and Behaviour: BARBARA A. HORWITZ
Plant Biology: DEBORAH DELMER

College of Engineering:

Applied Science: Chair. NEVILLE LUHMANN
Biological and Agricultural Engineering: Chair. DAVID HILLS
Chemical Engineering and Materials Science: SUBHASH RISBUD
Civil and Environmental Engineering: Chair. KARL ROMSTAD
Computer Science: Chair. BISWANATH MUKHERJEE

Electrical Engineering and Computer Engineering: Chair. BERNARD LEVI
Mechanical and Aeronautical Engineering: Chair. BAHRAM RAVANI

School of Law:
Law: REX PERSCHBACKER (Dean)

College of Letters and Science:
African-American and African Studies: Dir JOHN STEWART
American Studies: Dir PATRICIA TURNER
Anthropology: Chair. ROBERT BETTINGER
Art: Chair. ROBERT SOMMER
Asian American Studies: Dir DON PRICE
Chemistry: Chair. CLAUDE MEARES
Chicano/a Studies: Dir YVETTE FLORES-ORTIZ
Chinese and Japanese: Chair. MICHELLE YEH
Classics: Dir DAVID TRAILL
Comparative Literature: Dir KARI LOKKE
East Asian Languages and Cultures: Dir DON PRICE
Economics: Chair. MARTINE QUINZII
Education: Dir FRED GENESEE
English: Chair. KARL F. ZENDER
French and Italian: Chair. GEORGES VAN DEN ABBEELE
Geography: Chair. MICHAEL BARBOUR
Geology: Chair. JEFFREY F. MOUNT
German and Russian: Chair. PETER HAYS
History: Chair. TED MARGADANT
Humanities: Chair. (vacant)
Integrated Studies: Dir NORA A. MCGUINNESS
International Relations: Dir EMILY GOLDMAN
Italian: Dir JULIANA SCHIESARI
Linguistics: Dir STEVEN LAPOINTE
Mathematics: Chair. CRAIG TRACY
Medieval Studies: Dir WINFREID SCHLEINER
Music: Chair. WAYNE SLAWSON
Native American Studies: Chair. INES HERNANDEZ-AVILA
Philosophy: Chair. JEFFREY KING
Exercise Science: Chair. ED BERNAUER
Physics: Chair. BARRY KLEIN
Political Science: Chair. MIROSLAV NINCIC
Psychology: Chair. SALLY MENDOZA
Religious Studies: Dir NAOMI JANOWITZ
Rhetoric and Communication: Chair. CHARLES BERGER
Russian: Dir DANIEL RANCOUR-LAFERRIERE
Sociology: Chair. LYN LOFLAND
Spanish and Classics: Chair. ROBERT BLAKE
Statistics: Chair. GEORGE G. ROUSSAS
Theatre and Dance: Chair. JANELLE REINELT
Women's Studies: Dir SUAD JOSEPH

School of Management:
Management: ROBERT H. SMILEY (Dean)

School of Medicine:
Anaesthesiology: Chair. PETER MOORE
Biological Chemistry: Chair. JOHN W. B. HERSHEY
Dermatology: Chair. PETER J. LYNCH
Epidemiology and Preventive Medicine: Chair. MARC SCHENKER
Family Practice and Community Medicine: Chair. KLEA BERTAKIS
Cell Biology and Human Anatomy: Chair. KENT ERICKSON
Human Physiology: Chair. PETER M. CALA
Internal Medicine: Chair. FRED MEYERS (acting)
Medical Microbiology and Immunology: Chair. BLAINE L. BEAMAN
Medical Pharmacology and Toxicology: Chair. MANNFRED HOLLINGER
Neurology: Chair. WILLIAM J. JAGUST (acting)
Neurological Surgery: Chair. J. PAUL MUIZELAAR
Obstetrics and Gynaecology: Chair. LLOYD H. SMITH
Ophthalmology: Chair. JOHN L. KELTNER
Orthopaedic Surgery: Chair. ROBERT M. SZABO (acting)
Otolaryngology: Chair. HILARY A. BRODIE (acting)
Paediatrics: Chair. MARK PARRISH
Pathology: Chair. RALPH GREEN
Physical Medicine and Rehabilitation: Chair. ERNEST R. JOHNSON
Psychiatry: Chair. THOMAS ANDERS
Radiology: Chair. JAMES A. BRUNBERG
Surgery: Chair. JAMES GOODNIGHT, Jr
Urology: Chair. RALPH DEVERE WHITE

School of Veterinary Medicine:
Anatomy, Physiology and Cell Biology: Chair. CHARLES PLOPPER (acting)
Medicine and Epidemiology: Chair. GARY CARLSON (acting)
Molecular Biosciences: Chair. SHRI N. GIRI
Pathology, Microbiology and Immunology: Chair. N. JAMES MACLACHLAN
Population Health and Reproduction: Chair. ROBERT BONDURANT
Surgical and Radiological Sciences: Chair. TIMOTHY O'BRIEN

PROFESSORS

College of Agricultural and Environmental Sciences:

Faculty of Agricultural Economics:
ALSTON, J. M.
CAPUTO, M. R.
CARMAN, H. F.
CARTER, C. A.
CHALFANT, J. A.
GREEN, R. D.
HAVENNER, A.
HAZLETT, T. W.
HEIEN, D. M.
HOWITT, R. E.
JARVIS, L. S.
MARTIN, P. L.
MORRISON, C. J.
PARIS, Q.
SEXTON, R. J.
SHEPARD, L. E.
SUMNER, D. A.
TAYLOR, J. E.
WILEN, J. E.
WILLIAMS, S. J.

Faculty of Agronomy and Range Science:
DEMMENT, M. W.
DVORAK, J.
GENG, S.
GEPTS, P. L.
PHILLIPS, D. A.
PLANT, R. E.
RAINS, D. W.
TEUBER, L. R.
TRAVIS, R. L.
VAN KESSEL, C.

Faculty of Animal Science:
ADAMS, T. E.
ANDERSON, G. B.
BALDWIN, R. L.
BERGER, P. J.
CALVERT, C. C.
CHANG, E. S.
DE PETERS, E. J.
DOROSHOV, S.
FAMULA, T. R.
GALL, G. A. E.
HUNG, S. S. O.
KLASING, K. C.
LEE, Y. B.
MENCH, J. A.
MILLAM, J. R.
MOBERG, G. P.
MURRAY, J. D.
PRICE, E. O.
WEATHERS, W. W.
WILSON, B. W.
ZINN, R. A.

Faculty of Applied Behavioural Sciences:
BRUSH, S. B.
HARPER, L. V.
KENNEY, M. F.
MOMSEN, J.
SMITH, M. P.
WELLS, M. J.

Faculty of Avian Sciences:
KLASING, K. C.
WEATHERS, W. W.

Faculty of Entomology:
CAREY, J. R.
DINGLE, H.
EHLER, L. E.
ELDRIDGE, B. F.
GRANETT, J.
HAMMOCK, B. D.
KARBAN, R.
KAYA, H. K.
KIMSEY, L. S.
MATSAMURA, F.
PAGE, R. E.
PARRELA, M. P.
PENG, C. Y. S.
SCOTT, T. W.
SHAPIRO, A.
ULLMAN, D. E.
WARD, P. S.

Faculty of Environmental Design:
ALLAN, N. J.
FRANCIS, M.
GOTELLI, D.
LAKY, G.
MACCANNELL, E. D.
RIVERS, V. Z.
SHAWCROFT-GUARINO, B.
THAYER, R. L.

Faculty of Environmental Horticulture:
BARBOUR, M. G.
DURZAN, D. J.
HARDING, J. A.
MACDONALD, J. D.
PAREVA, M. P.
REID, M. S.
SEYMOUR, M. GOLD
WU, L. L.

Faculty of Environmental Studies:
FOIN, T. C.
GOLDMAN, C. R.
HASTINGS, A. M.
JOHNSTON, R. A.
ORLOVE, B. S.
QUINN, J. F.
RICHERSON, P. J.
SABATIER, P. A.
SCHOENER, T. W.
SCHWARTZ, S. I.
SPERLING, D.

Faculty of Environmental Toxicology:
HAMMOCK, B. D.
MATSUMURA, F.
RICE, R. H.
SHIBAMOTO, T.
WILSON, B. W.
WOOLEY, D. E.

Faculty of Food Science and Technology:
BANDMAN, E.
HAARD, N. F.
HUTCHENS, T. W.
KROCHTA, J. M.
MCCARTHY, M. J.
OGRYDZIAK, D. M.
O'MAHONY, M. A.
PRICE, C. W.
REID, D. S.
RUSSELL, G. F.
SCHNEEMAN, B. O.
SHOEMAKER, C. F.
SINGH, R. P.
SMITH, G. M.

Faculty of Land, Air and Water Resources:
BAHRE, C. J.
BLEDSOE, C. S.
CARROLL, J. J.
CASEY, W. H.
FLOCCHINI, R. G.
FOGG, G. E.

GRISMER, M. E.
GROTJAHN, R. D.
HOPMANS, J. W.
HSIAO, T. C.
LÄUCHLI, A. E.
MARINO, M. A.
NAVROTSKY, A.
PAW U, K. T.
PUENTE, C. E.
RICHARDS, J. M.
ROLSTON, D. E.
SHAW, R. H.
SHELTON, M. L.
SILK, W. K.
SINGER, M. J.
SOUTHARD, R. J.
WALLENDER, W. W.
WEARE, B. C.
ZASOSKI, R. J.

Faculty of Nematology:

FERRIS, H.
JAFFEE, B. A.
KAYA, H. K.
WILLIAMS, V. M.

Faculty of Nutrition:

ALLEN, L. H.
BROWN, K. G.
CLIFFORD, A. J.
DEWEY, K. G.
GRIVETTI, L. E.
KEEN, C. L.
LONNERDAL, B. L.
MCDONALD, R.
RUCKER, R. B.
SCHNEEMAN, B. O.
STERN, J. S.

Faculty of Plant Pathology:

BOSTOCK, R. M.
BRUENING, G.
DUNIWAY, J. M.
FALK, B. W.
GILCHRIST, D. G.
KADO, C. I.
MACDONALD, J. D.
TYLER, B. M.
VAN BRUGGEN, A. H. C.
WEBSTER, R. K.

Faculty of Pomology:

BLISS, F. A.
DEJONG, T. M.
KADER, A. A.
LABAVITCH, J. M.
POLITO, V. S.
SUTTER, E. G.
WEINBAUM, S. A.

Faculty of Textiles and Clothing:

HSIEH, Y.
JETT, S.
KAISER, S. B.
RUCKER, M. H.

Faculty of Vegetable Crops:

BAYER, D. E.
BENNETT, A. B.
BLOOM, A. J.
BRADFORD, K. J.
MICHELMORE, R. W.
NEVINS, D. J.
QUIROS, C. F.
SALTVEIT, Jr, M. E.
YODER, J. I.

Faculty of Viticulture and Enology:

BISSON, L. F.
BOULTON, R. B.
MEREDITH, C. P.
NOBLE, A. C.
WILLIAMS, L. E.

Faculty of Wildlife, Fish and Conservation Biology:

ANDERSON, D. W.
BOTSFORD, L. W.
CARO, T. M.
CECH, J. J.
ELLIOTT-FISK, D. L.
ERMAN, D. C.
MOYLE, P. B.

College of Engineering:

Faculty of Biological and Agricultural Engineering:

CHEN, P. P.
DELWICHE, M. J.
GILES, D. K.
GRISMER, M. E.
HARTSOUGH, B. R.
HILLS, D. J.
JENKINS, B. M.
KROCHTA, J. M.
MCCARTHY, M. J.
MARIÑO, M. A.
MILES, J. A.
PLANT, R. E.
RUMSEY, T. R.
SINGH, R. P.
UPADHYAYA, S. K.
WALLENDER, W. W.

Faculty of Applied Science:

BALDIS, H. A.
BLATTNER, M. M.
CRAMER, S. P.
FREEMAN, R. R.
HWANG, D. Q.
KOLNER, B. H.
KROL, D. M.
LUHMAN, N. C.
MAX, N.
MCCURDY, W.
OREL, A.
RODRIGUE, G.
VEMURI, R.
YEH, Y.

Faculty of Chemical Engineering and Materials Science:

BOULTON, R. B.
GATES, B. C.
GIBELING, J. C.
HIGGINS, B. G.
HOWITT, D. G.
JACKMAN, A. P.
MCCOY, B. J.
MUKHERJEE, A. K.
MUNIR, Z. A.
NAVROTSKY, A.
PALAZOGLU, A. N.
POWELL, R. L.
RISBUD, S. H.
RYU, D. D. Y.
SHACKELFORD, J. F.
STROEVE, P.
WHITAKER, S.

Faculty of Civil and Environmental Engineering:

ARULANANDAN, K.
CHANG, D. P. Y.
DAFALIAS, Y. F.
HERRMANN, L. R.
IDRISS, I. M.
KAVVAS, M. L.
KING, I. P.
KUTTER, B. L.
LAROCK, B. E.
LUND, J. R.
MARIÑO, M. A.
RAMEY, M. R.
ROMSTAD, K. M.
SCHROEDER, E. D.
SPERLING, D.

Faculty of Computer Science:

GUSFIELD, D.
LAUB, A. L.
LEVITT, K.
MARTEL, C. U.
MATLOFF, N. S.
MUKHERJEE, B.
OLSSON, R. A.
RUSCHITZKA, M. G.

Faculty of Electrical and Computer Engineering:

BOWER, R. W.
CHANG, T. S.
COLLINGE, J. P.
CURRENT, K. W.
DIENES, A. J.
FEHER, K.
FORD, G. E.
FRIEDLANDER, B.
GARDNER, W. A.
HAKIMI, S. L.
HALEY, S. B.
HERITAGE, J. P.
HSIA, T. C. S.
HUNT, C. E.
HURST, P. J.
KNOESEN, A.
KOLNER, H. B.
LAUB, A. J.
LEVY, B. C.
LUHMANN, Jr, N. C.
OKTOBDZIJA, V. G.
REDINBO, G. R.
SMITH, R. L.
SODERSTRAND, M. A.
WANG, S.

Faculty of Mechanical, Aeronautical and Materials Engineering

BAUGHN, J. W.
CHATTOT, J.-J.
DWYER, H. A.
FRANK, A. A.
HAFEZ, M. M.
HESS, R. A.
HUBBARD, M.
HULL, M. L.
KARNOPP, D. C.
KENNEDY, I. M.
KOLLMANN, W.
MARGOLIS, D. L.
RAVANI, B.
REHFIELD, L. W.
SARIGUL-KLIJN, N.
VAN DAM, C. P.
VELINSKY, S. A.
WHITE, B. R.
YAMAZAKI, K.

School of Law:

AYER, J. D.
BROWNSTEIN, A. E.
BRUCH, C. S.
DOBRIS, J. C.
DUNNING, H. C.
FEENEY, F. F.
GANDARA, A.
GLENNON, M. J.
GOODPASTER, G. S.
GROSSMAN, G. S.
HILLMAN, R. W.
IMWINKELRIED, E. J.
JOHNSON, K. R.
JORDAN, E. R.
JUENGER, F. K.
KURTZ, L. A.
LEWIS, E. A.
OAKLEY, J. B.
PERSCHBACHER, R. R.
POULOS, J. W.
SIMMONS, D. L.
WEST, M. S.
WOLK, B. A.
WYDICK, R. C.

College of Letters and Science:

Faculty of African American and African Studies:

OLUPONA, J. K.
STANFIELD, J. H.
STEWART, J. O.

Faculty of American Studies:

MECHLING, J.
TURNER, P.

Faculty of Anthropology:

BETTINGER, R. L.
HARCOURT, A. H.
JOSEPH, S.
MCHENRY, H. M.
RODMAN, P. S.
SKINNER, G. W.
SMITH, C. A.
SMITH, D. G.
SMITH, J. S.
YENGOYAN, A. A.

Art Studio:

ATKINSON, C.
CARNWATH, S.
HENDERSON, W.
HERSHMAN, L.
HIMELFARB, H.
HOLLOWELL, D.
PULS, L. A.
SCHULZ, C.

Faculty of Chemistry:

BALCH, A. L.
BRITT, R. D.
FAWCETT, W. R.
FINK, W. H.
JACKSON, W. M.
KAUZLARICH, S.
KELZER, J. E.
KURTH, M. J.
LAMAR, G. N.
LEBRILLA, C. B.
MEARES, C. F.
MILLER, R. B.
POWER, P. P.
ROCK, P. A.
SCHORE, N. E.
SMITH, K. M.
TINTI, D. S.
TRUE, N. S.

Faculty of Chicano Studies:

MONTOYA, M.

Faculty of East Asian Languages and Culture:

BORGEN, R.
LAI, W.
YEH, M.

Faculty of Comparative Literature:

BLANCHARD, M. E.
FINNEY, G.
SCHEIN, S. L.
SCHIESARI, J.
TORRANCE, R. M.

Faculty of Theatre and Dance:

ANDERSON, S. P.
CASE, S. E.
FOSTER, S.
REINELT, J.
WORTHEN, W. B.

Faculty of East Asian Studies:

BORGEN, R.
LAI, W. W.
MANN, S.
PRICE, D. C.
SKINNER, G. W.
SMITH, J. S.
YEH, M.

Faculty of Economics:

BONANNO, G.
CLARK, G.
FEENSTRA, R. C.
HOOVER, K. D.
LINDERT, P. H.
MAKOWSKI, L.
OLMSTEAD, A. L.
QUINZII, M.
ROEMER, J. E.
SHEFFRIN, S. M.
SILVESTRE, J.
WATTON, G. M.
WOO, W. T.

Faculty of Education:

DUGDALE, S. S.
FIGUEROA, R. A.
GANDARA, P. C.
MERINO, B. J.
MURPHY, S.
SANDOVAL, J. H.
WAGNER, J.
WATSON-GEGEO, K. A.

Faculty of English:

ABBOTT, D. P.
BYRD, M.
DALE, P. A.
DIEHL, J. F.
FERGUSON, M. W.
GILBERT, S. M.
HAYS, P. L.
HOFFMAN, M. J.
MAJOR, C.
MCPHERSON, S. J.
MORRIS, L. A.
OSBORN, M.
ROBERTSON, D. A.
SCHLEINER, W.
SIMPSON, D.
SNYDER, G.
VAN LEER, D.
WADDINGTON, R. B.
WILLIAMSON, A. B.
WORTHEN, W. B.
ZENDER, K. F.

Faculty of French and Italian:

BLANCHARD, M. E.
CANNON, J.
DUTSCHKE, D. J.
MANOLIU, M.
SCHIESARI, J.
VAN DEN ABBEELE, G.

Faculty of Geology:

CASEY, W. H.
DAY, H. W.
DOYLE, J. A.
FOGG, G. E.
MOORES, E. M.
MOUNT, J. F.
NAVROTSKY, A.
SCHIFFMAN, P.
TWISS, R. J.
VERMEIJ, G. J.
VEROSUB, K. L.
ZIERENBERG, R. A.

Faculty of German and Russian:

BERND, C. A.
DRUZHNIKOV, Y.
FINNEY, G.
KUHN, A. K.
MCCONNELL, W.
MENGES, K. R.
RANCOUR-LAFERRIERE, D.
SCHAEFFER, P. M.

Faculty of History:

BAUER, A. J.
BORGEN, R.
BROWER, Jr, D. R.
CADDEN, J.
HAGEN, W. W.
HALTTUNEN, K.
LANDAU, N. B.
MANN, S. L.
MARGADANT, T. W.
METCALF, B.
PRICE, D. C.
ROSEN, R. E.
SMITH, M. L.
SPYRIDAKIS, S.
TAYLOR, A. S.
WALKER, C. E.

Faculty of Integrated Studies:

GOODMAN, G. S.
LAST, J. A.
MECHLING, J.

Faculty of Linguistics:

BENWARE, W. A.
BLAKE, R.
MANOLIU, M.
MERINO, B. J.
SCHLEINER, W.
SMITH, J. S.
TIMM, L. A.
TORREBLANCA, M.
WATSON-GEGEO, K. A.
YENGOYAN, A.

Faculty of Mathematics:

BARNETTE, D. W.
BORGES, C. R.
CHEER, A. Y.
DIEDERICH, J. R.
EDELSON, A. L.
FUCHS, D. B.
HAAS, J.
HUNTER, J. K.
KRENER, A. J.
MILTON, E. O.
MULASE, M.
SALLEE, G. T.
SCHWARZ, A.
SILVIA, E. M.
TEMPLE, J. B.
THURSTON, W. P.
TRACY, C. A.
WETS, R. J. B.

Department of Military Science:

PORTER, R. R.

Faculty of Music:

BAUER, R.
BLOCH, R. S.
BUSSE BERGER, A. M.
FRANK, A. D.
HOLOMAN, D. K.
NUTTER, D. A.
REYNOLDS, C. A.
SLAWSON, A. W.

Faculty of Native American Studies:

LONGFISH, G. C.
VARESE, S.

Faculty of Philosophy:

COPP, D. I.
CUMMINS, R. C.
DWORKIN, G.
GRIESEMER, J. R.
JUBIEN, M.
TELLER, P.
WEDIN, M. V.

Faculty of Exercise Science:

MOLÉ, P. A.
RAMEY, M. R.

Faculty of Physics:

BECKER, R. H.
BRADY, F. P.
CHAU, L.
CHIANG, S.
COLEMAN, L. B.
CORRUCCINI, L. R.
COX, D. L.
FADLEY, C. S.
FONG, C.
GUNION, J. F.
KISKIS, J. E.
KLEIN, B. M.
KO, W. T.
LANDER, R. L.
PELLETT, D. E.
PICKETT, W. E.
SCALETTAR, R. T.
SHELTON, R. N.
SINGH, R. R. P.
YAGER, P. M.
ZIMANYI, G.

Faculty of Political Science:

BERMAN, L.
JACKMAN, R. W.
JENTLESON, B. W.

NINCIC, M.
PETERMAN, L. I.
ROTHCHILD, D. S.
SIVERSON, R. M.
WADE, L. L.

Faculty of Psychology:

ACREDOLO, L. P.
CHALUPA, L. M.
COSS, R. G.
ELMS, A. C.
EMMONS, R. A.
ERICKSEN, K. P.
GOODMAN, G. S.
HARRISON, A. A.
HENRY, K. R.
JOHNSON, J. T.
KROLL, N. E. A.
MENDOZA, S. P.
OWINGS, D. H.
PARKS, T. E.
POST, R. B.
SHAVER, P. R.
SIMONTON, D. K.
SOMMER, R.
SUE, S.
TOMLINSON-KEASEY, C.

Faculty of Religious Studies:

LAI, W. W.

Faculty of Communication:

BELL, R. A.
BERGER, C. R.
MOTLEY, M. T.

Faculty of Sociology:

BIGGART, N. W.
BLOCK, F.
COHEN, L. E.
GOLDSTONE, J. A.
HALL, J. R.
JACKMAN, M.
JOFFE, C. E.
LOFLAND, L. H.
STACEY, J.
STANFIELD, J. H.
WALTON, J. T.

Faculty of Spanish and Classics:

ARMISTEAD, S. G.
BLAKE, R.
GONZÁLEZ, C.
ROLLER, L. E.
SCARI, R. M.
SCHAEFFER, P. M.
SCHEIN, S. L.
TORREBLANCA, M.
TRAILL, D. A.
VERANI, H. J.

Faculty of Statistics:

BURMAN, P.
JOHNSON, W. O.
MACK, Y. P.
MUELLER, H. G.
ROUSSAS, G. G.
SAMANIEGO, F. J.
SHUMWAY, R. H.
UTTS, J. M.
WANG, J.-L.

Faculty of Women's Studies:

JOFFE, C.
JOSEPH, S.
NEWTON, J.
STACEY, J.

School of Management:

BIGGART, N. W.
BITTLINGMAYER, G.
CLARK, P.
GERSTNER, E.
GRIFFIN, P. A.
PALMER, D. A.
ROCKE, D. M.
TOPKIS, D. M.
TSAI, C.-L.
WALTON, G. M.

School of Medicine:

Department of Anaesthesiology:

FUNG, D.
GRONERT, G. A.
KIEN, N.
MOORE, D.
REITAN, J. A.
SEFWAT, A.

Department of Biochemistry:

BRADBURY, E. M.
HANLEY, M. R.
HERSHEY, J. W.
HOLLAND, M. J.
JUE, T.
MATTHEWS, H. R.
RUCKER, R.
SEBIN, M.
TROY, F. A.
WALSH, D. A.

Department of Community Health:

SCHENKER, M. B.
WINTEMUTE, G. J.

Department of Dermatology:

GRANDO, S. A.
ISSEROFF, R. R.
LAZARUS, G. S.
LYNCH, P. J.
ZIBOH, V. A.

Department of Family and Community Medicine:

BERTAKIS, K. D.
CALLAHAN, E. J.

Department of Cell Biology and Human Anatomy:

ERICKSON, K. L.
FITZGERALD, P.
HENDRICKX, A. G.
KUMARI, V.
MEIZEL, S.
PRIMAKOFF, P.
WILEY, L.

Department of Human Physiology:

CALA, P. M.
CARLSEN, R. C.
CURRY, F. E.
GRAY, S. D.
TURGEON, J. L.

Department of Internal Medicine:

AMSTERDAM, E. A.
AOKI, T. A.
CROSS, C. E.
DEPNER, T. A.
FITZGERALD, F. T.
GANDARA, D. R.
GERSHWIN, M. E.
HALSTED, C. H.
KAPPAGODA, C. T.
KAUFMAN, M. .P.
KAYSEN, G.
LAST, J. A.
LEUNG, J.
LOEWY, E.
LONGHURST, J. C.
PARSONS, G. H.
POWELL, J. S.
PIMSTONE, N. R.
ROBBINS, R. L.
SELDIN, M. F.
SIEGEL, D.
SILVA, J.
SOELDNER, J. S.
WILLIAMS, H. E.
WU, R.

Department of Medical Microbiology:

BEAMAN, B. L.
PAPPAGIANIS, D.
SYVANEN, M.
THEIS, J. H.

Department of Neurology:

JAGUST, W. J.
KNIGHT, R. T.
RAFAL, R. D.
REMLER, M. P.
RICHMAN, D. P.

Department of Neurosurgery:

BOGGAN, J. E.
BURMAN, R.
MUIZELAAR, J. P.
PANG, D.
WAGNER, F. C.

Department of Obstetrics and Gynaecology:

BOYERS, S.
LASLEY, B.
OVERSTREET, J. W.
SMITH, L.
WILEY, L. M.

Department of Ophthalmology

BURNS, M.
HJEIMELAND, L. M.
KELTNER, J. L.
MANNIS, M. J.
SCHWAB, I.

Department of Orthopaedic Surgery:

BENSON, D. R.
CHAPMAN, M. W.
MARTIN, R. B.
RAB, G. T.
REDDI, H.
RODRIGO, J. J.
SZABO, R. M.

Department of Otorhinolaryngology:

DONALD, P. J.
LEONARD, R.
SENDERS, C.

Department of Paediatrics:

GOETZMAN, B. W.
MAKKER, S. P.
MILSTEIN, J.
POLLITT, E.
STYNE, D. M.
WENMAN, W. M.

Department of Pathology:

CARDIFF, R. D.
CHEUNG, A.
ELLIS, W. G.
FINKBEINER
GREEN, R.
KOST, G. J.
LARKIN, E. C.
MILLER, C.
WALTERS, R. F.

Department of Plastic Surgery:

STEVENSON, T. R.

Department of Psychiatry:

AMARAL, D. G.
ANDERS, T. F.
BARGLOW, P.
FEINBERG, I.
HALES, R.
JONES, E.
KNAPP, P. K.
MORRISON, T. L.
SUE, S.
YARVIS, R.

Department of Radiology:

BOGREN, H. S.
BOONE, J.
BRUNBERG, J.
GREENSPAN, A.
KATZBERG, R. W.
LANTZ, B. M.
LINDFORS, K.
LINK, D. P.
MCGAHAN, J. P.
MOORE, E. H.
REICH, S.
ROSENQUIST, C. J.
SEIBERT, J. A.
STADAINIK, R. C.
VERA, D.
WEBER, D. A.

Department of Surgery:
BERKOFF, H. A.
BLAISDELL, F. W.
GOODNIGHT, J. E., Jr
GOURLEY, I.
HARNESS, J.
HOLCROFT, J. W.
ORGAN, C. H.
SCHNEIDER, P.
SEGEL, L. D.
STEVENSON, T. R.
SZABO, R. M.
WISNER, D. H.
WOLFE, B. M.

Department of Urology:
DAS, S.
DE VERE WHITE, R. W.
LEWIS, E.
PALMER, J. M.
STONE, A. R.

School of Veterinary Medicine:

Faculty of Anatomy, Physiology and Cell Biology:
BRUSS, M. L.
FAULKIN, Jr, L. J.
GIETZEN, D. W.
HART, B. L.
HINTON, D. E.
HYDE, D. M.
PINKERTON, K.
PLOPPER, C. G.
WU, R.

Faculty of Medicine and Epidemiology:
ARDANS, A. A.
CARLSON, G. P.
CARPENTER, T. E.
EAST, N. E.
FELDMAN, E.
GEORGE, L. W.
HEDRICK, R. P.
HIRD, D.
IHRKE, P. J.
KITTLESON, M. D.
LING, G. V.
MADIGAN, J.
NELSON, R. W.
PEDERSEN, N. C.
SMITH, B. P.
THOMAS, W. P.
THURMOND, M.
WILSON, W. D.

Faculty of Population Health and Reproduction:
BALL, B. A.
BONDURANT, R. H.
CLIVER, D. O.
CULLOR, J. A.
FARVER, T. B.
HOLMERG, C. A.
LAM, K. M.
LASLEY, W. L.
LIU, I. K. M.
MURRAY, J.

Faculty of Surgical and Radiological Sciences:
BAILEY, C. S.
BUYUKMIHCI, N. C.
GREGORY, C. R.
HASKINS, S. C.
HILDEBRAND, S. V.
HORNOF, W. J.
JONES, J. H.
KOBLIK, P. D.
LECOUTEUR, R. A.
MADEWELL, B. R.
NYLAND, T. G.
O'BRIEN, T. R.
PASCOE, J. R.
STEFFEY, E. P.
VASSEUR, P. B.

Faculty of Pathology, Microbiology and Immunology:
ANDERSON, M. L.
BARR, B. C.
BARTHOLD, S. W.
BICKFORD, A. A.
CONRAD, P. A.
GERSHWIN, L. J.
HIRSH, D. C.
LEFEBVRE
LOWENSTINE, L. J.
MACLACHLAN, N. J.
MOORE, P. F.
MURPHY, F. A.
OSBURN, B. I.
STOTT, J. L.
WILSON, D. W.
YILMA, T.
ZEE, Y. C.
ZINKI, J. G.

Faculty of Molecular Biosciences:
BUCKPITT, A. R.
GIRI, S. N.
HANSEN, R. J.
ROGERS, Q. R.
SEGALL, H. J.
VULLIET, P. R.
WITSCHI, H.

Division of Biological Sciences:

Evolution and Ecology:
DOYLE, J. A.
GILLESPIE, J. H.
GOTTLIEB, L. D.
GROSBERG, R. K.
LANGLEY, C. H.
PEARCY, R. W.
REJMANEK, M.
SCHOENER, T. W.
SHAFFER, H. B.
SHAPIRO, A. M.
STAMPS, J. A.
STANTON, M. L.
STRONG, D. R.
TOFT, C. A.
TURELLI, M.

Microbiology:
ARTZ, S. W.
BAUMANN, P.
KLIONSKY, D. J.
KOWALCZYKOWSKI, S. C.
MANNING, J. S.
MEEKS, J. C.
NELSON, D. C.
PRIVALSKY, M. L.
STEWART, V. J.
VILLAREJO, M. R.

Molecular and Cellular Biology:
ARMSTRONG, P. B.
BASKIN, R. J.
CARLSON, D. M.
CLEGG, J. S.
CRIDDLE, R. S.
CROWE, J. S.
DAHMUS, M. E.
DOI, R. H.
ERICKSON, C. A.
ETZLER, M. E.
GASSER, C. S.
GREY, R. D.
HAWLEY, R. S.
HEDRICK, J. L.
HJELMELAND, L. M.
KIGER, J. A.
LAGARIAS, J. C.
MCNAMEE, M. G.
MYLES, D.
NUCCITELLI, R. L.
RODRIGUEZ, R. L.
SCHMID, C. W.
SHOLEY, J. M.
SEGEL, I. H.
SHEN, C.-K. J.

Neurobiology, Physiology and Behaviour:
CARSTENS, E. E.
CHALUPA, L. M.
CHANG, E. S.
FULLER, C. A.
HORWITZ, B. A.
KEIZER, J. E.
MOBERG, G. P.
MULLONEY, B.
PAPPONE, P. A.
SILLMAN, A. J.
WEIDNER, W. J.
WILSON, M.
WOOLLEY, D. E.

Plant Biology:
DELMER, D. P.
FALK, R. H.
HARADA, J. J.
LUCAS, W. J.
MURPHY, T. M.
ROST, T. L.
STANTON, M. L.
STEMLER, A. J.
THEG, S. M.
VANDERHOEF, L. N.

University of California, Irvine

Irvine, CA 92697

Telephone: (714) 824-5011 until April 1998, (949) 824-5011 from April 1998

Opened 1965
State control
Three quarter terms
Chancellor: LAUREL L. WILKENING
Executive Vice-Chancellor: SIDNEY H. GOLUB
Vice-Chancellor (Student Services): MANUEL GOMEZ
Vice-Chancellor (Administrative and Business Services): WENDELL C. BRASE
Vice-Chancellor (Research): FREDERIC YUI-MING WAN
Vice-Chancellor (University Advancement): JERRY MANDEL
Registrar: CHARLENE N. BRADLEY
University Librarian: JOANNE R. EUSTER
Number of teachers: 998 professors (811 campus, 187 College of Medicine)
Number of students: 17,888 full-time

Publications: *UCI* General Catalogue (annually), *UCI Journal* (newspaper, quarterly), *UCI News Paper* (monthly), *New University* (weekly student newspaper) and numerous student publications.

DEANS

School of Biological Sciences: (vacant)
School of Arts: JILL BECK
School of Humanities: (vacant)
School of Physical Sciences: RALPH CICERONE
School of Social Ecology: DANIEL S. STOKOLS
School of Social Sciences: WILLIAM R. SCHONFELD
School of Engineering: NICOLAOS ALEXOPOULOS
Graduate School of Management: JOHN KING (acting)
College of Medicine: THOMAS CESARIO
Research and Graduate Studies: FREDERIC YUI-MING WAN
Undergraduate Education: JAMES DANZIGER
University Extension: PHILIP NOWLEN

DIRECTORS AND DEPARTMENT CHAIRPERSONS

Biological Sciences:
Developmental and Cell Biology: SUSAN BRYANT
Ecology and Evolutionary Biology: TIMOTHY BRADLEY
Molecular Biology and Biochemistry: JERRY MANNING
Psychobiology: HERBERT KILLACKEY

College of Medicine:
Anaesthesiology: CYNTHIA ANDERSON
Anatomy and Neurobiology: RICHARD ROBERTSON
Biological Chemistry: SUZANNE B. SANDMEYER

C and E Medicine: DANIEL MENZEL
Dermatology: GERALD D. WEINSTEIN
Family Medicine: JOHANNA SHAPIRO (acting)
Medicine: N. D. VAZIRI (acting)
Microbiology and Molecular Genetics: BERT L. SEMLER
Neurological Surgery: MARIO AMMIRATI (acting)
Neurology: STANLEY VAN DEN NOORT
Obstetrics and Gynaecology: THOMAS GARITE
Ophthalmology: BARUCH KUPPERMANN (acting)
Orthopaedic Surgery: HARRY SKINNER
Otolaryngology, Head and Neck Surgery: ROGER CRUMLEY
Pathology: Y. KIKKAWA
Paediatrics: IRA LOTT
Pharmacology: LARRY STEIN
Physical Medicine and Rehabilitation: JEN YU
Physiology and Biophysics: JANOS LANYI
Psychiatry and Human Behaviour: SIU TANG
Radiation Oncology: NILAM RAMSINGHANI
Radiological Sciences: ANTON HASSO
Surgery: SAMUEL E. WILSON

Engineering:
Chemical and Biochemical Engineering: (vacant)
Civil and Environmental Engineering: STEPHEN G. RITCHIE
Electrical and Computer Engineering: (vacant)
Mechanical and Aerospace Engineering: SAID ELGHOBASHI

Arts:
Dance: MARY COREY
Drama: GEORGE HARVEY
Music: BERNARD GILMORE
Studio Art: DAVID TREND

Humanities:
African American Studies Programme: THELMA FOOTE (acting)
Art History: DICKRAN TASHJIAN
Asian American Studies Programme: KETU KATRAK
Classics: PATRICK SINCLAIR
East Asian Language and Literatures: STEVEN D. CARTER
English and Comparative Literature: BROOK THOMAS
English as a Second Language: ROBIN SCARCELLA
Film Studies: RHONA BERENSTEIN
French and Italian: DAVID CARROLL
German: MEREDITH LEE
History: STEVEN K. TOPIK
Humanities Core Course: JOHN SMITH
Latin American Studies: JACOBO SEFAMI
Philosophy: (vacant)
Russian: (vacant)
Spanish and Portuguese: ALEJANDRO MORALES
Women's Studies: ELIZABETH GUTHRIE

Information and Computer Science: MICHAEL J. PAZZANI

Physical Sciences:
Chemistry: A. RICHARD CHAMBERLIN
Earth System Science: ELLEN R. M. DRUFFEL
Mathematics: ABEL KLEIN
Physics and Astronomy: JON M. LAWRENCE

Social Ecology:
Criminology, Law and Society: HENRY PONTELL
Environmental Analysis and Design: JOHN WHITELEY (acting)
Psychology and Social Behaviour: CAROL WHALEN
Urban Planning: MARK BALDASSARE

Social Sciences:
Anthropology: LEO CHAVEZ
Chicano and Latino Studies Programme: LOUIS MIRON
Cognitive Sciences: JACK YELLOTT
Economics: AMIHAI GLAZER
Global Peace and Conflict Studies: WAYNE SANDHOLTZ (acting)
Health and Philosophy of Science Programme: BRIAN SKYRMS
Linguistics: C. T. JAMES HUANG
Politics and Society: MARK PETRACCA
Sociology: FRANCESCA CANCIAN
Transportation Science Program: CHARLES A. LAVE (acting)

ATTACHED INSTITUTES

Cancer Research Institute: Dir HUNG FAN
Centre for Neurobiology of Learning and Memory: Dir JAMES L. MCGAUGH
Critical Theory Institute: Dir GABRIELLE SCHWAB
Developmental Biology Centre: Dir PETER BRYANT
Humanities Research Institute: Dir PAT O'BRIEN
Institute of Transportation Studies: Dir WILFRED W. RECKER
Center for Research on Information Technology and Organizations: Dir KENNETH L. KRAEMER
Institute for Surface and Interface Science: Dir ALEX MARADUDIN
Thesaurus Linguae Graecae: TED BRUNNER

University of California, Los Angeles (UCLA)

Los Angeles, CA 90024
Telephone: (310) 825-4321
Established 1919

Chancellor: ALBERT CARNESALE
Executive Vice-Chancellor: WYATT R. HUME
Administrative Vice-Chancellor: PETER W. BLACKMAN
Vice-Chancellor (Academic Affairs): CLAUDIA MITCHELL-KERNAN
Vice-Chancellor (External Affairs): THEODORE R. MITCHELL (acting)
Vice-Chancellor (Research Programs): C. KUMAR PATEL
Vice-Chancellor (Student Affairs): WINSTON C. DOBY
Vice-Chancellor (Academic Personnel): NORMAN ABRAMS
Vice-Chancellor (Legal Affairs): JOSEPH D. MANDEL
Registrar: (vacant)
Librarian: GLORIA S. WERNER
Number of teachers: 3,200
Number of students: 34,713

DEANS

School of the Arts and Architecture: DANIEL M. NEUMAN
College of Letters and Sciences: BRIAN COPENHAVER (Provost)
Humanities: PAULINE YU
Life Sciences: FREDERICK A. EISERLING
Physical Sciences: ROBERT PECCEI
Social Sciences: SCOTT WAUGH
School of Engineering and Applied Science: FRANK WAZZAN
Graduate School of Education and Information Studies: THEODORE R. MITCHELL
Anderson Graduate School of Management: JOHN MAMER (acting)
School of Dentistry: (vacant)
School of Law: JONATHAN VARAT
School of Medicine: GERALD LEVEY (Provost and Dean)
School of Nursing: MARIE J. COWAN
School of Public Health: ABDELMONEM AFIFI
School of Public Policy and Social Research: BARBARA J. NELSON
School of Theater, Film and Television: GILBERT CATES
International Studies and Overseas Programs: JOHN HAWKINS
University Extension: ROBERT LAPINER
Graduate Division: CLAUDIA MITCHELL-KERNAN

CHAIRPERSONS OF DEPARTMENTS

Arts:
Architecture and Urban Design: SYLVIA LAVIN
Art: MARY KELLY
Design: REBECCA ALLEN
Ethnomusicology and Systematic Musicology: TIM RICE
Music: JON ROBERTSON
World Arts and Cultures: CHRISTOPHER WATERMAN

Dentistry: (vacant)

Education and Information Studies:
Education: HAROLD G. LEVINE
Library and Information Sciences: MICHELE CLOONAN

Engineering and Applied Science:
Chemical Engineering: SELIM SENKAN
Civil and Environmental Engineering: MICHAEL STENSTROM
Computer Science: RICHARD MUNTZ
Electrical Engineering: WILLIAM J. KAISER
Materials Science and Engineering: K. N. TU
Mechanical and Aerospace Engineering: VIJAY DHIR

Law: JONATHAN VARAT

Letters and Science:
Aerospace Studies: Lt-Col DAVID TERRELL
Anthropology: JOAN SILK
Applied Linguistics and TESL: JOHN H. SCHUMANN
Art History: ANTHONY VIDLER
Atmospheric Sciences: ROGER WAKIMOTO
Biology: PARK S. NOBEL
Cesar Chavez Center: RAYMUND PAREDES (acting)
Chemistry and Biochemistry: EMIL REISLER
Classics: SARAH P. MORRIS
Earth and Space Sciences: T. MARK HARRISON
East Asian Languages and Cultures: ROBERT BUSWELL
Economics: BRYAN ELLICKSON
English: THOMAS WORTHAM
French: PATRICK COLEMAN
Geography: JOHN AGNEW
Germanic Languages: JAMES SCHULTZ
History: RICHARD VON GLAHN
Italian: MASSIMO CIAVOLELLA
Linguistics: EDWARD KEENAN
Mathematics: TONY F.-C. CHAN
Microbiology and Molecular Genetics: SHERIE L. MORRISON
Military Science: Lt-Col RITA SALLEY
Molecular, Cell and Developmental Biology: LUTZ BIRNBAUMER
Musicology: ROBERT A. WALSER
Naval Science: WILLIAM H. ALLEN
Near Eastern Languages and Cultures: ANTONIO LOPRIENO
Philosophy: BARBARA HERMAN
Physics and Astronomy: FERDINAND CORONITI
Physiological Science: ALAN GRINNELL
Political Science: RONALD ROGOWSKI
Psychology: ARTHUR WOODWARD
Slavic Languages and Literatures: OLGA YOKOYAMA
Sociology: ROBERT M. EMERSON
Spanish and Portuguese: RANDAL JOHNSON
Speech: NEIL MALAMUTH

Anderson Graduate School of Management: JOHN MCDONOUGH (acting)

Medicine:
Anaesthesiology: PATRICIA KAPUR
Biological Chemistry: ELIZABETH NEUFELD
Biomathematics: ELLIOT LANDAW
Family Medicine: JAMES PUFFER (acting)
Human Genetics: LEENA PELTONEN
Medicine: ALAN FOGELMAN

Microbiology and Immunology: SHERIE L. MORRISON
Molecular and Medical Pharmacology: MICHAEL PHELPS
Neurobiology: JACK FELDMAN
Neurology: ROBERT COLLINS
Obstetrics and Gynaecology: ALAN DECHERNEY
Ophthalmology: BARTLY MONDINO
Orthopaedic Surgery: GERALD FINERMAN
Pathology and Laboratory Medicine: JONATHAN BRAUN
Paediatrics: EDWARD MCCABE
Physiology: ERNEST WRIGHT
Psychiatry and Biobehavioural Sciences: PETER WHYBROW
Radiation Oncology: H. RODNEY WITHERS
Radiological Sciences: RICHARD STECKEL
Surgery: E. CARMACK HOLMES
Urology: JEAN DEKERNION

Nursing: MARIE J. COWAN

Public Health:
Biostatistics: WILLIAM G. CUMBERLAND
Community Health Sciences: GAIL G. HARRISON
Environmental Health Sciences: JOHN FROINES
Epidemiology: RALPH R. FRERICHS
Health Services: THOMAS H. RICE

Public Policy and Social Research:
Policy Studies: ARLEEN LEIBOWITZ
Social Welfare: JAMES LUBBEN
Urban Planning: (vacant)

Theatre, Film and Television:
Film and Television: ROBERT ROSEN
Theatre: RICHARD ROSE

DIRECTORS OF ORGANIZED RESEARCH INSTITUTES

School of the Arts and Architecture:
Fowler Museum of Arts and Cultures: DORAN ROSS
Grunwald Center for the Graphic Arts: DAVID RODES
Wight Art Galleries: HENRY HOPKINS

School of Dentistry:
Dental Research Institute: NOO-HEE PARK

Graduate School of Education and Information Studies:
Center for the Study of Evaluation: EVA BAKER
Corrine A. Seeds University Elementary School: DEBORAH STIPEK
Higher Education Research Institute: ALEXANDER ASTIN
Teachers' Education Laboratory: JEANNIE OAKES

College of Letters and Sciences:
Institute of Archaeology: RICHARD M. LEVENTHAL
Institute of Geophysics and Planetary Physics: MICHAEL GHIL
Center for the Study of Women: SANDRA HARDING
Molecular Biology Institute: ARNOLD J. BERK
Writing Program: CHERYL GIULIANO
Institute of Social Science Research: DAVID O. SEARS
Center for Medieval and Renaissance Studies: HENRY ANSGAR KELLY
Center for Modern and Contemporary Studies: VINCENT PECORA
Center for 17th- and 18th-Century Studies: PETER REILL
Clark Library: PETER REILL
Institute of Plasma and Fusion Research: MOHAMED ABDOU, ALFRED WONG

School of Medicine:
Aids Institute: IRVIN CHEN
Brain Research Institute: ALLAN TOBIN
Community Applications of Research: (vacant)
Crump Institute: MICHAEL PHELPS
Jerry Lewis Neuromuscular Research Center: ALAN D. GRINNELL
Jonsson Comprehensive Cancer Center: JUDITH GASSON
Jules Stein Eye Institute: BARTLY MONDINO
Mental Retardation Research Center: JEAN DEVELLIS
Neuropsychiatric Institute: PETER WHYBROW
UCLA-DOE Laboratory of Structural Biology and Molecular Medicine: DAVID EISENBERG

School of Public Policy and Social Research:
Institute of Industrial Relations: (vacant)

DIRECTORS OF INDEPENDENT UNITS

African-American Studies Center: RICHARD YARBOROUGH (acting)
American Indian Studies Center: DUANE CHAMPAGNE
Asian-American Studies Center: DON T. NAKANISHI
Chicano Studies Research Center: GUILLERMO HERNANDEZ

DIRECTORS OF INTERNATIONAL STUDIES AND OVERSEAS PROGRAMMES

James C. Coleman African Studies Center: EDMOND KELLER
Center for Latin American Studies: CARLOS TORRES
Center for European and Russian Studies: IVAN BEREND
Gustave Von Grunebaum Center for Near Eastern Studies: IRENE BIERMAN
Center for Japanese Studies: FRED NOTEHELFER
Center for Chinese Studies: BENJAMIN ELMAN
Center for International Relations: RICHARD ROSECRANCE
Education Abroad Program: VAL RUST
Center for Pacific Rim Studies: DEAN JAMISON
Center for Korean Studies: ROBERT BUSWELL
Joint East Asian Studies Center: JAMES TONG
Language Resource Program: RUSSELL CAMPBELL

University of California, Riverside

Riverside, CA 92521
Telephone: (909) 787-1012
Fax (909) 787-3866

Established 1954
State control
Academic year: September to June

Chancellor: RAYMOND L. ORBACH
Executive Vice-Chancellor: DAVID H. WARREN
Vice-Chancellor (Student Affairs): CARMEL MYERS
Vice-Chancellor (Administration): C. MICHAEL WEBSTER
Vice-Chancellor (Research): HARRY W. GREEN II
Vice-Chancellor (University Relations and Development): JAMES ERICKSON
Registrar: JAMES SANDOVAL
Librarian: JAMES C. THOMPSON

Library: see Libraries
Number of teachers: 483
Number of students: 8,865

DEANS

College of Natural and Agricultural Sciences: MICHAEL T. CLEGG
College of Humanities and Social Science: CARLOS VÉLEZ-IBÁÑEZ
Graduate School of Management: DAVID MAYERS
School of Education: ROBERT C. CALFEE
College of Engineering: SATISH TRIPATHI
Graduate Division: JEAN-PIERRE MILEUR

University of California, San Diego

La Jolla, CA 92093
Telephone: (619) 534-2230

Became part of the University 1960

Chancellor: ROBERT C. DYNES
Senior Vice-Chancellor (Academic Affairs): MARSHA A. CHANDLER
Vice-Chancellor (Business Affairs): STEVEN N. RELYEA
Vice-Chancellor (Resource Management and Planning): JOHN A. WOODS
Vice-Chancellor (Student Affairs): JOSEPH W. WATSON
Vice-Chancellor (Development and University Relations): JAMES LANGLEY
Vice-Chancellor (Research): RICHARD ATTIYEH
Vice-Chancellor (Health Sciences) and Dean of the School of Medicine: JOHN F. ALKSNE
Vice-Chancellor (Marine Sciences) and Director of Scripps Institution of Oceanography: CHARLES F. KENNEL
Provost of Revelle College: F. THOMAS BOND
Provost of John Muir College: PATRICK J. LEDDEN
Provost of Thurgood Marshall College: CECIL LYTLE
Provost of Earl Warren College: DAVID K. JORDAN
Provost of Eleanor Roosevelt College: ANN L. CRAIG
Registrar and Admissions Officer: RICHARD BACKER
Librarian: GERALD R. LOWELL

Number of teachers: 1,637
Number of students: 18,324

Publications: *UCSD General Catalog, UCSD Graduate Studies, UCSD School of Medicine Catalog, UCSD Summer Session* (all annual), *Explore* (University Extension Catalog), *USCD Perspectives.*

DEANS

Jacobs School of Engineering: ROBERT W. CONN
Graduate Studies: RICHARD ATTIYEH
Extended Studies and Public Services: MARY L. WALSHOK
Arts and Humanities: FRANTISEK DEAK
Natural Sciences: MARVIN GOLDBERGER
Social Sciences: PAUL DRAKE
Graduate School of International Relations and Pacific Studies: C. PETER TIMMER

CHAIRPERSONS OF DEPARTMENTS

Anthropology: T. LEVY
Applied Mechanics and Engineering Sciences: F. WILLIAMS
Bioengineering: S. CHIEN
Biology: W. MCGINNIS
Chemistry and Biochemistry: M. THIEMENS
Cognitive Science: G. FAUCONNIER
Communication: C. PADDEN
Computer Science and Engineering: J. FERRANTE
Economics: J. SOBEL
Electrical and Computer Engineering: W. COLES
Ethnic Studies: G. LIPSITZ
History: M. BERNSTEIN
Linguistics: M. CHEN
Literature: L. LOWE
Mathematics: J. REMMEL
Music: F. R. MOORE
Philosophy: G. ANAGNOSTOPOULOS
Physics: T. O'NEIL
Political Science: H. HIRSCH
Psychology: D. A. SWINNEY
Scripps Institution of Oceanography: K. MELVILLE
Sociology: C. WAISMAN
Theatre: W. JONES
Visual Arts: L. HOCK

School of Medicine:
Anaesthesiology: J. DRUMMOND
Family and Medicine: R. KAPLAN
Medicine: S. WASSERMAN
Neurosciences: L. THAL
Ophthalmology: S. BROWN
Orthopaedics: S. GARFIN
Pathology: D. BAILEY

Paediatrics: S. MENDOZA
Pharmacology: P. TAYLOR
Psychiatry: L. JUDD
Radiology: G. LEOPOLD
Reproductive Medicine: T. MOORE
Surgery: A. MOOSSA

University of California, San Francisco

3rd and Parnassus Aves, San Francisco, CA 94143
Telephone: (415) 476-9000
Fax: (415) 476-9634
Established 1873
Chancellor: H. T. DEBAS
Vice-Chancellor (Administration): S. BARCLAY
Vice-Chancellor (Academic Affairs): D. F. BAINTON
Vice-Chancellor (Research): Z. W. HALL
Vice-Chancellor (University Advancement and Planning): B. W. SPAULDING
Registrar: M. BLOS
Librarian: KAREN BUTTER (acting)
Library of 875,000 vols
Number of teachers: 855
Number of students: 3,589

DEANS

School of Dentistry: C. N. BERTOLAMI
School of Pharmacy: G. KENYON
School of Medicine: H. T. DEBAS
School of Nursing: J. S. NORBECK
Graduate Division: C. ATTKISSON

DIRECTOR

Langley Porter Neuropsychiatric Institute: C. VAN DYKE

University of California, Santa Barbara

Santa Barbara, CA 93106
Telephone: (805) 893-8000
Fax: (805) 893-8016
Established 1909; became part of the University 1944
Chancellor: HENRY T. YANG
Executive Vice-Chancellor (Academic Affairs): ILENE NAGEL
Vice-Chancellor (Institutional Advancement): JOHN M. WIEMANN
Vice-Chancellor (Administrative Services): DAVID N. SHELDON
Vice-Chancellor (Student Affairs): MICHAEL D. YOUNG
Vice-Chancellor (Research): FRANCE A. CÓRDOVA
Assistant Chancellor: ROBERT W. KUNTZ (Budget and Planning)
Associate Vice-Chancellors: RONALD W. TOBIN (Academic Programs), JULIUS M. ZELMANOWITZ (Academic Personnel), EVERETT R. KIRKELIE (Administrative and Auxiliary Services)
Assistant Vice-Chancellors: ANAND K. DYAL-CHAND (Student Academic Services), ERNEST A. LOPEZ (Public Affairs), CHERYL R. BROWN (Development), PETER STEINER (Alumni Affairs)
Registrar: BEVERLEY LEWIS
Librarian: (vacant)
Number of teachers: 901
Number of students: 18,940

DEANS

College of Letters and Science: EVERETT ZIMMERMAN (Provost, acting)
College of Engineering: GLENN LUCAS (acting)
College of Creative Studies: WILLIAM J. ASHBY (Provost)
Graduate School of Education: JULES ZIMMER
Graduate Division: CHARLES LI
Humanities and Fine Arts: DAVID MARSHALL
Mathematical, Life and Physical Sciences: DAVID J. CHAPMAN
Social Sciences: ED DONNERSTEIN (acting)
School of Environmental Science and Management: JEFF DOZIER

HEADS OF DEPARTMENT

College of Creative Studies: WILLIAM J. ASHBY
College of Engineering:
Chemical and Nuclear Engineering: GLENN FREDRICKSON
Electrical and Computer Engineering: HUA LEE
Materials: FRED LANGE
Mechanical and Environmental Engineering: ROBERT ODETTE
Computer Science: OSCAR IBARRA
College of Letters and Science:
Anthropology: KATHARINA SCHRIEBER
Art Museum: MARLA BERNS (Dir)
Art Studio: HARRY REESE
Asian American Studies: PAUL SPICKARD
Biochemistry and Molecular Biology: JAMES COOPER
Black Studies: GERARD PIGEON
Chemistry: DAN LITTLE
Chicano Studies: FRANCISCO LOMELI
Classics: ROBERT RENEHAN
Communication: DAVID SEIBOLD
Comparative Literature: SUSAN DERWIN
Dance: FRANK RIES (Dir)
Dramatic Art: PETER LACKNER
East Asian Languages and Cultural Studies: KUO-CHING TU
Ecology, Evolution and Marine Biology: SCOTT COOPER
Economics: ROBERT DEACON
English: MARK ROSE
Environmental Studies: JO-ANN SHELTON
Film Studies: CONSTANCE PENLEY
French and Italian: CATHERINE NESCI
Geography: MICHAEL GOODCHILD
Geological Sciences: BRUCE LUYENDYK
Germanic, Slavic and Semitic Languages: WOLF KITTLER
Global and International Studies: MARK JUERGENSMEYER (Dir)
History: JACK TALBOT
History of Art and Architecture: BRUCE ROBERTSON
Latin American and Iberian Studies: JOHN FORAN
Law and Society: DANIEL LINZ
Linguistics: SUSANNA CUMMING
Mathematics: MARTIN SCHARLEMANN
Medieval Studies: JOY ENDERS, SHARON FARMER
Molecular, Cellular and Developmental Biology: STUART FEINSTEIN
Music: WILLIAM PRIZER
Philosophy: ANTHONY BRUECKNER
Physics: ROLLIN MORRISON
Political Science: LORRAINE MCDONNELL
Psychology: AARON ETTENBERG
Religious Studies: RICHARD HECHT
Renaissance Studies: ROBERT J. WILLIAMS
Sociology: BETH SCHNEIDER
Spanish and Portuguese: GIORGIO PERISSINOTTO
Speech and Hearing Sciences: DAVID CHAPMAN (acting)
Statistics and Applied Probabilty: DAVID HINKLEY
Women's Studies: SHIRLEY LIM
Writing Program: JUDITH KIRSCHT (Dir)
Graduate School of Education:
Education: WILLIS COPELAND

ATTACHED RESEARCH INSTITUTES

ARPA Center for Optical Communications: Co-Dirs P. MICHAEL MELLIAR-SMITH, JOHN BOWERS
Center for Black Studies: Dir CLAUDINE MICHEL
Center for Chicano Studies: Dir DENISE SEGURA
Center for Computational Modeling Systems: TERENCE SMITH
Center for Control Engineering and Computation: Dir PETER KOKOTOVIC
Center for Educational Change in Mathematics: Dir JULIAN WEISSGLASS
Center for Macromolecular Science and Engineering: Dir GLENN FREDRICKSON
Center for Quantized Electronic Structures: Dir EVELYN HU
Center for Risk Studies and Safety: Dir THEOFANIS THEOFANOUS
Compound Semiconductor Research Center: Dir MARK RODWELL
David Simonett Center for Spatial Analysis (National Center for Geographic Information and Analysis): Dir KEITH CLARKE
Engineering Computer Infrastructure: Dir STEVE BUTNER
Geography Remote Sensing Unit: Dir JOHN ESTES
High-Performance Composites Center: Dir FREDERICK LECKIE
Institute for Computational Earth Systems Science: Dir CATHERINE GAUTIER
Institute for Crustal Studies: Dir RALPH ARCHULETA (acting)
Institute for Polymers and Organic Solids: Dir ALAN HEEGER
Institute for Social, Behavioural and Economic Research: Dir RICHARD APPELBAUM
Institute for Theoretical Physics: Dir DAVID GROSS
Interdisciplinary Humanities Center: Dir SIMON WILLIAMS
Linguistic Minority Research Institute: Dir REYNALDO MACIAS
Marine Science Institute: Dir STEVEN GAINES (interim)
Materials Research Laboratory: Dir ANTHONY CHEETHAM
Multidisciplinary Optical Switching Technology: Dir JOHN BOWERS
National Center for Ecological Analysis and Synthesis: Dir O. JAMES REICHMAN
National Nanofabrication Users' Network: Dir EVELYN HU
Neuroscience Research Institute: Dir STEVEN FISHER
Ocean Engineering Laboratory: Dir MARSHALL TULIN
Optoelectronics Technology Center: Dir LARRY A. COLDREN
Quantum Institute: Dir S. JAMES ALLEN
Institute for Nuclear Partical Astrophysics and Cosmology: Dir DAVID CALDWELL
Long-term Ecological Research on Antarctic Marine Eco Systems: Dir RAYMOND SMITH
Center for Non-Stoichiometric Semiconductors: Dir UMESH MISHRA
Southern California Earthquake Center: Dir RALPH ARCHULETA
Center for Robust Nonlinear Control of Aeroengines: Dir PETAR KOKOTOVIC (Co-ordinator)
Innovative Microwave Power Amplifier Consortium Center: Dir UMESH MISHRA

University of California, Santa Cruz

Santa Cruz, CA 95064
Telephone: (408) 459-2058
Chartered 1961; opened 1965
Chancellor: M. R. C. GREENWOOD
Executive Vice-Chancellor: R. MICHAEL TANNER
Librarian: ALLAN J. DYSON
Number of teachers: 551
Number of students: 10,200

DEANS

Arts: Edward F. Houghton
Engineering: Patrick Mantey
Graduate Studies: Ron Henderson
Humanities: Jorge Hankamer
Natural Sciences: David Kliger
Social Sciences: Martin Chemers

PROVOSTS

Cowell College: William Ladusaw
Adlai E. Stevenson College: Mark Cioc
Crown College: Leo Laporte
Merrill College: John Isbister
Porter College: Kathleen Foley
Kresge College: Paul Skenazy
Oakes College: David Anthony
College Eight: Walter L. Goldfrank

RESEARCH UNITS

Institute of Nonlinear Science: Dir Geoffrey Vallis.
Institute of Marine Sciences: Dir Gary Griggs.
Lick Observatory: Dir Joseph S. Miller.
Institute for Particle Physics: Dir Abraham Seiden.
Institute of Tectonics: Dir Eli Silver.

UNIVERSITY OF LA VERNE

1950 3rd St, La Verne, CA 91750

Telephone: (909) 593-3511
Fax: (909) 953-0965

Founded 1891 as Lordsburg College; became La Verne College in 1917; present name 1977
Private control
Academic year: September to June
President: Dr Stephen C. Morgan
Registrar: Marilyn Davies
Director of Admissions: Lisa Meyers
Librarian: Prof. Marlin Heckman

Library of 337,000 vols
Number of teachers: 145 full-time, 261 part-time
Number of students: 4,088

DEANS

College of Arts and Sciences: Prof. John Gingrich
School of Business and Global Studies: Prof. William Relf
College of Law: Prof. Kenneth Held
School of Organizational Management: Prof. Thomas Harvey
School of Continuing Education: Prof. James C. Manolis

UNIVERSITY OF REDLANDS

Redlands, CA 92373

Telephone: (714) 793-2121
Fax: (714) 793-2029

Founded 1907
Private

President: James R. Appleton
Provost and Vice-President for Academic Affairs: (vacant)
Vice-President for Finance and Administration: Phil Doolittle
Vice-President for University Relations: Ron Stephany
Registrar: Charlotte Lucey
Library Director: Klaus Musmann

Library of 233,882 vols
Number of teachers: 126
Number of students: 1,400

Publication: *Redlands.*

DEANS

College of Arts and Sciences: Dr Phillip Glotzbach
Whitehead College: Dr Mary Boyce

AFFILIATED CENTRES

Alfred North Whitehead Center for Lifelong Learning: f. 1976; 2,150 students; Dean Mary Boyce.

Johnston Center for Individualized Learning: f. 1969; 150 students; Dir Yasuyuki Owada.

UNIVERSITY OF SAN DIEGO

5998 Alcala Park, San Diego, CA 92110

Telephone: (619) 260-4600
Founded 1949

President: Alice B. Hayes
Vice-President and Provost: Dr Francis Lazarus
Vice-President for University Relations: John McNamara
Vice-President for Finance and Administration: Paul Bissonnette
Vice-President for Student Affairs: Thomas F. Burke
Librarian: Edward Starkey

Library of 596,600 vols
Number of teachers: 508
Number of students: 6,416

DEANS

School of Law: Daniel Rodriguez
College of Arts and Sciences: Dr Patrick Drinan
School of Education: Paula Cordeiro
School of Business: Dr Curtis Cook
School of Nursing: Dr Janet Rodgers

UNIVERSITY OF SAN FRANCISCO

2130 Fulton St, San Francisco, CA 94117-1080

Telephone: (415) 422-6762
Fax: (415) 422-2303
E-mail: schlegel@usfca.edu

Founded 1855
Private; Jesuit

President: Rev. John P. Schlegel
Vice-President for Academic Affairs: Dr John P. Gillespie (acting)
Vice-President for Student Affairs: Dr Carmen A. Jordan-Cox
Vice-President for Development: David F. MacMillan
Vice-President for Busines and Finance: Willard H. Nutting
Vice-President for University Relations: Aldred P. Alessandri
Vice-President for Legal Affairs and University Counsel: Rev. Robert F. Curran
Secretary: Rev. Philip P. Callaghan
Librarian: Dr Tyrone H. Cannon

Library of 593,543 vols
Number of teachers: 290
Number of students: 7,662

Publications: *USF Law Review* (quarterly), *USF Magazine* (quarterly).

DEANS AND DIRECTORS

Dean of Academic Services: B. J. Johnson
Colleges of Arts and Sciences: Stanley Nel
Business Administration: Gary Williams
School of Law: H. Jay Folberg
Nursing: Dr Stanley D. Nel (Administrator, acting)
School of Education: Paul Warren
College of Professional Studies: Betty Taylor

UNIVERSITY OF SOUTHERN CALIFORNIA

University Park, Los Angeles, CA 90089

Telephone: (213) 740-2311

Established 1879; incorporated and opened 1880

President: Steven B. Sample
Provost: Lloyd Armstrong, Jr
Senior Vice-Presidents: Lloyd Armstrong, Jr (Academic Affairs), Alan Kreditor (University Advancement), Dennis F. Dougherty (Administration), Stephen J. Ryan (Medical Affairs)
Vice-President, Business Affairs: Thomas H. Moran
Vice-President, Health Affairs: Joseph van der Meulen
Vice-President, Student Affairs: Michael Jackson
Vice-President and Comptroller: Fermin Vigil
Director of International Admissions: Mary E. Randall
Admissions and Financial Aid: Joseph Allen
Director of Admissions: Duncan Murdoch
Director of Academic Records and Registrar: Kenneth Servis
Treasurer: William C. Hromadka

Library: see Libraries
Number of teachers: 2,600
Number of students: 28,000

Publications: *USC Chronicle, USC Trojan Family* (quarterly).

DEANS

College of Letters, Arts and Sciences: Morton Schapiro
Graduate Studies: Jonathan Kotler
School of Accounting: Kenneth Merchant
School of Architecture: Robert Timme
School of Business Administration: Randolph Westerfield
School of Cinema and TV: Elizabeth Monk Daley
School of Dentistry: Howard M. Landesman
School of Education: Guilbert C. Hentschke
School of Engineering: Leonard M. Silverman
School of Fine Arts: Ruth Weisberg
School of Law: Scott H. Bice
School of Medicine: Stephen Ryan
School of Music: Larry J. Livingston
School of Pharmacy: Timothy Chan
School of Public Administration: Jane G. Pisano
School of Social Work: Rino J. Patti
School of Theatre: Robert Scales
School of Urban and Regional Planning: Edward Blakely
Annenberg School of Communications: Geoffrey Cowen
Fisher Gallery: Selma Holo
Leonard Davis School of Gerontology: Edward L. Schneider

UNIVERSITY OF THE PACIFIC

Stockton, CA 95211

Telephone: (209) 946-2011

Founded as California Wesleyan College 1851; name changed to University of the Pacific 1852; consolidated with Napa College 1896; name changed to College of the Pacific 1911; name changed to University of the Pacific 1961
Private control

President: Donald V. DeRosa
Provost: Philip N. Gilbertson
Financial Vice-President: Patrick Cavanaugh
Dean of Admissions: Janet S. Dial
Vice-President for Student Life: Judith M. Chambers
Librarian: Jean Purnell

Library of 475,000 vols
Number of teachers: 373
Number of students: 5,428

Publications: *Pacific Review, Pacific Historian, Pacifican, Contact Point* (Dental School), *De Minimus* (School of Law).

DEANS

Business and Public Administration: Mark Plovnick
Education: Fay B. Haisley

Engineering: Richard Turpin
Graduate School: Dennis Meerdink
International Studies: Margee Ensign
Liberal Arts: Robert Benedetti
Music: Carl E. Nosse
Pharmacy: Philip Oppenheimer
School of Dentistry: Arthur Dugoni
School of Law: Gerald Caplan
University College: (vacant)

UNIVERSITY OF WEST LOS ANGELES

1155 West Arbor Vitae St, Inglewood, CA 90301-2902

Telephone: (310) 342-5200
Fax: (310) 342-5298

Founded 1966
Private control

President: Ben Bycel
Director of Library Services: Linda Rauhauser

Library of 34,000 vols

DEANS

School of Law: Ben Bycel (acting)
School of Paralegal Studies: (vacant)

WEST COAST UNIVERSITY

440 Shatto Place, Los Angeles, CA 90020

Telephone: (213) 487-4433

Founded 1909

President: Dr Robert M. L. Baker, Jr
Provost: Dr Mary Elizabeth Shutler
Registrar: Roger Miller
Librarian: Michelle Stiles

Library of 25,000 vols
Number of teachers: 200
Number of students: 1,350

Campuses in Los Angeles, Orange, San Diego, Santa Barbara and Ventura Counties

WESTMONT COLLEGE

955 La Paz Rd, Santa Barbara, CA 93108

Telephone: (805) 565-6000
Fax: (805) 565-6234

Founded 1937

President: Dr David K. Winter
Provost: Dr Stan Gaede
Registrar: Dr W. Wright
Director of Learning Resources: John D. Murray

Library of 150,000 vols
Number of teachers: 82
Number of students: 1,250

WHITTIER COLLEGE

Whittier, CA 90608

Telephone: (562) 907-4200
Fax: (562) 907-4242

Founded 1887
Liberal Arts, Business and Law

President: James L. Ash, Jr
Provost and Dean of Academic Affairs: Richard S. Millman
Vice-President (College Advancement): Joseph M. Zanetta
Vice-President (Finance and Administration): Jo Ann Hankin
Vice-President (Legal Education) and Dean of Law School: John A. FitzRandolph
Librarian: Philip M. O'Brien

Library of 300,000 vols; special collections: John Greenleaf Whittier, Quakers
Number of teachers: 110
Number of students: 2,000

Publications: *The Rock* (quarterly), *Whittier Law Review, Cornerstone* (every 2 months).

COLORADO

ADAMS STATE COLLEGE OF COLORADO

Alamosa, CO 81102

Telephone: (719) 587-7011

Founded 1921

President: J. Thomas Gilmore
Vice-President for Academic Affairs: David Svald (acting)
Vice-President for Student Affairs: Lawrence T. Gomez
Dean of Education and Graduate Studies: Scott Baldwin
Dean of Academic Services: Cheryl Billingsley
Director of External Affairs: Shelly Andrews
Librarian: Dianne Machado

Library of 150,000 vols
Number of teachers: 120
Number of students: 2,600

COLORADO COLLEGE

Colorado Springs, CO 80903

Telephone: (719) 389-6000
Fax: (719) 389-6933

Chartered 1874

President: Kathryn Mohrman
General Secretary: Renee Rabinowitz
Vice-President for Business: Janice Cassin
Vice-President for Development: Donald W. Wilson
Vice-President for Student Life: Laurel McLeod
Librarian: John Sheridan

Number of teachers: 140
Number of students: 1,850

DEANS

College and Faculty: Timothy Fuller
Summer Session: William Hochman

COLORADO SCHOOL OF MINES

Golden, CO 80401

Telephone: (303) 273-3000

Founded 1874

A university of mineral resources

President: George S. Ansell
Vice-President for Business Affairs: Robert G. Moore
Vice-President for Academic Affairs and Dean of the Faculty: John U. Trefny
Vice-President for Development: Stephen P. Pougnet
Dean of Graduate Studies and Research: Arthur J. Kidnay
Vice-President for Student Affairs and Dean of Students: Harold R. Cheuvront
Director of Admissions: A. W. Young
Librarian: Joanne V. Lerud

Library of 250,344 vols
Number of teachers: 200
Number of students: 3,200

Publications: *Quarterly of the Colorado School of Mines, Mineral Industries Bulletin.*

COLORADO STATE UNIVERSITY

Fort Collins, CO 80523

Telephone: (970) 491-1101
Fax: (970) 491-0501

Founded 1870 as The Agricultural College of Colorado, became a State institution in 1876, a land-grant college in 1879

President: Albert Yates
Vice-President for Administration: Gerry J. Bomotti
Provost/Academic Vice-President: Loren Crabtree
Director of Admissions: M. R. Ontiveros
Director of Libraries: Camila Alire

Library of 1,700,000 vols
Number of teachers: 1,385
Number of students: 22,344

DEANS

College of Business: Dan Costello
College of Engineering: Johannes Gessler (interim)
College of Natural Resources: A. Allen Dyer
College of Natural Sciences: J. C. Raich
College of Agricultural Sciences: Kirvin L. Knox
College of Veterinary Medicine and Biomedical Sciences: J. L. Voss
College of Liberal Arts: Loren W. Crabtree
College of Applied Human Sciences: Nancy Hartley
Graduate School: D. Jaros

ASSOCIATED INSTITUTIONS

Colorado Agricultural Experiment Station: Lee E. Sommers.

Extension Service: Milan Rewerts.

Colorado State Forest Service: State Forester J. E. Hubbard.

Rocky Mountain Forest and Range Experiment Station: Dir Denver Buens.

Colorado Co-operative Fish and Wildlife Research Unit: Leader D. R. Anderson.

FORT LEWIS COLLEGE

1000 Rim Dr., Durango, CO 81301

Telephone: (303) 247-7184

Founded 1911

President: Joel M. Jones
Vice-President for Admissions: Harlan Steinle
Librarian: Margaret Landrum

Library of 175,000 vols
Number of teachers: 187
Number of students: 4,456

UNIVERSITY OF COLORADO

System Administration, Boulder, CO 80309

Telephone: (303) 492-6201

Incorporated 1861, opened 1877

President: John C. Buechner
Vice-President for Budget and Finance: Glen R. Stine
Vice-President for Academic Affairs and Research: Richard Byyny
Associate Vice-President for Budget and Finance: James Topping
Secretary of the University and Board of Regents: Milagros Caraballo

Library: see Libraries

Publications: *College Catalog* (annually), *Colorado Alumnus* (monthly for 10 months), *Colorado Business Review* (monthly), *Colorado Quarterly, English Language Notes, East European Quarterly, University of Colorado Law Review, Colorado Engineer, Arctic and Alpine Research* (quarterly), *Computer Newsletter* (9 times per year), and University of Colorado Studies series covering various subjects.

University of Colorado at Boulder

Boulder, CO 80309

Telephone: (303) 492-8908

Chancellor: Roderic Park (acting)
Vice-Chancellor for Administration: Pete Bardin (acting)
Vice-Chancellor for Academic Affairs and Dean of Faculties: Wallace Loh

Number of students: 25,571

DEANS

College of Environmental Design: PATRICIA O'LEARY
College of Business and Administration: LARRY SINGELL
School of Education: PHILIP DISTEFANO
School of Journalism: WILLARD ROWLAND
School of Law: HAROLD BRUFF
Graduate School: CAROL B. LYNCH
College of Arts and Sciences: PETER SPEAR
College of Engineering: ROSS COROTIS
College of Music: DANIEL SHER
Continuing Education: ANNE COLGAN
Health Sciences Center (Chancellor VINCENT FULGINITI):
School of Medicine: RICHARD D. KRUGMAN (acting)
School of Nursing: JUANITA TATE
School of Dentistry: ROBERT AVERBACH (acting)
School of Pharmacy: LOUIS DIAMOND

University of Colorado at Colorado Springs

Colorado Springs, CO 80933

Telephone: (303) 593-3000

Chancellor: LINDA BUNNELL SHADE

Number of students: 6,066

University of Colorado at Denver

Denver, CO 80217

Telephone: (303) 556-2400

Chancellor: GEORGIA LESH-LAURIE (acting)

Number of students: 10,932

UNIVERSITY OF DENVER

Denver, CO 80208

Telephone: (303) 871-2000
Telex: 910-931-0586
Fax: (303) 871-4000

Founded 1864
Private control
Academic year: September to May

Chancellor: DANIEL L. RITCHIE
Vice-Chancellor for Communications: CAROL FARNSWORTH
Vice-Chancellor for Institutional Advancement: JACK MILLER
Vice-Chancellor for Financial Affairs: CRAIG WOODY
Provost: WILLIAM ZARANKA
Vice-Provost for Undergraduate Studies: Dr SHEILA WRIGHT
Vice-Provost for Graduate Studies: Dr BARRY HUGHES
Registrar: J. POMMREHN
Librarian: NANCY ALLEN

Library of 1,897,000 vols
Number of teachers: 402 full-time, 18 part-time
Number of students: 8,667

Publications: *Denver Law Journal of International Law and Policy, Denver Law Journal* (quarterly), *Transportation Law Journal, The University of Denver Law Review, Family Law Quarterly, The Centre Report* (quarterly).

HEADS OF DEPARTMENTS

Faculty of Arts, Humanities and Social Sciences:
School of Art: BETHANY KRIEGSMAN
English: Dr ELEANOR MCNEES
History: Dr JOHN LIVINGSTON
Center for Judaic Studies: Dr STANLEY WAGNER
Languages and Literature: Dr HELGAR WATT
Music: Dr JOE DOCKSEY
Philosophy: FRANCIS SEEBURGER
Religious Studies: Dr FREDERICK GREENSPAHN

Faculty of Mathematical and Computer Sciences:
Mathematical and Computer Sciences: Dr JOEL COHEN

College of Education: Dr ELINOR KATZ (Bureau of Educational Services)

Graduate School of Professional Psychology: Dr PETER BUIRSKI

Faculty of Natural Sciences:
Biological Sciences: ROBERT DORES
Chemistry: GREGORY DEWEY
Engineering: Dr ALBERT J. ROSA
Geography: Dr DAVID LONGBRAKE
Physics: Dr FRANK MURCRAY

Faculty of Social Sciences:
Anthropology: Dr DEAN SAITTA
Economics: TRACY MOTT
Mass Communications: Dr MICHAEL WIRTH
Political Science: Dr STEVEN MCCAR
Psychology: Dr GEORGE POTTS
Public Affairs: RICHARD CALDWELL
Sociology: Dr NANCY REICHMAN
Human Communications: Dr ALTON BARBOUR

College of Law:
Masters of Taxation: Dr MARK VOGEL

College of Business Administration:
Accountancy: Dr RONALD KUCIC
Executive MBA: Dr PAUL STAMES
Finance: MACLYN CLOUSE
Hospitality Management and Tourism: Dr ROBERT O'HALLORAN
Legal Studies: MARK LEVINE
Management: Dr ROBERT MCGOWAN
Information Technology and Electronic Commerce: DON MCCUBBNEY
Marketing: JOHN BURNETT
Masters of International Management: Dr DAVID M. HOPKINS
Summit MBA Program: CAROLYN SHADLE
Real Estate and Construction Management: MARK LEVINE
Statistics/Operations Research: DARL BIEN
Weekend College: MICHELE BLOOM

ATTACHED INSTITUTE

Denver Research Institute.

UNIVERSITY OF NORTHERN COLORADO

Greeley, CO 80639

Telephone (970) 351-1890
Fax: (970) 351-1110

Founded 1889 as the State Normal School; name changed to Colorado State Teachers' College 1911, to Colorado State College of Education in 1935, to Colorado State College in 1957; present name adopted in 1970

President: HANK BROWN
Provost and Vice-President for Academic Affairs: Dr MARLENE STRATHE
Registrar: JEFFREY BUNKER
Vice-President for Administration: FRANCES L. SCHOENECK
Vice-President for Student Affairs: Dr STUART TENNANT
Librarian: GARY PITKIN

Number of teachers: 483
Number of students: 10,200

Publications: *Bulletin, Alumni Notes, Alumni News Letter, Journal of Research Services.*

DEANS

Graduate School: Dr RICHARD KING (acting)
College of Business Administration: ROBERT LYNCH
College of Continuing Education: NANCY REDDY (acting)
College of Education: Dr ALAN HUANG (acting)
College of Arts and Science: Dr SANDRA FLAKE
College of Performing and Visual Arts: Dr HOWARD SKINNER
College of Health and Human Sciences: VINCENT A. SCALIA

UNIVERSITY OF SOUTHERN COLORADO

2200 Bonforte Blvd, Pueblo, CO 81001-4901

Telephone: (719) 549-2100

Founded as Junior College 1933, Southern Colorado State College 1961, present name 1975

President: Dr ROBERT C. SHIRLEY
Librarian: Mrs B. MOORE

Library of 175,000 vols
Number of teachers: 200
Number of students: 4,343

WESTERN STATE COLLEGE OF COLORADO

Gunnison, CO 81231

Telephone: (303) 943-0120
Fax: (303) 943-7069

Founded 1911

President: HARRY PETERSON
Registrar: (vacant)
Librarian: SUSAN RICHARDS

Library of 120,000 vols
Number of teachers: 143
Number of students: 2,514

CONNECTICUT

ALBERTUS MAGNUS COLLEGE

New Haven, CT 06511

Telephone: (203) 777-8550

Coeducational liberal arts college

Founded 1925

President: JULIA MCNAMARA
Vice President (Academic Affairs): Sr CHARLES MARIE BRANTL
Director of Admissions: RICHARD LOLATTE
Director of Library Services: Dr ALAN BARTHOLOMEW

Library of 93,664 vols
Number of teachers: 55
Number of students: 565

CENTRAL CONNECTICUT STATE UNIVERSITY

New Britain, CT 06050

Telephone: (203) 832-3200
Telex: 9102505958
Fax: (203) 832-2522

Founded 1849

President: Dr RICHARD L. JUDD
Registrar: JAMES FOX
Director of Library Services: JEANNE SOHN

Library of 582,119 vols
Number of teachers: 387 full-time, 355 part-time
Number of students: 6,191 full-time, 5,561 part-time

Bachelor's and Master's in a wide variety of disciplines and Sixth-Year Certificate in Reading

CONNECTICUT COLLEGE

New London, CT 06320

Telephone: (860) 439-2000

Founded 1911

Coeducational liberal arts college

President: CLAIRE GAUDIANI

Registrar: Aileen Burdick
Dean of Planning and Enrolment Management: Mark Putnam
Office of Graduate Studies: John Burton
Dean of the College: Art Ferrari
Provost and Dean of the Faculty: David Lewis
Dean of Student Life: Catherine Wood Brooks
Librarian: Connie Dowell

Library of 475,000 vols
Number of teachers: 147 full-time
Number of students: 1,918

EASTERN CONNECTICUT STATE UNIVERSITY

83 Windham St, Willimantic, CT 06226-2295
Telephone: (860) 465-5221
Fax: (860) 465-4690
Founded 1889, refounded as Willimantic State College 1959, present name 1983
President: David G. Carter
Vice-President for Finance and Administration: Dennis Hannon
Vice-President for Academic Affairs: Dr Dimitrios Pachis
Vice-President for Institutional Advancement: Barbara Eshoo
Vice-President and Dean of Student Affairs: Dr Arvin Lubetkin
Registrar: Kathleen Fabian
Librarian: Tina Fu

Library of 226,000 vols
Number of teachers: 142 full-time, 190 part-time
Number of students: 4,527

FAIRFIELD UNIVERSITY

Fairfield, CT 06430-5195
Telephone: (203) 254-4000
Founded 1942
President: Rev. Aloysius P. Kelley
Academic Vice-President: Dr Robert E. Wall
Vice-President for Finance and Treasurer: William J. Lucas
Vice-President, Student Services: William P. Schimpf
Vice-President for Advancement: George E. Diffley
Vice-President for Administration: L. William Miles
University Registrar: Robert C. Russo
Library Director: James Estrada

Library of 326,000 vols
Number of teachers: 203 full-time, 181 part-time
Number of students: undergraduate 4,269, graduate 910

DEANS

College of Arts and Sciences: Dr Orin L. Grossman
School of Business: Dr Walter Ryba
Graduate School of Education and Allied Professions: Dr Margaret Deignan
School of Continuing Education: (vacant)
School of Nursing: Dr Theresa Valiga

HARTFORD GRADUATE CENTER

275 Windsor St, Hartford, CT 06120-2991
Telephone: (203) 548-2400
Fax: (203) 548-7887
Founded 1955
Affiliated with Rensselaer Polytechnic Institute
President: Dr Ann Stuart
Dean of Student Affairs: Rebecca M. Danchak
Library Director: Barbara J. Vizoyan

Library of 30,000 vols, 490 periodicals
Number of teachers: 35 full-time, 100 part-time
Number of students: 2,100

QUINNIPIAC COLLEGE

Hamden, CT 06518
Telephone: (203) 288-5251
Fax: (203) 281-8906
E-mail: admissions@quinnipiac.edu
Founded 1929
Independent
President: John L. Lahey
Provost and Vice-President for Academic Affairs: John B. Bennett
Registrar: Dorothy Lauria
Dean of Admissions: Joan Mohr
Librarian: Charles Getschell

Library of 466,000 vols
Number of teachers: 248 full-time, 321 part-time
Number of students: 4,167 full-time, 1,267 part-time

DEANS

School of Health Sciences: Joseph Woods
School of Business: Phillip Frese
School of Liberal Arts: David Stineback
School of Law: Neil Cogan
Students: Manuel C. Carreiro

SAINT JOSEPH COLLEGE

1678 Asylum Ave, West Hartford, CT 06117
Telephone: (860) 232-4571
Fax: (860) 233-5695
Founded 1932
President: Dr Winifred E. Coleman
Executive Vice-President: Maureen Reardon
Vice-President (Academic Affairs) and Dean: Dr Karen Ristau
Registrar: Irene Rios
Librarian: Linda Geffner

Library of 106,500 vols
Number of teachers: 119
Number of students: 1,794

SOUTHERN CONNECTICUT STATE UNIVERSITY

501 Crescent St, New Haven, CT 06515
Telephone: (203) 397-4275
Founded 1893
Liberal arts, career and teacher education
President: Michael J. Adanti
Vice-President for Academic Affairs: Dr Anthony V. Pinciaro, Jr
Vice-President for Finance and Administration: William R. Bowes
Vice-President for Student and University Affairs: Martin J. Curry (acting)
Dean of Student Affairs: David A. Pedersen
Registrar: Conrad S. Calandra
Librarian: Kenneth G. Walter

Library of 300,000 vols
Number of teachers: 400
Number of students: 13,000

DEANS

School of Arts and Sciences: Dr J. Philip Smith
School of Education: Dr Bernice Willis
School of Graduate Studies and Continuing Education: Dr Rodney A. Lane
School of Business: Dr Alan Leader
School of Library Science and Instructional Technology: Dr Edward C. Harris
School of Professional Studies: Fay Miller

TRINITY COLLEGE

Hartford, CT 06106
Telephone: (203) 297-2000
Fax: (203) 297-2257
Founded 1823
President: Evan S. Dobelle
Vice-President for Finance and Treasurer: Robert A. Pedemonti
Dean of the Faculty: Jill Reich
Secretary of the Faculty: Gerald Moshell
Librarian: Dr Steven L. Peterson

Library of 850,000 vols
Number of full-time teachers: 145, including 55 professors
Number of students: 2,100
Publications: *Tripod, Review, Trinity Papers, Reporter*.

UNITED STATES COAST GUARD ACADEMY

New London, CT 06320
Telephone: (801) 883-8724
Founded 1876
President: Rear-Admiral Paul E. Versaw
Director of Admissions: Capt. Robert Thorne
Librarian: Pat Daragan

Library of 136,000 vols
Number of teachers: 114
Number of students: 906

UNIVERSITY OF BRIDGEPORT

Bridgeport, CT 06601
Telephone: (203) 576-4000
Fax: (203) 576-4653
Founded 1927
President: Richard L. Rubenstein
Provost (acting) and Vice-President for Academic Affairs: Michael J. Grant
Vice-President for Administration and Finance: Thomas R. Klump
Vice-President for University Relations: (vacant)
Dean of Students: Janet S. Merritt
Dean of Admissions and Financial Aid: Suzanne D. Wilcox
Librarian: Karen Smiga

Library of 263,788 vols
Number of teachers: 83 full-time, 177 part-time
Number of students: 1,339 full-time, 808 part-time

DEANS

College of Graduate and Undergraduate Studies: Anthony J. Guerra
College of Chiropractice: Frank A. Zolli
College of Naturopathic Medicine: James Sensenic

UNIVERSITY OF CONNECTICUT

Storrs, CT 06269
Telephone: (860) 486-2000
State control
Language of instruction: English
Academic year: September to May
Established 1881 as The Storrs Agricultural School, present name 1939. Campuses in Farmington (Health Center) and Hartford (Law and Social Work); regional campuses at Avery Point, Hartford, Stamford, Torrington and Waterbury
President: Philip E. Austin
Chancellor and Provost for Academic Affairs: Mark A. Emmert
Chancellor and Provost for Health Affairs: Leslie S. Cutler
Vice-President for Institutional Advancement: T. Allenby
Vice-Chancellor for Student Affairs: Vicky L. Triponey
Vice-President for Finance and Administration: Wilbur R. Jones
Librarian: Paul J. Kobulnicky

Library: see Libraries
Number of teachers: 1,040 (full-time)

Number of students: 21,753

Publications: *Connecticut Alumnus* (quarterly), *University of Connecticut Directory of Classes* (2 a year), *Summer Sessions Bulletin* (annually), *University Advance* (weekly during academic year), *University of Connecticut, General Catalog* (annually), *The Graduate School Catalog* (annually), *School of Law Catalog* (annually), *School of Social Work Catalog* (annually), *School of Medicine Catalogue* (annually), *Student Handbook* (annually).

DEANS

College of Agriculture and Natural Resources: KIRKLYN M. KERR
College of Liberal Arts and Sciences: ROSS D. MACKINNON
School of Business Administration: THOMAS G. GUTTERIDGE
School of Dental Medicine: JAMES E. KENNEDY
School of Education: RICHARD SCHWAB
School of Engineering: AMIR FAGHRI
School of Extended and Continuing Education: ROBERT BALDWIN (acting)
School of Fine Arts: ROBERT H. GRAY
School of Family Studies: CHARLES M. SUPER
School of Law: HUGH C. MACGILL
School of Medicine: PETER J. DECKERS
School of Nursing: KATHLEEN A. BRUTTOMESSO (acting)
School of Pharmacy: MICHAEL C. GERALD
School of Allied Health Professions: JOSEPH SMEY
Ratcliffe Hicks School of Agriculture: SUMAN SINGHA (Director and Associate Dean)
School of Social Work: KAY DAVIDSON
Graduate School: ROBERT V. SMITH

DIRECTORS

Marine Science and Technology Center: RICHARD A. COOPER
Institute of Materials Science: HARRIS MARCUS
Institute for Social Inquiry: EVERETT C. LADD, Jr
Center for Academic Programs: MARIA MARTINEZ
Centre for Instructional Media and Technology: RICHARD GORHAM
International Services and Programs: MARK WENTZEL
Institute for Teaching and Learning: KEITH BARKER
Urban Semester Program: LOUISE SIMMONS
Study Abroad Programs: SALLY INNIS KLITZ
Computer Center: MALCOLM L. TOEDT
Office of Institutional Research: PAM ROELFS

PROFESSORS

College of Agriculture and Natural Resources:

ADAMS, Jr R. G., Entomology
ALLINSON, D. W., Agronomy
ASHLEY, R. A., Horticulture
BENDEL, R. B., Animal Science
BERKOWITZ, G., Plant Science
BIBLE, B. B., Horticulture
BRAVO-URETA, B. E., Agricultural Economics
BRIDGEN, M. P., Horticulture
BULL, N. H., Co-operative Extension
CLARK, R. M., Nutritional Sciences
COTTERILL, R. W., Agricultural Economics
FERRIS, A. G., Nutritional Sciences
GEARY, S. J., Pathobiology
HART, I. C., Animal Science
HILL, D. W., Clinical Chemistry
HOAGLUND, T. A., Animal Science
KERR, K. M., Pathobiology
LAMMI-KEEFE, C. J., Nutritional Sciences
LEE, T., Agricultural Economics
LOPEZ, R. A., Agricultural Economics
MILLER, D. R., Natural Resources
PAGOULATOS, E., Agricultural Economics
RIESEN, J. W., Animal Science
SCHROEDER, D. B., Natural Resources
SINGHA, S., Horticulture
VAN KRUININGEN, H. J., Pathobiology
WHITELY, H. E., Pathology

College of Liberal Arts and Sciences:

ABBOTT, J. L., English
ABE, K., Mathematics
ABIKOFF, W., Mathematics
ABRAHAMSON, M., Sociology
ALLEN, G. J., Psychology
ALLEN, J. L., Geography
ALLEN, P. R., Economics
ANDERSON, G. J., Ecology and Evolutionary Biology
ANDERSON, S., Philosophy
ANSELMENT, R. A., English
ASHER, R., History
AUSTIN, P. E., Economics
BAILEY, W. F., Chemistry
BARRECA, R. R., English
BARTH, P. S., Economics
BEE, R. L., Anthropology
BENSON, C. D., English
BENSON, D. R., Molecular and Cell Biology
BERENTSON, W., Geography
BERLEANT-SCHILLAR, R., Anthropology
BERTHELOT, A., Modern and Classical Languages (French)
BEST, P. E., Physics
BLEI R. C., Mathematics
BLOOM, L., English
BOHLEN, W. F., Marine Sciences
BOHN, R., Chemistry
BOSTER, J., Anthropology
BOWMAN, L. W., Political Science
BRASWELL, E. H., Molecular and Cell Biology
BRIDGES, J., Psychology
BROADHEAD, R. S., Sociology
BROWN, R. D., History
BUCK, R. W., Communication Sciences
BUCKLEY, R. N., History
BUDNICK, J. I., Physics
CAIRA, J. N., Ecology and Evolutionary Biology
CARELLO, C., Psychology
CARSTENSEN, F. V., Economics
CHAPPLE, W. D., Physiology and Neurobiology
CHARTERS, A., English
CHEN, T. T., Molecular Cell Biology
CIRURGIAO, A. A., Modern and Classical Languages (Spanish and Portuguese)
CLARK, A., Philosophy
CLIFFORD, J. G., Political Science
COHEN, M. F., Communication Sciences
COLLIER, C., History
COLWELL, R., Ecology and Evolutionary Biology
COONS, R. E., History
COOPER, R. A., Marine Sciences
CORMIER, V. F., Geology and Geophysics
CRAIN, R., Molecular and Cell Biology
CREEVEY, L., Political Science
CROMLEY, R., Geography
CROTEAU, M., Journalism
DASHEFSKY, A., Sociology
DAVID, C. W., Chemistry
DAVIS, J., History
DEBLAS, A. L., Physiology and Neurobiology
DENENBERG, V. H., Psychology
DESCH, Jr, C. E., Ecology and Evolutionary Biology
DEWAR, R. E., Anthropology
DEY, D. K., Statistics
DICKERSON, D. J., Psychology
DULACK, T., English
DUTTA, N., Physics
ELDER, C. L., Philosophy
EMMERT, M. A., Political Science
EPLING, G. A., Chemistry
EYLER, E. E., Physics
EYZAGUIRRE, L. B., Modern and Classical Languages (Spanish)
FARNEN, R. F., Political Science
FEIN, D., Psychology
FERREE, M. M., Sociology
FISHER, J. D., Psychology
FITZGERALD, W. F., Marine Sciences, Geology and Geophysics
FOWLER, C., Psychology
FRANK, H. A., Chemistry
GAI, M., Physics
GALLO, R. V., Physiology and Neurobiology
GATTA, J. J., English
GELFAND, A. E., Statistics
GIAMBALVO, V., Mathematics
GILBERT, H. R., Communication Sciences
GILBERT, M., Philosophy
GILMOUR, R. S., Political Science
GINE, E., Mathematics
GLASBERG, D., Sociology
GLAZ, J., Statistics
GLAZ, S., Mathematics
GOGARTEN, J. P., Molecular and Cell Biology
GOLDMAN, B. D., Physiology and Neurobiology
GOODWIN, P. B., History
GOULD, P. L., Physics
GRAY, N., Geology and Geophysics
GROCHENIG, K., Mathematics
GUGLER, J. N. M., Sociology
HAAS, A. H., Mathematics
HAHN, Y., Physics
HALLER, K., Physics
HALLWOOD, C. P., Economics
HALVORSON, P. L., Geography
HAMILTON, D., Physics
HANDWERKER, W. P., Anthropology
HANINK, D. M., Geography
HANSELL, R. W., Mathematics
HANSON, B. C., Political Science
HAYDEN, H. C., Physics
HECKATHORN, D., Sociology
HEFFLEY, D. R., Economics
HENRY, C., Ecology and Evolutionary Biology
HERZBERGER, D. K., Modern and Classical Languages (Spanish)
HIGHTOWER, L., Molecular and Cell Biology
HIGONETT, M. R., English
HINES, W. A., Physics
HISKES, R., Political Science
HOGAN, P. C., English
HOLSINGER, K., Ecology and Evolutionary Biology
HUANG, S. J., Chemistry
HURLEY, J. F., Mathematics
ISLAM, M. M., Physics
JACOBUS, L. A., English
JAVANAINEN, J., Physics
JOESTEN, R., Geology and Geophysics
JONES, S. P., English
KAPPERS, L. A., Physics
KATZ, L., Psychology
KEARNEY, R., Political Science
KELLY, J. A., Molecular and Cell Biology
KENDALL, D. A., Molecular and Cell Biology
KENNY, D. A., Psychology
KESSEL, Q. C., Physics
KIRSCH, I., Psychology
KNOX, J., Molecular and Cell Biology
KOLTRACHT, I., Mathematics
KREMER, J., Marine Sciences
KRIDER, H. M., Molecular and Cell Biology
KRIMERMAN, L. I., Philosophy
KRISCH, H., Political Science
KUO, L., Statistics
KUPPERMAN, J. J., Philosophy
LADD, E. C., Political Science
LANGLOIS, R. N., Economics
LASNIK, H., Linguistics
LEADBETTER, E. R., Molecular and Cell Biology
LERMAN, M., Mathematics
LEWIS, C. W., Political Science
LILLO-MARTIN, D., Linguistics
LINNEKIN, J., Anthropology
LOGAN, C. H., Sociology
LOWE, C. A., Psychology
LUYSTER, R. W., Philosophy
LYNES, M., Molecular and Cell Biology
MCEACHERN, W. A., Economics
MCKENNA, P., Mathematics
MACKINNON, R. D., Geography

MACLEOD, G., English
MADASCI, D., Physics
MADYCH, W. R., Mathematics
MAKOWSKY, V., English
MALLETT, R. L., Physics
MANNHEIM, P., Physics
MARCUS, P. I., Molecular and Cell Biology
MASCIANDARO, F., Modern and Classical Languages (Italian)
MAXON, A., Communication Sciences
MAXSON, S. C., Psychology
MEYER, J. W., Geography
MEYER, M., English
MEYERS, D. T., Philosophy
MICELI, T., Economics
MICHEL, R., Chemistry
MILLER, D. B., Psychology
MILLER, R. L., English
MILLER, S. M., Economics
MILLIKAN, R. G., Philosophy
MONAHAN, E. C., Marine Sciences
MUELLER-WESTERHOFF, U. T., Chemistry
MUKHOPADHYAY, N., Statistics
MURPHY, B., English
NELSON, M., English
NEUMANN, M., Mathematics
O'HARA, J. D., English
ORRINGER, N. R., Modern and Classical Languages (Spanish)
ORZA, A. T., English
PANAGROSSO, S. A., Military Science
PEASE, D. M., Physics
PETERSON, C. W., Physics
PETERSON, R., English
PHILLIPS, R., Philosophy
PHILPOTTS, A. R., Geology and Geophysics
PICKERING, S., English
POLLACK, E., Physics
RAWITSCHER, G. H., Physics
RAY, S. C., Economics
REITER, H. L., Political Science
RENFRO, J. L., Physiology and Neurobiology
RICKARDS, J., Psychology
RIGGIO, T. P., English
ROBBINS, G., Geology and Geophysics
ROBERTS, T. J., English
ROE, S. A., History
ROURKE, J., Political Science
RUSLING, J., Chemistry
SACKS, S. R., Economics
SALAMONE, J., Psychology
SANDERS, B., Psychology
SANDERS, C., Sociology
SCHAEFER, C. W., Ecology and Evolutionary Biology
SCHMERL, J. H., Mathematics
SCHWARZ, J. C., Psychology
SEGERSON, K., Economics
SEHULSTER, J. R., Psychology
SHANKWEILER, D. P., Psychology
SHAW, R. E., Psychology
SIDNEY, S. J., Mathematics
SILANDER, J. A., Ecology and Evolutionary Biology
SMITH, M. B., Chemistry
SMITH, W. W., Physics
SONSTROEM, D. A., English
SPALDING, K., History
SPENCER, D. E., Mathematics
SPEYER, J. F., Molecular and Cell Biology
SPIEGEL, E. S., Mathematics
STAVE, B. M., History
STEELE, S., Linguistics
STUART, J., Chemistry
STWALLEY, W., Physics
SUIB, S. L., Chemistry
SUNG, C. S. P., Chemistry
SWADLOW, H. A., Psychology
SWANSON, M., Physics
TANAKA, J., Chemistry
TAYLOR, R. L., Sociology
TEC, N., Sociology
TEPAS, D., Psychology
THOMAN, E., Psychology
THORSON, R. M., Geology and Physics
TOKES, R. L., Political Science
TOLLEFSON, J. L., Mathematics
TORGERSEN, T., Marine Sciences
TUCHMAN, G., Sociology
TURVEY, M., Psychology
VENGROFF, R., Political Science
VILLEMEZ, W., Sociology
VINSONHALER, C., Mathematics
VITALE, R. A., Statistics
WALKER, D. B., Political Science
WALLER, A., History
WATT, J. H., Communication Science
WELLS, K. D., Ecology and Evolutionary Biology
WHEELER, S. C., Philosophy
WHITLATCH, R., Marine Sciences
WICKLESS, W. J., Mathematics
WILKENFELD, R. B., English
WORCESTER, W., Journalism
WRIGHT, A. W., Economics
YARISH, C., Ecology and Evolutionary Biology
YPHANTIS, D. A., Molecular and Cell Biology
ZIRAKZADEH, C. E., Political Science

School of Allied Health Professions:

ADAMS, C. H.
BOHANNON, R. W.
HASSON, S.
SMEY, J. W.

School of Business Administration:

BIGGS, S. F., Accounting
CANN, W. A., Business Law
CARRAFIELLO, V. A., Business Law
CLAPP, J. M., Finance
FOX, K. H., Business Law
GARFINKEL, R. S., Operations Research and Information Management
GIACOTTO, C., Finance
GLASCOCK, J. L., Finance
GUTTERIDGE, T. G., Management
HEINTZ, J. A., Accounting
HEGDE, S., Finance
HUSSEIN, M., Accounting
JAIN, S. C., Marketing
KOCHANEK, R. F., Accounting
LUBATKIN, M. J., Management
MARSDEN, J. R., Operations Research and Information Management
O'BRIEN, T., Finance
POWELL, G. N., Management
SCOTT, G. M., Operations Research and Information Management
SEWALL, M. A., Marketing
SIRMANS, C. F., Finance and Real Estate
TUCKER, E. W., Business Law
VEIGA, J. F., Management

School of Education:

ARCHAMBAULT, F. X., Educational Psychology
BALDWIN, A., Curriculum and Instruction
BROWN, S. W., Educational Psychology
CASE, C. W., Educational Leadership
CHERKES-JULKOWSKI, M. D. G., Educational Psychology
DOYLE, M. A., Curriculum and Instruction
FOWLKES, M. R., Educational Leadership
GABLE, R. K., Educational Psychology
GARRETT, G. E., Sports, Leisure and Exercise Sciences
GOODKIND, T. B., Curriculum and Instruction
GREENSPAN, S., Educational Psychology
HARTLEY, H. J., Educational Leadership
IBRAHIM, F. A., Educational Psychology
IRWIN, J. W., Curriculum and Instruction
IWANICKI, E. F., Educational Leadership
KARAN, O. C., Educational Psychology
KEHLE, T. J., Educational Psychology
MCGUIRE, J., Educational Psychology
MCLEAN, L. K., Educational Psychology
MANNEBACH, A. J., Curriculum and Instruction
MARESH, C. M., Sports, Leisure and Exercise Sciences
MEAGHER, J. A., Curriculum and Instruction
MINAYA-PORTELLA-ROWE, L., Curriculum and Instruction
OWEN, S., Educational Psychology
REAGAN, T., Curriculum and Instruction
REIS, S. M., Educational Psychology
RENZULLI, J., Educational Psychology
SCHWAB, R., Educational Leadership
SHAW, S. F., Educational Psychology
SHECKLEY, B. G., Educational Leadership
SHIBLES, M. R., Educational Leadership
SHIVERS, J. S., Sports, Leisure and Exercise Sciences
WEINLAND, T. P., Curriculum and Instruction
WILBUR, M. P., Educational Psychology
YIANNAKIS, A., Sports, Leisure and Exercise Sciences

School of Engineering:

AMMAR, R. A., Computer Science and Engineering
BANSAL, R., Electrical and Systems Engineering
BAR-SHALOM, Y., Electrical and Systems Engineering
BARKER, K., Computer Science and Engineering
BELL, J. P., Chemical Engineering
BERGMAN, T., Mechanical Engineering
BRODY, H. D., Metallurgy
CHEO, P. K., Electrical and Systems Engineering
CLAPP, P. C., Metallurgy
COUGHLIN, R. W., Chemical Engineering
CUTLIP, M. B., Chemical Engineering
DAVIS, C. F., Civil and Environmental Engineering
DEVEREUX, O. F., Metallurgy
DEWOLF, J. T., Civil and Environmental Engineering
ENDERLE, J. D., Electrical and Systems Engineering
ENGEL, G., Computer Science and Engineering and Electrical and Systems Engineering
EPSTEIN, H., Civil and Environmental Engineering
FAGHIRI, A., Mechanical Engineering
FENTON, J., Chemical Engineering
FOX, M. D., Electrical and Systems Engineering
FRANTZ, G. C., Civil and Environmental Engineering
GALLIGAN, J., Metallurgy
GREENE, N. D., Metallurgy
HOWES, T., Metallurgy
JAIN, F. C., Electrical and Systems Engineering
JAVIDI, B., Electrical and Systems Engineering
JORDAN, D. J., Electrical and Systems Engineering and Computer Science and Engineering
JORDAN, E. H., Mechanical Engineering
KATTAMIS, T., Metallurgy
KAZEROUNIAN, K., Mechanical Engineering
KOBERSTEIN, J., Chemical Engineering
KOENIG, H. A., Mechanical Engineering and Orthodontics
LANGSTON, L. S., Mechanical Engineering
LEONARD, J. W., Civil and Environmental Engineering
LIPSKY, L., Computer Science and Engineering
LUH, P. B., Electrical and Systems Engineering
MARCUS, H. L., Metallurgy
MARYANSKI, F., Computer Science and Engineering
MORRAL, J. E., Metallurgy
MURTHA-SMITH, E., Civil and Environmental Engineering
OLGAC, N., Mechanical Engineering
PATTIPATI, K. R., Electrical and Systems Engineering
ROULIER, J. A., Computer Science and Engineering
SHAW, M., Chemical Engineering

TAYLOR, G. W., Electrical and Systems Engineering
TING, T. C., Computer Science and Engineering
WEISS, R. A., Chemical Engineering

School of Family Studies:

ANDERSON, S., Human Development and Family Relations
BLANK, T. O., Human Development and Family Relations
HARKNESS, S., Human Development and Family Relations
NAHEMOW, L., Human Development and Family Relations
O'NEIL, J. M., Human Development and Family Relations
RYDER, R., Human Development and Family Relations
SABATELLI, R., Human Development and Family Relations
SUPER, C. M., Human Development and Family Relations

School of Fine Arts:

ARM, T. E., Music
BAGLEY, P. B. E., Music
BASS, R., Music
BELLINGHAM, B. A., Music
CRAIG, J. D., Art
CROW, L. J., Dramatic Arts
ENGLISH, G., Dramatic Arts
FRANKLIN, J. F., Dramatic Arts
GRAY, R. H., Art
HILL, E., Dramatic Arts
MCDONALD, R. A., Dramatic Arts
MARTINEZ, A., Art
MAZZOCCA, A. N., Art
MILLER, R. F., Music
MOLETTE, C. W., Dramatic Arts
MUIRHEAD, D., Art
PATRYLAK, D. J., Music
SABATINE, J., Dramatic Arts
SOMER, A., Music
STEPHENS, R., Music
STERN, A. S., Dramatic Arts
TALVACCHIA, B. L., Art
THORNTON, R. S., Art
WERFEL, G., Art

School of Nursing:

BECK, C., Nursing
BERNAL, H.
CHIN, P., Nursing
CHURCH, O. M., Nursing
COLER, M. A., Nursing
FROMAN, R. D., Nursing
HARKNESS, G., Nursing
KOERNER, B. L., Nursing

School of Pharmacy:

CHOW, M. S. S., Clinical Pharmacy
COHEN, S. D., Toxicology
GERALD, M. C., Pharmacology
KRAMER, P. A., Pharmaceutics
LANGNER, R. O., Pharmacology
MAKRIYANNIS, A., Medicinal Chemistry
MORRIS, J. B., Toxicology
NIEFORTH, H. A., Medical Chemistry
PALMER, H., Clinical
PIKAL, M. J., Pharmaceutics
SMITH, R. V., Pharmacy

Health Center: 263 Farmington Ave, Farmington, Connecticut 06030

School of Dental Medicine:

BRYERS, J., BioStructure and Function
CUTLER, L. S., Oral Diagnosis
EISENBERG, E., Oral Diagnosis
FRANK, M. E., BioStructure and Function
GAY, T., BioStructure and Function
GOLDBERG, A. J., Prosthodontics
GRASSO, J. E., Prosthodontics
HAND, A., Paediatric Dentistry
KATZ, R., Behavioural Sciences and Community Medicine
KENNEDY, J. E., Periodontology
LURIE, A. G., Oral Diagnosis
NANDA, R., Orthodontics
NUKI, K., Oral Diagnosis
PAMEIJER, C. H., Prosthodontics
PETERSON, D. E., Oral Diagnosis
REISINE, S., Behavioural Sciences and Community Health
ROSSOMANDO, E. P., BioStructure and Function
SPANGBERG, L. S. W., Restorative Dentistry and Endontology
TANZER, J. M., Oral Diagnosis
TANZER, M. L., BioStructure and Function
TAYLOR, T., Prosthodontics
TINANOFF, N., Paediatric Dentistry
TRUMMEL, C. L., Periodontology
UPHOLT, W., BioStructure and Function

School of Medicine:

ADAMS, N. D., Medicine
AFFLECK, G. G., Community Medicine and Health Care
AGRAWAL, N. M., Medicine
ALTMAN, A. J., Paediatrics
ARNOLD, A., Medicine
BABOR, T. F., Community Medicine and Health Care
BAILIT, H., Community Medicine and Health Care
BARBARESE, E., Neurology
BAYER, M. J., Traumatology and Emergency Medicine
BENN, P. A., Paediatrics
BESDINE, R. W., Medicine
BIGAZZI, P. E., Pathology
BROWNER, B. O., Orthopaedic Surgery
BRUDER, M. E., Paediatrics
BULLOCK, W., Medicine
CAMPBELL, W. A., Obstetrics and Gynaecology
CARMICHAEL, G. G., Microbiology
CARSON, J. H., Biochemistry
CINTI, D. L., Pharmacology
CIVETTA, J. M., Surgery
CLOUTIER, M., Pediatrics
CONE, R. E., Pathology
CUSHMAN, R. A., Family Medicine
DAS, A. K., Microbiology
DAS, D. K., Surgery
DECKERS, P. J., Surgery
DONALDSON, III, J. O., Neurology
EISENBERG, S., Microbiology
FEDER, Jr, H. M., Family Medicine
FEIN, A., Physiology
FEINSTEIN, M. B., Pharmacology
FOROUHAR, F., Pathology
FRESTON, J. W., Medicine
GARIBALDI, R., Medicine
GERBER, M. A., Paediatrics
GLASEL, J. A., Biochemistry
GOLDSCHNEIDER, I., Pathology
GRANT-KELS, J. M., Dermatology
GRASSO, J. A., Anatomy
GREENBERG, B. R., Medicine
GREENSTEIN, R. M., Pediatrics
GROSS, J. B., Anaesthesiology
GRUNNET, M. L., Pathology
HAGER, W. D., Medicine
HANSEN, H., Community Medicine and Health Care
HESSELBROCK, V. M., Psychiatry
HOPFER, S. M., Laboratory Medicine
JAFFE, L., Physiology
KADDEN, R. M., Psychiatry
KAPLAN, A., Medicine
KATZ, A., Medicine
KIM, D. O., Surgery
KLOBUTCHER, L. A., Biochemistry
KOPPEL, D. E., Biochemistry
KOSHER, R. A., Anatomy
KREAM, B., Medicine
KREUTZER, D. L., Pathology
KUWADA, S., Anatomy
LE FRANCOIS, L., Medicine
LEONARD, G., Surgery
LEVINE, J. B., Medicine
LOEW, L. M., Physiology
LORENZO, J. A., Medicine
MOREST, D. K., Anatomy
MUKHOPADHYAY, B., Medicine
O'ROURKE, J. T., Pathology
OZOLS, J., Biochemistry
PAPERMASTER, D. S., Pharmacology
PAPPANO, A. J., Pharmacology
PARKE, A. L., Medicine
PELUSO, J. J., Obstetrics and Gynaecology
PESANTI, E. L., Medicine
PFEIFFER, S. E., Microbiology
PISCIOTTO, P. T., Laboratory Medicine
POTASHNER, S. J., Anatomy
RAISZ, L. G., Medicine
RAJAN, T. V., Pathology
RAMSBY, G. R., Diagnostic Imaging and Therapeutics
REIK, Jr, L., Neurology
ROSENKRANTZ, T. S., Paediatrics
ROWE, D. W., Paediatrics
ROWE, J. C., Paediatrics
RUSSELL, J.C., Surgery
RYAN, R. W., Laboratory Medicine
SCHENKMAN, J. B., Pharmacology
SETLOW, P., Biochemistry
SHA'AFI, R. I., Physiology
SHANLEY, J. D., Medicine
SHEEHAN, T. J., Community Medicine and Health Care
SIMON, R. H., Surgery
SPENCER, R. P., Diagnostic Imaging and Therapeutics
SRIVASTA, P. K., Medicine
TENNEN, H., Community Medicine and Health Care
TRAHIOTIS, C., Surgery
TSIPOURAS, P., Paediatrics
TUTSCHKA, P. J., Medicine
WELLER, S. K., Microbiology
WHITE, B. A., Anatomy
WHITE, W. B., Medicine
WOLFSON, L. I., Neurology
WU, G. Y., Medicine
YEH, H. H., Pharmacology

School of Law: 55 Elizabeth St, Hartford, CT 06105-2296

BAKER, T.
BARNES, R. D.
BECKER, L. E., Jr
BIRMINGHAM, R.
BRITTAIN, J. C.
CALLOWAY, D. A.
CULLISON, A. D.
DAILEY, A. C.
FERNOW, T. O.
GEORGAKOPOULOS, N.
JANIS, M.
JONES, C. C.
KAY, R. S.
KURLANTZICK, L. S.
MACGILL, H. C.
MCLEAN, W.
MORAWETZ, T. H.
OQUENDO, A.
ORLAND, L.
PAUL, J.
PAUL, J. R.
POMP, R. D.
SCHATZKI, G.
SILVERSTEIN, E.
STARK, J. H.
STRASSER, K. A.
TAIT, C. C.
TONDRO, T. J.
UTZ, S. G.
WEISBROD, C. A.
WHITMAN, R.
WOLFSON, N.

School of Social Work: University of Connecticut, 1798 Asylum Avenue, West Hartford, Connecticut 06117

ALISSI, A. S.
BLOOM, M.
BORRERO, M.
DAVIDSON, K.

HEALY, L.
HESSELBROCK, M. N.
HUMPHREYS, N.
JOHNSON, H.
KUTNER, S.
LEE, J.
MARTIN, R.
MORALES, J. A. B.
NEWMAN, J.
PINE, B.

ATTACHED INSTITUTES

Bureau of Educational Research: Dir FRANCIS ARCHAMBAULT
Center for Contemporary African Studies: Dir LARRY BOWMAN
Travelers Center on Aging: Dir NANCY SHEEHAN
Alcohol Research Center: Dir THOMAS BABOR
Center for Biochemical Toxicology: Dir STEVE COHEN
Biotechnology Center: Dir THOMAS T. CHEN
Booth Research Center for Computer Applications and Research: Dir PETER LUH (acting)
Center for International Business Programs: Dir SUBHASH JAIN
Connecticut Center for Economic Analysis: Dir FRED CARSTENSEN (acting)
Connecticut Small Business Development Center: Dir DENNIS GRUELL
Center for Conservation and Biodiversity: Dir KENT HOLSINGER
Center for Distance Learning: Dir JACK CONKLIN
Center for Economic Education: Dir EMMETT COTTER
Center for Environmental Health: Dir IAN HART (acting)
Electrical Insulation Research Center: Dir STEVEN BOGGS
Center for European Studies: Dirs BARBARA WRIGHT, MARVIN COX
Food Marketing Policy Center: Dir RONALD COTTERILL
Center for Grinding Research and Development: Dir OWEN DEVEREUX (acting)
Center for Judaic Studies and Contemporary Jewish Life: Dir ARNOLD DASHEFSKY
Labor Education Center: Dir MARK SULLIVAN
Center for Latin American and Caribbean Studies: Dir ELIZABETH MAHAN
Center for Materials Simulation: Dir PHILIP C. CLAPP
National Research Center on the Gifted and Talented: Dir JOSEPH RENZULLI
National Undersea Research Center: Dir IVAR BABB
Center for Oral History: Dir BRUCE STAVE
Pappanikou Center on Special Education and Rehabilitation: Dir LEE MCLEAN
Photonics Research Center: Dir CHANDRA ROYCHOUDHURI
Pollution Prevention and Research and Development Center: Dir JAMES FENTON
Advanced Technology Center for Precision Manufacturing: Dir HAROLD BRODY
Center for Real Estate and Urban Economic Studies: Dir C. F. SIRMANS
Center for International Social Work Studies: Dir LYNN HEALY
Center for the Study of Parental Acceptance and Rejection: Dir RONALD P. ROHNER
Center for Survey Research and Analysis: Dir KENNETH DAUTRICH
Northeastern Research Center for Wildlife Diseases: Dir HERBERT VAN KRUININGEN
Insurance Law Center: Dir TOM BAKER
Institute for African-American Studies: Dir RONALD TAYLOR
Asian American Studies Institute: Dir ROGER BUCKLEY
Institute of Cellular and Molecular Biology: Dir PHILIP YEAGLE
Environmental Research Institute: Dir GEORGE HOAG
Goethe Institute: Dir TERRY MCCORMICK
Management Information Systems Studies Institute: Dir GEORGE SCOTT
Marine Science and Technology Center: Dir RICHARD COOPER
Institute of Materials Science: Dir HARRIS MARCUS
Institute of Public and Urban Affairs: Dir ROBERT GILMOUR
Institute for the Advancement of Political Social Work Practice: Dir NANCY HUMPHREYS
Institute of Public Service: Dir ROLAND HOLSTEAD (acting)
Institute of Public Service International: Dir MOMAR NDIAYE
Puerto Rican and Latino Studies Institute: Dir SCOTT COOK (acting)
Small Business Institute: Dir WILLIAM SCHULZE
Institute for Social Inquiry (and The Roper Center for Public Opinion Research): Dir EVERETT C. LADD, Jr.
Connecticut Transportation Institute: Dir CHRISTIAN DAVIS
Institute for Violence Reduction: Dir MICHAEL BORRERO
Institute of Water Resources: Dir HUGO THOMAS

UNIVERSITY OF HARTFORD

200 Bloomfield Ave, West Hartford, CT 06117
Telephone: (860) 768-4417
Fax: (860) 768-5417

Founded 1877
Private control

President: Dr WALTER HARRISON
Provost: Dr ELIZABETH IVEY
Dean of the Faculty: Dr CATHERINE STEVENSON
Vice-President for Finance and Administration: BEVERLY P. MAKSIN
Dean of Students: Dr ANNE FITZMAURICE
Vice-President for Development: STEPHEN JEFFREY
Registrar: DOREEN LAY
Director of Admissions: RICHARD ZEISER
Director of Libraries and Learning Resources: RONALD EPP

Library of 561,000 vols
Number of teachers: 318
Number of students: 4,117 full-time undergraduates, 1,270 part-time undergraduates, 592 full-time graduates, 1,110 part-time graduates

DEANS

Hartford Art School: Dr STUART SCHAR
College of Arts and Sciences: Dr EDWARD GRAY
Barney School of Business and Public Administration: Dr CORINE NORGAARD
Hillyer College: Dr EDWARD GRAY
College of Education, Nursing and Health Professions: DAVID A. CARUSO
College of Engineering: ALAN J. HADAD
Hartt School: MALCOLM MORRISON
S. I. Ward College of Technology: ALAN J. HADAD
Hartford College for Women: Dr EDWARD GRAY

UNIVERSITY OF NEW HAVEN

West Haven, CT 06516
Telephone: (203) 932-7000
Fax: (203) 932-1469

Founded 1920

President: LAWRENCE J. DENARDIS
Vice-President for Academic Affairs and Provost: JAMES W. UEBELACKER
Vice-President for Student Affairs and Athletics: WILLIAM LEETE, Jr
Vice-President for University Advancement: DONALD J. IBSEN
Vice-President for Finance and Administration: DUNCAN P. GIFFORD
Dean of Admissions and Financial Aid: STEVEN BRIGGS
Librarian: HANKO DOBI

Library of 235,000 vols, 423,000 documents
Number of teachers: 157 full-time, 429 part-time
Number of students: 5,113

WESLEYAN UNIVERSITY

High St, Middletown, CT 06459
Telephone: (860) 685-3501
Fax (860) 685-0756

Chartered 1831

President: DOUGLAS J. BENNET
Vice-President (Academic Affairs): RICHARD W. BOYD
Vice-President and Treasurer: ROBERT TAYLOR
Vice-President and Secretary: (vacant)
Vice-President for University Relations: ROBERT B. BARTON
Dean of Admissions: BARBARA-JAN WILSON
Librarian: J. ROBERT ADAMS

Library of 1,000,000 vols
Number of teachers: 315
Number of students: 2,905

Publication: *Catalog Annual.*

WESTERN CONNECTICUT STATE UNIVERSITY

Danbury, CT 06810
Telephone: (203) 837-8200

Founded 1903

President: JAMES R. ROACH
Vice-President for Academic Affairs: EUGENE BUCCINI
Vice-President for Administration and Finance: RICHARD H. SULLIVAN
Vice-President for Student Affairs and Government Relations: FRANK J. MUSKA
Registrar: HENRY TRITTER
Director of Library Services: RALPH HOLIBAUGH

Number of teachers: 216
Number of students: 5,607

DEANS

Ancell School of Business: RONALD BENSON
School of Arts and Sciences: CAROL A. HAWKES
School of Professional Studies: WALTER B. BERNSTEIN

YALE UNIVERSITY

New Haven, CT 06520
Telephone: (203) 432-1333

Founded in 1701, named Yale College in 1718. Transition to University status took place from 1810 to 1861
Private control

President: RICHARD LEVIN
Provost: ALISON F. RICHARD
Secretary: LINDA K. LORIMER
Vice-President for Finance and Administration: JOSEPH P. MULLINEX
Vice-President for Development and Alumni Affairs: CHARLES J. PAGNAM
Librarian: SCOTT BENNETT

Library: see Libraries
Number of teachers: 2,747 (incl. research staff)
Number of students: 10,975

Publications: *Yale Review, Yale Journal of Biology and Medicine, Yale Law Journal, Yale Alumni Magazine, American Journal of Science, Library Gazette, Bulletin of Art Gallery Associates, American Scientist, Journal of American Oriental Society, Journal of Biological Chemistry, Yale Divinity News, Journal of the History of Medicine and Allied Sciences, Journal of Music Theory, Yale Forest School News, Yale Scientific Magazine, Yale French Studies, Yale Literary Magazine, Yale Journal of Criticism, Yale Journal of International*

Law, Yale Journal on Regulation, Yale Law & Policy Review.

DEANS

Yale College: RICHARD H. BRODHEAD
School of Architecture: FRED H. KOETTER
Graduate School: THOMAS APPELQUIST
Divinity School: Rev. RICHARD J. WOOD
School of Forestry and Environmental Studies: JOHN C. GORDON
Law School: ANTHONY T. KRONMAN
School of Medicine: Dr DAVID A. KESSLER
School of Music: ROBERT L. BLOCKER
School of Nursing: JUDITH B. KRAUSS
School of Drama: STAN WOJEWODSKI, Jr
Yale School of Management: JEFFREY E. GARTEN
School of Art: RICHARD BENSON

PROFESSORS

(Some staff serve in more than one faculty)
Faculty of Arts and Sciences (Yale College and Graduate School):

ADAMS, R. M., Philosophy
AGNEW, J.-C., American Studies and History
ALEXANDROV, V. E., Slavic Language and Literature
ALHASSID, Y., Physics
ALTMAN, S., Biology
AMANAT, A., History
ANDERSON, S. R., Linguistics
ANDREWS, D. W. K., Economics
APFEL, R. E., Mechanical Engineering
APPELQUIST, T. W., Physics
APTER, D. E., Comparative Political and Social Development
AVNI, O., French
BALTAY, C., Physics
BANAC, I., History
BARKER, R. C., Electrical Engineering and Applied Physics
BARNHART, R. M., History of Art
BARRON, A., Statistics
BARTLETT, B. S., History
BARTOSHUK, L. M., Psychology
BEALS, R. W., Mathematics
BENNETT, W. R. Jr, Physics
BERNER, R. A., Geology and Geophysics
BERNSTEIN, I. B., Mechanical Engineering and Physics
BERRY, S., Economics
BERS, V., Classics
BEWLEY, T., Economics
BLASSINGAME, J. W., History and African and African-American Studies
BLOCH, H., French
BLOOM, H. I., Humanities
BOER, F. P., Chemical Engineering
BOORMAN, S. A., Sociology
BÖWERING, G. H., Religious Studies
BRAINARD, W. C., Economics
BRISMAN, L., English
BRODHEAD, R. H., English
BROMLEY, D. A., Physics
BROMWICH, D., English
BROUDE, H. W., Economics and Economic History
BROWN, D., Economics
BROWN, T. H., Psychology
BURGER, R. L., Anthropology
BUSHKOVITCH, P. A., History
BUSS, L. W., Ecology and Evolutionary Biology, Geology and Geophysics
BUTLER, J., History and American Studies, Religious Studies
CAHN, W. B., History of Art
CAMERON, D. R., Political Science
CARBY, H. V., African and African-American Studies and American Studies
CAREW, T. J., Psychology and Biology
CHANG, K.-I., Chinese Literature and East Asian Languages and Literature
CHANG, R. K., Physics and Electrical Engineering
CHU, B.-T., Mechanical Engineering
CLARK, K., Comparative Literature and Slavic Languages and Literature
COIFMAN, R. R., Mathematics and Computer Science
COLE, A. T., Classics
COLLEY, L. J., History
COLTON, J., History of Art
CONSTANTINE-PATON, M., Biology
COTT, N. F., History and American Studies
CRABTREE, R. H., Chemistry
CROSS, R. J., Chemistry
CROTHERS, D. M., Chemistry and Molecular Physics and Biochemistry
CROWDER, R. G., Psychology
CROWLEY, J. B., History
DA COSTA, E. V., History
DAVIS, D. B., History
DE LA MORA, J. F., Mechanical Engineering
DELLAPORTA, S., Biology
DEMARQUE, P., Astronomy
DEMOS, J. P., History
DENNING, M., American Studies
DILLON, J. F., Jr, Applied Physics
DIMOCK, W. C., American Studies and English
DUPRE, L. K., Religious Studies
DUVAL, E. M., French
EIRE, C., History and Religious Studies
EISENSTAT, S. C., Computer Science
ERIKSON, K., Sociology and American Studies
ERRINGTON, J. J., Anthropology, East Asian Languages and Literatures
EVENSON, R. E., Economics
FAIR, R. C., Economics
FALLER, J. W., Jr, Chemistry
FEIT, W., Mathematics
FELMAN, S., French and Comparative Literature
FIRK, F. W., Physics
FISCHER, M., Computer Science
FLAVELL, R. A., Immunobiology and Biology
FOLTZ, W. J., African Studies and Political Science
FOSTER, B. R., Near Eastern Languages and Civilizations
FOWLER, C., Linguistics and Psychology
FRAADE, S. D., Religious Studies
FREEDMAN, P. H., History
FRENKEL, I. B., Mathematics
FRY, P. H., English
GADDIS, J. L., History
GAREN, A., Molecular Biophysics and Biochemistry
GARLAND, H., Mathematics
GARRETT, G., Political Science
GAUTHIER, J. A., Geology and Geophysics
GEANAKOPLOS, J., Economics
GELERNTNER, D., Computer Science
GILBERT, C. E., History of Art
GLIER, I., Germanic Languages and Literatures
GOLDBLATT, H., Medieval Slavic Language and Literature
GOLDSMITH, M. H., Biology
GOLDSMITH, T. H., Biology
GONZÁLEZ ECHEVERRÍA, R. O., Spanish and Portuguese
GOODYEAR, S. S., English
GORDON, R. B., Geophysics and Applied Mechanics
GORDON, R. W., History
GREEN, D., Political Science
GREENBERG, J. S., Physics
GRIFFITH, E. H., African and African-American Studies
GUICHARNAUD, J. E., French
GUTAS, D., Arabic Language and Literature
GUTZWILLER, M. C., Physics
HALLER, G. L., Chemical Engineering and Chemistry
HALLO, W. W., Assyriology and Babylonian Literature
HAMADA, K., Economics
HAMILTON, A. D., Chemistry
HAMLIN, C., German Languages and Literatures and Comparative Literature
HARMS, R. W., History
HARRIES, K., Philosophy
HARSHAV, B., Comparative Literature
HARTIGAN, J. A., Statistics
HENRICH, V. E., Applied Physics
HERSEY, G. L., History of Art
HICKEY, L. J., Geology and Geophysics
HIRSHFIELD, J., Physics
HOHENBERG, P. C., Applied Physics and Physics
HOLE, F., Anthropology
HOLLANDER, J., English
HOLQUIST, M., Comparative Literature and Slavic Languages and Literatures
HOMANS, M. B., English
HORN, L. R., Linguistics
HORVÁTH, C. G., Chemical Engineering
HOWE, R. E., Mathematics
HUDAK, P., Computer Science
HYMAN, P., Jewish History
IACHELLO, F., Physics
ILARDI, V., History
INSLER, S., Linguistics
JACKSON, K. D., Spanish and Portuguese
JACKSON, R. L., Slavic Languages and Literatures
JAYNES, G. D., Economics and African and African-American Studies
JOHNSON, M. A., Chemistry
JONES, P. W., Mathematics
JORGENSEN, W. L., Chemistry
JOSEPH, G. M., History
KAGAN, D., History and Classics
KAGAN, S., Philosophy
KANKEL, D. R., Biology
KANNAN, R., Computer Science
KASEVICH, M., Physics
KAZDIN, A. E., Psychology
KELLY, W. W., Anthropology
KENNEDY, P. M., History
KESSEN, W., Paediatrics
KIERNAN, B., History
KINDLMANN, P. J., Electrical Engineering
KLEIN, M. J., History of Science and Physics
KLEINER, D. E. E., Classics and History of Art
KUC, R., Electrical Engineering
KUTZINSKY, V., English, African-American Studies and American Studies
LANG, S., Mathematics
LAPALOMBARA, J., Political Science
LARSON, R. B., Astronomy
LASAGA, A. C., Geology and Geophysics
LAWLER, T., English
LAYTON, B. R., Religious Studies and Near Eastern Languages and Civilizations
LEE, R., Mathematics
LENGYEL, P., Molecular Biophysics and Biochemistry, and Genetics
LICHTEN, W. L., Physics, Engineering and Applied Science
LIKENS, G. E., Biology
LINZ, J. J., Political and Social Science
LONG, M., Mechanical Engineering and Applied Physics
LOVÁSZ, L., Computer Science and Mathematics
LUDMER, J., Spanish and Portuguese
MA, T.-P., Electrical Engineering and Applied Physics
MACDOWELL, S. W., Physics
MACNAB, R. M., Molecular Biophysics and Biochemistry
MCBRIDE, J. M., Chemistry
MCCLELLAN, E., East Asian Languages and Literatures, and Japanese Studies
MCDERMOTT, D. V., Computer Science
MCGUIRE, W. J., Psychology
MANDELBROT, B. B., Mathematics
MANLEY, L. G., English
MARCIANO, W. J., Physics
MARGULIS, G. A., Mathematics
MARSHALL, D. B., English
MATTHEWS, J., Classics and History

MAYER, E., Anthropology
MAYHEW, D. R., Political Science
MAZZOTTA, G., Italian Language and Literature
MEEKS, W. A., Religious Studies
MERRIMAN, J. M., History
MIDDLETON, J. F., Anthropology
MILLER, C. L., French, and African and African-American Studies
MILLER, M., History of Art
MIRANKER, W., Computer Science
MONCRIEF, V. E., Physics and Mathematics
MONTGOMERY, D., History
MOORE, G., Physics
MOORE, P. B., Chemistry and Molecular Biophysics and Biochemistry
MOOSEKER, M. S., Biology and Cell Biology
MORGAN, R. P., Theory of Music
MORSE, A. S., Electrical Engineering
MOSTOW, G. D., Mathematics
NARENDRA, K. S., Electrical Engineering
NEIMARK, A. V., Chemical Engineering
NORDHAUS, W. D., Economics
NOVICK, A., Biology
ODOM, W., Political Science
OEMLER, A., Jr, Astronomy
ONAT, E. T., Mechanical Engineering
ORNSTON, L. N., Biology
OUTKA, G., Philosophy and Christian Ethics
PAKES, A., Economics
PARKER, P. D. M., Physics
PATTERSON, A., English
PATTERSON, L., English
PEARCE, D. G., Economics
PECK, M. J., Economics
PERROW, C. B., Sociology
PETERSON, L. H., English
PEUCKER, B., German Languages and Literatures
PFEFFERLE, L., Chemical Engineering
PHILLIPS, P. C., Economics and Statistics
PIATETSKI-SHAPIRO, I., Mathematics
PINTO, M., Electrical Engineering
PLANTINGA, L. B., History of Music
POLLARD, D. B., Statistics
POLLITT, J. J., Classical Archaeology and History of Art
PORTER, C. A., French
POWELL, J. R., Biology
PRESTEGARD, J. H., Chemistry
PROBER, D. E., Applied Physics
PROWN, J. D., History of Art
QUINT, D. L., Comparative Literature and English
RAE, D. W., Political Science
RANIS, G., International Economics
RAWSON, C., English
READ, N., Physics and Applied Physics
REED, M. A., Electrical Engineering and Applied Physics
RICHARD, A. F., Anthropology and Environmental Studies
ROACH, J. R., English and Theatre Studies
ROBINSON, F. C., English
ROEDER, S., Biology
ROEMER, M. A., Filmmaking and American Studies
ROKHLIN, V., Computer Science and Mathematics
ROSENBAUM, J. L., Biology
ROSENBLUTH, F. M., Political Science
ROSNER, D. E., Chemical Engineering
RUDDLE, F. H., Biology and Genetics
RUDERMAN, D. B., Religious Studies and Jewish History
RUST, J., Economics
RUSSETT, B. M., Political Science and International Relations
RUSSETT, C. E., History
RYE, D. M., Geology and Geophysics
SACHDEV, S., Physics and Applied Physics
SALTZMAN, B., Geophysics
SAMMONS, J. L., Germanic Languages and Literatures
SANDWEISS, J., Physics
SANNEH, L., History
SAUNDERS, M., Chemistry
SCARF, H. E., Economics
SCHAEFER, B., Physics and Astronomy
SCHEFFLER, H. W., Anthropology
SCHEPARTZ, A., Chemistry
SCHMIDT, M. P., Physics
SCHULTZ, M. H., Computer Science
SCHULZ, T. P., Economics and Demography
SCHWARTZ, S. B., History
SCOTT, J. C., Political Science and Anthropology
SEILACHER, A., Geology and Geophysics
SHANKAR, R., Physics
SHAPIRO, I., Political Science
SHILLER, R. J., Economics
SHULMAN, R. G., Chemistry, Molecular Biophysics and Biochemistry
SIMPSON, W. K., Near Eastern Languages and Civilizations
SIMS, C. A., Economics
SINGER, J. L., Psychology
SIU, H. F., Anthropology
SKINNER, B. J., Geology and Geophysics
SKOWRONEK, S., Political Science
SMITH, G. G., History
SMITH, R. M., Political Science
SMITH, R. B., Geology and Geophysics
SMITH, S. B., Political Science
SNOWDEN, F. M., History
SOFIA, S., Astronomy
SÖLL, D. G., Molecular Biophysics and Biochemistry, Biology and Chemistry
SOMMERFIELD, C. M., Physics
SPENCE, J. D., History
SREENIVASAN, K. R., Mechanical Engineering, Physics and Applied Physics
SRINIVASAN, T. N., Economics
STEITZ, J. A., Molecular Biophysics and Biochemistry
STEITZ, T. A., Molecular Biophysics and Biochemistry
STEPTO, R. B., African and African-American Studies, American Studies and English
STERNBERG, R. J., Psychology and Education Psychology
STIMSON, H. M., Chinese Linguistics, East Asian Languages and Literatures
STONE, A. D., Physics and Applied Physics
STONE, R., English
STOUT, H. S., Religious Studies, History and American Studies
STOWE, B. B., Biology, and Forestry and Environmental Studies
SZCZARBA, R. H., Mathematics
SZWED, J. F., Anthropology, African and African-American Studies and American Studies
THOMPSON, R. F., History of Art
TRACHTENBERG, A., American Studies and English
TUFTE, E. R., Political Science, Computer Science and Statistics
TULLY, J. C., Chemistry
TUREKIAN, K. K., Geology and Geophysics
TURNER, F. M., History
TURNER, H. A. Jr, History
VAISNYS, J. R., Electrical Engineering
VALESIO, P., Italian Language and Literature
VAN ALTENA, W. F., Astronomy
VENCLOVA, T., Slavic Languages and Literatures
VERONIS, G., Geophysics and Applied Mathematics
VON STADEN, H. H., Classics and Comparative Literature
VRBA, E. S., Geology and Geophysics
WAGNER, A. R., Psychology
WAGNER, G. P., Biology
WEBER, R., Chemical Engineering
WEINER, A. M., Molecular Biophysics and Biochemistry
WEINSTEIN, S., Religious Studies, Buddhist Studies and East Asian Languages and Literatures
WEISS, H., Near Eastern Archaeology, Near Eastern Languages and Civilizations, and Anthropology
WELSH, A., English
WESTERFIELD, H. B., Political Science and International Studies
WIKSTROM, L. L., Chemical Engineering
WILLIAMS, G. W., Classics
WINKS, R. W., History
WOLF, B. J., American Studies and English
WOLF, W. P., Physics
WOOD, A., Philosophy
WRIGHT, C. M., History of Music
WYMAN, R. J., Biology
YEAZELL, R. B., English
ZELLER, M. E., Physics
ZELMANOV, E., Mathematics
ZIEGLER, F. E., Chemistry
ZIGLER, E. F., Psychology
ZILM, K. W., Chemistry
ZINN, R. J., Astronomy
ZUCKER, S. W., Computer Science and Electrical Engineering
ZUCKERMAN, G. J., Mathematics

School of Medicine:

AGHAJANIAN, G. K., Psychiatry and Pharmacology
ALEXANDER, J., Internal Medicine
ALLISON, T., Psychology
AMATRUDA, J. M., Internal Medicine
AMATRUDA, T. T., Internal Medicine
ANDIMAN, W. A., Paediatrics and Epidemiology and Public Health
ANDRIOLE, V. T., Internal Medicine
ANYAN, W. R., Paediatrics
ARIYAN, S., Surgery
ARNSTEIN, R. L., Psychiatry
ARONS, M. S., Surgery
ARONSON, P. S., Internal Medicine and Cellular and Molecular Physiology
ARTAVANIS-TSAKONAS, S., Cell Biology and Biology
ASIS, M. C., Obstetrics and Gynaecology
ASKENASE, P. W., Internal Medicine and Pathology
ATTERBURY, C. E., Internal Medicine
AWAD, I., Neurosurgery
BALTIMORE, R. S., Paediatrics and Epidemiology and Public Health
BARASH, P. G., Anaesthesiology
BARNSTABLE, C. J., Ophthalmology and Visual Science
BARON, R., Orthopaedics and Rehabilitation, and Cell Biology
BARRY, M., Internal Medicine and Epidemiology and Public Health
BARTOSHUK, L. M., Surgery
BATSFORD, W. P., Internal Medicine
BAUMGARTEN, A., Laboratory Medicine
BEARDSLEY, G. P., Paediatrics and Pharmacology
BEHRMAN, H. R., Obstetrics and Gynaecology, and Pharmacology
BELSKY, J. L., Internal Medicine
BIA, F. L., Internal Medicine and Laboratory Medicine
BIA, M. J., Internal Medicine
BINDER, H. J., Internal Medicine
BLATT, S. J., Psychiatry and Psychology
BOOSS, J., Neurology and Laboratory Medicine
BORON, W. F., Cellular and Molecular Physiology
BOTTOMLY, H. K., Immunobiology
BOULPAEP, E. L., Cellular and Molecular Physiology
BOWERS, M. B., Jr, Psychiatry
BOYER, J. L., Internal Medicine
BRACKEN, M. B., Epidemiology and Public Health
BRAVERMAN, I. M., Dermatology
BROADUS, A. E., Internal Medicine and Cellular and Molecular Physiology
BROWN, P. W., Orthopaedics and Rehabilitation, and Surgery

BROWN, T. H., Cellular and Molecular Physiology
BROWNELL, K. D., Psychology and Epidemiology and Public Health
BROWNSTEIN, D. G., Comparative Medicine
BRUNGER, A. T., Molecular Biophysics and Biochemistry
BUNNEY, B. S., Psychiatry and Pharmacology
BURRELL, M. I., Diagnostic Radiology
BYCK, R., Psychiatry and Pharmacology
BYRNE, T. N., Neurology and Medicine
CABIN, H., Internal Medicine
CADMAN, E. C., Internal Medicine
CARCANGIU, M. L., Pathology
CARTER, D., Pathology
CASTIGLIONE, F. M., Dermatology
CHANDLER, W. K., Cellular and Molecular Physiology
CHARNEY, D. S., Psychiatry
CHENG, Y.-C., Pharmacology
CIPRIANO, A. P., Dermatology
CLEARY, J. P., Internal Medicine
CLEMAN, M., Internal Medicine
COHEN, D. J., Child Psychiatry, Paediatrics and Psychology
COHEN, L. B., Cellular and Molecular Physiology
COHEN, L. S., Internal Medicine
COLEMAN, D., Medicine
COLEMAN, J. E., Molecular Biophysics and Biochemistry
COLLINS, J. G., Anaesthesiology
COMER, J. P., Child Psychiatry and Child Study Centre
COONEY, L. M., Jr, Internal Medicine
COOPER, J. R., Pharmacology
COPEL, J., Obstetrics and Gynaecology
COSTA, J. C., Pathology
CRESSWELL, P., Immunobiology
CULLEN, M. R., Internal Medicine, Epidemiology and Public Health
CURNEN, M. G., Epidemiology and Paediatrics
CURTIS, A. M., Diagnostic Radiology
DANNIES, P. S., Pharmacology
DAVEY, L. M., Neurosurgery
DAVIS, G. L., Pathology
DAVIS, M., Psychiatry and Psychology
DAW, N., Ophthalmology and Visual Science
DE CAMILLI, P. V., Cell Biology
DEISSEROTH, A. B., Internal Medicine
DELUCA, V. A., Internal Medicine
D'ESCOPO, N. D., Internal Medicine
DEVITA, V. T., Internal Medicine
DIMAIO, D., Genetics
DOBBINS, J. W., Internal Medicine
DONABEDIAN, R. K., Laboratory Medicine
DOWNEY, T. W., Child Psychiatry
DOWNING, S. E., Pathology
DUBOIS, A. B., Epidemiology and Public Health, and Cellular and Molecular Physiology
DUDRUCK, S. J., Surgery
DUFFY, T. P., Internal Medicine
DUNCAN, C., Neurosurgery and Paediatrics
DUNCAN, J., Diagnostic Radiology
EBERSOLE, J. S., Neurology
EDBERG, S. C., Laboratory Medicine
EDELSON, M., Psychiatry
EDELSON, R. L., Dermatology
EHRENKRANZ, R. A., Paediatrics
EHRENWERTH, J., Anaesthesiology
EHRLICH, B., Pharmacology and Cellular and Molecular Biology
EISENSTADT, J. M., Genetics
ELEFTERIADES, J., Surgery
ELIAS, J. A., Internal Medicine
ENGELMAN, D. M., Molecular Biophysics and Biochemistry
EVANS, R. W. W., Child Study Centre
FARBER, L. R., Internal Medicine
FEINSTEIN, A. R., Medicine and Epidemiology
FERRO-NOVICK, S., Cell Biology
FINKELSTEIN, F. O., Internal Medicine
FISCHER, D. S., Internal Medicine
FISCHER, J. J., Therapeutic Radiology
FLAMM, G. H., Psychiatry
FLOCH, M. H., Internal Medicine
FORBUSH, B., III, Cellular and Molecular Physiology
FORGET, B. G., Internal Medicine and Genetics
FORMAN, B. H., Internal Medicine
FORREST, J. N., Jr, Internal Medicine
FRIEDLAENDER, G. E., Orthopaedics and Rehabilitation
FRIEDLAND, G., Child Study Centre
GENEL, M., Paediatrics
GIEBISCH, G. H., Cellular and Molecular Physiology
GIFFORD, R. H., Internal Medicine
GIRANDI, N., Paediatrics
GLICKMAN, M. G., Diagnostic Radiology and Surgery
GOLDBERG, B., Paediatrics
GOLDMAN-RAKIC, P., Neurobiology
GOLDSMITH, T. H., Ophthalmology and Visual Science
GOLDSTEIN, P. S., Paediatrics
GONZALEZ, C., Ophthalmology and Visual Science
GORE, J. C., Diagnostic Radiology
GORELICK, F., Internal Medicine and Cell Biology
GRANGER, R. H., Child Study Center and Paediatrics
GREENFELD, D. G., Psychiatry
GREER, C., Neurosurgery
GRINDLEY, N. D., Molecular Biophysics and Biochemistry
GROSS, I., Paediatrics
GROSZMANN, R. J., Internal Medicine
GUSBERG, R. J., Surgery
HADDAD, G. G., Paediatrics
HAMMOND, G. L., Surgery
HAYDAY, A., Biology and Immunobiology
HAYSLETT, J. P., Internal Medicine
HELENIUS, A., Cell Biology
HELLENBRAND, W. S., Paediatrics
HENDLER, E. D., Internal Medicine
HENINGER, G., Psychiatry
HERBERT, P. N., Internal Medicine
HIERHOLZER, W. J., Internal Medicine and Epidemiology
HINES, R. L., Anaesthesiology
HOCHBERG, R. B., Obstetrics and Gynaecology
HOFFER, P. B., Diagnostic Radiology
HOFFMAN, J. F., Cellular and Molecular Physiology
HOLDER, A. R., Paediatrics
HOLFORD, T. R., Epidemiology and Public Health
HOLMES, F. L., History of Medicine
HORWICH, A., Genetics and Paediatrics
HORWITZ, R. I., Internal Medicine and Epidemiology
IANNINI, P. B., Internal Medicine
INNIS, R. B., Psychiatry and Pharmacology
JACOBS, S. C., Psychiatry
JACOBY, R. O., Comparative Medicine
JAFFE, C. C., Diagnostic Radiology and Internal Medicine
JAHN, R., Pharmacology and Cell Biology
JAMIESON, J. D., Cell Biology
JANEWAY, C., Immunobiology and Biology
JATLOW, P. I., Laboratory Medicine and Psychiatry
JOHNSON, M.-L., Dermatology
JOHNSTON, R., Paediatrics
JOHNSTON, W. D., Dental Surgery
JOINER, K. A., Medicine, Cell Biology and Epidemiology
JOKL, P., Orthopaedics and Rehabilitation
KACZMAREK, L. K., Cellular and Molecular Physiology and Pharmacology
KAETZ, H. W., Internal Medicine
KANTOR, F. S., Internal Medicine
KAPADIA, C. R., Internal Medicine
KASHGARIAN, M., Pathology and Biology
KASL, S. V., Epidemiology and Public Health
KAUFMAN, A. S., Child Study Center
KAUNITZ, P. E., Psychiatry
KEGGI, K. J., Orthopaedics and Rehabilitation
KELLER, M. S., Diagnostic Radiology and Paediatrics
KENNEY, J. D., Internal Medicine
KIDD, K. K., Genetics and Psychiatry
KIER, E. L., Diagnostic Radiology
KINDER, B., Surgery
KLIGER, A. S., Internal Medicine
KOCKIS, J. D., Neurology
KOHN, D., Dental Surgery and Paediatrics
KOHORN, E. I., Obstetrics and Gynaecology
KOMP, D. M., Paediatrics
KONIGSBERG, W., Molecular Biophysics, Biochemistry and Genetics
KOPF, G. S., Surgery
KOPRIVA, C. J., Anaesthesiology
KOSTEN, T. R., Psychiatry
LACAMERA, R. G., Paediatrics
LAMOTTE, C. C., Neurosurgery and Anaesthesiology
LAMOTTE, R. H., Anaesthesiology and Neurobiology
LAVIETES, S. R., Obstetrics and Gynaecology
LAWSON, J. P., Diagnostic Radiology, Orthopaedics and Rehabilitation
LEADERER, B. P., Epidemiology
LECKMAN, J. F., Child Psychiatry and Paediatrics
LENTZ, T. L., Cell Biology
LERANTH, C., Obstetrics and Gynaecology and Neurobiology
LEVANTHAL, J. M., Paediatrics and Child Study Center
LEVIN, L. S., Epidemiology and Public Health
LEVINE, R. A., Laboratory Medicine
LEVINE, R. J., Internal Medicine
LEVITIN, H., Internal Medicine
LEVY, L. L., Neurology
LEWIS, D. O., Child Study Center and Psychiatry
LEWIS, M., Child Study Center, Paediatrics and Child Psychiatry
LIFTON, R. P., Internal Medicine and Genetics
LISTER, G., Paediatrics and Anaesthesiology
LOFQUIST, A., Surgery
LORBER, M. I., Surgery
LOW, K. B., Therapeutic Radiology
LOWELL, D. M., Pathology
LYTTON, B., Surgery
MCCARTHY, P., Paediatrics
MCCARTHY, S., Diagnostic Radiology
MCCLENNAN, B. L., Diagnostic Radiology
MCCORMICK, D., Neurobiology
MCDONALD, B., Paediatrics
MCGLASHAN, T. H., Psychiatry
MCGOLDRICK, K., Anaesthesiology
MCKHANN, C. F., Surgery
MCMAHON-PRATT, D., Epidemiology
MCNAMARA, J. R., Paediatrics
MCPHEDRAN, P., Laboratory Medicine and Internal Medicine
MADRI, J. A., Pathology
MAHONEY, M. J., Genetics, and Obstetrics and Gynaecology, and Paediatrics
MAKUCH, R. W., Public Health
MALAWISTA, S. E., Internal Medicine
MANUELIDIS, L. M., Surgery and Pathology
MARCHESI, S. L., Pathology and Laboratory Medicine
MARCHESI, V. T., Pathology, Cell Biology and Molecular Medicine
MARIEB, N. J., Internal Medicine
MARKS, L. E., Epidemiology and Public Health, and Psychology
MARSH, J. C., Internal Medicine
MATTHAY, R. A., Internal Medicine
MATTSON, R. H., Neurology
MELLMAN, I. S., Cell Biology and Immunobiology
MENT, L. R., Paediatrics and Neurology
MERRELL, R. C., Surgery

MERSON, M. H., Epidemiology and Public Health
MILLER, I. G., Jr, Epidemiology and Public Health, and Molecular Biophysics and Biochemistry
MILLER, P. L., Anaesthesiology
MILSTONE, L., Dermatology
MODLIN, I. M., Surgery
MOLINOFF, P., Pharmacology and Psychiatry
MORROW, J. S., Pathology
MOSER, M., Internal Medicine
MUSTO, D. F., History of Medicine and Psychiatry
NADEL, E. R., Epidemiology and Public Health, and Cellular and Molecular Physiology
NAFTOLIN, F., Obstetrics and Gynaecology, and Biology
NAIR, S., Internal Medicine
NATH, R., Therapeutic Radiology
NELSON, J. C., Psychiatry
NESTLER, E. J., Psychiatry and Pharmacology
NOVICK, P., Cell Biology
NULAND, S. B., Surgery
OH, T.-H., Anaesthesiology
OLIVE, D. L., Obstetrics and Gynaecology
PATTON, C. L., Epidemiology and Public Health
PAULS, D. L., Child Study Center and Psychology
PEARSON, H. A., Paediatrics
PELKER, R. R., Orthopaedics and Rehabilitation
PERILLIE, P. E., Internal Medicine
PERSING, P., Surgery and Neurosurgery
PESCHEL, R., Therapeutic Radiology
PEZZIMENTI, J. F., Internal Medicine
PIEPMEIER, J., Neurosurgery
POBER, J. S., Pathology and Immunobiology
PRELINGER, E., Psychiatry
PRICHARD, J. W., Neurology
PRUETT, K. D., Child Study Center and Psychiatry
QUINLAN, D. M., Psychiatry and Psychology
RABINOVICI, R., Surgery
RADDING, C. M., Genetics and Molecular Biophysics and Biochemistry
RAFFERTY, T. D., Anaesthesiology
RAKIC, P., Neuroscience and Neurobiology
RAPPEPORT, J., Internal Medicine
RASTEGAR, A., Internal Medicine
REDMOND, D. E., Jr, Psychiatry and Neurosurgery
REGUERO, W., Obstetrics and Gynaecology
REINHOLD, R., Surgery
REISER, L. W., Psychiatry
RICHARDS, F. F., Internal Medicine
RIORDAN, C. E., Psychiatry
RITCHIE, B. R., Paediatrics
RITCHIE, J. M., Pharmacology
RITVO, S., Child Study Center
ROBINSON, F., Neurosurgery
ROBSON, K. S., Child Study Center
ROCKWELL, S. C., Therapeutic Radiology
ROONEY, S., Paediatrics
ROSE, J. K., Pathology and Cell Biology
ROSENBAUM, S., Anaesthesiology, Medicine and Surgery
ROSENFIELD, A. T., Diagnostic Radiology
ROSENHECK, R. A., Psychiatry
ROTH, R. H., Jr, Psychiatry and Pharmacology
ROUNSAVILLE, B. J., Psychiatry
RUBEN, H. L., Psychiatry
RUBIN, P., Surgery
RUDDLE, N. H., Epidemiology and Immunobiology
RUDNICK, G., Pharmacology
RUPP, W. D., Therapeutic Radiology and Molecular Biophysics and Biochemistry
RYDER, R. W., Epidemiology and Public Health
SACHS, H. S., Child and Adolescent Psychiatry
SACKS, F. L., Internal Medicine
SALOVEY, P., Epidemiology and Public Health
SANTOS-SACCHI, J., Surgery and Neurobiology
SARREL, P. M., Obstetrics and Gynaecology and Psychiatry
SARTORELLI, A. C., Pharmacology
SASAKI, C. T., Surgery
SAVIN, R. C., Dermatology
SCHIFFER, M. A., Obstetrics and Gynaecology
SCHOEN, R., Internal Medicine
SCHOWALTER, J. E., Child Study Center and Paediatrics
SCHWARTZ, I. R., Surgery and Neurobiology
SCHWARTZ, P. E., Obstetrics and Gynaecology
SEARS, M. L., Ophthalmology and Visual Science
SEASHORE, J. H., Surgery
SEASHORE, M. R., Paediatrics
SHAPIRO, E. D., Paediatrics and Epidemiology
SHAW, C., Diagnostic Radiology
SHAYWITZ, A. E., Paediatrics and Child Study Center
SHAYWITZ, B. A., Paediatrics and Child Study Center
SHEPHERD, G. M., Neuroscience and Neurobiology
SHERTER, C. B., Internal Medicine
SHERWIN, R. S., Internal Medicine
SHIELDS, M. B., Ophthalmology and Visual Science
SHULMAN, G. I., Endocrine Medicine, and Cellular and Molecular Physiology
SIEGEL, N. J., Paediatrics
SIGLER, P. B., Molecular Biophysics and Biochemistry
SIGWORTH, F. J., Cellular and Molecular Physiology
SILVERMAN, D., Anaesthesiology
SILVERSTONE, D. E., Ophthalmology and Visual Science
SLAYMAN, C. L., Cellular and Molecular Physiology
SLAYMAN, C. W., Genetics and Cellular and Molecular Physiology
SMITH, A. L., Comparative Medicine and Epidemiology
SMITH, B. R., Laboratory Medicine
SNOW, D. L., Psychiatry and Child Study Center
SNYDER, E. L., Laboratory Medicine
SON, Y. H., Therapeutic Radiology and Surgery
SOUTHWICK, S., Psychiatry
SPANGLER, S., Obstetrics and Gynaecology
SPARROW, S. S., Child Study Center and Psychology
SPENCER, D. D., Neurosurgery
SPENCER, S. S., Neurology
SPIESEL, S. Z., Paediatrics
SPIRO, H. M., Internal Medicine
STEWART, A., Endocrinology
STITT, J. T., Epidemiology and Physiology
STOLWIJK, J. A. J., Epidemiology and Public Health
STRAUSS, J. S., Psychiatry
SULAVIK, S. B., Internal Medicine
SUMMERS, W. C., Therapeutic Radiology, Molecular Biophysics and Biochemistry, and Genetics
SUMPIO, B., Surgery
TAMBORLANE, W. V., Paediatrics
TATTERSALL, P., Laboratory Medicine and Genetics
TAUB, A., Anaesthesiology
TAYLOR, K. J., Diagnostic Radiology
TIGELAAR, R. E., Dermatology and Immunobiology
TINETTI, M., Medicine and Epidemiology
TOULOUKIAN, R. J., Surgery
VAN DEN POL, A., Neurosurgery
WACKERS, F. J., Diagnostic Radiology and Internal Medicine
WAKSMAN, B. H., Pathology
WALSH, T. J., Ophthalmology
WARD, D. C., Genetics, Molecular Biophysics and Biochemistry
WARDLAW, S., Laboratory Medicine
WARSHAW, J. B., Paediatrics
WAXMAN, S. G., Neurology, Pharmacology and Neurobiology
WEIL, U. H., Orthopaedics and Rehabilitation
WEIR, E. C., Comparative Medicine
WEISS, R. M., Surgery
WEISSMAN, S. M., Genetics and Internal Medicine
WESSEL, M. A., Paediatrics
WESTCOTT, J. A., Diagnostic Radiology
WHITE, R. I., Jr, Diagnostic Radiology
WHITTEMORE, R., Paediatrics
WILLIAMS, K. R., Molecular Biophysics and Biochemistry
WONG, A. S., Ophthalmology and Visual Science
WRIGHT, F. S., Internal Medicine and Cellular and Molecular Physiology
YANAGISAWA, E., Surgery
ZARET, B. L., Internal Medicine
ZELSON, J. H., Paediatrics
ZELTERMAN, D., Epidemiology and Public Health
ZONANA, H. V., Psychiatry

School of Law:

ACKERMAN, B. A., Law and Political Science
ALSTOTT, A. L., Law
AMAR, A. R., Law
AYRES, I., Law
BURT, R. A., Law
CARTER, S. L., Law
COLEMAN, J., Law
CURTIS, D. E., Law
DALTON, H. L., Law
DAMASKA, M. R., Law
DAYS, D. S., III, Law
DEUTSCH, J. G., Law
DINEEN, F. X., Law
DUKE, S. B., Law of Science and Technology
ELLICKSON, R. C., Property and Urban Law
ELLIOTT, E. D., Jr, Law
FISS, O. M., Law
GEWIRTZ, P. D., Constitutional Law
GOLDSTEIN, A. S., Law
GOLDSTEIN, J., Law and Child Study Centre
GORDON, R. W., Law
GRAETZ, M. J., Law
HANSMANN, H. B., Law
KAHN, P. W., Law
KATZ, J., Law
KLEVORICK, A. K., Law and Economics
KOH, H. H., International Law
KRONMAN, A. T., Law
LANGBEIN, J. H., Law and Legal History
LUCHT, C. L., Law
MARSHALL, B., Law
MASHAW, J. L., Law
PETERS, E., Law
PETERS, J. K., Law
PRIEST, G. L., Law and Economics
REISMAN, W. M., Law
RESNIK, J., Law
ROMANO, R., Law
ROSE, C. M., Law and Organization
ROSE-ACKERMAN, S., Jurisprudence, Law and Political Science
RUBENFELD, J., Law
SCHUCK, P. H., Law
SCHULTZ, V., Law
SCHWARTZ, A., Law
SIEGEL, R., Law
SIMON, J. G., Law
SOLOMON, R., Law
STITH, K., Law
WEDGWOOD, R., Law
WHEELER, S., Law and Social Science
WHITMAN, J. Q., Comparative and Foreign Law
WINTER, R. K., Law
WIZNER, S., Law

Divinity School:
- ADAMS, H. B., Pastoral Theology
- ADAMS, M. MC., Historical Theology and Religious Studies
- ATTRIDGE, H. W., New Testament
- BARTLETT, D. L., Preaching and Communication
- CHILDS, B. S., Old Testament Interpretation and Criticism
- DITTES, J. E., Pastoral Theology and Psychology
- FARLEY, M. A., Christian Ethics
- HAWKINS, P. S., Religion and Literature
- KECK, L. E., Biblical Theology
- KELSEY, D. H., Theology
- OGLETREE, T. W., Theological Ethics
- RUSSELL, L. M., Theology
- SANNEH, L. O., Missions and World Christianity and History
- SEITZ, C. R., Old Testament
- SPINKS, B. D., Liturgical Studies
- WILSON, R. R., Old Testament and Religious Studies
- WOLTERSTORFF, N., Philosophical Theology
- WOOD, R. J., Philosophy

School of Forestry:
- BERLYN, G. P., Forestry and Environmental Studies
- BURCH, W. R., Jr, Natural Resource Management
- CLARK, T. W., Forestry and Environmental Studies
- GORDON, J. C., School of Forestry and Environmental Studies
- KELLERT, S. R., School of Forestry and Environmental Studies
- MENDELSOHN, R., Forest Policy
- SMITH, W. H., Forest Biology
- VOGT, K. A., Forest Ecology

School of Art:
- ALLEN, B., History of Art
- BENSON, R. M., Photography
- COOKE, E. S., Jr, History of Art
- CROW, T. E., History of Art
- DE BRETTEVILLE, S., Graphic Design
- FIELD, R. S., History of Art
- LYTLE, W. R., Painting
- PAPAGEORGE, T., Photography
- PEASE, D., Painting
- REED, R. J., Jr, Painting
- VOGEL, S. M., History of Art

School of Architecture:
- BEEBY, T. H., Architectural Design
- BLOOMER, K. C., Architectural Design
- FREW, R. S., Computer-Aided Design
- GARVIN, A., Urban Planning and Development
- GEHNER, M. D., Architectural Engineering
- HAYDEN, D., Architecture and Urbanism
- PURVES, A., Architectural Design
- RANALLI, G. J., Architectural Design
- SPIEGEL, H. D., Architectural Engineering

School of Music:
- AGAWU, K., Theory of Music
- AKI, S., Violin
- BERMAN, B., Piano
- BRESNICK, M. I., Composition
- CHOOKASIAN, L., Voice and Opera
- DUFFY, T. C.
- FASSLER, M. E.
- FORTE, A., Theory of Music
- FRANK, C., Piano
- FRIEDMAN, E., Violin
- GOTTLIEB, G., Percussion
- HARTH, S., Violin
- HAWKSHAW, P., History of Music
- LADERMAN, E., Composition
- LEVINE, J., Viola
- MURRAY, T., Organ
- OUNDJIAN, P., Violin
- PARISOT, A. S.
- REPHANN, R.
- ROSAND, E., History of Music
- ROSEMAN, R., Oboe
- RUFF, W. H., Jr.
- SHIFRIN, D., Clarinet
- SMITH, L. L.
- SWALLOW, J. W., Brass and Ensemble Performance
- TIRRO, F. P.
- YARICK-CROSS, D., Voice

School of Drama:
- FATA, W. W., Acting
- GISTER, E. R., Acting
- GREENWOOD, J., Design
- LEE, M. C., Design
- MORDECAI, B.
- ROGOFF, R., Dramaturgy and Drama Criticism
- SAMMLER, B., Technical Design

Yale School of Management:
- ANTLE, R., Accounting
- BRACKEN, P., Public Policy and Political Science
- FABOZZI, F. J.
- FEINSTEIN, J., Economics
- FRENCH, K., Management Studies and Finance
- GARSTKA, S., Practice of Management
- GARTEN, J. E., Practice of International Finance
- GOETZMANN, W., Finance and Real Estate
- IBBOTSON, R., Practice of Finance
- INGERSOLL, J. E., International Trade and Finance
- KAPLAN, E., Management Science
- LAPALOMBARA, J., Political Science
- LARDY, N. R., Management
- LEVIN, R., Economics
- LI, L., Production Management
- MACAVOY, P., Management Studies
- MARMOR, T. R., Public Management and Political Science
- NALEBUFF, B., Economics and Management
- OSTER, S. M., Management and Entrepreneurship
- RAE, D. W., Management
- ROSS, S. A., Economics and Finance
- SEN, S. K., Marketing
- SHUBIK, M., Economics and Management
- SWERSEY, A. J., Management
- VROOM, V. H., Management and Psychology

School of Nursing:
- AMELING, A. T., Psychiatric Mental Health Nursing
- BURST, H. V., Nursing
- DIERS, D. K., Nursing
- KRAUSS, J. B., Nursing
- SEXTON, D. L., Nursing
- WALD, F. S., Nursing
- WEAVER, D., Nursing

DELAWARE

DELAWARE STATE COLLEGE

Dupont Highway, Dover, DE 19901
Telephone: (302) 739-4924
Fax: (302) 739-5241

Founded 1891

President: Dr WILLIAM B. DELAUDER
Registrar: Dr RENFORD BREVETT
Librarian: GERTRUDE JACKSON

Library of 269,085 items
Number of teachers: 174
Number of students: 3,381

UNIVERSITY OF DELAWARE

Newark, DE 19716
Telephone: (302) 831-2000

Founded 1833 from the Newark Academy founded in 1765; chartered 1769

President: DAVID P. ROSELLE
Provost and Vice-President for Academic Affairs: R. BYRON PIPES
Vice-President for Student Affairs: STUART J. SHARKEY
Librarian: SUSAN BRYNTESON

Number of teachers: 911
Number of students: 18,200 undergraduates, 2,668 graduates

Publications: *Bibliography of Faculty Publications, Update, University Report, Catalog, Bulletins.*

DEANS

College of Agricultural Sciences: JOHN C. NYE
College of Arts and Science: MARY RICHARDS
College of Business and Economics: KENNETH BIEDERMAN
College of Education: FRANK BRUSH MURRAY
College of Engineering:
College of Human Resources: ALEXANDER DOBERENZ
College of Nursing: BETTY PAULANKA
College of Marine Studies: C. A. THOROUGHGOOD
College of Physical Education, Athletics and Recreation: ALLAN D. WATERFIELD
College of Urban Affairs and Public Policy: DANIEL RICH

PROFESSORS

- ABRAMS, B. A., Economics
- ACKERMAN, B. P., Psychology
- ALLEN, H. E., Civil Engineering
- ALLMENDINGER, D. F., History
- AMER, P. D., Computer and Information Sciences
- AMES, D. L., Urban Affairs and Public Policy
- AMSLER, M. E., English
- ANDERSON, E., Nursing
- ANDERSON, L., Marine Studies
- ANDERSON, M., Sociology
- ANDREWS, D. C., English
- ANGELL, T., Mathematical Sciences
- BAILEY, W., Educational Development
- BAKER, R. D., Mathematical Sciences
- BARNETT, A., Electrical Engineering
- BARNHILL, M. V., Physics and Astronomy
- BARTEAU, M. A., Chemical Engineering
- BASALLA, G., History
- BAXTER, W., Mathematical Sciences
- BEASLEY, J. C., English
- BELLAMY, D. P., Mathematical Sciences
- BENTON, W. J., Pathology
- BERSTEIN, J. A., History
- BILINSKY, Y., Political Science
- BILLON, S. A., Business Administration
- BISCHOFF, K., Engineering
- BOER, K., Engineering
- BOHNER, C. H., English
- BOORD, R. L., Life and Health Sciences
- BOULD, S., Sociology
- BOYER, J. S., Marine Studies
- BOYER, W. W., Jr, Political Science
- BRAUN, T. E. D., Languages and Literature
- BREUER, H. P., English
- BRILL, T. B., Chemistry
- BROCK, D. H., English
- BROCKENBROUGH, T. W., Civil Engineering
- BROWN, H., Art Conservation
- BROWN, J. L., Foreign Languages and Literatures
- BROWN, R. F., Philosophy
- BROWN, R. P., Theatre
- BUCKMASTER, D. A., Accounting
- BURMEISTER, J. L., Chemistry
- CALHOUN, T., English
- CALLAHAN, R., History
- CAMPBELL, L. L., Life and Health Sciences
- CARON, D. M., Entomology and Applied Ecology
- CARROLL, R., Plant Science
- CASE, J., Computer and Information Science
- CAVINESS, B. F., Computer and Information Sciences

CHOU, T. W., Mechanical and Aerospace Engineering
CHURCH, T., Marine Studies
CICALA, G., Psychology
CINCIN-SAIN, B., Marine Studies
COHEN, L. H., Psychology
COLE, G. L., Agriculture and Food Economics
COLMAN, R. F., Chemistry
COLTON, D., Mathematical Sciences
COOK-IOANNIDIS, P., Mathematical Sciences
COPE, M., Art History
CORNELL, H. V., Life and Health Sciences
COURTRIGHT, J. A., Communication
COX, R. L., English
CRAVEN, E. W., Art History
CRAWFORD, J. S., Art History
CROUSE, J. H., Educational Studies
CULLINGWORTH, J. B., Urban Affairs and Public Policy
CURTIS, J., History
CUSTER, J. F., Anthropology
DALRYMPLE, R., Civil Engineering
DANIELS, W. B., Physics and Astronomy
DAVISON, R., English
DAWSON, C., English
DAY, R. A., English
DEBESSAY, A., B&E Accounting
DEL FATTORE, J., English
DELEON, P. A., Life and Health Sciences
DENNIS, D., Chemistry
DENSON, C. D., Chemical Engineering
DEXTER, S. C., Marine Studies
DHURJATI, P., Chemical Engineering
DILLEY, F., Philosophy
DIRENZO, G., Sociology
DOBERENZ, A., Food Science and Human Nutrition
DONALDSON-EVANS, M. P., Foreign Languages and Literatures
DUGGAN, L. G., History
DURBIN, P., Philosophy
DYBOWSKI, C., Chemistry
DYNES, R. R., Sociology
EBERT, G. L., Mathematical Sciences
EISENBERG, R., Psychology
ELLIS, J. D., History
ELTERICH, G. J., Agriculture and Food Economics
EPIFANIO, C., Marine Studies
ERMANN, M. D., Sociology
EVANS, D. H., Chemistry
EXLINE, R. V., Psychology
FARNHAM-DIGGORY, S., Educational Studies
FLYNN, P. D., English
FOU, C., Physics and Astronomy
FRANCIS, D. W., Life and Health Sciences
FRAWLEY, W. J., Linguistics
FUTRELL, J. H., Chemistry and Biochemistry
GAERTNER, S. L., Psychology
GALLAGHER, J., Marine Studies
GARLAND, H., Business Administration
GARVINE, R. W., Marine Studies
GATES, B., English
GATES, B. C., Chemical Engineering
GEHRLEIN, W. V., Business Administration
GEIS, F., Psychology
GIBBS, R., Marine Studies
GILBERT, R. P., Mathematical Sciences
GLASS, B. P., Geology
GLYDE, H. R., Physics and Astronomy
GOLDEN, J. M., Educational Development
GOLDSTEIN, L., Political Science and International Relations
GOLINKOFF, R., Educational Studies
GRAHAM, A. K., Art
GRAHAM, F., Psychology
GRANDA, A. M., Life and Health Sciences
GREENBERG, M. D., Mechanical and Aerospace Engineering
GREENFIELD, I. G., Mechanical and Aerospace Engineering, Metallurgy
GUCERI, S., Mechanical Engineering
GUTIERREZ, C., Computer and Information Sciences
HADJIPANAYIS, G., Physics
HAENLEIN, G. F. W., Animal Science and Agricultural Biochemistry
HALIO, J., English
HALLENBECK, D. J., Mathematical Science
HALPRIN, A., Physics and Astronomy
HANS, V. P., Criminal Justice
HARDING, S. G., Philosophy
HAREVEN, T. K., Individual and Family Studies
HASLETT, B. J., Communication
HASLETT, D., Philosophy
HASTINGS, S., Food and Resource Economics
HAWK, J. A., Plant and Soil Sciences
HERMAN, H. D., Music
HIEBERT, J., Educational Development
HILDEBRANDT, J., Music
HILL, R. N., Physics
HOFFECKER, C. E., History
HOFFMAN, J. E.. Psychology
HOFFMAN, S. D., Economics
HOGAN, R. C., English
HOLMES, L. W., Art
HOMER, W. I., Art History
HOOPER, P., Accounting
HOOPER, R. L., Art
HSIAO, G. C., Mathematical Sciences
HUANG, C.-P., Civil Engineering
HUNSPERGER, R., Electrical Engineering
HURD, L. E., Life and Health Sciences
HUTCHINSON, H. D., Economics
IH, C., Electrical Engineering
INCIARDI, J. A., Sociology
INGERSOLL, D. E., Political Science
ISLAM, M. N., Food Science
IZARD, C., Psychology
JAIN, M. K., Chemistry
JONES, J. M., Psychology
JONES, R. C., Civil Engineering
KALER, E. W., Chemical Engineering
KALKSTEIN, L. S., Geography
KELLY, B. J., Physical Education
KEOWN, R. W., Food Science
KERNER, E. H., Physics and Astronomy
KERR, A., Civil Engineering
KERRANE, K., English
KING, N. R., Theatre
KINGSBURY, H. B., Mechanical and Aerospace Engineering
KLEIN, M. T., Chemical Engineering
KLEINMAN, R., Mathematical Sciences
KLEMAS, V., Marine Studies
KLOCKARS, C. B., Criminal Justice
KNECHT, R. W., Marine Studies
KNORR, D., Food Science
KOBAYASHI, N., Civil Engineering
KOLCHIN, P., History
KRAFT, J. C., Geology
KRAMER, J. J., Electrical Engineering
KRUM, J. R. , Business Administration
KUSHMAN, J. E., Textiles Design and Consumer Economics
LAMB, D. E., Computer and Information Sciences, Chemical Engineering
LEAVENS, P. B., Geology
LEITCH, T. M., English
LEMAY, J. A. L., English
LEWIS, K. R., Economics
LIBERA, R., Mathematical Sciences
LINK, C. R., Economics
LIU, TAI, History
LIVINGSTON, A., Mathematics
LUKASHEVICH, S., History
LURIE, E., Life and Health Sciences and History
LUTHER, G. W., Marine Studies
McCULLOUGH, R., Chemical Engineering
MANGONE, G., Marine Studies and Political Science
MARKELL, W., Accounting
MARTIN, R. E., English
MASON, D. M., Mathematical Sciences
MASTERSON, F., Psychology
MATHER, J. R., Geography
MEAKIN, J. D., Energy Conversion, Mechanical Engineering and Materials Science
MEHL, J. B., Physics and Astronomy
MELL, D., Jr, English
MERRILL, T., English
METZNER, A. B., Chemical Engineering
MEYER, D., History
MILLER, G. E., English
MILLS, D. L., Electrical Engineering
MOODY, W. B., Education Development
MOREHART, A. L., Plant Science
MORRISON, J., Textiles Design and Consumer Economics
MOSS, J. F., Art
MUNSON, M. S. B., Chemistry
MURPHY, L. C., Individual and Family Studies
MURRAY, F., Education
MURRAY, R. B., Physics and Astronomy
NASHED, M. Z., Mathematical Sciences
NEALE, D. C., Educational Sciences
NEES, L. P., Art History
NICHOLLS, R. L., Civil Engineering
NICHOLS, R. D., Art
NIGG, J. M., Sociology
NOGGLE, J., Chemistry
NORTON, D. L., Philosophy
OLIVER, J. K., Political Science
OLSON, J. H., Chemical Engineering
O'NEILL, J. B., Economics
ONN, D. G., Physics and Astronomy
PALLEY, M. L., Political Science
PALMER, L. M., Philosophy
PARKER, H., English
PAULAITIS, M. E., Chemical Engineering
PAULY, T., English
PETERS, D. L., Individual and Family Studies
PIFER, E., English
PIKULSKI, J. J., Educational Development
PILL, W. G., Plant and Soil Sciences
PIPES, R. B., Mechanical and Aerospace
PONG, D., History
POTTER, L. D., English
PUGLISI, D. J., B&E Finance
RAFFEL, J. A., Urban Affairs and Public Policy
RAYMOND, H. R., Physical Education
REIDEL, L., Theatre
REITNOUR, C. M., Animal Science and Agricultural Biochemistry
REYNOLDS, H. T., Political Science
RHEINGOLD, A. L., Chemistry
RICH, D., Urban Affairs and Public Policy
RIDGE, D., Chemistry
RITTER, W. F., Agricultural Engineering
ROBBINS, S., Theatre
ROBINSON, C. E., English
ROBINSON, D. M., Electrical Engineering
ROSENBERGER, J. K., Animal Science and Agricultural Biochemistry
ROTHMAN, R., Sociology
ROWE, C. A., Art
RUARK, G., English
RUSSELL, T. W. F., Chemical Engineering
RYLANDER, C. R., Physical Education
SANDLER, S. I., Chemical Engineering
SANIGA, E., Business Administration
SASOWSKY, N., Art
SAYDAM, T., Computer and Information Sciences
SCARPITTI, F. R., Sociology
SCHUENEMEYER, J. H., Mathematical Sciences
SCHULTZ, J., Chemical Engineering
SCHWARTZ, L. W., Mechanical Engineering
SCHWARTZ, N. E., Anthropology
SCHWEIZER, E., Chemistry
SCOTT, B. K., English
SEIDEL, B. S., Mechanical and Aerospace Engineering
SEIDMAN, L., Economics
SETTLE, R., Economics
SETTLES, B., Individual and Family Studies
SHARNOFF, M., Physics and Astronomy
SHARP, J. H., Marine Studies
SHIPMAN, H. L., Physics and Astronomy
SIEGEL, J., Life and Health Sciences
SKOPIK, S. D., Life and Health Sciences
SLOANE, A. A., Business Administration
SLOYER, C., Mathematical Sciences
SNODGRASS, W. D., English
SOLES, J., Political Science
SPARKS, D. L., Plant Science

SPINSKI, V., Art
STAKGOLD, I., Mathematics; Civil, Mechanical and Aerospace Engineering
STANLEY, W. B., Educational Development
STARK, R., Mathematical Sciences, Civil Engineering
STEINBERG, M., Music
STEINER, R., Languages and Literature
STEINMETZ, S. K., Individual and Family Studies
STETSON, M. H., Life and Health Sciences
STILLMAN, D., Art History
STRAIGHT, R., Arts
STRAKA, G., History
SUSSMAN, M. B., Individual and Family Studies
SVENDSON, I. B., Civil Engineering
SWAIN, F. M., Geology and Marine Studies
SYLVES, R. T., Political Science
TANIS, S., Art
TANNIAN, F. X., Urban Affairs and Public Policy
TAYLOR, H. M., Mathematical Sciences
THORPE, C., Chemistry
TINGEY, H., Mathematical Sciences
TOENSMEYER, U. C., Agriculture and Food Economics
TRIPP, M. R., Life and Health Sciences
VALBUENA, A. J., Languages and Literature
VENEZKY, R., Education
VIERA, B., Physical Education, Athletics and Recreation
VINSON, J. R., Mechanical and Aerospace Engineering; Marine Studies
WAGNER, R. C., Life and Health Sciences
WAITE, J. H., Marine Studies
WALKER, J. H., Theatre
WALKER, J. M., English
WARREN, R., Urban Affairs and Public Policy; Marine Studies
WARTER, P., Electrical Engineering
WEBSTER, F., Marine Studies
WEDEL, A. R., Linguistics
WEHMILLER, J. F., Geology
WEINACHT, R. J., Mathematical Sciences
WEISS, J. J., Art
WETLAUFER, D. B., Chemistry
WHITE, H. G., III, Chemistry
WILKINS, D. J., Mechanical Engineering
WILLIAMS, W. H., University Parallel
WILLMOTT, C. J., Geography
WIRTH, M. J., Chemistry and Biochemistry
WOLTERS, R. B., History
WOO, S.-B., Physics and Astronomy
WOOD, R. H., Chemistry
WOOD, T., Entomology and Applied Ecology
WU, J., Marine Studies and Civil Engineering
YANG, C. Y., Civil Engineering
ZIPSER, R. A., Languages and Literature
ZUCKERMAN, M., Psychology

WIDENER UNIVERSITY SCHOOL OF LAW

Delaware Campus:
P.O. Box 7474, 4601 Concord Pike, Wilmington, DE 19803-0474
Telephone: (302) 477-2100
Harrisburg Campus:
P.O. Box 69381, 3800 Vartan Way, Harrisburg, PA 17106-9381
Telephone: (717) 541-3900

President: ROBERT J. BRUCE
Dean: ARTHUR N. FRAKT

DISTRICT OF COLUMBIA

AMERICAN UNIVERSITY

4400 Massachusetts Ave, NW, Washington, DC 20016
Telephone: (202) 885-1000
Fax: (202) 885-3265

Chartered 1893

President: BENJAMIN LADNER
Provost: CORNELIUS KERWIN
Vice-President of Development: LINDA NELSON
Vice-President of Finance and Treasurer: DONALD L. MYERS
Vice-President of Enrolment Services: WILLIAM T. MYERS
Vice-President of Student Services: GAIL SHORT HANSON
Registrar: DONALD W. BUNIS
Librarian: PATRICIA WAND

Library of 867,000 vols, 8,712 special collections
Number of teachers: 546 full-time
Number of students: 11,093

DEANS

College of Arts and Sciences: HOWARD WACHTEL (acting)
Kogod College of Business Administration: MYRON J. ROOMKIN
Washington College of Law: CLAUDIO GROSSMAN
School of Public Affairs: WILLIAM LEO GRANDE (acting)
School of International Service: LOUIS GOODMAN
School of Communication: SANFORD J. UNGAR

CATHOLIC UNIVERSITY OF AMERICA

Washington, DC 20064
Telephone: (202) 319-5000

Incorporated 1887; chartered by the Congress of the United States 1889

Chancellor: JAMES Cardinal HICKEY
President: Very Rev. DAVID M. O'CONNELL
Provost: Dr JOHN CONVEY
Vice-President for Finance: RALPH H. BEAUDOIN
Vice-President for Administration: SUSAN D. PERVI
Vice-President for Student Affairs: Rev. ROBERT FRIDAY
Vice-President for Development: (vacant)
Secretary of University: VINCENT P. WALTER, Jr
Registrar: G. KENDALL RICE
Director of Libraries: ADELE CHWALEK

Number of teachers: *c.* 400
Number of students: *c.* 7,000

Publications: *The Anthropological Quarterly, The Catholic Historical Review* (quarterly), *Catholic Biblical Quarterly, Catholic University Law Review, Image: The Journal of Nursing Scholarship, Journal of Chinese Philosophy, Review of Metaphysics, Review of Religious Research.*

DEANS

School of Arts and Sciences: Dr ANTANAS SUZIEDELIS
School of Engineering: Dr WILLIAM E. KELLY
School of Architecture and Planning: GREGORY HUNT
Columbus School of Law: BERNARD DOBRANSKI
School of Library and Information Science: Dr ELIZABETH AVERSA
Benjamin T. Rome School of Music: Dr ELAINE R. WALTER
School of Nursing: Sister MARY JEAN FLAHERTY
School of Philosophy: Dr JUDE P. DOUGHERTY
School of Religious Studies: Rev. RAYMOND F. COLLINS
National Catholic School of Social Service: Sister ANN P. CONRAD
Metropolitan College: Dr JAMES S. PULA

GALLAUDET UNIVERSITY

800 Florida Ave, NE, Washington, DC 20002
Telephone: (202) 651-5000

Founded 1864

President: Dr. I. KING JORDAN
Vice-President, Academic Affairs: Dr ROSLYN ROSEN
Vice-President, Institutional Advancement: Dr MARGARET HALL
Vice-President, Administration and Business: PAUL KELLY
Vice-President, Pre-College National Mission Programs: Dr JANE KELLEHER FERNANDEZ
Librarian: JOHN DAY

Library of 200,000 vols
Number of teachers: 253

Publications: *Gallaudet Today, Perspectives in Education and Deafness, Preview, World Around You.*

DEANS

College of Arts and Sciences: Dr JANE DILLEHAY
College of Continuing Education: Dr REGINALD REDDING
Graduate School and Research: Dr MICHAEL KARCHMER
School of Communication: Dr PATRICK COX
School of Education and Human Services: Dr WILLIAM MCCRONE
School of Management: Dr RONALD SUTCLIFFE (acting)
School of Undergraduate Studies: Dr STEPHEN WEINER

ATTACHED INSTITUTE

Gallaudet Research Institute: research into deafness.

GEORGE WASHINGTON UNIVERSITY

Washington, DC 20052
Telephone: (202) 994-1000
Fax: (202) 994-9025

Founded 1821
Private control
Academic year: September to May

President: STEPHEN J. TRACHTENBERG
Vice-President for Academic Affairs: DONALD R. LEHMAN
Vice-President for Development and Alumni Affairs: MICHAEL J. WORTH
Vice-President and Treasurer: LOUIS H. KATZ
Vice-President for Medical Affairs: ALAN B. WEINGOLD
Vice-President for Student and Academic Support Services: ROBERT A. CHERNAK
Vice-President for Administrative and Information Services: WALTER BORTZ
Director of Undergraduate Admissions: KATHRYN M. NAPPER
Registrar: BRIAN SELINSKY
University Librarian: JACK SIGGINS

Library of 1,730,733 vols
Number of teachers: 4,470
Number of students: 18,986

DEANS

Columbian School of Arts and Sciences: LESTER A. LEFTON
Law School: J. H. FRIEDENTHAL
School of Medicine and Health Sciences: R. KEIMOWITZ
School of Public Health and Health Services: R. RIEGELMAN
Education: MARY HATWOOD FUTRELL
Engineering: THOMAS MAZZUCHI (acting)
Business and Public Management: JED KEE (acting)
Continuing Education: ROGER WHITAKER
International Affairs: HARRY HARDING

PROFESSORS

(many professors serve in more than one school)

Columbian School of Arts and Sciences and Elliott School of International Affairs:

ABRAMSON, F. P., Pharmacology
ABRAVANEL, E., Psychology

ALBRIGHT, J. W., Microbiology and Immunology
ALLEN, C. J., Anthropology
ALTMAN, A., Philosophy
ANDERSON, J. C., Art
ARTERTON, F. C., Political Management
ASCHHEIM, J., Economics
ATKINS, D. L., Biology
AZAR, I., Spanish and Human Sciences
BAILEY, J. M., Biochemistry and Molecular Biology
BECKER, W. H., History
BERGMANN, O., Physics
BERKOWITZ, E. D., History
BERMAN, B., Physics
BOULIER, B. L., Economics
BRADLEY, M. D., Economics
BROCK, G. W. Telecommunication
BROOKS, A. S., Anthropology
BURGESS, W. H., Biochemistry and Molecular Biochemistry
BURKS, J. F., French
BURNS, J. R., Zoology
CAPLAN, R. D., Psychology, Psychiatry and Behavioural Sciences
CARESS, E. A., Chemistry
CASSIDY, M. M., Physiology and Experimental Medicine
CAWS, P. J., Philosophy
CHAMBLISS, W. J., Sociology
CHANDRA, R. S., Pathology and Paediatrics
CHAVES, J., Chinese
CHIAPPINELLI, V. A., Pharmacology
CHURCHILL, R. P., Philosophy
CORDES, J., Economics and International Affairs
COSTIGAN, C. C., Design
COURTLESS, T. F., Law and Sociology
DEPALMA, L. A., Pathology and Anatomy, Cell Biology
DEPAUW, L. G., American History
DONALDSON, R. P., Biology
DUNN, R. M., Economics
EAST, M. A., International Affairs and Political Science
ETZIONI, A., Sociology
FILIPESCU, N., Chemistry, Obstetrics and Gynaecology
FISKUM, G. M., Biochemistry, Molecular Biology and Emergency Medicine
FOLKERTS, J., Journalism
FRENCH, R. S., Philosophy
GALLO, L. L., Biochemistry and Molecular Biology
GANZ, R. N., English
GASTWIRTH, J. L., Statistics and Economics
GILLETTE, H. F., Jr, American Civilization and History
GLICK, I. I., Mathematics
GOLDFARB, R. S., Economics
GOLDSTEIN, A. L., Biochemistry and Molecular Biology
GOW, D. D., Anthropology and International Affairs
GRIFFITH, W. B., Philosophy
GUENTHER, R. J., Music
GUPTA, M. M., Mathematics
HARDING, H., International Affairs and Political Science
HARSHBARGER, J. C., Pathology
HENIG, J. R., Political Science
HILTEBEITEL, A. J., Religion
HOLMAN, M. A., Economics
HOLMSTROM, R. W., Psychology
HORTON, J. O., American Civilization and History
HUFFORD, T. L., Botany
HUMPHREY, R. L., Anthropology
INGHAM, K. C., Biochemistry and Molecular Biology
JACOBSON, L. B., Theatre
JOHNSON, K. E., Health Care Sciences
JUNGHENN, H. D., Mathematics
KARCHER, P. S., Pathology
KARP, S. A., Psychology
KATZ, I. J., Mathematics
KENNEDY, K. A., Pharmacology and Genetics
KENNEDY, R. E., European History
KIM, Y. C., Political Science and International Affairs
KIM-RENAUD, Y. K., Korean Language and Culture, International Affairs
KING, M. M., Chemistry
KIRSCH, A. D., Statistics and Psychology
KLAREN, P. F., History and International Affairs
KLUBES, P., Pharmacology
KOERING, M. J., Anatomy and Cell Biology
KRULFELD, R. M., Anthropology
KUMAR, A., Biochemistry, Molecular Biology and Genetics
KWOKA, J. E., Jr, Economics
LABADIE, P. A., Economics
LACHIN, J. M., Statistics
LADER, M. P., Art
LAKE, J. L., Photography
LANGTON, P. A., Sociology
LEFTON, L. A., Psychology
LEHMAN, D. R., Physics
LEWIS, J. F., Geology
LILLIEFORS, H. W., Statistics
LINDEN, C. A., Political Science and International Affairs
LINEBAUGH, C. W., Speech and Hearing, Medicine
LIPSCOMB, D. L., Biology
LOGSDON, J. M., Political Science and International Affairs
LONGSTRETH, R. W., American Civilization
LOWE, J. C., Geography
LUDLOW, G., French, International Affairs
MCALEAVEY, D. W., English
MCCLINTOCK, C., Political Science, International Affairs
MCGRATH, D. C., Geography, Urban and Regional Planning
MADDOX, J. H., English
MAHMOUD, H. M., Statistics
MANDEL, H. G., Pharmacology
MANHEIM, J. B., Political Communications and Political Science
MERGEN, B. M., American Civilization
MILLAR, J. R., Economics and International Affairs
MILLER, J. C., Psychology
MILLER, J. H., Chemistry
MOLINA, S. B., Art
MONTASER, A., Chemistry
MOODY, S. A., Anatomy
NASR, S. H., Islamic Studies
NAU, H. R., Political Science and International Affairs
NAYAK, T. K., Statistics
OERTEL, Y. C., Pathology
O'REAR, C. E., Forensic Science
ORENSTEIN, J. M., Pathology
OZDOGAN, T., Ceramics
PACKER, R. K., Biology
PALMER, R. D., International Affairs
PARRIS, R., Music
PASTER, G. K., English
PATIERNO, S. R., Pharmacology
PECK, L. L., History
PELZMAN, J., Economics and International Affairs
PETERSON, R. A., Psychology, Psychiatry and Behavioural Sciences
PEUSNER, K. D., Anatomy and Cell Biology
PLOTZ, J. A., English
POST, J. M., Psychiatry and Behavioural Sciences, International Affairs and Engineering Management
QUITSLUND, J. A., English
RAMAKER, D. E., Chemistry
RASKIN, M., Policy Studies
REDDAWAY, P., Political Science and International Affairs
REICH, B., Political Science and International Affairs
RIBUFFO, L. P., History
RICE, C. E., Psychology
ROBERTS, S. V., Media and Public Affairs
ROBINSON, L. F., Art
ROMINES, M. A., English
ROSENAU, J. N. International Affairs
ROSENSTEIN, J. M., Anatomy and Cell Biology, Neurological Surgery
ROTHBLAT, L. A., Psychology, Anatomy
ROWE, W. F., Forensic Sciences
ROWLEY, D. A., Chemistry
SACHAR, H. M., Modern Jewish History, International Affairs
SAENZ, P. G., Spanish
SALAMON, L. B., English
SAPERSTEIN, M. E., Jewish History
SCHAFFNER, R. F., Medical Humanities and Philosophy
SCHLAGEL, R. H., Philosophy
SCHWARTZ, A. M., Pathology
SCOTT, D. W., Anatomy and Cell Biology
SEAVEY, O. A., English
SHAMBAUGH, D. L., Political Science and International Affairs
SIDAW, M. K., Pathology
SIDRANSKY, H., Pathology
SIEGEL, F. R., Geochemistry
SIGELMAN, C. K., Psychology
SIGELMAN, L., Political Science
SILBER, D. E., Psychology
SMITH, S. C., Economics, International Affairs
SMYTHE, R. T., Statistics
SODARO, M. J., Political Science and International Affairs
SPECTOR, R. H., History and International Affairs
STEN, C. W., English
STEPHENS, G. C., Geology
STEPHENS, R. W., Sociology
STERLING, C. H., Communication
STERN, C., Media and Public Affairs
STOKER, R. P., Political Science
STRICKLAND, D. K., Biochemistry and Molecular Biology
THIBAULT, J. F., French
THORNTON, R. C., History and International Affairs
TROPEA, J. L., Sociology
TROST, R. P., Economics
VANDERHOEK, J. Y., Biochemistry and Molecular Biology
VERMEER, D. E., Geography and Regional Science
VLACH, J. M., American Civilization, Anthropology
VON BARGHAHN-CALVETTI, B. A., Art
WADE, A. G., Theatre
WALKER, G. A., Biochemistry and Molecular Biology
WALLACE, D. D., Religion
WALLACE, R. A., Sociology
WALSH, R. J., Anatomy and Cell Biology
WARREN, C., Communication
WATSON, H. S., Economics
WHYTE, M. K., Sociology
WITHERS, M. R., Dance
WOLCHIK, S. L., Political Science and International Affairs
WOOD, B., Human Origins and Human Evolutionary Anatomy
WOODWARD, W. T., Painting
WRIGHT, J. F., Drawing and Graphics
WRIGHT, J. R., Political Science
YEIDE, H. E., Religion
YEZER, A., Economics
ZEIDNER, J., Administrative Sciences and Psychology
ZIOLKOWSI, J. E., Classics
ZOOK, B. C., Comparative Pathology
ZUCHELLI, A. J., Physics

Law School:

BANZHAF, J. F.
BARRON, J. A.
BLOCK, C. D.
BUERGENTHAL, T.
CHEH, M. M.
COTTROL, R. J.

CRAVER, C. B.
DIENES, C. T.
FRIEDENTHAL, J. H.
GABALDON, T. A.
HAMBURGER, P. A.
IZUMU, C. L.
JOHNSTON, G. P.
JONES, S. R.
LEES, F. J.
LUPU, I. C.
LYMAN, J. P.
MEIER, J. S.
MITCHELL, L. E.
MORGAN, T. D.
PARK, R. E.
PERONI, R. J.
PETERSON, T. D.
PIERCE, R. J.
POCK, M. A.
RAVEN-HANSEN, P.
REITZE, A. W.
ROBINSON, D.
SALTZBURG, S. T.
SCHECHTER, R. E.
SCHWARTZ, J. I.
SCHWARTZ, T. M.
SEIDELSON, D. E.
SIRULNIK, E. S.
SOLOMON, L. D.
SPANOGLE, J. A.
STARRS, J. E.
STEINHARDT, R. G.
STRAND, J. H.
TRANGSRUD, R. H.
TURLEY, J. R.
WEGNER, H. C.
ZUBROW, L. E.

School of Business and Public Management:

ACHROL, R. S., Marketing
ADAMS, W., Public Administration
AMLING, F., Business Finance
ASKARI, H. G., Global Management Research and International Finance
BABER, W. R., Accountancy
BAGCHI, P. K., Business Administration
BARNHILL, T. M., Finance
CARSON, J. H., Management Science
CATRON, B. L., Public Administration
CHERIAN, E. J., Information Systems
CHITWOOD, S. R., Public Administration
COYNE, J. P., Management Science
DAVIS, H. J., Strategic Management
DIVITA, S. F., Marketing
DYER, R. F., Business Administration
FORMAN, E. H., Management Science
FOWLER, F. D., Accountancy
FRAME, J. D., Management Science
GALLAGHER, M. G., Accountancy
HALAL, W. E., Management Science
HANDORF, W. C., Finance
HARMON, M. M., Public Administration
HARVEY, J. B., Management Science
HAWKINS, D. E., Tourism Studies, Tourism Policy and Research
HILMY, J., Accountancy
JORDAN, J. V., Finance
KEE, J. E., Public Administration
KLOCK, M. S., Finance
LAUTER, G. P., International Business
LENN, D. J., Strategic Management and Public Policy
LIEBOWITZ, J., Management Science
LOBUTS, J. F., Jr, Management Science
MCSWAIN, C. J., Public Administration
NEWCOMER, K. E., Public Administration
PAIK, C. M., Accountancy and Quantitative Methods
PARK, Y., International Business
PERRY, J. H., Business Administration
PITSVADA, B T., Public Administration
RAU, P. A., Business Administration
SEALE, W. E., Finance
SHELDON, D. R., Accountancy
SHERMAN, S. N., Business Administration
SOYER, R., Management Science
TIERNEY, C. E., Accountancy
TOLCHIN, S. J., Public Administration
TRACHTENBERG, S. J., Public Administration
UMPLEBY, S. A., Management Science
VAILL, P. B., Human Systems
WINSLOW, E. K,, Behavioural Science
WIRTZ, P. W., Management Science and Psychology

School of Medicine and Health Sciences:

AHLGREN, J. D., Medicine and Pharmacology
AUGUST, G. P., Paediatrics
AVERY, G. B., Paediatrics
BANK, W. O., Radiology and Neurological Surgery
BARTH, W. F., Medicine
BECKER, K. L., Medicine and Physiology, Experimental Medicine
BELMAN, A. B., Urology and Paediatrics
BERBERIAN, B. J., Dermatology
BINDER, H. W., Paediatrics
BOSCH, J. P., Medicine
CAMPOS, J. M., Paediatrics, Pathology, and Microbiology and Immunology
CHANOCK, R. M., Paediatrics
CHAPMAN, T. W., Health Care Sciences
CHATOOR-KOCH, I. M., Psychiatry and Behavioural Sciences and Paediatrics
CHENG, T. O., Medicine
COHEN, G. D., Health Care Sciences and Psychiatry and Behavioural Sciences
D'ANGELO, L. J., Paediatrics, Medicine and Health Care Sciences
DAVIS, D. O., Radiology, Neurology and Neurological Surgery
DEUTSCH, S., Anaesthesiology
DINNDORF, P. A., Paediatrics
DRUY, E. M., Radiology
EICHELBERGER, M. R., Surgery and Paediatrics
ELGART, M. L., Dermatology, Paediatrics and Medicine
FINKELSTEIN, J. D., Medicine
FROMM, H., Medicine
GARRISON, W. T., Psychiatry and Behavioural Sciences and Paediatrics
GEELHOED, G. W., International Medicine and Surgery
GINDOFF, P. R., Obstetrics and Gynaecology
GINSBERG, A. L., Medicine
GIORDANO, J. M., Surgery
GLASGOW, A. M., Paediatrics
GOODENHOUGH, D. J., Radiology
GREENBERG, L. W., Paediatrics
GRIFFITH, J. L., Psychiatry and Behavioural Sciences
GROSSMAN, J. H., Obstetrics and Gynaecology, Microbiology and Immunology, Prevention and Community Health
GUNTHER, S. F., Orthopaedic Surgery
HANNALLAH, R. S., Anaesthesiology and Paediatrics
HARISIADIS, L. A., Radiology
HARTMAN, C. R., Medicine
HAUDENSCHILD, C. C., Pathology and Medicine
HERER, G. R., Paediatrics
HICKS, J. M. B., Paediatrics and Pathology
HILL, M. C., Radiology
HIX, W. R., Surgery
HOLBROOK, P. R., Anaesthesiology and Paediatrics
HOLLAND, C. A., Paediatrics, Biochemistry and Molecular Biology and Microbiology and Immunology
HOUGEN, T. J., Paediatrics
HOWARD, W. J., Medicine
KATZ, R. J., Medicine and Emergency Medicine
KEIMOWITZ, R. I., Medicine and Health Care Sciences
KELLY, J. J., Neurology
KERZNER, B., Paediatrics
KIMMEL, P. L., Medicine
KUSHNER, D. C., Radiology and Paediatrics
LADISCH, S., Paediatrics and Biochemistry and Molecular Biology
LARSEN, J. W., Jr, Obstetrics and Gynaecology
LAURENO, R., Neurology
LEVINE, R. F., Medicine
LINDSAY, J., Medicine
LUBAN, N. C., Paediatrics and Pathology
LYNN, D. J., Health Care Sciences and Medicine
MACDONALD-GINZBURG, M. G., Paediatrics
MAJD, M., Radiology and Paediatrics
MALAWER, M. M., Orthopaedic Surgery
MANYAK, M. J., Urology
MARTIN, G. R., Paediatrics
MATERSON, R. S., Neurology
MCGILL, W. A., Anaesthesiology and Paediatrics
MCGRATH, M. H., Surgery
MERGNER, G. W., Anaesthesiology
MIDGLEY, F. M., Surgery and Paediatrics
MOAK, J. P., Paediatrics
MOVASSAGHI, N., Paediatrics
MRAZEK, D. A., Psychiatry, Behavioural Sciences and Paediatrics
NEVIASER, R. J., Orthopaedic Surgery
OCHSENSCHLAGER, D. W., Paediatrics and Emergency Medicine
OLMSTED, W. W., Radiology
OOI, B. S., Medicine
OSBORNE, C., Paediatrics
PACKER, R. J., Neurology and Paediatrics
PARROTT, R. H., Paediatrics
PATEL, R. I., Anaesthiology and Paediatrics
PAWLSON, L. G., Preventative Medicine, Healthcare Sciences, Medicine, Health Services Management and Policy
PHILLIPS, T. M., Medicine
PIEMME, T. E., Health Care Sciences, Medicine and Computer Medicine
PLATIA, E. V., Medicine
POLLACK, M. M., Anaesthesiology, Paediatrics
POTOLICCHIO, S. J., Neurology
POTTER, B. M., Radiology and Paediatrics
REAMAN, G. H., Paediatrics
REISS, D., Psychiatry and Behavioural Sciences, Medicine and Psychology
RIOS, J. C., Medicine, International Public Health and Computer Medicine
ROBBINS, D. C., Medicine
ROBERTSON, W. W., Orthopaedic Surgery and Paediatrics
RODRIGUEZ, W. J., Paediatrics and Microbiology and Immunology
ROGERS, C. C., Radiology and Obstetrics and Gynaecology
ROHATGI, P. K., Medicine
ROSENBERG, S. A., Surgery
ROSENQUIST, G. C., Paediatrics and Anatomy, Cell Biology
ROSENTHAL, R. E., Emergency Medicine, Biochemistry and Molecular Biology
ROSS, A. M., Medicine
RUCKMAN, R. N., Paediatrics
RUSHTON, H. G., Urology and Paediatrics
SACKIER, J. M., Surgery
SCHECHTER, G. P., Medicine
SCHEIDT, P. C., Paediatrics
SCHWARTZ, M. Z., Surgery and Paediatrics
SEKHAR, L. N., Neurological Surgery
SEVER, J. L., Paediatrics, Microbiology, and Immunology, Obstetrics and Gynaecology
SCHELBURNE, S. A., Neurology and Paediatrics
SHAN, J. A., Orthopaedic Surgery
SHESSER, R. F., Emergency Medicine and Medicine
SHORB, P. E., Surgery
SHORT, B. L., Paediatrics
SHUAIB, A., Neurology
SIDANY, A. N., Surgery
SILBER, T. J., Paediatrics, International Public Health and Health Care Sciences
SIMON, G. L., Medicine, Biochemistry and Molecular Biology

SLY, R. M., Paediatrics
SOLDIN, S. J., Paediatrics, Pathology
SOTSKY, S. M., Psychiatry and Behavioural Science
SPAGNOLO, S. V., Medicine
STEINBERG, W. M., Medicine
STILLMAN, R. J., Obstetrics and Gynaecology
SULICA, V. I., Dermatology
TSANGARIS, N. T., Surgery
TUAZON, C. U., Medicine
VARGHESE, P. J., Medicine and Paediatrics
VARMA, V. M., Radiology
VELASQUEZ, M. T., Medicine
WASSERMAN, A. G., Medicine
WEGLICKI, W. B., Medicine and Physiology
WELBORN, L. G., Anaesthesiology and Paediatrics
WESSELS, B. W., Radiology
WHITE, P. H., Medicine and Paediatrics
WIENER, J. M., Psychiatry and Behavioural Sciences and Paediatrics
WILLIAMS, C. M., Dermatology and Pathology
WILLIAMS, J. F., Anaesthesiology
WILSON, W. R., Surgery
WRIGHT, D. C., Neurological Surgery
ZALAL, G. H., Surgery and Paediatrics
ZIMMERMAN, H. J., Anaesthesiology and Medicine

Graduate School of Education and Human Development:

BELKNAP, N. J. , Special Education
BOSWELL, J. G., Education
CASTLEBERRY, M. S., Special Education
CONFESSORE, G. J., Higher Education Administration
DEW, D. W., Counselling, Psychiatry and Behavioural Sciences
FERRANTE, R., Education
FIFE, J. D., Education
FREUND, M. B., Special Education
GREENBERG, J. A., Education
HEDDESHEIMER, J. C., Counselling, Psychiatry and Behavioural Sciences
HOARE, C. H., Human Development and Human Resource Development
HOLMES, D. H., Education
HORRWORTH, G. L., Education
HOWERTON, E. B., Education
IANACONE, R. N., Special Education
KELLY, E. W., Counselling
LINKOWSKI, D. C., Counselling and Psychology and Behavioural Sciences
MAZUR, A. J., Special Education
MOORE, D. A., Education and International Affairs
PALEY, N. B., Elementary Education
PARATORE, S. R., Education
POWELL, L. E., Education Administration
RASHID, M. N., Education
RIST, R. C., Educational Leadership and Sociology
SASHKIN, M., Human Resource Development
SCHNANDT, D. R., Human Resource Development
SHOTEL, J. R., Special Education
TAYMANS, J. H., Special Education
WEST, L. L., Special Education
WORTH, M. J., Education

School of Engineering and Applied Science:

ALEXANDRIDIS, N. A., Engineering and Applied Science
BERKOVICH, S. Y., Engineering and Applied Science
BOCK, P. S., Engineering
BRIER, G. R., Engineering Management
CARROLL, R. L., Jr, Engineering and Applied Science
DEASON, J. P., Engineering and Applied Science
DELLA TORRE, E., Engineering and Applied Science
EISNER, H., Engineering Management
FALK, J. E., Operations Research
FELDMAN, M. B., Engineering and Applied Science
FRIEDER, G., Engineering, Applied Science and Statistics
FRIEDMAN, A. D., Engineering and Applied Science
GARRIS, C. A., Engineering
GILMORE, C. M., Engineering and Applied Science
HAQUE, M. I., Engineering and Applied Science
HARRALD, J. R., Engineering Management
HARRINGTON, R., Engineering and Applied Science
HELGERT, H. J., Engineering and Applied Science
HELLER, R. S., Engineering and Applied Science
HOFFMAN, L., Engineering and Applied Science
JONES, D. L., Engineering
KAHN, W. K., Engineering and Applied Science
KAUFMAN, R. E., Engineering
KYRIAKOPOULOS, N., Engineering
LANG, R. H., Engineering and Applied Science
LEE, J. D., Engineering and Applied Science
LEE, T. N., Engineering and Applied Science
LIEBOWITZ, H., Engineering and Applied Science
LOEW, M. H., Engineering
MAHMOOD, K., Engineering
MAURER, W. D., Engineering and Applied Science
MAZZUCHI, T. A., Operations Research and Engineering Management
MELTZER, A. C., Engineering and Applied Science
MURPHREE, E. L., Engineering Management
MYERS, M. K., Engineering and Applied Science
PARDAVI-HORVATH, M., Engineering and Applied Science
PICKHOLTZ, R. L., Engineering and Applied Science
SANDUSKY, R. R., Engineering and Applied Science
SARKANI, S., Civil Engineering
SHAMES, H. I., Engineering and Applied Science
SIBERT, J. L., Engineering and Applied Science
SILVERMAN, B. G., Engineering Management and Computer Medicine
SINGPURWALLA, N. D., Operations Research and Statistics
SOLAND, R. M., Operations Research
STEINER, H. M., Engineering Management
TOLSON, R. H., Engineering and Applied Science
TORIDIS, T. G., Engineering and Applied Science
WASYLKIWSKYJ, W., Engineering and Applied Science
WATERS, R. C., Engineering Management
WHITESIDES, J. L., Engineering and Applied Science
ZAGHLOUL, M. E., Engineering and Applied Science

School of Public Health and Health Services:

CAWLEY, J. F., Prevention and Community Health, Health Care Sciences
DARR, K. J., Hospital Administration, Health Care Sciences
EASTAUGH, S. R., Health Economics and Finance, Health Care Sciences
GREENBERG, W., Health Economics, Health Care Sciences
HIRSCH, R. P., Epidemiology and Biostatistics, Statistics
HOFFMAN, D. A., Epidemiology and Biostatistics, International Public Health
INFELD, D. L., Health Services Management and Policy, Health Care Sciences
PAUP, D. C., Prevention and Community Health
RIEGELMAN, R. K., Epidemiology and Biostatistics, Medicine, Health Care Sciences
RODRIGUEZ-GARCIA, R., International Public Health, Prevention and Community Health
ROSENBAUM, S., Health Services Management and Policy, Health Care Sciences
SOFAER, S., Prevention and Community Health, Health Care Sciences
SOUTHBY, R. M. F., International Health and Health Policy, Health Care Sciences

GEORGETOWN UNIVERSITY

37th and O Sts, NW, Washington, DC 20057
Telephone: (202) 687-5055

Founded in 1789 as the first Catholic University in the USA

President: LEO J. O'DONOVAN
Senior Vice-President: Dr JOHN J. DEGIOIA
Executive Vice-President for Health Sciences of the Medical Center: SAM WIESEL
Provost: Dr DOROTHY M. BROWN (acting)
Dean and Executive Vice-President for Law Center: JUDITH C. AREEN
Vice-President for Alumni and University Relations: KATHLEEN JONES
Vice-President for Planning and Institutional Research: JOSEPH PETTIT
Secretary: KATHLEEN SANTORA
Librarian: SUSAN K. MARTIN

Library of 2,123,000 vols
Number of teachers: 1,576 full-time, 509 part-time
Number of students: 12,629

Publications: *Georgetown Medical Bulletin* (3 a year), *The Georgetown Law Journal* (every 2 months), *Law and Policy in International Business* (3 a year), *Georgetown Magazine* (4 a year), *The Hoya* (2 a week), *Georgetown Law* (4 a year), *Domesday Book, The Voice* (weekly), *Hoya Review, The Blue and Gray* (2 a month).

DEANS

Georgetown College: Rev. ROBERT B. LAWTON
Graduate School: (vacant)
School of Nursing: (vacant)
Edmund A. Walsh School of Foreign Service: ROBERT GALLUCCI
School of Business: CHRISTOPHER PUTO
School for Summer and Continuing Education: MICHAEL J. COLLINS
Research and Graduate Education, Medical Center: KEN DRETCHEN

ATTACHED INSTITUTES

Center for Applied Research in the Apostolate: Dir GERALD EARLY.
Center for Clinical Bioethics: Dir DANIEL SULMASY.
Center for Contemporary Arab Studies: Dir BARBARA STOWASSER.
Center for German and European Studies: Dir SAMUEL H. BARNES.
Center for Eurasian, Russian and East European Studies: Dir MARCIA MORRIS (acting).
Center for Muslim-Christian Understanding: Dir JOHN ESPOSITO.
Institute for the Study of Diplomacy: Dir CASIMIR A. YOST.
Joseph and Rose Kennedy Institute of Ethics: Dir LEROY WALTERS.

HOWARD UNIVERSITY

2400 Sixth St, NW, Washington, DC 20059
Telephone: (202) 806-6100
Fax: (202) 806-5934

Founded 1867
Private control
Academic year: August to May (two terms)
President: Dr JOYCE A. LADNER (acting)

Vice-President for Academic Affairs: Dr ELBERT L. COX (acting)
Vice-President for Business and Fiscal Affairs: JAMES A. FLETCHER, II
Vice-President for Health Affairs: Dr WALTER F. LEAVELL
Vice-President for Institutional Management: BERT KING
General Counsel: HENRY RAMSEY, Jr (acting)
Vice-President for Student Affairs: Dr STEVE A. FAVORS
Secretary of the University and the Board of Trustees: ARTIS G. HAMPSHIRE-COWAN
Director of Libraries: Dr ANN RANDALL

Library of 1,900,000 vols
Number of teachers: 2,051
Number of students: 10,987

Publications: *Journal of Negro Education* (quarterly), *Journal of Religious Thought* (2 a year), *Howard Law Review* (quarterly), *The Howard Journal of Communications* (quarterly), *The Capstone* (weekly during academic terms).

DEANS

College of Dentistry: Dr ROBERT S. KNIGHT
College of Arts and Sciences: Dr CLARENCE M. LEE
College of Medicine: Dr CHARLES H. EPPS, Jr
College of Pharmacy: Dr WENDELL T. HILL, Jr
College of Fine Arts: Dr JEFF R. DONALDSON
College of Nursing: Dr DOROTHY L. POWELL
School of Social Work: Dr RICHARD A. ENGLISH
Graduate School of Arts and Sciences: Dr ORLANDO L. TAYLOR
College of Allied Health Sciences: Dr GENE E. GARY-WILLIAMS
School of Engineering: Dr M. LUCIUS WALKER
School of Law: HENRY RAMSEY, Jr
School of Architecture and Planning: HARRY G. ROBINSON, III
School of Communications: Dr JANNETTE DATES (acting)
School of Divinity: Dr CLARENCE O. NEWSOME
School of Education: Dr PORTIA H. SHIELDS
School of Business: Dr LAWRENCE A. JOHNSON
School of Continuing Education: Dr ELEANOR I. FRANKLIN

SOUTHEASTERN UNIVERSITY

501 Eye St, SW, Washington, DC 20024
Telephone: (202) 488-8162
Fax: (202) 488-8093

Founded 1879

Associate, Bachelor's and Master's degrees in Business and Government Management

President: EARL M. MITCHELL (acting)
Chief Operating Officer for Academic Affairs: Dr MOHAMMAD SAFA
Chief Operating Officer for External Affairs: JAMES H. ALLEN, Jr
Library Director: EUGENNIE BUCKLEY

Library of 46,000 vols
Number of teachers: 100
Number of students: 2,000

TRINITY COLLEGE

125 Michigan Ave NE, Washington, DC 20017
Telephone: (202) 884-9000
Fax: (202) 884-9229

Founded 1897

Roman Catholic liberal arts college for women, sponsored by Sisters of Notre Dame de Namur

President: PATRICIA MCGUIRE
Vice-President of Academic Affairs: Dr PATRICIA WEITZEL-O'NEILL
Dean of the School of Professional Studies and Adult Studies: (vacant)
Dean of Students: CAMILLE HAZEUR
Dean of Enrolment Management: (vacant)
Registrar: BURNESSE ROBERTS-BODDIE
Librarian: SUSAN CRAIG

Library of over 158,000 vols
Number of teachers: 55 full-time
Number of students: 581 full-time, 908 part-time

Publications: *Trinity College Record, Trinity Times, Trinilogue, Alumnae Journal, Trinity Today.*

UNIVERSITY OF THE DISTRICT OF COLUMBIA

4200 Connecticut Ave, NW, Washington, DC 20008

Telephone: (202) 274-5000

Founded 1851; a public urban land-grant university organized on three campuses from existing colleges; first degree programmes

President: TILDEN J. LEMELLE

Number of students: 9,660

Colleges of Arts and Sciences, and of Professional Studies.

FLORIDA

BARRY UNIVERSITY

11300 NE 2nd Ave, Miami Shores, FL 33161
Telephone: (305) 899-3000
Founded 1940

President: Sister JEANNE O'LAUGHLIN
Provost and Vice-President for Academic Affairs: Dr PATRICK LEE
Librarian: NANCY PINE

Library of 690,000 vols
Number of teachers: 248
Number of students: 7,218

DEANS

Business: Dr JACK SCARBOROUGH
Adult and Continuing Education: Sister LORETTA MULRY
Arts and Sciences: Dr LAURA ARMESTO
Nursing: Dr JUDITH BALCERSKI
School of Social Work: Dr STEPHEN M. HOLLOWAY
Education: Sister EVELYN PICHE
Natural and Health Sciences: Sister JOHN KAREN FREI
Graduate Medical Science: Dr CHESTER EVANS
Human Performance and Leisure Sciences: Dr G. JEAN CERRA

BETHUNE-COOKMAN COLLEGE

640 Dr Mary McLeod Bethune Blvd, Daytona Beach, FL 32114

Telephone: (904) 255-1401
Fax: (904) 257-7027
E-mail: bronsonp@cookman.edu

Founded 1904

President: Dr OSWALD P. BRONSON, Sr
Executive Vice-President: Dr J. S. FRINK
Vice-President for Academic Affairs and Dean of the Faculty: Dr ANN D. TAYLOR
Vice-President for Fiscal Affairs: CHARLES D. O'DUOR
Vice-President for Development: DIANE Y. JEFFERSON
Vice-President for Student Affairs: CLARENCE N. CHILDS
Vice-President for Governmental Affairs: Dr FREDERICK MILTON
Director of Admissions and Recruitment: WILLIAM BYRD
Director of Institutional Research: NARENDRA H. PATEL
Registrar: JAMES C. WYMES, Sr
Librarian: Dr BOBBY R. HENDERSON

Library of 156,861 vols
Number of teachers: 130 full-time, 84 part-time
Number of students: 2,343 full-time, 180 part-time

Publications: *The Clarion* (quarterly), *The Voice* (monthly), *Bethune-Cookman College Fact Book* (annually).

CHAIRMEN OF DIVISIONS

Business: Dr AUBREY E. LONG
Education: Dr EMMA W. REMBERT
Humanities: Dr S. LOUISE ROSEMOND
Science and Mathematics: Dr THEODORE R. NICHOLSON, Sr
Social Sciences: Dr SHEILA Y. FLEMMING
General Studies: Dr LOIS S. FENNELLY
Nursing: MARY EAVES (acting)

ECKERD COLLEGE

4200 54th Ave S, St Petersburg, FL 33711
Telephone: (813) 864-8331
Fax: (813) 866-2304

Founded 1958 as Florida Presbyterian College
Liberal arts college

President: PETER H. ARMACOST

Number of teachers: 130
Number of students: 1,500

FLORIDA AGRICULTURAL AND MECHANICAL UNIVERSITY

Tallahassee, FL 32307
Telephone: (904) 599-3000
Founded 1887

President: FREDERICK S. HUMPHRIES
Vice-President for University Relations and Public Affairs: DOROTHY P. WILLIAMS
Vice-President of Administration and Fiscal Affairs: ROBERT CARROLL
Vice-President for Academic Affairs: JAMES H. AMMONS
Vice-President for Student Affairs: A. DELORIES SLOAN
Vice-President for Sponsored Research: FRANKLIN HAMILTON
Director of Planning and Institutional Research: STERLIN ADAMS
Librarian: LAUREN SAPP

Library of 505,490 vols
Number of teachers: 550
Number of students: 9,933

DEANS

School of Architecture: RODNER WRIGHT
College of Arts and Sciences: Dr ARTHUR C. WASHINGTON
College of Education: Dr MELVIN GADSON
College of Engineering Sciences, Technology and Agriculture: Dr BOBBY R. PHILLS
School of Business and Industry: SYBIL C. MOBLEY
School of Nursing: MARGARET W. LEWIS
College of Pharmacy: HENRY LEWIS, III
School of General Studies: Dr BARBARA BARNES
School of Allied Health Sciences: JACQUELINE BECK
School of Journalism, Media and Graphic Arts: ROBERT RUGGLES
Division of Graduate Studies, Research and Continuing Education: Dr THEODORE HEMMINGWAY
FAMU/FSU College of Engineering: C. J. CHEN

FLORIDA ATLANTIC UNIVERSITY

Boca Raton, FL 33431
Telephone: (561) 297-3000
Founded 1961

President: Dr ANTHONY JAMES CATANESE

University Provost and Chief Academic Officer: Dr RICHARD L. OSBURN
Registrar: HARRY DE MIK
Librarian: Dr WILLIAM MILLER

Library of 665,000 volumes
Number of teachers: 778
Number of students: 19,699

Publication: *Journal of the Fantastic in the Arts*.

DEANS

College of Arts and Letters: Dr JAMES S. MALEK
College of Business: Dr BRUCE MALLEN
College of Education: Dr JERRY LAFFERTY
College of Engineering: Dr JOHN JUREWICZ (acting)
College of Liberal Arts: Dr CHARLES WHITE
College of Nursing: Dr ANNE BOYKIN
College of Science: Dr JOHN WIESENFELD
College of Architecture and Urban and Public Affairs: Dr ROSALYN CARTER

FLORIDA INSTITUTE OF TECHNOLOGY

150 W. University Blvd, Melbourne, FL 32901
Telephone: (407) 674-8000

President: LYNN E. WEAVER
Vice-President for Academic Affairs: ANDREW W. REVAY, Jr
Vice-President for Financial Affairs: RICHARD L. BARTREM
Vice-President for Research and Dean of Graduate School: NORINE E. NOONAN
Vice-President for Student Affairs and Dean of Students: MARSHA DUNCAN
Director of Admissions: JUDITH MARINO
Registrar: FRED BUYS
Director of Libraries: CELINE ALVEY

Number of students: 6,500

DEANS

College of Science and Liberal Arts: GORDON NELSON
College of Engineering: ROBERT L. SULLIVAN
School of Business : A. THOMAS HOLLINGSWORTH
School of Psychology: Dr CAROL PHILPOT
School of Aeronautics: Dr N. THOMAS STEPHENS
Graduate School: Dr NORINE E. NOONAN
School of Extended Graduate Studies: RONALD L. MARSHALL

FLORIDA INTERNATIONAL UNIVERSITY

University Park, Miami, FL 33199
Telephone: (305) 348-2000
Founded 1965; part of the State University System of Florida

President: MODESTO A. MAIDIQUE
Provost and Vice-President for Academic Affairs: JAMES MAU
Vice-President for Business and Finance: CYNTHIA W. CURRY
Vice-President for University Outreach and Athletics: MARY L. PANKOWSKI
Vice-President for University Advancement and Student Affairs: PAUL GALLAGHER
Vice-President for North Campus and Enrolment Services: RICHARD J. CORRENTI
Director of Libraries: LAURENCE A. MILLER

Degree programmes in arts and sciences, business administration, education, hospitality management, urban and public affairs, engineering, health sciences, nursing, accounting, computer science, journalism.

FLORIDA MEMORIAL COLLEGE

15800 NW 42nd Ave, Miami, FL 33054
Telephone: (305) 625-4141
Fax: (305) 623-4123
Founded 1879

President: Dr LEE E. MONROE
Librarian: Dr LABAN CONNOR

Library of 80,000 vols
Number of teachers: 116
Number of students: 1,960

FLORIDA SOUTHERN COLLEGE

111 Lake Hollingsworth Drive, Lakeland, FL 33801
Telephone: (941) 680-4111
Founded 1885

President: Dr THOMAS L. REUSCHLING
Admissions: ROBERT PALMER
Librarian: ANDREW L. PEARSON

Library of 190,000 vols
Number of teachers: 97
Number of students: 1,510 full-time, 537 part-time

FLORIDA STATE UNIVERSITY

Tallahassee, FL 32306
Telephone: (904) 644-1234
Founded 1851 as the Seminary West of the Suwannee River, and later became the Florida State College, became the Florida State College for Women 1905, became co-educational again and attained university status 1947
Academic year: August to April (two semesters)

Chancellor of the State University System: CHARLES REED
President: TALBOT D'ALEMBERTE
Provost and Vice-President for Academic Affairs: LAWRENCE ABELE
Dean of the Faculties and Deputy Provost: STEVE EDWARDS
Vice-President for Administration: JOHN CARNAGHI
Vice-President for Student Affairs: JON DALTON
Vice-President for Research: ROBERT M. JOHNSON
Vice-President for University Advancement: BEVERLEY B. SPENCER
Registrar: MAXWELL CARRAWAY
Librarian: CHARLES E. MILLER

Library: see Libraries
Number of teachers: 1,700
Number of students: 29,630

Publication: *Bulletin*.

DEANS

College of Arts and Sciences: F. LEYSIEFFER
College of Business: M. STITH
College of Communication: J. MAYO
School of Criminology: D. MAIER-KATKIN
College of Education: J. MILLER
College of Engineering: CHING-JEN CHEN
School of Human Sciences: PENNY A. RALSTON
College of Law: D. WEIDNER
School of Library and Information Studies: J. ROBBINS
School of Motion Picture, Television and Recording Arts: R. FIELDING
School of Music: J. PIERSOL
School of Nursing: EVELYN T. SINGER
College of Social Sciences: CHARLES F. CNUDDE
School of Social Work: D. MONTGOMERY
School of Theatre: GIL LAZIER
School of Visual Arts: JERRY DRAPER
Graduate Studies: A. MABE
Undergraduate Studies: E. MUHLENFELD
Panama City Campus: L. BLAND

JACKSONVILLE UNIVERSITY

Jacksonville, FL 32211-3394
Telephone: (904) 744-3950
Fax: (904) 744-0101
Founded 1934

President: PAUL S. TIPTON
Vice-President for Academic Affairs: Dr JESSE S. ROBERTSON
Director of Admissions: SUSAN HALLENBECK
Director of Student Financial Assistance: CATHERINE HUNTRESS
Registrar: CAROLYN BARRETT
Librarian: THOMAS H. GUNN

Library of 572,000 vols
Number of teachers: 113 full-time, 131 part-time
Number of students: 2,321

NEW COLLEGE OF THE UNIVERSITY OF SOUTH FLORIDA

5700 N Tamiami Trail, Sarasota, FL 34243-2197
Telephone: (941) 359-4320
Fax: (941) 359-4298
Founded 1960

Dean and Warden: Dr DOUGLAS C. LANGSTON
Admissions: KATHLEEN M. KILLION

Library of 200,000 vols
Number of teachers: 57
Number of students: 600

DIVISIONAL CHAIRMEN

Humanities: Dr STEPHEN T. MILES
Social Sciences: Dr GORDON B. BAUER
Natural Sciences: Dr LEO DEMSKI

NOVA SOUTHEASTERN UNIVERSITY

3301 College Ave, Fort Lauderdale, FL 33314
Telephone: (954) 262-7300
Founded 1964

President: RAY FERRERO Jr
Executive Vice-Chancellor and Provost, Health Professions Division: Dr FREDERICK LIPPMAN
Executive Provost and Vice-President, Academic Affairs: Dr ELIZABETH MCDANIEL
Vice-President for Finance: JEFFREY SCHNEIDER
Vice-President for Institutional Advancement: MARILYN JOHNSON
Vice-President for Student Affairs: JOE LAKOVITCH
Chancellor, Health Professions Division: Dr MORTON TERRY
Vice-President for Research and Planning: Dr JOHN LOSAK
Registrar: STANLEY CROSS

Number of students: 16,500

DEANS

Fischler Center for the Advancement of Education: Dr H. WELLS SINGLETON (Dean and Provost)
School of Computer and Information Sciences: Dr EDWARD LIEBLEIN
Family and School Center: Dr TIFFANY FIELD
Law Center: JOSEPH D. HARBAUGH
Farquar Center for Undergraduate Studies: Dr NORMA GOONEN
Oceanographic Center: Dr JULIAN MCCREARY
Center for Psychological Studies: Dr RONALD F. LEVANT
School of Social and Systemic Studies: Dr RON CHENAIL
School of Business and Entrepreneurship: RANDOLPH A. POHLMAN
Shepard Broad Law Center: JOSEPH HARBAUGH
College of Allied Health: Dr RAUL CUADRADO
College of Pharmacy: Dr WILLIAM HARDIGAN
College of Medical Sciences: Dr HAROLD LAUBACH
College of Optometry: Dr DAVID LOSHIN
College of Dental Medicine: Dr SEYMOUR OLIET
College of Osteopathic Medicine: Dr CYRIL BLAVO (acting)

ROLLINS COLLEGE

Winter Park, FL 32789

Telephone: (407) 646-2000
Fax: (407) 646-2600

Founded 1885

President: RITA BORNSTEIN
Vice-President for Academic Affairs and Provost: CHARLES M. EDMONDSON
Vice-President for Business and Finance and Treasurer: GEORGE HERBST
Vice-President for Development and College Relations: (vacant)
Dean of Student Affairs: STEVEN N. NEILSON
Dean of Admissions and Financial Aid: DAVID G. ERDMANN
Dean of Faculty: STEPHEN R. BRIGGS
Records: TONI STROLLO HOLBROOK
Librarian: GEORGE C. GRANT

Library of 274,000 vols
Number of teachers: 128
Number of students: 2,460 f.t.e.

Publications: *Sandspur* (weekly), *Alumni Record* (quarterly), *Brushing* (1 a year).

HEADS OF DEPARTMENT

Anthropology: CAROL LAUER
Art: ROBERT LEMON
Biology: PURSIS COLEMAN
Chemistry: PEDRO BERNAL
Computer Science: DOUG CHILD
Economics: KENNA TAYLOR
Education: J. SCOTT HEWITT
English: MAURICE O'SULLIVAN
Environmental Studies: BRUCE STEPHENSON
Foreign Languages: ROY KERR
History: JACK LANE
Latin American and Caribbean Affairs: PEDRO PEQUENO
Mathematics: MARK ANDERSON
Music: JOHN SINCLAIR
Organizational Communication: GREG GARDNER
Philosophy and Religion: J. THOMAS COOK
Physical Education: PHIL ROACH
Physics: ROBERT CARSON
Politics: THOMAS LAIRSON
Psychology: MARIA RUIZ
Sociology: LYNDA GLENNON
Theater, Dance, and Speech: S. JOSEPH NASSIF

SAINT LEO COLLEGE

POB 2187, Saint Leo, FL 33574

Telephone: (904) 588-8200
Fax: (904) 588-8654

Founded 1889
Private control, Catholic

President: ARTHUR F. KIRK, Jr
Vice-President for Academic Affairs: Dr DOUGLAS ASTOLFI
Vice-President for Student Affairs: Dr MAUREEN POWERS
Vice-President for Business Affairs: JOHN WEICHERDING
Director of Admissions: GARY BRACKEN
Registrar: KAREN HATFIELD
Librarian: KAY KOSUDA

Library of 90,000 vols
Number of teachers: 64
Number of students: 8,000

ST THOMAS UNIVERSITY

16400 NW 32nd Ave, Miami, FL 33054

Telephone: (305) 625-6000

Founded 1961

President: Mgr FRANKLYN M. CASALE
Vice-President, Academic Affairs: (vacant)
Vice-President for Administration: NORMAN BLAIR
Dean of School of Law: DANIEL J. MORRISSEY
Librarian: MARGARET ELLISTON

Library of 122,000 vols
Number of teachers: 72 full-time, 59 part-time
Number of students: 2,426

SCHILLER INTERNATIONAL UNIVERSITY – FLORIDA

For general details, see entry in Germany chapter

Florida Campus: 453 Edgewater Drive, Dunedin, FL 34698-7532; tel. (813) 736-5082; fax (813) 736-6263; Dir J. BROCK.

STETSON UNIVERSITY

421 N. Woodland Blvd, DeLand, FL 32720

Telephone: (904) 822-7000
Fax: (904) 822-8925
E-mail: sunews@stetson.edu

Established as DeLand Academy 1883; chartered as DeLand University 1887; name changed 1889.

Academic year: August to May

President: H. DOUGLAS LEE
Vice-President for University Relations: F. MARK WHITTAKER
Vice-President for Business and Finance: Dr JUDSON P. STRYKER
Vice-President for Information Technology: Dr SHAHRAM AMIRI
Vice-President and Dean of College of Law: LIZABETH A. MOODY
Vice-President for Campus Life: Dr JAMES BEASLEY

Libraries of 557,000 vols and 280,000 government documents
Number of teachers: 163 in DeLand; 34 at College of Law, St Petersburg
Number of students: 2,212 in DeLand; 645 at College of Law

Publications: *The Stetson University Bulletin, The Cupola, Stetson University Magazine, Commons*.

UNIVERSITY OF CENTRAL FLORIDA

Orlando, FL 32816

Telephone: (407) 823-2000

Founded 1963

President: Dr JOHN C. HITT
Registrar: Dr JOHN BUSH
Librarian: BARRY B. BAKER

Library of 1,000,000 vols
Number of teachers: 750
Number of students: 29,000

DEANS

Arts and Sciences: Dr KATHRYN SEIDEL
Business: Dr THOMAS KEON
Education: Dr SANDRA ROBINSON
Engineering: Dr MARTIN P. WANIELISTA
Health: Dr BELINDA MCCARTHY

CAMPUS DIRECTORS

Brevard Campus: Dr JAMES DRAKE
Daytona Beach Campus: Dr JACK ROLLINS (acting)
South Orlando Campus: Dr THOMAS SHOSTAK

UNIVERSITY OF FLORIDA

Gainesville, FL 32611

Telephone: (904) 392-3261

Founded 1853

President: JOHN V. LOMBARDI
Provost and Vice-President for Academic Affairs: ANDREW SORENSEN
Vice-President for Agricultural and Natural Resources: J. M. DAVIDSON (acting)
Vice-President for Health Affairs: D. R. CHALLONER
Vice-President for Administrative Affairs: GERALD SCHAFFER
Vice-President for Development: R. LINDGREN
Vice-President for Research: D. R. PRICE
Vice-President for Student Affairs: C. A. SANDEEN
University Registrar: B. FINCHER
Director of Libraries: D. CANELAS
Director, Florida State Museum: T. P. BENNETT

Library: see Libraries
Number of teachers: 3,531
Number of students: 35,753

Publications include: *Journal of Politics, Southern Folklore Quarterly, University of Florida Law Review, Florida Historical Quarterly, Latin American Studies Association Newsletter.*

DEANS

Architecture: W. DRUMMOND
Business Administration: J. KRAFT
Continuing Education: J. W. KNIGHT
Education: D. C. SMITH
Engineering: W. M. PHILLIPS
Fine Arts: D. MCGLOTHLIN
Graduate School: MADELYN LOCKHART
Journalism and Communications: R. L. LOWENSTEIN
Law: JEFFREY LEWIS
Liberal Arts and Sciences: W. W. HARRISON
Physical Education: P. BIRD
Medicine: A. NEIMS
Nursing: LOIS MALASANOS
Pharmacy: M. A. SCHWARTZ
Health Related Professions: RICHARD GUTEKUNST
Dentistry: DONALD LEGLER
Agriculture: L. J. CONNOR
Forestry: C. P. REID
Agriculture (Extension): J. T. WOESTE
Agriculture (Research): N. P. THOMPSON (acting)
Veterinary Medicine: R. DIERKS

HEADS OF DEPARTMENTS

Architecture:
- Architecture: LELAND SHAW (acting)
- Urban and Regional Planning: JAY M. STEIN
- Interior Design: JERRY NIELSON
- Landscape Architecture: HERRICK H. SMITH
- Building Construction: WEILIN CHANG

Business Administration:
- Accounting: DOUG SNOWBALL
- Decision and Information Sciences: GARY KOEHLER
- Economics: L. W. KENNY
- Finance and Insurance: H. C. SMITH, Jr
- Management: J. B. RAY
- Marketing: ALAN SAWYER

Dentistry:
- Community Dentistry: DONALD R. MCNEAL
- Dental Biomaterials: KENNETH J. ANUSAVICE
- Endodontics: FRANK J. VERTUZZI
- Operative Dentistry: G. E. SMITH
- Oral Biology: ARNOLD BLEIWEIS
- Oral Diagnostics Sciences: RONALD BAUGHMAN
- Oral Surgery: M. FRANKLIN DOLWICK
- Orthodontics: GREGORY J. KING
- Paediatric Dentistry: FRANK COURTS
- Periodontics: THOMAS HASSELL
- Prosthodontics: A. E. CLARK, Jr

Education:
- Counselor Education: GERARDO GONZALEZ
- Educational Leadership: R. CRAIG WOOD
- Foundations of Education: JAMES J. ALGINA
- Instruction and Curriculum: M. C. MAHLIOS
- Special Education: PAUL T. SINDELAR

Engineering:
- Aeronautical Engineering, Mechanics and Engineering Science: M. A. EISENBERG
- Chemical Engineering: T. S. ANDERSON
- Civil Engineering: PAUL Y. THOMPSON
- Coastal and Oceanographic Engineering: R. G. DEAN

Computer & Information Science: STEPHEN YAU
Electrical Engineering: MARTIN UMAN
Engineering Sciences: MARTIN EISENBERG
Environmental Engineering Science: JOSEPH J. DELFINO
Industrial and Systems Engineering: DONALD J. ELZINGA
Materials Science Engineering: GHOLAMREZA ABBASCHIAN
Mechanical Engineering: ROBERT B. GAITHER
Nuclear Engineering: JAMES TULENKO

Fine Arts:
Art: JOHN EDWARD CATTERALL
Music: J. R. GRIGSBY (acting)
Theatre: J. W. WILLIAMS

Florida State Museum:
Interpretation: M. A. NICKERSON
Anthropology: J. L. MILANICH
Natural Science: NORRIS H. WILLIAMS

Health Related Professions:
Clinical Psychology: NATHAN W. PERRY, Jr
Communicative Disorders: KENNETH R. BZOCH
Health and Hospital Administration: BARRY R. GREENE
Medical Laboratory Services: M. BRITT (acting)
Occupational Therapy: KAY WALKER
Physical Therapy: MARTHA A. CLENDENIN
Rehabilitation Counseling: HORACE W. SAWYER

Agriculture:
Agricultural Engineering: O. J. LOEWER
Agriculture, Education and Communication: CARL E. BEEMAN
Agronomy: CHARLES E. DEAN
Animal Science: F. G. HEMBRY
Dairy and Poultry Science: ROGER P. NATZKE
Entomology and Nematology: JOHN LOWELL CAPINERA
Environmental Horticulture: T. A. NEIL
Fisheries and Aquaculture: J. V. SHIREMAN
Food and Resource Economics: LARRY LIBBY
Food Science and Human Nutrition: J. F. GREGORY, III
Horticultural Science: D. J. CANTLIFFE
Microbiology and Cell Science: E. M. HOFFMAN
Plant Pathology: G. AGROIS
School of Forest Resources and Conservation: C. P. REID
Soil Science: G. A. O'CONNOR
Wildlife and Range Management: G. W. TANNER

Journalism and Communications:
Advertising: JOSEPH R. PISANI
Public Relations: JOHN DETWEILER
Telecommunications: GERALD P. SMEYAK
Journalism: JON A. ROOSENRAAD

Liberal Arts and Sciences:
African and Asian Languages and Literature: O. J. YAI
Anthropology: GEORGE ARMELAGOS
Astronomy: STEPHEN GOTTESMAN
Botany: DAVID JONES
Chemistry: MICHAEL ZERNER
Classics: GARETH SCHMELING
Communication Processes and Disorders: KENNETH GERHARDT
English: PATRICIA CRADDOCK
Geography: EDWARD MALECKI Jr
Geology: A. F. RANDAZZO
German and Slavic Languages and Literatures: A. F. STEPHAN
History: F. G. GREGORY
Philosophy: J. I. BIRO
Physics: NEIL SULLIVAN
Political Science: KENNETH WALD
Psychology: ROBERT SORKIN
Religion: A. A. NANJI
Romance Languages and Literature: RAYMOND GAY-CROSIER
Sociology: J. H. SCANZONI
Statistics: RONALD RANDLES
Zoology: FRANK NORDLIE

Medicine:
Anaesthesiology: JEROME H. MODELL
Anatomy and Cell Biology: MICHAEL H. ROSS
Biochemistry and Molecular Biology: D. L. PURICH
Community Health and Family Medicine: R. W. CURRY, Jr (acting)
Immunology and Medical Microbiology: RICHARD MOYER
Medicine: JAMES E. MCGUIGAN
Neurology: MELVIN GREER
Neuroscience: WILLIAM G. LUTTGE
Neurosurgery: ALBERT L. RHOTON
Obstetrics and Gynecology: BYRON J. MASTERSON
Ophthalmology: MELVIN RUBIN
Orthopaedic Surgery: ROY W. PETTY
Paediatrics: D. J. BARRETT
Pathology: NOEL MACLAREN
Pharmacology: STEPHEN BAKER
Physiology: MICHAEL I. PHILLIPS
Psychiatry: D. L. EVANS
Radiation Oncology: R. R. MILLION
Radiology: EDWARD V. STAAB
Surgery: EDWARD M. COPELAND

Pharmacy:
Health Care Administration: CHARLES DOUGLAS HELPER
Medicinal Chemistry: M. O. JAMES (acting)
Pharmacy Practice: DAVID ANGARAN
Pharmaceutics: H. C. DERENDORF
Pharmodynamics: MICHAEL J. KATOVICH

Health and Human Performance:
Exercise and Sport Science: ROBERT SINGER
Recreation, Parks and Tourism: PAUL R. VARNES
Health Science Education: R. MORGAN PIGG

Veterinary Medicine:
Comparative and Experimental Pathology: W. L. CASTLEMAN
Infectious Diseases: M. J. BURRIDGE
Large Animal Clinical Sciences: R. K. BRAUN
Physiological Science: DARYL BUSS
Small Animal Clinical Sciences: MARK S. BLOOMBERG

UNIVERSITY OF MIAMI

Coral Gables, FL 33124
Telephone: (305) 284-2211
Chartered 1925
Private control
Academic year: September to May (two terms)
President: EDWARD T. FOOTE, II
Provost and Executive Vice-President: Dr LUIS GLASER
Senior Vice-President: DAVID LIEBERMAN
Senior Vice-President for Medical Affairs and Dean, School of Medicine: Dr JOHN G. CLARKSON
Vice-President for University Advancement: Dr ROY J. NIRSCHEL, Jr
Vice-President and General Counsel: ROBERT BLAKE
Vice-President for Information Resources: Dr M. LEWIS TEMARES
Vice-President for Student Affairs: Dr PATRICIA A. WHITELY
Vice-President and Treasurer: DIANE COOK
Dean of Students: WILLIAM W. SANDLER, Jr
Vice-Provost for Enrollments: PAUL M. OREHOVEC
Director of Libraries: DON BOSSEAU
Library of 1,870,000 vols
Number of teachers: 1,853 full-time, 448 part-time
Number of students: 13,734
Publications: *The Miami Hurricane* (student bi-weekly newspaper), *Ibis* (yearbook), *Journal of Inter-American Studies* (quarterly), *World Affairs* (quarterly), *University Bulletins.*

DEANS
College of Arts and Sciences: Dr KUMBLE SUBBASWAMY
School of Business Administration: Dr PAUL K. SUGRUE
School of Education: Dr SAMUEL J. YARGER
College of Engineering: Dr M. LEWIS TEMARES
School of Architecture: ELIZABETH PLATER-ZYBERK
School of Law: SAMUEL J. THOMPSON
School of Medicine: Dr JOHN G. CLARKSON
School of Music: Dr WILLIAM HIPP
School of Nursing: Dr DIANE HORNER
School of Continuing Studies: Dr CAROL HOLDEN
Rosenstiel School of Marine and Atmospheric Sciences: Dr OTIS BROWN
Graduate School: Dr STEVEN ULLMAN (acting)
Graduate School of International Studies: Dr ROGER KANET
School of Communication: EDWARD PFISTER

UNIVERSITY OF NORTH FLORIDA

4567 St Johns Bluff Rd, South Jacksonville, FL 32224
Telephone: (904) 646-2500
President: ADAM W. HERBERT
Number of students: 10,500

UNIVERSITY OF SOUTH FLORIDA

4202 East Fowler Ave, Tampa, FL 33620
Telephone: (813) 974-2011
Founded 1956, classes commenced 1960
State control
Academic year: September to April (semester system) and summer sessions
President: Dr FRANCIS T. BORKOWSKI
Registrar: LINDA ERICKSON
Provost: Dr GERRY G. MEISELS
Executive Vice-President: ALBERT C. HARTLEY
Vice-President of Student Affairs: DANIEL R. WALBOLT
Vice-President for Public Affairs: Dr MARK LONO
Vice-President for Administrative Affairs: RICKARD C. FENDER
Vice-President for Development and Alumni Affairs: THOMAS L. TOBIN
Vice-President for Research: Dr GEORGE NEWKOME
Vice-President for Health Sciences: Dr RONALD KAUFMAN
Library of 1,351,547 vols
Number of teachers: 1,525
Number of students: 32,360

DEANS
College of Business Administration: Dr JAMES L. PAPPAS
College of Education: Dr WILLIAM G. KATZENMEYER
College of Engineering: Dr MICHAEL G. KOVAC
College of Fine Arts: Dr JOHN L. SMITH
College of Medicine: Dr RONALD KAUFMAN (acting)
College of Nursing: Dr JUDITH A. PLAWECKI
College of Arts and Sciences: Dr ROLLIN C. RICHMOND
College of Public Health: Dr PETER J. LEVIN
Graduate School: Dr JAMES M. ANKER
Undergraduate Studies: Dr WILLIAM SCHEUERLE
USF at Sarasota: Dr DAVID SCHENCK (acting)
USF at Fort Myers: Dr ROY I. MUMME (acting)
USF at St Petersburg: Dr WINSTON BRIDGES (acting)
New College of USF: Dr MARGARET BATES (acting, Provost)

UNIVERSITY OF TAMPA

Tampa, FL 33606
Telephone: (813) 253-3333
Founded 1931
President: RONALD L. VAUGHN
Vice-President for Administrative Affairs: ROBERT E. FORSCHNER
Vice-President for Development: DANIEL T. GURA
Librarian: MARLYN C. PETHE
Library of 250,000 vols
Number of teachers: 130 full-time
Number of students: 2,500 full-time

DEANS
College of Business: ALFRED N. PAGE
College of Liberal Arts and Sciences: JAN K. DARGEL

GEORGIA

AGNES SCOTT COLLEGE

141 E. College Avenue, Atlanta/Decatur, GA 30030
Telephone: (404) 638-6000
Fax: (404) 638-6177
Founded 1889
Liberal arts college for women
President: MARY BROWN BULLOCK
Vice-President for Business and Finance: WILLIAM GAILEY
Dean of College: EDMUND J. SHEEHEY
Dean of Students: GUÉ P. HUDSON
Registrar: MARY K. JARBOE
Director of Admission: STEPHANIE BALMER
Librarian: VIRGINIA MORELAND
Library of 201,000 vols
Number of teachers: 67
Number of students: 773
Publications: *Main Events, Agnes Scott Alumnae Magazine.*

ALBANY STATE COLLEGE

Albany, GA 31705
Telephone: (912) 430-4604
Founded 1903
President: Dr PORTIA HOLMES SHIELDS
Director of Admissions and Financial Aid: KATHLEEN CALDWELL
Vice-President for Academic Affairs: Dr ERNEST BENSON
Librarian: Dr DOROTHY HAITH
Library of 161,000 vols
Number of teachers: 150
Number of students: 2,405

BERRY COLLEGE

Mount Berry Station, Mount Berry, GA 30149
Telephone: (706) 236-2215
Founded 1902
President: J. SCOTT COLLEY
Dean of Students: THOMAS W. CARVER
Dean of the College: L. DOYLE MATHIS
Dean of Admissions: GEORGE GADDIE
Registrar: CHARLES GILBREATH
Library of 576,000 vols
Number of teachers: 126
Number of students: 1,856 undergraduates, 229 graduates
Publication: *Admissions Catalog.*

CLARK ATLANTA UNIVERSITY

223 James P. Brawley Drive SW, Atlanta, GA 30314
Telephone: (404) 880-8000
Founded 1988, following consolidation of Atlanta University (founded 1865) and Clark College (founded 1869); member of Atlanta University Center
President: THOMAS W. COLE, Jr
Provost and Vice-President for Academic Affairs: WINFRED HARRIS
Vice-President for Administration and Finance: CHARLES L. TEAMER
Vice-President and Dean of Students: DORIS WEATHER
Vice-President for Institutional Advancement and University Relations: RICHARD H. WHITE
Director of Admissions: ROSETTA GOODEN
Associate Provost and Dean of Graduate Studies: DAVID DORSEY
Dean of Undergraduate Studies: ALEXA HENDERSON
Librarian: ADELE S. DENDY
Library of 592,246 vols
Number of teachers: 330
Number of students: 5,912
Publication: *Clark Atlanta University Magazine* (4 a year).

DEANS
School of Arts and Sciences: LARRY EARVIN
School of Business: EDWARD DAVIS
School of Education: TREVOR TURNER
School of Library and Information Studies: ARTHUR GUNN
School of Public and International Affairs: HERSCHELLE S. CHALLENOR

EMORY UNIVERSITY

Atlanta, GA 30322
Telephone: (404) 727-6123
Chartered as Emory College 1836, University 1915
Related to the United Methodist Church
Chancellor: BILLY E. FRYE
President: WILLIAM M. CHACE
Executive Vice-President: JOHN L. TEMPLE
Provost: REBECCA S. CHOPP
Executive Vice-President for Health Affairs and Director of the Robert W. Woodruff Health Sciences Center: MICHAEL M. E. JOHNS
Vice-President for Arts and Sciences and Dean of Emory College: STEVEN E. SANDERSON
Vice-Provost and Dean of the Graduate School: DONALD G. STEIN
Vice-President for Finance and Treasurer: FRANK H. HUFF
Vice-President for Institutional Advancement: WILLIAM H. FOX
Vice-President and Dean for Campus Life: FRANCES LUCAS-TAUCHAR
Vice-President for Business: ROBERT E. WILLIAMS
Secretary of the University: GARY S. HAUK
Dean of Admissions: DANIEL WALLS
Registrar: CHARLES R. NICOLAYSEN
Director of Libraries: JOAN GOTWALS
Library of 2.3 m. vols
Number of teachers: 2,056 (full-time)
Number of students: 11,270
Publications: *Emory Magazine, Emory Law Journal, Medicine at Emory, Journal of Central European History, The Emory Lawyer, Emory University Journal of Medicine, New Vico Studies, Emory International Law Review, Lullwater Review.*

DEANS
Emory College: STEVEN E. SANDERSON
Oxford College (Oxford): WILLIAM H. MURDY
Business: RONALD E. FRANK
Graduate School: DONALD G. STEIN
School of Law: HOWARD O. HUNTER
School of Medicine: THOMAS J. LAWLEY
School of Nursing: DYANNE D. AFFONSO
School of Public Health: JAMES W. CURRAN
School of Theology: R. KEVIN LAGREE

FORT VALLEY STATE UNIVERSITY

Fort Valley, GA 31030
Telephone: (912) 825-6211
Fax: (912) 825-6394
Founded 1895
President: Dr OSCAR L. PRATER
Vice-President for Academic Affairs: Dr JOSEPHINE DAVIS
Registrar: EDWARD GRAENING
Librarian: Dr CAROLE R. TAYLOR
Library of 191,806 vols
Number of teachers: 147
Number of students: 2,978

DEANS
Arts and Sciences: Dr ISAAC CRUMBLY
Education, Graduate and Special Academic Programs: Dr CURTIS MARTIN
Agriculture and Special Allied Programs: Dr MELVIN WALKER

GEORGIA COLLEGE AND STATE UNIVERSITY

Milledgeville, GA 31061
Telephone: (912) 454-4444
Fax: (912) 454-2510
Chartered in 1889 as Georgia Normal and Industrial College; name changed 1922 to Georgia State College for Women and 1961 to The Woman's College of Georgia. Its present name dates from 1967 when it became a co-educational institution
President: Dr ROSEMARY DEPAOLO
Vice-President and Dean of Faculties: Dr RALPH W. HEMPHILL
Vice-President for Business and Finance: HARRY E. KEIM
Vice-President and Dean of Students: Dr BRUCE HARSHBARGER
Assoc. Vice-President for Enrolment Services: LARRY A. PEEVY
Executive Director of Institutional Advancement: MONICA WEBB
Director of Alumni Programs: NANCY H. KITCHENS
Library of 186,396 vols
Number of teachers: 277
Number of students: 5,800

GEORGIA INSTITUTE OF TECHNOLOGY

225 N Ave NW, Atlanta, GA 30332
Telephone: (404) 894-2000
Telex: 542507
Fax: (404) 894-5520
Chartered 1885
President: G. WAYNE CLOUGH
Provost and Vice-President for Academic Affairs: MICHAEL E. THOMAS
Senior Vice-President for Administration and Finance: ROBERT K. THOMPSON
Vice-President, External Affairs: JAMES M. LANGLEY
Vice-President, Student Affairs: LEE WILCOX
Vice-Provost of Research and Dean of Graduate Studies: JEAN-LOU CHAMEAU
Registrar: FRANK E. ROPER, Jr
Dean of Library: MIRIAM A. DRAKE
Library of 2,800,000 vols
Number of teachers: 732
Number of students: 12,901
Publications: *The Technique, Research Horizons, Georgia Tech Fact Book, Blue Print.*

DEANS
College of Architecture: THOMAS D. GALLOWAY
College of Computing: PETER A. FREEMAN
College of Engineering: JOHN WHITE

Ivan Allen College of Management, Public Policy and International Affairs: ROBERT G. HAWKINS
College of Sciences: GARY SCHUSTER

SCHOOL DIRECTORS

Aerospace Engineering: ROBERT LOEWY
Biology: ROGER M. WARTELL (acting)
Chemical Engineering: RONALD W. ROUSSEAU
Chemistry and Biochemistry: LOREN D. TOLBERT
Civil Engineering: MICHAEL MEYER
Earth and Atmospheric Sciences: DEREK CUNNOLD
Economics: CHRISTINE RIES
Electrical Engineering: ROGER WEBB
Industrial and Systems Engineering: JOHN J. JARVIS
Management: LLOYD BYARS (acting)
Materials Science and Engineering: ASHOK SAXENA
Mathematics: SHUI-NEE CHOW
Mechanical Engineering: WARD WINER
Physics: RAJ ROY
Psychology: RANDY ENGLE
Public Policy: BARRY BOZEMAN
Textile and Fibre Engineering: FRED L. COOK

ACADEMIC DEPARTMENT DIRECTORS

Air Force and Aerospace Studies: Col JERRY HOUSTON
Architecture Program: JOHN A. KELLY (acting)
Building Construction Program: ROOZBEH KANGARI
City Planning Program: STEVE FRENCH
Health and Performance Sciences: JAMES A. REEDY
History, Technology and Society: GREG NOBLES
Industrial Design Program: WILLIAM C. BULLOCK
International Affairs: LINDA BRADY
Literature, Communications and Culture: RICHARD GRUSIN
Military Science: Lt-Col JEFFREY A. KERN
Modern Languages: HEIDI M. ROCKWOOD (acting)
Music: JAMES G. JOHNSON
Naval Science: Capt. WILLIAM ROGERS

ATTACHED CENTERS AND INSTITUTES

Advanced Technology Development Center: Dir WAYNE HODGES.

Center for the Enhancement of Teaching and Learning: Dir DAVID J. MCGILL.

Continuing Education, Distance Learning and Outreach: Vice-Provost JOE DIGREGORIO

Economic Development Institute: Dir WAYNE HODGES (acting).

Georgia Tech Research Institute: Vice-Pres. and Dir ED REEDY (acting).

Georgia Tech Research Corporation: Vice-Pres. RONALD M. BELL.

Institute of Paper Science and Technology: Pres. JAMES FERRIS.

GEORGIA SOUTHERN UNIVERSITY

Statesboro, GA 30460
Telephone: (912) 681-5611
Fax: (912) 871-1409

Founded 1906

President: Dr HARRY CARTER (acting)
Provost and Vice-President for Academic Affairs: Dr LINDA BLEICKEN (acting)
Vice-President for Business and Finance: Dr RONALD J. CORE
Vice-President for Development and University Relations: Dr JAMES BRITT
Vice-President for Student Affairs: Dr JOHN F. NOLEN
Registrar: MIKE DEAL
Librarian: ANN HAMILTON (acting)

Library of 489,136 vols
Number of teachers: 620
Number of students: 13,965

GEORGIA STATE UNIVERSITY

University Plaza, Atlanta, GA 30303
Telephone: (404) 658-2000

Founded 1913

President: Dr CARL V. PATTON
Vice-President for Academic Affairs and Provost: Dr RONALD J. HENRY
Vice-President for Research: Dr CLEON C. ARRINGTON
Vice-President for Student Life: Dr JAMES E. SCOTT
Vice-President for Finance Administration: Dr WILLIAM DECATUR
University Librarian: (vacant)

Library of 1,602,457 vols, 1,943,554 microforms
Number of teachers: 1,179
Number of students: 24,024

Publications: *Business Review, Foreign Languages Beacon, Studies in Literary Imagination.*

DEANS

College of Health Sciences: Dr SHERRY GAINES
College of Arts and Sciences: Dr AHMED ABDELAL
College of Business Administration: Dr JOHN D. HOGAN
College of Education: Dr SAMUEL M. DEITZ
College of Law: Dr JANICE GRIFFITH
School of Policy Studies: Dr ROY BAHL (acting)

LA GRANGE COLLEGE

La Grange, GA 30240
Telephone: (706) 882-2911

Founded 1831

President: Rev. F. STUART GULLEY
Dean: Dr JAY SIMMONS
Registrar: JIMMY G. HERRING
Director of Admissions: ANDY GEETER
Librarian: LOREN PINKERMAN

Library of 105,000 vols
Number of teachers: 64
Number of students: 984

MEDICAL COLLEGE OF GEORGIA

Augusta, GA 30912
Telephone: (706) 721-0211

Founded 1828
Part of University System of Georgia

President: Dr FRANCIS J. TEDESCO
Registrar: JAMES L. MCLEOD
Librarian: Dr PAUL J. BRUCKER (acting)

Library of 194,000 vols
Number of teachers: 845
Number of students: 2,027

Publication: *Scope.*

DEANS

Allied Health Sciences: Dr BIAGIO J. VERICELLA
Dentistry: Dr DAVID R. MYERS
Medicine: Dr DARRELL G. KIRCH
Nursing: Dr VICKIE A. LAMBERT
Graduate Studies: Dr DARRELL G. KIRCH

MERCER UNIVERSITY

1400 Coleman Ave, Macon, GA 31207
Telephone: (912) 752-2700
Fax: (912) 752-4124

Chartered 1833
Private control (Baptist)

President: R. KIRBY GODSEY
Senior Vice-President for Finance and Administration: THOMAS G. ESTES
Senior Vice-President for University Advancement: EMILY P. MYERS
Vice-President for Public and Government Affairs: JOHN T. MITCHELL
Vice-President for Academic Affairs: HORACE FLEMING
Executive Vice-President and Provost: RUSSELL G. WARREN

Number of teachers: 653
Number of students: 6,800

Publications: *The Mercerian, Discoveries, Inside Mercer, The Business Advisor, The Mercer Engineer, TIFToday, The Law Letter.*

DEANS

Liberal Arts College: DOUGLAS W. STEEPLES
Director of Graduate Studies: PEGGY DUBOSE
Law: LARRY DESSEM
Medicine: DOUGLAS SKELTON
Pharmacy (Atlanta): TED MATTHEWS
School of Business and Economics: CARL JOINER
School of Engineering: MOGENS HENRIKSEN
School of Education: ANNE HATHAWAY
School of Theology: RICHARD A. CULPEPPER

MOREHOUSE COLLEGE

830 Westview Drive, SW, Atlanta, GA 30314
Telephone: (404) 681-2800

Founded 1867; member of Atlanta University Center

President: Dr WALTER MASSEY
Provost, and Senior Vice-President for Academic Affairs: Dr JOHN HOPPS
Librarian: BERNICE RAY

Library of 650,000 vols
Number of teachers: 167
Number of students: 2,889

MORRIS BROWN COLLEGE

634 Martin Luther King Drive, SW, Atlanta, GA 30314
Telephone: (404) 220-0270
Fax: (404) 659-4315

Founded 1881; member of Atlanta University Center and United Negro College Fund

President: Dr GLORIA L. ANDERSON (acting)
Vice-President for Academic Affairs: Dr REGINALD LINDSEY (acting)
Vice-President for Development: OLIVER DELK
Vice-President for Student Affairs: Dr LEVITA SMALL
Vice-President for Fiscal Affairs: DENISE SMITH-MOORE
Vice-President for Legal Affairs: DIONYSIA JOHNSON-MASSIE
Vice-President for Administration and Operations: JIM MARING
Registrar: LUCILLE S. WILLIAMS
Director of Alumni Affairs: (vacant)
Director for Institutional Research and Planning: KAREN BOWEN
Director of Admissions: VORY BILLUPS
Director for Student Financial Aid: WILLIE WILLIAMS

Library of 797,684 vols
Number of teachers: 143
Number of students: 2,154

Publications: *Bulletin, Wolverine Observer* (monthly).

NORTH GEORGIA COLLEGE AND STATE UNIVERSITY

Dahlonega, GA 30597
Telephone: (706) 864-1400

Founded 1873

President: SHERMAN R. DAY
Registrar: MARTHA TOMPKINS
Librarian: MARILYN LARY

Library of 115,000 vols
Number of teachers: 164
Number of students: 2,795

Publication: *North Georgia College Bulletin Series.*

OGLETHORPE UNIVERSITY

Atlanta, GA 30319
Telephone: (404) 261-1441
Fax: (404) 364-8500
Founded 1835
President: Donald S. Stanton
Registrar: Paul S. Hudson
Director of Admissions: Dennis Matthews
Director of Financial Aid: Patrick N. Bonones
Librarian: John A. Ryland
Library of 131,000 bound vols
Number of teachers: 116
Number of students: 1,230
Publications: *The Tower* (2 a year), *The Stormy Petrel* (fortnightly), *Yamacraw* (annually), *The Flying Petrel* (quarterly).

PAINE COLLEGE

1235 15th St, Augusta, GA 30901-3182
Telephone: (706) 821-8200
Founded 1882
President: Shirley A. R. Lewis
Registrar: Valerie Benson
Librarian: Cassandra Norman
Library of 73,000 vols
Number of teachers: 74
Number of students: 900
Publications: *The Paine Magazine* (quarterly), *The Windowpaine* (monthly), *The Lion* (annually), *The Paineite* (2 to 4 a year).

PIEDMONT COLLEGE

Demorest, GA 30535
Telephone: (706) 778-3000
Founded 1897
President: W. Ray Cleere
Admissions: Franklin Shumake
Registrar: Charlie Karcher
Dean: Carlton J. Adams
Librarian: Gene Ruffin
Library of 100,000 volumes
Number of teachers: 50
Number of students: 1,000

SAVANNAH STATE UNIVERSITY

Savannah, GA 31404
Telephone: (912) 356-2240
Founded 1890
President: Dr Carlton E. Brown
Registrar: Teria Sheffield
Librarian: Shamina Amin
Library of 162,810 vols
Number of teachers: 157
Number of students: 2,614

SHORTER COLLEGE

315 Shorter Ave, Rome, GA 30165
Telephone: (706) 291-2121
Fax: (706) 236-1515
E-mail: president@shorter.peachnet.edu
Founded 1873
President: Dr Larry L. McSwain
Provost: Dr Harold Newman
Senior Vice-President: Wayne Dempsey
Vice-President for Student Development: Dr Charles T. Hood
Registrar: Katharine Lovvorn
Director of Admissions: Wendy Sutton
Librarian: Kim Herndon

Library of 122,000 vols
Number of teachers: 65
Number of students: 1,593

SPELMAN COLLEGE

350 Spelman Lane SW, Atlanta, GA 30314
Telephone: (404) 681-3643
Fax: (404) 223-1428
Founded 1881; member of Atlanta University Center
President: Dr Audrey F. Manley
Registrar: Dr Fred Buddy
Number of teachers: 200
Number of students: 1,937

STATE UNIVERSITY OF WEST GEORGIA

Carrollton, GA 30118
Telephone: (770) 836-6442
Founded 1933; senior college status 1957, university status 1995
President: Dr Beheruz N. Sethna
Vice-President for Academic Affairs: Dr Thomas J. Hynes
Dean of Graduate School: Dr Jack O. Jenkins
Registrar: Bonnie Stevens
Director of Admissions: Dr Bobby Johnson
Director of Libraries: Charles E. Beard
Library of 1,481,407 vols and other articles
Number of teachers: 323
Number of students: 8,431
Publications: *Under Graduate Catalog, Graduate Catalog, West Georgia Fact Book, Studies in the Social Sciences, West Georgia College Faculty Research Review* (all annually).

UNIVERSITY OF GEORGIA

Athens, GA 30602
Telephone: (706) 542-3030
Incorporated by Act of General Assembly 1785, established 1801
President: Dr Michael F. Adams
Senior Vice-President for Finance and Administration: Dr Allan W. Barber
Senior Vice-President for Academic Affairs and Provost: Dr Karen A. Holbrook
Senior Vice-President for External Affairs: Larry Weatherford (acting)
Vice-President for Research and Associate Provost: Dr Joe L. Key
Vice-President for Public Service and Outreach, and Associate Provost: Dr S. Eugene Younts
Vice-President for Strategic Planning and Public Affairs: Dr Donald R. Eastman, III
Vice-President for Student Affairs: Dr Dwight Douglas
Registrar: (vacant)
Director of Libraries: Dr William G. Potter
Library of 3,458,000 vols
Number of teachers: 2,636
Number of students: 29,693
Publications: various faculty and departmental reviews, etc.

DEANS

Graduate School: Dr Gordhan L. Patel
College of Agricultural and Environmental Sciences: Dr Gale A. Buchanan
College of Arts and Sciences: Dr Wyatt W. Anderson
College of Business: Dr P. George Benson
College of Family and Consumer Sciences: Dr Sharon Y. Nickols
College of Education: Dr Russell H. Yeany, Jr
College of Journalism: Dr J. Thomas Russell
College of Pharmacy: Dr Stuart Feldman
School of Environmental Design: John F. Crowley III
School of Forest Resources: Dr Arnett C. Mace, Jr
School of Law: David E. Shipley
School of Veterinary Medicine: Dr Keith W. Prassee
School of Social Work: Dr Bonnie Yegidis

VALDOSTA STATE UNIVERSITY

North Patterson St, Valdosta, GA 31698
Telephone: (912) 333-5952
Founded 1906
President: Hugh C. Bailey
Vice-President for Academic Affairs: Dr Lloyd William Benjamin, III
Registrar: Gerald Wright
Librarian: George R. Gaumond
Library of 395,000 vols
Number of teachers: 512
Number of students: 9,749

WESLEYAN COLLEGE

Macon, GA 31297
Telephone: (912) 477-1110
Fax: (912) 757-4030
Founded 1836
President: Nora K. Bell
Dean of the College: Priscilla R. Danheiser
Dean of Admissions: John A. Thompson
Librarian: Catherine Lee
Library of 135,000 vols
Number of teachers: 50
Number of students: 550

HAWAII

BRIGHAM YOUNG UNIVERSITY, HAWAII CAMPUS

Laie, Oahu, HI 96762
Telephone: (808) 293-3211
Founded 1955
President: Eric B. Shumway
Vice-President for Academics: Olani Durrant
Vice-President for Student Affairs: Isileli T. Kongaika
Registrar: Vernelle Lakatani
Librarian: Rex Frandsen
Library of 163,000 vols
Number of teachers: 109
Number of students: 2,000

CHAMINADE UNIVERSITY OF HONOLULU

3140 Waialae Ave, Honolulu, HI 96816
Telephone: (808) 735-4711
Fax: (808) 735-4870
Founded 1955
President: Sue Wesselkamper
Vice-President for Finance and Operations: Ronald Rex
Dean of Arts and Sciences: Dr Richard Bordner
Dean of Professional Studies and Life Long Learning: Dr Michael Fassiotto
Registrar: John Morris
Librarian: Joan Flynn
Library of 67,000 vols
Number of teachers: 160
Number of students: 780 full-time
Publications: *Newsletter* (quarterly), *Silversword, Aulama, 'Ahinahina, Chaminade Literary Review.*

HAWAII PACIFIC UNIVERSITY

1166 Fort St Mall, Honolulu, HI 96813

Telephone: (808) 544-0200

Telex: 8881

Fax: (808) 544-9323

Founded 1965

President: CHATT G. WRIGHT
Senior Vice-President: DONALD S. GEDEON
Vice-President of Administration: RICK E. STEPIEN
Vice-President and Dean, Student Affairs: NANCY ELLIS
Vice-President and Academic Dean: JOHN FLECKLES
Dean for Graduate Studies: RICHARD T. WARD
Registrar: KELLY NASHIRO
Librarian: STEVE SIMPSON

Library of 180,000 vols and 3,000 periodicals
Number of teachers: 500
Number of students: 8,000

Publications: *Hawaii Pacific Review, Catalog* (annually), *Kalamalama* (monthly).

UNIVERSITY OF HAWAII

Hamilton Library, 2550 The Mall, Honolulu, HI 96822

Telephone: (808) 956-7205

Founded 1907, University of Hawaii 1920

Central administration for University of Hawaii System

President: Dr KENNETH P. MORTIMER
Senior Vice-President and Executive Vice-Chancellor: Dr DEAN O. SMITH (interim)
Senior Vice-President and Chancellor for the University of Hawaii at Hilo: Dr ROSE V. TSENG
Senior Vice-President and Chancellor for Community Colleges: JOYCE S. TSUNODA
Senior Vice-President for Research and Dean of the Graduate Division: Dr ALAN H. TERAMURA (interim)
Vice-President for Student Affairs: Dr DORIS CHING
Vice-President for Administration: EUGENE S. IMAI
Librarian: JOHN R. HAAK

Publications: *Bulletins*.

University of Hawaii at Hilo

Hilo, HI 96720-4091

Telephone: (808) 933-3444

Liberal Arts College

Chancellor: WILLIAM A. PEARMAN (acting)

DEANS

College of Arts and Sciences: PHILLIP A. TAYLOR
College of Agriculture: JACK K. FUJII
Provost, Hawaii Community College: SANDRA SAKAGUCHI
Number of students: 2,800

University of Hawaii at Manoa

2444 Dole St, Honolulu, HI 96822

Telephone: (808) 956-8111

Chancellor: KENNETH P. MORTIMER
Number of students: 18,252

DEANS

College of Arts and Sciences:
Faculty of Arts and Humanities: JUDITH R. HUGHES
Faculty of Languages, Linguistics and Literature: CORNELIA N. MOORE
Faculty of Natural Sciences: CHARLES HAYES (acting)
Faculty of Social Sciences: RICHARD DUBANOSKI
College of Business Administration: CHUCK GEE (interim)
College of Education: RANDY HITZ
College of Engineering: PAUL YUEN
College of Tropical Agriculture and Human Resources: CHARLES LAUGHLIN
Graduate Division: PETER GARROD
School of Architecture: RAYMOND YEH
School of Law: LAWRENCE FOSTER
School of Hawaiian, Asian and Pacific Studies: WILLA J. TANABE
School of Medicine: SHERREL HAMMAR (interim)
School of Nursing: ROSANNE HARRIGAN
School of Ocean and Earth Science and Technology: C. BARRY RALEIGH
School of Public Health: Dr WILLIAM WOOD (acting)
School of Social Work: PATRICIA L. EWALT
School of Travel Industry Management: CHUCK Y. GEE
Student Affairs: ALAN YANG
Outreach College: VICTOR KOBAYASHI (interim)

IDAHO

ALBERTSON COLLEGE

2112 Cleveland Blvd, Caldwell, ID 83605

Telephone: (208) 459-5000

Founded 1891

President: ROBERT L. HENDREN, Jr
Vice-President for Academic Affairs: Dr BONNIE BUZZA
Librarian: DALE I. CORNING

Library of 160,000 vols
Number of teachers: 60
Number of students: 651 undergraduate, 335 graduate

Publications: *Quest* (3 a year), *Catalog* (annually), *Annual Report*.

BOISE STATE UNIVERSITY

1910 University Drive, Boise, ID 83725

Telephone: (208) 385-1011

Founded 1932

President: Dr CHARLES P. RUCH
Registrar: SUSANNA B. YUNKER
Librarian: TIMOTHY BROWN

Library of 402,000 vols
Number of teachers: 500 full-time, 350 part-time
Number of students: 14,969

DEANS

College of Applied Technology: Dr LARRY BARNHART
College of Arts and Sciences: Dr PHIL EASTMAN
College of Business: Dr WILLIAM RUUD
College of Education: Dr ROBERT BARR
College of Engineering: Dr LYNN RUSSELL
College of Health Science: Dr JAMES TAYLOR
College of Social Sciences and Public Affairs: Dr JANE OLLENBURGER
Graduate College: Dr KENNETH HOLLENBAUGH

IDAHO STATE UNIVERSITY

Pocatello, ID 83209

Telephone: (208) 236-0211
Fax: (208) 236-4000

Founded 1901

President: Dr RICHARD L. BOWEN
Vice-President for Academic Affairs: Dr JONATHAN LAWSON
Vice-President for Financial Affairs: Dr ROBERT PEARCE
Dean of Student Affairs: Dr JANET C. ANDERSON
Registrar: MICHAEL STANDLEY
Librarian: KAY FLOWERS

Library of 886,000 vols
Number of teachers: 496
Number of students: 11,886

NORTHWEST NAZARENE COLLEGE

Nampa, ID 83686

Telephone: (208) 467-8011

Founded 1913

President: Dr RICHARD A. HAGOOD
Vice-President for Academic Affairs: Dr SAMUEL DUNN
Registrar: MERILYN THOMPSON
Director of Enrollment Management: BARRY SWANSON
Librarian: SHARON BULL

Library of 181,000 vols
Number of teachers: 78
Number of students: 1,231

UNIVERSITY OF IDAHO

Moscow, ID 83843

Telephone: (208) 885-6111

Chartered 1889

President: ROBERT A. HOOVER
Provost: BRIAN L. PITCHER
Vice-President for Research and Graduate Studies: JEANNE M. SHREEVE
Vice-President for Finance and Administration: JERRY N. WALLACE
Vice-President for Advancement: JOANNE B. CARR
Vice-President for Student Affairs and Vice-Provost for Recruitment: W HAL GODWIN
Registrar: RETA PIKOWSKY
Librarian: RONALD W. FORCE

Library of 2,000,000 vols
Number of teachers: 814
Number of students: 11,027

DEANS

Agriculture: DAVID R. LINEBACK
Business and Economics: BYRON DANGERFIELD
Education: N. DALE GENTRY
Engineering: RICHARD T. JACOBSEN
Forestry: CHARLES R. HATCH
Law: JOHN A. MILLER
Letters and Science: KURT O. OLSSON
Mines and Earth Resources: EARL BENNETT
Art and Architecture: PAUL G. WINDLEY

ILLINOIS

AUGUSTANA COLLEGE

Rock Island, IL 61201

Telephone: (309) 794-7000

Founded 1860

President: THOMAS TREDWAY
Dean of the College: RICHARD T. JURASEK
Director of Information Technology Services: CHRIS VAUGHAN
Director of Institutional Research: TIMOTHY SCHERMER
Director of Career Centre: KATHY WOLF
Librarian: JONATHAN MILLER

Library of 244,368 vols
Number of teachers: 132 full-time, 37 part-time (including 39 full professors)
Number of students: 2,075 full-time, 50 part-time, total 2,125

DEANS

Students: EVELYN S. CAMPBELL
Dean of Enrollment: JOHN W. HULLETT

BARAT COLLEGE

700 East Westleigh Rd, Lake Forest, IL 60045

Telephone: (847) 234-3000
Fax: (847) 615-5000

Founded 1904
President: Dr Lucy S. Morros
Dean of Academic Affairs: Dr David Throgmorton
Dean of Students: Janet Trzaska
Dean of Institutional Advancement: Peggy Froh
Dean of Admissions: Douglas Schacke
Librarian: Lourdes Mordini

Library of 100,000 vols
Number of teachers: 120
Number of students: 750

BENEDICTINE UNIVERSITY

Lisle, IL 60532-0900
Telephone: (630) 829-6000
Founded 1887 as St Procopius College
President: Dr William J. Carroll
Vice-President for Finance and Administration: Robert Head
Director of Library Services: Mary Joyce Pickett

Library of 164,079 vols
Number of teachers: 251
Number of students: 2,620

Publications: *Benedictine Voices Magazine* (quarterly and annually), *President's Annual Report*.

BLACKBURN COLLEGE

700 College Ave, Carlinville, IL 62626
Telephone: (217) 854-3231
Founded 1837
President: Miriam R. Pride
Dean: Dr George Banziger
Librarian: Carol Schaefer

Library of 81,250 vols
Number of teachers: 31 full-time, 11 part-time
Number of students: 570

BRADLEY UNIVERSITY

Peoria, IL 61625
Telephone: (309) 676-7611
Founded 1897
Independent comprehensive university
President: Dr John R. Brazil
Provost and Vice-President for Academic Affairs: Dr Sharon M. Murphy
Vice-President for Advancement: Dr John Shorrock
Vice-President for Business Affairs: Gary Anna
Associate Provost for Information Technologies and Resources: (vacant)
Associate Provost and Dean of the Graduate School: Dr Ahmad Fakheri (acting)
Associate Provost for Student Affairs: Dr Alan Galsky
Director of Enrolment Management: Dr Scott Friedhoff
Associate Director of Enrollment Management for Undergraduate Admissions: Angela Roberson
Associate Director of Enrollment Management and Director of Financial Assistance: David Pardieck
Registrar: Dr Suzanne Anderson
Executive Director of Library: Barbara Falik

Library of 1.2 m. items, including 521,000 books, bound periodicals and government documents; 737,000 microforms
Number of teachers: 298
Number of students: 6,200

DEANS

College of Liberal Arts and Sciences: Dr Claire Etaugh
Graduate School: Dr Ahmad Fakheri (acting)
College of Business Administration: Dr James R. Lumpkin
College of Education and Health Sciences: Dr Joan Sattler
College of Engineering and Technology: Dr John E. Francis
Slane College of Communications and Fine Arts: Dr Jeffrey H. Huberman

CHICAGO STATE UNIVERSITY

9501 S. King Drive, Chicago, IL 60628
Telephone: (312) 995-2000
Founded 1867
State control
Academic year: August to May (two terms)
President: Elnora Daniel
Provost and Academic Vice-President: Avan Billimoria
Librarian: Clarence Toomer

Number of teachers: 282
Number of students: 9,500

Publications: *Illinois Schools Journal*, *Tempo* (every 2 weeks), *Reflections* (monthly), annual catalogues, *CSU Excellence Magazine* (every 6 months).

COLUMBIA COLLEGE

600 S Michigan Ave, Chicago, IL 60605
Telephone: (312) 663-1600
Founded 1890
President: John B. Duff
Director of Admissions: Terry Miller
Librarian: Mary Schellhorn

Library of 178,928 vols
Number of teachers: 1,059
Number of students: 8,076

HEADS OF DEPARTMENTS

Photography and Art: John Mulvany
Film and Video: Michael Rabiger
Management: Dennis Rich
Theatre and Music: Sheldon Patinkin
Dance: Shirley Mordine
Radio/Sound: Al Parker
Liberal Education: Leslie van Marter
English: Garnett Kilberg-Cohen
Journalism: Ed Planer
Marketing: Margaret Sullivan
Television: Edward Morris
Fiction: Randall Albers
Science and Mathematics: Charles Cannon
Academic Computing: Rebecca Courington
Interpreter Training: Lynn Pena
Interdisciplinary Arts: Suzanne Cohan-Lange
Dance Movement Therapy: Jane Garnet-Sigel

DEPAUL UNIVERSITY

Chicago, IL 60604
Telephone: (312) 362-8000
Chartered as Saint Vincent's College 1898, as DePaul University 1907
President: Rev. John P. Minogue
Chancellor: Rev. John T. Richardson
Executive Vice-President for Academic Affairs: Richard J. Meister
Executive Vice-President and Vice-President for Business and Finance: Kenneth McHugh
Vice-President for Enrollment Management: David Kalsbeek
Vice-President for Student Affairs: James R. Doyle
Vice-President for Advancement: James Looney
Vice-President for University Planning and Information Technology: Helmut Epp
Registrar: Nancy Gall
Librarian: Doris Brown

Library of 906,794 vols
Number of teachers: 494
Number of students: 16,499

Publications: *De Paul Magazine* (quarterly), *De Paulia* (weekly), *Law Review* (2 a year), *Newsline* (monthly), *Journal of Health and Hospital Law* (monthly), *Philosophy Today* (quarterly), *Journal of Art and Entertainment* (2 a year), *Business Law Journal* (2 a year).

DEANS

College of Liberal Arts and Sciences: Dr Michael Mezey
Commerce: Ronald Patten
Law: Teree Foster
Music: Donald Casey
Education: Barbara Sizemore
School for New Learning: Susanne Dumbleton
Theatre School: Dr John Watts

DOMINICAN UNIVERSITY

River Forest, IL 60305
Telephone: (708) 366-2490
Fax: (708) 366-5360
Founded 1901
President: Donna M. Carroll
Vice-President of Academic Affairs: Norman Carroll
Registrar: Marilyn Benakis
Vice-President for Business Affairs: Amy McCormack
Vice-President for Institutional Advancement: (vacant)
Dean of Admissions: Hildegarde Schmidt
Dean of Graduate School of Library and Information Science: Prudence Dalrymple
Dean of Graduate School of Education: Colleen McNicholas
Dean of Students: Trudi Goggin
Librarian: Inez Ringland

Library of 310,000 vols
Number of teachers: 177
Number of students: 1,862

EASTERN ILLINOIS UNIVERSITY

Charleston, IL 61920-3099
Telephone: (217) 581-5000
Founded 1895
President: Dr David L. Jorns
Provost and Vice-President for Academic Affairs: Dr Teshome Abebe
Vice-President for Student Affairs: Louis Hencken
Vice-President for Business Affairs: Dr Morgan Olsen
Vice-President for Institutional Advancement: (vacant)

Number of teachers: 670
Number of students: 11,777

Publication: *Eastern Illinois University General Catalog*.

DEANS

College of Sciences: Dr Lida Wall
Lumpkin College of Business and Applied Sciences: Dr Ted Ivarie
College of Education and Professional Studies: Dr Elizabeth Hitch
College of Arts and Humanities: James Johnson
Graduate School: Dr Robert Augustine (acting)
Library Services: Dr Allen Lanham

ELMHURST COLLEGE

190 Prospect Ave, Elmhurst, IL 60126
Telephone: (630) 617-3500
Fax: (630) 617-3282
Founded 1871
President: Bryant L. Cureton

Vice-President for College Advancement: Kenneth E. Bartels
Vice-President of Academic Affairs and Dean of the Faculty: Michael Bell
Dean of Student Affairs: Kathleen Simons
Dean of Admission and Financial Aid: John R. Hopkins
Librarian: Susan Swords Steffen

Library of 200,000 vols
Number of teachers: 101 (Day Session)
Number of students: 1,750 Day Session, 1,000 Evening Session/Continuing Education

EUREKA COLLEGE

Eureka, IL 61530
Telephone: (309) 467-3721
Fax (309) 467-6386

Founded 1855

President: Dr George A. Hearne
Dean of the College: Dr Gary Gammon
Dean of Admissions and Financial Aid: Kurt Krile
Librarian: Virginia McCoy

Library of 72,000 vols
Number of teachers: 44
Number of students: 486

GOVERNORS STATE UNIVERSITY

University Park, IL 60466
Telephone: (708) 534-5000
Fax: (708) 534-8399

Founded 1969

President: Dr Paula Wolff
Provost: Dr Tobin Barrozo
Vice-President (Administration): Dr James Alexander
Registrar: Dora Hubbard
Librarian: Dr Richard Bradberry

Library of 230,000 vols
Number of teachers: c. 300
Number of students: 6,200

DEANS

College of Arts and Sciences: Dr Roger Oden
College of Education: Dr Lawrence Freeman (acting)
College of Health Professions: Dr Cecelia Rokusek
College of Business and Public Administration: Dr William Nowlin

ATTACHED INSTITUTE

Institute for Public Policy and Administration: Dir Dr Paul Green.

GREENVILLE COLLEGE

Greenville, IL 62246-0159
Telephone: (800) 345-4440

Founded 1892

President: Dr Robert E. Smith
Provost and Vice-President for Academic Affairs: Dr Jonathan S. Raymond
Director of Admissions: (vacant)

Library of 114,059 vols
Number of teachers: 54 full-time, 7 part-time
Number of students: 827

Publication: *Record* (quarterly).

ILLINOIS COLLEGE

Jacksonville, IL 62650
Telephone: (217) 245-3000
Fax: (217) 245-3034

Founded 1829

President: Richard A. Pfau
Director of Admissions: Richard L. Bystry
Librarian: Martin H. Gallas

Library of 130,000 vols
Number of teachers: 52
Number of students: 975

ILLINOIS INSTITUTE OF TECHNOLOGY

3300 S Federal St, Chicago, IL 60616
Telephone: (312) 567-3000

Formed 1940 by consolidation of Armour Institute of Technology (founded 1892), Lewis Institute (founded 1896)

President: Lewis M. Collens
Vice-President for International Affairs: Dr Darsh Wasan
Vice-President for External Affairs: David E. Baker
Vice-President for Business and Finance: John P. Collins
Vice-President for Institutional Advancement: Thomas Garrow
Vice-President for Main Campus: Dr Hassan Nagib
Vice-President for Downtown Campus: Henry Perritt
Dean of Admissions: Carole Snow
Registrar: Lourdes Silva (acting)

Libraries of 522,000 vols
Number of teachers: 295 full-time, 256 part-time
Number of students: 6,287

Publications: bulletins, research publications.

DEANS

College of Architecture: Donna Robertson
Armour College of Engineering: Hassan Nagib
Institute of Psychology: M. Ellen Mitchell
Institute of Design: Patrick Whitney
Chicago-Kent College of Law: Henry Perritt
Harold Leonard Stuart School of Management and Finance: M. Zia Hassan
Student Affairs: Lisa White-McNulty
Graduate College: Mohammed Shahidehpour
Undergraduate College: John Kallend

AFFILIATED INSTITUTES

IIT Research Institute: f. 1936.
Institute of Gas Technology: f. 1941.

ILLINOIS STATE UNIVERSITY

Normal, IL 61790
Telephone: (309) 438-5677

Founded 1857

President: Thomas P. Wallace
Vice-President and Provost: David Strand
Director of Admissions: David Snyder
Director of Libraries: Fred Peterson

Number of teachers: 947
Number of students: 21,129

DEANS

Undergraduate School: Alan Dillingham (acting)
Graduate School: Gregory Aloia
College of Applied Science and Technology: Elizabeth Chapman
College of Arts and Sciences: Paul Schollaert
College of Business: Robert Jefferson
College of Education: Sally Pancrazio
College of Fine Arts: Alvin Goldfarb
Summer Session: Sharon Stanford (acting)

ILLINOIS WESLEYAN UNIVERSITY

Bloomington, IL 61702
Telephone: (309) 556-3151
Fax: (309) 556-3411

Chartered 1850

President: Minor Myers, Jr
Provost and Dean of the Faculty: Janet M. McNew
Vice-President for Business and Finance: Kenneth C. Browning
Dean of Admissions: J. R. Ruoti
Dean of Student Affairs: Glenn J. Swichtenberg
Associate Dean of Academic Affairs: Roger H. Schnaitter
Director of Business and Economics Division: Mona J. Gardner
Director of Humanities Division: Larry W. Colter
Director of International Studies: Teodora Amoloza
Director of Natural Science Division: David Bailey
Director of Social Science Division: W. Michael Weis
Registrar: Jack Fields
Librarian: Susan E. Stroyan

Number of teachers: 143
Number of students: 1,809

Publication: *Illinois Wesleyan University Quarterly.*

JUDSON COLLEGE

1151 North State St, Elgin, IL 60123
Telephone: (847) 695-2500
Fax: (847) 695-0712

Founded 1963

President: Dr James W. Didier
Registrar: Brenda Atkinson
Librarian: Cathleen Zange

Library of 91,000 vols
Number of teachers: 40 full-time, 63 part-time
Number of students: 883

DEANS

Academic Affairs: Dr David O. Dickerson
Enrollment Services: Matthew S. Osborne
Business: William Wilson
Christian Religion and Philosophy: Robert D. Erickson
Communication Arts: Dr Stuart Ryder
Computer Information Science: Howard Myers
Teacher Education: William Peterson
Fine Arts: Dr Dale Voelker
Social Sciences: Theodore Hsieh
Physical Education: Karen Swanson
Science and Mathematics: Dr Frank Averill
Youth Ministry: Kimberley Budd, Dr Steve Gevali

KNOX COLLEGE

Galesburg, IL 61401
Telephone: (309) 343-0112
Fax: (309) 343-8921

Founded 1837

President: Frederick C. Nahm
Vice-President for Finance and Treasurer: Tracy Wagner
Dean of College and Vice-President for Academic Affairs: Lawrence B. Breitborde
Dean of Students: Yanina Vargas
Librarian: Jeffrey Douglas

Library of 266,503 vols
Number of teachers: 88, including 37 professors
Number of students: 1,047

Publications: *Knox Bulletin, Catalog and Report* (financial statement), *Knox Alumnus* (quarterly), *Catch.*

LAKE FOREST COLLEGE

Lake Forest, IL 60045
Telephone: (847) 234-3100
Fax: (847) 735-6291

Founded 1857

Four-year Liberal Arts College

President: David Spadafora
Provost and Dean of the Faculty: Steven P. Galovich

Registrar: Ruthane Bopp
Vice-President for Business Affairs: Leslie T. Chapman
Dean of the College: Elizabeth W. Fischer
Librarian: James R. Cubit

Number of teachers: 118
Number of students: 1,162

Publications: *The Stentor* (weekly), *Spectrum* (3 a year), *Tusitala* (annually).

LEWIS UNIVERSITY

Route 53, Romeoville, IL 60446
Telephone: (815) 838-0500
Fax: (815) 838-9456

Founded 1932

President: Br James Gaffney
Vice-President for Academic Affairs: Dr Henry Smorynski
Vice-President for Business and Finance: Wayne Draudt
Vice-President for Facilities Management: George Niemeyer
Vice-President for Mission and Development: Dr Stephany Schlachter
Vice-President for Student Affairs: Joseph Falese
Registrar: Robert Kempiak
Director of Libraries: Laura Patterson

Library of 165,000 vols
Number of teachers: 227
Number of students: 4,102

DEANS

College of Arts and Sciences: Dr Katherine Delaney
College of Business: James Perrone
College of Nursing: Dr Marilyn Bunt

LOYOLA UNIVERSITY CHICAGO

Chicago, IL 60611
Telephone: (312) 915-6000

Chartered as St Ignatius College 1870; incorporated as Loyola University 1909

President: Rev. John J. Piderit
Executive Vice-President: Dr Ronald E. Walker
President for the Medical Center: Dr Anthony L. Barbato
Senior Vice-President and Dean of Faculties: Dr James L. Wiser
Vice-President for Student Services: Dr Daniel Barnes (acting)
Vice-President for University Ministry: Rev. Lawrence Reuter
Assistant to the President: Rev. Ronald Ferguson
Vice-President for Advancement: Dr Joseph Sandman
Vice-President for Finance/Treasurer: David Meagher
Vice President for Human Resources: John B. Kambanis
Vice-President and General Counsel: Ellen Kane Munro
Vice-President for Administrative Co-ordination: Dr Marjorie Beane
Director of Registration and Records: Helen Hayes-Thomas
Vice-President for Facilities: Philip Kosiba

Library of 1,400,000 vols
Number of teachers: 1,600
Number of students: 13,759

Publications: *Stritch M.D., Loyola Law, Loyola World, Loyola Magazine.*

DEANS

Mundelein College: Dr Stephen Freedman
College of Arts and Sciences: Dr Kathleen M. McCourt
Rome Centre of Liberal Arts, Italy: John Felice
School of Business Administration: Dr William Bryan
Graduate School of Business: Dr John Kostolansky (Associate Dean)
Graduate School: Dr James Brennan
Institute of Industrial Relations: Dr Dow Scott
Institute of Pastoral Studies: Dr Camilla Burns (Director)
Parmly Hearing Institute: Dr William A. Yost (Director).
Erickson Institute of Early Education: Dr James Garbarino (President)
School of Law: Nina Appel
School of Medicine: Dr Daniel H. Winship
School of Social Work: Dr Joseph Walsh
School of Education: Dr Margaret Fong
School of Nursing: Dr Shirley Dooling
St Joseph Seminary of Loyola University: Rev. Patrick Rugen

MACMURRAY COLLEGE

Jacksonville, IL 62650
Telephone: (217) 479-7000
Fax: (217) 245-0405

Founded 1846

President: Edward J. Mitchell
Business Manager: Richard A. Marshall
Dean: James A. Goulding
Librarian: Ronald B. Daniels

Library of 145,000 vols
Number of teachers: 53, including 15 professors
Number of students: 715

Publications: *The Daily Other* (Student Newspaper), *Student Yearbook, Catalog* (every 2 years), *MacMurray College News, Montage.*

MILLIKIN UNIVERSITY

Decatur, IL 62522
Telephone: (217) 424-6211
Fax: (217) 424-3993

Founded 1901

President: Dr Curtis L. McCray
Provost and Vice-President for Academic Affairs: Dr Thomas F. Flynn
Dean of Student Life and Academic Development: Dr Sherilyn Poole
Vice-President for Business Affairs: John Hauser
Vice-President for University Development: Peggy S. Luy
Registrar: Walter Wessel
Director of the Library: Dr Charles Hale

Number of students: 1,878

Publications: *Millikin University Quarterly, The Decaturian* (fortnightly), *Quarterly Economic and Financial Forecast, Collage.*

DEANS

College of Arts and Sciences: Dr Mauri A. Ditzler
College of Fine Arts: Stephen Fiol
Tabor School of Business: Douglas E. Zemke
School of Nursing: Dr Sheryl Samuelson

MONMOUTH COLLEGE

700 East Broadway, Monmouth, IL 61462
Telephone: (309) 457-2311
Fax: (309) 457-2141

Founded 1853

President: Dr Richard Giese
Registrar: Erhard Saettler
Librarian: Janice Kemp

Library of 182,000 vols
Number of teachers: 62
Number of students: 990

NATIONAL-LOUIS UNIVERSITY

2840 Sheridan Rd, Evanston, IL 60201-1796
Telephone: (708) 475-1100
Fax: (708) 256-1057

Founded 1886

President: Orley R. Herron
Senior Vice-President for Academic Affairs: Katherine Delaney
Senior Vice-President for Administration: Lon Randall
Senior Vice-President for Finance: Delbert Stoner
Registrar: Adrienne McDay
Director of Admissions: Randall Berd
Librarian: Marilyn Lester

Library of 125,000 vols
Number of teachers: 218 full-time, 425 part-time
Number of students: 4,052 full-time, 3,523 part-time

DEANS

National College of Education: Linda Tafel
College of Arts and Sciences: Edward Risinger
College of Management and Business: Wayne Sander

NORTH CENTRAL COLLEGE

P.O. Box 3063, 30 N Brainard, Naperville, IL 60566-7063
Telephone: (630) 637-5100
Fax: (630) 637-5121

Founded 1861

President: Dr Harold Wilde
Vice-President of Business Affairs: Paul H. Loscheider
Dean of Faculty: Dr R. Devadoss Pandian
Librarian: Carolyn Sheehy

Library of 120,000 vols
Number of teachers: 189
Number of students: 2,617

NORTH PARK UNIVERSITY

3225 W. Foster Ave, Chicago, IL 60625
Telephone: (773) 244-6200

Founded 1891

President: David G. Horner
Vice-President for University Relations and Development: Melissa Morriss-Olson
Vice-President for Academic Affairs and Dean of Graduate and Professional Studies: I. Dean Ebner
Vice-President for Admission and Financial Aid: John Baworowsky
Dean of Undergraduate Studies and College of Arts and Sciences: Daniel deRoulet
Registrar: Dennis R. Bricault
Dean of the College Faculty: I. Dean Ebner
President and Dean of North Park Theological Seminary: John E. Phelan Jr
Director of Consolidated Library: Sonia E. Bodi

Library of 443,665 vols
Number of teachers: 87 full-time, 23 part-time (University); 17 full-time (Seminary)
Number of students: 1,938 (University), 188 (Seminary)

NORTHEASTERN ILLINOIS UNIVERSITY

5500 North St Louis Ave, Chicago, IL 60625
Telephone: (312) 583-4050

Founded 1961

President: Dr Salme H. Steinberg
Vice-President for Academic Affairs and Provost: Dr Estela López
Vice-President for Administrative Affairs: O. Cleve McDaniel

Vice-President for Student Affairs: Dr MELVIN C. TERRELL
Director of Development and Alumni Affairs: LEONARD IAQUINTA
Dean of Students: Dr R. KIPP HASSELL
Director for Admissions and Records: MIRIAM RIVERA
University Librarian: BRADLEY BAKER
Library of 651,005 vols (and Regional Archives Depository)
Number of teachers: 325 full-time, 163 part-time
Number of students: 10,386

DEANS

Graduate College: Dr MOHAN K. SOOD
College of Education: Dr MICHAEL E. CARL
College of Arts and Sciences: Dr JOHN BONI
College of Business and Management: Dr CHARLES F. FALK
Dean of Academic Development: Prof. MURRELL H. DUSTER

NORTHERN ILLINOIS UNIVERSITY

DeKalb, IL 60115-2854
Telephone: (815) 753-1271
Telex: 981417
Fax: (815) 753-8686
Founded 1895
President: JOHN E. LA TOURETTE
Vice-President of Administration: ANNE C. KAPLAN
Executive Vice-President and Provost: J. CARROLL MOODY
Senior Vice-President, Finance and Facilities: EDDIE R. WILLIAMS
Vice President, Development and University Relations: MICHAEL MALONE
Director, University Libraries: ARTHUR YOUNG
Library of 1.5 million vols and 1.2 million document items
Number of teachers: 1,203
Number of students: 19,993 (2,089 Extension)

DEANS

Graduate School: JERROLD H. ZAR
College of Business: DAVID K. GRAF
College of Education: ALFONZO THURMAN
College of Health and Human Studies: JAMES E. LANKFORD
College of Visual and Performing Arts: HAROLD KAFER
College of Engineering and Engineering Technology: ROMUALDAS KASUBA
College of Liberal Arts and Sciences: FREDERICK KITTERLE
College of Law: LEROY PERNELL

NORTHWESTERN UNIVERSITY

Evanston, IL 60208
Telephone: (847) 491-3741
Founded 1851
Private control
Academic year: September to June
President: HENRY S. BIENEN
Provost: LAWRENCE B. DUMAS
Senior Vice-President for Business and Finance: EUGENE S. SUNSHINE
Vice-President for Research: LYDIA VILLA-KOMAROFF
Vice-President for Student Affairs: MARGARET J. BARR
Vice-President for Development and Alumni Relations: RONALD D. VANDEN DORPEL
Vice-President for Administration and Planning: MARILYN MCCOY
Vice-President and General Counsel: MICHAEL C. WESTON
Vice-President for University Relations: ALAN K. CUBBAGE
Registrar: DONALD G. GWINN
Librarian: DAVID F. BISHOP
Library: see Libraries
Number of teachers (full-time): 2,072
Number of students (full-time): 13,920
Publications: *Tri-Quarterly* (3 a year), *Northwestern Perspective* (quarterly), *Journal of Criminal Law and Criminology* (quarterly), *Northwestern University Journal of International Law and Business* (3 a year), *The Reporter* (quarterly), *Northwestern University Law Review* (quarterly), *Northwestern Observer* (weekly).

DEANS

Graduate School: RICHARD I. MORIMOTO
Dental School: LEE M. JAMESON
Medical School: HARVEY R. COLTEN
Kellogg Graduate School of Management: DONALD P. JACOBS
School of Education: PENELOPE L. PETERSON
Medill School of Journalism: KEN BODE
School of Law: DAVID E. VAN ZANDT
School of Music: BERNARD J. DOBROSKI
School of Speech: DAVID ZAREFSKY
McCormick School of Engineering and Applied Science: JEROME B. COHEN
University College: DONALD E. COLLINS
College of Arts and Sciences: ERIC J. SUNDQUIST

HEADS OF DEPARTMENTS

College of Arts and Sciences:
- African-American Studies: SANDRA RICHARDS
- Anthropology: TIMOTHY EARLE
- Art Theory and Practice: WILLIAM CONGER
- Art History: SANDRA HINDMAN
- Biochemistry, Molecular Biology and Cell Biology: RICHARD MORIMOTO
- Chemistry: JAMES IBERS
- Classics: ROBERT W. WALLACE
- Economics: WILLIAM ROGERSON
- English: BETSY ERKKILA
- French and Italian: MICHAL GINSBURG
- Geological Sciences: ABRAHAM LERMAN
- German: GÉZA VON MOLNÁR
- Hispanic Studies: MARTIN MUELLER
- History: TIMOTHY GREEN
- Linguistics: BETH LEVIN
- Mathematics: CLARK ROBINSON
- Neurobiology and Physiology: LARRY PINTO
- Philosophy: RICHARD H. KRAUT
- Physics and Astronomy: RONALD TAAM
- Political Science: MICHAEL J. WALLERSTEIN
- Psychology: DOUGLAS L. MEDIN
- Religion: RICHARD KIECKHEFER
- Slavic Languages: ANDREW WACHTEL
- Sociology: ROBERT NELSON
- Statistics: BRUCE SPENCER

Kellogg Graduate School of Management:
- Accounting and Information Systems: RONALD DYE
- Finance: KATHLEEN HAGERTY
- Health Services Management: JOEL I. SHALOWITZ
- Management and Strategy: DAVID DRANOVE
- Managerial Economics and Decision Sciences: MORTON KAMIEN
- Marketing: LAKSHMAN KRISHNAMURTHI
- Organization Behavior: ROBERT B. DUNCAN
- Public and Non-Profit Management: DONALD HAIDER

Medill School of Journalism:
- Broadcast: PATRICIA DEAN
- Integrated Marketing Communications: CLARKE CAYWOOD
- Magazine: ABRAHAM PECK
- Newspaper: GEORGE H. HARMON

School of Music:
- Academic Studies and Composition: JOHN S. BUCCHERI
- Performance Studies: ROBERT A. BARRIS, MARCIA B. NORRMAN

School of Speech:
- Communication Studies: MICHAEL LEFF
- Communication Sciences and Disorders: DEAN C. GARSTECKI
- Performance Studies: CAROL SIMPSON STERN
- Radio, TV, Film: (vacant)
- Theatre: ERWIN F. BEYER

McCormick School of Engineering and Applied Science:
- Biomedical Engineering: ROBERT A. LINSENMEIER
- Chemical Engineering: JULIO OTTINO
- Civil Engineering: JOSEPH L. SCHOFER
- Computer Science: LAWRENCE BIRNBAUM
- Electrical and Computer Engineering: PRITHVIRAJ BANNERJEE
- Engineering Sciences and Applied Mathematics: BERNARD J. MATKOWSKY
- Industrial Engineering and Management Sciences: MARK S. DASKIN
- Materials Science and Engineering: KATHERINE T. FABER
- Mechanical Engineering: TED B. BELYTSCHKO

Dental School:
- Dental Basic and Behavioural Science: ARTHUR VEIS
- Dental Stomatology: KAREN SOLT
- Restorative Dentistry: DAN WILSON

Medical School:
- Anaesthesiology: BARRY SHAPIRO
- Cancer Center: STEVEN T. ROSEN
- Cell, Molecular and Structural Biology: ROBERT D. GOLDMAN
- Dermatology: DAVID WOODLEY
- Family Medicine: MARTIN S. LIPSKY
- Medicine: LEWIS LANDSBERG
- Microbiology-Immunology: PATRICIA SPEAR
- Molecular Pharmacology and Biological Chemistry: EUGENE SILINSKY
- Neurology: DAVID STUMPF
- Obstetrics and Gynaecology: JOHN J. SCIARRA
- Ophthalmology: LEE M. JAMPOL
- Orthopaedic Surgery: MICHAEL SCHAFER
- Otolaryngology and Maxillofacial Surgery: DAVID HANSON
- Paediatrics: MARTIN MYERS
- Pathology: JANARDAN K. REDDY
- Physical Medicine and Rehabilitation: ELLIOTT ROTH
- Physiology: JAMES C. HOUK
- Preventive Medicine: PHILIP GREENLAND
- Psychiatry and Behavioural Sciences: SHELDON I. MILLER
- Radiology: DIETER R. ENZMANN
- Surgery: DAVID NAHRWOLD
- Urology: ANTHONY J. SCHAEFFER

OLIVET NAZARENE UNIVERSITY

POB 592, Kankakee, IL 60901
Telephone: (815) 939-5011
Founded 1907
President: JOHN C. BOWLING
Registrar: JIM KNIGHT
Dean of Admissions: JOHN MONGERSON
Librarian: KATHY VANFOSSAN
Library of 300,000 items
Number of teachers: 100
Number of students: 2,246

PRINCIPIA COLLEGE

Elsah, IL 62028
Telephone: (618) 374-2131
Fax: (618) 374-5158
Founded 1910
President: Dr GEORGE D. MOFFETT
Dean of Faculty: Dr G. CURTIS MARTIN
Registrar: PATRICIA W. LANGTON
Director of Admissions and Enrollment: MARTHA QUIRK
Librarian: DAPHNE G. SELBERT
Library of 125,000 vols
Number of teachers: 93

Number of students: 525

QUINCY UNIVERSITY

1800 College Ave, Quincy, IL 62301-2699
Telephone: (217) 222-8020
Founded 1860; chartered 1873
President: Rev. Dr EUGENE R. KOLE
Executive Director for University Advancement: KEVIN RELLER
Vice-President for Enrollment Management: PATRICIA LAYTHAM
Vice-President of Academic Affairs: Dr GARY CARTER
Director of Admissions: JEFF VAN CAMP
Vice-President of Student Affairs: GREG WARREN
Registrar: EILLEEN HARRISON
Librarian: Rev. VICTOR KINGERY
Library of 235,000 vols
Number of teachers: 104
Number of students: 1,200

ROCKFORD COLLEGE

5050 East State St, Rockford, IL 61108
Telephone: (815) 226-4000
Fax: (815) 226-4119
Co-educational college founded 1847
President: Dr WILLIAM A. SHIELDS
Vice-President for Academic Affairs and Dean of the College: Dr WILLIAM T. O'HARE
Vice-President for Institutional Advancement: JOHN A. GALLAGHER
Vice-President for Finance and Administration: NOE A. MARINELLI
Vice-President for Student Affairs: KATHY ENGELKEN
Vice-President for Enrolment Management: CHRISTOPHER P. MODERSON
Associate Dean of the College: Dr SUSAN C. WHEALLER
Dean of Continuing and Graduate Education: WINSTON MCKEAN
Number of teachers: 83 full-time, 50 part-time
Number of students: 1,600
Publications: *Rockford Report* (quarterly), *Decus* (3 a year).
Rockford College Program in London:
Regent's College: Inner Circle, Regent's Park, London, NW1 4NS, England; tel. (071) 486-0141; telex 946240; Dir JOHN PAYNE.

ROOSEVELT UNIVERSITY

430 South Michigan Ave, Chicago, IL 60605
Telephone: (312) 341-3800
Founded 1945
Private control
President: THEODORE L. GROSS
Controller: JOHN ALLERSON
Registrar: JEAN LYNE
Librarian: A. JONES
Library of 374,000 vols
Number of teachers: 481 (169 full-time and 312 part-time)
Number of students: 6,300
Publications: *Business and Society, Annual Catalogs, Roosevelt University Magazine.*

DEANS

Faculties: STUART FAGAN
Graduate Division: ALICE ZIMRING
College of Arts and Science: RONALD TALLMAN
College of Business Administration: JAMES CICARELLI
Chicago Musical College: DON STEVEN
University College: GEORGE LOWERY
College of Education: LAURA EVANS

RUSH UNIVERSITY

1753 W Congress Parkway, Chicago, IL 60612
Telephone: (312) 942-5000
Founded 1972
Private control
Academic year: September to June (3 terms)
President: LEO M. HENIKOFF
Executive Vice-President: DONALD R. ODER
Vice-President Finance: KEVIN NECAS
Senior Vice-President Administration: TRUMAN ESMOND
Vice-President Philanthropy: JOHN BOHLEN
Vice-President Academic Resources: JOHN E. TRUFANT
Librarian: TRUDY GARDNER
Library of 59,451 vols, 2,003 periodicals
Number of teachers: 2,900
Number of students: 1,321

DEANS

Rush Medical College: ERIC E. BRUESCHKE
College of Nursing: KATHLEEN A. ANDREOLI
Graduate College: JOHN E. TRUFANT
College of Health Sciences: JOHN E. TRUFANT

HEADS OF DEPARTMENTS

Rush Medical College:

- Anatomy: RAYMOND SEALE (acting)
- Anaesthesiology: ANTHONY D. IVANKOVICH
- Biochemistry: KLAUS E. KUETTNER
- Cardiovascular-Thoracic Surgery: HASSAN NAJAFI
- Dermatology: ROGER W. PEARSON (acting)
- Diagnostic Radiology and Nuclear Medicine: JERRY PETASNICK
- Family Practice: WILLIAM SCHWER (acting)
- General Surgery: RICHARD A. PRINZ
- Immunology/Microbiology: HENRY GEWURZ
- Internal Medicine: STUART LEVIN
- Neurological Sciences: JACOB FOX
- Neurological Surgery: WALTER E. WHISLER
- Obstetrics and Gynaecology: GEORGE D. WILBANKS, Jr
- Ophthalmology: WILLIAM E. DEUTSCH
- Orthopaedic Surgery: GUNNAR B. ANDERSSON (acting)
- Otolaryngology and Bronchoesophagology: DAVID D. CALDARELLI
- Paediatrics: SAMUEL GOTTOFF
- Pathology: MERYL HABER
- Pharmacology: ASRAR B. MALIK
- Physical Medicine and Rehabilitation: JEFFREY NICHOLAS
- Physiology: ROBERT S. EISENBERG
- Plastic and Reconstructive Surgery: RANDALL MACNALLY
- Preventive Medicine: HENRY BLACK
- Psychiatry: JAN A. FAWCETT
- Psychology and Social Sciences: ROSALIND D. CARTWRIGHT
- Therapeutic Radiology: VIRENDRA SAXENA
- Urology: CHARLES F. MCKIEL, Jr

College of Nursing:

- Medical: DIANE LA ROCHELLE
- Community Health: CHERYL EASLEY
- Maternal/Child: KARREN KOWALSKI
- Psychiatric: JANE ULSAFER-VAN LANEN
- Surgical: JANE C. LLEWELLYN
- Geriatric/Gerontological: JOAN LESAGE

College of Health Sciences:

- Religion and Health: LAUREL BURTON
- Health Systems Management: JOHN E. TRUFANT (acting)
- Clinical Nutrition: REBECCA DOWLING
- Communication Disorders and Sciences: DIANNE H. MEYER
- Occupational Therapy: CYNTHIA HUGHES
- Medical Physics: JAMES CHU
- Medical Technology: RONALD HOIBERG (acting)

SAINT XAVIER UNIVERSITY

3700 West 103rd St, Chicago, IL 60655
Telephone: (773) 298-3000
Fax: (773) 779-9061
Founded 1847
President: Dr RICHARD A. YANIKOSKI
Vice-President for Academic Affairs: Dr GEORGE MATTHEWS
Vice-President for Enrolment Services: Sister EVELYN MCKENNA
Librarian: JOANN ELLINGSON
Library of 160,681
Number of teachers: 268
Number of students: 4,200
Schools of Arts and Sciences, Nursing, Education, Graham School of Management, Off-Campus International Program Development.

SCHOOL OF THE ART INSTITUTE OF CHICAGO

37 S. Wabash, Chicago, IL 60603
Telephone: (312) 899-5100
Fax: (312) 263-0141
Founded 1866
President: ANTHONY JONES
Dean: CAROL BECKER
Libraries of 325,000 vols, 450,000 slides, 4,000 video tapes, films, sound recordings
Number of teachers: 300
Number of students: 2,500
Four-year first degree courses, two-year master's degree courses, one-year advanced certificate courses.

SOUTHERN ILLINOIS UNIVERSITY AT CARBONDALE

Carbondale, IL 62901
Telephone: (618) 453-2121
Founded 1869
State control
Chancellor: JO ANN ARGERSINGER
Vice-Chancellor for Academic Affairs and Provost: JOHN S. JACKSON
Vice-Chancellor for Administration: JAMES A. TWEEDY
Vice-Chancellor for Institutional Advancement: TOM BRITTON
Vice-Chancellor for Student Affairs: HARVEY WELCH, Jr
Director of Admissions: WALKER ALLEN
Library of 2,247,503 vols, 3,537,477 microtext, 17,047 serials
Number of students: 23,881
Publication: *The Daily Egyptian.*

DEANS

Graduate School: RICHARD FALVO
College of Education: KEITH HILLKIRK
College of Liberal Arts: ROBERT JENSEN
College of Science: JACK PARKER
College of Agriculture: JAMES M. MCGUIRE
College of Business and Administration: SIVA BALASUBREMENIAN
College of Mass Communication and Media Arts: JOE S. FOOTE
College of Applied Sciences and Arts: ELAINE M. VITELLO
College of Engineering: JUH WA-CHEN
School of Law: THOMAS GUERNSEY
School of Medicine: CARL J. GETTO
Library Affairs: CAROLYN A. SNYDER

SOUTHERN ILLINOIS UNIVERSITY AT EDWARDSVILLE

Edwardsville, IL 62026
Telephone: (618) 650-2000
Fax: (618) 650-3837
Founded 1957

State control

Chancellor: DAVID WERNER
Provost and Vice-Chancellor for Academic Affairs: SHARON HAHS
Vice-Chancellor for Administration: KENNETH NEHER
Vice-Chancellor for Development and Public Affairs: (vacant)
Vice-Chancellor for Student Affairs: NARBETH EMMANUEL
Chief Executive Officer of the SIUE Foundation: BRAD HEWITT (acting)

Library of 736,000 vols
Number of students: 11,151

Publications: *Papers on Language and Literature, Sou'wester, Victorian Periodicals Review, Literati Internazionale.*

DEANS

School of Business: ROBERT CARVER
School of Education: GARY HULL
School of Engineering: HARLAN BENGTSON
School of Dental Medicine: PATRICK FERRILLO
College of Arts and Sciences: DIXIE ENGELMAN, DAVID STEINBERG
Graduate College: (vacant)
School of Nursing: FELISSA LASHLEY
Lovejoy Library: JAY STARRATT

UNIVERSITY OF CHICAGO

5801 S Ellis Ave, Chicago, IL 60637
Telephone: (773) 702-1234

Incorporated 1857 as the first University of Chicago, and 1890 as the University of Chicago (at the present site)

President: HUGO F. SONNENSCHEIN
Provost: GEOFFREY R. STONE
Vice-President and Chief Financial Officer: PATRICIA WOODWORTH
Vice-President for Community Affairs: HENRY WEBBER
Vice-President for Investments: PHILIP HALPERN
Registrar: MAXINE H. SULLIVAN

Library: see Libraries
Number of teachers: 1,747
Number of students: 11,297

DEANS

The College: JOHN W. BOYER
School of Business: ROBERT S. HAMADA
Divinity School: W. CLARK GILPIN
Law School: DOUGLAS G. BAIRD
School of Medicine: GLENN D. STEELE
School of Social Service Administration: EDWARD LAWLOR
Biological Sciences: GLENN D. STEELE
Humanities: PHILIP GOSSETT
Physical Sciences: DAVID W. OXTOBY
Social Sciences: RICHARD P. SALLER
Irving B. Harris School of Public Policy Studies: ROBERT MICHAEL

UNIVERSITY OF ILLINOIS

Urbana, IL 61801
Telephone: (217) 333-1000
Fax: (217) 333-9758

Chartered 1867
State control

President: JAMES J. STUKEL
Vice-President for Business and Finance: CRAIG S. BAZZANI
Vice-President for Academic Affairs: SYLVIA MANNING

Library: see Libraries
Number of teachers: 5,009 (full-time)
Number of students: 65,432

University of Illinois at Urbana-Champaign

Urbana, IL 61801
Telephone: (217) 333-1000

Chancellor: M. AIKEN
Provost and Vice-Chancellor for Academic Affairs: T. M. MENGLER (interim)
Vice-Chancellor for Administration and Human Resources: C. C. COLBERT
Vice-Chancellor for Student Affairs: P. E. ASKEW
Vice-Chancellor for Research: R. C. ALKIRE
Director of Admissions and Records: R. A. VEDVIK
Librarian: R. WEDGEWORTH

DEANS

College of Liberal Arts and Sciences: J. G. DELIA
College of Commerce and Business Administration: H. THOMAS
College of Engineering: W. R. SCHOWALTER
College of Agricultural, Consumer and Environmental Sciences: D. L. CHICOINE
College of Education: M. B. GRIGGS
College of Fine and Applied Arts: K. CONLIN
College of Law: J. COLOMBO (acting)
College of Communications: K. B. ROTZOLL
College of Applied Life Studies: (vacant)
School of Social Work: J. D. KAGLE
Graduate College: R. C. ALKIRE
College of Veterinary Medicine: V. E. VALLI
College of Medicine at Urbana-Champaign: T. WALDROP (Director)
Graduate School of Library and Information Science: L. S. ESTABROOK
Office of Continuing Education and Public Service: S. F. SCHOMBERG (Dir)
Institute of Aviation: H. L. TAYLOR (Director)
Institute of Labor and Industrial Relations: P. FEUILLE (Director)

HEADS OF DEPARTMENTS

College of Agricultural, Consumer and Environmental Sciences:

Agricultural and Consumer Economics: R. J. HAUSER
Agricultural Engineering: L. E. BODE
Animal Sciences: R. A. EASTER
Crop Sciences: G. H. HEICHEL
Food Science and Human Nutrition: B. M. CHASSY
Natural Resources and Environmental Science: G. L. ROLFE
Nutritional Sciences: J. W. ERDMAN, Jr
Veterinary Programs in Agriculture: V. E. VALLI
Vocational Agriculture Service: R. L. COURSON

College of Commerce and Business Administration:

Accountancy: E. WILLIS
Business Administration: K. B. MONROE
Economics: R. J. ARNOULD
Finance: M. J. LYNGE
Bureau of Economics and Business Research: G. OLDHAM

College of Education:

Educational Organization and Leadership: P. W. THURSTON
Educational Psychology: (vacant)
Curriculum and Instruction: (vacant)
Educational Policy Studies: J. D. ANDERSON
Special Education: A. RENZAGLIA
Vocational and Technical Education: T. L. WENTLING

College of Engineering:

Aeronautical and Astronautical Engineering: W. C. SOLOMON
Civil Engineering: D. E. DANIEL
Computer Science: D. A. REED
Electrical and Computer Engineering: S. M. KANG
General Engineering: H. E. COOK
Materials Science and Engineering: J. ECONOMY
Mechanical and Industrial Engineering: R. BUCKIUS
Nuclear Engineering: B. G. JONES
Physics: D. K. CAMPBELL
Theoretical and Applied Mechanics: H. AREF

College of Fine and Applied Arts:

School of Architecture: R. A. FORRESTER
School of Art and Design: D. WINKLER
Urban and Regional Planning: C. SILVER
Landscape Architecture: V. J. BELLAFIORE
School of Music: J. SCOTT
Dance: P. K. KNOWLES
Theatre: B. HALVERSON

College of Communications:

Advertising: J. HAEFNER
Institute of Communications Research: C. CHRISTIANS
Journalism: R. E. YATES
Media Studies: A. PRESS

College of Liberal Arts and Sciences:

Anthropology: J. KELLER
Astronomy: R. CRUTCHER
Biochemistry: J. A. GERLT
Biophysics: E. JAKOBSSON
Cell and Structural Biology: A. F. HORWITZ
Center for African Studies: P. T. ZELEZA
Chemical Engineering: C. F. ZUKOSKI
Chemistry: P. W. BOHN
Classics: D. SANSONE
Comparative Literature: J. L. SMARR (acting)
East Asian and Pacific Studies: G. T. YU
Ecology, Ethology and Evolution: A. DEVRIES
English: D. BARON (acting)
Entomology: M. R. BERENBAUM
French: D. KIBBEE
Geography: S. A. ISARD (acting)
Geology: J. D. BASS
Germanic Languages and Literature: M. KALINKE
History: J. R. BARRETT
Linguistics: J. MORGAN
Mathematics: P. TONDEUR
Microbiology: J. CRONAN
Philosophy: R. G. WENGERT
Plant Biology: C. A. SHEARER
Political Science: P. F. NARDULLI
Psychology: E. SHOBEN
Religious Studies: P. N. GREGORY
Russian and East European Center: M. FRIEDBERG
Slavic Languages and Literature: O. SOFFER
Sociology: J. LIE
South and West Asian Studies Program: M. G. WEINBAUM
Spanish, Italian and Portuguese: R. W. SOUSA
Speech Communication: D. L. SWANSON
Statistics: A. T. MARTINSEK

College of Applied Life Studies:

Community Health: L. A. CRANDALL
Kinesiology: J. E. MISNER
Leisure Studies: W. R. MCKINNEY
Rehabilitation Education Services: B. N. HEDRICK
Speech and Hearing Science: P. J. ALFONSO

College of Veterinary Medicine:

Clinical Medicine: H. F. TROUTT
Pathobiology: W. M. HASCHEK-HOCK
Biosciences: D. R. GROSS

University of Illinois at Chicago

601 S. Morgan St, Chicago, IL 60607-7128
Telephone: (312) 413-3350
Fax: (312) 413-3393

Founded 1894

Chancellor: DAVID C. BROSKI

Vice-Chancellor and Provost for Academic Affairs: ELIZABETH HOFFMAN
Vice-Chancellor for Health Services: R. K. DIETER HAUSSMANN
Vice-Chancellor for Administration: ARTHUR SAVAGE
Vice-Chancellor for Student Affairs: BARBARA HENLEY
Vice-Chancellor for Research: MI JA KIM
University Librarian: SHARON HOGAN

Library of 1,900,000 vols
Number of teachers: 2,237
Number of students: 24,583

DEANS

College of Architecture and the Arts: JUDITH R. KIRSHNER (acting)
College of Associated Health Professions: SAVITRI KAMATH
College of Business Administration: LAWRENCE H. OFFICER (acting)
College of Engineering: LAWRENCE KENNEDY
College of Liberal Arts and Sciences: ERIC A. GISLASON (acting)
College of Education: VICTORIA CHOU
College of Dentistry: ALLEN W. ANDERSON
College of Medicine: GERALD MOSS
College of Nursing: JOAN SHAVER
College of Pharmacy: ROSALIE SAGRAVES
College of Urban Planning and Public Affairs: WIM WIEWEL
Honors College: LANSINE KABA
Jane Addams College of Social Work: CREASIE FINNEY HAIRSTON
School of Public Health: SUSAN C. M. SCRIMSHAW
Graduate College: MI JA KIM
College of Medicine at Peoria: MICHAEL D. BAILIE
College of Medicine at Rockford: BERNARD P. SALAFSKY
College of Medicine at Urbana-Champaign: TONY WALDROP (acting)

HEADS OF DEPARTMENT

College of Architecture and the Arts:
- Architecture: K. RUEDI
- Art and Design: R. CARSWELL (acting)
- Art History: D. SOKOL
- Performing Arts: L. SALERNI

College of Associated Health Professions:
- Disability and Human Development: D. BRADDOCK
- Human Nutrition and Dietetics: S. K. KUMANYIKA
- Occupational Therapy: G. KIELHOFNER
- Physical Therapy: JULES ROTHSTEIN
- School of Biomedical and Health Information Sciences: W. B. PANKO
- School of Kinesiology: L. OSCAI

College of Business Administration:
- Accounting: R. RAMAKRISHNAN
- Economics: B. CHISWICK
- Finance: J. MCDONALD
- Information and Decision Sciences: R. ABRAMS
- Marketing: C. L. NARAYANA

College of Dentistry:
- Center for Molecular Biology of Oral Diseases: D. CHAMBERS
- Endodontics: N. A. REMEIKIS
- Oral Biology: R. SCAPINO
- Oral Surgery: L. HEFFEZ
- Orthodontics: C. EVANS
- Paediatric Dentistry: I. PUNWANI
- Periodontics: S. MUKHERJEE
- Restorative Dentistry: S. CAMPBELL
- Urban Health Program: M. DUNLAP
- Office of Continuing Education: J. BURGER

College of Education:
- Center for Literacy: T. SHANAHAN
- Center for Urban Educational Research and Development: L. ANDERSON
- Curriculum and Instruction: J. KNAFLE
- Early Childhood Research and Intervention Program: J. KAHN
- Educational Psychology: R. PEARL
- Policy Studies: S. TOZER
- Special Education: M. DONAHUE

College of Engineering:
- Bioengineering: R. L. MAGIN
- Chemical Engineering: J. H. KIEFER
- Civil and Materials Engineering: C.-H. WU
- Electrical Engineering and Computer Science: W.-K. CHEN
- Mechanical Engineering: S. GUCERI

College of Liberal Arts and Sciences:
- African-American Studies: D. HAWKINS
- Anthropology: L. KEELEY (acting)
- Biological Sciences: L. KAUFMAN (acting)
- Chemistry: E. A. GISLASON
- Classics: J. RAMSEY
- Communication: S. JONES
- Criminal Justice: D. ROSENBAUM
- Earth and Environmental Sciences: A. KOSTER VAN GROOS
- English: D. MARSHALL
- German: H. KRAFT
- History: M. PERMAN
- Latin American Studies: R. NUNEZ-CEDINO
- Mathematics, Statistics, and Computer Science: H. GILLET
- Philosophy: B. HART
- Physics: I. BATRA
- Political Science: A. MCFARLAND
- Psychology: A. ROSEN
- Slavic and Baltic Languages and Literatures: S. HOISINGTON
- Sociology: W. BRIDGES
- Spanish, Italian, French and Portuguese: R. AYERBE-CHAUX
- Women's Studies Progam: S. RIGER

College of Medicine at Chicago:
- Anaesthesiology: R. ALBRECHT
- Dermatology: V. FIELDER (acting)
- Emergency Medicine: G. STRANGE
- Family Practice: E. BURNS
- Medicine: L. FROHMAN
- Medical Education: L. J. SANDLOW
- Neurosurgery: J. AUSMAN
- Neurology: D. HIER
- Obstetrics and Gynaecology: S. ELIAS
- Ophthalmology: J. WILENSKY (acting)
- Orthopaedics: E. ABRAHAM
- Otolaryngology: E. L. APPLEBAUM
- Paediatrics: G. R. HONIG
- Pathology: J. MANALIGOD (acting)
- Physical Medicine and Rehabilitation: B. T. SHAHANI
- Psychiatry: J. FLAHERTY
- Radiology: M. MAFEE (acting)
- Surgery: H. ABCARIAN
- Surgical Oncology: T. DAS GUPTA
- Urology: L. ROSS

Basic Medical Sciences:
- Anatomy and Cell Biology: R. COHEN (acting)
- Biochemistry: D. CHAMBERS
- Genetics: R. DAVIDSON
- Microbiology and Immunology: B. PRABHAKAR
- Pharmacology: A. MALIK
- Physiology and Biophysics: R. J. SOLARO

College of Medicine at Peoria:
- Biomedical and Therapeutic Sciences: P. C. JOBE
- Dermatology: R. SWAMINATHAN
- Family and Community Medicine: J. G. HALVORSEN
- Medicine: S. L. RUSCH
- Neurology: J.C. KATTAH
- Neurosurgery: P. W. ELWOOD
- Obstetrics and Gynaecology: C. W. GIBSON
- Paediatrics: J. DILIBERTI
- Pathology: G. L. BARTLETT
- Psychiatry and Behavioural Medicine: S. A. SAEED
- Radiology: T. J. CUSACK
- Surgery: N. C. ESTES

College of Medicine at Rockford:
- Biomedical Sciences: F.-L. YU
- Family and Community Medicine: J. MIDTLING
- Medicine: R. CHRISTIANSEN
- Obstetrics and Gynaecology: J. MILLER
- Paediatrics: L. FRENKEL
- Pathology: G. ANDERSON (acting)
- Psychiatry: R. SLACK (acting)
- Surgery: R. C. WEBB

College of Medicine at Urbana-Champaign:
- Biochemistry: J. A. GERLT
- Cell and Structural biology: A. F. HOROWITZ
- Family Practice: T. SCHREPFER
- Internal Medicine: R. NELSON
- Medical Information Science: P. LAUTERBUR
- Microbiology and Immunology: J. E. CRONAN
- Molecular and Integrative Physiology: P. M. BEST
- Obstetrics and Gynaecology: S. TRUPIN
- Paediatrics: K. BUETOW
- Pathology: P. J. O'MORCHOE
- Pharmacology: B. KEMPER
- Psychiatry: J. GERGEN
- Surgery: U. OLIPHANT

College of Nursing:
- Maternal-Child Nursing: R. WHITE TRAUT
- Medical-Surgical Nursing: J. LARSON
- Public Health, Mental Health and Administrative Nursing: L. MARION

College of Pharmacy:
- Medical Chemistry and Pharmacognosy: G. A. CORDELL
- Pharmaceutics and Pharmacodynamics: R. F. SCHLEMMER (acting)
- Pharmacy Administration: B. LAMBERT (acting)
- Pharmacy Practice: J. BAUMAN (acting)

School of Public Health:
- Community Health Sciences: T. PROHASKA
- Environmental and Occupational Health Sciences: P. SCHEFF
- Epidemiology and Biostatistics: F. DAVIS
- Great Lakes Center for Occupational and Environmental Safety and Health: D. HRYHORCZUK
- Health Policy and Administration: P. FORMAN
- Health Research and Policy Centers: B. FLAY

Jane Addams College of Social Work:
- Bachelor of Social Work Program: F. BONECUTTER
- Doctoral Program: D. M. KILPATRICK
- Jane Addams Center for Social Policy and Research: C. F. HAIRSTON
- Master of Social Work Program: J. CATES
- Midwest Aids Training and Education Center: N. LINSK

College of Urban Planning and Public Affairs:
- Center for Urban Economic Development: W. HOWARD
- Great Cities Institute: W. WIEWEL
- Institute for Research on Race and Public Policy: (vacant)
- Nathalie P. Voorhees Center for Neighborhood and Community Improvement: P. WRIGHT
- Public Administration Program: G. BEAM
- Survey Research Laboratory: T. JOHNSON
- Urban Planning and Policy Program: C. R. WINKLE
- Urban Transportation Center: A. SEN

ATTACHED CENTRES AND INSTITUTES

Cancer Center: Dir Dr WILLIAM T. BECK.

Center for Narcolepsy Research: Dir Dr SHARON MERRITT.

Center for Pharmaceutical Biotechnology: Dir Dr MICHAEL JOHNSON.

Center for Research in Law and Justice: Dir Dr DENNIS ROSENBAUM.

Center for Research in Periodontal Diseases and Oral Molecular Biology: Dir Dr DONALD CHAMBERS.

Center for Research on Women and Gender: Dir Dr ALICE DAN.

Center for Urban Economic Development: Dir Dr WILLIAM HOWARD.

City Design Center: Dirs Dr ROBERTA FELDMAN, Dr GEORGE HEMMENS.

Craniofacial Center: Dir Dr JOHN W. POLLEY.

Electronic Visualization Laboratory: Dirs Dr THOMAS DEFANTI, DANIEL SADIN.

Energy Resources Center: Dir Dr WILLIAM WOREK.

Fracture Mechanics and Materials Durability Laboratory: Dir Dr ALEXANDER CHUDNOVSKY.

Gerontology Center: Dir Dr DONNA COHEN.

Institute for Tuberculosis Research: Dir Dr MICHAEL GROVES.

Institute on Disability and Human Development: Dir Dr DAVID BRADDOCK.

Integrated Systems Laboratory: Dir RAFFI TURIAN.

IVHS Laboratory: Dir Dr PETER NELSON.

Jane Addams Center for Social Policy and Research: Dir Dr DONALD BRIELAND.

Manufacturing Research Center: Dir Dr SABRI CETINKUNT.

MicroFabrication Laboratory: Dir Dr PETER HESKETH.

Nathalie P. Voorhees Center for Neighborhood and Community Improvement: Dir Dr PATRICIA WRIGHT.

Program for Collaborative Research in the Pharmaceutical Sciences: Dir Dr JOHN PEZZUTO.

Robotics and Automation Laboratory: Dir Dr JAMES LIN.

Urban Transportation Center: Dir Dr ASHISH SEN.

Virtual Reality Manufacturing Institute: Dir Dr PRASHANT BANERJEE.

UNIVERSITY OF ST FRANCIS

500 Wilcox St, Joliet, IL 60435
Telephone: (815) 740-3360
Founded 1920

President: Dr JAMES A. DOPPKE
Vice-President for Academic Affairs: Dr MARTIN LARREY
Director of Libraries: Sr CAROL ANN NOVAK

Library of 190,000 vols
Number of teachers: 285
Number of students: 4,096

DEANS

College of Arts and Sciences: Dr DENISE WILBUR
College of Business and Professional Studies: Dr LYLE HICKS
College of Nursing: Dr ALBERTTA DAVID
College of Health Arts: PHYLLIS THOMPSON
College of Graduate Studies: Dr F. WILLIAM KELLEY

WESTERN ILLINOIS UNIVERSITY

Macomb, IL 61455
Telephone: (309) 295-1414
Founded 1899

President: DONALD S. SPENCER
Provost and Academic Vice-President: BURTON WITTHUHN
Vice-President for Student Services: W. GARRY JOHNSON
Director of Admissions: KAREN HELMERS
Dean of University Libraries: THOMAS PETERS

Library of 700,000 vols
Number of teachers: 644
Number of students: 12,200

Publications: *Undergraduate Catalog, Graduate Catalog, Summer Sessions Bulletin, Mississippi Valley Review, Essays in Literature.*

DEANS

College of Arts and Sciences: PHYLLIS FARLEY RIPPEY
College of Business and Technology: M. DAVID BEVERIDGE
College of Education and Human Services: DAVID R. TAYLOR
College of Fine Arts and Communication: JAMES BUTTERWORTH
School of Extended and Continuing Education: LINDA STICKNEY-TAYLOR

WHEATON COLLEGE

Wheaton, IL 60187
Telephone: (630) 752-5000
Founded 1860

President: Dr DUANE LITFIN
Director of Admissions: DAN CRABTREE
Provost: Dr STANTON JONES
Vice-President for Finance: Dr DAVID JOHNSTON
Vice-President for Student Development: Dr SAMUEL A. SHELLHAMER
Vice-President for Advancement: Dr MARK DILLON
Dean of Conservatory: Dr GEORGE ARASIMOVICZ
Dean of Arts and Sciences: (vacant)
Registrar and Director of Academic Services: PAUL JOHNSON
Librarian: PAUL SNEZEK

Library of 1,000,000 items
Number of full-time teachers: 172, including 71 professors
Number of students: 2,675

Publications: *InForm* (5 a year), *Kodon Literary Magazine* (3 a year), *Record* (weekly), *Tower* (year book).

INDIANA

ANDERSON UNIVERSITY

Anderson, IN 46012
Telephone: (765) 649-9071
Founded 1917

President: Dr JAMES L. EDWARDS
Dean of the College: Dr CARL H. CALDWELL
Registrar: ARTHUR LEAK
Librarian: RICHARD SNYDER

Library of 210,000 vols
Number of teachers: 140
Number of students: 2,250

BALL STATE UNIVERSITY

Muncie, IN 47306
Telephone: (765) 289-1241
Founded 1918

President: JOHN E. WORTHEN
Vice-Presidents: Dr DOUGLAS MCCONKEY, DON PARK, WARREN VANDER HILL, THOMAS J. KINGHORN
Registrar: THOMAS BILGER
Librarian: Dr MICHAEL B. WOOD

Library of 1,420,000 vols
Number of teachers: 900
Number of students: 18,528

Publications: *International Journal of Social Education, Teacher Educator* (quarterly), *Proceedings of the Indiana Academy of Social Sciences* (annually), *Odyssey* (annually), *Indiana Mathematics Teacher* (2 a year), *Ball State Monographs* (irregularly).

BUTLER UNIVERSITY

4600 Sunset Ave, Indianapolis, IN 46208
Telephone: (317) 940-8000
Fax: (317) 940-9930
Founded 1855
Private control

President: GEOFFREY BANNISTER
Provost and Senior Vice-President for Academic Affairs: PAUL YU
Vice-President for Advancement: (vacant)
Registrar: SONDREA OZOLINS
Dean, Libraries: LEWIS MILLER

Number of teachers: 380
Number of students: 4,800

DEANS

Jordan College of Fine Arts: MICHAEL SELLS
College of Business Administration: LEE DAHRINGER
College of Education: SAUNDRA TRACY
College of Pharmacy: ROBERT A. SANDMANN
College of Liberal Arts and Sciences: MARGRIET LACY

CALUMET COLLEGE OF SAINT JOSEPH

2400 New York Ave, Whiting, IN 46394
Telephone: (219) 473-7770
Founded 1951

President: Dr DENNIS C. RITTENMEYER
Registrar: Bro. BENJAMIN BASILE
Librarian: JOANN ARNOLD

Library of 115,874 vols
Number of teachers: 44
Number of students: 1,000

DEPAUW UNIVERSITY

313 S. Locust St, Greencastle, IN 46135
Telephone: (765) 658-4800
Fax: (317) 658-4177

Chartered 1837 as Indiana Asbury University, name changed 1884

President: ROBERT G. BOTTOMS
Vice-President for Academic Affairs: Dr NEAL ABRAHAM
Vice-President for Finance and Administration: THOMAS E. DIXON
Vice-President for Development and Alumni Relations: PAUL HARTMAN
Vice-President for Admission and Financial Aid: MADELEINE R. EAGON
Vice-President for Public Affairs: THERESA F. BRYANT
Vice-President for Student Services: JAMES L. LINCOLN
Registrar: ELEANOR S. YPMA
Director of Libraries: KATHY DAVIS

Library of 287,000 volumes
Number of teachers: 164 full-time, 58 part-time
Number of students: 2,234

Publications: *DePauw Catalog* (every 2 years), *DePauw Magazine* (quarterly).

EARLHAM COLLEGE

Richmond, IN 47374
Telephone: (765) 983-1200
Telex: (765) 983-1304
Founded 1847

President: DOUGLAS BENNETT
Vice-President for Business Affairs: RICHARD K. SMITH
Vice-President for Institutional Advancement: JAMES THOMPSON
Provost and Dean of Academic Affairs: LEN CLARK
Librarian: TOM KIRK

Number of teachers: 91
Number of students: 1,005

Publications: *Earlhamite, Earlham Word* (weekly), *Crucible* (2 a year by students), *Sargasso* (annually by students).

DEANS

College: LEN CLARK
Students: ANNE WRIGHT

FRANKLIN COLLEGE

Franklin, IN 46131
Telephone: (317) 738-8000
Founded 1834
Chancellor: WILLIAM B. MARTIN
President: (vacant)
Vice-President for Academic Affairs and Dean of the College: ALLEN H. BERGER
Vice-President for Business and Finance: LARRY GRIFFITH
Vice-President for Development and Public Affairs: RICHARD V. SWINDLE
Dean of Enrolment Management: B. STEPHEN RICHARDS
Dean of Students: SUSAN B. GRIFFITH
Director of Library: CARLA JACOBS
Library of 113,680 vols
Number of teachers: 90
Number of students: 917

GOSHEN COLLEGE

Goshen, IN 46526
Telephone: (219) 535-7000
Fax: (219) 535-7660
Founded 1894
President: SHIRLEY H. SHOWALTER
Registrar: STANLEY MILLER
Librarian: DEVON YODER
Library of 155,000 vols
Number of teachers: 82 full-time, 30 part-time
Number of students: 890
Publication: *Mennonite Quarterly Review* (quarterly).

HANOVER COLLEGE

Hanover, IN 47243
Telephone: (812) 866-2151
First instruction 1827; chartered 1829
Private control (Presbyterian)
President: RUSSELL L. NICHOLS
Vice-President for Academic Affairs: STANLEY P. CAINE
Vice-President for Student Affairs: DAVID A. PALMER
Library of 267,000 vols, 1,184 periodicals
Number of teachers: 71
Number of students: 1,010

HUNTINGTON COLLEGE

Huntington, IN 46750
Telephone: (219) 356-6000
Fax: (219) 356-9448
Founded 1897
President: Dr G. BLAIR DOWDEN
Academic Dean: Dr GERALD D. SMITH
Dean of Enrolment: JEFF BERGGREN
Registrar: SARAH J. HARVEY
Librarian: ROBERT E. KAEHR
Library of 140,000 vols
Number of teachers: 52
Number of students: 614

INDIANA INSTITUTE OF TECHNOLOGY

1600 E. Washington, Fort Wayne, IN 46803
Telephone: (219) 422-5561
Fax: (219) 422-7696
Founded 1930
President: DONALD J. ANDORFER
Library of 45,000 volumes
Number of teachers: 50
Number of students: 1,425
Schools of engineering, business and computer science.

INDIANA STATE UNIVERSITY

Terre Haute, IN 47809
Telephone: (812) 237-6311
Fax: (812) 237-2291
Founded 1865
President: JOHN W. MOORE
Provost and Vice-President for Academic Affairs: RICHARD H. WELLS
Vice-President for Administration and Secretary of the University: ROBERT E. SCHAFER
Vice-President for Planning and Budgets: MARILYN SCHULTZ
Vice-President for University Advancement: J. ROBERT QUATROCHE
Vice-President for Student Affairs: PAUL T. EDGERTON
Registrar: DAVID P. RIDENOUR
Enrolment Services and Admissions: LEE YOUNG
Librarian: ELLEN WATSON
Library of 1,862,101 vols
Number of teachers: 568
Number of students: 10,934
Publications: *Contemporary Education* (quarterly), *African American Review* (quarterly), *Classical and Modern Literature* (quarterly), *Midwestern Journal of Language and Folklore* (2 a year), *The Hoosier Science Teacher* (quarterly), *Indiana English* (3 a year).

DEANS

College of Arts and Sciences: JOE WEIXLMANN
School of Business: DONALD BATES
School of Education: RICHARD ANTONAK
School of Graduate Studies: BERNICE BASS DE MARTINEZ
School of Health and Human Performance: BARBARA PASSMORE
School of Nursing: NANCY MCKEE (acting)
School of Technology: CLOIS E. KICKLIGHTER

INDIANA UNIVERSITY

Bloomington, IN 47405
Telephone: (812) 855-4848
Established 1820 as a State Seminary, opened 1824, became Indiana College 1828, attained university status 1838, became State University 1852
Campuses at Fort Wayne, Kokomo, Gary, South Bend, Indianapolis, New Albany, Richmond (see below)
President: MYLES BRAND
Chancellor: H. B WELLS
Vice-Presidents: K. R. R. GROS LOUIS, G. L. BEPKO, G. E. WALKER, J. G. PALMER, J. T. CLAPACS, M. A. MCROBBIE, J. C. SIMPSON
Registrar: R. G. PUGH
Director of Admissions: DON HOSSLER
Dean of Libraries: SUZANNE THORIN
Library: see Libraries
Number of teachers: 1,539 (Bloomington)
Number of students: 34,700 (Bloomington)
Publications: *American Historical Review* (5 a year), *American Journal of Semiotics* (quarterly), *American Sociological Review* (bimonthly), *Anthropological Linguistics* (quarterly), *Business Horizons* (bimonthly), *Folklore Research Journal* (3 a year), *Indiana Business Review* (bimonthly), *Indiana Law Journal* (quarterly), *Indiana Magazine of History* (quarterly), *Indiana University Mathematics Journal* (quarterly), *Journal of American History* (quarterly), *Journal of Personality and Social Psychology* (quarterly), *Journal of the Experimental Analysis of Behavior* (bimonthly), *Phi Delta Kappan* (10 a year), *Slavic and East European Journal* (quarterly), *Social Psychology Quarterly* (quarterly), *Sociological Methods and Research* (quarterly), *University Bulletin* (30 a year), *Victorian Studies* (quarterly).

DEANS

Dean for Budgetary Administration: MAYNARD THOMPSON
Dean of the Graduate School: GEORGE E. WALKER
Dean of Students: RICHARD MCKAIG
Dean of University Computing: CHRIS PEEBLES (acting)
Dean of the Faculties: DEBORAH FREUND
College of Arts and Sciences: MORTON LOWENGRUB
School of Business: JOHN RAU
School of Continuing Studies: JEREMY DUNNING (acting)
School of Education: DONALD WARREN
School of Health, Physical Education and Recreation: TONY A. MOBLEY
School of Journalism: TREVOR R. BROWN
School of Law: FRED AMAN
School of Library and Information Science: BLAISE CRONIN
School of Music: DAVID WOODS
School of Optometry: JACK W. BENNETT
School for Public and Environmental Affairs: A. JAMES BARNES

CHAIRMEN OF DEPARTMENTS

Afro-American Studies: JOHN MCCLUSKEY
Anthropology: ROBERT MEIER
Apparel Merchandising and Interior Design: KATHLEEN ROWOLD
Astronomy: STUART MUFSON
Biology: JEFF PALMER
Central Eurasian Studies: TOIVO RAUN
Chemistry: PAUL A. GRIECO
Classical Studies: TIMOTHY LONG
Comparative Literature: MATEI CALINESCU
Computer Science: DANIEL LEIVANT
Criminal Justice: EDMUND MCGARRELL
East Asian Languages and Cultures: GREGORY KASZA
Economics: ROBERT BECKER
English: KENNETH JOHNSTON
Fine Arts: JEFFREY WOLIN
Folklore: RUTH STONE
French and Italian: ROSEMARY LLOYD
Geography: DENNIS CONWAY
Geology: LEE SUTTNER
Germanic Studies: TERENCE THAYER
History: JAMES MADISON
History and Philosophy of Science: MICHAEL FRIEDMAN
Linguistics: PAUL NEWMAN
Mathematics: ROBERT GLASSEY
Middle Eastern Studies Program: FEDWA MALTI-DOUGLAS
Near Eastern Languages and Cultures: FEDWA MALTI-DOUGLAS
Philosophy: J. MICHAEL DUNN
Physics: ALAN KOSTELECKY
Polish Studies: TIMOTHY WILES
Political Science: EDWARD CARMINES
Psychology: JOSEPH STEINMETZ
Religious Studies: STEPHEN J. STEIN
Slavic Languages and Literature: RONALD F. FELDSTEIN
Sociology: J. SCOTT LONG
Spanish and Portuguese: DARLENE SODLIER
Speech Communication: ROBERT IVIE
Speech and Hearing Sciences: LARRY HUMES
Telecommunications: MICHAEL MCGREGOR
Theatre and Drama: LEON BRAUNER
West European Studies: PETER BONDANELLA

DIRECTORS OF RESEARCH INSTITUTES

Institute for Advanced Study: (vacant)
Afro-American Arts Institute: CHARLES SYKES
American Indian Studies Research Institute: RAYMOND J. DEMALLIE

Institute for Applied Mathematics and Scientific Computing: ROGER TEMAM
Indiana University Art Museum: ADELHEID GEALT
Glenn A. Black Laboratory of Archaeology: CHRISTOPHER SPALDING PEEBLES
School of Business Division of Research: MORTON MARCUS
School of Business Institute for Research on the Management of Information Systems: JO BASEY
Center for Research into the Anthropological Foundations of Technology: NICHOLAS TOTH, KATHY SCHICK
Institute for Child Study: RUSSELL SKIBA
Indiana University Cyclotron Facility: JOHN CAMERON
Institute for Study of Developmental Disabilities: DAVID MANK
Early Music Institute: WENDY GILLESPIE (acting)
East Asian Studies Center: GEORGE M. WILSON
East Asian Summer Language Institute: YASUKO ITO WATT
Center for Economic Education: W. PHILIP SAUNDERS
English Curriculum Study Center: EDWARD B. JENKINSON
Center for English Language Training: HARRY L. GRADMAN
Environmental Systems Applications Center: WILLIAM W. JONES
ERIC Clearinghouse for Social Studies/Social Science Education: JOHN PATRICK
Indiana Center for Evaluation: (vacant)
Folklore Institute: RUTH STONE
Indiana Geological Survey: NORMAN C. HESTER
Institute of German Studies: STEPHEN L. WAILES
Center for Health and Safety Studies: JAMES CROWE
High School Journalism Institute: JOHN E. DVORAK
Center for Human Growth: MICHAEL TRACY
Institute for Study of Human Capabilities: CHARLES WATSON
Inner Asian and Uralic National Resource Center: YURI BREGEL
International Development Institute: E. PHILIP MORGAN
Center for Italian Studies: EDOARDO A. LEBANO
Center for Research and Development in Language Instruction: ALBERT VALDMAN
Jewish Studies Center: ALVIN H. ROSENFELD
The Kinsey Institute for Research in Sex, Gender, and Reproduction: JOHN BANCROFT
Laboratory Animal Resources: RUSSELL L. SCHMIDT
Latin-American Music Center: CARMEN TELLEZ
Center for Latin American and Caribbean Studies: (vacant)
William Hammond Mathers Museum: GEOFFREY W. CONRAD
Indiana Molecular Institute: RUDOLPH A. RAFF
Medieval Studies Institute: (vacant)
Nuclear Theory Center: BRIAN SEROT
Population Institute for Research and Training: GEORGE ALTER
Center for Policy and Public Management: ROGER B. PARKS
Polish Studies Center: TIMOTHY WILES
Poynter Center: DAVID H. SMITH
Midwest Center for Public Sector Labor Relations: RICHARD S. RUBIN
Center for Reading and Language Studies: ROGER C. FARR
Russian and East European Institute: DAVID RANSEL
Center for Health and Safety Studies: JAMES CROWE
Seismic Laboratory: MICHAEL W. HAMBURGER
Institute of Social Research: ROBERT V. ROBINSON
Social Studies Development Center: JOHN J. PATRICK
Center for Survey Research: JOHN M. KENNEDY
Transportation Research Center: CLINTON V. OSTER
Institute for Urban Transportation: GEORGE M. SMERK
Workshop in Political Theory and Policy Analysis: ELINOR OSTROM
West European National Resource Center: NORMAN S. FURNISS

Indiana University East

Richmond, IN 47374
Telephone: (317) 966-8261
Chancellor: DAVID J. FULTON
Number of students: 2,351

Indiana University at Kokomo

Kokomo, IN 46902
Telephone: (317) 453-2000
Chancellor: EMITA B. HILL
Number of students: 2,965

Indiana University Northwest

Gary, IN 46408
Telephone: (219) 980-6700
Chancellor: HILDA RICHARDS
Number of students: 5,149

Indiana University at South Bend

South Bend, IN 46634
Telephone: (219) 237-4220
Chancellor: LESTER C. LAMON
Number of students: 7,088

Indiana University Southeast

New Albany, IN 47150
Telephone: (812) 945-2731
Chancellor: F. C. RICHARDSON
Number of students: 5,396

Indiana University — Purdue University at Fort Wayne

Fort Wayne, IN 46805
Telephone: (219) 482-5356
Chancellor: MICHAEL A. WARTELL
Number of students: 10,186

Indiana University — Purdue University at Indianapolis

Indianapolis, IN 46202
Telephone: (317) 274-4417
Chancellor: GERALD L. BEPKO
Number of students: 23,468

DEANS

School of Business: JOHN RAU
School of Education: DONALD WARREN
School of Journalism: TREVOR R. BROWN
School of Liberal Arts: JOHN D. BARLOW
School of Science: DAVID L. STOCUM
School of Nursing: ANGELA MCBRIDE
School of Law: NORMAN LEFSTEIN
School of Social Work: ROBERTA GREENE
Herron School of Art: ROBERT SHAY
School of Physical Education: PAUL N. KELLUM
School of Dentistry: H. WILLIAM GILMORE
School of Engineering and Technology: ALFRED R. POTRIN
School of Medicine: WALTER J. DALY
Division of Allied Health Sciences: JOHN R. SNYDER

CHAIRMEN OF DEPARTMENTS

Accounting: ED ALTHOFF
Business Economics and Public Policy: DAVID LEHR
Business Law: JORDAN LEIBMAN
Decision and Information Sciences: CAROL V. BROWN
Finance: (vacant)
Management: (vacant)
Marketing: (vacant)
Operations and Systems Management: (vacant)
Undergraduate Programs: C. DIANE BARTH
Anthropology: SUSAN B. SUTTON
Economics: ROBERT SANDY
English: RICHARD C. TURNER
French: ROSALIE VERMETTE
Geography: FREDERICK L. BEIN
Germanic Languages: GABRIELLE BERSIER
History: PHILLIP SCARPING
Philosophy: PAUL NAGY
Political Science: RICHARD FREDLAND
Religious Studies: E. THEODORE MULLEN
Biology: N. DOUGLAS LEES
Chemistry: DAVID J. MALIK
Computer and Information Science: RAYMOND C. Y. CHIN
Geology: ROBERT D. HALL
Mathematical Sciences: BARTHOLOMEW S. NG
Physics: B. D. NAGESWARA RAO
Psychology: JOHN T. HAZER
Oral Microbiology: CHRIS H. MILLER
Oral Pathology: (vacant)
Pediatric Dentistry: (vacant)
Preventive Dentistry: ARDEN G. CHRISTEN
Undergraduate Clinical Oral and Maxillofacial Surgery: JAMES H. DIRLAM
Orthodontics: (vacant)
Oral and Maxillofacial Surgery: (vacant)
Operative Dentistry: (vacant)
Periodontics: E. BRADY HANCOCK
Dental Practice Administration: DONALD RHES THARP
Computer Technology: THOMAS IM HO
Electrical Engineering Technology: BARRY BULLARD
Division of Engineering: H. ONER YURTSEVEN
Construction Technology/Supervision: EDGAR FLEENOR
Learn and Shop: JAMES R. EAST
Sociology: DAVID FORD
Spanish: NANCY NEWTON
Communication and Theatre: ROBERT C. DICK
Weekend College: JAMES R. EAST
Anatomy: DAVID B. BURR
Anaesthesiology: ROBERT STOELTING
Biochemistry: ROBERT A. HARRIS
Dermatology: EVAN FARMER
Family Medicine: DEBORAH I. ALLEN
Microbiology and Immunology: DIETRICH C. BAUER
Medicine: WALTER J. DALY
Medical Genetics: JOE C. CHRISTIAN
Neurology: JOSE BILLER
Obstetrics and Gynecology: MARILYN F. GRAHAM
Ophthalmology: ROBERT D. YEE
Orthopedic Surgery: RICHARD E. LINDSETH
Otolaryngology and Head and Neck Surgery: RICHARD D. MIYAMOTO
Pathology: JAMES W. SMITH
Pediatrics: RICHARD L. SCHREINER
Pharmacology and Toxicology: HENRY R. BESCH, JR
Physiology and Biophysics: RODNEY A. RHOADES
Psychiatry: HUGH C. HENDRIE
Radiation Oncology: NED B. HORNBACK
Radiology: ROBERT W. HOLDEN
Surgery: JAY L. GROSFELD
Urology: RANDALL G. ROWLAND

INDIANA WESLEYAN UNIVERSITY

Marion, IN 46953
Telephone: (765) 674-6901

Fax: (765) 677-2499

Founded 1920

President: JAMES BARNES

Vice-President for Financial Affairs: Dr WILLIAM R. MCDOWELL

Vice-President for Academic Affairs: Dr PAUL D. COLLARD

Librarian: (vacant)

Library of 211,000 vols

Number of teachers: 86

Number of students: 1,865

MANCHESTER COLLEGE

604 College Ave, North Manchester, IN 46962

Telephone: (219) 982-5000

Founded 1889

Four-year liberal arts and professional studies

President: Dr PARKER G. MARDEN

Vice-President for Academic Affairs: Dr JO YOUNG SWITZER

Vice-President and Dean of Student Development: WILLIAM RHUDY

Vice-President and Treasurer: NANCY E. KIN

Vice-President of Enrolment and Planning: Dr DAVID F. MCFADDEN

Registrar: LILA D. HAMMER

Director of the Library: ROBIN J. GRATZ

Library of 160,000 vols

Number of teachers: 72 full-time

Number of students: 1,054

Publications: *Manchester Magazine* (quarterly), *The Oak Leaves* (fortnightly), *The Aurora* (annually).

MARIAN COLLEGE

3200 Cold Spring Rd, Indianapolis, IN 46222-1997

Telephone: (317) 955-6000

Fax: (317) 955-6448

Founded 1851

Baccalaureate liberal arts college

President: DANIEL A. FELICETTI

Chief Advancement Officer: ANN RUNYON

Dean for Academic Affairs: Dr C. EDWARD BALOG

Dean for Student Affairs: WILLIAM H. WOODMAN

Chief Financial Officer: RUSSELL GLASSBURN

Librarian: KELLY GRIFFITH

Library of 129,638 vols

Number of teachers: 146

Number of students: 1,225

PURDUE UNIVERSITY

West Lafayette, IN 47907

Telephone: (765) 494-4600

Fax: (765) 494-7875

Founded 1869; instruction commenced 1874

State control

Academic year: August to May

President: STEVEN C. BEERING

Executive Vice-President and Treasurer: KENNETH P. BURNS

Executive Vice-President for Academic Affairs: ROBERT L. RINGEL

Vice President for State Relations: JOHN M. HUIE

Vice-President for Research and Dean of the Graduate School: LUIS M. PROENZA

Vice-President for Physical Facilities: WAYNE W. KJONAAS

Vice-President for Student Services: THOMAS B. ROBINSON

Vice-President for Housing and Food Services: JOHN A. SAUTTER

Vice-President for University Relations: JOSEPH L. BENNETT

Vice-President for Human Relations: ALYSA C. ROLLOCK

Vice-President for Business Services and Assistant Treasurer: JAMES S. ALMOND

Vice-President for Development: CHARLES B. WISE

Registrar: MARLESA A. RONEY

Director of Admissions: DOUGLAS L. CHRISTIANSEN

Dean of Libraries: EMILY R. MOBLEY

Dean of Students: L. TONY HAWKINS

Dean of International Programmes: MICHAEL J. STOHL

Libraries: See Libraries

Number of teachers: 2,204 West Lafayette campus; 1,382 regional campuses

Number of students: 35,715 (28,557 additional students at regional campuses)

Publications: *University Bulletins, Inside Purdue, Perspective.*

DEANS

School of Agriculture: VICTOR L. LECHTENBERG

School of Consumer and Family Sciences: DENNIS A. SAVAIANO

School of Education: MARILYN J. HARING

Schools of Engineering: RICHARD J. SCHWARTZ

School of Liberal Arts: MARGARET M. ROWE

School of Management and Krannert Graduate School of Management: DENNIS J. WEIDENAAR

Schools of Pharmacy, Nursing and Health Sciences: CHARLES O. RUTLEDGE

School of Science: HARRY A. MORRISON

School of Technology: DON K. GENTRY

School of Veterinary Medicine: ALAN H. REBAR

HEADS OF DEPARTMENT

School of Agriculture:

- Agricultural Economics: WALLACE E. TYNER
- Agricultural and Biological Engineering: VINCENT F. BRALTS
- Agricultural Statistics: RALPH W. GANN
- Agronomy: WILLIAM W. MCFEE
- Animal Sciences: JEFFREY D. ARMSTRONG
- Biochemistry: MARK A. HERMODSON
- Botany and Plant Pathology: RAYMOND D. MARTYN
- Entomology: CHRISTIAN Y. OSETO
- Food Science: PHILIP E. NELSON
- Forestry and Natural Resources: DENNIS C. LE MASTER
- Horticulture: EDWARD N. ASHWORTH (acting)

School of Consumer and Family Sciences:

- Child Development and Family Studies: DOUGLAS R. POWELL
- Consumer Sciences and Retailing: HEIKKI J. RINNE
- Foods and Nutrition: CONNIE M. WEAVER
- Restaurant, Hotel, Institutional and Tourism Management: RAPHAEL R. KAVANAUGH

School of Education:

- Curriculum and Instruction: JERRY L. PETERS
- Educational Studies: DALE H. SCHUNK

Schools of Engineering:

- Aeronautics and Astronautics: THOMAS N. FARRIS
- Chemical Engineering: GINTARAS V. REKLAITIS
- Civil Engineering: VINCENT P. DRNEVICH
- Construction Engineering and Management: DANIEL W. HALPIN
- Electrical and Computer Engineering: W. KENT FUCHS
- Freshman Engineering: VICTOR W. GOLDSCHMIDT
- Industrial Engineering: W. DALE COMPTON (interim)
- Interdisciplinary Engineering: DAVID P. KESSLER
- Materials Engineering: GERALD L. LIEDL
- Mechanical Engineering: FRANK P. INCROPERA
- Nuclear Engineering: ARDEN L. BEMENT

School of Liberal Arts:

- Audiology and Speech Sciences: ANNE SMITH
- Communication: CYNTHIA STOHL
- English: THOMAS P. ADLER
- Foreign Languages and Literatures: CHRISTIANE E. KECK
- Health, Kinesiology and Leisure Studies: THOMAS J. TEMPLIN
- History: GORDON R. MORK
- Philosophy: RODNEY J. BERTOLET
- Political Science: FRANK L. WILSON
- Psychological Sciences: THOMAS J. BERNDT
- Sociology and Anthropology: CAROLYN C. PERRUCCI
- Visual and Performing Arts: DAVID L. SIGMAN

School of Management:

- Accounting: ROBERT K. ESKEW, III
- Business Law: PHILLIP J. SCALETTA
- Economics: DANIEL J. KOVENOCK
- Finance: JOHN J. MCCONNELL
- Management Information Systems: KEMAL ALTINKEMER
- Marketing: MANOHAR U. KALWANI
- Organizational Behaviour/Human Resources: DAVID SCHOORMAN
- Operations Management: JAMES E. WARD
- Quantitative Methods: GORDON P. WRIGHT
- Strategic Management: DAN E. SCHENDEL

Schools of Pharmacy, Nursing, and Health Sciences:

- Health Sciences: PAUL L. ZIEMER
- Industrial and Physical Pharmacy: STEPHEN R. BYRN
- Medicinal Chemistry and Molecular Pharmacology: RICHARD F. BORCH
- Nursing: LINDA A. SIMUNEK
- Pharmacy Practice: STEVEN R. ABEL

School of Science:

- Biological Sciences: LOUIS A. SHERMAN
- Chemistry: RICHARD A. WALTON
- Computer Sciences: AHMED SAMEH
- Earth and Atmospheric Science: HARSHVARDHAN
- Mathematics: CARL C. COWEN, Jr
- Physics: ANDREW S. HIRSCH
- Statistics: MARY ELLEN BOCK

School of Technology:

- Aviation Technology: MICHAEL J. KROES
- Building Construction and Management Technology: STEPHEN D. SCHUETTE
- Computer Technology: JEFFREY L. WHITTEN
- Electrical Engineering Technology: LARRY D. HOFFMAN
- Industrial Technology: DENNIS R. DEPEW
- Mechanical Engineering Technology: MICHAEL A. MAGILL (acting)
- Organizational Leadership and Supervision: MICHAEL L. MENEFEE
- Technical Graphics: GARY R. BERTOLINE

School of Veterinary Medicine:

- Basic Medical Sciences: GORDON L. COPPOC
- Clinical Sciences: RALPH C. RICHARDSON
- Pathobiology: H. LEON THACKER (interim)

ROSE-HULMAN INSTITUTE OF TECHNOLOGY

5500 Wabash Ave, Terre Haute, IN 47803

Telephone: (812) 877-1511

Fax: (812) 877-9925

Founded 1874

President: Dr SAMUEL F. HULBERT

Associate Vice-President, Business and Finance: ROBERT A. COONS

Dean: BARRY A. BENEDICT

Registrar: L. W. HARMENING

Librarian: JOHN ROBSON (Director of the Library)

Library of 40,000 vols

Number of teachers: 120

Number of students: 1,420

Publication: *Bulletin* (every 2 years).

UNIVERSITY OF SAINT FRANCIS

2701 Spring St, Fort Wayne, IN 46808-3994
Telephone: (219) 434-3100
Fax: (219) 434-3183

Founded 1890

President: Sister M. ELISE KRISS
Vice-President for Academic Affairs: Sister M. ELAINE BROTHERS
Vice-President for Development: LOU ROSS
Vice-President for Student Services: SHARON MEJEUR
Vice-President for Administration: JOHN KESSEN

Number of teachers: 82
Number of students: 1,574

SAINT JOSEPH'S COLLEGE

Rensselaer, IN 47978
Telephone: (219) 866-6000

Founded 1889

President: ALBERT J. SHANNON
Registrar: CAROL BURNS
Librarian: CATHERINE SAYLERS

Library of 150,000 vols
Number of teachers: 64
Number of students: 1,000

SAINT MARY-OF-THE-WOODS COLLEGE

Saint Mary-of-the-Woods, IN 47876
Telephone: (812) 535-5151

Founded 1840

President: Sister BARBARA DOHERTY
Vice-President for Academic Affairs: Dr CONSTANCE BAUER
Registrar: SUSAN MEIER
Librarian: RITA LAWSON

Library of 148,000 vols
Number of teachers: 53 full-time, 14 part-time
Number of students: 645 f.t.e.

SAINT MARY'S COLLEGE

Notre Dame, IN 46556
Telephone: (219) 284-4000

Founded 1844

President: Dr MARILOU ELDRED
Vice-President and Dean of Faculty: Dr DOROTHY M. FEIGL
Vice-President for College Relations: (vacant)
Vice-President for Student Affairs: Dr LINDA L. TIMM
Vice-President for Fiscal Affairs: DANIEL F. OSBERGER

Library of 195,424 vols
Number of students: 1,435 full-time

Publications: *Courier, Blue Mantle, Chimes* (annually).

TAYLOR UNIVERSITY

236 W. Reade Ave, Upland, IN 46989-1001
Telephone: (317) 998-2751
Fax: (317) 998-4925

Founded 1846

Academic year: September to May (three terms)

President: Dr JAY KESLER
Executive Vice-President and Provost: Dr DARYL YOST
Registrar: BARBARA DAVENPORT
Director of Admissions: STEPHEN MORTLAND
Librarian: DAVID DICKEY

Library of 235,114 vols
Number of teachers: 145
Number of students: 2,254

Publications: *Profile, Taylor University Magazine, Taylor Club News.*

UNIVERSITY OF EVANSVILLE

1800 Lincoln Ave, Evansville, IN 47722
Telephone: (812) 479-2000
Telex: (810) 3530525
Fax: (812) 479-2320

Founded 1854

President: Dr JAMES S. VINSON
Registrar: KEITH KUTZLER
Vice-President for Academic Affairs: Dr STEPHEN GREINER
Vice-President for Fiscal Affairs: ROBERT E. GALLMAN
Vice-President for Development: W. SCOTT SHRODE

Number of teachers: 192, including 59 professors
Number of students: 3,264 (3,080 f.t.e.)

Publication: *The Crescent.*

DEANS

School of Business Administration: Dr DAVID B. REEDER
College of Arts and Sciences: Dr LARRY COLTER
College of Engineering and Computer Science: Dr PHILIP GERHART
College of Education and Health Sciences: Dr LYNN R. PENLAND
Learning Resources: WILLIAM LOUDEN

UNIVERSITY OF INDIANAPOLIS

1400 East Hanna Ave, Indianapolis, IN 46227
Telephone: (317) 788-3368

Founded 1902

President: Dr JERRY ISRAEL
Vice-President and Provost: Dr LYNN R. YOUNGBLOOD
Registrar: DIANE METHENY
Dean of Extended Programs: LOU HOLTZCLAW (acting)
Co-ordinator of Graduate Business Programs: Dr GERALD L. SPETH
Director of Admissions: MARK T. WEIGAND
Librarian: Dr PHILIP H. YOUNG

Library of 145,000 vols
Number of teachers: 165 full-time
Number of students: 1,888 full-time, 1,520 part-time

UNIVERSITY OF NOTRE DAME

Notre Dame, IN 46556
Telephone: (219) 631-5000

Founded 1842

President: Rev. EDWARD A. MALLOY
Executive Vice-President: Rev. E. WILLIAM BEAUCHAMP
Provost: NATHAN O. HATCH
Vice-President and Senior Associate Provost: Rev. TIMOTHY R. SCULLY
Vice-President for Graduate Studies and Research: Dr JAMES L. MERZ
Vice-President for Student Affairs: PATRICIA A. O'HARA
Vice-President for University Relations: Dr WILLIAM P. SEXTON
Registrar: HAROLD L. PACE
Director of Admissions: DANIEL J. SARACINO
Librarian: JENNIFER YOUNGER
Archivist: WENDY C. SCHLERETH

Library: see Libraries
Number of teachers: 986
Number of students: 10,275

Publications: *The Scholastic, American Midland Naturalist, Review of Politics, Publications in Medieval Studies, Notre Dame Law Review, Technical Review, The Juggler, Notre Dame Journal of Formal Logic, The Observer, The Dome, Notre Dame Magazine, The American Journal of Jurisprudence, Notre Dame Report, Science Quarterly, Texts and Studies in the History of Medieval Education, Religion and Literature, Notre Dame Journal of Law, Ethics and Public Policy.*

DEANS

Freshman Year of Studies: Dr EILEEN M. KOLMAN
College of Arts and Letters: Dr MARK W. ROCHE
College of Business Administration: Dr CAROLYN Y. WOO
College of Engineering: Dr FRANK P. INCROPERA
Law School: DAVID T. LINK
College of Science: Dr FRANCIS J. CASTELLINO

VALPARAISO UNIVERSITY

Valparaiso, IN 46383
Telephone: (219) 464-5000
Fax: (219) 464-5381

Founded 1859

President: ALAN F. HARRE
Registrar: ANN TROST
Vice-President for Admissions and Financial Aid: KATHARINE WEHLING
Vice-President for Academic Affairs: Dr ROY AUSTENSEN
Librarian: DONNA RESETAR

Library of 451,000 vols
Number of teachers: 228
Number of students: 3,603

WABASH COLLEGE

Crawfordsville, IN 47933
Telephone: (317) 362-1400

Founded 1832

President: Dr ANDREW T. FORD
Dean of the College: Dr P. DONALD HERRING
Registrar: LESTER L. HEARSON
Librarian: LARRY J. FRYE

Library of 224,000 vols
Number of teachers: 80
Number of students: 745

IOWA

BUENA VISTA UNIVERSITY

Storm Lake, IA 50588
Telephone: (712) 749-2351
Fax: (712) 749-2037

Founded 1891

President: FREDERICK V. MOORE
Dean of Faculty: Dr KAREN HALBERSLEBEN

Library of 146,000 vols
Number of teachers: 102
Number of students: 2,473

CENTRAL COLLEGE

Pella, IA 50219
Telephone: (515) 628-9000
Fax: (515) 628-5316

Founded 1853

President: DAVID H. ROE
Vice-President for Business and Finance: B. BOWZER
Dean of Faculty: V. COOMBS
Librarian: R. MARTIN

Library of 200,000 vols
Number of students: 1,102

Publications: *The Central Bulletin, The Central Ray, The Pelican.*

CLARKE COLLEGE

1550 Clarke Drive, Dubuque, IA 52001
Telephone: (319) 588-6300
Fax: (319) 588-6789
E-mail: clarke-info@clarke.edu

Founded 1843

President: CATHERINE DUNN
Vice-President for Academic Affairs: JOHN WOZNIAK
Vice-President for Student Life: KATE ZANGER
Vice-President for Enrollment Management: BOBBE AMES
Vice-President for Institutional Advancement: GAIL NAUGHTON
Vice-President for Business Affairs: JIM PRINCE
Registrar: EUGENA SULLIVAN
Librarian: PAUL ROBERTS

Library of 121,000 vols
Number of teachers: 120
Number of students: 1,200

COE COLLEGE

Cedar Rapids, IA 52402
Telephone: (319) 399-8000

Founded 1851

President: JAMES R. PHIFER
Registrar: EVELYN BENDA
Vice-President for Academic Affairs and Dean of Faculty: LAURA SKANDERA-TROMBLEY
Vice-President for Business Affairs: (vacant)
Vice-President for Development: DICK MEISTERLING
Vice-President for Student Affairs and Dean of Students: LOU STARK
Vice-President for Admission and Financial Aid: DENNIS TROTTER
Librarian: RICHARD DOYLE

Library of 193,000 vols
Number of teachers: 80
Number of students: 1,318

Publications: *Courier* (quarterly), *Bulletin* (every 2 years).

CORNELL COLLEGE

600 First St W., Mount Vernon, IA 52314-1098
Telephone: (319) 895-4000
Fax: (319) 895-4492

Founded 1853

President: Dr LESLIE H. GARNER, Jr
Vice-President for Academic Affairs and Dean of the College: Dr DENNIS D. MOORE
Vice-President for Business Affairs and Treasurer: GLENN W. DODD
Dean of Students: Dr JOAN M. CLAAR
Dean of Admissions and Enrollment Management: LARRY ERENBERGER
Director of Library Services: THOMAS M. SHAW

Library of 190,000 vols
Number of teachers: 78
Number of students: 1,166

DORDT COLLEGE

Sioux Center, IA 51250
Telephone: (712) 722-6000
Fax: (712) 722-1185

Founded 1955

President: Dr CARL ZYLSTRA
Vice-President for Business: BERNARD DEWIT
Vice-President for College Advancement: LYLE A. GRITTERS
Vice-President for Academic Affairs: Dr ROCKNE MCCARTHY
Vice-President for Student Affairs: CURTIS TAYLOR
Vice-President for Information Services: DAVID NETZ
Director of Admissions: QUENTIN VAN ESSEN

Library of 125,000 vols
Number of teachers: 75 full-time
Number of students: 1,300

Publications: *Pro Rege* (quarterly), *Voice* (quarterly).

DRAKE UNIVERSITY

2507 University Ave, Des Moines, IA 50311
Telephone: (515) 271-2011
Fax (515) 271-3977

Chartered 1881
Private control
Academic year: September to May (two semesters)

President: ROBERT D. RAY
Executive Vice-President and Provost: R. BARBARA GITENSTEIN
Associate Provost and Director of Research: MICHAEL S. CHENEY
Vice-President, Business and Finance: VICTORIA PAYSEUR
Vice-President, Institutional Advancement: RICHARD LUZE (acting)
Registrar: NANCY GEIGER
Director of Libraries: RODNEY HENSHAW

Library of 500,000 vols and 2,600 periodicals
Number of teachers: 275 full-time, 45 part-time
Number of students: 4,054 full-time, 2,279 part-time

Publications: *Drake Law Review*, *Drake Update*.

DEANS

Law School: C. PETER GOPLERUD III
School of Education: JAMES P. FERRARE
College of Business: ANTONE ALBER
School of Journalism and Mass Communication: JANET HILL KEEFER
College of Arts and Sciences: RONALD TROYER
College of Pharmacy and Health Sciences: STEPHEN G. HOAG

GRACELAND COLLEGE

Lamoni, IA 50140
Telephone: (515) 784-5000

Founded 1895

President: WILLIAM T. HIGDON
Vice-President for Academic Affairs and Dean of Faculty: DAVID L. CLINEFELTER
Vice-President for Financial Affairs: JAMES R. MCKINNEY, Sr
Vice-President for Student Life: THOMAS L. POWELL
Vice-President for Institutional Advancement: DENNIS D. PIEPERGERDES
Vice-President for Enrollment Management and Dean of Admissions: BONITA A. BOOTH
Vice-President and Dean of Nursing: SHARON M. KIRKPATRICK
Registrar: M. JOYCE LIGHTHILL
Librarian: DIANE E. SHELTON

Library of 111,464 vols
Number of teachers: 79 (full-time)
Number of students: 1,166

GRINNELL COLLEGE

Grinnell, IA 50112
Telephone: (515) 269-4000
Fax: (515) 269-3408

Founded 1846

President: RUSSELL K. OSGOOD
Vice-President for Academic Affairs and Dean of the College: JAMES E. SWARTZ
Vice-President and Dean of Student Affairs: THOMAS CRADY
Librarian: CHRISTOPER MCKEE

Library of 378,000 vols
Number of teachers: 141, including 47 professors
Number of students: 1,261

IOWA STATE UNIVERSITY

Ames, IA 50011
Telephone: (515) 294-4111
E-mail: admissions@iastate.edu

Founded 1858

President: MARTIN C. JISCHKE
Provost: JOHN J. KOZAK
Vice-Provost for Research and Advanced Studies: PATRICIA B. SWAN
Vice-Provost for Extension: STANLEY R. JOHNSON
Vice-President for External Affairs: MURRAY M. BLACKWELDER
Vice-President for Business and Finance: WARREN R. MADDEN
Vice-President for Student Affairs: THOMAS L. HILL
Dean of Library: OLIVIA MADISON

Library of 2,104,000 vols, 2,888,000 microforms
Number of students: 24,899

Publications: *The Agriculturist, The Iowa Engineer, Outlook, Ethos, Iowa State Daily, Iowa Stater, Inside Iowa State, Visions, Inquiry, Marston Muses, The Gentle Doctor, Iowa State University Veterinarian.*

DEANS

Agriculture: DAVID G. TOPEL
Business: BENJAMIN ALLEN
Design: MARK ENGELBRECHT
Education: WALTER GMELCH
Engineering: JAMES L. MELSA
Family and Consumer Sciences: CAROL MEEKS
Graduate College: PATRICIA B. SWAN
Liberal Arts and Sciences: JOHN DOBSON (acting)
Veterinary Medicine: RICHARD F. ROSS
Students: KATHLEEN A. MACKAY

HEADS OF DEPARTMENT

College of Agriculture:

BAKER, T. C., Entomology
BIRT, D., Food Science and Human Nutrition
BRAUN, E. J., Plant Pathology
CANTRELL, R. P., Agronomy
CARTER, R. I., Agricultural Education and Studies
CHAPLIN, M. H., Horticulture
ENGER, M. D., Zoology and Genetics
GOUDY, W. J., Sociology
ISAACSON, D. L., Statistics
KELLY, J. M., Forestry
MARPLE, D., Animal Science
MELVIN, S. W., Agricultural and Biosystems Engineering
MENZEL, B. W., Animal Ecology
MIRANOWSKI, J., Agricultural Economics
NILSEN-HAMILTON, M., Biochemistry and Biophysics
THOEN, C. O., Microbiology, Immunology and Preventive Medicine (acting)

College of Business:

RALSTON, A., Accounting and Finance (acting)
SHRADER, C. B., Management, Marketing, Transportation and Logistics

College of Design:

KELLER, J. T., Landscape Architecture
MAHAYNI, R., Community and Regional Planning
SEGREST, R. T., Architecture
STIEGLITZ, M., Art and Design

College of Education:

ANDERSON, D., Physical Education and Leisure Studies
DUGGER, J. C., Industrial Education and Technology
ROBINSON, D., Professional Studies (acting)
THOMPSON, E., Curriculum and Instruction

WOOD, S., Health and Human Performance (acting)
ZBARACKI, R., Curriculum and Instruction (acting)

College of Engineering:
AKINC, M., Materials Science and Engineering
DEVRIES, W. R., Mechanical Engineering
EGBELU, P. J., Industrial and Manufacturing Systems Engineering
GLATZ, C., Chemical Engineering
GREIMANN, L. F., Civil and Construction Engineering
RUDOLPHI, T. J., Aerospace Engineering and Engineering Mechanics
VENKATA, S. S., Electrical Engineering and Computer Engineering

College of Family and Consumer Sciences:
BIRT, D., Food Science and Human Nutrition
COWAN, D. L., Family and Consumer Sciences Education and Studies (acting)
GASKILL, L. A. R., Textiles and Clothing
MACDONALD, M. M., Human Development and Family Studies
WALSH, T. E., Hotel, Restaurant and Institution Management

College of Liberal Arts and Sciences:
CAKERICE, I., Air Force Aerospace Studies
CARPENTER, S. C., Military Science and Tactics
EIGHMEY, J., Journalism and Mass Communication
ENGER, M. D., Zoology and Genetics
EPPERSON, D. L., Psychology (acting)
FINNEMORE, D. K., Physics and Astronomy
GOUDY, W., Sociology
GUNZBURGER, M., Mathematics
HAUG, S. E., Music
HENRY, M., Foreign Languages and Literatures
ISAACSON, D. L., Statistics
JAMES, P., Political Science
KENT, T. L., English
KRAUS, G., Chemistry
MCJIMSEY, G. T., History
MAXEY, J. D., NavaL Science and Tactics
MIRANOWSKI, J., Economics
NILSEN-HAMILTON, M., Biochemistry and Biophysics
OLDEHOEFT, A. E., Computer Science
OLIVER, D., Botany
ROBINSON, W., Philosophy
SPRY, P. G., Geological and Atmospheric Sciences
WHITEFORD, M. B., Anthropology

College of Veterinary Medicine:
BROWN, C. M., Veterinary Clinical Sciences
CHEVILLE, N. F., Veterinary Pathology
ENGEN, R. L., Veterinary Physiology and Pharmacology
EVANS, L. E., Veterinary Clinical Sciences
GREER, M. H., Veterinary Anatomy
OSWEILER, G., Veterinary Diagnostic Laboratory
THOEN, C. O., Microbiology, Immunology and Preventive Medicine (acting)

ATTACHED RESEARCH INSTITUTES AND CENTRES

Agriculture and Home Economics Experiment Station: Dir DAVID G. TOPEL.

Alien and Hostile Environments Research Instrumentation Center: Dir MARC PORTER.

Ames Laboratory of US Department of Energy: Dir T. J. BARTON.

Bridge Engineering Center: Man. F. WAYNE KLAIBER.

Business Research Institute: Dir BENJAMIN ALLEN (acting).

Carrie Chapman Catt Center for Women and Politics: Dir DIANNE G. BYSTROM.

Center for Advanced Technology Development: Dir ROBERT HARRIS.

Center for Agricultural and Rural Development: Dir STANLEY R. JOHNSON.

Center for Building Energy Research: Dir HOWARD N. SHAPIRO.

Center for Coal and the Environment: Dir ROBERT C. BROWN.

Center for Crops Utilization Research: Prof. LAWRENCE A. JOHNSON.

Center for Designing Foods to Improve Nutrition: Dir DIANE BIRT.

Center for Historical Studies of Technology and Science: Dir ALAN MARCUS.

Center for Immunity Enhancement in Domestic Animals: Dir JAMES ROTH.

Center for Indigenous Knowledge for Agricultural and Rural Development: Dir MIKE WARREN.

Center for Industrial Research and Service: Dir RICHARD A. GRIEVE.

Center for Interfacial and Crystallization Technology: Dir GLENN L. SCHRADER.

Center for Nondestructive Evaluation: Dir R. BRUCE THOMPSON.

Center for Physical and Computational Mathematics: Dir JAMES CORONES.

Center for Professional and Executive Development: Dir GARY AITCHISON.

Center for Rare Earths and Magnetics: Dir R. W. MCCALLUM.

Center for Teaching Excellence: Dir L. ZACHARY.

Center for Transportation Research and Education: Dir T. H. MAZE.

Computation Center: Dir JAMES E. BERNARD (acting).

Computational Fluid Dynamics Center: Man. JOHN TANNEHILL.

Electric Power Research Center: Dir GLENN C. HILLESLAND.

Energy Analysis and Diagnostic Center: Dir H. N. SHAPIRO.

Engineering Research Institute: Dir GEORGE BURNET (acting).

FAA Center for Aviation Systems Reliability: Dir DONALD O. THOMPSON.

Family and Consumer Sciences Research Institute: Dir DIANNE DRAPER.

Fire Service Institute: Dir GEORGE OSTER.

Henry A. Wallace Center for Agricultural History and Rural Studies: (vacant).

Industrial Relations Center: Dir PAULA MORROW.

Institute for Design Research and Outreach: Dir MARK ENGELBRECHT.

Institute for Physical Research and Technology: Dir JOEL SNOW.

Instructional Research Center: Dir R. P. VOLKER.

Instructional Technology Center: Dir D. A. RIECK.

International Institute for Theoretical Physics: Dir J. P. VARY.

Iowa Center for Emerging Manufacturing Technology: Dir JAMES E. BERNARD.

Iowa Energy Center: Dir PATRICIA B. SWAN (acting).

Iowa Lakeside Laboratory: Dir ARNOLD VAN DER VALK.

Iowa Manufacturing Technology Center: Dir D. A. SHEPARD.

Iowa Small Business Development Center: Dir RONALD MANNING.

Iowa Space Grant Consortium: Dir W. J. BYRD.

ISU Pappajohn Center for Entrepreneurship: Dir STEVEN T. CARTER.

ISU Research Foundation: Dir ALAN PAAU.

ISU Research Park: Dir DAVID ROEDERER.

Leopold Center for Sustainable Agriculture: Dir DENNIS KEENEY.

Meat Export Research Center: DENNIS G. OLSON.

Media Resources Center: Dir DONALD RIECK.

Microanalytical Instrumentation Center: Dir M. D. PORTER.

Microelectronics Research Center: Dir DAVID W. LYNCH.

Midwest Agribusiness Trade Research and Information Center: Exec Dir WILLIAM MEYERS.

Midwest Transportation Center: Dir THOMAS MAZE.

Mining and Mineral Resources Research Institute: Dir WILLIAM BUTTERMORE (acting).

National Soil Tilth Laboratory: Dir JERRY HATFIELD.

North Central Regional Center for Rural Development: Dir PETER KORSCHING.

Rare-earth Information Center: Dir KARL GSCHNEIDNER.

Office of Biotechnology: Dir WALTER FEHR.

Program for Women in Science and Engineering: Dir M. A. EVANS.

Research Institute for Studies in Education: Dir (vacant).

Liberal Arts and Sciences Research Institute: Dir ELIZABETH HOFFMAN.

Seed Science Center: Dir M. K. MISRA.

Social and Behavioral Research Center for Rural Health: Dir RAND CONGER.

Statistical Laboratory: Dir DEAN L. ISAACSON.

Utilization Center for Agricultural Production: Dir DENNIS G. OLSON.

Veterinary Medical Research Institute: Dir RICHARD F. ROSS.

Water Resources Research Institute: Dir DENNIS KEENEY.

IOWA WESLEYAN COLLEGE

Mount Pleasant, IA 52641
Telephone: (319) 385-8021
Founded 1842
President: Dr ROBERT J. PRINS
Registrar: EDWARD L. KROPA
Director of Admissions: JAMES W. LYNES Jr (acting)
Director of Library Services: PAT NEWCOMER
Library of 108,427 vols
Number of teachers: 42
Number of students: 804

LORAS COLLEGE

1450 Alta Vista, Dubuque, IA 52004-0178
Telephone: (319) 588-7100
Founded 1839
President: JOACHIM FROEHLICH
Registrar: JON A. CHRISTY
Librarian: R. KLEIN
Library of 438,527 vols
Number of teachers: 136
Number of students: 1,809

LUTHER COLLEGE

Decorah, IA 52101
Telephone: (319) 387-2000
Founded 1861
President: JEFFREY D. BAKER
Registrar: MARY B. KLIMESH
Librarian: (vacant)
Library of 301,155 vols
Number of teachers: 220
Number of students: 2,410

MAHARISHI UNIVERSITY OF MANAGEMENT

Fairfield, IA 52557
Telephone: (515) 472-7000
Fax: (515) 472-1179

Founded 1971 as Maharishi International University; present name 1995
Private control
Academic year: August to July
President: Dr BEVAN MORRIS
Executive Vice-President: Dr KEITH WALLACE
Registrar: JANE TREVELYAN
Librarian: CRAIG SHAW

DEANS

College of Arts and Sciences: Dr CATHERINE GORINI, Dr JAMIE GRANT
College of the Science of Creative Intelligence: Dr GEOFFREY WELLS
Graduate School: Dr JOHN FAGAN
School of Business and Public Administration: Dr KURLEIGH KING
College of Maharishi Ayur-Veda: Dr RICHARD AVERBACH, Dr STUART ROTHENBERG

Library of 150,000 vols
Number of teachers: 161
Number of students: 1,025

MARYCREST COLLEGE

1607 West 12th St, Davenport, IA 52804
Telephone: (319) 326-9512
Founded 1939
President: Sister ANNE THERESE COLLINS
Registrar: Mrs ELIZABETH SHORE
Librarian: Sister JOAN SHEIL
Library of 89,000 vols
Number of teachers: 73
Number of students: 1,035

MORNINGSIDE COLLEGE

1501 Morningside Ave, Sioux City, IA 51106
Telephone: (712) 274-5000
Fax: (712) 274-5101
Founded 1894
President: Dr JERRY ISRAEL
Registrar: MARY PESHEK
Director of Admissions: LORA VANDER ZWAAG
Director of Library: DARIA BOSSMAN
Library of 158,281 items
Number of teachers: 75
Number of students: 1,374

MOUNT MERCY COLLEGE

1330 Elmhurst Drive NE, Cedar Rapids, IA 52402-4798
Telephone: (319) 363-8213
Founded 1928
President: Dr THOMAS. R. FELD
Academic Vice-President: Dr SUSAN E. PAULY
Financial Vice-President: JOHN GIBBONS Jr
Student Affairs Vice-President: Dr ROBERT M. NICHOLSON
Development Vice-President: Sr. CEPHAS WICHMAN
Enrollment Vice-President: Dr ALEX J. POPOVICS
Registrar: MARGARET M. JACKSON
Librarian: MARILYN MURPHY
Library of 100,000 vols
Number of teachers: 100
Number of students: 1,224

NORTHWESTERN COLLEGE

101 7th St S.W., Orange City, IA 51041-1996
Telephone: (712) 737-7000
Fax: (712) 737-7247
E-mail: postmaster@nwciowa.edu
Founded 1882
President: JAMES E. BULTMAN
Academic Dean: ROBERT ZWIER
Director of Admissions: RON DE JONG
Vice-President for Development: JOHN H. GRELLER
Vice-President for Financial Affairs: WAYNE KOOIKER
Director of Financial Aid: CAROL BOGAARD
Dean of Student Affairs: PAUL BLEZIEN
Registrar: (vacant)
Librarian: RICHARD REITSMA
Library of 160,000 items
Number of teachers: 64
Number of students: 1,177

ST AMBROSE UNIVERSITY

518 West Locust St, Davenport, IA 52803-2898
Telephone: (319) 333-6000
Fax: (319) 333-6243
Founded 1882
President: Dr EDWARD J. ROGALSKI
Provost: DONALD J. MOELLER
Dean of Admissions: PATRICK O'CONNOR
Librarian: JOHN POLLITZ
Library of 150,000 vols
Number of teachers: 223
Number of students: 2,776
Publication: *Ambrose Scene* (quarterly).
Colleges of arts and sciences, human services, business.

SIMPSON COLLEGE

Indianola, IA 50125-1299
Telephone: (515) 961-6251
Fax: (515) 961-1498
Founded 1860
President: BRUCE HADDOX (acting)
Academic Dean: NANCY ST. CLAIR (acting)
Librarian: C. DYER
Library of 155,761 vols
Number of teachers: 75
Number of students: 1,958
Publications: *The Simpson Magazine* (quarterly), *Viewbook* (annually), *Admissions Newsletter* (3 a year).

UNIVERSITY OF DUBUQUE

2000 University Ave, Dubuque, IA 52001
Telephone: (319) 589-3000
Founded 1852
President: Dr JEFFREY F. BULLOCK
Provost and Vice-President Academic Affairs: Dr PAUL KESSLER
Interim Vice-President and Dean of the School of Theology: Dr BRADLEY LONGFIELD
University Librarian: JOEL SAMUELS
Libraries of 65,000 vols (College), 76,723 vols (Seminary), 150,000 vols (Schools of Theology)
Number of students: College 944, Seminary 122

UNIVERSITY OF IOWA

Iowa City, IA 52242
Telephone: (319) 335-3549
Fax: (319) 335-0807
Founded 1847
State control
Academic year: August to May (two terms and summer session)
President: MARY SUE COLEMAN
Provost: JON WHITMORE
Vice-President of Student Services and Dean of Students: PHILLIP E. JONES
Vice-President for University Relations: ANN RHODES
Vice-President for Finance and University Services: DOUGLAS K. TRUE
Vice-President for Research: DAVID J. SKORTON
Treasurer: DOUGLAS K. TRUE
Registrar: JERALD W. DALLAM
Director of Admissions: MICHAEL BARRON
Continuing Education: EMMETT J. VAUGHAN
University Librarian: SHEILA CRETH
Number of teachers: 3,500
Number of students: 27,871

DEANS

Liberal Arts: LINDA MAXSON
Law: N. WILLIAM HINES
Medicine: ROBERT P. KELCH
Dentistry: DAVID C. JOHNSEN
Pharmacy: (vacant)
Graduate: LESLIE B. SIMS
Engineering: RICHARD K. MILLER
Education: RICHARD SHEPHARDSON (acting)
Business Administration: GARY C. FETHKE
Nursing: MELANIE C. DREHER
Continuing Education: EMMETT J. VAUGHAN

HEADS OF DEPARTMENT

Business Administration:
- Accounting: DANIEL COLLINS
- Economics: CHARLES WHITEMAN
- Finance: J. SA-AADU
- Management and Organizations: MICHAEL MOUNT
- Management Sciences: PHILIP C. JONES
- Marketing: JOHN DELANEY

College of Dentistry:
- Endodontics: ERIC RIVERA
- Family Dentistry (Comprehensive Care): PATRICK LLOYD
- Operative Dentistry: JOHN REINHARDT
- Oral Pathology, Radiology and Medicine: GILBERT E. LILLY
- Oral and Maxillofacial Surgery: DANIEL LEW
- Orthodontics: JOHN S. CASKO
- Paediatric Dentistry: JIMMY PINKHAM
- Periodontics: GEORGIA JOHNSON
- Preventive and Community Dentistry: HENRIETTA LOGAN (acting)
- Prosthodontics: FORREST SCANDRETT

College of Education:
- Counseling, Rehabilitation and Student Development: DENNIS MAKI
- Curriculum and Instruction: WILLIAM NIBBELINK
- Planning, Policy and Leadership Studies: DAVID BILLS
- Psychological and Quantitative Foundations: STEWART EHLY

College of Engineering:
- Biomedical Engineering: MALCOLM H. POPE
- Chemical and Biochemical Engineering: JONATHON S. DORDICK
- Civil and Environmental Engineering: FORREST M. HOLLY, Jr
- Electrical and Computer Engineering: SUDHAKAR REDDY
- Industrial Engineering: PETER O'GRADY
- Mechanical Engineering: LEA-DER CHEN

College of Liberal Arts:
- African-American World Studies: FREDRICK WOODARD
- American Studies: JOHN RAEBURN
- Aerospace Military Studies: STEVEN FULTON
- Anthropology: RUSSELL CIOCHON
- Art and Art History, School: DOROTHY JOHNSON
- Asian Languages and Literature: PHILIP LUTGENDORF
- Biological Sciences: GARY GUSSIN
- Chemistry: DARRELL EYMAN
- Classics: HELENA DETTMER
- Communication Studies: STEVEN DUCK
- Comparative Literature: STEVE UNGAR

Computer Science: STEVEN BRUELL
Dance: HELEN CHADIMA
English: ADALAIDE MORRIS
Exercise Science: JERRY MAYNARD
French and Italian: GEOFFREY HOPE
Geography: REBECCA ROBERTS
Geology: PHILIP HECKEL
German: SARAH FAGAN
History: SHELTON STROMQUIST
Journalism and Mass Communication, School: JOHN SOLOSKI
Library and Information Sciences: PADMINI SRINIVASAN
Linguistics: WILLIAM DAVIES
Literature, Science and the Arts: JON RINGEN
Mathematics: BOR-LUH LIN
Military Science: JACOB GARCIA
Museum of Natural History: GEORGE SCHRIMPER (Curator)
Music School: DAVID NELSON
Philosophy: GUENTER ZOELLER
Physics and Astronomy: WAYNE POLYZOU
Political Science: JOHN CONYBEARE
Psychology: MICHAEL O'HARA
Religion School: ROBERT BAIRD
Rhetoric Program: FREDERICK ANTCZAK
Russian: RAY PARROTT
Social Work: PATRICIA KELLEY
Sociology: ROSS MATSUEDA
Spanish and Portuguese: MARIA DUARTE
Speech Pathology and Audiology: RICHARD HURTIG
Sport, Health, Leisure and Physical Studies: YVONNE L. SLATTON
Statistics and Actuarial Sciences: JAMES BROFFITT
Theatre Arts: ALAN MACVEY
Women's Studies: MARGERY WOLF
Writers' Workshop: FRANK CONROY

College of Medicine:
Anatomy: MARY J. C. HENDRIX
Anaesthesia: DAVID L. BROWN
Biochemistry: ARTHUR SPECTOR
Dermatology: RICHARD SONTHEIMER
Family Medicine: EVAN W. KLIGMAN
Internal Medicine: FRANCOIS M. ABBOUD
Microbiology: MICHAEL A. APICELLA
Neurology: ANTONIO DAMASIO
Obstetrics and Gynaecology: JENNIFER NIEBYL
Ophthalmology: THOMAS WEINGEIST
Orthopaedic Surgery: REGINALD COOPER
Otolaryngology-Head and Neck Surgery: BRUCE GANTZ
Pathology: RICHARD G. LYNCH
Paediatrics: FRANK H. MORRISS, Jr
Pharmacology: GERALD F. GEBHART
Physical Therapy Program: DAVID H. NIELSEN
Physiology and Biophysics: ROBERT FELLOWS
Preventive Medicine and Environmental Health: JAMES MERCHANT
Psychiatry: ROBERT ROBINSON
Radiology: MICHAEL VANNIER
Surgery: CAROL SCOTT-CONNER
Urology: RICHARD WILLIAMS

College of Nursing:
Human Responses to Illness: MARTHA CRAFT-ROSENBERG
Organizations and Systems: MARION JOHNSON
Theory and Health Promotion: MARY BLEGEN

College of Pharmacy:
Center for Advanced Drug Development: ALTA BOTHA (Dir)
Clinical and Administrative Pharmacy: WILLIAM MILLER
Iowa Drug Information Service: HAZEL SEABA (Dir)
Medicinal and Natural Products Chemistry: JOHN ROSAZZA

Graduate College:
Urban and Regional Planning: JOHN FULLER

UNIVERSITY OF NORTHERN IOWA

Cedar Falls, IA 50614
Telephone: (319) 273-2311
Founded 1876
President: ROBERT D. KOOB
Registrar: PHILIP PATTON
Librarian: HERBERT D. SAFFORD
Library of 765,000 vols
Number of teachers: 643 full-time, 191 part-time
Number of students: 13,108

UPPER IOWA UNIVERSITY

Box 1857, Fayette, IA 52142
Telephone: (319) 425-5200
Founded 1857
President: RALPH L. MCKAY
Senior Vice-President for Residential University: PHILIP LANGERMAN
Senior Vice-President for Extended University: SUZANNE JAMES
Registrar: LORI HEYING
Library Director: BECKY WADIAN
Library of 147,000 vols
Number of teachers: 300
Number of students: 4,061

WARTBURG COLLEGE

Waverly, IA 50677
Telephone: (319) 352-8200
Fax: (319) 352-8514
Founded 1852
President: Dr ROBERT L. VOGEL
Vice-President for Administration and Finance: Dr MIKE BOOK
Vice-President for Development: Dr RICHARD TORGERSON
Vice-President for Student Life and Dean of Students: Dr ALEXANDER SMITH
Vice-President for Academic Affairs and Dean of Faculty: Dr MARY MARGARET SMITH
Registrar: Dr EDIE WALDSTEIN
Director of Admissions: DOUG BOWMAN
Librarian: GILLIAN GREMMELS
Library of *c.* 130,000 vols
Number of teachers: 85
Number of students: 1,450

WESTMAR UNIVERSITY

Le Mars, IA 51031
Telephone: (712) 546-2000
Founded 1890
Four-year liberal arts and science university
President: Dr GLENN M. BALCH, Jr
Dean: Dr JOSEPHINE AROGYASAMI
Registrar: MARY PESHEK
Library of 99,667 vols
Number of teachers: 43
Number of students: 500

KANSAS

BAKER UNIVERSITY

POB 65, Baldwin City, KS 66006
Telephone: (913) 594-6451
Chartered 1858
United Methodist
President: Dr DANIEL M. LAMBERT
Provost and Academic Dean: Dr STUART DORSEY
Vice-President and Dean of the School of Professional and Graduate Studies: Dr DONALD CLARDY
Vice-President for University Relations: JERRY WEAKLEY
Dean of Student Life: JAMES TRONA
Vice-President for Business and Finance and Treasurer: ROBERT LAYTON
Librarian: Dr JOHN FORBES
Library of 65,000 vols
Number of teachers: 128
Number of students: 2,012
Publications: *Orange, Pieces, Baker World.*

BENEDICTINE COLLEGE

Atchison, KS 66002-1499
Telephone: (913) 367-5340
Fax: (913) 367-6566
Founded 1858, name changed 1971 as result of merger of College of St Benedict's and Mount St Scholastica College
President: DANIEL J. CAREY
Vice-President of Academic Affairs and Dean of the College: AIDAN O. DUNLEAVY
Dean of Enrollment Management: KELLY J. VOWELS
Dean of Students and Vice-President for Student Affairs: ELMER FANGMAN
Library of 301,123 vols
Number of teachers: 52
Number of students: 730 full-time

BETHANY COLLEGE

Lindsborg, KS 67456
Telephone: (913) 227-3311
Founded 1881
President: Rev. CHRISTOPHER THOMFORDE
Vice-President and Academic Dean: Dr AMANDA GOLBECK
Registrar: SHARON BRUCE
Librarian: JOHN STRATTON
Library of 115,000 vols
Number of teachers: 54
Number of students: 672

BETHEL COLLEGE

300 E 27th St, North Newton, KS 67117
Telephone: (316) 283-2500
Founded 1887
President: Dr DOUGLAS PENNER
Academic Dean: Dr JOHN SHERIFF
Librarians: GAIL STUCKY, BARBARA THIESEN, JOHN THIESEN
Library of 125,000 vols
Number of teachers: 59 full-time, 13 part-time
Number of students: 610
Publications: *Bulletin, Mennonite Life.*

EMPORIA STATE UNIVERSITY

1200 Commercial, Emporia, KS 66801-5087
Telephone: (316) 341-1200
Fax: (316) 341-5073
Founded 1863, university status 1976
President: KAY K. SCHALLENKAMP
Library of 711,000 vols
Number of students: 4,476 undergraduates, 1,530 graduates
Publications: *ESU Business World* (quarterly), *Kansas School Naturalist* (quarterly), *Spotlight* (quarterly), *Flint Hills Review.*

FORT HAYS STATE UNIVERSITY

Hays, KS 67601
Telephone: (913) 628-4000
Founded 1902
President: Dr EDWARD H. HAMMOND
Provost: Dr JAMES L. FORSYTHE (acting)

Vice-President for Administration and Finance: BRUCE SHUBERT
Vice-President for Student Development: Dr HERBERT SONGER
Registrar: Dr PATRICIA MAHON
Office of Budget and Planning: Dir LARRY GETTY
Librarian: LAWRENCE CAYLOR

Library of 650,000 vols in govt document section, 482,000 in regular collection
Number of teachers: 278
Number of students: 5,620

Publications: *Leader, Reveille.*

DEANS

Arts and Sciences: Dr LARRY GOULD
Business: Dr RICHARD PETERS (acting)
Health and Life Sciences: Dr TONY FERNANDEZ
Education: Dr CHARLES LEFTWICH
Graduate Faculty: Dr JAMES L. FORSYTHE

FRIENDS UNIVERSITY

2100 University Ave, Wichita, KS 67213
Telephone: (316) 295-5000
Fax: (316) 262-5027

Founded 1898

President: Dr BIFF GREEN
Vice-President for Academic Affairs: Dr G. ROBERT DOVE
Registrar: MARCIA MORTON
Vice-President, Administration and Finance: RANDALL C. DOERKSEN
Vice-President for University Advancement: HERVEY WRIGHT III
Vice-President for Student Affairs: SHERYL WILSON
Dean of Enrollment Management: SHERYL WILSON
Librarian: DAVID PAPPAS

Library of 81,000 vols
Number of teachers: 65
Number of students: 2,715

Publication: *Focus* (quarterly).

DEANS

College of Business: AL SABER
College of Continuing Education: H. GRIFFIN WALLING

KANSAS STATE UNIVERSITY

Manhattan, KS 66506
Telephone: (785) 532-6250
Fax: (785) 532-6393
E-mail: kstate@ksu.edu

Founded 1863

President: JON WEFALD
Provost: JAMES R. COFFMAN
Vice-President, Administration and Finance: TOM RAWSON
Vice-President, Institutional Advancement: ROBERT KRAUSE
Librarian: BRICE HOBROCK

Library: see Libraries
Number of teachers: 1,049
Number of students: 20,306

Publications: *General Catalog, Student Catalog, Summer School Catalog, K-Stater,* Extension Bulletins, *Collegian,* Engineering Bulletins, *Dimensions.*

DEANS

Graduate School: RONALD TREWYN (acting)
Agriculture: MARC JOHNSON
College of Engineering: TERRY KING
College of Architecture and Design: DENNIS LAW
College of Arts and Sciences: PETER NICHOLLS
College of Human Ecology: CAROL KALLETT
College of Veterinary Medicine: NEIL ANDERSON (acting)
College of Education: MIKE HOLEN
College of Business Administration: YAR EBADI
College of Technology: DENNIS KUHLMAN
Continuing Education: ELIZABETH UNGER

KANSAS WESLEYAN COLLEGE

Salina, KS 67401
Telephone: (785) 827-5541
Fax: (785) 827-0927

Founded 1886

President: MARSHALL P. STANTON
Registrar: DENISE HOEFFNER
Librarian: RUTH COX

Library of 75,938 vols
Number of teachers: 40 full-time, 5 part-time
Number of students: 688

OTTAWA UNIVERSITY

10th & Cedar Sts, Ottawa, KS 66067
Telephone: (913) 242-5200
Fax: (913) 242-7429

Founded 1865

President: HAROLD D. GERMER
Campus Provost: Dr ROBERT G. DUFFETT
Provost, Kansas City: Dr JAMES BILLICK
Provost, Phoenix: Dr FRED ZOOK
Provost, International: VERNON LARSON
Vice-President of University Relations: ROSEANNE BECKER
Registrar: Dr CINDY DERRITT
Director of Enrollment Management: ANDY CARRIER
Librarian: JANE ANN NELSON

Library of 87,260 vols
Number of teachers: 65
Number of students: 2,579 full-time

PITTSBURG STATE UNIVERSITY

1701 South Broadway, Pittsburg, KS 66762
Telephone: (316) 231-7000
Fax: (316) 232-7515

Founded 1903

President: JOHN R. DARLING
Registrar: Dr LEE R. CHRISTENSEN
Librarian: BOB WALTER

Library of 545,000 vols
Number of teachers: 325
Number of students: 6,589

DEANS

College of Arts and Sciences: Dr ORVILLE L. BRILL
School of Education: Dr TOM BRYANT
School of Technology: Dr TOM BALDWIN
Graduate Studies: Dr OLIVER HENSLEY
Kelce School of Business: Dr RONALD CLEMENT

SAINT MARY COLLEGE

Leavenworth, KS 66048
Telephone: (913) 682-5151
Fax: (913) 758-6140

Founded 1923

Roman Catholic liberal arts college

President: Rev. RICHARD J. MUCOWSKI
Dean: Dr SANDRA VAN HOOSE
Registrar: MINDA WHITESIDE
Librarian: PENELOPE LONERGAN
Dean of Students: SHEILA PEDIGO

Library of 110,000 vols
Number of teachers: 36
Number of students: 561

SOUTHWESTERN COLLEGE

100 College St, Winfield, KS 67156-2499
Telephone: (316) 221-4150
Fax: (316) 221-8224

Founded 1885

Professional, Liberal Arts and Sciences and Teacher Preparatory College

President: Dr CARL E. MARTIN
Registrar: JILL L. MEGREDY
Dean of Faculty: Dr DAVID A. NICHOLS
Director of Admissions: BRENDA D. HICKS
Library Director: Dr GREGORY J. ZUCK

Library of 60,000 vols
Number of teachers: 46
Number of students: 750

STERLING COLLEGE

Sterling, KS 67579
Telephone: (316) 278-2173
Fax: (316) 278-3188

Founded 1887

President: Dr ED JOHNSON
Registrar: Miss FRANCES N. CALDERWOOD
Librarian: LARRY BLAZER

Library of 85,000 volumes
Number of teachers: 32
Number of students: 490

TABOR COLLEGE

400 South Jefferson, Hillsboro, KS 67063
Telephone: (316) 947-3121
Fax: (316) 947-2607

Founded 1908

Liberal arts college

President: Dr H. DAVID BRANDT
Vice-President of Academic Affairs: Dr LON FENDALL
Vice-President of Student Development: JUDY HIEBERT
Vice-President for Advancement: Dr JACK BRAUN
Vice-President for Business and Finance: KIRBY FADENRECHT
Vice-President for Enrollment Management: GLENN LYGRISSE

Library of 66,000 vols
Number of students: 500

UNIVERSITY OF KANSAS

Lawrence, KS 66045
Telephone: (785) 864-2700

Organized by the Legislature 1864; opened 1866

State University, under the Kansas Board of Regents

Academic year: August to May

Chancellor: ROBERT E. HEMENWAY
Registrar: RICHARD MORRELL
Librarian: WILLIAM CROWE

Number of teachers: 2,084
Number of students: 27,407

Lawrence Campus:

Provost: DAVID SHULENBERGER
Vice-Chancellor for Research and Public Service: ROBERT BARNHILL
Vice-Chancellor for Student Affairs: DAVID A. AMBLER
Vice-Chancellor for Information Services: WILLIAM CROWE

DEANS

Graduate School: ANDREW DEBICKI
College of Liberal Arts and Sciences: SALLY FROST MASON
Continuing Education: ROBERT SENECAL
Regents Center: ROBERT CLARK
School of Business: THOMAS SAROWSKI
School of Education: KAREN GALLAGHER
School of Engineering: CARL E. LOCKE
School of Architecture and Urban Design: JOHN GAUNT
School of Fine Arts: PETER G. THOMPSON
School of Journalism and Mass Communications: JAMES GENTRY

School of Law: MICHAEL HOEFLICH
School of Pharmacy: JACK FINCHAM
School of Social Welfare: ANN WEICK
Students: JAMES KITCHEN

Kansas University Medical Center (Kansas City and Wichita):

Executive Vice-Chancellor: DONALD F. HAGAN
Hospital Chief Executive Officer: IRENE CUMMING
Vice-Chancellor for Administration: ROGER O. LAMBSON
Vice-Chancellor for Academic Affairs: A. L. CHAPMAN

DEANS

Graduate Studies and Research: A. L. CHAPMAN
School of Medicine (Kansas City): DEBORAH POWELL (Exec.)
School of Medicine (Wichita): JOSEPH MEEK
School of Nursing: KAREN MILLER
School of Allied Health: KAREN MILLER

WASHBURN UNIVERSITY OF TOPEKA

1700 S. W. College, Topeka, KS 66621

Telephone: (913) 231-1010
Fax: (913) 233-2780

Founded 1865

President: Dr JERRY B. FARLEY
Vice-President for Academic Affairs and Provost: Dr WAYNE SHELEY
Vice-President for Administration and Treasurer: LOUIS E. MOSIMAN
Registrar: CARLA RASCH
Librarian: REBECCA BOSTIAN

Library of 315,293 vols
Number of teachers: 300
Number of students: 6,626

Publications: *Alumni Magazine, Annual Report, Circuit Rider, KAW, Washburn Review, Washburn Update.*

DEANS

Law: JAMES M. CONCANNON
School of Business: Dr LAWRENCE McKIBBIN
School of Applied Education: Dr WILLIAM S. DUNLAP
College of Arts and Sciences: Dr KAREN RAY
School of Nursing: Dr ALICE A. YOUNG
Division of Continuing Education: (vacant)

WICHITA STATE UNIVERSITY

Wichita, KS 67260

Telephone: (316) 978-3000
Fax: (316) 978-3174

Founded 1894 as Fairmount College (Congregational), control transferred to City of Wichita 1926, added to the Kansas state higher education system 1964

President: EUGENE M. HUGHES
Vice-President for Academic Affairs: BOBBY PATTON
Vice-President for Student Affairs and Dean of Students: (vacant)
Vice-President for Administration and Finance: R. D. LOWE
Vice-President for University Advancement: ELIZABETH KING
Dean of Libraries and Media Resources: J. G. SCHAD

Library of 1,150,000 vols
Number of teachers: 466 full-time, 163 part-time
Number of students: 14,568

Publications: *Sunflower*, *Wichita State University Magazine, Wichita State Alumni News.*

DEANS

Liberal Arts and Sciences: DAVID GLENN-LEWIN
Education: JON ENGELHARDT
Fine Arts: W. MYERS
Engineering: W. J. WILHELM
Business Administration: GERALD GRAHAM
Health Professions: (vacant)
Graduate: MICHAEL VINCENT
University College: JAMES KELLEY

KENTUCKY

BELLARMINE COLLEGE

2001 Newburg Rd, Louisville, KY 40205-0671

Telephone: (502) 452-8211
Fax: (502) 456-1844

Founded 1950

President: Dr JOSEPH J. McGOWAN, Jr
Vice-President for Enrolment Management and Dean of Admissions: ED WILKES
Library Director: DAVID CHATHAM

Library of 90,000 vols
Number of teachers: 98 full-time, 96 part-time
Number of students: 2,362

DEANS

College of Arts and Science: Dr THERESA SANDOK
Rubel School of Business: Dr ED POPPER
Allan and Donna Lansing School of Nursing: Dr SUSAN HOCKENBERGER

BEREA COLLEGE

Berea, KY 40404

Telephone: (606) 986-9341

Founded 1855

President: LARRY D. SHINN
Academic Vice-President and Provost: STEVE BOYCE
Vice-President for Business: JEFFREY G. EISENBARTH
Vice-President for Finance: DEBORAH NEWSOM
Vice-President for Alumni Relations and Development: RODNEY BUSSEY
Vice-President for Labor and Student Life: GAIL WOLFORD
Dean of the College: JOHN BOLIN
Director of Information Resources: ANNE CHASE

Library of 248,000 vols
Number of teachers: 123
Number of students: 1,488

CAMPBELLSVILLE COLLEGE

200 West College Street, Campbellsville, KY 42718-2799

Telephone: (502) 264-6014
Fax: (502) 789-5020

Founded 1906

President: Dr KENNETH W. WINTERS
Librarian: Dr RONALD E. BRYSON

Library of 95,000 vols
Number of teachers: 45
Number of students: 1,100

CENTRE COLLEGE

Danville, KY 40422

Telephone: (606) 238-5200
Fax: (606) 236-9610

Founded 1819

President: JOHN ROUSH
Vice-President and Dean: JOHN C. WARD

Library of 200,000 vols and 850 periodicals
Number of teachers: 90
Number of students: 1,000

CUMBERLAND COLLEGE

Williamsburg, KY 40769

Telephone: (606) 549-2200

Founded 1889

President: Dr JAMES H. TAYLOR
Registrar: EMILY MEADORS
Vice-President for Academic Affairs: JOSEPH E. EARLY
Dean of College Personnel: Dr J. P. DUKE
Librarian: LOIS WORTMAN

Library of 155,000 vols
Number of teachers: 112
Number of students: 1,900

EASTERN KENTUCKY UNIVERSITY

Richmond, KY 40475

Telephone: (606) 622-1000

Founded 1906

President: ROBERT KUSTRA
Vice-President for Academic Affairs and Research: RUSSELL ENZIE
Registrar: JILL ALLGIER
Librarian: MARCIA J. MYERS

Library of 875,000 vols
Number of teachers: 626
Number of students: 15,161

GEORGETOWN COLLEGE

Georgetown, KY 40324-1696

Telephone: (502) 863-8011
Fax: (502) 868-8891

Founded 1829

President: Dr WILLIAM H. CROUCH, Jr
Senior Vice-President for Academic Programs: Dr CHARLES BOEHMS
Executive Vice-President: Dr TOM E. BENBERG
Senior Vice-President: (vacant)
Librarian: RICHARD J. BURTT

Library of 123,000 vols
Number of teachers: 105
Number of students: 1,514

KENTUCKY STATE UNIVERSITY

Frankfort, KY 40601

Telephone: (502) 227-6000
Fax: (502) 227-6490

Founded 1886

President: Dr GEORGE W. REID
Vice-President for Academic Affairs: (vacant)
Vice-President for Student Affairs: Mrs BETTY GIBSON
Vice-President for Finance and Administration: (vacant)
Director of Records, Registration and Admissions: DEBORAH TILLETT
Director of Libraries: KAREN McDANIEL

Library of 304,000 bound vols
Number of teachers: 129
Number of students: 2,288

KENTUCKY WESLEYAN COLLEGE

3000 Frederica St, Owensboro, KY 42301

Telephone: (502) 926-3111
Fax: (502) 926-3196

Founded 1858

President: Dr WESLEY H. POLING
Dean: Dr M. MICHAEL FAGAN
Dean of Admission and Financial Aid: SCOT J. SCHAEFFER

Library of 150,000 vols
Number of teachers: 44 full-time, 21 part-time
Number of students: 711 full-time, 66 part-time

MOREHEAD STATE UNIVERSITY

Morehead, KY 40351

Telephone: (606) 783-2221
Fax: (606) 783-2678

Founded 1922

President: Dr RONALD G. EAGLIN
Executive Vice-President for Academic Affairs: Dr JOHN C. PHILLEY
Vice-President for Administration and Fiscal Services: PORTER DAILEY
Vice-President for Student Life: D. MICHAEL MINCEY
Vice-President for University Advancement: KEITH KAPPES
Director of Admissions: CHARLES MYERS
Director of Libraries: LARRY BESANT

Library of 483,730 vols
Number of teachers: 341
Number of students: 6,202 full-time, 2,252 part-time

MURRAY STATE UNIVERSITY

Murray, KY 42071-0009

Telephone: (502) 762-3011

Founded 1922

President: KERN ALEXANDER
Provost and Vice-President for Academic Affairs: (vacant)
Vice-President for Administrative Services: TOM DENTON
Vice-President for Student Affairs: DON ROBERTSON
Vice-President for Institutional Advancement: (vacant)
Dean of Admissions: PHIL BRYAN
Dean of Libraries: COY HARMON

Library of 891,000 vols
Number of teachers: 355
Number of students: 6,707 full-time, 2,104 part-time

PIKEVILLE COLLEGE

Pikeville, KY 41501

Telephone: (606) 432-9200

Founded 1889

President: HAROLD H. SMITH
Dean of the College: WALLACE CAMPBELL
Librarian: LEE ROBBINS

Library of 94,000 vols
Number of teachers: 55
Number of students: 771

SPALDING UNIVERSITY

851 South Fourth St, Louisville, KY 40203

Telephone: (502) 585-9911
Fax: (502) 585-7158

Founded 1814

President: THOMAS R. OATES
Vice-President for Administrative Services: ISHMON BURKS
Vice-President for Finance: ED GALANIF
Vice-President for University Advancement: MARY MERSHON REISERT
Provost and Dean of Graduate Studies: Dr M. JANICE MURPHY
Director of Admission: DOROTHY G. ALLEN
Director of Enrollment Management: C. BRIAN KESSE
Director of Financial Aid: BETTY HARLAN
Dean of Students: Dr DEBORAH FORD
Dean, College of Arts and Sciences: PHYLLIS PASSAFIUME
Dean, School of Education: Dr MARY T. BURNS
Dean, School of Nursing and Health Sciences: Dr CINDY CRABTREE
Dean, School of Professional Psychology and Social Work: Dr M. DUNCAN STANTON
Chair, School of Business: DAVID HUDSON

Library of 212,000 vols
Number of teachers: 86
Number of students: 1,423

THOMAS MORE COLLEGE

333 Thomas More Parkway, Crestview Hills, KY 41017

Telephone: (606) 341-5800

Founded 1921

President: Rev. Dr WILLIAM F. CLEVES
Registrar: PATSY KENNER
Librarian: JAMES MCKELLOGG

Library of 128,000 vols
Number of teachers: 68 full-time, 62 part-time
Number of students: 1,500

TRANSYLVANIA UNIVERSITY

300 N. Broadway, Lexington, KY 40508-1797

Telephone: (606) 233-8111

Founded 1780 as Transylvania Seminary, inc. as Transylvania University 1799

President: CHARLES L. SHEARER
Vice-President and Dean of the College: JAMES G. MOSELEY
Chief Financial Officer: JERRY RAY
Director of Admissions: JOHN GAINES
Registrar: JAMES MILLS
Librarian: KATHLEEN BRYSON

Library of 115,000 vols
Number of teachers: 64
Number of students: 926

UNION COLLEGE

Barbourville, KY 40906-1499

Telephone: (606) 546-4151
Fax: (606) 546-1217

Founded 1879

President: DAVID C. JOYCE
Registrar: BETTY LYNNE BERNHARDT
Vice-President for Academic Affairs: VERNON G. MILES
Vice-President for Planning and Human Resources: EDWARD H. BLACK
Vice-President for Business Affairs: CHERYL A. BROWN
Vice-President for Advancement: JODIE K. BARNES
Vice-President for Student Life and Dean of Students: EDWARD DE ROSSET
Dean of Graduate Academic Affairs: WILLIAM E. BERNHARDT
Dean of Admissions and Financial Aid: ROBERT W. BENNETT
Librarian: TARA L. COOPER

Library of 100,000 vols, 2,500 microfilm and 329,000 microfiche
Number of teachers: 56
Number of students: 1,016

UNIVERSITY OF KENTUCKY

Lexington, KY 40506

Telephone: (606) 257-9000
Telex: 204009
Fax: (606) 257-4000

Founded 1865

Academic year: August to May

President: Dr CHARLES T. WETHINGTON, Jr
Vice-President for Research and Graduate Studies: Dr FITZGERALD BRAMWELL
Vice-President for Information Systems: EUGENE R. WILLIAMS
Vice-President for University Relations: JOSEPH T. BURCH
Vice-President for Fiscal Affairs: GEORGE DEBIN
Vice-President for Management and Budget: EDWARD A. CARTER
Chancellor, Lexington Campus: Dr ELISABETH A. ZINSER
Vice-Chancellor for Minority Affairs: LAURETTA F. BYARS
Vice-Chancellor for Student Affairs: Dr JAMES M. KUDER
Vice-Chancellor for Administration: JACK C. BLANTON
Chancellor for the Albert B. Chandler Medical Center: Dr JAMES W. HOLSINGER
Assistant to the President for Administrative Affairs: Dr BEN W. CARR, Jr
Director of Admissions: PATRICK C. HERRING
Registrar: DONALD E. WITT
Director of Libraries: PAUL A. WILLIS

Library: see Libraries
Number of teachers: 1,924
Number of students: 29,090

Publications: *Agricultural Experimental Station Bulletin, Bureau of Business Research Bulletin, Bureau of Community Service Bulletin, Bureau of Government Research Bulletin, Bureau of School Service Bulletin, Engineering Experiment Station Bulletin, Kentucky Alumnus, Kentucky Engineer, Kentucky Law Journal, Report to Kentucky Schools, Romance Quarterly, The Kentuckian, University of Kentucky Bulletin.*

DEANS

College of Agriculture: Dr C. ORAN LITTLE
College of Arts and Sciences: Dr DONALD J. SANDS (acting)
College of Communications and Information Studies: Dr DOUGLAS A. BOYD
College of Engineering: Dr THOMAS W. LESTER
College of Fine Arts: Dr RHODA-GALE POLLACK
College of Human Environmental Sciences: Dr RETIA S. WALKER
College of Law: Dr DAVID E. SHIPLEY
College of Education: Dr SHIRLEY C. RAINES
College of Business and Economics: Dr RICHARD W. FURST
College of Pharmacy: Dr JORDAN L. COHEN
College of Medicine: Dr EMERY A. WILSON
College of Nursing: Dr C. A. WILLIAMS
College of Dentistry: Dr LEON A. ASSAEL
College of Allied Health Professions: Dr T. C. ROBINSON
College of Architecture: DAVID MOHNEY
College of Social Work: ED SAGAN (acting)
Graduate School: Dr MICHAEL T. NIETZEL
Undergraduate Studies: Dr LOUIS J. SWIFT
Lexington Community College: Dr JAMES P. CHAPMAN (acting)

UNIVERSITY OF LOUISVILLE

Louisville, KY 40292

Telephone: (852) 588-5555
Fax: (852) 588-5682

Founded 1798

President: JOHN W. SHUMAKER
University Provost: WALLACE V. MANN
Vice-President for Finance and Administration: LARRY L. OWSLEY
Vice-President for Student Affairs: DENISE D. GIFFORD (acting)
Vice-President for Development and Alumni: WILLIAM J. ROTHWELL
Vice-President for Health Affairs: DONALD R. KMETZ
Vice-President for Information Technology: RONALD MOORE
Vice-President for Research and Development: PATRICK W. FLANAGAN
Registrar: KATHY OTTO
University Librarian: RALZE DORR (acting)

Number of teachers: 1,154
Number of students: 21,218

Publications: *The Cardinal, Inside U of L.*

DEANS

Arts and Sciences: Dr DAVID HOWARTH
Medicine: DONALD KMETZ
Law: DON BURNETT, Jr

Graduate Programs and Research: PATRICK W. FLANAGAN
Dentistry: ROWLAND A. HUTCHINSON
Engineering (Speed Scientific School): THOMAS HANLEY
Music: HERBERT KOERSELMAN
School of Education: RAPHAEL NYSTRAND
Business School: ROBERT L. TAYLOR
Kent School of Social Work: THOMAS LAWSON (acting)
School of Allied Health Sciences: PATRICIA WALKER (acting)
School of Nursing: PAULETTE ADAMS (acting)

WESTERN KENTUCKY UNIVERSITY

College Heights, Bowling Green, KY 42101

Telephone: (502) 745-0111

Founded 1906

President: Dr THOMAS C. MEREDITH
Vice-President (Finance and Administration): Dr JAMES RAMSEY
Vice-President (Academic Affairs): Dr ROBERT V. HAYNES
Vice-President (Student Affairs): Dr JERRY WILDER
Registrar: Mrs FREIDA EGGLETON
Dean of Libraries: Dr MICHAEL BINDER
Library of 1,060,000 vols
Number of teachers: 554 full-time, 290 part-time
Number of students: 15,767

DEANS

Arts, Humanities, and Social Sciences: Dr DAVID LEE
Science, Technology and Health: Dr MARTIN HOUSTON
Business Administration: Dr J. MICHAEL BROWN
Education and Behavioural Sciences: Dr CARL R. MARTRAY
Student Life: HOWARD BAILEY
Academic Services: Dr RONNIE SUTTON

LOUISIANA

CENTENARY COLLEGE OF LOUISIANA

POB 41188, Shreveport, LA 71134-1188

Telephone: (318) 869-5011

Founded 1825

President: KENNETH L. SCHWAB
Dean of College: ROBERT BAREIKIS
Dean of Students: SCOTT GREENWOOD
Registrar: GARY YOUNG
Librarian: ROGER BECKER

Number of teachers: 70
Number of students: 743

Publications: *Yoncopin* (annually), *Conglomerate*, *Centenary Extra*, *Dimensions*, *This Is Centenary*.

DILLARD UNIVERSITY

2601 Gentilly Blvd, New Orleans, LA 70122

Telephone: (504) 283-8822

Founded 1869

President: Dr MICHAEL L. LOMAX
Registrar: CHARLES SAUNDERS
Director of Admissions: DARRIN RANKIN
Librarian: Dr THEODOSIA T. SHIELDS

Library of 140,000 vols
Number of teachers: 105 full-time, 23 part-time
Number of students: 1,488

ATTACHED CENTRE

National Center for Black–Jewish Relations

GRAMBLING STATE UNIVERSITY

Grambling, LA 71245

Telephone: (318) 247-3811
Fax: (318) 274-6172

Founded 1901

President: STEVE A. FAVORS
Registrar: KAREN LEWIS
Librarian: PAULINE W. LEE

Library of 294,000 vols

LOUISIANA COLLEGE

Pineville, LA 71359

Telephone: (318) 487-7011

Founded 1906

College of liberal arts and sciences under auspices of the Louisiana Baptist Convention

President: ROBERT L. LYNN
Academic Dean: STANLEY G. LOTT
Registrar: ALAN MOBLEY
Librarian: TERRY MARTIN

Library of 115,500 vols
Number of teachers: 109
Number of students: 1,245

LOUISIANA STATE UNIVERSITY SYSTEM

Baton Rouge, LA 70803

Telephone: (504) 388-2111

Founded 1860

President: ALLEN A. COPPING

Library of 3,600,000 vols
Number of students: 57,000

LOUISIANA STATE UNIVERSITY

Baton Rouge, LA 70803

Telephone: (504) 388-3202
Fax: (504) 388-5982

Founded 1860

Chancellor: WILLIAM L. JENKINS
Executive Vice-Chancellor and Provost: DANIEL FOGEL
Vice-Chancellor for Research: LYNN JELINSKI
Vice-Chancellor for Finance and Administrative Services: JERRY BAUDIN
Vice-Chancellor for Student Services: ART GOULAS (interim)
Chancellor of LSU Agriculture Center: WILLIAM RICHARDSON
Chancellor of Law Center: HOWARD L'ENFANT Jr (interim)
Director of Libraries: JENNIFER CARGILL

Number of students: 29,000

DEANS

Graduate School: JOHN LARKIN (interim)
Junior Division: CAROLYN COLLINS
General College: JACK B. PARKER
Division of Continuing Education: DANIEL WALSH Jr
College of Agriculture: KENNETH KOONCE
College of Arts and Sciences: KARL ROIDER
College of Basic Sciences: PETER RABIDEAU
College of Business Administration: THOMAS CLARK
College of Education: BARBARA FUHRMANN
College of Engineering: ADAM BOURGOYNE
School of Social Work: KENNETH MILLAR
School of Library and Information Science: BERT BOYCE
School of Music: RONALD ROSS
College of Design: CHRISTOS SACCOPOULOS
School of Veterinary Medicine: DAVID HUXSOLL

LOUISIANA STATE UNIVERSITY AT ALEXANDRIA

8100 Hwy 71, South, Alexandria, LA 71302-9633

Telephone: (318) 473-6444

Founded 1960

Chancellor: Dr BEN F. MARTIN
Director of Business Affairs and Comptroller: CHARLES HOLLOWAY

Library of 120,000 vols
Number of students: 2,404

DEANS

Academic Affairs: Dr J. ROBERT CAVANAUGH
Student Affairs: Dr CHARNIA CHEATWOOD

LOUISIANA STATE UNIVERSITY AT EUNICE

POB 1129, Eunice, LA 70535

Telephone: (318) 457-7311
Fax: (318) 546-6620

Founded 1964

Chancellor: Dr WILLIAM J. NUNEZ, III
Vice-Chancellor for Academic Affairs: Dr ROBERT J. DEGER, Jr
Vice-Chancellor for Business Affairs: ARLENE TUCKER
Director of Continuing Education: MONTY SULLIVAN
Vice-Chancellor for Student Affairs: Dr JOHN L. COUVILLION

Library of 100,000 vols
Number of teachers: 75
Number of students: 2,681

HEADS OF DIVISIONS

Liberal Arts: Dr STEPHEN R. GUEMPEL
Sciences: (vacant)
Nursing and Allied Health: THERESA A. DEBECHE
Business and Technology: (vacant)

LOUISIANA STATE UNIVERSITY MEDICAL CENTER

New Orleans, LA 70112-2784

Telephone: (504) 568-4800

Chancellor: MERVIN L. TRAIL (acting)

Number of students: 2,500

DEANS

School of Medicine (New Orleans): ROBERT DANIELS
School of Medicine (Shreveport): ARTHUR M. FREEMAN
School of Graduate Studies: MARILYN L. ZIMNY
School of Dentistry: ERIC J. HOVLAND
School of Allied Health Professions: STANLEY H. ABADIE
School of Nursing: HELEN A. DUNN

LOUISIANA STATE UNIVERSITY IN SHREVEPORT

One University Place, Shreveport, LA 71115

Telephone: (318) 797-5000

Founded 1965

Chancellor: Dr VINCENT J. MARSALA
Provost and Vice-Chancellor for Academic Affairs: Dr STUART MILLS (acting)
Vice-Chancellor for Business Affairs: MICHAEL T. FERRELL
Vice-Chancellor for Student Affairs: Dr GLORIA RAINES
Vice-Chancellor for University Relations: MARTIN E. ALBRITTON Jr
Librarian: LAURENE E. ZAPOROZHETZ

Library of 180,422 vols
Number of students: 4,400

Publications: *Bulletin of the Museum of Life Sciences* (2 a year), *North Louisiana Historical Journal* (quarterly).

LOUISIANA TECH UNIVERSITY

Ruston, LA 71272

Telephone: (318) 257-0211

Chartered 1894 as Louisiana Industrial Institute and College; name changed to Louisiana Industrial Institute 1898; became Louisiana Polytechnic Institute 1921, became Louisiana Tech University 1970

President: DANIEL D. RENEAU
Vice-President for Academic Affairs: Dr KENNETH REA
Vice-President for Administrative Affairs: (vacant)
Vice-President for Student and Alumni Affairs: Dr JEAN HALL
Vice-President for Research and Development and Dean of the Graduate School: Dr STUART DEUTSCH
Registrar: PHILLIP WASHINGTON
Director of Libraries: Dr REBECCA STENZEL

Library of 1,400,000 vols
Number of teachers: 400
Number of students: over 10,000

DEANS

College of Natural and Applied Sciences: Dr SHIRLEY REAGAN
College of Arts and Sciences: Dr ED JACOBS
College of Administration and Business: Dr JOHN EMERY
College of Education: Dr JERRY W. ANDREWS
College of Engineering and Science: Dr BARRY BENEDICT

LOYOLA UNIVERSITY

6363 St Charles Ave, New Orleans, LA 70118
Telephone: (504) 865-3847

Founded 1905 as Loyola College; chartered as University 1912

President: Rev. BERNARD P. KNOTH
Vice-President for Academic Affairs and Dean of Faculties: DAVID C. DANAHAR
Vice-President for Business and Finance: JOHN L. ECKHOLDT
Vice-President for Institutional Advancement: JOSEPH J. MANSFIELD
Vice-President for Student Affairs: (vacant)
Dean of Admissions: NAN MASSINGILL
Dean of Libraries: MARY LEE SWEAT

Library of 255,000 vols; Law Library of 123,000 vols
Number of teachers: 275
Number of students: 4,665

Publications: *New Orleans Review, Loyola Law Review, Loyola Magazine.*

DEANS

College of Arts and Sciences: Dr ROBERT ROWLAND
College of Business Administration: Dr J. PATRICK O'BRIEN
School of Law: MARCEL GARSAUD, Jr (acting)
College of Music: Dr DAVID SWANZY
City College: (vacant)
Dean of Campus Ministry: Fr JOSEPH CURRIE

McNEESE STATE UNIVERSITY

Lake Charles, LA 70609
Telephone: (318) 475-5000

Founded 1939

President: Dr ROBERT D. HEBERT
Registrar: Miss LINDA FINLEY
Librarian: NANCY KHOURY

Number of teachers: 292
Number of students: 8,444

Publications: *The Log, The McNeese Review, The Contraband* (weekly), *Alumni Newsletter* (3 a year), *The McNeese Arena* (1 a year), *The McNeese Update* (3 a year).

DEANS

College of Education: Dr HUGH FRUGÉ
Graduate School: Dr THOMAS G. WHEELER
College of Liberal Arts: Dr MILLARD T. JONES
College of Science: Dr GEORGE F. MEAD, Jr
College of Business: Dr ELDON R. BAILEY
College of Engineering and Technology: Dr CARROLL KARKALITS
College of Nursing: Dr ANITA FIELDS

NICHOLLS STATE UNIVERSITY

Thibodaux, LA 70310
Telephone: (504) 446-8111

Opened in 1948 as a junior college of Louisiana State University; became Francis T. Nicholls State College 1956, attained university status 1970

President: Dr DONALD J. AYO
Vice-President, Academic Affairs: Dr ALICE G. PECORARO (acting)
Vice-President, Business Affairs: LIONEL O. NAQUIN, Jr
Vice-President, Institutional Advancement: (vacant)
Vice-President, Student Affairs: Dr JOANNE FERRIOT
Library Director: MARK DAGANAAR

Library of 400,000 vols and periodicals and 380,000 microforms
Number of teachers: 308 (full-time)
Number of students: 7,184

DEANS

Dean of Freshman Division: Dr PETER B. STRAWITZ
College of Business Administration: Dr RIDLEY GROS
College of Education: Dr ROBERT J. CLEMENT
College of Arts and Sciences: Dr DAVID E. BOUDREAUX
College of Life Sciences and Technology: Dr GRACE MONK
Chef John Folse Culinary Institute: Dr JERALD CHESSER

NORTHEAST LOUISIANA UNIVERSITY

700 University Ave, Monroe, LA 71209
Telephone: (318) 342-1000
Fax: (318) 342-5161

Founded 1931 as college, attained university status 1970

President: LAWSON L. SWEARINGEN, Jr
Provost and Vice-President for Academic Affairs: Dr ARLEN R. ZANDER
Registrar: Dr JAMES ROBERTSON, Jr
Librarian: DONALD R. SMITH

Library of 1,054,000 vols
Number of teachers: 521
Number of students: 11,553

NORTHWESTERN STATE UNIVERSITY OF LOUISIANA

Natchitoches, LA 71497
Telephone: (318) 357-6441
Fax: (318) 357-4223

Founded 1884 as college, attained university status 1970

President: RANDALL J. WEBB
Registrar: LILLIE BELL
Librarian: ADA JARRED

Library of 313,000 vols
Number of teachers: 300
Number of students: 9,000

OUR LADY OF HOLY CROSS COLLEGE

4123 Woodland Drive, New Orleans, LA 70131-7399
Telephone: (504) 394-7744
Fax: (504) 391-2421

Founded 1916

President: Rev. THOMAS E. CHAMBERS
Vice-President of Academic Affairs: Dr GERALD F. DE LUCA
Registrar: JUNE AMUNDSON
Librarian: Sister HELEN FONTENOT

Library of 201,807 vols
Number of teachers: 87
Number of students: 1,300

SOUTHEASTERN LOUISIANA UNIVERSITY

University Station, Hammond, LA 70402
Telephone: (504) 549-2000
Fax: (504) 549-2061

Founded 1925 as college, attained university status 1970

President: SALLY CLAUSEN
Provost: Dr RANDY MOFFETT
Vice-President for Administration: STEPHEN SMITH
Vice-President for University Advancement: Dr JOE MILLER
Vice-President for Student Affairs: Dr PATSY CAUSEY
Director of Enrollment Services and Registrar: STEPHEN C. SOUTULLO
Librarian: KAY ADAMS

Library of 340,000 vols
Number of teachers: 447
Number of students: 15,330

SOUTHERN UNIVERSITY AND A & M COLLEGE SYSTEM

Baton Rouge, LA 70813
Telephone: (504) 771-4500

Founded 1880

President: LEON TARVER II
Executive Vice-President: EDWARD R. JACKSON
Vice-President for Planning and Evaluation: (vacant)
Vice-President for Finance and Business Affairs: TOLOR E. WHITE
Registrar: MARVIN ALLEN
Librarian: EMMA PERRY

Southern University and A & M College

Baton Rouge, LA 70813
Telephone: (504) 771-4500

Chancellor: MARVIN L. YATES
Vice-Chancellors: GERALD PEOPLES (Student Affairs), Dr WILLIAM MOORE (Academic Affairs)

Number of students: 9,172

Southern University in New Orleans

New Orleans, LA 70126
Telephone: (504) 286-5000

Chancellor: ROBERT B. GEX

Number of students: 4,323

Southern University at Shreveport

Shreveport, LA 71107
Telephone: (318) 674-3300

Chancellor: Dr JEROME GREENE

Number of students: 1,229

TULANE UNIVERSITY OF LOUISIANA

New Orleans, LA 70118
Telephone: (504) 865-5000

Founded 1834 as Medical College of Louisiana, became Tulane University of Louisiana 1884

President: EAMON M. KELLY
Provost: MARTHA W. GILLILAND
Chancellor: JOHN C. LAROSA

Senior Vice-President and General Counsel: RONALD MASON
Deputy Provost: ROBERT S. ROBINS
Vice-Presidents:
Institutional Advancement: JULIA I. WALKER
Institutional Program Development and Government/Agency Affairs: GENE D'AMOUR
Student Affairs: MARTHA SULLIVAN
Dean of Admissions and Enrolment Management: RICHARD WHITESIDE
Registrar: EARL D. RETIF
University Librarian: PHILIP LEINBACH

Library: see Libraries
Number of teachers: 926 full-time, 267 part-time
Number of students: 11,158

DEANS AND DIRECTORS

Dean of the Faculty of the Liberal Arts and Sciences: TERESA SUNTAR (acting)
College of Arts and Sciences: ANTHONY M. CUMMINGS
A.B. Freeman School of Business: JAMES W. MCFARLAND
School of Engineering: WILLIAM VANBUSKIRK
School of Architecture: DONALD GATZKE (acting)
School of Law: EDWARD SHERMAN
School of Medicine: JAMES CORRIGAN
School of Public Health and Tropical Medicine: ANNE ANDERSON (acting)
School of Social Work: SUZANNE ENGLAND
University College: RICK MARKSBURY (acting)
Tulane Regional Primate Research Center: PETER J. GERONE
Newcomb College: JEANIE WATSON

UNIVERSITY OF NEW ORLEANS

Lakefront, New Orleans, LA 70148
Telephone: (504) 280-6000
Fax: (504) 280-6872

Established in 1956 by Act 60 of Louisiana State Legislature

Metropolitan campus of the Louisiana State University System

Chancellor: GREGORY M. ST L. O'BRIEN
Vice-Chancellor for Academic Affairs and Provost: LOUIS PARADISE
Vice-Chancellor for Property and Facilities Management: PATRICK M. GIBBS
Vice-Chancellor for Governmental Affairs, Alumni and Development: ROBERT W. BROWN
Vice-Chancellor for Student Affairs and University Relations: DONALD A. PEKAREK
Vice-Chancellor for Financial Services, Comptroller and Chief Financial Officer: LINDA K. ROBISON
Vice-Chancellor for Research and Sponsored Programs: SHIRLEY LASKA
Dean of Academic Services and University Registrar: S. MARK STRICKLAND
Dean of Student Life: JANET CALDWELL
Dean of Library Services: JILL B. FATZER

Library of 1,100,000 vols
Number of teachers: 600
Number of students: 16,000

Publications: *Statistical Abstract of Louisiana* (3 a year), *Review of Business and Economics Research* (2 a year), *Metropolitan Report* (quarterly), *New Orleans Real Estate Market Survey* (2 a year), etc.

DEANS

College of Business Administration: TIMOTHY P. RYAN
College of Education: ROBERT WIMPELBERG
College of Sciences: JOE M. KING
College of Engineering: JOHN N. CRISP
College of Liberal Arts: PHILIP B. COULTER
College of Urban and Public Affairs: FREDERICK W. WAGNER
Metropolitan College: ROBERT L. DUPONT

UNIVERSITY OF SOUTHWESTERN LOUISIANA

USL Station, Lafayette, LA 70504
Telephone: (318) 482-1000
Fax: (318) 482-6195

Founded 1898

President: R. AUTHEMENT
Registrar: JAMES ROUGEAU (Associate Registrar)
Librarian: CHARLES TRICHE

Library of 733,000 vols
Number of teachers: 670
Number of students: 16,742

Publications: *The USL History Series*, *Southwestern Review* (annually), *Louisiana History* (quarterly), *Attakapas Gazette* (quarterly).

XAVIER UNIVERSITY OF LOUISIANA

7325 Palmetto St, New Orleans, LA 70125
Telephone: (504) 486-7411

Founded 1915

President: NORMAN C. FRANCIS
Vice-President for Academic Affairs: Dr DEIDRE D. LABAT
Director of Admissions: WINSTON BROWN
Director of Student Financial Aid: MILDRED HIGGINS
Librarian: ROBERT SKINNER

Library of 120,000 volumes
Number of teachers: 225
Number of students: 3,506

DEANS

College of Arts & Sciences: Dr HAROLD A. VINCENT
College of Pharmacy: Dr MARCELLUS GRACE
Graduate School: Dr ALVIN J. RICHARD

MAINE

BATES COLLEGE

Lewiston, ME 04240
Telephone: (207) 786-6100

Founded 1855

President: Dr DONALD W. HARWARD
Dean of Faculty: Dr MARTHA A. CRUNKLETON
Vice-President for Administrative Services and Dean of Admissions: WYLIE L. MITCHELL
Librarian: EUGENE WIEMERS

Library of 621,900 vols
Number of teachers: 174
Number of students: 1,672

BOWDOIN COLLEGE

Brunswick, ME 04011
Telephone: (207) 725-3000
Fax: (207) 725-3123

Incorporated 1794

President: ROBERT H. EDWARDS
Treasurer: KENT JOHN CHABOTAR
Dean for Academic Affairs: CHARLES R. BEITZ
Dean of Student Life: CRAIG W. BRADLEY
Vice-President for Development and College Relations: WILLIAM A. TORREY
Director of Research and Records: CHRISTINE BROOKS
Librarian: SHERRIE BERGMAN

Library of 760,000 vols
Number of teachers: 130
Number of students: 1,530

Publications: *Bowdoin Alumni Magazine* (quarterly).

COLBY COLLEGE

Waterville, ME 04901
Telephone: (207) 872-3000

Founded 1813

Undergraduate college of liberal arts

President: WILLIAM R. COTTER
Vice-President, Academic Affairs and Dean of Faculty: EDWARD H. YETERIAN
Administrative Vice-President: W. ARNOLD YASINSKI
Vice-President for Development and Alumni Relations: PEYTON RANDOLPH HELM
Dean of the College: EARL H. SMITH
Dean of Admissions and Financial Aid: PARKER J. BEVERAGE
Dean of Students: JANICE A. KASSMAN
Registrar: GEORGE L. COLEMAN II
Librarian: SUANNE MUEHLNER

Library of 500,000 volumes
Number of teachers: 160, including 44 professors
Number of students: 1,730

Publications: *Colby*, *President's Report*, *Report of Contributions*, *Colby Perspective*, *Colby Library Quarterly*, *Colby College Catalogue*.

SAINT JOSEPH'S COLLEGE

Standish, ME 04084-5263
Telephone: (207) 893-7746
Fax: (207) 893-7862

Founded 1912

President: Dr DAVID B. HOUSE
Registrar: TOM SAWYER
Vice-President of Academic Affairs: Dr DANIEL P. SHERIDAN
Librarian: Sister FLEURETTE KENNON

Library of over 50,000 vols
Number of teachers: 53 full-time, 43 part-time
Number of students: 750 full-time, 446 part-time (external 3,932)

UNIVERSITY OF MAINE

Orono, ME 04469
Telephone: (207) 581-1110

Founded 1865

President: PETER S. HOFF
Vice-President for Academic Affairs and Provost: JOHN A. ALEXANDER
Vice-President for Development: ROBERT J. HOLMES, Jr
Vice-President for Student Affairs: MARK W. ANDERSON (interim)
Vice-Provost for Undergraduate Education: DOUGLAS GELINAS
Vice-Provost for Research and Graduate Studies: DANIEL DWYER
Dean of Cultural Affairs and Libraries: ELAINE M. ALBRIGHT

Number of teachers: 608
Number of students: 9,213

Publications: *Bulletin*, *Maine Studies*, *Agricultural Experimental Station Publications*, *Co-operative Extension Bulletins*, *Technology Experiment Station Publications*.

DEANS

College of Liberal Arts and Sciences: Dr REBECCA EILERS
College of Public Policy and Health: Dr VIRGINIA GIBSON (acting)
College of Engineering: Dr JOHN FIELD (acting)
College of Education and Human Development: ROBERT COBB
College of Natural Sciences, Forestry and Agriculture: Dr G. BRUCE WIERSMA

UNIVERSITY OF MAINE AT FARMINGTON

86 Main St, Farmington, ME 04938
Telephone: (207) 778-7000

Founded 1864 as college, university status 1970

President: THEODORA J. KALIKOW
Vice-President for Academic Affairs and Provost: NANCY H. HENSEL
Vice President for Administration: ROGER G. SPEAR
Vice-President for Student and Community Services: WILLIAM W. GELLER
Director of Admissions: J. A. MCLAUGHLIN
Director of Library: FRANKLIN D. ROBERTS

Library of 105,000 vols
Number of teachers: 125
Number of students: 2,000

Publications: *Sandy River Review* (2 a year), *Salt* (quarterly).

DEANS

College of Education, Health and Rehabilitation: PAULA S. MORRIS
College of Arts and Sciences: ROBERT L. LIVELY

UNIVERSITY OF SOUTHERN MAINE

POB 9300, Portland, ME 04104-9300

Telephone: (207) 780-4141

Founded 1878

President: Dr RICHARD L. PATTENAUDE
Provost: Dr MARK LAPPING
Vice-President for Student Affairs: JUDITH RYAN
Vice-President for University Advancement: RICHARD STURGEON
Registrar: JOHN F. KEYSOR
Director of Admissions: DEBORAH JORDAN
Librarian: STEVEN C. BLOOM

Library of 371,000 volumes
Number of teachers: 425
Number of students: 10,230

MARYLAND

BOWIE STATE UNIVERSITY

14000 Jericho Park Rd, Bowie, MD 20715

Telephone: (301) 464-3000
Fax: (301) 464-7814

Founded 1865

President: Dr NATHANAEL POLLARD, Jr
Provost: Dr ESTHER WARD (acting)
Registrar: DHARMI CHAUDHARI
Librarian: COURTNEY FUNN

Library of over 180,000 vols
Number of teachers: 130
Number of students: 4,900

Publications: *BSU At A Glance* (monthly), *BSU Commuter* (monthly), *BSU Review* (2 a year).

DEPARTMENT CHAIRPERSONS

Behavioural Sciences and Human Services: Dr DORIS POLSTON (acting)
Business, Economics and Public Administration: Dr RICHARD BLALACK
Communications: Dr ELAINE BOURNE-HEATH
Computer Science: Dr NAGI WAKIM
Education: Dr O'DELL JACK
English and Modern Languages: Dr VIRGINIA GUILFORD
History, Politics and International Studies: Dr WILLIAM LEWIS
Fine and Performing Arts: Dr AMOS WHITE, IV
Natural Sciences and Mathematics: Dr KARL KIRKSEY (acting)
Nursing: Dr ELEANOR WALKER
ROTC: Maj. RODERICK ROBINSON

COLUMBIA UNION COLLEGE

Takoma Park, MD 20912

Telephone: (301) 891-4000

Founded 1904

Private (Seventh-day Adventist) liberal arts college

President: Dr CHARLES SCRIVEN
Dean: (vacant)
Vice-President, Finance: MARSHALL OGBURN
Director of Admissions: CINDY CARRENO
Registrar: Dr ANTHONY FUTCHER
Librarian: MARGARET VON HAKE

Library of 127,000 vols
Number of teachers: 53
Number of students: 1,212

Publications: *Reunion* (quarterly), *The Bulletin, Columbia Perspectives* (2 a year), *Golden Memories, Montage* (annually).

COPPIN STATE COLLEGE

2500 West North Ave, Baltimore, MD 21216

Telephone: (410) 383-5400
Fax: (410) 333-5369

Founded 1900; part of Univ. of Maryland System

President: CALVIN W. BURNETT
Provost and Vice-President for Academic Affairs: Dr HERMAN HOWARD
Vice-President for Business & Finance: GREGORY A. DAVIS
Vice-President for Student Life: Dr CLAYTON MCNEILL
Director, Institutional Research: TENDAI JOHNSON
Registrar: MARGARET TURNER
Librarian: MARY WANZA

Library of 101,000 vols, 266,000 microform titles, 688 current periodicals
Number of teachers: 110 full-time, 92 part-time
Number of students: 3,094 undergraduates, 496 postgraduates

FROSTBURG STATE UNIVERSITY

Frostburg, MD 21532

Telephone: (301) 687-4000
Fax: (301) 687-4737

Founded 1898; part of Univ. of Maryland System

President: Dr CATHERINE R. GIRA
Vice-Presidents:
Provost: CONSTANCE MCGOVERN
Student and Educational Services: ALICE R. MANICUR
University Advancement: Dr GARY HOROWITZ
Finance: ROGER BRUSZEWSKI
Registrar: RUTH CAMPBELL
Director of Admissions: EDGERTON DEUEL
Librarian: DAVID GILLESPIE

Library of 423,782 vols
Number of teachers: 305
Number of students: 5,295

GOUCHER COLLEGE

Baltimore, MD 21204

Telephone: (410) 337-6000

Founded 1885

President: JUDY JOLLEY MOHRAZ
Dean: ROBERT S. WELCH (acting)
Dean of Students: ELIZABETH NUSS
Registrar: DEIDRE L. PARISH
Vice-President for Enrollment Management: BARBARA FRITZE
Librarian: NANCY MAGNUSON

Number of teachers: 78
Number of students: 959

Publications: *Quindecim, Donnybrook Fair, Preface, The Goucher Quarterly, Goucher College Catalog, President's Bulletin.*

HOOD COLLEGE

Frederick, MD 21701-8575

Telephone: (301) 663-3131
Fax: (301) 694-7653

Founded 1893

President: SHIRLEY D. PETERSON
Vice-President and Dean of the Faculty: TOM SAMET
Vice-President for Administration and Finance: THOMAS M. BERGER
Vice-President for Development and College Relations: BRUCE E. BIGELOW
Vice-President and Dean of Students: OLIVIA WHITE
Vice-President for Enrollment Management: JOAN M. POWERS
Registrar: KATHY FARNSWORTH (acting)
Librarian: CHARLES KUHN

Library of 175,000 vols
Number of teachers: 90 f.t.e.

Publications: *Catalogue, Prospectus, Alumnae Magazine, Graduate Bulletin.*

DEANS

Academic Affairs: TOM SAMET
Graduate School: ANN BOYD

JOHNS HOPKINS UNIVERSITY

Baltimore, MD 21218

Telephone: (410) 516-8000

Founded 1876
Private control
Academic year: September to June

President: WILLIAM R. BRODY
Provost and Vice-President for Academic Affairs: STEVEN KNAPP
Senior Vice-President for Administration: JAMES T. MCGILL
Vice-President for Medicine: EDWARD D. MILLER
Vice-President for Development and Alumni Relations: ROBERT R. LINDGREN
Vice-President and General Counsel: ESTELLE A. FISHBEIN
Vice-President for Business Affairs: JOHN J. LORDAN
Registrar: HEDY SCHAEDEL

Library: see Libraries
Number of full-time teachers: 2,081
Number of students: 14,724

DEANS

School of Arts and Sciences: HERBERT KESSLER
School of Engineering: ILENE BUSCH-VISHNIAC
Faculty of Medicine: EDWARD D. MILLER Jr
School of Hygiene and Public Health: ALFRED SOMMER
School of Nursing: SUE K. DONALDSON
School of Continuing Studies: STANLEY C. GABOR
Paul Nitze School of Advanced International Studies: PAUL D. WOLFOWITZ
Peabody Conservatory of Music (Affiliated Institution): ROBERT SIROTA (Director)
Applied Physics Laboratory: GARY SMITH

PROFESSORS

School of Arts and Sciences:

ACHINSTEIN, P., Philosophy
ALEXANDER, K., Sociology
ANDERSON, W., French
ARRIGHI, G., Sociology
BAGGER, J., Physics and Astronomy
BALL, G., Psychology
BALL, L., Economics
BARKER, S. F., Philosophy
BARNETT, B., Physics and Astronomy
BEEMAN, K., Biology
BERRY, S., History
BESSMAN, M., Biology
BLUMENFELD, B. J., Physics and Astronomy
BOARDMAN, J. M., Mathematics
BOWEN, K., Chemistry
BRAND, L., Biology
BRIEGER, G., History of Science, Medicine and Technology
BROHOLM, C., Physics and Astronomy
BROOKS, J., History

BRYAN, B., Near Eastern Studies
BURZIO, L., Cognitive Science
CAMERON, S., English
CASTRO-KLAREN, S., Hispanic and Italian Studies
CHASE-DUNN, C., Sociology
CHERLIN, A., Sociology
CHIEN, C.-L., Physics and Astronomy
CHIEN, C.-Y., Physics and Astronomy
CHRISTENSEN, J., English
CONE, R. A., Biophysics
CONNOLLY, W., Political Science
COOPER, J., Political Science
COOPER, J. S., Near Eastern Studies
CORCES, V., Biology
CRENSON, M., Political Science
CROPPER, E., History of Art
CUMMINGS, M., Political Science
CURTIN, P., History
DAGDIGIAN, P., Chemistry
DAVID, S., Political Science
DAVIDSEN, A., Physics and Astronomy
DEFAUX, G., French
DEMPSEY, C., History of Art
DETIENNE, M., Classics
DIETZE, G., Political Science
DITZ, T., History
DIXON, S., Writing Seminars
DOERING, J., Chemistry
DOMOKOS, G., Physics and Astronomy
DRAPER, D., Chemistry, Biology, Biophysics
EBERT, J. D., Biology
EDIDIN, M., Biology
EGETH, H., Psychology
FAMBROUGH, D., Biology
FELDMAN, G., Physics and Astronomy
FELDMAN, P., Physics and Astronomy
FERGUSON, F., English
FERRY, J., Earth and Planetary Science
FISHER, G. W., Earth and Planetary Sciences
FLATHMAN, R. C., Political Science
FLEISHMAN, A., English
FORD, H., Physics and Astronomy
FORNI, P., Hispanic and Italian Studies
FREIRE, E., Biology, Biophysics
FRIED, M., Humanities and History of Art
FULTON, T., Physics and Astronomy
FYRBERG, E., Biology
GALAMBOS, L.P., History
GALLAGHER, M., Psychology
GARVEN, G., Earth and Planetary Sciences
GERSOVITZ, M., Economics
GINSBERG, B., Political Science
GOLDBERG, J., English
GOLDTHWAITE, R., History
GONZALEZ, E., Hispanic and Italian Studies
GORDON, R., Sociology
GREENE, J., History
GROSSMAN, A., English
HAMACHER, W., German
HAMILTON, B., Economics
HANNAWAY, O., History of Science, Medicine and Technology
HARDIE, L. A., Earth and Planetary Sciences
HARRINGTON, J., Economics
HECKMAN, T., Physics and Astronomy
HEDGECOCK, E., Biology
HENRY, R., Physics and Astronomy
HERTZ, N., Humanities Center
HOYT, A., Biology
HUANG, R. C., Biology
IRWIN, J., Writing Seminars, English
JOHNSON, M., History
JUSCZYK, P., Psychology
KAGAN, R., History
KARGON, R. H., History of Science, Medicine and Technology
KARLIN, K., Chemistry
KARNI, E., Economics
KATZ, R., Political Science
KEMPF, G., Mathematics
KESSLER, H., History of Art
KHAN, M. A., Economics
KIM, C. W., Physics and Astronomy
KINGSLAND, S., History of Science, Medicine and Technology

KNIGHT, F., History
KOHN, M., Sociology
KOLYVAGIN, V., Mathematics
KOSKI, W. S., Chemistry
KOVESI-DOMOKOS, S., Physics and Astronomy
KROLIK, J., Physics and Astronomy
LARRABEE, M. G., Biophysics
LATTMAN, E., Biophysics
LEE, Y. C., Biology
LEE, Y. K., Physics and Astronomy
LESLIE, S., History of Science, Medicine and Technology
LIDTKE, V., History
LOVE, W., Biophysics
MACCINI, L., Economics
MACKSEY, R., Humanities Center
MARSH, B., Earth and Planetary Sciences
MCCARTER, P. K., Near Eastern Studies
MCCARTY, R., Biology
MCCLOSKEY, M., Cognitive Science
MCGARRY, J., Writing Seminars
MELION, W., History of Art
MEYER, J. P., Mathematics
MICHAELS, W., English
MILLIS, A., Physics and Astronomy
MOFFITT, R., Economics
MOON, M., English
MOOS, H. W., Physics and Astronomy
MORAVA, J., Mathematics
MOUDRIANAKIS, E., Biology
NAGELE, R., German
NELSON, R., Psychology
NEUFELD, D., Physics and Astronomy
NICHOLS, S., French
NORMAN, C., Physics and Astronomy
OLSON, P. L., Earth and Planetary Sciences
ONO, T., Mathematics
OSBORN, T., Earth and Planetary Sciences
PAGDEN, A., History
PANDEY, G., Anthropology
PAULSON, R., English
PEVSNER, A., Physics and Astronomy
POLAND, D., Chemistry
POSNER, G. H., Chemistry
PRIVALOV, P., Biology
RANUM, O., History
REICH, D., Physics and Astronomy
ROBBINS, M., Physics and Astronomy
ROSEMAN, S., Biology
ROSS, D., History
ROWE, W., History
RUSSELL-WOOD, A. J. R., History
RYNASIEWICZ, R., Philosophy
SALAMON, L., Political Science
SCHLEIF, R., Biology
SCHNEEWIND, J. B., Philosophy
SCHWARTZ, G., Near Eastern Studies
SHALIKA, J., Mathematics
SHAPIRO, A., Classics
SHEARN, A., Biology
SHIFFMAN, B., Mathematics
SHOKUROV, V., Mathematics
SIEBER, H., Hispanic and Italian Studies
SILVERSTONE, H. J., Chemistry
SISSA, G., Classics
SMOLENSKY, P., Cognitive Science
SOGGE, C., Mathematics
SPIEGEL, G., History
SPRUCK, J., Mathematics
STANLEY, S., Earth and Planetary Sciences
STROBEL, D., Earth and Planetary Sciences
STRUEVER, N., Humanities and History
SVERJENSKY, D., Earth and Planetary Sciences
SWARTZ, M., Physics and Astronomy
SZALAY, A., Physics and Astronomy
TESANOVIC, Z., Physics and Astronomy
TOWNSEND, C., Chemistry
VALIS, N., Hispanic and Italian Studies
VEBLEN, D., Earth and Planetary Sciences
VISHNIAC, E., Physics and Astronomy
WALKER, J. C., Physics and Astronomy
WALKOWITZ, J., History
WALTERS, R., History
WELLBERY, D. P., German
WESTBROCK, R., Near Eastern Studies

WHITE, E. H., Chemistry
WILSON, G., Philosophy
WILSON, W. S., Mathematics
WOLF, S., Philosophy
WYSE, R., Physics and Astronomy
YANTIS, S., Psychology
YARKONY, D., Chemistry
YOUNG, H. P., Economics
ZELDICH, S., Mathematics
ZIFF, L., English
ZUCKER, S., Mathematics

GWC Whiting School of Engineering:

ANANDARAJAH, A., Civil Engineering
ANDREOU, A., Electrical and Computer Engineering
AWERBUCH, B., Computer Science
BARBARI, T., Chemical Engineering
BETENBAUGH, M. J., Chemical Engineering
BOLAND, J., Geography and Environmental Engineering
BOUWER, E. J., Geography and Environmental Engineering
BRUSH, G. S., Geography and Environmental Engineering
BUSCH-VISHNIAC, I. J., Mechanical Engineering
CAMMARATA, R., Materials Science and Engineering
DAVIDSON, F. M., Electrical and Computer Engineering
DONOHUE, M., Chemical Engineering
DOUGLAS, A. S., Mechanical Engineering
ELLINGWOOD, B. R., Civil Engineering
ELLIS, J. H., Geography and Environmental Engineering
FILL, J. A., Mathematical Sciences
FISHER, J., Geography and Environmental Engineering
FITZGERALD, E. R., Mechanical Engineering
GOLDMAN, A., Mathematical Sciences
GOODRICH, M. T., Computer Science
GOUTSIAS, J. I., Electrical and Computer Engineering
GREEN, R. E., Jr, Materials Science and Engineering
HAN, S.-P., Mathematical Sciences
HANKE, S., Geography and Environmental Engineering
HARVEY, D. W., Geography and Environmental Engineering
HOBBS, B. F., Geography and Environmental Engineering
JELINEK, F., Electrical and Computer Engineering
JONES, N. P., Civil Engineering
JOSEPH, R., Electrical and Computer Engineering
KAPLAN, A., Electrical and Computer Engineering
KATZ, J., Mechanical Engineering
KATZ, J. L., Chemical Engineering
KHURGIN, J., Electrical and Computer Engineering
KOSARAJU, S. R., Computer Science
LADE, P. V., Civil Engineering
MCHUGH, M. A., Chemical Engineering
MASSON, G. M., Computer Science
MENEVEAU, C. V., Mechanical Engineering
MEYER, G., Electrical and Computer Engineering
MILLER, M., Biomedical Engineering
NAIMAN, D. Q., Mathematical Sciences
O'MELIA, C. R., Geography and Environmental Engineering
PANG, J.-S., Mathematical Sciences
PARLANGE, M. B., Geography and Environmental Engineering
PAULAITIS, M. E., Chemical Engineering
PRINCE, J. L., Electrical and Computer Engineering
PROSPERETTI, A., Mechanical Engineering
RAMESH, J. T., Mechanical Engineering
REVELLE, C., Geography and Environmental Engineering

ROSEN, M., Materials Science and Engineering
RUGH, W. J., III, Electrical and Computer Engineering
SCHEINERMAN, E. R., Mathematical Sciences
SCHOENBERGER, E. J., Geography and Environmental Engineering
SEARSON, P. C., Materials Science and Engineering
SHARPE, W. N., Mechanical Engineering
STONE, A. T., Geography and Environmental Engineering
TAYLOR, R. H., Computer Science
WEINERT, H., Electrical and Computer Engineering
WESTGATE, C., Electrical and Computer Engineering
WIERMAN, J. C., Mathematical Sciences
WILCOCK, P. R., Geography and Environmental Engineering

Faculty of Medicine:

ABELOFF, M. D., Oncology and Medicine
ACHUFF, S. C., Medicine
ADKINSON, N. F., Jr, Medicine
ADLER, R., Ophthalmology and Neuroscience
AGNEW, W. S., Physiology and Neuroscience
AGRE, P. C., Medicine and Biological Chemistry
AMZEL, L. M., Biophysics and Biophysical Chemistry
ANDERSON, J. H., Radiology and Radiological Science, Diagnostic Radiology and Oncology
ANHALT, G. J., Dermatology and Pathology
ASKIN, F. B., Pathology
ATOR, N. A., Psychiatry and Behavioural Sciences
AUGUST, J. T., Pharmacology and Molecular Sciences, and Oncology
BACHORIK, P. S., Paediatrics
BARKER, L. R., Medicine
BARNHILL, R. L., Dermatology
BARTLETT, J. G., Medicine
BAUGHMAN, K. L., Medicine
BAUMGARTNER, W. A., Cardiac Surgery
BAYLESS, T. M., Medicine
BAYLIN, S. B., Oncology and Medicine
BECKER, L. C., Medicine
BELL, W. R., Medicine
BENZ, E. J., Jr, Medicine
BERG, J. M., Biophysics and Biophysical Chemistry
BIGELOW, G. E., Psychiatry and Behavioural Sciences
BLACKMAN, M. R., Medicine
BOEKE, J. D., Molecular Biology and Genetics
BOITNOTT, J. K., Pathology
BOROWITZ, M. J., Pathology and Oncology
BOTTOMLEY, P. A., Radiology, Biomedical Engineering and Medicine
BRADY, J. V., Psychiatry and Behavioural Sciences, and Neuroscience
BRANDT, J., Psychiatry and Behavioural Sciences
BREAKEY, W. R., Psychiatry
BREM, H., Neurosurgery and Oncology
BRESSLER, N. M., Ophthalmology
BRIEGER, G. H., History of Science, Medicine and Technology
BRINKER, J. A., Medicine
BRUSHART, T. M., Orthopaedic Surgery
BULKLEY, G. B., Surgery
BURDICK, J. F., Surgery
BURGER, P. C., Pathology, Oncology and Neurosurgery
BURKE, P. J., Oncology and Medicine
BURTON, J. R., Medicine
CAMERON, J. L., Surgery
CAMPBELL, J. N., Neurological Surgery
CAMPOCHIARO, P. A., Ophthalmology and Neuroscience
CAPUTE, A. J., Paediatrics
CASELLA, J. F., Paediatrics and Oncology
CATALDO, M. F., Behavioural Biology
CHAISSON, R. E., Medicine
CHANDRA, N., Medicine
CHAO, E. Y., Orthopaedic Surgery and Biomedical Engineering
CHARACHE, P., Pathology, Oncology and Medicine
CHATTERJEE, S. B., Paediatrics
CHERNOW, B., Medicine, Anaesthesiology and Critical Care Medicine
CHISOLM, J. J., Jr, Paediatrics
CINGOLANI, H., Medicine
CIVIN, C. I., Oncology and Paediatrics
CLEMENTS, J. E., Comparative Medicine and Neurology
COFFEY, D. S., Urology, Pharmacology and Molecular Sciences and Oncology
COLOMBANI, P. M., Paediatric Surgery and Oncology
CORNBLATH, D. R., Neurology
COTTER, R. J., Pharmacology and Molecular Sciences, and Biophysics
CRAIG, N. L., Molecular Biology and Genetics
CRAIG, S. W., Biological Chemistry and Pathology
CUMMINGS, C. W., Otolaryngology, Head and Neck Surgery and Oncology
DANG, C. V., Medicine, Oncology and Pathology
DANNALS, R. F., Radiology, Radiological Sciences and Nuclear Medicine
DEANGELIS, C., Paediatrics
DE JUAN, E., Jr, Ophthalmology
DELATEUR, B. J., Physical and Rehabilitation Medicine
DENCKLA, M. B., Neurology and Paediatrics
DEPAULO, J. R., Psychiatry and Behavioural Sciences
DESIDERIO, S. V., Molecular Biology and Genetics
DEVREOTES, P. N., Biological Chemistry
DICELLO, J. F., Oncology
DIEHL, A. M., Medicine
DONEHOWER, R. C., Oncology and Medicine
DONOWITZ, M., Medicine
DOVER, G. J., Paediatrics and Oncology
DRACHMAN, D. B., Neurology and Neuroscience
EGGLESTON, P. A., Paediatrics
EIPPER, E. A., Neuroscience and Physiology
ELKINS, T. E., Gynaecology and Obstetrics
ENGLUND, P. T., Biological Chemistry
EPSTEIN, J. I., Pathology, Urology and Oncology
EROZAN, Y. S., Pathology
ETTINGER, D. S., Oncology and Medicine
FERNBERG, A. P., Medicine and Oncology
FINKELSTEIN, D., Ophthalmology
FISHMAN, E. K., Radiology and Radiological Science, and Oncology
FORASTIERE, A. A., Oncology and Otolaryngology
FORTUIN, N. J., Medicine
FOX, H. E., Gynaecology and Obstetrics
FREEMAN, J. M., Neurology and Paediatrics
FRIED, L. P., Medicine
FROST, J. J., Radiology and Radiological Science, and Nuclear Medicine and Neuroscience
FUCHS, P. A., Otolaryngology and Biomedical Engineering
GEARHART, J. D., Gynaecology and Obstetrics, Comparative Medicine and Physiology
GEARHART, J. P., Urology and Paediatrics
GERSTENBLITH, G., Medicine
GIBSON, D. W., Pharmacology and Molecular Sciences
GOLDBERG, M. F., Ophthalmology
GOLDSTEIN, G. W., Neurology, Paediatrics
GORDIS, L., Paediatrics
GORDON, B., Neurology
GREEN, W. R., Ophthalmology and Pathology
GREENOUGH, W. B., III, Medicine
GREVER, M. R., Oncology
GRIFFIN, J. W., Neurology and Neuroscience
GRIFFITH, L. S., Medicine
GRIFFITHS, R. R., Psychiatry and Behavioural Sciences, and Neuroscience
GUGGINO, W. B., Physiology and Paediatrics
GUYTON, D. L., Ophthalmology
HANDLER, J. S., Medicine
HANLEY, D. F., Neurology, Anaesthesiology, Critical Care Medicine and Neurological Surgery
HARMON, J. W., Surgery
HARRIS, J. C., Jr, Psychiatry and Behavioural Sciences, and Paediatrics
HART, G. W., Biological Chemistry
HAWKINS, B. S., Ophthalmology
HAYWARD, G. S., Pharmacology and Molecular Sciences, Oncology and Pathology
HAYWARD, S. D., Pharmacology and Molecular Sciences, and Oncology
HELLMAN, D. B., Medicine
HENDRIX, T. R., Medicine
HEPTINSTALL, R. H., Pathology
HESS, A. D., Oncology and Pathology
HEYSSEL, R. M., Medicine
HIRSHMAN, C. A., Anaesthesiology and Critical Care Medicine
HOEHN-SARIC, R., Psychiatry and Behavioural Sciences
HOLTZMAN, N. A., Paediatrics
HUBBARD, A. L., Cell Biology, Anatomy and Physiology
HUGANIR, R. L., Neuroscience
HUGGINS, G. R., Gynaecology and Obstetrics
HUNGERFORD, D. S., Orthopaedic Surgery
HUTCHINS, G. M., Pathology
ISAACS, J. T., Oncology and Urology
ISAACS, W. B., Oncology and Urology
JABS, D. A., Ophthalmology and Medicine
JABS, E. W., Paediatrics, Surgery and Medicine
JACKSON, J. B., Pathology
JASINSKI, D. R., Medicine
JOHNS, R. J., Biomedical Engineering and Medicine
JOHNSON, K. O., Neuroscience and Biomedical Engineering
JOHNSON, R. T., Neurology, Molecular Biology and Genetics, and Neuroscience
JOHNSTON, M. V., Neurology and Paediatrics
JONES, B., Radiology and Radiological Sciences
KAN, J. S., Paediatrics
KASHIMA, H. K., Otolaryngology and Oncology
KASS, D. A., Medicine and Biomedical Engineering
KAVOUSSI, L. R., Urology
KELEN, G. D., Emergency Medicine
KELLY, T. J., Jr, Molecular Biology and Genetics
KICKLER, T. S., Pathology, Oncology and Medicine
KLAG, M. J., Medicine
KOEHLER, R. C., Anaesthesiology and Critical Care Medicine
KOSTUIK, J. P., Orthopaedic Surgery and Neurosurgery
KUNCL, R. W., Neurology
KURMAN, R. S., Gynaecology, Obstetrics and Pathology
KWITEROVICH, P. O., Jr, Paediatrics and Medicine
LADENSON, P. W., Medicine, Oncology and Pathology
LANE, M. D., Biological Chemistry
LEONG, K. W., Biomedical Engineering
LESSER, R. P., Neurology
LEVINE, D. M., Medicine
LEVINE, M. A., Medicine
LICHTENSTEIN, L. M., Medicine
LIETMAN, P. S., Medicine, Paediatrics, Pharmacology and Molecular Sciences

LILLEMOE, K. D., Surgery
LONG, D. M., Neurological Surgery
LOUGHLIN, G. M., Paediatrics
MCARTHUR, J. C., Neurology
MACGLASHAN, D. W., Medicine
MCHUGH, P. R., Psychiatry and Behavioural Sciences
MCKHANN, G. M., Neurology and Neuroscience
MCKUSICK, V. A., Medicine
MAINS, R. E., Neuroscience and Physiology
MALONEY, P. C., Physiology
MANN, R. B., Pathology and Oncology
MANSON, P. N., Plastic Surgery
MARBAN, E., Medicine and Physiology
MARGOLIS, S., Medicine and Biological Chemistry
MARSHALL, F. F., Urology and Oncology
MASSOF, R. W., Ophthalmology and Neuroscience
MAUGHAN, W. L., Medicine and Biomedical Engineering
MAUMENEE, I. E. H., Ophthalmology and Paediatrics
MEYER, R. A., Neurological Surgery and Biomedical Engineering
MEZEY, E., Medicine
MIGEON, B. R., Paediatrics
MIGEON, C. J., Paediatrics
MILDVAN, A. S., Biological Chemistry
MILLER, E. D., Anaesthesiology and Critical Care Medicine
MILLER, N. R., Ophthalmology and Neurology, Neurological Surgery
MOLLIVER, M. E., Neuroscience and Neurology
MONTZ, F. J., Gynaecology and Obstetrics
MORAN, T. H., Psychiatry and Behavioural Sciences
MOSER, H. W., Neurology and Paediatrics
MOSTWIN, J. L., Urology
MUNSTER, A. M., Surgery and Plastic Surgery
MURPHY, D. B., Cell Biology and Anatomy
MURPHY, P. A., Medicine and Molecular Biology, Genetics
NATHANS, D., Molecular Biology and Genetics
NATHANS, J., Molecular Biology and Genetics, Ophthalmology and Neuroscience
NESS, P. M., Pathology and Medicine
NIPARKO, J. K., Otolaryngology
NORMAN, P .S., Medicine
NORTH, R., Neurological Surgery, Anesthesiology and Critical Care Medicine
OFFERHAUS, G. J., Medicine and Pathology
PEARLSON, G. D., Psychiatry and Behavioural Sciences
PEDERSEN, P. L., Biological Chemistry
PERLER, B. A., Surgery
PERMUTT, S., Medicine
PITHA-ROWE, P. M., Oncology
POPEL, A. S., Biomedical Engineering
PRICE, D. L., Pathology and Neurology, Neuroscience
PROUD, D., Medicine
PROVOST, T. T., Dermatology
QUIGLEY, H. A., Ophthalmology
QUINN, T. C., Medicine
RABINS, P. V., Psychiatry and Behavioural Sciences
RAJA, R. R., Anaesthesiology and Critical Care Medicine
REED, R. R., Molecular Biology and Genetics and Neuroscience
REPKA, M. X., Ophthalmology
RICHARDSON, M. A., Otolaryngology
RIGAMONTI, D., Neurological Surgery
RILEY, L. H., Jr, Orthopaedic Surgery
ROSE, G. D., Biophysics and Biophysical Chemistry
ROSE, K. D., Cell Biology and Anatomy
ROSENSTEIN, B. J., Paediatrics
ROSENTHAL, D. L., Pathology and Oncology
ROSS, C. A., Psychiatry and Behavioural Sciences, and Neuroscience
RUFF, C. B., Cell Biology, Anatomy and Orthopaedic Surgery
SACHS, M. B., Biomedical Engineering and Neuroscience, Otolaryngology-Head and Neck Surgery
SANFILIPPO, A. P., Pathology
SAUDEK, C. D., Medicine
SCHACHAT, A. P., Ophthalmology and Oncology
SCHLEIMER, R. P., Medicine
SCHLUE, W., Medicine
SCHMIDT, C. W., Jr, Psychiatry and Behavioural Sciences
SCHNAAR, R. L., Pharmacology, Molecular Sciences and Neuroscience
SCHRAMM, L. P., Biomedical Engineering and Neuroscience
SCHUSTER, M. M., Medicine
SHAPER, J. H., Oncology
SHAPIRO, E. P., Medicine
SHARKIS, S. J., Oncology
SHIN, H. S., Molecular Biology and Genetics
SHORTLE, D. R., Biological Chemistry and Biophysics
SHOUKAS, A. A., Biomedical Engineering
SIDRANSKY, D., Otolaryngology and Oncology
SIEGELMAN, S. S., Radiology and Radiological Sciences
SINGER, H. S., Neurology and Paediatrics
SLAVNEY, P. R., Psychiatry and Behavioural Sciences, and Medicine
SMITH, P. L., Medicine
SNYDER, S. H., Neuroscience, Pharmacology and Molecular Sciences and Psychiatry and Behavioural Sciences
SOLLNER-WEBB, B. T., Biological Chemistry
SOMMER, A., Ophthalmology
SPIVAK, J. L., Medicine and Oncology
STARK, W. J., Jr, Ophthalmology
STITZER, M. L., Psychiatry and Behavioural Sciences
STRANDBERG, J. D., Comparative Medicine and Pathology
SYLVESTER, J. T., Medicine
TALALAY, P., Pharmacology and Molecular Sciences
TEAFORD, M. F., Cell Biology and Anatomy
TERRY, P. B., Medicine
THAKOR, N. V., Biomedical Engineering
THOMAS, G. H., Paediatrics and Pathology
TRAIL, T. A., Medicine
TRAYSTMAN, R. J., Anaesthesiology and Critical Care Medicine
VALLE, D. L., Paediatrics and Ophthalmology
VAN ZIJL, P. C., Radiology and Radiological Sciences, Nuclear Magnetic Resonance, Biophysics and Biophysical Chemistry
VOGELSTEIN, B., Oncology
VONDERHEYDT, R., Neuroscience
WALLACH, E. E., Gynaecology and Obstetrics
WALSER, M., Pharmacology and Molecular Sciences and Medicine
WATKINS, L., Jr, Cardiac Surgery
WEINMAN, E. J., Medicine
WEISHAMPEL, D. B., Cell Biology and Anatomy
WEISS, J. L., Medicine
WEST, S., Ophthalmology
WHARAM, M. D., Jr, Oncology, Paediatrics, Radiology and Neurosurgery
WIGLEY, F. M., Medicine
WILLIAMS, G. M., Surgery
WILLIAMS, J. R., Oncology
WILSON, M. E., Paediatrics
WINCHURCH, R. A., Surgery
WINKELSTEIN, J. A., Paediatrics
WISE, R. A., Medicine
WONG, D. F., Radiology and Radiological Science, and Nuclear Medicine
YARDLEY, J. H., Pathology
YAU, K., Neuroscience and Ophthalmology
YEO, C. J., Surgery and Oncology
YOLKEN, R. H., Paediatrics
YOUNG, E. D., Biomedical Engineering and Neuroscience, Otolaryngology-Head and Neck Surgery
ZACUR, H. A., Gynaecology and Obstetrics
ZEE, D. S., Neurology and Neuroscience, Ophthalmology and Otolaryngology
ZEIMER, R., Ophthalmology
ZERHOUNI, E. A., Radiology and Radiological Science, and Biomedical Engineering
ZIEVE, P. D., Medicine

School of Hygiene and Public Health:

ABBEY, H., Biostatistics
ALEXANDER, C. S., Maternal and Child Health
ANDERSON, G. F., Health Policy and Management
ANTHONY, J., Mental Hygiene
ARMENIAN, H., Epidemiology
BAKER, F., Environmental Health Sciences
BAKER, S., Health Policy and Management
BAKER, T. D., International Health
BEATY, T. H., Epidemiology
BLACK, R., International Health
BREITNER, J. C. S., Mental Hygiene
BRENNER, M. H., Health Policy and Management
BROOKMEYER, R., Biostatistics
BROWN, T. R., Population Dynamics
BRYANT, F. R., Biochemistry
BURKE, D. S., International Health
CABALLERO, B., International Health
CELENTANO, D., Epidemiology
CHOW, L. P., Population Dynamics
CLEMENTS, M. L., International Health
COHEN, B. H., Epidemiology
COMSTOCK, G. W., Epidemiology
DANNENBERG, A. M., Jr, Environmental Health Sciences
EATON, W., Mental Hygiene
FADEN, R. R., Health Policy and Management
FITZGERALD, R. S., Environmental Health Sciences
GILMAN, R., International Health
GITTELSOHN, A. M., Biostatistics
GOLDBERG, A. M., Environmental Health Sciences
GORDIS, L., Epidemiology
GOSTIN, L., Health Policy and Management
GRAY, R., Population Dynamics
GRIFFIN, D. E., Molecular Microbiology and Immunology
GROOPMAN, J., Environmental Health Sciences
GROSSMAN, L., Biochemistry
GUILARTE, T. R., Environmental Health Sciences
GUYER, B., Maternal and Child Health
HALSEY, N., International Health
HENDERSON, D. A., Epidemiology
HILL, K., Population Dynamics
HUANG, P. C., Biochemistry
JAKAB, G. J., Environmental Health Sciences
KATZ, J., International Health
KELLAM, S., Mental Hygiene
KENSLER, T. W., Environmental Health Sciences
KETNER, G. W., Molecular Microbiology and Immunology
KIM, Y. J., Population Dynamics
KRAG, S., Biochemistry
LAWRENCE, R. S., Health Policy and Management
LEAF, P., Mental Hygiene
LIANG, K. Y., Biostatistics
MACKENZIE, E., Health Policy and Management
MCMACKEN, R., Biochemistry
MANDELL, W., Mental Hygiene
MATANOSKI, G. M., Epidemiology
MEINERT, C. L., Epidemiology
MILLER, P., Biochemistry
MITZNER, W. A., Environmental Health Sciences

MORLOCK, L., Health Policy and Management
MORROW, R., International Health
MOSLEY, W. H., Population Dynamics
MUÑOZ, A., Epidemiology
NATHANSON, C. A., Population Dynamics
NAVARRO, V., Health Policy and Management
NELSON, K., Epidemiology
PAIGE, D. M., Maternal and Child Health
PICKART, C., Biochemistry
PIERCE, N. F., International Health
PIOTROW, P. T., Population Dynamics
REINKE, W. A., International Health
RISBY, T., Environmental Health Sciences
ROHDE, C. A., Biostatistics
ROSE, N., Molecular Microbiology and Immunology
ROSS, A., Biostatistics
ROTER, D., Health Policy and Management
ROYALL, R. M., Biostatistics
RUSSELL, P., International Health
SACK, D., International Health
SACK, R. B., International Health
SALKEVER, D. S., Health Policy and Management
SAMET, J., Epidemiology
SANTOSHAM, M., International Health
SCHOEN, R., Population Dynamics
SCHOENRICH, E. H., Health Policy and Management
SCHUETZ, A. W., Population Dynamics
SCOCCA, J., Biochemistry
SCOTT, A. L., Molecular Microbiology and Immunology
SHAH, K. V., Molecular Microbiology and Immunology
SIRAGELDIN, I. A., Population Dynamics
SOMMER, A., Epidemiology
SPANNHAKE, E., Environmental Health Sciences
STARFIELD, B. H., Health Policy and Management
STEINHOFF, M., International Health
STEINWACHS, D. M., Health Policy and Management
STRICKLAND, P. T., Environmental Health Sciences
STROBINO, D., Maternal and Child Health
SZKLO, M., Epidemiology
TERET, S., Health Policy and Management
TIELSCH, J. M., International Health
TONASCIA, J., Biostatistics
TRPIS, M., Molecular Microbiology and Immunology
TRUSH, M. A., Environmental Health Sciences
TS'O, P. O. P., Biochemistry
VLAHOV, D., Epidemiology
WAGNER, H. N., Environmental Health Sciences
WEINER, J. P., Health Policy and Management
WEST, K., International Health
WRIGHT, W. W., Population Dynamics
YAGER, J., Environmental Health Sciences
ZABIN, L. S., Population Dynamics
ZEGER, S., Biostatistics
ZIRKIN, B., Population Dynamics

School of Advanced International Studies (1730 Massachusetts Ave, Washington, DC 20036):

AJAMI, F., Middle East Studies
CALLEO, D. P., European Studies
COHEN, E. A., Strategic Studies
CORDEN, W. M., International Economics
DORAN, C. F., Canadian Studies and International Relations
FRANK, I., International Economics
GLEIJESES, P., US Foreign Policy and Latin American Studies
GOODELL, G. E., Social Change and Development
JACKSON, K. D., Asian Studies
LAMPTON, D. M., Asian Studies
MANDELBAUM, M., US Foreign Policy
PARROTT, B., Soviet Studies
PEARSON, C. S., International Economics
RIEDEL, J. C., International Economics
ROETT, R., Latin American Studies
SCHREVER, C. H., International Relations
THAYER, N. B., Asian Studies
ZARTMAN, I. W., African Studies

School of Nursing:

BERK, R. A., Psychometrics and Statistics
CAMPBELL, J., Community Health
DONALDSON, S., Physiology and Biophysics
HILL, M., Adult Health
VESSEY, J., Paediatrics

MARYLAND INSTITUTE, COLLEGE OF ART

1300 Mt Royal Ave, Baltimore, MD 21217
Telephone: (410) 669-9200
Fax: (410) 669-9206
E-mail: flazarus@mica.edu

Founded 1826

President: FRED LAZARUS IV
Registrar: Miss ANN HEETHER
Academic Dean: RAY ALLEN
Librarian: MARJORIE CHENOWETH

Library of 51,000 vols
Number of teachers: 178
Number of students: 1,143

MORGAN STATE UNIVERSITY

Hillen Rd and Coldspring Lane, Baltimore, MD 21239
Telephone: (410) 319-3333

Founded 1867

President: Dr EARL S. RICHARDSON
Vice-President for Academic Affairs: Dr CLARA ADAMS
Vice-President for Finance and Management: ABRAHAM MOORE
Registrar: HERBERT KLINGHOFFER
Director of Library: KAREN ROBERTSON

Library of 350,042 vols
Number of teachers: 278
Number of students: 5,034

DEANS

College of Arts and Sciences: Dr BURNEY HOLLIS
School of Education and Urban Studies: Dr PATRICIA MORRIS (acting)
School of Engineering: Dr EUGENE M. DELOATCH
School of Graduate Studies: Dr FRANK MORRIS
School of Business and Management: Dr OTIS THOMAS

MOUNT SAINT MARY'S COLLEGE

Emmitsburg, MD 21727
Telephone: (410) 447-6122
Fax: (301) 447-5755
E-mail: postmaster@msmary.edu

Founded 1808

President: GEORGE R. HOUSTON, Jr
Vice-President and Dean of College: Dr CAROL L. HINDS
Dean of Undergraduate Studies: Dr WILLIAM CRAFT
Registrar: JOHN C. GILL
Director of Library: Dr D. STEPHEN ROCKWOOD

Library of 200,000 vols
Number of teachers: 98 full-time, 22 part-time
Number of students: 1,798

Publication: *Mountaineer Briefing* (quarterly).

ST JOHN'S COLLEGE

POB 2800, Annapolis, MD 21404-2800
Telephone: (410) 263-2371

Founded as King William's School 1696

President: CHRISTOPHER B. NELSON
Vice-President for Advancement: JEFFREY A. BISHOP
Dean: EVA T. H. BRANN
Treasurer: FRED H. BILLUPS, Jr
Registrar: NANCY LEWIS
Director of Alumni Activities: ELIZABETH BLUME
Director of Admissions: JOHN CHRISTENSEN
Director of Development: PAMELA MCKEE
Librarian: KATHRYN KINZER

Library of 93,000 vols
Number of teachers: 69
Number of students: 415

For Santa Fe Branch see under New Mexico

ST MARY'S COLLEGE OF MARYLAND

St Mary's City, MD 20686
Telephone: (301) 862-0200
Fax: (301) 862-0462
E-mail: jmobrien@osprey.smcm.edu

Founded 1840

President: JANE MARGARET O'BRIEN
Provost: LARRY E. VOTE (acting)
Vice-President for Development: SALVATORE M. MERRINGOLO (acting)
Executive Vice-President for Administration: JOHN D. UNDERWOOD
Dean of Admissions: JAMES ANTONIO
Director of Library: (vacant)

Library of 120,000 vols
Number of teachers: 115 full-time, 56 part-time
Number of students: 1,656

ST MARY'S SEMINARY AND UNIVERSITY

5400 Roland Ave, Baltimore, MD 21210
Telephone: (410) 864-4000

Founded 1791

President and Rector: Rev. ROBERT F. LEAVITT
Vice-Rector: Rev. THOMAS J. BURKE
Vice-President for Administration and Finance: RICHARD G. CHILDS
Academic Dean: Rev. JAMES J. CONN
Treasurer: RICHARD G. CHILDS
Director of Financial Aid: PRISCILLA GORDON

Libraries of 95,281 vols
Number of teachers: 21 full-time, 24 part-time
Number of students: 75 full-time, 201 part-time

Publications: *St Mary's Bulletin* (quarterly), *Catalogues.*

SALISBURY STATE UNIVERSITY

Salisbury, MD 21801
Telephone: (410) 543-6000

Founded 1925; part of Univ. of Maryland System

President: WILLIAM C. MERWIN
Provost: Dr PHILLIP D. CREIGHTON
Registrar: AVERY SAULSBURY
Vice-President of Student Affairs: Dr CAROL WILLIAMSON
Vice-President of Business and Finance: RICHARD PUSEY
Vice-President for Institutional Advancement: MARTIN WILLIAMS
Dean of Admissions: JANE DANÉ
Librarian: J. R. THRASH

Library of 231,405 vols
Number of teachers: 245 full-time, 111 part-time
Number of students: 6,010

TOWSON UNIVERSITY

Towson, MD 21252-0001
Telephone: (410) 830-2000

Founded 1866; part of Univ. of Maryland System

President: Dr HOKE L. SMITH
Registrar: DAVID DECKER
Director of Admissions: ANGEL JACKSON
Provost and Vice-President: Dr JOHN D. HAEGER
Vice-President, Administration and Finance: RONALD GARRISON (acting)
Vice-President, Student Life: Dr PAUL PARKER
Vice-President, Institutional Advancement: JOANNE K. GLASSER
Librarian: Dr DEBORAH LEATHER

Library of 573,000 vols
Number of teachers: 678
Number of students: 15,105

Publications: *Towson Journal of International Affairs*, *Transitions* (annually), *Catalog* (annually), *Tower Echoes* (annually), *Towerlight* (weekly).

UNITED STATES NAVAL ACADEMY

Annapolis, MD 21402-5000

Telephone: (410) 293-1000
Fax: (410) 293-3734

Founded 1845

Superintendent: Vice Admiral JOHN R. RYAN
Commandant of Midshipmen: Rear Admiral GARY ROUGHEAD
Academic Dean: Dr WILLIAM C. MILLER
Vice Dean: Dr WILLIAM B. GARRETT
Dean of Admissions: DAVID VETTER
Registrar: Prof. R. L. DAVIS
Director of Museum: Prof. WILLIAM B. COGAR
Librarian: Prof. R. H. WERKING

Library of 653,600 vols
Number of teachers: 600
Number of students (midshipmen): 4,050

Publications: *USNA Catalogue*, *Lucky Bag*, *Shipmate*, *Trident*.

DIVISION DIRECTORS

Engineering and Weapons: Capt. WILLIAM R. RUBEL
Humanities and Social Sciences: Col. PAT HALTON
Mathematics and Science: Capt. H. J. HALLIDAY
Professional Development: Capt. WILLIAM R. MASON
Athletics: JACK LENGYEL

UNIVERSITY OF BALTIMORE

1420 North Charles St, Baltimore, MD 21201

Telephone: (301) 625-3000
Fax: (301) 539-3714

Founded 1925; part of Univ. of Maryland System

President: Dr H. MEBANE TURNER
Vice-Presidents:
Institutional Advancement: NEIL DIDRIKSEN
Administration and Finance: DON PADDY
Student and Academic Services: DENNIS PELLETIER
Provost: RONALD LEGON
Librarian: WANDA BREITENBACH

Library of 400,000 vols
Number of teachers: 167
Number of students: 5,000

DEANS

School of Law: JOHN SEBENT
Yale Gordon College of Liberal Arts: CARL STENBENG
Robert G. Merrick School of Business: JOHN HATFIELD
Admissions and Financial Assistance: ANNA BRELAND

DEPARTMENT CHAIRS

RGM School of Business:
Accounting: Dr KAREN FOR TIN
Economics and Finance: Dr SINAN CEBENOYAN
Information and Quantitative Sciences: Dr MARILYN OBLAK
Management: Dr SUSAN ZACUR
Marketing: Dr R. STIFF

YG College of Liberal Arts:
Criminal Justice: Dr JEFFERY SENSE
English and Communications Design: Dr STEPHEN MATANLE
Government and Public Administration: Dr L. THOMAS
History and Philosophy: Dr JEFFERY SAWYER
Psychology: Dr BILL CLEWELL

UNIVERSITY OF MARYLAND SYSTEM

3300 Metzerott Rd, Adelphi, MD 20783

Telephone: (301) 445-1900
Fax: (301) 445-4761

Founded 1988; comprises 11 state-supported instns: Univ. of Maryland at Baltimore, Univ. of Maryland Baltimore County, Univ. of Maryland College Park, Univ. of Maryland Eastern Shore, Univ. of Maryland Univ. College, Bowie State Univ., Coppin State College, Frostburg State Univ., Salisbury State Univ., Towson State Univ., Univ. of Baltimore; it also includes 2 research and service components: Center for Environmental and Estuarine Studies, Univ. of Maryland Biotechnology Inst.

Chancellor: Dr DONALD N. LANGENBERG
Vice-Chancellors: GEORGE L. MARX (Academic Affairs), JOHN K. MARTIN (Advancement), JOSEPH F. VIVONA (Administration and Finance)

University of Maryland at College Park

College Park, MD 20742

Telephone: (301) 405-1000

Founded 1859

President: Dr C. D. (DAN) MOTE Jr
Vice-President for Academic Affairs: Dr GREGORY L. GEOFFROY
Vice-President for Administrative Affairs: CHARLES F. STURTZ
Vice-President for University Advancement: REID W. CRAWFORD
Vice-President for Student Affairs: Dr WILLIAM L. THOMAS, Jr
Dean of Graduate School: Dr ILENE NAGEL
Registrar: WILLIAM C. SPANN
Director of Libraries: Dr CHARLES LOWRY

Library of 2,106,000 vols
Number of students: 33,889

Colleges of: Agriculture and Natural Resources, Arts and Humanities, Behavioural and Social Sciences, Business and Management, Computer, Mathematical and Physical Sciences, Education, Engineering, Journalism, Library and Information Services, Life Sciences, Health and Human Performance; Schools of Architecture and Public Affairs.

University of Maryland, Baltimore

522 W. Lombard St, Baltimore, MD 21201

Telephone: (410) 706-3100

Founded 1807

President: DAVID J. RAMSAY

Libraries of 613,407 vols
Number of students: 5,975

Schools of dentistry, law, medicine, nursing, pharmacy, social work, University of Maryland Medical System, University of Maryland Graduate School.

University of Maryland Baltimore County

1000 Hilltop Circle, Baltimore, MD 21250

Telephone: (410) 455-1000

Founded 1963

President: FREEMAN A. HRABOWSKI
Provost: ARTHUR T. JOHNSON (interim)
Vice-Presidents: MARK E. BEHM (Administration), CHARLES FEY (Student Affairs), SCOTT BASS (Graduate School), SHELDON CAPLIS (Institutional Advancement), CHARLES WOOLSTON (Vice-Provost)
Dean of Art and Sciences: RICK WELCH
Dean of Engineering: SHLOMO CARMI

Library of 684,000 vols and 4,000 journals
Number of teachers: 755
Number of students: 9,863

Publications: *Undergraduate Catalog*, *Graduate Catalog* (every 2 years).

University of Maryland, Eastern Shore

Princess Anne, MD 21853

Telephone: (410) 651-2200
Fax: (410) 651-6105

Founded 1886

President: DOLORES R. SPIKES
Vice-President for Academic Affairs: EUCHARIA NNADI
Vice-President for Administrative Affairs: RONNIE E. HOLDEN
Vice-President for Student Affairs: HERMAN FRANKLIN
Director, Admissions and Registration: ROCHELL PEOPLES
Librarian: JESSIE C. SMITH

Library of 161,000 vols
Number of teachers: 212
Number of students: 3,166

University of Maryland University College

University Blvd at Adelphi Rd, College Park, MD 20742-1600

Telephone: (301) 985-7000
Fax: (301) 985-7678

Founded 1947

President: T. BENJAMIN MASSEY
Executive Vice-President: VIDA J. BANDIS
Vice-President, Academic Affairs: MARY ELLEN PETRISKO
Librarian: KIM KELLEY

Number of teachers: 658
Number of students: 13,786

DEANS

Undergraduate Programs: PAUL HAMLIN
Graduate Studies: NICHOLAS H. ALLEN

WASHINGTON COLLEGE

300 Washington Ave, Chestertown, MD 21620-1197

Telephone: (410) 778-2800
Fax: (410) 778-7850

Founded 1782

President: JOHN S. TOLL
Senior Vice-President for Finance and Management: H. LOUIS STETTLER, III
Vice-President for Development and Alumni Affairs: ROBERT G. SMITH
Vice-President for Admissions and Enrollment Management: KEVIN COVENEY
Vice-President for College Relations: MEREDITH DAVIES HADAWAY
Vice-President for Administration: JOSEPH L. HOLT
Vice-President and Dean of Students: MAUREEN MCINTIRE
Registrar: JACK HAMILTON
Provost and Dean: JOACHIM J. SCHOLZ

Librarian: WILLIAM J. TUBBS
Library of 200,000 vols
Number of teachers: 75
Number of students: 1,053

WESTERN MARYLAND COLLEGE

Westminster, MD 21157-4390
Telephone: (410) 848-7000
Founded 1867
Liberal arts; first and master's degrees; training for teachers of the deaf
President: ROBERT H. CHAMBERS
Provost and Dean of the Faculty: JOAN DEVELIN COLEY
Vice-President for Administration and Finance: ETHAN A. SEIDEL
Vice-President for Institutional Advancement: RICHARD F. SEAMAN
Vice-President and Dean of Student Affairs: PHILIP R. SAYRE
Registrar: BARBARA SHAFFER
Librarian: HAROLD D. NEIKIRK
Library of 195,000 vols
Number of teachers: 204
Number of students: 2,795

MASSACHUSETTS

AMERICAN INTERNATIONAL COLLEGE

Springfield, MA 01109
Telephone: (413) 737-7000
Founded 1885
President: HARRY J. COURNIOTES
Director of Admissions: GERALD F. ROOT (acting)
Registrar: ROLAND AUBIN
Librarian: F. KNOWLTON UTLEY
Library of 189,000 vols
Number of teachers: 84 full-time, 83 part-time
Number of students: 1,350 undergraduates, 539 graduates

AMHERST COLLEGE

Amherst, MA 01002
Telephone: (413) 542-2000
Founded 1821; chartered 1825
President: TOM R. GERETY
Special Assistant to the President for Alumni Relations/Development: KENT W. FAERBER
Secretary for Public Affairs: D. C. WILSON
Registrar: G. M. MAGER
Dean of the Faculty: LISA A. RASKIN
Dean of Students: BENSON LIEBER
Dean of Admissions: JANE E. REYNOLDS
Library of 760,000 vols
Number of teachers: 161
Number of students: 1,612

ANNA MARIA COLLEGE

Paxton, MA 01612
Telephone: (800) 344-4586
Founded 1946
President: Dr BERNARD S. PARKER
Academic Dean: Dr CYNTHIA M. PATTERSON
Dean of Students: Dr JOSEPH FARRAGHER
Registrar: Sister ROLLANDE QUINTAL
Library of 95,000 vols
Number of teachers: 150
Number of students: 1,915

ASSUMPTION COLLEGE

500 Salisbury St, Worcester, MA 01615-0005
Telephone: (508) 767-7000
Founded 1904
President: THOMAS R. PLOUGH
Provost: CHARLES L. FLYNN
Co-Directors of Admissions: MARY BRESHAHAN, KATHLEEN MURPHY
Librarian: DAWN THISTLE
Library of 120,000 vols
Number of teachers: 216
Number of students: 2,636

ATLANTIC UNION COLLEGE

POB 1000, South Lancaster, MA 01561-1000
Telephone: (508) 368-2000
Fax: (508) 368-2015
Founded 1882
President: SYLVAN A. LASHLEY
Registrar: NORAH VALENTINE
Librarian: LETHIEL PARSON
Library of 119,000 vols
Number of teachers: 53
Number of students: 623

BABSON COLLEGE

Babson Park, (Wellesley), MA 02157
Telephone: (617) 235-1200
Fax: (617) 239-5614
Founded 1919
College of management
President: LEO I. HIGDON, Jr
Vice-President (Academic Affairs): Dr MICHAEL FETTERS
Vice-President (Business): JOHN ELDERT
Vice-President (Development): J. THOMAS KRIMMELL
Dean of Admissions: Dr CHARLES S. NOLAN
Librarian: HOPE N. TILLMAN
Library of 110,000 vols
Number of teachers: 200
Number of students: 3,336
Publications: *College Catalogs* (annually), *Alumni Bulletin* (quarterly).

BENTLEY COLLEGE

175 Forest St, Waltham, MA 02154
Telephone: (781) 891-2000
Telex: (910) 240-0945
Fax: (781) 891-2569
Founded 1917
President: Dr JOSEPH G. MORONE
Vice-President for Academic Affairs: H. LEE SCHLORFF
Vice-President for Marketing, Communication and Enrollment: (vacant)
Vice-President for Business and Finance, and Treasurer: JOANNE YESTRAMSKI
Vice-President for Information Services: SUSAN F. SCHWAB
Vice-President for Development and Alumni Affairs: JOHN M. SHUGERT
Vice-President for Student and Administrative Services: Dr ROBERT H. MINETTI
Library of 192,566 vols
Number of teachers: 369
Number of students: 6,169
Publication: *Business in the Contemporary World* (quarterly).
Courses in liberal arts, business management, accountancy, finance, computer information, systems, taxation, marketing, economics, international business, business communications.

BOSTON COLLEGE

Chestnut Hill, MA 02467
Telephone: (617) 552-8000
Fax: (617) 552-8828
Founded 1863 by the Society of Jesus
President: Rev. WILLIAM P. LEAHY
Financial Vice-President: PETER C. MCKENZIE
Academic Vice-President: DAVID R. BURGESS
Director of Libraries: JEROME YAVARKOVSKY
Library of 1,688,000 vols
Number of teachers: 892, including 199 full professors
Number of students: 14,652
Publications: *Stylus, Boston College Law School Magazine, Boston College Law Review, Boston College Magazine, Environmental Law Review, International and Comparative Law Review, Philosophy and Social Criticism, Third World Law Journal, Uniform Commercial Code Digest, Urban and Social Change Review.*

DEANS

College of Advancing Studies: Rev. J. A. WOODS
College of Arts and Sciences: Rev. J. ROBERT BARTH
Graduate School of Arts and Sciences: MICHAEL A. SMYER
School of Management: JOHN J. NEUHAUSER
School of Education: MARY M. BRABECK
School of Nursing: BARBARA H. MUNRO
Law School: JAMES S. ROGERS (interim)
Graduate School of Social Work: JUNE G. HOPPS
Summer Session: Rev. J. A. WOODS

BOSTON UNIVERSITY

147 Bay State Rd, Boston, MA 02215
Telephone: (617) 353-2000
Fax: (617) 353-2053
Founded 1839, Chartered 1869
Private control
Academic year: September to May (two semesters), June to August (summer session)
Chancellor: JOHN SILBER
President: JON WESTLING
Vice-Presidents:
- Executive Vice-President: JOSEPH MERCURIO
- Vice-President and General Counsel: TODD KLIPP
- Alumni Affairs and Development: CHRISTOPHER REASKE
- University Relations: DAVID LAMPE (Associate Vice-President)
- External Programs: RIAZ KHAN (Associate Vice-President)
- Academic Affairs, Health: RICHARD EGDAHL
- Administrative Services: RICHARD TOWLE
- Enrollment: ANNE SHEA
- International Graduate Programs: URBAIN DE WINTER (Assistant Provost)
- Business Affairs: PETER CUSATO
- Financial Affairs: KENNETH CONDON
- Publications and Video Production: PETER SCHWEICH
- Planning, Budgeting and Information: MARVIN COOK
- Student Affairs: W. NORMAN JOHNSON

Registrar: FLORENCE BERGERON
Director of Library: ROBERT HUDSON
Library: see Libraries
Number of teachers: 3,084
Number of students: 29,857
Publications: *Journal of Education, Boston University Law Review, Bostonia, Journal of Field Archaeology.*

DEANS

College of General Studies: BRENDAN GILBANE
College of Communication: BRENT BAKER
College of Engineering: CHARLES DELISI
College of Liberal Arts: DENNIS BERKEY
Graduate School: DENNIS BERKEY
Metropolitan College: ROMUALDAS SKVARCIUS
Sargent College of Health and Rehabilitation Sciences: ALLEN JETTE
School of Education: EDWIN DELATTRE
School for the Arts: BRUCE MACOMBIE

School of Graduate Dentistry: SPENCER FRANKL
School of Law: RONALD A. CASS
School of Management: LOUIS LATAIF
School of Medicine: ARAM CHOBANIAN
School of Social Work: WILMA PEEBLES WILKINS
School of Theology: ROBERT NEVILLE
The University Professors: CLAUDIO VELIZ

BRANDEIS UNIVERSITY

415 South St, Waltham, MA 02254-9110
Telephone: (781) 736-2000
Fax: (781) 736-8699
Founded 1948
President: Dr JEHUDA REINHARZ
Provost and Senior Vice-President for Academic Affairs: Dr IRVING EPSTEIN
Financial Affairs: PETER FRENCH
Development: NANCY K. WINSHIP
Administrative Affairs: SHELLEY M. KAPLAN
Admissions: DAVID GOULD
Library Director: BESSIE K. HAHN
Number of teachers: 361
Number of students: 2,929 undergraduate, 1,071 graduate

DEANS

Arts and Sciences: ROBIN F. MILLER
Florence Heller School for Advanced Studies in Social Welfare: Dr JACK SHONKOFF
Graduate School of International Economics and Finance: Dr PETER PETRI

DEPARTMENT CHAIRPERSONS

Creative Arts:
- Fine Arts: GRAHAM CAMPBELL
- Music: ERIC CHASALOW
- Theater Arts: MICHAEL MURRAY

Humanities:
- Classical and Oriental Studies: LEONARD MUELLNER
- English and American Literature: WILLIAM FLESCH
- German and Slavic: STEPHEN DOWDEN
- Near Eastern and Judaic Studies: JONATHAN SARNA
- Philosophy: PALLE YOURGRAU
- Romance and Comparative Literature: STEPHEN GENDZIER, LUIS YGLESIAS (Co-Chairs)

Science:
- Biochemistry: DANIEL OPRIAN
- Biology: JAMES HABER
- Chemistry: LU-YAM CHAN
- Computer Science: JAMES STORER
- Mathematics: DANIEL RUBERMAN
- Physics: JAMES BENSINGER

Social Science:
- African and Afro-American Studies: WELLINGTON NYANGONI
- American Studies: JOYCE ANTLER
- Anthropology: RICHARD PARMENTIER
- Economics: F. TRENERY DOLBEAR
- History: JACQUELINE JONES
- Politics: SIDNEY MILKIS
- Psychology: MALCOLM WATSON
- Sociology: PETER CONRAD

Physical Education: JUDITH HOUDE

BRIDGEWATER STATE COLLEGE

Bridgewater, MA 02325
Telephone: (508) 697-1200
Fax: (508) 697-1707
Founded 1840
President: Dr ADRIAN TINSLEY
Academic Vice-President: Dr ANN LYDECKER
Director of Libraries: DAVID CARLSON
Library of 352,500 units
Number of teachers: 259
Number of students: 8,400

CLARK UNIVERSITY

950 Main St, Worcester, MA 01610-1477
Telephone: (508) 793-7711
Founded by Jonas Gilman Clark; chartered 1887
President: RICHARD P. TRAINA
Senior Vice-President: THOMAS M. DOLAN
Exec. Vice-President: JAMES E. COLLINS
Vice-President for Public Affairs: ELAINE C. CINELLI
Vice-President for Advancement: DEBORAH BIERI
Provost: FREDERICK GREENAWAY
Associate Provost and Dean of College: SHARON KREFETZ
Associate Provost and Dean of Graduate School: DAVID ANGEL
Dean of Admissions: HAROLD WINGOOD
Dean of Graduate School of Management: MAURRY J. TAMARKIN
Director of Professional and Continuing Education: THOMAS MASSEY
Director, Institutional Studies and Student Records: ALBERT C. LEFEBVRE
Librarian: SUSAN S. BAUGHMAN
Library of 556,000 vols
Number of teachers: 172 full-time
Number of students: 1,869 undergraduates, 711 graduates, 446 professional and continuing-education students
Publications: catalogs, *Clark University News*, *Economic Geography*, *Idealistic Studies*.

COLLEGE OF OUR LADY OF THE ELMS

291 Springfield St, Chicopee, MA 01013-2839
Telephone: (413) 594-2761
Fax: (413) 592-4871
Founded 1928
Liberal arts college
President: Sister KATHLEEN KEATING
Academic Dean: Dr JOHN FREED
Dean of Students: DAWN ELLINWOOD
Co-Directors of Library: Sister MARY GALLAGHER, PATRICIA BOMBARDIER
Library of 103,000 vols, 684 periodicals
Number of teachers: 68
Number of students: 1,191

COLLEGE OF THE HOLY CROSS

Worcester, MA 01610
Telephone: (508) 793-2011
Fax: (508) 793-3030
Founded 1843
President: Rev. GERARD C. REEDY
Vice-President: Rev. WILLIAM J. O'HALLORAN
Vice-President for Academic Affairs and Dean of Students: JACQUELINE D. PETERSON
Vice-President for Student Affairs: (vacant)
Provost: FRANK VELLACCIO
Director of Library Services: JAMES E. HOGAN
Library of 550,000 vols
Number of teachers: 212
Number of students: 2,633

EASTERN NAZARENE COLLEGE

23 East Elm Ave, Quincy, MA 02170
Telephone: (617) 745-3000
Fax: (617) 745-3590
E-mail: admissions@enc.edu
Founded 1900
President: KENT R. HILL
Vice-President of Finance: KEN GORTON
Dean: DAVID KALE
Registrar: MYRNA GIBERSON
Dean of Students: ANITA HENCK
Director of Admissions: MARTIN TRICE
Librarian: SUSAN WATKINS
Library of 126,465 vols
Number of teachers: 52
Number of students: 1,260

EMERSON COLLEGE

100 Beacon St, Boston, MA 02116
Telephone: (617) 578-8500
Founded 1880
President: Dr JACQUELINE W. LIEBERGOTT (acting)
Academic Vice-President and Dean: Dr PHILIP AMATO (acting)
Vice-President for Administration and Student Services: JAMES VANDERPOL
Registrar: NEIL DAVIN
Librarian: MICKEY MOSKOVITZ
Library of 125,000 vols
Number of teachers: 225
Number of students: 2,640
Publications: *Emerson Review* (2 a year), *Omnivore* (2 a year), *Berkeley Beacon* (2 a week).

EMMANUEL COLLEGE

400 The Fenway, Boston, MA 02115
Telephone: (617) 735-9715
Fax: (617) 735-9871
E-mail: enroll@emmanuel.edu
Founded 1919
President: Sister JANET EISNER
Vice-President for Finance and Administration: TRICIA TOWER
Vice-President for Academic Affairs: Sister PATRICIA JOHNSON
Vice-President for Enrollment: JACQUELYN ARMITAGE
Vice-President for Development and Alumnae Relations: KIERAN MCTAGUE
Dean of Students: PATRICIA RISSMEYER
Library of 134,000 vols
Number of teachers: 80
Number of students: 1,300

FITCHBURG STATE COLLEGE

Fitchburg, MA 01420
Telephone: (508) 665-3112
Fax: (508) 665-3699
E-mail: mriccards@fsc.edu
Founded 1894
President: Dr MICHAEL P. RICCARDS
Vice-President for Academic Affairs: Dr PATRICIA SPAKES
Vice-President for Student Affairs: Dr CHARLES RATTO
Vice-President for Finance and Treasurer: MICHAEL T. RIVARD
Library of 215,000 vols
Number of teachers: 241 full-time, 208 part-time
Number of students: 5,800

FRAMINGHAM STATE COLLEGE

100 State Street, Framingham, MA 01701
Telephone: (508) 620-1220
Fax: (508) 626-4592
Founded 1839
President: Dr RAYMOND N. KIEFT
Vice-President, Academic Affairs: Dr HELEN HEINEMAN
Vice-President, Administration and Finance: JOHN J. HORRIGAN
Vice-President, Student Services: WENDY L. NOYES
Librarian: BONNIE MITCHELL (acting)
Library of 344,185 holdings
Number of teachers: 290
Number of students: 6,093

GORDON COLLEGE

255 Grapevine Rd, Wenham, MA 01984
Telephone: (978) 927-2300
Fax: (978) 524-3704
Founded 1889; merged with Barrington College, RI, 1985
President: R. JUDSON CARLBERG
Executive Vice-President: CRAIG HAMMON
Provost: MARK L. SARGENT
Vice-President for Finance: TIMOTHY D. STEBBINGS
Dean of Admissions: PAMELA B. LAZARAKIS
Registrar: CAROL HERRICK
Librarian: JOHN BEAUREGARD
Library of 285,000 vols
Number of teachers: 75
Number of students: 1,375

HAMPSHIRE COLLEGE

Amherst, MA 01002
Telephone: (413) 582-5521
Fax: (413) 582-5584
Founded 1965
Private control
President: GREGORY S. PRINCE, Jr
Director of Admissions: AUDREY Y. SMITH
Librarian: GAI CARPENTER
Library of 111,000 vols
Number of teachers: 100
Number of students: 1,100

DEANS
Communications and Cognitive Science: MARK H. FEINSTEIN
Humanities and Arts: MARY RUSSO
Natural Science: BRIAN SCHULTZ
Social Science: MICHAEL FORD, MARGARET CERULLO

HARVARD UNIVERSITY

Cambridge, MA 02138
Telephone: (617) 495-1000
Founded 1636; charter signed 1650
President: NEIL LEON RUDENSTINE
Radcliffe College President: LINDA S. WILSON
Vice-President for Administration: SALLY ZECKHAUSER
Vice-President for Financial Affairs: ELIZABETH HUIDEKOPER
Vice-President for Government, Community and Public Affairs: JANE CORLETTE (acting)
Vice-President for Alumni Affairs and Development: THOMAS REARDON
Vice-President and General Counsel: ANNE TAYLOR
Director of University Library: NANCY CLINE
Number of teachers: 2,142
Number of students: 18,597

DEANS
Harvard College: HARRY LEWIS
Divinity School: RONALD THIEMANN
Faculty of Arts and Sciences: JEREMY KNOWLES
Graduate School of Design: PETER G. ROWE
Law School: ROBERT C. CLARK
Medical School: JOSEPH MARTIN
Graduate School of Public Health: BARRY BLOOM
Graduate School of Business Administration: KIM CLARK
Graduate School of Education: JEROME MURPHY
J. F. Kennedy School of Government: JOSEPH NYE
Graduate School of Arts and Sciences: CHRISTOPH J. WOLFF
Continuing Education and University Extension: MICHAEL SHINAGEL
School of Dental Medicine: R. BRUCE DONOFF
Division of Engineering and Applied Science: VENKATESH NARAYANAMURTI

PROFESSORS
Divinity School:
ANDERSON, G., Hebrew Bible/Old Testament
BOVON, F., New Testament
BROOKS HIGGINBOTHAM, E., African American Religious History
CARMAN, J. B., Comparative Religion
COAKLEY, S., Theology
COX, H. G., Theology
DYCK, A., Ethics
ECK, D., Comparative Religion
FIORENZA, F. S., Roman Catholic Theological Studies
GILES, C., Pastoral Care and Counselling
GOMES, P. J., Christian Morals
HALL, D. D., American Religious History
HANSON, P. D., Hebrew Bible/Old Testament
HEHIR, J. B., Religion and Society
HUTCHISON, W. R., History of Religion in America
KIENZLE, B., Latin and Romance Languages
KING, K. L., New Testament Studies and Gnosticism
KOESTER, H. H., New Testament Studies and Ecclesiastical History
LEVENSON, J. D., Jewish Studies
NIEBUHR, R. R., Divinity
POTTER, R. B., Social Ethics
SCHÜSSLER FIORENZA, E., New Testament and Ministerial Studies
SULLIVAN, L., History of Religion
THIEMANN, R. F., Theology
WEST, C., Philosophy of Religion
WILLIAMS, P. N., Theology and Contemporary Change

Faculty of Arts and Sciences:
ABERNATHY, F. H., Mechanical Engineering
ALESINA, A., Economics and Government
ALEXIOU, M., Modern Greek Studies, Comparative Literature
ALT, J. E., Government
ANDERSON, D., Applied Mathematics
ANDERSON, J. G., Atmospheric Chemistry
APPIAH, K., Afro-American Studies and Philosophy
ASHTON, P. S., Forestry
AZIZ, M., Materials Science
BAR-YOSEF, O., Prehistoric Archaeology
BARANCZAK, S., Polish Language and Literature
BATES, R. H., Government
BAZZAZ, F. A., Biology
BENHABIB, S., Government
BENSON, L. D., English Literature
BERCOVITCH, S., English and American Literature and Language, Comparative Literature
BERG, H. C., Molecular and Cellular Biology, Physics
BIAGIOLI, M., History of Science
BIEWENER, A., Biology
BISSON, T. N., Medieval History
BLACKBOURN, D., History
BLIER, S., History of Art and Architecture
BLOXHAM, J., Geophysics
BOBO, L., Sociology and Afro-American Studies
BOIS, Y.-A., Modern Art
BOL, P., Chinese History
BOLITHO, H., Japanese History
BOSS, K. J., Biology
BOSSERT, W. H., Science
BOTT, R., Mathematics
BOYM, S., Slavic Languages and Literatures, Comparative Literature
BRANDT, A., History of Science
BRANTON, D., Biology
BRINKMANN, R., Music
BROCKETT, R. W., Electrical Engineering and Computer Science
BRYSON, W., History of Art and Architecture
BUELL, L., English
BURGARD, P., German
BUTLER, J. N., Applied Chemistry
CAMERON, A., Astrophysics
CAMPBELL, J. Y., Applied Economics
CARAMAZZA, A., Psychology
CATON, S., Contemporary Arab Studies
CAVANAGH, P., Psychology
CAVANAUGH, C., Biology
CAVES, R. E., Political Economy
CHAMBERLAIN, G., Economics
CHANDRA, P., Indian and South Asian Art
CHEATHAM, T. E., Computer Science
COATSWORTH, J., Latin American Affairs
COELHO, J.-F., Portuguese Language and Literature, Comparative Literature
COHEN, L., History
COLEMAN, K., Latin
COLEMAN, S. R., Science
COLTON, T., Government and Russian Studies
CONLEY, T., Romance Languages and Literature
COOPER, R., International Economics
COREY, E. J., Organic Chemistry
CRAIG, A. M., History
CRANSTON, E. A., Japanese Literature
CROMPTON, A. W., Natural History
CUTLER, D., Economics
DAMROSCH, L., Literature
DAVIDOVSKY, M., Music
DEMPSTER, A. P., Theoretical Statistics
DEVORE, B. I., Biological Anthropology
DOMINGUEZ, J. I., International Affairs
DONOGHUE, D., English and American Literature and Language
DONOGHUE, M., Biology
DOWLING, J., Natural Sciences
DUFFY, J., Byzantine Philology and Literature
DZIEWONSKI, A. M., Science
ECK, D. L., Comparative Religion and Indian Studies
ECKERT, C., Korean History
EHRENREICH, H., Science
EKSTROM, G., Geology and Geophysics
ELKIES, N., Mathematics
ELLISON, P., Anthropology
ENGELL, J., English and Comparative Literature
EPPS, B., Romance Languages and Literature
ERIKSON, R. L., Cellular and Developmental Biology
EVANS, A., Materials Engineering
EVANS, D. A., Chemistry
FANGER, D. L., Literature
FARRELL, B., Meteorology
FASH, W., Central American and Mexican Archaeology and Ethnology
FELDMAN, G., Science
FELDSTEIN, M. S., Economics
FERNANDEZ-CIFUENTE, L., Romance Languages and Literature
FIDO, F., Romance Languages and Literatures
FIELD, G. B., Applied Astronomy
FISHER, D., Physics
FISHER, P. J., English and American Literatures
FLEMING, D. H., American History
FLIER, M., Ukrainian Philology
FORD, P., Celtic Languages and Literatures
FRANKLIN, M., Physics
FREEMAN, R. B., Economics
FRIEDEN, J., Government
FRIEDMAN, B. M., Political Economy
FRIEND, C., Chemistry
FUDENBERG, D., Economics
GABRIELSE, G., Physics
GALISON, P., History of Science and of Physics
GARBER, M., English
GATES, H., Humanities
GAYLORD, M., Romance Languages and Literatures
GELBART, W. M., Molecular and Cellular Biology
GEORGI, H. M., Physics
GIENAPP, W., History

GILBERT, D., Psychology
GILBERT, W.
GLASHOW, S. L., Physics
GLAUBER, R. J., Physics
GOLDFARB, W., Modern Mathematics and Mathematical Logic
GOLDIN, C., Economics
GOLOVCHENKO, J., Physics
GORDON, A., History
GORDON, R. G., Chemistry
GOULD, S. J., Zoology, Geology
GRABOWICZ, G. G., Ukrainian Literature
GRAHAM, W. A., History of Religion and Islamic Studies
GREEN, J. R., Political Economy
GREENBLATT, S., English and American Literature and Language
GRILICHES, Z., Economics
GRINDLAY, J. E., Astronomy
GROSS, B. H., Mathematics
GROSZ, B., Computer Science
GUIDOTTI, G., Biochemistry
GUILLORY, J., English
GUTHKE, K. S., German Art and Culture
GUZZETTI, A. F., Visual Arts
HACKMAN, J., Social and Organizational Psychology
HALL, P., Government
HALPERIN, B. I., Mathematics and Natural Philosophy
HANKINS, J., History
HARDACRE, H., Japanese Religions and Society
HARRINGTON, A., History of Science
HARRINGTON, J. J., Environmental Engineering
HARRIS, J. C., English and Folklore
HARRIS, J. D., Mathematics
HARRIS, J. M., Jewish Studies
HARRISON, S. C., Biochemistry and Molecular Biology
HART, O., Economics
HARTL, D., Biology
HASTINGS, J., Natural Sciences
HEIMERT, A. E., American Literature
HEINRICHS, W. P., Arabic
HELLER, E., Physics
HELPMAN, E., Economics
HENRICHS, A. M., Greek Literature
HERSCHBACH, D. R., Science
HERZFELD, M., Anthropology
HIGGINBOTHAM, E. B., Afro-American Studies, History
HIGONNET, P. L.-R., French History
HO, Y. C., Engineering and Applied Mathematics
HOFFMAN, P., Geology
HOFFMANN, S. H.
HOLLAND, H. D., Geology
HOLM, R. H., Chemistry
HOOLEY, J., Psychology
HOROWITZ, P., Physics
HOWE, R., Engineering
HUEHNERGARD, J. D., Semitic Philology
HUNTINGTON, S. P.
HUTCHINSON, J. W., Applied Mechanics
HUTH, J., Physics
IRIYE, A., American History
JACOB, D., Atmospheric Chemistry, Environmental Engineering
JACOBSEN, E., Chemistry
JACOBSEN, S. B., Geochemistry
JAFFE, A. M., Mathematics and Theoretical Science
JARDINE, A., Romance Languages and Literatures
JASANOFF, J., Linguistics
JENKINS, F., Zoology and Biology
JOHNSON, B., Law and Psychiatry in Society
JONES, C. P., Classics and History
JONES, R. V., Applied Physics
JORGENSON, D. W., Economics
KAFADAR, C., Turkish Studies
KAGAN, J., Psychology
KAISER, W. J., English and Comparative Literature
KALAVREZOU, I., Byzantine Art
KATZ, L., Economics
KAZHDAN, D., Mathematics
KEENAN, E. L., History
KELLY, T., Music
KELMAN, H. C., Social Ethics
KIELY, R. J., English
KILLIP, C., Visual and Environmental Studies
KILSON, M. L., Government
KING, G., Government
KIRBY, W., History
KIRSHNER, R. P., Astronomy
KISHLANSKY, M., History
KLECKNER, N., Biochemistry and Molecular Biology
KLEINMAN, A. M., Medical Anthropology
KLEMPERER, W. A., Chemistry
KNOLL, A., Biology
KNOWLES, J. R., Chemistry
KOERNER, J., History of Art and Architecture
KORNAI, J., Economics
KORSGAARD, C., Philosophy
KOSSLYN, S. M., Psychology
KRONAUER, R. E., Mechanical Engineering
KRONHEIMER, P., Mathematics
KUGEL, J. L., Classical and Modern Jewish and Hebrew Literature and Comparative Literature
KUHN, P. A., History and East Asian Languages and Civilizations
KUNG, H., Electrical Engineering and Computer Science
KUNO, S., Linguistics
LAIOU, A. E., Byzantine History
LAMBERG-KARLOVSKY, C. C., Archaeology and Ethnology
LANGER, E. J., Psychology
LEE, L., Chinese Literature
LEVIN, R., Music
LEVINE, N., History of Art and Architecture
LEWALSKI, B., History and Literature, English Literature
LEWIN, D. B., Music
LEWIS, H. R., Computer Science
LEWONTIN, R. C., Biology
LIEBER, C., Chemistry
LIEBERSON, S., Sociology
LIEM, K., Ichthyology
LOCKWOOD, L. H., Music
LOEB, A., Astronomy
LOSICK, R. M., Biology
MACFARQUHAR, R., History and Political Science
MACHINIST, P., Hebrew and Other Oriental Languages
MAHER, B. A., Psychology of Personality
MAIER, C. S., European Studies
MALMSTAD, J., Slavic Languages and Literatures
MANIATIS, T. P., Molecular and Cellular Biology
MANKIW, N. G., Economics
MANSFIELD, H. C., Government
MARGLIN, S. A., Economics
MARSDEN, P. V., Sociology
MARTIN, L., Government
MARTIN, P. C., Pure and Applied Physics
MASKIN, E. S., Economics
MAY, E. R., American History
MAYBURY-LEWIS, D. H., Anthropology
MAZUR, B., Mathematics
MAZUR, E., Physics
MCCANN, D., Korean Literature
MCCARTHY, J. J., Biological Oceanography
MCCORMICK, M., History
MCDONALD, C., Romance Languages and Literatures
MCELROY, M. B., Environmental Studies
MCMAHON, A., Molecular and Cellular Biology
MCMAHON, T. A., Applied Mechanics and Biology
MCMULLEN, C., Mathematics
MCNALLY, R., Personality Psychology
MEDOFF, J. L., Labor and Industry
MEISTER, M., Molecular and Cellular Biology
MELTON, D. A., Molecular and Cellular Biology
MENDELSOHN, E. I., History of Science
MESELSON, M. S., Natural Sciences
MITCHELL, R., Applied Biology
MITCHELL, S. A., Scandinavian and Folklore
MITTEN, D. G., Classical Art and Archaeology
MORALEJO, S., Fine Arts
MORAN, R., Philosophy
MORRIS, C., Statistics
MOTTAHEDEH, R., History
MURDOCH, J. E., History of Science
MYERS, A., Chemistry and Chemical Biology
NAGY, G. J., Classical Greek Literature and Comparative Literature
NAKAYAMA, K., Psychology
NARAYAN, R., Astronomy
NECIPOGLU, G., Islamic Art
NELSON, D. R., Physics
NOZICK, R., Philosophy
O'CATHASAIGH, T., Irish Studies
O'CONNELL, R. J., Geophysics
OETTINGER, A., Applied Mathematics, Information Resources Policy
OWEN, E., Middle East History
OWEN, S.
OZMENT, S. E., Ancient and Modern History
PALUMBI, S., Biology
PARK, K., History of Science, Women's Studies
PARSONS, C., Philosophy
PATTERSON, O., Sociology
PAUL, W., Applied Physics
PEARSALL, D. A., English Literature
PEDERSON, S., History
PERALTA, E., Molecular Neurobiology
PERKINS, D. H., Political Economy
PERRY, E., Government
PERSHAN, P. S., Applied Physics
PERTILE, L., Romance Languages and Literature, Comparative Literature
PETERSON, P., Government
PFISTER, D. H., Systematic Botany
PHARR, S. J., Japanese Politics
PIERCE, N., Biology
PIERSON, P., Government
PILBEAM, D. R., Social Sciences
PINNEY, G., Classical Archaeology and Art
PRENTISS, M., Physics
PRESS, W. H., Astronomy, Physics
PUTNAM, H. W.
PUTNAM, R. D., Political Science
RABIN, M. O., Computer Science
RANDS, B., Music
RENTSCHLER, E., German
RESKIN, B., Sociology
RICE, J. R., Engineering Sciences and Geophysics
ROBERTSON, E., Molecular and Cellular Biology
ROBINSON, A. R., Geophysical Fluid Dynamics
ROGERS, P. P., Environmental Engineering
ROSEN, S., National Security and Military Affairs
ROSENTHAL, R., Social Psychology
RUBIN, D. B., Statistics
RUBIN, J., Japanese Humanities
RUDENSTINE, N., English and American Literature and Language
RUSSELL, J., Armenian Studies
RUVOLO, M., Anthropology
RYAN, J. L., German and Comparative Literature
SACHS, J. D., International Trade
SACKS, G. E., Mathematical Logic
SACKS, P., English and American Literature and Language
SANDEL, M. J., Government
SCANLON, T., Natural Religion, Moral Philosophy and Civil Policy
SCARRY, E., Aesthetics and the General Theory of Value
SCHACTER, D., Psychology

SCHMID, W., Mathematics
SCHOR, N., Romance Languages and Literature
SCHREIBER, S. L., Chemistry
SEGAL, C., Classics
SEN, A., Economics, Philosophy
SEPTIMUS, B., Jewish History and Sephardic Civilization
SHAKHNOVICH, E., Chemistry and Chemical Biology
SHAPIRO, I. I.
SHEARMAN, J.
SHELEMAY, K., Music
SHELL, M., English and Comparative Literature
SHEPSLE, K., Government
SHIEBER, S., Computer Science
SHLEIFER, A., Economics
SILVERA, I. F., Natural Sciences
SIMON, E., Germanic Languages and Literature
SIU, Y. T., Mathematics
SKJAERVO, P., Iranian
SKOCPOL, T. R., Government, Sociology
SOLBRIG, O. T., Biology
SOLLORS, W., English Literature, Afro-American Studies
SOMMER, D., Romance Languages and Literatures
SØRENSEN, A. B., Sociology
SPAEPEN, F. A., Applied Sciences
STAGER, L., Archaeology of Israel
STEINKELLER, P., Assyriology
STERNBERG, S. Z., Mathematics
STEVENS, P. F., Biology
STILGOE, J. R., History of Landscape
STONE, H. A., Applied Mathematics, Chemical Engineering
STONE, P. J., Psychology
STROMINGER, J. L., Biochemistry
SULEIMAN, S. R., Civilization of France, Comparative Literature
SZPORLUK, R., Ukrainian History
TAI, H., Sino-Vietnamese History
TAMBIAH, S. J., Anthropology
TARRANT, R. J., Latin Language and Literature
TATAR, M. M., German
TAUBES, C. H., Mathematics
TAYLOR, R. L., Mathematics
THERNSTROM, S., History
THOMAS, R., Greek and Latin
THOMPSON, D., Political Philosophy
TINKHAM, M., Physics
TODD, W. M., Slavic Languages and Literatures, Comparative Literature
TOMLINSON, P. B., Biology
TROMP, J., Geophysics
TU, W.-M., Chinese History and Philosophy
TUCK, R., Government
ULRICH, L., Early American History
VAFA, C., Physics
VAIL, H., History
VALIANT, L. G., Computer Science and Applied Mathematics
VAN DER KUIJP, L., Tibetan and Himalayan Studies
VAN DER MERWE, N. J., Scientific Archaeology
VENDLER, H.
VERBA, S.
VERDINE, G., Bio- and Organic Chemistry
VOGEL, E. F., Social Sciences
WANG, J. C., Biochemistry and Molecular Biology
WARREN, K., Anthropology
WATERS, M., Sociology
WATKINS, C. W., Linguistics and Classics
WATSON, J., Chinese Society
WEITZMAN, M., Economics
WEST, C., Afro-American Studies
WESTERVELT, R., Physics
WHITE, S. H., Psychology
WHITESIDES, G. M., Chemistry
WILEY, D. C., Biochemistry and Biophysics
WILLIAMSON, J. G., Economics
WILSON, R., Physics
WINSHIP, C., Sociology
WINTER, I. J., Fine Arts
WISSE, R., Yiddish Literature and Comparative Literature
WITZEL, E., Sanskrit
WOFSEY, S., Atmospheric and Environmental Studies
WOLFF, C., Music
WOMACK, J., Latin American History and Economics
WOOLLACOTT, R. M., Biology
WRANGHAM, R., Anthropology
WU, T. T., Applied Physics
YALMAN, N. O., Social Anthropology and Middle Eastern Studies
YANG, W., Electrical Engineering and Computer Science
YAU, S., Mathematics
ZIOLKOWSKI, J., Medieval Latin and Comparative Literature

Graduate School of Design:

ALTSHULER, A., Urban Policy and Planning
BAIRD, G., Architecture
FORMAN, R. T. T., Landscape Ecology
GOMEZ-IBAÑEZ, J. A., Urban Planning and Public Policy
HARGREAVES, G., Landscape Architecture
HAYS, M., Architectural Theory
KOOLHAAS, R., Architecture and Urban Design
KRIEGER, A., Urban Design
MACHADO, R., Architecture and Urban Design
MONEO, J. R., Architecture
MORI, T., Architecture
PEISER, R., Real Estate Development
POLLALIS, S. N., Design Technology and Management
ROWE, P. G., Architecture and Urban Design
SCHODEK, D. L., Architectural Technology
SILVETTI, J. S., Architecture
SMITH, C., Architectural History
STEINITZ, C. F., Landscape Architecture and Planning
STILGOE, J. R., History of Landscape Development
VAN VALKENBURGH, M., Landscape Architecture
VIGIER, F. C., Regional Planning

Law School:

ALFORD, W.
ANDREWS, W. D.
BARTHOLET, E., Public Interest
BEBCHUK, L. A., Law, Economics, Finance
BELLOW, G.
BREWER, S.
CHARNY, D.
CLARK, R. C.
DERSHOWITZ, A. M.
DESAN, C.
DONAHUE, C.
EDLEY, C. F.
ELHAUGE, E.
FALLON, R. H.
FIELD, M.
FISHER, W.
FRUG, G. E.
GLENDON, M. A.
GUINIER, L.
HALPERIN, D. I.
HANSON, J.
HAY, B. L.
HERWITZ, D. R.
HEYMANN, P. B.
HORWITZ, M. J., Legal History
JACKSON, H.
KAPLOW, L.
KAUFMAN, A. L.
KENNEDY, D. M.
KENNEDY, D. W., General Jurisprudence
KENNEDY, R. L.
KRAAKMAN, R. H.
LESSIG, L.
MANSFIELD, J. H.
MARTIN, H. S.
MELTZER, D. J.
MICHELMAN, F. I.
MILLER, A. R.
MINOW, M.
MNOOKIN, R.
NESSON, C. R.
OGLETREE, C., Jr
PARKER, R. D.
RAKOFF, T. D., Administrative Law
RAMSEYER, M.
ROSENBERG, M. D.
SANDER, F. E. A.
SARGENTICH, L. D.
SCOTT, H. S., International Financial Systems
SHAPIRO, D. L.
SHAVELL, S. M., Law and Economics
SINGER, J. W.
SLAUGHTER, A.-M.
STEIHER, C.
STEINER, H. J.
STONE, A. A., Law and Psychiatry
TRIBE, L. H., Constitutional Law
UNGER, R. M.
VAGTS, D. F., International Law
VISCUSI, W. K.
VORENBERG, J.
WARREN, A. C.
WARREN, E.
WEILER, J. H. H.
WEILER, P. C.
WEINREB, L. L.
WESTFALL, D.
WHITE, L.
WILKINS, D. B.
WOLFMAN, B.

Medical School:

ABBAS, A. K., Pathology
ABBOTT, W. M., Surgery
ADAMS, D. F., Radiology
ADELSTEIN, S. J., Medical Biophysics
AISENBERG, A. C., Medicine
AKINS, C. W., Surgery
ALBERT, M. S., Psychiatry
ALI, H. H., Anaesthesia
ALONSO, A. W., Psychiatry
ALPER, C., Paediatrics
ALT, F. W., Genetics
ANDERSON, E., Comparative Anatomy
APPLEBURY, M. L., Ophthalmology
ARKY, R., Medicine
ARNAOUT, M. A., Medicine
ARNDT, K. A., Dermatology
ATHANASOULIS, C. A., Radiology
AUSIELLO, D. A., Medicine
AUSTEN, K. F., Medicine
AUSTEN, W. G., Surgery
AUSUBEL, F., Genetics
AVRUCH, J., Medicine
BACH, F., Surgery
BADEN, H., Dermatology
BAIM, D., Medicine
BALDESSARINI, R. J., Psychiatry
BARBIERI, R., Obstetrics, Gynaecology and Reproductive Biology
BARLOW, C. F., Neurology
BARNETT, G. O., Medicine
BARSAMIAN, E. M., Surgery
BARSKY, A. J., III, Psychiatry
BEAL, M. F., Neurology
BEAN, B. P., Neurobiology
BEARDSLEE, W., Psychiatry
BECKWITH, J. R., Microbiology and Molecular Genetics
BELFER, M. L., Psychiatry
BENACERRAF, B. R., Obstetrics, Gynaecology and Reproductive Biology
BENDER, W. W., Biological Chemistry, Molecular Pharmacology
BENES, F. M., Psychiatry
BENJAMIN, T. L., Pathology
BERKOWITZ, R. S., Obstetrics, Gynaecology and Reproductive Biology
BERNFIELD, M., Paediatrics
BERSON, E. L., Ophthalmology

BIEDERMAN, J., Psychiatry
BIGGERS, J., Cell Biology
BIRD, E. D., Neuropathology
BISTRIAN, B. R., Medicine
BLACK, P. M., Neurosurgery
BLENIS, J., Cell Biology
BLOCH, K. J., Medicine
BONVENTRE, J. V., Medicine
BORUS, J. F., Psychiatry
BRADY, T., Radiology
BRANDT, A. M., History of Medicine
BRAUNWALD, E., Medicine
BREAKEFIELD, X. O., Neurology
BRENNAN, T., Medicine
BRENNER, B., Medicine
BRENNER, M. B., Medicine
BREWSTER, D., Surgery
BROTMAN, A. W., Psychiatry
BROWN, E. M., Medicine
BRUGGE, J. S., Cell Biology
BUCHANAN, J. R., Medicine
BUCKLEY, M. J., Surgery
BUNN, H. F., Medicine
BURAKOFF, S. J., Paediatrics
BURGESON, R. E., Dermatology
BURROWS, P. E., Radiology
CANELLOS, G. P., Medicine
CANTLEY, L. C., Medicine
CANTOR, H. I., Pathology
CAPLAN, D. N., Neurology
CAREY, M. C., Medicine
CARPENTER, C. B., Medicine
CASSEM, E. H., Psychiatry
CAVINESS, V. S., Jr, Child Neurology and Mental Retardation
CEPKO, C. L., Genetics
CHABNER, B., Medicine
CHEN, L. B., Pathology
CHIN, W. W., Medicine
CHRISTIANI, D. C., Medicine
CHURCH, G. H., Genetics
CHYLACK, L. T., Jr, Ophthalmology
CLAPHAM, D. E., Neurobiology
CLEARY, P. D., Medical Sociology
CLEVELAND, R. H., Radiology
CLOUSE, M. E., Radiology
COEN, D. M., Biological Chemistry, Molecular Pharmacology
COHEN, B. M., Psychiatry
COHEN, J. B., Neurobiology
COHN, L. H., Surgery
COLDITZ, G. A., Medicine
COLE, J. O., Psychiatry
COLEMAN, C. N., Radiation Oncology
COLES, R., Psychiatry and Medical Humanities
COLLIER, R. J., Microbiology and Molecular Genetics
COLLINS, J. J., Surgery
COLLINS, P., Pathology
COLODNY, A. H., Surgery
COLVIN, R. B., Pathology
COMPTON, C. C., Pathology
COOPER, G. M., Pathology
COREY, D. P., Neurobiology
CORSON, J. M., Pathology
COSIMI, A. B., Surgery
COTRAN, R., Pathology
COYLE, J. T., Psychiatry
CRONE, R., Anaesthesia
CROWLEY, W. F., Jr, Medicine
CRUM, C. P., Pathology
CRUMPACKER, C., Medicine
DAGGETT, W. M., Surgery
D'AMORE, P. A., Ophthalmology
DATTA, S., Anaesthesiology
DAVID, J. R., Medicine
DAVIDOVITCH, Z., Orthodontics
DAVIS, K. R., Radiology
DAWSON, D. M., Neurology
DELBANCO, T., Medicine
DEMLING, R. H., Surgery
DESANCTIS, R. W., Medicine
DESROSIERS, R. C., Microbiology, Molecular Genetics
DEUEL, T. F., Medicine
DEWOLF, W. C., Surgery
DIAMANDOPOULOS, G. T., Pathology
DOGON, I. L., Operative Dentistry
DONAHOE, P. K., Surgery
DONOFF, R. B., Oral and Maxillofacial Surgery
DORF, M. E., Pathology
DORSEY, J. L., Medicine
DORWART, R., Psychiatry
DOUGLASS, C. W., Dental Care Administration
DOWLING, J. E., Ophthalmology
DRAZEN, J. M., Medicine
DRETLER, S. P., Surgery
DRYJA, T. P., Jr, Ophthalmology
DVORAK, A. M., Pathology
DVORAK, H. F., Pathology
DZAU, V. J., Medicine
EARLS, F. J., III, Child Psychiatry
EBERLEIN, T. J., Surgery
EDELMAN, R., Radiology
EISENSTEIN, B., Medicine
EPSTEIN, A., Medicine
EPSTEIN, F., Medicine
ERIKSSON, E., Surgery
EZEKOWITZ, R. A. B., Paediatrics
FEDERMAN, D. D., Medicine and Medical Education
FEIN, R., Medical Economics
FINBERG, R. W., Medicine
FINK, M., Surgery
FISCHBACH, G. D., Neurobiology
FISHMAN, M. C., Medicine
FLEISHER, G. R., Paediatrics
FLETCHER, C., Pathology
FLETCHER, R., Ambulatory Care and Prevention
FLETCHER, S., Ambulatory Care and Prevention
FLIER, J. S., Medicine
FOLKMAN, M. J., Paediatric Surgery
FOSTER, C. S., Ophthalmology
FOX, I. H., Medicine
FRAENKEL, D. G., Microbiology
FRANK, R., Health Economics in Health Care Policy
FREI, E., III, Medicine
FRIED, M. P., Otology and Laryngology
FRIEDMAN, E., Ophthalmology
FRIGOLETTO, F. D., Jr, Obstetrics and Gynaecology
FURIE, B., Medicine
FURSHPAN, E. J., Neurobiology
GALABURDA, A., Neurology and Neuroscience
GALLI, J. J., Pathology
GARNICK, M. B., Medicine
GEHA, R. S., Paediatrics
GELBER, R. D., Paediatrics
GELMAN, S., Anaesthesia
GIMBRONE, M. A., Pathology
GIPSON, I. K., Ophthalmology
GLICKMAN, R. M., Medicine
GLIMCHER, L. H., Medicine
GLIMCHER, M. J., Orthopaedic Surgery
GOETINCK, P. F., Dermatology
GOITEIN, M., Radiation Therapy
GOLDBERG, A. L., Cell Biology
GOLDBERG, I. H., Pharmacology
GOLDHABER, P., Periodontology
GOLDMAN, H., Pathology
GOLDMAN, P., Biological Chemistry and Molecular Pharmacology
GOLDMANN, D. A., Paediatrics
GOLDSTEIN, D. P., Obstetrics, Gynaecology and Reproduction
GOLDWYN, R. M., Surgery
GOOD, B. J., Medical Anthropology
GOOD, M. J. D., Social Medicine
GOODENOUGH, D. A., Anatomy and Cell Biology
GOODMAN, H. M., Genetics
GOYAL, R. K., Medicine
GRAGOUDAS, E., Ophthalmology
GREEN, H., Cell Biology
GREENBERG, M. E., Neurology, Neuroscience
GREENBERG, R. M., Psychiatry
GREENE, R. E., Radiology
GREENES, R. A., Radiology
GRIFFIN, J., Medicine
GRILLO, H. C., Surgery
GRISCOM, N. T., Radiology
GROOPMAN, J. E., Medicine
GROWDON, J. H., Neurology
GRUNEBAM, H. U., Psychiatry
GUNDERSON, J. G., Psychiatry
GUREWICH, V., Medicine
GUSELLA, J. F., Genetics
GUTHEIL, T. G., Psychiatry
HABENER, J. F., Medicine
HABER, E., Medicine
HALES, C. A., Medicine
HALL, F. M., Radiology
HALL, J. E., Orthopaedic Surgery
HANDIN, R. I., Medicine
HARLOW, E. E., Genetics
HARRIS, J. R., Radiation Oncology
HARRIS, N. L., Pathology
HARRIS, W. H., Orthopaedic Surgery
HARRISON, S. C., Biological Chemistry and Molecular Biology
HAUSER, S. T., Psychiatry
HAVENS, L. L., Psychiatry
HAY, D. I., Oral Biology
HAY, E. D., Embryology
HAYES, W. C., Biomechanics
HAYNES, H. A., Dermatology
HEALY, G. B., Otolaryngology
HECHTMAN, H. B., Surgery
HEDLEY-WHYTE, E. T., Pathology
HEDLEY-WHYTE, J., Anaesthesia and Respiratory Therapy
HEMLER, M., Pathology
HENDREN, W. H., III, Paediatric Surgery
HENNEKENS, C. H., Ambulatory Care and Prevention
HERNDON, J. H., Orthopaedic Surgery
HERZOG, D. B., Psychiatry
HIATT, H. H., Medicine
HICKEY, P. R., Anaesthesia
HIROSE, T., Ophthalmology
HIRSCH, M. S., Medicine
HOBSON, J. A., Psychiatry
HOGLE, J. M., Biological Chemistry and Molecular Pharmacology
HOLLENBERG, N. K., Radiology
HOLMES, G. L., Neurology
HOLMES, L. B., Paediatrics
HORTON, E. S., Medicine
HOWLEY, P. M., Comparative Pathology
HUBEL, D. H., Neurophysiology
HUNT, R. D., Comparative Pathology
IEZZONI, L. I., Medicine
INGWALL, J. S., Medicine
INUI, T. S., Ambulatory Care and Prevention
ISSELBACHER, K. J., Medicine
IZUMO, S., Medicine
JACOBSON, A. M., Psychiatry
JAIN, R. K., Radiation Oncology
JAKOBIEC, F. A., Ophthalmology
JANDL, J. H., Medicine
JELLINCK, M. S., Paediatrics
JENIKE, M. A., Psychiatry
JOHNSON-POWELL, G., Child Psychiatry
JOLESZ, F. A., Radiology
JONAS, R., Surgery
JONES, H. R., Neurobiology
JOSEPHSON, M., Medicine
KABAN, L. B., Oral and Maxillofacial Surgery
KAHN, C. R., Medicine
KARCHMER, A. W., Medicine
KARNOVSKY, M. J., Pathological Anatomy
KASPER, D. L., Medicine
KASSER, J. R., Orthopaedic Surgery
KAUFMAN, D. S., Medicine
KAZEMI, H., Medicine
KESSLER, R., Health Care Policy
KHANTZIAN, E., Psychiatry
KHURI, S. F., Surgery
KIEFF, E. D., Medicine
KINET, J. P., Pathology
KING, G. L.
KINGSTON, R., Genetics

KIRSCHNER, M. W., Medicine and Cell Biology
KISSIN, I., Anaesthesia
KITZ, R. J., Research and Teaching in Anaesthetics and Anaesthesia
KLAGSBRUN, M., Surgery
KLEINMAN, A. M., Medical Anthropology
KLIBANSKI, A., Medicine
KNIPE, D. M., Microbiology and Molecular Genetics
KOLODNER, R. D., Biological Chemistry and Molecular Pharmacology
KOLTER, R. G., Microbiology and Molecular Genetics
KOMAROFF, A. L., Medicine
KOSIK, K. S., Neurology
KRANE, S. M., Clinical Medicine
KRAVITZ, E. A., Neurobiology
KRESSEL, H. Y., Radiology
KRIS, A., Psychiatry
KRONENBERG, H. M., Medicine
KUFE, D. W., Medicine
KUNKEL, L. M., Genetics
KUPPER, T., Dermatology
LAING, F. C.
LAMONT, J. T., Medicine
LARSEN, P. R., Medicine
LEBOWITZ, R. L., Radiology
LEDER, P., Genetics
LEFFERT, R. D., Orthopaedic Surgery
LESSELL, S., Ophthalmology
LETVIN, N., Medicine
LEVITON, A., Neurology
LEVITSKY, S., Surgery
LI, F. P., Medicine
LIANG, M., Medicine
LIBBY, P., Medicine
LIBERMAN, M. C., Physiology
LIN, E. C. C., Microbiology and Molecular Genetics
LIPSITT, D. R., Psychiatry
LIVINGSTON, D. M., Medicine
LIVINGSTONE, M. S., Neurobiology
LOCK, J. E., Paediatrics
LOEFFLER, J. S., Radiation Oncology
LOGERFO, F. W., Surgery
LOVEJOY, F. H. Jr, Paediatrics
LOWENSTEIN, E., Anaesthesia
LUX, S. E., IV, Paediatrics
MACK, J. E., Psychiatry
MANKIN, H. J., Orthopaedic Surgery
MANNICK, J. A., Surgery
MANSCHRECK, T. C., Psychiatry
MARGOLIES, M. N., Surgery
MARTIN, J. B., Neurology
MARTYN, J. A. J., Anaesthesia
MASLAND, R. H., Neuroscience
MATTHYSSE, S., Psychiatry
MAY, J., Surgery
MAYER, J. E., Jr, Surgery
MAYER, R. J., Medicine
MCCARLEY, R. W., Psychiatry
MCCORMICK, M. C., Paediatrics
MCDOUGAL, W. S., Surgery
MCINTOSH, K., Paediatrics
MCKEON, F. D., Cell Biology
MCLOUD, T. C., Radiology
MCNEIL, B. J., Health Care Policy
MEKALANOS, J. J., Microbiology and Molecular Genetics
MELLO, N. K., Psychology
MENDELSON, J. H., Psychiatry
MEYER, J. E., Radiology
MIHM, M. C., Jr, Dermatopathology
MILLER, K. W., Anaesthesiology
MIRIN, S. M., Psychiatry
MISHLER, E. G., Social Psychology
MITCHISON, T. J., Cell Biology
MODELL, A. H., Psychiatry
MOELLERING, R. C. Jr, Medical Research
MONACO, A. P., Surgery
MONGAN, J., Health Care Policy
MONTGOMERY, W. W., Otolaryngology
MONTMINY, M., Cell Biology
MOORE, G. T., Ambulatory Care and Prevention
MORGAN, J. P., Medicine
MORRIS, C. N., Health Care Policy
MORSE, W. H., Psychobiology
MORTON, C. C., Obstetrics and Gynaecology
MOSKOWITZ, M. A., Neurology
MULLIGAN, R., Genetics
MURPHY, J. M., Psychiatry
NADELSON, C., Psychiatry
NADLER, L. M., Medicine
NADOL, J. B. Jr, Otolaryngology
NATHAN, D. G., Paediatrics
NEEDLEMAN, H. L., Paediatric Dentistry
NEER, E. J., Medicine
NESSON, H. R., Medicine
NEUTRA, M. R., Paediatrics
NEWBURGER, J. W., Paediatrics
NEWHOUSE, J. P., Health Care Policy
NOTMAN, M. T., Psychiatry
NOVELLINE, R. A., Radiology
OJEMANN, R. G., Surgery
OLSEN, B. R., Anatomy
ORKIN, S. H., Paediatrics
PALFREY, J. S., Paediatrics
PARRISH, J. A., Dermatology
PAUL, D. L., Neurobiology
PENNEY, J. B., Jr, Neurology
PEPPERCORN, M. A., Medicine
PERRIMON, N., Genetics
PFEFFER, M. A., Medicine
PIER, G. B., Pathology
PINKUS, G. S., Pathology
PIZZO, P., Paediatrics
PLATT, O., Paediatrics
PLOEGH, H. L., Pathology
PODOLSKY, D. K., Medicine
POSS, R., Orthopaedic Surgery
POTTER, D. D., Neurobiology
POTTS, J. T., Jr, Clinical Medicine
POUSSAINT, A. F., Psychiatry
RABKIN, M. T., Medicine
RANDO, R. R., Biological Chemistry and Molecular Pharmacology
RAO, A., Pathology
RAPOPORT, T. A., Cell Biology
RAVIOLA, E., Neurobiology
REICH, P., Psychiatry
REID, L., Pathology
REINHERZ, E. L., Medicine
REMOLD, H. G., Medicine
REPPERT, S. M., Paediatrics
RETIK, A. B., Surgery
RICHARDSON, C. C., Biological Chemistry and Molecular Pharmacology
RICHIE, J. P., Surgery
RIORDAN, J. F., Biochemistry
RITZ, J., Medicine
ROBERTS, T. M., Pathology
ROBINSON, D. R., Medicine
ROSEN, F. S., Paediatrics
ROSEN, S. S., Pathology
ROSENBERG, R. D., Medicine
ROSENBLATT, M., Molecular Medicine
ROSENTHAL, D. I., Radiology
ROSENTHAL, D. S., Medicine
ROSNER, B. A., Medicine
ROTHENBERG, A., Psychiatry
RUDERMAN, J. V., Anatomy and Cell Biology
RUSSELL, P. S., Surgery
RUVKUN, G. B., Genetics
SACHS, B. P., Obstetrics, Gynaecology and Reproductive Medicine
SACHS, D. H., Surgery
SAITO, H., Biological Chemistry and Molecular Pharmacology
SALLAN, S. E., Paediatrics
SALZMAN, C., Psychiatry
SAMUELS, M. A., Neurology
SAPER, C. B., Neurology
SCHIFF, I., Gynaecology
SCHILDKRAUT, J. J., Psychiatry
SCHLOLLSMAN, S. F., Medicine
SCHNEEBERGER, E. E., Pathology
SCHNIPPER, L. E., Medicine
SCHOEN, F. J., Pathology
SCHUR, P. H., Medicine
SCOTT, R. M., Surgery
SEED, B., Genetics
SEIDMAN, C. E., Medicine
SEIDMAN, J. G., Genetics
SELKOE, D. J., Neurology
SELMAN, R. L., Psychology
SELTZER, S. E., Radiology
SELWYN, A., Medicine
SERHAN, C. N., Anaesthesia
SHANNON, D. C., Paediatrics
SHEFFER, A. L., Medicine
SHIPLEY, W. U., Radiation Therapy
SHKLAR, G., Oral Pathology
SHORE, M. F., Psychiatry
SIDMAN, R. L., Neuropathology
SILBERT, J. E., Medicine
SILEN, W., Surgery
SILVER, P. A., Biological Chemistry and Molecular Pharmacology
SIMEONE, J. F., Radiology
SIMON, B., Psychiatry
SKILLMAN, J. J., Surgery
SKLAR, J. L., Pathology
SLEDGE, C. B., Orthopaedic Surgery
SMITH, A. R., Radiation Oncology
SOBER, A. J., Dermatology
SODROSKI, J. G., Pathology
SONIS, S. T., Oral Medicine and Oral Pathology
SOUBA, W. W., Surgery
SPEALMAN, R. D., Psychobiology
SPECTOR, M., Orthopaedic Surgery
SPEIZER, F. E., Medicine
SPIEGELMAN, B. M., Biological Chemistry and Molecular Pharmacology
SPIRO, R. G., Biological Chemistry
SPRINGER, T. A., Pathology
STEER, M. L., Surgery
STEINMAN, T. I., Medicine
STERN, R. S., Dermatology
STILES, C. D., Microbiology and Molecular Genetics
STONE, A. A., Law and Psychiatry
STOSSEL, T. P., Medicine
STREILEIN, J. W., Ophthalmology
STREWLER, G. J., Medicine
STRICHARTZ, G. R., Anaesthesia
STROM, T. B., Medicine
STRUHL, K., Biological Chemistry and Molecular Pharmacology
SUIT, H. D., Radiation Oncology
SUKHATME, V. P., Medicine
SWARTZ, M. N., Medicine
SZOSTAK, J. W., Genetics
TABIN, C. J., Genetics
TASHJIAN, A. H. Jr, Biological Chemistry and Molecular Pharmacology
TAUBMAN, M. A., Oral Biology
TAYLOR, G. A., Radiology
TERHORST, C. P., Medicine
THIBAULT, G. E., Medicine
THIER, S. O., Medicine and Health Care Policy
THRALL, J. H., Radiology
TILNEY, N. L., Surgery
TOMKINS, R. G., Surgery
TOSTESON, D. C., Cell Biology
TREVES, S. T., Radiology
TSUANG, M. T., Psychiatry
TYLER, H. R., Neurology
UTIGER, R. D., Medicine
VACANTI, J. P., Surgery
VAILLANT, G. E., Psychiatry
VAN PRAAGH, R., Pathology
VOLPE, J. J., Neurology
WAGNER, G., Biological Chemistry and Molecular Pharmacology
WALKER, W. A., Nutrition and Paediatrics
WALSH, C. T., Biological Chemistry and Molecular Pharmacology
WARSHAW, A. L., Surgery
WEINBERG, A. N., Medicine
WEINBERGER, S. E., Medicine
WEINBLATT, M. E., Medicine
WEINER, H. L., Neurology
WEINSTEIN, H. J., Paediatrics
WEINSTEIN, M. C., Medicine

WEISS, S. T., Medicine
WEISSMAN, B. N., Radiology
WEIR, G. C., Medicine
WELLER, P. F., Medicine
WEYMAN, A. E., Medicine
WHITE, A. A. III, Orthopaedic Surgery
WHITTEMORE, A., Surgery
WILLETT, W. C., Medicine
WILLIAMS, G. H., Medicine
WILMORE, D. W., Surgery
WILSON, T. H., Cell Biology
WINKELMAN, J. W., Pathology
WINSTON, F. M., Genetics
WITTENBERG, J., Radiology
WOHL, M. E., Paediatrics
WOLF, G. L., Radiology
WOLF, M. A., Medicine
WOLFF, C., Anaesthesia
WOLFF, P. H., Psychiatry
WRAY, S. H., Neurology
YARMUSH, M., Surgery
YOUNG, A. B., Neurology
YOUNG, R. H., Pathology
YUNIS, E. J., Pathology
ZAPOL, W. M., Anaesthesia
ZERVAS, N. T., Neurosurgery
ZETTER, B. R., Surgery
ZINNER, M., Surgery

Graduate School of Public Health:

ALONSO, W., Population and International Health
BERKMAN, L. F., Health and Social Behaviour
BLENDON, R. J., Health Policy and Management
BLOOM, D. E., Population and International Health
BRAIN, J. D., Environmental Health
BRENNAN, T. A., Health Policy and Management
CHEN, L. C., Population and International Health
CHRISTIANI, D. C., Environmental Health
COOK, E. F., Epidemiology
DAVID, J. R., Tropical Public Health
DEGRUTTOLA, V. G., Biostatistics
DEMPLE, B. F., Toxicology
DYCK, A. J., Population and International Health
EARLS, F. J., Maternal and Child Health
EPSTEIN, A. M., Health Policy and Management
ESSEX, M. E., Cancer Biology
FINEBERG, H. V., Administration
FREDBERG, J. J., Environmental Health
GLIMCHER, L. H., Cancer Biology
GOLDMAN, P., Nutrition
GRAHAM, J. D., Health Policy and Management
HARN, D. A., Tropical Public Health
HARRINGTON, D. P., Biostatistics
HARRINGTON, J. J., Environmental Health
HEMENWAY, D., Health Policy and Management
HILL, A. G., Population and International Health
HSIAO, W. C., Health Policy and Management
KELSEY, K. T., Environmental Health
KOUTRAKIS, P., Environmental Health
LAGAKOS, S. W., Biostatistics
LAIRD, N. M., Biostatistics
LEE, T., Immunology and Infectious Diseases
LEVINS, R., Population and International Health
LI, F. P., Epidemiology
LITTLE, J. B., Cancer Biology
MCCORMICK, M. C., Maternal and Child Health
MONSON, R. R., Epidemiology and Environmental Health
MUELLER, N. E., Epidemiology
MURRAY, C., Population and International Health
NEWHOUSE, J. P., Health Policy and Management
PAGANO, M., Biostatistics
PIESSENS, W. F., Tropical Public Health
PROTHROW-STITH, D. B., Health Policy and Management
REICH, M. R., Population and International Health, and Health Policy and Management
ROBERTS, M. J., Health Policy and Management
ROBINS, J. M., Epidemiology and Biostatistics
RYAN, L. M., Biostatics
SAMSON, L. D., Molecular and Cellular Toxicology
SMITH, T. J., Environmental Health
SORENSON, G., Health and Social Behaviour
SPEIZER, F. E., Environmental Health
SPENGLER, J. D., Environmental Health
SPIELMAN, A., Tropical Public Health
STAMPFER, M. J., Nutrition and Epidemiology
TARLOV, A., Health Policy and Management
TASHJIAN, A. H., Jr, Toxicology
TRICHOPOULOS, D. V., Epidemiology
WALKER, A. M., Epidemiology
WARE, J. H., Biostatistics
WEI, L. J., Biostatistics
WEINSTEIN, M. C., Health Policy, Management and Biostatistics
WILLETT, W. C., Epidemiology and Nutrition
WIRTH, D. F., Tropical Public Health
ZELEN, M., Biostatistics

Graduate School of Education:

BOK, D. C.
CHAIT, R.
DUCKWORTH, E. R.
ELGIN, C. Z.
ELMORE, R. F.
FISCHER, K. W.
GARDNER, H. E.
GILLIGAN, C. F., Gender Studies and Education
GRAHAM, P. A., History of American Education
JOHNSON, S. M.
LAWRENCE-LIGHTFOOT, S.
LEVINE, R. A., Education and Human Development
LIGHT, R. J.
MURNANE, R.
MURPHY, J. T.
OLIVER, D. W.
ORFIELD, G., Education and Social Policy
SCHWARTZ, J.
SELMAN, R. L.
SINGER, J. D.
SNOW, C. E.
SUÁREZ-OROZCO, M.
WEISS, C. H.
WILLETT, J. B.
WILLIE, C. V., Education and Urban Studies

Graduate School of Business Administration:

AMABILE, T. M., Entrepreneurial Management
APPLEGATE, L. M., General Management
AUSTIN, J. E., Business, Government and International Economy
BADARACCO, J. L., General Management
BAKER, G. P., III, Organizations and Markets
BALDWIN, C. Y., Organizations and Markets
BARTLETT, C. A., General Management
BARTON, D. A., Technology and Operations Management
BEER, M., Organizational Behaviour
BELL, D. E., Marketing
BOWEN, H. K., Technology and Operations Management
BOWER, J. L., General Management
BRADLEY, S. P., Competition and Strategy
BRANDENBERGER, A. M., Competition and Strategy
BRUNS, W. J., Jr, Accounting and Control
CASH, J. I., Jr, Service Management
CAVES, R. E., Competition and Strategy
CHRISTENSEN, C. J., Control
CLARK, K. B., Dean of the Faculty
CRANE, D. B., Finance
CRUM, M. C., Finance
DATAR, S., Accounting and Control
DEIGHTON, J. A., Marketing
DESHPANDÉ, R., Marketing
DOLAN, R. J., Marketing
FROOT, K. A., Finance
FRUHAN, W. E., Jr, Finance
GABARRO, J. J., Organizational Behaviour
GARVIN, D. A., General Management
GHEMAWAT, P., Competition and Strategy
GREYSER, S. A., Marketing
HAMMOND, J. H., Technology and Operations Management
HAWKINS, D. F., Accounting and Control
HAYES, R. H., Technology and Operations Management
HEALY, P. M., Accounting and Control
HERZLINGER, R. E., Accounting and Control
HILL, L. A., Organizational Behaviour
IANSITI, M., Technology and Operations Management
IBARRA, H., Organizational Behaviour
JENSEN, M. C., Organizations and Markets
KANTER, R. M., General Management
KAPLAN, R. S., Accounting and Control
KESTER, W. C., Finance
KOHLBERG, E., Competition and Strategy
KOTTER, J. P., Organizational Behaviour
LIGHT, J. O., Finance
LORSCH, J. W., Organizational Behaviour
MASON, S. P., Finance
MCCRAW, T. K., Business, Government and International Economy
MCFARLAN, F. W., General Management
MCKENNEY, J. L., Management Information Systems
MERTON, R. C., Finance
MEYER, R. F., Managerial Economics
MILLS, D. Q., Human Resource Management
MONTGOMERY, C. A., Competition and Strategy
NOHRIA, N., Organizational Behaviour
NOLAN, R. L., General Management
PAINE, L. S., General Management
PALEPU, K. G., Accounting and Control
PEROLD, A. F., Finance
PIPER, T. R., Finance
PISANO, G., Technology and Operations Management
PORTER, M. E., Competition and Strategy
RANGAN, V. K., Marketing
REILING, H. B., Finance
ROTEMBERG, J. J., Business, Government and International Economy
ROTH, A. E., Negotiation and Decision Making.
RUBACK, R. S., Finance
SAHLMAN, W. A., Entrepreneurial Management
SALTER, M. S., Organizations and Markets
SASSER, W. E. Jr., Service Management
SCHLESINGER, L. A., Service Management
SCOTT, B. R., Business, Government and International Economy
SEBENIUS, J. K., Negotiation and Decision Making
SHAPIRO, R. D., Technology and Operations Management
SILK, A. J., Marketing
SIMONS, R. L., Accounting and Control
SLOANE, C. S., Organizational Behaviour
STEVENSON, H. H., Entrepreneurial Management
STOBAUGH, R. B., Production and Operations Management
TEDLOW, R. S., Business, Government and International Economy
TUFANO, P., Finance
TUSHMAN, M. L., Organizational Behaviour

UPTON, D. M., Technology and Operations Management
VIETOR, R. H. K., Business, Government and International Economy
WELLS, L. T., Jr, Business, Government and International Economy
WHEELWRIGHT, S. C., Technology and Operations Management
YOFFIE, D. B., Competition and Strategy
YOSHINO, M. Y., General Management
ZALTMAN, G., Marketing
ZUBOFF, S., Organizational Behaviour

J. F. Kennedy School of Government:

ALLISON, G. T., Government
ALTSHULER, A., Urban Policy and Planning
BANE, M. J., Domestic Social Policy
BATOR, F. M., International Political Economy
BOK, D., US Domestic Policy and Governance
BORJAS, G., Immigration
BRANSCOMB, L., Public Policy
BROOKS, H., Technology and Public Policy
CARTER, A. B., International and National Security
CLARK, W. C., International Science, Public Policy and Human Development
COOPER, R. N., International Economics
CUTLER, D. M., Public Finance and Health
DARMAN, R., Public Management
DOTY, P. M., Public Policy
ELLWOOD, D., Income Support and Social Welfare Policy
GERGEN, D., Public Management and Leadership
GOMEZ-IBANEZ, J. A., Public Policy and Urban Policy
GRINDLE, M. S., International Development
HEYMANN, P. B., Law
HIGGINBOTHAM, A. L., Race and Public Policy
HOGAN, W., Public Policy and Management
HOLDREN, J., Science and Energy Policy
JASANOFF, S., Science and Public Policy
JENCKS, C., US Domestic Social Policy
JORGENSON, D. W., Economics
KALB, M., Press and Public Policy
KALT, J., International Political Economy
KELMAN, S. J., Public Management
LAWRENCE, R. Z., International Trade
LEONARD, H., Public Management
LIGHT, R., Education
MANSBRIDGE, J., Democratic Governance
MAY, E., History
MEYER, J. R., Capital Formation, Economic Growth, Transportation
MONTGOMERY, J. D., International Studies
MOORE, M. H., Criminal Justice Policy and Management
NEUSTADT, R. E., Government
NEWHOUSE, J. P., Health Policy and Management
NEWMAN, K., Sociology of Labour Markets
NYE, J., International Affairs and Democratic Governance
ORREN, G. R., Public Policy
PATERSON, T., Press and Politics
PERKINS, D., Political Economy
PETERSON, P.E., American Government and Education
PORTER, R., Business and Government
PUTNAM, R., Democratic Governance
RAIFFA, H., Managerial Economics
RODRIK, D., International Trade and Development
SACHS, J., International Trade and Development
SAICH, A., International Affairs
SCHAUER, F., First Amendment
SCHERER, F. M., Business and Government
STAVINS, R. N., Environmental Economics
STOCK, J. H., Political Economy
THOMPSON, D. Political Philosophy
VERNON, R., International Affairs
VISCUSI, W. K., Risk Analysis and Environmental Regulation
WILLIAMS, S., Electoral Politics
WILSON, W. J., Urban Sociology
WISE, D., Political Economy
ZECKHAUSER, R. J., Political Economy

School of Dental Medicine:

DOGON, I. L., Restorative Dentistry
DONOFF, R. B., Oral and Maxillofacial Surgery
DOUGLASS, C. W., Oral Health Policy and Epidemiology
GOLDHABER, P., Periodontology
HAY, D. I., Oral Biology
KABAN, L. B., Oral and Maxillofacial Surgery
OLSEN, B. R., Oral Biology
SHKLAR, G., Oral Pathology
SONIS, S. S., Oral Medicine and Diagnostic Sciences
TAUBMAN, M. A., Oral Biology

HEBREW COLLEGE

43 Hawes St, Brookline, MA 02146
Telephone: (617) 232-8710
Fax: (617) 734-9769

Founded 1921

President: Dr DAVID GORDIS
Provost: Dr BARRY MESCH
Dean: Dr MICHAEL LIBENSON
Registrar: NORMA FRANKEL
Librarian: Dr MAURICE TUCHMAN

Library of 100,000 vols
Number of teachers: 43
Number of students: 730

Publication: *Hebrew College Today* (quarterly).

MASSACHUSETTS COLLEGE OF ART

621 Huntington Ave, Boston, MA 02215
Telephone: (617) 232-1555
Fax: (617) 232-0050

Founded 1873

President: WILLIAM O'NEIL
Vice-President of Academic Affairs: BETTY BUCHSBAUM
Vice-President of Administration and Finance: MARY SPOLIDORO
Vice-President of Students: PAUL MCCAFFREY
Librarian: GEORGE MORGAN

Library of 95,000 vols
Number of teachers: 70 full-time, 35 part-time
Number of students: 2,189 (day and evening)

MASSACHUSSETTS COLLEGE OF LIBERAL ARTS

375 Church St, North Adams, MA 01247
Telephone: (413) 662-5000

Founded 1894

Programmes in education, communications, business administration, liberal arts, computer science and medical technology

President: Dr THOMAS D. ACETO
Vice-President of Academic Affairs: Dr ASHIM K. BASU
Dean of Academic Studies: Dr ELAINE COLLINS
Dean of Students: Dr SCOTT KALICKI
Director of Counselling: Dr ELLEN DOYLE
Director of Career Development: SHARRON ZAVATTARO
Director of Financial Aid: ELIZABETH PETRI
Director of Admissions: DENISE RICHARDELLO
Vice-President of Administration and Finance: THOMAS M. JONES

Library of 172,000 vols
Number of full-time students: 1,600

MASSACHUSETTS INSTITUTE OF TECHNOLOGY

Cambridge, MA 02139
Telephone: (617) 253-1000

Founded 1861
Private institution
Academic year: September to May

President: CHARLES M. VEST
Chancellor: LAWRENCE S. BACOW
Provost: ROBERT A. BROWN
Associate Provost: PHILLIP L. CLAY
Associate Provost for the Arts: ALAN BRODY
Treasurer and Vice-President for Finance: G. P. STREHLE
Senior Vice-President: (vacant)
Vice-President, Research, and Dean for Graduate Education: J. DAVID LITSTER
Vice-President, Resource Development: BARBARA G. STOWE
Vice-President, Information Systems: J. D. BRUCE
Vice-President for Human Resources: JOAN F. RICE
Chairman of the Corporation: ALEXANDER V. D'ARBELOFF
Secretary of the Corporation, Secretary of the Executive Committee, Executive Assistant to the President, and Director of Public Relations: KATHRYN ADAMS WILLMORE
Controller: JAMES C. MORGAN
Registrar: J. D. NYHART (acting)
Director of Libraries: ANN J. WOLPERT

Teaching staff: 2,054, including 896 professors
Number of students: 9,947

Publications: *MIT Bulletin*, *Technology Review* (8 a year), *Tech Talk*, *Sloan Management Review*.

DEANS

School of Architecture and Planning: WILLIAM J. MITCHELL
School of Engineering: (vacant)
School of Humanities and Social Science: PHILLIP S. KHOURY
Alfred P. Sloan School of Management: RICHARD SCHMALENSEE (interim)
School of Science: ROBERT J. BIRGENEAU
Graduate School: J. DAVID LITSTER
Undergraduate Education and Student Affairs: ROSALIND H. WILLIAMS

PROFESSORS

(Some professors serve in more than one department)

School of Architecture and Planning:

Department of Architecture

ANDERSON, S., History and Architecture (Head)
BEINART, J., Architecture
DE MONCHAUX, J., Architecture and Urban Planning
DENNIS, M., Architecture
GLICKSMAN, L. R., Building Technology
LEVINE, E., Visual Arts
MITCHELL, W. J., Architecture, Media Arts and Sciences
PORTER, W. L., Architecture and Urban Planning
STINY, G., Architecture
WAMPLER, J., Architecture
WODICZKO, K., Visual Arts

Department of Media Arts and Sciences

BENTON, S. A., Media Arts and Sciences
MINSKY, M. L., Media Arts and Sciences
MITCHELL, W. J., Architecture, and Media Arts and Sciences
NEGROPONTE, N. P., Media Technology
PAPERT, S. A., Education and Technology
PENTLAND, A. P., Media Arts and Sciences
VERCOE, B., Media Arts and Sciences

Department of Urban Studies and Planning

AMSDEN, A.
BACOW, L., Law and Environmental Policy
CLAY, P., Urban Studies and Planning
DE MONCHAUX, J., Architecture and Urban Planning
FERREIRA, J., Urban Studies and Operations Research
FOGELSON, R. M., History and Urban Studies
FRIEDEN, B. J., City Planning
GAKENHEIMER, R. A., Urban Studies and Planning and Civil Engineering
KEYES, L. C., City and Regional Planning
LEVY, F. S., Urban Regional Planning and Economic Development
POLENSKE, K. R., Regional Political Economy and Planning
REIN, M., Sociology
SANYAL, B. (Head)
SUSSKIND, L. E., Urban Studies and Planning
TENDLER, J., Political Economy
WHEATON, W. C., Economics and Urban Studies

School of Engineering:

Department of Aeronautics and Astronautics

CRAWLEY, E. F., (Head)
DEYST, J. J.
EPSTEIN, A. H.
GREITZER, E. M.
HANSMAN, R. J.
HARRIS, W. L.
HASTINGS, D. E.
HOLLISTER, W. M.
KERREBROCK, J. L.
LAGACE, P. A.
LANDAHL, M. T.
MARKEY, W. R.
MARTINEZ-SANCHEZ, M.
MURMAN, E. M.
ODONI, A. R., Aeronautics and Astronautics and Civil Engineering
WIDNALL, S. E.
YOUNG, L. R.

Department of Chemical Engineering

ARMSTRONG, R. C.
BRENNER, H.
BROWN, R. A. (Head)
COHEN, R. E.
COLTON, C. K.
COONEY, C. L.
DEEN, W. M.
HATTON, T. A.
HOWARD, J. B.
JENSEN, K. J.
LANGER, R. S.
LAUFFENBERGER, D. A.
MCRAE, G. J.
MERRILL, E. W.
SAROFIM, A. F.
SAWIN, H. H.
SMITH, K. A.
STEPHANOPOULOS, GEO.
STEPHANOPOULOS, GRE.
TESTER, J. W.
WANG, D. I. C.

Department of Civil Engineering and Environmental Engineering

BEN-AKIVA, M.
BRAS, R. L. (Head)
BUYUKOZTURK, O.
CHISHOLM, S.
CONNOR, J. J., Jr
DE NEUFVILLE, R. L.
EINSTEIN, H. H.
GIBSON, L., Mechanical Engineering
GSCHWEND, P.
HEMOND, H. F.
KAUSEL, E.
LADD, C. C.
LERMAN, S. R.
LOGCHER, R. D.
MADSEN, O. S.
MARKS, D. H.
MCGARRY, F. J., Civil and Polymer Engineering
MCLAUGHLIN, D. B.
MEI, C. C.
MOAVENZADEH, F.
ODONI, A. R., Civil Engineering and Aeronautics and Astronautics
PERKINS, F. E.
ROOS, D.
SHEFFI, Y.
SUSSMAN, J. M.
VENEZIANO, D.
WHITMAN, R.
WILSON, N. H. M.

Department of Electrical Engineering and Computer Science

ABELSON, H., Computer Science and Engineering
AGARWAL, A., Computer Science and Engineering
ALLEN, J., Electrical Engineering and Computer Science
ANTONIADIS, D., Electrical Engineering
ARVIND, Computer Science and Engineering
BAGGEROER, A. B., Ocean Engineering and Electrical Engineering
BERS, A., Electrical Engineering
BERTSEKAS, D. P., Electrical Engineering
BERWICK, R. C., Computer Science and Engineering and Computational Linguistics
BOSE, A. G., Electrical Engineering
BRAIDA, L. B. D., Electrical Engineering
BROOKS, R. A., Computer Science and Engineering
BRUCE, J. D., Electrical Engineering
DAHLEH, M. A., Electrical Engineering
DAVIS, R., Computer Science and Engineering
DEL ALAMO, J. A., Electrical Engineering
DERTOUZOS, M. L., Computer Science and Electrical Engineering
DRAKE, A. W., Electrical Engineering
DRESSELHAUS, M. S., Electrical Engineering and Physics
FONSTAD, C. G., Jr, Electrical Engineering
FUJIMOTO, J. G., Electrical Engineering
GALLAGER, R. G., Electrical Engineering
GIFFORD, D. K., Computer Science and Engineering
GOLDWASSER, S., Computer Science and Engineering
GRAY, M. L., Electrical Engineering
GRAY, P. E., Electrical Engineering
GRIMSON, W. E. L., Computer Science and Engineering
GRODZINSKY, A. J., Electrical, Mechanical and Bioengineering
GUTTAG, J. V., Computer Science and Engineering
HAUS, H. A., Electrical Engineering
HENNIE, F. C. III, Computer Science and Engineering
HORN, B. K., Computer Science and Engineering
IPPEN, E. P., Electrical Engineering and Physics
KASSAKIAN, J. G., Electrical Engineering
KIRTLEY, J. L., Jr, Electrical Engineering
KONG, J. A., Electrical Engineering
LANG, J. H., Electrical Engineering
LARSON, R. C., Electrical Engineering
LEE, H. S., Electrical Engineering
LEISERSON, C. E., Computer Science and Engineering
LIM, J. S., Electrical Engineering
LISKOV, B. H., Computer Science and Engineering
LOZANO-PÉREZ, T., Computer Science and Engineering
LYNCH, N. A., Computer Science and Engineering
MAGNANTI, T. L., Management Science and Electrical Engineering
MARK, R. G., Health Sciences and Technology and Electrical Engineering
MEYER, A. R., Computer Science and Engineering
MICALI, S., Computer Science and Engineering
MINSKY, M. L., Media Arts and Sciences and Computer Science and Engineering
MITTER, S. K., Electrical Engineering
MOSES, J., Computer Science and Engineering
OPPENHEIM, A. V., Electrical Engineering
ORLANDO, T. P., Electrical Engineering
PARKER, R. R., Electrical Engineering
PEAKE, W. T., Electrical and Bioengineering
PENFIELD, P. L., Jr, Electrical Engineering
PRATT, G. W., Jr, Electrical Engineering
REIF, L. R., Electrical Engineering
RIVEST, R. L., Computer Science and Engineering
ROBERGE, J. K., Electrical Engineering
SALTZER, J. H., Computer Science and Engineering
SAWIN, H. H., Chemical Engineering and Electrical Engineering
SCHLECHT, M. F., Electrical Engineering
SCHMIDT, M. A., Electrical Engineering
SENTURIA, S. D., Electrical Engineering
SHAPIRO, J. H., Electrical Engineering
SMITH, A. C., Electrical Engineering
SMITH, H. I., Electrical Engineering
SODINI, C. G., Electrical Engineering
STAELIN, D. H., Electrical Engineering
STEVENS, K. N., Electrical Engineering
SUSSMAN, G. J., Electrical Engineering
SZOLOVITS, P., Computer Science and Engineering
THORNTON, R. D., Electrical Engineering
TROXEL, D. E., Electrical Engineering
TSITSIKLIS, J. N., Electrical Engineering
VERGHESE, G. C., Electrical Engineering
WARD, S. A., Computer Science and Engineering
WARDE, C., Electrical Engineering
WEISS, T. F., Electrical and Bioengineering
WHITE, J. K., Electrical Engineering
WILLSKY, A. S., Electrical Engineering
WILSON, G. L., Electrical and Mechanical Engineering
WINSTON, P. H., Computer Science and Engineering
WYATT, J. L., Electrical Engineering
ZAHN, M., Electrical Engineering

Department of Materials Science and Engineering

ALLEN, S. M., Physical Metallurgy
CHIANG, Y.-M., Ceramics
CIMA, M., Ceramics
CLARK, J. P., Materials Systems
EAGAR, T. W., Materials Engineering (Head)
FLEMINGS, M. C., Materials Processing
GIBSON, L., Materials Engineering
HOBBS, L. W., Ceramics
JENSEN, K. F., Chemical Engineering, Materials Science and Engineering
KIMERLING, L. C., Materials Science and Engineering
LATANISION, R. M., Materials Science
LECHTMAN, H., Archaeology and Ancient Technology
MCGARRY, F. J., Polymer Engineering and Civil Engineering
ROSE, R. M., Materials Science and Engineering
RUBNER, M. F., Polymer Materials Science
RUSSELL, K. C., Metallurgy and Nuclear Engineering
SADOWAY, D. R., Materials Chemistry
SURESH, S., Materials Science and Engineering
THOMAS, E. L., Materials Science and Engineering
THOMPSON, C. V., Electronic Materials
TULLER, H. L., Ceramics and Electronic Materials

VANDER SANDE, J. B., Materials Science
WITT, A. F., Materials Science and Engineering
WUENSCH, B. J., Ceramics
YANNAS, I. V., Polymer Science and Engineering

Department of Mechanical Engineering

ABEYARATNE, R., (Assoc. Head)
AKYLAS, T. R.
ANAND, L.
ARGON, A. S.
ASADA, H.
BATHE, K.-J.
CHENG, W. K.
CRAVALHO, E. G.
DEWEY, C. D., Jr
DUBOWSKY, S.
FLOWERS, W. C., Teaching Innovation
GHONIEM, A. F.
GIBSON, L.
GLICKSMAN, L.
GOSSARD, D. C.
GRODZINSKY, A. J., Electrical, Mechanical and Bioengineering
GUTOWSKI, T. G.
HARDT, D. E.
HEYWOOD, J. B.
HOGAN, N. J.
HUNTER, I. W.
KAMM, R. D.
MIKIC, B. B.
PARKS, D. M.
PATERA, A. T.
PROBSTEIN, R. F., Engineering
ROWELL, D.
SACHS, E. M.
SEERING, W. P.
SHERIDAN, T. B., Engineering and Applied Psychology
SLOCUM, A.
SLOTINE, J. E.
SMITH, J. L., Jr, Engineering
SONIN, A. A.
SUH, N. P., Manufacturing (Head)
SURESH, S.
TODREAS, N.
VEST, C. M.
WILLIAMS, J. H., Jr, Teaching Excellence
WILSON, G. L., Electrical and Mechanical Engineering
YANNAS, I. V., Polymer Science and Engineering
YOUCEF-TOUMI, K.

Department of Nuclear Engineering

APOSTOLAKIS, G.
CHEN, S.-H.
FREIDBERG, J. P. (Head)
GOLAY, M. W.
HANSEN, K. F.
HUTCHINSON, I. H.
KAZIMI, M. S.
LATANISION, R. M., Joint Materials Science and Engineering
LESTER, R. K.
LIDSKY, L. M.
RUSSELL, K. C., Joint Materials Science and Engineering
TODREAS, N. E., Nuclear Engineering and Mechanical Engineering
YIP, S.

Department of Ocean Engineering

BAGGEROER, A. B., Ocean and Electrical Engineering
CHRYSSOSTOMIDIS, C., Ocean Science and Engineering (Head)
KERWIN, J. E., Naval Architecture
MARCUS, H. S., Marine Systems
MASUBUCHI, K., Ocean Engineering and Materials Science
MILGRAM, J. H., Ocean Engineering
NYHART, J. D., Ocean Engineering and Management
PATRIKALAKIS, N. M., Ocean Engineering
SCHMIDT, H., Ocean Engineering
SCLAVOUNOS, P. D., Naval Architecture
TRIANTAFYLLOU, M. S., Ocean Engineering
VANDIVER, J. K., Ocean Engineering
WIERZBICKI, T., Applied Mechanics
YUE, D. K.-P., Hydrodynamics and Ocean Engineering

Division of Bioengineering and Environmental Health

DEEN, W. M.
DEWEY, C. F., Jr
ESSIGMAN, J. M.
FOX, J. G.
GRODZINSKY, A. J.
HOGAN, N. J.
HUNTER, I. W.
KAMM, R. D.
LANGER, R. S.
LAUFFENBURGER, D. A. (Co-Dir)
LODISH, H. F.
MATSUDAIRA, P. T.
TANNENBAUM, S. R. (Co-Dir)
THILLY, W. G.
WOGAN, G. N.
YANNAS, I. V.

Program in Science, Technology and Society:

BUCHWALD, J. Z., Bern Dibner Professor
FISCHER, M. J., Anthropology and Science and Technology Studies (Dir)
GRAHAM, L. R., History of Science
KELLER, E. F., History and Philosophy of Science
KENISTON, K., Human Development
MANNING, K. R., History of Science, Writing Program
POSTOL, T. A., Science, Technology and International Security
SMITH, M. R., History of Technology
TURKLE, S. R., Sociology of Science

School of Humanities and Social Science:

Department of Economics

ANGRIST, J.
BANERJEE, A.
BLANCHARD, O. J.
CABALLERO, R.
DIAMOND, P. A.
DORNBUSCH, R.
ELLISON, G.
FISHER, F. M.
GRUBER, J.
HARRIS, J.
HAUSMAN, J. A.
HOLMSTRÖM, B.
JOSKOW, P. L., Economics and Management (Head)
KREMER, M.
KRUGMAN, P.,
NEWEY, W. K.
PIORE, M. J., Economics and Management
POTERBA, J. M.
ROSE, N.
ROSS, S., Finance and Economics
SCHMALENSEE, R. L., Management and Economics
SNYDER, J. Political Science and Economics
TEMIN, P.
THUROW, L. C., Economics and Management
WHEATON, W. C., Economics and Urban Studies

Department of Humanities

BAMBERGER, J. S., Music
BRODY, A., Theatre Arts
CHILD, P., Music
DE COURTIVRON, I., French
DESAI, A., Writing
DONALDSON, P. S., Literature
DOWER, J. W., History
FISCHER, M. J., Anthropology and Science, Technology and Society
FLYNN, S., English as a Second Language and Linguistics
FOGELSON, R. M., History and Urban Studies
GARRELS, E., Spanish
GRAHAM, L., History and Science, Technology and Society
HARBISON, J., Music
HARRIS, E. T., Music
HILDEBIDLE, J., Literature
HOWE, J., Anthropology
JACKSON, J. E., Anthropology
JENKINS, H., III, Film Studies and Popular Literature
KELLER, E. F., Women's Studies and Science, Technology and Society
KHOURY, P. S., History
KIBEL, A. C., Literature
LIGHTMAN, A. P., Science and Writing
LINDGREN, L., Music
MAIER, P. R., History
MANNING, K. R., Science, Technology and Society, and Writing and Humanistic Studies
MAZLISH, B., History
MIYAGAWA, S., Japanese and Linguistics
PARADIS, J., Technical Communication
PERDUE, P., History
PERRY, R., Literature and Women's Studies
RITVO, H., History and Writing
SLYMOVICS, S., Anthropology and Women's Studies
SMITH, M. R., History of Technology and History
STEINBERG, A., Archaeology
TAPSCOTT, S. J., Literature
THOMPSON, M. A., Music
THORBURN, D., Literature
TURK, E. B., French
VERCOE, B. L., Music
WILLIAMS, R., Writing and History of Technology
WOLFF, C. G., Writing

Department of Linguistics and Philosophy

CHOMSKY, N. A., Linguistics
COHEN, J., Philosophy and Political Science
FLYNN, S., English as a Second Language and Linguistics
HALE, K. L., Linguistics
HALLE, M., Linguistics
HEIM, I., Linguistics
KENSTOWICZ, M., Linguistics
MARANTZ, A., Linguistics
MCGEE, V., Philosophy
MIYAGAWA, S., Linguistics and Japanese
O'NEIL, W., Linguistics
PESETSKY, D., Linguistics
SINGER, I., Philosophy
STALNAKER, R., Philosophy (Head)
THOMSON, J. J., Philosophy
WEXLER, K. N., Linguistics and Brain and Cognitive Science

Department of Political Science

BERGER, S., Comparative Politics and Political Economy
CHOUCRI, N., International Relations and Foreign Policy
COHEN, J., Philosophy and Political Science (Head)
MEYER, S. M., Defence and Arms Control Studies
POSEN, B. R., Defence and Arms Control Studies
SAMUELS, R. J., Comparative Politics and Political Economy
SAPOLSKY, H. M., Public Policy and Organization
SKOLNIKOFF, E. B., Public Policy
SNYDER, J. R., American Politics
WEINER, M.. Comparative Politics

Sloan School of Management:

ALLEN, T. J., Jr, Management
ANCONA, D. G., Organization Studies
ASQUITH, K. P., Accounting
BAILYN, L. L., Organizational Psychology and Management
BARNETT, A. I., Operations Research and Management
BERNDT, E. R., Applied Economics
BITRAN, G R., Management

CARROLL, J. S., Behavioural and Policy Sciences
COX, J. C., Finance
DORNBUSCH, R., Economics and Management
FINE, C.H., Management Science and Operations Research
FRANKEL, E. G., Management and Ocean Engineering
FREUND, R. M., Operations Research and Statistics
GIBBONS, R. S., Management Strategy and International Management
GRAVES, S. C., Manufacturing
HAUSER, J. R., Marketing
HAX, A. C., Management
JACOBY, H. D., Management
JOSKOW, P. L., Economics and Management
KAUFMAN, G. M., Operations Research and Management
KOCHAN, T. A., Management
LESSARD, D. R., International Management
LITTLE, J. D. C.
LO, A. W., Management
MCKERSIE, R. B., Management
MADNICK, S. E., Information Technology
MAGNANTI, T. L., Management Science
MALONE, T. W., Information Systems
MYERS, S. C., Finance
NYHART, J. D., Management and Ocean Engineering
ORLIN, J. B., Management Science and Operations Research
OSTERMAN, P.
PINDYCK, R. S., Finance
PIORE, M. J., Economics and Management
POUNDS, W. F., Management
ROBERTS, E. B., Management of Technology
SCHARFSTEIN, D., Finance
SCHMALENSEE, R. L., Management and Economics
SCOTT MORTON, M. S., Management
SHAPIRO, J. F., Operations Research and Management
STEIN, J. C., Management
STERMAN, J., Operations Research and Management
STOKER, T. M., Applied Economics
THUROW, L. C., Management and Economics
URBAN, G. L., Management
UTTERBACK, J., Management
VAN MAANEN, J. E., Organizational Studies
VON HIPPEL, E. A., Management
WANG, J., Finance
WEIN, L. M., Operations Research and Management
WELSCH, R. E., Manufacturing
WERNERFELT, B.
WESTNEY, D. E., International Management

School of Science:

Department of Biology

BROWN, G. M., Biochemistry
CHISOLM, S. W., Civil and Environmental Engineering and Biology
DEMAIN, A. L., Industrial Microbiology
FINK, G. R., Genetics
FOX, M. S., Molecular Biology
GUARENTE, L. P., Biology
HOPKINS, N. H., Biology
HORVITZ, H. R., Biology
HOUSMAN, D. E., Biology
HYNES, R. O., Biology
INGRAM, V. M., Biochemistry
JAENISCH, R., Biology
KIM, P. S., Biology
KING, J. A., Biology
KRIEGER, M., Molecular Genetics
LANDER, E., Biology
LODISH, H. F., Biology
MATSUDAIRA, P., Biology
ORR-WEAVER, T., Biology
PABO, C. O., Biology
PAGE, D., Biology
PARDUE, M. L., Biology
PENMAN, S., Cell Biology
QUINN, W., Neurobiology and Biology
RAJBHANDARY, U. L., Biochemistry
RICH, A., Biophysics
ROBBINS, P. W., Biochemistry
ROSENBERG, R. D., Medicine and Biology
SAUER, R. T., Biochemistry
SHARP, P. A., Biology (Head)
SINSKEY, A. J., Applied Microbiology
SOLOMON, F., Biology
STEINER, L. A., Immunology
STELLER, H., Biology
STUBBE, J., Chemistry and Biology
TONEGAWA, S., Biology
WALKER, G. C., Biology
WEINBERG, R. A., Biology
YOUNG, R. A., Biology

Department of Brain and Cognitive Sciences

ADELSON, E. H., Visual Sciences
BERWICK, R. C.,Computer Science and Engineering and Computational Linguistics
BIZZI, E., Brain Sciences and Human Behaviour (Head)
CORKIN, S. H., Psychology
GRAYBIEL, A. M., Neuroanatomy
HEIN, A., Experimental Psychology
HOGAN, N., Mechanical Engineering and Brain and Cognitive Science
JORDAN, M. I., Psychology
PINKER, S., Psychology
POGGIO, T. A., Vision Sciences and Biophysics
POTTER, M. C., Psychology
QUINN, W. G., Neurobiology
RICHARDS, W. A., Psychophysics
SCHILLER, P. H., Medical Engineering and Medical Physics
SCHNEIDER, G. E., Neuroscience
SPELKE, E., Psychology
STELLER, H., Neurobiology
SUR, M., Neuroscience
TONEGAWA, S., Biology
WEXLER, K. N., Psychology and Linguistics
WURTMAN, R. J., Neuropharmacology

Department of Chemistry

BAWENDI, M. G.
BUCHWALD, S. L.
CEYER, S. T.
CUMMINS, C. C.
DANHEISER, R. L. (Assoc. Head)
DAVISON, A.
DEUTCH, J. M.
ESSIGMANN, J. M., Chemistry and Toxicology
FIELD, R. W.
GRIFFIN, R. G.
KEMP, D. S.
KLIBANOV, A. M.
LIPPARD, S. J. (Head)
MASAMUNE, S.
MOLINA, M. J., Earth, Atmospheric and Planetary Sciences and Chemistry
NELSON, K. A.
NOCERA, D. G.
SCHROCK, R. R.
SEYFERTH, D.
SILBEY, R. J.
STEINFELD, J. I.
STUBBE, J., Chemistry and Biology
SWAGER, T. M.
TANNENBAUM, S. R., Chemistry and Toxicology
WOGAN, G. N., Chemistry and Toxicology

Department of Earth, Atmospheric and Planetary Sciences

BOYLE, E. A., Chemical Oceanography
BURCHFIEL, B. C., Geology
EDMOND, J. M., Oceanography
ELLIOT, J. L., Planetary Sciences
EMANUEL, K. A., Meteorology
EVANS, J. B., Geophysics
FLIERL, G. R., Oceanography
FREY, F. A., Geochemistry
GROTZINGER, J. P., Geology
GROVE, T. L., Geology
HAGER, B. H., Earth Sciences
HERRING, T. A., Geophysics
HODGES, K., Geology
JORDAN, T. H., Earth and Planetary Sciences
LINDZEN, R. S., Meteorology
MARSHALL, J., Physical Oceanography
MOLINA, M. J., Atmospheric Chemistry and Chemistry
MORGAN, F. D., Geophysics
NEWELL, R. E., Meteorology
PLUMB, R. A., Meteorology
PRINN, R. G., Atmospheric Chemistry (Head)
RIZZOLI, P. M., Oceanography
ROTHMAN, D. H., Geophysics
ROYDEN, L., Geology
SOUTHARD, J. B., Geology
STONE, P. H., Meteorology
TOKSÖZ, M. N., Geophysics
WISDOM, J., Planetary Sciences
WUNSCH, C. I., Physical Oceanography
ZUBER, M. T., Planetary Sciences

Department of Mathematics

ARTIN, M., Mathematics
BEILINSON, A., Mathematics
BENNEY, D. J., Applied Mathematics (Head)
CHENG, H., Applied Mathematics
DE JONG, A. J., Mathematics
DUDLEY, R. M., Mathematics
FREEDMAN, D. Z., Applied Mathematics
FRIEDMAN, S. D., Mathematics
GREENSPAN, H. P., Applied Mathematics
GUILLEMIN, V. W., Mathematics
HELGASON, S., Mathematics
HOPKINS, M. J., Mathematics
JERISON, D. S., Mathematics
KAČ, V., Mathematics
KLEIMAN, S., Mathematics
KLEITMAN, D. J., Applied Mathematics
LEIGHTON, F. T., Applied Mathematics
LUSZTIG, G., Mathematics
MATTUCK, A. P., Mathematics (Head)
MELROSE, R. B., Mathematics
MILLER, H. P., Mathematics
MROWHA, T., Mathematics
MUNKRES, J. R., Mathematics
PETERSON, F. P., Mathematics
ROGERS, H., Jr, Mathematics
ROSALES, R. R., Applied Mathematics
ROTA, G.-C., Applied Mathematics and Philosophy
SACKS, G. E., Mathematical Logic
SINGER, I. M., Mathematics
SIPSER, M., Applied Mathematics
STANLEY, R. P., Applied Mathematics
STRANG, W. G., Mathematics
STROOCK, D. W., Mathematics
TIAN, G., Mathematics
TOOMRE, A., Applied Mathematics
VOGAN, D. A., Mathematics

Department of Physics

BECKER, U. J.
BELCHER, J. W.
BENEDEK, G. B., Physics and Biological Physics
BERKER, A. N.
BERNSTEIN, A. M.
BERTOZZI, W.
BERTSCHINGER, E.
BIRGENEAU, R. J.
BRADT, H. VAN D.
BURKE, B. F.
BUSZA, W.
CANIZARES, C. R.
CHEN, M.
COPPI, B.
DRESSELHAUS, M. S., Physics and Electrical Engineering
ELLIOT, J. L., Physics and Earth, Atmospheric and Planetary Sciences
FARHI, E.
FELD, M. S.
FRIEDMAN, J. I.
GOLDSTONE, J.
GREYTAK, T. J.

GUTH, A. H.
HUANG, K.
JACKIW, R. W.
JAFFE, R. L.
JAVAN, A.
JOANNOPOULOS, J. D.
JOHNSON, K. A.
JOSS, P. C.
KARDAR, M.
KASTNER, M. A., Physics, Science
KENDALL, H. W.
KERMAN, A. K.
KETTERLE, W.
KLEPPNER, D.
KOSTER, G. F.
KOWALSKI, S. B.
LEE, P. A.
LEVITOR, L.
LEWIN, W. H. G.
LITSTER, J. D.
LOMON, E. L.
MATTHEWS, J. L.
MONIZ, E.
NEGELE, J. W.
PORKOLAB, M.
PRITCHARD, D. E.
RAPPAPORT, S. A.
REDWINE, R. P.
ROSENSON, L.
SCHECHTER, P.
SPHICAS, P.
TANAKA, T.
TING, S. C. C.
WEISS, R.
YAMAMOTO, R. K.

HEADS OF OTHER ACADEMIC ACTIVITIES

Alliance for Global Sustainability: C. M. VEST
Artificial Intelligence Laboratory: RODNEY BROOKS
Bates Linear Accelerator: RICHARD MILNER
Biotechnology Process Engineering Center: DANIEL I. C. WANG
Center for Advanced Educational Services: RICHARD C. LARSON
Center for Advanced Visual Studies: STEVE BENTON
Center for Cancer Research: RICHARD HYNES
Center for Coordination Science: THOMAS W. MALONE
Center for Energy and Environmental Policy Research: A. DENNY ELLERMAN
Center for Entrepreneurship: NADER T. TAVASSOLI
Center for Environmental Health Sciences: WILLIAM G. THILLY
Center for Global Change Science: RONALD G. PRINN
Center for Information Systems Research: JOHN F. ROCKART
Center for Innovation in Product Development: JOHN R. HAUSER
Center for International Studies: K. A. OYE
Center for Materials Science and Engineering: ROBERT J. SIBLEY
Center for Real Estate: WILLIAM WHEATON
Center for Space Research: CLAUDE R. CANIZARES
Center for Technology, Policy and Industrial Development: JOEL CLARK (interim)
Center for Transportation Studies: YOSSI SHEFFI
Clinical Research Center: R. J. WURTMAN
Energy Laboratory: JEFFERSON W. TESTER
Francis Bitter Magnet Laboratory: ROBERT G. GRIFFIN
Harvard-MIT Division of Health Sciences and Technology: MARTHA L. GRAY, JOSEPH V. BONVENTRE
Haystack Observatory: JOSEPH E. SALAH
Industrial Performance Center: RICHARD K. LESTER
Laboratory for Computer Science: MICHAEL L. DERTOUZOS
Laboratory for Electromagnetic and Electronic Systems: J. KASSAKIAN
Laboratory for Information and Decision Systems: S. K. MITTER, R. G. GALLAGER
Laboratory for Manufacturing and Productivity: T. G. GUTOWSKI
Laboratory for Nuclear Science: R. P. REDWINE
Leaders for Manufacturing Program: D. HARDT, W. HANSON, S. GRAVES
Lincoln Laboratory: DAVID L. BRIGGS
Management of Technology Program: LAURA ROBINSON
Man Vehicle Laboratory: CHARLES M. OMAN
Marine Hydrodynamics Laboratory: JUSTINE E. KERWIN
Massachusetts Space Grant Consortium: LAURENCE R. YOUNG
Materials Processing Center: LIONEL C. KIMERLING
Media in Transition: DAVID THORBURN, HENRY JENKINS
Media Laboratory: NICHOLAS P. NEGROPONTE
Microsystems Technology Laboratories: RAFAEL REIF
Mobile Robotics Group: RODNEY A. BROOKS
Multiscale Computing Project at LCS: CHARLES E. LEISERSON
NanoStructures Laboratory: HENRY I. SMITH
Nondestructive Evaluation Laboratory: SHI-CHANG WOOH
Nonlinear Systems Laboratory: JEAN-JACQUES E. SLOTINC
Nuclear Reactor Laboratory: JOHN A. BERNARD (interim)
NuMesh Group at LCS: STEPHEN WARD
Ocean Engineering Laboratory for Ship and Platform Flows: PAUL SCLAVOUNOS
Oceanography and Applied Ocean Sciences and Engineering: C. CHRYSSOSTOMIDIS
Operations Research Center: THOMAS MAGNANTI, ROBERT FREUND
Organizational Learning Center: PETER SENGE
Parallel and Distributed Operating Systems Group at LCS: FRANS KAASHOEK
Ralph M. Parsons Laboratory for Water Resources and Hydrodynamics: HAROD F. HEMOND
Plasma Science and Fusion Center: MIKLOS PORKOLAB
Power Engineering: JOHN G. KASSAKIAN
Precision Engineering Research Group: ALEXANDER H. SLOCUM
Production System Design Laboratory: DAVID S. COCHRAN
Program in Atmospheres, Oceans, and Climate: CARL WUNSCH
Program on Environmental Education and Research: JEFFREY STEINFELD
Program on the Pharmaceutical Industry: CHARLES COONEY, STAN FINKELSTEIN
Programming Methodology Group: BARBARA LISKOV
Research Development, School of Architecture and Planning: STANFORD ANDERSON
Research Laboratory of Electronics: JONATHAN ALLEN
Research Program on Communications Policy: HARVEY M. SAPOLSKY
Robot Hands Group: KENNETH SALISBURY
Sea Grant College Program: C. CHRYSSOSTOMIDIS
Sloan Automotive Laboratory: JOHN B. HEYWOOD
Software Devices and Systems: JOHN V. GUTTAG, DAVID L. TENNENHOUSE, STEPHEN J. GARLAND
Space Systems Laboratory: DAVID W. MILLER
Spatial NMR Laboratory: DAVID G. CORY
Special Interest Group in Urban Settlements: REINHARD GOETHERT
Spectrometry Laboratory: JEFFREY SIMPSON
Spectroscopy Laboratory: M. S. FELD
Spoken Language Systems Group: VICTOR ZUE
Supercomputer Center: CHARLES E. LEISERSON
Supercomputing Technologies Group at LCS: CHARLES E. LEISERSON
Switzerland (Project MAC): HAL ABELSON
System Design and Management Program: THOMAS MAGNANTI, JOHN R. WILLIAMS
System Dynamics Group: JOHN STERMAN
Technology, Business and Environment Program: JOHN R. EHRENFELD
Technology Laboratory for Advanced Composites: PAUL LAGACE
Technology, Management and Policy Program: DANIEL ROOS
Theory of Computation Group: (vacant)
Testing Tank (Tow Tank): MICHAEL TRIANTAFYLLOU
Three Dimensional Printing Project: EMANUEL SACHS
Undergraduate Research Opportunities Program: NORMA G. MCGAVERN
Virtual Wires Project at LCS: ANANT AGARWAL
Vision and Touch Guided Manipulation Group: KENNETH SALISBURY
Vortical Flow Research Lab: DICK YUE
Wallace Astrophysical Observatory: J. L. ELLIOTT
Whitehead Institute for Biomedical Research: GERALD FINK
Women's Studies: MICHELE OSHIMA
World Wide Web Consortium: TIM BERNERS-LEE

MERRIMACK COLLEGE

Turnpike St, North Andover, MA 01845
Telephone: (508) 683-7111
Founded 1947

President: RICHARD J. SANTAGATI
Registrar: SHIRLEY LAPOINTE
Librarian: STEPHEN A. BAHRE

Library of 131,000 vols, 900 periodicals
Number of teachers: 135 full-time, 60 part-time
Number of students: 2,129

MOUNT HOLYOKE COLLEGE

South Hadley, MA 01075
Telephone: (413) 538-2000
Telex: 6716465
Fax: (413) 538-2391
Founded 1837

President: JOANNE V. CREIGHTON
Treasurer: MARY JO MAYDEW
Dean of Faculty: PETER BEREK
Dean of College: SARAH MONTGOMERY
Dean of Students: REGINA MOONEY
Director of Admissions: ANITA SMITH
Registrar: ANNE COTTON
Librarian: SUSAN PERRY

Library of 618,967 vols
Number of teachers: 216
Number of students: 1,850 women

Publications: *Directory, Catalogue, Alumnae Quarterly.*

NEW ENGLAND CONSERVATORY OF MUSIC

290 Huntington Ave, Boston, MA 02115
Telephone: (617) 262-1120
Telex: 247316
Fax: (617) 262-0500
Founded 1867

President: ROBERT FREEMAN
Provost: ALAN FLETCHER
Registrar: ROBERT WINKLEY

The Spaulding Library contains 60,000 vols (books, scores, periodicals); the Firestone Library contains 20,000 sound and video recordings
Number of teachers: 180
Number of students: 750

Publications: *Notes* (2 a year), *Concert Calendar* (monthly during academic year).

NICHOLS COLLEGE

Dudley, MA 01571

Telephone: (508) 943-1560
Fax: (508) 943-1560, ext. 102

Founded 1815

President: JAMES J. DARAZSDI
Dean of Academic Affairs: DEBRA MURPHY
Registrar: PETER M. ENGH
Librarian: KAY K. LEE

Library of 67,000 vols
Number of teachers: 50
Number of students: 1,532 undergraduates, 415 graduates

NORTHEASTERN UNIVERSITY

360 Huntington Ave, Boston, MA 02115

Telephone: (617) 373-2000

Founded 1898

President: RICHARD M. FREELAND
Senior Vice-President for Administration and Finance: LAURENCE F. MUCCIOLO
Vice-President for Student Affairs: KAREN T. RIGG
Provost: DAVID HALL
Dean of Admissions: ALAN KINES
Librarian: ALAN BENENFELD

Library of 852,000 vols, 2,015,000 microforms, 8,285 serial titles, 18,900 audio and video items, 171,477 government documents
Number of teachers: 733 full-time, 1,439 part-time
Number of students: 14,674 full-time, 9,651 part-time

DEANS

College of Business Administration: IRA WEISS
College of Criminal Justice: JAMES A. FOX
College of Engineering: ALLEN L. SOYSTER
College of Arts and Sciences: JAMES R. STELLAR
School of Law: DANIEL GIVELBAR
Bouvé College of Pharmacy and Health Science: JAMES J. GOZZO
College of Nursing: EILEEN H. ZUNGOLO
University College: (vacant)
Department of Co-operative Education: (vacant)
College of Computer Science: LARRY FINKELSTEIN

RADCLIFFE COLLEGE

10 Garden St, Cambridge, MA 02138

Telephone: (617) 495-8608
Fax: (617) 495-8422

Founded 1879; chartered 1894

Instruction is provided by the Faculty of Arts and Sciences of Harvard University

President: LINDA S. WILSON

Library of 30,000 vols
Number of students: 2,711 women

Publications: *Radcliffe Quarterly*, *Radcliffe News* (3 a year), *Radcliffe Guide* (annually).

REGIS COLLEGE

235 Wellesley St, Weston, MA 02193

Telephone: (617) 768-7000

Founded 1927

President: SHEILA E. MEGLEY
Academic Dean: Sister LEILA HOGAN
Vice-President of Institutional Advancement: JOAN ARCHER
Vice-President for Planning and Enrollment: JUDITH CONLEY
Registrar: Sister PATRICIA MCDONOUGH
Chief Financial Officer: GORDON ANDERSON
Dean of Students: LYNN COLEMAN

Library of 125,000 vols
Number of teachers: 141
Number of students: 1,401

Publications: *Regis Today*, *Hemetera*, *Alumnae Bulletin*.

SALEM STATE COLLEGE

352 Lafayette St, Salem, MA 01970

Telephone: (508) 741-6000

Founded 1854

President: Dr NANCY D. HARRINGTON
Vice-Presidents:
Academic Affairs: Dr ALBERT HAMILTON
Student Life: Dr STANLEY P. CAHILL
Administration and Finance: JANYCE NAPORA
Institutional Advancement: RAMONE SEGREE
Director of Admissions: NATE BRYANT
Director of Library: LAVERNA SAUNDERS

Library of 225,000 vols
Number of teachers: 301
Number of students: 5,400

SIMMONS COLLEGE

300 The Fenway, Boston, MA 02115

Telephone: (617) 521-2000

Founded 1899

President: JEAN A. DOWDALL
Administrative Vice-President: CAROL LEARY
Treasurer: MICHAEL D. WEST
Registrar: DONNA DOLAN
Director of Libraries: ARTEMIS KIRK

Number of teachers: 184 full-time, 219 part-time
Number of students: 3,334

Publications: *Simmons Review*, *Now*, *Simmons News*, *Essays and Studies*.

DEANS

Undergraduate College: JUDITH WITTENBERG
Graduate School of Management: MARGARET HENNIG, ANNE JARDIM
Graduate Programs: JOHN A. ROBINSON
Library Science: ALUM JAMES MATARAZZO
Social Work: JOSEPH REGAN
Health Studies: HARRIET TOLPIN

SMITH COLLEGE

Northampton, MA 01063

Telephone: (413) 584-2700
Fax: (413) 585-2123
E-mail: admission@smith.edu

Founded 1871

President: RUTH J. SIMMONS
Provost: JOHN M. CONNOLLY
Dean of College: MAUREEN A. MAHONEY
Dean for Academic Development: DONALD C. BAUMER

Library of 1,201,000 vols
Number of teachers: 254 full-time, 22 part-time
Number of students: 2,630 undergraduate women, 120 graduate men and women

Publications: *NewsSmith*, *AcaMedia*, *Smith College Bulletin*, *Smith College Handbook*, annual report, bulletin and exhibition catalogues of the Museum of Art, *Alumnae Quarterly*.

SPRINGFIELD COLLEGE

263 Alden St, Springfield, MA 01109

Telephone: (413) 748-3000
Fax: (413) 748-3746

Founded 1885

President: Dr RANDOLPH W. BROMERY
Academic Dean/Provost: Dr GRETCHEN BROCKMEYER (acting)
Vice-President for Finance and Administration: WILLIAM D. MCGARRY
Vice-President for Institutional Advancement: DALLAS L. DARLAND
Vice-President for Student Affairs: Dr CORINNE P. KOWPAK

Library of 162,567 vols
Number of teachers: 194 full-time
Number of full-time students: 3,433

Publications: *Catalogs*, *Alumni Magazine*, *Presidential Newsletter*, *Admissions Viewbook*.

STONEHILL COLLEGE

North Easton, MA 02357

Telephone: (508) 238-1081
Fax: (508) 230-1432

Founded 1948

President: Rev. BARTLEY MACPHAIDÍN
Academic Vice-President and Dean: Rev. LOUIS MANZO
Dean of Admissions and Enrollment: BRIAN P. MURPHY

Library of 135,000 vols
Number of teachers: 200
Number of students: 3,000

SUFFOLK UNIVERSITY

Beacon Hill, Boston, MA 02108

Telephone: (617) 573-8000
Fax: (617) 573-8353

Founded 1906

President: DAVID J. SARGENT
Vice-President and Treasurer: FRANCIS X. FLANNERY
Dean of Students: NANCY C. STOLL
Director of Admissions—Colleges: KATHLEEN TEEHAN
Dean of Admissions—Law School: JOHN C. DELISO
Director of Law Library: BETSY MCKENZIE
Director of Graduate Admissions: MARSHA GINN
Registrar of College Departments: MARY A. HEFRON
Registrar of Law School: LORRAINE COVE
Director of Libraries: EDMUND HAMANN

Libraries of 241,000 vols, 2,070 periodicals, 396,250 microform units
Number of teachers: *c.* 400
Number of students: 6,203

Publications: *Suffolk Journal*, *Suffolk Law Review*, *The Advocate*, *Venture*, *Transnational Law Journal*.

DEANS

Colleges of Liberal Arts and Sciences: Dr MICHAEL R. RONAYNE
School of Management: JOHN F. BRENNAN
Law School: JOHN E. FENTON, Jr
Enrolment Management: MARGUERITE DENNIS

TUFTS UNIVERSITY

Medford, MA 02155

Telephone: (617) 628-5000

Chartered 1852

President: JOHN DIBIAGGIO
Executive Vice-President: STEVEN S. MANOS
Vice-Presidents: THOMAS MCGURTY (Finance), JOHN M. ROBERTO (Operations), KATHE CRONIN (Human Resources), I. MELVIN BERNSTEIN (Arts, Science and Technology)
Senior Vice-President and Provost: SOL GITTLEMAN
Senior Vice-President: THOMAS W. MURNANE
Dean of Undergraduate Admissions: DAVID D. CUTTINO
Dean of Students: BOBBIE KNABLE
Registrar: PAUL TRINGALE (acting)
Librarians: (Arts and Sciences: vacant), ELIZABETH EATON (Health Sciences), MELINDA SAFFER (School of Veterinary Medicine), NATALIE SCHATZ (Fletcher School)

Library of 927,900 vols

Number of teachers: 585 full-time, 478 part-time
Number of students: 8,089 full-time, 619 part-time

Publications: *Tufts Journal, Tuftonia.*

DEANS

Arts and Sciences: SUSAN ERNST, LEILA FAWAL
Dental Medicine (Boston): LONNIE NORRIS
Medicine (Boston): JOHN HARRINGTON
Veterinary Medicine (Boston/Grafton): PHILLIP KOBE KOSCH
Fletcher School of Law and Diplomacy: JOHN R. GALVIN
Sackler School of Graduate Biomedical Sciences: LOUIS LASAGNA
Nutrition School (Medford/Boston): IRWIN ROSENBERG
Graduate School of Arts and Sciences: ROBERT HOLLISTER

UNIVERSITY OF MASSACHUSETTS AT AMHERST

Amherst, MA 01003

Telephone: (413) 545-0111
Fax: (413) 545-2328

Chartered as Massachusetts Agricultural College 1863; name changed to Massachusetts State College 1931, to University 1947
Academic year: September to June

Chancellor: DAVID K. SCOTT
Vice-Chancellor for Administration and Finance: PAUL J. PAGE
Vice-Chancellor for Research: FREDERICK W. BYRON
Vice-Chancellor of Academic Affairs and Provost: CORA B. MARRETT
Vice-Chancellor for Student Affairs: THOMAS B. ROBINSON
Vice-Chancellor for University Advancement: ROYSTER C. HEDGEPETH
Director of Libraries: MARGARET CRIST

Library of 2,834,900 vols
Number of teachers: 1,154
Number of students: 24,884

Publication: *The Massachusetts Review* (quarterly).

DEANS

College of Humanities and Fine Arts: LEE R. EDWARDS
College of Social and Behavioral Sciences: GLEN GORDON
College of Natural Sciences and Mathematics: LINDA L. SLAKEY
College of Food and Natural Resources: ROBERT G. HELGESEN
College of Engineering: JOSEPH I. GOLDSTEIN
School of Public Health and Health Sciences: STEPHEN H. GELBACH
School of Nursing: EILEEN T. BRESLIN
School of Management: THOMAS O'BRIEN
School of Education: BAILEY W. JACKSON
Graduate School: CHARLENA M. SEYMOUR

ASSOCIATED INSTITUTE

Stockbridge School of Agriculture: Amherst, MA 01003; tel. (413) 545-2222; est. 1918; Dir RICHARD D. FLOYD.

UNIVERSITY OF MASSACHUSETTS BOSTON

100 Morrissey Blvd, Boston, MA 02125-3393

Telephone: (617) 287-5000
Fax: (617) 265-7173

Founded 1964

Chancellor: JEAN F. MACCORMACK
Vice-Chancellor for Academic Affairs and Provost: LOUIS ESPOSITO
Vice-Chancellor for Administration and Finance: DONALD D. BABCOCK (acting)
Vice-Chancellor for Student Affairs: CHARLES F. DESMOND
Vice-Chancellor for External Relations: EDWARD C. O'MALLEY, Jr.
Librarian: SHARON L. BOSTICK

Library of 547,846 vols
Number of teachers: 842
Number of students: 12,142

Liberal arts and professional undergraduate and graduate programmes.

UNIVERSITY OF MASSACHUSETTS DARTMOUTH

285 Old Westport Rd, North Dartmouth, MA 02747-2300

Telephone: (508) 999-8000

Founded 1895

Chancellor: Dr PETER H. CRESSY
Vice-Chancellor for Academic Affairs: Dr BENJAMIN F. TAGGIE
Vice-Chancellor for Student Affairs: Dr DIANA HACKNEY
Registrar: Dr RICHARD J. PANOFSKY
Director of Admissions: STEVEN T. BRIGGS
Dean of Library Services: (vacant)

Library of 430,200 vols
Number of teachers: 427
Number of students: 6,366

DEANS

College of Arts and Sciences: Dr JUDY SCHAAF
College of Engineering: Dr THOMAS J. CURRY
College of Nursing: Dr ELISABETH PENNINGTON
College of Visual and Performing Arts: Dr MICHAEL D. TAYLOR
College of Business and Industry: Dr RONALD D. MCNEIL

UNIVERSITY OF MASSACHUSETTS AT LOWELL

1 University Ave, Lowell, MA 01854

Telephone: (508) 934-4000

Founded 1973 by merger of Lowell State College and Lowell Technological Institute; current name 1991

Chancellor: WILLIAM T. HOGAN
Provost: ROBERT WAGNER
Vice-Chancellors: SUSAN A. GOODWIN (Administration and Finance), FREDERICK SPEROUNIS (University Relations and Development)

Library of 433,000 vols
Number of teachers: 406
Number of students: 8,913

WELLESLEY COLLEGE

Wellesley, MA 02181

Telephone: (617) 283-1000

Chartered 1870; opened 1875

President: Dr DIANA CHAPMAN WALSH
Vice-President for Finance and Administration: WILLIAM REED
Vice-President for Resources and Vice-President for Public Affairs: DAVID BLINDER
Dean of the College: NANCY KOLODNY
Dean of Students: MOLLY CAMPBELL
Dean of Admission: JANET LAVIN RAPEYLE
Librarian: MICHELINE JEDREY

Library of 687,000 vols
Number of teachers: 241 full-time, 72 part-time
Number of students: 2,136 full-time, 204 part-time

WESTERN NEW ENGLAND COLLEGE

1215 Wilbraham Rd, Springfield, MA 01119

Telephone: (413) 782-3111
Fax: (413) 782-1746

Founded 1919

President: ANTHONY S. CAPRIO
Provost and Vice-President for Academic Affairs: JERRY A. HIRSCH.
Vice-President for Financial Affairs: DAVID P. KRUGER.
Vice-President for Administration and Planning: JUDITH A. BRISSETTE
Vice-President for Advancement and Marketing: JANE E. ALBERT

Libraries of 440,000 vols
Number of teachers: 136 full-time, 137 part-time
Number of students: 4,732

Schools of arts and sciences, engineering, business, law; division of continuing education

WESTFIELD STATE COLLEGE

Westfield, MA 01086

Telephone: (413) 572-5200

Founded 1838

President: FREDERICK W. WOODWARD
Academic Dean: ROBERT A. MARTIN

Library of 136,000 vols
Number of teachers: 170
Number of students: 3,200

WHEATON COLLEGE

Norton, MA 02766

Telephone: (508) 285-8200
Fax: (508) 285-8270

Founded 1834

President: DALE ROGERS MARSHALL
Vice-President for Finance and Operations: EDWIN J. MERCK
Vice-President for Advancement: CATHERINE CONOVER
Provost: GORDON WEIL (acting)
Dean: SUE ALEXANDER
Dean of Admission and Financial Aid: GAIL BERSON
Librarian: PETER DEEKLE

Library of 352,700 vols
Number of teachers: 135
Number of students: 1,430

Publications: *Catalog, Quarterly Magazine, Wheaton Matters.*

WHEELOCK COLLEGE

200 The Riverway, Boston, MA 02215

Telephone: (617) 734-5200

Founded 1888

President: Dr MARJORIE BAKKEN
Vice-President: Dr MARCIA FOLSOM (acting)

Library of 85,000 vols
Number of teachers: 45 (full-time)
Number of students: 1,640

Publications: *Bulletin, Magazine.*

WILLIAMS COLLEGE

Williamstown, MA 01267

Telephone: (413) 597-3131

Chartered as Free School 1791; college charter granted 1793

President: HARRY C. PAYNE
Vice-President and Treasurer: DAVID G. HEALY
Provost: STUART J. B. CRAMPTON
Dean of the Faculty: DAVID L. SMITH
Dean of the College: PETER MURPHY
Director of Admission: THOMAS PARKER
Registrar: CHARLES R. TOOMAJIAN, Jr
Librarian: DAVID M. PILACHOWSKI

Library of 655,855 vols
Number of teachers: 173
Number of students: 2,021

WORCESTER POLYTECHNIC INSTITUTE

100 Institute Rd, Worcester, MA 01609
Telephone: (508) 831-5000
Fax: (508) 831-5753

Founded 1865

President: Dr EDWARD A. PARRISH
Provost and Vice-President for Academic Affairs: Dr JOHN F. CARNEY III
Vice-President for Student Affairs: BERNARD H. BROWN
Registrar: NIKKI ANDREWS (acting)
Librarian: HELEN M. SHUSTER

Library of 225,000 vols
Number of students: 4,000

WORCESTER STATE COLLEGE

486 Chandler St, Worcester, MA 01602-2597
Telephone: (508) 793-8000

Founded 1874

President: Dr KALYAN K. GHOSH

Library of 149,662 vols
Number of full-time teachers: 162
Number of students: 5,369

Publications: *The Student Voice* (weekly), *Communiqué* (monthly), *Worcester Statement, President's Newsletter, Annual Report.*

MICHIGAN

ADRIAN COLLEGE

110 S. Madison, Adrian, MI 49221-2575
Telephone: (517) 265-5161
Fax: (517) 264-3331

Founded 1859

President: STANLEY P. CAINE
Vice-President, Business Affairs: MICHAEL J. AYRE
Vice-President, Institutional Advancement: WILLIAM S. KENYON
Vice-President and Dean, Student Affairs: PAMELA M. BOERSIG
Vice-President and Dean, Academic Affairs: JAMES B. BORLAND
Admissions Director: JANEL A. SUTKUS
Registrar: DOUG BOYSE
Librarian: RICHARD D. GEYER

Library of 146,000 vols
Number of teachers: 70
Number of students: 1,001

ALBION COLLEGE

Albion, MI 49224
Telephone: (517) 629-1000
Fax: (517) 629-0509

Founded 1835

President: Dr PETER T. MITCHELL
Vice-President for Academic Affairs: Dr JEFFREY C. CARRIER
Vice-President for Enrollment Management: Dr ROBERT E. JOHNSON
Librarian: JOHN KONDELIK

Library of 562,000 vols
Number of teachers: 113
Number of students: 1,487

ALMA COLLEGE

Alma, MI 48801
Telephone: (517) 463-7111
Fax: (517) 463-7277

Founded 1886

President: ALAN J. STONE
Registrar: KAREN KLUMPP
Director of Admissions: (vacant)
Librarian: PETER DOLLARD

Library of 212,000 vols
Number of teachers: 86 full-time, 20 part-time
Number of students: 1,350

ANDREWS UNIVERSITY

Berrien Springs, MI 49104
Telephone: (616) 471-7771

Founded 1874

President: NIELS-ERIK ANDREASEN
Registrar: Dr EMILIO GARCIA-MARENKO
Librarian: Dr KEITH CLOUTEN

Library of 1,334,000
Number of teachers: 259
Number of students: 3,152

Publication: *Andrews University Seminary Studies* (2 a year).

DEANS

College of Arts and Sciences: Dr PATRICIA MUTCH
College of Technology: Dr M. WESLEY SHULTZ
Division of Architecture: LLEWELLYN D. SEIBOLD
Graduate Studies: Dr LISA M. BEARDSLEY
School of Business: Dr ANNE GIBSON
School of Education: Dr KAREN GRAHAM
SDA Theological Seminary: Dr WERNER VYHMEISTER

AQUINAS COLLEGE

1607 Robinson Rd, SE, Grand Rapids, MI 49506
Telephone: (616) 459-8281

Founded 1886

President: HARRY J. KNOPKE
Vice-Presidents: MARIBETH WARDROP (Development), GARY KONOW (Academic), MICHAEL KELLER (Enrollment Management), BILL SHEFFERLY (Finance and Operations), Sister MARY AQUINAS WEBER (Chancellor)
Registrar: LOIS B. KALMAN
Learning Resource Center Director: LARRY W. ZYSK

Library of 100,000 vols, 991 periodicals and over 16,000 non-print items
Number of teachers: 187
Number of students: 2,500

Publications: *Aquinas Magazine* (quarterly), *Presidential Perspectives* (2 a year).

CALVIN COLLEGE

3201 Burton, SE, Grand Rapids, MI 49546
Telephone: (616) 957-6000

Founded 1876

President: GAYLEN J. BYKER
Vice-Presidents: JEANETTE BULT DE JONG (Student Life), HENRY E. DEVRIES II (Information Services), JAMES KRAAI (Administration and Finance), THOMAS MCWHERTOR (Enrollment and External Relations)
Provost: Dr JOEL CARPENTER
Registrar: S. DEAN ELLENS
Director of the Library: GLENN A. REMELTS

Library of 600,000 vols
Number of teachers: 262 full-time, 75 part-time
Number of students: 4,085

AFFILIATED RESEARCH CENTRES

Calvin Center for Christian Scholarship: Sec. Dr RONALD WELLS.

H. H. Meeter Center for Calvin Studies: Dir Dr KARIN MAAG.

CENTRAL MICHIGAN UNIVERSITY

Mount Pleasant, MI 48859
Telephone: (517) 774-4000
Fax: (517) 774-4499

Founded 1892

President: LEONARD E. PLACHTA
Provost and Vice-President for Academic Affairs: RICHARD W. DAVENPORT
Vice-President: KIM ELLERTSON (Business and Finance)
Registrar: KAREN HUTSLAR
Dean of Students: BRUCE ROSCOE
Dean of Libraries: THOMAS J. MOORE

Number of teachers: 800
Number of students: 21,338

DEANS

College of Health Professions: STEPHEN KOPP
College of Communication and Fine Arts: SUE ANN MARTIN
College of Science and Technology: ROBERT KOHRMAN
College of Humanities and Social and Behavioural Sciences: GARY SHAPIRO
College of Extended Learning: DELBERT J. RINGQUIST
College of Graduate Studies: CAROLE A. BEERE
College of Business Administration: TERRY ARNELT
College of Education and Human Science: KELVIE CORNER

CRANBROOK ACADEMY OF ART

1221 N. Woodward Ave, POB 801, Bloomfield Hills, MI 48303-0801
Telephone: (248) 645-3300
Fax: (248) 646-0046

Founded 1932

Director: GERHARDT KNODEL
Dean of Admissions: KATHARINE WILLMAN
Registrar: KATHARINE WILLMAN
Librarian: JUDITH DYKI

Library of 25,000 vols
Number of teachers: 11 full-time
Number of students: 140

EASTERN MICHIGAN UNIVERSITY

Ypsilanti, MI 48197
Telephone: (313) 487-1849
Fax: (313) 487-7170

Founded 1849

President: WILLIAM E. SHELTON
Provost and Vice-President for Academic Affairs: RONALD W. COLLINS
Vice-President for Marketing and Student Affairs: LAURENCE N. SMITH
Vice-President for Business and Finance: PATRICK DOYLE
Vice-President for Enrolment Services: COURTNEY MCANUFF
Vice-President for University Relations: JUANITA REID
Registrar: JOY GARRETT
Librarian: MORELL BOONE

Library of 773,240 vols
Number of teachers: 851
Number of students: 23,557

Publications: *The Journal of Narrative Technique, Mosaics.*

DEANS

Business: STEWART L. TUBBS
Education: JERRY ROBBINS
Graduate School: RONALD E. GOLDENBERG
Arts and Science: BARRY FISH
Human Services: ELIZABETH C. KING
Students: (vacant)
Technology: THOMAS K. HARDEN
Continuing Education: PAUL T. MCKELVEY

FERRIS STATE UNIVERSITY

901 South State St, Big Rapids, MI 49307
Telephone: (616) 592-2000

Founded 1884

President: WILLIAM A. SEDERBURG

Vice-Presidents: RICHARD DUFFETT (Administration and Finance), DANIEL BURCHAM (Student Affairs), SUSAN REARDON (Advancement and Marketing)
Dean of Enrolment Services: DON MULLENS (acting)
Dean of Instructional Services and Library: GERI HURT (acting)

Library of 500,000 books and periodicals
Number of teachers: 477
Number of students: 9,767

GMI ENGINEERING & MANAGEMENT INSTITUTE

1700 West Third Ave, Flint, MI 48504-4898
Telephone: (810) 762-9500
Founded 1919

President: JAMES E. A. JOHN
Vice-President for International and Governmental Activities: DAVID J. DOHERTY
Vice-President for Business: SUSAN BOLT
Vice-President and Provost: JOHN D. LORENZ
Dean of Students: PATRICK DEESE

Library of 80,000 vols
Number of teachers: 135
Number of students: 3,200

First degree courses in electrical, mechanical, industrial and manufacturing systems engineering, management, environmental chemistry, computer engineering, applied optics and applied mathematics; master's degree in manufacturing management, and engineering; through a partnership with 500 corporations worldwide, GMI undergraduate students spend half of each year working with their corporate employer.

HILLSDALE COLLEGE

Hillsdale, MI 49242
Telephone: (517) 437-7341
Fax: (517) 437-0190
Founded 1844

President: Dr GEORGE ROCHE
Provost: Dr ROBERT BLACKSTOCK
Vice-President for Administration: F. LAMAR FOWLER
Vice-President for Student Affairs: CAROLANN BARKER
Vice-President for Development: JOHN CERVINI
Vice-President for External Programs and Communications: Dr RONALD L. TROWBRIDGE
Vice-President for Financial Affairs: H. KENNETH COLE
Registrar: KAY COSGROVE
Librarian: DANIEL JOLDERSMA

Library of 209,000 vols
Number of teachers: 89
Number of students: 1,170

Publication: *Imprimis* (monthly).

HOPE COLLEGE

POB 9000, Holland, MI 49422-9000
Telephone: (616) 395-7000
Fax: (616) 395-7922
Founded 1866

President: Dr JOHN H. JACOBSON
Vice-President for Admissions: JAMES A. BEKKERING
Vice-President of Student Development and Dean of Students: Dr RICHARD FROST
Provost: Dr JACOB E. NYENHUIS
Director of Admissions: GARY CAMP
Director of Libraries: DAVID P. JENSEN

Library of 317,100 vols
Number of teachers: 204 full-time, 71 part-time
Number of students: 2,911

Publication: *News from Hope College* (every 2 months).

KALAMAZOO COLLEGE

Kalamazoo, MI 49006-3295
Telephone: (616) 337-7000
Fax: (616) 337-7251

Chartered 1833 as Michigan and Huron Institute; name changed to Kalamazoo Literary Institute 1837, to Kalamazoo College 1855

President: JAMES F. JONES
Provost: GREGORY S. MAHLER
Business Manager: THOMAS PONTO
Vice-President for Advancement: BERNARD PALCHICK
Vice-President for Experiential Education: MARILYN J. LAPLANTE
Director, Information Services: LISA PALCHICK

Library of 280,000 vols
Number of teachers: 85
Number of students: 1,250

MADONNA UNIVERSITY

36600 Schoolcraft Rd, Livonia, MI 48150
Telephone: (313) 432-5300
Founded 1947

President: Sister MARY FRANCILENE
Vice-President for Academic Affairs: ERNEST NOLAN
Vice-President for Student Life: Sister NANCY MARIE
Director of Marketing and Admissions: LOUIS BROHL
Director of Financial Aid: CHRIS ZIEGLER
Director, Center for International Studies: DOUGLAS JULIUS
Registrar: Sister ALICIA BOMYA
Directors of Library Services: DAVID MURPHY, BRUCE BETT

Library of 139,584 vols
Number of teachers: 225
Number of students: 4,400

MARYGROVE COLLEGE

8425 West McNichols, Detroit, MI 48221
Telephone: (313) 862-8000
Founded 1905

Liberal arts college; two- and four-year undergraduate courses; master's courses; continuing education programme

President: Dr JOHN E. SHAY, Jr
Executive Vice-President: ANDREA LEE
Academic Dean: Dr JOHN NOVAK
Director of Development: CAROL QUIGLEY
Controller and Director of Finance: AMATA MILLER
Dean of Student Affairs: LISA JONES-HARRIS
Dean of Continuing Education: JOANN CUSMANO
Registrar: UJU EKE
Director of Admissions: CARLA MATHEWS
Librarian: Sister ANNA MARY WAICKMAN

Library of 160,000 vols
Number of teachers: 50
Number of students: 1,087 undergraduate, 1,423 graduate, 4,500 continuing education

MICHIGAN STATE UNIVERSITY

East Lansing, MI 48824
Telephone: (517) 355-1855
Telex: 810 251 0737

Founded 1855; the first college for teaching scientific agriculture and the forerunner of the American system of land-grant colleges
State control
Academic year: August to May (two terms)

President: M. PETER MCPHERSON
Provost and Vice-President for Academic Affairs: LOU ANNA KIMSEY SIMON
Vice-President for Finance and Operations and Treasurer: MARK MURRAY
Vice-President for University Development: CHARLES WEBB
Vice President for Research and Graduate Studies: ROBERT J. HUGGETT
Vice-President for Student Affairs and Services: LEE JUNE
Vice-President for University Relations: TERRY DENBOW
Vice-President for Legal Affairs and General Counsel: ROBERT NOTO
Vice-President for Governmental Affairs: STEVEN WEBSTER
Vice-President for University Projects: CHARLES GREENLEAF
Registrar: LINDA LOU SMITH (acting)
Director of Libraries: CLIFFORD H. HAKA

Library: see Libraries
Number of teachers: 2,705
Number of students: 42,603

Publications: *Centennial Review, University Catalog, MSU News Bulletin, MSU Alumni Magazine,* various college and departmental publs.

DEANS

Agriculture and Natural Resources: FRED POSTON (Dean and Vice-Provost)
Arts and Letters: WENDY WILKINS
Eli Broad College of Business and Eli Broad Graduate School of Management: JAMES HENRY
Communication Arts and Sciences: JAMES D. SPANIOLO
Education: CAROLE AMES
Engineering: GEORGE VAN DUSEN (acting)
Graduate Studies: KAREN KLOMPARENS
Human Ecology: JULIA R. MILLER
Human Medicine: WILLIAM ABBETT
International Studies and Programs: JOHN HUDZIK
James Madison College: NORMAN GRAHAM (acting)
Natural Science: GEORGE LEROI
Nursing: MARILYN ROTHERT
Osteopathic Medicine: ALLEN W. JACOBS
Social Science: KENNETH COREY
Urban Affairs Programs: DOZIER THORNTON (acting)
Veterinary Medicine: LONNIE J. KING

PROFESSORS

(C = Chairman of Department)

(Departments may be attached to more than one college)

Accounting

ARENS, A. A. (C)
BUZBY, S. L.
DILLEY, S. C.
GRAY, J.
HAKA, S.
MCCARTHY, W. E.
MEAD, G. C.
O'CONNOR, M. C.
OUTSLAY, E.
SOLLENBERGER, H. M.
WARD, D. D.

Advertising

GARRAMONE, G.
MIRACLE, G. E.
PRATT, C.
REECE, B. B.
SALMON, C.
VANDENBERGH, B. G. (C)

Agricultural and Extension Education

BOBBITT, J. F.
JAY, J. E.
LEVINE, S. J.
MOORE, E. A.
WHIMS, F.

Agricultural Economics

BATIE, S. S.
BERNSTEN, R. H.
BLACK, J. R.

CRAWFORD, E.
EICHER, C. K.
FERRIS, J. N.
HAMM, L. G. (C)
HARSH, S. B.
HARVEY, L. R.
HEPP, R. E.
HILKER, J. H.
HOEHN, J.
KELSEY, M. P.
MOSER, C. H.
NOTT, S. B.
PIERSON, T. R.
RICKS, D. J.
ROBISON, L. J.
ROCHIN, R. I.
SCHMID, A. A.
SCHWAB, G.
SHAFFER, J. D.
STAATZ, J. M.
VAN RAVENSWAAY, E.
WEBER, M.

Agricultural Engineering

BAKKER-ARKEMA, F. W.
BICKERT, W. G.
BROOK, R.
BURKHARDT, T. H.
GERRISH, J.
LOUDON, T. L.
MERVA, G. E.
MROZOWSKI, T.
SEGERLIND, L. J.
SRIVASTAVA, A. (C)
STEFFE, J. F.
SURBROOK, T. C.
VAN EE, G. R.
VON BERNUTH, R.

American Thought and Language

ABRAHAMS, E. C.
BECKWITH, G. M.
BRATZEL, J. N.
BRESNAHAN, R. J.
BUNGE, N. L.
CHAMBERLAIN, W.
D'ITRI, P. A.
ELLISTON, S. F.
FOX, H. B.
KORTH, P.
LADENSON, J. R.
LUNDE, E.
MCKINLEY, B. E.
NOVERR, D. A. (acting C)
OUSTERHOUT, A. M.
POWELL, M.
ROUT, K.
SLADE, J. A.
SOMERS, P. P., Jr
THOMAS, F. R.
ZIEWACZ, L. E.

Anatomy

FALLS, W. M.
GROFOVA, I.
JOHNSON, J. I., Jr
LEW, G.
RHEUBEN, M. B.
TANAKA, D.
VORRO, J. R. (C)
WALKER, B. E.

Animal Science

AULERICH, R. J.
BEEDE, D. K.
BENSON, M. E.
BUCHOLTZ, H. F.
BURSIAN, S.
ERICKSON, R. W.
FERRIS, T. A.
FOGWELL, R.
HAWKINS, D. R.
IRELAND, J.
MAO, I. L.
MELLENBERGER, R. W.
RAHN, A. P.
RITCHIE, H. D.
RUST, S. R.
SHELLE, J. E.
TUCKER, H. A.
VARGHESE, S. K.
WILSON, K. A.
YOKOYAMA, M. T.
WILSON, K. A.

Anthropology

CHARTKOFF, J.
CLELAND, C. E.
CLIMO, J.
DERMAN, W.
DWYER, D.
GALLIN, B.
GOLDSTEIN, L. G. (C)
LOVIS, W. A.
MORRISON, C.
POLLARD, H. P.
ROBBINS, L. H.
SAUER, N.
SNOW, L. F.
SPIELBERG, J.
WHITEFORD, S.

Art

DEUSSEN, P. W.
FAGAN, J. E.
FUNK, R.
GLENDINNING, P.
KILBOURNE, W. G.
KUSZAI, J. J.
LAWTON, J. L.
MACDOWELL
TARAN, I. Z.
VANLIERE, E. N.
VICTORIA, J. J.
WOLTER, K. H.

Audiology and Speech Sciences

CASBY, M.
EULENBERG, J. B.
MOORE, E. J.
PUNCH, J. L. (C)
RAKERD, B. S.
SMITH, L. L.
STOCKMAN, I. G.

Biochemistry

BIEBER, L. L.
DEAL, W. C., Jr
FERGUSON-MILLER, S.
FRAKER, P. J.
KAGUNI, J. M.
KAGUNI, L. S.
KINDEL, P. K.
MCCONNELL, D. G.
MCCORMICK, J. J.
MCGROARTY, E. J.
MCINTOSH, L.
MAHER, V. M.
PREISS, J.
RAIKHEL, N. V.
REVZIN, A.
SCHINDLER, M. S.
SMITH, W. L. (C)
TRIEZENBERG, S. J.
WANG, J. L.
WATSON, J. T.
WELLS, W. W.
WILSON, J. E.

Botany and Plant Pathology

DEZOETEN, G. A. (C)
EKERN, F. F.
EWERS, F. W.
FULBRIGHT, D. W.
HAMMERSCHMIDT, R.
HART, L. P.
HOLLENSEN, R.
JONES, A. L.
KEEGSTRA, K. G.
KENDE, H.
KLOMPARENS, K. L.
NADLER, K. D.
OHLROGGE, J. B.
POFF, K. L.
SAFIR, G. R.
SEARS, B.
TAGGART, R.
VARGAS, J. M., Jr
WEBBER, P. J.
WOLK, C. P.
ZEEVAART, J. A. D.

Center for Advanced Study of International Development

CARROLL, T. V. (Dir)

Chemical Engineering

BERGLUND, K.
DALE, B. (C)
DRZAL, L. T.
HAWLEY, M. C.
JAYARAMAN, K.
MILLER, D. J.
PETTY, C. A.

Chemistry

ALLISON, J.
BABCOCK, G. T. (C)
CHANG, C. K.
CROUCH, S. R.
CUKIER, R. I.
DUNBAR, K.
EICK, H. A.
FROST, J.
GALLOWAY, G. L.
HARRISON, J. F.
HUNT, K. C.
HUNT, P. M.
KANATZIDES, M. G.
KARABATSOS, G. J.
LEGOFF, E.
LEROI, G. E.
MCGUFFIN, V. L.
MCHARRIS, W. C.
MORRISSEY, D. J.
NOCERA, D. G.
PINNAVAIA, T. J.
RATHKE, M. W.
REUSCH, W. H.
SCHWENDEMAN, R.
WAGNER, P. J.

Civil and Environmental Engineering

BALADI, G.
HATFIELD, F.
LYLES, R. W.
MCKELVEY, F.
SAUL, W. E.
SOROUSHIAN, P.
TAYLOR, W. C.
VOICE, T. C.
WIGGERT, D. C.

Communication

ATKIN, C. K.
BOSTER, F. J.
DONOHUE, W.
JOHNSON, J. D. (C)

Computer Science

GREENBERG, L.
HUGHES, H. D.
JAIN, A. K. (C)
NI, L. M.
PRAMANIK, S.
REID, R. J.
STOCKMAN, G. C.
WEINSHANK, D. J.
WOJCIK, A. S.

Counseling, Educational Psychology and Special Education

ALONSO, L. J.
AMES, C.
BECKER, B. J.
BELL, N. T.
BYERS, J. L.
CLARIZIO, H. F.
CLARK, C. M.
CREWE, N. M.
DICKSON, W. P.
ENGLERT, C. S.
FLODEN, R. E.
HABECK, R. V.
HAMACHEK, D. E.

HAPKIEWICZ, W. C.
JUNE, L. N.
LEAHY, M. J.
LEHMANN, I. J.
LENT, R. W.
LOPEZ, F. G.
MCLEOD, R. J.
MEHRENS, W. A.
PERNELL, E.
PETERSON, P.
PHILLIPS, S. E.
PRAWAT, R. (C)
RAUDENBUSH, S.
SCHMIDT, W. H.
SMITH, G.
STEWART, D. A.
STEWART, N. R.
YELON, S. L.

Criminal Justice

BONNER, R. W.
BYNUM, T. S.
CARTER, D. L.
CHRISTIAN, K. E.
HORVATH, F. S.
HUDZIK, J. K.
MASTROFSKI
MORASH, M. A. (Dir)
SIEGEL, J.
STEWART, C. S.

Crop and Soil Sciences

BOYD, S. A.
CHRISTENSON, D. R.
COPELAND, L. O.
ELLIS, B. G. (C)
FOSTER, E. F.
FREED, R. D.
GAST, R. G.
HARWOOD, R. R.
HESTERMAN, O. B.
ISLEIB, D. R.
JACOBS, L. W.
JOHNSTON, T. J.
KELLS, J. D.
KELLY, J. D.
LEEP, R. H.
LENSKI, R. E.
MOKMA, D. L.
MOLINE, W. J.
PAUL, E. A.
PENNER, D.
PIERCE, F. J.
RENNER, K. A.
RIEKE, P. E.
RITCHIE, J. T.
ROBERTSON, G. P.
SMUCKER, A. J. M.
THOMASHOW, M.
TIEDJE, J. M.
VITOSH, M. L.
WARNCKE, D. D.

Economics

ALLEN, B. T.
BAILLIE, R. T.
BALLARD, C. L.
BIDDLE, J. E.
BOYER, K. D.
BROWN, B. W.
DAVIDSON, C.
FISHER, R. C.
GODDEERIS, J. H. (C)
HOLZER, H. J.
KANNAPPAN, S.
KREININ, M. E.
LADENSON, M. L.
LIEDHOLM, C. E.
MACKEY, M. C.
MARTIN, L. W.
MATUSZ, S. J.
MENCHIK, P. L.
MEYER, J.
NEUMARK, D. B.
OBST, N. P.
RASCHE, R. H.
SAMUELS, W. J.
SCHMIDT, P. J.
STRAUSS, J. A.
WOODBURY, S. A.
WOOLDRIDGE, J.

Educational Administration

CHURCH, R. L.
CUSICK, P. A. (acting C)
DAVIS, M.
FAIRWEATHER, J.
GRANDSTAFF, M. E.
IGNATOVICH, F. R.
JOSEPHS, M. J.
KAAGAN, S. S.
MCKEE, C.
MOORE, K. M.
ROMANO, L. G.
SIMON, L. A. K.
SYKES, G.
TURNER, M.
VAN DUSEN, G. M.
VOTRUBA, J. C.
WEILAND, S.

Electrical Engineering

ASMUSSEN, J., Jr (C)
BICKART, T. A.
CHEN, K.-M.
DELLER, J.
FISHER, P. D.
GOODMAN, E.
KHALIL, H.
NYQUIST, D. P.
PIERRE, P. A.
REINHARD, D. K.
SALAM, F. M.
SCHLUETER, R. A.
SHANBLATT, M.
SIEGEL, M.
TUMMALA, R. L.
WEY, C.-L.

English

ALFORD, J. A.
ANDERSON, H. P.
ATHANASON, A. N.
BANKS, J. S.
CRANE, M.
DULAI, S. S.
FISHBURN, K. R.
GASS, S. M.
GOCHBERG, D. S.
GOODSON, A. C.
GROSS, B. E.
HARROW, K.
HILL, J. L.
JOHNSEN, W.
LANDRUM, L. N.
LUDWIG, J. B.
MARTIN, R. A.
MCCLINTOCK, J. I.
MCGUIRE, P. C.
MEINERS, R. K.
O'DONNELL, P. J. (C)
PAANANEN, V. N.
PENN, W. S.
POGEL, N.
ROBINSON, R. F.
ROSENBERG, D. M.
SEATON, J.
SKEEN, A. C.
SMITHERMAN, G.
STALKER, J. C.
STOCK, P. L.
TAVORMINA, M. T.
UPHAUS, R. W.
VINCENT, W. A.
WAKOSKI, D.
WHALLON, W.

Entomology

AYERS, G. S.
BESAW, L. C.
BIRD, G. W.
GAGE, S.
GRAFIUS, E. J.
HOLLINGWORTH, R. M.
MERRITT, R. W.
MILLER, J. R.
POSTON, F. L.
RAIKHEL, A.
SCRIBER, J. M. (C)
STEHR, F. W.
VANTASSELL, E.
WHALON, M. E.
ZABIK, M. J.

Family and Child Ecology

AMES, B. D.
BOBBITT, N.
BOGER, R.
GRIFFORE, R.
IMIG, D. R.
IMIG, G. L.
KEITH, J. G.
KOSTELNIK, M. (C)
LUSTER, T. J.
MCADOO, H. P.
MILLER, J. R.
PHENICE, L.
SCHIAMBERG, L. B.
SODERMAN, A. K.
TAYLOR, C. S.
WALKER, R.
WHIREN, A. P.
YOUATT, J. P.

Family and Community Medicine

AGUWA, M. I.
KURTZ, M.
PAPSIDERO, J.

Family Practice

ALEXANDER, E.
BRODY, H.
GERARD, R.
GIVEN, C. W.
OGLE, K. S.
WADLAND, W. C. (C)

Finance

GRUNEWALD, A. E.
HENRY, J. B.
LASHBROOKE, E. C., Jr
O'DONNELL, J. L.
RAINEY, J. F.
SIMONDS, R. R. (C)
STENZEL, P.

Fisheries and Wildlife

BATIE, R. E.
D'ITRI, F.
DOBSON, T. A.
GARLING, D. L.
GIESY, J. P.
JOHNSON, D. I.
KING, D. L.
MCNABB, C. D.
PEYTON, R. B.
PRINCE, H. H.
TAYLOR, W. W. (C)

Food Science and Human Nutrition

BENNINK, M. R.
BOND, J. T.
BOOREN, A. M.
CASH, J. N.
CHENOWETH, W. L.
GRAY, I. J.
HEGARTY, P. V.
LINZ, J. E.
PESTKA, J. J.
PRICE, J. F.
ROMSOS, D. R.
SCHEMMEL, R. A.
SMITH, D. M.
UEBERSAX, M. A. (C)
ZABIK, M.
ZILE, M. H.

Forestry

DICKMANN, D. I.
KEATHLEY, D. E. (C)
KIELBASO, J. J.
KOELLING, M. R.
MCDONOUGH, M.

Geography

CAMPBELL, D. J.
CHUBB, M.
GROOP, R. E.
HARMAN, J. R.
HINOJOSA, R. (C)
MEHRETU, A.
OLSON, J. M.
WILLIAMS, J.
WITTICK, R. I.

Geological Sciences

ANSTEY, R. L.
CAMBRAY, F. W.
FUJITA, K.
HOLMAN, J. A.
LARSON, G. J.
LONG, D. T.
MERK, G.
SIBLEY, D. F.
TROW, J. W.
VELBEL, M. A.
VOGEL, T. A. (C)

History

ANDERSON, J. R.
EADIE, J. W.
FISHER, A.
GLIOZZO, C. A.
HINE, D. C.
KING, W.
LAURENCE, R. R.
LEVINE, P. D.
MARCUS, H. G.
MCKINNON, P.
MOCH, L. P.
POLLACK, N.
RADDING, C. M.
REED, H. A.
ROBINSON, D. W.
SCHOENL, W. J.
SILVERMAN, H. (C)
STEWART, G. T.
SWEENEY, J. M.
THOMAS, R. W.
THOMAS, S. J.
VIETH, J. K.
WILBUR, E.

Horticulture

CAMERON, A. C.
CARLSON, W. H.
DILLEY, D. R.
EWART, L. C.
FLORE, J. A.
HANCOCK, J. F.
HEINS, R. D.
HERNER, R. C.
HOWELL, G. S.
HULL, J., Jr
IEZZONI, A. F.
KELLY, J. F.
LOESCHER, W. H. (C)
PERRY, R. L.
SINK, K. C.
WIDDERS, I. E.
ZANDSTRA, B. H.

School for Hospitality Business

CICHY, R. (Dir)
KASAVANA, M. L.
NINEMEIER, J. D.
SCHMIDGALL, B. H.

Human Environment and Design

SONTAG, M. S.
SPRINGER, T. J. (C)
STERNQUIST, B.

Internal Medicine

CARNEGIE, D. E.
DEAN, H. A.
OTTEN, R. F.
PYSH, J. J.
RISTOW, G. E.

International Agriculture Institute

AXINN, G.
BARNES-MCCONNELL, P.
BREWER, F.
D'ITRI, F.
DODDS, J. H.
FREED, R. D.
ISLEIB, D. R. (Dir)
WILSON, K. A.

James Madison College

ALLEN, W. (Dean)
AYOOB, M.
BANKS, R. F.
DORR, R. F.
GRAHAM, N. A.
HOEKSTRA, D. J.
RUBNER, M.
SCHECHTER, M.
SEE, K. O.
WALTZER, K.
ZINMAN, M. R.

Journalism

DETJEN, J. T.
FICO, F.
HUDSON, R. V.
LACY, S. R.
MOLLOY, J. D.
SIMON, T. F.
SOFFIN, S. I. (Dir)
SPANIOLO, J. D.

Labor and Industrial Relations

BLOCK, R. N.
BRICKNER, D. G.
CURRY, T. H.
GLEASON, S. E.
KRUGER, D. H.
MOORE, M. L. (Dir)
REVITTE, J.
SMITH, P. R.
TOBEY, S. H.
VANDE VORD, N.
WOLKINSON, B. W.

Large Animal Clinical Sciences

AMES, N. K.
BAKER, J. C.
BARTLETT, P. C.
DERKSEN, F. J. (C)
HERDT, T.
KANEENE, J. B.
KING, L. J.
MATHER, E. C.
NACHREINER, R. F.
NICKELS, F. A.
ROBINSON, N. E.
SEARS, P. M.
SPRECHER, D. J.
STICK, J. A.
STRAW, B. E.

Linguistics and Germanic, Slavic, Asian and African Languages

ABBOTT, B. K.
BELGARDT, R.
DILL, H. J.
FALK, J. S.
HUDSON, G.
JUNTUNE, T. W.
LOCKWOOD, D. G.
MCCONEGHY, P.
PAULSELL, P.
PETERS, G. F. (C)
PRESTON, D.
SCHILD, K. W.
SENDICH, M.

Lyman Briggs School

INGRAHAM, E. (Dir)
SAYED, M. M. A.
SHEPARD, P. T.
SIMPSON, W. A.
SPEES, S. T.

Management

HOLLENBECK, J. R.
ILGEN, D. R.

Marketing and Supply Chain Management

ALLEN, J. W.
BOWERSOX, D. J.
CALANTONE, R. J.
CAVUSGIL, S. T.
CLOSS, D.
DROGE, C. L.
HARRELL, G. D.
MELNYK, S. A.
MONCZKA, R. M.
NARASIMHAN, R.
NASON, R. W. (C)
VICKERY, S. K.
WILSON, R. D.

Mathematics

AKBULUT, S.
ANDERSON, G. D.
AXLER, S.
BLAIR, D. E.
BROWN, W. C.
CHEN, B.-Y.
DRACHMAN, B.
DUNNINGER, D. R.
FINTUSHEL, R. A.
FITZGERALD, W. M.
FRAZIER, M. W.
FUCHS, M.
HALL, D. W.
HALL, J. I. (C)
HESTENES, M.
HILL, R. O.
IVANOV, N.
KUAN, W. E.
KURTZ, J. C.
LAMM, P. K.
LAPPAN, G.
LAPPAN, P. A.
LI, T. Y.
LO, C. Y.
LUDDEN, G. D.
MACCLUER, C. R.
MASTERSON, J. J.
MCCOY, T. L.
MEIERFRANKENFELD, U.
MORAN, D. A.
NEWHOUSE, S. E.
OW, W. H.
PALMER, E. M.
PARKER, T. H.
PHILLIPS, R. E.
PLOTKIN, J. M.
ROTTHAUS, C.
SAGAN, B. E.
SCHUUR, J. D.
SEEBECK, C. L.
SHAPIRO, J. H.
SINHA, I.
SLEDD, W. T.
SONNEBORN, L. M.
SREEDHARAN, V. P.
TSAI, C. E.
ULRICH, B.
VANCE, I. E.
VOLBERG, A.
WALD, J. W.
WANG, C.-Y.
WEIL, C. E.
WINTER, D. L.
WINTER, M. J. K.
WOLFSON, J. G.
WONG, P. K.
ZEIDAN, V. M.

Mechanical Engineering

BECK, J. V.
FOSS, J. F.
LLOYD, J. R.
MCGRATH, J.
MEDICK, M. A.
RADCLIFFE, C. J.
ROSENBERG, R. C. (C)
SCHOCK, H. J.
SHAW, S. W.
THOMPSON, B. S.

Medical Education Research and Development

ABBETT, W. S.
ANDERSON, W. A. (Dir)

HENRY, R. C.
TAVANO, D.

Medical Technology Program

DAVIS, G. L.

Medicine

ABELA, G. S.
BULL, R. W.
DIMITROV, N. V.
GOSSAIN, V. V.
HOLMES-ROVNER, M.
HOPPE, R.
JOHNSON, T. M.
JONES, J. W.
KUPERSMITH, J. (C)
MAYLE, J. E.
PENNER, J. A.
ROSENMAN, K. D.
SCHWARTZ, K. A.
SMITH, R. C.
SWANSON, G. M.

Materials Science and Mechanics

ALTIERO, N. J.
CLOUD, G. L.
HAUT, R. C.
HUBBARD, R. P.
MUKHERJEE, K. (C)
PENCE, T. J.
SOUTAS-LITTLE, R. W.
SUBRAMANIAN, K. N.

Microbiology

BAGDASARIAN, M.
BERTRAND, H.
BREZNAK, J. A.
BRUBAKER, R. R.
CONRAD, S. E.
CORNER, T.
DAZZO, F.
DEBRUIJN, F. J.
DODGSON, J. B. (C)
ESSELMAN, W.
FLUCK, M. M.
GARRITY, G. M.
HAUG, A.
HAUSINGER, R. P.
JACKSON, J. H.
KIERSZENBAUM, F.
MAES, R. K.
MULKS, M. H.
ORIEL, P. J.
PATTERSON, M. J.
PATTERSON, R.
REDDY, C. A.
SNYDER, L. R.
VELICER, L. F.
WALKER, R. D.
WILLIAMS, J. F.

Music

CARMAN, O. W.
CATRON, D. L.
DAN, R. M.
DONAKOWSKI, C.
ELL, F. W.
ERBES, R. L.
FORGER, D. M.
FORGER, J. B. (Dir)
GREGORIAN, L.
HUTCHESON, J. T.
JOHNSON, M. E.
JOHNSON, T. O.
LEBLANC, A.
LULLOFF, J. P.
NEWMAN, R.
OLSON, C.
RUGGIERO, C. H.
SINDER, P. N.
SMITH, C. K.
STOLPER, D.
TIMS, F. C.
VERDEBR, E. L.
VERDEBR, W.
VOTAPEK, R. J.
WARD, B. W.
WHITWELL, J. L.

National Superconducting Cyclotron Laboratory

BLOSSER, H. G.
GELBKE, C. K. (Dir)
HANSEN, P. G.
YORK, R. C.

Nursing

ALLEN, G. D.
COLLINS, C.
COURTNEY, G. A.
CURTIS, J. H.
GIVEN, B. A.
ROTHERT, M. L. (Dean)

Obstetrics, Gynecology and Reproductive Biology

DRUKKER, B. H. (C)

Osteopathic Manipulative Medicine

GREENMAN, P. E.
HRUBY, R., (C)
RECHTIEN, J. J.
REYNOLDS, H.
WARD, R. C.

Osteopathic Surgical Specialities

BECKMEYER, H. E. (C)
DOWNS, J. R.
HALLGREN, R.
HAUT, R. C.
HOGAN, M. J.
TEITELBAUM, H.
WALCZAK, J.

Packaging

BURGESS, C. J.
DOWNES, T. W.
GIACIN, J. R.
HARTE B. (Dir)
HUGHES, H. A.
LOCKHART, H. E.
SELKE, S. E. M.

Park, Recreation and Tourism Resources

BRISTOR, J. L.
FRIDGEN, J. (C)
HOLECEK, D. F.
RASMUSSEN, G. A.
STYNES, D. J.
VAN DER SMISSEN, B.

Pathology

BELL, T. G.
BOWMAN, H. E.
DUNSTAN, R. W.
HARKEMA, J. R.
JONES, M. Z.
KREHBIEL, J.
KUMAR, K.
LOVELL, K. L.
MACKENZIE, C. (C)
MARUSHIGE, K.
MULLANEY, T. P.
PADGETT, G. A.
REED, W. M.
SANDER, C. M.
SIEW, S.
TVEDTEN, H.
WILLIAMS, C. S. F.
YAMINI, B.

Pediatrics

BREITZER, G. M.
KAY, B. M.
MAGEN, M.
SCHNEIDERMAN, F. J.
SCHNEIDERMAN, L.

Pediatrics and Human Development

CHANG, C. C.
FISHER, R.
GORDON, R.
KALLEN, D. J.
KAUFMAN, D. B.
KULKARNI, R.
KUMAR, A.
MURRAY, D. L.
NETZLOFF, M. L.
PANETH, N.

SCOTT-EMUAKPOR, A.
SEAGULL, E. A.
SPARROW, A. W. (C)
TROSKO, J. E.

Pharmacology and Toxicology

ATCHISON, W. D.
BENNETT, J. L.
BRASELTON, W. E., Jr
FINK, G. D.
FISCHER, L. J.
GEBBER, G. L.
GOODMAN, J. I.
MICHELAKIS, A. M.
MOORE, K. E. (C)
ROTH, R. A.
THORNBURG, J.

Philosophy

ANDRE, J. A.
ASQUITH, P. D. (C)
BENJAMIN, M.
ESQUITH, S. L.
FLECK, L. M.
FRYE, M.
GARELICK, H. M.
HALL, R. J.
HANNA, J. F.
KOCH, D. F.
KOTZIN, R. H.
MCCRACKEN, C. J.
MILLER, B.
PETERSON, R. T.
SMITH, N. D.
SUTER, R.
TOMLINSON, T.
WALSH, H. T.

Physical Education and Exercise Science

DUMMER, G.
FELTZ, D. (C)
HAUBENSTRICKER, J. L.
MALING, R. M.

Physical Medicine and Rehabilitation

HINDS, W. C.
KAUFMAN, D.
STANTON, D. F. (C)

Physics and Astronomy

ABOLINS, M. A.
AUSTIN, S. M.
BASS, J.
BAUER, W. W.
BENENSON, W.
BORYSOWICZ, J.
BROCK, R. L.
BROMBERG, C. M.
BROWN, B. A.
CARLSON, E. H.
COWEN, J. A.
CRAWLEY, G. M.
DANIELEWICZ, P.
GALONSKY, A. I.
GOLDING, B.
HARRISON, M. J.
HARTMANN, W. M.
HETHERINGTON, J. H.
KASHY, E.
KEMENY, G.
KOVACS, J. S.
KUHN, J. R.
LINNEMAN, J. T.
LYNCH, W. G.
MAHANTI, S. D.
POLLACK, G. L.
POPE, B. G.
PRATT, W. P., Jr
PUMPLIN, J. C.
REPKO, W. W.
SIGNELL, P. S.
SIMKIN, S. M.
SMITH, H. A.
STEIN, R. F.
THORPE, M. F.
TUNG, W. K.
WEERTS, H. J.
WESTFALL, G. D.

ZELENVINSKY, V.

Physiology

ADAMS, T.
BARMAN, S.
CHIMOSKEY, J. E.
CHOU, C.-C.
DUKELOW, W. R.
HASLAM, S. Z.
HEIDEMANN, S.
HEISEY, S. R.
HOOTMAN, S. R.
JUMP, D. B.
MEYER, R. A.
PETROPOULOS, E. A.
RIEGLE, G. D.
ROOT-BERNSTEIN, R. S.
SPARKS, H.
SPIELMAN, W. S. (C)
TIEN, H. T.
ZIPSER, B.

Political Science

ABRAMSON, P. R.
BRATTON, M.
FINIFTER, A. W.
HALL, M. G.
HAMMOND, T. H.
HULA, R. C.
KNOTT, J. H. (C)
OSTROM, C. W., Jr
ROHDE, D. W.
SILVER, B. D.
SPAETH, H. J.
STEIN, B. N.
WAGMAN, J.
WEINBERGER, J. W.

Psychiatry

BIELSKI, R. J.
COLENDA, C. (C)
ENZER, N. B.
GUNNINGS, T.
OSBORN, G. G.
ROSEN, L. W.
STEIN, T.
STOFFELMAYR, B.
VAN EGEREN, L. F.
WERNER, A.
WILLIAMS, D. H.

Psychology

ABELES, N.
ARONOFF, J.
BARCLAY, A. M.
BOGAT, G. A.
CALDWELL, R. A.
CARR, T. H.
DAVIDSON, W., II
DONELSON, F. E.
FITZGERALD, H. E.
FORD, J. K.
HARRIS, L. J.
HUNTER, J. E.
HURLEY, J. R.
JACKSON, L. A.
KARON, B. P.
KERR, N. L.
KOSLOWSKI, S. W.
LEVINE, R. L.
LOMBARDI, V. L.
MCKINNEY, J. P.
MESSE, L. A.
NUNEZ, A. A.
PAULUS, G. S.
REYHER, J.
RILLING, M. E.
SCHMITT, N. W.
SISK, C. L.
STOLLAK, G. E.
THORNTON, D. W.
VONEYE, A. A.
WOOD, G. (C)
ZACKS, J. L.
ZACKS, R. T.

Radiology

GOTTSCHALK, A.
POTCHEN, E. J. (C)

Religious Studies

ANDERSON, R. T.
GREENE, J. T.
WELCH, A. T.

Resource Development

ANDERSON, R. C.
BARNES-MCCONNELL, P.
BARTHOLIC, J.
BRONSTEIN, D. A.
DERSCH, E.
EDENS, T.
FEAR, F. A.
KAKELA, P. J.
KAMRIN, M. A.
LEIGHTY, L. L.
NICKEL, P. E.
SCHULTINK, G.
VERBURG, K.
VLASIN, R. D.
WRIGHT, D.

Romance and Classical Languages

DONOHOE, J. I.
FIORE, R. L.
GRAY, E. F.
HARRISON, A. T.
JOSEPHS, H.
KOPPISCH, M. (C)
KRONEGGER, M. E.
LOCKERT, L. A.
MANSOUR, G. P.
MARINO, N. F.
PORTER, L. M.
SNOW, J. T.
TYRRELL, W. B.

Small Animal Clinical Sciences

ARNOCZKY, S. P.
BRADEN, T. D.
EVANS, A. T.
EYSTER, G. E.
FLO, G. L.
HAUPTMAN, J.
JOHNSON, C.
MOSTOSKY, U. V.
PROBST, C. W. (C)
SAWYER, D. C.
SCHALL, W. D.
WALSHAW, R.

Social Work

DUANE, E. A.
FLYNN, M. L. (Dir)
FREDDOLINO, P. P.
HERRICK, J. M.
LEVANDE, D. I.
WHITEMAN, V. L.

Sociology

BOKEMEIER, J.
BRIDGELAND, W.
BUSCH, L. M.
CONNER, T. L.
GALLIN, R. S.
HAMILTON, R. S.
HILL, R. C.
JOHNSON, N. E.
KAPLOWITZ, S.
MANNING, P. K.
RUMBAUT, R. G.
SCHWARZWELLER, H. K.
SHLAPENTOKH, V.
VANDERPOOL, C. K. (C)
WILEY, D.
ZINN, M. B.

Statistics and Probability

ERICKSON, R. V.
FABIAN, V.
FELDMAN, D.
FOX, M.
GARDINER, J. C.
GILLILAND, D. C.
HANNAN, J. F.
KOUL, H. L.
LEPAGE, R. D.
MANDREKAR, V.
PAGE, C. F.
SALEHI, H. (C)
STAPLETON, J.

Surgery

DEAN, R. E. (C)
DE LOS SANTOS, R. S.
HARKEMA, J.
OSUCH, J. R.

Teacher Education

ALLEMAN, J. E.
ANDERSON, C. W.
ANDERSON, K.
ANDERSON, L. M. (acting C)
BADER, L. A.
BARNES, H. L.
BOOK, C.
BROPHY, J. E.
BUCHMANN, M. B.
BURKE, J. B.
EDWARDS, P. A.
FEATHERSTONE, J.
FITZGERALD, S.
FLODEN, R.
FLORIO-RUANE, S.
GALLAGHER, J. J.
JOYCE, W. W.
KENNEDY, M. M.
LANIER, J. E.
LANIER, P. E.
LITTLE, T.
MCDIARMID, G. W.
MOON, R. A.
NEMSER, S. F.
PEARSON, P. D.
PUTNAM, J. G.
RAPHAEL, T. E.
RIETHMILLER, P. L.
ROEHLER, L. R.
SCHWILLE, J. R.
SEDLAK, M. W.
TSANG, M. C.
WEST, B. B.
WHEELER, C.

Telecommunication

BIOCCA, F. A.
GREENBERG, B. S.
LITMAN, B. R.
MODY, B.
MUTH, T. A. (acting C)
STEINFIELD, C.

Theatre

DURR, D. L. (C)
RUTLEDGE, F. C.
RUTLEDGE, G.
SCHUTTLER, G.

Urban and Regional Planning

COREY, K. E.
HAMLIN, R. E.
HINOJOSA, R.
LIM, G.-C.
THOMAS, J.

Urban Affairs

DARDEN, J. T. (Dean)
LANG, M.

W. K. Kellogg Biological Station

GROSS, K. L.
KLUG, M. J. (Dir)
KNEZEK, B. D.
MITTELBACH, G. G.

Zoology

AGGARWAL, S. K.
ATKINSON, J. W.
BALABAN, M.
BAND, R. N.
BEAVER, D. L.
BROMLEY, S. C.
BURTON, T. M. (C)
BUSH, G. L.
CATHEY, B.
CLEMENS, L. G.

COOPER, W. E.
EILAND, L. C.
FRIEDMAN, T. B.
HALL, D. J.
HETHERINGTON, M.
HILL, R. W.
MUZZALL, P. M.
OZAKI, H.
PAX, R. A.
PEEBLES, C.
RIVERA, E. M.
ROBBINS, L. G.
SNIDER, R. J.
STRANEY, D.
WEBBER, M. M.

MICHIGAN TECHNOLOGICAL UNIVERSITY

Houghton, MI 49931

Telephone: (906) 487-1885

Founded 1885: formerly Michigan College of Mining and Technology

President: Dr CURTIS J. TOMPKINS
Provost and Executive Vice-President: Dr FREDRICK DOBNEY
Secretary, Board of Control: Dr DALE TAHTINEN
Senior Vice-President for Advancement: J. D. SELLARS

Number of teachers: 400
Number of students: 6,390

Publication: *Catalog.*

DEANS

Engineering: Dr ROBERT O. WARRINGTON
Forestry: Dr WARREN E. FRAYER
Sciences and Arts: Dr MAX J. SEEL
Graduate School: Dr SUNG M. LEE
School of Business: Dr EUGENE KLIPPEL
School of Technology: TIMOTHY COLLINS
Director of Library: PHYLLIS JOHNSON

HEADS OF DEPARTMENTS

Metallurgical Engineering: Dr CAL WHITE
Mining Engineering: Dr FRANCIS OTUONYE
Physical Education: Prof. CHERYL DEPUYDT
Mathematics: Dr ALPHONSE H. BAARTMANS
Computer Sciences: Dr LINDA OTT
Electrical Engineering: Dr JON SOPER
Mechanical Engineering: Dr KLAUS WEINMANN
Humanities: Dr CYNTHIA L. SELFE
Social Sciences: Dr TERRY REYNOLDS
Chemical Engineering: Dr EDWARD R. FISHER
Forestry: Dr WARREN E. FRAYER
Geology and Geological Engineering: Dr WILLIAM I. ROSE
Biological Sciences: Dr JOHN ADLER
Physics: Dr J. BRUCE RAFERT
Civil Engineering: Dr C. ROBERT BAILLOD
Chemistry: Dr JAMES RIEHL

HEADS OF RESEARCH AGENCIES

Institute of Materials Processing: Dr JAMES HWANG
Institute of Wood Research: Dr GARY MCGINNIS
Keweenaw Research Center: Dr JAMES ROGERS

NORTHERN MICHIGAN UNIVERSITY

Marquette, MI 49855

Telephone: (906) 227-1000

Founded 1899

President: Dr JUDITH I. BAILEY
Vice-President for Academic Affairs: Dr PHILLIP L. BEUKEMA
Dean of Academic Information Services: THOMAS M. PEISCHL
Director of Admissions: GERRI DANIELS

Library of 521,280 vols
Number of teachers: 371
Number of students: 7,826

DEANS

College of Arts and Sciences: Dr MICHAEL T. MARSDEN
College of Business: Dr BRIAN G. GNAUCK
College of Behavioral Sciences and Human Services: Dr STEVEN B. CHRISTOPHER
College of Nursing and Allied Health: Dr BETTY J. HILL
College of Technology and Applied Sciences: Dr PHILLIP L. BEUKEMA (acting)

OAKLAND UNIVERSITY

Rochester, MI 48309-4401

Telephone: (248) 370-3500

Founded 1957

State control; Academic year: September to August (2 semesters, 2 sessions)

President: Dr GARY D. RUSSI
Vice-Presidents: DAGMAR CRONN (Academic Affairs), SUSAN GERRITS (General Counsel and Sec. to the Board of Trustees), SUSAN ALDRICH (Finance and Administration, acting), MARY BETH SNYDER (Student Affairs), DAVID DISEND (University Relations)
Librarian: SUZANNE O. FRANKIE

Number of teachers: 371 full-time
Number of students: 14,379

Publications: *Oakland University Undergraduate Catalog, Oakland University Graduate Catalog* (every 2 years), *Oakland University Magazine* (quarterly), *Inside Oakland* (fortnightly).

DEANS

School of Business Administration: JOHN GARDNER
School of Educational and Human Service: MARY L. OTTO
School of Engineering and Computer Science: MICHAEL POLIS
School of Health Sciences: RONALD E. OLSON
School of Nursing: JUSTINE J. SPEER
College of Arts and Sciences: DAVID J. DOWNING
Graduate Study and Research: Dr BRIAN GOSLIN (acting)

OLIVET COLLEGE

Olivet, MI 49076

Telephone: (616) 749-7000
Fax: (616) 749-7121

Founded 1844

President: MICHAEL S. BASSIS
Vice-President and Dean of the College: JAMES A. HALSETH
Vice-President for Finance and Administration: TIMOTHY J. NELSON
Vice-President for Institutional Advancement: (vacant)
Vice-President for Facilities, Planning, Operations and Technological Services: LARRY COLVIN
Vice-President for Enrollment Management: (vacant)
Director of Libraries: (vacant)

Number of students: 825

SIENA HEIGHTS COLLEGE

Adrian, MI 49221-1796

Telephone: (517) 264-7180
Fax: (517) 264-7702

Founded 1919

President: Dr RICHARD B. ARTMAN
Academic Dean: Dr SHARON WEBER
Dean of Graduate Studies and Lifelong Learning: Dr ROBERT W. GORDON
Director of Admissions and Enrollment: KEVIN KUCERA
Dean of Students: MICHELE BUKUL
Vice-President for Advancement: DON F. TAYLOR
Business Manager/Treasurer: SHARON ROBERTELLO
Registrar: ROBERT PARKER
Librarian: MARK DOMBROWSKI

Library of 136,082 vols
Number of teachers: 73
Number of students: 1,400

Publication: *Reflections.*

SPRING ARBOR COLLEGE

Spring Arbor, MI 49283

Telephone: (517) 750-1200
Fax: (517) 750-2108

Founded 1873

President: Dr JAMES CHAPMAN
Vice-Presidents: Dr MICHAEL CLYBURN (Academic Affairs), JONATHAN KULAGA (Advancement), JANET TJEPKEMA (Business Affairs), GEORGE KLINE (Program Development and Enrollment), EVERETT PIPER (Student Development)

Library of 107,000 vols
Number of students: 2,442

UNIVERSITY OF DETROIT MERCY

POB 19900, 4001 W. McNichols Rd, Detroit, MI 48219-0900

Telephone: (313) 993-1000

Founded 1877 as Detroit College and chartered as such 1881; chartered as a University 1911; merged with Mercy College of Detroit in 1990

President: Sister MAUREEN A. FAY
Vice-President for Academic Affairs: GEORGE F. LUNDY
Vice-President for Finance: DALE TUCKER
Vice-President for University Advancement: BARBARA MILBAUER
Vice-President for Contract Learning: BARBARA MILBAUER
Director of Admissions: (vacant)
Registrar: DIANE M. PRAET
Librarian: MARGARET AUER

Library of 508,000 vols
Number of full-time teachers: 360
Number of students: 7,000

DEANS

College of Liberal Arts: BRIAN P. NEDWEK
College of Business Administration: GARY A. GIAMARTINO
College of Engineering and Science: LEO C. HANIFIN
College of Education and Human Services: (vacant)
College of Health Professions: CYNTHIA ZANE
School of Architecture: STEPHEN VOGEL
School of Law: STEPHEN A. MAZURAK
School of Dentistry: BRUCE GRAHAM

UNIVERSITY OF MICHIGAN

Ann Arbor, MI 48109

Telephone: (313) 764-1817

Founded 1817

President: HOMER A. NEAL (acting)
Provost and Executive Vice-President for Academic Affairs: J. BERNARD MACHEN
Executive Vice-President and Chief Financial Officer: FARRIS W. WOMACK
Vice-President for Student Affairs: Dr MAUREEN HARTFORD
Vice-President for Development: THOMAS KINNEAR
Vice-President for University Relations: WALTER HARRISON
Vice-President for Research: Dr FREDERICK NEIDHART (acting)

Vice-Provost for Health Affairs: RHETAUGH G. DUMAS
Vice-Provost for Academic and Multicultural Affairs: Dr LESTER MONTS
Vice-Provost for Information Technology: DOUGLAS VAN HOUWELING
University Registrar: LAURA PATTERSON
Director of Admissions: THEODORE L. SPENCER

Library: see Libraries
Number of teachers: 3,923
Number of resident students: 36,687 (incl. extensions)

Publications: *Michigan Quarterly Review, The University of Michigan Today* (quarterly), *Research News* (monthly), *Michigan Alumnus.*

DEANS

College of Architecture and Urban Planning: ROBERT M. BECKLEY
School of Art: ALLEN J. SAMUELS
School of Business Administration: B. JOSEPH WHITE
School of Dentistry: WILLIAM KOTOWICZ (acting)
School of Education: CECIL G. MISKEL
College of Engineering: STEPHEN W. DIRECTOR
Graduate School: NANCY CANTOR
Law School: JEFFREY S. LEHMAN
School of Information: DANIEL ATKINS
College of Literature, Science and the Arts: EDIE N. GOLDENBERG
Medical School: A. LORRIS BETZ (acting)
School of Music: PAUL C. BOYLAN
School of Natural Resources: DANIEL A. MAZMANIAN
School of Nursing: ADA SUE HINSHAW
College of Pharmacy: JAMES RICHARDS
School of Public Health: NOREEN CLARK
School of Public Policy: EDWARD M. GRAMLICH
School of Social Work: PAULA ALLEN-MEARES
University Library: DONALD E. RIGGS

PROFESSORS

College of Architecture and Urban Planning:

BECKLEY, R. M.
BORKIN, H.
BRANDLE, K.
CARTER, B.
CHAFFERS, J.
CLIPSON, C.
CRANDALL, J. S.
CRANE, G.
DANDEKAR, H.
DARVAS, R.
DUKE, R.
JOHNSON, R.
KOWALEWSKI, H.
MARANS, R.
MARZOLF, K.
NYSTUEN, J.
OLVING, G.
PASTALAN, L.
RYCUS, M.
SNYDER, J.
SUTTON, S. E.
TURNER, J.
WERNER, W.

School of Art:

BAIRD, K.
CASTAGNACCI, V. E.
CHENG, M. Y.
HINTON, A.
LARSON, M. G.
LEE, D.
LEONARD, J.
PIJANOWSKI, E.
PIJANOWSKI, H. S.
RAMSAY, T.
RUSH, J.
SAMUELS, A.
SMITH, S.
STEWART, P.
TAKAHARA, T.
ZIRBES, G.

School of Business Administration:

ARNETT, H.
BAGOZZI, R. P.
BERNARD, V.
BREWER, G.
CAMERON, G.
CAPPOZZA, D.
DE SARBO, W.
DE WOSKIN, K.
DUFEY, G.
FORNELL, C.
GRIFFIN, C.
HILDEBRANDT, H.
HIRSHLEIFER, D.
HOSMER, L.
IMHOFF, E.
JACKSON, J.
JOHNSON, M. D.
KAUL, G.
KIM, H.
KINNEAR, T.
KON, S.
KORMENDI, R.
LEWIS, D.
LOVEJOY, W.
MARTIN, C.
MASTEN, S.
MILLER, E.
MIZRUCHI, M.
OLSON, J.
PRAHALAD, C.
QUINN, R.
REECE, J.
REILLY, R.
RYAN, M.
SCHRIBER, T.
SEVERANCE, D.
SEYHUN, N.
SIEDEL, G.
SLEMROD, J.
SNYDER, E.
SPIVEY, A.
TALBOT, B.
TAYLOR, J.
TICHY, N.
VARIAN, H.
WEICK, K.
WEISS, J.
WHEELER, J.
WHITE, J.
ZALD, M.

School of Dentistry:

BAGRAMIAN, R. A.
BRADLEY, R. M.
BROOKS, S. L.
BURGETT, F. G.
CHRISTIANSEN, R. L.
CLARKSON, B. H.
CLAYTON, J. A.
CLEWELL, D. B.
CORCORAN, J. F., Jr.
CORPRON, R. E.
DENNISON, J. D.
DRACH, J. C.
ELLISON, F. L.
FEIGAL, R. S.
GOBETTI, J. P.
HANKS, C. T.
HEYS, D. R.
HOLLAND, G. R.
JOHNSTON, L. E.
KELSEY, C. C.
KLEBE, R. J.
KORAN, A., III
KOTOWICZ, W. E.
KOWALSKI, C. J.
LANG, B. R.
LILLIE, J. H.
LOESCHE, W. J.
LOPATIN, D. E.
LOREY, R. E.
MACHEN, J. B.
MACKENZIE, I. C.
MCNAMARA, J. A.
MAKINEN, K. K.
MISTRETTA, C. M.
NANDA, S. K.
O'BRIEN, W. J.
POLVERINI, P. J.
ROBINSON, E.
ROWE, N. H.
RUTHERFORD, R.
SHIPMAN, C., Jr.
SMITH, F. N.
SOMERMAN, M. J.
STOHLER, C. S.
STRACHAN, D. S.
STRAFFON, L. H.
TEDESCO, A.
UPTON, L. G.
ZILLICH, R. M.

School of Education:

ANGUS, D. L.
BARRITT, L. S.
BATES, P.
BERGER, C. F.
BLACKBURN, R. T.
BLUMENFELD, P.
COHEN, D.
COXFORD, A. F.
ECCLES, J.
GERE, A. R.
GOODMAN, F. L.
HARRISON, D. K.
HIEBERT, E.
KEARNEY, C. P.
LAMPERT, M.
LOWTHER, M. A.
MARX, R. W.
MEISELS, S.
MISKEL, C. G.
MOODY, C. D.
NETTLES, M.
PALINSCAR, A.
PARIS, S. G.
PETERSON, M. W.
ROBINSON, J.
ROWAN, B.
SOLOWAY, E.
STARK, J. S.
SULZBY, E. F.
TICE, T. N.
TO, C.
WAGAW, T.
WIXSON, K. K.
WOMACK, F. W.

College of Engineering:

Aerospace Engineering:

ANDERSON, W. J.
DRISCOLL, J. F.
EISLEY, J. G.
FAETH, G. M.
HAYS, P. B.
KABAMBA, P. T.
KAUFFMAN, C. W.
MCCLAMROCH, N. H.
MESSITER, A. F.
ROE, P. L.
SICHEL, M.
TAYLOR, J. E.
VAN LEER, B.
VINH, N. X.

Atmospheric, Oceanic and Space Sciences:

ATREYA, S.
BANKS, P.
BARKER, J. R.
BOYD, J.
DRAYSON, S. R.
FISK, L.
GOMBOSI, T.
HAYS, P. B.
JACOBS, S. J.
KILLEEN, T.
KUHN, W. R.
NAGY, A. F.
SAMSON, P.
VESECKY, J.
WALKER, J. C. G.

Chemical Engineering:

Briggs, D. E.
Carnahan, B.
Curl, R. L.
Donahue, F. M.
Fogler, H. S.
Gland, J.
Gulari, E.
Schwank, J. W.
Wang, H. Y.
Wilkes, J. O.
Yang, R. T.
Yeh, G. S.

Civil and Environmental Engineering:

Hanson, R. D.
Li, V. C.
Naaman, A. E.
Nowak, A. S.
Weber, W. J., Jr
Wight, J. K.
Woods, R. D.
Wright, S. J.
Wylie, E. B.

Electrical Engineering and Computer Science:

Anderson, D. J.
Atkins, D. E.
BeMent, S. L.
Bhattacharya, P.
Birdsall, T. G.
Cain, C. A.
Calahan, D. A.
Conway, L. A.
Davidson, E. S.
England, A.
Getty, W. D.
Green, D. G.
Grizzle, J. W.
Gurevich, Y.
Haddad, G. I.
Hayes, J.
Holland, J.
Irani, K. B.
Jenkins, J. M.
Kabamba, P. T.
Kanicki, J.
Kaplan, S.
Katehi, P. B.
Khargonekar, P. P.
Leith, E. N.
Lomax, R. J.
McClamroch, N. H.
Meerkov, S. M.
Meyer, J. F.
Mourou, G.
Mudge, T. N.
Nagy, A. F.
Neuhoff, D. L.
O'Donnell, M.
Patt, Y.
Pavlidis, D.
Ribbens, W. B.
Rounds, W. C.
Senior, T. B. A.
Shin, K.
Singh, J.
Soloway, E.
Steel, D. G.
Stout, Q. F.
Teneketzis, D.
Teorey, T. J.
Ulaby, F. T.
Volakis, J. L.
White, C.
Williams, W. J.
Winful, H. G.
Wise, K. D.

Industrial and Operations Engineering:

Armstrong, T.
Bean, J.
Birge, J.
Chaffin, D.
Hancock, W.
Herrin, G.
Murty, K.
Nair, V.
Pollock, S.
Saigal, R.
Smith, R. L.
Teichroew, D.
White, C.
Wu, C.

Materials and Metallurgical Engineering:

Bilello, J.
Chen, I. W.
Filisko, F. E.
Ghosh, A.
Gibala, R.
Halloran, J. W.
Hosford, W. F.
Jones, J. W.
Pehlke, R. D.
Robertson, R. E.
Srolovitz, D. J.
Tien, T. Y.
Was, G. S.
Yee, A. F.

Mechanical Engineering:

Arpaci, V. S.
Assanis, D.
Barber, J. R.
Chen, M. M.
Comminou, M.
Farouki, R.
Goldstein, S.
Felbeck, D. K.
Kannatey-Asibou, E.
Kaviany, M.
Kikuchi, N.
Koren, Y.
Ludema, K. C.
Merte, H.
Papalambros, P. Y.
Schultz, A. B.
Scott, R. A.
Smith, G. E.
Sonntag, R. E.
Taylor, J. E.
Ulsoy, A. G.
Wineman, A. S.
Yang, W. H.
Yang, W. J.

Naval Architecture and Marine Engineering:

Beck, R. F.
Bernitsas, M. M.
Parsons, M. G.
Troesch, A. W.
Vorus, W. S.
Woodward, J. B.

Nuclear Engineering:

Duderstadt, J.
Fleming, R.
Gilgenbach, R.
Kammash, T.
Kearfott, K.
Knoll, G.
Larson, E. W.
Lau, Y.
Lee, J.
Martin, W.
Was, G.

Law School:

Aleinikoff, T.
Allen, L. E.
Alvarez, J. E.
Chambers, D. L.
Cooper, E. H.
Dehousse, R.
Eisenberg, R. S.
Ellsworth, P.
Fox, M.
Friedman, R.
Frier, B. W.
Green, T. A.
Gross, S. R.
Harris, S. L.
Herzog, D. J.
Higuchi, N.
Hilf, M. A.
Israel, J. H.
Jackson, J. H.
Jentes, W. R.
Kahn, D. A.
Kamisar, Y.
Kauper, T. E.
Krier, J. E.
Lehman, J. S.
Lempert, R. O.
MacKinnon, C. A.
Miller, W. I.
Miro, J. H.
Moravcik, J.
Payton, S.
Pildes, R. H.
Pooley, B. J.
Regan, D. H.
Reimann, M. W.
St Antoine, T. J.
Sandalow, T.
Schneider, C.
Schwartz, S. S.
Simma, B. E.
Simpson, A.
Sims, T. S.
Soper, P.
Stevenson, B.
Syverud, K. D.
Thomas, R. S.
Trimble, P. R.
Vining, J.
Waggoner, L. W.
Westen, P. K.
White, J. B.
White, J. J.
Whitman, C. B.

School of Information:

Atkins, D. E.
Blouin, F. X.
Dougherty, R. M.
Frost, C. O.
Furnas, G.
Hessler, D. W.
Pao, M. L.
Riggs, D. E.
Slavens, T. P.
Warner, R. M.

College of Literature, Science and the Arts:

American Culture:

McIntosh, J.
Wald, A.

Anthropology:

Behar, R.
Brace, C. L.
Caldwell, S.
Daniel, V.
Diamond, N.
Dirks, N.
Flannery, K. V.
Ford, R. I.
Frisancho, A. R.
Gingerich, P. D.
Humphreys, S. C.
Kelly, R. C.
Kottak, C. P.
Lansing, S.
Livingstone, F. B.
Lockwood, W. G.
Marcus, J. P.
O'Shea, J.
Owusu, M.
Parsons, J. R.
Rappaport, R. A.
Speth, J. D.
Stoler, A.
Trautman, T.
Whallon, R. W.
Williams, M.
Wolpoff, M. H.
Wright, H. T., III

Applied Physics:

ALLEN, J.
BHATTACHARYA, P. K.
BILELLO, J.
CLARKE, R.
GILGENBACH, R.
GLAND, J. L.
KOPELMAN, R.
LAU, Y. Y.
MERLIN, R.
MOUROU, G.
SANDER, L. M.
SINGH, J.
SROLOVITZ, D.
STEEL, D.
UHER, C.
WINFUL, H.
ZOM, J.

Asian Languages and Cultures:

DANLY, R. L.
DESHPANDE, M.
DEWOSKIN, K.
GÓMEZ, L. O.
HOOK, P.
LIN, S.
LOPEZ, D.
MUNRO, D.

Astronomy:

ALLER, H.
BREGMAN, J.
COWLEY, A.
MACALPINE, G.
RICHSTONE, D.

Biology:

ADAMS, J. P.
ALEXANDER, R. D.
ALLEN, S. L.
ANDERSON, W. R.
BENDER, R. A.
BROWN, W. M.
BURCH, J. B.
CARLSON, B. M.
EASTER, S. S., Jr
ESTABROOK, G. F.
FISHER, D.
FOGEL, R.
FORD, R.
FOSTER, D.
GANS, C.
HAZLETT, B. A.
HELLING, R. B.
HUME, R.
IKUMA, H.
KAUFMAN, P. B.
KLEINSMITH, L. J.
KLUGE, A. G.
LANGMORE, J. P.
LEHMAN, J.
MARTIN, M. M.
MOORE, T. E.
NOODEN, L. D.
NUSSBAUM, R. A.
OAKLEY, B.
PAYNE, R. B.
SHAPPIRIO, D. G.
SMITH, G. R.
TEERI, J.
TOSNEY, K.
VANDERMEER, J. H.
VOSS, E. G.
WEBB, P.
WERNER, E. E.
WYNNE, M. J.
YOCUM, C. F.

Chemistry:

ASHE, A. J.
BARKER, J.
BLINDER, S. M.
CORDES, G.
COUCOUVANIS, D.
COWARD, J.
CURTIS, M. D.
DUNN, T. M.
EGE, S. N.
EVANS, B. J.
FRANCIS, A. H.
GLAND, J.
GORDUS, A. A.
GRIFFIN, H. C.
KOPELMAN, R.
KOREEDA, M.
KUCZKOWSKI, R. L.
LAWTON, R. G.
LOHR, L. L.
LUBMAN, D. M.
MARINO, J. P.
MEYERHOFF, M. E.
MORRIS, M. D.
PECORARO, V. L.
PENNER-HAHN, J.
RASMUSSEN, P. G.
SACKS, R. D.
SHARP, R.
TOWNSEND, L.
WISEMAN, J. R.
YOCUM, C.

Classical Studies:

CAMERON, H. D.
CHERRY, J. F.
D'ARMS, J. H.
FRIER, B. W.
GARBRAH, K.
HERBERT, S.
HUMPHREY, J.
HUMPHREYS, S.
KNUDSVIG, G. M.
KOENEN, L.
MACCORMACK, S.
PEDLEY, J. G.
ROSS, D. O.
SCODEL, R.
WITKE, C.

Communication Studies:

HUESMANN, L. R.
STEVENS, J.
TRAUGOTT, M.

Economics:

ADAMS, W.
BERGSTROM, T.
BROWN, C.
COURANT, P.
CROSS, J.
DEARDORFF, A.
DUNCAN, G.
GORDON, R. H.
GRAMLICH, E.
HOLBROOK, R.
HOWREY, E. P.
HYMANS, S.
JOHNSON, G.
JUSTER, T.
LAITNER, J.
LEE, L. F.
PORTER, R.
SALANT, S. W.
SAXONHOUSE, G.
SHAPIRO, M.
SIMON, C.
SLEMROD, J.
SOLON, G.
STAFFORD, F.
STERN, R.
VARIAN, H.
WEISSKOPF, T.
WHITE, M.
WILLIS, R.

English Language and Literature:

AGEE, J.
ALEXANDER, W.
AWKWARD, M.
BAILEY, R.
BAXTER, C.
BORNSTEIN, G.
BRATER, E.
BROWN, J. R.
DELBANCO, N.
ELLISON, J.
ENGLISH, H.
FADER, D.
FALLER, L.
FULTON, A.
GERE, A.
GOLDSTEIN, L.
HOWES, A.
INGRAM, W.
JENSEN, E.
JOHNSON, L.
KNOTT, J.
KONIGSBERG, I.
KUCICH, J.
LENAGHAN, R.
LEVINSON, M.
LEWIS, R.
MCDOUGAL, S.
MCINTOSH, J.
MCNAMARA, L.
RABKIN, E.
ROBINSON, J.
SIEBERS, T.
TILLINGHAST, R.
VICINUS, M.
WALD, A.
WEISBUCH, R.
WHITE, J.
WILLIAMS, R.
WINN, J.

Film and Video Studies:

BEAVER, F.
KONIGSBERG, I.
PAUL, W.
STUDLAR, G.

Geological Sciences:

ESSENE, E. J.
FARRAND, W. R.
FISHER, D. C.
GINGERICH, P. D.
HALLIDAY, A. N.
KESLER, S. E.
LOHMANN, K. C.
MEYERS, P.
MOORE, T.
O'NEIL, J.
OUTCALT, S. I.
OWEN, R.
PEACOR, D. R.
POLLACK, H. N.
REA, D.
SMITH, G. R.
VAN DER VOO, R.
WALKER, J.
WALTER, L. M.
WILKINSON, B. H.

Germanic Languages and Literatures:

BAHTI, T. H.
COWEN, R. C.
KYES, R. L.
SCHELLE, H.
SEIDLER, I.
WEISS, H. F.

History:

ACHENBAUM, W.
BECKER, M. B.
BIEN, D. D.
BLOUIN, F. X.
BURBANK, J.
CHANG, C. S.
COHEN, D. W.
COLE, J. R.
COOPER, F.
DANN, J. C.
D'ARMS, J. V.
DIRKS, N. B.
ELEY, G. H.
ENDELMAN, T.
FEUERWERKER, A.
FINE, J. V. A.
FINE, S.
GREEN, T. A.
GREW, R.
HUMPHREYS, S.
LEWIS, E.

LIEBERMAN, V. B.
LINDNER, R. P.
MACCORMACK, S.
MACDONALD, M.
MCDONALD, T. J.
MACKAMAN, F.
MORANTZ-SANCHEZ, R.
PERKINS, B.
PERNICK, M. S.
ROSE, S. O.
ROSENBERG, W. G.
SCOTT, R. J.
SMITH-ROSENBERG, C.
STENECK, N. H.
STOLER, A.
TENTLER, T. N.
THORNTON, J. M.
TRAUTMANN, T. R.
VAN DAM, R. H.
VICINUS, M.
VINOVSKIS, M. A.
WARNER, R.
YOUNG, E. P.

History of Art:

BISSELL, R. W.
FORSYTH, I. H.
GAZDA, E.
ISAACSON, J.
KIRKPATRICK, D.
ROOT, M. C.
SPINK, W. M.

Linguistics:

DESHPANDE, M.
DWORKIN, S.
HEATH, J.
HOOK, P. E.
KELLER-COHEN, D.
MILROY, L.
MORLEY, J.
SHEVOROSHKIN, V.
SWALES, J.

Mathematics:

BARRETT, D. E.
BLASS, A. R.
BROWN, M.
BRUMFIEL, G.
BURNS, D. M., Jr
CONLON, J.
DOLGACHEV, I. V.
DUREN, P. L.
FEDERBUSH, P. G.
FORNAESS, J. E.
GEHRING, F. W.
GRIESS, R. L., Jr
HANLON, P. J.
HIGMAN, D. G.
HINMAN, P. G.
HOCHSTER, M.
HUNTINGTON, C. E.
KISTER, J. M.
KRAUSE, E. F.
LEWIS, D. J.
LODAY, J. L.
MILNE, J. S.
MONTGOMERY, H. L.
PRASAD, G.
RAMANUJAN, M. S.
RAUCH, J. B.
RAYMOND, F. A.
SCOTT, G. P.
SIMON, C.
SMOLLER, J. A.
SPATZIER, R. J.
STAFFORD, J.
STEMBRIDGE, J. R.
STORER, T. F.
TAYLOR, B. A.
URIBE, A.
WASSERMAN, A. G.
WEINSTEIN, M. I.
WINTER, D. J.

Near Eastern Studies:

COFFIN, E. A.
FOSSUM, J.
KRAHALKOV, C. R.
LEGASSICK, T. J.
LUTHER, K. A.
MICHALOWSKI, P.
RAMMUNY, R. M.
SCHRAMM, G. M.
STEWART-ROBINSON, J. M.
WINDFUHR, G. L.
YOFFEE, N.

Philosophy:

BERGMANN, F.
CURLEY, E.
DARWALL, S.
GIBBARD, A.
LOEB, L.
MEILAND, J.
MILLIKAN, R.
MUNRO, D.
RAILTON, P.
REGAN, D.
SKLAR, L.
VELLEMAN, D.
WALTON, K.

Physics:

AKERLOF, C. W.
ALLEN, J.
AXELROD, D.
BECCHETTI, F. D.
BRETZ, M.
BUCKSBAUM, P.
CHAPMAN, J. W.
CHUPP, T.
CLARKE, R.
COFFIN, C. T.
DONAHUE, T. M.
EINHORN, M. B.
FORD, G. W.
GIDLEY, D.
HECHT, K. T.
HEGYI, D.
JANECKE, J. W.
JONES, L. W.
KANE, G. L.
KRIMM, S.
KRISCH, A. D.
LONGO, M. J.
MERLIN, R.
MEYER, D. I.
NEAL, H.
ROE, B. P.
ROSS, M. H.
SANDER, L. M.
SANDERS, T. M.
SAVIT, R.
SINCLAIR, D.
STEEL, D. G.
TARLE, G.
THUN, R. P.
TICKLE, R. S.
TOMOZAWA, Y.
UHER, C.
VELTMAN, M. J. G.
WARD, J. F.
WILLIAMS, D. N.
WU, A. C. T.
YAO, Y.-P. E.
ZAKHAROV, V.
ZORN, J. C.

Political Science:

ACHEN, C.
AXELROD, S.
CAMPBELL, J.
CHAMBERLIN, T .
COHEN, M.
CORCORAN, M.
GITELMAN, Z.
GOLDENBERG, E.
HERZOG, D.
INGLEHART, R.
JACKSON, J.
JACOBSON, H.
JENNINGS, M.
KINDER, D.
KINGDON, J.
LEVINE, D.
LIEBERTHAL, K.
MARKUS, G.
MOHR, L.
ORGANSKI, A.
ROSENSTONE, S. J.
SAXONHOUSE, A.
SINGER, J.
TANTER, R.
WALTON, H.
ZIMMERMAN, W.

Psychology:

ADAMS, K.
ADELSON, J.
ANTONUCCI, T.
BARBARIN, O.
BERENT, S.
BERRIDGE, K.
BROWN, D.
BURNSTEIN, E.
BUSS, D.
BUTTER, C.
CAIN, A.
CROCKER, J.
DUTTON, J.
ECCLES, J.
ELLSWORTH, P.
FAST, I.
FEATHERMAN, D.
GELMAN, S.
GREEN, D.
GURIN, P.
HAGEN, J.
HOFFMAN, L.
HOLLAND, J.
HUESMANN, R.
JACKSON, J.
JONIDES, J.
KALTER, N.
KAPLAN, R.
KAPLAN, S.
KINDER, D.
KORNBLUM, S.
MCLOYD, V.
MAEHR, M.
MANIS, M.
MAYMAN, M.
MEYER, D.
MOODY, D.
MORRIS, C.
NISBETT, R.
OLSON, G.
OLSON, J.
PACHELLA, R.
PARIS, S.
PARK, D.
PERLMUTTER, M.
PETERSON, C.
POLLACK, I.
PRICE, R.
ROBINSON, T.
ROSENWALD, G.
SAMEROFF, A.
SCHWARZ, N.
SHATZ, M.
SHEVRIN, H.
SMITH, E.
SMITH, J. E. K.
SMUTS, B.
STEVENSON, H.
STEWART, A.
VEROFF, J.
WEICK, K.
WEINTRAUB, D.
WELLMAN, H.
WINTER, D.
WOLOWITZ, H.
WOODS, J.
YATES, F.
ZUCKER, R.

Romance Languages and Literatures:

CASA, F. P.
CHAMBERS, L. R.
DWORKIN, S. N.
GOIC, C.

GRAY, F. F., French
HAFTER, M. Z., Spanish
HUET, M.-H.
LÓPEZ-GRIGERA, L., Spanish
LUCENTE, G.
MERMIER, G. R.
PAULSON, W.
STANTON, D.

Slavic Languages and Literatures:

CARPENTER, B.
HUMESKY, A.
RONEN, O.
SHEVOROSHKIN, V.
STOLZ, B.
TOMAN, J.

Sociology:

ALWIN, D.
ANDERSON, B.
BIRTEK, F.
CHESLER, M.
DESKINS, D.
FARLEY, R.
GOLDBERG, D.
GROVES, R.
HERMALIN, A.
HOUSE, J.
KESSLER, R.
KNODEL, J.
LEMPERT, R.
MIZRUCHI, M.
NESS, G.
PAIGE, J.
ROSE, S.
SCHUMAN, H.
THORNTON, A.
ZALD, M.

Statistics:

ANDREWS, R.
CSÖRGÖ, S.
ERICSON, W. A.
HILL, B. M.
HOWREY, E. P.
HYMANS, S.
KEENER, R. W.
LITTLE, R.
MUIRHEAD, R. J.
NAIR, V.
ROTHMAN, E.
SMITH, J. E. K.
WOODROOFE, M.
WU, C. F. J.

Theatre and Drama:

BRATER, E.
BROWN, J. R.
FREDRICKSON, E.
JONES, B. J.
KERR, P.

Women's Studies:

BEHAR, R.
DOUVAN, E.
ECCLES, J.
GURIN, P.
JOHNSON, T.
LARIMORE, A.
ROSE, S.
SAXONHOUSE, A.
STANTON, D.
STEWART, A.
STOLER, A.
VICINUS, M.
WHITMAN, C.

Medical School:

Anatomy and Cell Biology:

ALTSCHILLER, R. A.
BURDI, A. R.
BURKEL, W. E.
CARLSON, B. M.
CHRISTENSEN, A. K.
COYLE, P.
ERNST, S. A.
HUELKE, D. F.
LILLIE, J. H.
MACCALLUM, D. K.
MCNAMARA, J. A.
NEWMAN, S. W.
RAYMOND, P. A.
SIPPEL, T. O.
WELSH, M. J.

Anaesthesiology:

LADU, B.
PANDIT, S. K.
SANFORD, T.
TREMPER, K.

Biological Chemistry:

ADELMAN, R. C.
AGRANOFF, B. W.
AMINOFF, D.
BALLOU, P.
COON, M. J.
DATTA, P.
DIXON, J. E.
GAFNI, A.
GOLDSTEIN, I. J.
HAJRA, A. K.
HULTQUIST, D. E.
IZUMO, S.
JOURDIAN, G. W.
KAUFMAN, R.
KENT, C.
LUDWIG, M. L.
MARLETTA, M. A.
MASSEY, V.
MATTHEWS, R. G.
MEDZIHRADSKY, F.
MENON, K. M. J.
NABEL, G. J.
PAYNE, A. H.
SCHACHT, J. H.
WEINHOLD, P. A.
WILLIAMS, C. H., Jr
ZAND, R.
ZUIDERWEG, E.

Cardiology:

ARMSTRONG, W.
BATES, E.
DAS, S.
IZUMO, S.
MORADY, F.
NABEL, B.
PITT, B.
RUBENFIRE, M.
STARLING, M.

Dermatology:

ELLIS, C. N.
HEADINGTON, J. T.
RASMUSSEN, J. E.
VOORHEES, J. J.

Endocrinology and Metabolism:

BARKAN, A. L.
GREENE, D. A.
GREKIN, R. J.
KNOPF, R. F.
PEK, S. B.
SCHTEINGART, D. F.
SIMA, A. E.

Family Practice:

COYNE, J. C.
SCHWENK, T. L.

Gastroenterology:

GUMUCIO, J. J.
HENLEY, K. S.
OWYANG, C.
YAMADA, T.

Geriatric Medicine:

GREEN, R.
HALTER, J.

Haematology:

ENSMINGER, W. D.
SCHMAIER, A.
WEISS, S.
WICHA, M.

Human Genetics:

BREWER, G. J.
GELEHRTER, T. D.
GINSBERG, D.
KURACHI, K.
KURNIT, D.
LEVINE, M.
MEISLER, M. H.
SING, C. F.
TASHIAN, R. E.

Hypertension:

JULIUS, S.
WEDER, A. B.
ZWEIFLER, A. J.

Microbiology and Immunology:

CLAFLIN, J. L.
CLEWELL, D. B.
COOPER, S.
DUNNICK, W.
FREIDMAN, D.
JUNI, E.
LOESCHE, W.
NEIDHARDT, F. C.
OLSEN, R.
SAVAGEAU, M. A.

Neurology:

ALBERS, J. W.
ALLEN, R. J.
BERENT, S.
BETZ, A.
CASEY, K. L.
GILMAN, S.
GREENBERG, H. S.
GROSSMAN, H. J.
MACDONALD, R. L.
SILVERSTEIN, F.
TROBE, J.

Neurosurgery:

BETZ, L.
CHANDLER, W.
HOFF, J.
MCGILLICUDDY, J.
TAREN, J.

Nuclear Medicine:

CORBETT, J. R.
GROSS, M.
KILBOURN, M. R.
KUHL, D. E.
ROGERS, W.
SHAPIRO, B.
SISSON, J. C.
WAHL, R. L.
WIELAND, D. M.

Obstetrics and Gynaecology:

ANSBACHER, R.
FOSTER, D.
HAYASHI, R.
JOHNSON, T.
MENON, K. M. J.
MORLEY, G.
ROBERTS, J.

Ophthalmology:

BERGSTROM, T. J.
FRUEH, B. R.
GREEN, D. G.
LICHTER, P. R.
MEYER, R. F.
PURO, D. G.
SIEVING, P. A.
SUGAR, A.
TROBE, J.
VINE, A. K.

Orthopaedic Surgery:

GOLDSTEIN, S. A.
HENSINGER, R. N.
LOUIS, D. S.
MATTHEWS, L. S.

Oto-rhino-laryngology:

BAKER, S.
KILENY, P. R.
KOOPMANN, C. F.
KRAUSE, C. J.
WOLF, G.

Pharmacology:

COUNSELL, R. E.
DOMINO, E. F.
ENSMINGER, W.
GNEGY, M. E.
HOLLENBERG, P. F.
HOLZ, R. W.
LUCCHESI, B. R.
MAYBAUM, J.
MEDZHIRADSKY, F.
NEUBIG, R. R.
PIPER, W.
PRATT, W. B.
SHLAFER, M.
SMITH, C. B.
SOMERMAN, M.
UEDA, T.
WEBER, W. W.
WOODS, J. H.

Physiology:

BRADLEY, R. M.
BRIGGS, J.
CARTER-SU, C.
CASEY, K. L.
D'ALECY, L. G.
DAWSON, D.
FAULKNER, J. A.
JULIUS, S.
KARSCH, F. J.
KEYES, P. L.
MACDONALD, R.
MCREYNOLDS, J. S.
MOISES, H. C.
NABEL, E. G.
PURO, D.
SCHNERMANN, B.
SCHWARTZ, J.
WEBB, R. C.
WILLIAMS, J.
YAMADA, T.

Psychiatry:

ADAMS, K.
AGRANOFF, B.
AKIL, H.
BERENT, S.
CAMERON, O.
COYNE, J.
CURTIS, G.
DREWNOWSKI, A.
GOMBERG, E.
GREDEN, J.
GROSSMAN, H.
GUYER, M.
KALTER, N.
KORNBLUM, S.
MARGOLIS, P.
MARSDEN, G.
NESSE, R.
POMERLEAU, O.
SHEVRIN, H.
TSAI, L.
UEDA, T.
WATSON, S.
ZUCKER, R.

Pulmonary and Critical Care Medicine:

LYNCH, J. P.
TOEWS, G. B.
WEG, J. G.

Radiology:

BLANE, C. E.
BREE, R. L.
CARSON, P. L.
CHAN, H. P.
CHO, K. J.
DUNNICK, N. R.
FRANCIS, I. F.
GABRIELSEN, T. O.
GROSS, B. H.
HERNANDEZ, R.
KOROBKIN, M.
KUHL, D. E.
KUHNS, L. R.
MARTEL, W.
RUBIN, J. M.
SILVER, T. M.
WAHL, R.

Surgery:

BARSAN, W., Emergency Medicine
CAMPBELL, D. A., Jr, General Surgery
CORAN, A. G., Paediatric Surgery
FEINBERG, S., Oral Surgery
HOFF, J. T., Neurosurgery
MATTHEWS, L., Orthopaedic Surgery
OESTERLING, J., Urology
ORRINGER, M., Thoracic Surgery
SMITH, D. Jr., Plastic Surgery
STANLEY, J., Vascular Surgery

School of Music:

Dance:

SPARLING, P.
WIDARYANTO, F.

Music:

ALBRIGHT, W. H.
BECKER, J. A.
BENGTSSON, E.
BOLCOM, W. E.
BOYLAN, P. C.
BUYSE, L.
CHUDACOFF, E. M.
COOPER, L. H.
CRAWFORD, D. E.
CRAWFORD, R.
CULVER, R.
CURTIS-SMITH, C.
DAPOGNY, J.
DERR, E.
ELLIOTT, A.
FROSETH, J. O.
GLASGOW, R. E.
GUINN, L. W.
HAYWOOD, L. M.
KAENZIG, F.
KANTOR, P.
KATZ, M.
KIESLER, K.
LEHMAN, P. R.
LEWIS, R. B.
MASON, M.
MEIER, G.
MONSON, I.
MONTS, L.
NADON-GABRION, C.
ORMAND, F.
PARMENTIER, E.
PATTERSON, W. C.
REYNOLDS, H. R.
SANKEY, S.
SARGOUS, H.
SHIRLEY, G.
SINTA, D. J.
SMITH, H. D.
STANDIFER, J. A.
UDOW, M.
WATKINS, G. E.
WILEY, R. J.

Division of Kinesiology

BORER, K. T.
EDINGTON, D. W.
FOSS, M. L.
KATCH, V. L.

School of Natural Resources:

ALLAN, D.
BARNES, B. V.
BREWER, G.
BULKLEY, J. W.
BURCH, J. B.
DRAKE, W. D.
FOWLER, G. W.
KAPLAN, R.
LOW, B. S.
MORTON, H. L.
OLSON, C. E., Jr
PATTERSON, R.
POLAKOWSKI, K. J.
STOERMER, E.
WEBB, P. W.
WITTER, J. A.
YAFFEE, S. L.

School of Nursing:

DUMAS, R.
HINSHAW, A. S.
KALISCH, B.
KALISCH, P.
KETEFIAN, S.
LUSK, S.
MISTRETTA, C.
OAKLEY, D.
PENDER, N.
REAME, N.
WHALL, A.

College of Pharmacy:

AMIDON, G. L.
BERARDI, R. R.
COUNSELL, R. E.
COWARD, J. K.
CRIPPEN, M.
DRACH, J. C.
FLYNN, G. L.
KOREEDA, M.
LEVY, R. J.
MARINO, J. P.
MARIETTA, M. A.
MOSBERG, H. I.
PAUL, A. G.
RICHARDS, J. W.
TOPLISS, J. G.
TOWNSEND, L. B.
WEINER, N. D.

School of Public Health:

Biostatistics:

BOEHNKE, M. L.
BROWN, M. B.
CORNELL, R. G.
KSHIRSAGAR, A. M.
LANGE, K.
LITTLE, R. J. A.
SCHORK, M. A.
WOLFE, R. A.

Dental Public Health:

BAGRAMIAN, R. A.
BURT, B. A.
ROBINSON, E.

Environmental and Industrial Health:

ALBERS, J. A.
ARMSTRONG, T. J.
BERENT, S.
CHAFFIN, D. B.
DEININGER, R. A.
DREWNOWSKI, A.
GRAY, R. H.
HARTUNG, R.
LEVINE, S. P.
MANCY, K. H.
MEIER, P. G.
PIPER, W.
RICHARDSON, R. J.
SAMSON, P. J.
WEBER, W.

Epidemiology:

BARLOW, R.
BURT, B. A.
JAMES, S. A.
KOOPMAN, J. S.
MAASSAB, H. F.
MONTO, A. S.
OSBORN, J. E.
PEYSER, P. A.
PORT, F. K.
SCHOTTENFELD, D.

Health Behaviour and Health Education:

CLARK, N. M.
HICKEY, T.
ISRAEL, B. A.
KRAUSE, N. M.
SIMONDS, S. K.
STRECHER, V.
TAKESHITA, Y. J.

Health Services Management and Policy:

ALEXANDER, J.
BASHSHUR, R.
BUTTER, I. H.
FRIES, B. E.
GRIFFITH, J. R.
HANCOCK, W. M.
LIANG, J.
MICK, S. S.
PENCHANSKY, R.
THOMAS, J. W.
WARNER, K. E.
WEISSERT, W. G.
WHEELER, J. R. C.

School of Social Work:

ALLEN-MEARES, P.
BARBARIN, O.
CHECKOWAY, B.
CHURCHILL, S.
CORCORAN, M.
CROXTON, T.
DANZIGER, S.
DUNKLE, R.
FALLER, K.
FELD, S.
FELLIN, P.
GARVIN, C.
GIBSON, R.
GOMBERG, E.
JAYARATNE, S.
JOHNSON, H.
LAUFFER, A.
MAPLE, F.
POWELL, T.
ROOT, L.
SIEFERT, K.
TROPMAN, J.
TUCKER, D.
ZALD, M.

SELECTED ATTACHED INSTITUTIONS

English Language Institute, Kresge Hearing Research Institute, Simpson Memorial Institute, Mental Health Research Institute, Institute for Human Adjustment, Institute for Social Research, Institute of Gerontology, Institute of Labor and Industrial Relations, Institute of Continuing Legal Education, Institute of Environmental and Industrial Health, Transportation Research Institute, Tauber Manufacturing Institute, Center for Chinese Studies, Center for Japanese Studies, Center for Near Eastern and North African Studies, Center for Russian Studies, Center for South and Southeast Asian Studies, Lawrence D. Buhl Genetics Research Center for Human Genetics, Center for Great Lakes and Aquatic Science, Center for Ergonomics, Center for Human Growth and Development, Center for the Study of Higher Education, Center for Research on Learning and Teaching, Automotive Research Center, Cancer Center, National Pollution Prevention Center, Information Technology Division, Biological Station, Botanical Gardens, University Herbarium, Museum of Anthropology, Museum of Paleontology, Museum of Zoology, University Observatories, Middle English Dictionary, Clinical Research Unit, Center for the Education of Women, Communicative Disorder Clinic, Michigan Memorial Phoenix Project, Center for Population Planning and Population Studies, Laboratory for Scientific Computation, Nuclear Resonance Laboratory, Mass Spectroscopy Laboratory, DNA Sequencing Laboratory, Electron Microbeam Analysis Laboratory.

There are more than one hundred other research units attached to the schools, colleges and departments.

University of Michigan—Dearborn

4901 Evergreen Rd, Dearborn, MI 48128-1491
Telephone: (313) 593-5000

Chancellor: JAMES C. RENICK
Provost: ROBERT SIMPSON
Vice-Chancellor for Business Affairs: ROBERT G. BEHRENS
Vice-Chancellor for Institutional Advancement: SUSAN L. MCCLANAHAN
Vice-Chancellor for Government Relations: EDWARD J. BAGALE
Vice-Chancellor for Student Affairs: DONNA L. MCKINLEY
Number of students: 8,214

DEANS

Arts, Sciences and Letters: JOHN PRESLEY
Education: JOHN B. POSTER
Engineering: SUBRATA SENGUPTA
Management: ERIC BRUCKER

University of Michigan—Flint

Flint, MI 48502-1950
Telephone: (313) 762-3000
Fax: (313) 762-3687
Founded 1956
Provides 61 Bachelor programs, 7 Master level programs
State control
Academic year: July to June
Chancellor: CHARLIE NELMS
Provost and Vice-Chancellor for Academic Affairs: RENATE MCLAUGHLIN
Vice-Chancellor for Administration: DOROTHY K. RUSSELL
Vice-Chancellor for Development: JOANNE SULLENGER
Vice-Chancellor for Student Services and Enrollment Management: VIRGINIA R. ALLEN
Librarian: ROBERT L. HOUBECK, Jr
Library of 708,800 vols
Number of teachers: 206 full-time
Number of students: 6,488

DEANS AND DIRECTORS

College of Arts and Sciences: HARRIET WALL (acting)
School of Management: FRED WILLIAMS
Nursing: ELLEN A. WOODMAN
School of Health Professions and Studies: MARY PERIARD
Graduate Programs: BEVERLY SCHMOLL
Extension and Continuing Education: CAROLYN COLLINS-BONDON

WAYNE STATE UNIVERSITY

Detroit, MI 48202
Telephone: (313) 577-2424
Fax: (313) 577-3200
Oldest antecedent college founded 1868, university 1933
State control
Academic year: August to May
President: IRVIN D. REID
Vice-President for Finance and Administrative Services: JOHN L. DAVIS
Vice-President for Academic Affairs: TILDEN G. EDELSTEIN
Vice-President for Marketing and Communications: JEFFREY STOLTMAN
Number of teachers: 1,692 full-time, 1,024 part-time
Number of students: 14,927 full-time, 17,222 part-time

DEANS

College of Education: PAULA C. WOOD
College of Engineering: CHIN KUO
College of Liberal Arts: SONDRA A. O'NEALE
College of Nursing: FREDERICKA SHEA (interim)
College of Pharmacy and Allied Health Professions: GEORGE C. FULLER
College of Science: JOHN D. PETERSEN
School of Social Work: LEON W. CHESTANG
College of Medicine: ROBERT J. SOKOL
Law School: JAMES K. ROBINSON
School of Business Administration: HARVEY KAHALAS
College of Lifelong Learning: ROBERT L. CARTER
College of Fine, Performing and Communication Arts: JACK KAY (interim)
Graduate Studies: DANIEL WALZ
College of Urban, Labor and Metropolitan Affairs: SUE MARX SMOCK
University Libraries and Library Science: PATRICIA SENN BREIVIK

PROFESSORS

(H = Head of Department)

School of Business Administration:

Accounting:

BILLINGS, B.
REINSTEIN, A.
SPAULDING, A. (H)
VOLZ, W.

Finance and Business Economics:

HAMILTON, J.
SOMERS, T. (H)
SPENCER, M.

Management:

MARTIN, J. E.
OSBORN, R. N.

Marketing:

BELTRAMINI, R.
CANNON, H.
JACKSON, G. (H)
KELLY, J.
RIORDAN, E.
RYMER, J.
YAPRAK, A.

College of Education:

Academic Services:

GREEN, J. (H)

Administrative and Organizational Studies:

DEMONT, R.
GIPSON-SIMPSON, J. H.
HALL, B. (H)
KRAJEWSKI, R.
RICHEY, R.

Health, Physical Education and Recreation:

ERBAUGH, S. (H)

Teacher Education:

BROWN, A.
ELLIOTT, S. (H)
HALE, J.
KAPLAN, L.
PETERSON, J. M.
SMITH, G.

Theoretical and Behavioural Foundations:

BROWN, A.
HILLMAN, S.
HOLBERT, J. A. (H)
MARCOTTE, D.
MARKMAN, B. S.
PIETROFESA, J.
SAWILOWSKY, S.

College of Engineering:

Auto Research Center:

HENEIN, N.

Chemical and Metallurgical Engineering and Materials Science:

GULARI, E. (H)
KUMMLER, R.
MANKE, C.
NG, S.
ROTHE, E. W.

Bioengineering Research Center:

KING, A.

Civil and Environmental Engineering:

AKTAN, H. M.
BEAUFAIT, F.
DATTA, T. K.
KHASNABIS, S.
KUO, C.
USMEN, M. (H)

Electrical and Computer Engineering:

HASSOUN, M.
MEISEL, J.
MITIN, V.
OLBROT, A.
SILVERSMITH, D.
SINGH, H.
WESTERVELT, F. (H)

Industrial Engineering and Manufacturing Engineering:

CHELST, K.
FALKENBURG, D. (H)
KNAPPENBURGER, H. A.
PLONKA, F.
SINGH, N.

Mechanical Engineering:

BERDICHEVSKY, V.
GIBSON, R.
HENEIN, N. A.
IBRAHIM, R.
KING, A.
KLINE, K. (H)
NEWAZ, G. M.
RIVIN, E.
SINGH, T.
TARAZA, D.
WHITMAN, A. B.

College of Fine, Performing and Communication Arts:

Art and Art History:

BILAITIS, R.
FIKE, P. G.
HEGARTY, J.
JACKSON, M.
NAWARA, J.
PARISH, T.
ROSAS, M.
UHR, H.
ZAJAC, J.

Dance:

POWERS, E. (H)

Music:

HARTWAY, J.
TINI, D.

Speech Communication and Journalism:

BROCK, B.
BURNS, B.
KAY, J.
PAPPAS, E. (H)
ZIEGELMUELLER, G. W.

Theatre:

CALARCO, N. J.
KAUSHANSKY, L.
MCGILL, R. E.
MAGIDSON, D.
PULLIN, N.
SCHMITT, A.
SCHRAEDER, T.
THOMAS, J. (H)

Law School:

ABRAMS, R. H.
ADAMANY, D. W.
ADELMAN, M. J.
BARTELL, L.
BOLDA, M.
BROWN, K.
BUCKERNER-INNISS, L.
BURNHAM, W.
BYRNES, L.
CALKINS, S.
CALLAHAN, K. R.
DANILENKO, G.
DEVANEY, D.
DOLAN, J. F.
FENTON, Z.
FINDLATER, J.
FRIEDMAN, J. M.
GRANO, J.
HENNING, P.
HETZEL, O.
KADES, E.
KELMAN, M.
LAMBORN, L.
LANNING, G.
LITMAN, J.
LITTLEJOHN, E.
LOMBARD, F. K.
MCFERREN, M.
MCINTYRE, M. J.
MOGK, J.
PETERS, S.
ROBINSON, J. (H)
SCHENK, A.
SCHULMAN, S.
SEDLER, R. A.
SLOVENKO, R.
VAN RHEE, C.
WEINBERG, J.
WELLMAN, V.
WHITE, K.
WISE, E. M.

College of Liberal Arts:

Africana Studies:

BOYD, M. (H)
HUTCHFUL, E.
MARTIN, M. (H)

Anthropology:

ASWAD, B. C.
BABA, M. (H)
KAPLAN, B. A.
MONTILUS, G.
ORTIZ DE MONTELLANO, B.
WEISS, M. L.

Classics, Greek and Latin:

MCNAMEE, K. (H)

Criminal Justice:

STACK, S. (H)
ZALMAN, M.

Economics:

BRAID, R.
GOODMAN, A. C.
LEE, L.
LEVIN, J. H.
ROSSANA, A. (H)

English:

BRILL, L.
BURGOYNE, R. (H)
COUTURE, B.
EDWARDS, W.
GOLEMBA, H.
HERRON, J.
LANDRY, D.
LELAND, C.
LINBERG, K.
MACLEAN, G.
MAROTTI, A.
O'NEALE, S.
RAPPORT, H.
REED, J. R.
SCRIVENER, M.
STROZIER, R.
VLASOPOLOS, A.
WASSERMAN, R.

History:

BONNER, T.
BRAZILL, W. J., Jr
BUKOWCZYK, J.
HYDE, C.
JOHNSON, C. H.
KRUMAN, M. (H)
MASON, P.
RAUCHER, A.
SCOTT, S. F.
SCHULER, M.
SMALL, M.

Near Eastern and Asian Studies:

ROUCHDY, A. (H)

Philosophy:

LOMBARD, L. (H)
MCKINSEY, T.
RUSSELL, B.
YANAL, R.

Political Science:

ABBOTT, P. R.
ADAMANY, D.
BROWN, R. (H)
DOWNING, R. G.
ELDER, C. (H)
ELLING, R.
FEINSTEIN, O.
PARISH, C. J.
PRATT, H.
TAPIA-VIDELA, J.
WOLMAN, H.

Romance Languages and Literatures:

DITOMMASO, A.
GUTIERREZ, J.
SPINELLI, D.
STIVALE, C. (H)

Sociology:

BRITT, D.
ESHLEMAN, J. R.
GELFAND, D. (H)
HANKINS, J.
SENGSTOCK, M.

College of Science:

Biological Sciences:

ARKING, R.
GANGWERE, S. K.
HEBERLEIN, G.
HOUGH, A.
LILIEN, J. (H)
MIZUKAMI, H.
MOORE, W. S.
NJUS, D. L.
PETTY, H.
SMITH, P. D.
TAYLOR, J.

Chemistry:

BRENNER, A.
ENDICOTT, J. F.
HASE, W. L.
JOHNSON, C. R. (H)
LINVELDT, R. (H)
MCCLAIN, W.
MOBASHERRY, S.
NEWCOMB, M.
OLIVER, J. P.
PETERSEN, J.
POOLE, C.
RABAN, J. P.
RECK, G.
RIGBY, J.
ROMANO, L.
RORABCHER, D.
SCHAAP, A. P.
SCHLEGEL, H.

Communication Disorders and Science:

BLISS, L. (H)
LEITH, W.
PANAGOS, J. M.

Computer Science:

CONRAD, M.
GOEL, N.
GROSKY, W. (H)
RAJLICH, V.
SETHI, I.

Geology:

FURLONG, R. B. (H)

Mathematics:

BACHELIS, G. F.
BERMAN, R.
BRENTON, L.
BROWN, L.
CHOW, P.-L. (H)

COHN, W.
DRUCKER, D.
FROHARDT, D.
GLUCK, D. H.
HANDEL, D.
HANSEN, L.
HOUH, C.
IRWIN, J. M.
KHAN, S.
KHASMINSKII, R.
KOROSTELEV, A.
MCGIBBON, C.
MAKAR-LIMANOV, L.
MENALDI, J. L.
MORDUKHOVICH, B.
OKOH, F.
PAK, J.
RHEE, C.
RODIN, Y.
SCHREIBER, B. H.
SCHOCHET, C. L.
SUN, T.-C.
WECHSLER, M. T.
YIN, G.

Nutrition and Food Science:

JEN, C.
KLURFELD, D. M. (H)
SHELEF, L.

Physics and Astronomy:

BERES, W.
CHANG, J. J.
CHEN, J. -T.
CORMIER, T. (H)
DUNIFER, G.
FAVRO, L.
GUPTA, S. N.
KARCHIN, P.
KAUPPILA, W. E.
KEYES, P. H.
KIM, Y. W.
KUO, P. K.
ROLNICK, W. B.
SAPERSTEIN, A. M.
STEIN, T. S.
WADEHRA, J.
WENGER, L.

Psychology:

ABEL, E.
AGER, J.
ALEXANDER, S.
BASS, A.
BERMAN, R.
COSCINA, D. (H)
FIRESTONE, I. J.
FITZGERALD, J.
JACOBSON, J.
JOHNSON, C.
KAPLAN, K.
KILBEY, M. M.
LABOUVIE-VIEF, G.
LEVY, S.
RATNER, H.
RICKEL, A.
SAITZ, E.
SHANTZ, C. A.
STETTNER, L.
TREIMAN, R.
WHITMAN, R.
YOUNG, A.

College of Lifelong Learning:

Interdisciplinary Studies Program:

ARONSON, A. R.
BAILS, J. G.
GLABERMAN, M.
KLEIN, J.
MAIER, C. L.
RASPA, R. N.
SCHINDLER, R. (H)
WRIGHT, R. H.

College of Medicine:

Anatomy:

BERNSTEIN, M.
GOODMAN, M.
GOSHGARIAN, H.
HAZLETT, L.
LASKER, G.
MAISEL, H. (H)
MEYER, D.
MITCHELL, J. A.
MIZERES, N. J.
POURCHO, R.
RAFOLS, J.
ROHER, A.
SKOFF, R.

Anaesthesiology:

BROWN, E. (H)

Audiology:

RINTELMANN, W. F. (H)

Biochemistry:

BROOKS, S.
BROWN, R. K.
EDWARDS, B.
EVANS, D.
JOHNSON, R.
LEE, C. P.
ROSEN, B. (H)
ROWND, R.
VINOGRADOV, S.

Cardiology:

KLONER, R.
WYNNE, J.

Community Medicine:

WALLER, J. (H)

Dermatology and Syphilology:

BIRMINGHAM, D.
HASHIMOTO, K. (H)

Family Medicine:

DALLMAN, J.
GALLAGHER, R. E.
WERNER, P. (H)

Immunology and Microbiology:

BERK, R.
BOROS, D. L.
BROWN, W. J.
DEGUISTI, D.
HAZLEH, L.
JEFFRIES, C.
KAPLAN, J.
KONG, Y.-C.
LEFFORD, M.
LEON, M.
LEVIN, S.
LISAK, R.
MONTGOMERY, P. C. (H)
PALCHAUDHURI, S.
SOBEL, J.
SUNDICK, R.
SWANBORG, R. H.
WEINER, L. M.

Internal Medicine:

AL-SARRAF, M.
BAGCHI, N.
BERGSMAN, K. L.
BISHOP, C. R.
BRENNAN, M.
CLAPPER, I.
CORBETT, T.
FERNÁNDEZ-MADRID, F. B.
GRUNBERGER, G.
HEILBRUN, L.
HEPPNER, G.
KESSEL, D.
LERNER, S.
LEWIS, B. M.
LUM, L.
LYNNE-DAVIS, P.
MCDONALD, F.
MACK, R.
MAJUMDAR, A.
MARSH, J.
MIGDAL, S.
MILLER, R.
MUTCHNICK, M.
NAKEFF, A.
PRASAD, A. S.
PURI, P.
RESNICK, L.
SAMSON, M. (H)
SANTEN, R.
SENSENBRENNER, L.
SOBEL, J.
SOWERS, J.
SPEARS, J.
TALMERS, F.
TRANCHIDA, L.
VAITKEVICIUS, V.
VALDIVIESO, M.
VALERIOTE, F.
WYNNE, J.

Neurology:

BENJAMINS, J. A.
CHUGANI, H.
DORE-DUFFY, P.
LEWITT, P.
LISAK, R. (H)
NIGRO, M.

Neurosurgery:

DIAZ, F. G. (H)
THOMAS, L. M.

Obstetrics and Gynaecology:

ABEL, E.
AGER, J.
BEHRMAN, S. J.
BERMAN, R.
COTTON, D. (H)
DEPPE, G.
EVANS, M.
FREEDMAN, R.
LANCASTER, W.
MAMMEN, E.
MARIONA, F.
MILLER, O.
MOGHISSI, K.
POLAND, M.
ROMERO, R.
SACCO, A. G.
SHERMAN, A.
SOBEL, J.
SOKOL, R.
STRYKER, J.
SUBRAMANIAN, M.

Ophthalmology:

ESSNER, E.
FRANK, R. N.
JAMPEL, R. S. (H)
PUKLIN, J.
SHICHI, H.
SHIN, D.
SPOOR, T.

Orthopaedic Surgery:

FITZGERALD, R. (H)
MANOLI II, A.
RYAN, J.

Otolaryngology:

COHN, A. M.
DRESCHER, D.
DWORKIN, J.
JACOBS, J.
MATHOG, R. H. (H)

Paediatrics:

BEN-YOSEPH, Y.
BRANS, Y. W.
CASH, R.
CHUGANI, H.
COHEN, S.
COLLINS, J.
DAJANI, A. S.
EPSTEIN, M.
FAROOKI, Z.
FLEISCHMANN, L.
GRUSKIN, A. (H)
GUTAI, J.
KAPLAN, J.
KAUFFMAN, R.
LUM, L.
LUSHER, J.

NIGRO, M.
OSTREA, E.
PINSKY, W. W.
RAUMDRANATH, Y.
ROBIN, A.
SAMAIK, A.
SARNAIK, A.
SENSENBRENNER, L.
SHANKARIAN, G.
SLOVIS, T.

Pathology:

BEDROSSIAN, C.
BROWN, W.
CRISSMAN, J. (H)
DALE, E.
EVANS, M.
GIACOMELLI, F. E.
HONN, K.
KURKINEN, M.
MAMMEN, E.
MILLER, D.
PALUTKE, M.
PERRIN, E. V.
RAZ, A.
SHEAHAN, D.
SPITZ, W. U.
THIBERT, R.
WEINER, L.
WIENER, J.
ZAK, B.

Pharmacology:

ANDERSON, G.
BANNON, M.
CHOPRA, D.
DUTTA, S.
GOLDMAN, H.
HIRATA, F.
HOLLENBERG, P. F. (H)
KESSEL, D.
MARKS, B.
NOVAK, R.
SLOANE, B.
WAKADE, A.

Physiology:

BARRACO, R.
CHURCHILL, P. C.
DUNBAR, J. C.
FOA, P.
GALA, R.
HONG, F. T.
LAWSON, D.
MCCOY, L. E.
MAMMEN, E.
NYBOER, J.
PENNEY, D.
PHILLIS, J. W. (H)
RAM, J.
RILLEMA, J. A.
SEEGERS, W.
WALZ, D. A. (H)

Psychiatry:

BANNON, M.
FISCHHOFE, J.
FREEDMAN, R.
GALLOWAY, M.
KAPATOS, G.
KUHN, D.
LEWITT, P.
LUBY, E.
LYCAKI, H.
POHL, R.
ROSENBAUM, A.
ROSENZWEIG, N.
SARWER-FONER, G.
SCHORER, C.
SITARAM, N.
UHDE, T. (H)

Radiation Oncology:

HERSKOVIC, A. M.
HONN, K. V.
MARUYAMA, Y.
ORTON, C. G.
PORTER, A. (H)

Radiology:

KLING, G. (H)
SOULEN, R.
WOLLSCHLAEGER, G.

Surgery:

BERGUER, R.
FROMM, D. (H)
KLEIN, M.
LEDGERWOOD, A. M.
LUCAS, C.
PHILIPPART, A.
ROSENBERG, J. C.
SILVA, Y. J.
STEPHENSON, L.
SUGAWA, C.
WALT, A. J.
WEAVER, A. W.
WILSON, R. F.

Urology:

JAFFER, D.
MONTIE, J.
PERLMUTTER, A. D.
PONTES, J. (H)

College of Nursing:

CAVANAGH, S. (H)
COVINGTON, C. (H)
ISENBERG, M.
JACOX, A.
MOOD, D.
OBERST, M. (H)
OERMANN, M.
RICE, V.

College of Pharmacy and Allied Health Professions:

Anaesthesia:

COOK, K. A.
CRAWFORTH, K. L.
HAGLUND, V. L.
MANGAHAS, P.
WALCZYK, M. L.
WORTH, P. A. (H)

Clinical Laboratory Science:

ALDRIGE, G. (H)
CASTILLO, J. B.
HARAKE, B.
WALLACE, A. M.

Mortuary Science:

BURDA-MASTROGIANIS, L.
FRADE, P.
FRITTS-WILLIAMS, M. L. (H)
HUNTOON, R.

Occupational and Environmental Health Sciences:

BASSETT, D. (H)
BHALLA, D.
KERFOOT, E. J.
TAFFE, B.
WARNER, P. O.

Occupational Therapy:

BROWN, K.
ESDAILE, S. (H)
LUBORSKY, M.
LYSACK, C.
POWELL, N.

Physical Therapy:

AMUNDSEN, L. (H)
CARLSON, C.
DROVIN, J.
DUNLEAVY, K.
MCNEVIN, N.
TALLEY, S.

Physician Assistant Studies:

FRICK, J.
NORMILE, H.
SIDDIQUE, M.
TODD, K.
WORMSER, H. (H)

Radiation Therapy Technology:

CHADWELL, D. (H)

KEMPA, A.

Pharmaceutical Sciences:

ABRAMSON, H.
BOLARIN, D.
COMMISSARIS, R.
CORCORAN, G. B. (H)
FULLER, G. C.
GIBBS, R.
HIRATA, F.
LINDBLAD, W.
LOUIS-FERDINAND, R. T.
PITTS, D. K.
SVENSSON, C. K.
WORMSER, H.
WOSTER, P. M.

Pharmacy Practice:

CAPPELLETTY, D.
EDWARDS, D. J.
FAGAN, S.
JABER, L. A.
KALE-PRADHAN, P. B.
KEYS, P.
MILLER, M.
MOSER, L. R.
MUNZENBERGER, P. J.
RHONEY, D.
RYBAK, M. J.
SCHUMANN, W.
SINGH, R.
SLAUGHTER, R. L. (H)
SMITH, G. B.
SMYTHE, M. A.
STEVENSON, J. G.
TISDALE, J. E.
VIVIAN, J. C.
WILSON, J.

College of Urban, Labor and Metropolitan Affairs:

Urban and Labor Studies:

BATES, T.
BROWN, D. R.
COOKE, W.
MASON, P.
SMOCK, S. M. (H)
WOLMAN, H.
YOUNG, H.

Clarence Hillberry Prof. of Urban Affairs:

GALSTER, G.

Coleman A. Young Prof. of Urban Affairs:

YOUNG, A. H.

Geography and Urban Planning:

BOYLE, R. M.
RESSE, L.
SINCLAIR, R.

School of Social Work:

BEVERLY, C.
BRANDALL, J.
CHESTANG, L. (H)

University Libraries:

Library and Information Science:

ALBRITTON, R. L.
BAKER, L. M.
BROWN-SYED, C. L.
EZELL, C. L.
FIELD, J. J.
HOLLEY, R. (H)
JOHNSON, N. B.
MIKA, J.
NEAVILL, G. B.
POWELL, R.
SPITERI, L. F.

ATTACHED RESEARCH INSTITUTES

Addiction Research Institute: Dir Dr EUGENE SCHOENER.

African American Film Institute: Dirs Dr MICHAEL MARTIN, Dr ROBERT BURGOYNE.

Asthma and Related Lung Disorders Research Center: Dir Dr GEORGE FULLER.

Bioengineering Center: Dir Dr ALBERT KING.

Barbara Anne Karmanos Cancer Institute: Dir Dr WILLIAM PETERS.

Center for Academic Ethics: Dir (vacant).

Center for Automotive Research: Dir Dr NAEIM HENEIN.

Center for Chicano-Boricua Studies: Dir Dr JOSE CUELLO.

Center for Health Research: Dir Dr ADA JACOX.

Center for International Business Education and Research: Dir Dr ATTILA YAPRAK.

Center for Legal Studies: Dir Dr JOHN FRIEDL.

Center for Molecular Medicine and Genetics: Dir Dr GEORGE GRUNBERGER.

Center for Peace and Conflict Studies: Dir Dr FREDERIC PEARSON.

Center for the Study of Arts and Public Policy: Dir Dr BERNARD BROCK.

Center for Urban Studies: Dir Dr DIANE BROWN.

Cohn-Haddow Center for Judaic Studies: Dir Dr DAVID WEINBERG.

C. S. Mott Center for Human Growth and Development: Dir Dr ERNEST ABEL.

Developmental Disabilities Institute: Dir Dr BARBARA LEROY.

Humanities Center: Dir Dr WALTER EDWARDS.

Institute of Chemical Toxicology: Dir Dr RAYMOND F. NOVAK.

Institute of Gerontology: Dir Dr JEFFREY W. DWYER.

Institute for Manufacturing Research: Dir Dr ROBERT L. THOMAS.

Institute of Maternal and Child Health: Dir Dr JOHN B. WALLER, Jr.

Labor Studies Center: Dir HAL STACK.

Merill-Palmer Institute for Family and Human Development: Dir Dr ELI SALTZ.

Skillman Center for Children: Dir Dr ERNESTINE MOORE.

Small Business Development Center—WSU: Dir RONALD HALL.

WESTERN MICHIGAN UNIVERSITY

Kalamazoo, MI 49008

Telephone: (616) 387-1000

President: ELSON S. FLOYD.
Provost and Vice-President for Academic Affairs: T. LIGHT
Vice-President for Business and Finance: R. M. BEAM
Vice-President for Student Affairs: T. A. POWELL
Vice-President for Research: D. E. THOMPSON
General Counsel and Vice-President for External Affairs: K. A. PRETTY
Executive Director for International Affairs: H. J. DOOLEY
Registrar: CATHY ZENZ
Librarian: LANCE QUERY

Number of students: 26,132

DEANS

Business: J. SCHMOTTER
Applied Sciences: L. LAMBERSON
Arts and Sciences: E. B. JORGENS
Education: F. E. RAPLEY
Graduate: S. SCOTT
Fine Arts: R. LUSCOMBE
Health and Human Services: J. PISANESCHI

MINNESOTA

AUGSBURG COLLEGE

2211 Riverside Ave, Minneapolis, MN 55454

Telephone: (612) 330-1000
Fax: (612) 330-1649

Founded 1869

President: WILLIAM V. FRAME
Registrar: PAUL SIMMONS
Director of Library: (vacant)

Library of 175,000 vols
Number of teachers: 125 full-time, 180 part-time
Number of students: 3,023

Publication: *Augsburg College Now* (quarterly).

BEMIDJI STATE UNIVERSITY

1500 Birchmont Drive NE, Bemidji, MN 56601-2699

Telephone: (218) 755-2000

Founded 1919

Part of Minnesota State Colleges and Universities system

President: Dr M. JAMES BENSEN
Dean of Graduate Studies, Library and Special Programs: Dr JON QUISTGAARD

Library of 184,000 vols
Number of teachers: 220 full-time
Number of students: 4,991

BETHEL COLLEGE AND SEMINARY

3900 Bethel Drive, St Paul, MN 55112

Telephone: (651) 638-6230
Fax: (651) 638-6008

Founded 1871

School of the churches of the Baptist General Conference

Liberal arts co-educational Christian college, offering baccalaureate and master's degree, and graduate theological seminary

President: GEORGE K. BRUSHABER
Provost (Seminary): LELAND ELIASON
Provost (College): JAMES H. BARNES
College Librarian: ROBERT C. SUDERMAN
Seminary Librarian: (vacant)

Seminary library of 135,000 vols, 2,400 periodicals; College library of 132,000 vols, 675 periodicals
Number of Seminary teachers: 29 full-time and part-time
Number of College teachers: 140 full-time, 50 part-time
Number of Seminary students: 545 men, 174 women
Number of College students: 1,051 men, 1,561 women

Publications: *College Catalog, Theological Seminary Catalog, Focus, Heart and Mind.*

CARLETON COLLEGE

1 North College St, Northfield, MN 55057

Telephone: (507) 646-4000

Founded 1866 by Board of Trustees appointed by the Minnesota Conference of Congregational Churches
Independent

President: STEPHEN R. LEWIS, Jr
Vice-President and Treasurer: CAROL N. CAMPBELL
Dean of the College: ELIZABETH MCKINSEY
Dean of Students: MARK W. GOVONI
Dean for Budget and Planning: (vacant)
Registrar: (vacant)

Library of 518,000 vols, 163,885 government documents, 82,918 bound periodicals
Number of teachers: 185
Number of students: 1,750

COLLEGE OF SAINT BENEDICT

37 S. College Ave, Saint Joseph, MN 56374-2099

Telephone: (612) 363-5011
Fax: (612) 363-6099

Chartered 1887

A Catholic liberal arts college for women partnered with Saint John's University for men; co-educational classes and social activities available to students on both campuses

President: MARY E. LYONS
Provost for Academic Affairs: Dr CLARK HENDLEY
Dean and Rector of Benedictine University: Dr CHARLES VILLETTE
Vice-President for Institutional Advancement: BARBARA CARLSON
Vice-President for Finance: S. MIRIAM ARDOLF
Vice-President for Student Development: Dr KATHLEEN ALLEN
Dean of the College: Dr RITA KNUESEL
Dean of Admissions: MARY MILBERT
Librarian: MICHAEL KATHMAN

Library of 535,400 vols
Number of teachers: 129 full-time, 29 part-time
Number of students: 1,940

Publications: *Saint Benedict's Today, Diotima, Studio I, Independent.*

COLLEGE OF ST CATHERINE

2004 Randolph Ave, St Paul, MN 55105

Telephone: (612) 690-6000
Fax: (612) 690-6024

Founded 1905

Roman Catholic liberal arts college for women

President: ANDREA J. LEE
Academic Dean: JEAN CAMERON (acting)
Vice President for Institutional Advancement: RANDI YODER
Vice-President for Business and Finance: WILLIAM HALLORAN
Vice-President for Student Affairs and Dean of Students: COLLEEN HEGRANES
Librarian: CAROL JOHNSON

Library of 231,021 vols
Number of teachers: 296
Number of students: 2,394

COLLEGE OF ST SCHOLASTICA

1200 Kenwood Ave, Duluth, MN 55811-4199

Telephone: (218) 723-6000
Fax: (218) 723-6290

Founded 1912

Private (Roman Catholic) liberal arts college; graduate programs in nursing, physical therapy, management, educational media, occupational therapy, science and mathematics education, exercise physiology and education

President: Dr LARRY GOODWIN (interim)
Dean of Faculty: Dr CECELIA M. TAYLOR (interim)
Registrar: GEORGE BEATTIE
Librarian: RACHEL APPLEGATE

Library of 127,400 vols
Number of teachers: 126 full-time, 40 part-time
Number of students: 2,030

CONCORDIA COLLEGE

Moorhead, MN 56562

Telephone: (218) 299-4000
Telex: (218)-299-3947

Founded 1891

Four-year liberal arts college, granting bachelor of arts and bachelor of music degrees
President: Dr PAUL J. DOVRE
Vice-President for Academic Affairs: Dr ELIZABETH BULL DANIELSON
Registrar: CHERIE HATLEM
Dean of Admissions: JAMES L. HAUSMANN
Librarian: V. ANDERSON

Library of 301,052 vols
Number of teachers: 200
Number of students: 2,928

CONCORDIA UNIVERSITY, ST PAUL

St Paul, MN 55104

Telephone: (612) 641-8278
Fax: (612) 659-0207

Founded 1893

President: Dr ROBERT HOLST
Executive Vice-President: Dr KAY MADSON
Vice-President for Academic Affairs: Dr CARL SCHOENBECK
Vice-President for Student Affairs: Dr PHILIP TESCH
Vice-President for Advancement: MICHAEL FLYNN
Director of Finance: FAY HARRE
Director of Operations: MARY ARNOLD
Librarian: G. OFFERMANN

Library of 125,000 vols
Number of teachers: 66
Number of students: 1,343

GUSTAVUS ADOLPHUS COLLEGE

St Peter, MN 56082

Telephone: (507) 933-8000

Founded 1862

President: AXEL D. STEUER
Registrar: DAVID WICKLUND
Dean of the Faculty: ELIZABETH R. BAER
Librarian: BARBARA FISTER

Library of 245,000 vols
Number of teachers: 190
Number of students: 2,240

HAMLINE UNIVERSITY

St Paul, MN 55104

Telephone: (612) 523-2202

Founded 1854

Related to the United Methodist Church

President: LARRY G. OSNES
Vice-Presidents: DAN LORITZ (University Relations), ORWIN CARTER (Finance and Administration)
Registrars: STEVE BJORK (Liberal Arts), JOYCE TRAYNOR (Law), DIANNE STIFFLER (Graduate)
Directors of Admissions: THERESA DECKER, SHELLEY HARKER (Law), LOUISE CUMMINGS (Liberal Arts)
Librarians: JULIE ROCHAT (Liberal Arts College), SUSAN KIEFER (School of Law)

Library of 230,000 vols
Number of teachers: 152
Number of students: 2,228

DEANS

College of Liberal Arts: JERRY GREINER
School of Law: RAYMOND KRAUSE
Graduate School: JOE GRABA
Students: MARILYN DEPPE

MACALESTER COLLEGE

St Paul, MN 55105-1899

Telephone: (612) 696-6000
Fax: (612) 696-6689

Founded 1874

Liberal arts college

President: MICHAEL S. MCPHERSON
Vice-Presidents: A. WAYNE ROBERTS (Provost), CRAIG H. AASE (Administration and Treasurer), RICHARD A. AMMONS (College Advancement), JOEL G. CLEMMER (Library and Information Services)
Dean of Admissions and Financial Aid: LORNE T. ROBINSON
Dean of Students: LAURIE B. HAMRE

Library of 400,000 vols
Number of teachers: 143 (f.t.e.)
Number of students: 1,742

Publications: *College Catalog, Prospectus, MacToday.*

MANKATO STATE UNIVERSITY

POB 8400, Mankato, MN 56002-8400

Telephone: (507) 389-2463

Founded 1867

Part of Minnesota State Colleges and Universities system

President: Dr RICHARD R. RUSH
Vice-President for Academic Affairs: Dr KAREN BOUBEL
Vice-President for Fiscal Affairs: H. DEAN TRAUGER
Vice-President for Student Affairs: Dr MARGARET HEALY
Registrar: DAVE GJERDE
Director of Library Services and Information Technology: Dr SYLVERNA FORD

Library of 693,973 vols
Number of teachers: 700
Number of students: 12,737

Publications: *MSU Today, MSU Reporter, MSU News Digest.*

METROPOLITAN STATE UNIVERSITY

700 E. 7th St, St Paul, MN 55106

Telephone: (616) 772-7777
Fax: (616) 772-7738

Founded 1971

Part of Minnesota State Colleges and Universities system

President: SUSAN A. COLE
Admissions Director: JANICE HARRING-HENDON
Librarian: VIRGINIA DUDLEY

Number of teachers: 85 full-time, 600 part-time
Number of students: 8,600

MINNEAPOLIS COLLEGE OF ART AND DESIGN

2501 Stevens Ave South, Minneapolis, MN 55404

Telephone: (612) 874-3700
Fax: (612) 874-3704
E-mail: admissions@mcad.edu

Founded 1886

President: JOHN S. SLORP
Director of Admissions: BECKY HAAS
Dean of Continuing Studies: BRIAN SZOTT
Treasurer: JAMES HOSETH
Director of Student Services: SUSAN CALMENSON
Dean of Academic Affairs: ANDREA NASSET
Library Director: SUZANNE DEGLER

Library of 60,000 vols
Number of teachers: 65
Number of students: 500

MINNESOTA STATE COLLEGES AND UNIVERSITIES

501 World Trade Center, 30 E. 7th St, St Paul, MN 55101

Telephone: (612) 296-8012
Fax: (612) 297-5550

Founded 1995

Incorporates 36 colleges and universities

Chancellor: MORRIS J. ANDERSON
Senior Vice-Chancellor for Academic and Student Affairs: LINDA BAER
Vice-Chancellor and Chief Financial Officer: LAURA M. KING
Vice-Chancellor for Human Resources: BILL TSCHIDA
Deputies to the Chancellor: JOHN OSTREM (Legislative Analysis), JOHN KAUL (Government Relations), LINDA KOHL (Public Affairs)

Number of students (system-wide): 145,000

MOORHEAD STATE UNIVERSITY

11th Street and 7th Ave South, Moorhead, MN 56563

Telephone: (218) 236-2011
Fax: (218) 236-2168

Founded 1887

Part of Minnesota State Colleges and Universities system

President: Dr ROLAND E. BARDEN
Vice-President for Academic Affairs: BETTE G. MIDGARDEN
Registrar: JOHN TANDBERG
Dean of Academic Resources: LAWRENCE L. REED

Library of 365,430 vols
Number of teachers: 300
Number of students 6,500

ST CLOUD STATE UNIVERSITY

St Cloud, MN 56301

Telephone: (612) 255-2122

Founded 1869

Part of Minnesota State Colleges and Universities system

President: ROBERT O. BESS
Vice-President for Academic Affairs: BARBARA GRACHEK
Dean of Learning Resources: JOHN G. BERLING

Library of 569,000 vols
Number of teachers: 650
Number of students: 16,000

SAINT JOHN'S UNIVERSITY

Collegeville, MN 56321

Telephone: (612) 363-2011

Founded 1857

Private liberal arts college for men; co-operates with the College of Saint Benedict

President: Bro. DIETRICH REINHART
Director of Admissions: MARY MILBERT
Librarian: MICHAEL KATHMAN

Library of 310,000 vols, 17,000 microforms, 123,000 government documents, over 1,200 periodicals
Number of teachers: 165
Number of students: 2,025

SAINT MARY'S UNIVERSITY

Winona, MN 55987

Telephone: (507) 452-4430
Fax: (507) 457-1633

Founded 1912

President: Bro. LOUIS DE THOMASIS
Vice-President for Student Development: SHARYN GOO
Vice-President for Academic Affairs: Dr JEFFREY HIGHLAND
Vice-President for Graduate and Special Programs: Dr DANIEL MALONY
Executive Vice-President for Admission: TONY M. PISCITIELLO
Vice-President for Financial Affairs: CYNTHIA MAREK
Vice-President for University Relations: MARY FOX
Vice-President for Corporate and Community Relations: LORAS SIEVE
Librarian: Bro. RICHARD LEMBERG

Library of 140,000 vols
Number of teachers: 440
Number of students: 8,000

SAINT OLAF COLLEGE

1520 St Olaf Avenue, Northfield, MN 55057-1098

Telephone: (507) 646-2222
Fax: (507) 646-3549

Founded 1874

President: MARK U. EDWARDS, Jr
Vice-Presidents: JAMES L. PENCE, ALAN NORTON, MARY SKORHEIM, BARBARA LUNDBERG, GORDON SOENKSEN
Librarian: KRIS MACPHERSON

Library of 486,000 vols
Number of teachers: 425
Number of students: 2,873

Publications: *Bulletin, St. Olaf.*

DEANS

Faculty: JAMES L. PENCE
Students: MARY SKORHEIM

SOUTHWEST STATE UNIVERSITY

1501 State St, Marshall, MN 56258-1598

Telephone: (507) 537-7021
Fax: (507) 537-7154

Founded 1963
Part of Minnesota State Colleges and Universities system

President: Dr DOUGLAS SWEETLAND
Vice-President: Dr RANDY ABBOTT
Registrar: PHIL COLTART
Library Director: JOHN BOWDEN

Library of 160,000 vols
Number of teachers: 108
Number of students: 3,000

UNIVERSITY OF MINNESOTA

100 Church St S.E., Minneapolis, MN 55455

Telephone: (612) 625-5000
Fax: (612) 624-6369

Founded 1851
State control
Academic year: September to June

President: MARK G. YUDOF
Executive Vice-President and Provost: ROBERT BRUININKS
Senior Vice-President: FRANK CERRA (Health Sciences)
Vice-Presidents: MICHAEL MARTIN (Agricultural Policy, acting), CAROL CARRIER (Human Resources) SANDRA GARDEBRING (Institutional Relations), CHRISTINE MAIZER (Research), MCKINLEY BOSTON (Student Development and Athletics), TERRY O'CONNOR (Finance, acting), ERIC KRUSE (Operations, acting)
Director of Libraries: THOMAS SHAUGHNESSY

Library: see Libraries
Number of teachers: 3,074 full-time, 2,336 part-time
Number of students 47,677

Publications: *Brief, Facts, Kiosk, Legislative Network, M, Minnesota Magazine, Minnesota Daily* (student newspaper).

DEANS

College of Agricultural, Food, and Environmental Sciences: MICHAEL MARTIN
College of Architecture and Landscape Architecture: THOMAS FISHER
College of Biological Sciences: ROBERT ELDE
School of Dentistry: MICHAEL TILL
College of Education and Human Development: STEVEN YUSSEN
General College: DAVID TAYLOR
Graduate School: CHRISTINE MAZIAR
College of Human Ecology: MARY HELTSLEY
Humphrey (Hubert H.) Institute of Public Affairs: JOHN BRANDL
Law School: E. THOMAS SULLIVAN
College of Liberal Arts: STEVEN ROSENSTONE
Carson School of Management: DAVID KIDWELL
Medical School: ALFRED MICHAEL
College of Natural Resources: ALFRED D. SULLIVAN
School of Nursing: SANDRA R. EDWARDSON
College of Pharmacy: MARILYN K. SPEEDIE
School of Public Health: EDITH D. LEYASMEYER
Institute of Technology: H. TED DAVIS
University College: GAIL SKINNER-WEST (interim)
College of Veterinary Medicine: DAVID THAWLEY

PROFESSORS

(Some staff serve in more than one department)
H = Head of Department

Accounting:

AMERSHI, A.
DAVIS, G.
DICKHART, J.
JOYCE, E.
KANODIA, C.
RAYBURN, J.

Adult Psychiatry:

CARROLL, M.
CLAYTON, P.
ECKERT, E.
EL-FAKAHANY, E.
HALIKAS, J.
HARTMAN, B.
HATSUKAMI, D.
KROLL, J.
MACKENZIE, T.

Aerospace Engineering and Mechanics:

BEAVERS, G. S.
FOSDICK, R. L.
GARRARD, W. L. (H)
JAMES, R. D.
JOSEPH, D. D.
LUNDGREN, T. S.
TEZDUYAR, T. E.
VANO, A. E.
WILSON, T. A.

Afro-American and African Studies:

FARAH, C.
ISAACMAN, A. F.
MCCURDY, R.
PORTER, P. W.
SCOTT, E.

Agricultural, Food and Environmental Education:

KRUEGER, R.
PETERSON, R. (H)

Agronomy and Plant Genetics:

BUSCH, R. H.
CARDWELL, V. B.
DURGAN, B. R.
EHLKE, N. J.
GENGENBACH, B. G. (H)
GRONWALD, J. W.
HARDMAN, L. L.
HICKS, D. R.
JONES, R. J.
JUNG, H. J.
LUESCHEN, W. E.
MARTIN, N. P.
OELKE, E. A.
ORF, J. H.
PHILLIPS, R. L.
RASMUSSON, D. C.
RINES, H. W.
SHEAFFER, C. C.
SIMMONS, S. R.
SOMERS, D. A.
STUTHMAN, D. D.
VANCE, C. P.
WYSE, D. L.

American Studies:

MAY, E. T.
NOBLE, D.
YATES, G. G.

Anaesthesiology:

BELANI, K. G.

Animal Science:

CROOKER, B. A.
DAYTON, W. R.
EL HALAWANI
EPLEY, R. J.
FOSTER, D. N.
HANSEN, L. B.
HAWTON, J. D.
HUNTER, A. G.
LINN, J. G.
NOLL, S. N.
O'GRADY, S. M.
OSBORNE, J. W.
PONCE DE LEON, F. A. (H)
RENEAU, J. K.
SEYKORA, A.
SHURSON, G. C.
STERN, M. D.
STEUERNAGEL, G. R.
WHEATON, J. E.
WHITE, M. E.

Anthropology:

GERLACH, L. P.
GIBBON, G.
GUDEMAN, S.
INGHAM, J. M.
MILLER, F. C.
WELLS, P.

Applied Economics:

APLAND, J. D.
EASTER, K. W.
EIDMAN, V. R. (H)
GARTNER, W. C.
HONADLE, B. W.
HOUCK, J. P.
KING, R. P.
KINSEY, J. L.
LEVINS, R. L.
MARTIN, M. V.
MORSE, G. W.
PARLIAMENT, C. D.
PEDERSON, E. D.
PETERSON, W. L.
ROE, T. L.
RUNGE, C. F.
RUTTAN, V. W.
SCHUH, G. E.
SENAUER, B. H.
WELSCH, D. E.

Applied Statistics:

BINGHAM, C.
CHALONER, K.
COOK, R. D.
GEISSER, S.
HAWKINS, D.
OEHLERT, G.
WEISBERG, S.

Architecture:

FISHER, T.
LAVINE, L.
MORRISH, W.
ROBINSON, J. W.
ROCKCASTLE, G.
SATKOWSKI, L.

Art:

BETHKE, K. E.
HOARD, C. C.
KATSIAFICAS, D.
MORGAN, C.
PHARIS, M.
PORTRATZ, W. E.
ROSE, T. A.

Art History:

ASHER, F. M.

COOPER, F.
MCNALLY, S.
MARLING, K. A. R.
POOR, R. J.
WEISBERG, G.

Astronomy:
DAVIDSON, K. D.
DICKEY, J. M.
GEHRZ, R. D.
HUMPHREYS, R. M.
JONES, T.
JONES, T. W.
KUHI, L.
RUDNICK, L.
SKILLMAN, E.
WOODWARD, P. R.

Biochemistry, Molecular Biology and Biophysics:
ALLEWELL, N. M.
ANDERSON, J. S.
ARMITAGE, I. M.
BANASZAK, L. J.
BERNLOHR, D. A.
BLOOMFIELD, V. A.
CONTI-FINE, B. M.
DAS, A.
DEMPSEY, M. E.
FLICKINGER, M. C.
FUCHS, J. A.
GOLDBERG, N. D.
HOGENKAMP, H. P. C.
HOOPER, A. B.
HOWARD, J. B.
KOERNER, J. F.
LA PORTE, D. C.
LISCOMB, J. D. (H)
LIVINGSTON, D. M.
LOUIS, C. F. (H)
LOVRIEN, R. E.
MAYO, K. H.
MESCHER, M. F.
NELSESTUEN, G. L.
OEGEMA, T. R.
OHLENDORFF, D. H.
ORR, H. T.
RAFTERY, M. A.
SCHOTTEL, J. S.
THOMAS, D. D.
TOWLE, H. C.
TSONG, T.
UGURBIL, K.
VAN NESS, B. G.
WACKETT, L. P.
WOODWARD, C. K.

Biostatistics:
CONNETT, J.
GOLDMAN, A.
LE, C.
LOUIS, T. (H)
NEATON, J.

Biosystems and Agricultural Engineering:
BHATTACHARYA, M.
JANNI, K. A.
MOREY, R. V.
NIEBER, J. L.

Business and Industry Education:
BROWN, J.
HOPKINS, C.
LAMBRECH, J.
LEWIS, T.
MCLEAN, G.
PUCEL, D.

Cell Biology and Neuroanatomy:
BAUER, G. E.
EGELMAN, E. H.
ELDE, R. P.
ERLANDSEN, S. L.
GIESLER, G. J.
HAMILTON, D. W.
KURIYAMA, R.
LETOURNEAU, P. C. (H)
LINCK, R. W.
MCLOON, S. C.
SEYBOLD, V. S.
SORENSON, R. L.
WYLIE, J. H.

Chemical Engineering and Materials Science:
BATES, F.
CARR, R. W.
CARTER, B.
CHELIKOWSKY, J. R.
CUSSLER, E. L.
DAHLER, J. S.
DAVIS, H. T.
DERBY, J.
EVANS, D. F.
FREDRICKSON, A. G.
GEANKOPLIS, C. J.
GERBERICH, W. W.
HU, W. S.
KELLER, K. H.
MACOSKO, C. W.
SCHMIDT, L. D.
SCRIVEN, L. E.
SEIDEL, R.
SHORES, D. A.
SMYRL, W. H.
SRIENC, F.
TIRRELL, M. V. (H)
TRANQUILLO, R.
URRY, D.
WARD, M. D.
WEAVER, J. H.

Chemistry:
BARANY, G.
BLOOMFIELD, V. A.
BRITTON, J. D.
CARR, P. W.
DAHLER, J. S.,
DAVIS, H. T.
ELLIS, J. E.
GENTRY, W. R. (H)
GLADFELTER, W. L.
GRAY, G. R.
HOYE, T.
KASS, S.
LEOPOLD, K.
LIPSKY, S.
LIU, H.-W.
LODGE, T.
MANN, K. R.
MILLER, L. L.
MILLER, W. G.
NOLAND, W. E.
PIGNOLET, L. H.
QUE, L.
RAFTERY, M.
STANKOVICH, M. T.
TOLMAN, W.
TRUHLAR, D. G.

Child Development:
COLLINS, W. A.
EGELAND, B. R.
GUNNAR, M. R.
MARATSOS, M. P.
MASTEN, A. S.
NELSON, C.
PICK, A. D.
PICK, H. L., Jr
SROUFE, L. A.
WEINBERG, R. A.
YONAS, A.

Civil Engineering:
ARNDT, R. E. A.
BREZONIK, P. L.
CROUCH, S. L.
DRESCHER, A.
FARELL, C.
FOUFOULA-GEORGIOU, E.
FRENCH, C. W.
GULLIVER, J. S.
MICHALOPOULOS, P.
PARKER, G. N.
REID, K. J.
SEMMENS, M. J.
SONG, C. C. S.
STEFAN, H.
STRACK, O. D. L.
VOLLER, V. R.

Classical and Near Eastern Studies:
ARIS, R.
BELFIORE, E.
CLAYTON, T.
COOPER, F.
HERSHBELL, J. P.
KELLY, T.
MCDONALD, W.
MCNALLY, S.
SONKOWSKY, R. P.
STAVROU, T.

Classical Civilization Program:
AKEHURST, F. R.
BELFIORE, E.
CLAYTON, T.
COOPER, F.
KELLY, T.
LIBERMAN, A.
SONKOWSKY, R.
STUEWER, R.
TRACY, J.
WILSON, L.

Clinical and Population Sciences:
AMES, T. R.
BLAHA, T. C.
DIAL, G. D.
FAHNING, M. L.
FARNSWORTH, R. J.
FETRO, J. P.
JOO, H. S.
MOLITOR, T. M.
PIJOQAN, C. J.
PULLEN, M. M.
SEGUIN, B. E.
THAWLEY, D. G.

Clinical Pharmacology:
HOLZMAN, J. L.
HUNNINGHAKE, D.
PENTEL, P.

Communications Disorders:
BROOKSHIRE, R. H.
CARNEY, A. E.
GUNDEL, J. K.
HAROLDSON, S.
MARGOLIS, R. H.
MOLLER, K. T.
NELSON, D. A.
REICHLE, J. E.
SPEAKS, C. E. (H)
STEMBERGER, J.
VIEMEISTER, N. F.

Community Health:
GARRAD, J.
JEFFREY, R. W.
LANDO, H. A.
LUEPKER, R. V.
PERRY, C. L.
PIRIE, P. L.
VENNINGA, R.
WAGENAAR, A. C.

Computer Science and Engineering:
DU, D.
DU, D. Z.
FOX, D.
GINI, M. L.
JANARDAN, R.
KUMAR, V.
NORBERG, A. L.
PARK, H.
SAAD, Y.
SHRAGROWITZ, E.
SLAGLE, J. R.
TSAI, W. T.
YEW, P.

Counselling and Student Psychology:
HANSEN, L. S.
HUMMEL, T.
SKOVHOLT, T.
VEACH, P.

Cultural Studies and Comparative Literature:
LEPPERT, R.
SARLES, H. B.
SCHULTE-SASSE, J.

Curriculum and Instruction:
BEACH, R. W.
COGAN, J.
FREEDMAN-NORBERG, K.
GRAVES, M.
JOHNSON, R.
LAMBRECHT, J.
LAWRENZ, F.
MANNING, J. C.
POST, T.
TAYLOR, B.

Dermatology:
DAHL, M. (H)
GORLIN, R.
KING, R.

Design, Housing, and Apparel:
ANGELL, W.
DELONG, M.
EICHER, J.
GUERIN, D.
JOHNSON, K.
OLSON, W.

East Asian Languages, Literatures, and Linguistics:
CHIN, Y.-S.
WANG, S.

Ecology, Evolution and Behaviour:
ALSTAD, D.
BARNWELL, F.
BIRNEY, E.
CORBIN, K.
CURTSINGER, J.
CUSHING, E.
DAVIS, M.
GORHAM, E.
LANYON, S.
MCKINNEY, D. F.
MEGARD, R.
MORROW, P., (H)
PACKER, C.
PHILLIPS, R.
PUSEY, A.
REGAL, P.
SCHMID, W.
SINIFF, D.
STARFIELD, A.
TESTER, J.
TILMAN, G. D.

Economics:
ALLEN, B.
CHARI, V. V.
CHIPMAN, J. S.
FELDMAN, R. D.
FOSTER, E.
GEWECKE, J. F.
HURWICZ, L.
JORDAN, J. S.
KEANE, M.
KEHOE, T.
KOCHERLAKOTA, N.
LEROY, S.
PRESCOTT, E. C.
RICHTER, M. K.
ROGERSON, R.
RUTTAN, V.
SANTOS, M.
SCHUH, G. E.
SWAN, C.

Education for Work and Community:
BROWN, J.
KRUEGER, R.
LEWIS, T.
PETERSON, R.
THOMAS, R.

Educational Policy and Administration:
AMMENTORP, W. M.
BAGLEY, A. L.
CHAPMAN, D. W.
COGAN, J. J.
DANIEL, P. T. K.
DOBBERT, M. L.
HERAN, J. C.
LANGE, D. L.
LEWIS, D. R.
LOUIS, K. S.
MESTENHAUSER, J. A.

Educational Psychology:
BART, W. M.
BRUININKS, R.
DAVISON, M. L.
DENO, S.
HANSEN, L. S.
HUMMEL, T.
HUPP, S.
JOHNSON, D. W.
LAWRENZ, F.
MCCONNELL, S.
MCEVOY, M.
MARUYAMA, G.
PELLEGRINI, A.
REST, J. R.
RYNDERS, J.
SAMUELS, S. J.
SKOVHOLT, T. M.
TENNYSON, R.
VAN DEN BROEK, P.
VEACH, P. M.
WILDERSON, F.
YSSELDYKE, J.

Electrical and Computer Engineering:
BAILEY, F. N.
CAMPBELL, S.
COHEN, P. I.
GEORGIOU, T.
GOPINATH, A.
JUDY, J. H.
KAVEH, M. (H)
KIEFFER, J. C.
KINNEY, L. L.
KUMAR, K. S. P.
LEE, E. B.
LEGER, J.
MAZIAR, C.
MOHAN, N.
NATHAN, M.
PARHI, K.
PERIA, W. T.
POLLA, D.
RIAZ, M.
ROBBINS, W. P.
RUDEN, P.
TANNENBAUM, A.
TEWFIK, A.
WOLLENBERG, B. F.

Emergency Medicine:
AMSTERDAM, J.
CLINTON, J.
KNOPP, R.
LING, L.
RUIZ, E.

English:
ANSON, C.
BALES, K.
BRIDWELL-BOWLES, L.
BROWNE, M. D.
CLAYTON, T.
COPELAND, R.
ESCURE, G.
FIRCHOW, P. E.
GARNER, S.
GRIFFIN, E. M.
HALEY, D.
HAMPL, P. M.
HANCHER, M.
HIRSCH, G.
KENDALL, C.
MCNARON, T.
MINER, V.
RABINOWITZ, P.
REED, P. J.
ROSS, D.
ROTH, M.
SOLOTAROFF, R.
SPRENGNETHER, M.
STEKERT, E. J.
WEINSHEIMER, J.

English as a Second Language:
COHEN, A.
TARONE, E.

Entomology:
ANDOW, D. A.
ASCERNO, M. E. (H)
FALLON, A. M.
HOLZENTAHAL, R. W.
KURTTI, T. J.
MOON, R. D.
RADCLIFFE, E. B.
RAGSDALE, D. W.
WALGENBACH, D. D.

Environmental and Occupational Health:
MANDEL, J. (H)
SEXTON, K.
VESLEY, D.
GERBERICH, S.

Epidemiology:
BROWN, J. E.
CROW, R. S.
FOLSOM, A. R.
GARRAD, J.
GLASSER, S. P.
HIMES, J. M.
JACOBS, D. R.
JEFFREY, R. W.
LANDO, H. A.
LUEPKER, R. V. (H)
MENOTTI, A.
PERRY, C. L.
PIRIE, P. L.
PRINEAS, R. J.
STORY, M. T.
VENINGA, R.
WAGENAAR, A. C.

Experimental and Clinical Pharmacology:
CLOYD, J. C.
FLETCHER, C. V.
GUAYL, D. R.
HANLON, J. T.
ROTSCHAFER, J. C.
ZASKE, D. E.

Family Education:
THOMAS, R.

Family Practice and Community Health:
BLAND, C. J.
COLEMAN, E.
KEENAN, J.
LURYE, N.
WIMAN, G.

Family Social Science:
BAUER, J.
BOSS, P.
DANES, S.
DETZNER, D.
DOHERTY, W.
GROTEVANT, H. D.
HOGAN, M. J.
MADDOCK, J.
OLSON, D. H.
RETTIG, K.
ROSENBLATT, P.
ZIMMERMAN, S.

Finance:
ALEXANDER, G.
BENVENISTE, L.
BOYD, J.
DOTHAN, M.
JAGANNATHAN, R.
NANTELL, T.

Fisheries and Wildlife:
ADELMAN, I. (H)
COHEN, Y.
CUTHBERT, F.

KAPUSCINSKI, A.
PANSHIN, D.
SORENSEN, P.
SPANGLER, G.

Food Science and Nutrition:
ADDIS, P. B.
ALLEN, C. E.
BHATTACHARYA, M.
BRADY, L. J.
BUSTA, F. F.
CSALLANY, A. S.
EPLEY, R. J.
FULCHER, R. G.
LABUZA, T. P.
LEVINE, A. S.
MCKAY, L. L.
REINECCIUS, G. A.
SLAVIN, J. L.
SMITH, D. E.
TATINI, S. R.
VICKERS, Z. M.
WARTHESEN, J. J. (H)

Forest Resources:
BAUER, M. E.
BAUGHMAN, M. J.
BLINN, C. R.
BROOKS, K. N.
BURK, T. E.
EK, A. R.
ELLEFSON, P. B.
GREGERSEN, H. M.
PERRY, J. A., II
REICH, P. B.
ROSE, D. W.
SUCOFF, E. I.

French and Italian:
AKEHURST, F. R. P.
NOAKES, S.
PAGANINI, M.
WALDAUER, J. L.

General College:
AMRAM, F. M.
BROTHEN, T. F.
COLLINS, T. G.
GIDMARK, J. B.
ROBERTSON, D. F.
YAHNKE, R. E.

Genetics and Cell Biology:
BROOKER, R. J.
CUNNINGHAM, W. P.
FAN, D. P.
GOLDSTEIN, S. F.
HACKETT, P. B.
HERMAN, R. K.
HERMAN, W. S.
JOHNSON, R. G.
LEFEBVRE, P. A.
MAGEE, P. T.
MCKINNELL, R. G.
O'CONNOR, M. B.
SILFLOW, C. D.
SIMMONS, M. J.
SNUSTAD, D. P.

Geography:
ADAMS, J. S.
BROWN, D. A.
GERSMEHL, P. J.
HART, J. F.
HSU, M. L.
LEITNER, H.
MARTIN, J. A.
PORTER, P. W.
RICE, J. G.
SCHWARTZBERG, J. E.
SCOTT, E. P.
SHEPPARD, E. S.
SKAGGS, R. H.

Geology and Geophysics:
ALEXANDER, E. C., Jr
BANERJEE, S. K.
HOOKE, R. L.
HUDLESTON, P.
KARATO, S.
KELTS, K.
KOHLSTEDT, D.
KOHLSTEDT, S. G.
MOREY, G. B.
MURTHY, V. R.
PAOLA, C.
PFANNKUCH, H. O.
SEYFRIED, W. E., Jr (H)
STOUT, J.
SOUTHWICK, D.
TEYSSIER, C.
YUEN, D.

German, Scandinavian and Dutch:
FIRCHOW, E. S.
HASSELMO, N.
HOUE, P.
JOERES, R. B.
LIBERMAN, A.
PARENTE, J., Jr
SCHULTE-SASSE, J.
STOCKENSTRÖM, G.
ZIPES, J. (H)

Gerontology:
BORN, D.
BOSS, P.
CLOYD, J.
DYSKEN, M.
EUSTIS, N.
GARRARD, J.
KANE, R.
KANE, R.
LASSMAN, F.
MCGUE, M.
MCTAVISH, D.
MEYERS, S.
MORTIMER, J.
QUAM, J.
RYDEN, M.
SNYDER, M.
WADE, M.
WIRTSCHAFTER, J.
ZIMMERMAN, S.

Health Computer Sciences:
CONNELLY, D.
FINKELSTEIN, S.
GATEWOOD, L.
SPEEDIE, S.

Health Ecology:
BEBEAU, M.
BORN, D.
DIANGELIS, A.
MARTENS, L.

Health Informatics:
CONNELLY, D.
CORCORAN-PERRY, S.
FAN, D.
FINKELSTEIN, S.
FRICTON, J.
GATEWOOD, L.
HARRIS, I.
JOHNSON, P.
MCQUARRIE, D.
PATTERSON, R.
SPEEDIE, S.
WILCOX, G.

Health Management and Policy:
MCBEAN, M. (H)
VENINGA, R.

Health Services Research and Policy:
CHRISTIANSON, J.
DOWD, B.
FELDMAN, R.
GARRARD, J.
HANLON, J.
KANE, R.
KANE, R.
KRALEWSKI, J.
LURIE, N.
MOSSCOVICE, I.
SWIONTKOWSKI, M.

Healthcare Management:
BEGUN, J.
CHRISTIANSON, J.
DORNBLASER, B.
LITMAN, TR.
WECKWERTH, V.

History:
ALTHOLZ, J. L.
BACHRACH, B. S.
BERMAN, H.
BRAUER, K. J.
EVANS, J.
EVANS, S.
FARMER, E. L.
GOOD, D.
HANAWALT, B.
HOWE, J. R.
ISAACMAN, A. F.
KELLY, T.
KOPF, D.
LEHMBERG, S. E.
MCCAA, R.
MAYNES, M. J.
MENARD, R. R.
METCALF, M.
MUNHOLLAND, J. K.
NOONAN, T. S.
PHILLIPS, C.
PHILLIPS, W.
REYERSON, K.
ROEDIGER, D.
RUDOLPH, R. L.
RUGGLES, S.
SAMAHA, J.
STAVROU, T. G.
THAYER, J. A.
TRACY, J. D.
VECOLI, R. J.
WALTNER, A.

History of Medicine:
EYLER, J. M.
WILSON, L. G.

History of Science and Technology:
KOHLSTEDT, S. G.
NORBERG, A. L.
SEIDEL, R. W.
SHAPIRO, A. E.
STUEWER, R. H.

Hormel Institute:
BROCKMAN, H. L.
KISS, Z.
SCHMID, H. H. O.

Horticultural Science:
ASCHER, P. D.
BRENNER, M. L.
BROWN, D. L.
CARTER, J. V.
GARDNER, G. M. (H)
HOOVER, E. E.
LI, P. H.
LUBY, J. J.
MARKHART, A. H., III
PELLETT, H. M.
ROSEN, C. J.
SOWOKINOS, J. R.
WHITE, D. B.

Hospital Pharmacy:
CANAFAX, D. M.
CIPOLLE, R. J.
CLOYD, J. C.
FLETCHER, C. V.
GUAY, D. R.
HALSTENSON, C. E.
ROTSCHAFER, J. C.
STRAND, L. M.
ZASKE, D. E.

Human Resource Development and Adult Education:
BROWN, J.
HOPKINS, C.
LEWIS, T.
MCLEAN, G.

PUCEL, D.
SWANSON, R.

Human Sexuality:

COLEMAN, E.

Humphrey (Hubert H.) Institute of Public Affairs:

ADAMS, J.
ARCHIBALD, S.
BRANDL, J.
BROOKINS, G.
BRYSON, J.
EUSTIS, N.
HOENACK, S.
KAPSTEIN, E.
KELLER, K.
KLEINER, M.
KUDRLE, R.
MYERS, S. L., Jr
SCHUH, G. E.

Information and Decision Sciences:

ADAMS, C. R.
CHERVANY, N. L.
DAVIS, G. B.
HOFFMAN, T. R.
JOHNSON, P. E.
MARCH, S. T.
WETHERBE, J. C.

Jewish Studies Center:

BACHRACH, B.
BERMAN, H.
COOPERMAN, D.
KRISLOV, S.
ZIPES, J.

Journalism and Mass Communication:

DICKEN-GARCIA, H.
FABER, R. J.
FANG, I. E.
LEE, C. C.
ROBERTS, N. L.
WACKMAN, D. B.
WELLS, W. D.

Kinesiology:

HANCOCK, P.
KANE, J.
LEON, A.
WADE, M.

Laboratory Medicine and Pathology:

ACKERMAN, E.
AHMED, K.
ANDERSON, R. E.
ANDERSON, W. R.
APPLE, F.
AZAR, M. M.
BALFOUR, H. J.
BENSON, E. S.
BROWN, D. M.
BRUNNING, R. D.
DALMASSO, A. P.
ECKFELDT, J.
EDSON, J. R.
ESTENSEN, R. D.
FERRIERI, P.
FINKELSTEIN, S.
FURCHT, L. T. (H)
GAJL-PECZALSKA, K.
GARRY, V.
GATEWOOD, L. C.
HALBERG, F.
HAUS, E.
HECHT, S.
HORWITZ, C.
KARNI, K.
KERSEY, J. H.
LEBIEN, T.
MCCARTHY, J.
MCCULLOUGH, J. J.
MCIVOR, S.
MALEJKA-GIGANTI, D.
MANIVEL, C.
MESCHER, M.
ORR, H.
POLESKY, H. F.

RAO, G.
ROSENBERG, A.
TSAI, M.
WATTENBERG, L. W.
WELLS, C.
WHITE, J.

Landscape Architecture:

MARTIN, R.
NECKAR, L.
PITT, D.

Law:

BEFORT, S.
BRYDEN, D. P.
BURKE, K.
COOPER, L. J.
COUND, J. J.
DRIPPS, D.
FARBER, D. A.
FELD, B. C.
FELLOWS, M. L.
FRASE, R. S.
FRICKEY, P.
GIFFORD, D. J.
HUDEC, R. E.
KOEPPEN, B.
LEVY, R. J.
MARSHALL, D. P.
MATHESON, J.
MORRIS, C. R.
MORRISON, F. L.
PAULSEN, M.
POWELL, J.
SCHOETTLE, F.
SHARPE, C.
SHERRY, S.
STEIN, R. A.
TONRY, M. H.
WEISSBRODT, D. S.
YOUNGER, J.
YUDOT, M.

Linguistics:

COHEN, A.
GUNDEL, J.
KAC, M.
TARONE, E. E.

Marketing and Logistics Management:

BEIER, F.
CARDOZO, R.
CHILDERS, T.
HARPER, D.
HOUSTON, M.
JOHN, D.
JOHN, G.
LOKEN, B.
MEYERS-LEVY, J.
ROERING, K.
RUDELIUS, W.
RUEKERT, R.
WALKER, O.

Mathematics:

AEPPLI, A.
AGARD, S.
ANDERSON, G.
ARONSON, D.
BAXTER, J.
BRAMSON, M.
COCKBURN, B.
EAGON, J.
EDELMAN, P.
FESHBACH, M.
FRIEDMAN, A.
FRISTEDT, B.
GARRETT, P.
GOLDMAN, J.
GRAY, L.
GULLIVER, R.
HARRIS, M.
HEJHAL, D.
JAIN, N. (H)
JODEIT, M.
KAHN, D.
KEYNES, H.
KRYLOV, N.

LITTMAN, W.
LUSKIN, M.
LYUBEZNIK, G.
MCCARTHY, C.
MCGEHEE, R.
MARDEN, A.
MESSING, W.
MEYERS, N.
MILLER, W., Jr
MOECKEL, R.
NI, W.-M.
NITSCHE, J.
OLVER, P.
POUR-EL, M.
PRIKRY, K.
REICH, E.
REJTO, P.
ROBERTS, J.
SATTINGER, D.
SAFONOV, M.
SELL, G.
SIBUYA, Y.
SPERBER, S.
STANTON, D.
STORVICK, D.
SVERAK, V.
WEBB, P.
WHITE, D.

Mechanical Engineering:

ARORA, S. R.
BAR-COHEN, A.
DONATH, M.
ERDMAN, A. G.
FROHRIB, D. A.
GIRSHICK, S.
GOLDSTEIN, R.
HEBERLEIN, J.
IBELE, W. E.
KITTLESON, D. B.
KUEHN, T. H.
KULACKI, F.
KVALSETH, T. O.
LEWIS, J.
LIU, B.
MCMURRY, P. H. (H)
MARPLE, V. A.
OGATA, K.
PATANKAR, S. V.
PFENDER, E.
PUI, D. Y.
RAMALINGAM, S.
RAMSEY, J. W.
RILEY, D. R.
SCHULMAN, Y.
SIMON, T. W.
SPARROW, E. M.
STARR, P.
STELSON, K.
STRYKOWSKI, P.
TAMMA, K.

Medical Technology:

KARNI, K.
WELLS, C.

Medicine:

ANAND, I.
ARCHER, S.
ASINGER, R.
BACHE, R.
BANTLE, J.
BENDITT, D.
BILLINGTON, C.
BITTERMAN, P.
BLUMENTHAL, M.
BOND, J.
CHESLER, E.
COHN, J. N.
CROSSLEY, K.
DAVIES, S.
DUANE, W.
FRANCIS, G.
FROHNERT, P.
FROM, A.
GEBHARD, R.
GOLDSMITH, S.

GOODMAN, J.
GRAY, R.
GRIMM, R.
HAASE, A.
HEBBEL, R.
HERTZ, M.
HOLTZMAN, J.
HOSTETTER, T.
HOWE, R.
HUNNINGHAKE, D.
INGBAR, D.
JACOB, H. S.
JANOFF, E.
JOHNSON, G.
JORDAN, M. C.
KASISKE, B.
KEANE, W.
KIANG, D.
KING, R.
LAKE, J.
LEVINE, A.
LEVITT, M. D.
LUEPKER, R.
LUIKART, S.
LURIE, N.
MCGLAVE, P.
MAHOWALD, M.
MARIASH, C.
MARINI, J.
MESSNER, R.
MILLER, L.
MOLDOW, C.
MURRAY, M.
NICHOL, K.
NIEWOEHNER, D.
NUTTALL, F. O.
PALLER, M.
PENTEL, P.
PETERSON, B.
PETERSON, P. K.
POPKIN, M.
RAIJ, L.
RAO, K.
RAVDIN, J.
SABATH, L. D.
SHAPIRO, F. L.
SHARP, B.
SIMON, G.
SKUBITZ, K.
STEER, C.
UGURBIL, K.
VERCELLOTTI, G.
VERFAILLIE, C.
WEIR, E. K.
WEISDORF, D.
WHITE, C.
WILLIAMS, D.
WILSON, L.

Microbiology:

CLEARY, P. P.
DUNNY, G.
DWORKIN, M.
FARAS, A. J.
HANSON, R.
JENKINS, M.
JOHNSON, R. C.
PLAGEMANN, P. G. W.
ROGERS, P.
SCHLIEVERT, P. M.
ZISSLER, J.

Music:

ANDERSON, J.
ARTYMIW, L.
BALDWIN, D.
BRAGINSKY, A.
GARRETT, M.
HAACK, P.
HEPOKOSKI, J.
JACKSON, D.
KIRCHHOFF, C.
KONKALL, K.
LANCASTER, T.
LUBET, A.
MCCURDY, R.
MAURICE, G.
O'REILLY, S.
REMENIKOVA, T.
SUTTON, V.
ZAIMONT, J. L.

Naval Science:

FREY, W.

Neurology:

ANDERSON, D.
ANSARI, K.
BIRNBAUM, G.
CRANFORD, R.
ETTINGER, M.
IADECOLA, C.
KENNEDY, W. R.
KLASSEN, A. C.
KRIEL, R.
LITCHY, W.
MAHOWALD, M.
NELSON, C.
PARRY, G. (H)
ROTTENBERG, D.
SWAIMAN, K. F.
TORRES, F.
WIRTSCHAFTER, J.

Neuroscience:

ANDERSON, J.
BEITZ, A.
BIRNBAUM, G.
BROWN, D.
BURKHARDT, D.
CARROLL, M.
CONTI-FINE, B.
EBNER, T.
ELDE, R.
EL-FAKAHANY, E.
FREY, W.
GEORGOPOULOS, A.
GIESLER, G., Jr
HARTMAN, B.
IACONO, W.
IADECOLA, C.
KENNEDY, W.
KERSTEN, D.
KOERNER, J.
LARSON, A.
LEGGE, G.
LETOURNEAU, P.
LEVINE, A.
LOH, H.
LOUIS, C.
LOW, W.
MANTYH, P.
MCLOON, S.
MILLER, R.
NELSON, C.
NEWMAN, E.
ORR, H.
OSBORN, J.
OVERMIER, J. B.
POPPELE, R.
PURPLE, R.
ROTTENBERG, D.
SANTI, P.
SAWCHUK, R.
SEYBOLD, V.
SOECHTING, J.
SORENSEN, P.
SPARBER, S.
THOMAS, D.
UGURBIL, K.
VIEMEISTER, N.
WILCOX G.

Neurosurgery:

EBNER, T. J.
KUCHARCZYK, J.
LOW, W. C.
MAXWELL, R. E. (H)
ROCKSWOLD, G. L.
WIRTSCHAFTER, J. D.

Nuclear Medicine:

BOUDREAU, R.
DU CRET, R.

Nursing:

CORCORAN-PERRY, S.
EDWARDSON, S.
RYDEN, M.
SNYDER, M.
TOMLINSON, P.
WYMAN, J.

Obstetrics, Gynaecology and Women's Health:

GAZIANO, E. P.
KNOX, G. E.
LEUNG, B. S.
MARTENS, M. G.
OKAGAKI, T.
POTISH, R.
THOMPSON, T. R.
TWIGGS, L. B. (H)
YEH, J.

Operations and Management:

ANDERSON, J. C.
CHERVANY, N.
HILL, A. V.
HOFFMANN, T.
NACHTSHEIM, C.
SCHROEDER, R. G.

Ophthalmology:

CAMERON, J. D.
DOUGHMAN, D. J.
GREGERSON, D. S.
HOLLAND, E. J.
KRACHMER, J. H. (H)
NELSON, J. D.
PULIDO, J. S.
SUMMERS, C. G.
WIRTSCHAFTER, J. D.

Oral Pathology:

VICKERS, R.

Oral Sciences:

ANDERSON, D. L.
CERVENKA, J.
COMBE, E.
DOUGLAS, W. H.
GERMAINE, G. R.
SCHACHTELE, C. F.
SHAPIRO, B. L.
VICKERS, R. A.

Orthodontics:

SPEIDEL, T. M.

Orthopaedic Surgery:

LEWIS, J. L.
OEGEMA, T.
OGILVIE, J.
SWIONTKOWSKI, M. (H)
THOMPSON, R. C.

Otolaryngology:

ADAMS, G. (H)
DUVALL, A. J.
GIEBINK, G. S.
JUHN, S. K.
MAISEL, R.
MARGOLIS, R.
NELSON, D.
SANTI, P.

Paediatrics:

BALFOUR, H.
BERRY, S.
BLAZER, B.
BLUM, R.
BLUMENTHAL, M.
BROWN, D. M.
CLAWSON, C. C.
FERRIERI, P.
FISH, A.
GEORGIEFF, M.
GIEBINK, G. S.
INGBAR, D.
JOHNSON, D.
KAPLAN, E.
KERSEY, J.
KIM, Y.
KING, R.
KRIEL, R.

KRIVIT, W.
LOCKMAN, L.
MAMMEL, M.
MAUER, S. M.
MICHAEL, A.
MOLLER, J. (H)
NELSON, C.
NESBIT, M.
NEVINS, T.
OGILVIE, J.
QUIE, P.
RAMSAY, N.
RESNICK, M.
ROBISON, L.
SHARP, H.
SINAIKO, A.
SUMMERS, G.
SWAIMAN, K.
THOMPSON, T.
TUCHMAN, M.
WANGENSTEEN, O. D.
WARWICK, W.
WHITE, J.
WHITLEY, C.
WYLIE, C.

Paediatric Dentistry:
MOLLER, K.
TILL, M.

Paediatric Neurology:
KRIEL, R.
LOCKMAN, L.
SWAIMAN, K.

Periodontology:
BAKDASH, B.
HERZBERG, M. C.
PHILSTROM, B. L.
WOLFF, L. F.

Pharmaceutics:
GRANT, D. J. W.
RAHMAN, Y. E.
SAWCHUK, R. J. (H)
SIEGEL, R. A.

Pharmacology:
CONTI-FINE, B.
EL-ZAKAHANY, E.
HANNA, P. E.
HOLTZMAN, J. L.
HUNNINGHAKE, D. B.
LAW, P.
LOH, H. H. (H)
PENTEL, P. R.
SINAIKO, A. R.
SLADEK, N. E.
SPARBER, S. B.
UCKUN, F. M.
WILCOX, G. L.
WOOD, W. G.
ZIMMERMAN, B. G.

Pharmacy Practice:
CIPOLLE, R. J.
JOHNSON, R. L.
MORLEY, P. C.
SCHONDELMEYER, S. W. (H)
STRAND, I. M.

Philosophy:
BOWIE, N.
DAHL, N. O.
EATON, M. M.
GIERE, R.
GUNDERSON, K.
HANSON, W. H.
HELLMAN, G.
HOPKINS, J. S.
KAC, M.
LEWIS, D.
MASON, H. E.
OWENS, J.
PETERSON, S.
SAVAGE, C. W.
SCHEMAN, N.
WALLACE, J. R.

Physical Medicine and Rehabilitation:
DI FABIO, R.
PATTERSON, R.

Physical Therapy:
FABIO, R.

Physics and Astronomy:
BAYMAN, B. F.
BROADHURST, J. H.
CAMPBELL, C. E.
DAHLBERG, E. D.
DEHNHARD, D. K.
ELLIS, P. J.
GIESE, C. F.
GLAZMAN, L.
GOLDMAN, A. M.
HALLEY, J. W.
HELLER, K. J.
HOSOTANI, Y.
HUANG, C. C.
JONES, R. S.
KAPUSTA, J. I.
LARKIN, A.
LYSAK, R. L.
MCLERRAN, L.
MARQUIT, E.
MARSHAK, M. L.
OLIVE, K.
PEPIN, R. O.
PETERSON, E. A.
POLING, K.
RUDAZ, S.
RUDDICK, K.
SHIFMAN, M.
SHKLOVSKII, B.
VAINSHTEIN, A.
VALLS, O. T.
VOLOSHIN, M.
WALSH, T. F.
WEYHMANN, W. V.
ZIMMERMANN, W.

Physiology:
BURKHARDT, D.
DI SALVO, J. (H)
EBNER, T.
GALLANT, E.
GEORGOPOULOS, A.
LEE, H. C.
LEVITT, D.
LOW, W.
MILLER, R. F. (H)
NEWMAN, E.
OSBORN, J.
POPPELE, R.
PURPLE, R.
SOECHTING, J.
WANGENSTEEN, O. D.

Plant Biology:
BIESBOER, D. D.
BRAMBL, R.
DOEBLEY, J. F.
GLEASON, F. K.
KOUKKARI, W. L.
MCLAUGHLIN, D. J.
RUBENSTEIN, I.
WETMORE, C. M.
WICK, S.

Plant Pathology:
BLANCHETTE, R. A.
BRAMBL, R.
GROTH, J. V.
KRUPA, S. V.
LARSEN, P. O.
LOCKHART, B. E.
MACDONALD, D. H.
MERONUCK, R. A.
NYVALL, R. F.
PERCICH, J. A.
PFLEGER, F. L. (H)
WINDELS, C. E.
YOUNG, N. D.
ZEYEN, R. J.

Political Science:
DIETZ, M.
DUVALL, R.
FARR, J.
FLANIGAN, W. H.
FOGELMAN, E.
FREEMAN, J.
GRAY, V.
HOLT, R. T.
KAPSTEIN, E.
KRISLOV, S.
KVAVIK, R.
ROSENSTONE, S.
SCOTT, T. M.
SHIVELY, W. P.
SIKKINK, K.
SMITH, S.
SULLIVAN, J. L.

Psychiatry Research:
CARROLL, M. E.
EL-FAKAHANY, E.
HARTMAN, B.
HATSUKAMI, D.

Psychological Foundations of Education:
BART, W.
DAVISON, M.
JOHNSON, D.
LAWRENZ, F.
MARUYAMA, G.
PELLEGRINI, A.
REST, J.
SAMUELS, S. J.
TENNYSON, R.
VAN DEN BROEK, P.

Psychology:
BERSCHEID, E.
BORGIDA, E.
BOUCHARD, T. J.
BURKHARDT, D. A.
BUTCHER, J. N.
CAMPBELL, J. P.
CUDECK, R.
DUNNETTE, M. D.
FOX, P. W.
HANSEN, J. I.
IACONO, W.
KERSTEN, D.
LEGGE, G. E.
LEON, G. R.
MCGUE, M.
MEEHL, P. E.
OVERMIER, J. B.
SACKETT, D.
SNYDER, M.
TELLEGEN, A.
VIEMEISTER, N. F.
WEISS, D. J.

Public Health Administration:
MCBEAN, M.
VENINGA, R.

Public Health Nutrition:
BROWN, J. E.
HIMES, J. H.
JEFFERY, R. W.
LUEPKER, R. V.
PERRY, C.
STORY, M. T.

Radiology:
AMPLATZ, K.
BOUDREAU, R.
DU CRET, R.
GARWOOD, M.
HU, X.
HUNTER, D.
KUCHARCZYK, J.
REINKE, D.
STEENSON, C.
THOMPSON, W. (H)
UGURBIL, K.
WALSH, J.

Recreation, Park and Leisure Studies:
KANE, M. J.

McAvoy, L.

Regulatory Biochemistry:

Bernlohr, D. A.
Conti-Fine, B. M.
Dempsey, M. E.
Goldberg, M. D.
Koerner, J. F.
Louis, C. F.
Mescher, M. F.
Nelsestuen, G. L.
Oegema, T. G.
Raftery, M. A.

Rhetoric:

Becker, S.
Duin, A. H.
Gross, A. G.
Horberg, R. O.
Lay, M. M.
Marchand, W. M.
McDowell, E. E.
Mikelonis-Paraskov, V. M.
Wahlstrom, B. J. (H)
Wharton, W. K.

School Psychology:

McConnell, S.
Ysseldyke, J.

Scientific Computation:

Allewell, N.
Anderson, R.
Boley, D.
Chelikowsky, J.
Cramer, C.
Davis, H. T.
Friedman, A.
Kelton, W. D.
Kumar, V.
Labuza, T.
Lowengrub, J.
Luskin, M.
Park, H.
Patankar, S.
Saad, Y.
Sell, G.
Song, C.
Stech, H.
Tezduyar, T.
Thomas, D.
Tierney, L.
Truhlar, D.
Woodward, P.
Yuen, D.

Slavic and Central Asian Languages and Literatures:

Bashiri, I.
Jahn, G.

Small Animal Clinical Sciences:

Armstrong, P. J.
Bistner, S.
Caywood, D.
Feeney, D.
Hardy, R.
Jessen, C.
Klausner, J.
Lipowitz, A.
Osborne, C.
Polzin, D.
Raffe, M.
Wallace, L.

Social and Administrative Pharmacy:

Canafax, D. M.
Cipolle, R. J.
Cloyd, J. C.
Fletcher, C. V.
Garrard, J. M.
Gatewood, L. C.
Litman, T. J.
Morley, P. C.
Schondelmeyer, S. W.
Speedie, S. M.
Strand, L. M.
Weaver, L. C.
Weckwerth, V. E.
Zaske, D. E.

Social Work:

Baizerman, M.
Beker, J.
Brookins, G. K.
Edleson, J.
Hollister, D.
Menanteau, D.
Meyers, S.
Quam, J.
Rooney, R.

Sociology:

Aminzade, R.
Anderson, R. E.
Brustein, W.
Cooperman, D.
Galaskiewicz, J.
Knoke, D.
Kruttschnitt, C.
Laslett, B.
Leik, R. K.
Malmquist, C.
Marini, M.
McTavish, D. G.
Mortimer, J.
Nelson, J. I.
Ward, D. A.

Soil, Water, and Climate:

Allmaras, R.
Anderson, J. L.
Bloom, P. R.
Clapp, C.
Cooper, T. H.
Dowdy, R. H.
Graham, P. H.
Grigal, D. F.
Gupta, S. C.
Halbach, T. R.
Koskinen, W. C.
Lemme, G. D.
Malzer, G.
Molina, J. A.
Moncrief, J. F.
Mulla, D. J.
Nater, E. A.
Randall, G. W.
Rehm, G. W.
Reicosky, D. C.
Robert, P. C.
Rosen, C.
Russelle, M. P.
Sadowski, M. J.
Seeley, M. W.
Voorhees, W. B.

South Asian and Middle Eastern Languages and Culture:

Junghare, I.

Spanish and Portuguese:

Jara, R.
Mirrer, L.
Ramos, A.
Spadaccini, N.
Vidal, H.
Zahareas, A. N.

Special Education Programs:

Deno, S.
Hupp, S.
McEvoy, M.
Rynders, J.
Wilderson, F.

Speech-Communication:

Browne, D. R.
Campbell, K.
Hewes, D.
Scott, R. L.
Sheldon, A.

Statistics:

Bingham, C.
Chaloner, K.
Cook, R. D.
Dickey, J.
Eaton, M. L.
Geisser, S.
Hawkins. D.
Meeden, G.
Oehlert, G.
Sudderth, W. D.
Tierney, L.
Weisberg, S.

Strategic Management and Organization:

Bowie, N.
Bromiley, P.
Chakravarthy, B.
Erickson, W. B.
Galaskiewicz, J.
Maitland, I.
Marcus, A.
Nichols, M.
Van de Ven, A.

Structural Biology and Biophysics:

Allewell, N. M.
Armitage, I. M.
Banaszak, L. J.
Bloomfield, V. A.
Hogenkamp, H. P.
Howard, J. B.
Lipscomb, J. D.
Lovrien, R. E.
Mayo, K. H.
Ohlendorf, D. H.
Thomas, D. D.
Tsong, T. Y.
Ugubril, K.

Surgery:

Bolman, R. M., III
Buchwald, H.
Caldwell, M.
Cerra, F.
Cunningham, B.
Delaney, J. P.
Dunn, D. (H)
Engeland, W.
Foker, J.
Goodale, R. L.
Lee, J. T.
Levine, A.
McQuarrie, D. G.
Matas, A.
Molina, E.
Payne, W.
Sako, Y.
Shumway, S.
Sutherland, D.
Weigelt, J.
Wells C.

Surgical Sciences:

Engeland, W.
Wells, C.

Theatre Arts and Dance:

Brockman, C. L.
Reid, B.

Theoretical Statistics:

Dickey, J.
Eaton, M.
Geisser, S.
Meeden, G.
Sudderth, W.
Tierney, L.

Therapeutic Radiology/Radiation Oncology:

Khan, F. M.
Lee, C. K.
Levitt, S. H. (H)
Potish, R. A.
Song, C. W.
Uckun, F.
Vallera, D.

TMJ/Orofacial Pain:

Fricton, J.

Toxicology:

Abul-Hajj, Y.
Brown, D.
Carlson, R.

DiSalvo, J.
Drewes, L.
Hanna, P.
Mirocha, C.
Nagasawa, H.
Niemi, G.
Prohaska, J.
Schook, L.
Shier, T.
Sparber, S.

Urban Studies:
Adams, J. S.
Berman, H.
Clemence, R.
Galaskiewicz, J.
Leitner, H.
Miller, R.
Ruggles, S.
Runge, C. F.
Scott, T.
Sheppard, E.
Wattenberg, E.
Zaidi, M.

Urologic Surgery:
Hulbert, J. (H)

Veterinary Diagnostic Medicine:
Collins, J.
Goyal, S.
Hayden, D.
Kurtz, H.
Walser, M.

Veterinary Pathobiology:
Beattie, C. W.
Beitz, A. J.
Bey, R. F.
Brown, D. R.
Duke, G. E.
Fletcher, T. F.
Gallant, E. M.
Halvorson, D. A.
Larson, A. A.
Louis, C. F.
Maheswaran, S. K.
Murtaugh, M. M.
Nagaraja, K. V.
Perman, V.
Schook, L. B.
Sharma, J. M.
Stromberg, B. E.
Weiss, D. J.

Women's Studies:
Faunce, P. S.
Geiger, S.
Kaminsky, A.
Longino, H.
Scheman, N.

Wood and Paper Science:
Bowyer, J.
Massey, J. (H)
Schmidt, E.

Work, Community and Family Education:
Hopkins, C.
Lambrecht, J.
McLean, G.
Peterson, R.
Pucel, D.
Swanson, R.
Thomas, R.

University of Minnesota, Duluth

Duluth, MN 55812
Telephone: (218) 726-8000

Chancellor: Kathryn Martin
Vice-Chancellors: Vincent Magnuson (Academic Administration), Bruce Gildseth (Academic Support and Student Life), Gregory Fox (Finance and Operations)

DEANS

School of Business and Economics: Tom Duff (acting)
College of Education and Human Service Professions: H. Mitzi Doane
School of Fine Arts: William Robert Bucker
College of Liberal Arts: Harold Hellenbrand
College of Science Engineering: Sabra Anderson
Duluth School of Medicine: Richard Ziegler (acting)

PROFESSORS

Anderson, A., Music
Anderson, C., Economics
Anderson, P. M., Biochemistry and Molecular Biology
Anderson, S. S., Mathematics and Statistics
Arthur, J., Sociology and Anthropology
Aufderheide, A., Pathology and Laboratory Medicine
Bacig, T., Sociology and Anthropology
Baria, D. N., Chemical Processing Engineering
Boman, T. G., Education
Brush, G., Art
Brush, L., Art
Burns, S. G., Electrical and Computer Engineering
Caple, R., Chemistry
Carlson, H., Education
Carlson, R. M., Chemistry
Castleberry, S., Management Studies
Crouch, D., Computer Science
Das, A., Psychology
De Rubeis, B. J., Industrial Engineering
Dorland, D., Chemical Engineering
Drewes, L., Biochemistry and Molecular Biology
Duff, T., Finance and Management Information Sciences
Eisenberg, R. M., Pharmacology
Evans, J., Chemistry
Falk, D., Social Work
Feroz, E., Accounting
Fetzer, J., Philosophy
Firling, C., Biology
Fischer, R. A., History
Fleischman, W., Sociology and Anthropology
Fugelso, M., Industrial Engineering
Fulkrod, J., Chemistry
Gallian, J. A., Mathematics and Statistics
Gaus, G., Philosophy
Gaus, G., Political Science
Gibson, W., Composition
Gordon, R., Psychology
Grahn, J., Management Studies
Grant, J. A., Geology
Green, J. C., Geology
Green, R., Mathematics and Statistics
Hafferty, F., Behavioural Science
Harriss, D. K., Chemistry
Hatten, J. T., Communication Sciences and Disorders
Hawk, A. M., Communication Sciences and Disorders
Hedin, T., Art
Hedman, S., Biology
Heller, L., Medical and Molecular Physiology
Hiller, J., Physics
Holst, T., Geology
Horse, J. R., Social Work
Huntley, J., Communication
James, B., Mathematics and Statistics
Jankofsky, K. P., English
Jesswein, W. A., Economics
Johnson, A. G., Medical Microbiology and Immunology
Johnson, J. M., Health, Physical Education and Recreation
Johnson, T., Industrial Engineering
Johnson, T. C., Geology
Jordan, T. F., Physics
Karim, M. R., Biology
Karp, J., Education
Kendall, L. A., Industrial Engineering
Kerrigan, T. L., Art
Klemer, A., Biology
Kramer, J., Social Work
Kritzmire, J., Music
Laundergan, J. C., Sociology-Anthropology-Geography
Lettenstrom, D., Art
Ley, E., Health, Physical Education and Recreation
Lichty, R. W., Economics
Linn, M. D., Composition
McCarthy, D. A., Education
McDonald, M., Chemical Engineering
Magnuson, V. R., Chemistry
Maiolo, J. C., English
Marchese. R., Sociology and Anthropology
Martin, K. A., Theatre
Matsch, C. L., Geology
Mayo, D., Philosophy
Maypole, D., Social Work
Merrier, P., Finance and Management Information Sciences
Miller, M., Aerospace Studies
Miller-Cleary, L., English
Morton, R., Geology
Newstrom, J. W., Management Studies
Niemi, G., Biology
Ojakangas, R. W., Geology
Pastor, J., Biology
Peterson, J. M., Economics
Pierce, J. L., Management Studies
Poe, D., Chemistry
Powless, R., American Indian Studies
Prohaska, J., Biochemistry and Molecular Biology
Raab, R. L., Economics
Red Horse, J., American Indian Studies
Regal, J., Pharmacology
Regal, R., Mathematics and Statistics
Riley, K., Composition
Roufs, T. G., Sociology and Anthropology
Rowley, C. S., Accounting
Rubenfeld, S., Management Studies
Severson, A. R., Anatomy and Cell Biology
Seybolt, R., Foreign Languages and Literatures
Sharp, G. P., International Studies
Sharp, P., Political Science
Shehadeh, N., Electrical and Computer Engineering
Smith, D., Sociology and Anthropology
Stachowitz, M., Electrical and Computer Engineering
Stech, H., Mathematics and Statistics
Steinnes, D. N., Economics
Storch, N. T., History
Stuecher, U., Psychology
Sunnafrank, M., Communication
Sydor, M., Physics
Thompson, L. C., Chemistry
Trachte, G., Pharmacology
Trolander, J., History
Tsai, B., Chemistry
Wallace, K., Biochemistry and Molecular Biology
Ward, P., Pathology and Laboratory Medicine
Wegren, T., Music
Whiteside, M. C., Biology
Williams, R. E., Music
Wong, S., Finance and Management Information Sciences
Zeitz, E., Foreign Languages and Literatures
Ziegler, R., Medical Microbiology and Immunology

University of Minnesota, Morris

Morris, MN 56267
Telephone (320) 589-2211

Chancellor: Samuel Schuman
Vice-Chancellors: Gary McGrath (Student Affairs), Samuel Schuman (Academic Affairs), Cathleen Brannen (Finance)

PROFESSORS

Ahern, W. H., History
Alstine, J. V., Science and Mathematics
Blake, E. S., Humanities
Cabrera, V., Modern Languages

CARLSON, J. A., Music
COTTER, J., Geology
DEMOS, V. P., Sociology
FARRELL, C. F., Modern Languages
FARRELL, E. R., Humanities
FRENIER, M. D., History
GOOCH, V., Biology
GREMMELS, J. C., English
HART, N. I., English
HINDS, H. E., History
HOPPE, D. M., Biology
IMHOLTE, J. Q., History
INGLE, J. S., Art Studio
JOHNSON, C. E., Music
KAHNG, S. M., Management
KISSOCK, C. M., Education
KLINGER, E., Psychology
LEE, J., Political Science
LEE, M.-L., Modern Languages
LOPEZ, A. A., Computer Science
NELLIS, J. G., Art Studio
O'REILLY, M. F., Mathematics
PAYNE, T. R., Theatre Arts
PETERSON, F. W., Art History
PURDY, D. H., English
TOGEAS, J. B., Chemistry
UEHLING, T. E., Philosophy
UNDERWOOD, T. L., History
VAN ALSTINE, J. B., Geology

University of Minnesota, Crookston

Crookston, MN 56716

Telephone: (218) 281-6510

Chancellor: DONALD G. SARGEANT
Vice-Chancellors: DOUGLAS KNOWLTON (Academic Affairs), DEAN MCCLEARY (Finance), ROBERT NELSON (Student Affairs)

PROFESSORS

KNOWLTON, D., Art and Sciences
MARX, G., Agricultural, Food, and Environmental Sciences
NEET, S., Art and Sciences
PETERSON, W. C., Art and Sciences
SELZLER, B., Art and Sciences
SVEDARSKY, W. D., Agricultural Management
WINDELS, C., Agricultural, Food and Environmental Sciences

UNIVERSITY OF ST THOMAS

2115 Summit Ave, St Paul, MN 55105

Telephone: (612) 962-5000
Fax: (612) 962-6504
E-mail: admissions@stthomas.edu

Founded 1885

President: Rev. DENNIS DEASE
Executive Vice-President: Dr JUDITH DWYER
Director of Admissions: MARLA FRIEDERICHS
Librarian: JEAN W. HALEY

Library of 421,000 vols
Number of teachers: 643
Number of students: 10,324

WINONA STATE UNIVERSITY

Winona, MN 55987

Telephone: (507) 457-5000
Fax: (507) 457-5586

Founded 1858

Part of Minnesota State Colleges and Universities system

President: Dr DARRELL KRUEGER
Vice-Presidents: Dr DENNIS NIELSEN (Academic), GARY EVANS (University Relations)
Dean of Library: RICHARD BAZILLION

Library of 262,692 vols, 772,500 microforms
Number of teachers: 325
Number of students: 7,068

MISSISSIPPI

ALCORN STATE UNIVERSITY

Lorman, MS 39096

Telephone: (601) 877-6100
Fax: (601) 877-2975

Founded 1871

President: Dr CLINTON BRISTOW, Jr
Vice-President for Academic Affairs: Dr MALVIN WILLIAMS
Vice-President for Business Affairs: WILEY JONES
Vice-President for Student Affairs: LAPLOSE JACKSON (acting)
Registrar: Dr ALICE GILL
Librarian: JESSIE ARNOLD

Library of 231,200 vols
Number of teachers: 191
Number of students: 3,073

Publications: *Alcorn State University Catalogue* (every 2 years), *The Alcorn Herald* (monthly), *Alcornite* (annually), *The Alcorn Report* (quarterly).

BELHAVEN COLLEGE

1500 Peachtree St, Jackson, MS 39202

Telephone: (601) 968-5919
Fax: (601) 968-9998
E-mail: admissions@belhaven.edu

Founded 1883

President: Dr ROGER PARROTT
Provost and Academic Dean: Dr DAN FREDERICKS
Vice-Provost and Dean of Adult Studies: Dr WILLIAM ANDERSON
Vice-Provost for Advancement: Dr STEPHEN LIVESAY
Vice-Provost for Development: JAMES FERGUSON
Vice-President for Finance and Campus Operations: TOM PHILLIPS
Associate Vice-President and Dean of Student Learning: Dr PAM JONES
Director of Financial Aid: LINDA PHILLIPS
Director of Admissions: LISA GREER
Librarian: GRETCHEN L. COOK

Library of 94,500 vols
Number of teachers: 79
Number of students: 1,317

BLUE MOUNTAIN COLLEGE

Box 338, Blue Mountain, MS 38610

Telephone: (601) 685-4771
Fax: (601) 685-4776

Founded 1873
Liberal arts college for women

President: E. HAROLD FISHER
Academic Dean: WILLIAM N. WASHBURN
Director of Admissions: CHARLOTTE LEWIS
Dean of Students: REBECCA BENNETT
Registrar: SHEILA FREEMAN
Librarian: CAROLYN MOUNCE

Library of 58,000 vols
Number of teachers: 33
Number of students: 552

DELTA STATE UNIVERSITY

Cleveland, MS 38733

Telephone: (601) 846-3000

Founded 1924

President: FOREST KENT WYATT
Registrar: JAMES DONALD COOPER
Librarian: TERRY LATOUR

Library of 213,000 vols
Number of teachers: 250
Number of students: 3,800

JACKSON STATE UNIVERSITY

1400 JR Lynch St, Jackson, MS 39217

Telephone: (601) 968-2121

Founded 1877

President: Dr JAMES E. LYONS, Sr
Executive Vice-President: Dr MILDRED ALLEN
Vice-President for Academic Affairs: Dr DORA WASHINGTON
Vice-President for Fiscal Affairs: KEVIN APPLETON
Vice-President for Student Affairs: Dr LEROY DURANT
Associate Director of Admissions: STEPHANIE CHATMAN
Registrar: BETTY GRAVES
Dean of Libraries: Dr LOU H. SANDERS

Library of 376,566 vols
Number of students: 6,224

Publications: *Blue and White Flash* (quarterly), *Alumni Newsletter* (quarterly).

DEANS

Graduate Dean: Dr BETTYE FLETCHER
School of Education: Dr JOHNNIE MILLS-JONES
Liberal Arts: Dr DOLLYE ROBINSON
School of Business: Dr GLENDA GLOVER
School of Science and Technology: Dr ABDUL MOHOMED
School of Social Work: Dr GWENDOLYN PRATER

MILLSAPS COLLEGE

Jackson, MS 39210

Telephone: (601) 354-5201

Founded 1890

President: Dr GEORGE M. HARMON
Dean of Faculty: Dr ROBERT H. KING
Librarian: J. F. PARKS, Jr

Library of 260,000 vols
Number of teachers: 89
Number of students: 1,410

MISSISSIPPI COLLEGE

Clinton, MS 39058

Telephone: (601) 925-3000

Founded: 1826

President: Dr HOWELL W. TODD
Vice-President for Academic Affairs: Dr BETTYE COWARD
Vice-President for Business Affairs: JEROLD MEADOWS
Vice-President for Student Personnel: Dr VAN D. QUICK
Vice-President for Institutional Advance: DANNY RUTLAND
Dean of Enrollment Services: JIM TURCOTTE

Library of 234,000 vols
Number of teachers: 150 (including 75 part-time)
Number of students: 3,400

MISSISSIPPI STATE UNIVERSITY

Mississippi State, MS 39762

Telephone: (601) 325-2323

Founded 1878

President: DONALD W. ZACHARIAS
Vice-President for Academic Affairs and Provost: DEREK J. HODGSON
Vice-President for Agriculture and Home Economics, Forestry and Veterinary Medicine: R. RODNEY FOIL
Vice-President for Business Affairs: LEAH NORMAN
Vice-President for Student Affairs: ROY H. RUBY
Vice-President for Research: MELVIN C. RAY (acting)
Vice-President for Administration: BILLY WARD
Registrar: W. S. SMITH, II
Librarian: FRANCES COLEMAN

Library of 873,000 vols, 2,108,000 microforms, 8,464 records and tapes, 7,500 periodicals
Number of teachers: 865
Number of students: 14,831

DEANS

Agriculture and Home Economics: WILLIAM R. FOX
Architecture: JOHN MCRAE
Arts and Sciences: FRANK E. SAAL
Business and Industry: HARVEY S. LEWIS
Continuing Education: BILL SMITH
Education: WILLIAM H. GRAVES
Engineering: WAYNE BENNETT
Forestry: JOHN E. GUNTER
Veterinary Medicine: DWIGHT MERCER

MISSISSIPPI UNIVERSITY FOR WOMEN

Columbus, MS 39701
Telephone: (601) 329-4750
Founded 1884
First State-supported college exclusively for women to be founded in the US
President: CLYDA S. RENT
Vice-President for Academic Affairs: SUSAN KUPISCH
Vice-President for Student Development: GAIL STEPHENS
Vice-President for Finance and Administration: MARK RICHARD (acting)
Assistant to the President: MARY MARGARET ROBERTS
Director of Library: FRIEDA M. DAVISON
Library of 426,900 vols
Number of teachers: 128
Number of students: 3,309
Publication: *Catalogue.*

HEADS OF DIVISIONS

Fine and Performing Arts: THOMAS SOVIK
Business and Communications: ANNE BALAZS
Education and Human Sciences: PAT DONAT (interim)
Health and Kinesiology: JO SPEARMAN
Humanities: BRIDGET PIESCHEL (interim)
Nursing: SHEILA ADAMS
Science and Mathematics: TAMMY MELTON
Interdisciplinary Studies: AUSTIN BUNCH

MISSISSIPPI VALLEY STATE UNIVERSITY

Itta Bena, MS 38941-1400
Telephone: (601) 254-9041
Founded 1946
President: WILLIAM W. SUTTON
Vice-President for Academic Affairs: W. ERIC THOMAS
Registrar: DARRELL L. JAMES
Librarian: ROBBYE R. HENDERSON
Library of 125,000 vols
Number of teachers: 112
Number of students: 2,168

TOUGALOO COLLEGE

Tougaloo, MS 39174
Telephone: (601) 977-7730
Fax: (601) 977-7739
Founded 1869
Private liberal arts college, affiliated with Disciples of Christ and United Church of Christ
President: Dr JOE A. LEE
Vice-President for Academic Affairs, and Provost: Dr LEWIS JONES
Vice-President for Student Affairs, and Dean of Students: FRED ALEXANDER
Vice-President for Institutional Advancement: DEJOYCE MCROY-MORGAN
Vice-President for Fiscal Affairs: Dr NAYYER HUSSAIN
Library of 139,600 vols
Number of teachers: 73
Number of students: 916
Publications: *Tougaloo News* (3 a year), *The Harambee* (monthly).

UNIVERSITY OF MISSISSIPPI

University, Lafayette Co, MS 38677
Telephone: (601) 232-7211
Chartered 1844
The School of Medicine, the School of Dentistry, the School of Nursing and the School of Health Related Professions are situated at Jackson, Mississippi
Chancellor: Dr ROBERT C. KHAYAT
Provost, and Vice-Chancellor for Academic Affairs: Dr GERALD WALTON
Vice-Chancellor for University Advancement: Dr DON FRUGE
Vice-Chancellor for Finance and Administration: REX DELOACH (acting)
Vice-Chancellor for Student Life: Dr RICHARD MULLENDORE
Vice-Chancellor for Health Affairs: Dr A. WALLACE CONERLY
Registrar: CHARLOTTE FANT (acting)
Dean of University Libraries: JOHN MEADOR
Library of 822,000 vols
Number of teachers: 595
Number of students: 10,280
Publications: *Catalogues:* Graduate School, Law School, Medical Center, Summer Session, Undergraduate.

DEANS

Accountancy: Dr JAMES W. DAVIS
Business Administration: Dr RANDY BOXX
Education: Dr JIM CHAMBLESS
Engineering: Dr ALLIE M. SMITH
Graduate School: Dr MICHAEL R. DINGERSON
Law School: Dr SAMUEL M. DAVIS
Liberal Arts: Dr H. DALE ABADIE
Pharmacy: Dr KENNETH B. ROBERTS
Dentistry: PERRY J. MCGINNIS, Jr (Jackson Campus)
Health Related Professions: Dr J. MAURICE MAHAN (Jackson Campus)
Medicine: Dr A. WALLACE CONERLY (Jackson Campus)
Nursing: Dr ANN G. PIERCE (Jackson Campus)

UNIVERSITY OF SOUTHERN MISSISSIPPI

Box 5001, Hattiesburg, MS 39406-5001
Telephone: (601) 266-5001
Fax: (602) 266-5756
Founded 1910
President: HORACE W. FLEMING
Vice-President for Administrative Affairs: CLYDE N. GINN
Vice-President for Academic Affairs: G. DAVID HUFFMAN
Vice-President for Research and Planning: KAREN M. YARBROUGH
Vice-President for Business and Finance: JAMES R. HENDERSON
Vice-President for Student Affairs: JOSEPH S. PAUL
Registrar: DANNY W. MONTGOMERY
Director of Institutional Planning and Analysis: ANN W. TOMLINSON
Library of 1,800,000 vols
Number of teachers: 577
Number of students: 11,570
Publications: *Business Insights* (2 a year), *Journal of Mississippi History, Mississippi Review, Notes on Mississippi Writers* (all quarterly).

DEANS

Arts: Dr PETER ALEXANDRA
Business Administration: H. TYRONE BLACK
Education and Psychology: JAMES O. SCHNUR
Health and Human Sciences: ALLISON YATES
Liberal Arts: GLENN T. HARPER
Nursing: GERRY CADENHEAD
Science and Technology: STEVEN DOBLIN
Social Work: EARLIE WASHINGTON
Honors: MAUREEN RYAN
Graduate School: ANSELM G. GRIFFIN
Library Services: JAMES MARTIN
Admissions: HOMER WESLEY

WILLIAM CAREY COLLEGE

498 Tuscan Ave, Hattiesburg, MS 39401-5499
Telephone: (601) 582-5051
Fax: (601) 582-6454
Founded 1906
Chancellor: JAMES W. EDWARDS
President: RORY LEE
Dean of Students: DAVID HESTER
Director of Admissions: STEWART BENNETT
Librarian: (vacant)
Library of 14,068 vols
Number of teachers: 80 full-time
Number of students: 2,172

MISSOURI

AVILA COLLEGE

11901 Wornall Rd, Kansas City, MO 64145
Telephone: (816) 942-8400
Fax: (816) 942-3362
Founded 1916
President: Dr LARRY KRAMER
Registrar: JEAN BINK
Librarian: KATHLEEN FINEGAN
Library of 73,200 vols
Number of teachers: 150 (full- and part-time)
Number of students: 1,600
Publication: *Avila College Catalog, Viewbook.*

CARDINAL GLENNON COLLEGE

5200 Glennon Drive, St Louis, MO 63119
Telephone: (314) 644-0266
Fax: (314) 644-3079
E-mail: frrice@kenrick.org
Founded 1931
Liberal arts college exclusively for candidates for Roman Catholic priesthood
President: Rev. Msgr GEORGE J. LUCAS
Director: Rev. EDWARD M. RICE
Librarian: Dr ANDREW J. SOPKO
Library of 75,000 vols
Number of students: 24

CENTRAL METHODIST COLLEGE

Fayette, MO 65248
Telephone: (660) 248-3391
Founded 1854
President: Dr MARIANNE INMAN
Dean of the College: Dr J. KEITH KEELING
Librarian: RITA GULSTAD
Library of 85,000 vols
Number of teachers: 58, including 15 professors
Number of students: 1,300
Publications: *Athenaeum Society Review, Bulletin, The Talon, Collegian.*

CENTRAL MISSOURI STATE UNIVERSITY

Warrensburg, MO 64093
Telephone: (660) 543-4111
Fax: (660) 543-8517

Founded 1871

President: ED M. ELLIOTT
Provost: Dr KYLE CARTER
Senior Vice-President for Information Services and Technology: TOM EDMUNDS
Vice-Presidents: JUDY VICKREY (Finance and Administration), STEPHEN PETERSEN (Student Affairs)
Vice-President for Planning and Policy and Executive Assistant to the President: Dr JOHN PAUL MEES
Director of Public Relations: JOHN INGLISH
Director of Admissions: DELORES HUDSON
Dean of Library Services: PAL RAO

Library of 1,153,000 vols
Number of teachers: 432
Number of students: 10,320

DEANS

College of Arts and Sciences: ROBERT SCHWARTZ
College of Applied Science and Technology: ARTHUR ROSSER
College of Business Administration: PAUL SHAFFER
College of Education and Human Services: JIM BOWMAN
School of Graduate Studies: STEPHEN WILSON

COLLEGE OF THE OZARKS

Point Lookout, MO 65726
Telephone: (417) 334-6411
Fax: (417) 335-2618

Founded 1906

President: Dr JERRY C. DAVIS
Vice-President: Dr HOWELL KEETER
Dean of the Work Program: Dr MAYBURN DAVIDSON
Dean of Institutional Advancement: RODNEY ARNOLD
Dean of the College: Dr KENTON C. OLSON
Dean of Students: Dr LARRY COCKRUM

Library of 112,000 vols
Number of teachers: 115
Number of students: 1,525

Publication: *Ozark Visitor* (quarterly).

CULVER-STOCKTON COLLEGE

Canton, MO 63435
Telephone: (217) 231-6000
Fax: (217) 231-6611

Founded 1853

President: Dr EDWIN B. STRONG, Jr
Registrar: BARBARA A. CONOVER
Vice-President for Academic Affairs: Dr C. THOMAS WILTSHIRE
Dean of Student Development: Dr DAVID WILSON
Librarian: SHARON UPCHURCH

Library of 143,890 vols
Number of teachers: 75
Number of students: 994

Publications: *Catalog*, *Chronicle* (quarterly), *Megaphone* (student newspapers, every 2 weeks).

DRURY COLLEGE

Springfield, MO 65802
Telephone: (417) 873-7879
Fax: (417) 873-7821

Founded 1873

President: Dr JOHN E. MOORE, Jr
Dean of the College: Dr STEPHEN H. GOOD
Registrar: GALE BOUTWELL
Librarian: STEVE STOAN

Library of 160,000 vols
Number of teachers: 118 full-time equivalent
Number of students: 2,467 full-time equivalent

EVANGEL UNIVERSITY OF THE ASSEMBLIES OF GOD

1111 N. Glenstone, Springfield, MO 65802
Telephone: (417) 865-2811
Fax: (417) 865-9599

Founded 1955

President: Dr ROBERT H. SPENCE
Vice-Presidents: Dr GLENN BERNET (Academic Affairs), GEORGE CRAWFORD (Business), JOAN CARGNEL (Student Development), JIM WILLIAMS (Institutional Advancement)

Library of 120,000 vols
Number of students: 1,616

Publication: *Vision* (College magazine, quarterly).

FONTBONNE COLLEGE

6800 Wydown Blvd, St Louis, MO 63105
Telephone: (314) 862-3456
Fax: (314) 889-1451

Founded 1917

President: DENNIS GOLDEN
Vice-President for Academic Affairs: SUSAN DUNTON (interim)
Vice-President for Student Affairs: GARY ZACK
Vice-President for Advancement: TIMOTHY WILLARD
Vice-President for Finance: CHERYL TURNER
Registrar: MARCIA COWER
Librarian: JOSEPH MCDONALD
Director of Admissions: PEGGY MUSEN

Library of 90,020 vols, 510 periodicals
Number of teachers: 45 full-time, 60 part-time
Number of students: 1,990

Publications: *Fontbonne College Magazine* (3 a year).

HEADS OF DEPARTMENT

Fine Arts: CATHERINE CONNOR
Business and Administration: HANS HELBLING
Communication Disorders: JANIE VON WOLFSECK
Education: JUDY FAILONI
Literature and Language Arts: JEAN WASKO
Home Economics: JANET CRITES
Mathematics and Computer Science: BETH NEWTON
Natural Sciences: TOMMIE FRISON
Philosophy, Religion and Social Science: DONALD P. BURGO

HARRIS-STOWE STATE COLLEGE

3026 Laclede Ave, St Louis, MO 63103
Telephone: (314) 340-3380
Fax: (314) 340-3399

Founded 1857

President: Dr HENRY GIVENS, Jr
Director of Admissions: Mrs VALERIE BEESON
Vice-President for Academic Affairs: Dr PATRICIA NICHOLS
Vice-President for Student Affairs: Dr PATRICIA NICHOLS
Vice-President for Business and Financial Services: ROCHELLE TILGHMAN
Vice-President for Institutional Support and Enrollment Management: Dr JAMES GORHAM
Registrar: Mrs MARY K. JONES
Librarian: MARTIN KNORR

Library of 87,000 vols
Number of teachers: 82
Number of students: 1,980

Publication: *The Harris-Stowe Vision* (every 6 months).

KANSAS CITY ART INSTITUTE

4415 Warwick Blvd, Kansas City, MO 64111-1874
Telephone: (816) 472-4852

Founded 1885

Four-year college of art and design
President: KATHLEEN COLLINS

Library of 33,000 vols and 60,000 slides
Number of students: 600

LINCOLN UNIVERSITY

Jefferson City, MO 65102
Telephone: (573) 681-5000
Fax: (573) 681-5566

Founded 1866

President: Dr DAVID B. HENSON
Vice-President for Academic Affairs: Dr ROSEMARY HEARN
Vice-President for Finance: Dr NATHAN COWL
Vice-President for Student Affairs: CONSTANCE WILLIAM
Counsel to the President: KEITH FULLER
Executive Director of University Relations: DEBRA WALKER
Librarian: ELIZABETH WILSON

Library of 164,800 vols
Number of teachers: 179
Number of students: 3,041

Publications: *Lincoln Clarion* (6 a year), *Alumni-Line* (3 a year).

DEANS

College of Agriculture, Applied Sciences and Technology: Dr MARY WYATT
College of Arts and Sciences: JAMES TATUM (acting)
College of Business: WAYNE LENHARDT (acting)

LINDENWOOD COLLEGE

209 S. Kingshighway, St Charles, MO 63301
Telephone: (314) 949-2000

President: DENNIS C. SPELLMANN
Provost: ARLENE TAICH
Dean of the College and Dean of Admissions and Financial Aid: DAVID R. WILLIAMS
Dean of Students: JOHN CREER
Librarian: JAN CZAPLA

Library of 132,000 books and pamphlets
Number of teachers: 100
Number of students: 5,000

Publication: *LindenWorld*.

MARYVILLE UNIVERSITY OF SAINT LOUIS

13550 Conway Road, St Louis, MO 63141-7299
Telephone: (314) 529-9300
Fax: (314) 542-9085
E-mail: admissions@maryville.edu

Founded 1872

President: Dr KEITH LOVIN
Vice-President for Planning, Information and Institutional Research and Special Assistant to the President: Dr EDGAR RASCH
Vice-President for Academic and Student Affairs: Dr PATRICIA THRO
Vice-President for Institutional Advancement: MARK BATES
Vice-President for Administration and Finance: Dr LARRY HAYS
Vice-President for Enrollment Management: Dr MARTHA WADE
Registrar: Dr ROBERT ADAMS
Librarian: Dr EUGENIA MCKEE

Library of 259,000 items
Number of teachers: 264
Number of students: 3,055

DEANS

College of Arts and Sciences: Dr THOMAS BRATKOWSKI
John E. Simon School of Business: Dr PAMELA HORWITZ
School of Education: Dr KATHE RASCH
School of Health Professions: Dr RAYMOND EDGE

MISSOURI VALLEY COLLEGE

500 East College, Marshall, MO 65340
Telephone: (816) 886-6924
Fax: (816) 886-9818
Founded 1889
President: J. KENNETH BRYANT
Registrar: MARSHA LASHLEY
Vice-President for Operations/Admissions: CHAD FREEMAN
Librarian: PAMELA REEDER
Library of 70,000 vols
Number of teachers: 55
Number of students: 1,212

NORTHWEST MISSOURI STATE UNIVERSITY

Maryville, MO 64468
Telephone: (660) 562-1212
Fax: (660) 562-1900
Founded 1905
President: Dr DEAN L. HUBBARD
Provost: Dr JOSEPH E. (TIM) GILMOUR
Vice-President for Finance and Support Services: RAY COURTER
Vice-President for Student Affairs: KENT PORTERFIELD
Dean of Graduate School: Dr FRANCES SHIPLEY
Dean of Libraries: Dr PATRICIA VANDYKE
Library of 221,200 vols
Number of teachers: 227
Number of students: 6,280
Publications: *Northwest Missourian* (weekly newspaper), *Tower* (student yearbook).

PARK COLLEGE

Parkville, MO 64152
Telephone: (816) 741-2000
Fax: (816) 741-4911
Founded 1875
President: Dr DONALD J. BRECKON
Registrar: EILEEN WEST
Vice-President of Academic Affairs: Dr Z. CLARA BRENNAN
Vice-President of Enrollment Management and Student Services: CLARINDA CREIGHTON
Director of Admissions: Dr RON CARRUTH
Librarian: ANN SCHULTIS
Library of 130,900 vols
Number of teachers: 100
Number of students: 1,194
Publications: *The Park Alumniad, Park College Partners* (both quarterly).

ROCKHURST COLLEGE

1100 Rockhurst Rd, Kansas City, MO 64110
Telephone: (816) 501-4000
Fax: (816) 501-4588
Founded 1910
President: Rev. EDWARD KINERK
Vice-President for Enrollment Management: Dr NAN TÖNJES
Vice-President for Business Affairs: ROGER MCCOY
Vice-President for Student Development: Dr LIZ KRAMER
Vice-President for Institutional Advancement: ROBIN STRACHAN
Registrar: ROSI REISIG
Librarian: JEANNE LANGDON
Library of 107,000 vols
Number of teachers: 192
Number of students: 2,867

DEANS

Arts and Sciences: COREY SIMMONDS (acting)
School of Management: Dr TOM LYON (acting)
School of Professional Studies: Dr NAN TÖNJES

SAINT LOUIS UNIVERSITY

221 North Grand Blvd, St Louis, MO 63103
Telephone: (314) 977-2222
Founded 1818; chartered 1832
Private control
Academic year: September to May (two terms)
President: Rev. LAWRENCE H. BIONDI
Chancellor: Rev. J. BARRY MCGANNON
Provost: SANDRA JOHNSON
Executive Vice-President: JAMES R. KIMMEY
Vice-President for Business and Finance: ROBERT ALTHOLZ
Vice-President for Student Development: PAUL V. STARK
Vice-President and General Counsel: WILLIAM KAUFFMAN
Vice-President for Human Resource Management: KATHY G. HAGEDORN
Vice-President for Development and University Relations: DONALD WHELAN
Vice-President for Madrid Campus: RICK L. CHANEY
Registrar: JOHN-HERBERT JAFFRY
Undergraduate Admissions Director: SCOTT BELOBRAJDIC
Controller: MARK C. SCHMOTZER
Director of Pius XII Memorial Library: FRANCES BENHAM
Library: see Libraries
Number of teachers: 1,209 full-time, 1,851 part-time
Number of students: 11,038
Publications: *The Modern Schoolman, Review for Religious, Theology Digest, Saint Louis University Law Journal, Seismological Bulletin, Manuscripta, Universitas, Chart, Eads Bridge Review, Challenge, Horizon, Healthline in Touch With You, Parameters, Institute of Jesuit Sources, Studies in the Spirituality of Jesuits, Symposium, Insight: Public Law Review, BALSA Reports, Parks Today, The University News.*

DEANS

College of Arts and Sciences: SHIRLEY DOWDY
Graduate School: DONALD G. BRENNAN
School of Medicine: PATRICIA L. MONTELEONE
School of Law: (vacant)
College of Philosophy and Letters: GARTH L. HALLETT
School of Business and Administration: NEIL SEITZ
School of Nursing: JOAN M. HRUBETZ
School of Public Health: RICHARD S. KURA
School of Allied Health Professions: FRANCES L. HORVATH
School of Social Service: WILLIAM J. HUTCHISON
Madrid Campus: RICK L. CHANEY
Parks College: CHARLES KIRKPATRICK

PROFESSORS

ABELL, B. F., Meteorology
ACETO, T., Jr, Paediatrics
AL-JUREIDINI, S. B., Paediatrics
ALBERT, S. G., Internal Medicine
ALDRIDGE, R. D., Biology
AMINE, L. S., Marketing
ANDERSON, E. L., Internal Medicine
ANDERSON, R. O., Communication
ARCHER, C. R., Radiology
ARKIN, I. M., Theological Studies
ARMBRECHT, H. J., Internal Medicine
ARTAL, R., Obstetrics and Gynaecology
ASPINWALL, N., Biology
ATTANASIO, J. B., Law
BACON, B. R., Internal Medicine
BAJAJ, S. P., Internal Medicine
BALDASSARE, J. J., Pharmacological and Physiological Science
BALFOUR, I. C., Paediatrics
BANKS, W. A., Internal Medicine
BARBER, M. D., Philosophy
BARENKAMP, S. J., Paediatrics
BARMANN, L. F., American Studies
BARRY, R. C., Paediatrics
BAUDENDISTEL, L. J., Anaesthesiology
BELLONE, C. J., Molecular Microbiology and Immunology
BELSHE, R. B., Internal Medicine
BENOFY, L. P., Physics
BENOIT, R. P., English
BENTLEY, D. W., Internal Medicine
BERNHARDT, P., Biology
BIONDI, L. H., Modern Languages
BJERREGAARD, P., Internal Medicine
BLACKWELL, R. J., Philosophy
BOHMAN, J. P., Philosophy
BOLL, R. W., Science and Mathematics
BOLLA, R. I., Biology
BRENNAN, D. G., Communication Disorders
BRENNAN, W. C., Social Work
BRESLIN, R. D., Education
BROCKHAUS, R. H., Management
BROWN, W. W., Internal Medicine
BROWNSON, R. C., Community Health
BUCHOLZ, R. D., Surgery
BURDGE, R. E., Orthopaedic Surgery
BURKE, W. J., Neurology
CANTWELL, J. C., Mathematics and Computer Science
CHAITMAN, B. R., Internal Medicine
CHAPNICK, B. M., Pharmacological and Physiological Science
CHARRON, W. C., Philosophy
CHEN, S.-C., Paediatrics
CHINNADURAI, G., Molecular Virology
CHU, J.-Y., Paediatrics
COE, R. M., Community and Family Medicine
COHEN, J. D., Internal Medicine
COMAS, M., Obstetrics and Gynaecology
CONNORS, N. A., Anatomy and Neurobiology
COOPER, M. H., Anatomy and Neurobiology
COSCIA, C., Biochemistry and Molecular Biology
COUNTE, M. A., Health Administration
CRITCHLOW, D. T., History
CROSSLEY, D. J., Geophysics
CZYSZ, P. A., Aerospace Engineering
DAVENPORT, G., Psychology
DAVIS, R. J., Jr Aerospace Studies
DEMELLO, D. E., Pathology
DIBISCEGLIE, A., Internal Medicine
DIECK, H. A., Chemistry
DIXIT, V. V., Physics, Science and Mathematics
DORE, I. I., Law
DOWDY, J., Mathematics and Computer Science
DOWDY, S., Research Methodology
DOYLE, J. P., Philosophy
DOYLE, R. E., Comparative Medicine
DUCKRO, P. N., Community and Family Medicine
DUNSFORD, J. E., Law
EASTWOOD, M. R., Psychiatry and Human Behaviour
ELICEIRI, G. L., Pathology
ELLSWORTH, M. L., Pharmacological and Physiological Science
FARRIS, B. E., Jr, Sociology
FEIR, D. J., Biology
FERMAN, M. A., Aerospace and Mechanical Engineering
FERNANDEZ-POL, J. A., Internal Medicine
FIORE, A. C., Surgery
FISHER, J. T., Theological Studies
FITCH, C. D., Internal Medicine
FITZGIBBON, S. A., Law
FLETCHER, J. W., Internal Medicine
FLICK, L. H., Community Health

FLIESLER, S. J., Ophthalmology
FLOOD, J. F., Internal Medicine
FORD, C. E., Mathematics and Computer Science
FORSBERG, J. H., Chemistry
FRANKOWSKI, S., Law
FREESE, R. W., Mathematics and Computer Sciences
FROST, C. W., Law
GANNON, P., Psychiatry and Human Behaviour
GARCIA, P., Modern Languages
GARVIN, P. J., Surgery
GEORGE, J. A., Aerospace and Mechanical Engineering
GIBBONS, J. L., Psychology
GILNER, F. H., Psychology
GILSINAN, J. F., Public Policy Studies
GOLD, A. H., Pharmacological and Physiological Science
GOLDMAN, R. L., Law
GOLDNER, J. A., Law
GOODGOLD, H. M., Internal Medicine
GORSE, G. J., Internal Medicine
GRADY, M. P., Education
GRAFF, R. J., Surgery
GRAHAM, M. A., Pathology
GRANDGENETT, D. P., Molecular Virology
GRAVISS, E. R., Radiology
GREANEY, T. L., Law
GREEN, MAURICE, Molecular Virology
GREEN, MICHAEL, Molecular Microbiology and Immunology
GROSSBERG, G. T., Psychiatry and Human Behaviour
GROSSMAN, L. J., Economics
GROSSWASSER, N., Modern Languages
GUITHUES, H. J., Finance
HALE, R. E., Research Methodology
HALLETT, G. L., Philosophy
HANDAL, P. J., Psychology
HARING, J. H., Anatomy and Neurobiology
HEANEY, R. M., Internal Medicine
HEBDA, J. J., Mathematics and Computer Science
HEIBERG, E., Radiology
HERRMANN, R. B., Geophysics, Earth and Atmospheric Sciences
HERRMANN, V. M., Surgery
HERTELENDY, F., Obstetrics and Gynaecology
HITCHCOCK, J. F., History
HOOVER, R. G., Pathology
HORVATH, F. L., Physician Assistant Education
HOWARD, A. J., Law
HOWLETT, A. C., Pharmacological and Physiological Science
HRUBETZ, J., Nursing
HUANG, J. S., Biochemistry and Molecular Biology
HUGHES, H. M., Psychology
HYERS, T. M., Internal Medicine
IKEDA, S., Anaesthesiology
JAMES, C. A., Finance
JANNEY, C. G., Pathology
JENNINGS, J. P., Accounting
JOHNSON, F. E., Surgery
JOHNSON, S. H., Law
JOHNSON, T. H., Modern Languages
JOHNSTON, M. F., Pathology
JOIST, J. H., Pathology
JOS, C. J., Psychiatry and Human Behaviour
KALLIONGIS, J. E., Mathematics and Computer Science
KAMINSKI, D. L., Surgery
KAO, M. S., Obstetrics and Gynaecology
KAPLAN, S. L., Psychiatry and Human Behaviour
KARUNAMOORTHY, S. N., Aerospace and Mechanical Engineering
KATZ, B. M., Research Methodology
KATZ, J. A., Management
KAUFMAN, N. H., Law
KAVANAUGH, J. F., Philosophy
KEENAN, W. J., Paediatrics
KEITHLEY, J. P., Accounting
KELLER, C. A., Internal Medicine
KENNEDY, D. J., Internal Medicine
KERN, M. J., Internal Medicine
KIM, S. H., Finance
KIM, Y. S., Pharmacological and Physiological Science
KIMMEY, J. R., Community Health
KLEIN, C., Biochemistry and Molecular Biology
KNUEPFER, M. M., Pharmacological and Physiological Science
KNUTSEN, A. P., Paediatrics
KOLMER, E., American Studies
KORN, J. H., Psychology
KORNBLUTH, J., Pathology
KOTAGEL, S., Neurology
KOWERT, B. A., Chemistry
KRAMER, T. J., Psychology
KURZ, R. S., Health Administration
KWAK, N. K., Decision Sciences and Management
KWON, I. W., Decision Sciences and Management
LABOVITZ, A. J., Internal Medicine
LAGUNOFF, D., Pathology
LANE, B. C., Theological Studies
LECHNER, A. J., Pharmacological and Physiological Science
LEIPPE, M. R., Psychology
LEVARY, R. R., Decision Sciences and Management
LIN, M. S., Internal Medicine
LIN, Y. J., Meteorology, Earth and Atmospheric Sciences
LIU, M.-S., Pharmacological and Physiological Science
LOMPERIS, T. J., Political Science
LONIGRO, A. J., Internal Medicine
LYNCH, R. E., Paediatrics
MCBRIDE, L. R., Surgery
MCDONALD, D. J., Orthopaedic Surgery
MCGAHEE, C. L., Psychiatry and Human Behaviour
MALONE, L. J., Jr, Chemistry
MANOR, D., Aerospace and Mechanical Engineering
MARGOLIS, R. B., Psychiatry and Human Behaviour
MARSKE, C. E., Sociology
MARTIN, K. J., Internal Medicine
MATTAMMAL, M. B., Internal Medicine
MATUSCHAK, G. M., Internal Medicine
MEDOFF, J., Biology
METHENY, N. A., Adult Health Nursing
MILLER, C. H., English
MILLER, D. D., Internal Medicine
MILLER, D. K., Internal Medicine
MILLER, S. W., Marketing
MILLER, T. A., Surgery
MITCHELL, B. J., Geophysics, Earth and Atmospheric Sciences
MODRAS, R. E., Theological Studies
MOISAN, T. E., English
MONFORT, C. E., III, Physics, Science and Mathematics
MONTELEONE, J. A., Paediatrics
MONTELEONE, P. L., Paediatrics
MOORADIAN, A. D., Internal Medicine
MOORE, J. T., Meteorology, Earth and Atmospheric Sciences
MOORE, T. L., Internal Medicine
MORLEY, J. E., Internal Medicine
MUNZ, D. C., Psychology
MURPHY, D. T., Modern Languages
MURRAY, R. L. E., Geriatric, Psychiatric and Mental Health Nursing
NAGABHUSHAN, B. L., Aerospace and Mechanical Engineering
NAUNHEIM, K. S., Surgery
NEDWEK, B., Public Policy Studies
NEELY, M. E., Jr, History
NEVINS, F. M., Law
NIKOLAI, R. J., Orthodontics
NOFFSINGER, J. E., Paediatrics
NOGUCHI, A., Paediatrics
NOURI, S., Paediatrics
O'BRIEN, J. C., Law
O'CONNOR, D. M., Paediatrics
O'ROURKE, K. D., Internal Medicine
OLIVER, J. M., Psychology
ORDOWER, H. M., Law
PADBERG, W. H., Social Work
PANNETON, W. M., Anatomy and Neurobiology
PARKER, G. E., Management
PARRA, R. O., Urology, Surgery
PARTRIDGE, N. C., Pharmacological and Physiological Science
PAULY, J. J., Communication
PENNEYS, N., Dermatology
PERMAN, W. H., Radiology
PERRY, H. M., Internal Medicine
PERRY, S. A., Medical-Surgical Nursing
PETERSON, G. J., Surgery
PETRUSKA, P. J., Internal Medicine
POLLARD, C. A., Community and Family Medicine
PUNZO, V. C., Philosophy
PURO, S., Political Science
RANA, W.-U.-Z., Anatomy and Neurobiology
RAO, G. V., Earth and Atmospheric Sciences
RAO, P. S., Paediatrics
RAVINDRA, K., Aerospace and Mechanical Engineering
RAY, C. G., Paediatrics
RENARD, G. J., Jr, Theological Studies
RIDDLE, I. I., Maternal and Child Health Nursing
RILES, J. B., Mathematics and Computer Sciences
ROHLIK, J., Law
ROMEIS, J. C., Health Services Research
ROSS, M. J., Psychology
RUCKDESCHEL, R. A., Social Work
RUDDY, T. M., History
RUH, M. F., Pharmacological and Physiological Science
RUH, T. S., Pharmacological and Physiological Science
RYERSE, J. S., Pathology
SALIMI, Z., Radiology
SALINAS-MADRIGAL, L., Pathology
SALSICH, P. W., Jr, Law
SANCHEZ, J. M., History
SANTHANAM, T. S., Physics, Science and Mathematics
SCALZO, A. J., Paediatrics
SCHLAFLY, D. L., Jr, History
SCHMITZ, H. H., Health Administration
SCHULZE, I. T., Molecular Microbiology and Immunology
SCOTT, J. F., English
SEARLS, E. H., Law Library
SEITZ, N. E., Finance
SELHORST, J. B., Neurology
SEVERSON, J. G., Jr, Biology
SHAPIRO, M. J., Surgery
SHEA, W. M., Theological Studies
SHEN, W. W., Psychiatry and Human Behaviour
SHIELDS, J. B., Radiology
SHIPPEY, T. A., English
SILBERSTEIN, M. J., Radiology
SILVERBERG, A. B., Internal Medicine
SLAVIN, R. G., Internal Medicine
SLY, W. S., Biochemistry and Molecular Biology
SMITH, K., Jr, Surgery
SOBKOWSKI, F. J., Orthodontics
SOTELO-AVILA, C., Pathology
SPAZIANO, V. T., Chemistry
SPRAGUE, R. S., Internal Medicine
STACEY, L. M., Physics
STANTON, C. M., Education
STARK, W., Biology
STEINHARDT, G. F., Urology, Surgery
STEVENS, C., Mathematics and Computer Science
STEVENSON, T. M., Economics
STOEBERL, P. A., Management
STOLZER, A. J., Aviation Science
STRATMAN, H. G., Internal Medicine
STRETCH, J. J., Social Work
STUMP, E. A., Philosophy
SUNDARAM, M., Radiology
TERRY, N., Law
THOMAS, C. W., Biomedical Engineering

THOMAS, D. R., Internal Medicine
THOMAS, J. M., Psychiatry and Human Behaviour
THOMAS, J. R., Otolaryngology
TOCE, S. S., Paediatrics
TOLBERT, D. L., Anatomy and Neurobiology
TOMAZIC, T. J., Research Methodology
TREADGOLD, W., History
TRUE, W. R., Community Health
TSAU, C. M., Mathematics and Computer Science
TUCHLER, D. J., Law
TYREE, D. A., Finance
VAGO, S., Sociology
VIEHLAND, L. A., Chemistry, Science and Mathematics
VOGLER, C. A., Pathology
VOGLER, G. A., Comparative Medicine
WACKER, W. D., Mathematics, Science and Mathematics
WARE, L., Law
WARREN, K. F., Political Science
WEBB, K., Community and Family Medicine
WEBER, T. R., Surgery
WEBSTER, R. O., Internal Medicine
WEINBERGER, A. M., Law
WELCH, P. J., Economics
WENDEL, G. D., Political Science
WERNET, S. P., Social Work
WESTFALL, T. C., Pharmacological and Physiological Science
WHITING, R. B., Internal Medicine
WHITMAN, B., Paediatrics
WIENER, R. L., Psychology
WIENS, R. D., Internal Medicine
WILLIAMS, A. L., Radiology
WINN, H. N., Obstetrics and Gynaecology
WOLD, W. S. M., Molecular Microbiology and Immunology
WOLFF, M. A., Law
WOLINSKY, F. D., Health Administration
WOLVERSON, M. K., Radiology
WONGSURAWAT, N., Internal Medicine
WOOD, E. G., Paediatrics
WOOD, T. T., Art and Art History
YEAGER, F., Finance
YOUNG, P. A., Anatomy and Neurobiology
ZAHM, D. S., Anatomy and Neurobiology
ZASSENHAUS, H. P., Molecular Microbiology and Immunology
ZENSER, T. V., Internal Medicine

SOUTHEAST MISSOURI STATE UNIVERSITY

Cape Girardeau, MO 63701
Telephone: (314) 651-2000
Fax: (314) 651-5061
Founded 1873
President: Dr DALE F. NITZSCHKE
Provost: Dr CHARLES KUPCHELLA
Director of Admissions: Dr ROBERT PARRENT
Registrar: PATRICIA KOGGE
Director of Library: Dr SARAH CRON
Library of 409,000 vols, 287,000 government documents and 1,174,000 microforms
Number of teachers: 378
Number of students: 8,234

SOUTHWEST MISSOURI STATE UNIVERSITY

901 South National, Springfield, MO 65804
Telephone: (417) 836-5000
Fax: (417) 836-6777
Founded 1905
President: JOHN H. KEISER
Director of Admissions: (vacant)
Dean of Library Services: KAREN HORNY
Library of 609,852 vols, 827,099 government documents, 871,618 units of microform, 29,373 audio-visual titles, 184,580 maps, 4,750 current periodicals
Number of teachers: 649 full-time, 167 part-time
Number of students: 16,439

STEPHENS COLLEGE

Columbia, MO 65215
Telephone: (573) 442-2211
Fax: (573) 876-7248
Founded 1833
President: MARCIA S. KIERSCHT
Vice-President for Academic and Student Affairs: ROBERT S. BADAL
Director of Admissions: JOHN FLUKE
Librarian: JACKIE HINSHAW
Library of 120,000 vols
Number of full-time teachers: 65
Number of students: 901

TARKIO COLLEGE

Tarkio, MO 64491
Telephone: (816) 736-4131
Founded 1883
Church-related liberal arts college
President: ROY MCINTOSH
Vice-President and Academic Dean: CHARLES YARBROUGH
Registrar: BARBARA WILMES
Librarian: CHARLES STELLING
Library of 65,695 vols
Number of teachers: 45
Number of students: 770

TRUMAN STATE UNIVERSITY

Kirksville, MO 63501
Telephone: (660) 785-4000
Fax: (660) 785-4181
E-mail: admissions@truman.edu
Founded 1867; formerly Northeast Missouri State University (until 1996)
President: Dr JACK MAGRUDER
Vice-President for Academic Affairs: GARRY GORDON (acting)
Director of Admission and Records: KATHY RIECK
Registrar: NANCY WEBER
Library of 370,000 vols
Number of teachers: 399
Number of students: 6,421
Publications: *Truman Review* (every 6 months), *Index* (weekly student newspaper), *Echo* (student yearbook), *Truman Today* (weekly during academic year).

UNIVERSITY OF MISSOURI SYSTEM

Columbia, MO 65211
Telephone: (573) 882-2011
Fax: (573) 882-2721
Founded 1839
President: MANUEL T. PACHECO
Vice-President for Administrative Affairs: R. KENNETH HUTCHINSON (interim)
Vice-President for Academic Affairs: STEPHEN W. LEHMKUHLE (acting)
Vice-President for University Outreach and Extension: RONALD TURNER
Libraries: see University Libraries

University of Missouri—Columbia

Columbia, MO 65211
Telephone: (573) 882-2121
Founded 1839
State control
Academic year: August to May
Chancellor: RICHARD L. WALLACE
Provost: BRADY DEATON (interim)
Vice-Chancellor for Student Affairs: CHARLES SHROEDER
Vice-Chancellor for Administrative Services: KEE GROSHONG
Vice-Chancellor for Development and Alumni Relations: HAROLD G. JEFFCOAT
Registrar and Director of Admissions: GARY L. SMITH
Number of teachers: 4,180
Number of students: 22,552

DEANS AND DIRECTORS

College of Agriculture, Food and Natural Resources: ROGER MITCHELL
College of Arts and Sciences: LARRY D. CLARK
College of Business and Public Administration: BRUCE J. WALKER
College of Education: RICHARD L. ANDREWS
College of Engineering: JAMES E. THOMPSON
College of Human and Environmental Sciences: BEA LITHERLAND
College of Veterinary Medicine: H. RICHARD ADAMS
Graduate School: CHARLES SAMPSON (interim)
School of Accountancy: EARL WILSON
School of Fine Arts: MELVIN PLATT
School of Health-Related Professions: RICHARD OLIVER
School of Journalism: R. DEAN MILLS
School of Law: TIMOTHY J. HEINSZ
School of Information Science and Learning Technologies: JOHN WEDMAN
School of Medicine: ROBERT CHURCHILL (interim)
School of Natural Resources: ALBERT VOGT
School of Nursing: TONI J. SULLIVAN
School of Social Work: CHARLES COWGER

University of Missouri—Kansas City

5100 Rockhill Rd, Kansas City, MO 64110
Telephone: (816) 235-1000
Founded 1929
State control
Academic year: August to July
Chancellor: ELEANOR BRANTLEY SCHWARTZ
Executive Vice-Provost/Executive Dean: MARVIN R. QUERRY
Vice-Chancellor for Administrative Affairs: J. JOSEPH DOERR
Vice-Chancellor for University Advancement: WILLIAM J. FRENCH
Vice-Chancellor for Student Affairs: LARRY DIETZ (interim)
Registrar: WILSON BERRY
Director, Admissions: MELVIN TYLER
Director, University Libraries: TED SHELDON
Library of 868,000 vols, 1,537,912 microforms
Number of teachers: 850
Number of students: 12,000

DEANS

College of Arts and Sciences: JAMES DURIG
Henry W. Bloch School of Business and Public Administration: WILLIAM B. EDDY
School of Dentistry: MICHAEL J. REED
School of Education: BERNARD OLIVER
School of Law: BURNELE V. POWELL
Conservatory of Music: TERRY APPLEBAUM
School of Pharmacy: ROBERT W. PIEPHO
School of Nursing: NANCY MILLS
School of Medicine: MARJORIE SIRRIDGE
School of Biological Sciences: MARINO MARTINEZ-CARRION
Extended Programs: JANET STRATTON (Dir)
Coordinated Undergraduate Engineering Programs: QUINTON BOWLES (Assoc. Dean)
Computer Science/Telecommunications Program: RICHARD HETHERINGTON (Dir)

University of Missouri—Rolla

Rolla, MO 65401
Telephone: (314) 341-4114

Fax: (314) 341-6306
Founded 1870
State control; Academic year: August to July
Chancellor: JOHN T. PARK
Vice-Chancellor for Academic Affairs: WALTER J. GAJDA, Jr
Vice-Chancellor for Administrative Affairs: Dr MOHAMMAD QAYOUMI
Vice-Chancellor for University Advancement: NEIL K. SMITH
Vice-Chancellor for Student Affairs: WENDELL R. OGROSKY
Registrar: MYRON G. PARRY
Director of Admissions and Student Financial Aid: MARTINA HAHN
Librarian: JEAN EISENMAN
Library of 464,000 vols
Number of teachers: 364
Number of students: 4,976

DEANS AND DIRECTORS

School of Engineering: O. ROBERT MITCHELL
School of Mines and Metallurgy: LEE W. SAPERSTEIN
College of Arts and Sciences: RUSSELL BUHITE

University of Missouri—St Louis

8001 Natural Bridge Rd, St Louis, MO 63121-4499
Telephone: (314) 553-5000
Founded 1963
State control
Academic year: August to July
Chancellor: BLANCHE M. TOUHILL
Vice-Chancellor for Academic Affairs: ROOSEVELT WRIGHT, Jr
Vice-Chancellor for Managerial and Technological Services: JAMES KREUGER
Vice-Chancellor for Student Affairs: LOWE S. MACLEAN
Vice-Chancellor for University Relations: KATHLEEN T. OSBORN
Registrar and Director of Admissions: MIMI LAMARCA
Library of 541,000 vols
Number of teachers: 420 full-time
Number of students: 13,161

DEANS AND DIRECTORS

College of Arts and Sciences: E. TERRENCE JONES
School of Business Administration: ROBERT M. NAUSS (acting)
School of Education: RICKEY LEE GEORGE (acting)
Evening College: EVERETT NANCE (acting)
Graduate School: DOUGLAS WARTZOK
School of Optometry: JERRY L. CHRISTENSEN
School of Nursing: SHIRLEY MARTIN
Honors College: FREDERICK FAUSZ

WASHINGTON UNIVERSITY

Saint Louis, MO 63130
Telephone: (314) 935-5000
Chartered 1853 as Eliot Seminary; charter altered to Washington University 1857
Private control
Academic year: August to May
Chancellor: MARK S. WRIGHTON
Executive Vice-Chancellors: EDWARD S. MACIAS, RICHARD A. ROLOFF
Executive Vice-Chancellor for Medical Affairs: WILLIAM A. PECK
Registrar: BILL D. SMITH
Librarian: SHIRLEY K. BAKER
Number of teachers: 3,069 full-time, 194 part-time
Number of students: 11,016
Publications: *Student Life, Washington University Record, Washington University Magazine, Alumni News.*

DEANS

Faculty of Arts and Sciences: EDWARD S. MACIAS
College of Arts and Sciences: JAMES E. MCLEOD
Graduate School of Arts and Sciences: ROBERT E. THACH
School of Architecture: CYNTHIA R. WEESE
John M. Olin School of Business: STUART I. GREENBAUM
School of Engineering and Applied Science: CHRISTOPHER I. BYRNES (includes the Sever Institute of Graduate Engineering)
School of Art: JOE DEAL
School of Law: DORSEY D. ELLIS, Jr
School of Medicine: WILLIAM A. PECK
George Warren Brown School of Social Work: SHANTI K. KHINDUKA

WEBSTER UNIVERSITY

470 East Lockwood Ave, St Louis, MO 63119
Telephone: (314) 968-6900
Founded 1915
President: Dr RICHARD S. MEYERS
Registrar: DON MORRIS
Librarian: LAURA REIN
Library of 249,000 vols
Number of teachers: 133 full-time, 2,441 part-time
Number of students: 14,628
Publications: *Annual Report, Webster World* (4 a year).

WESTMINSTER COLLEGE

Fulton, MO 65251
Telephone: (573) 642-3361
Fax: (573) 642-6356
Founded 1851
President: JAMES F. TRAER
Dean of Faculty and Vice-President: WALTER B. ROETTGER
Vice-President for Development: TRACY BRANSON
Registrar: PHYLLIS MASEK
Librarian: LORNA MITCHELL
Library of 103,000 vols
Number of teachers: 60
Number of students: 700

WILLIAM JEWELL COLLEGE

Liberty, MO 64068
Telephone: (816) 781-7700
Founded 1849
President: J. GORDON KINGSLEY
Registrar: ELAINE BARNES
Director of Admission: T. EDWIN NORRIS
Librarian: J. P. YOUNG
Library of 202,000 vols
Number of teachers: 99
Number of students: 1,880

WILLIAM WOODS UNIVERSITY

Fulton, MO 65251
Telephone: (314) 642-2251
Founded 1870
President: Dr JAHNAE H. BARNETT
Vice-President and Dean of Academic Affairs: Dr ANDRE COTE
Vice-President for Fiscal Affairs: LINDA KOCH
Dean of Student Services: DEBRA HACKMANN
Library of 160,000 vols
Number of teachers: 50 full-time, 25 part-time
Publications: *The Owl* (campus newspaper), *William Woods Magazine* (alumnae magazine).

MONTANA

CARROLL COLLEGE

Helena, MT 59625
Telephone: (406) 447-4300
Founded 1909
President: Dr MATTHEW J. QUINN
Academic Dean: Dr JAMES TRUDNOWSKI
Vice-President for Finance, Administration and Facilities: LYNN C. ETCHART
Registrar: MARY PAT DUTTON
Librarian: LOIS FITZPATRICK
Library of 94,000 vols
Number of teachers: 78
Number of students: 1,249

MONTANA STATE UNIVERSITY

Bozeman, MT 59717
Telephone: (406) 994-0211
Fax: (406) 994-2893
Founded 1893
President: MICHAEL MALONE
Provost and Vice-President for Academic Affairs: JOSEPH CHAPMAN
Vice-President for Research, Creative Activities and Technology Transfer: ROBERT SWENSON
Vice-President for Administration and Finance: ROBERT SPECTER
Vice-President for Student Affairs: ALLEN YARNELL
Registrar and Director of Admissions: CHARLES NELSON
Dean of Students: DENNIS KLEWIN
Number of students: 10,700

DEANS OF COLLEGES

Letters and Science: JAMES MCMILLAN
Agriculture: THOMAS MCCOY
Education, Health and Human Development: LARRY BAKER
Engineering: DAVID F. GIBSON
Arts and Architecture: JERRY BANCROFT
Graduate Studies: JOSEPH FEDOCK
Nursing: LEA ACORD
Business: MICHAEL OWEN

MONTANA STATE UNIVERSITY – BILLINGS

Billings, MT 59101
Telephone: (406) 657-2011
Fax: (406) 657-2051
Founded 1927
Chancellor: RONALD P. SEXTON
Provost and Academic Vice-Chancellor: JANIE C. PARK
Librarian: JANE HOWELL
Library of 138,356 vols
Number of teachers: 175
Number of students: 4,400

MONTANA STATE UNIVERSITY—NORTHERN

Havre, MT 59501
Telephone: (406) 265-3700
Founded 1929
Chancellor: MICHAEL RAO
Registrar: (vacant)
Librarian: WILL RAWN
Library of 84,000 vols
Number of teachers: 80
Number of students: 1,800
Baccalaureate courses in arts and sciences, teacher education, technology, business, nursing. Master's courses in education.

MONTANA TECH OF THE UNIVERSITY OF MONTANA

Butte, MT 59701-8931
Telephone: (406) 496-4101
Founded 1893
Chancellor: W. FRANKLIN GILMORE
Vice-Chancellor of Academic Affairs and Research: Dr THOMAS G. WARING
Vice-Chancellor of Administrative and Student Affairs: Dr JOHN A. HINTZ
Vice-Chancellor of Research and Graduate Studies: Dr JOSEPH F. FIGUEIRA
Registrar: EDWIN JOHNSON
Director of Admissions: RAY ROGERS
Director of Development: JAY VOGELSANG
Librarian: HENRY MCCLERMAN
Number of teachers: 88
Number of students: 1,823
Publications: *Catalog, The Magma, The Technocrat.*

ROCKY MOUNTAIN COLLEGE

1511 Poly Drive, Billings, MT 59102
Telephone: (406) 657-1000
Fax: (406) 259-9751
Founded 1878
President: Dr ARTHUR H. DEROSIER, Jr
Academic Vice-President: Dr SUSAN MCDANIEL
Librarian: JANET JELINEK
Library of 65,000 vols
Number of teachers: 45 full-time, 38 part-time
Number of students: 800

UNIVERSITY OF GREAT FALLS

1301 20th St South, Great Falls, MT 59405
Telephone: (406) 761-8210
Fax: (406) 791-5393
Founded 1932
Liberal arts college; 4-year and 2-year degree courses in Human Services, Professional Counselling, and Education
President: FREDERICK W. GILLIARD
Provost and Academic Vice-President: Dr B. LEE COOPER
Director of Admissions and Records: R. HENSLEY
Librarian: UNA M. KOONTZ
Library of 97,353 vols
Number of teachers: 80
Number of students: 1,400

UNIVERSITY OF MONTANA

Missoula, MT 59812
Telephone: (406) 243-0211
Fax: (406) 243-2797
Founded 1893
President: GEORGE M. DENNISON
Provost: ROBERT L. KINDRICK
Fiscal Affairs Vice-President: JAMES TODD
Associate Vice-President for Research: T. LLOYD CHESNUT
Registrar: PHILIP T. BAIN
Dean of Students: BARBARA B. HOLLMANN
Dean of Library Service: KAREN HATCHER
Library of *c.* 700,000 vols, plus 77,600 US Government documents
Number of teachers: 450
Number of students: 10,953

DEANS

College of Arts and Sciences: JAMES FLIGHTNER
College of Technology: DENNIS LERUM
School of Fine Arts: JAMES D. KRILEY
School of Business Administration: LARRY D. GIANCHETTA
Graduate School: ROBERT L. KINDRICK
School of Education: DONALD ROBSON
School of Forestry: PERRY BROWN
School of Journalism: JOSEPH DURSO (acting)
School of Law: EDWARD ECK
School of Pharmacy: DAVID FORBES
Division of Continuing Education: SHARON ALEXANDER

ASSOCIATED INSTITUTIONS

Montana Tech of The University of Montana
Western Montana College of The University of Montana
Helena Vocational Technical Center

WESTERN MONTANA COLLEGE

Dillon, MT 59725
Telephone: (406) 683-7011
Fax: (406) 683-7493
Founded 1893
State control
Academic year: September to June
Chancellor: Dr SHEILA M. STEARNS
Registrar: Dr FRED BUYS
Number of teachers: 50
Number of students: 1,200

NEBRASKA

CHADRON STATE COLLEGE

Chadron, NE 69337
Telephone: (308) 432-6000
Founded 1911
President: THOMAS L. KREPEL
Registrar: DALE WILLIAMSON
Librarian: TERRY BRENNAN
Library of 190,666 vols
Number of teachers: 101 full-time
Number of students: 3,206

CONCORDIA UNIVERSITY—NEBRASKA

800 North Columbia Ave, Seward, NE 68434
Telephone: (402) 643-3651
Fax: (402) 643-4073
Founded 1894
President: ORVILLE C. WALZ
Registrar: MATT HEIBAL
Director of Admissions: DONALD VOS
Librarian: MYRON BOETTCHER
Library of 230,000 vols
Number of teachers: 75
Number of students: 1,193
Publication: *Issues in Christian Education* (3 a year).

CREIGHTON UNIVERSITY

Omaha, NE 68178
Telephone: (402) 280-2700
Telex: 910-622-0287
Founded 1878
Chartered 1879
Private-Independent, associated with the Society of Jesus
President: Rev. MICHAEL G. MORRISON
Vice-President Academic Affairs: Dr CHARLES J. DOUGHERTY
Vice-President for Health Sciences: Dr RICHARD O'BRIEN
Vice-President for Administration and Finance: GEORGE A. GRIEB
Vice-President for University Relations: MICHAEL E. LEIGHTON
Vice-President for Student Services: Dr JOHN CERNECH
Vice-President for Information Systems: CONRAD P. DIETZ
Vice-President for University Ministry: Rev. ANDREW F. ALEXANDER
Director of Admissions: DENNIS J. O'DRISCOLL
Registrar: JOHN A. KRECEK
Director of Alumni Memorial Library: MICHAEL LACROIX
Library of 767,000 vols
Number of teachers: 1,361
Number of students: 6,297
Publications: *Creighton University Bulletin, The Creightonian, Bluejay, Creighton Law Review, Alumnews, Windows.*

DEANS

Arts and Sciences: Rev. MICHAEL PROTERRA
Business Administration: ROBERT E. PITTS
Dentistry: Dr WAYNE W. BARKMEIER
Graduate: BARBARA BRADEN
Law: LAWRENCE RAFUL
Medicine: M. ROY WILSON
Nursing: EDETH K. KITCHENS
Pharmacy and Allied Health Professions: SIDNEY J. STOHS
University College and Summer Sessions: C. TIMOTHY DICKEL
Students: JOHN CERNECH

DANA COLLEGE

Blair, NE 68008
Telephone: (402) 426-9000
Fax: (402) 426-7332
Founded 1884
President: Dr MYRVIN CHRISTOPHERSON
Registrar: Mrs NANCY PENNA
Dean: Dr PAUL FORNO
Librarian: DOROTHY WILLIS
Library of 190,000 vols
Number of teachers: 70
Number of students: 594

DOANE COLLEGE

Crete, NE 68333
Telephone: (402) 826-2161
Founded 1872
President: FRED BROWN
Dean of Admissions: DAN KUNZMAN
Dean of the College: GLEN DAVIDSON
Registrar: PAULA VALENTA
Librarian: PEGGY BROOKS SMITH
Library of 221,435 vols
Number of teachers: 104
Number of students: 885 (Crete Campus)

ATTACHED INSTITUTE

Midwest Institute for International Studies: Dir MAUREEN FRANKLIN

HASTINGS COLLEGE

Hastings, NE 68902-0269
Telephone: (402) 463-2402
Founded 1882
President: Dr RICHARD HOOVER
Academic Dean: Dr DWAYNE STRASHEIM
Registrar: JAMES SMITH
Librarian: ROBERT NEDDERMAN
Library of 115,000 vols
Number of teachers: 69
Number of students: 1,060
Publication: *Hastings College Today* (2 a year)

MIDLAND LUTHERAN COLLEGE

900 N. Clarkson St, Fremont, NE 68025
Telephone: (402) 721-5480
Fax: (402) 721-0250
E-mail: hansen@admin.mlc.edu
Founded 1883
President: CARL L. HANSEN
Vice-President for Finance and Treasurer: JOSEPH H. SJUTS
Vice-President for Institutional Advancement: FRED L. PYLE

Vice-President for Academic Affairs: DONALD L. KAHNK
Vice-President for Student Services and Dean of Students: NICKI J. MCINTYRE
Vice-President for Enrollment Services: ROLAND R. KAHNK
Registrar: TIMOTHY C. EBNER
Librarian: THOMAS E. BOYLE

Library of 112,000 vols
Number of teachers: 64
Number of students: 1,033

Publications: *The Midland* (weekly), *Observations* (4 a year).

NEBRASKA WESLEYAN UNIVERSITY

5000 St Paul Ave, Lincoln, NE 68504-2796

Telephone: (402) 466-2371
Fax: (402) 465-2179

Founded 1887

President: Dr JEANIE WATSON
Vice-President for Academic Affairs: Dr NORVAL KNETEN
Registrar: PATRICIA HALL
Director of Admissions: KEN SIEG

Library of 200,000 vols
Number of teachers: 86 full-time, 80 part-time
Number of students: 1,583

PERU STATE COLLEGE

Peru, NE 68421

Telephone: (402) 872-3815

Founded 1867

President: ROBERT L. BURNS
Vice-President, Administration and Finance: SUSAN UDEY
Vice-President, Academic Affairs: (vacant)
Vice-President, Student Affairs: DARYLL HERSEMANN
Registrar: KELLY LIEWER
Director of Continuing Education: ROBERT SMALLFOOT
Librarian: LORIN LINDSAY

Library of 100,000 vols
Number of teachers: 47
Number of students: 1,898

UNION COLLEGE

3800 South 48th St, Lincoln, NE 68506

Telephone: (402) 488-2331

Founded 1891

President: DAVE SMITH
Vice-President/Dean: LOWELL HAGELE
Vice-President for Finance: GARY BOLLINGER
Registrar: OSA CANTO
Director of Institutional Advancement: LUANN DAVIS
Librarian: CHLOE V. FOUTZ

Library of 112,283 vols
Number of teachers: 73
Number of students: 703

UNIVERSITY OF NEBRASKA

Lincoln, NE 68583-0745

Telephone: (402) 472-2111
Fax: (402) 472-1237

Founded 1869

President: Dr L. DENNIS SMITH
Executive Vice-President and Provost: Dr LEE B. JONES
Vice-President for Business and Finance: Dr JAMES C. VAN HORN
Vice-President and General Counsel: RICHARD R. WOOD
Vice-President for External Affairs and Corporation Secretary: (vacant)

University of Nebraska at Kearney

Kearney, NE 68849

Telephone: (308) 234-8208
Fax: (308) 234-8665

Founded 1903

Chancellor: Dr GLADYS STYLES JOHNSTON
Senior Vice-Chancellor for Academic Affairs: Dr JAMES ROARK
Vice-Chancellor for Student Affairs: Dr BARBARA SNYDER
Vice-Chancellor for Business and Finance: EARL E. RADEMACHER
Vice-Chancellor for University Relations: Dr WILLIAM R. LEWIS
Director of Libraries: MICHAEL HERBISON

Library of 228,625 vols
Number of teachers: 360 (f.t.e.)
Number of students: 8,045

DEANS

College of Fine Arts and Humanities: Dr HAROLD NICHOLS
College of Education: Dr JEAN RAMAGE
College of Natural and Social Sciences: Dr MICHAEL SCHUYLER
College of Business and Technology: Dr GALEN HADLEY
College of Continuing Education and External Programs: Dr BARBARA AUDLEY
College of Graduate Studies and Research: Dr KEN NIKELS

University of Nebraska—Lincoln

Lincoln, NE 68588

Telephone: (402) 472-2116
Fax: (402) 472-5110

Founded 1869

Chancellor: Dr JAMES MOESER
Senior Vice-Chancellor for Academic Affairs: Dr RICHARD EDWARDS
Vice-Chancellor for Student Affairs: Dr JAMES V. GRIESEN
NU Vice-President and Vice-Chancellor for Agriculture and Natural Resources: Dr IRVIN T. OMTVEDT
Director of Admissions: Dr LARRY R. ROUTH (acting)
Associate Vice-Chancellor for Information Services: KENT HENDRICKSON
Dean of Libraries: JOAN R. GIESECKE

Library: see Libraries
Number of teachers: 1,732 (full-time)
Number of students: 24,491

Publications: *Nebraska Law Review, University of Nebraska Studies, Nebraska Journal of Economics and Business, Prairie Schooner, University of Nebraska—Lincoln Daily Nebraskan.*

DEANS

College of Agricultural Sciences and Natural Resources: Dr DONALD M. EDWARDS
College of Architecture: W. CECIL STEWARD
College of Arts and Sciences: Dr BRIAN FOSTER
College of Business Administration: CYNTHIA H. MILLINGTON
College of Engineering and Technology: Dr JAMES HENDRIX
College of Human Resources and Family Sciences: Dr KAREN E. CRAIG
Graduate Studies: Dr MERLIN LAWSON
College of Law: NANCY RAPOPORT
Teachers' College: Dr JAMES P. O'HANLON
Division of Continuing Studies: Dr DONALD W. SWOBODA
College of Journalism: Dr WILL NORTON, Jr

University of Nebraska at Omaha

Omaha, NE 68182

Telephone: (402) 554-2311
Fax: (402) 554-3555

Founded 1908

Chancellor: Dr NANCY BLACK
Vice-Chancellor for Academic Affairs: Dr DEREK HODGSON
Vice-Chancellor for Business and Finance: GARY L. CARRICO
Vice-Chancellor for Student Services and Enrollment Management: Dr MARY A. MUDD
Vice-Chancellor for University Affairs and Communications: Dr JAMES R. BUCK
Registrar: WADE ROBINSON
Director of Admissions: JOHN J. FLEMMING
Librarian: JANICE S. BOYER

Library of 623,000 volumes and 1.7 million micro materials
Number of teachers: 519
Number of students: 15,899

Publications: *Gateway* (weekly), *Catalog* (annually).

DEANS

College of Arts and Sciences: Dr JOHN FLOCKEN
College of Business Administration: Dr STANLEY J. HILLE
College of Education: Dr RICHARD B. FLYNN
College of Continuing Studies: Dr MARY G. BRUNING
College of Human Resources and Family Sciences: Dr KAREN E. CRAIG
College of Public Affairs and Community Service: Dr DAVID W. HINTON
College of Fine Arts: Dr KAREN A. WHITE
Graduate Studies and Research: Dr CHRISTINE MARY REED
International Studies and Programs: THOMAS E. GOUTTIERRE

University of Nebraska Medical Center

42nd and Dewey Ave, Omaha, NE 68105

Telephone: (402) 559-4200
Fax: (402) 559-4396

Founded 1880

Chancellor: Dr WILLIAM O. BERNDT
Vice-Chancellor for Academic Affairs: Dr WILLIAM O. BERNDT
Vice-Chancellor for Business and Finance: DONALD S. LEUENBERGER
Director of Student Academic Services: Dr ARNOLD J. MENNING
Library Director: Dr NANCY N. WOELFL

Library of 196,313 vols
Number of teachers: 689
Number of students: 2,703

DEANS

Graduate Studies and Research: Dr DAVID A. CROUSE (interim)
College of Dentistry: Dr STEPHEN H. LEEPER
College of Medicine: Dr HAROLD M. MAURER
College of Pharmacy: Dr CLARENCE UEDA
College of Nursing: Dr ADA M. LINDSEY

ATTACHED INSTITUTIONS

Eppley Institute for Research in Cancer and Allied Diseases: Dir Dr BARRY GOLD (interim)
Meyer Rehabilitation Institute: Dir Dr BRUCE A. BUEHLER

WAYNE STATE COLLEGE

Wayne, NE 68787

Telephone: (402) 375-7000

Founded 1910

President: Dr DONALD J. MASH
Enrollment and Admissions: BONNIE SCRANTON
Librarian: STAN GARDNER

Library of 166,000 vols
Number of teachers: 166
Number of students: 4,000

NEVADA

UNIVERSITY AND COMMUNITY COLLEGE SYSTEM OF NEVADA

2601 Enterprise Road, Reno, NV 89512
Telephone: (702) 784-4901
Chancellor: RICHARD JARVIS

UNIVERSITY OF NEVADA, LAS VEGAS

4505 Maryland Parkway, Las Vegas, NV 89154-1021
Telephone: (702) 895-3011
Founded 1957
President: Dr CAROL C. HARTER
Provost: Dr DOUGLAS P. FERRARO
Vice-President for Finance and Administration: Dr NORVAL POHL
Vice-President for Student Services: Dr ROBERT ACKERMAN
Vice-President for University and Community Relations: FRED ALBRECHT
Registrar: JEFF HALVERSON
Dean of Enrollment Management: Dr JUANITA FAIN
Dean of Libraries: KENNETH MARKS
Library of 2,000,000 vols
Number of teachers: 612 (full-time), 447 (part-time)
Number of students: 20,272

DEANS

College of Business and Economics: Dr ELVIN LASHBROOKE
College of Hotel Administration: Dr DAVID CHRISTIANSON
College of Education: Dr JOHN READENCE
College of Health Sciences: Dr CAROLYN SABO
College of Law: Dr RICHARD MORGAN
College of Urban Affairs: Dr MARTHA WATSON
College of Liberal Arts: Dr JAMES FREY
College of Science and Mathematics: Dr RAYMOND ALDEN
College of Engineering: Dr WILLIAM WELLS
College of Fine Arts: Dr JEFF KOEP
College of Graduate Studies: Dr PENNY AMY
Honours College: Dr LEN JANE
Extended Studies: Dr PAUL AIZLEY

ATTACHED INSTITUTE

Desert Research Institute: 7010 El Barcho, Sparks, NV 89431; offices and laboratories in Reno, Stead, Las Vegas and Boulder City; research in energy, atmospheric environment, water resources, ecology, anthropology, socio-economics and demography; Pres. JAMES TARANIK.

UNIVERSITY OF NEVADA, RENO

Reno, NV 89557
Telephone: (702) 784-4636
Fax: (702) 784-1300
Founded 1874
President: JOSEPH N. CROWLEY
Vice-President for Administration and Finance: ASHOK K. DHINGRA
Vice-President for Academic Affairs: DAVID P. WESTFALL
Vice-President for University Advancement: PAUL A. PAGE
Vice-President for Student Services: PATRICIA K. MILTENBERGER
Registrar: MELISA N. CHOROSZY
Librarian: STEVEN ZINK
Library of 930,000 vols
Number of teachers: 649
Number of students: 12,000
Publications: *University Catalogue, Summer Sessions Bulletin, Independent Studies Bulletin, Scholarships and Prizes, Silver and Blue.*

DEANS

College of Agriculture: BERNARD M. JONES
College of Arts and Science: ROBERT MEAD
Extended Programs and Continuing Education: NEAL A. FERGUSON
College of Education: STEPHEN ROCK (acting)
College of Engineering: TED E. BATCHMAN
Graduate School: KENNETH W. HUNTER, Jr
College of Human and Community Sciences: JEAN PERRY
Mackay School of Mines: JANE C. S. LONG
School of Medicine: R. M. DAUGHERTY, Jr
College of Business Administration: H. MIKE REED
Orvis School of Nursing: JULIE JOHNSON (Dir)
School of Journalism: TRAVIS LINN (acting)

NEW HAMPSHIRE

DARTMOUTH COLLEGE

Hanover, NH 03755
Telephone: (603) 646-1110
Fax: (603) 646-2850
Founded 1769
Private control
President: JAMES O. FREEDMAN
Provost: LEE C. BOLLINGER
Vice-President for Development and Alumni Affairs: STANLEY A. COLLA, Jr
Registrar: THOMAS F. BICKEL
Dean of Admissions and Financial Aid: KARL M. FURSTENBERG
Librarian: MARGARET A. OTTO
Number of teachers: 430
Number of students: 4,700

DEANS

College: M. LEE PELTON
Faculty: JAMES WRIGHT
Freshmen: PETER D. GOLDSMITH
Medical School: ANDREW G. WALLACE
Thayer School of Engineering: ELSA GARMIRE
Amos Tuck School of Business Administration: PAUL P. DANOS

KEENE STATE COLLEGE

229 Main St, Keene, NH 03431
Telephone: (603) 352-1909
Founded 1909
President: STANLEY J. YAROSEWICK
Vice-President for Academic Affairs: ROBERT GOLDEN
Vice-President for Student Affairs: DELINA R. HICKEY
Vice-President for Finance and Planning: JAY V. KAHN
Librarian: PEGGY PARTELLO (acting)
Library of 258,181 vols
Number of teachers: 181
Number of students: 4,839

NEW ENGLAND COLLEGE

Henniker, NH 03242
Telephone: (603) 428-2211
Fax: (603) 428-7230
Founded 1946
President: JOHN S. MORRIS
Vice-President for Academic Affairs and Dean of Faculty: ZVI SZAFRAN
Registrar: FRANK L. HALL
Vice-President for Development: JEFFREY FULLER
Treasurer: ANN HARGRAVES
Vice-President for Student Development and Dean of Student Affairs: E. JOSEPH PETRICK
Director of Admissions: JOSEPH D. CONSIDINE
Librarian: (vacant)
Library of 103,000 vols
Number of teachers: 48
Number of students: 650

PLYMOUTH STATE COLLEGE

Plymouth, NH 03264
Telephone: (603) 535-5000
Fax: (603) 535-2654
E-mail: pscadmit@psc.plymouth.edu
Founded 1871
President: DONALD P. WHARTON
Dean of College: A. ROBIN BOWERS
Dean of Student Affairs: RICHARD T. HAGE
Director of Admissions: EUGENE FAHEY
Director of Financial Management: WILLIAM R. CRANGLE
Librarian: TODD TREVORROW
Library of 263,200 vols
Number of teachers: 168 full-time
Number of students: 4,228

RIVIER COLLEGE

Nashua, NH 03060
Telephone: (603) 888-1311
Founded 1933
President: Sister LUCILLE C. THIBODEAU
Vice-President for Academic Affairs: Sister THERESE LAROCHELLE
Vice-President for Student Development: LINDA JANSKY
Vice-President for Finance and Operations: JOSEPH A. FAGAN
Vice-President for Institutional Advancement: KENNETH P. BINDER
Librarian: Dr TRACEY LEGER-HORNBY
Library of 128,473 vols
Number of teachers: 71 full-time, 131 part-time
Number of students: 801 full-time, 2,127 part-time

DEANS

School of Arts and Sciences: Dr STEPHEN TRAINER
School of Professional Studies: Dr JUDITH HAYWOOD

SAINT ANSELM COLLEGE

100 St Anselm Drive, Manchester, NH 03102-1310
Telephone: (603) 641-7000
Fax: (603) 641-7116
Founded 1889
A liberal arts college with a baccalaureate program in nursing
President: Rev. JONATHAN DEFELICE
Dean of the College: Rev. PETER J. GUERIN
Registrar: MARY ANN ERICSON
Librarian: JOSEPH W. CONSTANCE, Jr
Library of 190,000 vols
Number of teachers: 117 full-time, 38 part-time
Number of students: 2,019

UNIVERSITY OF NEW HAMPSHIRE

Durham, NH 03824
Telephone: (603) 862-1234
Fax: (603) 862-3060
Founded 1866 as New Hampshire College of Agriculture and the Mechanic Arts, became university in 1923. In 1963, the State Colleges at Plymouth and Keene were added as separate campuses of the University System of New Hampshire. In 1985 Merrimack Valley College (est. 1967) became the University of New Hampshire at Manchester.
President: JOAN R. LEITZEL
Provost and Vice-President for Academic Affairs: WALTER EGGERS

Vice-President for Research and Public Service: DONALD C. SUNDBERG
Vice-President for Finance and Administration: CANDACE CORVEY
Vice-President for Student Affairs: LEILA MOORE
Registrar: WILLIAM MURPHY
Librarian: CLAUDIA MORNER

Library of 980,000 vols
Number of teachers: 589 (full-time)
Number of students: 12,400

Publications: *Catalog, Bulletin, Fact Sheet.*

DEANS

College of Life Sciences and Agriculture: WILLIAM MAUTZ
College of Liberal Arts: MARILYN HOSKIN
College of Engineering and Physical Sciences: ROY B. TORBERT
Graduate School: BRUCE MALLORY
School of Health and Human Services: RAYMOND COWARD
The Whittemore School of Business and Economics: J. BONNIE NEWMAN (interim)
University of New Hampshire at Manchester: KAROL LACROIX

NEW JERSEY

CALDWELL COLLEGE

9 Ryerson Ave, Caldwell, NJ 07006
Telephone: (973) 228-4424
Fax: (973) 228-2897
E-mail: mbackes@caldwell.edu

Founded 1939

President: Sister PATRICE WERNER
Registrar: Sister JUDITH RUDOLPH
Director of Library: LYNN RANDALL

Library of 116,000 volumes
Number of teachers: 130
Number of students: 1,131 f.t.e.

COLLEGE OF NEW JERSEY

POB 7718, Ewing, NJ 08628-0718
Telephone: (609) 771-1855

Founded 1855

President: HAROLD W. EICKHOFF
Vice-President for Academic Affairs: ANNE V. GORMLY
Vice-President for Administration and Finance: PETER L. MILLS
Vice-President for College Advancement: ALFRED BRIDGES
Vice-President for Student Life: (vacant)
Registrar: DONALD WORTHINGTON
Dean of the Library and Information Services: MARY BIGGS

Library of 450,000 vols
Number of teachers: 619
Number of students: 5,239 full-time, 1,467 part-time

DEANS

Arts and Sciences: Dr RICHARD KAMBER
Education: Dr SUZANNE PASCH
School of Business: Dr THOMAS BRESLIN (acting)
School of Technology: Dr ROBERT BITTNER
School of Nursing: Dr LAURIE SHERWEN
Graduate Studies: Dr SUZANNE PASCH

COLLEGE OF SAINT ELIZABETH

2 Convent Road, Morristown, NJ 07960-6989
Telephone: (973) 290-4000

Founded 1899

President: Sister FRANCIS RAFTERY
Dean of Studies: Dr JOHANNA GLAZEWSKI
Dean of Students: KATHERINE BUCK
Dean of Admissions and Financial Aid: DONNA YAMANIS
Librarian: Bro. PAUL CHERVENIE

Library of 188,000 vols
Number of teachers: 171
Number of students: 1,791

DON BOSCO COLLEGE

Swartswood Rd, Newton, NJ 07860
Telephone: (201) 383-3900

Founded 1928; primarily for men studying for the priesthood

President: Rev. KENNETH MCALICE
Dean of the College: Rev. DAVID G. MORENO
Treasurer: Rev. GENNARO SESTO

Library of 57,000 vols
Number of teachers: 20
Number of students: 50

DREW UNIVERSITY

Madison, NJ 07940
Telephone: (973) 408-3000
Fax: (973) 408-3080

Founded 1867

President: THOMAS H. KEAN
Vice-President for Administration: MARGARET E. L. HOWARD
Vice-President for Finance and Business: MICHAEL B. MCKITISH
Vice-President for Development: JOSEPH J. ANGELETTI, Jr
Registrar: HORACE TATE
Librarian: DEIRDRE STAM

Number of teachers: 200
Number of students: 2,127

Publication: *Drew Magazine.*

DEANS

College of Liberal Arts: PAOLO M. CUCCHI
Theological School: Dr LEONARD SWEET
Graduate School: JAMES PAIN

FAIRLEIGH DICKINSON UNIVERSITY

Teaneck, NJ 07666
Telephone: (201) 692-2000

Founded 1942

Campuses at Madison, NJ 07940 (tel. (201) 593-8500); Teaneck, NJ 07666 (tel. (201) 692-2000); and Wroxton, Oxon., England

President: FRANCIS J. MERTZ
Vice-President for Academic Affairs: Dr GEOFFREY WEINMAN
Vice-President for Institutional Advancement: Dr CHARLES R. DEES, Jr

Library of 650,000 vols
Number of teachers: 669
Number of students: 11,000

Publications: *The Literary Review, FDU Magazine, Journal of Psychology and the Behavioral Sciences.*

DEANS

Becton College of Arts and Sciences (Florham-Madison Campus): Dr PETER FALLEY
University College (Teaneck-Hackensack Campus): Dr DARIO CORTES
Silberman College of Business Administration: Dr PAUL LERMAN
Edward Williams College (Teaneck-Hackensack Campus): KENNETH T. VEHRKENS

INSTITUTE FOR ADVANCED STUDY

Olden Lane, Princeton, NJ 08540
Telephone: (609) 734-8000
Fax: (609) 924-8399

Founded 1930 for post-doctoral research in the fields of mathematics, theoretical physics, historical studies and social sciences

Private control
Academic year: September to April (two terms)

Chairman of the Board of Trustees: JAMES D. WOLFENSOHN
Director: PHILLIP A. GRIFFITHS
Librarians: MARCIA TUCKER, MOMOTA GANGULI

Library of 130,000 vols
Number of professors: 23
Number of visitors: *c.* 200

PROFESSORS

School of Historical Studies:

BOWERSOCK, G.
CONSTABLE, G.
CRONE, P.
GRABAR, O.
HABICHT, C.
LAVIN, I.
PARET, P.
VON STADEN, H.

School of Mathematics:

BOMBIERI, E.
BOURGAIN, J.
DELIGNE, P.
LANGLANDS, R.
MACPHERSON, R.
SPENCER, T.

School of Natural Sciences:

ADLER, S.
BAHCALL, J. N.
HUT, P.
SEIBERG, N.
WILCZEK, F.
WITTEN, E.

School of Social Science:

GEERTZ, C.
SCOTT, J.
WALZER, M.

JERSEY CITY STATE COLLEGE

2039 Kennedy Blvd, Jersey City, NJ 07305
Telephone: (201) 547-6000

Founded 1927

President: WILLIAM J. MAXWELL
Vice-President for Academic Affairs: Dr CARLOS HERNANDEZ
Vice-President for Development and Public Affairs: JOHN NEVIN
Vice-President for Student Affairs: JULIAN ROBINSON
Vice-President for Administration and Finance: EDWIN WEISMAN
Registrar: P. LA ROCHE
Director of Admissions: SAM MCGHEE
Chairman of Department of Library Services: R. NUGENT

Library of 250,000 vols
Number of teachers: 285
Number of students: 7,000

DEANS

Arts and Sciences: Dr JOSEPH WEISBERG
Professional Studies and Education: Dr FRED MEANS
Students: Dr MARCO CIRINCION

KEAN COLLEGE OF NEW JERSEY

Morris Ave, Union, NJ 07083
Telephone: (908) 527-2000

Founded 1855, present name 1973

Schools of: Education; Liberal Arts; Natural Sciences, Nursing and Mathematics; Business, Government and Technology

President: RONALD APPLBAUM
Academic Vice-President: SANDRA MARK
Vice-President of Academic Affairs: PATRICK COUGHLIN
Vice-President of Student Services: PATRICK J. IPPOLITO

Library of 270,000 vols
Number of teachers: 349 full-time, 11 part-time, 555 adjunct faculty
Number of students: 11,746

MONMOUTH UNIVERSITY

West Long Branch, NJ 07764-1898
Telephone: (732) 571-3400
Founded 1933
An independent, co-educational, non-sectarian, comprehensive university
President: REBECCA STAFFORD
Provost and Senior Vice-President for Academic Affairs: THOMAS PEARSON
Vice-President for Enrollment: MIRIAM E. KING
Librarian: SUSAN KUYHENDALL
Library of 252,500 vols, 1,250 periodicals
Number of teachers: 397 full-time and part-time
Number of students: 4,037 undergraduates, and 1,274 graduate students

MONTCLAIR STATE UNIVERSITY

Upper Montclair, NJ 07043
Telephone: (973) 655-4000
Fax: (973) 655-5455
Founded 1908
Liberal arts and professional studies
President: Dr GREGORY WATERS (interim)
Vice-President for Academic Affairs and Provost: Dr RICHARD A. LYNDE
Vice-President for Business and Finance: Dr PATRICIA HEWITT
Vice-President for Institutional Advancement: Dr GREGORY WATERS (acting)
Vice-President for Student Development and Campus Life: Dr KAREN PENNINGTON
Librarian: Dr JUDITH LIN HUNT
Library of 419,000 vols, 3,500 periodicals
Number of teachers: 472
Number of students: 12,993

NEW JERSEY INSTITUTE OF TECHNOLOGY

University Heights, 323 Martin Luther King Blvd, Newark, NJ 07102-1982
Telephone: (973) 596-3000
Fax: (973) 642-4380
E-mail: information@njit.edu
Founded 1881
President: SAUL K. FENSTER
Provost and Senior Vice-President for Academic Affairs: GARY THOMAS
Senior Vice-President for Administration, and Treasurer: HENRY MAUERMEYER
Vice-President for Research: ROBERT PFEFFER
Vice-President for Academic and Student Services: JOEL BLOOM
Vice-President for Development: JUDITH BOYD (acting)
Librarian: RICHARD T. SWEENEY
Library of 181,000 vols
Number of teachers: 354, part-time 233
Number of students: 7,837

DEANS

School of Architecture: URS GAUCHAT
College of Engineering: STEPHEN TRICAMO (acting)
School of Management: ALOK CHAKRABARTI
College of Science and Liberal Arts: JOHN POATE

HEADS OF DEPARTMENTS

Humanities and Social Sciences: N. ELLIOT
Civil and Environmental Engineering: W. SPILLERS
Chemical Engineering, Chemistry and Environmental Science: G. LEWANDOWSKI
Electrical and Computer Engineering: R. HADDAD
Mechanical Engineering: B. KOPLIK
Computer and Information Science: (vacant)
Mathematics: D. AHLUWALIA
Physics: A. JOHNSON
Aerospace Studies: Lt-Col W. CRAVER
Architecture: U. GAUCHAT
Industrial and Manufacturing Engineering: P. RANKY

PRINCETON UNIVERSITY

Princeton, NJ 08544
Telephone: (609) 258-3000
Founded 1746 as the College of New Jersey, became Princeton University 1896
Academic year: September to May
President: HAROLD T. SHAPIRO
Provost: JEREMIAH P. OSTRIKER
Financial Vice-President: RICHARD SPIES
Vice-President for Development: VAN ZANDT WILLIAMS, Jr
Vice-President for Public Affairs: ROBERT K. DURKEE
Vice-President for Facilities: EUGENE MCPARTLAND
Vice-President for Computing and Information Technology: IRA FUCHS
Vice-President for Human Resources: JOAN DOIG
Vice-President and Secretary: T. H. WRIGHT, Jr
Controller: HENRY J. MORPHY
Registrar: ANTHONY BROH
Librarian: KARIN TRAINER
Library: see Libraries
Number of teachers: 790 full-time
Number of students: 4,593 undergraduates, 1,747 graduates

Publications: *Annals of Mathematics* (every 2 months), *Library Chronicle, Population Index* (quarterly), *Princeton Weekly Bulletin, Record of the Art Museum* (2 a year), *World Politics* (quarterly). Publ. by Princeton University Press: *Philosophy and Public Affairs* (quarterly), *Princeton Alumni Weekly.*

DEANS

Faculty: JOSEPH TAYLOR
College: NANCY MALKIEL
Students: JANINA MONTERO
Graduate School: JOHN F. WILSON
School of Engineering and Applied Science: JAMES WEI
Admission: FRED HARGADON
Woodrow Wilson School of Public and International Affairs: MICHAEL ROTHSCHILD
School of Architecture and Urban Planning: RALPH LERNER
Religious Life and Chapel: JOSEPH C. WILLIAMSON

DIRECTORS

Industrial Relations Section: HENRY FARBER
Art Museum: A. ROSENBAUM
Plasma Physics Laboratory: ROBERT B. GOLDSTON
Index of Christian Art: JAMES MARROW
International Finance Section: P. B. KENEN
Shelby Cullom Davis Center for Historical Studies: WILLIAM JORDAN
Center of International Studies: (vacant)
University Research Board: SAM TREIMAN
University Health Services: PAMELA BOWEN
Office of Population Research: JAMES TRUSSELL
Econometric Research Program: G. C. CHOW
Center for Energy and Environmental Studies: R. H. SOCOLOW
Financial Research Center: BURTON MALKIEL
Princeton Urban and Regional Research Center: R. P. NATHAN
East Asian Linguistics Project: CHIH-PING CHOU
Geophysical Fluid Dynamics Program: JORGE SARMIENTO
Papers of Woodrow Wilson: ARTHUR S. LINK
Research Program in Criminal Justice: JAMESON W. DOIG
Research Program in Development Studies: JOHN P. LEWIS
Center for Human Values: GEORGE KATEB

PROFESSORS

AARSLEFF, H. C., English
ABBATE, C., Music
ABIEU, D. J., Economics
ACTON, F. S., Electrical Engineering and Computer Science
ADLER, S. L., Physics
ADORNO, R., Romance Languages and Literatures
AIZENMAN, M., Physics
AKSAY, I., Chemical Engineering
ALLEN, L. C., Chemistry
ALMGREN, F. J., Mathematics
ALYEA, H. N., Chemistry
ANDERSON, P. W., Physics
ARNOLD, R. D., Politics and Public Affairs
ASHBY, P. H., Religion
ASHENFELTER, O. C., Economics
ATKINS, S. D., Classics
AUSTIN, R. H., Physics
AXTMANN, R. C., Chemical Engineering
BABBITT, M. B., Music
BABBY, L. H., Slavic Language and Literature
BAHCALL, N., Astrophysical Science
BANKS, R. E., Council of Humanities and Creative Writing
BATES, B. W., Romance Languages and Literatures
BAUMOL, W. J., Economics
BENACERRAF, P., Philosophy
BENTLEY, G. E., English Literature
BENZIGER, J. B., Chemical Engineering
BERNANKE, B., Economics and Public Affairs
BERNASEK, S. L., Chemistry
BERNHEIM, B. D., Economics
BERRY, C. H., Economics and Public Affairs
BHATT, R. N., Electrical Engineering
BILLINGTON, D. P., Civil Engineering
BLEAKNEWY, W., Physics
BLINDER, A. S., Economics
BOGDONOFF, S. M., Aeronautical, Mechanical and Aerospace Engineering
BONINI, W. E., Geophysics and Geological Engineering, Civil Engineering
BONNER, J. T., Biology
BOON, J. A., Anthropology
BOWEN, W. G., Economics and Public Affairs
BOYER, M. C., Architecture
BRACCO, F., Mechanical and Aerospace Engineering
BRADFORD, D. F., Economics and Public Affairs
BRANSON, W. H., Economics and International Affairs
BRESSLER, M., Sociology
BROACH, J. R., Molecular Biology
BROADIE, S. W., Philosophy
BROMBERT, V. H., Romance Languages and Literatures and Comparative Literature
BROWDER, W., Mathematics
BROWN, C. F., Jr, Comparative Literature
BROWN, G. L., Mechanical and Aerospace Engineering
BROWN, L. C., Near Eastern Studies
BROWN, P. F., Art and Archaeology
BROWN, P. R., History
BRYAN, K., Geological and Geophysical Sciences and Atmospheric and Oceanic Sciences
BUNNELL, P. C., History of Photography and Modern Art; Art and Archaeology
BURGESS, J. P., Philosophy
BURGI, R. T., Slavic Languages and Literatures
CAKMAK, A. S., Civil Engineering
CALAPRICE, F. P., Physics
CALLAN, C. G., Jr, Physics
CAMPBELL, B. A., Psychology

CAMPBELL, J. Y., Economics; Economics and Public Affairs
CANTOR, N. E., Psychology
CARD, D. E., Economics
CARRASACO, D., Religion
CHAIKIN, P. M., Physics
CHALLENER, R. D., History
CHAMPLIN, E. J., Humanities; Classics
CHANCES, E. B., Slavic Languages and Literatures
CHASE, A. M., Biology
CHAZELLE, B. M., Computer Science
CHENG, S. I., Aeronautical Engineering
CHILDS, W. A. P., Art and Archaeology
CHOU, C.-P., East Asian Studies
CHOW, G. C., Economics, Political Economy
CHRISTODOULOU, D., Mathematics
CHURCH, A., Mathematics
CINLAR, E., Civil Engineering
CLARK, D., Computer Sciences
CLARK, R. J., Art and Archaeology
CLINTON, J. W., Near Eastern Studies
COALE, A. J., Economics and Public Affairs
COFFIN, D. R., Art and Archaeology
COHEN, M. R., Near Eastern Studies
COHEN, S. F., Politics
COLLCUTT, M. C., East Asian Studies
COLQUHOUN, A. H., Architecture
CONE, E. T., Music
CONNOR, W. R., Classics
CONWAY, J. H., Applied and Computational Mathematics
COOPER, J., Psychology
COOPER, J. M., Philosophy
CORNGOLD, S. A., Germanic Languages
COX, E. C., Biology
CRABB, D. W., Anthropology
CRERAR, D. A., Geological and Geophysical Sciences
CROSBY, H., Jr, Mechanical and Aerospace Engineering
ĆURČIĆ, S., Art and Archaeology
CURSCHMANN, M. J. H., Germanic Languages
DAHLEN, F. A., Geological and Geophysical Sciences
DANIELSON, M. N., Politics and Public Affairs
DANSON, L. N., English
DARLEY, J. M., Psychology
DARNTON, R. C., History
DAVIES, H. M., Religion
DAVIS, N. Z., History
DEATON, A. S., Economics and International Affairs
DEFFEYES, K. S., Geological and Geophysical Sciences
DIAMOND, M. L., Religion
DÍAZ-QUIÑONES, A., Romance Languages and Literatures
DI BATTISTA, M. A., English and Comparative Literature
DICKINSON, B. W., Electrical Engineering
DICKSON, M. B., Near Eastern Studies
DIIULIO, J. J., Politics and Public Affairs
DILLIARD, I., Journalism and Public Relations
DIMAGGIO, P. J., Sociology
DISMUKES, G. C., Chemistry
DIXIT, A. K., Economics and International Affairs
DOBKIN, D. P., Electrical Engineering and Computer Science
DOIG, J. W., Politics and Public Affairs
DOWNS, G. W., Politics
DOYLE, M. W., Public and International Affairs
DRAINE, B. T., Astrophysical Sciences
DRYER, F. L., Mechanical and Aerospace Engineering
DURBIN, E. J., Mechanical and Aerospace Engineering
DWORK, B. M., Mathematics
EBERT, R. P., Germanic Languages and Literatures
EISENBERGER, P. M., Physics
EMERSON, C. G., Slavic Languages and Literatures
ENGELSTEIN, L., History
ERINGEN, A. C., Civil Engineering
ERMOLAEV, H., Slavic Languages and Literatures
ESPENSHADE, T. J., Sociology
FAGLES, R., Comparative Literature
FALK, R. A., International Law, Politics, and International Affairs
FALTINGS, G., Mathematics
FANTHAM, R. E., Latin
FARBER, H. S., Economics
FEFFERMAN, C., Mathematics
FISCH, N. J., Astrophysical Sciences
FITCH, V. L., Physics
FLEMING, J. V., English and Comparative Literature
FLINT, S. J., Molecular Biology
FONG, W. C., Art History, Art and Archaeology
FORCIONI, A., Comparative Literature
FORREST, S. R., Electrical Engineering
FRANK, J. N., Comparative Literature
FRANKFURT, H. G., Philosophy
FRASSICA, P., Romance Languages and Literatures
FREEDMAN, R. W. B., Comparative Literature
FRESCO, J. R., Life Sciences
FURLEY, D. J., Greek Language and Literature, Classics
FURTH, H. P., Astrophysical Sciences
GAGER, J. G., Jr, Religion
GANDELSONAS, M. I., Architecture
GARVEY, G., Politics
GEDDES, R. L., Architecture
GEERTZ, H., Anthropology
GEISON, G. L., History and History of Science
GIBBS, N., Journalism and Council of Humanities
GILLHAM, J. K., Chemical Engineering
GILLISPIE, C. C., History, History of Science
GILPIN, R. G., Politics and International Affairs
GILVARG, C., Biochemical Sciences
GIRGUS, J. S., Psychology
GLASSMAN, I., Mechanical and Aerospace Engineering
GLUCKSBERG, S., Psychology
GOHEEN, R. F., Classics
GOLDFELD, S. M., Economics and Banking
GOLDMAN, M. P., English
GOLDMAN, N. J., Demography and Public Affairs
GOLDSTON, R. J., Astrophysical Sciences
GORDENKER, L., Politics
GOSSMAN, J. L., Romance Languages and Literatures
GOTT, J. R., III, Astrophysical Sciences
GOTTLIEB, M. B., Astrophysical Sciences
GOULD, J. L., Biology
GOWA, J., Politics
GRAESSLEY, W. W., Chemical Engineering
GRAFTON, A. T., History
GRANT, P., Biology
GRAVES, M., Architecture
GREENSTEIN, F. I., Politics
GROSS, C. G., Psychology
GROSS, D. J., Physics
GROSSMAN, G. M., Economics and Business Policy
GROTH, E. J., III, Physics
GROVES, J. T., Chemistry
GRUNER, S. M., Physics
GUNN, J. E., Astronomy
GUNNING, R. C.
GUTMAN, R., Architecture
GUTMANN, A., Politics
HALDANE, F. D. M., Physics
HALPERN, M., Politics
HAMMOUDI, A., Anthropology and Near East Studies
HAMORI, A. P., Near Eastern Studies
HAPPER, W., Physics
HARGRAVES, R. B., Geological and Geophysical Sciences
HARMAN, G. H., Philosophy
HARTOG, H. A., History
HAYES, W. D., Mechanical and Aerospace Engineering
HAZEN, D. C., Mechanical and Aerospace Engineering
HELD, I. M., Geological and Geophysical Sciences, Atmospheric and Oceanic Sciences
HEMPEL, C. G., Philosophy
HERRIN, J. E., History
HINDERER, W., Germanic Languages and Literatures
HOCHSCHILD, J. L., Politics and Public Affairs
HOEBEL, B. G., Psychology
HOFFMANN, L.-F., Romance Languages
HOLLANDER, R. B., Jr, European and Comparative Literature
HOLLISTER, L. S., Geological and Geophysical Sciences
HOLMES, P. J., Mechanical and Aerospace Engineering
HOOG, A., French Literature
HORN, H. S., Biology
HOWARTH, W. L., English
HSIANG, W.-C., Mathematics
HUBBELL, S. P., Ecology and Evolutionary Biology
HUNT, G. A., Mathematics
HUNTER, J. S., Civil Engineering
HUNTER, S., Art and Archaeology
HYNES, S., English
IRBY, J. E., Romance Languages and Literatures
ISSAWI, C., Near Eastern Studies
ITZKOWITZ, N., Near Eastern Studies
IWASAWA, K., Mathematics
JACKSON, R., Chemical Engineering
JACOBS, B. L., Psychology
JACOBS, W. P., Biology
JAFFEE, D. M., Economics
JAHN, R. G., Aerospace Sciences
JAMESON, A., Mechanical and Aerospace Engineering
JANDL, H. A., Architecture
JANSEN, M. B., History and East Asian Studies
JEFFREY, P., Music
JEFFREY, R., Philosophy
JEMMOTT, J. B., Psychology
JOHNSON, E. D. H., Belles-Lettres
JOHNSON, E. F., Chemical Engineering
JOHNSON, F. H., Biology
JOHNSON, M., Psychology
JOHNSON-LAIRD, P. N., Psychology
JOHNSTON, M., Philosophy
JONES, E. E., Psychology
JONES, M., Chemistry
JORDON, W. C., History
JUDSON, S., Geography, Geological and Geophysical Sciences
KAHN, A., Electrical Engineering
KAHN, V. A., English and Comparative Literature
KAHNEMAN, D., Psychology
KAO, Y. K., East Asian Studies
KARNEY, C. F. F., Astrophysical Sciences
KATEB, G., Politics
KATZ, N. M., Mathematics
KAUFMANN, T. D., Art and Archaeology
KAUZMANN, W. J., Chemistry
KEANEY, J. J., Classics
KEELEY, E. L., English and Creative Arts
KELLER, G., Geological and Geophysical Sciences
KELLER, S., Sociology
KELLEY, M., English
KELLEY, S., Politics
KENEN, P. B., Economics and International Finance
KERNAN, A. B., English
KINCHLA, R. A., Psychology
KING, E. L., Language, Literature, and Civilization of Spain
KLAINERMAN, S., Mathematics
KLOR DE ALVA, J. J., Anthropology
KNAPP, G. R., Astrophysical Sciences
KNAPP, J. M., Music
KNOEPFLMACHER, U. C., English
KOBAYASHI, H., Electrical Engineering and Computer Science
KOCH, R. A., Art and Archaeology
KOCHEN, S. B., Mathematics
KOHLI, A., Politics and International Affairs

KOHN, J. J., Mathematics
KORNHAUSER, A. L., Civil Engineering
KOSTIN, M. D., Chemical Engineering
KRIPKE, S., Philosophy
KROMMES, J. A., Astrophysical Sciences
KRUSKAL, M. D., Mathematics and Astrophysical Sciences
KUENNE, R. E., Economics
KUHN, H. W., Mathematical Economics
KULSRUD, R., Astrophysical Sciences
KUNG, S.-Y., Electrical Engineering
KURIHARA, Y., Geological and Geophysical Sciences
LAKE, P. G., History
LAKS, A., Classics
LAM, S.-H., Mechanical and Aerospace Engineering
LANGE, V., Modern Languages
LANSKY, P., Music
LAW, C. K., Mechanical and Aerospace Engineering
LEE, P. C. Y., Civil Engineering
LEIBLER, S., Physics and Molecular Biology
LEMONICK, A., Physics
LERNER, R., Architecture
LESTER, R. A., Economics
LEVIN, S. A., Ecology and Evolutionary Biology
LEVINE, A. J., Molecular Biology
LEVY, K., Music
LEVY, M. J., Jr, Sociology and International Affairs
LEWIS, B., Near Eastern Studies
LEWIS, D. K., Philosophy
LEWIS, J. P., Economics and International Affairs
LEWIS, W. A., Economics and International Affairs
LIEB, E. H., Mathematical Physics
LINK, A. S., American History
LINK, E. P., East Asian Studies
LIPTON, R. J., Computer Science
LISK, R. D., Biology
LITZ, A. W., Jr, Belles-Lettres and English
LIU, B., Electrical Engineering
LIU, J. T. C., East Asian Studies
LO, A. W., Electrical Engineering
LOCKARD, W. D., Politics
LOWRY, H. N., Ottoman and Modern Turkish Studies
LUCE, T. J., Jr, Latin Language and Literature, Classics
LUCHAK, G., Civil Engineering
LUDWIG, R. M., English
LUKER, K. C., Sociology
LYON, S. A., Electrical Engineering
MAHLMAN, J. D., Geological and Geophysical Sciences and Atmospheric and Oceanic Sciences
MAHONEY, M. S., History and History of Science
MAJDA, A. J., Mathematics
MAKINO, S., East Asian Studies
MALKIEL, B. G., Economics
MALKIEL, N. W., History
MAMAN, A., French, Romance Languages and Literatures
MANABE, S., Geological and Geophysical Sciences and Atmospheric and Oceanic Sciences
MARK, R., Civil Engineering and Architecture
MARKS, J. H., Near Eastern Studies
MARROW, J. H., Art and Archaeology
MARTIN, E., Anthropology
MARTIN, J. R., Art and Archaeology
MARTIN, R. B., English
MATHER, J. N., Mathematics
MAXWELL, B., Chemical Engineering
MAXWELL, R. M., Architecture
MAYER, A. J., History
MCCLURE, D. S., Chemistry
MCDONALD, K. T., Physics
MCFARLAND, T., English Literature
MCLANAHAN, S. S., Sociology and Public Affairs
MCLAUGHLIN, D. W., Mathematics
MCPHEE, J. A., Journalism and Public Relations
MCPHERSON, J. M., History
MELLOR, G. L., Mechanics, Mechanical and Aerospace Dynamics
MEYER, H., Art and Archaeology
MEYER, K. E., Writing and Council of Humanities
MIGDAL, A. A., Physics
MILES, R. B., Mechanical and Aerospace Engineering
MILLER, D. T., Psychology
MILLER, G. A., Psychology
MILLER, H. K., English
MINER, E., English and Comparative Literature
MISLOW, K., Chemistry
MITCHELL, L. G., English
MIYAKODA, K., Civil Engineering, Geological and Geophysical Sciences
MODARRESSI, H., Near Eastern Studies
MOORE, J. C., Mathematics
MORGAN, W. J., Geophysics
MORRISON, T., Humanities
MOTE, F. W., East Asian Studies
MOULTON, W. G., Linguistics and Germanic Languages and Literatures
MULVEY, J. M., Civil Engineering
MURPHY, W. F., Jurisprudence, Politics
MURRIN, J. M., History
NASH, S. C., Romance Languages and Literature
NAUMANN, R. A., Chemistry and Physics
NAVROTSKY, A., Geology
NEHAMAS, A., Humanities, Philosophy and Comparative Literature
NELSON, J., Mathematics
NEWTON, W. A., Molecular Biology
NOLET, A. M., Geological and Geophysical Sciences
NOLLNER, W. L., Music
NOTTERMAN, J. M., Psychology
OATES, J. C., Humanities
OBER, J., Classics
OBEYESEKERE, G., Anthropology
OKUDA, H., Astrophysical Sciences
O'NEILL, G. K., Physics
ONG, N.-P., Physics
ONO, M., Astrophysical Sciences
OORT, A. H., Geological and Geophysical Sciences and Atmospheric and Oceanic Sciences
ORLANSKI, I., Geological and Geophysical Sciences and Atmospheric and Oceanic Sciences
ORSZAG, S. A., Mechanical and Aerospace Engineering
OSTRIKER, J. P., Astrophysical Sciences
PACALA, S., Ecology
PACZYNSKI, B., Astrophysical Sciences
PAGELS, E. H., Religion
PAINTER, N. I., History
PAVEL, T., Comparative Literature and Romance Languages and Literatures
PEEBLES, P. J. E, Physics
PERKINS, C. D., Aerospace and Mechanical Sciences
PERKINS, F. W., Jr, Astrophysical Sciences
PETERSON, W. J., East Asian Studies
PHILANDER, S. G. H., Geological and Geophysical Sciences
PHINNEY, R. A., Geological and Geophysical Sciences
PINTO, J. A., Art and Archaeology
PIROUÉ, P. A., Physics
PITCHER, G. W., Philosophy
PLAKS, A. H., East Asian Studies
PLUMMER, J. H., Art and Archaeology
POLYAKOV, A., Physics
POOR, H. V., Electrical Engineering
POWELL, J. L., Economics
POWELL, W. B., Civil Engineering
POWERS, H. S., Music
PRELLER, V. S., Religion
PREVOST, J.-H., Civil Engineering
PRUCNAL, P. R., Electrical Engineering
PRUDHOMME, P. R., Chemical and Electrical Engineering
QUANDT, R. E., Economics
RABB, T. K., History
RABITZ, H. A., Chemistry
RABOTEAU, A. J., Religion
RAMPERSAD, A., Literature, English
RANDALL, J. K., Music
RAPKIN C., Architecture
REBENFELD, L., Chemical Engineering
REINHARDT, U. E., Economics and Public Affairs, Political Economy
REYNOLDS. G. T., Physics
RIGOLOT, F., Romance Languages and Literatures
ROCHE, T. P., Jr, English
RODGERS, D. T., History
ROGERSON, J. B., Jr, Astrophysical Sciences
ROGOFF, K., Economics and International Affairs
ROMER, T., Politics and Public Affairs
ROSE, M. D., Molecular Biology
ROSEN, H. S., Economics
ROSEN, L., Anthropology
ROSENTHAL, H., Social Sciences
ROSS, A., English
ROYCE, B. S. H., Mechanical and Aerospace Engineering
ROZMAN, G. F., Sociology
RUBENSTEIN, A., Economics
RUBENSTEIN, D. I., Ecology and Evolutionary Biology
RUDENSTEIN, N., English
RUSSEL, W. B., Chemical Engineering
RUTHERFORD, P. H., Astrophysical Sciences
RYAN, A. J., Politics
RYDER, N. B., Sociology
RUSKAMP, C. A., English
SANDERSON, W. C., Public and International Affairs
SARMIENTO, J. L., Geological and Geophysical Sciences
SARNAK, P. C., Mathematics
SAVILLE, D. A., Chemical Engineering
SCANLAN, R. H., Civil Engineering
SCANLON, R. H., Civil Engineering
SCHEDL, P. D., Molecular Biology
SCHORSKE, C. E., History
SCHWARTZ, J., Chemistry
SCHWARTZ, S. C., Electrical Engineering
SCOLES, G., Chemistry
SEAWRIGHT, J. L., Council of Humanities
SEDGEWICK, R., Computer Science
SEMMELHACK, M. F., Chemistry
SHEAR, T. L., Jr, Classical Archaeology
SHENK, T. E., Molecular Biology
SHERR, R., Physics
SHIMADA, S., Art and Archaeology
SHIMIZU, Y., Art and Archaeology
SHIMURA, G., Mathematics
SHINOZUKA, M., Civil Engineering
SHOEMAKER, F. C., Physics
SHOWALTER, E., English
SIGMUND, P. E., Politics
SILHAVY, T. J., Molecular Biology
SILVER, L. M., Molecular Biology
SINAI, Y. G., Mathematics
SITNEY, P. A., Council of Humanities
SLABY, S. M., Civil Engineering
SMITH, A. J., Physics
SMITH, J. W., Philosophy
SMITS, A., Mechanical and Aerospace Engineering
SMOLUCHOWSKI, R., Solid State Sciences
SOANES, S., Philosophy
SOCOLOW, R. H., Mechanical and Aerospace Engineering
SOLLENBERGER, N. S., Civil Engineering
SOOS, Z. G., Chemistry
SPENCER, D. C., Mathematics
SPIES, C. C., Music
SPIRO, T. G., Chemistry
SPITZER, L., Jr, Astronomy
STARR, P., Sociology
STEIGLITZ, K., Computer Science
STEIN, E. M., Mathematics
STEIN, S. J., History
STEINBERG, M., Biology

STENGEL, R. F., Mechanical and Aerospace Engineering
STIX, T. H., Astrophysical Sciences
STOCK, J. B., Molecular Biology
STOKES, D. E., Politics and Public Affairs
STONE, L., History
STOUT, J. L., Religion
SUBIRATS, E., Romance Languages and Literature
SUCKEWER, S., Mechanical and Aerospace Engineering
SULEIMAN, E. N., Politics
SULLIVAN, E. D., Humanities
SUMMERFIELD, M., Aeronautical Engineering
SUNDARESAN, S., Chemical Engineering
SUPPE, J. E., Geological and Geophysical Sciences
SURBER, W. H., Jr, Electrical Engineering
SURTZ, R. E., Romance Languages and Literatures
SZATHMARY, A., Philosophy
TANG, W. M., Astrophysical Sciences
TARJAN, R. E., Computer Science
TAYLOR, E. C., Chemistry
TAYLOR, H. F., Sociology
TAYLOR, J. H., Physics
THOMAS, J. B., Electrical Engineering
TIGNOR, R. L., History
TILGHMAN, S. M., Biology
TORQUATO, S., Civil Engineering
TOWNSEND, C. E., Slavic Languages and Literatures
TREIMAN, S. B., Physics
TREISMAN, A., Psychology
TROTTER, H. F., Mathematics
TRUSSELL, T. J., Economics and Public Affairs
TSUI, D. C., Electrical Engineering
TUCKER, A. W., Mathematics
TUCKER, R. C., International Studies
TUKEY, J. W., Science, Statistics
TUMIN, M. M., Sociology and Anthropology
TURKEVICH, J. N., Chemistry
TURNER, E. L., Astrophysical Sciences
TWITCHETT, D., East Asian Studies
UDOVITCH, A. L., Near Eastern Studies
UITTI, K. D., Modern Languages, Romance Languages and Literatures
ULLMAN, R., International Affairs
ULMER, B., Germanic Languages and Literature
VAN DE VELDE, R. W., Public and International Affairs
VAN FRAASSEN, B. C., Philosophy
VAN HOUTEN, F. B., Geological and Geophysical Sciences
VANMARCKE, E., Civil Engineering
VERDU, S., Electrical Engineering
VIDLER, A., Architecture
VOLKER, P. A., International and Economic Policy
VON GOELER, S. E., Astrophysical Sciences
VON HIPPEL, F. N., Public and International Affairs
WAGNER, S., Electrical Engineering
WALKER, T. R., Music
WALLACE, W. L., Sociology
WARREN, K. B., Anthropology
WARREN, S., Chemistry
WASHNITZER, G., Mathematics
WATERBURY, J., Politics and International Affairs
WATSON, G. S., Statistics
WEIGERT, M., Molecular Biology
WEISS, T. R., English and Creative Writing
WEITZMANN, K., Art and Archaeology
WEST, C. R., Religion
WESTERGAARD, P. T., Music
WESTOFF, C. F., Sociology, Demographic Studies
WHEELER, J. A.
WHITE, L. T., Politics
WHITE, R. B., Astrophysical Sciences
WHITWELL, J. C., Chemical Engineering
WIESCHAUS, E. F., Biology
WIGHTMAN, A. S., Mathematical Physics
WIGNER, E. P., Mathematical Physics
WILENTZ, R. S., History
WILES, A. J., Mathematics
WILKINSON, D. T., Physics
WILLIAMS, E. S., Humanities
WILLIG, R. D., Economics and Public Affairs
WILLIS, J. R., Near Eastern Studies
WILMERDING, J., American Art; Art and Archaeology
WILSON, J. F., Religion
WILSON, M. D., Philosophy
WISE, M. N., History
WOLFSON, S. J., English
WOLIN, S. S., Politics
WOLPERT, J., Geography, Public Affairs and Urban Planning
WOOD, E. F., Civil Engineering
WUTHNOW, R. J., Sociology
YAO, A. L.-L., Computer Science
YOSHIKAWA, S., Astrophysical Sciences
YU, Y. S., East Asian Studies
ZEITLIN, F. I., Classics
ZELIZER, V. A., Sociology
ZIOLKOWSKI, T. J., Germanic Languages and Literatures and Comparative Literature

RIDER UNIVERSITY

2083 Lawrenceville Rd, Lawrenceville, NJ 08648-3099

Telephone: (609) 896-5000
Fax: (609) 896-8029

Founded 1865

President: Dr J. BARTON LUEDEKE
Vice-President for Academic Affairs and Provost: (vacant)
Vice-President for Student Affairs: JAMES MCROBERTS
Vice-President for Development: NANCY GRAY
Dean of University Libraries: ELIZABETH S. SMITH

Library of 350,000 vols
Number of teachers: 200
Number of students: 5,519

ROWAN COLLEGE OF NEW JERSEY

Glassboro, NJ 08028

Telephone: (609) 256-4000

Founded 1923

President: HERMAN D. JAMES
Executive Vice-President and Provost: DONALD L. GEPHARDT (acting)
Registrar: EDWIN EIGENBROT
Librarian: (vacant)

Library of 339,000 vols
Number of teachers: 292
Number of students: 9,368

RUTGERS UNIVERSITY

POB 2101, New Brunswick, NJ 08903

Telephone: (908) 932-1766

Founded as Queen's College by Royal Charter 1766, name changed to Rutgers College 1825, Rutgers University 1924. Designated by legislature as State University of New Jersey 1945

Academic year: September to May

President: FRANCIS L. LAWRENCE
Senior Vice-President and Treasurer: JOSEPH P. WHITESIDE
Vice-President for Academic Affairs: JOSEPH SENECA
Vice-President for Institutional Research, Planning and Computing: CHRISTINE M. HASKA
Vice-President for Public Affairs and Development: DONALD B. EDWARDS
Vice-President for University Budgeting: NANCY S. WINTERBAUER
Vice-President for Administration and Associate Treasurer: RICHARD M. NORMAN
Vice-President for Undergraduate Education: SUSAN G. FORMAN
Vice-President for Student Affairs: ROSELLE L. WILSON
Vice-President for Research: JIM FLANAGAN
Vice-President for Continuing Education and Outreach: RAPHAEL CAPRIO
Secretary and Assistant to the President: MILDRED SCHILDKAMP
Newark Campus Provost: NORMAN SAMUELS
Camden Campus Provost: WALTER K. GORDON
Librarian: FRANK POLACH

Library: see Libraries
Number of teachers: 2,600
Number of students: 48,135

Publications: *Journal for International Law, Raritan Review, Journal for the History of Ideas, Public Productivity and Management Review, Journal of Research in Crime and Delinquency, Academic Questions, The American Sociologist, Child Welfare, Labor Studies Journal, Society, Women Studies* (quarterly), *North–South, Plant Molecular Biology Reporter, Public Budgeting and Finance.*

DEANS

New Brunswick Campus:
Business: P. GEORGE BENSON
Rutgers College: CARL KIRSCHNER
Cook College: BRUCE C. CARLTON
Douglass College: BARBARA SHAILOR
Education: LOUISE WILKINSON
Engineering: ELLIS H. DILL
Graduate School: RICHARD FOLEY
Livingston College: ARNOLD G. HYNDMAN
Pharmacy: JOHN COLAIZZI
Social Work: MARY E. DAVIDSON
University College: EMMET DENNIS
Library Service: RICHARD BUDD
Applied Professional Psychology: SANDRA HARRIS
Mason Gross School of the Arts: MARILYN SOMVILLE

Camden Campus:
Arts and Sciences: W. K. GORDON
Law: ROGER DENNIS
Graduate School: ROBERT CATLIN

Newark Campus:
Arts and Sciences: DAVID HOSFORD
Graduate School of Management: P. GEORGE BENSON
Law: ROGER ABRAMS
Nursing: HURDIS GRIFFITH
Criminal Justice: RONALD V. CLARKE
Graduate School: NORMAN SAMUELS

SAINT PETER'S COLLEGE

2641 Kennedy Blvd, Jersey City, NJ 07306-5997

Telephone: (201) 915-9000
Fax: (201) 451-0036

Founded 1872

President: JAMES N. LOUGHRAN
Academic Vice-President: Dr GEORGE E. MARTIN
Academic Dean: Dr PETER ALEXANDER
Associate Vice-President for Enrollment: NANCY P. CAMPBELL
Director of Admissions: BEN SCHOLZ
Registrar: JOAN Z. SHIELDS
Library Director: FREDERICK N. NESTA

Library of 282,000 vols
Number of teachers: 118 full-time, 242 part-time
Number of students: 3,477 full-time, 1,221 part-time

Undergraduate courses in the humanities, nursing, sciences, business studies; master's courses in education, international business, accountancy, management, management information systems, nursing.

SETON HALL UNIVERSITY

South Orange, NJ 07079

Telephone: (201) 761-9000

Founded 1856

Chancellor: Rev. THOMAS R. PETERSON
President: Rev. Mgr ROBERT SHEERAN
Provost: BERNHARD SCHOLZ
Executive Vice-Chancellor: JAMES O. ALLISON
Vice-President for University Affairs: CRAIG LEACH
Vice-President for Student Affairs: LAURA WANKEL
Vice-President for Planning: Rev. Mgr WILLIAM HARMS
Dean, University Libraries: ANITA TALAR (acting)

Number of teachers: 342 full-time, 375 part-time
Number of students: 9,630

Publications: *University Magazine, Precis, Alumni Network, Mid-Atlantic Journal of Business.*

DEANS

College of Arts and Sciences: JORENEE FORMICOLA
School of Education: SYLVESTER KOHUT, Jr
College of Nursing: BARBARA BEEKER
School of Business: JOHN SHANNON
School of Law (in Newark): RONALD RICCIO
School of Theology: Rev. JOHN FLESEY
Graduate Medical Education: JOHN PATERSON

STEVENS INSTITUTE OF TECHNOLOGY

Hoboken, NJ 07030

Telephone: (201) 420-5100

Founded 1870

President: HAROLD J. RAVECHÉ
Vice-President for University Relations: DAVID N. BARUS
Vice-President, Advancement: ELTON RENFROE
Vice-President, Operations: C. THOMAS LUNGHARD
Chief Financial Officer: CRAIG BECKER
Dean of Admissions and Financial Aid: PETER A. PERSUITTI
Dean of the Faculty: FRANCIS BOESCH
Dean of Graduate Studies: KEN DEROUCHER

Library of 105,000 vols
Number of teachers: 230
Number of students: 1,200 undergraduates, 500 full-time graduates

Publication: *The Annual Report.*

WESTMINSTER CHOIR COLLEGE OF RIDER UNIVERSITY

101 Walnut Lane, Princeton, NJ 08540-3899

Telephone: (609) 921-7100

Founded 1926

President: Dr J. BARTON LUEDEKE
Vice-President and Provost: Dr HELEN L. STEWART
Dean: ROBERT L. ANNIS
Registrar: Dr PETER D. WRIGHT
Librarian: JANE NOWAKOWSKI

Library of 55,000 vols; there is also a choral library with 5,000 titles and 300,000 copies
Number of teachers: 50
Number of students: 350

WILLIAM PATERSON UNIVERSITY OF NEW JERSEY

300 Pompton Rd, Wayne, NJ 07470

Telephone: (973) 720-2000

Founded 1855

President: Dr ARNOLD SPEERT
Executive Vice-President and Provost: Dr CHERNOH SESAY
Vice-President for Administration and Finance: STEPHAN BOLYAI
Vice-President for Institutional Advancement: RICHARD P. REISS
Dean of Students: Dr ROBERT ARIOSTO
Registrar: MARK EVANGELISTA
Librarian: Dr JOHN GABOURY

Library of 303,545 vols
Number of teachers: 318.5
Number of students: 9,669

Publication: *WPC Bulletin.*

DEANS

Humanities, Management and Social Science: (vacant)
Arts and Communication: OFELIA GARZIA
Education: Dr LESLIE AGARD-JONES
School of Science and Health: Dr ESWAR PHADIA

NEW MEXICO

COLLEGE OF SANTA FE

1600 St Michael's Drive, Santa Fe, NM 87505

Telephone: (505) 473-6133
Fax: (505) 473-6127

Founded 1947

President: Dr JAMES A. FRIES
Registrar: GERALD VINTHER
Librarian: SUSAN MYERS

Library of 135,000 vols
Number of teachers: 51 full-time, 117 part-time
Number of students: 1,518

EASTERN NEW MEXICO UNIVERSITY

Portales, NM 88130

Telephone: (505) 562-1011

Founded 1934

President: EVERETT L. FROST
Vice-President for Academic Affairs: Dr GEORGE MEHAFFY
Registrar: LARRY FUQUA
Librarian: C. EDWIN DOWLIN

Library of 699,847 vols
Number of teachers: 262
Number of students: 3,632

NEW MEXICO HIGHLANDS UNIVERSITY

Las Vegas, NM 87701

Telephone: (505) 425-7511

Founded 1893

President: Dr GILBERT SANCHEZ
Chief Fiscal Officer: ALLEN JAHNER
Academic Dean: Dr GILBERT RIVERA (acting)
Registrar: Dr CLARENCE SANCHEZ
Dean of Students: Dr JOHN JUAREZ
Librarian: Dr RAUL C. HERRERA

Number of teachers: 120, including 30 professors
Number of students: 2,300

NEW MEXICO INSTITUTE OF MINING AND TECHNOLOGY

Socorro, NM 87801

Telephone: (505) 835-5011

Founded 1889

President: DANIEL H. LOPEZ
Vice-President for Administration and Finance: W. DENNIS PETERSON
Vice-President for Academic Affairs: CARL J. POPP
Vice-President for Research and Economic Development: VAN D. ROMERO
Vice-President for Institutional Development: HERBERT M. FERNANDEZ
Librarian: KAY KREHBIEL

Library of 115,000 vols
Number of students: 1,500

DIRECTORS

New Mexico Bureau of Mines and Mineral Resources: CHARLES E. CHAPIN
New Mexico Petroleum Recovery Research Center: ROBERT L. LEE

NEW MEXICO STATE UNIVERSITY

Las Cruces, NM 88003-8001

Telephone: (505) 646-0111
Fax: (505) 646-1517

Founded in 1888 as Las Cruces College; became in 1889 the New Mexico College of Agriculture and Mechanic Arts and in 1960 New Mexico State University

President: WILLIAM B. CONROY
Executive Vice-President: JOHN C. OWENS (interim)
Vice-President–Business and Finance: JAMES MCDONOUGH
Vice-President–Student Affairs: PATRICIA R. WOLF
Vice-President–University Advancement: MARCIA G. MULLER
Vice-President–Economic Development: AVERETT S. TOMBES
Vice-President–Research: GARY CUNNINGHAM (interim)
Vice-President–Administration: JUAN N. FRANCO
Library Dean: CHARLES TOWNLEY

Library of 953,352 vols, plus 421,235 bound and unbound government documents and 1,337,979 microforms
Number of teachers: 1,072
Number of students: 15,127

Publications: *Graduate Catalog, Undergraduate Catalog,* Alumni newspaper.

DEANS

Graduate School: TIMOTHY J. PETTIBONE
College of Agriculture and Home Economics: JERRY SCHICKEDANZ (interim)
College of Arts and Sciences: RENE CASILLAS
College of Business Administration and Economics: DANNY R. ARNOLD
College of Education: PRENTICE BAPTISTE
College of Engineering: J. DERALD MORGAN
College of Health and Social Services: VIRGINIA HIGBIE

ATTACHED RESEARCH INSTITUTES

Agricultural Experiment Station: Dir GARY CUNNINGHAM.
Arts and Science Research Center: Dir REED DASENBROCK
Business Research and Services: Dir KATHLEEN BROOK.
Computing Research Laboratory: Dir SERGEI NIRENBURG
Educational Research Center: Dir ROY RODRIGUEZ.
Engineering Research Center: Dir LARRYL MATTHEWS.
Physical Science Laboratory: Dir DONALD BIRX.
Plant Genetic Engineering Laboratory: Dir JOHN D. KEMP.
Southwest Technical Development Institute: Dir RUDI SCHOENMACKERS.
Water Resources Research Institute: Dir THOMAS BAHR.

ST JOHN'S COLLEGE

Santa Fe, NM 87501

Telephone: (505) 984-6000
Fax: (505) 984-6003

Founded 1964

President: JOHN AGRESTO
Dean: A. JAMES CAREY
Registrar: DIANE MARTINEZ
Librarian: INGA M. WAITE

Library of 55,000 vols
Number of teachers: 61
Number of students: 400

For Annapolis branch see under Maryland.

UNIVERSITY OF NEW MEXICO

Albuquerque, NM 87131

Telephone: (505) 277-0111

Created by act of territorial legislation 1889; opened 1892

State control

Academic year: August to May

President: RICHARD E. PECK

Provost/Vice-President for Academic Affairs: WILLIAM C. GORDON

Vice-President for Student Affairs: ELISIO TORRES

Vice President for Business and Finance: DAVID MCKINNEY

Director of the Medical Centre: JANE E. HENNEY

Dean of Library Services: ROBERT MIGNEAULT

Library of 1,000,000 vols
Number of teachers: 1,250
Number of students: 25,009

Publications: various departmental publs.

DEANS

Graduate School: NASIR AHMED
Continuing Education: JERONIMO DOMINGUEZ
School of Architecture and Planning: RICHARD ERIBES
Students: KAREN M. GLASER
College of Arts and Sciences: MICHAEL FISCHER (acting)
College of Education: PEGGY BLACKWELL
College of Engineering: PAUL FLEURY
College of Fine Arts: THOMAS DODSON
School of Law: LEO ROMERO
Anderson Schools of Management: HOWARD L. SMITH
School of Medicine: PAUL B. ROTH
College of Nursing: KATHLEEN BOND
College of Pharmacy: WILLIAM M. HADLEY
Office of Undergraduate Studies: JANET ROEBUCK
Division of Dental Programs: JOSEPH SCALETTI (acting)

PROFESSORS

(C = Chairman of Department)

ABDALLA, R. N., Art and Art History
ABRAMS, J., Medicine
ADAMSON, G. W., Special Education
AHLUWALIA, H. S., Physics and Astronomy
AHMED, N., Electrical and Computer Engineering
ALLEN, F. S., Chemistry (C)
ALTENBACH, J. S., Biology
ALVERSON, D. C., Paediatrics
ANGEL, E. S., Electrical and Computer Engineering
ANGEL, R. M., Music
ANSPACH, J. F., Law
ATENCIO, A. C., Physiology
ATTERBOM, H. A., Health Promotion, Physical Education and Leisure Programmes
AVASTHI, P., Medicine
BACA, O. G., Biology
BAKER, W. E., Mechanical Engineering
BANKHURST, A. D., Medicine
BARBO, D. M., Obstetrics and Gynaecology
BARROW, T. F., Art and Art History
BARTLETT, L. A., English
BARTON, L. M., Biology
BASSALLECK, B., Physics and Astronomy
BASSO, K. H., Anthropology
BAWDEN, G. L., Anthropology
BEAR, D. G., Cell Biology
BEENE, L., English
BENNAHUM, D. A., Medicine
BENNAHUM, J., Theatre and Dance
BENNETT, M. D., Family and Community Medicine
BENZEL, E. C., Surgery
BERGEN, J. J., Spanish and Portuguese
BERGMAN, B. E., Law
BICKNELL, J. M., Neurology
BILLS, G. D., Linguistics
BIRKHOLZ, G. A., Nursing
BLACK, W. C., III, Pathology
BLACKWELL, P. J., Educational Foundations
BORDEN, T. A., Surgery
BORN, J. L., Pharmacy
BOWES, S., Educational Administration
BOYER, C. P., Mathematics and Statistics
BROGAN, J., Civil Engineering
BROOKSHIRE, D. S., Economics
BROWDE, M. B., Law
BROWN, F. L., Jr, Public Administration
BROWN, J., Biology
BRUECK, S. R. J., Electrical and Computer Engineering
BRYANT, H. C., Physics and Astronomy
BUCHNER, M. A., Mathematics and Statistics
BULLERS, W. I., Jr, Management
BURCHIEL, S. W., Pharmacy
BURNESS, H. S., Economics
BURR, S. L., Law
BURRIS, B. H., Sociology
BUSS, W., Pharmacology (C)
BYBEE, J. L., Linguistics
CAHILL, K. E., Physics and Astronomy
CAPUTI, J. E., American Studies
CARDENAS, A. J., Spanish and Portuguese
CARLOW, T. J., Neurology
CAVES, C. M., Physics and Astronomy
CECCHI, J. L., Chemical and Nuclear Engineering (C)
CHAMPOUX, J. E., Management
CHANDLER, C., Physics and Astronomy
CHANG, B. K., Medicine
CHAPDELAINE, M., Music
CHENG, J., Electrical and Computer Engineering
CHRISTENSEN, R. R., Mathematics and Statistics
CIVIKLY-POWELL, J. M., Communications and Journalism
CLARK, J. M., Music
CLOUGH, D. H., Nursing
COES, D. V., Management
COFER, L. F., Psychology
COHEN, E. B., Law Library
COLTON, D. L., Educational Administration
CONDON, J. C., Communication and Journalism
CONNELL-SZASZ, M., History
CORCORAN, G. B., Pharmacy
CORDOVA, I. R., Educational Administration
COUGHLIN, R., Sociology (C)
COUTSIAS, E. A., Mathematics and Statistics
CRAVEN, D. L., Art and Art History
CRAWFORD, M. H., Medicine
CURET, L. B., Obstetrics and Gynaecology
DAIL, W. G., Jr, Anatomy
DAMICO, H., English
DATYE, A. K., Chemical and Nuclear Engineering
DAVIDSON, R., Librarianship
DAVIS, G. L., American Studies
DAVIS, L., Neurology
DAVIS, M., Radiology
DEKEYSER, J., Music
DELANEY, H. D., Psychology
DESIDERIO, R. J., Law
DEVRIES, R. C., Electrical and Computer Engineering
DICKINSON, W. E., Surgery
DIELS, J.-C. M., Physics and Astronomy
DIETERLE, B., Physics and Astronomy
DILLARD, J. F., Management
DINIUS, A., Dental Program
DODSON, T. A., Music
DORATO, P., Electrical and Computer Engineering
DOUGHER, M. J., Psychology (C)
DRENNAN, J., Orthopaedics
DUBAN, S. L., Pediatrics
DUMARS, C., Law
DUNCAN, M. H., Paediatrics
DURYEA, P. J., Education
DUSZYNSKI, D. W., Biology
EATON, R. P., Medicine
EFROMOVICH, S., Mathematics and Statistics
EL-GENK, M. S., Chemical and Nuclear Engineering
ELIAS, L., Medicine
ELLIOTT, P. C., Management
ELLIS, J. W., Law
ELLISON, J. A., Mathematics and Statistics
ENGELBRECHT, G. A., Counselling and Family Studies
ENKE, C. G., Chemistry
ERIBES, R. A., Architecture and Planning
ESTRIN, J. A., Anaesthesiology (C)
ETULAIN, R., History
EVANS, W., Theatre and Dance
EWING, R. C., Earth Sciences
FEENEY, D., Psychology
FEINBERG, E. A., Art and Art History (C)
FELBERG, L., Music
FIELD, F. R., Training and Learning Technologies (C)
FINLEY, D., Physics and Astronomy
FISCHER, M. R., English
FISHBURN, W. R., Counselling and Family Studies
FLEMING, R. E., English
FLETCHER, M. P., General Library
FLEURY, P. A., Electrical and Computer Engineering
FORMAN, W. B., Medicine
FOUCAR, M. K., Pathology
FRANDSEN, K. D., Communication and Journalism
FRITZ, C. G., Law
FROELICH, J. W., Anthropology
FRONECH, D. K., Electrical and Computer Engineering
FRY, D., Surgery (C)
GAINES, B., English
GALEY, W. R., Jr, Physiology
GALLAGHER, P. J., English
GARCIA, F. C., Political Science
GARRY, P. J., Pathology
GEISSMAN, J. W., Earth Sciences
GELL-MAN, M., Physics and Astronomy
GERDES, D. C., Modern and Classical Languages (C)
GIBSON, A. G., Mathematics and Statistics
GILFEATHER, F., Mathematics and Statistics
GISSER, M., Economics
GLEW, R. H., Biochemistry (C)
GLUCK, J. P., Psychology (acting C)
GOMEZ-PALACIO, I., Law
GONZALES-BERRY, E., Modern and Classical Languages
GONZALES, R. A., Law
GOODMAN, R., Philosophy (C)
GORDON, W. C., Psychology
GOSZ, J. R., Biology
GRANT, D., Management
GREENBERG, R. E., Paediatrics
GRIFFIN, L. E., Health Promotion, Physical Education and Leisure Programmes
GWIN, M. C., English
HAALAND, K. Y., Psychiatry
HADLEY, W. M., Pharmacy
HAHN, B., Art and Art History
HAIMAN, F. S., General Honours
HALL, G. E., Law
HALL, J., Civil Engineering (C)
HALL, L. B., History
HARJO, J., Engineering
HARRIS, F., Political Science
HARRIS, M., Educational Foundations
HARRIS, R. J., Psychology
HART, F. M., Law
HARTSHORNE, M. F., Radiology
HASHIMOTO, F., Medicine
HAWKINS, C., Electrical and Computer Engineering

HEFFRON, W. A., Family and Community Medicine
HEGGEN, R. J., Civil Engineering
HENNEY, J. E., Medicine
HERMANN, M. S. G., Law
HERZON, F. S., Surgery
HEYWARD, V., Health Promotion, Physical Education and Leisure Programmes
HIGGINS, P. A., Nursing
HINTERBICHLER, K., Music
HOLDER, R. W., Chemistry
HOLLAN, J. D., Computer Science
HUACO, G. A., Sociology
HUMPHRIES, S., Jr, Electrical and Computer Engineering
JAFFE, I. S., Theatre and Dance
JAIN, R., Electrical and Computer Engineering
JAMSHIDI, M., Electrical and Computer Engineering
JEWELL, P. F., Surgery
JOHN-STEINER, V. P., Education
JOHNSON, D. M., English
JOHNSON, G. V., Biology
JOHNSON, J. D., Paediatrics
JOHNSON, P. J., Psychology
JONES, D., English
JOOST-GAUGIER, C., Art and Art History
JORDAN, S. W., Pathology
JUNGLING, K. C., Electrical and Computer Engineering (C)
KARLSTROM, K. E., Earth Sciences
KARNI, S., Electrical and Computer Engineering
KASSICIEH, S. K., Management
KAUFFMAN, D., Chemical and Nuclear Engineering
KAUFMAN, A., Family, Community and Emergency Medicine (C)
KEITH, S. J., Psychiatry (C)
KELLEY, R. O., Anatomy (C)
KELLY, H. W., Pharmacy
KELLY, S. G., Law
KELSEY, C. A., Radiology
KELSEY, C. W., Education
KENDALL, D. L., Electrical and Computer Engineering
KENKRE, V. M., Physics and Astronomy
KERN, R. W., History
KEY, C. R., Pathology
KISIEL, W., Pathology
KLEIN, C., Geology
KLEPPER, D. J., Medicine
KLINE, W., Education
KODRIC-BROWN, A., Biology
KOGOMA, T., Cell Biology
KORNFELD, M., Pathology
KOSTER, F. T., Medicine
KOVNAT, R., Law
KUCHARZ, W., Mathematics and Statistics
KUDO, A. M., Geology
KUES, B. S., Earth Sciences
LAFREE, G., Sociology (C)
LAMPHERE, L., Anthropology
LANCASTER, J. B., Anthropology
LEWIS, S. L., Nursing
LIGON, J. D., Biology (C)
LINDEMAN, R. D., Medicine
LINNELL, J., Theatre and Dance (C)
LIPSCOMB, M. F., Pathology (C)
LIPSKI, J., Modern Languages (C)
LONG, V., Counselling and Family Studies
LOPEZ, A. S., Law
LORENZ, J., Mathematics and Statistics
LOTFIELD, R. B., Biochemistry
LOVE, E. B., Librarianship
LUCKASSON, R. A., Special Education
LUGER, G. F., Computer Science
LUMIA, R., Mechanical Engineering
LUTZ, W., Chemical and Nuclear Engineering
MACIEL, D. R., History
MCCARTHY, D. M., Medicine
MCCLELLAND, C. E., III, History
MCCONNELL, T. S., Pathology
MCCULLOUGH-BRABSON, E., Music
MCDANIEL, M., Psychology
MCFARLANE, D. R., Public Administration
MCGRAW, J., Physics and Astronomy
MCGUFFEE, L. J., Pharmacology
MCIVER, J. K., Physics and Astronomy
MCLAUGHLIN, J. C., Pathology
MCNAMARA, P. A., Sociology
MCNEIL, J., Electrical and Computer Engineering
MCPHERSON, D., English
MACPHERSON, W. T., Law
MAKI, G., Electrical and Computer Engineering
MALOLEPSY, J., Theatre and Dance
MANN, B. M., Mathematics and Statistics
MARTINEZ, J. G. R., Special Education
MATTHEWS, J. A. J., Physics and Astronomy
MATTHEWS, O. P., Geography (C)
MATHEWSON, A. D., Law
MATWIYOFF, N. A., Cell Biology (C)
MAY, G. W., Civil Engineering
MAY, P. A., Sociology
MEIZE-GROCHOWSKI, R., Nursing
MELADA, I. P., English
MENNIN, S. P., Anatomy
MERKX, G. W., Sociology
METTLER, F. A., Jr, Radiology (C)
MIGNEAULT, R., Librarianship
MILLER, W. R., Psychology
MILSTEIN, M. M., Educational Administration
MOLD, C., Microbiology (C)
MONEIM, M. S., Orthopaedics (C)
MORAIN, S. A., Geography (C)
MORET, B. M., Computer Science
MORRIS, D. M., Surgery
MORRIS, M. M., Education
MORROW, C., Chemistry (C)
MOSELEY, P. L., Medicine
MURATA, G. H., Medicine
MURPHY, S. J., Paediatrics
NIEMCZYK, T. M., Chemistry
NORDHAUS, R. S., Architecture and Planning
NORWOOD, J. M., Law
NORWOOD, V. L., American Studies (C)
NURNBERG, H. G., Psychiatry
NUTTALL, H. E., Jr, Chemical and Nuclear Engineering
OBENSHAIN, S. S., Paediatrics
OCCHIALINO, M., Law
OGILBY, P. R., Chemistry
OLIVER, J. M., Pathology
OLLER, J. W., Jr, Linguistics
OMDAHL, J. L., Biochemistry
OMER, G., Jr., Orthopaedics
ONDRIAS, M. R., Chemistry
ONNEWEER, C., Mathematics and Statistics
ORRISON, W. W., Radiology
ORTIZ, A. A., Anthropology
ORTIZ, J. V., Chemistry
OVERTURF, G. D., Paediatrics
OWENS, L. D., English
PABISCH, P. K., Foreign Languages and Literature
PADILLA, R. S., Dermatology
PAINE, R. T., Jr, Chemistry
PANITZ, J. A., Physics and Astronomy
PAPADOPOULOS, E. P., Chemistry
PAPIKE, J. J., Geology
PAPILE, L. A., Paediatrics
PARK, S. M., Chemistry
PARKMAN, A. M., Management
PARNALL, T., Law
PARTRIDGE, L. D., Physiology
PATHAK, P. T., Mathematics and Statistics
PEABODY, D. S., Cell Biology
PECK, R. E., English
PEREZ-GOMEZ, J. R., Music
PETERSON, S. L., Pharmacy
PHAM, C., Economics
PIPER, J., Music
PORTER, J., History
PREDOCK-LINNELL, J., Theatre and Dance
PRICE, R. M., Physics and Astronomy
PRINJA, A. K., Chemical and Nuclear Engineering
PRIOLA, D. V., Physiology (C)
PYLE, R. R., Medicine
QUENZER, R. W., Medicine
RABINOWITZ, H., History
RADOSEVICH, R. R., Management
RAIZADA, V., Medicine
RAZANI, A., Mechanical Engineering
REBOLLEDO, T. D., Modern Languages
REED, W. D., Medicine
REES, B. L., Nursing
REEVES, T. Z., Public Administration
REHDER, R. R., Management
REID, R. A., Management
REMMER, K. L., Political Science
REYES, P., Biochemistry
RICHARDS, C. G., Mechanical Engineering
RIENSCHE, L. L., Comm. Disorders (C)
ROBBINS, R. G., History
ROBIN, D. M., Foreign Languages and Literature
RODERICK, N. F., Chemical and Nuclear Engineering
RODRIGUEZ, A., Modern and Classical Languages
ROEBUCK, J., History
ROGERS, E. M., Communication and Journalism
ROLL, S., Psychology
ROMERO, L. M., Law
ROSENBERG, G. A., Neurology (C)
ROSS, H. L., Sociology
ROSS, T. J., Civil Engineering
ROTH, P. B., Emergency Medicine
RUEBUSH, B. K., Psychiatry and Psychology
RUYBAL, S. E., Nursing
SAIERS, J. H., Medicine
SAIKI, J. H., Medicine
SALAND, L. C., Anatomy
SALVAGGIO, R., American Studies
SANTLEY, R. S., Anthropology
SARTO, G. E., Obstetrics and Gynaecology (C)
SAVAGE, D. D., II, Pharmacology
SCALES, A. C., Law
SCALETTI, J. V., Microbiology
SCALLEN, T. J., Biochemistry
SCHADE, D. S., Medicine
SCHARNHORST, G.F., English and American Studies
SCHAU, C. G., Educational Foundations
SCHREYER, H. L., Mechanical Engineering
SCHUELER, G.F, Philosophy (C)
SCHUETZ, J. E., Communication
SCHULTZ, C., Management
SCHUYLER, M. R., Medicine
SCHWARTZ, R. L., Law
SCHWERIN, K. H., Anthropology
SCOTT, P. B., Curriculum and Instruction in Multicultural Teacher Education
SEARLES, R.P., Medicine
SEMO, E., History
SEVERINO, S. K., Psychiatry
SHAHINPOOR, M., Mechanical Engineering
SHAMA, A., Management
SHANE, D. L., Nursing
SHELTON, S. P., Civil Engineering
SHIPMAN, V. C., Counselling and Family Studies
SHOMAKER, D. J., Nursing
SHULTIS, C. L., Music
SIBBITT, W. L., Jr, Medicine
SIEMBIEDA, W. J., Architecture and Planning
SIMONSON, D. G., Management
SKIPPER, B. J., Family, Community and Emergency Medicine
SKLAR, D. P., Emergency Medicine (C)
SKLAR, L. A., Pathology
SMITH, B. T., Computer Science
SMITH, D. D., Special Education
SMITH, D. M., Chemical and Nuclear Engineering
SMITH, H. L., Management
SMITH, M. M., Counselling and Family Studies
SMITH, P. J., Special Education
SMITH, W. S., Jr, Foreign Languages and Literature
SNYDER, R. D., Neurology
SONNENBERG, A., Medicine
SOUTHALL, T. W., Art and Art History
SRUBEK, J., Art Education

STARR, G. P., Mechanical Engineering
STEINBERG, S. L., Mathematics and Statistics
STONE, A. P., Mathematics and Statistics (C)
STRAUS, L. G., Anthropology
STRICKLAND, R. G., Medicine (C)
STURM, F. G., Philosophy
SUMMERS, J. W., Cell Biology
SUTHERLAND, R. J., Psychology
SWINSON, D., Physics and Astronomy
SZASZ, F. M., History
TANDBERG, W. D., Emergency Medicine
TAYLOR, A. P., Architecture and Planning
TAYLOR, S. A., Law
THOMPSON, D. E., Mechanical Engineering (C)
THOMSON, B. M., Civil Engineering
THORNHILL, A. R., Biology
THORSON, J. L., English
TIANO, S. B., Sociology
TOLMAN, J. M., Modern and Classical Languages
TOOLSON, E. C., Biology
TRINKAUS, E., Anthropology
TROTTER, J. A., Anatomy
TROUP, G. M., Pathology
TROUTMAN, W. G., Pharmacy
TUASON, V. B., Psychiatry
TURAN, M., Architecture and Planning
TURNER, P. H., Counselling and Family Studies (C)
TYLER, M., Music
TZAMALOUKAS, A., Medicine
UHLENHUTH, E. H., Psychiatry
USCHER, N. J., Music
USEEM, B., Sociology
UTTON, A. E., Law
VALDES, N., Sociology
VANDERJAGT, D., Biochemistry
VAN DONGEN, R. D., Curriculum and Instruction in Multicultural Teacher Education
VOGEL, K. G., Biology
WALDMAN, J. D., Paediatrics
WALKER, B. R., Physiology
WALTERS, E. A., Chemistry
WANG, M.-L., Civil Engineering
WATERMAN, R. E., Anatomy
WEIGLE, M. M., Anthropology (C)
WEISS, G. K., Physiology
WEISS, J. R., Nursing
WERNLEY, J. A., Surgery
WHEELAND, R. G., Dermatology (C)
WHIDDEN, M. B., English
WHITE, P., English
WIESE, W., Family, Community and Emergency Medicine
WILDIN, M. W., Mechanical Engineering
WILKINS, E. S., Chemical and Nuclear Engineering
WILLIAMS, R. H., Electrical and Computer Engineering
WILLIAMSON, M. R., Radiology
WILLIAMSON, S. L., Radiology
WILLMAN, C. L., Pathology
WINOGRAD, P., Law
WITEMEYER, H., English
WOFSY, C., Mathematics and Statistics
WOLF, S. S., Law
WOLFE, D. M., Physics and Astronomy (C)
WOLFE, J. D., Theatre and Dance
WOOD, C. J., Education Administration
WOOD, J. E., Mechanical Engineering
WOOD, W. F., Music
WOODWARD, L. A., Geology
WORRELL, R. V., Orthopaedics
WRIGHT, J. B., Library
YAGER, J., Psychiatry
YATES, T. L., Biology (C)
ZAGER, P. G., Medicine
ZANNES, E., Communication and Journalism
ZEILIK, M., II, Physics and Astronomy
ZIMMER, W. J., Mathematics and Statistics
ZONGOLOWICZ, H. M.
ZUMWALT, R. E., Pathology

WESTERN NEW MEXICO UNIVERSITY

Box 680, Silver City, NM 88062
Telephone: (505) 538-6011
Founded 1893
President: Dr RUDOLPH GOMEZ
Vice-President for Academic Affairs: Dr ALLAN DEGIULIO
Vice-President for Business Affairs: RICHARD LAWYER
Registrar: ERIC GUNNINK
Librarian: BEN WAKASHIGE
Library of 388,193 vols
Number of teachers: 65
Number of students: 1,600

NEW YORK

ADELPHI UNIVERSITY

Garden City, NY 11530
Telephone: (516) 877-3000
Founded 1896
President: (vacant)
Provost: IGOR WEBB
Registrar: JAMES OFSTROSKY
Librarian: EUGENE NEELY
Library of 452,172 vols, 589,581 microforms
Number of teachers: 310
Number of students: 9,000

DEANS

Arts and Sciences, Graduate and Undergraduate: IGOR WEBB (acting)
School of Social Work: JANICE WETZEL
School of Nursing: ELEANOR BARBA (acting)
Schools of Business: SYROUS KOOROS
Institute of Advanced Psychological Studies: GEORGE STRICKER
University College: DOMINICK CAVALLO
School of Education: JEFFREY KANE

ALBANY COLLEGE OF PHARMACY

106 New Scotland Ave, Albany, NY 12208
Telephone: (518) 445-7200
Founded 1881
President and Dean: JAMES G. GOZZO
Associate Dean for Academic Affairs: HOWARD D. COLBY
Associate Dean for Student Affairs: ALBERT M. WHITE
Director of Finance and Business Affairs: WILLIAM M. CRONIN
Director of Admissions: Mrs. JANIS L. FISHER
Librarian: DEBRA LOCASAIO
Number of teachers: 50
Number of students: 700

ALBANY LAW SCHOOL

80 New Scotland Ave, Albany, NY 12208
Telephone: (518) 445-2311
Founded 1851
Chairman of Board of Trustees: DONALD D. DE ANGELIS
Dean: THOMAS H. SPONSLER
Registrar: Dr CHARLES W. WALDROP
Librarian: ROBERT T. BEGG
Library of 256,000 vols
Number of teachers: 42 full-time, 29 adjunct
Number of students: 755

ALBANY MEDICAL COLLEGE

47 New Scotland Ave, Albany, NY 12208
Telephone: (518) 445-5544
Founded 1839
Dean: ANTHONY P. TARTAGLIA
Director of Admissions: SARA KREMER
Librarian: SHERRY HARTMAN
Library of 115,000 vols
Number of teachers: 431
Number of students: 512 medical, 105 graduate

ALFRED UNIVERSITY

26 North Main St, Alfred, NY 14802-1232
Telephone: (607) 871-2111
Founded 1836
President: EDWARD G. COLL, Jr
Provost: W. RICHARD OTT
Vice-President for Business and Finance: PETER C. FACKLER
Vice-President for University Relations: Dr WILLIAM F. STEPP
Director of Admissions: LAURIE RICHER
Librarian: AROLANA MEISSNER
Library of 234,466 vols
Number of teachers: 165
Number of students: 2,326
Publications: *Fiat Lux, Alfred Reporter, Kanakadea, University Catalogue.*

DEANS

College of Liberal Arts and Sciences: CHRISTINE GRONTKOWSKI
School of Ceramic Engineering and Sciences: ALASTAIR CORMACK
College of Business: DAVID SZCZERBACKI
College of Engineering and Professional Studies: W. RICHARD OTT
School of Art and Design: KATHLEEN COLLINS
Graduate Studies: W. RICHARD OTT (Dir)

BANK STREET COLLEGE OF EDUCATION

610 West 112th St, New York, NY 10025
Telephone: (212) 875-4400
Founded 1916
President: Dr AUGUSTA SOUZA KAPPNER
Vice-President for Finance and Administration: HOWARD BUXBAUM
Dean of External Affairs: THERESA KARAMANOS
Dean, Children's Programmes: REUEL JORDAN
Dean, Graduate School: PATRICIA A. WASLEY
Dean, Continuing Education: FERN KHAN
Director of Library: LINDA GREENGRASS
Library of 80,000 vols
Number of teachers: 150
Number of students: 850

BARD COLLEGE

Annandale-on-Hudson, NY 12504
Telephone: (914) 758-6822
Founded 1860
President: LEON BOTSTEIN
Registrar: ELLEN JETTO
Dean: STUART LEVINE
Director of Admissions: MARY BACKLUND
Director of Libraries: JEFFREY KATZ
Library of 190,000 vols
Number of teachers: 150
Number of students: 1,126

CANISIUS COLLEGE

2001 Main St, Buffalo, NY 14208
Telephone: (716) 883-7000
Fax: (716) 888-2525
Founded 1870
President: Rev. VINCENT M. COOKE
Chancellor: Rev. JAMES M. DEMSKE
Vice-President/Assistant to the President: Mrs. LILLIAN M. LEVEY
Vice-President for Academic Affairs: Dr JOAN CONNELL
Vice-President for Business and Finance: LAURENCE W. FRANZ

Vice-President for College Relations: J. PATRICK GREENWALD
Vice-President for Student Affairs: THOMAS E. MILLER
Librarian: GEORGE M. TELATNIK

Library of 350,361 vols
Number of teachers: 198 full-time, 160 part-time
Number of students: 4,944

CITY UNIVERSITY OF NEW YORK

535 East 80th St, New York, NY 10021
Telephone: (212) 794-5555
Founded 1847
A public institution comprising ten senior colleges, listed below, a Graduate School and University Center, a law school, a medical school, an affiliated medical school, Mount Sinai School of Medicine, a technical college and six community colleges: Borough of Manhattan Community College, Bronx Community College, Hostos Community College, Kingsborough Community College, Fiorello H. La Guardia Community College and Queensborough Community College
Chancellor: CHRISTOPH M. KIMMICH (interim)
Combined libraries of 6,000,000 vols

Graduate School and University Center

33 West 42nd St, New York, NY 10036
Telephone: (212) 642-1600
Established 1961
President: FRANCES DEGEN HOROWITZ
Number of teachers: 334 (full-time)
Number of students: 3,813

City University Medical School at The City College

Convent Ave and 138th St, New York, NY 10031
Telephone: (212) 690-8252
Founded 1984
Dean: STANFORD A. ROMAN, Jr

City University School of Law at Queens College

200-01 42nd Ave, Bayside, New York, NY 11361
Telephone: (718) 575-4200
Founded 1973
Dean: KRISTIN BOOTH GLEN
Number of teachers: 28 (full-time)
Number of students: 467

Bernard M. Baruch College

17 Lexington Ave, New York, NY 10010
Telephone: (212) 387-1000
Established 1919
President: LOIS S. CRONHOLM
Number of teachers: 409 (full-time)
Number of students: 15,071

Brooklyn College

Bedford Ave and Ave H, Brooklyn, NY 11210
Telephone: (718) 780-5485
Established 1930
President: VERNON LATTIN
Number of teachers: 496 (full-time)
Number of students: 14,964

City College

Convent Ave and 138th St, New York, NY 10031
Telephone: (212) 650-7000
Founded 1847
President: YOLANDA T. MOSES
Number of teachers: 457 (full-time)
Number of students: 12,083

College of Staten Island

2800 Victory Blvd, Staten Island, NY 10314
Telephone: (718) 982-2000
Founded 1976 by amalgamation of Staten Island Community College and Richmond College
President: MARLENE SPRINGER
Number of teachers: 266 (full-time)
Number of students: 12,023

Herbert H. Lehman College

Bedford Park Blvd West, Bronx, NY 10468
Telephone: (212) 960-8000
Founded 1931
President: RICARDO R. FERNANDEZ
Number of teachers: 266 (full-time)
Number of students: 9,283

Hunter College

695 Park Ave, New York, NY 10021
Telephone: (212) 772-4000
Founded 1870
President: DAVID A. CAPUTO
Number of teachers: 488 (full-time)
Number of students: 19,689

John Jay College of Criminal Justice

899 10th Ave, New York, NY 10019
Telephone: (212) 237-8000
Founded 1964
President: GERALD W. LYNCH
Number of teachers: 256 (full-time)
Number of students: 10,834

Medgar Evers College

1650 Bedford Ave, Brooklyn, NY 11225
Telephone: (718) 951-5000
Founded 1969
President: EDISON O. JACKSON
Number of teachers: 127 (full-time)
Number of students: 5,063

New York City Technical College

300 Jay St, Brooklyn, NY 11201
Telephone: (718) 240-4900
President: EMILIE A. COZZI (acting)
Number of teachers: 276 (full-time)
Number of students: 11,124

Queens College

65-30 Kissena Blvd, Flushing, NY 11367
Telephone: (718) 997-5411
Founded 1937
President: ALLEN LEE SESSOMS
Number of teachers: 514 (full-time)
Number of students: 16,381

York College

94-20 Guy R. Brewer Blvd, Jamaica, NY 11451
Telephone: (718) 262-2000
Founded 1966
President: CHARLES C. KIDD, Sr
Number of teachers: 144 (full-time)
Number of students: 6,030

CLARKSON UNIVERSITY

Potsdam, NY 13699-5500
Telephone: (315) 268-6400
President: DENNY G. BROWN
Fax: (315) 268-7993
Founded 1896
President: DENNY BROWN
Vice-President of Business and Financial Affairs/Treasurer: BRUCE T. H. KNILL
Dean of Admissions: SUZANNE A. LIBERTY
Registrar: LYNN C. BROWN, Jr.
Librarian: J. NATALIA STAHL
Library of 229,000 vols, 272,000 microforms
Number of teachers: 172, including 48 full professors
Number of students: 2,670
Publication: *Clarkson.*

DEANS

Graduate School: (vacant)
School of Engineering: ANTHONY G. COLLINS
School of Science: JAMES H. THORP III
School of Business: VICTOR P. PEASE
Summer Session and Special Programmes: STEPHEN NEWKOFSKY
Student Life: MICHAEL E. COOPER
Liberal Studies: JERRY GRAVANDER

COLGATE UNIVERSITY

13 Oak Drive, Hamilton, NY 13346
Telephone: (315) 228-1000
Fax: (315) 228-7798
First charter 1819; chartered as Madison University 1846, name changed to Colgate University 1890
President: NEIL R. GRABOIS
Vice-President for Business and Finance: ELIZABETH A. S. EISMEIER
Controller: THOMAS O'NEILL
Registrar: EDITH REILE
Secretary: GARY L. ROSS
Vice-President for Public Affairs: ROBERT L. TYBURSKI
Dean of the College: MICHAEL CAPPETO
Dean of Faculty: JANE L. PINCHIN
Director of Graduate Programs: GEORGE DEBOER
Librarian: JUDITH NOYES
Library of 500,000 vols
Number of teachers: 197 full-time, 76 part-time
Number of students: 2,675

COLLEGE OF MOUNT SAINT VINCENT

263rd St and Riverdale Ave, Riverdale, NY 10471
Telephone: (718) 405-3267
Founded 1847
President: Dr MARY C. STUART
Academic Vice-President: KATHLEEN KNOWLES
Librarian: Sister KATHLEEN N. CASSIDY
Library of 149,000 vols
Number of teachers: 80
Number of students: 1,150

COLLEGE OF NEW ROCHELLE

New Rochelle, NY 10805
Telephone: (914) 654-5000
Fax: (914) 654-5980
Founded 1904
President: Dr STEPHEN J. SWEENY
Senior Vice-President for Academic Affairs: Dr JOAN E. BAILEY
Registrar: CAROL BUCKINGHAM
Librarian: JAMES SCHLEIFER
Library of over 200,000 vols
Number of teachers: 774
Number of students: 6,475

DEANS

School of Arts and Sciences: Dr C. J. DENNE
School of New Resources: BESSIE BLAKE
Graduate School: LAURA ELLIS
School of Nursing: CONNIE VANCE

COLLEGE OF SAINT ROSE

432 Western Ave, Albany, NY 12203

Telephone: (518) 454-5111
Fax: (518) 458-5447

Founded 1920

President: Dr R. MARK SULLIVAN
Registrar: JUDITH KELLY
Vice-President of Finance and Administration: Dr KATHLEEN SINEL
Vice-President for Academic Affairs: Dr WILLIAM LOWE
Vice-President of Development and Alumni Relations: JEANNE KOBUSZEWSKI
Dean of Admissions and Enrollment Services: MARY M. GRONDAHL
Dean of Graduate and Adult and Continuing Education Admissions: ANNE TULLY
Director of Library Services: PETER KOONZ

Library of 195,000 vols
Number of teachers: 300
Number of students: 3,900

COLUMBIA UNIVERSITY

Morningside Heights, New York, NY 10027

Telephone: (212) 854-1754

Founded as King's College 1754; incorporated in 1784 and name changed to Columbia College. By order of the Supreme Court of State of New York, in 1912, title changed to Columbia University
Private control
Academic year: September to May

President: GEORGE RUPP
Provost: JONATHAN R. COLE
Executive Vice-President for Administration: EMILY C. LLOYD
Executive Vice-President for Finance: JOHN MASTEN
Treasurer and Controller: PATRICIA L. FRANCY
Vice-Presidents:
  Facilities Management: LAWRENCE R. KILDUFF
  Arts and Sciences: DAVID H. COHEN
  Development and Alumni Relations: RICHARD K. NAUM
  Public Affairs: ALAN J. STONE
  Information Services and University Librarian: ELAINE F. SLOAN
  Health Sciences: HERBERT PARDES
  Human Resources: COLLEEN CROOKER
Secretary: CORINNE H. RIEDER

Library: see Libraries
Number of teachers: 6,430
Number of students: undergraduate 5,600, graduate and professional 11,800, non-degree candidates 2,500 (excluding Barnard College and Teachers' College)

Publications: *Journal of the Ancient Near Eastern Society, The Astronomical Journal, Current Musicology, Germanic Review, Columbia Human Rights Law Review, Journal of International Affairs, Johnsonian News Letter, Columbia Journalism Review, Columbia Law Review, Journal of Philosophy, Renaissance Quarterly, Revista Hispánica Moderna, Romanic Review, Columbia Journal of Transnational Law, Columbia Journal of World Business, Chemical Highlights, Columbia Journal of Environmental Law, Columbia Studies in the Classical Tradition, Critical Texts, Global Political Assessment, Journal of Art and the Law, Prospects: The Annual for American Cultural Studies, Semiotext(e), Studies in American Indian Literature, Translation.*

DEANS

Columbia College: AUSTIN E. QUIGLEY
Graduate School of Arts and Sciences: EDUARDO MACAGNO
School of Law: LANCE LIEBMAN
School of Medicine: HERBERT PARDES
School of Engineering and Applied Science: ZVI GALIL
Graduate School of Architecture, Planning and Preservation: BERNARD TSCHUMI
Graduate School of Journalism: JOAN KONNER
Graduate School of Business: MEYER FELDBERG
School of Dental and Oral Surgery: ALLAN J. FORMICOLA
School of Public Health: ALLAN G. ROSENFIELD
School of Nursing: MARY O. MUNDINGER
General Studies: GILLIAN LINDT (acting)
School of International and Public Affairs: JOHN G. RUGGIE
School of Social Work: RONALD A. FELDMAN
School of the Arts: ROBERT FITZPATRICK

PROFESSORS

Anaesthesiology:
  FINCK, A. D.
  FINSTER, M.
  HILLEL, Z.
  HYMAN, A. I.
  MORISHIMA, H. O.
  ORNSTEIN, E.
  PANG, L.
  PANTUCK, E. J.
  SMILEY, R. M.
  STONE, J. G.
  THYS, D. M.
  TRINER, L.
  WEISSMAN, C.
  YOUNG, W. L.

Anatomy and Cell Biology:
  AMBRON, R.
  APRIL, E. W.
  BELLVE, A. R.
  BRANDT, P.
  BULINSKI, J. C.
  GERSHON, M. D.
  KESSIN, R. H.
  ROLE, L. W.
  SILVERMAN, A.-J.
  TENNYSON, V. M. S.
  TORAN-ALLERAND, C. D.

Anthropology:
  ALLAND, A., Jr
  COHEN, M. L.
  COMBS-SCHILLING, M. E.
  D'ALTROY, T.
  HOLLOWAY, R. L.
  MELNICK, D.
  NEWMAN, K.
  SKINNER, E. P.
  TAUSSIG, M.

Applied Physics:
  BOOZER, A. H.
  CHU, C. K.
  HERMAN, I. P.
  MARSHALL, T. C.
  MAUEL, M.
  NAVRATIL, G.

Architecture, Planning and Preservation:
  FRAMPTON, K.
  GRAVA, S.
  HERDEG, K.
  HOLL, S.
  MARCUSE, P.
  MCINTYRE, L.
  MCLEOD, M.
  PLUNZ, R.
  POLSHEK, J. S.
  SASSEN, S. J.
  SCLAR, E.
  STERN, R. A. M.
  TSCHUMI, B.
  WRIGHT, G.

Art History and Archaeology:
  BALLON, H. M.
  BECK, J. H.
  MYCK, A., Ethics
  BERGDOLL, B. G.
  BRILLIANT, R.
  CONNORS, J.
  FREEDBERG, D.
  KRAUSS, R.
  MIDDLETON, R.
  MURASE, M. C.
  MURRAY, S.
  PASZTORY, E.
  REFF, T.
  ROSAND, D.
  STALEY, A.

Arts:
  FORMAN, M., Film
  INSDORF, A., Film
  SARRIS, A., Film

Astronomy:
  APPLEGATE, J.
  BAKER, N.
  HALPERN, J. P.
  HELFAND, D.
  PATTERSON, J.
  PRENDERGAST, K. H.
  SPIEGEL, E. A.
  VAN GORKOM, J.

Biochemistry and Molecular Biophysics:
  FEIGELSON, P.
  GOFF, S.
  GOLD, A. M.
  GOLDBERGER, R. F.
  GOTTESMAN, M. E.
  GREENWALD, I. S.
  HENDRICKSON, W. A.
  HIRSH, D. I.
  HONIG, B.
  JESSELL, T.
  KRASNA, A. I.
  SRINIVASAN, P. R.

Biological Sciences:
  BOCK, W. J.
  CHALFIE, M.
  CHASIN, L. A.
  COHEN, D. H.
  KELLEY, D. B.
  MACAGNO, E. R.
  MANCINELLI, A.
  MANLEY, J.
  POLLACK, R.
  POO, M.
  PRIVES, C. L.
  TZAGOLOFF, A.
  ZUBAY, G. L.

Business:
  ADLER, M.
  ARZAC, E. R.
  BARTEL, A.
  BROCKNER, J.
  BURTON, J. C.
  CAPON, N.
  DONALDSON, J.
  EDWARDS, F.
  FEDERGRUEN, A.
  GIOVANNINI, A.
  GLASSERMAN, P.
  GLOSTEN, L. R.
  GREEN, L.
  GREENWALD, B. C. N.
  GUPTA, S.
  HAMBRICK, D.
  HARRIGAN, K.
  HARRIS, T.
  HEAL, G.
  HOLBROOK, M.
  HORTON, R.
  HUBBARD, R. G.
  HUBERMAN, G.
  HULBERT, J. M.
  ICHNIOWSKI, B. E.
  KOHLI, R.

KOLESAR, P.
LEFF, N.
LEHMANN, D.
LICHTENBERG, F. R.
MELUMAD, N. D.
MISHKIN, F.
NOAM, E.
OHLSON, J.
PATRICK, H.
SELDEN, L.
SEXTON, D.
STARR, M.
SUNDARESAN, S.
THOMAS, J. K.
TUSHMAN, M.
WARREN, E. K.
WILKINSON, M.
ZIPKIN, P.

Chemical Engineering and Applied Chemistry:
CHEH, H. Y.
DURNING, C.
GRYTE, C.
LEONARD, E. F.
O'SHAUGHNESSY, B.
SPENCER, J.

Chemistry:
BENT, B. E.
BERNE, B. J.
BERSOHN, R.
BRESLOW, R.
DANISHEFSKY, S. J.
EISENTHAL, K. B.
FLYNN, G. W.
FRIESNER, R.
KATZ, T. J.
NAKANISHI, K.
PARKIN, G. F. R.
PECHUKAS, P.
STILL, W. C.
TURRO, N. J.
VALENTINI, J.

Civil Engineering and Engineering Mechanics:
DASGUPTA, G.
DIMAGGIO, F. L.
FRIEDMAN, M. B.
GJELSVIK, A.
GRIFFIS, F. H.
MEYER, C.
STOLL, R. D.
TESTA, R. B.
VAICAITIS, R.

Classics:
BAGNALL, R. S.
CAMERON, A.
COULTER, J. A.
SAID, S.
TARÁN, L.
ZETZEL, J.

Computer Science:
AHO, A. V.
ALLEN, P. K.
FEINER, S. K.
GALIL, Z.
GROSS, J. L.
KAISER, G.
KENDER, J.
MCKEOWN, K.
STOLFO, S.
TRAUB, J. F.
UNGER, S.
WOZNIAKOWSKI, M.
YEMINI, Y.

Dental and Oral Surgery:
CANGIALOSI, T. J.
DAVIS, M. J.
EFSTRATIADIS, S. S.
FORMICOLA, A. J.
HASSELGREN, B. G.
HILLS, H. L.
ISRAEL, H. A.
KAHN, N.
KLYVERT, M.
LAMSTER, I. B.
MOSS-SALENTIJN, L.
MYERS, R.
ODRICH, J.
ROSER, S. M.
TROUTMAN, K. C.
ZEGARELLI, D. J.

Dermatology:
BICKERS, D. R.

East Asian Languages and Cultures:
ANDERER, P.
HYMES, R.
LEDYARD, G. K.
SHIRANE, H.
SMITH, H. D., II
WANG, D. D.-W.
ZELIN, M.

Economics:
BHAGWATI, J.
BLOOM, D.
CHICHILNISKY, G.
CLARIDA, R.
DESAI, P.
DHRYMES, P.
DUTTA, P. K.
ERICSON, R.
FINDLAY, R.
HAYASHI, F.
LANCASTER, K.
MUNDELL, R.
PHELPS, E.
WATTS, H.
WELLISZ, S. H.

Electrical Engineering:
ACAMPORA, A.
ANASTASSIOU, D.
DIAMENT, P.
HEINZ, T.
LAZAR, A.
MEADOWS, H. E.
OSGOOD, R.
SCHWARTZ, M.
SEN, A. K.
STERN, T. E.
TEICH, M. C.
TSIVIDIS, Y.
WANG, W.
YANG, E. S.
ZUKOWSKI, C. A.

English and Comparative Literature:
BLOUNT, M.
DAMROSCH, D.
DELBANCO, A.
DOUGLAS, A.
EDEN, K.
FERGUSON, R.
FERRANTE, J.
HANNING, R.
HOWARD, J.
KASTAN, D.
KOCH, J. K.
KROEBER, K.
MARCUS, S.
MEISEL, M.
MENDELSON, E.
MILLER, D. A.
MIROLLO, J. V.
MORETTI, F.
O'MEALLY, R. G.
PETERS, J. S.
QUIGLEY, A.
ROSENBERG, J. D.
ROSENTHAL, M.
SAID, E.
SEIDEL, M.
SHAPIRO, J.
SPIVAK, G. C.
STADE, G.
TAYLER, E. W.
YERKES, D.

French and Romance Philology:
BLOCH, R. H.
COMPAGNON, A.
CONDE, M.
FORCE, P.
LOTRINGER, S.
MAY, G.
MITTERAND, H.
RIFFATERRE, M.

Genetics and Development:
BESTOR, T.
CARLSON, M.
COSTANTINI, F.
EFSTRATIADIS, A.
GILLIAM, T. C.
OTT, J.
PAPAIOANNOU, V.
ROTHSTEIN, R. J.
SCHON, E. A.
STERN, C. D.
STRUHL, G.
WARBURTON, D.
WOLGEMUTH, D.

Geological Sciences:
BROECKER, W. S.
CHRISTIE-BLICK, N.
FAIRBANKS, R. G.
GORDON, A. L.
HAYES, D. E.
HAYS, J. O.
LANGMUIR, C.
MENKE, W.
MUTTER, J.
OLSEN, P.
RICHARDS, P. G.
SCHLOSSER, P.
SCHOLZ, C.
SIMPSON, H. J.
SYKES, L. R.
WALKER, D.

Germanic Languages:
ANDERSON, M. M.
HUYSSEN, A.
MULLER, H.
VON MUCKE, D. E.

History:
BILLOWS, R.
BLACKMAR, E.
BRINKLEY, A.
BULLIET, R.
BUSHMAN, R.
BYNUM, C.
CANNADINE, D.
DE GRAZIA, V.
DEAK, I.
FIELDS, B.
FONER, E.
GLUCK, C.
GOREN, A. A.
HAIMSON, L.
HARRIS, W. V.
HOWELL, M.
JACKSON, K. T.
KLEIN, H. S.
LYNCH, H. R.
MALEFAKIS, E. E.
MARABLE, M.
PAXTON, R.
ROTHMAN, D.
SCHAMA, S.
SHENTON, J. P.
SMIT, J. W.
STANISLAWSKI, M.
STEPAN, N.
STERN, F.
VON HAGEN, M. L.
WOLOCH, I.
WORTMAN, R.
WRIGHT, M.
YERUSHALMI, Y. H.

Industrial Engineering and Operations Research:
BIENSTOCK, D.
GALLEGO, G.
GOLDFARB, D.

KLEIN, M.
PINEDO, M.
SIGMAN, K.
YAO, D. D.-W.

International and Public Affairs:
MOLZ, R. K.
NELSON, R. R.
RODRIK, D.

Italian:
BAROLINI, T.
REBAY, L.

Journalism:
BELFORD, B.
BENEDICT, H.
CAREY, J. W.
GARLAND, P.
GOLDSTEIN, K. K.
ISAACS, S. D.
KONNER, J.

Krumb School of Mines:
BESHERS, D. N.
DUBY, P. F.
HARRIS, C. C.
SOMASUNDARAN, P.
THEMELIS, N. J.
YEGULALP, T. M.

Law:
BARENBERG, M.
BERGER, C. J.
BERGER, V.
BERMANN, G.
BLACK, B. A.
BLACK, B. S.
BLASI, V.
BRIFFAULT, R.
CHIRELSTEIN, M.
COFFEE, J. C.
CRENSHAW, K. W.
DAMROSCH, L.
EDGAR, H. S. H.
EDWARDS, R.
FARNSWORTH, E. A.
FINEMAN, M.
FLETCHER, G.
GARDNER, R.
GILSON, R. J.
GINSBURG, J. C.
GOLDBERG, V. P.
GOLDSCHMID, H. J.
GORDON, J. N.
GREENAWALT, R. K.
GREENBERG, J.
HOOVER, J.
JONES, W. K.
KORN, H. L.
LEEBRON, D. W.
LIEBMAN, J.
LIEBMAN, L.
LYNCH, G.
MOGLEN, E.
MONAGHAN, H.
NARASIMHAN, S.
NEUMAN, G. L.
PARKER, K. E.
RABB, H. S.
RAPACZYNSKI, A.
ROE, M. J.
SABEL, C. F.
SMIT, H.
SOVERN, M.
STONE, R.
STRAUSS, P. L.
THOMAS, K.
UVILLER, H. R.
WILLIAMS, P. J.
YOUNG, M.
YOUNG, W. F., Jr

Mathematics:
BASS, H.
FRIEDMAN, R.
GALLAGHER, P. X.
GOLDFELD, D.
JACQUET, H. M.
JORGENSEN, T.
KARATZAS, I.
KURANISHI, M.
MORGAN, J.
PHONG, D.
PINKHAM, H. C.

Mechanical Engineering:
CHEVRAY, R.
FREUDENSTEIN, F.
LONGMAN, R. W.
MODI, V.

Medicine:
AL-AWQATI, Q.
APPEL, G. B.
BAER, L. R.
BANK, A.
BIGGER, J. T.
BILEZIKIAN, J. P.
BUTLER, V. P., Jr
CALDWELL, L. P.
CANFIELD, R. E.
CANNON, P. J.
CHESS, L.
CIMINO, J. J.
CLAYTON, P. D.
CORTELL, S.
FIELD, M.
FRANCIS, C. K.
FRANTZ, A. G.
GIARDINA, E.-G.
GINSBURG, H. N.
GOLDBERG, I. J.
GRIECO, M. H.
HOLT, P. R.
JACOBS, T. P.
KEMP, H., Jr
LEGATO, M. J.
LEIFER, E.
LINDENBAUM, J.
LOEB, J.
MELCHER, G.
MORRIS, T. Q.
MORSE, J. E.
NEU, H. C.
PHILLIPS, G. B.
PI-SUNYER, F. X.
ROSNER, W.
SCHWARTZ, M. J.
TABAS, I. A.
TALL, A.
TAPLEY, D. F.
TAUB, R. N.
THOMSON, G. E.
TURINO, G. M.
WARDLAW, S.
WEINSTEIN, I. B.
WEISFELDT, M. L.
WEISS, H. J.

Microbiology:
CALAME, K. L.
FIGURSKI, D.
MITCHELL, A. P.
RACANIELLO, V. R.
SHORE, D. M.
SHUMAN, H. A.
SILVERSTEIN, S. J.
YOUNG, C.

Middle East and Asian Languages and Cultures:
BURRILL, K. R. F.
MADINA, M.
MIRON, D.
PRITCHETT, F.
RICCARDI, T.
SALIBA, G.
VAN DE MIEROOP, M.

Music:
BENT, I.
CHRISTENSEN, D.
EDWARDS, G.
FRISCH, W.
KRAMER, J.
LERDAHL, A. W.
PERKINS, L.
SISMAN, E.
TUCKER, M. T.

Neurological Surgery:
BRISMAN, R.
HOUSEPIAN, E. M.
MCMURTRY, J.
QUEST, D. O.
STEIN, B. M.

Neurology:
BRUST, J. C. M., Jr
COTE, L. J.
DE VIVO, D. C.
DI MAURO, S.
EMERSON, R. G.
FAHN, S.
GHEZ, C.
GOLD, A. P.
HALSEY, J., Jr
HAUSER, W. A.
KARLIN, A.
LATOV, N.
LOVELACE, R. E.
MAYEUX, R.
MOHR, J. P.
PEDLEY, T.
PENN, A. S.
ROWLAND, L. P.
SCHWARTZ, J.
SCIARRA, D.
STERN, Y.
WEXLER, N.

Nursing:
FULMER, T. T.
MUNDINGER, M. O.

Obstetrics and Gynaecology:
BOWE, E. T.
FERIN, M.
HEMBREE, W. C.
JAGIELLO, G.
LOBO, R. A.
NEUWIRTH, R. S.
TIMOR, I. E.
WILLIAMS, S. B.

Ophthalmology:
BEHRENS, M.
BITO, L.
DONN, A.
FARRIS, R. L.
FORBES, M.
GOURAS, P.
L'ESPERANCE, F., Jr
MOORE, S.
SPALTER, H.
SPECTOR, A.
SRINIVASAN, B.
TROKEL, S.
WORGUL, B. V.
YANNUZZI, L. A.

Orthopaedic Surgery:
DICK, H.
EFTEKHAR, N.
FIELDING, J. W.
GRANTHAM, S. A.
LAI, W. M.
MOW, V. C.
RATCLIFFE, A.
SHELTON, M. L.

Otolaryngology:
BLITZER, A.
CLOSE, L. G.
KHANNA, S. M.

Pathology:
AXEL, R.
DALLA-FAVERA, R.
GELLER, L. M.
GOLDMAN, J. E.
GREENE, L. A.
KAUFMAN, M.
KOHN, D. F.
LEFKOWITCH, J. H.
LIEM, R. K. H.

MASON, C. A.
PERZIN, K. H.
RICHART, R. M.
SHELANSKI, M. L.
SUCIU-FOCA, N.

Paediatrics:
COOPER, L. Z.
CUNNINGHAM, N.
DECKELBAUM, R. J.
DELL, R. B.
DRISCOLL, J. M.
GERSHON, A. A.
GERSONY, W. M.
HEAGARTY, M.
JACOBS, J.
KRONGRAD, E.
LEBLANC, W.
LEVINE, L.
MELLIN, G. W.
MELLINS, R. B.
NICHOLSON, J. F.
PIOMELLI, S.
SITARZ, A.
STARK, R.
WETHERS, D. L.
WINCHESTER, R. J.

Pharmacology:
BOYDEN, P.
GOLDBERG, D. J.
GRAZIANO, J. H.
HOFFMAN, B. F.
ROBINSON, R. B.
ROSEN, M. R.
SIEGELBAUM, S. A.
WIT, A. L.

Philosophy:
ALBERT, D.
BEROFSKY, B.
BILGRAMI, A.
GAIFMAN, H.
GOEHR, L. D.
LARMORE, C.
LEVI, I.
POGGE, T.
SIDORSKY, D.

Physical Education and Intercollegiate Athletics:
ROHAN, J. P.

Physics:
APRILE, E.
CHRIST, N. H.
GYULASSY, M.
HAILEY, C. J.
HARTMANN, S.
KAHN, S. M.
LEE, T. D.
LEE, W.
MUELLER, A.
NAGAMIYA, S.
RUDERMAN, M. A.
SCHWARTZ, M.
SCIULLI, F.
SHAEVITZ, M. H.
TUTS, P. M.
UEMURA, Y.
WEINBERG, E.
WILLIS, W. J.
ZAJC, W. A.

Physiology and Cellular Biophysics:
BLANK, M.
DODD, J.
FISCHBARG, J.
KANDEL, E. R.
LOW, M. G.
SCHACHTER, D.
SILVERSTEIN, S. C.
STERN, D.

Political Science:
ANDERSON, L.
BALDWIN, D.
BERNSTEIN, T. P.
BETTS, R. K.
BIALER, S.
CHALMERS, D. A.
COHEN, J. L.
CURTIS, G. L.
ELSTER, J.
FRANKLIN, J. H.
HAMILTON, C. V.
JERVIS, R. L.
JOHNSTON, D. C.
KATZNELSON, I. I.
KESSELMAN, M. J.
LEGVOLD, R.
MILNER, H.
NATHAN, A. N.
ROTHSCHILD, J.
RUGGIE, J.
SCHILLING, W. R.
SHAPIRO, R. Y.
SNYDER, J.
WESTIN, A. F.

Psychiatry:
BENNETT, R.
DEVANAND, D.
DOHRENWEND, B.
DUNTON, H. D.
EHRHARDT, A. A.
ENDICOTT, J.
ERLENMEYER-KIMLING, L.
FIEVE, R. R.
FISCHMAN, M. W.
FOLEY, A. R.
GLASSMAN, A. H.
GORMAN, J. M.
GURLAND, B. J.
HOFER, M.
JAFFE, J.
KLEBER, H. D.
KLEIN, D. F.
KLEIN, R. G.
KUPFERMANN, I.
PARDES, H.
PROHOVNIK, I.
RAINER, J.
RYAN, J.
SACKEIM, H. A.
SHAFFER, D.
SPITZER, R.
TAMIR, H.
WEISSMAN, M. M.

Psychology:
COOPER, L. A.
DWECK, C. S.
GALANTER, E. H.
GIBBON, J.
GRAHAM, N.
HIGGINS, E. T.
HOOD, D. C.
KRANTZ, D.
KRAUSS, R.
MATIN, L.
METCALFE, J.
MISCHEL, W.
TERRACE, H. S.

Public Health:
BAYER, R.
BRANDT-RAUF, P. W.
BROWN, L.
CHALLENOR, B. D.
COLOMBOTOS, J. L.
DAVIDSON, A.
DESPOMMIER, D. D.
FLEISS, J. L.
HASHIM, S. A.
HOWE, G. R.
KANDEL, D.
LEVIN, B.
LINK, B. G.
LO, S.-H.
MCCARTHY, J.
OTTMAN, R.
PEARSON, T. A.
PERERA, F. P.
ROSENFIELD, A. G.
SANTELLA, R. P.
SISK, J. E.
STRUENING, E. L.
TSAI, W.-Y.

Radiation Oncology:
AMOLS, H. I.
BRENNER, D. J.
GEARD, C.
HALL, E.
HEI, T. K.
SCHIFF, P. B.

Radiology:
ABLOW, R. C.
ALDERSON, P. O.
BERDON, W.
ESSER, P.
FELDMAN, F.
HILAL, S.
KING, D. L.
NEWHOUSE, J. H.
NICKOLOFF, E. L.
SILVER, A. J.

Rehabilitation Medicine:
DOWNEY, J. A.
EDELSTEIN, J. E.
LIEBERMAN, J. S.
MYERS, S. J.
NEUHAUS, B. E.
THORNHILL, H.

Religion:
AWN, J.
LINDT, G.
PROUDFOOT, W.
RUPP, G.
SOMERVILLE, R.
THURMAN, R.
WEISS-HALIVNI, D.

Slavic Languages:
BELKNAP, R. L.
GASPAROV, B.
MAGUIRE, R. A.
MILLER, F. J.
POPKIN, C.
REYFMAN, I.

Social Work:
AKABAS, S.
BLACK, R. B.
CLOWARD, R. A.
FELDMAN, R.
GARFINKEL, I.
GITTERMAN, A.
HESS, M. M.
IVANOFF, A.
KAMERMAN, S. B.
KIRK, S.
MCGOWAN, B.
MEYER, C. H.
MONK, A.
MULLEN, E. J.
POLSKY, H.
SCHILLING, R. F.
SCHINKE, S.
SIMON, B. L.
SOLOMON, R.

Sociology:
COLE, J. R.
GANS, H.
LITWAK, E.
RUGGIE, M.
SILVER, A. A.
SPILERMAN, S.
WHITE, H.

Spanish and Portuguese:
ALAZRAKI, J.
GRIEVE, P. E.
MARTINEZ-BONATI, F.
SILVER, P. W.
SOBEJANO, G.

Statistics:
DE LA PENA, V.
HEYDE, C. C.

Surgery:
ALTMAN, R. P.
CHIU, D. T. W.

Forde, K.
Hardy, M. A.
Hugo, N.
Lo Gerfo, P.
Markowitz, A.
Nowygrod, R.
Quaegebeur, J. M.
Reemtsma, K.
Rose, E. A.
Smith, C. R.
Spotnitz, H. M.
Stolar, C. J. H.
Tilson, M. D.

Urology:
Buttyan, R.
Hensle, T. W.
Olsson, C. A.
Puchner, P. J.
Romas, N. S.

AFFILIATED COLLEGES

Barnard College: 606 W. 120th St, New York, NY 10027; private liberal arts for women; Pres. Judith R. Shapiro.

Teachers College, Columbia University: 525 W. 120th St, New York, NY 10027; private, professional, graduate only; Pres. Arthur Elliott Levine.

ATTACHED INSTITUTES AND CENTRES

Accounting Research Center: Dirs Trevor Harris, Nahum Melumad.
Center for Chinese Business Studies: Dir Hoke Simpson.
Center for Chinese Legal Studies: Dir R. Randle Edwards.
Center for Climate Research: Dir Wallace Broecker.
Center for Human Resource Management Studies: Dir Ann Bartel.
Center for International Business Education: Dir Kathryn Harrigan.
Center for Israel and Jewish Studies: Dir Yosef H. Yerushalmi.
Center for Japanese Economy and Business: Dir Hugh Patrick.
Center for Japanese Legal Studies: Dir Michael K. Young.
Center for Law and the Arts: Dir John M. Kernochan.
Center for Law and Economic Studies: Dirs Victor P. Goldberg, Jeffrey N. Gordon.
Center for Molecular Recognition: Dir Arthur Karlin.
Center for Neurobiology and Behavior: Dir John Koester (acting).
Center for the Study of Operations: Dir Martin K. Starr.
Center for Population and Family Health: Dir James McCarthy.
Center for Preservation Research: Dir Martin Weaver.
Center for Psychoanalytic Training and Research: Dir Roger MacKinnon.
Center for Radiological Research: Dir Eric J. Hall.
Center for Research in Arts and Culture: Dir Joan Jeffri.
Center for Telecommunications Research: Dir Anthony Acampora.
Center for the Social Sciences: Dir Harrison White.
Center for the Study of Futures Markets: Dir Franklin R. Edwards.
Center for the Study of Geriatrics and Gerontology: Dir Barry J. Gurland.
Center for the Study of Human Rights: Dir J. Paul Martin.
Center for the Study of Innovation and Entrepreneurship: Dir Michael Tushman.
Center for the Study of Society and Medicine: Dir David J. Rothman.
Columbia Institute for Tele-Information: Dir Eli Noam.
Columbia-Presbyterian Cancer Center: Dir I. Bernard Weinstein.
Donald Keene Center of Japanese Culture: Dir Haruo Shirane.
East Asian Institute: Dir Madeleine Zelin.
Executive Leadership Research Center: Dir Donald Hambrick.
Fritz Reiner Center: Dir Alfred Lerdahl.
George T. Delacorte Center for Magazine Journalism: Dir (vacant).
Gertrude H. Sergievsky Center: Dir Richard P. Mayeux.
Harriman Institute: Dir Mark von Hagen.
Herbert and Florence Irving Center for Clinical Research: Dir Henry N. Ginsberg.
Institute for Marketing: Dir Donald Lehmann.
Institute for Not-for-Profit Management: Dir Raymond D. Horton.
Institute of African Studies: Dir George C. Bond.
Institute of Cancer Research: Dir Maxwell E. Gottesman.
Institute of Comparative Medicine: Dir Dennis S. Kohn.
Institute of Human Nutrition: Dir Richard J. Deckelbaum.
Institute of Latin American and Iberian Studies: Dir Douglas Chalmers.
Institute of War and Peace Studies: Dir Jack L. Snyder.
Institute for Research on Women and Gender: Dir Victoria De Grazia.
Institute on Aging: Dir Abraham Monk.
Institute on East Central Europe: Dir John S. Micgiel.
Institute on Western Europe: Dir Glenda G. Rosenthal.
International Institute for the Study of Human Reproduction: Dir Georgiana Jagiello.
Lamont-Doherty Earth Observatory: Dir John C. Mutter (acting).
Legislative Drafting Research Fund: Dir Richard Briffault.
Management Institute: Dir E. Kirby Warren.
Middle East Institute: Dir Richard W. Bulliet.
Parker School of Foreign and Comparative Law: Dir Hans Smit.
Southern Asian Institute: Dir Philip K. Oldenburg.
Temple Hoyne Buell Center for the Study of American Architecture: Dir Joan Ockman.

COOPER UNION FOR THE ADVANCEMENT OF SCIENCE AND ART

Cooper Square, New York, NY 10003
Telephone: (212) 353-4100
Founded 1859
President: John Jay Iselin
Chairman: Robert Bernhard
Vice-President for Business Affairs and Treasurer: Robert Hawks
Provost: (vacant)
Dean of Admissions: Richard L. Bory
Head Librarian: Elizabeth Vajda
Library of 88,900 vols
Number of teachers: 180
Number of students: 1,050
Publication: *At Cooper Union.*

DEANS

School of Art: Robert Rindler
School of Architecture: John Q. Hejduk
School of Engineering: Eleanor Baum
Faculty of Humanities and Social Sciences: John Harrington

CORNELL UNIVERSITY

Ithaca, NY 14853
Telephone: (607) 255-2000
Founded 1865
State and private control
Academic year: September to May
President: Hunter R. Rawlings III
Provost: Don R. Randel
Provost for Medical Affairs: Antonio Gotto
Senior Vice-President and Chief Financial Officer: Frederick A. Rogers
Vice-President for Alumni Affairs and Development: Inge Riechenbach
Vice-President for University Relations: H. N. Dullea
Vice-President for Student and Academic Services: S. H. Murphy
Vice-President for Information Technologies: (vacant)
Vice-President for Budget and Planning: Carolyn N. Ainslie
Vice-President for Facilities and Campus Services: Harold D. Craft Jr
Vice-President for Financial Affairs and Controller: Yoke San Reynolds
Vice-President for Human Resources: Mary G. Opperman
Vice-Provosts: Robert Richardson (Research), Cutberto Garza, Mary San Salone
Associate Provost: Winnie F. Taylor
Librarian: Sarah Thomas
Library: see Libraries
Number of teachers: 3,000
Number of students: 19,000
Publications: *Cornell Reports, Cornell Chronicle, Cornell Alumni, News, Administrative Science Quarterly, Cornell Law Review, Cornell Plantations, Cornell Veterinarian Quarterly, Cornell Engineering Quarterly, Cornell Hotel and Restaurant Administration Quarterly, Graduate School of Nutrition News, Industrial and Labor Relations Review, Library Journal Quarterly, Philosophical Review, Cornell Countryman, Campus Guide, Campus Walks, Cornell Desk Book, Cornell in Perspective, Cornellian, Cornell Daily Sun, Epoch, Facts About Cornell, Farm Research Quarterly, Food Topics, Human Ecology Forum, Introduction to Cornell, Music at Cornell, Cornell Alumni News, Cornell Enterprise (JGSM), Cornell International Law Journal, Cornell Law Forum, Cornell Engineering News, Northeast Indian Quarterly, Sapsucker Woods,* over 20 annual catalogues.

DEANS

University Faculty: J. R. Cooke
Graduate School: Walter I. Cohen (Vice-Provost and Dean)
Law School: C. W. Wolfram (interim)
Medical College: Antonio Gotto
Graduate School of Medical Sciences: David P. Hajjar
College of Architecture, Art and Planning: Porus D. Olpadwala (interim)
College of Arts and Sciences: Philip E. Lewis
College of Engineering: John E. Hopcroft
Division of Summer Session, Extra-mural Courses and Related Programs: Glenn C. Altschuler
New York State College of Veterinary Medicine: Donald Smith
New York State College of Agriculture and Life Sciences: Daryl B. Lund
New York State College of Human Ecology: F. M. Firebaugh
Graduate School of Management: Robert Swieringa
School of Hotel Administration: David A. Dittman
New York State School of Industrial and Labor Relations: Edward Lawler

PROFESSORS

Law School:
Abrams, K.
Alexander, G.
Barcelo, J., III
Clermont, K. M.
Cramton, R. C.
Eisenberg, T.
Farina, C.

Germain, C.
Hay, G. A.
Henderson, J., Jr
Hillman, R.
Johnson, S. L.
Lopucki, L.
McChesney, F.
Macey, J.
Martin, P. W.
Osgood, R.
Palmer, L. I.
Rossi, F. F.
Schwab, S.
Shiffrin, S.
Siliciano, J.
Simson, G. J.
Stone, K.
Summers, R. S.
Taylor, W.
Wolfram, C.

Medical Division:

(The Division comprises the Medical College (MC) and Graduate School of Medicine (GSM); professors serve only the Medical College unless otherwise indicated)

Anaesthesiology:

Blanck, T. J. J., Anaesthesiology (MC), Medicine (GSM)
Carlon, G. C., Anaesthesiology (Clinical)
Savarese, J. J., Anaesthesiology
Short, C. E., Anaesthesiology
Thomas, S. J., Anaesthesiology
Topkins, M. J., Anaesthesiology (Clinical)
Van Poznak, A., Anaesthesiology
Wilson, R. S., Anaesthesiology

Biochemistry:

Boskey, A. L., Biochemistry (MC & GSM)
Breslow, E. M., Biochemistry (MC & GSM)
Cooper, A. J. L., Biochemistry
Haschemeyer, R. H., Biochemistry (MC & GSM)
Horecker, B. L., Biochemistry (GSM)
Novogrodsky, A., Biochemistry (MC & GSM)
Rubin, A. L., Biochemistry (MC & GSM)
Stenzel, K. H., Biochemistry (MC & GSM)

Cell Biology:

Bachvarova, R. F., Cell Biology and Anatomy (MC), Cell Biology and Genetics (GSM)
Biedler, J. L., Cell Biology and Genetics (GSM)
Brooks, D. C., Cell Biology and Anatomy (MC), Cell Biology and Genetics (GSM)
Chao, M. V., Cell Biology and Anatomy (MC), Cell Biology and Genetics (GSM)
Fischman, D. A., Cell Biology and Anatomy (MC), Cell Biology and Genetics (GSM)
Gumbiner, B. M., Cell Biology and Genetics (GSM)
Hagamen, W. D., Jr, Cell Biology and Anatomy
Hutchison, D. J., Cell Biology and Genetics (GSM)
Massagu, J., Cell Biology and Genetics (GSM)
Moore, M. A. S., Cell Biology and Genetics (GSM)
Rodriguez-Boulan, E. J., Cell Biology and Anatomy (MC), Cell Biology and Genetics (GSM)
Rothman, J. E., Cell Biology and Genetics (GSM)
Sirlin, J. L., Cell Biology and Anatomy (MC), Cell Biology and Genetics (GSM)
Traktman, P., Cell Biology and Anatomy

Immunology:

Dupont, B., Immunology (GSM)
Hammerling, U., Immunology (GSM)
Lloyd, K. O., Immunology (GSM)
Old, L. J., Immunology (GSM)

Medicine:

Armstrong, D., Medicine
Bertino, J. R., Medicine (MC), Pharmacology (GSM)
Bockman, R. S., Medicine
Bogdonoff, M. D., Medicine
Borer, J. S., Medicine
Bosl, G. J., Medicine
Carter, D. M., Medicine
Charlson, M. E., Medicine
Cheigh, J. S., Medicine (Clinical)
Chiorazzi, N., Medicine (MC & GSM)
Christian, C. L., Medicine
Clarkson, B. D., Medicine
Crystal, R. G., Internal Medicine
De Vita, V. T., Jr, Medicine
Degnan, T. J., Medicine (Clinical)
Devereux, R. B., Medicine
Elkon, K. B., Endocrinology in Medicine
Ellois, J. R., Medicine (GSM)
Feinberg, A. W., Medicine (Clinical)
Friedman, S. M., Medicine
Fuks, Z. Y., Medicine (Radiation Oncology)
German, J. L., III, Medicine (GSM)
Gershengorn, M. C., Endocrinology in Medicine (MC), Physiology and Biophysics (GSM)
Gibofsky, A., Medicine (Clinical)
Gnlafi, S. C., Medicine
Golde, D. W., Medicine (MC), Pharmacology (GSM)
Hayes, J. G., Medicine
Houde, R. W., Medicine
Houghton, A. N., Medicine (MC), Immunology (GSM)
Imperato-McGinley, J. L., Medicine
Jaffe, E., Medicine (MC & GSM)
Johnson, W. D., Jr, Medicine
Kagen, L. J., Medicine
Kaplan, M. H., Medicine (Clinical)
Kappas, A., Medicine
Kelsen, D. P., Medicine
Kemeny, N. E., Medicine
Kiehn, T. E., Medicine (Clinical)
Kimberly, T. P., Medicine (MC & GSM)
Klein, H., Medicine (Clinical)
Klein, I. L., Medicine (MC & GSM)
Kligfield, P. D., Medicine
Kreis, W., Medicine
Kurtz, R. C., Medicine (Clinical)
Laragh, J. H., Medicine
Lerman, B. B., Medicine
Lipkin, M., Medicine (MC & GSM)
Marcus, A. J., Medicine
Margouleff, D., Medicine (Clinical)
Marks, P. A., Medicine (MC), Cell Biology and Genetics (GSM)
Mayer, K., Medicine (Clinical)
Mendelsohn, L., Medicine (MC), Pharmacology (GSM)
Murray, H. W., Medicine (MC & GSM)
Nachman, R. L., Medicine (MC & GSM)
Nathan, C., Medicine (MC & GSM)
Oettgen, H. F., Medicine
Pickering, T. G., Medicine
Pritchett, R. A. R., Medicine (Clinical)
Rifkind, R. A., Medicine (MC), Cell Biology and Genetics (GSM)
Riggio, R. R., Medicine (Clinical)
Rivlin, R. S., Medicine
Roberts, R. B., Medicine
Roe, D. A., Medicine (Nutrition)
Sanborn, T. A., Medicine
Scheidt, S., Medicine (Clinical)
Scherr, L., Medicine
Schulman, P., Medicine (Clinical)
Sealey, J. E., Medicine
Silver, J., Medicine (Cellular Biology)
Siskind, G. W., Medicine (MC & GSM)
Smith, K. A., Medicine (MC & GSM)
Soffer, R. L., Medicine (MC & GSM)
Sonenberg, M., Medicine (MC), Cell Biology and Genetics (GSM)
Steinberg, C. R., Medicine (Clinical)
Suthanthiran, M., Medicine
Thomas, M. H., III, Medicine (Clinical)
Timberger, R. J., Medicine (Clinical)
Vinciguerra, V. P., Medicine
Warrell, P., Jr, Medicine
Weinstein, A. M., Medicine
Weksler, B. B., Medicine (MC & GSM)
Weksler, M. E., Geriatrics in Medicine (MC & GSM)
Wilkes, B. M., Medicine
Winawer, S. J., Medicine (Clinical)
Young, C. W., Medicine
Zakim, D., Medicine (MC & GSM)

Microbiology:

Berns, K. I., Microbiology (MC & GSM)
Besmer, P., Molecular Biology (GSM)
Gilboa, E., Molecular Biology (GSM)
Hayward, W. S., Molecular Biology (GSM)
Holloman, W. K., Microbiology (MC), Molecular Biology (GSM)
Hurwitz, J., Molecular Biology (GSM)
Marians, K. J., Molecular Biology (GSM)
O'Donnell, M. E., Microbiology
O'Leary, W. M., Microbiology (MC), Molecular Biology (GSM)
Ravetch, J. A., Molecular Biology (GSM)
Senterfit, L. B., Microbiology (MC), Medicine (GSM)

Neurology and Neuroscience:

Blasberg, R. G., Neurology (MC), Neuroscience (GSM)
Blass, J. P., Neurology (MC), Medicine (GSM)
Caronna, J. J., Neurology (Clinical)
Foley, K. M., Neurology and Neuroscience
Gibson, G. E., Neuroscience (MC & GSM)
Halperin, J. J., Neurology
Hirsch, J., Neuroscience (MC), Pharmacology (GSM)
Joh, T. H., Neuroscience (MC & GSM)
McDowell, F. H., Neurology and Neuroscience
Pasternak, G. W., Neurology and Neuroscience
Petito, F. A., Neurology and Neuroscience (Clinical)
Pickel, V. M., Neuroscience (MC & GSM)
Plum, F., Neurology and Neuroscience
Posner, J. B., Neurology and Neuroscience
Reis, D. J., Neurology and Neuroscience
Victor, J. D., Neurology and Neuroscience
Wagner, J. A., Neurology and Neuroscience

Obstetrics and Gynaecology:

Bedford, J. M., Obstetrics and Gynaecology (Reproductive Biology)
Caputo, T. A., Obstetrics and Gynaecology (Clinical)
Chao, S., Obstetrics and Gynaecology (Clinical)
Chervenak, F. A., Obstetrics and Gynaecology
Fenton, A. N., Obstetrics and Gynaecology
Fuchs, S. A. R., Obstetrics and Gynaecology (Reproductive Biology)
Hoskins, W. J., Obstetrics and Gynaecology
Jones, W. B., Obstetrics and Gynaecology
Ledger, W. S., Obstetrics and Gynaecology
Lewis, J. J., Jr, Obstetrics and Gynaecology
Lovecchio, J. L., Obstetrics and Gynaecology (Clinical)
Rosenfeld, D. L., Obstetrics and Gynaecology (Clinical)
Rosenwaks, Z., Obstetrics and Gynaecology
Saxena, B. B., Obstetrics and Gynaecology (Endocrinology) (MC), Medicine (GSM)
Sicuranza, B. J., Obstetrics and Gynaecology (Clinical)
Witkin, S. S., Obstetrics and Gynaecology (Immunology)

Ophthalmology:

Chang, S., Ophthalmology
Coleman, D. J., Ophthalmology
Cooper, W. C., Ophthalmology (Clinical)
MacLeish, P. R., Ophthalmology (MC), Physiology and Biophysics (GSM)
Packer, S., Ophthalmology (Clinical)
Roberts, C. W., Ophthalmology (Clinical)

Pathology:

ALONSO, D. R., Pathology (MC), Medicine (GSM)
BROOME, J. D., Pathology
BULLOUGH, P. G., Pathology (MC), Medicine (GSM)
CAMPBELL, W. G., Jr, Pathology
CASALI, P., Pathology
CHAGANTI, R. S. K., Pathology (Genetics) (MC), Cell Biology and Genetics (GSM)
HAJDU, S. I., Pathology
HAJJAR, D. P., Pathology (MC), Biochemistry (GSM)
HUVOS, A. G., Pathology
KAHN, E. I., Pathology (Clinical)
LIEBERMAN, P. H., Pathology
MCNUTT, N. S., Pathology
MINICK, C. R., Pathology (MC), Medicine (GSM)
MOURADIAN, J. A., Pathology
ROSAI, J., Pathology
ROSEN, P. P., Pathology
SANTOS-BUCH, C. A., Pathology (MC), Medicine (GSM)
STERNBERG, S. S., Pathology (MC), Pharmacology (GSM)
SUN, T., Pathology (Clinical)
WOLF, C. F. W., Pathology (Clinical)
WOODRUFF, J. M., Pathology

Paediatrics:

AULD, P. A., Paediatrics
CHUTORIAN, A. B., Paediatrics
COOPER, R. S., Paediatrics (Clinical)
DAUM, F., Paediatrics
EHLERS, K. H., Paediatrics
FISHER, S. E., Paediatrics
FRIEDMAN, D. M., Paediatrics (Clinical)
GERTNER, J. M., Paediatrics
HAJJAR, K. A., Paediatrics
HARPER, R. G., Paediatrics (Perinatal Medicine)
HILGARTNER, M. W., Paediatrics
KAHN, E. I., Paediatrics (Clinical)
KLEIN, A. A., Paediatrics (Clinical)
KOCHEN, J. A., Paediatrics
LEHMAN, T. J. A., Paediatrics (Clinical)
LEIBEL, R. L., Paediatrics
LEVIN, A. R., Paediatrics
LEVY, J., Paediatrics (Clinical)
MARSHALL, F. N., Paediatrics (Clinical)
MULLER-EBERHARD, U., Paediatrics (MC), Pharmacology (GSM)
NEW, M. I., Paediatrics
O'REILLY, R. J., Paediatrics (MC), Immunology (GSM)
PAHWA, S. G., Paediatrics
SILVERBERG, M., Paediatrics
SIMONE, J. V., Paediatrics
STEINHERZ, P. G., Paediatrics
TAN, C. T. C., Paediatrics
WAPNIR, R. A., Paediatrics
WOLLNER-STERNBERG, N., Paediatrics

Pharmacology:

CHAN, W. W. Y., Pharmacology (MC & GSM)
CHOU, T. C., Pharmacology (GSM)
GUDAS, L. J., Pharmacology (MC & GSM)
INTURRISI, C. E., Pharmacology (MC & GSM)
LEVI, R., Pharmacology (MC & GSM)
OKAMOTO, M., Pharmacology (Anaesthesiology) (MC), Pharmacology (GSM)
REIDENBERG, M. M., Pharmacology (MC), Neuroscience (GSM)
RIFKIND, A. B., Pharmacology (MC & GSM)
RIKER, W. F., Jr, Pharmacology (GSM)
SCHWARTZ, M. K., Pharmacology (GSM)
SILAGI, S., Pharmacology (GSM)
SIROTNAK, F. M., Pharmacology (GSM)
STUTMAN, O., Pharmacology (GSM)
SZETO, H. H., Pharmacology
WATANABE, K. A., Pharmacology (GSM)

Physiology and Biophysics:

ANDERSEN, O. S., Physiology and Biophysics (MC & GSM)
GRAFSTEIN, B., Physiology and Biophysics (MC & GSM)
MAACK, T. M., Physiology and Biophysics (MC & GSM)
PALMER, L. G., Physiology and Biophysics (MC & GSM)
STEPHENSON, J. L., Physiology and Biophysics (Biomathematics) (MC), Physiology and Biophysics (GSM)
WINDHAGER, E. H., Physiology and Biophysics (MC & GSM)

Psychiatry:

ALEXOPOULOS, G. S., Psychiatry
BARCHAS, J. D., Psychiatry
BEMPORAD, J. R., Psychiatry (Clinical)
CLARKIN, J. F., Psychiatry (Clinical Psychology)
CLAYSON, M. D., Psychiatry (Clinical Psychology)
ESMAN, A., Psychiatry (Clinical)
FROSCH, W. A., Psychiatry
GAYLIN, S., Psychiatry (Clinical)
GIBBS, J. G., Jr, Psychiatry (MC), Neuroscience (GSM)
GILMAN, S., Psychiatry (History)
HALMI, K. A., Psychiatry
HOLLAND, J. C. B., Psychiatry
KATZ, J., Psychiatry (Clinical)
KERNBERG, O. F., Psychiatry
KOCSIS, J. H., Psychiatry
LORANGER, A. W., Psychiatry (Psychology)
MICHAELS, R., Psychiatry
MUNICH, R., Psychiatry (Clinical)
PFEFFER, C. R., Psychiatry
REDD, W. H., Psychiatry (Clinical Psychology) (MC), Pharmacology (GSM)
SACKS, M. H., Psychiatry
SAMITY, A. H., Psychiatry (Clinical Medicine)
SHAMOIAN, C. A., Psychiatry (Clinical)
SHAPIRO, T., Psychiatry (Clinical)
SMITH, G. P., Psychiatry (MC), Neuroscience (GSM)
STEIN, S. P., Psychiatry (Clinical)
STOKES, P. E., Psychiatry (MC), Medicine (GSM)
TARDIFF, K., Psychiatry
VIEDERMAN, M., Psychiatry (Clinical)

Public Health:

BEGG, C. B., Public Health (Biostatistics)
BOTVIN, G. J., Public Health (Psychology)
DRUSIN, L. M., Public Health (Clinical)
FINKEL, M., Public Health (Clinical)
HARLAP, S., Public Health (Epidemiology)
MILLMAN, R. B., Public Health (Psychology)
RUCHLIN, H. S., Public Health (Economics)

Radiology:

BATATA, H. A. E., Radiology (Clinical)
BECKER, D. V., Radiology
BRILL, P. W., Radiology
DECK, M. D. F., Radiology
FINN, R. D., Radiology (Physics)
FREIBERGER, R. H., Radiology
GOLDMAN, A. B., Radiology
GOLDSMITH, S. J., Radiology
HEELAN, R. T., Radiology
HENSCHKE, C. I., Radiology
HYMAN, R. A., Radiology
KAYE, J. J., Radiology
KAZAM, E., Radiology
LARSON, S. M., Radiology
LAUGHLIN, J. S., Radiology (Physics) (MC), Pharmacology (GSM)
LI, G. C., Radiology (Biophysics) (MC), Physiology and Biophysics (GSM)
LING, C. C., Radiology (Physics) (MC), Pharmacology (GSM)
MOHAN, R., Radiology (Physics)
NAIDICH, J. B., Radiology
NISCE, L. Z., Radiology
PAVLOV, H., Radiology
SOS, T. A., Radiology
WINCHESTER, P. H., Radiology
ZIMMERMAN, R. D., Radiology

Surgery:

ARBIT, E., Surgery (Neurosurgery)
BAINS, M., Surgery (Clinical)
BLUMGART, L. H., Surgery
BRADLOW, H. L., Surgery (Biochemistry)
BRENNAN, M., Surgery
BURSTEIN, A. H., Surgery (Applied Biomechanics)
CHASSIN, J. L., Surgery (Clinical)
COHEN, A. M., Surgery
CRAIG, E., Surgery (Orthopaedic)
DALY, J. M., Surgery
DECOSSE, J. J., Surgery
EISENBERG, M. M., Surgery
ENKER, W. E., Surgery (Clinical)
EXELBY, P. R., Surgery
FAIR, W. R., Surgery (Urology)
FISHMAN, J., Surgery (Biochemistry)
FORTNER, J. C., Surgery
FRASER, R. A. R., Surgery (Neurosurgery)
GALICICH, J. H., Jr, Surgery
GINSBERG, R. J., Surgery
GOLD, J. P., Surgery (Cardiothoracic)
GOLDSTEIN, M., Surgery (Urology)
GOULIAN, D., Jr, Surgery (Plastic Surgery)
ISOM, O. W., Surgery (Cardiothoracic)
KRIEGER, K. H., Surgery (Cardiothoracic)
LASKIN, R. S., Surgery (Clinical and Orthopaedic)
LEVINE, D. B., Surgery (Clinical and Orthopaedic)
LOWRY, S. F., Surgery
MCCORMICK, P., Surgery (Clinical)
MARTINI, N., Surgery
NAGLER, W., Surgery (Rehabilitation Medicine)
OSBORNE, M., Surgery
PATTERSON, R. H., Jr, Surgery (Neurosurgery)
PIZZI, W. F., Surgery (Clinical)
RANAWAT, C. S., Surgery (Clinical and Orthopaedic)
ROOT, L., Surgery (Clinical)
RUSCH, V. W., Surgery
SALVATI, E. A., Surgery (Clinical and Orthopaedic)
SCULCO, T. P., Surgery (Clinical and Orthopaedic)
SHAH, J. P., Surgery (Clinical)
SKINNER, D. B., Surgery (Cardiothoracic)
SPIRO, R. H., Surgery (Clinical)
STRONG, E. W., Surgery
STUBENBORD, W. T., Surgery
TURNBULL, A. D., Surgery (Clinical)
VAUGHAN, E. D., Jr, Surgery (Urology)
WARREN, R. F., Surgery (Orthopaedic)
WEILAND, A. J., Surgery (Orthopaedic and Plastic Surgery)
WESSON, D. E., Surgery
WHITMORE, W. F., Jr, Surgery (Urology)
WILSON, P. D., Surgery (Orthopaedic)
WISE, L., Surgery
WRIGHT, T. M., Surgery (Applied Biomechanics)
YURT, R. W., Surgery

College of Architecture, Art and Planning:

MCMINN, W.

Architecture:

GOSHNER, W.
GREENBERG, D. P.
HASCUP, G.
HUBBELL, K .
MILLER, J.
OTTO, C. F.
PEARMAN, C. W.
RICHARDSON, H.
SCHACK, M.
VIDLER, A.
WELLS, J.

Art:

BERTOIA, R.
BOWMAN, S.
KORD, V.
LOCEY, J.

POLESKIE, S.
SQUIER, J. L.

City and Regional Planning:

BENERIA, L.
CLAVEL, P.
DRENNAN, M.
FORESTER, J.
GOLDSMITH, W.
LEWIS, D.
OLPADWALA, P.
PARSONS, K. C.
SALTZMAN, S.

College of Arts and Sciences:

Anthropology:

ASCHER, R.
BESTOR, T.
GREENWOOD, D.
HENDERSON, J.
HOLMBERG, D.
KIRSCH, A.
LAMBERT, B.
SANGREN, P.
SIEGEL, J.
SMITH, R.

Asian Studies:

BRAZELL, K.
DEBARY, B.
GOLD, E.
GUNN, E.
MEI, T.-L.
SAKAI, N.
TAYLOR, K.

Astronomy:

CAMPBELL, D.
CORDES, J.
GIERASCH, P.
GIOVANELLI, R.
GOLDSMITH, P.
HAYNES, M.
HERTER, T.
HOUCK, J.
NICHOLSON, P.
SQUYRES, S.
TERZIAN, Y.
VEVERKA, J.
WASSERMAN, I.

Biochemistry, Molecular and Cell Biology:

BRETSCHER, A.
FEIGENSON, G.
HESS, G.
HINKLE, P.
WILSON, D

Chemistry:

ABRUNA, H.
ALBRECHT, A.
BAIRD, B.
BURLITCH, J.
CARPENTER, B.
CLARDY, J.
COLLUM, D.
DISALVO, F.
EZRA, G.
FAY, R.
FRECHET, J.
FREED, J.
GANEM, B.
HOFFMANN, R.
HOUSTON, P.
MCMURRY, J.
MEINWALD, J.
SOGAH, D.
WIDOM, B.
WILCOX, C., Jr
WOLCZANSKI, P.

Classics:

AHL, F.
CLINTON, K.
COLEMAN, J.
NUSSBAUM, A.
PUCCI, P.
RAWLINGS, H., III
RUSTEN, J.

SHANZER, D.

Comparative Literature:

APTER, E.
CARMICHAEL, C.
COHEN, W.
KENNEDY, W.
MONROE, J.

Ecology and Systematics:

HAIRSTON, N., Jr
KENNEDY, K.
PROVINE, W.

Economics:

BASU, K.
BLUME, L.
DAVIS, T.
EASLEY, D.
FRANK, R.
KIEFER, N.
MCCLELLAND, P.
MAJUMDAR, M.
MASSON, R.
MITRA, T.
POSSEN, U.
SHELL, K.
STALLER, G.
WAN, H., Jr

English:

ADAMS, B.
AMMONS, A.
BISHOP, J.
BOGEL, F.
BROWN, L.
CHASE, C.
CULLER, J.
FARRELL, R.
HERRIN, W.
HILL, T.
HITE, M.
JACOBUS, M.
JANOWITZ, P.
JEYIFO, B.
KASKE, C.
LEVY, C.
LURIE, A.
MCCALL, D.
MCCLANE, K., Jr
MCMILLIN, H.
MERMIN, D.
MOHANTY, S.
MORGAN, R.
MURRAY, T.
PARKER, A.
PORTE, J.
ROSENBERG, E.
SAWYER, P.,
SCHWARZ, D.
SELTZER, M.,
SHAW, H.
SIEGEL, S.
SPILLERS, H.
TESKEY, G.
VAUGHN, S.
WETHERBEE III, W.

Genetics and Development:

AQUADRO, C.
BLACKLER, A.
WOLFNER, M.

German Studies:

ADELSON, L.
DEINERT, H.
EZERGAILIS, I.
GROOS, A., Jr
HOHENDAHL, P.

Government:

ANDERSON, B.
BENSEL, R.
BERNAL, M.
BUCK-MORSS, S.
BUNCE, V.
HERRING, R.
KATZENSTEIN, P.
KRAMNICK, I.

LOWI, T.
SANDERS, M.
SHEFTER, M.
SHUE, V.
TARROW, S.
UPHOFF, N.

History:

ALTSCHULER, G.
BAUGH, D.,
BLUMIN, S.
COCHRAN, S.
HOLLOWAY, T.
HULL, I.
JOHN, J.
KAMMEN, M.
KAPLAN, S.
KOSCHMANN, J.
LA FEBER, W.
LACAPRA, D.
MOORE, R.
NAJEMY, J.
NORTON, M.
OKIHIRO, G.
PETERSON, C.
POLENBERG, R.
SHIRAISHI, T.
SILBEY, J.
STRAUSS, B.
USNER, D., Jr
WYATT, D.

History of Art:

CALKINS, R.
KUNIHOLM, P.
LAZZARO, C.
MEIXNER, L.
RAMAGE, A.
YOUNG, M.

Linguistics:

BOWERS, J.
HARBERT, W.
JASANOV, J.
MCCONNELL-GINET, S.
SUNA, M.

Mathematics:

BARBASCH, D.
BROWN, K.
CHASE, S.
COHEN, M.
CONNELLY, R.
DENNIS, R. K.
DIACONIS, P.
DURRETT, R.
DYNKIN, E.,
EARLE, C.
ESCOBAR, J.
FARRELL, R.
GROSS, L.
GUCKENHEIMER, J.
HATCHER, A.
HENDERSON, D.
HUBBARD, J.
HWANG, J.
KAHN, P.
KESTEN, H.
MORLEY, M.
NERODE, A.
ROTHAUS, O.
SALOFF-COSTE, L.
SCHATZ, A.
SEN, S.
SHORE, R.
SMILLIE, J.
SPEH, B.
STRICHARTZ, R.
SWEEDLER, M.
VOGTMANN, K.
WAHLBIN, L.
WEST, J.

Modern Languages and Linguistics:

GAIR, J.
LANTOLF, J.
ROSEN, C.
WAUGH, L.

WOLFF, J.

Music:

BILSON, M.
HSU, J.
RANDEL, D.
ROSEN, D.
SCATTERDAY, M.
STUCKY, S.
WEBSTER, J., Jr
ZASLAW, N.

Near Eastern Studies:

BRANN, S.
OWEN, D.
POWERS, D.
RENDSBURG, G.

Neurobiology and Behaviour:

BASS, A.
HOWLAND, H.
HOY, R.
PODLESKI, T.
SALPETER, M.
SEELEY, T.
SHERMAN, P.

Philosophy:

BOYD, R.
FINE, G.
GINET, C.
IRWIN, T
MACDONALD, S.
MILLER, R.
SHOEMAKER, S.
STURGEON, N.

Physics:

AMBEGAOKAR, V.
ASHCROFT, N.
BERKELMAN, K.
CASSEL, D.
COOPER, B.
DRELL, P.
DUGAN, G.
FITCHEN, D.
GALIK, R.
GITTELMAN, B.
GOTTFRIED, K.
GRUNER, S.
HAND, L.
HARTILL, D.
HO, W.
KALOS, M.
LEE, D.
LEPAGE, G.
LITTAUER, R.
MERMIN, N.
PARPIA, J.
POHL, R.
REPPY, J.
RICHARDSON, R.
SETHNA, J.
SIEVERS III, A.
SIGGIA, E.
STEIN, P.
TALMAN, R.
TEUKOLSKY, S.
TYE, S.-H.
YAN, T.-M.

Plant Biology:

TURGEON, E. G.

Program on Ethics and Public Life:

SHUE, H.

Psychology:

BEM, D.
BEM, S.
CUTTING, J.
DARLINGTON, R.
FINLAY, B.
GILOVICH, T.
HALPERN, B.
JOHNSTON, R.
KEIL, F.
KRUMHANSL, C.
MAAS, J.
NEISSER, U.
REGAN, E.

Romance Studies:

ARROYO, C.
BEREAUD, J.
CASTILLO, D.
FURMAN, N.
GREENBERG, M.
GROSSVOGEL, D.
KLEIN, R.
KRONIK, J.
LEWIS, P.
RESINA, J.
SEZNEC, A.
TITTLER, J.

Russian Literature:

CARDEN, P.
GIBIAN, G.
SENDEROVICH, S.
SHAPIRO, G.

Science and Technology Studies:

JASANOFF, S.
PINCH, T.
REPPY, J.
ROSSITER, M.

Sociology:

BREIGER, R.
MACY, M.
NEE, V.
STRANG, D.
WALKER, H.

Theatre Arts:

BATHRICK, D.
FELDSHUH, D.
LEVITT, B.

College of Engineering:

JELINSKI, L.

Applied and Engineering Physics:

BATTERMAN, B.
BUHRMAN, R.
COOL, T.
CRAIGHEAD, H.
FLEISCHMANN, H.
ISAACSON, M.
KUSSE, B.
LOVELACE, R.
SILCOX, J.
WEBB, W.

Chemical Engineering:

COHEN, C.
GUBBINS, K.
HARRIOTT, P.
OLBRICHT, W.
PANAGIOTOPOULOS, A.
RODRIGUEZ, F.
SALTZMAN, W.
SHULER, M.
STEEN, P.

Civil and Environmental Engineering:

ABEL, J.
BRUTSAERT, W.
DICK, R.
GOSSETT, J.
HOVER, K.
INGRAFFEA, A.
KULHAWY, F.
LION, L.
LIU, P.
LOUCKS, D.
MEYBURG, A.
O'ROURKE, T.
PEKOZ, T.
SANSALONE, M.
SCHULER, R.
SHOEMAKER, C.
STEDINGER, J.
TURNQUIST, M.
WHITE, R.

Computer Sciences:

BIRMAN, K.
COLEMAN, T.
CONSTABLE, R.
GRIES, D.
HALPERN, J.
HARTMANIS, J.,
HOPCROFT, J.
KOZEN, D.
SCHNEIDER, F.
TOUEG, S.
TREFETHEN, L.
VAN LOAN, C.

Electrical Engineering:

BALLANTYNE, J.
BERGER, T.
EASTMAN, L.
FARLEY, D., Jr
FINE, T.
HAMMER, D.
JOHNSON, C., Jr
KELLEY, M.
KINTNER, P., Jr
KRUSIUS, J.
LIBOFF, R.
MACDONALD, N.
MCISAAC, P.
NATION, J.
PARKS, T.
POLLOCK, C.
POTTLE, C.
SEYLER, C.
SUDAN, R.
TANG, C.-L.
THOMAS, R.
THORP, J.
TORNG, H.

Geological Sciences:

ALLMENDINGER, R.
BASSETT, W.
BIRD, J.
BROWN, L.
CATHLES, L.
CISNE, J.
ISACKS, B.
JORDAN, T.
KARIG, D.
KAY, R.
RHODES, F.
TRAVERS, W.
TURCOTTE, D.
WHITE, W.

Materials Science and Engineering:

AST, D.
BLAKELY, J.
DIECKMANN, R.
KRAMER, E.
LI, CH.-Y.
RUOFF, A.
SASS, S.

Mechanical and Aerospace Engineering:

AVEDISIAN, C.
BARTEL, D.
BOOKER, J.
CAUGHEY, D.
DAWSON, P.
DE BOER, P. C.
GEORGE, A.
GOULDIN, F.
LEIBOVICH, S.
LUMLEY, J.
MOON, F.
POPE, S.
TORRANCE, K.
VOELCKER, H.
WARHAFT, Z.

Operations Research and Industrial Engineering:

BILLERA, L.
BLAND, R.
HEATH, D.
MUCKSTADT, J.
RENEGAR, J.
RESNICK, S.
RUPPERT, D.
SCHRUBEN, L.
SHMOYS, D.

TARDOS, G.
TODD, M.
TROTTER, L., Jr
TURNBULL, B.

Theoretical and Applied Mechanics:

BURNS, J.
CADY, K.
HEALEY, T.
HUI, CH.-Y.
JENKINS, J.
LANCE, R.
MUKHERJEE, S.
PAO, Y.-HS.
PHOENIX, S.
RAND, R.
SACHSE, W.

New York State College of Veterinary Medicine:

Anatomy:

DELAHUNTA, A.
FARNUM, C.
NODEN, D.

Clinical Sciences:

AGUIRRE, G.
CENTER, S.
DIVERS, T.
DUCHARME, N.
ERB, H.
GROHN, Y.
HACKETT, R.
HORNBUCKLE, W.
KALLFELZ, F.
KOLLIAS, G., Jr
MILLER, W.
MOISE, N.
REBHUN, W.
SCOTT, D.
SHORT, C.
SMITH, D.
TENNANT, B.
WHITE, M.

Diagnostic Laboratory:

HENION, J.
REIMERS, T.

Microbiology, Immunology and Parasitology:

ANTCZAK, D.
AVERY, R.
BELL, R.
BLOOM, S.
BOWSER, P.
DIETERT, R.
LUST, G.
MCGREGOR, D.
MARSH, J.
NAQI, S.
SCHAT, K.

Pathology:

COOPER, B.
KING, J.
LEWIS, R.
MINOR, R.
PAULI, B.
PHEMISTER, R.
QUIMBY, F.
SCHLAFER, D.
SUMMERS, B.
YEN, A.

Pharmacology:

CERIONE, R.
OSWALD, R.
SCHWARK, W.
SHARP, G.

Physiology:

FORTUNE, J.
HOUPT, K.
HOUPT, T.
NATHANIELSZ, P.
ROBERTSHAW, D.
WOOTTON, J.

New York State College of Agriculture and Life Sciences:

Agricultural and Biological Engineering:

ALBRIGHT, L.
COOKE, J.
GEBREMEDHIN, K.
HAITH, D.
JEWELL, W.
PARLANGE, J.-Y.
PITT, R.
SCOTT, N.
STEENHUIS, T.
TIMMONS, M.
WALKER, L.
WALTER, M.

Agricultural Economics:

ALLEE, D.
BILLS, N.
BOISVERT, R.
CHAPMAN, L.
CHRISTY, R.
CONNEMAN, G., Jr
CONRAD, J.
GERMAN, G.
KANBUR, S.
KNOBLAUCH, W.
LADUE, E.
LEE, D.
LESSER, W.
MCLAUGHLIN, E.
MILLIGAN, R.
MOUNT, T.
NOVAKOVIC, A.
POLEMAN, T.
SCHULZE, W.
TAUER, L.
TOMEK, W.
WHITE, G.

Animal Science:

AUSTIC, R.
BAUMAN, D.
BEERMANN, D.
BELL, A.
BLAKE, R.
BUTLER, W.
CURRIE, W.
EVERETT, R.
FOX, D.
GALTON, D.
GOREWIT, R.
HINTZ, H.
OLTENACU, P.
POLLAK, E.
QUAAS, R.
THONNEY, M.

Bailey Hortorium:

BATES, D.
CREPET, W.
RODRIGUEZ, E.

Biochemistry, Molecular and Cell Biology:

CALVO, J.
EALICK, S.
LIS, J.
ROBERTS, J.
SHALLOWAY, D.
TYE, B.-KW.
VOGT, V.
WU, R.

Communication:

COLLE, R.
GLYNN, C.
OSTMAN, R.
SCHWARTZ, D.
YARBROUGH, J.

Cooperative Extension:

VIANDS, D.

Ecology and Systematics:

CHABOT, B.
DHONDT, A.
FEENY, P.
FITZPATRICK, J.
HARRISON, R.
HOWARTH, R.
MARKS, P.
MORIN, J.
ROOT, R.

Education:

DUNN, J.
MILLMAN, J.
MONK, D.
POSNER, G.
RIPPLE, R.
STRIKE, K.

Entomology:

ECKENRODE, C., Jr
LIEBHERR, J.
PECKARSKY, B.
REISSIG, W.
ROELOFS, W.
RUTZ, D.
SHELTON, A.
SODERLUND, D.
STRAUB, R.
TAUBER, M.
TINGEY, W.
WHEELER, Q.

Floriculture and Ornamental Horticulture:

ADLEMAN, M.
BASSUK, N.
GOOD, G.
LANGHANS, R.
MOWER, R.
PETROVIC, A.
TRANCIK, R.
TROWBRIDGE, P.
WEILER, T.

Food Science:

BARBANO, D.
GRAVANI, R.
HOTCHKISS, J.
LUND, D.
MILLER, D.
REGENSTEIN, J.
RIZVI, S.

Food Sciences:

ACREE, T.
DURST, R.
HANG, Y.
HRADZINA, G.
LEE, C.
MCLELLAN, M.
RAO, M.
SIEBERT, K.

Fruit and Vegetable Science:

BELLINDER, R.
CREASY, L.
PRITTS, M.
STILES, W.
TOPOLESKI, L.
WIEN, H.

Genetics and Development:

BRUNS, P.
FOX, T.
GOLDBERG, M.
HANSON, M.
KEMPHUES, K.
MACINTYRE, R.

Horticultural Sciences:

ANDERSEN, R.
HARMAN, G.
LAKSO, A.
POOL, R.
PRICE, H.
REISCH, B.
ROBINSON, R.
TAYLOR, A.

Landscape Architecture:

GOTTFRIED, H.

Microbiology:

GHIORSE, W.
MORTLOCK, R.
ZINDER, S.

Natural Resources:

BAER, R., Jr

DECKER, D.
FAHEY, T.
GILLETT, J.
HULLAR, T.
LASSOIE, J.
MCNEIL, R.
MOEN, A.

Neurobiology and Behaviour:

ADLER, K.
EISNER, T.
EMLEN, S.
HARRIS-WARRICK, R.
HOPKINS, C.
WALCOTT, C.

Nutrition:

ARION, W.
BENSADOUN, A.
COMBS, G., Jr
HABICHT, J.-P.
LATHAM, M.
LEVITSKY, D.
THORBECKE, E.

Physiology:

BEYENBACH, K.
QUARONI, A.

Plant Biology:

DAVIES, P.
NASRALLAH, J.
NASRALLAH, M.
NIKLAS, K.
PAOLILLO, D., Jr
PARTHASARATHY, M.
SPANSWICK, R.

Plant Breeding and Biometry:

ALTMAN, N.
CASELLA, G.
CASTILLO-CHAVEZ, C.
COFFMAN, W. R.
EARLE, E.
MCCULLOCH, C.
MUTSCHLER, M.
PARDEE, W.
RAMAN, K.
SORRELLS, M.
TANKSLEY, S.

Plant Pathology:

ABAWI, G.
AIST, J.
ALDWINCKLE, H.
BERGSTROM, G.
BURR, T.
COLLMER, A.
DILLARD, H.
FRY, W.
GONSALVES, D.
HOCH, H.
HUDLER, G.
HUNTER, J.
LORBEER, J.
LORIA, R.
SEEM, R.
SINCLAIR, W.
SLACK, S.
YODER, O.
ZITTER, T.

Rural Sociology:

BROWN, D.
EBERTS, P.
GEISLER, C.
GURAK, D.
LACEY, W.
LYSON, T.
MCMICHAEL, P.
STYCOS, J.

Soil, Crop and Atmospheric Sciences:

BRYANT, R.
CHERNEY, J.
COX, W.
DUXBURY, J.
FICK, G.
KNAPP, W.
MCBRIDE, M.
OBENDORF, R.
REID, W.
RIHA, S.
STEPONKUS, P.

New York State College of Human Ecology:

Design and Environmental Analysis:

BECKER, F.
EVANS, G.
HEDGE, A.
SIMS, W.

Human Development and Family Studies:

BRUMBERG, J.
CECI, S.
COCHRAN, M.
DEPUE, R.
ECKENRODE, J.
GABARINO, J.
HAMILTON, S.
LEE, L.
LUST, B.
MOEN, P.
ROBERTSON, S.
SAVIN-WILLIAMS, R.

Nutrition:

CAMPBELL, T.
GARZA, C.
HAAS, J.
OLSON, C
RASMUSSEN, K.
SAHN, D.
SANJUR, D.
STIPANUK, M.

Policy Analysis and Management:

BARR, D.
BATTISTELLA, R.
BRYANT, W. K.
CHI, P.
FIREBAUGH, F.
FORD, J.
GERNER, J.
HECK, R.
MCCLINTOCK, C.
SHAPIRO, C.
TROCHIM, W.

Textiles and Apparel:

CHU., CH.-CH.
LEMLEY, A.
LOKER, S.
OBENDORF, S.
SCHWARTZ, P.
WATKINS, S.

Johnson Graduate School of Management:

BENDANIEL, D.
BIERMAN, H., Jr
CONWAY, R.
DYCKMAN, T.
ELLIOTT, J.
HASS, J.
HILTON, R.
ISEN, A.
JARROW, R.
LEE, C.
LIBBY, R.
LIND, R.
MCCLAIN, J.
O'HARA, M.
RAO, V.
RUSSO, J.
SMIDT, S.
SWIERINGA, R.
THOMAS, L.
WALDMAN, M.
WITTINK, D.

School of Hotel Administration:

ARBEL, A.
BERGER, F.
BROWNELL, J.
CHASE, R.
CLARK, J.
DITTMAN, D.
EYSTER, J.
GELLER, A.
LUNDBERG, C.
MUTKOSKI, S.
PENNER, R.
REDLIN, M.

New York State College of Industrial and Labor Relations:

Collective Bargaining:

DANIEL, C.
GROSS, J.
KATZ, H.
LIPSKY, D.
ROSS, P.
SALVATORE, N.

Economics and Social Statistics:

HADI, A.

Extension and Public Service:

FARLEY, J.
HURD, R.

Labor Economics:

ABOWD, J.
BLAU, F.
EHRENBERG, R.
FIELDS, G.
HUTCHENS, R.
KAHN, L.
SMITH, R.

Organizational Behavior:

BACHARACH, S.
GRUENFELD, L.
HAMMER, T.
LAWLER, E.
STERN, R.

Personnel and Human Resource Management:

BRIGGS, V., Jr
DYER, L.
MILKOVICH, G.

Centres and Programmes:

Africana Studies and Research Center:

EDMONDSON, L.
TURNER, J.

Biological Sciences:

STINSON, H. Jr

DAEMEN COLLEGE

4380 Main St, Amherst, NY 14226
Telephone: (716) 839-3600
Fax: (716) 839-8516

Founded 1947 as Rosary Hill College; name changed 1976

Liberal arts and sciences

President: MARTIN J. ANISMAN
Dean of Admissions: MARIA P. DILLARD

Library of 135,000 vols
Number of teachers: 120
Number of students: 1,900

D'YOUVILLE COLLEGE

One D'Youville Sq, Buffalo, NY 14201
Telephone: (716) 881-3200
Fax: (716) 881-7790

Founded 1908 by the Grey Nuns of the Sacred Heart

President: Sister DENISE A. ROCHE
Senior Vice-President: RICHARD WIESEN
Vice-President for Student Affairs: ROBERT MURPHY
Registrar: BARRY SMITH
Admissions: RONALD DANNECKER
Librarian: MICHELE FARRELL

Library of 127,000 vols
Number of teachers: 85
Number of students: 1,900

First degree courses in business, education, humanities, management, natural sciences, nursing, occupational therapy, pre-professional programs, social sciences; graduate degrees in community health, nursing, physical therapy, physician assistance, occupational therapy

ELMIRA COLLEGE

Elmira, NY 14901

Telephone: (607) 735-1800

Founded 1855

President: Dr THOMAS K. MEIER
Academic Vice President: Dr BRYAN D. REDDICK
Vice President for Student Life: GERALD T. DEES
Vice President for Development: Dr MARY DEAN BREWER
Vice President for Business and Treasurer: JERRY B. GAPP
Vice-President for Public Relations: THOMAS K. RUTAN

Library of 335,506 vols
Number of students: 1,104 full-time, 753 part-time

FORDHAM UNIVERSITY

Fordham Rd, Bronx, NY 10458,
and at Lincoln Center, New York, NY 10023

Telephone: (718) 817-1000

Founded by Rt Rev. John Hughes, first Roman Catholic Archbishop of New York, in 1841 as St. John's College. Incorporated as a university 1846. Name changed to Fordham University 1907

President: Rev. JOSEPH A. O'HARE
Vice-President for Administration: Dr BRIAN J. BYRNE
Vice-President for Academic Affairs: Dr ROBERT CARRUBBA
Vice-President for Student Affairs: JEFFREY L. GRAY
Vice-President for Finance and Treasurer: DONALD CIPULLO
Vice-President for Development and University Relations: BRUNO M. SANTONOCITO
Vice-President for Enrollment: Dr PETER A. STACE
Vice-President for Lincoln Center: CHARLES D. HODULIK
Registrar: STEPHEN J. BORDAS
Director of Libraries: Dr JAMES MCCABE

Library of 1,528,559 vols
Number of teachers: 760
Number of students: 14,000

Publications: *International Philosophical Quarterly, Traditio* (annually).

DEANS

Fordham College: Rev. JEFFREY P. VON ARX
Graduate School of Arts and Sciences: Dr ROBERT HIMMELBURG
Graduate School of Business Administration: Dr ERNEST SCALBERG
Graduate School of Religion and Religious Education: Rev. VINCENT M. NOVAK
College of Business Administration: Dr SHARON SMITH
Graduate School of Education: Dr REGIS BERNHARDT
School of Law: JOHN D. FEERICK
Fordham College at Lincoln Center: Rev. ROBERT GRIMES
Graduate School of Social Service: Dr MARY ANN QUARANTA
Fordham College of Liberal Studies: Dr MICHAEL GILLAN

HAMILTON COLLEGE

Clinton, NY 13323
Telephone: (315) 859-4011
Fax: (315) 859-4648

Founded 1793 as Hamilton-Oneida Academy; chartered as Hamilton College 1812

President: EUGENE M. TOBIN
Dean: BOBBY FONG

Library of 500,000 vols
Number of teachers: 180
Number of students: 1,670

HARTWICK COLLEGE

Oneonta, NY 13820

Telephone: (607) 431-4200
E-mail: admissions@hartwick.edu

Founded 1797
Private liberal arts college
Academic year: August to May (three terms)

President: Dr RICHARD A. DETWEILER
Vice-President and Dean of Academic Affairs: Dr SUSAN GOTSCH
Vice-President for Institutional Advancement: (vacant)
Vice-President for Finance: JOHN M. PONTIUS, Jr
Dean of Student Life: GENEVA WALKER-JOHNSON
Dean of Admissions: KARYL CLEMENS
Director of Libraries: MARILYN DUNN

Library of 265,000 vols
Number of teachers: 125
Number of students: 1,497 full-time

HOBART AND WILLIAM SMITH COLLEGES

Geneva, NY 14456-3397

Telephone: (315) 781-3000
Fax: (315) 781-3400

Liberal arts colleges
Hobart founded 1822, William Smith founded 1908

President: RICHARD H. HERSH
Provost: SHEILA K. BENNETT
Treasurer: LOREN LOOMIS HUBBELL
Librarian: P. W. CRUMLISH

Library of 320,000 vols
Number of teachers: 134
Number of students: Hobart: 870 men; William Smith: 965 women

Publications: *Academic Catalogue, Admissions Viewbook, The Pulteney St. Survey, The Seneca Review.*

DEANS

Hobart: AARON SHATZMAN
William Smith: DEBRA K. DEMEIS

HOFSTRA UNIVERSITY

Hempstead, Long Island, NY 11549-1010

Telephone: (516) 463-6700
Fax: (516) 463-4848

Founded 1935

President: Dr JAMES M. SHUART
Provost and Dean of Faculties: Dr HERMAN A. BERLINER
Vice-President for Business Affairs and Treasurer: JAMES J. MCCUE
Vice-President for Planning and Liaison: Dr J. RICHARD BLOCK
Vice-President for Environment Services: MARY BETH CAREY
Vice-President for Development: CAROL A. BRONZO
Executive Director for University Relations: MICHAEL B. DELUISE
Executive Dean for Student Services: ROBERT L. CROWLEY
Dean of Library Services: Dr SUSAN S. LUKESH (acting)

Library of 1,400,000 vols
Number of teachers: 1,104
Number of students: 12,439

DEANS

Frank G. Zarb School of Business: Dr RALPH POLIMENI
School of Communication: Dr GARY L. KREPS
School of Education and Allied Human Services: Dr JAMES R. JOHNSON
College of Liberal Arts and Sciences: Dr BERNARD J. FIRESTONE (acting)
School of Law: STUART RABINOWITZ
New College and School for University Studies: DAVID C. CHRISTMAN
University College for Continuing Education: Dr DEANNA CHITAYAT

HOUGHTON COLLEGE

Houghton, NY 14744

Telephone: (716) 567-9200
Fax: (716) 567-9572

Founded 1883

President: Dr DANIEL R. CHAMBERLAIN
Academic Vice-President and Dean: Dr V. JAMES MANNOIA, Jr
Director of Records: MARGE AVERY
Librarian: Dr GEORGE BENNETT

Library of 221,000 vols
Number of teachers: 95
Number of students: 1,250

Houghton College Suburban Campus: 910 Union Rd, West Seneca, NY 14224; tel. (716) 674-6363; Co-ordinator JOHN DURBIN.

IONA COLLEGE

715 North Ave, New Rochelle, New York, NY 10801-1890

Telephone: (914) 633-2000
Fax: (914) 633-2018

Founded 1940

President: JAMES A. LIGUORI
Provost and Vice-President for Academic Affairs: JUDSON R. SHAVER
Vice-President for Finance: GREGORY PUCHALSKI
Vice Provost for Academic Affairs: JOHN BRAUNSTEIN
Librarian: JOY COLLINS

Library of 309,518 vols, 1,760 periodicals

Number of students: 7,466

DEANS

School of Arts and Sciences: WARREN ROSENBERG
School of Business: NICHOLAUS BEUTELL
Dean of Columba School: Dr GLORIA MOLDOW

ITHACA COLLEGE

100 Job Hall, Ithaca, NY 14850

Telephone: (607) 274-3124
Fax: (607) 274-1900
E-mail: admission@ithaca.edu

Founded 1892

President: PEGGY R. WILLIAMS
Provost: JAMES S. MALEK
Registrar: J. STANTON
Dean of Admissions: P. MITCHELL
Librarian: MARGARET JOHNSON

Library of 611,176 bound vols, and microforms, 2,541 periodical serial subscriptions
Number of teachers: 410 full-time, 103 part-time
Number of students: 5,897

Publications: *Admissions Prospectus, Undergraduate Catalog, Graduate Catalog, Ithaca College Quarterly.*

DEANS

School of Business: ROBERT ULLRICH
Roy H. Park School of Communications: THOMAS BOHN

School of Health Sciences and Human Performance: Richard Miller
School of Music: Arthur Ostrander
School of Humanities and Sciences: Howard Erlich
Athletics: Elizabeth A. Alden

JUILLIARD SCHOOL

60 Lincoln Center Plaza, New York, NY 10023
Telephone: (212) 799-5000
Founded 1905
President: Joseph W. Polisi
Registrar: Elizabeth Brummett
Library of 47,000 music scores and 18,000 books; the record library contains 15,000 long-playing records, compact discs and tape recordings, and 350 videocassettes
Number of teachers: 305 (incl. pre-college and evening division)
Number of students: 1,425 (incl. pre-college and evening division)

KEUKA COLLEGE

Keuka Park, NY 14478
Telephone: (315) 536-4411
Fax: (315) 536-5216
Founded 1890
Four-year liberal arts college
President: Joseph G. Burke
Dean of Admissions and Financial Aid: Joel Wincowski
Registrar: Linda M. Fleischman
Librarian: Sue E. Walker
Library of 85,000 vols
Number of teachers: 52
Number of students: 938

LE MOYNE COLLEGE

Syracuse, NY 13214
Telephone: (315) 445-4100
Fax: (315) 445-4540
Founded 1946
President: Rev. Robert A. Mitchell
Academic Vice-President: Dr Kurt F. Geisinger
Director of Admissions: David M. Pirani
Director of Library: James Simonis
Library of 222,000 vols
Number of teachers: 224
Number of students: 2,915

LONG ISLAND UNIVERSITY

Brookville, Long Island, NY 11548
Telephone: (516) 299-2000
Fax: (516) 299-2072
Founded 1926
President: Dr David J. Steinberg
Vice-President for Academic Affairs: Dr Michael Arons
Vice-President for Finance and Treasurer: Mary M. Lai
Vice-President for University Relations: Jerome A. Kleinman
Campus Provost, LIU-Brooklyn: Gale Stevens Haynes
Campus Provost, LIU-C.W. Post: Dr Joseph Schenker
Campus Provost, LIU-Westchester: Dr Dennis Payette
Campus Provost, LIU-Southampton: Timothy Bishop
Campus Provost, LIU-Brentwood: Dennis Payette
Campus Provost, LIU-Rockland: Dennis Payette
Libraries of 2,297,679 vols
Number of teachers: 1,205 full-time
Number of students: 23,540

MANHATTAN COLLEGE

Riverdale, Bronx, NY 10471
Telephone: (718) 862-8000
Fax: (212) 862-8014
Founded as Academy of the Holy Infancy 1853; chartered as Manhattan College 1863
Private, co-educational
President and Treasurer: Bro. Thomas J. Scanlan
Provost: Weldon Jackson
Vice-President for Student Services: E. Joseph Lee
Vice-President for Finance: John Daly
Bursar: Anthony Imperato
Vice-President for Advancement: Joseph Dillon
Registrar: Emile J. Letendre
Director of Library: Harry Welsh
Library of 240,000 vols
Number of teachers: 390
Number of students: 4,800
Publications: *Scientist, Humanist,* (annually), *Engineer, Chalk Dust, Journal of Business* (2 a year).

DEANS

Arts: Dr Mary Ann O'Donnell
Science: Dr Edward Brown
Engineering: Dr John Patterson
Business: James Suarez
Education: William Merriman
Graduate Division: James Suarez

MANHATTAN SCHOOL OF MUSIC

120 Claremont Ave, New York, NY 10027
Telephone: (212) 749-2802
Founded 1917
President: Marta Istomin
Vice-President and Dean: Richard Adams
Libraries of over 95,000 vols
Number of teachers: 250
Number of students: 850

MANHATTANVILLE COLLEGE

Purchase, NY 10577
Telephone: (914) 323-5230
Fax: (914) 694-6234
Founded 1841
President: Richard A. Berman
Provost: James B. Bryan
Library of over 250,000 vols
Number of teachers: 75 (full-time)
Number of students: 1,500

MARIST COLLEGE

290 North Rd, Poughkeepsie, NY 12601
Telephone: (914) 575-3000
Founded 1929
President: Dennis J. Murray
Executive Vice-President: Dr R. Mark Sullivan
Vice-President for Student Affairs: Gerard Cox
Vice-President for Academic Affairs: Dr Marc vanderHeyden
Vice-President for Admissions and Enrollment: Harry Wood
Vice-President for College Advancement: Shaileen Kopec
Vice-President for Information Services: Carl Gerberich
Vice-President for Business Affairs: Anthony Campilii
Registrar: Judy Ivankovic
Librarian: John McGinty
Library of 120,000 vols
Number of teachers: 250
Number of students: 4,025

MARYMOUNT COLLEGE

100 Marymount Ave, Tarrytown, NY 10591-3796
Telephone: (914) 631-3200
Fax: (914) 332-4956
Founded 1907
President: Sister Brigid Driscoll
Vice-President for Academic Affairs: Dr Roberta Matthews
Director of Admissions: Christine Richard
Librarian: Sister Virginia McKenna
Library of 118,000 vols
Number of teachers: 58 full-time
Number of students: 1,100

MARYMOUNT MANHATTAN COLLEGE

221 East 71st St, New York, NY 10021
Telephone: (212) 517-0400
Founded 1936, chartered 1961
President: Regina S. Peruggi
Vice-Presidents: Paula Hooper Mayhew (Academic Affairs), Arnold Dimond (Finance and Administration), Suzanne M. Murphy (External Affairs and Enrollment Services)
Library of 85,000 vols
Number of teachers: 142
Number of students: 537 full-time, 685 part-time

MOUNT SAINT MARY COLLEGE

330 Powell Avenue, Newburgh, NY 12550
Telephone: (914) 569-3259
Fax: (914) 562-6762
Founded 1960
Private control
President: Sister Ann Sakac
Registrar: Gerald Jilbert
Head Librarian: Mary Reed McTamany
Library of 113,000 vols
Number of teachers: 60 full-time, 45 adjunct
Number of students: 1,920

CHAIRPERSONS

Division of Arts and Letters: James Beard
Division of Business: Dr Jerome Picard
Division of Education: Dr Lucy DiPaola
Division of Mathematics and Computer Science: Vincent Kayes
Division of Natural Sciences: Dr Iris Turkenkopf
Division of Nursing: Dr Nancy Zweig
Division of Religion and Philosophy: Dr Kate Lindemann
Division of Social Sciences: Dr John Reilly

NAZARETH COLLEGE OF ROCHESTER

4245 East Ave, Rochester, NY 14618-3790
Telephone: (716) 389-2525
Fax: (716) 586-2452
Founded 1924
President: Rose Marie Beston
Vice-President for Academic Affairs: Dennis Silva
Registrar: Nancy Grear
Librarian: Richard A. Matzek
Library of 266,000 vols, 2,004 serials
Number of students: 2,723
Publications: *Gleaner, Verity, Sigillum.*

NEW SCHOOL FOR SOCIAL RESEARCH

66 West 12th St, New York, NY 10011
Telephone: (212) 229-5656
Fax: (212) 229-5330
Founded 1919

President: JONATHAN F. FANTON
Provost: JUDITH B. WALZER
Executive Vice-President: JOSEPH F. PORRINO
Senior Vice-President for External Affairs: RICHARD W. GORMAN
Vice-President for Development and Alumni Relations: JANE KARLIN
Vice-President and General Counsel: GREGORY K. SPENCE
Secretary of the Corporation: ROBERT A. GATES

Library of 4,130,688 vols
Number of teachers: 1,818
Number of students: 31,000

Publications: *Social Research* (quarterly), *Philosophy Journal* (2 a year), *World Policy Journal*.

DEANS

Graduate Faculty of Political and Social Science: JUDITH FRIEDLANDER
New School Adult Division: ELIZABETH DUNBAR DICKEY
Eugene Lang College: BEATRICE BANU
Graduate School of Management and Urban Policy: JAMES A. KRAUSKOPF
Parsons School of Design: CHARLES S. OLTON
Mannes College of Music: JOEL LESTER
School of Dramatic Arts: JAMES LIPTON

NEW YORK INSTITUTE OF TECHNOLOGY

POB 8000, Old Westbury, NY 11568-0170
Telephone: (516) 686-7516
Fax: (516) 626-6830
E-mail: admissions@acl.nyit.edu

Founded 1955

President: MATTHEW SCHURE
Vice-President and Treasurer: THOMAS VALLELY, III
Vice-President for Academic Affairs and Dean of Faculty: EDWARD GUILIANO
Vice-President for Student Affairs: MARYSE PREZEAU

Library of 202,000 vols, 3,667 periodicals
Number of teachers: 223 full-time, 699 part-time
Number of students: 5,635 undergraduates, 2,849 graduates, 912 first-time professionals

NEW YORK MEDICAL COLLEGE

Valhalla, NY 10595
Telephone: (914) 594-4000

Founded 1860
Private control

President: Rev. Msgr HARRY C. BARRETT
Registrar: BARBARA WINES
Librarian: DIANA CUNNINGHAM

Library of 149,000 vols, 2,100 journal titles
Number of teachers: 1,000 full-time, 1,500 part-time
Number of students: 780 medical, 565 graduate

DEANS

School of Medicine: RALPH A. O'CONNELL
Graduate School of Health Sciences: SHEILA M. SMYTHE
Graduate School of Basic Medical Sciences: FRANCIS L. BELLONI

NEW YORK UNIVERSITY

Washington Square, New York, NY 10012
Telephone: (212) 998-2310

Founded 1831

President: L. JAY OLIVA
Deputy Vice-Chancellor and Vice-President: DEBRA JAMES

Library: see Libraries
Number of teachers: 2,775
Number of students: 48,300

Publications: *Alumni News* (3 a year), *Drama Review* (quarterly), *Law Review* (6 a year), *Washington Square News* (daily), *Minetta Review* (2 a year), *Commentator* (fortnightly), *NYU Today* (fortnightly), *Vniversity* (3 a year), *Faculty Resource Network Newsletter, Physician* (2 a year), *Research News* (3 a year), *Brownstone* (3 a year), *Opportunity* (monthly), *Stern Business* (2 a year).

DEANS

Faculty of Arts and Science: PHILIP FURMANSKI
Graduate School of Arts and Science: CATHARINE STIMPSON
College of Arts and Science: MATTHEW S. SANTIROCCO
School of Law: JOHN E. SEXTON
School of Medicine and Post-Graduate Medical School: BOB GLICKMAN
College of Dentistry: EDWARD G. KAUFMAN
School of Education: ANN MARCUS
Stern School of Business: GEORGE C. DALY
Stern School of Business Undergraduate College: FREDERICK D. S. CHOI
School of Continuing Education: GERALD A. HEEGER
Wagner Graduate School of Public Service: JO IVY BOUFFORD
School of Social Work: TOM MEENAGHAN
Tisch School of the Arts: MARY SCHMIDT CAMPBELL
Gallatin Division: E. FRANCIS WHITE
Courant Institute of Mathematical Sciences: DAVID MCLAUGHLIN
Libraries: CARLTON C. ROCHELL

NIAGARA UNIVERSITY

NY 14109
Telephone: (716) 285-1212

Founded 1856

President: Rev. PAUL L. GOLDEN
Executive Vice-President for Academic Affairs: Dr SUSAN E. MASON
Dean of Admissions and Records: GEORGE C. PACHTER
Dean of Student Affairs: JOSEPH H. CUDA
Director of Libraries: LESLIE R. MORRIS

Library of 309,000 vols
Number of teachers: 240
Number of students: 2,753

Publications: *Index* (monthly), *Niagaran* (annually).

DEANS

College of Arts and Sciences: Dr NANCY MCGLEN
College of Business Administration: Dr KEITH T. MILLER
College of Education: Fr DANIEL F. O'LEARY
College of Nursing: Dr DOLORES A. BOWER
Institute of Travel, Hotel and Restaurant Administration: Dr CARL D. RIEGEL
Division of Lifelong Learning: JOANNE WRAY

NYACK COLLEGE

Nyack, NY 10960
Telephone: (914) 358-1710
Fax: (914) 358-1751

Founded 1882

Chancellor: Dr JAMES A. DAVEY
President: Dr DAVID E. SCHROEDER
Vice-President and Dean of the College: Dr RONALD W. RUEGSEGGER
Vice-President and Dean of Students: Rev. ANGEL ORTIZ
Vice-President and Treasurer: MARK WELLMAN
Dean of Faculty-Alliance Theological Seminary (Graduate School): Dr R. BRYAN WIDBIN
Vice-President for Advancement: DAVID C. JENNINGS
Registrar: DOROTHY R. ELLENBERGER
Librarian: LINDA POSTON

Library of 95,000 vols
Number of teachers: 120
Number of students: 1,433

PACE UNIVERSITY

Pace Plaza, New York, NY 10038
Telephone: (212) 346-1200

Founded 1906

Campuses at New York, Pleasantville and White Plains

President: Dr PATRICIA EWERS
University Registrar: MARCIA JACQUES
University Librarian: WILLIAM MURDOCK (acting)

Library of 938,158 vols, 5,100 periodicals
Number of teachers: 1,200
Number of students: 15,000

POLYTECHNIC UNIVERSITY

6 MetroTech Center, Brooklyn, NY 11201
Telephone: (718) 260-3600
Fax: (718) 260-3136

Founded 1854

Campuses at Brooklyn, Farmingdale and Westchester

President: Dr DAVID C. CHANG
Executive Vice-President and Provost: IVAN T. FRISCH
Senior Vice-President for Finance and Administration: LEONARD CUGICK
Senior Vice-President for Institutional and Alumni Relations: Dr RICHARD THORSEN
Vice-President for Academic Operations: ROGER ROESS
Vice-Provost for Academic Development: DEANE YANG
Vice-Provost for Research and Strategic Initiatives: DONALD HOCKNEY
Director of Library Services: JANA STEVENS-RICHMAN

Number of teachers: 185 full-time
Number of students: 3,282

DEANS

Engineering: R. ROESS (Associate Provost for Academic Affairs)
Research and Graduate Studies: R. THORSEN

PRATT INSTITUTE

200 Willoughby Ave, Brooklyn, NY 11205
Telephone: (718) 636-3600
Fax: (718) 636-3785

Founded 1887

President: Dr WARREN ILCHMAN
Vice-President for Finance: JULIE KARNS (acting)
Vice-President for Student Life: Dr KATHLEEN RICE
Vice-President for Research and Development: KIERAN MCTAGUE
Provost: Dr RICHARD BARSAM
Associate Director of Academic Records: WILLIAM MICKELSON
Dean of Libraries: F. WILLIAM CHICKERING

Library of 201,015 vols
Number of teachers: 519
Number of students: 3,384

Publications: *Pratt Institute Bulletin, Pratt Grad* (quarterly), *Gateway* (every 2 weeks), *Prattler* (every 2 weeks), *Prattonia* (annually).

DEANS

School of Art and Design: WILLIAM FASOLINO
School of Architecture: FRANCES HALSBAND
School of Liberal Arts and Sciences: Dr JACK MINKOFF

School of Professional Studies: Dr DONAL HIGGINS
Graduate School of Information and Library Science: Dr S. M. MATTA

RENSSELAER POLYTECHNIC INSTITUTE

110 8th St, Troy, NY 12181
Telephone: (518) 276-6000
Fax: (518) 276-6003
Founded 1824
President: C. J. BARTON (acting)
Vice-President for Administration: TOM YURKEWECZ
Vice-President for Finance: VIRGINIA GREGG
Vice-President for Student Life: DAVID HAVILAND
Vice-President for Institute Advancement: ROBBEE KOSAK
Vice-President for Government Relations: LARRY SNAVLEY
Director, Office of Contracts and Grants: RICHARD SCAMMELL
Registrar: SHARON KUNKEL
Librarian: H. LORETTA EBERT
Library of 469,000 vols, 3,283 periodicals
Number of teachers: 348 full-time
Number of students: 6,356 full-time, 483 part-time
Publications: *Graduate Catalogue, Undergraduate Catalogue* (annually).

DEANS AND DIRECTORS
Science: G. DOYLE DAVES
Engineering: JAMES TIEN (acting)
Humanities and Social Sciences: FAYE DUCHIN
Architecture: ALAN BALFOUR
Undergraduate and Continuing Education: JACK WILSON
Management: JOSEPH ECKER

ROBERTS WESLEYAN COLLEGE

Rochester, NY 14624-1997
Telephone: (716) 594-6000
Fax: (716) 594-6371
Founded 1866
President: WILLIAM C. CROTHERS
Provost: JOHN A. MARTIN
Vice-President for College Development: PETER L. MCCOWN
Vice-President for Finance: JAMES E. CUTHBERT
Vice-President for Administration: LANORA LAHTINEN
Vice-President for Academic Development: BURTON R. JONES
Registrar: WESLEY VANDERHOOF
Director of Financial Aid: STEPHEN FIELD
Librarian: ALFRED C. KROBER
Library of 103,400 vols
Number of teachers: 66
Number of students: 1,414
Publication: *Roberts Today* (quarterly).

ROCHESTER INSTITUTE OF TECHNOLOGY

Two Lomb Memorial Drive, Rochester, NY 14623
Telephone: (716) 475-2411
Founded 1829 as the Rochester Athenaeum
President: Dr ALBERT J. SIMONE
Provost and Vice-President for Academic Affairs: Dr STANLEY MCKENZIE
Vice-President for University Relations: NATHAN ROBFOGEL
Vice-President for Finance and Administration: Dr JAMES WATTERS
Vice-President for Student Affairs: Dr LINDA KUK
Secretary of the Institute and Assistant to the President: Dr FRED W. SMITH
Librarian: PATRICIA PITKIN
Library of 350,000 vols
Number of teachers: 1,100
Number of students: 12,900
Publications: *Undergraduate Bulletin* (annually), *Graduate Bulletin* (annually), *Admissions Bulletin* (annually), *Application, Course Description Catalog* (annually).

DEANS
College of Applied Science and Technology: WILEY R. MCKINZIE
College of Business: Dr LYN PANKOFF
College of Engineering: Dr PAUL PETERSEN
College of Imaging Arts and Sciences: Dr JOAN STONE
College of Liberal Arts: Dr DIANE HOPE
College of Science: Dr ROBERT CLARK
National Technical Institute for the Deaf: Dr ROBERT DAVILA

ROCKEFELLER UNIVERSITY

1230 York Ave, New York, NY 10021-6399
Telephone: (212) 327-8000
Founded 1901; became a graduate university in 1954; name changed from Rockefeller Institute to The Rockefeller University in 1965
President: TORSTEN WIESEL
Vice-Presidents: FRED BOHEN (Executive), DAVID J. LYONS (Financial), WILLIAM H. GRIESAR (and General Counsel)
Secretary: INGRID W. REED
Dean of Graduate and Postgraduate Studies: Dr NORTON ZINDER
Librarian: PATRICIA E. MACKEY
Library of 230,000 vols
Number of teachers: 250 professors, 69 heads of laboratory
Number of students: 148 graduates, 250 research fellows
Publications: *Journal of Experimental Medicine, Journal of General Physiology, Journal of Cell Biology, Journal of Clinical Investigation* (all monthly), *Scientific and Educational Programs* (annually) and occasional publications.

RUSSELL SAGE COLLEGE FOR WOMEN

45 Ferry St, Troy, NY 12180
Telephone: (518) 270-2000
Fax: (518) 244-6880
Founded 1916
President: Dr JEANNE H. NEFF
Vice-Presidents:
Finance and Administration: WILLIAM BECKMAN
External Relations: Dr DAVID MARCELL
Academic Affairs: Dr D'ANN CAMPBELL
Assistant Vice-President for Admissions: MICHAEL SPOSILI
Director of Libraries: KINGSLEY GREENE
Library of 350,000 vols, 1,200 periodicals
Number of teachers: 92 full-time, 47 part-time
Number of students: 1,000 full-time

ST BONAVENTURE UNIVERSITY

St Bonaventure, NY 14778
Telephone: (716) 375-2000
Fax: (716) 375-2005
Founded 1858
Chair, Board of Trustees: LESLIE C. QUICK, III
Vice-Chairs, Board of Trustees: SUSAN R. GREEN, WILLIAM E. SWAN
President: Dr ROBERT J. WICKENHEISER
Vice-President for Academic Affairs: Dr EDWARD K. ECKERT
Vice-President for Business: Dr DONALD L. ZEKAN
Vice-President for the Franciscan Charism: Rev. ANTHONY M. CARROZZO
Vice-President for Student Life: GEORGE F. SOLAN
Vice-President for University Advancement: DEAN BRUNO
Registrar: BARBARA RUSSELL
Librarian: PAUL SPAETH
Number of teachers: 181
Number of students: 2,822
Publications: *Cithara, Laurel, Bonadieu, Bonaventure, Cord, Franciscan Studies, The Works of William of Ockham.*

DEANS
School of Arts and Sciences: Dr JAMES P. WHITE
School of Business: Dr MICHAEL J. FISCHER
School of Journalism and Mass Communication: Dr LEE COPPOLA
School of Education: Dr CAROL ANN PIERSON
School of Graduate Studies: Dr EDWARD K. ECKERT
School of Franciscan Studies: Rev. MICHAEL BLASTIC

ST FRANCIS COLLEGE

180 Remsen St, Brooklyn, NY 11201
Telephone: (212) 522-2300
Chartered 1884
President: Dr FRANK J. MACCHIAROLA
Registrar: (vacant)
Librarian: WENDELL GUY
Library of 177,000 vols
Number of teachers: 155
Number of students: 1,633 full-time, 503 part-time

ST JOHN'S UNIVERSITY, NEW YORK

8000 Utopia Parkway, Jamaica, NY 11439
Telephone: (718) 990-6161
Fax: (718) 990-5723
Opened 1870; chartered 1871; re-chartered by Regents of the University of the State of New York 1906
Campuses at Queens, Staten Island and Rome
President: Rev. DONALD J. HARRINGTON
Executive Vice-President: ROBERT CRIMMINS
Provost: Dr TONY H. BONAPARTE
Vice-President for Campus Ministry: Rev. MICHAEL CARROLL
Vice-President for International Relations: Dr CECILIA CHANG
Vice-President for Administrative Services: JOHN P. CONNOLLY, Jr
Vice-President for Student Life: Dr SUSAN L. EBBS
Vice-President for Finance, and Treasurer: JAMES PELLOW
Vice-President for Human Resources: DENNIS MCAULIFFE
Vice-President for Government and Community Relations: JOSEPH SCIAME
Vice-President for Institutional Advancement: Rev. BERNARD TRACEY
Vice-President, Secretary to the University and Executive Director of Grants and Research: Dr DOROTHY E. HABBEN
Dean of Libraries: Dr JAMES BENSON
Library of 1,700,000 vols, 14,895 periodical subscriptions
Number of teachers: 1,088
Number of students: 18,523
Publications: *The Bankruptcy Law Review, The Forum, The Law Review/Catholic Lawyer, Journal of Legal Commentary, New York International Law Review, Recipe, Res Gestae, Sequoya Art and Literary Magazine, The Spectator, St. John's Today, Vincentian.*

DEANS
St John's College of Liberal Arts and Sciences: Sister MARGARET JOHN KELLY

School of Education and Human Services: Dr JERROLD ROSS
College of Business Administration: PETER J. TOBIN
College of Pharmacy and Allied Health Professions: Dr THOMAS WISER
Metropolitan College: Dr MARY MULVIHILL (acting)
St Vincent's College: Dr KATHLEEN MACDONALD
School of Law: Dr BRIAN TAMANAHA (acting)

BRANCH CAMPUSES

Staten Island Campus: 300 Howard Ave, Staten Island, NY 10301

Senior Vice-President for the Staten Island Campus: Rev. JAMES F. KIERNAN

Rome Campus (Italy): Graduate Center, Pontificio Oratorio San Pietro, Via Santa Maria Mediatrice 24, 00165 Rome, Italy

Vice-President for Rome Campus: Rev. MICHAEL J. CARROLL

ST LAWRENCE UNIVERSITY

Canton, NY 13617
Telephone: (315) 229-5011
Founded 1856
President: DANIEL F. SULLIVAN
Vice-President and Dean: THOMAS COBURN
Vice-President for University Advancement: LINDA R. PETTIT
Vice-President for Business Affairs: KATHRYN MULLANEY
Vice-President for Student Affairs: MARCIA LOU PETTY
Vice-President for Finance: KATHRYN MULLANEY
Vice-President for Administrative Operations: THOMAS COAKLEY
Secretary: ANGELA M. JOHNSTON
Registrar: JANET J. FLIGHT
Librarian: BART HARLOE
Library of over 472,300 vols
Number of teachers: 181
Number of students: 965 men, 932 women
Publications: *St Lawrence Magazine* (quarterly), *Hill News* (weekly), *Laurentian* (annually), *Gridiron* (annually).

SARAH LAWRENCE COLLEGE

Bronxville, NY 10708
Telephone: (914) 337-0700
Provisional charter 1926; absolute charter 1931
President: MICHELE TOLELA MYERS
Vice-President for Finance and Planning: DENNIS CROSS
Dean of College: BARBARA KAPLAN
Dean of Studies: ROBERT CAMERON (acting)
Dean of Admissions: THYRA BRIGGS
Director of Public Relations: DIANE FUSILLI
Registrar: MARY DRISCOLL
Library of 200,000 vols
Number of teachers: 238
Number of students: 1,111
Publications: *Sarah Lawrence Tribune, Sarah Lawrence Magazine, Sarah Lawrence Literary Review.*

SIENA COLLEGE

Loudonville, NY 12211
Telephone: (518) 783-2300
Fax: (518) 783-4293
Founded 1937
Independent liberal arts college
President: Rev. KEVIN E. MACKIN
Vice-President for Academic Affairs: Dr DOUGLAS ASTOLFI
Vice-President for Finance and Administration: ANTHONY G. PONDILLO
Vice-President for Development: Dr GREGORY J. STAHL
Vice-President for Student Affairs: Rev. JOHN FRAMBES
Dean of Residential and Judicial Services: JEANNE OBERMAYER
Director of Admissions: EDWARD J. JONES
Library Director: TIMOTHY G. BURKE
Library of 244,564 vols, 33,206 other items
Number of teachers: 171 full-time, 84 part-time
Number of students: 2,669 full-time, 767 part-time

SKIDMORE COLLEGE

Saratoga Springs, NY 12866
Telephone: (518) 580-5000
Founded 1903, chartered 1922
President: Dr DAVID H. PORTER
Vice-President for Business Affairs and Treasurer: KARL W. BROEKHUIZEN
Vice-President for Development and Alumni Affairs: CHRISTINE R. HOEK
Dean of the Faculty: PHYLLIS A. ROTH
Dean of Student Affairs: JOSEPH A. TOLLIVER
Dean of Special Programs: DONALD J. MCCORMACK
Dean of Enrollment and College Relations: KENT H. JONES
Director of Admissions: MARY LOU BATES
Director, Skidmore University Without Walls: CORNEL J. REINHART
Librarian: PEGGY SEIDEN
Library of 420,000 vols
Number of teachers: 184 full-time, 16 part-time
Number of students: 2,189

STATE UNIVERSITY OF NEW YORK

System Administration, State University Plaza, Albany, NY 12246
Telephone: (518) 443-5355
Chancellor: JOHN W. RYAN
Executive Vice-Chancellor: DONALD G. DUNN
Provost and Vice-Chancellor for Academic Affairs: PETER D. SALINS
University Counsel and Vice-Chancellor for Legal Affairs: GEORGE H. BUCHANAN
Senior Vice-Chancellor for Finance and Business: BRIAN T. STENSON
Vice-Chancellor for University Relations: SCOTT W. STEFFEY
Vice-Chancellor, and Secretary of the University: JOHN J. O'CONNOR
Number of teachers: 9,386 full-time
Number of students: 139,900 full-time

State University of New York at Albany

Albany, NY 12222
Telephone: (518) 442-3300
President: KAREN R. HITCHCOCK
Provost and Vice-President for Academic Affairs: JUDY GENSHAFT
Executive Vice-President and Vice-President for Finance and Business: CARL CARLUCCI
Vice-President for University Advancement: PAUL T. STEC (interim)
Vice-President for Research and Dean of Graduate Studies: DANIEL L. WULFF (interim)
Vice-President for Student Affairs: JAMES P. DOELLEFELD

State University of New York at Binghamton

Binghamton, NY 13902-6000
Telephone: (607) 777-2000
President: LOIS B. DEFLEUR
Provost and Vice-President for Academic Affairs: MARY ANN SWAIN
Vice-President for Administration: MICHAEL SCULLARD
Vice-President for Student Affairs: RODGER SUMMERS
Vice-President for External Affairs: THOMAS F. KELLY

State University of New York at Buffalo

Buffalo, NY 14260
Telephone: (716) 645-2000
President: WILLIAM R. GREINER
Provost: THOMAS E. HEADRICK
Vice-President for Research: DALE M. LANDI
Vice-President for Student Affairs: DENNIS R. BLACK
Senior Vice-President: ROBERT J. WAGNER
Vice-President for Health Affairs: MICHAEL BERNARDINO
Vice-President for University Advancement and Development: RONALD M. STEIN

State University of New York at Stony Brook

Stony Brook, NY 11794
Telephone: (516) 632-6000
President: SHIRLEY STRUM KENNY
Provost and Executive Vice-President for Academic Affairs: ROLLIN RICHMOND
Vice-President for Student Affairs: FREDERICK R. PRESTON
Vice-President for Administration: RICHARD MANN
Vice-President, Health Sciences Center: NORMAN EDELMAN
Vice-President for Research: GAIL HABICHT
Vice-President for Hospital Affairs: MICHAEL MAFFETONE
Vice-President for Brookhaven Affairs: FREDERICK PRESTON

HEALTH SCIENCE CENTERS

Health Science Center at Brooklyn: 450 Clarkson Ave, Brooklyn, NY 11203; Pres. EUGENE FEIGELSON.

Health Science Center at Syracuse: Syracuse, NY 13210; Pres. GREGORY L. EASTWOOD.

UNIVERSITY COLLEGES

State University College at Brockport: NY 14420; Pres. PAUL YU.

State University College at Buffalo: NY 14222; Pres. MURIEL A. MOORE.

State University College at Cortland: NY 13045; Pres. JUDSON H. TAYLOR.

State University College at Fredonia: NY 14063; Pres. DENNIS L. HEFNER.

State University College at Geneseo: NY 14454; Pres. CHRISTOPHER C. DAHL.

State University College at New Paltz: NY 12561; Pres. ROGER W. BOWEN.

State University College at Old Westbury: NY 11568; Pres. W. HUBERT KEEN (interim).

State University College at Oneonta: NY 13820; Pres. ALAN B. DONOVAN.

State University College at Oswego: NY 13126; Pres. DEBORAH FLEMMA STANLEY.

State University College at Plattsburgh: NY 12901; Pres. HORACE A. JUDSON.

State University College at Potsdam: NY 13676; Pres. JOHN A. FALLON III.

State University College at Purchase: NY 10577; Pres. BILL LACY.

State University Empire State College: Saratoga Springs, NY 12866; Pres. JANE W. ALTES (interim).

COLLEGES OF TECHNOLOGY

State University of New York College of Technology at Alfred: Alfred, NY 14802; Pres. WILLIAM D. REZAK.

State University of New York College of Technology at Canton: Canton, NY 13617; Pres. JOSEPH L. KENNEDY.

State University of New York College of Agriculture and Technology at Cobleskill: Cobleskill, NY 12043; Pres. KENNETH E. WING.

State University of New York College of Technology at Delhi: Delhi, NY 13753-1190; Pres. MARY E. RITTLING (interim).

State University of New York College of Technology at Farmingdale: Farmingdale, NY 11735; Pres. FRANK A. CIPRIANI.

State University of New York College of Agriculture and Technology at Morrisville: Morrisville, NY 13408-0636; Pres. RAYMOND W. CROSS.

SPECIALIZED COLLEGES

State University of New York College of Environmental Science and Forestry: Syracuse, NY 13210; Pres. ROSS S. WHALEY.

State University of New York College of Optometry at New York City: 100 E 24th St, New York, NY 10010; Pres. ALDEN N. HAFFNER.

State University Institute of Technology at Utica/Rome: POB 3050, Utica, NY 13504-3050; Pres. PETER J. CAYAN.

State University of New York Maritime College: Fort Schuyler, Bronx, NY 10465; Pres. DAVID C. BROWN.

SYRACUSE UNIVERSITY

Syracuse, NY 13244

Telephone: (315) 443-1870

Chartered 1870

Chancellor and President: Dr KENNETH A. SHAW
Vice-Chancellor for Academic Affairs: Dr GERSHON VINCOW
Executive Assistant to the Chancellor: ELEANOR GALLAGHER
Senior Vice-President for University Relations: Dr LANSING BAKER
Senior Vice-President, Business and Finance: LOUIS MARCOCCIA
Vice-President, Enrollment Management & Continuing Education: THOMAS CUMMINGS
Vice-President for Research and Computing: Dr BEN WARE
Vice-President for Student Affairs: Dr EDWARD GOLDEN
Director of Corporations and Foundations: Dr THOMAS HARBLIN
Executive Director of Government Relations: ELEANOR GALLAGHER
Dean of Admissions and Financial Aid: DAVID SMITH
Registrar: PETER DEBLOIS
University Librarian: DAVID STAM

Library: see Libraries
Number of teachers: 872
Number of students: 18,600

Publications: *Symposium* (quarterly on foreign languages and literature), *Syracuse Law Review* (quarterly), *Syracuse University Record* (weekly), *Syracuse University Magazine* (3 a year).

DEANS

School of Architecture: Prof. BRUCE J. ABBEY
College of Arts and Sciences: Dr ROBERT JENSEN
Maxwell Graduate School of Citizenship and Public Affairs: Dr JOHN PALMER
School of Education: Dr STEVEN T. BOSSERT
College of Engineering and Computer Science: Dr SAM CLEMENCE (acting)
State University of New York College of Environmental Science and Forestry: Dr ROSS WHALEY (President)
Graduate School: Dr HOWARD JOHNSON
Hendricks Memorial Chapel: RICHARD L. PHILLIPS
College for Human Development: Dr SUSAN J. CROCKETT
School of Information Studies: Dr RAYMOND F. VON DRAN
College of Law: Prof. DAAN BRAVEMAN
School of Management: Dr GEORGE R. BURMAN
College of Nursing: Dr GRACE CHICKADONZ
S. I. Newhouse School of Public Communications: Dr DAVID RUBIN
School of Social Work: Dr WILLIAM POLLARD
Summer Sessions: THOMAS M. O'SHEA
University College: THOMAS CUMMINGS
Utica College: Dr MICHAEL SIMPSON
College of Visual and Performing Arts: Prof. DONALD M. LANTZY

AFFILIATED INSTITUTIONS

Center of Hispanic Studies: f. 1945; co-operates closely with the faculties of geography and history.

Center on Human Policy.
Communications Research Center.
Institute for Energy Research.
Institute for Sensory Research.
All-University Gerontology Center.
Division of International Programs Abroad.
Center for Northeast Parallel Architectures.
Center for Computer Applications and Software Engineering.
Center for Membrane Science.
Global Affairs Institute.

UNION COLLEGE

Schenectady, NY 12308

Telephone: (518) 388-6000

Founded 1795; oldest non-denominational college in US

President: ROGER H. HULL
Vice-President (Finance and Administration): DIANE T. BLAKE
Vice-President (Academic Affairs) and Dean of Faculty: LINDA E. COOL
Vice-President (Admissions and Financial Aid) DANIEL M. LUNDQUIST
Vice-President (Alumni Affairs): JOSEPH L. MAMMOLA
Vice-President (College Relations): DAN C. WEST
Registrar: PENELOPE S. ADEY
Library Director: THOMAS MCFADDEN

Library of 515,000 vols
Number of teachers: 184 (full-time)
Number of students: 2,000 (full-time day)

Publications: *Catalogue, Concordiensis* (student weekly), *Chronicle* (college weekly), *Union College (Alumni), Union Book* (Senior Year Book), *Sentinel* (political magazine), *Idol* (student literary magazine).

DEANS

Faculty: LINDA COOL
Students: FREDERICK ALFORD

UNITED STATES MERCHANT MARINE ACADEMY

Kings Point, NY 11024-1699

Telephone: (516) 773-5000

Founded 1943

Superintendent: Rear-Admiral THOMAS T. MATTESON
Chief of Staff: Capt. JAMES ORMISTON
Academic Dean: Dr WARREN F. MAZEK
Commandant of Midshipmen: Capt. DONALD FERGUSON
Director, Office of External Affairs: Capt. ROBERT SAFARIK
Library: Dr GEORGE BILLY
Number of instructors: 80
Number of midshipmen: 951

HEADS OF ACADEMIC DEPARTMENTS

Marine Transportation: Capt. GEORGE SANDBERG
Engineering: Prof. JOSÉ FEMENIA
Humanities: Dr JANE BRICKMAN
Mathematics and Science: Dr LAURENCE CASSAR
Naval Science: Cdr ROBERT DIXON
Physical Education: Prof. SUSAN PETERSEN-LUBOW

UNITED STATES MILITARY ACADEMY

West Point, NY 10996

Telephone: (914) 938-4011

Founded 1802

Superintendent: Lt.-Gen. DANIEL W. CHRISTMAN
Commandant of Cadets: Brig.-Gen. ROBERT J. ST ONGE, Jr
Dean of the Academic Board: Brig.-Gen. FLETCHER M. LAMKIN, Jr
Director of Admissions: Col. MICHAEL L. JONES
Librarian: KENNETH W. HEDMAN

Library of 500,000 vols
Number of instructors: 562
Number of cadets: 4,112

HEADS OF DEPARTMENTS

Behavioral Science and Leadership: Col. CHARLES F. BROWER IV
Chemistry: Col. DAVID C. ALLBEE
Civil and Mechanical Engineering: Col. KIP P. NYGREN
Mathematical Sciences: Col. DAVID C. ARNEY
Geography and Environmental Engineering: Col. JOHN GRUBBS
Foreign Languages: Col. WILLIAM G. HELD
Law: Col. DENNIS R. HUNT
English: Col. PETER L. STROMBERG
Social Sciences: Col. JAMES R. GOLDEN
Physics: Col. RAYMOND J. WINKEL
Electrical Engineering and Computer Science: Col. DANIEL M. LITYNSKI
Systems Engineering: Col. JAMES L. KAYS
History: Col. ROBERT A. DOUGHTY
Military Instruction: Col. GREGORY K. WADE
Physical Education: Col. JAMES L. ANDERSON

UNIVERSITY OF ROCHESTER

Wilson Blvd, Rochester, NY 14627

Telephone: (716) 275-2121

Founded 1850
Private control
Academic year: September to May (two terms).

President: THOMAS JACKSON
Provost: CHARLES PHELPS
Executive Vice-President and Treasurer: RICHARD W. GREENE
Senior Vice-President and Chief Operating Officer: R. P. MILLER, Jr
Vice-President for Development: HOLLIS BUDD
Dean for Enrollment Policy and Management: NEILL F. SANDERS.
Registrar: (vacant)
Director of River Campus Libraries: RONALD DOW

Library: see Libraries
Number of teachers: 1,561
Number of students: 8,377

DEANS

The College: THOMAS J. LEBLANC
Graduate Studies: B. IGLEWSKI

School of Medicine and Dentistry: L. GOLDSMITH
Eastman School of Music: J. UNDERCOFLER (acting)
School of Nursing: S. RYAN
Graduate School of Management: CHARLES PLOSSER
Graduate School of Education and Human Development: P. WEXLER
Memorial Art Gallery: GRANT HOLCOMB

CHAIRMEN OF DEPARTMENTS

Psychiatry: E. CAINE
Health Services: R. MANCHESTER
Modern Languages and Cultures: B. JORGENSEN
Linguistics: M. TANENHAUS
Preventive Medicine and Community Health: T. PEARSON
Chemical Engineering: H. PALMER
Keyboard: N. TRUE, D. HIGGS
English: B. LONDON
Cancer Center: E. MESSING (interim)
Surgery: S. SCHWARTZ
Orthopaedics: R. BURTON
Computer Science: M. SCOTT
Radiology: A. ROBINSON
Theory: E. MARVIN
Optics: D. HALL
Anaesthesiology: D. WARD
Physics and Astronomy: P. SLATTERY
Musicology: J. THYM
Statistics: W. J. HALL
Anthropology: T. GIBSON
History: R. WESTBROOK
Biology: R. ANGERER
Conducting and Ensembles: S. HODKINSON
Medicine: R. DOLIN
Physiology: M. ANDERS
Psychology: M. ZUCKERMAN
Neurology: R. GRIGGS
Chemistry: J. FARRAR
Animal Medicine: J. WYATT
Philosophy: D. MODRAK
Biophysics: F. SHERMAN
Pharmacology and Toxicology: M. ANDERS
String Department: N. GOLUSES
Geological Sciences: A. BASU
Voice: J. MALOY
Biochemistry: F. SHERMAN
Microbiology: B. IGLEWSKI
Electrical Engineering: P. FAUCHET
Naval Science: (vacant)
Ophthalmology: G. BRESNICK
Art and Art History: M. A. HOLLY
Political Science: (vacant)
Biostatistics: D. OAKES
Economics: A. STOCKMAN
Pathology: A. ARVAN (acting)
Composition: D. LIPTAK
Mathematics: D. RAVENEL
Humanities (Eastman School of Music): J. BALDO
Music Education: D. BRINK FOX
Mechanical Engineering: J. LAMBROPOULOS
Paediatrics: E. MCANARNEY
Anatomy: (vacant)
Obstetrics and Gynaecology: D. GUZICK
Woodwind, Brass and Percussion: R. RICKER
Music: K. KOWALKE
Dental Research: L. TABAK
Jazz Studies: F. STURM

VASSAR COLLEGE

Poughkeepsie, NY 12601
Telephone: (914) 437-7000
Chartered 1861
President: FRANCES DALY FERGUSSON
Vice-President for Finance and Treasurer: ANTHONY STELLATO
Director of College Relations: SUSAN DEKREY
Vice-President for Development: KARIN L. GEORGE
Dean of the Faculty: NORMAN FAINSTEIN
Dean of the College: COLTON JOHNSON
Dean of Students: DAVID H. BROWN
Director of Libraries: SABRINA PAPE
Library of over 750,000 vols
Number of teachers: 248
Number of students: 2,250

WAGNER COLLEGE

Grymes Hill, Staten Island, NY 10301
Telephone: (718) 390-3100
Fax: (718) 390-3105
Founded 1883
President: Dr NORMAN R. SMITH
Dean of Admissions: ANGELO ARAIMO
Librarian: Y. JOHN AUH
Library of 285,000 vols
Number of teachers: 80 full-time, 110 part-time
Number of students: 1,800

WEBB INSTITUTE

Glen Cove, Long Island, NY 11542
Telephone: (516) 671-2213
Founded 1889
President: Dr JAMES J. CONTI
Registrar: WILLIAM G. MURRAY
Dean: Dr ROGER H. COMPTON
Librarian: PATRICIA PRESCOTT
Library of 50,000 vols
Number of teachers: 9 full-time, 14 part-time
Number of students: 94

WELLS COLLEGE

Aurora, NY 13026
Telephone: (315) 364-3440
Fax: (315) 364-3227
Founded 1868
Women's liberal arts college
President: LISA MARSH RYERSON
Vice-President and Treasurer: DIANE HUTCHINSON
Dean of the College: ELLEN HALL
Dean of Students: SUSAN RYAN
Director of Admissions: SUSAN SLOAN
Registrar: KARLA LEYBOLD-TAYLOR
Librarian: JERI VARGO
Library of 231,000 vols
Number of teachers: 49
Number of students: 325
Publication: *Wells College Express.*

YESHIVA UNIVERSITY

500 West 185th St, New York, NY 10033-3201
Telephone: (212) 960-5400
Telex: 220883
Fax: (212) 960-0055
Founded 1886
Independent control
Languages of instruction: English and Hebrew
President: NORMAN LAMM
Vice-President for Academic Affairs: S. R. GELMAN (interim)
Vice-President for Medical Affairs: D. P. PURPURA
Vice-President for Business Affairs: S. E. SOCOL
Vice-President for Development: D. T. FORMAN
Vice-President for University Affairs: H. C. DOBRINSKY
Director of Public Relations: D. M. ROSEN
General Counsel: M. H. BOCKSTEIN
Dean of University Libraries: P. BERGER
Six libraries of 1,000,000 vols
Number of teachers: 1,100
Number of students: 6,335
Publications: *Yeshiva University Review*, *Yeshiva University Today.*

DEANS

Yeshiva College: N. T. ADLER
Isaac Breuer College of Hebraic Studies: M. D. SHMIDMAN
James Striar School of General Jewish Studies: M. D. SHMIDMAN
Yeshiva Program and Mazer School of Talmudic Studies: Z. CHARLOP
Irving I. Stone Beit Midrash Program: M. D. SHMIDMAN
Stern College for Women: K. BACON
Sy Syms School of Business: H. NIERENBERG
Albert Einstein College of Medicine: D. P. PURPURA
Benjamin N. Cardozo School of Law: P. R. VERKUIL
Bernard Revel Graduate School and Harry Fischel School for Higher Jewish Studies: A. HYMAN
Ferkauf Graduate School of Psychology: L. J. SIEGEL
Wurzweiler School of Social Work: S. R. GELMAN
Azrieli Graduate School of Jewish Education and Administration: Y. S. HANDEL
Sue Golding Graduate Division of Medical Sciences: A. M. ETGEN

ATTACHED RESEARCH INSTITUTES

Irwin S. and Sylvia Chanin Institute for Cancer Research.

Rose F. Kennedy Center for Research in Mental Retardation and Human Development.

Jack and Pearl Resnick Gerontology Center.

Florence and Theodore Baumritter Kidney Dialysis and Research Center.

Marion Bessin Liver Research Center.

Ebrahim Ben Davood Eliahu Eshgaghian Transgenic Facility for Biomedical Research.

Samuel H. and Rachel Golding Center for Developmental Neurobiology.

Samuel H. and Rachel Golding Center for Molecular Genetics.

Cardiovascular Center.

Center for Diabetes Research.

Center for Research in Neuropsychopharmacology.

Institute for Human Communication Disorders.

NORTH CAROLINA

APPALACHIAN STATE UNIVERSITY

Boone, NC 28608
Telephone: (704) 262-2000
Founded 1899
Linked to the University of North Carolina
Chancellor: FRANCIS T. BORKOWSKI
Registrar: BROOKS MCLEOD
University Librarian: MARY REICHEL
Library of 550,000 vols
Number of teachers: 545
Number of students: 11,641

BARBER-SCOTIA COLLEGE

145 Cabarrus Ave, West, Concord, NC 28025
Telephone: (704) 789-2900
Fax: (704) 789-2958
Founded 1867
President: Dr SAMMIE POTTS
Vice-President for Academic Affairs: Dr ALEXANDER ERWIN

Vice-President for Student Affairs: ERIC JACKSON
Vice-President for Fiscal Affairs: NEMICHAND JAIN
Vice-President for Institutional Advancement: EUGENE C. PERRY Jr
Registrar: EMMA WITHERSPOON
Librarian: MINORA HICKS

Library of 68,374 vols
Number of teachers: 36
Number of students: 500

BARTON COLLEGE

Wilson, NC 27893
Telephone: (919) 399-6300
Fax: (919) 237-4957
Founded 1902
Private (Disciples of Christ)

President: Dr JAMES B. HEMBY, Jr
Registrar: Dr MURDINA MACDONALD
Academic Dean: Dr VERNON LINDQUIST

Library of 150,000 vols
Number of teachers: 82
Number of students: 1,300

BELMONT ABBEY COLLEGE

Belmont, NC 28012
Telephone: (704) 825-6700
Founded 1876

President: Dr ROBERT A. PRESTON
Provost and Dean of Faculty: Dr ARTIN ARSLANIAN
Vice-President for Business Affairs: JAMES SCHUPPENHAUER
Vice-President for Institutional Advancement: Dr JOHN MARSHALL
Vice-President for Student Affairs: Dr MICHAEL MCLEOD

Library of 100,000 vols
Number of teachers: 50
Number of students: 1,000

Publications: *Agora, Crossroads, Around Our Campus.*

BENNETT COLLEGE

Greensboro, NC 27401-3239
Telephone: (919) 370-8607
Founded 1873 (reorganized 1926)

President: GLORIA R. SCOTT
Director of Admissions: LINDA TORRENCE
Provost: CHARLOTTE ALSTON
Librarian: JUANITA PORTIS

Library of 100,000 vols
Number of teachers: 57
Number of students: 647

CAMPBELL UNIVERSITY

Buie's Creek, NC 27506
Telephone: (910) 893-1200
Founded 1887

President: Dr NORMAN A. WIGGINS
Vice-President for Business: Dr JAMES ELLERBE
Vice-President for Academic Affairs and Provost: Dr JERRY M. WALLACE
Vice-President for Institutional Advancement: Dr JACK BRITT
Registrar: J. DAVID MCGIRT
Dean of Admissions, Financial Aid and Veterans' Affairs: HERBERT KERNER
Director of Library Services: Dr RONNIE W. FAULKNER

Library of 466,899 vols
Number of teachers: 175 full-time, 253 part-time

Publications: *Prospect* (Alumni bulletin), *Campbell Times* (newspaper), *Pine Burr* (year book).

DEANS

School of Arts and Sciences: Dr WALTER S. BARGE
School of Law: Dr PATRICK HETRICK
School of Pharmacy: Dr RONALD W. MADDOX
School of Business: THOMAS H. FOLWELL
School of Education: Dr MARGARET GIESBRECHT
Divinity School: Dr MICHAEL G. COGDILL

CATAWBA COLLEGE

Salisbury, NC 28144
Telephone: (704) 637-4111
Founded 1851

President: Dr STEPHEN H. WURSTER
Registrar: CAROL GAMBLE
Director of Admissions: ROBERT BENNETT
Librarian: JOYCE DAVIS

Library of 200,000 vols
Number of teachers: 67
Number of students: 950

DAVIDSON COLLEGE

Davidson, NC 28036
Telephone: (704) 892-2000
Fax: (704) 892-2005
Founded 1837

President: ROBERT F. VAGT
Vice-President for Academic Affairs and Dean of the Faculty: CLARK G. ROSS
Vice-President for Institutional Advancement: JAMES W. MAY, Jr
Vice-President for Business and Finance: ROBERT C. NORFLEET
Director of College Relations: JERRY S. STOCKDALE
Director of Alumni Relations: EILEEN M. KEELEY
Dean of Admissions and Financial Aid: NANCY J. CABLE
Registrar: POLLY W. GRIFFIN
Director of Library: LELAND M. PARK

Library of 450,000 vols
Number of teachers: 152
Number of students: 1,623

Publications: *Davidson Journal* (quarterly), *Oak Row Report* (monthly), *The Davidsonian* (weekly student newspaper), *Quips and Cranks* (year book), *The Miscellany* (Literary Quarterly), *Hobart Park.*

DUKE UNIVERSITY

Durham, NC 27708
Telephone: (919) 684-8111

Union Institute Society founded in 1838 in Randolph County, North Carolina. In 1851 the Institute was reorganized as Trinity College, and in 1892 the College was removed to Durham. A new charter was issued in 1924, when, under the Duke Endowment, it became Duke University

President: NANNERL O. KEOHANE
Provost: JOHN W. STROHBEHN
Chancellor for Health Affairs and Dean of the Medical School: RALPH SNYDERMAN
Executive Vice-President for Administration: TALLMAN TRASK, III
Executive Vice-President (Asset Management): EUGENE J. MCDONALD
Senior Vice-President for Alumni Affairs and Development: JOHN J. PIVA, Jr
Senior Vice-President for Public Affairs: JOHN F. BURNESS
Vice-President and Corporate Controller: JOHN F. ADCOCK
Vice-President for Institutional Equity: MYRNA ADAMS
Vice-President and Director of Athletics: TOM A. BUTTERS
Vice-President for Student Affairs: JANET SMITH DICKERSON
Registrar: BRUCE CUNNINGHAM
Librarian: DAVID FERRIERO

Number of teachers: 2,122 full-time
Number of students: 11,511

DEANS

Dean of Trinity College and Vice-Provost for Undergraduate Education: RICHARD A. WHITE
Divinity School: DENNIS M. CAMPBELL
Medical Education: DAN G. BLAZER
School of Engineering: EARL H. DOWELL
School of the Environment: NORMAN CHRISTENSEN
School of Law: PAMELA B. GANN
Faculty of Arts and Sciences: WILLIAM CHAFE
Fuqua School of Business: REX ADAMS

EAST CAROLINA UNIVERSITY

Greenville, NC 27858
Telephone: (252) 328-6131
Fax: (252) 328-4155
Founded 1907
Constituent instn of the University of North Carolina System

Chancellor: RICHARD R. EAKIN
Vice-Chancellor for Health Sciences: Dr JAMES HALLOCK
Vice-Chancellor for Academic Affairs: Dr RICHARD D. RINGEISEN
Registrar: J. GILBERT MOORE
Director of Admissions: THOMAS E. POWELL, Jr
Director of Academic Library Services: CARROLL H. VARNER

Library of 1,156,000 volumes
Number of teachers: 1,167
Number of students: 17,567

ELON COLLEGE

Elon College, NC 27244
Telephone: (336) 584-9711
Fax: (336) 538-3986
Founded 1889
Related to the United Church of Christ

President: Dr JAMES FRED YOUNG
Provost: Dr GERALD L. FRANCIS
Vice-President for Academic Affairs: Dr JULIANNE MAHER
Co-ordinator of the Library: KATE D. HICKEY

Library of 200,000 vols
Number of teachers: 170 full-time, 81 part-time
Number of students: 3,700

FAYETTEVILLE STATE UNIVERSITY

1200 Murchison Rd, Fayetteville, NC 28301-4298
Telephone: (919) 486-1111
Founded 1867 as the Howard School, attained University status 1969
Part of University of North Carolina System

Chancellor: Dr WILLIS B. MCLEOD
Vice-Chancellor for Academic Affairs: Dr PERRY MASSEY
Vice-Chancellor for Business and Finance: FRANK TOLIVER
Vice-Chancellor for University Relations and Development: Dr DENISE MAHONE WYATT
Vice-Chancellor for Student Affairs: Dr HARRY GHEE
Registrar: MICHAEL HEARON
Librarian: BOBBY WYNN

Library of 198,000 vols
Number of teachers: 205 full-time
Number of students: 4,009

GREENSBORO COLLEGE

815 West Market St, Greensboro, NC 27401-1875

Telephone: (336) 272-7102
Fax: (336) 271-6634
Founded 1838
President: Dr CRAVEN E. WILLIAMS
Vice-President for Academic Affairs and Dean of the Faculty: Dr DANIEL N. KECK
Vice-President for Admissions: RANDY DOSS
Librarian: PAMELA MCKIRDY
Library of 91,290 vols
Number of teachers: 97
Number of students: 1,100

GUILFORD COLLEGE

5800 W. Friendly Avenue, Greensboro, NC 27410
Telephone: (910) 316-2000
Fax: (910) 316-2949
Founded 1837
Private (Society of Friends) co-educational liberal arts college
President: DONALD W. MCNEMAR
Dean: MARTHA H. COOLEY
Library Director: HERBERT L. POOLE
Library of over 335,000 vols
Number of teachers: 93
Number of students: 1,600
Publications: *Journal of Undergraduate Mathematics* (2 a year), *Journal of Undergraduate Research in Physics* (2 a year), *The Southern Friend* (2 a year).

HIGH POINT UNIVERSITY

High Point, NC 27262-3598
Telephone: (336) 841-9000
Founded 1924
President: Dr J. C. MARTINSON, Jr
Vice-President for Academic Affairs and Dean of Arts and Sciences: Dr E. VANCE DAVIS
Registrar: DIANA L. ESTEY
Dean of Admissions: JAMES SCHLIMMER
Librarian: Ms JUDY K. HITCHCOCK
Library of 153,400 vols
Number of teachers: 180
Number of students: 2,700

JOHNSON C. SMITH UNIVERSITY

100-152 Beatties Ford Rd, Charlotte, NC 28216
Telephone: (704) 378-1000
Fax: (704) 372-5746
Founded 1867
President: Dr DOROTHY COWSER YANCY
Vice-President for Academic Affairs: Dr LESTER C. NEWMAN
Vice-President for Business and Finance: ELLIOTT ROBINSON
Vice-President for Student Affairs: TREVA NORMAN
Vice-President for Development: GERALD WASHINGTON
Director of Admissions: BRIDGETT N. GOLMAN
Rector of Honors College: Dr MAXINE F. MOORE
Registrar: MOSES JONES
Librarian: LAURA D. TURNER
Library of 113,000 vols
Number of teachers: 80, including 10 professors
Number of students: 1,427

LENOIR-RHYNE COLLEGE

Hickory, NC 28603
Telephone: (828) 328-1741
Fax: (828) 328-7368
E-mail: admissions@lrc.edu
Founded 1891
Private control (Evangelical Lutheran Church in America)
President: RYAN A. LAHURD
Academic Dean: ROBERT L. SPULLER
Dean of Students: ANITA JOHNSON GWIN
Admissions Director: TIMOTHY JACKSON
Library of 124,000 vols
Number of teachers: 111
Number of students: 1,627

LIVINGSTONE COLLEGE

701 W. Monroe St, Salisbury, NC 28144
Telephone: (704) 638-5500
Founded 1879
President: Dr BURNET JOINER
Registrar: WENDY JACKSON
Dean for Student Affairs: Dr MICHELLE RELEFORD
Director of Admissions: (vacant)
Librarian: ELIZABETH MOSBEY
Library of 77,584 vols
Number of teachers: 60
Number of students: 777
Publications: *Alumni Bulletin* (quarterly), *Bears' Tale* (annually), *College Catalog* (annually), *The Livingstonian* (annually).

MARS HILL COLLEGE

Mars Hill, NC 28754
Telephone: (828) 689-1201
Fax: (828) 689-1478
Founded 1856
President: Dr A. MAX LENNON
Dean of Admissions: Dr JERRY JACKSON
Librarian: DEANNA DILLINGHAM (acting)
Library of 90,000 vols
Number of teachers: 78
Number of students: 1,200
First degree courses in arts, science, music, social work.

MEREDITH COLLEGE

Raleigh, NC 27607-5298
Telephone: (919) 829-8600
Founded 1891
President: JOHN E. WEEMS
Registrar: SUE TODD
Dean of Undergraduate Instruction: ALLEN PAGE
Director of Admissions: CAROL KERCHEVAL
Dean of Library Information Services: JANET L. FREEMAN
Library of 139,000 vols
Number of teachers: 101 full-time, 127 part-time
Number of students: 2,574

METHODIST COLLEGE

5400 Ramsey St, Fayetteville, NC 28311-1420
Telephone: (910) 630-7000
Chartered 1956; opened 1960
President: Dr M. ELTON HENDRICKS
Dean: Dr ANTHONY J. DELAPA
Business Manager: GENE CLAYTON
Secretary to the Board of Trustees: Dr FRANK P. STOUT
Library of 76,500 vols, 42,500 non-book holdings
Number of students: 1,324 full-time, 397 part-time

NORTH CAROLINA AGRICULTURAL AND TECHNICAL STATE UNIVERSITY

1601 East Market St, Greensboro, NC 27411
Telephone: (919) 334-7500
Founded 1891
Linked to the University of North Carolina
Chancellor: Dr EDWARD B. FORT
Vice-Chancellor for Academic Affairs: Dr HAROLD MARTIN
Vice-Chancellor for Business/Finance: CHARLES MCINTYRE
Vice-Chancellor for Student Affairs: Dr SULLIVAN WELBORNE
Vice-Chancellor for Development and University Relations: Dr ROBERT P. JENNINGS
Registrar: Ms DORIS GRAHAM
Librarian: WALTRENE CANADA
Library of 416,000 vols
Number of teachers: 519
Number of students: 7,533

NORTH CAROLINA CENTRAL UNIVERSITY

Durham, NC 27707
Telephone: (919) 560-6100
Founded 1910
Linked to the University of North Carolina
State control
Chancellor: JULIUS L. CHAMBERS
Vice-Chancellor for Financial Affairs: RUBY PITTMAN
Vice-Chancellor for Academic Affairs: Dr PATSY PERRY
Registrar: MILDRED MUNDINE
Librarian: FLOYD C. HARDY
Library of 600,422 vols
Number of teachers: 378
Number of students: 5,635
Publications: *Varia, Ex Umbra, Campus Echo, Bulletins.*

DEANS

College of Arts and Sciences: Dr BERNICE JOHNSON
School of Graduate Studies: Dr TED PARRISH
School of Library and Information Science: Dr BENJAMIN F. SPELLER
School of Law: PERCY LUNEY
School of Business: Dr SUNDAR FLEMING

NORTH CAROLINA WESLEYAN COLLEGE

3400 North Wesleyan Blvd, Rocky Mount, NC 27804
Telephone: (919) 985-5100
Fax: (919) 977-3701
Founded 1956
Co-educational, church-related liberal arts college
President: Dr JOHN B. WHITE
Dean: Dr MARY RUTH COX
Library of 75,000 vols
Number of teachers 66
Number of students: 1,500
Publication: *Bulletin* (quarterly).

PFEIFFER UNIVERSITY

Misenheimer, NC 28109
Telephone: (704) 463-1360
Founded 1885
Private (Methodist) control
President: Dr CHARLES M. AMBROSE
Registrar: LARRY DURRETT
Provost and Dean of Academic Affairs: J. MICHAEL RIEMANN
Librarian: N. B. WILSON
Library of 116,300 vols
Number of teachers: 51 full-time
Number of students: 1,814

QUEENS COLLEGE

1900 Selwyn Ave, Charlotte, NC 28274
Telephone: (704) 337-2200
Fax: (704) 337-2517

Founded 1857

Liberal arts college, undergraduate and graduate programmes; Presbyterian (USA) affiliation

President: Dr BILLY O. WIREMAN
Vice-President for Academic Affairs: (vacant)
Dean of Students: ERIC BALDWIN (acting)
Vice-President for Institutional Advancement: Dr RICHARD E. RANKIN
Vice-President for Administration and Finance: LAURIE GUY
Librarian: ROSEMARY ARNESON

Library of 117,000 vols
Number of teachers: 61 full-time, 24 part-time
Number of students: 1,550

Publication: *Odyssey* (4 a year).

ST ANDREWS PRESBYTERIAN COLLEGE

Laurinburg, NC 28352

Telephone: (910) 277-5000

Founded 1896
Private control
Academic year: September to June

President: Dr WARREN L. BOARD
Vice-President for Institutional Advancement: PAUL BALDASARE Jr
Registrar: Dr JAMES F. STEPHENS
Dean of the College: Dr LAWRENCE E. SCHULZ
Librarian: MARY MCDONALD

Library of 91,000 vols
Number of teachers: 51
Number of students: 748

Publication: *St Andrew's Review* (2 a year).

SALEM ACADEMY AND COLLEGE

Box 10548, Salem Station, Winston-Salem, NC 27108-0548

Telephone: (336) 721-2600
Fax: (336) 917-5339

Founded 1772
Private control

President: Dr JULIANNE STILL THRIFT
Director of Admissions and Financial Aid: KATHERINE KNAPP WATTS
Dean of the College: Dr EILEEN WILSON-OYELARAN
Director, School of Music: Dr DAVID SCHILDKRET
Librarian: Dr ROSE A. SIMON

Library of 128,500 vols
Number of teachers: 84
Number of students: 1,002

SHAW UNIVERSITY

Raleigh, NC 27601

Telephone: (919) 546-8200
Fax: (919) 546-8301

Founded 1865

President: Dr TALBERT O. SHAW
Academic Dean: Dr COLLIE COLEMAN
Executive Vice-President: Dr ERNEST L. PICKENS
Registrar: GENE PAGE
Librarian: SHEILA BOURNE

Library of 122,413 vols
Number of teachers: 242
Number of students: 2,418

UNIVERSITY OF NORTH CAROLINA

POB 2688, Chapel Hill, NC 27515-2688

Telephone: (919) 962-1000
Fax: (919) 962-2751

President: MOLLY CORBETT BROAD
Vice-President–Academic Affairs: ROY CARROLL
Vice-President–Finance: WILLIAM O. MCCOY
Vice-President–Planning: JUDITH P. PULLEY
Vice-President–Public Affairs and University Advancement: J. B. MILLIKEN
Vice-President–University/Schools Program: CHARLES COBLE
Vice-President–Program Assessment and Public Service: GARY BARNES
Secretary: ROSALIND FUSE-HALL

The University of North Carolina is a multi-campus university composed of sixteen institutions: University of North Carolina at Asheville, University of North Carolina at Chapel Hill, University of North Carolina at Greensboro, University of North Carolina at Charlotte, University of North Carolina at Wilmington, and North Carolina State University at Raleigh. Also Appalachian State University, East Carolina University, Elizabeth City State University, Fayetteville State University, North Carolina Agricultural and Technical State University, North Carolina Central University, North Carolina School of the Arts, University of North Carolina at Pembroke, Western Carolina University, Winston-Salem State University (q.v.)

University of North Carolina at Asheville

One University Heights, Asheville, NC 28804-3299

Telephone: (828) 251-6600

Established as Buncombe County Junior College 1927; later as Asheville-Biltmore College; made a unit of the University in 1969

Chancellor: Dr PATSY B. REED
Vice-Chancellor for Academic Affairs: Dr JAMES PITTS
Vice-Chancellor for Finance: ARTHUR FOLEY
Vice-Chancellor for Student Affairs: Dr ERIC V. IOVACCHINI
Vice-Chancellor for University Relations: BEVERLY MODLIN
Registrar: REBECCA SENSABAUGH
Librarian: JAMES R. KUHLMAN

Library of 243,800 vols
Number of teachers: 269
Number of students: 3,179

Publication: *Images.*

CHAIRMEN OF DEPARTMENTS

CAULFIELD, J., Literature
COOKE, T., Art
DAUGHTERTY, J., Computer Science
DOWNES, M., Humanities
FRIEDENBERG, L., Psychology
GALE, S., Mathematics
GUPTON, J., Chemistry
HAAS, W., Sociology
HUANG, A., Atmospheric Sciences
KORMANIK, G., Biology
LARSON, B., Economics
MAAS, R., Environmental Studies
MCDONALD, P., Foreign Languages
MCGLINN, J., Education
MCKENZIE, C., Management
MCKNIGHT, C., Music
MITCHELL, C., Mass Communication
MULLEN, D., Political Science
RAY, K., Health and Fitness
RUIZ, M., Physics
SPELLMAN, W., History
WALTERS, S., Drama
WILSON, G., Philosophy

University of North Carolina at Chapel Hill

Chapel Hill, NC 27599

Telephone: (919) 962-2211

Chartered 1789, opened 1795; since 1931 a unit of the University of North Carolina

Academic year: August to May

Chancellor: MICHAEL HOOKER
Provost: RICHARD RICHARDSON
Vice-Provost, Research and Graduate Studies: THOMAS MEYER
Vice-Chancellor, Administration: JAMES RAMSEY
Vice-Chancellor, University Advancement: MATTHEW KUPEC
Vice-Chancellor, Student Affairs: SUSAN KITCHEN
Registrar: DAVID C. LANIER
Director of Institutional Research: TIMOTHY R. SANFORD
Secretary of the Faculty: JOSEPH FERRELL
Director of Undergraduate Admissions: JEROME LUCIDO
University Librarian: JOE A. HEWITT

Library: see Libraries
Number of teachers: 2,421
Number of students: 24,189

Publications: *Southern Economic Journal* (quarterly), *Social Science Newsletter* (quarterly), *The High School Journal* (quarterly), *Current Contents* (quarterly), *Centerpieces* (monthly), *Baseline* (3 a year), *Dear Colleague* (2 a year), and numerous other faculty publications.

DEANS

College of Arts and Sciences and General College: RISA PALM
Graduate School of Business Administration: ROBERT SULLIVAN
School of Education: MADELEINE GRUMET
School of Law: JUDITH W. WEGNER
School of Medicine: JEFFREY HOUPT
School of Pharmacy: WILLIAM CAMPBELL
School of Public Health: WILLIAM ROPER
School of Information and Library Science: BARBARA B. MORAN
School of Dentistry: JOHN W. STAMM
School of Journalism: RICHARD R. COLE
School of Nursing: CYNTHIA FREUND
School of Social Work: RICHARD EDWARDS
Graduate School: LINDA DYKSTRA
Summer School: JAMES L. MURPHY

PROFESSORS

Allied Medical Programs:
MITCHELL, M. M.
MITCHELL, R. U.
PETERS, R. W.
SAKATA, R.
YODER, D. E.

American Studies Curriculum:
ALLEN, R. C.
KASSON, J. S.

Anaesthesiology:
BOYSEN, P. G.
GHIA, J. N.
KAFER, E. R.
MUELLER, R. A.
NORFLEET, E. A.
SPIELMAN, F. J.
SPRAGUE, D. H.
VAUGHAN, R. W.

Anthropology:
CRUMLEY, C. L.
EVENS, T. M.
FINKLER, K.
HOLLAND, D. C.
JOHNSON, N. B.
LARSEN, C. S.
LUTZ, C. A.
PEACOCK, J. L., III
STEPONAITIS, V. P.
WINTERHALDER, B.

Art:
FOLDA, J. T., III
GRABOWSKI, S. E.
KINNAIRD, R. W.
MARKS, A. S.
NOE, J. L.
SHERIFF, M. D.

STURGEON, C.
ZABOROWSKI, D. J.

Biochemistry:

CAPLOW, M.
CARTER, C. W., Jr
CHANEY, S. G.
ERREDE, B. J.
HERMANS, J.
LEE, D. C.
LENTZ, B. R.
MARZLUFF, W. F.
MEISSNER, G. W.
MORELL, P.
NAYFEH, S. N.
SANCAR, A.
SWANSTROM, R. I.
TIDWELL, P. F.
TRAUT, T. W.
VAN DYKE, T. A.
WOLFENDEN, R. V.

Biomedical Engineering Programme:

LUCAS, C. N.
TSUI, B. M.

Biostatistics:

DAVIS, C. E.
HELMS, R. W.
KALSBEEK, W. D.
KOCH, G. G.
KUPPER, L. L.
MARGOLIN, B. H.
QUADE, D. E.
SEN, P. K.
SUCHINDRAN, C. M.
SYMONS, M. J.

Biology:

BLOOM, K. S.
BOLLENBACHER, W. E.
DICKISON, W. C.
FEDUCCIA, J. A.
GENSEL, P. G.
GILBERT, L. I.
HARRIS, A. K., Jr
MATSON, S. W.
MATTHYSSE, A. G.
PARKS, C. R.
PEET, R. K.
PETES, T. D.
PRINGLE, J. R.
QUATRANO, R. S.
SALMON E. D.
SCOTT, T. K.
STAFFORD, D. W.
STIVEN, A. E.
WHITE, P. S.
WILEY, R. H., Jr

Business Administration:

ALDER, R. S.
ANDERSON, C. R.
ARMSTRONG, G. M.
BATEMAN, T. S.
BAYUS, B. L.
BETTIS, R. A.
BLOCHER, E. J.
BLOOM, P. N.
COLLINS, J. H.
CONRAD, J. S.
EDWARDS, J. R.
ELVERS, D. A.
EVANS, J. P.
FISCHER, W. A.
HARTZELL, D. J.
KASARDA, J. D.
KLOMPMAKER, J. E.
LANDSMAN, W. R.
MCENALLY, R. W.
MANN, R. A.
MARUCHECK, A. E.
NEEBE, A. W.
PEIRCE, E. R.
PERREAULT, W. D., Jr
PRINGLE, J. J.
RAVENSCRAFT, D. J.
RENDLEMAN, R. J.
ROBERTS, B. S.
RONDINELLI, D. A.
ROSEN, B.
RUBIN, D. S.
SHAPIRO, D. L.
SULLIVAN, R. S.
TILLMAN, R.
WAGNER, H. M.
WHYBARK, D. C.

Cell Biology and Anatomy:

BURRIDGE, K. W. T.
GRANGER, N. A.
HACKENBROCK, C. R.
HENSON, O. W., Jr
HERMAN, B.
JACOBSON, K. A.
KOCH, W. E.
LAUDER, J. M.
LEMASTERS, J. J.
MONTGOMERY, R. L.
O'RAND, M. G.
PENG, H. B.
PETRUSZ, P.
RUSTIONI, A.
SADLER, T. W.
SULIK, K. K.

Chemistry:

BAER, T.
BROOKHART, M. S.
BUCK, R. P.
COKE, J. L.
CRIMMINS, M. T.
DESIMONE, J. M.
ERICKSON, B. W.
EVANS, S. A., Jr
IRENE, E. A.
JICHA, D. C.
JOHNSON, C. S., Jr
JORGENSON, J. W.
KROPP, P. J.
MEYER, T. J.
MILLER, R. E.
MURRAY, R. W.
PEDERSEN, L. G.
SAMULSKI, E. T.
SORRELL, T. N.
SPREMULLI, L. L.
TEMPLETON, J. L.
THOMPSON, N. L.
WIGHTMAN, R. M.

City and Regional Planning:

GODSCHALK, D. R.
GOLDSTEIN, H. A.
KAISER, E. J.
LACEY, L.
LUGER, M. I.
MALIZIA, E. E.
MOREAU, D. H.
ROHE, W. M.

Classics:

BROWN, E. L.
HOUSTON, G. W.
LINDERSKI, J.
MACK, S.
RACE, W. H.
RECKFORD, K. J.
SAMS, G. K.
STADTER, P. A.
WEST, W. C., III
WOOTEN, C. W.

Communication Studies:

BALTHROP, V W.
COX, J. R., Jr
DYSON, M. E.
GROSSBERG, L.
HORNE, G. C.
KINDEM, G. A.
LONG, B. W.
ROSENFELD, L. B.
WOOD, J. T.

Comparative Literature:

FURST, L. R.

Computer Science:

BROOKS, F. P., Jr
FUCHS, H.
HALTON, J. H.
MAGO, G. A.
PIZER, S. M.
PLAISTED, D. A.
SMITH, J. B.
WEISS, S. F.

Curriculum, African and Afro-American Study:

NYANG'ORO, J. E.
SELASSIE, B. H.

Curriculum, Asian Studies:

SEATON, J. P.

Curriculum, Linguistics and Non-West Languages:

HENDRICK, R. J.
MELCHERT, H. C.
TSIAPERA, M.

Curriculum, Public Policy Analysis:

DILL, D. D.
STEGMAN, M. A.

Dentistry:

ARNOLD, R. R.
AUKHIL, I.
BAWDEN, J. W.
BAYNE, S. C.
BECK, J. D.
BURKES, E. J.
CRENSHAW, M. A.
HANKER, J. S.
HERSHEY, H. G.
HEYMANN, H. O.
HUNT, R. J.
HUTCHENS, L. H., Jr
JENZANO, J. W.
KUSY, R. P.
MCIVER, F. T.
MURRAH, V. A.
OFFENBACHER, S.
OLDENBURG, T. R.
PROFFIT, W. R.
ROBERSON, T. M.
SHUGARS, D. A.
SIMPSON, D. M.
STAMM, J. W.
STRAUSS, R. P.
TROPE, M.
TULLOCH, J. F. C.
TURVEY, T. A.
VANN, W. F., Jr
WARREN, D. W.
WHITE, R. P.
WHITE, R. P., Jr
WILLIAMS, R. C.
WRIGHT, J. T.
YAMAUCHI, M.
WOOD, M. T.

Dermatology:

BRIGGAMAN, R. A.
FINE, J. D.
O'KEEFE, E. J.

Dev. Disabilities Training Institute:

BAROFF, G. S.

Dramatic Art:

BARRANGER, M. S.
HAMMOND, D. A.
OWEN, R. A.
RAPHAEL, B. N.
TURNER, C. W.

Economics:

AKIN, J. S.
BENAVIE, A.
BLACK, S. W., III
BLAU, D. M.
CONWAY, P. J.
DARITY, W. A., Jr.
FIELD, A. J., Jr
FRIEDMAN, J. W.
FROYEN, R. T.

GALLANT, A. R.
GALLMAN, R. E.
GUILKEY, D. K.
MROZ, T. A.
MURPHY, J. L.
ROSEFIELDE, S. S.
SALEMI, M. K.
STEWART, J. F.
TARASCIO, V. J.
TAUCHEN, H. V.

Education:

BALLEW, J. H.
BRANTLEY, J. C.
BROWN, D.
BROWN, F.
BURKE, W. I.
COOP, R. H.
CUNNINGHAM, J.
DAY, B. D.
FITZGERALD, W. J.
FRIERSON, H. T.
GALASSI, J. P.
GALLAGHER, J. J.
HENNIS, R. S.
HUNTER, R. C.
LILLIE, D. L.
MARSHALL, C.
MORRISON, J. L.
NOBLIT, G. W.
ODOM, S. L., Jr
PALMER, W.
PRYZWANSKY, W. B.
SIMEONSON, R. J.
SPIEGEL, D. L.
STEDMAN, D J.
STUCK, G. B.
TOM, A. R.
UNKS, G.
WARE, W. B.
WASIK, B. H.
WHITE, K. P.

Emergency Medicine:

TINTINALLI, J. E.

English:

ANDREWS, W. L.
AVERY, L. G.
BETTS, D. W.
DESSEN, A. C.
EBLE, C. C.
FLORA, J. M.
GLESS, D. J.
GREENE, J. L.
GURA, P. F.
HARMON, W. R.
HARRIS, T.
HENDERSON, M. G.
HOBSON, F. C., Jr
KENNEDY, E. D.
KING, J. K.
LENSING, G. S., Jr
LINDEMANN, E.
LUDINGTON, C. T., Jr
MCGOWAN, J. P.
MOSKAL, J.
O'NEILL, P. P.
PATTERSON, D. W.
RAPER, J. R.
RUST, R. D.
SHAPIRO, A. R.
TAYLOR, B. W.
THOMPSON, J. P.
THORNTON, W.
WAGNER-MARTIN, L. C.
WHISNANT, D. E.
WITTING, J. S.
ZUG, C. G., III

Environmental Science and Engineering:

ANDREWS, R. N.
CHRISTAKOS, G.
CHRISTMAN, R. F.
CRAWFORD-BROWN, D. J.
DIGIANO, F. A.
FOX, D. L.
GLAZE, W. H.
GOLD, A.
JEFFRIES, H.
KAMENS, R. M.
LAURIA, D. T.
LEITH, D.
MILLER, C. T.
PFAENDER, F.
RAPAPORT, S. M.
REIST, P. C.
SINGER, P. C.
SOBSEY, M. D.
SWENBERG, J. A.
WATSON, J. E., Jr
WHITTINGTON, D.

Epidemiology:

HEISS, G.
HULKA, B.
IBRAHIM, M. A.
SAVITZ, D. A.
SEED, J. R.

Family Medicine:

CURTIS, P.
FIELDS, K. B.
GWYTHER, R. E.
LEA, J. W.
OLSON, P. R.
REEB, K. G.
SLOANE, P. D.

Geography:

BAND, L. E.
BIRDSALL, S. S.
FLORIN, J. W.
GESLER, W. M.
GREENLAND, D. E.
JOHNSON, J. H., Jr
MEADE, M.
MORIARTY, B. M.
PALM, R. I.
ROBINSON, P. J.
WALSH, S. J.
ZONN, L. E.

Geology:

BENNINGER, L. K.
CARTER, J. G.
DENNISON, J. M.
FULLAGAR, P. D.
POWELL, C. A.
TEXTORIS, D. A.

German:

KOELB, C. T.
MEWS, S. E.
PIKE, D. C.
ROBERGE, P. T.

History:

BARNEY, W. L.
BULLARD, M. M.
CHOJNACKI, S. J.
FILENE, P. G.
FINK, L. R.
FLETCHER, W. M.
GRIFFITHS, D. M.
HALL, J. D.
HARRIS, B. J.
HEADLEY, J. M.
HIGGINBOTHAM, R. D.
HUNT, M. H.
JARAUSCH, K. H.
KASSON, J. F.
KESSLER, L. D.
KOHN, R. H.
KRAMER, L. S.
LOTCHIN, R. W.
MATHEWS, D. G.
MCNEIL, G. R.
MCVAUGH, M. R.
NELSON, J. K.
PEREZ, L. A.
PFAFF, R. W.
SEMONCHE, J. E.
SOLOWAY, R. A.
TALBERT, R. J.
WATSON, H. L.
WILLIAMSON, J. R.

Information and Library Science:

CHATMAN, E. A.
DANIEL, E. H.
MORAN, B. B.
SHAW, W. M., Jr

Institute of Government:

ALLRED, S.
BELL, A. F. II
BRANNON, J. G.
CAMPBELL, W. A.
CLARKE, S. H.
DELLINGER, A. M.
DRENNAN, J. C.
FARB, R. L.
FERRELL, J. S.
JOYCE, R. P.
LAWRENCE, D. M.
LINER, C. D.
LOEB, B. F., Jr
MASON, J.
MESIBOV, L. L.
OWENS, D. W.
SMITH, M. R.
VOGT, A. J.
WHITAKER, G. P.

Journalism:

BLANCHARD, M. A.
BOWERS, T. A.
BROWN, J. D.
COLE, R. R.
ELAM, A. R.
LAUTERBORN, R. F.
LINDEN, T. R.
MEYER, P. E.
SHAVER, M. A.
SHAW, D. L.
SIMPSON, R. H.
STEVENSON, R. L.
STONE, C. S., Jr
WALDEN, R. C.

Law:

BILIONIS, L. D.
BLAKEY, W.
BOGER, J. C.
BROOME, L. L.
BROUN, K. S.
BROWN, C. N.
BRYAN, P. L.
BYRD, R. G.
CALMORE, J. O.
CLIFFORD, D. F., Jr
CONLEY, J. M.
CORRADO, M. L.
CRAIN, M. G.
DAYE, C. E.
GIBSON, S. E.
HASKELL, P. G.
HAZEN, T. L.
HORNSTEIN, D. T.
KALO, J. J.
LINK, R. C.
LOEWY, A. H.
MARKHAM, J. W.
MCUSIC, M. S.
ORTH, J. V.
ROSEN, R. A.
SHARP, S. B.
TURNIER, W. J.
WEGNER, J. W.
WEISBURD, A. M.
YARBROUGH, M. V.
ZELENAK, L. A.

Law Library:

GASAWAY, L. N.

Leisure Studies and Recreation Administration:

HENDERSON, K. A.

Marine Sciences:

BANE, J. M., Jr
FRANKENBERG, D.
HAY, M. E.
KOHLMEYER, J. J.

MARTENS, C. S.
NEUMANN, A. C.
PAERL, H. W.
PETERSON, C. H.
SCHWARTZ, F. J.
WELLS, J. T.
WERNER, P. E.

Maternal and Child Health Care:

BUEKENS, P.
KOTCH, J. B.
KOTELCHUCK, M.
TSUI, A. O.
UDRY, J. R.

Mathematics:

ASSANI, I.
BRYLAWSKI, T. H.
CIMA, J. A.
DAMON, J. N.
EBERLEIN, P. B.
FOREST, M. G.
GEISSINGER, L. D.
GOODMAN, S. E.
GRAVES, W. H.
HAWKINS, J. M.
KERZMAN, N.
KUMAR, S.
PETERSEN, K. E.
PFALTZGRAFF, J. A.
PLANTE, J. F.
PROCTOR, R. A.
SCHLESSINGER, M.
SMITH, W. W.
STASHEFF, J.
TAYLOR, M. E.
VARCHENKO, A.
WAHL, J. M.
WILLIAMS, M.
WOGEN, W. R.

Medical Allied Health Prof.:

BAILEY, D.
LEGRYS, V. A.
SAKATA, R.
YODER, D. E.

Medicine:

BERKOWITZ, L. R.
BERNARD, S. A.
BONDURANT, S.
BOUCHER, R. C., Jr
BOZYMSKI, E. M.
BRENNER, D. A.
BROMBERG, P. A.
CAREY, T. S.
CLEMMONS, D. R.
COHEN, M. S.
COHEN, P. L.
COLINDRES, R. E.
DEHMER, G. J.
DONOHUE, J. F.
DROSSMAN, D. A.
EARP, H. S., III
FALK, R. J.
FINN, W. F.
GABRIEL, D. A.
GETTES, L. S.
GONZALEZ, J. J.
GREGANTI, M. A.
GRIGGS, T. R.
HEIZER, W. D.
HOOLE, A. J.
HUANG, E. S.
KIZER, J. S.
KNOWLES, M. R.
LANE, T. W.
LIU, E. T.
MATTERN, W. D.
MITCHELL, B. S.
NUZUM, C. T.
ONTJES, D. A.
ORRINGER, E. P.
PAGANO, J. S.
RANSOHOFF, D. F.
ROBERTS, H.
ROGERS, C. S.
RUTALA, W. A.
SANDLER, R. S.
SARTOR, R. B.
SHEA, T. C.
SIMPSON, R. J., Jr
SMITH, S. C., Jr
SPARLING, P. F.
UNGARO, P. C.
WHITE, G. C., II
WILLIAMS, M. E.
WILLIS, P. W. IV
WINFIELD, J. B.
YOUNT, W. J.

Microbiology and Immunology:

BACHENHEIMER, S. L.
BOTT, K. F.
CANNON, J. G.
CLARKE, S. H.
EDGELL, M. H.
FRELINGER, J. A.
GILLIGAN, P. H.
GRIFFITH, J.
HAUGHTON, G.
HUTCHISON, C. A.
JOHNSTON, R. E.
KLAPPER, D. G.
NEWBOLD, J. E.
RAAB-TRAUB, N.
TING, J. P.
WYRICK, P. B.

Microelectronics—Chemistry:

IRENE, E. A.

Music:

BONDS, M. E.
FINSON, J. W.
KETCH, J. E.
MCKINNON, J. W.
NADAS, J. L.
NEFF, S.
OEHLER, D. L.
SMITH, B.
WARBURTON, T. A.
ZENGE, M. W.

Neurology:

GREENWOOD, R. S.
HALL, C. D.
HOWARD, J. N.
MANN, J. D.
SUZUKI, K.

Nursing:

DALTON, J. B.
DAVIS, D. H.
DOUGHERTY, M. C.
FOGEL, C. I.
FREUND, C. M.
FUNK, S. G.
GOEPPINGER, J.
HARRELL, J. S.
KJERVIK, D. K.
MILES, M. S.
MILIO, N.
MISHEL, M. H.
SANDELOWSKI, M. J.

Obstetrics and Gynaecology:

DROEGEMUELLER, W.
FOWLER, W. C., Jr
FRITZ, M. A.
GRANADOS
HASKILL, J. S.
PARISI, Y. M.
STEEGE, J. F.
WALTON, L. A.

Operations Research:

FISHMAN, G.
PROVAN, J. S.
STIDHAM, S., Jr.
TOLLE, J. W.

Ophthalmology:

COHEN, K. L.
EIFRIG, D. E.
GRIMSON, B. S.
PEIFFER, R. L., Jr.

Paediatrics:

AYLSWORTH, A. S.
BOSE, C. L.
CARSON, J. L.
COLLIER, A. M.
COOPER, H. A.
D'ERCOLE, A. J.
FERNALD, G. W.
FRENCH, F. S.
HAMRICK, H.
HENDERSON, F. W.
HENRY, G. W.
INGRAM, D. L.
KRAYBILL, E. N.
LAWSON, E. E.
LEIGH, M. W.
LEVINE, M. D.
LODA, F. A.
LOHR, J. A.
ROBERTS, K. B.
SCHALL, S. A.
SIMMONS, M. A.
STILES, A. D.
UNDERWOOD, L. E.
WILLIAMS, R. G.
WILSON, E. M.
WOOD, R. E.

Pathology and Laboratory Medicine:

ANDERSON, N. N.
BELLINGER, D. A.
BENTLEY, S. A.
BOULDIN, T. W.
CHAPMAN, J. F.
CROSS, R. E.
FARBER, R. A.
FOLDS, J. D.
FORMAN, D. T.
GRISHAM, J. W.
HAMMOND, J. E.
JENNETTE, J. C.
KAUFMAN, D. G.
LORD, S. T.
MAEDA, N.
REISNER, H. M.
SILVERMAN, L. M.
SMITH, G. J.
SMITHIES, O.
SUZUKI, K. I.
TIDWELL, R. R.
TOPAL, M. D.
WEISSMAN, B. E.

Pharmacology:

CREWS, F. T.
DER, C. J.
DUDLEY, K. H.
GATZY, J. T., Jr
GOZ, B.
HARDEN, T. K.
JULIANO, R. L.
KOLE, R.
MCCARTHY, K. D.
SCARBOROUGH, G. A.
THURMAN, R. G.

Pharmacy:

BROUWER, K. R.
CAMPBELL, W. H.
COCOLAS, G. H.
ECKEL, F. M.
HADZIJA, B. W.
HALL, I. H.
HARTZEMA, A. G.
LEE, K. H.
PIEPER, J. A.
THAKKER, D. R.

Philosophy:

ANTONY, L. M.
BLACKBURN, S. W.
BOXILL, B. R.
HILL, T. E., Jr
HOOKER, M.
LONG, D. C.
LYCAN, W. G.
MUNSAT, S. M.

POSTEMA, G. J.
RESNIK, M. D.
ROSENBERG, J. F.
SAYRE-MCCORD, G. D.
SCHLESINGER, G.
SMYTH, R. A.

Physical Education, Exercise and Sport Science:

BILLING, J. E.
HYATT, R. W.
MCMURRAY, R. G.
MUELLER, F. O.
PRENTICE, W. E., Jr
SILVA, J. M.

Physics/Astronomy:

CARNEY, B. W.
CHRISTIANSEN, W. A.
CLEGG, T. B.
DOLAN, L. A.
DY, K. S.
FRAMPTON, P. H.
HERNANDEZ, J.
KARWOWSKI, H. J.
LUDWIG, E. J.
MCNEIL, L. E.
NG, Y. J.
ROSE, J. A.
ROWAN, L. G.
SCHROEER, D.
THOMPSON, W. J.
VAN DAM, H.
YORK, J. W., Jr

Physiology:

ARENDSHORST, W. J.
FABER, J. E.
FAREL, P. B.
FAUST, R. G.
FROEHNER, S. C.
LIGHT, A. R.
LUND, P. K.
MCILWAIN, D. L.
OXFORD, G. S.
PERL, E. R.
REID, L. M.
SEALOCK, R. W.
STUART, A. E.
WHITSEL, B. L.

Political Science:

BEYLE, T. L.
CONOVER, P. J.
HARTLYN, J.
HUBER, E. H.
LOWERY, D. L.
MARKS, G. W.
PHAY, R. E.
RABINOWITZ, G.
RICHARDSON, R. J.
SCHOULTZ, L. G.
SCHWARTZ, J.
SEARING, D. D.
STEINER, J.
STEPHENS, J. D.
STIMSON, J. A.
WHITE, J. W.
WRIGHT, D. S.

Psychiatry:

BREESE, G. R., Jr
GOLDEN, R. N.
HOUPT, J. L.
JANOWSKY, D. S.
LIEBERMAN, J. A.
LIGHT, K. C.
MCCARTNEY, C. F.
MAILMAN, R. B.
MARCUS, L. M.
MESIBOV, G. B.
STABLER, B.
VAN BOURGONDIE, M. E.
WHITT, J. K.

Psychology:

BAUCOM, D. H.
CAIRNS, R. B.
CHAMBLESS, D. L.
DYKSTRA-HYLAND, L. A.
ECKERMAN, D. A.
FILLENBAUM, S.
GRAY-LITTLE, B.
HOLLINS, M.
INSKO, C. A.
JOHNSON, E. S.
ORNSTEIN, P.
SCHOPLER, J. H.
SHINKMAN, P. G.
THISSEN, D. M.
THOMPSON, V. D.
WALLSTEN, T. S.
YOUNG, F. W.

Public Health:

ROPER, W. L.

Public Health Nursing:

ATWOOD, J. R.
SALMON, M. E.

Health Policy and Administration:

JAIN, S.
KALUZNY, A. D.
KILPATRICK, K. E.
ROZIER, R. G.
VENEY, J. E.
ZELMAN, W. N.

Health Behaviour and Health Education:

BAUMAN, K. E.
DEVELLIS, B. M.
EARP, J. L.
MUTRAN, E.
SORENSON, J.
STECKLER, A. B.

Nutrition:

ANDERSON, J. J.
COLEMAN, R. A.
KOHLMEIER, L.
POPKIN, B. M.
ZEISEL, S. H.

Radiation Oncology:

CHANEY, E. L.
LEADON, S. A.
RALEIGH, J. A.
ROSENMAN, J. G.
TEPPER, J. E.
VARIA, M. A.

Radiology:

JAQUES, P. F.
JOHNSTON, R. E.
KWOCK, L.
LEE, J. K.
MAURO, M. A.
MCCARTNEY, W. H.
MITTELSTAEDT, C. A.

Religious Studies:

ERNST, C. W.
HALPERIN, D. J.
KAUFMAN, P. I.
SASSON, J. M.
TYSON, R. W., Jr.
VAN SETERS, J.

Romance Languages:

BANDERA, C.
CASADO, P. G.
CERVIGNI, D. S.
CILVETI, A. L.
CLARK, F. M.
DOMINGUEZ, F. A.
HAIG, I. R. S., II
ILLIANO, A.
KING, L. D.
MALEY, C. A.
MASTERS, G. M.
RECTOR, M. P.
SALGADO, M. A.
SHERMAN, C. L.
VOGLER, F. W.

Slavic Languages:

DEBRECZENY, P.
JANDA, L. A.
LEVINE, M. G.

Social Medicine:

CHURCHILL, L. R.
CROSS, A. W.
DE FRIESE, G. H.
ESTROFF, S. E.
MADISON, D. L.
MORRISSEY, J. P.
RUNYAN, D. K.

Social Work:

BOWEN, G. L.
COOKE, P. W.
DOBELSTEIN, A. W.
EDWARDS, R. L.
FRASER, M. W.
GALINSKY, M. J.
HENLEY, H. C.
NELSON, G. M.
ORTHNER, D. K.
USHER, C. L.
WEIL, M. O.

Sociology:

ALDRICH, H. E.
BEARMAN, P. S.
BLAU, J. R.
ELDER, G. H.
ENTWISLE, B.
KALLEBERG, A. L.
KLEINMAN, S.
NEILSEN, F. D.
OBERSCHALL, A. R.
REED, J. S., Jr
RINDFUSS, R. R.
SIMPSON, R. L.
UHLENBERG, P.

Statistics:

ADLER, R.
CARLSTEIN, E.
CHAKRAVARTI, I. M.
KALLIANPUR, G.
KARR, A. F.
KELLY, D. G.
LEADBETTER, M. R.
MARRON, J. S.
SIMONS, G.
SMITH, R. L.

Surgery:

BAKER, C. C.
BLIGHT, A. R.
BUNZENDAHL, H.
BURNHAM, S. J.
CARSON, C. C., III
HALL, J. W., III
KEAGY, B. A.
MANDEL, S. R.
MAXWELL, J. G.
MEYER, A. A.
NAKAYAMA, D. K.
OLLER, D. W.
PECK, M. D.
PILLSBURY, H. C., III
PRAZMA, J.
SHELDON, G. F.
SHOCKLEY, W. M.
SLOAN, G. M.
STAREK, P. J.
WEISSLER, M. C.
WILCOX, B. R.

Women's Studies Program:

BURNS, E. J.
HOFFERT, S. D.

University of North Carolina at Charlotte

9201 University City Blvd, Charlotte, NC 28223-0001

Telephone: (704) 547-2000
Fax: (704) 547-3219

Established as an extension centre of the University of North Carolina 1946; later Charlotte College; made a degree-granting institution in 1963; became part of UNC State System in 1965

Academic year: August to May

Chancellor: JAMES H. WOODWARD
Vice-Chancellor for Academic Affairs and Provost: Dr DENISE M. TRAUTH
Vice-Chancellor, Student Affairs: CHARLES F. LYNCH
Vice-Chancellor for Development and University Relations: R. EDWARD KIZER, Jr
Vice-Chancellor for Business Affairs: OLEN B. SMITH
Associate Vice-Chancellor for Undergraduate Programs: Dr TERREL L. RHODES
Registrar: KATHI M. BAUCOM
Associate Vice-Chancellor for Library and Information Services: RAYMOND A. FRANKLE

Library of 643,000 vols, 5,000 periodicals
Number of teachers: 643 full-time, 298 part-time
Number of students: 16,370

DEANS

College of Architecture: CHARLES C. HIGHT
College of Business Administration: Dr EDWARD M. MAZZE
College of Engineering: ROBERT D. SNYDER
College of Education: Dr JOHN M. NAGLE
College of Nursing and Health Professions: Dr SUE M. BISHOP
College of Arts and Sciences: SCHLEY R. LYONS

University of North Carolina at Greensboro

Greensboro, NC 27412

Telephone: (910) 334-5494

Established as a Normal College 1891; since 1931 a unit of the University of North Carolina; 1963 name changed to the University of North Carolina at Greensboro

Chancellor: PATRICIA A. SULLIVAN
Vice-Chancellor for Business Affairs: PHILIP H. RICHMAN
Vice-Chancellor for Administration and Planning: JAMES CLOTFELTER
Vice-Chancellor for University Advancement: RICHARD L. MOORE
Vice-Chancellor for Student Affairs: CAROL DISQUE
Provost: A. EDWARD UPRICHARD
Registrar: ELLEN H. ROBBINS
Library: DORIS L. HULBERT

Library of 2,400,000 vols
Number of teachers: 573 full-time, 145 part-time
Number of students: 12,323

DEANS

College of Arts and Sciences: Dr. WALTER H. BEALE
Bryan School of Business and Economics: Dr JAMES K. WEEKS
School of Education: DAVID G. ARMSTRONG
School of Health and Human Performance: Dr ROBERT W. CHRISTINA
School of Human Environmental Sciences: Dr HELEN SHAW
School of Music: Dr ARTHUR R. TOLLEFSON
School of Nursing: Dr LYNNE G. PEARCEY

HEADS OF DEPARTMENT

College of Arts and Sciences:
- Anthropology: Dr WILLIE L. BABER
- Art: Dr K. PORTER AICHELE
- Biology: Dr ROBERT E. GATTEN
- Broadcasting/Cinema and Theatre: Dr ROBERT HANSEN
- Chemistry: Dr MICHAEL F. FARONA
- Classical Studies: Dr JEFFREY S. SOLES
- Communication: Dr H. L. GOODALL, Jr
- English: Dr JAMES E. EVANS
- Geography: Dr GORDON BENNETT
- German and Russian: Dr JOACHIM BAER
- History: Dr STEVEN F. LAWSON
- Mathematical Sciences: Dr PAUL F. DUVALL
- Philosophy: Dr JOSHUA HOFFMAN
- Physics and Astronomy: Dr GAYLORD T. HAGESETH
- Political Science: Dr CHARLES L. PRYSBY
- Psychology: Dr TIMOTHY D. JOHNSTON
- Religious Studies: Dr HENRY S. LEVINSON
- Residential College: Dr FRANCES C. ARNDT
- Romance Languages: Dr KATHLEEN V. KISH
- Sociology: Dr DAVID J. PRATTO

Bryan School of Business and Economics:
- Accounting: Dr CHARLES D. MECIMORE
- Economics: Dr STUART D. ALLEN
- Information Systems and Operations Management: Dr GERALD R. HERSHEY
- Business Administration: Dr BENTON E. MILES

School of Education:
- Counselling and Educational Development: Dr L. DIANNE BORDERS
- Educational Leadership and Cultural Foundations: Dr H. SVI SHAPIRO
- Educational Research Methodology: Dr JOHN A. HATTIE
- Library and Information Studies: Dr KEITH C. WRIGHT (acting)
- Curriculum and Instruction: Dr GERALD PONDER

School of Health and Human Performance:
- Dance: Dr SUSAN W. STINSON
- Exercise and Sport Science: Dr DIANE L. GILL
- Leisure Studies: Dr STUART J. SCHLEIEN
- Public Health Education: Dr KEITH A. HOWELL

School of Human Environmental Sciences:
- Clothing and Textiles: Dr BETTY L. FEATHER
- Food, Nutrition and Food Service Management: Dr MARK FAILLA
- Housing and Interior Design: NOVEM M. MASON
- Human Development and Family Studies: Dr DAVID DEMO
- Social Work: Dr THOMAS B. SCULLION

University of North Carolina at Pembroke

Pembroke, NC 28372

Telephone: (910) 521-6000

Founded 1887 as College, attained University status 1969

Part of the University of North Carolina

Chancellor: Dr JOSEPH B. OXENDINE
Provost and Vice-Chancellor for Academic Affairs: Dr CHARLES R. JENKINS
Vice-Chancellor for Student Affairs: Dr JAMES B. CHAVIS
Dean of Graduate Studies: (vacant)
Registrar: Mrs JOYCE S. SINGLETARY
Director of Admissions: JACKIE CLARK
Vice-Chancellor for Business: R. NEIL HAWK
Librarian: (vacant)

Library of 200,000 vols
Number of teachers: 148 full-time, 65 part-time
Number of students: 3,034

North Carolina State University at Raleigh

Raleigh, NC 27695

Telephone: (919) 515-2011
Fax: (919) 515-2556

Founded 1887
State control
Language of instruction: English
Academic year: January to December (2 semesters)

Chancellor: LARRY K. MONTEITH
Provost: P. J. STILES
Vice-Chancellor for Institutional Advancement: J. MCNEILL
Vice-Chancellor for Finance and Business: G. WORSLEY
Vice-Chancellor for Research and Extension: CHARLES MORELAND
Vice-Chancellor for Student Affairs: T. H. STAFFORD, Jr
Vice-Provost for Enrollment Management and Director of Admissions: G. R. DIXON
Library Director: S. K. NUTTER

Library of 1,900,000 vols
Number of teachers: 1,613
Number of students: 27,169

DEANS

College of Agriculture and Life Sciences: D. F. BATEMAN
School of Design: MARVIN MALECHA
College of Education: J. J. MICHAEL
College of Engineering: NINO A. MASNARI
College of Forest Resources: L. W. TOMBAUGH
College of Humanities and Social Sciences: MARGARET ZAHN
College of Management: R. J. LEWIS
College of Physical and Mathematical Sciences: J. L. WHITTEN
College of Textiles: R. A. BARNHARDT
The Graduate School: D. W. STEWART
College of Veterinary Medicine: O. J. FLETCHER

HEADS OF DEPARTMENTS

Accounting: C. J. MESSERE
Adult and Community College Education: WILLIAM DEEGAN
Aerospace Studies, Air Force ROTC: Col ROBERT OSTRANDER
Agricultural Communications: THOMAS W. KNECHT (acting)
Anatomy, Physiological Sciences and Radiology: A. L. ARONSON
Animal Science: KENNETH L. ESBENSHADE
Architecture: C. SACCAUPOLOS
Biochemistry: JAMES MOYER (acting)
Biological and Agricultural Engineering: D. B. BEASLEY
Botany: ERIC DAVIES
Business Management: JACK W. WILSON
Chemical Engineering: RUBEN G. CARBONELL
Chemistry: ROBERT OSTERYOUNG
Civil Engineering: E. D. BRILL, Jr
Companion Animal and Special Species Medicine: ELIZABETH STONE
Computer Science: A. L. THARP
Counselor Education: STANLEY BAKER
Crop Science: DAVID KNAUFT
Curriculum and Instruction: C. L. CROSSLAND
Design: PERCY HOOPER (acting)
Economics: R. B. PALMQUIST
Electrical and Computer Engineering: ROBERT M. KOLBAS
English: THOMAS LISK
Entomology: J. D. HARPER
Food Animal and Equine Medicine: M. C. ROBERTS
Food Science: KENNETH SWARTZEL
Foreign Languages and Literatures: JOANN STEWART
Forestry: FREDERICK CUBBAGE
Genetics: S. CURTIS
Graphic Design: M. DAVIS
History: JOHN M. RIDDLE
Horticultural Science: T. J. MONACO
Industrial Design: G. E. LEWIS
Industrial Engineering: S. D. ROBERTS
Landscape Architecture: A. R. RICE
Marine, Earth and Atmospheric Sciences: L. J. PIETRAFESA
Materials Science and Engineering: J. J. HREN
Mathematics: R. H. MARTIN
Mathematics and Science Education: J. R. KOLB
Mechanical and Aerospace Engineering: F. R. DEJARNETTE
Microbiology: HOSNI HASSAN
Microbiology, Pathology and Parasitology: LANCE PERRYMAN

Military Science, Army ROTC: Lt JOHN F. MCINERNEY
Music: ROBERT B. PETTERS
Nuclear Engineering: D. J. DUDZIAK
Occupational Education: DEWEY ADAMS
Parks, Recreation and Tourism Management: P. S. REA
Philosophy and Religion: TOM REGAN
Physical Education: A. LYNN BERLE
Physics: C. R. GOULD
Plant Pathology: O. W. BARNETT
Political Science and Public Administration: M. S. SOROOS
Poultry Science: G. B. HAVENSTEIN
Psychology: D. W. MARTIN
Social Work: NELSON REID
Sociology and Anthropology: W. B. CLIFFORD
Soil Science: JOHN HAVLIN
Speech Communication: ROBERT ENTMAN
Statistics: THOMAS M. GERIG
Textile/Clothing Technology: JOSEPH W. A. OFF
Textile Engineering, Chemistry and Science: MANSUR MOHAMED
Textile and Apparel Management: T. J. LITTLE
Toxicology: E. HODGSON
Multidisciplinary Studies: C. D. KORTE
Wood and Paper Science: RICHARD J. THOMAS
Zoology: THURMAN GROVE

University of North Carolina at Wilmington

Wilmington, NC 28403-3297
Telephone: (910) 962-3000
Fax: (910) 962-3550

Established under the direction of the North Carolina College Conference and under the administration of the Directorate of Extension of the University of North Carolina in 1947; later organized as a county institution under the control of the New Hanover County Board of Education, known as Wilmington College; in 1969 made a unit of the University

Chancellor: JAMES R. LEUTZE
Provost and Vice-Chancellor for Academic Affairs: MARVIN K. MOSS
Vice-Chancellor for Student Affairs: PATRICIA LEONARD
Vice-Chancellor for Business Affairs: ROBERT O. WALTON, Jr
Vice-Chancellor for University Advancement: PATTON MCDOWELL (interim)
Vice-Chancellor for Public Service and Extended Education: MICHELLE HOWARD-VITAL
Librarian: SHERMAN HAYES

Library of 425,000 vols
Number of teachers: 527
Number of students: 9,176

WAKE FOREST UNIVERSITY

Box 7205, Winston-Salem, NC 27109
Telephone: (336) 758-5000
Fax: (336) 758-6074

Founded 1834

President: THOMAS K. HEARN, Jr
Registrar: MARGARET R. PERRY
Director of Admissions: W. G. STARLING
Librarian: RHODA K. CHANNING

Library of over 1 million vols
Number of teachers: 1,029 full-time, 638 part-time
Number of students: 5,841

WESTERN CAROLINA UNIVERSITY

Cullowhee, NC 28723
Telephone: (704) 227-7211
Fax: (704) 227-7202

Founded 1889
Linked to the University of North Carolina

Chancellor: JOHN W. BARDO
Vice-Chancellors: RICHARD J. COLLINGS (Academic Affairs), C. JOSEPH CARTER (Business Affairs), CLAIRE ELDRIDGE (Advancement and External Affairs), BONITA S. JACOBS (Student Development, acting)
Director of Admissions: DOYLE BICKERS
Registrar: CAROLYN CABE (acting)
Librarian: WILLIAM J. KIRWAN

Library of 436,041 vols
Number of teachers: 335
Number of students: 6,619

WINSTON-SALEM STATE UNIVERSITY

Winston-Salem, NC 27110
Telephone: (910) 750-2000

Founded 1892
Linked to the University of North Carolina

Chancellor: Dr CLEON F. THOMPSON, Jr
Registrar: WILLIAM CAIN
Director of Admissions: VAN C. WILSON
Librarian: Dr MAE RODNEY

Library of 158,858 vols
Number of teachers: 155
Number of students: 2,900

NORTH DAKOTA

DICKINSON STATE UNIVERSITY

Dickinson, ND 58601-4896
Telephone: (701) 227-2507
Fax: (701) 227-2006

Founded 1918

President: PHILIP W. CONN
Registrar: MARSHALL MELBYE
Librarian: BERNNETT REINKE

Library of 82,000 vols
Number of teachers: 106
Number of students: 1,601

Publications: *Catalog* (every 2 years), *Prospective Student View Book* (annually), *Western Concept* (student newspaper), *Prairie Smoke* (student yearbook), *Impressions* (student creative writing), *Alumni News* (quarterly), Departmental brochures (annually), *DSU Digest* (weekly), *Parents Newsletter* (quarterly), *Views* (quarterly).

JAMESTOWN COLLEGE

Jamestown, ND 58405
Telephone: (701) 252-3467
Fax: (701) 253-4318

Founded 1884
Private control

President: Dr JERRY COMBEE
Provost: Dr JIM STONE
Director of Admissions: CAROL SCHMEICHEL
Librarian: Mrs PHYLLIS BRATTON

Library of 100,000 vols
Number of teachers: 60
Number of students: 1,100

MAYVILLE STATE UNIVERSITY

Mayville, ND 58257
Telephone: (701) 786-2301
Fax: (701) 786-4748

Founded 1889

President: E. E. CHAFFEE
Vice-President for Academic Affairs: RAY C. BROWN
Registrar: MARY IVERSON
Librarian: BETTY KARAIM

Library of 83,964 vols
Number of teachers: 52
Number of students: 756

MINOT STATE UNIVERSITY

Minot, ND 58707
Telephone: (701) 858-3000

Founded 1913

President: Dr H. ERIK SHAAR
Registrar: Dr NANCY HALL
Librarian: LARRY GREENWOOD

Library of 335,000 vols
Number of teachers: 220
Number of students: 3,200

NORTH DAKOTA STATE UNIVERSITY

Fargo, ND 58105
Telephone: (701) 237-8011

Founded 1890

President: Dr J. L. OZBUN
Vice-President of Academic Affairs: SHARON A. WALLACE
Vice-President for Business and Finance: RICHARD RAYL
Vice-President for Student Affairs: GEORGE H. WALLMAN
Registrar: ALBERTA DOBRY
Librarian: JOHN BEECHER

Library of 344,663 vols
Number of teachers: 550
Number of students: 8,700

Publication: *The Bulletin*.

DEANS

Faculty of Agriculture: H. R. LUND
Faculty of Humanities and Social Sciences: THOMAS ISERN
Faculty of Science and Mathematics: ALLAN FISCHER
Faculty of Engineering and Architecture: JOSEPH STANISLAO
Faculty of Pharmacy: HARRY ROSENBERG
Faculty of Continuing Studies: RICHARD CHENOWETH (acting)
Faculty of Graduate School: CRAIG SCHNELL
Faculty of University Studies: ROGER D. KERNS
Faculty of Business Administration: HARRIETTE MCCAUL
Faculty of Human Development and Education: VIRGINIA CLARK

UNIVERSITY OF NORTH DAKOTA

Grand Forks, ND 58202
Telephone: (701) 777-2011
Fax: (701) 777-3650

Chartered 1883

President: KENDALL BAKER
Vice-President (Academic Affairs): MARLENE STRATHE
Vice-President (Finance): LYLE BEISWENGER
Vice-President (Student Affairs): GORDON HENRY
Vice-President (Operations): AL HOFFARTH
Registrar: ALICE C. POEHLS
Librarian: FRANK A. D'ANDRAIA

Library of 1,000,000 vols
Number of teachers: 711
Number of students: 11,300

DEANS

Graduate: HARVEY R. KNULL
Arts and Sciences: JOHN ETTLING
Business: DENNIS ELBERT
College of Education and Human Development: MARY HARRIS
Engineering: DON RICHARD
Fine Arts: BRUCE C. JACOBSEN
Law: W. JEREMY DAVIS
Medicine and Health Sciences: H. DAVID WILSON
Nursing: ELIZABETH NICHOLS
Extension: ROBERT BOYD

Center for Aerospace Sciences: JOHN D. ODEGARD

VALLEY CITY STATE UNIVERSITY

Valley City, ND 58072
Telephone: (701) 845-7990
Founded 1890
President: Dr ELLEN E. CHAFFEE
Academic Dean: DWIGHT CRABTREE
Vice-President for Business Affairs: STEVE BENSEN
Vice-President for Student Affairs: GLEN SCHMALZ
Librarian: DARRYL B. PODOLL
Library of 80,000 vols
Number of teachers: 56
Number of students: 986
Publication: *The Bulletin.*

OHIO

AIR FORCE INSTITUTE OF TECHNOLOGY

Wright-Patterson Air Force Base, OH 45433-7765
Telephone: (937) 255-2321
Fax: (937) 656-7600
Founded 1919
Commandant: Col. JOHN H. RUSSELL
Director of Admissions: Maj. BARBARA E. JOSEPH
Director of Academic Affairs: Dr JAMES M. HORNER
Library Director: JAMES T. HELLING
Library of 120,000 vols
Number of teachers: 134 civilian, 126 military

DEANS
Graduate School of Engineering: Dr ROBERT A. CALICO, Jr
Graduate School of Logistics and Acquisition Management: Dr JAN P. MUCZYK
School of Systems and Logistics: Dr RICHARD L. MURPHY
Civil Engineering and Services School: Col. JOSEPH H. AMEND
Civilian Institution Programs: Col. PAUL D. COPP

ANTIOCH UNIVERSITY

Yellow Springs, OH 45387
Telephone: (513) 767-7331
Fax: (513) 767-1891
Founded 1852
President: ALAN E. GUSKIN
Executive Vice-President: MICHAEL BASSIS
Financial Vice-President: PHYLLIS WILLIAMS
Number of teachers: 495
Number of students: 3,783
Publications: *Antioch Review* (quarterly), *The Record* (weekly), *The Antiochan* (quarterly), *Antioch Notes* (quarterly).

PROVOSTS
Antioch College: R. EUGENE RICE
Antioch New England: JAMES CRAIGLOW
School for Adult and Experiential Learning: ROBERT MILLER
Antioch Southern California: DALE JOHNSTON
Antioch Seattle: GARY ZIMMERMAN

ASHLAND UNIVERSITY

Ashland, OH 44805
Telephone: (419) 289-4142
Fax: (419) 289-5333
Founded 1878
President: G. WILLIAM BENZ
Provost: MARY ELLEN DRUSHAL
Registrar: RICHARD J. OBRECHT
Director of Libraries: WILLIAM B. WEISS
Library of 265,000
Number of teachers: 528
Number of students: 5,609

ATHENAEUM OF OHIO

6616 Beechmont Ave, Cincinnati, OH 45230
Telephone: (513) 231-2223
Founded 1829
Private control (Roman Catholic)
Academic year: September to June (three terms)
Chancellor: Archbishop DANIEL E. PILARCZYK
President: Rev. GERALD R. HAEMMERLE
Academic Dean: Dr TERRENCE CALLAN
Librarian: Sister DEBORAH HARMELING
Library of 77,000 volumes
Number of teachers: 20
Number of students: 290

BALDWIN-WALLACE COLLEGE

275 Eastland Rd, Berea, OH 44017
Telephone: (216) 826-2900
Founded 1845
President: Dr NEAL MALICKY
Dean of Enrollment Services: J. EDWARD WARNER
Librarian: Dr PATRICK SCANLAN
Library of 210,000 vols
Number of teachers: 152 full-time
Number of students: 4,700

BLUFFTON COLLEGE

280 W. College Ave, Bluffton, OH 45817-1196
Telephone: (419) 358-3000
Founded 1899
Private control
Academic year: September to May
President: LEE SNYDER
Vice-President for Fiscal Affairs: WILLIS J. SOMMER
Dean of Academic Affairs: JOHN KAMPEN
Librarian: JOANNE PASSET
Library of 130,000 vols; the Mennonite Historical Library contains 17,600 vols
Number of teachers: 56
Number of students: 1,000

BOWLING GREEN STATE UNIVERSITY

Bowling Green, OH 43403
Telephone: (419) 372-2531
Founded 1910
Academic year: August to May
President: SIDNEY A. RIBEAU
Provost, and Vice-President for Academic Affairs: CHARLES MIDDLETON
Vice-President for University Advancement: JOHN MOORE (acting)
Vice-President for Student Affairs: EDWARD G. WHIPPLE
Senior Vice-President for Finance: CHRISTOPHER DALTON
Library of 1.6 million vols and documents
Number of teachers: 690
Number of students: 17,249
Publications: Bulletins, Handbooks, *Philosopher's Index* (quarterly), *Alumni News Magazine* (quarterly), *Key* (annually), *Journal of Popular Culture* (quarterly).

DEANS
Arts and Sciences: CHARLES J. CRANNY
Education and Human Development: LES STERNBERG
Business Administration: JAMES SULLIVAN
Graduate College: LOUIS KATZNER
Health and Community Services: CLYDE WILLIS
Musical Arts: H. LEE RIGGINS
Firelands: DARBY WILLIAMS
Continuing Education, International and Summer Programmes: SUZANNE CRAWFORD
Libraries and Learning Resources: LINDA DOBB
College of Technology: THOMAS EREKSON

CAPITAL UNIVERSITY

Columbus, OH 43209-2394
Telephone: (614) 236-6011
Fax: (614) 236-6147
Founded 1850
A Lutheran institution
Academic year: August to May (two terms)
President: JOSIAH H. BLACKMORE
Vice-President for Academic Affairs: RONALD J. VOLPE
Vice-President for University Relations: JOSEPH JESTER
Vice-President for Resource Management: VERNON TRUESDALE
Registrar: JANET SCHWAB
Librarian: ALBERT MAAG
Library of 286,000 vols
Number of teachers: 170
Number of students: 3,680
Publications: *Chimes* (newspaper), *Capitalian* (yearbook), *Capital Literary Arts Magazine* (two a year), *Alumni Magazine* (quarterly).

DEANS
Arts and Sciences: DAINA MCGARY
Music: TERRY ZIPAY
College of Nursing: DORIS EDWARDS
Capital Law School: STEVEN BAHLS
Graduate School of Administration: (vacant)
Student Affairs: STEPHEN BELLER
Adult Learning and Assessment: GARY SMITH

CASE WESTERN RESERVE UNIVERSITY

10900 Euclid Ave, Cleveland, OH 44106
Telephone: (216) 368-2000
Founded 1967 from the Western Reserve University (f. 1826 as College) and the Case Institute of Technology (f. 1880 as Case School of Applied Science)
Private control
President: AGNAR PYTTE
Provost: RICHARD A. ZDANIS
Vice-President for Finance and Administration: NANCY D. SUTTENFIELD
Vice-President for Development: BRUCE A. LOESSIN
Vice-President for Public Affairs: RICHARD E. BAZNIK
Vice-President for Budgets and Planning: (vacant)
Vice-President for Institutional Planning and Analysis: KENNETH L. KUTINA
Vice-President for Medical Affairs: NATHAN A. BERGER
Vice-President for Information Services: RAYMOND K. NEFF
Vice-President for Student Affairs: GLENN NICHOLLS
Vice-President for Research and Technology Transfer: (vacant)
Secretary of the Corporation: SUSAN J. ZULL
Registrar: AMY HAMMETT
Director of University Library: JOANNE D. EUSTIS
Number of teachers: 1,949
Number of students: 9,948

DEANS
Graduate Studies: JOYCE E. JENTOFT
School of Dentistry: JEROLD S. GOLDBERG
School of Medicine: NATHAN A. BERGER
School of Law: GERALD KORNGOLD

Frances Payne Bolton School of Nursing: DOROTHY BROOTEN
Mandel School of Applied Social Sciences: DARLYNE BAILEY
Weatherhead School of Management: KIM S. CAMERON
Case School of Engineering: JAMES W. WAGNER
Arts and Sciences: JOHN E. BASSETT

HEADS OF DEPARTMENTS

Case School of Engineering:

Biomedical Engineering: GERALD M. SAIDEL
Chemical Engineering: NELSON C. GARDNER
Civil Engineering: ADEL S. SAADA
Electrical Systems and Computer Engineering and Science: ROBERT V. EDWARDS (acting)
Macromolecular Science: ALEXANDER JAMIESON
Materials Science and Engineering: GARY MICHAL
Mechanical and Aerospace Engineering: JOSEPH M. PRAHL

Arts and Sciences:

Anthropology: MELVYN C. GOLDSTEIN
Art History and Art: ELLEN LANDAU
Astronomy: R. EARLE LUCK
Biology: NORMAN B. RUSHFORTH
Chemistry: ANTHONY J. PEARSON
Classics: DONALD R. LAING, Jr
Communication Sciences: KATHY CHAPMAN
English: SUZANNE FERGUSON
Geological Sciences: PHILIP O. BANKS
History: CARROLL PURSELL
Mathematics: JAMES ALEXANDER
Modern Languages and Literatures: DAVID MARIE-PIERRE LEHIR
Music: ROSS W. DUFFIN
Philosophy: COLIN MCLARTY
Physics: LAWRENCE KRAUSS
Political Science: VINCENT E. MCHALE
Psychology: SANDRA W. RUSS
Religion: JAMES FLANAGAN
Sociology: EVA KAHANA
Statistics: JOSEPH SEDRANSK
Theatre Arts: JOHN ORLOCK

School of Dentistry:

Community Dentistry: JAMES A. LALUMANDIER
Endodontics: JEFFERSON J. JONES
General Practice Dentistry: RONALD L. OCCHIONERO
Oral Diagnosis/Radiology: DANNY R. SAWYER
Oral Pathology: EDWARD ROSSI
Oral Surgery: MICHAEL POWERS (acting)
Orthodontics: MARK HANS
Paediatric Dentistry: SETH CANION
Periodontics: NABIL F. BISSADA
Restorative Dentistry: LOUIS CASTELLARIN

Weatherhead School of Management:

Accountancy: DAVID R. CAMPBELL
Banking and Finance: DAVID A. BOWERS
Economics: WILLIAM PEIRCE
Information Systems: RICHARD J. BOLAND
Marketing and Policy Studies: LEONARD H. LYNN
Operations Research and Operations Management: HAMILTON EMMONS
Organizational Behaviour: RICHARD E. BOYATZIS

School of Medicine:

Anatomy: JOSEPH LAMANNA
Anaesthesiology: HELMUT F. CASCORBI
Biochemistry: RICHARD W. HANSON
Dermatology: KEVIN COOPER
Environmental Health Sciences: G. DAVID MCCOY
Epidemiology and Biostatistics: ALFRED RIMM
Family Medicine: C. KENT SMITH
General Medical Sciences: NATHAN A. BERGER
Genetics: HUNTINGTON F. WILLARD
Medicine: ADEL A. F. MAHMOUD
Molecular Biology and Microbiology: FRITZ M. ROTTMAN
Neurological Surgery: ROBERT A. RATCHESON
Neurology: DENNIS LANDIS
Neurosciences: LYNN LANDMESSER (acting)
Nutrition: HENRI BRUNENGRABER
Ophthalmology: JONATHAN LASS
Orthopaedics: VICTOR M. GOLDBERG
Otolaryngology: ANTHONY J. MANIGLIA
Pathology: MICHAEL E. LAMM
Paediatrics: ELLIS AVNER
Pharmacology: JOHN H. NILSON
Physiology and Biophysics: ANTONIO SCARPA
Psychiatry: S. CHARLES SCHULZ II
Radiology: JOHN R. HAAGA
Reproductive Biology: WULF H. UTIAN
Surgery: JERRY M. SHUCK
Urology: MARTIN RESNICK

RESEARCH CENTRES AND INSTITUTES

Center for Biomedical Ethics: Dir THOMAS H. MURRAY.

Center for Regional Economic Issues: Dir RICHARD SHATTAN (acting).

Center on Aging and Health: Dir MAY L. WYKLE.

Electronics Design Center: Dir C. C. LIU.

Mandel Center for Non-Profit Organizations: Dir JOHN PALMER SMITH.

Cancer Research Center: Dir JAMES A. WILLSON.

Yeager Center for Electrochemical Sciences: Dir ROBERT F. SAVINELL.

Center for Applied Polymer Research: Dir ANNE HILTNER.

Center for Automation and Intelligent Systems Research: Dir STEPHEN M. PHILLIPS

Center for Urban Poverty and Social Change: Dir CLAUDIA J. COULTON.

Geriatric Education Center: Dir JEROME KOWAL.

Law-Medicine Center: Dir MAXWELL J. MEHLMAN.

Health Systems Management Center: Dir J. B. SILVERS.

Center for International Health: Dir THOMAS M. DANIEL.

Center for Advanced Liquid Crystalline Optical Materials: Dir JACK L. KOENIG.

Alzheimer Center: Dir PETER WHITEHOUSE.

Applied Neural Control Laboratory: Dir J. THOMAS MORTIMER.

Cardiac Bioelectricity Research and Training Center: Dir YORAM RUDY.

Center for Adolescent Health: Dir FREDERICK C. ROBBINS.

Center for Bio-architectonics: Dir RAYMOND J. LASEK.

Center for Cardiovascular Biomaterials: Dir ROGER E. MARCHANT.

NSF Center for Molecular and Microstructure of Composites: Dir HATSUO ISHIDA.

Center on Hierarchical Structures: Dir ERIC BAER.

Edison Polymer Innovation Corporation: Dirs JEROME B. LANDO, ANNE HILTNER.

Macromolecular Modeling of Polymers Center: Dir JOHN BLACKWELL.

Center for the Environment: Dirs JOSEPH KOONCE, NORMAN ROBBINS

Center for Physical and Rehabilitation Medicine: Dir FREDERICK M. MAYNARD

National Centre for Microgravity Research on Fluids and Combustion: Dir SIMON OSTRACH

CENTRAL STATE UNIVERSITY

Wilberforce, OH 45384
Telephone: (216) 376-6332
Fax: (513) 376-6318

Founded 1887

President: JOHN W. GARLAND
Registrar: LARRY CANNON
Director of Admissions: THANDA B. MACEO
Librarian: GEORGE T. JOHNSON

Library of 130,000 vols
Number of teachers: 80
Number of students: 1,000

Publications: *Catalog, Alumni Journal* (quarterly).

DEANS

College of Arts and Sciences: Dr WILLIE HOUSTON
College of Business Administration: Dr C. H. SHOWELL
College of Education: Dr SHIRLI BILLINGS

CLEVELAND STATE UNIVERSITY

Euclid Ave at East 24th St, Cleveland, OH 44115
Telephone: (216) 687-2000
Telex: 810-421-8252
Fax: (216) 687-9366

Founded 1964

President: CLAIRE A. VAN UMMERSEN
Provost and Senior Vice-President for Academic and Student Affairs: HAROLD L. ALLEN
Vice-President for Finance and Administration: CHRISTINE A. JACKSON
Vice-President for Minority Affairs and Human Relations: NJERI NURU
Executive Director for Development and University Relations: ROBERT GORDON
Director of Libraries: (vacant)

Library of 856,978 vols, 4,005 periodicals, 625,191 microforms
Number of teachers: 531 full-time, 277 part-time
Number of students: 17,137

DEANS

College of Business Administration: ROBERT MINTER
College of Engineering: KENNETH KEYES
College of Arts and Sciences: KAREN STECKOL
College of Education: JAY MCLOUGHLIN
College of Graduate Studies: A. HARRY ANDRIST
Cleveland-Marshall College of Law: STEVEN STEINGLASS
Levin College of Urban Affairs: DAVID C. SWEET
Continuing Education: FERRIS F. ANTHONY

COLLEGE OF MOUNT ST JOSEPH

5701 Delhi Rd, Cincinnati, OH 45233-1670
Telephone: (513) 244-4200

Founded 1920

President: Sr FRANCIS MARIE THRAILKILL
Registrar: LEW RITA MOORE
Academic Dean: Sr JOHN MIRIAM JONES
Director of Business and Finance: ANNE MARIE WAGNER
Director of Admissions: EDWARD ECKEL
Dean of Students: JEFF LONG
Librarian: PAUL JENKINS

Library of 87,000 vols
Number of teachers: 104 full-time equivalent
Number of students: 2,594

Publications: *Catalog, Mount Magazine* (3 a year).

COLLEGE OF WOOSTER

Wooster, OH 44691
Telephone: (216) 263-2311

Founded 1866

Independent, founded by the Presbyterian Church (USA)
President: R. STANTON HALES
Vice-President for Academic Affairs: BARBARA HETRICK
Vice-President for Development: SARA L. PATTON
Vice-President for Finance and Business: WILLIAM H. SNODDY
Secretary: DEBORAH P. HILTY
Registrar: GLENN DAVIS
Director of Admissions: CAROL D. WHEATLEY
Librarian: DAMON D. HICKEY

Library of 319,200 vols
Number of teachers: 139
Number of students: 1,750

Publications: *Voice* (student newspaper), *Wooster* (alumni magazine), *Wooster Reports.*

DEANS

Faculty: SUSAN G. FIGGE
Students: KENNETH R. PLUSQUELLEC

DEFIANCE COLLEGE, THE

Defiance, OH 43512
Telephone: (419) 784-4010
Founded 1850
President: JAMES T. HARRIS
Vice-President for Academic Affairs/Academic Dean: Dr RICHARD W. STROEDE
Librarian: EDWARD WARNER
Library of 90,000 vols
Number of teachers: 55
Number of students: 1,030

DENISON UNIVERSITY

Granville, OH 43023-0603
Telephone: (740) 587-0810
Founded 1831
Private control
Academic year: September to June
President: DALE T. KNOBEL
Provost: CHARLES J. MORRIS , Jr
Vice-President for Finance and Management: SETH PATTON
Vice-President for Student Affairs and Dean of Students: SAMUEL J. THIOS
Registrar: LARRY R. MURDOCK
Director of Admissions: PERRY ROBINSON
Director of Libraries: MARY PROPHET (acting)
Number of teachers: 165 (f.t.e.)
Number of students: 2,108 (f.t.e)

FRANCISCAN UNIVERSITY OF STEUBENVILLE

1235 University Blvd, Steubenville, OH 43952-1763
Telephone: (740) 283-3771
Fax: (740) 283-6472
Founded 1946
President: Rev. MICHAEL SCANLAN
Dean of Faculty: Dr MICHAEL HEALY
Director of Admissions: MARGARET WEBER
Librarian: RUTH WALTER
Library of 200,000 vols
Number of teachers: 91 full-time, 56 part-time
Number of students: 1,605 full-time, 392 part-time
Publication: *Franciscan Way* (quarterly).

HEBREW UNION COLLEGE–JEWISH INSTITUTE OF RELIGION

3101 Clifton Ave, Cincinnati, OH 45220-2488; schools at Cincinnati, Los Angeles and New York (USA) and Jerusalem (Israel)
Telephone: (513) 221-1875
Founded 1875
President: Rabbi SHELDON ZIMMERMAN
Chancellor: Dr ALFRED GOTTSCHALK
Provost: Dr NORMAN COHEN
Dean of Cincinnati School: Rabbi KENNETH EHRLICH
Dean of Los Angeles School: Dr LEWIS M. BARTH
Dean of New York School: Rabbi AARON PANKEN
Dean of Jerusalem School: Rabbi MICHAEL MARMUR
Director of Libraries: Dr DAVID GILNER
Library of 500,000 vols and 6,000 ancient manuscripts
Number of teachers: 130
Number of students: 780
Publications: *American Jewish Archives, Hebrew Union College Annual, Studies in Bibliography and Booklore, Bibliographica Judaica, The Chronicle.*

HEIDELBERG COLLEGE

Tiffin, OH 44883
Telephone: (419) 448-2000
Fax: (419) 448-2124
Founded 1850
President: RICHARD H. OWENS
Vice-President for Academic Affairs: KENNETH J. PORADA
Vice-President for Institutional Advancement: EDWARD HYLAND
Dean of Admission: DAVID RHODES
Registrar: PAMELA FABER
Director of Library Services: EDWARD KRAKORA
Library of 200,000 vols
Number of teachers: 72 full-time, 30 part-time
Number of students: 1,400
Publications: *Heidelberg Alumni Magazine, Heidelberg College Catalogue.*

HIRAM COLLEGE

Hiram, OH 44234
Telephone: (216) 569-3211
Founded 1850
President: G. BENJAMIN OLIVER
Registrar: MARY ANN PAINLEY
Librarian: DAVID EVERETT
Library of 159,000 vols
Number of teachers: 89
Number of students: 1,150

JOHN CARROLL UNIVERSITY

Cleveland, OH 44118
Telephone: (216) 397-1886
Founded 1886
Private control (Roman Catholic affiliated)
Academic year: September to December, January to May, plus three five-week summer terms
President: Rev. EDWARD GLYNN
Academic Vice-President: Dr FREDERICK TRAVIS
Dean of College of Arts and Sciences: Dr NICK BAUMGARTNER
Dean of School of Business: Dr FRANK J. NAVRATIL
Dean of Graduate School: Dr SALLY H. WERTHEIM
Dean of Admissions and Financial Aid: JOHN J. GLADSTONE
Registrar: KATHLEEN DI FRANCO
Director of Library: Dr GORMAN L. DUFFETT
Library of 500,000 vols
Number of teachers: 310
Number of students: 4,500

KENT STATE UNIVERSITY

Kent, OH 44242
Telephone: (330) 672-3000
Founded 1910
President: Dr CAROL A. CARTWRIGHT
Vice-President for Business and Finance: Dr DAVID K. CREAMER
Provost: Dr MYRON S. HENRY
Vice-President for University Relations and Development: MARK D. LINDEMOOD
Vice-President for Human Resources: CHARLES L. GREENE
Vice-President for Enrollment Management and Student Affairs: Dr NANCY A. SCOTT
Director of Admissions: CHARLES E. RICKARD
Dean of Libraries and Media Services: DON L. TOLLIVER
Library of 2,225,000 vols
Number of teachers: 970
Number of students: 30,000
Publication: *Inside Kent.*

DEANS AND DIRECTORS

Education: Dr JOANNE R. WHITMORE
Arts and Sciences: Dr JOSEPH H. DANKS
Business Administration: Dr GEORGE STEVENS
Fine and Professional Arts: Dr SCOTT A. SULLIVAN
Honors College: Dr LARRY R. ANDREWS
School of Nursing: Dr DAVINA J. GOSNELL
Research and Graduate Studies: Dr M. THOMAS JONES
Liquid Crystals Institute: Dr JOHN WEST
College of Continuing Studies: Dr MARLENE DORSEY

KENYON COLLEGE

Gambier, OH 43022-9623
Telephone: (740) 427-5000
Founded 1824
President: ROBERT A. ODEN Jr
Provost: KATHERINE H. WILL
Dean of Admissions: JOHN W. ANDERSON
Dean of Students: DONALD J. OMAHAN
Dean for Academic Advising: JANE MARTINDELL
Vice-President for Library and Information Services: DANIEL TEMPLE
Library of 977,846 items
Number of teachers: 176
Number of students: 1,467

LAKE ERIE COLLEGE

Painesville, OH 44077
Telephone: (440) 352-3361
Fax: (440) 352-3533
E-mail: lrowe@lakeerie.edu
Founded 1856
Private control
Academic year: August to May (two semesters and one summer session)
Includes a four-year residential college with a programme of traditional courses, and an academic term abroad
President: Dr HAL LAYDON
Dean of College: (vacant)
Registrar: BARB EMCH
Director of Admissions: MARY ANN NASO
Library of 100,000 vols
Number of teachers: 58
Number of students: 700
Publication: *Bulletin*.

MALONE COLLEGE

515 25th St, NW, Canton, OH 44709
Telephone: (330) 471-8100
Fax: (330) 454-8478
Founded 1892
President: RONALD G. JOHNSON
Provost: ROBERT C. SUGGS
Library of 142,000 vols
Number of teachers: 89 (full-time)
Number of students: 2,239
Publication: *Horizon*.

MARIETTA COLLEGE

215 Fifth St, Marietta, OH 45750
Telephone: (740) 376-4643
Fax: (740) 376-4896

Founded 1797
Private control

President: LAUREN R. WILSON
Provost and Dean: EUGENE LUBOT
Dean of Students: MICHELLE DANIELS
Dean of Leadership Studies: STEPHEN SCHWARTZ
Librarian: SANDRA NEYMAN

Library of 287,493 vols
Number of teachers: 80 (full time)
Number of students: 1,108

Publications: *Marcolian, The BlueLine, The Navy Blue and White, The Blue and White.*

Courses in liberal arts and sciences, fine arts, computer science, environmental science, economics, management and accounting, sports medicine, international business, Asian and international studies, petroleum engineering.

MIAMI UNIVERSITY

Oxford, OH 45056
Telephone: (513) 529-1809
Fax: (513) 529-3841

Founded 1809
State control

President: JAMES C. GARLAND
Provost and Executive Vice-President for Academic Affairs: ANNE H. HOPKINS
Senior Vice-President for Finance and University Services: EDWARD J. DEMSKE
Vice-President for Student Affairs: MYRTIS H. POWELL
Vice-President for University Relations: KENNETH E. BURKE
University Registrar: KENNETH H. BOGARD
Secretary of the University: KAREN K. SHAFFER
Dean and University Librarian: JUDITH A. SESSIONS

Library of 2,340,000 vols
Number of teachers: 861 full-time, 504 part-time
Number of students: 20,517

DEANS

Arts and Science: KARL R. MATTOX
Business Administration: DANIEL G. SHORT
Education and Allied Professions: CURTIS W. ELLISON (acting)
Fine Arts: PAMELA FOX
Applied Science: DAVID C. HADDAD
Interdisciplinary Studies (Western College Program): BURTON KAUFMAN
Graduate School: ROBERT C. JOHNSON

MOUNT UNION COLLEGE

Alliance, OH 44601
Telephone: (330) 821-5320

Founded 1846

President: Dr HAROLD M. KOLENBRANDER
Dean: TRUMAN TURNQUIST (acting)
Registrar: STUART TERRASS
Librarian: ROBERT R. GARLAND

Number of teachers: 90 (full-time)
Number of students: 1,847

Publications: *Mount Union Magazine, Catalogues.*

MUSKINGUM COLLEGE

New Concord, OH 43762
Telephone: (614) 826-8211
Fax: (614) 826-8404

Founded 1837
Church related, liberal arts college

President: SAMUEL W. SPECK
Vice-President of Academic Affairs: DANIEL E. VAN TASSEL
Vice-President for Development: MATTHEW P. ELLI
Treasurer: F. B. THOMAS
Dean of Student Life: JANET HEETER-BASS
Dean of Enrollment: JEFF ZELLERS
Librarian: ROBIN HANSON

Library of 223,000 vols
Number of professors: 82 full-time
Number of students: 1,200

Publications: *Catalog, Alumni Bulletin, The Muskie Handbook, View Book.*

NOTRE DAME COLLEGE OF OHIO

4545 College Rd, South Euclid, OH 44121
Telephone: (216) 381-1680
Fax: (216) 381-3802

Founded 1922

President: ANNE L. DEMING
Vice-President for Academic Affairs: MARILYN JONES
Librarian: KAREN ZOLLER

Library of 88,159 vols
Number of teachers: 37 full-time, 64 part-time
Number of students: 634

OBERLIN COLLEGE

Oberlin, OH 44074
Telephone: (216) 775-8121
Fax: (216) 775-8886

Founded 1833

President: NANCY S. DYE
Vice-President for Finance: ANDREW EVANS
Vice-President for Development and Alumni Affairs: KAY THOMSON
Director of Admissions for the College of Arts and Sciences: DEBRA CHERMONTE
Director of Admissions for the Conservatory of Music: MICHAEL MANDEREN
Secretary: ROBERT A. HASLUN
Director of Libraries: RAY ENGLISH

Library of 1,100,000 vols
Number of teachers: 240
Number of students: 2,800

DEANS

College of Arts and Sciences: CLAYTON KOPPES
Conservatory of Music: KAREN L. WOLFF
Student Life and Services: DEB MCNISH (acting)

OHIO DOMINICAN COLLEGE

1216 Sunbury Rd, Columbus, OH 43219
Telephone: (614) 253-2741

Founded 1911 as College of St Mary of the Springs; name changed 1968
Four-year co-educational liberal arts college
Academic year: September to May (two terms and a summer session)

President: Sister MARY ANDREW MATESICH
Registrar: SALLY SIKORSKI
Vice-President for Student Affairs and Admissions: JAMES SAGONA
Director of the Library: MICHELLE ORT (acting)

Library of 154,000 vols
Number of teachers: 107
Number of students: 1,736

OHIO NORTHERN UNIVERSITY

Ada, OH 45810
Telephone: (419) 772-2000
Fax: (419) 772-1932

Founded 1871
Private (United Methodist); Academic year: September to May (summer sessions, June to August)

President: Dr DEBOW FREED
Registrar: R. G. CARPENTER
Librarian: P. LOGSDON

Library of 500,000 vols
Number of teachers: 200
Number of students: 2,870

DEANS

Arts and Sciences: Dr BYRON L. HAWBECHER
Engineering: Dr RUSSELL PRIMROSE
Pharmacy: Dr THOMAS A. GOSSEL
Law: Dr VICTOR STREIB
Business Administration: Dr TERRY L. MARIS

OHIO STATE UNIVERSITY

190 North Oval Mall, Columbus, OH 43210
Telephone: (614) 292-2424

Founded 1870
Campuses at Lima, Mansfield, Marion and Newark

President: E. GORDON GEE
Senior Vice-President for Academic Affairs and Provost: RICHARD SISSON
Vice-President for Agricultural Administration: BOBBY D. MOSER
Vice-President for Business and Administration: JANET G. PICHETTE
Vice-President for Development: JERRY MAY
Vice-President for Health Services: Dr MANUEL TZAGOURNIS
Vice-President for Research: EDWARD F. HAYES
Vice-President for Finance: WILLIAM J. SHKURTI

Library: see Libraries
Number of teachers: 4,310
Number of students: 54,781

Publications: *Bulletin of Business Research* (monthly), *College of Medicine Journal* (quarterly), *News in Engineering* (monthly), *Ohio Biological Survey Bulletin* (every 2 months), *Journal of Higher Education* (monthly), *Ohio Journal of Science* (every 2 months), *Journal of Money, Credit and Banking* (quarterly), *Ohio State Engineer* (student quarterly), *Ohio Theatre Collection Bulletin* (annually), *Speculum* (Veterinary Medicine, quarterly), *Theory into Practice* (5 a year), etc.

DEANS

College of Arts: JUDITH S. KOROSCIK
College of Biological Sciences: ALAN G. GOODRIDGE
Fisher College of Business: JOSEPH A. ALUTTO
College of Dentistry: HENRY W. FIELDS
College of Education: NANCY L. ZIMPHER
College of Engineering: JOSE B. CRUZ
College of Food, Agriculture and Environmental Sciences: BOBBY D. MOSER
College of Human Ecology: DENIS M. MEDEIROS (acting)
College of Humanities: KERMIT L. HALL
College of Law: GREGORY H. WILLIAMS
College of Mathematical and Physical Sciences: ROBERT GOLD
College of Medicine and Public Health: Dr BERNADINE P. HEALY
College of Nursing: CAROLE A. ANDERSON
College of Optometry: JOHN P. SCHOESSLER (acting)
College of Pharmacy: JOHN M. CASSADY
College of Social and Behavioural Sciences: RANDALL B. RIPLEY
College of Veterinary Medicine: GLEN F. HOFFSIS
College of Social Work: TONY TRIPODI
Graduate School: SUSAN L. HUNTINGTON
University College: MAC STEWART

ACADEMIC DIRECTORS

School of Allied Medical Professions: STEPHEN L. WILSON
School of Architecture: ROBERT S. LIVESEY
School of Educational Policy and Leadership: ROBERT DONMOYER

School of Journalism and Communication: DON DELL
School of Music: DONALD B. GIBSON
School of Natural Resources: FRED MILLER
School of Physical Activities and Human Services: MICHAEL SHERMAN
School of Public Health: RANDALL HARRIS
School of Public Policy and Management: C. RONALD HUFF
School of Teaching and Learning: ROBERT TIERNEY

DEPARTMENTS, ACADEMIC FACULTIES, DIVISION DIRECTORS

Accounting: LAWRENCE A. TOMASSINI
Adult Health and Illness Nursing: BONNIE J. GARVIN
Aerospace Engineering, Applied Mathematics and Aviation: GERALD M. GREGOREK
African-American and African Studies: ISAAC MOWOE (acting)
Agricultural Economics: STANLEY R. THOMPSON
Agricultural Education and Rural Sociology: N. L. MCCASLIN
Agricultural Engineering: ROBERT J. GUSTAFSON
Air Force and Aerospace Studies: Col GARY CHILCOTT
Anaesthesiology: JOHN MCDONALD
Animal Science: DAVID ZARTMAN
Anthropology: FRANK E. POIRIER
Art: GEORG HEIMDAL
Art Education: JAMES HUTCHENS
Astronomy: PATRICK OSMER
Biochemistry: GEORGE A. MARZLUF
Plant Biology: RALPH BOERNER
Cell Biology, Neurobiology and Anatomy: JAMES S. KING
Chemical Engineering: LIANG-SHIN FAN
Chemistry: MATTHEW PLATZ
Civil and Environmental Engineering and Geodetic Science: KEITH BEDFORD
Community Dentistry: PETER S. VIQ
Community Parent-Child and Psychiatric Nursing: NANCY A. RYEN-WENGER
Comparative Studies in the Humanities: THOMAS KASULAS
Computer and Information Science: STUART ZWEBEN
Consumer and Textile Sciences: KATHRYN A. JAKES
Continuing Education: MAC STEWART
Dance: KAREN BELL
East Asian Languages and Literatures: JAMES M. UNGER
Economics: MASANORI HASHIMOTO
Electrical Engineering: YUAN F. ZHENG
Emergency Medicine: DOUGLAS A. RUND
English: JAMES PHELAN
Entomology: DAVID DENLINGER
Family Medicine: GLEN AUKERMAN
Finance: STEPHEN A. BUSER
Food Science and Technology: KENNETH LEE
French and Italian: ROBERT COTTRELL
Geography: LAWRENCE BROWN
Geological Sciences: WILLIAM AUSICH
German: BERND FISCHER
Greek and Latin: WILLIAM W. BATSTONE
History: MICHAEL HOGAN
History of Art: MARK FULLERTON
Human Development and Family Science: ALBERT J. DAVIS
Human Nutrition and Food Management: TAMMY BRAY
Industrial, Interior and Visual Communication Design: LORRAINE JUSTICE (acting)
Industrial, Welding and Systems Engineering: R. ALLEN MILLER
Internal Medicine: ERNEST MAZZAFERRI
University Centre for International Studies: (vacant)
Linguistics: ROBERT D. LEVINE
Management and Human Resources: DAVID GREENBERGER
Management Sciences: GLENN W. MILLIGAN
Marketing: ROBERT E. BURNKRANT
Materials Science and Engineering: ROBERT L. SNYDEN
Mathematics: RUTH M. CHARNEY (acting)
Mechanical Engineering: KENNETH WALDRON
Medical Biochemistry: SAMSON T. JACOB (acting)
Medical Microbiology and Immunology: CAROLINE WHITACRE
Medieval and Renaissance Studies: NICHOLAS HOWE
Melton Center for Jewish Studies: TAMAR RUDAVSKY
Microbiology: JOHN N. REEVE
Military Science: Lt Col THOMAS E. WARD. II
Molecular Genetics: LEE F. JOHNSON
Naval Science: Capt. FREDERICK SPRUITENBURG
Near-Eastern Languages and Cultures: MARGARET MILLS
Neurology: JERRY R. MENDELL
Obstetrics and Gynaecology: LARRY COPELAND
Ophthalmology: PAUL A. WEBER
Otolaryngology: DAVID SCHULLER
Paediatrics: THOMAS HANSEN
Pathology: DANIEL D. SEDMAK
Pharmacology (Medicine): NORTON NEFF
Philosophy: DANIEL M. FARRELL
Physical Medicine and Rehabilitation: WILLIAM S. PEASE
Physics: FRANK C. DELUCIA
Physiology: JACK A. RALL
Plant Pathology: RANDALL C. ROWE
Political Science: PAUL A. BECK
Psychiatry: HENRY A. NASRALLAH
Psychology: JOHN T. CACIOPPO (acting)
Radiologic Technology: WILLIAM FINNEY
Radiology: DIMITRIOS SPIGOS
Slavic and East European Languages and Literatures: IRENE I. DELIC (acting)
Sociology: ELIZABETH MENAGHAN (acting)
Spanish and Portuguese: DIETER WANNER
Speech and Hearing Science: ROBERT FOX
Statistics: THOMAS J. SANTNER
Surgery: RONALD FERGUSON
Theatre: LESLIE FERRIS
Veterinary Biosciences: CHARLES CAPEN
Veterinary Clinical Sciences: ROBERT SHERDING
Veterinary Hospital: RICHARD BEDNARSKI
Veterinary Preventive Medicine: KENT H. HOBLET
Women's Studies: SALLY KITCH
Zoology: PETER PAPPAS

BRANCH CAMPUSES

Ohio State University Lima Campus: 100 Galvin Hall, 4240 Campus Drive, Lima, OH 45804; tel. (419) 221-1641; f. 1959; 2- and 4-year courses; Dean and Dir VIOLET I. MEEK.

Ohio State University Mansfield Campus: 103 Ovalwood Hall, 1680 University Drive, Mansfield, OH 44906; tel. (419) 755-4011; f. 1958; Dean and Dir JOHN O. RIEDL.

Ohio State University Marion Campus: 142A Morrill Hall, 1465 Mt Vernon Ave, Marion, OH 43302; tel. (614) 389-2361; f. 1957; 2- and 4-year courses; Dean and Dir DOMINIC DOTTAVIO.

Ohio State University Newark Campus: Founders Hall, 1179 University Drive, Newark, OH 43055; tel. (614) 366-3321; f. 1957; 2- and 4-year courses; Dean and Dir RAFAEL CORTADA.

Agricultural Technical Institute: Wooster, OH 44691; tel. (216) 264-3911; f. 1972; 2-year courses; Dir WILLIAM A. ANDERSON.

OHIO UNIVERSITY

Athens, OH 45701

Telephone: (614) 593-1000
Telex: 810-239-2992
Fax: (614) 593-4229

Founded 1804; the first land-grant college in the US; main campus in Athens, regional campuses in Chillicothe, Ironton, Lancaster, St Clairsville, Zanesville

President: ROBERT GLIDDEN
Provost: SHARON STEPHENS BREHM
Director of Admissions: N. KIP HOWARD
Librarian: HWA-WEI LEE

Library of 2,044,000 vols
Number of teachers: 1,600
Number of students: 27,386

Publications: *Ohio Review*, *Milton Quarterly*.

DEANS

Engineering and Technology: Dr W. KENT WRAY
Arts and Sciences: Dr LESLIE A. FLEMMING
Business Administration: GLENN CORLETT
Education: Dr KAREN J. VIECHNICKI (acting)
Fine Arts: Dr JAMES STEWART (acting)
University College: Dr PATRICIA RICHARD
Graduate Programs: Dr CAROL J. BLUM (acting)
Health and Human Services: Dr BARBARA K. CHAPMAN
Communications: Dr KATHY A. KRENDL
Osteopathic Medicine: Dr BARBARA ROSS-LEE
Honors Tutorial College: Dr JOSEPH H. BERMAN

OHIO WESLEYAN UNIVERSITY

Delaware, OH 43015

Telephone: (614) 368-2000

Founded by Methodist Episcopal Church 1841; chartered 1842

President: THOMAS B. COURTICE
Provost: W. C. LOUTHAN
Vice-President (Business Affairs) and Treasurer: GEORGE J. ELSBECK
Vice-President (University Relations): AUDRY K. CARTER
Dean of Academic Affairs: (vacant)
Chair, Division of Student Life: DAVID S. COZZENS
Registrar: M. J. ROACH
Librarian: THERESA BYRD

Number of teachers: 121.5
Number of students: 1,859

Publications: *OWU Bulletin* (annually), *Alumni Magazine* (quarterly).

OTTERBEIN COLLEGE

Westerville, OH 43081

Telephone: (614) 890-3000
Fax: (614) 823-1200

Founded 1847
Private control
Academic year: September to August

President: C. BRENT DE VORE
Registrar: DONALD FOSTER
Dean of Admissions and Financial Aid: THOMAS STEIN
Academic Dean: PATRICIA FRICK
Director of the Library: LOIS SZUDY

Library of 200,000 vols
Number of teachers: 140
Number of students: 2,500

Publications: *Otterbein Miscellany, Quiz and Quill*.

UNIVERSITY OF AKRON

302 E. Buchtel Ave, Akron, OH 44325

Telephone: (216) 375-7111

Founded 1870 by Ohio Universalist Convention; became Municipal University of Akron 1913; present title 1926; became State University 1967

President: MARION A. RUEBEL
Senior Vice-President and Provost: NOEL LEATHERS
Vice-President for Public Relations and Development: JOHN LA GUARDIA
Vice-President for Business and Finance: PAUL MCFARLAND
Registrar: GERALDINE CHITTY-HILL

Dean, University Libraries: DELMUS WILLIAMS
Library of 2,817,426 vols
Number of teachers: 2,900
Number of students: 24,000
Publications: *Bulletin* (annually), *UA News* (fortnightly), *Akron Magazine* (quarterly).

DEANS

Graduate Studies: CHARLES M. DYE
Buchtel College of Arts and Sciences: ROGER CREEL
College of Education: RITA SASLAUR (acting)
College of Engineering: IRVING F. MILLER
College of Business Administration: STEPHEN F. HALLAM
College of Fine and Applied Arts: LINDA L. MOORE
School of Law: RICHARD AYNEY
College of Nursing: CYNTHIA CAPERS
University College: KARLA MUGLER
Community and Technical College: DAVID SAMM
Wayne General and Technical College: JOHN KRISTOFCO

UNIVERSITY OF CINCINNATI

Cincinnati, OH 45221
Telephone: (513) 556-6000
Fax: (513) 556-2340

Chartered as Cincinnati College 1819; as University of Cincinnati and as a municipal institution 1870; became a municipally-sponsored state-affiliated institution in 1968; joined Ohio State University system 1977

Academic year: September to June

President: JOSEPH A. STEGER
Senior Vice-President for the Medical Center: DONALD C. HARRISON
Senior Vice-President and Provost: WALTER JONES
Vice-President and Dean for Graduate Studies and Research: ROBERT GESTELAND
Vice-President for Public Affairs: (vacant)
Vice-President for Student Services and Human Resources: MITCHELL LIVINGSTON
Vice-President for Finance: DALE MCGIRR
University Registrar: LYNN M. BARBER
Director of Admissions: JAMES WILLIAMS
Dean and University Librarian: DAVID F. KOHL
Library: see Libraries
Number of teachers: 2,391 full-time, 1,048 part-time
Number of students: 6,734 graduate, 991 professional, 27,226 undergraduate
Publications: *Horizon* (7 a year), *University Currents* (weekly during term), *News record* (3 a week during term), *College Bulletins* (every 2 years).

DEANS

McMicken College of Arts and Sciences: JOSEPH A. CARUSO
College of Engineering: (vacant)
College of Education: LOUIS A. CASTENELL, Jr
College of Business Administration: FREDRICK RUSS
College of Medicine: JOHN J. HUTTON, Jr
College of Law: JOSEPH P. TOMAIN
College of Nursing and Health: ANDREA R. LINDELL
College of Design, Architecture, Art and Planning: JAY CHATTERJEE
College of Pharmacy: DAN ACOSTA
College-Conservatory of Music: ROBERT WERNER
University College: (vacant)
School of Social Work: PHILLIP JACKSON (Director)
College of Evening and Continuing Education: JEANNETTE TAYLOR
Raymond Walters College: BARBARA BARDES
OMI College of Applied Science: (vacant)
Clermont College: JAMES MCDONOUGH

PROFESSORS

College of Arts and Sciences:

ALEXANDER, J. J., Chemistry
ALEXANDER, J. K., History
ARDEN, H. M., Romance Languages and Literatures
ARNER, R., English
ATKINSON, M., English
AULT, B. S., Chemistry
BEAVER, D., History
BELL, H., Mathematical Sciences
BENNETT, S., Political Science
BERRY, C. A., Economics
BERRYMAN-FINK, C. L., Communication Arts
BISHOP, G. F., Political Science
BOBST, A. M., Chemistry
BOWMAN, S., Judaic Studies
BRISKIN, M., Geology
BRYC, W., Mathematical Sciences
BURLEW, A. K. H., Psychology
CARROLL, R. L., Sociology
CARUSO, J., Biological Sciences
CHALKLEY, R., Mathematical Sciences
CHANG, T. C., Mathematical Sciences
CHARD, L., English
CHIMEZIE, A., Afro-American Studies
COHEN, G., Classics
COLLINS, P. H., Afro-American Studies
COUGHLIN, E. V., Romance Languages and Literatures
CRAYCRAFT, J. L., Economics
DANIELS, R., History
DAVIS, J. L., Classics
DAY, R. A., Chemistry
DEDDENS, J. A., Mathematical Sciences
DEMBER, W., Psychology
ELDER, A. A., English
ELDER, R. C., Chemistry
ENDORF, R. J., Physics
ERWAY, L. C., Biological Sciences
ESPOSITO, F. P., Physics
FAIRHURST, G., Communication Arts
FEINBERG, W. E., Sociology
FENICHEL, H., Physics
FISHBEIN, H., Psychology
FISHER, J. W., Mathematical Sciences
FOREMAN, M. E., Psychology
FRIEDRICHSMEYER, E., Germanic Languages
FRIEDRICHSMEYER, S. L., Germanic Languages
GALLO, J., Economics
GLENN, J. H., Germanic Languages
GODSHALK, W. L., English
GOTOFF, H. C., Classics
GRASHA, A. F., Psychology
GROETSCH, C., Mathematical Sciences
GROVER, J. E., Geology
GUSTAFSON, D., Philosophy
HALPERIN, R., Anthropology
HALPERN, H. P., Mathematical Sciences
HALSALL, B., Chemistry
HAMILTON, J. F., Romance Languages and Literatures
HARRIS, E. P., Germanic Languages and Literatures
HARRIS, N., Afro-American Studies
HARVEY, N., English
HEHMAN, R. F., Biological Sciences
HEINEMAN, W., Chemistry
HERMAN, E., Economics
HODGES, T., Mathematical Sciences
HONECK, R. P., Psychology
HORN, P. S., Mathematical Sciences
HUBBARD, A. T., Chemistry
HUDGINS, A. L., English
HUETHER, C., Biological Sciences
HUFF, W. D., Geology
HUGHES, J., English
ISAAC, B. L., Anthropology
JACKSON, H. E., Physics
JAMISON-HALL, A., Afro-American Studies
JENSEN, W. B., Chemistry
JOHNSON, N. R., Sociology
JOHNSON, R. A., Physics
JOINER, W. C. H., Physics
JOST, L. J., Philosophy
KAFKER, F. A., History
KAFTAL, V., Mathematical Sciences
KANE, T. C., Biological Sciences
KANESHIRO, E., Biological Sciences
KAPLAN, F., Chemistry
KARP, R., Biological Sciences
KILINC, A. I., Geology
KING, T., Mathematical Sciences
KLEIN, E. B., Psychology
KORMAN, P., Mathematical Sciences
KRAUT, B., Judaic Studies
KREISHMAN, G., Chemistry
LANGMEYER, D., Psychology
LANSKY, L. M., Psychology
LEAKE, L., Mathematical Science
LECLAIR, T. E., English
LEE, L., Communication Sciences
LEFTWICH, H. M., Economics
LEUNG, A., Mathematical Sciences
LEVINE, B. C., History
LEWIS, G., History
LUNDGREN, D., Sociology
MCEVOY, J., Philosophy
MACOMBER, R. S., Chemistry
MANSOURI, F., Physics
MARGOLIS, M. S., Political Science
MARK, H. B., Jr, Chemistry
MARK, J. E., Chemistry
MARTIN, J., Philosophy
MAYER, W., Economics
MAYNARD, J. B., Geology
MEADOWS, B. T., Physics
MEEKS, F., Chemistry
MELTON, R. S., Psychology
MERKES, E. P., Mathematical Sciences
MEYER, D. L., Geology
MEYER, K. R., Mathematical Sciences
MEYER, R. R., Biological Sciences
MEYERS, W., Psychology
MICHELINI, A. N., Classics
MILLER, A., Political Science
MILLER, A. I., Geology
MILLER, M. C., Biological Sciences
MILLER, Z., History
MILNE, F., English
MINDA, C. D., Mathematical Sciences
MITCHELL, O., History
MITRO, J., Mathematical Sciences
MUKKADA, A. J., Biological Sciences
MULLANE, H., Philosophy
MURIO, D. A., Mathematical Sciences
NASH, D. B., Geology
NEWROCK, R. S., Physics
NUSSBAUM, M. M., Physics
O'CONNOR, P. W., Romance Languages and Literatures
OSTERBURG, J., Mathematical Sciences
PARKER, D. B., Mathematical Sciences
PAYNE, P. A., Psychology
PELIGRAD, C., Mathematical Sciences
PELIGRAD, M., Mathematical Sciences
PINHAS, A. R., Chemistry
PINSKI, F., Physics
PORTE, M., Communication Arts
PRYOR, W. A., Geology
RALESCU, D., Mathematical Sciences
RAMUSACK, B. N., History
RAWLINGS, E. I., Psychology
RICHARDSON, R., Philosophy
RIDGWAY, T. H., Chemistry
ROBINSON, J., Philosophy
RODER, W., Geography
ROLWING, R., Mathematical Sciences
ROMERO, A., Romance Languages and Literatures
RUBENSTEIN, J., English
RUSSELL, J., Physics
RYAN, K., Geography
SAGE, M. M., Classics
SAKMYSTER, T., History
SCHADE, R., Germanic Languages and Literature
SCHLIPF, J. S., Computer Sciences

SCHUMSKY, D. A., Psychology
SCHWARTZ, M., Psychology
SEIGNEURET, J.-C., Romance Languages and Literatures
SELISKAR, C., Chemistry
SELYA, R. M., Geography
SHAPIRO, H., History
SLOTKIN, E., English
SNIDER, J. A., Biological Sciences
SPRAGUE, E. D., Chemistry
STAFFORD, H., Geography
STEPHENS, M., English
STEVER, J. A., Political Science
STUTZ, R. M., Psychology
STYER, D., Mathematical Sciences
SURANYI, P., Physics
THAYER, J., Chemistry
THOMAS, N., Political Science
TOLLEY, H. B., Political Science
TUAN, T.-F., Physics
UETZ, G. W., Biological Sciences
UNGAR, G. S., Mathematical Sciences
VANNOY, D., Sociology
VERDERBER, R., Communications Arts
VREDEVELD, G. M., Economics
WALBERG, G., Classics
WARM, J., Psychology
WEISS, G. M., Mathematical Sciences
WELLINGTON, D. C., Economics
WHITMORE, H. W., Economics
WILSON, R. M., Chemistry
WINGET, G., Biological Sciences
WOLFE, J. D., Political Science
WRIGHT, D. J., Mathematical Sciences

College of Engineering:

ABDALLAH, S. A., Aerospace Engineering and Engineering Mechanics
AKTAN, A. E., Civil and Environmental Engineering
ALLEMANG, R. J., Mechanical and Industrial Engineering
BERMAN, K. A., Computer Science
BISHOP, P. L., Civil and Environmental Engineering
BISWAS, P., Civil and Environmental Engineering
BODOCSI, A., Civil and Environmental Engineering
BOERIO, F. J., Materials Science and Engineering
BOOLCHAND, P., Electrical and Computer Engineering
BOYD, J. T., Electrical and Computer Engineering
BROWN, D. L., Mechanical and Industrial Engineering
BROWN, M. L., Mechanical and Industrial Engineering
BUCHANAN, R. C., Materials Science and Engineering
BUTLER, D. L., Aerospace Engineering and Engineering Mechanics
CARTER, H. W., Electrical and Computer Engineering
CHRISTENSON, J., Mechanical and Industrial Engineering
FAN, H. H., Electrical and Computer Engineering
FRIED, J. R., Chemical Engineering
GHIA, K. N., Aerospace Engineering and Engineering Mechanics
GHIA, U., Mechanical and Industrial Engineering
GOVIND, R., Chemical Engineering
GREENBERG, D. B., Chemical Engineering
GROOD, E. S., Aerospace Engineering and Engineering Mechanics
HALL, E. L., Mechanical and Industrial Engineering
HAMED, A., Aerospace Engineering and Engineering Mechanics
HENDERSON, H. T., Electrical and Computer Engineering
HERSHEY, D., Chemical Engineering
HUSTON, R. L., Mechanical and Industrial Engineering
HWANG, S.-T., Chemical Engineering
JAYARAMAN, N., Materials Science and Engineering
JENKINS, R. G., Chemical Engineering
KAO, Y. K., Chemical Engineering
KEENER, T. C., Civil and Environmental Engineering
KHANG, S. J., Chemical Engineering
KHOSLA, P. K., Aerospace Engineering and Engineering Mechanics
KINMAN, R. N., Civil and Environmental Engineering
KOSEL, P. B., Electrical and Computer Engineering
LIN, R. Y., Materials Science and Engineering
KROLL, R. J., Aerospace Engineering and Engineering Mechanics
MANTEI, T. D., Electrical and Computer Engineering
MINKARAH, I., Civil and Environmental Engineering
MITAL, A., Mechanical and Industrial Engineering
NAYFEH, A. H., Aerospace Engineering and Engineering Mechanics
NEVIN, J., Electrical and Computer Engineering
NOGAMI, T., Civil and Environmental Engineering
PANT, P. D., Civil and Environmental Engineering
PAUL, J. L., Computer Science
POLAK, A., Aerospace Engineering and Engineering Mechanics
POOL, M. J., Materials Science and Engineering
PRATSINIS, S. E., Chemical Engineering
PURDY, G. B., Computer Science
QUO, P. C., Mechanical and Industrial Engineering
RAMAMOORTHY, P., Electrical and Computer Engineering
RICHARDSON, D., Aerospace Engineering and Engineering Mechanics
ROE, R.-J., Materials Science and Engineering
ROENKER, K. P., Electrical and Computer Engineering
RUBIN, S. G., Aerospace Engineering and Engineering Mechanics
SAJBEN, M., Aerospace Engineering and Engineering Mechanics
SCARPINO, P. V., Civil and Environmental Engineering
SCHMIDT, D. S., Computer Science
SEKHAR, J. A., Materials Science and Engineering
SHAPIRO, A., Mechanical and Industrial Engineering
SHELL, R. L., Mechanical and Industrial Engineering
SIMITSES, G. J., Aerospace Engineering and Engineering Mechanics
SINGH, R. N., Materials Science and Engineering
SLATER, G., Aerospace Engineering and Engineering Mechanics
SONI, A. H., Mechanical and Industrial Engineering
STECKL, A., Electrical and Computer Engineering
STOUFFER, D. C., Aerospace Engineering and Engineering Mechanics
SUIDAN, M. T., Civil and Environmental Engineering
VAN OOIJ, W. J., Materials Science and Engineering
WAGNER, F. J., Computer Science
WANG I.-C., Mechanical and Industrial Engineering
WEE, W. G., Electrical and Computer Engineering

College of Education:

BARNETT, D. W., School Psychology and Counselling
BAUER, A. M., Early Childhood and Special Education
BERLOWITZ, M. J., Educational Foundation
COLLINS, R. L., Educational Foundation
CONYNE, R. K., School Psychology and Counselling
COOK, E. P., School Psychology and Counselling
COTTRELL, R., Health and Nutrition Sciences
CULLEN, F. T., Criminal Justice
DORSEY, A., Early Childhood and Special Education
EKVALL, S., Health and Nutrition Sciences
EVERS, N. A., Educational Administration
FLINCHBAUGH, R. W., Educational Administration
FOWLER, T. W., Curriculum and Instruction
FRANKEL, J., Educational Foundation
GORDON, J. S., Curriculum and Instruction
GRADEN, J. L., School Psychology and Counselling
HILL, J., Educational Administration
KRETSCHMER, R., Early Childhood and Special Education
LANGWORTHY, R. H., Criminal Justice
LATESSA, E. J., Criminal Justice
MARKLE, G. C., Curriculum and Instruction
MATRIANO, E., Curriculum and Instruction
MILGRAM, J. I., Educational Foundation
NAYLOR, D., Curriculum and Instruction
O'REILLY, P., Educational Foundation
STEVENS, J., Educational Foundation
SWAMI, P., Curriculum and Instruction
TANVEER, S. A., Curriculum and Instruction
TRAVIS, L. F., Criminal Justice
TRUAX, R. R., Early Childhood and Special Education
VANVOORHIS, P., Criminal Justice
WAGNER, D. I., Health and Nutritional Sciences
WILSON, B., Health and Nutritional Sciences
WILSON, F. R., School Psychology and Counselling
YAGER, G. G., School Psychology and Counselling
YINGER, R. J., Educational Foundation
ZINS, J., Early Childhood and Special Education

College of Business Administration:

ALLEN, C. T., Marketing
ANDERSON, D. R., Quantitative Analysis and Information Systems
ANGLE, H., Management
BAKER, N. R., Quantitative Analysis and Information Systems
BARNGROVER, C., Finance
BURNS, D., Accounting
CAMM, J. D., Quantitative Analysis and Information Systems
CURRY, D. J., Marketing
DEAN, M., Marketing
DWYER, F. R., Marketing
EVANS, J. R., Quantitative Analysis and Information Systems
GELTNER, D. M., Finance
GORE, G. J., Management
GRAEN, G. B., Management
HENDERSON, G. V., Finance
JOHNSON, T. E., Finance
KARDES, F., Marketing
KELTON, W. D., Quantitative Analysis and Information Systems
KIM, Y. H., Finance
LEVY, M. S., Quantitative Analysis and Information Systems
MACKLIN, M. C. W., Marketing
MAGAZINE, M., Quantitative Analysis and Information Systems
MILLER, N. G., Finance
SALE, T., Accounting
SCHNEE, J. E., Management

SWEENEY, D. J., Quantitative Analysis and Information Systems
WALKER, M. C., Finance
WYATT, S. B., Finance

College of Medicine:

ALBERT, R. E., Environmental Health
ASHRAF, M., Pathology and Laboratory Medicine
BANKS, R. O., Molecular and Cellular Physiology
BEHBEHANI, M. M., Molecular and Cellular Physiology
BEN-JONATHAN, N., Cell Biology
BHATTACHARYA, A., Environmental Health
BINGHAM, E. L., Environmental Health
BLUMENTHAL, K., Molecular Genetics and Biochemistry
BORNSCHEIN, R. L., Environmental Health
BRACKENBURY, R. W., Cell Biology
BRYANT, S. H., Pharmacology and Cell Biophysics
BUNCHER, C. R., Environmental Health
CHOROMOKOS, E. A., Ophthalmology
CLARK, C. S., Environmental Health
CLARK, K. E., Obstetrics and Gynaecology
CRUTCHER, K. A., Neurosurgery
CUPPOLETTI, J., Molecular and Cellular Physiology
DEDMAN, J. R., Molecular and Cellular Physiology
DOETSCHMAN, T. C., Molecular Genetics and Biochemistry
DRAKE, R. L., Cell Biology
FOULKES, E. C., Environmental Health
GRUENSTEIN, E. I., Molecular Genetics and Biochemistry
HARMONY, J., Pharmacology and Cell Biophysics
HORSEMAN, N., Molecular and Cellular Physiology
HUI, D. Y., Pathology and Laboratory Medicine
KAO, W. W. Y., Ophthalmology
KRANIAS, E. G., Pharmacy and Cell Biophysics
LARSEN, W. J., Cell Biology
LEHMAN, M. N., Cell Biology
LEMASTERS, G., Environmental Health
LIEBERMAN, M. A., Molecular Genetics and Biochemistry
LIGHT, I. J., Paediatrics
LINGREL, J. B., Molecular Genetics and Biochemistry
LOCKEY, J. E., Environmental Health
LOPER, J. C., Molecular Genetics and Biochemistry
MATLIB, M. A., Pharmacology and Cell Biophysics
MICHAEL, J. G., Molecular Genetics and Biochemistry
MILLARD, R., Pharmacology and Cell Biophysics
MILLHORN, D. E., Molecular and Cellular Physiology
MYATT, L., Obstetrics and Gynaecology
MYER, C., Otolaryngology
NEBERT, D. W., Environmental Health
PAUL, R. J., Molecular and Cellular Physiology
PERLSTEIN, P. H., Paediatrics
PESCE, A. J., Pathology and Laboratory Medicine
RAUH, J. L., Paediatrics
RUBINSTEIN, J. H., Paediatrics
SAELINGER, C., Molecular Genetics and Biochemistry
SCHWARTZ, A., Surgery
SIDMAN, C. L., Molecular Genetics and Biochemistry
SIGELL, L. T., Pharmacology and Cell Biophysics
SPECKER, B. L., Paediatrics
STAMBROOK, P. J., Cell Biology
STRINGER, J. R., Molecular Genetics and Biochemistry
SUSZKIW, J. B., Molecular and Cellular Pathology
TSO, P. P. W., Pathology and Laboratory Medicine
WALLICK, E. T., Pharmacology and Cell Biophysics
WARSHAWSKY, D., Environmental Health
WHITSETT, J. A., Paediatrics
WILLEKE, K., Environmental Health

College of Law:

APLIN, K. L.
APPLEGATE, J. S.
BIANCALANA, J.
BRAUCHER, J.
CARON, P.
CARRO, J. L.
CHRISTENSON, G. A.
EISELE, T. D.
FLETCHER, C. E.
LAUERMAN, N.
LOCKWOOD, B. B.
MURPHY, J. J.
RANDS, W.
SCHNEIDER, R.
SOLIMINE, M. E.
SQUILLANTE, A.
WEISSENBERGER, G.

College of Nursing and Health:

BUNYAN, R. M., Medical Surgical Nursing
DYEHOUSE, J. M., Physical and Mental Health Nursing
KENNER, C. A., Parent-Child Nursing
MARTIN, M. T., Medical Surgical Nursing
MCCRAKEN, A. L., Physical and Mental Health Nursing
MILLER, E. L., Medical Surgical Nursing
SCHARE, B. S., Medical Surgical Nursing
SPERO, J. R., Physical and Mental Health Nursing

Centre for Allied Health:

AGNELLO, J., Rehabilitation Sciences
CREAGHEAD, N., Communication Sciences
DONNELLY, K. G., Rehabilitation Sciences
FALCIGLIA, G., Health Sciences
KRETSCHMER, L. W., Rehabilitation Sciences
WEILER, E. M., Rehabilitation Sciences

College of Design, Architecture, Art and Planning:

ALLOR, D. J., School of Planning
BORN, G. C., Design
BOTTONI, J., Design
BURNHAM, R., Architecture and Interior Design
CARTWRIGHT, R., Art
CHAPAROS, N., Design
ELLISON, C. E., Planning
ENGELBRECHT, L. C., Art
ENSTICE, W. E., Art
FEINSTEIN, H., Art
GOSLING, D., Planning
HANCOCK, J. E., Architecture and Interior Design
HERRMANN, F. H., Art
HILDEBRANDT, H. P., Architecture and Interior Design
MANN, D. A., Architecture and Interior Design
MEACHAM, G. M., Design
NILAND D. L., Architecture and Interior Design
PREISER, W., Architecture and Interior Design
PUHALLA, D. M., Design
RENICK, P. A., Art
RIESS, J. B., Art
ROMANOS, M. C., School of Planning
SAILE, D., Architecture and Interior Design
SALCHOW, G. R., School of Design
SIMMONS, G. B., Architecture and Interior Design
SMITH, D. L., Architecture and Interior Design
STEWART, J. P., Art
STRICEVIC, G., Art
TUCKER, M., Art
VAMOSI, S. J., Architecture and Interior Design
VARADY, D., Planning
WAGNER, T., Planning
WIDDOWSON, W., Architecture and Interior Design
WOODHAM, D., Art

College of Pharmacy:

CACINI, W.
CAPERELLI, C. A.
CONRAD, W. F.
JANG, R.
RITSCHEL, W. A.,
SAKR, A.
SHENOUDA, L. S.
TAN, H. S. I.
WUEST, J. R.

College-Conservatory of Music:

ADAMS, D., Performance Studies
ANDERSON, S. V., History and Composition
BERG, A., Opera and Musical Theatre
BOYER-WHITE, R., Music Education
CALLAHAN, C., Performance Studies
CHILDS, S. G., Opera and Musical Theatre
CRABTREE, P., History and Composition
DEKANT, R., Performance Studies
DOAN, G. R., Music Education
EATON, J., Opera and Musical Theatre
FAABORG, K. K., Opera and Musical Theatre
FISHER, L. W., Performance Studies
FOSTER, D., History and Composition
FRASER, M., Opera and Musical Theatre
GARY, R., Keyboard
GIESBRECHT, P. M. B., Performance Studies
GRIFFITHS, K., Keyboard
HALE, N. K., Opera and Musical Theatre
HANANI, Y., Performance Studies
HANDEL, D. D., History and Composition
HASHIMOTO, E., Keyboard
HOFFMAN, J., History and Composition
HONN, B., Performance Studies
KALEVA, L., Opera and Musical Theatre
KENDALL, G., Performance Studies
LEMAN, J. W., Ensembles and Conducting
METZ, D., Music Education
MORRIS, R., Keyboard
MULBURY, D. G., Keyboard
OTTE, A. C., Performance Studies
PENDLE, K., History and Composition
PHILIPPE, J., Performance Studies
PRIDONOFF, E. A., Keyboard
RIVERS, E., Ensembles and Conducting
ROUSE, M. G., Broadcasting
SABLINE, O., Dance
SAMUEL, G., Ensembles and Conducting
SASSMANNSHAUS, K., Performance Studies
SHORTT, P., Opera and Musical Theatre
TOCCO, J. V., Keyboard
WAXLER, S., Opera and Musical Theatre
WEINSTOCK, F. M., Keyboard
WING, L., Music Education
WOLFRAM, M., Broadcasting
ZIEROLF, R. L., History and Composition

School of Social Work:

BORKIN, J.
SUNDERLAND, S. C.

OMI College of Applied Science:

BILL, H. L., Construction Science
BORONKAY, T. G., Mechanical Engineering Technology
BROWN, M. A., Humanities
DORSEY, R. W., Construction Science
DURBIN, D. J., Construction Science
GEONETTA, S. C., Humanities
GILLIGAN, L. G., Mathematics
MEAL, L., Chemical Technology
SUCKARIEH, G. G., Construction Science
SULLIVAN, J. F., Mathematics

Raymond Walters General and Technical College:

BAUGHIN, J. H., Foreign Languages
BAUGHIN, W., History

BROD, E. F., Foreign Languages
CALLAN, J., Business and Commerce
CEBULA, J. E., History
COOPER-FREYTAG, L., Biological Sciences
FLAVIN, L. A., English
GARNETT, W. B., Biological Sciences
GOODMAN, E., History
HANSEN, B. L., English
HEHMAN, R. G., Business and Commerce
LEAKE, J. A., History
LUTHER, P. A., English
MARSH, C. W., Mathematics, Physics
RNO, J., Mathematics, Physics
ROOS, M. E., English
SCHLECHT, P. A., Nursing
SCHULTZ, J. A., Biological Sciences
SULKES, S., English
THOMAS, G. P., Behavioural Sciences
WHEELER, S. G., History
YAKALI, E., Chemistry

University College:

CROCKER-LAKNESS, J. W., Language Arts
DZIECH, B., Language Arts
GARRETT, M. P., Language Arts
GRIESINGER, W. S., Humanities and Social Science
KAHN, S. R., Business and Commerce
MCGINNIS, J. W., Language Arts
MEEM, D. T., Language Arts
MURDOCH, N. H., Humanities and Social Science
NAPOLI, D., Humanities and Social Science
RUSH, S., Humanities and Social Science
SUMMERLIN, L., Language Arts
WHITE, L. M., Language Arts

Clermont General and Technical College:

CAREY, A. K.
DANAHY, L. K.
DEJONG, M. F.
FANKHAUSER, D. B.
HEIMBOLD, B. L.
WOLFF, G.

Collateral Department:

EVANS, B. T., Professional Practice

UNIVERSITY OF DAYTON

Dayton, OH 45469
Telephone: (513) 229-4122

Founded 1850

President: Bro. RAYMOND L. FITZ
Senior Vice-President for Administration: Bro. BERNARD J. PLOEGER
Provost: Rev. JAMES L. HEFT
Registrar: DANIEL F. PALMERT
Vice-President for University Advancement: FRANCES E. ARY
Vice-President and Treasurer: THOMAS E. BURKHARDT
Vice-President for Student Development: Dr WILLIAM C. SCHUERMAN
Vice-President for Athletic Programs and Facilities: THEODORE KISSELL
Vice-President for Graduate Studies and Research: Dr GORDON A. SARGENT
Dean of Libraries: Dr EDWARD D. GARTEN

Library of 1,304,000 vols
Number of teachers: 781
Number of students: 9,906

Publications: *University of Dayton Review* (quarterly), *Dimensions* (5 a year), *Law Review.*

DEANS

Arts and Sciences: PAUL J. HORMAN
Graduate Studies and Research: Dr GORDON A. SARGENT
School of Engineering: Dr JOSEPH LESTINGI
School of Business: Dr SAM B. GOULD
School of Education: Dr PATRICIA F. FIRST
School of Law: FRANCIS J. CONTE

DIRECTORS

Continuing Education: CAROL M. SHAW
Admissions: MYRON H. ACHBACH
Research Institute: Dr JOSEPH E. ROWE

UNIVERSITY OF FINDLAY

1000 North Main St, Findlay, OH 45840
Telephone: (419) 422-8313
Fax: (419) 424-4822

Founded 1882

President: Dr KENNETH E. ZIRKLE
Vice-President for Academic Affairs: Dr EDWARD W. ERNER
Vice-President for Business Affairs: MARTIN L. TERRY
Vice-President for Institutional Advancement: WILLIAM C. TRIGG, Jr
Vice-President for Student Services: FRANKLIN J. SCHULTZ
Registrar: TONY G. GOEDDE
Librarian: ROBERT W. SCHIRMER

Library of 127,000 vols
Number of teachers: 128
Number of students: 4,018

UNIVERSITY OF TOLEDO

Toledo, OH 43606-3390
Telephone: (419) 530-2696
Fax: (419) 530-4504

Founded 1872 as Toledo University of Arts and Trades; became Municipal University 1883, State University 1967

President: FRANK E. HORTON
Senior Vice-President for Academic Affairs: JUDY HAMPLE
Vice-President for Student Affairs: DAVID MEABON
Vice-President for Graduate Studies, Research and Economic Development: JAMES FRY
Vice-President for Administrative Affairs: THOMAS REPP
Director of Registration: JOSEPH DECHRISTOFORO
Dean of Libraries: LESLIE W. SHERIDAN

Library of over 1,000,000 vols
Number of teachers: 614 full-time, 702 part-time
Number of students: 20,307

Publications: *The Alumnus* (quarterly), *The Collegian,* and various departmental newsletters and journals.

DEANS

College of Arts and Sciences: PATRICIA CUMMINS
College of Business Administration: JAMES POPE
College of Education and Allied Professions: P. RUSCHE
College of Engineering: VIKRAM KAPOOR
College of Law: ALBERT QUICK
College of Pharmacy: N. F. BILLUPS
University College Programs: HENRY MOON
Graduate School: JAMES FRY
University Community College: JERRY SULLIVAN
Dean of Enrollment Management: KENT HOPKINS

PROFESSORS

College of Arts and Sciences:

Anthropology:

METRESS, S.

Art:

ATTIE, D.
BASTIAN, D.
BELL-AMES, L.
ELLOIAN, P.
GUIP, D.

Astronomy:

ANDERSON, L.
BOPP, B. W.
WITT, A. N.

Biology:

GOLDMAN, S. L.
JOHNSON, K.
KOMUNIECKI, P.
KOMUNIECKI, R. W.
LEE, H. H.
PRIBOR, D. B.
TRAMER, E. J.
WHEELOCK, M. J.

Chemistry:

CHRYSOCHOOS, J.
DAVIES, J. A.
DOLLIMORE, D.
EDWARDS, J. G.
FUNK, M. O., Jr
GANO, J. E.
PINKERTON, A. A.

Communications:

BENJAMIN, J. B.
KNECHT, R. J.
RUSSELL, C. G.
WILCOX, E. M.

Economics:

LESAGE, J.
MAGURA, M.
ROY, R.
WEISS, S. J.

English:

ABU-ABSI, S.
BARDEN, T.
BOENING, J.
DESSNER, L. J.
FREE, W. N.
LIPMAN, J.
REISING, R.
RUDOLPH, R. S.
SAUNDERS, J.
SZUBERLA, G. A.
WIKANDER, M. H.

Foreign Languages:

FEUSTLE, J. A.
NORMAND, G. M.
O'NEAL, W. J.
SCANLAN, T. M.
SCHAUB, U. T.

Geography:

FRANCKOWIAK, E. N.
MURACO, W. A.

Geology:

CAMP, M.
HARRELL, J.
HATFIELD, C.
PHILLIPS, M. W.

History:

BRITTON, D.
CAVE, A. A.
GLAAB, C. N.
HOOVER, W. D.
LINEBAUGH, P.
LONGTON, W. H.
LORA, R. G.
MENNING, C.
NATSOULAS, T.
O'NEAL, W.
RAY, R. D.
SMITH, R. F.
THOMPSON, G. E.
WILCOX, L. D.

Mathematics:

BENTLEY, H. L.
CARLSON, D.
KERTZ, G. J.
KUMMER, M.
LIN, E. B.
NAGISETTY, R. V.
PETTET, M. R.

SCHWARZ, F.
SHIELDS, P. C.
STEINBERG, S. A.
VAYO, H. W.
WENTE, H. C.
WHITE, D.
WOLFF, H. E.

Music:

DEYARMAN, R. M.
JEX, D.
KIHSLINGER, M. R.
RENZI, F. A.
RONDELLI, B.
VAN DER MERWE, R. A.
WEBSTER, R. M.

Nursing:

FABISZAK, A.

Philosophy:

BLATZ, C.
CAMPBELL, J.

Physics:

BOHN, R. G.
COMPAAN, A. D.
CURTIS, L. J.
ELLIS, D. G.
IWAMOTO, N.
JAMES, P. B.
KVALE, T.
LEE, S.
SIMON, H. J.
THEODOSIOU, C.
WILLIAMSON, W.

Political Science:

LINDEEN, J. W.
RANDALL, R.
WEISFELDER, R. F.

Psychology:

ARMUS, H.
ELLIOTT, R. K., Jr
HAAF, R. A.
HEFFNER, H.
HEFFNER, R.
HOROWITZ, I. A.
MCKEEVER, W. F.
PALMER, A.
SLAK, S.

Sociology:

ALKALIMAT, A.
KART, C. S.
KING, J. A.
METRESS, S.
MORRISSEY, M.

Theater:

HILL, J.
WATERMEIER, D. J.

College of Business Administration:

Accounting:

FINK, P. R.
GAFFNEY, D. J.
LAVERTY, B.
RAGUNATHAN, B.
SAFTNER, D.
SCHROEDER, N.

Information Systems and Operations Management:

AHMED, M. U.
KAMBUROWSKI, J.
KUNNATHUR, A.
MARCHAL, W. G.
RACHAMADUGU, R.
RAGHUNATHAN, T.
RAO, S. S.
SASS, C. J.
SMITH, A.
SUNDARARAGHAVAN, P. S.
VONDEREMBSE, M. A.

Finance:

SMOLEN, G. E.

Management:

BEEMAN, D. R.
BHATT, B. J.
DOLL, W. J.
KIM, K. I.
LONGNECKER, C.
NYKODYM, N.
SIMONETTI, J. L.
SPIRN, S.
TIMMINS, S. A.

Marketing:

DEKORTE, M. J.
FLASCHNER, A. B.
KOZLOWSKI, P. J.
LIM, J.
OKOROAFO, S.
THUONG, L.
ZALLOCCO, R.

College of Education:

Educational Administration and Supervision:

BALDWIN, G.
MERRITT, D.
PIPER, J.
RUSCH, E.
SULLIVAN, R.

Educational Psychology, Research and Social Foundation:

DAVISON, D. C.
DUNN, T. G.
GRAY, W. M.
HUDSON, L. M.
HURST, J.
JURS, S.
LOPEZ, T.
ZIMMER, J.

Elementary and Early Childhood Education:

AHERN, J.
BALZER, D. M.
CARR, E.
COOKE, G. E.
CRYAN, J. R.
DEBRUIN, J. E.
GRESS, J. R.
KOONTZ, F.
MCFARLAND, S. L.
SANDMAN, A.
SHIRK, G. B.

Counselor and Human Services Education:

PIAZZA, N.
RITCHIE, M.
WENDT, R. N.

Health Promotion and Human Performance:

ANDRES, F. F.
ARMSTRONG, C.
DROWATZKY, J.
FULTON, G. B.
GRENINGER, L. O.
METRESS, E.
OLSSON, R.
PRICE, J. H.
RANCK, S. L.

Educational Technology:

ELSIE, L. J.
PATTERSON, A. C.

Secondary Education:

DEMEDIO, D.
NATSOULAS, A.

Special Education:

BENJAMIN, B.
CARROLL, M. E.
MCINERNEY, W.

Vocational Education:

PIPER, J.

College of Engineering:

Bio-engineering:

CIOS, K.
DHAWAN, A.
FARISON, J.
FOURNIER, R.
LU, S.-Y.
MIKHAIL, W. E.

Chemical Engineering:

ABRAHAM, M.
CHANG, L.
DISMUKES, J.
JABARIN, S.

Civil Engineering:

ANGELBECK, D. I.
FU, K. C.
GUPTA, J.
KUMAR, A.
MOSTAGHEL, N.

Electrical Engineering:

ALAM, M.
ELTIMSAHY, A. H.
GHANDAKLY, A. A.
KING, R.
KWATRA, S. C.
LEDGARD, H.
SALARI, E.
SELIGA, T.
SMITH, E.
STUART, T. A.

Mechanical Engineering:

AFJEH, A.
BENNETT, R.
CHEN, F.
FATEMI, A.
HEFZY, M.
IREY, R. K.
KEITH, T. G.
KRAMER, S. N.
MCNICHOLS, R.
NAGANATHAN, N.
NG TSUNG, M.
WHITE, P.
WOLFE, K. R.

College of Law:

ANDERSON, R. W.
BERKOWITZ, R. L.
BOURGUIGNON, H. J.
CAMPBELL, B. A.
CHAPMAN, D. K.
CLOSIUS, P. J.
CRANDALL, T.
FRIEDMAN, H.
HARRIS, D.
HOPPERTON, R. J.
KADENS, M.
KENNEDY, B.
KLEIN, J. M.
LEAFFER, M. A.
MARTYN, S. R.
MERRITT, F. S.
MORAN, G. P.
RAITT, R.
RAY, D. E.
RICHMAN, W. M.
RIPPS, S. R.
STEINBOCK, D. J.
TIERNEY, J.

Library:

Library Administration:

BALDWIN, J. F.
HOGAN, A. D.
SHERIDAN, L.

Technological Media:

KALMBACH, J. A.

College of Pharmacy:

ALEXANDER, K.
BACHMANN, K. A.
BILLUPS, N. F.
BLACK, C. D.
DOLLIMORE, D.
ERHARDT, P.
HINKO, C.
HUDSON, R. A.
LIVELY, B. T.
MESSER, W.

PARKER, G.
SHERMAN, G. P.

University Community and Technical College:

General Studies:

GERLACH, J.
GLEN, M.
KRAUSE, T. J.
MILLER, K. J.

Technical Science and Mathematics:

GRECO, D.
PALMER, J.
STEIN, R. D.

Business Technologies:

DETTINGER, J. F.
LAWSHE, C. J.
POSTA, B.
RUDDY, M.

Engineering Technologies:

GALLAGHER, R.
KAMM, J.
KIME, E.
SOLAREK, D.

Health and Human Services:

LEWTON, J.
SULLIVAN, J.
TRABAND, M.
WEDDING, M. E.

Law Enforcement Technologies:

ROSSI, R.
TELB, J.

URSULINE COLLEGE

2550 Lander Rd, Pepper Pike, Cleveland, OH 44124
Telephone: (440) 449-4200
Fax: (440) 646-8318

Founded 1871

President: Sr DIANA STANO
Director of Admissions: (vacant)
Vice-President for Academic Affairs: Dr JOANNE PODIS
Vice-President for Student Services: (vacant)
Vice-President for Institutional Advancement: KEVIN GLADSTONE
Vice-President for Finance and Administration: VALERIE A. HUGHES
Registrar: ANN MARIE SICLARE
Librarian: BETSEY BELKIN

Library of 120,000 vols
Number of teachers: 125
Number of students: 1,220

WILBERFORCE UNIVERSITY

Wilberforce, OH 45384
Telephone: (937) 376-2911

Founded 1856

President: JOHN L. HENDERSON
Academic Dean: SANDRA CHAMBERS VAUGHN
Registrar: GAIL LASH
Director, Learning Resources Center: JEAN MULHERN
Executive Assistant to the President: MOSES GRIFFIN

Library of 62,000 vols
Number of teachers: 64
Number of students: 846

WILMINGTON COLLEGE

Wilmington, OH 45177
Telephone: (937) 382-6661

Founded 1870
Private control

President: DANIEL A. DIBIASIO
Vice-President for Academic Affairs and Dean of Faculty: PAUL MOKE
Vice-President for Business and Finance: KEVAN C. BUCK
Dean of Students: KENNETH PERESS
Dean of Admissions and Financial Aid: LAWRENCE T. LESICK
Registrar: KAREN M. GARMAN
Director of Library: JENNILOU S. GROTEVANT

Library of 106,000 vols
Number of teachers: 62 full-time
Number of students: 1,033

Publication: *The Link.*

WITTENBERG UNIVERSITY

POB 720, North Wittenberg Ave, Springfield, OH 45501-0720
Telephone: (937) 327-6231

Founded 1845
Private control
Academic year: August to May

President: BAIRD TIPSON
Provost: SAMMYE C. GREER
Vice-President for Business and Finance: P. GUS GEIL
Dean of Admissions: KENNETH G. BENNE
Registrar: F. E. ROLLER
Director of Library: KATHLEEN SCHULZ

Library of 360,000 vols, 1,500 periodicals
Number of teachers: 142 full-time, 54 part-time
Number of students: 1,924

Publications: *The Wittenberg Bulletin, Wittenberg Today, The Wittenberg Review: An Undergraduate Journal of the Liberal Arts.*

WRIGHT STATE UNIVERSITY

Dayton, OH 45435
Telephone: (937) 775-3333
Fax: (937) 775-3301

Founded 1967

President: Dr KIM GOLDENBERG
Registrar: GAIL FRED
Librarian: Dr V. MONTEVON

Library of 696,000 vols
Number of teachers: 676 f.t.e.
Number of students: 11,878 f.t.e.

DEANS

College of Business and Administration: RISHI KUMAR
College of Education and Human Services: GREGORY BERNHARDT
College of Liberal Arts: WILLIAM E. RICKERT
College of Science and Mathematics: ROGER K. GILPIN
School of Graduate Studies: JOSEPH A. THOMAS
School of Medicine: HOWARD PART
School of Nursing: JANE SWART
School of Professional Psychology: LEON VANDECREEK
School of Engineering and Computer Service: JAMES E. BRANDEBERRY
Lake Campus: DAN L. EVANS

ATTACHED INSTITUTES

Center for Economic Education: Dir ROGER SYLVESTER.

Bolinga Cultural Resources Center: Dir LILLIAN JOHNSON.

Center for Urban and Public Affairs: Dir MARY E. MAZEY.

Division of Professional Practice and Research: Dir JAMES TRENT.

Center for Small Business Assistance: Dir ROBERT SCHERER.

Conferences and Events: TERRI MILEO WEBB.

Center for Ground Water Management: Dir ROBERT W. RITZI, Jr.

Center for Labor-Management Co-operation: Dir SANDRA KENNEDY.

Statistical Consulting Center: Dir HARRY J. KHAMIS.

University Research Center: DAVID LOOK.

XAVIER UNIVERSITY

3800 Victory Parkway, Cincinnati, OH 45207
Telephone: (513) 745-3000
Fax: (513) 745-1954

Founded 1831

President: Rev. JAMES E. HOFF
Vice-President, Student Affairs: Dr RONALD A. SLEPITZA
Vice-President for Academic Affairs: Dr JAMES E. BUNDSCHUH
Vice-President, Financial Administration: Dr J. RICHARD HIRTÉ
Vice-President for University Relations: Rev. MICHAEL J. GRAHAM
Administrative Vice-President: JOHN F. KUCIA
Vice-President for Spiritual Development: Rev. J. LEO KLEIN.
Associate Vice-President for Enrollment Services: (vacant)
Director of Admission: (vacant)
Director of Financial Aid: PAUL CALME
Comptroller: JOHN D. VENNEMEYER
Librarian: Dr JOANNE L. YOUNG

Library of 355,000 vols
Number of teachers: 490
Number of students: 6,103

Publications: *Xavier University Newswire, Xavier Magazine, Xcerpts, Preview, Xtensions.*

DEANS

College of Arts and Sciences: Dr MAX J. KECK
Center for Adult and Part-time Students: SUSAN G. WIDEMAN
College of Business Administration: Dr MICHAEL A. WEBB
College of Social Sciences: Dr NEIL R. HEIGHBERGER

YOUNGSTOWN STATE UNIVERSITY

One University Plaza, Youngstown, OH 44555
Telephone: (330) 742-3000
Fax: (330) 742-1998

Founded 1908
State control
Academic year: September to August (four terms)

President: Dr LESLIE H. COCHRAN
Provost: Dr JAMES J. SCANLON
Executive Vice-President: Dr G. L. MEARS
Vice-President, Student Affairs: Dr CYNTHIA E. ANDERSON
Vice-President, Development and Community Affairs: VERN SNYDER
Executive Director, Administrative Services: PHILIP HIRSCH
Director, Public Relations and Marketing: LINDA LEWIS
Executive Director, Human Resources: SHIRLEY A. CARPENTER
Director of Library: THOMAS C. ATWOOD

Library of 887,000 vols
Number of teachers: 784
Number of students: 12,801

DEANS

College of Arts and Sciences: Dr BARBARA BROTHERS
College of Business Administration: Dr BETTY JO LICATA
College of Education: Dr CLARA M. JENNINGS
College of Engineering and Technology: Dr CHARLES A. STEVENS
College of Fine and Performing Arts: Dr GEORGE MCCLOUD
College of Health and Human Services: Dr JOHN J. YEMMA
School of Graduate Studies: Dr PETER J. KASVINSKY

OKLAHOMA

EAST CENTRAL UNIVERSITY

Ada, OK 74820

Telephone: (405) 332-8000

Founded 1909

President: BILL S. COLE
Registrar: PAMLA ARMSTRONG
Librarian: CHARLES PERRY

Library of 275,000 vols
Number of teachers: 168
Number of students: 4,378

LANGSTON UNIVERSITY

Langston, OK 73050

Telephone: (405) 466-2231

President: Dr ERNEST L. HOLLOWAY
Vice-President for Academic Affairs: Dr JEAN B. MANNING
Vice-President for Administrative and Fiscal Affairs: DEWEY W. CLAPP
Vice-President for Student Affairs: Dr ELBERT L. JONES
Vice-President for Institutional Advancement: Dr MAJOR MADISON

DEANS AND CHAIRMEN

School of Arts and Sciences: Dr CLYDE MONTGOMERY
Department of Music: Dr WILLIAM B. GARCIA
Department of Natural Sciences: Dr SARAH N. THOMAS
Department of English and Foreign Languages: Dr BENJAMIN BATES
Department of Mathematics: Dr SIVALINGAM SIVANESAN
Department of Social Science: Dr LAWRENCE GREAR
Department of Physical Science: Dr JOHN K. COLEMAN
School of Business: Dr LARZETTE G. HALE
School of Education and Behavioral Sciences: Dr DARLENE S. ABRAM
Department of Elementary Education: Dr LESTER CLARK
Department of Health, Physical Education and Recreation: ROZALYN L. WASHINGTON
School of Agriculture and Applied Sciences: Dr MARVIN BURNS
Department of Human Ecology: (vacant)
Department of Technology: CLARENCE HEDGE
School of Nursing and Health Professions: Dr CAROLYN T. KORNEGAY

NORTHEASTERN STATE UNIVERSITY (OKLAHOMA)

Tahlequah, OK 74464-2399

Telephone: (918) 456-5511
Fax: (918) 458-2015

Founded 1888 (state purchase 1909)

President: Dr LARRY B. WILLIAMS
Vice-President for Academic Affairs: Dr JAMES PATE
Vice-President for Business and Development: JAMES HOWARD
Vice-President for Administration: JOCELYN PAYNE
Registrar: BILL NOWLIN
Dean of Library: BÉLA FOLTIN, Jr

Library of 500,000 vols
Number of teachers: 290 full-time
Number of students: 8,750

Publications: *The Phoenix*, *The Redman*.

NORTHWESTERN OKLAHOMA STATE UNIVERSITY

709 Oklahoma Blvd, Alva, OK 73717-2799

Telephone: (580) 327-1700
Fax: (580) 327-1881

Founded 1897

President: Dr JOE J. STRUCKLE
Registrar: Mrs SHIRLEY MURROW
Librarian: RAY D. LAU

Library of 500,000 vols (including microforms)
Number of teachers: 124
Number of students: 1,905

OKLAHOMA BAPTIST UNIVERSITY

Shawnee, OK 74804

Telephone: (405) 275-2850
Fax: (405) 878-2069
E-mail: admissions@mail.okbu.edu

Founded 1910

President: Dr MARK A. BRISTER
Vice-President for Academic Affairs: Dr JOE BOB WEAVER
Executive Vice-President: JOHN PARRISH
Dean of Admissions: MICHAEL CAPPO
Dean of Students: DOUGLAS MELTON
Assistant Vice-President for Business Affairs: RON DEMPSEY
Vice-President for Religious Life: Dr DICK RADER
Director of Academic Records: PEGGY ASKINS
Dean of Library Sciences: Dr MARK HERRING

Library of 252,000 vols
Number of teachers: 140
Number of students: 2,000

DEANS

Arts and Sciences: Dr DEBORAH BLUE
Fine Arts: Dr PAUL HAMMOND
Business and Administration: Dr ROBERT BABB
Christian Service: Dr DICK RADER
Nursing: Dr CLAUDINE DICKEY

OKLAHOMA CITY UNIVERSITY

2501 North Blackwelder, Oklahoma City, OK 73106

Telephone: (405) 521-5000
Fax: (405) 521-5264

Founded 1904

President: Dr JERALD C. WALKER
Vice-President for Academic Affairs: Dr C. B. CLARK (acting)
Vice-President for Institutional Advancement: RONALD BOGLE
Vice-President for Student and Administrative Services: MARY E. COFFEY
Vice-President for University/Church Relations: Dr GLEN O. MILLER
Vice-President for Fiscal Affairs: DEBORAH MILLS
Registrar: GAYLE ROBERTSON
Librarian: DANELLE HALL

Library of 362,500 vols, 195,000 government documents
Number of teachers: 276
Number of students: 4,400

OKLAHOMA PANHANDLE STATE UNIVERSITY

Goodwell, OK 73939

Telephone: (405) 349-2611

Founded 1909

President: M. RAY BROWN (acting)
Vice-President for Academic Affairs: WILLIAM JONES (acting)
Vice-President for Business and Fiscal Affairs: HARRY ROSENGRANTS
Director of Student Activities: JEFF CHISUM
Registrar: EMMA SCHULTZ
Librarian: EDWARD BRYAN

Library of 91,000 vols
Number of teachers: 69
Number of students: 1,400

OKLAHOMA STATE UNIVERSITY

Stillwater, OK 74078

Telephone: (405) 744-5000

Founded 1890

President: Dr JAMES E. HALLIGAN
Executive Vice-President: Dr MARVIN S. KEENER
Vice-President for Business and External Relations: Dr HARRY W. BIRDWELL
Vice-President for Student Affairs: Dr RON S. BEER
Vice-President for Research: Dr THOMAS C. COLLINS
Registrar: Dr ROBIN H. LACY
Director of Admissions: Dr JOHN D. VITEK (acting)
Dean of Libraries: Dr EDWARD R. JOHNSON

Library of 1,724,000 vols
Number of teachers: 1,158
Number of students: 19,201

DEANS

College of Agricultural Sciences and Natural Resources: Dr SAMUEL E. CURL
College of Arts and Sciences: Dr SMITH L. HOLT
College of Business Administration: Dr GARY TRENNEPOHL
College of Education: Dr ANN CANDLER-LOTVEN
College of Engineering, Architecture and Technology: Dr KARL N. REID, Jr
College of Human Environmental Sciences: Dr PATRICIA K. KNAUB
Graduate College: Dr THOMAS C. COLLINS
College of Veterinary Medicine: Dr JOSEPH ALEXANDER
Undergraduate Studies: Dr BECKY JOHNSON
University Extension, International and Economic Development: Dr JAMES G. HROMAS

ORAL ROBERTS UNIVERSITY

7777 South Lewis, Tulsa, OK 74171

Telephone: (918) 495-6161
Fax: (918) 495-6033

Founded 1965

Chancellor: G. ORAL ROBERTS
President: RICHARD L. ROBERTS
Vice-Presidents: Dr CARL H. HAMILTON (Chief Academic Officer), JEFF GEUDER (Administrative Services), GEORGE FISHER (University Relations), DAVE ELLSWORTH (Operations), HARRY SALEM (Television Production)

Library of 1,000,000 items
Number of teachers: 200
Number of students: 4,500

DEANS

Arts and Sciences: Dr RALPH FAGIN
Business: Dr DAVID DYSON
Education: Dr CLARENCE OLIVER
Enrollment Management: Dr JEFF OGLE
Instructional Services: Dr ROBERT VOIGHT
Learning Resources: Dr WILLIAM W. JERNIGAN
Nursing: Dr KENDA JEZEK
Student Affairs: CLARENCE BOYD
Theology and Missions: Dr JERRY HORNER
School of Lifelong Education: JEFF OGLE

PHILLIPS UNIVERSITY

Enid, OK 73701

Telephone: (580) 237-4433

Founded 1906

President: Dr G. CURTIS JONES, Jr
Registrar: JOHN STAM
Librarian: RICK SAYRE

Library of 220,000 vols
Number of teachers: 75
Number of students: 1,000

Publications: *Haymaker*, *Inside Phillips*.

SOUTHEASTERN OKLAHOMA STATE UNIVERSITY

Durant, OK 74701
Telephone: (580) 924-0121
Founded 1909, refounded under present name 1974
Academic year: August to May (and summer session)
President: GLEN JOHNSON
Library Director: Dr DOROTHY DAVIS
Library of 180,000 vols
Number of students: 4,000

SOUTHERN NAZARENE UNIVERSITY

6729 NW 39th Expressway, Bethany, OK 73008
Telephone: (405) 789-6400
Fax: (405) 491-6381
Founded 1899
Church control
Academic year: August to June (two summer sessions and two terms)
President: Dr LOREN P. GRESHAM
Academic Dean: Dr DON DUNNINGTON
Registrar: GARY LANCE
Librarian: SHIRLEY PELLEY
Library of 105,000 vols, 13,000 periodicals, 339,000 microform items
Number of teachers: 70
Number of students: 1,499
Publication: *Southern Lights*.

SOUTHWESTERN OKLAHOMA STATE UNIVERSITY

Weatherford, OK 73096
Telephone: (405) 772-6611
Founded 1901
President: JOE ANNA HIBLER
Registrar: BOB KLAASSEN
Librarian: BEVERLY JONES
Library of 242,406 vols
Number of teachers: 222
Number of students: 5,226

UNIVERSITY OF CENTRAL OKLAHOMA

Edmond, OK 73034
Telephone: (405) 341-2980
Fax: (405) 359-5841
Founded 1890
President: GEORGE NIGH
Assistant to the President: ED PUGH
Vice-President for Academic Affairs: Dr CLYDE JACOB
Vice-President for Administration: Dr CORNELIUS WOOTEN
Vice-President for Student Services: Dr DUDLEY RYAN
Director of Public Relations: LINDA JONES
Director of Library Services: Dr JOHN LOLLEY
Library of 706,000 vols
Number of teachers: 730
Number of students: 15,400
Publications: *Alumni Newsletter*, (quarterly), *The Territory* (monthly), *Vista Newspaper* (twice weekly), *Bronze Catalog* (every two years), *Central State Review* (2 a year), *Tower Review* (2 a year), *CSU Alumni Newsletter* (quarterly).

DEANS

Graduate Studies and Research: Dr GEORGE AVELLANO
College of Business: Dr DAVID HARRIS (acting)
College of Education: Dr KEN ELSNER
College of Liberal Arts: Dr C. WARREN
College of Mathematics and Science: Dr GLENDA K. POWERS

UNIVERSITY OF OKLAHOMA

660 Parrington Oval, Norman, OK 73019-0390
Telephone: (405) 325-0311
Founded 1890; opened 1892
Campuses at Norman, Oklahoma City and Tulsa
State control
Academic year: August to May (summer session June and July)
President: DAVID L. BOREN
Vice-President for Administrative Affairs, Norman Campus: JERRY B. FARLEY
Vice-President for University Affairs, Norman Campus: FRED J. BENNETT
Vice-President for Administrative Affairs, Health Sciences Center: MARK LEMONS
Associate Vice-President for Health Sciences, Health Sciences Center: MARCIA M. MORRIS
Number of teachers: 1,552 full-time, 336 part-time
Number of students: 24,869
Publications: *University of Oklahoma Bulletin* (2 a month), *World Literature Today* (quarterly), *Oklahoma Law Review* (quarterly), *Oklahoma Business Bulletin* (monthly), *American Indian Law Review* (2 a year), *Genre* (quarterly), *Papers on Anthropology* (2 a year), *Comparative Frontiers Studies: An Interdisciplinary Newsletter* (quarterly), *Oklahoma Dentistry Magazine* (2 a year), *Vector* (monthly), *Better Babies* (quarterly), *Oklahoma Geriatric Newsnet* (monthly), *Chronicle* (quarterly).

Norman Campus
Senior Vice-President and Provost: JAMES F. KIMPEL
Registrar: PAUL B. BELL, Jr (acting)
Librarian: SUL LEE

DEANS

College of Architecture: DEBORAH DALTON
College of Arts and Sciences: DAVID A. YOUNG
College of Business Administration: RICHARD A. COSIER
College of Education: FREDERICK H. WOOD, Jr
College of Engineering: BILLY L. CRYNES
College of Fine Arts: DAVID G. WOODS
Graduate College: EDDIE C. SMITH
College of Law: C. PETER GOPLERUD III
College of Liberal Studies: DAN A. DAVIS
University College: PAUL B. BELL, Jr

University of Oklahoma Health Sciences Center

POB 26901, Oklahoma City, OK 73190
Telephone: (405) 271-4000
Founded 1890
Senior Vice-President and Provost: JAY H. STEIN
Registrar: WILLIE V. BRYAN
Librarian: MARTY M. THOMPSON

DEANS

College of Allied Health: LEE HOLDER
College of Dentistry: RUSSELL STRATTON
Graduate College: O. RAY KLING
College of Medicine: DOUGLAS VOTH
College of Nursing: PATRICIA R. FORNI
College of Public Health: BAILUS WALKER
College of Pharmacy: VICTOR YANCHICK
College of Medicine, Tulsa: HAROLD L. BROOKS

UNIVERSITY OF SCIENCE AND ARTS OF OKLAHOMA

POB 82345, Chickasha, OK 73018-0001
Telephone: (405) 224-3140
Fax: (405) 521-6244
Founded 1908
State-supported college
President: Dr ROY TROUTT
Vice-President for Academic Affairs: Dr JOHN FEAVER
Vice-President for Fiscal Affairs: NICK WIDENER
Vice-President for Administrative Affairs: TERRY WINN
Librarian: MARTHA WOLTZ
Library of 97,000 vols
Number of teachers: 55
Number of students: 1,393
Publication: *Trend*.

UNIVERSITY OF TULSA

600 South College Ave, Tulsa, OK 74104
Telephone: (918) 631-2305
Fax: (918) 631-2247
E-mail: elisso@centum.utulsa.edu
Founded as Henry Kendall College under Presbyterian control 1894, reorganized and name changed to University of Tulsa 1920; became non-denominational 1928
Independent control
Academic year: August to May
President: ROBERT W. LAWLESS
Provost and Senior Vice-President: LEWIS M. DUNCAN
Vice-Presidents: ROY A. RUFFNER (Business and Finance), ALLEN R. SOLTOW (Vice-President for Student Development, acting)
LARRY D. RICE (Vice-President for Institutional Advancement, acting)
Executive Director of Research, Sponsored Programs and Government Relations: ALLEN R. SOLTOW
Registrar: RUTH V. LANGSTON
Director of Libraries: ROBERT H. PATTERSON
Number of teachers: 408
Number of students: 4,236
Publications: *James Joyce Quarterly*, *University of Tulsa Magazine*.

DEANS

Henry Kendall College of Arts and Sciences: THOMAS A. HORNE
College of Business Administration: RODNEY H. MABRY
College of Engineering and Applied Science: STEVEN J. BELLOVICH
College of Law: MARTIN H. BELSKY
Research and Graduate Studies: JANET A. HAGGERTY
Continuing Education: MILLARD L. JARRETT

PROFESSORS

ADAMS, C. W., Law
ALLISON, G. D., Law
ARIMAN, T., Chemical Engineering
ARNOLD, M. T., Law
AZAR, J. J., Petroleum Engineering
BACKER, L. C., Law
BAILEY, G. A., Anthropology
BARKER, C. G., Geosciences
BEY, R. P., Finance
BOWEN, D. D., Management and Marketing
BRADLEY, J. C., History
BRILL, J. P., Petroleum Engineering
BUCKLEY, T. H., History
CAGLEY, J. W., Management and Marketing
CAIRNS, T. W., Mathematics and Computer Science
CAPALDI, N., Philosophy and Religion
CERRO, R. L., Chemical Engineering
CHRISTENSEN, J. M., Communication Disorders
CLARK, D. S., Law
COLLIER, G. E., Biological Science
COLLINS, J. M., Finance
COOK, D. B., Theatre
DE ALMEIDA, H. B., English
DIAZ, J. C., Mathematics and Computer Science
DONALDSON, R. H., Political Science
DUGGER, W. M., Economics

Durham, M. O., Electrical Engineering
Eisenach, E. J., Political Science
Feldman, S. M., Law
Frey, M. A., Law
Gilpin, G. H., English
Green, J. E., Education
Guruswamy, L. D., NELPI
Hall, R. L., Education
Hansson, R. O., Psychology
Hennessee, P. A., Accounting
Henry, D. O., Anthropology
Hicks, J. F., Law
Hipsher, W. L., Education
Hittinger, F. R., Philosophy and Religion
Hogan, R. T., Psychology
Holland, T. L., Law
Hollander, A. S., Accounting
Hollingsworth, W. G., Law
Howard, R. E., Chemistry
Hyatte, R. L., Languages
Johnson, D. M., Education
Kane, G. R., Electrical Engineering
Kelkar, B. G., Petroleum Engineering
Kestner, J. A., English
Kinsey, B. A., Sociology
Lacey, L. J., Law
Letcher, J. H., Mathematics and Computer Science
Lewicki, P., Psychology
Lindstrom, L. C., Anthropology
Luce, T. S., Psychology
Luks, K. D., Chemical Engineering
Manhart, T. A., Art
Manning, F. S., Chemical Engineering
Mansfield, M. E., NELPI
Martin, B. C., Nursing
Miska, S. Z., Petroleum Engineering
Monroe, R. J., Finance
Neidell, L. A., Management and Marketing
Norberg, A. H., Music
Odell, G. H., Anthropology
Parker, J. C., Law
Predl, R. E., Music
Rahe, P. A., History
Redner, R. A., Mathematics and Computer Science
Reeder, R. L., Biological Science
Resnick, M. C., Languages
Reynolds, A. C., Petroleum Engineering
Ronda, J. P., History
Russell, R. A., Management Information Systems
Rybicki, E. F., Mechanical Engineering
Samiee, S., Management and Marketing
Schmidt, Z., Petroleum Engineering
Schoenefeld, D. A., Mathematics and Computer Science
Schwartz, B., Law
Shadley, J. R., Mechanical Engineering
Shoham, O., Petroleum Engineering
Steib, S., Economics
Strattan, R. D., Electrical Engineering
Sublette, K. L., Chemical Engineering
Sumner, S. C., Art
Taylor, G. O., English
Thomas, J. C., Law
Tipton, S. M., Mechanical Engineering
Vozikis, G. S., Bovaird Chair
Wainwright, R. L., Mathematics and Computer Science
Watson, J. G., English
Whalen, M. E., Anthropology
Wolfe, J. A., Management and Marketing
Yasser, R. L., Law
Zedalis, R. J., NELPI

OREGON

EASTERN OREGON STATE COLLEGE

La Grande, OR 97850
Telephone: (503) 962-3672
Founded 1929

President: David E. Gilbert
Dean of Academic Affairs: James Hottois
Dean of Student Affairs: Richard Stenard
Dean of Administration: Mary Voves
Director of College Relations: Jerry Blanche
Director of Regional Services Institute: Terry Edvalson
Dean of Extended Programs: Dixie Lund
Director of Libraries: Patricia Cutright

Library of 103,000 vols
Number of teachers: 150
Number of students: 1,818

DEANS

School of Administrative Studies: Robert Larison
School of Arts and Sciences: Gerald E. Young
School of Education: Jens Robinson

GEORGE FOX UNIVERSITY

Newberg, OR 97132
Telephone: (503) 538-8383
Fax: (503) 537-3830

Founded 1891

President: H. David Brandt
Director of Admissions: Jeffrey Rickey
Vice-President for Academic Affairs: Jim Foster
Vice-President for Finance: Donald Millage
Vice-President for Development: Dana Miller
Vice-President for Enrollment Services: Andrea Cook
Vice-President for Student Life: Eileen Hulme
Executive Assistant to the President: Barry Hubbell
Librarian: Merrill Johnson

Library of 190,000 vols
Number of teachers: 110
Number of students: 2,300

Publication: *Life* (every 2 months).

LEWIS AND CLARK COLLEGE

Portland, OR 97219
Telephone: (503) 768-7055
Fax: (503) 768-7055

Founded 1867

President: Michael Mooney
Dean of College of Arts and Sciences: Jane Atkinson
Dean of Law School: James Huffman
Dean of Graduate School: Jay Casbon
Vice-President for Business and Finance: Wayne Pederson
Vice-President for College Relations: Scott Staff
Registrar: Anne Price
Librarian: Johanna Scherrer

Library of 609,485 vols
Number of teachers: 200
Number of students: 3,388

Publication: *Journal*.

LINFIELD COLLEGE

900 S.E. Baker St, McMinnville, OR 97128-6894

Telephone: (541) 434-2200
Fax: (541) 434-2215

Founded 1849

President: Dr Vivian A. Bull
Vice-President for Academic Affairs: Dr Marvin Henberg
Registrar: Robert Bosanac

Library of 135,000 vols
Number of teachers: 130 full-time, 135 part-time
Number of students: 2,204 (f.t.e.)

NORTHWEST CHRISTIAN COLLEGE

828 E. 11th, Eugene, OR 97401
Telephone: (541) 343-1641
Fax: (541) 343-9159

Founded 1895

President: James E. Womack
Director of Admissions: Randolph Jones
Librarian: Margaret Sue Rhee

Library of 65,000 vols
Number of teachers: 18
Number of students: 468

OREGON HEALTH SCIENCES UNIVERSITY

Portland, OR 97201
Telephone: (503) 494-8311

President: Dr Peter O. Kohler
Chief Financial Officer: James Walker
Director, University Hospital: Timothy Goldfarb
Dean, School of Dentistry: Dr Henry Van Hassel
Dean School of Medicine: Dr Joseph Bloom (acting)
Dean, School of Nursing: Dr Kate Potempa
Director, Crippled Children's Division: Dr Jerry Sells

Library of 180,000 vols

OREGON STATE UNIVERSITY

Corvallis, OR 97331
Telephone: (541) 737-0123
Fax: (541) 737-2400

Founded 1868
State control
Academic year: September to June

President: Paul G. Risser
Provost and Executive Vice-President: Roy G. Arnold
Vice-Provost for Student Affairs: Larry D. Roper
Vice-President for Finance and Administration: Mark E. McCambridge (interim)
Vice-Provost for Research: Wilson C. Hayes
Vice-President for University Advancement: Orcilia Zúñiga Forbes
Associate Provost for Academic Affairs: Andrew G. Hashimoto
Associate Provost for Information Services: Curt L. Pederson
Registrar: Barbara S. Balz
Librarian: Karyle Butcher (acting)

Library of 1,317,300 vols, 2,110,419 microfilms
Number of teachers: 2,270
Number of students: 14,127

Publications: *Oregon Stater, Yearbook of Asscn of Pacific Coast Geographers, OSU Bulletin* (quarterly), *OSU Fact Book, OSU Facts, OSU Enrollment Summary, OSU Graduation Summary, Beaver* (yearbook), *Fusser's Guide* (student directory), *Prism* (literary magazine), *The Daily Barometer* (newspaper).

DEANS

Graduate School: Thomas J. Maresh
College of Agricultural Sciences: Thayne R. Dutson
College of Business: Donald F. Parker
School of Education: Wayne Havorsen
College of Engineering: Thomas W. West (acting)
College of Forestry: George W. Brown
College of Health and Human Performance: Timothy P. White
College of Home Economics and Education: Kinsey B. Green
College of Liberal Arts: Kay F. Schaffer
College of Oceanic and Atmospheric Sciences: G. Brent Dalrymple
College of Pharmacy: Richard A. Ohvall

College of Science: FREDERICK H. HORNE
College of Veterinary Medicine: ROBERT C. WILSON
University Honors College: JON HENDRICKS

PACIFIC UNIVERSITY

College Way, Forest Grove, OR 97116
Telephone: (503) 357-6151
Founded 1849
President: Dr FAITH GABELNICK
Registrar: JOHN SNODGRASS
Dean of Enrollment Management: JESSE WELCH
Library Management Team Co-ordinator: ALEX TOTH
Library of 135,360 vols, 130,086 US documents, 1,670 Oregon documents
Number of teachers: 79 full-time
Number of students: 1,750 (f.t.e.)

PORTLAND STATE UNIVERSITY

POB 751, Portland, OR 97207-0751
Telephone: (503) 725-4433
Fax: (503) 725-4882
Founded 1946
Academic year: September to June (and Summer Session)
President: DANIEL O. BERNSTINE
Provost: MICHAEL F. REARDON
Vice-President for Finance and Administration: GEORGE PERNSTEINER
Vice-Provost: SHERWIN DAVIDSON
Vice-Provost for Academic Program Operations: RODERIC C. DIMAN
Vice-Provost for Graduate Studies and Research: WILLIAM FEYERHERM
Vice-Provost and Dean of Student and Enrollment Services: JANINE ALLEN
Director of Admissions: AGNES HOFFMAN (interim)
Director of Library: C. THOMAS PFINGSTEN
Library of 1,091,200 vols
Number of teachers: 766
Number of students: 14,863
Publications: *PSU General Catalog, PSU Magazine,* various school catalogues and brochures.

DEANS

College of Liberal Arts and Sciences: MARVIN KAISER
School of Business Administration: ROGER AHLBRANDT
Graduate School of Social Work: JAMES H. WARD
School of Education: PHYLLIS EDMONDSON
School of Fine and Performing Arts: ROBERT SYLVESTER
College of Urban and Public Affairs: NOHAD A. TOULAN
School of Engineering and Applied Science: ROBERT DRYDEN
School of Extended Studies: SHERWIN L. DAVIDSON

REED COLLEGE

3203 SE Woodstock Blvd, Portland, OR 97202-8199
Telephone: (503) 771-1112
Founded 1909
President: STEVEN S. KOBLIK
Dean of the Faculty: PETER STEINBERGER
Executive Vice-President: LARRY D. LARGE
Vice-President and Treasurer: EDWIN O. MCFARLANE
Vice-President and Dean of Student Services: JAMES S. TEDERMAN
Registrar: NORA MCLAUGHLIN
Director of Institutional Research: JON W. RIVENBURG
Director of Computing and Information Systems: MARTIN RINGLE
Dean of Admission: NANCY DONEHOWER
Librarian: VICTORIA HANAWALT
Library of 345,000 vols
Number of teachers: 130
Number of students: 1,200

SOUTHERN OREGON UNIVERSITY

Ashland, OR 97520
Telephone: (541) 552-6111
Fax: (541) 552-6337
Founded 1926
President: STEPHEN J. RENO
Registrar: CHARLOTTE YOUNG
Provost: SARA HOPKINS-POWELL
Librarian: SUE A. BURKHOLDER
Library of 375,000 vols including bound periodicals, 200,000 government documents, 600,000 items on microfilm
Number of teachers: 220
Number of students: 4,800

UNIVERSITY OF OREGON

Eugene, OR 97403-1242
Telephone: (541) 346-3111
Fax: (541) 346-2537
E-mail: fdyke@oregon.uoregon.edu
Established 1872; opened 1876
State control
Academic year: September to June
President: DAVID FROHNMAYER
Vice-President for Administration: DANIEL A. WILLIAMS
Vice-President for Academic Affairs: JOHN MOSELEY
Vice-President for Public Affairs and Development: DUNCAN MCDONALD
Vice-Provost for Research: TOM DYKE
Vice-Provost for Academic Affairs: LORRAINE DAVIS
Chancellor: JOSEPH COX
Registrar: HERB CHERECK
Librarian: GEORGE W. SHIPMAN
Library: see Libraries
Number of teachers: 1,168
Number of students: 17,207
Publications: *University of Oregon Bulletins, University of Oregon Books, Comparative Literature, Oregon Law Review, Oregon Business Review* (quarterly), *Physical Education Microcards, Governmental Research Bulletins, Imprint Oregon, Northwest Review, Bulletin of the Museum of Natural History.*

DEANS

Graduate School: MARIAN FRIESTAD
College of Arts and Sciences: JOE A. STONE
School of Architecture and Allied Arts: ROBERT MELNICK
College of Business Administration: DALE MORSE
College of Education: MARTIN KAUFMAN
School of Journalism: TIMOTHY GLEASON
School of Law: RENNARD STRICKLAND
School of Music: ANNE DHU MCLUCAS

PROFESSORS

ACRES, A. J., Art History
AGUIRRE, C. A., History
AIKENS, C. M., Anthropology
ALBAUM, G. S., Business
ALBERTGALTIER, A., Romance Languages
ALLEY, H. M., Honors College
ALPERT, L. J., Fine Arts
ALTMANN, B., Romance Languages
ANDERSON, F. W., Mathematics
ANDERSON, M. C., Psychology
ANDERSON, S. C., German
ANDERSON-INMAN, L., Education Policy and Management
AOKI, K., Law
ARIOLA, Z., Computer and Information Science
ASH, A. D., Political Science
AXLINE, M. D., Law
AYRES, W. S., Anthropology
BALDWIN, D. A., Psychology
BALDWIN, J. H., Planning Public Policy Management
BAMBURY, J. E., Architecture
BARACCHI, C., Philsophy
BARKAN, A., Biology
BARNES, B. A., Mathematics
BARNHARD, R. J., Chemistry
BARR, S. A., Dance
BARTLEIN, P., Geography
BARTON, R. F., Theatre Arts
BAUGH, W. H., Political Science
BAUMGOLD, D. J., Political Science
BAYLESS, M. J., English
BELITZ, D., Physics
BENDER, S. W., Law
BENGSTON, M. C., Fine Arts
BENNETT, R. W., Music
BENZ, M. R., Education Policy and Management
BERK, G. P., Political Science
BEST, R. J., Business
BEUDERT, M. C., Music
BIERSACK, A., Anthropology
BIRN, R. F., History
BIVINS, T. H., Journalism
BJERRE, C., Law
BLANDY, D. E., Arts and Administration
BLONIGEN, B. A., Economics
BOGEL, C. J., Art History
BOLTON, C. R., Recreation and Tourist Management
BONDS, A. B., Theatre Arts
BONINE, J. E., Law
BOREN, J. L., English
BOROVSKY, Z. P., German
BOSS, J. F., III, Music
BOTHUN, G. D., Physics
BOTVINNIK, B., Mathematics
BOUSH, D. M., Business
BOWDITCH, P. L., Classics
BOWERMAN, B. A., Biology
BOYNTON, S. L., Music
BRADSHAW, W. E., Biology
BRANCHAUD, B. P., Chemistry
BRAU, J. E., Physics
BRICK, H., History
BRICKER, D. D., Special Education
BRODIE, D. W., Law
BROKAW, C. J., History
BROWN, G. Z., Architecture
BROWN, S. T., East Asian Languages
BROWN, W. B., Business
BROX, R. M., Romance Languages
BULLIS, M. D., Education Policy and Management
BURRIS, V. L., Sociology
BUSTAMANTE, C. J., Chemistry
BYBEE, C. R., Journalism
BYRD, B. K., Labor Education Center
CALHOON, K. S., German
CALIN, F. G., Romance Languages
CAMPBELL, E. A., Music
CAPALDI, R. A., Biology
CARMICHAEL, H. J., Physics
CARNINE, D. W, Education Policy and Management
CARPENTER, G. M., Recreaction and Tourism Management
CARPENTER, K. L., Linguistics
CARROLL, G. C., Biology
CARTER, L. R., Sociology
CARTIER, C. L., Geography
CARTWRIGHT, V., Architecture
CASHMAN, K. V., Geological Sciences
CASTENHOLZ, R. W., Biology
CASTILLO, D., Romance Languages
CHALMERS, J. M., Business
CHANDLER, V. L., Biology
CHANEY, R. P., Anthropology
CHATFIELD, S. J., Dance

CHENG, N. YEN-WEN, Architecture
CINA, J., Chemistry
CLARK, R., Music
CLARK, S., English
COGAN, F. B., Honors College
COHEN, J. D., Physics
COHEN, S. E., Geography
COLEMAN, E. L., II, English
COLLIN, R. M., Law
COLLINS, P. F., Psychology
CONERY, J. S., Computer and Information Science
CONLEY, D. T., Education Policy and Management
CORNER, D. B., Architecture
CRAIG, J. P., Dance
CROSSWHITE, J. R., English
CRUMB, D. R., Music
CRUZ J., Romance Languages
CSONKA, P. L., Physics
CUNY, J., Computer and Information Science
DAHLQUIST, F. W., Chemistry
DANN, L. Y., Business
DARST, R. G., Political Science
DAVIE, W. E., Philosophy
DAVIES, P. H., Creative Writing
DAVIS, H., Architecture
DAVIS, R. L., Romance Languages
DAWSON, J. I., Political Science
DEGGE, R. M., Arts and Administration
DELANCEY, S. C., Linguistics
DELGUERCIO, D. G., Business
DENNIS, M., History
DESCUTNER, J. W., Dance
DESHPANDE, N. G., Physics
DEVRIES, P. J., Biology
DIAMOND, I., Political Science
DICKMAN, A. W., Biology
DIETHELM, J. K., Landscape Architecture
DISHION, T. J., Special Education
DOERKSEN, D. P., Music
DOERKSEN, P. F., Music
DOLEZAL, M.-L., Art History
DORSEY, R. J., Geological Science
DOUGLAS, S. A., Computer and Information Science
DOWD, C. R., Music
DOWNES, B. T., Planning Public Policy Management
DOXSEE, K. M., Chemistry
DREILING, M. C., Sociology
DUFEK, J. S., Exercise and Movement Sciences
DUFF, S. F., Architecture
DUGAW, D. M., English
DUNCAN, I. H., English
DURRANT, S., East Asian Languages
DYER, M. N., Mathematics
DYKE, T. R., Chemistry
EARL, J. W., English
EDSON, C. H., Education Policy and Management
EISEN, J. S., Biology
ELLIS, C. J., Economics
EMLET, R. B., Biology
ENGELKING, P. C., Chemistry
EPPLE, J. A., Romance Languages
EPPS, G., Law
EPSTEIN, M., East Asian Languages
ERLANDSON, J. M., Anthropology
ETTINGER, L. F., Arts and Administration
EVANS, G. W., Economics
EXTON, D., Chemistry
FAGOT, B. I., Psychology
FAIR, L. J., History
FANG, Y., Business
FARLEY, A. M., Computer and Information Science
FARWELL, M. R., English
FICKAS, S. F., Computer and Information Science
FIGLIO, D. N., Economics
FISHLEN, M. B., East Asian Languages
FLYNN, G. C., Chemistry
FORD, K. J., English
FORELL, C. A., Law
FOSTER, J. B., Sociology
FRACCHIA, J. G., Honors College
FRANK, D. A., Honors College
FRANKLIN, J. D., Journalism
FRAZIER, G. V., Business
FREINKEL, L. A., English
FREY, R. E., Physics
FREYD, J. J., Psychology
FRIESTAD, M. S., Business
FRISHKOFF, P., Business
FRY, G., International Studies
FUJII, N., East Asian Languages
FULLER, L. O., Sociology
GAGE, J. T., English
GALE, M. K., Planning Public Policy Management
GALL, M. D., Education Policy and Management
GARCIA-PABON, L., Romance Languages
GARY, S. N., Law
GASSAMA, I. J., Law
GAST, W. G., Architecture
GENASCI, D. B., Architecture
GEORGE, K. M., Anthropology
GEORGE, O., English
GERBER, T. P., Sociology
GERNON, H., Business
GERSTEN, R. M., Special Education
GILKEY, P. B., Mathematics
GILLAND, W. G., Architecture
GIRLING, C. L., Landscape Architecture
GIVON, T., Linguistics
GLADHART, A., Romance Languages
GLASER, S. R., Business
GLEASON-RICKER, M. M., Education Policy and Management
GLOVER, E., Special Education
GOBLE, A. E., History
GOLDMAN, M. S., Sociology
GOLDMAN, P., Education Policy and Management
GOLDRICH, D., Political Science
GOLDSCHMIDT, S. M., Education Policy and Management
GOLES, G. G., Geological Sciences
GOOD, R. H. III, Special Education
GOODMAN, B., History
GORDON-LICKEY, B., Psychology
GORDON-LICKEY, M., Psychology
GOULD, E., Romance Languages
GRAFF, R. J., Fine Arts
GRAY, J., Biology
GRAY, J. A., Economics
GREENE, F. D., Law
GREENE, R. A., Comparative Literature
GREENLAND, D. E., Geography
GREGORY, S., Physics
GRIFFITH, O. H., Chemistry
GROSENICK, J. K., Education Policy and Management
GRUDIN, R., English
GWARTNEY, P., Sociology
HACKMAN, R. M., Academic Affairs
HALEY, M. M., Chemistry
HANES, J. E., History
HARBAUGH, W. T., Economics
HARFORD, W. T., Business
HARRIS, L. J., Law
HARVEY, S. M., Anthropology
HASKETT, R. S., History
HATON, D. S., Music
HAUSHALTER, G. D., Business
HAWKINS, D. I., Business
HAWLEY, D. K., Chemistry
HAWN, A. W., Architecture
HAYDOCK, R., Physics
HAYNES, S. E., Economics
HECKER, S. F., Labor Education Center
HELPHAND, K. I., Landscape Architecture
HERRICK, D. R., Chemistry
HESSLER, J. M., History
HIBBARD, J., Planning Public Policy Management
HIBBARD, M. J., Planning Public Policy Management
HICKMAN, R. C., Fine Arts
HILDRETH, R. G., Law
HINTZMAN, D. L., Psychology
HO, S., Architecture
HODGES, S. D., Psychology
HOKANSON, K. E., Comparative Literature
HOLCOMB, J. M., Fine Arts
HOLLAND, M. J., Law
HOLLANDER, J. A., Sociology
HONGO, G. K., Creative Writing
HORNER, R. H., Center on Human Development
HOSAGRAHAR, J., Architecture
HOUSWORTH, E. A., Mathematics
HOWARD, D. R., Business
HUDSON, B. S., Chemistry
HUHNDORF, S. M., English
HULSE, D. W., Landscape Architecture
HUMMER, T. R., Creative Writing
HUMPHREYS, E. D., Geological Sciences
HURWIT, J. M., Art History
HURWITZ, R., Music
HUTCHINSON, J., Chemistry
HYMAN, R., Psychology
IMAMURA, J. N., Physics
ISENBERG, J., Mathematics
JACOBS, D., Political Science
JACOBSON, J. L., Law
JACOBSON-TEPFER, E., Art History
JAEGER, M. K., Classics
JEWETT, W. J., Architecture
JOHNSON, B. R., Landscape Architecture
JOHNSON, D. C., Chemistry
JOHNSON, L. B., Fine Arts
JOHNSON, L. T., Architecture
JOHNSON, M. L., Philosophy
JOHNSTON, A. D., Geological Sciences
JONES, B. J. K., Arts and Administration
JONES, S. I., Landscape Architecture
KAHLE, L. R., Business
KAMEENUI, E. J., Education Policy and Management
KANAGY, R., East Asian Languages
KANTOR, W. M., Mathematics
KARLYN, K., English
KATAOKA, H. C., East Asian Languages
KAYS, M. A., Geological Sciences
KEANA, J. F. W., Chemistry
KELLETT, R. W., Architecture
KELLMAN, M. E., Chemistry
KELSKY, K. L., Anthropology
KEMPNER, K. M., Education Policy and Management
KESSLER, L. J., Journalism
KEVAN, S. D., Physics
KEYES, P. A., Architecture
KIMBALL, R. A., History
KIMBLE, D. P., Psychology
KIMMEL, C. B., Biology
KING, R. D., Business
KINTZ, L. C., English
KIRKPATRICK, L. C., Law
KLESHCHEV, A., Mathematics
KLOPPENBERG, L. A., Law
KLUG, G. A., Exercise and Movement Sciences
KOCH, R. M., Mathematics
KOHL, S. W., East Asian Languages
KOKIS, G., Fine Arts
KOLPIN, V. W., Economics
KOREISHA, S. G., Business
KRAMER, D. F., Music
KRAUS, R. C., Political Science
KRUSOE, S., Fine Arts
KYR, R. H., Music
LAFER, G. C., Labour Education
LANDE, R., Biology
LARSON, S., Music
LARSON, S. J., English
LARSON, W. A., East Asian Languages
LASKAYA, C. A., English
LAUX, D. L., Creative Writing
LAVERY, R. M., Journalism
LAWRENCE, M. S., Law
LEAHY, J. V., Mathematics
LEE, C.-R., Creative Writing
LEES, C. A., English
LEFEVRE, H. W., Physics
LEONG, A., Russian

LESAGE, J. L., English
LEVI, D. S., Philosophy
LIBERMAN, K. B., Sociology
LIBESKIND, S., Mathematics
LIN, H., Mathematics
LIVELYBROOKS, D. W., Physics
LO, V. M., Computer and Information Science
LOCKERY, S. R., Biology
LONERGAN, M., Chemistry
LONG, J. W., Chemistry
LOVINGER, R. J., Landscape Architecture
LOWENSTAM, S. D., Classics
LUCKTENBERG, K., Music
LUEBKE, D. M., History
LUKACS, J. R., Anthropology
LUKS, E. M., Computer and Information Science
LYNCH, M. R., Biology
LYONS, R. M., Creative Writing
LYSAKER, J. T., Philosophy
MADDEX, J. P., Jr, History
MADRIGAL, R., Business
MAITLAND-GHOLSON, J. C., Arts and Administration
MALLE, B. F., Psychology
MALLINCKRODT, B. S., Counselling Psychology
MALONY, A., Computer and Information Science
MALSCH, D. L., Linguistics
MANCE, A. M., English
MANGA, M., Geological Sciences
MARCUS, A. H., Chemistry
MARROCCO, R. T., Psychology
MARTIN, G. M., Music
MARTINS, E., Biology
MATE, M., History
MATHAS, A., German
MATSUNAGA, S. R., Business
MATTHEWS, B. W., Physics
MATTHEWS, K. M., Architecture
MAURO, R., Psychology
MAVES, L. C., Jr, Music
MAXWELL, A., Journalism
MAY, B. D., Romance Languages
MAY, G. A., History
MCCOLE, J. J., History
MCDOWELL, P. F., Geography
MCGOWEN, R. E., History
MCKERNIE, G., Theatre Arts
MCLAUCHLAN, G., Sociology
MCWHIRTER, B. T., Behaviour and Communication Sciences
MCWHIRTER, E. H., Behaviour and Communication Sciences
MEDLER, J. F., Political Science
MEEKS-WAGNER, D. R., Biology
MELONE, N. P., Business
MERSKIN, D. L., Journalism
MEYER, A. D., Business
MEYER, G. W., Computer and Information Science
MIKKELSON, W. H., Business
MILLS, P. K., Business
MITCHELL, R. B., Political Science
MOHR, J. C., History
MONROE, S. M., Psychology
MOONEY, R. J., Law
MOORE, J. R., Music
MOORE, R. S., Music
MORENO-BLACK, G., Anthropology
MORGEN, S. L., Sociology
MORROGH, A., Art History
MORSE, D. C., Business
MOSES, L., Psychology
MOSS, M. L., Anthropology
MOSSBERG, T. W., Physics
MOURSUND, D. G., Education Policy and Management
MOURSUND, J. P., Counselling Psychology
MOWDAY, R. T., Business
MOYE, G. W., Architecture
MURPHY, A. B., Geography
MYAGKOV, M. G., Political Science
NATELLA, D. C., Fine Arts
NEAL, L. L., Recreation and Tourism Management

NEVILLE, H., Psychology
NICHOLSON, K., Art History
NICOLS, J., History
NIPPOLD., M. A., Special Education
NOVKOV, J. L., Political Science
O'BRIEN, R. M., Sociology
O'CONNELL, K. R., Fine Arts
O'FALLON, J. M., Law
O'KEEFE, T., Business
ORBELL, J. M., Political Science
OSTERNIG, L. R., Exercise and Movement Sciences
OSTLER, J., History
OVERLEY, J. C., Physics
OWEN, H. J., Music
OWEN, S. W., Music
PAGE, C. J., Chemistry
PAINTER, R. W., Law
PALMER, T. W., Mathematics
PAN, Y., Business
PARIS, M. L., Law
PARK, K., Physics
PARTCH, M. M., Business
PASCOE, P. A., History
PAUL, K. H., Fine Arts
PAYNE, D. L., Linguistics
PENA, R. B., Architecture
PEPPIS, P. W., English
PETING, D. L., Architecture
PETTINARI, J. A., Architecture
PHILLIPS, N. C., Mathematics
PICKETT, B. S., Fine Arts
PIELE, P. K., Education Policy and Management
POLOGE, S., Music
PONDER, S. E., Journalism
PONTO, R. D., Music
POPE, B. C., Women's Studies
POPE, D. A., History
POSNER, M. I., Psychology
POSTLETHWAIT, J. H., Biology
POVEY, D. C., Planning Public Policy Management
POWELL, D. T., Fine Arts
PRATT, S. L., Philosophy
PRENTICE, M. H., Fine Arts
PROSKUROWSKI, A., Computer and Information Science
PROUDFOOT, R. C., International Studies
PSAKI, F. R., Romance Languages
PYLE, F. B., III, English
RACETTE, G. A., Business
RAISKIN, J. L., Women's Studies
RAMIREZ, E. C., Theatre Arts
RAMSING, K. D., Business
RAVITS, M. A., Women's Studies
RAYFIELD, G. W., Physics
RAYMER, M. G., Physics
RECKER, G. W., Music
REED, M. H., Geological Sciences
REMINGTON, S. J., Physics
RETALLACK, G. J., Geological Sciences
REYNOLDS, J. S., Architecture
RIBE, R. G., Landscape Architecture
RICE, J. L., Russian
RICE, J. M., Geological Sciences
RICE, K. S., Physical Education and Recreation Services
RICHARDS, L. E., Business
RICHMOND, G. L., Chemistry
ROBERTS, W. M., Biology
ROBINSON, D. M., Journalism
ROCHA, E., Planning Public Policy Management
ROCKETT, G. W., English
RONDEAU, J. F., History
ROSE, J., Theatre Arts
ROSS, K. A., Mathematics
ROSSI, W. J., English
ROTH, L. M., Art History
ROTHBART, M. K., Psychology
ROTHBART, M., Psychology
ROWE, G. E., English
ROWELL, J., Architecture
RUSH, K. L., Behaviour and Communication Sciences

RUSSIAL, J. T., Journalism
RUSSO, M. V., Business
RYAN, C. C., Philosophy
RYAN, W. E., II, Journalism
SABRY, A., Computer and Information Science
SADOFSKY, H., Mathematics
SANG, T., East Asian Languages
SARANPA, K., German
SAUCIER, G. T., Psychology
SAYRE, G. M., English
SCHACHTER, J., Linguistics
SCHOMBERT, J. M., Physics
SCHULTZ, K. L., German
SCHUMAN, D., Law
SCHWARZ, I. E., Special Education
SEGALL, Z., Computer and Information Science
SEITZ, G. M., Mathematics
SELKER, E. U., Biology
SERCEL, P. C., Physics
SHANKMAN, S., English
SHANKS, A. L., Institute of Marine Biology
SHAO, Q. M., Mathematics
SHAPIRO, L., Biology
SHELTON, B. S., Mathematics
SHERER, P. D., Business
SHERIDAN, G. J., Jr, History
SHERMAN, S. R., English
SHINN, M. R., Special Education
SHURTZ, N. E., Law
SIERADSKI, A. J., Mathematics
SILVA, E. C., Economics
SILVERMAN, C. T., Anthropology
SIMMONS, D. C., Education Policy and Management
SIMMONS, W. S., Art History
SIMONDS, P. E., Anthropology
SIMONS, A. D., Psychology
SIMONSEN, W. S., Planning Public Policy Management
SINGELL, L. D., Jr, Economics
SISLEY, B. L., Physical Education and Recreation Services
SKALNES, L., Political Science
SLOVIC, P., Psychology
SMITH, J. R., Business
SMITH, M. E., Music
SOHLBERG, M. M., Behavioural and Communication Sciences
SOHLICH, W. F., Romance Languages
SOKOLOFF, D. R., Physics
SOPER, D. E., Physics
SOUTHWELL, P., Political Science
SPALTENSTEIN, J. N., Mathematics
SPRAGUE, G. F., Jr, Biology
SPRAGUE, K. U., Biology
STAHL, F. W., Biology
STAVITSKY, A. G., Journalism
STEEVES, H. L., Journalism
STEIN, A. J., Sociology
STEIN, R. L., English
STEINHARDT, V., Music
STEVENS, K. A., Computer and Information Science
STEVENS, T. H., Chemistry
STEVENSON, R. C., English
STOCKARD, A. J., Sociology
STOLET, J., Dance
STONE, J. A., Economics
STORMSHAK, E. A., Behaviour and Communication Sciences
STRAKA, L. M., Music
STROM, D. M., Physics
SUGAI, G. M., Education Policy and Management
SUNDT, R. A., Art History
SUTTMEIER, R. P., Political Science
SWAN, P. N., Law
SZURMUK, M., Romance Languages
TAKAHASHI, T. T., Biology
TAN, Y., Fine Arts
TAYLOR, M. E., Psychology
TAYLOR, Q., Jr, History
TEDARDS, A. B., Music
TEICH, N., English
TERBORG, J. R., Business
TERWILLIGER, N. B., Biology

THALLON, R., Architecture
THEODOROPOULOS, C., Architecture
THOMA, M. A., Economics
THOMAS, S., Mathematics
THOMPSON, A. C., Religious Studies
TICE, J. T., Architecture
TINDAL, G., Education Policy and Management
TIRAS, S. L., Business
TOKUNO, K., Religious Studies
TOMLIN, R., Linguistics
TONER, J., Physics
TOOMEY, D. R., Geological Sciences
TROMBLEY, R., Music
TUAN, M. H. C., Sociology
TUANA, N., Philosophy
TUBLITZ, N. J., Biology
TUCKER, D. M., Psychology
TYLER, D. R., Chemistry
UDOVIC, J. D., Biology
UNGSON, G. R., Business
UPSHAW, J. R., Journalism
UTSEY, G. F., Architecture
UTSEY, M. D., Architecture
VAKARELIYSKA, C., Russian
VANDENNOUWELAND, A., Economics
VANHEECKEREN, J.,Business
VAN HOUTEN, D. R., Sociology
VAN SCHEEUWIJCK, M., Music
VARGAS, M., Music
VERSACE, G. T., Music
VETRI, D. R., Law
VITULLI, M. A., Mathematics
VLATTEN, A., German
VONHIPPEL, P. H., Chemistry
WACHTER, C. L., Music
WAFF, H. S., Geological Sciences
WAGLE, K. E., Fine Arts
WALKER, H. M., Center on Human Development
WALKER, P. A., Geography
WANG, H., Physics
WANTA, W. M., Journalism
WARPINSKI, T. L., Fine Arts
WASKO, J., Journalism
WATSON, J. C., Theatre Arts
WEEKS, E. C., Planning Public Policy Management
WEEKS, J. C., Biology
WEINSTEIN, M. G., Business
WEISS, A. M., International Studies
WEISS, J., Romance Languages
WEISS, M. R., Exercise and Movement Sciences
WEISS, R. L., Psychology
WELCH, M. C., Architecture
WELDON, R. J., Geological Sciences
WELKE, B. Y., History
WESTERFIELD, M., Biology
WESTLING, L. H., English
WESTLING, W. T., Law
WESTON, J. A., Biology
WHEELER, T. H., Journalism
WHITELAW, W. E., Economics
WHITLOCK, C. L., Geography
WIDENOR, M. R., Labor Education Center
WILLIAMS, J. P., Music
WILLIAMS, J. R., Theatre Arts
WILLIS, J. H., III, Biology
WILSON, C. B., Computer and Information Science
WILSON, M. C., Classics
WILSON, W. W., Economics
WIXMAN, R., Geography
WOJCIK, D. N., English
WOLFE, A. S., East Asian Languages
WOLFE, J. M., Mathematics
WONHAM, H. B.,English
WOOD, A. M., Biology
WOOD, M. C., Law
WOOD, M. E., English
WOOLLACOTT, M. H., Exercise and Movement Sciences
WRIGHT, C. R. B., Mathematics
WRIGHT, P. L., Business
WYBOURNE, M. N., Physics
XU, D., Mathematics
XU, Y., Mathematics
YOUNG, J. E., Architecture
YOUNG, M. T., Computer Science
YOUNG, P. D., Anthropology
YUZVINSKY, S., Mathematics
ZILIAK, J. P., Economics
ZIMMER, L. K., Architecture
ZIMMERMAN, R. L., Physics
ZINBARG, R., Psychology
ZUCK, O. V., German

ATTACHED INSTITUTES

Institute of Molecular Biology: Dir FREDERICK DAHLQUIST.

Institute of Neurosciences: Dir MONTE WESTERFIELD.

Institute of Theoretical Science: Dir DAVISON SOPER.

Oregon Institute of Marine Biology: Dir LYNDA SHAPIRO.

Solar Energy Center: Dir JOHN S. REYNOLDS.

Advanced Science and Technology Institute: Dir ROBERT MCQUATE.

Oregon Humanities Center: Dir STEVEN SHANKMAN.

Center for the Study of Women in Society: Dir SANDRA MORGEN

Chemical Physics Institute: Dir DAVID HERRICK.

Materials Science Institute: Dir DAVID JOHNSON.

Center for Asian and Pacific Studies: Dir STEPHAN DURRANT.

Institute of Cognitive and Decision Sciences: Dir SARAH DOUGLAS.

Center for Housing Innovation: Dir DONALD B. CORNER.

Center for the Study of Work, Economy and Community: Dir DONALD VAN HOUTEN.

Institute for Sustainable Environment: Dir JOHN BALDWIN

Computational Intelligence Research Laboratory: Dir DAVID ETHERINGTON.

Computational Science Institute: Dirs JOHN S. CONERY, JANICE CLUNY.

International Institute for Sports and Human Performance: Dir HENRIETTE HEINY.

Institute on Violence and Destructive Behavior: Dir HILL WALKER.

Institute for Community Arts: Dir DOUG BRANDY.

Oregon Center for Optics: Dir MICHAEL RAYMER.

UNIVERSITY OF PORTLAND

5000 N Willamette Blvd, Portland, OR 97203
Telephone: (503) 283-7911
Fax: (503) 283-7399

Founded 1901
Private control
Language of instruction: English
Academic year: September to May (two terms and summer session)

President: Rev. DAVID T. TYSON
Academic Vice-President: Bro. DONALD J. STABROWSKI
Vice-President for Financial Affairs: Dr ROY HEYNDERICKX
Vice-President for University Relations: ANTHONY J. DISPIGNO
Vice-President for Student Services: Dr JOHN GOLDRICK
Registrar: MUFTI MCNASSAR
Librarian: RICHARD HINES

Library of 356,000 vols
Number of teachers: 138
Number of students: 2,721

Publications: *The Bulletin, The Log, The Beacon, The Writers, Portland Magazine.*

DEANS

Graduate School: Dr PATRICIA L. CHADWICK
College of Arts and Sciences: Dr MARLENE MOORE
School of Business Administration: Dr RONALD HILL
School of Nursing: Dr TERRY MISENER
School of Engineering: Dr ZIA YAMAYEE
School of Education: Sr MARIA CIRIELLO

PROFESSORS

ADRANGI, B., Business Administration
ALBRIGHT, R. J., Engineering
ARWOOD, E., Education
ASARNOW, H., English and Foreign Languages
ASKAY, R., Philosophy
BECKER, H., Business Administration
DANNER, D. G., Theology
DOYLE, R. O., Music
DRAKE, B. H., Business Administration
DUFF, R., Psychology and Social Science
FALLER, T., Philosophy
FREED, E., Business Administration
GAYLE, B., Communication Studies
GOVEIA, J., Business Administration
GRITTA, P. R., Business Administration
HICKS, F., Nursing
HOSINSKI, Rev. T., Theology
KHAN, K. H., Engineering
KOLMES, S., Biology
LINCOLN, S., Chemistry
LUM, L., Mathematics and Computer Science
MALE, J., Engineering
MASSON, L., English
MAYR, F. K., Philosophy
MURTY, D., Engineering
RUTHERFORD, H. R., Theology
SHERRER, Rev. C., English and Foreign Languages
SNOW, M., Physics
SOBOSAN, Rev. J., Theology
UTLAUT, M., Physics
WETZEL, K. J., Physics
ZIMMERMAN, L., History

WARNER PACIFIC COLLEGE

2219 SE 68th Ave, Portland, OR 97215
Telephone: (503) 775-4366
Fax: (503) 775-8853

Founded 1937

President: JAY A. BARBER, Jr
Provost: (vacant)
Registrar: JOHN BARBER
Dean of Faculty: JOHN W. HAWTHORNE
General Library Administrator: ALICE KIENBERGER

Library of 52,000 vols
Number of teachers: 50
Number of students: 693

WILLAMETTE UNIVERSITY

900 State St, Salem, OR 97301
Telephone: (503) 370-6300

Founded 1842

President: JERRY E. HUDSON
Registrar: PAUL OLSEN
Librarian: LARRY R. OBERG

Library of 215,000 vols, 1,355 periodicals
Number of teachers: 145 (full-time)
Number of students: 2,300

Publications: *Willamette University Bulletin, College of Law Bulletin, Willamette Scene, Willamette College of Law Journal, Atkinson Graduate School of Management Bulletin.*

DEANS

College of Liberal Arts: LAWRENCE D. CRESS
College of Law: ROBERT M. ACKERMAN

George H. Atkinson Graduate School of Management: DALE WEIGHT

PENNSYLVANIA

ALBRIGHT COLLEGE

Reading, PA 19612-5234

Telephone: (610) 921-2381

Fax: (610) 921-7530

Founded 1856

President: Dr ELLEN S. HURWITZ

Director of Admissions: GREGORY EICHHORN

Library Director: ROSEMARY DEEGAN

Library of 215,800 vols

Number of teachers: 130

Number of students: 1,130

ALLEGHENY COLLEGE

Meadville, PA 16335

Telephone: (814) 332-3100

Founded 1815

President: RICHARD J. COOK

Dean: BRUCE SMITH

Vice-President for Development: JOHN McCANDLESS

Vice-President for Administration and Treasurer: JOHN REYNDERS

Registrar: BENJAMIN HAYTOCK

Secretary: (vacant)

Librarian: CONSTANCE THORSON

Library of 681,000 vols

Number of teachers: 159, including 38 professors

Number of students: 1,890

Publications: *Campus, Bulletin, Kaldron, Literary Magazine.*

DEAN

Students: DAVID McINALLY

AMERICAN COLLEGE, THE

270 Bryn Mawr Ave, Bryn Mawr, PA 19010

Telephone: (610) 526-1000

Fax: (610) 526-1310

Founded 1927

Independent, non-traditional, distance-education institution; professional diplomas and designations, graduate degrees in the financial sciences and management

President: Dr SAMUEL H. WEESE

Vice-President for Academics: Dr GARY K. STONE

Vice-President and Treasurer: CHARLES S. DILULLO

Vice-President, Marketing and Communications: WILLIAM LOMBARDO

Librarian: JUDITH L. HILL

Library of 15,000 vols

Number of teachers: 30

Number of students: 60,000 (part-time and non-resident)

DIRECTORS

Graduate School of Financial Sciences: M. DONALD WRIGHT, Jr

BEAVER COLLEGE

Glenside, PA 19038-3295

Telephone: (215) 572-2900

Fax: (215) 572-0240

Founded 1853

President: BETTE E. LANDMAN

Vice-Presidents: MICHAEL BERGER, DAVID M. LARSEN, RICHARD SPELLER, DENNIS NOSTRAND, FRANK C. VOGEL, Jr

Registrar: HAROLD W. STEWART

Librarian: BENJAMIN WILLIAMS

Library of 129,000 vols, 46,000 microforms

Number of teachers: 298

Number of students: 2,750

Publications: *Beaver Bulletins, Beaver College Herald, Undergraduate Studies Catalog, Graduate Studies Catalog,* catalogue for Center for Education Abroad.

DEANS

Admissions: DENNIS NOSTRAND

Graduate Studies: A. RICHARD POLIS

Students: JANET WALBERT

Academic: MICHAEL BERGER

Continuing Education: NANCY ALLEN

BLOOMSBURG UNIVERSITY

400 E. Second St, Bloomsburg, PA 17815

Telephone: (717) 389-4000

Founded 1839

President: Dr JESSICA KOZLOFF

Provost: Dr WILSON BRADSHAW

Registrar: K. SCHNURE

Librarian: J. DANIEL VANN

Library of 376,800 vols

Number of teachers: 396

Number of students: 7,500

Courses in arts and sciences, business, teacher education, nursing and medical imaging, computer and information science.

BRYN MAWR COLLEGE

Bryn Mawr, PA 19010-2899

Telephone: (610) 526-5000

Incorporated 1885

President: NANCY J. VICKERS

Provost: ROBERT J. DOSTAL

Director of Admissions: NANCY L. MONNICH

Treasurer: JERRY BERENSON

Librarian: ELLIOTT SHORE

Library of 1,000,000 vols

Number of students: 1,826

DEANS

Undergraduate College: KAREN TIDMARSH

Graduate School of Arts and Sciences: JAMES C. WRIGHT

School of Social Work and Social Research: RUTH MAYDEN

CHAIRMEN OF DEPARTMENT

Anthropology: PHILIP KILBRIDE

Arts: MARK LORD

Biology: MARGARET HOLLYDAY

Chemistry: SHARON BURGMAYER

Classical/Near Eastern Archaeology: STELLA MILLER-COLLETT

Economics: DAVID ROSS

English: JANE HEDLEY

French (joint with Haverford College, *q.v.*): CATHERINE LAFARGE

Geology: MARIA LUISA CRAWFORD

German: IMKE MEYER

Greek: GREGORY DICKERSON

Growth and Structure of Cities: GARY McDONOGH

History: JANE CAPLAN

History of Art: DAVID CAST

Italian: NANCY DERSOFI

Latin: RUSSELL SCOTT

Mathematics: PAUL MELVIN (acting)

Philosophy: MICHAEL KRAUSZ

Physics: ALFONSO ALBANO

Political Science: MICHAEL ALLEN

Psychology: LESLIE RESCORLA

Russian: ELIZABETH ALLEN

Sociology: MARY OSIRIM

Spanish: (vacant)

Social Work/Research: RUTH MAYDEN

BUCKNELL UNIVERSITY

Lewisburg, PA 17837

Telephone: (717) 523-1271

Founded 1846

President: Dr WILLIAM D. ADAMS

Vice-President for Academic Affairs: Dr DANIEL LITTLE

Vice-President for Administration: Dr BARRY R. MAXWELL

Vice-President for University Relations: RICHARD W. JOHNSON II

Associate Vice-President for Information Services and Resources: RAY E. METZ

Library of 616,000 vols

Number of teachers: 261 full-time, 19 part-time, 84 professors

Number of full-time students: 3,661

Publications: *Catalogue, Bucknellian, L'Agenda, Student Handbook, Bucknell Engineer, Bucknell Review, Bucknell World.*

DEANS

College of Arts and Sciences: Dr EUGENIA P. GERDES

College of Engineering: Dr JOSEPH HUMPHREY

Student Life: RICHARD P. CHAPMAN

Admissions: MARK D. DAVIES

CABRINI COLLEGE

610 King of Prussia Rd, Radnor, PA 19087-3698

Telephone: (610) 902-8100

Fax: (610) 902-8539

Founded 1957 by the Missionary Sisters of the Sacred Heart

Four-year co-educational liberal arts and sciences college

President: Dr ANTOINETTE IADAROLA

Vice-President for Enrollment Management and Dean of the Graduate Division: Dr MARY ANN BILLER

Provost and Academic Dean: Dr THOMAS V. BOEKE

Vice-President for Institutional Advancement: AL MOLLICA

Vice-President for Student Development: ROBERT BONFIGLIO

Executive Director of Admissions and Financial Aid: NANCY GARDNER

College Relations Director: LISA C. BOGIA

Library Director: KRISTINE MUDRICK

Library of 101,290 vols

Number of teachers: 44 full-time, 74 part-time

Number of students: 2,014

CALIFORNIA UNIVERSITY OF PENNSYLVANIA

250 University Ave, California, PA 15419-1394

Telephone: (412) 938-4000

Founded 1852

President: Dr ANGELO ARMENTI, Jr

Dean of Admissions and Academic Records: NORMAN HASBROUCK

Dean of Library Services: WILLIAM L. BECK

Library of 739,395 vols (405,667 microform)

Number of teachers: 311

Number of students: 5,850

Publications: *Contribution to Scholarship* (annually), *Undergraduate Catalog* (2 a year), *Graduate Catalog* (2 a year).

DEANS

College of Liberal Arts: JESSE CIGNETTI

College of Education and Human Services: Dr STEPHEN PAVLAK

School of Graduate Studies and Research: Dr GEORGE CRANE

School of Science and Technology: Dr RICHARD HART

CARLOW COLLEGE

3333 Fifth Ave, Pittsburgh, PA 15213
Telephone: (412) 578-6000
Founded 1929

President: Dr GRACE ANN GEIBEL
Director, Adult Admissions: LINDA MADDEN-BRENHOLTS
Director of Admissions: CAROL DESCAK
Director of Weekend College: JACKIE BIES
Assistant Director, Special Undergraduate Programs: BETTY AQUINO
Vice-President for Academic Affairs: Dr MARIE IMMACULEE DANA
Librarian: ELAINE MISKO

Library of 115,000 vols
Number of teachers: 229
Number of students: 2,085

CARNEGIE MELLON UNIVERSITY

5000 Forbes Ave, Pittsburgh, PA 15213
Telephone: (412) 268-2000
Fax: (412) 268-7838

Founded 1900
Private control
Academic year: August to May

President: JARED L. COHON
Provost: P. P. CHRISTIANO
Senior Vice-President: (vacant)
Senior Vice-President for Legal Affairs: (vacant)
Vice-President for Planning and Budget: J. W. BOLTON
Vice-Provost for Computing Services: ALEX HILLS
Vice-President for Development: E. C. JOHNSON
Vice-President for Enrollment: W. F. ELLIOTT
Vice-President for University Relations: D. HALE
Vice-President for Business and Chief Financial Officer: P. J. KEATING
Vice-President for Applied Research: W. M. KAUFMAN
Director of University Libraries: E. C. LINKE (acting)

Library of 889,000 vols
Number of teachers: 829
Number of students: 7,758

DEANS AND DIRECTORS

Carnegie Institute of Technology: J. ANDERSON
College of Fine Arts: M. PREKOP
College of Humanities and Social Sciences: P. N. STEARNS
Graduate School of Industrial Administration: D. DUNN
Mellon College of Science: S. A. HENRY
School of Computer Science: R. REDDY
H. J. Heinz School of Public Policy and Management: M. KAMLET
Hunt Institute for Botanical Documentation: R. W. KIGER (Dir)
Carnegie Mellon Research Institute: W. M. KAUFMAN (Dir)
Software Engineering Institute: S. CROSS
Student Affairs: M. MURPHY

PROFESSORS

Mellon College of Science:

ANDREWS, P. B., Mathematical Sciences
BERRY, G. C., Chemistry
BROWN, W. E., Biology
COFFMAN, C. V., Mathematical Sciences
COLLINS, T., Chemistry
DADOK, J., Chemistry
EDELSTEIN, R. M., Physics
ENGLER, A., Physics
FEENSTRA, R., Physics
FERGUSON, T., Physics
FETKOVICH, J. G., Physics
FONSECA, I., Mathematical Sciences
FRIEZE, A. M., Mathematical Sciences
GAROFF, S., Physics
GILMAN, F., Physics
GREENBERG, J., Mathematical Sciences
GRIFFITHS, R. B., Physics
GURTIN, M. E., Mathematical Sciences
HENRY, S. A., Biology
HO, C., Biology
HRUSA, W. J., Mathematical Sciences
JONES, E. W., Biology
KAPLAN, M., Chemistry
KAROL, P., Chemistry
KEISTER, B. B., Physics
KINDERLEHRER, D., Mathematical Sciences
KISSLINGER, L. S., Physics
KRAEMER, R. W., Physics
LEVINE, M. J., Physics
LI, L.-F., Physics
LLINÁS, M., Chemistry
MCCLURE, W. R., Biology
MCCULLOUGH, R., Chemistry
MATYJASZEWSKI, K., Chemistry
MIZEL, V. J., Mathematical Sciences
MÜNCK, E., Chemistry
NAGLE, J. F., Physics
NICOLAIDES, R. A., Mathematical Sciences
OWEN, D. R., Mathematical Sciences
PATTERSON, G. D., Chemistry
PEDERSON, R. N., Mathematical Sciences
RUSS, J. S., Physics
SCHÄFFER, J. J., Mathematical Sciences
SCHUMACHER, R. T., Physics
SEKERKA, R. F., Physics
SHREVE, S. E., Mathematical Sciences
SONER, H. M., Mathematical Sciences
SORENSEN, R. A., Physics
STALEY, S. W., Chemistry
STATMAN, R., Mathematical Sciences
STEWART, R. F., Chemistry
SUTER, R., Physics
SWENDSEN, R. H., Physics
TARTAR, L., Mathematical Sciences
TAYLOR, D. L., Biology
VANDER VEN, N. S., Physics
VOGEL, H., Physics
WIDOM, M., Physics
WILLIAMS, J. F., Biology
WILLIAMS, W. O., Mathematical Sciences
WOLFENSTEIN, L., Physics
WOOLFORD, J., Biology
YOUNG, H., Physics

Carnegie Institute of Technology:

ADAMS, B., Materials Science Engineering
AKAY, A., Mechanical Engineering
ANDERSON, J., Chemical Engineering
BAUER, C. L., Materials Science Engineering
BAUMANN, D. M. B., Mechanical Engineering
BIEGLER, L. T., Chemical Engineering
BIELAK, J., Civil Engineering
CARLEY, L. R., Electrical and Computer Engineering
CASASENT, D., Electrical and Computer Engineering
CENDES, Z., Electrical and Computer Engineering
CHARAP, S. H., Electrical and Computer Engineering
CHIGIER, N. A., Mechanical Engineering
CHYU, M., Mechanical Engineering
CRAMB, A., Materials Science Engineering
DAVIDSON, C., Civil Engineering
DOMACH, M., Chemical Engineering
FENVES, S. J., Civil Engineering
FRUEHAN, R. J., Materials Science Engineering
GARRISON, W. M., Jr, Materials Science Engineering
GELLMAN, A., Chemical Engineering
GREVE, D. W., Electrical and Computer Engineering
GRIFFIN J. H., Mechanical Engineering
GROSSMANN, I. E., Chemical Engineering
HENDRICKSON, C. T., Civil Engineering
HOBURG, J. F., Electrical and Computer Engineering
JHON, M. S., Chemical Engineering
KHOSLA, P., Electrical and Computer Engineering
KO, E. I., Chemical Engineering
KROGH, B., Electrical and Computer Engineering
KRYDER, M. H., Electrical and Computer Engineering
KUMAR, B. V. K. V., Electrical and Computer Engineering
LAMBETH, D., Electrical and Computer Engineering
LAUGHLIN, D. E., Materials Science Engineering
LAVI, A., Electrical and Computer Engineering
LUTHY, R. G., Civil Engineering
MCMICHAEL, F. C., Civil Engineering
MCNEIL, S., Civil Engineering
MAHAJAN, S., Materials Science Engineering
MALY, W., Electrical and Computer Engineering
MASSALSKI, T. B., Materials Science Engineering
MORGAN, M. G., Engineering and Public Policy
MOURA, J. M., Electrical and Computer Engineering
NEUMAN, C. P., Electrical and Computer Engineering
OPPENHEIM, I. J., Civil Engineering
PIEHLER, H. R., Materials Science Engineering
POWERS, G., Chemical Engineering
PRIEVE, D. G., Chemical Engineering
REHAK, D. R., Civil Engineering
ROHRER, R. A., Electrical and Computer Engineering
ROLLETT, T., Materials Science Engineering
ROULEAU, W. T., Mechanical Engineering
RUBIN, E. S., Engineering and Public Policy
RUSSELL, T., Mechanical Engineering
RUTENBAR, R., Electrical and Computer Engineering
SAIGAL, S., Civil Engineering
SCHLESINGER, E., Electrical and Computer Engineering
SHEN, J., Electrical and Computer Engineering
SHIH, T., Mechanical Engineering
SIDES, P. J., Chemical Engineering
SIEWIOREK, D. P., Electrical and Computer Engineering
SINCLAIR, G. B., Mechanical Engineering
SIRBU, M., Engineering and Public Policy
SKOWRONSKI, M., Materials Science Engineering
SMALL, M. J., Civil Engineering
STANCIL, D. D., Electrical and Computer Engineering
STEIF, P. S., Mechanical Engineering
STERN, R., Electrical and Computer Engineering
STROJWAS, A., Electrical and Computer Engineering
TALUKDAR, S., Electrical and Computer Engineering
THOMAS, D. E., Jr, Electrical and Computer Engineering
WESTERBERG, A. W., Chemical Engineering
WHITE, R., Electrical and Computer Engineering
WYNBLATT, P., Materials Science Engineering
YAO, S.-C., Mechanical Engineering
YDSTIE, B. E., Chemical Engineering

College of Fine Arts:

AKIN, O., Architecture
ANDERSON, C. R., Drama
BALADA, L. I., Music
BALAS, E., Art
BALLAY, J. M., Design
BENNETT, R., Art
BOYARSKI, D., Design
BUCHANAN, R., Design

Burgess, L., Art
Cardenes, A., Music
Cooper, W. D., Architecture
Flemming, U., Architecture
Frisch, P., Drama
Giron, A., Drama
Hartkopf, V., Architecture
Highlands, D., Architecture
Izquierdo, J.-P., Music
Krishnamurti, R., Architecture
Kumata, C., Art
Loftness, V., Architecture
Mahdavi, A., Architecture
Maier, J., Art
Midani, A., Drama
Olds, H. T., Art
Oppenheim, I., Architecture
Orion, E., Drama
Prekop, M., Art
Rogers, B., Art
Santa Cruz, V., Drama
Slavick, S., Art
Thomas, M., Music
Weidner, M., Art

College of Humanities and Social Sciences:

Anderson, J. R., Psychology
Carpenter, J., Psychology
Carrier, D., Philosophy
Clark, M., Psychology
Cohen, S. A., Psychology
Costanzo, G., English
Daniels, J., English
Davis, O. A., Social and Decision Sciences
Dawes, R., Social and Decision Sciences
Eddy, W. F., Statistics
Enos, R. L., English
Evans, D., Philosophy
Feinberg, S. E., Statistics
Fischhoff, B., Social and Decision Sciences
Flower, L. S., English
Freed, B. F., Modern Languages
Glymour, C., Philosophy
Greenhouse, J., Statistics
Hayes, A. L., English
Hayes, J. R., Psychology
Hopper, P., English
Hounshell, D. A., History and Social and Decision Sciences
Just, M. A., Psychology
Kadane, J. B., Statistics
Kass, R. E., Statistics
Kaufer, D., English
Kennedy, A., English
Kiesler, S., Social and Decision Sciences
Klahr, D., Psychology
Klatzky, R., Psychology
Klepper, S., Social and Decision Sciences
Knapp, P., English
Kraut, R., Social and Decision Sciences
Lehoczky, J. P., Statistics
Lindemann, M., History
Loewenstein, G., Social and Decision Sciences
Lynch, K., History
MacWhinney, B., Psychology
McClelland, J., Psychology
Masters, H., English
Miller, D. W., History
Modell, J., History
Reder, L., Psychology
Resnick, D. P., History
Scheier, M. F., Psychology
Schervish, M., Statistics
Schlossman, S., History
Schoenwald, R. L., History
Seidenfeld, T., Philosophy
Sieg, W., Philosophy
Siegler, R. S., Psychology
Simon, H. A., Psychology
Steinberg, E. R., English
Sutton, D., History
Tarr, J. A., History
Trotter, J., History
Tucker, G. R., Modern Languages
Wasserman L., Statistics

Young, R. E., English

Graduate School of Industrial Administration:

Argote, L., Organizational Behaviour
Balas, E., Industrial Administration and Mathematics
Baybars, I., Industrial Administration
Cornuejols, G. P., Operations Research and Mathematics
Cyert, R. M., Economics and Industrial Administration
Dunn, D.
Epple, D., Economics
Goodman, P. S., Industrial Administration and Psychology
Green, R. C., Financial Economics
Hooker, J., Jr, Industrial Administration
Ijiri, Y., Industrial Administration
Kadane, J., Statistics and Social Science
Kekre, S., Industrial Administration
Kriebel, C. H., Industrial Administration
Kydland, F. E., Economics
Lave, L. B., Economics
McCallum, B. T., Economics
Meltzer, A. H., Economics, Industrial Administration and Public Policy
Miller, R.
Poole, K., Political Economy
Salancik, G. R., Industrial Administration and Organization
Simon, H. A., Administration and Psychology
Spatt, C. S., Economics and Finance
Spear, S., Economics
Srinivasan, K., Industrial Administration
Srivastava, S., Economics and Finance
Sunder, S., Management and Economics
Thompson, G. L., Industrial Administration and Mathematics
Williams, J., Industrial Administration

H. J. Heinz School of Public Policy and Management:

Blumstein, A., Urban Systems and Operations Research
Cyert, R., Economics and Industrial Management
Davis, O. A., Economics and Public Policy
Duncan, G., Statistics
Fischer, B., Labour Relations
Florida, R., Public Policy and Management
Gorr, W., Public Policy and Management Information Systems
Harrison, B., Political Economy
Kamlet, M., Economics and Public Policy
Klepper, S., Economics and Social Science
Larkey, P. D., Public Policy and Decision-making
Lave, L., Economics and Urban Affairs
Morgan, M. G., Electrical Engineering and Public Policy
Nagin, D., Management
Rousseau, D., Organization Behaviour
Stewman, S., Sociology and Demography
Strauss, R. P., Economics and Public Policy
Tarr, J. A., Urban and Environmental History and Policy

School of Computer Science:

Bryant, R. E.
Carbonell, J. G.
Clark, E. M., Jr
Furst, M.
Kanade, T.
Kannan, R.
Miller, G. L.
Morris, J.
Reynolds, J. C.
Scott, D. F., Computer Science, Mathematics and Philosophy
Shaw, M.
Sleator, D.
Witkin, A.

ATTACHED INSTITUTES

Hunt Institute for Botanical Documentation: Dir Dr Robert W. Kiger.

Carnegie Mellon Research Institute: Dir Dr William M. Kaufman.

Carnegie Bosch Institute: Exec. Dir Heinz Schulte.

Information Networking Institute: Dir Dr Bernard Bennington.

Robotics Institute: Dir Takeo Kanade.

Software Engineering Institute: Dir Stephen E. Cross.

Urban Systems Institute: Dir Prof. Alfred Blumstein.

Centre for Economic Development: Dir Prof. Richard Florida.

Engineering Design Research Center: Dir Daniel P. Siewiorek.

Data Storage Systems Center: Dir Mark H. Kryder.

Environmental Institute: Dir Cliff I. Davidson.

Center for Electronic Design Automation: Dir Roxann Martin.

SRC-CMU Research Center for Computer Aided Design: Dir Rob A. Rutenbar.

Pennsylvania SEMATECH Center of Excellence for Rapid Yield Learning: Dirs Wojciech Maly, Andrzej Strojwas.

Center for Excellence in Optical Data Processing: Dir David P. Casasent.

Laboratory for Networked and Mobile Computing Research: Dir John P. Shen *et al.*

Virtual Laboratory: Dir Dan Stancil.

Program on International Peace and Security: Dir Granger Morgan.

Center for Energy and Environmental Studies: Dir Edward S. Rubin.

Center for Integrated Study of the Human Dimensions of Global Change: Dirs Granger Morgan, Hadi Dowlatabadi.

Center for Iron and Steelmaking Research: Dirs Richard J. Fruehan, Alan W. Cramb.

Consortium for Advanced Deformation Processing Research: Dir Henry R. Piehler.

GUIde Consortium on the Forced Response of Bladed Disks: Dir Jerry H. Griffin.

Center for Entrepreneurial Development: Dir Dwight M. Baumann.

Pittsburgh Supercomputing Center: Dir Michael J. Levine.

Center for Nonlinear Analysis: Dir David Kinderlehrer.

Pittsburgh NMR Center for Biomedical Research: Dir Chien Ho.

NSF Science and Technology Center for Light Microscope Imaging and Biotechnology: Dir D. Lansing Taylor.

W. M. Keck Center for Advanced Training in Computational Biology: Dir William E. Brown.

Center for Integrated Manufacturing Decision Systems.

Field Robotics Center.

Center for Medical Robots and Computer-Assisted Surgery.

Vision and Autonomous Systems Center.

Robotics Engineering Consortium: Dir David M. Pahnos.

Language Technology Institute.

Center for Machine Translation: Dir Jaime G. Carbonell.

Human-Computer Interaction Institute: Dir Albert T. Corbett.

Information Technology Center: Dir Stephen E. Cross.

Interactive Multimedia Institute.

Studio for Creative Inquiry: Dir Bryan Rogers.

Center for Building Performance and Diagnostics: Dir VOLKER HARTKOPF.

Advanced Building Systems Integration Consortium.

Intelligent Workplace.

Carnegie Mellon/Building Industry Computer-Aided Design Consortium.

Institute for Gounod Studies: Dir KENNETH W. LANGEVIN.

Center for Cultural Analysis: Dir PETER N. STEARNS.

Center for the Study of Writing and Literacy: Dirs LINDA FLOWER, JOHN HAYES.

Center for History and Policy: Dir STEVEN SCHLOSSMAN.

Pittsburgh Center for Social History: Dir PETER STEARNS.

Center for Business, Technology and the Environment: Dir JOEL A. TARR.

Center for Research on African Americans in the Urban Economy: Dir JOE TROTTER.

Center for Historical Information Systems and Analysis: Dir DAVID MILLER.

Language Learning Research Center: Dir CHRISTOPHER JONES.

Laboratory for Computational Linguistics: Dir DAVID A. EVANS.

Center for the Advancement of Applied Ethics: Dirs PRESTON COVEY, PETER MADSEN.

Center for the Neural Basis of Cognition: Dir JONATHAN COHEN.

Carnegie Bosch Institute for Applied Studies in International Management: Pres. Dr BRUCE MCKERN.

Donald H. Jones Center for Entrepreneurship: Dir JOHN R. THORNE.

Center for Financial Analysis and Securities Training: Dir SANJAY SRIVASTAVA.

Center for the Management of Technology: Dir PAUL S. GOODMAN.

Center for Risk Perception and Communication.

Center for the Study of Public Policy: Dir ALLAN MELTZER.

Green Design Initiative: Dir LESTER LAVE.

National Consortium on Violence Research: Dir ALFRED BLUMSTEIN.

National Census Data Research Center: Dirs SETH SANDERS, STEVEN KLEPPER.

Decision Systems Research Institute: Dir GEORGE DUNCAN.

Center for Innovation in Learning: Dir JOHN R. HAYES.

Center for University Outreach.

Computer, Automation and Robotics Group: Dir Dr RONALD KRUTZ.

Computer Engineering Center: Dir Dr RONALD KRUTZ.

Advanced Devices and Materials Group: Dir Dr ALBERTO M. GUZMAN.

Industry Systems Group: Dir Dr RICHARD A. UHER.

High Speed Ground Transportation Center.

Biotechnology Group: Dir Dr EDWIN G. MINKLEY, Jr.

Center of Excellence in Environmental Microbiology: Dir Dr EDWIN G. MINKLEY, Jr.

ASTM Engine Test Monitoring Center: Dir JOHN ZALAR.

Center on the Materials of the Artist and Conservator: Dir Dr PAUL WHITMORE.

EPRI Center for Materials Production: Dir JOSEPH E. GOODWILL.

CMU-ITESM Institute for Strategic Development: Dir PAUL S. GOODMAN.

CEDAR CREST COLLEGE

Allentown, PA 18104-6196

Telephone: (610) 437-4471
Fax: (610) 437-5955

Founded 1867
Private control
Liberal arts college for women

President: DOROTHY GULBENKIAN BLANEY
Library Directors: DIANNE MELNYCHUK, MARY BETH FREEH

Library of 124,000 vols
Number of teachers: 65
Number of students: 1,527

Publications: *Alumnae Magazine*, *Exchange* (quarterly), *Catalog and Promotional Brochures.*

CHATHAM COLLEGE

Pittsburgh, PA 15232

Telephone: (412) 365-1100
Fax: (412) 365-1505

Founded 1869
Liberal arts undergraduate college for women; master's degree programmes open to women and men

President: ESTHER L. BARAZZONE
Vice-President for Institutional Advancement: MARY C. POPPENBERG
Vice-President for Academic Affairs: Dr ANNE STEELE
Dean of Students: LOUISE ANNE CALIGUIRI
Dean of Admissions and Financial Aid: Dr ANNETTE GIOVENGO
Librarian: (vacant)

Library of 120,000 vols
Number of teachers: 65
Number of students: 782

CHESTNUT HILL COLLEGE

Philadelphia, PA 19118

Telephone: (215) 248-7000
Fax: (215) 248-7056

Founded 1924

President: Sister CAROL JEAN VALE
Vice-President for Academic Affairs: WILLIAM T. WALKER
Librarian: MARY JOSEPHINE LARKIN

Library of 135,554 vols
Number of teachers: 120
Number of students: 1,543

CHEYNEY UNIVERSITY OF PENNSYLVANIA

Cheyney, PA 19319

Telephone: (610) 399-2220
Fax: (610) 399-2415

Founded 1837

President: W. CLINTON PETTUS
Director of Admissions: ELDRIDGE SMITH
Librarian: LUT NERO

Library of 238,699 vols
Number of teachers: 98
Number of students: 1,508

CLARION UNIVERSITY OF PENNSYLVANIA

Clarion, PA 16214

Telephone: (814) 226-2000

Founded 1867

President: DIANE L. REINHARD
Director of Admissions: JOHN SHROPSHIRE
Director of Libraries: RASHELLE KARP

Library of 363,000 vols
Number of teachers: 364
Number of students: 6,000

CURTIS INSTITUTE OF MUSIC, THE

1726 Locust St, Philadelphia, PA 19103

Telephone: (215) 893-5252
Fax: (215) 893-9065

Founded 1924

Chairman: MILTON L. ROCK
Vice-Chairs: A. MARGARET BOK, SHAUN F. O'MALLEY
Treasurer: BAYARD R. FIECHTER
Secretary: JAMES R. LEDWITH
Registrar: ELAINE KATZ
Librarian: ELIZABETH WALKER

Library of *c.* 60,000 vols, musical scores and recordings
Number of students: 166

DELAWARE VALLEY COLLEGE OF SCIENCE AND AGRICULTURE

Doylestown, PA 18901

Telephone: (215) 345-1500

Founded 1896

President: Dr THOMAS C. LEAMER
Dean: Dr NEIL J. VINCENT
Registrar: ROBERT P. MORAN
Director of Admissions: STEPHEN W. ZENKO
Librarian: PETER KUPPERSMITH

Library of 73,600 vols
Number of teachers: 81
Number of students: 1,380

DICKINSON COLLEGE

Carlisle, PA 17013

Telephone: (717) 243-5121

Founded 1773

President: A. LEE FRITSCHLER
Dean: NEIL B. WEISSMAN
Treasurer: MICHAEL L. BRITTON
Registrar: BRENDA K. BRETZ
Librarian: J. STEVEN MCKINZIE

Number of teachers: 151
Number of students: 1,875

Publications: *Catalogue, The Dickinson Magazine.*

DEANS

Academic Affairs: NEIL B. WEISSMAN
Educational Services: BETSY K. EMERICK

DREXEL UNIVERSITY

32nd and Chestnut Sts, Philadelphia, PA 19104

Telephone: (215) 895-2000
Fax: (215) 895-1414

Founded 1891 as Drexel Institute of Art, Science and Industry

President: Dr CONSTANTINE N. PAPADAKIS
Provost and Senior Vice-President for Academic Affairs: Dr RICHARD ASTRO
Senior Vice-President for Finance and Administration: FRANK BACHICH
Senior Vice-President for Institutional Advancement: BARBARA S. SPIRO
Vice-Provost for Student Life: ANTHONY CANERIS
Librarian: Dr EILEEN N. HITCHINGHAM

Library of 450,000 vols
Number of teachers: 295 full-time, 464 part-time
Number of students: 9,158

DEANS

College of Arts and Sciences: SAM BOSE
College of Business and Administration: STEVE BAJGIER
College of Engineering: Dr Y. T. SHAH
Nesbitt College of Design Arts: Dr J. MICHAEL ADAMS

College of Information Studies: Dr RICHARD H. LYTLE
Evening College: ROSE KETTERER

DUQUESNE UNIVERSITY

600 Forbes Ave, Pittsburgh, PA 15282
Telephone: (412) 396-6000
Founded 1878; chartered 1911
Private control
President: Dr JOHN E. MURRAY, Jr
Executive Vice-President for Management and Business: ISADORE R. LENGLET
Provost and Academic Vice-President: Dr MICHAEL P. WEBER
Executive Vice-President for Student Life: Rev. SEAN HOGAN
Registrar: PATRICIA JAKUB
Librarian: Dr PAUL J. PUGLIESE
Library of 583,500 vols and 179,424 units on microform
Number of teachers: 383 full-time, 426 part-time
Number of students: 9,500

DEANS
McAnulty College and Graduate School of Liberal Arts: Dr CONSTANCE RAMIREZ
Palumbo School of Business Administration: THOMAS J. MURRIN
Bayer School of Natural and Environmental Sciences: Dr HEINZ MACHATZKE
School of Education: Dr JAMES HENDERSON
Rangos School of Health Sciences: Dr JEROME L. MARTIN
School of Law: NICHOLAS P. CAFARDI
School of Music: MICHAEL KUMER
School of Nursing: Dr MARY DE CHESNAY
Mylan School of Pharmacy: Dr RANDALL L. VANDERVEEN
Division of Continuing Education: Dr BENJAMIN HODES

EASTERN COLLEGE

1300 Eagle Rd, St Davids, PA 19087-3696
Telephone: (610) 341-5967
Fax: (610) 341-1723
Founded 1952
Co-Presidents (acting): Dr HAROLD HOWARD, JOHN SCHAUSS
Chief Operating Officer: JOHN SCHAUSS
Provost: HAROLD HOWARD
Academic Dean (Undergraduate): SARAH MILES
Academic Dean (Graduate): VIVIAN NIX-EARLY
Vice-President of Student Development: THEODORE J. CHAMBERLAIN
Admissions Director: MARK SEYMOUR
Librarian: JAMES L. SAUER
Library of 209,000 vols
Number of teachers: 206
Number of students: 2,348

EDINBORO UNIVERSITY

Meadville St, Edinboro, PA 16444
Telephone: (814) 732-2000
Founded 1857
President: Dr FRANK G. POGUE
Provost and Vice-President for Academic Affairs: Dr ROBERT C. WEBER
Vice-President for Student Affairs and Student Success: Dr NAOMI T. JOHNSON
Vice-President for Financial Operations and Administration: RICHARD E. MORLEY
Assistant Vice-President for Admissions: TERRENCE CARLIN
Associate Vice-President for University Libraries and Academic Programs: Dr DONALD DILMORE
Library of 469,000 volumes
Number of teachers: 414
Number of students: 7,178

ELIZABETHTOWN COLLEGE

Elizabethtown, PA 17022-2298
Telephone: (717) 361-1000
Founded 1899
President: THEODORE E. LONG
Dean of Faculty: RONALD J. MCALLISTER
Treasurer: JOHN M. SHAEFFER
Library of 158,357 vols
Number of teachers: 105
Number of students: 1,525

FRANKLIN AND MARSHALL COLLEGE

POB 3003, Lancaster, PA 17604-3003
Telephone: (717) 291-3911
Franklin College founded in 1787, Marshall College founded in 1836; merged in 1853
President: A. RICHARD KNEEDLER
Dean: BRUCE PIPES
Treasurer: THOMAS J. KINGSTON Jr
Librarian: (vacant)
Library of 360,000 vols
Number of teachers: 152
Number of students: 1,800

GANNON UNIVERSITY

University Square, Erie, PA 16541
Telephone: (814) 871-7000
Founded 1925
President: Mgr DAVID RUBINO
Academic Vice-President: Dr THOMAS OSTROWSKI
Dean, Enrollment Services: RICHARD E. SUKITSCH
Librarian: Rev. Dr L. THOMAS SNYDERWINE
Library of 211,000 vols, 2,650 periodicals
Number of teachers: 202 full-time, 143 part-time
Number of students: 4,491

GENEVA COLLEGE

3200 College Ave, Beaver Falls, PA 15010
Telephone: (724) 846-5100
Fax: (724) 847-6687
Founded 1848
President: Dr JOHN H. WHITE
Provost: Dr JAMES N. BOELKINS
Academic Vice-President: Dr STAN CLARK
Registrar: ANN WOLLMAN
Librarian: GERALD MORAN
Library of 250,000 vols, including microforms
Number of teachers: 90
Number of students: 1,950

GETTYSBURG COLLEGE

Gettysburg, PA 17325
Telephone: (717) 337-6000
Fax: (717) 337-6008
E-mail: admiss@gettysburg.edu
Chartered 1832 as Pennsylvania College; name changed 1921
President: GORDON A. HAALAND
Provost: DANIEL DENICOLA
Dean of the College: JULIE L. RAMSEY
Director of Admissions: D. K. GUSTAFSON
Library of 350,000 vols
Number of teachers: 174
Number of students: 2,170
Publication: *Gettysburg Review.*

HAVERFORD COLLEGE

370 Lancaster Ave, Haverford, PA 19041
Telephone: (610) 896-1000
Fax: (610) 896-1224
An independent co-educational liberal arts college, founded in 1833 as the first American college established by the Society of Friends
President: THOMAS R. TRITTON
Vice-President for Institutional Advancement: G. HOLGER HANSEN
Treasurer and Vice-President for Administration and Finance: G. RICHARD WYNN
Director of Admissions: DELSIE PHILLIPS
Provost: ELAINE HANSEN
Dean of College: JOSEPH A. TOLLIVER
Librarian: MICHAEL FREEMAN
Library of 425,000 vols
Number of teachers: 95 full-time, 14 part-time
Number of students: 1,147
Publications: *Haverford Newsletter* (quarterly), *Haverford Magazine* (3 a year).

HOLY FAMILY COLLEGE

Grant and Frankford Aves, Philadelphia, PA 19114
Telephone: (215) 637-7700
Fax: (215) 824-2438
Founded 1954
President: Sister Dr FRANCESCA ONLEY
Director of Undergraduate Admissions: ROBERTA NOLAN
Director of Library Services: LORI SCHWABENBAUER
Library of 106,707 vols
Number of teachers: 215
Number of students: 2,485
Publications: *College Catalog*, *Familogue* (annually), *Tri-Lite*, *Folio*, *Bulletin Shield*, *The Family Tree.*
Degree programs in the liberal arts, business administration, education, medical technology, nursing, fire science administration, interdisciplinary programs, medical imaging. Master's programs in counselling psychology, education, nursing.

IMMACULATA COLLEGE

Immaculata, PA 19345
Telephone: (610) 647-4400
Fax: (610) 251-1668
Founded 1920
President: Sister MARIE ROSEANNE BONFINI
Registrar: Sister GEORGINE MARIE
Director of Admissions: KENNETH R. RASP
Librarian: PATRICIA CONNELL
Library of 115,000 vols
Number of teachers: 164
Number of students: 2,391

INDIANA UNIVERSITY OF PENNSYLVANIA

Indiana, PA 15705
Telephone: (412) 357-2100
Founded 1875, as Indiana State Normal School
State control
Academic year: September to May (2 sessions)
President: Dr LAWRENCE K. PETTIT
Provost and Vice-President for Academic Affairs: Dr MARK J. STASZKIEWICZ
Vice-President for Administration: C. EDWARD RECESKI
Vice-President for Finance: LOUIS SZALONTAI
Vice-President for Student Affairs: Dr HAROLD GOLDSMITH
Vice-President for Institutional Advancement: Dr JOAN FISHER
Dean of Graduate School: Dr DAVID LYNCH
Dean of Admissions: WILLIAM NUNN
Director of Libraries and Media Resources: Dr RENA FOWLER
Library of 765,000 vols
Number of teachers: 821

Number of students: 13,680

DEANS

College of Business: Dr ROBERT C. CAMP
School of Continuing Education: Dr NICHOLAS E. KOLB
College of Education: Dr JOHN BUTZOW
College of Fine Arts: Dr MICHAEL J. HOOD
College of Human Ecology and Health Sciences: Dr HAROLD E. WINGARD
College of Natural Sciences and Mathematics: Dr JOHN ECK
College of Humanities and Social Sciences: Dr BRENDA CARTER
Graduate School: Dr DAVID LYNCH
International Studies: LAILA DAHAN

KING'S COLLEGE

Wilkes-Barre, PA 18711

Telephone: (717) 208-5900

Founded 1946

President: Rev. JAMES LACKENMIER
Registrar: Dr JEAN P. ANDERSON
Dean of Enrollment Management: CHARLES O. BACHMAN
Library Director: Dr TERRENCE MECH

Library of 158,000 vols
Number of teachers: 171
Number of students: 2,152

KUTZTOWN UNIVERSITY

Kutztown, PA 19530

Telephone: (610) 683-4000
Fax: (610) 683-4010

Founded 1866

President: DAVID E. MCFARLAND
Provost, and Vice-President for Academic Affairs: L. GOLDBERG
Vice-President for Student Affairs: C. WOODARD
Vice-President for Administration and Finance: J. SUTHERLAND
Vice-President for University Advancement: W. SUTTON
Director of Admissions: R. MCGOWAN
Registrar: JOHN ERDMANN
Librarian: MARGARET DEVLIN

Library of 415,000 vols
Number of teachers: 441
Number of students: 7,920

DEANS

College of Visual and Performing Arts: ARTHUR BLOOM
College of Liberal Arts and Sciences: CARL BRUNNER
College of Education: HARRY M. TEITELBAUM (acting)
College of Graduate Studies and Extended Learning: W. B. EZELL, Jr
College of Business: TED HARTZ
Academic Services: Dr JOSEPH AMPREY

LAFAYETTE COLLEGE

Easton, PA 18042

Telephone: (215) 250-5000

Founded 1826

President: ARTHUR J. ROTHKOPF
Provost: JUNE SCHLUETER (acting)
Secretary, Board of Trustees: WILLIAM C. CASSEBAUM
Registrar: CYRUS S. FLECK, Jr
Clerk of the Faculty: RALPH L. SLAGHT
Director of Libraries: NEIL J. MCELROY

Library of 415,750 vols
Number of teachers: 175
Number of students: 2,015

Publications: *Announcement* (annually), *Mélange* (annually), *The Lafayette* (weekly), *The Lafayette Magazine* (3 a year), *The Alumni News* (3 a year).

LA SALLE UNIVERSITY

20th and Olney Ave, Philadelphia, PA 19141

Telephone: (215) 951-1000
Fax: (215) 951-1892

Founded 1863

President: Bro. JOSEPH BURKE
Provost: Dr DANIEL PANTALEO
Director of Admissions: Bro. GERALD FITZGERALD
Librarian: JOHN BAKY

Library of 375,000 vols
Number of teachers: 218 full-time, 260 part-time
Number of students: Day Division 3,200, Evening Division 1,800, Graduate Division 1,300

Publications: *La Salle Bulletin* (quarterly), *La Salle Magazine* (quarterly), *Four Quarters* (quarterly).

LEBANON VALLEY COLLEGE

Annville, PA 17003-0501

Telephone: (717) 867-6100
Fax: (717) 867-6018

Founded 1866

President: G. DAVID POLLICK
Registrar: KAREN D. BEST
Vice-President and Dean of Faculty: Dr STEPHEN C. MACDONALD
Dean of Admission: WILLIAM J. BROWN
Librarian: ROBERT PAUSTIAN

Library of 157,000 vols, 20,000 microfilms and recordings
Number of teachers: 75 (full-time)
Number of students: 1,370

LEHIGH UNIVERSITY

27 Memorial Drive West, Bethlehem, PA 18015-3089

Telephone: (610) 758-3155
Fax: (610) 758-3154

Founded 1865

President: GREGORY C. FARRINGTON
Provost and Vice-President for Academic Affairs: Dr NELSON G. MARKLEY
Vice-President for Finance and Administration: RHONDA I. GROSS
Vice-President for Public Affairs: KENNETH R. SMITH
Vice-President for Development and University Relations: JILL L. SHERMAN
Assistant Vice-President of Facilities Services and Campus Planning: ANTHONY L. CORALLO
Vice-Provost for Student Affairs: Dr JOHN W. SMEATON
Registrar: BRUCE S. CORRELL

Library of 1,324,500 Vols
Number of teachers: 397
Number of students: 6,316

Publications: *University Catalogue*, *Undergraduate Announcement Viewbook*.

DEANS

College of Arts and Science: Dr BOBB CARSON
College of Business and Economics: Dr PATTI T. OTA
College of Engineering and Applied Science: Dr HARVEY G. STENGER
College of Education: Dr ROLAND K. YOSHIDA

LINCOLN UNIVERSITY

PA 19352

Telephone: (610) 932-8300
Fax: (610) 932-8316

Founded 1854

President: Dr NIARA SUDARKASA
Vice-President for Academic Affairs: Dr RICHARD C. WINCHESTER
Vice-President for Fiscal Affairs: (vacant)
Vice-President for Development: ANTHONY FAIRBANKS
Vice-President for Enrollment Planning and Student Life: Dr ARNOLD HENCE
Registrar: (vacant)
Librarian: EMERY WIMBISH, Jr

Library of 180,000 vols
Number of teachers: 100 (full-time)
Number of students: 2,020

LOCK HAVEN UNIVERSITY OF PENNSYLVANIA

Lock Haven, PA 17745

Telephone: (717) 893-2000

Founded 1870

President: Dr CRAIG D. WILLIS
Director of Admissions: JOSEPH COLDREN
Director of Library Services: ROBERT S. BRAVARD

Library of 352,369 vols
Number of teachers: 218
Number of students: 3,690

Publication: *Lock Haven International Review* (annually).

LYCOMING COLLEGE

Williamsport, PA 17701

Telephone: (717) 321-4000
Fax: (717) 321-4337

Founded 1812

President: Dr JAMES E. DOUTHAT
Dean: Dr JOHN F. PIPER, Jr
Registrar: REBECCA L. HILE
Librarian: BRUCE M. HURLBERT

Library of 178,400 vols
Number of teachers: 92 (full-time)
Number of students: 1,546

MANSFIELD UNIVERSITY

Mansfield, PA 16933

Telephone: (717) 662-4000

Founded 1857

President: JOHN R. HALSTEAD
Director of Student Records: MARY JANE WATKINS
Director of Enrollment Services: BRIAN BARDEN
Director of Library Service and Instructional Resources: LARRY NESBIT

Library of 222,650 vols
Number of teachers: 180
Number of students: 2,891 undergraduate, 332 graduate

MARYWOOD UNIVERSITY

2300 Adams Ave, Scranton, PA 18509

Telephone: (717) 348-6211

Founded 1915

President: Sister MARY REAP
Academic Vice-President: Sister PATRICIA ANN MATTHEWS
Registrar: Sister DOLORES FILICKO
Director of Admissions: FRED BROOKS Jr
Director of Library: CATHERINE SCHAPPERT

Library of 208,000 vols
Number of teachers: 271
Number of students: 2,926

MESSIAH COLLEGE

1 College Ave, Grantham, PA 17027

Telephone: (717) 766-2511
Fax: (717) 691-6059

Founded 1909

Private control
Academic year: September to May

President: Dr RODNEY J. SAWATSKY
Provost: Dr DONALD B. KRAYBILL
Vice-President for Administration and Finance: Dr KENNETH M. MARTIN
Vice-President for Advancement: BARRY GOODLING
Vice-President for Enrollment Management: WILLIAM STRAUSBAUGH
Academic Dean: Dr KIM PHIPPS
Dean of Students: Dr CYNTHIA WELLS-LILLY

Library of 212,000 vols
Number of teachers: 135 full-time, 91 part-time
Number of students: 2,426 full-time, 91 part-time

Publications: *Messiah College Catalog* (1 a year), *The Bridge* (4 a year).

MILLERSVILLE UNIVERSITY OF PENNSYLVANIA

POB 1002, Millersville, PA 17551-0302
Telephone: (717) 872-3011
Fax: (717) 871-2251

Founded 1855

Associate, baccalaureate and masters degree programs in the liberal arts and sciences, teacher education, business, and professional studies

President: JOSEPH A. CAPUTO
Registrar: MARIANO GONZALEZ
Director of Admissions: DARRELL DAVIS
Librarian: Dr DAVID S. ZUBATSKY

Library of 991,500 vols incl. microfilm/ microfiche
Number of teachers: 332 full-time, 111 part-time
Number of students: 6,662 undergraduate, 902 graduate

MORAVIAN COLLEGE

1200 Main St, Bethlehem, PA 18018
Telephone: (610) 861-1300
Fax: (610) 861-3919

Founded 1742; men first admitted 1807

President: ERVIN J. ROKKE
Vice-President for Administration: F. ROBERT HUTH Jr
Vice-President for Planning and Enrollment: JOHN W. MCDERMOTT
Vice-President for Institutional Advancement: SUSANNE I. SHAW
Vice-President and Dean of Seminary: DAVID A. SCHATTSCHNEIDER
Vice-President and Dean: MARTHA REID
Vice-President and Dean of Students: BEVERLY J. KOCHARD

Library of 220,000 vols
Number of teachers: 88
Number of students: 1,234

MUHLENBERG COLLEGE

24th and Chew Sts, Allentown, PA 18104
Telephone: (610) 821-3100
Fax: (610) 821-3234

Founded 1848

President: ARTHUR R. TAYLOR
Dean of the Faculty: CURTIS G. DRETSCH
Dean of Academic Life: Dr CAROL SHINER WILSON
Library Director: MYRNA J. MCCALLISTER

Library of 290,000 vols
Number of teachers: 126
Number of students: 1,735

PENNSYLVANIA COLLEGE OF OPTOMETRY

1200 West Godfrey Ave, Philadelphia, PA 19141
Telephone: (215) 276-6200

Founded 1919

President: THOMAS L. LEWIS
Vice-President for Institutional Advancement: JOHN SCHLESINGER
Vice-President and Dean for Academic Advancement: ANTHONY F. DI STEFANO
Vice-President for Finance and Business Affairs: PATRICK J. SWEENEY
Vice-President and Dean for Student Affairs and Director of Admissions: ROBERT E. HORNE
Vice-President, and Executive Director of the Eye Institute: EUGENE WAYNE
Librarian: KEITH LAMMERS

Library of 19,200 vols
Number of teachers: 45 full-time, 28 part-time
Number of students: 668

PENNSYLVANIA STATE UNIVERSITY

University Park, PA 16802
Telephone: (814) 865-4700

Established 1855 by Act of the State legislature of Pennsylvania
Academic year: August to May

President: GRAHAM SPANIER
Executive Vice-President and Provost: JOHN A. BRIGHTON
Senior Vice-President for Administration: CAROL HERRMANN
Senior Vice-President for Finance and Business, and Treasurer: GARY C. SCHULTZ
Vice-President for Research and Dean of the Graduate School: RODNEY ERICKSON
Vice-Provost for Educational Equity: JAMES B. STEWART
Vice Provost: ROBERT SECOR
Vice-Provost and Dean for Undergraduate Education: JOHN J. CAHIR
Senior Associate Vice-President for Finance and Business: WILLIAM MCKINNON
Vice-President for Student Services: WILLIAM W. ASBURY
Vice-President for Development and Alumni Relations: RODNEY P. KIRSCH
Vice-President for Outreach and Cooperative Extension: JAMES H. RYAN
Registrar: J. JAMES WAGER
Dean of Libraries: NANCY EATON

Number of teachers: 4,023 (full-time)
Number of students: 73,427

DEANS

College of Agricultural Sciences: ROBERT D. STEELE
College of Business Administration: J. D. HAMMOND
College of Science: STEVE WEINREB (interim)
College of Education: EDWIN HERR (interim)
College of Engineering: DAVID N. WORMLEY
College of Health and Human Development: BARBARA M. SHANNON
College of the Liberal Arts: SUSAN WELCH
College of Earth and Mineral Sciences: JOHN A. DUTTON
College of Arts and Architecture: NEIL H. PORTERFIELD
College of Medicine: C. MCCOLLISTER EVARTS
Graduate School: RODNEY A. ERICKSON
Abington College: KAREN W. SANDLER
Altoona College: ALLEN C. MEADORS
Behrend College: JOHN M. LILLEY (Provost and Dean)
Berks–Lehigh Valley College: FREDERICK H. GAIGE
Capitol College: JOHN G. BRUHN (Provost and Dean)
Commonwealth College: JOSEPH C. STRASSER
College of Communications: JEREMY COHEN (interim)
Honors College: CHERYL L. ACHTERBERG
International Programs: BEVERLY LINDSAY

PROFESSORS

(Some professors serve in more than one department)

College of Agricultural Sciences:

Agricultural Economics and Rural Sociology:

ALTER, T. R., Agricultural Economics
BECKER, J. C., Agricultural Economics
BEIERLEIN, J. G., Agricultural Economics
DUNN, J. W., Agricultural Economics
EPP, D. J., Agricultural Economics
HALLBERG, M. C., Agricultural Economics
HEASLEY, D. K., Rural Sociology
HERRMANN, R. O., Agricultural Economics
HYMAN, D. W., Public Policy and Community Systems
JANSMA, J. D., Agricultural Economics
LEMBECK, S. M., Rural Sociology
LULOFF, A. E., Rural Sociology
MOORE, H. L., Agricultural Economics
SCHUTJER, W. A., Agricultural Economics
SHORTLE, J. S., Agricultural Economics
STEFANOU, S. E., Agricultural Economics
STOKES, C. S., Rural Sociology
VAN HORN, J. E., Rural Sociology
WARLAND, R. H., Rural Sociology
WEAVER, R. D., Agricultural Economics
WILLITS, F. K., Rural Sociology

Agricultural and Extension Education:

BOWEN, B. E., Agricultural and Extension Education
CAREY, H. A., Extension Information
LEWIS, R. B., 4-H Youth
MORTENSEN, J. H., Agricultural and Extension Education
SCANLON, D. C., Agricultural and Extension Education
SNIDER, B. A., Agricultural and Extension Education
YODER, E. P., Agricultural and Extension Education

Agricultural and Biological Engineering:

BUFFINGTON, D. E., Agricultural Engineering
ELLIOT, H. A., Agricultural Engineering
GRAVES, R.E.
JARRETT, A. R.
MANBECK, H. B.
MURPHY, D. J., Agricultural Engineering
PURI, V. M., Agricultural Engineering
WALKER, P. N.

Agronomy:

BEEGLE, D. B., Agronomy
BOLLAG, J. M., Soil Microbiology
CIOLKOSZ, E. J., Soil Genesis and Morphology
FALES, S. L., Crop Management
FOX, R. H., Soil Science
FRITTON, D. D., Soil Physics
HARTWIG, N. L., Weed Science
HATLEY, O. E., Agronomy
KOMARNENI, S., Clay Mineralogy
KRUEGER, C. R., Agronomy
LANYON, L. E., Soil Fertility
PETERSEN, G. W., Soil and Land Resources
RISIUS, M. L., Plant Breeding
SHANNON, J. C., Plant Physiology
SHENK, J. S., Plant Breeding
TURGEON, A. J., Agronomy
WATSCHKE, T. L., Turfgrass Science

Dairy and Animal Science:

BAUMRUCKER, C. R., Animal Nutrition-Physiology
CASH, E. H., Animal Science
CURTIS, S. E., Animal Science
DEAVER, D. R., Reproductive Physiology
ETHERTON, T. D., Animal Nutrition
HAGAN, D. R., Animal Science
HARGROVE, G. L., Dairy Science
HEALD, C. W., Dairy Science

HEINRICHS, A. J., Dairy and Animal Science
KILLIAN, G. J., Reproductive Physiology
MULLER, L. D., Dairy Science
O'CONNOR, M. L., Dairy Science
VARGA, G. A., Animal Science
WANGSNESS, P. J., Animal Nutrition
WILSON, L. L., Animal Science

Entomology:

CAMERON, E. A., Entomology
FRAZIER. J. L., Entomology
HELLER, P. R., Entomology
HOWER, A. A., Entomology
HULL, L. A., Entomology
KIM, K. C., Entomology
MULLIN, C. A., Entomology
PITTS, C. W., Entomology
SCHULTZ, J. C., Entomology
SMILOWITZ, Z., Entomology
SNETSINGER, R. J., Entomology

Food Science:

BEELMAN, R. B., Food Science
HOOD, L. F., Food Science
KILARA, A., Food Science
KROGER, M., Food Science
MARETZKI, A. N., Food Science and Nutrition
STEELE, R. D.

Horticulture:

ARTECA, R. N., Horticultural Physiology
CRAIG, R., Plant Breeding
CRASSWELLER, R. M., Tree Fruit
FERRETTI, P. A., Vegetable Crops
HOLCOMB, E. J., Floriculture
KOIDE, R. T., Horticultural Ecology
KUHNS, L. J., Ornamental Horticulture
NUSS, J. R., Ornamental Horticulture
ORZOLEK, M. D., Horticulture

Plant Pathology:

AYERS, J. E.
COLE, H., Jr, Agricultural Sciences
DAVIS, D. D.
FLORES, H. E.
HICKEY, K. D.
HOCK, W. K.
LUKEZIC, F. L.
MACNAB, A. A.
MERRILL, W., Jr
MOORMAN, G. W., Plant Pathology
PELL, E. J., Agriculture
PENNYPACKER, S. P., Plant Pathology
ROYSE, D. J., Plant Pathology
SKELLY, J. M.
STEWART, E. L., Plant Pathology
TRAVIS, J. W.
WUEST, P. J.

Poultry Science:

GAY, C. V., Cell Biology and Poultry Science
LEACH, R. M., Jr, Poultry Science
WEAVER, W. D., Poultry Science

Veterinary Science:

FERGUSON, F. G.
GRIEL, L. C., Jr
HUTCHINSON, L. J.
PERDEW, G. H.
REDDY, C. C.
SCHOLZ, R. W.
WILSON, R. A.

School of Forest Resources:

BLANKENHORN, P. R., Wood Technology
BOWERSOX, T. W., Silviculture
DEWALLE, D. R., Forest Hydrology
GERHOLD, H. D., Forest Genetics
GLOTFELTY, C., Forestry and Environmental Resource Conservation
LABOSKY, P., Jr, Wood Science and Technology
LYNCH, J. A., Forest Hydrology
MCCORMICK, L. H., Forest Resources
NIELSEN, L. A., Natural Resources
SAN JULIAN, G., Wildlife Resources
SHARPE, W. E., Forest Resources
STAUFFER, J. R., Ichthyology
STEINER, K. C., Forest Biology
STRAUSS, C. H., Forest Economics
YAHNER, R. H., Wildlife Management

College of Arts and Architecture:

Architecture:

FIFIELD, M. E., Architecture
GOLANY, G., Urban Design
HAIDER, J., Architecture
INSERRA, L. P., Architecture
LUCAS, J. P., Architecture

Art History:

CUTLER, A.
HAGER, H.

Landscape Architecture:

BATTAGLIA, A. M.
DICKIE, G.
JONES, D. R.
PENNYPACKER, E.
PORTERFIELD, N. H.

Theatre Arts:

DUQUE, M. R.
GIBSON, A. A.
LEONARD, R. E.
NICHOLS, R.

School of Music:

ARMSTRONG, D. C., Music
BROYLES, M., Music and American History
CARR, M. A., Music
DOSSE-PETERS, M.D., Music
MERRIMAN, L. C., Music
MILLER, D. D., Music
SMITH, S. H., Music
THOMPSON, K. P., Music Education
TOULSON, S. C., III, Music
WILLIAMS, E. V., Music
YODER, M. D., Music

School of Visual Arts:

AMATEAU, M., Art and Women's Studies
GRAVES, K., Art
HAMPTON, G., Art and Art Education
LANG, G., Art
LEUPP, L. G., Art
MADDOX, J., Art
PORTER, S., Art
SOMMESE, L. B., Art
STEPHENSON, J. E., Art
WILSON, B. G., Art Education

College of Business Administration:

Accounting:

DIRSMITH, M. W.
MCKEOWN, J. C.
MUTCHLER, J. F.
SMITH, C. H.

Business Logistics:

COYLE, J. J., Jr, Business Administration
HENSZEY, B. H., Business Law
SPYCHALSKI, J. C., Business Logistics
TYWORTH, J. E., Business Logistics

Finance:

EZZELL, J. R.
GHADAR, F.
KRACAW, W. A.
MILES, J. A.
WOOLRIDGE, J. R.

Insurance and Real Estate:

HAMMOND, J. D., Insurance
JAFFE, A. J., Business Administration
LUSHT, K. M., Business Administration
SHAPIRO, A. F., Business Administration

Management and Organization:

BAGBY, J. W., Business Law
BRASS, D. J., Organizational Behaviour
GIOIA, D. A., Organizational Behaviour
GRAY, B. L., Organizational Behaviour
SNOW, C. C., Business Administration
STEVENS, J. M.
SUSMAN, G. I., Management
TREVINO, L. K., Management

Management Science and Information Systems:

BALAKRISHNAN, A.
CHATTERJEE, K., Management Science
HARRISON, T. P., Management Science
HAYYA, J. C., Management Science
HOTTENSTEIN, M. P., Management
KOOT, R. S., Management Science
LILIEN, G. L., Management Science
MELANDER, E. R., Quantitative Business Analysis
ORD, J. K., Business Administration and Statistics
VERGIN, R. C., Business Administration

Marketing:

ANDERSON, P. F., Marketing
BITHER, S. W., Marketing
DESARBO, W. S., Marketing
GOLDBERG, M. E., Marketing
OLIVA, R. A., Marketing
OLSON, J. C., Marketing
SUJAN, M., Marketing
WILSON, D. T., Marketing

Business Administration Executive Education:

VICERE, A. A., Business Administration

College of Communications:

BERNER, R. T., Journalism and American Studies
BROOKS, T., Journalism
COHEN, J., Communications
DAVIS, D. K., Media Studies
FRIEDEN, R. M., Communications
PFAFF, D. W., Communications
SCHEMENT, J. R., Communications
SMITH, E. S., Communications
TAYLOR, R. D., Telecommunications Studies and Law

College of Earth and Mineral Sciences:

Geography:

CARLETON, A. M.
CRANE, R. G.
DOWNS, R. M.
ERICKSON, R. A., Geography and Business Administration
GLASMEIER, A. K., Geography and Regional Planning
GOULD, P. R.
HOLDSWORTH, D. W.
KNIGHT, C. G.
MACEACHREN, A. M., Geography
PEUQUET, D. J., Geography

Geosciences:

ALEXANDER, S. S., Geophysics
ALLEY, R. B., Geosciences
ARTHUR, M. A., Geosciences
BARRON, E. J., Geosciences
BRANTLEY, S. L., Geosciences
BURBANK, D. W., Geosciences
CUFFEY, R. J., Palaeontology
DAVIS, A., Geology
DEINES, P., Geochemistry
EGGLER, D. H., Petrology
ENGELDER, T. E., Geosciences
FURLONG, K. P., Geosciences
GOLD, D. P., Geology
GRAHAM, E. K., Geophysics
GREENFIELD, R. J., Geophysics
HATCHER, P. G., Fuel Science and Geosciences
KASTING, J. F., Geosciences and Meteorology
KERRICK, D. M., Petrology
KUMP, L. R., Geosciences
LANGSTON, C. A., Geophysics
NEWNHAM, R. E., Solid State Science
OHMOTO, H., Geochemistry
PARIZEK, R. R., Geology
ROY, R., Solid State Science and Geochemistry
SLINGERLAND, R. L., Geology
VOIGHT, B., Geology
WHITE, W. B., Geochemistry

Materials Science and Engineering:
ALLARA, D. L., Polymer Science and Chemistry
BROWN, P., Ceramic Science and Engineering
CHUNG, T.-C., Polymer Science
COLEMAN, M. M., Polymer Science
DEB ROY, T., Metallurgy
GREEN, D. J., Ceramic Science and Engineering
HARRISON, I. R., Polymer Science
HATCHER, P. G., Fuel Science and Geosciences
HOWELL, P. R., Metallurgy
KOSS, D. A., Metallurgy
KUMAR, S. K., Materials Science and Engineering
MACDONALD, D. D., Materials Science and Engineering
MESSING, G. L., Ceramic Science and Engineering
NEWNHAM, R. E., Solid State Science
OSSEO-ASARE, K., Metallurgy
PAINTER, P. C., Polymer Science
PANTANO, C. G., Materials Science and Engineering
PICKERING, H. W., Metallurgy
RUNT, J. P., Polymer Science
SCARONI, A. W., Fuel Science
SCHOBERT, H. H., Fuel Science
SPEAR, K. E., Ceramic Science
THROWER, P. A., Materials Science
TRESSLER, R. E., Materials Science and Engineering

Meteorology:
ACKERMAN, T. P.
BANNON, P.
BOHREN, C. F.
BRUNE, W. H.
CAHIR, J. J.
CARLSON, T. N.
DUTTON, J. A.
FRANK, W. M.
FRASER, A. B.
FRITSCH, J. M.
LAMB, D.
THOMSON, D. W.
WYNGAARD, J. C.

Mineral Economics:
ROSE, A. Z.

Mineral Engineering:
ADEWUMI, M. A., Petroleum and Natural Gas Engineering
BISE, C. J., Mining Engineering
CHANDER, S.
ELSWORTH, D., Geo-Environmental Engineering
ERTEKIN, T., Petroleum and Natural Gas Engineering
HARDY, H. R., Jr
HOGG, R.
LUCKIE, P. T.
MUTMANSKY, J. M.
RAMANI, R. V.

College of Education:

Education Policy Studies:
BAKER, D. P., Education
BOYD, W. L.
GEIGER, R. L.
GRESSON, A. D., Education
HARTMAN, W. T.
HENDRICKSON, R. M.
JOHNSON, H. C., Jr
LINDSAY, B.
PRAKASH, M. S., Education
RATCLIFF, J. L.
REED, R. J.
TERENZINI, P. T.
TIPPECONNIC, J. W., Education
WILLOWER, D. J.

Adult Education, Instructional Systems, and Workforce Education and Development:
ASKOV, E. N.
DWYER, F. M.
GRAY, K. C., Education
JONASSEN, D. H., Education
PASSMORE, D. L., Vocational Education
ROTHWELL, W. J., Education

Curriculum and Instruction:
GIROUX, H.
JOHNSON, J. E.
KINCHELOE, J. L.
LUNETTA, V. N.
NELSON, M. R., Education and American Studies
NICELY, R. F., Jr
RUBBA, P. A., Jr
SHANNON, P.
YAWKEY, T. C.

Counselor Education, Counseling Psychology, and Rehabilitation Services:
HERR, E. L., Education
KEAT, D. B., II, Education and Counseling Psychology
SLANEY, R. B., Counseling Psychology
SWISHER, J. D., Education

Educational and School Psychology and Special Education:
GAJAR, A. H., Special Education
HALE, R. L., Education
HUGHES, C. A., Education
MEYER, B. J. F., Educational Psychology
NEISWORTH, J. T., Special Education
ROBERTS, D. M., Educational Psychology
SALVIA, J. A., Special Education
SUEN, H. K., Educational Psychology

College of Science:

Astronomy and Astrophysics:
FEIGELSON, E. D.
GARMIRE, G. P.
MESZAROS, P. I.
RAMSEY, L. W.
USHER, P. D.
WEEDMAN, D. W.
WOLSZCZAN, A.

Biochemistry and Molecular Biology:
BRENCHLEY, J. E., Microbiology and Biotechnology
BRYANT, D. A., Biotechnology
DEERING, R. A.
FERRY, J. G., Biochemistry and Molecular Biology
FRISQUE, A. J., Molecular Virology
GAY, C. V., Cell Biology and Poultry Science
GOLBECK, J. H., Biochemistry and Biophysics
HAMMERSTEDT, R. H., Biochemistry
HARDISON, R. C., Biochemistry
HYMER, W. C., Biochemistry
JOHNSON, K. A., Biochemistry
KAO, T., Biochemistry and Molecular Biology
MASTRO, A. M., Microbiology and Cell Biology
PHILLIPS, A. T., Biochemistry
SCHLEGEL, R. A., Biochemistry and Molecular Biology
SIMPSON, R. T., Biochemistry and Molecular Biology
TAYLOR, W. D., Biophysics
TIEN, M., Biochemistry
TU, C. P. D., Biochemistry and Molecular Biology
UNZ, R. F., Environmental Microbiology

Biology (including Botany, Genetics and Zoology):
ANTHONY, A., Biology
ASSMANN, S. M.
BURSEY, C. R., Biology
CLARK, A. G., Biology
COSGROVE, D. J., Biology
FEDOROFF, N. V.
JEFFREY, W. R.
KEENER, C. S., Biology
MITCHELL, R. B.
NEI, M., Biology
SELANDER, R. K., Biology
STEPHENSON, A. G., Biology
WALKER, A., Anthropology and Biology
WOLFE, C. B., Jr, Biology

Chemistry:
ALLARA, D. L.
ALLCOCK, H. R.
ANDERSON, J. B.
BENKOVIC, S. J.
BERNHEIM, R. A.
BITTNER, E. R.
CASTLEMAN, A. W.
DE ROSA, M.
EWING, A. G.
FUNK, R. L.
GARRISON, B. J.
GOLD, L. P.
HARRISON, E. A.
HORROCKS, W. DE W.
JURS, P. C.
LOWE, J. P.
MALLOUK, T. E.
MARICONDI, C.
MARONCELLI, M.
MATTHEWS, C. R.
MERZ, K. M.
SEN, A.
WEINREB, S. M., Natural Products Chemistry
WINOGRAD, N.

Mathematics:
ANDERSON, J. H.
ANDREWS, G. E.
ARMENTROUT, S.
ARNOLD, D.
BANYAGA, A.
BARSHINGER, R. N.
BAUM, P.
BRONSHTEYN, I.
BROWNAWELL, W. D.
BRYLINSKI, J. L.
BRYLINSKI, R.
CALDERER, M. C.
DAWSON, J.
DEUTSCH, F.
FORMANEK, E.
HIGSON, N.
HUNTER, R. P.
JAMES, D. G.
JECH, T. J.
KATOK, A.
KATOK, S.
KRALL, A. M.
LALLEMENT, G. J.
LI, W. C. W.
MCCAMMON, M. L.
MASERICK, P. H.
MULLEN, G. L.
MYERS, R. E.
NISTOR, V.
NOURI-MOGHADAM, M. R.
OCNEANU, A.
PESIN, Y. B.
REGEV, A.
RUNG, D. C.
SIMPSON, S.
TSYGAN, B.
VASERSTEIN, L.
WARE, R. P.
WATERHOUSE, W. C.
WAYNE, C. E.
WELLS, R.
XU, J.
ZARHIN, Y.
ZEMYAN, S. M.

Physics:
ASHTEKAR, A. V.
BANAVAR, J. R.
CAMARDA, H. S.
CHAN, M. H. W.
COLE, M. W.
COLLINS, J. C.
COLLINS, R. W.
EIDES, M. J.

ERNST, W. E.
FREED, N.
GROTCH, H.
GUNAYDIN, M.
HERMAN, R. M.
HOULIHAN, J. F.
MAYNARD, J. D.
MILLER, D. E.
MONROE, J. L.
OBERMYER, R. T.
PATEL, J. S.
SMITH, G. A.
SMOLIN, L.
SOKOL, P. E.
STRIKMAN, M.
WHITMORE, J. J.
WILLIS, R. F.
WINTER, T. G.

Statistics:

AKRITAS, M. G.
BABU, G. J.
CHINCHILLI, V.
HARKNESS, W. L.
HETTMANSPERGER, T. P.
LINDSAY, B. G.
ORD, J. K.
PATIL, G. P.
RAO, C. R.
ROSENBERGER, J. L.
TEMPELMAN, A.

College of Engineering:

Acoustics:

ATCHLEY, A. A.
GARRETT, S. L.
LAUCHLE, G. C.

Aerospace Engineering:

AMOS, A. K.
LAKSHMINARAYANA, B.
MCLAUGHLIN, D. K.
MORRIS, P. J.

Agricultural and Biological Engineering:

BUFFINGTON, D. E.
ELLIOTT, H. A.
GRAVES, R. E.
JARRETT, A. R.
MANBECK, H. B.
MORROW, C. T.
MURPHY, D. J.
PURI, V. M.
WALKER, P. N.

Architectural Engineering:

BEHR, R. A.
BURNETT, E. F. P., Architectural and Civil Engineering
GESCHWINDER, L. F.
MUMMA, S. A.
SANVIDO, V. E.
YUILL, G. K.

Bioengineering:

GESELOWITZ, D. B., Bioengineering and Medicine
LIPOWSKY, H. H., Bioengineering and Engineering Science
ROSENBERG, G., Bioengineering and Surgery
SHUNG, K. K.

Chemical Engineering:

DANNER, R. P.
DAUBERT, T. E.
DUDA, J. L.
MCWHIRTER, J. R.
NAGARAJAN, R.
PHILLIPS, J.
TARBELL, J. M.
ULTMAN, J. S.
VANNICE, M. A.
VRENTAS, J. S.

Civil and Environmental Engineering:

ANDERSON, D. A.
BURNETT, E. F. P., Architectural and Civil Engineering
JOVANIS, P. P.
KILARESKI, W. P.
KRAUTHAMMER, T.
LOGAN, B. E.
MCDONNELL, A. J.
MASON, J. M.
MATSON, J. V.
MILLER, A. C.
REGAN, R. W.
SCANLON, A.
THOMAS, H. R.
UNZ, R. F., Environmental Microbiology
WANG, M. C.
YEH, G. T.

Computer Science and Engineering:

BARLOW, J.
DAS, C.
FENG, T.-Y.
GRIGORIEV, D.
IRWIN, M. J.
KOSTURI, R.
LAMBERT, J. M.
METZNER, J. J.
MILLER, D. A.
MILLER, W. C.

Electrical Engineering:

BOSE, N. K., Electrical Engineering
BREAKALL, J. K.
BURTON, L. C., Electrical and Computer Engineering
CROSKEY, C. L.
CROSS, L. E., Electrical Engineering
FERRARO, A. J., Electrical Engineering
GILDENBLAT, G., Electrical Engineering
HALL, D. L.
JACKSON, T. N., Electrical Engineering
KAVEHRAD, M.
KHOO, I. C., Electrical Engineering
KUNZ, K. S., Electrical Engineering
KURTZ, S. K., Electrical Engineering
LEE, K. Y., Electrical Engineering
LUEBBERS, R. J., Electrical Engineering
MATTHEWS, J. D., Electrical Engineering
MILLER, D. L., Electrical Engineering
MITCHELL, J. D., Electrical Engineering
PHILBRICK, C. R., Electrical Engineering
PHOHA, S., Electrical and Computer Engineering
ROBINSON, J. W., Electrical Engineering
RUZYLLO, J.
UCHINO, K., Electrical Engineering
VARADAN, V. K., Electrical Engineering
VARADAN, V. V., Electrical Engineering
WRONSKI, C. R., Microelectronic Materials and Devices
YU, F. T. S., Electrical Engineering

Engineering Science and Mechanics:

AMATEAU, M. F., Engineering Science and Mechanics
ASHOK, S., Engineering Science
CONWAY, J. C., Engineering Mechanics
FONASH, S. J., Engineering Sciences
GERMAN, R. M., Materials
HAYEK, S. I., Engineering Mechanics
HETTCHE, L. R., Engineering Research
LAKHTAKIA, A.
LENAHAN, P. M., Engineering Science and Mechanics
LIPOWSKY, H. H., Bioengineering and Engineering Science
MCGRATH, R. T.
MCNITT, R. P., Engineering Science and Mechanics
MESSIER, R. F., Engineering Science and Mechanics
PANGBORN, R. N., Engineering Mechanics
QUEENEY, R. A., Engineering Mechanics
ROSE, J. L., Engineering Design and Manufacturing
SALAMON, N. L., Engineering Science and Mechanics
THOMPSON, W., Jr, Engineering Science
TITTMANN, B. R., Engineering
VARADAN, V. K., Engineering Science and Mechanics
VARADAN, V. V., Engineering Science and Mechanics, and Electrical Engineering
VENTSEL, E. S., Engineering Science
WRONSKI, C. R., Microelectronic Devices and Materials
ZAMRIK, S. Y., Engineering Mechanics

School of Engineering Technology and Commonwealth Engineering:

BARTKOWIAK, R. A.
EISENBERG, E., Engineering
HAGER, W. R.
WALTERS
WEED, M. L.

Industrial and Manufacturing Engineering:

CAVALIER, T. M.
CHANDRA, M. J.
COHEN, P. H.
ENSCORE, E. E.
FREIVALDS, A.
JOSHI, S. B.
RAVINDRAN, A.
RUUD, C. O.
TIRUPATIKUMARA, S. R.
VENTURA, J. A.
VOIGHT, R. C.
WYSK, R. A.

Mechanical Engineering:

BENSON, R. C.
BRASSEUR, J. G.
BRIGHTON, J. A.
CHEUNG, F. B.
CIMBALA, J. M.
GILMORE, B. J.
HARRIS, T. A.
HEINSOHN, R. J.
HENRY, J. J.
KOOPMAN, G. H.
KULAKOWSKI, B. T.
KULKARNI, A. K.
KUO, K. K.
LITZINGER, T. A.
MERKLE, C. L.
MODEST, M. F.
RAY, A.
SANTAVICA, D. A.
SANTORO, R. J.
SETTLES, G. S.
SINHA, A.
SOMMER, H. J., III
STREIT, D. A.
THYNELL, S. T.
TRETHEWY, M. W.
TURNS, S. R.
WANG, K. W.
WEBB, R. L.
WORMLEY, D. N.
YANG, V.

Nuclear Engineering:

BARATTA, A. J.
CATCHEN, G. L.
HOCHREITER, L.
JESTER, W. A.
KLEVANS, E. H.

College of Health and Human Development:

Biobehavioural Health:

FINKELSTEIN, J. W.
GRAHAM, J. W., Biobehavioural Health and Human Development
JONES, B. C., Biobehavioural Health and Pharmacology
KOZLOWSKI, L. T.
MCCLEARN, G. E., Biobehavioural Health and Psychology
NICHOLSON, M. E., Health Education and Biobehavioural Health
SUSMAN, E. J., Biobehavioural Health, Human Development and Nursing
VICARY, J. R.

Communication Disorders:

BLOOD, G. W.
FRANK, T. A., Audiology
PROSEK, R. A.

Health Policy and Administration:
BRANNON, S. D.
SHORT, P. F.
YESALIS, C. E., III, Health Policy and Administration, and Exercise and Sport Science
YU, L. C.

Kinesiology:
CANNON, J. G.
CAVANAUGH, P. R., Locomotion Studies
ECKHARDT, R. B., Development Genetics
FARRELL, P. A., Applied Physiology
KENNY, W. L., Applied Physiology
KRAEMER, W. J., Applied Psychology
KRETCHMAR, R. S.
LARSSON, L. G., Physiology
LUNDEGREN, H. M., Physical Education and Leisure Studies
NEWELL, K. M.
PATERNO, J. V., Physical Education
THOMPSON, J. G.
YESALIS, C. E., III, Health Policy and Administration, and Exercise and Sport Science
ZATSIORSKY, V.

School of Hotel, Restaurant and Recreational Management:
GODBEY, G. C., Leisure Studies
LEE, R. D., Public Administration
LUNDEGREN, H. M., Physical Education and Leisure Studies
MANN, S. H., Operations Research
SHAFER, E. L., Environmental Management and Tourism

Human Development and Family Studies:
BARRY, K., Human Development
BELSKY, J.
BIRCH, L. L.
BURGESS, R. L.
BURTON, L. M., Sociology and Human Development
COLLINS, L. M.
CROUTER, A. C., Human Development
D'AUGELLI, A. R., Human Development
DRAPER, P., Anthropology and Human Development
EDELBROCK, C. S., Behavioural Health
GRAHAM, J. W., Biobehavioural Health and Human Development
GREENBERG, M. T.
HARPENDING, H. C., Anthropology and Human Development
MCHALE, S. M., Human Devlopment
SCHAIE, K. W., Human Development and Psychology
SPANIER, G. B., Human Development, Sociology and Family and Community Medicine
SUSMAN, E. J., Bio-behavioural Health, Human Development and Nursing
VERNON-FEAGANS, L.
VONDRACEK, F. W.
WILLIS, S. L.
ZARIT, S. H., Human Development

Nursing:
GUELDNER, S. H.
HOLT, F. M.
SUSMAN, E. J., Biobehavioural Health, Human Development and Nursing

Nutrition:
ACHTERBERG, C. L.
BEARD, J. L.
GREEN, M. H., Nutrition Science
KRIS-ETHERTON, P. M., Nutrition Science
MARETZKI, A. N., Food Science and Nutrition
MILNER, J. A., Nutrition
PICCIANO, M. F., Nutrition
ROLLS, B. J., Nutrition and Biobehavioural Health
ROSS, A. C., Nutrition
ST PIERRE, R., Nutrition Policy and Health Education
SHANNON, B. M., Nutrition
WRIGHT, H. S., Nutrition
YEH, Y.

College of the Liberal Arts:

African and African American Studies:
MCBRIDE, D.
STEWART, J. B.

American Studies:
BERNER, R. T., Journalism and American Studies
KESSLER, C. F., English, Women's Studies and American Studies
NELSON, M. R., Education and American Studies
SECOR, R. A., English and American Studies

Anthropology:
DRAPER, P.
DURRENBERGER, E.
HARPENDING, H. C.
HIRTH, K. G.
MILNER, G. R.
SNOW, D. R.
WALKER, A., Anthropology and Biology
WEBSTER, D. L.
WEISS, K. M., Anthropology and Genetics
WOOD, J. W.

Classics and Ancient Mediterranean Studies:
BALDI, P. H., Linguistics and Classics

Comparative Literature:
BEGNAL, M., English and Comparative Literature
DE ARMAS, F., Spanish and Comparative Literature
ECKHARDT, C. D., English and Comparative Literature
EDWARDS, R. R., English and Comparative Literature
GINSBERG, R. E., Philosophy
GROSSMAN, K., French
HALE, T. A., African, French, and Comparative Literature
LIMA, R. F., Spanish and Comparative Literature
MANN, C. W., English and Comparative Literature
STOEKL, A., French and Comparative Literature
STRASSER, G. F., German and Comparative Literature
WEINTRAUB, S., Arts and Humanities

Crime, Law and Justice:
BERNARD, T. J., Sociology, and Crime, Law and Justice
BLOCK, A. A.
GOODSTEIN, L. I., Administration of Justice, and Women's Studies
KRAMER, J. H., Sociology, and Administration of Justice
LEE, B. A., Sociology
OSGOOD, D. W.
RUBACK, R. B.
STEFFENSMEIER, D., Sociology, and Crime, Law and Justice

Economics:
BIERENS, H. J.
BOND, E. W.
FELLER, I.
FOX, T. G.
GHYSELS, E.
KLEIN, P. A.
KRISHNA, K.
KRISHNA, V.
LOMBRA, R. E.
MARSHALL, R. C.
NELSON, J. P.
ROBERTS, M. J.
RODGERS, J. D.
WELSH, A. L.
WALLACE, N.

English:
BEGNAL, M. H., English and Comparative Literature
BELL, B.
BIALOSTOSKY, D.
CLAUSEN, C.
CROWLEY, S.
DOWNS, R. C. S.
ECKHARDT, C. D., English and Comparative Literature
EDWARDS, R., English and Comparative Literature
HARRIS, S. K.
HUME, K.
HUME, R. D.
KESSLER, C. F., English, American Studies, and Women's Studies
MCCARTHY, W. B.
MANN, C. W., English and Comparative Literature
SECOR, R. A., English and American Studies
SORKIN, A. J.
SQUIER, S. M., Women's Studies and English
WATKINS, E.
WEIGL, B.
WEINTRAUB, S., Arts and Humanities
WEST, J. L. W.
WOODBRIDGE, L.

French:
BRAGGER, J. D.
BRAULT, G. J., French and Medieval Studies
GROSSMAN, K. M.
HALE, T. A., African, French and Comparative Literature
MAKWARD, C. J., French, and Women's Studies
STOEKL, A., French, and Comparative Literature

German and Slavic Languages:
EICHHOFF, J.
GENTRY, F. G.
NAYDAN, M. M.
SCHMALSTEIG, W.
SCHURER, E.
STRASSER, G. F., German and Comparative Literature

History:
AURAND, H. W., American History
BROYLES, M., Music and American History
CROSS, G. S., European History
GALLAGHER, G. W., American History
GOLDSCHMIDT, A., Jr, Middle East History
HALPERN, B., Ancient History and Religious Studies; Jewish Studies
JENKINS, P., Religious Studies and History
LANDES, J. B., Women's Studies and History
MCMURRY, S. A.
MADDOX, R. J., American History
MOSES, W. J., African-American History
MURPHY, B. A., History and Politics
PENCAK, W. A., History
PROCTOR, R. N., History of Science
ROEBER, A. G., Early Modern History and Religious Studies
ROSE, P. L., European History, Jewish Studies
SCHIEBINGER, L. L., European History and Women's Studies
SILVERMAN, D. P., European History
SWEENEY, J. R., Medieval History

Jewish Studies
HALPERN, B., Ancient History and Religious Studies
ROSE, P. L.

Labour Studies and Industrial Relations:
FILIPPELI, R. L.
STEWART, J. B.
WARDELL, M.

Linguistics:
BALDI, P. H., Linguistics and Classics
LYDAY, L. F., Spanish
SCHMALSTIEG, W. R., Slavic Languages

Philosophy:
COLAPIETRO, V.
GINSBERG, R. E.
GROSHOLZ, E. R.
JACQUETTE, D. L.

KERZBERG, P.
LINGIS, A. F.
MITCHAM, C.
SALLIS, J.
SCOTT, C. E.
STUHR, J. J.
VAUGHT, C. G.

Political Science:

ALBINSKI, H. S., Political Science, and Australian and New Zealand Studies
BREMER, S.
CIMBALA, S. J.
EISENSTEIN, J.
HARKAVY, R. E.
KEYNES, E.
KOCHANEK, S. A.
LAPORTE, R., Jr, Public Administration and Political Science
MARTZ, J. D.
SCAFF, L. A.
STRASSER, J.
WELCH, S.

Psychology:

BIERMAN, K. L.
BORKOVEC, T. D.
CARLSON, R.
COLE, P. M.
CRNIC, K. A.
FARR, J. L.
JACOBS, R. R.
JOHNSON, J. A.
KROLL, J. F.
LIBEN, L. S.
MCCLEARN, G. E., Human Development and Psychology
MARK, M. M.
MICHELSON, L.
NELSON, K. E.
RAY, W. J.
ROSENBAUM, D. A.
SCHAIE, K. W., Human Development and Psychology
SHIELDS, S. A., Women's Studies and Psychology
SHOTLAND, R. L.
STERN, R. M.
STREUFERT, S., Behavioural Science and Psychology
THOMAS, H.

Slavic and East European Languages:

NAYDAN, M. M.
SCHMALSTIEG, W. R.

Sociology:

BERNARD, T., Crime, Law and Justice, and Sociology
BOOTH, A.
BURTON, L., Human Development and Sociology
CLEMENTE, F. A.
DE JONG, G. F.
FIREBAUGH, G.
HAYWARD, M. D.
LEE, B. A.
LICHTER, D. T.
NELSEN, H. M.
SICA, A.
SPANIER, G. B., Human Development, Sociology, and Family and Community Medicine
STEFFENSMEIER, D. J., Sociology, and Crime, Law and Justice

Spanish, Italian and Portuguese:

DE ARMAS, F., Spanish and Comparative Literature
FITZ, E. E., Portuguese, Spanish and Comparative Literature
GONZALEZ-PÉREZ, A., Spanish
LIMA, R. F., Jr, Spanish and Comparative Literature
LYDAY, L. F., III, Spanish
PEAVLER, T. J., Spanish and Comparative Literature
WEISS, B., Italian

Speech Communication:

BENSON, T. W.
CANARY, D. J.
GOURAN, D. S.
GREGG, R. B.
HECHT, M.
HENNING, G. H.
HOGAN, J.
SAVIGNON, S.

Women's Studies:

GEORGE, D. H., English and Women's Studies
GOODSTEIN, L., Administration of Justice and Women's Studies
KESSLER, C. F., English, American Studies and Women's Studies
LANDERS, J. B., Women's Studies and History
MAKWARD, C . J., French and Women's Studies
MANSFIELD, P. K., Women's Studies and Health Education
SCHIEBINGER, L. L., European History and Women's Studies
SHIELDS, S.A., Women's Studies and Psychology
SQUIER, S. M., Women's Studies and English

Department of Military Science:

HANER, Lt-Col W.

Department of Naval Science:

ZIEBELL, Capt. G. G.

Department of Air Force Aerospace Studies:

PHILLIPS, Col R. D.

College of Medicine–Hershey:

ABER, R. C., Medicine
ABT, A. B., Pathology
AL-MONDHIRY, H. A. B., Haematology
APPELBAUM, P. C., Pathology
BALLARD, J. O., Haematology
BARNARD, D., Humanities
BELIS, J. A., Surgery
BERLIN, C. M., Paediatrics and Pharmacology
BHAVANANDAN, V. P., Biological Chemistry
BIEBUYCK, J. F., Anaesthesia and Biological Chemistry
BILLINGSLEY, M. L., Neuroscience
BIXLER, E. O., Psychiatry
BLANKENSHIP, G. W., Ophthalmology
BOAL, D. K., Radiology and Paediatrics
BOND, J. S., Biological Chemistry
BOTTI, J. J., Obstetrics and Gynaecology
BRENNAN, R. W., Medicine and Neurology
CAIN, J. M., Obstetrics and Gynaecology
CAMPBELL, D. B., Cardiothoracic Surgery
CAVANAUGH, P. R., Endocrinology, Diabetes, Metabolism
CHEUNG, J. Y. S., Nephrology, Cellular and Molecular Physiology
CHINCHILLI, V. M., Biostatistics
CLAWSON, G. A., Pathology and Biological Chemistry
CONNOR, J. D., Pharmacology
CONNOR, J. R., Anatomy
COURTNEY, R. J., Microbiology and Immunology
DAMIANO, R. J., Surgery, and Cellular and Molecular Physiology
DAVIS, D., Cardiology
DEMERS, L. M., Endocrinology and Pathology
DIAMOND, J. R.
DOSSETT, J. H., Paediatric Infectious Diseases
DWORKIN, B. R., Behavioural Science and Psychology
EHRLICH, H. P., Surgery
ESLINGER, P. J., Behavioural Science and Medicine
EVARTS, C. M., Surgery
EYSTER, M. E., Medicine and Haematology
FLOROS, F., Cellular and Molecular Physiology
GASCHO, J. A., Cardiology
GOLDMAN, J. N., Infectious Diseases and Immunology
GRIFFITHS, J. W., Jr, Comparative Medicine
HAMMOND, J. M., Endocrinology
HAMORY, B. H., Infectious Diseases and Epidemiology
HARTMAN, D. S., Radiology
HARVEY, H. A., Medical Oncology
HERMAN, J. M., Family and Community Medicine
HILL, C. W., Biological Chemistry
HOPPER, A. K., Biological Chemistry
HOPPER, J. E., Cell and Molecular Biology
HOPPER, K. D., Radiology
HOUTS, P. S., Behavioural Science
HOWETT, M. K., Microbiology and Immunology
HUFFORD, D. J., Family and Community Medicine and Behavioural Science
ISOM, H. C., Cell and Molecular Biology
JEFFERSON, L. S., Cell and Molecular Physiology
JEFFRIES, G. H., Medicine and Gastroenterology
JOHNSON, D. L., Surgery
JOHNSON, E. W., Cellular and Molecular Physiology
JONES, M. B., Behavioural Science and Psychology
KALES, A., Psychiatry
KALES, J. D., Community and Social Psychiatry
KAUFFMAN, G. L., Jr, Physiology and Surgery
KNUTSON, D. W., Medicine
KOCH, K. L., Gastroenterology
KREIDER, J. W., Pathology and Microbiology
KRUMMEL, T. M., Surgery and Paediatrics
KULIN, H. E., Endocrinology
LADDA, R. L., Paediatrics and Genetics
LANG, C. H., Physiology and Surgery
LANG, C. M., Comparative Medicine
LANGHOFF, E., Medicine
LA NOUE, K. F., Cell and Molecular Biology and Physiology
LEAMAN, D. M., Cardiology
LEHMAN, R. A., Neurosurgery
LEURE-DUPREE, A., Anatomy and Neuroscience
LEVENSON, R. G., Pharmacology
LEVENTHAL, R., Biology
LIPTON, A., Medicine and Medical Oncology
LLOYD, T. A., Reproductive Endocrinology
LONG, J. S., Pharmacology
LYDIC, R., Neuroscience
MADEWELL, J. E., Radiology
MALONEY, M. E., Medicine
MANNI, A., Endocrinology
MARKS, J. G., Dermatology
MARKS, K. H., Newborn Medicine
MILLER, B. A., Paediatrics
MILLER, K. L., Radiology
MILNER, R. J., Neuroscience and Anatomy
MORTEL, R., Obstetrics and Gynaecology
MOSER, R. P., Jr, Radiology
MUCHA, P., General Surgery
NACCARELLI, G. V., Cardiology
NAEYE, R. L., Pathology
NORGREN, R., Behavioural Science and Psychology
OUYANG, A., Medicine and Gastroenterology
PAE, W. E., Jr, Cardiothoracic Surgery
PAGE, R. B., Neuroscience and Anatomy
PEGG, A. E., Physiology and Pharmacology
PELLEGRINI, V. D., Orthopaedics
PHELPS, D. S., Paediatrics
POLAND, R. L., Paediatrics
POWERS, S. K., Neurosurgery
RANNELS, D. E., Physiology
REYNOLDS, H. Y., Medicine
ROSENBERG, G., Bioengineering and Surgery
RYBKA, W. B., Medicine
SALNESS, K. A., Emergency Medicine
SASSANI, J. W., Ophthalmology
SATYASWAROOP, P. G., Gynaecological Oncology
SCHENGRUND, C. L., Biological Chemistry

SCHWENTKER, E. P., Orthopaedics
SEVERS, W. B., Pharmacology and Neuroscience
SHIMAN, R., Biological Chemistry
SIMMS, G. R., Family and Community Medicine
SINOWAY, L. I., Cardiology
SPANIER, G. B., Human Development, Sociology and Family and Community Medicine
STAUFFER, J. L., Pulmonary and Critical Care
STREUFERT, S., Behavioural Science and Psychology
STRYKER, J. A., Radiology
TENSER, R. B., Medicine, Microbiology and Immunology
TEVETHIA, M. J., Microbiology and Immunology
TEVETHIA, S. S., Microbiology and Immunology
TOWFIGHI, J., Pathology
VANNUCCI, R. C., Paediatric Neurology
VARY, T. C., Physiology
VESELL, E. S., Pharmacology
WASSNER, S. J., Paediatrics and Paediatric Diabetes
WEISZ, J., Obstetrics and Gynaecology
WIDOME, M. D., Paediatrics
WIGDAHL, B., Microbiology and Immunology
WILLS, J. W., Microbiology and Immunology
YOUNG, M. J., Health Evaluation Science
ZAGON, I. S., Anatomy and Cell and Molecular Biology
ZAINO, R. J., Anatomic Pathology
ZELIS, R. F., Medicine, Cell and Molecular Biology and Cardiology

Harrisburg Capital College:
ASWAD, A., Engineering
BLUMBERG, M., Management
BRESLER, R. J., Public Policy
BRONNER, S. J., American Studies and Folklore
BRUHN, J. G., Sociology
CANTALUPO, C. R., English
CARDAMONE, M. J., Physics
CHISHOLM, R. F., Management
CIGLER, B. A., Public Policy and Administration
COLE, C. A., Engineering
COUCH, S. R., Sociology
DANDOIS, J. E., Engineering
DEXTER, C. R., Management and Marketing
DHIR, K. S., Business Administration
DISHNER, E. K., Education
FOXX, R., Psychology
HEISEY, R. M., Biology
HENK, W. A., Education and Reading
KAYNAK, E., Marketing
MAHAR, W. J., Humanities and Music
MARSICANO, A. J., Engineering
PETERSON, S. A., Public Affairs
PLANT, J. F., Public Policy and Administration
RABIN, J. M., Public Administration and Public Policy
RAY, G., Engineering
RICHMAN, I., American Studies and History
ROONEY, J. F., Sociology
SACHS, H. G., Biology
ZIEGENFUSS, J. T., Management and Health Care Systems

Erie Behrend College:
BALDWIN, D. R., English
FERNANDEZ-JIMENEZ, J., Spanish
FRANKFORTER, A. D., History
GAMBLE, J. K., Political Science and International Law
GEORGE, D. H., English and Women's Studies
KNACKE, R. F., Physics
LARSON, R. E., Mathematics
LILLEY, J. M., Music and Humanities
LOSS, A. K., English and American Studies
MAGENAU, J. M., III, Management
PROGELHOF, R. C., Mechanical Engineering
SALPER, R. L., Spanish and Women's Studies
SALVIA, A. A., Statistics
WOLFORD, C. L., English and Business

Penn State Abington:
ABT, V., Sociology and American Studies
AYOUB, A. B., Mathematics
COHN, P. N., Mathematics
JOHNSON, K. W., Mathematics
MILLER, L. P., English
MILLIS, M. C., Integrative Arts
MOORE, G. G., Chemistry
MUSTAZZA, L., English and American Studies
SANDLER, K. W., Romance Languages
SCHUSTER, I., Chemistry
SMITH, J. F., English and American Studies
STUTMAN, S., English, American Studies and Women's Studies

Penn State Altoona:
BECHTEL, L. J., Biobehavioural Health
MEADORS, A. C., Health Administration
MISKOVSKY, N. M., Physics
PILIONE, L. J., Physics
WINSOR, J. A., Biology

Penn State Berks–Lehigh Valley:
ACTOR, A. A., Physics
BARTKOWIAK, R. A., Engineering
GAIGE, F. H., History
LITVIN, D. B., Physics
LODWICK, K. L., History
MARCHALONIS, S., English and Women's Studies
MILAKOFSKY, L., Chemistry

ATTACHED RESEARCH INSTITUTES

Applied Research Laboratory: f. 1945; research and development in technical fields, especially underwater systems; Dir Dr L. RAYMOND HETTCHE..

Australia–New Zealand Studies Center: Dir Dr HENRY S. ALBINSKI.

Biotechnology Institute: f. 1984; Dir Dr NINA V. FEDOROFF.

Center for Applied Behavioural Sciences: Asst Dir Dr ROBERT J. VANCE

Center for Cell Research: f. 1987; a NASA center for commercial development of space; Dir Dr WESLEY C. HYMER.

Centre for Developmental and Health Genetics: Dir Dr GERALD E. MCCLEARN.

Particulate Materials Center: Dir Dr GARY L. MESSING.

Centre for Locomotion Studies: Dir Dr PETER R. CAVANAGH.

Center for the Study of Higher Education: Dir Dr JAMES L. RATCLIFF.

Environmental Resources Research Institute: Dir Dr ARCHIE J. MCDONNELL.

Gerontology Center: f. 1986; Dir Dr K. WARNER SCHAIE.

Health Physics Office: Dir RODGER W. GRANLUND.

Institute for the Arts and Humanistic Studies: Dir Dr ROBERT R. EDWARDS.

Institute for Policy Research and Evaluation: Dir Dr IRWIN FELLER.

Laboratory Animal Resources Program: f. 1966; Dir Dr FREDERICK G. FERGUSON.

Noll Physiological Research Center: Dir Dr WILLIAM J. EVANS.

Materials Research Laboratory: research into the science and technology of non-metallic materials; Dir Dr WILLIAM D. TAYLOR (acting).

Pennsylvania Transportation Institute: Dir Dr BOHDAN T. KULAKOWSKI.

Population Research Institute: Dir Dr DANIEL T. LICHTER.

PHILADELPHIA COLLEGE OF PHARMACY AND SCIENCE

600 South 43rd St, Philadelphia, PA 19104
Telephone: (215) 596-8800

Founded 1821

President: PHILIP P. GERBINO
Vice-President for Academic Affairs: BARBARA BYRNE
Dean of Students and Academic Support Services: JUANA REINA-LEWIS
Dean of Arts and Sciences: CHARLES W. GIBLEY, Jr
Dean of Pharmacy: GEORGE DOWNS
Financial Aid Officer: MICHAEL COLAHAN
Registrar: M. THERESE SCANLON
Librarian: MIGNON ADAMS

Library of 76,000 vols
Number of students: 2,000

Publication: *American Journal of Pharmacy* (quarterly).

DIRECTORS

Biological Sciences: MARGARET KASSCHAU
Biomedical Writing: LILI FOX VELEZ
Chemistry: EDWARD BIRNBAUM
Humanities: BEVERLEY ALMGREN (acting)
Mathematics, Physics and Computer Science: BERNARD BRUNNER
Medical Technology: MARGARET REINHART
Occupational Therapy: RUTH SCHEMM
Pharmaceutical Sciences: EDWIN T. SUGITA
Pharmacy Practice and Administration: REBECCA FINLEY
Physical Education: ROBERT MORGAN
Physical Therapy: ANNETTE IGLARSH
Physician Assistants: KENNETH HARBERT
Social Sciences: JOSEPH LAMBERT

PHILADELPHIA COLLEGE OF TEXTILES AND SCIENCE

School House Lane and Henry Ave, Philadelphia, PA 19144
Telephone: (215) 951-2700
Fax: (215) 951-2615

Founded 1884

President: JAMES P. GALLAGHER
Vice-President for Enrollment and Student Affairs: JANE H. ANTHEIL
Vice-President of Academic Affairs: CAROL S. FIXMAN
Vice-President for Business and Finance: RANDALL D. GENTZLER

Library of 88,000 vols, 16,000 periodicals, 5,500 microforms
Number of teachers: 90
Number of students: 3,400

ROSEMONT COLLEGE

1400 Montgomery Ave, Rosemont, PA 19010
Telephone: (215) 527-0200
Fax: (610) 527-1041

Founded 1921
Catholic liberal arts college

President: MARGARET M. HEALY
Registrar: JOSEPH T. ROGERS
Academic Dean: PAUL MOJZES
Director of Admissions: SANDRA ZERBY
Librarian: CATHERINE M. FENNELL

Library of 157,000 vols
Number of teachers: 141
Number of students: 361 full-time, 434 part-time, 152 graduate

SAINT FRANCIS COLLEGE

Loretto, PA 15940
Telephone: (814) 472-3000

Founded 1847

President: Rev. CHRISTIAN ORAVEC

Assistant to the President: Dr RICHARD CRAWFORD
Vice-President for Academic Affairs: Dr KATHLEEN OWENS
Vice-President for Finance: RICHARD GAJEWSKI
Vice-President for Student Affairs: Dr DENNIS RIEGELNEGG
Director of Development: RAYMOND PONCHIONE
Director of Library: PATRICIA SEROTKIN

Library of 199,000 vols
Number of teachers: 172
Number of students: 2,000

SAINT JOSEPH'S UNIVERSITY

5600 City Ave, Philadelphia, PA 19131
Telephone: (610) 660-1000
Fax: (610) 660-3300
Founded 1851

President: NICHOLAS S. RASHFORD
Assistant Vice-President for Enrollment Management: DAVID CONWAY
Vice-President for Academic Affairs: Dr DANIEL J. CURRAN
Registrar: GERARD DONAHUE
Librarian: EVELYN MINICK

Library of 335,000 vols
Number of teachers: 189 full-time, 239 part-time
Number of students: 3,076 day, 1,128 evening, 2,823 graduate.

Degree courses in the liberal arts, science, business administration and computer sciences.

SAINT VINCENT COLLEGE

Latrobe, PA 15650-2690
Telephone: (412) 539-9761
Founded 1846

President: Rev. MARTIN R. BARTEL
Provost: Bro. NORMAN HIPPS
Dean of Students: Rev. FRANK ZIEMKIEWICZ
Academic Dean: Dr BARBARA A. EDWARDS
Associate Academic Dean: ALICE KAYLOR
Director of Admission and Financial Aid: Rev. PAUL TAYLOR
Registrar: CELINE R. HAAS
Librarian: Rev. CHRYSOSTOM V. SCHLIMM

Library of 340,000 vols
Number of teachers: 90
Number of students: 1,200

Publication: *Saint Vincent Magazine* (quarterly).

SETON HILL COLLEGE

Greensburg, PA 15601
Telephone: (412) 834-2200
Founded 1883

President: JOANNE W. BOYLE
Vice-President for Enrollment Services: BARBARA HINKLE
Director of Library: DAVID STANLEY

Library of 118,400 vols
Number of teachers: 51 full-time, 47 part-time
Number of students: 1,095

SHIPPENSBURG UNIVERSITY OF PENNSYLVANIA

1871 Old Main Drive, Shippensburg, PA 17257
Telephone: (717) 532-9121
Fax: (717) 532-1273
Founded 1871

President: ANTHONY F. CEDDIA
Provost and Vice-President (Academic Affairs): JOANN C. FENTON
Associate Provost: Dr RICK RUTH
Vice-President for Student Affairs: Dr GEORGE F. HARPSTER Jr
Vice-President for Administration and Finance: GREIG MITCHELL
Dean of Special Academic Programs: Dr ELNETTA JONES
Dean of Admissions: JOSEPH CRETELLA
Librarian: Dr MADELYN VALUNAS

Library of over 2,000,000 items
Number of teachers: 375
Number of students: 6,603

DEANS

College of Arts and Sciences: JANET S. GROSS
College of Business: JAMES A. POPE, III
College of Education and Human Services: ROBERT B. BARTOS

SLIPPERY ROCK UNIVERSITY OF PENNSYLVANIA

Slippery Rock, PA 16057
Telephone: (724) 738-9000
Fax: (724) 738-2098
Founded 1889

President: Dr G. WARREN SMITH, II
Provost and Vice-President for Academic Affairs: Dr ANNE GRIFFITHS (interim)
Vice-President of Finance and Administrative Affairs: CHARLES CURRY
Vice-President for Student Affairs and Dean of Students: Dr SHARON JOHNSON
Vice-President of University Advancement: ROBERT J. MOLLENHAUER
Director of Academic Records and Summer School: ELIOTT BAKER
Director of Admissions: Dr DUNCAN SARGENT
Director of Library Services: Dr BARBARA FARAH

Library of 875,000 vols
Number of teachers: 400
Number of students: 7,038

Publications: *The Rock* (quarterly), *The Rocket* (weekly), *Saxigena* (annually), *Ginger Hill* (annually).

DEANS

College of Arts and Sciences: Dr CHARLES ZUZAK
College of Education: Dr CATHERINE MORSINK
College of Health and Human Services: Dr LEONA DA RASCENZO (interim)
College of Information Science and Business Administration: Dr FRANK MASTRIANNA
Graduate Studies and Research: (vacant)
Academic Services and Retention: Dr ROBERT WATSON

SUSQUEHANNA UNIVERSITY

Selinsgrove, PA 17870
Telephone: (717) 374-0101
Fax: (717) 372-4040
Founded 1858

President: Dr JOEL L. CUNNINGHAM
Dean of Faculty: Dr WARREN FUNK
Librarian: KATHLEEN GUNNING

Library of 244,000 vols
Number of teachers: 100
Number of students: 1,500

Publication: *Susquehanna University Studies*.

SWARTHMORE COLLEGE

500 College Avenue, Swarthmore, PA 19081
Telephone: (610) 328-8000
Fax: (610) 328-8673

Founded 1864 by members of the Religious Society of Friends

President: ALFRED H. BLOOM
Vice-President: PAUL ASLANIAN
Registrar: MARTIN O. WARNER
Provost: JENNIE KEITH
Dean: ROBERT GROSS
Librarian: PEGGY SEIDEN

Library of 776,000 vols
Number of teachers: 175
Number of students: 657 men, 787 women

Publication: *Bulletin*.

TEMPLE UNIVERSITY

Broad St and Montgomery Ave, Philadelphia, PA 19122
Telephone: (215) 787-7000
Founded 1884

President: PETER J. LIACOURAS
Provost: BARBARA L. BROWNSTEIN
Vice Presidents:
Financial Affairs: RICHARD A. CHANT (acting)
Development and Alumni Affairs: STEVEN R. DERBY
Health Sciences Center: LEON H. MALMUD
Administration: H. PATRICK SWYGERT
Secretary: WILLIAM C. SEYLER
Librarian: MAUREEN PASTINE

Library of *c.* 1,600,000 vols
Number of teachers: *c.* 2,600
Number of students: 31,001

Publications: *Law Quarterly, The American Journal of Legal History, Temple Review, Journal of Economics and Business,* etc.

DEANS

Tyler School of Art: GEORGE V. BAYLISS
Ambler Campus: JAMES H. BLACKHURST
College of Arts and Sciences: LOIS S. CRONHOLM
School of Business and Management: WILLIAM C. DUNKELBERG
College of Education: RICHARD M. ENGLERT
School of Medicine: MARTIN GOLDBERG
College of ECSA: FREDERICK B. HIGGINS
College of HPERD: DONALD R. HILSENDAGER
College of Music: HELEN L. LAIRD
College of Allied Health: MARY LEE SEIBERT
School of Communications and Theater: ROBERT R. SMITH
School of Law: JAMES STRAZZELLA
School of Dentistry: F. MARTIN TANSY
Graduate School: WILLIAM R. TASH
School of Pharmacy: ADELAIDE VAN TITUS
School of Social Administration: IONE D. VARGUS
Student Affairs Administration: KRISTL L. WIERNICKI

THIEL COLLEGE

Greenville, PA 16125
Telephone: (412) 589-2000
Founded 1866

President: C. CARLYLE HAALAND
Vice-President for Academic Affairs and Dean of College: Dr ROBERT C. OLSON
Vice-President for Administrative Services: Dr RICHARD H. RUGEN
Dean of Students: TRICIA L. HALLER (interim)
Director of Enrollment Management: STEPHEN EIDSON
Director of Financial Aid: CINDY FARRELL
Director of Development, External Affairs: DAVID J. GROBER (interim)
Director of Development, Internal Affairs: MARIANNE CALENDA (interim)
Librarian: DOUGLAS J. CERRONI

Library of 135,000 vols
Number of teachers: 57
Number of students: 965

THOMAS JEFFERSON UNIVERSITY

11th and Walnut Sts, Philadelphia, PA 19107
Telephone: (215) 955-6000
Founded 1824

President: Dr PAUL C. BRUCKER
Registrars: Dr JAMES B. ERDMANN (Jefferson Medical College), DIANE COLLINGS (College of Graduate Studies), MICHAEL J. PAQUET

(College of Allied Health Sciences), EDWARD W. TAWYEA
Librarian: EDWARD N. TAWYEA

Library of 167,504 vols
Number of teachers: 761
Number of students: 2,596

DEANS

Jefferson Medical College: JOSEPH S. GONNELLA
College of Graduate Studies: JUSSI J. SAUKKONEN
College of Allied Health Sciences: LAWRENCE ABRAMS

HEADS OF DEPARTMENTS

Jefferson Medical College:

Anatomy: E. MARSHALL JOHNSON
Anaesthesiology: JOSEPH L. SELTZER
Biochemistry: DARWIN J. PROCKOP
Dermatology: JOUNI J. UITTO
Family Medicine: JOHN L. RANDALL
Medicine: JOSÉ F. CARO
Microbiology and Immunology: CARLO M. CROCE
Neurology: ROBERT J. SCHWARTZMAN
Neurosurgery: JEWELL L. OSTERHOLM
Obstetrics and Gynaecology: RICHARD DEPP
Ophthalmology: WILLIAM S. TASMAN
Orthopaedic Surgery: RICHARD H. ROTHMAN
Otolaryngology: Dr WILLIAM M. KEANE
Pathology: EMANUEL RUBIN
Paediatrics: ROBERT L. BRENT
Pharmacology: Dr GERALD LITWACK
Physiology: ALLAN M. LEFER
Psychiatry: TROY L. THOMPSON II
Radiation Oncology and Nuclear Medicine: CARL M. MANSFIELD
Radiology: DAVID C. LEVIN
Rehabilitation Medicine: JOHN F. DITUNNO
Surgery: FRANCIS E. ROSATO
Urology: S. GRANT MULHOLLAND

College of Allied Health Sciences:

Nursing: PAMELA G. WATSON
Dental Hygiene: JO ANN GURENLIAN
Diagnostic Imaging: ALBERT D. HERBERT
General Studies: RAYMOND W. CAMPBELL
Laboratory Sciences: SHIRLEY E. GREENING
Occupational Therapy: RUTH LEVINE
Physical Therapy: ROGER NELSON

UNIVERSITY OF PENNSYLVANIA

Philadelphia, PA 19104
Telephone: (215) 898-5000

Founded 1740
Private control
Academic year: September to May, and two six-week summer terms

President: Dr JUDITH RODIN
Provost: MICHAEL L. WACHTER (interim)
Vice-Presidents: JOHN FRY, VIRGINIA CLARK, CAROL SCHEMAN, KATHRYN J. ENGEBRETSON, OMAR BLAIK, TOM SEAMON, MARIE WITT (interim)
Registrar: RONALD SANDERS
Librarian: PAUL H. MOSHER

Library: see Libraries
Number of teachers: 3,632
Number of students: 21,869

Publications: *Almanac* (weekly), *Compass* (fortnightly), *Daily Pennsylvanian, Pennsylvania Gazette* (8 a year), faculty and departmental publs.

DEANS AND DIRECTORS

School of Arts and Sciences: SAMUEL PRESTON (acting)
Wharton School: THOMAS P. GERRITY
School of Medicine: WILLIAM N. KELLEY
School of Veterinary Medicine: ALAN KELLY
School of Nursing: NORMA M. LANG
School of Dental Medicine: RAYMOND FONSECA
School of Engineering and Applied Science: GREGORY C. FARRINGTON
Law School: COLIN S. DIVER
Graduate School of Fine Arts: GARY A. HACK
Graduate School of Education: SUSAN FUHRMAN
School of Social Work: IRA SCHWARTZ
Annenberg School for Communication: KATHLEEN HALL JAMIESON
Dean of Admissions: W. J. STETSON, Jr

HEADS OF DEPARTMENT

School of Dental Medicine:

Microbiology: Prof. GARY COHEN
Oral Medicine: Prof. MARTIN GREENBERG
Periodontics: Prof. ALAN M. POLSON
Biochemistry: Prof. ELLIS GOLUB
Oral and Maxillofacial Surgery: Prof. PETER QUINN
Histology, Embryology and Anatomy: Prof. JOEL ROSENBLOOM
Dental Care Systems: Prof. SHELDON ROVIN
Pathology: Prof. BRUCE SHENKER
Endodontics: Prof. SYNGCUK KIM
General Restorative Dentistry: Prof. GERALD WEINTRAUB
Orthodontics: Prof. ROBERT VANARSDALL
Paediatric Dentistry: Prof. MARK L. HELPIN

Graduate School of Fine Arts:

City and Regional Planning: Prof. EUGENIE LADNER BIRCH
Architecture: Prof. RICHARD WESLEY (acting)
Landscape Architecture and Regional Planning: Prof. JOHN DIXON HUNT
Fine Arts: Prof. HITOSHI NAKAZATO (acting)

School of Arts and Sciences:

Economics: Prof. MARK ROSENZWEIG
Biology: Prof. ANDREW BINNS
German: Prof. SIMON RICHTER
English: Prof. WENDY STEINER
Romance Languages: IGNACIO J. LOPEZ
Folklore and Folklife: Prof. ROGER ABRAHAMS
Philosophy, Politics and Economics: Prof. SAMUEL FREEMAN
Asian American Studies: Prof. ROSANNE ROCHER
Philosophy: Prof. PAUL GUYER
Earth and Environmental Science: Prof. ROBERT GIEGENGACK
Asian and Middle Eastern Studies: Prof. DAVID SILVERMAN
South Asia Regional Studies: Prof. ALAN HESTON
Anthropology: Prof. GREGORY POSSEHL
Classical Studies: Prof. RALPH ROSEN
Slavic Languages and Literatures: Prof. FRANK TROMMLER (acting)
Psychology: Prof. ROBERT SEYFARTH
Sociology: Prof. DOUGLAS MASSEY
History: Prof. LYNN LEES
Linguistics: Prof. ANTHONY KROCH
Physics and Astronomy: Prof. PAUL LANGACKER
Chemistry: Prof. HAI-LUNG DAI
History and Sociology of Science: Prof. STEVEN FEIERMAN
Music: Prof. GARY TOMLINSON
Mathematics: Prof. DENNIS DETURCK
Italian Studies: Prof. STUART CURRAN
Latin American Studies: Prof. JORGE SALESSI
Religious Studies: Prof. STEPHEN DUNNING
Political Science: Prof. IAN LUSTICK
African Studies: Prof. SANDRA BARNES
Afro-American Studies: Prof. HERMAN BEAVERS
American Civilization: Prof. MELVYN HAMMARBERG
Biochemistry: Prof. PONZY LU
Biological Basis of Behaviour: Prof. STEPHEN FLUHARTY
Biophysics: Prof. LEE PEACHEY
Comparative Literature and Literary Theory: Prof. JOSEPH FARRELL
Communications: Prof. PAUL MESSARIS
Computer and Cognitive Science: Prof. MARK STEEDMAN
Design of the Environment: Prof. MARCO FRASCARI, RICHARD WESLEY
Elementary Education: Prof. JAMES LARKIN
Environmental Studies: Prof. ROBERT GIEGENGACK
Fine Arts: JULIE SCHNEIDER
History of Art: Prof. ELIZABETH JOHNS
International Relations: Prof. WALTER MCDOUGALL, Dr FRANK PLANTAN
International Studies and Business: Prof. ROGER ALLEN, Prof. JAMSHED GHANDHI
Jewish Studies: Prof. DAVID STERN
Theatre Arts: Prof. CARY MAZER
Urban Studies: Prof. ANN SPIRN (Co-Dir), Prof. ELAINE SIMON (Undergraduates)
Women's Studies: Prof. DREW FAUST, Dr DEMIE KURZ

Wharton School:

Legal Studies: Prof. G. RICHARD SHELL
Statistics: Prof. PAUL SHAMAN
Management: Prof. HARBIR SINGH
Marketing: Prof. DAVID SCHMITTLEIN
Insurance and Risk Management: Prof. JEAN LEMAIRE
Health Care Management and Policy: Prof. MARK PAULI
Public Policy and Management: Prof. ELIZABETH BAILEY
Finance: Prof. MICHAEL GIBBONS
Accounting: Prof. STANLEY BAIMAN
Operations and Information Management: Prof. PATRICK HARKER
Real Estate: Prof. SUSAN WACHTER

School of Veterinary Medicine:

Pathobiology: Prof. PHILLIP SCOTT
Animal Biology: Prof. MICHAEL KOLIKOFF
Clinical Studies, New Bolten Center: Prof. DAVID NUNAMAKER
Clinical Studies: Prof. PETER FELSBURG

School of Engineering and Applied Science:

Computer and Information Science: Prof. MITCHELL MARCUS
Systems Engineering: Prof. G. ANANDALINGAM
Electrical Engineering: Prof. SOHROB RABII (acting)
Chemical Engineering: Prof. RAYMOND GORTE
Bioengineering: Prof. GERSHON BUCHSBAUM
Materials Science and Engineering: Prof. WAYNE WORRELL
Mechanical Engineering and Applied Mechanics: Prof. JOHN BASSANI

School of Medicine:

Surgery: Prof. CLYDE F. BARKER
Radiology: Prof. REUBEN MEZRICH (acting)
Orthopaedic Surgery: Prof. ROBERT H. FITZGERALD Jr
Medicine: Prof. PETER TRABER
Rehabilitation Medicine: Prof. ALFRED P. FISHMAN
Molecular and Cellular Engineering: Prof. JIM WILSON
Emergency Medicine: Prof. WILLIAM G. BAXT
Neuroscience: Prof. ROBERT BARCHI
Neurosurgery: Prof. EUGENE FLAMM
Physiology: Prof. PAUL DE WEER
Radiation Oncology: Prof. W. GILLES MCKENNA
Pathology and Laboratory Medicine: Prof. LEONARD JARETT
Paediatrics: Prof. STEPHEN ALTSCHULER
Ophthalmology: Prof. STUART L. FINE
Dermatology: Prof. JOHN STANLEY (acting)
Anaesthesia: Prof. DAVID E. LONGNECKER
Obstetrics and Gynaecology: Prof. MICHAEL MENNUTI
Biochemistry and Biophysics: Prof. P. LESLIE DUTTON
Pharmacology: Prof. GARRET FITZGERALD (acting)
Microbiology: Prof. PRISCILLA SHAFFER

Cell and Developmental Biology: Prof. CHARLES P. EMERSON Jr
Genetics: Prof. HAIG KAZAZIAN
Neurology: Prof. ROBERT BARCHI
Otorhinolaryngology: Prof. DAVID KENNEDY
Psychiatry: Prof. DWIGHT EVANS

School of Nursing:
Adult Health and Illness: Prof. ROSALYN WATTS
Family and Community Health: Prof. ANN O'SULLIVAN
Health Care of Women: Prof. RUTH YORK
Psychiatric Mental Health: Prof. MARGARET COTRONEO
Science and Role Development: Prof. CAROL GERMAIN
Nursing of Children: Prof. JANET DEATRICK

School of Education:
Educational Leadership: Prof. REBECCA MAYNARD
Higher Education: Prof. ROBERT ZEMSKY
Language in Education: Prof. TERESA PICA
Psychology in Education: Prof. ERLING BOE, Prof. PAUL MCDERMOTT

ATTACHED INSTITUTIONS

African Studies Center
Alice Paul Research Center
Ancient Studies Center
Anspach Institute for Diplomacy and Foreign Affairs
Boettner Institute
Cancer Center
Center for Advanced Study of India
Center for Analysis of Developing Economies
Center for Analytic Research in Economics and Social Sciences
Center for Animal Health and Productivity
Center for Artificial Intelligence
Center for Bioethics
Center for Clinical Epidemiology and Biostatistics
Center for Communications and Information Science and Policy
Center for Comparative Genetics
Center for Computer Analysis of Texts
Center for Cultural Studies
Center for East Asian Studies
Center for Economic Studies in Technology
Center for Energy and the Environment
Center for Equine Sports Medicine
Center for Experimental Therapeutics
Center for Greater Philadelphia
Center for Health Service and Policy Research
Center for Human Resources
Center for Human Modeling and Simulation
Center for International Comparisons
Center for International Health and Development Communication
Center for Judaic Studies
Center for Manufacturing and Logistic Research
Center for Nursing Research
Center for Research and Evaluation of Social Policy
Center for Sensor Technologies
Center for School Study Councils
Center for Sleep and Respiratory Biology
Center for Study of Aging
Center for Study of Black Literature and Culture
Center for Study of the History of Nursing
Center for Study of Youth Policy
Center for Urban Ethnography
Center for Workplace Studies
Center for Advancing Care in Serious Illness
Clinical Research Center (Dental)
Diabetes Center
Emerging Economics Program
Fels Center of Government
Fishman-Davidson Center for the Study of the Service Sector
French Institute for Culture and Technology
S. S. Huebner Foundation for Insurance Education
Huntsman Center for Global Competition and Leadership
Institute for Economics Research
Institute for Environmental Medicine
Institute for Environmental Studies
Institute for Human Gene Therapy
Institute for Law and Economics
Institute for Medicine and Engineering
Institute for Research in Cognitive Science
Institute for Research on Higher Education
Institute on Aging
Italian Studies Center
Jones, Reginald H., Center for Management Policy & Strategy Organization
Krogman Center for Research in Child Growth and Development
Laboratory for Research on the Structure of Matter
Labor Relations Council
Lauder Institute of Management and International Studies
Lazarus-Goldman Research Center for Study of Social Work Practice
Leonard Davis Institute of Health Economics
Literacy Research Center
Low Birthweight Research Center
Mahoney, David, Institute for Neurological Sciences
Middle East Center
National Center on Adult Literacy
National Center on Educational Quality of the Workforce
Pennsylvania Muscle Institute
Pension Research Council
Philadelphia Center for Early American Studies
Plant Science Institute
Population Studies Center
Public Policy Center
Regional Laser Laboratory
Research Center in Oral Biology
Risk Management and Decision Processes Center
SEI Center for Advanced Studies in Management
Sellin Center for Studies in Criminology and Criminal Law
Snider, Sol C., Entrepreneurial Center
Transport Program
U.S.-Japan Management Center
Valley Forge Research Center
Weiss, George, Center for International Financial Research
Wharton Center for Quantitative Finance
Wharton Financial Institutions Center
Wharton Real Estate Center
Wharton Small Business Development Center
White, Rodney L., Center for Financial Research
Wurster, William H., Center for International Management Studies

UNIVERSITY OF PITTSBURGH

4200 Fifth Ave, Pittsburgh, PA 15260

Telephone: (412) 624-4141

Founded 1787 as Pittsburgh Academy; in 1819 became Western University of Pennsylvania, and in 1908 University of Pittsburgh

State-related

Academic year: two semesters

Chancellor: MARK A. NORDENBERG

Senior Vice Chancellor and Provost: JAMES V. MAHER

Senior Vice Chancellor for Health Sciences: ARTHUR S. LEVINE

Assistant Chancellor for Business and Administration: JEROME COCHRAN

Vice Chancellor for Finance: ARTHUR G. RAMICONE (acting)

Vice Chancellor for Student Affairs: ROBERT P. GALLAGHER (acting)

Vice Chancellor for Institutional Advancement: CAROL A. CARTER

Senior Vice Chancellor for Health Administration and President of University of Pittsburgh Medical Center: JEFFREY A. ROMOFF

Registrar: SAMUEL D. CONTE

Director of University Library System: RUSH G. MILLER

Library: see Libraries and Archives

Number of faculty (Pittsburgh campus): 2,848 full-time, 546 part-time

Number of students (Pittsburgh campus): 19,321 full-time, 6,140 part-time

DEANS

Faculty and College of Arts and Sciences: N. JOHN COOPER
Joseph M. Katz Graduate School of Business: FREDERICK W. WINTER
Graduate School of Public and International Affairs: CAROLYN BAN
Graduate School of Public Health: D. R. MATTISON
School of Social Work: D. E. EPPERSON
School of Dental Medicine: J. B. SUZUKI
School of Education: K. F. METZ
School of Engineering: G. D. HOLDER
College of General Studies: J. L. DANIEL
School of Health and Rehabilitation Sciences: C. E. BRUBAKER
School of Law: D. J. HERRING (acting)
School of Information Sciences: T. CARBO
School of Medicine: G. K. MICHALOPOULOS (acting)
School of Nursing: E. B. RUDY
School of Pharmacy: R. P. JUHL
University Honors College: G. A. STEWART
College of Business Administration: FREDERICK W. WINTER

CHAIRMEN OF DEPARTMENTS

Arts and Sciences:
Africana Studies: Y. A. LILLIE
Anthropology: R. D. DRENNAN
Architectural Studies: M. F. HEARN Jr
Biological Sciences: D. R. BURGESS
Chemistry: C. S. WILCOX
Classics: E. D. FLOYD (acting)
Communication: T. O. WINDT
Computer Science: S. TREU
East Asian Languages and Literatures: J. T. RIMER
Economics: J. N. OCHS
English: D. BARTHOLOMAE
Film Studies: L. FISCHER
French and Italian: D. O. LOONEY
Geology and Planetary Sciences: T. H. ANDERSON
Germanic Languages and Literatures: C. S. MUENZER
Hispanic Languages and Literatures: M. E. MORAÑA
History: G. R. ANDREWS
History and Philosophy of Science: M. H. SALMON
History of Art and Architecture: D. G. WILKINS
Intelligence Systems: J. D. MOORE
Jewish Studies: J. ROSENBERG
Linguistics: D. L. EVERETT
Mathematics: J. M. CHADAM
Music: D. BRODBECK
Neuroscience: E. M. STRICKER
Philosophy: K. L. MANDERS
Physics and Astronomy: F. TABAKIAN
Political Science: R. E. OWEN
Psychology: C. A. PERFETTI
Religious Studies: S. A. EDWARDS
Slavic Languages and Literatures: D. J. BIRNBAUM
Sociology: N. P. HUMMON
Statistics: A. R. SAMPSON
Studio Arts: M. L. MORRILL
Theatre Arts: W. S. COLEMAN
Urban Studies: C. CARSON

Engineering:
Bioengineering: J. S. SCHULTZ

Chemical and Petroleum: A. J. Russell
Civil and Environmental: R. G. Quimpo
Electrical: M. Simaan
Energy Resources: J. T. Cobb
Industrial: H. Wolfe
Materials Science and Engineering: W. A. Soffa
Mechanical: F. S. Petit (acting)

Education:
Administrative and Policy Studies: G. M. Nelson
Psychology in Education: A. J. Nitko
Instruction in Learning: N. P. Zigmond
Health, Physical and Recreation Education: J. D. Gallagher

Dental Medicine:
Dental Hygiene: A. Riccelli
Endodontics: J. A. Wallace
Orthodontics: J. J. Sciote
Periodontics: M. J. Novak
Prosthodontics: Y. H. Ismail

Information Sciences:
Information Science and Telecommunications: S. C. Hirtle
Library and Information Science: E. M. Rasmussen

Medicine:
Cell Biology and Physiology: R. A. Frizzell
Molecular Genetics and Biochemistry: J. C. Glorioso III
Neurobiology: P. R. Levitt
Pathology: G. Michalopoulos
Pharmacology: J. S. Lazo

Graduate School of Public Health:
Biostatistics: H. E. Rockette
Environmental and Occupational Health: H. S. Rosenkranz
Epidemiology: L. H. Kuller
Health Services Administration: E. M. Ricci
Human Genetics: D. R. Mattison (acting)
Infectious Diseases and Microbiology: C. R. Rinaldo

Health and Rehabilitation Sciences:
Clinical Dietetics and Nutrition: R. M. Onda (acting)
Communication Science and Disorders: M. R. McNeil
Health and Rehabilitation Sciences Interdisciplinary: C. E. Brubaker
Health Information Management: M. Abdelhak
Health Services Administration: E. M. Ricci
Occupational Therapy: J. K. Angelo
Physical Therapy: A. Delitto

Graduate School of Public and International Affairs:
Economic and Social Development: L. A. Picard
International Affairs: M. A. Staniland
Law and Justice: L. Weinberg
Public Management and Policy: (vacant)

Nursing:
Health Promotion and Development: S. N. Kobert
Health and Community Systems: A. Yurick
Acute Tertiary Care: L. A. Hoffman

RESEARCH CENTERS

Learning Research and Development Center: Dir L. B. Resnick.
Mid-Atlantic Technology Applications Center: Dir L. Hummel.
University of Pittsburgh Cancer Institute: Dir R. B. Herberman.
University Center for International Studies: Dir B. Holzner.
University Center for Social and Urban Research: Dir R. Schultz (acting).

REGIONAL CAMPUSES

University of Pittsburgh at Johnstown
President: Albert L. Etheridge
Number of faculty: 148 full-time, 26 part-time
Number of students: 2,691 full-time, 405 part-time

University of Pittsburgh at Greensburg
President: Frank A. Cassell
Number of faculty: 62 full-time, 32 part-time
Number of students: 1,203 full-time, 298 part-time

University of Pittsburgh at Titusville
President: Michael A. Worman
Number of faculty: 24 full-time, 13 part-time
Number of students: 265 full-time, 171 part-time

University of Pittsburgh at Bradford
President: Richard E. McDowell
Number of faculty: 70 full-time, 14 part-time
Number of students: 992 full-time, 287 part-time

UNIVERSITY OF SCRANTON

Scranton, PA 18510
Telephone: (717) 941-7400
Fax: (717) 941-6369
E-mail: admissions@uofs.edu

Founded 1888

President: Rev. Joseph M. McShane
Academic Vice-President: Dr Richard H. Passon
Vice-President for Finance and Treasurer: David E. Christiansen
Associate Provost for Enrollment Management: Susan Ikerd
Registrar: Robert E. Fetterhoff
Librarian: Charles E. Kratz

Number of teachers: 252
Number of students: 4,816

Publications: *The Scranton Journal* (quarterly), *Windhover* (yearbook), *Aquinas* (student newspaper), *The Record* (monthly), Diakonia.

DEANS

College of Arts and Sciences: Dr Joseph Dreisbach
Graduate School: Dr Robert E. Powell
Dexter Hanley College: Dr Shirley Adams
Arthur J. Kania School of Management: Dr Ronald Johnson
Panuska College of Professional Studies: Dr James Pallante

UNIVERSITY OF THE ARTS

320 South Broad St, Philadelphia, PA 19102
Telephone: (215) 875-4800
Fax: (215) 875-5467

Founded 1987 by merger of Philadelphia College of Art and Design (f. 1876) and Philadelphia College of Performing Arts (f. 1870)

President: Peter Solmssen
Provost: Virginia Red
Dean (Philadelphia College of Art and Design): Stephen Tarantal
Dean (Philadelphia College of Performing Arts): Stephen Jay
Dean of Students: Dr John Klinzing
Director of Admissions: Barbara Elliott
Director of Libraries: Stephen Bloom

URSINUS COLLEGE

POB 1000, Collegeville, PA 19426-1000
Telephone: (610) 409-3000

Founded 1869

President: John Strassburger
Director of Admissions: R. G. Di Feliciantonio
Librarian: Charles Jamison

Library of 200,000 vols
Number of teachers: 165
Number of students: 1,184 day, 1,300 evening

VILLANOVA UNIVERSITY

Villanova, PA 19085
Telephone: (610) 519-4500
Fax: (610) 519-5000

Founded 1842

President: Rev. Edmund J. Dobbin
Vice-President for Academic Affairs: Dr John Johannes
University Vice-President: Dr Helen K. Lafferty
Vice-President for Institutional Advancement: John M. Elizandro
Vice-President for Financial Affairs: Gary B. Fenner
Vice-President for Student Life: Dr Richard Neville
Senior Vice-President, Administration: Rev. William McGuire
Librarian: Dr James L. Mullins

Library of 604,000 vols, 2,998 periodicals, 247,700 microforms
Number of teachers: 558 full-time, 380 part-time
Number of students: 10,061

Publications: *Villanova University Bulletin, The Owl of Minerva, Horizons, The Theology Institute Proceedings, Journal for Peace and Justice Studies, Journal of South Asian and Middle Eastern Studies, Journal of Commerce and Finance, Villanova Law Review, Institute of Church and State Proceedings, Augustinian Studies.*

DEANS

Engineering: Dr Robert D. Lynch
Arts and Science: Rev. Kail C. Ellis
Commerce and Finance: Dr Thomas F. Monahan
Nursing: Dr M. Louise Fitzpatrick
Law: Dr Mark A. Sargent
Enrollment Management: Stephen Merritt
Students: Rev. John P. Stack
Graduate Studies for the College of Liberal Arts and Sciences: Dr Gerald Long

WASHINGTON AND JEFFERSON COLLEGE

Washington, PA 15301
Telephone: (724) 222-4400
Fax: (724) 223-5271

Washington Academy chartered 1787, rechartered as Washington College 1806; Jefferson Academy (Canonsburg) chartered 1794, rechartered as Jefferson College 1802; colleges united 1865

President: Brian C. Mitchell
Vice-President for Business and Finance: D. L. Lantz
Vice-President for Development: H. G. Moss
Vice-President for Academic Affairs and Dean of the College: G. A. Rembert
Vice-President for Enrollment Management: Thomas P. O'Connor
Assistant Dean and Registrar: A. J. Amendola
Librarian: P. Frisch

Library of 190,600 vols
Number of teachers: 111
Number of students: 1,097

Publications: *Topic, W & J Magazine, Catalogue.*

WAYNESBURG COLLEGE

Waynesburg, PA 15370
Telephone: (412) 627-8191

Founded 1849
Liberal arts and sciences

President: Timothy R. Thyreen
Vice-President for Academic Affairs: Dr Kathleen Davis

Vice-President for Institutional Advancement: MORT GAMBLE
Vice-President for Institutional Planning and Research: RICHARD L. NOFTZGER
Vice-President for Business and Finance: ROY R. BARNHART
Vice-President of Student Development: GERALD WOOD
Administrative Services: Ms BARBARA H. DUFFIELD
Registrar: RONALD D. COLTRANE
Librarian: SUZANNE WYLIE

Library of 126,098 vols
Number of teachers: 66 full-time, 48 part-time
Number of students: 1,351

WEST CHESTER UNIVERSITY

West Chester, PA 19383
Telephone: (610) 436-1000
Founded 1871
President: Dr MADELEINE WING ADLER
Director of Admissions: Ms MARSHA HAUG
Librarian: F. Q. HELMS

Library of 500,000 vols
Number of teachers: 539 full-time, 131 part-time
Number of students: 11,344
Publications: *Serpentine*, *College Literature*.

WESTMINSTER COLLEGE

New Wilmington, PA 16172
Telephone: (412) 946-8761
Founded 1852
Related to The Presbyterian Church (USA)
President: OSCAR E. REMICK
Vice-President for Academic Affairs and Dean of the College: JOHN DEEGAN, Jr
Vice-President for Student Affairs and Enrollment Management: (vacant)
Dean of Students: NEAL A. EDMAN (acting)
Dean of Admissions: R. DANA PAUL
Registrar: ELIZABETH E. HINES
Head Librarian: MOLLY P. SPINNEY

Library of 222,425 vols
Number of teachers: 96
Number of students: 1,540 undergraduates, 102 graduates
Publications: *Holcad* (newspaper), *Scrawl* (literary), *Argo* (yearbook).

WIDENER UNIVERSITY

One University Place, Chester, PA 19013-5792
Telephone: (610) 499-4000
Fax: (610) 876-9751
Founded 1821; formerly Widener College
President: Dr ROBERT J. BRUCE
Provost: Dr LAWRENCE P. BUCK

Library of 845,762 vols
Number of teachers: 310 full-time, 394 part-time
Number of students: 3,823 full-time, 3,532 part-time
Publications: *Bulletin, Summer Sessions Bulletin, Alumni Magazines, Law Review, Corporate Law Journal, Widener Law Symposium Journal.*

DEANS

College of Arts and Sciences: Dr LAWRENCE W. PANEK
School of Engineering: Dr FRED A. AKL
School of Hospitality Management: NICHOLAS J. HADGIS
School of Law: DOUGLAS E. RAY
School of Business Administration: Dr JOSEPH A. DIANGELO, Jr
School of Nursing: Dr MARGUERITE M. BARBIERE
School of Human Service Professions: Dr STEPHEN C. WILHITE
University College: Dr ARLENE DECOSMO

WILKES UNIVERSITY

Wilkes-Barre, PA 18766
Telephone: (717) 408-5000
Founded 1933
President: CHRISTOPHER N. BREISETH
Vice-President for Academic Affairs: Dr J. MICHAEL LENNON
Vice-President, Business Affairs and Auxiliary Enterprises: PAUL A. O'HOP
Vice-President, Development: PAUL J. STRUNK
Registrar: Dr JOHN F. MEYERS
Library Director: JON LINDGREN

Library of 198,000 vols
Number of teachers: 135 full-time
Number of students: 1,850 full-time

DEANS

School of Liberal Arts and Human Sciences: Dr BONNIE BEDFORD (interim)
School of Business, Society and Public Policy: Dr ANNE BATORY
School of Science and Engineering: Dr UMID R. NEJIB
School of Pharmacy: Dr BERNARD GRAHAM
Admissions: MICHAEL FRANTZ
Graduate Affairs: Dr WAGIHA TAYLOR
Student Affairs: Dr PAUL ADAMS

WILSON COLLEGE

Chambersburg, PA 17201
Telephone: (717) 264-4141
Fax: (717) 264-1578
Founded 1869
Private liberal arts college
President: Dr GWENDOLYN EVANS JENSEN
Director of Admissions: KAREN JEWELL
Librarian: SUSAN MATUSEK

Library of 170,000 vols, 450 periodicals
Number of teachers: 33 full-time, 56 part-time
Number of students: 821
Publications: *View Book* and *Catalogue*.

RHODE ISLAND

BROWN UNIVERSITY

Providence, RI 02912
Telephone: (401) 863-1000
Founded 1764
Private
Academic year: September to May
President: E. GORDON GEE
Provost: WILLIAM SIMMONS
Executive Vice-President for Finance and Administration: D. REAVES
Executive Vice-President for Public Affairs and University Relations: LAURA FREID
Dean of the College: NANCY DUNBAR
Director of Admission: MICHAEL GOLDBERGER
Registrar of the University: K. P. LEWIS
Librarian: MERRILY TAYLOR

Library of 3,000,000 vols
Number of teaching faculty: 540
Number of students: 7,641
Publications: *Catalogue of the University, Application to the College, The Graduate School, The Program in Medicine, Brown Alumni Magazine, George Street Journal.*

DEANS

Faculty: KATHRYN SPOEHR
Graduate School: PEDER ESTRUP
College: KENNETH SACKS
Medicine and Biological Sciences: D. J. MARSH

BRYANT COLLEGE

1150 Douglas Pike, Smithfield, RI 02917-1284
Telephone: (401) 232-6000
Fax: (401) 232-6319
Founded 1863
President: RONALD K. MACHTLEY
Vice-President for Institutional Advancement: LAURIE MUSGROVE
Vice-President for Student Affairs/Dean of Students: TOM EAKIN
Vice-President for Business Affairs/Treasurer: JOSEPH R. MEICHELBECK
Vice-President for Academic Affairs and Dean of Faculty: V. K. UNNI
Director of Undergraduate Programs: ELIZABETH A. POWERS
Director of Graduate Programs: W. DAYLE NATTRESS
Director of Library Services: MARY F. MORONEY

Library of over 127,000 vols
Number of students: 2,748 undergraduates, 584 graduates
Publication: *Bryant Review*.

PROVIDENCE COLLEGE

Providence, RI 02918
Telephone: (401) 865-1000
Founded 1917
President: Rev. PHILIP A. SMITH
Dean of Enrollment Management: CHRISTOPHER P. LYDON
Associate Registrar: ANN A. LOOMIS
Librarian: EDGAR C. BAILEY, Jr

Library of 342,000 vols
Number of teachers: 338
Number of undergraduate students: 3,597

RHODE ISLAND COLLEGE

600 Mount Pleasant Ave, Providence, RI 02908
Telephone: (401) 456-8000
Fax: (401) 456-8379
Founded 1854
President: JOHN NAZARIAN
Vice-President for Academic Affairs: JOHN J. SALESSES
Vice-President for Student Affairs: GARY M. PENFIELD
Vice-President for Administration and Finance: LENORE DELUCIA
Vice-President for Development and College Relations: (vacant)
Director of Records: BURT D. CROSS
Librarian: RICHARD A. OLSEN

Library of 360,000 vols
Number of teachers: 375
Number of students: 7,214 undergraduate, 1,852 graduate

DEANS

Arts and Sciences: RICHARD WEINER
Education and Human Development: DAVID E. NELSON
Graduate Studies: JAMES TURLEY
Social Work: GEORGE METREY
Student Affairs: GARY PENFIELD

RHODE ISLAND SCHOOL OF DESIGN

Providence, RI 02903
Telephone: (401) 454-6100
Founded 1877
President: ROGER MANDLE
Vice-Presidents: AMELIA KOCH (Finance, acting), HARDU KECK (Academic Affairs), FELICE BILLUPS (Planning and Research), T. NEIL SEVERANCE (Student Affairs)
Librarian: CAROL TERRY

Library of 70,000 vols
Museum of Art: 75,000 items

Number of teachers: 110 full-time, 180 part-time
Number of students: 1,912
Publications: *Annual Catalogue*, *RISD Views*, *Portfolio* (Student Year Book), *Bulletin of Rhode Island School of Design*, *Museum Notes*.

SALVE REGINA UNIVERSITY

Newport, RI 02840
Telephone: (401) 847-6650
Fax: (401) 847-0372
Founded 1947
Private control (Religious Sisters of Mercy)
President: Dr M. THERESE ANTONE
Vice-President for Business and Financial Affairs: WILLIAM B. HALL
Vice-President for Institutional Advancement: MICHAEL SEMENZA
Vice-President for Academic Affairs and Dean of Faculty: Dr JUDITH M. MILLS
Vice-President for Administrative Services and Community Relations: THOMAS P. FLANAGAN
Vice-President for Student Development: JOHN ROK
Executive Vice-President: DOMINIC C. VARISCO
Registrar: KATHLEEN H. WILLIS
Dean of Students: JOHN QUINN
Dean of Enrollment and Admissions: LAURA MCPHIE
Library of 116,000 vols
Number of teachers: 120
Number of students: 2,100

UNIVERSITY OF RHODE ISLAND

Kingston, RI 02881
Telephone: (401) 874-1000
Founded 1892 as Rhode Island College of Agriculture and Mechanic Arts; attained university status 1951
President: ROBERT L. CAROTHERS
Provost: M. BEVERLY SWAN
Vice-President for Business and Finance: KENNETH N. KERMES
Vice-President for Student Affairs: JOHN MCCRAY
Vice-President for University Relations: ROBERT L. BEAGLE
Registrar: ROBERT STROBEL
Dean of University Libraries: PAUL GANDEL
Library of 1,000,000 vols
Number of teachers: 721
Number of students: 13,698
Publications: *URI Commercial Fisheries Newsletter*, *URI Reporter* (Newsletter), *Pacer.*

DEANS

College of Arts and Sciences: WINIFRED BROWNELL (acting)
College of Business Administration: FRANK S. BUDNICK (acting)
College of Continuing Education: WALTER A. CROCKER, Jr
College of Engineering: THOMAS J. KIM
College of Human Science and Services: BARBARA BRITTINGHAM
University College: DIANE W. STROMMER
College of Pharmacy: LOUIS A. LUZZI
College of Resource Development: MARGARET LEINEN (acting)
College of Nursing: DAYLE JOSEPH (acting)
Graduate School of Oceanography: MARGARET LEINEN
Graduate School: THOMAS ROCKETT (acting)
Admissions and Student Financial Aid: DAVID G. TAGGART

ATTACHED RESEARCH PROGRAMS

Agricultural Experiment Station
Biotechnology Center
Center for Atmospheric Chemistry Studies
Center for Energy Study
Center for Ocean Management Studies
Coastal Resources Center
Consortium for the Development of Technology
Co-operative Extension Service
Institute for Advanced Manufacturing
Institute in Human Science and Services
Laboratories for Scientific Criminal Investigation
Marine Experiment Station
Marine Advisory Service
Research Center in Business and Economics
International Center for Marine Resource Development
National Sea Grant Depository
Division of Engineering Research and Development
Rhode Island Teachers' Center
RI Water Resources Center
Robotics Research Center

SOUTH CAROLINA

CITADEL, THE

171 Moultrie St, Charleston, SC 29409
Telephone: (803) 953-5000
Founded 1842
Controlled by State of South Carolina
President: JOHN GRINALDS
Executive Vice-President and Dean of the College: Brig.-Gen. R. CLIFTON POOLE
Vice-President for Facilities and Administration: Col DONALD M. TOMASIK
Commandant of Cadets: Col JOSEPH W. TREZ
Vice-President for Finance and Business Affairs: Col CALVIN G. LYONS
Director of Libraries: Lt Col ANGIE S. W. LE CLERCQ
Registrar: Col ISAAC S. METTS, Jr (acting)
Library of 182,000 vols
Number of teachers: 163 full-time, 53 part-time, 28 ROTC
Number of students: 7,500
Publications: *Sphinx, Brigadier, Guidon, Shako, Citadel Monograph Series, Citadel Review.*

CLEMSON UNIVERSITY

Clemson, SC 29634
Telephone: (864) 656-3311
Fax: (864) 656-4676
Founded 1889 as Clemson Agricultural College
President: CONSTANTINE W. CURRIS
Provost and Vice-President for Academic Affairs: STEFFEN ROGERS
Vice-President for Student Affairs: ALMEDA R. JACKS
Vice-President for Advancement: DEBORAH DU BOSE (acting)
Vice-President for Public Service and Agriculture: JOHN W. KELLY
Executive Secretary of the Board: J. THORNTON KIRBY
Librarian: J. F. BOYKIN
Library of 1,437,333 vols
Number of teachers: 1,227, including 1,070 full-time
Number of students: 16,500

DEANS

Vice-Provost and Dean of Graduate School: DEBORAH JACKSON (acting)
Vice-Provost and Dean of Undergraduate Studies: JEROME REEL
College of Agriculture, Forestry and Life Sciences: WILLIAM B. WEHRENBERG
College of Architecture, Arts and Humanities: JAMES F. BARKER
College of Health, Education and Human Development: HAROLD E. CHEATHAM
College of Engineering and Science: THOMAS M. KEINATH
College of Business and Public Affairs: JERRY TRAPNELL

COKER COLLEGE

Hartsville, SC 29550
Telephone: (803) 383-8000
Fax: (803) 383-8129
Founded 1908
President: JAMES D. DANIELS
Dean of the Faculty and College Provost: RONALD L. CARTER
Vice-President for Enrollment Management: Dr STEPHEN B. TERRY
Director of Financial Aid: HAL LEWIS
Librarian: NEAL A. MARTIN
Library of 70,000 vols
Number of teachers: 57
Number of students: 919

COLLEGE OF CHARLESTON

Charleston, SC 29424
Telephone: (803) 953-5500
Founded 1770; chartered 1785
President: ALEXANDER M. SANDERS, Jr
Senior Vice-President, Academic Affairs: CONRAD FESTA
Registrar: WILLIAM ANDERSON
Librarian: DAVID COHEN
Number of teachers: 624
Number of students: 10,600

COLUMBIA COLLEGE

Columbia, SC 29203
Telephone: (803) 786-3012
Founded 1854
President: PHYLLIS O. BONANNO
Provost: Dr LAURIE B. HOPKINS
Registrar: FRANCES S. OWENS
Librarian: JOHN C. PRITCHETT
Library of 168,100 vols
Number of teachers: 105
Number of students: 1,320

CONVERSE COLLEGE

Spartanburg, SC 29302
Telephone: (864) 596-9040
Fax: (864) 596-9225
Founded 1889
President: Dr SANDRA C. THOMAS
Director of Admissions: WANDA MOORE
Librarian: WADE WOODWARD
Library of 200,000 vols
Number of teachers: 85
Number of students: 1,200
Arts, sciences, music.

ERSKINE COLLEGE

Due West, SC 29639
Telephone: (803) 379-8833
Founded 1839
President: JOHN L. CARSON
Director of Admissions: JEFF CRAFT
Librarian: (vacant)
Library of 150,000 vols
Number of teachers: 62
Number of students: 831

FURMAN UNIVERSITY

Greenville, SC 29613
Telephone: (864) 294-2000
Founded 1826

President: DAVID E. SHI
Vice-President for Academic Affairs and Dean: A. V. HUFF
Vice-President for Business Affairs: WENDY LIBBY
Vice-President for Development: DONALD J. LINEBACK
Vice-President for Enrollment: BENNY WALKER
Vice-President for Intercollegiate Athletics: JOHN BLOCK
Vice-President for Marketing and Public Relations: GREGORY A. CARROLL
Vice-President for Student Services: HARRY B. SHUCKER
Registrar: PAUL H. ANDERSON
Librarian: JANIS BANDELIN

Library of 390,000 vols
Number of teachers: 200
Number of students: 2,840

Publications: *Studies* (2 a year), *Paladin* (weekly), *The Echo* (literary, 2 a year), *Furman Magazine* (1 a year), *Furman Reports* (4 a year), *Humanities Review* (1 a year).

DEANS

Graduate Studies: HAZEL W. HARRIS
Continuing Education: JOHN H. DICKEY

LANDER UNIVERSITY

Greenwood, SC 29649
Telephone: (864) 388-8300
Fax: (864) 388-8890
Founded 1872

President: WILLIAM C. MORAN
Vice-President for Academic Affairs: FRIEDERIKE WIEDEMANN
Vice-President for Business and Administration: W. E. TROUBLEFIELD, Jr
Vice-President for Student Affairs: RANDY BOUKNIGHT
Vice-President for University Advancement: ELEANOR S. TEAL
Registrar and Director of Institutional Research: R. THOMAS NELSON III
Director of Library: ANN T. HARE

Library of 256,464 vols
Number of teachers: 130
Number of students: 2,780

LIMESTONE COLLEGE

Gaffney, SC 29340-3799
Telephone: (864) 489-7151
Founded 1845

President: Dr WALT GRIFFIN
Academic Dean: Dr CHARLES J. CUNNING
Librarian: CAROLYN T. HAYWARD

Library of 60,000 vols
Number of teachers: 42 (full-time)
Number of students: 1,200

MEDICAL UNIVERSITY OF SOUTH CAROLINA

171 Ashley Ave, Charleston, SC 29425
Telephone: (803) 792-2300
Fax: (803) 792-0392
Founded 1824

President: Dr JAMES BURROWS EDWARDS
Vice-President (Academic Affairs): Dr RAYMOND S. GREENBERG
Vice-President (Business Affairs): ROBERT C. GALLAGER
Vice-President (Medical Affairs): Dr R. LAYTON MCCURDY
Librarian: Dr THOMAS P. BASLER

DEANS

College of Graduate Studies and University Research: Dr ROSALIE CROUCH
College of Medicine: Dr R. LAYTON MCCURDY
College of Dental Medicine: Dr RICHARD W. DECHAMPLAIN
College of Pharmacy: Dr JOHNNIE L. EARLY
College of Nursing: Dr MAUREEN KEEFE
College of Health Related Professions: Dr VALERIE T. WEST (interim)

NEWBERRY COLLEGE

Newberry, SC 29108
Telephone: (803) 276-5010
Fax: (803) 321-5627
Founded 1856

Private control (affiliated with the Evangelical Lutheran Church in America: South Carolina, Southeastern, Florida-Bahamas, and Caribbean Synods)

President: Dr PETER L. FRENCH
Librarian: LARRY ELLIS

Library of 86,992 vols
Number of teachers: 70
Number of students: 625

Publications: *Dimensions, Studies in Short Fiction* (quarterly), *The Indian* (fortnightly), *Kinnikinnick* (annually), *The Newberrian* (annually).

PRESBYTERIAN COLLEGE

Clinton, SC 29325
Telephone: (864) 833-2820
Fax: (864) 833-8481
Founded 1880

President: Dr JOHN V. GRIFFITH
Academic Dean: Dr J. DAVID GILLESPIE (acting)
Dean of Students: JOSEPH O. NIXON
Vice-President for Enrollment: R. DANA PAUL
Librarian: Dr N. DOUGLAS ANDERSON

Library of 157,000 vols
Number of teachers: 78 full-time, 41 part-time
Number of students: 1,116

SOUTH CAROLINA STATE UNIVERSITY

Orangeburg, SC 29117
Telephone: (803) 536-7000
Fax: (803) 533-3622
Founded 1896

President: Dr LEROY DAVIS
Director of Admissions: DOROTHY BROWN (acting)
Library Director: MARY L. SMALLS

Library of 1,279,800 vols
Number of teachers: 236
Number of students: 5,000

UNIVERSITY OF SOUTH CAROLINA

Columbia, SC 29208
Telephone: (803) 777-2001
Fax: (803) 777-3264

Chartered 1801; opened 1805

President: JOHN M. PALMS
Vice-President for Academic Affairs and Provost: JEROME D. ODOM
Vice-President for Business and Finance and Treasurer: JOHN FINAN
Vice-Provost for Research: MARSHA TORR
Vice-President for Human Resources: JANE M. JAMESON
Vice-President for Development: CHARLES D. PHLEGAR
Vice-President for Student Affairs: DENNIS A. PRUITT
Vice-Provost for Regional Campuses and Continuing Education: JOHN J. DUFFY
Vice-Provost for Libraries and Information Systems: GEORGE D. TERRY
Registrar: RICHARD L. BAYER
Chancellor, USC Aiken: ROBERT E. ALEXANDER
Chancellor, USC Spartanburg: JOHN C. STOCKWELL

Library of over 7,000,000 vols
Number of teachers: 1,810 full-time (8 campuses)
Number of students: 36,717 (8 campuses)

Publications: *Annual Bulletins.*

DEANS

College of Science and Mathematics: GERALD M. CRAWLEY
College of Business Administration: DAVID L. SHROCK
College of Education: HARVEY A. ALLEN (acting)
College of Engineering: CRAIG A. ROGERS
College of Liberal Arts: C. BLEASE GRAHAM (acting)
College of Journalism and Mass Communications: JUDY VANSLYKE TURK
College of Pharmacy: FARID SADIK (acting)
South Carolina Honors College: PETER C. SEDERBERG
School of Law: JOHN E. MONTGOMERY
School of Music: MANUEL ALVAREZ (interim)
College of Nursing: MARY ANN C. PARSONS
College of Applied Professional Sciences: JOHN J. DUFFY (acting)
College of Social Work: FRANK B. RAYMOND, III
College of Library and Information Science: FRED W. ROPER
College of Criminal Justice: C. BLEASE GRAHAM
Graduate School: CAROL Z. GARRISON
School of Medicine: LARRY R. FAULKNER
School of Public Health: HARRIS PASTIDES
USC Beaufort: CHRIS P. PLYLER
USC Lancaster: JOSEPH PAPPIN III
USC Salkehatchie: CARL A. CLAYTON
USC Sumter: C. LESLIE CARPENTER
USC Union: JAMES W. EDWARDS

WINTHROP UNIVERSITY

Rock Hill, SC 29733
Telephone: (803) 323-2236
Founded 1886

President: Dr ANTHONY DIGIORGIO
Vice-President for Academic Affairs: PATRICIA CORMIER
Vice-President for External Relations: BECKY MCMILLAN
Vice-President for Finance and Business: J. P. MCKEE
Vice-President for Student Life: FRANK P. ARDAIOLO
Registrar: KAREN C. JONES
Director of Admissions: DEBI BARBER

Library of 357,110 vols
Number of teachers: 401
Number of students: 5,107

Publications: *The Johnsonian* (weekly), *The Tatler, The Winthrop Anthology* (annually).

DEANS

Arts and Sciences: BETSY BROWN (acting)
Business Administration: JERRY H. PADGETT
Education: TOM POWELL
Library Services: PAUL DUBOIS
Visual and Performing Arts: BENNETT LENTCZNER
Admissions: JIM BLACK

WOFFORD COLLEGE

Spartanburg, SC 29303-3663
Telephone: (803) 597-4000
Fax: (803) 597-4019
Founded 1854

President: JOAB M. LESESNE, Jr

Vice-President for Academic Affairs/Dean of the College: DAN B. MAULTSBY
Vice-Presidents: LARRY MCGEHEE, B. G. STEPHENS
Vice-President for Business: EDWARD E. GREENE
Vice-President for Student Affairs: MICHAEL J. PRESTON
Executive Director of Development: DAVID BEACHAM
Director of Admissions: BRAND STILLE
Registrar: LUCY B. QUINN
Librarian: OAKLEY HERMAN COBURN

Library of 200,000 vols
Number of teachers: 57 full-time, 13 part-time
Number of students: 1,100

Publication: *Wofford Today* (newspaper).

SOUTH DAKOTA

AUGUSTANA COLLEGE

2001 So Summit, Sioux Falls, SD 57197
Telephone: (605) 336-0770
Fax: (605) 336-5299

Founded 1860

President: Dr RALPH H. WAGONER
Vice-President for Academic Services and Dean: Dr RICHARD A. HANSON
Vice-President for Administration and Finance: CHARLES BROWN
Vice-President for Advancement: KEITH CHRISTENSEN
Vice-President for Enrollment: ROBERT E. PRELOGER
Vice-President for Student Services: JAMES BIES
Registrar: Dr JOHN BYLSMA
Librarian: RONELLE THOMPSON

Library of 228,000 vols
Number of teachers: 121
Number of students: 1,475

BLACK HILLS STATE UNIVERSITY

Spearfish, SD 57783
Telephone: (605) 642-6011

Founded 1883

President: THOMAS O. FLICKEMA
Director of Records: APRIL MEEKER
Director of Library—Learning Center: Dr EDWIN ERICKSON

Library of 222,000 vols
Number of teachers: 122
Number of students: 2,773

DAKOTA STATE UNIVERSITY

Madison, SD 57042
Telephone: (605) 256-5111
Fax: (605) 256-5316

Founded 1881

President: Dr JERALD A. TUNHEIM
Academic Vice-President: Dr DAVID E. COOK
Vice-President for Student Affairs: TERRENCE RYAN
Vice-President for Business and Administrative Services: MARK O. LEE
Registrar: KATHRYN CALLIES
Director of Admissions: MICHAEL MUTZIGER
Librarian: ETHELLE BEAN

Library of 131,000 vols
Number of teachers: 75
Number of students: 1,326

Courses in teacher training, business management, mathematics, sciences, respiratory care, medical record, information systems and liberal arts

DAKOTA WESLEYAN UNIVERSITY

1200 West University, Mitchell, SD 57301-4398
Telephone: (605) 995-2600
Fax: (605) 995-2699

Founded 1885

President: Dr JOHN L. EWING, Jr
Registrar: JULIE PEAK
Vice-President for Academic Affairs: Dr BRUCE BLUMER
Vice-President for Campus Life: GWENDA KOCH
Director of Learning Resources: KEVIN KENKEL

Library of 66,000 vols
Number of teachers: 50
Number of students: 710

HURON UNIVERSITY

Huron, SD 57350
Telephone: (605) 352-8721

Founded 1883

President: Dr NORMAN L. STEWART
Vice-President for Academic Affairs: Dr GARY SMITH
Vice-President for Finance: ROBERT FISCHER
Registrar: PEGGY MANN
Librarian: KEVIN KENKEL

Library of 70,000 vols
Number of teachers: 61 full-time, 59 adjunct
Number of students: 1,088

Branch Campus: 2900 East 26th St, Sioux Falls, SD 57103; tel. (605) 331-5159.

Branch Campus in England: 3–5 Palace Gate, London, W8 5LS, England; tel. (171) 584-9696.

Branch Campus in Japan: 1-16-7 Kami-Ochiai, Shinjuku-ku, Tokyo, Japan; tel. (3) 3367-4141.

MOUNT MARTY COLLEGE

1105 West 8th, Yankton, SD 57078
Telephone: (605) 668-1011

Founded 1936

President: Dr MARK HURTUBISE
Registrar: GARY KLEIN
Librarian: SANDY BROWN

Library of 76,000 vols
Number of teachers: 65
Number of students: 1,000

NORTHERN STATE UNIVERSITY

Aberdeen, SD 57401
Telephone: (605) 626-3011

Founded 1901

President: JOHN HILPERT (acting)
Vice-President for Academic Affairs: ERIKA TALLMAN (interim)
Director of Graduate School: SHARON TEBBEN
Director of Libraries: J. PHILIP MULVANEY

Library of 250,000 vols
Number of teachers: 150
Number of students: 2,600

SOUTH DAKOTA SCHOOL OF MINES AND TECHNOLOGY

501 E. St Joseph, Rapid City, SD 57701-3995
Telephone: (605) 394-2511
Fax: (605) 394-6131

Founded 1885

President: RICHARD J. GOWEN
Vice-President for Academic Affairs: KAREN L. WHITEHEAD
Dean of Graduate Education and Research: SHERRY O. FARWELL
Director of Business and Administration: TIMOTHY G. HENDERSON
Dean of Students: DOUGLAS K. LANGE
Director of Library: PATRICIA M. ANDERSEN

Library of 179,000 vols
Number of teachers: 110 (full-time)
Number of students: 2,370

SOUTH DAKOTA STATE UNIVERSITY

College Station, Brookings, SD 57007
Telephone: (605) 688-4151

Founded as Dakota Agricultural College 1881, University 1964

President: Dr PEGGY GORDON ELLIOTT
Vice-President for Administration: Dr MICHAEL REGER
Director of Finance and Budget: W. G. TSCHETTER
Dean of Student Affairs: Dr ROBERT TOMLINSON
Vice-President for Academic Affairs: Dr CAROL PETERSON
Director of Library: Dr STEVE MARQUAROT

Library of 544,000 vols
Number of teachers: 479
Number of students: 8,162

UNIVERSITY OF SIOUX FALLS

Sioux Falls, SD 57105
Telephone: (800) 888-1047
Fax: (605) 331-6615

Founded 1883
Private (American Baptist)
Pre-professional liberal arts university

President: MARK BENEDETTO
Provost and Academic Dean: RICHARD MAYER
Registrar: PHYLLIS THOMPSON
Librarian: AILEEN MADDOX

Library of 75,000 vols
Number of teachers: 37 full-time, 28 part-time
Number of students: 950

UNIVERSITY OF SOUTH DAKOTA

Vermillion, SD 57069-2390
Telephone: (605) 677-5011
Fax: (605) 677-5073

Founded 1862

President: JAMES W. ABBOTT

Library of 445,215 vols
Number of teachers: 471
Number of students: 7,739

DEANS

College of Arts and Sciences: Dr JOHN CARLSON
School of Business: Dr JERRY JOHNSON
School of Education: Dr LARRY BRIGHT
College of Fine Arts: JOHN DAY
School of Law: BARRY VICKREY
School of Medicine: Dr ROBERT TALLEY
Graduate School: Dr CHARLES KAUFMAN
Continuing Education: Dr JANET LEWIS

TENNESSEE

AUSTIN PEAY STATE UNIVERSITY

Clarksville, TN 37044
Telephone: (615) 648-7566
Fax: (615) 648-5988

Founded 1927

President: Dr SAL D. RINELLA
Vice-President for Academic Affairs: STEVEN K. PONTIUS
Vice-President for Development: WENDELL GILBERT
Vice-President for Administration and Finance: JOYCE MOUNCE
Vice-President for Student Affairs: JOSEPH S. WHITE (acting)
Registrar: DENNIS DULNIAK
Director of Library: DONALD JOYCE

Library of 313,500 vols
Number of teachers: 283
Number of students: 7,803

BELMONT UNIVERSITY

1900 Belmont Blvd, Nashville, TN 37212-3757
Telephone: (615) 383-7001
Fax: (615) 385-6446

Founded 1951

President: WILLIAM E. TROUTT
Registrar: MARTHA L. KELLEY
Librarian: ERNEST W. HEARD

Library of 127,688 vols
Number of teachers: 141 full-time, 139 part-time
Number of students: 2,821

Publications: *The Tower* (annually), *Vision* (every 2 months), *Belmont Circle* (quarterly).

DEANS

Academic: JERRY WARREN
Students: SUZANNE MATHENY
Admissions: CLAUDE PRESSNELL

BETHEL COLLEGE

McKenzie, TN 38201
Telephone: (901) 352-4000

Founded 1842

President: ROBERT J. IMHOFF
Academic Dean: R. PAUL WILLIAMSON
Registrar: SHIRLEY MARTIN
Librarian: HAROLD KELLY

Library of 53,000 vols
Number of teachers: 26
Number of students: 490

Publications: *Bethel Beacon* (weekly), *Log Cabin* (annually), *Bethel Captions* (quarterly).

CARSON-NEWMAN COLLEGE

1646 Russell Ave, Jefferson City, TN 37760
Telephone: (615) 471-4000
Fax: (615) 471-3502

Founded 1851

President: J. CORDELL MADDOX
Vice-President for Finance: ROBERT DRINNEN

Library of 196,000 vols
Number of teachers: 122
Number of students: 2,200

Publications: *The Magazine for Alumni and Friends, Orange and Blue, Mossy Creek Journal, College Catalog.*

CHRISTIAN BROTHERS UNIVERSITY

650 East Parkway South, Memphis, TN 38104
Telephone: (901) 321-3000

Founded 1871
Private (Roman Catholic) control

President: Bro. MICHAEL MCGINNISS
Academic Vice-President: Dr MARK V. SMITH
Registrar: BARBARA HAVEY
Librarian: SHARON MADER

Library of 100,000 vols
Number of teachers: 150
Number of students: 1,800

Publication: *Catalog* (annually).

DAVID LIPSCOMB UNIVERSITY

Nashville, TN 37204-3951
Telephone: (615) 269-1000

Founded 1891
Four-year liberal arts college

President: STEPHEN F. FLATT
Executive Vice-President: CARL MCKELVEY
Provost: W. CRAIG BLEDSOE
Vice-President for University Relations: WILLIAM TUCKER
Librarian: CAROLYN WILSON

Library of 216,300 vols
Number of teachers: 194
Number of students: 2,555

EAST TENNESSEE STATE UNIVERSITY

Johnson City, TN 37614
Telephone: (423) 439-1000
Fax: (423) 439-4004

Founded 1911

President: Dr PAUL E. STANTON, Jr
Associate Vice-President for Admissions, Retention and Enrollment Management: Dr NANCY DISHNER
Registrar: RICHARD YOUNT
Provost, and Vice-President for Academic Affairs: Dr BERT C. BACH
Vice-President for University Advancement: Dr RICHARD MANAHAN
Vice-President for Health Affairs: Dr RONALD D. FRANKS
Vice-President for Business and Finance: JAMES BOWMAN
Vice-President for Student Affairs: Dr WAYNE ANDREWS (acting)
Dean of University Libraries: Dr FRED BORCHUCK

Library of 456,000 vols
Number of teachers: 660 (full-time)
Number of students: 11,840

DEANS

College of Arts and Sciences: Dr DONALD R. JOHNSON
College of Education: Dr MARTHA COLLINS
College of Business: Dr ALLAN D. SPRITZER
College of Public and Allied Health: Dr WILSIE BISHOP
James H. Quillen College of Medicine: Dr RONALD D. FRANKS
School of Continuing Studies: Dr GLENN BETTIS
School of Graduate Studies: Dr WESLEY BROWN
College of Applied Science and Technology: Dr JAMES HALES
College of Nursing: Dr JOELLEN EDWARDS

FISK UNIVERSITY

17th Ave North, Nashville, TN 37208-3051
Telephone: (615) 329-8500

Opened as Fisk School 1866; chartered as university 1867

President: CHARLES W. JOHNSON (acting)
Dean of Academic Affairs: Dr CARRELL P. HORTON
Executive Vice-President: Dr GEORGE NEELY, Jr
Librarian: JESSIE C. SMITH

Library of 203,000 vols
Number of teachers: 62 full-time, 32 part-time
Number of students: 765

Publications: *Fisk University Bulletin* (every 2 years), *Fisk News* (1 a year), *Fisk Reports* (4 a year).

KING COLLEGE

1350 King College Rd, Bristol, TN 37620
Telephone: (423) 652-1187
Fax: (423) 652-4456

Founded 1867

Provost and Acting President: Dr GREGORY D. JORDAN
Senior Vice-President: Dr JACK E. SNIDER
Vice-President for Academic Affairs: Dr WILLIAM J. WADE (acting)
Vice-President for Institutional Advancement: WILLIAM M. MCELROY
Vice-President for Student Development: ALBERT R. RAUSCH
Vice-President for Enrollment Management: ROGER L. KIEFFER
Vice-President for Christian Ministries: Dr ERROL G. ROHR
Vice-President for Financial Affairs: JOHN E. DILLOW
Librarian: DANIEL BOWELL

Library of 90,000 vols
Number of students: 537

Publication: *Tornado.*

KNOXVILLE COLLEGE

901 College St, Knoxville, TN 37921
Telephone: (615) 524-6500

Founded 1875
Liberal arts college

President: Dr JOE L. BOYER
Dean: Dr EVELYN HALLMAN
Registrar: Mrs BARBARA BOOKER
Librarian: Mrs PATTY COOPER

Library of 78,445 vols
Number of teachers: 51
Number of students: 633

LAMBUTH UNIVERSITY

Jackson, TN 38301
Telephone: (901) 425-2500
Fax: (901) 423-1990

Founded 1843

President: THOMAS F. BOYD
Vice-President and Dean of the College: WILLIAM J. SHUSTOWSKI, Jr
Vice-President for Institutional Advancement: J. DALTON EDDLEMAN
Vice-President for Business Affairs: CLARK B. MANOR
Vice-President for Student Life: STEPHEN M. CONDON
Director of Student Recruitment: NANCY TIPTON
Librarian: JUDITH HAZLEWOOD

Library of 155,554 vols
Number of teachers: 38 full-time, 27 part-time
Number of students: 819

LANE COLLEGE

545 Lane Ave, Jackson, TN 38301-4598
Telephone: (901) 426-7500
Fax: (901) 427-3987
E-mail: mcclure@lc.lane-college.edu

Founded 1882

President: Dr WESLEY CORNELIOUS MCCLURE
Registrar: WILLIE OZIER
Vice-President for Academic Affairs: Dr VICKI VERNON LOTT
Vice-President for Business and Finance: MELVIN R. HAMLETT
Vice-President for Institutional Advancement: DARLETTE CARVER SAMUELS
Vice-President for Student Affairs: Dr LEON HOWARD
Librarian: QUINTON JONES

Library of 125,000 vols
Number of teachers: 45
Number of students: 750

LE MOYNE-OWEN COLLEGE

807 Walker Ave, Memphis, TN 38126
Telephone: (901) 774-9090

Founded 1862

President: BURNETT JOINER
Registrar: SARAH BUFORD
Librarian: ANNETTE BERHE

Library of 82,043 vols
Number of teachers: 41
Number of students: 1,212

LINCOLN MEMORIAL UNIVERSITY

Harrogate, TN 37752
Telephone: (615) 869-3611
Fax: (615) 869-6426
Founded 1897

President: SCOTT D. MILLER
Senior Vice-President for Finance: D. D. THOMPSON
Vice-President for Development: CINDY COOKE-WHITT
Provost: RALPH EVANS
Vice-President for Student Affairs: WADE UNDERWOOD
Senior Vice-President for Administration: EARL BROOKS
Dean of Admissions and Institutional Research: CONRAD DANIELS
Head Librarian: WILMA PATTON

Library of 120,000 vols
Number of teachers: 71
Number of students: 2,000

Publication: *The Lincoln Herald* (quarterly).

MARYVILLE COLLEGE

Maryville, TN 37804
Telephone: (423) 981-8000
Fax: (423) 981-8010
Founded 1819

President: Dr GERALD W. GIBSON
Vice-President and Treasurer: RON APPUHN
Academic Vice-President: Dr NANCY SEDERBERG
Vice-President for College Advancement: ELTON JONES
Vice-President for Student Development: Dr WILLIAM SEYMOUR
Vice-President for Admissions and Enrollment Planning: DONNA DAVIS
Librarian: CHRIS NUGENT

Library of 112,000 vols
Number of teachers: 65
Number of students: 928

MEMPHIS COLLEGE OF ART

Overton Park, 1930 Poplar Avenue, Memphis, TN 38104-2764
Telephone: (901) 726-4085
Fax: (901) 272-6830
Founded 1936

President: JEFFREY D. NESIN
Executive Vice-President: PHILLIP S. MORRIS
Dean: ALONZO DAVIS
Director of Admissions: SUSAN MILLER
Librarian: WENDY TRENTHEM

Library of 19,000 vols
Number of teachers: 16 full-time, 30 part-time
Number of students: 285

Publication: *MCA Newsletter* (quarterly).

MIDDLE TENNESSEE STATE UNIVERSITY

Murfreesboro, TN 37132
Telephone: (615) 898-2300
Fax: (615) 898-5906
Founded 1911
Academic year: Mid-August to mid-May

President: JAMES E. WALKER
Vice-President for Finance and Administration: DUANE STUCKY
Provost and Vice-President for Academic Affairs: BARBARA S. HASKEW
Vice-President for Student Affairs: ROBERT C. LALANCE
Vice-President for Development and University Relations: LINDA HARE
Dean of Admissions: CLIFF GILLESPIE
Librarian: DON CRAIG

Library of 564,000 vols
Number of teachers: 642
Number of students: 17,000

DEANS

College of Business: DWIGHT BULLARD (acting)
College of Basic and Applied Sciences: EARL KEESE
College of Education: ROBERT EAKER
College of Liberal Arts: JOHN MCDANIEL
Graduate School: DONALD CURRY
College of Mass Communication: DERYL LEAMING

MILLIGAN COLLEGE

Milligan College, TN 37682
Telephone: (615) 929-0116
Founded 1866 (reorganized 1881)

President: MARSHALL J. LEGGETT
Academic Dean: GARY E. WEEDMAN
Library Director: STEVEN L. PRESTON

Library of *c.* 108,500 vols
Number of teachers: 46
Number of students: 811

RHODES COLLEGE

2000 North Parkway, Memphis, TN 38112
Telephone: (901) 843-3000
Fax: (901) 843-3718
Founded 1848
Liberal arts college

President: JAMES H. DAUGHDRILL, Jr
Chancellor: DAVID L. HARLOW
Dean of Academic Affairs: JOHN M. PLANCHON
Registrar: GLENN W. MUNSON
Dean of Admissions: DAVID J. WOTTLE
Dean of Students: MELODY HOKANSON-RICHEY
Assistant to the President for College Relations: LOYD C. TEMPLETON, Jr
Dean of Development: ARTHUR L. CRISCILLIS
Librarian: LYNNE M. BLAIR

Library of 230,000 vols
Number of teachers: 121 full-time
Number of students: 1,425

SOUTHERN ADVENTIST UNIVERSITY

Collegedale, TN 37315
Telephone: (423) 238-2111
Fax: (423) 238-3001
Founded 1892

President: Dr GORDON BIETZ
Registrar: JONI ZIER
Librarian: PEGGY BENNETT

Library of 180,000 vols
Number of teachers: 100
Number of students: 1,700

TENNESSEE STATE UNIVERSITY

3500 John A. Merritt Blvd, Nashville, TN 37209-1561
Telephone: (615) 963-5000
Founded 1912

President: Dr JAMES A. HEFNER
Vice-President: Dr AUGUSTUS BANKHEAD
Registrar: VICKIE HOLMES
Librarian: Dr YILDIZ BINKLEY

Library of 565,400 vols
Number of teachers: 518
Number of students: 8,625

TENNESSEE TECHNOLOGICAL UNIVERSITY

Cookeville, TN 38505
Telephone: (615) 372-3101
Fax: (615) 372-3898
Founded 1915

President: Dr ANGELO A. VOLPE
Vice-President for Student Services: MARC BURNETT
Academic Vice-President: MARVIN BARKER
Vice-President for Administration and Planning: DAVID L. LARIMORE
Vice-President for Business and Fiscal Affairs: TERRY RECTOR
Director of Library Services: WINSTON WALDEN

Library of 1,610,000 vols
Number of teachers: 380
Number of students: 8,275

TENNESSEE WESLEYAN COLLEGE

POB 40, Athens, TN 37371-0040
Telephone: (423) 745-7504
Founded 1857

President: Dr B. JAMES DAWSON
Dean: Dr PHILIP W. OTT
Director of Admissions: JOHN HEAD

Library of 75,000 vols
Number of teachers: 29
Number of students: 633

TUSCULUM COLLEGE

Greeneville, TN 37743
Telephone: (423) 636-7300
Founded 1794

President: ROBERT E. KNOTT
Vice-President: JOHN E. MAYS
Vice-President for Academic and Administrative Services: DAVID S. WOOD
Vice-President for Student and Auxiliary Services: MARK A. STOKES
Vice-President of Finance: BARBARA MORGAN
Associate Vice-President of Development: JAMES A. BARCO
Director of Admissions: DANNY HALL
Director of Campus Life: DAVID HENDRICKSEN

Library of 192,000 vols
Number of teachers: 120
Number of students: 1,508

UNION UNIVERSITY

Jackson, TN 38305
Telephone: (901) 668-1818
Fax: (901) 661-5444
Founded 1823

President: Dr DAVID S. DOCKERY
Director of Student Enlistment: CARROLL GRIFFIN
Provost: Dr CARLA SANDERSON
Vice-President of Information Services and Academic Resources: Dr HAL POE

Library of 167,629 vols
Number of teachers: 111
Number of students: 2,370

UNIVERSITY OF MEMPHIS

Memphis, TN 38152
Telephone: (901) 678-2000
Fax: (901) 678-3299
Founded 1912

President: Dr V. LANE RAWLINS
Provost: Dr J. IVAN LEGG
Vice-President for Business and Finance: Dr R. EUGENE SMITH
Vice-President for Student Educational Services: Dr DONALD K. CARSON
Vice-President for Advancement: KEVIN ROPER
Vice-President for Information Systems: Dr. JAMES I. PENROD
Librarian: Dr LESTER J. POURCIAU, Jr

Library of 1,021,000 vols
Number of teachers: 952 (full-time and part-time)
Number of students: 19,851

Publications: *The Southern Journal of Philosophy* (quarterly), *Educational Quest, Law*

Review, *The University of Memphis Magazine* (4 a year), *Bulletin of the University of Memphis* (4 a year), *Mid-South Business Journal*, *Memphis Economy*, *Memphis Housing Market Area Report*.

UNIVERSITY OF TENNESSEE SYSTEM

Knoxville, TN 37996

Telephone: (615) 974-1000

Chartered 1794 as Blount College; name changed by legislature 1840 to East Tennessee University, and in 1879 to The University of Tennessee

Major campuses at Chattanooga, Knoxville, Martin and Memphis

State control

Academic year: September to August

President: Dr JOSEPH E. JOHNSON

General Counsel and Secretary of Board of Trustees: BEAUCHAMP E. BROGAN

Senior Vice-President: HOMER S. FISHER, Jr

Vice President for Development: CHARLES F. BRAKEBILL

Vice-President for Agriculture: DORSEY M. GOSSETT

Vice-President for Public Service and Continuing Education: SAMMIE LYNN PUETT

Executive Vice-President and Vice-President for Business and Finance: EMERSON H. FLY

Vice-President of University of Tennessee Space Institute: T. DEWAYNE MCCAY

Library: see Libraries

Number of teachers: 3,189

Number of students: 41,927

Publications: *The University Record*, Extension Series (4 to 6 a year), *Tennessee Alumnus*, *Horizons* (both quarterly).

University of Tennessee at Chattanooga

Chattanooga, TN 37401

Telephone: (615) 755-4141

Chancellor: FREDERICK W. OBEAR

Assistant to the Chancellor: SUSAN CARDWELL

Provost: GRAYSON H. WALKER

Associate Provost for Academic Services: JANE W. HARBAUGH

Associate Provost for Academic Administration: WILLIAM AIKEN

Vice-Chancellor for Business and Finance: RALPH W. MOSER Jr (acting)

Vice-Chancellor for Development: VINCENT M. PELLEGRINO

Vice-Chancellor for Student Affairs: CHARLES RENNEISEN

Assistant Vice-Chancellor for Administration: RICHARD L. BROWN (acting)

DEANS

College of Arts and Sciences: CHARLES T. SUMMERLIN

Continuing Education: MARILYN WILLIS

School of Business Administration: LINDA P. FLETCHER

School of Education: MARY N. TANNER (acting)

College of Health and Human Services: RANDY WALKER (acting)

School of Engineering: RONALD B. COX

Library: SHEILA DELACROIX

University of Tennessee, Knoxville

Knoxville, TN 37996

Telephone: (615) 974-1000

Chancellor: Dr WILLIAM T. SNYDER

Executive Assistant to the Chancellor: MARIANNE R. WOODSIDE

Vice-Chancellor for Student Affairs: PHILIP A. SCHEURER

Vice-Chancellor for Computing and Telecommunications: (vacant)

Vice-Chancellor for Business and Finance; RAYMOND L. HAMILTON

Vice-Chancellor for Development and Alumni Affairs: JACK E. WILLIAMS

DEANS

Admissions and Records: SUSIE COLEMAN ARCHER

College of Agriculture: GERHARDT SCHNEIDER (acting)

School of Architecture: MARLEEN K. DAVIS

College of Business Administration: C. WARREN NEEL

College of Communications: DWIGHT L. TEETER, Jr

College of Education: RICHARD WISNIEWSKI

College of Engineering: JERRY E. STONEKING

College of Human Ecology: JACQUELYN O. DEJONGE

College of Law: RICHARD S. WIRTZ

College of Liberal Arts: LORMAN A. RATNER

College of Veterinary Medicine: MICHAEL H. SHIRES

Division of Continuing Education: LAVERNE B. LINDSEY

Graduate School of Social Work: EUNICE O. SHATZ

Graduate Studies: CLARENCE W. MINKEL

Research: LEO RIEDINGER

College of Nursing: (vacant)

Institute of Agriculture: DON O. RICHARDSON (Agricultural Experiment Stations), BILLY G. HICKS (Administration)

Graduate School of Library and Information Science: (vacant)

Space Institute: JOEL W. MUELHAUSER (Administration), KAPULURU C. REDDY (Academic Affairs)

Library: PAULA T. KAUFMAN

Students: W. TIMOTHY ROGERS

PROFESSORS

College of Liberal Arts:

ADCOCK, J. L., Chemistry
AIKEN, C. S., Geography
ALEXANDRATOS, S. D., Chemistry
ALEXIADES, V., Mathematics
ALIKAKOS, N., Mathematics
ANDERSON, D. F., Mathematics
AQUILA, R. E., Philosophy
ASP, C. W., Audiology and Speech Pathology
BAGBY, R. M., Zoology
BAKER, D. C., Chemistry
BAKER, G. A., Mathematics
BALL, C. H., Music
BARRETTE, P., Romance and Asian Languages
BARTMESS, J. E., Chemistry
BECKER, J. M., Microbiology
BELL, T. L., Geography
BERGERON, P. H., History
BETZ, M., Sociology
BINGHAM, C. R., Physics
BITZAS, G. C., Music
BLACK, J. A., Sociology
BLAIN, S. J., Arts
BLASS, W. E., Physics
BRADY, P. S., Romance and Asian Languages
BRAKKE, P. M., Arts
BRATTON, E. W., English
BREINIG, M., Physics
BRENKERT, G. G., Philosophy
BROADHEAD, T., Geological Sciences
BROCK, J. P., Jr, Music
BUGG, W. M., Physics
BUHITE, R. D., History
BULL, W. E., Chemistry
BUNTING, D. L., II, Ecology
BURGDOERFER, J. E., Physics
BURGHARDT, G. M., Psychology
BURSTEIN, A. G., Psychology
CALHOUN, W. H., Psychology
CALLCOTT, T. A., Physics
CAPONETTI, J. D., Botany
CARNEY, P. J., Audiology and Speech Pathology
CARROLL, D. A., English
CARRUTH, J. H., Mathematics
CEBIK, L. B., Philosophy
CHAMBERS, J. Q., Chemistry
CHEN, T. T., Zoology
CHILDERS, R. W., Physics
CHMIELEWSKI, E. V., History
CHURCHICH, J. E., Biochemistry
CLARK, C. E., Mathematics
COBB, C. W., Romance and Asian Languages
COBB, J. C., History
COHEN, C. P., Psychology
COHN, H. O., Physics
COKER, J., Music
COMBS, F. M., Music
CONDO, G. T., Physics
CONWAY, J. B., Mathematics
COOK, K. D., Chemistry
COOKE, T. P., Theatre
COTHRAN, R. M., Jr, Theatre
COX, D. R., English
CUNNINGHAM, R. B., Political Science
CUSTER, M., Theatre
CUTLER, E. W., History
DAEHNERT, R. H., Arts
DAVERMAN, R. J., Mathematics
DOBBS, D. E., Mathematics
DONGARRA, J., Computer Science
DRAKE, R. Y., Jr, English
DUNGAN, D. L., Religious Studies
DYDAK, J., Mathematics
ECHTERNACHT, A. C., Zoology
EDWARDS, R. B., Philosophy
EGUILUZ, A. G., Physics
ELSTON, S. B., Physics
ENSOR, A. R., English
ETNIER, D. A., Zoology
FALSETTI, J. S., Arts
FARRIS, W. W., History
FAULKNER, C. H., Anthropology
FIELD, R. C., Theatre
FINGER, J. R., History
FINNERAN, R. J., English
FITZGERALD, M. R., Political Science
FORESTA, R., Geography
FOX, K., Physics
FRANDSEN, H., Mathematics
GANT, M. M., Political Science
GEORGHIOU, S., Physics
GESELL, G. C., Classics
GOLDENSTEIN, M. B., Arts
GORMAN, R., Political Science
GOSLEE, N. M., English
GRABER, G. C., Philosophy
GRIMM, F. A., Chemistry
GROSS, L. J., Mathematics
GUIDRY, M. W., Physics
GUIOCHON, G. A., Chemistry
HAAS, A. G., History
HALLAM, T. G., Mathematics
HANDEL, M. A., Zoology
HANDEL, S. J., Psychology
HANDELSMAN, M. H., Romance and Asian Languages
HANDLER, L., Psychology
HANDLER, T., Physics
HAO, YEN-PING, History
HARRIS, W. F., Biology
HART, E. L., Physics
HASTINGS, D. W., Sociology
HATCHER, R. D., Zoology
HEFFERNAN, T. J., English
HEFLIN, W. H., Romance and Asian Languages
HICKOK, L. G., Botany
HINTON, D. B., Mathematics
HOLTON, R. W., Botany
HOOD, T. C., Sociology
HUGHES, K. W., Botany
HUSCH, L. S., Mathematics
JACKSON, C. O., Administration
JACOBS, K. A., Music
JACOBSON, H. C., Administration
JANTZ, R. L., Anthropology

JEON, K. W., Zoology
JOHANNSON, K., Mathematics
JONES, W. H., Psychology
JORDAN, G. S., Mathematics
JOSHI, J. G., Biochemistry
JOY, D. C., Zoology
JUMPER, S. R., Geography
KABALKA, G. W., Chemistry
KALLET, M., English
KAMYCHKOV, I. A., Physics
KARAKASHIAN, O., Mathematics
KEELING, K. A., Music
KEENE, M. L., English
KELLY, R. M., English
KENNEDY, J. R., Zoology
KENNEDY, W. C., Arts
KLEINFELTER, D. C., Chemistry
KLIPPEL, W. E., Anthropology
KOPP, O. C., Geology
KOVAC, J. D., Chemistry
LABOTKA, T. C., Geological Sciences
LANGSTON, M. A., Computer Science
LAWLER, J. E., Psychology
LAWLER, K., Psychology
LEE, B. S., Arts
LEGGETT, B. J., English
LEKI, I., English
LELAND, W. E., Arts
LENHART, S. M., Mathematics
LESTER, L. W., Administration
LEVY, K. D., Romance and Asian Languages
LINGE, D. E., Religious Studies
LIVINGSTON, P. R., Arts
LOFARO, M. A., English
LUBAR, J., Psychology
LYONS, W., Political Science
MACCABE, J. A., Zoology
MCCLELLAND, D. K., Music
MCCONNEL, R. M., Mathematics
MCCORMICK, J. F., Ecology
MCCRACKEN, G. F., Zoology
MACEK, J. H., Physics
MCSWEEN, H. Y., Geological Sciences
MAGDEN, N. E., Arts
MAGID, L. J., Chemistry
MAGID, R. M., Chemistry
MAHAN, G. D., Physics
MALAND, C., English
MALONE, J. C., Jr, Psychology
MARSH, F. H., Arts
MARTINSON, F. H., Arts
MASHBURN, R. R., Speech and Theatre
MATHEWS, H. T., Mathematics
MISRA, K. C., Geology
MONTIE, T.C., Microbiology
MONTY, K. J., Biochemistry
MOORE, M. C., Music
MOORE, R. N., Microbiology
MOSER, H. D., History
MULLIN, B. C., Botany
NABELEK, A. K., Audiology and Speech Pathology
NAZAREWICZ, W., Physics
NORMAN, R. V., Religious Studies
NORTHINGTON, D. B., Music
PAGNI, R. M., Chemistry
PAINTER, L. R., Physics
PEACOCK, D., Arts
PEDERSON, D. M., Music
PEGG, D. J., Physics
PENNER, A. R., English
PETERSEN, R. H., Botany
PETERSON, H. A., Audiology and Speech Pathology
PETERSON, J. R., Chemistry
PIMM, S. L., Zoology
PLAAS, H., Political Science
PLOCH, D. R., Sociology
PLUMMER, E. W., Physics
POLLIO, H. R., Psychology
POORE, J. H., Computer Science
POSTOW, B. C., Philosophy
PULSIPHER, L. M., Geography
QUINN, J. J., Physics
RAJPUT, B. S., Mathematics
RALSTON, B. A., Geography
REESE, J. E., English
REYNOLDS, C. H., Religious Studies
RIECHERT, S. E., Zoology
RIESING, T. J., Arts
RIGGSBY, W. S., Microbiology
RIVERA-RODAS, O., Romance and Asian Languages
ROMEISER, J. B., Romance and Asian Languages
ROSINSKI, J., Mathematics
ROTH, L. E., Zoology
RUTLEDGE, H. C., Classics
SAMEJIMA, F., Psychology
SANDERS, N. J., English
SAUDARGAS, R. S., Psychology
SAVAGE, D. C., Psychology
SAYLER, G. S., Microbiology
SCHAEFER, P. W., Mathematics
SCHEB, J. M., Political Science
SCHILLING, E., Botany
SCHMUDDE, T. H., Geography
SCHWEITZER, G. K., Chemistry
SCURA, D. M., English
SELLIN, I. A., Physics
SEPANIAK, M. J., Chemistry
SERBIN, S. M., Mathematics
SHIH, C. C., Physics
SHIVERS, C. A., Zoology
SHOVER, N. E., Sociology
SHURR, W. H., English
SILVERSTEIN, B., Audiology and Speech Pathology
SIMPSON, H. C., Mathematics
SMITH, T. A., Political Science
SMITH, W. O., Botany
SONI, K., Mathematics
SONI, R. P., Mathematics
SORENSEN, S. P., Physics
STACEY, G., Microbiology
STEPHENS, O. H., Jr, Political Science
STEPHENSON, K., Mathematics
STEWART, F. C., Arts
STUTZENBERGER, D. R., Music
SUNDBERG, C., Mathematics
SUNDELL, S. E., Physics
SUNDSTROM, E. D., Psychology
TAYLOR, L. A., Geology
THISTLETHWAITE, M. B., Mathematics
THOMAS, J. C., English
THOMASON, M. G., Computer Science
THOMPSON, J. R., Jr, Physics
THONNARD, N., Science Alliance
TIPPS, A. W., Music
TRAHERN, J. B., English
TRAVIS, C. B., Psychology
UNGS, T. D., Political Science
VAN DE VATE, D., Jr, Philosophy
VANHOOK, A., Chemistry
VAUGHN, G. L., Zoology
WADE, W. R., II, Mathematics
WAGNER, C. G., Mathematics
WAHLER, R. G., Psychology
WALKER, K. R., Geology
WALLACE, S. E., Sociology
WALNE, P. L., Botany
WARD, B. F. L., Physics
WARD, R. C., Computer Science
WASHBURN, Y. M., Romance and Asian Languages
WEHRY, E. L., Chemistry
WEIR, A., English
WELBORN, D. M., Political Science
WHEELER, T. V., English
WHEELER, W. B., History
WHITE, D. C., Microbiology
WHITSON, G. L., Zoology
WICKS, W. D., Biochemistry
WILLIAMS, T. F., Chemistry
WOODS, C., Chemistry
WUNDERLICH, B., Chemistry
YATES, S. A., Arts
ZAK, T., Mathematics
ZHANG, J. Y., Physics

College of Human Ecology:

BLANTON, P. W., Child and Family Studies
CAMPBELL, C. P., Human Resources Development
CARRUTH, B. R., Nutrition
CHEEK, G. D., Human Resources Development
COAXLEY, C. B., Human Resources Development
CRAIG, D. G., Human Resources Development
CUNNINGHAM, J. L., Child and Family Studies
DELONG, A. J., Textiles, Retailing and Int. Design
DRAKE, M. F., Textiles, Retailing and Int. Design
DUCKETT, K. E., Textiles, Retailing and Interior Design
FOX, G. L., Child and Family Studies
GORSKI, J. D., Health, Leisure and Safety Sciences
HAMILTON, C. B., Health, Leisure and Safety Sciences
HANSON, R. R., Human Resources Development
HASKELL, R. W., Human Resources Development
HAYES, G. A., Health, Leisure and Safety Sciences
KIRK, R. H., Health, Leisure and Safety Sciences
MORAN, J. D., Administration
NORDQUIST, V. M., Child and Family Studies
SACHAN, D. S., Nutrition
SKINNER, J. D., Nutrition
STEELE, C., Child and Family Studies
TWARDOSZ, S. L., Child and Family Studies
WADSWORTH, L. C., Textiles, Retailing and Int. Design
WALLACE, B. C., Health, Leisure and Safety Sciences
ZEMEL, M. B., Nutrition

College of Engineering:

ALEXEFF, I., Electrical Engineering
ARIMILLI, R. V., Mechanical and Aerospace Engineering
BAILEY, J. M., Electrical Engineering
BAKER, A. J., Engineering Science and Mechanics
BENNETT, R. M., Civil and Environmental Engineering
BIENKOWSKI, P. R., Chemical Engineering
BIRDWELL, J. D., Electrical Engineering
BISHOP, A. O., Jr, Electrical Engineering
BLALOCK, T. V., Electrical Engineering
BODENHEIMER, R. E., Electrical Engineering
BOGUE, D. C., Chemical Engineering
BONTADELLI, J. A., Industrial Engineering
BOSE, B. K., Electrical Engineering
BOULDIN, D. W., Electrical Engineering
BROOKS, C. R., Jr, Materials Science and Engineering
BUCHANAN, R. A., Materials Science and Engineering
BURDETTE, E. G., Civil and Environmental Engineering
CARLEY, T. G., Engineering Science and Mechanics
CHATTERJEE, A., Civil and Environmental Engineering
CLARK, E. S., Materials Science and Engineering
CLAYCOMBE, W. W., Industrial Engineering
COUNCE, R. M., Chemical Engineering
CUMMINGS, P. T., Chemical Engineering
DAVIS, W. T., Civil and Environmental Engineering
DEPORTER, E. L., Industrial Engineering
DODDS, H. L., Nuclear Engineering
DRUMM, E. C., Civil and Environmental Engineering
EDMONDSON, A. J., Mechanical and Aerospace Engineering
FELLERS, J. F., Materials Science and Engineering

FORRESTER, J. H., Engineering Science and Mechanics
FRAZIER, G. C., Chemical Engineering
GHOSH, M. M., Civil and Environmental Engineering
GONZALEZ, R. C., Electrical Engineering
GOODPASTURE, D. W., Civil and Environmental Engineering
GREEN, W. L., Electrical Engineering
HANSEN, M. G., Chemical Engineering
HODGSON, J. W., Mechanical and Aerospace Engineering
HOFFMAN, G. W., Electrical Engineering
HUNG, J. C., Electrical Engineering
JENDRUCKO, R. J., Engineering Science and Mechanics
JOHNSON, W. S., Mechanical and Aerospace Engineering
KENNEDY, E. J., Electrical Engineering
KERLIN, T. W., Jr, Nuclear Engineering
KIM, K. H., Engineering Science and Mechanics
KRANE, R. J., Mechanical and Aerospace Engineering
KRIEG, R. D., Engineering Science and Mechanics
LANDES, J. D., Engineering Science and Mechanics
LAWLER, J. S., Electrical Engineering
LIAW, P. K., Materials Science and Engineering
LUNDIN, C. D., Materials Science and Engineering
MILLER, L. F., Nuclear Engineering
MILLER, W. A., Civil and Environmental Engineering
MILLIGAN, M. W., Mechanical and Aerospace Engineering
MOORE, C. F., Chemical Engineering
NEFF, H. P., Jr, Electrical Engineering
OLIVER, B. F., Materials Science and Engineering
PACE, M. O., Electrical Engineering
PARANG, M., Mechanical and Aerospace Engineering
PARSONS, J. R., Mechanical and Aerospace Engineering
PEDRAZA, A. J., Materials Science and Engineering
PERONA, J. J., Chemical Engineering
PHILLIPS, P. J., Materials Science and Engineering
PITTS, D. R., Engineering—Administration
PRADOS, J. W., Chemical Engineering
REED, G. D., Civil and Environmental Engineering
ROBERTS, M. J., Electrical Engineering
ROBINSON, R. B., Civil and Environmental Engineering
ROTH, J. R., Electrical Engineering
SCHMITT, H. W., Industrial Engineering
SCOTT, W. E., Engineering Science and Mechanics
SHANNON, T. E., Nuclear Engineering
SMITH, G. V., Mechanical and Aerospace Engineering
SNIDER, J. N., Industrial Engineering
SOLIMAN, O., Engineering Science and Mechanics
SPECKHART, F. H., Mechanical and Aerospace Engineering
SPRUIELL, J. E., Materials Science and Engineering
SYMONDS, F. W., Electrical Engineering
TOMPKINS, F. D., Engineering Academic
TRIVEDI, M. M., Electrical Engineering
TSCHANTZ, B. A., Civil and Environmental Engineering
UHRIG, R. E., Nuclear Engineering
UPADHYAYA, B. R., Nuclear Engineering
WASSERMAN, J. F., Engineering Science and Mechanics
WEGMANN, F. J., Civil and Environmental Engineering
WEITSMAN, Y. J., Center of Excellence
WILKERSON, H. J., Mechanical and Aerospace Engineering
WILSON, C. C., Mechanical and Aerospace Engineering

College of Business Administration:

BARNABY, D. J., Marketing and Transportation
BLACK, H. A., Finance
BOEHM, T. P., Finance
BOHM, R. A., Economics
BOWLBY, R. L., Economics
CADOTTE, E. R., Marketing and Transportation
CARROLL, S. L., Economics
CHANG, H., Economics
CLARK, D. P., Economics
COLE, W. E., Economics
DAVIDSON, P., Economics
DAVIS, F. W., Jr, Marketing and Transportation
DEWHIRST, H. D., Management
DICER, G. N., Marketing and Transportation
FISHER, B. D., Accounting
FOX, W. F., Economics
GARRISON, C. B., Economics
HERRING, H. C., Accounting
HERZOG, H. W., Economics
JAMES, L. R., Management
KIGER, J. E., Accounting
LANGLEY, C. J., Jr, Marketing and Transportation
LEE, F.-Y., Economics
MAYHEW, A., Economics
MAYO, J. W., Economics
MENTZER, J. T., Marketing Logistics and Transportation
MUNDY, R. A., Marketing and Transportation
PARR, W. C., Statistics
PATTON, E. P., Marketing and Transportation
PHILIPPATOS, G. C., Finance
PHILPOT, J. W., Statistics
REEVE, J. M., Accounting
ROTH, H. P., Accounting
RUSH, M. C., Management
SANDERS, R. D., Statistics
SCHLOTTMANN, A., Economics
SHRIEVES, R. E., Finance
STAHL, M. J., Business Administration
STANGA, K. G., Accounting
SYLWESTER, D. L., Statistics
WACHOWICZ, J. M., Finance
WANSLEY, J. W., Finance
WILLIAMS, J. R., Accounting
WOODRUFF, R. B., Marketing Logistics and Transportation

College of Education:

ALEXANDER, J. E., Holistic Teaching/Learning
ALLISON, C. B., Cultural Studies in Education
BENNER, S. M., Inclusive Early Childhood Education
BLANK, K. J., Inclusive Early Childhood Education
BOGUE, E. G., Leadership Studies
BUTEFISH, W. L., Education in Science and Mathematics
CAMERON, W., Psychoeducational Studies
COLEMAN, L. J., Inclusive Early Childhood Education
DAVIS, A. R., Holistic Teaching/Learning
DAVIS, K. L., Counsellor Education and Counselling Psychology
DESSART, D. J., Curriculum and Instruction
DICKINSON, D. J., Education in Science and Mathematics
DOAK, E. D., Education in Science and Mathematics
FRENCH, R. L., Education in Science and Mathematics
GEORGE, T. W., Educational Administration
HARGIS, C. H., Holistic Teaching/Learning
HARRIS, G., Leadership Studies
HECTOR, M. A., Counsellor Education and Counselling Psychology
HIPPLE, T. W., Holistic Teaching/Learning
HOWLEY, E. T., Exercise Science
HUCK, S. W., Counsellor Education and Counselling Psychology
HUFF, P. E., Holistic Teaching/Learning
HULL, H. N., Language Communication and Humanities Education
JOST, K. J., Holistic Teaching/Learning
KASWORM, C. E., Bureau of Educational Research and Services
KNIGHT, L. N., Holistic Teaching/Learning
KOZAR, A. J., Exercise Science
KRONICK, R. F., Holistic Teaching/Learning
LIEMOHN, W. P., Exercise Science
MCCALLUM, R. S., Psychoeducational Studies
MCINTYRE, L. D., Education in Science and Mathematics
MALIK, A., Cultural Studies in Education
MEAD, B. J., Cultural Studies in Education
MERTZ, N. T., Leadership Studies
MILLER, J. H., Rehabilitation and Deafness Programs
MORGAN, W. J., Cultural Studies in Education
MYER, M. E., Jr, Education in Science and Mathematics
PAUL, M. J., Cultural Studies in Education
PETERS, J. M., Psychoeducational Studies
PETERSON, M. P., Counsellor Education and Counselling Psychology
POPPEN, W. A., Counsellor Education and Counselling Psychology
RAY, J. R., Education in Science and Mathematics
ROCKETT, I. R. H., Exercise Science
ROESKE, C. E., Education in Science and Mathematics
ROWELL, C. G., Educational Administration
SCHINDLER, W. J., Holistic Teaching/Learning
THOMPSON, C. L., Counsellor Education and Counselling Psychology
TURNER, T. N., Holistic Teaching/Learning
UBBEN, G. C., Leadership Studies
WELCH, O. M., Rehabilitation and Deafness Programs
WILEY, P. D., Language Communication and Humanities Education
WILLIAMS, R. L., Psychoeducational Studies
WOODRICK, W. E., Rehabilitation and Deafness Programs
WRISBERG, C. A., Cultural Studies in Education

College of Communications:

ASHDOWN, P. G., Journalism
BOWLES, D. A., Journalism
CROOK, J. A., Journalism
EVERETT, G. A., Journalism
HOWARD, H. H., Broadcasting
LITTMANN, M. E., Journalism
MILLER, M. M., Journalism
MOORE, B. A., Broadcasting
SINGLETARY, M. W., Journalism
SMYSER, R. D., Journalism
STANKEY, M. J., Advertising
SWAN, N. R., Jr, Broadcasting
TAYLOR, R. E., Advertising

College of Agriculture:

ALLEN, F. L., Plant and Soil Science
ASHBURN, E. L., Plant and Soil Science
BERNARD, E. C., Entomology and Plant Pathology
BLEDSOE, B. L., Agricultural Engineering
BOST, S. C., Entomology and Plant Pathology
BREKKE, C. J., Food Science and Technology
BROOKER, J. R., Agricultural Economics
BUCKNER, E. R., Forestry
BURGESS, E. E., Entomology and Plant Pathology
CALLAHAN, L. M., Ornamental Horticulture and Landscape Design

CARTER, C. E., Jr, Agricultural Extension Education
CHAMBERS, A. Y., Entomology and Plant Pathology
CLELAND, C. L., Agricultural Economics
COFFEY, D. L., Plant and Soil Science
COLLINS, J. L., Food Technology and Science
CONATSER, G. E., Animal Science
CONGER, B. V., Plant and Soil Science
COOK, O. F., Four-H Club
CRATER, G. D., Ornamental Horticulture and Landscape Design
DALY, R. T., Home Economics
DEARDEN, B. L., Forestry
DIMMICK, R. W., Forestry
DRAUGHON, F. A., Food Science and Technology
EASTWOOD, D. B., Agricultural Economics
ENGLISH, B. C., Agricultural Economics
FARMER, C. M., Agricultural Economics
FLINCHUM, W. T., Plant and Soil Science
FOSS, J. E., Plant and Soil Science
FRIBOURG, H. A., Plant and Soil Science
GARLAND, C. D., Agricultural Economics
GERHARDT, R. R., Entomology and Plant Pathology
GILL, W. W., Animal Science
GOAN, H. C., Animal Science
GODKIN, J. D., Animal Science
GRAHAM, E. T., Ornamental Horticulture and Landscape Design
GRAVES, C. R., Plant and Soil Science
GRESSHOFF, P. M., Ornamental Horticulture, Center of Excellence
HADDEN, C. H., Entomology and Plant Pathology
HALL, R. F., Extension Veterinary Medicine
HAYES, R. M., Plant and Soil Science
HENRY, Z. A., Agricultural Engineering
HILL, T. K., Forestry
HOPPER, G. M., Forestry
HOWARD, D. D., Plant and Soil Science
HUNTER, D. L., Agricultural Economics
JENKINS, R. P., Agricultural Economics
KIRKPATRICK, F. D., Animal Science
LAMBDIN, P. L., Entomology and Plant Pathology
LANE, C. D., Jr, Animal Science
LESSLY, R. R., Agricultural Extension Education
LEUTHOLD, F. O., Agricultural Economics
LITTLE, R. L., Forestry
LOCKWOOD, D. W., Plant and Soil Science
MCDANIEL, G. L., Ornamental Horticulture and Landscape Design
MCLEMORE, D. L., Agricultural Economics
MAYS, G. C., Communication
MEADOWS, D. G., Animal Science (Beef)
MELTON, C. C., Food Technology
MELTON, S. L., Food Technology and Science
MILLER, J. K., Animal Science
MILLER, R. D., Plant and Soil Science
MONTGOMERY, M. J., Animal Science
MORRIS, W. C., Food Science and Technology
MOTE, C. R., Agricultural Engineering
MULLINS, C. A., Plant and Soil Science
MUNDY, S. D., Agricultural Economics
NEEL, J. B., Animal Science
NEWMAN, M. A., Entomology and Plant Pathology
OLIVER, S. P., Animal Science
OSTERMEIER, D. M., Forestry
PARK, W. M., Agricultural Economics
PATRICK, C. R., Entomology and Plant Pathology
PELTON, M. R., Forestry
PENFIELD, M. P., Food Technology and Science
PLESS, C. D., Entomology and Plant Pathology
POWELL, B. T., Four-H
RAWLS, E. L., Agricultural Economics
RAY, D. E., Agricultural Economics
REINHARDT, C. A., Communication
RENNIE, J. C., Forestry
REYNOLDS, J. H., Plant and Soil Science
ROBBINS, K. R., Animal Science
ROBERTS, R. K., Agricultural Economics
RUTLEDGE, A. D., Plant and Soil
SAMS, C. E., Plant and Soil Science
SAMS, D. W., Plant and Soil Science
SANDERS, W. L., Statistics
SAXTON, A. M., Statistics
SIMMS, R. H., Animal Science
SMITH, G. F., Agricultural Economics
SOUTHARDS, C. J., Entomology and Plant Pathology
STRANGE, R. J., Forestry
TODD, J. D., Agricultural Extension and Education
TYLER, D. D., Plant and Soil Science
WEST, D. R., Plant and Soil Science
WESTBROOK, E. M., Home Economics and Family Economy
WILHELM, L. R., Agricultural Engineering
WILLIAMS, D. B., Ornamental Horticulture and Landscape Design
WILLIAMSON, H., Agricultural Economics
WILLS, J. B., Agricultural Engineering
WILSON, J. L., Forestry

College of Veterinary Medicine:

BRACE, J. J., Administration
BRIAN, D. A., Microbiology and Veterinary Medicine
BRIGHT, R. M., Small Animal Clinical Sciences
DORN, A. S., Small Animal Clinical Sciences
EDWARDS, D. F., Pathology
FARKAS, W. R., Comparative Medicine
GREEN, E. M., Large Animal Clinical Sciences
HENRY, R. W., Animal Science
HOPKINS, F. M., Large Animal Clinical Sciences
KRAHWINKEL, D. J., Jr, Small Animal Clinical Sciences
LEGENDRE, A. M., Small Animal Clinical Sciences
MCCORD, S. P., Comparative Medicine
MCDONALD, T. P., Animal Science and Veterinary Medicine
MCGAVIN, M. D., Pathology
OLIVER, J. W., Comparative Medicine
PATTON, C. S., Pathology
POTGIETER, L. N. D., Comparative Medicine
ROUSE, B. T., Microbiology and Veterinary Medicine
SCHULLER, H. M., Pathology
SHULL, R. M., Pathology
SHULTZ, T. W., Animal Science and Veterinary Medicine
SIMS, M. H., Animal Science and Veterinary Medicine
SLAUSON, D. O., Pathology

College of Law:

BLAZE, D. A.
COHEN, N. P.
COOK, J. G.
DESSEM, R. L.
HARDIN, P.,
HESS, A. M.
KING, J. H., Jr
LECLERQ, F. S.
LLOYD, R. M.
PHILLIPS, J. J.
RIVKIN, D. H.
SOBIESKI, J. L., Jr

School of Architecture:

ANDERSON, G.
GRIEGER, F.
KELSO, R. M.
KERSAVAGE, J. A.
KINZY, S. A.
LAUER, W. J.
LESTER, A. J.
LIZON, P.
ROBINSON, M. A.
RUDD, J. W.
SHELL, W. S.
WATSON, J. S.
WODEHOUSE, L. M.

School of Nursing:

ALLIGOOD, M. R.
GOODFELLOW, D. H.
MOZINGO, J.
THOMAS, S. P.

Graduate School of Social Work:

CETINGOK, M.
FAVER, C. A.
GLISSON, C. A.
HIRAYAMA, H.
NOOE, R. M.
RUBINSTEIN, H.

Graduate School of Bio-medical Sciences:

OLINS, A. L.
OLINS, D. E.
POPP, R. A.

Graduate School of Planning:

JOHNSON, D. A.
PROCHASKA, J. M.
SPENCER, J. A.

Graduate School of Library and Information Science:

ESTES, G. E.
TENOPIR, C.

Space Institute:

ANTAR, B. N.
COLLINS, F. G.
CRATER, H. W.
CRAWFORD, L. W.
CRAWFORD, R. A.
FLANDRO, G. A.
GARRISON, G. W.
KEEFER, D. R.
KUPERSCHMIDT, B. A.
LEWIS, J. W.
LO, C.
MCCAY, M. H.
PALUDAN, C. T. N.
PETERS, C. E.
PUJOL, A.
SCHULZ, R. J.
SHAHROKHI, F.
SHETH, A. C.
WU, J. M.

Center for Assessment Research:

MCGLASSON, N.

Library:

BAYNE, P. S.
BEST, R. A., Law
CRAWFORD, M. F.
FELDER-HOEHNE, F. H.
GRADY, A. M.
LECLERCQ, A. W.
PHILLIPS, L. L.
PIQUET, D. C., Law
RADER, J. C.

Learning Research Center:

WALTER L. HUMPHREYS

Energy, Environment and Resources Center:

COLGLAZIER, E. M.

University of Tennessee Center for Health Sciences

Memphis, TN 38103
Telephone: (902) 528-5500
Chancellor: WILLIAM R. RICE
Executive Assistant to the Chancellor: MARTHA J. YOUNG
Vice-Chancellor for University Relations: JESSE F. MCCLURE
Vice-Chancellor for Student Affairs: WILLIAM C. ROBINSON
Vice-Chancellor for Development: GLENDA A. O'CONNOR
Vice-Chancellor for Business and Finance: ROBERT L. BLACKWELL
Vice-Chancellor for Administration: RAYMOND H. COLSON

DEANS

College of Allied Health Sciences: WILLIAM G. HINKLE
College of Medicine: ROBERT L. SUMMITT
College of Dentistry: WILLIAM F. SLAGLE
College of Pharmacy: DICK R. GOURLEY
College of Nursing: MICHAEL A. CARTER
College of Graduate Health Sciences: ROBERT FREEMAN

DEPARTMENT CHAIRMEN

College of Medicine:

Anatomy and Neurobiology: STEPHEN T. KITAI
Biochemistry: JOHN FAIN
Microbiology and Immunology: TERRANCE G. COOPER
Pharmacology: MURRAY HEIMBERG
Physiology and Biophysics: LEONARD R. JOHNSON
Anaesthesiology: JOHN ZANELLA
Family Medicine: WILLIAM M. RODNEY
Neurology: WILLIAM A. PULSINELLI
Obstetrics and Gynaecology: FRANK LING
Paediatrics: RUSSELL W. CHESNEY
Preventive Medicine: WILLIAM B. APPLEGATE
Psychiatry: NEAL B. EDWARDS
Radiology: BARRY E. GERALD
General Surgery: LOUIS G. BRITT
Urology: CLAIR E. COX, II
Neurosurgery: JAMES T. ROBERTSON
Ophthalmology: BARRETT G. HAIK
Orthopaedic Surgery: ALLEN S. EDMONSON
Otolaryngology: KEVIN T. ROBBINS
Pathology: ROBERT E. SCOTT
Internal Medicine: DENNIS R. SCHABERG
Family Medicine (Knoxville Unit): GEORGE S. SHACKLETT
Biostatistics and Epidemiology: GRANT W. SOMES
Comparative Medicine: DAVID M. RENQUIST
Biomedical Engineering: FRANK A. DIBIANCA
Emergency Medicine: KEVIN S. MERIGIAN
Human Values and Ethics: TERRENCE F. ACKERMAN

College of Dentistry:

Prosthodontics: WILLIAM F. BOWLES, III
General Dentistry: RUSSELL GILPATRICK
Biologic and Diagnostic Sciences: JAMES E. TURNER
Oral and Maxillofacial Surgery: JIMMY E. ALBRIGHT
Orthodontics: ROLF G. BEHRENTS
Pediatric Dentistry: SANFORD J. FENTON
Periodontics: MARK R. PATTERS

College of Allied Health Sciences:

Clinical Laboratory Sciences: BRENTA G. DAVIS
Dental Hygiene: (vacant)
Health Information Management: (vacant)
Physical Therapy: (vacant)

College of Pharmacy:

Pharmaceutical Sciences: MARVIN C. MEYER
Clinical Pharmacy: LAWRENCE J. HAK

College of Nursing:

Primary Care: CAROL L. PANICUCCI
Acute Care: CAROL L. THOMPSON
Health Care Systems: NANCY R. LACKEY

University of Tennessee at Martin

Martin, TN 38328

Telephone: (901) 587-7000

Chancellor: MARGARET N. PERRY
Vice-Chancellor for Academic Affairs: FRANK S. BLACK
Vice-Chancellor for Financial Affairs: PHILLIP W. DANE
Vice-Chancellor for Student Affairs: PHILIP W. WATKINS
Executive Vice-Chancellor for Development: NICK DUNAGAN

DEANS

School of Agriculture and Home Economics: JAMES L. BYFORD
School of Business Administration: GARY F. YOUNG
School of Education: GARY RUSH
School of Arts and Sciences: ROBERT M. SMITH
School of Engineering: TROY F. HENSON
Student Affairs: DONALD G. SEXTON
Intensive English Language Programs: JOHN A. EISTERHOLD

UNIVERSITY OF THE SOUTH

Sewanee, TN 37383-1000

Telephone: (615) 598-1000

Chartered 1858

Private (Protestant Episcopal Church)

President: SAMUEL R. WILLIAMSON, Jr
Provost: FREDERICK H. CROOM
Director of Summer College: JOHN V. REISHMAN
Director of Graduate School of Theology: Rev. DONALD S. ARMENTROUT
Director of Admissions: ROBERT M. HEDRICK
Registrar: STEVENS ANDERSON
Librarian: TOMMY G. WATSON

Library of 469,000 vols
Number of teachers: College 151, Seminary 9
Number of students: College 1,246, Seminary 83

Publications: *Sewanee Review, Sewanee Theological Review.*

DEANS

College of Arts and Sciences: ROBERT L. KEELE
Dean of Students: ROBERT W. PEARIGEN
School of Theology: Very Rev. Dr GUY F. LYTLE, III

VANDERBILT UNIVERSITY

Nashville, TN 37240

Telephone: (615) 322-7311
Telex: 554323
Fax: (615) 343-5555

Founded 1873

Chancellor: JOE B. WYATT
Provost: CHARLES A. KIESLER
Vice-Chancellors: J. S. BEASLEY II, JEFF CARR, W. A. JENKINS, R. R. ROBINSON
Treasurer: WILLIAM T. SPITZ
Secretary: JEFF CARR
Registrar: R. G. GIBSON
Librarian: M. GETZ

Number of teachers: 1,525 full-time, 1,029 part-time
Number of students: 9,236

DEANS

College of Arts and Science: DAVID L. TULEEN (acting)
Graduate School: R. G. HAMILTON, Jr
Blair School of Music: J. F. SAWYER
Divinity School: JOSEPH C. HOUGH, Jr
School of Engineering: EDWARD A. PARRISH
School of Law: JOHN J. COSTONIS
Owen Graduate School of Management: MARTIN S. GEISEL
School of Medicine: J. E. CHAPMAN
School of Nursing: COLLEEN CONWAY-WELCH
George Peabody College: JAMES W. PELLIGRINO

PROFESSORS

ABBEY, J. C., Medical-Surgical Nursing
ABERNETHY, V. D., Psychiatry
ABKOWITZ, M. D., Civil and Environmental Engineering
ADKINS, R. B., Jr, Surgery and Cell Biology
ALBRIDGE, R. G., Physics
ALLEN, G. S., Neurosurgery
ALLISON, F., Jr, Medicine
ANDERSON, W. F., Biochemistry
ANDREWS, J. R., Spanish and Portuguese
APPELBAUM, M. I., Psychology
ARENSTORF, R. F., Mathematics
AUBREY, R. F., Psychology and Education
BAN, T. A., Psychiatry
BARACH, J. P., Physics
BARR, J., Hebrew Bible
BASU, P. K., Civil and Environmental Engineering
BAUCH, J. P., Education
BAUMEISTER, A. A., Psychology and Special Education
BAYUZICK, R. J., Materials Science and Engineering
BELL, C. L. G., Economics
BELL, V. M., English
BELTON, R., Law
BENDER, H. W., Jr, Surgery
BERMAN, M. L., Anaesthesiology
BESS, F. H., Audiology, Otolaryngology
BICKMAN, L., Psychology
BIGLER, H. F., Nursing
BIRKBY, R. H., Political Science
BLACKBURN, J. D., Jr, Management
BLAIR, I. A., Pharmacology and Chemistry
BLAKE, R., Psychology
BLANNING, R., Management
BLASER, M. J., Medicine
BLOCH, F. S., Law
BLUMSTEIN, J. F., Law
BOEHM, F. H., Obstetrics and Gynaecology
BÖER, G. B., Management
BOGITSH, B. J., Biology
BONDS, A. B., III, Electrical Engineering
BOUCEK, R. J., Jr, Paediatrics
BOURNE, J. R., Electrical Engineering and Biomedical Engineering
BOWEN, B. C., French
BRANSFORD, J. D., Psychology and Education
BRASH, A. R., Pharmacology
BRAU, C. A., Physics
BRIGHAM, K. L., Experimental Medicine and Biomedical Engineering
BRODERSEN, A. J., Electrical Engineering
BRUCE, J. W., Law
BURISH, T. G., Psychology and Medicine
BURK, R. F., Medicine
BURNETT, L. S., Obstetrics and Gynaecology
BURR, I. M., Paediatrics
BURT, A. M., III, Cell Biology
BUTTRICK, D. G., Homilectics and Liturgics
CADZOW, J. A., Electrical Engineering
CAMPBELL, E. Q., Sociology
CAPDEVILA, J. H., Medicine
CARPENTER, G. F., Biochemistry
CARTER, C. E., Biology
CASAGRANDE, V. A., Cell Biology and Psychology
CASTELNUOVO-TEDESCO, P., Psychiatry
CAUL, W. F., Psychology
CHALKLEY, G. R., Molecular Physiology and Biophysics, Biochemistry
CHAPMAN, J. E., Pharmacology, Medical Administration
CHARNEY, J. I., Law
CHERRINGTON, A. D., Physiology
CHYTIL, F., Biochemistry and Nutrition
CLAYTON, K. N., Psychology
COBB, P. A., Education
COHEN, S., Biochemistry
COLLEY, D. G., Microbiology and Medicine
COLLIER, S., History
COLLINS, R. D., Pathology
COMPTON, J. J., Philosophy
CONDER, J. J., English
CONKIN, P. K., History
CONWAY-WELCH, C., Nursing
COOK, A. J., English
CORBIN, J. D., Molecular Physiology and Biophysics
CORDRAY, D. S., Public Policy and Psychology
COSTONIS, J. J., Free Enterprise
COTTON, R. B., Paediatrics
COVINGTON, R. N., Law
CRISPIN, J., Spanish
CRIST, L. S., French

CROFFORD, O. B., Jr, Medicine, Diabetes and Metabolism
CROOKE, P. S., III, Mathematics
CRUSE, T. A., Mechanical Engineering
CUNNINGHAM, L. W., Biochemistry
DAFT, R. L., Management
DAMON, W. W., Economics and Business Administration, Management
DANZO, B. J., Obstetrics and Gynaecology
DAVIDSON, J. L., Electrical Engineering
DAVIDSON, J. M., Pathology
DEAL, T. E., Education
DEMAREST, A. A., Anthropology
DEMETRIOU, A. A., Surgery
DENNIS, H. F., Jr, Special Education
DES PREZ, R. M., Medicine
DETTBARN, W., Pharmacology, Neurology
DODGE, K. A., Psychology
DOKECKI, P., Psychology and Special Education
DONALDSON, M. L., Nursing
DOODY, M. A., Humanities, English
DOWNING, J. W., Anaesthesiology; Obstetrics and Gynaecology
DOYLE, D. H., History
DREWS, R., Classics and History
DRISKEL, R. A., Economics
DUPONT, W. D., Preventive Medicine
EBERT, M. E., Psychiatry and Pharmacology
EDNER, F. F., Psychology
EDWARDS, K. M., Paediatrics
EDWARDS, W. H., Sr, Surgery
EISERT, D. R., Radiology and Radiological Sciences
ELLEDGE, W. P., English
ELLIOTT, J. H., Ophthalmology
ELSHTAIN, J. B., Political Science
ELY, J. W., Jr, Law and History
ENTMAN, S. S., Obstetrics and Gynaecology
ERNST, D. J., Physics
EVERTSON, C. M., Education
EXTON, J. H., Molecular Physiology and Biophysics, Pharmacology
FARLEY, E., Theology
FEDERSPIEL, C. F., Preventative Medicine (Biostatistics)
FEMAN, S. S., Ophthalmology
FENICHEL, G. M., Neurology and Paediatrics
FINEGAN, T. A., Economics
FINN, C. E., Jr, Education and Public Policy
FISCHER, C. F., Computer Science, Mathematics, Chemistry and Physics
FISCHER, P. C., Computer Science
FLANAGAN, W. F., Materials Science
FLEISCHER, A. A., Radiology and Radiological Sciences
FLEISCHER, B., Molecular Biology
FLEISCHER, S., Molecular Biology
FLEXNER, J. M., Medicine and Oncology
FORSTMAN, H. J., Theology
FORT, T., Chemical Engineering
FOSTER, J. E., Economics
FOX, R., Psychology and Biomedical Engineering
FRANKLIN, J. L., History
FRANKS, J. J., Psychology
FREEDMAN, P. H., History
FREEMAN, J. A., Cell Biology and Ophthalmology
FREEMON, F. R., Neurology
FRIEDMAN, B., Law
FRIESINGER, G. C., II, Medicine
FUCHS, D. H., Special Education
FUCHS, L. S., Special Education
GAVISH, B., Management
GAY, V. P., Religious Studies
GEISEL, M. S., Management
GHISHAN, F., Paediatrics, Molecular Physiology and Biophysics
GIBBS, J. P., Sociology
GIRGUS, S. B., English
GLASSMAN, A. B., Pathology
GOLDBERG, R. R., Mathematics
GOLDMAN, S. R., Psychology
GORSTEIN, F., Pathology
GOTTERER, G. S., Medical Administration
GOULD, M., Mathematics
GOVE, A. F., Slavic Languages and Literature
GOVE, W. R., Sociology
GRAHAM, G. J., Jr, Political Science
GRAHAM, H. D., History
GRAHAM, T. P., Jr, Paediatrics
GRANNER, D. K., Molecular Physiology and Biophysics; Medicine
GRAY, G. F., Pathology
GRECO, F. A., Medicine
GREEN, N. E., Orthopaedics and Rehabilitation
GREGOR, T. A., Anthropology
GRIFFIN, L. J., Sociology and Political Science
GUENGERICH, F. P., Biochemistry
HAHN, G. T., Metallurgical Engineering
HAKIM, R. M., Medicine
HALL, D. J., Law
HALL, D. S., Physics and Astronomy
HALL, H. D., Oral Surgery
HALPERIN, J., English
HAMILTON, J. H., Physics
HANCOCK, M. D., Political Science
HANDE, K. R., Medicine
HARDMAN, J. G., Pharmacology
HARGROVE, E. C., Political Science and Education
HARLEY, R. K., Special Education
HARPER, M. C., Orthopaedics and Rehabilitation
HARRAWOOD, P., Civil Engineering
HARRIS, T. M., Chemistry
HARRIS, T. R., Biomedical Engineering, Chemical Engineering, Medicine
HARROD, H. L., Social Ethics and Sociology of Religion, Religious Studies
HARSHMAN, S., Microbiology
HASH, J. H., Microbiology
HASSEL, R. C., Jr, English
HAWIGER, J., Microbiology
HAWLEY, W. D., Education and Political Science
HAYWOOD, H. C., Psychology and Neurology
HAZLEHURST, F. H., Fine Arts
HELDERMAN, J. H., Medicine
HELLER, R. M., Jr, Radiology and Radiological Sciences, Paediatrics
HEMMINGER, R. L., Mathematics
HESS, B. A., Jr, Chemistry
HOADLEY, P. G., Civil Engineering
HODGES, M. P., Political Science
HODGSON, P. C., Theology
HOFFMAN, L. H., Cell Biology
HOGAN, B. L. M., Cell Biology
HOGGE, J. H., Psychology
HOLADAY, B. J., Nursing
HOLADAY, D. A., Anaesthesiology
HOLLADAY, W. G., Physics
HOLLON, S. D., Psychology
HOOVER, R. L., Pathology
HOUGH, J. C., Jr, Divinity
HOWARD, M., Law
HUANG, C. J., Economics
HUANG, R. D., Management
ICHIKAWA, I., Paediatrics
INAGAMI, T., Biochemistry
ISHERWOOD, R. M., History
JACOBSON, H. R., Medicine and Nephrology
JAMES, A. E., Radiology and Radiological Sciences; Medical Administration; Obstetrics and Gynaecology
JARMAN, M. F., English
JENSEN, G. F., Sociology
JOESTEN, M. D., Chemistry
JOHNSON, D. A., Church History
JOHNSON, L. E., Electrical Engineering and Biomedical Engineering
JOHNSTON, J. S., Law
JONES, C. D., Jr, Theatre
JONES, H. W., III, Obstetrics and Gynaecology
JONES, M. M., Chemistry
JÓNSSON, B., Mathematics
KAAS, J. H., Psychology
KAHANE, C. S., Mathematics
KAISER, A. B., Medicine
KAISER, A. P., Special Education
KAMBAM, J., Anaesthesiology
KARZON, D. T., Paediatrics
KATAHN, E., Piano
KAVASS, I. I., Law
KAWAMURA, K., Electrical Engineering and Management of Technology
KERNS, D. V., Jr, Electrical and Biomedical Engineering
KERNS, S. E., Electrical Engineering
KIESLER, C. A., Psychology
KING, L. E., Jr, Medicine
KINSER, D. L., Materials Science
KIRCHNER, S., Radiology and Radiological Sciences
KIRKMAN, R. E., Higher Education
KIRSHNER, H. S., Neurology and Psychiatry
KNIGHT, D. A., Hebrew Bible
KOURY, M. J., Medicine
KRAL, R., Biology
KRANTZ, S. B., Medicine
KREYLING, M., English
LABEN, J. K., Nursing
LACHS, J., Philosophy
LANGEVOORT, D. C., Law
LAPPIN, J. S., Psychology
LAWTON, A. R., Paediatrics, Paediatric Physiology and Cell Metabolism, and Microbiology
LEBLANC, L. J., Management
LEE, D. A., Musicology
LEFKOWITZ, L. B., Jr, Preventive Medicine
LEGAN, H. L., Dentistry
LENHERT, P. G., Physics
LENT, J. R., Special Education
LERNER, L. D., English
LESTOURGEON, W. M., Molecular Biology
LEVINSON, L. H., Law
LICHTER, B.D., Materials Science and Management of Technology
LIMBIRD, L. E., Pharmacology
LIPSEY, M. W., Education
LOOSEN, P. T., Psychiatry and Medicine
LOVE, R. J., Hearing and Speech Sciences
LUKEHART, C. M., Chemistry
LUKENS, J. N., Jr, Paediatrics
LYNCH, J. B., Plastic Surgery
MAGUIRE, C. F., Physics
MAHONEY, T. A., Organizational Studies
MAIER, H. G., Law
MARGO, R. A., Economics
MARNETT, L. J., Biochemistry and Cancer Research
MARTIN, J. C., Chemistry
MARTIN, P. R., Psychiatry
MASULIS, R. W., Management
MAURER, C. H., Spanish
MAYER, S. E., Pharmacology
MCCARTHY, J. A., German
MCCOY, T. R., Law
MCDOUGAL, W. S., Urology
MCFAGUE, S., Theology
MEGIBBEN, C. K., Mathematics
MELLOR, A. M., Mechanical Engineering
MEYRICK-CLARRY, B. O., Pathology and Medicine
MILLER, C. F., Geology
MILLER, J. W., Education
MILLS, L. O., Pastoral Theology and Counselling
MITCHELL, W. M., Pathology
MONGA, L., French and Italian
MORLEY, S. A., Economics
MOSES, H. L., Cell Biology and Pathology
MOSIG, G., Molecular Biology
MURPHY, J. F., Educational Leadership
NEWBROUGH, J. R., Psychology, Education, Special Education
NEWMAN, J. H., Pulmonary Medicine
NURCOMBE, B., Psychiatry
OATES, J. A., Medicine and Pharmacology
O'DAY, D. M., Ophthalmology
ODOM, R. D., Psychology
OLIVER, R. L., Management (Marketing)
OLSON, G. E., Cell Biology
ONG, D. E., Biochemistry
ORGEBIN-CRIST, M. C., Obstetrics and Gynaecology, Reproductive Physiology and Family Planning, Cell Biology
ORTH, D. N., Medicine

OSSOFF, R. H., Otolaryngology, Hearing and Speech Sciences
OVERHOLSER, K. A., Biomedical and Chemical Engineering
PAGE, D. L., Pathology
PAGE, T. L., Biology
PALMER, R. E., Jr, English
PANVINI, R. S., Physics
PARK, J. H., Molecular Physiology and Biophysics
PARKER, F. L., Environmental and Water Resources Engineering, Management of Technology
PARL, F. F., Pathology
PARRIS, W., Anaesthesiology
PARRISH, E. A., Jr, Electrical Engineering
PARTAIN, C. L., Radiology and Radiological Sciences, Biomedical Engineering
PARTLETT, D. F., Law
PATTE, D. M., Religious Studies, New Testament and Early Christianity
PATTON, J. A., Radiology and Radiological Sciences
PELLEGRINO, J. W., Cognitive Studies
PENDERGRASS, H. P., Radiology and Radiological Sciences
PERRY, L. C., History
PETERSON, R. A., Sociology
PFANNER, H. F., German
PHILLIPS, J. A. III, Paediatrics and Biochemistry
PICHOIS, C., French
PINCUS, T., Medicine and Microbiology
PINKSTON, W. T., Physics
PINSON, C. W., Surgery
PLEDGER, W. J., Cell Biology
PLUMMER, M. D., Mathematics
PORTER, R. H., Psychology
POST, J. F., Philosophy
POST, R. K., Molecular Physiology and Biophysics
POWERS, M. K., Psychology
PRICE, R. R., Radiology
PUPO-WALKER, C. E., Spanish
QUERTERMOUS, T., Medicine
RACE, W. H., Classics
RADOS, D. L., Management
RAMAYYA, A. V., Physics
RAMSEY, L. H., Medicine
RAY, O. S., Psychology and Psychiatry
RAY, W. A., Preventive Medicine
REGEN, D. M., Molecular Physiology and Biophysics
REICHMAN, J., Law
REYNOLDS, V. H., Surgery
RICHIE, R. E., Surgery
RIESER, J. J., Psychology
RIETH, H. J., Jr, Special Education
RILEY, H. D., Jr, Paediatrics
ROBACK, H. B., Psychiatry and Psychology
ROBERTS, L. J., II, Pharmacology and Medicine
ROBERTSON, D. H., Medicine and Pharmacology
ROBERTSON, R. M., Medicine
ROBINSON, R. R., Medicine
RODEN, D. M., Pharmacology
ROOS, C. E., Physics, Radiology and Radiological Sciences
ROSELLI, R. J., Biomedical Engineering
ROSS, J. C., Medicine
ROTH, J. A., Chemical Engineering and Environmental Engineering
ROWAN, W. H., Jr, Computer Science
RUBIN, C., Mechanical Engineering
RUBIN, D. H., Medicine
RUIZ-RAMON, F., Spanish
RULEY, H. E., Microbiology and Immunology
RUSHING, W. A., Sociology
RUSSELL, C. S., Economics, Education and Human Development
RUST, R. T., Management
SALLIS, J., Philosophy
SALMON, W. D., Jr, Medicine
SANDERMANN, H., Molecular Biology
SANDERS-BUSH, E., Pharmacology and Psychiatry
SANDLER, H. M., Psychology
SANDLER, M. P., Radiology and Radiological Sciences
SASTRY, B. V. R., Pharmacology
SAWYERS, J. L., Surgery
SCHAAD, L. J., Chemistry
SCHAFFNER, W., Preventative Medicine and Medicine
SCHAPIRA, M., Pathology
SCHEFFMAN, D. T., American Competitive Enterprise
SCHNELLE, K. B., Jr, Chemical and Environmental Engineering
SCHOENBLUM, J. A., Law
SCHUMAKER, L. L., Mathematics
SCOTT, C. E., Philosophy
SCUDDER, G. D., Management (Operations Management)
SEGOVIA, F. F., Theology
SERGENT, J. S., Medicine
SEVERINO, A. E., Portuguese
SEVIN, D. H. O., Germanic Languages and Literatures
SHERBURNE, D. W., Philosophy
SHIAVI, R. G., Biomedical Engineering and Electrical Engineering
SIEGFRIED, J. J., Economics
SIESSER, W. G., Geology
SKEEL, D. J., Social Studies Education
SLOAN, F. A., Economics
SLOVIS, C. M., Emergency Medicine
SMITH, B. E., Anaesthesiology
SMITH, H. E., Chemistry
SMITH, J. A., Jr, Urology
SMITH, R., Medicine
SMITH, W. P., Psychology
SNAPPER, J. R., Medicine
SNELL, J. D., Jr, Medicine
SODERQUIST, L. D., Law
SPECTOR, S., Psychiatry and Pharmacology
SPEECE, R. E., Civil and Environmental Engineering
SPENGLER, D. M., Orthopaedics and Rehabilitation
SPICKARD, W. A., Jr, Medicine
SPORES, R., Anthropology
STAHLMAN, M. T., Paediatrics and Pathology
STAROS, J. V., Molecular Biology
STEAD, W. W., Medicine
STEARNS, R. G., Geology
STOLL, H. R., Finance
STONE, W. J., Medicine
STRAUSS, A. M., Mechanical Engineering
STRUPP, H. H., Psychology
STUBBS, G. J., Microbiology
SULLIVAN, W. L., English
SULSER, F., Psychiatry and Pharmacology
SUNDELL, H. W., Paediatrics
SUNDQUIST, E. J., English
SWEETMAN, B. J., Anaesthesiology
SWIFT, L. L., Pathology
SZTIPANOVITS, J., Electrical Engineering
TAM, J. P., Microbiology and Immunology
TANNER, R. D., Chemical Engineering
TEAL, C., Violin
TELLINGHUISEN, J., Chemistry
TELOH, H. A., Philosophy
TESCHAN, P. E., Medicine
TESELLE, E., Church History and Theology
THACKSTON, E. L., Civil and Environmental Engineering
THOITS, P. A., Sociology
THOMPSON, T., Psychology
TIBBETS, C., Microbiology
TICHI, C., English
TOLBERT, M. A., Theology
TOLK, N. H., Physics
TOUSTER, O., Molecular Biology and Biochemistry
TOWNES, A. S., Medicine
VOEGELI, V. J., History
WALKER, N. A., English
WALLSTON, K. A., Psychology in Nursing, Psychology
WALTER, B., Political Science
WANG, T. G., Materials Science
WARNER, J. S., Neurology
WATERMAN, M. R., Biochemistry
WATTERSON, D. M., Pharmacology
WEATHERBY, H. L., Jr, English
WEBB, G. F., Mathematics
WEBSTER, M. S., Physics
WEIL, P. A., Molecular Physiology and Biophysics
WEINGARTNER, H. M., Finance
WELLS, J. N., Pharmacology
WERT, J. J., Metallurgy
WESTFIELD, F. M., Economics
WHETSELL, W. O., Jr, Pathology, Psychiatry, Cell Biology
WHITE, E. J., Electrical Engineering
WHITTIER, D. P., Biology
WIKSWO, J. P., Jr, Physics
WILKINSON, G. R., Pharmacology
WILLIAMS, H. E., Mathematics, Computer Science
WILLIAMS, L. F., Jr, Surgery
WILLIAMS, R. C., Jr, Molecular Biology
WILLIAMSON, J. W., Mechanical Engineering
WILSON, D. J., Chemistry and Environmental Chemistry
WILTSHIRE, S. F., Classics
WINFIELD, A. C., Radiology and Radiological Sciences
WINTERS, D. L., History
WOLRAICH, M. L., Paediatrics
WOOD, A. J. J., Medicine and Pharmacology
WOOD, M., Anaesthesiology
WOODWARD, S. C., Pathology
WRIGHT, P. F., Paediatrics
XIA, D., Mathematics
ZANER, R. M., Medicine, Philosophy, Medical Ethics
ZEPPOS, N. S., Jr, Law

TEXAS

ABILENE CHRISTIAN UNIVERSITY

ACU Box 29100, Abilene, TX 79699
Telephone: (915) 674-2000
Fax: (915) 674-2958

Founded 1906
Private (Church of Christ) liberal arts

President: ROYCE L. MONEY
Executive Vice-President: JACK RICH
Provost: DWAYNE VAN RHEENEN
Librarian: MARSHA HARPER

Library of 449,000 vols
Number of teachers: 278
Number of students: 4,397

Publication: *ACU Today.*

DEANS

College of Biblical Studies: JACK REESE
College of Business Administration: JACK GRIGGS
College of Arts and Sciences: COLLEEN DURRINGTON
Graduate School: CARLEY DODD
Director of Research: CARLEY DODD

ANGELO STATE UNIVERSITY

POB 11007, ASU Station, San Angelo, TX 76909
Telephone: (915) 942-2073
Fax: (915) 942-2038

Founded 1928

President: Dr E. JAMES HINDMAN
Vice-President for Academic Affairs: Dr RUTH J. PERSON
Vice-President for University Relations and Development: MICHAEL P. RYAN
Vice-President for Fiscal Affairs: ROBERT L. KRUPALA
Director of Admissions: MONIQUE COSSICK
Registrar: ANITA LOSHBOUGH
Librarian: MAURICE FORTIN

Library of 1,247,600 items
Number of teachers: 228 (full-time)
Number of students: 6,234

AUSTIN COLLEGE

Sherman, TX 75092
Telephone: (903) 813-2000
Fax: (903) 813-3199
Founded 1849
Four-year liberal arts co-educational Christian college
President: OSCAR C. PAGE
Vice-President for Academic Affairs and Dean of the Faculty: DAVID JORDAN
Treasurer and Vice-President for Business Affairs: GEORGE ROWLAND
Vice-President for Institutional Advancement: JAMES LEWIS
Vice-President for Student Affairs: TIMOTHY P. MILLERICK
Vice-President for Institutional Enrollment: JONATHAN STROUD
Library of 315,000 vols
Number of teachers: full-time 85, part-time 15
Number of students: full-time 1,071, part-time 22

BAYLOR UNIVERSITY

Waco, TX 76798
Telephone: (254) 710-1011
Chartered 1845 under Republic of Texas by Texas Baptist Educational Society at Independence, Texas; consolidated 1886 with Waco University and is affiliated with Baptist General Convention of Texas
President: Dr ROBERT B. SLOAN, Jr
Secretary: ANGELA BAILEY
Director of Admissions: DIANA RAMEY
Librarian: Dr AVERY SHARP
Number of teachers: 600
Number of students: 12,000
Publications: *Law Review, Baylor Business Review, Baylor Line, Baylor Geological Studies, Journal of Church and State, Baylor News, The Lariat.*

EAST TEXAS BAPTIST UNIVERSITY

1209 N Grove St, Marshall, TX 75670-1498
Telephone: (903) 935-7963
Fax: (903) 938-1705
Founded 1912
President: BOB E. RILEY
Registrar: DAVID MOHN
Librarian: Dr ROSE MARY MAGRILL
Library of 100,000 vols
Number of teachers: 55
Number of students: 1,200
Courses in the liberal arts.

HARDIN-SIMMONS UNIVERSITY

Box 16000, HSU Station, Abilene, TX 79698
Telephone: (915) 670-1000
Founded 1891
President: Dr LANNY HALL
Vice-President for Academic Affairs: Dr CRAIG TURNER
Associate Vice-President, Enrollment Services: SHANE DAVIDSON
Registrar: DOROTHY KISER
Director of University Libraries: ALICE W. SPECHT
Library of 415,752 vols
Number of teachers: 140
Number of students: 2,312

HOWARD PAYNE UNIVERSITY

Brownwood, TX 76801
Telephone: (915) 646-2502
Fax: (915) 649-8900
Founded 1889
President: Dr RICK GREGORY
Chancellor: Dr DON NEWBURY
Provost: Dr ROBERT BICKNELL
Registrar: DON JACKSON
Librarian: NANCY ANDERSON
Library of 125,000 vols
Number of teachers: 127
Number of students: 1,470

HUSTON-TILLOTSON COLLEGE

900 Chicon St, Austin, TX 78702
Telephone: (512) 505-3000
Fax: (512) 505-3190
Founded 1876
President: Dr JOSEPH T. MCMILLAN, Jr
Vice-President for Academic Affairs: Dr LENORA D. WATERS
Registrar: EARNESTINE STRICKLAND
Librarian: PATRICIA QUARTERMAN
Library of 73,164 vols
Number of teachers: 49
Number of students: 641

LAMAR UNIVERSITY

Lamar University-Beaumont, POB 10001, Beaumont, TX 77710
Telephone: (409) 880-7011
Telex: (409) 880-2335
Fax: (409) 880-8404
Founded 1923 as South Park Junior College
Chancellor: (vacant)
Vice-Chancellor for Academic Affairs: Dr BILL NYLIN
Assistant Chancellor for Development: W. S. LEONARD
President: REX L. COTTLE
Executive Vice-President for Academic and Student Affairs: BEHERUZ SETHAN (acting)
Vice-President for Finance and Operations: BERTIN HOWARD (acting)
Dean of Admissions and Registrar: ELMER G. RODE
Dean of Library Services: PETER B. KAATRUDE
Library of 964,543 vols
Number of teachers: 507
Number of students: 10,671

DEANS

Graduate Studies: Dr ROBERT MOULTON
College of Education: Dr LEBLAND MCADAMS
College of Arts and Sciences: Dr KENDALL BLANCHARD
College of Business: ROBERT SWERDLOW (acting)
College of Fine and Applied Arts: Dr JIMMY SIMMONS
College of Engineering: Dr FRED M. YOUNG
Institute of Technology: Dr KENNETH E. SHIPPER

McMURRY UNIVERSITY

McMurry Station, Abilene, TX 79697
Telephone: (915) 691-6200
Founded 1923
President: ROBERT E. SHIMP
Vice-President for Academic Affairs: PAUL LACK
Vice-President for Financial Affairs: CARL BROWN
Vice-President for Institutional Advancement: JAMES DOTHEROW
Vice-President for Enrollment Management and Student Relations: RUSSELL WATJEN
Director of Library: JOE W. SPECHT
Library of 200,000 vols
Number of teachers: 119
Number of students: 1,400

MIDWESTERN STATE UNIVERSITY

3410 Taft Boulevard, Wichita Falls, TX 76308
Telephone: (940) 397-4000
Fax: (940) 397-4302
Founded 1922
President: Dr LOUIS J. RODRIGUEZ
Vice-President for Academic Affairs: Dr JESSE W. ROGERS
Vice-President for Business Affairs: ALVIN G. HOOTEN
Vice-President for Student and Administrative Services: Dr HOWARD FARRELL
Registrar: BILLYE J. TIMS
Librarian: MELBA S. HARVILL
Number of teachers: 172
Number of students: 5,832
Publications: *The Wichitan* (weekly), *The Wai-Kun* (annually), *MSU News and Views* (2 a year), *Voices* (annually), *Faculty Forum Papers* (annually).

OUR LADY OF THE LAKE UNIVERSITY OF SAN ANTONIO

411 SW 24th St, San Antonio, TX 78207-4689
Telephone: (210) 434-6711
Fax: (210) 436-0824
Founded 1883
President: SALLY MAHONEY
Executive Vice-President: ROBERT E. GIBBONS
Vice-President and Dean of Academic Affairs: HOWARD BENOIST
Vice-President for Finance and Facilities: ALLEN R. KLAUS
Vice-President for Institutional Advancement: MICHAEL MULNIX
Vice-President and Dean of Student Life: MARY ELLEN SMITH
Dean of Enrollment and Management: LORETTA A. SCHLEGEL
Institutional Research Officer: FRED D. SCOTT
Library of 254,419 vols
Number of teachers: 140
Number of students: 3,666

PAUL QUINN COLLEGE

3837 Simpson-Stuart Rd, Dallas, TX 75241
Telephone: (214) 376-1000
Founded 1872
President: LEE MONROE
Vice-President for Academic Affairs: Dr CHARLES HUMPHREY
Registrar: J. D. HURD
Librarian: Ms. MACHIE
Number of teachers: 48
Number of students: 780
Publication: *Paul Quinn Gazette*.

RICE UNIVERSITY

POB 1892, Houston, TX 77251
Telephone: (713) 527-8101
Founded 1891
Private control
President: MALCOLM GILLIS
Provost: DAVID H. AUSTON
Vice-President for Information Technology: G. ANTHONY GORRY
Vice-President for Finance and Administration: DEAN W. CURRIE
Vice-President for Student Affairs: ZENAIDO CAMACHO
Vice-President for University Advancement: KATHRYN R. COSTELLO
Vice-President for Investments and Treasurer: S. W. WISE
Registrar: JAMES WILLIAMSON

Librarian: CHARLES HENRY

Library of over 1,400,000 vols
Number of teachers: 463
Number of students: 4,000

Publications: *Journal of Southern History, Studies in English Literature 1500–1900, Rice University Studies* (quarterly).

DEANS

Humanities: J. C. BROWN
Wiess School of Natural Sciences: K. S. MATTHEWS
Social Sciences: R. M. STEIN
Architecture: LARS LERUP
Shepherd School of Music: MICHAEL HAMMOND
George R. Brown School of Engineering: C. S. BURRUS
Jesse H. Jones School of Administration: G. R. WHITAKER, Jr
Continuing Studies: M. MCINTIRE
Admission and Records: R. N. STABELL

PROFESSORS

AAZHANG, B., Electrical and Computer Engineering
AKERS, W. W., Chemical Engineering
AKIN, J. E., Mechanical Engineering
ALCOVER, M., French
AMBLER, J. S., Political Science
ANDERSON, J. B., Geology and Geophysics
ANTOULAS, A. C., Electrical and Computer Engineering
APPLE, M., English
ARESU, B., French Studies
ARMENIADES, C. D., Chemical Engineering
AVE-LALLEMANT, H. G., Geology and Geophysics
BAKER, S. D., Physics
BARRON, A., Chemistry
BAYAZITOGLU, Y., Mechanical Engineering
BEARDEN, F. W., Health and Physical Education
BECKINGHAM, K., Biochemistry and Cell Biology
BEDIENT, P. B., Environmental Engineering
BENNETT, G., Biochemistry and Cell Biology
BILLUPS, W. E., Chemistry
BLACK, E., Political Science
BOLES, J. B., History
BONNER, B. E., Physics
BOSHERNITZAN, M., Mathematics
BRACE, P., Political Science
BRELSFORD, J. W., Psychology
BRITO, D. L., Political Economy
BRODY, B. A., Philosophy
BROKER, K. L., Art and Art History
BROOKS, P. R., Chemistry
BROWN, B. W., Economics and Statistics
BROWN, J. N., Economics
BROWN, L., Sociology
BRYANT, J., Economics
BUYSE, L., Music
CAMFIELD, W. A., Fine Arts
CAMPBELL, J. W., Biology
CANNADY, W. T., Architecture
CARROLL, M. M., Computational and Applied Mathematics
CARTWRIGHT, R. S., Computer Science
CASBARIAN, J. J., Architecture
CASTAÑEDA, J. A., Spanish
CHANCE, J., English
CITRON, M., Music
CIUFOLINI, M., Chemistry
CLARK, J. W., Jr, Electrical and Computer Engineering
CLOUTIER, P. A., Space Physics, Astronomy
COCHRAN, T., Mathematics
COOK, W. J., Computational and Applied Mathematics
COPELAND, J., Linguistics
CORCORAN, M., Physics
COX, D., Statistics
CROWELL, S., Mathematics
CURL, R. F., Jr, Chemistry
CUTHBERTSON, G. M., Political Science
DAVIDSON, C., Sociology
DAVIS, P. W., Anthropology
DAVIS, S. H., Jr, Chemical Engineering, Mathematical Sciences
DENNIS, J. E., Mathematical Sciences
DHARAN, B. G., Administrative Science
DIPBOYE, R., Administrative Science and Psychology
DOODY, T., English
DOUGHTIE, E. O., English
DRISKILL, L., English
DUCK, I., Physics
DUFOUR, R. J., Space Physics and Astronomy
DUNNING, F. B., Space Physics and Astronomy
DURRANI, A. J., Civil Engineering
DYSON, D. C., Chemical Engineering
EIFLER, M., German
EL-GAMAL, M., Economics
ELLISON, P., Music
ENGEL, P. S., Chemistry
ENGELHARDT, T., Philosophy
FARWELL, J., Music
FELLEISEN, M., Computer Science
FEW, A., Space Physics
FISCHER, N., Music
FISHER, F. M., Biology
FREEMAN, J. W., Space Science
GLANTZ, R. M., Biology
GLASS, G. P., Chemistry
GOLDMAN, R. N., Computer Science
GOLDSMITH, K., Music
GORDON, C., Sociology
GORDON, R., Geology and Geophysics
GOUX, J., French
GRANDY, R. E., Philosophy and Linguistics
GROB, A., English
GRUBER, I. D., History
HAMM, K. E., Political Science
HANNON, J. P., Physics
HARCOMBE, P., Biology
HARDT, R. M., Mathematics
HARTLEY, P. R., Economics
HARVEY, F. R., Mathematics
HASKELL, T., History
HAVENS, N., Drama
HELLUMS, J. D., Chemical Engineering
HEMPEL, J., Mathematics
HIGHTOWER, J. W., Chemical Engineering
HIRASAKI, G., Chemical Engineering
HOLLOWAY, C., Music
HUANG, H. W., Physics
HULET, R., Physics
HUSTON, J. D., English
IAMMARINO, N., Human Performance and Health Sciences
ISLE, W., English
JOHNSON, D. H., Electrical and Computer Engineering
JONES, B. F., Mathematics
JUMP, J. R., Electrical and Computer Engineering
KANATAS, G., Administrative Science
KATZ, M., Music
KATZ, P., Music
KAUN, K., Music
KELBER, W. H., Religious Studies
KENNEDY, K. W., Computer Science
KIMMEL, M., Statistics
KINSEY, J. L., Chemistry
KLEIN, A., Religious Studies
KLINEBERG, S. L., Sociology
KONISKY, J., Biochemistry
KULSTAD, M., Philosophy
LAUGHERY, K. R., Psychology
LEAL, M. T., Spanish
LEE, B., Anthropology
LEE, E., Human Performance and Health Sciences
LEEMAN, W. P., Geology and Geophysics
LEVANDER, A. R., Geology and Geophysics
LIANG, E., Space Physics and Astronomy
LUCA, S., Music
MCINTIRE, L. V., Chemical Engineering
MCINTOSH, R. J., Anthropology
MCINTOSH, S. K., Anthropology
MCLELLAN, R. B., Materials Science
MARCUS, G. E., Anthropology
MARGRAVE, J. L., Chemistry
MARTIN, R. C., Psychology
MARTIN, W. C., Sociology
MATUSOW, A., History
MERWIN, J. E., Civil Engineering
MICHEL, F. C., Space Science
MICHIE, H., English
MIELE, A., Astronautics and Mathematical Sciences
MIESZKOWSKI, P., Economics
MIETTINEN, H. E., Physics
MILBURN, E., Music
MILLER, C. A., Chemical Engineering
MINTER, D., English
MORGAN, T. C., Political Science
MORRIS, W. A., English
MUTCHLER, G. S., Physics
NELSON, D., French
NORDGREN, R. P., Civil Engineering
NORDLANDER, P., Physics
O'DELL, C. R., Space Physics and Astronomy
ODHIAMBO, A., History
OLSON, J. S., Biochemistry
OSHERSON, D., Psychology
PALMER, G. A., Biochemistry
PARRY, R. J., Chemistry
PATTEN, R. L., English
PEARSON, J. B., Electrical and Computer Engineering
PHILLIPS, G., Biochemistry and Cell Biology
PHILPOTT, C. W., Biology
PIPER, W. B., English
POLKING, J. C., Mathematics
POULOS, B., Art and Art History
QUELLER, D. C., Ecology and Evolutionary Biology
RABSON, T. A., Electrical and Computer Engineering
RAU, C., Physics
REIFF, P., Space Physics and Astronomy
ROBERT, M., Chemical Engineering
ROBERTS, J. B., Physics
RUDOLPH, F. B., Biochemistry
SAN, K. Y., Chemical Engineering
SASS, R. L., Biology
SAWYER, D., Geology and Geophysics
SCHNEIDER, D. J., Psychology
SCHNOEBELEN, A. M., Music
SCHROEPFER, G. J., Biochemistry
SCOTT, D. W., Mathematical Sciences
SCUSERIA, G., Chemistry
SEED, P., History
SEMMES, S. W., Mathematics
SHER, G., Philosophy
SICKLES, R., Economics
SKURA, M., English
SMALLEY, R. E., Chemistry
SMITH, G., Art and Art History
SMITH, G. W., Economics
SMITH, R. J., History
SNOW, E. A., English
SOLIGO, R., Economics
SORENSEN, D. C., Mathematical Sciences
SPANOS, P. D., Mechanical Engineering and Civil Engineering
SPENCE, D. W., Health and Physical Education
STEVENSON, P. M., Physics
STEWART, C. R., Biology
STOKES, G., History
STOLL, R. J., Political Science
STONG, R., Mathematics
STRASSMAN, J., Ecology and Evolutionary Biology
STROUP, J. M., Religious Studies
SUBTELNY, S., Biology
SYMES, W. W., Mathematical Sciences
TALWANI, M., Geophysics
TAPIA, R. A., Mathematical Sciences
TAYLOR, R. N., Administration and Psychology
TEMKIN, L., Philosophy
TEZDUYAR, T. E., Mechanical Engineering and Materials Science
THOMPSON, E. M., Russian
THOMPSON, J. R., Mathematical Sciences
TITTEL, F., Electrical and Computer Engineering

TOMSON, M. B., Environmental Science and Engineering
TYLER, S. A., Anthropology and Linguistics
UECKER, W. C., Accounting
VAIL, P. R., Geology and Geophysics
VAN HELDEN, A., History
VARDI, M. Y., Computer Science
VEECH, W. A., Mathematics
VELETSOS, A. S., Engineering
WALTERS, G. K., Physics and Space Science
WANG, C. C., Mathematical Sciences
WARD, C. H., Environmental Science and Engineering
WATKINS, M. J., Psychology
WEISHEIT, J. C., Space Physics
WEISMAN, R. B., Chemistry
WEISSENBERGER, K. H., German
WELLS, R. O., Mathematics
WESTBROOK, R. A., Administrative Science
WHITMIRE, K. H., Chemistry
WIENER, M. J., History
WIESNER, M., Environmental Science and Engineering
WILLIAMS, E. E., Administrative Science
WILSON, L. J., Chemistry
WILSON, R. K., Political Science
WILSON, W. L., Electrical and Computer Engineering
WINDSOR, D., Administrative Science
WINKLER, K., Music
WINKLER, M., German
WINNINGHAM, G. L., Art
WITTENBERG, G., Architecture
WOLF, R. A., Space Physics
WOLIN, R., History
WOOD, S., English
WYSCHOGROD, E., Religious Studies
YOUNG, J. F., Electrical and Computer Engineering
YUNIS, H., Hispanic and Classical Studies
ZEFF, S. A., Accounting
ZODROW, G., Economics
ZWAENEPOEL, W., Computer Science
ZYGOURAKIS, K., Chemical Engineering

ST EDWARDS UNIVERSITY

3001 South Congress Ave, Austin, TX 78704
Telephone: (512) 448-8400
Fax: (512) 448-8492

Founded 1885

Private, co-educational; four-year liberal arts; graduate courses in business, human services; also New College (non-traditional undergraduate courses)

President: Dr ROBERT N. FUNK (interim)
Vice-President for Financial Affairs: DAVID A. DICKSON, Jr
Vice-President and Academic Dean: DONNA JURICK
Vice-President for University Relations: CHRIS READ
Director of Admissions: MEGAN MURPHY
Librarian: EILEEN SHOCKETT

Library of 140,000 vols
Number of teachers: 234
Number of students: 3,100

ST MARY'S UNIVERSITY OF SAN ANTONIO

San Antonio, TX 78228-8572
Telephone: (210) 436-3011

Founded 1852

President: Rev. JOHN J. MODER
Academic Vice-President: Dr CHARLES L. COTRELL
Vice-President for Student Development: RUTH R. RODGERS
Vice-President for University Advancement: THOMAS B. GALVIN
Vice-President for Financial Administration: DANIEL J. WHITE
Assistant to President for Planning: Dr GERARD DIZINNO
Registrar: LOUISA AVITUA-TREVINO
Librarian: H. PALMER HALL

Library of 324,000 vols
Number of students: 4,166

DEANS

School of Humanities and Social Sciences: Rev. CHARLES H. MILLER
School of Science, Engineering and Technology: Dr ANTHONY KAUFMANN
Graduate School: Dr RON MERRELL
Law School: ROBERT WILLIAM PIATT
School of Business Administration: Dr DAVID MANUEL

SAM HOUSTON STATE UNIVERSITY

POB 2026, Huntsville, TX 77341
Telephone: (409) 294-1111
E-mail: adm_smm@shsu.edu

Founded 1879 as Sam Houston Normal Institute

Academic year: August to May, with two summer sessions

President: BOBBY K. MARKS
Vice-President for Academic Affairs: DAVID K. PAYNE
Vice-President for Finance: JACK PARKER
Associate Vice-President for Academic Affairs: DONALD COERS
Director of Admissions: JOEY CHANDLER
Registrar: ROBERT DUNNING
Director of Libraries: RICHARD WOOD

Library of 1,500,000 vols, 3,028 periodicals, 938,054 microforms, 11,568 records/tapes
Number of teachers: 488 full-time
Number of students: 12,709 (10,120 full-time)

Publications: *Journal of Business Strategies, Texas Review* (2 a year).

DEANS

College of Arts and Sciences: CHRISTOPHER BALDWIN
College of Business Administration: JAMES E. GILMORE
College of Education and Applied Science: KENNETH CRAYCRAFT
College of Criminal Justice: TIMOTHY FLANAGAN

DIRECTORS OF DIVISIONS

English and Foreign Languages: EUGENE YOUNG
Dance and Drama: JAMES MILLER
Public Communication: DON RICHARDSON
Mathematical and Information Sciences: GLENN MATTINGLY
Consumer Services, Fashion and Design: BETTY E. WEATHERALL
Psychology and Philosophy: A. J. BRUCE
Health and Kinesiology: ROBERT CASE
Agricultural Scienes and Vocational Education: WILLIAM HARRELL

DIRECTORS OF DEPARTMENTS

Art: JIMMY BARKER
Music: (vacant)
Political Science: R. H. PAYNE
Sociology: W. H. BENNETT
Accounting: ROSS QUARLES
General Business and Finance: LEROY ASHORN
Economics and Business Analysis: WILLIAM GREEN
Management and Marketing: ROGER ABSHIRE
History: JAMES OLSON
Biological Sciences: ANDREW DEWEES
Physics: RUSSELL PALMA
Chemistry: MARY PLISHKER
Geography and Geology: ALLEN WILLIAMS
Technology and Photography: EMMETT JACKSON
Library Science: RICHARD WOOD

SOUTHERN METHODIST UNIVERSITY

Dallas, TX 75275
Telephone: (214) 768-2000
Fax: (214) 768-1001

Chartered 1911

President: Dr R. GERALD TURNER
Provost: Dr ROSS C. MURFIN
Vice-President for Student Affairs: Dr JAMES E. CASWELL
Vice-President for Business and Finance, and Treasurer: Ms ELIZABETH C. WILLIAMS
Vice-President for External Affairs: WILLIAM H. LIVELY
Vice-President for Executive Affairs: Dr THOMAS BARRY
Vice-President for Legal Affairs and Government Relations, General Counsel, and University Secretary: S. LEON BENNETT
Admissions: RON MOSS
Registrar: JOHN A. HALL

Library of 1,449,000 vols, 255,000 bound periodicals
Number of teachers: 493 full-time, 295 part-time
Number of students: 9,464

Publications: *Southwest Review* (quarterly), *Journal of Air Law and Commerce* (quarterly), *SMU Law Review, The International Lawyer, Perkins Perspective.*

DEANS

Dedman College: Dr JASPER NEEL
Arts: Dr CAROLE BRANDT
Business: Dr ALBERT W. NIEMI, Jr
Engineering and Applied Science: Dr ANDRE G. VACROUX
Law: HARVEY WINGO
Theology: Dr ROBIN W. LOVIN, Jr

SOUTHWEST TEXAS STATE UNIVERSITY

601 University Drive, San Marcos, TX 78666
Telephone: (512) 245-2111
Fax: (512) 245-2033

Founded 1899

President: Dr JEROME H. SUPPLE
Executive Vice-President: Dr MICHAEL ABBOTT
Vice-President for Academic Affairs: Dr ROBERT GRATZ
Vice-President for Finance and Support Services: BILL NANCE
Vice-President for Student Affairs: Dr JAMES STUDER
Vice-President for University Advancement: GERALD HILL
Director for Alumni Affairs: BART HARST
Librarian: JOAN HEATH

Library of 1,075,200 vols, 1,638,500 microforms, 5,400 serials, 246,200 audiovisual items
Number of teachers: 939
Number of students: 20,652

Publications: *University Star* (4 a week), *Pedagog* (annually), *Hillside Scene* (monthly), *Persona* (literary journal, annually).

DEANS

College of General Studies: Dr RONALD C. BROWN
School of Liberal Arts: Dr G. JACK GRAVITT
School of Science: Dr STANLEY ISRAEL
School of Applied Arts and Technology: Dr G. EUGENE MARTIN
School of Education: Dr JOHN J. BECK
School of Business: Dr PAUL GOWENS
School of Fine Arts: Dr T. RICHARD CHEATHAM
School of Health Professions: Dr RUMALDO Z. JUAREZ
Graduate School: Dr J. MICHAEL WILLOUGHBY

SOUTHWESTERN UNIVERSITY

Box 770, Georgetown, TX 78627-0770

Telephone: (512) 863-6511
Fax: (512) 863-5788

Opened 1873 by merging of Rutersville College (Chartered 1840), Wesleyan College (1844), McKenzie College (1848), and Soule University (1856)

President: ROY B. SHILLING, Jr
Vice-President for Fiscal Affairs: RICHARD L. ANDERSON
Vice-President for Enrollment Management: JOHN W. LIND
Vice-President for Development: RICHARD B. EASON
Vice-President for University Relations: MARILYN MOCK
Provost and Dean of the Faculty: DALE T. KNOBEL
Registrar: GEORGE BRIGHTWELL
Librarian: LYNNE M. BRODY

Library of 261,000 vols
Number of teachers: 105
Number of students: 1,261

Publications: *Bulletin* (monthly), *The Megaphone* (weekly), *Southwestern Magazine* (quarterly), *The Sou' Wester* (annually).

DEANS

Fine Arts: CAROLE LEE
Students: SHERRI H. BABCOCK

STEPHEN F. AUSTIN STATE UNIVERSITY

Box 6078, Nacogdoches, TX 75962

Telephone: (713) 468-2011

Founded 1923

President: DANIEL D. ANGEL
Vice-President for Academic Affairs: JANELLE ASHLEY
Vice-President for Business Affairs: ROLAND SMITH
Vice-President for University Affairs: BAKER PATTILLO
Vice-President for University Advancement: JERRY HOLBERT
Library Director: ALVIN CAGE

Library of 1,465,322 vols
Number of teachers: 599
Number of students: 12,500 full-time

DEANS

College of Applied Arts and Sciences: JAMES STANDLEY
College of Business: MARLIN YOUNG
College of Education: THOMAS FRANKS
College of Fine Arts: RON JONES
College of Forestry: SCOTT BEASLEY
College of Liberal Arts: JIM SPEER (acting)
College of Sciences and Mathematics: THOMAS ATCHISON

SUL ROSS STATE UNIVERSITY

Alpine, TX 79832

Telephone: (915) 837-8032
Fax: (915) 837-8334
E-mail: rvmorgan@sulross.edu

Founded 1917

President: Dr R. VIC MORGAN, Jr
Vice-President for Academic and Student Affairs: Dr DAVE COCKRUM
Dean of Admissions and Records: ROBERT CULLINS
Librarian: GILDA ORTEGO

Library of 760,700 vols
Number of teachers: 117
Number of students: 3,144

DEANS

Arts and Sciences: Dr BRUCE GLASRUD
Professional Studies: Dr CHET SAMPLE
Range Animal Science: Dr ROB KINUCAN
Rio Grande College: Dr FRANK ABBOTT

TEXAS A & M UNIVERSITY SYSTEM

College Station, TX 77840-7896

Telephone: (409) 845-4331
Fax: (409) 845-2490

Founded 1876
Academic year: September to August

Chancellor: Dr BARRY B. THOMPSON
Deputy Chancellor for Finance and Operations: RICHARD LINDSAY
Deputy Chancellor for Academic Institutions and Agencies: Dr LEO SAYAVEDRA
Vice-Chancellor for Agriculture: Dr EDWARD HILER
Vice-Chancellor for Engineering: Dr C. ROLAND HADEN
Vice-Chancellor for Business Services: TOM KALE
Vice-Chancellor for Research, Planning and Continuing Education: Dr J. CHARLES LEE
Vice-Chancellor for Facilities Planning and Construction: Gen. WESLEY PEEL

Texas A & M International University

5201 University Blvd, Laredo, TX 78041-1900

Telephone: (956) 326-2001
Fax: (956) 326-2346

Founded 1969 as part of Texas A & I University

Upper level college, junior, senior and graduate courses

President: Dr J. CHARLES JENNETT
Director of Admissions and Advisement: MARÍA DEL REFUGIO ROSILLO
Vice-President for Finance and Administration: JOSÉ GARCÍA
Vice-President for Academic Affairs and Provost: (vacant)
Vice-President for Advancement and External Affairs: MICHELLE ALEXANDER
Registrar: BARBARA LUNCE
Librarian: RODNEY WEBB

Library of 130,000 vols
Number of students: 2,800

DEANS

College of Arts and Humanities: Dr JERRY THOMPSON
College of Business Administration: Dr KHOSROW FATEMI
College of Science and Technology: (vacant)
College of Education: Dr ROSA MARIA VIDA
Student Affairs: Dr STEPHEN BROWN

Texas A & M University

College Station, TX 77843

Telephone: (409) 845-3211

Founded 1876, University 1963

President: Dr RAY M. BOWEN
Vice-Presidents: Dr RONALD R. DOUGLAS (Academic Affairs), Dr JERRY GASTON (Administration), BILL KRUMM (Finance), ROBERT L. WALKER (Development), Dr J. MALON SOUTHERLAND (Student Affairs).
Executive Director, Admissions and Records: GARY ENGELGAU
Director of Library: Dr FRED M. HEATH

Library of 2,500,000 vols
Number of teachers: 2,327
Number of students: 41,461

DEANS

College of Engineering: Dr C. ROLAND HADEN
College of Agriculture and Life Sciences: Dr EDWARD A. HILER
College of Veterinary Medicine: Dr H. RICHARD ADAMS
College of Education: Dr JANE C. CONOLEY
College of Geosciences: Dr DAVID PRIOR
College of Science: Dr RICHARD E. EWING
College of Liberal Arts: Dr WOODROW JONES, Jr
College of Business Administration and Graduate School of Business: Dr A. BENTON COCANOUGHER
College of Architecture: WARD WELLS (interim)
College of Medicine: Dr MICHAEL L. FRIEDLAND

Texas A & M University—Commerce

Commerce, TX 75429

Telephone: (903) 886-5014

Founded 1889

President: KEITH W. MCFARLAND (interim)
Vice-President for Academic Affairs: Dr DONNA ARLTON
Vice-President for Student and University Services: GENE LOCKHART

Library of 1,544,588 vols and microfilms
Number of teachers: 250 full-time
Number of students: 7,260

Texas A & M University—Corpus Christi

6300 Ocean Drive, Corpus Christi, TX 78412

Telephone: (512) 994-5700

Founded 1971; part of University System of South Texas

President: ROBERT R. FURGASON
Vice-President for Institutional Advancement: KEN DEDOMINICIS
Provost/Vice-President for Academic Affairs: SANDRA S. HARPER
Executive Vice-President for Finance and Administration: C. RAY HAYES
Librarian: BENJAMIN WAKASHIGE

DEANS

Arts and Humanities: PAUL HAIN
Science and Technology: DIANA I. MARINEZ
Teacher Education: ROBERT L. COX
Business Administration: MOUSTAFA ABDELSAMAD

Texas A & M University—Kingsville

Kingsville, TX 78363

Telephone: (512) 595-2111

Founded 1917
Established as South Texas Normal School; name changed to South Texas State Teachers' College by law in 1923, to Texas College of Arts and Industries by law in 1929, and to Texas A & I University by law in 1967; part of the Texas A & M University System

President: MANUEL L. IBAÑEZ
Vice-President for Academic Affairs and Provost: ROBERT KIRBY
Vice-President for Student Affairs: KAY CLAYTON
Director of Research: SUSAN SEDWICK
Director of Continuing Education: MARK M. WALSH
Registrar: JOE ESTRADA
Librarian: ROBERTA PITTS

Library of 748,000 vols and 2,122 periodicals
Number of teachers: 329
Number of students: 5,876

DEANS

Agriculture: CHARLES DEYOUNG
Arts and Sciences: MARY MATTINGLY
Business Administration: (vacant)
Engineering: PHIL V. COMPTON
Education: FRANCISCO HIDALGO
Graduate Studies: ALBERTO M. OLIVARES

ATTACHED INSTITUTES

Texas A & M University Citrus Center: Weslaco, Texas; Dir JOSE AMADOR.

Caesar Kleberg Wildlife Research Institute: Kingsville, Texas; Dir Dr FRED BRYANT.

Prairie View A & M University

POB 188, Prairie View, TX 77446
Telephone: (409) 857-3311
Fax: (409) 857-3928

Founded 1876, University 1973

President: JULIUS W. BECTON, Jr
Registrar: ROBERT FORD
Provost and Vice-President for Academic Affairs: FLOSSIE M. BYRD
Vice-President for Administration and Finance: HAROLD S. BONNER
Director of Institutional Development: HARVEY G. DICKERSON
Vice-President for Student Affairs: JILES P. DANIELS
Director of Library: DUDLEY YATES
Director of Public Information Services: BRYAN BARROWS

Library of 260,000 vols
Number of teachers: 315
Number of students: 5,600

DEANS

Graduate School: WILLIE F. TROTTY
Banneker Honors College: JEWEL L. PRESTAGE
College of Arts and Sciences: EDWARD W. MARTIN
College of Engineering and Architecture: JOHN FOSTER
College of Applied Sciences and Engineering Technology: HAKUMAT ISRANI
College of Education: M. PAUL MEHTA
College of Nursing: DOLLIE BRATHWAITE
College of Business: BARBARA A. JONES

Tarleton State University

Stephenville, TX 76402
Telephone: (817) 968-9000
Fax: (817) 968-9920

Founded 1899, University 1973

President: Dr DENNIS P. MCCABE
Provost and Vice-President for Academic Affairs: Dr B. J. ALEXANDER
Vice-President for Institutional Advancement: Dr KOY FLOYD
Vice-President for Student Services: Dr WANDA L. MERCER
Vice-President for Finance and Administration: JERRY GRAHAM
Director of Admissions: GAIL MAYFIELD
Registrar: DON ROSS
Librarian: Dr KENNETH W. JONES

Library of 310,000 vols
Number of teachers: 356
Number of students: 6,381

DEANS

College of Arts and Sciences: Dr LAMAR JOHANSON
College of Education and Fine Arts: Dr JOE GILLESPIE
College of Agriculture and Technology: Dr DON KNOTTS (interim)
College of Business Administration: Dr DAN COLLINS
College of Graduate Studies: Dr RON BRADBERRY
Students: RUSTY JERGINS

West Texas A & M University

West Texas Station, Canyon, TX 79016-0001
Telephone: (806) 651-2100
Fax: (806) 651-2126
E-mail: cbarnes@wtamu.edu

Founded: 1910

President: Dr RUSSELL C. LONG
Provost and Vice-President for Academic Affairs: Dr FLAVIUS KILLEBREW

Library of 1,086,936 vols
Number of teachers: 245
Number of students: 6,640

Publication: *The Prairie* (Newspaper).

TEXAS CHRISTIAN UNIVERSITY

2800 S. University Drive, Fort Worth, TX 76129
Telephone: (817) 257-7000
Fax: (817) 257-7333

Founded 1873

Chancellor: MICHAEL R. FERRARI
Vice-Chancellor for Finance and Business: JAMES A. MCGOWAN
Provost and Vice-Chancellor for Academic Affairs: WILLIAM H. KOEHLER
Vice-Chancellor for Student Affairs: DONALD B. MILLS
Vice-Chancellor for University Advancement: BRONSON C. DAVIS
Vice-Chancellor for Administrative Services: EDD E. BIVIN
Registrar: PATRICK MILLER
Librarian: ROBERT A. SEAL

Library of 1,799,000 vols
Number of teachers: 428
Number of students: 7,273

Publications: *Bulletins* (every 2 years).

DEANS

AddRan College of Arts and Sciences: MICHAEL D. MCCRACKEN
Brite Divinity School: LEO G. PERDUE
Harris College of Nursing: KATHLEEN BOND
M. J. Neeley School of Business: H. KIRK DOWNEY
School of Education: DOUGLAS J. SIMPSON
College of Fine Arts and Communication: ROBERT P. GARWELL

TEXAS LUTHERAN COLLEGE

Seguin, TX 78155
Telephone: (210) 372-8000
Fax: (210) 372-8096

Founded 1891

A church-related, co-educational, liberal arts, undergraduate college with programs in business administration, teacher education, computer science, and the health-related fields

President: Dr JON N. MOLINE
Academic Dean: Dr LEONARD G. SCHULZE
Registrar: KRISTIN PLAEHN
Librarian: PATRICK HSU

Library of 151,402 vols
Number of teachers: 95
Number of students: 1,268

TEXAS SOUTHERN UNIVERSITY

3100 Cleburne Ave, Houston, TX 77004
Telephone: (713) 527-7011

Founded 1947
State control

President: JAMES M. DOUGLAS
Provost/Vice-President for Academic Affairs: Dr KENNETH JACKSON
Vice-President for Administration: BOBBY YOUNG (acting)
Vice-President for Development: HARRY MILLER
Vice-President for Student Services: Dr WILLIE MARSHALL
Registrar: WILLIE CRIDDLE (acting)
Director of Libraries: ADELE DENDY

Libraries of 820,912 vols
Number of teachers: 390
Number of students: 11,000

Publications: *Ex-Press* (quarterly), *Inside TSU* (monthly), *Urban Notebook* (quarterly).

DEANS

School of Technology: Dr JOSHUA HILL (acting)
School of Business: Dr PRISCILLA SLADE
School of Education: Dr IRMA MALLOY
School of Law: MCKEW CARRINGTON (acting)
College of Arts and Sciences: Dr MERLINE PITRE
Graduate School: Dr JOSEPH JONES
School of Pharmacy and Health Sciences: Dr PEDRO LECCA

TEXAS TECH UNIVERSITY

Box 42013, Lubbock, TX 79409-2013
Telephone: (806) 742-2011

Founded by Texas Legislature 1923

President: Dr DONALD HARAGAN
Registrar: DON WICKARD
Director of Libraries: E. DALE CLUFF

Library of 1,614,148 vols
Number of teachers: 1,574
Number of students: 24,007

DEANS

College of Agricultural Sciences and Natural Resources: Dr SAMUEL E. CURL
College of Architecture: Dr MARTIN HARMS
College of Arts and Sciences: Dr JANE WINER
College of Business Administration: Dr CARL H. STEM
College of Education: Dr ELAINE JARCHOW
College of Engineering: Dr JORGE AUNON
College of Human Sciences: Dr ELIZABETH HALEY
Graduate School: Dr DAVID SCHMIDLEY
School of Law: FRANK NEWTON

ATTACHED INSTITUTES AND CENTRES

Agricultural Finance Institute: Dir PHILLIP N. JOHNSON
Insitute for Research in Plant Stress: Dir ROBERT ALBIN
Pork Industry Institute for Research and Education: Dir JOHN MCGLONE
Wildlife and Fisheries Management Institute: Dir RON SOSEBEE
Center for Agricultural Technology Transfer: Dir PAUL VAUGHN
Center for Applied International Development Studies: Dir GARY S. ELBOW
Center for Applied Systems Analysis: Dir CLYDE F. MARTIN
Center for Feed and Industry Research and Education: Dir REED RICHARDSON
Center for Historic Preservation and Technology: Dir JOE KING
Center for Petroleum Mathematics: Dir WAYNE FORD
Center for Forensic Studies: Dir E. ROLAND MENZEL
Center for Public Service: Dir CHARLES FOX
Center for the Study of the Vietnam Conflict: Dir JAMES R. RECKNER
Southwest Center for German Studies: Dir MEREDITH MCCLAIN
Center of Sports Health and Human Performance: Chair. ELIZABETH HALL
State Affiliate Census Data Center: Dir EVANS W. CURRY
Institute for Communications Research: Dir JERRY HUDSON
Institute for Design and Advanced Technology: Dir A. ERTAS
Institute for Environmental Sciences: Dir MICHAEL WILLIG
Institute for Studies in Pragmaticism: Dir KENNETH KETNER
Center for Professional Development: Dir DAVID ANDERSON

Small Business Development Center: Dir CRAIG BEAN
Small Business Institute: Dir ALEX STEWART
Texas Center for Productivity and Quality of Work Life: Dir BARRY MACY
Institute for Banking and Financial Studies: Dir STEVE SEARS
Institute for Management and Leadership Research: Dir ROBERT L. PHILLIPS
Institute for Marketing Studies: Dir ROY D. HOWELL
Institute for Studies in Organizational Automation: Dir KATHLEEN HENNESSEY
Center for Improvement of Teaching Effectiveness: Dir A. L. SMITH
Center for Excellence in Education: Dir BILL SPARKMAN
Science and Mathematics Education Center: Dir GERALD SKOOG
Center for Energy Research: Dir WALT J. OLER
Center for Hazardous and Toxic Waste Studies: Dir RAGHU NARAYAN
Water Resources Center: Dir LLOYD V. URBAN
Center for Applied Research in Industrial Automation and Robotics: Dir WILLIAM KOLARIK
Wind Engineering Research Center: Dir KISHOR C. MEHTA
Institute for Disaster Research: Dir JAMES R. MCDONALD
Institute for Ergonomics Research: Dir M. M. AYOUB
Institute for Multicomputer Processing and Controls: Dir WILLIAM J. B. OLDHAM
Murdough Center for Engineering Professionalism: Dir JIMMY SMITH
Child Development Research Center: Dir CATHY NATHAN
Home Economics Instructional Curriculum Center: Dir MARILYN WRAGG
Institute for Multidisciplinary Research on Adolescent and Adult Risk-Taking Behavior: Dir NANCY BELL
Institute for Nutritional Sciences: Dir STEVE JORGENSON
Texas Wine Marketing Research Institute: Dir TIM H. DODD
Center for Study of Addiction: Dir CARL ANDERSEN
Leather Research Institute: Dir JINGER EBERSPACHER
Center for Applied Petrophysical Studies: Co-Dirs GEORGE ASQUITH, MARION ARNOLD
International Center for Arid and Semiarid Land Studies: Dir KARY MATHIS
International Center for Textile Research and Development: Dir DEAN ETHRIDGE
Institute for Child and Family Studies: Dir MARY TOM RILEY
Institute for the Gifted: Dir MARTHA HISE
Institute for Biotechnology: Dir DAVID KNAFF

Texas Tech University Health Sciences Center

POB 4349, Lubbock, TX 79409
Telephone: (806) 743-3111
President: Dr DONALD HARAGAN

DEANS

School of Medicine: Dr BERNHARD MITTEMEYER
School of Nursing: Dr PAT YODER WISE
School of Allied Health: Dr SHIRLEY MCMANIGAL
School of Pharmacy: ARTHUR NELSON

TEXAS WESLEYAN UNIVERSITY

Fort Worth, TX 76105-1536
Telephone: (817) 531-4444
Fax: (817) 531-4425
E-mail: http:info@txwesleyan.edu
Founded 1890
President: JAKE B. SCHRUM
Provost: THOMAS F. ARMSTRONG
Vice-Presidents: DAVE VOSKUIL, CAREN HANDLEMAN, STEVE MARTIS
Registrar: PATI ALEXANDER
Librarian: CINDY SWIGGER
Library of 281,500 vols
Number of teachers: 129
Number of students: 3,172

TEXAS WOMAN'S UNIVERSITY

Denton, TX 76204
Telephone: (940) 898-3201
Fax: (940) 898-3198
Founded 1901
President: Dr CAROL D. SURLES
Vice-President for Academic Affairs: Dr BEVERLEY BYERS-PEVITTS
Vice-President for Finance and Administration: Dr BRENDA FLOYD
Vice-President for Institutional Advancement: Mrs KATHLEEN C. GIGL
Vice-President for Student Life: Dr RICHARD NICHOLAS (acting)
Librarian: ELIZABETH SNAPP
Library of 788,271 vols
Number of teachers: 500
Number of students: 9,356

TRINITY UNIVERSITY

715 Stadium Drive, San Antonio, TX 78212-7200
Telephone: (210) 736-7011
Fax: (210) 736-7696
Founded 1869
President: Dr RONALD K. CALGAARD
Vice-President for Academic Affairs: Dr EDWARD C. ROY
Registrar: RICHARD C. ELLIOTT
Librarian: RICHARD W. MEYER
Library of 821,000 vols
Number of teachers: 220
Number of students: 2,560
Publications: *Trinitonian, Mirage.*

DEANS

Faculty of Humanities and Arts: Dr WILLIAM O. WALKER, Jr
Faculty of Science, Mathematics and Engineering: Dr DONALD F. BAILEY (acting)
Faculty of Behavioral and Administrative Studies: Dr MARY STEFL

UNIVERSITY OF DALLAS

1845 E. Northgate Drive, Irving, TX 75062-4799
Telephone: (214) 721-5000
Founded 1956
President: Mgr MILAM J. JOSEPH (acting)
Vice-President for Administration: ROBERT M. GALECKE
Provost and Dean of the College: Dr GLEN THUROW
Graduate Dean: Dr GLEN THUROW
Registrar: JAN BURK
Librarian: SUE KENDALL (acting)
Library of 259,261 vols
Number of teachers: 188
Number of students: 3,008

UNIVERSITY OF HOUSTON

Houston, TX 77204-2162
Chancellor and President: ARTHUR K. SMITH
Provost: EDWARD P. SHERIDAN
Library Director: DANA ROOKS
Library of 1.8 million vols
Number of teachers: 933 full-time, 1,537 part-time
Number of students: 30,774
Publications: *UHouston, Experts Directory.*

DEANS

College of Architecture: BRUCE C. WEBB
College of Business Administration: SARA FREEDMAN
College of Education: ALLEN WARNER
Conrad N. Hilton College of Hotel and Restaurant Management: ALAN T. STUTTS
Cullen College of Engineering: JOHN C. WOLFE
Continuing Education: LOIS PHILLIPS
College of Humanities, Fine Arts and Communication: LOIS PARKINSON ZAMORA
U H Law Center: STEPHEN ZAMORA
College of Natural Sciences and Mathematics: JOHN BEAR
College of Optometry: JERALD STRICKLAND
College of Pharmacy: MUSTAFA LOKHANDWALA
College of Social Sciences: RICHARD M. ROZELLE
College of Technology: BERNARD MCINTYRE
Graduate School of Social Work: KAREN A. HOLMES

ATTACHED INSTITUTIONS

Center for Public Policy: Dir RICHARD MURRAY.
Energy Laboratory: Dir GLENN AUMANN.
Allied Geophysical Laboratories: Assoc. Dir Dr DAN EBROM.
Coastal Center: Dir GLENN AUMANN.
Blaffer Gallery: Dir DONALD BACIGALUPI.
West Houston Institute: Dir SANDY FREIDMAN.
Institute for Higher Education Law and Governance: Dir MICHAEL OLIVAS.
Health Law and Policy Institute: Dir MARK ROTHSTEIN.
Sasakawa International Center for Space Architecture: Dir LARRY BELL.
Institute for Corporate Environmental Management: Dir BETH BELOFF.
Space Vacuum Epitaxy Center: Dir ALEX IGNATIEV.
Texas Center for Superconductivity at the University of Houston: Dir PAUL CHU.

UNIVERSITY OF HOUSTON–CLEAR LAKE

2700 Bay Area Blvd, Houston, TX 77058-1098
Telephone: (281) 283-7600
Fax: (281) 283-2010
Founded 1974
President: Dr WILLIAM A. STAPLES
Senior Vice-President and Provost: EDWARD J. HAYES
Vice-President for Administration and Finance: MICHELLE DOTTER
Librarian: JOE MCCORD
Library of 382,400 vols
Number of teachers: 192 full-time, 254 part-time
Number of students: 6,947
Publications: *The University Catalog, Forte, Snapshot, Egret.*

DEANS

School of Education: Dr DENNIS W. SPUCK
School of Natural and Applied Sciences: Dr CHARLES MCKAY
School of Human Sciences and Humanities: Dr SPENCER A. MCWILLIAMS
School of Business and Public Administration: Dr WILLIAM T. CUMMINGS

UNIVERSITY OF HOUSTON–DOWNTOWN

One Main Street, Houston TX 77002
Telephone: (713) 221-8000
Fax: (713) 221-8157
Founded 1974; adopted present name in 1983
President: Dr MAX CASTILLO
Vice-President for Academic Affairs and Provost: Dr MOLLY R. WOODS

Vice-President for Administration: CHANEY ANDERSON
Executive Assistant to the President and Director of Constituent Relations: MILICENT LARSON
Executive Director of Institutional Advancement: Dr ANNE MURPHY
Dean of Student Affairs: Dr ANN MCDONALD
Librarian: (vacant)

Library of 230,000 vols
Number of teachers: 394
Number of students: 8,194

DEANS

College of Humanities and Social Sciences: Dr MICHAEL DRESSMAN
College of Sciences and Technology: Dr GEORGE PINCUS
College of Business: Dr BOBBY BIZZELL
University College: Dr DAN JONES (interim)

UNIVERSITY OF HOUSTON–VICTORIA

2506 Red River, Victoria, TX 77901
Telephone: (512) 576-3151
Fax: (512) 573-0017
Founded 1973
President: Dr KAREN HAYNES
Provost and Vice-President for Academic Affairs: Dr DON SMITH
Executive Director, Enrollment Management: RICHARD D. PHILLIPS
Director, Computer Services: JOSEPH S. FERGUSON
Vice-President, Administration and Finance: WAYNE B. BERAN
Executive Director, Institutional Advancement: CAROLE OLIPHANT
Director, Library: Dr JOE F. DAHLSTROM

Library of 170,000 vols
Number of teachers: 40
Number of students: 1,491

CHAIRMEN

Division of Education: Dr CHERYL HINES
Division of Arts and Sciences: Dr CINDY SCHNEBLY
Division of Business Administration: Dr CHARLES BULLOCK

UNIVERSITY OF MARY HARDIN-BAYLOR

Belton, TX 76513
Telephone: (817) 939-8642
Fax: (817) 939-4535
Founded 1845
President: Dr JERRY G. BAWCOM
Vice-President for Administrative and Academic Affairs: Dr KENNETH W. JOHNSON
Registrar: R. W. MONTGOMERY
Director of Admissions: BOBBY JOHNSON
Librarian: ROBERT A. STRONG

Library of 145,000 vols
Number of teachers: 102
Number of students: 2,300

UNIVERSITY OF NORTH TEXAS

Denton, TX 76203-3826
Telephone: (817) 522-7911
Founded 1890
Chancellor and President: Dr ALFRED F. HURLEY
Provost and Vice-President for Academic Affairs: Dr BLAINE A. BROWNELL
Vice-President for Fiscal Affairs: PHILIP C. DIEBEL
Vice-President for External Affairs: WALTER E. PARKER
Vice-President for Administrative Affairs: FREDERICK R. POLE
Vice-President for Development: Dr PETER LANE
Vice-President for Student Affairs: Dr JOE G. STEWART
Vice-President and General Counsel: Dr RICHARD RAFES
Director of Admissions: MARCILLA COLLINSWORTH
Registrar: JONEEL J. HARRIS
Librarian: Dr B. DONALD GROSE

Library of 2,164,427 vols, 2,190,831 microforms
Number of teachers: 800 full-time, 540 teaching assistants and teaching fellows
Number of students: 25,605

DEANS

Graduate School: Dr ROLLIE SCHAFER
Education: Dr PAUL DIXON
Arts and Sciences: Dr NORA KIZER BELL
Music: Dr DAVID SHRADER
Business Administration: (vacant)
Library Science: (vacant)
Community Service: Dr DANIEL M. JOHNSON
Merchandising and Hospitality Management: Dr SUZANNE LA BRECQUE
School of Visual Arts: Dr D. JACK DAVIS

UNIVERSITY OF ST THOMAS

3800 Montrose Blvd, Houston, TX 77006
Telephone: (713) 522-7911
Founded 1947
Private control
President: Rev. J. MICHAEL MILLER
Vice-President for Finance: JAMES BOOTH
Vice-President for Academic Affairs: Dr LEE WILLIAMES
Director, Community Services: Rev. WILLIAM J. YOUNG
Dean of Admissions: ELSIE BIRON
Librarian: JAMES PICCININNI

Library of 203,000 vols
Number of teachers: 222
Number of students: 2,506
Publications: *Cauldron, St Thomas Magazine.*

DEANS

School of Arts and Sciences: Dr JEROME A. KRAMEN
School of Theology: Fr LOUIS BRUSATTI
School of Business: Dr YHI-MIN HO
School of Education: Dr ANNA DEWALD
Evening/Summer: Dr JANICE GORDON KELTER

UNIVERSITY OF TEXAS PAN AMERICAN

Edinburg, TX 78539
Telephone: (512) 381-2100
Founded 1927, reorganized 1952
President: Dr MIGUEL A. NEVAREZ
Director of Admissions: DAVID ZUNIGA
Director of Financial Aid: ARNOLD TREJO
Librarian: Dr ELINOR BRIDGES

Library of 549,266 vols
Number of teachers: 550
Number of students: 13,747

UNIVERSITY OF TEXAS SYSTEM

601 Colorado St, Austin, TX 78701
Telephone: (512) 499-4201
Founded 1883
Chancellor: WILLIAM H. CUNNINGHAM
Executive Vice-Chancellor for Academic Affairs: FRANCIE A. FREDERICK (acting)
Executive Vice-Chancellor for Health Affairs: CHARLES B. MULLINS
Vice-Chancellor and General Counsel: RAY FARABEE
Vice-Chancellor for Governmental Relations: MICHAEL D. MILLSAP
Executive Vice-Chancellor for Business Affairs: R. D. BURCK
Vice-Chancellor for Development and External Relations: SHIRLEY BIRD PERRY
Vice-Chancellor for Telecommunications and Information Technology: MARIO J. GONZALEZ
Vice-Chancellor for Health Affairs: JAMES C. GUCKIAN

University of Texas at Austin

Austin, TX 78712
Telephone: (512) 471-3434
Founded 1883; formerly University of Texas, Main University
State control
Academic year: September to May (two terms) with two summer sessions
President: LARRY R. FAULKNER
Senior Vice-President: WILLIAM S. LIVINGSTON
Vice-President for Student Affairs: JAMES W. VICK
Provost: STEPHEN A. MONTI (interim)
Vice-President for Research: JUAN M. SANCHEZ
Vice-President for Business Affairs: G. CHARLES FRANKLIN
Vice-President and Dean of Graduate Studies: TERESA A. SULLIVAN
Vice-President for Administration and Legal Affairs: PATRICIA C. OHLENDORF
Vice-President for Development: JOHNNIE D. RAY
Vice-President for Human Resources and Community Relations: JAMES L. HILL
Librarian: HAROLD W. BILLINGS

Library: see Libraries
Number of teachers: 2,687
Number of students: 48,857

DEANS

College of Business Administration: ROBERT G. MAY
College of Communication: ELLEN ANN WARTELLA
College of Education: MANUEL J. JUSTIZ
College of Engineering: BEN G. STREETMAN
College of Fine Arts: DAVID L. DEMING
College of Liberal Arts: SHELDON EKLAND-OLSON
College of Natural Sciences: MARY ANN RANKIN
College of Pharmacy: JAMES T. DOLUISIO
School of Law: M. MICHAEL SHARLOT
Graduate School of Library and Information Science: E. GLYNN HARMON (interim)
School of Architecture: LAWRENCE W. SPECK
Graduate School of Social Work: BARBARA W. WHITE
LBJ School of Public Affairs: EDWIN DORN
Continuing Education: THOMAS M. HATFIELD
School of Nursing: DOLORES SANDS

PROFESSORS

College of Liberal Arts:

ABBOUD, P. F., Middle Eastern Languages
ABZUG, R. H., History
ALBRECHT, D. G., Psychology
ALLAIRE, E. B., Philosophy
AMSEL, A., Psychology
ANGEL, R. J., Sociology
ANGELELLI, I. A., Philosophy
ARENS, K. M., Germanic Studies
ARMSTRONG, D., Classics
ASHER, N. M., Philosophy
AYRES, J. B., English
BAKER, M.-F. J., French and Italian
BAR-ADON, A., Middle Eastern Languages
BARNOUW, J., English
BEAN, F. D., Jr, Sociology
BONEVAC, D. A., Philosophy
BOYD, C. P., History
BRAMBLETT, C. A., Anthropology
BRAYBROOKE, D., Government

BRODY, R., Spanish and Portuguese
BRONARS, S. G., Economics
BROW, J. B., Anthropology
BROWN, J. C., History
BROWN, N. D., History
BROWNING, G. D., Philosophy
BUCHANAN, B., II, Government
BUMP, J. F., English
BURNHAM, W. D., Government
BUSS, A. H., Psychology
BUSS, D. M., Psychology
BUTLER, J. S., Sociology
BUTZER, K. W., Geography
CABLE, T. M., English
CARTER, J. C., Classics
CARTON, E. B., English
CARVER, L. D., English
CAUSEY, R. L., Philosophy
CAUVIN, J.-P. B., French and Italian
CHARNEY, D. H., Rhetoric
CLAYTON, J. D., Slavic Languages
CLEAVES, P. S., Latin American Studies
COHEN, D. B., Psychology
COHEN, L. B., Psychology
CROSBY, A. W., Jr, American Studies
CRUNDEN, R. M., History
CULLINGFORD, E., English
CUSHING, R. G., Sociology
DACY, D. C., Economics
DAVIES, C. S., Geography
DAWSON, R. L., French and Italian
DELAGARZA, R. O., Government
DIEHL, R. L., Psychology
DOMJAN, M. P., Psychology
DONAHUE, F. E., Germanic Studies
DOOLITTLE, W., Geography
DOUGHTY, R. W., Geography
DULLES, J. W. F., American Studies
DUSANSKY, R., Economics
EDWARDS, D. V., Government
ENELOW, J. M., Government
ENGLISH, P. W., Geography
FAIGLEY, L. L., Rhetoric
FALOLA, O. O., History
FARMAYAN, H., History
FARMER, N. K., Jr, English
FARRELL, J. P., English
FAUROT, J. L., Asian Studies
FERNEA, E. W., English
FERNEA, R. A., Anthropology
FISHKIN, J. S., Government
FISHKIN, S. F., American Studies
FLOWERS, B. M., English
FREEMAN, G. P., Government
FREEMAN, S. J., Economics
FRIEDMAN, A. W., English
FRISBIE, W. P., Sociology
FULLERTON, D., Economics
GAGARIN, M., Classics
GALINSKY, G. K., Classics
GALLE, O. R., Sociology
GARRISON, J. D., English
GEISLER, W. S., III, Psychology
GERACI, V. J., Economics
GHOSE, Z. A., English
GLADE, W. P., Economics
GLENN, N. D., Sociology
GOETZMANN, W. H., History
GONZALEZ-GERTH, M., Spanish and Portuguese
GONZALEZ-LIMA, F., Psychology
GOUGH, P. B., Psychology
GOULD, L. L., History
GRAHAM, D. B., English
GRAHAM, L. S., Government
GRAHAM, R., History
GUTMANN, M. P., History
HALL, M. G., History
HALL, S. A., Geography
HAMERMESH, D. S., Economics
HANCOCK, I. F., Linguistics
HANKINSON, R. J., Philosophy
HANSEN, N. M., Economics
HARDGRAVE, R. L., Government
HARLOW, B. J., English
HARMS, R. T., Linguistics
HEINEN, H. P., Germanic Studies
HEINZELMAN, K. O., English
HELMREICH, R. L., Psychology
HENRY, C. M., Government
HESTER, T. R., Anthropology
HIGGINS, K. M., Philosophy
HIGLEY, J. C., Government
HILFER, A. C., English
HILL, F. G., Economics
HILLMANN, M. C., Middle Eastern Languages
HINICH, M. J., Government
HINOJOSASMITH, R., English
HOBERMAN, J. M., Germanic Studies
HOCHBERG, H. I., Philosophy
HOLAHAN, C. J., Psychology
HOLZ, R. K., Geography
HORN, J. M., Psychology
IHONVBERE, J. O., Government
JANNUZI, F. T., Economics
JELAVICH, P. C., History
JORDAN, T. G., Geography
KANE, R. H., Philosophy
KAPPELMAN, J. W., Jr, Anthropology
KATZ, M. R., Slavic Languages
KAULBACH, E. N., English
KELLEY, T. M., English
KELLNER, D. M., Philosophy
KELLY, W. R., Sociology
KENDRICK, D. A., Economics
KIBLER, W. W., French and Italian
KING, R. D., Linguistics
KOLSTI, J. S., Slavic Languages
KROLL, J. H., Classics
KRUPPA, J. E., English
KURTZ, L. R., Sociology
LAMPHEAR, J. E., History
LANGLOIS, J. H., Psychology
LARIVIERE, R. W., Asian Studies
LASALLE, P. N., English
LASBY, C. G., History
LEVACK, B. P., History
LIMON, J. E., English
LINDFORS, B. O., English
LINDSTROM, N. E., Spanish and Portuguese
LIPPMANN, J. N., French and Italian
LITVAK, L., Spanish and Portuguese
LOPREATO, J., Sociology
LOUIS, W. R., History
LUJAN, M. E., Spanish and Portuguese
MCAFEE, R. P., Economics
MCFADDEN, D., Psychology
MACKEY, L. H., Philosophy
MACNEILAGE, P. F., Linguistics
MALOF, J. F., English
MANNERS, I. R., Geography
MARCUS, L., English
MARCUS, M. J., French and Italian
MARSHALL, S. E., Sociology
MARTINICH, A. P., Philosophy
MAY, J. C., Government
MEACHAM, S., Jr, History
MEIKLE, J. L., American Studies
MIDDLETON, J. C., Germanic Studies
MINAULT, G., History
MOLDENHAUER, J. J., English
MORGAN, D. C., Jr, Economics
MORGAN, M. G., Classics
MOURELATOS, A., Philosophy
NEELY, J. A., Anthropology
NETHERCUT, W. R., Classics
NORMAN, A. L., Economics
OLIVELLE, J. P., Asian Studies
PALAIMA, T. G., Classics
PARKER, D. S., Classics
PELLS, R. H., History
PENA, M. H., Anthropology
PENNEBAKER, J. W., Psychology
PHILLIPS, S. H., Philosophy
POLOMÉ, E. C., Germanic Studies
POTTER, J. E., Sociology
PRENTICE, N. M., Psychology
PRINDLE, D. F., Government
PULLUM, T. W., Sociology
RAMIREZ, M., III, Psychology
REBHORN, W. A., Jr, English
ROBERTS, B. R., Sociology
ROSSMAN, C. R., English
ROSTOW, W. W., Economics
RUMRICH, J. P., English
RUSZKIEWICZ, J. J., Anthropology
SCHADE, G. D., Spanish and Portuguese
SCHAEDEL, R. P., Anthropology
SCHALLERT, T. J., Psychology
SCHEICK, W. J., English
SCHOPEN, G., Asian Studies
SELBY, H. A., Anthropology
SEUNG, T. K., Philosophy
SHELMERDINE, C. W., Classics
SHERZER, D. M., French and Italian
SHERZER, J. F., Anthropology
SHUMWAY, N., Spanish and Portuguese
SIBLEY, D. S., Economics
SJOBERG, G. A., Sociology
SLESNICK, D. T., Economics
SMITH, B. D., Economics
SMITH, C. S., Linguistics
SOLE, C. A., Spanish and Portuguese
SOLE, Y., Spanish and Portuguese
SOLOMON, R. C., Philosophy
STAFFORD, M. C., Sociology
STAHL, D. O., II, Economics
STOTT, W. M., American Studies
STROSS, B. M., Anthropology
SUSSMAN, H. M., Linguistics
SUTHERLAND, W., Jr, English
SWAFFAR, J. K., Germanic Studies
SWANN, W. B., Jr, Psychology
TELCH, M. J., Psychology
THIESSEN, D. D., Psychology
TRIMBLE, J. R., English
TYLER, R. C., History
UGALDE, A., Sociology
UMBERSON, D. J., Sociology
VANOLPHEN, H. H., Asian Studies
VARELA, J. L., Spanish and Portuguese
WADLINGTON, W. P., English
WAGNER, R. H., Government
WALKER, S. S., Anthropology
WALL, R. E., Linguistics
WARD, P., Sociology
WARR, E. M., Sociology
WEINSTOCK, J. M., Germanic Studies
WESTBROOK, M. R., English
WEVILL, D. A., English
WHIGHAM, F. F., Jr, English
WHITBREAD, T. B., English
WHITE, L. M., Classics
WHITE, P. L., History
WILCZYNSKI, W., Psychology
WINSHIP, M. B., English
WOLITZ, S. L., French and Italian
WOODBURY, A. C., Linguistics
WOODRUFF, P. B., Philosophy
ZIMIC, S., Spanish and Portuguese

College of Natural Sciences:

ANTONIEWICZ, P. R., Physics
APPLING, D. R., Chemistry and Biochemistry
ARMENDARIZ, E. P., Mathematics
ARTZT, K. J., Zoology
BACKUS, M. M., Geological Sciences
BAJAJ, C. L., Computer Sciences
BARD, A. J., Chemistry and Biochemistry
BARKER, D. S., Geological Sciences
BATORY, D. S., Computer Sciences
BAULD, N. L., Chemistry and Biochemistry
BECKNER, W., Mathematics
BENGTSON, R. D., Physics
BERK, H. L., Physics
BICHTELER, K. R., Mathematics
BITTNER, G. D., Zoology
BOGGS, J. E., Chemistry and Biochemistry
BOHM, A. R., Physics
BONA, J. L., Mathematics
BOSE, H. R., Jr, Microbiology
BOYER, R. E., Geological Sciences
BOYER, R. S., Computer Sciences
BRAND, J. J., Botany
BRILEY, M. E., Human Ecology
BRONSON, F. H., Zoology
BROWN, R. M., Jr, Botany

Browne, J. C., Computer Sciences
Buffler, R. T., Geological Sciences
Bull, J. J., Zoology
Caffarelli, L. A., Mathematics
Campion, A., Chemistry and Biochemistry
Candelas, P., Physics
Carlson, W. D., Geological Sciences
Cheney, E. W., Mathematics
Chiu, C. B., Physics
Clarke, S. D., Human Ecology
Cline, A. K., Computer Sciences
Cloos, M. P., Geological Sciences
Coker, W. R., Physics
Cowley, A. H., Chemistry and Biochemistry
Crews, D. P., Zoology
Daniel, J. W., Mathematics
Davis, R. E., Chemistry and Biochemistry
Delozanne, A. L., Physics
Dewitt, B. S., Physics
Dewitt, C. M., Physics
Dicus, D. A., Physics
Dijkstra, E. W., Computer Sciences
Dollard, J. D., Mathematics
Douglas, J. N., Astronomy
Downer, M. W., Physics
Drummond, W. E., Physics
Dudley, J. P., Microbiology
Durbin, J., Mathematics
Earhart, C. F., Microbiology
Eaton, W. T., Mathematics
Emerson, E. A., II, Computer Sciences
Erskine, J. L., Physics
Evans, N. J., II, Astronomy
Fink, M., Physics
Fischler, W., Physics
Fisher, W. L., Geological Sciences
Forrest, H. S., Zoology
Fowler, N. L., Botany
Freed, D. S., Mathematics
Freeland, J. H., Human Ecology
Freeman, G. L., Zoology
Frommhold, L. W., Physics
Fussell, D. S., Computer Sciences
Galloway, W. E., Geological Sciences
Gamba, I. M., Mathematics
Gardiner, W. C., Chemistry and Biochemistry
Gavenda, J. D., Physics
Gentle, K. W., Physics
Gerth, F. E., III, Mathematics
Gilbert, J. C., Chemistry and Biochemistry
Gilbert, J. E., Mathematics
Gilbert, L. E., Zoology
Gleeson, A. M., Physics
Gompf, R. E., Mathematics
Gordon, C. M., Mathematics
Gottlieb, P. D., Microbiology
Gouda, M. G., Computer Sciences
Griffy, T. A., Physics
Guy, W. T., Jr, Mathematics
Hackert, M. L., Chemistry and Biochemistry
Hamrick, G. C., Mathematics
Hardesty, B. A., Chemistry and Biochemistry
Harshey, R. M., Microbiology
Harvey, P. M., Astronomy
Hazeltine, R. D., Physics
Heitmann, R. C., Mathematics
Hillis, D. M., Zoology
Hoffmann, G. W., Physics
Holcombe, J. A., Chemistry and Biochemistry
Horton, C. W., Jr, Physics
Huston, A. C., Human Ecology
Huston, T. L., Human Ecology
Ivash, E. V., Physics
Jaffe, D. T., Astronomy
Jayaram, M., Microbiology
Jefferys, W. H., Astronomy
John, P. W. M., Mathematics
Jones, R. A., Chemistry and Biochemistry
Kalthoff, K. O., Zoology
Keto, J. W., Physics
Kirkpatrick, M. A., Zoology
Kitto, G. B., Chemistry and Biochemistry
Kleinman, L., Physics
Koch, H. A., Mathematics
Kocurek, G. A., Geological Sciences
Kodadek, T. J., Chemistry and Biochemistry
Krieg, P. A., Zoology
Kuipers, B. J., Computer Sciences
Kyle, J. R., Geological Sciences
Lacy, J. H., Astronomy
Lagow, R. J., Chemistry and Biochemistry
Lagowski, J. J., Chemistry and Biochemistry
Lagowski, J. M., Zoology
Lam, S. S., Computer Sciences
Lambert, D. L., Astronomy
Lambowitz, A., Chemistry and Biochemistry
Land, L. S., Geological Sciences
Larimer, J. L., Zoology
Laude, D. A., Chemistry and Biochemistry
Levin, D. A., Botany
Lifschitz, V., Computer Sciences
Llave, R., Mathematics
Long, L. E., Geological Sciences
Loop, R., Human Ecology
Luecke, J. E., Mathematics
Lundelius, E. L., Jr, Geological Sciences
Mabry, T. J., Botany
McAdam, S. J., Mathematics
McBride, E. F., Geological Sciences
Magnus, P. D., Chemistry and Biochemistry
Maguire, B., Jr, Zoology
Maguire, M. P., Zoology
Martin, S. F., Chemistry and Biochemistry
Matzner, R. A., Physics
Mauseth, J. D., Botany
Meyer, R. J., Microbiology
Misra, J., Computer Sciences
Mok, A. K., Computer Sciences
Molineux, I. J., Microbiology
Moore, C. F., Physics
Moore, J. S., II, Computer Sciences
Morrison, P. J., Physics
Mosher, S., Geological Sciences
Nakamura, Y., Geological Sciences
Nather, R. E., Astronomy
Ne'eman, Y., Physics
Oakes, M. E. L., Physics
Odell, E. W., Mathematics
Palka, B. P., Mathematics
Payne, S. M., Microbiology
Pianka, E. R., Zoology
Pollak, G. D., Zoology
Prigogine, I., Physics
Radin, C. L., Mathematics
Ramachandran, V., Computer Sciences
Reichl, L. E., Physics
Richardson, R. H., Zoology
Riggs, A. F., II, Zoology
Riley, P. J., Physics
Robertson, W. W., Physics
Robertus, J. D., Chemistry and Biochemistry
Robinson, E. L., Astronomy
Rosenthal, H. P., Mathematics
Rossky, P. J., Chemistry and Biochemistry
Roux, S. J., Jr, Botany
Rowe, T. B., Geological Sciences
Ryan, M. J., Zoology
Saltman, D. J., Mathematics
Sanders, B. G., Zoology
Scalo, J. M., Astronomy
Schelter, W., Mathematics
Scherr, C. W., Physics
Schieve, W. C., Physics
Schwitters, R. F., Physics
Sessler, J. L., Chemistry and Biochemistry
Shapiro, P. R., Astronomy
Sharp, J. M., Jr, Geological Sciences
Shields, G. A., Astronomy
Showalter, R. E., Mathematics
Simpson, B. B., Botany
Singer, M. C., Zoology
Smith, D., Geological Sciences
Smith, M. K., Mathematics
Sneden, C. A., Astronomy
Sprinkle, J. T., Geological Sciences
Starbird, M. P., Mathematics
Starr, R. C., Botany
Sudarshan, G., Physics
Sutton, H. E., Zoology
Swift, J. B., Physics
Swinney, H. L., Physics
Szaniszlo, P. J., Microbiology
Tajima, T., Physics
Tate, J. T., Mathematics
Thomas, P., Marine Science
Thompson, G. A., Jr, Botany
Thompson, W. J., Zoology
Tucker, P. W., Microbiology
Turner, B. L., Botany
Udagawa, T., Physics
Uhlenbeck, K., Mathematics
Vaaler, J. D., Mathematics
Vishniac, E. T., Astronomy
Walker, J. R., Microbiology
Wang, K., Chemistry and Biochemistry
Webber, S. E., Chemistry and Biochemistry
Weinberg, S., Physics
Wheeler, J. C., Astronomy
White, J. M., Chemistry and Biochemistry
Whitesell, J. K., Chemistry and Biochemistry
Whitledge, T. E., Marine Science
Williams, R. F., Mathematics
Willis, R. A., Human Ecology
Wills, D., Astronomy
Wilson, C. R., Geological Sciences
Winget, D. E., Astronomy
Wyatt, R. E., Chemistry and Biochemistry
Young, D. M., Jr, Mathematics
Zakon, H. H., Zoology

College of Business Administration:

Allison, J. R., Management Science and Information Systems.
Alpert, M. I., Marketing Administration
Anderson, U. L., Accounting
Arnold, V. L., Management
Atiase, R., Accounting
Bagchi, U., Management
Beyer, J. M., Management
Brockett, P. L., Management Science and Information Systems
Cox, E. P., III, Marketing Administration
Cross, F. B., Management Science and Information Systems
Davenport, T. H., Management Science and Information Systems
Deitrick, J. W., Accounting
Doenges, R. C., Finance
Dyer, J. S., Management Science and Information Systems
Fitzsimmons, J. A., Management
Fowler, A. C., Accounting
Freeman, R. N., Accounting
Gau, G. W., Finance
George, E. I., Management Science and Information Systems
Golden, L. L., Marketing Administration
Graham-Moore, B. E., Management
Granof, M. H., Accounting
Green, R. T., Marketing Administration
Henion, K. E., II, Marketing Administration
Hoyer, W. D., Marketing Administration
Huber, G. P., Management
Huff, D. L., Marketing Administration
Jaillet, P., Management Science and Information Systems
Jarvenpaa, S. L., Management Science and Information Systems
Jemison, D. B., Management
Jentz, G. A., Management Science and Information Systems
Jordan, E. W., Management Science and Information Systems
Kinney, W. R., Jr, Accounting
Kohli, A. K., Marketing Administration
Kotabe, M., Marketing Administration
Lasdon, L. S., Management Science and Information Systems
Limberg, S. T., Accounting
McAlister, L. M., Marketing Administration

McDaniel, R. R., Jr, Management Science and Information Systems
Magee, S. P., Finance
Mahajan, V., Marketing Administration
Martin, J. D., Finance
Matsuo, H., Management
Mettlen, R. D., Finance
Newman, D. P., Accounting
Peterson, R. A., Marketing Administration
Prentice, R. A., Management Science and Information Systems
Rao, R. K. S., Finance
Robertson, J. C., Accounting
Ronn, E. I., Finance
Ruefli, T. W., Management Science and Information Systems
Sager, T. W., Management Science and Information Systems
Senchack, A. J., Jr, Finance
Shaw, B. M., Management Science and Information Systems
Spellman, L. J., Finance
Srivastava, R. K., Marketing Administration
Starks, L. T., Finance
Stokes, S. L., Management Science and Information Systems
Sullivan, R. S., Management Science and Information Systems
Summers, E. L., Accounting
Titman, S., Finance
Whinston, A. B., Management Science and Information Systems

College of Communication:

Alves, R. C., Journalism
Berg, C. E., Radio-Television-Film
Brooks, R. D., Radio-Television-Film
Burns, N. M., Advertising
Cherwitz, R. A., Speech Communication
Colson, J. B., Journalism
Cunningham, I. C., Advertising
Dalston, R. M., Speech Communication
Daly, J. A., Speech Communication
Danielson, W. A., Journalism
Downing, J. D., Radio-Television-Film
Gray, P. H., Speech Communication
Hart, R. P., Speech Communication
Hopper, R. W., Speech Communication
Jeffrey, R. C., Speech Communication
Kalupa, F. B., Journalism
Knapp, M. L., Speech Communication
Korbus, W. E., Journalism
Leckenby, J. D., Advertising
McCombs, M. E., Journalism
Marquardt, T. P., Speech Communication
Martin, F. N., Speech Communication
Maxwell, M. M., Speech Communication
Murphy, J. H., Advertising
Newcomb, H. M., Radio-Television-Film
Olasky, M. N., Journalism
Quinn, J. M., Journalism
Reese, S. D., Journalism
Schatz, T. G., Radio-Television-Film
Staiger, J., Radio-Television-Film
Tankard, J. W., Jr, Journalism
Todd, R. G., Journalism
Whitney, D. C., Journalism
Wilcox, G. B., Advertising
Williams, F. D., Speech Communication

College of Education:

Ainslie, R. C., Educational Psychology
Barufaldi, J. P., Curriculum and Instruction
Benitez, M. A., Curriculum and Instruction
Borich, G. D., Educational Psychology
Brown, R. M., Educational Administration
Cardozier, V. R., Educational Administration
Carlson, C. I., Educational Psychology
Carry, L. R., Curriculum and Instruction
Confrey, J., Curriculum and Instruction
Coyle, E. F., Kinesiology and Health Education
Davis, O. L., Jr, Curriculum and Instruction
Emmer, E. T., Educational Psychology
Estes, N., Educational Administration
Falbo, T. L., Educational Psychology
Farrar, R. P., Kinesiology and Health Education
Foley, D. E., Curriculum and Instruction
Frost, J. L., Curriculum and Instruction
Gilbert, L. A., Educational Psychology
Gottlieb, N. H., Kinesiology and Health Education
Guszak, F. J., Curriculum and Instruction
Hoffman, J. V., Curriculum and Instruction
Ivy, J. L., Kinesiology and Health Education
Jennings, E., Educational Psychology
Jensen, J. M., Curriculum and Instruction
Kennamer, L. G., Curriculum and Instruction
King, J. D., Educational Administration
Koch, W. R., Educational Psychology
Lindfors, J. W., Curriculum and Instruction
Manaster, G. J., Educational Psychology
Marion, R. L., Special Education
Mink, O. G., Curriculum and Instruction
Moore, W., Educational Administration
Ortiz, A. A., Special Education
Parker, R. M., Special Education
Phelps, D. G., Educational Administration
Phillips, B. N., Educational Psychology
Resta, P. E., Curriculum and Instruction
Reyes, P., Educational Administration
Rieth, H. J., Special Education
Roser, N. L., Curriculum and Instruction
Roueche, J. E., Jr, Educational Administration
Schallert, D. L., Educational Psychology
Scribner, J. D., Educational Administration
Spirduso, W. W., Kinesiology and Health Education
Thomas, M. P., Jr, Educational Administration
Vaughn, S., Special Education
Veldman, D. J., Educational Psychology
Wagstaff, L. H., Educational Administration
Weinstein, C. E., Educational Psychology
Wicker, F. W., Educational Psychology
Yates, J. R., Educational Administration

College of Engineering:

Abraham, J. A., Electrical and Computer Engineering
Aggarwal, J. K., Electrical and Computer Engineering
Allen, D. T., Chemical Engineering
Ambler, A. P., Electrical and Computer Engineering
Arapostathis, A., Electrical and Computer Engineering
Armstrong, N. E., Civil Engineering
Babuska, I. M., Aerospace Engineering
Baker, L. E., Electrical and Computer Engineering
Banerjee, S. K., Electrical and Computer Engineering
Bard, J. F., Mechanical Engineering
Barlow, J. W., Chemical Engineering
Barnes, J. W., Mechanical Engineering
Barr, R. E., Mechanical Engineering
Baughman, M. L., Electrical and Computer Engineering
Beaman, J. J., Jr, Mechanical Engineering
Becker, E. B., Aerospace Engineering
Becker, M. F., Electrical and Computer Engineering
Bedford, A., Aerospace Engineering
Blackstock, D. T., Mechanical Engineering
Bostick, F. X., Jr, Electrical and Computer Engineering
Bourell, D. L., Mechanical Engineering
Bovik, A. C., Electrical and Computer Engineering
Breen, J. E., Civil Engineering
Brock, J. R., Chemical Engineering
Broucke, R. A., Aerospace Engineering
Bryant, M. D., Mechanical Engineering
Buckman, A. B., Electrical and Computer Engineering
Burns, N. H., Civil Engineering
Busch-Vischniac, I. J., Mechanical Engineering
Campbell, J. C., Electrical and Computer Engineering
Carey, G. F., Aerospace Engineering
Carrasquillo, R. L., Civil Engineering
Caudle, B. H., Petroleum and Geosystems
Charbeneau, R. J., Civil Engineering
Cogdell, J. R., Electrical and Computer Engineering
Craig, R. R., Jr, Aerospace Engineering
Crawford, M. E., Mechanical Engineering
Crawford, M. M., Mechanical Engineering
Diller, K. R., Mechanical Engineering
Dolling, D. S., Aerospace Engineering
Driga, M. D., Electrical and Computer Engineering
Dupuis, R. D., Electrical and Computer Engineering
Ekerdt, J. G., Chemical Engineering
Eliezer, Z., Mechanical Engineering
Fair, J. R., Chemical Engineering
Flake, R. H., Electrical and Computer Engineering
Fowler, D. W., Civil Engineering
Fowler, W. T., Aerospace Engineering
Frank, K. H., Civil Engineering
Furlong, R. W., Civil Engineering
Georgiou, G., Chemical Engineering
Gloyna, E. F., Civil Engineering
Goodenough, J. B., Mechanical Engineering
Grady, W. M., Electrical and Computer Engineering
Gray, K. E., Petroleum and Geosystems Engineering
Hallock, G. A., Electrical and Computer Engineering
Hamilton, M. F., Mechanical Engineering
Hayes, L. J., Aerospace Engineering
Heller, A., Chemical Engineering
Hill, A. D., Petroleum and Geosystems Engineering
Himmelblau, D. M., Chemical Engineering
Hixson, E. L., Electrical and Computer Engineering
Ho, P. S., Mechanical Engineering
Holley, E. R., Civil Engineering
Howell, J. R., Mechanical Engineering
Hudson, W. R., Civil Engineering
Hull, D. G., Aerospace Engineering
Jensen, P. A., Mechanical Engineering
Jirsa, J. O., Civil Engineering
Johnston, K. P., Chemical Engineering
Jones, J. W., Mechanical Engineering
Juricic, D., Mechanical Engineering
Kennedy, T. W., Civil Engineering
Klingner, R. E., Civil Engineering
Koen, B. V., Mechanical Engineering
Koros, W. J., Chemical Engineering
Kreger, M. E., Civil Engineering
Kwong, D.-L., Electrical and Computer Engineering
Kyriakides, S., Aerospace Engineering
Lake, L. W., Petroleum and Geosystems Engineering
Lamb, J. P., Jr, Mechanical Engineering
Landsberger, S., Mechanical Engineering
Lawler, D. F., Civil Engineering
Lee, C. E., Civil Engineering
Lee, J. C., Electrical and Computer Engineering
Liechti, K. M., Aerospace Engineering
Liljestrand, H. M., Civil Engineering
Ling, F. F., Mechanical Engineering
Ling, H., Electrical and Computer Engineering
Lipovski, G. J., Electrical and Computer Engineering
Lloyd, D. R., Chemical Engineering
Loehr, R. C., Civil Engineering
McCullough, B. F., Civil Engineering
Machemehl, R. B., Civil Engineering
Mahmassani, H. S., Civil Engineering
Maidment, D. R., Civil Engineering
Malina, J. F., Jr, Civil Engineering
Mark, H. M., Aerospace Engineering

Marshek, K. M., Mechanical Engineering
Masada, G. Y., Mechanical Engineering
Matthews, R. D., Mechanical Engineering
Maziar, C. M., Electrical and Computer Engineering
Neikirk, D. P., Electrical and Computer Engineering
O'Connor, J. T., Civil Engineering
Oden, J. T., Aerospace Engineering
Olson, R. E., Civil Engineering
Panton, R. L., Mechanical Engineering
Paul, D. R., Chemical Engineering
Pearce, J. A., Electrical and Computer Engineering
Peters, E. J., Petroleum and Geosystems Engineering
Podio, A. L., Petroleum and Geosystems Engineering
Pope, G. A., Petroleum and Geosystems Engineering
Powers, E. J., Jr, Electrical and Computer Engineering
Ralls, K. M., Mechanical Engineering
Rase, H. F., Chemical Engineering
Rochelle, G. T., Chemical Engineering
Roesset, J. M., Civil Engineering
Roth, C. H., Jr, Electrical and Computer Engineering
Runge, T. M., Biomedical Engineering
Rylander, H. G., III, Electrical and Computer Engineering
Sanchez, I. C., Chemical Engineering
Sanchez, J. M., Mechanical Engineering
Sandberg, I. W., Electrical and Computer Engineering
Schapery, R. A., Aerospace Engineering
Schmidt, P. S., Mechanical Engineering
Schutz, B. E., Aerospace Engineering
Sepehrnoori, K., Petroleum and Geosystems Engineering
Sharma, M. M., Petroleum and Geosystems Engineering
Smith, H. W., Electrical and Computer Engineering
Stearman, R. O., Aerospace Engineering
Steinfink, H., Chemical Engineering
Stern, M., Aerospace Engineering
Stokoe, K. H., II, Civil Engineering
Swartzlander, E. E., Jr, Electrical and Computer Engineering
Tapley, B. D., Aerospace Engineering
Tasch, A. F., Jr, Electrical and Computer Engineering
Tassoulas, J. L., Civil Engineering
Tesar, D., Mechanical Engineering
Thurston, G. B., Mechanical Engineering
Trachtenberg, I., Chemical Engineering
Tucker, R. L., Civil Engineering
Valvano, J. W., Electrical and Computer Engineering
Vanrensburg, W. C. J., Petroleum and Geosystems Engineering
Varghese, P. L., Aerospace Engineering
Vliet, G. C., Mechanical Engineering
Wagner, T. J., Electrical and Computer Engineering
Walser, R. M., Electrical and Computer Engineering
Walton, C. M., Civil Engineering
Wehring, B. W., Mechanical Engineering
Welch, A. J., Electrical and Computer Engineering
Weldon, W. F., Electrical and Computer Engineering
Westkaemper, J. C., Aerospace Engineering
Wheeler, M. F., Aerospace Engineering
Willson, C. G., Chemical Engineering
Wise, G. L., Electrical and Computer Engineering
Womack, B. F., Electrical and Computer Engineering
Wright, S. G., Civil Engineering
Yura, J. A., Civil Engineering

College of Fine Arts:

Allen, G. D., Music
Antokeletz, E. M., Music
Baltzer, R. A., Music
Barnitz, J. E., Art and Art History
Barrington, G. H., Music
Barrington, W. R., Music
Behague, G. H., Music
Bloom, M., Theatre and Dance
Brockett, O. G., Theatre and Dance
Brokaw, J. W., Theatre and Dance
Brooks, R. L., Art and Art History
Clarke, J. R., Art and Art History
Cohen, D. M., Theatre and Dance
Coles, T. R., Art and Art History
Crisara, R. D., Music
Crutcher, R. A., Music
Daly, S. J., Art and Art History
Deatherage, M. M., Music
Desimone, R. A., Music
Dietz, H.-B., Music
Duke, R. A., Music
Erlmann, V. F., Music
Frock, G. A., Music
Garrett, N. B., Music
Geringer, J. M., Music
Gonzo, C. L., Music
Grantham, D. J., Music
Green, D. M., Music
Grieder, T., Art and Art History
Guerra, L. A., Music
Hale, K. J., Art and Art History
Henderson, L. D., Art and Art History
Hilley, M. F., Music
Isackes, R. M., Theatre and Dance
Jellison, J. A., Music
Jennings, C. A., Theatre and Dance
Junkin, J. F., Music
Knaub, D. L., Music
Kostka, S. M., Music
Lauhakaikul, T., Art and Art History
Lawn, R. J., Music
McCreless, P. P., Music
Mariani, V. A., Art and Art History
Martin, D. J., Music
Milliken, G., Art and Art History
Nancarrow, D. A., Theatre and Dance
Olefsky, P., Music
Peacock, G. B., Theatre and Dance
Pittel, H. C., Music
Preyer, B. I., Art and Art History
Race, W. C., Music
Richter, G. A., Music
Saul, P. A., Art and Art History
Schmandt-Besserat, D., Art and Art History
Shiff, R. A., Art and Art History
Smith, J. C., Art and Art History
Tsu, S., Theatre and Dance
Tusa, M. C., Music
Vasquez, S. V., Theatre and Dance
Welcher, D. E., Music
Wiley, D. C., Music
Wiman, L. R., Art and Art History
Young, P. C., Music
Zeder, S. L., Theatre and Dance

College of Pharmacy:

Abell, C. W.
Combs, A. B.
Crismon, M. L.
Davis, P. J.
Delgado, J. N.
Ereshefsky, L.
Erickson, C. K.
Hurley, L. H.
Kehrer, J. P.
Koeller, J. M.
Kuhn, J. G.
Lau, S. S.
Leslie, S. W.
Littlefield, L. C.
McGinity, J. W.
Monks, T. J.
Pearlman, R.
Rascati, K. L.
Shepherd, M. D.
Stavchansky, S. A.
Talbert, R. L., Jr
Wilcox, R. E.

School of Law:

Anderson, D. A.
Baade, H. W.
Baker, L. A.
Blais, L. E.
Bobbitt, P. C.
Carson, L. C., II
Churgin, M. J.
Dawson, R. O.
Dix, G. E.
Dodge, J. M., II
Dzienkowski, J. S.
Estlund, C. L.
Evans, T. L.
Forbath, W. E.
Gergen, M. P.
Getman, J. G.
Gibson, W. W., Jr
Goode, S. J.
Graglia, L. A.
Hamilton, R. W.
Hazel, J. P.
Hu, H. T. C.
Issacharoff, S.
Johanson, S. M.
Johnson, C. H.
Laycock, H. D.
Leiter, B. R.
Levinson, S. V.
McGarity, T. O.
Markovits, I.
Markovits, R. S.
Mullenix, L. S.
Powe, L. A., Jr
Powers, W. C., Jr
Rabban, D. M.
Ratliff, J. T., Jr
Ratner, S. R.
Rau, A. S.
Robertson, D. W.
Robertson, J. A.
Russell, T. D.
Sampson, J. J.
Silver, C. M.
Smith, E. E.
Steiker, J. M.
Sturley, M. F.
Sutton, J. F., Jr
Tigar, M. E.
Torres, G.
Treece, J. M.
Weinberg, L.
Weintraub, R. J.
Wellborn, O. G.
Westbrook, J. L.
Wiseman, Z. B.
Wright, C. A.

Graduate School of Library and Information Science:

Davis, D. G., Jr
Gracy, D. B., II
Hallmark, J.
Immroth, B. F.
Lukenbill, W. B.
Miksa, F. L.
Sheldon, B. E.
Wyllys, R. E.

School of Architecture:

Alofsin, A.
Arumi, F. N.
Atkinson, S. D.
Benedikt, M. L.
Black, J. S.
Box, J. H.
Coote, R. J.
Dodge, R. L., Jr
Kahn, T. D.
Leiding, G.
Mugerauer, R. W., Jr
Swallow, R. P.
Tatum, L. E.

School of Social Work:

Austin, D. M.

BOUNOUS, R. C.
DINITTO, D. M.
HEFFERNAN, W. J., Jr
LAUDERDALE, M. L.
MCROY, R. G.
RUBIN, A.
SCHWAB, A. J., Jr
SHORKEY, C. T.

LBJ School of Public Affairs:
BOSKE, L. B.
EATON, D. J.
GALBRAITH, J. K.
HAMILTON, D. S.
MARSHALL, F. R.
RHODES, L.
SCHMANDT, J.
SCHOTT, R. L.
SHERMAN, M.
TOLO, K. W.
WARNER, D. C.
WILSON, R. H.

School of Nursing:
BROWN, S. A.
GROBE, S. J.
HALL, B. A.
WALKER, L. O.

ATTACHED RESEARCH ORGANIZATIONS

Academic Computing and Instructional Technology Services: Dir THOMAS F. EDGAR
Institute for Advanced Technology: Dir HARRY D. FAIR
Animal Resources Center: Dir JERRY FINEG
Applied Research Laboratories: Dir MICHAEL PESTORIUS
Bureau of Economic Geology: Dir NOEL TYLER
Center for Electromechanics: Dir JOHN H. GULLY
Harry Huntt Ransom Humanities Research Center: Dir THOMAS F. STALEY
IC[2] Institute: Dir GEORGE KOZMETSKY (interim)
Institute for Technology and Learning: Dir JOHN M. SLATIN
Urban Issues Program: Dir ROBERT H. WILSON

ATTACHED TO THE COLLEGE OF COMMUNICATION

Center for Research on Communication Technology and Society: Dir FREDERICK WILLIAMS

ATTACHED TO THE COLLEGE OF BUSINESS ADMINISTRATION

C. Aubrey Smith Center for Auditing Education and Research: Dir WILLIAM R. KINNEY
Bureau of Business Research: Dir RAJ SRIVASTAVA
Center for Business Decision Analysis: Dir TIMOTHY W. RUEFLI
Center for Computational Finance: Dir Dr PATRICK JAILLET (Center is attached also to College of Engineering and College of Natural Sciences)
Center for Legal and Regulatory Studies: Dir JOHN ALLISON
Center for Management of Operations and Logistics: Dir GANG YU
Manufacturing Systems Center: Dir GEORGE KOZMETSKY (interim)
Center for Research in Electronic Commerce: Dir ANDREW WHINSTON
Center for International Business Education and Research: Dir ROBERT T. GREEN
Center for Organizations Research: Dir JANICE M. BEYER

ATTACHED TO THE COLLEGE OF ENGINEERING

Center for Aeromechanics Research: Dir JEFFREY K. BENNIGHOF
Computer Engineering Research Center: Dir JACOB A. ABRAHAM
Construction Industry Institute: Dir RICHARD L. TUCKER
Electrical Engineering Research Laboratory: Dir DEAN P. NEIKIRK
Centre for Electromechanics: Dir STEVEN P. NICHOLS (acting)
Electronics Research Center: Dir EDWARD J. POWERS
Center for Energy Studies: Dir STEVEN P. NICHOLS
Bureau of Engineering Research: Dir BEN G. STREETMAN
Geotechnical Engineering Center: Dir STEPHEN G. WRIGHT
Center for Materials Science and Engineering: Dir DONALD R. PAUL
Center for Mechanics of Solids, Structures and Materials: Dir STELIOS KYRIAKIDES
Microelectronics Research Center: Dir JOE C. CAMPBELL (interim)
Offshore Technology Research Center: Dir JOSE M. ROESSET
Center for Petroleum and Geosystems Engineering: Dir GARY A. POPE
Phil M. Ferguson Structural Engineering Laboratory: Dir RICHARD E. KLINGNER
Center for Space Research: Dir BYRON D. TAPLEY
Texas Institute for Computational and Applied Mathematics: Dir J. T. ODEN (Institute is attached jointly to College of Natural Sciences)
Center for Research in Water Resources: Dir DAVID MAIDMENT

ATTACHED TO THE COLLEGE OF NATURAL SCIENCES

Artificial Intelligence Laboratory: Dir GORDON S. NOVAK
Institute for Biomedical Research: Dir RICHARD WILLIS (acting)
Center for Biotechnology: Dir G. BARRIE KITTO
Brackenridge Field Laboratory: Dir LAWRENCE E. GILBERT
Cell Research Institute: Dir DENNIS T. BROWN
Biochemical Institute: Dir MARVIN L. HACKERT
Culture Collection of Algae: Dir RICHARD C. STARR
Center for Developmental Biology: Dir GARY L. FREEMAN
Laboratory of Electrochemistry: Dir ALLEN J. BARD
Fusion Research Center: Dir ALAN J. WOOTTON
Institute for Fusion Studies: Dir RICHARD D. HAZELTINE
Genetics Institute: Dir H. ELDON SUTTON
Institute for Geophysics: Dir PAUL STOFFA
Center for Materials Chemistry: Dir JOHN M. WHITE
Institute for Cellular and Molecular Biology: Dir ALAN LAMBOWITZ
Marine Science Institute: Dir WAYNE S. GARDNER
McDonald Observatory: Dir FRANK N. BASH
Center for Nonlinear Dynamics: Dir HARRY L. SWINNEY
Center for Numerical Analysis: Dir DAVID M. YOUNG
Center for Particle Physics: Dir ROY F. SCHWITTERS
Plant Resources Center: Dir B. L. TURNER
Ilya Prigogine Center for Studies in Statistical Mechanics and Complex Systems: Dir ILYA PRIGOGINE
Center for Relativity: Dir RICHARD A. MATZNER
Center for Statistical Sciences: Co-Dirs PETER W. M. JOHN, THOMAS W. SAGER
Center for Structural Biology: Dir JON ROBERTUS
Institute of Reproductive Biology: Dir FRANK H. BRONSON
Research Institute – Weinberg Theory Group: Dir STEVEN WEINBERG
Center for Synthesis, Growth and Analysis of Electronic Materials: Dir JOHN M. WHITE
Institute for Theoretical Chemistry: Dir ROBERT E. WYATT
Vertebrate Paleontology and Radiocarbon Laboratory: Dir ERNEST L. LUNDELIUS
Charles A. Dana Center for Science and Mathematics Education: Dir P. URI TREISMAN

ATTACHED TO THE COLLEGE OF PHARMACY

Drug Dynamics Institute: Dir JAMES W. MCGINITY
Institute for Neuroscience: Dir CREED W. ABELL

ATTACHED TO THE COLLEGE OF FINE ARTS

Center for Advanced Studies in the Arts: Dir RICHARD J. LAWN

ATTACHED TO THE COLLEGE OF LIBERAL ARTS

Institute for Classical Archaeology: Dir JOSEPH C. CARTER
Center for Applied Research in Economics: Dir DANIEL HAMERMESH
Center for Criminology and Criminal Justice Research: Dir WILLIAM R. KELLY
Center for Deliberative Polling: Dir JAMES S. FISHKIN
Institute of Human Development and Family Studies: Dir GEORGE W. HOLDEN
Institute of Latin American Studies: Dir NICOLAS SHUMWAY (interim)
Linguistics Research Center: Dir WINFRED P. LEHMANN
Population Research Center: Dir FRANK BEAN
Texas Archaeological Research Laboratory: Dir THOMAS R. HESTER
Center for Studies in Texas History: Dir RON C. TYLER
Center for Vision and Image Sciences: Dir WILSON S. GEISLER

ATTACHED TO THE LBJ SCHOOL OF PUBLIC AFFAIRS

Center for the Study of Human Resources: Dir CHRISTOPHER T. KING
Policy Research Institute: Dir EDWIN DORN

ATTACHED TO THE SCHOOL OF SOCIAL WORK

Center for Social Work Research: Dir RUTH G. MCCOY

University of Texas at Arlington

POB 19125, Arlington, TX 76019
Telephone: (817) 272-2101

Founded 1895 Arlington College, reorganized as a component of the University of Texas 1965

President: Dr ROBERT E. WITT
Provost: Dr GEORGE C. WRIGHT
Senior Vice-President for Finance and Administration: M. DAN WILLIAMS
Vice-President for Undergraduate Academic and Student Affairs: Dr MARY RIDGWAY
Vice-President for Student Enrollment Services: SHIRLEY BINDER
Vice-President for Development: ANNE ABBE
Librarian: THOMAS WILDING

Library of 1,000,000 vols
Number of teachers: 997
Number of students: 21,200

DEANS

Liberal Arts: Dr RUTH GROSS (acting)
Science: Dr VERNE COX (acting)
Business: Dr DAN WORRELL (acting)
Engineering: Dr RON BAILEY
Science: Dr NEAL SMATRESK
Graduate School: Dr DALE ANDERSON
School of Social Work: Dr SANTOS HERNANDEZ
Architecture: EDWARD BAUM
Nursing: Dr ELIZABETH POSTER
School of Urban and Public Affairs: Dr RICHARD L. COLE
Center for Professional Teacher Education: Dr JEANNE GERLACH

University of Texas at Dallas

Box 830688, Richardson, TX 75083-0688
Telephone: (972) 883-2111
Fax: (972) 883-2237

Founded 1969; formerly Southwest Center for Advanced Studies

Academic year: September to August

President: Dr FRANKLYN G. JENIFER
Provost and Vice-President for Academic Affairs: Dr B. HOBSON WILDENTHAL
Vice-Provost: Dr PRISCILLA BEADLE
Vice-President for Business Affairs: ROBERT L. LOVITT
Vice-President for Student Affairs: Dr MARY SIAS
Director of Budget: CHERYL O'STEEN
Director of Enrollment Services: BARRY SAMSULA
Director of Admissions and Records: JEAN STUART
Director of Libraries: Dr EDWARD WALTERS

Library of 545,000 vols
Number of teachers: 294
Number of students: 9,378

Publications: *Common Knowledge, Issues in Science and Technology.*

DEANS

Graduate Studies: Dr AUSTIN CUNNINGHAM
Undergraduate Studies: Dr S. MICHAEL COLEMAN
School of Arts & Humanities: Dr DENNIS M. KRATZ
School of General Studies: Dr GEORGE FAIR
School of Human Development: Dr BERT MOORE
School of Management: Dr HASAN PIRKUL
School of Natural Sciences & Mathematics: Dr RICHARD CALDWELL
School of Social Sciences: Dr RITA MAE KELLY
Erik Jonsson School of Engineering and Computer Science: Dr WILLIAM OSBORNE

PROGRAM HEADS

(Graduate Programs except where indicated)

American Studies (Undergraduate): Dr DACHANG CONG
Biology: Dr RON YASBIN
Chemistry: Dr JOHN FERRARIS
Communication Disorders: Dr ROBERT D. STILLMAN
Computer Science: Dr IVOR PAGE
Geosciences: Dr KENT NIELSEN
Applied Cognition and Neuroscience: Dr W. JAY DOWLING
Humanities: Dr GERALD SOLIDAY
Interdisciplinary Studies: Dr GEORGE FAIR
International Management Studies: Dr STEPHEN E. GUISINGER
Management and Administrative Sciences: FRANK BASS
Mathematical Sciences: Dr JOHN WIORKOWSKI
Physics: Dr JOHN H. HOFFMAN
Political Economy: Dr ANTHONY CHAMPAGNE
Science/Mathematics Education: Dr FRED FIFER
Human Development and Early Childhood Disorders: Dr MIKE COLEMAN
Electrical Engineering: Dr WILLIAM FRENSLEY
Human Development and Communications Sciences: Dr ROBERT STILLMAN

DIRECTORS

Center for International Accounting Development: Dr ADOLPH ENTHOVEN
International Business Center: Dr STEPHEN E. GUISINGER
Center for Continuing Education: (vacant)
Center for Lithospheric Studies: Dr GEORGE McMECHAN
Center for Quantum Electronics and its Application: Dr CARL COLLINS
William B. Hanson Center for Space Sciences: Dr RODERICK HEELIS
Center for Translation Studies: Dr RAINER SCHULTE
Morris Hite Center for Product Development and Marketing Science: Dr FRANK BASS
Center for Engineering Mathematics: Dr LOUIS J. HUNT
Teacher Education Certification Officer: (vacant)
Center for Applied Optics: Dr CYRUS D. CANTRELL
Center for Research in Genetic Technology: Dr DONALD S. GRAY
Center for Teaching and Learning: Dr FREDERICK L. FIFER
Center for Communications and Learning: Dr GEORGE FAIR
Bruton Center for Development Studies: Dr BRIAN BERRY
Cecil and Ida Green Center for the Study of Science and Society: (vacant)

ATTACHED INSTITUTE

Callier Center for Communication Disorders: 1966 Inwood Rd, Dallas, TX 75235; Dir Dr ROSS ROESER.

University of Texas at El Paso

El Paso, TX 79968-0500
Telephone: (915) 747-5000

Founded 1913 as Texas School of Mines and Metallurgy; name changed to Texas Western College 1949; current name adopted 1967

President: Dr DIANA NATALICIO
Vice-President for Academic Affairs: Dr STEPHEN RITER
Vice-President for Finance and Administration: JUAN SANDOVAL
Director of Admissions: DIANA GUERRERO
Librarian: PATRICIA A. PHILLIPS (acting)

Library: see Libraries
Number of teachers: 819
Number of students: 15,176

Publications: *Southwest Journal of Business and Economics* (occasionally), *Nova* (monthly, Sept. to May), *Southwestern Studies* (occasionally), *The Prospector* (2 a week).

DEANS

Students: Dr WILLIAM SCHAFER
Education: Dr ARTURO PACHECO
Engineering: Dr ANDREW H. SWIFT
Liberal Arts: Dr HOWARD DAUDISTEL
Sciences: Dr THOMAS E. BRADY
Business Administration: Dr FRANK HOY
Graduate School: Dr CHARLES G. GROAT
Nursing: Dr PATRICIA CASTIGLIA

University of Texas Medical Branch at Galveston

301 University Blvd, Galveston, TX 77555
Telephone: (409) 761-1011

Founded 1891; formerly Medical Branch, Galveston

President: THOMAS N. JAMES
Executive Vice-President for Administration and Business Affairs: E. J. PEDERSON
Director of Library: EMIL FREY

Number of teachers: 873
Number of students: 1,692

DEANS

Medicine: GEORGE T. BRYAN
Graduate School of Biomedical Sciences: K. LEMONE YIELDING
School of Allied Health Sciences: JOHN G. BRUHN
School of Nursing: MARY V. FENTON

University of Texas Southwestern Medical Center at Dallas

5323 Harry Hines Blvd, Dallas, TX 75235
Telephone: (214) 648-3111
Fax: (214) 648-8690

Founded 1949; formerly Southwestern Medical School founded 1943

President: KERN WILDENTHAL
Executive Vice-President for Academic Affairs: WILLIAM B. NEAVES
Executive Vice-President for Business Affairs: PETER H. FITZGERALD
Executive Vice-President for Clinical Affairs: WILLIS C. MADDREY
Dean, Southwestern Medical School: ROBERT J. ALPERN
Dean, Graduate School of Biomedical Sciences: JOHN P. PERKINS
Dean, School of Allied Health Sciences: H. GORDON GREEN
Associate Dean for Student Affairs: BARBARA WALLER
Associate Dean for Academic Affairs: Dr JAMES GRIFFIN
Associate Vice-President of Student Services: J. WESLEY NORRED
Librarian: MARTY ADAMSON

Number of teachers: 1,149
Number of students: 800 medical, 499 graduate, 397 allied health

Publications: *Southwestern Magazine* (annually), *Newsletter* (monthly).

University of Texas Health Science Center at San Antonio

7703 Floyd Curl Drive, San Antonio, TX 78284
Telephone: (210) 567-7000

Founded 1959 as South Texas Medical School, a part of The University of Texas System, name changed to University of Texas Medical School at San Antonio 1967, present name 1972

President: Dr JOHN P. HOWE, III
Executive Vice-President for Administration and Business Affairs: ROBERT B. PRICE
Vice-President for University Relations: JUDY P. WOLF
Vice-President for Academic Services: Dr JOHN A. THOMAS
Executive Assistant to the President: MARY G. ETTLINGER
President and Chief Executive Officer, University Health System: JOHN A. GUEST
Director of Student Services: (vacant)

Library of 192,576 vols

DEANS

Medical School: Dr JAMES J. YOUNG
Dental School: KENNETH L. KALKWARF
Graduate School of Biomedical Sciences: Dr SANFORD A. MILLER
School of Allied Health Sciences: Dr JAMES G. VAN STRATEN
School of Nursing: Dr PATTY L. HAWKEN

University of Texas Health Science Center at Houston School of Public Health

POB 20186, Houston, TX 77225
Telephone: (713) 792-4315

Founded 1967

President: Dr M. DAVID LOW

Number of teachers: 113
Number of students: 700

University of Texas of the Permian Basin

Odessa, TX 79762
Telephone: (915) 552-2000

Founded 1969

President: CHARLES A. SORBER

Library of 763,000 vols
Number of students: 2,217

DEANS

College of Arts and Sciences: Dr JAMES OLSON
School of Education: Dr PETE IENATSCH
School of Business: Dr GARY KLEIN

UNIVERSITY OF THE INCARNATE WORD

4301 Broadway, San Antonio, TX 78209
Telephone: (210) 829-6000
Chartered 1881
Chancellor: Sister MARGARET PATRICE SLATTERY
President: Dr LOUIS J. AGNESE, Jr
Registrar: BOBBYE G. FRY
Librarian: MENDELL MORGAN, Jr
Library of 177,000 vols
Number of teachers: 268
Number of students: 3,287

WAYLAND BAPTIST UNIVERSITY

Plainview, TX 79072
Telephone: (806) 296-5521
Founded 1906, chartered 1908
President: Dr WALLACE E. DAVIS
Vice-President for Institutional Advancement: (vacant)
Vice-President for Academic and Student Services: Dr BILL HARDAGE
Vice-President for Finance and Administrative Services: ERNIE CLARK
Chief Financial Officer: ERNESTINE CLARK
Registrar: JUDY WILLIAMS
Librarian: POLLY LACKEY
Library of 149,000 vols
Number of teachers: 79
Number of students: 4,190
Publications: *The Trail Blazer* (newspaper, every 2 weeks), *The Traveler* (yearbook, annually), *Footprints* (quarterly).

WILEY COLLEGE

Marshall, TX 75670
Telephone: (903) 927-3300
Fax: (903) 938-8100
Founded 1873
President: Dr JULIUS S. SCOTT, Jr
Dean of Faculty: Dr JOSEPH W. CAPERS
Executive Assistant to President: LORETTA J. THOMPSON MARTIN
Dean for Student Affairs: ABBIE STALLWORTH
Librarian: FRANK FRANCIS
Library of 85,000 vols
Number of teachers: 58
Number of students: 647

DIVISION CHAIRS

Chair of Natural and Computational Sciences: Dr JOHN STUART
Chair of Education: Dr WILLIE BARNES
Chair of Social and Behavioural Sciences: Dr LLOYD THOMPSON
Chair of Humanities: Dr T. BERNARD CLAYTON

UTAH

BRIGHAM YOUNG UNIVERSITY

Provo, UT 84602
Telephone: (801) 378-4636
Fax: (801) 378-5972
Founded 1875 by President Brigham Young of the Church of Jesus Christ of Latter-day Saints
President: MERRILL J. BATEMAN
Academic Vice-President: ALAN L. WILKINS
Administrative Vice-President: BRAD W. FARNSWORTH
Student Life Vice-President: ALTON L. WADE
Advancement Vice-President: R. J. SNOW
General Counsel: EUGENE H. BRAMHALL
Dean of Admissions and Records: ERLEND D. PETERSON
Director of Libraries: STERLING J. ALBRECHT
Library of over 2 million volumes, pamphlets and bulletins
Number of teachers: 1,381 full-time, 321 part-time; does not include graduate assistants
Number of students: 30,465

DEANS

School of Law: H. REESE HANSEN
College of Biology and Agriculture: CLAYTON S. HUBER
School of Management: K. FRED SKOUSEN
School of Education: ROBERT S. PATTERSON
College of Family, Home and Social Sciences: CLAYNE L. POPE
College of Fine Arts and Communications: BRUCE L. CHRISTENSEN
College of Humanities: VAN C. GESSEL
College of Engineering and Technology: DOUGLAS M. CHABRIES
College of Nursing: SANDRA ROGERS
College of Physical and Mathematical Sciences: BILL R. HAYS
College of Health and Human Performance: ROBERT CONLEE
Honors and General Education: PAUL A. COX
Graduate Studies: ADDIE FUHRIMAN
Religious Education: ROBERT L. MILLET
Student Life: JANET S. SCHARMAN
Continuing Education: RICHARD C. EDDY

UNIVERSITY OF UTAH

Salt Lake City, UT 84112
Telephone: (801) 581-7200
Telex: 3789459
Fax: (801) 581-3007
Incorporated 1850 as University of Deseret; chartered 1892 as University of Utah
Academic year: September to June
President: JERILYN S. MCINTYRE (acting)
Vice-Presidents: DAVID W. PERSHING (acting) (Academic Affairs), JOHN M. MATSEN (Health Sciences), RICHARD K. KOEHN (Research), THOMAS G. NYCUM (Administrative Services), TED R. CAPENER (University Relations), J. MICHAEL MATTSSON (Development), RICHARD G. WEIGEL, (Student Affairs, acting)
General Counsel: JOHN K. MORRIS
Registrar: RALPH O. BOREN
Librarian: SARAH C. MICHALAK
Number of teachers: 3,702
Number of students: 26,359
Publications: *Utah Law Review* (quarterly), *Western Humanities* (quarterly), *Western Political Quarterly*.

DEANS

Architecture: WILLIAM C. MILLER
Business: JOHN W. SEYBOLT
Education: COLLEEN KENNEDY
Engineering: K. LARRY DEVRIES (acting)
Fine Arts: PHYLLIS A. HASKELL
Health: JOHN M. DUNN
Humanities: PATRICIA L. HANNA
Law: LEE E. TEITELBAUM
Medicine: PETER HEILBRUN (acting)
Mines & Mineral Industries: FRANCIS H. BROWN
Nursing: LINDA K. AMOS
Pharmacy: JOHN W. MAUGER
Science: BENNY RUSHING
Social & Behavioral Science: DONNA M. GELFAND
Social Work: KAY L. DEA
Graduate School: ANN W. HART
Liberal Education: JOHN G. FRANCIS
Continuing Education: CLIFFORD J. DREW

CHAIRMEN OF DEPARTMENTS

Business:
- Accounting: LEROY FAERBER
- Finance: CALVIN M. BOARDMAN
- Management: BILL HESTERLY
- Marketing: TERESA M. PAVIA

Education:
- Educational Administration: D. J. SPERRY
- Educational Psychology: W. R. JENSON
- Educational Studies: R. E. REYNOLDS
- Special Education: JOHN MCDONNELL

Engineering:
- Bioengineering: RICHARD NORMANN
- Chemical Engineering: TERRY RING
- Civil Engineering: LAWRENCE REAVELEY
- Computer Science: THOMAS C. HENDERSON
- Electrical Engineering: OM P. GANDHI
- Materials Science and Engineering: GERALD STRINGFELLOW
- Mechanical Engineering: ROBERT B. ROEMER

Fine Arts:
- Art: NATHAN B. WINTERS
- Ballet: B. J. HAMBLIN
- Modern Dance: SCOTT MARSH
- Music: E. J. THOMPSON
- Theatre: WILLIAM C. SISKA

Health:
- Communication Disorders: MARY LOU WILLBRAND
- Exercise and Sport Science: S. K. BEVERIDGE
- Foods and Nutrition: WAYNE ASKEW
- Health Education: I. R. GROSSHANS
- Parks, Recreation and Tourism: GARY ELLIS (acting)
- Physical Therapy: CAROLEE MONCUR, SCOTT WARD

Humanities:
- Communication: CONNIE BULLIS
- English: R. STEPHEN TATUM
- History: RAY GUNN
- Languages and Literature: CAROLYN MORROW
- Philosophy: DON GARRETT

Medicine:
- Anatomy: THOMAS N. PARKS
- Anaesthesiology: K. C. WONG
- Biochemistry: D. CARROLL, M. C. RECHSTEINER
- Cellular, Viral and Molecular Biology: RAY WHITE
- Family and Preventive Medicine: MICHAEL MAGILL
- Human Genetics: R. L. WHITE
- Internal Medicine: MERLE A. SANDE
- Medical Informatics: REED M. GARDNER
- Neurology: J. R. BARINGER
- Neurosurgery: RONALD APFELBAUM
- Obstetrics and Gynaecology: ELI Y. ADASHI
- Ophthalmology: R. J. OLSON
- Pathology: CARL KJELDSBERG
- Paediatrics: EDWARD B. CLARK
- Physical Medicine and Rehabilitation Division: JAMES R. SWENSON
- Pharmacology: J. W. GIBB
- Physiology: SALVADOR FIDONE
- Psychiatry: B. I. GROSSER
- Radiation Oncology: FREDERIC A. GIBBS
- Radiology: B. J. MANASTER (acting)
- Surgery: EDWARD W. NELSON

Mines and Earth Sciences:
- Fuels Engineering: TERRY RING
- Geology and Geophysics: JOHN M. BARTLEY
- Metallurgy and Metallurgical Engineering: J. G. BYRNE
- Meteorology: KUO-NAN LIOU
- Mining Engineering: M. K. MCCARTER

Pharmacy:
- Medicinal Chemistry: GLENN D. PRESTWICH
- Pharmaceutics and Pharmaceutical Chemistry: W. I. HIGUCHI
- Pharmacology and Toxicology: J. W. GIBB

Pharmacy Practice: GARY M. ODERDA

Science:

Biology: SANDY PARKINSON (acting)
Chemistry: C. DALE POULTER
Mathematics: JAMES A. CARLSON
Physics: P. C. TAYLOR

Social and Behavioural Science:

Aerospace Studies: PATRICK J. COLLSON
Anthropology: KRISTEN HAWKES
Economics: E. K. HUNT
Family and Consumer Studies: CATHLEEN ZICK
Geography: ROGER M. MCCOY
Military Science: JEFFREY H. NEWEY
Naval Science: DONALD C. BROWN
Political Science: SUSAN OLSON
Psychology: TIMOTHY W. SMITH
Sociology: LEE BEAN

UTAH STATE UNIVERSITY

Logan, UT 84322

Telephone: (435) 797-1000

Chartered 1888

Academic year: September to June (and Summer Session)

President: GEORGE H. EMERT
Provost: G. JAY GOGUE
Vice-President, Research: PETER F. GERITY
Vice-President, Administrative Affairs: LYNNE E. JANES (interim)
Vice-President, Extension and Continuing Education: ROBERT L. GILLILAND
Vice-President, Student Services: PATRICIA S. TERRELL
Vice-President, University Relations: PAUL M. NORTON

Number of teachers: 787
Number of students: 21,234

Publications: *Outlook* (every 2 months), *Outreach* (monthly), *Utah Science* (quarterly), *Western Historical Quarterly, Western American Literary Journal* (quarterly).

DEANS

School of Graduate Studies: JAMES P. SHAVER
College of Agriculture: RODNEY J. BROWN
College of Business: DAVID B. STEPHENS
College of Education: GERALD R. GIORDANO
College of Engineering: A. BRUCE BISHOP
College of Family Life: BONITA W. WYSE
College of Humanities, Arts and Social Sciences: STAN L. ALBRECHT
College of Natural Resources: FRANK E. BUSBY
College of Science: JAMES A. MACMAHON
Learning Resources Program: BYRON R. BURNHAM (acting)
University Extension: ROBERT L. GILLILAND

HEADS OF DEPARTMENTS

College of Agriculture:

Nutrition and Food Sciences: ANN W. SORENSON
Animal, Dairy and Veterinary Science: ROBERT C. LAMB
Agricultural Systems, Technology and Education: GARY S. STRAQUADINE
Plants, Soils and Biometeorology: V. PHILIP RASMUSSEN
Biotechnology Center: WILLIAM H. SCOUTEN

College of Business:

Business Information Systems and Education: LLOYD W. BARTHOLOME
Business Administration: PHILIP R. SWENSEN
Economics: HERBERT H. FULLERTON (acting)
Accounting: CLIFFORD R. SKOUSEN
Management/Human Resources: JOHN R. CRAGUN

College of Education:

Elementary Education: JAY A. MONSON
Communicative Disorders and Deaf Education: THOMAS S. JOHNSON
Special Education and Rehabilitation: CHARLES L. SALZBERG
Secondary Education: WILLIAM S. STRONG
Instructional Technology: DON C. SMELLIE
Health, Physical Education and Recreation: ARTHUR R. JONES
Psychology: DAVID M. STEIN

College of Engineering:

Electrical and Computer Engineering: RICHARD W. HARRIS
Civil and Environmental Engineering: LOREN R. ANDERSON
Biological and Irrigation Engineering: WYNN R. WALKER
Industrial Technology and Education: MAURICE G. THOMAS
Mechanical and Aerospace Engineering: JOSEPH C. BATTY
Utah Water Research Laboratory: RONALD C. SIMS

College of Family Life:

Family and Human Development: BRENT C. MILLER
Human Environments: JOAN R. MCFADDEN

College of Humanities, Arts and Social Sciences:

Music: NICHOLAS MORRISON (acting)
Theatre Arts: COLIN JOHNSON
Art: CRAIG S. LAW
Landscape Architecture and Environmental Planning: RICHARD E. TOTH
Political Science: RANDY T. SIMMONS
English: JEFFREY SMITTEN
Sociology, Social Work and Anthropology: GARY H. KIGER
Communication: EDWARD C. PEASE
History: NORMAN L. JONES
Languages and Philosophy: DIANE MICHELFELDER

College of Natural Resources:

Forest Resources: TERRY L. SHARIK
Rangeland Resources: JOHN C. MALECHEK
Fisheries and Wildlife: CHRIS LUECKE (acting)
Ecology Center: FREDERICK H. WAGNER
Geography and Earth Resources: TED J. ALSOP (acting)

College of Science:

Physics: W. JOHN RAITT
Mathematics and Statistics: JERRY RIDENHOUR
Geology: DONALD W. FIESINGER
Computer Science: DONALD H. COOLEY
Biology: EDMUND D. BRODIE, Jr
Chemistry and Biochemistry: VERNON PARKER

WEBER STATE UNIVERSITY

Ogden, UT 84408

Telephone: (801) 626-6000
Fax: (801) 626-7922

Founded 1889

Liberal arts, vocational, technical 4-year university

President: Dr PAUL H. THOMPSON
Registrar: Dr WINSLOW L. HURST
Director of Library: JOAN G. HUBBARD

Library of 580,000 vols
Number of teachers: 442
Number of students: 14,000

Publications: *University Times, Annual Catalog*.

WESTMINSTER COLLEGE OF SALT LAKE CITY

1840 South 1300 East St, Salt Lake City, UT 84105

Telephone: (801) 484-7651
Fax: (801) 466-6916

Founded 1875

President: Dr PEGGY A. STOCK
Vice-President for Information Technology: Dr SHERYL PHILLIPS
Executive Vice-President and Treasurer: STEPHEN MORGAN
Vice-President for Institutional Advancement: JANET GLAESER
Vice-President for Student Development and Enrollment Planning: PHIL ALLETTO
Vice-President for Academic Affairs and Dean of the Faculty: Dr STEPHEN R. BAAR
Dean of Students: CAROLYN PERKINS
Librarian: CAROLYN PERKINS

Library of 84,000 vols
Number of teachers: 216
Number of students: 2,140

DEANS

School of Arts and Sciences: Dr RAY OWNBEY
School of Business: Dr JAMES SEIDELMAN
School of Education: Dr JANET DYNAK
School of Nursing and Health Sciences: Dr GRETCHEN MCNEELY

VERMONT

BENNINGTON COLLEGE

Bennington, VT 05201

Telephone: (802) 442-5401
Fax: (802) 442-6164
E-mail: admissions@bennington.edu

Chartered 1925

President: ELIZABETH COLEMAN
Dean of Admissions and the First Year: ELENA BACHRACH
Director of Financial Aid: MEG WOOLMINGTON
Dean of the College: ROBERT WALDMAN
Vice-President for Finance and Administration: LAWRENCE LEE
Director of Development: DAVID REES
Director of Student Affairs: DONNA BOURASSA
Librarian: ROBERT WALDMAN

Library of 108,000 vols
Number of teachers: 70
Number of students: 400

Publications: *Bennington, Silo, Ben Belitt Chapbooks in Literature*.

CASTLETON STATE COLLEGE

Castleton, VT 05735

Telephone: (802) 468-5611

Founded 1787

Liberal arts, career education

President: Dr MARTHA K. FARMER
Dean of the College: Dr JOSEPH T. MARK
Director of Admissions: VICTORIA ANGIS (interim)
Registrar: HOPE SWANSON
Librarian: PATRICK MAX

Library of 124,400 vols
Number of teachers: 92
Number of students: 1,840

GODDARD COLLEGE

Plainfield, VT 05667

Telephone: (802) 454-8311
Fax: (802) 454-8017

Founded 1938

President: BARBARA MOSSBERG
Registrar: HERVENA MARTIN
Librarian: CLARA BRUNS

Library of 72,000 vols
Number of teachers: 24 full-time, 8 part-time
Number of students: 500

JOHNSON STATE COLLEGE

Johnson, VT 05656

Telephone: (802) 635-2356
Fax: (802) 635-9745

Founded 1828
President: Dr ROBERT HAHN
Academic Dean: Dr VINCENT CROCKENBERG
Director of Graduate Programs: (vacant)
Registrar: JOHN LORD
Librarian: JOE FARARA

Library of 84,000 vols
Number of teachers: 68 full-time, 50 part-time
Number of students: 1,672

DIVISION CHAIRMEN

Humanities: GERALD ANDERSON
Mathematics: CHARLES EYLER
Education: ALICE WHITING
Fine and Performing Arts: RUSSELL LONGTIN
Behavioral Sciences: DAVID FINK
Environmental and Health Sciences: PETER KRAMER
English and Writing: ANDREA PERHAM
Business and Economics: EUGENIE WILLIAMS

LYNDON STATE COLLEGE

Lyndonville, VT 05851
Telephone: (802) 626-6200
Fax: (802) 626-9770

Founded 1911

College of the liberal arts and professional programs

President: Dr ROBERT A. BURNHAM
Dean of Administration: WAYNE T. HAMILTON
Dean of Students: KIRK A.MANNING
Dean of Academic Affairs: PAUL F. TERO
Director of Admissions: R. JOSEPH BELLAVANCE
Librarian: LAUREL STANLEY

Library of 102,520 vols, 588 periodicals
Number of teachers: 63 (full-time)
Number of students: 1,137

MARLBORO COLLEGE

Marlboro, VT 05344
Telephone: (802) 257-4333
Fax: (802) 257-4154

Founded 1946

President: PAUL J. LEBLANC
Dean of Faculty: JOHN HAYES
Dean of Students: AMY GRILLO ANGELL
Admissions Director: KATE HALLAS
Librarian: MOLLY BRENNAN

Library of 60,000 vols
Number of teachers: 36
Number of students: 275

MIDDLEBURY COLLEGE

Middlebury, VT 05753
Telephone: (802) 443-5000

Founded 1800

President: JOHN M. MCCARDELL, Jr
Executive Vice-President and Provost: RONALD D. LIEBOWITZ
Executive Vice-President and Treasurer: DAVID W. GINEVAN
Dean of Students: ANN CRAIG HANSON

Library of 791,000 vols
Number of teachers: 216 full-time, 27 part-time
Number of students: 2,176

NORWICH UNIVERSITY

Northfield, VT 05663
Telephone: (802) 485-2000
Fax: (802) 485-2580

Founded 1819

President: RICHARD W. SCHNEIDER
Provost and Dean of Faculty: JOSEPH BYRNE (acting)
Senior Vice-President: RICHARD S. HANSEN
Commandant of Cadets: CRAIG LIND
Vice-President and Dean of Vermont College: JACKSON KYTLE
Dean of Admissions: FRANK GRIFFIS
Head Librarian: PAUL HELLER

Library of 260,000 vols and microfilms; military history collection
Number of teachers: 142
Number of students: 2,619

ST MICHAEL'S COLLEGE

Colchester, VT 05439
Telephone: (802) 654-2000
Fax: (802) 655-4079

Founded 1904

President: Dr MARC A. VANDERHEYDEN
Vice-President Academic Affairs: Dr JOHN J. MCDONALD
Vice-President Administration and Business: JOHN T. GUTMAN
Vice-President Student Life: MICHAEL SAMARA
Vice-President Institutional Advancement: (vacant)
Vice-President for Admission and Enrollment Management: JERRY FLANAGAN
Dean of the College: Dr JOHN KENNEY
Dean of the Prevel School: Dr SUSAN KUNTZ
Dean of the School of International Studies: Dr BONNIE TANGALOS
Registrar: JOHN D. SHEEHEY
Librarian: PATRICIA SUOZZI

Library of 175,000 vols, 1,400 periodicals
Number of teachers: 141 full-time
Number of students: 2,689

TRINITY COLLEGE OF VERMONT

Colchester Ave, Burlington, VT 05401
Telephone: (802) 658-0337
Fax: (802) 658-5446

Founded 1925

President: Dr LORNA DUPHINEY EDMUNDSON
Registrar: ALICE ROULEAU
Academic Dean: BRUCE BERGLAND
Director of Admissions: DOROTHY WATSON
Director of Public Relations: KATHY O'DELL-THOMPSON

Library of 65,000 vols
Number of teachers: 49
Number of students: 1,500

UNIVERSITY OF VERMONT

Burlington, VT 05405
Telephone: (802) 656-3480
Fax: (802) 658-5446

Founded 1791

President: THOMAS P. SALMON
Provost and Senior Vice-President: GERALD P. FRANCIS (acting)
Registrar: C. C. HOWE
Librarian: REBECCA R. MARTIN

Library of 1,050,000 vols
Number of teachers: 985
Number of students: 11,338

Publication: *Annual Bulletin.*

DEANS

Graduate College: DELCIE DURHAM
College of Arts and Sciences: JOAN SMITH
College of Agriculture: LAWRENCE FORCIER
College of Engineering and Mathematics: ROBERT C. ARNS (acting)
School of Business Administration: MICHAEL SESNOWITZ
College of Medicine: JOHN W. FRYMOYER
School of Nursing: MARIE MCGRATH (acting)
School of Allied Health Sciences: LOUIS M. IZZO (acting)
College of Education and Social Services: JILL TARULE
School of Natural Resources: L. K. FORCIER

VIRGINIA

BRIDGEWATER COLLEGE

Bridgewater, VA 22812
Telephone: (540) 828-2501
Fax: (540) 828-5479
E-mail: admissions@bridgewater.edu

Founded 1880

Liberal arts courses

President: Dr PHILLIP C. STONE
Executive Assistant to the President, Director of Planning: Col. JAMES H. BENSON
Librarian: R. GREENAWALT

Library of 162,000 vols
Number of teachers: 64
Number of students: 1,007

COLLEGE OF WILLIAM AND MARY IN VIRGINIA

Williamsburg, VA 23187-8795
Telephone: (757) 253-4000

Founded 1693

President: TIMOTHY J. SULLIVAN
Provost: GILLIAN T. CELL
Vice-President for Management and Budget: SAMUEL E. JONES
Vice-President for Development: DENNIS SLON
Registrar: MONICA AUGUSTIN
Librarian: CONNIE K. MCCARTHY

Libraries of 1,343,000 vols
Number of teachers: 578 full-time, 135 part-time
Number of students: 7,571

Publications: *The William and Mary Quarterly, Law Review, Business Review.*

DEANS

Faculty of Arts and Sciences: P. GEOFFREY FEISS
Graduate Studies: FRANZ GROSS
School of Education: VIRGINIA MCLAUGHLIN
School of Marine Science: L. DONELSON WRIGHT
School of Business Administration: LAWRENCE PULLEY
Marshall-Wythe School of Law: W. TAYLOR REVELEY III
Students: W. S. SADLER

EASTERN MENNONITE UNIVERSITY

Harrisonburg, VA 22802-2462
Telephone: (540) 432-4000
Fax: (540) 432-4444

Founded 1917

Liberal arts college affiliated with the Mennonite Church, with programs in 50 subject areas; emphasis on international education

President: Dr JOSEPH L. LAPP
Director of Admissions: ELLEN B. MILLER
Registrar: DAVID A. DETROW
Librarian: BOYD T. REESE

Library of 148,000 vols
Number of teachers: 88
Number of students: 1,325

GEORGE MASON UNIVERSITY

4400 University Drive, Fairfax, VA 22030-4444
Telephone: (703) 993-1000

Founded 1957

President: Dr ALAN G. MERTEN
Senior Vice-President for Finance and Planning: MAURICE W. SCHERRENS
Vice-President for University Life: Dr KAREN ROSENBLUM
Provost: Dr DAVID L. POTTER

Library of 2,734,000 vols
Number of teachers: 765 full-time, 543 part-time
Number of students: 24,368

Publication: *Faculty Bibliography* (annually).

HAMPDEN-SYDNEY COLLEGE

Hampden-Sydney, VA 23943

Telephone: (804) 223-6000

Founded 1776

Men's college of the liberal arts and sciences

President: Samuel V. Wilson
Vice-President for Business Affairs: Norm Krueger
Dean of the Faculty: Lawrence H. Martin
Dean of Admissions: Anita H. Garland
Registrar: Florence C. Watson
Librarian: Sharon I. Goad

Library of 160,000 vols
Number of teachers: 100
Number of students: 960

HAMPTON UNIVERSITY

Hampton, VA 23668

Telephone: (804) 727-5000
Fax: (804) 727-5746

Founded 1868

President: Dr William R. Harvey
Executive Vice-President/Provost: Dr Demetrius D. Venable
Vice-President for Health: Dr Elnora D. Daniel
Vice-President for Business Affairs and Treasurer: Leon Scott
Vice-President for Development: Laron J. Clark
Dean of Students: Dr Rodney Smith
Director of Admissions: Leonard Jones
Registrar: Jorsene Cooper

Library of 331,727 vols
Number of students: 5,305

HOLLINS COLLEGE

Roanoke, VA 24020

Telephone: (540) 362-6000

Founded 1842

President: Janet R. Rasmussen
Vice-President for Academic Affairs: L. Wayne Markert
Director of Admissions: Stuart K. Trinkle
Director of Financial Aid: Rebecca Eckstein
Registrar: Nancy T. Hostetter
Librarian: Diane J. Graves

Library of 212,000 vols
Number of teachers: 90 (84 f.t.e.)
Number of students: 1,094; graduate students 236 (of total number)

Publications: *Alumnae Magazine*, *Hollins Critic*.

JAMES MADISON UNIVERSITY

Harrisonburg, VA 22807

Telephone: (703) 568-6211

Founded 1908, name changed from Madison College 1977

President: Dr Ronald E. Carrier
Executive Vice-President: Dr Linwood Rose
Vice-President for Academic Affairs: Dr Bethany Oberst
Vice-President for Student Affairs: Dr Robert Scott
University Librarian: Dennis Robison

Library of 507,000 vols
Number of teachers: 505 (full-time)
Number of students: 11,500

Schools of letters and sciences, integrated science, fine arts and communication, business, education and human services, nursing and graduate studies

LONGWOOD COLLEGE

Farmville, VA 23909-1899

Telephone: (804) 395-2000
Fax: (804) 395-2635

Founded 1839 as comprehensive college

President: Patricia P. Cormier
Vice-President for Academic Affairs: Norman Bregman
Vice-President for Business Affairs: Richard V. Hurley
Vice-President for Institutional Advancement: Bobbie Burton
Vice-President for Student Affairs: Phyllis L. Mable
Director of Public Relations: Dennis Sercombe
Associate Vice-President for Research and Information Systems: Richard Bratcher
Director of Financial Aid: Lisa Tumer
Registrar: Judy Vogt

Library of 288,175 vols
Number of teachers: 158 full-time, 90 adjunct
Number of students: 2,891 full-time, 343 part-time

HEADS OF DEPARTMENTS

Art: Randall Edmondson
Business & Economics: Berkwood Farmer
Education: David Smith
English, Philosophy & Foreign Languages: McRae Amoss
Health, Physical Education & Recreation: Bette L. Harris
History & Government: William Harbour
Library Science: Calvin Boyer
Mathematics & Computer Science: Robert Webber
Military Science: (vacant)
Music: Donald Trott
Natural Sciences: Carolyn Wells
Education, Special Education and Social Work: Frank Howe
Sociology & Anthropology: Douglas Dalton
Speech & Dramatic Arts: Gene Muto
Psychology: Linda Tennison

LYNCHBURG COLLEGE

1501 Lakeside Drive, Lynchburg, VA 24501-3199

Telephone: (804) 544-8100

Founded 1903

President: Dr Charles O. Warren, Jr
Registrar: Jay Webb
Vice-President for Enrollment Management: Dr David Behrs
Dean of the College: Dr Jacqueline W. Asbury
Librarian: Christopher Millson-Martula

Library of 243,300 vols
Number of teachers: 130
Number of students: 2,000

MARY BALDWIN COLLEGE

Staunton, VA 24401

Telephone: (540) 887-7000

Founded 1842

President: Cynthia H. Tyson
Dean: James Lott
Registrar: Lewis D. Askegaard
Librarian: Lisabeth Chabot

Library of 180,000 items
Number of teachers: 125
Number of students: 2,161

MARY WASHINGTON COLLEGE

1301 College Ave, Fredericksburg, VA 22401-5358

Telephone: (540) 654-1000
Fax: (540) 654-1073

Founded 1908

President: Dr William M. Anderson, Jr

Vice-President for Academic Affairs and Dean of the Faculty: Dr Philip L. Hall
Librarian: Leroy S. Strohl, III
Number of teachers: 177
Number of students: 3,700

OLD DOMINION UNIVERSITY

Norfolk, VA 23529

Telephone: (757) 683-3000
Fax: (757) 683-4505

Founded 1930 as a college

President: James V. Koch
Registrar: Carolyn S. Eakin
Assistant Vice-President for Enrollment Services: (vacant)
Librarian: Jean A. Major

Library of 2,065,000 items
Number of teachers: 632
Number of students: 17,077

PRESBYTERIAN SCHOOL OF CHRISTIAN EDUCATION

1205 Palmyra Ave, Richmond, VA 23227

Telephone: (804) 359-5031
Fax: (804) 254-8060

Founded 1914

President: Wayne G. Boulton
Registrar: Joan Daniel
Librarian: John Trotti

Library of 260,000 vols
Number of teachers: 14
Number of students: 139

RADFORD UNIVERSITY

Radford, VA 24142

Telephone: (540) 831-5000
Fax: (540) 831-6619

Founded 1910

President: Dr Douglas Covington
Vice-President for Academic Affairs: Ann S. Ferren
Vice-President for Student Affairs: Paul W. Harris
Vice-President for Business Affairs: David A. Burdette
Vice-President for University Advancement: Charles A. Wood

Library of 303,950 vols
Number of students: 8,500

RANDOLPH-MACON COLLEGE

POB 5005, Ashland, VA 23005-5505

Telephone: (804) 798-8372

Founded 1830

President: Dr Roger H. Martin
Registrar: Dr Marilyn J. Gibbs
Dean of Admissions: John C. Conkright
Librarian: Dr Dan T. Bedsole

Library of 160,000 vols
Number of teachers: 92 full-time
Number of students: 1,093

RANDOLPH-MACON WOMAN'S COLLEGE

Lynchburg, VA 24503

Telephone: (804) 947-8000
Fax: (804) 947-8138

Founded 1891

President: Kathleen Gill Bowman
Vice-President for Development, Admissions and Public Relations: James C. Kughn, Jr
Treasurer: William A. Burns
Librarian: Theodore J. Hostetler

Library of 150,000 vols
Number of teachers: 90
Number of students: 750

Publications: *Catalogue, Student's Handbook, Pictorial Bulletin, R-MWC Today, Randolph-Macon Alumnae Bulletin.*

ROANOKE COLLEGE

Salem, VA 24153

Telephone: (703) 375-2500

Founded 1842

President: DAVID M. GRING
Vice-President and Dean: KENNETH R. GARREN
Vice-President for Business Affairs: RICHARD C. HEMBERGER
Vice-President for Resource Development: JUDITH L. NELSON
Vice-President for Student Affairs: MCMILLAN JOHNSON
Vice-President for Admissions Services: MICHAEL C. MAXEY
Librarian: STANLEY F. UMBERGER

Library of 170,000 vols
Number of teachers: 150
Number of students: 1,700

SWEET BRIAR COLLEGE

Sweet Briar, VA 24595

Telephone: (804) 381-6142
Fax: (804) 381-6173
E-mail: admissions@sbc.edu

Chartered 1901
Liberal arts and sciences college

President: Dr ELISABETH S. MUHLENFELD
Vice-President for College Relations: MITCHELL L. MOORE
Dean: Dr GEORGE H. LENZ
Associate Dean of Academic Affairs: Dr ALIX S. INGBER
Dean of Co-Curricular Life: Dr VALDRIE N. WALKER
Director of Alumnae Affairs: LOUISE S. ZINGARO
Director of Admissions: NANCY E. CHURCH
Registrar: PAUL WILEY
Librarian: JOHN JAFFE

Library of 236,000 vols
Number of teachers: 67 full-time, 39 part-time
Number of students: 731

Publications: *Catalog* (annually), *Newsletter, Alumnae Magazine*.

UNIVERSITY OF RICHMOND

Richmond, VA 23173

Telephone: (804) 289-8000

Chartered as Richmond College 1830; as University of Richmond 1920

President: Dr RICHARD L. MORRILL
Chancellor: E. BRUCE HEILMAN
Vice-President for Business and Finance: L. W. MOELCHERT
Vice-President and Provost: ZEDDIE P. BOWEN
Vice-President for University Relations: H. G. QUIGG
Vice-President for Student Affairs: LEONARD S. GOLDBERG
Registrar: W. VON KLEIN
Librarian: (vacant)

Library of 421,000 vols
Number of teachers: 222 full-time, 179 part-time
Number of students: 3,270 full-time, 1,435 part-time

DEANS

Faculty of Arts and Sciences: F. SHELDON WETTACK
Richmond College (Men): R. A. MATEER
Westhampton College (Women): PATRICIA C. HARWOOD
Business Administration: T. L. REUSCHLING
Law: JOSEPH D. HARBAUGH
Graduate: JOHN L. GORDON, Jr
University College, Summer School, Continuing Education: M. C. GRAEBER

UNIVERSITY OF VIRGINIA

Charlottesville, VA 22903

Telephone: (804) 924-0311
Fax: (804) 924-0938

Founded by act of General Assembly of Virginia, 1819

Academic year: September to May (two semesters)

President: JOHN T. CASTEEN, III
Provost: PETER W. LOW
Executive Vice-President and Chief Financial Officer: LEONARD W. SANDRIDGE, Jr
Registrar: ANN R. ANTROBUS
Dean of Students: R. T. CANEVARI
Dean of Admissions: JOHN A. BLACKBURN
Librarian: KARIN WITTENBORG

Library: see Libraries
Number of teachers: 2,126
Number of students: 18,417

Publications: *Virginia Quarterly Review, Virginia Law Review, Virginia Law Weekly, News Letter, Alumni News, Register, University Topics.*

DEANS

College and Graduate School of Arts and Sciences: MELVYN P. LEFFLER
School of Architecture: WILLIAM A. MCDONOUGH
School of Education: DAVID W. BRENEMAN
School of Engineering and Applied Science: RICHARD W. MIKSAD
The Graduate School of Business Administration: EDWARD A. SNYDER
School of Law: ROBERT E. SCOTT
School of Medicine: ROBERT M. CAREY
School of Nursing: B. JEANETTE LANCASTER
McIntire School of Commerce: CARL P. ZEITHAML
Division of Continuing Education: SONDRA STALLARD

PROFESSORS

School of Arts and Sciences:

ADLER, P. N., Biology
ALLEN, R. O., Chemistry
ALLINSON, G. D., History
ANDREWS, L. S., Chemistry
ARNOLD, A. J., French
ARRAS, J. D., Philosophy
AYERS, E. L., History
BAKER, P. S., English and English Literature
BALBUS, S., Astronomy
BARNETT, M. A., French Literature and General Linguistics
BAROLSKY, P., Art
BATTESTIN, M. C., English and English Literature
BAUERLE, R. H., Biology
BAXTER, M., Economics
BEIZER, J. L., French Literature and General Linguistics
BELANGER, T., Classics
BELL, M., Art
BENNETT, B. K., German Language and Literature
BERLANSTEIN, L. R., History
BERTENTHAL, B. I., Psychology
BEST, T. W., German Language and Literature
BLACK, D., Sociology
BLOCK, G. D., Biology
BLOOMFIELD, L. A., Physics
BOLLERSLEV, T. P., Economics
BRADEN, G. M., English and English Literature
BRINKLEY, E. S., French Literature and General Linguistics
BRUNJES, P. C., Psychology
BRYAN, R. F., Chemistry
BRYANT, R. G., Chemistry
BRYDGES, D., Mathematics
BURNETT, R. E., Chemistry
BURTON, E. T., Economics
CAFISO, D. S., Chemistry
CANO, J., Spanish, Italian and Portuguese
CANTOR, P. A., English and English Literature
CAPLOW, T., Sociology
CAREY, F. A., Chemistry
CARGILE, J., Philosophy
CEASER, J. W., Government and Foreign Affairs
CELLI, V., Physics
CHANG, T. C., Mathematics
CHAPEL, R. C., Drama
CHASE-LEVENSON, K. S., English and English Literature
CHASE-LEVENSON, M. H., English and English Literature
CHEVALIER, R. A., Astronomy
CHILDRESS, J. F., Religious Studies
CLAY, J. S., Classics
COHEN, R., English and English Literature
COLKER, M. L., Classics
COLLINS, M., Mathematics
COLOMB, G. G., English and English Literature
CONNETTI, S., Physics
CONNOLLY, J. W., Slavic Languages and Literature
COOK, R. F., French
COSBY, B. J., Environmental Sciences
COSTA, D. L., Mathematics
COURTNEY, E., Classics
COX, B. B., Physics
CROCKER, J. C., Anthropology
CROSBY, E. U., History
CROZIER, R. L., Art
CUSHMAN, S. B., English and English Literature
DAMON, F. H., Anthropology
DAY, D., English and English Literature
DEAVER, B. S., Physics
DEETZ, J. F., Anthropology
DEMAS, J. N., Chemistry
DEPAULO, B. M., Psychology
DERTHICK, M. A., Government and Foreign Affairs
DEVEREUX, D. T., Philosophy
DIAMOND, C. A., Philosophy
DOBBINS, J., Art
DOLAN, R., Environmental Sciences
DOVE, R. F., English and English Literature
DUGGAN, H. N., English and English Literature
DUNKL, C. F., Mathematics
EDMUNDSON, M. W., English and English Literature
EDSALL, N. C., History
EISENBERG, D., English and English Literature
ELSON, M. J., Slavic Languages and Literature
ELZINGA, K. G., Economics
EMERY, R. E., Psychology
EPPS, T. W., Economics
FATTON, R., Government and Foreign Affairs
FAULKNER, J. R., Mathematics
FELSKI, R., English and English Literature
FERREIRA, M. J., Religious Studies
FINKEL, S. E., Government and Foreign Affairs
FISHBANE, P. M., Physics
FOGARTY, G. P., Religious Studies
FOWLER, A. D., English and English Literature
FOWLER, M., Physics
FRIESEN, W. O., Biology
GALLAGHER, T. F., Physics
GALLOWAY, J. N., Environmental Science
GAMBLE, H. Y., Religious Studies
GARRETT, G. P., English and English Literature
GARRETT, R. H., Biology
GARSTANG, M., Environmental Sciences

GIES, D. T., Spanish, Italian, and Portuguese
GOEDDE, L. O., Art
GOLD, P. E., Psychology
GOODELL, H. G., Environmental Sciences
GOODFRIEND, M. S., Economics
GOTTESMAN, I. I., Psychology
GRAEBNER, N. A., History
GRAINGER, R. M., Biology
GRIMES, R. N., Chemistry
GRISHAM, C. M., Chemistry
GRONER, P. S., Religious Studies
HABERLY, D. T., Spanish, Italian and Portuguese
HADDEN, J. K., Sociology
HAGAN, J. G., Art
HANDLER, R., Anthropology
HARMAN, W., Chemistry
HARMS, I., German Language and Literature
HAVRAN, M. J., History
HAYDEN, B. P., Environmental Science
HECHT, S. M., Chemistry
HERBST, I. W., Mathematics
HERMAN, J. S., Environmental Sciences
HERRERO, J. S., Spanish, Italian and Portuguese
HESS, G. B., Physics
HETHERINGTON, E. M., Psychology
HILL, D. L., Psychology
HIRSCH, E. D., English and English Literature
HIRSH, J., Biology
HOH, L. G., Drama
HOLDEN, M., Government and Foreign Affairs
HOLT, C. A., Economics
HOLT, M. F., History
HOPKINS, P. J., Religious Studies
HORNBERGER, G. M., Environmental Sciences
HOWARD, A., Environmental Sciences
HOWLAND, J. S., Mathematics
HUMPHREYS, P. W., Philosophy
HUNG, P. Q., Physics
HUNT, D. F., Chemistry
HUNTER, J. D., Sociology
HYMES, D. H., Anthropology
IANNA, P. A., Astronomy
IMBRIE, J. Z., Mathematics
INNES, S., History
ISIN, A., Physics
ISRAEL, J., History
JAMES, J. A., Economics
JOHNSON, W. R., Economics
JORDAN, D. C., Government and Foreign Affairs
JUSTICE, C. O., Environmental Sciences
KABIR, P. K., Physics
KELLER, G. E., Mathematics
KELLER, R. E., Biology
KELLOGG, R. L., English
KETT, J. F., History
KHARE, R. S., Anthropology
KING, R. G., Economics
KIRSCH, A. C., English and English Literature
KLOSKO, G., Government and Foreign Affairs
KOLB, H. H., English and English Literature
KOVACS, P. D., Classics
KRETSINGER, R. H., Biology
KRIETE, T. L., Mathematics
KUBOVY, M., Psychology
KUHN, N. J., Mathematics
KUMAR, J. K., Sociology
LANE, A. J., History
LANGBAUM, R. W., English and English Literature
LARSON, D. J., Physics
LEFFLER, M. P., History
LEVENSON, J. C., English and English Literature
LICHSTEIN, N. N., History
LYONS, J. D., French
MCARDLE, J. J., Psychology
MCCARTHY, J. S., Physics
MCCARTY, R. C., Psychology
MCCLAIN, P. D., Government and Foreign Affairs
MCCLELLAN, W. D., History
MCCLESKEY, H. C., Government and Foreign Affairs
MCCLURE, P. A., Environmental Sciences
MCCRIMMON, K. M., Mathematics
MACDONALD, T. L., Chemistry
MCDONALD, W. C., German Language and Literature
MCDOWELL, D. E., English and English Literature
MCGANN, J. J., English and English Literature
MCKINLEY, M. B., French Literature and General Linguistics
MACKO, S. A., Environmental Sciences
MARSHALL, J. A., Chemistry
MASSAM, H. M., Statistics
MAUS, K. E., English and English Literature
MEGILL, A. D., History
MELLON, D., Biology
MENAKER, M., Biology
METCALF, P. A., Anthropology
MICHAELS, P. J., Environmental Science
MIDELFORT, H. E., History
MIKALSON, J. D., Classics
MILLER, J. C., History
MILLER, O. L., Biology
MILLER, W. L., Rhetoric and Communication Studies
MILLS, A. L., Environmental Sciences
MILLS, D. E., Economics
MILNER, M., Sociology
MINEHART, R. C., Physics
MIRMAN, L. J., Economics
MOOMAW, W., Government and Foreign Affairs
MORFORD, M. P., Classics
MURRAY, J. J., Biology
NALLE, S. T., History
NELSON, B. W., Environmental Sciences
NELSON, R. J., English and English Literature
NESSELROADE, J. R., Psychology
NEWSOM, D. D., Government and Foreign Affairs
NOBLE, J. V., Physics
NOBLE, T. F., History
NOCK, S. L., Sociology
NOHRNBERG, J. C., English and English Literature
NOLAN, B., English and English Literature
NORUM, B. E., Physics
O'BRIEN, D. M., Government and Foreign Affairs
OCHS, P. W., Religious Studies
O'CONNELL, R. W., Astronomy
OLSEN, E. O., Economics
OLTMANNS, T. F., Psychology
ONUF, P. S., History
ORR, G. S., English and English Literature
OSHEIM, D. J., History
PARSHALL, B. J., Mathematics
PATTERSON, C. J., Psychology
PERDUE, C. L., Anthropology
PERKOWSKI, J. L., Slavic Languages and Literature
PITT, L. D., Mathematics
PLOG, S. E., Anthropology
POON, J., Physics
PROFFITT, D. R., Psychology
PROSSER, M. H., Rhetoric and Communication Studies
PURYEAR, P. L.
QUANDT, W. D., Government and Foreign Affairs
RAILTON, S. F., English and English Literature
RAMAZANI, R., English and English Literature
RAMAZANI, R. K., Government and Foreign Affairs
RAMIREZ, D. E., Mathematics
RAY, B. C., Religious Studies
RAY, G., Environmental Sciences
REPPUCCI, N. D., Psychology
RHOADS, S. E., Government and Foreign Affairs
RICHARDS, D. S., Mathematics
RICHARDSON, F. S., Chemistry
RIOPEL, J. L., Biology
RITTER, R. C., Physics
ROOD, R. T., Astronomy
RORTY, R., English and English Literature
ROSENBLUM, M., Mathematics
ROSS, W. B., Music
ROVNYAK, J. L., Mathematics
ROWELL, C. H., English and English Literature
RUBIN, D. L., French
RUDDIMAN, W. F., Environmental Sciences
RUVALDS, J., Physics
SABATO, L. J., Government and Foreign Affairs
SACHEDINA, A. A., Religious Studies
SAPIR, J. D., Anthropology
SARAZIN, C. L., Astronomy
SASLAW, W. C., Astronomy
SAWAIE, M., Asian and Middle Eastern Linguistics
SCHNATTERLY, S. E., Physics
SCHUKER, S. A., History
SCHUTTE, A. J., History
SCOTT, L. L., Mathematics
SHATIN, J., Music
SHAW, D. L., Spanish, Italian and Portuguese
SHERMAN, R., Economics
SHOUP, P. S., Government and Foreign Affairs
SHUGART, H. H., Environmental Sciences
SIMMONS., A. J., Philosopohy
SPACKS, P. M., English and English Literature
SPEARING, A. C., English and English Literature
STAGG, J., History
STEIN, R. B., Art
STERN, S. N., Economics
STONG, R. E., Mathematics
STUBBS, K. L.
SUMMERS, J. D., Art
SUNDBERG, R. J., Chemistry
THACKER, H. B., Physics
THOMAS, L. E., Mathematics
THOMPSON, K. W., Government and Foreign Affairs
THORNTON, S. T., Physics
THUAN, T. X., Astronomy
TIMKO, M. P., Biology
TOLBERT, C. R., Astronomy
TUCKER, H., English and English Literature
VANDER MEULEN, D. L., English and English Literature
VON HOFSTEN, C., Psychology
VORIS, R. L., German Literature
WAGNER, R., Anthropology
WARD, H. N., Mathematics
WEBER, H., Physics
WEGNER, D. M., Psychology
WEICKER, L. P., Government and Foreign Affairs
WHITAKER, J., Economics
WILBUR, H. M., Biology
WILKEN, R. L., Religious Studies
WILSON, T. D., Psychology
WINNER, A., English and English Literature
WLASSICS, T., Spanish, Italian and Portuguese
WOMACK, B., Government and Foreign Affairs
WRIGHT, C. P., English and English Literature
WRIGHT, H. M., Art
ZIEMAN, J. C., Environmental Sciences
ZUNZ, O., History

School of Architecture:

BOESCHENSTEIN, W. C.

BYRD, W. T.
CLARK, W. G.
COLLINS, R. C.
DI VALMARANA, M.
DRIPPS, R. D.
HARRIS, W. M.
LAY, K.
LUCY, W. H.
MCDONOUGH, W. A.
MOCKBEE, S.
RAINEY, R. M.
SPAIN, D. G.
WALDMAN, P. D.
WESTFALL, C. W.
WILSON, R. G.

School of Education:

ABIDIN, R. R., Human Services
BRENEMAN, D. W., Leadership and Policy Studies
BROWN, R. S., Human Services
BUNKER, L. K., Human Services
BURBACH, H. J., Leadership, Foundations and Policy
CALLAHAN, C. M., Educational Studies
CANADY, R. L., Leadership and Policy Studies
CHRONISTER, J. L., Leadership and Policy Studies
COOPER, J. M., Curriculum, Instruction and Special Education
DEWITZ, P. A., Curriculum, Instruction and Special Education
DUKE, D. L., Leadership and Policy Studies
ESTES, T. H., Curriculum, Instruction and Special Education
GANSNEDER, B., Leadership, Foundations and Policy
GIBBS, A., Leadership and Policy Studies
GIECK, J. H., Human Services
HALLAHAN, D. P., Curriculum, Instruction and Special Education
JUEL, C. L., Curriculum, Instruction and Special Education
KAUFFMAN, J. M., Curriculum, Instruction and Special Education
LEE, C. C., Human Services
MACDOUGALL, M. A., Educational Studies
MCNERGNEY, R. F., Educational Studies
MOORE, J. R., Curriculum, Instruction and Special Education
MORINE DERSHIMER, G., Curriculum, Instruction and Special Education
PATE, R. H., Human Services
PERRIN, D. H., Human Services
RICHARDS, H. C., Educational Studies
SHORT, J. G., Educational Studies
SNELL, M. E., Curriculum, Instruction and Special Education
STRANG, H. R., Educational Studies
TAYLOR, A. L., Leadership and Policy Studies
THOMPSON, E., Curriculum, Instruction and Special Education
WAGONER, J. L., Leadership and Policy Studies
WEISS, M., Human Services
WELTMAN, A. L., Human Services
YEAKEY, C. C., Leadership and Policy Studies

School of Engineering and Applied Science:

ADAMS, J. M., Biomedical Engineering
ALLAIRE, P. E., Mechanical Engineering
AYLOR, J. H., Electrical Engineering
BARKER, R. E., Materials Science
BARRETT, L. E., Mechanical, Aerospace and Nuclear Engineering
BARTON, F. W., Civil Engineering
BATSON, A. P., Computer Sciences
BEAN, J. C., Electrical Engineering
BROWN, D. E., Systems Engineering
CARTA, G., Chemical Engineering
CHERNO, M., General Engineering
CROWE, T. W., Electrical Engineering
DEMETSKY, M. J., Civil Engineering
DORNING, J. J., Nuclear Engineering
DUGAN, J. B., Electrical Engineering
FARMER, B. L., Materials Science
FISHER, S. S., Mechanical Engineering
FLACK, R. D., Mechanical Engineering
GAINER, J. L., Chemical Engineering
GANGLOFF, R. P., Materials Science
GARBER, N. J., Civil Engineering
GIANNAKIS, G. B., Electrical Engineering
GILLIES, G. T., Mechanical, Aerospace and Nuclear Engineering
GUNTER, E. J., Mechanical Engineering
HAIMES, Y. Y., Science and Systems
HERAKOVICH, C. T., Civil Engineering
HOEL, L. A., Civil Engineering
HORGAN, C. O., Applied Mathematics
HUDSON, J. L., Chemical Engineering
HUTCHINSON, T. E., Biomedical Engineering
IGNIZIO, J. P., Science and Systems
JESSER, W. A., Materials Science
JOHNSON, B. W., Electrical Engineering
JOHNSON, R. A., Materials Science
JOHNSON, R. E., Nuclear Engineering
JOHNSON, W. C., Materials Science and Engineering
JONES, A. K., Computer Sciences
KAUZLARICH, J. J., Mechanical Engineering
KELLY, J. L., Nuclear Engineering
KIRWAN, D. J., Chemical Engineering
KNIGHT, J. C., Computer Sciences
KRZYSZTOFWICZ, R., Science and Systems
LASIECKA, I., Applied Mathematics
LEE, J., Biomedical Engineering
LUNG, W., Civil Engineering
MCDANIEL, J. C., Mechanical, Aerospace and Nuclear Engineering
MANSFIELD, L. E., Applied Mathematics
MIKSAD, R. W., Mechanical, Aerospace and Nuclear Engineering
MORRIS, D., Civil Engineering
MORTON, J. B., Mechanical Engineering
NOOR, A. K., Civil Engineering
O'CONNELL, J. P., Chemical Engineering
ORTEGA, J. M., Applied Mathematics
PFALTZ, J. L., Computer Sciences
PILKEY, W. D., Mechanical Engineering
PINDERA, M., Civil and Applied Mechanics
ROBERTS, W. W., Applied Mathematics
SCOTT, J. E., Mechanical Engineering
SHIFLET, G. J., Materials Science
SIMMONDS, J. G., Applied Mathematics
SKALAK, T. C., Biomedical Engineering
STANKOVIC, J. A., Computer Sciences
STARKE, E. A., Materials Science
STONER, G. E., Materials Science
THACKER, J. G., Mechanical Engineering
THORNTON, E. A., Mechanical Engineering
THORNTON, K. C., Technology, Culture
TOWNSEND, M. A., Mechanical Engineering
TRIGGIANI, R., Applied Mathematics
WADLEY, H. N., Mechanical Engineering
WEAVER, A. C., Computer Sciences
WERT, J. A., Materials Science
WILSDORF, D., Materials Science
WILSON, S. G., Electrical Engineering
WULF, W. A., Computer Sciences
YU, S. L., Civil Engineering

Darden School (Graduate School of Business Administration):

ALLEN, B. R.
BECKENSTEIN, A. R.
BODILY, S. E.
BOURGEOIS, L. J.
BROWNLEE, E. R.
BRUNER, R. F.
COLLEY, J. L.
CONROY, R. M.
DAVIS, E. W.
DUNN, W. E.
EAKER, M. R.
FARRIS, P. W.
FREELAND, J. R.
FREEMAN, R. E.
FREY, S. C.
GALE, C.
GRAYSON, L. E.
HARRIS, R. S.
HASKINS, M. E.
HORNIMAN, A. B.
LANDEL, R. D.
MACAVOY, T. C.
MEIBURG, C. O.
PFEIFER, P. E.
ROTCH, W.
SACK, R. J.
SIHLER, W. W.
SMITH, C. R.
SPEKMAN, R. E.
WERHANE, P. H.

School of Law:

ABRAHAM, K. S.
BALNAVE, R. D.
BEVIER, L. R.
BONNIE, R. J.
CASE, M. C.
COHEN, G. M.
COUGHLIN, A. A.
DOOLEY, M. P.
DUDLEY, E. C.
GILLETTE, C. P.
GOETZ, C. J.
HENDERSON, S. D.
HOWARD, A. D.
IBBEKEN, D. H.
JEFFRIES, J. C.
JOHNSON, A. M.
KARLAN, P. S.
KITCH, E. W.
KLARMAN, M. J.
KRAUS, J. S.
LESLIE, D. L.
LEVMORE, S. X.
LILLY, G.
LOW, P. W.
MAHONEY, P. G.
MARTIN, D. A.
MERRILL, R. A.
MONAHAN, J. T.
MOORE, J. N.
O'CONNELL, J.
O'NEIL, R. M.
ORTIZ, D. R.
ROBINSON, G. O.
ROBINSON, M. W.
ROIN, J. A.
RUTHERGLEN, G. A.
SCOTT, E.
SCOTT, R. E.
SINCLAIR, K.
STEPHAN, P. B.
STUNTZ, W. J.
TRIANTIS, G. G.
TURNBULL, A. R.
WADLINGTON, W. J.
WALKER, W. L.
WALT, S. D.
WENGER, L. B.
WHITE, G. E.
WHITE, T. R., III
YIN, G. K.

School of Medicine:

ABBOTT, R. D., Internal Medicine
AGARWAL, S. K., Radiology
ALFORD, B. A., Radiology
APPREY, M., Psychiatry
AYERS, C. R., Internal Medicine
BALIAN, G., Orthopaedics and Rehabilitation
BANKER, G. A., Neuroscience
BARNETT, B. L., Family and Community Medicine
BARRETT, E. J., Internal Medicine
BARTH, J. T., Psychiatry
BATEMAN, B. G., Obstetrics and Gynaecology
BECKER, D. M., Internal Medicine
BELLER, G. A., Internal Medicine
BENJAMIN, D. C., Microbiology
BENNETT, J. P., Neurology
BERRY, F. A., Anaesthesiology
BEYER, A. L., Microbiology
BILTONEN, R. L., Pharmacology
BLACKMAN, J. A., Paediatrics
BLECK, T. P., Neurology
BLOODGOOD, R. A., Anatomy

BOGGESS, H. P., Family and Community Medicine
BOLTON, W. K., Internal Medicine
BRACIALE, T. J., Pathology
BRADBEER, C., Biochemistry
BRAUTIGAN, D. L., Microbiology
BROOKEMAN, J. R., Radiology
BROWN, G. L., Psychiatry
BROWN, J. C., Microbiology
BRUNNER, C. M., Internal Medicine
BRUNS, D. E., Pathology
BUCKMAN, J., Psychiatry
BURWELL, L. R., Internal Medicine
CAIL, W. S., Radiology
CANTERBURY, R. J., Psychiatry
CANTRELL, R. W., Otolaryngology
CAREY, R. M., Internal Medicine
CASTLE, J. D., Anatomy and Cell Biology
CHAN, D., Orthopaedic Surgery
CHAPMAN, M. D., Internal
CHEVALIER, R. L., Paediatrics
CHUNG, L. W., Urology
CLARKE, W. L., Paediatrics
COATES, M. L., Family and Community Health
COMINELLI, F., Internal Medicine
CONNELLY, J.
CONSTABLE, W. C., Radiology
CONWAY, B. P., Ophthalmology
CORBETT, E. C., Emergency Medicine
CORWIN, J. T., Otolaryngology
COX, D. J., Psychiatry
CRAMPTON, R. S., Internal Medicine
CREUTZ, C. E., Pharmacology
DANIEL, T. M., Surgery
DAVIS, J. S., Internal Medicine
DEALARCON, P. A., Paediatrics
DEE, P. M., Radiology
DE LANGE, E. E., Radiology
DEREWENDA, Z. S., Physiology
DESIMONE, D. W., Cell Biology
DETMER, D. E., Surgery
DIBENEDETTO, M., Physical Medicine and Rehabilitation
DIFAZIO, C. A., Anaesthesiology
DIMARCO, J. P., Internal Medicine
DION, J., Radiology
DONOWITZ, G. R., Internal Medicine
DONOWITZ, L. G., Paediatrics
DULING, B. R., Physiology
DUNN, J. T., Internal Medicine
DURBIN, C. G., Anaesthesiology
DUSSAULT, R. G., Radiology
DWYER, S. J., Radiology
EDLICH, R. F., Plastic Surgery
ENGELHARD, V. H., Microbiology
EPSTEIN, R. M., Anaesthesiology
EVANS, W. S., Internal Medicine
FAJARDO, L. L., Radiology
FARR, B. M., Internal Medicine
FECHNER, R. E., Pathology
FELDER, R. A., Pathology
FELDMAN, P. S., Pathology
FERGUSON, J. E., Obstetrics and Gynaecology
FLETCHER, J. C., Internal Medicine
FLICKINGER, C. J., Anatomy
FOX, J. W., Microbiology
FRIERSON, H. F., Pathology
FU, S., Internal Medicine
GAL, T. J., Anaesthesiology
GARRISON, J. C., Pharmacology
GASKIN, F., Psychiatry
GEAR, A. L., Biochemistry
GIBSON, R. S., Internal Medicine
GILLENWATER, J. Y., Urology
GOMEZ, R. A., Paediatrics
GONIAS, S. L., Pathology
GREER, K. E., Dermatology
GREYSON, C. B., Psychiatry
GROSS, C. W., Otolaryngology
GUERRANT, R. L., Internal Medicine
GUTGESELL, H. P., Paediatrics
GUTH, L., Neuroscience
GUYENET, P. G., Pharmacology
GWALTNEY, J. M., Internal Medicine
HACKETT, J. T., Physiology
HAGY, J. A., Family and Community Medicine
HALEY, E. C., Neurology
HAMLIN, J. L., Biochemistry
HANKS, J. B., Surgery
HARRELL, F. E., Health Evaluation Sciences
HAYDEN, F. G., Internal Medicine
HAYDEN, G. F., Paediatrics
HAYS, R. B., Family and Community
HEIMER, L., Otolaryngology
HENDLEY, J. O., Paediatrics
HERR, J. C., Anatomy
HESS, C. E., Internal Medicine
HEWLETT, E., Internal Medicine
HILLMAN, B. J., Radiology
HINTON, B. T., Anatomy
HOBBS, W. R., Psychiatry
HOLLOWAY, P. W., Biochemistry
HOOK, E. W., Internal Medicine
HOSTLER, S. L., Paediatrics
HOWARDS, S. S., Urology
HUANG, C.-H., Biochemistry
INNES, D. J., Pathology
JAGGER, J. C., Neurosurgery
JAHRSDOERFER, R. A., Otolaryngology
JANE, J. A., Neurosurgery
JOHNS, R. A., Anaesthesiology
JOHNSON, M. L., Pharmacology
JONES, R. S., Surgery
KADNER, R. J., Microbiology
KAPLAN, P. A., Radiology
KASSELL, N. F., Neurosurgery
KATTWINKEL, J., Paediatrics
KAUL, S., Internal Medicine
KEATS, T. E., Radiology
KELLY, T. E., Paediatrics
KESLER, R. W., Paediatrics
KIM, Y. I., Neurology
KITCHIN, J. D., Obstetrics and Gynaecology
KNAUS, W. A., Health Evaluation Sciences
KRON, I. L., Surgery
KUTCHAI, H. C., Physiology
LAMBERT, P. R., Otolaryngology
LARNER, J., Pharmacology
LAWRENCE, J. C., Pharmacology
LAWS, E. R., Neurosurgery
LEE, K. S., Neurosurgery
LEVINE, P. A., Otolaryngology
LEVY, W. B., Neurosurgery
LINDEN, J. M., Internal Medicine
LINDSAY, R. W., Internal Medicine
LOGIN, I. S., Neurology
LYNCH, C., Anaesthesiology
LYNCH, K. R., Pharmacology
MACARA, I. G., Pharmacology
MCCUE, F. C., Orthopaedics and Rehabilitation
MCLAUGHLIN, R. E., Orthopaedics and Rehabilitation
MANDELL, G., Internal Medicine
MARTIN, M. L., Emergency Medical Services
MASSARO, T. A., Paediatrics
MEIXEL, S. A., Family and Community Medicine
MILLER, C. W., Orthopaedic Surgery
MILLER, J. Q., Neurology
MILLS, S. E., Pathology
MINTZ, P. D., Pathology
MOHRMANN, M. E., Paediatrics
MORGAN, R. F., Plastic Surgery
MORSE, R. M., Family and Community
MURPHY, R. A., Physiology
MYERS, C. E., Internal Medicine
NOLAN, S. P., Surgery
NORMANSELL, D. E., Pathology
OLDER, R. A., Radiology
OWENS, G. K., Physiology
PARKER, W. D., Neurology
PARLETTE, H. L., Dermatology
PARSONS, J. T., Microbiology
PARSONS, S. J., Microbiology
PATTERSON, J. W., Pathology
PEARSON, R. D., Internal Medicine
PEARSON, W. R., Biochemistry
PETRI, W. A., Internal Medicine
PEURA, D. A., Internal Medicine
PHILBRICK, J. T., Internal Medicine
PHILLIPS, L. H., Neurology
PLATTS-MILLS, T. A., Internal Medicine
PORTERFIELD, P. B., Psychiatry
POWERS, E. R., Internal Medicine
PRUETT, T., Surgery
REIN, M. F., Internal Medicine
REKOSH, D., Microbiology
REYNOLDS, R. E., Internal Medicine
RHEUBAN, K., Paediatrics
RICH, T. A., Radiology
RODEHEAVER, G. T., Plastic Surgery
RODGERS, B. M., Surgery
ROGOL, A. D., Paediatrics
ROSE, C. E., Internal Medicine
ROSS, M., Internal Medicine
ROSS, W. T., Anaesthesiology
ROWLINGSON, J. C., Anaesthesiology
ROY, R. C., Anaesthesiology
RUTH, R. A., Otolaryngology
SANDO, J. J., Pharmacology
SANTEN, R. J., Internal Medicine
SAULSBURY, F. T., Paediatrics
SAVORY, J., Pathology
SCHELD, W. M., Internal Medicine
SCHIRMER, B., Surgery
SHAFFER, H. A., Radiology
SHUPNICK, M. A., Internal Medicine
SMITH, M., Microbiology
SOJKA, N. J., Comparative Medicine
SOMLYO, A. P., Physiology
SOMLYO, A. V., Physiology
SPOTNITZ, W. D., Surgery
STEERS, W. D., Urology
STEINER, L., Neurosurgery
STEINER, M., Neurosurgery
STEVENSON, I. P., Psychiatry
STEWARD, O., Neurosurgery
STOLER, M. H., Pathology
STURGILL, B. C., Pathology
STURGILL, T. W., Internal Medicine
SURATT, P., Internal Medicine
SUTHERLAND, W. M., Biochemistry
SUTPHEN, J. L., Paediatrics
SZABO, G., Physiology
TAYLOR, P.-T., Obstetrics and Gynaecology
TAYLOR, R. P., Biochemistry
TEATES, C. D., Radiology
THIAGARAJAH, S., Obstetrics and Gynaecology
THOMPSON, T. E., Biochemistry
THORNER, M. O., Internal Medicine
TILLACK, T. W., Pathology
TRIBBLE, C. G., Surgery
TUNG, K. S., Pathology
TURNER, T. T., Urology
UNDERWOOD, P. B., Obstetrics and Gynaecology
VANCE, M. L., Internal Medicine
VANDENBERG, S. R., Pathology
VELDHUIS, J. D., Internal Medicine
VILLAR PALASI, C., Pharmacology
VOLKAN, V. D., Psychiatry
WAGNER, D. P., Health Evaluation Sciences
WALLACE, K. K., Radiology
WANG, G. J., Orthopaedics and Rehabilitation
WATERS, D. B., Family and Community Medicine
WATSON, D. D., Radiology
WEARY, P. E., Dermatology
WEBER, M. J., Microbiology
WHEBY, M. S., Internal Medicine
WHITE, J. M., Anatomy
WHITEHILL, R., Orthopaedics and Rehabilitation
WILHELM, M. C., Surgery
WILLIAMS, M. E., Internal Medicine
WOODE, M. K., Medical Education
WOOTEN, G. F., Neurology
WYKER, A. W., Urology
YAZEL, J. J., Psychiatry

School of Nursing:

ABRAHAM, I. L.
BRODIE, B.

Fox, J.
Lancaster, B. J.
Novak, J. C.
Ozbolt, J. G.
Parker, B. J.
Taylor, A. G.

McIntire School of Commerce:

Atchison, M. D.
Awad, E. M.
Broome, O. W.
Croll, D. B.
De Mong, R. F.
Haas, R. M.
Kehoe, W. J.
Lindgren, J. H.
Maloney, D. M.
Morin, B. A.
Nelson, R. R.
Overstreet, G. A.
Ruppel, A. C.
Schmidt, S.
Scott, C. H.
Scott, R. A.
Shenkir, W. G.
Snyder, N. H.
Trent, R. H.
Williams, T. H.
Zeithaml, C. P.

AFFILIATED COLLEGE

Clinch Valley College: Wise, VA 24293; Chancellor: Jay Lemons; Vice-Chancellor for Student Affairs: Gary W. Juhan; 58 teachers; 1,515 students.

PROFESSORS

Baird, J. R., Sciences
Ball, R. A., English
Blackburn, J. G., History and Sociology
Culbertson, G. E., Business
Daniel, V. W., Sciences
Davidson, R. A., Education and Psychology
Donathan, D. M., Humanities
Ellsworth, L. F., Dean's Office
Elosser, P. D., Mathematics
Ely, R. W., Dean's Office
Johnson, B. M., Nursing
Mahony, M. J., English
Peake, R. H., English
Portuondo, A. A., English
Rouse, D. L., History and Sociology
Scolnick, J. M., Education and Psychology
Sheldon, G. W., Education and Psychology
Shelton, P. C., Sciences
Wheatley, F. W., Education and Psychology
Yun, P. S., Business
Zylawy, R. I., English

VIRGINIA COMMONWEALTH UNIVERSITY

910 West Franklin St, Richmond, VA 23284
Telephone: (804) 828-0100

Founded 1838 as the medical department of Hampden-Sydney College. Richmond Professional Institute and Medical College of Virginia merged in 1968 to form this University

State control

President: Dr Eugene P. Trani
Vice-President for Finance and Administration: Paul W. Timmreck
Provost and Vice-President for Academic Affairs: Grace E. Harris
Vice-President for Health Sciences: Hermes A. Kontos
Vice-President for Advancement: Peter L. Wyeth
Vice-President for External Relations: Donald C. Gehring
Vice-President for Research and Graduate Studies: William L. Dewey
Director of University Library Services: Barbara J. Ford

Library of 1,500,000 vols, 2,800,000 microforms, 260,000 govt documents
Number of teachers: 1,560 full-time
Number of students: 22,702

DEANS

College of the Humanities and Sciences: Stephen D. Gottfredson
School of the Arts: Richard E. Toscan
School of Business: Howard P. Tuckman
School of Education: J. S. Oehler
School of Social Work: Frank R. Baskind
School of Allied Health Professions: Cecil B. Drain
School of Dentistry: L. M. Hunt, Jr
School of Engineering: Henry A. McGee, Jr
School of Medicine: Dr Hermes A. Kontos
School of Nursing: Nancy F. Langston
School of Pharmacy: Victor A. Yanchick

VIRGINIA MILITARY INSTITUTE

Lexington, VA 24450
Telephone: (540) 464-7207
Founded 1839

Superintendent: Maj.-Gen. Josiah Bunting III
Dean: Col Alan F. Farrell
Business Executive: Col John L. Rowe, Jr
Commandant: Col Keith D. Dickson
Treasurer: Lt-Col. Gary R. Knick
Librarian: Lt-Col Donald H. Samdahl, Jr (acting)

Library of 248,000 vols
Number of teachers: 99 full-time, 16 part-time, 26 military
Number of students: 1,300 men and women

Publication: *Catalogue.*

VIRGINIA POLYTECHNIC INSTITUTE AND STATE UNIVERSITY

Blacksburg, VA 24061
Telephone: (703) 231-6000
Established 1872; opened to women 1921
State control
Academic year: August to May

President: Dr Paul E. Torgersen
Provost: Peggy S. Meszaros
Executive Vice-President and Chief Business Officer: M. E. Ridenour
Vice-President, Development: Charles W. Steger
Vice-President, Information Systems: Earving Blythe
Vice-President, Student Affairs: Landrum Cross
Director of Admissions: David Bousquet
Librarian: Eileen Hitchingham

Number of teachers: 1,530
Number of students: 22,702

Publications: *The Techgram, Virginia Tech Magazine, Extension Division Series, Research Division Series.*

DEANS

Agriculture: L. A. Swiger
Architecture: P. K. Edwards
Arts and Sciences: Robert C. Bates
Business: R. E. Sorensen
Engineering: William Stephenson
Forestry: G. N. Brown
Human Resources and Education: Janet M. Johnson
Graduate: Leonard Peters
Veterinary Medicine: P. Eyre
Extension: Clark Jones
Research: L. Peters

VIRGINIA STATE UNIVERSITY

Petersburg, VA 23806
Telephone: (804) 524-5000
Fax: (804) 524-6505

Founded by State of Virginia as Virginia Normal and Collegiate Institute 1882; opened 1883; name changed to Virginia Normal and Industrial Institute 1902; to Virginia State College for Negroes 1930; to Virginia State College 1946; to Virginia State University 1979

President: Eddie N. Moore, Jr

Library of 245,731 vols
Number of teachers: 191
Number of students: 4,007

DEANS

School of Agriculture Sciences and Technology: Dr Lorenza W. Lyons
School of Business: Dr Sadie R. Gregory
School of Liberal Arts and Education: Dr Samuel L. Creighton
School of Continuing Education and Graduate Studies: Dr Wayne F. Virag

VIRGINIA UNION UNIVERSITY

1500 North Lombardy St, Richmond, VA 23220
Telephone: (804) 257-5600
Fax: (804) 257-5818

Founded 1865

President: Dr S. Dallas Simmons
Vice-President for Academic Affairs: Dr W. Weldon Hill
Vice-President for Financial Affairs: Kevin W. Davenport
Director of University Services: Gilbert L. Carter
Vice-President for Student Affairs: Wilbert D. Talley
Registrar: Mrs Janice D. Bailey
Librarian: Dr Vonita W. Foster

Library of 155,900 vols
Number of teachers: 98
Number of students: 1,696

DEANS

Sydney Lewis School of Business: Dr Patrick R. Liverpool
School of Arts and Sciences: Dr Phillip W. Archer
School of Theology: Dr John W. Kinney

WASHINGTON AND LEE UNIVERSITY

Lexington, VA 24450
Telephone: (540) 463-8400

Founded as Augusta Academy 1749, chartered as Liberty Hall Academy 1782, name changed to Washington Academy 1798, to Washington College 1813, and to present name 1871

President: John W. Elrod
Treasurer: Lawrence W. Broomall
Registrar: D. Scott Dittman
Librarian: Barbara J. Brown

Undergraduate library of 464,000 vols; law library of 350,000 vols
Number of teachers: 197
Number of students: 2,000

Publications: *Shenandoah* (literary quarterly), *Washington and Lee Law Review, Journal of Science, Political Review.*

DEANS

Arts and Sciences: Laurent Boetsch
Commerce, Economics and Politics: Larry C. Peppers
Law: Barry Sullivan

WASHINGTON

CENTRAL WASHINGTON UNIVERSITY

Ellensburg, WA 98926

Telephone: (509) 963-2111

Founded 1891

President: IVORY V. NELSON
Registrar: CAROLYN L. WELLS
Librarian: GARY A. LEWIS
Provost and Vice-President for Academic Affairs: DAVID DAUWALDER
Vice-President for Business Affairs: ABDUL NASSER
Dean of Academic Services: JAMES PAPPAS
Vice-President for Student Affairs: SARAH SHUMATE
Vice-President for University Advancement: MARK YOUNG

Library of 485,417 vols
Number of teachers: 370
Number of students: 7,367 (f.t.e.)

CITY UNIVERSITY

335 116th Avenue S.E., Bellevue, WA 98004

Telephone: (425) 637-1010
Fax: (425) 637-9689

Founded 1973 as City College; present name 1982
Private control
Sites in states of Washington and California, and in Canada, Denmark, Germany, Slovakia, Spain and Switzerland

President: Dr MICHAEL A. PASTORE
Vice-President for External Relations, and Accreditation Liaison Officer: Dr WINSTON C. ADDIS
Vice-President for Institutional Assessment and Planning: Dr DOUGLAS G. ARNOLD
Vice-President for Admissions and Student Affairs: NABIL EL-KHATIB
Vice-President for Academic Affairs: Dr STEVEN STARGARDTER
Vice-President for Business and Finance: DENNIS E. PAGE
Vice-President for Student Relations, Compliance and Military Affairs: WILLIAM J. KRAMER
Vice-President for Human Resources: MELINDA E. WILSON
Vice-President for Site Administration: MARIETA JOHNSON

Number of students: 14,600

EASTERN WASHINGTON UNIVERSITY

Cheney, WA 99004

Telephone: (509) 359-6200
Fax: 359-6946

Founded 1882

President: STEPHEN M. JORDAN
Associate Registrar: DEBBIE FOCKLER
Director of Enrollment Management: BRIAN LEVIN-STANKEVICH
Director of Libraries: PATRICIA KELLEY

Library of 483,152 vols
Number of teachers: 365
Number of students: 8,000

GONZAGA UNIVERSITY

Spokane, WA 99258-0001

Telephone: (509) 328-4220
Fax: (509) 484-2818

Founded 1887
Private control
Academic year: September to May, and summer session

Chancellor: Rev. BERNARD J. COUGHLIN
President: Rev. ROBERT SPITZER
Vice-President: Rev. FRANK COSTELLO
Academic Vice-President: Rev. PATRICK FORD
Vice-President for University Relations: MARGOT STANFIELD
Vice-President, Student Life: SUE WEITZ
Vice-President, Finance: CHARLES J. MURPHY
Vice-President, Administration and Planning: HARRY H. SLADICH
Dean of Admissions: PHILLIP BALLINGER
Librarian: ROBERT BURR

Library of 425,000 vols
Number of teachers: 275
Number of students: 5,572

Publications: *Signum* (quarterly), *Gonzaga Bulletin* (weekly), *Charter* (annually), *Reflections* (annually), *Spires* (annually).

DEANS

Arts and Sciences: MICHAEL MCFARLAND
Law: JOHN E. CLUTE
Engineering: DENNIS HORN
Graduate School: LEONARD DOOHAN
Education: CORINNE MCGUIGAN
Business Administration: CLARENCE BARNES
Dean of Students: SUE WEITZ
Professional Studies: RICHARD WOLFE

HERITAGE COLLEGE

Toppenish, WA 98948

Telephone: (509) 865-2244
Fax: (509) 865-4469

Founded 1907; present name 1982
Liberal arts college

President: Dr KATHLEEN ROSS
Controller: MIKE SORAN
Vice-President for Administration, and Chief Operating Officer: Dr RICHARD WUESTE
Vice-President for Academic Affairs: (vacant)
Dean of Student Records: MARGO PERROTTI
Director of Financial Aid: CARLA LAMKA
Director of Omak Campus: JAMES DETERS

Library of 55,000 vols (main campus)
Number of teachers: 37 full-time, 125 part-time
Number of students: 1,142

PACIFIC LUTHERAN UNIVERSITY

Tacoma, WA 98447

Telephone: (206) 531-6900
Fax: (206) 535-8320

Founded 1890

President: LOREN J. ANDERSON
Provost: PAUL T. MENZEL
Librarian: SHERRY J. TONN

Library of 366,800 vols
Number of teachers: 250
Number of students: 3,600

SAINT MARTIN'S COLLEGE

Lacey, WA 98503

Telephone: (206) 491-4700
Fax: (206) 459-4124

Founded 1895

President: Dr DAVID R. SPANGLER
Vice-President for Academic Affairs: Dr LILIAN CADY (acting)
Executive Vice-President: JACK S. THOMPSON
Registrar: Ms MARY LAW
Librarian: Ms DALIA HAGAN

Library of 85,000 vols
Number of teachers: 70
Number of students: 958

SEATTLE PACIFIC UNIVERSITY

3307 Third Ave West, Seattle, WA 98119

Telephone: (206) 281-2111

Founded 1891

President: PHILIP W. EATON
Vice-President for Academic Affairs: BRUCE G. MURPHY
Vice-President for Business and Planning: DONALD W. MORTENSON
Vice-President for Campus Life: STEVEN G. W. MOORE
Vice-President for University Advancement: ROBERT D. MCINTOSH
Vice-President for University Relations: MARJORIE R. JOHNSON
Dean of Enrollment Services: JANET L. WARD
Registrar: RUTH ADAMS
Director of Learning Resources: RAY DOERKSEN

Library of 275,000 vols
Number of teachers: 215
Number of students: 3,500

SEATTLE UNIVERSITY

Seattle, WA 98122

Telephone: (206) 296-6000
Fax: (206) 296-6136

Founded 1891

President: Fr WILLIAM J. SULLIVAN
Dean of Admissions: LEE GERIG
Provost: Dr JOHN D. ESHELMAN
Assistant Provost for Academic Administration: Dr EDWARD JENNERICH
Assistant Provost for Programs and Planning: Dr TULLISSE MURDOCK
Controller: STEVE OH
Librarian: LAWRENCE THOMAS

Library of 196,904 vols
Number of teachers: 312
Number of students: 4,800

Publication: *Bulletin of Information*.

DEANS

College of Arts and Sciences: Dr JOSEPH GOWER
Matteo Ricci College: Dr BERNARD STECKLER
School of Business: Dr JERRY VISCIONE
School of Education: Dr MARGARET HAGGERTY
School of Science and Engineering: Dr KATHLEEN MAILER
School of Nursing: Dr LUTH TENORIO
Graduate School: Dr EDWARD JENNERICH

UNIVERSITY OF PUGET SOUND

Tacoma, WA 98416

Telephone: (253) 756-3100

Founded 1888
Private control

President: SUSAN RESNECK PIERCE
Academic Vice-President: TERRY A. COONRY
Dean of Students: JUDITH W. KAY
Vice-President for Finance: MICHAEL ROTHMAN
Vice-President for Enrollment: GEORGE H. MILLS
Registrar: JOHN FINNEY
Librarian: MARILYN MITCHELL

Number of teachers: 220
Number of students: 2,650 full-time.

UNIVERSITY OF WASHINGTON

Seattle, WA 98195

Telephone: (206) 543-2100

Established by legislature 1861

President: WILLIAM P. GERBERDING
Provost: L. L. WILKENING
Executive Vice-President: T. TRASK, III
Vice-President for Health Sciences: J. N. LEIN
Vice-President for Minority Affairs: W. BAKER (acting)
Vice-President for Student Affairs: E. R. MORRIS
Vice-President for University Relations: J. R. COLLIER

Executive Director, Admissions and Records: W. W. WASHBURN
Director of Libraries: CHARLES E. CHAMBERLIN
Library: see Libraries
Number of teachers: 2,572 full-time
Number of students: 30,227
Publications: *American Journal of Human Genetics, Biochemistry, Journal of Limnology and Oceanography, Modern Language Quarterly, Pacific Northwest Quarterly, Poetry Northwest, Trends in Engineering, Washington Law Review, Journal of Financial and Quantitative Analysis, Papers of Regional Science Association.*

DEANS

Graduate School: G. L. WOODRUFF
College of Architecture and Urban Planning: G. B. VAREY
College of Arts and Sciences: J. G. NORMAN
School of Business Administration: A. N. PAGE (acting)
College of Education: (vacant)
College of Engineering: J. R. BOWEN
College of Ocean and Fishery Sciences: G. R. HEATH
College of Forest Resources: D. B. THORUD
School of Pharmacy: M. GIBALDI
School of Dentistry: K.-A. OMNELL
School of Law: J. R. PRICE
School of Medicine: M. E. WHITCOMB
School of Nursing: S. T. HEGYVARY
School of Social Work: N. HOOYMAN
School of Public Health and Community Medicine: G. S. OMENN
Graduate School of Public Affairs: M. GORDON
Graduate School of Library and Information Science: PHYLLIS VAN ORDEN

DIRECTORS

Alcoholism and Drug Abuse Institute: H. H. SAMSON
Applied Physics Laboratory: R. C. SPINDEL
Center for Bioengineering: L. HUNTSMAN
Center for Inherited Diseases: A. G. MOTULSKY
Center for Research in Oral Biology: R. C. PAGE
Friday Harbor Laboratories: A. O. D. WILLOWS
Center for Law and Justice: J. G. WEIS
Center for Studies in Demography and Ecology: C. HIRSCHMAN
Institute on Aging: I. B. ABRASS (acting)
Institute for Environmental Studies: C. B. LEOVY
Institute for Marine Studies: E. L. MILES
Quaternary Research Center: S. C. PORTER
Child Development and Mental Retardation Center: M. J. GURALNICK
Fisheries Research Institute: R. C. FRANCIS
Regional Primate Center: D. M. BOWDEN

PROFESSORS

College of Architecture and Urban Planning:

BELL, E. J., Urban Planning
BOSWORTH, T. L., Architecture
BUCHANAN, R. T., Landscape Architecture
GREY, A. L., Jr, Urban Planning
HAAG, R., Landscape Architecture
HANCOCK, J. L., Urban Planning
HILDEBRAND, G., Architecture and Art
JACOBSON, P. L., Architecture, Urban Design and Planning
KELBAUGH, D. S., Architecture
KOLB, K. R., Architecture
LUDWIG, R. L., Urban Design and Planning
MILLER, D. H., Urban Planning
NYBERG, F. E., Architecture, Urban Design and Planning
PUNDT, H. G., Architecture and Art History
SELIGMAN, C. A., Architecture
SMALL, R. E., Architecture and Landscape Architecture
THIEL, P., Architecture, Urban Design and Planning
UNTERMANN, R., Landscape Architecture, Urban Design and Planning
VAREY, G. B., Architecture and Building Construction
VERNEZ-MOUDON, A., Architecture, Urban Design and Planning
ZARINA, A., Architecture, Urban Design and Planning

College of Arts and Sciences:

ADAMS, H. S., English
ADAMS, J. B., Geological Sciences
ADELBERGER, E. D., Physics
ALDEN, D., History and International Studies
ALEXANDER, E., English
ALTIERI, C. F., English
AMES, W. E., Communications
AMMIRATI, J., Botany
ANDERSEN, N. H., Chemistry
ANDERSON, F. F., Romance Languages and Literatures
ANDREWS, W. G., Near East Languages and Civilization
ARNOLD, R. R., Art
AUGEROT, J., Slavic Languages and Literatures and International Studies
BACHARACH, J. L., History
BAER, J.-L., Computer Science
BAKER, M., Geophysics and Atmospheric Sciences
BAKER, M., Physics
BALICK, B., Astronomy
BARASH, D. P., Psychology
BARDEEN, J. M., Physics
BARZEL, Y., Economics
BASS, R., Mathematics
BEACH, L. R., Psychology
BEALE, J. M., Music
BECKER, J., Psychiatry and Psychology
BECKMANN, G. M., School of International Studies
BEECHER, M., Psychology
BEHLER, D. E., Germanics and Comparative Literature
BEHLER, E., Germanics and Comparative Literature
BENDICH, A. J., Botany
BENNETT, W. L., Political Science
BENTLEY, G. N., English
BERNSTEIN, I., Psychology
BEYERS, W. B., Geography
BLAKE, K. A., English
BLALOCK, H. M., Jr, Sociology
BLIQUEZ, L. J., Classics and Art
BLISS, L. C., Botany
BLUMENTHAL, R. M., Mathematics
BLUMSTEIN, P., Sociology
BOBA, I., School of International Studies and History
BODANSKY, D., Physics
BOERSMA, P. D., Environmental Studies
BOHM, K.-H., Astronomy
BOHM-VITENSE, E., Astronomy
BOLER, J. F., Philosophy
BOLLES, R. C., Psychology
BONJOUR, L. A., Philosophy
BOOKER, J. R., Geophysics
BORDEN, W. T., Chemistry
BORGATTA, E. F., Sociology
BOSMAJIAN, H. A., Speech
BOSTROM, R. C., Geological Sciences and Geophysics
BOULWARE, D. G., Physics
BOYNTON, P. E., Astronomy and Physics
BRAME, M. K., Linguistics
BRASS, P. R., Political Science and Asian Studies in School of International Studies
BRAVMANN, R. A., Art History
BRIDGMAN, J. M., History
BROWN, F. C., Physics
BROWN, G. M., Economics
BROWN, L. S., Physics
BROWNLEE, D. E., Astronomy
BURKE, R., History
BURNETT, T., Physics
BUTOW, R. J. C., School of International Studies and History
BYERS, B. E., Genetics
CALLIS, J. B., Chemistry
CAMPBELL, F. L., Sociology
CARLSEN, J. C., Music
CARR, J. E., Psychology and Psychiatry
CARRAHER, R. G., Art
CARTER, R. F., Communications
CATTOLICO, R. A., Botany
CELENTANO, F., Art
CHAN, H.-L., International Studies
CHARLSON, R. F., Environmental Studies, Geophysics and Atmospheric Sciences
CHIROT, D., Sociology and International Studies
CHRISTIAN, G. D., Chemistry
CHRISTOFIDES, C. G., Romance Languages and Literature, Comparative Literature and Art
CIRTAUTAS, I. D., Near Eastern Languages and Civilization
CLARK, K. C., Physics and Geophysics
CLAY, J. D., Drama
CLELAND, R. E., Botany
CLONEY, R. A., Zoology
COBURN, R. C., Philosophy
COHEN, S. M., Philosophy
COMTOIS, M. E., Drama
CONLON, F. F., History
CONTRERAS, H., Linguistics
COOK, K. S., Sociology
COOK, V., Physics
CORSON, H. H., Mathematics
COSTNER, H. L., Sociology
COWAN, D. S., Geological Sciences
CRAMER, J. G., Jr, Physics
CREAGER, J. S., Oceanography and Geological Sciences
CRIMINALE, W. O., Jr, Oceanography, Geophysics and Applied Mathematics
CROSSON, R. S., Geophysics
CURJEL, C. R., Mathematics
CURTIS, E. B., Mathematics
CURTIS-VERNA, M., Music
DAHLSTROM, R. A., Drama
DAHN, R. F., Art
DAILEY, M. D., Art
DASH, J. G., Physics
DEHMELT, H. G., Physics
DELMORAL, R., Botany
DEMPSTER, S., Music
DENTON, M. F., Botany
DEVIN, R. M., Drama
DEYRUP-OLSEN, I. J., Zoology
DIETRICHSON, P., Philosophy
DILLON, G. L., English
DOERR, H. O., Psychology and Psychiatry
DUNN, R. J., English
DUNNE, T., Geological Sciences
DUNNELL, R. C., Anthropology
EASTMAN, C. M., Anthropology
EDELSTEIN, A. S., Communications
EDWARDS, J. S., Zoology
EGGERS, D. F., Jr, Chemistry
EICHINGER, B. E., Chemistry
ELLIS, S. D., Physics
ELLISON, H. J., School of International Studies and History
ENGEL, T., Chemistry
EPIOTIS, N., Chemistry
ERICKSON, K. B., Mathematics
EVANS, B. W., Geological Sciences
FAIN, S. C., Physics
FANGMAN, W. L., Genetics
FEIST, R., Music
FELSENSTEIN, J., Genetics
FERRILL, A. L., History
FIEDLER, F. E., Psychology
FLEMING, D. K., Geography
FOLLAND, G. B., Mathematics
FORTSON, E. N., II, Physics
FOWLER, D., English
FOWLER, W. B., History
FREY, C., English
FRIEDMAN, L. J., Romance Languages and Literature
GALLANT, J. A., Genetics

GANGOLLI, R. A., Mathematics
GERBERDING, W. P., Political Science
GERHART, J. B., Physics
GERSTENBERGER, D. L., English
GHIORSO, M., Geological Sciences
GHOSE, S., Geological Sciences
GIFFARD, C. A., Communications
GOLDE, H., Computer Science
GOLDSTEIN, A. A., Mathematics
GORE, W. J., Political Science
GOTTMAN, J. M., Psychology
GOUTERMAN, M. P., Chemistry
GRAYSON, D. K., Anthropology
GREENBERG, R., Mathematics
GREENWALD, A. G., Psychology
GREGORY, N. W., Chemistry
GROSSMAN, A. J., Music
GRUNBAUM, B., Mathematics
GUARRERA, F. P., Music
GUEST, A. M., Sociology
GURALNIK, M. J., Psychology and Paediatrics
HALL, B. D., Genetics
HALLET, B., Geological Sciences
HALPERIN, C. S., Botany
HALPERN, I., Physics
HALSEY, G. D., Jr, Chemistry
HALVORSEN, R., Economics
HANEY, J. V., Slavic Languages and Literatures and International Studies
HANKINS, T. L., History
HANLEY, S. B., International Studies
HARMON, D. P., Classics and Comparative Literature
HARRELL, C. S., Anthropology and International Studies
HARTMANN, D., Atmospheric Sciences
HARTWELL, L. H., Genetics
HASKINS, E. F., Botany
HEER, N. L., Near Eastern Languages and Literature
HELLER, E. J., Chemistry and Physics
HELLMANN, D. C., Political Science and School of International Studies
HENLEY, E. M., Physics
HERTLING, G. H., Germanics
HILDEBRAND, G., Art History and Architecture
HIRSCHMAN, C., Sociology
HIXSON, W. J., Art
HOBBS, P. V., Atmospheric Sciences
HODGE, P. W., Astronomy
HOLTON, J. R., Atmospheric Sciences
HOSTETLER, P. S., Drama
HOUZE, R. A., Atmospheric Physics
HU, M., Art
HUEY, R. B., Zoology
HUNN, E. S., Anthropology
HUNT, E. B., Psychology
HUTTON, R. S., Psychology
INGALLS, R. L., Physics
IRVING, R., Mathematics
JACKSON, W. A. D., Geography and School of International Studies
JACOBSON, N., Psychology
JAEGER, C. S., German
JANS, J. P., Mathematics
JOHNSON, C. R., English
JONES, R. C., Art
KAPETANIC, D., Slavic Languages and Literature, and International Studies
KAPLAN, A., Music
KARTIGANER, D. M., English
KENAGY, G. J., Zoology
KEYES, C. F., Anthropology
KEYT, D., Philosophy
KLAUSENBURGER, J., Romance Languages and Literature
KINGSBURY, M., Art History
KNAPP, J. S., Dance
KNECHTGES, D. R., Asian Languages and Literature
KLEE, V. M., Jr, Mathematics
KOBLITZ, N., Mathematics
KOHN, A. J., Zoology
KORG, J., English
KOTTLER, H. W., Art
KOTTWITZ, R., Mathematics
KOWALSKI, B. R., Chemistry
KRUMME, G., Geography
KUHL, P. K., Speech and Hearing
KWIRAM, A. L., Chemistry
LADNER, R. E., Computer Science
LAIRD, C. D., Zoology
LANG, G. E., Communications, Political Science and Sociology
LANG, K., Communications
LARDY, N., International Studies
LAZOWSKA, E., Computer Science
LEGTERS, L. H., School of International Studies
LEOPOLD, E. B., Botany and Forest Resources
LEOVY, C. B., Atmospheric Sciences and Geophysics
LEV, D. S., Political Science
LEVI, M. A., Political Science
LEVY, F. J., History
LEWIS, B., Geophysics and Oceanography
LIND, D. A., Mathematics
LISTER, C. R. B., Geophysics and Oceanography
LOCKARD, J. S., Psychology and Neurosurgery
LOCKWOOD, T. F., English
LOFTUS, E. J., Psychology
LOFTUS, G. R., Psychology
LOPER, R. B., Drama
LORD, J. J., Physics
LUBATTI, H. J., Physics
LUJAN, H. D., Political Science
LUNDIN, N. K., Art
LUNDQUIST, B. R., Music
LUNNEBORG, C., Psychology and Statistics
MACKAY, P. A., Classics, Comparative Litrature and, Near Eastern Language and Civilization
MCCALLUM, I. S., Geological Sciences
MCCOLL, W. D., Music
MCCRACKEN, J. D., English
MCCRONE, D. J., Political Science
MCDERMOTT, L. C., Physics
MCDERMOTT, M. N., Physics
MCELROY, C. W., English
MCGEE, J. S., Economics
MCHUGH, H., English
MARGON, B., Astronomy
MARKS, C. E., Philosophy
MARLATT, G. A., Psychology
MARSHALL, D., Mathematics
MARSHALL, J. C., Art
MARTIN, R. D., Statistics
MATTHEWS, D. R., Political Science
MAYER, J., Geography
MELTZOFF, A., Psychology
MERRILL, R. T., Geophysics and Geological Sciences
MICHAEL, E. A., Mathematics
MICKLESEN, L. R., Slavic Languages and Literature, Linguistics and International Studies
MIGDAL, J. S., International Studies
MILLER, G., Physics
MILLER, R. A., Asian Languages and Literature
MINIFIE, F. D., Speech and Hearing Sciences
MITCHELL, T. R., Management and Organization and Psychology
MODELSKI, G., Political Science
MODIANO, R., English and Comparative Literature
MORRILL, R. L., Geography and Environmental Studies
MORROW, J. A., Mathematics
MOSELEY, S., Art
NAMIOKA, I., Mathematics
NASON, J. D., Anthropology
NELSON, C. R., Economics
NELSON, T. O., Psychology
NEUMAN, D. M., Art
NEWMEYER, F. J., Linguistics
NEWELL, L. L., Anthropology
NOE, J. D., Computer Science
NORMAN, J. G., Chemistry
NORMAN, J. L., Asian Languages and Literatures
NUNKE, R. J., Mathematics
NUTE, P. E., Anthropology
ODELL, G. M., Zoology
O'DOAN, N. D., Music
OLSON, D. J., Political Science
OPPERMAN, H. N., Art
ORIANS, G. H., Zoology and Environmental Studies
OSBORNE, M. S., Mathematics
OTTENBERG, S., Anthropology
PAINE, R. T., Jr, Zoology
PALAIS, J. B., International Studies and History
PALKA, J. M., Zoology
PALMER, J. M., Prosthodontics and Speech and Hearing Sciences
PARKS, G. K., Geophysics
PARKS, R. W., Economics
PASCAL, P., Classics
PEASE, O. A., History
PEMBER, D. R., Communication
PERLMAN, M. D., Statistics
PERRY, E., International Studies
PETERS, P. C., Physics
PHELPS, R. R., Mathematics
PIZZUTO, E., Art
POCKER, Y., Chemistry
PORTER, S. C., Geological Sciences
POTTER, K. H., International Studies and Philosophy
PRINS, D., Speech and Hearing Sciences
PUFF, R. D., Physics
PUNDT, G. H., Art and Architecture
PYKE, R., Mathematics
PYLE, K. B., International Studies and History
RAGOZIN, D., Mathematics
RAHN, J., Music
RAYMOND, C. F., Geophysics
REED, R., Atmospheric Sciences
REHR, J. J., Physics
REID, B. R., Chemistry
REINERT, O., English and Comparative Literature
RENSBERGER, J. M., Geological Sciences
RESHETAR, J. S., Jr, Political Science
RICHMAN, R. J., Philosophy
RIDDIFORD, L. M., Zoology
RIEDEL, E. K., Physics
ROCKAFELLAR, R. T., Mathematics
ROHWER, S. A., Zoology
RORABAUGH, W. J., History
ROSE, N. J., Chemistry
ROSSEL, S. H., Scandinavian Languages and Literatures
ROTHBERG, J. E., Physics
RUBIN, J., Asian Languages and Literatures
RUSS, J., English
RUTHERFOORD, J. P., Physics
RUZICKA, J., Chemistry
SACKETT, G. P., Psychology
SALE, R. H., English
SAPORTA, S., Linguistics and Romance Languages
SARASON, I. G., Psychology
SARASON, L., Mathematics
SAUM, L. O., History
SAX, G., Education
SCHEIDEL, T. M., Speech
SCHEINGOLD, S. A., Political Science
SCHICK, M., Physics
SCHIFFMAN, H. F., Asian Languages and Literatures
SCHMITT, D. R., Sociology
SCHOMAKER, V., Chemistry
SCHUBERT, W. M., Chemistry
SCHUBIGER, G. A., Zoology
SCHURR, J. M., Chemistry
SCHWARTZ, P., Sociology
SCOTT, J. W., American Ethnic Studies, Sociology
SEGAL, J., Mathematics
SHAW, A. C., Computer Science

SHORACK, G. R., Statistics
SHULMAN, R., English
SIKI, B., Music
SILBERBERG, E., Economics
SILBERGELD, J. L., Art
SIMONSON, H. P., English
SIMPSON, J. B., Psychology
SKOWRONEK, F. E., Music
SLUTSKY, L. J., Chemistry
SMITH, C. W., Art
SMITH, J. D., Oceanography, Geophysics and Geological Sciences
SMITH, R. E., Psychology
SMITH, S. W., Geophysics
SMITH, W. O., Music
SNYDER, L., Computer Science
SNYDER, R., Zoology
SPAFFORD, M. C., Art
STADLER, D. R., Genetics
STAMM, K., Communications
STARK, R., Sociology
STARYK, S. S., Music
STEELE, C. M., Psychology
STEENE, B., Scandinavian Languages and Literature and Comparative Literature
STERN, E. A., Physics
STEVICK, R. D., English
STORCH, L., Music
STOUT, E. L., Mathematics
STRATHMANN, R. R., Zoology
STREITBERGER, W., English
STUIVER, M., Geological Sciences
SUGAR, P. F., History and International Studies
SULLIVAN, J. B., Mathematics
SULLIVAN, W., Astronomy
SWINDLER, D. R., Anthropology
TANIMOTO, S. L., Computer Science
TAYLOR, M. J., Political Science
TELLER, D. Y., Psychology and Physiology
THOMAS, C. S., History
THOMAS, M. D., Geography
THOMPSON, E. A., Statistics
THOMPSON, G., Speech and Hearing Sciences
THORNTON, J., Economics
THOULESS, D. J., Physics
TOWNSEND, J. R., International Studies and Political Science
TREADGOLD, D. W., International Studies and History
TRUMAN, J. W., Zoology
TSUKADA, M., Botany
TUFTS, P. D., Music
UHLMANN, G. A., Mathematics
ULLMAN, J. C., History
UNTERSTEINER, N., Atmospheric Sciences and Geophysics
VANDENBOSCH, R., Chemistry
VAN DEN BERGHE, P. L., Sociology
VANDYCK, R. S., Physics
VELIKONJA, J., Geography
VILCHES, O. E., Physics
VOYLES, J. B., Germanics
WAALAND, J. R., Botany
WADDEN, D. J., Art
WAGER, L. W., Sociology
WAGONER, D. R., English
WALLACE, J. M., Atmospheric Sciences
WALLERSTEIN, G., Astronomy
WAN, F. Y., Applied Mathematics
WANG, C. H., Asian Languages and Literature and Comparative Literature
WARASHINA, P. B., Art
WARD, P., Geological Sciences
WARFIELD, R. B., Mathematics
WARNER, G. W., Jr, Mathematics
WATTS, R. O., Chemistry
WEBB, E., International Studies and Comparative Literature
WEIS, J. G., Sociology
WELLNER, J. A., Statistics
WESTWATER, M. J., Mathematics
WHISLER, H. C., Botany
WHITEHILL-WARD, J., Art
WILETS, L., Physics
WILEY, H., Dance
WILLEFORD, W., English and Comparative Literature
WILLIAMS, R. W., Physics
WILLOWS, A. O. D., Zoology
WILSON, W. R., Speech and Hearing Sciences
WINANS, E. V., Anthropology
WINGFIELD, J., Zoology
WITHERSPOON, G., Anthropology
WOODS, S. C., Psychology
YAMAMURA, K., International Studies
YANTIS, P. A., Speech and Hearing Sciences
YOUNG, K. K., Physics
YOUNG, P. R., Computer Science
ZOLLER, W. H., Chemistry

School of Business Administration:
ALBERTS, W. W., Finance, Business Economics and Quantitative Methods
BOURQUE, P. J., Finance, Business Economics and Quantitative Methods
CHIU, J. S. Y., Management Science
D'AMBROSIO, C. A., Finance, Business Economics
DUKES, R. E., Accounting
ETCHESON, W. W., Marketing
FAALAND, B. H., Finance, Business Economics and Quantitative Methods
FROST, P. A., Finance, Business Economics and Quantitative Methods
HALEY, C. W., Finance, Business Economics and Quantitative Methods
HEATH, L. C., Accounting
HENNING, D. A., Management and Organization
HESS, A. C., Finance, Business Economics and Quantitative Methods
HIGGINS, R. C., Finance, Business Economics and Quantitative Methods
INGENE, C., Marketing and International Business
JACOB, N. L., Finance, Business Economics and Quantitative Methods
JIAMBALVO, J., Accounting
JOHANSSON, J. K., Marketing, Transportation, and International Business
JOHNSON, D. W., Finance, Business Economics and Quantitative Methods
KLASTORIN, T., Management Science
KNUDSON, H. R., Management and Organization
LATHAM, G., Management and Organization
MACLACHLAN, D. L., Marketing
MITCHELL, T. R., Management and Organization
MOINPOUR, R., Marketing, Transportation and International Business
MUELLER, G. G., Accounting
NARVER, J. C., Marketing, Transportation and International Business
NEWELL, W. T., Management and Organization, Management Science
NOREEN, E. W., Accounting
PAGE, A. N., Finance, Business Economics and Quantitative Methods
PETERSON, R. B., Finance, Business Economics and Quantitative Methods
RAMANATHAN, K. V., Accounting
ROLEY, V. V., Finance and Business Economics
SAXBERG, B. O., Management and Organization
SCHALL, L. D., Finance, Business Economics and Quantitative Methods
SCOTT, W. G., Management and Organization
SPRATLEN, T. H., Marketing, Transportation and International Business
SUMMER, C. E., Management and Organization
SUNDEM, G. L., Accounting
WHEATLEY, J. J., Marketing, Transportation and International Business
YALCH, R., Marketing

College of Education:
ABBOTT, R. D.
AFFLECK, J. Q.
ANDERSON, R.
ANDREWS, R. L.
BANKS, J. A.
BILLINGSLEY, F. F.
BOLTON, D. L.
BRAMMER, L. M.
BURGESS, C. O.
BUTTERFIELD, E. C.
DOI, J. I.
EDGAR, E. B.
EVANS, E. D.
GOODLAD, J. I.
HARING, N. G.
HUNKINS, F. P.
JENKINS, J. R.
KALTSOUNIS, T.
KERR, D. H.
KERR, S. T.
KLOCKARS, A. J.
LIEBERMAN, A.
LOVITT, T. C.
LOWENBRAUN, S.
MADSEN, D. L.
MCCARTIN, R. E.
MORISHIMA, J. K.
NEEL, R. S.
OLSTAD, R. G.
PECKHAM, P. D.
RYCKMAN, D. B.
SAX, G.
SCHILL, W. J.
SEBESTA, S. L.
THOMPSON, M. D.
TOSTBERG, R. E.
WHITE, O.
WINN, W. D.

College of Engineering:
AKSAY, I. A., Materials Science Engineering
ALBRECHT, R. W., Electrical and Nuclear Engineering
ALEXANDER, D. E., Mechanical Engineering
ALEXANDRO, F., Electrical Engineering
ALLAN, G. G., Forest Resources and Chemical Engineering
ANDERSEN, J., Electrical Engineering
ARCHBOLD, T. F., Mining, Metallurgical and Ceramic Engineering
BABB, A. L., Chemical and Nuclear Engineering
BALISE, P. L., Mechanical Engineering
BEREANO, P., Interdepartmental Curricular Programme
BERG, J. C., Chemical Engineering
BOGAN, R. H., Civil Engineering
BOLLARD, R. J. H., Aeronautics and Astronautics
BOWEN, J. R., Chemical Engineering
BRADT, R. C., Mining, Metallurgical and Ceramic Engineering
BROWN, C. B., Civil Engineering
BURGES, S. J., Civil Engineering
CHALUPNIK, J. D., Mechanical Engineering
CHEUNG, P. W., Electrical Engineering and Bioengineering
CHRISTIANSEN, W. H., Aeronautics and Astronautics
CLARK, R. N., Electrical Engineering
COLCORD, J. E., Civil Engineering
CORLETT, R. C., Mechanical Engineering
DALY, C. H., Mechanical Engineering
DAVIS, E. J., Chemical Engineering
DECHER, R., Aeronautics and Astronautics
DEPEW, C. A., Mechanical Engineering
DOW, D. G., Electrical Engineering
ELIAS, Z. M., Civil Engineering
EMERY, A. F., Mechanical Engineering
EVANS, R. J., Civil Engineering
FERGUSON, J. F., Civil Engineering
FINLAYSON, B. A., Chemical Engineering
FISCHBACH, D. B., Materials Science and Engineering
FYFE, I. M., Aeronautics and Astronautics
GARLID, K. L., Chemical and Nuclear Engineering
GESSNER, F., Mechanical Engineering

HARALICK, R. M., Electrical Engineering
HAWKINS, N. M., Civil Engineering
HEIDEGER, W. J., Chemical Engineering
HERTZBERG, A., Aeronautics and Astronautics
HOFFMAN, A. S., Chemical Engineering and Bioengineering
HOLDEN, A., Electrical Engineering
HOLSAPPLE, K. A., Aeronautics and Astronautics
HSU, C.-C., Electrical Engineering
ISHIMARU, A., Electrical Engineering
JOHNSON, D. E., Bioengineering
JOHNSON, D. L., Electrical Engineering
JOPPA, R. G., Aeronautics and Astronautics
JORGENSEN, J. E., Mechanical Engineering
KEVORKIAN, J. K., Aeronautics and Astronautics
KIPPENHAM, C. J., Mechanical Engineering
KOBAYASHI, A. S., Mechanical Engineering
KOSALY, G., Nuclear and Mechanical Engineering
KUROSAKA, M., Aeronautics and Astronautics
LAURITZEN, P. O., Electrical Engineering
LYTLE, D. W., Electrical Engineering
MCCORMICK, N. J., Nuclear Engineering
MCKEAN, W. T., Chemical Engineering and Forest Resources
MALTE, P. C., Mechanical Engineering
MAR, B. W., Civil Engineering
MARKS, R. J., Electrical Engineering
MATTOCK, A. H., Civil Engineering
MEDITCH, J. S., Electrical Engineering
MONTGOMERY, D. C., Industrial Engineering
MORITZ, W. E., Electrical Engineering
NECE, R. E., Civil Engineering
NIHAN, N. L., Civil Engineering
NOGES, E., Electrical Engineering
PARMETER, R. R., Aeronautics and Astronautics
PEARSON, C. E., Aeronautics and Astronautics, Applied Mathematics
PEDEN, I., Electrical Engineering
PILAT, M. J., Civil Engineering
PINTER, R. E., Electrical Engineering
POLONIS, D. H., Mining, Metallurgical and Ceramic Engineering
PORTER, R. P., Electrical Engineering
PRATT, D. T., Mechanical Engineering
RAO, Y. K., Mining, Metallurgical and Ceramics Engineering
RATNER, B., Bioengineering and Chemical Engineering
RIBE, F. L., Nuclear Engineering
RILEY, J., Mechanical Engineering
ROBKIN, M. A., Nuclear Engineering
ROEDER, C. W., Civil Engineering
RUSSELL, D. A., Aeronautics and Astronautics
SCHNEIDER, J. B., Urban Planning and Civil Engineering
SCOTT, W. D., Mining, Metallurgical and Ceramic Engineering
SEFERIS, J. C., Chemical Engineering
SIGELMANN, R. A., Electrical Engineering
SLEICHER, C. A., Jr, Chemical Engineering
SPINDEL, R. C., Electrical Engineering
STEAR, E. B., Electrical Engineering
STENSEL, H. D., Civil Engineering
STOEBE, T. G., Mining, Metallurgical and Ceramic Engineering
TAGGART, R., Mechanical Engineering
TSANG, L., Electrical Engineering
VAGNERS, J., Aeronautics and Astronautics
VENKATA, S. S., Electrical Engineering
VERESS, S. A., Civil Engineering
VESPER, K. H., Mechanical Engineering and Management and Organization, Marine Studies
VLASES, G. C., Nuclear Engineering
WELCH, E. B., Civil Engineering
WOLAK, J., Mechanical Engineering
WOODRUFF, G. L., Nuclear Engineering
YEE, S. S., Electrical Engineering
ZICK, G. L., Electrical Engineering

College of Ocean and Fishery Science:

School of Oceanography:

BANSE, K.
CARPENTER, R.
COACHMAN, L.
CREAGER, H. S.
DELANEY, J.
EMERSON, S.
ERIKSEN, C.
FROST, B. W.
HEATH, G. R.
HEDGES, J.
HERSHMAN, M. J.
JUMARS, P. A.
LEWIS, B.
LISTER, C. R. B.
MCMANUS, D. A.
MERRILL, R. T.
MILES, E. L.
MURPHY, S. R.
MURRAY, J.
NOWELL, A. R. M.
RHINES, P. B.
RICHARDS, F. A.
SMITH, J. D.
STERNBERG, R. W.
WELANDER, P.
WINTER, D. R.
WOOSTER, W. S.

School of Fisheries:

BRANNON, E. L.
BROWN, G. W.
CHEW, K. K.
FORD, E. D.
FRANCIS, R. C.
GALLUCCI, V. F.
HALVER, J. D.
HILBORN, R. W.
LANDOLT, M.
LISTON, J.
MATCHES, J. R.
MATHEWS, S. B.
MILLER, B. S.
PIETSCH, T. W.
PIGOTT, G. M.
SCHELL, W. R.
SMITH, L. S.
STICKNEY, R. R.
TAUB, F.
WHITNEY, R. R.

College of Forest Resources:

ADAMS, D. M.
AGEE, J. K.
ALLAN, G. G., Forest Resources and Chemical Engineering
BARE, B. B.
BETHEL, J. S.
BRUBAKER, L. B.
COLE, D. W.
DOWDLE, B.
EDMONDS, R. L.
FIELD, D. R.
FRITSCHEN, L. J.
GARA, R. I.
HATHEWAY, W. H.
HINCKLEY, T. M.
HRUTFIORD, B. F.
LEE, R. G.
MANUWAL, D. A.
OLIVER, C.
PICKFORD, S. G.
SARKENEN, K., Forest Resources and Chemical Engineering
SCHREUDER, G. F.
SHARPE, G. W.
STETTLER, R. F.
THORUD, D. B.
TUKEY, H. B.
UGOLINI, F. C.
WAGGENER, T. R.
WOTT, J. A.

Graduate School of Library and Information Science:

CHISHOLM, M. E., Library and Information Science

Graduate School of Public Affairs:

DENNY, B. C.
KROLL, M., Public Affairs and Political Science
LOCKE, H. G.
LYDEN, F. J.
WILLIAMS, W.
ZERBE, R. O.

School of Dentistry:

AMMONS, W. F., Periodontics
BOLENDER, C. L., Prosthodontics
BRUDVIK, J. S., Prosthodontics
CANFIELD, R. C., Restorative Dentistry
CLAGETT, J. A., Periodontics and Microbiology
CONRAD, D. A., Dental Public Health Sciences and Health Services
DERONEN, T. A., Dental Public Health Services, Biostatistics
DWORKIN, S. F., Oral Surgery
ENGEL, D., Periodontics
FRANK, R. P., Prosthodontics
GEHRIG, J. D., Oral Surgery
HARRINGTON, G. W., Endodontics
JOHNSON, R. H., Periodontics
KOKICH, V., Orthodontics
LEWIS, T. M., Restorative Dentistry
LITTLE, R. M., Orthodontics
MILGROM, P. M., Dental Public Health Services
MOFFETT, B. C., Orthodontics
MYALL, R. W., Oral Surgery
NATKIN, E., Endodontics
NICHOLLS, J. I., Restorative Dentistry
OMNELL, K.-A., Oral Medicine
PAGE, R. C., Pathology and Periodontics
PALMER, J. M., Speech and Hearing Sciences and Prosthodontics
ROBINOVITCH, M. R., Oral Biology
SHAPIRO, P., Orthodontics
SMITH, D. E., Prosthodontics
TAMARIN, A., Oral Biology
WARNICK, M. E., Restorative Dentistry
WORTHINGTON, P., Oral and Maxillofacial Surgery
YUODELIS, R. A., Restorative Dentistry

School of Law:

ANDERSON, W. R.
ARONSON, R. H.
BURKE, W. T.
CHISUM, D. S.
FITZPATRICK, J. F.
FLETCHER, R. L.
HALEY, J. O.
HARDISTY, J. H.
HAZELTON, P. A.
HENDERSON, D. F.
HJORTH, R. L.
HUME, L. S.
HUSTON, J. C.
JAY, S. M.
JOHNSON, R. W.
JUNKER, J. M.
KUMMERT, R. O.
LOH, W. D.
MORRIS, A.
PECK, C. J.
PRICE, J. R.
PROSTERMAN, R. L.
RODDIS, R. S.
RODGERS, W. H.
ROMBAUER, M.
SMITH, F. W., Jr
STOEBUCK, W. B.
TRAUTMAN, P. A.

School of Medicine:

ABELSON, H. T., Paediatrics
ABRASS, I., Medicine
ADAMSON, J. W., Medicine

ALBERT, R., Medicine
ALMERS, W., Physiology and Biophysics
ALVORD, E. C., Pathology
ANDERSON, M. E., Rehabilitation Medicine and Physiology
ANSELL, J. S., Urology
APPELBAUM, F., Medicine
BARNES, G. W., Urology
BASSINGTHWAIGHTE, J. B., Bioengineering
BEAVO, J., Pharmacology
BECKER, J., Psychiatry, Psychology
BELKNAP, B. H., Medicine
BENEDETTI, T. J., Obstetrics and Gynaecology
BEN-MENACHEM, Y., Radiology
BERGER, A. J., Physiology and Biophysics
BERGMAN, A. B., Paediatrics
BERNSTEIN, I. D., Paediatrics
BIERMAN, E. L., Medicine
BINDER, M., Physiology and Biophysics
BIRD, T., Medicine
BLACKMON, J. R., Medicine
BLAGG, C. R., Medicine
BLEYER, W. A., Paediatrics
BORNSTEIN, P., Medicine and Biochemistry
BOWDEN, D. M., Psychiatry
BREMNER, W. J., Medicine
BRENGELMANN, G., Physiology and Biophysics
BROWN, B. G., Medicine
BRUNZELL, J. D., Medicine
BUCHANAN, T. M., Medicine and Pathobiology
BUCKNER, C. D., Medicine
BUNT-MILAM, A. H., Ophthalmology
BUTLER, J., Medicine
BYERS, P., Medicine and Pathology
CARR, J. E., Psychiatry and Psychology
CARRICO, C. J., Surgery
CATTERALL, W. A., Pharmacology
CHAIT, A., Medicine
CHAMPOUX, J. J., Microbiology
CHAPMAN, C. R., Anaesthesiology and Psychiatry
CHAPMAN, W. H., Urology
CHATRIAN, G. E., Laboratory Medicine and Neurological Surgery
CHEEVER, M. A., Medicine
CHENEY, F. W., Anaesthesiology
CHESNUT, C. H., Radiology and Medicine
CLARREN, S., Paediatrics
COBB, L. A., Medicine
COPASS, M. K., Medicine
COUNTS, G. W., Medicine
COUSER, W. G., Medicine
COREY, L., Laboratory Medicine and Microbiology
COUNTS, G. W., Medicine
CRILL, W. E., Medicine, Physiology and Biophysics
CROAKE, J. S., Psychiatry
CULLEN, B. F., Anaesthesiology
CUMMINGS, C. W., Otolaryngology
DALE, D. C., Medicine
DAVIE, E. W., Biochemistry
DEISHER, R. W., Paediatrics
DELATEUR, B. J., Rehabilitation Medicine
DETTER, J. C., Laboratory Medicine
DETWILER, P., Physiology and Biophysics
DILLARD, D. H., Surgery
DOBIE, R. A., Otolaryngology
DODGE, H. T., Medicine
DODRILL, C. B., Neurological Surgery
DOERR, H. O., Psychiatry and Psychology
DOHNER, C. W., Medicine and Education
DONALDSON, J. A., Otolaryngology
DUNNER, D. L., Psychiatry
EISENBERG, M., Medicine
EMANUEL, I., Epidemiology and International Health and Paediatrics
ENSINCK, J. W., Medicine
ESCHENBACH, D., Obstetrics and Gynaecology
EYRE, D. R., Orthopaedics
FARRELL, D. F., Medicine
FEFER, A., Medicine
FEIGL, E., Physiology and Biophysics
FETZ, E. E., Physiology and Biophysics
FIALKOW, P. J., Medicine and Genetics
FIGGE, D. C., Obstetrics and Gynaecology
FIGLEY, M. M., Radiology
FISCHER, E. H., Biochemistry
FRENCH, J. W., Paediatrics
FUCHS, A., Physiology and Biophysics
FUJIMOTO, W. Y., Medicine
GARTLER, S. M., Medicine, Genetics
GEYMAN, J. P., Family Medicine
GILLILAND, B., Laboratory Medicine and Medicine
GLOMSET, J. A., Medicine and Biochemistry
GODWIN, J. D., Radiology
GOLDMAN, M. L., Radiology
GOODNER, C. J., Medicine
GORDON, A. M., Physiology and Biophysics
GORDON, M., Biochemistry
GRAHAM, C. B., Radiology and Paediatrics
GREENBERG, P., Medicine
GREENE, H. L., Medicine
GREER, B. E., Obstetrics and Gynaecology
GRIFFIN, T. W., Radiation Oncology
GROMAN, N. B., Microbiology
GROUDINE, M., Radiation Oncology
GUNTHEROTH, W. G., Paediatrics
GUY, A., Rehabilitation Medicine and Bioengineering
HAGGITT, R. C., Pathology
HAKOMORI, S., Pathobiology and Microbiology
HALAR, E. M., Rehabilitation Medicine
HANDSFIELD, H. H., Medicine
HANSEN, J. A., Medicine
HANSEN, S., Orthopaedics
HARLEY, J. D., Radiology
HARRIS, A. B., Neurological Surgery
HAUSCHKA, S. D., Biochemistry
HAYDEN, P., Paediatrics
HEIMAN, J., Psychiatry and Behavioural Sciences
HEIMBACH, D. M., Surgery
HELLSTROM, I. E., Microbiology
HELLSTROM, K. E., Pathology
HENDERSON, M., Medicine and Epidemiology
HENDRICKSON, A. E., Ophthalmology and Biological Structure
HERMAN, C. M., Surgery
HILLE, B., Physiology and Biophysics
HILDEBRANDT, J., Physiology and Medicine
HLASTALA, M. P., Physiology and Biophysics and Medicine
HODSON, W. A., Paediatrics
HOLBROOK, K. A., Biological Structure
HOLMES, K. K., Medicine
HORITA, A., Pharmacology
HORNBEIN, T. F., Anaesthesiology, Physiology and Biophysics
HUDSON, L. D., Medicine
HUNTSMAN, L. L., Bioengineering
INUI, T. S., Medicine and Health Services
IVEY, T. D., Surgery
JOHANSEN, K. H., Surgery
JOHNSON, M. H., Psychiatry
JONES, R. F., Surgery
JONSEN, A. R., Medical History and Ethics
JUCHAU, M. R., Pharmacology
KALINA, R. E., Ophthalmology
KEHL, T. H., Physiology, Biophysics and Computer Science
KELLY, W. A., Neurological Surgery
KENNEDY, J. W., Medicine
KENNY, M. A., Laboratory Medicine
KLEBANOFF, S. J., Medicine
KNOPP, R. H., Medicine
KOEHLER, J. K., Biological Structure
KOERKER, D. J., Physiology and Biophysics and Medicine
KRAFT, G. H., Rehabilitation Medicine
KREBS, E. G., Pharmacology and Biochemistry
KROHN, K., Radiology
LABBE, R. F., Laboratory Medicine
LAKSHMINARAYAN, S., Medicine
LANDESMAN, S., Psychiatry
LARAMORE, G., Radiation Oncology
LARSON, E., Medicine
LEHMANN, J. F., Rehabilitation Medicine
LEIN, J. N., Obstetrics and Gynaecology
LEMIRE, R. J., Paediatrics
LIVINGSTON, R. B., Medicine
LOCKARD, J. S., Neurological Surgery
LOEB, L. A., Pathology
LOESER, J. B., Neurological Surgery
LOGERFO, J. P., Medicine and Health Services
LOOP, J. W., Radiology
LUFT, J. H., Biological Structure
MACK, L. A., Radiology
MACKLER, B., Paediatrics
MANNIK, M., Medicine
MARAVILLA, K. R., Radiology and Neurological Surgery
MARCHIORO, T. L., Surgery
MARTIN, G. M., Pathology
MARTIN, J. C., Psychiatry
MATSEN, F. A., Orthopaedics
MAYO, M. E., Urology
MCARTHUR, J. R., Medicine
MCDONALD, G. B., Medicine
MEYERS, J., Medicine
MILLS, R. P., Ophthalmology
MONSEN, E. R., Medicine
MORRIS, D. R., Biochemistry
MOSS, A. A., Radiology
MOTTET, N. K., Pathology and Environmental Health
MOTULSKY, A., Genetics and Medicine
MURPHY, T. M., Anaesthesiology
NEFF, J. M., Paediatrics
NEIMAN, P. E., Medicine
NELP, W. B., Medicine and Radiology
NELSON, J. A., Radiology
NESTER, E. W., Microbiology
NORWOOD, T., Pathology
NOVACK, A. H., Paediatrics
OCHS, H. D., Paediatrics
ODLAND, G. F., Medicine, Biological Structure
OJEMANN, G. A., Neurological Surgery
OMENN, G. S., Medicine and Environmental Health
PAGE, R. C., Pathology and Periodontics
PALMER, J., Medicine
PALMITER, R. D., Biochemistry
PAPAYANNOPOULOU, T., Medicine
PARSON, W. W., Biochemistry
PAULSEN, C. A., Medicine
PETRA, P. H., Obstetrics and Gynaecology and Biochemistry
PHILLIPS, T. J., Family Medicine
PIERSON, D., Medicine
PIOUS, D. A., Paediatrics
PLORDE, J. J., Laboratory Medicine
POLLACK, G. H., Bioengineering
POPE, C. E., Medicine
PORTE, D., Medicine
PRESTON, T. A., Medicine
PRINZ, P., Psychiatry
RAISYS, V., Laboratory Medicine
RASEY, J. S., Radiation Oncology
RASKIND, M. A., Psychiatry
RAUSCH, R. L., Animal Medicine and Pathobiology
REICHENBACH, D. D., Pathology
REICHLER, R. J., Psychiatry
REID, B. R., Biochemistry and Chemistry
RICE, C. L., Surgery
RITCHIE, J. L., Medicine
ROBERTS, T. S., Neurological Surgery
ROBERTSON, W. O., Paediatrics
ROBINSON, N. L., Psychiatry
RODIECK, R. W., Ophthalmology
ROHRMAN, C. A., Radiology
ROOS, B. A., Medicine
ROSENBLATT, R. A., Family Medicine
ROSS, R., Pathology
ROSSE, C., Biological Structure
ROWELL, L. B., Physiology and Biophysics
RUBELL, E. W., Otolaryngology
RUBIN, C. E., Medicine

Ruvalcaba, R., Paediatrics
Saari, J. C., Ophthalmology and Biochemistry
Sale, G., Pathology
Saunders, D. R., Medicine
Scher, A. M., Physiology and Biophysics
Schmer, G., Laboratory Medicine
Schoenknecht, F. D., Laboratory Medicine and Microbiology
Schuffler, M., Medicine
Schwartz, S. M., Pathology
Schwartzkroin, P., Neurological Surgery and Physiology, Biophysics
Schwindt, P. C., Physiology and Biophysics
Scott, C. R., Paediatrics
Scribner, B. H., Medicine
Sells, C. J., Paediatrics
Shapiro, B. M., Biochemistry
Shaw, C., Pathology
Shepard, T. H., Paediatrics
Sherrard, D. J., Medicine
Sherris, J. C., Microbiology
Shurtleff, D. B., Paediatrics
Silverstein, F., Medicine
Simkin, P. A., Medicine
Singer, J., Medicine
Slichter, S., Medicine
Smith, A. L., Paediatrics
Smith, O. A. Jr, Physiology and Biophysics
Snyder, J. M., Otolaryngology
Soules, M. R., Obstetrics and Gynaecology
Spadoni, L. R., Obstetrics and Gynaecology
Spence, A. M., Medicine
Staheli, L. T., Orthopaedics
Stahl, W., Medicine, Physiology and Biophysics
Staley, J. T., Microbiology
Stamatoyannopoulos, G., Medicine
Stamm, W., Medicine
Steiner, R., Obstetrics and Gynaecology, Physiology and Biophysics
Stenchever, M. A., Obstetrics and Gynaecology
Stevenson, J. G., Paediatrics
Stirling, C. E., Physiology and Biophysics
Stolov, W. C., Rehabilitation Medicine
Storm, D. R., Pharmacology
Strandjord, P. E., Laboratory Medicine
Strandness, D. E., Surgery
Streissguth, A. P., Psychiatry
Sumi, S. M., Medicine and Pathology
Swanson, P. D., Medicine
Tapper, D., Surgery
Teller, D. C., Biochemistry
Teller, D. Y., Physiology and Psychology
Thomas, E. D., Medicine
Thompson, A. R., Medicine
Towe, A. L., Physiology and Biophysics
Townes, B. D., Psychiatry
Trier, W. C., Surgery
Truog, W. E., Paediatrics
Tucker, G. J., Psychiatry
Turck, M., Medicine
VanArsdel, P. P., Medicine
VanCitters, R. L., Physiology and Biophysics, Medicine
VanHoosier, G. L., Animal Medicine
Vestal, R., Medicine
Vincenzi, F. F., Pharmacology
Vontver, L., Obstetrics and Gynaecology
Vracko, R., Pathology
Walker, R. D., Psychiatry and Behavioural Science
Wallace, J. F., Medicine
Walsh, K. A., Biochemistry
Ward, R. J., Anaesthesiology
Wedgwood, R. J., Paediatrics
Westrum, L. E., Neurological Surgery and Biological Structure
Weymuller, E. A., Otolaryngology
Whiteley, H. R., Microbiology
Whorton, J. C., Biomedical History
Wight, T., Pathology
Winn, H. R., Neurological Surgery
Winterscheid, L. C., Surgery
Woodrum, D. E., Paediatrics
Wooton, P., Radiation Oncology
Young, E. T., Biochemistry
Zager, R., Medicine

School of Nursing:

Barnard, K. E., Parent and Child Nursing
Batey, M. V., Community Health Care Systems
Benoliel, J. Q., Community Health Care Systems
Chrisman, N. J., Community Health Care Systems
De Tornyay, R., Community Health Care Systems
Eyres, S. J., Parent and Child Nursing
Gallucci, B. J., Physiological Nursing
Goertzen, I. E., Community Health Care Systems
Horn, B. J., Community Health Care Systems
Hegyvary, S. T., Community Health Care Systems
Kogan, H., Psychosocial Nursing
Kuramoto, A., Physiological Nursing
Lewis, F. M., Community Health Care Systems
Mitchell, P. H., Physiological Nursing
Osborne, O. H., Psychosocial Nursing
Patrick, M. I., Physiological Nursing
Rose, M. H., Parent and Child Nursing
Wolf-Wilets, V. C., Psychosocial Nursing
Woods, N. A., Physiological Nursing

School of Pharmacy:

Baillie, T., Medicinal Chemistry
Brady, L. R., Medicinal Chemistry
Campbell, W. H., Pharmacy Practice
Gibaldi, M., Pharmaceutics
Kradjan, W., Pharmacy Practice
Levy, R. H., Pharmaceutics
Nelson, S. D., Medicinal Chemistry
Nelson, W. L., Medicinal Chemistry
Plein, J. B., Pharmacy Practice
Trager, W. F., Medicinal Chemistry

School of Social Work:

Briar, S.
Gottlieb, N. R.
Hawkins, J. D.
Jaffee, B.
Levy, R. L.
Patti, R. J.
Resnick, H.
Takagi, C. Y.
Whittaker, J. K.

School of Public Health and Community Medicine:

Breslow, N. E., Biostatistics
Buchanan, T. L., Pathobiology and Medicine
Crowley, J. J., Biostatistics
Daling, J. R., Epidemiology
Davis, K. A., Biostatistics
Day, R. W., Health Services
De Rouen, T., Biostatistics
Diehr, P. K., Biostatistics
Emanuel, I., Epidemiology and Paediatrics
Feigl, P., Biostatistics
Fisher, L. D., Biostatistics
Fleming, T. R., Biostatistics
Foy, H. M., Epidemiology
Gale, J. I., Epidemiology
Grayston, J. T., Epidemiology
Hakomori, S., Pathobiology and Microbiology
Henderson, M. M., Epidemiology and Medicine
Inui, T. S., Health Services and Medicine
Jackson, K. L., Environmental Health
Kenny, G. E., Pathobiology
Koepsell, T., Health Services, Epidemiology
Kronmal, R. A., Biostatistics
Kuo, C.-C., Pathobiology
Lee, J. A., Environmental Health
Logerfo, J. P., Health Services and Medicine
Martin, D. C., Biostatistics
Moolgavkar, S. H., Epidemiology
Mottet, N. K., Environmental Health and Pathology
Murphy, S. D., Environmental Health
Omenn, G. S., Environmental Health and Medicine
Patrick, D. L., Health Services
Perine, P. L., Epidemiology
Perrin, E. B., Health Services
Peterson, A. V., Biostatistics
Prentice, R. L., Biostatistics
Rausch, R. L., Pathobiology
Robkin, M. A., Environmental Health and Nuclear Engineering
Thomas, D. B., Epidemiology
Van Belle, G., Biostatistics
Wagner, E. H., Health Services
Wahl, P. W., Biostatistics
Wang, S., Pathobiology
Weiss, N. S., Epidemiology
Wilson, J. T., Environmental Health
Worthington-Roberts, B., Epidemiology

WALLA WALLA COLLEGE

204 South College Avenue, College Place, WA 99324

Telephone: (509) 527-2615

Founded 1892

President: W. G. Nelson
Vice-President for Academic Administration: John Brunt
Vice-President for Student Administration: Nelson Thomas
Vice-President for Financial Administration: Manford Simcock
Vice-President for College Advancement: Karen Johnson
Registrar: Carolyn Denney
Vice-President for Admissions and Marketing: Stephen Payne
Director of Libraries: Carolyn Gaskell

Library of 170,000 vols
Number of teachers: 125
Number of students: 1,650

WASHINGTON STATE UNIVERSITY

Pullman, WA 99164

Telephone: (509) 335-3564

Founded (as college) 1890; university 1959
Academic year: August to May

President: Samuel H. Smith
Provost: Gretchen M. Bataille
Vice-President for Business Affairs: Sallie A. Giffen
Vice-President for Extended University Affairs: Thomas L. Purce
Registrar: Monty Nielsen
Director, Libraries: Nancy Baker

Library of 1,888,000 vols
Number of teachers: 1,253 including 382 professors
Number of students: 20,020

DEANS

College of Agriculture and Home Economics: James J. Zuiches
College of Economics and Business: A. Gale Sullenberger
College of Education: Walt Gmelch (interim)
College of Engineering: Robert Altenkirch
Graduate School: Karen de Pauw (interim)
Intercollegiate Center for Nursing Education, Spokane: Dorothy Detlor-Langan
College of Pharmacy: Mahmoud M. Abdel-Monem
College of Sciences: Leon Radziemski
College of Veterinary Medicine: Borje Gustafsson
College of Liberal Arts: Gail Chermak (interim)

WESTERN WASHINGTON UNIVERSITY

Bellingham, WA 98225

Telephone: (206) 650-3000

Founded 1893 as Bellingham Normal School, name changed to Western Washington College of Education 1937, finally Western Washington University 1977

President: Dr Karen Morse
Provost/Vice-President for Academic Affairs: Dr Roland L. De Lorme
Vice-President for Business and Financial Affairs: Dr George A. Pierce
Vice-President for Student Affairs: Dr Eileen V. Coughlin
Vice-President for External Affairs: Dr Albert J. Froderberg
Librarian: Dr Judith Segal

Library of 593,644 vols
Number of teachers: 507
Number of students: 11,039

WHITMAN COLLEGE

345 Boyer Ave, Walla Walla, WA 99362

Telephone: (509) 527-5111

Founded 1859

President: Dr Thomas Cronin
Vice-President for Development: Stephen Becker
Dean of Faculty: Patrick Keef
Dean of Students: Charles Cleveland
Registrar: Ronald Urban
Librarian: Henry Yaple

Library of 325,000 vols
Number of teachers: 101 full-time
Number of students: 1,300

WHITWORTH COLLEGE

300 West Hawthorne Rd, Spokane, WA 99251

Telephone: (509) 777-1000
Fax: (509) 777-3221

Founded 1890
Christian liberal arts college in the Reformed tradition

President: Dr William P. Robinson
Vice-President of Academic Affairs: Dr Tammy Reid
Library Director: Dr Hans Bynagle

Library of 165,000 vols
Number of teachers: 267
Number of students: 2,100

WEST VIRGINIA

ALDERSON-BROADDUS COLLEGE

Philippi, WV 26416

Telephone: (304) 457-1700
Fax: (304) 457-6239

Founded 1871
Four-year liberal arts college
Academic year: August to May (two semesters) plus summer sessions

President: Dr Stephen E. Markwood
Provost and Academic Dean: Dr Kenneth Yount
Director of Admissions: Eric Ruf
Director of Financial Aid: Michael Short
Dean of External Education: Dr Donald A. Smith
Director of Development: (vacant)
Dean of Student Life: Dr Dennis Stull
Business Manager: Marsha Denniston
Registrar: Saundra Hoxie
Librarian: David E. Hoxie

Library of 107,651 vols
Number of teachers: 51 full-time, 15 part-time
Number of students: 703

BETHANY COLLEGE

Bethany, WV 26032

Telephone: (304) 829-7000
Fax: (304) 829-7108

Founded 1840
Private control

President: D. Duane Cummins
Vice-President for Institutional Advancement: William N. Johnston
Vice-President for Academic Affairs and Dean: Pamela M. Balch
Vice-President for Student Affairs and Dean: John S. Cunningham
Vice-President for Finances and Treasurer: Joseph M. Kurey
Registrar: John Giesmann
Librarian: Mary E. Halford

Library of 200,000 vols
Number of teachers: 58 full-time, 3 part-time
Number of students: 758

Publications: *Folio* (annually), *Harbinger* (annually), *Bethanian* (annually), *Tower* (weekly), *Bethany College Bulletin* (annually), *Bethany Bulletin* (quarterly), *The Campbell Light* (quarterly).

BLUEFIELD STATE COLLEGE

219 Rock St, Bluefield, WV 24701

Telephone: (304) 327-4000
Fax: (304) 325-7747

Founded 1895

President: Robert E. Moore
Provost: Betty Rader
Registrar: E. Ralph Patsel
Manager of Library Services: Joanna Thompson

Library of 69,300 vols
Number of teachers: 77
Number of students: 2,506

CONCORD COLLEGE

Vermillion St, POB 1000, Athens, WV 24712

Telephone: (304) 384-3115
Fax: (304) 384-9044

Founded 1872

President: Dr Jerry L. Beasley
Vice-President and Academic Dean: Dr Dean W. Turner
Registrar: R. Mull
Librarian: Robert Turnbull

Library of 112,000 vols
Number of teachers: 95
Number of students: 2,631

DAVIS AND ELKINS COLLEGE

Elkins, WV 26241

Telephone: (304) 637-1900

Founded 1904

President: Dr Dorothy I. MacConkey
Dean of the Faculty: Dr Clarence L. Coffindaffer
Vice-President for Development: Charles Blewett
Vice-President for Enrollment Management: Victor Thacker
Director of Admissions: Kevin D. Chenoweth
Registrar: Dr Russell Shepherd
Director of the Library: Ellis Hodges

Library of 116,000 vols
Number of teachers: 52 full-time, 25 part-time
Number of students: 787

FAIRMONT STATE COLLEGE

Locust Avenue, Fairmont, WV 26554

Telephone: (800) 641-5678
Fax: (304) 366-4870

Founded 1867

President: Janet Dudley-Eshbach
Vice-President for Academic Affairs: Fred Fidura
Vice-President for Administration and Finance: Frederick Schaupp
Vice-President for Student Affairs: (vacant)
Provost for the Community and Technical College: Vicki Riley (interim)
Registrar: John G. Conaway (acting)
Librarian: Robert Masters

Library of 265,000 vols
Number of teachers: 190
Number of students: 6,500

GLENVILLE STATE COLLEGE

Glenville, WV 26351

Telephone: (304) 462-7361

Founded 1872

President: Dr William K. Simmons
Dean of Academic Affairs: Dr James L. Peterson
Librarian: Dr Richard Tubesing

Library of 150,000 vols
Number of teachers: 89
Number of students: 2,096

MARSHALL UNIVERSITY

Huntington, WV 25755

Telephone: (304) 696-2300
Fax: (304) 696-6453

Founded 1837

President: J. Wade Gilley
Vice-President for Academic Affairs: Dr Sarah Denman
Vice-President, Financial Affairs: Herbert Karlet
Vice-President, Health Sciences/Dean, School of Medicine: Dr Charles McKown
Vice-President, Development: Frank P. Justice
Vice-President for Operations: Dr Ed Grose
Dean of Student Affairs: Donnalee Cockrille
Director of Libraries: Ms Josephine Fidler
Director of University Relations: C. T. Mitchell

Library of 426,200 vols
Number of teachers: 584 full-time
Number of students: 15,696

DEANS

Community College: Dr Betty Kyger
College of Education: Dr Larry Froehlich
College of Fine Arts: Donald van Horn
College of Liberal Arts: Dr Joan T. Mead
College of Business: Dr Calvin Kent
College of Science: Dr Thomas Sporch
Graduate School: Dr Leonard Deutsch
School of Nursing: Dr Lynne B. Welch

SALEM-TEIKYO UNIVERSITY

223 West Main Street, POB 500, Salem, WV 26426-0500

Telephone: (304) 782-5011
Fax: (304) 782-5395

Founded 1888

President: Dr Ronald E. Ohl
Vice-President for Academic Affairs and Provost: Dr Wayne H. England
Registrar: Cynthia J. Calise
Librarian: Dr Phyllis D. Freedman

Library of 200,000 vols
Number of teachers: 55 full-time and 25 part-time
Number of students: 810

SHEPHERD COLLEGE

Shepherdstown, WV 25443

Telephone: (304) 876-5000
Fax: (304) 876-3101

Founded 1871

President: Dr DAVID L. DUNLOP
Vice-President for Academic Affairs: Dr MARK STERN
Librarian: Dr JOSEPH BARNES

Library of 210,000 vols
Number of teachers: 127
Number of students: 4,000

UNIVERSITY OF CHARLESTON

2300 MacCorkle Ave, SE, Charleston, WV 25304

Telephone: (304) 357-4800
Fax: (304) 357-4715

Founded 1888 as Morris Harvey College, present name 1979

President: EDWIN H. WELCH
Vice-President for Academic Life and Dean of Faculty: Dr ROBERT FREY
Vice-President for Finance and Administration: JERRY FORSTER
Vice-President for Enrollment Management and Dean of Student Life: BETH CICCARELLO
Director of Admissions: (vacant)
Librarian: DONNA LEWIS

Library of 106,000 vols
Number of teachers: 65 full-time
Number of students: 1,500

CHAIRMEN OF DIVISIONS

Morris Harvey Division of Arts and Sciences: Dr EUGENE HARPER
Division of Health Sciences: Dr SANDRA BOWLES
Jones-Benedum College of Business: DENNIS A. MCMILLEN
Carleton Varney School of Art and Design: JOELLEN A. KERR
Charleston Conservatory of Music and Fine Arts: THOMAS BOOKHOUT

WEST LIBERTY STATE COLLEGE

West Liberty, WV 26074

Telephone: (304) 336-5000

Founded 1837

President: Dr RONALD M. ZACCARI
Provost and Vice-President for Academic Affairs: Dr JOHN P. MCCULLOUGH
Executive Assistant to the President and Director of Enrollment Services: E. NELSON CAIN
Vice-President for Finance and Administration: MICHAEL TURBANIC
Librarian: NANCY SANDERCOX

Library of 210,000 vols
Number of teachers: 120
Number of students: 2,397

WEST VIRGINIA STATE COLLEGE

Institute, WV 25112

Telephone: (304) 766-3000

Founded 1891 as a land-grant college by West Virginia Legislature

President: Dr HAZO W. CARTER, Jr
Vice-President for Academic Affairs: Dr BARBARA J. ODEN
Vice-President for Administrative Affairs: Dr CASSANDRA WHYTE
Vice-President for Student Affairs: Dr ERVIN V. GRIFFIN
Vice-President for Planning and Institutional Advancement: Dr STEPHEN W. BATSON
Director of Fiscal Affairs: LAURENCE J. SMITH
Director of Registration: JOHN L. FULLER
Director of Library: Dr RAVINDRA N. SHARMA

Library of 195,000 vols
Number of teachers: 137 full-time, 116 part-time
Number of students: 4,545

WEST VIRGINIA UNIVERSITY

POB 6201, Morgantown, WV 26506-6201

Telephone: (304) 293-0111
Fax: (304) 293-3080
E-mail: wvuadmissions@arc.wvu.edu

Founded 1867

President: DAVID C. HARDESTY, Jr
Provost and Vice-President for Academic Affairs and Research: Dr GERALD E. LANG
Vice-President for Administration and Finance: SCOTT C. KELLEY
Vice-President for Health Sciences: Dr ROBERT M. D'ALESSANDRI
Vice-President for Institutional Advancement: DAVID C. SATTERFIELD
Vice-President for Student Affairs: KENNETH D. GRAY
Director of Admissions and Records: CHENG KHOO

Library: see Libraries
Number of faculty: 1,575
Number of students: 22,238

Publications: *Victorian Poetry, Journal of Small Business Management, West Virginia Law Review, The AUBER Bibliography, West Virginia Business and Economics Review, Inquiry, West Virginia Public Affairs Quarterly Reporter, West Virginia University Alumni Magazine, Parents Newsletter, Minelands, Small Flows, On Tap, E-Train, Pipeline, Water Resources, Mountaineer Spirit.*

DEANS

College of Agriculture, Forestry and Consumer Science: Dr ROSEMARY HAGGETT
Eberly College of Arts and Sciences: Dr M. DUANE NELLIS
College of Business and Economics: Dr SYDNEY STERN
College of Creative Arts: PHILIP FAINI
School of Dentistry: Dr ROBERT H. HORNBROOK (interim)
College of Engineering and Mineral Resources: Dr ALLEN C. COGLEY
College of Human Resources and Education: Dr WILLIAM L. DEATON
Perley Isaac Reed School of Journalism: Dr WILLIAM T. SLATER
College of Law: JOHN W. FISHER II
Library Services: Dr RUTH M. JACKSON
School of Medicine: Dr ROBERT M. D'ALESSANDRI
School of Pharmacy: Dr GEORGE R. SPRATTO
School of Nursing: Dr E. JANE MARTIN
School of Physical Education: Dr DANA BROOKS
Student Life: HERMAN L. MOSES

WEST VIRGINIA UNIVERSITY INSTITUTE OF TECHNOLOGY

Montgomery, WV 25136

Telephone: (304) 442-3071
Fax: (304) 442-3059

Founded 1895

President: Dr JOHN P. CARRIER
Registrar: ROBERT P. SCHOLL, Jr
Director of Admissions: DONNA VARNEY
Librarian: V. C. YOUNG

Library of 160,000 vols
Number of teachers: 198
Number of students: 2,554

WEST VIRGINIA WESLEYAN COLLEGE

Buckhannon, WV 26201

Telephone: (304) 473-8000
Fax: (304) 473-8187

Founded 1890

President: WILLIAM R. HADEN
Chairman of the Board of Trustees: WILLIAM E. WATSON
Secretary of the Board of Trustees: Rev. JOHN R. CAMPBELL
Vice-President for Academic Affairs and Dean of the College: RICHARD G. WEEKS Jr
Vice-President for Finance: G. MICHAEL GOINS
Vice-President for External Relations: JOANNE SOLIDAY
Dean of Students: TRINA DOBBERSTEIN
Director of Admission: ROBERT SKINNER
Director of Student Aid: LANA GOLDEN

Library of 149,085 vols
Number of teachers: 136
Number of students: 1,680 (undergraduates)

Publications: *Mosaic, Pharos, College Bulletin, Sundial, Murmurmontis.*

WHEELING JESUIT UNIVERSITY

Wheeling, WV 26003-6295

Telephone: (304) 243-2000
Fax: (304) 243-2243

Founded 1954

Jesuit Liberal Arts College

President: Rev. THOMAS S. ACKER
Executive Vice-President and Chief Financial Officer: CAROLE T. COLEMAN
Vice-President for Advancement, Public Relations and Marketing: ALVIN E. HALL Sr
Chief Academic Officer and Dean: Dr DEBRA B. HULL
Dean of Students: ELLIS F. HALL, III
Director of Admissions: THOMAS M. PIÉ
Registrar: BRENT A. KOEBER
Librarian: EILEEN R. CARPINO

Library of 139,000 vols
Number of students: 1,527

WISCONSIN

ALVERNO COLLEGE

POB 343922, Milwaukee, WI 53234-3922

Telephone: (414) 382-6000
Fax: (414) 382-6354

Founded 1887

President: Sister JOEL READ
Registrar: PATRICIA HARTMANN
Vice-President for Academic Affairs: AUSTIN DOHERTY
Vice-President for Finance and Management Services: JAMES OPPERMANN
Vice-President for Institutional Advancement: DIANE SIMONS
Director of Library/Media Center: MARY GEORGIA MATLOCK (interim)

Library of 350,037 vols
Number of teachers: 107 full-time, 84 part-time
Number of students: 1,070 full-time, 1,087 part-time

BELOIT COLLEGE

700 College St, Beloit, WI 53511

Telephone: (608) 363-2000

Chartered 1846

President: VICTOR E. FERRALL, Jr
Vice-President for Academic Affairs and Dean of the College: DAVID J. BURROWS
Vice-President for Administration and Treasurer: JOHN M. NICHOLAS
Vice-President for Student Affairs and Dean of Students: WILLIAM J. FLANAGAN
Vice-President for Enrollment Services: ALAN G. MCIVOR
Vice-President for External Affairs: BRUCE D. WYATT

Library of 250,000 vols
Number of teachers: 90
Number of students: 1,200

Publications: *The Round Table* (weekly), *Avatar* (annually), *Beloit Magazine* (3 a year).

CARDINAL STRITCH UNIVERSITY

6801 N Yates Rd, Milwaukee, WI 53217
Telephone: (414) 410-4000
Founded 1937
President: Sister MARY LEA SCHNEIDER
Vice-President for Academic Affairs: Dr MARNA E. BOYLE
Vice-President for Business and Finance: KAREN L. WALRATH
Libraries of 605,000 vols
Number of teachers: 176
Number of students: 5,600

CARROLL COLLEGE

100 North East Ave, Waukesha, WI 53186
Telephone: (414) 547-1211
Fax: (414) 524-7139
Founded 1846
President: FRANK S. FALCONE
Vice-President for Academic Affairs and Dean of the Faculty: ROBERT G. BLACK
Vice-President for College Advancement: DEAN A. REIN
Senior Vice-President for Administration and Dean of Professional Studies: REBECCA L. SHERRICK
Library of 196,000 vols
Number of teachers: 74 full-time, 104 part-time
Number of students: 1,631 full-time
Publications: *Carroll College Catalog, The Quarterly Report.*

EDGEWOOD COLLEGE

855 Woodrow St, Madison, WI 53711
Telephone: (608) 257-4861
Fax: (608) 259-6717
Founded 1927
Four-year liberal arts college; coeducational
President: Dr JAMES A. EBBEN
Registrar: Ms ELLEN FEHRING
Academic Dean: Dr JUDITH WIMMER
Librarian: Dr MARY JANE SCHERDIN
Library of 93,000 vols
Number of teachers: 72 full-time, 87 part-time
Number of students: 2,082

LAKELAND COLLEGE

POB 359, Sheboygan, WI 53082-0359
Telephone: (414) 565-2111
Fax: (414) 565-1206
Founded 1862
President: Dr STEPHEN A. GOULD
Dean: Dr REINHARD ULRICH
Librarian: ANN PENKE
Library of 70,000 vols
Number of teachers: 41
Number of students: 954

LAWRENCE UNIVERSITY

Appleton, WI 54912
Telephone: (414) 832-7000
Founded 1847
President: RICHARD WARCH
Vice-President for Business Affairs: WILLIAM F. HODGKISS
Vice-President for Development and External Affairs: GREGORY A. VOLK
Dean of Students: NANCY TRUESDELL
Dean of Admissions and Financial Aid: STEVEN T. SYVERSON
Registrar: ANNE S. NORMAN
Librarian: DENNIS N. RIBBENS
Library of 310,000 vols
Number of teachers: 117
Number of students: 1,243
Publications: *Bulletin, Annual Report,* etc.

DEANS

University Faculty: (vacant)
Conservatory: ROBERT K. DODSON

MARIAN COLLEGE OF FOND DU LAC

45 South National Ave, Fond du Lac, WI 54935
Telephone: (920) 923-7600
Fax: (920) 923-7154
E-mail: admit@mariancoll.edu
Founded 1936
President: Dr RICHARD I. RIDENOUR
Vice-President of Student Life: CAROL REICHENBERGER
Academic Dean: Dr KATHLEEN MAILER
Director of Admissions: STACEY AKEY (acting)
Librarian: MARY ELLEN GORMICAN (acting)
Library of 94,000 vols
Number of teachers: 135
Number of students: 2,099

MARQUETTE UNIVERSITY

POB 1881, Milwaukee, WI 53201-1881
Telephone: (414) 288-7302
Fax: (414) 288-3300
Founded 1864 as Marquette College; chartered as a university in 1907
President: Rev. ROBERT A. WILD
Executive Vice-President: Dr JERRY A. VISCIONE
Vice-Presidents: Dr DAVID R. BUCKHOLDT, Rev. ANDREW J. THON, JOHN L. HOPKINS, GREGORY J. KLEINBAUM, KENNETH H. SMITS, JAMES P. LIDDY
Registrar: ANTHONY TORTORELLA
Library of 1,044,000 vols
Number of teachers: 996
Number of students: 10,539
Publications: *Marquette News and Views* (every 2 weeks), *Medieval Philosophical Texts in Translation,* (irregular), *Aquinas Lecture, Jesuit Lecture, Pere Marquette Lectures* (all annually), *The Marquette Law Review* (quarterly), *The Marquette Tribune* (2 a week), *Renascence* (quarterly), *Marquette* (quarterly), *Marquette Journal* (quarterly), *Philosophy and Theology* (quarterly), *Review of the Social Economy* (3 a year), *National Sports Law Institute Journal* (2 a year).

DEANS AND DIRECTORS

College of Arts and Sciences: THOMAS E. HACHEY
College of Business Administration: LEWIS MANDELL
College of Communication: WILLIAM R. ELLIOTT
School of Dentistry: Dr WILLIAM K. LOBB
School of Education: MARY P. HOY
College of Engineering: Dr G. E. O WIDERA
Graduate School: Rev. THADDEUS J. BURCH
Law School: HOWARD B. EISENBERG
College of Health Sciences: JACK C. BROOKS
College of Nursing: MADELINE M. WAKE
College of Professional Studies: ROBERT J. DEAHL.

MOUNT MARY COLLEGE

2900 North Menomonee River Parkway, Milwaukee, WI 53222
Telephone: (414) 258-4810
Founded 1913
President: PATRICIA O'DONOGHUE
Academic Dean: DIANA BEAUDOIN
Co-ordinator of Admissions: MICHAEL ISTWAN
Librarian: DAVID WEINBERG-KINSEY
Library of 111,000 vols
Number of teachers: 144
Number of students: 1,300

NORTHLAND COLLEGE

1411 Ellis Ave, Ashland, WI 54806
Telephone: (715) 682-1699
Fax: (715) 682-1308
Founded 1892
President: ROBERT RUE PARSONAGE
Vice-President for Institutional Advancement: DON CHASE
Vice-President of Finance and Administration: HAROLD VANSELOW (interim)
Vice-President and Dean of Student Development and Enrollment: JAMES MILLER
Vice-President and Academic Dean: DAVID FULLER
Vice-President and Executive Director, SOEI: KIM BRO
Chief Librarian: MARY FENNESSEY
Library of 76,500 vols
Number of teachers: 65
Number of students: 875
Publications: *Northlight, Highway, Horizons, New Student News, Inside/Outlook, View Book, Northland Report, Family Focus, Profile.*

RIPON COLLEGE

POB 248, Ripon, WI 54971
Telephone: (920) 748-8118
Founded 1851
President: PAUL B. RANSLOW
Vice-President and Dean of Faculty: DAVID B. SELIGMAN
Vice-President and Dean of Students: ROBERT H. YOUNG
Vice-President for Admissions and Financial Aid: SCOTT J. GOPLIN
Director of Libraries: CHARLENE H. SHULTS
Library of 150,000 vols
Number of teachers: 75
Number of students: 750

ST NORBERT COLLEGE

De Pere, WI 54115
Telephone: (414) 337-3181
Fax: (414) 337-4073
Founded 1898
President: THOMAS A. MANION
Dean of the College: THOMAS TREBOR
Registrar: JON CURTIS
Librarian: JEROME LOM
Library of 175,000 vols
Number of teachers: 115 full-time, 25 part-time
Number of students: 1,938

SILVER LAKE COLLEGE OF THE HOLY FAMILY

2406 South Alverno Rd, Manitowoc, WI 54220
Telephone: (414) 684-6691
Founded 1935
President: Sister BARBARA BELINSKE
Dean: Sister MAUREEN ANNE SHEPARD
Registrar: Sister JANICE STINGLE
Librarian: Sister MARY GABRIEL VAN DREEL
Library of 66,000 vols
Number of teachers: 40 full-time, 99 part-time
Number of students: 1,060
Publications: *SLC Update* (weekly), *New Directions* (quarterly), *Silver Reflections.*

UNIVERSITY OF WISCONSIN SYSTEM

Madison, WI 53706-1559
Telephone: (608) 262-2321
Fax: (608) 262-3985
Founded 1848
In 1971 the University of Wisconsin System merged with the Wisconsin State Universities system. There are 13 four-year institutions (see below) and 13 two-year centers
President: KATHARINE C. LYALL
Senior Vice President for Administration: DAVID W. OLIEN (interim)
Senior Vice President for Academic Affairs: DAVID J. WARD
Vice President for Finance: MARCIA BROMBERG
Vice President for University Relations: MARGARET LEWIS (acting)
Number of students (26 campuses): 150,600

UNIVERSITY OF WISCONSIN—EAU CLAIRE

Eau Claire, WI 54702-4004
Telephone: (715) 836-2637
Founded 1916
Chancellor: DONALD MARSH
Provost and Vice-Chancellor: THOMAS MILLER (interim)
Vice-Chancellor for Business and Student Services: CHARLES BAUER
Assistant Chancellor for Information and Technology Management: DAVID HART
Dean of Students: ANN LAPP
Registrar: SUE SHELTON
Librarian: ROBERT ROSE
Library of 574,000 vols
Number of teachers: 700
Number of students: 10,500

DEANS

College of Arts and Sciences: CARL HAYWOOD
College of Professional Studies: RONALD SATZ
College of Business: THOMAS DOCK
School of Education: STEVE KURTH
School of Human Sciences and Services: CAROL KLUN
School of Nursing: SUSAN JOHNSON

UNIVERSITY OF WISCONSIN EXTENSION

Madison, WI 53706
Chancellor: ALBERT J. BEAVER (interim)
Provost and Vice-Chancellor: KEVIN P. REILLY

DEANS

Continuing Education Extension: M. J. OFFERMAN
Co-operative Extension: C. O. O'CONNOR
Extension Communications: L. J. DICKERSON

UNIVERSITY OF WISCONSIN—GREEN BAY

Green Bay, WI 54311-7001
Telephone: (920) 465-2000
Fax: (920) 465-2032
E-mail: uwgb@uwgb.edu
Founded 1968
Liberal arts
Chancellor: Dr MARK L. PERKINS
Provost and Vice-Chancellor: Dr HOWARD COHEN
Assistant Chancellor for Planning and Budget: Dr DEAN RODEHEAVER
Assistant Chancellor for Fiscal Services: THOMAS MAKI
Library of over 1 million bibliographic items
Number of students: 5,500
Publications: *Undergraduate Catalog* (every 2 years), *Undergraduate Prospectus* (annually), *Inside UW-Green Bay* (3 a year), *Graduate Catalog* (every 2 years).

UNIVERSITY OF WISCONSIN—LA CROSSE

1725 State St, La Crosse, WI 54601
Telephone: (608) 785-8000
Fax: (608) 785-8809
Founded 1909
Chancellor: JUDITH KUIPERS
Vice-Chancellor: JULIUS E. ERLENBACH
Director of Admissions and Records: GALE GRIMSLID
Library Director: DALE MONTGOMERY
Library of 520,000 vols
Number of teachers: 430
Number of students: 8,500

UNIVERSITY OF WISCONSIN—MADISON

Madison, WI 53706
Telephone: (608) 262-1234
Telex: (608) 263-5595
Founded 1849
Chancellor: DAVID WARD
Provost and Vice-Chancellor for Academic Affairs: JOHN WILEY
Vice-Chancellor for Health Sciences: (vacant)
Vice-Chancellor for Administration: JOHN TORPHY
Registrar: THOMAS JOHNSON (acting)
Director of Admissions: KEITH WHITE (acting)
Secretary of the Faculty: DAVID MUSOLF
Dean of Libraries: KENNETH FRAZIER
Library: see Libraries
Number of students: 40,196

DEANS

College of Letters and Science: PHILLIP R. CERTAIN
College of Engineering: JOHN G. BOLLINGER
College of Agriculture and Life Sciences: ELTON ABERLE
School of Education: CHARLES READ
School of Business: ANDREW POLICANO
School of Pharmacy: MELVIN WEINSWIG
Law School: KENNETH DAVIS
Medical School: PHILIP FARRELL
School of Nursing: VIVIAN LITTLEFIELD
Graduate School: VIRGINIA HINSHAW
School of Veterinary Medicine: DARYL BUSS
School of Human Ecology: HAMILTON MCCUBBIN
Institute for Environmental Studies: THOMAS M. YUILL
Division of Continuing Studies: HOWARD MARTIN

UNIVERSITY OF WISCONSIN—MILWAUKEE

Milwaukee, WI 53201
Telephone: (414) 229-1122
Founded 1885
Chancellor: NANCY L. ZIMPHER
Provost and Vice-Chancellor: KENNETH L. WATTERS
Assistant Chancellors: DONALD G. MELKUS, WILLIAM MAYRL, SANDRA HOEH-LYON, CHARMAINE CLOWNEY
Secretary of the University: GEORGE BAKER
Number of teachers: 817 full-time, 564 part-time
Number of students: 22,251

DEANS AND DIRECTORS

Graduate School: WILLIAM REED RAYBURN
College of Letters and Science: MARSHALL R. GOODMAN
School of Allied Health Professions: RANDALL LAMBRECHT (acting)
School of Architecture and Urban Planning: ROBERT C. GREENSTREET
School of Education: WILLIAM B. HARVEY
School of Fine Arts: CATHERINE A. DAVY
College of Engineering and Applied Science: S. H. CHAN (acting)
School of Social Welfare: JAMES BLACKBURN
School of Business Administration: CHARLES O. KRONCKE
School of Nursing: SHARON ELIZABETH DAVIDSON HOFFMAN
School of Library and Information Science: MOHAMMED M. AMAN
Division of Outreach and Continuing Education: SUSAN KELLY
Director of Libraries: PETER WATSON-BOONE
Student Affairs: WILLIAM MAYRL
Director of Enrollment Services: BETH WECKMUELLER
Director of Office of International Studies: Dr YENBO WU

CHAIRS OF DEPARTMENT

College of Letters and Science:
- Africology: WINSTON A. VAN HORNE
- Anthropology: TRUDY TURNER
- Art History: Prof. KENNETH BENDINER
- Biological Sciences: JAMES COGGINS
- Chemistry: Prof. JAMES COOK
- Communication: KATHRYN DINDIA
- Economics: Prof. M. BAHMANI-OSKOOEE
- English: MICHAEL NOONAN
- Foreign Languages and Linguistics: CHARLES WARD
- French, Italian and Comparative Literature: RACHEL SKALITZKY
- Geography: Prof. MARK SCHWARTZ
- Geosciences: MARK HARRIS
- History: Prof. BRUCE FETTER
- Mass Communication: Prof. DAVID PRITCHARD
- Mathematical Sciences: Prof. DAVID SCHULTZ
- Philosophy: Prof. MARK KAPLAN
- Physics: JOHN NORBURY
- Political Science: Prof. MARCUS ETHRIDGE
- Psychology: Prof. RAYMOND FLEMING
- Sociology: Prof. DONALD GREEN
- Spanish and Portuguese: Prof. JULIO RODRIGUEZ-LUIS

School of Education:
- Administrative Leadership: Prof. LARRY MARTIN
- Educational Policy and Community Studies: WALTER FARRELL
- Curriculum and Instruction: Prof. LINDA POST
- Educational Psychology: Prof. DOUG MICKELSON
- Exceptional Education: ANN HAINS

School of Architecture and Urban Planning:
- Architecture: Prof. MICHAEL UTZINGER
- Urban Planning: Prof. WILLIAM HUXHOLD

College of Engineering and Applied Science:
- Civil Engineering and Mechanics: Prof. KWANG LEE
- Electrical Engineering: Prof. DEVENDRA MISRA
- Computer Science: Prof. K. VAIRAVAN
- Industrial and Manufacturing Engineering: Prof. HAMID SEIFODDINI
- Materials Engineering: Prof. D. VENUGOPALAN
- Mechanical Engineering: DILIP KOHLI

School of Allied Health Professions:
- Health Sciences: Prof. RENE GRATZ
- Human Kinetics: Prof. ANN SYNDER
- Communication Sciences and Disorders: Prof. PAULA RHYNER

School of Fine Arts:
- Art: LANE HALL
- Film: Prof. RICHARD BLAU
- Music: WILL SCHMID
- Theatre and Dance: LEROY STONER

School of Nursing:

Foundations of Nursing: Prof. JOAN WILK
Health Maintenance: FLORENCE SELDER
Health Restoration: Prof. SUZANNE FALCO

UNIVERSITY OF WISCONSIN—OSHKOSH

800 Algoma Blvd, Oshkosh, WI 54901

Telephone: (920) 424-1234
Fax: (920) 424-7317

Founded 1871

Chancellor: JOHN E. KERRIGAN
Provost and Vice-Chancellor: VICKI LORD LARSON
Associate Vice-Chancellor: WILLIAM C. WRESCH
Assistant Chancellor, Student Affairs: ELLIOTT L. GARB
Assistant Vice-Chancellor, Academic Support: MURIEL A. HAWKINS
Assistant Vice-Chancellor, Graduate School and Research: PATRICIA J. KOLL
Registrar: DANIEL EDLEBECK
Assistant Vice-Chancellor, Information Technology: JOHN F. BERENS

Library of 1,140,000 vols
Number of teachers: 535
Number of students: 10,619

DEANS

College of Education and Human Services: DONALD W. MOCKER
College of Business Administration: E. ALAN HARTMAN
College of Letters and Science: MICHAEL ZIMMERMAN
College of Nursing: MERRITT E. KNOX
Students: (vacant)

UNIVERSITY OF WISCONSIN—PARKSIDE

Box 2000, 900 Wood Road, Kenosha, WI 53141-2000

Telephone: (414) 595-2355

Founded 1968

Chancellor: ELEANOR J. SMITH
Provost/Vice-Chancellor: JOHN M. OSTHEIMER
Assistant Chancellor for Student Affairs: G. GARY GRACE
Assistant Chancellor for Administration and Fiscal Affairs: WILLIAM STREETER
Assistant Chancellor for University Relations: MARILYN FOSTER KIRK

Library of 365,000 vols
Number of students: 5,000

UNIVERSITY OF WISCONSIN—PLATTEVILLE

1 University Plaza, Platteville, WI 53818

Telephone: (608) 342-1491
Fax: (608) 342-1232

Founded 1866

Chancellor: DAVID J. MARKEE
Vice-Chancellor: CAROL SUE BUTTS
Assistant Chancellor for Business Affairs: STEPHEN ZIELKE
Assistant Chancellor for Student Affairs: SHARON WALKER
Dean of the School of Graduate Studies: JUDITH PAUL
Dean and Director of Admissions and Enrollment Management: RICHARD SCHUMACHER
Registrar: EDWARD DENEEN
Director of Library: PAUL MORIARTY

Library of 195,000 vols
Number of teachers: 270
Number of students: 5,100

DEANS

College of Engineering, Mathematics and Science: RICHARD SHULTZ
College of Business, Industry, Life Science and Agriculture: JERRY STROHM
College of Liberal Arts and Education: CHARLOTTE STOKES

UNIVERSITY OF WISCONSIN—RIVER FALLS

River Falls, WI 54022

Telephone: (715) 425-3911
Fax: (715) 425-4487

Founded 1874
State control

Chancellor: GARY THIBODEAU
Provost and Vice-Chancellor: ROBERT MILAM
Vice-Chancellor, Administration and Finance: VIRGIL NYLANDER
Dean of Students: ROGER BALLOU
Registrar: JUDITH GEORGE
Librarian: CHRISTINA BAUM

Library of 212,000 vols
Number of teachers: 280
Number of students: 5,422

DEANS

College of Agriculture, Food and Environmental Sciences: G. E. ROHDE
College of Arts and Sciences: GORDEN HEDAHL
College of Education and Graduate Studies: KAREN VIECHNICKI

UNIVERSITY OF WISCONSIN—STEVENS POINT

2100 Main St, Stevens Point, WI 54481

Telephone: (715) 346-0123
Fax: (715) 346-3957

Founded 1894

Chancellor: THOMAS F. GEORGE
Vice-Chancellor: HOWARD THOYRE

Library of 1,500,000 items
Number of teachers: 391

UNIVERSITY OF WISCONSIN—STOUT

Menomonie, WI 54751

Telephone: (715) 232-1431
Fax: (715) 232-1416

Founded 1891
State control
Academic year: September to May

Chancellor: Dr CHARLES W. SORENSEN
Provost and Vice-Chancellor for Academic and Student Affairs: Dr ROBERT SEDLAK
Assistant Chancellor for Administrative and Student Life Services, and Budget, Planning and Analysis: DIANE MOEN
Assistant Vice-Chancellor for Academic and Student Affairs: Dr JULIE FURST-BOWE
Director, Library Learning Center: J. JAX

Library of 226,000 vols
Number of teachers: 435
Number of students: 7,545

DEANS

College of Arts and Sciences: Dr JOHN MURPHY
College of Technology, Engineering and Management: Dr BRUCE SIEBOLD
College of Human Development: Dr JOHN WESOLEK
Dean of Students: Dr PINCKNEY HALL

UNIVERSITY OF WISCONSIN—SUPERIOR

Superior, WI 54880

Telephone: (715) 394-8396

Founded 1893

Chancellor: BETTY J. YOUNGBLOOD
Director of Admissions: J. WOJCIECHOWSKI
Librarian: BOB CARMACK

Library of 240,000 vols
Number of teachers: 135
Number of students: 2,600

UNIVERSITY OF WISCONSIN—WHITEWATER

Whitewater, WI 53190

Telephone: (414) 472-1918

Founded 1868

Chancellor: H. GAYLON GREENHILL
Provost and Vice-Chancellor for Academic Affairs: DAVID PRIOR
Assistant Chancellor for Administrative Services: JAMES W. FREER
Assistant Chancellor for Student Affairs: ROGER B. LUDEMAN
Assitant Vice-Chancellor for Technology and Information Resources: HSI-PING SHAO

Library of 330,000 vols
Number of teachers: 584
Number of students: 9,946

VITERBO COLLEGE

815 South 9th St, La Crosse, WI 54601

Telephone: (608) 796-3000

Founded 1890

Liberal arts college, coeducational

President: Dr WILLIAM J. MEDLAND
Director of Admission: Dr ROLAND W. NELSON
Academic Vice-President: Dr JACK HAVERTAPE
Vice-President for Student Life: Sister JEAN MOORE
Librarian: JOHN HEMPSTEAD

Library of 84,000 vols
Number of teachers: 87 full-time, 64 part-time
Number of students: 1,548

WYOMING

UNIVERSITY OF WYOMING

Laramie, WY 82071

Telephone: (307) 766-1121

Founded 1886

President: PHILIP L. DUBOIS
Registrar: REBECCA MACON
Provost and Vice-President, Academic Affairs: (vacant)
Vice-President, Student Affairs: JAMES C. HURST
Vice-President, Finance: DANIEL BACCARI
Vice-President, Research: WILLIAM GERN
Librarian: KEITH COTTAM

Library of 1,151,000 vols
Number of teachers: 700
Number of students: 11,251

Publications: *University Bulletin* (quarterly), *Agricultural Experimental Station Bulletin* (12 to 20 a year), *Geological Survey Bulletins.*

DEANS

College of Agriculture: STEVEN HORN
College of Business: BRUCE FORSTER
College of Education: DAN KING
College of Engineering: KYNRIC PELL
College of Law: JOHN BURMAN
College of Arts and Sciences: OLIVER WALTER
College of Health Sciences: MARTHA WILLIAMS
Graduate School: DON WARDER

GUAM

Universities and Colleges

UNIVERSITY OF GUAM

UOG Station, Mangilao, GU 96923

Telephone: (671) 734-9435
Fax: (671) 734-2296

Founded 1952; formerly the College of Guam; the only American university in the Western Pacific

President: Dr JOSE T. NEDEDOG
Director, Admissions and Records: Dr CATALINA LOWE
Academic Vice-President: Dr JUDITH GUTHERTZ
Vice-President for Student Affairs: Dr RICHARD WITTENBACK-SANTOS
Vice-President for Administration and Finance: Dr CARMEN FERNANDEZ

Library of 1,050,000 items
Number of teachers: 221
Number of students: 3,476

Publications: *Micronesica* (2 a year), *Coral Reef Newsletter* (annually), *Isla* (2 a year), *Micronesian Educator* (annually), *Storyboard: A Journal of Pacific Imagery.*

DEANS

College of Agriculture: Dr JEFF BARCINAS
College of Arts and Sciences: Dr MARY SPENCER
College of Education: Dr JAMES L. CRAIG
College of Business and Public Administration: Dr CLYDE SAUGET
College of Nursing and Health Sciences: Dr MAUREEN FOCHTMAN
Graduate School: Dr JOYCE CAMACHO
Learning Resources: Dr CHIH WANG

UNITED STATES VIRGIN ISLANDS

Universities and Colleges

UNIVERSITY OF THE VIRGIN ISLANDS

St Thomas, VI 00802

Telephone: (340) 776-9200

Founded 1962

Four-year liberal arts college with professional programmes.

Branch campus at St Croix

President: Dr ORVILLE KEAN
Vice-President for Academic Affairs: Dr DENIS PAUL
Vice-President for Business and Financial Affairs: MALCOLM C. KIRWAN
Vice-President for Research and Public Service: Dr LAVERNE RAGSTER
Vice-President for Student Affairs: Dr RONALD HARRIGAN
Vice-President for Institutional Advancement: Dr GWEN-MARIE MOOLENAAR
Director of Admissions: Dr JUDITH EDWIN
Director of Libraries: JENNIFER JACKSON

Library of 102,000 vols
Number of teachers: 266
Number of students: 2,610 (1,212 full-time)

URUGUAY

Learned Societies

AGRICULTURE, FISHERIES AND VETERINARY SCIENCE

Asociación Rural del Uruguay (Rural Association): Avda Uruguay 864, Montevideo; tel. 902-04-84; fax 902-04-89; f. 1871; 3,000 mems; library of 3,000 vols; Pres. Dr JUAN MIGUEL SILVA Y ROSAS; publs *Revista* (monthly).

ARCHITECTURE AND TOWN PLANNING

Sociedad de Arquitectos del Uruguay (Society of Architects): Gonzalo Ramírez 2030, 11200 Montevideo; tel. 41-95-56; fax 41-95-56; f. 1914; 2,000 mems; library of 2,000 vols; Pres. Arq. CARLOS A. DEBELLIS; Sec.-Gen. Arq. MARÍA CARMEN BRUSCO; publs *Boletín, Arquitectura*.

BIBLIOGRAPHY, LIBRARY SCIENCE AND MUSEOLOGY

Agrupación Bibliotecológica del Uruguay (Library Association): Cerro Largo 1666, 11200 Montevideo; activities include library science, archives, documentation, bibliography, history and numismatics; Pres. LUIS ALBERTO MUSSO; publs *Bibliografía uruguaya sobre Brasil*, *Aportes para la historia de la bibliotecología en el Uruguay*, *Bibliografía y documentación en el Uruguay*, *Bibliografía bibliográfica y bibliotecología*, *Bibliografía básica de la historia de la República Oriental del Uruguay*, *Legislación Uruguaya sobre Brasil*, etc.

Asociación de Bibliotecólogos del Uruguay (Library Science Association of Uruguay): Eduardo V. Haedo 2255, CC 1315, 11200 Montevideo; fax 4099989; e-mail ab@adinet.com.uy; f. 1978; 430 mems; Pres. ROSA FERIA; publ. *Panel de noticias* (monthly).

HISTORY, GEOGRAPHY AND ARCHAEOLOGY

Instituto Histórico y Geográfico del Uruguay: Convención 1366, 3° piso, Montevideo; f. 1843; 40 academicians; Pres. Prof. EDMUNDO M. NARANCIO; publ. *Revista*.

Sociedad de Amigos de Arqueología (Archaeological Society): Buenos Aires 652, Casilla 399, Montevideo; f. 1926; 70 mems, 16 foreign mems; publ. *Revista*.

LANGUAGE AND LITERATURE

Academia Nacional de Letras (National Academy of Literature): Ituzaingó 1255, 11000 Montevideo; tel. 915-23-74; fax 016-74-60; f. 1946; 10 mems; Pres. ANTONIO CRAVOTTO; Sec. CARLOS JONES GAYE; publs *Boletín, Ensayos Literarios*.

MEDICINE

Academia Nacional de Medicina del Uruguay: 18 de Julio 2175, 5° piso, Montevideo; tel. 401444; f. 1976; 27 mems; publ. *Boletín* (annually).

Asociación Odontológica Uruguaya (Odontological Association): Avda Durazno 937-39, Montevideo; tel. 901572; f. 1946; 3,000 mems; comprises 8 depts and 6 sections; museum; library of 6,000 vols; Pres. Dr LUIS P. LAUKO; Sec. Dr JOSÉ LLAGUNO; publs *Odontología Uruguaya* (2 a year), *Boletín Informativo* (monthly).

Sociedad de Cirugía del Uruguay (Surgical Society): CC 10972, Montevideo; tel. and fax (2) 47-42-79; f. 1930; 420 mems; library of 3,400 vols; Pres. Dr ALBERTO DEL CAMPO; Sec.-Gen. Dr HERNÁN PARODI; publ. *Cirugía del Uruguay* (4 a year).

Sociedad de Radiología e Imagenología del Uruguay: Brito del Pino 1227, Ap. 602, 11300, Montevideo; tel. 792016; telex 22314; fax 491603; f. 1923; scientific activity linked to the Médicos Imagenólogos; holds conferences and seminars; 150 mems; Pres. Dr EDUARDO TISCORNIA; publ. *Revista de Imagenología del Uruguay*.

Has attached:

Gremial Uruguaya de Médicos Radiólogos: Montevideo; f. 1972; 70 mems; Pres. Dr ERNESTO H. CIBILS.

Sociedad Uruguaya de Historia de la Medicina: Casilla de Correo 157, Montevideo; f. 1971; research on history of medicine and allied sciences; 80 mems; Pres. Prof. Dr FERNANDO MAÑÉ GARZÓN; Sec. Dr JUAN I. GIL; publ. *Sesiones de la Sociedad Uruguaya*.

Sociedad Uruguaya de Pediatría (Paediatrics Society): Casilla de Correo 10906, Montevideo; f. 1927; 500 mems, affiliated to the Asociación Latino Americana de Pediatría; library of 3,500 vols, 6,500 periodicals; Pres. Prof. Dr ANTONIO NAIRAC; Sec. Dra GRACIELA SEHABIAQUE; publ. *Archivos de Pediatría del Uruguay* (quarterly).

NATURAL SCIENCES

Biological Sciences

Sociedad Malacológica del Uruguay (Malacological Society): Casilla 1401, 11000 Montevideo; f. 1957; 210 mems; Pres. JORGE BROGGI; Sec. JUAN CARLOS ZAFFARONI; publs *Comunicaciones* (2 a year) and specialized articles.

Sociedad Zoológica del Uruguay: Casilla 399, Montevideo; f. 1961; Pres. Prof. MIGUEL A. KLAPPENBACH; publ. *Boletín*.

TECHNOLOGY

Academia Nacional de Ingeniería: Cuareim 1492, Montevideo; f. 1965; 40 full mems; Pres. Ing. ANDRÉS TIERNO ABREU; Sec. Ing. AURELIO TILVE.

Asociación de Ingenieros del Uruguay (Association of Uruguayan Engineers): Cuareim 1492, Montevideo; f. 1905; 1,400 mems, also hon. and corresp. abroad; Pres. Ing. EDUARDO CRISPO AYALA; Sec. Ing. PONCIANO J. TORRADO; affiliated to the Unión Panamericana de Asociaciones de Ingenieros; library of 2,000 vols; publ. *Revista de Ingeniería*.

Research Institutes

GENERAL

Consejo Nacional de Investigaciones Científicas y Técnicas (CONICYT): Paraguay 1470, 2° piso, 11100 Montevideo; tel. (2) 901-42-85; fax (2) 902-48-70; e-mail info@conicyt.gub.uy; f. 1961; to stimulate research in all branches of knowledge; library of 5,000 vols, 60 periodicals; Pres. Ing. ANDRÉS LALANNE; Dir Ec. MARÍA JULIANA ABELLA; publs *Ciencia y Tecnología para el Desarrollo de Uruguay* (6 a year), *Boletín Bibliográfico en CYT* (4 a year).

Oficina Regional de Ciencia y Tecnología de la Unesco para América Latina y el Caribe/Unesco Regional Office for Science and Technology in Latin America and the Caribbean: Av. Brasil 2697, Casilla 859, 11000 Montevideo; tel. 707-20-23; fax 707-21-40; f. 1949; co-ordinates Unesco's programme in the region, particularly: science and technology for development, environment and natural resources management, science, technology and society, earth sciences and natural hazards, marine sciences, water sciences, information science, informatics, education; organizes meetings and conferences; computer directories with 5,000 entries of instns engaged in science and technology in the region; Dir Dr FRANCISCO JOSÉ LACAYO; publs *Infomab, Waterway, Unesco Bulletin of Montevideo*.

AGRICULTURE, FISHERIES AND VETERINARY SCIENCE

Instituto Nacional de Investigación Agropecuaria (National Agricultural Research Institute): La Estanzuela, CC 39173, 70000 Colonia; tel. (522) 40-60 ext. 136; fax (522) 40-61; e-mail bib_le@inia.org.uy; f. 1914; library of 12,000 vols, 1,000 periodicals; Dir FERNANDO CERRI; publs *Serie Técnica, Boletín de Divulgación, Serie Actividades de Difusión, Hojas de Divulgación*.

Instituto Nacional de Pesca (National Fishery Institute): Constituyente 1497, 11200 Montevideo; tel. 48-31-80; fax 41-32-16; f. 1975; 196 staff; library of 1,200 vols; Dir Gral. JUAN JOSÉ FERNANDEZ PARES.

ECONOMICS, LAW AND POLITICS

Centro de Estadísticas Nacionales y Comercio Internacional del Uruguay (CENCI Uruguay): Misiones 1361, Casilla de Correo 1510, Montevideo; tel. 915-29-30; fax 915-45-78; f. 1956 to provide economic and statistical information on all American countries; to operate computer programmes handling the import tariffs on commodities; 1,200 mems; library of over 550 vols; Dirs C. VERTESI, K. BRUNNER; publs *Boletines: Noticias Latinoamericanas, Industrias por sectores de actividad, Anuario estadístico sobre el intercambio comercial, Manuales prácticos del Importador, del Exportador, Aduanero y del Contribuyente, Estudios del Mercado*.

Instituto Nacional de Estadística (Statistical Office): Río Negro 1520, Montevideo; tel. (2) 93-28-78; fax (2) 93-28-81; f. 1829; library of 4,000 vols; Dir-Gen. ORUAL ANDINA; publs *Síntesis Estadística, Boletín Trimestral* (4 a year), *Encuesta Continua de Hogares, Anuario Estadístico*.

HISTORY, GEOGRAPHY AND ARCHAEOLOGY

Servicio Geográfico Militar (Military Geographical Institute): Avda 8 de Octubre 3255, Montevideo; tel. 81-68-10; f. 1913; geodesy, photogrammetry, geophysics and cartography; library of 3,500 vols; Dir Col IVHO R. ACUÑA; publs *Boletín*, scale aeronautic and aerial maps.

MEDICINE

Instituto de Endocrinología 'Profesor Dr Juan C. Mussio Fournier' (Institute of Endocrinology): Hospital Pasteur, Calle Larravide 74, Montevideo; f. 1937; under Ministry of Health; Dir Prof. Dr ALFREDO NAVARRO; publs *Archivos* and learned treatises and articles.

Instituto de Oncología: Avda 8 de Octubre 3265, Montevideo; f. 1960; Dir Prof. Dr ALFONSO FRANGELLA.

Liga Uruguaya contra la Tuberculosis (Anti-Tuberculosis League): Magallanes 1320, 11200 Montevideo; tel. 408-35-70; f. 1902; specializes in combating tuberculosis in children and the elderly; library of 3,000 vols; Pres. MÁXIMO A. SAAVEDRA; Sec. NORVAL SILVERA DE LEÓN.

NATURAL SCIENCES

Biological Sciences

Instituto de Investigaciones Biológicas Clemente Estable: Avda Italia 3318, Montevideo; fax 47-54-61; f. 1927; 12 divisions, 3 depts; biological research; library of 12,000 vols.

Physical Sciences

Dirección Nacional de Meteorología del Uruguay (National Meteorological Directorate): Javier Barrios Amorín No 1488, Casilla de Correo 64, 11200 Montevideo; tel. (2) 40-56-55; fax (2) 49-73-91; f. 1895; library of 6,000 vols, 13,800 documents; Dir IVONNE DUTRA MAISONNAVE; publs *Boletín Agrometeorológico*, *Anuario Climatológico*, *Notas Técnicas*, *Boletín Pluviométrico*.

Observatorio Astronómico de Montevideo (Montevideo Astronomical Observatory): Casilla de Correo 867, 11000 Montevideo; tel. (2) 48-58-25; f. 1928; library of 5,000 vols; Dir Prof. LUIS HERMIDA.

RELIGION, SOCIOLOGY AND ANTHROPOLOGY

Instituto Interamericano del Niño (Inter-American Children's Institute): Avda 8 de Octubre 2904, Montevideo; tel. (2) 487-21-50; fax (2) 487-32-42; e-mail iin@chasque.apc.org; f. 1927; specialized organization of the OAS; specialized library of 50,000 vols, open to the public; computerized information centre; Pres. Dr FERNANDO TOMÉ ABARCA; Dir-Gen. Dr RODRIGO QUINTANA MELÉNDEZ; publs *Boletín* and specialized books and pamphlets.

TECHNOLOGY

Dirección Nacional de Minería y Geología: Calle Hervidero 2861, Montevideo; tel. 209-31-96; fax 209-49-05; e-mail dinamige@adinet.com.uy; f. 1912; library of 3,000 vols; Dir Dr GONZALO ILLARRAMENDI TARABAL; publs *Industria Extractiva de la ROU, Boletín Informativo, Boletines DINAMIGE,* geological maps.

Dirección Nacional de Tecnología Nuclear: Mercedes 1014, Montevideo; tel. 90-69-19; fax 92-16-19; f. 1955 as Comisión Nacional de Energía Atómica; controls activities involving the use of radioactive materials or equipment producing ionizing radiation; prepares technical and safety rules for activities involving nuclear technology; liaises with national and international institutions on procedural aspects of nuclear technology; library of 3,500 vols; collection of microfiches; Dir Col WALTER CIBILS; publs *Revista* (1 a year), *Memoria* (1 a year).

Instituto Uruguayo de Normas Técnicas (Uruguayan Standards Institution): p. 7° Galería Elysée, San José 1031; tel. 921680; fax 921681; e-mail unit@adinet.com.uy; f. 1939; standardization, certification, information on standards, training in high-level management; library of 280,000 vols; Dir Eng. PABLO BENIA; publ. *UNIT Standards*.

Libraries and Archives

Florida

Biblioteca Pública Municipal: Florida; f. 1889; 42,000 vols; Dir JOSÉ ALBERTO DIBARBOURIE.

Montevideo

Archivo General de la Nación (National Archives): Calle Convención 1474, Montevideo; f. 1926; 14,000 vols; Dir Prof. JUAN E. PIVEL DEVOTO; publ. *Revista*.

Biblioteca Central y Publicaciones del Consejo de Educación Secundaria: Eduardo Acevedo 1427, Montevideo; tel. 484273; f. 1885; secondary and higher education; 105,000 vols; collection of rare books; Librarian DAVID YUDCHAK.

Biblioteca del Museo Histórico Nacional (Library of the National Historical Museum): Rincón 437, C.P. 11.000, Montevideo; f. 1940; 150,000 vols, 4,000 vols of MSS; specialization in the history of America and history of art; iconography, engravings, maps, numismatics; the entire library and Uruguayan collections of Dr Pablo Blanco Acevedo; Dir ELISA SILVA CAZET.

Biblioteca del Palacio Legislativo: Avda Libertador Brigadier Gral Lavelleja y Avda Gral Flores, Montevideo; tel. 409111; f. 1929; legal deposit library in conjunction with National Library; 322,000 vols; specializes in jurisprudence; Dir LUIS H. BOIONS POMBO; publs *Bibliografía Uruguaya*, *Boletín Bibliográfico* (monthly).

Biblioteca Municipal 'Dr Francisco Albero Schinca': 8 de Octubre 4210, Montevideo; f. 1929; 14,000 vols; Dir ROSARIO CRUZ DE SESOVIA.

Biblioteca Municipal 'Dr Joaquín de Salterain': Ciudadela 1225, Montevideo; 36,000 vols; includes a slide library; Librarian ROLANDO BRIANES.

Biblioteca Nacional del Uruguay (National Library): 18 de Julio 1790, CC 452, Montevideo; tel. (2) 408-50-30; fax (2) 409-69-02; f. 1816; 900,000 vols, 20,000 periodicals; comprises reference service, copyright office, legal deposit, Uruguayan and special materials, restoration of printed works, National Information System project, cultural extension; Dir-Gen. LUIS ALBERTO MUSSO; publ. *Revista de la Biblioteca Nacional*.

Has attached:

Centro Nacional de Documentación Científica, Técnica y Económica: 18 de Julio 1790, CC 452, Montevideo; tel. 484172; fax 496902; f. 1953; part of National Library; Dir (vacant).

Biblioteca Pedagógica Central (Pedagogic Library): Plaza Cagancha 1175, Montevideo; f. 1889; library of 117,630 vols; Dir ANAIR MARTINOL; publs *Información Bibliográfica* (2 a year), *Temas*, *Traducciones*, *Bibliografía Uruguaya sobre Educación*.

Museums and Art Galleries

Montevideo

Museo de Descubrimiento: Zabala y Piedras, Montevideo; evokes the journeys of Cristobal Colon, the meeting of the two worlds; maps, dioramas and photographs.

Museo Histórico Nacional (National Historical Museum): Casa Rivera, Calle Rincón 437, Montevideo; tel. 95-10-51; f. 1900; sectional collections of local Indian cultures (prehistoric, colonial epoch, development and political history of the country); portraits, relics, arms, documents, coins, medals, etc., relating to the Wars of Independence, British invasion, early revolutions, etc.; Dir ELISA SILVA CAZET; publs *Revista Histórica*, catalogues, related leaflets.

Museo Municipal de Bellas Artes: Avda Millán 4015, Montevideo; tel. 38-54-20; f. 1928; paintings, drawings, wood-carvings, sculptures; Dir MARIO C. TEMPONE.

Museo Nacional de Bellas Artes (National Museum of Fine Arts): Tomás Giribaldi 2283, Parque Rodó, Montevideo; f. 1911; 4,217 paintings, engravings, drawings, sculptures, ceramics; Dir ANGEL KALENBERG.

Museo Nacional de Historia Natural (Natural History Museum): Casilla 399, 11000 Montevideo; fax 97-02-13; f. 1837 as National Museum; zoology, botany, palaeontology, archaeology; library of 200,000 vols; Dir HÉCTOR S. OSORIO; publs *Anales*, *Comunicaciones Zoológicas*, *Comunicaciones Botánicas*, *Comunicaciones Antropológicas*, *Comunicaciones Paleontológicas*, *Flora del Uruguay*.

Museo Pedagógico (Pedagogic Museum): Plaza Cagancha 1175, Montevideo; f. 1888; Dir Sra NILDA BARBAGELATA DE RITTER; publ. *Boletín* (weekly).

Museo y Archivo Histórico Municipal: Palacio del Cabildo, Calle Juan Carlos Gómez 1362, Montevideo; tel. 98-28-26; f. 1915; permanent exhibition of the history of Montevideo from 1726; furniture, icons, paintings, jewellery and maps; library of 9,000 vols; Hon. Dir JORGE R. DELUCCHI; publ. *Anales*.

Museo y Jardin Botánico de Montevideo: Avda 19 de Abril 1181, Montevideo; tel. 39-44-22; f. 1902; Dir Ing. Agr. PABLO B. ROSS.

Museo Zoológico 'Dámaso Antonio Larrañaga': Rambla República de Chile 4215, Montevideo; f. 1956; instruction on national and exotic fauna; library of 2,000 specialized vols; 2,000 species of fauna and molluscs, etc.; Dir JUAN PABLO CUELLO.

San José de Mayo

Museo de Bellas Artes Departamental de San José: Calle Dr Julián Becerro de Bengoa 493, 80000 San José de Mayo; paintings, drawings, sculptures, ceramics; tel. 3642; f. 1947; school of art; library of 3,000 vols; Dir CÉSAR BERNESCONI; publ. *Notimuseo* (monthly).

Tacuarembó

Museo del Indio y del Gaucho: Calle 25 de Mayo 315, Tacuarembó; affilated to the Museo Histórico de Montevideo; large collection representing ancient native crafts, weapons and other implements of the aboriginal Indians and gauchos; Founder and Dir WASHINGTON ESCOBAR.

Universities

UNIVERSIDAD CATÓLICA DEL URUGUAY

Avda 8 de Octubre 2738, 11600 Montevideo
Telephone: 47-27-17
Fax: 47-03-23

Founded 1985
Private control
Academic year: March to November

Chancellor: Archbishop JOSÉ GOTTARDI
Vice-Chancellor: Fr ARMANDO RAFFO
President: Fr JOSÉ LUIS MENDIZÁBAL

Vice-Presidents: Esc. GUILLERMO PÉREZ DEL CASTILLO (Development), Dr JOSÉ AROCENA (Academic), Ing. JOHN G. MILES (Administrative)

General Director: Mag. FERNANDO SORONDO BATALLER

Librarian: Dr JOSÉ AROCENA

Number of teachers: 603
Number of students: 5,000

Publications: *Prisma, Relaciones Laborales en el Uruguay, Cuadernos de Negocios Internacionales e Integración.*

DEANS

Faculty of Social Sciences and Communication: Dr PABLO MIERES
Faculty of Psychology: Psic. LILIÁN DASET
Faculty of Law: Dr AUGUSTO DURÁN MARTÍNEZ
Faculty of Business Administration: Ec. ROBERTO HORTA
Faculty of Engineering: MANUEL BURGOS

ATTACHED INSTITUTES

Institute of Philosophy: Dir Fr EDUARDO CASAROTTI.
Institute of Distance Theology Education: Dir Fr RAÚL GONZÁLEZ.
Institute of Religious Sciences: Dir Fr ANDRÉS ASSANDRI.
Institute of Entrepreneur Management: Dir PABLO SERÉ.
Institute of Ethics and Bioethics: Dir Fr OMAR FRANÇA.
Institute of Agricultural Management: Dir Fr JORGE CROVARA.
Institute of Forestry and Wood Processing: Dir Ing. DIEGO CASTELLS.
Institute of Agriculture and Veterinary Medicine: Dir Ing. MARIANO LASTRETO.

UNIVERSIDAD DE LA REPÚBLICA

Avda 18 de Julio 1968 (2° piso), 11200 Montevideo

Telephone: (2) 408-49-01
Fax: (2) 408-03-03
E-mail: secretar@oce.edu.uy
Founded 1849
State control
Language of instruction: Spanish
Academic year: March to December
Rector: Ing. Qco RAFAEL GUARGA
Vice-Rector: Cr. MIGUEL GALMÉS
Libraries with 1,000,000 vols
Number of teachers: 4,982
Number of students: 59,436
Publication: faculty bulletins.

DEANS

Faculty of Agronomy: Ing. Agr. GONZALO GONZÁLEZ
Faculty of Architecture: Arq. RUBEN OTERO
Faculty of Economics: Cr. MIGUEL GALMÉS
Faculty of Social Sciences: Lic. JORGE LANDINELLI
Faculty of Science: Dr RICARDO EHRLICH
Faculty of Engineering: Ing. MARÍA SIMÓN
Faculty of Medicine: Dr LUIS CALIGARI
Faculty of Dentistry: Dr PABLO PEBÉ
Faculty of Chemistry: Dr ALBERTO NIETO
Faculty of Veterinary Medicine: Dr PABLO PESCE
Faculty of Humanities: Prof. ADOLFO ELIZAINCÍN
Faculty of Law: Esc. TERESA GNAZZO
Faculty of Psychology: Dr ALEJANDRO SCHERZER

DIRECTORS

School of Librarianship and Related Sciences: see below
School of Music: Prof. ANTONIO MASTROGIOVANNI
School of Fine Arts: Prof. FERNANDO ODRIOZOLA
Research and Postgraduate Centre: Cr. RAÚL TRAJTEMBERG
Insititute of Social Sciences: Prof. ALFREDO ERRANDONEA

Colleges

Escuela Universitaria de Bibliotecología y Ciencias Afines 'Ing. Federico E. Capurro': Emilio Frugoni 1427, 11200 Montevideo; tel. 41-07-88; fax (2) 40-58-10; f. 1945; attached to Univ. de la República; 4-year courses in librarianship, 3-year courses in archive studies; 50 teachers; 500 students; postgraduate course: 50 students; library of 11,000 vols; Dir Lic. MARIO BARITÉ; publs *Revista* (annually), *Informatio*† (annually).

Instituto Superior de Electrotecnía, Electrónica y Computación: Calle Joaquín Requena 1931, Montevideo; tel. 492520; f. 1922; electrical engineering, electronics and computing; 300 teachers; library of 6,000 vols; Dir Ing. AMÉRICO HARTMANN.

Universidad del Trabajo del Uruguay: Calle San Salvador 1674, Montevideo; f. 1878; offers 220 different courses at 81 colleges in agriculture, handicrafts, industry and commerce; lower- and intermediate-level education and training; 4,500 full-time teachers; 50,000 students; Dir Dr HÉCTOR G. LÓPEZ ESTREMADOURO; publs *UTU Visión*, *Anales*.

UZBEKISTAN

Learned Societies

GENERAL

Uzbek Academy of Sciences: 700047 Tashkent, Ul. Gogolya 70; tel. (3712) 133-38-02; fax (3712) 133-49-01; divisions of Physical-Mathematical Sciences (Chair. U. Kh. Rasulev), Mechanics, Process Control and Informatics (Chair. Y. N. Muborakov), Chemical-Technological Sciences (Chair. N. A. Parpiev), Earth Sciences (Chair. Kh. A. Akbarov), Biological Sciences (Chair. B. A. Tashmukhamedov), Medical Sciences (Chair. K. Yuldashev), Historical, Linguistic and Literary Sciences (Chair. A. A. Askarov), Philosophical, Economic and Juridical Sciences (Chair. A. R. Mukhamedjanov), Agricultural Sciences (Chair. A. A. Abdullaev), Karakalpak Division of Sciences (Chair. (vacant)), Samarkand Division of Sciences (Chair. T. Sh. Shirinkulov); 78 mems, 86 corresp. mems; attached research institutes: see Research Institutes; library: see Libraries and Archives; Pres. Prof. D. A. Djuraev; Chief Scientific Sec. Prof. K. G. Gulamov; publs *Doklady* (Reports), *Uzbekskii Geologicheskii Zhurnal* (Uzbek Geological Journal), *Uzbekskii Khimicheskii Zhurnal* (Uzbek Chemical Journal), *Obshchestvennye Nauki v Uzbekistane* (Social Sciences in Uzbekistan), *Uzbekskii Fizicheskii Zhurnal* (Uzbek Journal of Physics), *Uzbekskii Matematicheskii Zhurnal* (Uzbek Journal of Mathematics), *Uzbekskii Zhurnal—Problemy Mekhaniki* (Uzbek Journal—Problems of Mechanics), *Uzbekskii Zhurnal—Problemy Informatiki i Energetiki* (Uzbek Journal—Problems of Informatics and Energetics), *Izvestiya Uzbekskogo Geograficheskogo Obshchestva Akademii Nauk RUz* (Uzbek Geographical Society Review).

Research Institutes

AGRICULTURE, FISHERIES AND VETERINARY SCIENCE

Institute of Fertilizers: 700000 Tashkent, Ul. Okhunbabaeva 18; tel. (3712) 33-39-50; fax (3712) 33-74-48; f. 1992; attached to Uzbek Acad. of Sciences; library of 39,000 vols; Dir Prof. S. Usmanov; publ. *Collection of Scientific Works* (1 a year).

Institute of Soil Research and Agrochemistry: 700109 Tashkent, Ul. Kamarniso 3; tel. (3712) 46-02-63; attached to Uzbek Acad. of Sciences; Dir D. S. Sattarov.

Research Institute of Karakul Sheep Breeding: Samarkand, Ul. Karla Marksa 47; tel. 33-32-79; f. 1930; library of 55,807 vols; Dir R. G. Valiev.

BIBLIOGRAPHY, LIBRARY SCIENCE AND MUSEOLOGY

Sulaimonov, Kh., Institute of Manuscripts: 700011 Tashkent, Ul. Navoi 69; tel. (3712) 44-01-71; attached to Uzbek Acad. of Sciences; Dir A. P. Kayumov.

ECONOMICS, LAW AND POLITICS

Abu Raihon Beruni Institute of Oriental Studies: 700170 Tashkent, Ul. Abdullaeva 81; tel. (3712) 62-52-77; attached to Uzbek Acad. of Sciences; Dir M. M. Khairullaev.

Institute of Economics: 700060 Tashkent, Ul. Borovskogo 5; tel. (3712) 33-86-03; attached to Uzbek Acad. of Sciences; Dir O. Khikmatov.

Muminov, I., Institute of Philosophy and Law: 700170 Tashkent, Ul. Muminova 9; tel. (3712) 62-38-87; attached to Uzbek Acad. of Sciences; Dir A. M. Jalolov.

HISTORY, GEOGRAPHY AND ARCHAEOLOGY

Institute of Archaeology: 703051 Samarkand, Ul. Abdullaeva 3; tel. (3662) 35-55-13; fax (3662) 31-06-94; e-mail shirinov@archeo.samuni.silk.org; f. 1970; attached to Uzbek Acad. of Sciences; Dir T. Shirinov; publ. *History of the Material Culture of Uzbekistan* (1 a year).

Institute of History: 700170 Tashkent, Ul. Muminova 9; tel. (3712) 62-38-73; attached to Uzbek Acad. of Sciences; Dir A. Askarov.

LANGUAGE AND LITERATURE

Institute of Linguistics: 700170 Tashkent, Ul. Muminova 9; tel. (3712) 62-43-24; attached to Uzbek Acad. of Sciences; Dir A. P. Khojiev.

Institute of Literature: 700170 Tashkent, Ul. Muminova 9; tel. (3712) 62-94-34; attached to Uzbek Acad. of Sciences; Dir T. M. Mirzaev.

MEDICINE

Institute for Dermatology and Venereology: 700109 Tashkent, Farabi 3; tel. 46-08-07; f. 1932; library of 14,000 vols; Dir Prof. V. A. Akovbyan; publ. *Pathogenesis and Therapy for Skin and Venereal Diseases* (annually).

Institute of Vaccines and Sera: 700084 Tashkent, Ul. Timiryazeva 37; tel. 43-79-53; Dir B. A. Shevchenko.

Institute of Virology: 700194 Tashkent, Yunus Obod, Ul. Murodova, Block 3, Bldg 7; tel. (3712) 24-83-26; attached to Uzbek Acad. of Sciences; Dir Prof. Shabat Hodjaev.

Isaev, L.M., Research Institute of Medical Parasitology: 703005 Samarkand, Isaeva 38; tel. 37-42-42; f. 1923; library of 45,000 vols; Dir Sh. A. Razakov; publ. *Current Problems of Medical Parasitology* (annually).

Research Institute of Cardiology: 700109 Tashkent, Ul. Farabi 2; tel. 46-59-81.

Research Institute of Clinical and Experimental Medicine: 742000 Nukus, Ul. M. Gorkogo 185; tel. 4-50-41.

Research Institute of Clinical and Experimental Surgery: 700015 Tashkent, Farkhadskaya 10; tel. 77-25-22.

Research Institute of Epidemiology, Microbiology and Infectious Diseases: 700133 Tashkent, Reshetova 2; tel. 43-36-05; e-mail shamasir@epid.silk.ord; f. 1961; Dir Sh. Sh. Shavakhabov.

Uzbek Blood Transfusion Institute: Tashkent, Yaselnaya ul. 51.

Uzbek Institute of Rehabilitation and Physiotherapy (Semashko Institute): Tashkent, Khurshida 4; tel. 34-55-00; f. 1919; physiotherapy in cardiology, arthropology, neurology and pulmonology, oriental medicine, phytotherapy; library of 16,210 vols; Dir Prof. Karim U. Uldashev; publ. *Collection of Scientific Works* (1 a year).

Uzbek Institute of Sanitation and Hygiene: Tashkent, Ul. Khamza 85.

Uzbek Orthopaedics and Traumatology Research Institute: Tashkent, Khamza 78; tel. 33-10-30; f. 1946; library of 28,000 vols; Dir Prof. T. Ungbaev; publ. *Works of the Institute* (annually).

NATURAL SCIENCES

General

Kitob International Latitude Station: 731740 Kitob Qashqadaryo v.; tel. 21-3-50; attached to Uzbek Acad. of Sciences; Dir B. Matmagaziev.

Biological Sciences

Institute of Biochemistry: 700143 Tashkent, Ul. Abdullaeva 56; tel. (3712) 62-24-41; fax (3712) 62-32-56; attached to Uzbek Acad. of Sciences; Dir T. S. Saatov.

Institute of Botany: 700143 Tashkent, Ul. Khodzhaeva 32; tel. (371) 162-70-65; fax (371) 162-79-38; e-mail post@botany.org.uz; attached to Uzbek Acad. of Sciences; Dir Prof. Dr Ozodbek A. Ashurmetov.

Institute of Microbiology: 700128 Tashkent, Pr. Abdulla Kadiri 7A; tel. (3712) 44-25-19; fax (3712) 41-71-29; attached to Uzbek Acad. of Sciences; Dir A. G. Khalmuradov.

Institute of Physiology and Biophysics: 700095 Tashkent, Ul. A. Niyazova 1; tel. (3712) 46-95-17; attached to Uzbek Acad. of Sciences; Dir P. B. Usmanov.

Institute of Plant Chemistry: 700170 Tashkent, Ul. Abdullaeva 77; tel. (3712) 62-59-13; attached to Uzbek Acad. of Sciences; Dir Kh. N. Aripov.

Institute of Zoology: 700095 Tashkent, Ul. A. Niyazova 1; tel. (3712) 46-07-18; attached to Uzbek Acad. of Sciences; Dir J. Azimov.

Sodiqov, A., Institute of Bio-organic Chemistry: 700143 Tashkent, Ul. Abdullaeva 83; tel. (3712) 62-70-71; attached to Uzbek Acad. of Sciences; Dir Sh. I. Salikhov.

Mathematical Sciences

Romanovskii, V. I., Institute of Mathematics: 700143 Tashkent, Akademia Shaharchasi, Ul. Khodzhaeva 29; tel. (3712) 62-56-94; attached to Uzbek Acad. of Sciences; Dir Sh. A. Ayupov.

Physical Sciences

Abdullaev, Kh. M., Institute of Geology and Geophysics: 700017 Tashkent, Ul. A. K. Suleimanovoi 33; tel. (3712) 33-46-59; attached to Uzbek Acad. of Sciences; Dir F. A. Usmanov.

Astronomical Institute: 700052 Tashkent, Astronomicheskaya ul. 33; tel. (3712) 35-06-38; fax (371) 136-00-37; attached to Uzbek Acad. of Sciences; Dir Sh. A. Egamberdiev.

Central Asian Institute of Geology and Mineral Raw Materials: 700000 Tashkent GSP, Ul. T. Shevchenko 15; tel. 33-62-17; Dir A. A. Abdumazhitov.

Institute of Chemistry: 700170 Tashkent, Ul. Kh. Abdullaeva 77A; tel. (371) 162-56-60; fax (371) 162-76-57; attached to Uzbek Acad. of Sciences; Dir Z. S. Salimov.

Institute of Nuclear Physics: 700132 Tashkent oblast, Ulugbek Poselok; tel. (3712) 64-15-52; telex 116108; fax (3712) 44-26-03; attached to Uzbek Acad. of Sciences; Dir B. S. YULDASHEV.

Institute of Seismology: 700128 Tashkent, Ul. Khurshida 3; tel. (3712) 41-51-70; fax (3712) 41-53-14; f. 1966; attached to Uzbek Acad. of Sciences; library of 43,000 vols; Dir Prof. K. N. ABDULLABEKOV; publ. *Uzbek Geological Journal* (6 a year).

Institute of the Chemistry and Physics of Polymers: 700128 Tashkent, Ul. A. Kadiri 7B; tel. (3712) 41-70-80; fax (3712) 44-26-61; attached to Uzbek Acad. of Sciences; Dir S. SH. RASHIDOVA.

TECHNOLOGY

Central Asian Research Institute of the Silk Industry: Tashkent oblast, Kalinin raion, Dzhar-Aryk; Dir M. P. GANIEVA.

Institute of Cybernetics: 700187 Tashkent, Ul. Khodzhaeva 34; tel. (3712) 62-74-93; fax (3712) 62-73-21; e-mail allamiyar@vega.tashkent.su; f. 1966; attached to Uzbek Acad. of Sciences; library of 100,000 vols; Dir KH. N. NIGMATOV; publs *Problemy Informatiki i Energetiki* (6 a year), *Voprosy Kibernetiki* (3 a year), *Voprosy Vychislitelnoi i Prikladnoi Matematiki* (3 a year), *Algoritmy* (3 a year), *Voprosy Modelirovaniya i Informatizatsii Ekonomiki* (3 a year).

Institute of Hydrogeology and Engineering Geology: 700041 Tashkent, Ul. Hodjibaeva 64; tel. 62-62-15; fax 62-45-53; f. 1960; library of 18,000 vols; Dir R. A. NIAZOV.

Institute of Power Engineering and Automation: 700143 Tashkent, Akademia Shaharchasi; tel. (3712) 62-05-26; attached to Uzbek Acad. of Sciences; Dir R. A. ZAKHIDOV.

Institute of the Geology and Exploration of Oil and Gas Deposits: 700059 Tashkent, Ul. Sh. Rustaveli 114; tel. 53-09-08; Dir S. T. TALINOV.

Institute of Water Problems: 700000 Tashkent, Ul. Ya. Kolasa 24; tel. (3712) 33-83-88; fax (3712) 33-89-24; f. 1992; attached to Uzbek Acad. of Sciences; Dir N. R. KHAMRAEV.

Oripov, U. A., Institute of Electronics: 700143 Tashkent, Akademia Shaharchasi, Ul. Khodzhaeva 33; tel. (371) 162-79-40; fax (371) 162-87-67; e-mail root@ariel.tashkent.su; attached to Uzbek Acad. of Sciences; Dir U. KH. RASULEV.

Research Institute of Chemical Technology: 700143 Tashkent, Akademgorodok; tel. 62-59-22; Dir K. KH. RAZIKOV.

Research Institute of the Chemistry and Technology of Cotton Cellulose: 700710 Tashkent, Pr. M. Gorkogo 1A; tel. 62-57-12; Dir YU. T. TASHPULATOV.

Scientific and Production Association 'Akademasbob': 700143 Tashkent, Akademia Shaharchasi; tel. (3712) 162-72-73; fax (3712) 65-42-50; e-mail bahramov@apr.tashkent.su; f. 1962; attached to Uzbek Acad. of Sciences; design of scientific instruments; Dir-Gen. S. A. BAKHRAMOV.

Scientific Industrial Association 'Biolog': 700125 Tashkent, Ul. Khodzhaeva 28; tel. (3712) 62-58-21; attached to Uzbek Acad. of Sciences; Dir O. JALILOV.

Scientific Industrial Association 'Solar Physics': 700084 Tashkent, Ul. Gh. Mavlonova 2B; tel. (3712) 33-12-71; telex 116120; attached to Uzbek Acad. of Sciences; Dir K. G. GULAMOV.

Urozboev, M. T., Institute of the Mechanics and Seismic Stability of Structures: 700143 Tashkent, Akademia Shaharchasi; tel. (3712) 62-72-97; f. 1959; attached to Uzbek Acad. of Sciences; Dir YA. N. MUBAREKOV; publ. *Problems of Mechanics* (6 a year).

Uzbeknipineftegas (Uzbekistan Research and Design Institute of the Gas and Oil Industry): Tashkent 700029, Ul. T. Shevchenko 2; Dir N. KH. ALIMUKHAMEDOV.

Libraries and Archives

Samarkand

Samarkand State University Central Library: 703004 Samarkand, Bulvar Gorkogo 15; tel. 3-24-06; 1,632,000 vols; spec. collns incl. ancient oriental literature; Dir M. VALYEVA.

Tashkent

Alisher Navoi State Public Library of Uzbekistan: 700000 Tashkent, Alleya Narodova 5; tel. 33-05-47; f. 1870; 4,157,500 vols; Dir D. TADZHIEVA.

Central Library of the Uzbek Academy of Sciences: 700127 Tashkent, Ul. A. Tukaeva 1; tel. 33-83-68; f. 1934; 1,500,000 vols; Dir N. G. UMAROV.

Republican Library for Science and Technology: 700000 Tashkent, Buyuk Turon kuch. 17; tel. (3712) 33-09-22; f. 1957; technical and agricultural; 2,000,000 vols; Dir MUNIRA A. MAKSUMOVA; publs *Pakhtachilik* (Cotton), *Ipak* (Silk), *Bulletin of Small and Medium Private Business*.

Tashkent V. I. Lenin State University Central Library: 700095 Tashkent, Vozgorodok; tel. 2-91-45; 2,460,000 vols; Dir L. S. YUGAI.

Museums and Art Galleries

Nukus

Karakalpak Art Museum: 742000 Karakalpakstan, Nukus, Pr. Doslyka 127; tel. (36122) 2-24-56; fax (36122) 2-59-69; e-mail rashkhal@miras.nukus.silk.org; f. 1966; archaeology of ancient Khorezm, Karakalpak folk art, Russian avant-garde art 1910–1935; library of 8,000 vols; Dir M. BABANAZAROVA.

Karakalpak Historical Museum: Nukus, Ul. Rakhmatova 3; illustrates the part played by the Uzbek people in the October Socialist Revolution, the Civil War and the Second World War.

Samarkand

Museum of Uzbek History, Culture and Arts: Samarkand, Sovetskaya ul. 51; f. 1874; Dir N. S. SADYKOVA.

Tashkent

Museum of Literature: 700011 Tashkent, Ul. Navoi 69; tel. (3712) 41-02-75; Dir S. R. KHASANOV.

Oibek, M. T., Historical Museum of Uzbekistan: 700047 Tashkent, Ul. Sh. Rashidova 3; tel. (3712) 39-10-83; attached to Uzbek Acad. of Sciences; Dir K. KH. INOYATOV.

Rusanov, F. N., Botanical Garden: 700053 Tashkent, Ul. Abidovoi 232; tel. (3712) 35-06-13; attached to Uzbek Acad. of Sciences; Dir P. K. ZAKIROV.

Tashkent Historical Museum of the People of Uzbekistan: 700047 Tashkent, Ul. Kuibysheva 15; tel. 33-57-33; f. 1876; Dir G. R. RASHIDOV.

Uzbek State Museum of Art: 700060 Tashkent, Proletarskaya 16; tel. 32-34-44; f. 1918; library of 22,700 vols; Dir D. S. RUSIBAEV.

Universities

NUKUS STATE UNIVERSITY

742012 Nukus, Universitetskaya ul. 1

Telephone: 3-23-72

Founded 1979

Rector: Prof. K. ATANIYAZOV

Number of students: 7,000

Faculties of agricultural economics, history and geography, philology, Russian language and literature, romance and Germanic philology, mathematics, physics, chemistry and biology, physical training

SAMARKAND STATE UNIVERSITY

703004 Samarkand, Bul. University 15

Telephone: 35-19-38

Fax: 35-03-40

Founded 1933

State control

Languages of instruction: Uzbek, Russian, Tajik

Academic year: September to June

Rector: Prof. T. M. MUMINOV

Pro-Rectors: Prof. M. NUSHAROV, A. NASIMOV, I. SAIDOV, SH. SAFAROV.

Librarian: G. VALIEVA

Number of teachers: 1,275

Number of students: 16,000

Faculties of history, geography, foreign languages, mathematics, applied mathematics, physics, chemistry, biology, Uzbek, Tajik and Russian philology, law, economics, sociology, management, physical training, musical education, pre-school and primary education

TASHKENT STATE UNIVERSITY

700095 Tashkent, Vuzgorodok, Universitetskaya ul. 95

Telephone: 46-02-24

Founded 1920

Rector: Dr S. K. SIRAZHDINOV

Pro-Rectors: E. N. KUTSENKO, P. B. AZIZOV, SH. M. SHAMUKHAMEDOV

Head of Teaching Department: A. N. POTEKHIN

Library Director: L. S. YUGAI

Number of teachers: 1,480

Number of students: 19,300

Faculties of history, Uzbek philology, Russian philology, Romance and Germanic philology, oriental studies, journalism, philosophy and economics, law, mathematics, applied mathematics, physics, chemistry, biology and soil science, geology, geography

Other Higher Educational Institutes

Andizhan Cotton Institute: 711520 Andizhan oblast, Andizhan raion, poselok Kuigan-Yar; tel. 5-54-34.

Andizhan Medical Institute: 710000 Andizhan, Pr. Navoi 136; tel. 2-36-82; library of 105,000 vols.

Andizhan Pedagogical Institute of Languages: 710011 Andizhan, Pr. Zhdanova 5; tel. 4-42-50; f. 1966; faculties: Russian language and literature, foreign languages (English, German, French); Rector K. M. ISHANOVICH; publ. *Scientific Proceedings*.

Bukhara Medical Institute: 705018 Bukhara, Ul. Navoi 1; tel. 3-00-50; f. 1990; library of 32,000 vols; Rector Prof. AKRAM IBRAHIMOVICH MUMINOV.

Bukhara Technological Institute of Food and Light Industry: 705017 Bukhara, Pr. Leninskogo Komsomola 15; tel. 3-04-02; faculties: engineering and pedagogical, food industry technology, light industry, bread technology, engineering economics.

Central Asian Medical Paediatrics Institute: 700140 Tashkent, Ul. Chermet 103; tel. 62-53-50.

Ferghana Polytechnic Institute: 712022 Fergana, Ferganskaya ul. 86; tel. 2-13-33; fax 22-72-81; e-mail nodir@ferpi.vodiy.uz; f. 1967; faculties: civil engineering, chemical technology, power, mechanical construction, engineering economics; library of 290,000 vols; Rector Prof. TOJIEV R. JUMABOEVICH; publ. *Scientific-Technical Journal* (4 a year).

Financial Institute: Tashkent; 3,815 students; Rector M. SHARIFKHODZHAEV.

First Tashkent State Medical Institute: 700048 Tashkent, Ul. Khamza 103; tel. 67-63-07; f. 1920; trains general practitioners and stomatologists; library of 600,000 vols; Rector Prof. T. A. DAMINOV.

Samarkand Agricultural Institute: 703003 Samarkand, Ul. K. Marksa 77; tel. 4-33-20; f. 1929; depts: agronomy, animal husbandry, veterinary; library of 250,000 vols.

Samarkand Co-operative Institute: 703000 Samarkand, Kommunisticheskaya ul. 41; tel. 3-12-85, 3-37-74; f. 1931; faculties: engineering technology, trade economics, trade, accounting; 210 teachers; 7,000 students; library of 205,718 vols; Rector A. S. SOLIEV.

Samarkand I. P. Pavlov State Medical Institute: 703000 Samarkand, Ul. Amir Temur 18; tel. 33-07-66; f. 1930; faculties of general practice and paediatrics; library of 330,000 vols; Rector N. M. KAMALOV.

Samarkand State Architectural and Civil Engineering Institute: 703047 Samarkand, Lolazor 70; tel. (3662) 37-15-93; fax (3662) 31-04-52; e-mail info@techun.samuni.silk.org; depts: architecture, economics, building, building technology; library of 400,000 vols; Rector SOBIR M. BOBOEV.

Second Tashkent State Medical Institute: 704109 Tashkent, Ul. Farobi 2; tel. 46-82-05; f. 1990.

Tashkent State Technical University: 700095 Tashkent, Vuzgorodok, Universitetskaya 2; tel. (3712) 46-46-00; fax (3712) 294836; f. 1929; faculties: oil and gas, electronics, automation and computer hardware, power engineering, mechanical engineering and machine building, mining and geology, humanities; 2,000 teachers; 20,000 students.

Tashkent Electrotechnical University of Communications: 700084 Tashkent, Ul. Amir Temur 108; tel. 35-09-34; fax (3712) 35-10-40; f. 1955; faculties: radio communication, television and broadcasting, automatic electrical communication, multi-channel communication, special communication, management and marketing of telecommunication; 225 teachers; 3,100 students; library of 500,000 vols; Rector Prof. Dr T. D. RAJABOV.

Tashkent Engineering Institute: 700011 Tashkent, Ul. Pakhtorskaya 17; f. 1989.

Tashkent Institute of Agricultural Engineering and Irrigation: 700000 Tashkent, Ul. Kary Niyazova 39; tel. (3712) 33-46-85; telex 116108; fax (3712) 44-26-03; f. 1934; depts: mechanization, electrification, mechanization of irrigation, land exploitation, hydrotechnical construction, economics of water production; 684 teachers; 4,914 students; library of 864,000 vols; Rector Prof. S. I. IBADULLAEV.

Tashkent Institute of Political Science and Management: Tashkent; Rector M. ISKANDROV.

Tashkent Institute of Railway Engineers: 700045 Tashkent, Oboronnaya ul. 1; tel. 91-14-40; f. 1931; faculties: engineering, automation, telemechanics and communication, traffic management, industrial and civil construction, construction, economics; f. 1931; 400 teachers; 12,000 students; library of 500,000 vols; Rector M. F. PRASOLOV.

Tashkent Institute of Textile and Light Industry: 700100 Tashkent, Shokhyahon 5; tel. (3712) 53-06-06; fax (3712) 53-36-17; f. 1932; faculties: cotton technology, mechanical technology, technology for light industry, engineering economics, chemical technology; 242 teachers; 2,214 students; library of 644,000 vols; Rector Prof. KH. ALIMOVA.

Tashkent Law Institute: Tashkent; Rector A. AGZAMKHODZHAEV.

Tashkent Pharmaceutical Institute: 700015 Tashkent, Ul. Kafanova 35; tel. 56-38-39; library of 100,000 vols.

Tashkent Road and Road Transport Institute: 700047 Tashkent, Ul. Karla Marksa 32; tel. 33-08-27; faculties: road building machinery, roads, road transport, road transport management, engineering economics; br. in Termez; Rector S. P. PULATOV.

Tashkent State Agrarian University: 700183 Tashkent, Selkhozinstitut; tel. 63-76-00; depts: agrochemistry and soil science, agronomy, fruit and vegetable growing, viticulture, plant protection, silkworm breeding, economics and management, forestry, accounting; library of 196,000 vols; Rector E. T. SHAIKHOV.

Tashkent State Conservatoire: 700000 Tashkent, Ul. Pushkina 31; tel. 33-52-74; fax 33-52-74; f. 1936; piano, orchestral, Uzbek folk instruments, singing, choral conducting, composition, musicology, sound production; library of 242,723 vols; Rector O. Y. YUSUPOVA.

Tashkent State Economics University: 700063 Tashkent, Ul. Almazar 183; tel. 45-26-62; f. 1931; faculties: economic planning, agricultural economics, trade economics, financial economics, accounting, economic cybernetics; 400 teachers; 11,000 students; library of 300,000 vols; br. in Andizhan; Rector S. GULYAMOV.

Tashkent State Institute of Culture: 700164 Tashkent, Massiv vysokovoltnyi, sektor 3, 127-A; tel. 62-03-23; librarianship, educational and cultural work; br. in Namangan.

Tashkent State Pedagogical Institute of Foreign Languages: 700115 Tashkent, Ul. Mukimi 104; tel. 56-08-75.

Tashkent State Theatrical and Art Institute: 700031 Tashkent, Ul. Germana Lopatina 77; tel. 56-28-80; f. 1945; acting, stage directing, cinema, painting, graphic arts, history and theory of art, monumental decorative art, interior design, museum studies, protection of monuments, architectural restoration; 190 teachers; 900 students; Rector T. T. TURSUNOV.

VATICAN CITY

Learned Societies

GENERAL

Accademia Romana di S. Tommaso d'Aquino e di Religione Cattolica (Roman Academy of St Thomas Aquinas): Piazza della Cancelleria 1, 00186 Rome, Italy; f. 1879; 70 mems; theological, philosophical and juridico-economic sections; Pres. Cardinal MARIO LUIGI CIAPPI; Vice-Pres. Mgr ANTONIO PIOLANTI; Sec. D. LUIGI BOGLIOLO.

FINE AND PERFORMING ARTS

Pontificia Insigne Accademia di Belle Arti e Lettere dei Virtuosi al Pantheon: Palazzo della Cancelleria Apostolica, Piazza della Cancelleria 1, Rome, Italy; f. 1543; Pres. Dott. VITALIANO TIBERIA; Sec. Prof. ERNESTO LAMAGNA.

HISTORY, GEOGRAPHY AND ARCHAEOLOGY

Pontificia Accademia Romana di Archeologia (Pontifical Roman Academy of Archaeology): Palazzo della Cancelleria Apostolica, 00186 Rome, Italy; f. 1810; 105 mems; Pres. VICTOR SAXER; Sec. SILVIO PANCIERA; publs *Rendiconti*, *Memorie*.

NATURAL SCIENCES

General

Pontificia Academia Scientiarum (Pontifical Academy of Sciences): Casina Pio IV, 00120 Vatican City State; tel. 06-69883451; fax 06-69885218; e-mail academy.sciences@acdscience.va; f. 1603; mathematical and experimental sciences; 80 acads chosen worldwide; Pres. Prof. NICOLA CABIBBO; Chancellor Prof. GIUSEPPE PITTAU; publs *Scripta Varia*, *Commentarii*, *Documenta*.

RELIGION, SOCIOLOGY AND ANTHROPOLOGY

Collegium Cultorum Martyrum: Via Napoleone III 1, 00185 Rome, Italy; f. 1879; *c.* 750 mems; Master Mgr EMANUELE CLARIZIO; Sec. LUIGI CIOTTI.

Pontificia Academia Mariana Internationalis (Pontifical International Marian Academy): Via Merulana 124, 00185 Rome, Italy; premises in Vatican City; tel. 06-70373235; fax 06-70373234; e-mail pami@ofm.org; f. 1946, Pontifical since 1959; studies on Our Lady; 75 mems, 155 corresp. mems, 134 hon. mems; Pres. GASPAR CALVO MORALEJO; Sec. STEFANO CECCHIN; publs Scientific collections.

Pontificia Accademia dell'Immacolata (Academy of the Immaculate Conception): Via del Serafico 1, 00142 Rome, Italy; f. 1835; 15 mems; promotes Marian studies and culture, especially the doctrine of the Immaculate Conception in the fields of theology, literature and art; Pres. Cardinal ANDREA M. DESKUR; Sec. and Archivist Fr LORENZO DI FONZO.

Pontificia Accademia Teologica Romana: Piazza della Cancelleria 1, 00186 Rome, Italy; f. 1718; attached to the Pontifical University of the Lateran; 34 hon. mems, 40 ordinary mems; 20 being normally resident in Rome, 10 from the rest of Italy and 10 from other countries, and 12 corresp. mems; Protector Cardinal PIO LAGHI; Sec. Rt Rev. Mgr ANTONIO PIOLANTI; publ. *Divinitas*.

Research Institutes

NATURAL SCIENCES

Physical Sciences

Vatican Observatory, The: 00120 Vatican City; tel. 06-6983411; telex 5042020; f. 1889; 11 staff; galactic structure, relativistic astrophysics; library of 33,000 vols; Dir GEORGE V. COYNE; publs *Vatican Observatory Publications*, *Annual Report*.

Libraries and Archives

Rome

Archivio Segreto Vaticano (Papal Archives): 00120 Vatican City; f. 1611; attached school: see Schools; Prefect SERGIO PAGANO; publs *Collectanea Archivi Vaticani*, *Varia*.

Biblioteca Apostolica Vaticana (Vatican Apostolic Library): 00120 Vatican City; tel. 69883302; fax 69884795; e-mail bav@librs6k.vatlib.it; f. 1450 as a public library by Pope Nicholas V, and provided with staff and a structure by Sixtus IV in 1475; at the present time it contains some 75,000 MSS, 80,000 archival files, 100,000 engravings, 8,000 incunabula, and 1,000,000 other vols; among famous collections which have helped to build up the Library are those of the Dukes of Urbino (1657), of Queen Christina of Sweden (1690), of the Florentine Marquis Capponi (1745), of Barberini (1902), of Chigi (1923), and the Borghese collection, which included many items housed in the Papal Library at Avignon; the Sistine Chapel collection is of the greatest importance to historians of music; among the many rare and precious MSS in the Library are a Greek Bible of the 4th century, Vergils of the 4th and 6th centuries, a 4th–5th-century palimpsest of Cicero's *Republic*, autographs of St Thomas Aquinas, Tasso, Petrarch, Boccaccio, Poliziano, Michelangelo, and Luther; houses numismatic colln; attached museums: see Museums and Art Galleries; attached school: see Schools; Protector Cardinal LUIGI POGGI; Prefect Prof. Don RAFFAELE FARINA; publs *Studi e Testi*, catalogues and facsimile editions.

Museums and Art Galleries

Vatican City

Museo Profano: Vatican City; f. 1767 by Pope Clement XIII; administered by Vatican Apostolic Library; bronze sculptures and minor arts of the classical era; Curator Dr GIOVANNI MORELLO.

Museo Sacro: Vatican City; f. 1756 by Pope Benedict XIV; administered by Vatican Apostolic Library; contains objects of liturgical art, historical relics and curios from the Lateran, objects of palaeolithic, medieval and Renaissance minor arts, paintings of the Roman era; Curator Dr GIOVANNI MORELLO.

Vatican Museums and Galleries: 00120 Vatican City; tel. 06-69883333; telex 2024; fax 06-69885061; Dir-Gen. Dr FRANCESCO BURANELLI; Administrator Dr FRANCESCO RICCARDI; Sec. Dr EDITH CICERCHIA; publs *Bollettino dei Monumenti, Musei e Gallerie Pontificie*.

Contain the following sections:

Historical Museum: 00120 Vatican City; f. 1973; divided into the Historical Museum proper, housed in the Lateran Palace, containing arms, uniforms and armour of the pontifical court and Army Corps (disbanded 1970), and the Carriage Museum, in the Vatican gardens, containing carriages, berlins and the first cars used by the Popes; Dir Asst Mons. PIETRO AMATO.

Museo Pio Clementino: 00120 Vatican City; f. by Pope Clement XIV (1769–74), and enlarged by his successor, Pius VI (1775–1799); exhibits include the Apollo of Belvedere, Roman copies of the Apoxyomenos by Lysippus, of the Meleager by Skopas and of the Apollo Sauroktonous by Praxiteles; the original Vatican Collection was begun with the Apollo—already in possession of Pope Julius II when he was still a Cardinal, at the end of the 15th century—and the Laocoon Group, found in 1506; Curator Dott. PAOLO LIVERANI.

Museo Chiaramonti e Braccio Nuovo: 00120 Vatican City; f. by Pope Pius VII at the beginning of the 19th century, to house the many new findings excavated in that period; exhibits include the statues of the Nile, of Demosthenes and of the Augustus 'of Prima Porta'; Curator Dott. PAOLO LIVERANI.

Museo Gregoriano Etrusco: 00120 Vatican City; f. by Pope Gregory XVI in 1837; contains objects from the Tomba Regolini Galassi of Cerveteri, the Mars of Todi, bronzes, terracottas and jewellery, and Greek vases from Etruscan tombs; Curator Dott. MAURIZIO SANNIBALE.

Museo Gregoriano Egizio: 00120 Vatican City; f. 1839 by Pope Gregory XVI; contains Egyptian antiquities (statues, stelae, sarcophagi, etc.), many of which were discovered in Rome, and Roman imitations of Egyptian statues from Hadrian's villa in Tivoli; Consultant Prof. JEAN-CLAUDE GRENIER.

Museo Gregoriano Profano: 00120 Vatican City; f. by Gregory XVI in 1844 and housed in the Lateran Palace, it was transferred to a new building in the Vatican and opened to the public in 1970; Roman sculptures from the Pontifical States; portrait-statue of Sophocles, the Marsyas of the Myronian group of Athena and Marsyas, the Flavian reliefs from the Palace of the Apostolic Chancery; Curator Dott. PAOLO LIVERANI.

Museo Pio Cristiano: 00120 Vatican City; f. by Pius IX in 1854 and housed in the Lateran Palace; transferred to a new building in the Vatican and opened to the public in 1970; large collection of sarcophagi; Latin and Greek inscriptions from Christian cemeteries and basilicas; the Good Shepherd; Curator Dott. GIANDOMENICO SPINOLA.

Museo Missionario Etnologico: 00120 Vatican City; f. by Pius XI in 1926 and housed in the Lateran Palace; transferred to a new building in the Vatican and opened to the public in 1973; ethnographical collections from all over the world; Curator Rev. ROBERTO ZAGNOLI.

Pinacoteca Vaticana: 00120 Vatican City; inaugurated by Pope Pius XI in 1932; includes paintings by Giotto, Fra Angelico, Raphael, Leonardo da Vinci, Titian and Caravaggio, and the Raphael Tapestries; Curator Dott. ARNOLD NESSELRATH.

Collezione d'Arte Religiosa Moderna: 00120 Vatican City; f. 1973 by Pope Paul VI; paintings, sculptures and drawings offered to the Pope by over 200 artists and donors; Curator Dott. MARIO FERRAZZA.

Vatican Palaces: 00120 Vatican City; Nicoline Chapel decorated by Beato Angelico (1448–1450); Sistine Chapel restructured by Sixtus IV (1477–1483): frescoes by Perugino, Botticelli, Cosimo Rosselli, Ghirlandaio, Luca Signorelli, Michelangelo; Borgia Apartment: decorated by Pinturicchio and his workshop; Chapel of Urban VIII (1631–1635); Raphael Stanze and loggias decorated by Raphael and his assistants; Gallery of Maps (1580–83), Gallery of Tapestries, etc.; Curator Dott. ARNOLD NESSELRATH.

Universities

PONTIFICIA UNIVERSITAS GREGORIANA
(Pontifical Gregorian University)

Piazza della Pilotta 4, 00187 Rome, Italy
Telephone: 06-67011
Fax: 67-015-413

Founded by St Ignatius Loyola and St Francis Borgia, and constituted by Pope Julius III in 1553; confirmed and established by Pope Gregory XIII in 1582

The central university for ecclesiastical studies under the direction of the Jesuit Order; Pontificium Institutum Biblicum and Pontificium Institutum Orientalium Studiorum are autonomous colleges associated with the University (see below)

Languages of instruction: Italian, English, German, French, Spanish, Portuguese
Academic year: October to June (two terms)

Grand Chancellor: Cardinal PIO LAGHI
Vice-Grand Chancellor: Most Rev. Father PETER-HANS KOLVENBACH
Rector Magnificus: Most Rev. Father GIUSEPPE PITTAU
Vice-Rector: Rev. Fr FRANCO IMODA
Secretary-General: Rev. ALEJANDRO ANGULO
Librarian: Rev. MAXIMILIAN ZITNIK

Library of 900,000 vols
Number of teachers: 380
Number of students: 3,600

Publications: *Gregorianum*, *Periodica de re morali canonica liturgica*, *Studia Missionalia*, *Archivum Historiae Pontificiae*, *Analecta Gregoriana*, *Miscellanea Historiae Pontificiae*, *Saggi ISR*, *Studia Spiritualia*, *Documenta Missionalia*, *Studia Socialia*, *Acta Nuntiaturae Gallicae*, *Studi Critici sulle Scienze*, *Tesi Gregoriana*, *Studia Missionalia*, *Inculturation.*

DEANS AND DIRECTORS

Faculty of Theology: S. BASTIANEL
Faculty of Canon Law: G. GHIRLANDA
Faculty of Philosophy: C. HUBER
Faculty of Ecclesiastical History: J. BENITEZ
Faculty of Missionary Work: A. WOLANIN
Faculty of Social Sciences: A. ANGULO
Institute of Psychology: F. IMODA
Institute of Spirituality: H. ALPHONSO
Institute of Religious Sciences: M. SZENTMÁRTONI
School of Advanced Latin Studies: S. GRASSO
Interdisciplinary Centre on Social Communication: R. WHITE
Cultural Heritage of the Church: H. PFEIFFER

PROFESSORS

Faculty of Theology:

BASTIANEL, S., Moral Theology
BECKER, K. J., Dogmatic Theology
BRÉTON, S., New Testament Exegesis
BRODEUR, S., New Testament Exegesis
CABA, J., Old Testament Exegesis
CALDUCH BENAGES, N., Old Testament Exegesis
CHAPPIN, M., Church History
CONROY, C., Old Testament Exegesis
COSTACURTA, B., Exegesis
DE FIORES, S., Mariology
DEMMER, K., Moral Theology
FERRER, J., Moral Theology
GRILLI, M., Exegesis
GROTH, B., Fundamental Theology
HALL, J. M., Liturgy
HENN, W., Dogmatic Theology
LADÁRIA, L., Dogmatic Theology
LUBOMIRSKI, M., Dogmatic Theology
MCDERMOTT, J., Dogmatic Theology
MEYNET, R., New Testament Exegesis
MILLÁS, J. M., Dogmatic Theology
MULLER, E., Dogmatic Theology
O'COLLINS, G., Dogmatic Theology
O'DONNELL, J., Dogmatic Theology
PASTOR, F., Dogmatic Theology
PELLAND, G., Patristics
POTTIE, C., Liturgy
ROSATO, P., Dogmatic Theology
SCHMITZ, P., Moral Theology
VANNI, U., Exegesis
VERCRUYSSE, J., Church History and Ecumenical Theology
WICKS, J., Fundamental Theology

Faculty of Law:

FERME, B., Canon Law and Sacraments
FERRARI DA PASSANO, P., Public Church Law
GHIRLANDA, G., Canon Law and Theology of Church Law
HILBERT, M., Text of Canon Law
KOWAL, J., Canon Law and Sacraments
SUGAWARA, Y., Canon Law and Religious Life

Faculty of Philosophy:

BABOLIN, S., Aesthetics and Philosophy of Human Culture
CARUANA, L., World Philosophy
DI MAIO, A., Medieval Philosophy
FABROCINI, PH., Logic
FLANNERY, K., Greek Philosophy
GILBERT, P., Metaphysics
GORCZYCA, J., Ethics
HUBER, C., Philosophy of Knowledge
LECLERC, M., History of Modern Philosophy
LUCAS LUCAS, R., Philosophical Anthropology
MCNELLIS, P. W., Social Ethics
MAGNANI, G., Phenomenology and Philosophy of Religion
PANGALLO, M., History of Medieval Philosophy
SPROKEL, N., General Ethics
WALSH, T., Philosophy of Religion

Faculty of Church History:

BENITEZ, J. M., Modern Church History
DE LASALA CLAVER, F., History of the Roman Curia
GUTIERREZ, A., Church History (Latin America)
INGLOT, M., History of the Roman Curia
JANSSENS, J., Christian Archaeology– Historical Methodology
MEZZADRI, L., Modern Church History
PFEIFFER, H., Christian Art

Faculty of Missiology Work:

FARAHIAN, E., Missionary Biblical Theology
FUSS, M., Buddhism
LÓPEZ-GAY, J., Missiology and Japanese Buddhism
ROEST CROLLIUS, A., Mission Spirituality
SHELKE, C., Comparative Study of Religions
WOLANIN, A., Mission Dogmatics

Faculty of Social Sciences:

ANGULO NOVOA, A., Ethics, Political Sociology
BAUGH, L., Film and Television Language
BERNAL RESTREPO, S., Sociology, Church Social Doctrine
CARBONELL DE MASY, R., Economics
SCARVAGLIERI, G., General Religious Sociology
SCHÜHLY, G., Methodology, Research
SPILLANE, J., Ethics of Economics
SUAREZ, R. W., Philosophy of Social Science
WHITE, R., Social Communication

Institute of Spirituality:

ALPHONSO, H., Spiritual Theology
COSTA, M., Spiritual Theology
GARCÍA MATEO, R., Spiritual Theology
MARTINEZ, E. R., Biblical Spirituality
MORILLA DELGADO, J., Spiritual Theology
NAVONE, J., Biblical Spirituality
ORSUTO, D., Spiritual Theology
RUIZ-JURADO, M., Spiritual Theology
SECONDIN, B., Pastoral Theology
SERVAIS, J., Spiritual Theology
SZENTMÁRTONI, M., Pastoral Psychology

Institute of Psychology:

DOLPHIN, B., Psychology and Statistics
HEALY, T., Psychology and Statistics
IMODA, F., Psychology
KIELY, B., Psychopathology
VERSALDI, G., Psychology and Psychotherapy

Institute of Religious Sciences:

BAGGIO, A. M., Political Ethics
BARLONE, S., Fundamental Theology
BASTIANEL, S., Moral Theology
ELBERTI, A., Dogmatic Theology
FINAMORE, R., Religious Didactics
GIACOVELLI, C., Methodology
GISMONDI, G., Fundamental Theology
GRILLI, M., Biblical Theology
LACHENSCHMID, R., Dogmatic Theology
SALATIELLO, G., Anthropology
SZENTMÁRTONI, M., Psychology of Religion
TENACE, M., Dogmatic Theology
VALENTINI, A., New Testament Exegesis
VANNI, U., New Testament Exegesis
VANZAN, P., Pastoral Theology

School of Advanced Latin Studies:

BARTOLA, A., Latin Fundamental Institutions
FOGAZZA, D., Latin Fundamental Institutions
FOSTER, R., Stylistics
GRASSO, S., Latin Letters
MAGGI, F., Latin Letters
PICCIONE, R. M., Latin Fundamental Institutions
RIZZO, M. C., Latin Fundamental Institutions
SALVADORE, M., Latin Fundamental Institutions

Interdisciplinary Centre on Social Communication:

BABOLIN, S., Symbology
BAUGH, L., Film and TV Language
CABASES, F., Religious Communication
CARNICELLA, M. C., Religious Communication
DINI, A., Sociology
EHRAT, J., Semiotics
MARTINEZ, J., Pastoral Communication

MASINI, E., Futurology
ROSSETTI, A., Economic History
WHITE, R., Pastoral Planning

Cultural Heritage of the Church:
BABOLIN, S., Symbology
JANSSENS, J., Church History
LASALA, F. DE, Palaeography
PFEIFFER, H., Art History
RUPNIK, I. M., Art History

AFFILIATED INSTITUTES

Filozofsko-Teološki Institut Družbe Isusove: Jordanovac 110, 41001 Zagreb, Croatia; Pres. N. STANKOVIČ; Sec. I. CINDORI.

Institut de Philosophie St Pierre Canisius: Kimwenza, BP 3724, Kinshasa, Gombe, Zaire; Rector S. DECLOUX; Sec. E. STIENNON.

Instituto Latinoamericano de Doctrina y Estudios Sociales (ILADES): Almirante Barroso 6, Casilla 1446, Correo 21, Santiago, Chile; Dir T. MIFSUD.

Instituto Superior de Ciencias Religiosas: En la Arquidiócesis de Montevideo, Uruguay; Dir P. I. PERALTA ANSORENA.

Instituto Superior de Direito Canônico do Brasil: Rua Benjamin Constant 23, 20241 Rio de Janeiro, Brazil; Dir L. MADERO LOPEZ.

Instituto Teologico del Uruguay 'Mariano Soler': Avda S. Fructuoso 1019, Montevideo, Uruguay; Rector J. C. DELPIAZZO; Sec. A. BONZANI.

Istituto di Filosofia 'Aloysianum': Via Donatello 24, 35123 Padua, Italy; Dir P. G. NARDONE.

Istituto di Scienze Religiose 'Beato Ippolito Galantini': Via Cosimo il Vecchio 26, 50139 Florence, Italy; Dir G. MAZZANTI.

Istituto Superiore di Scienze Religiose 'Giuseppe Toniolo': Via S. Benedetto da Norcia 2, 65127 Pescara, Italy; Pres. G. CILLI.

Istituto Superiore di Scienze Umane e Religiose: Via Ignatianum 23, 98100 Messina, Italy; Dir A. SFERRAZZA.

Istituto Superiore per i Formatori: Seminario Vescovile, Viale Timavo 93, 42100 Reggio Emilia, Italy; Dir A. MANENTI.

Jesuit School of Philosophy and Humanities 'Arrupe College': POB MP320, Mount Pleasant, Harare, Zimbabwe; Pres. V. SHIRIMA.

Pontificio Istituto Regina Mundi: Lungotevere Tor di Nona 7, 00186 Rome, Italy; Dir F. BARBIERO; Sec. J. VANHOOF.

PONTIFICIA UNIVERSITAS LATERANENSIS
(Pontifical Lateran University)

Piazza S. Giovanni in Laterano 4, 00184 Rome, Italy
Telephone: 06-69886401
Fax: 06-69886508

Founded 1773
Languages of instruction: Italian, Latin

Grand Chancellor: HE Card. CAMILLO RUINI
Rector: H. E. Mgr ANGELO SCOLA
General Secretary: Rev. Dr DANIELE MICHELETTI
Administrator: Dr RAFFAELE LOMONACO
Librarian: Rev. Mgr LUIGI FALCONE

Library of 550,000 vols
Number of teachers: 113
Number of students: 1,650

Publications: *Apollinaris*, *Aquinas*, *Lateranum*, *Studia et Documenta Historiae et Juris*.

DEANS

Faculty of Theology: Rev. Mgr RENZO GERARDI
Faculty of Canon Law: Rev. Prof. IGNACIO PEREZ DE HEREDIA
Faculty of Civil Law: Prof. GIAN LUIGI FALCHI
Faculty of Philosophy: Dr ANGELA ALES BELLO

INCORPORATED INSTITUTES

Institutum Theologiae Moralis 'Accademia Alfonsiana': Via Merulana 31, 00185 Rome, Italy; Pres. Rev. Fr BRUNO HIDBER.

Institutum Patristicum 'Augustinianum': Via Paolo VI 25, 00193 Rome, Italy; Pres. Rev. Fr ANGELO DI BERNARDINO.

Institutum Theologiae Vitae Religiosiae 'Claretianum': Largo Lorenzo Mossa 4, 00165 Rome, Italy; Pres. Rev. Fr JOSÉ ROVIRA.

AGGREGATED INSTITUTES

Institut Supérieur de la Sagesse de Beyrouth: Rue de la Sagesse, Achrafieh, Beirut, Lebanon; teaching of law; Pres. Fr PAUL AKL.

Istituto Teologico di Assisi: Piazza S. Francesco 1, 06082 Assisi, Italy; Prefect of Studies Rev. Fr BRUNO PENNACCHINI.

AFFILIATED INSTITUTES

Istituto Teologico Abruzzese-Molisano di Chieti: Via Nicoletto Vernia 1, 66100 Chieti, Italy; Rector Rev. Fr MARCO TRIVISONNE.

Istituto Teologico Marchigiano: sections in Ancona and Fermo; Prefect of Studies Mgr DUILIO BONIFAZI.

Istituto Teologico Marchigiano (Ancona Section): Via Monte d'Ago 87, 60131 Ancona, Italy; Rector Rev. VINCENZO BAIOCCO.

Istituto Teologico Marchigiano (Fermo Section): Seminario Arcivescovile, 62023 Fermo (Ascoli Piceno), Italy; Rector Rev. Fr PAOLO DE ANGELIS.

Studio Filosofico e Teologico del Seminario Patriarcale Latino di Gerusalemme: POB 14152, Beit Jala, Jerusalem, Israel; Prefect of Studies Dr WILLIAM SHOMALY.

Studio Teologico 'S. Zeno': Via Seminario 8, 37100 Verona, Italy; Rector Most Rev. Mgr GIUSEPPE VALENSISE.

Institut de formation théologique, Grand Séminaire de Montréal: 2065 rue Sherbrooke Ouest, Montréal, Qué. H3H 1G6, Canada; Rector Rev. Fr LIONEL GENDRON.

Oratory Church of the Holy Family 'St Philip Neri': 1372 King St, West Toronto, Ont. MGK 1H3, Canada; Prefect of Studies Rev. Fr JONATHAN ROBINSON.

INSTITUTES WITHIN THE PREMISES

Pontificium Institutum Pastorale: Piazza S. Giovanni in Laterano 4, 00184 Rome, Italy; Pres. Rev. Prof. SERGIO LANZA.

Istituto Superiore di Scienze Religiose 'Ecclesia Mater': Piazza S. Giovanni in Laterano 4, 00184 Rome, Italy; Pres. Most Rev. Mgr PAOLO SEWADAGI.

PONTIFICIA UNIVERSITÀ SALESIANA
(Salesian Pontifical University)

Piazza Ateneo Salesiano 1, 00139 Rome, Italy
Telephone: 06-872901
Fax: 06-87290318
E-mail: rettore@ups.urbe.it

Founded by the Holy See 1940; university status granted 1973 by Pope Paul VI
Language of instruction: Italian
Academic year: October to June (2 semesters)

Chancellor: Very Rev. JUAN E. VECCHI
Rector: Very Rev. MICHELE PELLEREY
Vice-Rector: Rev. ANGELO AMATO
Administrator: Very Rev. CARLO LIEVORE
Secretary-General: Very Rev. JAROSŁAW ROCHOWIAK
Librarian: Very Rev. JUAN PICCA

Library of 670,000 vols
Number of teachers: 186
Number of students: 1,918

Publications: *Salesianum* (quarterly), *Orientamenti Pedagogici* (every 2 months), *Tuttogiovani Notizie* (quarterly).

DEANS

Faculty of Canon Law: Very Rev. PIERO GIORGIO MARCUZZI
Faculty of Theology: Very Rev. ANGELO AMATO
Faculty of Philosophy: Very Rev. MARIO TOSO
Faculty of Education: Very Rev. CARLO NANNI
Faculty of Letters (Christian and Classics): Very Rev. ENRICO DAL COVOLO
Faculty of Social Communication Sciences (ISCOS): Very Rev. FRANCO LEVER
Department of Youth Pastoral Theology and Catechetics: Very Rev. RICCARDO TONELLI
Higher Institute of Religious Sciences (ISSR): Very Rev. MARIO CIMOSA
Postgraduate School of Clinical Psychology: Very Rev. CARLO NANNI

PROFESSORS

Faculty of Canon Law:
ARDITO, S., Text of Canon Law
MARCUZZI, P. G., Text of Canon Law

Faculty of Theology:
AMATO, A., Dogmatics
BERGAMELLI, F., Patrology
BUZZETTI, C., New Testament Literature
CARLOTTI, P., Moral Theology
CAVIGLIA, G., Fundamental Theology
CIMOSA, M., Old Testament
COFFELE, G., Fundamental Theology
FARINA, R., Ancient Church History
FRIGATO, S., Moral Theology
GALLO, L., Dogmatics
GATTI, G., Moral Theology
GOZZELINO, G., Dogmatics
MARITANO, M., Ancient Church History and Patrology
MERLO, P., Moral Theology
MOSETTO, F., New Testament
PASQUATO, O., Medieval and Modern Church History
PERRENCHIO, F., New Testament
PICCA, J., New Testament
SEMERARO, C., Contemporary Church History
SODI, M., Liturgy
STRUS, A., Old Testament
TONELLI, R., Pastoral Theology
TRIACCA, A., Liturgy
VICENT, R., Old Testament
VINCENT, A. F., Pastoral Theology
ZEVINI, G., New Testament

Faculty of Philosophy:
ABBÀ, G., Ethics
ALESSI, A., Metaphysics
CHENIS, C., Philosophy
PALUMBIERI, S., Anthropology
TOSO, M., Social and Political Philosophy

Faculty of Education:
ALBERICH SOTOMAYOR, E., Fundamental Catechetics
ARTO, A., Developmental Psychology
BAJZEK, J., Sociology of Religion
BISSOLI, C., Bible, Pastoral and Catechesis
COMOGLIO, M., Didactics
FIZZOTTI, E., Psychology of Religion
GEVAERT, J., Anthropology and Catechesis
MACARIO, L., Pedagogical Developmental Methodology
MALIZIA, G., Sociology and School Politics
MION, R., Sociology of Family and Youth
NANNI, C., Philosophy of Education
PELLEREY, M., General Didactics
POLACEK, K., Projective Techniques
POLIZZI, V., Biology and Philosophy of Nature
PRELLEZO GARCIA, J., History of Modern and Contemporary Education and Pedagogy
SARTI, S., Statistics

TRENTI, Z., Pastoral and Catechesis
ZANNI, N., Didactics

Faculty of Letters (Christian and Classics):
AMATA, B., Greek and Latin Patristics
BRACCHI, R., History of the Greek and Latin Languages
DAL COVOLO, E., Ancient Christian Greek Literature
PAVANETTO, A., Classical Greek Language and Literature

Faculty of Social Communication Sciences:
GIANNATELLI, R., Media Education
LEVER, F., Theory and Technique of Television/Mass Media and Catechesis

ATTACHED RESEARCH INSTITUTES

Historical Institute of Canon Law.

Institute of Dogmatic Theology.

Institute of Pastoral Theology.

Institute of Spirituality.

Institute of Liturgical Studies.

Institute of Theory and History of Education.

Institute of Pedagogic Methodology.

Institute of Didactics.

Institute of Catechetics.

Institute of Psychology.

Studies on Don Bosco Centre.

Psychopedagogical Research Centre.

Institute of Sociology of Education.

Observatory on Youth.

Studies on the Missions Centre.

ATTACHED INSTITUTES

Département de Philosophie de l'Université Catholique de l'Afrique Centrale: BP 11628, Yaoundé, Cameroon; Dean Rev. CLAUDE PEIRAULT.

Departamento de Filosofía del Instituto de Teología para Religiosos: Avda Rómulo Gallegos, Apdo 70.913, Los Ruices, Caracas 1071-A, Venezuela; Dean Rev. JOSÉ C. AYESTARÁN.

Don Bosco International Institute: Via Caboto 27, 10129 Turin, Italy; section of Roman Faculty of Theology; Vice-Dean Very Rev. FRANCESCO MOSETTO.

Institut de Philosophie 'Saint-Joseph-Mukasa': BP 339, Yaoundé, Cameroon; Dean Rev. JOSEF BÖCKENHOFF.

Instituto 'Santo Tomás de Aquino': Rua Itutinga 240, 30350 Belo Horizonte, MG, Brazil; Dean Rev. CLETO CALIMAN.

Philosophisch-Theologische Hochschule der Salesianer: Don Bosco-Str. 1, 83671 Benediktbeuern, Germany; Rector Very Rev. ALOIS KOTHGASSER.

Salesian House Philosophical Studies: 10 Avda 36–73, Zona 11, Guatemala, CA; Dean ROLAND ECHEVERRÍA.

Salesian House Philosophical Studies: Avda El Liceo, Apdo 43, Los Teques, Venezuela; Dean MARINO MENINI.

Salesian House Philosophical Studies: Divya Daan, College Rd, Nasik 422005, India; Dean ALBANO FERNANDES.

Salesian House Philosophical Studies: The Retreat, Yercaud 636601, India; Dean SUSAI AMALRAJ.

Salesian House Philosophical Studies: Centro di Studi 'Paolo VI', Via S. Giovanni Bosco 1, 25075 Nave, Italy; Dean PAOLO ZINI.

Salesian House Philosophical Studies: Av. Lo Cañas s/n, Casilla 53, La Florida, Santiago, Chile; Dean SEPÚLVEDA ÁNGEL MERCADO.

Salesian House Theological Studies: Calle Torelló 8, 08035 Barcelona, Spain; Dean JORDI LATORRE I CASTILLO.

Salesian House Theological Studies: POB 160, Bethlehem-Cremisan, Israel; Dean GIOVANNI CAPUTA.

Salesian House Theological Studies: 20 Avenida 13–45, Zona 11, Guatemala City, Guatemala, CA; Dean ALEJANDRO HERNÁNDEZ.

Salesian House Theological Studies: Via del Pozzo, CP 256, 98100 Messina, Italy; Dean NUNZIO CONTE.

Salesian House Theological Studies: Paseo de las Delicias 20, 28045 Madrid, Spain; Dean PAULINO MONTERO.

Salesian House Theological Studies: Rua Pio XI 1100 (Lapa), 05060-001 São Paulo, Brazil; Dean RONALDO ZACHARIAS.

Salesian House Theological Studies: Kristu Jyoti College, Krishnarajapuram, Bangalore 560036, India; Dean DOMINIC VELIATH.

Salesian House Theological Studies: Mawlai, Shillong 793008, Meghalaya, India; Dean SEBASTIAN PALLISSERY.

Salesian House Theological Studies: Tonalá 344, Ap. p. 66, Tlaquepaque, 45500 Guadalajara, Mexico; Dean JUAN BOSCO JIMÉNEZ.

Salesian House Theological Studies: POB 1756, MCC PO 1299, Makati, Manila, Philippines; Dean JOHN CABRIDO.

Centre Saint-Augustin: Villa contigue au Village S.O.S., BP 15222, Dakar, Senegal; Dean PAUL VERBRUGGEN.

Instituto de Teología para Religiosos – ITER: Avda Romulo Gallegos, Apdo 70.913, Los Ruices, Caracas 1071-A, Venezuela; Dean JOSÉ AYESTARÁN.

Institut de Théologie 'S. François de Sales': BP 372, Lubumbashi, Democratic Republic of the Congo; Dean GABRIEL NGENDAKURYIO.

PONTIFICIA UNIVERSITÀ S. TOMMASO D'AQUINO
(St Thomas Aquinas Pontifical University)

Largo Angelicum 1, 00184 Rome, Italy
Telephone: 06-67021
Fax: 06-6790407

College founded 1580; became University 1909; present title conferred 1963
Languages of instruction: Italian, English
Academic year: October to June

Grand Chancellor: Rev. TIMOTHY RADCLIFFE
Rector Magnificus: Rev. EDWARD KACZYŃSKI
Vice-Rector (Academic): Rev. F. RAMOS
Vice-Rector (Administrative): Rev. J. MCGUIRE
Secretary-General (Registrar): Rev. RINALDO GIULIANI
Librarian: Rev. MIGUEL ITZA

Library of 200,000 vols
Number of teachers: 111
Number of students: 1,737

Publications: *Angelicum*, *Rassegna di Letteratura Tomistica*, *Studia Univ. S. Thomae In Urbe*, *Istituto S. Tommaso: Studi*.

DEANS

Faculty of Theology: Rev. J. AGIUS
Faculty of Canon Law: Rev. A. URRU
Faculty of Philosophy: Rev. A. WILDER
Faculty of Social Sciences: Rev. F. COMPAGNONI

DIRECTORS

Institute of Spirituality: Rev. FABIO GIARDINI
'Mater Ecclesiae' Institute: Rev. M. SALVATI
Institute of St Thomas: Rev. G. GRASSO

PONTIFICIA UNIVERSITAS URBANIANA
(Pontifical Urban University)

Via Urbano VIII 16, 00165 Rome, Italy
Telephone: 06-69882351
Fax: 06-69881871
E-mail: puusegre@pcn.net

Founded 1627 by Pope Urban VIII
State control
Language of instruction: Italian
Academic year: October to June

Chancellor: Cardinal JOZEF TOMKO
Vice-Chancellor: Bishop MARCELLO ZAGO
Rector Magnificus: Rev. Mgr AMBROGIO SPREAFICO
Vice-Rector: Rev. Mgr GUIDO MAZZOTTA
Secretary-General: Rev. P. GIOVANNI MARCONCINI
Librarian: Rev. Fr WILLI HENKEL

Number of teachers: 130 (incl. 27 full-time)
Number of students: 1,238

Publications: *Euntes Docete*, *Bibliografia Missionaria*, *Annales*, *Urbaniana*.

DEANS

Faculty of Theology: Rev. Prof. ERICH SCHMID
Faculty of Philosophy: Rev. Prof. GUIDO MAZZOTTA
Missiology: Rev. Prof. GIUSEPPE CAVALLOTTO
Canon Law: Rev. Prof. VELASIO DE PAOLIS

PROFESSORS

Faculty of Theology:
BIGUZZI, G., New Testament Exegesis
CICCIMARRA, F., Canon Law
COLOMBO, G., Moral Theology
DEIANA, G., Biblical Languages and Scriptures
EGBULEFU, J., Sacramental Theology
GONZALEZ FERNANDEZ, F., Church History
LAVATORI, R., Christology
NOCE, C., Patrology
PIRC, J., Ecclesiology
SCHMID, E., Moral Theology
SPADA, D., Dogmatic Theology
SPREAFICO, A., Old Testament Exegesis

Faculty of Philosophy:
MAZZOTTA, G., Metaphysics
MICCOLI, P., Modern and Contemporary History
MURA, G., Hermeneutics
ONAH, I. G., Methodology, Anthropology
VENDEMIATI, A.

Faculty of Missiology:
BARREDA, J., Ecumenism
CAVALLOTTO, G., Catechesis
DINH DUC DAO, , Missiography
ESQUERDA BIFET, J., Missionary Spirituality
GIGLIONI, P., Liturgical Spirituality
KAROTEMPREL, S., Theology of Mission
TREVISIOL, A.

Faculty of Canon Law:
DE PAOLIS, V., Matrimony and Canon Law
SALACHAS, D., Oriental Canon Law
SASTRE SANTOS, E., History of Canon Law

DIRECTORS

Institute for the Study of Atheism: Dr GASPARE MURA
Institute for Missionary Catechesis: Rev. GIUSEPPE CAVALLOTTO
Department of Languages: Rev. GIOVANNI DEIANA
Department of Social Communication: BERNARDO CERVELLERA
Chinese Study Centre: Rev. PAUL PANG
Affiliated Institutes: Rev. P. GIUSEPPE IULIANO

Colleges

PONTIFICIA FACOLTÀ DI SCIENZE DELL'EDUCAZIONE 'AUXILIUM'

Via Cremolino 141, 00166 Rome, Italy
Telephone: 06-61550790
Fax: 06-61564640

Founded 1954

Grand Chancellor: Rev. D. EGIDIO VIGANÒ
President: ENRICA ROSANNA
Secretary: CARLA SARTORIO

Publication: *Rivista di Scienze dell' Educazione* (3 a year).

PONTIFICIA FACOLTÀ TEOLOGICA DI S. BONAVENTURA DEI FRATI MINORI CONVENTUALI

Via del Serafico 1, 00142 Rome, Italy
Telephone: 06-51503206
Fax: 06-5192067
E-mail: seraphicum1@ofmconv.org

Founded 1587, re-founded 1905

Grand Chancellor: Most Rev. AGOSTINO GARDIN
President: Rev. Fr GIOVANNI IAMMARRONE
Vice-President: Rev. Fr MAURIZIO WSZOLEK
Secretary: Rev. Fr JULIAN ZAMBANINI
Librarian: Rev. Fr BONAVENTURA DANZA

Library of 210,000 vols
Number of professors: 41
Number of students: 130

Publication: *Miscellanea Francescana* (quarterly).

PONTIFICIA FACOLTÀ TEOLOGICA 'MARIANUM'

Viale Trenta Aprile 6, 00153 Rome, Italy
Telephone: 06-5839161
Fax: 06-5880292
E-mail: 106614.2716@compuserve.com

Founded 1950

Grand Chancellor: Rev. Fr H. M. MOONS
President: Rev. Fr I. M. CALABUIG
Secretary: Sister ORNELLA DI ANGELO

Library of 102,000 vols on Mariological studies

Publication: *Marianum* (2 a year).

PONTIFICIA FACOLTÀ TEOLOGICA TERESIANUM

Piazza San Pancrazio 5A, 00152 Rome, Italy
Telephone: 06-585401

Founded 1935

Academic year: October to June

Grand Chancellor: Most Rev. Fr CAMILO MACCISE
President: Very Rev. Fr JESÚS CASTELLANO CERVERA
Secretary: Rev. Fr DARIO CUMER
Librarian: Rev. Fr EUGENIO DUQUE

Library of 280,000 vols (open to the public)
Number of teachers: 40
Number of students: 450

Publications: *Teresianum* (specialist review, 2 a year), *Bibliographia Internationalis Spiritualitatis*, *Studia Theologica*.

ATTACHED INSTITUTE

Pontificio Istituto di Spiritualità: f. 1957; 30 teachers; 300 students; centre for bibliographical research in field of spiritual theology; Moderator Very Rev. Fr CARLO LAUDAZI.

PONTIFICIO ATENEO S. ANSELMO

Piazza Cavalieri di Malta 5, 00153 Rome, Italy
Telephone: 06-57911
Fax: 06-5746863
Telegraphic Address: Santanselmo Aventino, Rome

Founded 1687

Language of instruction: Italian

Grand Chancellor: Most Rev. Fr FRANCIS ROSSITER
Rector Magnificus: Rev. Fr P. R. TRAGAN
Secretary: Rev. Fr V. TOBIN
Librarian: Rev. Fr GREGOR BUCHER
Treasurer: Rev. Fr MARIO RAVIZZOLI

Library of 83,000 vols
Number of professors: 32
Number of students: 338

Publications: *Studia Anselmiana*, *Rerum Ecclesiasticarum Documenta* (Critical Editions of Liturgical Texts), *Corpus Consuetudinum Monasticarum*, *Ecclesia Orans* (Liturgical Inst. Review).

DEANS

Faculty of Theology: Rev. Fr P. ENGELBERT
Faculty of Philosophy: Rev. Fr E. SALMANN
Pontifical Liturgical Institute: Rev. Fr A. CHUPUNGCO

PONTIFICIO ATENEO ANTONIANUM

Via Merulana 124, 00185 Rome, Italy
Telephone: 06-70373502
Fax: 06-70373604
E-mail: segreteriapaa@ofm.org

Founded 1933

Franciscan International University

Grand Chancellor: Most Rev. J. BINI
Rector Magnificus: Rev. Fr J. A. MERINO
Vice-Rector: Rev. Fr V. BATTAGLIA
Secretary-General: Rev. Fr J. B. XUEREB
Librarian: Rev. Fr M. PORTILLO

Library of 500,000 vols
Number of professors: 130

Publication: *Antonianum*.

DEANS

Faculty of Theology: Rev. Fr CZESLAW TEKLAK
Faculty of Canon Law: Rev. Fr V. PAPEŽ
Faculty of Philosophy: Fr A. NGUYEN VAN SI

DIRECTORS

Biblical Studies: Rev. Fr FRÉDÉRIC MANNS
Institute of Spirituality: Rev. Fr L. PADOVESE
Institute of Ecumenical Studies: Rev. Fr R. GIRALDO
Higher School of Medieval and Franciscan Studies: Rev. Fr A. CACCIOTTI
Higher Institute of Religious Studies: E. MARCHITIELLI
International Centre for Environmental Studies: Rev. Fr J. A. MERINO

PONTIFICIO ISTITUTO DI ARCHEOLOGIA CRISTIANA (Pontifical Institute of Christian Archaeology)

Via Napoleone III 1, 00185 Rome, Italy
Telephone: 06-4465574
Fax: 06-4469197
E-mail: piac1@pelagus.it

Founded 1925 by Pope Pius XI

Grand Chancellor: Cardinal PIO LAGHI
Rector: Mgr PATRICK SAINT-ROCH
Secretary: Mgr JOSEP MARTÍ AIXALÀ
Librarian and Prefect of Collections: Dr GIORGIO NESTORI

Library of 60,000 vols

Publications: *Rivista di Archeologia Cristiana*, *Roma Sotterranea Cristiana*, *Studi di Antichità Cristiana*, *Monumenti dell'Antichità Cristiana*, *Inscriptiones Christianae*, *Sussidi allo Studio delle Antichità Cristiane*.

PROFESSORS

BISCONTI, F., Christian Iconography
DATTRINO, L., Patristics
FIOCCHI NICOLAI, V., Christian Cemeteries and Topography of Ancient Rome
GUIDOBALDI, F., Ancient Sacred Architecture
MAZZOLENI, D., Classical and Christian Epigraphy
PERGOLA, PH., 'Orbis Christianus'
RAMIERI, A. M., Art History
SAINT-ROCH, P., Hagiography and Liturgy of the Early Church

PONTIFICIUM INSTITUTUM BIBLICUM (Pontifical Biblical Institute)

Via della Pilotta 25, 00187 Rome, Italy
Telephone: 06-6796453
Fax: 06-67016211

Founded 1909 by Pope Pius X for scriptural studies; Faculty of Ancient Oriental Studies added 1932; Pontifical Biblical Institute of Jerusalem founded 1927 (branch of Roman Institute)

Associated with the Pontifical Gregorian University (see above)

Rector: Rev. R. O'TOOLE
Secretary: CARLO VALENTINO
Librarian: Rev. H. BERTELS

Number of teachers: 40
Number of students: 380

Publications: *Biblica* (quarterly), *Orientalia* (quarterly), *Elenchus of Biblica* (annually), *Acta Pont. Inst. Biblici* (annually), *Analecta Biblica*, *Analecta Orientalia*, *Biblica et Orientalia*, *Subsidia Biblica*, *Studia Pohl*.

DEANS

Biblical Faculty: Rev. S. PISANO
Faculty of Ancient Oriental Studies: Rev. J. SWETNAM

PROFESSORS

Faculty of Biblical Studies:

ALETTI, J.-N., New Testament Exegesis
ALTHANN, R., Biblical Aramaic and Hebrew
BOVATI, P., Old Testament Exegesis
BRENK, F., History of Greek Religion and Philosophy
FORTE, A., Biblical Greek
GILBERT, M., Old Testament Exegesis
KILGALLEN, J., New Testament Exegesis
LUZARRAGA, J., New Testament Exegesis
MANKOWSKI, P., Biblical Hebrew
NEUDECKER, R., Rabbinic Literature
O'TOOLE, R. F., New Testament Exegesis
PISANO, S., Textual Criticism
PLÖTZ, K., Hebrew
SIEVERS, J., History and Literature of the Intertestamental Period
SIMIAN-YOFRE, H., Old Testament Exegesis
SKA, J. L., Old Testament Exegesis
STOCK, K., New Testament Exegesis
SWETNAM, J., Biblical Greek
VANHOYE, A., New Testament Exegesis

Faculty of Ancient Oriental Studies:

ARNOLD, L., Arabic Language
GIANTO, A., North-West Semitic and Hebrew
MARAZZI, M., Hittite Language and Literature
MAYER, W., Accadian Language and Literature
MORRISON, C., Syriac and Targumic-Aramaic Languages
VOTTO, S., Sumerian and Greek

AFFILIATED INSTITUTE

Pontifical Biblical Institute: Jerusalem, Israel; (See under Israel.).

PONTIFICIO ISTITUTO DI MUSICA SACRA

Via di Torre Rossa 21, 00165 Rome, Italy
Telephone: 06-6638792
Fax: 06-6622453

Founded 1911 by Pope Pius X

Grand Chancellor: Cardinal PIO LAGHI
President: Mgr VALENTINO MISERACHS
Secretary: AUGUSTO FANTINI
Librarian: ANTONIO ADDAMIANO

Library of 30,000 vols
Number of teachers: 15
Number of students: 75

Publication: *Calendar*.

PONTIFICIUM INSTITUTUM ORIENTALE
(Pontifical Oriental Institute)

Piazza Santa Maria Maggiore 7, 00185 Rome, Italy
Telephone: 06-4465589

Founded 1917 by Pope Benedict XV for the benefit of Eastern and Western scholars both Catholic and non-Catholic, interested in Oriental ecclesiastical questions

Associated with the Pontifical Gregorian University (see above)

Rector: Rev. CLARENCE GALLAGHER
Secretary: Rev. JAKOV KULIČ
Librarian: Rev. FRANÇOIS GICK

Library of 148,000 vols
Number of teachers: 63
Number of students: 375

Publications: *Orientalia Christiana Periodica*, *Orientalia Christiana Analecta*, *Concilium Florentinum* (Documenta et Scriptores), *Anaphorae Syriacae*, *Kanonika*.

DEANS

Faculty of Oriental Ecclesiastical Studies: Rev. V. POGGI
Faculty of Oriental Canon Law: Rev. C. GALLAGHER

PROFESSORS

ARRANZ, L. M., Oriental Liturgy
CAPIZZI, C., Byzantine Church History and Greek Palaeography
FARRUGIA, E., Oriental Theology
GALLAGHER, C., Oriental Canon Law
GARGANO, G., Oriental Patrology
LAVENANT, R., Syriac Patrology
LESKOVEC, P., Dogmatic Theology
MARCHESI, G., Christology
NEDUNGATT, G., Oriental Canon Law
POGGI, V., Church History of the Near East
SENYK, S., Slavic Church History
TAFT, R., Oriental Liturgy
TROLL, C., Islamic Institutions
ŽUŽEK, I., Oriental Canon Law

PONTIFICIO ISTITUTO DI STUDI ARABI E D'ISLAMISTICA

Viale di Trastevere 89, 00153 Rome, Italy
Telephone: 06-5882676
Fax: 06-5882595
E-mail: pisai@flashnet.it

Founded 1949

Director: Fr ETIENNE RENAUD
Librarian: Fr ALDO GIANNASI

Library of 20,000 vols
Number of teachers: 11
Number of students: 60

Publications: *Islamochristiana* (annually), *Etudes Arabes* (2 a year), *Encounter* (Documents for Christian-Muslim Understanding, 10 a year).

Schools

Scuola Vaticana di Biblioteconomia (Vatican Library School): 00120 Vatican City; attached to Vatican Apostolic Library; 100 students a year; Dir Prof. Don RAFFAELE FARINA.

Scuola Vaticana di Paleografia, Diplomatica e Archivistica: 00120 Vatican City; attached to Papal Archives; Dir SERGIO PAGANO; publ. *Littera Antiqua*.

VENEZUELA

Learned Societies

GENERAL

Academia Venezolana (Academy of Venezuela): Bolsa a San Francisco, Caracas 1010; tel. (2) 481-87-16; f. 1883; corresp. of the Real Academia Española (Madrid); 24 mems; library: see Libraries and Archives; Dir LUIS PASTORI; Sec. LUIS BELTRAN GUERRERO; publs *Boletín* (quarterly), *Clásicos Venezolanos*.

ARCHITECTURE AND TOWN PLANNING

Asociación de Agrimensores de Venezuela (Surveyors' Association): c/o Colegio de Ingenieros de Venezuela, Apdo 2006, Bosque Los Caobos, Caracas 1010; Pres. Agm. GERMÁN AÑEZ OTERO; Sec. Agm. RAFAEL ELSTER NODA.

Colegio de Arquitectos de Venezuela (Venezuela Architects' Association): Avda Colegio de Arquitectos, Urb. La Urbina, Sector Norte, Prolongación Antigua Carretera Petare-Guarenas, Caracas 1070; tel. 2418007; f. 1945 as Sociedad Venezolana de Arquitectos; 3,600 mems; Pres. Arq. ITALO BALBI; Sec. Arq. HENRY SAAD; publ. *Revista del CAV*.

BIBLIOGRAPHY, LIBRARY SCIENCE AND MUSEOLOGY

Colegio de Bibliotecólogos y Archivólogos de Venezuela (Venezuelan Librarians' and Archivists' Association): Apdo 6283, Caracas; tel. (2) 572-18-58; f. 1989; 419 mems; Pres. Lic. ELSI JIMENEZ DE DÍAZ; Vice-Pres. Lic. FLOR MARINA LUNA; publs *AB Te Informa* (quarterly), *CBActualidad* (irregular).

ECONOMICS, LAW AND POLITICS

Academia de Ciencias Políticas y Sociales (Academy of Political and Social Sciences): Palacio de las Academias, Bolsa a San Francisco, Caracas 1010; tel. (2) 483-26-74; f. 1917; 33 mems; Pres. Dr GONZALO PARRA ARANGUREN; Sec. Dr JOSÉ G. SARMIENTO NÚÑEZ; publ. *Boletín*.

Colegio de Abogados del Distrito Federal (Lawyers' Association): Apdo 347, Caracas; f. 1788; 2,000 mems; Pres. Dr LUIS GONZÁLEZ BERTI; Sec. Dr ADÁN FEBRES CORDERO; publ. *Revista*.

EDUCATION

Consejo Nacional de Universidades (National University Council): Avda Urdaneta, Edif Bco Italo, 4° piso, Caracas; f. 1946; consists of staff and student representatives of all universities and representatives from the Ministry of Finance and the Science Council; library of 2,000 vols; Pres. The MINISTER OF EDUCATION; Perm. Sec. ALBERTO DRAYER B.; publ. *Boletín Informativo* (quarterly).

Grupo Universitario Latinoamericano de Estudio para la Reforma y el Perfeccionamiento de la Educación (Latin American University Group for Reform and Improvement in Education): Apdo 62532, Caracas 1060-A; tel. (2) 527064; telex 28381; fax 524247; f. 1965; higher education, research, and educational planning; 115 mems; Pres. Dra ELIZABETH DE CALDERA; Exec. Sec. Prof. FELIPE BEZARA; publ. *Universitas 2000* (quarterly).

FINE AND PERFORMING ARTS

Asociación Venezolana Amigos del Arte Colonial (Venezuelan Association of Friends of Colonial Art): Museo de Arte Colonial, Quinta de 'Anauco', Avda Panteón y Calle Gamboa, San Bernardino, Caracas; preservation and collection of period furniture, paintings, architectural forms, music, silver, etc. up to 1810; Pres. GLORIA S. DE EGUI; Vice-Pres. CARLOS F. DUARTE; publ. *Revista*.

Consejo Nacional de la Cultura (CONAC) (National Cultural Council): Torre Norte, piso 16 – Centro Simón Bolívar, Apdo 50995, Caracas; f. 1990 for the planning, promotion, dissemination and formation of human resources in the fields of music, theatre, dancing, plastic arts, literature, libraries, historic and artistic resources, museums, cinema and folklore; Pres. Dr JOSÉ ANTONIO ABREU; Sec. GUSTAVO ARNSTEIN; publs *Revista Nacional de Cultura* (quarterly), *Revista 'IMAGEN'* (monthly), *Revista de Cine 'ENCUADRE'* (quarterly).

Has attached:

Fundación de Etnomusicología y Folklore del CONAC (Foundation for Ethnomusicology and Folklore): Apdo 81015, Caracas 1080; f. 1990; consists of: Instituto Nacional de Folklore (INAF, f. 1950), Instituto Interamericano de Etnomusicología y Folklore (INIDEF, f. 1970), Museo Nacional de Folklore (f. 1971), Centro Interamericano de Etnomusicología y Folklore (CIDEF, f. 1973) for the OAS Regional Development Programme; aims to preserve and protect the American cultural heritage; annual courses in ethnomusicology, folklore, handicrafts, ethnohistory, anthropolinguistic studies; PRA/OAS scholarships; archive of ethnomusic, slides and photographs; specialized library of 2,700 vols, 308 periodicals; Dir Dra ISABEL ARETZ; publ. *Anuario FUNDEF*.

Instituto Zuliano de la Cultura 'Andrés E. Blanco': Gobernación del Estado Zulia, Academia de Bellas Artes 'Neptali Rincón', Maracaibo; f. 1972; administers all the cultural institutes in the state; Dir CARMEN DELGADO PEÑA; Administrator DOMINGO GUZMÁN RAMOS.

Sociedad Amigos del Museo de Bellas Artes (Society of the Friends of the Museum of Fine Arts): Museo de Bellas Artes, Parque los Caobos, Caracas; f. 1957; 250 mems; Pres. MIMI DE HERRERA USLAR; Exec. Sec. ANA DE BESSON.

HISTORY, GEOGRAPHY AND ARCHAEOLOGY

Academia de Historia del Zulia: Academia de Bellas Artes, Maracaibo; f. 1940; 12 mems; Pres. ABRAHÁN BELLOSO; Sec.-Gen. ANICETO RAMÍREZ Y ASTIER; Librarian JOSÉ A. BUTRÓN OLIVARES; publ. *Boletín*.

Academia Nacional de la Historia (National Academy of History): Palacio de las Academias, Bolsa a San Francisco, Caracas 1010; tel. and fax (2) 482-67-20; f. 1888; library: see Libraries and Archives; Dir RAFAEL FERNÁNDEZ HERES; Sec. MARIANELA PONCE; publs *Boletín*, *Memorias*.

Centro de Historia del Táchira (Historical Centre): Carrera 4, No 13-68, San Cristóbal; f. 1942; Dir Mons. RAÚL MÉNDEZ-MONCADA; Sec. Lic. HORACIO MORENO; publ. *Boletín*.

Centro de Historia Larense (Lara Historical Centre): Casa Colonial, Calle 22, diagonal a Plaza Lara, Apdo 406, Barquisimeto, Distrito Iribarren; f. 1941; 12 mems; publ. *Boletín*; library of *c.* 1,000 vols.

Centro Histórico Sucrense (Historical Centre): Cumaná; f. 1945; 24 national and 14 foreign corresp. mems; Dir R. P. Fray CAYETANO DE CARROCERA; Sec.-Gen. Br. ALBERTO SANABRIA; publ. *Boletín*.

Junta Nacional Protectora y Conservadora del Patrimonio Histórico y Artístico de la Nación (Commission for the Protection and Preservation of the Historical and Artistic Heritage of the Nation): Palacio de Miraflores, Avda Urdaneta, Caracas; there is a subsidiary office in each State; authorizes exploration and excavation of sites; mems are nominated by the Government for five-year terms, and may be re-elected; Dir Dr RAFAEL ARMANDO ROJAS.

Sociedad Bolivariana de Venezuela (Bolivar Society): Apdo 874, Caracas; to promote by all available media the knowledge of Simón Bolívar's life and works, as well as his political, cultural and social ideas and publishes about 15,000 volumes of historical works per year; 300 mems; library of 6,000 vols; Pres. Gral CANDIDO PEREZ MENDEZ; Sec. Gral ADOLFO ROMERO LUENGO; publ. *Revista*.

MEDICINE

Academia de Medicina del Zulia: Apdo 1725, Maracaibo, Zulia 4001A; tel. and fax (61) 42-34-42; f. 1927; 150 mems; library of 950 vols; Pres. Dr GILBERTO OLIVARES; Sec. Dr JOSÉ A. COLINA-CHOURIO; publ. *Revista*.

Academia Nacional de Medicina (National Academy of Medicine): Bolsa a San Francisco, Apdo 804, Caracas 1010; tel. 42-18-68; f. 1904; 40 mems, 50 nat. corresp. mems, 30 foreign corresp. mems; library: see Libraries and Archives; Pres. Dr AUGUSTO LEÓN C.; Sec. Dr JULIAN MORALES R.; publ. *Gaceta Médica de Caracas* (quarterly).

Colegio de Farmacéuticos del Distrito Federal y Estado Miranda (Association of Pharmacists): Urbanización Las Mercedes, Caracas 1060; deals with all aspects of the pharmaceutical industry; 1,200 mems; library of 600 vols; Pres. Dr PEDRO RODRÍGUEZ MURILLO; Sec. Dra ESTHER VALERA DE PÉREZ B.; Librarian Dra CARMEN ELENA GARCIA; publ. *Revista 'Colfar'*.

Colegio de Médicos del Distrito Federal (Doctors' Association): Plaza de Bellas Artes, Avda Bellas Artes, Los Chaguaramos, Caracas; f. 1942; 2,800 mems; Pres. Dr NÉSTOR BRACHO SEMPRÚN; Sec. Dr HERNÁN VALERO DÍAZ; publ. *Acta Médica Venezolana*.

Colegio de Médicos del Estado Miranda (Doctors' Association): Avda El Golf, Qta La Setentiseis, El Bosque, Caracas; f. 1944; 3,100 mems; professional and scientific association; Pres. Dr HERNÁN VÁSQUEZ RIGUAL; Gen. Sec. Dr RUBEN HERNÁNDEZ SERRANO; publ. *Cuadernos Medicos*.

Instituto J. I. Baldó: El Algodonal, Antímano, Caracas; f. 1937; lung diseases; Pres. Dr MANUEL ADRIANZA.

Sociedad de Obstetricia y Ginecología de Venezuela (Society of Obstetrics and Gynaecology): Maternidad Concepción Palacios, Avda San Martín, Apdo 20081, Caracas 1020-A; tel. and fax 4510895; f. 1940; 1,200 mems; Pres. Dr Luzardo Canache Campos; publ. *Revista de Obstetricia y Ginecología de Venezuela*.

Sociedad Venezolana de Anestesiología (Society of Anaesthesiology): Colegio de Médicos, Apdo 40 217, Caracas; Pres. Oscar Loynaz-Reverón.

Sociedad Venezolana de Cardiología (Society of Cardiology): Torre del Colegio, 15°, Oficina B-1, Avda José María Vargas, Urb. Santa Fé, Apdo 80.917 (Prados del Este), Caracas 1080; 196 mems; Pres. Dr Simón Muñoz Armas; Sec. Dr Domingo Navarro Dona.

Sociedad Venezolana de Cirugía (Society of Surgery): Torre del Colegio, 15°, Oficina A, Avda José María Vargas, Urb. Santa Fé, Caracas 1080; f. 1945; Pres. Dr Augusto Diez; Sec.-Gen. Dr Ismael J. Salas M.

Sociedad Venezolana de Cirugía Ortopédica y Traumatología (Society of Orthopaedics and Traumatological Surgery): Colegio de Médicos del DF, Plaza Las Tres Gracias, Los Chaguaramos, Caracas; f. 1949; 197 mems; Pres. Dr Alberto J. Jacir S.; publ. *Boletín de Ortopedia y Traumatología* (quarterly).

Sociedad Venezolana de Dermatología (Society of Dermatology): Colegios de Médicos del DF, 2° piso, Caracas; Pres. Dr Antonio José Rondón Lugo.

Sociedad Venezolana de Gastroenterología (Venezuelan Society of Gastroenterology): Apdo 81245, Prados del Este, Caracas 1050-A; tel. and fax 9799380; f. 1945; 606 mems; Pres. Dr Carlos E. Paradisi; Sec. Dr Pascual Candia; publ. *GEN* (quarterly).

Sociedad Venezolana de Hematología (Society of Haematology): Av. José María Vargas, Edif. Torre del Colegio, Piso 2, Local E–2 Urb. Santa Fé Norte, Caracas 1080; tel. (2) 9795664; f. 1959; library of 527 vols, 14 periodicals; Pres. Dr Carlos Goldstein.

Sociedad Venezolana de Historia de la Medicina (History of Medicine Society): Palacio de las Academias, Bolsa a San Francisco, Caracas 101; Pres. Dr Tulio Briceño Maaz.

Sociedad Venezolana de Medicina Interna (Society of Internal Medicine): Hospital Universitaria, Ciudad Universitaria, Caracas; Pres. Dr Adolfo Starosta.

Sociedad Venezolana de Oftalmología (Society of Ophthalmology): Avda Papal de Los Ruices, Centro Empresarial Los Ruices, (Piso 5, Oficina 507), Apdo del Este 50-150, Caracas 1050; fax (2) 2398127; e-mail j3002596-1@enntvw1.enntv.ve; f. 1953; 600 mems; Pres. Dra Silvia Salinas; Sec.-Gen. Dr Roseado Castellanos; publ. *Revista Oftalmológica Venezolana* (quarterly).

Sociedad Venezolana de Otorinolaringología (Society of Oto-Rhino-Laryngology): Avda Cajigal, San Bernardino, Caracas 1011; Pres. Dr François Conde Jahn; Sec. Dr Germán Tovar Bustamante; publ. *Acta Venezolana de ORL* (annually).

Sociedad Venezolana de Psiquiatría (Society of Psychiatry): Apdo 3380, Caracas 1010A; tel and fax (2) 731-20-24; f. 1942; 600 mems; library of 1,650 vols; Pres. Dr Manuel Matute; Sec.-Gen. Dr Edgard Belfort; publ. *Archivos Venezolanos de Psiquiatría y Neurología* (2 a year).

Sociedad Venezolana de Puericultura y Pediatría (Society of Puericulture and Paediatrics): Avda Libertador, Edif. La Linea, 9° piso, Ofc. 93A, Caracas 1050; Pres. Dr Xavier Mugarra T.

Sociedad Venezolana de Radiología (Society of Radiology): Policlínica Méndez Gimón, Avda Andrés Bello, Caracas; Pres. Dr Sebastián Nuñez Mier y Terán.

NATURAL SCIENCES

General

Academia de Ciencias Físicas, Matemáticas y Naturales (Academy of Physical, Mathematical and Natural Sciences): Bolsa a San Francisco, Apdo 1421, Caracas 1010; tel. (2) 483-41-33; fax (2) 484-66-11; f. 1917; 30 mems, 20 Venezuelan corresp. mems, 30 foreign corresp. mems; Pres. Ignacio Iribarren; Sec. José M. Carrillo; publ. *Boletín* (quarterly).

Asociación Venezolana para el Avance de la Ciencia (ASOVAC) (Venezuelan Association for the Advancement of Science): Apdo del Este 61843, Caracas 107; f. 1950; 3,000 mems; publ. *Acta Científica Venezolana* (every 2 months).

Fundación La Salle de Ciencias Naturales (La Salle Foundation of Natural Sciences): Edificio Fundación La Salle, Avda Boyacá, Apdo 1930, Caracas 1010A; tel. 782-87-11; fax 793-74-93; f. 1957; oceanography, anthropology, limnology, aquaculture, agronomy, mining and forestry; runs stations for marine, agricultural and hydrobiological research, the *Instituto Universitario de Tecnología del Mar* on the island of Margarita, *Instituto de Tecnología Agropecuaria* at San Carlos and at Boconó, and *Instituto de Tecnología Industrial* at San Félix; library (see under Libraries); 970 mems; Pres. Hno. Ginés; Exec. Vice-Pres. Gilberto Velarde; publs *Monografías* (irregular), *Antropológica* (quarterly review), *Memoria* (oceanography and natural science studies, 2 a year), *Presencia* (3 a year).

Biological Sciences

Sociedad de Ciencias Naturales 'La Salle' ('La Salle' Society of Natural Sciences): Edificio Fundación La Salle, Avda Boyacá, Apdo 1930, Caracas 1010A; tel. (2) 21-76-53; fax (2) 22-48-12; f. 1940; 504 mems; 17 hon., 42 national and 30 foreign corresps, 500 associates; comprises three depts: Botany, Zoology and Publications; the Museum contains more than 100,000 exhibits; Dir Lic. Jesús Hoyos; Pres. Dr Luis Rivas L.; Sec. Dr Carlos Acevedo; publs *Memoria* (2 a year), *Natura* (quarterly).

Sociedad Venezolana de Ciencias Naturales (Venezuelan Society of Natural Sciences): Calle Arichuna y Cumaco, El Marqués, Apdo 1521, Caracas 1010A; tel. (2) 21-76-53; fax (2) 22-48-12; f. 1931; 1,100 mems; library of 12,000 vols, 400 periodicals; annual exhibitions, lectures, films on nature conservation; department of speleology for study and exploration of caves throughout the country; biological station for research on flora and fauna, soil science and crop studies, ecology of neotropical savannas; dept for education on environmental protection; depts for the study of tropical orchids, bromeliads and astronomy; studies in environmental pollution; Pres. R. Aveledo Hostos; Gen. Sec. Dr Ricardo Muñoz Tébar; publs *Boletín de la SVCN*, *Boletín Informativo*.

Physical Sciences

Sociedad Venezolana de Geólogos (Venezuelan Geological Society): Apdo 17493, Caracas 1015A; tel. (2) 234-07-16; fax (2) 908-20-53; f. 1955; 1,050 mems; Pres. María A. Lorente; Sec. Roberto Arnstein; publs *Geología de Venezuela, Boletín* (3 a year), memoirs, maps.

PHILOSOPHY AND PSYCHOLOGY

Asociación Latinoamericana de Análisis y Modificación del Comportamiento (Latin American Asscn of Analysis and Behavioural Modification): Apdo 66126, Caracas 1061A; f. 1974; professional society for psychology in research and teaching on experimental analysis of behaviour; 1,583 mems; Pres. Miguel A. Escotet; Vice-Pres. Carlos M. Quirce; publs *Learning and Behavior* (2 a year), *Alamoc Newsletter* (quarterly).

TECHNOLOGY

Asociación Venezolana de Ingeniería Sanitaria y Ambiental (Sanitary and Environmental Engineering Association): c/o Colegio de Ingenieros de Venezuela, Apdo 2006, Caracas 1010; Pres. Ing. Octavio Jelambi.

Colegio de Ingenieros de Venezuela (Engineers' Association): Apdo 2006, Bosque Los Caobos, Caracas 101; f. 1861; 7,000 mems; library of 4,000 vols; Pres. Darío Brillembourg; Sec. Julio Urbina; publ. *Boletín* (monthly).

Sociedad Venezolana de Ingeniería Hidráulica (Society of Hydraulic Engineering): c/o Colegio de Ingenieros de Venezuela, Apdo 2006, Caracas; f. 1960; Pres. Federico Lovera.

Sociedad Venezolana de Ingenieros Agrónomos (Society of Agricultural Engineers): c/o Colegio de Ingenieros de Venezuela, Apdo 2006, Caracas; f. 1944; Pres. Ing. Agr. Humberto Fontana.

Sociedad Venezolana de Ingenieros Civiles (Society of Civil Engineers): c/o Colegio de Ingenieros de Venezuela, Apdo 2006, Caracas; Pres. Manuel Fernando Mejías.

Sociedad Venezolana de Ingenieros de Petróleo (Society of Petroleum Engineers): c/o Colegio de Ingenieros de Venezuela, Apdo 2006, Caracas; Pres. Rubén A. Carlo.

Sociedad Venezolana de Ingenieros Forestales (Society of Forestry Engineers): c/o Colegio de Ingenieros de Venezuela, Apdo 2006, Caracas; tel. 5713122, ext. 167; f. 1960; 1,122 mems; library of 8,000 vols; Pres. Rafael Viloria; Sec. Lourdes Altuve; publ. *Revista Forestal* (quarterly).

Sociedad Venezolana de Ingenieros Químicos (Society of Chemical Engineers): c/o Colegio de Ingenieros de Venezuela; Apdo 2006, Caracas; f. 1958 to promote the chemical engineering profession and exchange information with similar orgs in Venezuela and abroad; 1,000 mems; Exec. Dir Yolanda de Osorio; publ. *Boletín* (quarterly).

Research Institutes

GENERAL

Consejo Nacional de Investigaciones Científicas y Tecnológicas (CONICIT) (National Council for Scientific and Technological Research): Apdo 70617, Los Ruices, Caracas; telex 25205; fax 2398677; f. 1967 for the promotion of scientific and technological research, and for co-ordinating the activities of organizations involved in the science and technology sector, and of organizations of the national executive; Pres. Dr Ignacio Avalos Gutierrez; Vice-Pres. Dr Michael Suarez F.

Institut Français de Recherche Scientifique pour le Développement en Coopération (ORSTOM) Mission Venezuela: Apdo 68.183, Caracas 1062A; f. 1974; pedology, socio-economics, anthropology, oceanography; 8 mems; Dir Jean-Marie Hetier. (See main entry under France.)

Instituto Venezolano de Investigaciones Científicas (IVIC) (Venezuelan Scientific Research Institute): Apdo 21827, Caracas 1020A; tel. (2) 501-1122; fax (2) 571-2557; telex 21657; f. 1959; 120 staff; research in biology, medicine, chemistry, physics, mathematics and technology, atomic research, archaeology, anthropology, sociology of science; postgraduate studies; library: see Libraries; Dir EGIDIO ROMANO.

AGRICULTURE, FISHERIES AND VETERINARY SCIENCE

Centro Nacional de Investigaciones Agropecuarias (Agricultural Research Centre): Apdo A4653, Maracay 2101, Estado Aragua; fax 454320; f. 1937; attached to the National Foundation for Agricultural Research; Dir Dr CLAUDIO CHICCO; publs *Agronomía tropical, Zootecnia Tropical, Veterinaria Tropical* (every 2 months), *Caña de Azucar*.

Consejo Nacional de Investigaciones Agrícolas (National Council for Agricultural Research): Torre Norte, 14° piso, Centro Simón Bolívar, Apdo 5662, Caracas; f. 1959; functions include administration of the National Foundation for Agricultural Research; Pres. Dr RAFAEL ISIDRO QUEVEDO; Sec. Dr LUIS V. FRÓMETA BELLO.

Estación Experimental Tachira: Bramón, Rubio, Edo Táchira; tel. (76) 66783; telex 76340; f. 1953; agricultural research; library of 1,100 vols; Dir JOSÉ ROSARIO MANRIQUE; publ. *Annual Report*.

Instituto Agrario Nacional (Agrarian Institute): Quinta Barrancas, Avda San Carlos, Vista Alegre, Caracas 102; f. 1949; concerned with agrarian reform activities; Pres. ANTONIO MERCHAN; publ. *Memoria y Cuenta*.

Instituto de Investigaciones Veterinarias (Veterinary Research Institute): Apdo 70, Maracay, Estado Aragua; f. 1940; small specialized library; 55 mems; Dir Dr CLAUDIO FUENMAYOR F.

ARCHITECTURE AND TOWN PLANNING

Dirección General de Desarrollo Urbanistico del Ministerio del Desarrollo Urbano (Bureau of Urban Development of the Ministry of Urban Development): Edificio Banco de Venezuela, 5° piso, Caracas; f. 1946; 350 mems; library of 20,000 vols; Dir Arq. DANIEL BARREIRO DELGADO.

ECONOMICS, LAW AND POLITICS

Centro de Estudios del Desarrollo (Development Studies Center): POB 47604, Caracas 1041A; tel. (2) 752-34-75; fax (2) 751-26-91; e-mail cendes@reaccion.ve; f. 1961; centre for research and graduate studies on problems relating to economic, social, educational, regional, political, ecological, environmental and scientific-technological development of Venezuela and Latin America; library of 36,000 vols specializing in development problems and planning; Dir HELIA ISABEL DEL ROSARIO; publs *Cuadernos del CENDES* (3 a year), *CENDES Newsletter* (3 a year).

Instituto Iberoamericano de Derecho Agrario y Reforma Agraria: Facultad de Ciencias Jurídicas y Políticas, Universidad de los Andes, Mérida; tel. (74) 402646; fax (74) 402644; f. 1973; 12 mem. countries; training and research in agrarian law, agricultural economics, rural sociology, etc.; postgraduate courses; library of 4,000 vols; Pres. RAMÓN VICENTE CASANOVA; publ. *Revista de Derecho Agrario y Reforma Agraria*.

Oficina Central de Estadística e Informática (Central Office of Statistics and Informatics); Apdo 4593, Caracas 1010; tel (02) 782-11-33; telex 21241; f. 1978; Dir Dr MIGUEL J. BOLÍVAR CHOLLETT; publs *Anuario Estadistico de Venezuela, Anuario del Comercio Exterior de Venezuela, etc.*

EDUCATION

Centro Regional para la Educación Superior en América Latina y el Caribe/ Unesco Regional Centre for Higher Education in Latin America and the Caribbean: Apdo 68394, Caracas 1062-A; tel. 284-50-75; fax 283-14-11; f. 1978; promotes co-operation in the field of higher education among all the countries of Latin America and the Caribbean region; exchange of information and experience; conducts research and provides information and documentation at regional level; serves as secretariat of regional cttee for validation of courses and diplomas; library of 20,000 vols, 300 periodicals; Dir LUIS YARZABAL; publs *Educación Superior y Sociedad, Bibliografías Selectivas*.

Instituto Latinoamericano de Investigaciones Científicas en Educación a Distancia (Latin American Institute of Scientific Research on Distance Education): Calle California, Qta. Las Churrucas, Apdo 69680, Las Mercedes 1060A, Caracas; f. 1980; research, teaching and planning in distance and open education; library of 8,000 vols; Pres. MIGUEL A. ESCOTET; publ. *ILICED Newsletter* (quarterly).

HISTORY, GEOGRAPHY AND ARCHAEOLOGY

Centro de Historia del Estado Carabobo: Valencia, Edo de Carabobo; f. 1979 to conduct research into national and regional history, preserve and improve regional archives, conserve monuments, encourage and publicize celebrations of national historic events, and establish cultural relations with similar Venezuelan and foreign organizations; 24 mems; Pres. Lic. LUIS CUBILLÁN; Sec. Dr MARCO TULIO MÉRIDA; publ. *Boletín*.

Instituto de Geografía y Conservación de Recursos Naturales (Institute of Geography and Conservation of Natural Resources): Vía Chorros de Milla, Mérida; f. 1959; library of 20,236 vols and 44,555 periodicals; research in theoretical geography, applied geography and geographical techniques; committees for research and teaching technical co-ordination; documentation and information; Dir Prof. CARLOS A. MUÑOS LAGO; publs *Revista Geográfica Venezolana* (2 a year), *Cuadernos Geográficos* (irregular).

Ministerio del Ambiente y de los Recursos Naturales Renovables, Servicio Autónomo del Geografía y Cartografía Nacional: Avda Este 6, Esquina de Camejo, Edificio Camejo, Piso 2–220, Centro Simón Bolívar, Caracas; tel. (2) 408-12-10; fax (2) 542-03-74; e-mail sagecan@marnr.gov.ve; f. 1935; Dir Grl. Lic. ALICIA MOREAU D.

MEDICINE

Instituto de Medicina Experimental (Institute of Experimental Medicine): POB 50.587, Sabana Grande, Ciudad Universitaria, Caracas 1051; tel. 693-18-62; telex 27495; fax 693-12-60; f. 1940; research in biochemistry, pharmacology, physiology, neurology, general and applied pathology; 130 staff; library of 30,176 vols, 4,100 periodicals; Dir Dra ITALA LIPPO DE BECEMBERG; Librarian Lic. TRINA YANES DE RAMÍREZ; publ. *Boletín Informativo Sistema Nacional de Documentación e Información Biomédica*. (See also under the Universidad Central de Venezuela.)

Instituto Nacional de Nutrición (Institute of Nutrition): Apdo 2049, Caracas; f. 1949; library of 10,000 vols; Dir Dr LUIS BERMÚDEZ CHAURIO; publ. *Archivos Latinoamericanos de Nutrición*.

NATURAL SCIENCES

General

Estación de Investigaciones Marinas (EDIMAR): Apdo 144, Porlamar, Punta de Piedras, Isla de Margarita, Edo Nueva Esparta; tel. 98051; affiliated to the Fundación La Salle de Ciencias Naturales (see under Learned Societies); tel. 98051; telex 21553; fax 98061; f. 1958; 52 staff; fisheries, marine biology, oceanography, marine geology, aquaculture, marine food processing; library 'H. Ginés' of 17,800 vols, 1,200 periodicals; Dir Dr JOAQUÍN BUITRAGO; publ. *Memoria Sociedad de Ciencias Naturales*.

Biological Sciences

Estación Biológica de los Llanos (Biological Station): Calabozo, Estado Guárico; f. 1961; library of 3,200 vols; Dirs F. TAMAYO, R. A. HOSTOS, L. ARISTEGUIETA.

Fundación Instituto Botánico de Venezuela (Botanical Institute): Apdo 2156, Jardín Botánico de Caracas, Avda Salvador Allende, Caracas 1010A; tel. (2) 605-93-83; fax (2) 662-90-81; e-mail monteroe@camelot.rect.ucv.ve; f. 1991; library of 2,000 vols, 1,100 periodicals; Pres. Dra ZORAIDA LUCES DE FEBRES; publs *Acta Botánica Venezuela* (2 a year), *Flora de Venezuela*.

Physical Sciences

Dirección de Geología del Ministerio de Energía y Minas (Department of Geology of the Ministry of Energy and Mines): Torre Oeste, 4° piso, Parque Central, Caracas 1010; f. 1936; conducts national geological surveys, and research in geotechnics, marine geology and mineralogy; library of 120,000 vols; Dir SIMÓN E. RODRIGUEZ; publs *Boletín de Geología* (2 a year), *Cuadernos Geológicos* (3 a year), *Boletín Informativo del Centro de Análisis de Información Geológica-Minera (CAIGEOMIN)* (2 a year), research bulletins, statistical and other data (annually).

Estación Meteorológica (Meteorological Station): Ciudad Bolívar; f. 1940; undertakes meteorological research and hydrographical surveys of the River Orinoco and its tributaries; Dir E. SIFONTES; numerous publications on meteorology and climatology of Venezuela.

Observatorio Naval 'Juan Manuel Cagigal' (Juan Manuel Cagigal Naval Observatory): Apdo 6745, La Planicie, 23 Enero, Caracas; tel. (2) 481-22-66; fax (2) 483-58-78; e-mail dhn@truevision.net; f. 1888; astronomy, meteorology, oceanography, hydrography, planetarium; Dir GREGORIO PÉREZ MORENO; publs *Boletín Meteorologico* (monthly and annually), *Boletín Avisos a los Navegantes, Almanaque Astronomico Venezolano, Boletín Climatológico Anual*.

RELIGION, SOCIOLOGY AND ANTHROPOLOGY

Fundación 'Lisandro Alvarado': Apdo 4518, Maracay 2101A, Estado Aragua; tel. (43) 453420; f. 1965; archaeological and historical research; museums of history and anthropology, specialized library (in preparation); brs in Valencia (museums of art, history, anthropology, historical archives) and Puerto Cabello (museum of art and history); 40 mems; Pres. Dra ADELAIDA DE DÍAZ UNGRÍA; Dir HENRIQUETA PEÑALVER GÓMEZ.

Instituto Caribe de Antropología y Sociología: Apdo 1930, Caracas 1010A; tel. 782-8711 ext. 226; telex 21553; department of the Fundación La Salle de Ciencias Naturales (see under Learned Societies); f. 1962; anthropological research and development programmes among Indian populations of Venezuela; 6 mems; library of 3,000 vols; Dir WERNER WILBERT; publ. *Antropológica* (2 a year).

TECHNOLOGY

Dirección de Minas del Ministerio de Minas e Hidrocarburos (Department of Mining of the Ministry of Mines and Hydrocarbons): Torre Norte, 20° piso, Caracas 101; f. 1936; Dir BRÍGIDO R. NATERA.

PDUSA-INTEVEP, Centro de Investigación y Apoyo Tecnológico: Apdo 76343, Caracas 1070A; tel. (2) 908-6111; fax (2) 908-6447; f. 1974; research and development branch of Petróleos de Venezuela, concerned with hydrocarbons and petrochemicals; Information Centre of 30,000 publs, 1,600 periodicals, connected to int. online systems; Pres. FRANCISCO PRADAS; publs *Visión Tecnológica* (2 a year), reports, etc.

Libraries and Archives

Barquisimeto

Biblioteca Pública 'Pio Tamayo' (Public Library): Calle 26, entre Carreras 20 y 21, Barquisimeto; f. 1911; 21,943 vols; Librarian GERMÁN HURTADO REYES.

Biblioteca Técnica Científica Centralizada 'Froilan Alvarez Yepez' (Central Scientific and Technical Library): Apdo 254, Barquisimeto; telex 51314; fax 544394; f. 1966; specializes in social sciences, economic development and technology; 50,000 vols, 800 periodicals; Librarian Lic. CECILIA VEGA F.; publ. *Indice Bibliográfico de los estudios de FUDECO*.

Caracas

Archivo de Música Colonial Venezolano (Archives of Colonial Music): Escuela Superior de Música, Veroes a Santa Capilla, Caracas; Librarian GARCÍA LAZO.

Archivo General de la Nación (National Archives): Santa Capilla a Carmelitas, Caracas; f. 1910; sections: La Colonia (1498–1810), La Revolución (1810–21), La Gran Colombia (1821–30), La República (1830 to present day); comprises Seminario de Investigación Archivística and courses on palaeography; Dir Dr MARIO BRICEÑO PEROZO; publs *Boletín* (2 a year), *Biblioteca Venezolana de Historia* (2 a year).

Biblioteca Central de la Universidad Católica 'Andrés Bello' (Central Library of the 'Andrés Bello' Catholic University): Urb. Montalbán, La Vega, Apdo 29068, Caracas; f. 1953; 111,558 vols; Librarian Lic. EMILIO PÍRIZ PÉREZ; publ. *Montalbán*.

Biblioteca Central de la Universidad Central de Venezuela (Central University Library): Ciudad Universitaria, Los Chaguaramos, Caracas; tel. 6628427; telex 28479; f. 1850; sections on social science, the humanities, pure science and technology; official publications; reference section; 280,000 vols; 3,500 periodicals; Dir Prof. MANUEL RODRIGUEZ CAMPOS.

Biblioteca Central del Ministerio de Agricultura y Cría (Library of the Ministry of Agriculture): Avda Lecuna, Parque Central, Torre Este, 1° piso, Caracas; f. 1936; 70,000 vols; Librarian TUSNELDA CRESPO PIETRI.

Biblioteca Central del Ministerio del Trabajo (Library of the Ministry of Labour): Centro Simón Bolívar, Edificio Sur, 5° piso, Caracas; f. 1988; 3,200 vols; Librarian MARCELA GARCÍA JORDAN; publ. *Boletín Legislativo*.

Biblioteca Central 'Juan Pablo Pérez Alfonzo' (Library of the Ministry of Energy and Mines): Avda Lecuna, Torre Oeste, 2° piso, Parque Central, Caracas; tel. 5075206; telex 21692; fax 5754386; f. 1950; specializes in mines, petroleum, gas, geology, refinement, petrochemicals; 20,000 vols; Librarian Lic. SILVIA PERNIA C; publs *Boletín de Geología*, *Memoria y Cuenta del Ministerio de Energía y Minas*, *Petróleo y otros Datos Estadísticos*, *Anuario Estadisticos Mineros*, *Carta Semanal*, *Compendia Estadística del Sector Eléctrico*.

Biblioteca de la Academia Nacional de la Historia (Library of the National Academy of History): Palacio de las Academias, Avda Universidad, Bolsa a San Francisco, Caracas; tel. (2) 482-38-49; fax (2) 482-67-20; f. 1888; 120,000 vols; Dir Dr RAFAEL FERNÁNDEZ HERES; publ. *Boletín de la Academia Nacional de la Historia*.

Biblioteca de la Academia Nacional de Medicina (Library of the National Academy of Medicine): Palacio de las Academias, Bolsa a San Francisco, Apdo 804, Caracas 1010; tel. 481-89-39; f. 1893; 4,000 vols; Librarian Dr TULIO BRICEÑO MAAZ; publ. *Gaceta Médica de Caracas*.

Biblioteca de la Academia Venezolana (Library of the Academy of Venezuela): Palacio de las Academias, Bolsa a San Francisco, Caracas 1010; f. 1883; 25,000 vols; special collections: Venezuelan classics, dictionaries, Ayacucho collection, 'El Coyo Ilustrado'; Librarian MARIO TORREALBA LOSSI.

Biblioteca de la Corte Suprema de Justicia (Law Courts Library): Esquina de la Bolsa, Caracas; f. 1942; 4,500 vols; Dir Br FERNANDO ARAUJO M.

Biblioteca de los Tribunales del DF 'Fundación Rojas Astudillo' (Law Library): Apdo 344, Gradillas a San Jacinto, Edif. Gradillas, entrada B, 3° piso, Caracas 1010; tel. 82-34-56; f. 1950; bibliographical services and studies; 52,100 vols; Librarian Lic. AURA C. LÓPEZ RIVAS; publ. *Boletín*.

Biblioteca del Congreso (Congress Library): Plaza del Capitolio, Caracas; f. 1915; 9,000 vols; Librarian LOURDES GARCÍA.

Biblioteca del Ministerio de Fomento (Library of the Ministry of Development): Centro Simón Bolívar, Edificio Sur, 5° piso, Oficina 535, Caracas; f. 1953; 6,000 vols; Librarian ROSARIO BARNOLA.

Biblioteca del Ministerio de Obras Públicas (Library of the Ministry of Public Works): Centro Simón Bolívar, Edificio Camejo, Mezzanina, Caracas; f. 1948; 4,312 vols; Dir CARLOS A. ARREAZA F.

Biblioteca del Ministerio de Relaciones Exteriores (Library of the Ministry of Foreign Affairs): Caracas; 5,000 vols; specializes in international law; Librarian ALICIA CURIEL.

Biblioteca del Ministerio de Relaciones Interiores (Library of the Ministry of the Interior): Esquina de Carmelitas, 2° piso, Caracas; 3,585 vols; Librarian Dr RUIZ LANDER.

Biblioteca del Ministerio de Sanidad y Asistencia Social (Library of the Ministry of Health): Instituto Nacional de Higiene, Ciudad Universitaria, Apdo 61.153, Correos del Este, Caracas; f. 1936; 9,411 vols; Librarian ESPERANZA REYES BAENA; publs *Revista Venezolana de Sanidad y Asistencia Social*, *Memorias del MSAS*.

Biblioteca 'Dr M. A. Sánchez Carvajal' de la Sociedad de Obstetricia y Ginecología de Venezuela: Maternidad Concepción Palacios, Avda San Martín, Apdo 20081, Caracas 1020A; tel. and fax 451-08-95; f. 1940; over 8,500 vols; also MSS and medical history collection; Librarian Dra JUDITH TORO MERLO.

Biblioteca 'Ernesto Peltzer' del Banco Central de Venezuela: Torre Financiera, 16° piso, Esq. de Santa Capilla, Avda Urdaneta, Apdo 2017, Caracas 1010; tel. 801-51-11; telex 28250; fax 861-00-48; f. 1940; economics and finance; 96,891 vols, 1,000 periodicals; Dir SILVIO CASTELLANOS.

Biblioteca Fundación La Salle de Ciencias Naturales (Library of the 'La Salle' Foundation for Natural Sciences): Avda Boyacá, Cota Mil., Edif. Fundación La Salle, Apdo 1930, Caracas 1010A; tel. (2) 793-42-55; fax (2) 793-74-93; f. 1942; 100,000 vols; special collection: cultural anthropology, local languages, Venezuelan Indians, zoology, botany, natural resources contamination; Librarian MIREYA VILORIA.

Biblioteca 'Marcel Roche' del Instituto Venezolano de Investigaciones Científicas (Library of the Venezuelan Institute for Scientific Research): Altos de Pipe, Km 11, Carretera Panamericana, Apdo 21827, Caracas 1020A; tel. (2) 504-15-15; fax (2) 504-14-23; e-mail xjayaro@ivic.ivic.ve; f. 1955; 500,000 vols, 5,817 periodicals; Librarian XIOMARA JAYARO Y.

Biblioteca Nacional (National Library): Apdo 6525, Final Avda Panteón Esq. Fé a Remedios, Caracas; tel. 505-91-41; fax 505-91-59; e-mail vbetanc@reaccium.ve; f. 1883; 2,300,000 items; Rare Books and MSS collection; Dir Lic. VIRGINIA BETANCOURT; publs include *Bibliografía Venezolana*, *ISBN*, *Boletín Bibliotécnico*, *Informe Anual*.

Biblioteca Pública 'Mariano Picón Salas' (Public Library): Parque Arístides Rojas, Avda Andrés Bello, Caracas; f. 1965; 23,689 vols; Dir Lic. ROMULO NAVEA SOTO.

Cumaná

Biblioteca General de la Universidad de Oriente (General Library of the Universidad de Oriente): Apdo 245, Cerro Colorado, Cumaná; 154,000 vols; Librarian Lic. ROSA GONZÁLEZ DE LÓPEZ.

Maracaibo

Biblioteca 'Baralt' (Public Library): Avda 3 E No 71-15, Apdo 1340, Maracaibo; f. 1961; founded and maintained by Fundación Belloso; 35,000 vols; Librarian MERCEDES BERMÚDEZ DE BELLOSO.

Biblioteca de la Universidad del Zulia: Apdo de Correos 526, Maracaibo; f. 1946; 19,000 vols; Librarian Lic. EGLA ORTEGA.

Biblioteca Pública del Estado Zulia: Maracaibo; administered by the Instituto Zuliano de la Cultura (*q.v.*); Dir FERNANDO GUERRERO MATHEUS.

Maracay

Biblioteca Central del Centro Nacional de Investigaciones Agropecuarias (Library of the National Agricultural Research Centre): Apdo A4653, Maracay 2101, Edo Aragua; tel. 452491; fax 454320; f. 1937; 200,000 vols; Library Assistant NANCY GARCÉS DE HERNÁNDEZ.

Mérida

Servicios Bibliotecarios Universidad de los Andes (Los Andes University Library Services): Edificio Administrativo de la Universidad de los Andes, 2° piso, Mérida 5101; tel. (74) 402731; telex 74206; fax (74) 402507; f. 1889; *c.* 250,000 vols, 7,817 periodical titles; reference books for all subjects taught in the University; small collection of 16th- and 17th-century books; Co-ordinator Lic. MARÍA E. CHÁVEZ DE BURGOS.

Trujillo

Biblioteca '24 de Julio' (Public Library): Trujillo; f. 1930; 12,000 vols; Librarian ITALA BRICEÑO RUMBOS.

Valencia

Biblioteca Central de la Universidad de Carabobo: Valencia; 11,000 vols; Librarian ANTONIETA PINTO DE KATZ.

Museums and Art Galleries

Caracas

Casa Natal del Libertador Simón Bolívar (Simón Bolívar's Birthplace): San Jacinto a Traposos, Caracas; tel. (2) 541-25-63; murals by Tito Salas depicting the life of Bolívar and events of the Independence Movement; Curator JOSEFINA DE SANDOVAL.

Colección Ornitológica Phelps (Phelps Ornithological Collection): Blvd Sabana Grande, Edif. Gran Sabana, 3° piso, Apdo 2009, Caracas 1010A; tel. (2) 719-238; fax (2) 762-5921; f. 1938; library of 10,000 vols; Pres. KATHLEEN PHELPS; Curator M. LENTINO R.

Fundación Museo de Ciencias: Avenida Mexico, Plaza de los Museos, Los Caobos, Apartado Postal 5883, Caracas 1010; tel. (2) 577-50-94; fax (2) 571-12-65; e-mail mciencia@reacciun.ve; f. 1875 as Museo Nacional, subsequently Museo de Ciencias Naturales; archaeology, palaeontology, geology, zoology, anthropology, entomology, ethnology; library of 2,100 vols; Pres. Ing. SERGIO ANTILLANO ARMAS.

Galería de Arte Nacional: Plaza de los Museos, Los Caobos, Apdo 6729, Caracas 1010; tel. (2) 578-18-18; fax (2) 578-16-61; e-mail fgan@infoline.wtfe.com; f. 1976; Venezuelan visual art from pre-Hispanic time to the present; Pres. CLEMENTINA VAAMONDE B.; Exec. Dir RAFAEL A. ROMERO DIAZ.

Museo Bolivariano (Bolívar Museum): San Jacinto a Traposos, Caracas; f. 1911 and inaugurated in present building 1960; contains 1,546 exhibits; mementos, portraits, personal relics and historical paintings of Simón Bolívar and his fellow-workers in the Independence Movement; library of 1,200 vols; Dir FLOR ZAMBRANO DE GENTILE.

Museo de Arte Colonial (Museum of Colonial Art): Quinta de Anauco, Avda Panteón, San Bernardino, Caracas 1011; tel. (2) 51-86-50; fax (2) 51-85-17; f. 1942; painting, sculpture, decorative arts; library; under the supervision of the Asociación Venezolana de Amigos del Arte Colonial (*q.v.*); Dir CARLOS F. DUARTE.

Museo de Bellas Artes de Caracas (Museum of Fine Arts): Plaza Morelos, Los Caobos, Caracas 105; fax (2) 571-01-69; f. 1938, enlarged 1957, 1963, 1974; paintings and sculpture by national and foreign artists; library of 6,000 vols; Dir MARIA ELENA RAMOS.

Ciudad Bolívar

Museo 'Talavera': Calle Bolívar 103, Ciudad Bolívar; f. 1940; pre-Columbian and Colonial period exhibits, religious art, natural science, numismatics; Dir Dr J. GABRIEL MACHADO; publ. *Museo Talavera*.

El Tocuyo

Museo Colonial (Historical Museum): El Tocuyo; f. 1945.

Maracaibo

Museo 'Urdaneta' Histórico Militar (Museum of Military History): Apdo 814, Maracaibo 4001A; tel. 226778; telex 61111; f. 1936; Dir Prof. J. C. BORGES ROSALES.

Trujillo

Museo 'Cristóbal Mendoza' (Historical Museum): Trujillo.

Universities

UNIVERSIDAD NACIONAL ABIERTA (Open University)

Apdo 2096, Caracas 1010A
Telephone: (2) 5741322
Telex: 2611

Founded 1977 on the 'open university' principle, using modern methods of communication and educational technology. One national centre in Caracas and 20 regional centres
State control
Language of instruction: Spanish

Rector: Dr ORLANDO ARMITANO B. (acting)
Academic Vice-Rector: Dr ARMANDO VILLARROEL V.
Administrative Vice-Rector: Dr ORLANDO ARMITANO B.
Secretary: Dr MILTON GRANADOS
Librarian: Lic. SILA RINCÓN FINOL

Number of teachers: 473
Number of students: 29,032

Publications: *Una Opinión, Una Documenta, Una Voz a Distancia.*

COURSE CO-ORDINATORS

Academic Co-ordinator: Prof. GUILLERMO CEDEÑO
Basic Science and Technology: Ing. RAFAEL ARRAIZ E.
Science of Man: Prof. RAMÓN IGNACIO LUNAR
Administration and Accountancy: Lic. HILDA SAYAGO
Student Services: Lic. LUIS FERRETO
University Extension: Prof. HILDA ORTEGA
Academic Evaluation Unit: Dr FABIO CHACÓN
Planning and Evaluation: Dra LAURA BOYER
General Studies: Prof. ROSE MARY DIAZ DEL VALLE
Mathematics: Lic. JOSÉ RAMÓN ORTIZ
Industrial Engineering: Ing. MARÍA B. FERNÁNDEZ
Systems Engineering: Ing. MARÍA A. PÉREZ DE O.
Education: Lic. SARA LEÓN
Administration: Lic. HILDA SAYAGO
Accountancy: Lic. JUÁN E. GUERRA
Regional and Local Centres: Lic. NELLY RUÍZ DE T.

LOCAL CENTRES

Anzoátegui: Dir Lic. MARIANELLYS SALAZAR DE G.
Aragua: Dir Lic. AMBROSIO NORIEGA
Apure: Dir Lic. IMELDA DE SILVA
Barinas: Dir Lic. HEIVA PALMA
Bolivar: Dir Prof. HAYDEÉ DE PORRAS
Carabobo: Dir Lic. FELIX SÁNCHEZ
Cojedes: Dir Lic. BERNABÉ CASTILLO
Falcón: Dir Prof. ANGEL FERRER
Guarico: Dir Lic. LILY PÉREZ DE PÉREZ
Lara: Dir Prof. ARNALDO ESCALONA P.
Mérida: Dir Lic. JAVIER BERBESÍ
Metropolitano: Dir Prof. LUIS RAMOS ESCOBAR
Monagas: Dir Lic. MARIA ANGELICA ARVELAEZ
Nueva Esparta: Dir Prof. JESÚS LARES
Portuguesa: Dir Lic. NAPOLEÓN SÁNCHEZ
Sucre: Dir Prof. GILBERTO REYES
Táchira: Dir Lic. JOSÉ CASTRO MORA
Trujillo: Dir Prof. GUILLERMO YUGURÍ
Yaracuy: Dir Lic. MARÍA ISABEL HERNÁNDEZ
Zulia: Dir Prof. PROSPERO CARDENAS
T.F. Delta Amacuro: Dir Prof. HERMÁN VAZQUEZ

UNIVERSIDAD DE CARABOBO

Avda Bolívar 125-39, Apdo Postal 129, Valencia 2001
Telephone: (41) 215044
Telex: 41478

Founded 1852
State control
Academic year: September to February, March to July

Rector: Dr GUSTAVO HIDALGO-VITALE
Academic Vice-Rector: Dr ELIS MERCADO MATUTE
Administrative Vice-Rector: Ing. JOSÉ BOTELLO WILSON
Secretary: Dr RUBÉN BALLESTEROS
Librarian: ANTONIETA PINTO DE KATZ

Library: see Libraries
Number of teachers: 2,585
Number of students: 44,654

Publications: *Boletín Universitario, Utopia y Praxis*, etc.

DEANS

Faculty of Economics and Social Sciences: Econ. LIONEL AGUDO
Faculty of Engineering: Ing. GIOVANNI NANI
Faculty of Law: Ab. ELOY RUTMAN CISNEROS
Faculty of Health Sciences: Dr CLAUDIO ROMANO
Faculty of Education: Lic. CARLOS HERRERA
Postgraduate Studies: Dr ALEJANDRO SUE MACHADO

UNIVERSIDAD CATÓLICA 'ANDRÉS BELLO'

Urb. Montalbán, La Vega, Apdo 1020, Caracas 1020
Telephone: (2) 407-44-44
Fax: (2) 407-43-49
E-mail: webmaster@ucab.edu.ve

Founded 1953
Private control (Society of Jesus)
Academic year: October to July
Campuses in San Cristóbal, Táchira

Chancellor: Mgr IGNACIO VELASCO
Rector: Dr LUIS UGALDE
Academic Vice-Rector: Dra MIRIAM LÓPEZ DE VALDIVIESO
Administrative Vice-Rector: Ing. LORENZO CALDENTEY
Secretary-General: Econ. GUSTAVO SUCRE
Librarian: Lic. EMILIO PÍRIZ PÉREZ

Library: see Libraries
Number of professors: 750
Number of students: 9,600, also 2,000 postgraduate

Publications: *Revista Montalbán, Revista de la Facultad de Derecho, Revista de Relaciones Industriales y Laborales, Temas de Coyuntura, Cuadernos Venezolanos de Filosofía, Pensamiento Agustiniano, Temas de Comunicación Social, Espacios, Analogías del Comportamiento, Encuentro EAC y Cuadernos UCAB-Educación*, etc.

DEANS

Faculty of Law: Dr ADÁN FEBRES CORDERO
Faculty of Social and Economic Sciences: Dr CHI YI CHEN
Faculty of Humanities and Education: Lic. ORLANDO ALVAREZ
Faculty of Engineering: Ing. RAFAEL HERNÁNDEZ SÁNCHEZ-OCAÑA
Postgraduate Studies: Lic. MIGUEL A. GÓMEZ

DIRECTORS

School of Law: Dr JOSÉ RAFAEL HERNÁNDEZ
School of Economics: Econ. MARÍA ISABEL MARTÍNEZ A.
School of Business Administration and Accounting: Lic. ARMANDO VOLPE
School of Philosophy: Lic. CORINA YORIS
School of Letters: Lic. MAREYA VÁSQUEZ
School of Social Communication: Lic. MAX RÖMER

School of Education: Lic. RAFAEL ESTRADA
School of Psychology: Lic. SILVANA CAMPAGNARO DE SOLÓRZANO
School of Civil Engineering: Ing. WICKARD MIRALLES
School of Industrial Engineering: Ing. DIEGO CASAÑAS
School of Technology: Ing. LOURDES ORTIZ
School of Social Sciences: Lic. JESÚS CIVIT
Institute of Economic and Social Research: Dr EDUARDO ORTIZ
Centre of Legal Research: Dra. MARÍA GRACIA MORAIS DE GUERRERO
Centre of Philosophical Studies: MASSIMO DESIATO
Centre of Communication Research: CAROLINE DE OTEYZA
Centre of Religious Studies: P. JOSÉ AYESTARÁN
Centre of Engineering Research: RAFAEL HERNÁNDEZ
Centre of Research and Institutional Evaluation: ERCILIA VÁZQUEZ
Centre of Literary Studies: MIREYA VÁZQUEZ
Centre of Behavioural Studies: ANDRÉS MIÑARRO
Institute of History: MANUEL DONIS

UNIVERSIDAD CATÓLICA DEL TÁCHIRA

Calle 14 con Carrera 14, Apdo 306, San Cristóbal 5001, Edo Táchira
Telephone: (76) 430510
Fax (076) 446183

Founded 1982

Rector: JOSÉ DEL REY FAJARDO
Vice-Rector: ASTRID RICO DE MÉNDEZ
Chief Administrative Officer: CONRADO CONTRERAS PULIDO
Librarian: GLORIA RUIZ DE UGARTE

Number of teachers: 336
Number of students: 5,000

Publications: *Paramillo* (annually), *Revista Tachirense de Derecho* (monthly).

DEANS

Faculty of Law and Political Science: VICTOR HUGO MORA CONTRERAS
Faculty of Economics and Social Sciences: ANSELMO VILLASMIL SOULES
Faculty of Humanities and Education: GERARDO COLMENARES
Faculty of Religion: EDUARDO FAJARDO RUEDA

HEADS OF DEPARTMENTS

Faculty of Humanities and Education:
- Professional Practice: VICTOR OMAÑA
- Social Sciences: JOSÉ GREGORIO PÉREZ ROJAS
- Computer Science: PATRICIA HENRÍQUEZ
- Biological Sciences: MERCEDES ESCALANTE LABRADOR

Faculty of Economics and Social Sciences:
- Mathematics and Systems: E. YAÑEZ
- Legislation and Basic Support: ABDA HERINA MORA
- Accounting: PEDRO PARRA
- Administration: BETTY TOSCANO
- Economics: UBENN DE CONTRERAS

Faculty of Law and Political Science:
- Public Law: GABRIEL DE SANTIS TEBALDINI
- Private Law: FÉLIDA ROA DE ROA
- Basic and Complementary Disciplines: ANDRÉS OCHOA DE PATIÑO
- Tutorials and Research: GERARDO PATIÑO VASQUEZ
- Practical Work: ELIS PEREIRA

UNIVERSIDAD CENTRAL DE VENEZUELA

Ciudad Universitaria, Los Chaguaramos, Zona Postal 104, Caracas 1051
Telephone: 61-98-11
Telex: 29482
Fax: 6622486

Founded 1721
State control
Language of instruction: Spanish
Academic year: January to December

Rector: Dr LUIS D. FUENMAYOR
Academic Vice-Rector: Dr ROBERTO RUIZ
Administrative Vice-Rector: Dr TRINO ALCIDES DÍAZ
Registrar: Dr GLADYS FERNANDEZ
General Co-ordinator: Dr LIRIO CAMERO
Secretary: Dr ALEXIS RAMOS
Librarian: Dr EUDIS BORRA
Number of teachers: 6,987
Number of students: 45,000

Publications: *Memoria y Cuenta, Gaceta Universitaria, Correo Ucevista, Hora Universitaria, Aula Magna, Boletín del Archivo Histórico,* faculty bulletins etc.

DEANS

Faculty of Agriculture (in Maracay): Dr FREDDY GILL
Faculty of Architecture and Town Planning: Dr MARCO NEGRON
Faculty of Science: Dr IVAN ESCALONA
Faculty of Engineering: Dr GASPARE LAVEGA
Faculty of Medicine: Dr SIMON MUÑOZ
Faculty of Dentistry: Dr FRANCISCO BECHARA
Faculty of Veterinary Science (in Maracay): Dr RAFAEL INFANTE
Faculty of Law and Political Science: Dr NELSON RODRIGUEZ
Faculty of Economic and Social Sciences: Dr ELIAS ELJURI
Faculty of Pharmacy: Dr NELSON FERRIGNI
Faculty of Humanities and Education: Dr IGOR COLINA

UNIVERSIDAD CENTRO-OCCIDENTAL 'LISANDRO ALVARADO'

Apdo 400, Barquisimeto, Lara
Telephone: (51) 51001
Telex: 51304
Fax: 516087

Founded 1963 as Experimental Centre of Higher Education; university status 1968
State control
Language of instruction: Spanish
Academic year: January to December

Rector: Dr RICARDO GARCÍA DE LONGORIA
Academic Vice-Rector: Dra GADRA SÁNCHEZ DE PÉREZ
Administrative Vice-Rector: Dr GUÉDEZ CORTEZ
Secretary-General: Dr RICARDO GÁSPERI MAGO
Librarian: Lic. MORELLA BARRANCOS

Number of teachers: 930
Number of students: 9,665

Publications: *Memoria y Cuenta* (annually), *Tarea Común* (quarterly), *El Veterinario* (monthly), *Boletín Científico, Escuela de Agronomía, Boletín Informativo, Escuela de Administración.*

DEANS

Faculty of Administration and Accountancy: Lic. CÉSAR MORENO
Faculty of Agronomy: Ing. JOSÉ PASTOR GUTIÉRREZ
Faculty of Sciences: Dr JOSÉ BETHELMY
Faculty of Medicine: Dr RÉGULO CARPIO
Faculty of Civil Engineering: Ing. HERMES ESPINOZA
Faculty of Veterinary Medicine: Dr RAMÓN SALCEDO

ATTACHED INSTITUTES

Consejo Asesor de Investigación y Servicios (Advisory Council on Research and Services): assessment and consultation on the planning of research; Pres. Dr FRANCISCO MONTES DE OCA.

Instituto de la Uva (Institute for Research on Grapes): research on grape cultivation and advisory service to wine growers; Dir MARIA LUISA DE PIRE.

UNIVERSIDAD DE LOS ANDES

Avda 3, Independencia, Edif. Rectorado, Mérida 5101
Telephone: (74) 401111
Telex: 74137
Fax: (74) 527704
E-mail: rector@rector.ula.ve

Founded 1785 as the Real Colegio Seminario de San Buenaventura de Mérida, became University 1810
Campuses at Trujillo and Táchira
State control
Language of instruction: Spanish
Academic year: January to June, July to December

Rector: FELIPE H. PACHANO RIVERA
Academic Vice-Rector: CARLOS GUILLERMO CÁRDENAS D.
Administrative Vice-Rector: EDILIO VILLEGAS DÍAZ
Secretary: LÉSTER RODRÍGUEZ HERRERA
Registrar: FREDY UZCÁTEGUIZ
Librarian: MARÍA EUGENIA CHÁVEZ DE BURGOS

Library: see Libraries
Number of teachers: 2,947
Number of students: 34,294

Publications: faculty yearbooks, etc.

DEANS

Táchira Campus: Dr ROMÁN HERNÁNDEZ D.
Rafael Rangel Campus: Dr JUAN C. DELGADO B.
Faculty of Law and Political Science: ANDREY GROMIKO URDANETA
Faculty of Humanities and Education: FRANCISCO GAVIDIA
Faculty of Pharmacy: Dr ALFREDO CARABOT CUERVO
Faculty of Odontology: Dra MELVA DÍAZ DE LEÓN
Faculty of Medicine: Dr ANIBAL MUSSA
Faculty of Engineering: Ing. JOSÉ ANDÉREZ
Faculty of Forestry: Prof. DOUGLAS ROJAS
Faculty of Architecture: Arq. VÍCTOR BLANCO
Faculty of Sciences: SPYRIDON RASSIA SOULI
Faculty of Economic and Social Sciences: MANUEL ARANGUREN

UNIVERSIDAD METROPOLITANA

Apdo 76819, Caracas 1070
Telephone: (2) 2414833
Fax: (2) 2419575

Founded 1970
Private control
Language of instruction: Spanish
Academic year: October to February, March to July, August to September

President: Ing. JULIO SOSA RODRIGUEZ
Rector: Prof. IGNACIO IRIBARREN TERRERO
Academic Vice-Rector: Prof. JUAN LACUNA
Administrative Vice-Rector: Prof. JOSÉ ABDALA
Registrar: Lic. LOLITA PONTE DÁVILA
Librarian: Lic. CARMEN DE CARDENAS

Number of professors: 461
Number of students 4,600

Publications: *Noticias* (every 2 months), *Metrovoz* (quarterly), *Gerencio* (3 a year), *Reflejos* (3 a year), *Nobel* (3 a year).

DEANS

Engineering: Prof. MARIO PAPARONI
Arts and Sciences: Prof. JUAN ALMECIJA
Economics and Social Sciences: Prof. FREDDY ARREAZA
Research and Graduate Study: Prof. ELEIDA DE CANESTRARI

HEADS OF DEPARTMENTS

School of Engineering:

Chemical Engineering: Prof. ALICIA DE DIENES
Civil Engineering: Prof. CRISTINA MALDONADO DE CAMPOS
Electrical Engineering: Prof. JOSE LUIS GIMENEZ
Systems Engineering: Prof. EDNA DE MILLAN
Mechanical Engineering: Prof. FRANCISCO ALVAREZ

School of Arts and Sciences:

Mathematics: Prof. SILVIA VILLEGAS
Modern Languages: Prof. BARBARA ZANDER
Pre-School Education: Prof. IRMA MATUT
Humanities: Prof. MARIA ELENA CAPRILES
Physics: Prof. CARMEN DE CALATRONI
Chemistry: Prof. ELISA DE FIGARELLA

School of Economics and Social Sciences:

Management: Prof. MIGDALIA MONTES DE OCA
Banking and Finance: Prof. LUIS FERNANDO DE LIMA

School of Graduate Study:

Continuing Education: Prof. ROSALIND DE PULIDO
Engineering Management: Prof. JULIO MOTTOLA
Finance: Prof. JUAN ANTONIO LOVERA
Real Estate Management: Prof. ELIAS ALVAREZ
Oil Refining, Gas and Petrochemicals: Prof. XAVIER FIGARELLA

CENDIF (research centre for the child and the family): Prof. MARIA A. DE LEIGHTON

METROPOLIS (supervision and support of the use of the micro-computer as academic tool): Prof. ADELAIDE BIANCHINI

UNIVERSIDAD NACIONAL EXPERIMENTAL FRANCISCO DE MIRANDA

Calle Norte, Edif. Universitario, Coro, Estado Falcón 4101

Telephone: (68) 519732
Telex: 56184

Founded 1977
Academic year: January to December (2 semesters)

Chancellor: SIMON ALBERTO CONSALVI
Rector: Dr PEDRO BORREGALES P.
Academic Vice-Rector: Dr OSCAR ABREU
Administrative Vice-Rector: Dr JULIO LOPEZ P.
Administrator: Lic. CESAR VELASQUEZ
Librarian: Lic. NIDYA PETIT DE MOTTA

Number of teachers: 350
Number of students: 3,000

Publications: *Gaceta Universitaria* (quarterly), *Boletín* (weekly), *Cultura Falconiana* (quarterly), etc.

DEANS

Faculty of Medicine: Dr ROBERTO GRAND L.
Faculty of Veterinary Medicine and Agriculture: Dr DIOGENES RODRIGUEZ
Faculty of Civil and Industrial Engineering: Ing. ORANGEL NUÑEZ.

UNIVERSIDAD 'ROMULO GALLEGOS'

102A San Juan de los Morros, Estado Guárico 2301A

Telephone: (46) 310831
Fax: (46) 312670

Founded 1977
State control
Language of instruction: Spanish
Academic year: March to December (2 semesters)

President and Rector: Ing. GIOVANNI NANI R.
Academic Vice-Rector: Ing. ENRIQUE MUJICA ALVAREZ
Administrative Vice-Rector: Lic. GHENRY J. NAVARRO U.
Librarian: Lic. RHAIZA MARQUEZ

Number of teachers: 367
Number of students: 5,306

Publication: *Horizontes Universitarios*.

DEANS

Faculty of Odontology: Dr OMAR SCOVINO
Faculty of Education: Lic. CECILIA REQUENA R.
Faculty of Engineering: Ing. NELSON MARTE
Faculty of Health: Dra MARTHA CANTAVELLA
Faculty of Veterinary Medicine: Méd. Vet. SALVADOR DE J. PÉREZ ALEMÁN
Faculty of Economics: Lic. CARLOS HERRERA
Continuing Education: Lic. YOLANDA VILLASMIL
Postgraduate Studies: Lic. GLADYS MORENO V.
Research and Extension: Prof. GEOMAIRA MONTENEGRO

ATTACHED INSTITUTES

Centre for Minimal Intervention in Farming: Dir Prof. RAFAEL SÁNCHEZ.
Centre for Legal Studies: Dir Abog. GLADYS BOYER.
Centre for the Study of Grain: Dir Prof. ANGEL DAVID RIVILLO.

UNIVERSIDAD NACIONAL EXPERIMENTAL DE LOS LLANOS OCCIDENTALES 'EZEQUIEL ZAMORA'

Apdo Postal 19, Barinas 5201

Telephone: (73) 41201/09
Telex: 73171
Fax: (73) 41858

Founded 1975
Language of instruction: Spanish
Academic Year: January to December (2 semesters)

An experimental government-sponsored institute of higher education, serving the Los Llanos Occidentales region, and the States of Apure, Barinas, Cojedes and Portuguesa

Rector: Dr RICARDO J. CASTRO ALVAREZ
Vice-Rector: Dr JOSÉ ALFREDO GUERRERO SOSA
Secretary: Dr LUIS A. SUÁREZ CORDERO
Librarian: Dra MIGDALIA DE LARA

Number of teachers: 600
Number of students: 8,000

Publications: *Revista UNELLEZ de Ciencia y Tecnología*, *Biollania*.

Courses in agriculture and mechanization, economics, social development, regional planning, human ecology.

UNIVERSIDAD NACIONAL EXPERIMENTAL POLITECNICA 'ANTONIO JOSÉ DE SUCRE'

Apdo Postal 539, Barquisimeto, Edo Lara

Telephone: (51) 42-01-33
Fax: (51) 41-38-80

Founded 1962
Private control

Rector: Dr IVÁN OLAIZOLA D'ALESSANDRO
Vice-Rector (Secretarial): Dr RAMÓN VIELMA
Regional Vice-Rectors: Ing. AMAEL CASTELLANO (Barquisimeto campus), Ing. ILDELFONSO MEJÍA ZAMBRANO (Caracas campus), Ing. LUIS CÁRDENAS CASTILLO (Puerto Ordaz campus)
Academic Co-ordinator: Ing. EDUARDO CABRÉ TRUJILLO
Administrative Co-ordinator: Lic. XIOMARA DE BARRA

Library of 19,200 vols, 9,000 periodicals
Number of teachers: 900
Number of students: 10,000

Publications: *Información General de la Universidad* (annually), *Boletín Bibliográfico de Publicaciones Recibidas* (2 a year), *Avance Universitario* (2 a year).

Mechanical, electrical, electronic, systems, metallurgical, chemical, and industrial engineering faculties.

UNIVERSIDAD NACIONAL EXPERIMENTAL SIMÓN RODRÍGUEZ

Apdo Postal 3690, Carmelitas, Caracas 1010A

Telephone: 979-10-22
Telex: 21910

Founded 1974
Regional centres in 13 towns

President: Dr GUSTAVO GONZÁLEZ ERASO
Rector: Dra ELIZABETH Y. DE CALDERA
Academic Vice-Rector: Prof. RICARDO SZIKORA
Administrative Vice-Rector: Dr EUDES HERNANDEZ
Secretary: Dra DAISE CASTILLO BELLO

Number of teachers: 387
Number of students: 12,859

Publications: *Memoria y Cuenta de la Universidad* (annually), *Gaceta Universitaria* (quarterly), *Revista de Cultura* (quarterly).

Faculties of education, administration and food technology.

UNIVERSIDAD NACIONAL EXPERIMENTAL DEL TÁCHIRA

Apdo 436, Avda Universidad, Paramillo, San Cristóbal, Táchira

Telephone: (76) 56-44-22
Telex 76196
Fax: (76) 56-58-96

Founded 1974
State control
Language of instruction: Spanish
Academic year: February to July, August to December

Rector: Ing. HUMBERTO ACOSTA
Academic Vice-Rector: Ing. TRINO GUTIÉRREZ NIETO
Administrative Vice-Rector: Ing. GUSTAVO SERRANO
Secretary: Ing. RAFAEL USECHE
Dean of Teaching: Ing. JOSÉ ROA
Dean of Research: Ing. MARTÍN PAZ
Dean of Extension: Zoot. FREDDY DÍAZ DÍAZ
Dean of Graduate Studies: Ing. RODRIGO SAYAGO
Dean of Undergraduate Studies: Lic. ISIDRO PERNIA
Librarian: Lic. MARIZA VILLEGAS DE MOROS

Number of teachers: 401
Number of students: 4,596 undergraduate, 800 propaedeutic, 900 graduate

Publications: *Gaceta*, *Vocero Universitario*, *Boletín*, *Aleph sub cero*, *Boletín Estadístico*, *Revista Científica UNET*.

HEADS OF DEPARTMENTS

Agricultural Engineering: Ing. JOSÉ CLEMENTE LINARES
Industrial Engineering: Ing. ELIZABETH CASTILLO
Mechanical Engineering: Ing. FREDDY QUIROZ
Electronic Engineering: Ing. RAFAEL CHACÓN
Architecture: Arq. NANCY BECERRA DE PADRÓN
Physics: Arq. CARLOS CH. PARDO
Biochemistry: Prof. LUIS VERGARA
Mathematics: Dr RAMÓN MIRABAL
Social Sciences: Prof. IRIS HEVIA
Earth and Environment: Ing. ANÍBAL MUÑOZ
Laboratories and Projects: Ing. SAMUEL JAIMES
Computer Science: Ing. MIGUEL URBINA
Educational Development: Lic. REINALDO TOVAR
Animal Production Engineering: Zoot. IRAIDA DE ACOSTA

UNIVERSIDAD DE ORIENTE

Edificio Rectorado, Apdo 094, Cumaná, Estado Sucre
Telephone: (93) 23366
Telex: 93152
Founded 1958
State control
Academic year: February to December
Rector: Dr Andrés Pastrana Vásquez
Academic Vice-Rector: Dr Oswaldo Betancourt
Administrative Vice-Rector: Dr Diogenes Figueroa Lugo
Secretary-General: Dr Cesar A. Boada Salazar
Library: see Libraries
Number of teachers: 1,382
Number of students: 23,084
Publications: *Oriente Universitario* (monthly bulletin), *Boletín del Instituto Oceanográfico, Lagena, Oriente Agropecuario, La UDO Investiga, Directorio del Personal Docente e Investigación* (annually), *Catálogo de la UDO* (annually).

Universidad de Oriente, Nucleo Anzoátegui

(Anzoátegui Campus)

Apdo postal 4327, Puerto La Cruz, Anzoátegui
Telephone: 663827
Telex: 81240
Founded 1965
Dean: Prof. Manuel López Farías
Number of teachers: 418
Number of students: 9,000

HEADS OF SCHOOLS

Basic Courses: Prof. Pedro Jiménez
Engineering and Applied Science: Prof. Rubén Aular
Administrative Sciences: Prof. Juan D. Guaicain

ATTACHED INSTITUTES

Centro de Desarrollo Tecnológico: Dir Prof. René P. Cabrera.
Centro de Investigación Tecnológica Oriente: Dir Dr Clemente Vallenilla.

Universidad de Oriente, Nucleo Bolívar

(Bolívar Campus)

La Sabanita, Ciudad Bolívar
Dean: Dr Arturo Raul Lara Rojas

DIRECTORS

Medicine: Prof. Victor Espinoza León
Geology and Mines: Prof. Oscar García Cachazo
Basic Courses: Prof. Margoth Siso de San Martin

ATTACHED INSTITUTES

Centre for Biomedical Research: Dir Dr Otto Sánchez.
Geosciences Centre: Dir Prof. Manuel Funes Ariza.

Universidad de Oriente, Nucleo de Monagas

(Los Guaritos Campus)

Avda Universidad, Maturín, Edo Monagas
Telex: 91180
Founded 1961
Dean: Dr José Jiménez Tiamo
Academic Co-ordinator: Ing. Luis Arismendi
Administrative Co-ordinator: Ing. Marcial Viñas de la Hoz
Librarian: Lic. Ramón José Núñez
Publication: *Oriente Agropecuario* (2 a year).

HEADS OF SCHOOLS

Basic Courses: Prof. José Vicente Andérico
School of Agricultural Engineering: Nilda Alcorces de Guerra
School of Animal Husbandry: (vacant)
Programme of Administrative Science: Prof. Arnaldo Rojas
Programme of Human Resources: Prof. Luis Márquez

ATTACHED INSTITUTE

Instituto de Investigaciones Agropecuarias: Dir Dr Tomás Rodríguez

Universidad de Oriente, Nucleo Nueva Esparta

(Nueva Esparta Campus)

Apdo Postal 147, Guatamare, Nueva Esparta
Telephone and fax: (95) 610131
Founded 1958
State control
Dean: Ing. Casto González M.
Academic Co-ordinator: Prof. José G. Marcano
Administrative Co-ordinator: Ing. Luis Marcano

HEADS OF SCHOOLS

Basic Courses: Prof. Esteban Obando
Hotel and Tourism: Prof. José M. Velásquez
Applied Ocean Sciences: Prof. José Luis Fuentes

ATTACHED INSTITUTE

Instituto de Investigaciones Científicas: Dir Prof. Domingo González.

Universidad de Oriente, Nucleo de Sucre

(Sucre Campus)

Cumaná
Dean: Prof. Francia Padilla de Korchoff

HEADS OF SCHOOLS

Basic Courses: Prof. Fortunato Malan
Humanities and Education: Prof. Ezequiel Salazar
Sciences: Prof. Elsie Romero de Bellorin
Social Sciences: Prof. María Elena Zajía
Administration and Accountancy: Prof. José Antonio Aristimuño

ATTACHED INSTITUTES

Instituto Oceanográfico: Dir Prof. Anibal Velez.
Centro de Microscopía Electrónica: Dir Prof. Susan Tai de Díaz.
Centro de Tecnología Educativa: Dir Lic. Mary Plazas de N.
Centro de Sismología: Dir Prof. Juan de Martín Marfil.

UNIVERSIDAD RAFAEL URDANETA

Apdo 614, Maracaibo, Edo Zulia
Telephone: (61) 922655
Fax: (61) 922659
Founded 1974
Private control
Language of instruction: Spanish
Academic year: February to June, September to January
Rector: Dr Eloy Párraga Villamarín
Academic Vice-Rector: Dr José León García Díaz
Administrative Vice-Rector: Econ. Jorge Sánchez Meleán
Librarian: Lic. Norka Portillo de Gutiérrez
Number of teachers: 258
Number of students: 2,310

DEANS

Faculty of Political and Social Sciences: Dra Beatriz Aparicio
Faculty of Stockbreeding: Ing. Romulo Rincón
Faculty of Engineering: Ing. Fernando Urdaneta

UNIVERSIDAD DE SANTA MARIA

Avda Páez, Frente Plaza Madariaga, El Paraiso, Caracas
Founded 1953
Private control
Rector: Dr Juan Bautista Fuenmayor Rivera
Vice-Rector: Dr José Ramón Berrizbeitia
Number of teachers: *c.* 300
Number of students: *c.* 4,500

DEANS

Faculty of Economics: Dr César Balestrini
Faculty of Engineering: Dr Humberto Ache Ramos
Faculty of Law: Dr Humberto Bello Lozano
Faculty of Pharmacy: Dr Raúl Sojo Bianco

UNIVERSIDAD SIMÓN BOLÍVAR

Apdo 89.000, Caracas 1080
Telephone: (2) 906-31-11
Telex: 21910
Fax: (2) 962-16-15
Founded 1970
State control
Language of instruction: Spanish
Academic year: September to July
Rector: Ing. Freddy Malpica
Academic Vice-Rector: Dr Osmar Issa
Administrative Vice-Rector: Ing. Juan Leon
General Secretary: Dr Pedro María Aso.
Librarian: Dra Rosario Gassol de Horowitz
Number of teachers: 850
Number of students: 10,000
Publications: *Atlántida, Argos, Perfiles*

DEANS

General Studies: Juan Carlos Rodríguez
Professional Studies: Raul Goncalves
Postgraduate Studies: Carlos Pérez
Research: Benjamín Scharifker

DIVISION DIRECTORS

Physics and Mathematics: Roberto Réquiz
Humanities and Social Sciences: Ana María Rajkay
Biological Sciences: Daisy Pérez de Acosta
Technological Studies (Núcleo Universitario del Litoral): Enrique López Contreras

RESEARCH INSTITUTES

Instituto de Tecnologías Ciencias Marinas: Dir David Bone.
Instituto de Altos Estudios de América Latina: Dir Miguel Angel Burelli Rivas.
Instituto de Recursos Naturales Renovables: Dir Haymara Alvarez.
Instituto de Estudios Regionales y Urbanos: Dir Nelson Geigel Lope-Bello.
Instituto de Investigaciones Históricas 'Bolivarium': Dir Juan Manuel Morales.

UNIVERSIDAD TECNOLÓGICA DEL CENTRO

Vía Aragüita (2 kms de la Carretera Nacional), Apdo 1620, Valencia 2001
Telephone: (45) 646677
Fax: (45) 646666
E-mail: unitecl@telcel.net.ve
Founded 1979
Private control
Rector: Ing. César Peña Vigas

Academic Vice-Rector: Ing. CORINA ETTEDGUI DE BETANCOURT
Administrative Vice-Rector: Ing. REINALDO PLAZ
Administrator: Lic. IDERMA JIMÉNEZ
Librarian: Ing. OSVALDO CRUZ

Number of teachers: 129
Number of students: 1,500

Publication: *El Innovador.*

Courses in information science, mechanical engineering, administration, business studies, electrical engineering, productivity and knowledge management.

UNIVERSIDAD DEL ZULIA

Apdo de Correos 526, Maracaibo 4011, Estado Zulia

Telephone: (61) 517697
Telex: 62172
Fax: (61) 512525

Founded 1891, closed 1904, reopened 1946
State control
Academic year: January to July, September to December

Rector: Dr ANGEL LOMBARDI LOMBARDI
Academic Vice-Rector: Lic. ANTONIO CASTEJÓN
Administrative Vice-Rector: Econ. NEURO VILLALOBOS
Secretary: Ing. ANGEL LARREAL
Librarian: Lic. EGLA ORTEGA

Library: see Libraries
Number of teachers: 3,652
Number of students: 47,590

Publications: *Memoria y Cuenta de LUZ* (annually), *Gaceta* (quarterly), *Publicaciones de la Unidad de Estadísticas.*

DEANS

Faculty of Law: Dr HERMANN PETZOLD PERNÍA
Faculty of Humanities and Education: Prof. NERÍO VÍLCHEZ
Faculty of Economic and Social Sciences: Prof. JULIANA FERRER
Faculty of Medicine: Dr RAFAEL MARTÍNEZ
Faculty of Agriculture: Prof. ALONSO FERNÁNDEZ
Faculty of Dentistry: Prof. EXEQUIADES PAZ A
Faculty of Architecture: Prof. IGNACIO DE OTEIZA
Faculty of Veterinary Sciences: Prof. GUSTAVO SOTO
Faculty of Experimental Sciences: Prof. TERESITA ALVAREZ DE FERNANDEZ
Faculty of Engineering: Prof. NELSON MOLERO

ATTACHED RESEARCH INSTITUTES

Instituto de Investigaciones de Arquitectura y Sistemas Ambientales (Institute of Research on Architecture and Environmental Systems): Dir Arq. EDGARDO IBAÑEZ.
Unidad Coordinadora de Proyectos Conjuntos (Co-ordinating Unit for Related Projects): research on inter-relation between social sciences, agriculture and veterinary science in rural development; Dir Econ. JOSÉ E. FUENTES.
Instituto de Medicina del Trabajo e Higiene Industrial (Institute of Industrial Medicine and Hygiene): Dir Dra NORA VARGAS DE PINEDA.
Instituto de Investigaciones Clínicas (Institute of Clinical Research): Dir Dr HUMBERTO MARTINEZ.
Instituto de Cálculo Aplicado (Institute of Applied Calculus): Dir Ing. CARLOS MORALES.
Centro de Estadísticas e Investigación de Operaciones (Centre for Statistics and Operations Research): Dir Econ. IGOR GARCÍA.
Instituto de Investigaciones de la Facultad de Ciencias Económicas y Sociales (Institute of Economic Research): Dir Econ. JOSÉ MORENO.
Instituto Criminología del Derecho (Institute for Criminology): Dir FRANCISCO DELGADO.
Centro de Estudios Literarios (Centre for Literary Studies): Dir Prof. LUIS OQUENDO.
Centro de Documentación e Investigación Pedagógica (Centre for Educational Documentation and Research): Dir Prof. VIRGINIA PIRELA.
Instituto de Investigaciones Biológicas (Biological Research Institute): basic and applied research in biology and experimental medicine; Dir Dra CONSUELO VALERO.
Centro de Investigaciones y Estudios Laborales y Disciplinas Afines (Centre for Research on Labour and Related Disciplines): Dir Dr LUIS EDUARDO DÍAZ.
Centro de Estudios Históricos (Centre for Historical Studies): Dir Dr RUTILIO ORTEGA.
Centro de Investigaciones Biológicas (Centre for Biological Research): Dir Prof. JOAQUIN LEÓN.
Instituto de Filosofía del Derecho (Institute of Legal Philosophy): Dir Dra BRIGITTE BERNARD.
Unidad de Genética Médica (Unit for Medical Genetics): Dir Dra LENNIE PINEDA DE DELVILLAR.
Instituto de Investigaciones Petroleras (Centre for Petroleum Research): Dir Ing. RENATO ACOSTA.
Centro de Estudios de la Empresa (Centre for Business Studies): Dir Lic. JESÚS DANIEL BORGES.
Centro de Estudios Filosóficos (Centre for Philosophical Studies): Dir Dr ANGEL BUSTILLOS.
Instituto de Investigaciones Agronómicas (Institute of Agricultural Research): Dir Ing. ISIDRO MELÉNDEZ.
Centro Experimental de Producción Animal (Experimental Centre for Animal Production): Dir Dr WILLIAM ISEA.
Centro Experimental de Estudios Latinoamericanos (Experimental Centre for Latin American Studies): Dir Dr GASTÓN PARRA LUZARDO.

College

INSTITUTO UNIVERSITARIO POLITÉCNICO 'LUIS CABALLERO MEJÍAS'

Apdo 20955, San Martin, Caracas 1020–A
Telephone: 49-89-17

Founded 1974

Director: Ing. RAFAEL DUQUE SALINAS
Deputy Director (Academic): Ing. IDELFONSO MEJÍAS
Deputy Director (Administrative): Lic. RAMÓN PELLES
Librarian: Lic. MYRIAM LÓPEZ ACOSTA

Number of teachers: 216
Number of students: 2,017

HEADS OF DEPARTMENTS

Professional Studies: Lic. PEDRO LECUE
Systems Engineering: Lic. PEDRO LECUE
Industrial Engineering: Lic. OSWALDO GUILLERMO
Mechanical Engineering: Lic. CALÓGERO SALVO
Foundation Courses: Lic. LIADA RONDON DE MOSQUERA
General Courses: Lic. RAFAEL RENÉ RAMIREZ
Basic Sciences: Lic. FRANKLIN PIRELA

Schools of Art and Music

Academia de Música 'Padre Sojo' (Padre Sojo Academy of Music): 4A Avda—Transv. 8A y 9A, Apdo 60479 Este, Caracas; Dir Prof. BETHANIA OLAVARRIETA.

Academia de Música Fischer (Fischer Academy of Music): Edif. Léon de San Marco, Avda Ciencias y Calle Risquez, Los Chaguaramos, Caracas; Dir CARMEN DE FISCHER.

Centro de Bellas Artes (Center for Fine Arts): Apdo 10015, Bella Vista, Maracaibo; tel. (61) 912950; fax (61) 920195; f. 1954 to promote cultural activities; theatre, two art galleries, school of ballet and modern dance, Maracaibo Contemporary Dance Troupe, Maracaibo Symphony Orchestra, National Youth Theatre, Goajiro Indian workshop, *Colegio Bellas Artes,* library; Dir OSCAR D'EMPAIRE.

Conservatorio de Música 'José Luis Paz': Edif. Secretaría de Cultura, 3° piso, Avda 2, Maracaibo; tel. 223868; Dir Prof. OSCAR FACCIO.

Conservatorio Italiano de Música (Italian Conservatoire of Music): Edif. Centro Venezolano-Italiano de Cultura, Avda Anauco, Colinas de Bello Monte, Caracas; Dir C. GALZIO.

Escuela de Artes Visuales 'Cristóbal Rojas' (Cristóbal Rojas School of Visual Arts): Avda Lecund-Este 10 bis, El Conde, Caracas; f. 1936; Dir CARMEN JULIA NEGRÓN DE VALERY.

Escuela Superior de Arte 'Neptali Rincón': Centro Vocacional Dr O. Hernández, Avda El Milagro Diagonal al Hospital Central, Maracaibo; tel. (61) 223868; f. 1957; courses in painting, sculpture, ceramics, etc.; 12 teachers, 300 students; Dir Prof. ANIBAL LARES M.

Escuela Superior de Música 'José Angel Lamas' (Lamas High School of Music): Veroes a Santa Capilla, Caracas; f. 1887; Dir VICENTE EMILIO SOJO.

Fundación Teresa Carreño: Teatro Teresa Carreño, Plaza Morelos, Apdo 5431; Caracas 1010; tel. 5749122; telex 28149; fax 5711398; f. 1983; concerts, opera, ballet, master classes and courses for opera singers; Dir-Gen. BEATRICE RANGEL MANTILLA.

VIET NAM

Learned Societies

GENERAL

Hanoi Union of Science and Technology: Tran Xuan Soan St, Hanoi; tel. 57149; Sec.-Gen. TA QUANG DAN.

Viet Nam Union of Scientific and Technical Associations: 30B Ba Trieu St, Hanoi; tel. 56781; f. 1983; 17 mem. socs.; Pres. TRAN DAI NGHIA; Vice-Pres. LE KHAC, DUONG HONG DAT, NGUYEN VAN HIEU, DAO VAN TAP.

Writers and Artists Union: 51 Tran Hung Dao St, Hanoi; tel. 52694; f. 1957; 7 mems socs; Pres. CU HUY CAN; Vice-Pres. NGUYEN DINH THI, TRAN VAN CAN, LUU HUU PHUOC.

AGRICULTURE, FISHERIES AND VETERINARY SCIENCE

Forestry Association: 123 Lo Duc St, Hanoi; tel. 53236; Sec.-Gen. TRAN DUC HAU.

Gardeners' Association: Nguyen Cong Tru St, Hanoi; f. 1985; Sec.-Gen. NGHIEM XUAN YEM.

ARCHITECTURE AND TOWN PLANNING

Builders' Association: 34 Hang Chuoi St, Hanoi; Sec.-Gen. LE QUANG BAU.

ECONOMICS, LAW AND POLITICS

Economics Association: 27 Tran Xuan Soan St, Hanoi.

Law Association: Nguyen Thuong Hien, Hanoi; tel. 57149; Sec.-Gen. PHAN ANH.

HISTORY, GEOGRAPHY AND ARCHAEOLOGY

History Association: C/o Viet Nam Union of Scientific and Technical Associations, 30B Ba Trieu St, Hanoi.

MEDICINE

General Association of Medicine: 68 Ba Trieu St, Hanoi; tel. 52323; f. 1955; 21 mem. socs; Pres. (vacant); Vice-Pres HOANG DINH CAU, PHAM KHAC QUANG, NGUYEN TANG GI TRONG, NGUYEN TRINH CO, DANG DINH HUAN, TRAN THI AN, NGUYEN VAN DAN, TRAN HUU NGHIEP.

Traditional Medicine Association: C/o Viet Nam Union of Scientific and Technical Associations, 30B Ba Trieu St, Hanoi; Sec.-Gen. TRAN NGOC SUNG.

NATURAL SCIENCES

Biological Sciences

Biology Association: C/o Viet Nam Union of Scientific and Technical Associations, 30B Ba Trieu St, Hanoi; tel. 58333; Sec.-Gen. LE XUAN TU.

Mathematical Sciences

Mathematics Association: C/o Viet Nam Union of Scientific and Technical Associations, 30B Ba Trieu St, Hanoi; tel. 58331; Sec.-Gen. HOANG VY.

Physical Sciences

Geology Association: 6 Pham Ngu Lao, Hanoi; tel. 54261; Sec.-Gen. NGUYEN TIEN THANH.

Physics Association: C/o Viet Nam Union of Scientific and Technical Associations, 30B Ba Trieu St, Hanoi; Pres. NGUY NHU CONG TUM; Sec.-Gen. VU XUAN OANH.

TECHNOLOGY

Casting and Metallurgy Association: C/o Viet Nam Union of Scientific and Technical Associations, 30B Ba Trieu St, Hanoi; Sec.-Gen. PHAN TU PHUNG.

Mechanics Association: C/o Viet Nam Union of Scientific and Technical Associations, 30B Ba Trieu St, Hanoi; Sec.-Gen. PHAM HIEN.

Mining Association: 54 Hai Ba Trung, Hanoi; Sec.-Gen. TRAN ANH VINH.

Research Institutes

GENERAL

Institute of Culture: O Cho Dua, Hanoi; tel. 56415; f. 1971; 50 staff; study of Vietnamese culture in all its aspects and relations with other countries; library of 5,000 vols; Dir Prof. LE ANH TRA; Sec. Dr LAM TO LOC; publ. *Culture Research Information*.

AGRICULTURE, FISHERIES AND VETERINARY SCIENCE

Animal Husbandry Research Institute: Chem, Tu Liem, Hanoi; tel. 43971; f. 1969; research on domestic animals; extension service; Dir Dr LE VIET LY, publ. *Scientific and Technical Journal on Animal Husbandry*.

Centre for Research on Inland Aquatic Products: Tien Son District, Ha Bac Province; f. 1975.

Centre for Research on the Mechanization of Agriculture and the Food Industry: 10A, 55 Tran Nhat Duat St, 1st Dist, Ho Chi Minh City; tel. 8444233; fax 8440437; f. 1976; 100 mems; library of 3,000 vols; Dir TRAN QUAN; publ. *Agricultural Electro-Mechanization* (irregular).

Dalat Centre for Scientific Research: 116 Xo Viet Nghe Tinh St, Da Lat, Lam Dong Province; tel. 2078; f. 1978; development and reproduction of animals, cow and buffalo embryo transplantation, cryobiology, chemistry of natural substances, introduction and acclimatization of plants; 18 scientists; Dir Dr NGUYEN DANG KHOI.

Food Crops Research Institute: Gialoc, Hai Duong Province; tel. (32) 826463; fax (32) 826385; f. 1968; research on varietal and technological improvement of rice, root and tuber crops, legumes, vegetables and fruit-tree crops; library of 1,600 vols and 150 journals; Dir Prof. Dr VU TUYEN HOANG: publ. *Research Bulletin of Food Crops* (every 2–3 years).

Forest Science Institute: Chem, Tu Liem District, Hanoi; tel. and fax 345722; f. 1961.

Institute of Agricultural Land Planning and Arrangement: Hanoi.

Institute of Agricultural Science of Southern Vietnam: 121 Nguyen Binh Khiem St, 1st District, Ho Chi Minh City; tel. (8) 8291746; fax (8) 8297650; f. 1981; research on pedology, crop sciences and animal sciences; library of 10,000 vols; collection of insects; Dir Prof. PHAM VAN BIEN; publ. *Annual Report of Research Results*.

Institute of Agro-Chemistry and Pedology: Tu Liem District, Hanoi; f. 1968.

Institute of Forestry: Tu Liem District, Hanoi; f. 1974.

Institute of Fruit-tree and Industrial Crop Research: Phong Chau, Vinh Phu Province; f. 1969.

Institute of Veterinary Research: Dong Da Precinct, Hanoi; f. 1968.

National Institute of Plant Protection: POB Chem, Tu Liem District, Hanoi; tel. 344723; telex 441266; fax (4) 8363563; f. 1968; plant protection research and development with emphasis on biological and genetic control, integrated pest management of food and vegetable and specific tropical crops; library of 700 vols; Dir LE VAN THUYET; publ. *Plant Protection Bulletin* (every 2 months).

Research Institute of Marine Products: 170 Le Lai St, 35000 Haiphong; tel. (31) 836664; fax (31) 836812; f. 1961; study, training and research in fisheries biology, stock assessment, brackish water aquaculture, mariculture, oceanography, technology of fishing and processing; library of 12,000 vols; Dir Prof. Dr BUI DINH CHUNG; publ. *Fisheries Research Bulletin*.

Rubber Research Institute of Viet Nam: 177 Hai Ba Trung St, Ho Chi Minh City; tel. (8) 294139; fax (8) 298599; f. 1975; library of 3,000 vols; Gen. Dir MAI VAN SON.

Viet Nam Institute of Agricultural Engineering: Phuong Mai, Dong Da, Hanoi; tel. (4) 8523187; fax (4) 8521131; f. 1968; research machinery for agricultural production and food processing; library of 3,000 vols; Dir Prof. Dr PHAM VAN LANG; publ. *Agricultural and Food Industries* (monthly, in Vietnamese with a summary in English).

Viet Nam Institute of Agricultural Science and Technology: Thanh Tri District, Hanoi; f. 1978; Dir Prof. DAO THE TUAN.

ECONOMICS, LAW AND POLITICS

Institute of Economic Management: 68 Phan Dinh Phung St, Hanoi; tel. 256254; fax 256795; f. 1978.

Institute of Economics: 27 Tran Xuan Soan St, Hanoi; tel. 254774; fax 259071; f. 1960; library of 8,000 vols; Dir VU TUAN ANH; publ. *Nghien Cuu Kinh Te* (Economic Studies Review, fortnightly in Vietnamese, every 6 months in English).

Institute of Finance: 8 Phan Huy Chu St, Hanoi; tel. 58111-301, 279; f. 1961.

Institute of International Relations: Lang Thuong, Dong Da, Hanoi; tel. and fax (4) 8343543; f. 1959; library of 25,000 vols; publ. *International Studies* (6 a year in Vietnamese, 2 a year in English).

Institute of Labour Science and Social Affairs: 2 Dinh Le St, Hanoi; tel. 269733; fax 254728; f. 1978; labour relations, working conditions, wages and living standards, levels of skill, social security; Dir Dr DO MINH CUONG.

Institute of Law: 27 Tran Xuan Soan St, Hanoi; tel. 54774-49; f. 1960.

Institute of Planning Research: 6 Hoang Dieu St, Hanoi; tel. 58171; f. 1975.

Institute of Social Sciences: Ho Chi Minh City; f. 1978.

Institute of Statistical Science and Economic Information: 66 Hoang Dieu St, Hanoi; tel. 58171; f.1976; 27 staff; library of 2,600 foreign books, 1,100 Vietnamese; special collections in field of statistics; Dir NGUYEN XUAN TUONG (acting); publs *Bulletin of Statistical Science, Selection of Information Dissemination Periodicals.*

Institute of Trade Economics and Technology: 28 Nguyen Thuong Hien St, Hanoi; tel. 52388, 52234, 52191; f. 1975.

EDUCATION

Institute of Higher and Secondary Vocational Education Research: Dai Co Viet St, Hanoi; tel. 57944, 56943; f. 1977.

Institute of Physical Culture and Sports: Hang Day, Hanoi; tel. 53112; f. 1979.

National Institute for Educational Science: 101 Tran Huan Dao St, Hanoi; tel. (4) 8256978; fax (4) 8223213; e-mail vienk.h.g.d@hn.vnn.vn; f. 1961; library of 40,000 vols; Dir Assoc. Prof. Dr TRAN KIEU; publ. *Information on Educational Sciences* (6 a year).

FINE AND PERFORMING ARTS

Institute of Stage Arts: O Cho Dua, Hanoi; tel. 56415; f. 1978.

Viet Nam Musicology Institute: 32 Nguyen Thai Hoc St, Ba Dinh District, Hanoi; tel. (4) 8457368; fax (4) 8434953; f. 1976; research in the national heritage of music, song, dance, costumes; Dir Prof. NGUYEN PHUC LINH.

HISTORY, GEOGRAPHY AND ARCHAEOLOGY

Institute of Archaeology: 61 Phan Chu Trinh St, Hanoi; tel. 53203; f. 1960.

Institute of History: 38 Hang Chuoi St, Hanoi; tel. 53200; f. 1960.

LANGUAGE AND LITERATURE

Institute of Linguistics: 20 Ly Thai To St, Hanoi; tel. (4) 257406; fax (4) 259071; f. 1968; library of 12,000 vols; Dir Dr LY TOAN CHANG; publ. *Ngon Ngu* (quarterly).

Institute of Literary Studies: 20 Ly Thai To St, Hanoi; tel. (4) 8253548; fax (4) 8250385; f. 1959; library of 150,000 vols; Dir Prof. HA MINH DUC; publ. *Tap Chi Van Hoc* (literary review, monthly).

Institute of Research on Chinese and Demotic Characters: 26 Ly Thuong Kiet St, Hanoi; tel. 57795; f. 1970.

MEDICINE

Central Institute of Ophthalmology: 38 Tran Nhan Tong, Hanoi; tel. 53967; f. 1957.

High Plateaux (Tay Nguyen) Institute of Hygiene and Epidemiology: Buon Ma Thuoc, Dac Lac Province; f. 1976.

Ho Chi Minh City Institute of Hygiene: 159 Hung Phu St, Ho Chi Minh City; tel. 59501; f. 1977.

Ho Chi Minh City Institute of Hygiene and Epidemiology: 167 Nguyen Thi Minh Khai St, Ho Chi Minh City; tel. 40909, 90352; f. 1977.

Ho Chi Minh City Institute of National Medicine: 273 Nam Ky Khoi St, Ho Chi Minh City; tel. 45954, 41308; f. 1975.

Institute for the Protection of the Mother and Newborn Child: 43 Trang Thi St, Hanoi; tel. (4) 8252161; fax (4) 8254638; f. 1966; obstetrics, gynaecology, care of the newborn child and family planning; library of 5,000 vols; Dir Prof. DUONG THI CUONG; publs *Nội san Sản Phụ Khoa* (internal journal of obstetrics and gynaecology, annually), *Tổng kêt công trình nghiên cúu khoa học* (review of scientific studies, annually).

Institute of Child Care: Bach Mai, Hanoi; f. 1969.

Institute of Malariology, Entomology and Parasitology: Tu Liem District, Hanoi; tel. 54847; f. 1957.

Institute of Materia Medica: 3B Quang Trung St, Hanoi; tel. 52644; fax (4) 254357; f. 1961; multidisciplinary research on pharmaceutical materials, mainly medicinal plants; postgraduate training; library of 6,000 vols; Dir Prof. NGUYEN GIA CHAN; publ. *Materia Medica Bulletin* (quarterly).

Institute of Occupational Health Research: 14 Tran Binh Trong St, Hanoi; tel. 58181, 54883; f. 1971.

Institute of Odonto-Maxillo-Facial Research: Hanoi.

Institute of Vaccine and Serum Production Research: 9 Phan Thanh Gian St, Nha Trang; also 18 Le Hong Phong St, Da Lat; f. 1979.

National Institute of Drug Quality Control: 48 Hai Ba Trung St, Hanoi; tel. (4) 8255341; fax (4) 8256911; f. 1971; publ. *Drug Quality Control Newsletter* (quarterly).

National Institute of Hygiene and Epidemiology: 1 Yersin St, 10000 Hanoi; tel. (4) 8213241; fax (4) 8210853; e-mail nihe@netnam.org.vn; f. 1924; epidemiology of communicable diseases, vaccine development; library of 12,000 vols; Dir Prof. HOANG THUY LONG; publ. *Tap Chi Ve Sinh Phong Dich* (Journal, in Vietnamese with abstract in English, quarterly).

National Institute of Nutrition: 48 Tang Bat Ho St, Hanoi; tel. (4) 9717090; fax (4) 9717885; e-mail nin@netnam.org.vn; f. 1980; depts of basic nutrition, community nutrition, applied nutrition, clinical nutrition, food science, food safety, dietetics, experiment workshop, library; Dir Prof. HÀ HUY KHÔI; publ. nutrition newsletter (quarterly).

National Institute of Otorhinolaryngology: Bachmai Hospital Centre, Hanoi; tel. 254706; fax 253525; f. 1969; 200 staff; library of 1,000 vols; Dir Prof. LUONG SY CAN; publs *Noi San Tai Mui Hong* (annually), *Thong Tin Tai Mui Hong* (annually).

National Institute of Traditional Medicine: 29 Nguyen Binh Khiem St, Hanoi; tel. 262850; f. 1957; traditional medicine; library of 19,343 vols, special collection of books on Chinese medicine and medicine in Viet Nam since 15th century; Dir Prof. Dr HŌANG BÁO CHÂU; publ. *Thông tin y hoc cô truyên dan toc* (quarterly).

National Institute of Tuberculosis and Respiratory Diseases: 120 Hoang Hoa Tham St, Hanoi; tel. (4) 8326249; fax (4) 8326162; f. 1957; research on tuberculosis, lung cancer, chronic bronchitis, asthma, occupational lung diseases; operates two national programmes: National Tuberculosis Control Programme, Acute Respiratory Infections in Children; library of 10,000 vols; Dir Prof. N. V. Co; publ. *Lao và bệnh phôi* (4 a year).

Nha Trang Institute of Hygiene and Epidemiology: 10 Tran Phu St, Nha Trang, Phu Khanh Province; tel. 20405, 20410; f. 1976.

NATURAL SCIENCES

General

National Centre for Scientific Research of Viet Nam, Ho Chi Minh City Branch: 1 Mac Dinh Chi St, Ho Chi Minh City; tel. 95814; telex 8268; f. 1975; fundamental and applied research in biology, chemistry, physics, mathematics, geoscience; Pres. Prof. Dr HO SI THOANG; Sec. Prof. Dr NGUYEN VAN TRONG.

Biological Sciences

Institute of Biology: Nghia Do, Tu Liem District, Hanoi; tel. 58333-551; f. 1975; biochemistry and molecular biology of nitrogen fixation; plant genetics; Dir Prof. LE XUAN TU; publs *Annual Scientific Reports, Journal of Biology.*

Mathematical Sciences

Institute of Mathematics: POB 631, Bo Ho, 10000 Hanoi; tel. 361317; fax 343303; f. 1969; operations research, optimal control theory, dynamic systems, probability and mathematical statistics, discrete mathematics, functional analysis, numerical analysis, partial differential equations, methods of mathematical physics, algebra, geometry and topology; 90 staff; library of 11,000 vols, 350 periodicals; Dir Prof. TRAN DUC VAN; publ. *Acta Mathematica Vietnamica* (2 a year).

Physical Sciences

Institute of Chemistry, National Centre for Natural Science and Technology of Viet Nam: Nghia Do, Tu Liem District, Hanoi; tel. 343312; telex 411525; fax 361283; f. 1978; applied research and engineering in inorganic, physicochemical, analytical and polymer chemistry and natural chemical compounds; library of 5,420 vols; Dir Prof. Dr DANG VU MINH; Scientific Sec. Dr PHAM HUU LY; publ. *Tap chí Hóa hoc* (Journal of Chemistry, quarterly).

Institute of Earth Science: Tu Liem District, Hanoi; tel. 58331-372; f. 1967.

Institute of Geology and Minerals: Thanh Xuan, Hanoi; tel. 54315; f. 1976.

Institute of Meteorology and Hydrology: Lang Trung, Dong Da, Hanoi; tel. (4) 8343538; fax (4) 8355993; f. 1977; Dir Dr NGUYEN TRONG HIEU (acting).

Institute of Oceanography: 01 Cau Da, Nha Trang, Khanh Hoa Province; tel. (58) 881153; fax (58) 881152; e-mail haiduong@nhatrang.teltic.com.vn; f. 1923; library of 60,000 vols; museum, aquarium: Dir VO VAN LANH.

Institute of Physics: Tu Liem District, Hanoi; tel. 52129; f. 1969.

PHILOSOPHY AND PSYCHOLOGY

Institute of Philosophy: 25 Lang Ha St, Ba Dinh District, Hanoi; tel. and fax (4) 5140530; f. 1962; library of 50,000 vols; Dir Prof. NGUYEN TRONG CHUAN; publ. *Philosophy* (6 a year).

RELIGION, SOCIOLOGY AND ANTHROPOLOGY

Institute of Ethnology: 27 Tran Xuan Soan St, Hanoi; tel. 54771; f. 1968; research in cultural history and social structure of the nationalities in Viet Nam and Southeast Asia; 62 staff; library of 10,000 vols; Dir BE VIET DANG; publ. *Ethnographical Studies* (quarterly).

TECHNOLOGY

Broadcast Research and Application Center: 171 Ly Chinh Thang St, Dist. 3, Ho Chi Minh City; tel. (8) 8298427; fax (8) 8293487; f. 1978; 150 staff; library of 3,000 vols; Dir Prof. NGUYEN KIM SACH.

Food Industries Research Institute: Km. 8 Nguyen Trai Rd, Dong Da, Hanoi; tel. and fax (4) 8584554; f. 1967; microbiology, biotechnology, food processing, quality control of food; Dir Prof. Dr NGO THI MAI.

Hydraulic Engineering Consultants Corporation No. 1: 299 Tay Son St, Dong Da,

Hanoi; tel. (4) 8530209; fax (4) 8522374; f. 1956; library of 9,000 vols; Dir-Gen. PHAM NHU HAI.

Institute for Building Science and Technology: Nghia Tan, Tu Liem, Hanoi; tel. (4) 8344196; fax (4) 8361197; f. 1963; geotechnical and foundation engineering, structural engineering, concrete, structural testing, environmental engineering, construction chemistry, construction technology, water supply and drainage technology; library of 20,000 vols; Dir Prof. Dr NGUYEN TIEN DICH; publ. *Building Science and Technology* (quarterly).

Institute for Standardization in Construction: 303 Doi Can St, Hanoi; tel. 343689; f. 1979; library of 5,000 vols; Dir Dr PHAM KINH CUONG; publs *Vietnamese Standards* (TCVN), *National Typification Design in Construction.*

Institute of Building Materials: 25B Cat Linh St, Hanoi; tel. 52521; f. 1975.

Institute of Construction Mechanization and Industry: 303 Doi Can St, Hanoi; tel. 53267; f. 1979.

Institute of Cybernetics and Computing Technology: Tu Liem District, Hanoi; f. 1976.

Institute of Electrical Research: Dong Da Precinct, Hanoi; f. 1979.

Institute of Engineering and Processing Technology: Dong Da Precinct, Hanoi; tel. 55220; f. 1977.

Institute of Farm Machinery Research: Thanh Xuan, Hanoi; tel. 544429; fax (34) 26677; f. 1970; research, machinery design; library of 5,500 vols; Dir NGUYEN VAN HOI.

Institute of Ferrous Metal: Thuong Tinh District, Hanoi; f. 1977.

Institute of General Construction Programming: 34 Hang Chuoi St, Hanoi; f. 1979.

Institute of Industrial Chemistry: 1 Pham Ngu Lao St, Hanoi; tel. 53903; f. 1959.

Institute of Machine-Building: Tu Liem District, Hanoi; tel. 42312; f. 1962.

Institute of Machinery and Industrial Instruments: 34 Lang Ha St, Dong Da District, Hanoi; tel. 344565; fax 344975; f. 1973; library of 10,000 vols; Dir Dr TRAN VIET HUNG.

Institute of Mechanics: 224 Doi Can St, Ba Dinh, Hanoi; tel. 263641; telex 411526; f. 1979; basic and applied research in the fields of fluids, deformable solids and vibration mechanics; library of 14,182 vols; Dir Prof. NGUYEN VAN DIEP; publs *Journal of Mechanics* (quarterly), institute's reports.

Institute of Motor Transport: 28 Tran Hung Dao St, Hanoi; tel. 56064; f. 1978.

Institute of Oil and Gas Research: Hung Yen, Hai Hung Province; f. 1976.

Institute of Paper and Cellulose Research: Viet Tri, Vinh Phu Province; f. 1970.

Institute of Research on Mining Technology: Yen Vien, Hanoi; tel. 271481; f. 1979; research on underground and opencast mining, mine development and construction, excavating and tunnelling, environmental mine safety, ventilation, electro-mechanization, transport, coal preparation and processing; library of 9,000 vols; Dir TRAN TRONG KIEN; publs *Mining Technology Information* (quarterly), *Works Collection* (every 5 years).

Institute of Ship Design: Cau Giay, Hanoi; tel. 42357; f. 1979.

Institute of the Science and Technology of Capital Construction: 303 Doi Can St, Hanoi; tel. 53267; f. 1979.

Institute of Tropical Technology: Nghia do-Tuliem, Hanoi; tel. and fax (43) 44696; f. 1980; corrosion testing and metal protection, concrete protection, testing of non-metallic materials, their resistance to tropical climates and lifetime prediction, development of new material, tropic-proofing of electrical and electronic equipment; small library; Dir Dr BUI THI AN.

Institute of Water Conservation: Dong Da Precinct, Hanoi; f. 1965.

National Food Industries Research Institute (FIRI): Km. 8 Nguyen Trai Road, Thanh Xuan, Dong Da, Hanoi; tel. 244318; telex 411417; f. 1967; carries out research in biotechnology, food processing technology using local raw materials, and other areas connected with food; Dir Prof. Dr NGO THI MAI.

National Research Institute of Mining and Metallurgy: 30B Doan Thi Diem St, Hanoi; tel. (4) 8233775; fax (4) 8456983; e-mail vimluki@netnam.org.vn; f. 1967; library of 10,000 vols; Dir NGUYEN ANH.

Research Institute of Posts and Telecommunications (RIPT): Nghia Tan, Tu Liem, Hanoi; tel. 344254; telex 411521; fax 345485; Dir Prof. Dr NGUYEN CANH TUAN; publ. *Ket Qua Nghien Cuu Khoa Hoc* (annually).

Scientific and Technological Institute for Communications and Transport: 2 Lang Thuong, Cau Giay, Dong Da, Hanoi; tel. 343404; fax 343403; f. 1956; Dir Asst Prof. Dr NGUYEN VAN LAP.

Textile Research Institute: 326D Minhkhai St, Hanoi; tel. 62873; f. 1969; research in material technology, machinery for spinning, weaving and finishing; 215 staff; library of 3,500 vols; Dir PHAM HOANG NINH; publs *Textiles Magazine* (every 2 months), *Textile Research Journal* (annually).

Viet Nam Atomic Energy Commission: 59 Ly Thuong Kiet St, Hanoi; tel. 256479; telex 411518; fax 266133; f. 1979; nuclear science and technology; Chair. NGUYEN DINH TU; Dir NGUYEN TIEN NGUYEN; publs nuclear news-briefs, *Nuclear Science and Technology.*

Libraries and Archives

Hanoi

Central Institute for Medical Science Information: 13–15 Lê Thánh Tông, Hanoi; tel. (4) 8264040; fax (4) 8242668; e-mail vttyh@hn.vnn.vn; f. 1979 to succeed fmr Central Library for Medical Sciences; attached to Ministry of Health; 50,000 vols; Dir Eng. NGUYEN TUAN KHOA; publs *Vietnam Medical Information* (quarterly, in English), *Bibliography of Vietnamese Medical Literature* (annually, in Vietnamese).

Central Institute of Scientific and Technical Information: 39 Tran Dung Dao St, Hanoi; tel. 52731; f. 1972.

Central Library for Science and Technology: 24–26 Lý Thuòng Kiêt, Hanoi; tel. 263491; telex 412287; fax 263127; f. 1960; attached to the National Centre for Scientific and Technological Information and Documentation; 230,000 vols, 4,500 periodicals; Dir VU VAN SON.

Institute of Social Sciences Information — Central Social Sciences Library: 26 Lý Thuòng Kiêt, Hanoi; f. 1975 by amalgamation of Dept. of Social Sciences Information and Central Social Sciences Library; attached to the National Centre of Social Sciences and Humanities; 300,000 vols; Dir Prof. LAI VAN TOAN; publs *Review of Social Sciences Information* (monthly), *Bibliography of Social Sciences* (annually).

National Library of Viet Nam: 31 Tràng Thi, 10000 Hanoi; tel. (4) 8252643; fax (4) 253357; e-mail tdung@nlv01.gov.vn; f. 1919; attached to Ministry of Culture and Information; 1,200,000 vols, 7,300 periodical titles; Dir TRAN ANH DUNG (acting); publs *National Bibliography* (monthly and quarterly), *Bibliography of Periodical Articles, Bibliography of Newspaper Articles* (monthly), *Information on Culture and Arts, Library and Bibliographical Work* (quarterly).

Ho Chi Minh

General Scientific Library of Ho Chi Minh City: 69 Lý Tu Trọng, BP 341, Ho Chi Minh City; tel. (8) 8225055; fax (8) 8299318; f. 1976; fmrly National Library II; attached to Ho Chi Minh City Cultural Office; 800,000 vols, 4,500 periodical titles; Dir HUYNH NGOC SUONG.

Social Sciences Library: 34 Ly-Tú-Trong, Ho Chi Minh City; tel. (8) 8296744; fax (8) 223735; f. 1975; the collections of the fmr Archaeological Research Institute have been added to the library; provides facilities for research in philosophy, sociology, literature, linguistics, archaeology, ethnology, history, economics, law; 145,000 vols; Dir TRAN MINH DUC.

Museums and Art Galleries

Haiphong

Haiphong Museum: Haiphong; f. 1959; local history.

Hanoi

Ho Chi Minh Museum: Hanoi; tel. 58261; f. 1977; study of the President's life and work; Dir HA HUY GIAP.

National Art Gallery: 66 Nguyên Thái Học St, Hanoi; tel. 233084; f. 1966; preservation and presentation of national cultural heritage; research on ancient and modern fine arts, ceramics, handicrafts; specialized library of 1,100 vols; Dir NGUYEN VAN CHUNG.

People's Army Museum: Dien Bien Phu St, Hanoi; f. 1959; Dir LE CHIEU.

Viet Nam History Museum: 1 Trang Tien, Hanoi; tel. 53518; f. 1958; research and conservation, history of Viet Nam from palaeolithic period to 1945; Dir NGUYEN MANH LOI (acting); publs *Bulletin* (annually), monographs.

Viet Nam Revolution Museum: 25 Tong Dan St, Hanoi; tel. (4) 8254323; f. 1959; study of revolutionary history of Viet Nam; library of 21,000 vols and historical documents, 17,900 documentary photographs; Dir Prof. Dr PHAM MAI HUNG.

Ho Chi Minh

Ho Chi Minh City Museum: Botanical Gardens, Ho Chi Minh City; f. 1977; two sections: one devoted to the revolution, the other to ancient arts.

Hue

Hue Museum: Hue; history of the old capital.

Thai Nguyen

Viet Bac Museum: Thai Nguyen, Bac Thai province; f. 1965; history of the revolution.

Vinh

Nghe-Tinh Museum: Vinh, Nghe Tinh Province; study of the Nghe-Tinh 'Soviet' Uprising, 1930-31.

Universities

CANTHO UNIVERSITY

Duong 30–4, Cantho City, Cantho Province

Telephone: 20237
Fax: 25474

Founded 1966
State control

Rector: TRAN PHUOC DUONG
Vice-Rectors: VO TONG XUAN, LE THE DONG, TRAN THUONG TUAN

Library of 30,000 vols
Number of teachers: 934
Number of students: 5,900

Publications: annual scientific and technology reports.

DEANS

Faculty of Agronomy: Prof. Dr TRAN THUONG TUAN
Faculty of Animal and Veterinary Science: Prof. Dr CHAU BA LOC
Faculty of Food Science and Technology: BUI HUU THUAN
Faculty of Fisheries: NGUYEN ANH TUAN
Faculty of Agricultural Engineering: VU QUANG THANH
Faculty of Water Management and Land Reclamation: LE QUANG MINH
Faculty of Economics: NGUYEN TAN NHAN
Faculty of History and Geography: DO THI CHINH
Faculty of Mathematics and Physics: Dr NGUYEN THANH DAO
Faculty of Information Technology: VO VAN CHIN
Faculty of Chemistry and Biology: Dr TRAN SON
Faculty of Foreign Languages: HUYNH TRUNG TIN
Faculty of Literature: NGUYEN HOA BANG
Faculty of Medical Sciences: PHAM HUNG LUC

ATTACHED INSTITUTES

Biotechnology Research and Development Centre: Dir Prof. Dr TRAN PHUOC DUONG

Mekong Delta Farming System Research and Development Centre: Dir Prof. Dr VO TONG XUAN

Renewable Energy Centre: Dir Dr DO NGOC QUYNH

Foreign Languages Centre: Dir Prof. Dr TRAN PHUOC DUONG

Shrimp-Artemia Research and Development Centre: Dir Dr VU DO QUYNH

COLLEGE OF TECHNICAL TEACHER TRAINING

1 Vo van Ngan St, Thu Duc, Ho Chi Minh City

Telephone: (8) 8968641
Fax: (8) 8964922

Founded 1962 as Ho Chi Minh City Pedagogical University of Technology; new name *c.* 1996
State control
Academic year: September to August

Rector: Assoc. Prof. Dr PHUNG RAN
Vice-Rectors: Assoc. Prof. Dr THAI BA CAN, NGUYEN VAN THUC
Director of Office for Personnel and Administration: NGUYEN VAN MINH
Librarian: NGO THI HOA

Library of 220,000 vols
Number of teachers: 250
Number of students: 6,500

Publication: *Tap san Su Pham Ky Thuat* (quarterly).

DEANS

Department of Electrical and Electronic Engineering: TRAN SUM
Department of Mechanical Engineering: Dr NGUYEN TIEN DUNG
Department of Automotive Engineering: PHAN VAN DAO
Department of Fundamental Techniques: DANG THANH TAN
Department of Agricultural Mechanization: NGUYEN LE TRUNG
Department of Printing Engineering: NGUYEN VAN QUYEN
Department of Home Economics: LUONG THI KIM TUYEN
Department of Technical Education: NGUYEN THI VIET THAO
Center for Computer Science: BUI HUY QUYNH
Center for Foreign Languages: TRAN HUU LICH
Vietnamese-German Center: Dr DO DUC TUY

TRUONG DAI HOC BACH KHOA HANOI (Hanoi University of Technology)

Hanoi

Telephone: 62222
Telex: 412262

Founded 1956

Rector: Prof. Dr NGUYEN MINH HIEN
Vice-Rectors: Prof. Dr HOANG VAN PHONG (Academic), Dr BANH TIEN LONG (Research), Prof. Dr PHAM MINH HA (International Relations)
Chief Administrative Officer: DUONG VAN NGHI
Librarian: GIAN HUU CAN

Library of 700,000 vols
Number of teachers: 920
Number of students: 16,000

HEADS OF DEPARTMENT

Applied Mathematics: TRAN XUAN HIEN
Applied Mechanics: NGUYEN HUU CHI
Automation Engineering: NGUYEN CONG HIEN
Chemical Processes and Equipment: NGUYEN BIN
Cutting Machines and Tools: PHAM DAP
Electric Machinery: NGUYEN MANH DUY
Electrical Systems: TRAN DINH LONG
Electronic Engineering: DO XUAN THU
Engines and Automobiles: DU QUOC THINH
Food Engineering: NGUYEN DUY THINH
Foundry and Thermal Treatment: NGUYEN VAN THAI
General Chemistry: LE CONG HOA
Hydraulic Machinery and Automation: NGUYEN PHU VINH
Industrial Management: NGUYEN MINH DUE
Informatics: DO XUAN LOI
Inorganic Chemistry Technology and Electrochemical Engineering: NGUYEN HOA TOAN
Measurement and Control: NGUYEN THE THANG
Mechanical Construction Technology: NGUYEN VIET TIEP
Metallurgical Engineering: BUI VAN MUU
Organic Chemistry Technology: DAO VAN TUONG
Refrigerating Devices and Thermal Machinery: DANG QUOC PHU
Telecommunications: PHAM MINH HA
Textile Technology: TRAN MINH NAM

RESEARCH CENTRES AND INSTITUTES

Centre for Biotechnology: Dir LE VAN NHUONG
Centre for Inorganic Materials: Dir LA VAN BINH
Centre for Polyester Technology: Dir TRAN VINH DIEU
Institute of Physical Engineering: Dir NGUYEN XUAN CHANH

TRUONG DAI-HOC TONG-HO'P HANOI (University of Hanoi)

90 Nguyen Trai St, Dong Da, Hanoi

Telephone: 243061
Telex: 411556
Fax: 243061

Re-founded 1956
State control
Academic year: September to July

Rector: Prof. Dr DAO TRONG THI
Vice-Rectors: Prof. Dr PHUNG HUU PHU, Prof. Dr TRAN VAN NHUNG, Prof. Dr NGUYEN HUU XY, Prof. Dr DANG UNG VAN

Number of teachers: 800
Number of students: 10,000
Library of 800,000 vols, 3,000 periodicals

The University engages in research on natural resources, and theoretical and applied research in related fields.

Publication: *Tạp Chí Khoa Học* (Scientific Journal).

Faculties: mathematics/mechanics/informatics, physics, chemistry, biology, geography and geology, philosophy, economics, law, history, journalism, philology, foreign languages (Russian, French, English, Chinese), Vietnamese language (for foreigners).

Research centres: applied microbiology, mycology, environment, scientific equipment, industrial mineralogy, Asia Pacific studies, co-operative Vietnamese studies, international cultures, foreign languages.

UNIVERSITY OF HO CHI MINH CITY

227, Nguyen van Cu St, 5th District, Ho Chi Minh City

Telephone: (8) 353193
Fax: (8) 222360

Founded 1977, university status *c.* 1990
State control
Academic year: September to July

Rector: Prof NGUYEN NGOC GLAO
Vice-Rectors: NGUYEN VAN DEN, NGUYEN THANH HUONG

Number of teachers: 500
Number of students: 8,000

Faculties of mathematics, physics, chemistry, biology, geology, geography, literature and linguistics, history, economics, philosophy, English, French, Russian, librarianship, law, oriental studies.

RESEARCH CENTRES

Centre for Viet Nam and South-East Asia Studies
Centre for Foreign Languages
Centre for Computer Science
Centre for Plants and Breeding Research
Centre for Applied Chemistry
Centre for Applied Biology
Centre for Scientific and Technical Creativity
Centre for Natural Resources and Environmental Studies
Centre for Electronics
Centre for Materials Technology

UNIVERSITY OF HUE

SRV, 03 Le Loi, Hue, Binh Tri Thien Province

Founded 1957, university status 1988

Rector: THANH NGUYEN

There are eight faculties.

Colleges

GENERAL

Da Lat College: Da Lat, Lam Dong Province; there are 5 faculties.

Tay Nguyen College: Dai hoc Tay, Buon Ma Thuot, Daclak Province; tel. 52290; f. 1977; animal sciences, medicine, forestry and agriculture; 198 teachers; library of 32,000 vols; Dir Dr Y NGONG NIE KDAM; publ. *Tay Nguyim Scientific Journal* (monthly).

AGRICULTURE, FORESTRY AND MARINE PRODUCTS

Hanoi Agricultural University No. 1: Gia Lam District, Hanoi; tel. 271654; telex 412262; fax 263243; f. 1956; 500 teachers, 800 students; library of 10,000 vols; Rector Prof. CU XUAN DAN; publ. *Agricultural Science Information* (monthly bulletin).

Agricultural University No. 2: Viet Yen District, Ha Bac Province; there are 5 faculties.

Agricultural University No. 3: Thai Nguyen City, Bac Thai Province; there are 4 faculties.

University of Agriculture and Forestry: Thu Duc District, Ho Chi Minh City; tel. 966780; fax 960173; f. 1959; 320 teachers; library of 66,000 vols; Rector Prof. DUONG THANH LIEM.

University of Fisheries: 2 Nguyen Dinh Chieu, Nhatrang City, Khanh Hoa Province; tel. (58) 831145; fax (58) 831147; f. 1959; faculties of Marine Mechanics, Navigation and Marine Exploitation, Aquaculture, Marine Products Processing, and Fishery Economics; 180 teachers; 7,000 students; library of 18,000 vols, 500 periodicals; Rector Prof. Dr NGUYEN TRONG CAN; Vice-Rectors Prof. Dr NGUYEN TRONG NHO, Prof. PHAN NGOC DIEP; publ. a fisheries journal (4 a year).

College of Forestry: Dong Trieu District, Quang Ninh Province; there are 5 faculties.

ART AND SOCIAL ARTS AND CONSERVATOIRES

College of Law: Thuong Tin, Ha Son Binh Province.

College of Stage Arts and Cinematography: 33 Hong Hoa Tham St, Hanoi.

Conservatoire of Hanoi: O Cho Dua, Hanoi.

Conservatoire of Ho Chi Minh City: 112 Nguyen Du St, District 1, Ho Chi Minh City; tel. (8) 2992362; fax (8) 220916; f. 1956; theory, composition, conducting, singing, national and orchestral instruments, electric instruments; 136 teachers, 600 students; Dir Prof. Dr QUANG HAI.

Hanoi Cultural Workers College: O Cho Dua, Hanoi; there are 4 faculties.

Ho Chi Minh City University of Fine Arts: 5 Phan Dang Luu St, Ho Chi Minh City; tel. (8) 412691; fax (8) 412695; f. 1913; painting, sculpture, graphic arts, graphic design; 58 teachers; Dir Prof. NGUYEN VAN HOANG.

Viet Nam College of Fine Arts: Yet Kieu St, Hanoi; there are 3 faculties.

ECONOMICS AND PLANNING

College of Commerce: Tu Liem District, Hanoi; there are 5 faculties.

Foreign Trade College: Tu Liem District, Hanoi; there are 3 faculties.

Hanoi College of Economics and Planning: Nam Bo St, Hanoi; there are 12 faculties.

Hanoi University of Finance and Accountancy: Tú Liêm, Hanoi; tel. (4) 343326; f. 1963; training graduate and postgraduate cadres in public finance, corporate finance, money and credit and accountancy, insurance and auditing; 350 teachers; 20,000 students (5000 full time, 15,000 part-time); library of 25,000 vols; Rector Prof. Dr HOXUÂN PHUONG; publ. *Finance and Accountancy* (quarterly).

Ho Chi Minh City College of Economics: 17 Duy Tan St, Ho Chi Minh City; there are 6 faculties.

Ho Chi Minh City College of Finance: 229 Dong Khoi St, Ho Chi Minh City; there are 3 faculties.

MEDICINE, PHYSICAL EDUCATION AND SPORTS

College of Physical Training and Sports: Tu Son, Bac Ninh Province; there are 8 faculties.

Hanoi College of Pharmacy: 13 Le Thanh Tong St, Hanoi; tel. 54539; f. 1961; 160 teachers; 780 students; library of 20,000 vols; Dean Prof. Dr NGUYEN THANH DO.

Hanoi Medical School: Ton That Tung St, Dong Da, Hanoi; tel. (4) 8524752; fax (4) 8525115; f. 1902; graduate and postgraduate courses; 926 staff; library of 50,000 vols; Dir Prof. TON THAT BACH.

University of Medicine and Pharmacy of Ho Chi Minh City: 217 An Duong Vuong St, District 5, Ho Chi Minh City; tel. (8) 8558411; fax (8) 8552304; f. 1947; faculties of medicine, pharmacy, dentistry.

Bac Thai Medical College: Thai Nguyen City, Bac Thai Province; tel. (28) 52671; fax (28) 55710; f. 1968; there are 22 faculties; library of 25,000 vols; Rector Dr HOANG KHAI LAP.

Thai Binh College of Pharmacy: Thai Binh, Thai Binh Province; there are 33 faculties.

TECHNICAL AND INDUSTRIAL

Da Nang Polytechnic: Hoa Vang, Quang Nam-Da Nang Province; there are 7 faculties.

Ho Chi Minh City University of Technology: 268 Ly Thuong Kiet St, Ho Chi Minh City; tel. 652442; fax 653823; f. 1957; faculties of basic sciences, electrical engineering, civil engineering, chemical engineering, mechanical engineering, applied geology, industrial management, industrial art design; 550 teachers; 16,641 students; library of 45,000 vols; Rector Prof. Dr TRUONG MINH VE; Sec.-Gen. Prof. Dr DAO VAN LUONG.

College of Water Conservancy: Dong Da Precinct, Hanoi; there are 6 faculties.

Geology and Mining College: Tu Liem District, Hanoi; there are 8 faculties.

Hanoi College of Architecture: Kilometre No. 7, Hanoi-Ha Dong Highway; there are 4 faculties.

Hanoi University of Civil Engineering: 5 Giaiphong Road, Hanoi; tel. and fax 691684; f. 1966; construction engineering, engineering economics, technology of construction materials, hydraulic engineering, architecture and urban planning, bridges and roads, machinery and equipment for construction, environmental engineering, offshore engineering; postgraduate dept; informatics centre; 495 teachers; library of 380,000 vols; Rector Prof. NGUYEN NHU KHAI.

Ho Chi Minh City College of Architecture: 196 Nguyen Thi Minh Khai St, Ho Chi Minh City; there are 2 faculties.

Industrial Decorative Arts College: O Cho Dua, Hanoi; f. 1965; there are 5 faculties.

Viet Nam Maritime University: 484 Lach Tray St, Haiphong; tel. (31) 845930; fax (31) 845117; f. 1956; there are 10 faculties; br. in Ho Chi Minh City; Rector Prof. Dr LE DUC TOAN.

Posts and Telecommunications Training Center No. 1: Km M.10, Hadong Rd, Ha Tay, Hanoi; tel. (4) 8544256; fax (34) 825523; f. 1953; library of 7,000 vols; Dir Dr NGUYEN KIM LAN.

Road and Rail Transport College: Tu Liem District, Hanoi; there are 5 faculties.

Thai Nguyen College of Industrial Technology: Thai Nguyen, Bac Thai Province; there are 5 faculties.

YEMEN

Libraries and Archives

Aden

Miswat Library: Aden; previously called Lake Library; administered by Aden Municipality; *c.* 30,000 vols, in English, Arabic and Urdu.

Teachers' Club Library: Aden; over 2,000 vols.

Travelling Library: Aden; ancillary to Miswat Library; administered by Aden Municipality; *c.* 9,500 vols, in English and Arabic.

San'a

British Council Library: POB 2157, Beit al-Mottahar, Harat Handhal, San'a; tel. 275584; fax 274128; 10,000 vols, 36 periodicals.

Library of the Great Mosque of San'a: San'a; f. 1925; the collection of 10,000 MSS and printed vols is not at present accessible to the public; Librarian Zaid Bin Ali Enan.

Universities

UNIVERSITY OF ADEN

POB 6312, Khormaksar, Aden

Telephone: 234433
Fax: 234426
E-mail: adenuniversity@y.net.ye

Founded 1975
State control
Languages of instruction: Arabic and English
Academic year: September to June

Rector: Prof. Dr Saleh Ali Basurra
Vice-Rector for Academic Affairs: Assoc. Prof. Dr Saeed Abdo Gabali
Vice-Rector for Scientific Research and Postgraduate Studies: Dr Ahmed Ali Al-Hamdani
Vice-Rector for Students' Affairs: Assoc. Prof. Dr Abdul Aziz Saleh bin Habtoor
General Registrar: Abdul Rahman Mahfooth
General Director for Libraries, Documentation and Translation: Rasheed A. Hameed A. Samad
General Director for the Rector's Office: Nabeel A. Kareem Makawee
General Director for Planning and Development: Abdelmageed Abdulla Arasi
Number of teachers: 750
Number of students: 15,000

Publications: *Law*, *Agricultural Journal* (annually), *Saba* (2 a year), *The Economist*, *The Yemen Engineer* (annually), *Theses* (6 a year), *Theses Summaries and Abstracts* (2 a year), *Al-Yemen Magazine*, *Journal of Natural and Applied Sciences* (2 a year), *Journal of Human and Social Sciences* (2 a year).

DEANS

Educational Affairs: Asst Prof. Dr Abdul Rahman Sabri
Faculty of Arts: Assoc. Prof. Dr Khadri Abdul Baqi Ahmed
Faculty of Law: Assoc. Prof. Dr Saleh Ba-Muallem
Faculty of Economics and Administration: Asst Prof. Ahmed Saleh Munasser
Faculty of Agriculture: Assoc. Prof. Dr Hussein A. Rahman Alkaff
Faculty of Engineering: Asst Prof. Ahmed Saeed Saroor
Faculty of Medicine: Assoc. Prof. Dr Hussain M. Alkaff
Faculty of Education (Zingibar): Asst Prof. Dr Ahmed Saleh Haidara
Faculty of Education (Sabr): Asst Prof. Dr Mehdi A. Salam
Faculty of Education (Mukalla): Assoc. Prof. Dr Muhammed Ahmed Falhoom
Faculty of Education (Aden): Asst Prof. Ali Abdulla Fakhri
Faculty of Education (Shabwa): Asst Prof. Dr Saeed Ba-Faiyad
Faculty of Petroleum and Minerals: Asst Prof. Ali Mugawar

SAN'A UNIVERSITY

POB 1247, San'a

Telephone: 200514
Telex: 2468

Founded 1970
State control; financial support from Kuwait
Languages of instruction: Arabic and English
Academic year: October to June

Rector: Dr Abdul Aziz S. Al Maghaleh
Vice-Rector: Dr Abubaker Al Qirbi
Assistant Vice-Rector: Dr Ahmed O. Bam-ashmus
Dean of Student Affairs: Dr Abdo A. Othman
Librarian: Ahmad Al Yadumi
Number of teachers: 332
Number of students: 10,715

Publications: faculty research journals.

DEANS

Faculty of Arts: Dr Ahmed Al Saydi
Faculty of Law and Sharia: Dr Abdul Munim Al Badrawi
Faculty of Commerce and Economics: Dr Nasser Aulaqi
Faculty of Science: Dr Ali Al Shukai
Faculty of Education: Dr Mohamed Al Khader
Faculty of Medicine and Health Sciences: Dr Abdallah Al-Huraybi
Faculty of Engineering: Dr Awad Saleh
Faculty of Agriculture: Dr Nasser Aulaqi (acting)

HEADS OF DEPARTMENTS

Faculty of Arts:
- Arabic: Dr W. Romia
- English: Prof. Dr K. S. Misra
- History: Dr S. M. Salem
- Geography: Dr A. H. Rasol
- Philosophy: Dr A. Salam Nor Al Deen
- Islamic Studies: Dr H. Helwah
- Archaeology: Dr A. Noor Al Deen

Faculty of Science:
- Chemistry: Prof. Dr A. Al-Abbadi
- Biochemistry: Prof. Dr M. Ramadan
- Biology: Dr G. M. Hagag
- Mathematics: Dr M. A. Kandeel
- Geology: Dr H. Al Saturi
- Physics: Dr A. Farghali
- Oceanography: (vacant)

Faculty of Sharia and Law:
- Criminal Law: Dr A. A. Alafi
- Civil Law: Dr A. Al Badrawi
- Islamic Law: Dr H. Ismail
- Private International Law: Dr M. Al Sadawi
- Commercial Law: Dr K. Abu Saria
- Procedural Law: Dr N. Omar
- Public International Law: Dr H. Bazaraa

Faculty of Commerce and Economics:
- Accounting: Dr S. Isa
- Business Administration: Prof. K. Zatar
- Economics: Dr S. Abdul-Mabood
- Political Science: Dr A. Awda
- Statistics and Insurance: Dr A. Al Sayed

College

Kulliat Asshari'a Wa Alqanun (Faculty of Islamic Law): San'a; f. 1970.

YUGOSLAVIA

(Republics of Montenegro and Serbia)

Learned Societies

GENERAL

Crnogorska Akademija Nauka i Umjetnosti (Montenegrin Academy of Sciences and Arts): 81000 Podgorica, Rista Stijovića 5; tel. (81) 631-095; depts of Natural Sciences, of Social Sciences, of Arts; 37 mems; Pres. DRAGUTIN VUKOTIĆ; Sec.-Gen. MILINKO ŠARANOVIĆ; publs *Godišnjak CANU* (annually), *Glasnik* (Review), *Posebna izdanja* (Special Editions), *Posebni radovi* (Special Works), *Bibliografije* (Bibliographies), *Istorijski izvori* (Historical Issues), *Naučni skupovi* (Symposia), *Zbornici radova* (Works).

Matica srpska (Serbian Society): 21000 Novi Sad, Matice Srpske 1; tel. (21) 27-622; fax (21) 28-901; f. 1826; literary, scientific, cultural and publishing society; 2,000 mems; library of 1,000,000 vols; Pres. BOŠKO PETROVIĆ; Sec. DRAGAN STANIĆ; publs *Letopis Matice srpske* and *Proceedings* (in the following series: natural sciences, history, social sciences, literature and language, philology and linguistics, art, Slavonic studies, theatre and music).

Srpska Akademija Nauka i Umetnosti (Serbian Academy of Sciences and Arts): 11000 Belgrade, Knez Mihailova 35, POB 366; tel. (11) 187-144; fax: (11) 182-825; f. 1886; sections of Natural Sciences and Mathematics (Sec. STEVAN KOIČKI), Technical Sciences (Sec. PETAR MILJANIĆ), Medical Sciences (Sec. IVAN SPUŽIĆ), Literature and Language (Sec. PREDRAG PALAVESTRA), Social Sciences (Sec. KOSTA MIHAILOVIĆ), Historical Sciences (Sec. BOŽIDAR FERJANČIĆ), Fine Arts (Sec. STANOJLO RAJIČIĆ); 116 mems, 42 corresp. mems; Pres. ALEKSANDAR DESPIĆ; Gen. Sec. MIROSLAV PANTIĆ; Exec. Sec. VLADIMIR DAVIDOVIĆ; publs *Godišnjak* (Yearbook), *Glas* (Review), *Posebna izdanja* (Monographs), *Spomenik* (Monument), *Srpski etnografski zbornik* (Serbian Ethnographic Collection), *Srpski dijalektološki zbornik* (Serbian Dialectology Collection), *Naučni skupovi* (Scientific Conferences), *Muzička izdanja* (Musical Editions), *Bulletin*, *Galerija* (Gallery), *Iz teorije prava* (Theory of Law), *Ekonomski zbornik* (Collection of Economic Works).

BIBLIOGRAPHY, LIBRARY SCIENCE AND MUSEOLOGY

Bibliotekarsko društvo Srbije (Library Association of Serbia): 11000 Belgrade, Skerlićeva 1; tel. (11) 451-242; telex 12208; fax (11) 452-952; f. 1947; Pres. DOBRIVOJE MLADENOVIĆ; Sec. VERA CRLJIĆ; publ. *Bibliotekar* (The Librarian, 2 a year).

Savez Muzejskih društava Jugoslavije (Federation of Museums Associations): Belgrade, Istorijski Muzej Srbije, Nemanjina 24/VII.

ECONOMICS, LAW AND POLITICS

Association of Jurists of Serbia: Belgrade, Proleterskih brigada 74; f. 1946; Pres. Prof. Dr MIODRAG ORLIĆ; publ. *Pravni život*.

Economists' Society of Serbia: Belgrade, Nusićeva 6/III, POB 490; f. 1944; Pres. BOGOLJUB STOJANOVIĆ; publ. *Ekonomika preduzeća* (monthly).

Jurists' Association of Yugoslavia: Belgrade, Proleterskih brigada 74, POB 179; tel. (11) 444-8459; f. 1947; 30,000 mems; Pres. Prof. Dr SLOBODAN PEROVIĆ; Sec.-Gen. Prof. Dr STEVAN LILIĆ; publ. *Arhiv*.

EDUCATION

Savez pedagoških društava Srbije (Federation of Pedagogical Societies of Serbia): 11000 Belgrade, Terazije 26; tel. and fax (11) 687-749; f. 1923, reorganized 1950 and 1977; 2,000 mems; Pres. MIRJANA MARKOVIĆ; Sec. VERA SPASENOVIĆ; publs *Nastava i vaspitanje* (Teaching and Education, 5 a year), *Pedagoška Biblioteka* (Pedagogical Library, occasionally).

Zajednica Universiteta Jugoslavije (Association of Yugoslav Universities): 11000 Belgrade, Palmotićeva 22; tel. (11) 334-524; f. 1957; science and higher education; 19 mem. universities; Pres. Prof. Dr DRAGUTIN RILKE; Sec.-Gen. Dr SULEJMAN RESULOVIĆ; publ. *University Today* (quarterly).

HISTORY, GEOGRAPHY AND ARCHAEOLOGY

Historical Society of Serbia: Belgrade, Faculty of Philosophy, Čika Ljubina 18–20; f. 1948; 1,500 mems; Pres. Prof. Dr LJUBOMIR MAKSIMOVIĆ; publ. *Istoriski glasnik* (2 a year).

Serbian Geographical Society: Belgrade, Studenski trg 3/III; f. 1910; 1,500 mems; library of 4,500 vols; Chair. Prof. Dr STEVAN M. STANKOVIĆ; Sec. BORKA RADOVANOVIĆ; publs *Bulletin* (2 a year), *Terre et Hommes* (annually), *Globus* (annually), *Editions Spéciales* (1 or 2 a year), *Mémoires, Géographique Actualité*.

LANGUAGE AND LITERATURE

Društvo za Srpski Jezik i Književnost (Society of Serbian Language and Literature): Belgrade University, Studenski trg 1; f. 1910; Pres. P. STEVANOVIĆ; Sec. D. PAVLOVIĆ; publ. *Pritozi za knjizevnost, jezik, istorija i folklor*.

PEN Montenegrin Centre: 81250 Cetinje, Njegoševa 7, POB 117; tel. (86) 21-303; f. 1990; Pres. PAVLE MIJOVIC; Sec. MLADEN LOMPAR; publ. *PEN Montenegro* (annually).

Serbian PEN Centre: 11000 Belgrade, Francuska 7; f. 1926, re-f. 1962; 83 mems; Pres. MIODRAG PERIŠIĆ; Sec. KOSTA ČAVOŠKI; publ. *Relations* (quarterly, in English, with Asscn of Serbian Writers).

Srpska književna zadruga (Serbian Literary Association): 11000 Belgrade, Srpskih vladara 19/I; tel. 330–305; f. 1892; publishing of literary, historical and other learned works; *c.* 2,500 mems; library of 12,000 vols; special collection of 19th-century periodicals; Pres. (vacant); Sec.-Gen. RADIVOJE KONSTANTINOVIĆ; publ. *Glasnik* (annually).

MEDICINE

Serbian Society for the Fight against Cancer: Belgrade 11000, Pasterova 14; tel. and fax (11) 656-386; e-mail ebrzakov@ubbg.etf.bg.ac.yu; f. 1927; 30,000 mems; Pres. Dr PREDRAG BRZAKOVIĆ; publ. *Bolje Sprečiti nego Lečiti* (The Best Cure is Prevention, quarterly).

NATURAL SCIENCES

Biological Sciences

Srpsko biološko društvo (Serbian Biological Society): 11000 Belgrade, Kneza Miloša 101/111; f. 1947; 800 mems; Pres. Prof. Dr RADOMIR KONJEVIĆ; Sec. KAĆA PAUNOVIĆ; publs *Arhiv bioloških nauka* (Archives of Biological Sciences), *Nauka i Priroda* (Science and Nature), *Bios*.

Mathematical Sciences

Society of Mathematicians of Serbia: Belgrade, Knez Mihailova 35; tel. (11) 638263; f. 1948; Pres. Dr DJORDJE KARAPANDŽIĆ; publ. *Matematički Vesnik* (quarterly).

Physical Sciences

Serbian Chemical Society: 11001 Belgrade, Karnegijeva 4, POB 462; f. 1897 to promote chemical research and education; 2,500 mems; Pres. Prof. Dr ŽIVORAD ČEKOVIĆ; Sec. Prof. Dr NIKOLA BLAGOJEVIĆ; publs *Journal* (monthly), *Hemijski pregled* (every 2 months).

Serbian Geological Society: Belgrade, Kamenička 6, POB 227; f. 1891; 500 mems; library of 3,500 vols; Pres. Dr NIKOLA PANTIĆ; publ. *Zapisnici srpskog geološkog društva* (Reports, annually).

TECHNOLOGY

'Nikola Tesla' Association of Societies for Promotion of Technical Sciences in Yugoslavia: Belgrade, POB 359; organizes an international festival of scientific and technical films, held every two years.

Union of Engineers and Technicians of Serbia: Belgrade, 7a Kneza Miloša; tel. 330067; f. 1945; 32 mem. organizations; Pres. R. ČOLIĆ; Sec. S. PANTOVIĆ.

Union of Engineers and Technicians of Yugoslavia: Belgrade, Kneza Miloša 9/II; tel. (11) 32-43-653; fax (11) 32-43-652; e-mail internet@eunet.yu; f. 1919; mem. assocs in most brs of engineering; Chair. Prof. Dr Ing. MIHAILO MILOJEVIĆ; Gen. Sec. Prof. Dr Ing. MILORAD TERZIĆ; publs *Tehnika* (6 a year), *It Bulletin* (6 a year).

Research Institutes

AGRICULTURE, FISHERIES AND VETERINARY SCIENCE

Institute for Agricultural Mechanization: Belgrade, Zemun, POB 41; f. 1947; 30 mems; library of 6,000 vols; Dir DJORDJE

DJURDJEVIĆ; publ. *Poljoprivredna Tehnika* (Agricultural Engineering, annually).

Institute for Plant Protection and the Environment: 11000 Belgrade, T. Drajzera 9, POB 936; tel. 660-049; f. 1945; depts of Phytopathology, Phytopharmacy, Biological Control, Toxicology and Environmental Protection; library of 7,000 books and 12,650 periodicals; Dir Dr DIMITRIJE MATIJEVIĆ; publ. *Zaštita bilja* (Plant Protection; quarterly).

BIBLIOGRAPHY, LIBRARY SCIENCE AND MUSEOLOGY

Jugoslovenski Bibliografsko-Informacijski Institut (Yugoslav Institute for Bibliography and Information): Belgrade, Terazije 26; tel. (11) 687-836; fax (11) 687-760; f. 1949; publishes the Bibliography of Yugoslavia, which includes books, pamphlets, music scores and articles of literary, scientific interest, philology, art and sport, translations and official publications; 50 mems; Dir Dr RADOMIR GLAVIČKI.

Republički Zavod za Zaštitu Spomenika Kulture (Institute for the Protection of Cultural Monuments): 81250 Cetinje, Bajova 150; tel. (86) 31-182; fax (86) 31-753; f. 1948; research, registration and protection of cultural property in Montenegro; library of 2,500 vols; Dir Dr ČEDOMIR MARKOVIČ; publ. *Starine Crne Gore* (annually).

Republički zavod za zaštitu spomenika kulture (Institute for the Protection of Cultural Monuments of Serbia): Belgrade, Božidara Adžije 11; tel. (11) 454-786; fax (11) 444-98-46; f. 1947; research, documentation, conservation and restoration, legal protection and maintenance of central registers of immovable cultural property; specialized training of personnel, publication of books and periodicals; Dir MILETA MILIĆ; Head, Architecture Dept BRANA STOJKOVIĆ PAVELKA; Head, Paintings Dept ZVONIMIR ZEKOVIĆ; Head, Physical and Chemical Laboratory (vacant); Head of Dept of History of Art, Ethnology and Archaeology MARKO OMČIKUS; Depts of Law, Documentation, Photographic Laboratory; library of 20,000 vols; publs *Saopštenja* (Communications), annuals, summaries in French, studies, research material, reviews.

ECONOMICS, LAW AND POLITICS

Institute of International Politics and Economics: 11000 Belgrade, POB 750, Makedonska 25; tel. (11) 3225-611; fax (11) 3224-013; f. 1947; international relations, world economy, international law, social, economic and political development in all countries; library of 250,000 vols; Dir MILENKO KREĆA; publs *International Problems* (4 a year), *Pregled evropskog zakonodavstva* (Survey of European Legislations, 6 a year).

FINE AND PERFORMING ARTS

Institute of Musicology of the Serbian Academy of Sciences and Arts: 11000 Belgrade, Knez Mihailova 35; tel. 639-033; f. 1948; history of Serbian and Yugoslav music, Balkan folk music and medieval church music, music theory and aesthetics; 7 mems; library of 5,500 vols; Dir D. STEFANOVIĆ; publs monographs.

HISTORY, GEOGRAPHY AND ARCHAEOLOGY

Arheološki Institut (Archaeological Institute): Belgrade, Knez Mihailova 35/IV; tel. (11) 637-191; fax (11) 180-189; e-mail biblioteka@ai.sanu.ac.yu; f. 1947; study of prehistoric, classical and medieval archaeology in the Central Balkan area; library of 13,000 vols, 22,000 vols of periodicals; Dir Dr MILOJL VASIĆ; publs *Starinar* (annually), *Djerdapske sveske – Cahiers des Portes de Fer.*

Istoriski Institut Crne Gore (Historical Institute): Podgorica, Naselje Kruševac.

MEDICINE

Institut za Istraživanje Mozga (Brain Research Institute): 85330 Kotor, Dobrota 66; tel. (82) 25-429; fax (82) 25-119; f. 1966; Dir Prof. NIKOLAS KOVAČEVIĆ; publ. *Studia Marina* (2 or 3 a year).

Zavod za zaštitu zdravlja Srbije (Institute of Public Health of Serbia) (formerly Institute of Hygiene): Belgrade, Dr Subotića 5; tel. (11) 685-476; fax (11) 685-735; e-mail info@batut .org.yu; f. 1924; library of 40,000 vols; Dir Asst Prof. Dr DRAGOLJUB DJOKIĆ; publ. *Glasnik* (2 a year).

NATURAL SCIENCES

Biological Sciences

Botanical Institute and Garden of the University of Belgrade: 11000 Belgrade, Takovska 43; tel. (11) 767-988; fax (11) 638-500; f. 1874; library of 7,000 vols; Dir Prof. Dr JELENA BLAŽENČIĆ; publ. *Bulletin* (annually).

Physical Sciences

Astronomska Opservatorija u Beogradu (Astronomical Observatory of Belgrade): Belgrade, Volgina 7; tel. (11) 419-357; fax (11) 419-553; f. 1887, re-formed 1932; astrometry, astrophysics; library of 13,100 vols; Dir M. S. DIMITRIJEVIĆ; publs *Bulletin, Publications.*

Hidrometeorološki Zavod Republike Srbije (Hydrometeorological Service of Serbia): 11000 Belgrade, Kneza Višeslava 66; Dir NIKOLA DUTINA.

Has attached:

Meteorološka opservatorija Beograd (Belgrade Meteorological Observatory): 11000 Belgrade, Bul. JNA 8; f. 1887; Chief Officer SLOBODAN HADŽIVUKOVIĆ; publ. *Observations Météorologiques à Belgrade.*

Seismological Institute: Belgrade, Tašmajdan, POB 351; f. 1906; Dirs Dr B. A. SIKOŠEK, Dr M. N. VUKAŠINOVIČ; 12 mems; publs *Annuaire macroséismique et microséismique, Bulletin mensuel, Studies.*

TECHNOLOGY

Institut za nuklearne nauke 'Vinča' (Vinča Institute of Nuclear Sciences): 11001 Belgrade, Vinča, POB 522; tel. (11) 4440-871; telex 11563; fax 4440-195; f. 1948; basic and applied research in natural, technological and nuclear sciences, and consulting and research programmes in physics, chemistry, physical chemistry, biology, technical sciences, nuclear energy, electronics, computing, material sciences; production and application of radio isotopes; information systems and data processing; library of 30,000 vols; Dir Gen. Dr MIROSLAV KOPEČNI.

Institut za Tehnologiju Nuklearnih i Drugih Mineralnih Sirovina (Institute for Technology of Nuclear and Other Mineral Raw Materials): 11000 Belgrade, Franše D'Epere 86, POB 390; tel. (11) 648-455; telex 11581; f. 1948; research and application of technology in the field of processing nuclear, metallic and non-metallic mineral raw materials; environmental protection; training; 168 staff; library of *c.* 3,600 vols, 30,000 periodicals; Dir-Gen. Dr RADE ĆOSOVIĆ.

Libraries and Archives

Belgrade

Arhiv Jugoslavije: 11000 Belgrade, Vase Pelagića 33, POB 65; tel. (11) 650-755; fax (11) 652-740; f. 1950; 14,000 vols; Dir JOVAN POPOVIĆ.

Arhiv Srbije: 11000 Belgrade, Karnegijeva 2; tel. 33-70-781; fax 33-70-246; f. 1900; history of Serbia; 75,000 vols; Dir MILORAD M. RADEVIĆ; publ. *Arhivski pregled* (1 a year).

Biblioteka grada Beograda (Belgrade City Library): Belgrade, Zmaj Jovina 1; tel. (11) 639-518; f. 1929; 400,000 vols, 399 MSS; Head SIMEON BABIĆ.

Biblioteka Srpske akademije nauka i umetnosti (Library of the Serbian Academy of Sciences and Arts): 11001 Belgrade, Knez Mihailova 35; tel. (11) 639-120; telex 72593; fax 182-825; e-mail admin@bib.sanu.ac.yu; f. 1842 by the Serbian Learned Society; information service, inter-library loan scheme; prepares bibliographies and edits special publications; 1,100,000 vols; Dir Dr NIKŠA STIPČEVIĆ.

Narodna biblioteka Srbije (National Library of Serbia): Belgrade, Skerlićeva 1; tel. (11) 451-242; telex 12208; f. 1832; 1,224,527 vols, 250,413 periodicals, 129,001 vols of newspapers, 329 old MSS, 75,022 MSS and archives, 89 incunabulae and 16,400 old and rare books; rich collection of diverse library and archive materials; federal copyright and deposit library; Dir MILOMIR PETROVIĆ; publs *Izveštaj o radu, Arheografski prilozi, Godišnjak, Srpska bibliografija, Stručna bibliotekarska literatura* (series), *Živa prošlost* (series), etc.

Univerzitetska biblioteka 'Svetozar Marković' (University Library 'Svetozar Marković'): Belgrade, Bulevar revolucije 71; tel. (11) 33-70-509; fax (11) 33-70-354; its forerunner was the library of the Serbian Lyceum (1844); centre of the network of university libraries in Serbia; 1,428,000 vols (books, periodicals, newspapers), 548 Serbian and other MSS 12th–18th centuries, 5,000 old documents; Head IVAN GADJANSKI.

Cetinje

Biblioteka Državnog muzeja Crne Gore (Library of the National Museum of Montenegro): Cetinje, Titov trg 7; f. 1926; over 20,000 vols.

Centralna narodna biblioteka Crne Gore (Central National Library of Montenegro): 81250 Cetinje, Pf. 57, Bulevar crnogorskih junaka 163; tel. (86) 31-143; fax (86) 31-726; e-mail jelena@ubtg.cis.cg.ac.yu; f. 1946; about 1,350,000 vols; special collection of MSS, maps, picture postcards, photographs, records, exhibition catalogues; Federal copyright and deposit library; Dir Dr ČEDOMIR DRAŠKOVIĆ; publ. *Bibliografski vjesnik.*

Kragujevac

Narodna biblioteka (Public Library): Kragujevac; f. 1866; about 50,000 vols.

Niš

Narodna Biblioteka 'Stevan Sremac' ('Stevan Sremac' Public Library): 18000 Niš, Dušana Kostića 9; tel. 22-060; collection of the Serbian Academy of Science and Art; library of 218,834 vols; Dir SRBOBRAN DJORDJEVIC.

Novi Sad

Arhiv Vojvodine: 21000 Novi Sad, Dunavska 35; tel. (21) 21-244; fax (21) 22-332; f. 1926; library of 30,000 vols; Dir PAVLE STANOJEVIĆ; publs *Naučno-informativna sredstva o arhivskoj gradji u arhivima Vojvodine* (Scientific information on the Vojvodina archives, quarterly), *Izveštaji o naučno-istraživačkom radu u inostranstvu* (Research reports from archives abroad).

Biblioteka Matice Srpske (Matica Srpska Library): 21000 Novi Sad, Ul. Matice srpske 1; tel. (21) 420-199; fax (21) 28574; e-mail bms@bms.ns.ac.yu; f. 1826 in Budapest, opened 1838 and transferred to Novi Sad in 1864; 865,000 books; 200,000 vols of periodicals, 17 incunabula, 600 manuscript books, 500 paleotype, 30,000 old and rare books, 475,000 units of special library material (maps, posters, leaflets, music records, cassettes, etc.); copyright and deposit library for Yugoslavia; regional information centre of Science and Technology Information Network; depository library for FAO and UNESCO; Dir MIRO VUKSANOVIĆ; publs incl. *Godišnjak Biblioteke Matice srpske* (Matica srpska Library Yearbook, annually), *Bibliografija knjiga u Vojvodini* (Bibliography of Books in Vojvodina, annually), *Vesti* (Newsletter, quarterly).

Podgorica

Biblioteka Istorijskog Instituta Crne Gore (Library of the Historical Institute of Montenegro): 8100 Podgorica, Naselje Kruševac; f. 1948; 38,000 vols.

Požarevac

Narodna biblioteka (Public Library): Požarevac; f. 1847; about 30,000 vols.

Priština

Biblioteka Popullore dhe Universitare e Kosovës (National and University Library of Kosovo): 38000 Priština, POB 136, 'Ramiz Sadiku' p.n.; tel. (38) 25-605; f. 1944; *c.* 600,000 vols; Dir BEDRI HYSA.

Sabac

Narodna biblioteka 'Žika Popovič' (Public Library 'Žika Popović'): 15000 Sabac, Masarikova 18; f. 1847; *c.* 200,000 vols.

Museums and Art Galleries

Belgrade

Etnografski muzej (Ethnographical Museum): Belgrade, Studentski trg. 13, p.p. 357; tel. (11) 328-18-88; fax (11) 621-284; f. 1901; library of 30,000 vols; Dir MITAR MIHIĆ; publ. *Glasnik etnografskog muzeja*.

Josip Broz Tito Memorial Centre: 11000 Belgrade, Užička 11-15; tel. 660-322; telex 11133; f. 1982 as a collection of museums and buildings connected with the life and work of Tito; Dir RANKO BUGARČIĆ.

Museum of Contemporary Art: 11070 Belgrade, Ušće Save b.b.; tel. (11) 145-900; fax (11) 2222-955; f. 1958; opened 1965; exhibitions of Yugoslav and foreign art; library of 4,500 vols, 22,000 catalogues; Dir RADISLAV TRKULJA; publ *World Art Critics* (1 a year).

Muzej grada Beograda (Belgrade City Museum): 11000 Belgrade, Zmaj Jovina St 1, POB 87; tel. 637-954; f. 1903; history of the city from prehistory to the present; depts of archaeology, numismatics, history, art, literature, science; library (15,580 vols, 300 rare books) and documentation centre; conservation laboratory; Dir BOŽIDAR ŠUJICA; publ. *Godišnjak Grada Beograda* (annually).

Muzej Nikole Tesle (Nikola Tesla Museum): Belgrade, Proleterskih brigada 51; tel. and fax (11) 433-886; e-mail ntmuseum@eunet.yu; f. 1952; life and work of Nikola Tesla; library of 1,570 vols, *c.* 150,000 documents which belonged to Nikola Tesla; Dir Dr BRANIMIR JOVANOVIĆ.

Muzej Pozorišne Umetnosti Srbije (Museum of Performing Arts of Serbia): 11000 Belgrade, Gospodar Jevremova 19; tel. (11) 626-630; fax (11) 628-920; e-mail mpus@eunet.yu; f. 1950; documents, photos, newspaper cuttings on the theatre, costumes, decorations, audiovisual documentation; library of *c.* 7,500 vols; Dir MIODRAG DJUKIĆ; publ. *Teatron* (4 a year).

Muzej primenjene umetnosti (Museum of Applied Arts): Belgrade, Vuka Karadžića 18; tel. (11) 626-841; fax (11) 629-121; f. 1950; ceramics, porcelain, glass, metalwork, jewellery, furniture, woodwork, textiles and costume, photography, book layout, architecture, design; library of 21,660 vols; Dir SVETLANA ISAKOVIĆ; publ. *Muzej primenjene umetnosti-Zbornik* (irregular).

Narodni muzej (National Museum): Belgrade, Trg Republike 1A; tel. (11) 624-322; fax (11) 627-721; f. 1844; archaeological collections and an art gallery (Yugoslav and foreign collections and a medieval art gallery); library of 45,000 vols; Dir JEVTA JEVTOVIĆ; publs *Zbornik, Numizmatičar, Kovčežić*, various catalogues.

Prirodnjački muzej u Beogradu (Belgrade Natural History Museum): Belgrade, Njegoševa 51, POB 401; tel. (11) 444-22-63; fax (11) 444-22-63 ext. 14; f. 1895; botanical, environmental, geological, mineralogical, palaeontological, petrological and zoological studies and collections; library of 61,000 vols; Dir Dr VOJISLAV VASIĆ; publ. *Bulletin* (separate series on biology and geology).

Vojni Muzej (Military Museum): Belgrade-Kalemegdan; f. 1878; military history of Yugoslav peoples; library of 15,500 vols; Dir Col MILOJE ŠĆEKIĆ; publ. *Vesnik* (annually).

Zeljeznicki Muzej (Railway Museum of Yugoslavia): Belgrade, 6 Nemanjina ul.; f. 1950; library of 20,000 vols; archives section being formed; Dir MILAN RADIVOJEVIĆ.

Cetinje

Narodni muzej Crne Gore (National Museum of Montenegro): 81250 Cetinje, Novice Cerovića b.b.; depts of history, ethnography, archaeology, arts; library of 30,000 vols; Dir PETAR ČUKOVIĆ; publ. *Glasnik Cetinjskih Muzeja*.

Njegošev muzej (Njegoš's Museum): Cetinje; local exhibits; Dir JANKO LEPIČIČ.

Kotor

Pomorski muzej (Maritime Museum): 81330 Kotor; f. 1900; 10,000 vols; Dir JOVAN MARTINOVIĆ; publ. *Godišnjak Pomorskog Muzeja u Kotoru* (Yearbook).

Novi Sad

Art Gallery of Matica Srpska: 21000 Novi Sad, Trg Galerija; tel. (21) 24-155; f. 1847; collection of Serbian art in Vojvodina from the end of the 17th century to the present; Dir LEPOSAVA ŠELMIĆ.

Muzej Vojvodine (Museum of Vojvodina): 21000 Novi Sad, Dunavska 35–37; tel. (21) 26766; fax (21) 25059; f. 1947; sections: archaeology, ethnology, history, applied art; library of 80,000 vols; Dir LJUBIVOJE CEROVIĆ; publs *Rad vojvodjanskih muzeja* (annually), *Posebna izdanja* (occasionally).

Subotica

Gradski muzej—Városi Múzeum: 24000 Subotica, Trg Slobode 1; tel. (24) 22-128; f. 1892; sections: archaeology, local history, art, ethnology (collections from Africa and Southeast Asia and Oceania), biology, coins (Hungarian and Roman); library of 12,000 vols; Dir M. A. MILKA MIKUSKA.

Universities

UNIVERZITET U BEOGRADU (University of Belgrade)

11001 Belgrade 6, Studentski trg 1

Telephone: (11) 635-153

Founded 1863; reorganized 1905 and 1954

Academic year: October to September

Rector: Prof. Dr DRAGUTIN VELIČKOVIĆ

Vice-Rectors: Prof. Dr DRAGAN KUBUROVIĆ, Prof. Dr DRAGOSLAV MLADENOVIĆ, Prof. Dr DJORDJE PAUNOVIĆ, DEJAN JOVANOVIĆ (student)

Secretary-General: SILVIA ZDRAVKOVIĆ

Librarian: IVAN GADJANSKI

Library: see Libraries

Number of teachers: 3,201

Number of students: 49,890

DEANS

Faculty of Agriculture: Prof. Dr V. KOLJAJIĆ
Faculty of Architecture: Prof. Dr M. RAKOČEVIĆ
Faculty of Biology: Prof. Dr I. RADOVIĆ
Faculty of Chemistry: Prof. Dr I. JURANIĆ
Faculty of Civil Engineering: Prof. Dr Ž. PERIŠIĆ
Faculty of Defectology: Prof. Dr P. IVANOVIĆ
Faculty of Economics: Prof. Dr M. ŽIŽIĆ
Faculty of Electrical Engineering: Prof. Dr B. LAZIĆ
Faculty of Forestry: Prof. Dr D. JOVIĆ
Faculty of Geography: Prof. Dr B. ATANACKOVIĆ
Faculty of Law: Prof. Dr M. PETROVIĆ
Faculty of Mechanical Engineering: Prof. Dr D. ZRNIĆ
Faculty of Medicine: Prof. Dr R. GRBIĆ
Faculty of Mining and Geology: Prof. Dr R. SIMIĆ
Faculty of National Defence: Prof. Dr D. VOJČIĆ
Faculty of Organizational Sciences: Prof. Dr P. JOVANOVIĆ
Faculty of Pharmacy: Prof. Dr S. SPASIĆ
Faculty of Philology: Prof. Dr S. GRUBAČIĆ
Faculty of Philosophy: Prof. (vacant)
Faculty of Physical Chemistry: (vacant)
Faculty of Physical Education: (vacant)
Faculty of Physics: (vacant)
Faculty of Political Sciences: Prof. Dr M. STOJKOVIĆ
Faculty of Stomatology: Prof. Dr D. BELOICA
Faculty of Technical Engineering, Bor: Prof. Dr N. MAGDALINOVIĆ
Faculty of Technology and Metallurgy: Prof. Dr V. MILENKOVIĆ
Faculty of Transport and Traffic Engineering: Prof. Dr V. ČOLIĆ
Faculty of Veterinary Medicine: Prof. Dr B. MARKOVIĆ

PROFESSORS

Faculty of Agriculture:

ANDRIĆ, J., Costs and Cost Accounting Methods
ANOJČIĆ, B., Veterinary Science
BABOVIĆ, M., Phytopathology
BOGAVAC, M., Farm Organization
BOGDANOVIĆ, V., Soil Microbiology
BOGOJEVIĆ, J., Zoology and Ecology
BOŽIĆ, D., General Agronomy
CRNOBRNJA, J., Financial Analysis
CVETKOVIĆ, R., Agroecology
ČANAK, M., Mathematics
ČAVOŠKI, D., Meat Technology
DANIČIĆ, M., Wine Technology
DJOROVIĆ, M., Marketing
DOBRIVOJEVIĆ, K., Entomology
DŽAMIĆ, R., Plant Physiology and Agrochemistry
EREMIĆ, M.. Economics
FURUNDŽIĆ, M., Farm Organization
GAJIĆ, I., Animal Science
GAJIĆ, Ž., Animal Science

GUGUŠEVIĆ-DJAKOVIĆ, M., Technology of Precooked Food
JAKOVLJEVIĆ, M., Soil Chemistry
JAKŠIĆ, M., Physical and Colloidal Chemistry
JELIĆ, M., Mathematics
JOKIĆ, A., Organic Chemistry
JOVANOVIĆ, B., Plant Breeding
JOVANOVIĆ, M., General Fruticulture
KILIBARDA, K., Sociology
KOLARSKI, D., Basic Nutrition
KOLJAJIĆ, V., Feed Science and Technology
KRNJAJIĆ, S., Entomology
KRSTIĆ, B., Farm Organization
KRSTIĆ-PAVLOVIĆ, N., Medicinal Plants
LAZAREVIĆ, LJ., Animal Selection
LOVIĆ, R., Viticulture
MILUTINOVIĆ, M., Fruit and Vine Breeding Selection
MIŠOVIĆ, M., Crop Production
MITROVIĆ-TUTUNDŽIĆ, V., Fish Production
MOŠORINSKI, N., Chemistry
NAKALAMIĆ, A., General Viticulture
NEDIĆ, M., Special Field Crop Production
NENADIĆ, N., Field Crop Production
NENIĆ, P., Agricultural Machinery
PANIĆ, M., Phytopathology
PAVASOVIĆ, V., Unit Operations
PAVEŠIĆ-POPOVIĆ, J., Field Crops
PAVLIČEVIĆ, A., Animal Nutrition
PERIĆ, V., Meat Processing
PEŠIĆ, M., Organic Chemistry
RADOJEVIĆ, R., Economics
RADOVANOVIĆ, R., Technology of Meat By-products
RAHOVIĆ, D., Fruticulture
RAIČEVIĆ, D., Agricultural Machinery
RANDJELOVIĆ, V., Agricultural Economics
RODIĆ, J., Financial Analysis
RUDIĆ, D., Land Drainage
SIMIĆ, J., Economic Systems
SIMOVA-TOŠIĆ, D., Entomology
STANKOVIĆ, J., Statistics
STANOJEVIĆ, D., Physics
STANOJEVIĆ, S., Meteorology and Climatology
STEVANOVIĆ, D., Agrochemistry and Fertilization
STOJADINOVIĆ, D., Principles of Economics
STOJANOVIĆ, M., Microbiology
STOJANOVIĆ, S., Pedology
ŠESTOVIĆ, M., Special Phytopharmacy
ŠINŽAR, B., Botany and Plant Ecology
ŠUTIĆ, M., Microbiology
TANČIĆ, N., Pedology
TODOROVIĆ, M., Thermodynamics
TODOROVIĆ, N., Meteorology and Climatology
TOŠIĆ, M., Agricultural Machinery
TOŠIĆ, M., Phytopathology
VELIČKOVIĆ, D., Biochemistry
VEREŠ, M., Food Canning
VITOROVIĆ, S., Agricultural Toxicology
VUKOJEVIĆ, M., Farm Organization

Faculty of Architecture:

CAGIĆ, P., Architectural Design
GRUJIĆ, M., Practical Art Education
GRUJIĆ, N., Descriptive Geometry
KEKOVIĆ, A., Theory of Architecture
KUJUNDŽIĆ, V., Laminated Timber Construction Design
LJUBOJEVIĆ, D., Practical Art Education
LOJANICA, M., Process of Design
MARTINKOVIĆ, K., Construction Design
MILJKOVIĆ, S., Urban Reconstruction
MLADENOVIĆ, D., Urban Techniques and Composition
NEŠKOVIĆ, J., History and Conservation
PEROVIĆ, M., Contemporary Architecture
RADOJEVIĆ, A., Architectural Draughtsmanship
STJEPANOVIĆ, A., Architectural Design of Housing
VULOVIĆ, P., Architectural Design
ZUROVAC, J., Seismic Constructions
ŽIVADINOVIĆ, M., Architectural Design

Faculty of Biology:

ANDJELKOVIĆ, M., Genotoxicology
BLAZENČIĆ, J., Systematics of Algae, Fungi and Lichens
CULAFIĆ, LJ., Plant Physiology
CURČIĆ, B., Animal Development
DAVIDOVIĆ, V., Comparative Physiology
KONJEVIĆ, R., Plant Physiology
KRUNIĆ, M., Comparative Morphology and Systematics of Invertebrates
MARINČEK, M., General and Systematic Zoology
MARINKOVIĆ, D., Genetics
MARTINOVIĆ, J., Neurophysiology and Neurochemistry
RADOVANOVIĆ, J., Cytology and Histology
SAVIĆ, A., Principles of Molecular Biology
SAVIĆ, D., Molecular Genetics
SAVIĆ, I., Animal Ecology and Zoogeography
SIMIĆ, D., Microbiology
TOPISIROVIĆ, LJ., Biochemistry
TUČIĆ, N., Theory of Evolution

Faculty of Chemistry:

ČEKOVIĆ, Ž., Principles of Organic Chemistry
GAŠIĆ, M., Organic Chemistry
MILOSAVLJEVIĆ, S., Structure Determination by Instrumental Methods
MILOVANOVIĆ, G., Analytical Chemistry, Separation Methods
PASTOR, T., Analytical Chemistry, Instrumental Analysis
VUČETIĆ, J., Biochemistry

Faculty of Civil Engineering:

AĆIĆ, M., Concrete Structures
ANAGNOSTI, P., Geotechnical Engineering
ANDJUS, V., Roads and Airports
AVAKUMOVIĆ, D., Irrigation and Drainage
BATINIĆ, B., Hydraulics
CVETANOVIĆ, A., Pavement Engineering
DJORDJEVIĆ, B., Hydraulic Engineering
JOKSIĆ, D., Photogrammetry
KONTIĆ, S., Geodesy
MAKSIMOVIĆ, Č., Fluid Mechanics
MALETIN, M., Roads and Airports
MIĆIĆ, V., Mathematics
MURAVLJOV, M., Testing of Materials
MUŠKATIROVIĆ, D., River Hydraulics, Inland Navigation and Ports
NIKOLIĆ, D., Structural Analysis, Statics of Structures
PAKVOR, A., Concrete Structures
PERIŠIĆ, Ž., Concrete Structures
PETROVIĆ, P., Hydraulic Engineering Structures
PETROVIĆ-LAZAREVIĆ, S., Economics
PRAŠČEVIĆ, Ž., Management and Technology of Building
RANKOVIĆ, S., Structural Analysis, Statics of Structures
SEKULOVIĆ, M., Theory of Structures
VUKMIROVIĆ, V., Hydrology

Faculty of Defectology:

BOJANIN, S., Neuropsychology with Re-educative Methods
BRAJOVIĆ, LJ., Audiology
BUKELIĆ, J., Social Psychiatry
ĆORDIĆ, A., Pedagogy of the Mentally Retarded
DIKIĆ, S., Pathology of Sight
DJURIČIĆ, Z., Sociology
IVANOVIĆ, P., Principles of Defectology
JAKULIĆ, S., Professional Rehabilitation of the Mentally Retarded
JAŠEVIĆ, Ž., Criminology
JOVANOVIĆ, T., Medical Psychology
KANDIĆ-POPOVIĆ, Z., Criminal Law
KRAJINČANIĆ, B., Clinical Genetics
LUKIĆ, M., Ethics
MACIĆ, D., Education
MITROVIC, M., Rehabilitation and Sight Correction
STAKIĆ, D. J., Resocialization
STEFANOVIĆ, B., Ophthalmology
STOŠLJEVIĆ, L., Methods of Work with Physically Disabled Children
ŠPADIJER-DŽINIĆ, J., Social Pathology
VLAJIĆ, Ž., Audiology
ŽIVKOVIĆ, M., Psychology of Persons with Speech Disorders

Faculty of Economics:

ADAMOVIĆ, LJ., International Economic Relations I
ALEKSIĆ, P., Sociology
BARALIĆ, Ž., Cost Accounting and Analysis in Commerce
ČIROVIĆ, M., Monetary Economy
CVIJETIĆ, L., Economic History
DINIĆ, J., Economic Geography
DRAGIŠIĆ, D., Political Economy
DRAŠKIĆ, M., International Business Law
EREMIĆ, M., Economic Statistics
KONSTANTINOVIĆ, G., Microeconomic Analysis
KORAĆ, M., Contemporary Economic Theories under Socialism
KOVAČ, O., Foreign Trade Economics
KOVAČEVIĆ, M., Accounting II
KOVAČEVIĆ, ML., Foreign Trade-Organization and Performance
KRASULJA, D., Business Finance and Financial Analysis
LEKIĆ, M., Economic Geography
MADŽAR, LJ., Theory and System of Planning
MARSENIĆ, D., Economics of Yugoslavia
MILISAVLJEVIĆ, M., Planning and Development Policy
PAVLOVIĆ, M., Political Economy
PERIĆ, A., Finance II
PETKOVIĆ, V., Sociology
PILIĆ, V., Marx's Method of Economic Analysis
PJANIĆ, Z., Theory and Policy of Prices
POPOVIĆ, B., Economics of Associated Labour
RADIĆ, M., Agricultural Economics
RADUNOVIĆ, D., Economics of Trade
RAKOČEVIĆ, K., Mathematics I
RALEVIĆ, R., Financial and Actuarial Mathematics
RANKOVIĆ, J., Theory and Analysis of Balances
RAŠKOVIĆ, V., Sociology
SOŠKIĆ, B., Economic Doctrines
STOJANOVIĆ, D., Economic Mathematical Methods and Models
SUBOTIĆ, N., Business Law
TOURKI, M., Mathematical Methods and Models
TRIČKOVIĆ, V., Market Research
UNKOVIĆ, S., Economics of Tourism
UROŠEVIĆ, S., Technology
VUČENOVIĆ, V., Theory and Methodology of Self-Managing Decision-making
ZEČEVIĆ, T., Theory of Sampling and Planning of Experiments
ZEKOVIĆ, V., Economics of Industry
ŽIŽIĆ, M., Outlines of Statistical Analysis

Faculty of Electrical Engineering:

ÇVETKOVIĆ, D., Mathematics
ĆALOVIĆ, M., Power System Analysis and Control
DJORDJEVIĆ, A., Microwave Theory and Technology
DRAGOVIĆ, M., Electromagnetic Field Theory
DRAJIĆ, D., Statistical Communication Theory
IĆEVIĆ, D., Sociology and Economics
JANIĆ, R., Mathematics
JOVANOVIĆ, M., Electrical Plants
KALIĆ, DJ., Electrical Machines
LACKOVIĆ, I., Mathematical Analysis
LAZAREVIĆ, I., Mathematics
MARINČIĆ, A., Telecommunications
MARJANOVIĆ, S., Electronics
MATAUŠEK, M., Process Identification and Control
MIKIČIĆ, D., Mechanics and Hydraulics
NAHMAN, J., Electrical Energy Transmission
PAUNOVIĆ, DJ., Radio-engineering
PETROVIĆ, D., Electrical Machines

Petrović, G., Digital and Computer Communications
Petrović, M., Electromechanical Energy Conversion
Popović, B., Electromagnetic Field Theory
Pravica, P., Electroacoustics
Savić, M., High-voltage Equipment and Networks
Simić, N., Radio Relay Links
Stanić, B., Physics
Stanković, D., Principles of Meteorology, Sensors
Stanković, S., Control Systems
Stojanović, Z., Telecommunications
Stojić, M., Control Systems
Teodosić, V., Nuclear Engineering
Tošić, D., Numerical Analysis
Vasić, P., Mathematics
Velašević, D., Systems Programming
Zatkalik, J., Radar Theory and Systems
Zlatanović, M., Plasma Technology
Živković, D., Computer-based Control Systems

Faculty of Forestry:

Aleksov, I., Organization of Production
Banković, S., Dendrometry
Dimitrijević, M., Principles of Arts
Djorović, M., Agricultural Land Reclamation
Djukanović, M., Environmental Protection
Gburčik, P., Forest Ecoclimatology
Jevtić, Lj., Flood Control and Forest Reclamation
Jović, D., Forest Management
Jović, N., Forest Pedology
Kršljak, B., Machines and Tools in Wood Processing
Lalić, M., Forest Transportation Vehicles
Macura, V., Town Planning
Malešević, J., Mathematics
Marković, Z., Marxism and Self-Management
Mijanović, O., Floriculture
Miljković, J., Particle-boards, Fibre-boards and Wood-plastic Masses
Nikolić, M., Sawmill Wood Processing
Nikolić, M., Veneer and Veneer Boards
Nikolić, S., Forest Utilization
Petković, S., Hydraulics with Hydrology
Popović, M., Hydrogeology, Geomorphology
Potrebić, M., Wood Constructions
Redžić, A., Economics of Wood Industry
Stamenković, V., Increment Study
Stojanović, Lj., Silviculture
Šašić, M., Forest Management
Šelmić, V., Wildlife Management
Šoškić, B., Properties of Wood
Todorović, T., Fundamentals of Geotechnics in Torrent Control
Tomanić, L., Forest Management
Tomić, Z., Forest Plant Communities
Trifunović, M., Mathematics
Vasić, M., Forest Protection

Faculty of Geography:

Gavrilović, D., Geomorphology
Gavrilović, Lj., Hydrology
Ilić, J., Economic Geography
Marković, M., Sociology
Perišić, M., Spatial Planning
Rakićević, T., Physical Geography
Ristić, K., Regional Geography
Stanković, S., Tourist Geography
Subotić, S., Tourist Geography

Faculty of Law:

Aleksić, Z., Criminology
Atanacković, D., Criminal Law
Avramović, S., History of Law
Basta, D., Philosophy of Law
Besarović, V., Commercial Law, Law of Intellectual Property
Brajić, V., Labour Law
Čavoški, K., Introduction to Law
Dimitrijević, V., International Public Law, International Relations
Jekić, Z., Criminal Procedure
Jevtić, D., National History of State and Law
Kavran, D., Administrative Law, Theory of Organization
Košutić, B., Introduction to Law
Kreća, M., International Public Law
Labus, M., Political Economy
Lazarević, Lj., Criminal Law
Lukić, M., Forensic Medicine
Marković, R., Administrative Law
Milić, V., General Sociology
Milojević, M., International Public Law, International Organizations
Orlić, M., Civil Law
Pak, M., International Private Law
Pečujlić, M., General Sociology
Perović, S., Civil Law
Petrović, M., Public Finance and Tax Law
Popović, D., Public Finance and Tax Law
Rajović, V., Civil Procedure
Stanković, O., Introduction to Civil Law, Real Estate
Stanković, V., Economic System of Yugoslavia
Stanojević, O., Roman Law
Stojanović, R., International Public Law, International Organizations
Šoškic, D., Political Economy
Šulejić, P., Insurance Law
Taboroši, S., Economic System of Yugoslavia
Trajković, M., Transportation Law
Vasiljević, M., Commercial Law, Transportation Law

Faculty of Mechanical Engineering:

Antić, M., Theory of Traction, Industrial Furnaces, Drying Plants, Locomotives
Banić, M., Strength of Materials and Structures
Borisavljević, M., Utilization of Motor Vehicles
Bulat, V., Scientific Labour Management
Deljer, S., Material Handling Machinery
Djaković, B., Chemical Engineering Equipment
Djordjević, V., Dynamics of Gases
Dragović, T., High-Speed Aerodynamics, Computer Technology
Džordžo, B., Ship Installations
Gajić, D., Aerodynamics Structure
Grujić, L., Discrete and Nonlinear Systems
Janićijević, N., Motor Vehicle Design
Jankov, R., Piston Compressors
Janković, D., Calculation of Motor Vehicles
Janković, S., Dynamics of Projectile Flight
Jojić, K., Strength of Materials
Josifović, M., Theory of Elasticity, Aeroelasticity
Jovanović, D., Scientific Labour Management
Jovanović, S., Engineering Economics
Jovanović, T., Quantitative Analysis Methods
Jovičić, M., Descriptive Geometry
Jovičić, M., Tools and Tooling
Kolendić, I., Internal Combustion Engines
Krsmanović, Lj., Turbomachines, Hydraulic Transmissions
Lovrić, D., National Defence
Mamuzić, Z., Mathematics
Manojlović, B., Engineering Materials
Marcikić, N., Aircraft Equipment
Marković, S., Railway Vehicles
Milačić, V., Machine Tools
Milinčić, D., Heat and Mass Transfer
Miljanić, P., Electrical Engineering
Milojković, B., Automatic Control, Linear Systems
Milović, P., Building and Mining Machinery
Novaković, V., Agricultural Machinery
Ostrić, D., Metal Structures
Pantelić, T., Theory of Mechanisms
Pejović, S., Hydraulic Installations
Pilić, B., Sociology and Economics
Pivko, S., Engineering Mechanics
Popović, D., Factory Layout, Processing Apparatus, Operations Equipment
Protić, Z., Hydraulic Machinery
Radosavljević, L., Engineering Mechanics, Theory of Oscillations
Radovanović, M., Fuels and Lubricants
Ristić, M., Nuclear Engineering
Saljnikov, V., Hydromechanics, Fluid Mechanics
Šašić, M., Pipe Conveyance
Šolaja, V., Machine Tools
Stanić, J., Engineering Metrology, Metal Working Processes
Stanojević, D., Aircraft Design and Construction
Stojanović, D., Steam Turbines, Power Plant Installations
Stojanović, Ž., Pumps, Compressors and Fans
Todorović, B., Heating and Air Conditioning
Todorović, J., Calculation and Testing of Motor Vehicles
Trifunović, T., Internal Combustion Engine Testing
Urošević, M., Heating and Ventilating
Verčon, J., Lubrication Techniques
Veriga, S., Machine Elements
Vesović, M., Railway Engineering
Voronjec, D., Basic Industrial Processes
Vujić, M., Jet and Rocket Engines, Jet Propulsion
Vujić, S., Refrigeration Engineering, Design of Air-Conditioning Equipment
Vušković, I., Hydraulic Machines, Engineering Metrology
Zarić, S., Automation of Production Processes
Živković, C. M., Internal Combustion Engines
Živković, S. M., Aircraft Design and Construction
Živojinov, J., Engineering Physics
Zrnić, N., Design and Construction of Ships

Faculty of Medicine:

Antić, R., Internal Medicine
Arambašić, M., Pathological Anatomy
Beleslin, D., Pharmacology
Blagojević, M., Ophthalmology
Budisavljević, M., Phthisiology
Bugarski, O., Chemistry
Bumbaširević, Ž., Orthopaedic Surgery
Conić, Z., Physical Medicine and Rehabilitation
Cvetković, M., Biochemistry
Čalić-Perišić, N., Paediatrics
Davidović, M., Biology
Đurić, D., Internal Medicine
Drndarski, K., Bacteriology
Funtek, M., Military Education
Gerzić, Z., Surgery
Glidžić, V., Surgery
Gospavić, J., Neuropsychiatry
Išvaneski, M., Pathological Anatomy
Japundžic, I., Biochemistry
Jokanović, D., Forensic Medicine
Jokanović, R., Paediatrics
Josipović, V., Internal Medicine
Jovanović, S., Anatomy
Kilibarda, M., Professional Diseases
Korać, D., Paediatrics
Kostić-Simonović, J., Physics
Krajinović, S., Epidemiology
Lalević, P., Surgery
Lambić, I., Internal Medicine
Marković, A., Surgery
Mićović, P., Social Medicine
Milanović, V., Sociology
Milosević, M., Pharmacology
Mladenović, D., Gynaecology
Morić-Petrović, S., Neuropsychiatry
Mršević, D., Histology
Najdanović, B., Internal Medicine
Nikolić, M., Neuropsychiatry
Pavlović, D., Surgery

PERIŠIĆ, S., Dermatology
PERIŠIĆ, V., Internal Medicine
PETROVIĆ, F., Medical Statistics
POPOVIĆ, S., Child Surgery
RADMANOVIĆ, B., Pharmacology
RADOJIČIĆ, B., Neuropsychiatry
RADULOVIĆ, B., Orthopaedic Surgery
RAKIĆ, C., Orthopaedic Surgery
RAKIĆ, LJ., Biochemistry
SAVIČ, D., Oto-Rhino-Laryngology
SAVIĆEVIĆ, M., Hygiene
ŠIMIĆ, B., Hygiene
ŠKEROVIĆ, D., Physiology
STEFANOVIĆ, B., Oto-Rhino-Laryngology
STEFANOVIĆ, D., Dermatology
ŞTEFANOVIĆ, P., Oto-Rhino-Laryngology
ŠULOVIĆ, V., Gynaecology
ŠUVAKOVIĆ, V., Infectious Diseases
TOMIĆ, M., Gynaecology
VARAGIĆ, V., Pharmacology
VUJADINOVIĆ, B., Surgery

Faculty of Mining and Geology:

ANDJELKOVIĆ, M., Historical Geology
CVETIĆANIN, R., Coal Deposits
DIMITRIJEVIĆ, M., Geological Mapping
DJORDJEVIĆ, V., Petrography
DRAŠKIĆ, D., Ore Processing
EREMIJA, M., Palaeogeography
FILIPOVIĆ, B., Hydrogeology
GENČIĆ, B., Underground Methods applied to Bedded Deposits
GRUBIĆ, A., Historical Geology
JANJIĆ, M., Engineering Geology
JANKOVIĆ, S., Prospecting of Ore Deposits
JOVANOVIĆ, P., Mine Development
JOVIČIĆ, V., Safety in Mines
KAČKIN, D., Mine Fans, Pumps and Compressors
KARAMATA, S., Petrogenesis
KRSTANOVIĆ, I., Crystallography
MAKSIMOVIĆ, Z., Geochemistry
MANOJLOVIĆ-GIFING, M., Elements of Ore Dressing
MARKOVIĆ, S., Geotectonics
MILOSAVLJEVIĆ, R., Mineral Dressing
MILOVANOVIĆ, D., Economic Geology
MITROVIĆ, J., Palaeozoology
NIKOLIĆ, P., General Geology
OBRADOVIĆ, J., Sedimentology
PANTIĆ, N., Palaeobotany
PARADANIN, L., Oil and Gas Field Development
PAVLOVIĆ, M., Palaeogeology
PETKOVIĆ, M., Prospecting of Ore Deposits
PETROVIĆ, B., Structural Geology
PROTIĆ, M., Petrology of Sedimentary Rocks
SIMONOVIĆ, M., Open-cast Mining Equipment
SPAJIĆ, O., Historical Geology
STEFANOVIĆ, D., Geophysical Prospecting
SUTIĆ, M., Elements of Civil Engineering
TERZIĆ, M., Petrology of Magmatic Rocks
TOPOLAC, Ž., Physics
VAKANJAC, B., Non-metallic Ore Deposits
VUKOVIĆ, M., Hydraulics

Faculty of National Defence:

ATANACKOVIĆ, Z., Political System of Yugoslavia
JOVIĆ, C. R., Defence and Protection
KANDIĆ, B. D., Introduction to Philosophy and Ethics
LUKIĆ, P., National and International Law of War
VOJČIĆ, A. D., Methodology of Defence and Protection

Faculty of Organizational Sciences:

BOGOSAVLJEVIĆ, S., Statistics
BOŽIĆ, V., Managerial Economics and Business Planning
ÇAMILOVIĆ, S., Personnel Management
ĆIRIĆ, V., Principles of Computer Programming
ČUPIĆ, M., Theory of Decision-Making
DAJOVIĆ, S., Mathematics
DULANOVIĆ, Z., Organization
FILIPOVIĆ, V., Marketing
GEREKE, Z., Ecology Management
JAUKOVIĆ, M., Management Information Systems
JOVANOVIĆ, P., Project and Investment Management
KRČEVINAC, S., Operations Research and Econometrics
LAZAREVIĆ, B., Information Systems
LEVI-JAKŠIĆ, M., Technology Management
MILIĆEVIĆ, D., Economics
MILIĆEVIĆ, V., Managerial Economics and Business Planning
MITROVIĆ, Ž., Quality Management
PEJOVIĆ, P., Numerical Analysis
PERIĆ, A., German and English Language
PETRIĆ, J., Operations Research
PETROVIĆ, B., Work Study
PETROVIC, M., Manpower Planning
RADENKOVIĆ, B., Simulation
RADOVIĆ, M., Production Systems
RAJKOV, M., Systems Dynamics
ROGLIĆ, V., French Language
STARČEVIĆ, D., Expert Systems
TERZIĆ, B., Russian Language
TODOROVIĆ, J., Production Management
VUJČIĆ, V., Mathematics
VUKOVIĆ, N., Statistics
ŽARKIĆ-JOKSIMOVIĆ, N., Accounting and Finance

Faculty of Pharmacy:

ALEKSIĆ, M., Sociology
BOGAVAC, M., Organic Chemistry
DJURIĆ, Z., Pharmaceutical Technology and Biopharmacy, Industrial Pharmacy and Cosmeticology
DRAŠKOVIĆ, B., Physics
GORUNOVIĆ, M., Pharmacognosy
HORVAT, J., Immunochemistry
JOVANOVIĆ, M., Pharmaceutical Technology and Biopharmacy, Industrial Pharmacy and Cosmeticology
KEČKIĆ, J., Mathematics
MAJKIĆ-SINGH, N., Medical Biochemistry, Clinical Enzymology
MIRIĆ, M., Bromatology
PETROVIĆ, M., Physiology
POKRAJAC, M., Pharmacokinetics
POPOVIĆ, A., Physiology
RADOVIĆ, Z., Physical Chemistry
RADULOVIĆ, D., Pharmaceutical Chemistry
STANKOVIĆ, B., Analytical Chemistry
STUPAR, M., Pharmaceutical Technology and Biopharmacy, Industrial Pharmacy and Cosmeticology
VUKOJEVIĆ, N., Organic Chemistry
ŽIVANOV-STAKIĆ, D., Pharmaceutical Chemistry
ŽIVANOVIĆ, P., Botany

Faculty of Philology:

BABIĆ, S., Hungarian Language and Literature
BOJOVIĆ, Z., History of Yugoslav Literature from the Renaissance to the Age of Enlightenment
BOZOVIĆ, R., Arabian Literature
BOZOVIĆ, Z., Russian Literature
BUGARSKI, R., Theory of Translation, English Language
DERETIĆ, J., Serbian Literature
DESIĆ, M., Serbian Language
DIMITRIJEVIĆ, N., Methodology of English Language Teaching
DJINDJIĆ, S., Turkish Language and Literature
DJORDJEVIĆ, R., English Language
DJUKANOVIĆ, J., German Language
GEORGIJEVSKI, H., Macedonian Literature
GORTAN-PREMK, D., Contemporary Serbo-Croat
GRUBAČIĆ, S., German Literature
HLEBEC, B., English Language
IRICANIN, G., German Language
JANKOVIĆ, V., Literary Criticism
JOVANOVIĆ, G., Polish Language
JOVANOVIĆ, M., Russian Literature
KLAJN, I., Italian Language and History of Language
KONSTANTINOVIĆ, R., French Literature
KOSTIĆ, V., English Literature
KRIVOKAPIĆ, M., German Literature
KRSTIĆ, D., Pedagogical Psychology
LEOVAC, S., 20th-century Serbian Literature
MAROJEVIĆ, R., Russian Language
MILINČEVIĆ, V., 19th-century Serbian Drama
MILOŠEVIĆ, N., Literary Criticism
MILOŠEVIĆ-DJORDJEVIĆ, N., Folk Literature
MITROVIĆ, M., Slovenian Literature
NESKOVIĆ, R., Introduction to Philosophy
NIKOLIĆ, M., Methods of Teaching Yugoslav Literature
PAVLOVIĆ SAMUROVIĆ, LJ., Spanish Language and Literature
PETKOVIĆ, N., 20th-century Serbian Literature
PETROVIĆ, S., Introduction to Literature
PETROVIĆ, S., Sociology of Culture and Art
PIPER, P., Russian Language
SIBINOVIĆ, M., Russian Literature and Theory of Translation
SIMIĆ, R., Contemporary Serbo-Croatian
STANKOVIĆ, B., Russian Language
STANOJČIĆ, Z., Contemporary Serbo-Croatian
STIPČEVIĆ, N., Italian Literature
STOJANOVIĆ, D., Literary Criticism
TANASKOVIĆ, D., Arabian Language
TARTALJA, I., Theory of Literature
TRIFUNOVIĆ, DJ., Medieval Literature
TRNAVČI, H., Albanian Language and Literature
TURKONI, S., Italian Literature
VUKOMANOVIĆ, S., History of Serbo-Croatian
ŽILETIĆ, Z., German Language

Faculty of Philosophy:

ARANDJELOVIĆ, J., General Methodology
BERGER, J., Methods of Clinical Psychology
BOJANOVIĆ, R., Psychology of Interpersonal Relations
BULATOVIĆ, R., Special Andragogy
CERMANOVIĆ-KUZMANOVIĆ, A., Classical Archaeology
ĆIRKOVIĆ, S., Medieval National History
CREPAJAC, LJ., Greek Language
CVETKOVIĆ, Z., Mathematics Teaching
DJORDJEVIĆ, J., Didactics
DJURIĆ, V., History of Medieval Art
DRAGIĆEVIĆ, C., Statistics in Psychology
FERJANČIĆ, B., Byzantology
FLAŠAR, M., Classical Literature
GUZINA, M., Industrial Psychology
HAVELKA, N., Social Psychology
IVIĆ, I., Developmental Psychology
JEREMIĆ, D., Aesthetics
JOVANOVIĆ, M., History of Modern Art
JOVANOVIĆ, V., Medieval Archaeology
KALIĆ, J., General Medieval History
KNEŽEVIĆ, S., World Ethnology
KORAĆ, V., History of Architecture
KOVAČEVIĆ, P., Psychometrics
KRESTIĆ, V., Modern History of Yugoslavia
KRON, A. Logic
MAKSIMOVIĆ, J., History of Medieval Art
MARJANOVIĆ, S., Pre-School Education
MIRKOVIĆ, M., Ancient History
OGNJENOVIĆ, P., General Psychology
PAVKOVIĆ, N., General Ethnology
PETKOVIĆ, S., History of Art of the New Era
PETRANOVIĆ, B., History of Yugoslavia
PETROVIĆ, DJ., Ethnology of Yugoslavia
PETROVIĆ, V., Psychotherapy and Counselling
POPOVIĆ, B., Psychology of Personality
POPOVIĆ, MIH., General Sociology
POPOVIĆ, MIL., Social Pathology
POTKONJAK, N., General Education Science
RADONJIĆ, S., General Psychology
RANKOVIĆ, M., General Sociology
ŠALABALIĆ, R., Latin Language

SAMARDŽIĆ, R., General History of the New Era
SAVIĆEVIĆ, D., Andragogy
SMILJANIĆ, V., Psychology of Development
SREJOVIĆ, D., Prehistoric Archaeology
STAJNBERGER, I., Engineering Psychology, Ergonomics
TEŠIĆ, V., History of Education
TUTUNDŽIĆ, S., Oriental Archaeology
VLAHOVIĆ, P., Ethnology of the Yugoslav People
VUČIĆ, L., Educational Psychology

Faculty of Physical Chemistry:

JOVANOVIĆ, A., Spectroscopy
PETRANOVIĆ, N., Thermodynamics
RIBNIKAR, S., Nuclear Chemistry
STAMATOVIĆ, A., Experimental Electronics
VESELINOVIĆ, D., Physical Chemistry
VUČELIĆ, D., Biophysical Chemistry

Faculty of Physical Education:

ALEKSIĆ, I., Hygiene
ALEXSIĆ, V., Association Football
DJORDJEVIĆ, D., Field Activities, Psychomotor Studies
ILIĆ, S., History of Physical Culture
KOTUROVIĆ, LJ., Kinestherapeutics
MATIĆ, M., Methodology of Schools
MATKOVIĆ, I., Swimming and Water Polo
MRVALJEVIĆ, D., Anatomy
OPAVSKI, P., Biomechanics
PETROVIĆ, D., Track and Field Athletics
PETROVIĆ, J., Gymnastics (Men)
POKRAJAC, B., Handball, Basketball
POPOVIĆ, S., Boxing, Wrestling and Judo
RADISAVLJEVIĆ, L., Dance
RADOJEVIĆ, J., Sports, Gymnastics (women)
STEFANOVIĆ, V., Pedagogy, Methodology of Recreation
STOJANOVIĆ, M., Human Developmental Biology and Introduction to Sports Medicine
TODOROVIĆ, B., Physiology
TOKOVIĆ, LJ., Common National Defence
TOMIĆ, D., Games and Sports

Faculty of Political Sciences:

BOŽOVIĆ, R., Sociology of Culture and Cultural Policy
BULAT, S., Introduction to Political Economy
ĆETKOVIĆ, V., General Sociology
DAMJANOVIĆ, M., Organization and Administration in Self-Management Society
FIRA, A., Constitutional Law
GUDAC, Ž., Contemporary Political History
JAKŠIĆ, S., Sociology of the Family
LAZIN, S., Social Psychology and Psychology of Political Behaviour
MARINKOVIĆ, R., Sociology of Local Communities
MARJANOVIĆ, J., Introduction to Political Science
MARKOVIĆ, D., Sociology of Work, Social Ecology
MATIĆ, M., Political Systems and Political Life
MILETIĆ, A., International Relations
MILOSAVLJEVIĆ, M., Social Pathology
MILOSAVLJEVIĆ, S., Methodology
MITROVIĆ, D., International Business Relations, International Private Law and International Commercial Law
NEDELJKOVIĆ, I., Theory of Social Work
PAVLOVIĆ, V., Political Sociology of Contemporary Society
PEJANOVIĆ, O., Contemporary Philosophy
PEŠIĆ, M., General Sociology
PODUNAVAC, M., Theory of Political Systems
PRIBIĆEVIĆ, B., Contemporary Labour Movements
PRNJAT, B., Sociology of Culture and Cultural Policy
RAČIĆ, O., International Law, International Organizations
RADOJKOVIĆ, M., Public Opinion and Mass Communication
RAKOČEVIĆ, Ž., Contemporary Political Economy
STANOVČIĆ, V., History of Political Theories
STOJKOVIĆ, M., Yugoslav Foreign Policy, Diplomacy and Diplomatic History
ŠTRAHINJIĆ, Č., Introduction to Law
ŠPADIJER, B., Socio-political System of Yugoslavia, Constitutional Law
ŠTAMBUK, V., Informatics and Cybernetics
TARTALJA, S., History of Political Theories
VASOVIĆ, V., Contemporary Political Systems
VESELINOV, D., Introduction to Political Economy
VUKMIRICA, V., Contemporary Economic Systems
ZEČEVIĆ, M., Normative Legal Proceedings, Constitutional Law
ŽIVANOV, S., Contemporary Labour Movements
ŽIVOTIĆ, R., Stylistics and Rhetoric

Faculty of Stomatology:

ANDJIĆ, J., Biochemistry
BELOICA, D., Children's and Preventive Dentistry
DIMITRIJEVIĆ, B., Maxillofacial Surgery
DJUKANOVIĆ, D., Oral Diseases
DOVIJANIĆ, P., Social Medicine
FILIPOVIĆ, V., Dental Diseases
JOJIĆ, B., Oral Surgery
KARADŽOV, O., Dental Diseases
KEZELE, D., Dental Diseases
KNAJTNER, I., Dermatovenereology
KOLAK, Ž., Dental Diseases
KOSOVČEVIĆ, M., Prosthodontics
KRSTIĆ, M., Prosthodontics
KUBUROVIĆ, D., Dental Diseases
LEKOVIĆ, V., Oral Diseases
MIJALKOVIĆ, D., Internal Medicine
MILENKOVIĆ, P., Physiopathology
PAJIĆ, M., Dental Diseases
PAP, K., Dental Diseases
PEROVIĆ, J., Oral Surgery
PESOVIĆ, G.
PETROVIĆ, V., Oral Surgery
PIŠČEVIĆ, A., Maxillofacial Surgery
POPOV, S., Physics
POPOVIĆ, V., Children's and Preventive Dentistry
SEDLECKI, S., Dental Diseases
SIMOVIĆ, V., Orthodontics
SINOBAD, D., Prosthodontics
SJEROBABIN, I., Maxillofacial Surgery
SOKOLOVIĆ, M., Oral Surgery
ŠUŠIĆ, D., Physiology
ŠĆEPAN, V., Microbiology
TERZIĆ, M., Pharmacology
TRIFUNOVIĆ, D., Prosthodontics
UNKOVIĆ, S., Anatomy
VUJOŠEVIĆ, LJ., Prosthodontics
VULOVIĆ, M., Children's and Preventive Dentistry
ZELIĆ, O., Oral Diseases

Faculty of Technical Engineering—Bor:

BUDIĆ, I., Ore Dressing Raw Minerals
DOSTANIĆ, Č., Industrial Plant in Processing Metallurgy
KOVAČEVIĆ, P., Elements of Mechanical Engineering
LJUBIĆ, Z., Surface Mining
MAGDALINOVIĆ, N., Ore Reduction in Minerals Processing
MARJANOVIĆ, R., Mechanics
MILIĆEVIĆ, Ž., Elements of Exploitation of Ore Deposits
MILJKOVIĆ, M., Accident Prevention (Labour Protection)
RISTIĆ, B., General and Inorganic Chemistry
STANKOVIĆ, Z., Physical Chemistry
STANOJLOVIĆ, R., Physical Methods of Mineral Concentration
STJEPANOVIĆ, M., Mining Equipment and Facilities
ZDRAVKOVIĆ, R., Economics
ŽIVKOVIĆ, Ž., Extractive Metallurgy, Light Metals and Theory of Metallurgical Processes

Faculty of Technology and Metallurgy:

AST, T., Instrumental Methods
BAJIĆ, D., Electronics
BANINA-OSTOJIĆ, A., Industrial Microbiology and Enzymology
BARAS, J., Brewing Technology
BASTIĆ, M., Instrumental Methods in Organic Chemistry
BLAGOJEVIĆ, N., Glass Technology
BOGOSAVLJEV, P., Iron Metallurgy
BOGUNOVIĆ, LJ., General Chemistry
BONČIĆ-CARIČIĆ, G., Organic Chemistry
BREKIĆ, M., Material Science
CVIJOVIĆ, R., Air Pollution
CVIJOVIĆ, S., Transport Phenomena
DEDIJER, A., Ch.E. Process Design
DESPIĆ, A., Physical Chemistry
DIMIĆ, G., Physics
DJOKIĆ, D., Mineral Fertilizers Technology
DJORDJEVIĆ, B., Thermodynamics
DJURKOVIĆ, B., Metallurgy of Rare Metals
DRAGOJEVIĆ, M., General Chemistry
DRAŽIĆ, D., Physical Chemistry
DRAŽIĆ, V., Physical Chemistry
DROBNJAK, DJ., Physical Metallurgy
DŽOKIĆ, D., Textile Dyeing
FILIPOVIĆ, J., Organic Synthesis
GALOGAŽA, V., Organic Chemical Technology
GROZDANIĆ, D., Numerical Methods in Chemical Engineering
ILIĆ, I., Theory of Metallurgical Processes
ILIĆ, M., English Language
JAKOVLJEVIĆ-HALAI, N., Non-metal Coatings
JAĆOVIĆ, M., Macromolecular Chemistry
JANAĆKOVIĆ, T., Building Materials Technology
JANČIĆ, M., Materials Science
JOKSIMOVIĆ-TJAPKIN, S., Combustion and Kilns
JOVANOVIĆ, B., Organic Chemistry
JOVANOVIĆ, D., Electrochemical Kinetics
JOVANOVIĆ, G., Process Design
JOVANOVIĆ, J., Petrochemical Technology
JOVANOVIĆ, M., Analytical Chemistry
JOVANOVIĆ, R., Textile Fibres
JOVANOVIĆ, S., Colloidal Chemistry
KNEŽIĆ, L., Water Technology
KOSTIĆ-GVOZDENOVIĆ, LJ., Inorganic Chemical Technology
KONJAJEV-MIHAILIDI, T., Physics
KRSTIĆ, D., Automatics
KRSTIĆ, V., Organic Chemistry
KRSMANOVIĆ, M., Mathematics
KUKIĆ, G., Food Technology
LAUŠEVIĆ, M., Instrumental Analysis
LAZIĆ, M., Mathematics
LJUBOJEVIĆ, R., Engineering Drawing
MAJDANAC, LJ., Pulp and Paper Technology
MARKOVIĆ, S., Iron and Steel Casting
MAKSIMOVIĆ, M., Galvanizing Technology
MATIĆ, S., Textile Quality Analysis
MATIJAŠEVIĆ, S., Theory of Casting
MILENKOVIĆ, V., Theory of Plastic Deformation of Metals
MIŠKOVIĆ, B., Plastic Treatment of Metals
MITROVIĆ, M., Process Dynamics
MIŠIĆ-VUKOVIĆ, M., Native Organic Compounds Chemistry
MIŠKOVIĆ, J., Instrumental Analysis
MIŠKOVIĆ, N., Plastic Treatment of Metals
MIĆIĆ, J., Reactor Design
MIHAILOVIĆ, D., Metallography
MILOSAVLJEVIĆ, S., Textile Yarn Production
MIJOVIĆ, V., Textile Quality Analysis
MILAČIĆ, N., Mathematics
MITRAKOVIĆ, D., Electronics
MLADENOVIĆ, S., Corrosion and Protection
MUŠKATIROVIĆ, M., Organic Chemistry
NEDELJKOVIĆ, LJ., Steel Metallurgy
NIKOLIĆ, B., Physical Chemistry
NIKOLIĆ, M., Textile Fabric Design
NINKOVIĆ, R., Inorganic Acid Technology

Novović-Simović, N., Heat Treatment of Metals
Obradović, M., Mathematics
Pavlović, B., Physics
Petrović-Djakov, D., Chemical Thermodynamics
Petrović, D., Physics
Petrović, S., Organic Chemistry
Petrovski, B., Mechanical Equipment Design
Plavšić, M., Rubber Technology
Popović, G., Computer Modelling in Chemical Engineering
Popović, Z., Kiln Design in Metallurgy
Popović, M., General Chemistry
Popov, K., Electrometallurgy
Radenović, P., Sociology
Radmilović, V., Heat Treatment of Metals
Radovanović, D., Chemical Thermodynamics
Radojković-Veličković, M., Organic Chemistry
Rekalić, V., Analytical Chemistry
Rogulić, M., Physical Metallurgy
Romhanji, E., Theory of Plastic Deformation of Metals
Sadibašić, A., Process Control
Savković-Stevanović, J., Statistical Methods in Chemical Engineering
Sedmak, S., Mechanical Equipment Design
Simonović, D., Transport Phenomena
Simić, D., Physics
Sinadinović, D., Metallurgy of Non-ferrous Metals
Skala, D., Reactor Design
Sokić, M., Organic Synthesis
Stojanović, O., Organic Chemistry
Stavrić, B., Economics
Stojaković, Dj., Inorganic Chemistry
Stević, S., General Chemistry
Stojanović, N., Organic Chemistry
Šurčurlija, Ž., Sociology
Šaper, R., Process Control
Šćepanović, V., General Chemistry
Šepa, D., Physical Chemistry
Šerbanović, S., Thermodynamics
Šiler-Marinković, S., Biochemistry
Škundrić, P., Textile Fibres
Tadić, Ž., Organic Chemistry
Tasić, A., Transport Phenomena
Tecilazić-Stevanović, M., Ceramics Technology
Tomović, M., Non-ferrous metals Casting
Trajković, R., Textile Finishing Technology
Trifunović, D., Material Science
Uščumlić, M., Mathematics
Uščumlić, S., Mathematics
Valčić A., Materials Science
Valent, V., Thermodynamics
Veličković, J., Polymer Technology
Vidojević, N., Physical Metallurgy of Welding
Vitorović, O., Analytical Chemistry
Vojnović, M., Electrochemistry
Vrhovac, Lj., Organic Chemical Technology
Vračar, R., Theory of Metallurgical Processes
Vučurović, B., Electroanalytical Methods
Vučurović, D., Theory of Metallurgical Processes
Vuković, D., Chemical Engineering Equipment Design
Vunjack-Novaković, G., Chemical Engineering Equipment Design
Zdanski, F., Fluid Mechanics
Zec, J., Russian Language
Zečević, S., Electrochemical Engineering

Faculty of Transport and Traffic Engineering:

Banković, R., Urban Public Transport
Bojković, Z., Electrical Engineering
Čičak, M., Railway Transport and Traffic Management
Cvetković, P., Technical Mechanics, Fluid Mechanics
Ćućuz, N., Dynamics of Vehicles
Čolić, Resistance and Ship Propulsion, Vessels
Dragač, R., Road Safety
Eror, S., Railway Transport and Traffic Management
Gabriel, Z., Aircraft Engines, Aircraft Equipment and Instruments
Jovanović, N., Transport Planning
Kuzović, Lj., Traffic Flow Theory
Lazić, V., Technical Mechanics
Lazović, S., Communication Systems
Lenasi, J., Motor Vehicles
Milošević, S., Traffic Psychology
Perišić, R., Intermodal Transport, Freight Terminals
Petrović, R., Logistics Systems
Putnik, N., Transport and Traffic
Radoš, J., Traffic Flow Control
Šelmić, R., Technical Thermodynamics
Špagnut, D., Transport Freight Characteristics
Teodorović, D., Transportation Networks, Airline Planning and Operations
Tomić, M., Urban Planning
Topenčarević, Lj., Road Transport Management and Operations
Tošić, V., Airports, Air Navigation
Vešović, V., Transport and Traffic Management
Vukadinović, S., Statistics and Operations Research
Vukobrat, M., Technical Mechanics
Zorić, D., Aircraft, Flight Mechanics

Faculty of Veterinary Medicine:

Aleksić, N., Parasitic Diseases
Baltić, M., Food Control, Fish Meat Hygiene
Blaženić, Z., Edible and Toxic Plants
Božić, T., Pathological Physiology
Dakić, M., Meat Hygiene
Dimitrijević, S., Parasitic Diseases
Dragonović, B., Radiology and Physical Therapy, Radiation Hygiene
Džinić, F., Sociology, Ethics
Ivanov, I., Clinical Diagnostics
Jovanović, M., Pathological Morphology
Jovanović, S., Animal Husbandry
Katić Radivojević, S., Parasitology
Kepčija, Dj., Food Analysis
Kulišić, Z., Parasitology
Lolin, M., Infectious Diseases of Animals and Diseases of Bees
Marković, B., Fish Diseases, Microbiology and Immunology
Mihailović, M., Biochemistry
Mijačević, V., Milk Technology
Mrvoš, G., Obstetrics, Sterility and Artificial Insemination
Nikolovski, Z., Clinical Diagnostics
Palić, T., Diseases of Ungulates, Poultry and Wild Animals
Pejin, I., Statistics
Popović, D., Physics
Popović, N., Diseases of Rabbits, Wild and Fur Animals
Popović, S., Veterinary Anatomy
Radenković, B., Animal Hygiene
Sinovec, Z., Nutrition
Slavić, M., Chemistry
Smiljanić, D., Unit Operations in the Food Industry
Soldatović, B., Biology
Stojić, V., Physiology
Šamanc, H., Diseases of Cloven-Footed Animals
Šimić, M., Histology and Embryology
Tešić, M., Organization of Production and Turnover of Animals and Food
Trailović, D., Diseases of Ungulates and Carnivores
Trbojević, G., Economics and Organization of Animal Production and Health Protection
Vasić, J., Surgery and Ophthalmology
Vicković, D., Legal Provisions in Veterinary Medicine, Forensic Veterinary Medicine Hygiene
Vuković, I., Meat Technology
Živanov, D., Pharmacology and Toxicology

ATTACHED INSTITUTE

Institute for Regional Geology and Palaeontology: Kamenička 6, POB 227, Belgrade; tel. 632-166; f. 1880; 34 staff; library of 77,000 vols; Chief Dr Luka Pešić; publ. *Geološki anali Balkanskoga poluostrva* (annually).

UNIVERZITET UMETNOSTI U BEOGRADU
(University of Arts in Belgrade)

11000 Belgrade, Kosančićev venac 29
Telephone: (11) 625-166
Fax: (11) 629-785

Founded 1957 as Academy of Arts; became University 1973
Academic year: October to September

Rector: Prof. Radmila Bakočević
Vice-Rectors: Prof. Zoran Vuković, Prof. Gradimir Petrovic
Secretary-General: Dobrila Šoškić-Petrović

Number of teachers: 415
Number of students: 2,048

DEANS

Faculty of Music: Prof. Ljubiša Petrusevski (acting)
Faculty of Fine Arts: Prof. Momčilo Antonović
Faculty of Applied Arts and Design: Prof. Dr Branko Vujović
Faculty of Dramatic Arts: Prof. Dr Ljiljana Mrkić-Popović

PROFESSORS

Faculty of Music:

Arsikin, I., Solo Singing
Bakočević, R., Solo Singing
Cetković, Z., Chamber Music
Dimitrijević, Z., Piano
Djurković, B., Conducting
Erić, Z., Composition
Galun, A., Organ
Hofman, S., Composition
Ignjatović, N., Contrabass
Ivanović, A., Solo Singing
Ivanović, M., Methodology of Music Teaching
Ivanović, M., Piano
Ivanović, P., Viola
Kambasković, R., Theory
Kosanović, M., Violin
Kostović, Lj., Chamber Music
Kulenović, T., Flute
Lazin, S., Sociology
Maksimović, R., Composition
Matić-Marović, D., Chorus and Conducting
Mihailović, D., Piano
Mihailović, D., Violin
Mihailović, J., Piano
Mihajlović, M., Composition
Pantović, Lj., Singing
Pešić, U., Chamber Music
Petruševski, Lj., Oboe
Rabuzin, S., Horn
Rackov, N., Piano
Rašković, F., Violin
Smiljanić, R., Solo Singing
Šainović, J., Conducting
Šepić, S., Conducting
Trajković, V., Composition
Valdma, A., Piano
Vukdragović, M., Piano
Živković, M., Harmony with Harmony Analysis

Faculty of Fine Arts:

Antonović, M., Painting and Drawing
Bojović, A., Painting and Drawing
Čvorović, S., Painting and Drawing

DRAGULJ, E., Graphics
GROZDANIĆ, M., Graphics and Drawing
JOVANOVIĆ, D., Painting and Drawing
KOMAD, V., Sculpture
LUBARDA, D., Painting and Drawing
MILJUŠ, B., Mosaic
PANIĆ, V., Psychology
RADOJČIĆ, S., Sculpture and Drawing
RELJIĆ, R., Painting and Drawing
STEVANOVIĆ, M., Painting and Drawing
TEPAVAC, M., Sculpture and Drawing
TODORIĆ, V., Painting and Drawing
VASIĆ, C., Painting and Drawing
VUKOSAVLJEVIĆ, N., Sculpture and Drawing
VUKOVIĆ, Z., Painting and Drawing
ŽIVKOVIĆ, I., Painting Technologies
ŽIVKOVIĆ, V., Plastic Anatomy

Faculty of Applied Arts and Design:

BERBEROVIĆ, M., Scene Costume
BLANUŠA, M., Drawing and Painting
DODIG, A., Lettering
ISAKOVIĆ, M., Ceramics
KIŠ, S., Ceramics Technology
KUKIĆ, Ž., Film and TV Scenography
KUZMANOVIĆ, N., Descriptive Geometry and Perspective
LALIĆ, R., Painting and Drawing
PAJVANČIĆ, A., Graphics Communication
PETROVIĆ, G., Applied Painting
RAKIĆ, B., Nudes
STAJEVIĆ, B., Pot Ceramics
STUPAR, S., Furniture
TODOROVIĆ, V., Applied Painting
VIDIĆ, M., Drawing and Modelling
VUCKOVIĆ, M., Graphics
VUJOVIĆ, B., History of Art
VUKOVIĆ, S., Interior Architecture
ZEGARAC DELJA, LJ., Contemporary Fashion

Faculty of Dramatic Arts:

BABAC, M., Film Editing
BAJČETIĆ, P., Acting
BARAC, S., Dance
DJOKIĆ, J., Film Editing
DJOKIĆ, R., Sociology of Arts
DJUKIĆ, A., Film and TV Directing
DRAGIĆEVIĆ-ŠEŠIĆ, M., Culture Management
GADJANSKI, M., Stage Combat
HARAŠIĆ, S., Theatre Directing
HRISTIĆ, J., Dramaturgy
IMAMI, P., Film and Screenplay
JEVTIĆ, N., Theatre Directing
JEVTOVIĆ, V., Acting
JEZERKIĆ, V., Dramaturgy
JOVANOVIĆ, S., Film Production
KARANOVIĆ, S., Film Directing
KORAĆ, A., Radio Production
LORENCIN, N., Film Directing
MANDIĆ, T., Psychology
MANDŽUKA, D., Theatre Production
MANDŽUKA, L., Make-up
MARJANOVIĆ, P., History of Yugoslav Theatre
MARKOVIĆ, G., Film Directing
MERC, R.
MIJAČ, D., Theatre Directing
MRKIĆ-POPOVIĆ, LJ., Diction
PAJKIĆ, N., Film and TV Screenplay
PAVLOVIĆ, Ž., Film and TV Screenplay
POPOVIĆ, P., Film Camera
POPOVIĆ, Z., TV Production
PRNJAT, S., Film Technology
RAPAJIĆ, S., Theatre Directing
SALETOVIĆ, S., Theatre Directing
SAVIN, E., Theatre Directing
SIJAN, S., Film Directing
TABAČKI, M., Stage and Costume Design
TATIĆ, D., Radio Directing
VASIĆ, C., Fine Art Culture

ATTACHED INSTITUTES

Centre for Electronic Art: Head ALEKSANDAR KAJEVIĆ.

Centre for Graphic and Visual Research: Dir Prof. VELIZAR KRSTIĆ.

Institute for Theatre, Film, Radio and Television: Head Dr ALEKSANDRA JOVICEVIĆ.

UNIVERZITET CRNE GORE, PODGORICA
(University of Montenegro, Podgorica)

81000 Podgorica, Cetinjski put b.b.

Telephone: (81) 14484
Fax: (81) 11301

Founded 1974 from existing faculties and high schools in Podgorica, Nikšić and Kotor
State control
Academic year: October to July

Rector: Prof. Dr RATKO DUKANOVIĆ
Vice-Rectors: Prof. Dr JANKO GOGIĆ, Prof. Dr SRETEN ŠKULETIĆ
Secretary-General: DRAGIŠA IVANOVIĆ
Librarian: Dr VASO JOVOVIĆ

Number of teachers: 833
Number of students: 8,828

DEANS

Law: Dr RANKO MUJOVIĆ
Economics: Dr PREDRAG IVANOVIĆ
Electrical Engineering: Prof. Dr MILUTIN OSTOJIĆ
Metallurgy and Technology: Prof. Dr DRAGOLJUB BLEČIĆ
Mechanical Engineering: Prof. Dr. RADOŠ BULATOVIĆ
Philosophy: Dr MILADIN VUKOVIĆ
Maritime Faculty, Kotor: Prof. Dr STEVAN POPOVIĆ
Civil Engineering: Dr RADENKO PEJOVIĆ
Academy of Music: Prof. VOJIN KOMADINA
Faculty of Arts, Cetinje: MILIVOJE BABOVIĆ
Mathematical and Natural Sciences: Prof. Dr ŽARKO PAVIĆEVIĆ
College of Physiotherapy: Dr VUKAŠIN MIHAJLOVIĆ

ATTACHED RESEARCH INSTITUTES

Historical Institute of Montenegro: 81000 Podgorica, Bul. revolucije 3; tel. (81) 41-336; fax (81) 41-624; Dir Prof. BRANISLAV KOVAČEVIĆ.
Agricultural Institute: 81000 Podgorica, Cetinjski put bb; tel. (81) 14-988; fax (81) 14-849; Dir Dr LJUBOMIR PEJOVIĆ.
Institute for Foreign Languages: 81000 Podgorica, J. Tomaševića 37; tel. (81) 45-345; fax (81) 52-043; Dir Dr SLAVICA PEROVIĆ.
Medical Institute: 81000 Podgorica, Ljubljanska bb; tel. and fax (81) 45-157; Dir Prof. BOŽIDAR RASPOPOVIĆ.
Institute of Marine Biology: 85330 Kotor, Dobrota bb; tel. and fax (82) 25-119; Dir SRETEN MANDIĆ.

UNIVERZITET U KRAGUJEVCU
(Kragujevac University)

34000 Kragujevac

Telephone: (34) 370-270
Fax: (34) 370-168

Founded 1976
State control
Academic year: October to June

Rector: Prof. Dr RADOSLAV SENIĆ
Vice-Rectors: Prof. Dr SLOBODAN TANASIJEVIĆ, Prof. Dr SLAVICA DUKIĆ DEJANOVIĆ, Prof. Dr TOMISLAV PRODANOVIĆ
General Secretary: MIROSLAV MIJAILOVIĆ
Foreign Contacts: OLIVERA MIJATOVIĆ
Librarian: RUŽICA IGNJATOVIĆ

Number of teachers: 600
Number of students: 9,000

Publication: *Bulletin* (every 2 months), and several faculty publications.

DEANS

Faculty of Mechanical Engineering: Prof. Dr RATKO MITROVIĆ
Faculty of Mechanical Engineering at Kraljevo: Prof. Dr MILOMIR GAŠIĆ
Faculty of Economics: Prof. Dr STEVO KOVAČEVIĆ
Faculty of Law: Prof. Dr BORA ČEJOVIĆ
Faculty of Science and Mathematics: Prof. Dr RADOSLAV ŽIKIĆ
Faculty of Medicine: Prof. Dr SRECKO DJORDJEVIĆ
Faculty of Agriculture: Prof. Dr DRAGUTIN DJUKIĆ
Technical Faculty at Čačak: Prof. Dr DRAGIŠA RANDJIĆ
Teacher-Training Faculty at Jagodina: Prof. Dr MILAN NEDELJKOVIĆ
Teacher-Training Faculty at Užice: Prof. Dr LAKETA NOVAK

ATTACHED INSTITUTES

Institute for Fruit Research at Čačak: Dir MILOJKO RANKOVIĆ.

Institute for Crops Research at Kragujevac: Dir MILANKO PAVLOVIĆ.

UNIVERZITET U NIŠU
(University of Niš)

18000 Niš, Univerzitetski trg 2

Telephone: (18) 547-970
Fax: (18) 547-950

Founded 1965
State control

Rector: Prof. Dr BRANIMIR DJORDJEVIĆ
Vice-Rectors: Prof. Dr NENAD RADOJKOVIĆ, Prof. Dr DUŠAN ZDRAVKOVIĆ, Prof. Dr GORDANA STANKOVIĆ, Prof. Dr SLOBODAN MILENKOVIĆ
Secretary-General: DRAGOSLAV DJOKIĆ

Number of teachers: 1,193
Number of students: 17,009

Publications: *Pregled predavanja* (Calendar, annually), *Glasnik Univerziteta u Nišu* (Review, irregular), *Univerzitet u Nišu* (information booklet, irregular), *Vodič za brucoše* (student guide, annually), *Naučni podmladak* (student scientific journal, quarterly), *Facta Universitatis* (Scientific Journal, irregular).

DEANS

Faculty of Civil Engineering and Architecture: Prof. Dr DUŠAN ILIĆ
Faculty of Economics: Prof. Dr BORKO KRSTIĆ
Faculty of Electronic Engineering: Prof. Dr MIODRAG ARSIĆ
Faculty of Law: Prof. Dr VOJISLAV DJURDJIĆ
Faculty of Mechanical Engineering: Prof. Dr ZORAN BORIČIĆ
Faculty of Medicine: Prof. Dr BRANKO LOVIĆ
Faculty of Occupational Safety: Prof. Dr MIROSLAV MIJAILOVIĆ
Faculty of Philosophy: Prof. Dr VESELIN ILIĆ
Faculty of Technology: Prof. Dr VLADA VELJKOVIĆ
Teacher-Training Faculty: Prof. Dr BORA STANIMIROVIĆ

PROFESSORS

Faculty of Civil Engineering:

ANDJELKOVIĆ, H., Descriptive Geometry
ANDJELKOVIĆ, M., Industrial Facilities Design, Public Design
ARANDJELOVIĆ, D., Hydraulic Engineering
DAMNJANOVIĆ, D., Road Engineering
DAMNJANOVIĆ, M., Building Construction, Structural Steelwork
DRENIĆ, D., Structure Testing
IGIĆ, T., Technical Mechanics, Strength of Materials
ILIĆ, D., Housing Design, Project Development
MARKOVIĆ, M., Descriptive Geometry
MARKOVIĆ, V., Dams and Water Potential Utilization

MILENKOVIĆ, S., Urban Water Supply and Sewerage Systems Engineering
MILIĆEVIĆ, M., Structure Statics, Theory of Surface Girders
POPOVIĆ, B., Structure Statics
PROTIĆ, P., Mathematics
RADOJIČIĆ, T., Concrete Bridges and Concrete Structures
SPASOJEVIĆ, N., Concrete Bridges, Concrete Structures
STOJIĆ, D., Timber Structures and Scaffolds, Timber and Wall Structures
TRAJKOVIĆ, D., Organization of Construction Work
VALJAREVIĆ, R., Elements of Geology
VELIČKOVIĆ, D., Metal Structures
ZDRAVKOVIĆ, S., Structural Stability and Dynamics, Theory of Surface Girders

Faculty of Economics:

ARANDJELOVIĆ, Z., Yugoslav Economy
BOGDANOVIĆ, S., Mathematics
BUBANJA, P., Philosophy
GROZDANOVIĆ, D., Business Economics
JEZDIMIROVIĆ, M., Financial Accounting, Book-keeping
JOVANOVIĆ, M., Financial Theory and Policy
MILOŠEVIĆ, V., Business Economics
NIKOLIĆ, S., Business Organization
PREDIĆ, B., Planning and Development Policy
SEKULOVIĆ, M., Economic Doctrines
SIMONOVIĆ, D., Agricultural Economics
TODOROVIĆ, O., Operations Research
ZDRAVKOVIĆ, D., Theory of Prices and Pricing Policy

Faculty of Electronics:

ARSIĆ, M., Measurements in Electronics, Process Information Systems
DANKOVIĆ, B., Process Control
DIMITRIJEVIĆ, B., Electrical Measurements, Measurements in Microelectronics
DJORDJEVIĆ, B., Digital Electronics and Electronic Circuits
DJORDJEVIĆ, L., Programming, Software Development Tools
DJORDJEVIĆ, R., Mathematics I
DJURIĆ, B., Electronics II
GMITROVIĆ, M., Electric Network Synthesis, Circuit Theory
KOCIĆ, L., Mathematics II, Mathematical Methods
KRSTIĆ, D., Radiotechnology, Radiocommunication Systems
LITOVSKI, V., Electronics I, Electronic Circuit Design
MILOSAVLJEVIĆ, Č., Automatic Control, Electric Motor Drive Regulation
MILOŠEVIĆ, M., Electroacoustics
MILOVANOVIĆ, B., Microwave Technology and Systems, Optic Communications
MILOVANOVIĆ, G., Mathematics I, Numerical Mathematics
MILOVANOVIĆ, I., Mathematics I, Discrete Mathematics
MITIĆ, D., Elements of Electrical Engineering
NIKOLIĆ, Z., Quality Control and Reliability
PEJOVIĆ, M., Physics
PETKOVIĆ, M., Mathematics II
PETKOVIĆ, R., Elements of Electrical Engineering, Theory of Electric Circuits
RADENKOVIĆ, V., Measurements in Electric Power Engineering
RANČIĆ, P., Electrical Installations and Illumination
RISTIĆ, S., Electronic Components, Semiconducting Components
STANKOVIĆ, R., Logic Design, Pattern Recognition
STEFANOVIĆ, D., Materials for Electronics, Optoelectronics and Integrated Optics
STEFANOVIĆ, M., Telecommunication Theory, Optical Telecommunications
STOJADINOVIĆ, N., Physics of Microelectronic Components, Elements of Microelectronics
STOJANOVIĆ, V., Television, Analogue Electronics
STOJČEV, M., Microprocessors and Microcomputers, Microprocessor Technology, Data Acquisition Systems
STOJILKOVIĆ, S., Materials in Electrical Engineering
TOŠIĆ, Ž., Microcomputer Programming and Systems, Computer Organization, Elements of Computer Engineering, Artificial Intelligence
VELIČKOVIĆ, D., Electromagnetics, Elements of Electrical Engineering
ŽIVKOVIĆ, LJ., Electrotechnical Materials

Faculty of Mechanical Engineering:

BORIČIĆ, Z., Fluid Mechanics, Hydraulic and Pneumatic Systems of Automatic Control
ĆOJBAŠIĆ, L., Elements of Processing Technology
DJOKIĆ, V., Theory and Methodology of Mechanical Systems Design, Elements of Construction Theory
DOMAZET, D., Modelling and Optimization of Production Systems, Computer-Aided Production Design
HEDRIH, K., Elastodynamics
ILIĆ, G., Measurement Technology, Thermodynamics, Mechanical and Hydromechanical Operations
JEVTIĆ, V., Mining and Building Machinery, Continuous Transport Machinery
LAKOVIĆ, S., Thermal Power Plants, Steam Boilers
MARINKOVIĆ, V., Machine Processing, Machine Tools I
MIJAJLOVIĆ, R., Interrupted Transport Machinery, Internal Transport and Storage Systems
MILOVANČEVIĆ, D., Mathematics
MILTENOVIĆ, V., Elements of Machines, Reliability of Machine Systems
NIKODIJEVIĆ, D., Hydraulic Components, Fluid Mechanics
NIKOLIĆ, V., Automatic Control, Dynamics and Identification of Automatic Control Processes, Discrete and Multivariate Systems of Automatic Control
PAVLOVIĆ, N., Technical Optics, Theory of Machines and Mechanisms
PETKOVIĆ, LJ., Numerical Mathematics and Programming
PETROVIĆ, T., Measurement Techniques, Apparatus and Device Design, Element and Systems Design, Fine Mechanical Element Design
PREDIĆ, B., Descriptive Geometry
RADOJKOVIĆ, N., Thermodynamics, Chemical Thermodynamics, Thermal and Diffusing Apparatus
STANOJEVIĆ, M., Mathematics
STOILJKOVIĆ, V., Machine-Building Technology
STOJILJKOVIĆ, M., Automation of Production, Technological Systems
STOKIĆ, D., Mechanics
TASIĆ, Ž., Electromechanics and Applied Electronics, Electrical Engineering and Electronics, Power Conveyors
VUKIĆEVIĆ, D., Machine Materials
VULIĆ, A., Quality Measurement and Standardization, Power Conveyors
ŽIVKOVIĆ, Ž., Theory of Machines and Mechanisms, Technical Drawing

Faculty of Medicine:

BABIĆ, R., Radiology
BAKIĆ, M., Internal Medicine, Haematology
BAŠIĆ, H., Pathological Anatomy
BJELAKOVIĆ, G., Biochemistry
BOŠKOVIĆ, Ž., Epidemiology
BUDIĆ, Z., Surgery, Anaesthesiology
ĆIRIĆ, V., Internal Medicine, Cardiology
DENOVIĆ, B., Forensic Medicine
DIMOV, D., Pathological Anatomy
DJORDJEVIĆ, K., Medical Chemistry
DJORDJEVIĆ, V., Biochemistry
DJUKNIĆ-PEJOVIĆ, M., Histology, Embryology
DREZGIĆ, LJ., Epidemiology
HADŽI-PEŠIĆ, LJ., Internal Medicine, Cardiology
IGIĆ, LJ., Stomatological Prosthetics
ILIĆ, R., Pathological Anatomy
ILIĆ, S., Internal Medicine, Cardiology
JOVANOVIĆ, D., Physiology
JOVANOVIĆ, S., Dermatovenereology
KATIĆ, V., Pathological Anatomy
KOJOVIĆ, Z., Physical Medicine and Rehabilitation
KORAĆEVIĆ, D., Biochemistry
KOSTIĆ, OB., Physiology
KOSTIĆ, OL., Physical Medicine and Rehabilitation
KUTLEŠIĆ, Č., Pathological Anatomy
LOVIĆ, B., Internal Medicine, Cardiology
MALOBABIĆ, Z., Pharmacology and Toxicology
MARJANOVIĆ, S., Anatomy
MARKOVIĆ, V., Internal Medicine, Cardiology
MARKOVIĆ, Z., Internal Medicine, Rheumatology
MIHAJLOVIĆ, M., Physiology
MIHAJLOVIĆ, P., Biophysics
MILENKOVIĆ, Z., Surgery, Neurosurgery
MIRKOVIĆ, B., Diseases of the Mouth and Periodontal Tissue
MITIĆ, M., Medical Chemistry
MITIĆ, N., Dental Pathology
MITIĆ, S., Pre-Clinical Dental Pathology
MITROVIĆ, R., Hygiene, Medical Ecology
MLADENOVIĆ, Z., Maxillofacial Surgery
MRČARICA, E., Biology, Human Genetics
NOVOTIN, D., Surgery, Orthopaedics
ORLOV, S., Diseases of the Mouth and Periodontal Tissue
OTAŠEVIĆ, V., Forensic Medicine
PARAVINA, M., Dermatovenereology
PAVLOVIĆ, V., Pre-Clinical Dental Pathology
PENEV, G., Pathological Anatomy
PEROŠEVIĆ, Z., Epidemiology
PEROVIĆ, M., Histology, Embryology
PETROVIĆ, J., Paediatrics
PETROVIĆ, S., Histology, Embryology
POPOVIĆ, V., Industrial Medicine
RADIĆ, S., Pathological Physiology
RAIČEVIĆ, R., Internal Medicine, Nephrology
RANKOVIĆ, Ž., Infectology
SAVIĆ, M., Paedodontics and Preventive Stomatology
SKOČAJIĆ, S., Dental Pathology
SOKOLOVIĆ, B., Pre-Clinical Stomatological Prosthetics
SPALEVIĆ, M., Forensic Medicine
STAMENKOVIĆ, I., Internal Medicine, Gastroenterology
STANKOVIĆ, A., Internal Medicine, Rheumatology
STEFANOVIĆ, V., Internal Medicine, Nephrology
STOJANOVIĆ, D., Pathological Anatomy
STOJILJKOVIĆ, M., General Surgery
STOJILJKOVIĆ, S., Pathological Physiology
STOJKOVIĆ, M., Internal Medicine, Gastroenterology
TASIĆ, T., Internal Medicine, Gastroenterology
TIJANIĆ, LJ., Orthodontics
VIDOVIĆ, Ž., Orthodontics
VUJIČIĆ, B., Oral Surgery
VUKUŠIĆ, Z., Pathological Physiology
ZDRAVKOVIĆ, J., Neuropsychiatry

Faculty of Law:

BOŽIĆ, M., Economic Policy
GORČIĆ, J., Financial Law
JOCIĆ, L., Roman Law
KOVAČEVIĆ, R., Introduction to Civil and Property Law
MIJAČIĆ, M., Law of Obligation
MILADINOVIĆ, V., Criminal Law
MILENOVIĆ, D., Business Law

PARAVINA, D., Labour Law
PETROVIČ, M., Administrative Law
ROČKOMANOVIĆ, M., Private International Law
STANIMIROVIĆ, D., Sociology
STANKOVIĆ, G., Civil Procedural Law
STOJIČIĆ, S., National History of Law

Faculty of Philosophy:

BOGDANOVIĆ, N., Dialectology of Serbo-Croat, Linguistic Culture, Linguistics and Stylistics
BRANKOVIĆ, M., Athletics
DIMITRIJEVIĆ, P., Physics II
DJORDJEVIĆ, D., Sociology and Philosophy of Natural Sciences, Sociology of Work Economics
DJORDJEVIĆ, M., Psychology
IGOV, R., Analytical Chemistry I
ILIĆ, V., Sociology of Religion, Sociology of Culture and Arts with Serbian National History
IVKOVIĆ, M., Sociology of Education
JABLAN, S., Descriptive Geometry
JOKSIMOVIĆ, S., Football, Skiing
JOVANOVIĆ, I., Basketball
JOVANOVIĆ, M., Serbian Romantic and Realist Literature
KOČINAC, LJ., Mathematical Logic, Theory of Measures and Integrals, Linear Algebra and Analytical Geometry
KOSTIĆ, R., Volleyball
KOVAČEVIĆ, M., Serbian Language Syntax with Semantics, Stylistics and Analysis of Discourse
LAINOVIĆ, R., French Language
LETIĆ, B., Medieval Literature, Literature from Renaissance to Rationalism, Literature of the Coastal Region
MADIĆ, B., Theory and Teaching of Physical Education
MILETIĆ, G., Instrumental Analytical Chemistry
MILETIĆ, S., Chemistry of Natural Products
MILJKOVIĆ, LJ., Solid State Physics, Physics of Materials
MITROVIĆ, LJ., General Sociology
OBRADOVIĆ, M., Physical Chemistry
PALIĆ, R., Organic Chemistry
PAVLOVIĆ, T., Physics I
PECEV, T., Analytical Chemistry II
PEJČIĆ, M., Philosophy and Sociology
PETROVIĆ, Č., Political Economy
PIVAČ, M., Handball, Swimming
PREMOVIĆ, P., General and Inorganic Chemistry
PURENOVIĆ, M., Industrial Chemistry
RADOVIĆ, B., Instrumental Organic Chemistry, Instrumental Methods of Structural Analysis, Mechanisms of Organic Reactions
RAKOČEVIĆ, M., Chemistry Teaching Methodology
RAKOČEVIC, V., Functional Analysis, Theory of Measures and Integrals
RISTIĆ, R., English Literature of the 18th and 19th centuries, Culture and Civilization of the Commonwealth, Canadian and Australian Studies
STOJANOVIĆ, M., Macedonian and Slovenian Literature
STOJKOVIĆ, M., Sociology of Morals, Labour Sociology
VIDANOVIĆ, DJ., Teaching of English Language, Morphology, Introduction to Linguistics and History of English Language
VUČKOVIĆ, S., Recreation Theory and Teaching Methods, Activities and Nature
ŽIVANOVIĆ, N., Theory and History of Physical Education
ZUNIĆ, Sociology of Culture and Arts, Serbian Cultural History

Faculty of Occupational Safety:

DJUKANOVIĆ, M., Urban Ecology and Town Planning, Living Environment and Elements of Protection
IVANJAC, M., Labour Law, Sociology of Occupational Safety, Training for Safety at Work and Environmental Protection
MARKOVIĆ, P., Psycho-Physiology of Work and Psycho-Physiological Changes
MIJAILOVIĆ, M., Planning and Programming of Occupational Safety, Living Environment Quality Planning and Programming
MILENOVIĆ, B., Essential Economics, Social Evolution and Living Environment
NEDELJKOVIĆ, V., Ventilation and Air-Conditioning Systems, Energy and Living Environment
NIKOLIĆ, B., Protection in Technological Processes, Technological Processes in the Home
STANKOVIĆ, M., Mathematics, Mathematical Modelling
VELIČKOVIĆ, D., Noise in the Living Environment, Noise and Vibration

Faculty of Technology:

CAKIĆ, M., Physical Chemistry, Instrumental Analysis
CVETKOVIĆ, D., Organic Chemistry II, Organo-Chemical Technology
CVETKOVIĆ, M., Electrical Engineering with Electronics, Automatic Control
DIMITRIJEVIĆ, S., Political Economy
DJORDJEVIĆ, S., Organic Chemistry I
ILIĆ, P., General Chemistry
KOCIĆ, M., Physics
RANDJELOVIĆ, N., Biology, Essential Microbiology
RAŠKOVIĆ, LJ., Elements of Polymer Engineering, Textile Raw Materials
STANKOVIĆ, M., Biochemistry, Industrial Practice, Technology of Natural Organic Products
VELJKOVIĆ, V., Technological Operations

Teacher-Training Faculty:

DEDIC, DJ., School and Family Pedagogy
ZLATANOVIĆ, M., Literature, Rhetorical Art

UNIVERZITET U NOVOM SADU
(University of Novi Sad)

21000 Novi Sad, Trg Dositeja Obradovića 5
Telephone: (21) 350-622
Fax: (21) 611-725

Founded 1960
State control
Academic year: October to June

Rector: Prof. Dr DRAGOSLAV HERCEG
Vice-Rectors: Prof. Dr VELIMIR SOTIROVIĆ, Prof. Dr RADMILO TODOSIJEVIĆ
General Secretary: PETAR RADONJANIN

Number of teachers: 2,050
Number of students: 21,000

Publications: *Glas Univerziteta* (journal, monthly), *Glasnik* (Review, irregular), *Bulletin* (irregular).

DEANS

Faculty of Agriculture: Prof. Dr MARIJA KRALJEVIĆ-BALALIĆ
Faculty of Civil Engineering: Prof. Dr SAM ATILA
Faculty of Economics: Prof. Dr VOJIN KALINIĆ
Faculty of Engineering Sciences: Prof. Dr DUŠAN PETROVAČKI
Faculty of Law: Prof. Dr DRAGAN MILKOV
Faculty of Medicine: Prof. Dr PAVLE BUDAKOV
Faculty of Natural Sciences and Mathematics: Prof. Dr RADE DAVIDOVIĆ
Faculty of Philosophy: Prof. Dr TOMISLAV BEKIĆ
Faculty of Physical Education: Prof. Dr DARKO KALAJDŽIĆ
Faculty of Technology: Prof. Dr JOVAN JAKOVLJEVIĆ
Faculty of Education: Prof. Dr NENAD PETROVIĆ
Technical Faculty 'Mihajlo Pupin': Prof. Dr DUŠAN LIPOVAC
Academy of Art: Prof. NENAD OSTOJIĆ

PROFESSORS

Faculty of Agriculture:

BOŠNJAK, DJ., Crop Irrigation
BOŠNJAKOVIĆ, A., Agricultural Machinery
BOŽIDAREVIĆ, D., Marketing and Turnover of Food Products
BRANKOVIĆ, D., Concrete Constructions
ÇINDRIĆ, P., Ampelography
ČOBANOVIĆ, K., Statistics
DOKIĆ, P., Plant Improvement
DJUKIĆ, N., Agricultural Machinery
DJUROVKA, M., Vegetable Growing
DRAGOVIĆ, S., Crop Irrigation
GVOZDENOVIĆ, D., Pomology
HADŽIĆ, V., Pedology
JASNIĆ, S., Phytopathology
JOVANOVIĆ, B., Mechanics
JOVANOVIĆ, B., Fishery
JOVANOVIĆ, M., Economics of Agricultural Estates
JOVANOVIĆ, R., Nutrition of Domestic Animals
KASTORIE, R., Plant Physiology
KIŠGECI, J., Cultivation of Special Crops
KORAĆ, M., Pomology
KOVČIN, S., Nutrition of Nonruminant Animals
KRAJINOVIĆ, M., Animal Husbandry
KRALJEVIĆ-BALALIĆ, M., Genetics
LAZIĆ, B., Vegetable Growing
LAZIĆ, V., Agricultural Machinery
MARKOVIĆ, V., Vegetable Cultivation
MIHAILOVIĆ, D., Meteorology
MIHAJLOVIĆ, L., Agricultural Economics, Farm Organization
MIHALJEV, I., Plant Improvement
MIJATOVIĆ, B., Geology with Hydrology
MILOJKOVIĆ, N., Pedology
MIŠIĆ, T., Genetics
MOLNAR, I., General Farming
NIKOLIĆ, R., Agricultural Tractors, Agricultural Machinery
OBRENOVIĆ, D., Business Analysis
PEJIĆ, N., Nutrition of Ruminant Animals
PETROVIĆ, M., Plant Physiology
PETROVIĆ, N., Plant Physiology
PETROVIĆ, S., Genetics
POTKONJAK, S., Economics of Melioration and Mechanization, Economics of Water Resources
SAVIĆ, M., Agricultural Machines
SAVIĆ, S., Fodder Technology
SEKULIĆ, R., Entomology
SRDIĆ, Z., Entomology
STAMENKOVIĆ, S., Entomology
STANČIĆ, B., Breeding of Domestic Animals
STARČEVIĆ, LJ., Special Farming
STEVANOVIĆ, M., General Farming
STOJANOV, M., Sociology
STOJANOVIĆ, Z., Veterinary Science and Zoo Hygiene
ŠIJAČKI, N., Anatomy and Histology
ŠKORIĆ, D., Plant Improvement
TEODOROVIĆ, M., Special Livestock Breeding
UBAVIĆ, M., Agrochemistry
VAPA, M., Psychology of Domestic Animals
VIDOVIĆ, V., Animal Breeding
VUJANIĆ-VARGA, D., Pomology
VUJČIĆ, I., Dairy Technology
ŽIVANOVIĆ, M., Phytopharmacology

Faculty of Civil Engineering:

DETKI, J., Mathematics
FERENCI, F., Mathematics
GOSTOVIĆ, M., Engineering Geodesy
MIHAILOVIĆ, V., Concrete Structures
SAM, A., Social Sciences
SAVIĆ, M., Farming Organization
SEBENJI, F., Building Physics
SKENDEROVIĆ, B., Building Materials I
VENEČANIN, S., Concrete Structures, Concrete Bridges
ZELENHASIĆ, E., Hydrology and Elements of Hydrotechnology

Faculty of Economics:

ACIN, DJ., International Economic Relations
BALABAN, N., Principles of Informatics
BANDIN, J., Accountancy and Bookkeeping
BANDIN, T., Business Enterprise
BJELICA, B., Finance
BUHA, J., Contemporary Economic Systems
JAKOVČEVIĆ, K., Business Economics
JOSIFIDIS, K., Macroeconomics
KALINIĆ, V., Trade Company Management
LAKI, L., Sociology
ŞTOJKOVIĆ, M., Statistics
ŞAGI, A., Microeconomics
ŞUVAKOV, T., Microeconomics
VASILJEV, S., Marketing

Faculty of Engineering Sciences:

ATANACKOVIĆ, T., Material Resistance
BABIN, N., Transport Machines
BAČLIĆ, B., Mechanics and Thermodynamics of Continuum
BAJIĆ, M., Organization of Industrial Systems
ĐUKUROV, Ž., Fluid Mechanics
ÇIRIĆ, D., Physics
ÇOMIĆ, I., Mathematics
ĆOSIĆ, I., Production Systems
CVETIĆANIN, L., Mechanics
DIMIĆ, M., Mass Transfer, Heat Apparatus
DJUKIĆ, DJ., Mechanics
DOVNIKOVIC, L., Descriptive Geometry
FOLIĆ, R., Concrete Structures and Structural Theory
GATALO, R., Machine Tools, Flexible Technological Systems
GRKOVIĆ, V., Turbines
GVOZDENAC, D., Thermal Energy and Measurement in Thermal Engineering
INIĆ, M., Traffic Safety
KAKAŠ, D., Heat Treatment
KOVAČ, P., Welding
KOVAČEVIĆ, I., Mathematics
KOVAČEVIĆ, V., Computing Systems
LALOVIĆ, M., Power Systems
MARIĆ, M., Heat Science, Drying Technology
MARIĆ, V., Mathematical Methods
MILATOVIĆ, Ž., Political Economy
MILIDRAG, S., Motor Vehicles
MILIKIĆ, D., Treatment Methods by Material Removal
MILINSKI, N., Physics
MILORADOV, M., Hydrotechnic Elements
MOGIN, P., Databases
NOVAK, L., Circuit and Systems Theory
OBRADOVIĆ, D., Computer Programming
OBRADOVIĆ, M., Digital Communications
PERUNOVIĆ, P., Boilers
PETKOVSKI, DJ., Automation Control Systems
PETROVAČKI, D., Automatic Control
PLANČAK, M., Technology of Plasticity and Cold Extrusion
PLAVŠIĆ, M., Machine Construction
POPOV, R., Theory of Machines and Mechanisms
PRODANOVIĆ, M., City and Spatial Planning
RADOJKOVIĆ, Z., Roads and Infrastructure
SATARIĆ, M., Physics
SAVIĆ, V., Logistic Technical Systems
ŞEKULIĆ, S., Working Processes
ŞEŠIĆ, Ž., SUS Motors
SIDJANIN, L., Materials Science I, Engineering Materials
STANIVUKOVIĆ, D., Logistic Technical Systems
STOJANKOVIĆ, M., Mathematics
TEŠIĆ, M., Agricultural Machinery
VUJANOVIĆ, B., Mechanics
VUJOVIĆ, V., Technology of Plasticity
VUKOVIĆ, V., Fluid Mechanics
VULANOVIĆ, V., Quality Control
ZLOKOLICA, M., Theory of Mechanisms and Machines

Faculty of Law:

ARSIĆ, Z., Economic Law
CARIĆ, S., Economic Law
DJURDJEV, A., Constitutional Law
ETINSKI, R., International Public Law
GRUBAČ, M., Criminal Procedural Law
JANČIĆ-CVEJIĆ, O., Family Law
JOVANOVIĆ, PA., Contemporary Political Systems
JOVANOVIĆ, PR., Labour Law
KRKLJUŠ, LJ., History of Yugoslav State and Law
MALENICA, A., Roman Law
MILKOV, D., Administrative Law
MUNĆAN, J., Social Law
PAJVANČIĆ, M., Constitutional Law
PERIĆ, O., Criminal Law
PIHLER, S., Criminal Law
POPOV, DJ., Introductory Economics
POPOVIĆ, M., Theory of State and Law
RADULOVIĆ, R., Defence
RELIĆ, J., Criminology, Penology
SALMA, J., Law of Obligation
STANKOVIĆ, F., Introductory Economics
STAROVIĆ, B., Civil Procedural Law
ŞTOJANOVIĆ, Z., Criminal Law
ŞARKIĆ, S., History of State and Law
ŠOGOROV, S., Economic Law
TRKLJA, M., Financial Law
VRANJEŠ, M., Financial Law
VUČKOVIĆ, M., Law of Obligation
VUKADINOVIĆ, G., Theory of State and Law
VUKIĆEVIĆ, M., Introductory Economics

Faculty of Medicine:

ALEKSIĆ, S., Gynaecology and Obstetrics
BANIĆ, B., Pharmacology and Toxicology
BOROTA, R., Pathological Physiology
BUDAKOV, P., Pathological Anatomy
BURANJ, B., Epidemiology
DANIČIĆ, B., Surgery, War Surgery
DEVEČERSKI, V., Histology and Embryology
DJAKOVIĆ-ŠVARCER, K., Pharmacology and Toxicology
DJURIĆ, B., Internal Medicine
DOKMANOVIĆ-DJORDJEVIĆ, M., Gynaecology and Obstetrics
FELLE, D., Internal Medicine
GEBAUER, E., Paediatrics
GUDURIĆ, B., Surgery
HADŽIĆ, M., Pathological Anatomy
HILLIER-KOLAROV, V., Oral Diseases
HRUBIK, O., Physiology
JAKOVLJEVIĆ, DJ., Social Medicine
KOVAČEVIĆ, Z., Biochemistry
KRAJČINOVIĆ, J., Surgery
KRISTIFOROVIĆ-ILIĆ, M., Hygiene
KRSTIĆ, A., Paediatrics
KULAUZOV, M., Pathological Physiology
LATINOVIĆ, S., Ophthalmology
LAŽETIĆ, B., Physiology
LEPŠANOVIĆ, L., Internal Medicine
LUČIĆ, A., Pathological Physiology
MARINKOVIĆ, R., Anatomy
MARKOVIĆ, N., Oncology
MIKIĆ, Ž., Surgery, War Surgery
MIKOV, M., Occupational Medicine
MILIN, J., Histology and Embryology
MILOŠEVIĆ, D., Otorhinolaryngology
MILUTINOVIĆ, B., Physiology
MIRILOV, M., Hygiene
MOMČILOVIĆ, A., Surgery
MUDRINIĆ, P., Occupational Medicine
NADJ-KOŠA, V., Neurology and Psychiatry
NIKOLIĆ, V., Internal Medicine
NIKOLIĆ-DOVAT, V., Paediatrics
NOVAKOV, S., Social Medicine
PAJIĆ, D., Surgery
PECIĆ, J., Microbiology with Parasitology and Immunology
PEJIN, D., Internal Medicine
PETROVIĆ, P., Surgery
POLZOVIĆ, A., Anatomy
POPOV, I., Psychiatry
POPOVIĆ, D., Forensic Medicine
PROTIĆ, M., Stomatology
RADOVANOVIĆ, N., Surgery, War Surgery
RISTIĆ, D., Surgery, War Surgery
RISTIĆ, J., Surgery, War Surgery
RONČEVIĆ, N., Paediatrics
SAVIĆ, K., Medical Rehabilitation
SAVIĆ, M., Occupational Medicine
STAMENKOVIĆ, Ž., Internal Medicine
STANIŠIĆ, M., Rehabilitation
STANULOVIĆ, M., Pharmacology and Toxicology
STEFANOVIĆ, LJ., Internal Medicine
ŞTOJANOVIĆ, S., Surgery
ŠLJAPIĆ, N., Pathological Anatomy
TASIĆ, M., Forensic Medicine
VUJKOV, V., Microbiology with Parasitology and Immunology
VUKOVIĆ, B., Epidemiology
ŽEČEVIĆ, D., Internal Medicine
ŽIVANOVIĆ, M., Internal Medicine

Faculty of Natural Sciences and Mathematics:

ABRAMOVIĆ, B., Microanalysis
BIKIT, I., Nuclear Physics
BJELICA, L., Physical Chemistry
BOGDANOVIĆ, Ž., Geography
BUGARSKI, D., Geography
ÇRVENKOVIĆ, S., Mathematics
ĆURČIĆ, S., Social Geography
DAVIDOVIĆ, R., Regional Geography
DIVJAKOVIĆ, V., Physics of Condensed Matter
DJUKIĆ, N., Agricultural Zoology
GAAL, F., Analytical Chemistry
GAJIĆ, LJ., Analysis and Probability
GAJIN, S., Microbiology
GAŠIĆ, O., Biochemistry
GILEZAN, N., Mathematics
GLUMAC, S., Morphology and Systematization of Invertebrates
HADŽIĆ, O., Probability and Statistics, Mathematics
HALAŠI, R., Organic Analysis
HERCEG, D., Numerical Mathematics
JANIĆ, I., Atomic Physics
JANJATOVIĆ, V., Botany
JANJIĆ, J., Physics
KAPOR, A., Physics of Condensed Matter
KAPOR, D., Theoretical Physics
KOSANIĆ, M., General Chemistry
KOVAČEVIĆ, R., Biochemistry
KRSTIĆ, B., Plant Physiology
LEOVAC, V., Inorganic Chemistry
MALIĆ, S., Formal Languages, Mathematics
MARIĆ, D., General Physiology
MILJKOVIĆ, D., Theoretical Organic Chemistry
NIKOLIĆ, A., Physical Chemistry
NIKOLIĆ-DESPOTOVIĆ, D., Analysis and Probability
PAP, E., Mathematics
PAVLOV, M., Electronics
PENOV, K., Organic Chemistry
PERIŠIĆ-JANJIĆ, N., General and Inorganic Chemistry
PETROVIĆ, D., Physics of Condensed Matter
PETROVIĆ, J., Organic Chemistry
PILIPOVIĆ, S., Analysis and Probability
RATAJAC, R., Agricultural Zoology
RIBAR, B., Electromagnetism, Measuring Techniques
RONČEVIĆ, S., Biology
SIMONOVIĆ, I., Comparative Physiology
STANKOVIĆ, Ş., Physics of Condensed Matter
STANKOVIĆ, Ž., Plant Physiology
STEVANOVIĆ, D., Morphology and Taxonomy of Invertebrates
STOJAKOVIĆ, Z., Linear Algebra
STOJANOVIĆ, S., Theoretical Mechanics and Electrodynamics
STOJANOVIĆ, S., Botany
SURLA, D., Computer Science
ŞURLA, K., Numerical Mathematics
ŞEŠELJA, B., Mathematics
ŠKRINJAR, M., Theoretical Physics
ŞURANJI, T., Analytical Chemistry
TAKAČI, A., Mathematics
TOMIĆ, P., Geography
TOŠIĆ, B., Theoretical Physics
TOŠIĆ, R., Combinatorics
UŠAN, J., Mathematics

VOJINOVIĆ-MILORADOV, M., General Chemistry
VOJVODIĆ, G., Algebra and Logic
VRBAŠKI, Ž., Chemical Technology
ŽDERIĆ, M., Biology
ŽIGRAI, I., Analytical Chemistry

Faculty of Philosophy:

BANJAI, J., Literary Theory
BEKIĆ, T., German Literature
BERIĆ, V., History of German Language
BIRO, M., Elements of Clinical Psychology, Elements of Psychotherapy and Consulting
BOŠNJAK, I., Hungarian Literature
BRUKNER, B., Archaeology
BURZAN, M., Serbian Language
ČOVIĆ, B., Russian Literature
DINIĆ-KNEŽEVIĆ, D., General Medieval History of Yugoslav Nations
DOSTANIĆ, R., History of Pedagogy
DUDOK, D., History of Slovak Language and Literature
EGERIĆ, M., Modern Serbian Literature
GENC, L., Genetics and Educational Psychology
GEROLD, L., Hungarian Literature
GRKOVIĆ, M., History of Serbian and Comparative Grammar of Slavic Languages
HARPANJ, M., Slovak Literature, Literary Theory
IGNJATOVIĆ, I., General Psychology, Psychology of Personality
IVANOVIĆ, R., History of Yugoslav Literatures
JERKOVIĆ, V., Old Slavonic Language
KAIĆ, K., History of Hungarian Culture
KAMENOV, E., Pre-School Education
KAPOR-STANULOVIĆ, P., Development Psychology, Mental Health
KLEUT, M., Serbian Literature
KMEĆ, J., Slovak Literature and Yugoslav-Slovak Ties
KOKOVIĆ, D., Sociology and Sociology of Culture
KONSTANTINOVIĆ, I., French Literature
KOSANOVIĆ, B., Russian Literature
KRKLJUŠ, S., Didactics
KULIĆ, M., History of Philosophy
MAGDU, L., Romanian Language
MARICKI-GADJANSKI, K., Classical Languages, Ancient History
MARINKOVIĆ, B., 18th-century Serbian Literature
MATIJAŠEVIĆ, J., Modern Russian Language
MILOSAVLJEVIĆ, P., Methodology of Literary Studies
MOMČILOVIĆ, B., English Literature
OLJAČA, M., Educational System
PETROVIĆ, D., Dialectology of Serbian and Standard Serbian Language
PIŽURICA, M., History of Serbian Language
POPOV, Č., Modern History
RADOVANOVIĆ, M., General Linguistics
RADOVIĆ, M., Comparative Literature
REDJEP, J., Medieval Literature
RISTIĆ, Ž., Methodology of Psychology
RODIĆ, R., School Education
ROKAI, P., Medieval History
SAVIĆ, S., Sociolinguistics and Discourse Analysis
SIMEUNOVIĆ, V., Philosophy
STOJAKOV, S., Introduction to Education Science
STRAJNIĆ, N., Comparative Literature
ŠIPKA, M., Statistical Psychology
TAMAŠ, J., Ruthenian Literature, Ukrainian Literature
TOČANAC, D., Modern French Language
TRIPKOVIĆ, M., Sociology and Sociological Theories
UZELAC, M., Aesthetics
VUKOVIĆ, G., Modern Serbian Language

Faculty of Physical Education:

BALA, G., Kinesiology of Individual Sports
BJELICA, S., Sociological and Psychological Elements of Kinesiology
BLAGAJAC, M., Kinesiology of Recreational Sports
DIMOVA, K., Kinesiology of Individual Sports
DUNDJEROVIĆ, R., Kinesiology of Individual Sports
KALAJDŽIĆ, D., Kinesiology of Sports Games
KOVAČ, J., Kinesiology of Sports Games
MALACKO, J., Kinesiology of Sports
RADOVANOVIĆ, DJ., Kinesiology of Physical Education
RAIČ, A., Economical and Political Elements of Kinesiology
STEJIĆ, M., Kinesiology of Individual Sports
TONČEV, I., Kinesiology of Individual Sports

Faculty of Technology:

CARIĆ, M., Milk and Dairy Technology
CURAKOVIĆ, M., Wrapping and Packaging
DJURIĆ, M., Engineering Thermodynamics
GAĆEŠA, S., Technology of Malt and Beer
JAKOVLJEVIĆ, J., Starch Technology
KALUDJERSKI, G., Flour and Baking
KARLOVIĆ, DJ., Technology of Plant Oils, Fats and Margarine
KIŠ, E., Catalysis
LAJŠIĆ, S., Chemistry and Processing of Natural Products
LESKOVAC, V., Biochemistry
MARJANOVIĆ, N., Food Analysis
MILIĆ, B., Organic Chemistry
PAVLOVIĆ, O., Electrochemical Engineering
PEJIN, D., Yeast and Alcohol Technology
PEKIĆ, B., Chemistry and Technology of Pharmaceutical Products
PERIČIN, D., Biochemistry of Industrial Enzymology
PETROVIĆ, S., Biochemistry
PETROVIĆ, S., Analytical Chemistry
RADONJIĆ, LJ., Corrosion and Protection
REDE, R., Technology of Meat Processing and Production
RUŽIĆ, N., Technology of Wine Production
SOVILJ, M., Unit Operations
ŠIMON, V., Elements of Mechanical Engineering and Technical Drawing
TEKIĆ, M., Process-Plant Design
TOJAGIĆ, S., Ready-Made Food Technology
TURKULOV, J., Technology of Plant Oils, Fats and Margarine
VUJIČIĆ, B., Technology of Fruit and Vegetable Products

Faculty of Education:

DJURIĆ, DJ., Educational Psychology
GRUBOR, A., Education
LIPOVAC, M., Didactics and Education
PETROVIĆ, N., Mathematics and Teaching of Mathematics

Technical Faculty 'Mihajlo Pupin':

DIMITRIJEVIĆ, Ž., Physics, Measurements
HOTOMSKI, P., Informatics
LIPOVAC, D., Informatics
MALBAŠA, V., Electronic Systems and Networks
MITROVIĆ, Ž., Mathematical Numerical Analysis
NADRLJANSKI, DJ., Programming and Computers
NEDIMOVIĆ, B., Technical Design and Descriptive Geometry
NIKOLIĆ, M., Sociology
RISTIĆ, D., Organization Science
SOTIROVIĆ, V., Informatics

Academy of Art:

BANIĆEVIĆ, P., Acting
BRUČI, R., Composition
ČERNOGUBOV, B., Choir
ĆETKOVIĆ, V., Art History
DENKOVIĆ, LJ., Sculpture
DJAK, Ž., Graphics
DOBANOVAČKI, B., Graphic Communications
DRAŠKOVIĆ, B., Directing
EGIĆ, M., Flute
GILIĆ, V., Directing
HORVAT, L., Viola
IVANOVIĆ, K., Contrabass
JAGUŠT, M., Conducting
JAJČANIN-CVIJANOVIĆ, A., Acting
JOVANOVIĆ, Z., Chamber Music
JUHAS, G., History of Hungarian Drama and Theatre
KARANOVIĆ, B., Photography
KELBLI, M., Clarinet
KOVAČEK, B., History of Yugoslav Drama and Theatre
LAZIĆ, R., Directing
MARKOVIĆ, R., Acting
MIHAILOVIĆ, D., Dramaturgy
MIŠIĆ, LJ., Dance
NAGORNI, M., Graphics
PETIN, N., Harmony
PLEŠA, B., Acting
POZNANOVIĆ, B., Intermedia Research
RADIĆ, D., Composition
RAKIDŽIĆ, J., Painting
RNJAK, D., History of World Drama and Theatre
STANOJEV, M., Graphics
STAŠEVIĆ, M., Drawing
TIKVEŠA, H., Drawing
TODOROVIĆ, D., Painting
TOPLAK, I., Playing of Scores
VALDMA, A., Piano

There are research institutes attached to each faculty

UNIVERZITET U PRIŠTINI
(University of Priština)

38000 Priština, Vidovdanska b.b.

Telephone: (38) 24-970
Fax: (38) 27-628

Founded 1970
State control
Academic year: September to June

Rector: Prof. Dr RADIVOJE PAPOVIĆ
Vice-Rectors: Prof. Dr LJUBOMIR ŠĆEPANOVIĆ, Prof. Dr STANOJE DOGANDŽIĆ
Secretary-General: RANKO DJOKIĆ
Head of Library: Prof. Dr SLOBODAN KOSTIĆ

Number of teachers: 756
Number of students: 10,300

Publications: *Univerzitetska Misao, Acta Biologiae et Medicinae Experimentalis, Pregled Predavanja.*

DEANS

Faculty of Agriculture: Prof. Dr BRANISLAV BRKIĆ
Faculty of Philosophy: Prof. Dr RADENKO KRULJ
Faculty of Law: Prof. Dr MILOVAN MARKOVIĆ
Faculty of Economics: Prof. Dr RADISLAV ANDJELKOVIĆ

Faculty of Civil Engineering and Architecture: Prof. Dr VUKOMIR SAVIĆ

Faculty of Medicine: Prof. Dr TOMISLAV DJOKIĆ

Faculty of Mining and Metallurgy: Prof. Dr DRAGOSLAV ELEZOVIĆ

Faculty of Natural Sciences and Mathematics: Prof. Dr SLOBODAN GLIGORIJEVIĆ

Faculty of Arts: Prof. ZORAN KARALEJIĆ

Faculty of Physical Education: Prof. Dr MIROSLAV MEKIĆ

Faculty of Philology: Prof. Dr BORISLAV VUKOVIĆ

Faculty of Electrical Engineering: Prof. Dr ĆEMAL DOLIČANIN

Faculty of Mechanical Engineering: Prof. Dr VLADIMIR RAIČEVIĆ

Faculty of Teacher Training: Prof. Dr MOMIR JOVIĆ

College

Higher School of Economics: Belgrade; f. 1956; two-year course leading to a diploma in economics, finance and commerce; 63 professors, 1,630 students; library of 10,066 vols; Dir Prof. N. POTKONJAK.

ZAMBIA

Learned Societies

BIBLIOGRAPHY, LIBRARY SCIENCE AND MUSEOLOGY

Zambia Library Association: POB 32839, Lusaka; Chair. Mrs C. ZULU; Hon. Sec. W. C. MULALAMI; publs *Journal* (quarterly), *Newsletter* (every 2 months).

MEDICINE

Zambia Medical Association: POB RW 148, Lusaka; Chair. Dr S. SIKANETA; Sec. Dr D. LEVITT; publ. *Medical Journal of Zambia* (every 2 months).

NATURAL SCIENCES

Biological Sciences

Wildlife Conservation Society of Zambia: POB 30255, Lusaka; tel. (1) 254226; fax (1) 222906; f. 1953; wildlife and natural resource conservation, environmental education; 1,500 mems; Pres. G. R. KAYUKWA; Exec. Dir M. SICHILONGO; publs *Kobus* (monthly), *Chongololo Chipembele for Schools, Teacher's Guide* (both every 2 months).

TECHNOLOGY

Engineering Institution of Zambia: POB 34730, Lusaka; f. 1955; 2,600 mems; Pres. G. K. CHIBUYE; Vice-Pres. Dr K. AKAPELWA; publ. *Journal* (quarterly).

Research Institutes

GENERAL

National Council for Scientific Research: POB 310158, Chelston, Lusaka 15302; tel. 281081; telex 40005; fax 283502; f. 1967; statutory body to advise the government on scientific research policy, to promote and coordinate research and to collect and disseminate scientific information; incorporates Livestock and Pest Research Centre, Tree Improvement Research Centre, Radioisotopes Research Unit, Food Technology Research Unit, Water Resources Research Unit, Building and Industrial Minerals Research Unit; 90 research staff; library of 9,200 vols, 100 periodicals; Chair. the Minister of Science, Technology and Vocational Training; Sec.-Gen. Prof. M. N. SIAMWIZA; publs *Zambia Journal of Science and Technology* (irregular), *Zambia Science Abstracts* (annually), *NCSR Annual Report, Proceedings of Seminars, Workshops etc.*

AGRICULTURE, FISHERIES AND VETERINARY SCIENCE

Central Fisheries Research Institute: POB 350100, Chilanga; tel. 278680; f. 1965; hydrobiological research directed towards increasing fish production; library of 4,500 vols; Chief Fisheries Research Officer Dr R. MUBAMBA; publs *Fisheries Statistics, Annual Report*.

Central Veterinary Research Station: POB 50, Mazabuka; f. 1926; directed by the Ministry of Lands and Agriculture; general veterinary diagnosis and research; Asst Dir, Veterinary Research Dr M. A. Q. AWAN.

Division of Forest Products Research: POB 20388, Kitwe; tel. 227088; telex 52051; f. 1963; controls research into wood utilization, timber properties preservation, engineering, forest products and wood composite studies; Chief Officer S. M. MUTEMWA; publs *Bulletin, Records* (irregular).

Division of Forest Research: POB 22099, Kitwe; tel. 220456; telex 52051; fax 224110; f. 1956; ecological and botanical studies; soil and site assessment investigations; silvicultural research, exotic plantations and indigenous forests and woodlands; mensurational studies of plantation growth; tree breeding and selection; agroforestry and fuelwood projects; forest pathology and entomology; seed collection, processing, testing and low-temperature storage; staff of 24; library of 7,800 vols, 150 periodicals and 100 serials; Chief Forest Research Officer F. M. MALAYA; publs *Research Notes, Research Pamphlets, Research Bulletins, Research Newsletter*.

International Red Locust Control Organisation for Central and Southern Africa: POB 240252, Ndola; tel. (2) 614284; telex 30072; fax (2) 614285; e-mail locust@zamnet.zm; f. 1970; to prevent plagues of red locust by controlling incipient outbreaks, to assist mem. countries in the management of army worm and grain-eating birds and to carry out research and training; member countries: Kenya, Malawi, Mozambique, Swaziland, Tanzania, Uganda, Zambia, Zimbabwe; library of 3,000 vols, 35 periodicals; Dir E. K. BYARUHANGA; publs *Annual Report, Quarterly Reports, Scientific Papers*.

Mount Makulu Agricultural Research Station: Private Bag 7, Chilanga; f. 1952; Headquarters of Research Branch of Department of Agriculture, Ministry of Agriculture and Water Development, and 11 regional and specialist research stations; research on soils, soil classification, vegetation types and land classification; agronomy; chemistry; ecology; entomology; pasture research; phytosanitary services; plant breeding; plant pathology; Seeds Control and Certification Institute; stored products entomology; cotton entomology; main crops under investigation: maize, groundnuts, cotton, tobacco, pastures and pasture legumes, beans, wheat, sorghum, soyabeans; library of 28,000 vols, 18,000 reports, 12,000 reprints; Chief Agricultural Research Officer I. KALIANGILE; publs *Accessions List* (every 2 months), *Research Branch Memoranda* (occasional), *Annual Report, Reprints of Articles by Staff Members, Production Farming in Zambia* (monthly).

ECONOMICS, LAW AND POLITICS

Pan-African Institute for Development, East and Southern Africa: POB 80448, Kabwe; tel. 223651; telex 81290; f. 1979; training, research, surveys, follow-up action; 34 staff; library of 7,000 vols; Dir ANTHONY LINDSAY HAGAN; Registrar PATRICK A. MUSOKWA.

MEDICINE

National Food and Nutrition Commission: POB 32669, Lusaka; tel. 227803; f. 1967; statutory body to improve the nutritional status of the people of Zambia; 98 mems; Chair. Prof. C. CHINTU; Exec. Dir ALLEN RUNETA; publ. *Nutrition News* (3 a year).

Pneumoconiosis Medical and Research Bureau: Independence Ave, POB 20205, Kitwe; f. 1950; research on pneumoconiosis and related chest diseases; library of 300 vols; Dir Dr C. M. MUSOWE.

Tropical Diseases Research Centre: POB 71769, Ndola; tel. 610961; telex 30180; fax 612837; f. 1976; research in communicable diseases, support for disease control and primary health care programmes; trains Zambian scientists in the field of bio-medical research, serves as international research and training centre; epidemiological research, clinical trials, research in malaria, schistosomiasis, trypanosomiasis, diarrhoeal diseases, etc.; 32 researchers, 98 support staff; library of 2,200 vols, 219 periodicals; Dir Dr M. MUKUNYANDELA; publs *Annual Report, Tropical Diseases Research Centre Newsletter*.

NATURAL SCIENCES

Physical Sciences

Geological Survey of Zambia (Ministry of Mines and Minerals Development): POB 50135, Lusaka; tel. (1) 250174; e-mail gsd@zamnet.zm; f. 1951; statutory depository for all mining and prospecting records and reports; responsible for geological mapping, economic mineral investigations, assisting the public on mineral matters, and advising the Ministry on all mineral and geological matters; library of 89,346 vols; Dir D. MULELA; publs *Annual Report, Records, Bulletins, Memoirs, Reports, Occasional Papers, Economic Reports, Annotated Bibliography and Index of the Geology of Zambia*, and maps.

Libraries and Archives

Kitwe

Hammarskjöld Memorial Library: POB 21493, Kitwe; tel. (2) 211488; telex 52050; fax (2) 211001; f. 1963; 45,000 vols; collection of films, filmstrips, slides, microfiche, videotapes, tape-recordings on local history; rare book collection on the history of central Africa; specializes in social sciences; research library and archives of the Mindolo Ecumenical Foundation; Head Librarian E. F. SAKALA.

Kitwe Public Library: POB 20070, Kitwe; tel. 213685; f. 1954; 33,000 vols; one branch library; publs *Annual Report*, list of new books (irregular).

Lusaka

Lusaka City Libraries: POB 31304, Katondo Rd, Lusaka; tel. 227282; f. 1943; 3 br. libraries and a mobile library; 145,000 vols, 200 periodicals, 320 maps; Librarian J. C. NKOLE; publs *Library Bulletin* (quarterly), *Annual Report*.

National Archives of Zambia: POB 50010, Lusaka; tel. 254081; fax 254080; f. 1947; covers national literature from 1890 to the present day in the forms of national archives, historical MSS, microfilms, cartographic, philatelic, currency, pictorial and printed publication collections; 18,000 linear metres of records; depository and reference library of 17,000 vols and 11,000 periodicals; the National Archives Library is a reference and legal deposit library for all printed publications published in Zambia; Dir M. N. MUTITI;

Senior Archivist T. M. Suuya; Senior Librarian H. K. Nyendwa; publs *Annual National Bibliography, Annual Reports, Calendars of District Note Books, vols I and IV, Information About the National Archives of Zambia, List of Periodicals,* vols I and II.

Zambia Library Service: POB 30802, Lusaka; tel. and fax (1) 254993; f. 1962; 6 regional libraries, 18 branch libraries and a central library of 500,000 vols; aims to provide a countrywide free public library service; Librarian E. M. Moadabwe; publ. *Zambia Library Service Newsletter* (irregular).

Ndola

Ndola Public Library: POB 70388, Independence Way, Ndola; tel. 617173; telex 30270; f. 1934; 90,000 vols, 140 periodicals; public library services in Lusaka serving Ndola City Council Community; central library, four brs, two prison library centres; centre for American Circulating Library from American Cultural Center; Librarian Dr K. Mumba Chisaka; publ. *Copperbelt Library Bulletin* (irregular).

Museums and Art Galleries

Livingstone

Livingstone Museum: Mosi-oa-Tunya Rd, POB 60498, Livingstone; tel. (3) 324427; fax (3) 320991; e-mail livmus@zamnet.zm; f. 1934; ethnology of the peoples of Zambia; prehistory, history and natural history of Zambia; autograph, letters and relics of David Livingstone; library of *c.* 20,000 vols, 200 periodicals, including special collection of *c.* 2,000 vols on prehistory, history, ethnography and Africana; supporting depts of taxidermy, conservation and education; Dir K. V. Katanekwa; publs *Zambia Museum Journal, The Livingstone Museum Newsletter.*

Mbala

Moto Moto Museum: POB 420230, Mbala; tel. (4) 450098; fax (4) 450243; e-mail motomoto@zamnet.zm; f. 1974; research in ethnography, pre-history and history; educational and exhibition programmes; library of 2,000 vols; Dir Stanford M. Siachoono; publs *Zambia Museums Journal, Annual Report, Museum Newsletter.*

Ndola

Copperbelt Museum: POB 71444, Buteko Ave, Ndola; tel. 613591; fax 617450; f. 1962; collection, conservation, preservation, documentation and exhibit of geological and historical items, ethnography and natural history; Dir Sibanyama Mudenda.

Universities

COPPERBELT UNIVERSITY

POB 21692, Kitwe

Telephone: (2) 222066
Telex: 53270
Fax: (2) 222469

Founded 1979 as Ndola Campus of University of Zambia; present status 1987
State control
Language of instruction: English
Academic year: January to September (3 terms)

Chancellor: (vacant)
Vice-Chancellor: (vacant)
Deputy Vice-Chancellor: Dr J. Lungu
Registrar: K. K. Kapika (acting)
Librarian: Prof. M. C. Lundu

Number of teachers: 150
Number of students: 1,580

DEANS

School of Business: Prof. T. E. Gilling
School of Built Environment: Dr H. M. Silengo
School of Technology: Capt. F. Kanungwa
School of Forestry and Wood Science: P. Moonga

HEADS OF DEPARTMENTS

School of Business:

- Accounting and Finance: Prof. N. Ronan
- Business Administration: D. M. Chilipamushi
- Postgraduate Programme: Dr J. N. Nyirenda
- Production Management: E. A. Mukula

School of Built Environment:

- Building Science: W. Shakantu
- Architecture and Building Science: Prof. W. Hill
- Urban and Regional Planning: E. Boakye
- Construction and Civil Engineering: G. C. Ngoma

School of Technology:

- Chemical Engineering: T. Kooma
- Electrical Engineering: G. Mwangana
- Mining: W. S. Samiselo
- Computer Science: B. P. Chondoka

ATTACHED INSTITUTES

Institute of Consultancy, Applied Research and Extension Studies: Dir Dr T. K. Taylor.

Institute of Environmental Management: Dir Dr K. K. D. Maseka.

UNIVERSITY OF ZAMBIA

POB 32379, Lusaka

Telephone: (1) 291777
Telex: 44370
Fax: 253952
E-mail: registra@unza.zm

Founded 1965
State control
Language of instruction: English
Academic year: November to September

Chancellor: (vacant)
Vice-Chancellor: Dr E. C. Mumba (acting)
Registrar: M. Tandeo
Librarian: Dr H. Mwacalimba

Number of teachers: 535
Number of students: 3,464

Publications: *African Social Research, Zambian Papers, Zango, Zambia Law Journal, Journal of Humanities, Journal of Medicine, Journal of Sciences and Technology.*

DEANS

Agricultural Sciences: Dr F. Mwape
Natural Sciences: Dr D. Theo
Humanities and Social Sciences: Dr J. D. Chileshe
Distance Education: Prof. R. Siaciwena (Dir)
Education: Dr I. W. Chikalanga (acting)
Law: Dr N. Simbyakula
Engineering: Dr S. B. Kanyanga
Medicine: Prof. Munkonge
Veterinary Medicine: Dr K. L. Samui
Mines: Dr F. Kamona
Research and Graduate Studies: Dr G. Lungwangwa (Dir)

HEADS OF DEPARTMENTS

Agricultural Sciences:

- Animal Sciences: Dr E. S. K. Yambayamba
- Crop Science: Dr M. S. Mwala
- Agricultural Economics and Extension Education: Dr E. C. Musaba
- Soil Science: Dr A. C. Chipeleme

Education:

- Educational Administration and Policy Studies: Dr A. Sikwibele
- Educational Psychology, Sociology and Special Education: Dr O. C. Chakulimba
- Language and Social Sciences Education: Dr C. M. Namafe
- Mathematics and Science Education: B. Nkhata
- In-Service Education and Advisory Science Education: G. Tambulukani
- Adult Education and Extension Studies: Dr D. M. Sibalwa
- Library and Information Studies: V. Shifwepa

Engineering:

- Agricultural Engineering: Dr N. J. Kwendakwema
- Civil Engineering: Dr M. N. Mulenga
- Electrical and Electronic Engineering: Prof. S. Karim
- Mechanical Engineering: Dr A. N. Ng'andu
- Surveying: Prof. A. Bujakiewicz

Humanities and Social Sciences:

- Development Studies: Dr F. Mutesa
- Economics: Dr M. C. Ndulo
- Gender Studies: Dr M. C. Milimo
- History: F. E. Mulenga
- Literature and Languages: S. B. Hirst
- Political and Administrative Studies: Dr N. M. Mulikita
- Philosophy: Prof. C. Dillon-Malone
- Psychology: G. Mwape
- Social Development Studies: Dr A. Kapungwe

Medicine:

- Anatomy: Prof. J. T. Karashani
- Community Medicine: Dr L. Chiwele (acting)
- Internal Medicine: Dr P. Matondo (acting)
- Obstetrics and Gynaecology: Dr Y. Ahmed
- Paediatrics and Child Health: Dr G. Shakankale (acting)
- Physiological Sciences: Dr C. V. Prasana
- Post-Basic Nursing: L. Lambwe (acting)
- Psychiatry: Prof. A. Haworth
- Surgery: Prof. K. Erzingatsian
- Pathology and Microbiology: Dr C. J. Shinondo

Mines:

- Geology: Dr I. Nyambe
- Metallurgy and Mineral Processing: Dr S. Simukanga
- Mining Engineering: Prof. R. Krishna

Natural Sciences:

- Biological Sciences: Dr L. E. Mumba
- Chemistry: Dr S. F. Banda
- Geography: Dr M. C. Mulenga
- Mathematics and Statistics: Dr J. C. Chikunji
- Physics: Dr H. V. Mweene

Veterinary Medicine:

- Biomedical Sciences: Dr J. N. Siulapwa
- Clinical Studies: Dr I. K. Phiri (acting)
- Paraclinical Studies: Dr H. Chitambo
- Disease Control: Dr A. Nambota

ATTACHED INSTITUTES

Centre for the Arts: Dir Dr M. Mtonga (acting).

Computer Centre: Dir M. P. Bennett.

Institute for African Studies: Dr O. Saasa.

Institute for Economic and Social Research: Dir Prof. O. S. SAASA.

Rural Development Studies: Dr J. T. MILIMO.

Educational Research Bureau: Dir Prof. E. K. WADDIMBA.

Institute for Human Relations: Dir Dr M. C. MUSAMBACHIME.

Colleges

Evelyn Hone College of Applied Arts and Commerce: POB 30029, Lusaka; tel. 211557; f. 1963; Principal J. P. KALUNGA; Senior Registrar A. P. CHITSULO; Librarian R. SHULA; library of 20,000 vols; 200 teachers; 1,200 full-time, 1,500 part-time students; publs *Beacon Newspaper* (quarterly), *College Prospectus* (annually).

National Institute of Public Administration: POB 31990, 10101 Lusaka; tel. 228802; telex 40523; f. 1963; trains government administrators and accounting personnel for central and local government; library of 28,000 vols; 75 teachers; 1,270 students (including some on in-training courses); Principal Dr KANGANJA; Registrar G. H. MOONO (acting); Librarian A. G. KASONSO; publs *Administration for Rural Development* (research papers), teaching pamphlets, *NIPA Review*.

Natural Resources Development College: POB 310099, Lusaka; fax (1) 224639; f. 1964; 3-year diploma courses in agriculture, agricultural education and engineering, nutrition, fisheries, water engineering; library of 32,000 vols; 48 teachers; 430 students; Principal T. F. F. MALUZA; Librarian M. M. MISENGO.

Northern Technical College: POB 250093, Ndola; tel. 680141; f. 1964; automotive, electrical, heavy duty and mechanical engineering, business studies and communication skills; library of 16,000 vols; 64 full-time, 28 part-time teachers; 500 full-time, 480 part-time students; Principal M. G. NYIRENDA; Registrar F. M. SUSU; Librarian M. C. BANDA.

Zambia College of Agriculture: POB 53, Monze; f. 1947; 2-year certificate course; 42 staff, 240 students; library of 3,000 vols; Principal D. H. MCCLEERY.

ZIMBABWE

Learned Societies

AGRICULTURE, FISHERIES AND VETERINARY SCIENCE

Crop Science Society of Zimbabwe: POB UA 409, Union Ave, Harare; f. 1970; 200 mems.

Zimbabwe Agricultural Society: POB 442, Harare; tel. 705641; fax 705644; f. 1895; 5,400 mems; Gen. Man. J. R. PEARCE.

Zimbabwe Veterinary Association: POB CY 168, Causeway, Harare; f. 1920; 175 mems; Pres. Dr G. GWAZE; Sec. Dr R. MADEKUROZVA; publ. *Zimbabwe Veterinary Journal* (quarterly).

BIBLIOGRAPHY, LIBRARY SCIENCE AND MUSEOLOGY

Zimbabwe Library Association: POB 3133, Harare; f. 1959; 254 mems; Chair. DRIDEN KUNAKA; Sec. ALBERT MASHEKA; tel. (4) 792641; fax (4) 703050; publ. *Zimbabwe Librarian*.

FINE AND PERFORMING ARTS

Arts Association Harare: POB 4011, Harare; f. 1968; Chair. HAROLD MARSH; Sec. EVE STRANNIX.

HISTORY, GEOGRAPHY AND ARCHAEOLOGY

Geographical Association of Zimbabwe: c/o Dept of Geography, University of Zimbabwe, Box MP167, Mount Pleasant, Harare; tel. (4) 303211; fax (4) 883264; e-mail scumming@esanet.zw; f. 1967; 600 mems; Chair. R. S. BURRETT; Sec. Dr C. KUNAKA; publs *Geographical Journal of Zimbabwe*, *Geographical Education Magazine*.

Prehistory Society of Zimbabwe: POB 876, Harare; f. 1958; promotion of the study of early history, pre-history and archaeology in Africa, with particular reference to Zimbabwe; 100 mems; library of 1,000 vols; Chair. LORRAINE SWAN; publs. *Zimbabwean Prehistory* (irregular), *Newsletter* (quarterly).

LANGUAGE AND LITERATURE

Literature Bureau, Zimbabwe: POB CY 749, Causeway, Harare; f. 1954; a br. of Ministry of Education; encourages, advises and sponsors African authors, finds publishers for their work and establishes markets for their books; also active in language studies, workshops, seminars, etc.; Matabeleland branch: POB 828, Bulawayo; Chief Publications Officer B. C. CHITSIKE; publ. *Bureau Bulletin* (quarterly).

Zimbabwe Writers Union: Gloag High School, POB 61, Turk Mine; Pres. CONT MHLANGA; Sec.-Gen. PATHISA NYATHI.

MEDICINE

Dental Association of Zimbabwe: POB 3303, Harare; tel. (4) 702234; Pres. Dr T. D. MUKURAZHIZHA; publ. *Journal* (annually).

Pharmaceutical Society of Zimbabwe: POB 1476, Harare; tel. and fax (4) 706967; Pres. G. N. MAHLANGY; Sec. Dr F. CHINYANGANYA.

Zimbabwe Medical Association: POB 3671, Harare; tel. 720731; Pres. B. G. MAUCHAZA; Sec. E. VUSHE.

NATURAL SCIENCES

General

Zimbabwe Scientific Association: POB 978, Harare; f. 1899; 350 mems; Pres. Prof. J. P. LOVERIDGE; Sec. Dr K. T. MANISODZA; publs *Transactions* (annually), *Zimbabwe Science News* (quarterly).

Biological Sciences

Botanical Society of Zimbabwe: POB 461, Harare; tel. 735163; f. 1934; Hon. Sec. J. R. JAMES.

Kirk Biological Society: Dept of Biological Sciences, University of Zimbabwe, POB MP167, Mount Pleasant, Harare; tel. (4) 303211; telex 26580; fax (4) 333407; e-mail jmugodo@yahoo.com; f. 1969; botany, zoology, ecology, microbiology; Chair. JAMES MUGODO.

Lowveld Natural History Branch, Wildlife Society of Zimbabwe: POB 81, Chiredzi; f. 1968; promotion of conservation and natural history education; 186 mems; Chair. J. TAYLER; Sec. A. WILLIAMSON; publs *Newsletter* (monthly), *The Hartebeest* (annually).

Ornithological Association of Zimbabwe: POB CY 161, Causeway, Harare; tel. 794611; e-mail birds@harare.iafrica.com; Pres. JOHN PAXTON; publ. *Honeyguide* (quarterly).

Wildlife Society of Zimbabwe: Mukuvisi Environment Centre, POB HG 996, Highlands, Harare; tel. 747648; fax 747174; e-mail zimwild@harare.iafrica.com; f. 1927; all aspects of wild life conservation and environmental awareness; 2,500 mems; Pres. SHIRLEY CORMACK; CEO Dr IAN CORMACK; publ. *Zimbabwe Wildlife*.

Physical Sciences

Geological Society of Zimbabwe: POB CY1719, Causeway, Harare; e-mail hjelsma@geology.uz.zw; f. 1981; 320 mems; Chair. M. L. VINYU; Sec. H. A. JELSMA.

Mennel Society: Dept of Geology, University of Zimbabwe, POB MP167, Mount Pleasant, Harare; f. 1964; to promote the understanding of earth sciences through lectures, films, field trips; 40 mems; Pres. H. MUNYANYIWA; Chair J. B. CHAUMBA; publ. *Detritus*.

TECHNOLOGY

Institution of Mining and Metallurgy (Zimbabwe Section): POB 405, Harare; fax 46504; f. 1931; Chair. J. L. NIXON; Hon. Sec. M. R. RICHARDSON.

Survey Institute of Zimbabwe: POB 3869, Harare; f. 1967; 80 mems; voluntary asscn of surveyors in the fields of land, engineering, topographical and mine surveying; Pres. S. Z. ZHOU; Hon. Sec. J. BIRKETT.

Zimbabwe Institution of Engineers: POB 660, Harare; tel. 746821; fax 746652; e-mail zie@harare.iafrica.com; f. 1944; 2,568 mems; Pres. Eng. J. C. GOLDSMITH; Chief Exec. Eng. R. E. G. OFFORD; publs *The Zimbabwe Engineer* (monthly), *Year Book, Proceedings* (1 a year).

Research Institutes

GENERAL

Research Council of Zimbabwe: POB CY 294, Causeway, Harare; tel. 703001; telex 22141; fax (4) 728799; f. 1964, reconstituted 1984; advisory body to the Government on general scientific policy and official channel for exchange of national and international scientific and technical information; Chair. Dr E. ZWANGOBANI; Sec. I. C. CHIRI; publs *Directory of Organizations concerned with Scientific Research and Services in Zimbabwe* (every 2 years), *Zimbabwe Research Index* (annually), *Symposium Proceedings* (every 2 years), *Research Council of Zimbabwe Bulletin* (quarterly).

AGRICULTURE, FISHERIES AND VETERINARY SCIENCE

Agricultural Research Council of Zimbabwe: POB CY 594, Causeway, Harare; f. 1970; advises on agricultural research policy and programmes in Zimbabwe; administers regional research institutes and stations through the Department of Research and Specialist Services (Dir Dr N. R. GATA); Chair. Prof. M. RUKUNI; publs *Annual Report*, *Zimbabwe Agricultural Journal* (6 a year), *Zimbabwe Journal of Agricultural Research* (2 a year), *Kirkia – Journal of Botany of Zimbabwe* (1 a year).

Research institutes and stations:

Agronomy Institute: POB CY 550, Causeway, Harare; f. 1976; formerly Salisbury Research Station; research into crop agronomy, crop ecology and crop production; Head D. HIKWA.

Chemistry and Soil Research Institute: POB CY 550, Causeway, Harare; f. 1909; research and advisory work on soils and agricultural chemistry; registration and regulation of fertilizers and foodstuffs; crop nutrition, chemistry, pedology, soil physics and soil productivity research sections; Head C. F. MUSHAMBI.

Cotton Research Institute: POB 530, Kadoma; f. 1925; all aspects of cotton agronomy, breeding and pest research; Head G. G. RABEY.

Crop Breeding Institute: POB CY 550, Causeway, Harare; f. 1976; formerly Salisbury Research Station; responsible for breeding programmes on maize, soya beans, groundnuts, wheat, barley, potatoes, sorghum, pearl millet and sunflowers; Head Dr A. MASHIRIGWANI (acting).

Plant Protection Research Institute: POB CY 550, Causeway, Harare; f. 1964; research and advisory work on plant pests and diseases; entomology, pathology and nematology sections; Head Dr A. MASHIRIGWANI (acting).

Biometrics Bureau: POB 594, Causeway, Harare; f. 1968; undertakes applied biometrical research, provides professional advice and a computer service to other research workers; Head J. KANGAI.

Farming Systems Research Unit: POB 550, Causeway, Harare; f. 1984; responsible for adapting, developing and testing on farms improved crop and livestock production technologies and systems, and a model for farm systems research acceptable to the Department of Research and Specialist Services and suitable for wide-scale application in Zimbabwe; Team Leader B. MOMBESHORA.

Grasslands Research Station: Private Bag 3701, Marondera; f. 1929; research on pasture, animal and crop production for the high-rainfall sandveld area; selection and testing of Rhizobium strains and commercial production of legume inoculants; Head P. R. HATENDI.

Henderson Research Station: Private Bag 2004, Mazowe; f. 1949; pasture work on the introduction and screening of grasses and legumes for suitability as fertilized pastures; research in ruminant nutrition; herbicide and weed control research; Head Mr MUPETA.

Lowveld Research Station: POB 97, Chiredzi; f. 1967; research in irrigation agronomy in South-Eastern Lowveld; subtropical horticulture and vegetable crops; Head I. MHARAPARA.

Matopos Research Station: Private Bag K5137, Bulawayo; f. 1903; research in veld management, ecology of regional soil types, bush encroachment, cattle breeding, and beef production; Head Dr T. SMITH.

Makoholi Experiment Station: Private Bag 9182, Masvingo; f. 1942; research into problems of animal and crop production for sandveld and medium rainfall districts of Zimbabwe; crop agronomy, cattle production (indigenous breeds) and natural grazing management; Head J. GAMBIZA.

Horticultural Research Centre: located on Grasslands Research Station, Private Bag 3701, Marondera; f. 1968; responsible for all aspects of horticultural research; Officer-in-Charge Dr J. JACKSON.

Coffee Research Station: POB 61, Chipinge; f. 1964; research into all aspects of coffee management, growth, pest and disease control; tea research projects; Officer-in-Charge (vacant).

Rhodes-Inyanga Experiment Station: Private Bag 8044, Rusape; f. 1910; Pome fruit research; Officer-in-Charge C. B. PAYNE.

Agricultural Research Trust: POB MP 84, Mount Pleasant, Harare; tel. (4) 860412; fax (4) 726062; e-mail artfarm@africaonline.co.zw; f. 1980; research into cereals, grains, oilseed and horticultural crops and the provision of research field sites for crop breeders, agronomists and the crop chemical industry; Dir R. A. WINKFIELD.

Department of Veterinary Services; Tsetse and Trypanosomiasis Control Branch: POB 8283, Causeway, Harare; under the Ministry of Agriculture; f. 1909; for the control of trypanosomiasis and tsetse fly and the investigation of methods of control; laboratory at Harare and one research station in Zambezi Valley; Asst Dir V. CHADENGA.

Attached laboratory:

Veterinary Research Laboratory: POB 8101, Causeway, Harare; f. 1906; diagnostic centre and research institute for animal diseases; 30 mems; library of 1,200 vols; Asst Dir Dr G. STEWART.

Forestry Commission: POB 8111, Causeway, Harare; tel. 48430; telex 48323; fax 47066; f. 1954; state forest authority, responsible for formulating forest policy in Zimbabwe; engaged in large-scale plantation operations; research and advisory services, forestry extension and wildlife utilization.

Attached centre:

Forest Research Centre: POB HG 595, Highlands, Harare; conducts research into many aspects of forestry, principally high-yielding plantations, with special emphasis on tree genetics and the production of progressively improved pine and eucalypt seed, wood quality, general plantation management and fertilizer research; screening of multi-purpose tree species for use in fuel-wood plantations and social forestry.

Tobacco Research Board: POB 1909, Harare; tel. 575289; fax 575288; e-mail tobres@kutsaga.co.zw; f. 1950; board mems represent growers, buyers, and Ministry of Agriculture; conducts research into all types of tobacco, agronomy, breeding, engineering and pest control; operates three research stations; library of 12,000 vols, 250 periodicals; Chair. A. F. RAVENSCROFT; Dir L. T. V. COUSINS; publs technical bulletins, *Annual Report and Accounts*.

ECONOMICS, LAW AND POLITICS

Central Statistical Office: POB 8063, Causeway, Harare; f. 1927; co-ordinated statistical service for the Government; staff of 400; Dir G. MANDISHONA.

Institute of Development Studies: University of Zimbabwe, POB 880, Harare; tel. (4) 333341; telex 26422; fax (4) 333345; f. 1982 to undertake policy-oriented research, consultancy and training; three research departments: agrarian and labour studies, economics and technology studies and international relations and social development studies; library of 10,000 vols, 17,000 documents; Dir Dr DONALD P. CHIMANIKIRE.

MEDICINE

Public Health Laboratory: POB 8079, Causeway, Harare; f. 1909; Dir Dr P. G. DAVIES; Pathologist Dr R. F. LOWE; Chief Medical Technologist D. A. MVERE.

NATURAL SCIENCES

Physical Sciences

Geological Survey of Zimbabwe: POB CY 210, Causeway, Harare; tel. 726342; telex 22416; fax: 739601; f. 1910; geological mapping and survey of mineral resources; library of 1,400 vols, 800 symposia, 11,900 periodicals, 2,600 technical files; museum displaying Zimbabwean geology and economic minerals; Dir W. MAGALELA; publs *Annals, Bulletins, Mineral Resources Series* (irregular), short reports and maps.

Meteorological Service: POB BE 150, Belvedere, Harare; tel. 704955; telex 4004; fax 733156; f. 1897; Dir M. C. ZINYOWERA; publs *Monthly Meteorological Summaries, Rainfall Handbook Supplements, Climate Handbook Supplements, Agromet Bulletin* (October–March), daily weather reports and forecasts, weekly rainfall maps during rainy season November–March.

Affiliated institute:

Goetz Observatory: POB A C 65, Ascot, Bulawayo; tel. 66197; also seismology; publ. *Seismological Bulletin, Agricultural Meteorological Bulletin* (monthly).

TECHNOLOGY

Department of Metallurgy: Ministry of Mines, POB 1375, Causeway, Harare; tel. (4) 726629; telex 2141; fax (4) 793065; f. 1962; 88 staff; library of 280 vols; conducts investigations on methods of economic extraction from precious, base-metal and non-metallic ores and industrial minerals evaluation, also on physical metallurgy, e.g. non-destructive testing, impact testing, etc.; Dir T. I. NYATSANGA; publ. *Testwork Reports*.

Standards Association of Zimbabwe: POB 2259, Harare; tel. 885511; fax 882020; e-mail sazinfo@samara.co.zw; f. 1957; encourages high standards; has laboratory facilities for testing and operates certification marking schemes; compiles Standards Asscn of Zimbabwe Standards; library service; Dir-Gen. Eng. P. S. KUPAKUWANA; Chair. E. JINDA; publs *Annual Report, Fulcrums* (official bulletin).

Libraries and Archives

Bulawayo

National Library and Documentation Service National Free Library of Zimbabwe: POB 1773, Bulawayo; tel. 62359; telex 33128; fax 77662; f. 1943 as national lending library for educational, scientific and technical books; national centre for inter-library loans; maintains National Union Catalogue; 100,000 vols; Librarian H. R. NCUBE.

Public Library: POB 586, Bulawayo; tel. 60966; f. 1896; reference, lending, junior library; mobile library; postal service to rural readers; African and Zimbabwe collections; Zimbabwe map collection; legal deposit library for Zimbabwe; brs at Ascot, Bradfield and Waterford; 150,000 vols; Librarian R. W. DOUST; publs *Bulawayo Book News* (quarterly), *Triennial Report*.

Harare

Harare City Library: POB 1087, Harare; f. 1902; 60,000 vols; Librarian and Sec. M. ROSS-SMITH.

Library of Parliament: POB CY 298, Causeway, Harare; tel. (4) 700181 ext. 2131; telex 24064; fax (4) 795548; f. 1923; 115,000 vols; wide range of parliamentary and government documents obtained from Zimbabwe Parliament and from several Commonwealth countries; general collection specializing in political science, history, political biography, economics, sociology, public administration and management, education, foreign relations; separate law collection, separate archival and reference collection and Zimbabweana; Librarian N. MASAWI.

National Archives of Zimbabwe: Private Bag 7729, Causeway, Harare; tel. (4) 792741; fax (4) 792398; f. 1935 as the Government Archives of Southern Rhodesia; incorp. archives of Northern Rhodesia and Nyasaland and designated the Central African Archives 1947; became National Archives of Rhodesia and Nyasaland 1958–63; reverted January 1964 to Rhodesian Government and responsibility for Northern Rhodesia and Nyasaland archives ceased; also serves Zimbabwean municipalities and some parastatal bodies and holds archives of Federation of Rhodesia and Nyasaland; comprises sections of Records Management, Research (Public Archives, Historical Manuscripts), Library (nat. historical reference colln, incl. Photographic and Map Collns; legal deposit, depository for Unesco publications) and Technical (Reprographic Unit, Conservation Unit, Oral History, Automation, Audio-Visual Archives Unit); exhibition gallery; four provincial records centres; Dir I. J. JOHNSTONE; publs *Oppenheimer Series, Bibliographical Series, Occasional Papers, Zimbabwe National Bibliography* (annually), *Guide to the Public Archives of Rhodesia, Vol. 1, 1890–1923, Guide to the Historical Manuscripts in the National Archives, Report of the Director* (annually), *Current Periodicals, Directory of Libraries,* various histories and monographs.

University of Zimbabwe Library: POB MP45, Mount Pleasant, Harare; tel. (4) 303211; telex 26580; fax (4) 307773; f. 1956; 500,000 vols; 5,250 periodicals; Medical library; Mpilo Hospital library; Law library; Education library; Institute of Development

Studies Library; Lake Kariba Research Station library; Map library; Veterinary library; Africana (Zimbabweana) collection; collection of African languages; U.Z. Theses Collection; Librarian S. M. MADE.

Zimbabwe National Library and Documentation Service: POB 758, Harare; tel. 774943; f. 1972; co-ordinates all libraries in govt depts, colleges of education, agriculture and technology, public libraries; combined stock (100 libraries): 1,000,000 vols; Dir S. R. DUBE; publs *Directory of Zimbabwean Libraries*, *Government Library Service Newsletter*.

Mutare

City of Mutare Public Libraries: POB 48, Mutare; incorporates Sakubva Public Library (f. 1972, 27,000 vols), Dangamvura Public Library (f. 1988, 18,000 vols), Turner Memorial Library (f. 1902, 40,000 vols); Head of Library Services: D. MANDOWO.

Museums and Art Galleries

Bulawayo

Natural History Museum of Zimbabwe: Leopold Takawira Ave and Park Rd, POB 240, Bulawayo; tel. 960045; fax 964019; e-mail natmuse@acacia.samara.co.zw; f. 1901; geological, palaeontological, entomological and zoological; study collections and exhibits covering Ethiopian region, with special reference to southern Africa; historical, ethnographical and prehistorical exhibits appertaining to Zimbabwe and adjacent regions; Dir A. KUMIRAI; Curator of Mammals F. P. D. COTTERILL; Curator of Entomology R. SITHOLE; Curator of Arachnology M. FITZPATRICK; Curator of Ornithology A. MSIMANGA; Curator of Herpetology R. L. CHIDAVAENZI; Curator of Palaeontology D. MUNYIKWA; Curator of Ichthyology P. MAKONI; publs *Arnoldia (Zimbabwe)*, *Syntarsus*, occasional natural history papers.

Gweru

Military Museum of Zimbabwe: Lobengula Ave, POB 1300, Gweru; f. 1972; history of Zimbabwe Midlands and military history of Zimbabwe; Dir T. TSOMONDO.

Harare

National Gallery of Zimbabwe: 20 Julius Nyerere Way, POB CY 848, Causeway, Harare; tel. 704666; f. 1957; national collection of sculpture, paintings, drawings, prints, ceramics and artefacts by Zimbabwean and other Southern African artists; also includes European works of art dating from 16th century, and traditional and contemporary African art; regular exhibition programme; education programme; BAT studio for emerging young artists; library of 6,500 vols; Dir Prof. GEORGE P. KAHARI; publ. *Annual Report*.

National Herbarium and Botanic Garden: POB CY 550, Causeway, Harare; tel. (4) 744170; fax (4) 708938; f. 1909; attached to Agricultural Research Ccl of Zimbabwe; maintains a comprehensive collection of 500,000 specimens, provides an identification service for workers in agriculture and related fields and contributes to knowledge of the flora of South-Central Africa; taxonomic and ecological research, and research on medicinal and poisonous plants; library of 544 vols; Head (National Herbarium and Botanic Garden) N. NOBANDA; publ. *Kirkia* (1 a year).

Zimbabwe Museum of Human Sciences: Civic Centre, POB CY33, Causeway, Harare; tel. 751797; fax 774207; e-mail nmmz@pci.co.zw; f. 1902; zoological, ethnographical, archaeological and historical exhibits, study collections of archaeological, ethnographical material, rock art appertaining to Zimbabwe and adjacent areas; Dir T. MASONA; publs *Zimbabwea*, *Cookeia*, occasional human science papers.

Masvingo

Great Zimbabwe National Monument: PB 1060, Masvingo; tel. (39) 62080; fax (39) 63310; ruins of medieval dry stone buildings representing the Zimbabwe culture; history and development of Great Zimbabwe shown in site museum; Dir E. MATENGA.

Mutare

Mutare Museum: Aerodrome Rd, POB 920, Mutare; f. 1959; archaeological, zoological and historical exhibits, appertaining to the Eastern Districts in particular; national collection of road transport and firearms; Dir J. H. CHIPOKA.

Universities

NATIONAL UNIVERSITY OF SCIENCE AND TECHNOLOGY

POB 346, Bulawayo

Telephone: 76833
Fax: 76804

Founded 1990
State control
Language of instruction: English
Academic year: August to December, January to May

Chancellor: R. G. MUGABE
Vice-Chancellor: Prof. P. M. MAKHURANE
Pro Vice-Chancellor: Prof. C. B. NYATHI
Registrar: M. T. KARIWO
Librarian: K. MATSIKA

Number of teachers: 100 full-time
Number of students: 1,600

Publication: *University Year Book*.

DEANS

Faculty of Industrial Technology: Dr L. SIHWA
Faculty of Applied Sciences: T. S. DLODLO
Faculty of Commerce: E. RAZEMBA

Departments of Accounting, Applied Biology, Applied Chemistry, Applied Mathematics, Applied Physics, Banking, Business Management, Chemical Engineering, Computer Science, Civil and Water Engineering, Electronic Engineering, Finance, Industrial Engineering, Insurance.

UNIVERSITY OF ZIMBABWE

POB MP167, Mount Pleasant, Harare

Telephone: (4) 303211
Fax: (4) 333407

Founded 1955 as University College of Rhodesia; became University of Rhodesia in 1970, and University of Zimbabwe in 1980.

Language of instruction: English
Academic year: August to June

Chancellor: HE The President of the Republic of Zimbabwe
Vice-Chancellor: Prof. GRAHAM HILL
Registrar: W. MUKONDIWA
Librarian: S. M. MADE

Number of teachers: 900
Number of students: 13,000

Publications: *Zambezia*, *UZ-News*, *Journal of Applied Science in Southern Africa*, *Central African Journal of Medicine*.

DEANS

Faculty of Agriculture: Dr L. R. NDLOVU
Faculty of Arts: Dr H. CHIMHUNDU
Faculty of Commerce: H. MUKWENHA
Faculty of Education: Dr M. N. PERESUH
Faculty of Engineering: Prof. A. ZINGONI
Faculty of Law: J. ZOWA
Faculty of Medicine: Dr J. MUFUNDA
Faculty of Science: Prof. H. A. M. DZINOTYIWEYI
Faculty of Social Studies: Prof. E. G. MUKONOWESHURO
Faculty of Veterinary Science: Prof. M. J. OBWOLO

CHAIRMEN OF DEPARTMENTS

Agriculture:

Animal Science: Dr C. MUTISI
Crop Science: Dr I. K. MARIGA
Agricultural Economics and Extension: G. D. MUDIMU
Soil Science and Agricultural Engineering: D. A. SANZANJE

Arts:

African Languages and Literature: Dr D. A. MARAIRE
English: Dr R. ZHUWARARA
Geography: Prof. L. M. ZINYAMA
Economic History: Dr S. A. MLAMBO
History: Dr I. PIKIRAYI
Linguistics: K. G. MKANGANWI
Modern Languages: P. S. E. O'FLAHERTY
Religious Studies, Classics and Philosophy: A. J. CALLINCOS
Theatre Arts: M. B. ZIMUNYA

Commerce:

Accountancy: J. T. CHIKONDO
Business Studies: Z. MURANDA

Education:

Educational Foundations: Dr F. ZINDI
Curriculum and Arts Education: S. J. NONDO
Science and Mathematics Education: P. S. NGWAZIKAZANA
Technical Education: S. GWERU
Teacher Education: T. BOURDILLON
Educational Administration: S. CHITEKUTEKU
Adult Education: C. S. NONDO
Centre for Educational Technology: K. N. HUNGWE

Engineering:

Civil Engineering: K. MAWIRE
Electrical Engineering: Dr E. T. KAPUYA
Mechanical Engineering: Dr G. RUKWEZA
Metallurgy: Dr D. J. SIMBI
Mining Engineering: Prof. J. G. VOSS
Surveying: P. MATAMBANADZO

Law:

Public Law: B. MATSHWAYO
Private Law: A. J. MANASE
Procedural Law: J. T. NYAPADI

Medicine:

Anaesthetics: Dr A. Z. HATENDI
Anatomy: Dr G. MAWERA
Chemical Pathology: Dr W. B. MUJAJI
Clinical Pharmacology: Prof. C. F. B. NHACHI
Community Medicine: Dr R. MATCHABA
Haematology: Dr A. M. COUTTS
Histopathology: Dr R. MAKUNIKE
Institute of Continuing Health Education: C. A. SAMKANGE
Medical Laboratory Technology: A. MANDISODZA
Medical Microbiology: Dr S. A. TSWANA
Medicine: Dr J. A. MATENGA
Nursing Science: R. J. NDLOVU
Obstetrics and Gynaecology: Dr T. CHIPATO
Paediatrics and Child Welfare: R. GLYN-JONES
Pharmacy: Dr O. MUNJERI
Physiology: Dr C. T. MUSABAYANE
Psychiatry: Dr I. V. S. CHAGWEDERA

Radiology: I. C. HARID
Rehabilitation: D. MADZIVIRE
Surgery: I. C. HARID

Science:

Biochemistry: Dr B. MASOLA
Biological Science: N. B. DUBE
Chemistry: Dr S. SIBANDA
Computing Science: Dr E. S. MHLANGA
Geology: Dr T. BLENKINSOP
IMR: T. R. C. FERNANDES
Mathematics: D. VUMA
Physics: Dr M. F. MUSHAYANDEBVU
Statistics: Dr P. CHAREKA
Food, Nutrition and Family Science: Dr L. T. MAROVATSANGA

Social Studies:

Centre for Applied Social Science: Dr C. NHIRA
Economics: Dr T. MOYO
Political and Administrative Studies: Dr A. NHEMA
Psychology: R. P. BUNDY
Rural and Urban Planning: T. MUBVAMI
Sociology: V. N. MUZVIDZIWA

Veterinary Science:

Preclinical Veterinary Studies: Dr J. CHAMUNORWA
Paraclinical Veterinary Studies: Dr P. HOVE
Clinical Veterinary Studies: Dr R. M. BUSAYI

ATTACHED INSTITUTES

Institute of Water and Sanitation: Dir Dr P. TAYLOR.

Development Technology Centre: Dir T. RUKUNI.

University Lake Kariba Research Station: Dir Dr C. H. D. MAGADZA.

University Teaching and Learning Centre: Dir Dr C. T. NZIRAMASANGA.

Institute of Developmental Studies: Dir Dr P. CHIMANIKIRE (acting).

Human Resources Research Centre: Co-ordinator Dr C. M. NHERERA.

Colleges

Bulawayo Polytechnic: Park Rd, 12th Ave, POB 1392, Bulawayo; tel. 63181; f. 1927; tertiary education in technical, commercial, scientific, design and catering fields; 210 full-time, 150 part-time teachers; 5,448 students; library of 37,170 vols; Principal A. MWADIWA.

Chibero College of Agriculture: Private Bag 901, Norton; tel. 2230; f. 1960; 2-year national diploma in agriculture; library of 6,000 vols; 15 teachers; 120 students; Principal M. E. NYAMANGARA; publ. *Agricultural Education*.

Gwebi College of Agriculture: Private Bag 376B, Harare; tel. 304515; fax (4) 304522; f. 1950; 3-year diploma in agriculture; library of 2,300 vols; 14 teachers; 120 students; Chief Officer W. MATIZHA.

Esigodini Agricultural Institute: Private Bag 5808, Esigodini; f. 1921; 2-year certificate course for African students; Principal ROBERT GAKA CHISORO.

Harare School of Art: Corner Rhodes Avenue/Eighth-Street, Harare.

Harare Polytechnic: POB CY 8074, Causeway, Harare; tel. 752311; f. 1927; 500 teachers (incl. 280 part-time); *c.* 9,000 students; full-time and sandwich courses for technicians and craftsmen; courses in printing and adult education; full-time and part-time courses in library and information science, computer studies; library of 68,000 vols; Principal C. G. CHIVANDA.

Kushinga-Phikelela Agricultural Institute: Private Bag 3705, Marondera; tel. 4329; f. 1982; 15 teachers; 160 students; 2-year certificate courses in engineering, animal science, field crops; library of 3,100 vols; Principal J. DICKENS.

Mlezu Institute of Agriculture: POB 8062, Kwekwe; f. 1982; 2-year course; Principal J. K. D. MARIPFONDE (acting).

School of Social Work: Private Bag 66022, Kopje, Harare; tel. 752965; f. 1964; library of 9,500 vols; 13 teachers; 210 students; first degrees, certificate, master's degree and diploma courses; Principal Dr E. KASEKE.

Zimbabwe College of Music: Civic Centre, Rotten Row, Harare C.3; tel. 723803; f. 1948; library of 3,000 vols; Chair. B. ZULU; Dir NEIL CHAPMAN; Registrar C. E. ASCROFT.

INDEX OF INSTITUTIONS

B

BIBLIOTECA

C

D

F

G

H

I

J

K

L

M

O

P

Q

R

S

T

U

V

W

X

Y

Z